CONTENTS

Table of Contents v

Preface vii

How To Use the *Directory of Corporate Affiliations: U.S. Private Companies* x

Abbreviations xv

New Listings xvii

Breakdown of Privately Held Companies by State xxvi

Mergers, Acquisitions and Name Changes 1992 xxvii

Public Stock Offerings xxxi

Mergers, Acquisitions, Name Changes and Public Stock Offerings 1988-92 xxxii

Section 1
Index of Company Names A-1

Section 2
U.S. Private Companies 1

Geographic Index to U.S. Private Companies 1223

Alphabetical Compendium of S.I.C. Codes 1363

Numerical Compendium of S.I.C. Codes 1375

S.I.C. Index 1385

Corporate Responsibilities Index 1511

1993

DIRECTORY OF CORPORATE AFFILIATIONS

VOLUME
3

U.S. PRIVATE COMPANIES

"WHO OWNS WHOM"

National Register Publishing
A Reed Reference Publishing Company
New Providence, New Jersey

Published by National Register Publishing, A Reed Reference Publishing Company.

Printed and bound in the United States of America.
International Standard Book Number: 0-87217-201-5
Directory of Corporate Affiliations Five-vol. Set: 0-87217-048-9

Library of Congress Catalog Card Number: 87-659005

ISBN 0-87217-201-5
9 780872 172012

PREFACE

THE DIRECTORY OF CORPORATE AFFILIATIONS LIBRARY

This edition of the *Directory of Corporate Affiliations: U.S. Private Companies* (formerly the *Directory of Leading Private Companies*) incorporates major revisions that reflect National Register Publishing's continuing commitment to provide its customers with the most comprehensive, current and easy to use corporate information available. Recognizing the inter-relatedness of companies throughout the world and the increasing difficulty of keeping track of companies that may be public or private and whose organizational structures cross national boundaries, the editors have reorganized the information previously contained in the *Directory of Corporate Affiliations, Leading Private Companies,* and the *International Directory of Corporate Affiliations* into the five volume *Directory of Corporate Affiliations* set.

The *Directory of Corporate Affiliations* is a clearly organized, comprehensive set that covers public and private businesses in the United States and throughout the world. The basic principle of organization for the volumes in the set is the location of the parent company. All subsidiaries of the parent company, no matter where they are located, can now be found in the same title as the parent. Companies headquartered in the United States have been further subdivided into public and private volumes. Duplication of information between titles has been eliminated, and a master index has been provided for the set. The *Directory of Corporate Affiliations* consists of the following: *Master Index*; *U.S. Public Companies*, Volumes I and II; *U.S. Private Companies*, Volume III; and *International Public and Private Companies*, Volume IV.

The *Master Index* alphabetically lists all companies, both headquarters and subsidiaries, that are located anywhere in the set. A reference is given to the volume and page number where the company's full listing can be found. With the increasing internationalization of business and the constant change in corporate structures, it is frequently difficult to know whether a company is American or foreign owned or whether it is public or private. The *Master Index* solves this problem by directing the user to the appropriate volume where the company will be found. The *Master Index* also contains a useful Brand Name Index that lists well known brand names for all the companies listed in the set. A user knowing a brand name but not the name of the manufacturer can consult this index and again be led to the volume and page where full information on the company that produces the product will be found.

Volumes I and II contain information on U.S. Public Companies. Volume I contains the company listings while volume II contains geographic, Standard Industrial Classification, and personnel indexes to those companies. Companies contained in the U.S. Public volumes are public companies headquartered in the United States as well as all of their subsidiaries, no matter where they are located.

Volume III contains information on U.S. Private Companies. Listed here are U.S.-based private companies and all of their subsidiaries no matter where they are located.

Volume IV contains listings for all non-U.S. based companies, whether they are public or private, and all of their subsidiaries whether they are located in the United States or overseas.

CONTENT, COVERAGE AND ARRANGEMENT of *U.S. PRIVATE COMPANIES*

There are entries for 9,799 parent companies and 12,044 subsidiaries listed in the *Directory of Corporate Affiliations: U.S. Private Companies*. In addition to company name, address, telephone number and key personnel, entries include a description of the company's lines of business with Standard Industrial Classification (SIC) codes; approximate annual sales; number of employees; and names and addresses of the firm's outside legal counsel, accounting firm, major banker and insurance carrier. See the sample entry on page xi for a comprehensive guide to the information that can be found in each entry.

Companies are arranged alphabetically by the name of the parent company. Subsidiary companies follow the listing for the parent in order of reporting hierarchy. Numbers in parentheses show who reports to whom.

Indexes

Index of Company Names
An alphabetical index is located in the front of the book, which lists all parent and subsidiary company names included in the *Directory of Corporate Affiliations: U.S. Private Companies* with a reference to the page where the company will be found. Parent companies are listed in bold type; subsidiary company listings include the name of the parent company of which they are a part.

Geographic Index
The geographic index lists companies arranged by city within state.

S.I.C. Index
Providing access to the listed companies by industry, the Standard Industrial Classification index arranges companies alphabetically within their S.I.C. codes.

Corporate Responsibilities Index
This index lists all personnel included in the directory alphabetically by last name within job responsibility groups. It includes the name and location of an individual's company and refers the user to the page on which the company can be found.

Other Useful Business Information
Included in the frontmatter is a list of *Mergers, Acquisitions and Name Changes* and *Public Stock Offerings*, as well as *New Listings* appearing for the first time in this publication.

COMPILATION METHOD
The *Directory of Corporate Affiliations: U.S. Private Companies* is compiled and updated from information supplied by the companies themselves and business publications. All companies are sent questionnaires prior to inclusion, and each company receives its listing for updating prior to appearing in each edition.

RELATED SERVICES
Mailing lists of companies found in the *Directory of Corporate Affiliations: U.S. Private Companies* may be ordered from Susan Knuth, 1350 E. Touhy Ave., Des Plaines, IL 60018, telephone (708) 390-2358. Database tapes are available from Yvette Berthel, Reed Reference Electronic Publishing, 121 Chanlon Road, New Providence, NJ 07974, telephone (908) 665-2854.

The *Directory of Corporate Affiliations* set is also available in CD-ROM format. For more information, please call (800) 521-8110.

3. If you cannot find the name in the index

If the company name does not appear in the index, try the *Mergers, Acquisitions & Name Changes* or *Public Stock Offerings* sections. The former section alphabetically lists the previous names of companies along with their new names and/or owners. The latter section lists companies which are no longer found in this book, as they are now publicly owned. To find information on these companies, see the *Directory of Corporate Affiliations: U.S. Public Companies*, also published by National Register Publishing. Immediately following these two special sections is a cumulative history of such changes, listing mergers, acquisitions, name changes and public stock offerings back to 1988.

Basic components of a listing

1. Parent Company Information

The following is an example of a parent company listing and an explanation of its basic components.

Philosopher's Stone, Inc.	**Company Name**
1420 S. Brady St.	**Company Address**
South Bend, IN 46601	
Tel: 219-234-7121 **(IN)**	**Telecommunications Data &**
Fax: 219-516-0192	**State of Incorporation**
Year Founded: 1966	**Year the Company was Founded**
Assets: $12,000,000	**Financial Information**
Liabilities: $6,000,000	
Net Worth: $6,000,000	
Approx. Sls.: $50,000,000	
Emp.: 300	**Number of Employees, Including Subsidiaries**
Fiscal Year End: 12/31/91	
Book Publisher	**Business Description**
S.I.C.: 2731	**Standard Industrial Classification Codes**
Cynthia Croy (Chm. Bd.)	**Key Personnel**
H. Peter Steeves (Pres. & Chief Oper. Officer)	
Amy Sorensen (Exec. V.P.)	
Bates & Gilbert (Auditors)	**Name, City and State of Service Firm**
Elkhart, IN	

U.S. company entries will also contain a two letter state abbreviation to the right of the telephone number indicating the state in which the company is incorporated.

2. Subsidiary Company Information

Following each parent company listing are the entries for each of that company's divisions, subsidiaries, affiliates, and joint ventures. These company designations are defined as follows:

Division	Internal organization of the company, not incorporated
Subsidiary	A chartered business owned by the company 50% or above
Affiliate	A chartered business owned by the company 49% or less
Joint Venture	Two or more companies sharing responsibility & ownership of entity

Parent Company entries will be followed by their U.S. Holdings, then Non-U.S. Holdings.

Understanding Levels of Reportage

Each division, subsidiary, affiliate and joint venture entry will have a number in parentheses following the company name. This number represents the level of reportage for that particular company. Any company with a level (1) reports directly to the parent company. Level (2) companies report to the level (1) company immediately above them. Level (3) companies report to the level (2) directly above them.

In the example below, Manchester Industries, Quantum, Ink, and Ikenberry North, Inc. all report directly to the parent company, Philosopher's Stone, Inc. Star Newspapers is a subsidiary of, and reports directly to, Manchester Industries.

Following is a sample list of subsidiary information and an explanation of the components.

Subsidiaries:

Manchester Industries **(1)** ——— **Reports to Parent Company (Philosopher's Stone, Inc.)**
R.R. 1, Box 817
North Manchester, IN 46962
Tel: 219-982-1011 **(IN)**
Fax: 219-982-1012
Printer of Books, Newspapers
S.I.C.: 2731
Thomas Boebel (Pres.)

Subsidiary:

Star Newspapers **(2)** ——— **Reports to Level 1 Company Above (Manchester Industries)**
11 Wabash St.
Attica, IN 47918 (100%) ——— **Percent of Ownership**
Tel: 317-762-4000 **(IN)**
Emp.: 50
Newspaper publishers
S.I.C.: 2711
Steve Devitt (Pres.)

Quantum, Ink **(1)** ——— **Reports to the Parent Company (Philosopher's Stone, Inc.)**
18 Morris Ave.
Corydon, IN 47991 (79%)
Tel: 812-289-1235 **(KY)**
Emp: 10
Desktop Publisher
S.I.C.: 2731
Clarence Boley (Chief Oper. Officer)

Non-U.S. Holding:

Ikenberry North, Inc. **(1)** ——— **Subsidiary not Located in the U.S. Reports to Parent Company (Philosopher's Stone, Inc.)**
2 Karrington Ave.,
Windsor, Ontario, Canada
Tel: 516-211-8912
Emp.: 11
Desktop Publisher
S.I.C.: 2731
Jeffery Gilbert (Pres.)

Percent of ownership in each of these companies is shown in parentheses across from the address. If both parent companies of a joint venture are listed in the directory, the joint venture will be listed twice, once under each of its parent companies.

How to locate companies in a given geographical area

The Geographic Index following Section 2 has been provided to assist you in searching for companies in a specific city or state. Simply turn to the city and state and you will find an alphabetical list of companies with their page numbers in Section 2 and street address, if known. An example follows:

INDIANA

Alexandria

RAM GRAPHICS, INC., State Rd. 9 S. (46601), pg. 591

Anderson

Commercial Service Printing, 1200 E. Fifth St. (46018), pg. 753

PAY LESS SUPER MARKETS, INC., First Savings Tower (46015), pg. 551

WARNER PRESS, INC., 1200 E. Fifth St. (46018), pg. 753

Warner Press Publishers, 1200 E. Fifth St. (46018), pg. 753

Angola

Mid West Correct Craft, Inc., P.O. Box 216 (46703), pg. 187

How to locate companies in a given line of business

If you are using the directory to identify companies who manufacture a certain product, or are in a specific area of business, the S.I.C. index will simplify your search. The index is preceded by two compendia. If you know the S.I.C. code of a company and need to know what the code represents, use the Numerical Compendium. If you know the product or service and do not know its S.I.C. code, start with the Alphabetical Compendium.

The S.I.C. index groups all of the companies in the book by area of business. The index itself is arranged numerically by S.I.C. code, and then alphabetically by company. As in the Index of Company Names, parent companies are represented in bold type, and subsidiary entries contain a reference to the parent. Page numbers refer you to the company's listing in Section 2. "NEC" in a category heading stands for "Not Elsewhere Classified."

2731—BOOKS: PUBLISHING, OR PUBLISHING & PRINTING

ADVANCE PUBLICATIONS INC., pg. 12

AMERICAN BIBLE SOCIETY, pg. 32

AMERICAN KENNEL CLUB, INC., pg. 37

AMERICAN TECHNICAL PUBLISHERS, INC., pg. 40

AMWAY CORPORATION, pg. 44

ARBOR HOUSE—The Hearst Corporation, pg. 338

ARCATA CORPORATION, pg. 50

ARCATA GRAPHICS HALLIDAY—Arcata Corporation, pg. 50

How to locate executive personnel

If you are looking for lists of executives with certain titles or functions, consult the Corporate Responsibilities Index. This index will direct you to personnel listed in the directory who work, for example, in **personnel**.

Abbott, Tom, Dir.-Human Resources—
Zollner Corporation, Fort Wayne, IN, pg. 789
Abrams, Michael, Dir.-Personnel—Telkee Inc.,
Media, PA, pg. 689
Abrams, Michael, Dir-Personnel—Sunroc
Corporation, Media, PA, pg. 689
Abramson, Betty, Dir.-Personnel & Acctg.—
Starcrest Products of California, Perris,
CA, pg. 676

How to find the company behind the brand name

The Brand Name Index located in the *Master Index* volume presents major tradenames in common use by national advertisers. While the index is by no means complete, it is a reference for obtaining product descriptions and directs the user to the companies that produce them.

P

PENNY FROM HEAVEN--Stuffed Toy Figures;
Canisters; Towels; T-shirts--AMERICAN GREETING
CORPORATION, *U.S. Private*, pg. 67
PENNZOIL—Oil Products—PENNZOIL COMPANY,
U.S. Public, pg. 823
PENSTAR--Electronic Anesthesia Machine--BTR PLC.,
Int'l, pg. 204

Comments or suggestions regarding the content and format of these books are encouraged and can be directed to *Directory of Corporate Affiliations*, National Register Publishing, 121 Chanlon Rd., New Providence, NJ 07974.

ABBREVIATIONS

PERSONNEL ABBREVIATIONS

Chm. Bd.	Chairman of the Board	Sec.	Secretary
Vice Chm.	Vice Chairman	Gen. Counsel	General Counsel
Pres.	President	Dir.-Pur.	Purchasing Director
Exec. V.P.	Executive Vice President	Dir.-Personnel	Personnel Director
Sr. V.P.	Senior Vice President	Dir.-Human Resources	Human Resources Director
Grp. V.P.	Group Vice President	Dir.-Data Processing	Data Processing Director
V.P.	Vice President	Dir.-Pub. Rels.	Public Relations Director
Asst. V.P.	Assistant Vice President	Dir.-Pub. Information	Public Information Director
Chief Exec. Officer	Chief Executive Officer	Dir.-Investor Rels.	Investor Relations Director
Chief Oper. Officer	Chief Operating Officer	Dir.-Corp. Affairs	Corporate Affairs Director
Chief Fin. Officer	Chief Financial Officer	Gen. Mgr.	General Manager
Chief Admin. Officer	Chief Administrative Officer	Mng. Dir.	Managing Director
Treas.	Treasurer		

BUSINESS DESCRIPTION ABBREVIATIONS

Access.	Accessories	Mdse., Mdsg.	Merchandise, Merchandising
Admin.	Administrative, Administration	Mfr., Mfg.	Manufacturer, Manufacturing
Adv.	Advertising	Mktg.	Marketing
Assoc.	Associate	Mng., Mngmt.	Managing, Management
Brdcst.	Broadcast	Matl., Matls.	Material, Materials
Comml.	Commercial	Natl.	National
Corp.	Corporate, Corporation	Oper., Opers.	Operation, Operating, Operations
Devel.	Development	Pkgng.	Packaging
Dir.	Director	Plng.	Planning
Distr.	Distribution	Prod., Prods.	Product, Products
Engrng.	Engineering	Pub.	Public
Fin.	Finance, Financial	Pub. Rels.	Public Relations
Govt.	Government	Pur.	Purchasing
Grp.	Group	Reg.	Regional
Indus.	Industry, Industrial	Rels.	Relations
Intl.	International	Sls.	Sales

COMPANY DESIGNATIONS

The following designations indicate the forms of business enterprise in various countries; these forms usually represent the organizations for large enterprises.

AB	Aktiebolag	Finland, Sweden
AG	Aktiengesellschaft	Austria, Germany, Switzerland, Liechtenstein
A/S	Aksjeselskap	Norway
	Aktieselskab	Denmark
B.V.	Besloten Vennootschap	Holland
C.V.	Commanditaire Vennootschap	Holland
Cie.	Compagnie	France, Luxembourg
Co.	Company	United States, France, Luxembourg, South Africa
Ets.	Etablissement(s)	France, Luxembourg
GmbH	Gesellschaft mit beschrankter Haftung	Austria, Germany, Switzerland
I/S	Interessantelskab	Denmark, Norway
KG	Kommanditgesellschaft	Austria, Germany, Switzerland
KK	Kabushiki Kaisha	Japan
K/S	Kommanditselskab	Denmark
Ltd.	Limited	United Kingdom, United States, South Africa
Ltda.	Limitada	Brazil, Portugal
Ltee.	Limitee	Canada
Mij.	Maatschappij	Holland
N.V.	Naamloze Vennootschap	Belgium, Holland
OHG	Offene Handelsgesellschaft	Austria
Oy	Osakeyhtiot	Finland
PLC	Public Limited Company	United Kingdom
P.T.	Perusahaan Terbatas	Indonesia
Pte.	Private	Singapore
Pty.	Proprietary	Australia, South Africa
Pvt.	Private	India, Rhodesia
S.A.	Societe Anonyme	Belgium, France, Luxembourg, Switzerland
	Sociedad Anonima	Spain, Latin America
S.A.C.I.	Sociedad Anonima Comercial e Industrial	Latin America
S.A. de C.V.	Sociedad Anonima de Capital Variable	Mexico
S.A.E.	Sociedad Anonima Espanola	Spain
S.A.I.C.	Sociedad Anonima Industrial y Comercial	Latin America
S.A.R.L.	Sociedad Anonima de Responsabilidade Limitada	Brazil, Portugal
	Sociedade a Responsabilitie Limitee	France, Luxembourg
S.A.S.	Societa in Accomandita Semplice	Italy
S.C.	Societe en Commandite	France, Luxembourg
S.p.A.	Societa per Azioni	Italy
S.P.R. L.	Societe de Personnes a Responsabilitie Limitee	Belgium
S.R.L.	Societa a Responsabilita Limitada	Italy
Sdn. Bhd.	Sendirian Berhad	Malaysia
Ste.	Societe	France, Luxembourg, Switzerland
Ste.Cve.	Societe Cooperative	Belgium
V.o.F.	Vennootschap onder firma	Holland

BUSINESS TERMS ACRONYMS

CAD	Computer Assisted Design
CAE	Computer Aided Engineering
CAID	Computer Assisted Industrial Design
CAM	Computer Aided Manufacturing
COM	Computer Output Micrographics
CPE	Customer Precise Equipment
CPU	Central Processing Unit
DBA	Doing Business As
DISC	Domestic International Sales Corporation
DIY	Do-It-Yourself Products
DRAM	Dynamic Random Access Memory
FIFO	First-In, First-Out Method of Accounting
FSC	Foreign Sales Corporation
HPLC	High Performance Liquid Chromotography
HUD	Heads-Up Display Systems
HVAC	Heating, Venting, Air Conditioning
IC	Integrated Circuit
IR	Infrared
ISDN	Integrated Services Digital Network
KM	Kilometer
LAN	Local Area Network
LCS	Liquid Crystal Displays
LED	Light-Emitting Diode
LIFO	Last-In, First Out Method of Accounting
MB	Megabit
MFPM	Made From Purchased Materials
MITSE	Made in the Same Establishment as the Basic Materials
MRO	Maintenance and Repair Organizations
NA	National Association; Not Applicable
NEC	Not Elsewhere Classified
OECD	Organization for Economic Cooperation
OEM	Original Equipment Manufacturer
OREO	Other Real Estate Owned
PACS	Pictures Archiving and Communications Systems
PBX	Private Brand Exchange
PC	Personal Computer
PCC	Photo Conducting Cells
PEMS	Porcelain Enameled Metal Substrates
PET	Positron Emission Tomography
PVC	Polyvinyl Chloride
RDBMS	Relational Database Management System
REIT	Real Estate Investment Trust System
RFI	Radio Frequency Interference
RISC	Reduced Instruction Set Computing
RTC	Resolution Trust Corporation, under the Office of Thrift Supervision, Formerly Federal Home Loan Administration
SAW	Surface Acoustic Wave
SCSI	Small Computer Systems Interface
SFAS	Statement of Financial Accounting Standards
TDMA	Time Dimension Multiple Access
VIS	Voice Information Services

NEW LISTINGS

Appearing for the first time in this publication

ALABAMA

Birmingham
Saunders, Inc.
Mobile
Gulf Lumber Company, Inc.
McConnell Automotive
Turner Supply Company
Montgomery
Piknik Products Company, Inc.
Smith Industries, Inc.
Pritchard
Autry Greer & Sons, Inc.
Red Bay
Tiffin Motor Homes, Inc.
South Lafayette
Tallapoosa River Electric Co-Op
Tuscaloosa
Harco Drug, Inc.

ALASKA

Anchorage
Carr Gottstein Foods
Nana Regional Corporation, Inc.
Healy
Usibelli Coal Mine, Inc.

ARIZONA

Glendale
Sands Motor Company, Inc.
Phoenix
ASH, Inc. d/b/a Auto Safety House
Messenger Corporation
Redburn Tire Company
United Producers & Consumers Co-Op
Wincup
Scottsdale
Fender Musical Instruments
Tucson
Holmes Tuttle Ford, Inc.
Quebedeaux Pontiac, Inc.
Trico Electric Co-Op

ARKANSAS

Earle
Earle Industries, Inc.
Fayetteville
Continental Ozark, Inc.
Northwest Tobacco & Candy Co.
Pace Industries, Inc.
Forest City
Woodruff Electrical Co-Op
Fort Smith
Flanders Industries, Inc.
Little Rock
Orbit Value International, Inc.
Russellville
Bibler Brothers, Inc.
Texarkana
Buhrman-Pharr Hardware Company
West Memphis
Elite Lamp, Inc.

CALIFORNIA

Alameda
IA Corp.
Bakersfield
Casey Co.
Bell Gardens
Bell Gardens Bicycle Club
Beverly Hills
Capucci Creations International, Inc.
First Gray Line Corporation
M.L. Stern & Company, Inc.
Brea
Bristol Industries
Burbank
J.H. McCormick, Inc.
Oroamerica, Inc.
UniHealth America
World Title Company
Calabasas
Environmental Industries, Inc.
Griffin Homes, Inc.
Cerritos
California Panel & Veneer Company
City of Commerce
Kold Kist Brands, Inc.
City of Industry
Bentley Mills, Inc.
Cacique Cheese Co., Inc.
Guaranteed Products, Inc.
La Victoria Foods, Inc.
Smarty Pants N Tops Too, Inc.
Yum Yum Donut Shop, Inc. d/b/a Donut Equipment & Supply Co.
Compton
Houston Fearless 76 Inc.
Concord
Earl Goldman Insurance Co.
Costa Mesa
Del Taco, Inc.
Griswold Industries, Inc.
Downey
Duary/J.F. Duncan Industries, Inc.
Encino
First Financial Group, Inc. d/b/a American Beauty Homes
Folsom
Whitmire Distribution
Fremont
Inkel Technology
Fresno
Germain's Inc.
Gardena
Die Cast Products, Inc.
Lorber Industries of California
Overton Moore & Associates
Glendora
Caltrol, Inc.
Rain Bird Sprinkler Mfg. Corp.
Inglewood
IBM Foods d/b/a Overhill Farms
Irvine
McGaw, Inc.
Irwindale
Davis Wire Corporation
Superior Fast Freight
Lawndale
La Computer Center
Long Beach
Beach City Chevrolet Co.
Cormier Chevrolet Company, Inc.
Maness Industries, Inc.
Los Angeles
Bandini Fertilizer Company
Ben Myerson Candy Company, Inc.
Beno's
Bergelectric Corporation
Cecil Saydah Company
A.D. Clark, Inc.
Echevarria Angel Co., d/b/a Somma Mattress
Ernst Paper Products, Inc.
Evy of California, Inc.
First Computer Corporation
Fortifiber Corporation
Good Stuff Food Company, Inc.
Harden Industries, Inc.
Leonard Green & Partners
Los Angeles Smoking Curing Company
Madison Graham Colorgraphics, Inc.
Nadel Partnership, Inc.
Norden Fruit Company, Inc.
Organically Grown Corporation

Paramount Fitness Equipment Corp.
Poly Pak America, Inc.
Potato Sales Company, Inc.
Purcell Group, Inc.
Raleigh Enterprises, Inc.
Service Packing Company
Shield Security, Inc.
Theodore Barry & Associates
Tulip Corporation
The Zippertubing Co.

Monterey Park
Camino Real Chevrolet
Refrigeration Supplies Distributors

Newport Beach
J.M. Peters Co.

Pasadena
Converse Professional Group, Inc.
James M. Montgomery Consulting Engineers
Pacifica Services, Inc.

Rancho Santa Fe
Frank Raymond Warren

Redondo Beach
Bobit Publishing Company

Sacramento
Twenty-First Century Publishing Co.

Salinas
Pacifica Capital Bancorp

San Bernadino
Gate City Beverage Distributors

San Diego
Arnolds Interiors, Inc.
Deans Photo Service, Inc.
Expo Industries, Inc.
H.G. Fenton Material Company
Laser Power Corporation
McKellar Development of La Jolla
Nelson Photo Supplies
Old Stone of California, Inc.
Robinhood Homes
Wavetek Corporation

San Fernando
Cordova Laboratories
Oh Boy Corporation

San Francisco
Carpenter Rigging
Chemoil
Gump's, Inc.

San Gabriel
Howards Appliances, Inc.

San Jose
Actrix Systems, Inc.
Trace Products

Santa Ana
Belgrave Industries
Transico International

Santa Barbara
Pacifica Real Estate Group

Santa Fe Springs
Riccobon & Company, Inc

Santa Monica
A-Mark Financial
Candle Corporation
Carlsberg Financial Corp.
Morley Group
Psomas & Associates

Saugas
Blue Cross Laboratories
John Paul Mitchell Systems

Sherman Oaks
Mrs. Goochs Natural Food Markets

Soquel
Network Real Estate of California, Inc.

South Gate
Schultz Steel Company

Sunland
The Cherokee Group

Sunnyvale
Quality Technologies Corporation

Sylmar
Cordova Enterprise

Thousand Oaks
Consolidated Electrical Distributors

Upland
New Bedford Panoramex Corporation

Van Nuys
Continental Coin Corporation
Industrial Electronic Engineers, Inc.
Keyes Motors, Inc.
Shapco, Inc.

Vernon
Jazz Holding Corporation

West Sacramento
MTS, Inc.

Whittier
Cal-Air, Inc.

Woodland Hills
Catalina Yachts, Inc.

COLORADO

Colorado Springs
Maxcor Manufacturing, Inc.
Mountain States Pipe & Supply Company
National Systems & Research Co.
Wigand Corporation

Cortez
Empire Electric Association

Denver
Johnson Storage & Moving Company

Glenwood Springs
Holy Cross Electric Association

Lamar
Carder, Inc.

Monte Vista
Monte Vista Co-Op Association, Inc.

CONNECTICUT

Bloomfield
Graphic Center, Inc.

Bramford
Arcola Wire Company

Bridgeport
Moore Special Tool Co., Inc.

Brookfield
Rapid Power Technologies, Inc.

Danbury
Danbury Printing & Lithograph, Inc.

Greenwich
R.L. Albert & Son, Inc.
American Institute for Foreign Study
Decorative Crafts, Inc.
Strategic Distribution Inc.

Hamden
Condere Corporation

Hartford
New England Dairies, Inc.

Norwalk
MBI, Inc.
New Hermes Incorporated
Rex Machine Center, Inc.
Vallerie's Transport Service, Inc.
Vectron Labs, Inc.

Plainville
Peck Spring Company

Riverside
Grand Union Holdings Corporation

Shelton
Landstar Holding
Rudel Machinery Company, Inc.

Stamford
Conestoga Holdings, Inc.
Geneve Corporation
Mormac Marine Transport, Inc.
Service America Corp.
Victoria Station Incorporated

Wallingford
Novametrix Medical Systems, Inc.

Waterbury
Abrams Publishing Inc.

West Hartford
Abbott Ball Company

DELAWARE

Bridgefield
Delagra Corporation
Greenwood
Delaware Electric Co-Op
Middletown
Quaker City Motor Parts Company
Milford
Burris Foods, Inc.
Smyrna
Metal Masters Foodservice Equipment

DISTRICT OF COLUMBIA

Washington
American Enterprise Institute for Public Policy Research
Forman Brothers, Inc.
National Academy of Sciences, USA
National Geographic Society

FLORIDA

Casselberry
Royal Jeep Eagle Chrysler Plymouth, Inc.
TOC Retail, Inc.
Clearwater
National Equipment Manufacturing Corporation
Coral Springs
Continental Plastic Card Co.
Deerfield Beach
Deerfield Builders Supply, Inc.
Kitchens of the Ocean, Inc.
List Industries, Inc.
Jacksonville
Coggin-O'Steen Investment Corp.
Harry Pepper & Associates
Largo
Overstreet Paving Company
Merritt Island
Island Lincoln-Mercury
Miami
International Airline Support Group
Med-Lab Supply Company, Inc.
Orlando
Daniels Manufacturing Corporation
Safety Harbor
Jacobsen Manufacturing, Inc.
Sarasota
Kalin Enterprises, Inc.
Tampa
Gulf Coast Lead Company, Inc.
Lazy Days RV Center, Inc.
West Palm Beach
Overseas Service Corporation

GEORGIA

Americus
Sheffield Hardware Company
Atlanta
Academy Insurance Group, Inc.
General Wholesale Company, Inc.
H. Kessler & Company
TDA
United Parking, Inc.
Willen Manufacturing Company, Inc.
Augusta
Southeastern Equipment Company, Inc.
Southern Beverage Packers, Inc.
Bainbridge
Elberta Crate & Box Company
Flint River Mills
Stones, Inc.
Cairo
Ira Higdon Grocery, Inc.
Carrolton
Southwire Co.
Columbus
American Selfcare Corporation
Georgia Crown Distibuting Co.
Fitzgerald
Lowell Packing Company
Moultrie
Beadles Lumber Company, Inc.
Norcross
AGCO Inc.
Pameco Corp.
Savannah
Aminco, Inc.
Derst Baking Company, Inc.
Thomasville
Industrial Boiler Company, Inc.

HAWAII

Hilo
Isevato Contracting Co. Ltd.
Puna Plantation Hawaii Ltd.
Honolulu
Aloha Airgroup, Inc.
Kahului
Valley Isle Produce, Inc.
Princeville
Princeville Corporation

IDAHO

Alene
Idaho Forest Industry, Inc.
Boise
Peterson Motor Company
Buhl
Rangen, Inc.
Coeur D'Alene
Advanced Input Devices, Inc.
Idaho Falls
Electrical Wholesale Supply Company, Inc.
Industrial Contractors, Inc.
Ketchum
Scott U.S.A.
Laclede
Riley Creek Lumber Company

ILLINOIS

Arlington Heights
F.H. Bonn Company
Aurora
BRK Electronics, Inc.
Carbondale
Vogler Motor Company, Inc.
Chicago
Acme Continental Foods, Inc.
American Decal & Mfg. Co.
Baker & McKenzie International
Brewer Electric Mfg. Co.
Bruss Company
Cloverhill Bakery
Dudek & Bock Spring Manufacturing Company
Electro Brand, Inc.
H. Group Holding Inc.
Harris Steel Co.
Industrial Steel & Wire Company
Milton Industries, Inc.
Putman Publishing Co.
Ready Metal Manufacturing Company
Spurgeon Mercantile Company
Tab Chemicals, Inc.
Telco Capital Corporation
Ultimo Ltd.
Des Plaines
Distribution America
Tash, Inc.
Effingham
LWMCK Corporation
Hoffman Estates
Dataron Incorporated
Itasca
Tennessee Restaurant Corporation
Lake Forest
Eon Labs, Inc.
Lemont
Folger Adam Company

Lile
Volvo Sales & Service Center
Lincolnwood
London Litho Aluminum Co., Inc.
Madison
Spectrulite Consortium, Inc.
Melrose Park
Kreher Steel Company, Inc.
Niles
Jarke Corporation
Northwestern Industrial Piping
Rosemont
McCain Foods Inc.
Russell
Camosy, Inc.
South Holland
Goodheart-Willcox Co., Inc.
Springfield
Egizii Electric, Inc.
Roberts Foods, Inc.
Villa Park
Wozniak Industries

INDIANA

Carmel
Evergreen Healthcare Ltd.
Covington
Covington Foods, Inc.
Elkhart
Homan Lumber Mart
Fort Wayne
Essex Group, Inc.
SBN System Inc.
Indianapolis
The Associated Group
Melvin Simon & Associates
Jasper
Wharfside Restaurants, Inc.
Lafayette
Egyptian Lacquer Manufacturing Company, Inc.
Fauber Construction Company
Rostone Corporation
Monticello
White County Farm Bureau Co-Op Association
New Albany
Kaiser Tobacco Company, Inc.
Tell City
Tell City Chair Co.
Winchester
OMCO Mould, Inc.

IOWA

Carter Lake
Owen Industries, Inc.
Cedar Rapids
Apache Hose & Belting Company
Gazette Company, Inc.
Loomis Brothers, Inc.
Clinton
Carstensen Freight Line, Inc. d/b/a Clinton Disposal Co.
Custom Park, Inc.
Davenport
Bawden Corporation
Brammer Manufacturing Company, Inc.
Sieg Company
Huff
Foreign Candy Co., Inc.
Keokuk
The Hubinger Company
Pella
Vermeer Manufacturing Co.

KANSAS

Great Bend
Doonan & Sons, Inc.
Wakeeney
Western Electric Utility Association
Wichita
Associated Company, Inc.
Chance Industries Inc.
EVCON Holdings
Foley Holding Company, Inc.
Goldsmiths, Inc.

KENTUCKY

Cold Spring
Griffin Industries, Inc.
Cresent Springs
Blue Grass Foods, Inc.
Erlanger
Tressa, Inc.
Florence
Keco Industry, Inc.
Fort Mitchell
Paul Hemmer Construction Company
Hopkinsville
Hopkinsville Elevator Company
Horse Cave
Bale of Kentucky, Inc.
Lexington
Mason Company
Louisville
Progress Paint Manufacturing Co.
Newport
NS Group, Inc.
National Band & Tag Company

LOUISIANA

Baton Rouge
Barber Brothers Contracting Company
Distributors Oil Company, Inc.
Lafayette
Schad Industries, Inc.
Oak Grove
Ruffin Building Systems, Inc.

MAINE

Auburn
Pioneer Plastics Holding, Inc.
Bangor
Darling's
Warren
Crowe Rope Company
Winslow
Laverdiere's Enterprises

MARYLAND

Baltimore
Collman Graphics, Inc.
Parks Sausage Company
Scotsman Group d/b/a Williams Mobile Offices, Inc.
Stop Shop Save
Beltsville
Office Environmental Corporation
Hunt Valley
Fair Lanes Inc.
Lanham
Columbia C & W, Inc.
Rowman & Littlefield Publishers
Owings Mills
Lion Brothers Co.
Potomac
Caterair Holdings Corp.
Taneytown
The Taney Corporation

MASSACHUSETTS

Andover
The Frye Company
Billerica
IDE Corporation
Boston
Advent International
Brockton
Christy's Markets, Inc.
Cambridge
Praxis International Inc.
Chelsea
American Finish & Chemical Company
Dorchester
Swift Instruments, Inc.
Everett
Helpern Joan & David, Inc.
Fall River
Quaker Fabric Corporation
Indian Orchard
Heat Bath Park Metallurgical, Inc.

Lawrence
Agri-Mark, Inc.
Lynn
Scangas Brothers Holdings, Inc.
New Bedford
Brittany Dyeing & Printing Corporation
Epec, Inc.
Northborough
Electro Fiberoptics Corporation
Somerset
Alden Auto Parts Wholesale, Inc.
Parks Corporation
Tewksbury
Market Basket, Inc.

MICHIGAN

Battle Creek
United Steel & Wire Co.
Chelsea
Chelsea State Bank
Detroit
First Fed Michigan Corporation
Durand
Premarc Corporation
Farmington
Mechanical Heat & Cold, Inc.
Farmington Hills
Marketing Displays International, Inc.
Fowlerville
Bent Tube, Inc.
Grand Haven
Challenge Graphics Equipment Co.
Grand Rapids
Dickinson Press, Inc.
Magheilse Tool Corporation
Michigan Lithographing, Inc.
Jackson
Dawn Food Products, Inc.
Kalkaska
Wayne Wire Cloth Products, Inc.
Livonia
Perfection Automotive Products Corporation
Lowell
King Milling Company
Mason
Dart Container Corp.
Saginaw
U.S. Graphite, Inc.
Stevensville
Wollin Products, Inc.
Traverse City
Venturi Inc.
Warren
Manufacturers Products Company

MINNESOTA

Austin
Astrup Drugs, Inc.
Eden Prairie
Argosy Electronics, Inc.
Garden Valley
J.H. Larson Electrical Company
Minneapolis
Bank MF & Company, Inc.
Banner Engineering Corp.
CBM Industries, Inc.
Diversified Dynamics Inc.
Morcestco, Inc.
Minnetonka
Scicom Data Services, Ltd.
Princeton
Crystal Cabinet Works, Inc.
Savage
Continental Machines, Inc.
St. Paul
AmClyde Engineered Products, Inc.
Minnesota Brewing Company
Peoples Electric Company, Inc.
Specialty Manufacturing Company
Wayzata
Schott Corporation
Winsted
Littfin Lumber Company

MISSISSIPPI

Jackson
Capitol Street Corp.
Dewey Corporation
Forestry Suppliers, Inc.
Jackson Paper Company
Trend Line Corporation
Moundridge
Bradbury Company, Inc.

MISSOURI

Joplin
Contract Freighters, Inc.
Kansas City
Gamey Holding Company, Inc.
Thermal Technology Industries
Mountain Grove
Richards Brothers of Mountain Grove
Springfield
Bass Pro Shops, Inc.
Erickson Transport Corporation
Positronic Industry, Inc.
Reyco Industries
St. Joseph
News-Press & Gazette Company
St. Louis
Bekins Distribution Services Co.
Clark Oil & Refining Corporation

MONTANA

Billings
Ryan Oldsmobile
Bozeman
Country Classic Dairies, Inc. d/b/a Darigold Farms
Kalispell
Equity Supply Company

NEBRASKA

Clay Center
Dahlsten Truck Line, Inc.
Hastings
Dulton-Lainson Co.
Lexington
Lexington Co-Op Oil Co.

NEW HAMPSHIRE

Bedford
Eckman Construction Company
Concord
Automotive Supply Assoc., Inc.
Hampton
The Henley Group, Inc.
Manchester
Colonial Supply Corporation
Granite State Packing Co. d/b/a Jac Pac Food

NEW JERSEY

Bayonne
Bookazine Company
Beverly
Phoenix International, Inc.
Cedar Knolls
Carmick Labs., Inc.
Chatham
Magla Products
Edison
Michael Stevens Ltd.
Elizabeth
Pharmacaps Inc.
Emerson
Tri-K Industries, Inc.
Fairfield
Microbond Companies, Inc.
Fort Lee
Couristan, Inc.
Hackensack
Superior Linen & Drapery Company
Leonia
Kulite Semiconductor Products, Inc.

Lodi
Interplast Universal Industries, Inc.
Marlton
RMS Techs, Inc.
Moonachie
Magicsilk, Inc.
Morris Plains
Weichert Company
Newark
Daidone Electric, Inc.
Fiske Brothers Refining Company
North Branch
Structural Foam Plastics, Inc.
Northvale
Aerco International, Inc.
Old Tappan
Parlux Fragrances Inc.
Oradell
John H. Graham & Co., Inc.
Paterson
Mona Industries, Inc.
Phillipsburg
Orbel Corporation
Randolph
John Dusenbery Co., Inc.
Rutherford
Paper Sources International
Teaneck
Ajinmoto U.S.A. Inc.
Wayne
Corber Corporation
Whippany
RI Holdings

NEW MEXICO

Albuquerque
Furr's Supermarkets
Mountain States Constructors, Inc.
Plains Electric Generation Transmission Co-Op, Inc.
Science & Engineering Associates
Anthony
Sharp Oil Company
Roswell
Bell Gas, Inc.

NEW YORK

Batavia
P.W. Minor & Son, Inc.
Bronx
Coat, Apron & Linen Supply
Savemart, Inc.
Brooklyn
Chem-Tainer Corporation
Gussco Manufacturing, Inc.
Buffalo
Carton-Craft Corporation
Carmel
Guideposts Associates, Inc.
Deer Park
Global Steel Products Corporation
East Bloomfield
Crossman Corp.
Elmira
Chemung Ford, Inc.
Hilliard Corporation
Elmsford
Commons Bros. Inc.
Flushing
Anglers Roslyn Group Ltd.
Garden City
Hughes-Treitler Manufacturing Corporation
Great Neck
Shogyo International Corporation
Hauppauge
Floral Glass & Mirror, Inc.
Hawthorne
Metric & Multistandard Compenents
Wolfe & Munier, Inc.
Hicksville
Structural Industries, Inc.
Ithaca
Therm, Inc.
Jamaica
Green Bus Lines, Inc.
King Wire & Cable Corporation
Long Island City
Durlacher & Co., Inc.
Pace Collection, Inc.
Mamaroneck
Cine Magnetics, Inc.
Melville
MidCoast Mortgage Corporation
Mineola
Great Neck Saw Manufacturers, Inc.
Mount Kisco
Curtis Instruments, Inc.
Mount Vernon
Magnetic Analysis Corp.
Sigmund Cohn Corp.
New York
American Arbitration Association
Amsco School Publications, Inc.
Arnav Industries, Inc.
Baby Togs, Inc.
Baris Shoe Company, Inc.
Berkliff Corporation
Bonhomme Shirtmakers Ltd.
Commonwealth Toy & Novelty Company
Cox & Company, Inc.
Dancker, Sellew & Douglas, Inc.
Fairfield Maxwell Ltd.
Fiduciary Trust Company International
Financial World Partners
First City Industries, Inc.
Hagen & Sawyer
Hartz Group
Integrated Resources, Inc.
Japan Travel Bureau International, Inc.
Johnson & Higgins
Perry H. Koplik & Sons
Land N Sea, Inc.
Perfect Pearl Company, Inc.
Potomac Graphic Industries, Inc.
Pyramid Handbags, Inc.
October Films, Inc.
Rabco Health Service
Rockville Fabrics Corporation
S. Rothchild & Co., Inc.
Sally Lou Fashions Corporation
Silverman Products & Textiles
Standard Garment Company, Inc.
Thomas Publishing Co.
Tishman Realty & Construction
Tony Lambert Company
Torino Fashions, Inc.
Track Data
Trian Group
Carole Wren, Inc.
Orangeburg
Innovative Plastics Corporation
Plainview
Veeco Instrumentations, Inc.
Queens Village
Bellacicco & Sons
Reno
Hamilton Co., Inc.
Rochester
ALP/Freddy's
Alleson of Rochester, Inc.
Caldwell Manufacturing Company
Mathews & Boucher
Ronkonkoma
Quality King Distributors
Schenectady
Lawrence Group, Inc.
Seaford
Bast Chevrolet, Inc.
Syracuse
Syracuse Supply Company
Troy
Standard Manufacturing Company
Valhalla
Ruhl Companies, Inc.

Tollman/Hundley Hotels
White Plains
American Savings Bank
Browning Chemical Corporation
Brunschwig & Fils, Inc.
Corham, Inc.
M. Kamenstein, Inc.
Wyoming
Markin Tubing, Inc.
Yonkers
Precision Value Corporation

NORTH CAROLINA

Burlington
Star Food Products, Inc.
Cliffside
Colonial Petroleum Co.
Hickory
Alex Lee, Inc.
High Point
Air Power, Inc.
Marsh Furniture Company
Slane Hosiery Mills, Inc.
Raleigh
Daniel Industries Inc.
Research Triangle Park
CompuChem Corporation
Wilmington
Block Industries, Inc.

NORTH DAKOTA

Bismarck
Basin Electric Power Co-Op
Finley
Finley Farmers Grain Elevator Company
Minot
Minot Builders Supply Association
Westlie Motor Company
Rugby
Rugby Farmers Union Elevator Company

OHIO

Alliance
The Genie Company
Blue Ash
Chester Oak Financial Corporation
Canton
Summit Environmental Group
Cincinnati
Cincinnati Gear Company
Ficks Reed Company
Ford Development Corporation
Hamilton Mutual Insurance Company of Cincinnati
Monarch Construction Company
Al Neyer, Inc.
Planes Moving & Storage, Inc.
Random Corporation
Reece-Campbell, Inc.
Riemeir Lumber Company, Inc.
Warm Brothers Construction Company
Wellington Industries Inc.
Cleveland
Adec International Automation Corp.
Brittany Corporation
Emerald Corporation
Freeman Manufacturing & Supply Company
Reese Chemical Co., Inc.
Unger Company
Voss Industries, Inc.
Columbus
Decor Corporation
Homewood Corporation
Dayton
Woolpert Consultants
Elyria
Elyria Foundry Company
Harrison
Hubert Company
Loveland
Cincinnati United Contractors
Massillon
Republic Engineered Steels
Miamisburg
Dieitron Tool Co., Inc.
Milford
Bigg's Hyper Shoppes, Inc.
Solon
Crawford Fittings Co.
Seegot Inc.
Toledo
Prestolite Electric Incorporated
Urbana
Champaign Landmark
West Chester
Schumacher-Dugan Constructions
Willoughby
Metal Seal & Products, Inc.

OKLAHOMA

Clinton
Elk Supply Company d/b/a Clinton Lumber Co.
Duncan
Duncan Equipment Company
Kingfisher
Kingfisher Co-Op Elevator Association
Oklahoma City
American Fidelity Corp.
Kimray, Inc.
United Engines, Inc.
Perry
Charles Machine Works, Inc.
Walters
Cotton Electric Co-Op

OREGON

Beaverton
Plaid Industries, Inc.
Brookings
C&K Markets, Inc.
Eugene
Guard Publishing Company
Vitus Electrical Supply Company
Medford
Sherms Thunderbird Market
Springfield
Timber Products Company, LP

PENNSYLVANIA

Aston
Phonetics, Inc.
Bluebell
Crown Textile Company
Bristol
Jones Apparel Group, Inc.
Chambersburg
Nibble with Gibble's, Inc.
Oliver Oil Co., Inc.
Collegeville
Collegeville/Imagineering L.P.
Columbia
Colonial Metals Co.
Conestoga
Safe Harbor Water Power Corporation
Denver
Kalas Manufacturing, Inc.
Sunline Coach Co., Inc.
Derry
Industrial Ceramics, Inc.
Drums
Eastern Environmental Services, Inc.
Earl
Conestoga Wood Specialties, Inc.
Ephrata
Hamilton Equipment, Inc.
Erie
Erie Family Life Insurance Company
Harrisburg
Schaedler Brothers, Inc.
United Techtronic Industry
Leola
Ross Engineering Co., Inc.

Manheim
Lift-Tech
Mount Joy
First Mount Joy Corporation
New Oxford
Round Hill Foods, Inc.
Pittsburgh
Pittsburgh Brewing Company
Royersford
American Machine & Tool Company
Williamsport
MHB, Inc.
York
Tighe Industries, Inc.
Youngstown
Phar-Mor, Inc.

RHODE ISLAND

Cranston
Jan-Co., Inc.
Greenville
Hart Engineering Corporation
Providence
Imperial Pearl Company, Inc.

SOUTH CAROLINA

Columbia
Bearing Distributors, Inc.
CMI Industries, Inc.
Consolidated Systems, Inc.
Gaffney
Peelers Rug Company
Greenville
Wunda Weve Carpet Co.
Kingtree
Farmers Telephone Co-Op

SOUTH DAKOTA

Alcester
Alkota Cleaning Systems, Inc.
Madison
East River Electrical Power Co.

TENNESSEE

Athens
Athens Furniture, Inc.
Germantown
Ezon Products, Inc.
Memphis
Allen & Ohara, Inc.
Bryce Corporation
Bud Davis Cadillac, Inc.
Bulab Holdings, Inc.
Cummings Mid-South, Inc.
Dealers Transport Company, Inc.
Delta Life Corporation
Econocom-USA Inc.
Fred P. Gattas Company, Inc.
Ideal Chemical & Supply Company
John J. Campbell Co., Inc.
Leader Federal Bank For Savings
Manufacturers Consolidation Service
Martin, Cole, Dando & Robertson
Memphis Group, Inc.
Metro Foods, Inc.
Mid America International Trucks, Inc.
National Marketing Company
Ozark Motor Lines
Plant Maintenance Service Corporation
Seessel Holdings, Inc.
Standard Welders Supply Co.
Tri-State Armature Electric Works
Tri-State Mack Distributors
Nashville
Central Parking Corp.
Tennessee Wholesale Drug Company

TEXAS

Arlington
Berryman Products, Inc.
Shoreline Products, Inc.
Beaumont
Helena Laboratories Corporation
Corsicana
Regal International, Inc.
Dallas
Duggan Industries, Inc.
Epic Healthcare Group
Ferguson Industries
The Figaro Company, Inc.
First Southwest Company
INDRESCO, Inc.
Listing Products, Inc.
Overhead Door Corporation
Pacific Enterprises Oil Company (USA)
Republic Supply Company
Sterling Jewelry & Distributing Co.
Wholesale Electronic Supply
Wing Industries, Inc.
El Paso
Pasotex Corporation
Fort Worth
Buffton Corporation
Garland
Metro Label Corp.
Houston
American Capital Management & Research, Inc.
General Homes Corporation
MMI Products, Inc.
Vista Chemical Co.
Lufkin
Perry Brothers, Inc.

UTAH

Ogden
Anderson Lumber Company
Standard Corporation
Salt Lake City
Cummins Intermountain Diesel
Huntsman Corporation
PST Vans, Inc.
St. George
Rocky Mountain Company, d/b/a RMC Foods

VERMONT

Center Rutland
Carris Reels, Inc.

VIRGINIA

Herndon
Perot Systems Corporation
Marion
Marley Mouldings, Inc.
Mount Crawford
Riddleberger Brothers, Inc.
Portsmouth
Peck Iron & Metal Company, Inc.
Richmond
Estes Express Lines, Inc.
William H. Goodwin Trust
Mactavish Machine Manufacturing Company
Sulfolk
Birdsong Corporation
Virginia Beach
Stihl Inc.

WASHINGTON

Everett
Certified Holding Corp.
Millstone Coffee, Inc.
Kent
Pacific Foods, Inc.
Seattle
Alaska Pulp Corporation
Dairygold Inc.
Hallidie Machinery Company, Inc.
Seattle Lighting Fixture Co.
Seattle Times Company
Totem Resources Corporation

WEST VIRGINIA

Charles Town
Charles Town Races, Inc.

Charleston
- Industrial Rubber Products Company
- Kanawha Steel & Equipment Co.

Fairmont
- Browns Lumber & Supply Company
- Helmick Corporation

Morgantown
- King Prime, Inc.

Parkersburg
- Marmac Corporation

Ravenswood
- Ravenswood Aluminum Corp.

WISCONSIN

Arcadia
- Arcadia Fryers

Germantown
- The F. Dohmen Company

Grantsburg
- McNally Industries, Inc.

La Cross
- Inland Printing Company, Inc.

Madison
- University Book Store

Menomonee Falls
- Kuhlman, Inc.

Milwaukee
- Lappin Electric Company

New Berlin
- G & L Products, Inc.

Racine
- Racine Federated, Inc.

Ripon
- Lyke Corporation d/b/a Ripon Community Printers

Sheboygan
- Polar Ware Company

Sheboygan Falls
- Richardson Industries, Inc.

Stevens Point
- First Financial Corporation

WYOMING

Casper
- Rissler & McMurry Company
- Wyoming Machine Company

Cheyenne
- Unicover Corporation

Riverton
- Gilpatrick Construction Company

Breakdown of Privately Held Companies by State

	Parent Cos.	Non-Parent Cos.
Alabama	78	120
Alaska	10	13
Arizona	99	139
Arkansas	64	65
California	1,002	1,011
Colorado	91	154
Connecticut	246	171
Delaware	19	44
Dist. of Columbia	43	58
Florida	296	361
Georgia	229	315
Hawaii	20	69
Idaho	23	21
Illinois	832	831
Indiana	214	267
Iowa	80	118
Kansas	109	131
Kentucky	129	116
Louisiana	105	91
Maine	49	46
Maryland	140	156
Massachusetts	328	296
Michigan	493	383
Minnesota	300	251
Mississippi	38	66
Missouri	493	383
Montana	21	12

	Parent Cos.	Non-Parent Cos.
Nebraska	58	86
Nevada	23	28
New Hampshire	47	46
New Jersey	456	361
New Mexico	22	8
New York	1,062	925
North Carolina	200	260
North Dakota	29	14
Ohio	502	478
Oklahoma	54	93
Oregon	82	93
Pennsylvania	544	442
Puerto Rico	1	22
Rhode Island	52	32
South Carolina	124	110
South Dakota	29	17
Tennessee	204	220
Texas	402	593
Utah	46	46
Vermont	33	26
Virgin Islands	0	4
Virginia	139	171
Washington	149	164
West Virginia	25	29
Wisconsin	243	231
Wyoming	19	12

TOTAL COMPANIES LISTED:

Number of U.S. Parent Companies: 9,799
Number of U.S. Non-Parent Companies: 10,032
Number of Foreign Non-Parent Companies: 2,012

Mergers, Acquisitions and Name Changes 1992

A

A & E Business Products—acquired by Taylor Corporation
AFCG—name changed to ASCG, Inc.
A-G Co-Operative Creamery, Inc.—merged into Arcadia Fryers
AGCO Corporation—acquired by AGCO Inc.
Access Medical Systems—name changed to Environetics
Ackerman Advertising—acquired by Greenstone Roberts Advertising
Acme Appliance Corp.—name changed to Acme Kitchen Products, Inc.
Admiration Hosiery Mills, Inc.—merged into Highland Mills Inc.
Alliance Telecommunications, Inc.—acquired by The Allen Group, Inc.
Allied Stores Corporation—name changed to Federated Department Stores, Inc.
American Transportation Corporation—name changed to AmTran Corporation
American Western Corporation—acquired by Carlisle Plastics, Inc.
Ardell Industries Inc.—acquired by American Safety Razor, a subsidiary of Jordan Company
Arizona Television, KTVK Channel 3—name changed to Media America Corp.
Associated Mills, Inc.—name changed to Odyssey Partners
Atex Gas, Inc.—merged with Bell Gas, Inc.
Autoland Chevrolet, Inc.—name changed to Ocean Chevrolet, Inc.

B

Baylor Company—acquired by Royal Begemann Group
Be-Lo Markets, Inc.—acquired by Camellia Food Stores Co-Op Inc.
Benjamin Air Rifle—name changed to Benjamin Sheridan Corp. & acquired by Crossman Corp.
The Berkline Corporation—acquired by Corber Corporation
Biochem International Inc.—name changed to BCI International
E.E. Black, Ltd.—acquired by Morrison Knudsen Corp.
Blinn Wholesale Drug Co., Inc.—acquired by Commons Bros., Inc.
Braun Cadillac, Inc.—acquired by Don Massey Cadillac Inc.
Brower Company—acquired by Bay Industries
Brown Cadillac, Inc.—acquired by Massey Cadillac, a subsidiary of Don Massey Cadillac Inc.
Byron Elevator Company—name changed to Argiland Company

C

CNC Holding Corporation—name changed to Cole National Corp.
Cabot Communications—merged with Arnold Fortuna Lane to form Arnold Fortuna Lane & Cabot, Inc.
Cabot Farmers Co-Op Creamery Company—name changed to Cabot Creamery Co-Operative Inc. & acquired by Agri-Mark, Inc.
Cedar Valley Products, Inc.—acquired by G & L Products, Inc.
Challenge Machinery Co.—name changed to Challenge Technologies & acquired by Challenge Graphics Equipment Co.
Charter Oak Financial Corporation—acquired by Guarantee Title Co., Inc.
B.C. Christopher & Co.—acquired by Fahnestock & Co., a subsidiary of Fahnestock Viner Holdings Inc.
Clinton Mills Inc.—acquired by CMI Industries, Inc.
Combined Communications Services—acquired by R.R. Donnelley & Sons Company
CompuChem Corporation—acquired by Roche Holding Ltd.
Cordova Laboratories—acquired by Cordova Enterprise
Craig-Hallum Corporation—acquired by Hamilton Investments

D

Dairy Stores, Inc.—name changed to National Food Stores, Inc. T/A Krauzer's
Dayton Superior Corporation—name changed to Danis Industries Corporation
Det. Division of National Guardian & Beechwood Security of Cleveland—acquired by Guardian Alarm Co.
Devon Tape Corporation—name changed to American Tape Corporation
Digital Development Corporation—name changed to DDC Pertec
DineLite Corp.—acquired by Po Folks, Inc.
Dubrowsky & Perlbinder, Inc.—name changed to P.D. Fashions

E

EECO International—name changed to Transico Incorporated
Economy Printing Concern, Inc.—name changed to E.P. Graphics, Inc.
Ehrig & Associates—acquired by Evans Communications, Inc.
Electronic Tel Communication—acquired by Electronic Telecommunications, Inc.
Emb-Tex Corp.—name changed to Swiss-M-Tex, L.P.
Ever Ready Corp.—acquired by Metro Label Corp.

F

FTI Industries, Inc.—name changed to Fluidic Technologies, Inc.
Fanny May Candies—name changed to Jordan Company
Fashion Bar, Inc.—acquired by Specialty Retailers, Inc.
Fayette Energy Corp.—acquired by Arcadian Power Corp.
William Feather Printers, Inc.—merged into Alden Press
Fisher Camuto Retail Corporation—name changed to Nine West Group, Inc.
Frank Parra Chevrolet—name changed to F.P.A., Inc., d/b/a Frank Parra Chevrolet

G

General Binding Corporation—name changed to Lane Industries
General Processors, Inc.—acquired by W.A. Adams Inc., a subsidiary of Standard Commercial Corporation
J. E. Goold & Company—acquired by Bindley Western Industries, Inc.
Gradison & Company, Inc.—name changed to Gradison Div. & acquired by McDonald & Company Investments, Inc.
Graphics Holding Company—name changed to Bell South Enterprises

H

HMC Corporation—name changed to Mark Machine Inc.
Harpers—acquired by Kimball International
Harris Wholesale Company—name changed to Fox Meyer Harris & acquired by National Intergroup, Inc.
Havens and Emerson—merged with Lawler, Matusky & Skelly to form Lawler-Havens, Inc.
HealthChicago, Inc.—acquired by Hamona, Inc.
Hemar Group—name changed to EduServ
Henry's Safety Supply—name changed to Safety Master Corporation & acquired by Strategic Distribution Inc.
Heurikon Corporation—acquired by Computer Products, Inc.
Hitachi Zosen Clearing, Inc.—name changed to Clearing International, Inc.
Homestead Products—acquired by Seattle Lighting Fixture Co.
Hub City Inc.—acquired by Regal-Beloit Corporation
Hudson International Conductors—acquired by Phelps Dodge Corporation
Hudson Valley Apple Products Company—name changed to Brooklyn Bottling Co.

I

Industrial Boiler Company—acquired by Aqua Chem, a subsidiary of Lyonnaise des Eaux S.A.
Institute for Scientific Information—acquired by Thompson Financial Service, a subsidiary of The Thompson Corporation
InterAmerican Zinc—acquired by IMCO Recycling
Invest West Financial Corporation—acquired by Pacifica Real Estate Group
Isidore & Paulson, Inc.—acquired by Warwick, Baker & Fiore, Inc.

K

Kenwood Dealer Group, Inc.—name changed to Kings Toyota Suzuki
Kimtron Corporation—name changed to Sherwood Corporation & acquired by Inkel Corp.
Klein Brothers Ltd.—acquired by ConAgra Trading Companies, a subsidiary of ConAgra, Inc.

L

L B International, Inc.—name changed to Leathers Best
Lamar Life Corporation—name changed to Capitol Street Corp.
Landegger Industries, Inc.—name changed to Black Clawson Co.
Leisure Arts, Inc.--acquired by Southern Progress Corporation, a subsidiary of Time Warner Inc.
Leone Enterprises—name changed to Aqua Purity Sentinel Services
Longwood Toyota—name changed to Bruce Rossmeyer's Toyotaland
John D. Lucas Printing Company—acquired by Collman Graphics, Inc.

M

Macrodyne Industries, Inc.—name changed to Phoenix International
The Management Group—name changed to Hostmark Management Group
Mari Hube Ltd.—name changed to Muscum Boutique Intercontinental, Ltd.
Martin Instruments Co.—merged into Martin Universal Design, Inc.
May Centers, Inc.—name changed to CenterMark Properties, Inc.
Merchants Distributors, Inc.—acquired by Alex Lee, Inc.
Michaels, Stern & Co.—name changed to Heather Crolie, Inc.
Micro Dynamics, Inc.—acquired by Herley Industries, Inc.
Mount Vernon Realty, Inc.—name changed to Weichert Realty, Inc. & acquired by Weichert Company
MultiQuip, Inc.—acquired by C Itoh & Co. Ltd.

N

National Business Systems, Inc.—name changed to SBN System Inc.
National Heritage, Inc.—acquired by Evergreen Healthcare Ltd.
Newspaper Printing Corp. Inc.—name changed to World Publishing Company
Norick Brothers, Inc.—name changed to Reynolds &

Reynolds Business Forms Division & merged with Reynolds & Reynolds Company
Northview Corporation—name changed to The Vagabond Inns
Northwestern Drug Company—acquired by The F. Dohmen Company

O

Officemax—acquired by K-Mart Corporation
Ohio Grain Company—acquired by Champaign Landmark
Oklahoma Publishing Company—acquired by Gaylord Entertainment Co.
Organizational Dynamics, Inc.—name changed to ODI

P

Peter Piper, Inc.—acquired by SIB Nominees, a subsidiary of The Bank of Tokyo
Pinkerton & Laws Co.—name changed to SAE-Pinkerton & Laws Inc.
Pixley Richards West, Inc.—name changed to Intesys Technologies
Pneumo Abex Holdings Co.—name changed to The Henley Group, Inc.
Pocahontas Food Group, Inc.—acquired by Performance Food Group, Inc.
Porteous Mitchel & Braun Company—acquired by The Dunlap Companies
S. Prawer & Co.—name changed to S.P.C. Transport
Primary Industries Corporation—acquired by Primary Industries Ltd.
Pritikin Programs, Inc.—acquired by The Quaker Oaks Company
Professional Lithographers—acquired by R.R. Donnelly & Sons, Company

R

R/K Agri Services, Inc.—name changed to Hydro/Kirby Agri Service, Inc.
R.R. & R.R. Evans Company—name changed to Brown Evans Company
Raybro Electric Supplies—acquired by Consolidated Electrical Distributors
William Recht Company—name changed to Durex Industries, Inc.
The Record Bar, Inc.—name changed to Super Club Music Corp.
Reflector Hardware Corporation—name changed to RHC/Spacemaster Corporation
Remy Martin Amerique, Inc.—name changed to Kuug Remy Cointreau Amerique, Inc.
Harry Rosenblatt & Sons, Inc.—name changed to Fortune Fashion
Rowe International Inc.—acquired by R I Holdings
Rubloff Real Estate & Capital—name changed to Orix Real Estate Equities, Inc.
The Russell Corporation—name changed to Food & Gas, Inc.

S

SGI Inc.—acquired by ERO Industries, Inc.
Sacramento Union Publishing—acquired by Twenty-First Century Publishing Co.
Sanel Auto Supply Associates—name changed to Automotive Supply Assoc., Inc.
Sargent-Sowell, Inc.—acquired by The SArgent-SOwell Company
The Schram Advertising Company—name changed to Temkin & Temkin
Scott's Food Stores, Inc.—acquired by SUPERVALV, INC.
Sea Nymph Inc.—acquired by Outboard Marine Corp.
Security Van Line, Inc.—acquired by Johnson Storage & Moving Company
Service Control Corp.—name changed to Western Linen Corp.
Sidal Aluminum Corp.—name changed to Hoogovens Aluminum Corp.
Dr. I.C. Smith Co. Inc.—acquired by Bergen Brunswig Corporation
South Bend Drug Co., Inc.—name changed to Health Care Distributors of Indiana, Inc.
Starmark, Inc.—acquired by Grant/Jacoby, Inc.
Stella D'Oro Biscuit Co.—acquired by The Nabisco Foods Group, a subsidiary of R.J.R. Nabisco Holdings Corp.
Summit Holding Company—name changed to United National Bank & acquired by United Bankshares

T

Techsteel, Inc.—acquired by W.C. Caye & Company, Inc.
Tower Records—acquired by MTS, Inc.
Townhouse Penthouse Industries, Inc.—name changed to Simmons Upholstered Furniture, Inc.
TransLogic Corporation—acquired by Thyssen AG
Trettco, Inc.—name changed to HDS Services
TrueForm Intimate Apparel—acquired by Maidenform, Inc.
Tuscany Kolcraft Industries—name changed to Creative Salon Furniture Inc.

U

U.S. Metal Container Company—name changed to Blitz U.S.A.
Union Equity Cooperative Exchange—acquired by Farmland Industries, Inc.

V

Van Munching & Co.—acquired by Heinekin NV
Vectron Labs, Inc.—acquired by Dover Corporation
Video Training Corporation—name changed to Resource, Inc.
Vinnell Corporation—acquired by BDM International, Inc.
Virginia Fibre Corporation—acquired by Greif Bros. Corp.

Vitarine Pharmaceuticals, Inc.—acquired by Eon Labs, Inc.
Volkart, Inc.—name changed to Paul Reinhart Inc, & acquired by Paul Reinhart AG

W

WW Engineering & Science Inc.—acquired by Summit Environmental Group
Frank Raymond Warren—name changed to Warren Properties
Watkins Manufacturing Corp.—acquired by Masco Corporation
Western Oil Tool & Manufacturing Co.—name changed to Wotco Inc.
Whiting Patterson Co.—acquired by American Envelope Company, a subsidiary of CC Industries, Inc.
Worldwide Volkswagon Corp.—acquired by Volkswagon of America, Inc., a subsidiary of Volkswagon AG

Public Stock Offerings

Companies Deleted Since Last Edition

COMPANY NAME	EXCHANGE
Affiliated Food Stores	NASDAQ
Alden Press	NASDAQ
Allied Clinical Laboratories	NASDAQ
American Healthcorp Inc.	OTC
Broadway & Seymour	NASDAQ
Buehler International Inc.	NYSE, Bo, MW & Ph
CRI, Inc.	NYSE
Chicago & North Western Transportation Company	NYSE
Dyersburg Fabrics Inc.	NYSE
ERO Industries, Inc.	NYSE
Electronic Tel Communication, Inc.	NASDAQ
Foodmaker, Inc.	NYSE
Greyhound Lines, Inc.	ASE
Harbor Bancorp	OTC
IBC Holding Corp.	NASDAQ
Infinity Broadcasting Corporation	NASDAQ
Kohl's Department Stores	NASDAQ
Lifetime Hoan Corp.	OTC
Morning Star Foods	NASDAQ
National Components, Inc.	NASDAQ
Old Dominion Freight Line, Inc.	NASDAQ
Salton/Maxim Housewares Group	NASDAQ
Sholodge, Inc.	OTC
Smart & Final	NYSE
SportsTown, Inc.	NASDAQ
The Taubman Company, Inc.	NYSE
Toastmaster, Inc.	NYSE
Tracor, Inc.	NASDAQ

Mergers, Acquisitions, Name Changes and Public Stock Offerings 1988-1992

A

ARC American Corp.—acquired by Consolidated Gold Fields plc
Admiral Cruises—merged into Royal Caribbean Cruise Ltd.
Advanced Logic Research, Inc.—now OTC
Advanced Systems Applications, Inc.—acquired by Policy Management Systems Corporation
Advanced Technology Inc.—acquired by Emhart Corp.
Aerovent, Inc.—acquired by Flakt AB, Stockholm, Sweden
Affholder, Inc.—now OTC
Albany International—now OTC
Alco Gravure Industries, Inc.—merged into Maxwell Communications
Aldix International Corporation—merged into Automatic Equipment Corporation
Alexander Proudfoot Co.—now London exchange
Allegheny Ludlum Steel—now OTC
Allied Broadcast Equipment—acquired by Harris Corp.
Allied Van Lines, Inc.—acquired by National Freight Consortium plc
Allomatic Products Company—acquired by Raytech Corporation
Altschiller Reitzfeld Inc.—acquired by Tracy-Locke
Alumax, Inc.—acquired by AMAX, Inc.
The Amalgamated Sugar Co.—acquired by Valhi, Inc.
Amerace Corporation—acquired by Great American Management & Investment
Amarlite Architectural Co.—acquired by Pony Industries, Inc.
American Bakeries Company—merged into Interstate Bakeries Corporation
American Bank Stationery Co.—merged with MB Group plc
American Bros. Co.—acquired by Outokumpu Oy, Helsinki Finland
American Cablesystems—now ASE
American Consumers Inc.—now OTC
American Forest Products Company—acquired by Georgia-Pacific Corporation
American Natural Beverage Co.—acquired by Seagram Beverage Company
American Nursing Resources—acquired by Kimberly Nursing Care
American Recreation Products, Inc.—acquired by Kellwood Company
American Rice—now OTC
American Seaway Foods Inc.—acquired by Riser Foods Inc.
Ammco Tools, Inc.—acquired by Danaher Corporation
AMSCO International, Inc.—now NYSE & ASE
Amscomatic, Inc.—acquired by All-Pak Machinery Systems, Inc.
Analytics Incorporated—acquired by Computer Science Corporation
Anchor Packaging Co.—acquired by Pony Industries Inc.
Anderson Communications Companies, Inc.—acquired by Thompson Recruitment Adv. Inc.
Anvil Products, Inc.—acquired by Tyco Laboratories, Inc.
Applied Engineering Co.—acquired by Jacobs Engineering Group
Applied Powers Inc.—now OTC
Aquidneck Data Corp.—acquired by Eastman Kodak Company
Arkansas Freightways Corporation—now NASDAQ
Arrow Industries, Inc.—acquired by ConAgra, Inc.
Arundel Asphalt Products, Inc.—acquired by Genstar Corporation
Arvey Corp.—acquired by International Paper Co.
Aspen Airways, Inc.—acquired by Air Wis Services, Inc.
Astro Wire & Cable Corporation—acquired by Carol Cable Co.
Atlanta Dairies Co-Operative Inc.—acquired by Pet Dairy
Audiovox—now OTC
Avondale Industries Inc.—now OTC
Arthur Young—merged into Ernst & Young

B

B&B International Holdings, Inc.—now NASDAQ
BEI Electronics, Inc.—now NASDAQ
BH Holding—acquired by PNC Financial Corp.
Backer & Spielvogel—merged with Ted Bates
L.G. Balfour Co., Inc.—acquired by Town & Country Corporation
Ball Industries—acquired by W.W. Grainger, Inc.
B-Bar-B, Inc.—acquired by Liqui-Box Corporation
Barber-Colman Co.—acquired by Siebe plc
Beatrice Company—acquired by ConAgra, Inc.
Berkshire Furniture Co.—acquired by Leggett-Platt
Arnold Bernhard & Co.—now OTC
L.M. Berry & Co.—acquired by BellSouth Corp.
Billboard Publications—acquired by Affiliated Publications
Billings & Gage Mfg. Co.—acquired by Diamond Crystal Specialty Foods Inc.
Billy The Kid, inc.—acquired by Unilever plc
Blake Steel Service Inc.—acquired by Klockner Namasco Co.
Blue Bird Baking Co.—merged into Rich Products Corp.
Botto, Roessner, Horne & Messinger—acquired by Ketchum Communications
Bresler's 33 Flavors Inc.—acquired by Oberweis Dairy, Inc.
Bright of America, Inc.—acquired by Russ Berrie and Company, Inc.
Broughton Foods Co.—now OTC
Brudi, Inc.—acquired by Tredagar Industries
Budget Rent-a-Car—now OTC

Buitoni Foods Corporation—acquired by Carnation Company
Burdick Corp.—acquired by Siemens Medical Systems Inc.
Burns & McDonnell Energy—now OTC
Burrel Belting Company—acquired by Verseidog, Krefeld, Federal Republic of Germany
Byer & Bowman Advertising Agency, Inc.—acquired by Homeroff/Milenthall

C

CPB—now OTC
Cablec Corporation—acquired by BICC plc (UK)
Cabletron, Inc.—now NYSE
California Micro Solutions d/b/a Computerland of San Francisco—merged into Infomax, Inc.
Carey-McFall Corporation—acquired by Springs Industries
Carnival Cruise Lines—now OTC
Carolina Mill, Inc.—now OTC
Caron International—acquired by Great American Management & Investment
The Ceco Corporation—merged into H.H. Robertson Corporation
Cedar Fair Limited Partnership—now NYSE
Cellu-Craft Inc.—acquired by Alusuisse
Challenger Electrical Equipment Corp.—acquired by Westinghouse Electric Corporation
Charms Co.—acquired by Tootsie Roll Co.
Chartway Technologies—acquired by ICF Information Technology, Inc.
Chase Packaging Corporation—acquired by Union Camp
Chem-Trend Incorporated—acquired by Burmah Oil Trading Limited
Cherokee Group—now OTC
B.C. Christopher & Co.—acquired by Fahenstock Co., Inc.
Citrus Central, Inc.—acquired by Crown Cork & Seal Co., Inc.
Coca-Coca Bottling or Arkansas—acquired by Coca-Cola Enterprises, Inc.
Coca Cola/Dr Pepper Bottling Co. of Memphis—acquired by Coca-Cola Enterprises
Cohen & Greenbaum Inc.—acquired by BBDO
Collier-Jackson Inc.—acquired by H & R Block Inc.
Collingwood Grain, Inc.—acquired by Archer Daniels Midland Company
Comart Associates Inc.—acquired by KLP Group plc
Communications Corporation of America—acquired by Contel Customer Support, Inc.
Computer Maintenance—now OTC
Computer Systems Research, Inc.—acquired by Macmillan/McGraw-Hill School Publishing Company
Consolidated Coatings Corp.—acquired by RPM, Inc.
Continental Can Company—acquired by Crown Cork & Seal Co., Inc.
Con-Way Eastern Express Inc.—acquired by Freightway Company
Creative Industries Group, Inc.—acquired by Mosco Industries, Inc.

D

Dart Drugs—now OTC
Data Technology Corp.—now OTC
Dave Cook Sporting Goods Co.—merged into Gart Brothers, a sub. of Pacific Enterprises
Dayton Extruded Plastics—now OTC
Denny's—acquired by TW Services, Inc.
DeVry Institutes—now OTC
Digital Research, Inc.—acquired by Novell Inc.
Dining & Kitchen Administration Inc. d/b/a Daka Inc.—acquired by Fuddruckers, Inc.
Dinwiddie Construction Co.—acquired by Fletcher Construction Co. of New Zealand
Distribix, Inc.—acquired by Paper Corporation of America a sub of Alco Standard Corporation
Dixie Container Corp.—acquired by Packaging Corporation of America
Dixie Electronics—acquired by NCH Inc.
Dixie Furniture Co.—acquired by Masco Corp.
Dixon Paper Co.—acquired by International Paper Co.
Doelz—acquired by Timplex/Unisys
Doktor Pet Centers, Inc.—acquired by American Equine Products
Dollar Rent A Car Systems, Inc.—acquired by Chrysler Corporation
Donnelly Corporation—now ASE
Doubleday & Co.—acquired by Bertelsman Publishing Group, Inc.
Robert Douglass Associates—name changed to The Douglas Group & merged with Deloitte Haskins and Sells
Duracell International, Inc.—now NYSE
Drug Emporium—now OTC
Dryden Oil of New England—acquired by Castrol Oil Company
R.G. Dun Cigar Corp.—merged into National Cigar Corporation

E

E-Z Serve, Inc.—acquired by Harken Oil & Gas Inc.
Eastex Energy, Inc.—now OTC
Eberhard Faber, Inc.—merged into Faber/Castell Corp.
Econo Lodges of America, Inc.—acquired by Choice Hotels International
Eesco, Inc.—acquired by Bunzi Corporation
Einson Freeman, Inc.—acquired by WPP Group plc
Ekco Housewares, Inc.—acquired by Centronics Inc.
El International Incorporated—acquired NUS Corporation
El Paso Products Co.—acquired by Roxene Products
Electrical Equipment Co.—merged into Flori Corp.
Elgin National Industries, Inc.—acquired by The Jupiter Corp.

The Enro Shirt Company, Inc.—merged into The Apparel Group, Ltd.
Ephron, Raboy & Tsao—acquired by Bergelt Litchfield Raboy & Tsao Inc.
Epsilon—now OTC
Essef Corp.—now OTC
Everfresh Juice Co.—acquired by John Labatt of Canada
Exide Electronics, Inc.—now NASDAQ

F

FL Industries, Inc.—acquired by Thomas & Betts Corporation
FLM Building Products, Inc.—acquired by Meyer International Forest Products Limited
Famolare—acquired by U.S. Shoe Corp.
Fastenal Co.—now OTC
Favorite Plastic Corp.—acquired by Sportech Corporation
Feature Enterprises Inc.—acquired by Towne & Country Linen Corp.
Federal-Cartridge Co.—acquired by Pentair, Inc.
Fiberchem, Inc.—acquired by M.A. Hanna Company
Fifth Season Travel—acquired by the Getz Corp.
First Brands—now NYSE
First National Supermarkets Inc.—acquired by Koninklyke Ahold NV
Fletcher Oil & Refining—acquired by Honde Oil & Gas Co.
Flextronics, Inc.—now OTC
Font & Vaamonde Associates, Inc.—acquired by Grey Advertising, Inc.
Formica Corp.—now NYSE
Fox & Associates of New York—acquired by Horizon Media, Inc.
Frasse-Bassett, Inc.—acquired by U.S. Steel Supply, Inc.
Frawley Corp.—now PSE
Charles Freihofer Baking Co., Inc.—acquired by General Foods Corp.
Frontier Oil Corporation—acquired by Wainoso Oil Corporation
Frost Brothers, Inc.—merged into Sakowitz, Inc.
Fruehauf Corporation—now NYSE

G

GNC Energy Corporation—now OTC
The GT Group—acquired by Carey Winston Co.
Garst Seed Co.—acquired by ICI Agricultural
Geers Gross Advertising Inc.—acquired by McCann-Erickson Worldwide
Gehl Company—now OTC
Gemini Research—acquired by Lams Research Corporation
Giant Industries, Inc.—now NYSE
Gilmore Steel Corporation—now ASE
Girvin, Conrad, Girvin—merged into DDB Needham
Goal Systems International, Inc.—now NASDAQ
Gold Bond-Good Humor Ice Cream, Inc.—acquired by Thomas J. Lipton Company, a subsidiary of Unilever Group
Goldome Federal Savings Bank—now OTC
Government Technology Services, Inc.—now NASDAQ
Go-Video, Inc.—now OTC
Granite Construction Incorporated—now NASDAQ
Grant Oil Country Tubular Corporation—now NASDAQ
Gray & Rogers, Inc.—acquired by Foote, Cone & Belding Communications, Inc.
Graybow-Daniels Company—acquired by United Westburne
Greenstone Rabasca Roberts Inc.—now NASDAQ
Group 243 Incorporated—acquired by Ross Roy Group, Inc.
Guild Wineries & Distilleries—acquired by Canadaigua Wine Company
S. Gumpert Co., Inc.—acquired by Rich Products Inc.

H

HHB Systems, Inc.—now OTC
Hall Financial Group—now NYSE
Health-Tex Inc.—acquired by VF Corporation
Healthtrust, Inc.—now NYSE
Heckthorn Mfg. Co.—acquired by 3900 Corporation
The Higbee Co.—acquired by Dillard Dept. Stores Inc.
Holiday of Orlando, Inc.—now OTC
Holladay Tyler Printing Corp.—acquired by Southam Ltd., Canada
Holm Industries Inc.—acquired by The Standard Products Co.
Holmberg Electronics Corporation—acquired by Thomas & Betts Corporation
Homart Development Co.—acquired by Coldwell-Banker
Homedco Group, Inc.—now NYSE
Homer & Durham—merged with Lowe Tucker Metcalf, Inc.
Hooker U.S. Holdings, Ltd.—now on Sydney exchange
Houston Wire & Cable Distribution—acquired by ALLTEL Corporation

I

IDEX Corporation—now NYSE
Illinois Coil Spring Co.—merged into Kokomo Spring Company, Inc.
Imperial Holly Corp.—now AMEX
Incom International, Inc.—merged into IMO Delaval
Indiana Farm Bureau Cooperative Association, Inc.—acquired by The Maxwell Communication Corporation plc
Industrial Components—acquired by Sterling Electronics Corporation
Ingles Markets, Inc.—now OTC
Inspeech, Inc.—now OTC
Intermec South Inc.—acquired by Intermec Corporation
International Tool & Supply Co.—acquired by Ensco Company

J

J & J Snack Foods Corp.—now OTC
Jackson Jordan, Inc.—acquired by Charter Consolidated
Jarl Extrusions, Inc.—acquired by Allan Aluminum Corporation
Javelin Software Corporation—acquired by Information Resources, Inc.
Jepson Corp.—now NYSE
Johnson Hill's, Inc.—acquired by Kline Brothers Co.
Johnson March Corp.—acquired by Laporte Industries (Holdings) plc
Jones Electric of Sanford, Inc.—merged into Southern Electric Supply Company, Inc.

K

Keystone Cement Co.—acquired by Giant Group, Ltd.
King Bearing, Inc.—acquired by Bearings, Inc.
King Broadcasting Co.—merged into Providence Journal Company
Kornhauser & Calene Inc.—merged into Partners & Shevak, Inc.
Kropp Forge Co.—acquired by TIC Investment Corp.
Kroy Inc.—acquired by Heller Financial
Kusan, Inc.—merged into Stolle Corporation

L

A. Lakin & Sons—acquired by Southwestern General
Lamina, Inc.—acquired by Anchor Machine & Manufacturing Ltd.
Lawyers Cooperative—acquired by The Thomson Corporation
Layton Label Manufacturing Company—acquired by Engraph, Inc.
Lechters, Inc.—now OTC
Leslie Company—acquired by Watts Industries, Inc.
Leslie Paper—acquired by International Paper
Letco, Inc.—acquired by Builders Design, Inc.
Alfred M. Lewis, Inc.—acquired by The Price Co.
Lily of France—acquired by Bestforms
Logo Paris—acquired by Essilor Company
Luckie & Forney, Inc.—merged into Tucker Wayne/Luckie Co.
Lufkin Industries, Inc.—now NASDAQ
Lyons Group, Inc.—acquired by Sherwin Williams

M

MMR Holding Corporation—now OTC
MPI, Incorporated—acquired by Leggett & Platt
MRI Advertising—merged into McAdams Richman & Ong
Magna Copper Co.—now OTC
Magnetek, Inc.—now NYSE
Malone & Hyde, Inc.—acquired by The Fleming Cos.
Mann Theaters—acquired by Gulf + Western
Marine Group, Inc.—acquired by Brunswick Corp.
Marquette Electronics, Inc.—now NASDAQ
Mattatuck Manufacturing Co.—acquired by Teleflex, Inc.
Maynard Electronics—acquired by Archive Corporation
Mayville Metal Products—acquired by Connell Ltd. Partnership
McCaw Cellular Communications—now OTC
McClatchey Newspapers, Inc.—now ASE
McGarvey Coffee, Inc.—acquired by Sara Lee Corporation
McLane Company—acquired by Wal-Mart Stores, Inc.
McLouth Steel Products—acquired by Tang Industries
Meyers Arnold Company—merged into Upton Department Stores
Miami Carey Corp.—acquired by NuTone, Inc.
Microage, Inc.—now OTC
Micropolis Corp.—now OTC
Microscience International Corporation—now NASDAQ
Microtel, Inc.—merged into Advanced Telecommunications
Microwave Products of America Inc.—acquired by Litton Industries
Midwest Communications Corp.—now OTC
Midwest Grain Products, Inc.—now OTC
Milprint, Inc.—acquired by Bemis Company, Inc.
Mini Mart, Inc.—acquired by Dillon Cos. Inc. of The Kroger Co.
Mr. Coffee—now OTC
Monumental Paper Company—acquired by Paper Corporation of America
Morris Creameries, Inc.—merged into Country Lake Foods
Moore & Munger, Inc.—acquired by Rosow & Company, Inc.
Monogram Models, Inc.—now ASE
Moorco International, Inc.—now NASDAQ
Mortell Co.—acquired by Essex Chemical
Mueller Co.—acquired by Tyco Laboratories, Inc.
Multiple Technologies Corp.—acquired by Nynex Corporation

N

NAAS Foods, Inc.—acquired by RHM Holding Co., United Kingdom
Nasco Holdings, Inc.—acquired by Innovo
The National Guardian Corporation—acquired by LEP Group plc
National Medical Care, Inc.—acquired by W.R. Grace & Co.
Nes, Inc.—merged into Weschler Instruments
Neslab Instruments, Inc.—acquired by Life Sciences International plc
Network Publishing Company—acquired by News America Publishing, Inc.
New Hampshire Ball Bearings, Inc.—acquired by Minebea Co. Ltd.
New Jersey Publishing—merged into Gannett Company Directories of New Jersey
Newport Steel Corporation—now ASE
The J.M. Ney Company—acquired by Andersen Group, Inc.

Northern Supply Co., Inc.—merged into Auto Wares, Inc.
Nova Publishing Co.—merged with Worchester County Newspapers
Nu-West, Inc.—now OTC
The Nucleus, Inc.—acquired by UEL plc
Nutech, Inc.—acquired by Pacific Nuclear Systems

O

Office Depot—now OTC
Oil Recovery Systems—now OTC
Outlet Communications—now OTC
Outlook Graphics—now NASDAQ

P

PEI Associates Inc.—acquired by IT Corp.
Palm Beach Holdings, Inc.—acquired by Crystal Brands, Inc.
Pamida Holdings Corporation—now ASE & Midwest Stock exchange
Pat Fashions Industries, Inc.—now ASE
Patrick Media Group—acquired by General Electric Capital Corporation
The W.M. Pattison Supply Co.—acquired by W.W. Grainger, Inc.
Penn Traffic Company—now OTC
Pester Marketing Co.—acquired by The Coastal Corp.
Pet Dairy—now on NYSE
Pierre Frozen Foods, Inc.—acquired by Hudson Foods, Inc.
Piggly Wiggly Southern—acquired by Bruno's, Inc.
Pillsbury Chemical & Oil, Inc.—acquired by Novamox USA
Pinkerton's, Inc.—now OTC
Polaris Industries, Inc.—now ASE
Pony Industries, Inc.—acquired by Baker Hughes Incorporated
Porter Paint Co.—acquired by Portor Courtaulds Coating Inc.
Preferred Risk Life—now OTC
Pretty Neat Products Corp.—acquired by Goody Products, Inc.
Price Pfister, Inc.—now OTC
ride Refining, Inc.—now NYSE
incess Hotels International, Inc.—now London & Tokyo exchanges
ulse Engineering, Inc.—now OTC

Q

Quality Steel Corp.—acquired by All Meadows Co.
Quintron Corporation—acquired by Glenayre Electronics, Ltd.

R

RJR Nabisco Holdings Corporation—now NYSE
Ralph & Kacoo's Restaurant of Bluebonnet—acquired by Piccadilly Cafeterias, Inc.
The Reader's Digest Association, Inc.—now NYSE
Red Owl Stores, Inc.—acquired by Supervalu North Annex
Reeves Brothers, Inc.—acquired by Schick Inc.
Relay Communications—acquired by Microcom, Inc.
Relief Printing Corp.—acquired by Taylor Corp.
Restaurant Associates Industries, Inc.—acquired by Kyotaru Co., Ltd., Japan
Revell, Inc.—now ASE
Rex Plastics, Inc.—now NYSE
Riedel International—now OTC
Rini Supermarkets, Inc.—merged into Riser Foods, Inc.
Robec, Inc.—now NASDAQ
Rocky Rococo Pizza Corp.—acquired by Public Storage, Inc.
Ross Systems, Inc.—now NYSE
Royal Appliance Mfg. Co.—now NASDAQ

S

Saalfeld Paper Corp.—acquired by International Paper Co.
Safeway, Inc.—now NYSE
St. Joe Paper Company—now OTC
Sanderson Farms—now OTC
Sandvik, Inc.—now on Sweden & London exchanges
John B. Sanfilippo & Son, Inc.—now NASDAQ
Schlegel Corporation—now part of BTR plc, London
Schlott Realtors—acquired by Coldwell Banker Real Estate
Thomas A. Schutz—merged with The Omnicom Group
Scripps Howard—now OTC
Seamco,Inc.—acquired by Sandviks Process Systems
Seitz Foods, Inc.—acquired by Sara Lee Corp.
Semoran Management Corporation—acquired by Pizza Hut
Seneca Balance, Inc.—acquired by Intrex, Inc.
Service America Corporation—now OTC
Sevenson Environmental Services, Inc.—now NASDAQ
The Sharper Image—now OTC
The Shaw-Walker Company—acquired by Westinghouse Electric Corporation
Simon Brothers, Inc.—acquired by Clark Foodservice Corp.
Six Flags Corporation—acquired by Time Warner, Inc.
Sloan Paper Co.—acquired by Alco Standard Corporation
Smith Barney, Inc.—acquired by Primerica
Snappy Care Rental, Inc.—acquired by Thrifty Care Rental, Inc.
Softsel Computer Products, Inc.—now OTC
Solectron—now OTC
The Southland Corporation—now NASDAQ
Southwestern Ohio Steel—acquired by Armco Inc.
Stanwich Industries—now OTC
Stern-Leach Company—acquired by Cookson America, Inc.
The Stop & Shop Companies, Inc.—now NYSE
Summagraphics Corp.—now OTC
Sun Distributors—now NYSE
Sundor Brands, Inc.—acquired by Procter & Gamble
Supracote—acquired by The Broken Hill Proprietary

Company
Swift Transportation Corporation—now OTC

T

Tanner Southwest—acquired by Ashland Oil
Tecnol, Inc.—now NASDAQ
Telco Research Corp.—acquired by Nynex Corp.
Telecom*USA—merged into MCI Communications Corp.
Temporaries, Inc.—acquired by Blue Arrow plc
Don Tennant Co., Inc.—merged into Noble Communications Co.
Terminix International—acquired by Service Master
Tessco—acquired by Code-Alarm, Inc.
Texas Oil & Chemical Corp.—acquired by Arabian Shield Development Co.
Thetford Systems, Inc.—acquired by The Dyson-Kissner-Moran Corp.
Thrift Rent-a-Car—now OTC
Ticor Title Insurance Company of California—acquired by Chicago Title & Trust of Alleghany Corporation
The Timberland Co.—now NYSE
The Times Journal Company—acquired by The Gannett Co.
Topps Chewing Gum, Inc.—now OTC
The Trailways Corp.—acquired by GLI Holdings
Trax Holding Company, Inc.—acquired by Marubeni Corporation
Tri Data Systems, Inc.—merged into Avatar Corporation
Tudor Engineering Company—acquired by American Capital & Research Corp.

U

Union Machinery, Inc.—acquired by AMF, Inc.
Union National Life Insurance Company—acquired by United Companies of America
Uniroyal Goodrich Tire Co.—acquired by Michelin Tire Group
U.S. Plywood—acquired by Georgia Pacific
U.S. Robotics—now NASDAQ
Unitog Company—now OTC
University Industries—now NYSE
Uno Restaurants, Inc.—now ASE
Utica-Duxbak Corp.—acquired by Duxbak, Inc.

V

Valley Grain Products, Inc.—acquired by Archer Daniels Midland Company (ADM)
Verifone, Inc.—now OTC
Vermont Castings, Inc.—acquired by PacifiCorp
Vinson Supply Co.—acquired by Sammons Enterprises
Vital Signs, Inc.—now NASDAQ
Vonnegut Industrial Products, Inc.—acquired by W.W. Grainger, Inc.
The Vons Companies, Inc.—now NYSE

W

WLR Foods, Inc.—now NASDAQ
Wabash National Corporation—now NYSE
Warnaco, Inc.—now NYSE
Weaver Bros., Inc.—merged into Bank One Mortgage Corp.
Weirton Steel—now NYSE
West Indies Advertising Co.—acquired by Grey Advertising Co.
Whiteford Transport Systems, Inc.—merged into Lend Lease Trucks, Inc.
Williams & Company, Inc.—acquired by CAWSL Corp.
Wilson & George Meyer & Co.—acquired by Norsk Hydro A/S, Oslo, Norway
W.K.P. Wilson & Son, Inc.—acquired by Corroon & Black
Windmere Corp.—now OTC

X

Xilinx, Inc.—now OTC
Xscribe Corp.—now OTC

Z

Zions Co-Operative Mercantile Institution—now OTC
Zoom Telephonics, Inc.—now NASDAQ

PUT YOUR HANDS ON VITAL

BUSINESS INFORMATION YOU

WON'T FIND IN ANY ANNUAL REPORT —

WITH THE MOST COMPREHENSIVE

DATABASE OF PRIVATELY HELD

COMPANIES IN THE U.S.

121 Chanlon Road • New Providence, New Jersey 07974
1-800-521-8110

The Only Comprehensive Source for Facts from Inside U.S. Private Companies.

Now Available on Database!

Look inside the corporate suite of nearly 8,000 privately held businesses and 9,500 subsidiaries, divisions and affiliates with the Directory of Corporate Affiliations/U.S. Private database. Unlike state business directories and other non-discriminating directories, the foundation for this important database is comprehensive information on a *select* group of companies. With this definitive and well-defined database, you can:

- Access basic business and financial data on the top privately held companies, including the *Forbes* 400, the 1,000 largest private businesses nationwide, and the top 100 companies in major urban markets.
- Make contact with more than 30,000 prime executives and decision makers.
- Locate solid sales leads, prospective clients and new investment opportunities within private companies.

If these companies were public, you could get *some* of this information from reading their annual reports. But there's only one way to access *all* the facts on privately held companies — the Directory of Corporate Affiliations/ U.S. Private database.

Make more informed business decisions and extend your understanding of the total U.S. corporate environment with the Directory of Corporate Affiliations/U.S. Private database — the discriminating source for solid, comprehensive electronic intelligence from inside America's private executive boardrooms.

1993

DIRECTORY OF CORPORATE AFFILIATIONS

This edition of the *Directory of Corporate Affiliations: U.S. Private Companies* was prepared by National Register Publishing's Database Publishing Group in collaboration with the Publications Systems Department.

Managing Editor: Thomas Bachmann
Senior Editor: Brian-Kent Proffitt
Senior Production Editor: Kerrie Beckner
Associate Editor: Sharon B. Simon
Contributing Editor: Jan Badamo
Assistant Editors: Lori Davidson, Lainie M. Herman
Research: Judy Redel, Director; Claudette Stecher, Senior Research Editor; Patricia Flinsch, Associate Research Editor; John Platt, Assistant Research Editor
Editorial Systems: John Roney, Director; Gary Aiello, Manager; Robert Grant, Project Leader; Lynne Mauro, Senior Programmer Analyst; Victoria Mauer, Programmer; Daniel Benner, Consultant

Senior Vice President, Database Publishing Group: Peter Simon
Publisher: Kathy Banks
Director, Database Planning: Dean Hollister
Editorial Director: Stephen L. Torpie

INDEX OF COMPANY NAMES

A

A BAR A RANCH—See The Gates Corporation, pg. 445
A+ PUBLISHING—See International Data Group, pg. 576
A & A ASSOCIATES—See Zimmerman Holdings, Inc., pg. 1220
A & A MANUFACTURING CO., pg. 1
A & E BUSINESS PRODUCTS—See Taylor Corporation, pg. 1081
A & E STORES, INC., pg. 1
A-1 TRANSMISSIONS—See Cottman Transmission Systems, Inc., pg. 288
A & S TRIBAL INDUSTRIES, pg. 1
A & W FOODS, INC., pg. 1
A & W RESTAURANTS, INC., pg. 1
A & Z HAYWARD, INC., pg. 1
A A CATER TRUCK MANUFACTURING COMPANY, INC., pg. 1
AA JAPAN CO.—See American Appraisal Associates, Inc., pg. 48
AAA PLUMBING POTTERY CORP.—See Gerber Plumbing Fixtures Corporation, pg. 454
AAI INTERNATIONAL LTD.—See Datron Incorporated, pg. 317
AAL CAPITAL MANAGEMENT CORP.—See Aid Association For Lutherans, pg. 26
AAL DISTRIBUTORS INC.—See Aid Association For Lutherans, pg. 26
A.B. DATA, LTD., pg. 1
A-B EMBLEM DIV. OF CONRAD INDUSTRIES, INC., pg. 2
AB SONIC INTERNATIONAL APS—See Dukane Corporation, pg. 352
ABB ENVIRONMENTAL SYSTEMS, pg. 2
A B C APPLIANCE INC., pg. 2
ABC SUPPLY COMPANY, INC., pg. 2
ABC TRANSPORTATION CO.—See American Buildings Co., pg. 50
ABI FOOD SERVICES, INC.—See Coca Cola Bottling Co. United, Inc., pg. 258
ABI MANAGEMENT, INC.—See American Financial Corporation, pg. 53
ABI NATIONAL ACCOUNTS—See American Business Information, Inc., pg. 50
ABI NATIONAL ACCOUNTS—See American Business Information, Inc., pg. 50
ABI NATIONAL ACCOUNTS—See American Business Information, Inc., pg. 50
ABI NATIONAL ACCOUNTS—See American Business Information, Inc., pg. 50
ABI NATIONAL ACCOUNTS—See American Business Information, Inc., pg. 50
A.B.P. MIDWEST, INC., pg. 2
ABS INDUSTRIAL VERIFICATION, INC.—See American Bureau of Shipping, pg. 50
AC LEASING CORPORATION—See Action Equipment, pg. 14
ACF INDUSTRIES, INC.—See Icahn & Co., Inc., pg. 561
ACFC CORPORATE FINANCE LIMITED—See Metropolitan Life Insurance Co., pg. 745
ACI FINANCIAL CORP., pg. 2
ACL TECHNOLOGIES, pg. 2
ACO INC., pg. 2
ACR INDUSTRIES INC., pg. 2
ACR MECHANICAL CORPORATION, pg. 2
A.D. CONTROLS—See Synergism, Inc., pg. 1070
AD PLASTICS LTD.—See Dentsply International Inc., pg. 330
ADD, INC.—See Journal Communications Inc., pg. 607
A-DEC, INC., pg. 1
ADI WAREHOUSE DIVISION, CARQUEST CORP.—See Carquest Corporation, pg. 224
ADL MANAGEMENT EDUCATION INSTITUTE, INC.—See Arthur D. Little, Inc., pg. 678
ADS/TMP WORLDWIDE—See TMP Worldwide, Inc., pg. 1073
ADV MARKETING GROUP, INC., pg. 2
A. E. DEVELOPMENT CORP.—See McLaughlin Gormley King Company, pg. 731
A-E DIVISION—See Central Allied Enterprises, pg. 232
AEA, INC., pg. 3
AEA INC./AUTO PARTS—See AEA, Inc., pg. 3
AEA OF COLUMBIA—See AEA, Inc., pg. 3
AEA OF RALEIGH—See AEA, Inc., pg. 3
AEC, pg. 3
AEC, INC.—See Sterling, Inc., pg. 1047
AEI HOLDING CO., INC., pg. 3
AES—See Eastern Technologies Ltd, pg. 364
AFG GLASS INC.—See AFG Industries, Inc., pg. 4
AFG INDUSTRIES, INC., pg. 3
AFG INTERNATIONAL, INC.—See AFG Industries, Inc., pg. 3
AFI EXPORT, INC.—See JMB Realty Corporation, pg. 585
AFS INSURANCE SERVICES, INC.—See Associated Food Stores Inc., pg. 89
A-G CO-OP CREAMERY, pg. 4
AG COMPONENTS DIV.—See Weasler Engineering Inc., pg. 1169
AGCO CORPORATION—See AGCO Inc., pg. 4
AGCO INC., pg. 4
AGCO MANUFACTURING GROUP—See AGCO Inc., pg. 4
AGI INC., pg. 4
AGR INTERNATIONAL, INC., pg. 4
AGSCO, INC., pg. 4
AIM COMMUNICATIONS—See Leo Burnett Company, Inc., pg. 192
AJC INTERNATIONAL, INC., pg. 4
A J M PACKAGING CORPORATION, pg. 4
A K H COMPANY, INC., pg. 4
A.L E. SYSTEMS, INC.—See Berwind Corporation, pg. 145
ALP/FREDDY'S, pg. 4
A & M ASSOCIATES, INC.—See Amerco, A Nevada Corporation, pg. 48
AM ENTERTAINMENT—See Allied Advertising Agency, pg. 37
AM GENERAL CORPORATION—See Renco Group, pg. 926
AM GENERAL CORPORATION—See Renco Group, pg. 926
AM GENERAL CORPORATION—See Renco Group, pg. 926
AM GENERAL CORPORATION—See Renco Group, pg. 926
AM GENERAL CORPORATION—See Renco Group, pg. 926
AM GENERAL CORPORATION—See Renco Group, pg. 926
AM REAL CORP.—See Insignia Financial Group, Inc., pg. 571
AMA LEO BURNETT—See Leo Burnett Company, Inc., pg. 192
A-MARK FINANCIAL, pg. 1
AMC—See Associated Merchandising Corp., pg. 91
AMD INDUSTRIES INC., pg. 5
AMF AZALEA BOWL—See William H. Goodwin Trust, pg. 471
AMF BAKERY SYSTEMS, pg. 5
AMF BOWLING CENTERS INC.—See William H. Goodwin Trust, pg. 471
AMF BOWLING CENTERS INC.—See William H. Goodwin Trust, pg. 471
AMF LANG'S BOWLARAMA INC.—See William H. Goodwin Trust, pg. 471
AMGRO, INC.—See All America Financial, pg. 34
AMI INDUSTRIES, INC., pg. 5
AMPI INVESTMENT CORP.—See Associated Milk Producers, Inc., pg. 91
AMPI RESEARCH CORP.—See Associated Milk Producers, Inc., pg. 91
AMPI VENTURE, INC.—See Associated Milk Producers, Inc., pg. 91
AMR (AUDIO MEDIA RESEARCH)—See Peavey Electronic Corp., pg. 854
AMSPEC CHEMICAL CORPORATION, pg. 5
AMW INDUSTRIES INC.—See Harbour Group Ltd., pg. 507
A & N LEASING—See Service Motor Company, pg. 992
ANS INSURANCE AGENCY—See American SelfCare Corporation, pg. 61
AP PARTS MANUFACTURING COMPANY—See Charter House Group, pg. 240
AP TECHNOLOGY MANAGEMENT INC.—See Adolfson & Peterson, Inc., pg. 18
A-P-A TRANSPORT CORP., pg. 5
APG SECURITY, INC., pg. 5
API GROUP INC., pg. 5
API, INC.—See JMB Realty Corporation, pg. 585
APPX SOFTWARE—See Kennedy Associates, pg. 623
A.P.S., INC., pg. 5
A.P.S. SUPPLY, INC.—See A.P.S., Inc., pg. 5
AQHI, INC., pg. 5
ARA BELGIUM, S.A.—See ARA Group, pg. 7
ARA/CORY REFRESHMENT SERVICES, INC.—See ARA Group, pg. 6
ARA ENVIRONMENTAL SERVICES, INC.—See ARA Group, pg. 6
ARA EUROPE HEADQUARTERS—See ARA Group, pg. 7
ARA FOOD SERVICES, LTD.—See ARA Group, pg. 7
ARA GROUP, pg. 5
ARA HEALTHCARE NUTRITION SERVICES, INC.—See ARA Group, pg. 6
ARA LEISURE CONVENTION SERVICES, INC.—See ARA Group, pg. 6
ARA LEISURE SERVICES GROUP, FLORIDA—See ARA Group, pg. 6
ARA LEISURE SERVICES, HAWTHORNE RACE COURSE—See ARA Group, pg. 6
ARA LEISURE SERVICES, INC.—See ARA Group, pg. 6
ARA LEISURE SERVICES, NEW ORLEANS CONVENTION CENTER—See ARA Group, pg. 6
ARA LEISURE SERVICES OF TEXAS, INC.—See ARA Group, pg. 6
ARA LEISURE SERVICES, RIVERGATE—See ARA Group, pg. 6
ARA LEISURE SERVICES, SOLDIER FIELD—See ARA Group, pg. 6
ARA LEISURE SERVICES, WRIGLEY FIELD—See ARA Group, pg. 6
ARA MAGAZINE & BOOK DIVISION, INC.—See ARA Group, pg. 6
ARA N.V.—See ARA Group, pg. 7
ARA SERVICES, GMBH—See ARA Group, pg. 7
ARA SERVICES, INC.—See ARA Group, pg. 5
ARA SERVICES, JOHN HANCOCK CENTER—See ARA Group, pg. 6
ARA SERVICES, LOYOLA UNIVERSITY—See ARA Group, pg. 6
ARA SERVICES, LTD.—See ARA Group, pg. 7
ARA SERVICES OF TEXAS, INC.—See ARA Group, pg. 6
ARA SERVICES, ROSEMONT HORIZON—See ARA Group, pg. 6
ARA SERVICES, S.A.—See ARA Group, pg. 7
ARA VENDING SERVICES LTD.—See ARA Group, pg. 7
ARA VIRGINIA SKY-LINE CO., INC.—See ARA Group, pg. 6
ASA PROPERTIES HAWAII INC.—See Persis Corporation, pg. 863
ASC/CANADA INCORPORATED—See ASC Incorporated, pg. 7
ASC INCORPORATED, pg. 7
ASC PROTOCRAFT—See ASC Incorporated, pg. 7
ASC TRIM—See ASC Incorporated, pg. 7
ASC WEINSBERG KAROSSERIEWERKE WEINSBERG GMBH—See ASC Incorporated, pg. 7
ASCG, INC., pg. 7
THE ASCII GROUP, INC., pg. 8
A S H, INC., pg. 8
ASI MARKET RESEARCH, INC.—See IDC Services, Inc., pg. 560
ASI MARKET RESEARCH, INC.—See IDC Services, Inc., pg. 560
ASICS TIGER CORPORATION, pg. 8
A.S.M. INDUSTRIES—See Serfilco, Ltd., pg. 991
ASM INTERNATIONAL, pg. 8
ATC AG—See American Tool Companies, Inc., pg. 64
ATC AIR, INC.—See American Tool Companies, Inc., pg. 64
ATI INDUSTRIES, pg. 8
AT&L RAILROAD—See Wheeler Brothers Grain Co., pg. 1185
ATL TERMINAL CORP.—See Atlas Van Lines, Inc., pg. 97
ATZ PLASTIC MOLDERS, INC.—See Zenith Products Corp., pg. 1217
AVA-AUTOMATIC VENDORS OF AMERICA, pg. 8
AVW AUDIOVISUAL, INC.—See Freeman Decorating Co., pg. 431
AXIA INCORPORATED, pg. 8
A.Y.M. INC.—See A. Y. McDonald Industries, Inc., pg. 728
AALLIED DIE CASTING MFG., INC.—See RCM Industries, pg. 906
THE AARQUE COMPANIES, pg. 9
AARQUE MANAGEMENT CORP.—See The Aarque Companies, pg. 9
AARQUE STEEL CORPORATION—See The Aarque Companies, pg. 9
ABACUS PACKAGING CORP.—See Mid-Continent Screw Products Co., pg. 750
ABBELL ASSOCIATES, pg. 9

ABBEY ETNA MACHINE CO. GMBH—See Abbey Etna Machine Company, pg. 9
ABBEY ETNA MACHINE COMPANY, pg. 9
ABBOTT BALL COMPANY, pg. 9
J.R. ABBOTT CONSTRUCTION, INC., pg. 9
ABBOTT ELECTRONICS, INC., pg. 9
ABBOTT GLASS CO., INC., pg. 9
ABBOTT GROUP LTD., pg. 9
ABBOTT INDUSTRIAL SUPPLY—See Abbott Group Ltd., pg. 9
ABBOTT LABORATORIES/ASHLAND, pg. 9
ABBOTT PRODUCTS INC.—See Abbott Group Ltd., pg. 9
ABBYLAND FOODS, INC., pg. 10
ABBYLAND PORK RACK—See Abbyland Foods, Inc., pg. 10
ABCO MARKETS, INC., pg. 10
ABDALLA'S LAFAYETTE, INC., pg. 10
ABELSON-TAYLOR, INC., pg. 10
ABERDEEN MFG. CORP. CONWAY PLANT—See CC Industries, Inc., pg. 200
ABERDEEN MFG. CORP. KAUFMAN PLANT—See CC Industries, Inc., pg. 200
ABERDEEN MFG. CORP. LOUIS HAND PLANT—See CC Industries, Inc., pg. 200
ABERDEEN MFG. CORP. SAVOY PLANT—See CC Industries, Inc., pg. 200
ABERDEEN MFG. CORPORATION—See CC Industries, Inc., pg. 200
ABINGDON PRESS, pg. 10
ABLE TRANSLATIONS LIMITED—See Berlitz International, Inc., pg. 142
ABRAMS PUBLISHING INC., pg. 10
ABRAMSON EHRLICH MANES, INC., pg. 10
ABRASIVE ENGINEERING & MANUFACTURING DIV.—See Acrometal Companies, Inc., pg. 14
ABRASIVES, INC.—See Prime Technology, Inc., pg. 889
ABROS, INC.—See Art Iron, Inc., pg. 86
ACACIA FINANCIAL CORPORATION—See The Acacia Group, pg. 10
THE ACACIA GROUP, pg. 10
ACACIA INSURANCE SALES CORPORATION—See The Acacia Group, pg. 10
ACACIA MORTGAGE CORPORATION—See The Acacia Group, pg. 10
ACACIA NATIONAL LIFE INS. CO.—See The Acacia Group, pg. 11
ACADEMY ENTERTAINMENT, INC.—See Artec Distributing, Inc., pg. 86
ACADEMY ENTERTAINMENT INC.—See Artec Distributing, Inc., pg. 86
ACADEMY INSURANCE GROUP, INC., pg. 11
ACADEMY LIFE INSURANCE CO.—See Academy Insurance Group, Inc., pg. 11
ACCELERATED CLAIMS PROCESSING, INC.—See Health Management Systems, Inc., pg. 521
ACCESS EQUIPMENT LTD.—See Up-Right, Inc., pg. 1139
ACCOUNTING FORMS COMPANY, INC.—See Safeguard Business Systems, Inc., pg. 966
ACCRA PAC GROUP, pg. 11
ACCU-CAST, INC.—See Stockham Valves & Fittings, Inc., pg. 1050
ACCU-SORT SYSTEMS, INC., pg. 11
ACCU-SORT TIME SYSTEM—See Accu-Sort Systems, Inc., pg. 11
ACCUCARE DIV.—See Medline Industries, Inc., pg. 736
ACCURATE BOX CO., INC., pg. 11
ACCURATE BUSHING CO., INC., pg. 11
ACCURATE PERFORATING CO., pg. 11
ACCURATE THREADED FASTENERS, INC., pg. 11
ACCUTRONICS, INC.—See The Marmon Group, Inc., pg. 711
ACE GLASS INCORPORATED, pg. 11
ACE HARDWARE CORPORATION, pg. 12
ACE NOVELTY COMPANY, INC., pg. 12
ACE NOVELTY FUN SERVICE DIVISION—See Ace Novelty Company, Inc., pg. 12
ACE OFFICE PRODUCTS, pg. 12
ACESS ENERGY CORPORATION, pg. 12
ACHESON A.N.Z. PTY. LTD.—See Acheson Industries, Inc., pg. 12
ACHESON COLLOIDEN B.V.—See Acheson Industries, Inc., pg. 12
ACHESON COLLOIDS (CANADA) LTD.—See Acheson Industries, Inc., pg. 12
ACHESON COLLOIDS COMPANY—See Acheson Industries, Inc., pg. 12
ACHESON COLLOIDS COMPANY—See Acheson Industries, Inc., pg. 12
ACHESON DO BRASIL IND. E COM LTDA.—See Acheson Industries, Inc., pg. 12
ACHESON FRANCE S.A.—See Acheson Industries, Inc., pg. 12
ACHESON INDUSTRIES (EUROPE) LTD.—See Acheson Industries, Inc., pg. 12
ACHESON INDUSTRIES, INC., pg. 12
ACHESON INTERNATIONAL S.A.-EQUIPMENT DIV.—See Acheson Industries, Inc., pg. 12
ACHESON ITALIANA S.R.L.—See Acheson Industries, Inc., pg. 12
ACHESON (JAPAN) LTD.—See Acheson Industries, Inc., pg. 12
ACHESON KOREA LTD.—See Acheson Industries, Inc., pg. 12
ACKER DRILL CO. INC., pg. 12
ACKERMAN MCQUEEN, INC., pg. 12
ACME BOOT CO., INC.—See Farley Industries, pg. 400
ACME CANVAS CO., INC., pg. 13
ACME CHEMICALS & INSULATION CO.—See Insulating Materials, Inc., pg. 572
ACME CONTINENTAL FOODS, INC., pg. 13
ACME FOUNDRY, INC., pg. 13
ACME MILLS CO. INC., pg. 13
ACME POULTRY COMPANY, INC., pg. 13
ACME REFRIGERATION OF BATON ROUGE INC., pg. 13
ACME TRIM—See Acme Mills Co. Inc., pg. 13
ACME TRUCK LINE, INC., pg. 13
ACME VISIBLE RECORDS, pg. 13
THE ACORDIA, INC.—See The Associated Group, pg. 90
ACORN BUILDING COMPONENTS INC., pg. 13
ACORN DISTRIBUTING CO.—See Acorn Building Components Inc., pg. 14
ACORN ENGINEERING COMPANY, pg. 14
ACORN OF ILLINOIS—See Acorn Building Components Inc., pg. 14
ACOUSTI ENGINEERING CO. OF FLORIDA, pg. 14
ACOUSTIC RESEARCH—See International Jensen Inc., pg. 578
ACRAGAGE—See Sycon Corporation, pg. 1069
ACRISON, INC., pg. 14
ACROMETAL COMPANIES, INC., pg. 14
ACTION CLINTON—See Action Technology Company, pg. 15
ACTION COMMODITIES CORPORATION—See Tennessee Dressed Beef Company, pg. 1087
ACTION CONTROLS PTY. LTD.—See Action Instruments, Inc., pg. 14
ACTION EQUIPMENT, pg. 14
ACTION INDUSTRIE COMPUTER, GMBH—See Action Instruments, Inc., pg. 14
ACTION INSTRUMENTS (CHINA) LTD.—See Action Instruments, Inc., pg. 14
ACTION INSTRUMENTS, INC., pg. 14
ACTION INSTRUMENTS, LTD.—See Action Instruments, Inc., pg. 15
ACTION INSTRUMENTS, S.A.—See Action Instruments, Inc., pg. 15
ACTION LIFT—See Medico Industries, Inc., pg. 735
ACTION MANUFACTURING CO., pg. 15
ACTION ROCKAWAY—See Action Technology Company, pg. 15
ACTION SUPPLY—See Action Equipment, pg. 14
ACTION TECHNOLOGY COMPANY, pg. 15
ACTION TIRE—See Action Equipment, pg. 14
ACTIVE ELECTRICAL SUPPLY COMPANY, pg. 15
ACTIVE HOMES CORP.—See Active Tool & Manufacturing Co., Inc., pg. 15
ACTIVE INDUSTRIES, INC.—See Active Tool & Manufacturing Co., Inc., pg. 15
ACTIVE QUILTING DIV.—See Rockville Fabrics Corporation, pg. 942
ACTIVE TOOL & MANUFACTURING CO., INC., pg. 15
ACTRON MANUFACTURING COMPANY, pg. 15
ACUREX CORP. AEROTHERM DIVISION—See Acurex Environmental Corporation, pg. 15
ACUREX CORP. AEROTHERM PRODUCTS DIVISION—See Acurex Environmental Corporation, pg. 16
ACUREX CORP. AUTODATA DIVISION—See Acurex Environmental Corporation, pg. 16
ACUREX ENVIRONMENTAL CORPORATION, pg. 15
ACUREX EXPORT SALES, LTD.—See Acurex Environmental Corporation, pg. 16
AD/PRODUCTIONS—See Young & Rubicam Inc., pg. 1211
THE AD TEAM OF FLORIDA INC., pg. 16
AD-TECH COMMUNICATIONS, pg. 16
ADA BEEF, INC., pg. 16
ADAIR FEED & GRAIN COMPANY, pg. 16
ADAIR GREENE ADVERTISING, pg. 16
ADAM MELDRUM & ANDERSON CO., INC., pg. 16
ADAMS BUSINESS FORMS, pg. 16
ADAMS COLWAY & ASSOCIATES, pg. 16
R. P. ADAMS COMPANY, INC., pg. 16
ADAMS EXTRACT CO., INC., pg. 16
ADAMS INTERNATIONAL—See TLC Beatrice International Holdings Inc., pg. 1073
ADAM'S MARK HOTELS—See HBE Corporation, pg. 496
ADAMS NATURAL PEANUT BUTTER—See Agway, Inc., pg. 26
RALPH & PAUL ADAMS, INC.—See Jones Dairy Farm, pg. 603
ADAMS RITE (EUROPE) LTD.—See Adams Rite Manufacturing Co., pg. 17
ADAMS RITE MANUFACTURING CO., pg. 16
ADAMS RITE PRODUCTS INC.—See Certified Holding Corp., pg. 237
ADAMS WINE CO., pg. 17
ADAMSON ADVERTISING, INC., pg. 17
ADAPT, INC.—See Lawrence Group, Inc., pg. 662
ADDISON STEEL INC., pg. 17
ADDRESSES UNLIMITED—See New Jersey Press, Inc., pg. 801
ADEC AUTOMATION—See Adec International Automation Corp., pg. 17
ADEC INTERNATIONAL AUTOMATION CORP., pg. 17
ADELPHIA LAMP & SHADE INC., pg. 17
ADEPT TECHNOLOGY, INC., pg. 17
ADHESIVE RESEARCH, INC.—See Topflight Corp., pg. 1102
ADJUSTABLE LIFE INSURANCE COMPANY—See The Minnesota Mutual Life Insurance Company, pg. 758
ADLAND ADVERTISING, INC., pg. 17
ADLER BOSCHETTO PEEBLES & PARTNERS, INC., pg. 17
ADLER & SHAYKIN, pg. 17
ADMARK, INC., pg. 18
ADMARKETING, INC., pg. 18
ADMINISTRATIVE SERVICES, INC.—See National Life Insurance Company, pg. 791
ADMIRAL MAINTENANCE SERVICE L.P., pg. 18
ADMIRAL PACKAGING, INC.—See Union Industries, Inc., pg. 1128
ADMIRATION HOSIERY MILLS, INC.—See Highland Mills Inc., pg. 534
ADOLFSON & PETERSON, INC., pg. 18
ADPLAN ASSOCIATES, pg. 18
ADPLUS GMBH—See The Lowe Group, pg. 685
ADRA SYSTEMS, INC., pg. 18
ADRAY APPLIANCE & PHOTO CENTER, INC., pg. 18
ADSHOP—See Backer Spielvogel Bates Worldwide, Inc., pg. 109
ADVANCE BUSINESS GRAPHICS, pg. 18
ADVANCE MACHINE COMPANY, pg. 18
ADVANCE MECHANICAL SYSTEMS, INC., pg. 19
ADVANCE PACKAGING CORPORATION, pg. 19
ADVANCE POWER CO. LTD.—See Panduit Company, pg. 845
ADVANCE PUBLICATIONS INC., pg. 19
ADVANCE STEEL CO., pg. 20
ADVANCE THERMAL CORP.—See Transco Inc., pg. 1107
ADVANCED AROMATICS, INC.—See Chemical Exchange Industries, pg. 242
ADVANCED CIRCUIT TECHNOLOGY, pg. 20
ADVANCED CONTROLS, INC., pg. 20
ADVANCED DETECTION SYSTEMS—See Venturedyne, Ltd., pg. 1148
ADVANCED DZIGN SYSTEMS—See Day & Zimmermann, Inc., pg. 320
ADVANCED ENERGY INDUSTRY, pg. 20
ADVANCED INPUT DEVICES, INC., pg. 20
ADVANCED INSTRUMENTS, INC., pg. 20
ADVANCED MANUFACTURING & DEVELOPMENT, pg. 20
ADVANCED MARINE ENTERPRISES, INC., pg. 20
ADVANCED TECHNOLOGY, INC., pg. 20
ADVANCED TECHNOLOGY SYSTEMS, INC.—See Commercial Light Company, pg. 268
ADVANSTAR COMMUNICATIONS, pg. 21
ADVANTAGE MOVING & STORAGE CO., INC.—See Mayflower Transit, Inc., pg. 724
ADVENT INTERNATIONAL, pg. 21
ADVENT LOUDSPEAKERS—See International Jensen Inc., pg. 578
ADVENTURE LANDS OF AMERICA, INC., pg. 21
ADVENTURE TOURS USA, INC., pg. 21
ADVERTIMING INC.—See Vitt Media International, Inc., pg. 1154
ADVERTISING AGE—See Crain Communications, Inc., pg. 295
ADVERTISING AGE INTERNATIONAL—See Crain Communications, Inc., pg. 296
ADVERTISING, BOELTER & LINCOLN, pg. 21
ADVERTISING CHECKING BUREAU INCORPORATED, pg. 21
ADVERTISING DISTRIBUTORS OF MARYLAND, INC.—See Harte-Hanks Communications, Inc., pg. 513
ADVERTISING TO WOMEN, INC., pg. 21
ADVICO YOUNG & RUBICAM AG—See Young & Rubicam Inc., pg. 1211
ADVISERS CAPITAL MANAGEMENT INC., pg. 21
ADVISORS ADVERTISING, pg. 21
ADVOCATE SERVICES, INC.—See Servistar Corporation, pg. 993
ADWORKS, INC., pg. 21
AERCO INTERNATIONAL INC., pg. 21
AERO BODY & TRUCK EQUIPMENT, INC.—See Tri-State Motor Transit Co., pg. 1111
AERO DATA METAL CRAFTERS, pg. 22
AERO ENTERPRISES, INC.—See ARA Group, pg. 6
AERO PERU CORPORATION, pg. 22
AEROCLO METAL PRODUCTS—See Precision Valve Corporation, pg. 886
AERO-FINISH INC.—See Kleco Corp., pg. 635
AEROGLIDE AMERICAS INTERNATIONAL, INC.—See Aeroglide Corporation, pg. 22
AEROGLIDE CORPORATION, pg. 22
AEROLYTE SYSTEMS—See Clemco Industries, pg. 254
AEROLYTE SYSTEMS—See Clemco Industries, pg. 254
AEROMAIL, INC.—See City Postal, Inc., pg. 251
AEROMOTIVE SYSTEMS CO.—See ASC Incorporated, pg. 7
AERONAUTICAL RADIO, INC.—See Arinc Inc., pg. 82
AEROPAK—See DeMert & Dougherty, Inc., pg. 328
AEROS INSTRUMENTS, INC.—See Squire-Cogswell Company, pg. 1034
THE AEROSPACE CORPORATION, pg. 22
AEROTRON, INC., pg. 22
AEROVIRONMENT, INC., pg. 22
AETNA BEARING COMPANY, pg. 23
AETNA HEALTH PLANS, pg. 23
AETNA INDUSTRIES, INC., pg. 23
AETNA PLYWOOD, INC., pg. 23
AFFILIATED COMPUTER SERVICES, INC., pg. 23
AFFILIATED OF FLORIDA INC., pg. 23
AFFILIATED FOOD DISTRIBUTORS, pg. 23
AFFILIATED FOOD STORES, pg. 23
AFFILIATED FOODS COOPERATIVE INC., pg. 23
AFFILIATED FOODS, INC., pg. 24
AFFILIATED FOODS SOUTHWEST, pg. 24
AFFILIATED GENERAL AGENCY, INC.—See Affiliated Food Stores, pg. 23
AFFILIATES GROUP INC., pg. 24
AFTER SIX ACCESS—See After Six, Incorporated, pg. 24
AFTER SIX, INCORPORATED, pg. 24
AG PROCESSING INC A COOPERATIVE, pg. 24
AGEMA INFRARED SYSTEMS, INC., pg. 24
AGENCIAS USA, pg. 24
AGMET LTD.—See Electro-Science Laboratories, Inc., pg. 375
AGRA TECH SEEDS, INC.—See Gold Kist, Inc., pg. 465
AGRATRADE FINANCING, INC.—See Gold Kist, Inc., pg. 465
AGRI-GRAPHICS, INC.—See Altair Corporation, pg. 45
AGRI INTERNATIONAL, INC.—See Gold Kist, Inc., pg. 465
AGRI-MARK, INC., pg. 25
AGRI-SERVICE AGENCIES, INC.—See Dairylea Cooperative Inc., pg. 311
AGRICULTURAL INSURANCE COMPANY—See American Financial Corporation, pg. 53
AGRINET FARM RADIO NETWORK—See Ray Communications, Inc., pg. 914
AGRINORTHWEST, INC., pg. 25
AGRIPAC INC., pg. 25

AGUILARES RANCHES—See Sebastian Cotton & Grain Corp., pg. 987
AGVESTMENTS, INC.—See Gold Kist, Inc., pg. 465
AGWAY DATA SERVICES, INC.—See Agway, Inc., pg. 25
AGWAY FINANCIAL CORPORATION—See Agway, Inc., pg. 25
AGWAY GENERAL AGENCY—See Agway, Inc., pg. 25
AGWAY, INC., pg. 25
AGWAY INDEMNITY INSURANCE COMPANY—See Agway, Inc., pg. 25
AGWAY INSURANCE CO.—See Agway, Inc., pg. 25
AGWAY PETROLEUM CORP.—See Agway, Inc., pg. 25
AHERN NEW YORK, pg. 26
AID ASSOCIATION FOR LUTHERANS, pg. 26
AID AUTO STORES, INC., pg. 26
AIKEN ELECTRIC COOPERATIVE INC., pg. 26
ROBERT B. AIKENS & ASSOCIATES INC., pg. 26
AIM SERVICES CO., LTD.—See ARA Group, pg. 7
AIN PLASTICS, INC., pg. 26
AIR CONDITIONING CO., INC., pg. 26
AIR ENGINEERING CO., INC.—See Amelco Corporation, pg. 47
AIR FRESH TRUCKING—See Wilsey Bennett Co., pg. 1193
AIR GAGE COMPANY, pg. 27
AIR INDUSTRIES CORPORATION, pg. 27
AIR JAMAICA LTD., pg. 27
AIR LAND FORWARDERS, INC.—See The Suddath Companies, pg. 1056
AIR MASTER CORPORATION, pg. 27
AIR-O-MATIC POWER STEER CO.—See Sycon Corporation, pg. 1069
AIR POWER, INC., pg. 27
AIR-SCENT INTERNATIONAL—See Surco Products, Inc., pg. 1065
AIRCAP INDUSTRIES CORP.—See MTD Products, Inc., pg. 694
AIRCO COMMERCIAL SERVICES, INC.—See Airco Mechanical Inc., pg. 27
AIRCO MECHANICAL INC., pg. 27
AIRCRAFT GEAR CORPORATION, pg. 27
AIRCRAFT INSURANCE AGENCY—See Hawthorne Corp., pg. 519
AIRCRAFT PRODUCTS COMPANY—See The Pullman Company, pg. 899
AIRCRAFT PRODUCTS COMPANY—See The Pullman Company, pg. 899
AIRCRAFT SUPPORT GROUP, INC.—See International Airline Support Group, Inc., pg. 575
AIRGUARD INDUSTRIES INC., pg. 27
AIRLINE HYDRAULICS CORPORATION, pg. 27
AIRLINE MANUFACTURING COMPANY, INC., pg. 27
AIRMASTER FAN CO., pg. 28
THE AIROLITE COMPANY, pg. 28
AIRPORT '82 ASSOCIATES LTD.—See Family Inns of America, Inc., pg. 398
AIRTEX PRODUCTS—See UIS, Inc., pg. 1123
AIRTROL, INC., pg. 28
AIRWAYS RENT A CAR—See Ridgeview Motors, Inc., pg. 934
AJAX MANUFACTURING COMPANY, INC., pg. 28
AJAX PAVING INDUSTRIES INC., pg. 28
AKARD CONSTRUCTION CO., INC.—See Zale Corporation, pg. 1215
AKERS PACKAGING SERVICE INC., pg. 28
AKRA TOOL—See UDT Sensors, Inc., pg. 1122
THE AKRO CORPORATION—See Collins & Aikman Group Inc., pg. 262
ALABAMA ELECTRIC COOPERATIVE, INC., pg. 28
ALABAMA FARMERS CO-OP, pg. 28
ALABAMA METAL INDUSTRIES CORPORATION, pg. 28
ALABAMA OIL COMPANY—See Spencer Companies Inc., pg. 1030
ALABAMA WHOLESALE DRUG CO.—See Tennessee Wholesale Drug Company, pg. 1088
ALACON, pg. 29
ALADDIN INDUSTRIES, INCORPORATED, pg. 29
ALADDIN INDUSTRIES PTY. LTD.—See Aladdin Industries, Incorporated, pg. 29
ALADDIN INTERNATIONAL CORP. S.A.R.L.—See Aladdin Industries, Incorporated, pg. 29
ALADDIN INTERNATIONAL CORPORATION (UK)—See Aladdin Industries, Incorporated, pg. 29
ALADDIN MILLS INC., pg. 29
ALADDIN PETROLEUM CORPORATION, pg. 29
ALADDIN RESOURCES, INC.—See Aladdin Industries, Incorporated, pg. 29
ALADDIN SYNERGETICS, INC.—See Aladdin Industries, Incorporated, pg. 29
ALAMO GROUP, INC., pg. 29
ALAMO INDUSTRIAL GROUP, pg. 29
ALAMO IRON WORKS—See Alamo Industrial Group, pg. 29
THE ALAMO LEARNING SYSTEMS, INC., pg. 29
ALAMO RENT-A-CAR INC., pg. 30
THE ALAN & GRAY CO.—See Alling & Cory Company, pg. 40
ALAN LITHOGRAPH, INC., pg. 30
ALARON ELECTRONICS FAR EAST LTD., HONG KONG—See Alaron Inc., pg. 30
ALARON INC., pg. 30
ALAS/D.P.P.—See Backer Spielvogel Bates Worldwide, Inc., pg. 109
ALAS/DPP BARCELONA S.A.—See Backer Spielvogel Bates Worldwide, Inc., pg. 109
ALAS/DPP VALENCIA S.A.—See Backer Spielvogel Bates Worldwide, Inc., pg. 109
ALASKA BOAT CO.—See Wards Cove Packing Company, pg. 1163
ALASKA INDUSTRIAL HARDWARE INC., pg. 30
ALASKA MARINE LINES, INC.—See Lynden Incorporated, pg. 689
ALASKA PUBLISHING PROPERTIES, INC.—See Yankee Publishing Incorporated, pg. 1207
ALASKA PULP CORPORATION, pg. 30
ALASKA TOOL & EQUIPMENT SERVICE—See Alaska Industrial Hardware Inc., pg. 30
ALASKA-WEST EXPRESS, INC.—See Lynden Incorporated, pg. 689
ALASKAN COPPER COMPANIES, pg. 30
ALASKAN COPPER COMPANIES—See Alaskan Copper Companies, pg. 30
ALATEC PRODUCTS, INC., pg. 30
ALBA FORWARDING CO., INC., pg. 30
ALBAN TRACTOR CO. INC., pg. 30
ALBANY LIFE ASSURANCE COMPANY LIMITED—See Metropolitan Life Insurance Co., pg. 745
ALBANY TIMES UNION—See The Hearst Corporation, pg. 523
J. S. ALBERICI CONSTRUCTION CO., INC., pg. 31
ALBEROY DIVISION—See Beldoch Industries Corporation, pg. 133
MIKE ALBERT LEASING, INC., pg. 31
R.L. ALBERT & SON, INC., pg. 31
ALBERTA NATIONAL GAS COMPANY LTD.—See ANGUS Chemical Company, pg. 75
ALBI MANUFACTURING DIVISION—See Stanchem Inc., pg. 1035
ALBION WIRE, INC.—See Group Dekko International Inc., pg. 489
THE FRED W. ALBRECHT GROCERY CO., pg. 31
ALBUQUERQUE METALS CO.—See CF&I Steel Corporation, pg. 201
ALCO HEALTH SERVICES CORPORATION, pg. 31
ALCO INDUSTRIES, INC., pg. 32
ALCO MANAGEMENT, INC.—See Jemison, Inc., pg. 592
ALCO PROPERTIES, INC.—See Jemison, Inc., pg. 592
ALCO/BELGIUM FOUNDRIES—See Heico Inc., pg. 525
ALCOHOLISM TREATMENT CENTER—See Central DuPage Health System, pg. 232
ALCOM PRINTING GROUP, INC., pg. 32
ALCOR ENVELOPE CO.—See Alling & Cory Company, pg. 40
ALCOSA/SUNWISE—See Hanover Foods Corporation, pg. 506
ALDAN RUBBER CO., pg. 32
ALDEN AUTO PARTS WHOLESALE, INC., pg. 32
THE ALDEN GROUP LTD., pg. 32
J.S. ALDEN PUBLIC RELATIONS, INC.—See The Alden Group Ltd., pg. 32
JOHN ALDEN FINANCIAL CORPORATION, pg. 32
JOHN ALDEN LIFE INSURANCE COMPANY—See John Alden Financial Corporation, pg. 33
ALDEN SHOE CO., INC., pg. 33
ALDI INC., pg. 33
ALDINE TECHNOLOGIES, pg. 33
ALESSI INCORPORATED—See Dukane Corporation, pg. 352
ALEX FOODS, INC., pg. 33
ALEX FRIES—See Land O'Lakes, Inc., pg. 654
ALEX LEE, INC., pg. 33
ALEXANDER DOLL CO., INC., pg. 33
ALEXANDER MARKETING SERVICES/CHICAGO—See Alexander Marketing Services, Inc., pg. 33
ALEXANDER MARKETING SERVICES/DETROIT—See Alexander Marketing Services, Inc., pg. 33
ALEXANDER MARKETING SERVICES, INC., pg. 33
ALEXANDRA DE MARKOFF, LTD.—See MacAndrews & Forbes Holdings Inc., pg. 695
ALFORD INDUSTRIES, INC., pg. 33
ALFORD PACKAGING—See Alford Industries, Inc., pg. 34
ALFORD REFRIGERATED WAREHOUSE, INC., pg. 34
ALGIERS IRON WORKS & DRY DOCK, INC.—See Bollinger Machine Shop And Shipyard, Inc., pg. 163
ALGOOD FOOD COMPANY, pg. 34
ALICEVILLE CASTING CO.—See Stockham Valves & Fittings, Inc., pg. 1050
ALIMAK ELEVATOR COMPANY, pg. 34
ALIMED, INC., pg. 34
ALINABAL, INC., pg. 34
M. ALKALAY AGENCIES, LTD.—See Newly Weds Foods Inc., pg. 804
ALKCO LIGHTING COMPANY—See Jac Jacobsen Industries, Inc., pg. 588
ALKOTA CLEANING SYSTEMS, INC., pg. 34
ALL ABOUT SPORTS—See Van Leunens Inc., pg. 1144
ALL AMERICA FINANCIAL, pg. 34
ALL AMERICA INSURANCE COMPANY—See Central Mutual Insurance Co., pg. 233
ALL AMERICAN BOTTLING CORP., pg. 35
ALL AMERICAN ENGINEERING CO.—See Datron Incorporated, pg. 316
ALL AMERICAN FINANCIAL—See All America Financial, pg. 34
ALL AMERICAN HOME CENTER, pg. 35
ALL AMERICAN INDUSTRIES, INC.—See Datron Incorporated, pg. 316
ALL-LUMINUM PRODUCTS, INC., pg. 35
ALL NATION INSURANCE CO., pg. 35
ALL-PHASE ELECTRIC SUPPLY CO. INC., pg. 35
ALL-SEASONS, INC.—See Washington Homes, Inc., pg. 1166
ALL SEASONS SERVICES, INC., pg. 35
ALL-STATE FORD TRUCK SALES—See Hesco Parts Corporation, pg. 532
ALL WORLD TRAVEL SERVICE, INC.—See The Elder-Beerman Stores Corp., pg. 373
ALLBRITTON COMMUNICATIONS COMPANY—See Perpetual Corporation, pg. 862
ALLBRITTON NEWS BUREAU, INC.—See Perpetual Corporation, pg. 862
ALLBRITTON TELEVISION PRODUCTIONS, INC.—See Perpetual Corporation, pg. 862
ALLECO INC., pg. 35
ALLEGHENY INTERNATIONAL CREDIT CORP.—See Sunbeam-Oster Company, Inc., pg. 1059
ALLEN CANNING COMPANY, pg. 35
ALLEN & COMPANY INCORPORATED, pg. 35
ALLEN-EDMONDS SHOE CORP., pg. 36
ALLEN FOODS, INC., pg. 36
ALLEN & HOSHALL, INC., pg. 36
IVAN ALLEN COMPANY, INC., pg. 36
J.W. ALLEN & COMPANY, pg. 36
ALLEN & OHARA, INC., pg. 36
ALLEN-ROGERS CO.—See Davis Mining & Manufacturing, pg. 319
ALLEN STEEL CO., pg. 36
ALLEN'S CONCRETE, INC.—See Ritchie Corporation, pg. 936
ALLENS OF HASTINGS, INC., pg. 36
ALLESON OF ROCHESTER, INC., pg. 37
ALLEY-CASSETTY COAL CO., pg. 37
ALLFAST FACILITY—See Allfast Fastening Systems, Inc., pg. 37
ALLFAST FASTENING SYSTEMS, INC., pg. 37
ALLFORMS PACKAGING CORP.—See Rock-Tenn Company, pg. 941
ALLHABO AKTIEBOLAG—See Panduit Company, pg. 845
ALLIANCE AMERICA, pg. 37
ALLIANCE AUTOMATION SYSTEMS, pg. 37
ALLIANCE MANAGEMENT, INC., pg. 37
ALLIED ADVERTISING—See Allied Advertising Agency, pg. 37
ALLIED ADVERTISING AGENCY, pg. 37
ALLIED BUILDING PRODUCTS CORPORATION, pg. 37
ALLIED BUS SALES, INC.—See Mayflower Transit, Inc., pg. 725
ALLIED CHUCKER & ENGINEERING COMPANY, pg. 37
ALLIED CONTAINER CORP.—See Specialty Industries, Inc., pg. 1027
ALLIED EASTERN CO.—See Zeller Corp., pg. 1217
ALLIED FOODS, INC., pg. 38
ALLIED GROUP INC.—See Allied Mutual Insurance Company, pg. 38
ALLIED MERCANTILE COMPANY, pg. 38
ALLIED MINERAL PRODUCTS, INC., pg. 38
ALLIED MUTUAL INSURANCE COMPANY, pg. 38
ALLIED OIL & SUPPLY, INC., pg. 38
ALLIED OLD ENGLISH, INC., pg. 38
ALLIED PAPER INCORPORATED, pg. 38
ALLIED PLYWOOD CORP., pg. 38
ALLIED PRINTING SERVICES, INC., pg. 38
ALLIED PRODUCTS—See Consolidated Cigar Corporation, pg. 276
ALLIED SECURITY, INC., pg. 39
ALLIED SECURITY, INTERNATIONAL, pg. 40
ALLIED SPORTING GOODS INC., pg. 40
ALLIED STEEL PRODUCTS—See Great American Industries, Inc., pg. 480
ALLIED SYSTEMS, LTD., pg. 40
ALLIED TIRE CO.—See Allied Oil & Supply, Inc., pg. 38
ALLIED TIRE SALES, pg. 40
ALLING & CORY COMPANY, pg. 40
ALLISON CORPORATION, pg. 40
ALLISON-ERWIN CO. INC., pg. 40
ALLISON PAYMENT SYSTEMS DIV.—See Cummins-American Corp., pg. 305
ALLMETAL SCREW PRODUCTS CORP., pg. 40
ALLNEWSCO, INC.—See Perpetual Corporation, pg. 862
ALLOWAY MANUFACTURING, pg. 41
ALLOY PRODUCTS CORPORATION, pg. 41
ALLOY TECHNOLOGY INTERNATIONAL INC., pg. 41
ALLRIGHT BALTIMORE, INC.—See Allright Corporation, pg. 41
ALLRIGHT BATON ROUGE, INC.—See Allright Corporation, pg. 41
ALLRIGHT BEAUMONT CO.—See Allright Corporation, pg. 41
ALLRIGHT BIRMINGHAM, INC.—See Allright Corporation, pg. 41
ALLRIGHT BIRMINGHAM INC.—See Allright Corporation, pg. 41
ALLRIGHT BOSTON PARKING, INC.—See Allright Corporation, pg. 41
ALLRIGHT CAL. INC.—See Allright Corporation, pg. 41
ALLRIGHT CAROLINA, INC.—See Allright Corporation, pg. 41
ALLRIGHT CARPARK, INC.—See Allright Corporation, pg. 41
ALLRIGHT CINCINNATI, INC.—See Allright Corporation, pg. 41
ALLRIGHT COLORADO, INC.—See Allright Corporation, pg. 41
ALLRIGHT COLUMBUS PARKING, INC.—See Allright Corporation, pg. 41
ALLRIGHT CORPORATION, pg. 41
ALLRIGHT CORPORATION—See Allright Corporation, pg. 41
ALLRIGHT CORPORATION—See Allright Corporation, pg. 41
ALLRIGHT CORPORATION OF DELAWARE—See Allright Corporation, pg. 41
ALLRIGHT CORPUS CHRISTI, INC.—See Allright Corporation, pg. 41
ALLRIGHT DAYTON PARKING, INC.—See Allright Corporation, pg. 41
ALLRIGHT FLORIDA, INC.—See Allright Corporation, pg. 41
ALLRIGHT JACKSONVILLE, INC.—See Allright Corporation, pg. 41
ALLRIGHT LITTLE ROCK, INC.—See Allright Corporation, pg. 41
ALLRIGHT LONG BEACH PARKING, INC.—See Allright Corporation, pg. 41
ALLRIGHT LOUISVILLE CO., INC.—See Allright Corporation, pg. 41
ALLRIGHT MIAMI, INC.—See Allright Corporation, pg. 41
ALLRIGHT MISSOURI, INC.—See Allright Corporation, pg. 41
ALLRIGHT NASHVILLE PARKING, INC.—See Allright Corporation, pg. 41

ALLRIGHT NEW ORLEANS, INC.—See Allright Corporation, pg. 42
ALLRIGHT NEW YORK PARKING, INC.—See Allright Corporation, pg. 42
ALLRIGHT PARKING CHARLOTTE, INC.—See Allright Corporation, pg. 42
ALLRIGHT PARKING CHICAGO, INC.—See Allright Corporation, pg. 42
ALLRIGHT PARKING CORPORATION—See Allright Corporation, pg. 42
ALLRIGHT PARKING EL PASO, INC.—See Allright Corporation, pg. 42
ALLRIGHT PARKING MINNESOTA, INC.—See Allright Corporation, pg. 42
ALLRIGHT PARKING OF AUSTIN, INC.—See Allright Corporation, pg. 42
ALLRIGHT PARKING OF CLEVELAND, INC.—See Allright Corporation, pg. 42
ALLRIGHT PARKING OF GEORGIA—See Allright Corporation, pg. 42
ALLRIGHT PARKING OF GEORGIA, INC.—See Allright Corporation, pg. 42
ALLRIGHT PARKING OF INDIANAPOLIS, INC.—See Allright Corporation, pg. 42
ALLRIGHT PARKING OF MILWAUKEE, INC.—See Allright Corporation, pg. 42
ALLRIGHT PARKING OF TEXAS, INC.—See Allright Corporation, pg. 42
ALLRIGHT PARKING SYSTEM, INC.—See Allright Corporation, pg. 42
ALLRIGHT PARKING VIRGINIA, INC.—See Allright Corporation, pg. 42
ALLRIGHT PARKING VIRGINIA, INC.—See Allright Corporation, pg. 42
ALLRIGHT PARKING VIRGINIA, INC.—See Allright Corporation, pg. 42
ALLRIGHT PARKING WASHINGTON, INC.—See Allright Corporation, pg. 42
ALLRIGHT PENSACOLA PARKING—See Allright Corporation, pg. 42
ALLRIGHT ROANOKE PARKING, INC.—See Allright Corporation, pg. 42
ALLRIGHT SACRAMENTO—See Allright Corporation, pg. 42
ALLRIGHT SAN ANTONIO PARKING, INC.—See Allright Corporation, pg. 42
ALLRIGHT SAN DIEGO PARKING, INC.—See Allright Corporation, pg. 42
ALLRIGHT SAN FRANCISCO PARKING, INC.—See Allright Corporation, pg. 42
ALLRIGHT SHREVEPORT, INC.—See Allright Corporation, pg. 42
ALLRIGHT SIERRA PARKING, INC.—See Allright Corporation, pg. 42
ALLRIGHT SIERRA PARKING INC.—See Allright Corporation, pg. 42
ALLRIGHT SPRINGFIELD—See Allright Corporation, pg. 42
ALLRIGHT SYSTEM PARKING, INC.—See Allright Corporation, pg. 42
ALLRIGHT TENN. INC.—See Allright Corporation, pg. 42
ALLRIGHT TOLEDO, INC.—See Allright Corporation, pg. 42
ALLRIGHT WEST PALM BEACH, INC.—See Allright Corporation, pg. 42
ALLSOP, INC., pg. 43
ALLSTATE CAN CORPORATION, pg. 43
ALLSUPS CONVENIENCE STORES INC., pg. 43
ALLURE—See Advance Publications Inc., pg. 19
ALMA INDUSTRIES, pg. 43
ALMAY, INC.—See MacAndrews & Forbes Holdings Inc., pg. 695
ALMO CORP., pg. 43
ALMOND ROCA INTERNATIONAL—See Brown & Haley, pg. 182
ALOHA AIRGROUP, INC., pg. 43
ALOHA AIRLINES, INC.—See Aloha Airgroup, Inc., pg. 43
ALOHA ISLANDAIR—See Aloha Airgroup, Inc., pg. 43
ALPHA ASSOCIATES, INC., pg. 43
ALPHA BOLT COMPANY—See Washers, Inc., pg. 1165
THE ALPHA CORPORATION OF TENNESSEE, pg. 43
ALPHA DISTRIBUTORS LTD.—See AmeriServ Food Company, pg. 66
ALPHA ELECTRONIC SIGNAL TECHNOLOGIES, INC., pg. 43
ALPHA MILLS CORP., pg. 43
ALPHA ONE EXCHANGE, pg. 43
ALPHA Q, INC.—See AQHI, Inc., pg. 5
ALPHA RESIN SUPPLY—See Great Lakes Terminal & Transport Corp., pg. 482
ALPHA SHIRT CO., pg. 44
ALPHA UNITED—See Lytron Incorporated, pg. 690
ALPINE CENTER, S.R.L. (BERLITZ)—See Berlitz International, Inc., pg. 142
ALPS INSTITUTE—See Berlitz International, Inc., pg. 142
ALPS INSTITUTE S.R.L. (BERLITZ)—See Berlitz International, Inc., pg. 142
ALRA LABORATORIES, INC., pg. 44
ALRO GROUP, pg. 44
ALRO GROUP, ALPENA—See Alro Group, pg. 44
ALRO GROUP, BENTON HARBOR—See Alro Group, pg. 44
ALRO GROUP, BOCA RATON—See Alro Group, pg. 44
ALRO GROUP, DAYTON—See Alro Group, pg. 44
ALRO GROUP, DETROIT—See Alro Group, pg. 44
ALRO GROUP, FLINT—See Alro Group, pg. 44
ALRO GROUP, FORT WAYNE—See Alro Group, pg. 44
ALRO GROUP, GRAND RAPIDS—See Alro Group, pg. 44
ALRO GROUP, INDIANAPOLIS—See Alro Group, pg. 44
ALRO GROUP, JACKSON—See Alro Group, pg. 44
ALRO GROUP, JACKSON PLASTICS—See Alro Group, pg. 44
ALRO GROUP, JACKSON TOOL-PAC—See Alro Group, pg. 44
ALRO GROUP, LOUISVILLE—See Alro Group, pg. 44
ALRO GROUP, MUNCIE—See Alro Group, pg. 44
ALRO GROUP, PERRYSBURG—See Alro Group, pg. 44
ALRO GROUP, SOUTH BEND—See Alro Group, pg. 44
ALRO SPECIALTY METALS, CHARLOTTE—See Alro Group, pg. 44
ALRO SPECIALTY METALS, MENOMONEE FALLS—See Alro Group, pg. 44
ALRO SPECIALTY METALS, NASHVILLE—See Alro Group, pg. 44
ALRO SPECIALTY METALS, REDFORD—See Alro Group, pg. 44
ALRO SPECIALTY METALS, TALLMADGE—See Alro Group, pg. 44
ALRO SPECIALTY METALS, TONAWANDA—See Alro Group, pg. 44
ALRO SPECIALTY METALS, VILLA PARK—See Alro Group, pg. 44
ALSTIN ADVERTISING, INC., pg. 45
ALTAIR CORPORATION, pg. 45
ALTAMA DELTA CORP., pg. 45
ALTEC INDUSTRIES EASTERN DIVISION—See Altec Industries, Inc., pg. 45
ALTEC INDUSTRIES, INC., pg. 45
ALTEC INDUSTRIES, LTD.—See Altec Industries, Inc., pg. 45
ALTEC LANSING CONSUMER PRODUCTS—See Sparkomatic Corporation, pg. 1025
THE HARRY ALTER COMPANY, pg. 45
THE HARRY ALTER COMPANY—See Temperature Equipment Corporation, pg. 1086
ALTERMAN TRANSPORT LINES, INC., pg. 45
ALTIER & SONS SHOES INC., pg. 45
ALTO DAIRY COOPERATIVE, pg. 45
ALTO PAPERS—See Bradner Central Company, pg. 171
ALTO SHAAM INC., pg. 46
THE ALTON & SOUTHERN RAILWAY CO.—See Anschutz Corporation, pg. 76
ALTUS FEDERAL SAVINGS BANK, pg. 46
ALTUS MORTGAGE CORPORATION—See Altus Federal Savings Bank, pg. 46
ALTUS REAL ESTATE SERVICES, INC.—See Altus Federal Savings Bank, pg. 46
ALTUS SERVICES, INC.—See Altus Federal Savings Bank, pg. 46
ALUMA SHIELD INDUSTRIES, INC., pg. 46
ALUMINUM FORGE COMPANY—See The Marmon Group, Inc., pg. 711
THE ALUMINUM POWDER COMPANY—See Metallurg, Inc., pg. 742
ALUMINUM SHAPES, INC., pg. 46
ALVA/AMCO PHARMACAL COMPANIES, INC., pg. 46
ALVEY INC., pg. 46
AMADOR MOTORS—See Prospect Motors, Inc., pg. 895
AMALLOY, pg. 46
AMANA FARMS, INC.—See Amana Society, pg. 46
AMANA-NORDSTROM MOTEL CO.—See Amana Society, pg. 46
AMANA SOCIETY, pg. 46
AMANA SOCIETY SERVICE CO.—See Amana Society, pg. 46
AMANO CINCINNATI, INC., pg. 46
AMARILLO GEAR COMPANY—See The Marmon Group, Inc., pg. 711
AMARLITE ARCHITECTURAL PRODUCTS, pg. 47
AMBAC INTERNATIONAL CORP., pg. 47
AMBASSADAIR TRAVEL CLUB, INC.—See Amtran, Inc., pg. 69
AMBASSADOR CARDS—See Hallmark Cards, Inc., pg. 502
AMBASSADOR STEEL CO., pg. 47
AMBER TOURS, INC.—See Amtran, Inc., pg. 69
AMBER TRAVEL, INC.—See Amtran, Inc., pg. 70
AMBRIA—See Lettuce Entertain You Enterprises, Inc., pg. 669
AMBULATORY ONE AMERICA INC., pg. 47
AMCELL CORPORATION, pg. 47
AMCLYDE ENGINEERED PRODUCTS, INC., pg. 47
AMCO FOLDING CARTONS, INC., pg. 47
AMEDCO HEALTH CARE, INC.—See Huntco Inc., pg. 554
AMELCO CORPORATION, pg. 47
AMELCO, INC.—See Amelco Corporation, pg. 47
AMERBELLE CORPORATION, pg. 47
AMERCO, A NEVADA CORPORATION, pg. 47
AMERCO LEASING COMPANY—See Amerco, A Nevada Corporation, pg. 48
AMERICA OUTDOORS LTD, pg. 48
AMERICAN AIRCRAFT PARTS MANUFACTURING CO., pg. 48
AMERICAN ALLOY CASTINGS COMPANY—See American Foundry Group, Inc., pg. 54
AMERICAN ANTENNA CORP—See Capsonic Group, Inc., pg. 216
AMERICAN APPRAISAL ASSOCIATES, INC., pg. 48
AMERICAN APPRAISAL CANADA, INC.—See American Appraisal Associates, Inc., pg. 48
AMERICAN APPRAISAL CAPITAL SERVICES, INC.—See American Appraisal Associates, Inc., pg. 48
THE AMERICAN APPRAISAL CO.—See American Appraisal Associates, Inc., pg. 48
AMERICAN APPRAISAL ESPANA, S.A.—See American Appraisal Associates, Inc., pg. 48
AMERICAN APPRAISAL ESPANA, S.A.—See American Appraisal Associates, Inc., pg. 48
AMERICAN APPRAISAL ESPANA, S.A.—See American Appraisal Associates, Inc., pg. 48
AMERICAN APPRAISAL ESPANA, S.A.—See American Appraisal Associates, Inc., pg. 48
AMERICAN APPRAISAL FRANCE—See American Appraisal Associates, Inc., pg. 48
AMERICAN APPRAISAL HONG KONG LTD.—See American Appraisal Associates, Inc., pg. 48
AMERICAN APPRAISAL HUNGARY CO. LTD.—See American Appraisal Associates, Inc., pg. 49
AMERICAN APPRAISAL ITALIA S.R.L.—See American Appraisal Associates, Inc., pg. 49
AMERICAN APPRAISAL ITALIA S.R.L.—See American Appraisal Associates, Inc., pg. 49
AMERICAN APPRAISAL ITALIA S.R.L.—See American Appraisal Associates, Inc., pg. 49
AMERICAN APPRAISAL ITALIA S.R.L.—See American Appraisal Associates, Inc., pg. 49
AMERICAN APPRAISAL ITALIA, S.R.L.—See American Appraisal Associates, Inc., pg. 49
AMERICAN APPRAISAL POLAND SP. Z.O.O.—See American Appraisal Associates, Inc., pg. 49
AMERICAN APPRAISAL PORTUGAL CONSULTORES DE. AVALIACAO S.A.—See American Appraisal Associates, Inc., pg. 49
AMERICAN APPRAISAL (PORTUGAL) LTD.—See American Appraisal Associates, Inc., pg. 49
AMERICAN APPRAISAL THAILAND LTD.—See American Appraisal Associates, Inc., pg. 49
AMERICAN APPRAISAL (U.K.) LTD.—See American Appraisal Associates, Inc., pg. 49
AMERICAN APPRAISAL (U.K.) LTD.—See American Appraisal Associates, Inc., pg. 49
AMERICAN ARBITRATION ASSOCIATION, pg. 49
AMERICAN ARGO CORP.—See Coordinated Apparel, Inc., pg. 283
AMERICAN AUTOMOBILE ASSOCIATION, NATIONAL TRAVEL DEPARTMENT, pg. 49
AMERICAN BALER CO.—See Avis Industrial Corporation, pg. 102
AMERICAN BALL MANUFACTURING—See Prince Manufacturing, Inc., pg. 890
THE AMERICAN BANKERS ASSOCIATION, pg. 49
AMERICAN BAR & BUSHING STOCK—See American Foundry Group, Inc., pg. 54
AMERICAN BARMAG CO., pg. 49
AMERICAN BEARING & POWER—See Invetech Co., pg. 582
AMERICAN BIBLE SOCIETY, pg. 49
AMERICAN BINDRY-EAST—See The American Companies, Inc., pg. 51
AMERICAN BINDRY-MIDWEST—See The American Companies, Inc., pg. 51
AMERICAN BIO SYNTHETICS—See Bell Flavors & Fragrances, pg. 134
AMERICAN BREAD CO. OF ALABAMA INC.—See American Bread Company - Sunbeam Bakery, pg. 49
AMERICAN BREAD COMPANY - SUNBEAM BAKERY, pg. 49
AMERICAN BROKERAGE CORPORATION—See Phoenix Home Life Mutual Insurance Company, pg. 868
AMERICAN BUILDINGS CO., pg. 49
AMERICAN BUREAU OF SHIPPING, pg. 50
AMERICAN BUSINESS DIRECTORIES—See American Business Information, Inc., pg. 50
AMERICAN BUSINESS INFORMATION, INC., pg. 50
AMERICAN CAPITAL MANAGEMENT & RESEARCH, INC., pg. 50
AMERICAN CAST IRON PIPE CO., pg. 50
AMERICAN CASTINGS CO.—See American Foundry Group, Inc., pg. 54
AMERICAN CHEMICAL SOCIETY, pg. 50
AMERICAN COLOR—See Sullivan Holding Company, pg. 1056
THE AMERICAN COMPANIES, INC., pg. 50
AMERICAN COUNCIL FOR INTERNATIONAL STUDIES—See American Institute For Foreign Study, pg. 56
AMERICAN CRANE & EQUIPMENT CORP., pg. 51
AMERICAN CRYSTAL SUGAR COMPANY, pg. 51
AMERICAN DECAL & MFG. CO., pg. 51
AMERICAN DEVELOPMENT CORPORATION, pg. 51
AMERICAN DIRECTORY PUBLISHING—See American Business Information, Inc., pg. 50
AMERICAN DRUGGIST—See The Hearst Corporation, pg. 522
AMERICAN EAGLE AIRLINES, pg. 51
AMERICAN ECONO-THERM—See Petro Chem Development Company, pg. 865
AMERICAN ELECTRIC CO., LTD.—See Amelco Corporation, pg. 47
AMERICAN ELECTRONICS, INC.—See AEI Holding Co., Inc., pg. 3
AMERICAN EMPIRE SURPLUS LINES INSURANCE COMPANY—See American Financial Corporation, pg. 53
AMERICAN ENTERPRISE INSTITUTE FOR PUBLIC POLICY RESEARCH, pg. 51
AMERICAN ENVELOPE COMPANY—See CC Industries, Inc., pg. 199
AMERICAN ENVELOPE COMPANY-KRUYSMAN DIV.—See CC Industries, Inc., pg. 199
AMERICAN ENVELOPE OF BUFFALO—See CC Industries, Inc., pg. 199
AMERICAN ENVELOPE OF CHICAGO-DIE CUT DIV.—See CC Industries, Inc., pg. 199
AMERICAN ENVELOPE OF CHICAGO-WEB DIV.—See CC Industries, Inc., pg. 199
AMERICAN ENVELOPE OF DALLAS—See CC Industries, Inc., pg. 199
AMERICAN ENVELOPE OF DENVER—See CC Industries, Inc., pg. 199
AMERICAN ENVELOPE OF LOS ANGELES—See CC Industries, Inc., pg. 199
AMERICAN ENVELOPE OF NASHVILLE—See CC Industries, Inc., pg. 199
AMERICAN ENVELOPE OF OMAHA—See CC Industries, Inc., pg. 199
AMERICAN ENVELOPE OF PHILADELPHIA—See CC Industries, Inc., pg. 199
AMERICAN ENVELOPE OF SAN ANTONIO—See CC Industries, Inc., pg. 199
AMERICAN ENVELOPE OF SEATTLE—See CC Industries, Inc., pg. 200
AMERICAN ENVELOPE OF ST. LOUIS—See CC Industries, Inc., pg. 199
AMERICAN EXCELSIOR COMPANY, pg. 51

AMERICAN EXPORT REGISTER—See Thomas Publishing Co., pg. 1093
AMERICAN FABRICS COMPANY, pg. 51
AMERICAN FACTORS ASSOC. AUSTRALIA PTY., LTD.—See JMB Realty Corporation, pg. 585
AMERICAN FAMILY FINANCIAL SERVICES, INC.—See American Family Mutual Insurance Co., pg. 52
AMERICAN FAMILY LIFE INSURANCE CO.—See American Family Mutual Insurance Co., pg. 52
AMERICAN FAMILY MUTUAL INSURANCE CO., pg. 51
AMERICAN FAMILY MUTUAL INSURANCE CO.—See American Family Mutual Insurance Co., pg. 52
AMERICAN FAST PRINT, LIMITED, pg. 52
AMERICAN FASTENERS—See Jupiter Industries, Inc., pg. 609
AMERICAN FELT & FILTER, pg. 52
AMERICAN FENCE CO. AZ—See American Fence Company, pg. 52
AMERICAN FENCE CO. LTD.—See American Fence Company, pg. 52
AMERICAN FENCE CO. OF MIDWEST—See American Fence Company, pg. 52
AMERICAN FENCE COMPANY, pg. 52
AMERICAN FIDELITY CORP., pg. 52
AMERICAN FINANCE GROUP, pg. 52
AMERICAN FINANCIAL CORPORATION, pg. 52
AMERICAN FINANCIAL ENTERPRISES, INC.—See American Financial Corporation, pg. 53
AMERICAN FINANCIAL SECURITY—See American Finance Group, pg. 52
AMERICAN FINE FOODS, INC.—See Steiner Corporation, pg. 1045
AMERICAN FINE FOODS, INC. (NYSSA PLANT)—See Steiner Corporation, pg. 1045
AMERICAN FLUORESCENT CORPORATION, pg. 54
AMERICAN FOODS GROUP, pg. 54
AMERICAN FOODS GROUP, INC., pg. 54
AMERICAN FOODSERVICE—See American Produce & Vegetable Co., pg. 60
AMERICAN FOODSERVICE CORP., pg. 54
AMERICAN FOUNDRY GROUP, INC., pg. 54
AMERICAN FROZEN FOODS, INC., pg. 55
AMERICAN FUEL CELL & COATED FABRICS CO. (AMFUEL), pg. 55
AMERICAN FUNDS ADVISOR INC., pg. 55
AMERICAN FURNITURE COMPANY, pg. 55
AMERICAN GASKET & RUBBER—See Action Technology Company, pg. 15
AMERICAN GILSONITE CO., pg. 55
AMERICAN GRAIN & RELATED INDUSTRIES, pg. 55
AMERICAN GRANBY, INC.—See Amtrol Inc., pg. 70
AMERICAN HARDWARE MUTUAL INSURANCE CO., pg. 55
AMERICAN HEALTH COMPANIES, INC., pg. 55
AMERICAN HEALTH & SECURITY INSURANCE CO., INC.—See American SelfCare Corporation, pg. 61
AMERICAN HOSPITAL EQUIPMENT CORP.—See Randolph Medical Inc., pg. 912
AMERICAN INDUSTRIAL SERVICES—See Steiner Corporation, pg. 1045
AMERICAN INDUSTRIES INC., pg. 55
AMERICAN INKS & COATINGS CORP., pg. 56
AMERICAN INSTITUTE FOR FOREIGN STUDY, pg. 56
AMERICAN INSTITUTE FOR FOREIGN STUDY—See American Institute For Foreign Study, pg. 56
AMERICAN INSTITUTE OF C.P.A.'S INC., pg. 56
AMERICAN INSTITUTIONAL FOODS—See AJC International, Inc., pg. 4
AMERICAN INSULATED WIRE CORP.—See Leviton Mfg. Co., Inc., pg. 671
AMERICAN INTERNATIONAL CONTAINER, INC., pg. 56
AMERICAN INVESTMENT CASTING CO.—See American Foundry Group, Inc., pg. 54
AMERICAN JOURNAL OF NURSING COMPANY, pg. 57
AMERICAN KENNEL CLUB, INC., pg. 57
AMERICAN LAUBSCHER CORP., pg. 57
AMERICAN LAUNDRY MACHINERY INC., pg. 57
AMERICAN LEARNING CORP.—See Encyclopaedia Britannica, Inc., pg. 381
AMERICAN LEGEND CORPORATE, pg. 57
AMERICAN LIBERTY FINANCIAL CORP., pg. 57
AMERICAN LIBRARY ASSOCIATION, pg. 57
AMERICAN LIFE INSURANCE COMPANY OF NEW YORK—See Mutual of America, pg. 778
AMERICAN LINEN SUPPLY COMPANY, pg. 57
AMERICAN LITERATURE REVIEW—See Thomas Publishing Co., pg. 1093
AMERICAN LOCK & SUPPLY INC., pg. 57
AMERICAN LOUVER CO., pg. 57
AMERICAN MACHINE & TOOL COMPANY, pg. 57
AMERICAN MANAGEMENT GROUP, pg. 57
AMERICAN MANUFACTURING CO. (TN), pg. 58
AMERICAN MANUFACTURING COMPANY, INC. (LA), pg. 58
AMERICAN MARKETING INDUSTRIES, INC., pg. 58
AMERICAN MARKETING WORKS & INTERNATIONAL CORPORATION, pg. 58
AMERICAN MARKING SYSTEMS, pg. 58
AMERICAN MATHEMATICAL SOCIETY, INC., pg. 58
THE AMERICAN MEAT PACKING CORP.—See Kane-Miller Corp., pg. 616
AMERICAN MERCHANTS LIFE INSURANCE CO.—See American Hardware Mutual Insurance Co., pg. 55
AMERICAN METAL & PLASTICS, pg. 58
AMERICAN MILITARY ARMS CORPORATION, pg. 58
AMERICAN MITAC CORPORATION, pg. 58
AMERICAN MONEY MANAGEMENT CORPORATION—See American Financial Corporation, pg. 53
AMERICAN MOTIVATION (N.Z.) LTD.—See Carlson Companies, Inc., pg. 221
AMERICAN MUTUAL LIFE INSURANCE COMPANY, pg. 58
AMERICAN NATIONAL CAN CO.—See Poly-Seal Corporation, pg. 880
AMERICAN NATIONAL FIRE INSURANCE COMPANY—See American Financial Corporation, pg. 53
AMERICAN NUT CO.—See Clements Foods Co., pg. 255
AMERICAN OFFICE EQUIPMENT, pg. 58
AMERICAN OPTICAL CORP., pg. 59
AMERICAN OPTICAL CORP.—See American Optical Corp., pg. 59
AMERICAN PACKAGING CORPORATION, pg. 59
AMERICAN PACKAGING CORPORATION—See American Packaging Corporation, pg. 59
AMERICAN PAPER PRODUCTS GROUP, LTD., pg. 59
AMERICAN PASSAGE MEDIA CORPORATION, pg. 59
AMERICAN PLASTIC TOYS INC., pg. 59
AMERICAN PRINTERS & LITHOGRAPHERS, pg. 59
AMERICAN PRODUCE & VEGETABLE CO., pg. 59
AMERICAN PROTECTION INDUSTRIES, INC., pg. 60
AMERICAN RED BALL INTERNATIONAL, INC.—See Red Ball Corporation, pg. 918
AMERICAN RED BALL WORLD WIDE MOVERS—See Red Ball Corporation, pg. 918
AMERICAN REFRACTORIES CO.—See Belmont Industries, Inc., pg. 136
AMERICAN REPUBLIC INSURANCE CO., pg. 60
AMERICAN RESTAURANT GROUP, INC., pg. 60
AMERICAN RUG CRAFTSMEN INC., pg. 60
AMERICAN SAFETY RAZOR COMPANY—See Jordan Company, pg. 604
AMERICAN SAVINGS BANK, pg. 60
AMERICAN SAW & MANUFACTURING CO., pg. 60
AMERICAN SEATING COMPANY, pg. 60
AMERICAN SELECT INSURANCE CO.—See All America Financial, pg. 35
AMERICAN SELFCARE CORPORATION, pg. 60
AMERICAN SENTINEL INSURANCE COMPANY—See Erin Group Administrators, Inc., pg. 387
AMERICAN SHEAR KNIVE CO.—See Asko, Inc, pg. 88
AMERICAN SIGN & INDICATOR CORPORATION—See Winko-Matic Signal Co./Multisonics Corp., pg. 1196
AMERICAN SIGN & MARKETING SERVICES, INC., pg. 61
AMERICAN SNACKS, INC., pg. 61
AMERICAN SPECIALTIES INC., pg. 61
AMERICAN SPECIALTY DISTRIBUTING—See Portland Food Products Company, pg. 881
AMERICAN SPECIALTY DISTRIBUTING—See Portland Food Products Company, pg. 881
AMERICAN SPECIALTY FOODS—See Dan Dee Pretzel & Potato Chip Co., pg. 313
AMERICAN SPECIALTY FOODS—See Portland Food Products Company, pg. 881
AMERICAN SPEEDY PRINTING CENTERS, INC., pg. 61
AMERICAN STABILIS, INC., pg. 61
AMERICAN STANDARD AIR CONDITIONING PRODUCTS—See American Standard Inc., pg. 61
AMERICAN STANDARD INC., pg. 61
AMERICAN STANDARD INSURANCE COMPANY OF WISCONSIN—See American Family Mutual Insurance Co., pg. 52
AMERICAN STANDARD SANITARYWARE (THAILAND) LTD.—See American Standard Inc., pg. 62
AMERICAN STANDARD TRANSPORTATION PRODUCTS—See American Standard Inc., pg. 61
AMERICAN STEEL CORP.—See National Steel Corporation, pg. 794
AMERICAN STEEL FOUNDRIES—See Amsted Industries Incorporated, pg. 69
AMERICAN STEEL & WIRE CORPORATION—See Chicago West Pullman Corporation, pg. 246
THE AMERICAN STOCK EXCHANGE, pg. 62
AMERICAN STOCK EXCHANGE CLEARING CORP.—See The American Stock Exchange, pg. 63
AMERICAN STOCK EXCHANGE REALTY ASSOCIATES INC.—See The American Stock Exchange, pg. 63
AMERICAN STOCK TRANSFER & TRUST CO.—See North Atlantic Industries, Inc., pg. 812
AMERICAN STONE-MIX, INC., pg. 63
AMERICAN STRIP STEEL INC., pg. 63
AMERICAN SUNROOF COMPANY—See ASC Incorporated, pg. 7
AMERICAN SYSTEMS CORPORATION, pg. 63
AMERICAN SYSTEMS ENGINEERING CORPORATION—See Science Applications International Corporation, pg. 981
AMERICAN TANK & FABRICATING CO., pg. 63
AMERICAN TAPE CORPORATION, pg. 63
AMERICAN TARA CORPORATION, pg. 63
AMERICAN TECHNICAL PUBLISHERS, INC., pg. 63
AMERICAN TECHNICAL SERVICES GROUP, INC., pg. 63
AMERICAN TIRE RECLAMATION—See Rao Wholesale Tire Centers, Inc., pg. 913
AMERICAN TOOL COMPANIES, INC., pg. 64
AMERICAN TRADING AND PRODUCTION CORPORATION, pg. 64
AMERICAN TRADING AND PRODUCTION CORPORATION, OIL & GAS DIV.—See American Trading and Production Corporation, pg. 64
AMERICAN TRADING AND PRODUCTION CORPORATION, OIL & GAS DIV.—See American Trading and Production Corporation, pg. 64
AMERICAN TRADING & PRODUCTION CORP., CANADIAN OIL & GAS OPERATIONS—See American Trading and Production Corporation, pg. 65
AMERICAN TRADING & PRODUCTION CORPORATION, OIL & GAS DIV.—See American Trading and Production Corporation, pg. 64
AMERICAN TRADING REAL ESTATE PROPERTIES, INC.—See American Trading and Production Corporation, pg. 65
AMERICAN TRADING REAL ESTATE PROPERTIES, INC.—See American Trading and Production Corporation, pg. 65
AMERICAN TRADING REAL ESTATE PROPERTIES, INC.—See American Trading and Production Corporation, pg. 65
AMERICAN TRADING REAL ESTATE PROPERTIES, INC.—See American Trading and Production Corporation, pg. 65
AMERICAN TRADING TRANSPORTATION CO., INC.—See American Trading and Production Corporation, pg. 65
AMERICAN TRANS AIR EXECUJET, INC.—See Amtran, Inc., pg. 70
AMERICAN TRANS AIR, INC.—See Amtran, Inc., pg. 70
AMERICAN TRANS AIR TRAINING CORP.—See Amtran, Inc., pg. 70
AMERICAN TRANSFER & STORAGE CO.—See Mayflower Transit, Inc., pg. 724
AMERICAN TV & APPLIANCE OF MADISON, INC., pg. 65
AMERICAN UNIFORM CO.—See Steiner Corporation, pg. 1045
AMERICAN UNITED LIFE INSURANCE COMPANY, pg. 65
AMERICAN VISION CENTERS, INC., pg. 65
AMERICAN WATER WORKS ASSOCIATION, pg. 65
AMERICAN WELDING & MANUFACTURING CO., pg. 65
AMERICAN WELDING & MANUFACTURING CO.—See Freedom Forge Corporation, pg. 431
AMERICAN WHITE CROSS LABORATORIES, INC., pg. 65
THE AMERICAN-WORLD LIFE INSURANCE CO.—See Zale Corporation, pg. 1215
AMERICAN WYOTT CORPORATION, pg. 65
AMERICO MANUFACTURING CO., INC., pg. 66
AMERIDATA, INC., pg. 66
AMERISERV FOOD COMPANY, pg. 66
AMERISURE COMPANIES, pg. 66
AMERITAS LIFE INSURANCE CORP., pg. 66
AMES AUTOMOTIVE WAREHOUSE—See Aid Auto Stores, Inc., pg. 26
AMES SAFETY ENVELOPE COMPANY, INC., pg. 66
AMES TAPING TOOL SYSTEMS CO.—See AXIA Incorporated, pg. 8
AMES TAPING TOOLS CO. OF CANADA LIMITED—See AXIA Incorporated, pg. 8
AMEX COMMODITIES CORPORATION—See The American Stock Exchange, pg. 63
AMFAC AGRIBUSINESS, INC.—See JMB Realty Corporation, pg. 585
AMFAC AMYCEL, INC.—See JMB Realty Corporation, pg. 585
AMFAC DEVELOPMENT CORP.—See JMB Realty Corporation, pg. 585
AMFAC DISTRIBUTION CORPORATION—See JMB Realty Corporation, pg. 585
AMFAC ENERGY, INC.—See JMB Realty Corporation, pg. 585
AMFAC FINANCIAL INC.—See JMB Realty Corporation, pg. 585
AMFAC FOODS, INC.—See JMB Realty Corporation, pg. 585
AMFAC GARDEN HAWAII—See JMB Realty Corporation, pg. 585
AMFAC HEALTH CARE—See JMB Realty Corporation, pg. 585
AMFAC, INC.—See JMB Realty Corporation, pg. 585
AMFAC/JMB HAWAII, INC.—See JMB Realty Corporation, pg. 585
AMFAC NURSERIES COLE, INC.—See JMB Realty Corporation, pg. 585
AMFAC PROPERTY DEVELOPMENT CORP.—See JMB Realty Corporation, pg. 585
AMFAC PROPERTY INVESTMENT CORP.—See JMB Realty Corporation, pg. 585
AMFAC RESORTS, INC.—See JMB Realty Corporation, pg. 585
AMFAC RETAIL CORP.—See JMB Realty Corporation, pg. 585
AMFAC SILVERADO CORP.—See JMB Realty Corporation, pg. 585
AMFAC SUGAR AND AGRIBUSINESS, INC.—See JMB Realty Corporation, pg. 585
AMFAC TROPICAL PRODUCTS—See JMB Realty Corporation, pg. 585
AMFAM, INC.—See American Family Mutual Insurance Co., pg. 52
AMICA MUTUAL INSURANCE CO., pg. 66
AMICALE INDUSTRIES, INC., pg. 66
AMICK CONSTRUCTION LTD., pg. 67
AMICO-HOUSTON DISTR. CENTER—See Alabama Metal Industries Corporation, pg. 29
AMINCO, INC., pg. 67
AMITY LEATHER PRODUCTS COMPANY, pg. 67
AMKOR ELECTRONICS, INC., pg. 67
AMLINGS FLOWERLAND, pg. 67
AMLINGS LANDSCAPE CO.—See Amlings Flowerland, pg. 67
AMLOID CORPORATION, pg. 67
AMMIRATI & PURIS INC., pg. 67
AMOL DICALITE LTD.—See Belmont Industries, Inc., pg. 137
AMPACET CORPORATION, pg. 67
AMPCO METAL INC., DALLAS DIV.—See Ampco Metal Incorporated, pg. 68
AMPCO METAL INCORPORATED, pg. 67
AMPCO METAL LTD.—See Ampco Metal Incorporated, pg. 68
AMPCO METAL NEDERLANDS B.V.—See Ampco Metal Incorporated, pg. 68
AMPCO METAL NORDISKA AB—See Ampco Metal Incorporated, pg. 68
AMPCO METAL S.A.—See Ampco Metal Incorporated, pg. 68
AMPERIF CORPORATION, pg. 68
AMPEX COMPUTER PRODUCTS DIVISION—See Sherborne Group, Inc., pg. 998
AMPEX CORPORATION MARKETING, SALES & SERVICE—See Sherborne Group, Inc., pg. 998

AMPEX CORPORATION, VIDEO SYSTEMS DIV.—See Sherborne Group, Inc., pg. 998
AMPEX MAGNETIC TAPE DIVISION—See Sherborne Group, Inc., pg. 998
AMPEX RECORDING SYSTEMS DIVISION—See Sherborne Group, Inc., pg. 998
AMPHENOL CORPORATION—See LPL Technologies, Inc., pg. 648
AMRAY, INC., pg. 68
AMRECORP REALTY INC., pg. 68
AMSCO SCHOOL PUBLICATIONS, INC., pg. 68
AMSTAR CORPORATION—See ESSTAR Incorporated, pg. 361
AMSTAR TECHNICAL PRODUCTS CO., INC.—See ESSTAR Incorporated, pg. 361
AMSTED INDUSTRIES INCORPORATED, pg. 68
AMSTED INDUSTRIES INTERNATIONAL—See Amsted Industries Incorporated, pg. 69
AMSTORE CORPORATION, pg. 69
AMTRAK-NATIONAL RAILROAD PASSENGER CORP., pg. 69
AMTRAN CORPORATION, pg. 69
AMTRAN, INC., pg. 69
AMTROL INC., pg. 70
AMURCON CORPORATION, pg. 70
AMURCON EQUITIES—See Amurcon Corporation, pg. 70
AMURCON MANAGEMENT—See Amurcon Corporation, pg. 70
AMURCON SECURITIES CORP.—See Amurcon Corporation, pg. 70
AMWAY ARGENTINA, INC.—See Amway Corporation, pg. 70
AMWAY BELGIUM CO.—See Amway Corporation, pg. 70
AMWAY CORPORATION, pg. 70
AMWAY DE ESPANA, S.A.—See Amway Corporation, pg. 70
AMWAY DE GUATEMALA, S.A.—See Amway Corporation, pg. 70
AMWAY DE MEXICO, S.A. DE C.V.—See Amway Corporation, pg. 70
AMWAY DE PANAMA S.A.—See Amway Corporation, pg. 70
AMWAY DE PORTUGAL, INC.—See Amway Corporation, pg. 70
AMWAY DO BRASIL LTDA.—See Amway Corporation, pg. 70
AMWAY (EUROPE) LTD.—See Amway Corporation, pg. 70
AMWAY FRANCE—See Amway Corporation, pg. 70
AMWAY GESSELLSCHAFT M.B.H.—See Amway Corporation, pg. 70
AMWAY GMBH—See Amway Corporation, pg. 70
AMWAY HOTEL CORPORATION—See Amway Corporation, pg. 70
AMWAY HUNGARIA MARKETING KFT.—See Amway Corporation, pg. 70
AMWAY INDONESIA—See Amway Corporation, pg. 71
AMWAY INTERNATIONAL, INC.-HONG KONG BRANCH—See Amway Corporation, pg. 71
AMWAY ITALIA S.R.L.—See Amway Corporation, pg. 71
AMWAY (JAPAN) LIMITED—See Amway Corporation, pg. 71
AMWAY KOREA, LTD.—See Amway Corporation, pg. 71
AMWAY (MALAYSIA) SDN. BHD.—See Amway Corporation, pg. 71
AMWAY NEDERLAND LTD.—See Amway Corporation, pg. 71
AMWAY OF AUSTRALIA PTY. LTD.—See Amway Corporation, pg. 71
AMWAY OF CANADA, LTD.—See Amway Corporation, pg. 71
AMWAY OF NEW ZEALAND LIMITED—See Amway Corporation, pg. 71
AMWAY (SCHWEIZ) AG—See Amway Corporation, pg. 71
AMWAY TAIWAN, LTD.—See Amway Corporation, pg. 71
AMWAY (THAILAND) LIMITED—See Amway Corporation, pg. 71
AMWAY (U.K.) LIMITED—See Amway Corporation, pg. 71
ANAHEIM MANUFACTURING COMPANY, pg. 71
ANCHOR CONTINENTAL INCORPORATED, pg. 71
ANCHOR DARLING INDUSTRIES INC.—See Cawsl Corporation, pg. 230
ANCHOR DARLING VALVE CO.—See Cawsl Corporation, pg. 230
ANCHOR FENCE COMPANY—See PPA Industries, Inc., pg. 836
ANCHOR FINANCIAL CORPORATION, pg. 71
ANCHOR GASOLINE CORPORATION, pg. 71
ANCHOR INDUSTRIES INC., pg. 71
ANCHOR METALS, INC.—See Datron Incorporated, pg. 316
ANCHOR OPTICAL CO., INC.—See Edmund Scientific Company, pg. 369
ANCHOR POST PRODUCTS-WASHINGTON DIV.—See PPA Industries, Inc., pg. 836
ANCHOR TOOL & DIE COMPANY, pg. 71
ANCHORLOK CORP.—See Lear Siegler Diversified Holdings Corp., pg. 664
ANCO INSULATIONS, INC., pg. 72
ANCO TRANSPORTATION SERVICE, INC.—See C. R. Anthony Company, pg. 77
ANCRA CINCINATTI—See Ancra Corporation, pg. 72
ANCRA CORPORATION, pg. 72
ANDAMIOS ATLAS, S.A.—See AXIA Incorporated, pg. 8
ARTHUR ANDERSEN—See Arthur Andersen & Co., S.C., pg. 72
ARTHUR ANDERSEN & CO.—See Arthur Andersen & Co., S.C., pg. 72
ARTHUR ANDERSEN & CO., S.C., pg. 72
ANDERSEN CONSULTING—See Arthur Andersen & Co., S.C., pg. 72
ANDERSEN WINDOWS INC., pg. 72
ANDERSON ADVERTISING, INC., pg. 72
ANDERSON BROTHERS CONSTRUCTION BRAINERD, pg. 72
ANDERSON COPPER & BRASS COMPANY—See The Marmon Group, Inc., pg. 711
ANDERSON DIE CASTINGS, INC., pg. 72
ANDERSON, DUSENBURY & ALBAN, pg. 72
ANDERSON INDUSTRIES, INC., pg. 72
ANDERSON INDUSTRIES INC., pg. 73
ANDERSON & LEMBKE INC.—See Chiat/Day/Mojo Inc. Advertising, pg. 244
ANDERSON & LEMBKE INC., pg. 73
ANDERSON LITHOGRAPH COMPANY, pg. 73
ANDERSON LUMBER COMPANY, pg. 73
MARK ANDERSON ASSOCIATES, INC., pg. 73
MARK ANDERSON ASSOCIATES, INC.—See Mark Anderson Associates, Inc., pg. 73
THE ANDERSON NEWS—See Landmark Communications, Inc., pg. 655
ANDERSON-PARRISH ASSOCIATES, INC.—See Lawler-Havens Inc., pg. 661
ANDERSON, ROTHSTEIN & FIQUA, pg. 73
ANDERSON TRUCKING SERVICE INC., pg. 73
ANDERSON-TULLY CO., pg. 73
W.E. ANDERSON DIV.—See Dwyer Instruments Inc., pg. 356
ANDERSON WHOLESALE COMPANY, pg. 73
THE ANDERSONS INVESTMENT SERVICES CORP.—See The Andersons, pg. 74
THE ANDERSONS, pg. 73
THE ANDERSONS WHITE PIGEON TERMINAL—See The Andersons, pg. 74
ANDERSSON MEDIA AKTIEBOLAG—See Young & Rubicam Inc., pg. 1211
ANDIAMO, INC., pg. 74
ANDIS COMPANY, pg. 74
ANDMORE SPORTSWEAR CORPORATION, pg. 74
ANDREA INTERNATIONAL—See Ardell International, Inc., pg. 81
ANDREAS GALLERIES, INC.—See Lantzsch-Andreas Enterprises, Inc., pg. 658
ANDREWS GROUP, INCORPORATED, pg. 74
ANDREWS/MAUTNER, INC., pg. 74
ANDY FRAIN AVIATION SERVICES, INC.—See Andy Frain Services, Inc., pg. 428
ANDYS RENTAL INC.—See X-A Cabinet Corporation, pg. 1206
ANGELO BROTHERS CO., pg. 74
ANGLERS ROSLYN GROUP LTD., pg. 75
ANGLO FABRICS COMPANY, INC., pg. 75
ANGLO-AUSTRIAN MAGNESITE, LTD.—See Belmont Industries, Inc., pg. 137
ANGUS CHEMICAL COMPANY, pg. 75
ANGUS CHEMIE GMBH—See ANGUS Chemical Company, pg. 75
ANGUS FINE CHEMICALS LTD.—See ANGUS Chemical Company, pg. 75
ANIMAL FAIR—See Guy Schoenecker, Inc., pg. 978
ANN ARBOR ASSEMBLY CORPORATION—See Edgewood Tool & Manufacturing Company, pg. 368
ANN ARBOR COMPUTER—See Jervis B. Webb Company, pg. 1170
ANNABELLE CANDY COMPANY, pg. 75
ANNIN & COMPANY, pg. 75
ANNING-JOHNSON COMPANY—See Anson Industries, Inc., pg. 76
ANO-COIL CORPORATION, pg. 75
ANSCHUTZ CORPORATION, pg. 75
ANSCO PHOTO-OPTICAL PRODUCTS CORP., pg. 76
BENJAMIN ANSEHL COMPANY, pg. 76
ANSER (ANALYTIC SERVICES INC.), pg. 76
MOSES ANSHELL, INC., pg. 76
ANSON INDUSTRIES, INC., pg. 76
ANSON-STONER, INC., pg. 76
ANTARES GROUP INC., pg. 76
ANTENNA PRODUCTS CORP., pg. 76
ANTHEM COMPANIES, INC.—See The Associated Group, pg. 90
ANTHEM HEALTH PLANS OF FLORIDA INC.—See The Associated Group, pg. 90
ANTHEM LIFE INSURANCE COMPANIES, INC.—See The Associated Group, pg. 90
C. R. ANTHONY COMPANY, pg. 77
ANTHONY DIVISION—See MidWest Body Corporation, pg. 752
ANTHONY FOREST DIV.—See Anthony Forest Products Co., Inc., pg. 77
ANTHONY FOREST PRODUCTS CO., INC., pg. 77
ANTHONY INTERNATIONAL—See Anthony Forest Products Co., Inc., pg. 77
C. R. ANTHONY INTERNATIONAL, LTD.—See C. R. Anthony Company, pg. 77
ANTHONY'S OF SANDPOINT, INC.—See C. R. Anthony Company, pg. 77
ANTHONY'S OF SLEEPY EYE, INC.—See C. R. Anthony Company, pg. 77
ANTHONY'S OF SPRING VALLEY, INC.—See C. R. Anthony Company, pg. 77
ANTIQUES & COLLECTIBLES—See Landmark Communications, Inc., pg. 656
ANTWERP DIAMOND DISTRIBUTORS INC., pg. 77
APACHE HOSE & BELTING COMPANY, pg. 77
APACHE PLASTICS, L.P., pg. 77
APCO ARGENTINA INC., pg. 77
APCOM INC.—See State Industries Inc., pg. 1041
APEX BROACH & MACHINE CO., pg. 77
APEX CORPORATION, pg. 78
APEX GALVANIZING CORP.—See Victaulic Company of America, pg. 1149
APEX MFG. CO., INC.—See Soundesign Corporation, pg. 1018
APEX MILLS CORPORATION, pg. 78
APEX OIL COMPANY, INC., pg. 78
APEX SUPPLY CO. INC., pg. 78
APOLLO COLORS, INC., pg. 78
APOLLO INDUSTRIES—See Theochem Labs., Inc., pg. 1090
APPALACHIAN REALTY CO.—See The H. T. Hackney Co., pg. 498
APPAREL AMERICA, INC., pg. 78
THE APPAREL GROUP, LTD., pg. 78
APPAREL INDUSTRIES, INC., pg. 78
APPAREL VENTURES, INC., pg. 78
I. APPEL CORPORATION, pg. 78
APPERSON BUSINESS FORMS, INC., pg. 78
APPLE LINES, INC., pg. 79
APPLE VACATIONS WEST INC., pg. 79
APPLETREE MARKETS, pg. 79
APPLICATION AUTOMATION, INC.—See Sterling, Inc., pg. 1047
APPLICATION ENGINEERING CORPORATION—See Sterling, Inc., pg. 1047
APPLICATOR CO.—See Plastek Group, pg. 875
APPLIED COATINGS—See Bel-Art Products, pg. 133
APPLIED GRAPHICS TECHNOLOGY—See U.S. News & World Report, pg. 1136
APPLIED HOLOGRAPHICS, INC.—See SBN System Inc., pg. 960
APPLIED INDUSTRIAL MATERIALS CORPORATION, pg. 79
APPLIED MICROSYSTEMS CORPORATION, pg. 79
APPLIED SCIENCES DIVISION—See Caddock Electronics, Inc., pg. 207
APPLIED SOLAR ENERGY CORPORATION, pg. 79
APPLIED GRAPHICS TECHNOLOGIES—See U.S. News & World Report, pg. 1136
APRIL HILL, INC.—See Grocers Baking Co., pg. 488
AQUA FAB INDUSTRIES, INC., pg. 79
AQUIDNECK DATA COMPANY—See Day & Zimmermann, Inc., pg. 320
ARACLEAN SERVICES, INC.—See ARA Group, pg. 6
ARAMIS, INC.—See Estee Lauder, Inc., pg. 389
ARAMONT PROPERTIES, INC.-DELAWARE—See ARA Group, pg. 6
ARANDELL-SCHMIDT CORPORATION, pg. 79
ARASERVE, INC.—See ARA Group, pg. 6
ARATEX OF PUERTO RICO—See ARA Group, pg. 6
ARBOR HOUSE—See The Hearst Corporation, pg. 522
ARBURG, INC., pg. 79
ARCADE INC., pg. 80
ARCADIA FRYERS, pg. 80
ARCADIAN POWER CORP., pg. 80
ARCATA CORPORATION, pg. 80
ARCATA GRAPHICS BAIRD WARD, INC.—See Arcata Corporation, pg. 80
ARCATA GRAPHICS BUFFALO, INC.—See Arcata Corporation, pg. 80
ARCATA GRAPHICS COMPANY—See Arcata Corporation, pg. 80
ARCATA GRAPHICS FAIRFIELD INC.—See Arcata Corporation, pg. 80
ARCATA GRAPHICS HALLIDAY—See Arcata Corporation, pg. 80
ARCATA GRAPHICS KINGSPORT—See Arcata Corporation, pg. 80
ARCATA GRAPHICS SHERWOOD—See Arcata Corporation, pg. 80
ARCHER/MALMO ADV., INC., pg. 80
ARCHIBALD CANDY COMPANY—See Jordan Company, pg. 604
THE ARCHITECTS COLLABORATIVE, INC. (TAC), pg. 80
ARCHITECTURAL INTERIORS, INC.—See A. Epstein and Sons, Intl., Inc., pg. 384
ARCHWAY COOKIES, INC., pg. 81
ARCINCO, INC., pg. 81
ARCOLA WIRE COMPANY, pg. 81
ARCON CONSTRUCTION CO., INC., pg. 81
ARCTIC ALASKA DRILLING—See Markair, Inc., pg. 708
ARCTIC ALASKA TESTING LABORATORIES—See Shannon & Wilson, Inc., pg. 995
ARCTIC PACKAGING & LOGISTICS INC.—See Lynden Incorporated, pg. 689
ARDCO, INC., pg. 81
ARDELL INDUSTRIES INC.—See Jordan Company, pg. 604
ARDELL INTERNATIONAL, INC., pg. 81
THE ARDMORE DAILY ARDMOREITE—See Stauffer Communications, Inc., pg. 1042
ARELLANO/BSB PUBLICIDAD—See Backer Spielvogel Bates Worldwide, Inc., pg. 109
DONALD L. ARENDS INC., pg. 81
ARGILAND COMPANY, pg. 81
ARGO INTERNATIONAL—See Decal Enterprises, Inc., pg. 323
ARGO INTERNATIONAL CORP., pg. 81
ARGO-TECH CORPORATION, pg. 82
ARGO TERMINAL CO.—See Great Lakes Terminal & Transport Corp., pg. 482
THE ARGOS GROUP—See Barton-Malow Enterprises, Inc., pg. 123
ARGOSY ELECTRONICS, INC., pg. 82
ARIAN, LOWE, TRAVIS & GUSICK, INC., pg. 82
ARINC INC., pg. 82
ARINC RESEARCH CORP.—See Arinc Inc., pg. 82
ARISTERA—See The Renovator's Supply, Inc., pg. 927
ARISTO MANUFACTURING CO.—See The Metal Ware Corp., pg. 742
ARIZONA AUCTION SERVICES, INC. D/B/A ARIZONA AUTO AUCTION—See Cox Enterprises, Inc., pg. 293
ARIZONA AUCTION SERVICES, INC., D/B/A SOUTHWEST AUTO AUCTION—See Cox Enterprises, Inc., pg. 293
ARIZONA GRAINS INC., pg. 82
ARIZONA LOTTERY, pg. 82
ARIZONA SASH & DOOR CO.—See Foxworth-Galbraith Lumber Co., pg. 428
ARIZONA SUPERMARKETS, INC., pg. 82
ARIZONA WHOLESALE SUPPLY COMPANY, pg. 82
ARK-LES CORPORATION, pg. 82
ARKANSAS ALUMINUM ALLOYS—See A. Tenenbaum Co. Inc., pg. 1087

THE ARKANSAS CITY DAILY TRAVELER—See Stauffer Communications, Inc., pg. 1042
ARKANSAS ELECTRIC COOPERATIVES INC., pg. 83
ARKANSAS FARM BUREAU FEDERATION, pg. 83
ARKANSAS INDUSTRIAL DEVELOPMENT COMMISSION, pg. 83
ARKANSAS INVESTMENT CASTING—See American Military Arms Corporation, pg. 58
ARKANSAS & MEMPHIS RAILWAY BRIDGE AND TERMINAL CO.—See Anschutz Corporation, pg. 76
ARKANSAS OAK FLOORING, pg. 83
ARKANSAS VALLEY DISTRIBUTING—See Hale-Halsell Company, pg. 500
ARKAY PACKAGING CORPORATION, pg. 83
ARLEN ADVERTISING, pg. 83
ARLEY MERCHANDISE CORPORATION, pg. 83
ARLO GROUP, BATTLE CREEK—See Alro Group, pg. 44
ARLO GROUP, CLEARWATER—See Alro Group, pg. 44
ARLO GROUP, KALAMAZOO—See Alro Group, pg. 44
ARLO GROUP, ORLANDO—See Alro Group, pg. 44
ARMSTRONG AIR CONDITIONING INC.—See Lennox International Inc., pg. 667
ARMSTRONG-HUNT, INC.—See Armstrong International, Inc., pg. 83
ARMSTRONG INTERNATIONAL, INC., pg. 83
ARMSTRONG MACHINE WORKS—See Armstrong International, Inc., pg. 83
ARMSTRONG MACHINE WORKS, S.A.—See Armstrong International, Inc., pg. 84
ARMSTRONG PRODUCE LTD., pg. 84
ARMSTRONG-YOSHITAKE, INC.—See Armstrong International, Inc., pg. 84
ARNAV INDUSTRIES, INC., pg. 84
ARNHOLD AND S. BLEICHROEDER, INC., pg. 84
BEN ARNOLD CO., INC., pg. 84
TRUMAN ARNOLD COMPANIES, pg. 84
ARNOLD CONCRETE PRODUCTS-GREENSBORO—See Carolina Steel Corporation, pg. 223
ARNOLD CONCRETE PRODUCTS-RALEIGH DIV.—See Carolina Steel Corporation, pg. 223
ARNOLD FORTUNA LAWNER & CABOT, pg. 84
ARNOLD FORTUNA LAWNER & CABOT—See Arnold Fortuna Lawner & Cabot, pg. 84
ARNOLD FORTUNA LAWNER & CABOT—See Arnold Fortuna Lawner & Cabot, pg. 84
ARNOLD FORTUNA LAWNER & CABOT—See Arnold Fortuna Lawner & Cabot, pg. 84
ARNOLD MACHINERY CO., pg. 84
ARNOLD MACHINERY COMPANY OF ARIZONA—See Arnold Machinery Co., pg. 85
ARNOLD STEEL COMPANY, INC., pg. 85
ARNOLDS INTERIORS, INC., pg. 85
AROCOM DIRECT, INC.—See Meldrum & Fewsmith Communications Inc., pg. 737
AROCOM MARKETING GROUP, INC.—See Meldrum & Fewsmith Communications Inc., pg. 737
AROCOM MARKETING GROUP, INC.—See Meldrum & Fewsmith Communications Inc., pg. 737
AROCOM MARKETING GROUP, INC.—See Meldrum & Fewsmith Communications Inc., pg. 737
J. ARON & COMPANY (U.K.), LIMITED—See Goldman, Sachs & Co., pg. 468
J. ARON & COMPANY (U.K.), LIMITED—See Goldman, Sachs & Co., pg. 468
PAUL ARPIN VANLINES, INC., pg. 85
ARRINGTON-HILLGATE INTERNATIONAL—See Arrington Travel Center Inc., pg. 85
ARRINGTON TRAVEL CENTER INC., pg. 85
ARROW BUILDING CENTERS—See Consolidated Lumber Co., pg. 276
ARROW CHEVROLET, INC., pg. 85
ARROW FASTENER CO., INC., pg. 85
ARROW GROUP INDUSTRIES, INC.—See The Dyson-Kissner-Moran Corporation, pg. 357
ARROW INDUSTRIES, INC., pg. 85
ARROW METAL PRODUCTS CORPORATION, pg. 85
ARROW PNEUMATICS CO. INC., pg. 85
ARROW SINTERED PRODUCTS—See Arrow Pneumatics Co. Inc., pg. 85
ARROW TANK & ENGINEERING CO., pg. 85
ARROW THOMPSON METALS—See Thompson Steel Co., Inc., pg. 1095
ARROW TYPOGRAPHERS, INC.—See Delaware North Companies, Inc., pg. 326
ARROWHEAD MILLS, INC., pg. 86
ART IRON, INC., pg. 86
ART PUBLISHING CO.—See Goldmark Industries, Ltd., pg. 468
ART VAN FURNITURE INC., pg. 86
ARTCO-BELL CORPORATION, pg. 86
ARTCO-BELL STEEL CORP.—See Artco-Bell Corporation, pg. 86
ARTEC DISTRIBUTING, INC., pg. 86
ARTECON, INC.—See Nordic Group of Companies, Ltd., pg. 809
ARTESIAN DEVELOPMENT CORPORATION—See Artesian Resources Corporation, pg. 86
ARTESIAN LABORATORIES, INC.—See Artesian Resources Corporation, pg. 86
ARTESIAN RESOURCES CORPORATION, pg. 86
ARTESIAN WATER COMPANY, INC.—See Artesian Resources Corporation, pg. 86
ARTHUR CHEESE COMPANY, pg. 87
ARTHUR TREACHER'S, INC., pg. 87
ARTIC N.V. S.A.—See TLC Beatrice International Holdings Inc., pg. 1073
ARTICHOKE INDUSTRIES, INC., pg. 87
ARTIST GRAPHICS—See Control Systems Inc., pg. 281
ARTISTIC CARTON COMPANY, pg. 87
ARTPLAN PUBLICIDADE—See TBWA Advertising, Inc., pg. 1072
ARTS & COMMUNICATIONS COUNSELORS, INC., NY—See Ruder, Finn, Inc., pg. 954
ARTS & CRAFTS PRESS—See Continental Graphics Holdings, Inc., pg. 279
ARTS & ENTERTAINMENT NETWORK—See The Hearst Corporation, pg. 523
ARVIDA—See JMB Realty Corporation, pg. 586
ASAHI/AMERICA, INC., pg. 87
ASBURY CARBONS, INC., pg. 87
ASBURY FERST, INC.—See Asbury Carbons, Inc., pg. 87
ASBURY GRAPHITE MILLS, INC.—See Asbury Carbons, Inc., pg. 87
ASBURY PARK PRESS, INC.—See New Jersey Press, Inc., pg. 801
ASCO MUSIC—See Cox Enterprises, Inc., pg. 292
ASER PUBLICIDAD/Y&R—See Young & Rubicam Inc., pg. 1213
ASH GROVE CEMENT—See Ash Grove Cement Company, pg. 87
ASH GROVE CEMENT—See Ash Grove Cement Company, pg. 87
ASH GROVE CEMENT—See Ash Grove Cement Company, pg. 87
ASH GROVE CEMENT—See Ash Grove Cement Company, pg. 87
ASH GROVE CEMENT CO., DURKEE PLANT—See Ash Grove Cement Company, pg. 87
ASH GROVE CEMENT COMPANY, pg. 87
ASH INSTRUMENTS DIVISION, DENTSPLY LTD.—See Dentsply International Inc., pg. 330
ASH, U.S.A.—See Dentsply International Inc., pg. 330
ASHER CANDY COMPANY—See MacAndrews & Forbes Holdings Inc., pg. 695
ASHER/GOULD ADVERTISING, INC., pg. 88
THE ASHER WINER COMPANY, pg. 88
ASHMAN ENTERPRISES, INC., pg. 88
ASHTON/SCHOLASTIC PTY. LTD.—See SI Holdings Inc., pg. 962
ASHWORTH BROS., INC., pg. 88
ASIA COMPUTERWORLD—See International Data Group, pg. 577
ASIA COMPUTERWORLD COMMUNICATIONS—See International Data Group, pg. 577
ASKO, INC, pg. 88
ASPENRISE PROPERTIES, INC.—See Society for Savings Bancorp, Inc., pg. 1016
ASPLUNDH TREE EXPERT CO., pg. 88
ASSET MARKETING, LTD.—See Backer Spielvogel Bates Worldwide, Inc., pg. 109
ASSOCIATED ADVERTISING AGENCY, INC., pg. 89
ASSOCIATED AIR FREIGHT, INC., pg. 89
ASSOCIATED AIRCRAFT SUPPLY COMPANY, pg. 89
ASSOCIATED COMPANY, INC., pg. 89
ASSOCIATED DIESEL SERVICE & EQUIPMENT COMPANY, pg. 89
ASSOCIATED DRUGGISTS—See Cullman Ventures, Inc., pg. 304
ASSOCIATED ELECTRIC CO-OP INC., pg. 89
ASSOCIATED EQUIPMENT COMPANY, INC., pg. 89
ASSOCIATED FOOD STORES INC., pg. 89
ASSOCIATED FOODS INC.—See Associated Grocers of New England, Inc., pg. 90
ASSOCIATED GROCERS, INC., pg. 89
ASSOCIATED GROCERS, INC., pg. 90
ASSOCIATED GROCERS OF ALABAMA, INC., pg. 90
ASSOCIATED GROCERS OF NEW ENGLAND, INC., pg. 90
ASSOCIATED GROUP—See MacAndrews & Forbes Holdings Inc., pg. 694
ASSOCIATED GROUP INC.—See The Associated Group, pg. 90
THE ASSOCIATED GROUP, pg. 90
ASSOCIATED INDUSTRIAL RUBBER—See Flexfab, Inc., pg. 418
ASSOCIATED INDUSTRIAL SUPPLY, INC., pg. 90
ASSOCIATED LEASE CORP.—See Associated Grocers of New England, Inc., pg. 90
ASSOCIATED OF LOS ANGELES, pg. 90
ASSOCIATED MACHINECRAFT CORPORATION, pg. 90
ASSOCIATED MATERIALS INC., pg. 91
ASSOCIATED MERCHANDISING CORP., pg. 91
ASSOCIATED MERCHANDISING CORP. (FRANCE) S.A.—See Associated Merchandising Corp., pg. 91
ASSOCIATED METALS & MINERALS CORP., pg. 91
ASSOCIATED MILK PRODUCERS, INC., pg. 91
ASSOCIATED MUSIC PUBLISHERS—See Music Sales Corporation, pg. 777
ASSOCIATED PETROLEUM CARRIERS, pg. 91
THE ASSOCIATED PRESS A/S—See The Associated Press, pg. 92
THE ASSOCIATED PRESS AB—See The Associated Press, pg. 92
THE ASSOCIATED PRESS (BELGIUM) S.A.—See The Associated Press, pg. 92
THE ASSOCIATED PRESS DE VENEZUELA, S.A.—See The Associated Press, pg. 92
THE ASSOCIATED PRESS GMBH—See The Associated Press, pg. 92
THE ASSOCIATED PRESS, LTD.—See The Associated Press, pg. 92
THE ASSOCIATED PRESS, pg. 91
ASSOCIATED PROCESS CONTROLS, pg. 92
ASSOCIATED WHOLESALE GROCERS, INC., pg. 92
ASSOCIATION OF CREDIT UNION LEAGUE EXECUTIVES—See Credit Union National Association, pg. 298
ASSURANCE GLASS CO. OF ALABAMA—See Globe-Amerada Glass Company, pg. 463
ASTER NUT PRODUCTS INC., pg. 92
ASTON MARTIN LAGONDA OF NORTH AMERICA, INC., pg. 92
ASTRE CONSULTING CORP.—See Astre Corporate Group, pg. 92
ASTRE CORPORATE GROUP, pg. 92
ASTRO WIRE & CABLE CORPORATION, pg. 92
ASTRONAUTICS C.A. LTD.—See Astronautics Corp. of America, pg. 93
ASTRONAUTICS CORP. OF AMERICA, pg. 93
ASTRUP DRUGS, INC., pg. 93
AT HOME RESPIRATORY AND MEDICAL, INC.—See Syracuse Supply Company, pg. 1070
ATAG ALLGEMEINE TREUHAND AG—See Ernst & Young, pg. 387
ATAG FIDUCIAIRE GENERALE SA—See Ernst & Young, pg. 387
ATAL SA—See Joyce International, Inc., pg. 608
ATAPCO AZTECA, S.A. DE C.V.—See American Trading and Production Corporation, pg. 65
ATAPCO OFFICE PRODUCTS GROUP—See American Trading and Production Corporation, pg. 64
ATARI GAMES CORPORATION, pg. 93
ATCHISON COUNTY CO-OP ASSOCIATION, pg. 93
ATCOM, INC., pg. 93
ATERON CORP., pg. 93
ATEX OIL CO. OF TEXAS, INC., pg. 93
ATHENS PAPER CO. INC., pg. 93
THE ATHLETE'S FOOT GROUP, INC., pg. 94
ATHLETIC ATTIC PROPERTIES INC., pg. 94
THE ATKINS AGENCY, pg. 94
ATLANTA AUTO AUCTION, INC.—See Cox Enterprises, Inc., pg. 293
ATLANTA BEVERAGE CO., pg. 94
ATLANTA CASUALTY COMPANY—See American Financial Corporation, pg. 53
ATLANTA HILL RESTAURANT CORP.—See Specialty Restaurants Corporation, pg. 1028
ATLANTA MARKET CENTER, pg. 94
ATLANTA MFG. FACILITY—See L. M. Scofield Company, pg. 982
ATLANTA MOTOR LINES, INC., pg. 94
ATLANTA NEWSPAPERS—See Cox Enterprises, Inc., pg. 292
ATLANTA SOUTHEASTERN DEVELOPMENT CORP.—See Ideal Pool Corp., pg. 562
ATLANTA STRUCTURAL CONCRETE DIV.—See Bristol Steel & Iron Works, Inc., pg. 177
ATLANTA WIRE WORKS, INC., pg. 94
ATLANTIC AVIATION CORP., pg. 94
ATLANTIC BUILDERS GROUP INC., pg. 94
ATLANTIC COAST ASPHALT—See Hubbard Construction Co., pg. 549
ATLANTIC MUTUAL COMPANIES, pg. 94
ATLANTIC CONCRETE PRODUCTS, INC., pg. 94
ATLANTIC DAIRY COOPERATIVE, pg. 94
ATLANTIC GULF COMMUNITIES CORPORATION, pg. 95
ATLANTIC HEALTH CARE RESOURCES, INC.—See Syracuse Supply Company, pg. 1070
ATLANTIC HOMES CORP.—See The Great Atlantic Companies, pg. 480
ATLANTIC LUMBER COMPANY—See Sabbeth Industries Ltd, pg. 965
ATLANTIC METALS CORPORATION, pg. 95
THE ATLANTIC MONTHLY MAGAZINE, pg. 95
ATLANTIC MUTUAL INSURANCE CO.—See Atlantic Mutual Companies, pg. 94
ATLANTIC NATIONAL CORPORATION—See Hawthorne Corp., pg. 519
ATLANTIC PLUMBING SUPPLY COMPANY, pg. 95
ATLANTIC STEEL COMPANY, pg. 95
ATLANTIC SUGAR ASSOCIATION, INC., pg. 95
ATLANTIC TO PACIFIC BEDDING CORP., pg. 95
ATLAS BOLT & SCREW COMPANY—See The Marmon Group, Inc., pg. 712
ATLAS CITRON HALIGMAN & BEDECARRE, pg. 96
ATLAS CO. OF BOSTON, INC.—See Skyway Luggage Co., pg. 1009
THE ATLAS CONSTRUCTION CO., pg. 96
ATLAS FOUNDRY & MACHINE CO.—See TIC United Corporation, pg. 1073
ATLAS HOTELS, INC., pg. 96
ATLAS LEDERER CO.—See Columbia National Group, Inc., pg. 265
ATLAS LIFT TRUCK RENTALS & SALES, INC., pg. 96
ATLAS PATTERN WORKS—See Stockham Valves & Fittings, Inc., pg. 1050
ATLAS PEN & PENCIL CORPORATION, pg. 96
ATLAS POWER EQUIPMENT COMPANY, pg. 96
ATLAS REFINERY, pg. 96
ATLAS/SOUNDOLIER—See American Trading and Production Corporation, pg. 64
ATLAS SPECIALIZED TRANSPORTATION—See Atlas Van Lines, Inc., pg. 97
ATLAS SUPPLY COMPANY, pg. 96
ATLAS TAG & LABEL INC.—See Bissell Inc., pg. 153
ATLAS TOOL INC., pg. 96
ATLAS VAN LINES, INC., pg. 96
ATLAS WIRE CORPORATION, pg. 97
ATLAS WORLD-CLASS TRAVEL—See Atlas Van Lines, Inc., pg. 97
ATLITE LIGHTING EQUIP, INC., pg. 97
ATOLS TOOL AND MOLD CORP., pg. 97
ATTORNEY'S TITLE INSURANCE FUND, pg. 97
ATWOOD AUTOMOTIVE INC.—See Atwood Industries, Inc., pg. 97
ATWOOD DISTRIBUTING, INC., pg. 97
ATWOOD INDUSTRIES, INC., pg. 97
AU PAIR IN AMERICA—See American Institute For Foreign Study, pg. 56
W.E. AUBUCHON CO., INC., pg. 97
AUBURN FAITH COMMUNITY HOSPITAL, pg. 97
AUBURNDALE STAR—See Stauffer Communications, Inc., pg. 1042
GEORGE W. AUCH CO., pg. 97
THE AUCHTER COMPANY, pg. 98
AUDIO SPECIALIST, INC., pg. 98
AUGSBURG FORTRESS, PUBLISHERS, pg. 98
AUNT NELLIE'S FARM KITCHENS, INC., pg. 98
AURORA CASKET COMPANY, pg. 98
AURORA NATIONAL BANK—See GreatBanc, Inc., pg. 483

AURORA PACKING CO., INC., pg. 98
AUSHERMAN CONSTRUCTION COMPANY, pg. 98
THE AUSTAD COMPANY, pg. 98
AUSTIN ASSOCIATES, INC., pg. 98
AUSTIN-AUSTRALIA—See National Gypsum Company, pg. 790
AUSTIN BRIDGE & RD. CO.-ASPHALT DIV.—See Austin Industries, Inc., pg. 99
AUSTIN BRIDGE & RD.-CONCRETE DIV.—See Austin Industries, Inc., pg. 99
AUSTIN CAROLINA CO.—See Austin Co., Inc., pg. 99
THE AUSTIN CO.—See National Gypsum Company, pg. 790
THE AUSTIN CO. OF CANADA—See National Gypsum Company, pg. 790
AUSTIN CO., INC., pg. 98
THE AUSTIN CO. S.A.—See National Gypsum Company, pg. 790
THE AUSTIN CO. OF U.K. LTD.—See National Gypsum Company, pg. 790
THE AUSTIN COMPANY—See National Gypsum Company, pg. 790
AUSTIN CONSULTING—See National Gypsum Company, pg. 790
AUSTIN INDUSTRIES, INC., pg. 99
AUSTIN ITALIA S.P.A.—See National Gypsum Company, pg. 790
JAMES AUSTIN CO., pg. 99
AUSTIN KELLEY ADVERTISING, INC., pg. 99
AUSTIN-NEDERLAND B.V.—See National Gypsum Company, pg. 791
J. AUSTIN OIL CO., pg. 99
AUSTIN POWDER CO., pg. 99
AUSTIN SCULPTURE, pg. 99
AUSTRALIAN COLEMAN, INC.—See MacAndrews & Forbes Holdings Inc., pg. 695
AUSTRIA III—See TBWA Advertising, Inc., pg. 1072
AUSTRIAN AIRLINES, pg. 100
AUTO CRANE COMPANY, pg. 100
AUTO DIREKT VERSICHERUNGS AG—See Nationwide Mutual Insurance Company, pg. 795
AUTO DRIVEAWAY CO., pg. 100
AUTO GLASS SPECIALISTS, pg. 100
AUTO JECTORS, INC.—See Group Dekko International Inc., pg. 489
AUTO-OWNERS INSURANCE, pg. 100
AUTO-OWNERS LIFE INSURANCE CO.—See Auto-Owners Insurance, pg. 100
AUTOLIFT INDUSTRIAL LIFT TRUCKS—See Plymouth Locomotive International, Inc., pg. 877
AUTOMANAGE, pg. 100
AUTOMATED MARKETING SYSTEMS, INC., pg. 100
AUTOMATIC LIQUID PACKAGING, INC., pg. 100
AUTOMATIC MACHINE PRODUCTS COMPANY, pg. 100
AUTOMATIC METAL BLANKING, INC.—See Amtrol Inc., pg. 70
AUTOMATIC SERVICE CO.—See AVA-Automatic Vendors of America, pg. 8
AUTOMATIC SERVICE CO. OF VIRGINIA, LYNCHBURG BRANCH—See AVA-Automatic Vendors of America, pg. 8
AUTOMATIC SERVICE CO. OF VIRGINIA, NO. VIRGINIA BRANCH—See AVA-Automatic Vendors of America, pg. 8
AUTOMATIC TIMING & CONTROLS, INC.—See Desco Corporation, pg. 332
AUTOMATION INTELLIGENCE, INC., pg. 101
AUTOMATION INTELLIGENCE UK LTD.—See Automation Intelligence, Inc., pg. 101
AUTOMATION PRODUCTS GROUP—See The ISI Manufacturing, Inc., pg. 560
AUTOMATION RESOURCES—See Effective Management Systems, pg. 370
AUTOMOBILE AUCTION DIVISION—See Cox Enterprises, Inc., pg. 293
AUTOMOBILE MAGAZINE—See K-III Communications Corporation, pg. 611
AUTOMOBILE SPECIALTY CO.—See ASC Incorporated, pg. 7
AUTOMOTIVE ACCESSORY CO., LTD.—See UIS, Inc., pg. 1124
AUTOMOTIVE AFTERMARKET DIVISION—See Freudenberg-NOK (MI), pg. 432
AUTOMOTIVE CHEMICAL CORPORATION—See Findley Adhesives, Inc., pg. 410
AUTOMOTIVE MARKETING ASSOC.—See Carquest, pg. 224
AUTOMOTIVE MARKETING GROUP—See R. L. Polk & Co., pg. 879
AUTOMOTIVE MOULDING COMPANY, pg. 101
AUTOMOTIVE NEWS, pg. 101
AUTOMOTIVE NEWS—See Crain Communications, Inc., pg. 295
AUTOMOTIVE PLASTIC TECHNOLOGIES, INC., pg. 101
AUTOMOTIVE PRODUCTS GROUP—See American Standard Inc., pg. 62
AUTOMOTIVE RENTALS, INC., pg. 101
AUTOMOTIVE SUPPLY ASSOC., INC., pg. 101
AUTOMOTIVE WAREHOUSE, INC.—See Carquest Corporation, pg. 224
AUTONET, INC.—See Landmark Communications, Inc., pg. 656
AUTOROLL MACHINE CORP., pg. 101
AUTOSWAGE PRODUCTS, INC., pg. 101
AVADYNE, INC., pg. 101
THE AVALON HILL GAME COMPANY—See Monarch Avalon, Inc., pg. 765
AVALON HILL/SPORTS ILLUSTRATED GAMES—See Monarch Avalon, Inc., pg. 765
AVANZARE—See Lettuce Entertain You Enterprises, Inc., pg. 669
AVATAR CORPORATION, pg. 101
AVERY MAYS CONSTRUCTION CO.—See The Hunt Corporation, pg. 553
AVES ADVERTISING, INC., pg. 102
AVEX ELECTRONICS, INC.—See J.M. Huber Corporation, pg. 550
AVEX ELECTRONICS LTD.—See J.M. Huber Corporation, pg. 550
AVEX ELECTRONICS PTE. LTD.—See J.M. Huber Corporation, pg. 550
AVIATION CONSTRUCTORS, INC.—See Cleveland Group, Inc., pg. 255
AVIATION PRODUCT SUPPORT INC.—See Kleco Corp., pg. 635
AVIBANK MFG., INC., pg. 102
AVIS FORD INC., pg. 102
AVIS, INC., pg. 102
AVIS INDUSTRIAL CORPORATION, pg. 102
AV-KONTAKT A/S—See Backer Spielvogel Bates Worldwide, Inc., pg. 109
AVON BOOKS—See The Hearst Corporation, pg. 522
AVONDALE FOREIGN SALES CORPORATION—See Avondale Mills, Inc., pg. 103
AVONDALE MILLS, INC., pg. 103
AVRETT, FREE & GINSBERG, INC., pg. 103
A.W. LAWRENCE & COMPANY, INC.—See Lawrence Group, Inc., pg. 662
AWREY BAKERIES, INC., pg. 103
AXELBAND & BROWN & ASSOCIATES INC., pg. 103
AXELSON, INC., pg. 103
AXIOS, LTDA.—See The Pullman Company, pg. 900
AYDLOTTE & CARTWRIGHT, INC., pg. 103
AYER CHICAGO—See N W Ayer Incorporated, pg. 104
AYER EUROPE—See N W Ayer Incorporated, pg. 104
AYER FRANKFURT—See N W Ayer Incorporated, pg. 104
N W AYER INCORPORATED, pg. 103
AYER LTD.—See N W Ayer Incorporated, pg. 104
AYER MILANO—See N W Ayer Incorporated, pg. 104
AYER/NEDERLAND B.V.—See N W Ayer Incorporated, pg. 104
AYER PORTUGAL—See N W Ayer Incorporated, pg. 104
AYER PUBLIC RELATIONS—See N W Ayer Incorporated, pg. 104
AYER ROMA—See N W Ayer Incorporated, pg. 104
AYER VAZQUEZ S.A. DE PUBLICIDAD—See N W Ayer Incorporated, pg. 104
AYERDIRECT, DIRECT RESPONSE—See N W Ayer Incorporated, pg. 104
AZCON CORP.—See Blue Tee Corporation, pg. 161
AZON CORPORATION, pg. 105
AZTECA FOODS, INCORPORATED, pg. 105

B

B. DALTON BOOKSELLER, INC.—See Barnes & Noble Bookstores, Inc., pg. 120
B & B CASH GROCERY STORE, pg. 105
B & B HOMES CORPORATION, pg. 105
B & B MOTOR & CONTROL CORPORATION, pg. 105
B & K STEEL & SUPPLY, INC., pg. 105
BA ADVERTISING, pg. 105
BAC-PRITCHARD, INC.—See Amsted Industries Incorporated, pg. 69
B.A.S.S., INC., pg. 105
B C PUBLISHING—See International Data Group, pg. 576
BC HYDROTILE MACHINERY CO.—See The Black Clawson Co., pg. 154
BCI TALENT PAYMENTS—See IDC Services, Inc., pg. 560
BCM ENGINEERS INC., pg. 106
BCP TECHNICAL SERVICE, INC., pg. 106
B&E GRAIN COMPANY—See Land O'Lakes, Inc., pg. 654
BEC ADVERTISING, pg. 106
BEC INC., pg. 106
B-E HOLDINGS INC., pg. 106
BE & K, INC., pg. 106
B & G WHOLESALERS, INC., pg. 106
BGW SYSTEMS, INC., pg. 106
B. H. AIRCRAFT CO., INC., pg. 106
BIW CABLE SYSTEMS-CONNECTOR SYSTEMS DIV.—See BIW Cable Systems, Inc., pg. 107
BIW CABLE SYSTEMS, INC., pg. 106
BJ ACQUISITION CORP., pg. 107
B & J SUPPLY, INC.—See American Tara Corporation, pg. 63
BKM ENTERPRISES, INC., pg. 107
B&L JEWELRY CO.—See Reliable Stores, Inc., pg. 925
BLH ELECTRONICS, pg. 107
BMB COMPANY—See Alamo Group, Inc., pg. 29
BMR CORPORATION—See Energy Minerals Corporation, pg. 381
BNA BOOKS DIV.—See The Bureau of National Affairs, Inc., pg. 189
BNA COMMUNICATIONS, INC.—See The Bureau of National Affairs, Inc., pg. 189
BNA ENVIRONMENT & SAFETY SERVICES DIV.—See The Bureau of National Affairs, Inc., pg. 189
BNA INTERNATIONAL INC.—See The Bureau of National Affairs, Inc., pg. 190
BNA LEGAL SERVICES DIV.—See The Bureau of National Affairs, Inc., pg. 189
BNA PLUS—See The Bureau of National Affairs, Inc., pg. 189
BNA SOFTWARE—See The Bureau of National Affairs, Inc., pg. 189
BNE LAND & DEVELOPMENT CO.—See Boddie-Noell Enterprises Inc., pg. 161
BNZ MATERIALS, INC.—See McNeel International Corp., pg. 732
BPC DIVISION—See Bristol Products, L.P., pg. 176
B & R FOODS—See Performance Food Group, Inc., pg. 861
B & R PET SUPPLIES, INC.—See The Andersons, pg. 74
BRAC CREDIT CORP.—See Beech Holdings Corp., pg. 131
BS & B SAFETY SYSTEMS—See International Systems & Controls Corp., pg. 579
BSA ADVERTISING, INC., pg. 107
BSB/ADAPTUS AB—See Backer Spielvogel Bates Worldwide, Inc., pg. 109
BSB AMSTERDAM—See Backer Spielvogel Bates Worldwide, Inc., pg. 109
BSB ATHENS ADVERTISING S.A.—See Backer Spielvogel Bates Worldwide, Inc., pg. 109
BSB BATES-GRUPPEN A/S—See Backer Spielvogel Bates Worldwide, Inc., pg. 109
BSB BRUSSELS SA/NV—See Backer Spielvogel Bates Worldwide, Inc., pg. 109
BSB CHILE PUBLICIDAD—See Backer Spielvogel Bates Worldwide, Inc., pg. 109
BSB CITY—See Backer Spielvogel Bates Worldwide, Inc., pg. 109
BSB DINFO—See Backer Spielvogel Bates Worldwide, Inc., pg. 109
BSB DORLAND LIMITED—See Backer Spielvogel Bates Worldwide, Inc., pg. 109
BSB EUROPE—See Backer Spielvogel Bates Worldwide, Inc., pg. 109
BSB EUROPE/THE EUROCENTRE—See Backer Spielvogel Bates Worldwide, Inc., pg. 109
BSB FINNAD OY—See Backer Spielvogel Bates Worldwide, Inc., pg. 109
BSB FINNAD WEST—See Backer Spielvogel Bates Worldwide, Inc., pg. 109
BSB FRANCE—See Backer Spielvogel Bates Worldwide, Inc., pg. 109
BSB FRANKFURT WERBEAGENTUR GMBH—See Backer Spielvogel Bates Worldwide, Inc., pg. 109
BSB/GHERSY-QUINTERO, C.A. PUBLICIDAD—See Backer Spielvogel Bates Worldwide, Inc., pg. 109
BSB GOTEBORG AB—See Backer Spielvogel Bates Worldwide, Inc., pg. 109
BSB GRAFFIX LIMITED—See Backer Spielvogel Bates Worldwide, Inc., pg. 110
BSB HELSINGBORG AB—See Backer Spielvogel Bates Worldwide, Inc., pg. 110
BSB HONG KONG—See Backer Spielvogel Bates Worldwide, Inc., pg. 110
BSB HUNTER ADVERTISING—See Backer Spielvogel Bates Worldwide, Inc., pg. 110
BSB INDONESIA—See Backer Spielvogel Bates Worldwide, Inc., pg. 110
BSB ITALIA—See Backer Spielvogel Bates Worldwide, Inc., pg. 110
BSB JAPAN LTD.—See Backer Spielvogel Bates Worldwide, Inc., pg. 110
BSB MADCO—See Backer Spielvogel Bates Worldwide, Inc., pg. 110
BSB MALAYSIA SDN. BHD.—See Backer Spielvogel Bates Worldwide, Inc., pg. 110
BSB MEDIA & RESEARCH—See Backer Spielvogel Bates Worldwide, Inc., pg. 110
BSB MEDICAL—See Backer Spielvogel Bates Worldwide, Inc., pg. 110
BSB/MEZA, LTDA.—See Backer Spielvogel Bates Worldwide, Inc., pg. 110
BSB NAESS & MORCH A/S—See Backer Spielvogel Bates Worldwide, Inc., pg. 110
BSB NEW ZEALAND—See Backer Spielvogel Bates Worldwide, Inc., pg. 110
BSB PORTUGAL—See Backer Spielvogel Bates Worldwide, Inc., pg. 110
BSB PUBLICIDAD S.A.—See Backer Spielvogel Bates Worldwide, Inc., pg. 110
BSB SEPTEMBER AB—See Backer Spielvogel Bates Worldwide, Inc., pg. 110
BSB SINGAPORE—See Backer Spielvogel Bates Worldwide, Inc., pg. 110
BSB STOCKHOLM AB—See Backer Spielvogel Bates Worldwide, Inc., pg. 110
BSB SWEDEN—See Backer Spielvogel Bates Worldwide, Inc., pg. 110
BSB/TAIWAN COMPANY LIMITED—See Backer Spielvogel Bates Worldwide, Inc., pg. 110
BSB THAILAND—See Backer Spielvogel Bates Worldwide, Inc., pg. 110
B.T. EQUIPMENT CO., INC.—See Gilbane Building Company, pg. 457
BTD/TMP WORLDWIDE—See TMP Worldwide, Inc., pg. 1073
B.T.F. CORPORATION, pg. 107
BTG, INC., pg. 107
B & V WASTE SCIENCE & TECHNOLOGY CORP.—See Black & Veatch, pg. 154
BVD LICENSING CORPORATION—See Farley Industries, pg. 400
B-W ADVERTISING AGENCY, pg. 107
B-W ADVERTISING AGENCY—See Best Western International, Inc., pg. 147
B&W CO-OP, INC., pg. 107
B & W FARM CENTER—See B&W Co-op, Inc., pg. 107
B-W INSURANCE AGENCY—See Best Western International, Inc., pg. 147
B-W SUPPLY, INC.—See Best Western International, Inc., pg. 147
BWP DISTRIBUTORS, INC.—See Carquest Corporation, pg. 224
BAAR & BEARDS, pg. 107
BABCOCK LUMBER COMPANY, pg. 107
THE BABCOCK & WILCOX COMPANY, pg. 107
BABY TOGS, INC., pg. 107
BACARDI IMPORTS, INC., pg. 108
BACCO CONSTRUCTION CO., pg. 108
BACHARACH INC., pg. 108
BACHMAN COMPANY, pg. 108
BACHMANN INDUSTRIES, INC., pg. 108
BACHMAN'S, INC., pg. 108
BACK BAY ADVISORS, INC.—See The New England, pg. 799
BACKER SPIELVOGEL BATES, INC.—See Backer Spielvogel Bates Worldwide, Inc., pg. 108

BACKER SPIELVOGEL BATES WORLDWIDE, INC., pg. 108
BACKUS TURNER & PARTNERS, INC., pg. 112
HENRY BACON BUILDING MATERIALS, INC., pg. 113
BACON GROCERY CO., INC.—See Jones Company, Inc., pg. 603
W.S. BADCOCK CORPORATION, pg. 113
BADER & CO., pg. 113
BADER RUTTER & ASSOC., INC., pg. 113
BADGER AIR BRUSH COMPANY, pg. 113
BADGER CONSTRUCTION EQUIPMENT CO., INSLEY DIV., pg. 113
BADGER EQUIPMENT COMPANY—See Avis Industrial Corporation, pg. 102
BADGER NORTHLAND INC., pg. 113
BADGER TRUCK CENTER, INC., pg. 113
BAGNASCO S.R.L.—See Hollingsworth & Vose Co., pg. 539
BAHLSEN INC., pg. 114
GORDON BAILEY & ASSOCIATES, INC., pg. 114
BAILEY, KLEPINGER & MEDRICH, INC., pg. 114
BAILEY LAUERMAN & ASSOCIATES, INC., pg. 114
BAIRD, PATRICK & CO., INC., pg. 114
BAIRD RAY NISSAN, INC., pg. 114
THE U.S. BAIRD CORPORATION, pg. 114
BAIRD & WARNER INC., pg. 114
BAKE-LINE PRODUCTS, INC., pg. 114
H.J. BAKER & BRO., INC., pg. 114
BAKER BROS. DE PUERTO RICO—See Systems Engineering & Manufacturing Corp., pg. 1071
BAKER BROTHERS/MICRO-PLATE—See Systems Engineering & Manufacturing Corp., pg. 1071
BAKER COMMODITIES, INC., pg. 115
BAKER CONCRETE CONSTRUCTION, INC., pg. 115
BAKER-HAMILTON—See Distribution America, pg. 340
BAKER INDUSTRIES, INC.—See Borg-Warner Corporation, pg. 166
BAKER MATERIAL HANDLING CORP., pg. 115
BAKER & MCKENZIE INTERNATIONAL, pg. 115
R. J. BAKER ADVERTISING, INC.—See Stone, August, Baker Communications Companies, pg. 1051
THE BAKERSFIELD CALIFORNIAN, pg. 115
BALCO, INC. (MA), pg. 115
BALCRANK PRODUCTS—See New Hampshire Oak, pg. 801
BALDI, BLOOM & WHELAN ADVERTISING, pg. 115
BALDT, INC., pg. 115
BALDWIN CONSTRUCTION, INC., pg. 115
BALE OF KENTUCKY, INC., pg. 115
GEO. J. BALL, INC., pg. 115
BALL SEED CO.—See Geo. J. Ball, Inc., pg. 116
BALL SUPERIOR LTD.—See Geo. J. Ball, Inc., pg. 116
BALLANTINE BOOKS—See Advance Publications Inc., pg. 19
BALLENGER PAVING COMPANY, INC., pg. 116
Y.C. BALLENGER ELECTRICAL CONTRACTORS, pg. 116
BALLET MAKERS, INC., pg. 116
B.A. BALLOU & CO. INC., pg. 116
BALTIC LINEN COMPANY, INC., pg. 116
BALTIMORE AIRCOIL COMPANY—See Amsted Industries Incorporated, pg. 69
BALTIMORE BOOK—See Landmark Communications, Inc., pg. 655
BALTIMORE LUGGAGE COMPANY, pg. 116
BALTIMORE ORIOLES, INC., pg. 116
BALTIMORE STATIONERY CO., pg. 116
BAM PUBLICATIONS, INC., pg. 117
BAMBINAGGINE—See Doe Spun, Inc., pg. 343
BANANA SERVICES INC., pg. 117
BANANZA AIR MANAGEMENT SYSTEMS, INC.—See Rapid Engineering Inc., pg. 913
BANDINI FERTILIZER COMPANY, pg. 117
BANDY CARROLL HELLIGE ADVERTISING, pg. 117
BANGOR PUNTA DO BRAZIL LTDA.—See Lear Siegler Diversified Holdings Corp., pg. 664
BANGOR PUNTA OVERSEAS, S.A.—See Lear Siegler Diversified Holdings Corp., pg. 664
BANK OF HOMEWOOD—See Great Lakes Financial Resources, Inc., pg. 481
BANK OF LINCOLNWOOD—See GSC Enterprises, Inc., pg. 441
BANK M F & COMPANY, INC., pg. 117
BANK MARKETING ASSOCIATION—See The American Bankers Association, pg. 49
BANK OF NORTH DAKOTA, pg. 117
BANK SHARES, INC., pg. 117
BANKCRAFTERS, INC., pg. 117
BANKERS BOX/RECORDS STORAGE SYSTEMS—See Fellowes Manufacturing Co., pg. 406
BANKERS SYSTEMS INC., pg. 117
BANKHEAD ENTERPRISES INC., pg. 117
BANKMANAGERS CORP., pg. 118
W. O. BANKSTON ENTERPRISES INC., pg. 118
W. O. BANKSTON LEASING INC.—See W. O. Bankston Enterprises Inc., pg. 118
W. O. BANKSTON LINCOLN MERCURY—See W. O. Bankston Enterprises Inc., pg. 118
BANKSTON NISSAN IN IRVING, INC.—See W. O. Bankston Enterprises Inc., pg. 118
W. O. BANKSTON NISSAN INC.—See W. O. Bankston Enterprises Inc., pg. 118
BANNER ASSOCIATES INC., pg. 118
BANNER ENGINEERING CORP., pg. 118
BANNER RADIO—See Katz Communications, Inc., pg. 618
BANNER WHOLESALE GROCERS, INC., pg. 118
BAR-S FOODS CO., pg. 118
BARANCORP, pg. 118
BARANSKI & ASSOCIATES—See Barancorp, pg. 118
D. A. BARANSKI & CO.—See Barancorp, pg. 118
BARANSKI ENERGY COMPANY—See Barancorp, pg. 118
JOSEPH A. BARANSKI LITERARY AGENCY—See Barancorp, pg. 118
BARANSKI PUBLISHING COMPANY—See Barancorp, pg. 118
THE BARBAR GROUP, INC., pg. 119
BARBAR REALTY, INC.—See The Barbar Group, Inc., pg. 119
BARBER BROTHERS CONTRACTING COMPANY, pg. 119
BARBER DAIRIES, INC., pg. 119
BARBER ICE CREAM COMPANY—See Barber Dairies, Inc., pg. 119
BARCLAY & SONS—See Reliable Stores, Inc., pg. 925
BARCLAY WHITE INCORPORATED, pg. 119
BARD MFG. CO., pg. 119
BARDEN & ROBESON CORPORATION, pg. 119
BARDES CORP., pg. 119
BARDONS & OLIVER, INC., pg. 119
BARGE-WAGENER, INC., pg. 119
BARGER BUILDER & DEVELOPERS, pg. 119
BARIS SHOE COMPANY, INC., pg. 119
BARKER CAMPBELL & FARLEY, pg. 120
BARKLEY & EVERGREEN ADVERTISING, INC., pg. 120
A. BARLETTA & SONS, pg. 120
BARLOW & EATON—See Reliable Stores, Inc., pg. 925
JOHN S. BARNES CORP., pg. 120
BARNES DE COLOMBIA—See The Pullman Company, pg. 900
BARNES DE MEXICO—See The Pullman Company, pg. 900
BARNES, MORRIS, PARDOE & FOSTER MANAGEMENT SERVICES—See The Kaempfer Company, Investment Builders, pg. 613
BARNES & NOBLE—See Rowman & Littlefield Publishers, Inc., pg. 953
BARNES & NOBLE BOOKSTORES, INC., pg. 120
BARNES PUMPS, INC.—See Harbour Group Ltd., pg. 507
BARNETT MILLWORKS, INC., pg. 120
BARNEYS NEW YORK, pg. 120
BARNHARDT MANUFACTURING CO., pg. 120
BARNHART ADVERTISING, MARKETING & PUBLIC RELATIONS, INC., pg. 120
BARNHILL CONTRACTING COMPANY, pg. 121
BARNSTORM AVIATION—See International Airline Support Group, Inc., pg. 575
BARON-ABRAMSON, INC., pg. 121
BARON ADVERTISING, INC., pg. 121
BARON & ZARETSKY ADVERTISING, INC., pg. 121
BARONE SAUSAGE COMPANY—See City Meats & Provisions Co., pg. 251
BAROUM EATON ALLEN CORPORATION, pg. 121
BARQ'S, INC., pg. 121
BARR & BARR, INC., pg. 121
BARR BROTHERS & CO., INC., pg. 121
W. M. BARR & CO., INC., pg. 121
BARR ELECTRIC CORPORATION, pg. 122
BARREL O'FUN SNACK FOODS CO., pg. 122
BARRY-CARTER MILLING CO.—See Windmill Holdings Corp., pg. 1195
BARRY MANUFACTURING COMPANY LTD. (BEMAC)—See Jomac, Inc., pg. 602
BARRY SERVICES COMPANY—See Day & Zimmermann, Inc., pg. 320
THEODORE BARRY & ASSOCIATES, pg. 122
BARRY-WEHMILLER COMPANY, pg. 122
BARRY-WEHMILLER PACKAGING SYSTEMS—See Barry-Wehmiller Company, pg. 122
BARRY-WEHMILLER PACKAGING SYSTEMS—See Barry-Wehmiller Company, pg. 122
THE BARTELL DRUG COMPANY, pg. 122
E.J. BARTELLS CO., pg. 122
BARTLETT BRAINARD & EACOTT, INC., pg. 122
BARTLETT AND COMPANY, pg. 122
THE F.A. BARTLETT TREE EXPERT CO., pg. 123
BARTON BEERS, LTD.—See Barton Brands, Ltd., pg. 123
BARTON BRANDS, LTD., pg. 123
BARTON BRANDS OF CALIFORNIA, INC.—See Barton Brands, Ltd., pg. 123
BARTON BRANDS OF GEORGIA, INC.—See Barton Brands, Ltd., pg. 123
BUZZ BARTON & ASSOCIATES, INC., pg. 123
E.C. BARTON & CO., pg. 123
BARTON-MALOW COMPANY—See Barton-Malow Enterprises, Inc., pg. 123
BARTON-MALOW ENTERPRISES, INC., pg. 123
BARTON-MALOW RIGGING CO.—See Barton-Malow Enterprises, Inc., pg. 123
BARTON PRESS, INC., pg. 123
BASALT PRECAST DIVISION—See Dillingham Construction Corporation, pg. 338
THE BASES GROUP, pg. 124
THE BASES GROUP—See The Bases Group, pg. 124
BASES INTERNATIONAL—See The Bases Group, pg. 124
BASHAS, pg. 124
BASIC AMERICAN FOODS, pg. 124
BASIC COMPUTER, pg. 124
BASIC CONSTRUCTION COMPANY, pg. 124
BASIC FOOD INTERNATIONAL INC., pg. 124
BASIC INDUSTRIES—See Insilco Corporation, pg. 571
PETER A. BASILE SONS INC., pg. 124
BASIN ELECTRIC POWER CO-OP, pg. 125
BASLER ELECTRIC CIRCUITS, INC.—See Basler Electric Company, pg. 125
BASLER ELECTRIC COMPANY, pg. 125
BASS ENTERPRISES PRODUCTION COMPANY, pg. 125
BASS PRO SHOPS, INC., pg. 125
THE W.E. BASSETT COMPANY, pg. 125
BASSMASTER MAGAZINE—See B.A.S.S., Inc., pg. 105
BASSO & ASSOCIATES INC. ADV. & PUBLIC RELATIONS, pg. 125
BAST CHEVROLET INC., pg. 125
BATA SHOE CO., INC.—See CHB Corp., pg. 201
BATEMAN BROTHERS LUMBER CO., INC., pg. 125
BATES ADVERTISING A/S—See Backer Spielvogel Bates Worldwide, Inc., pg. 110
TED BATES A/S—See Backer Spielvogel Bates Worldwide, Inc., pg. 110
BATES BACKER & SPIELVOGEL A/S—See Backer Spielvogel Bates Worldwide, Inc., pg. 111
BATES BENJAMIN A/S—See Backer Spielvogel Bates Worldwide, Inc., pg. 111
BATES BERGEN A/S—See Backer Spielvogel Bates Worldwide, Inc., pg. 111
BATES CONTAINER, INC., pg. 125
BATES FABRICS, INC., pg. 125
BATES FILM—See Backer Spielvogel Bates Worldwide, Inc., pg. 111
TED BATES GREENHOUSE—See Backer Spielvogel Bates Worldwide, Inc., pg. 111
THE BATES MFG. CO., pg. 125
BATES STAVANGER A/S—See Backer Spielvogel Bates Worldwide, Inc., pg. 111
BATES TELEMARKETING—See Backer Spielvogel Bates Worldwide, Inc., pg. 111
TED BATES-VESTFOLD—See Backer Spielvogel Bates Worldwide, Inc., pg. 111
BATESCO QUARRIES DIV.—See Ash Grove Cement Company, pg. 88
BATEY/POINDEXTER, pg. 126
BATH IRON WORKS, pg. 126
BATON ROUGE WATER WORKS COMPANY, pg. 126
BATSON-COOK COMPANY, pg. 126
BATTEAST CONSTRUCTION COMPANY, INC., pg. 126
BATTELLE DEVELOPMENT CORP.—See Battelle Memorial Institute, pg. 126
BATTELLE MEMORIAL INSTITUTE, pg. 126
BATTENBERG, FILLHARDT & WRIGHT, INC., pg. 126
BATTENFELD GLOUCESTER ENGINEERING CO. INC., pg. 126
BATTERY ST. ENTERPRISES, RUNNING GEAR DIV.—See Levi Strauss & Co., pg. 670
BATTEY MACHINERY COMPANY, pg. 127
BAUERLEIN INC., pg. 127
BAUGH CONSTRUCTION COMPANY, pg. 127
BAUGHER CHEVROLET-BUICK-GEO, INC., pg. 127
W. A. BAUM COMPANY, INC., pg. 127
BAUMGARTEN STAMP CO.—See American Marking Systems, pg. 58
BAVARIA AVIONIK TECHNOLOGIE GMBH—See Rogerson Aircraft Corporation, pg. 944
BAVARIA CARGO TECHNOLOGIE GMBH—See Rogerson Aircraft Corporation, pg. 944
BAVARIA KEYTRONIC TECHNOLOGIE GMBH—See Rogerson Aircraft Corporation, pg. 944
BAWDEN CORPORATION, pg. 127
BAWDEN PRINTING, INC.—See Bawden Corporation, pg. 127
BAWDEN, TORREY & ASSOCIATES—See Bawden Corporation, pg. 127
BAXTER ADVERTISING, INC., pg. 127
J.H. BAXTER & COMPANY, pg. 127
BAXTER HODELL DONNELLY PRESTON INC., pg. 127
BAXTER SHIRK DESIGN COLLABORATIVE—See Baxter Hodell Donnelly Preston Inc., pg. 127
BAXTER/PEAS—See Baxter Hodell Donnelly Preston Inc., pg. 127
BAY CITIES AUTO AUCTION—See Cox Enterprises, Inc., pg. 293
BAY FAIR SHOPPING CTR.—See R. H. Macy & Co., Inc., pg. 699
BAY INDUSTRIES INC., pg. 127
BAY PARK, INC.—See Allright Corporation, pg. 42
BAY SAVINGS BANK, FSB—See FirstFed Michigan Corporation, pg. 414
BAY STATE MILLING CO., pg. 127
BAYDALE, INC.—See JMB Realty Corporation, pg. 585
BAYER BESS VANDERWARKER INC., pg. 128
ROBERT E. BAYLEY CONSTRUCTION, pg. 128
THE WILLIAM BAYLEY CO., pg. 128
BAYOU STATE OIL CORPORATION, pg. 128
BAYSIDE FUEL OIL CORP.—See Bayside Fuel Oil Depot Corp., pg. 128
BAYSIDE FUEL OIL DEPOT CORP., pg. 128
BE-LO MARKETS INC.—See Camellia Food Stores Co-op Inc., pg. 212
BEACH CITY CHEVROLET CO., pg. 128
BEACH MOLD & TOOL INC., pg. 128
BEACON GAGE—See Sycon Corporation, pg. 1069
BEACON GROUP, pg. 128
BEACON INDUSTRIES, INC.—See Beacon Group, pg. 128
BEACON INSURANCE CO. OF AMERICA—See All America Financial, pg. 34
BEACON MFG. CO., pg. 129
THE BEACON-NEWS—See The Copley Press, Inc., pg. 284
BEACON SALES CORPORATION, pg. 129
BEACON WINCH COMPANY—See Beacon Group, pg. 129
BEAD INDUSTRIES INC., pg. 129
BEADLES LUMBER COMPANY, INC., pg. 129
BEALL'S, INC., pg. 129
D. D. BEAN & SONS (CANADA) LTD.—See D. D. Bean & Sons Co., pg. 129
D. D. BEAN & SONS CO., pg. 129
D. D. BEAN & SONS (N.C.) INC.—See D. D. Bean & Sons Co., pg. 129
THE LEWIS BEAR COMPANY, pg. 129
BEARDEN LUMBER COMPANY, INC., pg. 129
BEARING DISTRIBUTORS, INC., pg. 130
BEARING SERVICE COMPANY, pg. 130
BEAUCHAMP DISTRIBUTING COMPANY, pg. 130
BEAUDRY FORD, INC., pg. 130
BEAUMONT ENTERPRISE—See The Hearst Corporation, pg. 523
BEAUT-EASE CORPORATION—See Hyde Manufacturing Co., pg. 556
BEAUTIFUL & LANDOR ASSOCIATES—See Young & Rubicam Inc., pg. 1211
BEAUTY ENTERPRISES INC., pg. 130
BEAUTY HANDBOOK CORPORATION, pg. 130
BEAUTY-PROFESSIONAL—See DeMert & Dougherty, Inc., pg. 328

BEST HOSPITAL SUPPLY DIV.—See Best Manufacturing, Inc., pg. 146
BEST INSURORS, INC.—See Walter Industries, Inc., pg. 1162
BEST MANUFACTURING, INC., pg. 146
BEST PRODUCTS CO., INC.—See Adler & Shaykin, pg. 17
BEST PROVISION CO., INC., pg. 146
BEST TEXTILE CO. DIV.—See Best Manufacturing, Inc., pg. 146
BEST WESTERN INTERNATIONAL, INC., pg. 146
BESTEEL INDUSTRIES, pg. 147
BESTFORM FOUNDATIONS, INC., pg. 147
BESTOP, INC., pg. 147
BESTPAK, INC.—See Ivex Packaging Corporation, pg. 583
BETAC CORPORATION—See Betac International Corporation, pg. 147
BETAC INTERNATIONAL CORPORATION, pg. 147
CHANNING L. BETE CO., INC., pg. 147
THE BETHAM CORPORATION, pg. 147
BETHEL MILLS, INC., pg. 148
BETTCHER MANUFACTURING CORP., pg. 148
BETTER BAKED FOODS, INC., pg. 148
BETTER BRANDS OF ATLANTA, INC., pg. 148
BETTER LIVING INC., pg. 148
BETTERBRANDS, LTD.—See Young's Market Company, pg. 1214
BETTERWAY PUBLICATIONS INC.—See F & W Publications, Inc., pg. 394
BEUTLER HEATING & AIR CONDITIONING INC., pg. 148
BEVERAGE-AIR CO.—See Specialty Equipment Companies Inc., pg. 1027
BEVERAGE CANNERS INTERNATIONAL CORP., pg. 148
BEVERAGE MANAGEMENT, INC.—See Brooks Beverage Management, Inc., pg. 179
BEVERIDGE PAPER CO.—See Simkins Industries, Inc., pg. 1005
THE BEVERLY HILLS HOTEL, pg. 148
DOUGLAS BEWICK ASSOCIATES/TMP WORLDWIDE—See TMP Worldwide, Inc., pg. 1074
BI-METAL BEARING—See The Pullman Company, pg. 900
THE BIBB COMPANY-BRUCKNELL PLANT—See NTC Group, pg. 781
THE BIBB COMPANY-ROANOKE RAPIDS PLANT—See NTC Group, pg. 781
THE BIBB COMPANY-WHITE HORSE RD. PLANT—See NTC Group, pg. 781
BIBB-DISC, INC.—See NTC Group, pg. 781
BIBLER BROTHERS, INC., pg. 148
BIBLIO DISTRIBUTION CTR.—See Rowman & Littlefield Publishers, Inc., pg. 953
BIDDLE INSTRUMENTS, pg. 148
BIDDLE SAWYER CORPORATION, pg. 148
BIDDULPH OLDSMOBILE, pg. 149
BIEDERMAN, KELLY & SHAFFER, INC., pg. 149
BIG BEAR SUPERMARKETS NO. 3, pg. 149
BIG BOWL CAFE—See Lettuce Entertain You Enterprises, Inc., pg. 669
BIG BOY RESTAURANT SYSTEM—See Elias Brothers Restaurants, Inc., pg. 376
BIG CHEESE PIZZA CORPORATION—See Godfather's Pizza, Inc., pg. 464
BIG FOOT CATTLE CO.—See Vienna Sausage Mfg. Co., pg. 1151
BIG HORN CO-OP MARKETING ASSOCIATION, pg. 149
BIG J SUPER STORES, INC.—See Jones Company, Inc., pg. 603
BIG JOE MANUFACTURING CO., pg. 149
BIG RED RC & 7-UP OF LAGRANGE, TX—See Grant-Lydick Beverage Co., pg. 477
BIG V SUPERMARKETS, INC., pg. 149
BIG Y FOODS INC., pg. 149
BIGGS GILMORE COMMUNICATIONS, pg. 149
BIGG'S HYPER SHOPPES, INC., pg. 150
BIGSBY & KRUTHERS, INC., pg. 150
BIJUR LUBRICATING CORPORATION, pg. 150
BIKE ATHLETIC CO., pg. 150
BILL COMMUNICATIONS, INC., pg. 150
BILLCOM AUTOMOTIVE—See Bill Communications, Inc., pg. 150
BILLCOM EXPOSITION & CONFERENCE—See Bill Communications, Inc., pg. 150
BILLCOM EXPOSITION & CONFERENCE GROUP—See Bill Communications, Inc., pg. 150
BILL'S DOLLAR STORES, INC., pg. 150
THE BILTRITE CORPORATION, pg. 151
BINDICATOR COMPANY—See Berwind Corporation, pg. 145
BING STEEL INC., pg. 151
BINGHAM, pg. 151
BINKLEY COMPANY, pg. 151
BINNEY & SMITH INC.—See Hallmark Cards, Inc., pg. 502
BINNING'S BUILDING PRODUCTS, INC., pg. 151
THE BINSWANGER COMPANY, pg. 151
BINSWANGER DEVELOPMENT—See The Binswanger Company, pg. 152
BINSWANGER INDUSTRIAL—See The Binswanger Company, pg. 152
BINSWANGER INVESTMENT—See The Binswanger Company, pg. 152
BINSWANGER MANAGEMENT CORP.—See The Binswanger Company, pg. 152
BINSWANGER REALTY—See The Binswanger Company, pg. 152
BIO MEDIC CORPORATION, pg. 152
BIO-TEK INSTRUMENTS, INC., pg. 152
BIOPRODUCTS, INC., pg. 152
WILLIAM M. BIRD & CO., INC., pg. 152
BIRDSALL VOSS & KLOPPENBURG, INC., pg. 152
BIRDSONG CORPORATION, pg. 153
BIRMINGHAM HILL RESTAURANT CORP.—See Specialty Restaurants Corporation, pg. 1028
DAMIAN BISCH & PARTNERS, INC. ADVERTISING, pg. 153
BISCO INDUSTRIES, pg. 153
BISHOPSGATE CORP.—See Shepaug Corporation, pg. 998
BISON BASEBALL INC.—See Rich Products Corp., pg. 932
BISON CANNING CO., INC.—See Goya Foods, Inc., pg. 474
BISSELL INC., pg. 153
BISSELL LTD.—See Bissell Inc., pg. 153
BISTRO SOUPS, LTD.—See Vienna Sausage Mfg. Co., pg. 1151
BITREK CORPORATION, pg. 153
BITUMINOUS ROADWAYS, INC., pg. 153
BIXBY INTERNATIONAL CORP., pg. 153
BIZZACK INC., pg. 153
BLACK ANGUS, INC.—See Son Chief Electrics, Inc., pg. 1018
BLACK BOX CORPORATION—See MICOM Communications Corp., pg. 748
BLACK CADILLAC OLDS, INC., pg. 153
THE BLACK CLAWSON CO., pg. 154
BLACK & CO., pg. 154
BLACK FIN YACHT CORPORATION, pg. 154
BLACK GILLOCK & LANGBERG, pg. 154
BLACK HILLS TRUCKING CO.—See True Companies, pg. 1117
WALTER J. BLACK, INC., pg. 154
BLACK MILLWORK CO., INC., pg. 154
BLACK PENCIL S.A.R.L.—See Leo Burnett Company, Inc., pg. 192
BLACK & VEATCH, pg. 154
BLACK & VEATCH ARCHITECTS, INC.—See Black & Veatch, pg. 154
BLACK & VEATCH INTERNATIONAL—See Black & Veatch, pg. 154
WALTER J. BLACK, INC. FULFILLMENT SERVICES—See Walter J. Black, Inc., pg. 154
STANLEY BLACKER, INC., pg. 155
BLACK'S READERS SERVICE—See Walter J. Black, Inc., pg. 154
BLACKSTONE PARTNERSHIP (NYC), pg. 155
BLADE COMMUNICATIONS, INC., pg. 155
TIM & DIANE BLAGGE INC., pg. 155
ALGERNON BLAIR INTERNATIONAL, pg. 155
JOHN BLAIR COMMUNICATIONS, INC., pg. 155
WILLIAM BLAIR & COMPANY, pg. 155
WHITNEY BLAKE COMPANY OF VERMONT, INC., pg. 155
BLANCETT—See Racine Federated, Inc., pg. 909
WM. BLANCHARD CO., pg. 155
BLAND CADILLAC COMPANY, pg. 155
BILL BLASS, INC.—See MacAndrews & Forbes Holdings Inc., pg. 695
BLATTNER/BRUNNER INC., pg. 156
D.H. BLATTNER & SONS, INC., pg. 156
BARRY BLAU & PARTNERS, INC., pg. 156
BLAUER MANUFACTURING CO., INC., pg. 156
BLAW KNOX CORP., pg. 156
BLAW KNOX - DURALOY DIVISION—See Blaw Knox Corp., pg. 156
BLAW KNOX FOOD & CHEMICAL EQUIPMENT COMPANY—See Blaw Knox Corp., pg. 156
BLAW KNOX ROLLS DIVISION—See Blaw Knox Corp., pg. 156
BLUE GRASS CHRYSLER-PLYMOUTH, pg. 156
BLESSINGS CORP.—See Williamson-Dickie Mfg. Co., pg. 1192
BLEVINS CONCESSION SUPPLY CO., pg. 156
BLEVINS INC., pg. 156
BLEVINS POPCORN—See Agway, Inc., pg. 26
BLEYCO PAPER CO. OF MICHIGAN—See A. W. Mendenhall Co., Inc., pg. 739
BLISH-MIZE CO.—See Distribution America, pg. 340
BLISS-SALEM, INC., pg. 156
WILLIAM B. BLISS DIV.—See Falcon Safety Products Inc., pg. 398
BLISSFIELD MANUFACTURING COMPANY, pg. 157
BLISTEX, INC., pg. 157
BLISTEX LIMITED—See Blistex, Inc., pg. 157
BLITZ U.S.A., INC.—See Blitz USA, pg. 157
BLITZ USA, pg. 157
BLITZ-WEINHARD BREWING—See G. Heileman Brewing Co., Inc., pg. 526
BLOCK DISTRIBUTING COMPANY, pg. 157
BLOCK INDUSTRIES, INC., pg. 157
BLOCK & NARDIZZI, pg. 157
BLOCKHOUSE CO., INC., pg. 157
G.S. BLODGETT CORPORATION, pg. 157
BLOMMER CHOCOLATE CO., pg. 157
BLONDER-TONGUE LABORATORIES, INC., pg. 157
BLOOM ELECTRIC SERVICES, INC., pg. 157
BLOOMFIELD INDUSTRIES CANADA LTD.—See Specialty Equipment Companies Inc., pg. 1027
BLOOMFIELD REFINING CO.—See The Gary-Williams Company, pg. 444
BLOOMHORST STORY O'HARA INC., pg. 158
BLOOMSBURG MILLS INC., pg. 158
BLOUNT LUMBER COMPANY, pg. 158
BLUE ANCHOR, INC., pg. 158
BLUE BELL CREAMERIES, INC., pg. 158
BLUE BELL/KING KOIL, INC., pg. 158
BLUE BELL POTATO CHIP CO.—See GF Industries, Inc., pg. 439
BLUE BIRD COACH LINES INC., pg. 158
BLUE BIRD CORPORATION, pg. 158
BLUE BOAR CAFETERIA CO., pg. 158
BLUE CORAL, INC., pg. 159
BLUE CORAL INTERNATIONAL—See Blue Coral, Inc., pg. 159
BLUE CRAB LOUNGE—See Lettuce Entertain You Enterprises, Inc., pg. 669
BLUE CROSS AND BLUE SHIELD OF OKLAHOMA, pg. 159
BLUE CROSS AND BLUE SHIELD ASSOCIATION, pg. 159
BLUE CROSS AND BLUE SHIELD OF MASSACHUSETTS, pg. 159
BLUE CROSS & BLUE SHIELD OF ILLINOIS, pg. 160
BLUE CROSS & BLUE SHIELD OF OREGON, pg. 160
BLUE CROSS & BLUE SHIELD OF TEXAS, INC., pg. 160
BLUE CROSS & BLUE SHIELD OF VIRGINIA, pg. 160
BLUE CROSS LABORATORIES, pg. 160
BLUE DIAMOND GROWERS, pg. 160
BLUE FOX TACKLE CO.—See Normark Corporation, pg. 810
BLUE GRASS FOODS, INC., pg. 160
BLUE LINE DISTRIBUTING—See Little Caesar Enterprises, Inc., pg. 678
BLUE RIBBON PEN & PENCIL CO.—See Pen Holdings, Inc., pg. 856
BLUE RIDGE FINANCE CO., INC.—See Fairway Ford, Inc., pg. 398
BLUE RIDGE TRANSFER CO., pg. 161
BLUE SHIELD OF CALIFORNIA, pg. 161
BLUE SPRINGS EXAMINER—See Stauffer Communications, Inc., pg. 1042
BLUE TEE CORPORATION, pg. 161
BLUELINES HMO—See Blue Cross and Blue Shield of Oklahoma, pg. 159
BLUEWATER—See Bluewater Marine, pg. 161
BLUEWATER MARINE, pg. 161
BLUEWATER MARINE INC.—See Klapmeier Management Company, pg. 634
BLUFF CITY CIGARETTE SERVICE—See Samelson-Leon Company, Inc., pg. 968
BLUFF CITY DISTRIBUTING CO., INC., pg. 161
BLUMENTHAL PRINT WORKS, INC., pg. 161
BLUMHARDT MANUFACTURING COMPANY—See TIC United Corporation, pg. 1073
BLYTHEVILLE CANNING COMPANY, INC.—See Bush Brothers & Company, pg. 196
BOAM CHEMICALS CO., INC.—See MacAndrews & Forbes Holdings Inc., pg. 694
BOAM PRODUCE (OVERSEAS) LTD.—See MacAndrews & Forbes Holdings Inc., pg. 694
BOASBERG VALENTINE-RADFORD, INC.—See Valentine-Radford, Inc., pg. 1143
BOAT TRANSIT, INC.—See Jupiter Industries, Inc., pg. 609
BOBIT PUBLISHING COMPANY, pg. 161
BOBST GROUP INC., pg. 161
BOCA HAMPTONS MANAGEMENT, INC.—See Cenvill Development Corp., pg. 236
BOCA RATON FINANCIAL CENTER—See The Barbar Group, Inc., pg. 119
BODDIE-NOELL ENTERPRISES INC., pg. 161
THE BODINE CORP., pg. 161
BODINE ELECTRIC COMPANY, pg. 162
E. H. BOECKH CO.—See American Appraisal Associates, Inc., pg. 48
BOGUE ELECTRIC MANUFACTURING CO., pg. 162
BOH BROTHERS CONSTRUCTION COMPANY, INC.—See Boh Corporation, pg. 162
BOH CORPORATION, pg. 162
BOHBOT COMMUNICATIONS, INC., pg. 162
BOHLE WERKZEUGMASCHINEN GMBH—See Ingersoll International Inc., pg. 568
DAVID BOLAND, INC., pg. 162
M. R. BOLIN INC., pg. 162
BOLLIGER, INC., pg. 163
BOLLINGER HEALTH CARE—See Bollinger Industries Inc., pg. 163
BOLLINGER INDUSTRIES INC., pg. 163
BOLLINGER MACHINE SHOP AND SHIPYARD, INC., pg. 163
BOLTON-EMERSON EQUIPMENTOS INDUSTRIAS LTDA.—See Bolton-Emerson, Inc., pg. 163
BOLTON-EMERSON, INC., pg. 163
BOLTON-EMERSON-MCNIECE, INC.—See Bolton-Emerson, Inc., pg. 163
BOLTON-EMERSON PAPER MACHINERY DIV.—See Bolton-Emerson, Inc., pg. 163
BOLTON-EMERSON S.A.—See Bolton-Emerson, Inc., pg. 163
BOLTON-EMERSON-SOUTHERN, INC.—See Bolton-Emerson, Inc., pg. 163
BOLTON-EMERSON TALAMAC MAQUINAS E EQUIPAMENTOS LTDA.—See Bolton-Emerson, Inc., pg. 163
BOMAN & KEMP STEEL & SUPPLY COMPANY—See B & K Steel & Supply, Inc., pg. 105
BOMMER INDUSTRIES, INC., pg. 164
THE BOMSTEIN AGENCY, pg. 164
BON JOUR INTERNATIONAL LTD., pg. 164
BON TON FOODS, INC., pg. 164
BONANZA BUS LINES, INC., pg. 164
BONANZA RESTAURANTS—See Metromedia Company, pg. 744
BOND'S JEWELERS, INC.—See Zale Corporation, pg. 1215
BONES/LINCOLNWOOD—See Lettuce Entertain You Enterprises, Inc., pg. 669
BONGARDS CREAMERIES INC., pg. 164
BONHOMME SHIRTMAKERS, LTD., pg. 164
BONKERS, INC.—See Victoria Station Incorporated, pg. 1150
BONLAND INDUSTRIES, INC., pg. 164
F.H. BONN COMPANY, pg. 164
BONNEVILLE COMMUNICATIONS, pg. 164
BONNEVILLE INTERNATIONAL CORP.—See Deseret Management Corporation, pg. 332
BONNEY FORGE CORPORATION, pg. 164
BONNIE BAKING CO.—See Lewis Brothers Bakeries, Inc., pg. 673
BONSIB INC., pg. 164
BOOKAZINE COMPANY, INC., pg. 164
BOOKSTOP, INC.—See Barnes & Noble Bookstores, Inc., pg. 120
BOONVILLE MINING SERVICES, INC.—See Bucyrus-Erie Company, pg. 186
JOHN BOOS & COMPANY, pg. 165
BOOTH AMERICAN, pg. 165

BOOTH NEWSPAPERS, INC., pg. 165
BOOTH SEAFOOD SALES CORP.—See Rich Products Corp., pg. 932
BOOZ ALLEN & HAMILTON INC., pg. 165
BOOZ, ALLEN & HAMILTON INTERNATIONAL (UK) LTD.—See Booz Allen & Hamilton Inc., pg. 165
BORCHERS BROS., pg. 165
BORDELAIS, LEMEUNIER & LEO BURNETT—See Leo Burnett Company, Inc., pg. 192
BORDER STATES INDUSTRIES, INC., pg. 165
BORDER STATES PAVING, INC., pg. 165
BORDERS, PERRIN & NORRANDER, INC., pg. 165
BORG-WARNER AUTOMOTIVE (CANADA) LIMITED—See Borg-Warner Corporation, pg. 166
BORG-WARNER AUTOMOTIVE CONTROL SYSTEMS-BLYTHEVILLE—See Borg-Warner Corporation, pg. 166
BORG-WARNER AUTOMOTIVE, INC.—See Borg-Warner Corporation, pg. 166
BORG WARNER AUTOMOTIVE, INC.—See Borg-Warner Corporation, pg. 166
BORG-WARNER AUTOMOTIVE, INC., CONTROL SYSTEMS—See Borg-Warner Corporation, pg. 166
BORG-WARNER AUTOMOTIVE, INC., TRANSMISSION SYSTEMS—See Borg-Warner Corporation, pg. 166
BORG-WARNER AUTOMOTIVE-MICHIGAN POWDERED METAL PRODUCTS, INC.—See Borg-Warner Corporation, pg. 166
BORG-WARNER CORPORATION, pg. 165
BORG-WARNER DE MEXICO, S.A.—See Borg-Warner Corporation, pg. 166
BORG-WARNER-SPRING/BRUMMER DIVISION—See Borg-Warner Corporation, pg. 166
HUGO BOSCA CO., INC., pg. 166
BOSCOV'S DEPARTMENT STORES, INC., pg. 167
BOSE A/S—See Bose Corporation, pg. 167
BOSE CORPORATION, pg. 167
BOSTON CHICKEN, INC., pg. 167
BOSTON DISTRIBUTORS, INC., pg. 167
BOSTON INSULATED WIRE & CABLE CO. LTD.—See BIW Cable Systems, Inc., pg. 107
BOSTON MUTUAL LIFE INSURANCE CO., pg. 167
BOSTON SCIENTIFIC CORP., pg. 167
BOSTON TRADING LTD. INC., pg. 168
BOSTROM DISTRIBUTION CENTER—See Bostrom Seating, Inc., pg. 168
BOSTROM SEATING, INC., pg. 168
BOTTO, ROESSNER, HORNE & MESSINGER, INC.—See Ketchum Communications Inc., pg. 625
BOUCHARD FIRE PROTECTION—See John Bouchard & Sons Company, pg. 168
JOHN BOUCHARD & SONS COMPANY, pg. 168
BOULDER ENTERPRISE, INC.—See The New Yorker Magazine, pg. 803
BOURNS AG & BOURNS (SCHWEIZ) AG—See Bourns, Inc., pg. 168
BOURNS BENELUX B.V.—See Bourns, Inc., pg. 168
BOURNS ELECTRONICS, LTD.—See Bourns, Inc., pg. 168
BOURNS, GMBH—See Bourns, Inc., pg. 168
BOURNS, INC., pg. 168
BOURNS INSTRUMENTS INC.—See Bourns, Inc., pg. 168
BOURNS-OHMIC S.A.—See Bourns, Inc., pg. 168
BOURY INCORPORATED, pg. 168
BOVAIRD SUPPLY CO., pg. 168
BOVAY, pg. 169
BOWEN BROTHERS FRUIT CO., INC., pg. 169
BOWHEAD EQUIPMENT COMPANY—See Lynden Incorporated, pg. 689
BOWLERAMA LANES, INC.—See Great Lakes Recreation Co., pg. 482
BOWLING CORP. OF AMERICA—See Charan Industries, Inc., pg. 239
BOX INNARDS, INC.—See Rock-Tenn Company, pg. 941
BOYD, TAMNEY & CROSS ADVERTISING/MARKETING, pg. 169
BOYER BROS. INC., pg. 169
BOYLE ENGINEERING CORP., pg. 169
BOYLSTON CAPITAL ADVISORS—See The New England, pg. 799
BOZOF DINETTES, INC., pg. 169
E.J. BRACH CORPORATION, pg. 169
E.J. BRACH, INC.—See E.J. Brach Corporation, pg. 169
E.J. BRACH, INC.—See E.J. Brach Corporation, pg. 169
E.J. BRACH, INC.—See E.J. Brach Corporation, pg. 169
E.J. BRACH, INC.—See E.J. Brach Corporation, pg. 169
BRAD FOOTE GEAR WORKS, INC., pg. 169
BRADBURY COMPANY, INC., pg. 169
BRADFORD COMPANY, pg. 170
BRADFORD EXCHANGE LTD., pg. 170
J. C. BRADFORD & CO., pg. 170
BRADFORD OIL COMPANY, INC., pg. 170
W. C. BRADLEY CO., pg. 170
BRADLEY COMMUNICATIONS, INC., pg. 170
BRADLEY CORPORATION, pg. 170
BRADLEY PRINTING COMPANY—See Graphisphere Holding Company, pg. 478
BRADLEY SPECIALTY RETAILING, INC.—See W. C. Bradley Co., pg. 170
BRADNER CENTRAL COMPANY, pg. 170
BRADNER SMITH & CO.—See Bradner Central Company, pg. 171
BRADSHAW ASSOCIATES IN ADVERTISING, INC., pg. 171
THE BRADY COMPANY, pg. 171
BRADY ENTERPRISES, INC., pg. 171
THE BRADY MARKETING COMPANY, pg. 171
BRAID ELECTRIC COMPANY, pg. 171
BRAINARD STRAPPING, pg. 171
BRAINERD DAILY DISPATCH—See Stauffer Communications, Inc., pg. 1042
BRAINSTORM ADVERTISING & SALES PROMOTIONS, pg. 171
BRAKE SUPPLY CO.—See George Koch Sons, Inc., pg. 639
BRAMAN WORLD CAR CENTER, pg. 171
DAVID A. BRAMBLE, INC., pg. 171
BRAMMER MANUFACTURING COMPANY, pg. 171
BRANCE KRACHY COMPANY, INC., pg. 171
BRAND, SHICK & WESLEY, pg. 172
BRANDAU Y COMPANIA S.A.—See Metallurg, Inc., pg. 742
BRANDYWINE RACEWAY ASSN., INC.—See Brandywine Sports, Inc., pg. 172
BRANDYWINE REALTY & DEVELOPMENT, INC.—See Brandywine Sports, Inc., pg. 172
BRANDYWINE SPORTS, INC., pg. 172
BRANT ALLEN INDUSTRIES, INC., pg. 172
BRAUM ICE CREAM STORES INC., pg. 172
BRAUN-BRUMFIELD, INC.—See The Sheridan Group, pg. 998
W. BRAUN COMPANY, pg. 172
W. BRAUN INTERNATIONAL—See W. Braun Company, pg. 172
BRAUN/KETCHUM PUBLIC RELATIONS—See Ketchum Communications Inc., pg. 625
BRAUNS FASHIONS, INC., pg. 172
THE BRAVO GROUP—See Young & Rubicam Inc., pg. 1210
BRAYTON INTERNATIONAL INC.—See Steelcase Inc., pg. 1044
BRAZIER FOREST INDUSTRIES, INC., pg. 172
BRAZIER FOREST PRODUCTS OF OREGON—See Brazier Forest Industries, Inc., pg. 173
BRECK OPERATING CORP.—See States, Inc., pg. 1041
BRECKENRIDGE MATERIAL COMPANY, pg. 173
BRECKS—See Foster & Gallagher Inc., pg. 426
BREGG DATA FORMS, INC., pg. 173
BREMER FINANCIAL CORPORATION, pg. 173
BREMS EASTMAN GLADE, INC., pg. 173
BRENCAL CONTRACTORS INC.—See BEC Inc., pg. 106
BRENDAMOUR'S SPORTING GOODS CO., pg. 173
THE BRENLIN GROUP, pg. 173
BRENNAN COLLEGE SERVICE, INC.—See Follett Corporation, pg. 422
BRESLER'S INDUSTRIES, INC., pg. 174
BRETON CONSTRUCTION, INC., pg. 174
DAVID BRETT, INC., pg. 174
BREUER ELECTRIC MFG. CO., pg. 174
C. BREWER & COMPANY, LIMITED, pg. 174
BREWER ENVIRONMENTAL INDUSTRIES, INC.—See C. Brewer & Company, Limited, pg. 174
C. BREWER PROPERTIES, INC.—See C. Brewer & Company, Limited, pg. 174
BRIAN CENTER MANAGEMENT CORPORATION, pg. 175
BRIAN UNLIMITED DISTRIBUTION COMPANY, INC., pg. 175
BRIDAL ORIGINALS, INC., pg. 175
BRIDE'S—See Advance Publications Inc., pg. 19
BRIDGEMAN'S RESTAURANTS INC., pg. 175
BRIDGEPORT FITTINGS, INC., pg. 175
BRIDGEPORT MACHINES, INC., pg. 175
BRIDGES & COMPANY, INC., pg. 175
BRIDGEWATER RESOURCES CORPORATION, pg. 175
BRIERLEY & PARTNERS, pg. 175
BRIGGS INDUSTRIES, INC., pg. 175
R.A. BRIGGS & CO.—See Home Innovations, Inc., pg. 541
BRIGGS WEAVER—See Sammons Enterprises, Inc., pg. 968
BRIM, INC., pg. 176
BRIM SERVICES GROUP—See Brim, Inc., pg. 176
BRIMMS INC., pg. 176
BRINK ELECTRIC CONSTRUCTION COMPANY, pg. 176
BRINK EQUIPMENT & SUPPLY COMPANY—See Brink Electric Construction Company, pg. 176
BRINK'S, INC.—See The H. T. Hackney Co., pg. 498
FRANK BRISCOE CO. INC., pg. 176
BRISK WATERPROOFING—See The Western Group, pg. 1179
BRISTOL CONCRETE PRODS. CORP.—See Bristol Steel & Iron Works, Inc., pg. 177
BRISTOL INDUSTRIES, pg. 176
BRISTOL LINGERIE—See House of Ronnie, Inc., pg. 546
BRISTOL PRODUCTS, L.P., pg. 176
BRISTOL RECREATION SYSTEMS, INC.—See Connecticut Mutual Life Insurance Company, pg. 275
BRISTOL STEEL & IRON WORKS, INC., pg. 176
BRISTOLIPE DIVISION—See Bristol Products, L.P., pg. 176
BRITANNICA HOME LIBRARY SERVICES—See Encyclopaedia Britannica, Inc., pg. 381
BRITCOM TELEMARKETING DIVISION—See Encyclopaedia Britannica, Inc., pg. 381
BRITISH KNIGHTS—See Jack Schwartz Shoes, Inc., pg. 980
BRITT INDUSTRIES, INC.—See Kurdziel Industries, Inc., pg. 646
BRITTANY CORPORATION, pg. 177
BRITTANY DYEING & PRINTING CORPORATION, pg. 177
BRIX MARITIME BARGING, INC.—See Brix Maritime Co., pg. 177
BRIX MARITIME CO., pg. 177
BRIX MARITIME TOWING, INC.—See Brix Maritime Co., pg. 177
BROAD VOGT & CONANT INC., pg. 177
BROADCAST AND VIDEO ENTERPRISES DIV.—See Landmark Communications, Inc., pg. 654
BROADCAST ELECTRONICS, INC., pg. 177
BROADCAST SUPPLY WEST, pg. 177
BROADCAST TIME, INC., pg. 177
BROADCASTERS OF MISSISSIPPI, INC.—See News-Press & Gazette Company, pg. 804
BROADMOOR HOTEL, INC., pg. 177
BROADSTREET PLAZA—See F. L. Roberts & Co. Inc., pg. 938
R.F. BROADUS & ASSOCIATES, INC., pg. 177
BROADWAY & SEYMOUR—See Effective Management Systems, pg. 370
BROCK CANDY COMPANY, pg. 177
BROCK CONTROL SYSTEMS, INC., pg. 178
J. C. BROCK CANADA, LTD—See J. C. Brock Corp., pg. 178
J. C. BROCK CORP., pg. 178
M. J. BROCK & SONS, INC., pg. 178
BROCK MANUFACTURING—See CTB Inc., pg. 205
GEORGE F. BROCKE & SONS, INC., pg. 178
BRODBECK ENTERPRISES, INC., pg. 178
BRODER BROS. CO., pg. 178
BRODER BROS. CO. OF FLORIDA, INC.—See Broder Bros. Co., pg. 178
BRODERICK COMPANY, INC.—See Goldman Financial Group, pg. 468
BRODHEAD-GARRETT CO., pg. 178
BROGAN & PARTNERS ADVERTISING/PUBLIC RELATIONS INC., pg. 178
WILLIAM BROJACK LUMBER COMPANY, pg. 179
BROKAY PRODUCTS, INC.—See Caravan Products Company, Inc., pg. 217
BROMAR INC., pg. 179
BRONNER SLOSBERG HUMPHREY, pg. 179
BRONSON LEIGH WEEKS, pg. 179
BRONZE HEADQUARTERS—See Headco Industries, Inc., pg. 520
BROOKFIELD ENGINEERING LABORATORIES, INC., pg. 179
BROOKHURST, INC., pg. 179
BROOKLYN BOTTLING CO., pg. 179
BROOKS BEVERAGE MANAGEMENT, INC., pg. 179
BROOKS BEVERAGES INC.—See Brooks Beverage Management, Inc., pg. 179
E. J. BROOKS COMPANY, pg. 179
BROOKS COUNTY PACKING CO.—See Sunnyland Foods, Inc., pg. 1061
BROOKS FOODS—See Agway, Inc., pg. 26
JOHN W. BROOKS INC., pg. 180
BROOKS PRODUCTS, ARLINGTON—See Brooks Products, Inc., pg. 180
BROOKS PRODUCTS, INC., pg. 180
BROOKS PRODUCTS, ORLANDO—See Brooks Products, Inc., pg. 180
BROOKS PRODUCTS, STOCKTON—See Brooks Products, Inc., pg. 180
BROOKS PROVISIONS INC., pg. 180
BROOKS RESOURCES CORPORATION, pg. 180
BROOKSHIRE BROS., INC., pg. 180
BROOKSHIRE GROCERY, pg. 180
BROOKSTONE COMPANY, INC., pg. 180
BROUGHER AGENCY, INC.—See VASA Insurance Group, Inc., pg. 1146
BROUGHTON FOODS COMPANY, pg. 180
BROWER COMPANY—See Bay Industries Inc., pg. 127
BROWERPEASE, INC., pg. 181
E.H. BROWN ADVERTISING, INC., pg. 181
BROWN & BIGELOW, INC., pg. 181
BROWN BROTHERS, HARRIMAN & CO., pg. 181
BROWN BROTHERS, HARRIMAN (HONG KONG) LTD.—See Brown Brothers, Harriman & Co., pg. 181
BROWN BROTHERS HARRIMAN LIMITED—See Brown Brothers, Harriman & Co., pg. 181
BROWN BROTHERS HARRIMAN (LUXEMBOURG) S.A.—See Brown Brothers, Harriman & Co., pg. 181
BROWN BROTHERS HARRIMAN SERVICES AG—See Brown Brothers, Harriman & Co., pg. 181
BROWN BROTHERS, HARRIMAN & CO., TOKYO—See Brown Brothers, Harriman & Co., pg. 181
BROWN BROTHERS HARRIMAN TRUST CO. (CAYMAN) LTD.—See Brown Brothers, Harriman & Co., pg. 181
BROWN BROTHERS HARRIMAN TRUST CO. OF FLORIDA—See Brown Brothers, Harriman & Co., pg. 181
BROWN BROTHERS HARRIMAN TRUST CO. OF NEW YORK—See Brown Brothers, Harriman & Co., pg. 181
BROWN BROTHERS HARRIMAN TRUST CO. OF TEXAS—See Brown Brothers, Harriman & Co., pg. 181
BROWN & CALDWELL CONSULTING ENGINEERS, pg. 181
BROWN DERBY, INC., pg. 181
BROWN DISC PRODUCTS COMPANY—See Genevar Enterprises, pg. 451
EARLE PALMER BROWN, pg. 182
EARLE PALMER BROWN/BETHESDA—See Earle Palmer Brown, pg. 182
EARLE PALMER BROWN/KALAMAZOO—See Earle Palmer Brown, pg. 182
EARLE PALMER BROWN/NEW YORK—See Earle Palmer Brown, pg. 182
EARLE PALMER BROWN/NORFOLK—See Earle Palmer Brown, pg. 182
EARLE PALMER BROWN/RICHMOND—See Earle Palmer Brown, pg. 182
BROWN EVANS COMPANY, pg. 182
BILL BROWN FORD INC., pg. 182
BROWN & HADLEY & PARTNERS, pg. 182
BROWN & HALEY, pg. 182
BROWN HARRIMAN CORPORATION—See Brown Brothers, Harriman & Co., pg. 181
BROWN, HARRIS, STEVENS, INC.—See Helmsley Enterprises, Inc., pg. 527
BROWN-MINNEAPOLIS TANK & FABRICATING CO., pg. 182
BROWN MOTORS, pg. 182
H.H. BROWN SHOE COMPANY, INC., pg. 182
F.M. BROWN SONS, INC., pg. 183
BROWN-STRAUSS STEEL, INC.—See Blue Tee Corporation, pg. 161
BROWN WOOD PRESERVING COMPANY, pg. 183
E.T. BROWNE DRUG CO., INC., pg. 183
BROWNE MEDICAL SYSTEMS, INC.—See Phillips Plastics Corporation, pg. 867
BROWNING CHEMICAL CORPORATION, pg. 183
BROWNS LUMBER & SUPPLY COMPANY, pg. 183
THE BROWNSTEIN GROUP, pg. 183
BROYLES, ALLEBAUGH & DAVIS, INC., pg. 183
BRUBAKER TOOL CORP., pg. 183

BRUCE-ANDERSEN COMPANY, INC., pg. 183
BRUCE FOODS CORP., pg. 183
BRUCE HARDWOOD FLOORS—See Triangle Pacific Corporation, pg. 1112
BRUCE INDUSTRIES, INC., pg. 183
T. BRUCE SALES, INC., pg. 183
BRUCKNER MACHINE & TOOL CORP., pg. 183
M. A. BRUDER & SONS, INC., pg. 184
M. BRUENGER & CO., INC., pg. 184
DICK BRUHN INC., pg. 184
THE BRULIN CORPORATION, pg. 184
BRUNER CORPORATION, pg. 184
BRUNER-IVORY HANDLE COMPANY—See O.P. Link Handle Company, pg. 677
BRUNING PAINT COMPANY, pg. 184
BRUNNER & LAY, INC., pg. 184
BRUNSCHWIG & FILS, INC., pg. 184
BRUNSWICK SQUARE—See R. H. Macy & Co., Inc., pg. 699
BRUSH RESEARCH MANUFACTURING COMPANY, pg. 184
BRUSS COMPANY, pg. 184
BRUTGER EQUITIES, INC., pg. 185
BRYANT ELECTRIC COMPANY, INC., pg. 185
BRYANT GRINDER CORP.—See Goldman Financial Group, pg. 468
BRYANT MUNGO DIVISION—See Temperature Equipment Corporation, pg. 1086
BRYANT SUGAR HOUSE—See United States Sugar Corporation, pg. 1137
BRYANT SUPPLY COMPANY, INC., pg. 185
BRYANT UNIVERSAL ROOFERS INC., pg. 185
BRYCE CORPORATION, pg. 185
BUB CITY CRABSHACK & BAR-B-Q—See Lettuce Entertain You Enterprises, Inc., pg. 669
BUCHANAN CONSTRUCTION PRODUCTS, INC.—See Ideal Industries, Inc., pg. 562
BUCILLA CORPORATION, pg. 185
BUCK KNIVES, INC., pg. 185
BUCK & PULLEYN, INC., pg. 185
BUCKMAN LABORATORIES, pg. 185
BUCKMAN LABORATORIES, INC.—See Bulab Holdings, Inc., pg. 188
BUCYRUS (AFRICA) PROPRIETARY LTD.—See Bucyrus-Erie Company, pg. 186
BUCYRUS (AUSTRALIA) PROPRIETARY LTD.—See Bucyrus-Erie Company, pg. 186
BUCYRUS BLADES DE MEXICO—See Esco Corporation, pg. 388
BUCYRUS BLADES INC.—See Esco Corporation, pg. 388
BUCYRUS BLADES OF CANADA LTD.—See Esco Corporation, pg. 388
BUCYRUS BLADES OF GEORGIA—See Esco Corporation, pg. 388
BUCYRUS (BRASIL) LTDA.—See Bucyrus-Erie Company, pg. 186
BUCYRUS CHILE LTDA.—See Bucyrus-Erie Company, pg. 186
BUCYRUS-ERIE CO. OF CANADA LTD.—See Bucyrus-Erie Company, pg. 186
BUCYRUS-ERIE COMPANY, pg. 186
BUCYRUS-EUROPE LTD.—See Bucyrus-Erie Company, pg. 186
BUD INDUSTRIES, INC., pg. 186
BUD WEST, INC.—See Bud Industries, Inc., pg. 186
BUDCO GROUP INC., pg. 186
BUDDE & WESTERMANN—See Fleming Packaging Corp., pg. 417
CARL BUDDIG & COMPANY, pg. 186
BUDGET MARKETING, INC., pg. 186
BUDGET RENT A CAR CORPORATION—See Beech Holdings Corp., pg. 131
BUERKLE BUICK-HONDA CO., pg. 186
BUFFALO COLOR CORPORATION, pg. 187
BUFFALO COLOR CORPORATION—See Buffalo Color Corporation, pg. 187
BUFFALO HOSPITAL SUPPLY CO., INC., pg. 187
BUFFALO ROCK COMPANY, pg. 187
BUFFALO WATERFRONT RESTAURANT CORP.—See Specialty Restaurants Corporation, pg. 1029
BUFFALO WHITE GMC, INC., pg. 187
BUFFELEN WOODWORKING COMPANY, pg. 187
BUFKOR, INC., pg. 187
BUGLE BOY INDUSTRIES, INC., pg. 187
BUHLER INC., pg. 187
BUHRMAN-PHARR HARDWARE COMPANY, pg. 187
BUILDER MARTS OF AMERICA, pg. 187
BUILDERS DEVELOPMENT INC.—See Garvey Industries, Inc., pg. 444
BUILDERS EMPORIUM—See Collins & Aikman Group Inc., pg. 262
BUILDERS INC.—See Garvey Industries, Inc., pg. 444
BUILDING PLASTICS, INC., pg. 188
BUILDING PRODUCTS INC., pg. 188
BUILDING PRODUCTS INC. OF S.D.—See Building Products Inc., pg. 188
BUILT ENVIRONMENT SERVICES—See Effective Management Systems, pg. 370
BULAB HOLDINGS, INC., pg. 188
BULK SYSTEMS—See Jervis B. Webb Company, pg. 1170
BULL, INC.—See Science Applications International Corporation, pg. 981
E. D. BULLARD COMPANY, pg. 188
CURT BULLOCK BUILDERS, INC., pg. 188
BULLOCK'S—See R. H. Macy & Co., Inc., pg. 699
BULTMAN FUNERAL HOME—See Ourso Investment Corporation, pg. 832
BUNDY PROPERTIES—See American Protection Industries, Inc., pg. 60
BUNGEY MEDICAL—See Backer Spielvogel Bates Worldwide, Inc., pg. 111
BUNN-O-MATIC CORP. OF CANADA LTD.—See Bunn-O-Matic Corporation, pg. 188
BUNN-O-MATIC CORPORATION, pg. 188
BUNTIN ADVERTISING, INC., pg. 188
BUNTON COMPANY, pg. 188
BUQUET & LE BLANC INC., pg. 189
BURC ELECTRONICS & MACHINERY CORP.—See Panduit Company, pg. 845
BURD & FLETCHER COMPANY, pg. 189
BUREAU OF ENGRAVING, pg. 189
THE BUREAU OF NATIONAL AFFAIRS, INC., pg. 189
C.F. BURGER CREAMERY COMPANY, pg. 190
BURGESS & NIPLE, INC.—See Burgess & Niple, Limited, pg. 190
BURGESS & NIPLE, LIMITED, pg. 190
BURGESS-NORTON MFG. CO.—See Amsted Industries Incorporated, pg. 69
BURGESS PIGMENT CO., pg. 190
BURGOYNE, INC., pg. 190
BURK ROYALTY CO., pg. 190
BURKE COMMUNICATION INDUSTRIES, INC., pg. 190
BURKE ENGINEERING COMPANY, pg. 190
BURKE FLOORING PRODUCTS DIV.—See Burke Industries, Inc., pg. 191
BURKE FUEL & HEATING CO.—See Meenan Oil Co. Limited Partnership, pg. 736
BURKE INDUSTRIES, INC., pg. 191
THE BURKE INSTITUTE—See The Bases Group, pg. 124
BURKE RUBBER CO.—See Burke Industries, Inc., pg. 191
E. J. BURKE SECURITY SYSTEMS, INC.—See Borg-Warner Corporation, pg. 166
BURKHARDT & CHRISTY ADVERTISING, INC., pg. 191
BURKS PROSSER/ENPO INDUSTRIES, INC.—See Harbour Group Ltd., pg. 507
BURKS PUMPS, INC.—See Harbour Group Ltd., pg. 507
BURLINGTON BASKET CO., pg. 191
BURLINGTON MOTOR CARRIERS—See Burlington Motor Carriers Inc., pg. 191
BURLINGTON MOTOR CARRIERS INC., pg. 191
BURMOT AUSTRALIA PTY., LTD.—See Burns & Roe Enterprises, Inc., pg. 194
DAVID K. BURNAP ADVERTISING AGENCY, INC., pg. 191
BURNER SYSTEMS INTERNATIONAL, INC.—See The Dyson-Kissner-Moran Corporation, pg. 357
WM. T. BURNETT & CO., INC., pg. 191
LEO BURNETT CHILE—See Leo Burnett Company, Inc., pg. 192
LEO BURNETT CO., INC. SUCURSAL ARGENTINA—See Leo Burnett Company, Inc., pg. 192
LEO BURNETT CO., S.R.L.—See Leo Burnett Company, Inc., pg. 192
LEO BURNETT COMPANY, INC., pg. 191
LEO BURNETT COMPANY LTD.—See Leo Burnett Company, Inc., pg. 192
LEO BURNETT COMPANY, LTD.-TAIWAN BRANCH—See Leo Burnett Company, Inc., pg. 192
LEO BURNETT DENMARK—See Leo Burnett Company, Inc., pg. 192
LEO BURNETT INC.—See Leo Burnett Company, Inc., pg. 192
LEO BURNETT INTL., ASIA HDQTRS.—See Leo Burnett Company, Inc., pg. 192
LEO BURNETT INTERNATIONAL, LATIN AMERICAN HDQTRS.—See Leo Burnett Company, Inc., pg. 192
LEO BURNETT-KYODO CO. LTD.—See Leo Burnett Company, Inc., pg. 192
LEO BURNETT LIMITED—See Leo Burnett Company, Inc., pg. 193
LEO BURNETT LTD.—See Leo Burnett Company, Inc., pg. 193
LEO BURNETT LTD., EUROPE/MIDDLE EAST HDQTRS.—See Leo Burnett Company, Inc., pg. 193
LEO BURNETT LTD. THAILAND—See Leo Burnett Company, Inc., pg. 193
LEO BURNETT PTE. LTD.—See Leo Burnett Company, Inc., pg. 193
LEO BURNETT PUBLICIDADE, LTDA.—See Leo Burnett Company, Inc., pg. 193
LEO BURNETT S.A. DE C.V.—See Leo Burnett Company, Inc., pg. 193
LEO BURNETT SDN. BHD.—See Leo Burnett Company, Inc., pg. 193
LEO BURNETT VENEZUELA, C.A.—See Leo Burnett Company, Inc., pg. 193
BURNHAM BROADCASTING COMPANY, pg. 193
JOHN BURNHAM & CO., pg. 194
BURNS INTERNATIONAL SECURITY SERVICES, INC.—See Borg-Warner Corporation, pg. 166
BURNS & MCDONNELL ENGINEERS-ARCHITECTS-CONSULTANTS, pg. 194
BURNS & MCDONNELL WASTE CONSULTANTS, INC.—See Burns & McDonnell Engineers-Architects-Consultants, pg. 194
BURNS & ROE ENTERPRISES, INC., pg. 194
BURNS & ROE ENVIRONMENTAL SERVICES—See Burns & Roe Enterprises, Inc., pg. 194
BURNS & ROE INDUSTRIAL SERVICES COMPANY—See Burns & Roe Enterprises, Inc., pg. 194
BURNS & ROE PACIFIC COMPANY—See Burns & Roe Enterprises, Inc., pg. 194
BURNS & ROE SOUTHEAST—See Burns & Roe Enterprises, Inc., pg. 194
BURNSIDE CONSTRUCTION CO., pg. 194
BURNSTAD BROTHERS, INC., pg. 194
BURNSTEAD CONSTRUCTION COMPANY, pg. 194
W. ATLEE BURPEE CO.—See Geo. J. Ball, Inc., pg. 116
BURRELL COMMUNICATIONS GROUP INC., pg. 195
BURRELL GROUP, pg. 195
THE BURRIS AGENCY, INC., pg. 195
BURRIS CHEMICAL INC., pg. 195
BURRIS FOODS, INC., pg. 195
BURRISS BUILDING SYSTEMS—See B. Burriss Companies, pg. 195
B. BURRISS COMPANIES, pg. 195
BURRO CRANE CO.—See Badger Construction Equipment Co., Insley Div., pg. 113
BURROWS PAPER CORPORATION, pg. 195
BURSON-MARSTELLER—See Young & Rubicam Inc., pg. 1210
F.N. BURT COMPANY, INC., pg. 195
BURT EQUIPMENT COMPANY, INC., pg. 195
BURTCO METAL SYSTEMS—See Burt Equipment Company, Inc., pg. 195
BURTMAN IRON WORKS, INC., pg. 195
BURTON-DIXIE OF BLACKSBURG INC.—See CC Industries, Inc., pg. 200
BURTON MEDICAL PRODUCTS CORPORATION—See Jac Jacobsen Industries, Inc., pg. 588
THE BUSCHMAN CO., pg. 196
BUSH BROTHERS & COMPANY, pg. 196
BUSH DEVELOPMENT CORP., pg. 196
BUSINESS GUIDES INC.—See Lebhar-Friedman, Inc., pg. 665
BUSINESS INFORMATION TECHNOLOGY, pg. 196
BUSINESS INSURANCE—See Crain Communications, Inc., pg. 295
BUSINESS MARKETING—See Crain Communications, Inc., pg. 295
BUSINESS MENS INSURANCE CORPORATION, pg. 196
BUSINESS TRAVEL MANAGEMENT, INC.—See Mary Kay Corporation, pg. 717
BUTCHER & CO., INC., pg. 196
THE BUTCHER CO., pg. 196
M. BUTEN & SONS INC., pg. 196
BUTERA FINER FOODS INC., pg. 196
BUTLER AUTOMATIC, INC., pg. 197
BUTLER DESIGN SERVICES, INC.—See Butler International, pg. 197
BUTLER FLEET MAINTENANCE SERVICES—See Butler International, pg. 197
BUTLER FOODS, INC., pg. 197
BUTLER INSTALLATION SERVICES, INC.—See Butler International, pg. 197
BUTLER INTERNATIONAL, pg. 197
BUTLER QUALITY SERVICES, INC.—See Butler International, pg. 197
BUTLER SERVICE GROUP, INC.—See Butler International, pg. 197
BUTLER TELECOMMUNICATIONS GROUP—See Butler International, pg. 197
BUTLER TELECOMMUNICATIONS SERVICES—See Butler International, pg. 197
BUTLER UTILITIES SERVICES, INC.—See Butler International, pg. 197
LAWRENCE BUTNER ADVERTISING, INC., pg. 197
H. E. BUTT GROCERY CO., pg. 197
BUTTER KERNEL PRODUCTS—See Faribault Foods Inc., pg. 399
BUTTERICK COMPANY, INC., pg. 197
BUXTON COMPANY, pg. 197
BUYER ADVERTISING, INC., pg. 197
BYER CALIFORNIA, pg. 197
BYERLY FORD-NISSAN INC., pg. 198
BYERLY'S INC., pg. 198
JACK BYRNE FORD & MERCURY, INC., pg. 198
JACK BYRNE MINUTEMAN LUBE—See Jack Byrne Ford & Mercury, Inc., pg. 198
BYRNES & KIEFER COMPANY, pg. 198
BYRON'S, INC.—See Rich Products Corp., pg. 932

C

C & K MARKETS, INC., pg. 198
C & L MARKETING INC.—See Capitol Industries-EMI Inc., pg. 216
C-LINE PRODUCTS, INC., pg. 198
C & M CORPORATION, pg. 198
C & S WHOLESALE GROCERY INC., pg. 198
C&A AUTOMOTIVE GROUP—See Collins & Aikman Group Inc., pg. 262
C&A FLOOR COVERINGS—See Collins & Aikman Group Inc., pg. 262
C&A WALLCOVERINGS—See Collins & Aikman Group Inc., pg. 262
C&A YARN DIVISION—See Collins & Aikman Group Inc., pg. 262
CAC MICROCIRCUITS, INC., pg. 198
CAE LINK ALLEN DIVISION, pg. 198
CAI—See Recon/Optical, Inc., pg. 917
CB COMMERCIAL REAL ESTATE GROUP CENTRAL DIVISION—See Carlyle Holding Corporation, pg. 222
CB COMMERCIAL REAL ESTATE GROUP EASTERN DIVISION—See Carlyle Holding Corporation, pg. 222
CB COMMERCIAL REAL ESTATE GROUP, INC.—See Carlyle Holding Corporation, pg. 222
CB COMMERCIAL REAL ESTATE GROUP, NEW YORK—See Carlyle Holding Corporation, pg. 222
C-B CORPORATION, pg. 198
CB NORTH AMERICA, INC., pg. 199
C B J ENTERPRISES, INC., pg. 199
CBM AMERICA CORP., pg. 199
CBM INDUSTRIES, INC., pg. 199
CBP RESOURCES, INC., pg. 199
C B R CEMENT CORPORATION, pg. 199
CBS SIGNS, INC.—See Gordon Sign Company, pg. 472
C&C ASSOCIATES—See Couristan Inc., pg. 290
CC INDUSTRIES ESTIA DIV.—See CC Industries, Inc., pg. 200
CC INDUSTRIES, INC., pg. 199
CC INDUSTRIES, KAYWOOD DIV.—See CC Industries, Inc., pg. 200
CC INDUSTRIES, KAYWOOD-SOUTHERN DIV.—See CC Industries, Inc., pg. 200
CC SERVICES—See Country Companies Insurance Group, pg. 289
CCC INFORMATION SERVICES—See Financial Protection Services Inc., pg. 410

CCI CORPORATION, pg. 200
CCW STAMP CO.—See American Marking Systems, pg. 58
C&D/HIT INC.—See Cosco Industries, pg. 288
CDA/TURK GROUP, pg. 200
CDM FEDERAL PROGRAMS CORPORATION—See Camp Dresser & McKee Inc., pg. 212
CEC INC.—See The Chardon Rubber Co., pg. 239
CEI CONSTRUCTION, INC., pg. 200
C.E.M. DIV. SPIROL INTL. CORP.—See Spirol International Corp., pg. 1031
CEM SOUTH—See T. L. Smith Machine, pg. 1013
CF INDUSTRIES, INC., pg. 200
CFB INDUSTRIES, INC., pg. 201
CF & I FABRICATORS OF COLORADO—See CF&I Steel Corporation, pg. 201
CF & I FABRICATORS OF UTAH—See CF&I Steel Corporation, pg. 201
CF&I STEEL CORPORATION, pg. 201
CGF INDUSTRIES, pg. 201
CGRW ADVERTISING, INC., pg. 201
CGS INDUSTRIES, INC., pg. 201
CHB CORP., pg. 201
CHC ADVERTISING, pg. 201
CHF INDUSTRIES, INC.—See CC Industries, Inc., pg. 200
CH2M HILL COMPANIES, LTD., pg. 202
CH2M HILL, INC.—See CH2M Hill Companies, Ltd., pg. 202
CH2M HILL INDUSTRIAL DESIGN CORP.—See CH2M Hill Companies, Ltd., pg. 202
CH2M HILL INTERNATIONAL, LTD.—See CH2M Hill Companies, Ltd., pg. 202
CIA KETCHUM—See Ketchum Communications Inc., pg. 625
C.I.C.S.A.—See Maxon Corporation, pg. 723
CIO PUBLISHING CORP.—See International Data Group, pg. 576
C-J EXTRUDERS INC.—See Nexus Plastics, Inc., pg. 805
CJC HOLDINGS, INC., pg. 202
CKS PARTNERS, pg. 202
CM CHAIN DIVISION—See Columbus McKinnon Corp., pg. 266
CM FURNITURE, INC.—See Carolina Mills, Inc., pg. 223
CM HOIST DIVISION—See Columbus McKinnon Corp., pg. 266
CM LIFE INSURANCE COMPANY—See Connecticut Mutual Life Insurance Company, pg. 275
CM MECHANICAL HANDLING SYSTEMS—See Columbus McKinnon Corp., pg. 266
CM SHREDDER DIV.—See Columbus McKinnon Corp., pg. 266
CM TRANSNATIONAL—See Connecticut Mutual Life Insurance Company, pg. 275
CMCI CORP.—See CUNA Mutual Insurance Society, pg. 205
CMD-KEITH CO.—See Ben E. Keith Company, pg. 620
CME-KHBB ADVERTISING, pg. 202
CMI INDUSTRIES, INC., pg. 202
CMI INTERNATIONAL INC., pg. 202
CMI LLOYDS—See Central Mutual Insurance Co., pg. 233
C M P PRINTING COMPANY—See C M P Publications, Inc., pg. 203
C M P PUBLICATIONS, INC., pg. 202
CMS CHEMICAL COMPANY—See Harwick Chemical Corp., pg. 515
C.M.W. LABORATORIES DENTSPLY, LTD.—See Dentsply International Inc., pg. 330
CNJ DISTRIBUTING—See Corner Pockets of America, pg. 286
CORS, pg. 203
C P CONVERTERS, INC., pg. 203
CP ILLINOIS, INC.—See Container Products Inc., pg. 278
CPI PLASTICS, INC.—See Container Products Inc., pg. 278
CPM, INC., pg. 203
CPS CORPORATION—See Fox Valley Corporation, pg. 428
CRC INDUSTRIES INC.—See Berwind Corporation, pg. 145
CRE, INC., pg. 203
CRK ADVERTISING, pg. 203
CRL, INC., pg. 203
CRN INTERNATIONAL, INC., pg. 203
CRP HOSE DIVISION—See Radiator Specialty Company, pg. 909
CS FIRST BOSTON ASSET MANAGEMENT LIMITED—See CS First Boston Group, Inc., pg. 204
CS FIRST BOSTON AUSTRALIA (HOLDINGS) LIMITED—See CS First Boston Group, Inc., pg. 204
CS FIRST BOSTON FINANCIERE, INC.—See CS First Boston Group, Inc., pg. 204
CS FIRST BOSTON GROUP, INC., pg. 203
CS FIRST BOSTON (HONG KONG) LIMITED—See CS First Boston Group, Inc., pg. 204
CS FIRST BOSTON NEW ZEALAND HOLDINGS LIMITED—See CS First Boston Group, Inc., pg. 204
CS FIRST BOSTON PACIFIC, INC.—See CS First Boston Group, Inc., pg. 204
CS FIRST BOSTON (SINGAPORE) LIMITED—See CS First Boston Group, Inc., pg. 204
CS FIRST BOSTON SINGAPORE LTD.—See CS First Boston Group, Inc., pg. 204
CS FIRST BOSTON USA, INC.—See CS First Boston Group, Inc., pg. 204
CSA, INC., pg. 204
CSC ERECTORS, INC.—See Carolina Steel Corporation, pg. 223
CSE CORPORATION, pg. 204
CSE SERVICES INSURANCE BROKERAGE—See CSE Corporation, pg. 205
CSFB-EFFECTENBANK AKTIENGESELLSCHAFT—See CS First Boston Group, Inc., pg. 204
CSFB FINANCE B.V.—See CS First Boston Group, Inc., pg. 204
CSFB FUND MANAGEMENT LIMITED—See CS First Boston Group, Inc., pg. 204
CSFB (GILTS) LIMITED—See CS First Boston Group, Inc., pg. 204
CSFB INVESTMENT MANAGEMENT LIMITED—See CS First Boston Group, Inc., pg. 204
CSI ADVERTISING INC., pg. 205
CSI INTERNATIONAL CORPORATION, pg. 205
CTB, INC.—See The Dickerson Group, Inc., pg. 336
CTB INC., pg. 205
CT&I CORP. OF WISCONSIN—See Chicago Tube & Iron Co., pg. 246
CUDIS INSURANCE SOCIETY, INC.—See CUNA Mutual Insurance Society, pg. 205
CUMIS INSURANCE SOCIETY, INC.—See CUNA Mutual Insurance Society, pg. 205
CUNA MUTUAL FINANCIAL SERVICES CORP.—See CUNA Mutual Insurance Society, pg. 205
CUNA MUTUAL INSURANCE SOCIETY, pg. 205
CUNA MUTUAL INVESTMENT CORP.—See CUNA Mutual Insurance Society, pg. 205
C. V. INVESTMENTS, INC.—See Cenvill Development Corp., pg. 236
C.V. SUMBER SAKTI—See Panduit Company, pg. 846
CVC PRODUCTS, INC., pg. 206
C.V.W. LTD. PARTNERSHIP—See Cenvill Development Corp., pg. 236
CW COMMUNICACACIONES S/A—See International Data Group, pg. 577
CW/COMMUNICATIONS AB—See International Data Group, pg. 577
CW PUBLIKATIONEN AG—See International Data Group, pg. 577
CW PUBLISHING, INC.—See International Data Group, pg. 576
C & W RAILWAY CO.—See CF&I Steel Corporation, pg. 201
C&W REFRACTORIES, LTD.—See CFB Industries, Inc., pg. 201
CWT SPECIALTY STORES, INC.—See Peter W. Smith & Company, Inc., pg. 1011
CYB YASUMURA DESIGN—See Young & Rubicam Inc., pg. 1210
CABANA FOODS, INC., pg. 206
CABELL CONSTRUCTION COMPANY—See Jupiter Industries, Inc., pg. 609
CABLECRAFT INC.—See Tuthill Corporation, pg. 1120
CABLEREP, INC.—See Cox Enterprises, Inc., pg. 294
CABLEVISION INDUSTRIES CORP., pg. 206
CABLEWARE TECHNOLOGY DIV.—See Loos & Co., Inc., pg. 683
CABLEWAVE SYSTEMS, INC., pg. 206
CABOT CREAMERY CO-OPERATIVE INC.—See Agri-Mark, Inc., pg. 25
SAMUEL CABOT, INC., pg. 206
CACIQUE CHEESE CO., INC., pg. 206
CACTUS FEEDERS, INC., pg. 207
CADACO—See Rapid Mounting & Finishing Co., pg. 913
CADDOCK ELECTRONICS, INC., pg. 207
CADDOCK NETWORK DIVISION—See Caddock Electronics, Inc., pg. 207
CADENCE CAPITAL MANAGEMENT—See Pacific Mutual Life Insurance Company, pg. 841
CADET MANUFACTURING COMPANY, pg. 207
CADILLAC PIPE—See Premarc Corporation, pg. 886
CADILLAC PRODUCTS, INC., pg. 207
THE CADMAN COMPANIES—See C B R Cement Corporation, pg. 199
THE CAFARO CO., pg. 207
CAFCO—See Central Mutual Insurance Co., pg. 233
CAFE BA-BA-REEBA—See Lettuce Entertain You Enterprises, Inc., pg. 669
CAIN & BULTMAN, INC., pg. 207
CAIRNS & BROTHER, INC., pg. 207
CAJUN ELECTRIC POWER CO-OP, pg. 207
CAL-AIR INC., pg. 208
CAL/EMBLEM LABELS, INC., pg. 208
CAL GRAPHICS DIVISION—See The Hearst Corporation, pg. 521
CAL-MAINE EGG PRODUCTS INC.—See Cal-Maine Foods, Inc., pg. 208
CAL-MAINE FARMS—See Cal-Maine Foods, Inc., pg. 208
CAL-MAINE FOODS, INC., pg. 208
CALABASH LTD.—See Doe Spun, Inc., pg. 343
CALAVERAS CEMENT CORPORATION—See C B R Cement Corporation, pg. 199
CALAVO FOODS, INC.—See Calavo Growers of California, pg. 208
CALAVO GROWERS OF CALIFORNIA, pg. 208
CALCASIEU LUMBER COMPANY, pg. 208
CALCOR SPACE FACILITY, INC., pg. 208
CALCOT, LTD., pg. 208
CALDWELL MANUFACTURING—See Chief Industries, Inc., pg. 247
CALDWELL MANUFACTURING COMPANY, pg. 208
CALDWELL TANKS, INC., pg. 209
CALDWELL VANRIPER INC., pg. 209
CALET, HIRSCH & FERRELL, INC.—See Ross Roy Group, Inc., pg. 949
CALET, HIRSCH & FERRELL, INC./FLORIDA—See Ross Roy Group, Inc., pg. 949
CALICO CAT PRESS, INC., pg. 209
CALICO CORNERS, pg. 209
CALIENTE CHILI, INC.—See William B. Reily & Co., Inc., pg. 923
CALIFORNIA ANGELS BASEBALL CLUB—See Golden West Broadcasters, pg. 467
CALIFORNIA APRICOT ADVISORY BOARD, pg. 209
CALIFORNIA ARTICHOKE & VEGETABLE GROWERS CORP., pg. 209
CALIFORNIA AUTO DEALERS EXCHANGE, INC.—See Cox Enterprises, Inc., pg. 293
CALIFORNIA AUTO DEALERS EXCHANGE, INC.—See Cox Enterprises, Inc., pg. 293
CALIFORNIA AVOCADO COMMISSION, pg. 209
CALIFORNIA CEDAR PRODUCTS, INC., pg. 209
CALIFORNIA CUSTOM FOODS—See Pacific Coast Producers, pg. 840
CALIFORNIA ELECTRIC SERVICE, pg. 209
CALIFORNIA-GYM EQUIPMENT CO.—See Bollinger Industries Inc., pg. 163
CALIFORNIA HARDWARE CO.—See Distribution America, pg. 340
CALIFORNIA HARDWARE CO., pg. 209
CALIFORNIA & HAWAIIAN SUGAR COMPANY, pg. 210
CALIFORNIA MANUFACTURING ENTERPRISES, pg. 210
CALIFORNIA MICRO DEVICES, pg. 210
CALIFORNIA MILK PRODUCERS, pg. 210
CALIFORNIA OFFSET PRINTERS, INC., pg. 210
CALIFORNIA PACIFIC RESEARCH, INC., pg. 210
CALIFORNIA PAINT DIV.—See California Products Corp., pg. 210
CALIFORNIA PANEL & VENEER COMPANY, pg. 210
CALIFORNIA PHYSICIANS INSURANCE CORP.—See Blue Shield of California, pg. 161
CALIFORNIA PRODUCTS CORP., pg. 210
CALIFORNIA SCHOOL BOOK FAIRS, INC.—See SI Holdings Inc., pg. 962
CALIFORNIA STATE LOTTERY, pg. 210
CALIFORNIA STRAWBERRY ADVISORY BOARD, pg. 210
THE CALIFORNIAN—See Landmark Communications, Inc., pg. 656
THE CALKINS MANUFACTURING COMPANY, pg. 210
CALMARK ASSET MANAGEMENT CO.—See Calmark Investment Company, pg. 211
CALMARK COMMUNITIES, INC.—See Calmark Investment Company, pg. 211
CALMARK DEVELOPMENT CORP.—See Calmark Investment Company, pg. 211
CALMARK HOSPITALITY SYSTEMS—See Calmark Investment Company, pg. 211
CALMARK INVESTMENT COMPANY, pg. 211
CALMARK PROPERTIES, INC.—See Calmark Investment Company, pg. 211
CALMARK REALTY MANAGEMENT, INC.—See Calmark Investment Company, pg. 211
CALTEX PETROLEUM CORPORATION, pg. 211
CALTROL, INC., pg. 211
CALUMET CONSTRUCTION CORPORATION, pg. 211
CALUMET CONTRUCTION CORPORATION-INDIANAPOLIS DIVISION—See Calumet Construction Corporation, pg. 211
CALUMET PHOTOGRAPHIC, INC., pg. 211
CALVERT GROUP, LTD.—See The Acacia Group, pg. 11
CALVERT SECURITIES CORPORATION—See The Acacia Group, pg. 11
CALVIN KLEIN SPORT, INC.—See Calvin Klein, Inc., pg. 635
CALYPSO FOODS—See Agway, Inc., pg. 26
CAMALLOY, INC., pg. 211
CAMBIO EQUITIES CORP., pg. 211
CAMBRIDGE ASSOCIATES—See The Dartnell Corporation, pg. 316
CAMBRIDGE CONSULTANTS LIMITED—See Arthur D. Little, Inc., pg. 679
CAMBRIDGE STREET METAL CO., INC., pg. 211
CAMBRO MANUFACTURING COMPANY, pg. 211
CAMELLIA FOOD STORES CO-OP INC., pg. 211
CAMELOT COMMUNICATIONS, INC., pg. 212
CAMELOT MUSIC, INC., pg. 212
CAMEO CURTAINS—See CC Industries, Inc., pg. 200
WALTER F. CAMERON ADVERTISING INC., pg. 212
CAMERON & BARKLEY COMPANY, INC., pg. 212
CAMERON-NEWELL ADVERTISING, INC., pg. 212
CAMILLUS CUTLERY CO., pg. 212
CAMINO REAL CHEVROLET, pg. 212
CAMOSY, INC., pg. 212
CAMP AMERICA—See American Institute For Foreign Study, pg. 56
CAMP DRESSER & MCKEE INC., pg. 212
CAMP DRESSER & MCKEE INTERNATIONAL INC.—See Camp Dresser & McKee Inc., pg. 212
CAMP HOSIERY—See Farley Industries, pg. 400
CAMPA PRODUCTS B.V.—See The Dyson-Kissner-Moran Corporation, pg. 358
THE CAMPAIGN PALACE—See Backer Spielvogel Bates Worldwide, Inc., pg. 111
JOHN J. CAMPBELL CO., INC., pg. 212
CAMPBELL CONSTRUCTION CO., pg. 213
THE CAMPBELL GROUP, pg. 213
CAMPBELL INDUSTRIES, INC.—See Marine Construction & Design Co., pg. 707
CAMPBELL OIL CO., pg. 213
CAMPBELL AND WAGMAN, pg. 213
CAMPING WORLD HOLDINGS, INC., pg. 213
CAMPMOR INC., pg. 213
CAMPTEL INTERNATIONAL SPA—See The Dyson-Kissner-Moran Corporation, pg. 358
CAMPUS POINT REALTY CORPORATION—See Science Applications International Corporation, pg. 981
THE CANADIAN COLEMAN CO., LTD.—See MacAndrews & Forbes Holdings Inc., pg. 695
CANADIAN HARDINGE BROTHERS MACHINE TOOLS INC.—See Hardinge Brothers, Inc., pg. 508
CANADIAN LYNDEN TRANSPORT LTD.—See Lynden Incorporated, pg. 690
CANADIAN MINI-WAREHOUSE PROPERTIES, LTD.—See Public Storage, Inc., pg. 898
CANADIAN NORTHERN SHIELD—See CUNA Mutual Insurance Society, pg. 206
CANADIAN SHADE TREE SERVICE, LTD.—See The Davey Tree Expert Company, pg. 317
CANADIAN STEBBINS ENGINEERING & MFG. CO. LTD.—See Stebbins Engineering & Mfg. Co., pg. 1044
CANAL INDEMNITY COMPANY—See Canal Insurance Co., pg. 213
CANAL INSURANCE CO., pg. 213
CANAL REFINING CO.—See Anchor Gasoline Corporation, pg. 71
D. CANALE FOOD SERVICES, INC., pg. 213
CANBERRA INDUSTRIES, INC., pg. 213

CANCER INDUSTRIES—See Joseph, Littlejohn & Levy, pg. 607
CANDLE CORPORATION, pg. 214
CANDLE CORPORATION OF AMERICA, pg. 214
CANDLESTICK WATERFRONT REST. CORP.—See Specialty Restaurants Corporation, pg. 1028
CANEFCO LIMITED—See Electric Furnace Co., pg. 373
A. J. CANFIELD CO., pg. 214
CANNON, pg. 214
CANTERBURY HOTEL—See Taj International Hotels, pg. 1076
CANTON AGGREGATE DIVISION—See Central Allied Enterprises, pg. 232
CANTON DROP FORGE, pg. 214
CANYON CAPITAL INC.—See KOA Holdings, pg. 612
CAPELETTI BROS., INC., pg. 214
CAPENER, MATTHEWS & WALCHER, pg. 214
CAPEZIO BALLET MAKERS, INC.—See Ballet Makers, Inc., pg. 116
CAPISTAR, INC.—See Spartan Stores Inc., pg. 1026
CAPITAL BANCORP, pg. 214
CAPITAL BANK—See Capital Bancorp, pg. 214
CAPITAL BANK, N.A.—See Capital Bancorp, pg. 214
CAPITAL BANK OF CALIFORNIA—See Capital Bancorp, pg. 214
CAPITAL CITY MANUFACTURING COMPANY—See House of Perfection, Inc., pg. 546
CAPITAL CITY PRESS, INC., pg. 214
CAPITAL CONTROLS COMPANY INC., pg. 215
CAPITAL CONTROLS LTD.—See Capital Controls Company Inc., pg. 215
CAPITAL DEVELOPMENT CO., pg. 215
CAPITAL ELECTRIC GROUP, INC., pg. 215
CAPITAL FACTORS, INC.—See Capital Bancorp, pg. 214
CAPITAL FUNDING CO.—See Lantzsch-Andreas Enterprises, Inc., pg. 658
CAPITAL-GAZETTE COMMUNICATIONS, INC.—See Landmark Communications, Inc., pg. 656
CAPITAL INDUSTRIES, INC., pg. 215
CAPITAL MARBLE & GRANITE CO. INC.—See Cold Spring Granite Company, pg. 260
CAPITAL NEWSPAPERS—See The Hearst Corporation, pg. 523
CAPITAL PANTS CO., pg. 215
CAPITAL RESOURCES—See Alex Lee, Inc., pg. 33
CAPITAL TIRE, INC., pg. 215
CAPITOL BROADCASTING CO., INC., pg. 215
CAPITOL CADILLAC, CORP.—See Don Massey Cadillac Inc., pg. 719
CAPITOL CHEVROLET CADILLAC GEO, INC., pg. 215
CAPITOL CITY PUBLISHING CO., INC.—See Journal Register Company, pg. 608
CAPITOL CONSTRUCTION GROUP, INC., pg. 215
CAPITOL GROUP, pg. 215
CAPITOL INDUSTRIES-EMI INC., pg. 216
CAPITOL METALS PROCESSING, INC., pg. 216
CAPITOL RECORDS, INC.—See Capitol Industries-EMI Inc., pg. 216
CAPITOL STREET CORP., pg. 216
CAPP, INC., pg. 216
CAPPELLI MILES WILTZ & KELLY, pg. 216
CAPPER'S—See Stauffer Communications, Inc., pg. 1043
CAPPER'S INSURANCE SERVICE, INC.—See Stauffer Communications, Inc., pg. 1043
CAPSONIC GROUP, INC., pg. 216
CAPTIVE-AIRE SYSTEMS, INC., pg. 216
CAPTIVE PLASTICS, pg. 216
CAPUCCI CREATIONS INTERNATIONAL, INC., pg. 216
CAR BRITE DISTRIBUTING, INC.—See E & A Industries, Inc., pg. 358
CAR BRITE, INC.—See E & A Industries, Inc., pg. 358
CARAUSTAR INDUSTRIES, INC., pg. 217
CARAVAN PRODUCTS COMPANY, INC., pg. 217
CARBIDE INTERNATIONAL INC.—See Harbour Group Ltd., pg. 507
CARBIDIE CORPORATION—See Spreckles Industries, Inc., pg. 1032
THE CARBIDE/GRAPHITE GROUP, INC., pg. 217
CARCO ELECTRONICS, pg. 217
CARCO INTERNATIONAL, INC., pg. 217
CARCOMP SERVICES, INC.—See Globe Glass & Mirror Co., pg. 464
CARD TECHNOLOGY CORP.—See SBN System Inc., pg. 960
CARD TECHNOLOGY CORPORATION—See SBN System Inc., pg. 960
CARDEM INSURANCE CO., LTD.—See Walter Industries, Inc., pg. 1162
CARDEN & CHERRY, INC., pg. 217
CARDER, INC., pg. 217
CARDINAL ALUMINUM CO., pg. 217
CARDINAL INC., pg. 217
CARDINAL REALTY SERVICES INC., pg. 218
CARDIS CORPORATION—See Carquest Corporation, pg. 224
CAREER BLAZERS AGENCY, INC.—See Career Blazers Inc., pg. 218
CAREER BLAZERS INC., pg. 218
CAREER BLAZERS LEARNING CENTER—See Career Blazers Inc., pg. 218
CAREER BLAZERS SERVICE COMPANY, INC.—See Career Blazers Inc., pg. 218
CAREER BLAZERS TEMPORARY PERSONNEL—See Career Blazers Inc., pg. 218
CAREER BLAZERS OF WHITE PLAINS, INC.—See Career Blazers Inc., pg. 218
CAREERS USA INC., pg. 218
CAREERTRACK INC., pg. 218
CARELLI, GLYNN & WARD, pg. 218
W. P. CAREY & CO., INC., pg. 218
CAREY MACHINERY & SUPPLY COMPANY, pg. 218
CARGILL AGRICOLA S.A.—See Cargill Inc., pg. 219
CARGILL CITRO-AMERICA, INC.—See Cargill Inc., pg. 219
CARGILL DETROIT CORP., pg. 219
CARGILL FERTILIZER, INC.—See Cargill Inc., pg. 219
CARGILL FINANCIAL MARKETS DIV.—See Cargill Inc., pg. 219
CARGILL FLOUR MILLING DIV.—See Cargill Inc., pg. 219
CARGILL INC., pg. 219
CARGILL INTERNATIONAL S.A.—See Cargill Inc., pg. 219
CARGILL INVESTOR SERVICES, INC.—See Cargill Inc., pg. 219
CARGILL LTD.—See Cargill Inc., pg. 219
CARGILL MARINE & TERMINAL—See Cargill Inc., pg. 219
CARGILL NUTRENA FEED—See Cargill Inc., pg. 219
CARGILL NV—See Cargill Inc., pg. 219
CARGILL PETROLEUM, INC.—See Cargill Inc., pg. 219
CARGILL SALT, pg. 219
CARGILL SALT DIVISION—See Cargill Inc., pg. 219
CARGILL SEED DIV.—See Cargill Inc., pg. 219
CARGILL TRADING LTD.—See Cargill Inc., pg. 219
CARGILL UK LTD.—See Cargill Inc., pg. 219
CARGOCAIRE ENGINEERING CORPORATION, pg. 220
CARHARTT, INC., pg. 220
CARIBBEAN MOVING & STORAGE, INC.—See The Suddath Companies, pg. 1056
CARIBE EXPRESS, pg. 220
CARIBE EXPRESS—See Caribe Express, pg. 220
CARIBE EXPRESS LATIN AMERICAN DIV.—See Caribe Express, pg. 220
CARIBE EXPRESS PACE AIR FREIGHT—See Caribe Express, pg. 220
CARIBE FREIGHT—See Caribe Express, pg. 220
CARIPLANT S.A.—See Margo Nursery Farms, Inc., pg. 707
CARLES INC., pg. 220
THE P.J. CARLIN CONSTRUCTION COMPANY, pg. 220
CARLISLE EQUIPMENT COMPANY, pg. 220
CARLISLE RETAILERS, INC., pg. 220
JOHN CARLO INC., pg. 220
CARL'S DRUG COMPANY, INC.—See Victory Markets Inc., pg. 1150
CARLSBERG FINANCIAL CORP., pg. 220
DICK CARLSON ASSOCIATES—See Austin Sculpture, pg. 100
CARLSON COMPANIES, INC., pg. 220
CARLSON, DELGADO, HOAG, MATTHEI ADVERTISING, INC., pg. 222
CARLSON INTERNATIONAL DIVISION—See Carlson Companies, Inc., pg. 221
CARLSON LEARNING COMPANY—See Carlson Companies, Inc., pg. 221
CARLSON LEASING, INC.—See Carlson Companies, Inc., pg. 221
CARLSON MARKETING GROUP (AUST.) PTY. LIMITED—See Carlson Companies, Inc., pg. 221
CARLSON MARKETING GROUP, INC.—See Carlson Companies, Inc., pg. 221
CARLSON MARKETING GROUP JAPAN CO. LTD.—See Carlson Companies, Inc., pg. 221
CARLSON MARKETING GROUP JAPAN KK—See Carlson Companies, Inc., pg. 221
CARLSON MARKETING GROUP LTD.—See Carlson Companies, Inc., pg. 221
CARLSON MARKETING GROUP SCANDINAVIA MOTIVATION SERVICE AB—See Carlson Companies, Inc., pg. 221
CARLSON MARKETING GROUP (U.K.) LIMITED—See Carlson Companies, Inc., pg. 221
CARLSON & PARTNERS, INC., pg. 222
CARLSON PROMOTION DIVISION—See Carlson Companies, Inc., pg. 221
CARLSON REAL ESTATE COMPANY—See Carlson Companies, Inc., pg. 221
CARLSON RETAIL MARKETING—See Carlson Companies, Inc., pg. 221
CARLSON TRAVEL GROUP, INC.—See Carlson Companies, Inc., pg. 221
CARLSON TRAVEL NETWORK INTERNATIONAL—See Carlson Companies, Inc., pg. 221
CARLSON TRAVEL NETWORK RETAIL—See Carlson Company, Inc., pg. 221
CARLSON TRAVEL NETWORK-COMMERCIAL—See Carlson Companies, Inc., pg. 221
CARLSON TRAVEL NETWORK-RETAIL—See Carlson Companies, Inc., pg. 221
CARLTON MANUFACTURING, INC., pg. 222
CARLYLE & CO. JEWELERS, pg. 222
THE CARLYLE GROUP—See Carlyle Holding Corporation, pg. 222
CARLYLE HOLDING CORPORATION, pg. 222
CARMICHAEL LYNCH, INC., pg. 222
CARNEGIE ASSOCIATES, INC., pg. 222
CARNES COMPANY, INC.—See Venturedyne, Ltd., pg. 1148
CARNEY/MOHLIN & COMPANY, pg. 222
CARNIVAL CREATIONS, pg. 222
CARNRICK LABS., INC., pg. 222
CARO PRODUCE & INSTITUTIONAL FOODS—See Performance Food Group, Inc., pg. 861
CAROLINA ABSORBENT COTTON CO.—See Barnhardt Manufacturing Co., pg. 120
CAROLINA BIOLOGICAL SUPPLY CO., pg. 222
CAROLINA BUILDERS CORPORATION, pg. 223
CAROLINA BY-PRODUCTS CO.—See CBP Resources, Inc., pg. 199
CAROLINA GLOVE CO., pg. 223
CAROLINA MAIDEN CORP.—See Carolina Mills, Inc., pg. 223
CAROLINA MILLS, INC., pg. 223
CAROLINA MIRROR COMPANY, pg. 223
CAROLINA MOUNTAIN WATER—See Sammons Enterprises, Inc., pg. 968
CAROLINA SHOE COMPANY—See H.H. Brown Shoe Company, Inc., pg. 182
CAROLINA STEEL CORPORATION, pg. 223
CAROLINA STEEL-GREENVILLE PLANT—See Carolina Steel Corporation, pg. 223
CAROLINA STEEL-HICKORY PLANT—See Carolina Steel Corporation, pg. 223
CAROLINA STEEL-SALEM PLANT—See Carolina Steel Corporation, pg. 223
CAROLINA STEEL SERVICE CENTER PLANT—See Carolina Steel Corporation, pg. 223
CAROLINA TRACTOR & EQUIPMENT CO., pg. 223
DANIEL CARON LTD., pg. 224
CAROUSEL SNACK BARS OF MINNESOTA, pg. 224
CARPARK—See The Oliver Carr Co., pg. 225
E. R. CARPENTER CO., pg. 224
CARPENTER MANUFACTURING, INC.—See Servaas, Inc., pg. 991
CARPENTER RIGGING, pg. 224
CARPETERIA, INC., pg. 224
CARPRO, INC.—See Caravan Products Company, Inc., pg. 217
CARQUEST, pg. 224
CARQUEST CORPORATION, pg. 224
CARR GOTTSTEIN FOODS, pg. 225
THE OLIVER CARR CO., pg. 225
CARRAFIELLO, DIEHL & ASSOCIATES, INC., pg. 225
CARRIAGE HOUSE MANOR—See Meritcare, Inc., pg. 740
CARRIER VIBRATING EQUIPMENT, INC., pg. 225
CARRINGTON PARFUMS LTD.—See MacAndrews & Forbes Holdings Inc., pg. 695
CARRIS REELS, INC., pg. 225
CARROLL COUNTY TIMES—See Landmark Communications, Inc., pg. 655
CARROLL'S FOODS, INC., pg. 225
CARROLS CORPORATION, pg. 225
CARROWS RESTAURANTS, INC.—See Restaurant Enterprises Group, Inc., pg. 929
CARRYORE, LIMITED—See National Steel Corporation, pg. 794
CARSE OIL CO. INC., pg. 225
CARSON PRODUCTS COMPANY—See Aminco, Inc., pg. 67
CARSTENS HEALTH INDUSTRIES, INC., pg. 225
CARSTENSEN FREIGHT LINE, INC., pg. 226
CARTALL DIV.—See Peco Inc., pg. 854
CARTER, pg. 226
CARTER CHAMBERS SUPPLY, INC., pg. 226
CARTER COMPANIES, pg. 226
THE WILLIAM CARTER COMPANY, pg. 226
CARTER DAY CO.—See Carter Day Industries, Inc., pg. 226
CARTER DAY INDUSTRIES, INC., pg. 226
CARTER DAY INDUSTRIES (CANADA) LTD.—See Carter Day Industries, Inc., pg. 226
CARTER DAY INTERNATIONAL, INC.—See Carter Day Industries, Inc., pg. 226
J. C. CARTER COMPANY, INC., pg. 226
JERRY C. CARTER, INC., pg. 226
CARTER-JONES LUMBER COMPANY, pg. 226
CARTON-CRAFT CORPORATION, pg. 226
CARTWRIGHT COMMUNICATIONS CO., pg. 227
CARUS CHEMICAL COMPANY, CHEMICAL DIV.—See Carus Corporation, pg. 227
CARUS CORPORATION, pg. 227
CARUS PUBLISHING COMPANY—See Carus Corporation, pg. 227
CARVER, INC., pg. 227
CASA DI BERTACCHI—See Rich Products Corp., pg. 932
CASA GRANDE WEST WATER COMPANY, INC.—See JMB Realty Corporation, pg. 585
CASA LUPITA RESTAURANTS, INC.—See Metromedia Company, pg. 744
CASANOVA PENDRILL PUBLICIDAD INC., pg. 227
CASCADE CONTROLS, INC.—See Synergism, Inc., pg. 1070
CASCADE STEEL ROLLING MILLS, INC.—See Schnitzer Steel Industries, Inc., pg. 977
CASCADIA TECHNOLOGY CORPORATION—See Novametrix Medical Systems Inc., pg. 817
CASCHEM INC., pg. 227
CASCINO PURCELL FREEBAIRN, pg. 227
CASCO CABLE TELEVISION INC.—See Susquehanna Pfaltzgraff, pg. 1065
CASE FARMS, INC.—See Case Foods, Inc., pg. 228
CASE FARMS OF OHIO—See Case Foods, Inc., pg. 228
CASE FOLEY SACKETT, INC., pg. 227
CASE FOODS, INC., pg. 227
CASE-SWAYNE CO. INC., pg. 228
CASEY CO., pg. 228
CASEY CO.—See Casey Co., pg. 228
THE CASEY COUNTY NEWS—See Landmark Communications, Inc., pg. 655
CASH & CARRY GROCER INC., pg. 228
CASH PLUS, INC., pg. 228
CASHCO, INC., pg. 228
CASKET SHELLS, INC., pg. 228
CASS-CLAY CREAMERY, pg. 228
CASSANO'S INC., pg. 228
CASSENS TRANSPORT COMPANY, pg. 228
CASTCRAFT INDUSTRIES, INC., pg. 228
CASTCRAFT SOFTWARE OPTIFONT—See Castcraft Industries, Inc., pg. 228
CASTEX INDUSTRIES INC., pg. 228
CASTING MATERIAL COMPANY, pg. 229
CASTLE-HARLAN, INC., pg. 229
CASTLEBERG'S—See Reliable Stores, Inc., pg. 925
CASTLEBERRY'S FOOD COMPANY, pg. 229
CASTOR ADVERTISING CORP., pg. 229
CASTRO CONVERTIBLE CORPORATION, pg. 229
CASUDA CANYON RESTAURANT CORP.—See Specialty Restaurants Corporation, pg. 1028
CASWELL/MASSEY CO. LTD., pg. 229
CAT PUMPS AG—See Diversified Dynamics Inc., pg. 340
CAT PUMPS CORPORATION—See Diversified Dynamics Inc., pg. 340
CAT PUMPS DEUTSCHLAND GMBH—See Diversified Dynamics Inc., pg. 340

CAT PUMPS INTERNATIONAL N.V.—See Diversified Dynamics Inc., pg. 340
CAT PUMPS (UK) LTD.—See Diversified Dynamics Inc., pg. 340
CATALINA YACHTS, INC., pg. 229
CATALOGUE MARKETING, INC.—See Hickory Farms, Inc., pg. 533
CATALYST ENERGY CORPORATION—See United Thermal Corporation, pg. 1137
CATCHER—See Wyse Advertising, Inc., pg. 1206
CATERAIR HOLDINGS CORP., pg. 229
CATERAIR INTERNATIONAL—See Caterair Holdings Corp., pg. 229
CATHOLIC ORDER OF FORESTERS, pg. 229
CATO JOHNSON FRANKFURT—See Young & Rubicam Inc., pg. 1211
CATO JOHNSON LIMITED—See Young & Rubicam Inc., pg. 1212
CATO JOHNSON-NEW YORK—See Young & Rubicam Inc., pg. 1210
CATO JOHNSON SWITZERLAND—See Young & Rubicam Inc., pg. 1212
CATO JOHNSON WORLDWIDE—See Young & Rubicam Inc., pg. 1210
CATO YASUMURA BEHAEGHEL (CYB)—See Young & Rubicam Inc., pg. 1212
L. D. CAULK CO. OF CANADA DIV.—See Dentsply International Inc., pg. 330
L. D. CAULK DIV.—See Dentsply International Inc., pg. 330
CAUSA PUBLICIDAD—See Leo Burnett Company, Inc., pg. 192
JIM CAUSLEY PONTIAC GMC INC., pg. 229
CAVALIER CORPORATION, pg. 229
CAVE CITY CHEVROLET—See Don Massey Cadillac Inc., pg. 719
CAWSL CORPORATION, pg. 229
THE CAXTON PRINTERS LTD., pg. 230
W.C. CAYE & COMPANY, INC., pg. 230
CCC CONVEYORS, INC.—See The Dyson-Kissner-Moran Corporation, pg. 357
CE DE CANDY, INC., pg. 230
CEBCOR (CONSOLIDATED EMPLOYMENT BENEFITS CORP.), pg. 230
CEDAR CREEK PROPERTIES INC.—See Ash Grove Cement Company, pg. 88
CEDAR CREEK REALTY CO., INC.—See Ash Grove Cement Company, pg. 88
CEDAR FARMS COMPANY, INC., pg. 230
CEDARBURG DAIRY—See Roundy's, Inc., pg. 952
THE CEDARWOOD COMPANIES, pg. 230
CEILING & PARTITIONS, INC., pg. 230
CELEBRITY BOATS, INC.—See Jupiter Industries, Inc., pg. 609
CELENTANO BROTHERS, pg. 231
CELESTIAL SEASONINGS, pg. 231
CELLO BAG COMPANY, INC., pg. 231
CELLULAR SERVICE, INC., pg. 231
CENCOM CABLE TELEVISION—See Gaylord Entertainment Co., pg. 446
CENEX (FARMERS UNION CENTRAL EXCHANGE, INC.), pg. 231
CENEX/LAND O'LAKES, INC.—See CENEX (Farmers Union Central Exchange, Inc.), pg. 231
CENTENNIAL CAPITAL CORPORATION—See Massachusetts Mutual Life Insurance Co., pg. 719
CENTENNIAL INSURANCE CO.—See Atlantic Mutual Companies, pg. 94
CENTERMARK PROPERTIES, INC., pg. 231
CENTIMARK CORPORATION, pg. 231
CENTRAL ADVERTISING AGENCY, pg. 231
CENTRAL ALL PRO—See AEA, Inc., pg. 3
CENTRAL ALLIED ENTERPRISES, pg. 232
CENTRAL BEAUTY EQUIPMENT—See Belvedere Company, pg. 138
CENTRAL CALIFORNIA TRACTION CO.—See Anschutz Corporation, pg. 76
CENTRAL COCA-COLA BOTTLING COMPANY, INC., pg. 232
CENTRAL COMMISSARY, INC.—See Cornucopia, Inc., pg. 287
CENTRAL COMMUNICATIONS COMPANY—See Illinois Consolidated Telephone Co., pg. 563
CENTRAL DATA CORPORATION, pg. 232
CENTRAL DE INDUSTRIAS, S.A.—See Lear Siegler Diversified Holdings Corp., pg. 664
CENTRAL DUPAGE HEALTH SYSTEM, pg. 232
CENTRAL DUPAGE HOSPITAL ASSOCIATION—See Central DuPage Health System, pg. 232
CENTRAL FEED MILLS, INC., pg. 232
CENTRAL FREIGHT LINES INC., pg. 232
CENTRAL GROCERS CO-OP, pg. 232
CENTRAL ILLINOIS PERIODICALS, INC.—See The Charles Levy Company, pg. 672
CENTRAL ILLINOIS STEEL COMPANY, pg. 232
CENTRAL KENTUCKY NEWS-JOURNAL—See Landmark Communications, Inc., pg. 655
CENTRAL LIFE ASSURANCE CO., pg. 232
CENTRAL LIVESTOCK ASSOCIATION, INC., pg. 233
CENTRAL LIVESTOCK ORDER BUYING COMPANY—See Central Livestock Association, Inc., pg. 233
CENTRAL MAINE MORNING NEWSPAPERS—See Guy Gannett Publishing Company, pg. 442
CENTRAL MARYLAND HOMES—See Landmark Communications, Inc., pg. 655
CENTRAL MEDIA, S.A.—See Backer Spielvogel Bates Worldwide, Inc., pg. 111
CENTRAL MICHIGAN CONTAINER CORPORATION—See Advance Packaging Corporation, pg. 19
CENTRAL MUTUAL INSURANCE CO., pg. 233
CENTRAL NATIONAL-GOTTESMAN INC., pg. 233
CENTRAL PAPER COMPANY, pg. 233
CENTRAL PARKING CORP., pg. 234
CENTRAL PARKING CORP.—See Central Parking Corp., pg. 234
CENTRAL PHARMACEUTICALS, INC., pg. 234
CENTRAL POINT SOFTWARE, INC., pg. 234
CENTRAL REALTY CORP.—See Union Holdings, Inc., pg. 1128
CENTRAL/SHIPPEE, INC., pg. 234
CENTRAL STATES DIVERSIFIED, INC., pg. 234
CENTRAL STATES ENTERPRISES, INC., pg. 234
CENTRAL SUPPLY CO., INC., pg. 234
CENTRAL TEXTILE DIV.—See Masters, Inc., pg. 720
CENTRAL TRANSPORT INC., pg. 234
CENTRAL-UNITED LIFE INSURANCE CO.—See Central Mutual Insurance Co., pg. 233
CENTRE FOUNDRY & MACHINE CO.—See The Dyson-Kissner-Moran Corporation, pg. 357
CENTRE LIME & STONE CO., INC.—See Glenn O. Hawbaker, Inc., pg. 517
CENTRIFUGAL & MECHANICAL INDUSTRIES—See Jupiter Industries, Inc., pg. 609
CENTRIFUGAL & MECHANICAL INDUSTRIES, INC.—See Jupiter Industries, Inc., pg. 609
CENTRO DE IDIOMAS BERLITZ DE VENEZUELA—See Berlitz International, Inc., pg. 143
CENTURY AMERICA CORPORATION, pg. 234
CENTURY AUTOLINE, pg. 235
CENTURY BOATS BY GENERAL MARINE INDUSTRIES—See General Marine Industries, Inc., pg. 450
CENTURY BUSINESS CREDIT CORPORATION, pg. 235
CENTURY COMPUTER MARKETING, pg. 235
CENTURY CONCRETE, INC.—See Ash Grove Cement Company, pg. 88
CENTURY DATA SERVICES, INC.—See Century Business Credit Corporation, pg. 235
CENTURY DATA SYSTEMS, pg. 235
CENTURY FENCE COMPANY, pg. 235
CENTURY FINANCIAL SERVICES—See Cenvill Development Corp., pg. 236
CENTURY FURNITURE INDUSTRIES, pg. 235
CENTURY GOLF COURSES, INC.—See Cenvill Development Corp., pg. 236
CENTURY PRODUCTS CO., pg. 235
CENTURY PRODUCTS INC.—See Acme Canvas Co., Inc., pg. 13
CENTURY PUBLICATIONS, INC.—See Harte-Hanks Communications, Inc., pg. 513
CENTURY PUBLISHING COMPANY, pg. 235
CENTURY REAL ESTATE, INC.—See Cenvill Development Corp., pg. 236
CENTURY SEAFOOD INC., pg. 235
CENTURY 21 AGMONT REAL ESTATE, INC., pg. 235
CENTURY 21 HOMES MAGAZINE-YORK, PA—See Landmark Communications, Inc., pg. 655
CENTURY 21 KRISS & ASSOCIATES—See Realty One, pg. 917
CENTURY 21 REAL ESTATE CORP.—See Metropolitan Life Insurance Co., pg. 744
CENTURY UTILITIES, INC.—See Cenvill Development Corp., pg. 236
CENVILL DEVELOPMENT CORP., pg. 235
CENVILL MANAGEMENT, INC.—See Cenvill Development Corp., pg. 236
CENVILL RECREATION, INC.—See Cenvill Development Corp., pg. 236
CENVILL SERVICES—See Cenvill Development Corp., pg. 236
CEPCO—See Collins & Aikman Group Inc., pg. 263
CERAMCO—See Dentsply International Inc., pg. 330
CERAMIC COOLING TOWER CO.—See Amsted Industries Incorporated, pg. 69
CERAS JOHNSON DE PORTUGAL, LDA.—See S. C. Johnson & Son, Inc., pg. 599
CERAS JOHNSON LTDA.—See S. C. Johnson & Son, Inc., pg. 599
CERCA GMBH—See Backer Spielvogel Bates Worldwide, Inc., pg. 111
CERCOM TECHNOLOGIES, INC.—See Intertrade Industries, pg. 581
CERRITOS FORD, INC., pg. 236
CERRO COPPER PRODUCTS CO.—See The Marmon Group, Inc., pg. 711
CERRO METAL PRODUCTS COMPANY—See The Marmon Group, Inc., pg. 711
CERRO SALES CORPORATION—See The Marmon Group, Inc., pg. 711
CERRO WIRE & CABLE CO., INC.—See The Marmon Group, Inc., pg. 711
CERTIFIED CORP., pg. 236
CERTIFIED DIV.—See Lear Siegler Diversified Holdings Corp., pg. 664
CERTIFIED GROCERS ADVERTISING CO., pg. 236
CERTIFIED GROCERS MIDWEST, INC., pg. 236
CERTIFIED GROCERS OF CALIFORNIA, pg. 237
CERTIFIED GROCERS OF FLORIDA, INC., pg. 237
CERTIFIED HOLDING CORP., pg. 237
CERTIFIED WHOLESALERS INC.—See Associated Grocers of New England, Inc., pg. 90
CERTRONICS, INC.—See Synergism, Inc., pg. 1070
CERWIN VEGA, INC., pg. 237
CHADWICK-HELMUTH COMPANY, INC., pg. 237
CHADWICK-MILLER INC., pg. 237
CHADWICK-MILLER INTL. LTD.—See Chadwick-Miller Inc., pg. 237
CHAFFEE CASE & PARTNERS, pg. 237
CHAGNON LUMBER COMPANY, INC., pg. 238
CHAIRWORLD, INC.—See Globe Business Furniture, Inc., pg. 463
CHAITRA LEO BURNETT ADVERTISING PRIVATE LTD.—See Leo Burnett Company, Inc., pg. 192
D. CHAKLIN, DIR. EUROPEAN OPERATIONS—See Astronautics Corp. of America, pg. 93
CHALEK & CHALEK, INC., pg. 238
CHALK & PARTNERS, LTD., pg. 238
CHALLENGE GRAPHICS EQUIPMENT CO., pg. 238
CHALLENGE TECHNOLOGIES—See Challenge Graphics Equipment Co., pg. 238
CHALLENGER CONSTRUCTION, INC.—See The DeMars Corp., pg. 328
THE CHAMBERLAIN GROUP, INC.—See Duchossois Industries, Inc., pg. 350
CHAMBERLAIN HEALTH & BEAUTY AIDS COMPANY, pg. 238
CHAMBERLAIN MANUFACTURING CORP.—See Duchossois Industries, Inc., pg. 350
M.S. CHAMBERS & SON, INC.—See The Dyson-Kissner-Moran Corporation, pg. 357
CHAMELEON TECHNOLOGIES INCORPORATED—See Veda International, Inc., pg. 1146
CHAMPAIGN LANDMARK, pg. 238
CHAMPAIGN LANDMARK—See Champaign Landmark, pg. 238
CHAMPION ALUMINUM CORPORATION, pg. 238
CHAMPION BOXED BEEF, pg. 238
CHAMPION BUSINESS FORMS, pg. 238
CHAMPION, INC., pg. 238
CHAMPION LABORATORIES, INC.—See UIS, Inc., pg. 1123
CHAMPION PNEUMATIC MACHINERY CO., INC., pg. 238
CHAMPLAIN LIFE INSURANCE COMPANY—See National Life Insurance Company, pg. 791
CHANCE INDUSTRIES, INC., pg. 238
CHANDLER PRODUCTS, INC.—See Jupiter Industries, Inc., pg. 609
CHANGE-O-MATIC/WESCO—See Steiner Corporation, pg. 1045
CHANLON VIDEO ARTS—See SB Entertainment Inc., pg. 960
CHANNEL HOME CENTERS INC., pg. 238
CHANNEL INDUSTRIES, INC.—See Channel Technologies, Inc., pg. 239
CHANNEL PRODUCTS, INC.—See Channel Technologies, Inc., pg. 239
CHANNEL TECHNOLOGIES, INC., pg. 239
CHANNELLOCK, INC., pg. 239
CHAPMAN DIRECT ADVERTISING—See Young & Rubicam Inc., pg. 1210
CHAPMAN PRINTING COMPANY, pg. 239
CHARAN INDUSTRIES, INC., pg. 239
CHARAN REALTY GROUP—See Charan Industries, Inc., pg. 239
THE CHARDON RUBBER CO., pg. 239
CHARING CROSS GROUP, pg. 239
CHARITABLE GAMING DIV.—See Michigan State Lottery Bureau, pg. 747
CHARLES CURTAIN COMPANY, INC., pg. 239
CHARLES MACHINE WORKS, INC., pg. 240
CHARLES OF THE RITZ GROUP LTD.—See MacAndrews & Forbes Holdings Inc., pg. 695
CHARLES RIVER DATA SYSTEMS, INC., pg. 240
CHARLES RIVER FOODS, INC., pg. 240
CHARLES TOWN RACES, INC., pg. 240
CHARLESTON INDUSTRIES—See Petersen Aluminum Corporation, pg. 864
CHARMGLOW INDUSTRIES, INC., pg. 240
CHARRON, SCHWARTZ & PARTNERS, INC., pg. 240
CHARTER HOUSE GROUP, pg. 240
CHARTER HOUSE INCORPORATED—See Stainless Incorporated, pg. 1035
CHARTER INVESTMENT CO.—See Academy Insurance Group, Inc., pg. 11
CHARTER OAK FINANCIAL CORPORATION—See Guarantee Title Co., Inc., pg. 491
CHARTWAY TECHNOLOGIES, pg. 240
CHASE CHEVROLET CO., pg. 240
CHASE CHRYSLER/PLYMOUTH—See Chase Chevrolet Co., pg. 240
F. H. CHASE, INC., pg. 240
CHATHAM EIGHT CORPORATION—See The Prudential Insurance Company of America, pg. 896
CHATHAM IMPORTERS—See Peerless Importers, Inc., pg. 855
CHATHAM MANUFACTURING COMPANY—See CMI Industries, Inc., pg. 202
CHATHAM SMITH CORP.—See CMI Industries, Inc., pg. 202
CHATHAM TOWING COMPANY, INC.—See Colonial Oil Industries, pg. 264
THE CHATHAM WATER CO.—See Woolrich, Inc., pg. 1201
CHATSWORTH DATA CORPORATION, pg. 241
CHATTAHOOCHEE VALLEY RAILWAY COMPANY—See Farley Industries, pg. 400
CHATTANOOGA CHOO-CHOO HOLIDAY INN, pg. 241
CHATTANOOGA GROUP, pg. 241
CHEF ITALIA, INC., pg. 241
CHELSEA MILLING CO., pg. 241
CHELSEA MOORE COMPANY, pg. 241
CHELSEA STATE BANK, pg. 241
CHEM-TAINER CORPORATION, pg. 241
CHEMCENTRAL/ATLANTA—See CHEMCENTRAL Corporation, pg. 241
CHEMCENTRAL/BUFFALO—See CHEMCENTRAL Corporation, pg. 241
CHEMCENTRAL/CHICAGO—See CHEMCENTRAL Corporation, pg. 241
CHEMCENTRAL/CINCINNATI—See CHEMCENTRAL Corporation, pg. 241
CHEMCENTRAL/CLEVELAND—See CHEMCENTRAL Corporation, pg. 241
CHEMCENTRAL CORPORATION, pg. 241
CHEMCENTRAL/DALLAS—See CHEMCENTRAL Corporation, pg. 241
CHEMCENTRAL/DETROIT—See CHEMCENTRAL Corporation, pg. 241
CHEMCENTRAL/FORT WAYNE—See CHEMCENTRAL Corporation, pg. 241
CHEMCENTRAL/GRAND RAPIDS—See CHEMCENTRAL Corporation, pg. 241

CHEMCENTRAL/GREENSBORO—See CHEMCENTRAL Corporation, pg. 241
CHEMCENTRAL/HOUSTON—See CHEMCENTRAL Corporation, pg. 241
CHEMCENTRAL/INDIANAPOLIS—See CHEMCENTRAL Corporation, pg. 242
CHEMCENTRAL/KANSAS CITY—See CHEMCENTRAL Corporation, pg. 242
CHEMCENTRAL/LOS ANGELES—See CHEMCENTRAL Corporation, pg. 242
CHEMCENTRAL/LOUISVILLE—See CHEMCENTRAL Corporation, pg. 242
CHEMCENTRAL/MILWAUKEE—See CHEMCENTRAL Corporation, pg. 242
CHEMCENTRAL/MINNESOTA—See CHEMCENTRAL Corporation, pg. 242
CHEMCENTRAL/NEW ORLEANS—See CHEMCENTRAL Corporation, pg. 242
CHEMCENTRAL/ODESSA—See CHEMCENTRAL Corporation, pg. 242
CHEMCENTRAL/OKLAHOMA CITY—See CHEMCENTRAL Corporation, pg. 242
CHEMCENTRAL/ORLANDO—See CHEMCENTRAL Corporation, pg. 242
CHEMCENTRAL/PITTSBURGH—See CHEMCENTRAL Corporation, pg. 242
CHEMCENTRAL/PORTLAND—See CHEMCENTRAL Corporation, pg. 242
CHEMCENTRAL/ST. LOUIS—See CHEMCENTRAL Corporation, pg. 242
CHEMCENTRAL/SALT LAKE CITY—See CHEMCENTRAL Corporation, pg. 242
CHEMCENTRAL/SAN ANTONIO—See CHEMCENTRAL Corporation, pg. 242
CHEMCENTRAL/SAN FRANCISCO—See CHEMCENTRAL Corporation, pg. 242
CHEMCENTRAL/SEATTLE—See CHEMCENTRAL Corporation, pg. 242
CHEMCENTRAL/SPOKANE—See CHEMCENTRAL Corporation, pg. 242
CHEMCENTRAL/TOLEDO—See CHEMCENTRAL Corporation, pg. 242
CHEMCENTRAL/TULSA—See CHEMCENTRAL Corporation, pg. 242
CHEMICAL EXCHANGE INDUSTRIES, pg. 242
CHEMICAL SPECIALTIES CORP.—See Syndet Products, Inc., pg. 1069
CHEMIFAX—See Blue Coral, Inc., pg. 159
CHEMIONICS CORPORATION—See Chessco Industries, Inc., pg. 244
CHEMOIL, pg. 242
CHEMROCK CORPORATION—See Belmont Industries, Inc., pg. 136
CHEMROCK CORPORATION—See Belmont Industries, Inc., pg. 137
CHEMROCK CORPORATION—See Belmont Industries, Inc., pg. 137
CHEMROCK CORPORATION—See Belmont Industries, Inc., pg. 137
CHEMROCK CORPORATION—See Belmont Industries, Inc., pg. 137
CHEMSTONE CORP., pg. 242
CHEMTECH INDUSTRIES, INC., pg. 242
CHEMUNG FORD, INC., pg. 242
CHENEY COMPANY, pg. 242
CHERAW YARN MILLS, INC., pg. 242
CHERCO COMPRESSORS, INC.—See Minstar, Inc., pg. 758
THE CHERENSON GROUP, pg. 243
CHERNIN'S SHOES, pg. 243
CHERNOFF/SILVER & ASSOCIATES, pg. 243
CHEROKEE APPAREL CORP.—See The Cherokee Group, pg. 243
CHEROKEE BRICK & TILE CO., pg. 243
THE CHEROKEE GROUP, pg. 243
CHEROKEE SHOE COMPANY, INC.—See The Cherokee Group, pg. 243
CHERRY CENTRAL COOPERATIVE, pg. 243
CHESAPEAKE FINANCIAL CORP., pg. 243
THE CHESAPEAKE LIFE INSURANCE CO., pg. 243
CHESCO PRODUCTS, INC.—See American Tool Companies, Inc., pg. 64
CHESSCO CAPITAL CORP.—See Chessco Industries, Inc., pg. 244
CHESSCO INDUSTRIES, INC., pg. 243
CHESTER NEWS AND REPORTER—See Landmark Communications, Inc., pg. 655
CHESTERFIELD INDUSTRIAL PARK, INC.—See Watlow Electric Manufacturing Company, pg. 1167
A.W. CHESTERTON COMPANY, pg. 244
CHEVY CHASE CARS & GEO, pg. 244
CHEYENNE OUTFITTERS, INC., pg. 244
CHI SYSTEMS, INC., pg. 244
CHIAT/DAY/MOJO/ATLANTA—See Chiat/Day/Mojo Inc. Advertising, pg. 244
CHIAT/DAY/MOJO/CHICAGO—See Chiat/Day/Mojo Inc. Advertising, pg. 244
CHIAT/DAY/MOJO/DALLAS—See Chiat/Day/Mojo Inc. Advertising, pg. 244
CHIAT/DAY/MOJO INC. ADVERTISING, pg. 244
CHIAT/DAY/MOJO/SAN FRANCISCO—See Chiat/Day/Mojo Inc. Advertising, pg. 245
CHIAT/DAY/MOJO—See Chiat/Day/Mojo Inc. Advertising, pg. 245
CHICAGO—See Landmark Communications, Inc., pg. 656
CHICAGO BLASTING COMPANY—See Graycor, Inc., pg. 480
CHICAGO BOAT YARD, INC.—See CFB Industries, Inc., pg. 201
CHICAGO CONVENTION & TOURISM BUREAU, pg. 245
CHICAGO CORP.—See Chicorp, Inc., pg. 247
CHICAGO EXTRUDED METALS CO., pg. 245
THE CHICAGO FAUCET CO., pg. 245
CHICAGO FIRE BRICK COMPANY—See CFB Industries, Inc., pg. 201
CHICAGO FIRE BRICK OF DELAWARE, INC.—See CFB Industries, Inc., pg. 201
CHICAGO HEIGHTS STEEL, pg. 245
CHICAGO HOLDINGS, INC., pg. 245
CHICAGO LOCK COMPANY, pg. 245
CHICAGO MECHANICAL, INC., pg. 245
CHICAGO MERCANTILE EXCHANGE, pg. 245
CHICAGO RAIL LINK—See Chicago West Pullman Corporation, pg. 246
CHICAGO READER, INC., pg. 245
CHICAGO SHOW PRINTING CO., pg. 246
CHICAGO STEEL & WIRE—See MCM Enterprises, Inc., pg. 691
CHICAGO SUN TIMES—See Adler & Shaykin, pg. 18
CHICAGO TRANSIT AUTHORITY—See Regional Transportation Authority (RTA), pg. 922
CHICAGO TUBE & IRON CO., pg. 246
CHICAGO TUBE & IRON COMPANY OF MINNESOTA—See Chicago Tube & Iron Co., pg. 246
CHICAGO UNION STATION COMPANY—See Amtrak-National Railroad Passenger Corp., pg. 69
CHICAGO WEST PULLMAN CORPORATION, pg. 246
CHICAGO WEST PULLMAN FINANCIAL CORPORATION—See Chicago West Pullman Corporation, pg. 246
CHICAGO WEST PULLMAN HEAVY INDUSTRIES—See Chicago West Pullman Corporation, pg. 246
CHICAGO WEST PULLMAN & SOUTHERN R.R. CO.—See Chicago West Pullman Corporation, pg. 246
CHICAGO WEST PULLMAN TRANSPORTATION CORPORATION—See Chicago West Pullman Corporation, pg. 246
CHICAGO WHITE METAL CASTING, INC., pg. 246
CHICK-FIL-A, INC., pg. 247
CHICORP FINANCIAL SERVICES—See Chicorp, Inc., pg. 247
CHICORP, INC., pg. 247
CHICORP MANAGEMENT INC.—See Chicorp, Inc., pg. 247
CHIEF CONSTRUCTION—See Chief Industries, Inc., pg. 247
CHIEF ETHANOL FUELS, INC.—See Chief Industries, Inc., pg. 247
CHIEF E-Z BREAKER, INC.—See Chief Industries, Inc., pg. 247
CHIEF FINANCIAL SERVICES—See Chief Industries, Inc., pg. 247
CHIEF INDUSTRIES, INC., pg. 247
CHIEF INDUSTRIES UK LTD.—See Chief Industries, Inc., pg. 247
CHILDREN'S BETTER HEALTH INSTITUTE—See Benjamin Franklin Literary & Medical Society, Inc., pg. 139
THE CHILDREN'S PLACE RETAIL STORES, INC., pg. 247
CHILDREN'S WORLD LEARNING CENTERS, INC.—See ARA Group, pg. 7
CHILEWICH PARTNERS, pg. 248
CHILI PEPPER OF ROCKY POINT, INC.—See Specialty Restaurants Corporation, pg. 1028
CHINA COMPUTERWORLD—See International Data Group, pg. 577
CHINA TRAVEL BUREAU LTD.—See Orbitair International Ltd., pg. 828
CHIP SUPPLY INC., pg. 248
CHIPICO PICKLES—See Vienna Sausage Mfg. Co., pg. 1151
CHIPMAN-UNION, INC., pg. 248
CHIQUITA BRANDS, INC.—See American Financial Corporation, pg. 53
CHIQUITA BRANDS INTERNATIONAL, INC.—See American Financial Corporation, pg. 53
CHISHOLM, BOYD & WHITE CO.—See Venturedyne, Ltd., pg. 1148
CHISWICK TRADING INC., pg. 248
CHITTENDEN & EASTMAN CO., pg. 248
CHIVAS PRODUCTS LTD., pg. 248
CHOCTAW ELECTRIC CO-OP, pg. 248
CHOCTAW, INC., pg. 248
CHORE-TIME/BROCK INTERNATIONAL—See CTB Inc., pg. 205
CHORE-TIME CAGE SYSTEMS—See CTB Inc., pg. 205
CHORE-TIME EQUIPMENT—See CTB Inc., pg. 205
CHORUS LINE, INC.—See Jazz Holding Corporation, pg. 591
LENA CHOW, INC., pg. 248
CHRISTAL RADIO—See Katz Communications, Inc., pg. 618
CHRISTENSON, BARCLAY & SHAW, INC., pg. 248
CHRISTENSON ELECTRIC, INC., pg. 248
CHRISTIAN CHILDREN'S FUND, INC., pg. 248
CHRISTIAN DIOR—See Jones Apparel Group, Inc., pg. 602
CHRISTIAN MEMORIAL CULTURAL CENTER, pg. 249
CHRISTIANITY TODAY, INC., pg. 249
CHRISTIANSBURG GARMENT CO. INC.—See Donnkenny, Inc., pg. 345
CHRISTIANSEN & FRITSCH, INC., pg. 249
CHRISTIE ELECTRIC CORPORATION, pg. 249
CHRISTMAS & THINGS, INC.—See H. C. Prange Company, pg. 884
CHRISTOPHER THOMAS ASSOCIATES INC., pg. 249
CHRISTY HALSEY OIL CO.—See Meenan Oil Co. Limited Partnership, pg. 736
CHRISTY'S MARKETS, INC., pg. 249
CHROMA CORPORATION, pg. 249
CHUO SENKO ADVERTISING CO., LTD.—See N W Ayer Incorporated, pg. 103
CHURCH & CHURCH INC., pg. 249
CHURCHMANS ROAD ASSOCIATES, L.P.—See Artesian Resources Corporation, pg. 87
CHURCH'S FRIED CHICKEN, INC.—See Al Copeland Enterprises, Inc., pg. 284
CICERO/BSB PUBLICIDAD S.A.—See Backer Spielvogel Bates Worldwide, Inc., pg. 111
CIGAR SUPPLY CO.—See Austin Co., Inc., pg. 99
CIMARON GRAIN CO.—See Union Holdings, Inc., pg. 1128
CIMARRON AMERICAN FIDELITY—See American Fidelity Corp., pg. 52
CIMINELLI DEVELOPMENT COMPANY, INC., pg. 249
CIMLINC INC., pg. 249
CINAMERICA THEATRES, L.P., pg. 249
THE CINCINNATI CORDAGE & PAPER COMPANY, pg. 249
CINCINNATI GEAR COMPANY, pg. 250
CINCINNATI INCORPORATED, pg. 250
CINCINNATI LIMOUSINE SERVICE INC.—See Bill Woeste Dealer Group, pg. 1198
CINCINNATI SUB-ZERO PRODUCTS, INC., pg. 250
CINCINNATI UNITED CONTRACTORS, pg. 250
CINCOM SYSTEMS, INC., pg. 250
CINE MAGNETICS, INC., pg. 250
CIOCIOLA & COMPANY ADVERTISING, INC., pg. 250
CIPRIANI KREMER DESIGN—See Arnold Fortuna Lawner & Cabot, pg. 84
CIQYA/BRAVO FOODS DE MEXICO—See Newly Weds Foods Inc., pg. 804
CIRCLE A.W. PRODUCTS, CO., pg. 250
CIRRUS SYSTEM, INC.—See Mastercard International, Inc., pg. 720
CISSELL MANUFACTURING COMPANY—See The Dyson-Kissner-Moran Corporation, pg. 357
CITADEL LAND, INC.—See Washington Homes, Inc., pg. 1166
CITATION COMPANIES, INC., pg. 250
CITIZENS GAS & COKE UTILITY, pg. 250
CITIZENS INSURANCE COMPANY OF AMERICA—See All America Financial, pg. 35
CITIZENS NATIONAL BANCSHARES INC., pg. 250
CITIZENS NATIONAL BANK—See Citizens National Bancshares Inc., pg. 251
CITIZENS REALTY & INSURANCE INC., pg. 251
CITRUS COUNTY CHRONICLE—See Landmark Communications, Inc., pg. 655
CITRUS WORLD INC., pg. 251
CITY BEVERAGE CO., pg. 251
CITY MACHINE TOOL & DIE COMPANY, pg. 251
CITY MEATS & PROVISIONS CO., pg. 251
CITY POSTAL, INC., pg. 251
CITY & STATE—See Crain Communications, Inc., pg. 295
CIVES CORP., pg. 251
CIVIC FOOD CENTER, INC.—See So-Lo-Food, Inc., pg. 1016
CIVIL SERVICE EMPLOYEES INSURANCE CO.—See CSE Corporation, pg. 205
CIVIL SERVICE EMPLOYEES LIFE INSURANCE CO.—See CSE Corporation, pg. 205
CLAIRE MANUFACTURING CO.—See Carlyle Holding Corporation, pg. 222
CLANTON'S AUTO AUCTION—See Cox Enterprises, Inc., pg. 293
CLAREMONT FLOCK CORPORATION, pg. 251
THE CLARINDA COMPANY COLOR DIVISION—See Whitestar Graphics, Inc., pg. 1187
THE CLARINDA COMPANY—See Whitestar Graphics, Inc., pg. 1187
CLARION ENTERPRISES, INC.—See Montgomery Elevator Company, pg. 767
CLARITY COVERDALE RUEFF ADVERTISING, pg. 251
TJ CLARK ADVERTISING/PR, pg. 251
CLARK CONSTRUCTION GROUP, pg. 252
DAVID CLARK COMPANY, INC., pg. 252
CLARK DOOR CO., INC., pg. 252
CLARK ENTERPRISES, INC.—See Clark Construction Group, pg. 252
CLARK FOODSERVICE, INC., pg. 252
CLARK GUM COMPANY, pg. 252
A.D. CLARK, INC., pg. 252
KEITH CLARK—See Cullman Ventures, Inc., pg. 304
CLARK OIL & REFINING CORPORATION, pg. 252
CLARK OIL & REFINING CORPORATION--BLUE ISLAND REFINERY—See Clark Oil & Refining Corporation, pg. 253
CLARK OIL & REFINING CORPORATION--WOOD RIVER REFINERY—See Clark Oil & Refining Corporation, pg. 253
CLARK & POPE, INC., pg. 253
CLARK-SIMON, INC.—See Clark Foodservice, Inc., pg. 252
CYRUS CLARK CO., INC., pg. 253
CLARKE GOWARD FITTS MATTESON, INC., pg. 253
P. J. CLARKE'S—See Lettuce Entertain You Enterprises, Inc., pg. 669
CLARKLIFT OF MINNESOTA, INC., pg. 253
CLARKSON CONSTRUCTION COMPANIES, pg. 253
CLASSIC BATH PRODUCTS—See Triangle Pacific Corporation, pg. 1112
CLASSIC CHEVROLET—See Libertyville Lincoln-Mercury Sales, Inc., pg. 674
CLASSIC MARKETS CORP., pg. 253
CLASSIC RESIDENCE BY HYATT—See H. Group Holding Inc., pg. 495
THE CLASSICS CLUB—See Walter J. Black, Inc., pg. 154
CLASSIFIED INSURANCE COMPANY, INC.—See Millers' Mutual Insurance Assn. Of Illinois, pg. 755
CLAUD S. GORDON COMPANY—See Watlow Electric Manufacturing Company, pg. 1167
CLAY-PARK LABS, INC., pg. 253
CLAYSON KNITTING CO. INC., pg. 253
A.T. CLAYTON & COMPANY, INC., pg. 253
CLAYTON CORPORATION, pg. 253
CLAYTON-DAVIS & ASSOCIATES, INCORPORATED, pg. 253
CLAYTON INDUSTRIES CO., pg. 253
CLAYTON MANUFACTURING DIV., DYNAMIC EQUIPMENT—See Clayton Industries Co., pg. 254
CLAYTON MARK—See Amtrol Inc., pg. 70
CLAYTON METALS CORP.—See Clayton Corporation, pg. 253

CLAYTON PLASTICS CORP.—See Clayton Corporation, pg. 253
CLAYTON, WILLIAMS & SHERWOOD, INC., pg. 254
CLEANERS HANGER CO., pg. 254
CLEAR CREEK, INC.—See National Cooperative Refinery Association, pg. 787
CLEAR SHIELD NATIONAL, INC.—See Envirodyne Industries, Inc., pg. 383
CLEAR SPRINGS FOODS, INC., pg. 254
CLEARING INTERNATIONAL, INC., pg. 254
CLEARPOINT RESEARCH CORPORATION, pg. 254
CLEARWATER PHILLIES—See The Phillies-A Limited Partnership, pg. 867
CLEARY LANE ASSOCIATES, INC.—See Society for Savings Bancorp, Inc., pg. 1016
CLEMCO INDUSTRIES, pg. 254
CLEMENS MARKETS INC., pg. 254
CLEMENTS FOODS CO., pg. 254
CLEMENTS NUT CO.—See Clements Foods Co., pg. 255
CLEMENTS VINEGAR COMPANY—See Clements Foods Co., pg. 255
CLEVELAND BROTHERS EQUIPMENT CO., pg. 255
THE CLEVELAND BUILDERS SUPPLY CO.—See Standard Lafarge, pg. 1036
CLEVELAND CHAIR COMPANY, pg. 255
CLEVELAND CONSOLIDATED INC.—See Cleveland Group, Inc., pg. 255
CLEVELAND ELECTRIC CO.—See Cleveland Group, Inc., pg. 255
CLEVELAND ELECTRIC COMPANY OF ARKANSAS—See Cleveland Group, Inc., pg. 255
CLEVELAND GROUP, INC., pg. 255
CLEVELAND MACHINE CONTROLS, pg. 255
CLEVELAND WRECKING COMPANY, pg. 255
CLEVITE DE MEXICO—See The Pullman Company, pg. 900
CLEVITE SRL—See The Pullman Company, pg. 900
CLEWISTON SUGAR HOUSE—See United States Sugar Corporation, pg. 1137
CLIFFORD METAL—See Lapham-Hickey Steel Corp., pg. 658
CLIGGOT PUBLISHING, pg. 255
THE CLIMATIC CORP., pg. 255
CLIMCO COILS CO.—See Furnas Electric Company, pg. 437
CLIMET INSTRUMENTS CO.—See Venturedyne, Ltd., pg. 1148
CLINCH RIVER CORP.—See Jupiter Industries, Inc., pg. 609
CLINE, DAVIS & MANN, INC., pg. 255
CLINICARE SYSTEMS, INC.—See Gaymar Industries, Inc., pg. 447
THE CLINIPAD CORPORATION, pg. 255
CLINTON MILLS—See CMI Industries, Inc., pg. 202
CLINTON MILLS INC.—See CMI Industries, Inc., pg. 202
CLINTON MILLS SALES CO.—See CMI Industries, Inc., pg. 202
CLIPPER EXXPRESS CO., pg. 256
THE CLOISTER—See Sea Island Company, pg. 983
CLOUD CORPORATION, pg. 256
CLOVER FINANCIAL CORPORATION, pg. 256
CLOVER YARNS, INC.—See Steiner & Company, pg. 1045
CLOVERDALE EQUIPMENT CO., pg. 256
CLOVERHILL BAKERY, pg. 256
CLOVERLANES, INC.—See Great Lakes Recreation Co., pg. 482
CLOW CORPORATION—See McWane, Inc., pg. 733
CLOW VALVE DIV.—See McWane, Inc., pg. 733
CLOW WATER SYSTEMS CORP.—See McWane, Inc., pg. 733
CLOW WATER SYSTEMS CORP.—See McWane, Inc., pg. 733
CLUB CORP REALTY—See Club Corporation International, pg. 256
CLUB CORPORATION INTERNATIONAL, pg. 256
CLUB CORPORATION OF AMERICA—See Club Corporation International, pg. 256
CLUB RESORTS, INC.—See Club Corporation International, pg. 256
CLUBMAN—See Ardell International, Inc., pg. 81
CMI SCHNEIBLE CO.—See CMI International Inc., pg. 202
CO-EX PLASTICS, INC.—See Huntsman Chemical Corporation, pg. 555
THE COAKLEY HEAGERTY COMPANIES, LTD., pg. 256
COAKLEY & WILLIAMS INC., pg. 256
COAST CATAMARAN FRANCE—See MacAndrews & Forbes Holdings Inc., pg. 695
COAST GRAIN COMPANY, INC., pg. 256
COAST MANUFACTURING COMPANY, pg. 257
COAST PACKING COMPANY, pg. 257
COAST TO COAST—See Servistar Corporation, pg. 993
COAST TO COAST STORES, INC., pg. 257
COASTAL DAIRY PRODUCTS, INC., pg. 257
COASTAL LUMBER COMPANY, pg. 257
COASTAL WHOLESALE, INC., pg. 257
COAT, APRON & LINEN SUPPLY, pg. 257
THE COATES AGENCY, pg. 257
COBANK—See Federal Farm Credit Banks Funding Corporation, pg. 405
COBAR MACHINE & TOOL CO.—See Republic Fastener Products Corp., pg. 928
THE COBB GROUP—See Ziff Communications Company, pg. 1218
COBLE DAIRY PRODUCTS CO-OP, pg. 257
COBRA TOOL, INC.—See American Tool Companies, Inc., pg. 64
COCA-COLA BOTTLING CO. OF CHICAGO, pg. 257
COCA-COLA BOTTLING CO. OF THE SOUTHWEST, pg. 257
COCA COLA BOTTLING CO. UNITED, INC., pg. 257
COCA-COLA BOTTLING COMPANY OF ELIZABETHTOWN, pg. 258
COCA-COLA/DR. PEPPER BOTTLING CO. OF SOUTH ARKANSAS—See Ouachita Coca-Cola Bottling Company, pg. 831
GEORGE W. COCHRAN CO., INC., pg. 258
COCHRANE FURNITURE CO., INC., pg. 258
BARTLETT COCKE JR. CONSTRUCTION CO., pg. 258
CODE-A-PHONE CORP., pg. 258
CODE, HENNESSY & SIMMONS, pg. 258
CODI INTERNATIONAL B.V.—See Farley Industries, pg. 400
CODISCO INC., pg. 258
THE COE MFG. CO., pg. 258
COFINCO, INC.—See Norfoods, Inc., pg. 810
COGENTRIX INCORPORATED, pg. 258
COGGIN-O'STEEN INVESTMENT CORP., pg. 259
COGGIN PONTIAC-GMC INC.—See Coggin-O'Steen Investment Corp., pg. 259
LESTER COGGINS TRUCKING, pg. 259
COGIFER INC., pg. 259
COGSDILL TOOL PRODUCTS, INC., pg. 259
COGSDILL-NUNEATON, LTD.—See Cogsdill Tool Products, Inc., pg. 259
COHEN/JOHNSON, INC., pg. 259
M. M. COHN CO., INC.—See The Dunlap Companies, pg. 353
SIGMUND COHN CORP., pg. 259
COILCRAFT, INC., pg. 259
COKEN COMPANY, INC., pg. 259
COLAD GROUP INC., pg. 259
COLD HEADING CO., pg. 259
COLD SPRING GRANITE COMPANY, pg. 259
COLDWATER SEAFOOD CORPORATION, pg. 260
COLDWELL BANKERS/SCHLOTT REALTORS, pg. 260
COLE BUSINESS FURNITURE—See Joyce International, Inc., pg. 608
COLE HENDERSON DRAKE, INC., pg. 260
COLE HERSEE COMPANY, pg. 260
COLE KEY CORPORATION—See Cole National Corporation, pg. 260
COLE-LAYER-TRUMBLE COMPANY (CLT)—See Day & Zimmermann, Inc., pg. 320
COLE NATIONAL CORPORATION, pg. 260
COLE PAPERS INC., pg. 260
COLE TAYLOR BANK—See Cole Taylor Financial Group, pg. 260
COLE TAYLOR FINANCIAL GROUP, pg. 260
COLE TAYLOR/YORKTOWN—See Cole Taylor Financial Group, pg. 260
COLEMAN CABLE SYSTEMS, INC., pg. 260
COLEMAN CADILLAC INC., pg. 261
COLEMAN & CHRISTISON, INC., pg. 261
THE COLEMAN COMPANY—See MacAndrews & Forbes Holdings Inc., pg. 695
THE COLEMAN COMPANY—See MacAndrews & Forbes Holdings Inc., pg. 695
THE COLEMAN COMPANY—See MacAndrews & Forbes Holdings Inc., pg. 695
THE COLEMAN COMPANY, INC.—See MacAndrews & Forbes Holdings Inc., pg. 695
COLEMAN DAIRY INC., pg. 261
COLEMAN (DEUTSCHLAND) GMBH—See MacAndrews & Forbes Holdings Inc., pg. 695
COLEMAN EVCON SUPPLY LIMITED—See MacAndrews & Forbes Holdings Inc., pg. 695
COLEMAN INTERNATIONAL OPERATION—See MacAndrews & Forbes Holdings Inc., pg. 695
COLEMAN JAPAN LTD.—See MacAndrews & Forbes Holdings Inc., pg. 695
COLEMAN OUTDOOR PRODUCTS—See MacAndrews & Forbes Holdings Inc., pg. 695
COLEMAN SPAS, INC.—See MacAndrews & Forbes Holdings Inc., pg. 695
COLEMAN U.K., INC.—See MacAndrews & Forbes Holdings Inc., pg. 695
COLEMAN WATER RECREATION OPERATIONS—See MacAndrews & Forbes Holdings Inc., pg. 695
COLES EXPRESS, pg. 261
COLFAX ENVELOPE CORPORATION, pg. 261
COLFAX, INC., pg. 261
COLIN SERVICE SYSTEMS, INC., pg. 261
COLLE & MCVOY, INC., pg. 261
COLLEGE DIVISION—See American Institute For Foreign Study, pg. 56
COLLEGEVILLE FLAG MFG. COMPANY, pg. 261
COLLEGEVILLE/IMAGINEERING L.P., pg. 262
COLLEGIATE CONCEPTS INC., pg. 262
E.D. COLLIER & SON—See Bateman Brothers Lumber Co., Inc., pg. 125
THE COLLIGAN GROUP—See Ross Roy Group, Inc., pg. 949
COLLIN STREET BAKERY, pg. 262
COLLINS & AIKMAN GROUP INC., pg. 262
COLLINS & AIKMAN INC.—See Collins & Aikman Group Inc., pg. 263
COLLINS & AIKMAN TEXTILE GROUP—See Collins & Aikman Group Inc., pg. 262
COLLINS CHEVROLET, GEO, pg. 263
COLLINS ELECTRIC COMPANY, INC., pg. 263
BILL COLLINS FORD INC., pg. 263
WARREN E. COLLINS, INC., pg. 263
COLLINS OLDSMOBILE INC., pg. 263
COLLMAN GRAPHICS, INC., pg. 263
COLMAN TOYOTA, pg. 263
COLOMBO BAKING CO.—See San Francisco French Bread Company, pg. 969
COLONIAL BEEF CO., pg. 263
COLONIAL DODGE INC., pg. 263
COLONIAL DRILLING & EXPLORATION CORPORATION—See Colonial Oil Industries, pg. 264
COLONIAL HOMES—See The Hearst Corporation, pg. 523
COLONIAL MARINE INDUSTRIES, INC.—See Colonial Oil Industries, pg. 264
COLONIAL METALS CO., pg. 263
COLONIAL MILLWORK, INC.—See Marmac Corporation, pg. 710
COLONIAL OIL INDUSTRIES, pg. 263
COLONIAL PETROLEUM CO., pg. 264
COLONIAL PIPELINE COMPANY, pg. 264
COLONIAL SAND & STONE CO.—See Shepaug Corporation, pg. 998
COLONIAL SUPPLY CORPORATION, pg. 264
COLONIAL TERMINALS, INC.—See Colonial Oil Industries, pg. 264
COLONIAL WILLIAMSBURG FOUNDATION, pg. 264
COLONNA BROS., INC., pg. 264
COLONY COMMUNICATIONS INC.—See Providence Journal Company, pg. 896
COLONY HOTELS & RESORTS, INC.—See Carlson Companies, Inc., pg. 221
COLONY LIQUOR DISTRIBUTORS, INC., pg. 264
COLONY PRESS INC.—See Jupiter Industries, Inc., pg. 609
COLOR ARTS, INC., pg. 264
COLOR COSMETICS—See Plastek Group, pg. 875
COLOR CUSTOM, INC., pg. 264
COLOR DATA EAST—See Schawk, Inc., pg. 975
COLOR GRAPHICS, INC., pg. 264
COLOR YOUR WORLD, INC.—See 21 International Holdings, Inc., pg. 1121
COLORADO AIR RESTAURANT CORP.—See Specialty Restaurants Corporation, pg. 1028
COLORADO AUCTION SERVICES CORPORATION—See Cox Enterprises, Inc., pg. 293
COLORADO BOXED BEEF CO., pg. 265
COLORADO LOTTERY, pg. 265
COLORCON—See Berwind Corporation, pg. 145
COLORCON LTD.—See Berwind Corporation, pg. 145
COLORFORMS, pg. 265
COLORIZER PAINT DIV.—See California Products Corp., pg. 210
COLORTYME, INC., pg. 265
COLSKY MEDIA, INC., pg. 265
COLSON CASTER CORPORATION—See The Marmon Group, Inc., pg. 711
COLSON EQUIPMENT, INC.—See The Marmon Group, Inc., pg. 711
THE COLSON GROUP, INC.—See The Marmon Group, Inc., pg. 711
COLSON TRANSPORTWIELEN B.V.—See The Marmon Group, Inc., pg. 711
COLUMBIA CORPORATION, pg. 265
THE COLUMBIA CORPORATION—See Yorktowne Paper Mills, Inc., pg. 1209
COLUMBIA FALLS ALUMINUM COMPANY, pg. 265
COLUMBIA FARMS INC., pg. 265
COLUMBIA GENERAL LIFE INSURANCE CO.—See UniHealth America, pg. 1127
COLUMBIA IRON & METAL CO.—See Columbia National Group, Inc., pg. 265
COLUMBIA LUMBER & MANUFACTURING CO., pg. 265
COLUMBIA MALL—See R. H. Macy & Co., Inc., pg. 699
THE COLUMBIA MFG. COMPANY, INC., pg. 265
COLUMBIA NATIONAL GROUP, INC., pg. 265
COLUMBIA PAINT CO., pg. 265
COLUMBIA PARCAR CORP.—See Nordic Group of Companies, Ltd., pg. 809
COLUMBIA PIPE & SUPPLY COMPANY, pg. 266
COLUMBIA SERVICES, INC.—See Washington Mutual Savings Bank, pg. 1166
COLUMBIA SUSSEX CORPORATION, pg. 266
COLUMBIAN ADVERTISING INC., pg. 266
COLUMBIAN DIRECT MARKETING—See Columbian Advertising Inc., pg. 266
COLUMBIAN LIFE INSURANCE COMPANY—See Columbian Mutual Life Insurance Co., pg. 266
COLUMBIAN MUTUAL LIFE INSURANCE CO., pg. 266
COLUMBIAN PHILIPPINES INC.—See Columbian Rope Company, pg. 266
COLUMBIAN ROPE COMPANY, pg. 266
COLUMBINE SYSTEMS INC., pg. 266
COLUMBUS LIFE INSURANCE CO.—See Western & Southern Life Insurance Co., pg. 1181
COLUMBUS MCKINNON CORP., pg. 266
COLUMBUS MILLS, INC., pg. 267
COLUMBUS PIPE & EQUIPMENT COMPANY, pg. 267
COLUMBUS SHOW CASE COMPANY, pg. 267
COLUMBUS SHOWCASE, ASHLAND DIVISION—See Columbus Show Case Company, pg. 267
COLUMBUS STEEL DRUM COMPANY, pg. 267
COLUMBUS VERSICHERUNGS VERMITTLUNGS—See Nationwide Mutual Insurance Company, pg. 795
COLUSA ELEVATOR CO., pg. 267
COLUSON TECHNOLOGIES—See Strategic Distribution Inc., pg. 1053
COLWELL INDUSTRIES, INC., pg. 267
COLWOOD CO., INC.—See Columbia Lumber & Manufacturing Co., pg. 265
COM CORP FACTORS, INC.—See Kennington Ltd., Inc., pg. 623
COMARK, pg. 267
COMARK, INC.—See Cenvill Development Corp., pg. 236
COMBE INCORPORATED, pg. 267
COMBS & HEATHCOTT, pg. 267
COMBUSTION POWER COMPANY, pg. 267
COMED COMMUNICATIONS DIVISION—See Ted Thomas Associates Inc., Advertising, pg. 1092
COMED MANAGEMENT INC.—See New York Life Insurance Company, pg. 802
COMFORTO GROUP—See Haworth, Inc., pg. 518
COMLINEAR CORPORATION, pg. 268
COMMAND PLASTIC CORPORATION, pg. 268
COMMAND WEB OFFSET CO.—See MacNaughton Einson Graphics, pg. 698
COMMANDER OIL CORPORATION, pg. 268
COMMERCIAL & ARCHITECTURAL PRODUCTS INC., pg. 268
THE COMMERCIAL BANK, pg. 268

COMMERCIAL DESIGN ARCHITECTS/HEPY, INC.—See Harley Ellington Pierce Yee Associates, Inc., pg. 509
COMMERCIAL ESPANOLA DE COMPONENTES S.A.—See Panduit Company, pg. 845
COMMERCIAL & INDUSTRIAL ADMINISTRATION CO. INC, pg. 268
COMMERCIAL LIGHT COMPANY, pg. 268
COMMERCIAL PARTS, LTD.—See Rocor Transportation Companies Inc., pg. 942
COMMERCIAL PLASTICS & SUPPLIES CORP., pg. 268
COMMERCIAL PRINTERS OF CONNECTICUT, pg. 268
COMMERCIAL PRODUCTS, INC.—See The Dickerson Group, Inc., pg. 336
COMMERCIAL REAL ESTATE—See Landmark Communications, Inc., pg. 655
COMMERCIAL RESOURCE INSURANCE CO.—See Lawrence Group, Inc., pg. 662
COMMERCIAL SERVICE PRINTING—See Warner Press, Inc., pg. 1164
COMMERCIAL TRAVELERS MUTUAL INSURANCE COMPANY, pg. 269
COMMODORE CRUISE LINE, LTD., pg. 269
COMMONS BROS., INC., pg. 269
COMMONS METRO INC.—See Commons Bros., Inc., pg. 269
COMMONWEALTH BUILDING COMPANY—See Landmark Communications, Inc., pg. 656
COMMONWEALTH DIRECT MARKETING—See Landmark Communications, Inc., pg. 656
COMMONWEALTH PRINTING COMPANY—See Landmark Communications, Inc., pg. 656
COMMONWEALTH TOY & NOVELTY COMPANY, pg. 269
COMMTEK COMMUNICATIONS, pg. 269
COMMTRON CORPORATION—See Ingram Industries Inc., pg. 569
COMMUNICATION & DESIGN AGENCY INC., pg. 269
COMMUNICATION TRENDS, INC., pg. 269
COMMUNICATIONS CONCEPTS, pg. 269
COMMUNICATIONS DATA SERVICES, INC.—See The Hearst Corporation, pg. 523
COMMUNICATIONS DIVERSIFIED, pg. 269
COMMUNICATIONS INTERNATIONAL, pg. 269
COMMUNICATIONS INTERNATIONAL, pg. 269
COMMUNICATIONS PLANNING CORPORATION/TMP WORLDWIDE—See TMP Worldwide, Inc., pg. 1074
COMMUNICATIONS PLUS, INC., pg. 269
COMMUNICATIONS & SIGNALING, INC.—See Stauffer Communications, Inc., pg. 1043
COMMUNICO, pg. 270
COMMUNITY BANK OF HOMEWOOD-FLOSSMOOR—See Great Lakes Financial Resources, Inc., pg. 481
COMMUNITY CASH STORES, pg. 270
COMMUNITY TIMES EXTRA—See Landmark Communications, Inc., pg. 656
COMO GRAIN CO.—See Tom Wade Co., pg. 1157
COMPACT SOUND SERVICES—See Andrews Group, Incorporated, pg. 74
COMPACT VIDEO SERVICES, INC.—See Andrews Group, Incorporated, pg. 74
COMPAGNIE FISCHBEIN, S.A.—See AXIA Incorporated, pg. 8
COMPAGNIE INTERNATIONALE DES PRODUITS SANITAIRES (CIPS) JACOB DELAFON—See Kohler Company, pg. 640
COMPANIA GENERAL DE ESENCIAS GRUPO FLORASYNTH S.A.—See Florasynth Inc., pg. 420
COMPANIA MINERA RAURA S.A.—See The Marmon Group, Inc., pg. 712
COMPANION LIFE INSURANCE CO.—See Mutual of Omaha Insurance Company, pg. 779
COMPEL MARKETING, INC., pg. 270
COMPENDIUM SYSTEMS, pg. 270
COMPILERS PLUS—See American Business Information, Inc., pg. 50
COMPLETE INTERIORS INC., pg. 270
COMPLEX INDUSTRY CORPORATION, pg. 270
COMPONENT TECHNOLOGY CORP., pg. 270
B. W. COMPONENTES MEXICANOS DE TRANSMISSIONES, S.A. DE C.V.—See Borg-Warner Corporation, pg. 166
COMPONENTS CORPORATION OF AMERICA, pg. 270
COMPOSITE RESEARCH & MANAGEMENT COMPANY—See Washington Mutual Savings Bank, pg. 1166
COMPREHENSIVE BUSINESS SERVICES INC.—See KOA Holdings, pg. 612
COMPTON'S NEW MEDIA INC.—See Encyclopaedia Britannica, Inc., pg. 381
COMPU NEWS PUBLISHING—See International Data Group, pg. 577
COMPUADD CORPORATION, pg. 271
COMPUTER BUYING PUBLISHING, INC.—See International Data Group, pg. 576
COMPUTER CIRCUITRY GROUP—See Insilco Corporation, pg. 571
COMPUTER CORPORATION OF AMERICA—See Praxis International Inc., pg. 884
COMPUTER DYNAMICS, INC., pg. 271
COMPUTER ENTERPRISES, INC.—See Technical Aid Corporation, pg. 1083
COMPUTER INFORMATION SERVICES, INC.—See Oxford First Corporation, pg. 834
COMPUTER INSTRUMENTS CORPORATION, pg. 271
COMPUTER INTELLIGENCE—See Ziff Communications Company, pg. 1219
COMPUTER LIBRARY—See Ziff Communications Company, pg. 1219
COMPUTER METHODS CORPORATION, pg. 271
THE COMPUTER PATCH OF JOPLIN—See Stauffer Communications, Inc., pg. 1043
COMPUTER PRINTING DIV.—See National Reproductions Corporation, pg. 793
COMPUTER SALES INTERNATIONAL INC., pg. 271
COMPUTER SERVICE COMPANY—See Steiny & Company, Inc., pg. 1049
COMPUTER STOCK FORMS, INC.—See Rotary Forms Press, Inc., pg. 951
COMPUTER SYSTEMS OF LONG ISLAND—See Effective Management Systems, pg. 370
COMPUTER TECHNOLOGIES, INC.—See Effective Management Systems, pg. 370
COMPUTER TECHNOLOGY MANAGEMENT INC.—See A. Epstein and Sons, Intl., Inc., pg. 384
COMPUTERLAND—See ComputerLand Corporation, pg. 271
COMPUTERLAND CANADA LTD.—See ComputerLand Corporation, pg. 271
COMPUTERLAND CORPORATION, pg. 271
COMPUTERWORLD-COLUMBIA—See International Data Group, pg. 577
COMPUTERWORLD DE BRAZIL—See International Data Group, pg. 577
COMPUTROL, INC.—See Armstrong International, Inc., pg. 83
COMPUWARE CORPORATION, pg. 271
COMSTOCK FOODS—See Agway, Inc., pg. 25
COMSTOCK MICHIGAN FRUIT—See Agway, Inc., pg. 25
COMTOOL TECHNOLOGIES—See Intertrade Industries, pg. 581
COMUNICA LEO BURNETT—See Leo Burnett Company, Inc., pg. 192
COMUNICA LEO BURNETT-COSTA RICA—See Leo Burnett Company, Inc., pg. 192
COMUNICA LEO BURNETT PUBLICIDAD—See Leo Burnett Company, Inc., pg. 192
CONAIR CORPORATION, pg. 272
THE CONAIR GROUP, INC., pg. 272
CONAIR PACIFIC EQUIPMENT PTE. LTD.—See Conair Corporation, pg. 272
CONBRACO INDUSTRIES INC., pg. 272
CONCEPTOS INTERNATIONAL—See Tinsley Advertising, pg. 1099
CONCESSION AIR CORPORATION—See Delaware North Companies, Inc., pg. 326
CONCORCO LDA.—See 21 International Holdings, Inc., pg. 1121
CONCORD ASSETS GROUP, INC., pg. 272
CONCORD LITHO CO., INC., pg. 272
CONCORD MINIATURES—See Cardinal Inc., pg. 218
CONCORD WATCH CO.—See North American Watch Corporation, pg. 812
CONCORD WATCH COMPANY, S.A.—See North American Watch Corporation, pg. 812
CONCORDIA CUSTOM YACHTS—See Sauer Industries, Inc., pg. 972
CONCORDIA PUBLISHING HOUSE, pg. 272
CONCORP, INC., pg. 272
CONCRETE ACCESSORIES COMPANY, INC.—See Ritchie Corporation, pg. 936
CONCRETE CONSTRUCTION COMPANY, pg. 273
CONCRETE PIPE & PRODUCTS CO. INC., pg. 273
CONCRETE PIPE & PRODUCTS CO., INC. OF CALIFORNIA—See Concrete Pipe & Products Co. Inc., pg. 273
CONCRETE TECHNOLOGY CORP., pg. 273
THE CONDE NAST PUBLICATIONS INC.—See Advance Publications Inc., pg. 19
CONDE NAST TRAVELER—See Advance Publications Inc., pg. 19
CONDERE CORPORATION, pg. 273
CONDON OIL COMPANY, INC., pg. 273
CONDOR D.C. POWER SUPPLIES INC., pg. 273
CONDOR PACIFIC INDUSTRIES, INC., pg. 273
CONDOR TOOL & DIE, INC.—See Anchor Tool & Die Company, pg. 72
CONDUCTORS UNLIMITED—See Electrical Insulation Suppliers, pg. 374
CONE-BLANCHARD MACHINE COMPANY, pg. 273
CONE, LDA.—See Panduit Company, pg. 845
CONESTOGA HOLDINGS, INC., pg. 273
CONESTOGA WOOD SPECIALTIES, INC., pg. 273
CONGAREE CONSTRUCTION CO., INC., pg. 274
CONGOLEUM CORPORATION, pg. 274
CONILL ADVERTISING, INC., pg. 274
CONKLIN CO. INC., pg. 274
CONKLIN INSTRUMENT CORPORATION, pg. 274
C.C. CONLEY & SONS, INC.—See Green Holdings, Inc., pg. 484
CONLEY FROG & SWITCH COMPANY, pg. 274
CONNECTICUT CONTAINER CORPORATION, pg. 274
CONNECTICUT DRIVE SHAFT, INC., pg. 274
CONNECTICUT MUTUAL FINANCIAL SERVICES—See Connecticut Mutual Life Insurance Company, pg. 275
CONNECTICUT MUTUAL LIFE INSURANCE COMPANY, pg. 274
CONNECTICUT SPRING & STAMPING CORPORATION, pg. 275
CONNECTICUT STATE LOTTERY, pg. 275
CONNELL BROTHERS CO. PHILIPPINES INC.—See Wilbur-Ellis Company & Connell Brothers Company, pg. 1189
CONNELL BROTHERS COMPANY LTD.—See Wilbur-Ellis Company & Connell Brothers Company, pg. 1189
CONNELL BROTHERS (HONG KONG) LTD.—See Wilbur-Ellis Company & Connell Brothers Company, pg. 1189
CONNELL LIMITED PARTNERSHIP, pg. 275
CONNELL RICE & SUGAR CO., pg. 275
CONNELLY CONTAINERS, INC., pg. 275
CONNELLY CONTAINERS, INC. OF PHILADELPHIA—See Connelly Containers, Inc., pg. 275
CONNOR FOREST INDUSTRIES, INC.—See Bridgewater Resources Corporation, pg. 175
CONNORS BRUNSWICK, INC., pg. 275
CONQUEST CARPET MILLS, pg. 276
MICHAEL CONRAD & LEO BURNETT GMBH & CO. KG—See Leo Burnett Company, Inc., pg. 192
CONSENSUS RESEARCH PTY., LTD.—See Backer Spielvogel Bates Worldwide, Inc., pg. 111
CONSO PRODUCTS COMPANY, pg. 276
CONSOLIDATED BEVERAGES, INC., pg. 276
CONSOLIDATED CIGAR CORPORATION, pg. 276
CONSOLIDATED COMMUNICATIONS DIRECTORIES, INC.—See Illinois Consolidated Telephone Co., pg. 563
CONSOLIDATED COMMUNICATIONS MOBILE SERVICES, INC.—See Illinois Consolidated Telephone Co., pg. 563
CONSOLIDATED COMMUNICATIONS OPERATOR SERVICES, INC.—See Illinois Consolidated Telephone Co., pg. 563
CONSOLIDATED COMMUNICATIONS PUBLIC SERVICES, INC.—See Illinois Consolidated Telephone Co., pg. 563
CONSOLIDATED COMPANIES INC. (CONCO), pg. 276
CONSOLIDATED CO-OP, pg. 276
CONSOLIDATED DISTILLED PRODUCTS—See NWS, Inc., pg. 782
CONSOLIDATED ENGRAVERS-EAST, INC.—See The Dyson-Kissner-Moran Corporation, pg. 357
CONSOLIDATED GROUP, INC.—See The Dyson-Kissner-Moran Corporation, pg. 357
CONSOLIDATED INDUSTRIAL CORPORATION, pg. 276
CONSOLIDATED INDUSTRIES, INC., pg. 276
CONSOLIDATED LUMBER CO., pg. 276
CONSOLIDATED METAL PRODUCTS, INC., pg. 276
CONSOLIDATED METCO, INC., pg. 277
CONSOLIDATED MIDWEST, INC., pg. 277
CONSOLIDATED NETWORK, INC.—See Illinois Consolidated Telephone Co., pg. 563
CONSOLIDATED PIPE & SUPPLY COMPANY, pg. 277
CONSOLIDATED PUBLISHING COMPANY, pg. 277
CONSOLIDATED SCREEN-MAKERS, INC.—See The Dyson-Kissner-Moran Corporation, pg. 357
CONSOLIDATED SYSTEMS, INC., pg. 277
CONSOLIDATED TELEMARKETING AMERICA, INC.—See Illinois Consolidated Telephone Co., pg. 563
CONSOLIDATED WHOLESALE COMPANY DIVISION—See GSC Enterprises, Inc., pg. 440
CONSOLIDATED WHOLESALE LUMBER CO.—See Calcasieu Lumber Company, pg. 208
CONSTRUCTION COUNSELLORS, INC., pg. 277
CONSTRUCTION MACHINERY COMPANY, pg. 277
CONSTRUCTION MANAGEMENT SERVICE, pg. 277
CONSTRUCTION SPECIALTIES, INC., pg. 277
CONSTRUCTION SPECIALTIES OF CALIFORNIA—See Construction Specialties, Inc., pg. 277
CONSULTANTS CORP.—See Washington Homes, Inc., pg. 1166
CONSULTEC, INC.—See General American Life Insurance Co., pg. 448
CONSULTING SERVICES, INC.—See Guardian Industries Corp., pg. 492
CONSUMERS MARKETS INC., pg. 277
CONTAINER PORT GROUP—See World Shipping, Inc., pg. 1203
CONTAINER PRODUCTS INC., pg. 278
CONTAINER PRODUCTS INC.—See Container Products Inc., pg. 278
CONTAINER PRODUCTS INC.—See Container Products Inc., pg. 278
CONTAINER PRODUCTS INC.—See Container Products Inc., pg. 278
CONTEC INTERNATIONAL, pg. 278
CONTEMPORARY LONG TERM CARE—See Bill Communications, Inc., pg. 150
CONTICO INTERNATIONAL, INC., pg. 278
CONTINENTAL AMERICAN CORP. D/B/A PIONEER BALLOON COMPANY, pg. 278
CONTINENTAL AMERICAN LIFE INSURANCE CO.—See Provident Mutual Life Insurance Co., pg. 896
CONTINENTAL CABLEVISION, pg. 278
CONTINENTAL CIRCUITS CORP., pg. 278
CONTINENTAL COIN CORPORATION, pg. 278
CONTINENTAL CONAIR, LTD.—See Conair Corporation, pg. 272
CONTINENTAL CONVEYOR & EQUIPMENT COMPANY—See NESCO, Inc., pg. 798
CONTINENTAL DEVELOPMENT COMPANY—See Burrell Group, pg. 195
CONTINENTAL EAGLE CORPORATION, pg. 278
CONTINENTAL ELECTRIC INDUSTRIES, LTD.—See Conair Corporation, pg. 272
CONTINENTAL FORGE COMPANY, pg. 279
CONTINENTAL GENERAL CORPORATION—See Western & Southern Life Insurance Co., pg. 1181
CONTINENTAL GRAIN COMPANY, pg. 279
CONTINENTAL GRAPHICS CORPORATION—See Continental Graphics Holdings, Inc., pg. 279
CONTINENTAL GRAPHICS HOLDINGS, INC., pg. 279
CONTINENTAL MACHINES, INC., pg. 279
CONTINENTAL/MIDLAND, INC., pg. 279
CONTINENTAL MILLS, INC., pg. 279
CONTINENTAL MORTGAGE INVESTORS—See Guardian Industries Corp., pg. 492
CONTINENTAL NATIONAL AMERICAN REAL ESTATE INC., pg. 280
CONTINENTAL OZARK, INC., pg. 280
CONTINENTAL PAPER & SUPPLY CO., pg. 280
CONTINENTAL PLASTIC CARD CO., pg. 280
CONTINENTAL WATER COMPANY, pg. 280
CONTINENTAL WEB PRESS, INC., pg. 280
CONTRACT FREIGHTERS, INC., pg. 280
CONTRACT FURNISHINGS & SYSTEMS, LTD., pg. 280
CONTRACT INTERIORS INC., pg. 280
CONTRACTORS STEEL COMPANY, pg. 280
CONTRACTORS SUPPLIES, INC., pg. 280
CONTRACTORS SUPPLY COMPANY, INC., pg. 281
CONTRAN CORPORATION, pg. 281
CONTROL ENGINEERING CO.—See Jervis B. Webb Company, pg. 1170
CONTROL SYSTEMS INC., pg. 281
CONTROLLED SYSTEMS OF WISCONSIN, INC., pg. 281

CONUS COMMUNICATION COMPANY LIMITED PARTNERSHIP—See Hubbard Broadcasting, Inc., pg. 549
CONVENIENCE PRODUCTS, INC.—See Clayton Corporation, pg. 253
CONVENIENT FOOD MART, INC., pg. 281
CONVERSE PROFESSIONAL GROUP, INC., pg. 281
CONWAY CORPORATION, pg. 281
CONWAY IMPORT CO. INC., pg. 281
CONWOOD COMPANY L.P., pg. 281
B.C. COOK & SONS ENTERPRISES, INC.—See Cook Holding Corporation, pg. 282
COOK CHOCOLATE CANADA LTD.—See World's Finest Chocolate, Inc., pg. 1203
COOK HOLDING CORPORATION, pg. 282
COOK MANUFACTURING CORPORATION, pg. 282
COOK MOVING SYSTEMS, INC., pg. 282
DAVID C. COOK PUBLISHING CO., pg. 282
THE WILLIAM COOK AGENCY, INC., pg. 282
JACK KENT COOKE, INC., pg. 282
COOKE MEDIA GROUP, INC.—See Jack Kent Cooke, Inc., pg. 282
COOKIN' GOOD DISTRIBUTION CTR.—See Showell Farms, Inc., pg. 1000
COOLEY, INC., pg. 282
THE COON-DE VISSER CO., pg. 282
COOPER COMMUNITIES, INC., pg. 283
COOPER INSTRUMENT CORP., pg. 283
COOPER LEDER MARCOMM, pg. 283
COOPER VENTURES, INC.—See Cooper Communities, Inc., pg. 283
THE COOPERATIVE FINANCE ASSN., INC.—See Farmland Industries, Inc., pg. 402
COOPERATIVE SERVICE CO.—See Farmland Industries, Inc., pg. 402
COOPERHEAT, INC., pg. 283
COOPERS & LYBRAND, pg. 283
COORDINATED APPAREL, INC., pg. 283
COPCO—See Wilton Industries, Inc., pg. 1195
AL COPELAND ENTERPRISES, INC., pg. 283
COPELAND LUMBER YARD, INC., pg. 284
JOHN COPES FOOD PRODUCTS, INC., pg. 284
COPETRO, S.A.—See Horsehead Industries, Inc., pg. 545
COPLAND FABRICS, INC., pg. 284
THE COPLEY PRESS, INC., pg. 284
COPLEY REAL ESTATE ADVISORS, INC.—See The New England, pg. 799
COPPER & BRASS SALES, INC., pg. 284
COPPERWELD STEEL COMPANY, pg. 284
THE COPPS CORP., pg. 285
COPPUS ENGINEERING CORP., pg. 285
COPYHOLDER DIVISION—See Fellowes Manufacturing Co., pg. 406
CORA TEXAS MANUFACTURING CO., pg. 285
CORAL PETROLEUM CORPORATION, pg. 285
CORAL PETROLEUM DEVELOPMENT—See Coral Petroleum Corporation, pg. 285
CORAL PETROLEUM INTERNATIONAL, INC.—See Coral Petroleum Corporation, pg. 285
CORBER CORPORATION, pg. 285
CORCORAN MFG. CO., INC., pg. 285
CORCORAN TRUCKING COMPANY, pg. 285
CORDLEY TEMPRITE—See Elkay Manufacturing Company, pg. 377
CORDOVA ENTERPRISE, pg. 285
CORDOVA LABORATORIES—See Cordova Enterprise, pg. 286
CORDOVA LABORATORIES-I.A.F. DIV.—See Cordova Enterprise, pg. 286
CORHAM, INC., pg. 286
CORINTHIAN DIRECT—See Corinthian Media, Inc., pg. 286
CORINTHIAN MEDIA, INC., pg. 286
CORMIER CHEVROLET COMPANY, INC., pg. 286
CORMIER RICE MILLING COMPANY, INC., pg. 286
CORN STATES HYBRID SERVICE, INCORPORATED, pg. 286
CORNELL DUBILIER ELECTRONICS—See Kaplan Electronics, pg. 616
CORNELL FORGE COMPANY, pg. 286
CORNELL IRON WORKS, INC., pg. 286
CORNELL MANUFACTURING COMPANY—See Jupiter Industries, Inc., pg. 609
CORNELL STOREFRONT SYSTEMS, INC.—See Cornell Iron Works, Inc., pg. 286
CORNER BAKERY—See Lettuce Entertain You Enterprises, Inc., pg. 669
CORNER POCKETS OF AMERICA, pg. 286
CORNERSTONE, pg. 286
CORNNUTS INC., pg. 286
CORNUCOPIA, INC., pg. 287
THE CORNWALL & PATTERSON CO.—See Pratt-Read Corporation, pg. 884
CORPORATE, EDP—See Rotterdam Ventures Inc., pg. 951
CORPORATE FINANCE MAGAZINE—See Financial World Partners, pg. 410
CORPORATE HEALTH STRATEGIES, INC.—See Metropolitan Life Insurance Co., pg. 744
CORPORATE•TECHNOLOGY•PUBLIC AFFAIRS—See Ruder, Finn, Inc., pg. 954
CORPORATE TRAVEL SERVICES, pg. 287
CORPOREX COMPANIES, INC., pg. 287
CORPUS CHRISTI CALLER-TIMES—See Harte-Hanks Communications, Inc., pg. 513
CORPUS CHRISTI TRANSFER COMPANY—See Mayflower Transit, Inc., pg. 725
R.J. CORR NATURALS, INC., pg. 287
CORRECT CRAFT, INC., pg. 287
CORRIGAN BROS., INC., pg. 287
CORRIGAN COMPANY MECHANICAL CONTRACTORS—See Corrigan Bros., Inc., pg. 287
CORRUGATED METALS, INC., pg. 287
CORTAL-SELDEX—See Haworth, Inc., pg. 518
CORTEC GROUP, pg. 287
CORTLAND LINE CO., INC., pg. 287
CORUM WATCH CORPORATION—See North American Watch Corporation, pg. 812
COSCO, INC., pg. 287
COSCO INDUSTRIES, pg. 288
COSMETIQUE, INC., pg. 288
COSMOLAB DIV.—See Koh-I-Noor, Inc., pg. 639
COSMOPOLITAN—See The Hearst Corporation, pg. 523
COSMOPULOS CROWLEY DALY/CKG, pg. 288
COSMOS COMMUNICATIONS, INC., pg. 288
COST CARE, INC.—See John Hancock Mutual Life Insurance Company, pg. 596
COSTA CRUISE LINES, N.V., pg. 288
COSTAIN/LIFE SCIENCES INTERNATIONAL—See Day & Zimmermann, Inc., pg. 321
COSTAL WOOD PRODUCTS, INC.—See McConnell Cabinets, Inc., pg. 727
H. COTLER COMPANY, pg. 288
COTO WABASH—See The Dyson-Kissner-Moran Corporation, pg. 357
COTTER ACCEPTANCE CO., INC.—See Cotter & Company, pg. 288
COTTER & COMPANY, pg. 288
COTTER FINANCE CO., INC.—See Cotter & Company, pg. 288
COTTMAN TRANSMISSION SYSTEMS, INC., pg. 288
COTTON ELECTRIC CO-OP, pg. 288
F.X. COUGHLIN CO., pg. 289
COUGLE COMMISSION COMPANY, INC., pg. 289
COULTER CORPORATION, pg. 289
COUNTRY CASUALTY INSURANCE COMPANY—See Country Companies Insurance Group, pg. 289
COUNTRY CLASSIC DAIRIES, INC., pg. 289
COUNTRY COMPANIES INSURANCE GROUP, pg. 289
COUNTRY FRESH, INC., pg. 289
COUNTRY HOME BAKERY, INC., pg. 290
COUNTRY INVESTORS LIFE ASSURANCE COMPANY—See Country Companies Insurance Group, pg. 289
COUNTRY LIVING—See The Hearst Corporation, pg. 523
COUNTRY MUTUAL INSURANCE COMPANY—See Country Companies Insurance Group, pg. 289
COUNTRY MUTUAL NORTHWEST REGIONAL OFFICE—See Country Companies Insurance Group, pg. 289
COUNTRY NOTEBOOK—See The Renovator's Supply, Inc., pg. 927
COUNTRY PREFERRED INSURANCE COMPANY—See Country Companies Insurance Group, pg. 289
COUNTRYMARK CO-OP INC.—See Countrymark Cooperative, Inc., pg. 290
COUNTRYMARK COOPERATIVE, INC., pg. 290
COUNTRYSIDE—See The Hearst Corporation, pg. 523
COUNTY MORTGAGE CORPORATION—See FirstFed Michigan Corporation, pg. 414
COUNTY SEAT STORES, INC., pg. 290
COUNTY TOOL & ABRASIVE—See Buck Knives, Inc., pg. 185
COURI CARPET CO.—See Couristan Inc., pg. 290
COURI-MURAD & CO.—See Couristan Inc., pg. 290
COURISTAN INC., pg. 290
THE COURT COMPANY, pg. 290
COURTESY CHEVROLET & IMPORTS INC., pg. 290
WILLIAM E. COUTTS, CO. LTD.—See Hallmark Cards, Inc., pg. 502
COVALENT SYSTEMS CORPORATION, pg. 290
COVE PETROLEUM—See Anchor Gasoline Corporation, pg. 71
COVE SHOE COMPANY—See H.H. Brown Shoe Company, Inc., pg. 182
COVENTRY HOMES OF COLORADO—See Del Webb's Coventry, pg. 1171
COVENTRY HOTELS ASSOCIATION, pg. 290
COVINGTON FOODS, INC., pg. 290
COVINGTON INDUSTRIES, pg. 290
COWBOY OIL COMPANY, pg. 290
COWDEN METAL SPECIALTIES, INC., pg. 291
COWEN & COMPANY, pg. 291
COWIN & COMPANY, INC., pg. 291
COWLES BUSINESS MEDIA, INC.—See Cowles Media Company, pg. 291
COWLES MAGAZINES, INC.—See Cowles Media Company, pg. 291
COWLES MAGAZINES, INC., pg. 291
COWLES MEDIA COMPANY, pg. 291
COWLES SYNDICATE, INC.—See The Hearst Corporation, pg. 524
COWPER & SIEGFRIED, pg. 291
COWTOWN BOOT COMPANY, pg. 291
COX ADVERTISING, pg. 292
COX ARIZONA PUBLICATIONS, INC.—See Cox Enterprises, Inc., pg. 292
COX CABLE BAKERSFIELD, INC.—See Cox Enterprises, Inc., pg. 294
COX CABLE CEDAR RAPIDS, INC.—See Cox Enterprises, Inc., pg. 294
COX CABLE CLEVELAND AREA, INC.—See Cox Enterprises, Inc., pg. 294
COX CABLE GREATER HARTFORD, INC.—See Cox Enterprises, Inc., pg. 294
COX CABLE GREATER OCALA, INC.—See Cox Enterprises, Inc., pg. 294
COX CABLE HAMPTON ROADS, INC.—See Cox Enterprises, Inc., pg. 294
COX CABLE HUMBOLDT, INC.—See Cox Enterprises, Inc., pg. 294
COX CABLE JEFFERSON PARISH, INC.—See Cox Enterprises, Inc., pg. 294
COX CABLE LUBBOCK, INC.—See Cox Enterprises, Inc., pg. 294
COX CABLE MIDDLE GEORGIA, INC.—See Cox Enterprises, Inc., pg. 294
COX CABLE NEW ORLEANS, INC.—See Cox Enterprises, Inc., pg. 294
COX CABLE OKLAHOMA CITY, INC.—See Cox Enterprises, Inc., pg. 294
COX CABLE OMAHA, INC.—See Cox Enterprises, Inc., pg. 294
COX CABLE PENSACOLA, INC.—See Cox Enterprises, Inc., pg. 294
COX CABLE QUAD CITIES, INC.—See Cox Enterprises, Inc., pg. 294
COX CABLE RHODE ISLAND, INC.—See Cox Enterprises, Inc., pg. 294
COX CABLE ROANOKE, INC.—See Cox Enterprises, Inc., pg. 294
COX CABLE SAGINAW, INC.—See Cox Enterprises, Inc., pg. 294
COX CABLE SAN DIEGO, INC.—See Cox Enterprises, Inc., pg. 294
COX CABLE SANTA BARBARA, INC.—See Cox Enterprises, Inc., pg. 294
COX CABLE SOUTH CAROLINA, INC.—See Cox Enterprises, Inc., pg. 294
COX CABLE SPOKANE, INC.—See Cox Enterprises, Inc., pg. 294
COX CABLE STATEN ISLAND (PARTNERSHIP)—See Cox Enterprises, Inc., pg. 294
COX CABLE UNIVERSITY CITY, INC.—See Cox Enterprises, Inc., pg. 294
COX COMMUNICATIONS, INC.—See Cox Enterprises, Inc., pg. 292
COX & COMPANY, INC., pg. 292
COX ENTERPRISES, INC., pg. 292
COX FURNITURE, pg. 294
COX HOBBIES, INC., pg. 294
COX LANDEY AND PARTNERS, INC., pg. 294
COX LUMBER CO., pg. 294
COX TEXAS PUBLICATIONS, INC.—See Cox Enterprises, Inc., pg. 292
COX WOOD PRESERVING CO., pg. 295
J.B. COXWELL CONTRACT, INC., pg. 295
COYOTE RESTAURANT CORP.—See Specialty Restaurants Corporation, pg. 1028
CRADDOCK DEVELOPMENT CO., INC., pg. 295
CRAFCO, INC.—See Ergon, Inc., pg. 386
CRAFTEX MILLS INC. OF PENNSYLVANIA, pg. 295
CRAFTY BEAVER HOME CENTER, pg. 295
CRAGAR INDUSTRIES—See Mr. Gasket Company, pg. 761
CRAIG SYSTEMS—See Eastern Technologies Ltd, pg. 364
CRAIN COMMUNICATIONS, INC., pg. 295
CRAIN'S CHICAGO BUSINESS—See Crain Communications, Inc., pg. 295
CRAIN'S CLEVELAND BUSINESS—See Crain Communications, Inc., pg. 295
CRAIN'S DETROIT BUSINESS—See Crain Communications, Inc., pg. 295
CRAIN'S NEW YORK BUSINESS—See Crain Communications, Inc., pg. 295
CRAMER COMPANY, pg. 296
CRAMER INC., pg. 296
CRAMER-KRASSELT, pg. 296
CRANE CARRIER COMPANY, pg. 296
CRANE & CO., INC., pg. 296
CRANE CONSTRUCTION CO., pg. 296
CRANE PLASTICS COMPANY, pg. 296
CRANFORD JOHNSON ROBINSON WOODS, pg. 296
CRANKSHAFT MACHINE COMPANY—See Avis Industrial Corporation, pg. 102
CRANSTON MANUFACTURING FACILITY—See Pakula & Company, pg. 843
CRANSTON PRINT WORKS COMPANY, pg. 296
CRANSTON PROPERTIES, INC.—See Society for Savings Bancorp, Inc., pg. 1016
CRAWFORD FITTINGS & CO., pg. 297
THE CRAWFORD GROUP, pg. 297
CRAWFORD INDUSTRIES—See American Trading and Production Corporation, pg. 64
CRAY COMMUNICATIONS INC., pg. 297
CRAYOLA PRODUCTS DIV.—See Hallmark Cards, Inc., pg. 502
CREAM PRODUCTS CO., INC., pg. 297
CREATION WINDOWS OF INDIANA, INC., pg. 297
CREATIVE ALLIANCE, INC., pg. 297
CREATIVE COMMUNICATIONS WERBEGESELLSHAFT, M.B.H.—See Backer Spielvogel Bates Worldwide, Inc., pg. 111
CREATIVE DIRECT MARKETING GROUP, INC., pg. 297
CREATIVE HAIRDRESSERS, pg. 297
CREATIVE MARKETING ALLIANCE INC., pg. 297
CREATIVE MARKETING GROUP, INC.—See The Curtis Publishing Company, pg. 306
CREATIVE MARKETING INTERNATIONAL CORP., pg. 297
CREATIVE MARKETING RESOURCE, INC., pg. 297
CREATIVE PLAYTHINGS LTD., pg. 297
CREATIVE PRODUCTIONS, pg. 297
CREATIVE PUBLICATIONS—See Educational Publishing Corporation, pg. 369
CREATIVE SALON FURNITURE INC., pg. 297
CREATIVE TECHNICAL SERVICES—See The Direct Marketing Group Inc., pg. 339
CREDIT CARD SERVICE CORPORATION—See Financial Protection Services Inc., pg. 410
CREDIT SUISSE FINANCIAL PRODUCTS—See CS First Boston Group, Inc., pg. 204
CREDIT SUISSE FIRST BOSTON AG—See CS First Boston Group, Inc., pg. 204
CREDIT SUISSE FIRST BOSTON BUDAPEST RT—See CS First Boston Group, Inc., pg. 204
CREDIT SUISSE FIRST BOSTON CZECHOSLOVAKIA A.S.—See CS First Boston Group, Inc., pg. 204
CREDIT SUISSE FIRST BOSTON ESPANA S.A.—See CS First Boston Group, Inc., pg. 204
CREDIT SUISSE FIRST BOSTON FRANCE S.A.—See CS First Boston Group, Inc., pg. 204

CREDIT SUISSE FIRST BOSTON ITALIA (COMPAGNIA MOBILIARE) SPA—See CS First Boston Group, Inc., pg. 204
CREDIT SUISSE FIRST BOSTON LTD.—See CS First Boston Group, Inc., pg. 204
CREDIT SUISSE FIRST BOSTON NEDERLAND N.V.—See CS First Boston Group, Inc., pg. 204
CREDIT SUISSE FIRST BOSTON UK LIMITED—See CS First Boston Group, Inc., pg. 204
CREDIT UNION BENEFITS SERVICES, INC.—See Credit Union National Association, pg. 298
CREDIT UNION NATIONAL ASSOCIATION, pg. 298
CREEDMOOR MANUFACTURING DIVISION—See Altec Industries, Inc., pg. 45
CRENLO, INC., pg. 298
CRES-COR/CROWN-X, pg. 298
CRESCENT ELECTRIC SUPPLY CO., pg. 298
CRESCIVE DIE & TOOL, INC., pg. 298
CRESIVE MILAN DIVISION—See Crescive Die & Tool, Inc., pg. 298
CRESMER, WOODWARD, O'MARA & ORMSBEE, pg. 298
CREST CADILLAC COMPANY, pg. 298
CREST CADILLAC, INC.—See Don Massey Cadillac Inc., pg. 719
CREST DISTRIBUTING COMPANY, INC., pg. 298
CREST-MAYFLOWER INTERNATIONAL, INC.—See Mayflower Transit, Inc., pg. 725
CRESTED BUTTE MOUNTAIN RESORT, INC., pg. 299
CRESTLINER, INC.—See Minstar, Inc., pg. 758
CRESWELL, MUNSELL, FULTZ & ZIRBEL—See Young & Rubicam Inc., pg. 1211
CRESWELL, MUNSELL, FULTZ & ZIRBEL—See Young & Rubicam Inc., pg. 1211
CRESWELL, MUNSELL, FULTZ & ZIRBEL—See Young & Rubicam Inc., pg. 1211
CRESWELL, MUNSELL, FULTZ & ZIRBEL—See Young & Rubicam Inc., pg. 1211
CRETE CARRIER CORP., pg. 299
THE CRETEX COMPANIES, pg. 299
CRICKET MAGAZINE—See Carus Corporation, pg. 227
CRISA CORPORATION, pg. 299
THE CRISPIN COMPANY, pg. 299
CRISPIN & PORTER ADVERTISING INC., pg. 299
THE CRITERION GROUP, INC., pg. 299
THE CROCKER-FELS COMPANY, pg. 299
H. S. CROCKER CO., INC., pg. 299
CROFT METAL INC., pg. 300
CROFT METALS, INC. OF NC—See Croft Metal Inc., pg. 300
HEATHER CROLIE, INC., pg. 300
CROLL-REYNOLDS COMPANY, pg. 300
CRONIN & COMPANY, INC., pg. 300
CROOKS SUPERMARKET INC., pg. 300
BING CROSBY PRODUCTIONS, INC.—See Cox Enterprises, Inc., pg. 292
CROSBY & OVERTON, INC., pg. 300
CROSBY & OVERTON TRANSPORTATION CO.—See Crosby & Overton, Inc., pg. 300
CROSCILL, INC., pg. 300
CROSMAN CORPORATION—See MacAndrews & Forbes Holdings Inc., pg. 695
CROSS & BROWN COMPANY—See Metropolitan Life Insurance Co., pg. 744
W.W. CROSS, INC.—See D. D. Bean & Sons Co., pg. 129
CROSS MOTORS CORP., pg. 300
THE CROSSET COMPANY INC., pg. 300
CROSSMAN CORP., pg. 300
CROTON WATCH COMPANY, pg. 300
CROUCH SUPPLY COMPANY, INC., pg. 301
CROWDER CONSTRUCTION CO., pg. 301
CROWE ROPE COMPANY, pg. 301
CROWELL, WEEDON & CO., pg. 301
CROWLEY MARITIME CORPORATION, pg. 301
CROWLEY WEBB & ASSOCIATES, pg. 301
CROWN AMERICAN CORPORATION, pg. 301
CROWN BUICK, INC., pg. 302
CROWN CABLE INC.—See Hallmark Cards, Inc., pg. 502
CROWN CENTER REDEVELOPMENT CORP.—See Hallmark Cards, Inc., pg. 502
CROWN COAL & COKE CO. INC., pg. 302
CROWN COAT, INC.—See Jupiter Industries, Inc., pg. 609
CROWN CRUISE LINE—See Commodore Cruise Line, Ltd., pg. 269
CROWN DRUG—See Eon Labs, Inc., pg. 384
CROWN FENCE CO., pg. 302
CROWN FOODS INC., pg. 302
CROWN GROCERS, INC.—See Certified Grocers Of California, pg. 237
CROWN HOLDINGS, INC., pg. 302
CROWN INTERNATIONAL, INC., pg. 302
CROWN IRON WORKS COMPANY—See Crown Holdings, Inc., pg. 302
CROWN LANCE, INC.—See Bolliger, Inc., pg. 163
CROWN LANCE ITALIA SRL—See Bolliger, Inc., pg. 163
CROWN LEISURE PRODUCTS—See CC Industries, Inc., pg. 200
CROWN MEDIA INC.—See Hallmark Cards, Inc., pg. 502
CROWN PRINCE DIVISIONAL OFFICE—See Crown Prince, Inc. (CA), pg. 302
CROWN PRINCE, INC. (CA), pg. 302
CROWN PUBLISHERS, INC.—See Advance Publications Inc., pg. 20
CROWN STORE EQUIPMENT—See Jupiter Industries, Inc., pg. 609
CROWN TEXTILE COMPANY, pg. 302
CRUCIBLE MATERIALS CORP., pg. 302
CRUM ELECTRIC SUPPLY CO., INC., pg. 303
CRUSTBUSTER, INC., pg. 303
CRUSTEEL LTD.—See Crucible Materials Corp., pg. 303
CRYSTAL CABINET WORKS, INC., pg. 303
CRYSTAL CLEAR INDUSTRIES COMPANY, pg. 303
CRYSTAL CREAM & BUTTER COMPANY, pg. 303
CRYSTAL FLASH PETROLEUM CORP., pg. 303
CRYSTAL GEYSER, pg. 303
CRYSTAL REFINING—See Lakeside Refining Co. Inc., pg. 651
THE CRYSTAL TISSUE CO., pg. 303
CUBIX CORPORATION, pg. 303
CUE INDUSTRIES, INC.—See Guardian Industries Corp., pg. 492
CUIBS PTY. LTD.—See CUNA Mutual Insurance Society, pg. 206
CUISINARTS INC.—See Conair Corporation, pg. 272
CUIZINA ITALIA, INC.—See National Frozen Foods Corp., pg. 789
CULCO, INC.—See Randall's Food Markets, Inc., pg. 912
VINCE CULLERS ADVERTISING INC., pg. 304
CULLIGAN INTERNATIONAL COMPANY—See E-II Holdings, Inc., pg. 358
CULLMAN PRODUCTS CORPORATION, pg. 304
CULLMAN VENTURES, INC., pg. 304
CULLUM DEVELOPMENT CO.—See Randall's Food Markets, Inc., pg. 912
CULLUM DISTRIBUTION CENTER, INC.—See Randall's Food Markets, Inc., pg. 912
CULVER & ASSOCIATES, INC., pg. 304
CULVER TEXTILE CORPORATION, pg. 304
CUMBERLAND FARMS, INC., pg. 304
CUMBERLAND FREIGHT LINE, INC.—See Cumberland-Swan, Inc., pg. 304
CUMBERLAND PACKING CORP., pg. 304
CUMBERLAND-SWAN, INC., pg. 304
CUMIS GENERAL INSURANCE CO.—See CUNA Mutual Insurance Society, pg. 206
CUMIS GROUP INSURANCE—See CUNA Mutual Insurance Society, pg. 206
THE CUMIS GROUP LTD.—See CUNA Mutual Insurance Society, pg. 206
CUMIS LIFE INSURANCE CO.—See CUNA Mutual Insurance Society, pg. 206
CUMMINGS INC., pg. 304
CUMMINS-ALLISON CORP.—See Cummins-American Corp., pg. 305
CUMMINS-AMERICAN CORP., pg. 304
CUMMINS CUMBERLAND INC., pg. 305
CUMMINS INTERMOUNTAIN DIESEL, pg. 305
CUMMINS MID-SOUTH, INC., pg. 305
CUMMINS SOUTHWEST INC., pg. 305
CUNA CARIBBEAN INSURANCE SOCIETY LTD.—See CUNA Mutual Insurance Society, pg. 206
CUNA FOUNDATION—See Credit Union National Association, pg. 298
CUNA MORTGAGE CORPORATION—See Credit Union National Association, pg. 298
CUNA MUTUAL INSURANCE CO.—See CUNA Mutual Insurance Society, pg. 206
CUNA MUTUAL INSURANCE SOC.—See CUNA Mutual Insurance Society, pg. 206
CUNA SERVICE GROUP, INC.—See Credit Union National Association, pg. 298
CUNNINGHAM ENGINEERS, INC.—See Cunningham-Limp Development Co., pg. 305
CUNNINGHAM-LIMP DEVELOPMENT CO., pg. 305
CUPERTINO ELECTRIC, INC.—See Synergism, Inc., pg. 1070
CUPLEX, INC., pg. 305
CURON—See 21 International Holdings, Inc., pg. 1121
CURRAN CONTRACTING CO., pg. 305
CURRIES COMPANY—See ESSTAR Incorporated, pg. 361
THE CURRY CORPORATION, pg. 305
CURTICE-BURNS FOODS, INC.—See Agway, Inc., pg. 25
CURTICE BURNS MEAT SNACKS, INC.—See Agway, Inc., pg. 26
CURTIS EQUIPMENT CO., INC.—See Hale-Halsell Company, pg. 500
CURTIS INSTRUMENTS, INC., pg. 305
CURTIS INTL. LTD.—See The Curtis Publishing Company, pg. 306
CURTIS LUMBER COMPANY, pg. 305
CURTIS MANUFACTURING COMPANY, INC.—See Insilco Corporation, pg. 571
CURTIS MEDIA GROUP INC., pg. 305
THE CURTIS PUBLISHING COMPANY, pg. 306
CURTIS SCREW CO., INC., pg. 306
L.N. CURTIS & SONS, pg. 306
CURTIS SWANN—See Burgoyne, Inc., pg. 190
CURTIS-TOLEDO, INC., pg. 306
CURTMAN DIVISION—See Uncas Manufacturing Company, pg. 1125
CURVCRAFT, pg. 306
CUSTOM AD-PLANNER—See Multi-Ad Services, Inc., pg. 775
CUSTOM CASTING—See Esco Corporation, pg. 388
CUSTOM CONTROL SENSORS, INC., pg. 306
CUSTOM DECOR, INC., pg. 306
CUSTOM DISTRIBUTORS, INC.—See Aqua Fab Industries, Inc., pg. 79
CUSTOM EVENT MARKETING, INC.—See Backer Spielvogel Bates Worldwide, Inc., pg. 109
CUSTOM FOOD PRODUCTS INC.—See Griffith Laboratories Worldwide, Inc., pg. 487
CUSTOM PAK, INC., pg. 306
CUSTOM PRODUCT DIV.—See Chief Industries, Inc., pg. 247
CUSTOM PRODUCTS DIVISION—See Chief Industries, Inc., pg. 247
CUSTOM SHOP SHIRTMAKERS INC., pg. 306
H.H. CUTLER COMPANY, pg. 306
CUTLER MANUFACTURING CORPORATION, pg. 307
CUTLERY WORLD—See Hoffritz for Cutlery, pg. 538
CUTTER FLYING SERVICE, INC., pg. 307
CYBER SYSTEMS, INC., pg. 307
CYBEREX, INC., pg. 307
CYBORG SYSTEMS OF CANADA—See Cyborg Systems, Inc., pg. 307
CYBORG SYSTEMS, INC., pg. 307
CYBORG SYSTEMS (UK) LTD.—See Cyborg Systems, Inc., pg. 307
CYCLO-GARD—See Sycon Corporation, pg. 1069
CYNTHIANA DEMOCRAT—See Landmark Communications, Inc., pg. 655

D

D & D NEWSPAPER CIRCULATORS, INC.—See The Charles Levy Company, pg. 672
D&H DISTRIBUTING COMPANY, pg. 307
D & K OPTICAL, INC., pg. 307
D&L VENTURE CORP., pg. 307
D & R ADVERTISING, pg. 307
D & W FOOD CENTERS, INC., pg. 308
DAQ ELECTRONICS INC., pg. 308
D/B CAMERAS MICROCHECK DIVISION—See AEI Holding Co., Inc., pg. 3
DBM HATCH, INC., pg. 308
D.C. LOTTERY & CHARITABLE GAMES CONTROL BOARD, pg. 308
D.C.I., INC., pg. 308
DCI MARKETING, pg. 308
D & D BEAN COMPANY—See Trinidad/Benham Corporation, pg. 1114
D & D WHOLESALE LIQUORS—See Haas Brothers, pg. 498
DDC PERTEC, pg. 308
DDF&M INC. DUDRECK DEPAUL FICCO & MORGAN INC., pg. 308
DDF&M DIRECT—See DDF&M Inc. Dudreck DePaul Ficco & Morgan Inc., pg. 308
DDM/TMP WORLDWIDE—See TMP Worldwide, Inc., pg. 1074
DEC AG—See DEC International, Inc., pg. 309
DEC ALKAR DIV.—See DEC International, Inc., pg. 309
DEC/BOU-MATIC—See DEC International, Inc., pg. 309
DEC INTERNATIONAL, INC., pg. 308
D.F.A. ADVERTISING, pg. 309
DG TRIM PRODUCTS DIV.—See Indian Head Industries Inc., pg. 565
DGWB, INC., pg. 309
DH MEDICAL SUPPLY INC.—See Taylor Medical Inc., pg. 1081
D & H PIPING—See Dombrowski & Holmes, Inc., pg. 343
D & H TOOL AND DIE—See United States Ceramic Tile Co., pg. 1135
DHL AIRWAYS, INC.—See DHL Corporation, pg. 309
DHL CORPORATION, pg. 309
DHL HANDLING MEXICANA, S.A. DE C.V.—See DHL Corporation, pg. 309
DHL INTERNATIONAL AB—See DHL Corporation, pg. 309
DHL INTERNATIONAL BV—See DHL Corporation, pg. 309
DHL INTERNATIONAL COURIER SERVICE GMBH—See DHL Corporation, pg. 309
DHL INTERNATIONAL EXPRESS LTD.—See DHL Corporation, pg. 309
DHL INTERNATIONAL (HONG KONG) LTD.—See DHL Corporation, pg. 309
DHL INTERNATIONAL N.V.—See DHL Corporation, pg. 309
DHL INTERNATIONAL S.A.—See DHL Corporation, pg. 309
DHL INTERNATIONAL (U.K.) LTD.—See DHL Corporation, pg. 309
DKM BUILDING ENTERPRISES, L.P.—See The Dyson-Kissner-Moran Corporation, pg. 357
DKM, LTD.—See The Dyson-Kissner-Moran Corporation, pg. 357
DKM PROPERTIES CORPORATION—See The Dyson-Kissner-Moran Corporation, pg. 357
DKM RESOURCES, INC.—See The Dyson-Kissner-Moran Corporation, pg. 357
DLS DIV.—See Takatta Inc., pg. 1077
D. M. MANAGEMENT COMPANY, pg. 309
D.M.A. ASSOCIATES—See Synergism, Inc., pg. 1070
DMI THE HEALTHCARE AGENCY, pg. 309
DMI, INC., pg. 309
DNN GALVANIZING CORPORATION—See National Steel Corporation, pg. 794
DRI INDUSTRIES—See Leichtung, Inc., pg. 666
DRK INC., pg. 309
D & S MARKETING—See Bel-Art Products, pg. 133
DSI/TMP WORLDWIDE—See TMP Worldwide, Inc., pg. 1074
DSI/TMP WORLDWIDE—See TMP Worldwide, Inc., pg. 1074
DSIC/TMP WORLDWIDE—See TMP Worldwide, Inc., pg. 1074
DSU LEASING, INC.—See D.S.U.-Peterbilt & GMC, Inc., pg. 310
D.S.U.-PETERBILT & GMC, INC., pg. 309
DVC INDUSTRIES, pg. 310
D.V.F. INC.—See MacAndrews & Forbes Holdings Inc., pg. 695
DWC COMPUTER SOLUTIONS INC.—See Mason Company, pg. 718
D&Z, INC.—See Day & Zimmermann, Inc., pg. 320
DACOR CORPORATION, pg. 310
DADDY DID IT—See New Texas Tumbleweed, pg. 802
DAD'S COOKIES—See Mrs. Alison's Cookie Company, pg. 760
DAD'S PRODUCTS CO., INC., pg. 310
D'AGOSTINO SUPERMARKETS INC., pg. 310
DAHLEM COMPANY, INC., pg. 310
DAHLIN SMITH WHITE, INC., pg. 310
DAHLSTEN TRUCK LINE, INC., pg. 310
DAHLSTROM OF CANADA LTD.—See The Aarque Companies, pg. 9
DAHLSTROM MANUFACTURING B.V.—See Dahlstrom Manufacturing Company, Inc., pg. 310
DAHLSTROM MANUFACTURING CO., INC.-SAFEWAY DIVISION—See Dahlstrom Manufacturing Company, Inc., pg. 310

DAHLSTROM MANUFACTURING COMPANY, INC., pg. 310
DAHMS ELECTRONIK GMBH—See Panduit Company, pg. 845
DAIDONE ELECTRICAL INC., pg. 310
DAIGLE OIL CO., pg. 310
THE DAILY BREEZE—See The Copley Press, Inc., pg. 284
DAILY COURIER-NEWS—See The Copley Press, Inc., pg. 284
THE DAILY JOURNAL (IL)—See The Copley Press, Inc., pg. 284
DAILY RACING FORM, INC.—See K-III Communications Corporation, pg. 611
DAILY RACING FORM, INC. (MIDWEST)—See K-III Communications Corporation, pg. 611
DAILY RACING FORM, INC. (NORTHWEST)—See K-III Communications Corporation, pg. 611
DAILY RACING FORM, INC. PACIFIC—See K-III Communications Corporation, pg. 611
DAILY RACING FORM, INC. (TORONTO)—See K-III Communications Corporation, pg. 611
THE DAILY & SUNDAY OKLAHOMAN—See Gaylord Entertainment Co., pg. 446
DAIRY EXPORT CO., INC.—See Darigold, Inc., pg. 315
DAIRY EXPRESS, INC.—See Lynden Incorporated, pg. 689
DAIRY FRESH CORP., pg. 310
DAIRY FRESH ICE CREAM—See Dairy Fresh Corp., pg. 311
DAIRY TECHNOLOGY LTD.—See Wisconsin Dairies Cooperative, pg. 1198
DAIRYGOLD INC., pg. 311
DAIRYGOLD, INC.—See Dairygold Inc., pg. 311
DAIRYLAND INSURANCE CO.—See Sentry Insurance, A Mutual Company, pg. 990
DAIRYLAND POWER COOPERATIVE, pg. 311
DAIRYLEA COOPERATIVE INC., pg. 311
DAIRYMEN, INC., pg. 311
DAISY DE VENEZUELA C.A.—See Farley Industries, pg. 400
DAKCO DISTRIBUTORS, INC., pg. 311
DAKIN, INC., pg. 311
DAKOTA BAKE-N-SERV—See Rhodes International, Inc., pg. 931
DAKOTA DRUG, INC.—See Dakco Distributors, Inc., pg. 311
DAKOTA ELECTRIC ASSOCIATION, pg. 312
DAKOTA PORK INDUSTRIES—See American Foods Group, pg. 54
DAKOTAH, INC., pg. 312
DAKTRONICS, INC., pg. 312
DAL-TILE CORP., pg. 312
DALE FOODS—See Vincent Food Industries, Inc., pg. 1152
DALE INDUSTRIES INC., pg. 312
DALFORT CORP., pg. 312
DALLAS FLOWER MARKET, INC.—See Denver Wholesale Florists Company, pg. 331
DALLAS & MAVIS FORWARDING CO., INC. (D & M)—See Jupiter Industries, Inc., pg. 609
DALLAS PETERBILT, INC., pg. 312
DALLAS TERMINAL RAILWAY AND UNION DEPOT CO.—See Anschutz Corporation, pg. 76
DALLY ADVERTISING, INC., pg. 312
WAYNE DALTON CORPORATION, pg. 312
LEO A. DALY COMPANY, pg. 313
M.J. DALY & SONS, INC., pg. 313
DAMART/TMP WORLDWIDE—See TMP Worldwide, Inc., pg. 1074
DAN DEE PRETZEL & POTATO CHIP CO., pg. 313
DAN RIVER APPAREL FABRICS MARKETING DIV.—See Dan River Inc., pg. 313
DAN RIVER COTTON CO., INC.—See Dan River Inc., pg. 313
DAN RIVER DANVILLE MFG. DIV.—See Dan River Inc., pg. 313
DAN RIVER INC., pg. 313
DAN RIVER INC.-HOME FURNISHINGS & RELATED PRODS., DIV. I—See Dan River Inc., pg. 313
DANA COMMUNICATIONS, INC., pg. 313
DANA PERFUMES CORP., pg. 313
DANAFILMS, INC., pg. 313
DANBURY PHARMACAL INC.—See Henry Schein, Inc., pg. 975
DANBURY PRINTING & LITHOGRAPH, INC., pg. 313
DANCKER, SELLEW & DOUGLAS, INC., pg. 314
JOHN W. DANFORTH CO., pg. 314
DANFOSS DUKES FLUID POWER INC., pg. 314
THE DANIEL CO. OF SPRINGFIELD, pg. 314
C.R. DANIELS, INC., pg. 314
DANIEL'S JEWELRY CO. OF ARIZONA, INC.—See Zale Corporation, pg. 1215
DANIELS MANUFACTURING CORPORATION, pg. 314
DANIELS PRINTING COMPANY, pg. 314
DANIS BUILDING CONSTRUCTION GROUP—See Danis Industries Corporation, pg. 314
DANIS HEAVY CONSTRUCTION GROUP—See Danis Industries Corporation, pg. 314
DANIS HIGHWAY CONSTRUCTION GROUP—See Danis Industries Corporation, pg. 314
DANIS INDUSTRIES CORPORATION, pg. 314
DANLY DIE SET DIVISION—See Connell Limited Partnership, pg. 275
DANN DEE DISPLAY FIXTURES, pg. 314
DAN'S SUPREME SUPER MARKETS INC., pg. 314
DANUSER MACHINE CO., pg. 315
DANVILLE MARKETING—See Dan River Inc., pg. 313
DANZIG/ROSENBERG—See Austin Sculpture, pg. 100
DARBY & ASSOCIATES—See Backer Spielvogel Bates Worldwide, Inc., pg. 111
DARDA INC. (USA), pg. 315
DARIEN & KILBURG, INC., pg. 315
DARIGOLD, INC., pg. 315
DARIN & ARMSTRONG, INC.—See Walbridge Aldinger Company, pg. 1159
DARLENE JEWELRY MANUFACTURING COMPANY, pg. 315
L. A. DARLING COMPANY—See The Marmon Group, Inc., pg. 711
DARLING-DELAWARE CO., INC., pg. 315
DARLING ENVELOPE CORPORATION, pg. 315
DARLING'S, pg. 315
DARLINGTON VENEER COMPANY, pg. 315
DART CONTAINER CORP., pg. 316
DART TRANSIT COMPANY, INC., pg. 316
THE DARTNELL CORPORATION, pg. 316
DARWIN DATA SYSTEMS—See Effective Management Systems, pg. 370
DASCIT/WHITE & WINSTON, INC.—See Integrated Resources, Inc., pg. 573
DATA AIRE, INC.—See Construction Specialties, Inc., pg. 277
DATA DOCUMENTS HOLDINGS, INC., pg. 316
DATA DOCUMENTS, INC.—See Data Documents Holdings, Inc., pg. 316
DATA INSTRUMENTS, INC., pg. 316
DATA PREFERENCE, INC.—See The Marmon Group, Inc., pg. 712
DATA SOURCES—See Ziff Communications Company, pg. 1218
DATA STORAGE CENTER—See The Suddath Companies, pg. 1056
DATA TRANSPORTATION COMPANY—See The Bekins Company, pg. 133
DATABASE AMERICA COMPANIES, pg. 316
DATABILITY, INC., pg. 316
DATACOMM—See Bill Communications, Inc., pg. 150
DATAMEDIA CORPORATION, pg. 316
DATASPHERE, INC.—See Construction Specialties, Inc., pg. 277
DATRON INCORPORATED, pg. 316
DATRON SYSTEMS, INC.—See Datron Incorporated, pg. 317
DAUBERT CHEMICAL COMPANY, INC.—See Daubert Industries, Inc., pg. 317
DAUBERT COATED PRODUCTS, INC.—See Daubert Industries, Inc., pg. 317
DAUBERT INDUSTRIES, INC., pg. 317
DAUMAN DISPLAYS, INC.—See Continental Graphics Holdings, Inc., pg. 279
DAV-EL SERVICES, INC., pg. 317
DAV-EL WASHINGTON D.C., INC.—See Dav-El Services, Inc., pg. 317
DAV-EL WEST—See Dav-El Services, Inc., pg. 317
J.T. DAVENPORT & SONS, INC., pg. 317
THE DAVEY TREE EXPERT COMPANY, pg. 317
DAVEY TREE SURGERY CO.—See The Davey Tree Expert Company, pg. 317
D.A. DAVIDSON & CO., pg. 318
DAVIDSON MARKETING, INC., pg. 318
DAVIDSON PRINTING COMPANY—See Advanstar Communications, pg. 21
DAVIS ADVERTISING INC., pg. 318
DAVIS, BALL & COLOMBATTO ADVERTISING, INC., pg. 318
BUD DAVIS CADILLAC, INC., pg. 318
DAVIS COMPANIES, pg. 318
DAVIS ELECTRICAL CONSTRUCTORS, INC., pg. 318
JIMMY DAVIS ENTERPRISES, INC., pg. 318
JOSEPH DAVIS, INC., pg. 318
DAVIS INDUSTRIES INC., pg. 318
DAVIS MECHANICAL CONTRACTORS, INC., pg. 318
DAVIS MINING & MANUFACTURING, pg. 319
DAVIS MOLDING CO.—See Heico Inc., pg. 525
DAVIS-MOORE OLDSMOBILE, INC., pg. 319
DAVIS-MOORE RECREATIONAL VEHICLE CENTER—See Davis-Moore Oldsmobile, Inc., pg. 319
DAVIS-NEWMAN-PAYNE, pg. 319
DAVIS PAINT COMPANY, pg. 319
DAVIS & PHILLIPS, INC., pg. 319
DAVIS TOOL & ENGINEERING CO.—See Davis Industries Inc., pg. 318
DAVIS WALKER CORP.—See Heico Inc., pg. 525
DAVIS WIRE CORPORATION, pg. 319
DAVLIN PAINT COMPANY, INC., pg. 319
DAW TECHNOLOGIES, INC., pg. 319
DAWAHARES, INC., pg. 319
DAWN FOOD PRODUCTS, INC., pg. 319
DAWN JOY FASHIONS, INC., pg. 319
DAXUS CORPORATION, pg. 319
DAY DATA SYSTEMS—See Day & Zimmermann, Inc., pg. 320
DAY ENGINEERING—See Day & Zimmermann, Inc., pg. 320
DAY INDUSTRIES—See The Rawlplug Company, Inc., pg. 914
DAY MAINTENANCE—See Day & Zimmermann, Inc., pg. 320
DAY PRODUCTS—See Day & Zimmermann, Inc., pg. 320
DAY & ZIMMERMANN, INC., pg. 320
DAY & ZIMMERMANN, INC.—See Day & Zimmermann, Inc., pg. 321
DAYCON PRODUCTS COMPANY, INC., pg. 321
DAYLUX, INC.—See Sillcocks Plastics International, Inc., pg. 1004
DAYS INNS OF AMERICA, INC.—See Tollman/Hundley Hotels, pg. 1100
DAYS INNS OF AMERICA, INC.—See Tollman/Hundley Hotels, pg. 1100
DAYTON NEWSPAPERS, INC.—See Cox Enterprises, Inc., pg. 292
DAYTON ROGERS MFG. CO., pg. 321
DAYTON ROGERS OF OHIO—See Dayton Rogers Mfg. Co., pg. 321
DAYTON ROGERS OF TEXAS—See Dayton Rogers Mfg. Co., pg. 321
DAZEY CORPORATION, pg. 321
DE ART S.R.L.—See Dentsply International Inc., pg. 330
DE FRANCISCI MACHINE CORP.(DEMACO), pg. 321
PAUL A. DE JESSE, INC. ADVERTISING, pg. 321
DE NOVO CORPORATION, pg. 321
DE VONS JEWELERS, pg. 321
DEACON DAY ADVERTISING AND THE MCLAUCHLAN GROUP—See The Lowe Group, pg. 685
DEAD RIVER COMPANY, pg. 321
DEAD RIVER FOREST PRODUCTS—See Dead River Company, pg. 322
DEAD RIVER PETROLEUM CO.—See Dead River Company, pg. 322
DEAD RIVER PROPERTIES—See Dead River Company, pg. 322
DEALERS AUTO AUCTION OF DALLAS, INC.—See Cox Enterprises, Inc., pg. 293
DEALERS ELECTRICAL SUPPLY CO., pg. 322
DEALERS MANUFACTURING COMPANY, pg. 322
DEALERS TRANSPORT COMPANY, INC., pg. 322
DEAN OPERATIONS INC., pg. 322
DEANS PHOTO SERVICE, INC., pg. 322
DEARBORN GAGE COMPANY, pg. 322
THE DEARBORN GROUP, pg. 322
DEARDEN'S, INC., pg. 322
DEARDORFF-JACKSON COMPANY, pg. 323
DEARE MARKETING INC./MATTHEW-LAWRENCE ADVERTISING & SALES PROMOTION INC., pg. 323
DEB HOLDINGS, INC., pg. 323
THE EDWARD J. DEBARTOLO CORPORATION, pg. 323
ED DEBEVIC'S OF ARIZONA—See Lettuce Entertain You Enterprises, Inc., pg. 669
ED DEBEVIC'S/SHORT ORDERS DELUXE/ PHOENIX—See Lettuce Entertain You Enterprises, Inc., pg. 669
ED DEBEVIC'S/SHORT ORDERS DELUXE/ TORRANCE—See Lettuce Entertain You Enterprises, Inc., pg. 669
DEBRUCE GRAIN INC., pg. 323
DECAL ENTERPRISES, INC., pg. 323
DECATUR NEWS PUBLISHING COMPANY, INC., pg. 323
DECHERT PRICE & RHOADS, pg. 323
DECISION DATA—See Decision Data Inc., pg. 324
DECISION DATA COMPUTER (BELGIUM) S.A.—See Decision Data Inc., pg. 324
DECISION DATA COMPUTER (GB) LTD.—See Decision Data Inc., pg. 324
DECISION DATA COMPUTER GMBH—See Decision Data Inc., pg. 324
DECISION DATA COMPUTER INTL. S.A.—See Decision Data Inc., pg. 324
DECISION DATA COMPUTER (S.A.)—See Decision Data Inc., pg. 324
DECISION DATA DIRECT—See Decision Data Inc., pg. 324
DECISION DATA INC., pg. 323
THE DECISION SHOP—See Backer Spielvogel Bates Worldwide, Inc., pg. 111
DECK HOUSE INC., pg. 324
DECKER RICKARD, pg. 324
DECO CONTAINER—See Forever Living Products, pg. 424
DECO PRODUCTS CO., pg. 324
DECO PURCHASING CO.—See Helmsley Enterprises, Inc., pg. 527
DECOR CORPORATION, pg. 324
DECORATIVE CRAFTS, INC., pg. 324
DECORATIVE FABRICS - CAVEL—See Collins & Aikman Group Inc., pg. 262
DECORATIVE FABRICS - MASTERCRAFT—See Collins & Aikman Group Inc., pg. 262
DEDERT CORPORATION, pg. 324
JESSICA DEE COMMUNICATIONS PUBLIC RELATIONS—See Chiat/Day/Mojo Inc. Advertising, pg. 244
DEE PAPER COMPANY, pg. 324
DEEN WHOLESALE MEAT COMPANY, INC., pg. 324
DEERFIELD MANUFACTURING CO., INC., pg. 324
DEERSKIN TRADING POST, INC., pg. 324
DEFENDER SERVICES, INC., pg. 324
DEFENSE CREDIT UNION COUNCIL—See Credit Union National Association, pg. 298
J.L. DEGRAFFENREID & SONS, INC.—See Vincent Food Industries, Inc., pg. 1152
DEITSCH PLASTIC EXPORT CO.—See Deitsch Plastics Company, pg. 325
DEITSCH PLASTICS COMPANY, pg. 325
MARCEL DEKKER, INC., pg. 325
DEKKO WIRE DIV., KENDALLVILLE—See Group Dekko International Inc., pg. 489
DEKTAS & EGER, INC., pg. 325
DEL AMERICAN PROPERTIES, INC., pg. 325
DEL MAR AVIONICS, pg. 325
DEL MONTE CORP.—See Del Monte Foods, pg. 325
DEL MONTE FOODS, pg. 325
DEL REY RESTAURANT CORP.—See Specialty Restaurants Corporation, pg. 1028
DEL TACO, INC., pg. 325
DEL-VAL MANUFACTURING COMPANY, pg. 325
DELAGRA CORPORATION, pg. 325
DELAIR GROUP, INC.—See Aluminum Shapes, Inc., pg. 46
DELAWARE CHARTER GUARANTEE & TRUST CO.—See The Principal Financial Group, pg. 890
DELAWARE ELECTRIC CO-OP, pg. 325
DELAWARE LOTTERY, pg. 326
DELAWARE NORTH COMPANIES, INC., pg. 326
DELAWARE RIBBON MANUFACTURERS, INC., pg. 326
DELIMATIC REFRESHMENT SERVICES—See Tom's Foods, pg. 1101
DELLA CONSTRUCTION CO. INC., pg. 326
DELMAR PHOTOGRAPHIC AND PRINTING COMPANY—See Continental Graphics Holdings, Inc., pg. 279
DELMAR STUDIOS—See Continental Graphics Holdings, Inc., pg. 279
DELMONT DIV.—See Parkdale Mills, pg. 849
DELOITTE & TOUCHE, pg. 326
DELORE—See Ardell International, Inc., pg. 81

THE DELPHI GLASS CORP. DELPHI STAINED GLASS CENTERS, pg. 326
DELTA EDUCATION, INC., pg. 326
DELTA FOREMOST CHEMICAL CORP., pg. 327
DELTA INDUSTRIES, pg. 327
DELTA LIFE CORPORATION, pg. 327
DELTA & PINE LAND COMPANY—See Southwide, Inc., pg. 1024
DELTA PRIDE CATFISH, INC., pg. 327
DELTA QUEEN STEAMBOAT COMPANY—See Equity Group Investments, pg. 385
DELTA RESINS & REFRACTORIES, INC., pg. 327
DELTA RUBBER COMPANY, pg. 327
DELTA SUGAR CORPORATION, pg. 327
DELTA SURPRENANT WIRE & CABLE, INC., pg. 327
DELUCA VALVE & INSTRUMENT CO.—See Harley Industries, Inc., pg. 510
DELUXE HOMES OF PENNSYLVANIA, INC., pg. 327
DELVICO/BATES, S.A.—See Backer Spielvogel Bates Worldwide, Inc., pg. 111
DEMAND GRAPHICS RESEARCH—See Kwik-Kopy Corp., pg. 647
DEMARIA BUILDING CO. INC., pg. 327
THE DEMARS CORP., pg. 327
DEMARS HAKA DEVELOPMENT, INC.—See The DeMars Corp., pg. 328
DEMARS PROGRAM MANAGEMENT, INC.—See The DeMars Corp., pg. 328
DEMCO INC., pg. 328
DEMERT & DOUGHERTY, INC., pg. 328
DEMETER, INC., pg. 328
JACK DEMMER FORD, INC., pg. 328
DEMOCRAT PRINTING & LITHOGRAPH COMPANY, pg. 328
DEMOULAS SUPER MARKETS, pg. 328
DEMPSEY & SIDERS INSURANCE AGENCY—See American Financial Corporation, pg. 53
DEMPSTER, INC., pg. 328
DEN-MAT CORPORATION, pg. 328
DENA CORPORATION, pg. 329
DENISE LINGERIE—See House of Ronnie, Inc., pg. 546
DENISON/BSB—See Backer Spielvogel Bates Worldwide, Inc., pg. 111
DENLINGER, INC., pg. 329
DENNIS CHEMICAL COMPANY, INC., pg. 329
W.J. DENNIS CO., pg. 329
DE NOOYER CHEVROLET INC., pg. 329
C.S. DENT & CO.—See Grandpa Brands Company, pg. 476
DENTEC CORPORATION, pg. 329
DENTON ENTERPRISES INC., pg. 329
DENTSPLY ARGENTINA S.A.C.I.—See Dentsply International Inc., pg. 330
DENTSPLY (AUSTRALIA) PTY. LTD.—See Dentsply International Inc., pg. 330
DENTSPLY CANADA LTD.—See Dentsply International Inc., pg. 330
DENTSPLY CAULK DE MEXICO, S.A. DE C.V.—See Dentsply International Inc., pg. 330
DENTSPLY GMBH—See Dentsply International Inc., pg. 330
DENTSPLY/IMPLANT DIVISION—See Dentsply International Inc., pg. 330
DENTSPLY INDUSTRIA E COMERCIO LTDA.—See Dentsply International Inc., pg. 330
DENTSPLY INTERNATIONAL INC., pg. 329
DENTSPLY LTD.—See Dentsply International Inc., pg. 330
DENTSU, SUDLER & HENNESSEY—See Dentsu, Young & Rubicam Partnerships, pg. 330
DENTSU WUNDERMAN DIRECT INC.—See Young & Rubicam Inc., pg. 1213
DENTSU, YOUNG & RUBICAM, ALCANTARA/ MANILA—See Dentsu, Young & Rubicam Partnerships, pg. 330
DENTSU, YOUNG & RUBICAM/BANGKOK—See Dentsu, Young & Rubicam Partnerships, pg. 330
DENTSU, YOUNG & RUBICAM/BEIJING—See Dentsu, Young & Rubicam Partnerships, pg. 330
DENTSU, YOUNG & RUBICAM/HONG KONG—See Dentsu, Young & Rubicam Partnerships, pg. 330
DENTSU, YOUNG & RUBICAM/KUALA LUMPUR—See Dentsu, Young & Rubicam Partnerships, pg. 330
DENTSU, YOUNG & RUBICAM PARTNERSHIPS, pg. 330
DENTSU, YOUNG & RUBICAM/SEOUL—See Dentsu, Young & Rubicam Partnerships, pg. 330
DENTSU, YOUNG & RUBICAM/SHANGHAI—See Dentsu, Young & Rubicam Partnerships, pg. 330
DENTSU, YOUNG & RUBICAM/SINGAPORE—See Dentsu, Young & Rubicam Partnerships, pg. 330
DENTSU, YOUNG & RUBICAM/TAIPEI—See Dentsu, Young & Rubicam Partnerships, pg. 330
DENTSU, YOUNG & RUBICAM/TOKYO—See Dentsu, Young & Rubicam Partnerships, pg. 330
DENVER AUTO AUCTION—See Cox Enterprises, Inc., pg. 293
DENVER AUTOMETRICS—See Denver Equipment Company, pg. 331
DENVER BABY DOE'S REST. CORP.—See Specialty Restaurants Corporation, pg. 1028
DENVER EQUIPMENT COMPANY, pg. 331
DENVER EQUIPMENT PTY., LTD.—See Denver Equipment Company, pg. 331
DENVER FREEWAY RESTAURANT CORP.—See Specialty Restaurants Corporation, pg. 1028
DENVER METALS CO.—See CF&I Steel Corporation, pg. 201
DENVER PROCESS EQUIPMENT, LTD.—See Denver Equipment Company, pg. 331
DENVER & RIO GRANDE WESTERN RAILROAD CO.—See Anschutz Corporation, pg. 75
DENVER SERVICE CENTER/INTEC—See T.D. Williamson, Inc., pg. 1192
DENVER THOMAS, INC.—See Denver Equipment Company, pg. 331
DENVER WHOLESALE FLORISTS COMPANY, pg. 331
DEPEW DEVELOPMENT INC., pg. 331
A.N. DERINGER, INC., pg. 331
DERST BAKING COMPANY, INC., pg. 331
DES MOINES TIRE—See Rott-Keller Supply Co., pg. 951
DESA INTERNATIONAL, INC., pg. 331
DESCO ADVERTISING & MARKETING—See Desco Corporation, pg. 332
DESCO CORPORATION, pg. 332
DESERET BOOK CO.—See Deseret Management Corporation, pg. 332
DESERET MANAGEMENT CORPORATION, pg. 332
DESERET NEWS—See Deseret Management Corporation, pg. 332
DESERT MEDICAL SUPPLY INC.—See Taylor Medical Inc., pg. 1081
DESERT PRODUCTION SERVICES—See Media America Corp., pg. 734
DESIGN-BUILD WEST—See RNL Facilities Corporation, pg. 907
DESIGN CENTER—See Del Webb's Coventry, pg. 1171
DESIGN 1 INTERIORS, pg. 332
DESIGN USA—See Jacmar Companies, Inc., pg. 587
DESIGNED CONTRACTS, INC.—See Washington Homes, Inc., pg. 1166
DESOTO HARDWOOD FLOORING COMPANY—See National Bedding & Furniture Industries, pg. 786
DESPATCH INDUSTRIES, pg. 332
DESTINY INDUSTRY INC., pg. 332
DET. DIVISION OF NATIONAL GUARDIAN & BEECHWOOD SECURITY OF CLEVELAND—See Guardian Alarm Co., pg. 491
DETAILS—See Steelcase Inc., pg. 1044
DETAILS MAGAZINE—See Advance Publications Inc., pg. 19
THE DETECTIVE BOOK CLUB—See Walter J. Black, Inc., pg. 154
DETECTO SCALE COMPANY, pg. 332
DETEX CORPORATION, pg. 333
DETREY DENTSPLY—See Dentsply International Inc., pg. 330
DETREY DENTSPLY AG—See Dentsply International Inc., pg. 330
DETREY DENTSPLY S.A.—See Dentsply International Inc., pg. 330
DETROIT CITY DAIRY, INC., pg. 333
DETROIT COIL COMPANY, pg. 333
DETROIT DIESEL ALLISON CO.—See Western Diesel Services Inc., pg. 1179
DETROIT DIESEL CORP.—See Penske Corporation, pg. 859
DETTRA FLAG COMPANY, pg. 333
DEUTSCH/DWORIN, INC., pg. 333
DEUTSCH, SHEA & EVANS, INC., pg. 333
THE DEUTSCH COMPANY, pg. 333
DEUTSCHE ACHESON GMBH—See Acheson Industries, Inc., pg. 12
DEUTSCHE HERAKLITH A.G.—See Belmont Industries, Inc., pg. 137
DEVAULT FOODS, pg. 333
DEVELOPERS DIVERSIFIED, pg. 333
DEVELOPERS INVESTORS, INC.—See W. C. Bradley Co., pg. 170
DEVINE & PEARSON, INC., pg. 333
DEVLIEG BULLARD SERVICES GROUP, pg. 333
DEVLIN LUMBER & SUPPLY CORP., pg. 334
DEVOE PAINT CORPORATION, pg. 334
DEVON DIRECT MARKETING & ADVERTISING, INC., pg. 334
DEWBERRY & DAVIS, pg. 334
DEWCO MILWAUKEE SALES—See Don E. Williams Co., pg. 1190
DEWEESE INC., pg. 334
DEWEY CORPORATION, pg. 334
E.C. DEWITT & COMPANY (AUST.) PTY. LTD.—See C.B. Fleet Company, Incorporated, pg. 417
E.C. DEWITT & COMPANY LIMITED—See C.B. Fleet Company, Incorporated, pg. 417
DEWITT INTERNATIONAL (SINGAPORE) PTE. LTD.—See C.B. Fleet Company, Incorporated, pg. 417
DEWITT MEDIA, INC., pg. 334
DEWOLFE & FISKE INC.—See Chadwick-Miller Inc., pg. 237
DEXOL INDUSTRIES, INC., pg. 334
DEXTER CHEMICAL CORP., pg. 334
DEXTER COMPANY, pg. 334
DEXTER SHOE COMPANY, pg. 334
DI GIORGIO CORPORATION, pg. 334
DIADORA AMERICA, INC., pg. 335
DIAGRAPH CORPORATION, pg. 335
DIAL TUBE COMPANY—See J. H. Roberts Industries Inc., pg. 939
DIAMETER PAPER CO.—See Bradner Central Company, pg. 171
DIAMOND AD LTD.—See Backer Spielvogel Bates Worldwide, Inc., pg. 111
DIAMOND BRANDS, INC., pg. 335
DIAMOND CHAIN COMPANY—See Amsted Industries Incorporated, pg. 69
DIAMOND CHEMICAL CO., INC., pg. 335
T.L. DIAMOND COMPANY, pg. 335
DIAMOND CRYSTAL SPECIALTY FOODS, INC., pg. 335
DIAMOND ELECTRONICS, INC., pg. 335
DIAMOND HILL PLYWOOD COMPANY—See Darlington Veneer Company, pg. 316
DIAMOND MOTORS INC., pg. 335
DIAMOND PAPER BOX CO.—See Dee Paper Company, pg. 324
DIAMOND PRODUCTS COMPANY—See Havatampa Incorporated, pg. 517
DIAMOND WALNUT GROWERS, INC.—See Sun Diamond Growers of California, pg. 1058
DICALITE CORPORATION—See Belmont Industries, Inc., pg. 136
DICALITE HOLDING B.V.—See Belmont Industries, Inc., pg. 137
DICASER S.A. DE C.V.—See Belmont Industries, Inc., pg. 137
DICK CORPORATION, pg. 335
DICKERSON CAROLINA, INC.—See The Dickerson Group, Inc., pg. 336
THE DICKERSON GROUP, INC., pg. 335
DICKERSON, INC.—See The Dickerson Group, Inc., pg. 336
DICKERSON REALTY CORP.—See The Dickerson Group, Inc., pg. 336
DICKERSON REALTY FLORIDA, INC.—See The Dickerson Group, Inc., pg. 336
DICKIES INDUSTRIAL WARE—See Williamson-Dickie Mfg. Co., pg. 1192
DICKINSON PRESS, INC., pg. 336
DICKTEN & MASCH MANUFACTURING CO., pg. 336
DIDDE WEB PRESS, pg. 336
DIE CAST PRODUCTS, INC., pg. 336
DIEBEL MANUFACTURING CO., pg. 336
DIEHL, INC.—See Diehl Specialties Intl., pg. 336
DIEHL SPECIALTIES INTL., pg. 336
DIELINE CORPORATION, pg. 336
DIEMAKERS, INC., pg. 336
DIEMASTERS—See Schawk, Inc., pg. 975
DIEMOLDING CORP., pg. 336
DIERBERGS MARKETS INC., pg. 337
DIESEL MARINE NORSHIPCO—See Norfolk Shipbuilding & Drydock Corporation, pg. 810
DIET CENTER, INC.—See American Health Companies, Inc., pg. 55
DIETRICH'S MILK PRODUCTS, INC., pg. 337
DIETZGEN CORPORATION, pg. 337
DIETZGEN DE MEXICO S.A. DE C.V.—See Dietzgen Corporation, pg. 337
DIFCO, INC., pg. 337
DIFEO AUTOMOTIVE NETWORK, pg. 337
J.D. DIFFENBAUGH, INC., pg. 337
DIFRANZA WILLIAMSON, INC.—See Ketchum Communications Inc., pg. 625
DIGICOURSE, INC.—See The Laitram Corporation, pg. 651
DIGITAL ELECTRONIC AUTOMATION, pg. 337
DIGITAL NEWS PUBLISHING COMPANY, INC.—See International Data Group, pg. 576
DIGITAL PATHWAYS INC., pg. 337
DIGITEC—See Sycon Corporation, pg. 1069
DIGITRON TOOL CO., INC., pg. 337
DILKS STAMP CO.—See American Marking Systems, pg. 58
DILLINGHAM CONSTRUCTION CORPORATION, pg. 337
DILLINGHAM CONSTRUCTION (H.K.) LIMITED—See Dillingham Construction Corporation, pg. 338
DILLINGHAM CONSTRUCTION N.A., INC.—See Dillingham Construction Corporation, pg. 338
DILLINGHAM CONSTRUCTION PACIFIC, LTD.—See Dillingham Construction Corporation, pg. 338
DIMAC CORPORATION, pg. 338
DIMAC DIRECT—See DIMAC Corporation, pg. 338
DIMAC DIRECT—See DIMAC Corporation, pg. 338
DIMAC DIRECT—See DIMAC Corporation, pg. 338
DIMAC DIRECT—See DIMAC Corporation, pg. 338
DIMCO-GRAY COMPANY, pg. 338
DIMEO CONSTRUCTION COMPANY, pg. 338
DINAIRE CORP., pg. 338
DINE OUT ADVERTISING CORP., pg. 338
DINGS DYNAMICS CO.—See Venturedyne, Ltd., pg. 1148
DINGS MAGNETIC CO.—See Venturedyne, Ltd., pg. 1148
DINNER BELL FOODS, INC.—See American Financial Corporation, pg. 53
DINWIDDIE CONSTRUCTION CO., pg. 338
DIRECT COMMUNICATIONS CORPORATION, pg. 339
DIRECT DELIVERY SEVICE—See H & H Advertising, pg. 496
DIRECT DENTAL SUPPLY CO.—See Patterson Dental Company, pg. 851
THE DIRECT MARKETING GROUP INC., pg. 339
DIRECT PRESS MODERN LITHO CORPORATION, pg. 339
DIRECT RESPONSE BROADCASTING NETWORK, INC., pg. 339
DIRECTORY DATA MANAGEMENT—See TMP Worldwide, Inc., pg. 1074
DIRECTORY DISTRIBUTING ASSOCIATES, INC., pg. 339
DISCOUNT DRUG MART INC., pg. 339
DISCOVERY PLASTIC—See RHC/Spacemaster Corporation, pg. 907
DISPATCH CONSUMER SERVICES—See The Dispatch Printing Company, pg. 339
THE DISPATCH PRINTING COMPANY, pg. 339
DISPLAY TECHNOLOGIES, INC., pg. 339
DISPOSAL URBAN MAINTENANCE PROCESSION CO., INC.—See Silver State Disposal Service, Inc., pg. 1004
DISPOSAMED DIV.—See Medline Industries, Inc., pg. 736
THE DISSTON CO., pg. 339
DISTRIBUTION AMERICA, pg. 340
DISTRIBUTION UNLIMITED, INC.—See Rotterdam Ventures Inc., pg. 951
DISTRIBUTOR CONCEPTS—See King Group, Inc., pg. 630
DISTRIBUTORS OIL COMPANY, INC., pg. 340
DISTRICT PETROLEUM PRODUCTS, INC., pg. 340
DIVANE BROS. ELECTRIC CO., pg. 340
DIVERSIFIED COMMUNICATIONS, pg. 340
DIVERSIFIED COMPOUNDERS—See Dennis Chemical Company, Inc., pg. 329
DIVERSIFIED DYNAMICS INC., pg. 340
DIVERSIFIED GROUP, INC., pg. 340
DIVERSIFIED INSURANCE SERVICES OF AMERICA—See Connecticut Mutual Life Insurance Company, pg. 275
DIVERSIFIED STEEL—See American Industries Inc., pg. 56
DIVERSIFIED WOOD PRODUCTS—See Sabbeth Industries Ltd, pg. 965
DIVERSION—See The Hearst Corporation, pg. 522
DIX & EATON INCORPORATED, pg. 341

DIXICO, INC.—See Bell Packaging Corporation, pg. 135
DIXIE BREWING CO., INC., pg. 341
DIXIE BUILDING SUPPLIES, INC.—See Walter Industries, Inc., pg. 1162
DIXIE DAIRY COMPANY, pg. 341
DIXIE ELECTRIC COOPERATIVE, pg. 341
DIXIE INDUSTRIES, INC.—See Columbus McKinnon Corp., pg. 267
DIXIE INSURANCE COMPANY—See American Financial Corporation, pg. 53
DIXIE OIL COMPANY, pg. 341
DIXIE ROYAL HOMES, INC.—See Family Inns of America, Inc., pg. 398
DIXON VALVE & COUPLING COMPANY, pg. 341
DIXONWEB PRINTING COMPANY—See Sleepeck Printing Company, pg. 1010
DIXSON, INC., pg. 341
D'JESCO, INC.—See AJC International, Inc., pg. 4
DOALL COMPANY, pg. 341
DOANE PRODUCTS CO., pg. 342
DOBBS BROTHERS MANAGEMENT, pg. 342
DOBLES CHEVROLET, INC., pg. 342
DOBSON & JOHNSON, INC., pg. 342
DOBSON MOVING & STORAGE, INC.—See Mayflower Transit, Inc., pg. 725
DOCK FOUNDRY COMPANY, pg. 342
DR PEPPER COMPANY—See Dr Pepper/Seven-Up Companies, Inc., pg. 342
DR PEPPER JAPAN CO.—See Dr Pepper/Seven-Up Companies, Inc., pg. 342
DR PEPPER/SEVEN-UP COMPANIES, INC., pg. 342
DOCUMAIL SYSTEMS DIVISION—See Bell & Howell Company, pg. 135
DODGE CITY DAILY GLOBE—See Stauffer Communications, Inc., pg. 1042
DODGE CITY SHOPPER'S WEEKLY—See Stauffer Communications, Inc., pg. 1042
DODGEN FEED BODIES—See Hagie Manufacturing Co., pg. 499
DODSON GROUP, pg. 342
DOE-ANDERSON ADVERTISING AGENCY, INC., pg. 342
DOE SPUN, INC., pg. 343
DOEHLER-JARVIS—See ICM Industries, Inc., pg. 559
DOESKIN CO.—See Statler Industries, pg. 1042
THE F. DOHMEN COMPANY, pg. 343
DOLLAR BARGAIN STORES—See Schottenstein Stores Corporation, pg. 978
DOLPHIN, INC.—See Karsten Manufacturing Corporation, pg. 617
DOLRIIS, GORM LARSEN & PARTNER—See N W Ayer Incorporated, pg. 104
DOMBROWSKI & HOLMES, INC., pg. 343
DOMECQ IMPORTERS INC., pg. 343
DOMESTIC CIGARS—See Consolidated Cigar Corporation, pg. 276
DOMESTIC LINEN SUPPLY CO.—See Domestic Linen Supply & Laundry Co., pg. 343
DOMESTIC LINEN SUPPLY & LAUNDRY CO., pg. 343
DOMINICK & DOMINICK, INCORPORATED, pg. 343
DOMINICK FUTURES CORPORATION—See Dominick & Dominick, Incorporated, pg. 343
DOMINICK'S FINER FOODS, pg. 343
DOMINO'S PIZZA DISTRIBUTION CORP.—See Domino's Pizza Inc., pg. 344
DOMINO'S PIZZA INC., pg. 344
DOMINO'S PIZZA INTERNATIONAL, INC.—See Domino's Pizza Inc., pg. 344
DON AND CHARLIE'S—See Lettuce Entertain You Enterprises, Inc., pg. 669
EDWARD DON & COMPANY OF ILLINOIS, pg. 344
DON MASSEY CADILLAC, INC.—See Don Massey Cadillac Inc., pg. 719
DONAHOE & PUROHIT, INC., pg. 344
DONAHUE, INC., ADVERTISING, pg. 344
JON DONAIRE PASTRIES, INC.—See Presto Food Products, Inc., pg. 888
DONALDSON GROUP, pg. 344
DONER & COMPANY LIMITED—See W.B. Doner & Company, pg. 344
DONER SCHUR PEPPLER—See W.B. Doner & Company, pg. 344
W.B. DONER & COMPANY, pg. 344
DONINO & PARTNERS, INC., pg. 344
DONLEE TECHNOLOGIES INC., pg. 344
DONLEN CORP., pg. 345
DONLEY'S, INC., pg. 345
DONNELLEY MARKETING DATA PROCESSING OPERATIONS—See Peter W. Smith & Company, Inc., pg. 1011
DONNELLEY MARKETING, INC.—See Peter W. Smith & Company, Inc., pg. 1011
DONNELLEY MARKETING INFORMATION SERVICES—See Peter W. Smith & Company, Inc., pg. 1011
DONNKENNY, INC., pg. 345
THE DONOHOE COMPANIES, INC., pg. 345
DONREY INC. TX—See Donrey Media Group, pg. 345
DONREY MEDIA GROUP, pg. 345
DONTECH, pg. 345
DOONAN & SONS, INC., pg. 346
DOOR STORE, INC., pg. 346
ACE DORAN HAULING & RIGGING COMPANY, pg. 346
DORAN MILL CO.—See Doran Textiles Inc., pg. 346
DORAN TEXTILES INC., pg. 346
DORLAND BUSINESS COMMUNICATIONS—See Backer Spielvogel Bates Worldwide, Inc., pg. 111
DORLAND SWEENEY JONES, pg. 346
DORMAN-ROTH FOODS, INC., pg. 346
DORMEYER INDUSTRIES, pg. 346
EDWARD G. DORN & ASSOCIATES, INC., pg. 346
ERNST W. DORN CO., INC., pg. 346
DORON PRECISION SYSTEMS, INC., pg. 346
DORR-OLIVER INCORPORATED, pg. 346
THE DORRIS LUMBER & MOULDING CO., pg. 347
DORRITIE LYONS & NICKEL, INC., pg. 347
DORSEY TRAILERS, INC., pg. 347
DOT PRINTER, INC., pg. 347
DOTHAN UNDERWEAR—See Host Apparel, Inc., pg. 545
DOUBLE AA BUILDERS, LTD., pg. 347
THE DOUBLE-COLA COMPANY, pg. 347
DOUBLE D FERTILIZER—See Jasper County Farm Bureau Co-op Association, Inc., pg. 590
DOUBLE DIAMOND DIST. INC.—See Wotco Inc., pg. 1204
DOUBLE H WEST SHOE WHOLESALE—See H.H. Brown Shoe Company, Inc., pg. 182
DOUBLEDAY BOOK SHOPS, INC.—See Barnes & Noble Bookstores, Inc., pg. 120
JON DOUGLAS COMPANY, pg. 347
DOUGLAS ELLIMAN-GIBBONS & IVES, INC., pg. 347
DOUGLAS MANAGEMENT COMPANY—See Lynden Incorporated, pg. 689
DOUGLAS STEEL FABRICATING CORPORATION, pg. 347
DOUGLAS STEPHEN PLASTICS, INC., pg. 347
DOUGLASTON ELECTRIC—See Turtle & Hughes, Inc., pg. 1120
DOVE EUROPE—See Mars, Incorporated, pg. 713
DOVE INTERNATIONAL, INC.—See Mars, Incorporated, pg. 713
DOVER CHEMICAL CORP.—See ICC Industries, Inc., pg. 558
DOVER HANDBAG CO., INC.—See Michael Stevens Ltd., pg. 1048
DOVRE SKI PRODUCTS—See The Shelburne Corporation, pg. 996
DOWN EAST TIMBERLANDS DIVISION—See The Hearst Corporation, pg. 524
DOWN PRODUCTS DIV.—See Woolrich, Inc., pg. 1201
DOWNEY DESIGNS INTERNATIONAL, INC., pg. 348
DOWNEY, INC.—See K & G Of Wisconsin, Inc., pg. 610
DOWNEY PRINTING, pg. 348
TONY DOWNS FOODS COMPANY, pg. 348
THE DOWNS GROUP, INC., pg. 348
DOYLE MCKENNA BAYER BROWN, pg. 348
DRACKETT & LAVIDGE, INC., pg. 348
DRAFTING GRAPHICS, INC., pg. 348
DRAGON INTERNATIONAL—See Bugle Boy Industries, Inc., pg. 187
DRAKE PETROLEUM COMPANY, INC.—See Warren Equities Inc., pg. 1165
DRAPER CORPORATION, pg. 348
DRAPER DANIELS MEDIA SERVICES, INC., pg. 348
DRAPER DE MEXICO S.A. DE C.V.—See Draper Corporation, pg. 348
DRAPER ERIN LTD.—See Draper Corporation, pg. 348
DRAW CO.—See Interbath, Inc., pg. 574
DRAYCOTT PARTNERS, LTD.—See The New England, pg. 800
DREISBACH & SONS CADILLAC COMPANY, pg. 348
DRESSEN-BARNES ELECTRONICS DIV.—See AEI Holding Co., Inc., pg. 3
LOUIS DREYFUS CORPORATION, pg. 348
DRI MARK PRODUCTS, INC., pg. 349
DRI-PRINT FOILS, pg. 349
DRIBECK IMPORTERS, INC., pg. 349
L.F. DRISCOLL CO., pg. 349
DRIVE TRAIN INDUSTRIES, pg. 349
ROBERT F. DRIVER CO., INC., pg. 349
DRUCKER PRINTING—See Meehan Tooker, pg. 736
DRUG EMPORIUM OF ARIZONA, INC., pg. 349
DRUG GUILD DISTRIBUTORS, INC., pg. 349
DRUMHELLER BAG & SUPPLY—See Norfoods, Inc., pg. 810
DRUMM & ASSOCIATES, INC., pg. 349
DRUMMOND COMPANY, INC., pg. 349
DRUTHER'S INTERNATIONAL, INC., pg. 350
DRY STORAGE CORPORATION, pg. 350
DRYDEN & CO., INC.—See The Prudential Insurance Company of America, pg. 897
DRYDEN & PALMER COMPANY—See Gravymaster Inc., pg. 479
DUAL MANUFACTURING & ENGINEERING, INC.—See Corber Corporation, pg. 285
DUALITE INC., pg. 350
DUALITE SALES & SERVICE, INC.—See Dualite Inc., pg. 350
DUANE READE, pg. 350
DUARY/J.F. DUNCAN INDUSTRIES, INC., pg. 350
DUBIN-CLARK & COMPANY, pg. 350
DUCHOSSOIS INDUSTRIES, INC., pg. 350
DUCKWALL-ALCO STORES, INC., pg. 351
A. DUDA & SONS INC., pg. 351
DUDEK & BOCK SPRING MANUFACTURING COMPANY, pg. 351
DUDLEY SPORTS CO. DIVISION—See Spalding & Evenflo Companies, Inc., pg. 1025
DUDNYK ADVERTISING, pg. 351
DUFF MIX DIV.—See Gilster Mary Lee Corp., pg. 460
DUFF-NORTON—See Spreckles Industries, Inc., pg. 1032
DUFFY & SHANLEY, INC., pg. 351
DUGAN & MEYERS CONSTRUCTION CO.—See Dugan & Meyers Interests, Inc., pg. 351
DUGAN & MEYERS INTERESTS, INC., pg. 351
DUGAN, VALVA ASSOCIATES, pg. 351
DUGGAN INDUSTRIES, INC., pg. 351
DUKANE CANADA LTD.—See Dukane Corporation, pg. 352
DUKANE CORPORATION, pg. 351
DUKE MANUFACTURING CO., INC., pg. 352
DULING OPTICAL CORPORATION, pg. 352
DUMORE CORPORATION, pg. 352
DUNAVANT ENTERPRISES, INC., pg. 352
DUNCAN EQUIPMENT COMPANY, pg. 352
DUNCAN HEATH ASSOCIATES—See Josephson International Inc., pg. 607
DUNCAN TOYS COMPANY—See Nordic Group of Companies, Ltd., pg. 810
DUNCO REALTY & EQUIP. CORP.—See Victory Markets Inc., pg. 1150
DUNDEE MILLS, INC., pg. 352
DUNES HOTELS AND CASINOS INC., pg. 352
DUNGEY & ASSOCIATES—See Harbor Financial Mortgage Corp., pg. 506
S. P. DUNHAM & CO., pg. 353
DUNHAM'S ATHLEISURE CORPORATION, pg. 353
DUNKIRK ICE CREAM CO., INC., pg. 353
DUNLAP & CO. INC., pg. 353
THE DUNLAP COMPANIES, pg. 353
DUNLOP MANUFACTURING CO.—See The Vernon Company, pg. 1148
DUNMORE CORPORATION, pg. 353
DUNMORE CORPORATION/BREWSTER—See Dunmore Corporation, pg. 353
CHARLES DUNN COMPANY-REALTORS, pg. 353
J.E. DUNN CONSTRUCTION CO.—See Dunn Industries Inc., pg. 354
DUNN-EDWARDS CORPORATION, pg. 353
DUNN INDUSTRIES INC., pg. 354
DUNN REBER GLENN MARZ, pg. 354
DUNSTON LEATHERS, INC.—See United States Luggage Company, pg. 1136
DUO-FAST CORPORATION, pg. 354
DUPEY MANAGEMENT CORP., pg. 354
G.B. DUPONT CO., INC., pg. 354
DUPPS COMPANY, pg. 354
DURA CONVERTIBLE SYSTEMS DIV.—See Collins & Aikman Group Inc., pg. 262
DURACO PRODUCTS, INC., pg. 354
DURACO PRODUCTS INC. OF SOUTH CAROLINA—See Duraco Products, Inc., pg. 354
DURALAM, INC.—See Sargento Incorporated, pg. 971
DURAND CANNING CO.—See Faribault Foods Inc., pg. 399
DURANT ELECTRONICS, INC.—See Strombecker Corporation, pg. 1054
DUREX INDUSTRIES INC., pg. 354
DURHAM TRANSPORTATION, INC., pg. 354
DURLACHER & CO., INC., pg. 354
A. K. DURNIN CHRYSLER PLYMOUTH, INC., pg. 355
DURO DYNE CORPORATION, pg. 355
DURO-LAST ROOFING, INC., pg. 355
DURO LITE LAMPS, INC.—See Duro-Test Corporation, pg. 355
DURO PAPER BAG MANUFACTURING CO., pg. 355
DURO-TEST CANADA—See Duro-Test Corporation, pg. 355
DURO-TEST CORPORATION, pg. 355
DURO-TEST INTL. CORP.—See Duro-Test Corporation, pg. 355
DURO-TEST DE MEXICO, S.A.—See Duro-Test Corporation, pg. 355
DURON, INC., pg. 355
JOHN DUSENBERY CO., INC., pg. 355
DUTCH PARKING, INC.—See Allright Corporation, pg. 42
DUTCH PARKING INC.—See Allright Corporation, pg. 42
DUTCH PARKING INC.—See Allright Corporation, pg. 42
DUTTON-LAINSON CO., pg. 356
DUVAL & PARTNERS, pg. 356
DWECK & CAMPBELL, INC., pg. 356
DWYER INSTRUMENTS INC., pg. 356
DYATRON/BONDO CORPORATION, pg. 356
DYER GRAIN CO.—See Tom Wade Co., pg. 1157
DYER-LAUDERDALE FARMERS CO-OP—See Tennessee Farmers Co-op, pg. 1087
THOMAS K. DYER, INC.—See Howard Needles Tammen & Bergendoff, pg. 547
DYKE INDUSTRY, INC., pg. 356
DYNABILT PRODUCTS—See Burtman Iron Works, Inc., pg. 196
DYNACOR DIV.—See Medline Industries, Inc., pg. 736
DYNAMIC CONTROLS CORP., pg. 356
DYNAMIC METAL PRODUCTS COMPANY, pg. 356
DYNASTY DOLLS—See Cardinal Inc., pg. 218
DYNECOL, INC.—See PVS Chemicals, Inc., pg. 838
DYNISCO GERATE G.M.B.H.—See Berwind Corporation, pg. 145
DYNISCO, INC.—See Berwind Corporation, pg. 145
DYNISCO INSTRUMENT SARL.—See Berwind Corporation, pg. 145
DYNISCO (U.K.) LIMITED—See Berwind Corporation, pg. 145
THE DYSON-KISSNER-MORAN CORPORATION, pg. 357

E

E & A INDUSTRIES, INC., pg. 358
E-B ADVERTISING DISPLAY INC., pg. 358
E & D GRAIN MARKETING CO—See EDI International, Inc., pg. 359
E & G FOODS, pg. 358
E-II HOLDINGS, INC., pg. 358
EAC CORPORATION, pg. 359
E B 5 CORPORATION, pg. 359
EB (NA)—See Encyclopaedia Britannica, Inc., pg. 381
EBM SYSTEMS, INC., pg. 359
EBSC CORPORATION, pg. 359
E.C.D., INC., pg. 359
ECP INCORPORATED—See Daubert Industries, Inc., pg. 317
ECRM, pg. 359
EDI INTERNATIONAL, INC., pg. 359
EDP/TEMPS INC.—See Technical Aid Corporation, pg. 1083
EEMCO DIV.—See Datron Incorporated, pg. 317
EFCO CORPORATION, pg. 359
E F INDUSTRIES, pg. 359
EGC MEDIA GROUP, INC., pg. 359
ELE INTERNATIONAL, INC., pg. 359
ELS EDUCATIONAL SERVICES—See American Institute For Foreign Study, pg. 56

ELS EDUCATIONAL SERVICES—See American Institute For Foreign Study, pg. 56
EMI-MANHATTAN RECORDS—See Capitol Industries-EMI Inc., pg. 216
EMI MUSIC PUBLISHING NORTH AMERICA—See Capitol Industries-EMI Inc., pg. 216
EMS CENTRAL REGIONAL OFFICE (CORPORATE)—See Effective Management Systems, pg. 370
EMS EASTERN REGIONAL OFFICE—See Effective Management Systems, pg. 370
EMS-ILLINOIS—See Effective Management Systems, pg. 370
EMS SOUTHWEST REGION OFFICE—See Effective Management Systems, pg. 370
EMS-WEST—See Effective Management Systems, pg. 370
ENI, pg. 360
ENI ENGINEERING COMPANY—See Jupiter Industries, Inc., pg. 609
E.P. GRAPHICS, INC., pg. 360
EPG/TBWA—See TBWA Advertising, Inc., pg. 1072
ERA GENERAL AGENCY CORP.—See ERA Real Estate, pg. 360
ERA REAL ESTATE, pg. 360
ERB LUMBER COMPANY, pg. 360
ERM-COMPUTER SERVICES, INC.—See The ERM Group, pg. 360
ERM-ENVIROCLEAN—See The ERM Group, pg. 360
THE ERM GROUP, pg. 360
ERM-MIDWEST, INC.—See The ERM Group, pg. 360
ERM-NEW ENGLAND, INC.—See The ERM Group, pg. 360
ERM-NORTH CENTRAL, INC.—See The ERM Group, pg. 360
ERM-NORTHEAST, INC.—See The ERM Group, pg. 360
ERM-NORTHWEST, INC.—See The ERM Group, pg. 360
ERM-ROCKY MOUNTAIN, INC.—See The ERM Group, pg. 360
ERM-SOUTH, INC.—See The ERM Group, pg. 360
ERM-SOUTHEAST, INC.—See The ERM Group, pg. 360
ERM-SOUTHWEST, INC.—See The ERM Group, pg. 360
ERM-WEST, INC.—See The ERM Group, pg. 361
ERS ADVERTISING, INC., pg. 361
ESI MEATS, INC.—See Metromedia Company, pg. 744
ESL-NIPPON CO. LTD.—See Electro-Science Laboratories, Inc., pg. 375
ESL S.N.C.—See Electro-Science Laboratories, Inc., pg. 375
ESSTAR INCORPORATED, pg. 361
ETL TESTING LABORATORIES, INC, pg. 361
EV SERVICES INC.—See Resort Condominiums International, pg. 929
EWI, INC., pg. 361
E-Z CLOR/KRATZ—See Aqua Fab Industries, Inc., pg. 79
E Z LOADER BOAT TRAILERS, INC., pg. 361
E-Z MART STORES, INC., pg. 361
E-Z SERVE CORP., pg. 361
EAGER BEAVER, pg. 362
EAGLE BUTTON CO., INC., pg. 362
EAGLE ELECTRIC MFG. CO., INC., pg. 362
EAGLE LINCOLN MERCURY INC., pg. 362
EAGLE-OTTAWA LEATHER CO.—See Albert Trostel & Sons Company, pg. 1116
SID EAGLE ASSOCIATES—See House of Ronnie, Inc., pg. 546
EAGLE ZINC CO.—See T.L. Diamond Company, pg. 335
R.W. EAKEN, INC., pg. 362
EARLE INDUSTRIES, INC., pg. 362
THE EARLY & DANIEL COMPANY, INC.—See EDI International, Inc., pg. 359
EARNHARDT'S AUTO CENTER, pg. 362
EARP MEAT COMPANY, pg. 362
EARTHMOVING EQUIPMENT DIV.—See Esco Corporation, pg. 388
EASLEY TEXTILE—See Swirl, Inc., pg. 1068
EAST ASCENSION TELEPHONE COMPANY—See Eatel Corporation, pg. 364
EAST COAST SERVICE CTR.—See T.D. Williamson, Inc., pg. 1192
EAST JORDAN IRON WORKS, pg. 362
EAST KENTUCKY POWER CO-OP, pg. 362
EAST MOLINE METAL PRODUCTS COMPANY, pg. 363
EAST RIVER ELECTRICAL POWER CO., pg. 363
EASTERN AIR DEVICES, INC., pg. 363
EASTERN AMERICAN ENERGY CORP.—See Eastern American Energy Corporation, pg. 363
EASTERN AMERICAN ENERGY CORPORATION, pg. 363
EASTERN CANVAS PRODUCTS, INC., pg. 363
EASTERN COLOR PRINTING COMPANY, pg. 363
EASTERN FINE PAPER, INCORPORATED, pg. 363
EASTERN FLAT BED SYSTEMS, pg. 363
EASTERN LOBBY SHOPS—See The Levy Organization, pg. 672
EASTERN MILK PRODUCERS COOPERATIVE ASSN., INC., pg. 363
EASTERN NEWS DISTRIBUTORS, INC.—See The Hearst Corporation, pg. 523
EASTERN SMELTING & REFINING CORPORATION, pg. 363
EASTERN STEEL & METAL COMPANY—See Olympic Steel Inc., pg. 825
EASTERN TECHNOLOGIES LTD, pg. 364
EASTERN TOBACCO CO.—See A.C. Monk Co., Inc., pg. 766
EASTLAND NATIONAL BANK—See First Abilene Bankshares, Inc., pg. 412
EASTLAND SHOE MANUFACTURING CORPORATION, pg. 364
EASTMAN MACHINE CO., pg. 364
EASTMAN RADIO, INC.—See Katz Communications, Inc., pg. 618
EASTON PRESS BOOKS—See MBI Inc., pg. 691
EASTON PRESS VIDEOS—See MBI Inc., pg. 691
EASTWAY AIR CARTAGE, INC.—See Eastway Delivery Service of Houston, Inc., pg. 364
EASTWAY DELIVERY SERVICE OF AUSTIN, INC.—See Eastway Delivery Service of Houston, Inc., pg. 364
EASTWAY DELIVERY SERVICE OF DALLAS, INC.—See Eastway Delivery Service of Houston, Inc., pg. 364
EASTWAY DELIVERY SERVICE OF HOUSTON, INC., pg. 364
EASTWAY TRANSPORTATION SERVICES, INC.—See Eastway Delivery Service of Houston, Inc., pg. 364
EASY DAY MANUFACTURING COMPANY, INC., pg. 364
EAT N PARK RESTAURANTS, pg. 364
EATEL CORPORATION, pg. 364
EATON EQUIPMENT CORP., pg. 364
EATON LEONARD TECHNOLOGIES, INC.—See Zimmerman Holdings, Inc., pg. 1220
EATON OFFICE SUPPLY CO., INC., pg. 364
EBCO MFG. COMPANY, pg. 365
EBELING & REUSS COMPANY, pg. 365
BRUCE W. EBERLE & ASSOCIATES—See Eberle Direct Marketing Group, Inc., pg. 365
EBERLE DIRECT MARKETING GROUP, INC., pg. 365
EBONY FASHIONS—See Johnson Publishing Company, Inc., pg. 599
EBSCO GRAPHICS—See Ebsco Industries, Inc., pg. 365
EBSCO INDUSTRIES, INC., pg. 365
EBSCO INVESTMENT SERVICES, INC.—See Ebsco Industries, Inc., pg. 365
EBY BROWN CO., pg. 365
EBY BROWN CO.—See Eby Brown Co., pg. 365
MARTIN K. EBY CONSTRUCTION COMPANY, INC.—See Eby Corporation, pg. 365
EBY CORPORATION, pg. 365
THE ECCENTRIC/BIG BOWL—See Lettuce Entertain You Enterprises, Inc., pg. 669
ECCO SERVICES, INC.—See Cooper Communities, Inc., pg. 283
ECHEVARRIA ANGEL CO., INC., pg. 365
ECHO DESIGN GROUP, INC., pg. 365
PAUL ECKE RANCH, INC., pg. 366
JACK ECKERD CORPORATION, pg. 366
ECKERD DRUG CO.—See Jack Eckerd Corporation, pg. 366
ECKMAN CONSTRUCTION COMPANY, pg. 366
ECLIPSE-COMBUSTION—See Eclipse, Inc., pg. 366
ECLIPSE COMBUSTION & INDUSTRIAL EQUIPMENT PTY.—See Eclipse, Inc., pg. 366
ECLIPSE-CONTROLS—See Eclipse, Inc., pg. 366
ECLIPSE, INC., pg. 366
ECLIPSE MANUFACTURING COMPANY, pg. 367
ECLIPSE THERMAL SYSTEMS—See Eclipse, Inc., pg. 366
ECLIPSE THERMAL SYSTEMS—See Eclipse, Inc., pg. 366
ECLIPSE THERMAL SYSTEMS—See Eclipse, Inc., pg. 366
ECLIPSE THERMAL SYSTEMS, LTD.—See Eclipse, Inc., pg. 366
ECO WATER SYSTEMS, pg. 367
ECO WATER SYSTEMS, INC.—See The Marmon Group, Inc., pg. 712
ECODYNE MRM, INC.—See The Marmon Group, Inc., pg. 712
ECODYNE WATER SYSTEMS, INC.—See The Marmon Group, Inc., pg. 712
ECONO-CLAD BOOKS—See The American Companies, Inc., pg. 51
ECONOCOM-USA INC., pg. 367
ECONOLITE CANADA, INC.—See Econolite Control Products, Inc., pg. 367
ECONOLITE CONTROL PRODUCTS, INC., pg. 367
THE ECONOMICS PRESS, INC., pg. 367
ECONOMY FOLDING BOX CORP., pg. 367
ECONOMY INTERNATIONAL SERVICE INC.—See AJC International, Inc., pg. 4
ECONOMY MECHANICAL INDUSTRIES, INC.—See Jupiter Industries, Inc., pg. 609
ECUATORIANA AIRLINES, pg. 367
EDDINS-WALCHER COMPANY, pg. 367
EDELBROCK CORP., pg. 367
EDELMANN DIV. OF STANT, INC., pg. 368
EDELMANN SCOTT, INC., pg. 368
EDELSON & SONS CORPORATION, pg. 368
EDELSTEIN ASSOCIATES ADVERTISING INC., pg. 368
EDELWEISS—See White Stag Manufacturing Company, pg. 1186
EDERER CRANES—See Ederer Inc., pg. 368
EDERER INC., pg. 368
EDGAR B. FURNITURE CO., pg. 368
EDGERTON FORGE, INC.—See Avis Industrial Corporation, pg. 102
EDGEWATER CORPORATION, pg. 368
EDGEWATER STEEL CO.—See Edgewater Corporation, pg. 368
EDGEWOOD TOOL & MANUFACTURING COMPANY, pg. 368
EDITORS PRESS, INC.—See The Kiplinger Washington Editors, Inc., pg. 632
EDLON PRODUCTS, INC.—See Pfaudler-U.S., Inc., pg. 866
EDLUND COMPANY, INC., pg. 368
EDMONSON WHEAT GROWERS, INC., pg. 369
EDMUND SCIENTIFIC COMPANY, pg. 369
ED'S DEERFIELD—See Lettuce Entertain You Enterprises, Inc., pg. 669
EDUCATIONAL INSIGHTS, INC., pg. 369
EDUCATIONAL PUBLISHING CORPORATION, pg. 369
EDUSERV, pg. 369
EDWAL SCIENTIFIC PRODUCTS DIV.—See Falcon Safety Products Inc., pg. 398
EDWARD DON & COMPANY OF GEORGIA-CLARKSTON BRANCH—See Edward Don & Company of Illinois, pg. 344
EDWARDS BAKING CO., pg. 369
EDWARDS BROTHERS - CAROLINA—See Edwards Brothers, Inc., pg. 370
EDWARDS BROTHERS, INC., pg. 369
EDWARDS ENGINEERING CORPORATION, pg. 370
J.D. EDWARDS & COMPANY, pg. 370
EDWARDSTONE & COMPANY, INC., pg. 370
EDWARDSVILLE INTELLIGENCER—See The Hearst Corporation, pg. 524
EFFECTIVE MANAGEMENT SYSTEMS, pg. 370
EFFEMS AG—See Mars, Incorporated, pg. 713
EFFICIENT ENGINEERING CO., pg. 371
EFFINGHAM-CLAY SERVICE CO., pg. 371
EFFRON FUEL OIL CO., INC.—See Meenan Oil Co. Limited Partnership, pg. 736
EGAN COS., pg. 371
EGAN MCKAY ELECTRICAL CONTRACTORS—See Egan Cos., pg. 371
EGAN & SONS AIR CONDITIONING CO.—See Egan Cos., pg. 371
EGAN & SONS CO.—See Egan Cos., pg. 371
EGAN & SONS INSULATION—See Egan Cos., pg. 371
EGG HARBOR YACHT CO., INC., pg. 371
EGGLAND'S BEST, INC., pg. 371
EGIZII ELECTRIC, INC., pg. 371
EGYPTIAN LACQUER MANUFACTURING COMPANY, INC., pg. 371
EGYPTIAN LACQUER MFG. CO.—See Egyptian Lacquer Manufacturing Company, Inc., pg. 371
800-FLOWERS, pg. 371
EIGHTY EIGHT OIL CO.—See True Companies, pg. 1117
84 LUMBER CO., pg. 371
EINSTEIN MOOMJY INC., pg. 371
EIRE PARTNERS, INC., pg. 372
EISAMAN, JOHNS & LAWS ADVERTISING, INC., pg. 372
LEO EISENBERG & CO., INC., pg. 372
EISNER & ASSOCIATES, INC., pg. 372
WILLIAM EISNER & ASSOCIATES INC., pg. 372
EKTELON CORP.—See Prince Manufacturing, Inc., pg. 890
THE EL-BEE CHARGIT CORP.—See The Elder-Beerman Stores Corp., pg. 373
EL CAMINO RESOURCES, LTD., pg. 372
EL DORADO TIRE CO., pg. 372
EL PASO RESTAURANT CORP.—See Specialty Restaurants Corporation, pg. 1028
EL TORITO RESTAURANTS, INC.—See Restaurant Enterprises Group, Inc., pg. 929
EL TORITO RESTAURANTS, INC., pg. 372
ELAN FOODS, pg. 372
ELASTIC FABRICS OF AMERICA—See CMI Industries, Inc., pg. 202
ELASTIC MATERIALS, INC., pg. 372
ELASTIC STOP NUT—See Harvard Industries, Inc., pg. 514
ELASTOMERIC TECHNOLOGIES, INC., pg. 372
ELBECO INCORPORATED, pg. 372
ELBERTA CRATE & BOX COMPANY, pg. 372
THE ELDER-BEERMAN STORES CORP., pg. 373
ELDER MANUFACTURING COMPANY, pg. 373
ELDER MOVING & STORAGE CO.—See Mayflower Transit, Inc., pg. 725
ELDORADO CHEMICAL COMPANY, pg. 373
ELEC-TROL MEXICO—See Hamlin, Inc., pg. 503
ELECTRIC FURNACE CO., pg. 373
ELECTRIC FURNACE FRANCE S.A.R.L.—See Electric Furnace Co., pg. 373
ELECTRIC FURNACE GERMANY, GMBH—See Electric Furnace Co., pg. 373
ELECTRIC MOBILITY CO.—See Eager Beaver, pg. 362
ELECTRIC POWER EQUIPMENT CO., pg. 373
ELECTRIC RESEARCH AND MANUFACTURING COOPERATIVE, INC. (ERMCO)—See Arkansas Electric Cooperatives Inc., pg. 83
ELECTRIC SPECIALTY & SUPPLY CORP., pg. 374
ELECTRICAL CONDUCTORS, INC.—See Coleman Cable Systems, Inc., pg. 261
ELECTRICAL EQUIPMENT COMPANY, pg. 374
ELECTRICAL EQUIPMENT COMPANY—See Electrical Equipment Company, pg. 374
ELECTRICAL INSULATION SUPPLIERS, pg. 374
ELECTRICAL WHOLESALE SUPPLY COMPANY, INC., pg. 374
ELECTRO AD AGENCY, INC., pg. 374
ELECTRO BRAND, INC., pg. 374
ELECTRO-COATINGS, INC., pg. 374
ELECTRO DYNAMICS CRYSTAL CORPORATION, pg. 374
ELECTRO FIBEROPTICS CORPORATION, pg. 374
ELECTRO-MATIC PRODUCTS INC., pg. 374
ELECTRO MECHANICAL DESIGN SERVICES, INC., pg. 375
ELECTRO-MECHANICAL INSTRUMENTS DIV.—See AEI Holding Co., Inc., pg. 3
ELECTRO METHODS INC., pg. 375
ELECTRO OPTICAL IND.—See Channel Technologies, Inc., pg. 239
ELECTRO-SCIENCE DEUTSCHLAND—See Electro-Science Laboratories, Inc., pg. 375
ELECTRO-SCIENCE LABORATORIES, INC., pg. 375
ELECTRO-SPRAY ENAMELING—See Hofley Manufacturing Company, pg. 538
ELECTRO-WIRE PRODUCTS, INC., pg. 375
ELECTRO-WIRE PRODUCTS, INC.—See Electro-Wire Products, Inc., pg. 375
ELECTROCATALYTIC, INC., pg. 375
ELECTROCHEMICAL INDUSTRIES (FRUTAROM) LTD.—See ICC Industries, Inc., pg. 558
ELECTROID CORP.—See Valcor Engineering Corp., pg. 1142
THE ELECTRON CORP., pg. 375
ELECTRONIC DATA MAGNETICS, INC., pg. 375
ELECTRONIC DISPLAY SYSTEMS (KALLEGO)—See Chief Industries, Inc., pg. 247
ELECTRONIC DRIVES AND CONTROLS, pg. 375
ELECTRONIC ENGINEERS MASTER—See The Hearst Corporation, pg. 522
ELECTRONIC MEASUREMENTS, INC.—See Berwind Corporation, pg. 145
ELECTRONIC MEDIA—See Crain Communications, Inc., pg. 295
ELECTRONIC NEWS PUBLISHING—See International Data Group, pg. 576

ELECTRONIC PLATING SERVICE, INC.—See KDI Corporation, pg. 612
ELECTRONIC PRODUCTS MAGAZINE—See The Hearst Corporation, pg. 522
ELECTRONICA CONDOR DE MEXICO—See Condor D.C. Power Supplies Inc., pg. 273
ELECTRONICA DEL PACIFICO—See Panduit Company, pg. 845
ELECTRONICS STAMPING CORP., pg. 375
ELECTRONIK (PTY) LTD.—See Panduit Company, pg. 845
ELEK-TEK, INC., pg. 375
ELEKTRO METALL EXPORT GMBH—See Datron Incorporated, pg. 317
ELEKTROWERK WEISWEILER GMBH—See Metallurg, Inc., pg. 742
ROBERT ELEN & ASSOCIATES, pg. 376
ELEVEN-O-ONE CORP.—See Zale Corporation, pg. 1216
ELFIN INDUSTRIES, LTD.—See Ancra Corporation, pg. 72
ELGIN-HONEY HILL CORPORATION, pg. 376
ELGIN NATIONAL INDUSTRIES, INC.—See Jupiter Industries, Inc., pg. 609
ELGIN WATCH INTERNATIONAL, INC., pg. 376
ELIAS BROTHERS RESTAURANTS, INC., pg. 376
ELI'S CHICAGO'S FINEST, INC., pg. 376
ELITE LAMP, INC., pg. 376
ELIXIR INDUSTRIES, pg. 376
ELIZABETHTON TWINS BASEBALL CLUB—See Minnesota Twins Baseball Club, pg. 758
ELK SUPPLY COMPANY, pg. 376
ELKAY MANUFACTURING—See Elkay Manufacturing Company, pg. 377
ELKAY MANUFACTURING COMPANY, pg. 377
ELKAY PLASTICS COMPANY, INC., pg. 377
ELKAY PRODUCTS, INC., pg. 377
ELKINGTON REALTY & DEVELOPMENT, pg. 377
ELKINS CONSTRUCTORS, INC., pg. 377
ELKMAN ADVERTISING & PUBLIC RELATIONS, pg. 377
ELLERBE BECKET CONSTRUCTION SERVICES—See Ellerbe Becket, Inc., pg. 378
ELLERBE BECKET, INC., pg. 378
ELLICOTT MACHINE CORP., pg. 378
ELLIOTT COMPANY, pg. 378
ELLIOTT TURBOMACHINERY CANADA, INC.—See Elliott Company, pg. 378
ELLIOTT TURBOMACHINERY LTD.—See Elliott Company, pg. 378
ELLIOTT TURBOMACHINERY S.A.—See Elliott Company, pg. 378
ELLIS PHARMACEUTICALS—See Eon Labs, Inc., pg. 384
ELLIS & ROSS ADVERTISING & DESIGN—See EvansGroup, pg. 391
ELLISON GRAPHICS—See Herlin Press, pg. 531
RAY ELLISON HOMES—See Rayco, pg. 914
MICHAEL R. ELLISON INC., pg. 378
ELLWOOD CITY FORGE, pg. 378
ELMER'S WEIGHTS—See Bollinger Industries Inc., pg. 163
ELMIRA LITHO—See Meehan Tooker, pg. 736
ELOMETA CORPORATION—See Treadwell Corporation, pg. 1108
ELSER & AUCONE, INC., pg. 378
ELTON COAL CO.—See Berwind Corporation, pg. 145
THE ELWELL-PARKER ELECTRIC CO., pg. 378
ELYRIA FOUNDRY COMPANY, pg. 378
EMERALD CORPORATION, pg. 378
EMERY WATERHOUSE COMPANY, pg. 379
EMGE PACKING CO., INC.—See Cargill Inc., pg. 219
EMIGRANT SAVINGS BANK, pg. 379
EMKAY, INC., pg. 379
JOHN EMMERLING INC., pg. 379
EMPIRE AIRLINES, pg. 379
EMPIRE BEROL U.S.A.—See Pen Holdings, Inc., pg. 856
EMPIRE BLUE CROSS & BLUE SHIELD, pg. 379
EMPIRE BRUSHES, INC., pg. 379
EMPIRE CLOTHING—See Excelled Sheepskin & Leather Coat Corporation, pg. 392
EMPIRE DIAMOND CORPORATION, pg. 379
EMPIRE ELECTRIC ASSOCIATION, pg. 379
EMPIRE KOSHER POULTRY, INC., pg. 379
EMPIRE LIFE INSURANCE COMPANY—See Washington Mutual Savings Bank, pg. 1166
EMPIRE NATIONAL BANK, pg. 379
EMPIRE PETROLEUM, INC., pg. 379
EMPIRE PRESS—See Cowles Magazines, Inc., pg. 291
EMPIRE SOUTHWEST CO., pg. 379
EMPIRE STEEL TRADING COMPANY, pg. 380
EMPIRE WEST COMPANIES, INC., pg. 380
EMPLOYEE BENEFITS AMERICA—See Pacific Mutual Life Insurance Company, pg. 841
EMPLOYERS INSURANCE OF WAUSAU A MUTUAL CO., pg. 380
EMPLOYERS INSURANCE OF WAUSAU A MUTUAL CO.—See Nationwide Mutual Insurance Company, pg. 795
EMPRESA DE REFRACTARIOS COLOMBIANOS S.A.—See Belmont Industries, Inc., pg. 137
EMRICK CHEVROLET SALES CORPORATION, pg. 380
EMSON RESEARCH, INC., pg. 380
EN-COM PROPERTIES, INC.—See The Hoyt Group, pg. 548
EN-PAK, INC.—See Invetech Co., pg. 582
ENABLING TECHNOLOGIES COMPANY, pg. 380
ENCO-JOHNSON CITY DIVISION—See Enco Materials, Inc., pg. 380
ENCO MATERIALS, INC., pg. 380
ENCORE MARKETING INTERNATIONAL, pg. 380
ENCORE SHOE CORPORATION, pg. 380
ENCYCLOPAEDIA BRITANNICA EDUCATIONAL CORPORATION—See Encyclopaedia Britannica, Inc., pg. 381
ENCYCLOPAEDIA BRITANNICA EDUCATIONAL CORPORATION, pg. 380
ENCYCLOPAEDIA BRITANNICA, INC., pg. 381
ENDLESS VACATION PUBLISHING—See Resort Condominiums International, pg. 929
ENDURO INDUSTRIES, INC.—See J. H. Roberts Industries Inc., pg. 939
ENDURO-NIAGARA LTD.—See J. H. Roberts Industries Inc., pg. 939
ENERFAB INC., pg. 381
ENERGY AND TECHNOLOGY MANAGEMENT CORPORATION—See Science Applications International Corporation, pg. 981
ENERGY BROKERS GUILD, pg. 381
ENERGY & ENVIRONMENTAL RESEARCH CORP., pg. 381
ENERGY FUELS DEVELOPMENT CORPORATION, pg. 381
ENERGY MINERALS CORPORATION, pg. 381
ENGER-KRESS COMPANY, pg. 381
ENGINEERED POLYMERS CORPORATION—See Harbour Group Ltd., pg. 507
ENGINEERED PRODUCTS, INC., pg. 382
ENGINEERING SERVICE, INC., pg. 382
ENGINEERING TECHNOLOGY LTD. (E.T.), pg. 382
ENGINEERS & FABRICATORS CO.—See The Marley Company, pg. 710
ENGLEFIELD, INC., pg. 382
ENIDINE INCORPORATED, pg. 382
ENMARK STATIONS, INC.—See Colonial Oil Industries, pg. 264
THE ENRO SHIRT COMPANY, INC.—See The Apparel Group, Ltd., pg. 78
ENSONIQ CORPORATION, pg. 382
THE ENSTAR GROUP, INC., pg. 382
THE ENTERPRISE GROUP—See The Mutual Life Insurance Company of New York (MONY), pg. 778
ENTERPRISE PRESS, INC., pg. 382
ENTERPRISE PRODUCTS COMPANY, pg. 382
ENTERPRISE RENT-A-CAR COMPANY, pg. 382
ENTERPRISE S.A. DE C.V.—See Eclipse, Inc., pg. 366
ENTERPRISES INTERNATIONAL INC., pg. 382
ENTERTAINMENT PARTNERS—See IDC Services, Inc., pg. 560
ENTRON INDUSTRIES LIMITED PARTNERSHIP, pg. 383
THE ENTWISTLE COMPANY, pg. 383
ENTWISTLE DEFENSE TECHNOLOGY DIV.—See The Entwistle Company, pg. 383
THE ENTWISTLE EXPORT CO., INC.—See The Entwistle Company, pg. 383
ENVIROCON INTERNATIONAL CORP.—See McNeel International Corp., pg. 732
ENVIRODYNE INDUSTRIES, INC., pg. 383
ENVIRODYNE LIMITED—See Envirodyne Industries, Inc., pg. 383
ENVIRONETICS, pg. 383
ENVIRONMENTAL INDUSTRIES, INC., pg. 383
ENVIRONMENTAL RESORTS INC.—See Greenwood Mills, Inc., pg. 486
EON LABS, INC., pg. 383
EPEC, INC., pg. 384
EPIC HEALTHCARE GROUP, pg. 384
EPOXYLITE CORPORATION, pg. 384
A. EPSTEIN AND SONS, INTL., INC., pg. 384
EPSTEIN CIVIL ENGINEERING, INC.—See A. Epstein and Sons, Intl., Inc., pg. 384
EPSTEIN CONSTRUCTION INC.—See A. Epstein and Sons, Intl., Inc., pg. 384
EPSTEIN ENGINEERING EXPORT, LTD.—See A. Epstein and Sons, Intl., Inc., pg. 384
EPSTEIN ENGINEERING EXPORT (WARSAW), LTD.—See A. Epstein and Sons, Intl., Inc., pg. 384
EPSTEIN ENGINEERING, INC.—See A. Epstein and Sons, Intl., Inc., pg. 384
EPSTEIN MATERIAL HANDLING ENGINEERING, INC.—See A. Epstein and Sons, Intl., Inc., pg. 384
EPSTEIN PROCESS ENGINEERING, INC.—See A. Epstein and Sons, Intl., Inc., pg. 384
A. EPSTEIN & SONS (CALIFORNIA) INC.—See A. Epstein and Sons, Intl., Inc., pg. 384
A. EPSTEIN & SONS (FRANCE) INC.—See A. Epstein and Sons, Intl., Inc., pg. 384
A. EPSTEIN & SONS, INC.—See A. Epstein and Sons, Intl., Inc., pg. 384
A. EPSTEIN & SONS (ISRAEL) LTD.—See A. Epstein and Sons, Intl., Inc., pg. 384
A. EPSTEIN & SONS (U.K.) LTD.—See A. Epstein and Sons, Intl., Inc., pg. 384
EQUINOX ADVERTISING, INC., pg. 384
THE EQUION CORPORATION, pg. 385
EQUIPMENT ASSURANCE LTD.—See Bucyrus-Erie Company, pg. 186
EQUIPMENT MANUFACTURING, INC., pg. 385
EQUIPO AUTOMOTRIZ AMERICANA S.A. DE C.V.—See Takatta Inc., pg. 1077
EQUITABLE BAG COMPANY, pg. 385
EQUITABLE BANK OF LITTLETON, N.A.—See Equitable Bankshares of Colorado, Inc., pg. 385
EQUITABLE BANKSHARES OF COLORADO, INC., pg. 385
EQUITY CONSTRUCTION CO., INC.—See Prime Hospitality Corp., pg. 889
EQUITY COUNTRY INC.—See Farmland Industries, Inc., pg. 402
EQUITY EXPORT, OIL & GAS, INC.—See Farmland Industries, Inc., pg. 402
EQUITY FUND ADVISORS INC., pg. 385
EQUITY GROUP INVESTMENTS, pg. 385
EQUITY SERVICES, INC.—See National Life Insurance Company, pg. 791
EQUITY SUPPLY COMPANY, pg. 385
ERB LUMBER CO. OF INDIANA—See Erb Lumber Company, pg. 360
ERDLE PERFORATING OF CAROLINA—See Erdle Perforating Co., pg. 385
ERDLE PERFORATING CO., pg. 385
ERDLE PERFORATING CO. LTD.—See Erdle Perforating Co., pg. 385
MARSHALL ERDMAN AND ASSOCIATES, INC., pg. 385
ERGON, INC., pg. 386
ERIC MOWER AND ASSOCIATES/ROCHESTER, INC.—See Eric Mower and Associates, Inc., pg. 774
ERICKSON DIVERSIFIED CORP., pg. 386
ERICKSON OIL PRODUCTS, INC., pg. 386
ERICKSON TRANSPORT CORPORATION, pg. 386
ERICO INTERNATIONAL, pg. 386
ERICSON MARKETING COMMUNICATIONS, pg. 386
ERIE BRONZE & ALUMINUM CO.—See McInnes Steel Company, pg. 730
ERIE FAMILY LIFE INSURANCE COMPANY, pg. 386
ERIE INDEMNITY COMPANY—See Erie Family Life Insurance Company, pg. 386
ERIE INSURANCE EXCHANGE—See Erie Family Life Insurance Company, pg. 386
ERIE INSURANCE GROUP—See Erie Family Life Insurance Company, pg. 386
ERIE PRESS SYSTEMS, pg. 386
ERIEZ MAGNETICS, pg. 386
ERIEZ PRODUCTS MAGNETICOS E METALURGICOS, LTDA.—See Sunbeam-Oster Company, Inc., pg. 1059
THE ERIN COMPANY, pg. 387
ERIN GROUP ADMINISTRATORS, INC., pg. 387
N. ERLANGER, BLUMGART & COMPANY, INC., pg. 387
THE (ERLE STANLEY) GARDNER MYSTERY LIBRARY—See Walter J. Black, Inc., pg. 154
ERMCO, INC., pg. 387
ERNEST PAPER PRODUCTS, INC., pg. 387
E. C. ERNST—See The Philadelphia Bourse, Inc., pg. 866
ERNST HOME CENTER, INC., pg. 387
ERNST & YOUNG, pg. 387
ERNST & YOUNG—See Ernst & Young, pg. 387
ERSHIGS, INC., pg. 387
ERVIN AMASTEEL DIV.—See Ervin Industries, Inc., pg. 387
ERVIN INDUSTRIES, INC., pg. 387
ERVING PAPER MILLS, pg. 388
ESCO CORPORATION, pg. 388
ESCO ELEVATORS, INC., pg. 388
ESCO, EUROPE S.A.—See Esco Corporation, pg. 388
ESCO INTERNATIONAL—See Esco Corporation, pg. 388
ESCO LTD.—See Esco Corporation, pg. 388
ESCO, S.A.—See Esco Corporation, pg. 388
ESCOD INDUSTRIES—See Insilco Corporation, pg. 571
ESCUELAS DE IDIOMAS BERLITZ DE ESPANA, S.A.—See Berlitz International, Inc., pg. 143
ESPRIT ACCESSORIES—See Esprit de Corp., pg. 388
ESPRIT DE CORP., pg. 388
ESPRIT KIDS—See Esprit de Corp., pg. 388
ESPRIT SPORT—See Esprit de Corp., pg. 388
ESQUIRE—See The Hearst Corporation, pg. 523
ESQUIRE CANADA, INC.—See Strombecker Corporation, pg. 1054
ESQUIRE NOVELTY CO.—See Strombecker Corporation, pg. 1054
ESROCK ADVERTISING, pg. 388
ESSEX GRAIN PRODUCTS, INC., pg. 389
ESSEX GROUP, INC., pg. 389
ESSEX INDUSTRIES—See ESSTAR Incorporated, pg. 361
ESSKAY MANUFACTURING CO., pg. 389
ESTABLISSEMENT MESNEL, S.A.—See 21 International Holdings, Inc., pg. 1121
THE ESTEE CORPORATION, pg. 389
ESTEE LAUDER, INC., pg. 389
ESTEE LAUDER K.K.—See Estee Lauder, Inc., pg. 389
ESTEE LAUDER N.V.—See Estee Lauder, Inc., pg. 389
ESTEE LAUDER, INTL.—See Estee Lauder, Inc., pg. 389
ESTES EXPRESS LINES, INC., pg. 389
ESTES INDUSTRIES, INC.—See Peter W. Smith & Company, Inc., pg. 1011
ESTHER WILLIAMS SWIMMING POOL CO., pg. 389
ETHAN ALLEN, INC.—See Green Mountain Holding Corporation, pg. 485
ETHICAL COMMUNICATIONS—See Backer Spielvogel Bates Worldwide, Inc., pg. 111
A.J. ETKIN CONSTRUCTION CO.—See Alex J. Etkin, Inc., pg. 390
ALEX J. ETKIN, INC., pg. 389
OY ETRA AB—See Panduit Company, pg. 845
EUCLID CRANE DIVISION—See Kranco, Inc., pg. 644
EUREKA MANUFACTURING CO., INC.—See Reed & Barton Corporation, pg. 920
EUROFLEX SCREEN PRINT SUPPLIES LTD.—See Flexible Products Company, pg. 419
EUROFORM S.R.L.—See The Forum Corporation, pg. 426
EUROMARKET DESIGNS, INC., pg. 390
EUROPE LANGUAGE CENTER SRL—See Berlitz International, Inc., pg. 143
EUROPEAN PLUMBING PRODS. GROUP—See American Standard Inc., pg. 62
EUROPEAN TRAVEL & LIFE—See K-III Communications Corporation, pg. 611
EUSTON STATION, INC.—See Victoria Station Incorporated, pg. 1150
EVA-TONE INC., pg. 390
EVANA AUTOMATION, pg. 390
EVANGELINE MEDICAL & X-RAY DISTRIBUTORS, pg. 390
EVANS ADHESIVE CORP., pg. 390
EVANS BROTHERS COMPANY, INC., pg. 390
EVANS ELECTRIC SUPPLY, INC.—See Reily Electric Supply, Inc., pg. 923
EVANS FABRICATION, INC., pg. 390
EVANS FOOD GROUP—See EvansGroup, pg. 391
EVANS, HARDY & YOUNG, INC., pg. 390
EVANS INDUSTRIES, INC., pg. 390
STU EVANS LINCOLN-MERCURY INC., pg. 390
EVANSGROUP, pg. 390
EVANSGROUP—See EvansGroup, pg. 391
EVANSGROUP—See EvansGroup, pg. 391
EVANSGROUP—See EvansGroup, pg. 391
EVANSGROUP—See EvansGroup, pg. 391
EVANSGROUP—See EvansGroup, pg. 391
EVANSGROUP—See EvansGroup, pg. 391

EVANSGROUP—See EvansGroup, pg. 391
EVANSGROUP—See EvansGroup, pg. 391
EVANSTON BANK—See GreatBanc, Inc., pg. 483
EVANSVILLE BREWING COMPANY, pg. 391
EVCON HOLDINGS, pg. 391
EVENFLO JUVENILE FURNITURE CO.—See Spalding & Evenflo Companies, Inc., pg. 1024
EVENFLO MEXICO S.A.—See Spalding & Evenflo Companies, Inc., pg. 1025
EVENFLO PRODUCTS CO.—See Spalding & Evenflo Companies, Inc., pg. 1024
EVENFLO PRODUCTS DIVISION—See Spalding & Evenflo Companies, Inc., pg. 1025
EVENING POST PUBLISHING CO., pg. 391
EVERBRITE, INC., pg. 391
EVERBRITE LACROSSE—See Everbrite, Inc., pg. 391
EVEREST—See Lettuce Entertain You Enterprises, Inc., pg. 669
EVERFRESH BEVERAGES INC., pg. 391
EVERGREEN HEALTHCARE LTD., pg. 391
EVERGREEN INTERNATIONAL AVIATION, INC., pg. 392
EVERGREEN MILLS INC.—See Varied Investments, Inc., pg. 1145
L. G. EVERIST INC., pg. 392
EVERLAST SPORTS MANUFACTURING CORP., pg. 392
EVERLASTING VALVE CO.—See Armstrong International, Inc., pg. 83
EVERPURE INC.—See E-II Holdings, Inc., pg. 358
EVSWATER INDUSTRIAL SYSTEMS—See The Marmon Group, Inc., pg. 712
EVY OF CALIFORNIA, INC., pg. 392
EWI, INC.-STAMPING & DIE DIV.—See EWI, Inc., pg. 361
EXACT EQUIPMENT CORPORATION, pg. 392
EXCEL CORP.—See Cargill Inc., pg. 219
EXCEL INDUSTRIES, INC., pg. 392
EXCEL MEDIA SERVICES INC.—See Meldrum & Fewsmith Communications Inc., pg. 737
EXCELL MANUFACTURING COMPANY, pg. 392
EXCELLED SHEEPSKIN & LEATHER COAT CORPORATION, pg. 392
EXCELSIOR MANUFACTURING & SUPPLY CORP., pg. 392
EXCELSIOR PRINTING CO.—See Crane & Co., Inc., pg. 296
EXCELSIOR PROCESS & ENGRAVING CO.—See Crane & Co., Inc., pg. 296
EXECU-FIT HEALTH PROGRAMS, INC.—See UniHealth America, pg. 1127
EXECUTIVE CAPITAL CORP., pg. 392
EXECUTIVE CAR LEASING COMPANY—See Executive Car Leasing, Inc., pg. 393
EXECUTIVE CAR LEASING, INC., pg. 393
EXECUTIVE ENTERPRISES, INC., pg. 393
EXECUTIVE ENTERPRISES PUBLICATIONS CO., INC.—See Executive Enterprises, Inc., pg. 393
EXECUTIVE JET AVIATION, INC., pg. 393
EXECUTIVE TELECOM SYSTEMS, INC.—See The Bureau of National Affairs, Inc., pg. 189
EXIDE CORPORATION, pg. 393
EXOTHERMICS-ECLIPSE, INC.—See Eclipse, Inc., pg. 366
EXPERIENCE IN SOFTWARE, INC., pg. 393
EXPO INDUSTRIES, INC., pg. 393
EXPRESS STEEL AND PLASTICS—See Hickinbotham Bros., Ltd, pg. 532
EXPRESS 1 STOP—See Sullivan Oil Company, pg. 1057
EYECESSORIES—See The Hilsinger Corp., pg. 535
EZON PRODUCTS, INC., pg. 393

F

F & B MANUFACTURING CO., pg. 393
F & M DISTRIBUTORS INC., pg. 393
F & W PUBLICATIONS, INC., pg. 394
F C L GRAPHICS, pg. 394
FCN ADVERTISING, pg. 394
FCS FORUM S.S.R.O.—See The Forum Corporation, pg. 426
FCW PUBLISHING CORP.—See International Data Group, pg. 576
FDL FOODS, INC., pg. 394
FEL CORPORATION, pg. 394
F & F PRODUCTIONS, INC.—See Hubbard Broadcasting, Inc., pg. 549
F & F SHOE COMPANY—See Mason Shoe Mfg. Co., pg. 718
FGI, pg. 394
FGMC, INC.—See General Homes Corporation, pg. 449
F J M CORPORATION, pg. 394
FKG OIL COMPANY—See Moto, Inc., pg. 773
FKQ ADVERTISING INC., pg. 394
FMI PROPERTIES CORP.—See American Financial Corporation, pg. 53
FM INDUSTRIES, INC., pg. 394
FMR CORP.—See Fidelity Investments (FMR Corp.), pg. 408
FMS MANAGEMENT SYSTEMS, INC., pg. 394
FP CAMEOCOLOR, INC.—See Fleming Packaging Corp., pg. 417
F.P.A., INC., pg. 394
F. R. MANUFACTURING CORPORATION, pg. 395
FTD/FLORISTS' TRANSWORLD DELIVERY ASSOCIATION, pg. 395
FTZ INDUSTRIES, INC.—See Bardes Corp., pg. 119
F.W.D.C., INC.—See Cenvill Development Corp., pg. 236
FWD CORPORATION, pg. 395
FAB-KNIT MANUFACTURING CO.—See Anderson Industries, Inc., pg. 73
FABDEC LTD.—See DEC International, Inc., pg. 309
FABER/CASTELL CANADA LTD.—See Faber/Castell Corporation, pg. 395
FABER/CASTELL CORPORATION, pg. 395
FABER, COE & GREGG, INC., pg. 395
FABER, COE & GREGG OF CHICAGO, INC.—See Faber, Coe & Gregg, Inc., pg. 395
FABER, COE & GREGG OF PENNSYLVANIA, INC.—See Faber, Coe & Gregg, Inc., pg. 395
FABER ENTERPRISES, INC., pg. 395
NEIL FABER MEDIA INC., pg. 395
FABEX INC., pg. 395
FABIANAC, STROPES & ARMSTRONG, INC., pg. 395
FABICK BROTHERS EQUIPMENT—See John Fabick Tractor Company, pg. 396
FABICK & COMPANY—See John Fabick Tractor Company, pg. 396
FABICK MACHINERY—See John Fabick Tractor Company, pg. 396
FABICK TRACTOR—See John Fabick Tractor Company, pg. 396
JOHN FABICK TRACTOR COMPANY, pg. 396
FABREEKA INTERNATIONAL, INC., pg. 396
FABRIC WHOLESALERS, INC., pg. 396
FABRICA DE VALVULAS—See Farley Industries, pg. 400
M. FABRIKANT & SONS, INC., pg. 396
FABWEL INC., pg. 396
FACEMATE CORPORATION, pg. 396
FACEMATE POND LILT GREAT FALLS—See Facemate Corporation, pg. 396
FADAL ENGINEERING COMPANY, INC., pg. 396
FADDALEY ENTERPRISES INC.—See Daniel Caron Ltd., pg. 224
FADLER, INC.—See Hale-Halsell Company, pg. 500
FAHLGREN MARTIN, INC., pg. 396
FAIR HARBOR PROPERTIES, INC.—See Society for Savings Bancorp, Inc., pg. 1016
FAIR LANE BOWLING DIV.—See Fair Lanes Inc., pg. 396
FAIR LANES INC., pg. 396
FAIRBANKS MORSE PUMP CORPORATON, pg. 397
FAIRFAX LUMBER & MILLWORK COMPANY INC., pg. 397
FAIRFIELD BUILDING SYSTEMS—See Fairfax Lumber & Millwork Company Inc., pg. 397
FAIRFIELD ELECTRIC CO-OP, pg. 397
FAIRFIELD FOODS—See Mrs. Fields' Inc., pg. 761
FAIRFIELD INDUSTRIES, INC.—See Fairfield Maxwell Ltd., pg. 397
FAIRFIELD INTERNATIONAL CORPORATION—See Fairfield Maxwell Ltd., pg. 397
THE FAIRFIELD LUMBER & SUPPLY COMPANY, pg. 397
FAIRFIELD MAXWELL LTD., pg. 397
FAIRLANES BOWL, INC.—See Great Lakes Recreation Co., pg. 482
FAIRMONT ELECTRONICS—See RS Electronics, pg. 908
FAIRMONT HOMES, INC., pg. 397
THE FAIRMONT HOTELS, pg. 397
FAIRMOUNT MORTGAGE, INC.—See Del Webb's Coventry, pg. 1171
FAIRVIEW CONSTRUCTION, INC, pg. 397
FAIRVIEW PROPERTIES, INC.—See The Kiplinger Washington Editors, Inc., pg. 632
FAIRVIEW WINE CO.—See White Rock Distilleries Inc., pg. 1186
FAIRWAY DISTRICT—See Hunt Oil Company, pg. 554
FAIRWAY FOODS, INC.—See Holiday Companies, pg. 539
FAIRWAY FORD, INC., pg. 397
FAJEN & BLAIR DIVISION—See Crossman Corp., pg. 300
FALCON ASSOCIATES, LTD.—See Science Applications International Corporation, pg. 981
FALCON CANDY COMPANY, pg. 398
FALCON SAFETY PRODUCTS INC., pg. 398
FALCONER GLASS INDUSTRIES, INC.—See Guardian Industries Corp., pg. 492
PETE FALL FORD INC., pg. 398
FALLEK CHEMICAL COMPANY (UK) LTD.—See ICC Industries, Inc., pg. 558
FALLEK CHEMICAL CORP.—See ICC Industries, Inc., pg. 558
FALLEK CHEMICAL S.A.—See ICC Industries, Inc., pg. 558
FALLEY'S INC.—See The Yucaipa Companies, pg. 1214
FALLON COMMUNITY HEALTH PLAN, pg. 398
FAMILY INNS OF AMERICA, INC., pg. 398
FAMILY INNS OF NEW ORLEANS, INC.—See Family Inns of America, Inc., pg. 398
THE FAMILY INSURANCE AGENCY, INC.—See The Troy Savings Bank, pg. 1117
THE FAMILY INVESTMENT SERVICES CO., INC.—See The Troy Savings Bank, pg. 1117
THE FAMILY MORTGAGE BANKING CO., INC.—See The Troy Savings Bank, pg. 1117
FAMILY PHARMACY GENERAL OFFICE—See Alco Health Services Corporation, pg. 32
FAMTEC AG—See FamTec International, Inc., pg. 398
FAMTEC INTERNATIONAL, INC., pg. 398
FANCHEM, LTD.—See PVS Chemicals, Inc., pg. 838
FANNER-PLP—See Preformed Line Products, pg. 886
FANNIE MAY CANDY SHOPS, INC.—See Jordan Company, pg. 604
FANTA FURNITURE—See All-Luminum Products, Inc., pg. 35
FANTASTIC SAM'S INTERNATIONAL, INC., pg. 398
FAR WEST CONCEPTS, INC.—See Restaurant Enterprises Group, Inc., pg. 929
FAR WEST PRODUCTS, INC.—See Al Copeland Enterprises, Inc., pg. 284
FARADAY, INC., pg. 399
FARAGO ADVERTISING, pg. 399
FARALLON COMPUTING, INC., pg. 399
FARBEST INC.—See Countrymark Cooperative, Inc., pg. 290
FARE DEVELOPMENT CORP.—See Holly's Inc., pg. 540
FAREWAY STORES, INC., pg. 399
FARGO CLINIC LTD., pg. 399
FARGO GLASS & PAINT COMPANY, pg. 399
FARIBAULT FOODS INC., pg. 399
FARIBAULT WOOLEN MILL CO., pg. 399
FARLEY CANDY COMPANY, pg. 399
FARLEY, INC.—See Farley Industries, pg. 400
FARLEY INDUSTRIES, pg. 399
FARM BUREAU CASUALTY INSURANCE CO.—See Arkansas Farm Bureau Federation, pg. 83
FARM BUREAU MUTUAL INSURANCE CO. OF ARKANSAS—See Arkansas Farm Bureau Federation, pg. 83
FARM CREDIT BANK OF BALTIMORE—See Federal Farm Credit Banks Funding Corporation, pg. 405
FARM CREDIT BANK OF COLUMBIA—See Federal Farm Credit Banks Funding Corporation, pg. 405
FARM CREDIT BANK OF LOUISVILLE—See Federal Farm Credit Banks Funding Corporation, pg. 405
FARM CREDIT BANK OF OMAHA—See Federal Farm Credit Banks Funding Corporation, pg. 405
FARM CREDIT BANK OF ST. LOUIS—See Federal Farm Credit Banks Funding Corporation, pg. 405
FARM CREDIT BANK OF ST. PAUL—See Federal Farm Credit Banks Funding Corporation, pg. 405
FARM CREDIT BANK OF SPOKANE—See Federal Farm Credit Banks Funding Corporation, pg. 405
FARM CREDIT BANK OF SPRINGFIELD—See Federal Farm Credit Banks Funding Corporation, pg. 405
FARM CREDIT BANK OF TEXAS—See Federal Farm Credit Banks Funding Corporation, pg. 405
FARM CREDIT BANK OF WICHITA—See Federal Farm Credit Banks Funding Corporation, pg. 405
FARM FAMILY MUTUAL INSURANCE CO., pg. 401
FARM FRESH, INC., pg. 401
FARM & HOME LIFE INSURANCE CO.—See The Chesapeake Life Insurance Co., pg. 243
FARM & HOME OIL COMPANY, pg. 401
FARM JOURNAL, INC., pg. 401
FARM STORE NO. 1—See Steiner Corporation, pg. 1045
FARM STORES, INC., pg. 401
FARMAN'S PICKLE COMPANY—See Agway, Inc., pg. 26
FARMASTER/BIG VALLEY DIV.—See Behlen Mfg. Co., pg. 132
FARMERS AND TRADERS LIFE INSURANCE CO., pg. 401
FARMERS CHEMICAL CO.—See Farmland Industries, Inc., pg. 402
FARMERS CO-OP MARKET INC., pg. 401
FARMER'S COPPER & INDUSTRIAL SUPPLY—See Farmers Marine Copper Works, pg. 401
FARMERS INVESTMENT COMPANY, INC.—See Bale Of Kentucky, Inc., pg. 115
FARMERS MARINE COPPER WORKS, pg. 401
FARMERS MARKETING ASSOCIATION—See Manna Pro Partners, pg. 704
FARMERS MUTUAL HAIL INSURANCE CO., pg. 401
FARMERS NATIONAL COMPANY—See Metropolitan Life Insurance Co., pg. 744
FARMER'S PRIDE, INC., pg. 401
FARMERS RICE COOPERATIVE, pg. 401
FARMERS TELEPHONE CO-OP, pg. 402
FARMERS UNION MARKETING & PROCESSING ASSOCIATION, pg. 402
FARMHAND, INC., pg. 402
FARMINGTON HILLS HOLDING COMPANY, pg. 402
FARMLAND INDUSTRIES, INC., pg. 402
FARMLAND INDUSTRIES, INC.—See Farmland Industries, Inc., pg. 402
FARMLAND INDUSTRIES U.K. LTD.—See Farmland Industries, Inc., pg. 402
FARMLAND INSURANCE AGENCY, INC.—See Farmland Industries, Inc., pg. 402
FARMSTEAD FOODS, INC., pg. 402
FARMWAY CO-OP INC., pg. 402
FARNAM COMPANIES, INC., pg. 403
FARNSWORTH COMPANIES, pg. 403
FARNSWORTH CONSTRUCTION—See Farnsworth Companies, pg. 403
FARNSWORTH DEVELOPMENT CO.—See Farnsworth Companies, pg. 403
MEL FARR FORD, INC., pg. 403
FARRAND CONTROLS—See Ruhl Companies, Inc., pg. 955
FARRAR, STRAUS & GIROUX, INC., pg. 403
FARRELL CMA, pg. 403
FARRELL LINES INCORPORATED, pg. 403
FARWELL, OZMUN, KIRK & CO.—See United Hardware Distributing Co., pg. 1133
FASFAX CORPORATION—See International Shoe Machine Corp., pg. 579
FASHION BAR INC.—See Specialty Retailers, Inc., pg. 1029
FASHION SHOP OF KENTUCKY INC., pg. 403
FASTCUT TOOL CORPORATION—See Brubaker Tool Corp., pg. 183
FASTEC INDUSTRIAL, pg. 403
FASTEC SW CORPORATION—See Fastec Industrial, pg. 403
FAUBER CONSTRUCTION COMPANY, INC., pg. 403
FAWCETT BOOKS—See Advance Publications Inc., pg. 19
FAWN INDUSTRIES, INC., pg. 404
FAXON CANADA—See The Faxon Company, Inc., pg. 404
THE FAXON COMPANY, INC., pg. 404
FAXON EUROPE—See The Faxon Company, Inc., pg. 404
FAY, SPOFFORD & THORNDIKE, INC., pg. 404
FAYVA—See Morse Shoe, Inc., pg. 772
FEDCO, INC., pg. 404
FEDERAL BUSINESS PRODUCTS, INC., pg. 404
FEDERAL CHICAGO CORPORATION, pg. 404
FEDERAL COMPRESS & WAREHOUSE COMPANY, INC., pg. 404
FEDERAL DATA CORPORATION, pg. 404
FEDERAL DISTILLERS—See White Rock Distilleries Inc., pg. 1186
FEDERAL DISTRIBUTING CORPORATION, pg. 404
FEDERAL FARM CREDIT BANKS FUNDING CORPORATION, pg. 404
FEDERAL HOSE MANUFACTURING CORP.—See Flexfab, Inc., pg. 418

FEDERAL INTERMEDIATE CREDIT BANK OF JACKSON—See Federal Farm Credit Banks Funding Corporation, pg. 405
FEDERAL SAVINGS BANK—See Kemmons Wilson Companies, pg. 1194
FEDERAL STAMPINGS OF CALIFORNIA—See Dayton Rogers Mfg. Co., pg. 321
FEDERAL STAMPINGS OF FLORIDA—See Dayton Rogers Mfg. Co., pg. 321
FEDERAL STAMPINGS OF NEW YORK—See Dayton Rogers Mfg. Co., pg. 321
FEDERAL STAMPINGS OF OREGON—See Dayton Rogers Mfg. Co., pg. 321
FEDERATED MUTUAL INSURANCE COMPANY, pg. 405
C. R. FEDRICK, INC.—See Sundt Corp., pg. 1060
FEED SERVICE CORP., pg. 405
FEL-PRO INCORPORATED, pg. 405
FELLERS & COMPANY, pg. 405
FELLOWES MANUFACTURING CO., pg. 405
FELLOWS CORPORATION—See Goldman Financial Group, pg. 468
THE FELTERS COMPANY, pg. 406
FELTON BRUSH INC., pg. 406
FENDER MUSICAL INSTRUMENTS, pg. 406
FENESTRA CORPORATION—See The Marmon Group, Inc., pg. 711
FENNER MANHEIM, pg. 406
H.G. FENTON MATERIAL COMPANY, pg. 406
FENTON PRESS, INC., pg. 406
FERGUSON ELECTRIC CONSTRUCTION CO., INC., pg. 406
FERGUSON INDUSTRIES, pg. 406
FERGUSON INDUSTRIES INTERNATIONAL—See Ferguson Industries, pg. 406
FERGUSON MANUFACTURING & EQUIPMENT COMPANY, pg. 406
FERMAN OLDSMOBILE, pg. 406
GEORGE E. FERN COMPANY—See Budco Group Inc., pg. 186
FERN/HANAWAY, INC. ADVERTISING/PUBLIC RELATIONS, pg. 407
FERRALLOY—See ICM Industries, Inc., pg. 559
FERRARA FOODS & CONFECTIONS, INC., pg. 407
JAMES FERRERA & SONS, INC., pg. 407
FERRELL COMPANIES INC./FERRELLGAS, pg. 407
FERRELL NORTH AMERICA—See Ferrell Companies Inc./Ferrellgas, pg. 407
FERRELLGAS, INC.—See Ferrell Companies Inc./Ferrellgas, pg. 407
FERRO METAL & CHEMICAL CORPORATION LTD.—See Philipp Brothers Chemicals, Inc., pg. 867
FERRO UNION, INC., pg. 407
AB FERROLEGERINGAR—See Metallurg, Inc., pg. 742
FERROLEGERINGAR AG—See Metallurg, Inc., pg. 742
FERROUS PROCESSING & TRADING CO., pg. 407
FERRY-MORSE SEED COMPANY, pg. 407
FESSEL, SIEGFRIEDT & MOELLER, INC., pg. 407
FEUER LEATHER CORPORATION, pg. 407
FEY MFG. CO., INC.—See Standun, Inc., pg. 1038
FIBELCO S.A./N.V.—See AXIA Incorporated, pg. 8
FIBER MATERIALS, INC., pg. 408
FIBERESIN INDUSTRIES INC., pg. 408
FIBERTEC INC.—See Dyatron/Bondo Corporation, pg. 356
FIBRE GLASS-EVERCOAT COMPANY INC., pg. 408
THE FIBRE-METAL PRODUCTS COMPANY, pg. 408
FIBREBOND CORPORATION, pg. 408
FIBREWEB INTERNATIONAL, LTD.—See Gould Paper Corporation, pg. 473
FICKS REED COMPANY, pg. 408
FICOMET S.A.R.L.—See AXIA Incorporated, pg. 8
FIDELITY ACCEPTANCE CORPORATION—See Society for Savings Bancorp, Inc., pg. 1016
FIDELITY EXPRESS MONEY ORDER COMPANY DIVISION—See GSC Enterprises, Inc., pg. 440
FIDELITY INVESTMENTS (FMR CORP.), pg. 408
FIDUCIARY TRUST CO. INTERNATIONAL, pg. 408
FIDUCIARY TRUST COMPANY OF NEW YORK LTD.—See Fiduciary Trust Company International, pg. 409
FIDUCIARY TRUST (INTERNATIONAL) S.A.—See Fiduciary Trust Company International, pg. 409
FIE TRADING CORPORATION—See Fastec Industrial, pg. 403
FIELD CONTAINER COMPANY, L.P., pg. 409
THE FIELD CONTROLS COMPANY—See Heico Inc., pg. 525
FIELD PACKING COMPANY, pg. 409
FIELD PUBLICATIONS—See K-III Communications Corporation, pg. 611
FIELDALE CORPORATION, pg. 409
FIELDING TRAVEL BOOKS—See The Hearst Corporation, pg. 521
FIELDS & DEVEREAUX/HEPY, INC.—See Harley Ellington Pierce Yee Associates, Inc., pg. 509
FIESTA MART INC., pg. 409
FIFTH AVENUE HOSPITAL—See Brim, Inc., pg. 176
57TH FIGHTER GROUP OF ATLANTA, INC.—See Specialty Restaurants Corporation, pg. 1028
56TH FIGHTER GROUP OF LONG ISLAND, INC.—See Specialty Restaurants Corporation, pg. 1029
THE FIGARO COMPANY, INC., pg. 409
FIKE CORPORATION, pg. 409
FILA FITNESS LTD.—See MacAndrews & Forbes Holdings Inc., pg. 695
FILBERT CORP. (MAIN OFFICE)—See Vilter Manufacturing Corporation, pg. 1152
FILCO, INC., pg. 409
FILENE RESEARCH INSTITUTE—See Credit Union National Association, pg. 298
FILKO/COBRA, INC.—See F & B Manufacturing Co., pg. 393
FILL-RITE DIVISION—See Tuthill Corporation, pg. 1120
FILMCO INDUSTRIES, INC.—See Envirodyne Industries, Inc., pg. 383
FILMCO INDUSTRIES INC.—See Thermwell Products Co., Inc., pg. 1092
FIMBEL DOOR CORPORATION, pg. 409
FINAGRAIN, CIE COMMERCIALE AGRICOLE ET FINANCIERE S.A.—See Continental Grain Company, pg. 279
FINAL ART—See Backer Spielvogel Bates Worldwide, Inc., pg. 111
THE FINALS, LTD.—See Andmore Sportswear Corporation, pg. 74
FINANCIAL AIMS CORPORATION—See D.A. Davidson & Co., pg. 318
FINANCIAL ASSOCIATES, pg. 410
FINANCIAL LIFE COMPANIES, INC.—See North Central Life Insurance Companies, pg. 813
FINANCIAL NETWORK INVESTMENT, pg. 410
FINANCIAL PROTECTION SERVICES INC., pg. 410
FINANCIAL RESOURCES GROUP—See Globe Mortgage Company, pg. 464
FINANCIAL WORLD PARTNERS, pg. 410
FINANCIERE CREDIT SUISSE-FIRST BOSTON—See CS First Boston Group, Inc., pg. 204
FINCH, PRUYN & CO., INC., pg. 410
FINDLAY INDUSTRIES, INC., pg. 410
WALLY FINDLAY GALLERIES INTERNATIONAL, pg. 410
FINDLEY ADHESIVES, INC., pg. 410
FINDLEY EURO BV—See Findley Adhesives, Inc., pg. 410
FINDLEY FRANCE SA—See Findley Adhesives, Inc., pg. 411
J.H. FINDORFF & SON, INC., pg. 411
FINE ORGANICS CORP., pg. 411
M. FINE & SONS MANUFACTURING CO., INC., pg. 411
FINELPAC B.V.—See AXIA Incorporated, pg. 8
FINESILVER MANUFACTURING COMPANY, pg. 411
FINGER FURNITURE COMPANY, INC., pg. 411
FINGER LAKES PRINTING COMPANY—See Independent Publications, Inc., pg. 565
FINGERLE LUMBER CO., pg. 411
FINISHLINE INDUSTRIES INC. OF ARIZONA—See John S. Frey Enterprises, pg. 433
FINISHLINE INDUSTRIES INC. OF GEORGIA—See John S. Frey Enterprises, pg. 433
FINKEL OUTDOOR PRODUCTS OF CALIFORNIA—See CC Industries, Inc., pg. 200
FINKEL OUTDOOR PRODUCTS OF FLORIDA—See CC Industries, Inc., pg. 200
FINKEL OUTDOOR PRODUCTS, INC.—See CC Industries, Inc., pg. 200
A. FINKL & SONS CO., pg. 411
FINLAY ENTERPRISES, INC., pg. 411
FINLAY FINE JEWELRY—See Finlay Enterprises, Inc., pg. 411
FINLEY FARMERS GRAIN ELEVATOR COMPANY, pg. 411
FINNAD COMMUNICATIONS—See Backer Spielvogel Bates Worldwide, Inc., pg. 111
FINNAREN & HALEY, INC., pg. 411
FINOPAC APS—See AXIA Incorporated, pg. 8
FINORA COMPANY, INC.—See Norfoods, Inc., pg. 810
FIRE CONTROL INSTRUMENTS, INC., pg. 411
FIRELINE CO.—See Plibrico Co., pg. 877
FIRET, B.V.—See Farley Industries, pg. 400
FIROILLO A. CO. INC.—See Seaboard Flour Corporation, pg. 984
FIRST ABILENE BANKSHARES, INC., pg. 411
FIRST ADVANTAGE MORTGAGE CORPORATION—See First American Bankshares, Inc., pg. 412
FIRST AMERICAN BANK OF APOSTLE ISLANDS—See Bremer Financial Corporation, pg. 173
FIRST AMERICAN BANK OF GEORGIA, N.A.—See First American Bankshares, Inc., pg. 412
FIRST AMERICAN BANK OF MARYLAND—See First American Bankshares, Inc., pg. 412
FIRST AMERICAN BANK METRO—See Bremer Financial Corporation, pg. 173
FIRST AMERICAN BANK, N.A., WASHINGTON, D.C.—See First American Bankshares, Inc., pg. 412
FIRST AMERICAN BANK OF NEW YORK—See First American Bankshares, Inc., pg. 412
FIRST AMERICAN BANK OF VIRGINIA—See First American Bankshares, Inc., pg. 412
FIRST AMERICAN BANK SOUTHWEST—See Bremer Financial Corporation, pg. 173
FIRST AMERICAN BANK & TRUST—See Bremer Financial Corporation, pg. 173
FIRST AMERICAN BANK & TRUST—See Bremer Financial Corporation, pg. 173
FIRST AMERICAN BANKSHARES, INC., pg. 412
FIRST AMERICAN CAPITAL BANK—See Southern California Bancorp, pg. 1020
FIRST AMERICAN INFORMATION SERVICES, INC.—See Bremer Financial Corporation, pg. 173
FIRST AMERICAN INSURANCE AGENCIES, INC.—See Bremer Financial Corporation, pg. 173
FIRST AMERICAN INTERNATIONAL BANK—See First American Bankshares, Inc., pg. 412
FIRST AMERICAN METRO CORP.—See First American Bankshares, Inc., pg. 412
FIRST AMERICAN TRUST COMPANY OF MINNESOTA—See Bremer Financial Corporation, pg. 173
FIRST BOSTON ASSET MANAGEMENT CORPORATION—See CS First Boston Group, Inc., pg. 204
FIRST BOSTON CANADA LIMITED—See CS First Boston Group, Inc., pg. 204
THE FIRST BOSTON CORPORATION—See CS First Boston Group, Inc., pg. 203
FIRST BOSTON INTERNATIONAL LIMITED—See CS First Boston Group, Inc., pg. 204
FIRST BOSTON (JAPAN) LIMITED—See CS First Boston Group, Inc., pg. 204
FIRST BOSTON (PUERTO RICO), INC.—See CS First Boston Group, Inc., pg. 204
FIRST BOSTON SECURITIES CORPORATION—See CS First Boston Group, Inc., pg. 204
FIRST CHOICE HOMES—See Jewell Building Systems, pg. 594
FIRST CITIZENS BANK, N.A.—See Horizon Bancorp, pg. 544
FIRST COLUMBIA ESCROW, INC.—See Washington Mutual Savings Bank, pg. 1166
FIRST COMPUTER CORPORATION, pg. 412
FIRST CONNECTICUT SBIC, pg. 412
FIRST DATABANK—See The Hearst Corporation, pg. 522
FIRST DISTRICT ASSOCIATION, pg. 412
FIRST ELECTRIC COOPERATIVE, pg. 412
1ST FAMILY TRAVELERS HAWAII, pg. 412
FIRST FEDERAL OF MICHIGAN—See FirstFed Michigan Corporation, pg. 414
FIRST FEDERAL SAVINGS AND LOAN ASSN. OF ROCHESTER, pg. 413
FIRST FINANCIAL GROUP, INC., pg. 413
FIRST FLORIDA EQUITIES, LTD., pg. 413
FIRST FRANKLIN FINANCIAL CORP.—See 1st Franklin Corporation, pg. 413
1ST FRANKLIN CORPORATION, pg. 413
FIRST GRAY LINE CORPORATION, pg. 413
FIRST INTERNATIONAL REINSURANCE COMPANY—See Geneve Corporation, pg. 451
FIRST KENTUCKY TRUST COMPANY—See First National Bank of Louisville, pg. 413
FIRST LAND & DEVELOPMENT, INC.—See Adler & Shaykin, pg. 18
FIRST MOUNT JOY CORPORATION, pg. 413
FIRST NATIONAL BANK IN CLEBURNE—See First Abilene Bankshares, Inc., pg. 412
FIRST NATIONAL BANK IN CHICAGO HEIGHTS—See GreatBanc, Inc., pg. 483
FIRST NATIONAL BANK OF ABILENE—See First Abilene Bankshares, Inc., pg. 412
FIRST NATIONAL BANK OF BLUE ISLAND—See Great Lakes Financial Resources, Inc., pg. 481
FIRST NATIONAL BANK OF CENTRAL CALIFORNIA—See Pacific Capital Bancorp, pg. 839
FIRST NATIONAL BANK OF LOUISVILLE, pg. 413
FIRST NATIONAL BANK OF SWEETWATER—See First Abilene Bankshares, Inc., pg. 412
FIRST PYRAMID LIFE INSURANCE COMPANY OF AMERICA—See Victory Financial Group, Inc., pg. 1150
FIRST SIGNATURE BANK & TRUST CO.—See John Hancock Mutual Life Insurance Company, pg. 596
FIRST SOUTHWEST COMPANY, pg. 413
FIRST STATE FEDERAL SAVINGS & LOAN, pg. 413
FIRST STATE PAPER, INC.—See Central Paper Company, pg. 234
FIRST TRUST SAVINGS BANK—See Guarantee Title Co., Inc., pg. 491
FIRST UNITED SMALL BUSINESS INVESTMENT CO.—See James Ferrera & Sons, Inc., pg. 407
FIRST WORTHING, pg. 414
FIRSTATE SERVICES, INC.—See First State Federal Savings & Loan, pg. 414
FIRSTFED MICHIGAN CORPORATION, pg. 414
FISAX—See AXIA Incorporated, pg. 9
FISCA OIL CO., INC., pg. 414
FISCHBACH & DOUGHERTY, INC., pg. 414
DAVE FISCHBEIN CO.—See AXIA Incorporated, pg. 8
GEORG FISCHER AMASTEEL S.A.—See Ervin Industries, Inc., pg. 388
FISCHER LIME & CEMENT COMPANY, pg. 414
L. FISH CORPORATION, pg. 414
FISH ENGINEERING & CONSTRUCTION, INC., pg. 414
FISH INTERNATIONAL CO.—See Fish Engineering & Construction, Inc., pg. 414
FISH INTERNATIONAL ENGINEERS—See Fish Engineering & Construction, Inc., pg. 414
FISH SERVICE CORPORATION—See Fish Engineering & Construction, Inc., pg. 414
FISHER BROADCASTING, INC.—See Fisher Companies, Inc., pg. 415
FISHER COMPANIES, INC., pg. 414
FISHER GRAPHIC INDUSTRIES, pg. 415
FISHER MILLS, INC.—See Fisher Companies, Inc., pg. 415
FISHER PEN CO. OF NEVADA—See Fisher Pen Company, pg. 415
FISHER PEN COMPANY, pg. 415
FISHER PROPERTIES INC.—See Fisher Companies, Inc., pg. 415
FISHER SKYLIGHTS, INC., pg. 415
FISHERIES SUPPLY COMPANY, pg. 415
FISHERS BIG WHEEL INC., pg. 415
FISHING TACKLE RETAILER—See B.A.S.S., Inc., pg. 105
FISHKING PROCESSORS, INC., pg. 415
FISHMAN & TOBIN, INC., pg. 415
FISKE BROTHERS REFINING COMPANY, pg. 415
FITTS-LAWRENCE, INC.—See Lawrence Group, Inc., pg. 662
FITZGERALD ADVERTISING INC., pg. 416
FITZGERALD & CO., pg. 416
FITZGERALD & COMPANY, INC., pg. 416
FITZPATRICK & WELLER, INC., pg. 416
FITZSIMONS MANUFACTURING CO.—See Copper & Brass Sales, Inc., pg. 284
FIVE CROWNS—See Lawry's Restaurants, Inc., pg. 663
FIVE DOLLAR CLOTHING STORES, pg. 416
FIVE STAR HOMES—See Atlantic Gulf Communities Corporation, pg. 95
FLAGSHIP CITY INSURANCE COMPANY—See Erie Family Life Insurance Company, pg. 386
FLAIR COMMUNICATIONS AGENCY, INC., pg. 416
FLAIR COMMUNICATIONS AGENCY, INC.—See Flair Communications Agency, Inc., pg. 416
FLAKT INC., BAHNSON DIV., pg. 416
FLAMBEAU CORPORATION—See Nordic Group of Companies, Ltd., pg. 809

FRANKLIN FEDERAL SAVINGS ASSOCIATION, pg. 429
THE FRANKLIN MINT—See American Protection Industries, Inc., pg. 60
FRANKLIN PRESS—See Continental Graphics Holdings, Inc., pg. 279
FRANKLIN SECURITIES, INC.—See 1st Franklin Corporation, pg. 413
FRANKLIN SPORTS INDUSTRIES, pg. 429
FRANKLIN STEEL COMPANY, pg. 429
FRANKS SUPPLY COMPANY, INC., pg. 429
FRANKULIN TOOL & MFG. CO.—See Wrought Washer Mfg., Inc., pg. 1205
FRANTZ BEARING DIV.—See Frantz Manufacturing Co., pg. 430
FRANTZ EXPORT CORP.—See Frantz Manufacturing Co., pg. 430
FRANTZ MANUFACTURING CO., pg. 429
FRANZ BAKERY—See United States Bakery, pg. 1134
FRASER PAPER, LTD., pg. 430
FRAZIER-WILLIAMS CHEVROLET GEO, pg. 430
FREDERIC PRINTING COMPANY, pg. 430
FREDERICK TRADING COMPANY, pg. 430
FREDERICKSBURG AUTO AUCTION—See Cox Enterprises, Inc., pg. 293
FREDRICKSON MOTOR EXPRESS CORP., pg. 430
FREED & ASSOCIATES, pg. 430
FREEDLAND INDUSTRIES CORPORATION, pg. 430
FREEDMAN, GIBSON & WHITE INC., pg. 430
S. FREEDMAN & SONS, INC., pg. 430
FREEDOM FORGE CORPORATION, pg. 430
FREEDOM NEWSPAPERS INC., pg. 431
CARL M. FREEMAN ASSOCIATES, INC., pg. 431
FREEMAN BLANSHEI PARTNERS, pg. 431
FREEMAN COSMETIC CORP., pg. 431
FREEMAN DECORATING CO., pg. 431
FREEMAN MANUFACTURING & SUPPLY COMPANY, pg. 431
FREEMAN SHOES COMPANY, pg. 431
H. FREEMAN & SON, INC., pg. 431
FREESON ADVERTISING AGENCY, pg. 431
FREEWAY CORPORATION, pg. 432
FREEWAY ROANOKE—See Freeway Corporation, pg. 432
FREEWAY ROCKFORD—See Freeway Corporation, pg. 432
FREHNER CONSTRUCTION COMPANY, INC., pg. 432
FREMONT CANNING CO.—See The Fremont Co., pg. 432
THE FREMONT CO., pg. 432
FREMONT ELECTRIC COMPANY—See Carquest Corporation, pg. 224
FREMONT FOREST PRODUCTS, pg. 432
FRENCH & BEAN—See Associated Grocers of New England, Inc., pg. 90
I. H. FRENCH & CO. INC., pg. 432
JIM FRESARD PONTIAC BUICK, INC., pg. 432
FRESH MARK, INC., pg. 432
FRESINBRA INDUS. S.A.—See American Standard Inc., pg. 62
FRESNO AUTO DEALERS AUCTION—See Cox Enterprises, Inc., pg. 293
FREUDENBERG-NOK (MI), pg. 432
JOHN S. FREY ENTERPRISES, pg. 433
FRICKS & ASSOCIATES/ADVERTISING INC., pg. 433
FRIEDMAN BENJAMIN INC. ADV., pg. 433
FRIEDMAN, EISENSTEIN, RAEMER & SCHWARTZ, pg. 433
FRIENDLY CHEVROLET CO. INC., pg. 433
FRIENDLY HOLIDAYS INC., pg. 433
FRIENDLY ICE CREAM CORP.—See Tennessee Restaurant Corp., pg. 1087
FRIERSON MEE & HERMAN, pg. 433
FRIGID FOOD PRODUCTS, INC., pg. 433
BOB FRINK CHEVROLET G.E.O. MANAGEMENT, pg. 433
FRIONA AGRICULTURE CREDIT CORP.—See Friona Industries, L.P., pg. 434
FRIONA FEED YARD DIV.—See Friona Industries, L.P., pg. 434
FRIONA INDUSTRIES, L.P., pg. 434
FRITZ CHEMICAL COMPANY, pg. 434
FRITZ CO. INC., pg. 434
FRITZ COMPANIES, INC., pg. 434
PHILIP FRITZE & SONS, INC., pg. 434
FROG SWITCH & MANUFACTURING COMPANY, pg. 434
FRONTIER CHEVROLET CO.—See Roundtree Automotive Group, pg. 952
FRONTIER FOUNDRIES, INC., pg. 434
FRONTIER LUMBER COMPANY, INC., pg. 434
FRONTIER TRANSPORT CORPORATION—See Overland Transportation System, Inc., pg. 833
FROST COMPANY, pg. 435
FROST INC., pg. 435
JACK FROST, INC.—See JFC Inc., pg. 584
FROZEN SPECIALTIES, INC.—See Windmill Holdings Corp., pg. 1195
FRU-CON CONSTRUCTION CORPORATION, pg. 435
FRU-CON ENGINEERING INC.—See Fru-Con Construction Corporation, pg. 435
FRUIT OF THE LOOM—See Farley Industries, pg. 400
FRY/HAMMOND/BARR INCORPORATED, pg. 435
THE FRYE COMPANY, pg. 435
FT. DEARBORN LITHOGRAPH GRAPHIC ARTS DIVISION—See Fort Dearborn Lithograph Company, pg. 425
FUEL SOUTH, INC., pg. 435
FUEL SOUTH INC.—See Jones Company, Inc., pg. 603
FUGAZY INTERNATIONAL CORPORATION, pg. 435
FUGAZY LIMOUSINES—See Fugazy International Corporation, pg. 435
FUGAZY TRAVEL—See Fugazy International Corporation, pg. 435
FUGRO-MCCLELLAND HONG KONG, LTD.—See Fugro-McClelland, Inc., pg. 435
FUGRO-MCCLELLAND, INC., pg. 435
FUGRO-MCCLELLAND, LTD.—See Fugro-McClelland, Inc., pg. 436
FUGRO-MCCLELLAND MIDDLE EAST—See Fugro-McClelland, Inc., pg. 435
FUJI TRUCOLOR FOTO—See Deans Photo Service, Inc., pg. 322
FULFILLMENT UNLIMITED—See Professional Book Distributors, Inc., pg. 894
FULL CIRCLE—See CENEX (Farmers Union Central Exchange, Inc.), pg. 231
FULL CIRCLE COMMUNICATIONS—See Full Circle Media Corp., pg. 436
FULL CIRCLE MEDIA CORP., pg. 436
FULL SERVICE BEVERAGE COMPANY, pg. 436
FULL SERVICE BEVERAGE COMPANY OF COLORADO—See Full Service Beverage Company, pg. 436
THE FULLER BRUSH COMPANY, pg. 436
GEORGE A. FULLER COMPANY, pg. 436
FULLERTON METALS CO., pg. 436
FUNCTIONS—See Granger Construction Co., pg. 476
FUND MANAGEMENT CO.—See Mutual of Omaha Insurance Company, pg. 779
FUNDAMENTAL MANAGEMENT, INC.—See Industrial Wire Products Corporation, pg. 567
FUNDING SERVICES INC.—See American Office Equipment, pg. 59
FUNDSNET, INC.—See SBN System Inc., pg. 960
FUNERAL SECURITY PLANS, INC.—See D. W. Newcomer's Sons, Inc., pg. 804
FUNK & WAGNALLS CORP.—See K-III Communications Corporation, pg. 611
FURIGAS NV—See The Dyson-Kissner-Moran Corporation, pg. 358
FURMAN FOODS, INC., pg. 436
FURMAN LUMBER COMPANY, pg. 436
FURMAN, ROTH ADV., pg. 437
FURNAS ELECTRIC COMPANY, pg. 437
FURNITURE CONSULTANTS, pg. 437
FURNIVAL/STATE MACHINERY CO., pg. 437
FURR'S SUPERMARKETS, pg. 437
THE FUSCO CORPORATION, pg. 437
LOU FUSZ AUTOMOTIVE NETWORK, pg. 437
LOU FUSZ MOTOR COMPANY—See Lou Fusz Automotive Network, pg. 437
FUTTER LUMBER CORPORATION, pg. 437
FUTURE FOAM, INC., pg. 437
FUTURE FORD/HUGO INC., pg. 437
FUTURES PERSONNEL SERVICES, pg. 438
FUZERE MANUFACTURING COMPANY INC.—See Schawk, Inc., pg. 975
FYRNETICS, INC., pg. 438

G

G & A COMMUNICATIONS, pg. 438
G & L PRODUCTS—See G & L Products, Inc., pg. 438
G & L PRODUCTS, INC., pg. 438
G & W ELECTRIC CO., pg. 438
GACC HOLDING COMPANY—See American Financial Corporation, pg. 53
GAF (AUSTRALASIA) PTY. LTD.—See GAF Corporation, pg. 438
GAF (BELGIUM) N.V.—See GAF Corporation, pg. 438
GAF BROADCASTING CO., INC.—See GAF Corporation, pg. 438
GAF BUILDING MATERIALS CORPORATION—See GAF Corporation, pg. 438
GAF (CANADA) INC.—See GAF Corporation, pg. 438
GAF CORP. DE MEXICO S.A. DE C.V.—See GAF Corporation, pg. 438
GAF CORPORATION, pg. 438
GAF (DANMARK) A/S—See GAF Corporation, pg. 438
GAF (DEUTSCHLAND) GMBH—See GAF Corporation, pg. 438
GAF DO BRASIL INDUSTRIA E COMMERCIO, LTDA.—See GAF Corporation, pg. 438
GAF EXPORT CORP.—See GAF Corporation, pg. 438
GAF (FRANCE) S.A.—See GAF Corporation, pg. 438
GAF (GREAT BRITAIN) CO. LTD.—See GAF Corporation, pg. 438
GAF HULS CHEMIE GMBH—See GAF Corporation, pg. 438
GAF INSURANCE LTD.—See GAF Corporation, pg. 438
GAF INTERNATIONAL CORP.—See GAF Corporation, pg. 438
GAF (ITALIA) S.P.I.—See GAF Corporation, pg. 438
GAF (JAPAN) LTD.—See GAF Corporation, pg. 438
GAF (NEDERLAND) N.V.—See GAF Corporation, pg. 438
GAF (NEW ZEALAND) PTY., LTD.—See GAF Corporation, pg. 438
GAF NORDEN AB—See GAF Corporation, pg. 439
GAF (OSTERREICH) GMBH—See GAF Corporation, pg. 439
GAF (SINGAPORE) PTE. LTD.—See GAF Corporation, pg. 439
GAF SOUTH AFRICA (PTY.), LTD.—See GAF Corporation, pg. 439
GAF SUCURSAL EN ESPANA—See GAF Corporation, pg. 439
GAF (SWITZERLAND) AG—See GAF Corporation, pg. 439
GAI CONSULTANTS, INC., pg. 439
GAI CONSULTANTS, INC.—See GAI Consultants, Inc., pg. 439
GAI CONSULTANTS-SOUTHEAST, INC.—See GAI Consultants, Inc., pg. 439
G B STORES—See Schottenstein Stores Corporation, pg. 978
GBF/AYER—See N W Ayer Incorporated, pg. 104
GCC, INC.—See Gillett Holdings, Inc., pg. 459
G.D.C. BUSINESS SYSTEMS, INC.—See Cenvill Development Corp., pg. 236
GDE SYSTEMS—See Carlyle Holding Corporation, pg. 222
GES ENVIRONMENTAL, INC.—See W. B. Goode Company, Inc., pg. 470
GES INC., pg. 439
GF INDUSTRIES, INC., pg. 439
GF OFFICE FURNITURE—See GF Office Furniture Ltd., pg. 439
GF OFFICE FURNITURE LTD., pg. 439
GF PROPERTIES, INC.—See GF Industries, Inc., pg. 439
GFA BRANDS, INC., pg. 440
GFM INTERNATIONAL INVESTORS, LIMITED—See Metropolitan Life Insurance Co., pg. 745
GHN—See Everbrite, Inc., pg. 391
G.I. JOE'S INC., pg. 440
G.I.C. FINANCIAL SERVICES CORPORATION—See Guardian Industries Corp., pg. 492
G.L. ADVERTISING, pg. 440
G L SUB COMPANY—See The Marmon Group, Inc., pg. 712
GMI, INC.-GLASSTREAM—See General Marine Industries, Inc., pg. 450
GNC CORP—See Goshen Rubber Co., Inc., pg. 472
GNG-1, INC.—See Gillett Holdings, Inc., pg. 459
GNG-3, INC.—See Gillett Holdings, Inc., pg. 459
GNWC WIRE, CABLE & NETWORK PRODUCERS, pg. 440
GPD LIMITED, pg. 440
G&R PUBBLICITA/SUDLER & HENNESSEY—See Young & Rubicam Inc., pg. 1212
GRC RESTAURANTS, INC.—See Restaurant Enterprises Group, Inc., pg. 929
GRN CORP.—See Goshen Rubber Co., Inc., pg. 472
GS&B-LINTAS ADVERTISING, pg. 440
GSC DISTRIBUTING COMPANIES DIVISION—See GSC Enterprises, Inc., pg. 440
GSC ENTERPRISES, INC., pg. 440
GSC ENTERPRISES, INC., pg. 440
GSD&M, pg. 441
GSH CORP.—See Goshen Rubber Co., Inc., pg. 472
GSL SOLAR CONSULTANTS & ADVISORS, INC.—See Great Salt Lake Minerals & Chemicals Corp., pg. 482
GSP MARKETING SERVICES, INC., pg. 441
GWC PROPERTIES, INC.—See McCall Oil & Chemical Corp., pg. 727
GWP, INC., pg. 441
GABBERT'S, INC., pg. 441
THE GAGE COMPANY, pg. 441
GAGE FOOD PRODUCTS COMPANY—See Vincent Food Industries, Inc., pg. 1152
GAGE MARKETING GROUP, pg. 441
GAGGENAU USA CORPORATION, pg. 441
GAI'S SEATTLE FRENCH BAKING CO., INC., pg. 441
GALARDI GROUP, INC., pg. 441
GALAXY BUSINESS PRODUCTS—See Metpac, Ltd., pg. 742
GALENPHARMA, INC.—See GenDerm Corporation, pg. 448
GALESI ENTERPRISES—See Rotterdam Ventures Inc., pg. 951
R. J. GALLAGHER CO., pg. 441
GALLAGHER-KAISER CORP., pg. 441
E & J GALLO WINERY, pg. 441
GAME TIME, INC., pg. 442
GAMEPRO—See International Data Group, pg. 576
GAMMA ONE, INC., pg. 442
GANAHL LUMBER COMPANY, pg. 442
GANNETT FLEMING AFFILIATES, INC., pg. 442
GUY GANNETT PUBLISHING COMPANY, pg. 442
GANNETT TRANSIT, pg. 442
GANS INK & SUPPLY COMPANY, INC., pg. 442
THE GARBER COMPANY, pg. 442
GARBER, GOODMAN ADVERTISING, INC., pg. 443
GARCY CORPORATION—See RHC/Spacemaster Corporation, pg. 907
GARCY SPECIALTY FIXTURES—See RHC/Spacemaster Corporation, pg. 907
GARCY/SLP—See RHC/Spacemaster Corporation, pg. 907
GARDEN CITY COMPLEX—See Sunflower Electric Power Corporation, pg. 1060
GARDEN STATE CONVERTERS—See Triangle Marketing Corp., pg. 1112
THE GARDEN STATE PLAZA CORP.—See R. H. Macy & Co., Inc., pg. 699
GARDEN WAY, INC., pg. 443
GARDINER METAL COMPANY, pg. 443
GARDINER SOLDER COMPANY—See Gardiner Metal Company, pg. 443
GARDNER COMMUNICATIONS, INC., pg. 443
GARDNER PUBLICATIONS, INC., pg. 443
GARED SPORTS INC.—See Nixdorff Krein Industries Inc., pg. 807
GARELICK FARMS, INC., pg. 443
GARIBOLDI PARISI VERGA/INTERAD—See The Lowe Group, pg. 685
GARNAC GRAIN CO., INC.—See Norfoods, Inc., pg. 810
GARNEY COMPANIES, INC.—See Garney Holding Company, Inc., pg. 443
GARNEY HOLDING COMPANY, INC., pg. 443
GARRISON-LONTINE ADVERTISING, pg. 443
GARSITE/TSR, INC., pg. 443
GARSITE/TSR, INC.—See Garsite/TSR, Inc., pg. 443
GARTNER GROUP, INC., pg. 443
GARVEY ELEVATORS INC., pg. 443
GARVEY GRAIN—See Garvey Industries, Inc., pg. 444
GARVEY INDUSTRIES, INC., pg. 443
GARVEY INTERNATIONAL, INC.—See Garvey Industries, Inc., pg. 444
GARVIN FIRE PROTECTION SYSTEMS, pg. 444
THE GARY GROUP, pg. 444
GARY METALS CO., INC.—See Primary Industries Corporation, pg. 889
THE GARY-WILLIAMS COMPANY, pg. 444
GARY-WILLIAMS ENERGY CORPORATION—See The Gary-Williams Company, pg. 444
GAS EQUIPMENT COMPANY, INC., pg. 444
GAS-FIRED PRODUCTS, INC., pg. 444

GAS-FIRED PRODUCTS (U.K.) LTD.—See Gas-Fired Products, Inc., pg. 444
GASE BAKERY CO.—See Perfection Bakeries Inc., pg. 861
GAST MFG. CORP., pg. 444
GASTON COUNTY CARPET DIV.—See Gaston County Dyeing Machine Co., pg. 444
GASTON COUNTY DYEING MACHINE CO., pg. 444
GATE CITY BEVERAGE DISTRIBUTORS, pg. 444
GATE PETROLEUM COMPANY, pg. 445
GATES CANADA INC.—See The Gates Corporation, pg. 445
THE GATES CORPORATION, pg. 445
GATES DO BRASIL IND. E COM. LTDA.—See The Gates Corporation, pg. 445
GATES ENERGY PRODUCTS, INC.—See The Gates Corporation, pg. 445
GATES EUROPE N.V.—See The Gates Corporation, pg. 445
GATES FORMED-FIBRE PRODUCTS—See The Gates Corporation, pg. 445
GATES HYDRAULICS LTD.—See The Gates Corporation, pg. 445
GATES LAND CO.—See The Gates Corporation, pg. 445
GATES, MCDONALD & CO.—See Nationwide Mutual Insurance Company, pg. 795
GATES POWER DRIVE PRODUCTS, INC.—See The Gates Corporation, pg. 445
THE GATES RUBBER COMPANY—See The Gates Corporation, pg. 445
THE GATES RUBBER COMPANY LIMITED—See The Gates Corporation, pg. 445
THE GATES RUBBER COMPANY—See The Gates Corporation, pg. 445
GATES RUBBER DE MEXICO—See The Gates Corporation, pg. 445
GATES VULCA AUTOMOTIVE PRODUCTS DIVISION—See The Gates Corporation, pg. 445
GATEWAY APPAREL, INC., pg. 445
GATEWAY COMMUNICATIONS—See Macromedia Inc., pg. 698
GATEWAY PRESS, INC., pg. 446
GATEWAY SAFETY SYSTEMS CO.—See Takatta Inc., pg. 1077
GATEWAY 2000, pg. 446
GATOR FREIGHTWAYS, INC., pg. 446
GATOR INDUSTRIES INC., pg. 446
FRED P. GATTAS COMPANY, INC., pg. 446
GAY JOHNSON'S INC., pg. 446
GAYLORD BROADCASTING CO.—See Gaylord Entertainment Co., pg. 446
GAYLORD CENTRAL PRINTING & PUBLISHING DIV.—See Gaylord Printing, Inc., pg. 447
GAYLORD ENTERTAINMENT CO., pg. 446
GAYLORD LITHOGRAPH DIV.-DETROIT—See Gaylord Printing, Inc., pg. 447
GAYLORD PRINTING, INC., pg. 446
GAYMAR INDUSTRIES, INC., pg. 447
GAZETTE COMPANY, INC., pg. 447
THE GAZETTE—See Landmark Communications, Inc., pg. 655
GEAR HEADQUARTERS INC.—See Headco Industries, Inc., pg. 520
GEARON HOFFMAN CONLON & NYE ADVERTISING, INC., pg. 447
GEBHARDT INDUSTRIAL REFRIGERATION, INC.—See Vilter Manufacturing Corporation, pg. 1152
GEBO DISTRIBUTING CO., INC., pg. 447
GEE BEE DEPARTMENT STORES—See Schottenstein Stores Corporation, pg. 978
GEE BEE JR. FAMILY APPAREL STORE—See Schottenstein Stores Corporation, pg. 978
GEE CEE CAP COMPANY—See The Vernon Company, pg. 1148
GREEN INTERNATIONAL, INC.—See Green Holdings, Inc., pg. 484
GEER, DUBOIS INC., pg. 447
GEIGER BROTHERS, pg. 447
GEINDRE MARKETING SERVICES—See Backer Spielvogel Bates Worldwide, Inc., pg. 111
STEPHEN L. GELLER INC., pg. 447
GELMART INDUSTRIES PHILIPPINES, INC.—See Playtex Apparel Inc., pg. 876
GEM-DANDY, INC., pg. 447
GEM, INCORPORATED, pg. 447
GEM INDUSTRIES FINANCE CORPORATION, pg. 447
GEM INDUSTRIES, INC.—See Gem Industries Finance Corporation, pg. 447
GEM SOUTHEAST, INC.—See Gem Industries Finance Corporation, pg. 447
GEM TOP EAST INC—See Gem Top Mfg., Inc., pg. 448
GEM TOP MFG., INC., pg. 448
GEMINI ALUMINUM CORPORATION, pg. 448
GEMINI CONSULTING, pg. 448
GEMINI CONSULTING-LONDON—See Gemini Consulting, pg. 448
GENCON SERVICES, INC.—See George W. Auch Co., pg. 98
GENDERM CORPORATION, pg. 448
GENELCO, INC.—See General American Life Insurance Co., pg. 448
GENERAL AEROSPACE MATERIALS CORPORATION, pg. 448
GENERAL ALUM & CHEMICAL, pg. 448
GENERAL AMERICAN DOOR COMPANY—See Merchant Capital Group Ltd, pg. 739
GENERAL AMERICAN LIFE INSURANCE CO., pg. 448
GENERAL AUTOMATION, INC., pg. 448
GENERAL AUTOMOTIVE CORPORATION, pg. 448
GENERAL AUTOMOTIVE SPECIALTY CO., INC., pg. 449
GENERAL BINDING CORPORATION—See Lane Industries, Inc., pg. 656
GENERAL BINDING CORPORATION—See Lane Industries, Inc., pg. 657
GENERAL BUSINESS SERVICES, INC., pg. 449
GENERAL CHEMICAL CORPORATION—See New Hampshire Oak, pg. 801
GENERAL COMMERCIAL PACKAGING, INC.—See The Suddath Companies, pg. 1056
GENERAL COMPUTER CORP. INC., pg. 449
GENERAL DRUG CO., pg. 449
GENERAL ELECTRIC MASTER RETIREMENT TRUST, pg. 449
GENERAL FELT INDUSTRIES, INC.—See 21 International Holdings, Inc., pg. 1121
GENERAL FELT INDUSTRIES, INC.—See 21 International Holdings, Inc., pg. 1121
GENERAL GENERIC TRUCKING DIV.—See Accra Pac Group, pg. 11
GENERAL GROWTH CENTER COMPANIES, INC.—See General Growth Companies, Inc., pg. 449
GENERAL GROWTH COMPANIES, INC., pg. 449
GENERAL GROWTH OF CALIFORNIA, INC.—See General Growth Companies, Inc., pg. 449
GENERAL HARDWARE DISTRIBUTORS—See Alaska Industrial Hardware Inc., pg. 30
GENERAL HOMES CORPORATION, pg. 449
GENERAL HOSPITAL—See Brim, Inc., pg. 176
GENERAL IMPLEMENT DISTRIBUTORS—See Arnold Machinery Co., pg. 85
GENERAL INSTALLATION CO.—See J. S. Alberici Construction Co., Inc., pg. 31
GENERAL INSTRUMENT CORPORATION—See Forstmann Little & Co., pg. 425
GENERAL LATEX & CHEMICAL CORPORATION, pg. 449
GENERAL MACHINERY CO.—See Wheaton Inc., pg. 1184
GENERAL MARINE INDUSTRIES, INC., pg. 449
GENERAL MEDIA PUBLISHING GROUP, pg. 450
GENERAL MEDIA SERVICES, INC., pg. 450
GENERAL METALCRAFT, INC., pg. 450
GENERAL PARTS, INC.—See Carquest Corporation, pg. 224
GENERAL POWER EQUIPMENT CO.—See Cotter & Company, pg. 288
GENERAL REFRACTORIES CO. OF CANADA, LTD.—See Belmont Industries, Inc., pg. 137
GENERAL REFRACTORIES CO., U. S. REFRACTORIES DIV.—See Belmont Industries, Inc., pg. 136
GENERAL SAFETY CORPORATION, pg. 450
GENERAL SCIENCES CORP.—See Science Applications International Corporation, pg. 981
GENERAL SERVICES CORPORATION, pg. 450
GENERAL SHIP CORPORATION, pg. 450
GENERAL SPORTCRAFT COMPANY LTD., pg. 450
GENERAL SPRING, INC., pg. 450
GENERAL TEXTILES, pg. 451
GENERAL TIME CORP., pg. 451
GENERAL TOOLS MFG., pg. 451
GENERAL TRAVEL SERVICES, INC.—See Washington Mutual Savings Bank, pg. 1166
GENERAL WELDING SUPPLY CORPORATION, pg. 451
GENERAL WHOLESALE COMPANY, INC., pg. 451
GENERAL WIG MANUFACTURERS, INC.—See MacAndrews & Forbes Holdings Inc., pg. 695
GENERATION METALS CORP., pg. 451
GENERRA SPORTSWEAR COMPANY, INC., pg. 451
GENERRA SPORTSWEAR (HONG KONG) LTD.—See Generra Sportswear Company, Inc., pg. 451
GENESEE METAL STAMPINGS, INC., pg. 451
GENEVA CORPORATION, pg. 451
GENEVAR ENTERPRISES, pg. 451
GENEVE CAPITAL GROUP INC.—See Geneve Corporation, pg. 451
GENEVE CORPORATION, pg. 451
THE GENIE COMPANY, pg. 452
GENIE MANUFACTURING CORP., pg. 452
GENOVA HARTWICK JULIANO, INC., pg. 452
GENOVA PRODUCTS, INC., pg. 452
GENTEX OPTICS, INC., pg. 452
GENTLEMEN'S QUARTERLY—See Advance Publications Inc., pg. 19
GENTRY INSURANCE AGENCY, INC.—See Mayflower Transit, Inc., pg. 725
GENTZ INDUSTRIES INC.—See Freedom Forge Corporation, pg. 431
GENUARDI SUPER MARKETS INC., pg. 452
GEO-CENTERS, INC., pg. 452
GEOGRAPHIC MARKETING GROUP (GMG), pg. 452
GEOMEDIA S.A.—See Backer Spielvogel Bates Worldwide, Inc., pg. 111
GEORGE LITHOGRAPH, pg. 452
GEORGE TRANSFER, INC., pg. 453
GEORGETOWN INDUSTRIES, INC., pg. 453
GEORGETOWN MARBURY HOTEL—See Taj International Hotels, pg. 1076
GEORGETOWN PARTNERS, INC.—See Gould Investors, L.P., pg. 473
GEORGIA AUCTION SERVICES, INC.—See Cox Enterprises, Inc., pg. 293
GEORGIA AUCTION SERVICES, INC. D/B/A COMMUNITY AUTION RESALE SERVICES—See Cox Enterprises, Inc., pg. 293
GEORGIA CROWN DISTRIBUTING, pg. 453
GEORGIA DEALERS AUTO AUCTION—See Cox Enterprises, Inc., pg. 293
GEORGIA DUCK & CORDAGE MILLS, pg. 453
GEORGIA IRON WORKS CO., pg. 453
THE GEORGIA MARBLE COMPANY, pg. 453
GEORGIA STONE INDUSTRIES, INC.—See New England Stone Industries, Inc., pg. 800
GEORGIA TELEVISION COMPANY—See Cox Enterprises, Inc., pg. 292
GEORGIA WOODLANDS RAILROAD CO.—See Chicago West Pullman Corporation, pg. 246
GEORGIAN PRESS, INC., pg. 453
GEORGIE BOY MANUFACTURING, INC., pg. 453
GEOSAFE CORPORATION—See Battelle Memorial Institute, pg. 126
GEO-YOUNG & RUBICAM—See Young & Rubicam Inc., pg. 1212
GERBER ADVERTISING, pg. 453
GERBER AGRI-EXPORT INC.—See J. Gerber & Co. Inc., pg. 454
J. GERBER & CO. INC., pg. 453
GERBER PLUMBING FIXTURES CORPORATION, pg. 454
GERBIG, SNELL/WEISHEIMER & ASSOC., INC., pg. 454
GERLAND CORP., pg. 454
GERRARD AND COMPANY, pg. 454
GERRITY CO., INC., pg. 454
GERRITY LUMBER CO.—See Gerrity Co., Inc., pg. 454
GERSON & GERSON, INC., pg. 454
THE GERSTENSLAGER COMPANY, pg. 454
GESELLSCHAFT FUR ELEKTROMETALLURGIE M.B.H.—See Metallurg, Inc., pg. 742
GESSNER INDUSTRIES, pg. 455
GESTRO HORNE—See Backer Spielvogel Bates Worldwide, Inc., pg. 111
GETMAN CORPORATION, pg. 455
THE GETZ CORPORATION—See The Marmon Group, Inc., pg. 712
GEUPEL DEMARS, INC.—See The DeMars Corp., pg. 328
GEYER-MCALLISTER PUBLICATIONS, INC., pg. 455
GHAFARI ASSOCIATES, INC., pg. 455
GHAFARI ASSOCIATES, INC.—See Ghafari Associates, Inc., pg. 455
GHENT MANUFACTURING, INC., pg. 455
GIANETTINO & MEREDITH ADVERTISING, pg. 455
GIANT EAGLE, INC., pg. 455
GIANT EAGLE MARKET CO.—See Giant Eagle, Inc., pg. 456
GIANT MARKETS INC., pg. 456
THE GIANTS OF LITERATURE SERIES—See Walter J. Black, Inc., pg. 154
THE GIARDINI/RUSSELL GROUP, pg. 456
ROBERT GIBB & SONS, INC., pg. 456
GIBBS DIECASTING ALUMINUM CORP.—See George Koch Sons, Inc., pg. 639
GIBBS & HILL, INC.—See Hill International Inc., pg. 535
GIBBS WIRE & STEEL COMPANY, INC., pg. 456
GIBBS WIRE & STEEL COMPANY OF CANADA LTD.—See Gibbs Wire & Steel Company, Inc., pg. 456
GIBRALTAR CASUALTY CO.—See The Prudential Insurance Company of America, pg. 897
GIBRALTAR STEEL CORP., pg. 456
GIBSON CONTINER DIVISON—See Weston Paper & Manufacturing Co., pg. 1183
THE GIBSON GROUP INC., pg. 456
GIBSON GUITAR CORPORATION, INC., pg. 456
THE GIBSON-HOMANS COMPANY, pg. 457
GIBSON-HOMANS CONYERS DIV.—See The Gibson-Homans Company, pg. 457
GIBSON-HOMANS OF CANADA LTD.—See The Gibson-Homans Company, pg. 457
GIBSON WINE COMPANY, pg. 457
GIFFELS ASSOCIATES, INC., pg. 457
GIFFELS HOYEM BASSO, INC.—See Giffels Associates, Inc., pg. 457
GIFTREPS NORTHWEST—See Austin Sculpture, pg. 100
GIGANTE VAZ & PARTNERS ADVERTISING, INC., pg. 457
GIGI—See Ardell International, Inc., pg. 81
GILBANE BUILDING COMPANY, pg. 457
GILBANE PROPERTIES, INC.—See Gilbane Building Company, pg. 457
GILBERT & BENNETT, pg. 457
N. G. GILBERT CORPORATION, pg. 458
GILBERT MFG. CORP., pg. 458
GILBERT/ROBINSON, INC., pg. 458
GILBERT, WHITNEY & JOHNS, INC., pg. 458
GILCREST STORAGE—See The Fred W. Albrecht Grocery Co., pg. 31
GILES & RANSOME, INC., pg. 458
M.C. GILL CORPORATION, pg. 458
GILLESPIE ADVERTISING, INC.—See The Gillespie Organization, Inc., pg. 458
THE GILLESPIE ORGANIZATION, INC., pg. 458
GILLESPIE PUBLIC RELATIONS, INC.—See The Gillespie Organization, Inc., pg. 458
GILLETT BROADCASTING, INC.—See Gillett Holdings, Inc., pg. 459
GILLETT BROADCASTING OF MARYLAND, INC. WMAR-TV—See Gillett Holdings, Inc., pg. 459
GILLETT BROADCASTING OF TENNESSEE, INC.—See Gillett Holdings, Inc., pg. 459
GILLETT CORPORATION—See Gillett Holdings, Inc., pg. 459
GILLETT-GP CORPORATION—See Gillett Holdings, Inc., pg. 459
GILLETT GROUP, INC.—See Gillett Holdings, Inc., pg. 459
GILLETT GROUP MANAGEMENT, INC.—See Gillett Holdings, Inc., pg. 459
GILLETT HOLDINGS, INC., pg. 458
GILLETT PRODUCTIONS, INC.—See Gillett Holdings, Inc., pg. 459
GILLIS ADVERTISING & PUBLIC RELATIONS, pg. 459
GILLOGLY CHEVROLET INC., pg. 459
MARTY GILMAN, INC., pg. 459
GILMAN PAPER CO., pg. 459
GILMORE BROS., INC., pg. 459
GILMORE ENVELOPE CORP., pg. 460
GILPATRICK CONSTRUCTION COMPANY, pg. 460
GILSTER MARY LEE CORP., pg. 460
GILVIN-TERRILL INC., pg. 460
GINGISS INTERNATIONAL, pg. 460
GINO'S EAST/ROLLING MEADOWS—See Lettuce Entertain You Enterprises, Inc., pg. 669
GINSBERG'S INSTITUTIONAL FOODS, INC., pg. 460
GIRGENTI, HUGHES, BUTLER & MCDOWELL, pg. 460
GISH, SHERWOOD & FRIENDS, INC., pg. 460
GISMO INC.—See Guarantee Electrical Company, pg. 491
GIT N GO, INC.—See Hale-Halsell Company, pg. 501

GITANO BOY'S & MEN'S DIVISION—See Gitano Group Inc., pg. 460
GITANO GIRL'S DIVISION—See Gitano Group Inc., pg. 460
GITANO GROUP INC., pg. 460
GIUMARRA VINEYARDS, pg. 460
GLAMORISE FOUNDATIONS, INC., pg. 460
GLAMOUR—See Advance Publications Inc., pg. 19
GLASS PRODUCTS, INC.—See AFG Industries, Inc., pg. 3
GLASSEAL PRODUCTS, INC.—See HCC Industries, pg. 496
GLASTEEL INDUSTRIAL LAMINATES, pg. 461
GLASTEEL TENNESSEE, INC.—See Glasteel Industrial Laminates, pg. 461
GLASTRON BOATS—See Minstar, Inc., pg. 759
GLAZERS WHOLESALE DRUG CO. INC., pg. 461
GLEN ELLEN WINERY, pg. 461
GLEN OAKS INDUSTRIES, INC., pg. 461
GLEN RAVEN MARKETING CORP.—See Glen Raven Mills, Inc., pg. 461
GLEN RAVEN MARKETING CORPORATION—See Glen Raven Mills, Inc., pg. 461
GLEN RAVEN MARKETING CORPORATION—See Glen Raven Mills, Inc., pg. 461
GLEN RAVEN MILLS, INC., pg. 461
GLEN RAVEN MILLS, INC.—See Glen Raven Mills, Inc., pg. 461
GLEN RAVEN MILLS, INC.-KINSTON PLANT—See Glen Raven Mills, Inc., pg. 461
GLEN RAVEN MILLS, INC.-CONSUMER PRODUCTS DIVISION—See Glen Raven Mills, Inc., pg. 461
GLEN RAVEN MILLS, INC.-CONSUMER PRODUCTS DIVISION—See Glen Raven Mills, Inc., pg. 461
GLEN RAVEN MILLS, INC.-CUSTOM FABRICS DIV.—See Glen Raven Mills, Inc., pg. 462
GLEN RAVEN MILLS, INC.-CUSTOM FABRICS DIV., EQUINOX PLANT—See Glen Raven Mills, Inc., pg. 462
GLEN RAVEN MILLS, INC.-CUSTOM FABRICS DIV., EQUINOX FINISHING PLANT—See Glen Raven Mills, Inc., pg. 462
GLEN RAVEN MILLS, INC.-CUSTOM FABRICS DIVISION—See Glen Raven Mills, Inc., pg. 461
GLEN RAVEN MILLS, INC.-CUSTOM FABRICS DIVISION-EQUINOX PLANT—See Glen Raven Mills, Inc., pg. 461
GLEN RAVEN MILLS, INC.-CUSTOM FABRICS DIVISION-EQUINOX FINISHING PLANT—See Glen Raven Mills, Inc., pg. 461
GLEN RAVEN MILLS, INC.-FILAMENT FABRICS DIV.—See Glen Raven Mills, Inc., pg. 462
GLEN RAVEN MILLS, INC.-GLEN TOUCH PLANT—See Glen Raven Mills, Inc., pg. 461
GLEN RAVEN MILLS, INC.-GLEN TOUCH PLANT—See Glen Raven Mills, Inc., pg. 462
GLEN RAVEN MILLS, INC.-GLENSPUN DIV.—See Glen Raven Mills, Inc., pg. 462
GLEN RAVEN MILLS, INC.-GLENSPUN DIVISION—See Glen Raven Mills, Inc., pg. 461
GLEN RAVEN MILLS, INC.-KINGSTON PLANT—See Glen Raven Mills, Inc., pg. 462
GLEN RAVEN MILLS, INC.-NORLINA PLANT—See Glen Raven Mills, Inc., pg. 461
GLEN RAVEN MILLS, INC.-NORLINA PLANT—See Glen Raven Mills, Inc., pg. 462
GLEN RAVEN MILLS, INC.-PARK AVE. FINISHING DIVISION—See Glen Raven Mills, Inc., pg. 461
GLEN RAVEN MILLS, INC.-TEXTURED MILLS GROUP, GLEN TOUCH DIV.—See Glen Raven Mills, Inc., pg. 462
GLEN RAVEN MILLS, INC.-TEXTURED YARN GROUP, NORLINA DIV.—See Glen Raven Mills, Inc., pg. 462
GLEN RAVEN MILLS, INC.-TEXTURED YARN GROUP-GLEN TOUCH DIVISION—See Glen Raven Mills, Inc., pg. 461
GLEN RAVEN MILLS, INC.-TEXTURED YARN GROUP-NORLINA DIVISION—See Glen Raven Mills, Inc., pg. 461
GLEN RAVEN MILLS, INC.-TRANSPORTATION DIV.—See Glen Raven Mills, Inc., pg. 462
GLEN RAVEN MILLS, INC.-TRANSPORTATION DIVISION—See Glen Raven Mills, Inc., pg. 462
GLEN RAVEN MILLS, INC.-ULTRASPUN PLANT—See Glen Raven Mills, Inc., pg. 461
GLEN RAVEN MILLS, INC.-ULTRASPUN PLANT—See Glen Raven Mills, Inc., pg. 462
GLEN RAVEN MILLS MARKETING CORP.—See Glen Raven Mills, Inc., pg. 461
GLEN RAVEN MILLS, INC.-FILAMENT FABRICS DIVISION—See Glen Raven Mills, Inc., pg. 461
GLENAYRE TURNKEY TECHNOLOGIES, INC., pg. 462
GLENCRAFT LINGERIE, INC., pg. 462
GLENDALE MEMORIAL HOSPITAL AND MEDICAL CENTER—See UniHealth America, pg. 1127
THE GLENNON COMPANIES, pg. 462
GLENOIT MILLS, INC., pg. 462
GLENROY CONSTRUCTION CO. INC., pg. 462
GLENSHAW GLASS CO. INC., pg. 462
GLENVIEW STATE BANK—See Cummins-American Corp., pg. 305
GLENWOOD POST—See Stauffer Communications, Inc., pg. 1042
GENE B. GLICK COMPANY, INC., pg. 462
GLICO HARMONY FOODS CORPORATION, pg. 462
GLINES & RHODES, INC., pg. 463
GLOBAL FINANCIAL SERVICES, INC.—See Globe Mortgage Company, pg. 464
GLOBAL FOOD CORPORATION—See Basic Food International Inc., pg. 124
GLOBAL INSURANCE COMPANY—See Lawrence Group, Inc., pg. 662
GLOBAL MARKETING RESOURCES, pg. 463
GLOBAL PETROLEUM CORP., pg. 463
GLOBAL STEEL PRODUCTS CORPORATION, pg. 463
GLOBAL TURNKEY SYSTEMS INC., pg. 463
GLOBE-AMERADA GLASS COMPANY, pg. 463
GLOBE BUSINESS FURNITURE, INC., pg. 463
GLOBE GLASS & MIRROR CO., pg. 463
GLOBE INDUSTRIES, INC., pg. 464
GLOBE INTERNATIONAL INC., pg. 464
GLOBE MORTGAGE COMPANY, pg. 464
GLOBE SECURITY SYSTEMS, INC.—See Borg-Warner Corporation, pg. 166
GLOBE VALVE CORPORATION—See Gerber Plumbing Fixtures Corporation, pg. 454
GLOBUS-GATEWAY/COSMOS TOURAMA, pg. 464
GLORIA JEAN'S COFFEE BEAN CORP., pg. 464
GLORIA VANDERBILT DIVISION—See Gitano Group Inc., pg. 460
GLOSSER BROS. DEPARTMENT STORE—See Schottenstein Stores Corporation, pg. 978
GLOSSER BROTHERS, INC.—See Schottenstein Stores Corporation, pg. 978
GODDESS BRA COMPANY, pg. 464
GODFATHER'S PIZZA, INC., pg. 464
GODFREY ADVERTISING, pg. 464
GODWIN ADVERTISING AGENCY, INC., pg. 464
GOEBEL ART, INC., pg. 464
GOER MANUFACTURING CO.—See RHC/Spacemaster Corporation, pg. 907
GOHMANN ASPHALT & CONSTRUCTION INC., pg. 465
GOHMANN ASPHALT & CONSTRUCTION OF KY., INC.—See Gohmann Asphalt & Construction Inc., pg. 465
GOHMANN ASPHALT & CONSTRUCTION OF TEXAS, INC.—See Gohmann Asphalt & Construction Inc., pg. 465
GOLD BOND BUILDING PRODUCTS—See National Gypsum Company, pg. 790
GOLD BOND GYPSUM PRODUCTS—See National Gypsum Company, pg. 790
GOLD COAST ADVERTISING, pg. 465
GOLD KIST, INC., pg. 465
GOLD MEDAL PRODUCTS CO., pg. 465
GOLD'N PLUMP, INC.—See JFC Inc., pg. 584
MORTON GOLDBERG ASSOCIATES, INC., pg. 465
GOLDBERG FOSSA SEID ADVERTISING, INC., pg. 465
GOLDBERG MARCHESANO KOHLMAN INC., pg. 465
GOLDBERG MOSER O'NEILL, pg. 465
GOLDBERGER DOLL MFG. COMPANY, INC., pg. 466
GOLDEN CAT CORPORATION—See Knightbridge Partners, pg. 637
GOLDEN CORRAL CORPORATION, pg. 466
GOLDEN EAGLE DISTRIBUTORS, INC., pg. 466
GOLDEN FLEECE OUTERWEAR CO.—See I. Spiewak & Sons, Inc., pg. 1031
GOLDEN GATE UNIVERSITY, pg. 466
GOLDEN GEM GROWERS INC., pg. 466
THE GOLDEN GIANTS SERIES—See Walter J. Black, Inc., pg. 154
GOLDEN PEANUT COMPANY—See Gold Kist, Inc., pg. 465
GOLDEN POULTRY CO., INC.—See Gold Kist, Inc., pg. 465
GOLDEN STATE FLOORING COMPANY—See J. E. Higgins Lumber Co., pg. 533
GOLDEN STATE FOODS CORP., pg. 466
GOLDEN STATE MUTUAL LIFE INSURANCE COMPANY, pg. 467
GOLDEN SUN FEEDS, INC., pg. 467
GOLDEN TRIANGLE PLASTICS, INC.—See Plastic Engineering Components Inc., pg. 875
GOLDEN WEST BROADCASTERS, pg. 467
GOLDEN WEST HOMES, pg. 467
GOLDEN WEST HOMES PERRIS DIV.—See Golden West Homes, pg. 467
GOLDEN WEST REFINING COMPANY—See Thrifty Oil Company, pg. 1096
GOLDFARB & COMPANY ADVERTISING, pg. 467
THE GOLDHIRSH GROUP INC., pg. 467
GOLDING INDUSTRIES—See Joseph, Littlejohn & Levy, pg. 607
S. I. GOLDMAN CO., pg. 467
GOLDMAN FINANCIAL GROUP, pg. 468
GOLDMAN SACHS (ASIA) LIMITED—See Goldman, Sachs & Co., pg. 468
GOLDMAN SACHS (AUSTRALIA) LIMITED—See Goldman, Sachs & Co., pg. 468
GOLDMAN SACHS CANADA—See Goldman, Sachs & Co., pg. 468
GOLDMAN, SACHS & CO., pg. 468
GOLDMAN SACHS EQUITY SECURITIES (U.K.) LIMITED—See Goldman, Sachs & Co., pg. 468
GOLDMAN SACHS FINANZ AG—See Goldman, Sachs & Co., pg. 468
GOLDMAN SACHS FUTURES LIMITED—See Goldman, Sachs & Co., pg. 468
GOLDMAN SACHS GOVERNMENT SECURITIES (U.K.) LIMITED—See Goldman, Sachs & Co., pg. 468
GOLDMAN SACHS INTERNATIONAL FINANCE LIMITED—See Goldman, Sachs & Co., pg. 468
GOLDMAN SACHS INTERNATIONAL LIMITED—See Goldman, Sachs & Co., pg. 468
GOLDMAN SACHS INTERNATIONAL LIMITED ET CIE.—See Goldman, Sachs & Co., pg. 468
GOLDMAN SACHS (JAPAN) CORP.—See Goldman, Sachs & Co., pg. 468
GOLDMAN SACHS LIMITED—See Goldman, Sachs & Co., pg. 468
GOLDMAN SACHS MONEY MARKETS INC.—See Goldman, Sachs & Co., pg. 468
GOLDMARK INDUSTRIES, LTD., pg. 468
GOLDMARK PARTNERS—See Goldmark Industries, Ltd., pg. 469
GOLDSMITH/JEFFREY, INC., pg. 469
GOLDSMITHS, INC., pg. 469
JOEL GOLDSTEIN MARKETING COMMUNICATIONS, pg. 469
GOLF HOST RESORTS, INC.—See Golf Hosts, Inc., pg. 469
GOLF HOSTS, INC., pg. 469
LEON SHAFFER GOLNICK ADVERTISING, INC., pg. 469
GOLODETZ CORPORATION, pg. 469
M. GOLODETZ EXPORT CORP.—See Golodetz Corporation, pg. 469
GOLUB & CO., pg. 469
GOLUB CORPORATION, pg. 469
GOMAR MANUFACTURING CO., INC., pg. 469
GONNELLA BAKING CO., pg. 469
GOOCH PACKING CO., INC.—See Randall's Food Markets, Inc., pg. 912
GOOD COMPANIES, pg. 470
GOOD HOUSEKEEPING—See The Hearst Corporation, pg. 523
SHELDON GOOD & CO., INC., pg. 470
SHELDON GOOD & COMPANY OF FLORIDA—See Sheldon Good & Co., Inc., pg. 470
SHELDON GOOD & COMPANY OF COLORADO, INC.—See Sheldon Good & Co., Inc., pg. 470
GOOD STUFF FOOD COMPANY, INC., pg. 470
W. B. GOODE COMPANY, INC., pg. 470
W. B. GOODE COMPANY, INC.—See W. B. Goode Company, Inc., pg. 470
W. B. GOODE COMPANY, INC.—See W. B. Goode Company, Inc., pg. 470
W. B. GOODE COMPANY, INC.—See W. B. Goode Company, Inc., pg. 470
GOODHEART-WILLCOX CO., INC., pg. 470
GOODKIND & O'DEA, INC.—See Dewberry & Davis, pg. 334
GOODMAN EQUIPMENT CORP., pg. 470
GOODMANS, INC., pg. 471
GOODPASTURE, INC., pg. 471
GOODRUM LEONARD & ASSOCIATES, INC., pg. 471
GOODWAY TOOL CORPORATION, pg. 471
GOODWILL INDUSTRIES OF AMERICA, INC., pg. 471
WILLIAM H. GOODWIN TRUST, pg. 471
GOOLSBY FOODS, INC., pg. 471
GORDON BROTHERS, pg. 471
GORDON BROTHERS CORPORATION—See Gordon Brothers, pg. 471
GORDON & FERGUSON OF DELAWARE, INC., pg. 471
GORDON FOOD SERVICE INC., pg. 472
GORDON JEWELRY CORPORATION—See Zale Corporation, pg. 1215
KENNETH GORDON NEW ORLEANS, LTD., pg. 472
GORDON PLASTICS DIV.—See Plastigage Corporation, pg. 876
GORDON SIGN COMPANY, pg. 472
GORDON & SMITH, INC., pg. 472
GORDY'S, INC., pg. 472
W. L. GORE & ASSOCIATES, INC., pg. 472
CHESTER GORE COMPANY INC., pg. 472
GORE GRAPHICS, INC., pg. 472
GOSHEN RUBBER CO., INC., pg. 472
GOSHEN RUBBER OF CANADA LTD.—See Goshen Rubber Co., Inc., pg. 472
GOSIGER INC., pg. 472
GOSNELL BUILDERS, pg. 472
GOUCHENOUR ADV., INC., pg. 473
GOUGLER INDUSTRIES, INC., pg. 473
GOULD CENTRAL FLORIDA—See Stephen Gould Paper Co., Inc., pg. 473
GOULD INVESTORS, L.P., pg. 473
GOULD PACKAGING, INC., pg. 473
GOULD PACKAGING, INC.—See Gould Packaging, Inc., pg. 473
GOULD PAPER CORPORATION, pg. 473
GOULD SOUTHERN—See Stephen Gould Paper Co., Inc., pg. 474
STEPHEN GOULD OF ARIZONA, INC.—See Stephen Gould Paper Co., Inc., pg. 474
STEPHEN GOULD OF CALIFORNIA—See Stephen Gould Paper Co., Inc., pg. 474
STEPHEN GOULD OF CALIFORNIA-NORTH BAY—See Stephen Gould Paper Co., Inc., pg. 474
STEPHEN GOULD OF CAROLINA, INC.—See Stephen Gould Paper Co., Inc., pg. 474
STEPHEN GOULD OF CAROLINA, INC.—See Stephen Gould Paper Co., Inc., pg. 474
STEPHEN GOULD OF COLORADO, INC.—See Stephen Gould Paper Co., Inc., pg. 474
STEPHEN GOULD OF CONNECTICUT CORP.—See Stephen Gould Paper Co., Inc., pg. 474
STEPHEN GOULD CORPORATION (PLAINVIEW, NY)—See Stephen Gould Paper Co., Inc., pg. 474
STEPHEN GOULD CORPORATION (ROCHESTER, NY)—See Stephen Gould Paper Co., Inc., pg. 474
STEPHEN GOULD OF FLORIDA, INC.—See Stephen Gould Paper Co., Inc., pg. 474
STEPHEN GOULD OF FLORIDA, INC.—See Stephen Gould Paper Co., Inc., pg. 474
STEPHEN GOULD OF ILLINOIS, INC.—See Stephen Gould Paper Co., Inc., pg. 474
STEPHEN GOULD IN—See Stephen Gould Paper Co., Inc., pg. 474
STEPHEN GOULD OF INDIANA, INC.—See Stephen Gould Paper Co., Inc., pg. 474
STEPHEN GOULD MD—See Stephen Gould Paper Co., Inc., pg. 474
STEPHEN GOULD MI—See Stephen Gould Paper Co., Inc., pg. 474
STEPHEN GOULD/MIDHUDSON—See Stephen Gould Paper Co., Inc., pg. 474
STEPHEN GOULD MIDWEST—See Stephen Gould Paper Co., Inc., pg. 474
STEPHEN GOULD OF NEW ENGLAND, INC.—See Stephen Gould Paper Co., Inc., pg. 474
STEPHEN GOULD OH—See Stephen Gould Paper Co., Inc., pg. 474
STEPHEN GOULD OF OHIO, INC.—See Stephen Gould Paper Co., Inc., pg. 474
STEPHEN GOULD PAPER CO., INC., pg. 473

STEPHEN GOULD PAPER CO., INC.—See Stephen Gould Paper Co., Inc., pg. 474
STEPHEN GOULD OF PENNSYLVANIA CORP.—See Stephen Gould Paper Co., Inc., pg. 474
STEPHEN GOULD OF PUERTO RICO, INC.—See Stephen Gould Paper Co., Inc., pg. 474
STEPHEN GOULD OF TENNESSEE—See Stephen Gould Paper Co., Inc., pg. 474
STEPHEN GOULD OF TEXAS, INC.—See Stephen Gould Paper Co., Inc., pg. 474
GOURMET—See Advance Publications Inc., pg. 19
GOYA FOODS, INC., pg. 474
GOYA FOODS OF FLORIDA—See Goya Foods, Inc., pg. 474
GPS HEALTHCARE—See Berwind Corporation, pg. 145
A. GRACE DEVELOPMENT, pg. 474
W. M. GRACE DEVELOPMENT, pg. 474
GRACE & ROTHSCHILD, pg. 474
THE GRADALL CO.—See ICM Industries, Inc., pg. 559
GRAF BERTEL, pg. 474
GRAFALLOY INC.—See Prince Manufacturing, Inc., pg. 890
JOHN H. GRAHAM & CO., INC., pg. 475
GRAHAM GROUP, INC., pg. 475
GRAHAM MAGNETICS, INC., pg. 475
GRAHAM MFG. CO.—See ESSTAR Incorporated, pg. 361
GRAHAM PAINT AND VARNISH COMPANY, pg. 475
GRAIN PROCESSING CORP.—See Varied Investments, Inc., pg. 1145
GRAMEX CORPORATION, pg. 475
THE GRANADA GROUP, pg. 475
GRAND BANKS YACHTS, LTD., pg. 475
GRAND ISLAND CONTRACT CARRIERS & BROKERAGE, INC.—See Chief Industries, Inc., pg. 247
THE GRAND ISLAND DAILY INDEPENDENT—See Stauffer Communications, Inc., pg. 1042
GRAND JUNCTION NEWSPAPERS, INC.—See Cox Enterprises, Inc., pg. 292
GRAND PRAIRIE CO-OP, INC., pg. 475
GRAND PRAIRIE CO-OP, INC.—See Grand Prairie Co-op, Inc., pg. 475
GRAND PRAIRIE CO-OP, INC.—See Grand Prairie Co-op, Inc., pg. 475
GRAND PRAIRIE CO-OP, INC.—See Grand Prairie Co-op, Inc., pg. 475
GRAND PRAIRIE CO-OP, INC.—See Grand Prairie Co-op, Inc., pg. 475
GRAND PRAIRIE CO-OP, INC.—See Grand Prairie Co-op, Inc., pg. 475
GRAND PRAIRIE CO-OP, INC.—See Grand Prairie Co-op, Inc., pg. 475
GRAND PRAIRIE CO-OP, INC.—See Grand Prairie Co-op, Inc., pg. 475
GRAND PRARIE CO-OP, INC.—See Grand Prairie Co-op, Inc., pg. 475
GRAND UNION CAPITAL CORPORATION—See Grand Union Holdings Corporation, pg. 476
THE GRAND UNION COMPANY—See Grand Union Holdings Corporation, pg. 476
GRAND UNION HOLDINGS CORPORATION, pg. 475
THE GRANDOE CORPORATION, pg. 476
GRANDPA BRANDS COMPANY, pg. 476
GRANDPA SOAP CO.—See Grandpa Brands Company, pg. 476
GRANDVILLE PRINTING COMPANY, pg. 476
GRANDY'S, INC., pg. 476
GRANGER CONSTRUCTION CO., pg. 476
GRANIT-BRONZ, INC.—See Cold Spring Granite Company, pg. 260
GRANITE STATE MANUFACTURING CO., pg. 476
GRANITE STATE PACKING CO., pg. 476
GRANITEVILLE CO., pg. 476
GRANT COUNTY NEWS—See Landmark Communications, Inc., pg. 655
GRANT DESIGN—See Grant Marketing Communications Inc., pg. 477
GRANT/JACOBY, INC., pg. 477
GRANT-LYDICK BEVERAGE CO., pg. 477
GRANT MARKETING COMMUNICATIONS INC., pg. 477
GRANT PROMOTION—See Grant Marketing Communications Inc., pg. 477
GRANT PUBLIC RELATIONS—See Grant Marketing Communications Inc., pg. 477
GRANT STEEL CORP.—See Columbia National Group, Inc., pg. 265
GRANT THORNTON, pg. 477
GRANTHAM COMPANY, pg. 477
GRANTREE CORPORATION, pg. 477
GRAPHIC ARTS CENTER—See Continental Graphics Holdings, Inc., pg. 279
GRAPHIC CENTER, INC., pg. 478
GRAPHIC CONTROLS, CORP., pg. 478
GRAPHIC CONTROLS INDUSTRIAL PRODUCTS DIV.—See Graphic Controls, Corp., pg. 478
GRAPHIC CONTROLS MEDICAL PRODUCTS DIV.—See Graphic Controls, Corp., pg. 478
GRAPHIC LEARNING—See Abrams Publishing Inc., pg. 10
GRAPHIC PRODUCTIONS COMPANY, pg. 478
GRAPHICS INTERNATIONAL INC.—See Hallmark Cards, Inc., pg. 502
GRAPHISPHERE HOLDING COMPANY, pg. 478
THE GRAVER CHEMICAL DIV.—See The Marmon Group, Inc., pg. 712
THE GRAVER COMPANY—See The Marmon Group, Inc., pg. 712
GRAVER WATER DIVISION—See The Marmon Group, Inc., pg. 712
EARL G. GRAVES, LTD., pg. 478
EARL G. GRAVES PUBLISHING CO., INC.—See Earl G. Graves, Ltd., pg. 478
GRAVES-HUMPHREYS COMPANY—See Jeld-Wen, Inc., pg. 592
GRAVYMASTER INC., pg. 478
GRAY BAUMGARTEN LAYPORT, INC., pg. 479
JAMES N. GRAY CONSTRUCTION CO., INC., pg. 479
THE EDWARD GRAY CORP.—See Graycor, Inc., pg. 480
GRAY INTERNATIONAL—See Graycor, Inc., pg. 480
GRAY & KILGORE, INC.—See Ross Roy Group, Inc., pg. 950
GRAY KIRK/VANSANT ADVERTISING, INC., pg. 479
GRAY PRINTING CO., pg. 479
GRAY-PRO, INC., pg. 479
JACK GRAY TRANSPORT, INC., pg. 479
GRAYBAR ELECTRIC COMPANY, INC., pg. 479
GRAYBAR INTERNATIONAL, INC.—See Graybar Electric Company, Inc., pg. 479
GRAYCOR, INC., pg. 479
GRAYLINE HOUSEWARES, pg. 480
GRAYMILLS CORP., pg. 480
GREAT AMERICAN BREADED VEGETABLE CO.—See Westin, Inc., pg. 1183
GREAT AMERICAN BROADCASTING COMPANY—See American Financial Corporation, pg. 53
GREAT AMERICAN BROADCASTING COMPANY—See American Financial Corporation, pg. 52
GREAT AMERICAN COMMUNICATIONS COMPANY—See American Financial Corporation, pg. 53
THE GREAT AMERICAN ENTERTAINMENT COMPANY—See American Financial Corporation, pg. 53
GREAT AMERICAN FOOD STORES, INC.—See Victory Markets Inc., pg. 1150
GREAT AMERICAN HOLDING CORPORATION—See American Financial Corporation, pg. 53
GREAT AMERICAN INDUSTRIES, INC., pg. 480
GREAT AMERICAN INSURANCE COMPANY—See American Financial Corporation, pg. 53
GREAT AMERICAN MANAGEMENT SERVICES, INC.—See American Financial Corporation, pg. 53
GREAT AMERICAN TELEVISION & RADIO COMPANY, INC.—See American Financial Corporation, pg. 53
THE GREAT ATLANTIC COMPANIES, pg. 480
GREAT ATLANTIC HOSPITALITY CO. INC.—See The Great Atlantic Companies, pg. 480
GREAT ATLANTIC MANAGEMENT CO. INC.—See The Great Atlantic Companies, pg. 480
GREAT BOOKS OF THE WESTERN WORLD—See Encyclopaedia Britannica, Inc., pg. 381
THE GREAT FRAME UP SYSTEMS, INC., pg. 480
GREAT LAKES BANCORP, pg. 480
GREAT LAKES BOWLING CENTRE, INC.—See Great Lakes Recreation Co., pg. 482
GREAT LAKES CARBON CORP.—See Horsehead Industries, Inc., pg. 545
THE GREAT LAKES CHEESE CO., pg. 481
GREAT LAKES CHEESE OF NEW YORK, INC.—See The Great Lakes Cheese Co., pg. 481
GREAT LAKES CONSTRUCTION CO., pg. 481
GREAT LAKES DREDGE & DOCK, pg. 481
GREAT LAKES FILTER—See Acme Mills Co. Inc., pg. 13
GREAT LAKES FINANCIAL RESOURCES, INC., pg. 481
GREAT LAKES LITHOGRAPH CO., pg. 481
GREAT LAKES OF WISCONSIN—See The Great Lakes Cheese Co., pg. 481
GREAT LAKES RECREATION CO., pg. 481
GREAT LAKES SPORTSWEAR MANUFACTURING INDUSTRIES, pg. 482
GREAT LAKES TECHNOLOGIES CORP., pg. 482
GREAT LAKES TERMINAL & TRANSPORT CORP., pg. 482
GREAT LAKES TERMINAL & TRANSPORT OF PENNSYLVANIA—See Great Lakes Terminal & Transport Corp., pg. 482
GREAT NECK SAW MANUFACTURERS, INC., pg. 482
GREAT PLAINS MANUFACTURING, INC., pg. 482
GREAT SALT LAKE MINERALS & CHEMICALS CORP., pg. 482
GREAT SCOTT ADVERTISING CO. INC., pg. 482
GREAT SCOTT FOOD MARKETS, INC.—See James Ferrera & Sons, Inc., pg. 407
GREAT VIBRATIONS DIV.—See Interbath, Inc., pg. 574
GREATBANC, INC., pg. 482
GREATER CHICAGO AUTO AUCTION—See Cox Enterprises, Inc., pg. 293
GREATER CONSTRUCTION CORP., pg. 483
GREATER HOUSTON MAILING SERVICE, INC.—See Harte-Hanks Communications, Inc., pg. 513
GREATER NEW YORK BOX CO., pg. 483
GREATER NEW YORK MUTUAL INSURANCE COMPANY, pg. 483
GREATER ORLANDO AUTO AUCTION, pg. 483
GREATER TAMPA BAY AUTO AUCTION—See Cox Enterprises, Inc., pg. 293
GREDE FOUNDRIES, INC., pg. 483
GREDE NEW CASTLE, INC—See Grede Foundries, Inc., pg. 483
GREDE PERMCAST, INC.—See Grede Foundries, Inc., pg. 483
GREDE TRANSPORT, INC.—See Grede Foundries, Inc., pg. 483
GREDE VASSAR, INC.—See Grede Foundries, Inc., pg. 483
GREECO BROTHERS, INC., pg. 483
GREEFF FABRICS—See Collins & Aikman Group Inc., pg. 262
GREELEY GAS CO., pg. 483
GREEN BAY DRESSED BEEF COMPANY—See American Foods Group, pg. 54
GREEN BAY PACKAGING INC., pg. 483
GREEN BUS LINES, INC., pg. 483
THOMAS L. GREEN & CO., INC., pg. 484
B. GREEN & CO., pg. 484
GREEN CONSTRUCTION OF INDIANA, INC., pg. 484
DANIEL GREEN CO., pg. 484
GREEN GARDE—See H.D. Hudson Manufacturing Company, pg. 551
GREEN HOLDINGS, INC., pg. 484
GREEN INTERNATIONAL-GUYANA, INC.—See Green Holdings, Inc., pg. 484
JOHN E. GREEN CO., pg. 484
GREEN LEAF VENTURES, INC., pg. 484
GREEN MINING, INC.—See Green Holdings, Inc., pg. 484
GREEN MOUNTAIN HOLDING CORPORATION, pg. 485
LEONARD GREEN & PARTNERS, pg. 485
GREEN SPOT PACKAGING INC., pg. 485
JACK GREENBERG INC., pg. 485
M. H. GREENEBAUM, INC., pg. 485
ALBERT M. GREENFIELD & COMPANY—See Helmsley Enterprises, Inc., pg. 527
GREENFIELD INDUSTRIES INC.—See Harbour Group Ltd., pg. 507
GREENGAGE ASSOCIATES, INC., pg. 485
GREENHORNE & O'MARA, INC., pg. 485
GREENPOINT DIVISION—See J. H. France Refractories Co., pg. 428
GREENSBORO NEWS & RECORD—See Landmark Communications, Inc., pg. 655
GREENSTONE ROBERTS ADVERTISING, pg. 485
GREENSTRIPE MEDIA, INC., pg. 485
GREENTREE RECORDS—See The Benson Music Group, pg. 140
GREENVIEW GARDEN SUPPLY—See Lebanon Chemical Corp., pg. 665
GREENWAY CO-OP SERVICE, pg. 485
GREENWICH AIR SERVICES, pg. 485
GREENWILLOW BOOKS—See The Hearst Corporation, pg. 521
GREENWOOD COTTON CO.—See Greenwood Mills, Inc., pg. 486
GREENWOOD DEVELOPMENT CO.—See Greenwood Mills, Inc., pg. 486
GREENWOOD MILLS, INC., pg. 485
GREENWOOD PACKING PLANT, pg. 486
GREENWOOD WAREHOUSE CO.—See Greenwood Mills, Inc., pg. 486
AUTRY GREER & SONS, INC., pg. 486
GREER STEEL CO., pg. 486
GREFCO, INC.—See Belmont Industries, Inc., pg. 136
GREFCO, INC.—See Belmont Industries, Inc., pg. 137
GREFCO, INC.—See Belmont Industries, Inc., pg. 137
GREFCO, INC.—See Belmont Industries, Inc., pg. 137
GREFCO, INC.—See Belmont Industries, Inc., pg. 137
GREGG APPLIANCES INC., pg. 486
GREGG INDUSTRIES, INC., pg. 486
GREGORY AFFILIATES, INC., pg. 486
GREGORY & CLYBURNE, INC., pg. 486
GREMAC INC.—See Macromedia Inc., pg. 698
GRESS FOODS INC., pg. 486
GREY EAGLE DISTRIBUTORS INC., pg. 486
GREYSTONE REALTY CORPORATION—See New York Life Insurance Company, pg. 802
THE GRIEVE CORPORATION, pg. 486
GRIFFIN AG PRODUCTS INC.—See Griffin Corporation, pg. 487
GRIFFIN BACAL INC., pg. 486
GRIFFIN CANADA INC.—See Amsted Industries Incorporated, pg. 69
GRIFFIN CORPORATION, pg. 487
GRIFFIN ENVELOPE, INC., pg. 487
GRIFFIN HOMES, INC., pg. 487
GRIFFIN INDUSTRIES, INC., pg. 487
GRIFFIN INTERNATIONAL—See Griffin Corporation, pg. 487
GRIFFIN MANUFACTURING CO., pg. 487
GRIFFIN MINING CO.—See Griffin Corporation, pg. 487
GRIFFIN PIPE PRODUCTS CO.—See Amsted Industries Incorporated, pg. 69
GRIFFIN WHEEL CO.—See Amsted Industries Incorporated, pg. 69
GRIFFITH COLOMBIA S.A.—See Griffith Laboratories Worldwide, Inc., pg. 487
GRIFFITH LABORATORIES (H.K.) LTD.—See Griffith Laboratories Worldwide, Inc., pg. 487
GRIFFITH LABORATORIES IBERIA S.A.—See Griffith Laboratories Worldwide, Inc., pg. 487
GRIFFITH LABORATORIES IRELAND LIMITED—See Griffith Laboratories Worldwide, Inc., pg. 487
GRIFFITH LABORATORIES ITALIA S.R.L.—See Griffith Laboratories Worldwide, Inc., pg. 487
GRIFFITH LABORATORIES, K.K.—See Griffith Laboratories Worldwide, Inc., pg. 487
GRIFFITH LABORATORIES LIMITED—See Griffith Laboratories Worldwide, Inc., pg. 487
THE GRIFFITH LABORATORIES, LTD.—See Griffith Laboratories Worldwide, Inc., pg. 487
GRIFFITH LABORATORIES (PHILS.) INC.—See Griffith Laboratories Worldwide, Inc., pg. 488
GRIFFITH LABORATORIES PTY., LTD.—See Griffith Laboratories Worldwide, Inc., pg. 488
N.V. GRIFFITH LABORATORIES S.A.—See Griffith Laboratories Worldwide, Inc., pg. 488
GRIFFITH LABORATORIES WORLDWIDE, INC., pg. 487
GRIFFITH MICRO SCIENCE INTERNATIONAL INC.—See Griffith Laboratories Worldwide, Inc., pg. 487
GRIFFITH PANAMA S.A.—See Griffith Laboratories Worldwide, Inc., pg. 488
JACK GRIGGS INC., pg. 488
GRIMMER REALTY CO. INC., pg. 488
GRINDMASTER CORPORATION, pg. 488
GRINNELL STREET ASSOCIATES, INC.—See Society for Savings Bancorp, Inc., pg. 1016
GRISANTI, INC., pg. 488
GRISWOLD, INC.—See Ross Roy Group, Inc., pg. 950
GRISWOLD INDUSTRIES, INC., pg. 488
GRIT PRINTING CO.—See Stauffer Communications, Inc., pg. 1043
GRIT PUBLISHING COMPANY—See Stauffer Communications, Inc., pg. 1043
GRIZZARD ADVERTISING, INC., pg. 488
GROCERS & MERCHANTS INSURANCE SERVICE—See Certified Grocers Of California, pg. 237
GROCERS BAKING CO., pg. 488
GROCERS CAPITAL CO.—See Certified Grocers Of California, pg. 237

GROCERS DEVELOPMENT CENTER—See Certified Grocers Of California, pg. 237
GROCERS EQUIPMENT CO.—See Certified Grocers Of California, pg. 237
GROCERS GENERAL MERCHANDISE COMPANY—See Certified Grocers Of California, pg. 237
GROCERS SPECIALTY CO.—See Certified Grocers Of California, pg. 237
GROCERS SUPPLY CO. INC., pg. 488
GROCERS SUPPLY INSTITUTION—See Grocers Supply Co. Inc., pg. 489
GROCERS SUPPLY INTERNATIONAL—See Grocers Supply Co. Inc., pg. 489
GROCERS SUPPLY SMALL BUSINESS—See Grocers Supply Co. Inc., pg. 489
GROCERY SUPPLY COMPANY DIVISION—See GSC Enterprises, Inc., pg. 440
GROENDYK MFG. CO., INC.—See Great American Industries, Inc., pg. 480
GROENDYKE TRANSPORTS, INC., pg. 489
GROESBECK LUMBER & SUPPLY, INC., pg. 489
GROMER SUPER MARKETS, INC., pg. 489
JOHN GROSS & CO., pg. 489
GROSSENBURG IMPLEMENTS, INCORPORATED, pg. 489
GROSSMAN IRON & STEEL COMPANY, pg. 489
M. GROSSMAN SON, INC., pg. 489
GROTON RUN PROPERTIES, INC.—See Society for Savings Bancorp, Inc., pg. 1016
THE JOHN C. GROUB COMPANY INC., pg. 489
GROUND WATER ASSOCIATES, INC.—See Hydro Group, Inc., pg. 556
GROUP DEKKO INTERNATIONAL INC., pg. 489
GROUP INSURANCE INC., pg. 490
GROUP INSURANCE OF COLORADO—See Group Insurance Inc., pg. 490
GROUP LIFE & HEALTH INSURANCE COMPANY—See Blue Cross & Blue Shield of Texas, Inc., pg. 160
GROUP 3 DESIGN—See GWP, Inc., pg. 441
GROUP TWO ADVERTISING, INC., pg. 490
GROUPAMERICA INSURANCE CO.—See Connecticut Mutual Life Insurance Company, pg. 275
GROVE VALVE & REGULATOR COMPANY, pg. 490
S. J. GROVES & SONS COMPANY, pg. 490
GROWMARK, INC., pg. 490
GROWTH MANAGEMENT CORP.—See Family Inns of America, Inc., pg. 398
R.J. GRUNTS/CHICAGO—See Lettuce Entertain You Enterprises, Inc., pg. 669
GRUPO BSB SA—See Backer Spielvogel Bates Worldwide, Inc., pg. 111
GRYBAUSKAS & PARTNERS, pg. 490
GSC DISTRIBUTION OF HOUSTON—See GSC Enterprises, Inc., pg. 440
GUARANTEE AMERICAN LIFE COMPANY—See Guarantee Mutual Life Co., pg. 491
GUARANTEE ELECTRICAL COMPANY, pg. 490
GUARANTEE INTERIORS—See Guarantee Electrical Company, pg. 491
GUARANTEE MUTUAL LIFE CO., pg. 491
GUARANTEE TITLE CO., INC., pg. 491
GUARANTEED PRODUCTS, INC., pg. 491
GUARANTY CORPORATION, pg. 491
GUARANTY SAVINGS INSURANCE COMPANY—See Victory Financial Group, Inc., pg. 1150
GUARD PUBLISHING COMPANY, pg. 491
GUARDIAN ALARM CO., pg. 491
GUARDIAN ASSET MANAGEMENT CORP. (GAMCORP)—See The Guardian Life Insurance Company of America, pg. 492
GUARDIAN BAILLIE GIFFORD, LTD.—See The Guardian Life Insurance Company of America, pg. 492
GUARDIAN GLASS INC.—See Guardian Industries Corp., pg. 492
GUARDIAN INDUSTRIES CORP., pg. 491
GUARDIAN INDUSTRIES CORP.—See Guardian Industries Corp., pg. 492
THE GUARDIAN INSURANCE & ANNUITY CO. (GIAC)—See The Guardian Life Insurance Company of America, pg. 492
GUARDIAN INVESTOR SERVICES CORP.—See The Guardian Life Insurance Company of America, pg. 492
THE GUARDIAN LIFE INSURANCE COMPANY OF AMERICA, pg. 492
GUARDIAN TRANSPORTATION CORP.—See Guardian Industries Corp., pg. 492
GUARDSMARK, INC., pg. 492
GUERNICA ESPECTACULOS & TURISMO, S.A.—See World Jai-alai, pg. 1203
GUESS ?, INC., pg. 493
GUEST QUARTERS SUITE HOTELS, pg. 493
GUEST SERVICES, INC., pg. 493
GUIDEPOSTS ASSOCIATES, INC., pg. 493
GUILD MUSIC CORPORATION—See U.S. Music Corporation, pg. 1136
GUILFORD TRANSPORTATION INDUSTRIES INC., pg. 493
GUILLORY TANK TRUCK SERVICE—See Charles Holston, Inc., pg. 541
GULF COAST JEWELRY & SPECIALTY CO., INC.—See Zale Corporation, pg. 1216
GULF COAST LEAD COMPANY, INC., pg. 493
GULF COAST LEAGUE TWINS—See Minnesota Twins Baseball Club, pg. 758
GULF CONSTRUCTORS INTERNATIONAL, INC.—See Walbridge Aldinger Company, pg. 1159
GULF DISTRIBUTION INC., pg. 493
GULF EXPLORATION, pg. 493
GULF FOUNDATION INC.—See Misener Marine Construction, pg. 760
GULF LUMBER COMPANY, INC., pg. 493
GULF OIL—See Cumberland Farms, Inc., pg. 304
GULF SEAL SPECIALTIES, INC.—See Gulf States Asphalt Company, Inc., pg. 494
GULF STATES ASPHALT COMPANY, INC., pg. 493
GULF STATES MANUFACTURERS, INC., pg. 494
GULF STATES PAPER CORPORATION, pg. 494
GULF STATES TOYOTA, pg. 494
GULFSTREAM AEROSPACE CORP.—See Gulfstream Holdings Corporation, pg. 494
GULFSTREAM AEROSPACE CORP.—See Gulfstream Holdings Corporation, pg. 494
GULFSTREAM AEROSPACE CORP.—See Gulfstream Holdings Corporation, pg. 494
GULFSTREAM AEROSPACE CORP.—See Gulfstream Holdings Corporation, pg. 494
GULFSTREAM AEROSPACE CORP.—See Gulfstream Holdings Corporation, pg. 494
GULFSTREAM AEROSPACE TECHNOLOGIES CORP.—See Gulfstream Holdings Corporation, pg. 494
GULFSTREAM HOLDINGS CORPORATION, pg. 494
GULFSTREAM MARKETING MIDWEST REGION—See Gulfstream Holdings Corporation, pg. 494
S. GUMPERT CO., INC.—See Rich Products Corp., pg. 932
GUMPS—See Gump's, Inc., pg. 494
GUMP'S, INC., pg. 494
GUNDER & ASSOCIATES, INC., pg. 494
CURTIS C. GUNN, INC., pg. 494
GUNNEBO FASTENING CORP., pg. 494
GUNTHER NASH MINING CONSTR.—See J. S. Alberici Construction Co., Inc., pg. 31
VINOD GUPTA COMPANY, INC., pg. 494
GURLEY MOTOR COMPANY, pg. 494
GURNEY INDUSTRIES INC., pg. 495
GUSHER PUMPS INC.—See Ruthman Pump & Engineering Co., pg. 957
GUSSINI SHOE STORES—See The Kobacker Company & Affiliates, pg. 638
GUSSO MANUFACTURING, INC., pg. 495
GUSTAFSON, INC.—See Uniroyal Chemical Company, Inc., pg. 1129
GUTH LIGHTING COMPANY—See Jac Jacobsen Industries, Inc., pg. 588
THE GUTHRIE GROUP, pg. 495
GUTMANN CUTLERY, INC.—See Hyde Manufacturing Co., pg. 556
THE GUTTMAN GROUP, pg. 495
GUYAN CORP.—See Logan & Kanawha Coal Co., pg. 681

H

H. E. SARGENT CONSTRUCTOR INC.—See H. E. Sargent, Inc., pg. 971
H. HACKFELD & CO. LTD.—See JMB Realty Corporation, pg. 585
H & S FRUIT CO.—See Stadelman Fruit Inc., pg. 1034
H & C, LEO BURNETT—See Leo Burnett Company, Inc., pg. 192
H & D STEEL SERVICE, INC., pg. 495
H. GROUP HOLDING INC., pg. 495
H & H DISTRIBUTING COMPANY, INC., pg. 495
H & H TUBE & MANUFACTURING CO., pg. 495
H.A.T. HOLDING COMPANY—See Havatampa Incorporated, pg. 517
H.B.A. KING INC.—See Boston Distributors, Inc., pg. 167
HBC INTERNATIONAL SALES CORP.—See Hobart Brothers Co., pg. 537
HBE ADAM'S RIB—See HBE Corporation, pg. 496
HBE BANK FACILITIES—See HBE Corporation, pg. 496
HBE CORPORATION, pg. 495
HBE MEDICAL BUILDINGS—See HBE Corporation, pg. 496
HBE RETIREMENT COMMUNITIES—See HBE Corporation, pg. 496
H.B.L., INC.—See Lantzsch-Andreas Enterprises, Inc., pg. 658
HCB CONTRACTORS, pg. 496
HCC INDUSTRIES, pg. 496
HLC INDUSTRIES, pg. 496
HDS SERVICES, pg. 496
H. G. PRODUCTIONS—See Stone, August, Baker Communications Companies, pg. 1051
H & H ADVERTISING, pg. 496
H.H. FOODS, INC.—See Hale-Halsell Company, pg. 501
H&H INTERNATIONAL—See Harriet & Henderson Yarns, Inc., pg. 511
H & H PRINTING—See H & H Advertising, pg. 496
HHCC INTERNATIONAL, INC.—See Hill, Holliday, Connors, Cosmopulos, Inc., pg. 534
HI SERVICE ENTERPRISES, INC.—See Home Interiors & Gifts, Inc., pg. 541
H & K REALTY CO. INC.—See E & A Industries, Inc., pg. 358
HKM OF CALIFORNIA CORP.—See UIS, Inc., pg. 1123
HKM OF DELAWARE CORP.—See UIS, Inc., pg. 1123
HLB COMMUNICATIONS, INC., pg. 496
H M K ENTERPRISES, INC., pg. 497
HMK ADVERTISING, INC., pg. 497
HMO IOWA, INC.—See The Principal Financial Group, pg. 890
HOH ARCHITECTS, INC.—See The HOH Organizations, pg. 497
HOH ENGINEERS, INC.—See The HOH Organizations, pg. 497
HOH INTERNATIONAL, INC.—See The HOH Organizations, pg. 497
HOH-OHIO—See The HOH Organizations, pg. 497
THE HOH ORGANIZATIONS, pg. 497
HP DIRECT, pg. 497
H.P.H. INDUSTRIES LTD., pg. 497
HPM CORPORATION, pg. 497
HPS, INC., pg. 497
HRR ENTERPRISES, INC.—See Kane-Miller Corp., pg. 616
H S DIE & ENGINEERING, INC., pg. 497
HTB, INC., pg. 497
HT&T COMPANY, INC.—See C. Brewer & Company, Limited, pg. 174
HVC/DALY COMPANY—See KDI Corporation, pg. 612
H W ELECTRONICS, INC., pg. 497
HWH ARCHITECTS ENGINEERS PLANNERS INC., pg. 498
HWI BUILDING CORP.—See Hardware Wholesalers, Inc., pg. 508
H.A. SAMOUHOS PUB. LTD.—See International Data Group, pg. 577
HAAS BROTHERS, pg. 498
THE HABAND CO., pg. 498
THE HABEGGER CORPORATION, pg. 498
HABITS, INC.—See Saul Bros. & Company, Inc., pg. 972
THE ALLAN R. HACKEL ORGANIZATION, pg. 498
J. LEE HACKETT CO., pg. 498
HACKNEY BROTHERS, INC., pg. 498
THE H. T. HACKNEY CO., pg. 498
HACKNEY & SONS, INC., pg. 498
HADDON CRAFTSMEN, INC., pg. 499
HADEN EQUITY, LTD.—See Haden, Inc., pg. 499
HADEN, INC., pg. 499
HADEN INVESTMENT, LTD.—See Haden, Inc., pg. 499
HADEN SCHWEITZER CORPORATION—See Haden, Inc., pg. 499
HAEGER INDUSTRIES, INC., pg. 499
HAEGER POTTERIES, INC.—See Haeger Industries, Inc., pg. 499
HAEGER POTTERIES OF MACOMB, INC.—See Haeger Industries, Inc., pg. 499
BARRETT HAENTJENS & COMPANY, pg. 499
HAGER GESELLSCHAFT—See The Lowe Group, pg. 685
HAGGAR APPAREL COMPANY, pg. 499
HAGGEN'S, INC., pg. 499
HAGIE MANUFACTURING CO., pg. 499
C.F. HAGLIN & SONS, pg. 499
THE HAHN CO.—See Trizec Properties, Inc., pg. 1115
J.R. HAHN CO., INC., pg. 500
HAHN JUNG CHEMICAL, INC.—See Uniroyal Chemical Company, Inc., pg. 1130
W. L. HAILEY & COMPANY, INC., pg. 500
HAINES CITY CITRUS GROWERS ASSOCIATION, pg. 500
HAINES CITY HERALD & RIDGE SHOPPER—See Stauffer Communications, Inc., pg. 1042
HAINES & CO., INC., pg. 500
HAINES LUNDBERG WAEHLER, pg. 500
THE HAIR CUTTERY—See Creative Hairdressers, pg. 297
HAJOCA CORP., pg. 500
HALE BROTHERS, INC.—See Performance Food Group, Inc., pg. 861
HALE-HALSELL COMPANY, pg. 500
HALE MOTORS—See Dairy Fresh Corp., pg. 311
THE C. P. HALL COMPANY, pg. 501
THE HALL CHEMICAL COMPANY—See Goldman Financial Group, pg. 468
THE HALL CHINA COMPANY, pg. 501
HALL CONTRACTING CORP., pg. 501
HALL, HAERR, PETERSON & HARNEY, INC., pg. 501
HALL & KNIGHT HARDWARE CO.—See Distribution America, pg. 340
HALL SIGN, INC., pg. 501
HALLIDIE MACHINERY COMPANY, INC., pg. 501
HALLMARK ADVERTISING, INC., pg. 501
HALLMARK ART PRODUCTS & INTERNATIONAL DIV.—See Hallmark Cards, Inc., pg. 502
HALLMARK CARDS AUSTRALIA LTD.—See Hallmark Cards, Inc., pg. 502
HALLMARK CARDS, INC., pg. 501
HALLMARK CARDS LTD., EUROPEAN DIV.—See Hallmark Cards, Inc., pg. 502
HALLMARK CARDS NZ LTD.—See Hallmark Cards, Inc., pg. 502
HALLMARK EDUCATIONAL PRODUCTS DIV.—See Hallmark Cards, Inc., pg. 502
HALLMARK LITHO CO.—See Pacific Envelope Company, pg. 840
HALLS MERCHANDISING INC.—See Hallmark Cards, Inc., pg. 502
HALOCARBON PRODUCTS CORP., pg. 502
HALPER BROS.—See Reliable Knitting Works, pg. 925
HALSEY DRUG CO., INC., pg. 502
HALSTEAD INDUSTRIAL PRODS. DIV.—See Halstead Industries, Inc., pg. 502
HALSTEAD INDUSTRIES, INC., pg. 502
HALSTEAD METAL PRODS. DIV.—See Halstead Industries, Inc., pg. 502
HAMAMATSU CORP., pg. 502
HAMBURG BROTHERS INC., pg. 502
HAMBURGER HAMLETS INC.—See Weatherly Financial Group, pg. 1169
HAMER PROPERTIES, INC.—See Walter Industries, Inc., pg. 1162
HAMEROFF/MILENTHAL/SPENCE, INC., pg. 503
HAMILTON BONADUZ AG—See Hamilton Co., Inc., pg. 503
HAMILTON, CARVER & LEE, INC., pg. 503
HAMILTON CO., INC., pg. 503
HAMILTON COLLECTION—See MBI Inc., pg. 691
HAMILTON EQUIPMENT, INC., pg. 503
HAMILTON, INC.—See AFG Industries, Inc., pg. 3
HAMILTON MUTUAL INSURANCE COMPANY OF CINCINNATI, pg. 503
HAMILTON STORES, INC., pg. 503
HAMILTON SWEENEY ADVERTISING, INC., pg. 503
HAMILTON WHOLESALE JEWELRY CO., INC.—See Zale Corporation, pg. 1216
HAMLIN ELECTRONICS EUROPE LTD.—See Hamlin, Inc., pg. 503
HAMLIN ELECTRONICS GMBH—See Hamlin, Inc., pg. 503
HAMLIN, INC., pg. 503
HAMLIN S.A. DE C.V.—See Hamlin, Inc., pg. 503
JERRY HAMM CHEVROLET INC., pg. 503
HAMMACHER, SCHLEMMER & CO., INC., pg. 503
HAMMEL, GREEN & ABRAHAMSON, INC., pg. 504
THE HAMMERBLOW CORP., pg. 504

J. L. HAMMETT COMPANY, pg. 504
HAMMOND FARRELL INC., pg. 504
HAMMOND LEAD PRODUCTS, INC., pg. 504
HAMPSHIRE HOTEL—See Taj International Hotels, pg. 1076
HAMPTON PRINT WORKS, INC., pg. 504
HAMPTON RESOURCES INC., pg. 504
HANCOCK LUMBER, INC., pg. 504
HANCOCK PEANUT COMPANY, pg. 504
LOUIS HAND DIV.—See CC Industries, Inc., pg. 200
HANDEL & COMPANY, HANTEX MILLS—See Handel & Company, Inc., pg. 504
HANDEL & COMPANY, INC., pg. 504
HANDGARDS INC., pg. 504
HANDLEY & MILLER, INC., pg. 505
HANDLING SYSTEMS ENGINEERING, pg. 505
HANDSCHY INDUSTRIES—See Field Container Company, L.P., pg. 409
HANDSOME REWARDS—See Starcrest Products of California, pg. 1040
HANDY MANUFACTURING CO., INC., pg. 505
HANDY STORE FIXTURES, INC.—See Handy Manufacturing Co., Inc., pg. 505
HANDY WACKS CORPORATION, pg. 505
HANEL LUMBER CO., INC., pg. 505
HANES COMPANIES, INC., pg. 505
HANKINS LUMBER COMPANY, INC., pg. 505
HANNA-BARBERA PRODUCTIONS, INC.—See American Financial Corporation, pg. 53
HANNA CAR WASH INTERNATIONAL, INC., pg. 505
HANNA CORPORATION, pg. 505
HANNAFORD SEEDMASTER SERVICES AUSTRALIA (PTY) LTD.—See Uniroyal Chemical Company, Inc., pg. 1129
CLIFFORD B. HANNAY & SON INC., pg. 505
THE HANNIBAL COURIER-POST—See Stauffer Communications, Inc., pg. 1042
HANO BUSINESS FORMS, INC., pg. 505
HANOVER FOODS CORP.—See Hanover Foods Corporation, pg. 506
HANOVER FOODS CORP.—See Hanover Foods Corporation, pg. 506
HANOVER FOODS CORPORATION, pg. 506
THE HANOVER INSURANCE COMPANY—See All America Financial, pg. 34
HANOVER LLOYD'S INSURANCE COMPANY—See All America Financial, pg. 35
HANS FOLSGAARD, AGENTUR A/S—See Panduit Company, pg. 845
HANSEN COUPLING DIVISION—See Tuthill Corporation, pg. 1120
A. L. HANSEN MFG. CO., pg. 506
HANSEN PLASTICS DIVISION—See Tuthill Corporation, pg. 1120
HAPCO/AMERICAN DIV.—See The Dyson-Kissner-Moran Corporation, pg. 357
HAPPY HOLIDAY TREE FARMS, pg. 506
HARBERT CORPORATION, pg. 506
HARBISON-WALKER REFRACTORIES—See INDRESCO, Inc., pg. 565
HARBOR BANCORP, pg. 506
HARBOR FINANCIAL INSURANCE AGENCY—See Harbor Financial Mortgage Corp., pg. 506
HARBOR FINANCIAL MORTGAGE CORP., pg. 506
HARBOR FINANCIAL PROPERTY MANAGEMENT CO.—See Harbor Financial Mortgage Corp., pg. 506
HARBOR FINANCIAL TITLE CORP.—See Harbor Financial Mortgage Corp., pg. 506
HARBOUR CASUALS, LTD.—See Milady Brassiere & Corset Co., Inc., pg. 753
HARBOUR CONTRACTORS, INC., pg. 506
HARBOUR GROUP LTD., pg. 506
HARBOUR INDUSTRIES, INC., pg. 507
HARCO DRUG, INC., pg. 507
HARCO TECHNOLOGIES CORPORATION, pg. 507
THE HARDAWAY COMPANY, pg. 507
HARDAWAY CONCRETE CO., INC., pg. 507
HARDAWAY CONSTRUCTION COMPANY, INC., pg. 508
HARDEN FURNITURE COMPANY, pg. 508
HARDEN GALLERIES—See Harden Furniture Company, pg. 508
HARDEN INDUSTRIES, INC., pg. 508
HARDIE IRRIGATION-LANDSCAPE DIV., pg. 508
HARDIN CONSTRUCTION GROUP, INC., pg. 508
HARDINGE BROTHERS, INC., pg. 508
HARDINGE MACHINE TOOLS, LTD.—See Hardinge Brothers, Inc., pg. 508
HARDWARE WHOLESALERS, INC., pg. 508
BRYAN HARDWICK ASSOCIATES, pg. 508
HARDWICK CLOTHES INC., pg. 508
HARDWOOD VISUALS—See Howe Furniture Corporation, pg. 547
HARDWOODS OF MICHIGAN, INC., pg. 509
HARFORD SYSTEMS, INC.—See Bio Medic Corporation, pg. 152
HARGRO ENTERPRISES, INC., pg. 509
HARIG GRINDERS—See Bridgeport Machines, Inc., pg. 175
HARKER'S INC., pg. 509
HARKINS BUILDERS, INC., pg. 509
HARKINS CARPENTRY—See Harkins Builders, Inc., pg. 509
HARLAN ELECTRIC CO., pg. 509
HARLEY ELLINGTON PIERCE YEE ASSOCIATES, INC., pg. 509
HARLEY INDUSTRIES, INC., pg. 509
HARMAN AUTOMOTIVE—See Harvard Industries, Inc., pg. 514
HARMESON MANUFACTURING COMPANY, INC., pg. 510
HARMON CITY, INC., pg. 510
HARMON SMITH INC., pg. 510
HARMONY ENGINEERING CORPORATION, pg. 510
HARMONY HOUSE RECORDS & TAPES, pg. 510
THE HARODITE FINISHING COMPANY INC., pg. 510
HARPER BROS., INC., pg. 510
HARPER INDUSTRIES, INC., pg. 510
HARPER SHIRT COMPANY—See Harper Industries, Inc., pg. 510
HARPER'S BAZAAR—See The Hearst Corporation, pg. 523
HARP'S FOOD STORES, INC., pg. 510
HARRIET & HENDERSON COTTON CO.—See Harriet & Henderson Yarns, Inc., pg. 511
HARRIET & HENDERSON YARNS, INC., pg. 511
HARRIMAN RECORD—See Landmark Communications, Inc., pg. 655
HARRINGTON & KING, pg. 511
HARRINGTON & KING, SOUTH, INC.—See Harrington & King, pg. 511
HARRINGTON MARKET RESEARCH—See Biggs Gilmore Communications, pg. 149
HARRIS ADVERTISING, INC., pg. 511
HARRIS, BAIO & MCCULLOUGH INC., pg. 511
HARRIS DRURY COHEN, pg. 511
HARRIS & DRUTT INC., pg. 511
HARRIS ENTERPRISES INC., pg. 511
HARRIS FARMS, INC., pg. 511
HARRIS FEEDING CO.—See Harris Farms, Inc., pg. 512
HARRIS FORD, INC., pg. 512
HARRIS-KAYOT, INC., pg. 512
HARRIS AND LOVE, INC., pg. 512
HARRIS MECHANICAL CONTRACTING CO., pg. 512
HARRIS RANCH BEEF CO.—See Harris Farms, Inc., pg. 512
HARRIS RANCH RESTAURANT—See Harris Farms, Inc., pg. 512
HARRIS STEEL CO., pg. 512
HARRIS WALDINGER, INC.—See Harris Mechanical Contracting Co., pg. 512
HARRISBURG STAMP CO.—See American Marking Systems, pg. 58
HARRISON CONSTRUCTION CORP., pg. 512
HARRISON DIV.—See Sierracin Corporation, pg. 1003
HARRISON PAINT CORPORATION, pg. 512
HARRISON, STAR, WIENER & BEITLER, INC., pg. 512
HARRISONBURG AUTO AUCTION—See Cox Enterprises, Inc., pg. 293
HARRISS & COVINGTON HOSIERY MILLS, pg. 512
HARROD DEVITT SOCIEDAD ANONIMA—See The Prudential Insurance Company of America, pg. 897
HARROP INDUSTRIES, INC., pg. 512
KARL M. HARROP CO., INC.—See Arcata Corporation, pg. 80
HART-CARTER CO.—See Carter Day Industries, Inc., pg. 226
HART CROWSER, INC., pg. 512
HART DISTRIBUTION SERVICES—See Hart Graphics Inc., pg. 513
HART ENGINEERING CORPORATION, pg. 512
HART FORMS & SERVICES—See Hart Graphics Inc., pg. 513
HART GRAPHICS INC., pg. 513
HART SERVICES, INC., pg. 513
HARTE-HANKS COMMUNICATIONS, INC., pg. 513
HARTE-HANKS COMMUNITY NEWSPAPERS, INC.—See Harte-Hanks Communications, Inc., pg. 513
HARTE-HANKS DATA TECHNOLOGIES—See Harte-Hanks Communications, Inc., pg. 513
HARTE-HANKS DIRECT MAIL/CALIFORNIA—See Harte-Hanks Communications, Inc., pg. 513
HARTE-HANKS GRAPHICS—See Harte-Hanks Communications, Inc., pg. 513
HARTE-HANKS MARKETING SERVICES—See Harte-Hanks Communications, Inc., pg. 513
HARTE-HANKS TELEVISION, INC. (KENS-TV)—See Harte-Hanks Communications, Inc., pg. 513
HARTE-HANKS TRANSPORTATION SERVICES—See Harte-Hanks Communications, Inc., pg. 513
THE HARTER GROUP, pg. 513
HARTER SYSTEMS DIV.—See The Harter Group, pg. 514
HARTFORD DISTRIBUTORS INC., pg. 514
HARTFORD-WOOD RIVER TERMINAL—See Piasa Motor Fuels Inc., pg. 869
HARTWELL COMMERCIAL DIVISION—See The Hartwell Corporation, pg. 514
THE HARTWELL CORPORATION, pg. 514
HARTZ GROUP, pg. 514
THE HARTZ MOUNTAIN CORP., pg. 514
HARTZ MOUNTAIN GROUP—See Hartz Group, pg. 514
HARTZ MOUNTAIN INDUSTRIES—See Hartz Group, pg. 514
HARTZELL CORPORATION, pg. 514
HARVARD INDUSTRIES, INC., pg. 514
HARVARD INTERIORS MANUFACTURING CO.—See Harvard Industries, Inc., pg. 514
HARVE BENARD LTD. MANUFACTURING, pg. 514
HARVEST BRANDS, INC.—See Altair Corporation, pg. 45
HARVEST EQUITY INC.—See Farmland Industries, Inc., pg. 402
HARVEST INDUSTRIES, INC.—See Altair Corporation, pg. 45
HARVEST STATES COOPERATIVES, pg. 514
J.H. HARVEY COMPANY, pg. 515
HARVEY CONSTRUCTION COMPANY, INC., pg. 515
FRED HARVEY TRANSPORTATION COMPANY—See JMB Realty Corporation, pg. 585
SID HARVEY INC., pg. 515
HARVEY INDUSTRIES, INC., pg. 515
HARWICK CHEMICAL CORP., pg. 515
THE HARWOOD COMPANIES, INC., pg. 515
HARZA ENGINEERING CO., pg. 516
HARZA ENVIRONMENTAL SERVICES, INC.—See Harza Engineering Co., pg. 516
HARZA NORTHWEST, INC.—See Harza Engineering Co., pg. 516
HASELOW & ASSOCIATES, INC., pg. 516
HASKEL ENERGY SYSTEMS LTD.—See Haskel, Inc., pg. 516
HASKEL, INC., pg. 516
HASPER EQUIPMENT CO.—See Cloverdale Equipment Co., pg. 256
JOHN HASSALL, INC., pg. 516
THE HASSINGER COMPANIES, pg. 516
HASSLOCHER ENTERPRISES, INC., D/B/A FRONTIER ENTERPRISES, pg. 516
HASTINGS CO-OP CREAMERY COMPANY, pg. 516
HAT DANCE—See Lettuce Entertain You Enterprises, Inc., pg. 669
HATCH GRINDING COMPANY—See Carquest Corporation, pg. 225
HATFIELD QUALITY MEATS, INC., pg. 517
HATTERAS YACHTS—See Minstar, Inc., pg. 758
HATZEL & BUEHLER, INC.—See Construction Management Service, pg. 277
HAUCK MFG. CO., pg. 517
HAUENSTEIN & BURMEISTER, INC., pg. 517
THE HAUGHEY GROUP, INC., pg. 517
HAULPAK DIVISION, KOMATSU DRESSER COMPANY—See INDRESCO, Inc., pg. 565
HAVATAMPA INCORPORATED, pg. 517
HAVENS & EMERSON, INC.—See Lawler-Havens Inc., pg. 661
HAVENS STEEL CO., pg. 517
HAVILAND ENTERPRISES, pg. 517
HAVILAND-KALAMAZOO—See Haviland Enterprises, pg. 517
HAVILAND/WILBUR-ELLIS AGRICULTURAL, pg. 517
HAWAIIAN BITUMULS & PAVING COMPANY—See Dillingham Construction Corporation, pg. 338
HAWAIIAN DISCOVERY TOURS, INC.—See JMB Realty Corporation, pg. 585
HAWAIIAN DREDGING & CONSTRUCTION COMPANY—See Dillingham Construction Corporation, pg. 338
GLENN O. HAWBAKER, INC., pg. 517
GERTRUDE HAWK CHOCOLATES, INC., pg. 517
HAWKEYE STEEL PRODUCTS, INC., pg. 518
HAWKINS MARKETS, INC., pg. 518
HAWLEY MARTIN PARTNERS, INC., pg. 518
HAWORTH GROUP INC., pg. 518
HAWORTH, INC., pg. 518
HAWORTH LTD.—See Haworth, Inc., pg. 518
HAWORTH U.K. LTD.—See Haworth, Inc., pg. 518
HAWS DRINKING FAUCET CO., pg. 518
HAWTHORNE ADV., INC., pg. 518
HAWTHORNE AIRPORT SERVICES, INC.—See Hawthorne Corp., pg. 519
HAWTHORNE AVIATION—See Hawthorne Corp., pg. 519
HAWTHORNE COMMUNICATIONS, INC., pg. 518
HAWTHORNE CORP., pg. 518
HAWTHORNE LIFT SYSTEMS, pg. 519
HAWTHORNE MACHINERY COMPANY, pg. 519
HAWTHORNE POWER SYSTEMS—See Hawthorne Machinery Company, pg. 519
HAWTHORNE PROPERTIES, INC.—See Hawthorne Corp., pg. 519
HAWTHORNE SERVICES, INC.—See Hawthorne Corp., pg. 519
HAY & FORAGE INDUSTRIES—See AGCO Inc., pg. 4
HAYDEN, INC.—See The Equion Corporation, pg. 385
HAYES/HARWOOD, pg. 519
C. I. HAYES, INC., pg. 519
HAYES MICROCOMPUTER PRODUCTS (CANADA)—See Hayes Microcomputer Products, Inc., pg. 519
HAYES MICROCOMPUTER PRODUCTS, INC., pg. 519
HAYES MICROCOMPUTER PRODUCTS, INC.—See Hayes Microcomputer Products, Inc., pg. 519
HAYES MICROCOMPUTER PRODUCTS LTD.—See Hayes Microcomputer Products, Inc., pg. 519
HAYES, SEAY, MATTERN & MATTERN, INC., pg. 519
HAYS FLOOD CONTROLS—See Romac Industries, Inc., pg. 945
HAYWIN TEXTILE PRODUCTS, INC., pg. 520
HAZEL BISHOP CORPORATION, pg. 520
HAZELNUT GROWERS OF OREGON—See Sun Diamond Growers of California, pg. 1058
HAZEN PAPER COMPANY, pg. 520
HAZEN & SAWYER, pg. 520
HEAD SPORTS, INC., pg. 520
HEADCO INDUSTRIES, INC., pg. 520
HEADCO MACHINE WORKS, INC.—See Headco Industries, Inc., pg. 520
HEADER PRODUCTS INC., pg. 520
J. H. HEAFNER CO. INC., pg. 520
HEALTH AMERICA/CAPITALCARE, INC.—See Mutual of Omaha Insurance Company, pg. 779
HEALTH CARE DISTRIBUTORS OF INDIANA, INC., pg. 520
HEALTH CARE, INC.—See Accra Pac Group, pg. 11
HEALTH CARE LODGES, pg. 520
HEALTH CARE PREFERRED—See The Principal Financial Group, pg. 890
HEALTH MAINTENANCE OREGON—See Blue Cross & Blue Shield of Oregon, pg. 160
HEALTH MANAGEMENT SYSTEMS, INC., pg. 521
HEALTH SERVICES PLUS, INC.—See Alco Health Services Corporation, pg. 32
HEALTH VITAMIN COMPANY, INC., pg. 521
HEALTH WATERS, INC.—See Sammons Enterprises, Inc., pg. 968
HEALTHCARE GROUP—See The Hearst Corporation, pg. 522
BILL HEARD ENTERPRISES, INC., pg. 521
HEARST BOOK GROUP—See The Hearst Corporation, pg. 522
HEARST BOOKS/BUSINESS PUBLISHING GROUP—See The Hearst Corporation, pg. 521
HEARST BROADCASTING DIVISION—See The Hearst Corporation, pg. 522
HEARST BUSINESS COMMUNICATIONS, INC.—See The Hearst Corporation, pg. 522
HEARST CABLEVISION OF CALIFORNIA, INC.—See The Hearst Corporation, pg. 523

THE HEARST CORPORATION, pg. 521
HEARST ENTERPRISES DIVISION—See The Hearst Corporation, pg. 523
HEARST ENTERTAINMENT—See The Hearst Corporation, pg. 523
HEARST ENTERTAINMENT PRODUCTIONS, INC.—See The Hearst Corporation, pg. 523
HEARST ENTERTAINMENT & SYNDICATION—See The Hearst Corporation, pg. 523
HEARST MAGAZINES DIVISION—See The Hearst Corporation, pg. 523
HEARST MAGAZINES SPECIAL PUBLICATIONS—See The Hearst Corporation, pg. 523
HEARST MARINE BOOKS—See The Hearst Corporation, pg. 521
HEARST NEWSPAPERS DIVISION—See The Hearst Corporation, pg. 523
HEARST PROFESSIONAL MAGAZINES, INC.—See The Hearst Corporation, pg. 522
HEARST REAL ESTATE DIVISION—See The Hearst Corporation, pg. 524
HEARTHSONG, INC.—See Foster & Gallagher Inc., pg. 426
HEAT BATH PARK METALLURGICAL, INC., pg. 524
HEAT BATH PARK METALLURGICAL PRODUCTS—See Heat Bath Park Metallurgical, Inc., pg. 524
HEAT CONTROLLER, INC., pg. 524
HEAT TECH, INC.—See Group Dekko International Inc., pg. 489
HEATCRAFT INC.—See Lennox International Inc., pg. 667
HEATCRAFT REFRIGERATION PRODUCTS DIVISION—See Lennox International Inc., pg. 667
HEATERS ENGINEERING, INC.—See Group Dekko International Inc., pg. 489
HEATH CONSULTANTS INCORPORATED, pg. 524
JOHN HEATH & CO. LIMITED—See American Trading and Production Corporation, pg. 65
HEAVY MACHINES, INC., pg. 524
HEBREW NATIONAL KOSHER FOODS DIV.—See National Foods Inc., pg. 788
HECK ENTERPRISES, INC., pg. 524
HECKETHORN MFG. COMPANY, pg. 524
HECTOR & CO. A.B.—See Belmont Industries, Inc., pg. 137
HEDBERG DATA SYSTEMS, INC.—See Steelcase Inc., pg. 1044
HEDLAND—See Racine Federated, Inc., pg. 909
HEERY INTERNATIONAL, INC., pg. 525
HARRY O. HEFTER-ASSOCIATES, INC.—See The HOH Organizations, pg. 497
HEHR INTERNATIONAL INC., pg. 525
HEICO INC., pg. 525
HEIDTMAN STEEL PRODUCTS, INC., pg. 525
HEIGHTS HEATING & COOLING, pg. 525
HEIL-BRICE RETAIL ADVERTISING, pg. 525
HEIL BULK TRAILER CO.—See The Heil Co., pg. 525
THE HEIL CO., pg. 525
HEIL REFUSE & DUMP BODY CO.—See The Heil Co., pg. 525
HEIL ROTOMOLD, INC.—See The Heil Co., pg. 526
HEIL STEEL FABRICATING, INC.—See The Heil Co., pg. 526
HEIL TANK SERVICES, INC.—See The Heil Co., pg. 526
HEIL WEST, INC.—See The Heil Co., pg. 526
HEILEMAN AIR SERVICES, LTD.—See G. Heileman Brewing Co., Inc., pg. 526
G. HEILEMAN BREWING CO., INC., pg. 526
G. HEILEMAN BREWING COMPANY, INC.—See G. Heileman Brewing Co., Inc., pg. 526
HEINEN'S INC., pg. 526
HEINTZELMAN'S TRUCK CENTER INC., pg. 526
HELENA LABORATORIES CORPORATION, pg. 526
HELIKON FURNITURE CO., INC., pg. 526
HELLER BROS. PACKING CORP., pg. 526
HELLER INTERNATIONAL, pg. 526
HELLER SEASONINGS & INGREDIENTS, INC., pg. 526
J. HELLMAN PRODUCE, INC., pg. 527
HELM, INC., pg. 527
HELMICK CORPORATION, pg. 527
EDD HELMS ELECTRICAL CONTRACTING, pg. 527
EDD HELMS ELECTRICAL SERVICE, INC.—See Edd Helms Electrical Contracting, pg. 527
HELMSLEY ENTERPRISES, INC., pg. 527
HELMSLEY HOTELS INC.—See Helmsley Enterprises, Inc., pg. 527
HELMSLEY-NOYES CO., INC.—See Helmsley Enterprises, Inc., pg. 527
THE HELMSLEY PALACE HOTEL—See Helmsley Enterprises, Inc., pg. 527
HELMSLEY-SPEAR CONVERSION SALES CORP.—See Helmsley Enterprises, Inc., pg. 527
HELMSLEY-SPEAR INC.—See Helmsley Enterprises, Inc., pg. 527
HELMSMAN MANAGEMENT SERVICES, INC.—See Liberty Mutual Insurance Co., pg. 674
HELP MANAGEMENT CORPORATION, pg. 527
HELP SERVICE CORPORATION—See Help Management Corporation, pg. 528
HELPERN JOAN & DAVID, INC., pg. 528
HELWIG CARBON PRODUCTS, INC., pg. 528
HELZBERG'S DIAMOND SHOPS, INC., pg. 528
HEMISPHERE-LEO BURNETT, INC.—See Leo Burnett Company, Inc., pg. 192
PAUL HEMMER CONSTRUCTION COMPANY, pg. 528
HEMPT BROTHERS, INC., pg. 528
HENCO, INC., pg. 528
HENDERSON & BAIRD HARDWARE CO., INC.—See Distribution America, pg. 340
HENDERSON ADVERTISING, INC., pg. 528
HENDERSON AUCTIONEERS, pg. 528
HENDERSON ELECTRIC CO., INC., pg. 529
JOSEPH J. HENDERSON & SON, INC., pg. 529
HENDERSON MFG.—See Willmar Manufacturing, pg. 1193
HENDRICK IMPORTS—See Hendrick Management Corporation, pg. 529
HENDRICK MANAGEMENT CORPORATION, pg. 529
HENDRICK MOTORSPORTS—See Hendrick Management Corporation, pg. 529
LEON HENDRICKSON, pg. 529
HENEBRYS—See Reliable Stores, Inc., pg. 925
HENKELS & MCCOY, INC., pg. 529
THE HENLEY GROUP, INC., pg. 529
HENLEY PAPER COMPANY, pg. 529
THE HENNEGAN COMPANY, pg. 529
HENNELLS, INC., pg. 530
HENNINGSEN FOODS, INC.—See Kifuki U.S.A. Co., Inc., pg. 629
HENNINGSEN FOODS LTD.—See Kifuki U.S.A. Co., Inc., pg. 629
HENNINGSEN NEDERLAND B.V.—See Kifuki U.S.A. Co., Inc., pg. 629
HENNINGSEN & SONS, INC.—See A. Teichert & Son, Inc., pg. 1084
HENNINGSEN-VAN DEN BURG—See Kifuki U.S.A. Co., Inc., pg. 629
HENRI'S FOOD PRODUCTS CO., INC., pg. 530
E.P. HENRY CORPORATION, pg. 530
HENRY COUNTY LOCAL—See Landmark Communications, Inc., pg. 655
HENRY GILL SILVERMAN ADVERTISING, pg. 530
HENRY RUSSELL BRUCE, INC., pg. 530
HENRYS, INC., pg. 530
HENSCHEL CORP.—See SPD Technologies, pg. 964
HENSEL PHELPS CONSTRUCTION CO., pg. 530
HENSLEY & CO., pg. 530
HENSON TIMBER PRODUCTS CORP.—See Stonecutter Mills Corp., pg. 1051
HER MAJESTY, pg. 530
HERALD-NEWS—See The Copley Press, Inc., pg. 284
THE HERALD—See Blade Communications, Inc., pg. 155
HERBAL ENTERPRISES INC., pg. 530
G. R. HERBERGER'S, INC., pg. 530
HERCULES ENGINES, INC., pg. 531
THE HERCULES TIRE & RUBBER COMPANY, pg. 531
HERCULES TIRE & RUBBER COMPANY, pg. 531
HEREFORD STATE BANK—See First Abilene Bankshares, Inc., pg. 412
HERESITE PROTECTIVE COATINGS INC., pg. 531
HERFF JONES INC., pg. 531
HERITAGE CUTLERY, INC.—See Rogers, Lunt & Bowlen Co., pg. 943
HERITAGE LINCOLN-MERCURY—See Fairway Ford, Inc., pg. 398
HERITAGE SERVICE CORPORATION—See Guarantee Title Co., Inc., pg. 491
HERLIN PRESS, pg. 531
A.D. HERMAN CONSTRUCTION CO.—See The Atlas Construction Co., pg. 96
HERMAN ASSOCIATES, INC., pg. 531
JOS. M. HERMAN SHOE CO., pg. 531
HERMES AUTOMOTIVE MANUFACTURING CORP., pg. 531
HERMETIC SEAL CORP.—See HCC Industries, pg. 496
HERMETITE CORP.—See HCC Industries, pg. 496
HERRAMIENTAS KLEIN S.A. DE C.V.—See Klein Tools Inc., pg. 635
HERRING NEWMAN, pg. 531
HERSHEY CREAMERY COMPANY, pg. 531
THE HERTZ CORPORATION—See Park Ridge Corporation, pg. 849
HERTZ EQUIPMENT RENTAL CORP.—See Park Ridge Corporation, pg. 849
HESCO PARTS CORPORATION, pg. 531
HESCO SUPPLY CO., INC.—See The Hearst Corporation, pg. 524
HESS ENGINEERING INC., pg. 532
HESS'S DEPARTMENT STORES, INC.—See Crown American Corporation, pg. 302
HESSTON—See AGCO Inc., pg. 4
HEWITT-ROBINS CORP., pg. 532
HEWITT SOAP CO.—See Jordan Company, pg. 604
HEYMAN CORPORATION, pg. 532
HI NABOR SUPERMARKET INC., pg. 532
HI-PRO ANIMAL HEALTH DIV.—See Friona Industries, L.P., pg. 434
HI-PRO FEED DIV.—See Friona Industries, L.P., pg. 434
HI TECH INFORMATION INC.—See International Data Group, pg. 577
HIBBERT GROUP, pg. 532
HICKERSON PHELPS KIRTLEY & ASSOCIATES, pg. 532
HICKEY-MITCHELL COMPANY—See Nationwide Mutual Insurance Company, pg. 795
HICKINBOTHAM BROS., LTD, pg. 532
HICKMAN WILLIAMS & CO. INC., pg. 532
HICKORY CONSTRUCTION COMPANY, pg. 532
HICKORY FARMS, INC., pg. 532
HICKORY HILL FURNITURE CORPORATION—See Norwalk Furniture Corporation, pg. 816
HICKORY PRINTING GROUP, INC., pg. 533
HICKS & ASSOCIATES INC.—See Science Applications International Corporation, pg. 982
HICKS OIL-HICKS GAS, INC., pg. 533
RONI HICKS & ASSOCIATES, INC., pg. 533
HIDDEN VALLEY RESORT—See Kettler Brothers, Inc., pg. 626
THE HIEBING GROUP, INC., pg. 533
IRA HIGDON GROCERY, INC., pg. 533
HIGGINBOTHAM-BARTLETT CO., pg. 533
J. E. HIGGINS LUMBER CO., pg. 533
HIGH INDUSTRIES INC., pg. 533
HIGH POINT EQUITIES, INC.—See Society for Savings Bancorp, Inc., pg. 1016
HIGH POINT FINANCIAL CORP., pg. 533
HIGH POINT INVESTMENT ADVISORY SERVICES—See High Point Financial Corp., pg. 534
HIGH POINT OIL CO., pg. 534
HIGH POINT VENTURES, INC.—See Rotterdam Ventures Inc., pg. 951
HIGH SCHOOL DIVISION—See American Institute For Foreign Study, pg. 56
HIGH TREE SERVICES LTD.—See The Davey Tree Expert Company, pg. 317
HIGHER EDUCATION ASSISTANCE FOUNDATION—See Help Management Corporation, pg. 528
HIGHER EDUCATION LOAN PROGRAM OF KANSAS—See Help Management Corporation, pg. 528
HIGHER EDUCATION LOAN PROGRAM OF WASHINGTON, D.C.—See Help Management Corporation, pg. 528
HIGHER EDUCATION LOAN PROGRAM OF WEST VIRGINIA—See Help Management Corporation, pg. 528
THE HIGHLAND GROUP, INC., pg. 534
HIGHLAND MILLS INC., pg. 534
HIGHLIGHTS FOR CHILDREN, INC., pg. 534
HIGH-LITES, INC.—See Jac Jacobsen Industries, Inc., pg. 588
HIGHWOOD SERVICE, INC.—See Ralph C. Wilson Enterprises, pg. 1194
HILAND DAIRY COMPANY—See Prairie Farms Dairy, Inc., pg. 884
HILL-BEHAN LUMBER COMPANY, pg. 534
HILL & GRIFFITH COMPANY, pg. 534
HILL, HOLLIDAY, CONNORS, COSMOPULOS, INC., pg. 534
HILL, HOLLIDAY/LOS ANGELES—See Hill, Holliday, Connors, Cosmopulos, Inc., pg. 534
HILL, HOLLIDAY/NEW YORK—See Hill, Holliday, Connors, Cosmopulos, Inc., pg. 534
HILL, HOLLIDAY/TORONTO—See Hill, Holliday, Connors, Cosmopulos, Inc., pg. 534
HILL INTERNATIONAL INC., pg. 534
HILL & WANG—See Farrar, Straus & Giroux, Inc., pg. 403
HILLEND ENVIRONMENTAL INDUSTRY, LTD.—See The Heil Co., pg. 526
HILLERICH & BRADSBY CO., INC., pg. 535
HILLHOUSE ASSOCIATES INSURANCE, INC.—See New York Life Insurance Company, pg. 802
HILLIARD CORPORATION, pg. 535
HILL-LOMA, INC.—See Goldman Financial Group, pg. 468
HILLMAN COMPANY, pg. 535
HILLS MATERIALS CO.—See Northwestern Engineering Co., pg. 815
HILLSDALE DAILY NEWS—See Stauffer Communications, Inc., pg. 1042
HILLSIDE CAPITAL, INC., pg. 535
HILLSIDE INDUSTRIES, INC.—See Hillside Capital, Inc., pg. 535
THE HILSINGER CORP., pg. 535
HINDERLITER HEAT TREATING, INC.—See Hinderliter Industries, Inc., pg. 535
HINDERLITER INDUSTRIES, INC., pg. 535
HINIKER COMPANY, pg. 535
HINKLE EASTER PRODUCTS—See Darda Inc. (USA), pg. 315
HINKLEY LIGHTING INC., pg. 535
HIPPOCRATES PARTNERS, pg. 535
HIROSS INC., pg. 536
HIRSCHFELD, INC., pg. 536
HIRSCHFELD STEEL COMPANY, INC.—See Hirschfeld, Inc., pg. 536
HIRSH COMPANY—See Code, Hennessy & Simmons, pg. 258
HITACHI ZOSEN SYSTEMS, INC—See Effective Management Systems, pg. 371
HITCHCOCK CHAIR COMPANY LTD, pg. 536
HITCHCOCK-FLEMING & ASSOCIATES, INC., pg. 536
HITCHCOCK INDUSTRIES, INC., pg. 536
HITCHINER MANUFACTURING COMPANY, INC., pg. 536
THE HIVELY AGENCY INC., pg. 536
HLI HOLDINGS, INC.—See Howell Laboratories, Inc., pg. 548
HOBART BROTHERS CO., pg. 536
HOBART BROTHERS OF CANADA LTD.—See Hobart Brothers Co., pg. 536
HOBART TAFA TECHNOLOGIES, INC.—See Hobart Brothers Co., pg. 537
HOBOKEN FLOORS-ADIRONDACK DIVISION—See Hoboken Wood Flooring Corporation, pg. 537
HOBOKEN FLOORS-A.S.T. DIVISION—See Hoboken Wood Flooring Corporation, pg. 537
HOBOKEN FLOORS-CAPITOL DIVISION—See Hoboken Wood Flooring Corporation, pg. 537
HOBOKEN FLOORS-CONNECTICUT DIV.—See Hoboken Wood Flooring Corporation, pg. 537
HOBOKEN FLOORS-EASTERN FLOORING DIVISION—See Hoboken Wood Flooring Corporation, pg. 537
HOBOKEN FLOORS-NEW ENGLAND DIVISION—See Hoboken Wood Flooring Corporation, pg. 537
HOBOKEN WOOD FLOORING CORPORATION, pg. 537
HODGSON MILL, INC.—See Siemer Milling Company, pg. 1002
HODSKINS SIMONE & SEARLS, INC., pg. 537
HOECHST CERAMTEC NORTH AMERICA, INC., pg. 537
HOFFCO, INC., pg. 537
HOFFER PLASTICS CORPORATION, pg. 537
HOFFMAN BROTHERS PACKING CO., pg. 537
HOFFMAN CONSTRUCTION COMPANY OF ALASKA—See Hoffman Corporation, pg. 537
HOFFMAN CONSTRUCTION COMPANY OF CALIFORNIA—See Hoffman Corporation, pg. 537
HOFFMAN CONSTRUCTION COMPANY OF OREGON—See Hoffman Corporation, pg. 537
HOFFMAN CONSTRUCTION COMPANY OF WASHINGTON—See Hoffman Corporation, pg. 537
HOFFMAN CORPORATION, pg. 537
HOFFMAN HOMES, INC.—See The Hassinger Companies, pg. 516
A. H. HOFFMAN, INC., pg. 538
HOFFMAN/LEWIS, pg. 538

HOFFMAN MECHANICAL CORPORATION—See Hoffman Corporation, pg. 538
HOFFMAN SEEDS, INC.—See A. H. Hoffman, Inc., pg. 538
HOFFMAN STRUCTURES, INC.—See Hoffman Corporation, pg. 538
HOFFMAN YORK & COMPTON, pg. 538
HOFFRITZ FOR CUTLERY, pg. 538
HOFFRITZ INTERNATIONAL—See Hoffritz for Cutlery, pg. 538
HOFLEY MANUFACTURING COMPANY, pg. 538
HOGAN TRANSFER & STORAGE CORPORATION, INC.—See Mayflower Transit, Inc., pg. 724
MICHAEL HOGG-YOUNG & RUBICAM (PVT.) LTD.—See Young & Rubicam Inc., pg. 1214
HOH ASSOCIATES—See Post Buckley Schuh & Jernigan, pg. 882
HOHNER/HSS INC., pg. 538
HOLBROOK LUMBER COMPANY, pg. 538
HOLCOMB & HOKE MFG. COMPANY, INC., pg. 538
HOLCOMB STATION—See Sunflower Electric Power Corporation, pg. 1060
HOLDER CORPORATION, pg. 538
ED HOLDERNESS SUPPLIES, pg. 538
HOLIDAY COMPANIES, pg. 539
HOLIDAY HOUSE, INC.—See Washington Mutual Savings Bank, pg. 1166
HOLIDAY INN—See Benson's, Inc., pg. 140
HOLIDAY STATIONS, INC.—See Holiday Companies, pg. 539
RON HOLLAND ADVERTISING INC., pg. 539
HOLLAND MARK MARTIN, pg. 539
THE HOLLAND SENTINEL—See Stauffer Communications, Inc., pg. 1042
A. J. HOLLANDER CO., INC., pg. 539
ROGER HOLLER CHEVROLET CO., pg. 539
JOHN R. HOLLINGSWORTH CO., pg. 539
HOLLINGSWORTH OIL CO. INC., pg. 539
HOLLINGSWORTH & VOSE CO., pg. 539
HOLLINGSWORTH & VOSE CO. U.K. LTD.—See Hollingsworth & Vose Co., pg. 539
HOLLINGSWORTH & VOSE EUROPE NV—See Hollingsworth & Vose Co., pg. 539
HOLLISTER ADVERTISING, pg. 539
HOLLY MILK PLANT—See Atlantic Dairy Cooperative, pg. 95
HOLLYMATIC CORPORATION, pg. 539
HOLLY'S INC., pg. 540
HOLLYTEX—See 21 International Holdings, Inc., pg. 1121
HOLLYTEX CARPET MILLS, INC., pg. 540
HOLLYTEX-WESTERN DIV.—See 21 International Holdings, Inc., pg. 1121
HOLLYWOOD ALLOY CASTING COMPANY, pg. 540
HOLLYWOOD PARK, INC., pg. 540
HOLMAN ENTERPRISES, pg. 540
HOLMATIC, INC.—See Barry-Wehmiller Company, pg. 122
HOLMES PROTECTION GROUP, INC., pg. 540
HOLMES PROTECTION OF LONG ISLAND, INC.—See Holmes Protection Group, Inc., pg. 540
HOLMES PROTECTION OF NEW JERSEY, INC.—See Holmes Protection Group, Inc., pg. 540
HOLMES PROTECTION OF NEW YORK, INCORPORATED—See Holmes Protection Group, Inc., pg. 540
HOLMES PROTECTION OF PHILADELPHIA, INC.—See Holmes Protection Group, Inc., pg. 540
HOLMES TUTTLE FORD, INC., pg. 540
HOLMQUIST GRAIN & LUMBER CO., pg. 540
HOLOPHANE, S.A. DE C.V.—See McNeel International Corp., pg. 732
HOLOUBEK INC., pg. 540
HOLSTEIN ASSOCIATION OF AMERICA, pg. 541
CHARLES HOLSTON, INC., pg. 541
HOLSUM BAKERY, INC., pg. 541
HOLSUM OF FORT WAYNE, INC.—See Lewis Brothers Bakeries, Inc., pg. 673
HOLT HOSIERY MILLS, INC., pg. 541
HOLTON NAMIOTKA JONES, INC., pg. 541
FRANK HOLTON CO.—See G. Leblanc Corporation, pg. 665
HOLY CROSS ELECTRIC ASSOCIATION, pg. 541
HOLZER WATCH CO., INC., pg. 541
HOMAN LUMBER MART, INC., pg. 541
HOME CARE P.R.N., INC.—See Technical Aid Corporation, pg. 1083
HOME CURTAIN CORPORATION—See Home Innovations, Inc., pg. 541
HOME HEATING & AIR CONDITIONING—See EVCON Holdings, pg. 391
HOME INNOVATIONS BED FASHIONS—See Home Innovations, Inc., pg. 541
HOME INNOVATIONS, INC., pg. 541
HOME INTERIORS & GIFTS, INC., pg. 541
HOME JUICE CO. OF FLORIDA—See Home Juice Company, pg. 542
HOME JUICE COMPANY, pg. 541
HOME-OWNERS INSURANCE CO.—See Auto-Owners Insurance, pg. 100
HOMELAND STORES, INC., pg. 542
HOMEMAKER SHOPS, INC., pg. 542
HOMES BY DAVE BROWN, pg. 542
HOMES OF MERIT INC., pg. 542
HOMES & SON CONTRACTORS, INC., pg. 542
HOMES OF YORK-ADAMS COUNTY—See Landmark Communications, Inc., pg. 655
HOMESTEAD HOUSE INC., pg. 542
HOMESTEAD PRODUCTS—See Seattle Lighting Fixture Co., pg. 986
HOMETOWN PUBLICATIONS—See Journal Communications Inc., pg. 607
HOMEWOOD CORPORATION, pg. 542
HONEYMEAD PRODUCTS CO., pg. 542
HONOLULU ADVERTISER, INC.—See Persis Corporation, pg. 863
HONORBUILT INDUSTRIES, INC., pg. 542
HOOD COMMUNICATIONS, INC.—See Hood Corporation, pg. 543
HOOD & COMPANY, pg. 542
HOOD CORPORATION, pg. 542
H. P. HOOD INC.—See Agway, Inc., pg. 25
HOOD INDUSTRIES INC.—See Carpenter Rigging, pg. 224
HOOF PRODUCTS COMPANY, pg. 543
HOOGOVENS ALUMINUM CORP., pg. 543
V. B. HOOK & CO., INC., pg. 543
J. G. HOOK, INC., pg. 543
HOOKER FURNITURE CORPORATION, pg. 543
HOOKER INDUSTRIES, pg. 543
HOOSIER WIRE, INC.—See Group Dekko International Inc., pg. 489
HOOVER GROUP, INC., pg. 543
HOPE DESIGN GROUP, pg. 543
HOPE'S ARCHITECTURAL PRODUCTS INC., pg. 543
HOPKINSVILLE ELEVATOR COMPANY, INC., pg. 543
HOPKINSVILLE MILLING CO., pg. 543
HOPPER INC., pg. 543
HOPPLE PLASTICS, INC., pg. 544
THOMAS R. HOPSON BROKER, INC., pg. 544
HORIZON BANCORP, pg. 544
HORIZON MEDIA ENTERTAINMENT—See Horizon Media, Inc., pg. 544
HORIZON MEDIA, INC., pg. 544
HORIZON PAPER CO., INC., pg. 544
HORLICK LEVIN ADVERTISING INC., pg. 544
HORN PACKAGING CORPORATION, pg. 544
HORNADY AMMUNITION—See Hornady Manufacturing Company, pg. 544
HORNADY MANUFACTURING COMPANY, pg. 544
HORNER RAUSCH COMPANY, pg. 544
HORSEHEAD INDUSTRIES, INC., pg. 545
HORSEHEAD RESOURCE DEVELOPMENT COMPANY, INC.—See Horsehead Industries, Inc., pg. 545
HORTON HOMES, INC., pg. 545
HOSPITAL AFFILIATES DEVELOPMENT CORPORATION—See Affiliates Group Inc., pg. 24
HOSPITAL BUILDING & EQUIPMENT CO.—See HBE Corporation, pg. 496
HOSPITALITY PROCUREMENT DIVISION—See Carlson Companies, Inc., pg. 221
HOST APPAREL, INC., pg. 545
HOST FOR HER—See Host Apparel, Inc., pg. 545
HOSTMARK MANAGEMENT GROUP, pg. 545
HOT SHOT DELIVERY INC., pg. 545
THE HOTSY CORPORATION, pg. 545
HOTTMAN EDWARDS, pg. 545
HOUCHENS INDUSTRIES INC., pg. 545
HOUCK INDUSTRIES, INC., pg. 545
HOUGEN MANUFACTURING INC., pg. 546
HOUGHTON A.G. SWITZERLAND—See E. F. Houghton & Co., pg. 546
E. F. HOUGHTON & CO., pg. 546
E. F. HOUGHTON CO. OF CANADA LTD.—See E. F. Houghton & Co., pg. 546
E. F. HOUGHTON DO BRAZIL—See E. F. Houghton & Co., pg. 546
HOUGHTON ITALIA S.P.A.—See E. F. Houghton & Co., pg. 546
HOUGHTON VAUGHN PLC—See E. F. Houghton & Co., pg. 546
HOUGHTON-BENELUX B.V.—See E. F. Houghton & Co., pg. 546
HOUSE BEAUTIFUL—See The Hearst Corporation, pg. 523
HOUSE OF BIANCHI, pg. 546
HOUSE & GARDEN—See Advance Publications Inc., pg. 19
HOUSE OF PERFECTION, INC., pg. 546
HOUSE OF RAEFORD FARMS, INC., pg. 546
HOUSE OF RONNIE, INC., pg. 546
HOUSING-HOME SALES, INC.—See Washington Homes, Inc., pg. 1166
HOUSTON CHRONICLE—See The Hearst Corporation, pg. 524
HOUSTON EFFLER & PARTNERS, pg. 546
HOUSTON ENGINEERS—See Wilson Industries Inc., pg. 1194
HOUSTON FEARLESS 76 INC., pg. 546
HOUSTON FOODS COMPANY, pg. 547
HOVOMEX S.A. DE C.V.—See Hollingsworth & Vose Co., pg. 539
THE DEE HOWARD COMPANY, pg. 547
HOWARD INDUSTRIES, INC., pg. 547
HOWARD MANUFACTURING, pg. 547
HOWARD, MERRELL & PARTNERS, INC., pg. 547
HOWARD NEEDLES TAMMEN & BERGENDOFF, pg. 547
HOWARD PAPER—See Fox Valley Corporation, pg. 428
HOWARD PAPER MILLS—See Fox Valley Corporation, pg. 428
HOWARDS APPLIANCES, INC., pg. 547
HOWDEN SIROCCO INC., pg. 547
HOWE FURNITURE CORPORATION, pg. 547
E. W. HOWELL COMPANY, INC., pg. 547
HOWELL EXPORTS—See Howell Instruments Corp., pg. 548
HOWELL INSTRUMENTS CORP., pg. 547
HOWELL LABORATORIES, INC., pg. 548
HOWES LEATHER COMPANY, INC., pg. 548
HOYLE PRODUCTS—See Brown & Bigelow, Inc., pg. 181
THE HOYT COMPANY—See Vinyl Therm, Inc., pg. 1152
HOYT CORPORATION, pg. 548
HOYT DEVELOPMENT—See Vinyl Therm, Inc., pg. 1152
THE HOYT GROUP, pg. 548
HOYT SECURITIES, INC.—See The Hoyt Group, pg. 548
RONALD HSU CONSTRUCTION, pg. 548
HUB FURNITURE CO.—See Reliable Stores, Inc., pg. 925
HUB FURNITURE STORE—See Reliable Stores, Inc., pg. 925
HUB INC., pg. 548
HUBACHER CADILLAC INC., pg. 548
HUBBARD BROADCASTING, INC., pg. 548
HUBBARD COMMUNICATIONS—See Hubbard Broadcasting, Inc., pg. 549
HUBBARD CONSTRUCTION CO., pg. 549
HUBBARD HALL INC., pg. 549
HUBBARD MILLING COMPANY, pg. 549
HUBBARD PETFOOD—See Hubbard Milling Company, pg. 549
HUBBS IMPORTING CORP., pg. 550
J.M. HUBER CORPORATION, pg. 550
HUBER, HUNT & NICHOLS, INC.—See The Hunt Corporation, pg. 553
J.M. HUBER, CALCIUM CARBONATE DIV.—See J.M. Huber Corporation, pg. 550
J.M. HUBER, CHEMICALS DIVISION—See J.M. Huber Corporation, pg. 550
J.M. HUBER, CLAY DIV.—See J.M. Huber Corporation, pg. 550
J.M. HUBER, ENGINEERED CARBONS DIV.—See J.M. Huber Corporation, pg. 550
J.M. HUBER, FLOW CONTROL DIV.—See J.M. Huber Corporation, pg. 550
J.M. HUBER, OIL & GAS DIV.—See J.M. Huber Corporation, pg. 550
J.M. HUBER, POLYMER SERVICES DIV.—See J.M. Huber Corporation, pg. 550
J.M. HUBER, PRINTING INK DIV.—See J.M. Huber Corporation, pg. 550
J.M. HUBER, SOLEM DIV.—See J.M. Huber Corporation, pg. 550
J.M. HUBER, WOOD PRODUCTS DIV.—See J.M. Huber Corporation, pg. 550
HUBERT COMPANY, pg. 550
THE HUBINGER COMPANY, pg. 550
HUBLER CHEVROLET INC., pg. 550
HUDEPOHL-SCHOENLING BREWING COMPANY, pg. 550
HUDSON & AFFILIATED CO., pg. 551
J. H. HUDSON CONSTRUCTION CO.—See J. S. Alberici Construction Co., Inc., pg. 31
H.D. HUDSON MANUFACTURING COMPANY, pg. 551
JIM HUDSON, PONTIAC, OLDSMOBILE GMC, pg. 551
HUDSON VALLEY PAPER COMPANY, pg. 551
HUDSON VALLEY TREE, INC., pg. 551
BARRY HUEY, BULLOCK & COOK ADVERTISING, INC., pg. 551
S. E. HUFFMAN CORP., pg. 551
HUFFMAN KOOS CO., pg. 551
NEIL HUFFMAN CHRYSLER PLYMOUTH DODGE—See Neil Huffman Nissan Inc., pg. 551
NEIL HUFFMAN VOLKSWAGON MAZDA SUBURU—See Neil Huffman Nissan Inc., pg. 551
NEIL HUFFMAN NISSAN INC., pg. 551
HUGHES ADVERTISING INC., pg. 551
R. S. HUGHES CO., INC., pg. 551
E.H. HUGHES COMPANY, INC., pg. 552
HERMAN HUGHES & SONS, INC., pg. 552
HUGHES MARKETS INC., pg. 552
HUGHES-TREITLER MANUFACTURING CORPORATION, pg. 552
HUITT-ZOLLARS, INC., pg. 552
HULL CORPORATION, pg. 552
HULMAN & COMPANY, pg. 552
HULT FRITZ MATUSZAK & ASSOCIATES, INC., pg. 552
HUMBOLDT EXPRESS, INC., pg. 552
HUMISTON-KEELING, INC., pg. 552
HUMPHREY FLUID POWER LTD.—See Humphrey Products Company, pg. 553
HUMPHREY PRODUCTS COMPANY, pg. 553
HUMPHREYS PRICE/COCHRAN & SANFORD ADVERTISING, pg. 553
HUNT BUILDING CORPORATION, pg. 553
CAROLINE HUNT TRUST ESTATE, pg. 553
RODNEY HUNT COMPANY, pg. 553
THE HUNT CORPORATION, pg. 553
HUNT OIL CENTRAL EXPLORATION DIVISION—See Hunt Oil Company, pg. 554
HUNT OIL COMPANY, pg. 553
HUNT OIL COTTON VALLEY DISTRICT—See Hunt Oil Company, pg. 554
HUNT OIL FAIRWAY GAS PLANT—See Hunt Oil Company, pg. 554
HUNT OIL GULF COAST DISTRICT—See Hunt Oil Company, pg. 554
HUNT OIL GULF COAST EXPLORATION DIVISION—See Hunt Oil Company, pg. 554
HUNT OIL INTERNATIONAL EXPLORATION-FOUNTAIN PLACE—See Hunt Oil Company, pg. 554
HUNT OIL INTERNATIONAL EXPLORATION-LONDON OFFICE—See Hunt Oil Company, pg. 554
HUNT OIL INTERNATIONAL PRODUCTION-FOUNTAIN PLACE—See Hunt Oil Company, pg. 554
HUNT OIL LAFAYETTE LAND OFFICE—See Hunt Oil Company, pg. 554
HUNT OIL SHREVEPORT LAND OFFICE—See Hunt Oil Company, pg. 554
HUNT OIL SOUTHWESTERN OFFICE—See Hunt Oil Company, pg. 554
THE HUNT PAVING COMPANY, INC.—See The Hunt Corporation, pg. 553
HUNT REFINING COMPANY—See Hunt Oil Company, pg. 554
HUNTCO ACQUISITIONS HOLDINGS, INC.—See Huntco Inc., pg. 554
HUNTCO HEALTH CARE CO.—See Huntco Inc., pg. 554
HUNTCO INC., pg. 554
HUNTCO STEEL CO.—See Huntco Inc., pg. 554
HUNTCOR INC.—See The Hunt Corporation, pg. 553
HUNTER CONTRACTING COMPANY, pg. 554
HUNTER CORP., pg. 554
HUNTER ENGINEERING CO., INC., pg. 554
HUNTER MARINE CORPORATION, pg. 555
HUNTINGTON TILE, INC.—See Pacific Holding Corporation, pg. 840
HUNTSINGER & JEFFER, pg. 555
HUNTSMAN CHEMICAL CORPORATION, pg. 555

HUNTTING ELEVATOR CO., pg. 555
HURD LOCK & MANUFACTURING CO.—See Avis Industrial Corporation, pg. 102
HURD MILLWORK COMPANY, INC.—See UIS, Inc., pg. 1123
HURLETRON INC.—See Altair Corporation, pg. 45
MIKE DAUGHERTY'S HURLING CHEVROLET, INC., pg. 555
HURON DAILY TRIBUNE—See The Hearst Corporation, pg. 524
HURON VALLEY STEEL CORP., pg. 555
HURST PERFORMANCES, INC.—See Mr. Gasket Company, pg. 761
HUSSEY CORPORATION, pg. 555
HUSSEY PLASTICS CO.—See Hussey Corporation, pg. 555
HUSSEY SEATING CO. (CANADA) LTD.—See Hussey Corporation, pg. 555
HUSSEY SEATING SYSTEMS (EUROPE) LTD.—See Hussey Corporation, pg. 555
HUTCHENS INDUSTRIES INC., pg. 555
HUTCHINS MANUFACTURING COMPANY, pg. 555
HUTCHINSON WIL-RICH MANUFACTURING CO.—See TIC United Corporation, pg. 1073
HUTCHINS/YOUNG & RUBICAM—See Young & Rubicam Inc., pg. 1211
CHUCK HUTTON CHEVROLET COMPANY, pg. 556
HVIDE SHIPPING, INC., pg. 556
HY-VEE FOOD STORES INCORPORATED, pg. 556
HYATT AIR, INC.—See H. Group Holding Inc., pg. 495
HYATT CORPORATION—See H. Group Holding Inc., pg. 495
HYATT HOTELS CORPORATION—See H. Group Holding Inc., pg. 495
HYATT INTERNATIONAL CORPORATION—See H. Group Holding Inc., pg. 495
HYDE MANUFACTURING CO., pg. 556
HYDE POINT FASHIONS—See Target Sportswear, Inc., pg. 1079
HYDRAULICS INTERNATIONAL, INC., pg. 556
HYDRECO—See ICM Industries, Inc., pg. 559
HYDRIL COMPANY, pg. 556
HYDRIL COMPANY—See Hydril Company, pg. 556
HYDRIL PRODUCTION TECHNOLOGY DIV.—See Hydril Company, pg. 556
HYDRIL RUBBER OPERS.—See Hydril Company, pg. 556
HYDRITE CHEMICAL COMPANY, pg. 556
HYDRO GROUP, INC., pg. 556
HYDRO/KIRBY AGRI SERVICE, INC., pg. 556
HYDRO-MILL CO., pg. 557
HYER INDUSTRIES INC./THAYER SCALE, pg. 557
HYGEIA DAIRY CO., INC., pg. 557
HYGRADE METAL MOULDING MFG. CORP., pg. 557
HYMAN FREIGHTWAYS INC., pg. 557
HYNES INDUSTRIES INC., pg. 557
HYOSUNG ASC—See ASC Incorporated, pg. 7
HYPERTRONICS CORPORATION, pg. 557
HYPLAINS DRESSED BEEF, INC., pg. 557
HYPRO CORPORATION, pg. 557
HYSPAN PRECISION PRODUCTS, INC., pg. 557

I

I. MAGNIN & CO.—See R. H. Macy & Co., Inc., pg. 699
I SKI SKI GOGGLES, pg. 557
IA CONSTRUCTION CORP., pg. 558
IA CORP., pg. 558
I B DIFFUSION, LP, pg. 558
I.B.C. ROOT BEER COMPANY—See Dr Pepper/Seven-Up Companies, Inc., pg. 342
IBM FOODS, pg. 558
IBT, INC., pg. 558
I.C. SYSTEM, INC., pg. 558
ICC CHEMICAL (UK) LIMITED—See ICC Industries, Inc., pg. 558
ICC COMERCIO E INDUSTRIA LTDS.—See ICC Industries, Inc., pg. 558
ICC HANDELS AG—See ICC Industries, Inc., pg. 558
ICC (HONG KONG) LTD.—See ICC Industries, Inc., pg. 559
ICC IBERICA S.A.—See ICC Industries, Inc., pg. 559
ICC INDUSTRIES, B.V.—See ICC Industries, Inc., pg. 559
ICC INDUSTRIES, INC., pg. 558
ICC (ISRAEL) CHEMICALS LTD.—See ICC Industries, Inc., pg. 559
ICC ITALIA S.R.L.—See ICC Industries, Inc., pg. 559
I.C.C. TRADING, INC.—See ICC Industries, Inc., pg. 558
ICC TRADING (TAIWAN) LTD.—See ICC Industries, Inc., pg. 559
ICE COMMUNICATIONS, INC., pg. 559
ICM ARTISTS, LTD.—See Josephson International Inc., pg. 607
ICM INVESTMENT CO.—See ICM Industries, Inc., pg. 559
ICM INDUSTRIES, INC., pg. 559
I.C.S.A.-FLORASYNTH—See Florasynth Inc., pg. 420
ICW COPARTNER—See N W Ayer Incorporated, pg. 104
ID SOLUTIONS—See Intelligent Controls Inc., pg. 574
IDAB INTERNATIONAL INCORPORATED, pg. 559
IDAB WAMAC AB—See IDAB International Incorporated, pg. 559
IDAB WAMAC PACIFIC—See IDAB International Incorporated, pg. 559
IDAB WAMAC PACIFIC LIMITED—See IDAB International Incorporated, pg. 559
IDC ARGENTINA—See International Data Group, pg. 577
IDC AUSTRALIA—See International Data Group, pg. 577
IDC AUSTRIA—See International Data Group, pg. 577
IDC BEIJING—See International Data Group, pg. 578
IDC BRAZIL—See International Data Group, pg. 578
IDC CANADA—See International Data Group, pg. 578
IDC CHINA/HONG KONG LTD.—See International Data Group, pg. 578
IDC DEUTSCHLAND GMBH—See International Data Group, pg. 578
IDC EUROPEAN RESEARCH CENTER—See International Data Group, pg. 578
IDC FINLAND—See International Data Group, pg. 578
IDC FRANCE—See International Data Group, pg. 578
IDC GREECE—See International Data Group, pg. 578
IDC HUNGARY—See International Data Group, pg. 578
IDC INDIA—See International Data Group, pg. 578
IDC IRVINE—See International Data Group, pg. 577
IDC ITALIA S.R.L.—See International Data Group, pg. 578
IDC JAPAN—See International Data Group, pg. 578
IDC KOREA, INC.—See International Data Group, pg. 578
IDC MEXICO—See International Data Group, pg. 578
IDC NEDERLAND—See International Data Group, pg. 578
IDC NEW JERSEY—See International Data Group, pg. 577
IDC NEW ZEALAND—See International Data Group, pg. 578
IDC NORGE—See International Data Group, pg. 578
IDC POLAND—See International Data Group, pg. 578
IDC RUSSIA—See International Data Group, pg. 578
IDC SCANDINAVIA A/S—See International Data Group, pg. 578
IDC SERVICES, INC., pg. 559
IDC SINGAPORE—See International Data Group, pg. 578
IDC SPAIN—See International Data Group, pg. 578
IDC SWEDEN—See International Data Group, pg. 578
IDC SWITZERLAND—See International Data Group, pg. 578
IDC TAIWAN—See International Data Group, pg. 578
IDC TEXAS—See International Data Group, pg. 577
IDC THAILAND—See International Data Group, pg. 578
IDC UNITED KINGDOM—See International Data Group, pg. 578
IDC VENEZUELA—See International Data Group, pg. 578
IDC VIRGINIA—See International Data Group, pg. 577
IDC WEST—See International Data Group, pg. 577
I D E CORPORATION, pg. 560
IDG BOOKS WORLDWIDE—See International Data Group, pg. 576
IDG COMMUNICACIONES C.A.—See International Data Group, pg. 577
IDG COMMUNICACIONES S.A. DE C.V.—See International Data Group, pg. 577
IDG COMMUNICATIONS—See International Data Group, pg. 576
IDG COMMUNICATIONS—See International Data Group, pg. 577
IDG COMMUNICATIONS FRANCE—See International Data Group, pg. 577
IDG COMMUNICATIONS, INC.—See International Data Group, pg. 577
IDG COMMUNICATIONS ITALIA SRL—See International Data Group, pg. 577
IDG COMMUNICATIONS/JAPAN—See International Data Group, pg. 577
IDG COMMUNICATIONS LIST SERVICES—See International Data Group, pg. 576
IDG COMMUNICATIONS LTD.—See International Data Group, pg. 577
IDG COMMUNICATIONS LTD.—See International Data Group, pg. 577
IDG COMMUNICATIONS NEDERLAND BV—See International Data Group, pg. 577
IDG COMMUNICATIONS NORGE AS—See International Data Group, pg. 577
IDG COMMUNICATIONS PTY LTD.—See International Data Group, pg. 577
IDG COMMUNICATIONS RESEARCH—See International Data Group, pg. 576
IDG COMMUNICATIONS, S.A.—See International Data Group, pg. 577
IDG COMMUNICATIONS VERLAGSGES.MBH—See International Data Group, pg. 577
IDG COMMUNICATIONS (W. AFRICA) LTD.—See International Data Group, pg. 577
IDG CZECHOSLOVAKIA—See International Data Group, pg. 577
IDG DENMARK A/S—See International Data Group, pg. 577
IDG HIGH TECH COMPANY—See International Data Group, pg. 577
IDG INTERNATIONAL NEWS GROUP—See International Data Group, pg. 576
IDG MAGYAROSZAGI LAPLADO KFT.—See International Data Group, pg. 577
IDG (MALAYSIA) SDN BHD—See International Data Group, pg. 577
IDG POLAND S.A.—See International Data Group, pg. 577
IDG-TECHNIKA COMMUNICATIONS, LTD.—See International Data Group, pg. 577
IDG/UFT—See International Data Group, pg. 577
IDG/WORLD EXPO CORPORATION—See International Data Group, pg. 578
THE IDI GROUP COMPANIES, pg. 560
IDM CONTROLS, pg. 560
IDM EQUIPMENT COMPANY—See IDM Controls, pg. 560
I-E PROPRIETARY, LTD.—See The Pullman Company, pg. 900
IFP HYDRAULICS INC.—See ICM Industries, Inc., pg. 559
IFS FINANCIAL SERVICES, INC.—See Western & Southern Life Insurance Co., pg. 1181
IFS SYSTEMS, INC.—See Western & Southern Life Insurance Co., pg. 1181
IG CONSEIL S.A.—See Ketchum Communications Inc., pg. 625
IGA, INC. (INDEPENDENT GROCERS ALLIANCE), pg. 560
IGI RESOURCES, INC.—See Intermountain Industries, Inc., pg. 575
ILC DATA DEVICE—See ILC Industries, Inc., pg. 560
ILC DOVER, INC.—See ILC Industries, Inc., pg. 560
ILC INDUSTRIES, INC., pg. 560
IMT—See National Forge Company, pg. 789
ISI FLUID POWER, INC.—See The ISI Manufacturing, Inc., pg. 560
THE ISI MANUFACTURING, INC., pg. 560
ITA GROUP, pg. 560
ITI MARKETING SERVICES, INC., pg. 561
IVI TRAVEL—See Frank Consolidated Enterprises Inc., pg. 428
IXL FURNITURE—See Triangle Pacific Corporation, pg. 1112
IAMS COMPANY, pg. 561
ICAHN & CO., INC., pg. 561
ICE CRAFT—See Specialty Equipment Companies Inc., pg. 1027
ICE CREAM SPECIALTIES, INC.—See Prairie Farms Dairy, Inc., pg. 884
ICELAND SEAFOOD CORPORATION, pg. 561
ICELANDAIR, pg. 561
ICICLE SEAFOODS, INC., pg. 561
IDAHO FOREST INDUSTRY, INC., pg. 561
IDAHOAN FOODS, pg. 561
IDAHO LOTTERY, pg. 561
IDAHO SUPREME COMPANY, pg. 561
IDEA COURIER, INC.—See I D E Corporation, pg. 560
IDEA ENGINEERING & FABRICATING, pg. 562
IDEA MAN, INC., pg. 562
IDEAL CHEMICAL & SUPPLY COMPANY, pg. 562
IDEAL FORGING CORPORATION, pg. 562
IDEAL INDUSTRIES, INC., pg. 562
IDEAL MACARONI COMPANY, pg. 562
IDEAL PARKING, INC.—See Allright Corporation, pg. 43
IDEAL POOL CORP., pg. 562
IDEAL SCHOOL SUPPLY COMPANY—See Educational Publishing Corporation, pg. 369
IDEAL SCHOOL SUPPLY CORPORATION—See Educational Publishing Corporation, pg. 369
IDEAL-STANDARD—See American Standard Inc., pg. 62
IDEAL-STANDARD—See American Standard Inc., pg. 62
IDEAL-STANDARD—See American Standard Inc., pg. 62
IDEAL-STANDARD—See American Standard Inc., pg. 62
IDEAL-STANDARD BRAZIL—See American Standard Inc., pg. 62
IDEAL-STANDARD GMBH—See American Standard Inc., pg. 62
IDEAL-STANDARD LTD.—See American Standard Inc., pg. 62
IDEAL-STANDARD, S.A. DE C.V.—See American Standard Inc., pg. 62
IDEAL-STANDARD S.A.I.—See American Standard Inc., pg. 62
IDEAL-STANDARD S.P.A.—See American Standard Inc., pg. 62
IDEAL-STANDARD WABCO IND. E COM. LTDA—See American Standard Inc., pg. 62
IDEALEASE OF MEMPHIS—See Mid America International Trucks, Inc., pg. 750
IDENTIFICATION SYSTEMS DIV.—See Matthews International Corp., pg. 721
IDLE WILD FOODS—See Union Holdings, Inc., pg. 1128
IDLE WILD MANAGEMENT CORPORATION—See Union Holdings, Inc., pg. 1128
IDYLWILD CORPORATION—See Silicon Valley Development, pg. 1004
IGLOO CORPORATION, pg. 562
ILLINIOS AUTO ELECTRIC MIDWEST ENGINE WAREHOUSE DIV.—See Illinois Auto Electric Co., pg. 562
ILLINOIS AUTO CENTRAL DIV.—See Illinois Auto Electric Co., pg. 562
ILLINOIS AUTO ELECTRIC CO., pg. 562
ILLINOIS CEREAL MILLS, INC., pg. 562
ILLINOIS CONSOLIDATED TELEPHONE CO., pg. 563
ILLINOIS HOME MORTGAGE CORP.—See The Hassinger Companies, pg. 516
ILLINOIS HYDRAULIC CONSTRUCTION COMPANY, pg. 563
ILLINOIS LIMITED PARTNERSHIP—See Martin Exploration Management Company, pg. 715
ILLINOIS RANGE COMPANY, pg. 563
ILLINOIS STATE LOTTERY, pg. 563
JOHN ILTIS ASSOCIATES, pg. 563
IMAGE DYNAMICS, INCORPORATED, pg. 563
IMAGE TRANSFORM—See Andrews Group, Incorporated, pg. 74
IMAGE TRANSFORM LAB—See Andrews Group, Incorporated, pg. 74
IMAGES WOODWORKING, INC.—See Robert E. Bayley Construction, pg. 128
IMAGING SYSTEMS DIVISION—See SBN System Inc., pg. 960
IMC, INC.—See ZBS Industries, Inc., pg. 1215
IMPACT COMUNICACOES—See Young & Rubicam Inc., pg. 1213
IMPARTS—See Vic Manufacturing, pg. 1149
IMPERIA BROS., INC., pg. 563
IMPERIAL CLEVITE DO BRAZIL—See The Pullman Company, pg. 900
IMPERIAL DIE CASTING—See RCM Industries, pg. 906
IMPERIAL DIVISION—See The Pullman Company, pg. 899
IMPERIAL, INC., pg. 564
IMPERIAL LITHO/GRAPHICS, INC., pg. 564
IMPERIAL MANUFACTURING COMPANY, pg. 564
IMPERIAL PEARL COMPANY, INC., pg. 564
IMPERIAL POOLS, INC., pg. 564
IMPERIAL SCHRADE CORP., pg. 564
IMPERIAL SCHRADE CORP.—See Imperial Schrade Corp., pg. 564
IMPERIAL SCHRADE (EUROPE) G.M.B.H.—See Imperial Schrade Corp., pg. 564
IMPERIAL STAG LTD.—See Imperial Schrade Corp., pg. 564
THE IMPEX GROUP LIMITED—See Goldman Financial Group, pg. 468
IMPO GLAZTILE, pg. 564
IMPRESSIONS INC.—See Edwards Brothers, Inc., pg. 370
IMPRINT PRODUCTS, L.P., pg. 564

IMPROVED BLOW MOLDING EQUIPMENT COMPANY, INC.—See Goodman Equipment Corp., pg. 471
THE IN-HOUSE AGENCY, pg. 564
IN-N-OUT BURGERS, pg. 564
IN-OFFICE COFFEE COMPANY—See Wechsler Coffee Corp., pg. 1172
INCENTIVE—See Bill Communications, Inc., pg. 150
INCOR, INC.—See Dale Industries Inc., pg. 312
INDECK ENERGY SERVICES, INC.—See Indeck Power Equipment Company, pg. 564
INDECK POWER EQUIPMENT COMPANY, pg. 564
INDECO, INC.—See Johnson Bros. Corp., pg. 597
INDECO PERUANA S.A.—See The Marmon Group, Inc., pg. 712
THE INDEPENDENCE EXAMINER—See Stauffer Communications, Inc., pg. 1042
INDEPENDENCE HOLDING COMPANY—See Geneve Corporation, pg. 451
INDEPENDENCE INVESTMENT ASSOCIATES, INC.—See John Hancock Mutual Life Insurance Company, pg. 596
INDEPENDENCE SQUARE PROPERTIES—See The Penn Mutual Life Insurance Company, pg. 858
INDEPENDENT CAN COMPANY, pg. 564
INDEPENDENT CELLULAR NETWORK, INC.—See CC Industries, Inc., pg. 200
INDEPENDENT INSURANCE AGENTS OF AMERICA, pg. 565
INDEPENDENT METALS, pg. 565
INDEPENDENT NAIL COMPANY—See Maze Nails, pg. 725
INDEPENDENT PUBLICATIONS, INC., pg. 565
INDEPENDENT PUBLISHING COMPANY—See Harte-Hanks Communications, Inc., pg. 513
INDEPENDENT TOOL & DIE—See Oberg Industries Co., pg. 819
INDIAN HEAD GASKET DIV.-DETROIT—See Indian Head Industries Inc., pg. 565
INDIAN HEAD INDUSTRIES INC., pg. 565
INDIANA FINANCIAL INVESTORS, INC.—See Libco Corporation, pg. 674
INDIANA INSULATED WIRE—See Group Dekko International Inc., pg. 489
INDIANA KENTUCKY ELECTRIC CORPORATION—See Ohio Valley Electric Corporation, pg. 823
INDIANA RECORDS MANAGERS, pg. 565
INDIANA SEED CO., INC.—See Land O'Lakes, Inc., pg. 654
INDIANA SERVICE CENTER/SATELLITE LOCATION—See T.D. Williamson, Inc., pg. 1192
INDIANHEAD GOLF CLUB—See Chief Industries, Inc., pg. 247
INDRESCO, INC., pg. 565
INDUPLEX, INC.—See Belmont Industries, Inc., pg. 137
INDUSTRIA CENTROAMERICANA DE SANITARIOS, S.A.—See American Standard Inc., pg. 62
INDUSTRIA CERAMICA CENTROAMERICANA, S.A.—See American Standard Inc., pg. 62
INDUSTRIA CERAMICA COSTARRICENSE, S.A.—See American Standard Inc., pg. 62
INDUSTRIAL ACOUSTICS COMPANY GMBH—See Industrial Acoustics Company, Inc., pg. 566
INDUSTRIAL ACOUSTICS COMPANY, INC., pg. 565
INDUSTRIAL ACOUSTICS COMPANY, LTD.—See Industrial Acoustics Company, Inc., pg. 566
INDUSTRIAL ACOUSTICS COMPANY S.C. INC.—See Industrial Acoustics Company, Inc., pg. 566
INDUSTRIAL ALLOYS, INC.—See Industrial Wire Products Corporation, pg. 567
INDUSTRIAL & AUTOMOTIVE FASTENERS—See Key Manufacturing Group, Inc., pg. 627
INDUSTRIAL BOOKSTORE—See Manufacturers' News, Inc., pg. 705
INDUSTRIAL CERAMICS, INC., pg. 566
INDUSTRIAL CHEMICAL LABORATORIES—See Rochester Midland Corporation, pg. 941
INDUSTRIAL COATINGS GROUP, INC., pg. 566
INDUSTRIAL COATINGS GROUP (SALES OFFICE)—See Industrial Coatings Group, Inc., pg. 566
INDUSTRIAL CONTRACTORS, INC., pg. 566
INDUSTRIAL DESIGN ASSOCIATES—See Astre Corporate Group, pg. 92
INDUSTRIAL DIELECTRICS, INC., pg. 566
INDUSTRIAL ELECTRONIC ENGINEERS, INC., pg. 566
INDUSTRIAL EQUIPMENT NEWS—See Thomas Publishing Co., pg. 1093
INDUSTRIAL GENERAL CORPORATION, pg. 566
INDUSTRIAL INFORMATION HEADQUARTERS CO.—See Headco Industries, Inc., pg. 520
INDUSTRIAL LIFT TRUCKS—See Syracuse Supply Company, pg. 1070
INDUSTRIAL MATERIALS TECHNOLOGY—See National Forge Company, pg. 789
INDUSTRIAL METALS OF THE SOUTH, pg. 566
INDUSTRIAL MICROGENICS—See Astre Corporate Group, pg. 92
INDUSTRIAL RUBBER GOODS—See The Chardon Rubber Co., pg. 239
INDUSTRIAL RUBBER PRODUCTS COMPANY, pg. 566
INDUSTRIAL STEEL & WIRE COMPANY, pg. 567
INDUSTRIAL TOOLS DIV.—See INDRESCO, Inc., pg. 565
INDUSTRIAL TOWEL & UNIFORM, pg. 567
INDUSTRIAL TRUST COMPANY—See The Prudential Insurance Company of America, pg. 897
INDUSTRIAL WIRE PRODUCTS CORPORATION, pg. 567
INDUSTRIAS KOLMEX, S.A.—See MacAndrews & Forbes Holdings Inc., pg. 696
INDUSTRIAS METALICAS SUD AMERICANAS LTDA. (IMSA)—See The Marmon Group, Inc., pg. 712
INEX VISION SYSTEMS—See Barry-Wehmiller Company, pg. 122
INEX VISION SYSTEMS—See Barry-Wehmiller Company, pg. 122
INFINITY BROADCASTING CORPORATION, pg. 567
INFOCORP—See Ziff Communications Company, pg. 1219
INFORMATION ACCESS CO.—See Ziff Communications Company, pg. 1219
INFORMATION BUILDERS, pg. 567
INFORMATION COMPUTER ENTERPRISE—See International Data Group, pg. 577
INFORMATION DIMENSIONS, INC.—See Battelle Memorial Institute, pg. 126
INFORMATION PROCESSING PRODUCTS—See Fellowes Manufacturing Co., pg. 406
INFORMATION STRATEGIES GROUP—See International Data Group, pg. 578
INFORMATION SYSTEMS—See Database America Companies, pg. 316
INFORMATION SYSTEMS & NETWORK CORPORATION, pg. 567
INFOTEC DEVELOPMENT, INC., pg. 567
INFOWORLD PUBLISHING, INC.—See International Data Group, pg. 576
INGALLS, QUINN & JOHNSON, pg. 567
INGERSOLL BOHLE INGERSOLL GMBH INC.—See Ingersoll International Inc., pg. 568
INGERSOLL CM SYSTEMS INC.—See Ingersoll International Inc., pg. 568
INGERSOLL CUTTING TOOL CO.—See Ingersoll International Inc., pg. 568
INGERSOLL ENGINEERS—See Ingersoll Engineers Inc., pg. 568
INGERSOLL ENGINEERS—See Ingersoll Engineers Inc., pg. 568
INGERSOLL ENGINEERS—See Ingersoll Engineers Inc., pg. 568
INGERSOLL ENGINEERS—See Ingersoll Engineers Inc., pg. 568
INGERSOLL ENGINEERS GMBH—See Ingersoll Engineers Inc., pg. 568
INGERSOLL ENGINEERS INC., pg. 568
INGERSOLL ENGINEERS LIMITED—See Ingersoll Engineers Inc., pg. 568
INGERSOLL ENGINEERS PTY. LTD.—See Ingersoll Engineers Inc., pg. 568
INGERSOLL ENGINEERS PTY. LTD.—See Ingersoll Engineers Inc., pg. 568
INGERSOLL ENGINEERS S.A.—See Ingersoll Engineers Inc., pg. 568
INGERSOLL GMBH INC.—See Ingersoll International Inc., pg. 568
INGERSOLL INTERNATIONAL INC., pg. 568
INGERSOLL MASCHINEN UND WERKZEUGE GMBH—See Ingersoll International Inc., pg. 568
INGERSOLL MILLING MACHINE CO.—See Ingersoll International Inc., pg. 568
THE INGERSOLL MILLING MACHINE CO.—See Ingersoll International Inc., pg. 568
INGERSOLL MILLING MACHINES OVERSEAS LTD.—See Ingersoll International Inc., pg. 568
INGLES MARKETS, INC., pg. 568
INGRAM BARGE COMPANY—See Ingram Industries Inc., pg. 569
INGRAM COAL COMPANY—See Ingram Industries Inc., pg. 569
INGRAM INDUSTRIES INC., pg. 568
INGRAM LIBRARY SERVICES, INC.—See Ingram Industries Inc., pg. 569
INGRAM MERCHANDISING SERVICE INC.—See Ingram Industries Inc., pg. 569
INGRAM PAPER COMPANY, pg. 569
INGRAM PERIODICALS INC.—See Ingram Industries Inc., pg. 569
INGRAM PRODUCTION COMPANY—See Ingram Industries Inc., pg. 569
INGRID-SEVKO, INC., pg. 569
INJECTION FOOTWEAR CORP., pg. 569
INJECTRON CORPORATION, pg. 569
INK SPECIALTIES CO.—See Weber Marking Systems, Inc., pg. 1171
INKEL CORP., pg. 569
INKEL TECHNOLOGY—See Inkel Corp., pg. 570
INKOM, IDAHO PLANT—See Ash Grove Cement Company, pg. 87
INLAND ASSOCIATES, pg. 570
INLAND ASSOCIATES, INC., pg. 570
INLAND CONSTRUCTION COMPANY—See Graycor, Inc., pg. 480
INLAND DIE CASTING—See RCM Industries, pg. 906
THE INLAND GROUP, INC., pg. 570
INLAND PRINTING CO., INC., pg. 570
INLAND TOOL & MANUFACTURING, INC.—See Ralph C. Wilson Enterprises, pg. 1194
INLANDER-STEINDLER PAPER, pg. 570
INMAN CONSTRUCTION CORPORATION, pg. 570
INMAN MILLS, pg. 570
PAUL INMAN ASSOCIATES INC., pg. 570
INN AT HARRIS RANCH—See Harris Farms, Inc., pg. 512
INNCO MANAGEMENT CORP.—See Family Inns of America, Inc., pg. 398
INNER SECRETS, INC., pg. 570
INNOVATIVE PLASTICS CORPORATION, pg. 570
INPUT, pg. 571
INPUT, INC.—See INPUT, pg. 571
INPUT, K.K.—See INPUT, pg. 571
INPUT, LTD.—See INPUT, pg. 571
INPUT, SARL—See INPUT, pg. 571
INSECT CONTROL & RESEARCH CORP.—See McLaughlin Gormley King Company, pg. 731
INSIDE SPORTS, INC.—See Century Publishing Company, pg. 235
INSIGHT COMMUNICATIONS LTD.—See Backer Spielvogel Bates Worldwide, Inc., pg. 111
INSIGNIA FINANCIAL GROUP, INC., pg. 571
INSIGNIA MANAGEMENT GROUP—See Insignia Financial Group, Inc., pg. 571
INSIGNIA MORTGAGE & INVESTMENT CORP.—See Insignia Financial Group, Inc., pg. 571
INSILCO CORPORATION, pg. 571
INSTA-FOAM PRODUCTS, INC.—See Flexible Products Company, pg. 419
INSTA-PRO INTERNATIONAL, LTD.—See Triple F, Inc., pg. 1114
INSTANT S.R.L.—See Up-Right, Inc., pg. 1139
THE INSTANT WEB COMPANIES, pg. 571
INSTITUTION FOOD HOUSE, INC.—See Alex Lee, Inc., pg. 33
INSTITUTIONAL FINANCING SERVICES, pg. 571
INSTITUTO DE IDIOMAS COLOMBIA, S.A.—See Berlitz International, Inc., pg. 143
INSTRUCTIONAL FAIR, INC.—See Educational Publishing Corporation, pg. 369
INSTRUMENT SPECIALTIES COMPANY, pg. 572
INSTRUMENT SPECIALTIES EUROPE, S.A. - EUROPEAN DIVISION—See Instrument Specialties Company, pg. 572
INSTRUMENTARIUM IMAGING, INC., pg. 572
INSULATING MATERIALS, INC., pg. 572
INSURANCE CORP. OF AMERICA, pg. 572
INSURANCE INTERMEDIARIES, INC.—See Nationwide Mutual Insurance Company, pg. 795
INSURANCE MANAGEMENT ASSOCIATES, pg. 572
INTECH ADVANCED ANALOG, pg. 572
INTEGRA TECHNOLOGIES CORP., pg. 572
INTEGRAL SYSTEMS, pg. 572
INTEGRAL SYSTEMS—See Integral Systems, pg. 573
INTEGRAL SYSTEMS—See Integral Systems, pg. 573
INTEGRAL SYSTEMS, INC.—See Integral Systems, pg. 573
INTEGRATEC, pg. 573
INTEGRATED ACQUISITION, INC.—See Integrated Resources, Inc., pg. 573
INTEGRATED BENEFIT SYSTEMS—See Integrated Resources, Inc., pg. 573
INTEGRATED BUSINESS SYSTEMS—See Effective Management Systems, pg. 370
INTEGRATED CIRCUITS MASTER CATALOG—See The Hearst Corporation, pg. 522
INTEGRATED ENERGY CONTROLS CORP., pg. 573
INTEGRATED FINANCIAL—See Integrated Resources, Inc., pg. 573
INTEGRATED FUNDING, INC.—See Integrated Resources, Inc., pg. 573
INTEGRATED MEDIA, INC.—See International Data Group, pg. 576
INTEGRATED RESOURCES ASSET MANAGEMENT CORP.—See Integrated Resources, Inc., pg. 573
INTEGRATED RESOURCES CAPITAL SERVICES, INC.—See Integrated Resources, Inc., pg. 573
INTEGRATED RESOURCES EQUIPMENT GROUP, INC.—See Integrated Resources, Inc., pg. 573
INTEGRATED RESOURCES EQUITY CORP.—See Integrated Resources, Inc., pg. 573
INTEGRATED RESOURCES, INC., pg. 573
INTEGRATED RESOURCES INSURANCE & INVESTMENT SERVICES, LTD.—See Integrated Resources, Inc., pg. 573
INTEGRATED RESOURCES INTERNATIONAL, LTD.—See Integrated Resources, Inc., pg. 573
INTEGRATED RESOURCES (JAPAN), INC.—See Integrated Resources, Inc., pg. 573
INTEGRATED RESOURCES LIFE INSURANCE CO.—See Integrated Resources, Inc., pg. 573
INTEGRATED RESOURCES MARKETING, INC.—See Integrated Resources, Inc., pg. 573
INTEGRATED SYSTEMS ANALYSTS, INC., pg. 573
INTELLIGENT CONTROLS INC., pg. 573
INTER-MOUNTAIN RENTALS—See ROC Properties Inc., pg. 908
INTERBATH, INC., pg. 574
INTERCOLE, INC., pg. 574
INTERCOMMUNICATIONS INC., pg. 574
INTERCONTINENTAL MFG. CO.—See Datron Incorporated, pg. 316
INTERCOUNTY TITLE CO. OF ILLINOIS, pg. 574
INTERELECTRONIC OERTLI AG—See Panduit Company, pg. 845
INTERFACE ELECTRONICS CORPORATION, pg. 574
INTERFORM CORPORATION, pg. 574
INTERGY, INC.—See Ashman Enterprises, Inc., pg. 88
INTERIOR DESIGN INC.—See A. Epstein and Sons, Intl., Inc., pg. 384
INTERIOR SPACE DESIGN INC., (ISD)—See A. Epstein and Sons, Intl., Inc., pg. 384
INTERLAKEN CAPITAL, INC., pg. 574
INTERLOCK INDUSTRIES, INC., pg. 574
INTERMATIC INC., pg. 575
INTERMOUNTAIN FARMERS ASSOCIATION, pg. 575
INTERMOUNTAIN GAS CO.—See Intermountain Industries, Inc., pg. 575
INTERMOUNTAIN INDUSTRIES, INC., pg. 575
INTERNACIONAL MONTEREY, S.A.—See Sealy Corporation, pg. 986
INTERNATIONAL AGRICULTURAL MARKET DEVELOPMENT CO.—See Sunkist Growers, Inc., pg. 1061
INTERNATIONAL AIRLINE SUPPORT GROUP, INC., pg. 575
THE INTERNATIONAL BOILER WORKS COMPANY, pg. 575
INTERNATIONAL BUSINESS INTERIORS INC., pg. 575
INTERNATIONAL CHEESE COMPANY, INC.—See International Cheese Company Limited Partnership, pg. 576
INTERNATIONAL CHEESE COMPANY LIMITED PARTNERSHIP, pg. 575
INTERNATIONAL CHEMICAL COMPANY, pg. 576
INTERNATIONAL CIRCULATION DISTRIBUTORS—See The Hearst Corporation, pg. 523
INTERNATIONAL COLD STORAGE CO., INC., pg. 576
INTERNATIONAL COMMUNICATIONS GROUP, INC., pg. 576

INTERNATIONAL COMPONENTS CORPORATION, pg. 576
INTERNATIONAL CREATIVE MANAGEMENT, INC.—See Josephson International Inc., pg. 607
INTERNATIONAL CREATIVE MANAGEMENT LTD.—See Josephson International Inc., pg. 607
INTERNATIONAL DATA CORP.—See International Data Group, pg. 577
INTERNATIONAL DATA GROUP, pg. 576
INTERNATIONAL DESIGNER ACCESSORIES, INC., pg. 578
INTERNATIONAL EDITIONS—See The Hearst Corporation, pg. 523
INTERNATIONAL FURNITURE DIV.—See Schnadig Corporation, pg. 977
INTERNATIONAL GEAR CORPORATION, pg. 578
INTERNATIONAL JENSEN INC., pg. 578
INTERNATIONAL LEARNING SYSTEMS (JAPAN) LTD.—See Berlitz International, Inc., pg. 143
INTERNATIONAL MANAGEMENT GROUP (IMG), pg. 578
INTERNATIONAL MARINE HOLDINGS, INC., pg. 579
INTERNATIONAL MARKETING SERVICES—See International Data Group, pg. 576
INTERNATIONAL METALS & MACHINES, INC.—See CRL, Inc., pg. 203
INTERNATIONAL MICROCIRCUITS, INC., pg. 579
INTERNATIONAL MICROWAVE CORPORATION—See Communications International, pg. 269
INTERNATIONAL MILL CONSTRUCTION, INC.—See Tippins Incorporated, pg. 1099
INTERNATIONAL MILL CONSTRUCTION, INC.—See Tippins Incorporated, pg. 1099
INTERNATIONAL PERMALITE, INC., pg. 579
INTERNATIONAL SEAWAY TRADING CORPORATION, pg. 579
INTERNATIONAL SHOE MACHINE CORP., pg. 579
INTERNATIONAL SPECIALTY PRODUCTS, INC.—See GAF Corporation, pg. 438
INTERNATIONAL STEEL WOOL CORPORATION—See F.H. Bonn Company, pg. 164
INTERNATIONAL SYSTEMS & CONTROLS CORP., pg. 579
INTERNATIONAL TABLES DIV.—See Schnadig Corporation, pg. 977
INTERNATIONAL TABLETING—See Pharmavite Corp., pg. 866
INTERNATIONAL TRANSDUCER CORPORATION—See Channel Technologies, Inc., pg. 239
INTEROLIVA—See Westin, Inc., pg. 1183
INTEROP, INC.—See Ziff Communications Company, pg. 1219
INTERPLAN—See RNL Facilities Corporation, pg. 907
INTERPLAST UNIVERSAL INDUSTRIES, INC., pg. 579
INTERPLASTIC CORP., pg. 579
INTERROYAL CORPORATION, pg. 580
INTERSTATE BRICK COMPANY—See Pacific Coast Building Products Inc., pg. 839
INTERSTATE COMMODITIES INC., pg. 580
INTERSTATE CONTAINER CORPORATION—See Interstate Resources, Inc., pg. 580
INTERSTATE DISTRIBUTOR COMPANY, pg. 580
INTERSTATE DISTRIBUTORS INC., pg. 580
INTERSTATE DRUG EXCHANGE, INC., pg. 580
INTERSTATE ELECTRIC SUPPLY COMPANY, INC., pg. 580
INTERSTATE JITNEY JUNGLE STORES, INC.—See Jitney-Jungle Stores of America, Inc., pg. 594
INTERSTATE PAPER CORPORATION—See Interstate Resources, Inc., pg. 580
INTERSTATE PAYCO SEED COMPANY, pg. 580
INTERSTATE PRODUCERS LIVESTOCK ASSOCIATION, pg. 580
INTERSTATE RESOURCES, INC., pg. 580
INTERSTATE STEEL SUPPLY CO., pg. 580
INTERSTATE STEEL SUPPLY CO. OF MARYLAND—See Interstate Steel Supply Co., pg. 581
INTERSTATE VAN LINES, INC., pg. 581
INTERTEC LIMITED—See ICC Industries, Inc., pg. 559
INTERTEC PUBLISHING—See K-III Communications Corporation, pg. 611
INTERTRADE INDUSTRIES, pg. 581
INTEX—See Playtex Apparel Inc., pg. 876
INTEX CHEMICAL INC., pg. 581
INTRA-ACOUSTICS COMPANY, LTD.—See Industrial Acoustics Company, Inc., pg. 566
INTRALOX A/S—See The Laitram Corporation, pg. 651
INTRALOX EUROPEAN—See The Laitram Corporation, pg. 651
INTRALOX, INC.—See The Laitram Corporation, pg. 651
INTRALOX, INC. GMBH—See The Laitram Corporation, pg. 651
INTRALOX ITALIA S.R.L.—See The Laitram Corporation, pg. 651
INTRALOX LTD.—See The Laitram Corporation, pg. 651
INTREPID CORP., pg. 581
INTREPID ENTERPRISES, INC., pg. 581
INVERNESS CORP., pg. 581
INVEST WEST FINANCIAL CORPORATION—See Pacifica Real Estate Group, pg. 842
INVESTOR'S MANAGEMENT CORP., pg. 581
INVETECH CO., pg. 581
INVINCIBLE METAL FURNITURE CO., pg. 582
INVIRECHEM—See Pace International Corporation, pg. 838
INVISTA CAPITAL MANAGEMENT CORP.—See The Principal Financial Group, pg. 891
IOWA ASSEMBLIES, INC.—See Group Dekko International Inc., pg. 490
IOWA INDUSTRIAL HYDRAULICS, INC.—See ICM Industries, Inc., pg. 559
IOWA LOTTERY, pg. 582
IOWA PAINT MFG. COMPANY, INC., pg. 582
IPMC, INC.-DETROIT—See Ivex Packaging Corporation, pg. 583
IRELAND COFFEE TEA, INC., pg. 582
IRELAND GOURMET SHOP—See Ireland Coffee Tea, Inc., pg. 582
IROQUOIS DIE & MFG. CO., pg. 582
IROQUOIS POPCORN—See Blevins Concession Supply Co., pg. 156
IRVINE COMPANY, pg. 582
IRVINE WORLD NEWS NEWSPAPER COMPANY—See Irvine Company, pg. 582
THE ROBERT IRSAY COMPANY—See Jupiter Industries, Inc., pg. 609
ISELCO SF—See Panduit Company, pg. 845
ISEMOTO CONTRACTING CO. LTD., pg. 582
ISFEL COMPANY, INC., pg. 582
ISLAND HOLIDAYS, LTD.—See JMB Realty Corporation, pg. 585
ISLAND LINCOLN-MERCURY, pg. 582
ISOMEX, S.A.—See Schenectady Chemicals, Inc., pg. 975
ITALIA/GAL ADVERTISING, pg. 582
ITHACA INDUSTRIES INC., pg. 582
ITRAN CORPORATION, pg. 583
ITS: INTERTRADE SCIENTIFIC, INC.—See Micro Component Technology Inc., pg. 748
H. B. IVES, pg. 583
IVEX PACKAGING CORPORATION, pg. 583
IVEX PACKAGING CORPORATION-AVENEL—See Ivex Packaging Corporation, pg. 583
IVEX PACKAGING CORPORATION-BRIDGEVIEW—See Ivex Packaging Corporation, pg. 583
IVEX PACKAGING CORPORATION-CANADIAN REGION—See Ivex Packaging Corporation, pg. 583
IVEX PACKAGING CORPORATION-ENGINEERING GROUP—See Ivex Packaging Corporation, pg. 583
IVEX PACKAGING CORPORATION-FLORAL AND NURSERY PRODUCTS—See Ivex Packaging Corporation, pg. 583
IVEX PACKAGING CORPORATION-FOOD PACKAGING DIVISION—See Ivex Packaging Corporation, pg. 583
IVEX PACKAGING CORPORATION-GRANT PARK—See Ivex Packaging Corporation, pg. 583
IVEX PACKAGING CORPORATION-GROVE CITY—See Ivex Packaging Corporation, pg. 583
IVEX PACKAGING CORPORATION-HILLSIDE—See Ivex Packaging Corporation, pg. 583
IVEX PACKAGING CORPORATION-INDUSTRIAL PRODUCTS DIVISION—See Ivex Packaging Corporation, pg. 583
IVEX PACKAGING CORPORATION-JOLIET—See Ivex Packaging Corporation, pg. 583
IVEX PACKAGING CORPORATION-KEELE STREET—See Ivex Packaging Corporation, pg. 583
IVEX PACKAGING CORPORATION-LONGUEUIL—See Ivex Packaging Corporation, pg. 584
IVEX PACKAGING CORPORATION-MADISON—See Ivex Packaging Corporation, pg. 583
IVEX PACKAGING CORPORATION-MANTENO—See Ivex Packaging Corporation, pg. 583
IVEX PACKAGING CORPORATION-MILL DIVISION—See Ivex Packaging Corporation, pg. 583
IVEX PACKAGING CORPORATION-PEORIA—See Ivex Packaging Corporation, pg. 583
IVEX PACKAGING CORPORATION-POLYMERIZATION AND EXTRUSION DIVISION—See Ivex Packaging Corporation, pg. 583
IVEX PACKAGING CORPORATION-TROY—See Ivex Packaging Corporation, pg. 583
IVEX PACKAGING CORPORATION-VISALIA—See Ivex Packaging Corporation, pg. 583
FRANK IX & SONS, INC., pg. 584

J

J. CREW GROUP, INC., pg. 584
J & M ADVERTISING—See My Own Meals, Inc., pg. 780
J. & W. SELIGMAN & COMPANY, pg. 584
J & J FURNITURE CO, INC.—See Warehouse Home Furnishings Distributor, pg. 1163
J & L METROLOGY COMPANY, INC.—See Goldman Financial Group, pg. 468
JAG NORTHWEST INC.—See Pickering Industries Inc., pg. 870
J B LABS, INC., pg. 584
J & B PRODUCTS—See Bristol Products, L.P., pg. 176
J & C ADVERTISING—See N W Ayer Incorporated, pg. 104
JCI DATA PROCESSING, INC., pg. 584
JFC INC., pg. 584
JFG COFFEE COMPANY—See William B. Reily & Co., Inc., pg. 923
J.F.P. & ASSOCIATES OF FLORIDA, INC., pg. 584
J H COLLECTIBLES, pg. 584
JII/SALES PROMOTION ASSOCIATES, INC.—See Jordan Industries, Inc., pg. 604
JJJ REALTY TRUST—See Action Equipment, pg. 14
JL TOOL & PROCESSING, INC.—See Ring Technologies, Inc., pg. 935
JM CLIPPER CORPORATION D/B/A ACADIA—See Harbour Group Ltd., pg. 507
JM FAMILY ENTERPRISES INC., pg. 584
JMB REALTY CORPORATION, pg. 584
JMC CREATIVIDAD ORIENTADA/YOUNG & RUBICAM—See Young & Rubicam Inc., pg. 1213
JMCT/DIRECT—See Jordan, McGrath, Case & Taylor Inc., pg. 604
JMCT HEALTH—See Jordan, McGrath, Case & Taylor Inc., pg. 604
JMCT PUBLICIDAD—See Jordan, McGrath, Case & Taylor Inc., pg. 604
J.M.P. BAKERY CO., INC., pg. 586
JNY—See Jones Apparel Group, Inc., pg. 602
J P FOODSERVICE, INC., pg. 586
JPM COMPANY, pg. 586
THE JPM COMPANY OF SOUTH CAROLINA, INC.—See JPM Company, pg. 586
JPS AUTOMOTIVE—See JPS Textile Group, Inc., pg. 586
JPS CONVERTER & INDUSTRIAL CORP.—See JPS Textile Group, Inc., pg. 586
JPS ELASTOMERICS CORP.—See JPS Textile Group, Inc., pg. 586
JPS TEXTILE GROUP, INC., pg. 586
J & R FILM COMPANY, pg. 586
JRN, INC., pg. 586
JS&A ADVERTISING, pg. 586
JS&A GROUP, INC., pg. 586
J.W. WINDOW COMPONENTS, INC.—See Walter Industries, Inc., pg. 1162
JWG ASSOCIATES, pg. 586
JWK INTERNATIONAL CORP., pg. 586
JABIL CIRCUIT INC., pg. 587
JACKES-EVANS MFG. CO., pg. 587
GENE JACKSON FARMS—See A. Duda & Sons Inc., pg. 351
JACKSON HOLE SKI RESORT, pg. 587
JACKSON MILLS, INC., pg. 587
JACKSON PACKING CO. INC., pg. 587
JACKSON PAPER COMPANY, pg. 587
JACKSON PRODUCTS CORP., pg. 587
JACKSONVILLE CRAWDADDY CORP.—See Specialty Restaurants Corporation, pg. 1028
JACKSONVILLE VENTURES, INC.—See Rotterdam Ventures Inc., pg. 951
JACMAR COMPANIES, INC., pg. 587
JACMAR DEVELOPMENT CORP.—See Jacmar Companies, Inc., pg. 587
JACOBS & GERBER, INC., pg. 587
JAC JACOBSEN INDUSTRIES, INC., pg. 587
JACOBSEN MANUFACTURING, INC., pg. 588
K.F. JACOBSON CO.—See R. B. Pamplin Corp., pg. 845
JACOBSON METAL COMPANY—See Money Point Diamond Co., pg. 765
JACOBSON ROST, INC., pg. 588
JACQUES/MCCLELLAND GEOSCIENCES, INC.—See Fugro-McClelland, Inc., pg. 436
JACQUES MORET, INC., pg. 588
CHARLES JACQUIN ET CIE, INC., pg. 588
JAFFREY FIRE PROTECTION CO.—See D. D. Bean & Sons Co., pg. 129
DON JAGODA ASSOCIATES, INC., pg. 588
JAKE SWEENEY AUTO LEASING, INC.—See Jake Sweeney Automotive Inc., pg. 1067
JAKE SWEENEY JEEP EAGLE, INC.—See Jake Sweeney Automotive Inc., pg. 1067
JAKSON-A CHF COMPANY—See CC Industries, Inc., pg. 200
JAMAICA WATER PROPERTIES—See Welsbach Electric Corp., pg. 1175
JAMECO INDUSTRIES, INC., pg. 588
JAMES BUILDING CORPORATION, pg. 588
JAMES CHEVROLET INC., pg. 588
T.L. JAMES & COMPANY, pg. 588
ROBERT JAMES SALES INC., pg. 589
JAMES STEEL & TUBE COMPANY—See Avis Industrial Corporation, pg. 102
TOM JAMES COMPANY, pg. 589
JAMESWAY CO.—See The Marmon Group, Inc., pg. 712
JAMISON BEDDING, INC., pg. 589
JAMISON, CAWDREY, BENJAMIN, pg. 589
JAMISON DOOR COMPANY, pg. 589
JAMISON PLASTIC CORPORATION, pg. 589
JAMTEX LTD.—See Gitano Group Inc., pg. 460
JAN-CO., INC., pg. 589
JANDY INDUSTRIES, pg. 589
JANI KING OF CALIFORNIA, INC.—See Jani King International, Inc., pg. 589
JANI KING, INC.—See Jani King International, Inc., pg. 589
JANI KING INTERNATIONAL, INC., pg. 589
JANIK & ASSOCIATES, INC., pg. 589
JANLIN PLASTIC INC.—See Plastic Engineering Components Inc., pg. 875
JANLYNN CORPORATION, pg. 589
JANNEY MONTGOMERY SCOTT INC.—See The Penn Mutual Life Insurance Company, pg. 858
JAPAN DIRECTORY ADVERTISING COMPANY, LTD. (JDAC)—See TMP Worldwide, Inc., pg. 1074
JAPAN TRAVEL BUREAU INTERNATIONAL, INC., pg. 590
JAPS-OLSON COMPANY, pg. 590
JARCHEM INDUSTRIES, INC., pg. 590
JARCHEM SPECIALTY CHEMICAL DIVISION—See Jarchem Industries, Inc., pg. 590
THE JASON GROUP, INC., pg. 590
JASON INDUSTRIAL, INC., pg. 590
JASPER COUNTY FARM BUREAU CO-OP ASSOCIATION, INC., pg. 590
JASPER NEWS-BOY—See The Hearst Corporation, pg. 524
JASPER TEXTILE—See House of Ronnie, Inc., pg. 546
JAVELIN ELECTRONICS—See American Trading and Production Corporation, pg. 64
JAVELIN/YOUNG & RUBICAM—See Young & Rubicam Inc., pg. 1212
JAY INCORPORATED, pg. 590
JAY INSTRUMENT & SPECIALTY CO., pg. 590
JAYCO INC., pg. 590
JAYDON INCORPORATED, pg. 590
THE JAYDOR CORPORATION, pg. 591
THE JAYME ORGANIZATION, INC., pg. 591
J. M. JAYSON & CO., INC., pg. 591
JAZZ HOLDING CORPORATION, pg. 591
JAZZERCISE, INC., pg. 591
THE JEANS COMPANY—See Levi Strauss & Co., pg. 670
JEANNEAU CONSTRUCTIONS NAUTIQUES S.A.—See Lear Siegler Diversified Holdings Corp., pg. 664
JEFFERSON CHEVROLET—See Jefferson Chevrolet Co., pg. 591
JEFFERSON CHEVROLET CO., pg. 591
JEFFREY BUICK-NISSAN INC., pg. 591
JEFFREY DIVISION—See INDRESCO, Inc., pg. 565

JEFFREY MICHAEL, pg. 591
THE JEL SERT CO., pg. 591
JELD-WEN, INC., pg. 591
JELMAR COMPANY, pg. 592
JEMISON, INC., pg. 592
JENKINS SPIRITS CORP. LTD., pg. 592
JENNIFER CONVERTIBLES INC., pg. 592
JENNIFER DALE, INC., pg. 592
JENSEN ELECTRIC COMPANY, pg. 592
IRVING F. JENSEN CO., INC., pg. 593
JEPSON-MURRAY ADVERTISING, pg. 593
JERELL, INC., pg. 593
JERGENS INC., pg. 593
JERNBERG INDUSTRIES, INC., pg. 593
JEROME-DUNCAN FORD, pg. 593
JEROME FOODS INC., pg. 593
JERRICO, INC.—See Castle-Harlan, Inc., pg. 229
JERSEY PRINTING COMPANY, INC., pg. 593
JESCO, INC., pg. 593
JESSE BRANCH COAL CO.—See Berwind Corporation, pg. 145
JET, INC.—See Jayco Inc., pg. 590
JET SPRAY CORP., pg. 593
JET SPRAY INTERNATIONAL—See Jet Spray Corp., pg. 593
JETSTREAM SYSTEMS—See Barry-Wehmiller Company, pg. 122
JETSTREAM SYSTEMS—See Barry-Wehmiller Company, pg. 122
JETSTREAM SYSTEMS—See Barry-Wehmiller Company, pg. 122
JEWELER'S FINANCIAL SERVICE, INC.—See Zale Corporation, pg. 1215
JEWELERS MUTUAL INSURANCE COMPANY, pg. 593
JEWELL BUILDING SYSTEMS, pg. 594
JEWELL INSTRUMENTS, INC., pg. 594
JEWELMONT CORPORATION, pg. 594
THE JEWETT REFRIGERATOR CO., INC.—See Ruslander & Sons, Inc., pg. 957
JIMLAR CORPORATION, pg. 594
JITACHI ZOSEN SYSTEMS, INC.—See Effective Management Systems, pg. 371
JITNEY-JUNGLE STORES OF AMERICA, INC., pg. 594
JITNEY JUNGLE WHOLESALE CO., INC.—See Jitney-Jungle Stores of America, Inc., pg. 594
CURT G. JOA, INC., pg. 594
JOAN & DAVID, INC.—See Helpern Joan & David, Inc., pg. 528
JOAN FABRICS CORP., pg. 594
JOANNA—See CC Industries, Inc., pg. 200
G. JOANNOU CYCLE CO. INC., pg. 595
JOBBER RETAILER—See Bill Communications, Inc., pg. 150
JOCKEY INTERNATIONAL, INC., pg. 595
JOFCO INC., pg. 595
JOFFKO CAMEROON CORPORATION—See Joffko International, pg. 595
JOFFKO INTERNATIONAL, pg. 595
JOFFKO PHILIPPINES, INC.—See Joffko International, pg. 595
JOHANSON MANUFACTURING CORPORATION, pg. 595
JOHN HANCOCK ADVISERS, INC.—See John Hancock Mutual Life Insurance Company, pg. 596
JOHN HANCOCK ADVISERS INTERNATIONAL, LTD.—See John Hancock Mutual Life Insurance Company, pg. 596
JOHN HANCOCK CAPITAL CORPORATION—See John Hancock Mutual Life Insurance Company, pg. 596
JOHN HANCOCK CAPITAL GROWTH MANAGEMENT, INC.—See John Hancock Mutual Life Insurance Company, pg. 596
JOHN HANCOCK INSURANCE COMPANY OF BERMUDA LTD.—See John Hancock Mutual Life Insurance Company, pg. 596
JOHN HANCOCK INTL. SERVICES S.A.—See John Hancock Mutual Life Insurance Company, pg. 596
JOHN HANCOCK LEASING CORPORATION—See John Hancock Mutual Life Insurance Company, pg. 596
JOHN HANCOCK MUTUAL FUNDS—See John Hancock Mutual Life Insurance Company, pg. 596
JOHN HANCOCK MUTUAL LIFE INSURANCE COMPANY, pg. 595
JOHN HANCOCK SERVICOS INTERNACIONAIS S/C., LTDA.—See John Hancock Mutual Life Insurance Company, pg. 596
JOHN HANCOCK SUBSIDIARIES, INC.—See John Hancock Mutual Life Insurance Company, pg. 596
JOHN PEEL LTD.—See Target Sportswear, Inc., pg. 1079
JOHN RICH & SONS—See Woolrich, Inc., pg. 1201
JOHN WIELAND HOMES OF CHARLESTON, INC.—See John Wieland Homes Inc., pg. 1189
JOHN WIELAND HOMES OF CHARLOTTE, INC.—See John Wieland Homes Inc., pg. 1189
JOHN WIELAND HOMES OF JACKSONVILLE, INC.—See John Wieland Homes Inc., pg. 1189
JOHNNY APPLESEED'S, INC., pg. 597
JOHNSON ACOUSTICAL & SUPPLY CO., pg. 597
AL JOHNSON CONSTRUCTION CO., pg. 597
JOHNSON BROS. CORP., pg. 597
C. S. JOHNSON CO., pg. 597
THE JOHN JOHNSON CO., pg. 597
RICK JOHNSON & COMPANY, INC., pg. 597
JOHNSON COMPANY, LTD.—See S. C. Johnson & Son, Inc., pg. 599
G. E. JOHNSON CONSTRUCTION CO., INC., pg. 597
THE JOHNSON CORPORATION, pg. 597
JOHNSON COUNTY FARM BUREAU CO-OP, pg. 598
E.F. JOHNSON COMPANY, pg. 598
JOHNSON & HIGGINS, pg. 598
BERNARD JOHNSON INCORPORATED, pg. 598
THE JOHNSON INDUSTRIES CORP., pg. 598
LA JOHNSON FRANCAISE S.A.—See S. C. Johnson & Son, Inc., pg. 599
LEGRAND JOHNSON CONSTRUCTION CO., pg. 598
JOHNSON MANUFACTURING CO.—See Gardiner Metal Company, pg. 443
JOHNSON MOVING & STORAGE, NEW ORLEANS—See Johnson Storage & Moving Company, pg. 601
JOHNSON NEWSPAPER CORPORATION, pg. 598
W.B. JOHNSON PROPERTY, INC., pg. 598
JOHNSON PUBLISHING COMPANY, INC., pg. 598
JOHNSON & QUIN, INC., pg. 599
S. C. JOHNSON COMPANY LIMITED—See S. C. Johnson & Son, Inc., pg. 600
S. C. JOHNSON DE CENTROAMERICA S.A.—See S. C. Johnson & Son, Inc., pg. 600
S. C. JOHNSON, LTD.—See S. C. Johnson & Son, Inc., pg. 600
S. C. JOHNSON & SON COLOMBIANA S.A.—See S. C. Johnson & Son, Inc., pg. 600
S. C. JOHNSON & SON DE ARGENTINA S.A.I.C.—See S. C. Johnson & Son, Inc., pg. 599
S. C. JOHNSON & SON DE VENEZUELA, C.A.—See S. C. Johnson & Son, Inc., pg. 600
S. C. JOHNSON & SON (HELLAS) E.P.E.—See S. C. Johnson & Son, Inc., pg. 600
S. C. JOHNSON & SON, INC., pg. 599
S. C. JOHNSON & SON, LIMITED—See S. C. Johnson & Son, Inc., pg. 600
S. C. JOHNSON & SON, LTD.—See S. C. Johnson & Son, Inc., pg. 600
S. C. JOHNSON & SON OF SOUTH AFRICA (PTY.) LTD.—See S. C. Johnson & Son, Inc., pg. 600
S. C. JOHNSON & SON PTE. LIMITED—See S. C. Johnson & Son, Inc., pg. 600
S. C. JOHNSON & SON PTY. LTD.—See S. C. Johnson & Son, Inc., pg. 600
S. C. JOHNSON & SON, S.A. DE C.V.—See S. C. Johnson & Son, Inc., pg. 600
S. C. JOHNSON & SON TAIWAN LTD.—See S. C. Johnson & Son, Inc., pg. 600
S. C. JOHNSON KIEV CORP.—See S. C. Johnson & Son, Inc., pg. 600
JOHNSON STORAGE & MOVING, AURORA—See Johnson Storage & Moving Company, pg. 601
JOHNSON STORAGE & MOVING, BOULDER/LONGMONT—See Johnson Storage & Moving Company, pg. 601
JOHNSON STORAGE & MOVING, CHEYENNE—See Johnson Storage & Moving Company, pg. 601
JOHNSON STORAGE & MOVING, CLEBURNE—See Johnson Storage & Moving Company, pg. 601
JOHNSON STORAGE & MOVING, COLORADO SPRINGS—See Johnson Storage & Moving Company, pg. 601
JOHNSON STORAGE & MOVING COMPANY, pg. 600
JOHNSON STORAGE & MOVING, DENVER—See Johnson Storage & Moving Company, pg. 601
JOHNSON STORAGE & MOVING, ENGLEWOOD—See Johnson Storage & Moving Company, pg. 601
JOHNSON STORAGE & MOVING, SAN DIEGO—See Johnson Storage & Moving Company, pg. 601
JOHNSON STORAGE & MOVING, SANTA FE—See Johnson Storage & Moving Company, pg. 601
JOHNSON SUPPLY & EQUIPMENT CORP., pg. 601
JOHNSON TECHNOLOGY—See Freedom Forge Corporation, pg. 431
JOHNSON & TOWERS, INC., pg. 601
JOHNSON VENTURE CAPITAL, INC.—See S. C. Johnson & Son, Inc., pg. 599
JOHNSON WAX AG—See S. C. Johnson & Son, Inc., pg. 600
JOHNSON WAX A/S—See S. C. Johnson & Son, Inc., pg. 600
JOHNSON WAX DEVELOPMENT CORP.—See S. C. Johnson & Son, Inc., pg. 599
JOHNSON WAX (EGYPT)—See S. C. Johnson & Son, Inc., pg. 600
JOHNSON WAX GMBH—See S. C. Johnson & Son, Inc., pg. 600
JOHNSON WAX (IRELAND) LIMITED—See S. C. Johnson & Son, Inc., pg. 600
JOHNSON WAX LIMITED—See S. C. Johnson & Son, Inc., pg. 600
JOHNSON WAX MOROCCO S.A.—See S. C. Johnson & Son, Inc., pg. 600
JOHNSON WAX NEDERLAND B.V.—See S. C. Johnson & Son, Inc., pg. 600
JOHNSON WAX NEW ZEALAND LTD.—See S. C. Johnson & Son, Inc., pg. 600
JOHNSON WAX NIGERIA LIMITED—See S. C. Johnson & Son, Inc., pg. 600
N.V. JOHNSON WAX BELGIUM S.A.—See S. C. Johnson & Son, Inc., pg. 600
JOHNSON WAX S.P.A.—See S. C. Johnson & Son, Inc., pg. 600
JOHNSON'S WAX (EAST AFRICA) LTD.—See S. C. Johnson & Son, Inc., pg. 600
JOHNSON'S WAX ESPANOLA, S.A.—See S. C. Johnson & Son, Inc., pg. 600
JOHNSON'S WAX, GES. M.B.H.—See S. C. Johnson & Son, Inc., pg. 600
JOHNSON'S WAX LTD.—See S. C. Johnson & Son, Inc., pg. 600
JOHNSONVILLE FOODS, INC., pg. 601
JOHNSONVILLE SAUSAGE, INC.—See Johnsonville Foods, Inc., pg. 601
JOHNSONWAX DEL ECUADOR S.A.—See S. C. Johnson & Son, Inc., pg. 600
ERNEST S. JOHNSTON ADVERTISING, INC., pg. 601
FRED B. JOHNSTON COMPANY, INC., pg. 601
JOHNSTON, LEMON & CO. INC., pg. 601
JOHNSTOWN CORPORATION, pg. 601
JOHNSTOWN KNITTING MILL CO., pg. 602
JOINER ROWLAND SERIO KOEPPEL, pg. 602
JOJOS RESTAURANTS, INC.—See Restaurant Enterprises Group, Inc., pg. 929
THE JOLT COMPANY, pg. 602
JOMAC, INC., pg. 602
JONATHAN MANUFACTURING CORP., pg. 602
JONBIL INC., pg. 602
JONES, ANASTASI & BIRCHFIELD, pg. 602
JONES APPAREL GROUP, INC., pg. 602
JONES APPAREL GROUP, INC. CANADA—See Jones Apparel Group, Inc., pg. 602
JONES BLAIR COMPANY, pg. 602
JONES BLAIR ENERGY, INC.—See Jones Blair Company, pg. 603
JONES BUSINESS SYSTEM—See Decision Data Inc., pg. 324
CAROLINE JONES ADVERTISING, INC., pg. 603
JONES CHEMICALS, INC., pg. 603
EDWARD D. JONES & CO., pg. 603
JONES COMPANY, INC., pg. 603
JONES DAIRY FARM, pg. 603
JONES, DAY, REAVIS & POGUE, pg. 603
JONES HOLDING CORPORATION—See Jones Apparel Group, Inc., pg. 602
JONES INFORMATION MANAGEMENT, INC.—See Jones International Ltd., pg. 603
JONES INTERCABLE, INC.—See Jones International Ltd., pg. 604
JONES INTERNATIONAL LTD.—See Jones Apparel Group, Inc., pg. 602
JONES INTERNATIONAL LTD., pg. 603
JONES INVESTMENT CO., INC.—See Jones Apparel Group, Inc., pg. 602
JONES & LAMSON WATERBURY FARREL CORP.—See Goldman Financial Group, pg. 468
JONES OPTICAL COMPANY—See Totes Incorporated, pg. 1103
JONES PROPERTIES, INC.—See Jones International Ltd., pg. 603
R. A. JONES & CO. INC., pg. 604
JONES SPACELINK, LTD.—See Jones International Ltd., pg. 603
JONES & THOMAS, INC., pg. 604
JONESWEAR—See Jones Apparel Group, Inc., pg. 602
JORDACHE ADVERTISING, pg. 604
JORDACHE ENTERPRISES, INC., pg. 604
JORDAN ASSOCIATES, pg. 604
JORDAN COMPANY, pg. 604
JORDAN DENNIS COMPANY, INC.—See Harte-Hanks Communications, Inc., pg. 513
JORDAN INDUSTRIES, INC., pg. 604
JORDAN, MCGRATH, CASE & TAYLOR INC., pg. 604
JORDAN MOTORS, INC., pg. 605
JORDAN TAMRAZ CARUSO ADVERTISING, INC., pg. 605
JORDAN'S MEATS, pg. 605
JORDAN'S FOODS-BANGOR DIVISION—See Jordan's Meats, pg. 605
JORDAN'S FOODS-FAIRFIELD DIVISION—See Jordan's Meats, pg. 605
JORDAN'S FOODS-WESTBROOK DIVISION—See Jordan's Meats, pg. 605
JORDAN'S FOODS-CARIBOU DIVISION—See Jordan's Meats, pg. 605
JORDAN'S FOODS-COLCHESTER DIVISION—See Jordan's Meats, pg. 605
JORDON COMMERCIAL REFRIGERATOR CO., pg. 605
EARLE M. JORGENSEN COMPANY, pg. 605
JORGENSEN STEEL & ALUMINUM—See Earle M. Jorgensen Company, pg. 605
JORGENSEN STEEL & ALUMINUM/BALTIMORE—See Earle M. Jorgensen Company, pg. 605
JORGENSEN STEEL & ALUMINUM/BIRMINGHAM—See Earle M. Jorgensen Company, pg. 605
JORGENSEN STEEL & ALUMINUM/BOSTON—See Earle M. Jorgensen Company, pg. 605
JORGENSEN STEEL & ALUMINUM/CHARLOTTE—See Earle M. Jorgensen Company, pg. 605
JORGENSEN STEEL & ALUMINUM/CHICAGO—See Earle M. Jorgensen Company, pg. 605
JORGENSEN STEEL & ALUMINUM/CINCINNATI—See Earle M. Jorgensen Company, pg. 605
JORGENSEN STEEL & ALUMINUM CLEVELAND—See Earle M. Jorgensen Company, pg. 605
JORGENSEN STEEL & ALUMINUM/DALLAS—See Earle M. Jorgensen Company, pg. 605
JORGENSEN STEEL & ALUMINUM/DAYTON—See Earle M. Jorgensen Company, pg. 605
JORGENSEN STEEL & ALUMINUM/DETROIT—See Earle M. Jorgensen Company, pg. 605
JORGENSEN STEEL & ALUMINUM/HARTFORD—See Earle M. Jorgensen Company, pg. 606
JORGENSEN STEEL & ALUMINUM/INDIANAPOLIS—See Earle M. Jorgensen Company, pg. 606
JORGENSEN STEEL & ALUMINUM/KANSAS CITY—See Earle M. Jorgensen Company, pg. 606
JORGENSEN STEEL & ALUMINUM/LOS ANGELES—See Earle M. Jorgensen Company, pg. 606
JORGENSEN STEEL & ALUMINUM/MINNEAPOLIS—See Earle M. Jorgensen Company, pg. 606
JORGENSEN STEEL & ALUMINUM/PHILADELPHIA—See Earle M. Jorgensen Company, pg. 606
JORGENSEN STEEL & ALUMINUM/SEATTLE—See Earle M. Jorgensen Company, pg. 606
JORGENSEN STEEL & ALUMINUM/ST. LOUIS—See Earle M. Jorgensen Company, pg. 606
JORGENSEN STEEL & ALUMINUM/TULSA—See Earle M. Jorgensen Company, pg. 606
JORGENSEN STEEL & ALUMINUM/DENVER—See Earle M. Jorgensen Company, pg. 605
JOSAM COMPANY, pg. 607
JOSEPH KIRSCHNER CO.—See Jordan's Meats, pg. 605
JOSEPH, LITTLEJOHN & LEVY, pg. 607
J. JOSEPHSON, INC., pg. 607
JOSEPHSON INTERNATIONAL INC., pg. 607
JOURNAL COMMUNICATIONS INC., pg. 607
THE JOURNAL-DEMOCRAT—See Landmark Communications, Inc., pg. 655

JOURNAL REGISTER COMPANY, pg. 608
JOURNAL/SENTINEL INC.—See Journal Communications Inc., pg. 607
JOY SERVICE—See Lakeside Refining Co. Inc., pg. 651
JOY TOY, CO.—See Strombecker Corporation, pg. 1054
JOYCE INTERNATIONAL, INC., pg. 608
JOYKIST/GSC DISTRIBUTING—See GSC Enterprises, Inc., pg. 440
JPS CARPET CORP.—See JPS Textile Group, Inc., pg. 586
J.R. SIMPLOT CO.-AGRICULTURE GROUP—See J.R. Simplot Company, pg. 1007
J.R. SIMPLOT CO.-DIVERSIFIED PRODUCTS GROUP—See J.R. Simplot Company, pg. 1007
J.R. SIMPLOT CO.-FOOD GROUP—See J.R. Simplot Company, pg. 1007
J.R. SIMPLOT CO.-MINERALS & CHEMICAL GROUP—See J.R. Simplot Company, pg. 1007
J.R. TECHNICAL—See Arrow Pneumatics Co. Inc., pg. 85
JUDD'S INCORPORATED, pg. 608
JUDSON-ATKINSON CANDIES, INC., pg. 608
JUDY BOND, INC., pg. 608
JACQUES JUGEAT, INC., pg. 608
JUHL MARKETING COMMUNICATIONS, pg. 608
JUNIATA OFFICE SUPPLIES, pg. 608
JUNIOR GALLERY LTD., pg. 609
JUNO TOOL & PLASTIC CORPORATION—See The Cretex Companies, pg. 299
JUPITER CORP. TRANSPORTATION SYSTEM—See Jupiter Industries, Inc., pg. 609
JUPITER INDUSTRIES, INC., pg. 609
THE JUPITER CORPORATION—See Jupiter Industries, Inc., pg. 609
JUPITER ENERGY CORP.—See Jupiter Industries, Inc., pg. 609
JUPITER TRANSPORTATION CORP.—See Jupiter Industries, Inc., pg. 609
JOHN R. JURGENSEN CO.—See Valley Asphalt Corporation, pg. 1143
JUST BORN, INC., pg. 610
JUST PANTS, pg. 610
JUSTISS OIL CO., INC., pg. 610
JUSTRITE MANUFACTURING COMPANY, pg. 610

K

K & W TRANSPORTATION—See Anderson Trucking Service Inc., pg. 73
K & G OF WISCONSIN, INC., pg. 610
K-PROMOTIONS, INC.—See Carlson Companies, Inc., pg. 221
K & R DELIVERY, INC., pg. 610
K-III COMMUNICATIONS CORPORATION, pg. 610
K-III INFORMATION—See K-III Communications Corporation, pg. 611
K-III MAGAZINES CORPORATION—See K-III Communications Corporation, pg. 611
KATV TELEVISION, INC.—See Perpetual Corporation, pg. 862
KB ALLOYS, INC.—See Harbour Group Ltd., pg. 507
K&B DBM MARKETING OY—See Backer Spielvogel Bates Worldwide, Inc., pg. 111
K & B, INC., pg. 611
KBAK-TV—See Burnham Broadcasting Company, pg. 194
KC FOODS—See Hulman & Company, pg. 552
KCL CORPORATION, pg. 611
KCOY-TV—See Stauffer Communications, Inc., pg. 1043
KCS ENERGY INC., pg. 612
K&D ADAPTUS DIRECT—See Backer Spielvogel Bates Worldwide, Inc., pg. 112
K&D ASIA-HONG KONG—See Backer Spielvogel Bates Worldwide, Inc., pg. 112
K&D BOND DIRECT—See Backer Spielvogel Bates Worldwide, Inc., pg. 112
K&D HELLAS—See Backer Spielvogel Bates Worldwide, Inc., pg. 112
K&D ITALIA—See Backer Spielvogel Bates Worldwide, Inc., pg. 112
K-D LAMP COMPANY, pg. 612
K&D WERBEAGENTUR—See Backer Spielvogel Bates Worldwide, Inc., pg. 112
KDA/HEPY, P.C.—See Harley Ellington Pierce Yee Associates, Inc., pg. 509
KDI AMERICAN PRODUCTS, INC.—See KDI Corporation, pg. 612
KDI CORPORATION, pg. 612
KDI ELECTRO-TEC CORP.—See KDI Corporation, pg. 612
KDI ELECTRONICS—See KDI Corporation, pg. 612
KDI PARAGON, INC.—See KDI Corporation, pg. 612
KDI PRECISION PRODUCTS, INC.—See KDI Corporation, pg. 612
KDI SYLVAN POOLS, INC.—See KDI Corporation, pg. 612
KEZ—See Media America Corp., pg. 734
KFI, INC.—See Cox Enterprises, Inc., pg. 292
KGFF-AM—See Stauffer Communications, Inc., pg. 1043
KGNC-AM & FM—See Stauffer Communications, Inc., pg. 1043
KGWC-TV—See Stauffer Communications, Inc., pg. 1043
KGWN-TV—See Stauffer Communications, Inc., pg. 1043
KHON-TV—See Burnham Broadcasting Company, pg. 194
KIKK AM/FM—See National Amusements, Inc., pg. 785
K-J DISTRIBUTORS, INC., pg. 612
K & L FEEDS—See Empire Kosher Poultry, Inc., pg. 379
KLAS-TV—See Landmark Communications, Inc., pg. 654
KMBC DIVISION—See The Hearst Corporation, pg. 522
KMBC-TV—See The Hearst Corporation, pg. 522
KMIZ-TV—See Stauffer Communications, Inc., pg. 1043
KOA HOLDINGS, pg. 612
KOB-TV, INC.—See Hubbard Broadcasting, Inc., pg. 549
KPMG PEAT MARWICK, pg. 613
K & R RENTALS, INC.—See K & R Delivery, Inc., pg. 610
KRBS RADIO—See Multi-Ad Services, Inc., pg. 775
KSBW, INC.—See Gillett Holdings, Inc., pg. 459
KSBY, INC.—See Gillett Holdings, Inc., pg. 459
KSFY-TV—See News-Press & Gazette Company, pg. 805
KSG INC., pg. 613
KSK COMMUNICATIONS, LTD., pg. 613
KSL RADIO—See Deseret Management Corporation, pg. 332
KSL-TV—See Deseret Management Corporation, pg. 332
KSNC—See SJL of Kansas Corp., pg. 963
KSNG—See SJL of Kansas Corp., pg. 963
KSNT—See SJL of Kansas Corp., pg. 963
KSTF-TV—See Stauffer Communications, Inc., pg. 1043
KSTP-AM, INC.—See Hubbard Broadcasting, Inc., pg. 549
KSTP-FM, INC.—See Hubbard Broadcasting, Inc., pg. 549
KSTP-TV—See Hubbard Broadcasting, Inc., pg. 549
KTUL TELEVISION, INC.—See Perpetual Corporation, pg. 862
KTVS-TV—See Stauffer Communications, Inc., pg. 1043
K&W, A DIV. OF STANDCO INDUSTRIES, INC.—See Standco Industries, Inc., pg. 1038
KYB CORPORATION OF AMERICA, pg. 613
KYB INDUSTRIES INC.—See KYB Corporation of America, pg. 613
KAANAPALI WATER CORPORATION—See JMB Realty Corporation, pg. 585
THE KAEMPFER COMPANY, INVESTMENT BUILDERS, pg. 613
KAEPA INC., pg. 613
KAHLER FRIENDT & PARTNERS, INC., pg. 613
ALBERT KAHN ASSOCIATES, INC., pg. 613
M. B. KAHN CONSTRUCTION CO., INC., pg. 614
KAIBAB INDUSTRIES, pg. 614
KAIBAB METALS, INC.—See Kaibab Industries, pg. 614
KAISER AEROSPACE & ELECTRONICS CORP., pg. 614
KAISER FOUNDATION HEALTH & HOSPITALS GROUP, pg. 614
KAISER MCEUEN INC., pg. 615
KAISER PERMANENTE, COLORADO DIVISION—See Kaiser Foundation Health & Hospitals Group, pg. 614
KAISER PERMANENTE, GEORGIA DIVISION—See Kaiser Foundation Health & Hospitals Group, pg. 614
KAISER PERMANENTE, HAWAII DIVISION—See Kaiser Foundation Health & Hospitals Group, pg. 614
KAISER PERMANENTE, KANSAS/MISSOURI DIVISION—See Kaiser Foundation Health & Hospitals Group, pg. 614
KAISER PERMANENTE, MID-ATLANTIC STATES DIVISION—See Kaiser Foundation Health & Hospitals Group, pg. 614
KAISER PERMANENTE, NORTH CAROLINA DIVISION—See Kaiser Foundation Health & Hospitals Group, pg. 614
KAISER PERMANENTE, NORTHEAST DIVISION—See Kaiser Foundation Health & Hospitals Group, pg. 614
KAISER PERMANENTE, NORTHERN CALIFORNIA REGION—See Kaiser Foundation Health & Hospitals Group, pg. 614
KAISER PERMANENTE, NORTHWEST DIVISION—See Kaiser Foundation Health & Hospitals Group, pg. 614
KAISER PERMANENTE, OHIO DIVISION—See Kaiser Foundation Health & Hospitals Group, pg. 614
KAISER PERMANENTE, SOUTHERN CALIFORNIA DIVISION—See Kaiser Foundation Health & Hospitals Group, pg. 614
KAISER PERMANENTE, TEXAS DIVISION—See Kaiser Foundation Health & Hospitals Group, pg. 614
KAISER TOBACCO COMPANY, INC., pg. 615
KAL KAN FOODS, INC.—See Mars, Incorporated, pg. 713
KALAMAZOO HOLDINGS, INC., pg. 615
KALAMAZOO LABEL CO., pg. 615
KALAMAZOO SCRAP & PROCESSING—See Sturgis Iron & Metal Company, Inc., pg. 1055
KALAS MANUFACTURING, INC., pg. 615
KALB VOORHIS & CO., pg. 615
KALIN ENTERPRISES, INC., pg. 615
KALLISTA, INC.—See Kohler Company, pg. 640
KALMBACH PUBLISHING CO., pg. 615
KALSEC, INC.—See Kalamazoo Holdings, Inc., pg. 615
KAMENSTEIN EUROPE, LTD.—See M. Kamenstein, Inc., pg. 615
M. KAMENSTEIN, INC., pg. 615
KAMPGROUNDS OF AMERICA (CANADA) LTD.—See KOA Holdings, pg. 613
KAMSTRA COMMUNICATIONS, INC., pg. 615
KANAWHA STEEL & EQUIPMENT CO., pg. 615
SAM KANE BEEF PROCESSORS, INC., pg. 616
KANE-MILLER CORP., pg. 616
KANEX, pg. 616
KANGAROOS, USA INC., pg. 616
KANGOL LTD.—See The Marmon Group, Inc., pg. 712
KANSAS AGRICULTURE NETWORK—See Stauffer Communications, Inc., pg. 1043
KANSAS CITY AUTO AUCTION—See Cox Enterprises, Inc., pg. 293
KANSAS CITY CHIEFS FOOTBALL CLUB, pg. 616
KANSAS CITY ROYALS RADIO NETWORK—See Stauffer Communications, Inc., pg. 1043
KANSAS CITY TERMINAL RAILWAY CO.—See Anschutz Corporation, pg. 76
KANSAS INFORMATION NETWORK—See Stauffer Communications, Inc., pg. 1043
KANSAS METALS CO.—See CF&I Steel Corporation, pg. 201
KAPLAN ELECTRONICS, pg. 616
KAPPLER EUROPE, LTD.—See KSG Inc., pg. 613
KAPPLER, INC.—See KSG Inc., pg. 613
KAPRIELIAN/O'LEARY, pg. 616
KARAKAS, VANSICKLE OUELLETTE ADVERTISING & PUBLIC RELATIONS, pg. 616
KARGES FURNITURE COMPANY, pg. 616
KARLER PACKING COMPANY, INC., pg. 617
KARNAK CORPORATION, pg. 617
L. KARP & SONS, INC., pg. 617
KARPEN FURNITURE DIV.—See Schnadig Corporation, pg. 977
KARSH & HAGAN, INC., pg. 617
KARSTEN ENGINEERING CORP.—See Karsten Manufacturing Corporation, pg. 617
KARSTEN MANUFACTURING CORPORATION, pg. 617
KARTRET SWITCHGEAR LTD.—See O'Brien Energy Systems Inc., pg. 820
THE KARTRIDG PAK CO., pg. 617
KARTRIDG PAK CO.—See Barry-Wehmiller Company, pg. 122
KASANEN TRAINING/BTC FORUM—See The Forum Corporation, pg. 426
M.W. KASCH COMPANY, pg. 617
KASH N KARRY FOOD STORES, INC., pg. 617
KASLE STEEL CORPORATION, pg. 617
KASPAR WIRE WORKS, INC., pg. 617
KASPER MACHINE COMPANY, pg. 618
KASSEL & ZOLL PROVISIONS, INC., pg. 618
KASSER/LAIRD DISTILLING CO.—See Laird & Company, pg. 650
KASSON & KELLER—See Keymark Corporation, pg. 627
KATSIN/LOEB ADVERTISING, pg. 618
KASTLE SYSTEMS, INC., pg. 618
KASTNER & PARTNER GMBH WERBEAGENTUR—See Leo Burnett Company, Inc., pg. 192
KATHE-K SHOE STORES—See The Kobacker Company & Affiliates, pg. 638
KATZ AMERICAN TELEVISION—See Katz Communications, Inc., pg. 618
KATZ COMMUNICATIONS, INC., pg. 618
KATZ CONTINENTAL TELEVISION—See Katz Communications, Inc., pg. 618
KATZ HISPANIC RADIO SALES—See Katz Communications, Inc., pg. 618
KATZ, INC., pg. 618
KATZ INDEPENDENT TELEVISION—See Katz Communications, Inc., pg. 618
KATZ RADIO—See Katz Communications, Inc., pg. 618
KA'U AGRIBUSINESS CO., INC.—See C. Brewer & Company, Limited, pg. 174
KAUAI SUGAR STORAGE CO.—See JMB Realty Corporation, pg. 585
KAUFFMAN PRODUCTS, INC., pg. 618
KAUFFMAN STEWART ADVERTISING, pg. 618
KAUKAUNA CHEESE, pg. 619
KAWAGUCHI TRAVEL SERVICES, INC.—See Washington Mutual Savings Bank, pg. 1166
DAVID KAY, INC.—See Foster & Gallagher Inc., pg. 426
KAYE INSTRUMENTS, INC., pg. 619
KAYEM FOODS, INC., pg. 619
KAYENESS, INC.—See Berwind Corporation, pg. 145
KAYSAM CORPORATION OF AMERICA—See Norcross Industries, Inc., pg. 809
KAYSER COLL. TECHNISCHE UBERSETZER—See Berlitz International, Inc., pg. 143
KAYSER-ROTH CORPORATION—See Collins & Aikman Group Inc., pg. 263
KAYSER-ROTH HOSIERY, INC.—See Collins & Aikman Group Inc., pg. 262
KAYWOODIE—See S. M. Frank & Co., Inc., pg. 429
KAZ, INC., pg. 619
KEARFOTT GUIDANCE & NAVIGATION CORP.—See Astronautics Corp. of America, pg. 93
KEARNEY—See The Dyson-Kissner-Moran Corporation, pg. 357
KEARNEY DIV.—See The Dyson-Kissner-Moran Corporation, pg. 357
KEARNEY-NATIONAL CANADA LTD.—See The Dyson-Kissner-Moran Corporation, pg. 358
KEARNEY-NATIONAL, INC.—See The Dyson-Kissner-Moran Corporation, pg. 357
KEARNEY-WESTERN POWER PRODUCTS, INC.—See The Dyson-Kissner-Moran Corporation, pg. 357
P.J. KEATING COMPANY, pg. 619
DANIEL J. KEATING CONSTRUCTION CO.—See Daniel J. Keating Co., pg. 619
DANIEL J. KEATING CO., pg. 619
KEATING MATERIALS CORPORATION—See P.J. Keating Company, pg. 619
KECO AEROSPACE GROUND EQUIPMENT DIV.—See Keco Industry, Inc., pg. 619
KECO INDUSTRY, INC., pg. 619
KECO MILLING CO.—See Windmill Holdings Corp., pg. 1195
KEEN COMPRESSED GAS CO., INC., pg. 619
KEEN PROPANE DIVISION—See Keen Compressed Gas Co., Inc., pg. 619
KEEN WELDING DIVISION—See Keen Compressed Gas Co., Inc., pg. 619
KEENELAND ASSOC., INC., pg. 620
KEENERS, INC., pg. 620
KEENEY MANUFACTURING CO., pg. 620
ROBERT KEESHAN ASSOCIATES, INC.—See Josephson International Inc., pg. 607
KEHNE ELECTRIC COMPANY, INC., pg. 620
KEILER & COMPANY, pg. 620
KEIPER RECARO, INC., pg. 620
BEN E. KEITH CO. OF OKLAHOMA—See Ben E. Keith Company, pg. 620
BEN E. KEITH COMPANY, pg. 620
GEO. E. KEITH COMPANY, pg. 620
KEKAHA SUGAR COMPANY, LIMITED—See JMB Realty Corporation, pg. 585
J. J. KELLER & ASSOCIATES, INC., pg. 620
KELLER CONSTRUCTION COMPANY LTD., pg. 620
KELLER CRESCENT CO., pg. 620
KELLER & GANNON—See Lester B. Knight & Associates, Inc., pg. 637
THE KELLER MANUFACTURING CO., INC., pg. 621
KELLER MOTOR CAR COMPANY, INC., pg. 621
KELLEY & WALLWORK INC., pg. 621
KELLEY BEAN CO., INC., pg. 621
KELLIHER/SAMETS MARKETING COMMUNICATIONS, pg. 621
KELLY MICHENER INC., pg. 621
KELLY-MOORE PAINT COMPANY, INC., pg. 621

KELLY, SCOTT AND MADISON, INC., pg. 621
KELSEY CONSTRUCTION, INC., pg. 621
KELSEY DEVELOPMENT—See Kelsey Construction, Inc., pg. 622
KELSO-BURNETT COMPANY, pg. 622
KELSO-BURNETT ZION BRANCH—See Kelso-Burnett Company, pg. 622
KELSO OIL COMPANY, pg. 622
KEM KREST CORP.—See Accra Pac Group, pg. 11
KEMMERER BOTTLING GROUP INC., pg. 622
KEMP FURNITURE CO.—See Coastal Lumber Company, pg. 257
KEN-MAC METAL, INC., pg. 622
KENCO—See Sparkomatic Corporation, pg. 1025
KENDALE INDUSTRIES, INC., pg. 622
KENDALL AUSTRALIA PTY. LTD.—See Kendall Healthcare Products Co., pg. 622
KENDALL CANADA LTD.—See Kendall Healthcare Products Co., pg. 622
THE KENDALL CO.—See Kendall Healthcare Products Co., pg. 622
THE KENDALL CO. (UK) LTD.—See Kendall Healthcare Products Co., pg. 622
KENDALL DE MEXICO S.A. DE D.V.—See Kendall Healthcare Products Co., pg. 622
KENDALL GMBH—See Kendall Healthcare Products Co., pg. 622
KENDALL HEALTHCARE PRODUCTS CO., pg. 622
KENDALL HEALTHCARE PRODUCTS COMPANY—See Kendall Healthcare Products Co., pg. 622
KENDALL S.A.—See Kendall Healthcare Products Co., pg. 622
KENDALL SINGAPORE—See Kendall Healthcare Products Co., pg. 622
KENDALL THAILAND—See Kendall Healthcare Products Co., pg. 622
KENNEDY ASSOCIATES, pg. 623
KENNEDY COMPANY—See Shugart Corporation, pg. 1001
KENNEDY MANUFACTURING COMPANY, pg. 623
KENNEDY VALVE, pg. 623
KENNEDY VAN SAUN CORP.—See McNally Wellman Company, pg. 732
KENNESAW LIFE & ACCIDENT INSURANCE COMPANY—See Regan Holding Corporation, pg. 921
KENNEY MANUFACTURING COMPANY, pg. 623
KENNINGTON LTD., INC., pg. 623
KENNINGTON PROPERTIES, INC.—See Kennington Ltd., Inc., pg. 623
KENOSHA TWINS BASEBALL CLUB—See Minnesota Twins Baseball Club, pg. 758
KENOSIA PROPERTIES, INC.—See Society for Savings Bancorp, Inc., pg. 1016
KENT FEEDS INC.—See Varied Investments, Inc., pg. 1146
THE KENT MANUFACTURING CO., pg. 623
KENT SUSSEX TIRE SERVICE—See Burris Foods, Inc., pg. 195
KENTILE FLOORS INC., pg. 623
KENTON GRAIN CO.—See Tom Wade Co., pg. 1157
KENTUCKY BERWIND LAND COMPANY—See Berwind Corporation, pg. 145
KENTUCKY DEPARTMENT OF TRAVEL DEVELOPMENT, pg. 623
KENTUCKY INDIANA LUMBER CO.—See Kentucky Indiana Lumber Co. Inc., pg. 624
KENTUCKY INDIANA LUMBER CO.—See Kentucky Indiana Lumber Co. Inc., pg. 624
KENTUCKY INDIANA LUMBER CO. INC., pg. 623
KENTUCKY MANUFACTURING CO., pg. 624
KENTUCKY OPTICAL—See Optical Corp. of America, pg. 828
KENTUCKY STANDARD—See Landmark Communications, Inc., pg. 655
KENWAL PRODUCTS CORP., pg. 624
KENWORTH OF INDIANAPOLIS INC., pg. 624
KENYON OIL COMPANY, INC.—See Warren Equities Inc., pg. 1165
KERN INDUSTRIES, pg. 624
KERN LIVESTOCK SUPPLEMENT CO., INC.—See Altair Corporation, pg. 45
KERN'S BAKERIES, INCORPORATED, pg. 624
KEROFF & ROSENBERG ADVERTISING INC., pg. 624
KERRISON DRY GOODS COMPANY, INC., pg. 624
KERVICK ENTERPRISES, INC., pg. 624
H. KESSLER & COMPANY, pg. 624
H. KESSLER & COMPANY—See H. Kessler & Company, pg. 624
H. KESSLER & COMPANY—See H. Kessler & Company, pg. 624
H. KESSLER & COMPANY—See H. Kessler & Company, pg. 624
KESTERSON FOOD COMPANY, INC., pg. 624
KETCHUM ADVERTISING/CHICAGO—See Ketchum Communications Inc., pg. 625
KETCHUM ADVERTISING (JAPAN) LTD.—See Ketchum Communications Inc., pg. 626
KETCHUM ADVERTISING/LOS ANGELES—See Ketchum Communications Inc., pg. 625
KETCHUM ADVERTISING/NEW YORK—See Ketchum Communications Inc., pg. 625
KETCHUM ADVERTISING/PHILADELPHIA—See Ketchum Communications Inc., pg. 625
KETCHUM ADVERTISING/PITTSBURGH—See Ketchum Communications Inc., pg. 625
KETCHUM ADVERTISING/SAN FRANCISCO—See Ketchum Communications Inc., pg. 625
KETCHUM ADVERTISING SINGAPORE—See Ketchum Communications Inc., pg. 625
KETCHUM ADVERTISING/USA—See Ketchum Communications Inc., pg. 625
KETCHUM ADVERTISING/USA—See Ketchum Communications Inc., pg. 625
KETCHUM COMMUNICATIONS INC., pg. 625
KETCHUM DIRECTORY ADVERTISING/EXECUTIVE—See Ketchum Communications Inc., pg. 625
KETCHUM DIRECTORY ADVERTISING/USA—See Ketchum Communications Inc., pg. 625
KETCHUM, INC., pg. 626
KETCHUM INTERNATIONAL INC.—See Ketchum Communications Inc., pg. 625
KETCHUM PUBLIC RELATIONS/ATLANTA—See Ketchum Communications Inc., pg. 625
KETCHUM PUBLIC RELATIONS/CHICAGO—See Ketchum Communications Inc., pg. 625
KETCHUM PUBLIC RELATIONS/NEW YORK—See Ketchum Communications Inc., pg. 625
KETCHUM PUBLIC RELATIONS/PHILADELPHIA—See Ketchum Communications Inc., pg. 625
KETCHUM PUBLIC RELATIONS/PITTSBURGH—See Ketchum Communications Inc., pg. 625
KETCHUM PUBLIC RELATIONS PLC—See Ketchum Communications Inc., pg. 625
KETCHUM PUBLIC RELATIONS/SAN FRANCISCO—See Ketchum Communications Inc., pg. 625
KETCHUM PUBLIC RELATIONS/WASHINGTON, DC—See Ketchum Communications Inc., pg. 625
KETCHUM WERBEAGENTUR GMBH—See Ketchum Communications Inc., pg. 625
KETTENBURG MARINE CORPORATION, pg. 626
KETTENBURG MARINE/NEWPORT BEACH RETAIL—See Kettenburg Marine Corporation, pg. 626
KETTENBURG MARINE/NEWPORT ENGINES—See Kettenburg Marine Corporation, pg. 626
KETTERING ADVERTISING DISPLAY CO., pg. 626
KETTLE RESTAURANTS, pg. 626
KETTLER BROTHERS, INC., pg. 626
KEUFFEL & ESSER—See Azon Corporation, pg. 105
KEWAUNEE ENGINEERING CORP.—See Marine Travelift, Inc., pg. 707
KEX PRODUCTS, INC.—See Berwind Corporation, pg. 145
KEY CADILLAC, INC., pg. 626
KEY CONTAINER CORPORATION, pg. 626
KEY FOOD STORES CO-OPERATIVE, INC., pg. 626
KEY HANDLING SYSTEMS, INC., pg. 627
KEY HEALTH PLAN—See The Associated Group, pg. 90
KEY INDUSTRIES, INC., pg. 627
KEY MANUFACTURING GROUP, INC., pg. 627
KEY PLASTICS, INC., pg. 627
KEYES COMPANY, pg. 627
KEYES INVESTMENTS—See Keyes Company, pg. 627
KEYES MANAGEMENT—See Keyes Company, pg. 627
KEYES MARTIN, pg. 627
KEYES MOTORS, INC., pg. 627
KEYMARK CORPORATION, pg. 627
KEYSOR CENTURY CORPORATION, pg. 627
KEYSTONE AUTOMOTIVE INDUSTRIES, INC., pg. 627
KEYSTONE AUTOMOTIVE INDUSTRIES, INC.-JACKSON—See Keystone Automotive Industries, Inc., pg. 628
KEYSTONE AUTOMOTIVE INDUSTRIES, INC.-HUNTSVILLE—See Keystone Automotive Industries, Inc., pg. 628
KEYSTONE AUTOMOTIVE INDUSTRIES, INC-JACKSONVILLE—See Keystone Automotive Industries, Inc., pg. 628
KEYSTONE AUTOMOTIVE INDUSTRIES, INC.-LITTLE ROCK—See Keystone Automotive Industries, Inc., pg. 628
KEYSTONE AUTOMOTIVE INDUSTRIES, INC.-LOUISVILLE—See Keystone Automotive Industries, Inc., pg. 628
KEYSTONE AUTOMOTIVE INDUSTRIES, INC.-MACON—See Keystone Automotive Industries, Inc., pg. 628
KEYSTONE AUTOMOTIVE INDUSTRIES, INC.-ORLANDO—See Keystone Automotive Industries, Inc., pg. 628
KEYSTONE AUTOMOTIVE INDUSTRIES, INC.-TIJUANA—See Keystone Automotive Industries, Inc., pg. 628
KEYSTONE BRUSH & CONTACT CO.—See Kirkwood Industries, Inc., pg. 633
KEYSTONE CARBON COMPANY, pg. 628
KEYSTONE COFFEE, pg. 628
KEYSTONE FOODS CORPORATION, pg. 628
KEYSTONE GROUP INC.—See Sovereign Group Inc., pg. 1024
KEYWELL CORPORATION, pg. 629
SAMUEL G. KEYWELL CO.—See Keywell Corporation, pg. 629
SAMUEL G. KEYWELL CO.—See Keywell Corporation, pg. 629
KGAN-TV—See Guy Gannett Publishing Company, pg. 442
KIDVERTISER, pg. 629
KIEWIT CONSTRUCTION GROUP, INC.—See Peter Kiewit Sons Inc., pg. 629
KIEWIT MINING GROUP, INC.—See Peter Kiewit Sons Inc., pg. 629
PETER KIEWIT SONS INC., pg. 629
KIFUKI U.S.A. CO., INC., pg. 629
KILAUEA AGRONOMICS, INC.—See C. Brewer & Company, Limited, pg. 174
KILSBY-JORGENSEN STEEL & ALUMINUM INC.—See Earle M. Jorgensen Company, pg. 606
KILSBY-JORGENSEN STEEL & ALUMINUM INC.—See Earle M. Jorgensen Company, pg. 606
KILSBY-JORGENSEN STEEL & ALUMINUM LTD.—See Earle M. Jorgensen Company, pg. 606
KILSBY-JORGENSEN STEEL & ALUMINUM SA DE CV—See Earle M. Jorgensen Company, pg. 606
KILSBY-ROBERTS—See Earle M. Jorgensen Company, pg. 606
KILSBY-ROBERTS/BALTIMORE—See Earle M. Jorgensen Company, pg. 606
KILSBY-ROBERTS/BIRMINGHAM—See Earle M. Jorgensen Company, pg. 606
KILSBY-ROBERTS/BOSTON—See Earle M. Jorgensen Company, pg. 606
KILSBY-ROBERTS/CHARLOTTE—See Earle M. Jorgensen Company, pg. 606
KILSBY-ROBERTS/CHICAGO—See Earle M. Jorgensen Company, pg. 606
KILSBY-ROBERTS/CLEVELAND—See Earle M. Jorgensen Company, pg. 606
KILSBY-ROBERTS CUTTING CENTER/HONING/TULSA—See Earle M. Jorgensen Company, pg. 606
KILSBY-ROBERTS CUTTING CENTER/INDIANAPOLIS—See Earle M. Jorgensen Company, pg. 606
KILSBY-ROBERTS/DALLAS—See Earle M. Jorgensen Company, pg. 606
KILSBY-ROBERTS/DAVENPORT—See Earle M. Jorgensen Company, pg. 606
KILSBY-ROBERTS/DENVER—See Earle M. Jorgensen Company, pg. 606
KILSBY-ROBERTS/DETROIT—See Earle M. Jorgensen Company, pg. 606
KILSBY-ROBERTS/HAYWARD—See Earle M. Jorgensen Company, pg. 606
KILSBY-ROBERTS HONING/BLUE ISLAND—See Earle M. Jorgensen Company, pg. 606
KILSBY-ROBERTS/HOUSTON—See Earle M. Jorgensen Company, pg. 606
KILSBY-ROBERTS/INDIANAPOLIS—See Earle M. Jorgensen Company, pg. 606
KILSBY-ROBERTS/KANSAS CITY—See Earle M. Jorgensen Company, pg. 606
KILSBY-ROBERTS/LITTLE ROCK—See Earle M. Jorgensen Company, pg. 606
KILSBY-ROBERTS/LOS ANGELES—See Earle M. Jorgensen Company, pg. 606
KILSBY-ROBERTS/MEMPHIS—See Earle M. Jorgensen Company, pg. 606
KILSBY-ROBERTS/MILWAUKEE—See Earle M. Jorgensen Company, pg. 606
KILSBY-ROBERTS/PHILADELPHIA—See Earle M. Jorgensen Company, pg. 606
KILSBY-ROBERTS/PORTLAND—See Earle M. Jorgensen Company, pg. 606
KILSBY-ROBERTS/ST. LOUIS—See Earle M. Jorgensen Company, pg. 606
KILSBY-ROBERTS/SEATTLE—See Earle M. Jorgensen Company, pg. 606
KILSBY-ROBERTS/TULSA—See Earle M. Jorgensen Company, pg. 606
KILSBY-ROBERTS/TWIN CITIES—See Earle M. Jorgensen Company, pg. 606
L. ROBERT KIMBALL & ASSOCIATES, pg. 629
KIMBALL BAGGAGE TAG DIVISION—See Rand McNally & Company, pg. 911
KIMGLASS DIVISION—See Kimstock, Inc., pg. 630
KIMRAY, INC., pg. 629
KIMSTOCK, INC., pg. 630
KINDEL FURNITURE COMPANY, pg. 630
KINDY OPTICAL—See Duling Optical Corporation, pg. 352
KINETIC SYSTEMS CORPORATION, pg. 630
KINETICS, INC.—See Haworth, Inc., pg. 518
VICTOR KING ADVERTISING, pg. 630
KING BEAR AUTO CENTERS—See King Bear Enterprises, Inc., pg. 630
KING BEAR ENTERPRISES, INC., pg. 630
THE KING COMPANY, pg. 630
KING FEATURES SYNDICATE DIVISION—See The Hearst Corporation, pg. 524
KING FUELS INC., pg. 630
KING GROUP, INC., pg. 630
KING INDUSTRIES, INC., pg. 630
KING KOIL LICENSING COMPANY INC., pg. 630
KING KULLEN GROCERY CO., INC., pg. 630
KING LOUIE INTERNATIONAL, INC., pg. 631
KING MICHIGAN SUNDRIES DIV.—See King Group, Inc., pg. 630
KING MILLING COMPANY, pg. 631
KING OF THE ROAD DIV.—See Chief Industries, Inc., pg. 247
KING PRIME, INC., pg. 631
KING & PRINCE SEAFOOD CORPORATION, pg. 631
KING WIRE & CABLE CORPORATION, pg. 631
KINGFISHER CO-OP ELEVATOR ASSOCIATION, pg. 631
E. B. KINGMAN COMPANY, pg. 631
KINGS FOODSERVICE—See Unifax, Inc., pg. 1126
KINGS ISLAND COMPANY—See American Financial Corporation, pg. 53
KINGS PLAZA SHOPPING CTR. & MARINA—See R. H. Macy & Co., Inc., pg. 699
KINGS TOYOTA SUZUKI, pg. 631
KINGSBRIDGE MEDIA & MARKETING, INC., pg. 631
KINGSBURY ASSEMBLY MACHINE DIV.—See Kingsbury Corporation, pg. 632
KINGSBURY CANADA, INC.—See Kingsbury Corporation, pg. 632
KINGSBURY CORPORATION, pg. 631
KINGSBURY, INC., pg. 632
KINGSBURY SERVICE CORP.—See Kingsbury Corporation, pg. 632
KINGSBURY WORLD SALES—See Kingsbury Corporation, pg. 632
KINGSDOWN, INC., pg. 632
KINGSLEY MACHINE CO., pg. 632
KINGSTON MARKETING CO.—See Topco Associates, Inc., pg. 1101
KINGSWOOD ADVERTISING, INC., pg. 632
KINGTOOL DIVISION—See Kingsbury Corporation, pg. 632
KINKO'S CORPORATION, pg. 632
KINNEAR DOOR—See Wayne Dalton Corporation, pg. 313
KINNEY SYSTEM, INC., pg. 632
KINNING & REIL OF WYOMING—See RK Mechanical, Inc., pg. 907
KIPLINGER EDITORS—See The Kiplinger Washington Editors, Inc., pg. 632
THE KIPLINGER WASHINGTON EDITORS, INC., pg. 632
KIPP GROUP, pg. 632

KIRBY BUILDING SYSTEMS, INC., pg. 632
WILLIAM J. KIRCHER & ASSOCIATES, pg. 633
THE KIRK & BLUM MFG. CO., pg. 633
KIRK & MATZ LTD., pg. 633
KIRK-MAYER, INC., pg. 633
KIRKPATRICK PETTIS—See Mutual of Omaha Insurance Company, pg. 779
KIRKWOOD CARBON—See Kirkwood Industries, Inc., pg. 633
KIRKWOOD COMMUTATOR—See Kirkwood Industries, Inc., pg. 633
KIRKWOOD FOREIGN SALES CORP.—See Kirkwood Industries, Inc., pg. 633
KIRKWOOD INDUSTRIES, INC., pg. 633
MORRIS KIRSCHMAN & COMPANY, INC., pg. 633
KIRSHENBAUM & BOND, pg. 633
THE KISLAK COMPANY, INC.—See J. I. Kislak Inc., pg. 633
J. I. KISLAK INC., pg. 633
J. I. KISLAK AGENCY, INC.—See J. I. Kislak Inc., pg. 633
J. I. KISLAK MORTGAGE CORPORATION—See J. I. Kislak Inc., pg. 633
KISSIMMEE TOYOTA INC., pg. 633
A. C. KISSLING, INC., pg. 634
KITCHELL CEM, INC.—See Kitchell Corporation, pg. 634
KITCHELL CONTRACTORS, INC. OF ARIZONA—See Kitchell Corporation, pg. 634
KITCHELL CORPORATION, pg. 634
KITCHELL DEVELOPMENT COMPANY—See Kitchell Corporation, pg. 634
KITCHEN KOMPACT, INC., pg. 634
KITCHENS OF THE OCEAN, INC., pg. 634
KLAPMEIER MANAGEMENT COMPANY, pg. 634
KLAUS RADIO INC., pg. 634
KLAUSEN & PARTNERS A/S—See Young & Rubicam Inc., pg. 1212
KLAUSSNER CORPORATION, pg. 634
KLAUSSNER FURNITURE INDUSTRY—See Klaussner Corporation, pg. 634
KLEAR KNIT INC., pg. 634
KLECO CORP., pg. 634
KLEER PAK CORPORATION, pg. 635
KLEIN ADVERTISING INC., pg. 635
JOHN KLEIN & ASSOC., INC., pg. 635
CALVIN KLEIN, INC., pg. 635
CALVIN KLEIN SPORT—See Calvin Klein, Inc., pg. 635
KLEIN TOOLS INC., pg. 635
KLEINSCHMIDT INC., pg. 635
KLEMTNER ADVERTISING INC., pg. 635
THE KLINE FURNITURE CO.—See Reliable Stores, Inc., pg. 925
KLINE IRON & STEEL CO., INC., pg. 635
GEORGETTE KLINGER, INC., pg. 635
KLIPSCH & ASSOCIATES INC., pg. 635
KLOCK CO.—See Collins & Aikman Group Inc., pg. 263
KLOCKNER-MOELLER NORSK A/S—See Panduit Company, pg. 845
KLOSTERMAN'S BAKING COMPANY, pg. 636
KLUENER FOODS CO.—See Kluener Packing Company, pg. 636
KLUENER PACKING COMPANY, pg. 636
KNAPE & KNAPE, pg. 636
THE KNAPHEIDE MFG. CO., pg. 636
KNAPP COMMUNICATIONS CORPORATION, pg. 636
KNAPP SHOES INC., pg. 636
KNAR GOLD & SILVER EXCHANGE, pg. 636
E.W. KNAUSS & SON, INC., pg. 636
KNIGHT ARCHITECTS ENGINEERS PLANNERS, INC.—See Lester B. Knight & Associates, Inc., pg. 637
KNIGHT/EMERSON CONSULTING, INC.—See Lester B. Knight & Associates, Inc., pg. 637
KNIGHT EQUIPMENT CORP., pg. 636
KNIGHT KOREA—See Lester B. Knight & Associates, Inc., pg. 637
LESTER B. KNIGHT & ASSOCIATES, INC., pg. 637
KNIGHT MANAGEMENT CONSULTING, INC.—See Lester B. Knight & Associates, Inc., pg. 637
KNIGHT PMD, INC.—See Lester B. Knight & Associates, Inc., pg. 637
KNIGHT WENDLING AG—See Lester B. Knight & Associates, Inc., pg. 637
KNIGHT WENDLING LTD.—See Lester B. Knight & Associates, Inc., pg. 637
KNIGHTBRIDGE PARTNERS, pg. 637
KNIK CONSTRUCTION CO., INC.—See Lynden Incorporated, pg. 689
KNITMAKER DIVISION—See Beldoch Industries Corporation, pg. 133
KNOLL INTERNATIONAL, INC.—See 21 International Holdings, Inc., pg. 1121
KNOLL INTERNATIONAL ITALIA S.P.A.—See 21 International Holdings, Inc., pg. 1121
KNOLL INTL., INC.—See 21 International Holdings, Inc., pg. 1121
KNOLLOFFICE, INC.—See 21 International Holdings, Inc., pg. 1121
ALFRED A. KNOPF, INC.—See Advance Publications Inc., pg. 20
KNOTH & MEADS COMPANY, pg. 637
KNOTT'S BERRY FARM, pg. 637
KNOUSE FOODS INC., pg. 637
KNOWLES ELECTRONICS, INC., pg. 637
KNOX ALLRIGHT, INC.—See Allright Corporation, pg. 42
KNOX INTERNATIONAL CORP., pg. 638
KNOX LUMBER CO.—See Payless Cashways, Inc., pg. 853
KNOX OIL OF TEXAS INC., pg. 638
KNOXVILLE JOURNAL CORPORATION—See Persis Corporation, pg. 863
KNURLET TOOL CO.—See Kasper Machine Company, pg. 618
KNUTSON CONSTRUCTION CO., pg. 638
KO-REC-TYPE—See Baroum Eaton Allen Corporation, pg. 121
THE KOBACKER COMPANY & AFFILIATES, pg. 638
KOBRA INTERNATIONAL LTD, pg. 638
KOBS & DRAFT—See Backer Spielvogel Bates Worldwide, Inc., pg. 112
KOBS & DRAFT—See Backer Spielvogel Bates Worldwide, Inc., pg. 112
KOBS & DRAFT—See Backer Spielvogel Bates Worldwide, Inc., pg. 112
KOBS & DRAFT ADVERTISING—See Backer Spielvogel Bates Worldwide, Inc., pg. 112
KOBS & DRAFT ADVERTISING, INC.—See Backer Spielvogel Bates Worldwide, Inc., pg. 109
KOBS & DRAFT ASIA-MALAYSIA—See Backer Spielvogel Bates Worldwide, Inc., pg. 112
KOBS & DRAFT ASIA-THAILAND—See Backer Spielvogel Bates Worldwide, Inc., pg. 112
KOBS & DRAFT BELGIUM—See Backer Spielvogel Bates Worldwide, Inc., pg. 112
KOBS & DRAFT BV—See Backer Spielvogel Bates Worldwide, Inc., pg. 112
KOBS & DRAFT EUROPE—See Backer Spielvogel Bates Worldwide, Inc., pg. 112
KOBS & DRAFT S.A.—See Backer Spielvogel Bates Worldwide, Inc., pg. 112
KOCH ENGINEERING CO., INC.—See Koch Industries, Incorporated, pg. 639
KOCH ENGINEERING COMPANY, INC., pg. 638
GEORGE KOCH SONS, INC., pg. 639
H. KOCH & SONS—See Collins & Aikman Group Inc., pg. 262
KOCH INDUSTRIES, INCORPORATED, pg. 639
KOCH MEMBRANE SYSTEMS—See Koch Industries, Incorporated, pg. 639
KOCH REFINING COMPANY—See Koch Industries, Incorporated, pg. 639
KOCH SUPPLIES INC., pg. 639
KOCIDE CHEMICAL CO.—See Griffin Corporation, pg. 487
KOCOLENE OIL CORP., pg. 639
KOEHLER MANUFACTURING COMPANY, pg. 639
KOH-I-NOOR, INC., pg. 639
KOHLER COMPANY, pg. 639
KOHLER DE MEXICO, S.A. DE C.V.—See Kohler Company, pg. 640
KOHLER JAPAN K.K.—See Kohler Company, pg. 640
KOHLER JAPAN K.K.—See Kohler Company, pg. 640
KOHLER LTD.—See Kohler Company, pg. 640
KOHLER LTD.—See Kohler Company, pg. 640
KOHLER LTD.—See Kohler Company, pg. 640
KOHLER LTD.—See Kohler Company, pg. 640
KOHM ASSOCIATES, INC., pg. 640
KOKOMO GRAIN CO., INC., pg. 640
KOKOMO SANITARY POTTERY CORP., pg. 640
KOKOMO SPRING COMPANY, INC., pg. 640
KOKOSING CONSTRUCTION COMPANY, INC., pg. 640
KOKOSING MATERIALS, INC.—See Kokosing Construction Company, Inc., pg. 641
KOLD KIST BRANDS, INC., pg. 641
KOLD-TV—See News-Press & Gazette Company, pg. 805
KOLESAR & HARTWELL INC., pg. 641
KOLL CO., pg. 641
KOLLER ENTERPRISES, INC., pg. 641
JOHN F. KOLODY INC., pg. 641
KOLON, BITTKER & DESMOND, INC., pg. 641
KOLON-MET LIFE INSURANCE COMPANY LIMITED—See Metropolitan Life Insurance Co., pg. 745
CHARLES KOMAR & SONS, INC., pg. 641
KOMATSU DRESSER COMPANY—See INDRESCO, Inc., pg. 565
KOMBI, LTD., pg. 641
KOMLINE-SANDERSON ENGINEERING CORP., pg. 641
KOMPLETTBURO GMBH, INTERNATIONALE KOMMUNIKATION—See Ketchum Communications Inc., pg. 625
KONTORSERVICE INC.—See Western Temporary Services, Inc., pg. 1182
KOOL SEAL, INC., pg. 641
KOOLVENT ALUMINUM PRODUCTS, INC., pg. 641
PERRY H. KOPLIK & SONS, pg. 641
J. KORBER & COMPANY, pg. 641
KOREA JOHNSON CO., LTD.—See S. C. Johnson & Son, Inc., pg. 600
KORES NORDIC USA CORP., pg. 642
KORET OF CALIFORNIA, pg. 642
KORET GIVENCHY, pg. 642
KORET OF CALIFORNIA—See Koret of California, pg. 642
KOREY, KAY & PARTNERS, pg. 642
KORMAN CO., pg. 642
KORN/FERRY INTERNATIONAL, pg. 642
KORN/FERRY INTERNATIONAL—See Korn/Ferry International, pg. 642
KORN/FERRY INTERNATIONAL—See Korn/Ferry International, pg. 642
KORN/FERRY INTERNATIONAL—See Korn/Ferry International, pg. 642
KORN/FERRY INTERNATIONAL—See Korn/Ferry International, pg. 642
KORN/FERRY INTERNATIONAL—See Korn/Ferry International, pg. 642
KORN/FERRY INTERNATIONAL—See Korn/Ferry International, pg. 642
KORN/FERRY INTERNATIONAL—See Korn/Ferry International, pg. 642
KORN/FERRY INTERNATIONAL—See Korn/Ferry International, pg. 642
KORN/FERRY INTERNATIONAL—See Korn/Ferry International, pg. 642
KORN/FERRY INTERNATIONAL—See Korn/Ferry International, pg. 642
KORN/FERRY INTERNATIONAL—See Korn/Ferry International, pg. 642
KORN/FERRY INTERNATIONAL—See Korn/Ferry International, pg. 642
KORN/FERRY INTERNATIONAL—See Korn/Ferry International, pg. 642
KORN/FERRY INTERNATIONAL—See Korn/Ferry International, pg. 642
KORN/FERRY INTERNATIONAL—See Korn/Ferry International, pg. 642
KORN/FERRY INTERNATIONAL—See Korn/Ferry International, pg. 642
KORN/FERRY INTERNATIONAL—See Korn/Ferry International, pg. 642
KORN/FERRY INTERNATIONAL—See Korn/Ferry International, pg. 642
KORN/FERRY INTERNATIONAL—See Korn/Ferry International, pg. 642
KORN/FERRY INTERNATIONAL—See Korn/Ferry International, pg. 643
KORN/FERRY INTERNATIONAL—See Korn/Ferry International, pg. 643
KORN/FERRY INTERNATIONAL—See Korn/Ferry International, pg. 643
KORN/FERRY INTERNATIONAL—See Korn/Ferry International, pg. 643
KORN/FERRY INTERNATIONAL—See Korn/Ferry International, pg. 643
KORN/FERRY INTERNATIONAL—See Korn/Ferry International, pg. 643
KORN/FERRY INTERNATIONAL—See Korn/Ferry International, pg. 643
KORN/FERRY INTERNATIONAL—See Korn/Ferry International, pg. 643
KORN/FERRY INTERNATIONAL—See Korn/Ferry International, pg. 643
KORN/FERRY INTERNATIONAL—See Korn/Ferry International, pg. 643
KORN/FERRY INTERNATIONAL—See Korn/Ferry International, pg. 643
KORN/FERRY INTERNATIONAL—See Korn/Ferry International, pg. 643
KORN/FERRY INTERNATIONAL—See Korn/Ferry International, pg. 643
KORN/FERRY INTERNATIONAL—See Korn/Ferry International, pg. 643
KORN/FERRY INTERNATIONAL—See Korn/Ferry International, pg. 643
KORN/FERRY INTERNATIONAL—See Korn/Ferry International, pg. 643
KORN/FERRY INTERNATIONAL—See Korn/Ferry International, pg. 643
KORN/FERRY INTERNATIONAL—See Korn/Ferry International, pg. 642
KORN/FERRY INTERNATIONAL—See Korn/Ferry International, pg. 643
KORN/FERRY INTERNATIONAL—See Korn/Ferry International, pg. 643
KORN/FERRY INTERNATIONAL—See Korn/Ferry International, pg. 643
KORN/FERRY INTERNATIONAL—See Korn/Ferry International, pg. 643
KORN/FERRY INTERNATIONAL—See Korn/Ferry International, pg. 643
KORN/FERRY INTERNATIONAL—See Korn/Ferry International, pg. 643
KORN/FERRY ORGANIZATIONAL CONSULTING—See Korn/Ferry International, pg. 642
KOVA FERTILIZER INC., pg. 643
GEORGE KOVACS LIGHTING, INC., pg. 643
KOWALSKI SAUSAGE CO., INC., pg. 643
KOYKER MFG. CO.—See Sioux Steel Company, pg. 1008
KOYO-MATTISON—See Mattison Machine Works, pg. 721
KRACO ENTERPRISES, INC., pg. 643
KRAFCOR UNLIMITED—See Specialty Industries, Inc., pg. 1027
KRAFT HARDWARE, INC., pg. 643
WARD KRAFT, INC., pg. 643
KRAGIE/NEWELL, pg. 643
KRAMES COMMUNICATIONS—See K-III Communications Corporation, pg. 611
KRANCO, INC., pg. 643
KRANSCO, pg. 644
KRASDALE FOODS INC., pg. 644
KRAUS-ANDERSON CONSTRUCTION—See Kraus-Anderson, Inc., pg. 644
KRAUS-ANDERSON, INC., pg. 644
KRAUS-ANDERSON MORTGAGE CO.—See Kraus-Anderson, Inc., pg. 644
KRAUS-ANDERSON REALTY CO.—See Kraus-Anderson, Inc., pg. 644
KRAUSE, NADUREK & EICKMEYER, pg. 644
KRAUSE PLOW CORP., pg. 644
KRAUSE'S SOFA FACTORY, INC., pg. 644
KREHER STEEL COMPANY, INC., pg. 644
KRENGEL MFG. CO.—See American Marking Systems, pg. 58
KREONITE, INC., pg. 644
KREPS-WISE ASSOCIATES, pg. 644
KRESSER/CRAIG, pg. 644
LEONARD KREUSCH, INC., pg. 645
KRIER FOODS, INC., pg. 645
KROCH'S & BRENTANO'S, INC., pg. 645
KROEHLER FURNITURE MANUFACTURING COMPANY, INC., pg. 645
KROH OPERATING L.P., pg. 645
KROMMENHOEK MCKEOWN ASSOCIATES, pg. 645
KROPP FORGE CO.—See TIC United Corporation, pg. 1073
KRUSE HARDWARE COMPANY, pg. 645
KRUSE INTERNATIONAL, pg. 645
KRYSTAL COMPANY, pg. 645
KTVU INC.—See Cox Enterprises, Inc., pg. 292
KUHLMAN, INC., pg. 646
KUHN & WITTENBORN, INC., pg. 646
KUKLA PRESS, INC., pg. 646
KULITE SEMICONDUCTOR PRODUCTS, INC., pg. 646

KUNER-EMPSON COMPANY—See Faribault Foods Inc., pg. 399
PETER KUNTZ COMPANY—See Erb Lumber Company, pg. 360
KUNZLER & COMPANY, INC., pg. 646
KUONI TRAVEL, INC., pg. 646
KUPPER PARKER COMMUNICATIONS INC., pg. 646
KURDZIEL INDUSTRIES, INC., pg. 646
KURDZIEL IRON OF ROTHBURY—See Kurdziel Industries, Inc., pg. 646
KURDZIEL IRON OF WAUSEON—See Kurdziel Industries, Inc., pg. 646
KURFEES COATINGS, INC., pg. 646
KURT MANUFACTURING CO. INC., pg. 646
KURTZ BROS., INC., pg. 646
KURTZMAN/SLAVIN/LINDA, INC., pg. 646
KWICKIE/FLASH FOODS, INC.—See Jones Company, Inc., pg. 603
KWIK-KOPY CORP., pg. 647
KWIKEE SYSTEMS—See Multi-Ad Services, Inc., pg. 775
KYANITE MINING CORPORATION, pg. 647
KYBER COAL CO.—See Berwind Corporation, pg. 145

L

L&J TECHNOLOGIES, pg. 647
L & L NURSERY SUPPLY, INC., pg. 647
L & L OIL COMPANY, INC., pg. 647
L & R COMMUNICATIONS, LIMITED, pg. 647
L&R MANUFACTURING CO., pg. 647
LB INDUSTRIES INC., pg. 647
LDI, LTD., pg. 647
LFC HOLDING CORPORATION, pg. 647
THE LINC GROUP, INC., pg. 648
LINC SCIENTIFIC LEASING INC.—See The LINC Group, Inc., pg. 648
LISC MANAGEMENT SERVICES—See Union Holdings, Inc., pg. 1128
LKI—See Leonard Kreusch, Inc., pg. 645
L.L. BEAN, INC., pg. 648
L & L/JIROCH DISTRIBUTING CO.—See Spartan Stores Inc., pg. 1026
L & L PLANT SOIL DIVISION—See L & L Nursery Supply, Inc., pg. 647
LNR COMMUNICATIONS, pg. 648
LOPC—See Joyce International, Inc., pg. 608
LPL TECHNOLOGIES, INC., pg. 648
LSC-MARKETING, INC.—See The Chesapeake Life Insurance Co., pg. 243
LSI/KALA—See Schawk, Inc., pg. 975
LSI TRUCK PRODUCTS CORP.-NEWAY/ANCHOR LOCK—See Lear Siegler Diversified Holdings Corp., pg. 664
LTI, INC.—See Lynden Incorporated, pg. 689
LWMCK CORPORATION, pg. 648
LA BELLE INDUSTRIES, INC., pg. 648
LA-CO INDUSTRIES, INC., pg. 648
LA COMPUTER CENTER, pg. 648
LA FRANCE CORPORATION, pg. 649
LA MARCHE MFG. CO., pg. 649
LA MESA R V CENTER, INC., pg. 649
LA PALMA INTERCOMMUNITY HOSPITAL—See UniHealth America, pg. 1127
LA PETITE BOULANGERIE, INC.—See Mrs. Fields' Inc., pg. 761
LA PREFERIDA, INC., pg. 649
LA PRENSA ASOCIADA, INC.—See The Associated Press, pg. 92
LA REINA, INC., pg. 649
LA ROSA'S, INC., pg. 649
LA SALLE COUNTY FARM SUPPLY, pg. 649
LA SOCIETE VS LIMITEE—See ARA Group, pg. 7
LA VICTORIA FOODS, INC., pg. 649
LAB PRODUCTS, INC.—See Bio Medic Corporation, pg. 152
LABARGE PIPE & STEEL COMPANY, pg. 649
LABEL-AIRE INC., pg. 649
LABEL PRODUCTS & DESIGN DIVISION—See Journal Communications Inc., pg. 608
LABELON CORPORATION, pg. 649
LABORATORIES GRIFFITH DE MEXICO, S.A. DE C.V.—See Griffith Laboratories Worldwide, Inc., pg. 488
LABORATORIOS GRIFFITH DE CENTRO AMERICA S.A.—See Griffith Laboratories Worldwide, Inc., pg. 488
LABORATORY SUPPLY COMPANY, INC., pg. 649
LABSCO—See Laboratory Supply Company, Inc., pg. 650
LACKLAND CITY WATER CO.—See Rayco, pg. 914
LACKMAN FOOD SERVICE, pg. 650
LADDIN & COMPANY, INC., pg. 650
LADISH MALTING CO.—See Cargill Inc., pg. 219
LADY MARLENE SALES CORP., pg. 650
LADY ROSE DIV.—See Masters, Inc., pg. 720
LADYBUG MAGAZINE—See Carus Corporation, pg. 227
RAY LAETHEM PONTIAC GMC TRUCK CO., pg. 650
LAFAYETTE MANUFACTURING, INC., pg. 650
LAFAYETTE PRECISION PRODUCTS INC.—See RDI, Inc., pg. 906
LAFAYETTE STEEL CO., pg. 650
LAIDLAW CORPORATION, pg. 650
LAIRD & COMPANY, pg. 650
THE LAITRAM CORPORATION, pg. 650
LAITRAM MACHINERY INC.—See The Laitram Corporation, pg. 651
LAKE CATHERINE—See Munro & Company, Inc., pg. 776
LAKE COUNTY PRESS, pg. 651
LAKE ERIE ELECTRIC, INC., pg. 651
LAKE GEORGE VENTURES, INC.—See Rotterdam Ventures Inc., pg. 951
LAKE MICHIGAN CONSTRUCTION, INC.—See Orix Real Estate Equities, Inc., pg. 829
LAKE MICHIGAN CONSTRUCTION III, INC.—See Orix Real Estate Equities, Inc., pg. 829
LAKE MICHIGAN CONSTRUCTION II, INC.—See Orix Real Estate Equities, Inc., pg. 829
LAKE MICHIGAN PROPERTIES IV, INC.—See Orix Real Estate Equities, Inc., pg. 829
LAKE MICHIGAN PROPERTIES, INC.—See Orix Real Estate Equities, Inc., pg. 829
LAKE MICHIGAN PROPERTIES III, INC.—See Orix Real Estate Equities, Inc., pg. 829
LAKE MICHIGAN PROPERTIES II, INC.—See Orix Real Estate Equities, Inc., pg. 829
LAKE PLACID GRANITE CO.—See Cold Spring Granite Company, pg. 260
LAKE REGION MANUFACTURING COMPANY, INC., pg. 651
LAKE SHORE, INC.—See The Oldenburg Group Companies, pg. 824
LAKE TO LAKE DAIRY—See Land O'Lakes, Inc., pg. 653
LAKE WALES DAILY HIGHLANDER—See Stauffer Communications, Inc., pg. 1042
LAKELAND AUTO AUCTION—See Cox Enterprises, Inc., pg. 293
LAKESIDE COAL COMPANY—See Alabama Electric Cooperative, Inc., pg. 28
LAKESIDE ENTERPRISES, INC.—See Barton Press, Inc., pg. 124
LAKESIDE FOODS, INC., pg. 651
LAKESIDE INDUSTRIES, pg. 651
LAKESIDE REFINING CO. INC., pg. 651
LAKEWOOD ENGINEERING & MANUFACTURING CO., pg. 652
LAKIN GENERAL CORPORATION, pg. 652
LAMAR CORP.—See Premarc Corporation, pg. 886
LAMAR CORPORATION, pg. 652
LAMAR FINANCIAL SERVICES INSURANCE COMPANY—See Capitol Street Corp., pg. 216
LAMAR INVESTMENT MANAGEMENT COMPANY—See Capitol Street Corp., pg. 216
LAMAR LEASING CO., INC.—See Capitol Street Corp., pg. 216
LAMAR LIFE INVESTORS—See Capitol Street Corp., pg. 216
LAMARCA DIRECT MARKETING—See LaMarca Group Inc., pg. 652
LAMARCA GROUP INC., pg. 652
LAMASTER FARMER, ET AL, pg. 652
LAMB AG—See Enterprises International Inc., pg. 383
LAMB ENGINEERING & CONSTRUCTION CO., pg. 652
ROBERT E. LAMB, INC., pg. 652
LAMB LEASING & LAMB BROTHERS GENERAL—See Lamb Engineering & Construction Co., pg. 652
TONY LAMBERT COMPANY, pg. 652
LAMBESIS COMMUNICATIONS, pg. 652
LAMINAIRE CORPORATION, pg. 652
LAMINATED BEAM DIV.—See Anthony Forest Products Co., Inc., pg. 77
LAMP POST FRANCHISE CORPORATION, pg. 652
LAMPERT YARDS, INC., pg. 653
LAMSON AND GOODNOW MFG. CO.—See Rogers, Lunt & Bowlen Co., pg. 943
LAMSTON—See Plymouth Lamston Stores, Corp., pg. 877
LAN-CHILE AIRLINES, pg. 653
LAN-O-SHEEN, INC., pg. 653
LANCASTER HOST RESORT, pg. 653
LANCASTER MALLEABLE CASTINGS COMPANY, pg. 653
THE LANCASTER NEWS—See Landmark Communications, Inc., pg. 655
LANCE CAMPER MANUFACTURING CORPORATION, pg. 653
LAND N SEA, INC., pg. 653
LAND O'LAKES, INC., pg. 653
LAND O'LAKES FINANCE CO.—See Land O'Lakes, Inc., pg. 654
LAND O'LAKES FARM CENTERS—See Land O'Lakes, Inc., pg. 654
LAND O'LAKES INTERNATIONAL DEVELOPMENT CORP.—See Land O'Lakes, Inc., pg. 654
LAND O'LAKES SEED DIVISION—See Land O'Lakes, Inc., pg. 653
LANE PRESS, INC., pg. 654
LAND SPAN INC.—See Watkins Associated Industries Inc., pg. 1167
LANDAU BUILDING CO., pg. 654
LANDAU & HEYMAN INC., pg. 654
LANDISC SYSTEMS—See Day & Zimmermann, Inc., pg. 320
LANDMARK COMMUNICATIONS, INC., pg. 654
LANDMARK COMMUNITY NEWSPAPERS, INC.—See Landmark Communications, Inc., pg. 655
LANDMARK HOTEL CORPORATION, pg. 656
LANDMARK SPECIAL PUBLICATIONS—See Landmark Communications, Inc., pg. 656
E. B. LANE & ASSOCIATES, INC., pg. 656
LANE BROADCASTING, INC.—See Lane Industries, Inc., pg. 657
THE LANE CONSTRUCTION CORP., pg. 656
LANE FILM PRODUCTS DIVISION—See Lane Industries, Inc., pg. 657
LANE GRAPHICS PRODUCTS DIV.—See Lane Industries, Inc., pg. 657
LANE HONDA/HYUNDAI—See Rosenthal Automotive Organization, pg. 949
LANE HOTELS, INC.—See Lane Industries, Inc., pg. 657
LANE INDUSTRIES, INC., pg. 656
LANE LIMITED, pg. 657
LANE PROPERTIES, INC.—See Lane Industries, Inc., pg. 657
LANGENDORF BAKING COMPANY OF SEATTLE, INC.—See Gai's Seattle French Baking Co., Inc., pg. 441
C.J. LANGENFELDER & SON, INC., pg. 657
DAVID LANGER & CO., INC., pg. 657
HAL LANGERMAN CO., pg. 657
LANGERT GOLF CO., INC.—See Prince Manufacturing, Inc., pg. 890
LANGLEY & MORGAN CORP.—See Jupiter Industries, Inc., pg. 609
LANGSTON COMPANIES, pg. 657
LANGUAGE INSTITUTE FOR ENGLISH (L.I.F.E.)—See Berlitz International, Inc., pg. 142
LANMAN & KEMP-BARCLAY CO. INC., pg. 657
LANSDALE, CARR & BAUM, pg. 658
LANSING DAIRY, INC.—See Melody Foods, Inc., pg. 738
LANTECH INC., pg. 658
LANTZSCH-ANDREAS ENTERPRISES, INC., pg. 658
LANZ, INC., pg. 658
LAPEYRE STAIR, INC.—See The Laitram Corporation, pg. 651
LAPHAM-HICKEY STEEL CORP., pg. 658
LAPHAM-HICKEY STEEL CORP. (MO)—See Lapham-Hickey Steel Corp., pg. 658
LAPHAM HICKEY STEEL (WI)—See Lapham-Hickey Steel Corp., pg. 658
LAPPIN ELECTRIC COMPANY, pg. 658
LARAMIE TIRE DISTRIBUTORS INC., pg. 658
LAREDO MORNING TIMES—See The Hearst Corporation, pg. 523
LOU LARICHE CHEVROLET-SUBARU INC., pg. 658
LARIO ENTERPRISES, INC.—See Lario Oil & Gas Company, pg. 659
LARIO OIL & GAS COMPANY, pg. 658
LARK LUGGAGE COMPANY, INC.—See E-II Holdings, Inc., pg. 359
LARKEN INC., pg. 659
LARKIN, INC.—See Lennox International Inc., pg. 667
LARKIN MEEDER & SCHWEIDEL, pg. 659
LAROCHE CHEMICALS INC.—See Laroche Holdings, Inc., pg. 659
LAROCHE HOLDINGS, INC., pg. 659
LAROCHE INDUSTRIES INC.—See Laroche Holdings, Inc., pg. 659
LARRYS, INC., pg. 659
LARRY'S INDUSTRIES, INC.—See Bresler's Industries, Inc., pg. 174
LARSEN COLBY ADVERTISING, pg. 659
JACK LENOR LARSEN, INC., pg. 659
AL LARSON BOAT SHOP, INC., pg. 659
LARSON BOATS—See Minstar, Inc., pg. 758
J.H. LARSON ELECTRICAL COMPANY, pg. 659
LARSON MANUFACTURING COMPANY, pg. 659
LARWIN COMPANY, pg. 659
LAS PLUMAS LUMBER NORTH DIVISION—See Di Giorgio Corporation, pg. 335
LAS PLUMAS LUMBER SOUTH DIVISION—See Di Giorgio Corporation, pg. 335
LAS VEGAS SUN, INC., pg. 659
LASALLE-DEITCH CO., INC., pg. 660
LASALLE LIGHTING—See LaSalle-Deitch Co., Inc., pg. 660
LASALLE PARTNERS, pg. 660
LASER POWER CORPORATION, pg. 660
LASER PRECISION CORP., pg. 660
LASKEY ASSOCIATES, pg. 660
LASKO METAL PRODUCTS, INC., pg. 660
LASKY COMPANY, pg. 660
LASTING PRODUCTS, INC., pg. 660
THE LATHROP COMPANY, pg. 660
LAUBECK CORPORATION, BECKLEY DIVISION—See Laubeck Corporation/Cross, pg. 660
LAUBECK CORPORATION/CROSS, pg. 660
LAUBECK CORPORATION, LAUBENSTEIN DIVISION—See Laubeck Corporation/Cross, pg. 660
LAUERER MARKIN GIBBS, INC., pg. 660
THE HOMER LAUGHLIN CHINA COMPANY, pg. 661
LAUNEY, HACHMANN & HARRIS, INC., pg. 661
LAURENTIAN TECHNOMEDIA INC.—See International Data Group, pg. 577
LAURIAT INC.—See Chadwick-Miller Inc., pg. 237
LAUTIER FLORASYNTH S.A.—See Florasynth Inc., pg. 420
LAUTIER S.A.—See Florasynth Inc., pg. 420
LAVELLE AIRCRAFT COMPANY, pg. 661
LAVELLE INDUSTRIES INC., pg. 661
LAVERDIERE'S ENTERPRISES, pg. 661
LAVIDGE & ASSOCIATES INC., pg. 661
LAW CO. SCROOP INC.—See Law Engineering, Inc., pg. 661
THE LAW COMPANY, INC., pg. 661
LAW ENGINEERING, INC., pg. 661
LAWLER-HAVENS INC., pg. 661
LAWLER, MATUSKY & SKELLY ENGINEERS—See Lawler-Havens Inc., pg. 661
JACK LAWLOR ADVERTISING, INC., pg. 661
LAWNWARE PRODUCTS, INC., pg. 661
LAWRENCE AGENCY CORPORATION—See Lawrence Group, Inc., pg. 662
LAWRENCE & COMPANY—See White Rock Distilleries Inc., pg. 1186
THE F. D. LAWRENCE ELECTRIC CO., pg. 661
LAWRENCE GENERAL CORPORATION—See Lawrence Group, Inc., pg. 662
LAWRENCE GROUP, INC., pg. 662
LAWRENCE HEALTHCARE ADMINISTRATIVE SERVICES—See Lawrence Group, Inc., pg. 662
LAWRENCE INSURANCE GROUP, INC.—See Lawrence Group, Inc., pg. 662
LAWRENCE MANAGEMENT GROUP, INC.—See Lawrence Group, Inc., pg. 662
LAWRENCE METAL PRODUCTS, INC., pg. 662
LAWRENCE PAPER COMPANY, pg. 662
LAWRENCE PUMPS, INC., pg. 662
LAWRENCE RISK SERVICES CORPORATION—See Lawrence Group, Inc., pg. 662
LAWRENCE & SCHILLER, INC., pg. 663
LAWRENCE UNITED CORP.—See Lawrence Group, Inc., pg. 662
LAWRY'S RESTAURANTS, INC., pg. 663
LAWSON ASSOCIATES INC., pg. 663

LAWSON MECHANICAL CONTRACTORS, pg. 663
P. LAWSON TRAVEL, LTD.—See Carlson Companies, Inc., pg. 221
LAY PACKING COMPANY INC., pg. 663
LAYMAN CANDY COMPANY, INC., pg. 663
LAYNE & BOWLER—See The Marley Company, pg. 710
LAYNE-WESTERN CO., INC.—See The Marley Company, pg. 710
LAZY DAYS R V CENTER, INC., pg. 663
LE CIRQUE OPTIQUE—See Tuckerman Optical Co., pg. 1118
LEACH CORPORATION, pg. 663
LEACH & GARNER COMPANY, pg. 663
LEADER FEDERAL BANK FOR SAVINGS, pg. 663
LEADER INSTRUMENTS CORPORATION, pg. 664
LEADER LEASING, INC.—See Leader Federal Bank For Savings, pg. 664
LEADER NATIONAL CORPORATION—See The Dyson-Kissner-Moran Corporation, pg. 357
LEADER SERVICES, INC.—See Leader Federal Bank For Savings, pg. 664
LEAGUE GENERAL INSURANCE CO.—See CUNA Mutual Insurance Society, pg. 205
LEAGUE LIFE INSURANCE CO.—See CUNA Mutual Insurance Society, pg. 205
LEAMINGTON PLANT—See Ash Grove Cement Company, pg. 87
LEANN, INC.—See Fresh Mark, Inc., pg. 432
LEAR SIEGLER ACCURATE CORP.—See Lear Siegler Diversified Holdings Corp., pg. 664
LEAR SIEGLER DIVERSIFIED HOLDINGS CORP., pg. 664
LEAR SIEGLER DIVERSIFIED HOLDINGS CORP.—See Forstmann Little & Co., pg. 424
LEAR SIEGLER HAWAIIAN PROPERTIES DIV.—See Lear Siegler Diversified Holdings Corp., pg. 664
LEAR SIEGLER INDUSTRIES LTD., GEN. SEATING DIV.—See Lear Siegler Diversified Holdings Corp., pg. 664
LEAR SIEGLER MEASUREMENT CONTROLS CORP.—See Lear Siegler Diversified Holdings Corp., pg. 664
LEAR SIEGLER PLASTICS CORP.—See Lear Siegler Diversified Holdings Corp., pg. 664
LEAR SIEGLER SEATING CORP.—See Lear Siegler Diversified Holdings Corp., pg. 664
LEAR SIEGLER SEYMOUR CORP.—See Lear Siegler Diversified Holdings Corp., pg. 664
LEAR SIEGLER TELECOMMUNICATIONS DIV.—See Lear Siegler Diversified Holdings Corp., pg. 664
LEASAMETRIC, INC.—See The Marmon Group, Inc., pg. 712
LEASING SERVICES CORP.—See Novar Electronics, pg. 817
LEATHER CENTER, INC., pg. 664
LEATHER WAREHOUSE, INC., pg. 664
LEATHERS BEST, pg. 664
THE LEAVELL COMPANY, pg. 664
LEAVELL MINERAL RESOURCES, INC.—See The Leavell Company, pg. 665
LEBANON CHEMICAL CORP., pg. 665
THE LEBANON ENTERPRISE—See Landmark Communications, Inc., pg. 655
LEBANON TOTAL TURF CARE—See Lebanon Chemical Corp., pg. 665
LEBHAR-FRIEDMAN, INC., pg. 665
LEBLANC CASE CO.—See G. Leblanc Corporation, pg. 665
G. LEBLANC CORPORATION, pg. 665
G. LEBLANC—See G. Leblanc Corporation, pg. 665
LEBRIJA RUBIO PUBLICIDAD S.A.—See N W Ayer Incorporated, pg. 104
LECHMERE, INC., pg. 665
LECO FEED MILLS, INC.—See Fred Webb Inc., pg. 1170
LEDONNE, WILNER & WEINER, INC., pg. 665
LEE COMPANY, pg. 665
LEE CONSTRUCTION CO.—See National Engineering & Contracting Co., pg. 788
LEE DAVIS AYER—See N W Ayer Incorporated, pg. 104
LEE GROCERY COMPANY, pg. 665
LEE HYDRAULISCHE MINIATURKOMPONENTEN—See Lee Company, pg. 665
LEE INDUSTRIES—See Fleet Engineers, Inc., pg. 417
LEE-MOORE OIL CO., INC., pg. 665
LEE MYLES ASSOCIATES CORPORATION, pg. 666
LEE NATIONAL CORPORATION, pg. 666
LEE PRODUCTS LTD.—See Lee Company, pg. 665
LEE & RILEY, INC., pg. 666
LEE SPRING CO., LTD.—See The Unimax Corporation, pg. 1127
LEE SPRING COMPANY—See The Unimax Corporation, pg. 1127
LEECE-NEVILLE DE MEXICO S.A. DE C.V.—See 21 International Holdings, Inc., pg. 1121
LEEWARDS CREATIVE CRAFTS, INC., pg. 666
CARLOS R. LEFFLER INC., pg. 666
LEFRAK ORGANIZATION INC., pg. 666
AL PAUL LEFTON CO., INC., pg. 666
LEGACY GIFTS—See Bucilla Corporation, pg. 185
A.C. LEGG PACKING COMPANY, INC., pg. 666
LEGIS CORPORATION—See Siegel Corp., pg. 1002
LEHIGH-LEOPOLD—See Joyce International, Inc., pg. 608
GEO. H. LEHLEITNER & CO., INC., pg. 666
A. J. LEHMAN CO.—See Grandpa Brands Company, pg. 476
LEHMAN ASSOCIATES, INC.—See United States Realty & Investment Co., pg. 1137
LEICHTUNG, INC., pg. 666
LEISURE TIME GAMES—See Monarch Avalon, Inc., pg. 765
LEN RON MFG. CO. INC.—See Estee Lauder, Inc., pg. 389
LENAC, WARFORD, STONE, INC., pg. 667
LENAPE FORGE, INC., pg. 667
LENNOX INDUSTRIES (CANADA) LTD.—See Lennox International Inc., pg. 667
LENNOX INDUSTRIES (CANADA) LTD.—See Lennox International Inc., pg. 667
LENNOX INDUSTRIES INC.—See Lennox International Inc., pg. 667
LENNOX INTERNATIONAL INC., pg. 667
LENSCLEAN, INC.—See Aldine Technologies, pg. 33
LEO BUNETT TURIN—See Leo Burnett Company, Inc., pg. 193
LEO BURNETT COLOMBIA, S.A.—See Leo Burnett Company, Inc., pg. 192
LEO BURNETT CONNAGHAN & MAY PTY. LTD.—See Leo Burnett Company, Inc., pg. 192
LEO BURNETT PRAGUE—See Leo Burnett Company, Inc., pg. 193
LEO BURNETT S.A.—See Leo Burnett Company, Inc., pg. 193
LEO BURNETT SONYON, INC.—See Leo Burnett Company, Inc., pg. 193
LEO BURNETT SP. Z.O.O., UL.—See Leo Burnett Company, Inc., pg. 193
LEO BURNETT SWEDEN A.B.—See Leo Burnett Company, Inc., pg. 193
S. R. LEON COMPANY, INC., pg. 667
LEON-FERENBACH COMPANY, pg. 667
HAROLD LEONARD & COMPANY, INC., pg. 667
LEONARD & HARRAL PACKING CO., pg. 667
CHARLES LEONARD, INC., pg. 668
LEONARD KREUSCH GMBH & CO.—See Leonard Kreusch, Inc., pg. 645
LEONARD MONAHAN LUBARS & KELLY, pg. 668
LEONARD WHOLESALE, INC., pg. 668
J. N. LEOUSSIS ADVERTISING & MARKETING S.A.—See TBWA Advertising, Inc., pg. 1072
LEPAGE'S, INC.—See Cortec Group, pg. 287
L'ERMITAGE HOTELS, pg. 668
LES APPAREILLAGER ELECTRIQUES KEARNEY-NATIONAL—See The Dyson-Kissner-Moran Corporation, pg. 358
LESCHEN WIRE ROPE—See Wire Rope Corp. of America, Inc., pg. 1197
LESHNER MILLS. INC., pg. 668
LESLIE ADVERTISING, pg. 668
LESLIE PUBLIC RELATIONS—See Leslie Advertising, pg. 668
LESON CHEVROLET COMPANY, INC., pg. 668
LESTER B. KNIGHT CAST METALS, INC.—See Lester B. Knight & Associates, Inc., pg. 637
J.L. LESTER & SON, INC., pg. 668
KENNETH O. LESTER, INC.—See Performance Food Group, Inc., pg. 862
LET THEM EAT CAKE—See Wilton Industries, Inc., pg. 1195
LETICA CORPORATION, pg. 668
LETTS INDUSTRIES, INC., pg. 668
LETTS INDUSTRIES, PIONEER DIV.—See Letts Industries, Inc., pg. 668
LETTUCE ENTERTAIN YOU ENTERPRISES, INC., pg. 668
LETVEN-DICCICCO, INC., pg. 669
LEUPOLD & STEVENS, INC., pg. 669
LEVEL EXPORT SALES CORP., pg. 670
LEVEL FIVE RESEARCH INC.—See Information Builders, pg. 567
LEVELAC—See Sycon Corporation, pg. 1069
LEVENSON & HILL, INC., pg. 670
KENNETH LEVENTHAL & COMPANY, pg. 670
LEVI STRAUSS (AUSTRALIA) PTY. LTD.—See Levi Strauss & Co., pg. 670
LEVI STRAUSS BELGIUM, S.A.—See Levi Strauss & Co., pg. 670
LEVI STRAUSS & CO., pg. 670
LEVI STRAUSS & CO. (CANADA), INC.—See Levi Strauss & Co., pg. 670
LEVI STRAUSS & CO. (EUROPE) S.A.—See Levi Strauss & Co., pg. 670
LEVI STRAUSS DE ESPANA, S.A.—See Levi Strauss & Co., pg. 670
LEVI STRAUSS DE MEXICO, S.A. DE C.V.—See Levi Strauss & Co., pg. 671
LEVI STRAUSS EMPLOYEE PURCHASE PLAN, INC.—See Levi Strauss & Co., pg. 670
LEVI STRAUSS EXIMCO (LTD.)—See Levi Strauss & Co., pg. 670
LEVI STRAUSS (FAR EAST), LTD.—See Levi Strauss & Co., pg. 670
LEVI STRAUSS FRANCE, S.A.—See Levi Strauss & Co., pg. 671
LEVI STRAUSS (GENEVA) S.A.—See Levi Strauss & Co., pg. 671
LEVI STRAUSS GERMANY G.M.B.H.—See Levi Strauss & Co., pg. 671
LEVI STRAUSS INTERNATIONAL—See Levi Strauss & Co., pg. 670
LEVI STRAUSS ITALIA, S.P.A.—See Levi Strauss & Co., pg. 671
LEVI STRAUSS JAPAN K.K.—See Levi Strauss & Co., pg. 671
LEVI STRAUSS (MALAYSIA) SDN. BHD.—See Levi Strauss & Co., pg. 671
LEVI STRAUSS NEDERLAND B.V.—See Levi Strauss & Co., pg. 671
LEVI STRAUSS (NEW ZEALAND) LTD.—See Levi Strauss & Co., pg. 671
LEVI STRAUSS NORWAY, A/S—See Levi Strauss & Co., pg. 671
LEVI STRAUSS (PHILIPPINES) INC.—See Levi Strauss & Co., pg. 671
LEVI STRAUSS SPORTSWEAR—See Levi Strauss & Co., pg. 670
LEVI STRAUSS (SUISSE) S.A.—See Levi Strauss & Co., pg. 671
LEVI STRAUSS (U.K.) LTD.—See Levi Strauss & Co., pg. 671
LEVIMEX DE BAJA CALIFORNIA S.A. DE C.V.—See Leviton Mfg. Co., Inc., pg. 671
LEVITON MFG. CO., INC., pg. 671
LEVITZ CREDIT CORPORATION—See LFC Holding Corporation, pg. 648
LEVITZ FURNITURE CORPORATION—See LFC Holding Corporation, pg. 647
LEVLAD, INC., pg. 671
LEVLANE ADVERTISING, INC., pg. 671
THE LEVOLOR CORPORATION, pg. 671
LEVONIAN BROTHERS INC., pg. 671
A. LEVY & J. ZENTNER CO., pg. 671
NORMAN LEVY ASSOCIATES, INC., pg. 672
JACK LEVY ASSOCIATES, pg. 672
CHARLES LEVY TRANSPORTATION CO.—See The Charles Levy Company, pg. 672
THE CHARLES LEVY COMPANY, pg. 672
EDWARD C. LEVY CO., INC., pg. 672
LEVY HOME ENTERTAINMENT—See The Charles Levy Company, pg. 672
JACOB LEVY & BROS., INC., pg. 672
THE LEVY ORGANIZATION, pg. 672
LEVY REAL ESTATE PARTNERS—See The Levy Organization, pg. 672
LEVY RESTAURANTS—See The Levy Organization, pg. 672
LEVY SECURITY CONSULTANTS, LIMITED, pg. 672
B. LEVY & SONS, pg. 672
LEVY UNITED NEWS—See The Charles Levy Company, pg. 672
LEWALLYN ENGINEERING—See Textile Rubber & Chemical Company, pg. 1090
LEWIS ADVERTISING AGENCY, pg. 672
DONALD D. LEWIS ADVERTISING, pg. 672
LEWIS ADVERTISING, INC., pg. 673
LEWIS BROS. BAKERIES—See Lewis Brothers Bakeries, Inc., pg. 673
LEWIS BROS. BAKERIES (MO)—See Lewis Brothers Bakeries, Inc., pg. 673
LEWIS BROS. BAKERIES (TN)—See Lewis Brothers Bakeries, Inc., pg. 673
LEWIS BROTHERS BAKERIES, INC., pg. 673
LEWIS BUILDING CO., INC.—See Lewis Homes Management Corp., pg. 673
LEWIS, CLARK & GRAHAM, pg. 673
LEWIS & COKER SUPER MARKETS, pg. 673
LEWIS COMMUNICATIONS, INC., pg. 673
LEWIS CONSTRUCTION CO., INC.—See Lewis Homes Management Corp., pg. 673
LEWIS DEVELOPMENT CO.—See Lewis Homes Management Corp., pg. 673
LEWIS DRUG, INC., pg. 673
LEWIS & GACE, INC., pg. 673
LEWIS HOMES MANAGEMENT CORP., pg. 673
LEWIS HOMES OF CALIFORNIA—See Lewis Homes Management Corp., pg. 673
LEWIS HOMES OF NEVADA—See Lewis Homes Management Corp., pg. 673
LEWIS VINCENNES, INC.—See Lewis Brothers Bakeries, Inc., pg. 673
LEXINGTON CO-OP OIL CO., pg. 673
LEXINGTON EQUIPMENT CO.—See Castle-Harlan, Inc., pg. 229
LEXMARK AUSTRALIA—See Lexmark International, Inc., pg. 674
LEXMARK CANADA INC.—See Lexmark International, Inc., pg. 674
LEXMARK FRANCE—See Lexmark International, Inc., pg. 674
LEXMARK INTERNATIONAL, INC., pg. 673
LEXMARK INTERNATIONAL, INC.—See Lexmark International, Inc., pg. 674
LEXMARK INTERNATIONAL, INC.—See Lexmark International, Inc., pg. 674
LEXMARK INTERNATIONAL, INC.—See Lexmark International, Inc., pg. 674
LEXMARK INTERNATIONAL, INC.—See Lexmark International, Inc., pg. 674
LEXMARK INTERNATIONAL, INC.—See Lexmark International, Inc., pg. 674
LEXMARK INTERNATIONAL, INC.—See Lexmark International, Inc., pg. 674
LEXMARK INTERNATIONAL, INC.—See Lexmark International, Inc., pg. 674
LEYSE—See The Vollrath Company Inc., pg. 1155
W.S. LIBBEY COMPANY, pg. 674
LIBCO CORPORATION, pg. 674
LIBERAL BY-PRODUCTS—See Union Holdings, Inc., pg. 1128
LIBERAL INTERNATIONAL SALES CORP.—See Union Holdings, Inc., pg. 1128
LIBERAL INTERNATIONAL SALES V.I. INC.—See Union Holdings, Inc., pg. 1128
LIBERTY AUTO PARTS—See Sturgis Iron & Metal Company, Inc., pg. 1055
LIBERTY DISTRIBUTORS INC.—See Liberty Mutual Insurance Co., pg. 674
LIBERTY FINANCIAL COMPANIES—See Liberty Mutual Insurance Co., pg. 674
LIBERTY GLASS COMPANY, pg. 674
LIBERTY HOUSE—See JMB Realty Corporation, pg. 585
LIBERTY HOUSE, INC.—See JMB Realty Corporation, pg. 585
LIBERTY LIFE ASSURANCE COMPANY OF BOSTON—See Liberty Mutual Insurance Co., pg. 674
LIBERTY MILITARY SALES CO., pg. 674
LIBERTY MUTUAL FIRE INSURANCE CO.—See Liberty Mutual Insurance Co., pg. 674
LIBERTY MUTUAL INSURANCE CO., pg. 674
LIBERTY NORTHWEST INSURANCE CORP.—See Liberty Mutual Insurance Co., pg. 674
LIBERTY TOOL CORPORATION, pg. 674
LIBERTYVILLE LINCOLN-MERCURY SALES, INC., pg. 674
LIDA ADVERTISING COMPANY, pg. 674
LIEBERMAN-APPALUCCI, pg. 675

LIFE CARE SERVICES CORPORATION—See The Weitz Corporation, pg. 1174
LIFE INSURANCE CO. OF ARIZONA—See The Chesapeake Life Insurance Co., pg. 243
LIFE LINE NUTRITIONALS, INC., pg. 675
LIFE SCIENCES INTERNATIONAL—See Day & Zimmermann, Inc., pg. 320
LIFE SCIENCES INTERNATIONAL-CALIFORNIA—See Day & Zimmermann, Inc., pg. 320
LIFESHARES GROUP, INC.—See The Chesapeake Life Insurance Co., pg. 243
LIFESHARES SERVICES CO.—See The Chesapeake Life Insurance Co., pg. 243
LIFESURANCE CORPORATION—See Victory Financial Group, Inc., pg. 1150
LIFESURANCE CORPORATION—See Regan Holding Corporation, pg. 921
LIFETIME DOORS INC., pg. 675
LIFETIME TELEVISION—See The Hearst Corporation, pg. 523
LIFETOUCH, INC., pg. 675
LIFETOUCH NATIONAL SCHOOL STUDIOS INC.—See Lifetouch, Inc., pg. 675
LIFETOUCH PORTRAIT STUDIOS INC.—See Lifetouch, Inc., pg. 675
LIFETOUCH PUBLISHING INC.—See Lifetouch, Inc., pg. 675
LIFETOUCH SENIOR PORTRAITS INC.—See Lifetouch, Inc., pg. 675
LIFETOUCH VIDEO CREATIONS, INC.—See Lifetouch, Inc., pg. 675
LIFT-ALL CO., INC., pg. 675
LIGGETT-STASHOWER, INC., pg. 675
LIGHTS OF AMERICA, INC., pg. 675
THE LIHUE PLANTATION COMPANY, LIMITED—See JMB Realty Corporation, pg. 585
THE CHAS. H. LILLY CO., pg. 675
LIMA ELECTRIC CO., INC.—See Marathon Electric Manufacturing Corp., pg. 706
LIN & ROE COMPANY—See Burns & Roe Enterprises, Inc., pg. 194
LINBECK CORP., pg. 675
LINC CAPITAL CORPORATION—See The LINC Group, Inc., pg. 648
LINC CAPITAL MANAGEMENT—See The LINC Group, Inc., pg. 648
LINC EQUIPMENT SERVICES—See The LINC Group, Inc., pg. 648
LINC MANAGEMENT SERVICES—See The LINC Group, Inc., pg. 648
LINC MEDICAL IMAGING—See The LINC Group, Inc., pg. 648
LINC QUANTUM ANALYTICS—See The LINC Group, Inc., pg. 648
LINCOLN COURIER—See The Copley Press, Inc., pg. 284
LINCOLN ELECTRIC SYSTEMS, pg. 675
LINCOLN INDUSTRIES, pg. 676
LINCOLN INDUSTRIES, INC.—See Zoeller Co., pg. 1221
LINCOLN PROPERTY CO., NORTHERN CALIFORNIA—See Lincoln Property Company, pg. 676
LINCOLN PROPERTY COMPANY, pg. 676
LINCOLN PROVISION COMPANY, INC., pg. 676
LINDENMEYR CENTRAL—See Central National-Gottesman Inc., pg. 233
LINDENMEYR MUNROE—See Central National-Gottesman Inc., pg. 233
LINDENMEYR MUNROE—See Central National-Gottesman Inc., pg. 233
LINDENMEYR MUNROE—See Central National-Gottesman Inc., pg. 233
LINDENMEYR MUNROE—See Central National-Gottesman Inc., pg. 233
LINDENMEYR MUNROE—See Central National-Gottesman Inc., pg. 233
LINDENMEYR MUNROE—See Central National-Gottesman Inc., pg. 233
LINDENMEYR MUNROE—See Central National-Gottesman Inc., pg. 233
LINDENMEYR MUNROE—See Central National-Gottesman Inc., pg. 233
LINDENMEYR MUNROE—See Central National-Gottesman Inc., pg. 233
LINDENMEYR NATIONAL—See Central National-Gottesman Inc., pg. 233
LINDENMEYR PAPER—See Central National-Gottesman Inc., pg. 233
LINDENMEYR PAPER—See Central National-Gottesman Inc., pg. 233
LINDENMEYR PAPER—See Central National-Gottesman Inc., pg. 233
LINDENMEYR PAPER—See Central National-Gottesman Inc., pg. 233
LINDENMEYR PAPER—See Central National-Gottesman Inc., pg. 233
LINDER & ASSOCIATES, INC., pg. 676
LINDSAY HOSPITAL MEDICAL CENTER—See UniHealth America, pg. 1127
LINDSAY MANUFACTURING INC., pg. 676
LINDSAY OLIVE GROWERS, pg. 676
LINDSAY, STONE & BRIGGS ADVERTISING, INC., pg. 676
LINE EQUIPMENT SALES CO., INC.—See Utilities Construction Co., Inc. Of South Carolina, pg. 1141
LINEAR DYNAMICS INC., pg. 676
LINENS & MORE—See Homemaker Shops, Inc., pg. 542
LINETT & HARRISON, pg. 676
O.P. LINK HANDLE COMPANY, pg. 676
LINK RESOURCES—See International Data Group, pg. 578
LINKOUS CONSTRUCTION COMPANY, INC., pg. 677
LINN PRODUCTS, INC., pg. 677
LINOTYPE-HELL COMPANY, pg. 677
LINZER PRODUCTS CORP., pg. 677
LION BROTHERS COMPANY, INC., pg. 677
THE LION, INC. (GIBBONS-STEGMAIER BREWERY), pg. 677
LION RIBBON COMPANY—See C.M. Offray & Son Inc., pg. 822
LIONEL TRAINS, INC., pg. 677
MARK LIPMAN DIV.—See Guardsmark, Inc., pg. 493
LIPMAN, RICHMOND, GREENE, pg. 677
THE LIPSITT DESIGN GROUP—See Ross Roy Group, Inc., pg. 950
LIQUID CONTROLS CORPORATION, pg. 677
LIST INDUSTRIES, INC., pg. 677
LITECONTROL CORPORATION, pg. 677
LITHO COLORPLATE—See Schawk, Inc., pg. 975
LITHO-KROME COMPANY—See Hallmark Cards, Inc., pg. 502
LITHOGRAPH PRINTING COMPANY, INC., pg. 678
LITHOGRAPHIX, INC., pg. 678
LITHOTYPE COMPANY, INC., pg. 678
RONALD LITOFF, LTD., pg. 678
LITTELFUSE AG—See Littelfuse, Inc., pg. 678
LITTELFUSE B.V.—See Littelfuse, Inc., pg. 678
LITTELFUSE, INC., pg. 678
LITTELFUSE LTD.—See Littelfuse, Inc., pg. 678
LITTELFUSE S.A. DE C.V.—See Littelfuse, Inc., pg. 678
LITTFIN LUMBER COMPANY, pg. 678
LITTLE AMERICA HOTELS—See Sinclair Oil Corp., pg. 1008
LITTLE AMERICA REFINING—See Sinclair Oil Corp., pg. 1008
ARTHUR D. LITTLE OF CANADA LTD.—See Arthur D. Little, Inc., pg. 679
LITTLE CAESAR ENTERPRISES, INC., pg. 678
ARTHUR D. LITTLE ENTERPRISES, INC.—See Arthur D. Little, Inc., pg. 679
LITTLE FALLS COLOR PRINT—See Sullivan Paper Company, pg. 1057
ARTHUR D. LITTLE FAR EAST, INC.—See Arthur D. Little, Inc., pg. 679
ARTHUR D. LITTLE, INC., pg. 678
ARTHUR D. LITTLE INTL., INC.—See Arthur D. Little, Inc., pg. 679
ARTHUR D. LITTLE INTL., INC.—See Arthur D. Little, Inc., pg. 679
ARTHUR D. LITTLE (JAPAN), INC.—See Arthur D. Little, Inc., pg. 679
LITTLE LADY FOODS, INC., pg. 679
ARTHUR D. LITTLE LIMITADA—See Arthur D. Little, Inc., pg. 679
ARTHUR D. LITTLE LTD.—See Arthur D. Little, Inc., pg. 679
ARTHUR D. LITTLE MEXICANA, S.A. DE C.V.—See Arthur D. Little, Inc., pg. 679
ARTHUR D. LITTLE PROGRAM SYSTEMS MANAGEMENT CO.—See Arthur D. Little, Inc., pg. 678
ARTHUR D. LITTLE S.R.C.—See Arthur D. Little, Inc., pg. 679
LITTLEFORD DAY, TAYLOR-STILES DIVISION, pg. 679
LITTLETON COIN CO., INC., pg. 679
LIVERIGHT PUBLISHING CORP.—See W.W. Norton & Company, Inc., pg. 816
LIVERNOIS ENGINEERING COMPANY, pg. 679
LIVERNOIS VEHICLE CO.—See Livernois Engineering Company, pg. 679
LIVINGSTON & COMPANY, pg. 679
LIVINGSTON + KEYE—See Livingston & Company, pg. 679
LLOYD CONTROLS, INC., pg. 679
LLOYD ELECTRIC APPARATUS CO.—See Lloyd Controls, Inc., pg. 680
LLOYD PROPERTIES, pg. 680
LOBDELL-EMERY MANUFACTURING COMPANY, pg. 680
LOCKARD CONSTRUCTION, INC., pg. 680
LOCKHART CADILLAC INC., pg. 680
LOCKHART & PETTUS, INC., pg. 680
LOCKLEY MANUFACTURING DIVISION—See The Entwistle Company, pg. 383
LOCKS ADVERTISING AGENCY, pg. 680
LOCKWOOD CORPORATION, pg. 680
LOCKWOOD FOLDING BOX—See H. S. Crocker Co., Inc., pg. 300
LOCUS COMPUTING CORP., pg. 680
LODAL, INC., pg. 680
LOEBER MOTORS, INC., pg. 680
LOEFFLER KETCHUM MOUNTJOY, pg. 680
LOEHMANN'S, INC., pg. 681
LOFT'S SEEDS, INC., pg. 681
LOGAN & KANAWHA COAL CO., pg. 681
LOGGHE STAMPING COMPANY, pg. 681
LOGIC WORLD, INC.—See Lawrence Group, Inc., pg. 662
LOGICAL OPERATIONS—See Ziff Communications Company, pg. 1219
LOGISTICS SYSTEMS ARCHITECTS—See Science Applications International Corporation, pg. 982
LOGISTIX, pg. 681
LOHMEYER SIMPSON COMMUNICATIONS, INC., pg. 681
LOIS/USA, pg. 681
LOMBARD COMPANY, pg. 681
LOMBARD LINCOLN-MERCURY & LEASING, INC., pg. 681
LOMBARDI FOODSERVICE, INC., pg. 681
LONDON LITHO ALUMINUM CO., INC., pg. 681
LONDON & SCANDINAVIAN METALLURGICAL CO. LIMITED—See Metallurg, Inc., pg. 742
LONDONTOWN CORPORATION—See Londontown Holdings Corporation, pg. 682
LONDONTOWN HOLDINGS CORPORATION, pg. 681
LONE STAR CADILLAC CO., pg. 682
LONE STAR CORRUGATED CONTAINER CORPORATION, pg. 682
LONE STAR DIVISION—See Day & Zimmermann, Inc., pg. 320
LONE STAR FORGE COMPANY—See TIC United Corporation, pg. 1073
LONG-AIRDOX COMPANY—See The Marmon Group, Inc., pg. 711
LONG BEACH COMMUNITY HOSPITAL—See UniHealth America, pg. 1127
LONG EQUIPMENT CO.—See Long MFG. NC, Inc., pg. 682
THE LONG & FOSTER COMPANIES, INC., pg. 682
THE LONG & FOSTER REAL ESTATE, INC.—See The Long & Foster Companies, Inc., pg. 682
THE LONG ISLAND RAIL ROAD CO.—See Metropolitan Transportation Authority, pg. 745
LONG ISLAND WATER CORPORATION, pg. 682
LONG JOHN SILVER'S, INC.—See Castle-Harlan, Inc., pg. 229
LONG MFG. NC, INC., pg. 682
LONG PRAIRIE PACKING CO.—See Rosens Diversified, Inc., pg. 948
W. E. LONG COMPANY, pg. 682
LONGYEAR (AUSTRALIA) PTY. LTD.—See Longyear Company, pg. 682
LONGYEAR CANADA INC.—See Longyear Company, pg. 682
LONGYEAR CENTROAMERICANA S.A.—See Longyear Company, pg. 682
LONGYEAR CHILE LTDA.—See Longyear Company, pg. 683
LONGYEAR COMPANY, pg. 682
LONGYEAR DE MEXICO S.A. DE C.V.—See Longyear Company, pg. 683
LONGYEAR DEUTSCHLAND GMBH—See Longyear Company, pg. 683
LONGYEAR DIAMOND PRODS. (PHILIPPINES) INC.—See Longyear Company, pg. 683
LONGYEAR FRANCE—See Longyear Company, pg. 683
LONGYEAR IBERICA S.A.—See Longyear Company, pg. 683
LONGYEAR (NEDERLAND) B.V.—See Longyear Company, pg. 683
LONGYEAR NEW ZEALAND LTD.—See Longyear Company, pg. 683
LONGYEAR U.K. LTD.—See Longyear Company, pg. 683
LOOMIS BROTHERS, INC., pg. 683
LOOMIS, SAYLES & CO.—See The New England, pg. 799
LOOS & CO., INC., pg. 683
LOOSE LEAF METALS COMPANY INC.—See Lane Industries, Inc., pg. 657
LORALYN FASHION—See I. Appel Corporation, pg. 78
LORBER INDUSTRIES OF CALIFORNIA, pg. 683
LORD BIBB DIV.—See Masters, Inc., pg. 720
LORD CORP., INDUSTRIAL ADHESIVES & COATINGS DIV.—See Lord Corporation, pg. 683
LORD CORP., INDUSTRIAL PRODUCTS DIV.—See Lord Corporation, pg. 683
LORD CORP. (U.K.) LTD.—See Lord Corporation, pg. 683
LORD CORPORATION, pg. 683
LORD FAR EAST, INC.—See Lord Corporation, pg. 683
LORD INDUSTRIAL LTDA.—See Lord Corporation, pg. 683
LORD KOREA LTD.—See Lord Corporation, pg. 683
LORD RESEARCH CORPORATION—See Lord Corporation, pg. 683
LORD, SULLIVAN & YODER, INC. ADVERTISING, pg. 683
LORSCH CREATIVE NETWORK, pg. 684
LORTZ DIRECT MARKETING INC., pg. 684
THE LORVIC CORP., pg. 684
LOS ALAMOS MONITOR—See Landmark Communications, Inc., pg. 655
LOS ALAMOS TECHNICAL ASSOCIATES, INC., pg. 684
LOS ANGELES DEALERS AUTO AUCTIONS—See Cox Enterprises, Inc., pg. 293
LOS ANGELES DIE MOLD—See Plastic Engineering Components Inc., pg. 875
LOS ANGELES SMOKING CURING COMPANY, pg. 684
LOS ANGELES UNION TERMINAL, INC.—See Anschutz Corporation, pg. 75
LOST ARROW CORPORATION, pg. 684
LOSURDO FOODS, INC., pg. 684
LOTAS MINARD PATTON MCIVER, pg. 684
LOTHROP, LEE & SHEPARD BOOKS—See The Hearst Corporation, pg. 521
A.E. LOTTES COMPANY—See Carquest Corporation, pg. 225
LOTUS CARPET DIVISION—See Columbus Mills, Inc., pg. 267
LOTUS PUBLISHING CORPORATION—See International Data Group, pg. 576
LOU ANA FOODS, INC.—See Schad Industries, Inc., pg. 974
LOU ANA FOODS OF TEXAS, INC.—See Schad Industries, Inc., pg. 974
LOUIS DREYFUS NATURAL GAS—See Louis Dreyfus Corporation, pg. 349
LOUIS LONDON ADVERTISING & SALES PROMOTION, pg. 684
LOUISIANA DOWNS—See The Edward J. DeBartolo Corporation, pg. 323
LOUISIANA NATIONAL LIFE INSURANCE COMPANY—See Victory Financial Group, Inc., pg. 1150
LOUISIANA UTILITIES SUPPLY COMPANY, pg. 684
LOUISVILLE BEDDING COMPANY, pg. 684
LOUISVILLE SCRAP MATERIAL CO., INC., pg. 684
THE LOUISVILLE TRANSPORTATION COMPANY—See Interlock Industries, Inc., pg. 574
LOUV-AIRE, INC.—See The Airolite Company, pg. 28
LOVE BOX COMPANY, INC., pg. 685
LOVE CONTROLS CORPORATION—See Dwyer Instruments Inc., pg. 356
LOVE MORTGAGE COMPANY, pg. 685
LOVEJOY INC., pg. 685
LOVE'S ENTERPRISES, INC., pg. 685
T. A. LOVING COMPANY, pg. 685
LOWE & ASSOCIATES—See The Lowe Group, pg. 685
LOWE COMMUNICATION GROUP—See The Lowe Group, pg. 685

LOWE FMS—See The Lowe Group, pg. 685
THE LOWE GROUP, pg. 685
THE LOWE GROUP—See The Lowe Group, pg. 685
LOWE HOWARD-SPINK LIMITED—See The Lowe Group, pg. 685
LOWE KUIPER & SCHOUTEN B.V.—See The Lowe Group, pg. 685
LOWE LUERZER GMBH—See The Lowe Group, pg. 685
LOWE LUERZER GMBH—See The Lowe Group, pg. 685
LOWE MBAC—See The Lowe Group, pg. 685
LOWE PAPER CO.—See Simkins Industries, Inc., pg. 1005
LOWE TROOST S.A.—See The Lowe Group, pg. 685
LOWELL PACKING COMPANY, pg. 685
LOWELL SHOE, INC.—See Morse Shoe, Inc., pg. 772
LOWE'S FOOD STORES, INC.—See Alex Lee, Inc., pg. 33
LOXCREEN COMPANY, pg. 686
LOZIER CORPORATION, pg. 686
LOZIER STORE FIXTURES, INC.—See Lozier Corporation, pg. 686
LSJ SPORTSWEAR INC.—See Merchant Capital Group Ltd, pg. 739
LUBECON SYSTEMS, INC., pg. 686
LUBER-FINER, EUROPE, N.V./S.A.—See UIS, Inc., pg. 1124
LUBER-FINER, INC.—See UIS, Inc., pg. 1123
LUBRICATION ENGINEERS, INC., pg. 686
JOHN D. LUCAS PRINTING COMPANY—See Collman Graphics, Inc., pg. 263
LUCCA PACKING DIV., NALLEY'S FINE FOODS—See Agway, Inc., pg. 25
LUCEDALE SPORTSWEAR COMPANY—See Harper Industries, Inc., pg. 510
LUCKY FRUIT & PRODUCE, INC., pg. 686
LUCKY INNS OF AMERICA, INC.—See Family Inns of America, Inc., pg. 398
LUCKY WINNER, INC., pg. 686
LUDINGTON NEWS CO. INC., pg. 686
LUDLOW COMPOSITES CORPORATION, pg. 686
LUDLOW TEXTILES CO., INC., pg. 686
LUGBILL BROTHERS, INC., pg. 686
LUGENE OPTICIANS—See Optical Corp. of America, pg. 828
LUKENHEIMER CO., pg. 687
LUKENHEIMER CO.-ENERGO VALVES—See Lukenheimer Co., pg. 687
LUKER ENGINEERING & FABRICATION GROUP—See Gold Kist, Inc., pg. 465
LUMAS REALTY, INC., pg. 687
LUMBER SYSTEMS, INC., pg. 687
LUMBERMENS MERCHANDISING CORPORATION, pg. 687
LUMCO INDUSTRIES, INC., pg. 687
LUND BOATS—See Minstar, Inc., pg. 759
LUNDBERG AND ASSOCIATES—See Lawrence Group, Inc., pg. 662
LUNDIA DIV. OF MII, INC., pg. 687
LUNDY CONSTRUCTION CO., INC., pg. 687
LUNDY PACKING CO. INC., pg. 687
LUNSTEAD, A HAWORTH PORTFOLIO CO.—See Haworth, Inc., pg. 518
LUNTZ CORPORATION, pg. 687
JIM LUPIENT ENTERPRISES, pg. 687
LURIA BROS. DIVISION—See Connell Limited Partnership, pg. 275
LUSCOMBE AND PARTNERS PTY. LTD.—See W.B. Doner & Company, pg. 344
THE LUSK COMPANY, pg. 687
LUSK INTERIORS, INC.—See The Lusk Company, pg. 688
LUSKEYS WESTERN STORES, INC., pg. 688
LUSTINE OLDSMOBILE & BUICK, INC., pg. 688
LUTHERAN BROTHERHOOD, pg. 688
LUTHERAN BROTHERHOOD FAMILY FOR MUTUAL FUNDS—See Lutheran Brotherhood, pg. 688
LUTHERAN BROTHERHOOD FINANCIAL CORPORATION—See Lutheran Brotherhood, pg. 688
LUTHERAN BROTHERHOOD FOUNDATION—See Lutheran Brotherhood, pg. 688
LUTHERAN BROTHERHOOD REAL ESTATE PRODUCTS COMPANY—See Lutheran Brotherhood, pg. 688
LUTHERAN BROTHERHOOD RESEARCH CORP.—See Lutheran Brotherhood, pg. 688
LUTHERAN BROTHERHOOD SECURITIES CORP.—See Lutheran Brotherhood, pg. 688
LUTHERAN BROTHERHOOD VARIABLE INSURANCE PRODUCTS COMPANY—See Lutheran Brotherhood, pg. 688
LUXOR CORPORATION—See Ebsco Industries, Inc., pg. 365
LUZIANNE BLUE PLATE FOODS—See William B. Reily & Co., Inc., pg. 923
LYALL ASSEMBLIES, INC.—See Group Dekko International Inc., pg. 490
LYKE CORPORATION, pg. 688
LYKES BROTHERS INC. OF FLORIDA, pg. 688
LYKES BROS. STEAMSHIP CO., INC., pg. 688
LYKES DISPENSER DIV.—See Lykes Brothers Inc. of Florida, pg. 688
LYKES ENERGY, INC., pg. 689
LYKES LINES AGENCY, INC.—See Lykes Bros. Steamship Co., Inc., pg. 689
LYM-TECH SCIENTIFIC—See John R. Lyman Company, pg. 689
JOHN R. LYMAN COMPANY, pg. 689
LYMAN LUMBER COMPANY, pg. 689
LYNCHBURG SERVICE CENTER—See Carolina Steel Corporation, pg. 223
LYNDEN AIR FREIGHT, INC.—See Lynden Incorporated, pg. 689
LYNDEN FINANCIAL SERVICES, INC.—See Lynden Incorporated, pg. 689
LYNDEN FORWARDING, INC.—See Lynden Incorporated, pg. 689
LYNDEN INCORPORATED, pg. 689
LYNDEN LOGISTICS, INC.—See Lynden Incorporated, pg. 689
LYNDEN TRANSPORT, INC.—See Lynden Incorporated, pg. 689
ED J. LYNG COMPANY—See Trinidad/Benham Corporation, pg. 1114
LYON CONKLIN & COMPANY, pg. 690
LYON COUNTY CO-OP OIL CO., pg. 690
LYON METAL PRODUCTS, INC., pg. 690
WILLIAM LYON COMPANY, pg. 690
LYON'S RESTAURANTS, INC., pg. 690
LYTRON INCORPORATED, pg. 690

M

M & C SPECIALTIES COMPANY, pg. 690
M&H ADVERTISING, pg. 690
M&M/MARS—See Mars, Incorporated, pg. 713
M & M RESTAURANT SUPPLY—See Keystone Foods Corporation, pg. 629
M & T INCORPORATED, pg. 690
M&W GEAR COMPANY, pg. 690
M A C GROUP (JAPAN), INC.—See Gemini Consulting, pg. 448
MADD (MOTHERS AGAINST DRUNK DRIVING), pg. 691
MAF COTE SPECIALTIES CO., INC.—See MacAndrews & Forbes Holdings Inc., pg. 694
M-B COMPANY INC. OF WISCONSIN, pg. 691
MBI INC., pg. 691
MBL HOLDING CORPORATION—See Mutual Benefit Life Insurance Company, pg. 778
MBL LIFE ASSURANCE CORP.—See Mutual Benefit Life Insurance Company, pg. 778
MBS HOLDING, INC., pg. 691
MBT ASSOCIATES, INC., pg. 691
MCC, INC., pg. 691
MCC GROUP, INC., pg. 691
MCM ENTERPRISES, INC., pg. 691
MCRB FULFILLMENT CO.—See MCRB Service Bureau, Inc., pg. 692
MCRB FULFILLMENT CO.—See MCRB Service Bureau, Inc., pg. 692
MCRB SERVICE BUREAU, INC., pg. 691
MD PNEUMATICS, INC.—See Tuthill Corporation, pg. 1120
MDC SYSTEMS—See Day & Zimmermann, Inc., pg. 320
M & E MANUFACTURING CO.—See Plastek Group, pg. 875
M.E.D. COMMUNICATIONS, pg. 692
MEPC AMERICAN PROPERTIES INCORPORATED, pg. 692
MFA OIL COMPANY, pg. 692
MFA INCORPORATED, pg. 692
MFG SYSTEMS—See Effective Management Systems, pg. 370
M.G.C. COMPANY—See Underground Construction Company, Inc., pg. 1126
MGIC INVESTMENT CORPORATION—See Northwestern Mutual Life Insurance Co., pg. 815
MGM BRAKES DIV.—See Indian Head Industries Inc., pg. 565
MGR EQUIPMENT CORP., pg. 692
MGTB AYER—See N W Ayer Incorporated, pg. 104
MHB INC., pg. 692
MI FUND INCORPORATED, pg. 692
MIMLIC CORP.—See The Minnesota Mutual Life Insurance Company, pg. 758
M K DIAMOND PRODUCTS, INC., pg. 692
MLT VACATIONS, INC.—See NWA, Inc., pg. 782
M M SYSTEMS CORPORATION, pg. 692
M M I COMPANIES, INC., pg. 692
MML BAY STATE LIFE INSURANCE COMPANY—See Massachusetts Mutual Life Insurance Co., pg. 718
MML INVESTORS SERVICES, INC.—See Massachusetts Mutual Life Insurance Co., pg. 718
MML PENSION INSURANCE COMPANY—See Massachusetts Mutual Life Insurance Co., pg. 718
MML REAL ESTATE CORPORATION—See Massachusetts Mutual Life Insurance Co., pg. 719
MML REALTY MANAGEMENT CORP.—See Massachusetts Mutual Life Insurance Co., pg. 719
MML SERIES INVESTMENT FUND—See Massachusetts Mutual Life Insurance Co., pg. 718
M M M SALES, INC., pg. 692
M M S DESIGN—See Measured Marketing Services, pg. 734
MNP CORP., pg. 693
MPC WORLD—See International Data Group, pg. 576
MPD, INC., pg. 693
MPH & CMI—See MPD, Inc., pg. 693
MPO VIDEOTRONICS, INC., pg. 693
MRC TELECOMMUNICATIONS INC.—See Journal Communications Inc., pg. 607
M/S FISCHBEIN PACKAGING (SINGAPORE) PTE. LTD.—See AXIA Incorporated, pg. 9
MSC INDUSTRIAL SUPPLY CO., pg. 693
MSD, INC., pg. 693
MSI INSURANCE COMPANIES, pg. 693
MSI SERVICES, INC., pg. 693
MSR (MOUNTAIN SAFETY RESEARCH)—See Recreational Equipment, Inc., pg. 917
MTC CORPORATION—See The Carbide/Graphite Group, Inc., pg. 217
MTC REMCO TAPE PRODUCTS CO.—See M & C Specialties Company, pg. 690
MTD PRODUCTS, INC., pg. 694
MTD PRODUCTS LIMITED—See MTD Products, Inc., pg. 694
MTI LEASING, LTD.—See Marine Travelift, Inc., pg. 707
MTI VACATIONS, INC., pg. 694
MTS, INC., pg. 694
MTV NETWORKS—See National Amusements, Inc., pg. 785
MWC LIGHTING SYSTEMS, INC.—See Jac Jacobsen Industries, Inc., pg. 588
M.W.O.S. TRADE SHOW—See I. Spiewak & Sons, Inc., pg. 1031
MAACO ENTERPRISES INC., pg. 694
MAC PAPERS, INC., pg. 694
MACANDREWS & FORBES CO.—See MacAndrews & Forbes Holdings Inc., pg. 694
MACANDREWS & FORBES GROUP, INC.—See MacAndrews & Forbes Holdings Inc., pg. 695
MACANDREWS & FORBES HOLDINGS INC., pg. 694
MACANDREWS & FORBES LTD.—See MacAndrews & Forbes Holdings Inc., pg. 694
MACCABEES MUTUAL LIFE INSURANCE, pg. 696
MACCO CONSTRUCTORS, INC., pg. 696
MACDANIELS, HENRY & SPROUL, INC., pg. 696
THE E. F. MACDONALD VERKAUFSFORDERUNG GMBH—See Carlson Companies, Inc., pg. 221
E. F. MACDONALD MOTIVATION DIV.—See Carlson Companies, Inc., pg. 221
THE MACERICH CO., pg. 696
MACHADO & CO. INC., pg. 696
GUS MACHADO ENTERPRISES, pg. 696
MACHINING ENTERPRISES INC., pg. 696
MACK MOLDING COMPANY, pg. 697
MACK PRINTING COMPANY, pg. 697
MACK PUBLISHING CO.—See Mack Printing Company, pg. 697
MACKAY-SHIELDS FINANCIAL CORP.—See New York Life Insurance Company, pg. 803
MACKENZIE, KUTH & KLEIN DIV.—See Ghafari Associates, Inc., pg. 455
MACKINNON-PARKER, INC., pg. 697
MACKLANBURG-DUNCAN CO., pg. 697
MACKLANBURG-DUNCAN CO. OF CALIFORNIA, INC.—See Macklanburg-Duncan Co., pg. 697
MACLEAN-FOGG CO., pg. 697
MACMILLAN OIL CO., INC.—See Graham Group, Inc., pg. 475
MACNAMARA, KLEIN & SOLIN INC., pg. 698
MACNAUGHTON EINSON GRAPHICS, pg. 698
MACRISTY INDUSTRIES, INC., pg. 698
MACRO COMPUTER PRODUCTS INC., pg. 698
MACRODYNE ENGINEERING SERVICES—See Phoenix International, Inc., pg. 869
MACROMEDIA INC., pg. 698
MACROMEDIA LEASING—See Macromedia Inc., pg. 698
MACROMEDIA PUBLISHING INC.—See Macromedia Inc., pg. 698
MAC'S MACHINERY & SUPPLY—See DoAll Company, pg. 341
MACTAVISH MACHINE MANUFACTURING COMPANY, pg. 698
MACUSER—See Ziff Communications Company, pg. 1218
MACWHYTE CO.—See Amsted Industries Incorporated, pg. 69
MACWORLD—See International Data Group, pg. 576
MACY CREDIT CORP.—See R. H. Macy & Co., Inc., pg. 699
R. H. MACY & CO., INC., pg. 698
THE MAD BUTCHER, INC., pg. 699
MADDAK INC.—See Bel-Art Products, pg. 133
MADEMOISELLE—See Advance Publications Inc., pg. 19
MADER CONSTRUCTION GROUP INC., pg. 699
MADIGAN BROTHERS, INC., pg. 699
MADISON DAIRY PRODUCE COMPANY, pg. 699
MADISON ELECTRIC CO., pg. 699
MADISON GRAHAM COLORGRAPHICS, INC., pg. 699
MADISON GROCERY CO., INC., pg. 699
MADISON, INC.—See John S. Frey Enterprises, pg. 433
MADISON INDUSTRIES—See John S. Frey Enterprises, pg. 433
MADISON INDUSTRIES INC. OF ARIZONA—See John S. Frey Enterprises, pg. 433
MADISON INDUSTRIES INC. OF GEORGIA—See John S. Frey Enterprises, pg. 433
MADISON NATIONAL LIFE INSURANCE CO., INC.—See Geneve Corporation, pg. 451
MAECORP INC., pg. 699
MAERZ OFENBAU AG—See Belmont Industries, Inc., pg. 137
MAERZ OFENBAU G.M.B.H.—See Belmont Industries, Inc., pg. 137
CHAS. V. MAESCHER & CO., INC.—See Maescher Industries, Inc., pg. 700
MAESCHER CONSTRUCTION CO.—See Maescher Industries, Inc., pg. 700
MAESCHER INDUSTRIES, INC., pg. 699
MAGAZINE MARKET PLACE, INC.—See Foster & Gallagher Inc., pg. 426
MAGAZINE MARKETING, INC.—See The Gillespie Organization, Inc., pg. 458
MAGAZINE SERVICES INC.—See The Kiplinger Washington Editors, Inc., pg. 632
THE MAGEE CARPET COMPANY, pg. 700
MAGGIANO'S LITTLE ITALY—See Lettuce Entertain You Enterprises, Inc., pg. 669
MAGHIELSE TOOL CORPORATION, pg. 700
MAGIC CIRCLE MANUFACTURING DIV.—See Acme Foundry, Inc., pg. 13
MAGIC MAID DIVISION—See Son Chief Electrics, Inc., pg. 1018
MAGIC MARKET CONVENIENCE STORES—See E-Z Serve Corp., pg. 362
MAGIC PAN INTERNATIONAL INC., pg. 700
MAGIC VALLEY FOODS, INC., pg. 700
MAGICSILK, INC., pg. 700
MAGIKITCH'N, INC.—See G.S. Blodgett Corporation, pg. 157
MAGLA PRODUCTS, pg. 700
MAGLINE, INC., pg. 700
MAGNA MEDIA ADVERTISING—See Macromedia Inc., pg. 698
MAGNA-POW'R INC.—See ICM Industries, Inc., pg. 559

MAGNASYNC MOVIOLA CORPORATION—See J & R Film Company, pg. 586
MAGNECO/METREL, INC., pg. 700
MAGNEDYNE DIV.—See Sierracin Corporation, pg. 1003
MAGNETIC ANALYSIS CORP., pg. 700
MAGNETIC DATA, INC., pg. 700
MAGNETIC TECHNOLOGIES CORPORATION, pg. 701
MAGNETICS—See Spang & Company, pg. 1025
MAGNETROL INTERNATIONAL, pg. 701
MAGNOLIA DIVISION—See Sanderson Plumbing Products Inc., pg. 970
MAGNOLIA HI-FI, INC., pg. 701
MAGNOMIN-GENERAL MINING S.A.—See Belmont Industries, Inc., pg. 137
MAGNUM BUILDING SYSTEMS—See W. B. Goode Company, Inc., pg. 470
MAGNUS METALS—See Farley Industries, pg. 400
MAGUIRE GROUP ARCHITECTS, INC.—See Maguire Group Inc., pg. 701
MAGUIRE GROUP INC., pg. 701
MAGUIRE OIL CO., pg. 701
MAGUIRE THOMAS PARTNERS, pg. 701
MAHARAM FABRIC CORPORATION, pg. 701
MAIDENFORM, INC., pg. 701
MAIN BROTHERS OIL COMPANY, INC., pg. 702
MAIN LINE MANAGEMENT SERVICES, INC.—See Chicago West Pullman Corporation, pg. 246
MAINE BOTTLERS—See White Rock Distilleries Inc., pg. 1186
MAINE POTATO GROWERS, INC., pg. 702
MAINE PRINTING & BUSINESS FORMS CO., pg. 702
MAINE STATE LOTTERY COMMISSION, pg. 702
MAINTAIN—See The Maxima Corporation, pg. 723
MAJESTIC MOLDED PRODUCTS, INC., pg. 702
MAJESTIC PINES CARE CENTER—See Meritcare, Inc., pg. 740
MAJOR FOODS LTD.—See ARA Group, pg. 7
MAJOR PHARMACEUTICALS CORP.—See Eon Labs, Inc., pg. 384
MAJOR VIDEO CONCEPTS, INC.—See LDI, Ltd., pg. 647
MAKERS OF KAL, INC., pg. 702
MAKI CORPORATION, pg. 702
MAKI HOME CENTER, INC.—See Maki Corporation, pg. 702
MAKO CONSTRUCTION CO.—See Henkels & McCoy, Inc., pg. 529
MAL TOOL & ENGINEERING CO.—See Collins & Aikman Group Inc., pg. 263
MALCO PRODUCTS, INC., pg. 702
MALDEN MILLS INDUSTRIES, INC., pg. 702
MALESON NAYLOR, pg. 702
MALIBU GRAND PRIX CORPORATION, pg. 702
MALL ENTERTAINMENT USA—See Specialty Restaurants Corporation, pg. 1028
MALLARD PEN & PENCIL CO.—See Pen Holdings, Inc., pg. 856
MALLERY LUMBER CORP., pg. 702
MALLET & CO., pg. 703
MALLORY, INC., pg. 703
MALLOY LITHOGRAPHING INC., pg. 703
MALONE ADVERTISING, INC., pg. 703
MALT-O-MEAL COMPANY, pg. 703
MAMA TISH'S ITALIAN SPECIALTIES, pg. 703
MAMMALIAN TOXICOLOGY DIVISION—See Springborn Laboratories, Inc., pg. 1033
MAN-GILL CHEMICAL COMPANY, pg. 703
MANAGEMENT DYNAMICS, pg. 703
MANAGING AUTOMATION—See Thomas Publishing Co., pg. 1093
MANCHESTER TANK & EQUIPMENT COMPANY, pg. 703
B.T. MANCINI CO., INC., pg. 703
MANDELBAUM MOONEY ASHLEY, pg. 703
MANESS INDUSTRIES, INC., pg. 703
MANHATTAN AND BRONX SURFACE TRANSIT OPERATING AUTHORITY—See Metropolitan Transportation Authority, pg. 745
MANHATTAN BUILDING COMPANIES, pg. 703
MANHATTAN CONSTRUCTION COMPANY—See Manhattan Building Companies, pg. 704
MANHATTAN ELECTRIC CABLE CORPORATION—See Edwardstone & Company, Inc., pg. 370
MANHATTAN LIFE INSURANCE COMPANY—See The Union Central Life Insurance Co., pg. 1128
MANHATTAN NATIONAL CORPORATION—See The Union Central Life Insurance Co., pg. 1128
MANHATTAN STORE INTERIORS, INC., pg. 704
MANHEIM'S OSHAWA DEALERS EXCHANGE—See Cox Enterprises, Inc., pg. 294
MANKE LUMBER COMPANY, INC., pg. 704
MANN HUGHES GERRISH—See Backer Spielvogel Bates Worldwide, Inc., pg. 112
MANNA PRO CORPORATION, pg. 704
MANNA PRO PARTNER L.P. (LIMITED PARTNERSHIP)—See Manna Pro Corporation, pg. 704
MANNA PRO PARTNERS, pg. 704
MANNING EQUIPMENT, INC., pg. 704
MANNING & LEWIS ENGINEERING CO., pg. 704
MANNINGTON CARPET CORP.—See Mannington Mills, Inc., pg. 704
MANNINGTON CERAMIC TILE—See Mannington Mills, Inc., pg. 704
MANNINGTON MILLS, INC., pg. 704
MANOSTAT CORPORATION, pg. 704
MANS-STEEL DIV.—See Hutchens Industries Inc., pg. 555
MANS-STEEL FOUNDRY—See Hutchens Industries Inc., pg. 555
MANSFIELD OIL COMPANY, pg. 704
E. L. MANSURE DIV.—See CC Industries, Inc., pg. 200
MANTECADOS PAYCO—See TLC Beatrice International Holdings Inc., pg. 1073
MANUFACTURE LEVITON DU CANADA—See Leviton Mfg. Co., Inc., pg. 671
MANUFACTURERA THERMON DE MEXICO, S.A.—See Thermon Manufacturing Company, pg. 1092
MANUFACTURERS CONSOLIDATION SERVICE, pg. 705
MANUFACTURERS' JUNCTION RAILROAD COMPANY—See Chicago West Pullman Corporation, pg. 246
MANUFACTURERS' NEWS, INC., pg. 705
MANUFACTURERS PRODUCTS COMPANY, pg. 705
MANUFACTURERS TECHNOLOGIES, INC., pg. 705
MAPLEHURST FARMS, INC., pg. 705
MAPLETON DEVELOPMENT, INC.—See Belmont Industries, Inc., pg. 136
MAQUILADORA CLAMAQ S.A. DE C.V.—See Clayton Industries Co., pg. 254
MAR-JAC FARMS, INC.—See Mar-Jac Inc., pg. 705
MAR-JAC INC., pg. 705
MAR-JAC PROCESSING, INC.—See Mar-Jac Inc., pg. 705
MAR-MAC MANUFACTURING COMPANY, INC., pg. 705
MARATHON CHEESE CORP., pg. 705
MARATHON ELECTRIC MANUFACTURING CORP., pg. 705
MARATHON SPECIAL PRODS.—See Marathon Electric Manufacturing Corp., pg. 706
THE MARBLE COMPANY—See Blevins Inc., pg. 156
MARBORO BOOKS INC.—See Barnes & Noble Bookstores, Inc., pg. 120
MARC ADVERTISING, pg. 706
MARCAL PAPER MILLS, INC., pg. 706
MARCH MANUFACTURING INC., pg. 706
MARCO COLOR LABS, INC., pg. 706
MARCO MARINE SAN DIEGO—See Marine Construction & Design Co., pg. 707
MARCO SEATTLE, INC.—See Marine Construction & Design Co., pg. 707
MARCUS ADVERTISING, INC., pg. 706
MARCUS BROTHERS TEXTILES, INC., pg. 706
MARDEN-KANE, INC., pg. 706
MARGEOTES FERTITTA & WEISS, INC., pg. 706
MARGO FARMS DEL CARIBE, INC.—See Margo Nursery Farms, Inc., pg. 706
MARGO IMPORTS B.V.—See Margo Nursery Farms, Inc., pg. 707
MARGO NURSERY FARMS, INC., pg. 706
MARGO'S LA MODE, INC.—See The Elder-Beerman Stores Corp., pg. 373
MARIANA CORPORATION—See Gohmann Asphalt & Construction Inc., pg. 465
MARINE AIR SYSTEMS, INC.—See Nelson A. Taylor Co., Inc., pg. 1081
MARINE CONSTRUCTION & DESIGN CO., pg. 707
MARINE TECH—See Minstar, Inc., pg. 758
MARINE TERMINAL SHIPPING CO.—See Farmland Industries, Inc., pg. 402
MARINE TRANSPORT LINES, INC., pg. 707
MARINE TRAVELIFT, INC., pg. 707
MARINE WORLD AFRICA USA, pg. 707
MARINER CONSTRUCTORS NAUTICAS, S.A.—See Lear Siegler Diversified Holdings Corp., pg. 664
MARINETTE MARINE CORPORATION, pg. 707
MARION MACHINE COMPANY DIVISION—See Superior Machine Company Of South Carolina, Inc., pg. 1064
MARION POWER SHOVEL DIVISION—See INDRESCO, Inc., pg. 565
MARIS, WEST & BAKER, INC., pg. 707
MARISA CHRISTINA INC., pg. 707
MARITIME LIFE ASSURANCE CO.—See John Hancock Mutual Life Insurance Company, pg. 597
MARITZ COMMUNICATIONS CO.—See Maritz Inc., pg. 707
MARITZ INC., pg. 707
MARITZ LIMITED—See Maritz Inc., pg. 708
MARITZ MARKETING RESEARCH, INC.—See Maritz Inc., pg. 707
MARITZ PERFORMANCE IMPROVEMENT COMPANY—See Maritz Inc., pg. 708
MARITZ TRAVEL CO.—See Maritz Inc., pg. 708
MARK ANDY, INC., pg. 708
MARK CHEVROLET INC., pg. 708
MARK FABRICKS, INC., pg. 708
MARK LIGHTING FIXTURE CO., INC., pg. 708
MARK MACHINE INC., pg. 708
MARK I MOLDED PLASTICS, INC.—See Atwood Industries, Inc., pg. 97
MARK III INDUSTRIES, pg. 708
MARKAIR, INC., pg. 708
MARKDATA INC., pg. 708
MARKEM CORPORATION, pg. 708
MARKET DEVELOPMENT CO.—See Spartan Stores Inc., pg. 1026
MARKET DEVELOPMENT GROUP, INC., pg. 709
MARKET DEVELOPMENT GROUP INC., pg. 709
MARKET DIRECTIONS, INC.—See Valentine-Radford, Inc., pg. 1143
MARKET WYSE—See Wyse Advertising, Inc., pg. 1206
MARKETFORCE ADVERTISING PHILIPPINES INC.—See Dentsu, Young & Rubicam Partnerships, pg. 330
MARKETFORCE AUSTRALIA—See Backer Spielvogel Bates Worldwide, Inc., pg. 112
MARKETING ALTERNATIVES, INC., pg. 709
MARKETING COMMUNICATIONS, pg. 709
THE MARKETING CONTINUUM, INC., pg. 709
MARKETING CORP. OF AMERICA, pg. 709
MARKETING DISPLAYS INTERNATIONAL, INC., pg. 709
MARKETING MAGIC INC., pg. 709
MARKETING RESEARCH GROUP—See American Business Information, Inc., pg. 50
MARKETING RESOURCES OF AMERICA, INC., pg. 709
MARKETING SERVICES UNLTD., pg. 709
MARKETING SUPPORT, INCORPORATED, pg. 709
MARKETPULSE—See Praxis International Inc., pg. 884
THE MARKEY COMPANY—See A & W Foods, Inc., pg. 1
MARKHON INDUSTRIES, INC—See Kennedy Manufacturing Company, pg. 623
MARKIN TUBING, INC., pg. 709
MARKOM/LEO BURNETT A.S.—See Leo Burnett Company, Inc., pg. 193
MARKS-FITZGERALD FURNITURE CO.—See Rhodes, Inc., pg. 931
MARKWOOD INC., pg. 710
MARLAN VALVES CO.—See Stockham Valves & Fittings, Inc., pg. 1050
MARLBOROUGH CAPITAL ADVISORS, INC.—See The New England, pg. 799
THE MARLEY COMPANY, pg. 710
THE MARLEY COOLING TOWER CO.—See The Marley Company, pg. 710
MARLEY ELECTRIC HEATING CO.—See The Marley Company, pg. 710
MARLEY PUMP CO.—See The Marley Company, pg. 710
THE MARLIN COMPANY, pg. 710
ED MARLING STORES, INC., pg. 710
MARLOW INDUSTRIES, pg. 710
MARMAC CORPORATION, pg. 710
MARMON CORPORATION—See The Marmon Group, Inc., pg. 711
THE MARMON GROUP, INC., pg. 710
THE MARMON GROUP, INC.—See The Marmon Group, Inc., pg. 711
MARMON-HERRINGTON COMPANY—See The Marmon Group, Inc., pg. 711
MARMON INDUSTRIAL CORPORATION—See The Marmon Group, Inc., pg. 712
MARMON/KEYSTONE CANADA-MONTREAL—See The Marmon Group, Inc., pg. 712
MARMON/KEYSTONE CANADA-TORONTO—See The Marmon Group, Inc., pg. 712
MARMON/KEYSTONE CORP.—See The Marmon Group, Inc., pg. 711
MARONTATE & CO., pg. 713
MAROTTA SCIENTIFIC CONTROLS, INC., pg. 713
MARQUARDT & CO.—See Central Paper Company, pg. 234
MARQUARDT & ROCHE INC., pg. 713
MARQUETTE BANK MINNEAPOLIS, NATIONAL ASSOCIATION—See Bank Shares, Inc., pg. 117
MARQUETTE BANK ROCHESTER—See Bank Shares, Inc., pg. 117
MARQUETTE COPPERSMITHING CO., INC., pg. 713
MARRINER MARKETING COMMUNICATIONS, INC., pg. 713
MARS ADVERTISING CO., pg. 713
MARS CONFECTIONERY—See Mars, Incorporated, pg. 713
MARS, INCORPORATED, pg. 713
MARS PETFOODS (UNISABI)—See Mars, Incorporated, pg. 714
MARS SUPER MARKETS, INC., pg. 714
MARSH FURNITURE COMPANY, pg. 714
MARSH LUMBER COMPANY—See Interstate Resources, Inc., pg. 580
MARSH PRODUCTS CO.—See Premarc Corporation, pg. 886
MARSHALL & WILLIAMS CO., pg. 714
R. J. MARSHALL CO., pg. 714
MARSHALL CONTRACTORS INC., pg. 714
MARSHALL JACCOMA MITCHELL ADVERTISING, pg. 714
MARSTRAT, INC., pg. 714
MARTHA WHITE MILLS OF W.VA., INC.—See Windmill Holdings Corp., pg. 1195
ALBERT C. MARTIN & ASSOCIATES, pg. 714
MARTIN BAND INSTRUMENT CO.—See G. Leblanc Corporation, pg. 665
MARTIN & BAYLEY INC., pg. 714
MARTIN & BENEDICT INC., pg. 714
MARTIN, COLE, DANDO & ROBERTSON, pg. 714
MARTIN DOOR MFG., INC., pg. 714
MARTIN ELECTRONICS, INC.—See KDI Corporation, pg. 612
MARTIN EXPLORATION MANAGEMENT COMPANY, pg. 715
MARTIN FOREST INDUSTRIES, pg. 715
MARTIN GAS CORPORATION, pg. 715
MARTIN INDUSTRIES (AL), pg. 715
J.B. MARTIN COMPANY, pg. 715
MARTIN LUTHER HOSPITAL—See UniHealth America, pg. 1127
MARTIN PAINT STORES, pg. 715
SHERRI MARTIN—See Dawn Joy Fashions, Inc., pg. 319
MARTIN SPROCKET & GEAR, INC., pg. 715
MARTIN UNIVERSAL DESIGN, INC., pg. 715
MARTIN/UNIVERSAL INDUSTRIES—See Martin Universal Design, Inc., pg. 716
MARTINS ABBATOIR & WHOLESALE MEATS INC., pg. 716
MARTINY & COMPANY, pg. 716
MARTRADE LTD., pg. 716
MARTZ & WADAS, pg. 716
MARUCHAN INC., pg. 716
MARVAL INDUSTRIES, INC., pg. 716
MARVEL ENTERTAINMENT GROUP—See MacAndrews & Forbes Holdings Inc., pg. 695
MARVIN ENGINEERING COMPANY, INC., pg. 716
MARVIN LUMBER & CEDAR COMPANY, pg. 716
GILDA MARX INC., pg. 716
MARX/KNOLL, DENIGHT & DODGE, INC., pg. 716
MARY KAY CORPORATION, pg. 716
MARY KAY COSMETICOS DE MEXICO PTY., S.A. DE C.V.—See Mary Kay Corporation, pg. 717
MARY KAY COSMETICS, GMBH—See Mary Kay Corporation, pg. 717
MARY KAY COSMETICS INC.—See Mary Kay Corporation, pg. 716
MARY KAY COSMETICS, INC.—See Mary Kay Corporation, pg. 717
MARY KAY COSMETICS LTD.—See Mary Kay Corporation, pg. 717
MARY KAY COSMETICS PTY. LTD.—See Mary Kay Corporation, pg. 717

MARY KAY COSMETICS, S.A.—See Mary Kay Corporation, pg. 717
MARYLAND & VIRGINIA MILK PRODUCERS ASSOCIATION, pg. 717
MARYLAND PAPER BOX COMPANY, pg. 717
MARYLAND PLASTICS, INC., pg. 717
MARYLAND PLASTICS, INC.—See Bio Medic Corporation, pg. 152
MARYLAND RIBBON COMPANY—See C.M. Offray & Son Inc., pg. 822
MARYLAND STATE LOTTERY, pg. 717
MARYLAND VIRGINIA MILK PRODUCERS ASSOCIATION, INC., pg. 717
MARYLAND WOOD PRESERVING CORP.—See Devlin Lumber & Supply Corp., pg. 334
MARYVILLE-ALCOA NEWSPAPERS, INC.—See Persis Corporation, pg. 863
MASBACK HARDWARE CO.—See Distribution America, pg. 340
MASEK DISTRIBUTING INC., pg. 717
MASHBURN CONSTRUCTION COMPANY, pg. 717
MASLAND INDUSTRIES, pg. 717
MASON COMPANY, pg. 718
MASON DISTRIBUTORS, INC., pg. 718
MASON & HANGER ENGINEERING INC.—See Mason Company, pg. 718
MASON & HANGER NATIONAL INC.—See Mason Company, pg. 718
MASON & HANGER SERVICES INC.—See Mason Company, pg. 718
MASON HANGER-SILAS MASON CO.—See Mason Company, pg. 718
MASON & MADISON, INC., pg. 718
MASON OIL COMPANY, pg. 718
MASON SHOE MFG. CO., pg. 718
MASON TECHNOLOGIES INC.—See Mason Company, pg. 718
MASSACHUSETTS CONTAINER CORPORATION—See Connecticut Container Corporation, pg. 274
MASSACHUSETTS ENVELOPE CO., pg. 718
MASSACHUSETTS MUTUAL LIFE INSURANCE CO., pg. 718
MASSACHUSETTS STATE LOTTERY, pg. 719
MASSACHUSETTS STEEL TREATING—See The Presmet Corp., pg. 887
DON MASSEY BUICK, INC.—See Don Massey Cadillac Inc., pg. 719
MASSEY CADILLAC, INC.—See Don Massey Cadillac Inc., pg. 719
MASSEY CADILLAC, INC.—See Don Massey Cadillac Inc., pg. 719
DON MASSEY CADILLAC INC., pg. 719
MASSMAN CONSTRUCTION COMPANY, pg. 719
MASSMUTUAL HOLDING COMPANY—See Massachusetts Mutual Life Insurance Co., pg. 719
MASTER APPLIANCE CORP., pg. 719
MASTER COLLECTORS INC., pg. 719
MASTER FOODS—See Mars, Incorporated, pg. 713
MASTER FOODS AB—See Mars, Incorporated, pg. 714
MASTER FOODS AUSTRIA GMBH—See Mars, Incorporated, pg. 714
MASTER FOODS NV—See Mars, Incorporated, pg. 714
MASTER INDUSTRIES CORP., pg. 719
MASTER MOLDED PRODUCTS CORPORATION, pg. 720
MASTER PLANS CORPORATION—See Society for Savings Bancorp, Inc., pg. 1016
MASTER SKIIS—See MacAndrews & Forbes Holdings Inc., pg. 694
MASTER TROUSER/ MASTER APPAREL/ BOTANY 500 SLACKS LTD.—See Master Industries Corp., pg. 720
MASTERBILT FIXTURES, INC.—See Grocers Supply Co. Inc., pg. 489
MASTERCARD INTERNATIONAL, INC., pg. 720
MASTERCARD INTERNATIONAL, INC.—See Mastercard International, Inc., pg. 720
MASTERCRAFT BOAT COMPANY—See MacAndrews & Forbes Holdings Inc., pg. 695
MASTERCRAFT CORPORATION—See Minstar, Inc., pg. 759
MASTERCRAFT FURNITURE CORP., pg. 720
MASTERFOODS LTD.—See Mars, Incorporated, pg. 714
MASTERFOODS OY—See Mars, Incorporated, pg. 714
MASTERITE INDUSTRIES, INC.—See KDI Corporation, pg. 612
MASTERS INC., pg. 720
MASTERS, INC., pg. 720
MASTERSON ROTHBERG ADVERTISING, pg. 720
MASTICO INDUSTRIES, LTD.—See Globe Industries, Inc., pg. 464
MATARI ADVERTISING—See N W Ayer Incorporated, pg. 104
MATECO ELECTRONICS CORP., pg. 720
MATERIAL HANDLING EQUIPMENT CO.—See Modern Group Ltd., pg. 763
MATERIAL TRANSPORT CO.—See Ash Grove Cement Company, pg. 88
MATERIALES INDUSTRIALES S.A.—See Belmont Industries, Inc., pg. 137
MATHEMATICAL REVIEWS—See American Mathematical Society, Inc., pg. 58
CURTIS MATHES CORPORATION, pg. 720
MATHEWS & BOUCHER, pg. 720
MATHIES COAL CO.—See National Steel Corporation, pg. 794
MATHIEU CORPORATION, pg. 720
MATHIEU, DONOVAN & ASSOCIATES, INC., pg. 721
MATRIX BUILDING CO., INC.—See Maescher Industries, Inc., pg. 700
MATRIX ESSENTIALS, INC., pg. 721
THE F. X. MATT BREWING CO., pg. 721
MATTER GALBUCCI LEO BURNETT, WERBEAGENTUR—See Leo Burnett Company, Inc., pg. 193
MATTERN HATCHERY—See Empire Kosher Poultry, Inc., pg. 379
MATTHEWS CANADA LTD.—See Matthews International Corp., pg. 721
MATTHEWS INTERNATIONAL CORP., pg. 721
MATTHEWS INTL. CORP.-GRAPHIC SYSTEMS DIV.—See Matthews International Corp., pg. 721
MATTHEWS INTERNATIONAL MARKING SYSTEMS DIV.—See Matthews International Corp., pg. 721
MATTHEWS INTERNATIONAL MEMORIAL DIVISION—See Matthews International Corp., pg. 721
MATTHEWS INTL. TRADING CORP.—See Matthews International Corp., pg. 721
MATTINGLY & PARTNERS/AUCKLAND—See Dentsu, Young & Rubicam Partnerships, pg. 331
MATTINGLY & PARTNERS GROUP PTY LTD.—See Dentsu, Young & Rubicam Partnerships, pg. 330
MATTINGLY & PARTNERS/MELBOURNE—See Dentsu, Young & Rubicam Partnerships, pg. 331
MATTINGLY & PARTNERS/SYDNEY—See Dentsu, Young & Rubicam Partnerships, pg. 331
MATTISON MACHINE WORKS, pg. 721
MAUI DIVERS OF HAWAII, LTD., pg. 721
MAUI VARIETIES, LTD., pg. 721
MAULDIN MFG. CO., INC.—See Whitin Roberts Co., pg. 1187
MAUNA KEA AGRIBUSINESS CO., INC.—See C. Brewer & Company, Limited, pg. 174
MAUNA LOA MACADAMIA NUT CO.—See Foster & Gallagher Inc., pg. 426
MAUNA LOA MACADAMIA NUT CORPORATION—See C. Brewer & Company, Limited, pg. 174
MAUNA LOA ORCHIDS, LTD.—See Flowers of Hawaii, pg. 421
MAUNA LOA ORCHIDS, LTD., D/B/A HAWAIIAN EXOTIC FLOWERS—See Flowers of Hawaii, pg. 421
MAUNA LOA RESOURCES INC.—See C. Brewer & Company, Limited, pg. 174
MAUNEY HOSIERY MILLS, INC., pg. 722
MAUREXCO EXPORTERS—See Maurice Electric Supply Company, pg. 722
MAUREY MANUFACTURING CORP., pg. 722
MAURICE ELECTRIC SUPPLY COMPANY, pg. 722
THE MAURIN-OGDEN COMPANIES, pg. 722
MAURIN-OGDEN MANAGEMENT CORPORATION—See The Maurin-Ogden Companies, pg. 722
MAUTZ PAINT COMPANY, pg. 722
MAVERIK COUNTRY STORES, INC., pg. 722
MAVIS INDUSTRIES, INC.—See General Computer Corp. Inc., pg. 449
MAX WARD-DELMAR STUDIOS—See Lifetouch, Inc., pg. 675
MAXCOR MANUFACTURING, INC., pg. 722
MARY MAXIM, INC., pg. 722
MARY MAXIM, LTD.—See Mary Maxim, Inc., pg. 723
MAXIMA BUSINESS SYSTEMS—See The Maxima Corporation, pg. 723
MAXIMA COMPUTER SYSTEMS CORP.—See The Maxima Corporation, pg. 723
THE MAXIMA CORPORATION, pg. 723
MAXIMA DATA SYSTEMS—See The Maxima Corporation, pg. 723
MAXIMET—See Karsten Manufacturing Corporation, pg. 617
MAXINE OF HOLLYWOOD, INC., pg. 723
MAXITROL CO., pg. 723
MAXON COMBUSTION SYSTEMS, LTD.—See Maxon Corporation, pg. 723
MAXON CORPORATION, pg. 723
MAXON GMBH—See Maxon Corporation, pg. 723
MAXON GMBH—See Maxon Corporation, pg. 723
N.V. MAXON INTERNATIONAL S.A.—See Maxon Corporation, pg. 723
N.V. MAXON INTERNATIONAL S.A.—See Maxon Corporation, pg. 723
MAXON MARINE, INC.—See Chicago West Pullman Corporation, pg. 246
MAXON S.A.R.L.—See Maxon Corporation, pg. 723
MAXUM EXTERIOR COATINGS—See Premier Coatings, Inc., pg. 886
THE MAY APPAREL GROUP, INC., pg. 723
GEORGE S. MAY CANADA, LTD.—See George S. May International Company, pg. 724
GEORGE S. MAY INTERNATIONAL COMPANY, pg. 723
GEORGE S. MAY INTERNATIONAL, S.P.A.—See George S. May International Company, pg. 724
EARL MAY SEED & NURSERY L.P., pg. 724
MAY & SPEH, INC., pg. 724
MAYER BERKSHIRE CORPORATION, pg. 724
MAYER MYERS PAPER COMPANY, pg. 724
PETER A. MAYER ADVERTISING, INC., pg. 724
MAYFAIR INDUSTRIES, INC.—See Apparel America, Inc., pg. 78
MAYFAIR MILLS, INC., pg. 724
MAYFAIR SUPER MARKETS, INC., pg. 724
MAYFIELD BUILDING SUPPLY CO.—See MBS Holding, Inc., pg. 691
MAYFLOWER CONTRACT SERVICES, INC.—See Mayflower Transit, Inc., pg. 725
MAYFLOWER MOTOR COACH, INC.—See Mayflower Transit, Inc., pg. 725
MAYFLOWER OF TEXAS—See Mayflower Transit, Inc., pg. 725
MAYFLOWER TRANSIT, INC., pg. 724
MAYNARD STEEL CASTING COMPANY, pg. 725
MAYS CHEMICAL COMPANY, pg. 725
MAYVILLE ENGINEERING CO., INC., pg. 725
MAYVILLE METAL PRODUCTS DIVISION—See Connell Limited Partnership, pg. 275
MAYWOOD, INC., pg. 725
MAZE NAILS, pg. 725
MAZO LERCH COMPANY, INC., pg. 725
MBANK NEW BRAUNFELS—See MCorp, pg. 733
MCADAMS, RICHMAN & ONG, INC., pg. 725
WILLIAM DOUGLAS MCADAMS INC., pg. 726
MCAFEE CONSOLIDATED INC., pg. 726
MCANALLY ENTERPRISES, INC., pg. 726
MCARDLE PRINTING CO., INC.—See The Bureau of National Affairs, Inc., pg. 189
MCCAFFERY & RATNER, INC., pg. 726
MCCAFFREY AND MCCALL, pg. 726
MCCAIN CITRUS INC., pg. 726
MCCAIN MANUFACTURING CORP., pg. 726
MCCALL OIL & CHEMICAL CORP., pg. 726
MCCALL OIL REAL ESTATE CORPORATION—See McCall Oil & Chemical Corp., pg. 727
MCCALL PROPERTIES, INC.—See McCall Oil & Chemical Corp., pg. 727
MCCARTHY BROTHERS CO.—See McCarthy Building Companies, pg. 727
MCCARTHY BUILDING COMPANIES, pg. 727
MCCARTY FARMS, pg. 727
MCCARTY FOODS, INC.—See McCarty Farms, pg. 727
MCCARTY PROCESSORS, INC.—See McCarty Farms, pg. 727
MCCLAIN FINLON ADVERTISING, pg. 727
MCCLEAN-ANDERSON—See Price Brothers Co., pg. 888
MCCLELLAND CONSULTANTS MIDWEST, INC.—See Fugro-McClelland, Inc., pg. 436
MCCLELLAND & DUFF, INC.—See Erb Lumber Company, pg. 360
MCCLELLAND-SUHAIMI, LTD.—See Fugro-McClelland, Inc., pg. 436
MCCOLLS DAIRY—See Crystal Cream & Butter Company, pg. 303
MCCOMMUNICATIONS INC., pg. 727
MCCONNAUGHY STEIN SCHMIDT BROWN, pg. 727
MCCONNELL AUTOMOTIVE, pg. 727
MCCONNELL CABINETS, INC., pg. 727
J.H. MCCORMICK, INC., pg. 727
MCCORMICK PAINT WORKS COMPANY, pg. 727
MCCOURT LABEL CO., pg. 727
MCCRACKEN BROOKS COMMUNICATIONS, INC., pg. 728
MCCRORY CONSTRUCTION CO., INC., pg. 728
MCCRORY CORPORATION—See Riklis Family Corporation, pg. 934
MCCRORY STORES DIV.—See Riklis Family Corporation, pg. 934
MCCURDY & CO., INC., pg. 728
MCDONALD DAVIS & ASSOCIATES, INC., pg. 728
MCDONALD EQUIPMENT CO., pg. 728
A. Y. MCDONALD INDUSTRIES, INC., pg. 728
A. Y. MCDONALD MFG. CO.—See A. Y. McDonald Industries, Inc., pg. 728
MCDONALD PRODUCTS COMPANY—See Smith Metal Arts Company, Inc., pg. 1014
A. Y. MCDONALD SUPPLY CO. INC.—See A. Y. McDonald Industries, Inc., pg. 728
MCDOUGAL, LITTELL & COMPANY, pg. 728
MCDOUGALL ASSOCIATES, INC., pg. 728
MCDOWELL MFG. CO.—See Alco Industries, Inc., pg. 32
MCFARLAND & DRIER, INC., pg. 729
MCFARLAND & DRIER INTERNATIONAL—See McFarland & Drier, Inc., pg. 729
MCFARLING FOODS, INC., pg. 729
MCGAW, INC., pg. 729
MCGEAN-ROHCO, INC., pg. 729
MCGRATH & ASSOCIATES—See Nooter Corporation, pg. 808
MCGRAW/KOKOSING, INC.—See Kokosing Construction Company, Inc., pg. 641
MCGUFFEY'S RESTAURANTS, INC., pg. 729
JAMES MCHUGH CONSTRUCTION CO., pg. 729
MCILHENNY COMPANY, pg. 729
MCILHENNY RESOURCES—See McIlhenny Company, pg. 729
J. GIBSON MCILVAIN CO., pg. 729
MCINERNEY INC., pg. 729
MCINERNEY-MILLER BROTHERS INC., pg. 729
MCINNES ROLLED RINGS—See McInnes Steel Company, pg. 730
MCINNES STEEL COMPANY, pg. 729
MCJUNKIN CORPORATION, pg. 730
MCKEAN OLDSMOBILE COMPANY, pg. 730
MCKEE BAKING CO., INC., pg. 730
MCKEE DOOR, INC., pg. 730
MCKEE FOODS CORPORATION, pg. 730
MCKELLAR DEVELOPERS OF LA JOLLA, pg. 730
JOHN MCKENZIE PACKING CO., INC., pg. 730
MCKENZIE TANK LINES, INC., pg. 730
MCKINLAY & PARTNERS, INC., pg. 730
MCKINNEY INC. ADVERTISING & PUBLIC RELATIONS, pg. 730
MCKINNEY & SILVER, pg. 730
MCKINNON BRIDGE CO., pg. 731
MCKINSEY & COMPANY, INC., pg. 731
MCKONE & CO., INC., pg. 731
MCLAUGHLIN GORMLEY KING COMPANY, pg. 731
MCLAUGHLIN INDUSTRIAL DISTRIBUTORS, INC., pg. 731
MCLAUGHLIN MFG. COMPANY, pg. 731
MCLEAN ENTERPRISES, INC., pg. 731
MCLEAN-THOMAS INC., pg. 731
MCLOUTH STEEL, pg. 731
MCMASTER CARR SUPPLY CO. INC., pg. 731
MCNALLY INDUSTRIES, INC., pg. 731
MCNALLY PITTSBURG MFG. CORP.—See McNally Wellman Company, pg. 732
MCNALLY WELLMAN COMPANY, pg. 732
MCNAMARA PONTIAC INC., pg. 732
MCNAUGHTON & GUNN, INC., pg. 732
MCNAUGHTON-MCKAY ELECTRIC CO., pg. 732
MCNEEL INTERNATIONAL CORP., pg. 732
MCNEIL & NRM., INC., pg. 732
MCNEILUS COMPANIES, pg. 732
MCNEILUS COMPANIES—See McNeilus Companies, pg. 732

MCORP, pg. 732
MCRAE'S, INC., pg. 733
MCROBERT SPRINGS CO.—See The Marmon Group, Inc., pg. 712
MCSWAIN CARPETS INC., pg. 733
MCWANE CAST IRON PIPE CO.—See McWane, Inc., pg. 733
MCWANE, INC., pg. 733
MCWILLIAMS FORGE CO., pg. 733
D. J. MEAD-HUBBS & HOWE—See Sofco-Mead, Inc., pg. 1016
MEADE GROUP, INC., pg. 733
MEADE ULLMAN ADVERTISING & PUBLIC RELATIONS, pg. 733
MEADOWBROOK CO.—See T.L. Diamond Company, pg. 335
MEADOWCRAFT, INC., pg. 733
MEADOWLANDS HOSPITAL MEDICAL CENTER—See UniHealth America, pg. 1127
R.G. MEADOWS, INC., pg. 733
MEADVILLE FORGING CO., pg. 733
DON MEALEY CHEVROLET INC., pg. 733
MEARS TRANSPORTATION GROUP, pg. 734
MEASURED MARKETING SERVICES, pg. 734
MECHANICAL HEAT & COLD, INC., pg. 734
MECO—See Sycon Corporation, pg. 1069
MECO CORPORATION, pg. 734
MED-LAB SUPPLY COMPANY, INC., pg. 734
MEDCREST DIV.—See Medline Industries, Inc., pg. 736
MEDECINE ET SYSTEMES INFORMATIQUES INTERGRES—See Science Applications International Corporation, pg. 982
MEDECORE DIV.—See Medline Industries, Inc., pg. 736
MEDIA AMERICA CORP., pg. 734
MEDIA BUYERS, INC.—See Asher/Gould Advertising, Inc., pg. 88
MEDIA BUYING SERVICES INTL. INC., pg. 734
MEDIA CONCEPTS CORPORATION, pg. 734
MEDIA DECISIONS—See Backer Spielvogel Bates Worldwide, Inc., pg. 112
MEDIA GRAPHICS—See Spectrum Industries, Inc., pg. 1029
MEDIA LOGIC, INC., pg. 734
MEDIA MANAGEMENT—See Meyer & Wallis, Inc., pg. 746
MEDIA MANAGEMENT ASSOCIATES, pg. 734
MEDIA MARKETING RESEARCH—See Backer Spielvogel Bates Worldwide, Inc., pg. 112
MEDIA PLUS, pg. 734
MEDIA POWER, INC., pg. 734
MEDIA PRINTING CORPORATION, pg. 734
MEDIA STORE INC., pg. 735
MEDIA THAT WORKS, pg. 735
MEDIA TRANSIA INDIA LTD.—See International Data Group, pg. 577
MEDIA TRANSIA THAILAND LTD.—See International Data Group, pg. 577
MEDIACOMP, INC., pg. 735
MEDIACOMP MEDIA MANAGEMENT SERVICES—See Mediacomp, Inc., pg. 735
MEDIANEWS GROUP, EASTERN OPERATIONS—See MediaNews Group Inc., pg. 735
MEDIANEWS GROUP INC., pg. 735
MEDIATEX COMMUNICATIONS CORPORATION, pg. 735
MEDICAL ANALYSIS SYSTEMS INC., pg. 735
MEDICAL LABORATORY AUTOMATION, INC., pg. 735
THE MEDICAL PROTECTIVE COMPANY, pg. 735
MEDICALODGES, INC.—See Health Care Lodges, pg. 520
MEDICO, INC.—See S. M. Frank & Co., Inc., pg. 429
MEDICO INDUSTRIES, INC., pg. 735
MEDIEVAL DINNER & TOURNAMENT, INC., pg. 735
THE MEDISCUS GROUP, pg. 736
MEDLINE INDUSTRIES, INC., pg. 736
MEDRAD, INC., pg. 736
MEDTECH LABORATORIES, INC., pg. 736
MEEHAN TOOKER, pg. 736
MEENAN LI DIV.—See Meenan Oil Co. Limited Partnership, pg. 736
MEENAN OIL CO. LIMITED PARTNERSHIP, pg. 736
MEER CORPORATION, pg. 736
MEGAPULSE, INC., pg. 737
MEGAS BEAUTY AIDS, INC., pg. 737
JOSHUA MEIER CORP., pg. 737
MEIER METAL SERVICE CENTERS, INC., pg. 737
MEIJER, INC., pg. 737
MELARD MANUFACTURING CORPORATION, pg. 737
MELARD PLASTICS INC.—See Melard Manufacturing Corporation, pg. 737
MELDRUM & FEWSMITH ADVERTISING INC.—See Meldrum & Fewsmith Communications Inc., pg. 737
MELDRUM & FEWSMITH COMMUNICATIONS INC., pg. 737
MELDRUM & FEWSMITH YELLOW PAGES INC.—See Meldrum & Fewsmith Communications Inc., pg. 737
MELE MANUFACTURING CO., INC., pg. 737
MELLING FORGING COMPANY—See Avis Industrial Corporation, pg. 102
MELLON CORPORATION, pg. 738
H.B. MELLOTT ESTATE, INC., pg. 738
MELLOY BROS. ENTERPRISES, pg. 738
MELLOY NISSAN—See Melloy Bros. Enterprises, pg. 738
MELODY FOODS, INC., pg. 738
MEMBER SERVICE LIFE INSURANCE CO.—See Blue Cross and Blue Shield of Oklahoma, pg. 159
MEMBERS ONLY BY EUROPE CRAFT, pg. 738
MEMPHIS GROUP, INC., pg. 738
MEMPHIS LIGHT, GAS & WATER, pg. 738
MEMPHIS PUBLISHING COMPANY, pg. 738
MENARD ELECTRIC COOPERATIVE, pg. 738
MENASHA CORPORATION, pg. 738
MENASHA DEVELOPMENT CORPORATION—See Menasha Corporation, pg. 739
MENASHA FOREIGN SALES CORPORATION—See Menasha Corporation, pg. 739
MENASHA TRANSPORT INC.—See Menasha Corporation, pg. 739
MENDELSOHN/ZIEN ADVERTISING, INC., pg. 739
A. W. MENDENHALL CO., INC., pg. 739
MENDENHALL & LEISTRA, pg. 739
MENNEN MEDICAL INC., pg. 739
MENOMINEE PAPER CO.—See Bell Packaging Corporation, pg. 135
MEN'S JOURNAL—See Straight Arrow Publishers, Inc., pg. 1052
MENSWEAR DIV.—See Levi Strauss & Co., pg. 670
MENTOR AGVS, INC.—See Production Machinery Corporation, pg. 893
MENU FOODS, INC., pg. 739
MEPPS S.A.—See Sheldons' Inc., pg. 997
MERCANTILE BANK—See MCorp, pg. 733
MERCATOR ASSET MANAGEMENT CO., INC.—See The Prudential Insurance Company of America, pg. 897
MERCER FORGE, INC.—See Rotterdam Ventures Inc., pg. 952
MERCER PAPER TUBE CO.—See Yorktowne Paper Mills, Inc., pg. 1209
MERCER TRANSPORTATION CO., pg. 739
MERCHANDISING EQUIPMENT GROUP, pg. 739
MERCHANT CAPITAL GROUP LTD, pg. 739
MERCHANTS DISTRIBUTORS, INC.—See Alex Lee, Inc., pg. 33
MERCHANTS INSURANCE AGENCY—See U.R.M. Stores, Inc., pg. 1124
MERCHANTS PUBLISHING CO., pg. 739
MERCHANTS RENT A CAR, INC., pg. 739
MERCHANTS TRANSPORT OF HICKORY—See Alex Lee, Inc., pg. 33
MERCHANTS TRUCK LINE, INC., pg. 740
MERCOID DIV.—See Dwyer Instruments Inc., pg. 356
MERCURY COMPUTER SYSTEMS, INC., pg. 740
MERCURY DISTRIBUTING CO., INC., pg. 740
MERIDIAN COMMUNICATIONS, pg. 740
MERIDIAN INDUSTRIES, INC., pg. 740
MERIDIAN MFG. CO., INC.—See Roytex, Inc., pg. 953
MERIDIAN TECHNOLOGY LEASING SERVICES, pg. 740
MERITCARE, INC., pg. 740
MERLE NORMAN COSMETICS, INC., pg. 740
MERLING, MARX & SEIDMAN, INC., pg. 741
MERMOD, JACCARD & KING JEWELRY CO. OF IOWA, INC.—See Zale Corporation, pg. 1216
MERMOD, JACCARD & KING JEWELRY CO. OF NEBRASKA—See Zale Corporation, pg. 1216
MERRIAM-WEBSTER, INC.—See Encyclopaedia Britannica, Inc., pg. 381
STAN MERRITT INC./ADVERTISING, pg. 741
MERSMAN FURNITURE, pg. 741
MESA CITRUS GROWERS, pg. 741
MESABA-CLIFFS MINING CO.—See National Steel Corporation, pg. 794
MESCO METAL BUILDINGS CORP.—See Anderson Industries, Inc., pg. 73
MESIROW FINANCIAL, pg. 741
MESSENGER CORPORATION, pg. 741
FRANK MESSER & SONS CONSTRUCTION CO., pg. 741
META FARM—See Triple F, Inc., pg. 1114
META PLANT FOOD—See Fisca Oil Co., Inc., pg. 414
META SERVICES INC.—See Ederer Inc., pg. 368
METABO CORPORATION, pg. 741
METAL CUTTING TOOLS CORP.—See Harbour Group Ltd., pg. 507
METAL LEVE S.A.—See The Pullman Company, pg. 900
METAL MASTERS FOODSERVICE EQUIPMENT, pg. 741
METAL SALES MANUFACTURING CORPORATION—See Interlock Industries, Inc., pg. 575
METAL SEAL & PRODUCTS, INC., pg. 741
METAL TRADES, INC., pg. 741
THE METAL WARE CORP., pg. 741
METALCENTER, INC., pg. 742
METALCHIMICA SRL—See Metallurg, Inc., pg. 742
METALL UND ROHSTOFF AG—See Associated Metals & Minerals Corp., pg. 91
METALLOY CORPORATION, pg. 742
METALLURG (CANADA) LIMITED—See Metallurg, Inc., pg. 742
METALLURG DO BRAZIL LTDA.—See Metallurg, Inc., pg. 742
METALLURG (FAR EAST) LIMITED—See Metallurg, Inc., pg. 742
METALLURG, INC., pg. 742
METALLURG MEXICO, S.A. DE CV—See Metallurg, Inc., pg. 742
METALTECH, INC., pg. 742
METALURGICA DETROIT—See The Pullman Company, pg. 900
METFORM, INC.—See Maclean-Fogg Co., pg. 698
METLIFE CAPITAL CORPORATION—See Metropolitan Life Insurance Co., pg. 744
METLIFE CAPITAL CREDIT CORP.—See Metropolitan Life Insurance Co., pg. 744
METLIFE FUNDING CO.—See Metropolitan Life Insurance Co., pg. 744
METLIFE HEALTHCARE MANAGEMENT CORP.—See Metropolitan Life Insurance Co., pg. 745
METLIFE SECURITIES, INC.—See Metropolitan Life Insurance Co., pg. 745
METLIFE SECURITY INSURANCE COMPANY OF LOUISIANA—See Metropolitan Life Insurance Co., pg. 745
METLIFE-STATE STREET INVESTMENT SERVICES, INC.—See Metropolitan Life Insurance Co., pg. 744
METLIFE (UK) LIMITED—See Metropolitan Life Insurance Co., pg. 745
METMOR FINANCIAL, INC.—See Metropolitan Life Insurance Co., pg. 745
METPAC, LTD., pg. 742
METPAR CORPORATION, pg. 742
METPON—See Metromedia Company, pg. 743
METRA, COMMUTER RAIL SERVICE BOARD—See Regional Transportation Authority (RTA), pg. 922
METRIC & MULTISTANDARD COMPONENTS, pg. 743
METRIC REALTY, INC.—See Metropolitan Life Insurance Co., pg. 745
METRO—See Dentsu, Young & Rubicam Partnerships, pg. 331
METRO ATLANTA PROPERTIES—See Fischbach & Dougherty, Inc., pg. 414
METRO CELL, INC.—See Rao Wholesale Tire Centers, Inc., pg. 913
METRO FOODS, INC., pg. 743
METRO FORD INC., pg. 743
METRO FORD SALES, INC., pg. 743
METRO INFORMATION SERVICES, pg. 743
METRO LABEL CORP., pg. 743
METRO LABEL CORP.—See Metro Label Corp., pg. 743
METRO MEDICAL RESOURCES, INC.—See Syracuse Supply Company, pg. 1070
METRO-NORTH COMMUTER RAILROAD COMPANY—See Metropolitan Transportation Authority, pg. 745
METRO PARKING SYSTEMS—See Metropolitan Properties Inc., pg. 745
METRO 25 TIRE CENTERS, INC.—See Rao Wholesale Tire Centers, Inc., pg. 913
METROLOGIC INSTRUMENTS, INC., pg. 743
METROLOGIC INSTRUMENTS-MIDWEST—See Metrologic Instruments, Inc., pg. 743
METROLOGIC INSTRUMENTS-NORTHEAST—See Metrologic Instruments, Inc., pg. 743
METROLOGIC INSTRUMENTS-WESTERN REGION—See Metrologic Instruments, Inc., pg. 743
METROMEDIA COMMUNICATION CORP.—See Metromedia Company, pg. 744
METROMEDIA COMPANY, pg. 743
METROMEDIA STEAKHOUSES, INC.—See Metromedia Company, pg. 744
METRON STEEL CORP., pg. 744
METROPOLITAN ARIZONA CORPORATION—See JMB Realty Corporation, pg. 585
METROPOLITAN ASPHALT, INC.—See Peter A. Basile Sons Inc., pg. 124
METROPOLITAN FURNITURE CORPORATION—See Steelcase Inc., pg. 1044
METROPOLITAN INSURANCE AND ANNUITY COMPANY, TAIWAN BRANCH—See Metropolitan Life Insurance Co., pg. 745
METROPOLITAN INSURANCE & ANNUITY CO.—See Metropolitan Life Insurance Co., pg. 744
METROPOLITAN LIFE HOLDINGS, LTD.—See Metropolitan Life Insurance Co., pg. 745
METROPOLITAN LIFE INSURANCE CO., pg. 744
METROPOLITAN LIFE INSURANCE COMPANY OF CANADA—See Metropolitan Life Insurance Co., pg. 745
METROPOLITAN PROPERTIES INC., pg. 745
METROPOLITAN PROPERTY & CASUALTY INSURANCE CO.(MET P&C)—See Metropolitan Life Insurance Co., pg. 744
METROPOLITAN SUBURBAN BUS AUTHORITY—See Metropolitan Transportation Authority, pg. 745
METROPOLITAN SUNDAY NEWSPAPERS, INC., pg. 745
METROPOLITAN TOWER LIFE INSURANCE CO.—See Metropolitan Life Insurance Co., pg. 744
METROPOLITAN TRANSPORTATION AUTHORITY, pg. 745
METROPOLITAN TRUST COMPANY OF CANADA—See Metropolitan Life Insurance Co., pg. 745
METSA, INC.—See Metromedia Company, pg. 744
METTOWEE LUMBER & PLASTIC CO., INC.—See Telescope Casual Furniture, Inc., pg. 1085
MEXICAN INDUSTRIES IN MICHIGAN, pg. 745
MEYER BROADCASTING COMPANY, pg. 746
MEYER JEWELERS, pg. 746
MEYER MATERIAL COMPANY—See The Marmon Group, Inc., pg. 711
MEYER & WALLIS, INC., pg. 746
THE MEYERCORD COMPANY, pg. 746
GERHARDT F. MEYNE CO., pg. 746
MEYOCKS BENKSTEIN ASSOCIATES, pg. 746
MI-JACK PRODUCTS, INC., pg. 746
MIA BAMBINI—See Doe Spun, Inc., pg. 343
THE MIAMI MARGARINE CO., pg. 746
MIAMI PAPER COMPANY—See WWF Paper Corporation, pg. 1157
MIAMI SYSTEMS CORPORATION, pg. 746
MIAMI VALLEY BROADCASTING CORPORATION, D/B/A WHIO-TV—See Cox Enterprises, Inc., pg. 292
MICHAEL, BOLGER, REINSCHMIEDT, KING (MBRK), pg. 746
MICHAEL BUSINESS MACHINES CORPORATION, pg. 747
DAVID MICHAEL & CO. INC., pg. 747
MICHAEL FOODS, INC., pg. 747
MICHAEL'S DEVELOPMENT COMPANY, pg. 747
MICHAELS GROUP INC., pg. 747
MICHIGAN BAKERY SUPPLY CO.—See Best Brands, pg. 146
MICHIGAN BLUEBERRY GROWERS ASSN., pg. 747
MICHIGAN MILK PRODUCERS ASSOCIATION, pg. 747
MICHIGAN PHARMACAL—See Eon Labs, Inc., pg. 384
MICHIGAN STATE LOTTERY BUREAU, pg. 747
MICHIGAN TRACTOR AND MACHINERY CO., pg. 747
MICHIGAN WHEEL CORPORATION, pg. 747
MICKEY & COMPANY—See Donnkenny, Inc., pg. 345
MICO INC., pg. 748
MICO, INC., pg. 748
MICO WEST—See Mico Inc., pg. 748
MICOM CARIBE, INC.—See MICOM Communications Corp., pg. 748
MICOM COMMUNICATIONS CORP., pg. 748
MICOM COMMUNICATIONS CORP.—See MICOM Communications Corp., pg. 748
MICRO-AIRE SURGICAL INSTRUMENTS, INC.—See The Marmon Group, Inc., pg. 711

MICRO COMPONENT TECHNOLOGY INC., pg. 748
MICRO ELECTRONICS, pg. 748
MICRO-GEN EQUIPMENT CORP.—See S. C. Johnson & Son, Inc., pg. 599
MICRO-MET L CORP., pg. 748
MICROBAND COMPANIES, INC., pg. 748
MICROCOMPUTER GAMES—See Monarch Avalon, Inc., pg. 765
MICRODOT AEROSPACE FASTENING SYSTEMS GROUP—See MICRODOT, Inc., pg. 749
MICRODOT AEROSPACE LIMITED—See MICRODOT, Inc., pg. 749
MICRODOT, INC., pg. 749
MICRODYNAMICS, INC., pg. 749
MICROFLECT COMPANY, INC., pg. 749
MICROMEDIA LIMITED—See Bell & Howell Company, pg. 135
MICRON SEPARATIONS, INC., pg. 749
MICROPHASE CORPORATION, pg. 749
MICROPUMP—See Micropump Corporation, pg. 749
MICROPUMP CORPORATION, pg. 749
MICROPURE MEDICAL, INC.—See Phillips Plastics Corporation, pg. 867
MICROTEMPS SYSTEMS & PROGRAMMING—See Technical Aid Corporation, pg. 1083
MICROVENA CORPORATION—See Phillips Plastics Corporation, pg. 867
MICROWAVE NETWORKS INCORPORATED, pg. 749
MID-AM BUILDING SUPPLY, INC., pg. 749
MID-AMERICA CDM, INC.—See Harte-Hanks Communications, Inc., pg. 513
MID-AMERICA DAIRYMEN, INC., pg. 750
MID AMERICA INTERNATIONAL TRUCKS, INC., pg. 750
MID AMERICA STEEL, INC., pg. 750
MID ATLANTIC CONSTRUCTION, INC.—See Rodgers Builders, Inc., pg. 943
MID-ATLANTIC CORRECT CRAFT, INC.—See Correct Craft, Inc., pg. 287
MID-CONTINENT CASUALTY CO.—See American Financial Corporation, pg. 53
MID-CONTINENT CASUALTY CO.—See American Financial Corporation, pg. 53
MID-CONTINENT CASUALTY COMPANY—See American Financial Corporation, pg. 53
MID-CONTINENT SCREW PRODUCTS CO., pg. 750
MID-KANSAS CO-OP ASSOCIATION, pg. 750
MID PACIFIC AIR—See KOA Holdings, pg. 613
MID PACIFIC AIR CORPORATION—See KOA Holdings, pg. 613
MID RES SERVICE DIV.—See Midwesco Inc., pg. 751
MID-SOUTH FORD TRUCK SALES, INC., pg. 750
MID-SOUTH MFG. CO.—See UIS, Inc., pg. 1123
MID-SOUTH MILLING COMPANY, INC., pg. 750
MID SOUTH SALES, pg. 750
MID-STATE HOMES, INC.—See Walter Industries, Inc., pg. 1162
MID STATE PRODUCTS CO.—See Osco Industries Inc., pg. 830
MID-STATE WIRE COMPANY—See MCM Enterprises, Inc., pg. 691
MID-STATES FORGING DIE & TOOL CO.—See Modern Drop Forge Co., pg. 762
MID-STATES MORTGAGE CORP.—See Seligman & Associates, Inc., pg. 988
MID-STATES PETROLEUM INC., pg. 750
MID-VALLEY OIL COMPANY, INC.—See Warren Equities Inc., pg. 1165
MID-VALLEY PETROLEUM CORPORATION—See Warren Equities Inc., pg. 1165
MID-WEST AUTOMATION SYSTEMS, pg. 750
MID-WEST COMPANY—See J. H. Roberts Industries Inc., pg. 939
MID WEST CORRECT CRAFT, INC.—See Correct Craft, Inc., pg. 287
MID-WEST PAPER PRODUCTS COMPANY, pg. 750
MIDCO DATA SYSTEMS, INC.—See Dakco Distributors, Inc., pg. 311
MIDCO INTERNATIONAL INC., pg. 751
MIDCOAST INDUSTRIAL SERVICES CORPORATION, pg. 751
MIDCOAST MORTGAGE CORPORATION, pg. 751
MIDDLE WEST SERVICE COMPANY—See SC Companies, Inc., pg. 961
MIDDLESEX INSURANCE CO.—See Sentry Insurance, A Mutual Company, pg. 990
MIDDLESEX INSURANCE CO.—See Middlesex/Patriot General Insurance Companies, pg. 751
THE MIDDLESEX NEWS—See Harte-Hanks Communications, Inc., pg. 513
MIDDLESEX/PATRIOT GENERAL INSURANCE COMPANIES, pg. 751
MIDLAND DAILY NEWS—See The Hearst Corporation, pg. 524
MIDLAND FORGE DIVISION—See Columbus McKinnon Corp., pg. 266
MIDLAND MUTUAL LIFE INSURANCE CO., pg. 751
MIDLAND NATIONAL LIFE INSURANCE CO.—See Sammons Enterprises, Inc., pg. 968
MIDLAND PAPER CO., pg. 751
MIDLAND REPORTER-TELEGRAM—See The Hearst Corporation, pg. 524
MIDLAND SHIRT COMPANY—See Harper Industries, Inc., pg. 510
MIDSOUTH ICE CO.—See Spencer Companies Inc., pg. 1030
MIDSOUTH OIL CO.—See Spencer Companies Inc., pg. 1030
MIDWAY FORD TRUCK CENTER INC., pg. 751
MIDWAY PRODUCTS CORPORATION, pg. 751
MIDWESCO ENERGY SYSTEMS DIV.—See Midwesco Inc., pg. 751
MIDWESCO INC., pg. 751
MIDWESCO MECHANICAL—See Midwesco Inc., pg. 751
MIDWEST AGRI-COMMODITIES—See Southern Minnesota Beet Sugar Cooperative, pg. 1022
MIDWEST AUTO PARTS DISTRIBUTORS, INC., pg. 751
MIDWEST BODY CORPORATION, pg. 752
MIDWEST BOTTLE GAS COMPANY—See Consolidated Midwest, Inc., pg. 277
MIDWEST COAST TRANSPORT L.P., pg. 752
MIDWEST DIVISION—See Hippocrates Partners, pg. 536
MIDWEST EQUIPMENT CO.—See L. Fish Corporation, pg. 414
MIDWEST FASHIONS, INC.—See H.H. Cutler Company, pg. 307
MIDWEST FASTENERS CORPORATION, pg. 752
MIDWEST INDUSTRIES, INC., pg. 752
MIDWEST LITHO ARTS—See Graphisphere Holding Company, pg. 478
MIDWEST MECHANICAL CONTRACTORS INC., pg. 752
MIDWEST MICA—See Kirkwood Industries, Inc., pg. 633
MIDWEST MOTEL SUPPLY—See Super 8 Motels, Inc., pg. 1063
MIDWEST MUTUAL INSURANCE CO.—See Preferred Risk Mutual Insurance, pg. 886
MIDWEST PETROLEUM CO., pg. 752
MIDWEST POLY—See Custom Pak, Inc., pg. 306
MIDWEST PRODUCTS, INC.—See Huntco Inc., pg. 554
MIDWEST TIRE & MUFFLER, INC., pg. 752
MIDWEST VISION CENTERS, pg. 752
MIGHTY DISTRIBUTING SYSTEM, pg. 752
MARILYN MIGLIN, INC., pg. 752
MIKEN COMPANIES, INC., pg. 752
MIL-MOR MEDIA, INC., pg. 753
MILADY BRASSIERE & CORSET CO., INC., pg. 753
MILDRUM MANUFACTURING CO.—See The Napier Company, pg. 783
MILE HIGH ENTERPRISES, INC.—See ARA Group, pg. 6
MILES METAL COMPANY—See The Marmon Group, Inc., pg. 712
MILES SAND & GRAVEL COMPANY, pg. 753
MILEX OF AMERICA, INC., pg. 753
THE MILFORD AGENCY, pg. 753
MILK MARKETING INC., pg. 753
MILK SPECIALTIES COMPANY, pg. 753
MILKY WAY, INC.—See Lynden Incorporated, pg. 689
MILL MAPLE PROPERTIES, INC.—See Washington Mutual Savings Bank, pg. 1166
MILL PLAIN FOUR, INC.—See Washington Mutual Savings Bank, pg. 1166
MILL PLAIN ONE, INC.—See Washington Mutual Savings Bank, pg. 1166
MILL PLAIN THREE, INC.—See Washington Mutual Savings Bank, pg. 1166
MILL PLAIN TWO, INC.—See Washington Mutual Savings Bank, pg. 1166
GEORGE W. MILLAR CO.—See Central Paper Company, pg. 234
MILLBANK ELECTRONICS GROUP LTD.—See American Trading and Production Corporation, pg. 65
MILLER ADVERTISING AGENCY INC., pg. 753
MILLER BROS. INDUSTRIES, INC., pg. 753
MILLER BUILDING CORP., pg. 753
MILLER BUSINESS SYSTEMS, INC., pg. 753
MILLER CHEMICAL & FERTILIZER CORP.—See Alco Industries, Inc., pg. 32
MILLER & CO., pg. 753
MILLER COMPANY, pg. 754
MILLER CURTAIN CO., INC., pg. 754
MILLER ELECTRIC COMPANY, pg. 754
MILLER ELECTRIC MFG. CO., pg. 754
MILLER FLUID POWER CORP., pg. 754
THE MILLER GROUP (UK) LTD.—See Miller Electric Mfg. Co., pg. 754
H. C. MILLER COMPANY, pg. 754
MILLER HARNESS, INC.—See MPO Videotronics, Inc., pg. 693
HOWARD MILLER CLOCK COMPANY, pg. 754
MILLER & LONG CO. INC., pg. 754
MILLER MEESTER ADVERTISING INC., pg. 754
MILLER OIL CO., INC., pg. 754
MILLER PERSONNEL, INC., pg. 755
MILLER PRODUCTS COMPANY, INC., pg. 755
MILLER-ST. NAZIANZ, INC., pg. 755
MILLER & SMITH, INC., pg. 755
MILLER TRANSPORTERS, INC.—See Dewey Corporation, pg. 334
MILLERS' GENERAL INSURANCE COMPANY—See Millers' Mutual Insurance Assn. Of Illinois, pg. 755
MILLERS' MUTUAL INSURANCE ASSN. OF ILLINOIS, pg. 755
THE MILLGARD CORP., pg. 755
MILLIKEN & CO., INC., pg. 755
MILLMASTER ONYX GROUP, INC., pg. 755
MILLS HALL WALBORN & ASSOCIATES, pg. 756
OLAN MILLS, INC., pg. 756
W.G. MILLS, INC., pg. 756
MILLSTEIN INDUSTRIES, pg. 756
MILLSTONE COFFEE, INC., pg. 756
MILLTECH-HOH, INC.—See The HOH Organizations, pg. 497
MILNE FRUIT PRODUCTS—See Ocean Spray Cranberries, Inc., pg. 821
THE MILNOT COMPANY, pg. 756
MILTON CAN CO., INC., pg. 756
MILTON INDUSTRIES, INC., pg. 756
MILTON SHOE MANUFACTURING COMPANY, INC., pg. 756
MILWAUKEE BUCKS, INC., pg. 756
MILWAUKEE ELECTRIC TOOL (CANADA) LTD.—See ESSTAR Incorporated, pg. 361
MILWAUKEE ELECTRIC TOOL CORP.—See ESSTAR Incorporated, pg. 361
THE MILWAUKEE JOURNAL—See Journal Communications Inc., pg. 607
MILWAUKEE SENTINEL—See Journal Communications Inc., pg. 607
MIMLIC ASSET MANAGEMENT COMPANY—See The Minnesota Mutual Life Insurance Company, pg. 758
MIMLIC SALES CORPORATION—See The Minnesota Mutual Life Insurance Company, pg. 758
MINARIK ELECTRIC COMPANY, pg. 756
MINCO PRODUCTS, INC., pg. 756
A. MINDEL & SON, INC.—See Seton Company, pg. 993
MINDGAMES, INC., pg. 756
MINER ENTERPRISES INC., pg. 756
MING SURVEYORS, INC.—See Hoffman Corporation, pg. 538
THE MINGO GROUP, INC., pg. 757
MINI MART, INC., pg. 757
ED MINIAT, INC., pg. 757
MINIATURE PRECISION COMPONENTS, pg. 757
MINING CONTROLS, INC.—See Jupiter Industries, Inc., pg. 609
MINISTERS LIFE INSURANCE COMPANY, pg. 757
MINN-DAK GROWERS, LTD., pg. 757
MINNEAPOLIS AUTO AUCTION—See Cox Enterprises, Inc., pg. 293
MINNESOTA BREWING COMPANY, pg. 757
MINNESOTA ELECTRIC SUPPLY COMPANY, pg. 757
THE MINNESOTA MUTUAL LIFE INSURANCE COMPANY, pg. 757
MINNESOTA SUN PUBLICATIONS—See Guy Gannett Publishing Company, pg. 442
MINNESOTA TWINS BASEBALL CLUB, pg. 758
MINNETONKA BOAT WORKS—See Minstar, Inc., pg. 758
P.W. MINOR & SON, INC., pg. 758
MINOR RUBBER CO., INC., pg. 758
MINOT BUILDERS SUPPLY ASSOCIATION, pg. 758
MINSERCO, INC.—See Bucyrus-Erie Company, pg. 186
MINSTAR, INC., pg. 758
MINSTER AUTOMATION INC.—See The Minster Machine Company, pg. 759
THE MINSTER MACHINE COMPANY, pg. 759
MINTZ & HOKE INC., pg. 759
MINUTEMAN PRESS INTERNATIONAL, pg. 759
MINYARD FOOD STORES, pg. 759
MINYARD PROPERTIES, INC.—See Minyard Food Stores, pg. 759
MISCO INDUSTRIES, pg. 759
MISENER MARINE CONSTRUCTION, pg. 759
MISENER MARINE P.R.—See Misener Marine Construction, pg. 760
MISS ELAINE INC., pg. 760
MISS ELLIETTE, INC., pg. 760
MISSILE SUPPLY CO.—See Electrical Insulation Suppliers, pg. 374
MISSION HILLS RESTAURANT CORP.—See Specialty Restaurants Corporation, pg. 1028
MISSION INDUSTRIES, pg. 760
MISSION SHOPPING CTR.—See R. H. Macy & Co., Inc., pg. 699
MISSION VALLEY MILLS, INC.—See Farley Industries, pg. 400
MISSISSIPPI CHEMICAL CORPORATION, pg. 760
MISSISSIPPI ENERGIES, INC.—See Yazoo Investment Corporation, pg. 1208
MISSISSIPPI LIME CO., pg. 760
MISSISSIPPI PHOSPHATES CORP.—See Mississippi Chemical Corporation, pg. 760
MISSISSIPPI VALLEY GAS CO.—See Yazoo Investment Corporation, pg. 1208
MISSOURI AUCTION SERVICES CORP. D/B/A 166 AUTO ACTION—See Cox Enterprises, Inc., pg. 293
MISSOURI BOILER & TANK CO.—See Nooter Corporation, pg. 808
MISSOURI LOTTERY, pg. 760
MRS. ALISON'S COOKIE COMPANY, pg. 760
MRS. BAIRD'S BAKERIES, INC., pg. 760
MRS. FIELDS' INC., pg. 761
MRS. GOOCHS NATURAL FOOD MARKETS, pg. 761
MRS. GRIMES FOODS—See Faribault Foods Inc., pg. 399
MRS. SCHLORER'S, INC.—See Connelly Containers, Inc., pg. 275
MRS. WINNER'S CHICKEN & BISCUIT RESTAURANTS, pg. 761
MR. ARTICHOKE PACKING CO., INC.—See California Artichoke & Vegetable Growers Corp., pg. 209
MR. CHRISTMAS INC., pg. 761
MR. GASKET COMPANY, pg. 761
MISTER TWISTER—See Sheldons' Inc., pg. 997
MITCHEL & SCOT MACHINE CO., INC., pg. 761
MITCHELL & ASSOC., INC., pg. 761
MITCHELL-BRADFORD INTERNATIONAL—See Hubbard Hall Inc., pg. 549
MITCHELL BUSINESS EQUIPMENT—See The Philadelphia Bourse, Inc., pg. 866
MITCHELL CO.—See Stonecutter Mills Corp., pg. 1051
MITCHELL COACH MANUFACTURING, pg. 761
MITCHELL CORPORATION, CLARE DIV.—See Mitchell Corporation of Owosso, pg. 761
MITCHELL CORPORATION, HANCHETT MANUFACTURING CO.—See Mitchell Corporation of Owosso, pg. 762
MITCHELL CORPORATION OF OWOSSO, pg. 761
JOHN PAUL MITCHELL SYSTEMS, pg. 762
MITCHELL SHACKLETON & CO. LTD.—See National Forge Company, pg. 789
MITEK, INC., pg. 762
MITRE CORPORATION, pg. 762
MO-CAR INTERNACIONAL, S.A.—See 21 International Holdings, Inc., pg. 1121
MOARK MOLD, INC.—See Plastic Engineering Components Inc., pg. 875
MOBILE DRILLING COMPANY, INC.—See Zimmerman Holdings, Inc., pg. 1220
MOBILE TECHNOLOGY INC., pg. 762
MOBILIER INTERNATIONAL—See Haworth, Inc., pg. 518
MODEL GLASS, INC., pg. 762
MODEL MILL CO.—See Windmill Holdings Corp., pg. 1195
HENRY MODELL & COMPANY, INC., pg. 762

MODELS COAT—See Swirl, Inc., pg. 1068
MODERN BUILDING CLEANING INC.—See ARA Group, pg. 7
MODERN CONCRETE SEPTIC TANK COMPANY, pg. 762
MODERN DROP FORGE CO., pg. 762
MODERN EQUIPMENT CO., INC.—See Alco Industries, Inc., pg. 32
MODERN EQUIPMENT RENTALS INC.—See Modern Group Ltd., pg. 763
MODERN FORGE/TENNESSEE—See Modern Drop Forge Co., pg. 762
MODERN GROUP LTD., pg. 762
MODERN HANDLING EQUIPMENT CO. OF NY—See Modern Group Ltd., pg. 763
MODERN HANDLING EQUIPMENT CO.—See Modern Group Ltd., pg. 763
MODERN HANDLING EQUIPMENT OF N.J., INC.—See Modern Group Ltd., pg. 763
MODERN HEALTHCARE—See Crain Communications, Inc., pg. 295
MODERN HILIFT EQUIPMENT CO.—See Modern Group Ltd., pg. 763
MODERN HOME CARE PRODUCTS PVT. LTD.—See S. C. Johnson & Son, Inc., pg. 600
MODERN PACKAGING CORP.—See Superior Container, Inc., pg. 1063
MODERN TALKING PICTURE SERVICE, INC.—See KDI Corporation, pg. 612
MODERN TIRE DEALER—See Bill Communications, Inc., pg. 150
MODERN WELDING CO., INC., pg. 763
MODERN WOOD PRODUCTS, INC.—See Cowden Metal Specialties, Inc., pg. 291
MODERN WOODMEN OF AMERICA, pg. 763
MODULITE CORPORATION, pg. 763
MOELLER MARINE PRODUCTS—See Moore Company, pg. 768
MOGAS INDUSTRIES, INC., pg. 763
MOHAWK DISTILLED PRODUCTS, pg. 763
MOHAWK FURNITURE, INC.—See Gem Industries Finance Corporation, pg. 447
MOHAWK PAPER MILLS, INC., pg. 763
MOHAWK PLASTICS, INC., pg. 763
MOHAWK TOOLS—See Precision Twist Drill Co., pg. 885
WALLACE MOIR CO., pg. 763
MOJ MIKRO—See International Data Group, pg. 577
MOL-BEE, INC.—See Plastic Engineering Components Inc., pg. 875
MOLDCRAFT PLASTICS INC.—See Poly-Seal Corporation, pg. 880
MOLDED FIBER GLASS COMPANIES, pg. 763
MOLDED FIBER GLASS TRAY CO.—See Molded Fiber Glass Companies, pg. 764
MOLDED FIBER GLASS/WEST—See Molded Fiber Glass Companies, pg. 764
MOLESPHINI & TOBIN, INC., pg. 764
MOLIN AUTO PARTS INC., pg. 764
MOLINE ACCESSORIES COMPANY—See Montgomery Elevator Company, pg. 767
MOLINE ACCESSORIES CORPORATION—See Montgomery Elevator Company, pg. 767
MOLINE CORPORATION, pg. 764
MOLLENBERG-BETZ INC., pg. 764
MOLON MOTOR & COIL CORP., pg. 764
MOLTRUP STEEL PRODUCTS COMPANY, pg. 764
MONA INDUSTRIES, INC., pg. 764
EDWARD V. MONAHAN INC., pg. 765
MONARCH AVALON, INC., pg. 765
THE MONARCH COMPANY, INC., pg. 765
MONARCH CONSTRUCTION COMPANY, pg. 765
MONARCH FOODS, INC.—See Shakey's Incorporated, pg. 994
MONARCH IMPORT CO., INC., pg. 765
MONARCH LUGGAGE CO. INC., pg. 765
MONARCH TOY CO., LTD.—See Monarch Avalon, Inc., pg. 765
MONARK EGG CORPORATION, pg. 765
MONEX INTERNATIONAL, LTD., pg. 765
MONEY POINT DIAMOND CO., pg. 765
MONFRIED OPTICAL—See Duling Optical Corporation, pg. 352
MONGOLD LUMBER CO.—See Marmac Corporation, pg. 710
MONICO ALLOYS, INC., pg. 765
MONIER ROOF TILE, INC., pg. 765
MONITOR AEROSPACE CORPORATION, pg. 765
MONITOR CAPITAL ADVISORS INC.—See New York Life Insurance Company, pg. 803
MONITOR CONSTRUCTION CO.—See Dugan & Meyers Interests, Inc., pg. 351
MONITOR LIFE INSURANCE COMPANY OF NEW YORK—See Commercial Travelers Mutual Insurance Company, pg. 269
A.C. MONK CO., INC., pg. 766
MONK-HENDERSON TOBACCO CO.—See A.C. Monk Co., Inc., pg. 766
MONKEM COMPANY, INC.—See Burlington Motor Carriers Inc., pg. 191
MONORAIL, INC.—See Columbian Rope Company, pg. 266
MONROC, INC., pg. 766
MONROE FOODS/DESSERT MASTERS—See B. Green & Co., pg. 484
MONROE PRINTING COMPANY—See Mack Printing Company, pg. 697
MONROE SYSTEMS FOR BUSINESS, INC., pg. 766
MONROVIA NURSERY CO., pg. 766
MONSEY PRODUCTS COMPANY, pg. 766
F.G. MONTABERT, pg. 766
B. L. MONTAGUE CO., pg. 766
MONTANA CITY PLANT—See Ash Grove Cement Company, pg. 88
MONTANA LOTTERY, pg. 766
MONTE VISTA CO-OP ASSOCIATION, INC., pg. 766
MONTEBELLO BRANDS INC., pg. 767
MONTEREY MECHANICAL COMPANY, pg. 767
MONTEREY MUSHROOMS, INC.—See JMB Realty Corporation, pg. 585
MONTEREY'S TEX MEX CAFE, pg. 767
BOB MONTGOMERY CHEVROLET/HONDA, pg. 767
MONTGOMERY ELEVATOR COMPANY, pg. 767
MONTGOMERY ELEVATOR EXPORT CORPORATION—See Montgomery Elevator Company, pg. 767
MONTGOMERY-GREEN CO.—See Edward Don & Company of Illinois, pg. 344
JAMES M. MONTGOMERY CONSULTING ENGINEERS, pg. 767
MONTGOMERY WARD & CO., INC., pg. 767
MONTGOMERY, ZUKERMAN, DAVIS, INC., pg. 768
MONTICELLO TANK, INC.—See Chicago Tube & Iron Co., pg. 246
MONTREAL FAST PRINT—See American Fast Print, Limited, pg. 52
MONTRES MOVADO, S.A.—See North American Watch Corporation, pg. 812
MONUMENTAL MILLWORK, INC., pg. 768
MONY ADVISERS, INC.—See The Mutual Life Insurance Company of New York (MONY), pg. 778
MONY BROKERAGE, INC.—See The Mutual Life Insurance Company of New York (MONY), pg. 778
MONY CREDIT CORPORATION—See The Mutual Life Insurance Company of New York (MONY), pg. 778
MONY CS, INC.—See The Mutual Life Insurance Company of New York (MONY), pg. 778
MONY FUNDING, INC.—See The Mutual Life Insurance Company of New York (MONY), pg. 778
MONY LIFE INSURANCE CO. OF AMERICA—See The Mutual Life Insurance Company of New York (MONY), pg. 778
MONY REALTY PARTNERS, INC.—See The Mutual Life Insurance Company of New York (MONY), pg. 778
MONY SECURITIES CORP.—See The Mutual Life Insurance Company of New York (MONY), pg. 778
MONY SECURITIES CORP.—See The Mutual Life Insurance Company of New York (MONY), pg. 778
MONY TAX CONSULTING SERVICES, INC.—See The Mutual Life Insurance Company of New York (MONY), pg. 778
M. D. MOODY & SONS INC., pg. 768
MOONEY AIRCRAFT CORPORATION, pg. 768
MOONEY CHEMICALS, pg. 768
MOORE BEARING CO.—See Invetech Co., pg. 582
MOORE COMPANY, pg. 768
E. R. MOORE CO., pg. 768
MOORE, EPSTEIN, MOORE, pg. 768
THE J.W. MOORE GROUP, pg. 768
HAROLD MOORE & ASSOCIATES, INC., pg. 768
REX MOORE ELECTRICAL CONTRACTORS & ENGINEERS, pg. 768
MOORE SPECIAL TOOL AG—See Moore Special Tool Co., Inc., pg. 768
MOORE SPECIAL TOOL CO., INC., pg. 768
MOORGATE ADVERTISING AGENCY, pg. 768
MOORMAN MFG. COMPANY, pg. 769
MORADPOUR, DALSACE, LANGLOIS, PIZANTI—See Young & Rubicam Inc., pg. 1212
MORAN INDUSTRIES, INC., pg. 769
ART MORAN PONTIAC-GMC INC., pg. 769
MORAN TOWING OF FLORIDA—See Moran Towing & Transporation Co. Inc, pg. 769
MORAN TOWING OF MAINE—See Moran Towing & Transporation Co. Inc, pg. 769
MORAN TOWING OF MARYLAND—See Moran Towing & Transporation Co. Inc, pg. 769
MORAN TOWING OF PENNSYLVANIA, INC.—See Moran Towing & Transporation Co. Inc, pg. 769
MORAN TOWING OF TEXAS—See Moran Towing & Transporation Co. Inc, pg. 769
MORAN TOWING & TRANSPORATION CO. INC, pg. 769
MORAN TOWING OF VIRGINIA—See Moran Towing & Transporation Co. Inc, pg. 769
MORECO INC.—See Modern Group Ltd., pg. 763
MORFLEX, INC.—See Reilly Industries, Inc., pg. 923
MORGAN CONSTRUCTION COMPANY, pg. 769
MORGAN COUNTY NEWS—See Landmark Communications, Inc., pg. 655
MORGAN FOOD PRODUCTS—See Morgan Manufacturing Company, Inc., pg. 770
MORGAN FOODS, INC., pg. 770
MORGAN INDUSTRIES INC., pg. 770
MORGAN MANUFACTURING COMPANY, INC., pg. 770
MORGAN REALTY ASSOCIATES, pg. 770
MORGAN TECHNICAL SERVICES, INC—See Morgan Construction Company, pg. 770
MORGUARD INVESTMENTS LIMITED, TORONTO—See Metropolitan Life Insurance Co., pg. 745
MORITZ CADILLAC-SAAB INC., pg. 770
MORLEY CONSTRUCTION CO., INC.—See Morley Group, pg. 770
MORLEY GROUP, pg. 770
MORLEY SHIRT COMPANY—See Custom Shop Shirtmakers Inc., pg. 306
MORMAC MARINE TRANSPORT, INC., pg. 770
MORNING GLORY FARMS REGION, pg. 770
MOROCH & ASSOC., INC., pg. 770
MOROCH, INC.—See Moroch & Assoc., Inc., pg. 771
MORONI FEED CO.—See Norbest, Inc., pg. 809
JOHN MORRELL & CO.—See American Financial Corporation, pg. 54
WILLIAM MORRIS AGENCY, INC., pg. 771
E.K. MORRIS & CO., INC.—See Art Iron, Inc., pg. 86
T.J. MORRIS COMPANY, INC., pg. 771
MORRIS CORPORATION—See Shivers Trading & Operating Co., pg. 999
MORRIS COUPLING CO., pg. 771
MORRIS NEWSPAPER CORPORATION, pg. 771
THE ROBERT E. MORRIS COMPANY, pg. 771
THE MORRISON AGENCY, pg. 771
MORRISON, INC., pg. 771
MORRISON TEXTILE MACHINERY CO., pg. 771
WILLIAM MORROW & CO., INC.—See The Hearst Corporation, pg. 521
MORROW JUNIOR BOOKS—See The Hearst Corporation, pg. 522
MORSE AUTOMOTIVE PRODUCTS—See Borg-Warner Corporation, pg. 166
ED MORSE CHEVROLET INC.—See Morse Operations Inc., pg. 772
MORSE DIESEL INTERNATIONAL, pg. 771
ED MORSE DODGE, INC.—See Morse Operations Inc., pg. 772
MORSE OPERATIONS INC., pg. 772
MORSE SHOE, INC., pg. 772
MORSE SHOE LEASED DIV.—See Morse Shoe, Inc., pg. 772
M. A. MORTENSON COMPANY, pg. 772
MORTON'S JEWELRY CO.—See Reliable Stores, Inc., pg. 925
TOM MOSER PORSCHE AUDI—See Bill Woeste Dealer Group, pg. 1198
MOSLER CANADA—See American Standard Inc., pg. 62
MOSLER COUNTER SYSTEMS DIV.—See Mosler Inc., pg. 772
MOSLER DROPOSITORY DIV.—See Mosler Inc., pg. 772
MOSLER ELECTRONIC SYSTEMS DIV.—See Mosler Inc., pg. 772
MOSLER INC., pg. 772
MOSLER, INC.—See Mosler Inc., pg. 772
MOSLER SA DE C.D.—See Mosler Inc., pg. 772
MOSS AND COMPANY, INC., pg. 772
MOSS & LOWENHAUPT CIGAR CO.—See Faber, Coe & Gregg, Inc., pg. 395
MOSS TELECOMMUNICATIONS SERVICES, pg. 772
MOSSBERG INDUSTRIES, INC., pg. 772
O. F. MOSSBERG & SONS, INC., pg. 773
MOTEK ENGINEERING & MANUFACTURING COMPANY, pg. 773
MOTHER EARTH NEWS, pg. 773
MOTHERS BACK ISSUES, INC.—See Mother Earth News, pg. 773
MOTHER'S BOOKSHELF—See Mother Earth News, pg. 773
MOTIVATION S.P.A.—See Carlson Companies, Inc., pg. 221
MOTIVATIONAL INCENTIVES GROUP—See Western International Media Corporation, pg. 1180
MOTO, INC., pg. 773
MOTOR BOATING & SAILING—See The Hearst Corporation, pg. 523
MOTOR CONSUMER BOOKS—See The Hearst Corporation, pg. 522
MOTOR CRASH ESTIMATING GUIDE—See The Hearst Corporation, pg. 522
MOTOR MAGAZINE—See The Hearst Corporation, pg. 522
MOTOR MASTER PRODUCTS—See Zeller Corp., pg. 1217
MOTOR PUBLICATIONS—See The Hearst Corporation, pg. 522
MOTOR WHEEL CORPORATION, pg. 773
MOTORISTS MUTUAL INSURANCE CO., pg. 773
THE MOTORLEASE CORP., pg. 773
MOULTON CUTTING CO.—See J. H. Roberts Industries Inc., pg. 939
MOUNT BACHELOR VILLAGE CORP.—See Brooks Resources Corporation, pg. 180
MOUNT JACKSON PRESS, INC.—See Judd's Incorporated, pg. 608
MOUNT VERNON DEMOCRAT—See Landmark Communications, Inc., pg. 655
MOUNT VERNON DRYER FABRICS—See R. B. Pamplin Corp., pg. 845
MOUNT VERNON MILLS, INC.—See R. B. Pamplin Corp., pg. 844
MOUNT VERNON MILLS, INC.—See R. B. Pamplin Corp., pg. 844
MOUNT VERNON MILLS, INC., CLARKTON, NC—See R. B. Pamplin Corp., pg. 844
MOUNT VERNON MILLS, INC., CONSUMER PRODUCTS DIV. (MCCORMICK)—See R. B. Pamplin Corp., pg. 844
MOUNT VERNON MILLS, INC., LAFRANCE INDUSTRIES—See R. B. Pamplin Corp., pg. 844
MOUNT VERNON MILLS, INC., MOUNT VERNON FORMING FABRICS—See R. B. Pamplin Corp., pg. 844
MOUNT VERNON MILLS, INC., RIEGEL CONSUMER PRODUCTS DIV.—See R. B. Pamplin Corp., pg. 844
MOUNT VERNON MILLS, INC., RIEGEL TEXTILE DIV.—See R. B. Pamplin Corp., pg. 844
MOUNT VERNON MILLS, INC., RIEGEL TEXTILE DIV. (ALTO)—See R. B. Pamplin Corp., pg. 844
MOUNT VERNON MILLS, INC., RIEGEL TEXTILE DIV. (TRION)—See R. B. Pamplin Corp., pg. 844
MOUNT VERNON MILLS, INC., TALLASSEE, AL—See R. B. Pamplin Corp., pg. 844
MOUNT VERNON MILLS, INC., WILLIAMSTON—See R. B. Pamplin Corp., pg. 844
MOUNT VERNON MILLS, INC., WOODRUFF—See R. B. Pamplin Corp., pg. 845
MOUNT VERNON MILLS, SMITH & WATERS, INC.—See R. B. Pamplin Corp., pg. 845
MOUNT VERNON NEON—See Everbrite, Inc., pg. 391
MT. WALDO OPERATIONS—See Gerrity Co., Inc., pg. 454
MOUNTAIN AIR DELIVERY, pg. 773
MOUNTAIN STATES CONSTRUCTORS, INC., pg. 773
MOUNTAIN STATES PIPE & SUPPLY COMPANY, pg. 773
MOUNTAIN VALLEY SPRING COMPANY—See Sammons Enterprises, Inc., pg. 968
MOUNTAINEER MEDICAL/PRIMACARE I.V.—See Syracuse Supply Company, pg. 1070
MOVADO MUSEUM DESIGNS INTERNATIONAL LTD.—See North American Watch Corporation, pg. 812
MOVADO WATCH COMPANY, S.A.—See North American Watch Corporation, pg. 812

ERIC MOWER AND ASSOCIATES/BUFFALO, INC.—See Eric Mower and Associates, Inc., pg. 774
ERIC MOWER AND ASSOCIATES, INC., pg. 774
MOYER MITCHELL COMPANY, INC., pg. 774
MOYER PACKING COMPANY, pg. 774
MOYER PRODUCTS, INC., pg. 774
MOZEL DEVELOPMENT CORP., pg. 774
MTV ASIA—See National Amusements, Inc., pg. 785
MTV AUSTRALIA—See National Amusements, Inc., pg. 785
MTV BRAZIL—See National Amusements, Inc., pg. 785
MTV EUROPE—See National Amusements, Inc., pg. 785
MTV JAPAN—See National Amusements, Inc., pg. 785
MTV: MUSIC TELEVISION—See National Amusements, Inc., pg. 785
MUBEN REALTY CO.—See Mutual Benefit Life Insurance Company, pg. 778
MUEBLES FINO BUENO—See Good Companies, pg. 470
MUELHENS, INC., pg. 774
MUELLER, A HAWORTH PORTFOLIO CO.—See Haworth, Inc., pg. 518
MUELLER MACK, pg. 774
R.A. MUELLER, INC., pg. 774
MUELLER SPORTS MEDICINE, INC., pg. 774
MUENCH-KREUZER CANDLE COMPANY, pg. 774
C. A. MUER CORP., pg. 774
MUFFLER WAREHOUSE, INC.—See Carquest Corporation, pg. 225
MUHLHAUSER & YOUNG, pg. 774
MULACH PARKING STRUCTURES CORP.—See Mulach Steel Corporation, pg. 775
MULACH STEEL CORPORATION, pg. 775
MULBERRY METAL PRODUCTS, INC., pg. 775
MULDER HARDENBERG B.V.—See Panduit Company, pg. 845
MULHERN BELTING, INC., pg. 775
MULLE/BREEN ADVERTISING, pg. 775
MULLEN ADVERTISING, INC., pg. 775
ED MULLINAX FORD, INC., pg. 775
MULLINS LEAF TOBACCO CO.—See Austin Co., Inc., pg. 99
MULTI-AD SERVICES, INC., pg. 775
MULTI LANGUAGE CENTER SRL—See Berlitz International, Inc., pg. 143
MULTI-LINE CAN CO.—See Lykes Brothers Inc. of Florida, pg. 688
MULTI-MEDIA MARKETING COMMUNICATIONS, INC. (M.M.M.C., INC.), pg. 775
MULTI MEDIA SERVICES CORP., pg. 775
MULTI-PLEX, INC.—See Davis Industries Inc., pg. 318
MULTICONTACT—See Young & Rubicam Inc., pg. 1212
MULTIFORM ENTERPRISES, INC.—See GranTree Corporation, pg. 478
MULTIMATIC CORPORATION, pg. 775
MULTIPLE ALLIED SERVICES, INC., pg. 775
MULTIPLE PARKING SERVICES, INC.—See Allright Corporation, pg. 42
MULTISERV INTERNATIONAL LTD.—See The Dyson-Kissner-Moran Corporation, pg. 358
MUNCIE DIVISION—See Witt Company, pg. 1198
MICHAEL J. MUNGO COMPANY, INC., pg. 775
MUNIGLE CORPORATION, pg. 775
MUNITIONS TECHNOLOGY DIVISION—See Day & Zimmermann, Inc., pg. 320
MUNRO & COMPANY, INC., pg. 775
MUNROE, INC., pg. 776
MUNSEN'S DISCOVERY ENTERPRISES, pg. 776
MUNSEN'S DISCOVERY TRAVEL—See Munsen's Discovery Enterprises, pg. 776
MURALO CO., INC., pg. 776
MURDOCK, INC., pg. 776
MURO PHARMACEUTICAL, INC., pg. 776
MURPHY COMPANY, pg. 776
MURPHY FARMS INC., pg. 776
MURPHY FAVRE HOUSE MANAGERS, INC.—See Washington Mutual Savings Bank, pg. 1166
MURPHY FAVRE, INC.—See Washington Mutual Savings Bank, pg. 1166
MURPHY FAVRE PROPERTIES, INC.—See Washington Mutual Savings Bank, pg. 1166
MURPHY FAVRE SECURITIES SERVICES, INC.—See Washington Mutual Savings Bank, pg. 1166
MURPHY INTERNATIONAL—See Murphy Company, pg. 776
MURPHY PLYWOOD—See Murphy Company, pg. 776
MURPHY PROPERTIES, INC.—See Murphy Company, pg. 776
MURPHY TIMBER—See Murphy Company, pg. 776
MURRAY-CARVER, pg. 776
MURRAY DRUG—See Eon Labs, Inc., pg. 384
ARTHUR MURRAY ENTERPRISES, INC.—See Arthur Murray Intl., Inc., pg. 776
ARTHUR MURRAY INTL., INC., pg. 776
JOHN F. MURRAY ADVERTISING AGENCY INC., pg. 776
MURRAY TURBOMACHINERY CORPORATION—See Coppus Engineering Corp., pg. 285
MURRAY'S DISCOUNT AUTO STORES, pg. 777
MURRY'S, INC., pg. 777
MUSCUM BOUTIQUE INTERCONTINENTAL, LTD., pg. 777
MUSE CORDERO CHEN, INC., pg. 777
MUSIC SALES CORPORATION, pg. 777
MUSKA ELECTRIC COMPANY, pg. 777
MUSKEGON CONSTRUCTION COMPANY—See Owen-Ames-Kimball Co., pg. 833
MUSKIN LEISURE PRODUCTS, INC., pg. 777
MUSTANG INDUSTRIAL EQUIPMENT CO.—See Mustang Tractor & Equip. Co., pg. 777
MUSTANG MANUFACTURING COMPANY, INC., pg. 777
MUSTANG POWER SYSTEMS—See Mustang Tractor & Equip. Co., pg. 777
MUSTANG TRACTOR & EQUIP. CO., pg. 777
MUTUAL OF AMERICA, pg. 777
MUTUAL OF AMERICA FINANCIAL SERVICES CORP.—See Mutual of America, pg. 778
MUTUAL BENEFIT FINANCIAL SERVICE CO.—See Mutual Benefit Life Insurance Company, pg. 778
MUTUAL BENEFIT LIFE INSURANCE COMPANY, pg. 778
MUTUAL DISTRIBUTORS LTD., pg. 778
THE MUTUAL LIFE INSURANCE COMPANY OF NEW YORK (MONY), pg. 778
MUTUAL MANUFACTURING & SUPPLY CO., pg. 778
MUTUAL OF OMAHA—See Mutual of Omaha Insurance Company, pg. 779
MUTUAL OF OMAHA FUND MANAGEMENT CO.—See Mutual of Omaha Insurance Company, pg. 779
MUTUAL OF OMAHA INSURANCE COMPANY, pg. 779
MUTUAL SAVINGS FIRE INSURANCE COMPANY—See Victory Financial Group, Inc., pg. 1150
MUTUAL SAVINGS LIFE INSURANCE COMPANY—See Victory Financial Group, Inc., pg. 1150
MUTUAL SERVICE CORPORATION—See Pacific Mutual Life Insurance Company, pg. 841
MUTUAL TRADING CO., INC., pg. 779
MUTUAL TRAVEL, INC.—See Washington Mutual Savings Bank, pg. 1166
MUTUAL WELDING CO., LTD, pg. 779
MY OWN MEALS, INC., pg. 779
MYERS & ASSOCIATES, INC., pg. 780
F.W. MYERS & CO.—See The Myers Group (U.S) Inc., pg. 780
THE MYERS GROUP (U.S) INC., pg. 780
MYERS GROUP U.S., INC.—See The Myers Group (U.S) Inc., pg. 780
C. C. MYERS, INC., pg. 780
BEN MYERSON CANDY COMPANY, INC., pg. 780
MYONNE PANTIES—See I. Appel Corporation, pg. 78
MYRICK CONSTRUCTION INC., pg. 780
MYRON MANUFACTURING CORPORATION, pg. 780
MYSTIC STAMP COMPANY—See Littleton Coin Co., Inc., pg. 679

N

N.A. TRADING LTD.—See North American Watch Corporation, pg. 812
N.B. JACKETS DIVISION—See Bell & Howell Company, pg. 135
NBBJ, pg. 780
NBBJ/LPA—See NBBJ, pg. 780
NBBJ-ROSENFIELD—See NBBJ, pg. 780
N.B.K. GEOSCIENCES, LTD.—See Fugro-McClelland, Inc., pg. 436
NBO STORES INC., pg. 780
NBS CARD SERVICES, INC.—See SBN System Inc., pg. 960
NBS IMAGING SYSTEMS, INC.—See SBN System Inc., pg. 960
NBS LIMITED-CARD SERVICES DIVISION—See SBN System Inc., pg. 960
NBS LIMITED-CARD SYSTEMS DIVISION—See SBN System Inc., pg. 960
NBS SOUTHERN, INC.—See SBN System Inc., pg. 960
NBSC INVESTMENT CO.—See High Point Financial Corp., pg. 534
NCM DECORATION, INC.—See NMC of North America, Inc., pg. 781
NAP-LTD.—See TMP Worldwide, Inc., pg. 1074
NDAP/TMP WORLDWIDE—See TMP Worldwide, Inc., pg. 1074
NDC CO. LTD.—See The Pullman Company, pg. 900
NDC DISTRIBUTORS, INC.—See National Distributing Co., Inc., pg. 787
N E D CORP., pg. 780
NER HOLDINGS, INC.—See Hargro Enterprises, Inc., pg. 509
NFM CREATIVE COMMUNICATIONS, pg. 780
NFO RESEARCH, INC., pg. 780
NJF INVESTMENT GROUP, INC.—See Pacific Mutual Life Insurance Company, pg. 841
NKH&W, INC., pg. 781
NMC OF NORTH AMERICA, INC., pg. 781
NPG OF ARIZONA, INC.—See News-Press & Gazette Company, pg. 805
NPS CORPORATION, pg. 781
NPS ENERGY SERVICES, INC.—See Day & Zimmermann, Inc., pg. 321
NPS, INC.—See Day & Zimmermann, Inc., pg. 321
NRM CORPORATION, pg. 781
NS LAND COMPANY—See National Steel Corporation, pg. 794
NSK-WARNER K.K.—See Borg-Warner Corporation, pg. 166
N&T LEO BURNETT A/S—See Leo Burnett Company, Inc., pg. 193
NTC APPAREL FABRICS DIVISION—See NTC Group, pg. 781
NTC CONSUMER PRODUCTS DIV.—See NTC Group, pg. 781
NTC ENGINEERED PRODUCTS DIV.—See NTC Group, pg. 781
NTC GROUP, pg. 781
NTH CONSULTANTS, LTD., pg. 781
NTH CONSULTANTS, LTD.—See NTH Consultants, Ltd., pg. 781
NTH CONSULTANTS, LTD.—See NTH Consultants, Ltd., pg. 781
NTS CORPORATION, pg. 781
N.W. TRANSPORT SERVICE, INC., pg. 781
NWA, INC., pg. 782
NWS, INC., pg. 782
NABHOLZ CONSTRUCTION CORP., pg. 782
NA-CHURS PLANT FOOD COMPANY, pg. 782
NACOMA CONSOLIDATED, INC., pg. 782
JACK NADEL, INC. DIV.—See Measured Marketing Services, pg. 734
NADEL PARTNERSHIP, INC., pg. 782
THE NADEL PARTNERSHIP, INC.—See Nadel Partnership, Inc., pg. 783
THE NADEL PARTNERSHIP, INC.—See Nadel Partnership, Inc., pg. 783
NADY SYSTEMS, INC., pg. 783
FRANK C. NAHSER INC., pg. 783
NALLEYS FINE FOODS—See Agway, Inc., pg. 25
NAMICO, INC., pg. 783
NANA DEVELOPMENT CORPORATION—See Nana Regional Corporation, Inc., pg. 783
NANA REGIONAL CORPORATION, INC., pg. 783
THE NAPIER COMPANY, pg. 783
NARRAGANSETT CAPITAL INC., pg. 783
NARROW FABRIC INDUSTRIES, INC., pg. 783
NASCO—See Geneve Corporation, pg. 452
NASH DO BRASIL BOMBAS LTDA.—See The Nash Engineering Company, pg. 784
NASH ENGINEERING CO. (GREAT BRITAIN) LTD.—See The Nash Engineering Company, pg. 784
THE NASH ENGINEERING COMPANY, pg. 783
THE NASH ENGINEERING COMPANY OF CANADA, LTD.—See The Nash Engineering Company, pg. 784
NASHUA HOMES OF IDAHO INC., pg. 784
NASHVILLE MACHINE CO. INC., pg. 784
NASHVILLE STEEL CORP., pg. 784
NASHVILLE TEXTILE CORP.—See House of Ronnie, Inc., pg. 546
NASHVILLE WIRE PRODUCT CO., pg. 784
NASON AND CULLEN, INC., pg. 784
NASON AUTOMOTIVE—See The O'Brien Corporation, pg. 820
NATHAN'S FAMOUS INC., pg. 784
THE NATION—See Shepaug Corporation, pg. 998
NATIONAL ACADEMY SCIENCES USA, pg. 784
NATIONAL AMUSEMENTS, INC., pg. 784
NATIONAL ATLAS LIFE INSURANCE CO.—See Zale Corporation, pg. 1216
NATIONAL ATTORNEYS TITLE INSURANCE COMPANY, pg. 786
NATIONAL AUTO DEALERS EXCHANGE—See Cox Enterprises, Inc., pg. 293
NATIONAL AUTO RESEARCH—See The Hearst Corporation, pg. 522
NATIONAL BAND & TAG CO., pg. 786
THE NATIONAL BANK OF SUSSEX COUNTY—See High Point Financial Corp., pg. 534
NATIONAL BANNER COMPANY, pg. 786
NATIONAL BASKETBALL ASSOCIATION, pg. 786
NATIONAL BEDDING & FURNITURE INDUSTRIES, pg. 786
NATIONAL BEEF PACKING COMPANY—See Union Holdings, Inc., pg. 1128
NATIONAL BOOK COMPANY INC.—See W.W. Norton & Company, Inc., pg. 816
NATIONAL BRANDS BEVERAGE DIV.—See Agway, Inc., pg. 25
NATIONAL BRANDS, INC., pg. 786
NATIONAL BUILDING SYSTEMS—See LWMCK Corporation, pg. 648
NATIONAL BULK CARRIERS, INC., pg. 786
NATIONAL CAR RENTAL SYSTEM, INC., pg. 786
NATIONAL CARRIERS, INC.—See Union Holdings, Inc., pg. 1128
NATIONAL CASUALTY CO.—See Nationwide Mutual Insurance Company, pg. 795
NATIONAL CLEANING CONTRACTORS, INC., pg. 786
NATIONAL COMPUTER PRINT, INC., pg. 786
NATIONAL COMPUTER SUPPLIES—See Riccobon & Company, Inc., pg. 931
NATIONAL CONCRETE PRODUCTS COMPANY, pg. 787
NATIONAL COOPERATIVE REFINERY ASSOCIATION, pg. 787
NATIONAL CORSET SUPPLY HOUSE, pg. 787
NATIONAL DEVELOPMENT CO., INC.—See Sunstates Realty Group Inc., pg. 1062
NATIONAL DIECASTING MACHINERY—See Racine Federated, Inc., pg. 909
NATIONAL DISTRIBUTING CO., INC., pg. 787
NATIONAL DISTRIBUTING CO., INC.—See National Distributing Co., Inc., pg. 787
NATIONAL DISTRIBUTING CO., INC.—See National Distributing Co., Inc., pg. 787
NATIONAL DISTRIBUTING CO., INC.—See National Distributing Co., Inc., pg. 787
NATIONAL DISTRIBUTING CO., INC.—See National Distributing Co., Inc., pg. 787
NATIONAL DISTRIBUTING CO., INC.—See National Distributing Co., Inc., pg. 787
NATIONAL DISTRIBUTING CO., INC.—See National Distributing Co., Inc., pg. 787
NATIONAL DISTRIBUTING CO., INC.—See National Distributing Co., Inc., pg. 787
NATIONAL DISTRIBUTING CO., INC.—See National Distributing Co., Inc., pg. 787
NATIONAL DISTRIBUTING CO., INC.—See National Distributing Co., Inc., pg. 787
NATIONAL DISTRIBUTING CO., INC.—See National Distributing Co., Inc., pg. 787
NATIONAL EMERGENCY SERVICES, INC., pg. 788
NATIONAL ENGINEERING & CONTRACTING CO., pg. 788
THE NATIONAL ENQUIRER, pg. 788
NATIONAL FEDERATION OF COMMUNITY DEVELOPMENT CREDIT UNIONS—See Credit Union National Association, pg. 298
NATIONAL FINANCIAL INSURANCE COMPANY, pg. 788
NATIONAL FIRE PROTECTION ASSOCIATION, pg. 788
NATIONAL FOOD STORES, INC. T/A KRAUSZER'S, pg. 788
NATIONAL FOODS INC., pg. 788
NATIONAL FOOTBALL LEAGUE PROPERTIES, INC., pg. 788
NATIONAL FORGE COMPANY, pg. 788

NATIONAL FORGE ENGINEERED SYSTEMS DIV.—See National Forge Company, pg. 789
NATIONAL FORGE EUROPE NV—See National Forge Company, pg. 789
NATIONAL FORGE EXPORT CORP.—See National Forge Company, pg. 789
NATIONAL FROZEN FOODS CORP., pg. 789
NATIONAL FRUIT PRODUCT COMPANY, pg. 789
NATIONAL-GENERAL SUPPLY, INC.—See Carl Weissman & Sons, Inc., pg. 1174
NATIONAL GEOGRAPHIC SOCIETY, pg. 789
NATIONAL GRAPE CO-OP ASSOCIATION, INC., pg. 789
NATIONAL GROUP, INC., pg. 789
NATIONAL GYPSUM COMPANY, pg. 790
NATIONAL HEALTH CARE AFFILIATES, INC., pg. 791
NATIONAL HEALTH LABORATORIES INC.—See MacAndrews & Forbes Holdings Inc., pg. 696
NATIONAL HEALTH PRODUCTS, pg. 791
NATIONAL HERITAGE, INC.—See Evergreen Healthcare Ltd., pg. 392
NATIONAL HOTEL CORP.—See Carlson Companies, Inc., pg. 221
NATIONAL LABEL COMPANY, pg. 791
NATIONAL LAMINATION CO.—See Tang Industries Inc., pg. 1078
THE NATIONAL LATEX PRODUCTS CO., pg. 791
NATIONAL LIBERTY, pg. 791
NATIONAL LIFE INSURANCE COMPANY, pg. 791
NATIONAL LIFE INVESTMENT MANAGEMENT CO., INC.—See National Life Insurance Company, pg. 791
NATIONAL LIVE STOCK & MEAT BOARD, pg. 792
NATIONAL LUMBER CO., pg. 792
NATIONAL MACHINERY ADV. SERVICES, pg. 792
NATIONAL MACHINERY COMPANY, pg. 792
THE NATIONAL MAGAZINE COMPANY LTD.—See The Hearst Corporation, pg. 524
NATIONAL MARINE, INC.—See Vectura Group, Inc., pg. 1146
NATIONAL MATERIAL LIMITED PARTNERSHIP—See Tang Industries Inc., pg. 1078
NATIONAL MEDIA MAIL, INC., pg. 792
NATIONAL MEDIA SERVICES, INC.—See TMP Worldwide, Inc., pg. 1074
NATIONAL MEDIA SERVICES, INC., pg. 792
NATIONAL MERCHANDISE CO., INC., pg. 792
NATIONAL METAL PRODUCTS CO.—See Tang Industries Inc., pg. 1078
NATIONAL MINES CORP.—See National Steel Corporation, pg. 794
NATIONAL MORTGAGE COMPANY, pg. 792
NATIONAL OATS CO.—See Agway, Inc., pg. 25
NATIONAL OUT-OF-HOME MEDIA/METRO 8, pg. 792
NATIONAL PENSION LIFE INSURANCE COMPANY—See Mutual of America, pg. 778
NATIONAL PLASTICS CORPORATION—See Millstein Industries, pg. 756
NATIONAL POSTERS, INC.—See National Group, Inc., pg. 790
NATIONAL PROPERTY ANALYSTS, INC., pg. 792
NATIONAL R.V., INC., pg. 792
NATIONAL REALTY CORP.—See Helmsley Enterprises, Inc., pg. 527
NATIONAL REPRODUCTIONS CORPORATION, pg. 793
NATIONAL RESEARCH BUREAU—See Automated Marketing Systems, Inc., pg. 100
NATIONAL RESTAURANT SUPPLY COMPANY, pg. 793
NATIONAL RETAIL HARDWARE ASSN., pg. 793
NATIONAL RIVET & MANUFACTURING COMPANY, pg. 793
NATIONAL SAFETY ASSOCIATES, pg. 793
NATIONAL SAVINGS LIFE INSURANCE COMPANY—See Victory Financial Group, Inc., pg. 1150
NATIONAL SEATING CO., pg. 793
NATIONAL SECURITIES CLEARING CORP.—See The American Stock Exchange, pg. 63
NATIONAL SILICATES LTD.—See PQ Corporation, pg. 837
NATIONAL SOLVENT CORPORATION, pg. 793
NATIONAL SPINNING CO., INC., pg. 793
NATIONAL STEEL CORPORATION, pg. 793
NATIONAL STEEL GREAT LAKES DIV.—See National Steel Corporation, pg. 794
NATIONAL STEEL MIDWEST DIV.—See National Steel Corporation, pg. 794
NATIONAL STEEL & SHIPBUILDING COMPANY, pg. 794
THE NATIONAL SUPER SERVICE CO., pg. 794
NATIONAL SYSTEMS & RESEARCH CO., pg. 794
NATIONAL TECHNICAL SERVICES—See American Technical Services Group, Inc., pg. 64
NATIONAL THERMAL INSULATION—See Transco Inc., pg. 1107
NATIONAL TOOL & MANUFACTURING COMPANY, pg. 794
NATIONAL TRANSPORT SERVICES CO.—See Wakefern Food Corporation, pg. 1158
NATIONAL TRAVELERS LIFE CO., pg. 794
NATIONAL TRUCK LEASING SYSTEM, pg. 794
NATIONAL UTILITY SERVICE, INC., pg. 794
NATIONAL VAN LINES, INC., pg. 794
NATIONAL VIDEO, INC.—See West Coast National Video, pg. 1177
NATIONAL WELDERS SUPPLY CO. INC., pg. 794
NATIONAL WOOD PRODUCTS, CO.—See Saunders Brothers, pg. 972
NATIONAL YARN CRAFTS—See National Spinning Co., Inc., pg. 793
NATIONAL YELLOW PAGES MONITOR (NYPM)—See NFO Research, Inc., pg. 781
NATION'S BUSINESS, pg. 794
NATIONWIDE BEEF, INC., pg. 795
NATIONWIDE COMMERCIAL CO.—See Amerco, A Nevada Corporation, pg. 48
NATIONWIDE CORPORATION—See Nationwide Mutual Insurance Company, pg. 795
NATIONWIDE FINANCIAL SERVICES, INC.—See Nationwide Mutual Insurance Company, pg. 795
NATIONWIDE FUNDING INC.—See Nationwide Mutual Insurance Company, pg. 795
NATIONWIDE HEALTH CARE CORP.—See Nationwide Mutual Insurance Company, pg. 795
NATIONWIDE HOMES, INC., pg. 795
NATIONWIDE LIFE INSURANCE CO.—See Nationwide Mutual Insurance Company, pg. 795
NATIONWIDE MUTUAL INSURANCE COMPANY, pg. 795
NATIONWISE AUTOMOTIVE, INC., pg. 795
NATURE MADE NUTRITIONAL PRODUCTS INC.—See Pharmavite Corp., pg. 866
NATURE'S RECIPE PET FOODS, pg. 796
NAUGATUCK GLASS COMPANY, pg. 796
NAUTILUS, pg. 796
NAUTILUS VIRGINIA INC.—See Nautilus, pg. 796
NAVAJO FOREST PRODUCTS INDUSTRIES, pg. 796
NAVAJO WESTERN LAND CO.—See Watkins Associated Industries Inc., pg. 1167
NAVCOM DEFENSE ELECTRONICS, INC., pg. 796
NAYLOR PIPE COMPANY, pg. 796
NAZ-DAR COMPANY—See Thrall Enterprises, Inc., pg. 1095
M.F. NEAL & CO.,INC.—See MacAndrews & Forbes Holdings Inc., pg. 694
NEAL & STEPHENS ADVERTISING, INC., pg. 796
NEAPCO, INC.—See UIS, Inc., pg. 1123
NEBRASKA BOOK CO.—See Lincoln Industries, pg. 676
NEBRASKA DEPT. OF ECONOMIC DEVELOPMENT, pg. 796
NEBRASKA ENGINEERING CO.—See TIC United Corporation, pg. 1073
NEBRASKA-IOWA SUPPLY COMPANY, pg. 796
NEBRASKA PUBLIC POWER DISTRICT, pg. 796
NEBRASKA TURKEY GROWERS—See Norbest, Inc., pg. 809
NEEB CORPORATION, pg. 797
NEENAH FOUNDRY COMPANY, pg. 797
NEER MANUFACTURING COMPANY, pg. 797
NEHRING ELECTRICAL WORKS COMPANY—See Coleman Cable Systems, Inc., pg. 261
NEILL-LAVIELLE SUPPLY CO., pg. 797
NEKURA VERSICHERUNGS AG—See Nationwide Mutual Insurance Company, pg. 795
NELLA OIL COMPANY, pg. 797
NELMOR CO., INC.—See Sterling, Inc., pg. 1047
NELSEN STEEL & WIRE CO., pg. 797
NELSON BROTHERS FURNITURE CO., pg. 797
NELSON COMMUNICATIONS, INC., pg. 797
L. R. NELSON CORPORATION, pg. 797
NELSON PHOTO SUPPLIES, pg. 797
NELSON & SCHMIDT, INC., pg. 797
NELSON & SMALL INC., pg. 798
JEFFREY NEMETZ & ASSOCIATES, INC., pg. 798
NEMSCHOFF CHAIRS, INC., pg. 798
THE NEOGARD CORPORATION—See Jones Blair Company, pg. 603
THE NERLAND AGENCY, INC., pg. 798
NESCO, INC., pg. 798
NESLAB INSTRUMENTS, INC., pg. 798
NESOTA CO.—See The Minnesota Mutual Life Insurance Company, pg. 758
G.L. NESS AGENCY, INC., pg. 798
NESSEN LAMPS—See Jac Jacobsen Industries, Inc., pg. 588
NESTAWAY CO.—See AXIA Incorporated, pg. 8
NETWORK CAPITAL GROUP—See Network Real Estate of California, Inc., pg. 798
NETWORK HOME SERVICES, INC.—See Network Real Estate of California, Inc., pg. 798
NETWORK REAL ESTATE OF CALIFORNIA, INC., pg. 798
NETWORK REAL ESTATE OF CENTRAL CALIFORNIA, INC.—See Network Real Estate of California, Inc., pg. 798
NETWORK REAL ESTATE, INC.—See Network Real Estate of California, Inc., pg. 798
NETWORK REAL ESTATE OF LOS ANGELES, INC.—See Network Real Estate of California, Inc., pg. 798
NETWORK REAL ESTATE OF NORTHERN CALIFORNIA, INC.—See Network Real Estate of California, Inc., pg. 798
NETWORK REAL ESTATE OF SOUTHERN CALIFORNIA, INC.—See Network Real Estate of California, Inc., pg. 798
NETWORK SERVICES COMPANY OF CHICAGO, pg. 798
NETWORK WORLD, INC.—See International Data Group, pg. 576
NETWORKS AMERICA—See Western International Media Corporation, pg. 1180
NETZSCH, INC., pg. 798
NEUHOFF FARMS, INC.—See Valleydale Packers Inc., pg. 1143
NEW ALBANY GAZETTE—See Landmark Communications, Inc., pg. 655
NEW BALANCE ATHLETIC SHOE, INC., pg. 798
NEW BALANCE CANADA INC.—See New Balance Athletic Shoe, Inc., pg. 799
NEW BEDFORD PANORAMEX CORPORATION, pg. 799
NEW CENTURY FREIGHT TRAFFIC ASSOCIATION, INC.—See The Marmon Group, Inc., pg. 712
NEW COOPERATIVE INC., pg. 799
NEW DIMENSIONS IN EDUCATION—See Abrams Publishing Inc., pg. 10
THE NEW ENGLAND, pg. 799
NEW ENGLAND AUTO AUCTION, INC.—See Cox Enterprises, Inc., pg. 293
NEW ENGLAND CO. DIV.—See Best Manufacturing, Inc., pg. 146
NEW ENGLAND COFFEE COMPANY, pg. 800
NEW ENGLAND COLLECTORS SOCIETY—See Reed & Barton Corporation, pg. 920
THE NEW ENGLAND COMPANIES, INC.—See The New England, pg. 799
NEW ENGLAND CONFECTIONERY CO.—See UIS, Inc., pg. 1123
NEW ENGLAND CORPORATION, pg. 800
NEW ENGLAND CORRECT CRAFT, INC.—See Correct Craft, Inc., pg. 287
NEW ENGLAND DAIRIES, INC., pg. 800
NEW ENGLAND FROZEN FOODS, pg. 800
NEW ENGLAND INVESTMENT COMPANIES, INC.—See The New England, pg. 799
NEW ENGLAND INVESTMENT MARKETING, INC.—See The New England, pg. 799
NEW ENGLAND LIFE MORTGAGE FUNDING CORP.—See The New England, pg. 799
NEW ENGLAND LOG HOMES, INC.—See New England Corporation, pg. 800
NEW ENGLAND MACHINERY, INC., pg. 800
NEW ENGLAND NEWSPAPER SUPPLY COMPANY, INC., pg. 800
NEW ENGLAND PENSION & ANNUITY CO.—See The New England, pg. 800
NEW ENGLAND PETROLEUM CORPORATION—See American Financial Corporation, pg. 54
NEW ENGLAND PORTFOLIO ADVISORS, INC.—See The New England, pg. 799
NEW ENGLAND RESEARCH, INC.—See McLaughlin Gormley King Company, pg. 731
NEW ENGLAND SECURITIES CORP.—See The New England, pg. 799
NEW ENGLAND STONE INDUSTRIES, INC., pg. 800
NEW ENGLAND TAP CORPORATION (NETCO)—See Brubaker Tool Corp., pg. 183
NEW ENGLAND VARIABLE LIFE INSURANCE CO—See The New England, pg. 800
NEW FOOD INGREDIENTS, LTD.—See Newly Weds Foods Inc., pg. 804
NEW FORTIS CORP., pg. 800
NEW HAMPSHIRE OAK, pg. 800
NEW HAMPSHIRE SWEEPSTAKES COMMISSION, pg. 801
NEW HAMPTON, INC., pg. 801
NEW HAVEN MFG. CORP., pg. 801
NEW HAVEN SAVINGS BANK, pg. 801
NEW HERMES INC.-SOUTHEAST—See New Hermes Incorporated, pg. 801
NEW HERMES INC-SOUTH—See New Hermes Incorporated, pg. 801
NEW HERMES INCORPORATED, pg. 801
NEW HERMES, LTD.—See New Hermes Incorporated, pg. 801
NEW JERSEY FLOAT GLASS, INC.—See AFG Industries, Inc., pg. 3
NEW JERSEY PRESS, INC., pg. 801
NEW JERSEY STATE LOTTERY, pg. 801
NJ TRANSIT, pg. 801
NJ TRANSIT BUS OPERATIONS—See NJ Transit, pg. 802
NJ TRANSIT CORPORATION—See NJ Transit, pg. 802
NJ TRANSIT RAIL OPERATIONS—See NJ Transit, pg. 802
NEW MECH COMPANIES, INC., pg. 802
NEW ORLEANS PELICANS—See Minnesota Twins Baseball Club, pg. 758
NEW ORLEANS WATERFRONT REST. CORP.—See Specialty Restaurants Corporation, pg. 1028
NEW PARK MALL—See R. H. Macy & Co., Inc., pg. 699
NEW STANDARD CORPORATION, pg. 802
NEW TEXAS TUMBLEWEED, pg. 802
NEW WOMAN MAGAZINE—See K-III Communications Corporation, pg. 611
NEW WORLD ENTERTAINMENT, INC.—See Andrews Group, Incorporated, pg. 74
NEW YORK CARPET WORLD INC., pg. 802
NEW YORK CITY DEPT. OF GENERAL SERVICES, pg. 802
NEW YORK CITY OFF TRACK BETTING CORP., pg. 802
NEW YORK CITY TRANSIT AUTHORITY—See Metropolitan Transportation Authority, pg. 745
NEW YORK FINANCIAL CORP.—See Shepaug Corporation, pg. 998
NEW YORK LANGUAGE CENTER—See Berlitz International, Inc., pg. 143
NYLIFE ADVISERS, INC.—See New York Life Insurance Company, pg. 803
NYLIFE DEPOSITARY CORPORATION—See New York Life Insurance Company, pg. 803
NYLIFE EQUITY INC.—See New York Life Insurance Company, pg. 803
NEW YORK LIFE & HEALTH INSURANCE COMPANY—See New York Life Insurance Company, pg. 802
NEW YORK LIFE INSURANCE AND ANNUITY CORPORATION—See New York Life Insurance Company, pg. 802
NEW YORK LIFE INSURANCE COMPANY, pg. 802
NEW YORK LIFE INSURANCE CO. OF CANADA—See New York Life Insurance Company, pg. 803
NEW YORK LIFE INSURANCE WORLDWIDE LTD.—See New York Life Insurance Company, pg. 803
NEW YORK LIFE INTERNATIONAL INVESTMENT—See New York Life Insurance Company, pg. 803
NYLIFE LEASING INC.—See New York Life Insurance Company, pg. 803
NYLIFE MORTGAGE INC.—See New York Life Insurance Company, pg. 803
NYLIFE REALTY INC.—See New York Life Insurance Company, pg. 803
NYLIFE SECURITIES INC.—See New York Life Insurance Company, pg. 803
NEW YORK LIFE WORLDWIDE HOLDING, INC.—See New York Life Insurance Company, pg. 803
NEW YORK MAGAZINE COMPANY—See K-III Communications Corporation, pg. 611
THE NEW YORK OBSERVER—See Shepaug Corporation, pg. 998

NEW YORK RACING ASSOCIATION, pg. 803
NEW YORK SYSTEMS EXCHANGE CORP.—See Syracuse Supply Company, pg. 1070
NEW YORK WIRE CO., TEXTILE MILL—See Root Corporation, pg. 947
NEW YORK WIRE CO., WIRE DRAWING MILL—See Root Corporation, pg. 947
NEW YORK WIRE CO., WIRE WEAVING MILL—See Root Corporation, pg. 947
THE NEW YORKER MAGAZINE, pg. 803
NEW ZEALAND LAMB CO., INC., pg. 803
NEWAGE INDUSTRIES INC., pg. 803
NEWARK REHABILITATION, INC.—See The Prudential Insurance Company of America, pg. 896
GUST K. NEWBERG CONSTRUCTION CO., pg. 803
J. J. NEWBERRY CANADIAN LTD. C/O GAULT BROTHERS DIV.—See Riklis Family Corporation, pg. 935
J. J. NEWBERRY CO.—See Riklis Family Corporation, pg. 934
NEWBRIDGE COMMUNICATIONS—See K-III Communications Corporation, pg. 611
NEWBROOK PAPER—See Triangle Marketing Corp., pg. 1112
NEWBURGH AUTO AUCTION—See Cox Enterprises, Inc., pg. 293
NEWBURGH & SOUTH SHORE RAILROAD COMPANY—See Chicago West Pullman Corporation, pg. 246
NEWBURY INDUSTRIES, INC., pg. 803
NEWBURY INSURANCE CO.—See The New England, pg. 800
D. W. NEWCOMER'S SONS, INC., pg. 804
NEWELL PAPER CO. OF MERIDIAN—See Jackson Paper Company, pg. 587
NEWFIELD PUBLICATIONS—See K-III Communications Corporation, pg. 611
NEWFOUNDLAND GEOSCIENCES, LTD.—See Fugro-McClelland, Inc., pg. 436
HENRY NEWGARD & COMPANY, pg. 804
NEWHOUSE BRAKE DIVISION—See Connecticut Drive Shaft, Inc., pg. 274
NEWHOUSE NEWSPAPERS METRO-SUBURBIA, INC.—See Advance Publications Inc., pg. 19
NEWLY WEDS FOODS ASIA/PACIFIC—See Newly Weds Foods Inc., pg. 804
NEWLY WEDS FOODS INC., pg. 804
NEWLY WEDS FOODS, INC.—See Newly Weds Foods Inc., pg. 804
NEWLY WEDS FOODS THAILAND—See Newly Weds Foods Inc., pg. 804
NEWMAN, SAYLOR & GREGORY, pg. 804
NEWMAN'S OWN, INC., pg. 804
NEWMARK, POSNER & MITCHELL, INC., pg. 804
NEWPORT/CAPE DORY YACHTS, INC., pg. 804
THE NEWS—See Landmark Communications, Inc., pg. 655
THE NEWS-DEMOCRAT—See Landmark Communications, Inc., pg. 655
NEWS-ENTERPRISE—See Landmark Communications, Inc., pg. 655
THE NEWS-PILOT—See The Copley Press, Inc., pg. 284
NEWS-PRESS & GAZETTE COMPANY, pg. 804
THE NEWS PRINTING COMPANY—See Perpetual Corporation, pg. 862
THE NEWS-SUN—See The Copley Press, Inc., pg. 284
NEWSPAPER ADVERTISING SPECIALISTS, INC. (N.A.S.), pg. 805
NEWSPRINT SOUTH, INC.—See Mississippi Chemical Corporation, pg. 760
NEWSPRINT SOUTH SALES CORP.—See Mississippi Chemical Corporation, pg. 760
THE NEWTON KANSAN—See Stauffer Communications, Inc., pg. 1042
O. A. NEWTON & SON CO., pg. 805
NEWTRON GROUP INC., pg. 805
NEXT, INC., pg. 805
NEXUS PLASTICS, INC., pg. 805
THE J. M. NEY COMPANY, pg. 805
AL NEYER, INC., pg. 805
NIAGARA BLOWER COMPANY, pg. 805
NIAGARA CUTTER, INC., pg. 805
NIAGARA ENVELOPE CO., INC.—See Niagara Envelope Company, Inc., pg. 806
NIAGARA ENVELOPE CO. OF FLORIDA—See Niagara Envelope Company, Inc., pg. 806
NIAGARA ENVELOPE COMPANY, INC., pg. 805
NIAGARA FRONTIER TRANSPORATION METRO SYSTEM, INC., pg. 806
NIAGARA THERAPY MFG. CORP., pg. 806
NIAGARA TRANSFORMER CORP., pg. 806
NIBBLE WITH GIBBLE'S, INC., pg. 806
NIBCHEM INC.—See Nibco, Inc., pg. 806
NIBCO, INC., pg. 806
NIBCO PIPING PRODUCTS EAST—See Nibco, Inc., pg. 806
NIBCO SWM MARKETING CORP.—See Nibco, Inc., pg. 806
NIC SAND—See Blue Coral, Inc., pg. 159
NICKELODEON/NICK AT NITE—See National Amusements, Inc., pg. 785
NICKERSON LUMBER COMPANY, pg. 806
ALFRED NICKLES BAKERY, INC., pg. 806
NICKLES BAKERY, INC.—See Alfred Nickles Bakery, Inc., pg. 807
NICKLES BAKERY INC., ELKHART—See Alfred Nickles Bakery, Inc., pg. 807
NICKLES BAKERY INC., LIMA—See Alfred Nickles Bakery, Inc., pg. 807
THE NIELSEN COMPANY, pg. 807
NIELSEN CONSTRUCTION COMPANY, pg. 807
NIGHTINGALE-CONANT CORP., pg. 807
NIHON FAXON—See The Faxon Company, Inc., pg. 404
NIHON READY SYSTEMS—See Ready Systems, pg. 916
THE NIKKEL CORPORATION, pg. 807
NIMNICHT CHEVROLET COMPANY, pg. 807
NINE WEST GROUP, INC., pg. 807
94TH AERO SQUADRON OF COLUMBUS, INC.—See Specialty Restaurants Corporation, pg. 1029
94TH AERO SQUADRON OF MIAMI, INC.—See Specialty Restaurants Corporation, pg. 1028
94TH AERO SQUADRON OF ORLANDO, INC.—See Specialty Restaurants Corporation, pg. 1028
94TH AERO SQUADRON OF PALWAUKEE, INC.—See Specialty Restaurants Corporation, pg. 1028
94TH AERO SQUADRON OF PINELLAS COUNTY, INC.—See Specialty Restaurants Corporation, pg. 1028
94TH AERO SQUADRON RESTAURANT, INC.—See Specialty Restaurants Corporation, pg. 1028
94TH AERO SQUADRON OF SAN JOSE, INC.—See Specialty Restaurants Corporation, pg. 1028
94TH AERO SQUADRON OF SARASOTA, INC.—See Specialty Restaurants Corporation, pg. 1028
94TH AERO SQUADRON OF TORRANCE, INC.—See Specialty Restaurants Corporation, pg. 1028
94TH AS OF WEST PALM BEACH, INC.—See Specialty Restaurants Corporation, pg. 1028
94TH OF COLLEGE PARK, INC.—See Specialty Restaurants Corporation, pg. 1028
NINETY-FOURTH OF ST. LOUIS, INC.—See Specialty Restaurants Corporation, pg. 1028
92 Q WERQ AM/FM—See United Broadcasting Inc., pg. 1131
NINTEMAN CONSTRUCTION COMPANY, INC.—See Sundt Corp., pg. 1060
NIPPON FLOUR MILLS CO., LTD.—See Newly Weds Foods Inc., pg. 804
NISSHOKU SCHENECTADY CHEMICALS, INC.—See Schenectady Chemicals, Inc., pg. 975
NITRAM ENERGY INC., pg. 807
NIXDORFF KREIN INDUSTRIES INC., pg. 807
NOB HILL GENERAL STORE, INC., pg. 807
NOBART, INC., pg. 808
NOBLE & ASSOCIATES, pg. 808
NOBLES INDUSTRIES, INC., pg. 808
NODAK DISTRIBUTOR—See Dakco Distributors, Inc., pg. 311
NODAK ELECTRIC CO-OP, pg. 808
NODAK MUTUAL INSURANCE COMPANY, pg. 808
NOEL CANNING CORPORATION, pg. 808
NOEL OF JAMAICA LTD.—See Gitano Group Inc., pg. 460
NOEL-JOANNA, INC., pg. 808
THE C. W. NOFSINGER COMPANY—See Burns & McDonnell Engineers-Architects-Consultants, pg. 194
NOLL PRINTING CORPORATION—See Our Sunday Visitor, Inc., pg. 832
NOMA-INTERNATIONAL, INC., pg. 808
NOORDERVLIET & WINNINGHOFF/LEO BURNETT B.V.—See Leo Burnett Company, Inc., pg. 193
NOOTER CONSTRUCTION CO.—See Nooter Corporation, pg. 808
NOOTER CORPORATION, pg. 808
NOOTER/ERIKSEN COGENERATION SYSTEMS, INC.—See Nooter Corporation, pg. 808
NOR-CAL BEVERAGE CO., INC., pg. 808
NORANDEX INC., pg. 809
NORBEST, INC., pg. 809
NORBRAN LEASING—See The Charles Levy Company, pg. 672
NORCAM CONSTRUCTION COMPANY—See Ritter Bros., Inc., pg. 937
NORCOSTCO, INC., pg. 809
NORCRAFT COMPANIES—See Norcraft Companies, Inc., pg. 809
NORCRAFT COMPANIES, INC., pg. 809
NORCROSS INDUSTRIES, INC., pg. 809
NORDEN FRUIT COMPANY, INC., pg. 809
NORDIC CONTROLS CO.—See Furnas Electric Company, pg. 437
NORDIC GROUP OF COMPANIES, LTD., pg. 809
NORDSKAR & THORKILDSEN LEO BURNETT A/S—See Leo Burnett Company, Inc., pg. 193
NOREL PAPER CORPORATION, pg. 810
NORELL PERFUMES, INC.—See MacAndrews & Forbes Holdings Inc., pg. 696
NORFOLK SHIPBUILDING & DRYDOCK CORPORATION, pg. 810
NORFOODS, INC., pg. 810
NORGARD MIKKELSEN REKLAMEBUREAU A/S—See Backer Spielvogel Bates Worldwide, Inc., pg. 112
NORLIGHT—See Journal Communications Inc., pg. 607
NORMAG CORPORATION—See Berwind Corporation, pg. 145
NORMAN BROTHERS NISSAN INC., pg. 810
NORMANDALE PROPERTIES—See Opus South Corporation, pg. 828
NORMARK CORPORATION, pg. 810
NORPAC FOODS, INC. COOPERATIVE, pg. 810
NORRELL CORPORATION, pg. 810
NORRELL HEALTH CARE INC.—See Norrell Corporation, pg. 811
NORRIS SCREEN & MFG., INC.—See Jupiter Industries, Inc., pg. 609
NORSHIPCO INDUSTRIAL ENTERPRISES—See Norfolk Shipbuilding & Drydock Corporation, pg. 810
NORSK JOHNSON'S WAX A/S—See S. C. Johnson & Son, Inc., pg. 600
NORTH AMERICAN ACCEPTANCE CORPORATION—See Washington Mutual Savings Bank, pg. 1166
NORTH AMERICAN COMPANY, pg. 811
NORTH AMERICAN ENCLOSURES, INC., pg. 811
NORTH AMERICAN FINANCIAL CORP.—See Carlson Companies, Inc., pg. 221
THE NORTH AMERICAN MANUFACTURING CO., pg. 811
NORTH AMERICAN PRODUCTS CORP., pg. 811
NORTH AMERICAN PUBLISHING COMPANY, pg. 811
NORTH AMERICAN REFRACTORIES COMPANY, pg. 811
NORTH AMERICAN ROOFING COMPANY, INC., pg. 811
NORTH AMERICAN ROYALTIES, INC., pg. 811
NORTH AMERICAN SAFETY PROGRAM ADMINISTRATORS—See Lawrence Group, Inc., pg. 662
NORTH AMERICAN SALT COMPANY, pg. 812
NORTH AMERICAN WATCH CORPORATION, pg. 812
NORTH AMERICAN WATCH OF CANADA, LTD.—See North American Watch Corporation, pg. 812
NORTH & JUDD, pg. 812
NORTH ATLANTIC INDUSTRIES, INC., pg. 812
NORTH ATLANTIC INDUSTRIES SYSTEMS DIVISION—See North Atlantic Industries, Inc., pg. 812
NORTH CAROLINA EQUIPMENT CO., pg. 812
NORTH CAROLINA FOAM INDUSTRIES, INC.—See Barnhardt Manufacturing Co., pg. 120
NORTH CAROLINA MUTUAL LIFE INSURANCE CO., pg. 813
NORTH CAROLINA MUTUAL WHOLESALE DRUG CO., pg. 813
NORTH CENTRAL LIFE INSURANCE COMPANIES, pg. 813
NORTH CENTRAL SUGAR MARKETING CO-OP—See Southern Minnesota Beet Sugar Cooperative, pg. 1022
NORTH COAST BEHAVIORAL RESEARCH—See Wyse Advertising, Inc., pg. 1206
NORTH COAST ELECTRIC COMPANY, pg. 813
NORTH DAKOTA MILL & ELEVATOR ASSOCIATION, pg. 813
NORTH DENVER HILL CORP.—See Specialty Restaurants Corporation, pg. 1028
NORTH ELECTRIC SUPPLY, INC., pg. 813
NORTH PACIFIC LUMBER COMPANY, pg. 813
NORTH PARK LINCOLN MERCURY INC., pg. 813
NORTH PIER ASSOCIATES—See Specialty Restaurants Corporation, pg. 1028
NORTH RIVER HOMES, INC.—See ROC Properties Inc., pg. 908
NORTH SHORE MOVERS, pg. 813
NORTH STAR STEEL CO.—See Cargill Inc., pg. 219
NORTH STAR STEEL HOUSTON—See Cargill Inc., pg. 219
NORTH STAR STEEL KENTUCKY, INC.—See Cargill Inc., pg. 219
NORTH STAR STEEL TEXAS, INC.—See Cargill Inc., pg. 219
NORTHEAST TEXAS FARMERS CO-OP, pg. 813
NORTHEASTERN GRAPHIC SUPPLY, INC., pg. 814
NORTHERN AUTOMOTIVE CORPORATION—See The Trump Group, pg. 1118
NORTHERN COMPUTERS INC.—See American Trading and Production Corporation, pg. 65
NORTHERN CROSS, LTD.—See Barancorp, pg. 118
NORTHERN DRUG COMPANY, pg. 814
NORTHERN MICHIGAN VENEERS, INC., pg. 814
NORTHERN PACIFIC CORPORATION—See The Trump Group, pg. 1118
NORTHERN WIRE & CABLE, INC., pg. 814
NORTHFIELD CHEESE CO.—See Interlaken Capital, Inc., pg. 574
NORTHLAND ALASKA, INC.—See Green Holdings, Inc., pg. 484
NORTHLAND ALUMINUM PRODUCTS, INC., pg. 814
NORTHLAND CONTAINER CORP., pg. 814
NORTHLAND ELECTRIC SUPPLY COMPANY, pg. 814
NORTHLAND SPORTS INC.—See Dakco Distributors, Inc., pg. 311
NORTHLICH STOLLEY LAWARRE, pg. 814
NORTHRIDGE INDUSTRIES, INC.—See H. Group Holding Inc., pg. 495
NORTHVILLE INDUSTRIES CORP., pg. 814
NORTHWAY MOTORCAR CORPORATION, pg. 814
NORTHWEST AEROSPACE TRAINING CORPORATION—See NWA, Inc., pg. 782
NORTHWEST AIRCRAFT INC.—See NWA, Inc., pg. 782
NORTHWEST AIRLINES, INC.—See NWA, Inc., pg. 782
NORTHWEST FARM BUREAU INSURANCE COMPANY—See Country Companies Insurance Group, pg. 289
NORTHWEST FENCE PRODUCTS CO.—See Carl Weissman & Sons, Inc., pg. 1174
NORTHWEST MARINE, INC.—See Southwest Marine, Inc., pg. 1023
NORTHWEST MEDIA, INC.—See Persis Corporation, pg. 863
NORTHWEST PAPER CONVERTING COMPANY, pg. 814
NORTHWEST PARKING SERVICES INC.—See Allright Corporation, pg. 42
NORTHWEST PIPE FITTINGS, INC., pg. 815
NORTHWEST SERVICE, INC.—See Food Services of America, pg. 423
NORTHWEST TOBACCO & CANDY CO., pg. 815
NORTHWESTERN DRUG COMPANY—See The F. Dohmen Company, pg. 343
NORTHWESTERN ENGINEERING CO., pg. 815
NORTHWESTERN GOLF COMPANY, pg. 815
NORTHWESTERN INDUSTRIAL PIPING, pg. 815
NORTHWESTERN MEATS INC., pg. 815
NORTHWESTERN MUTUAL LIFE INSURANCE CO., pg. 815
NORTHWESTERN PACIFIC RAILROAD CO.—See Anschutz Corporation, pg. 75
NORTHWESTERN STEEL & WIRE CO., pg. 815
NORTON ASSOCIATES, INC., pg. 815
W.W. NORTON & COMPANY, INC., pg. 815
J. R. NORTON COMPANY, pg. 816
NORTOWN OLDSMOBILE INC., pg. 816
NORWALK CO., INC., pg. 816
NORWALK FURNITURE CORPORATION, pg. 816
NORWALK POWDERED METALS, INC., pg. 816
NORWECO, INC., pg. 816
NORWEGIAN CRUISE LINE, pg. 816
NORWESCO, INC., pg. 816
NORWICH RECYCLING CORP.—See Victory Markets Inc., pg. 1150
NORWOOD INDUSTRIES, INC.—See Seton Company, pg. 993

NORWOOD SHOE CORPORATION, pg. 816
THE NOTEWORTHY COMPANY, pg. 816
NOVA POWER, INC., pg. 816
NOVAMETRIX MEDICAL SYSTEMS INC., pg. 817
NOVAQUIM S.A. DE C.V.—See Uniroyal Chemical Company, Inc., pg. 1130
NOVAR CONTROLS CORP.—See Novar Electronics, pg. 817
NOVAR CORP.—See Novar Electronics, pg. 817
NOVAR ELECTRONICS, pg. 817
NOVILLE ESSENTIAL OIL CO., INC., pg. 817
NOW HEAR THIS (NHT)—See International Jensen Inc., pg. 578
NU-MERICS INC.—See Republic Fastener Products Corp., pg. 928
NU-SAFE REPORTING—See Gerber Advertising, pg. 453
NU SKIN INTERNATIONAL, pg. 817
NUARC COMPANY, INC., pg. 817
NUCLEAR DATA SYSTEMS—See Canberra Industries, Inc., pg. 213
NUEAR ELECTRONICS—See Starkey Laboratories, Inc., pg. 1040
NUEMANN (USA)—See Sennheiser Electronic Corp., pg. 990
NUGGET MOTORS—See Don Massey Cadillac Inc., pg. 719
NUHAHN, INC., pg. 817
NULAID FOODS, pg. 817
#1 COCHRAN, INC., pg. 817
NUTECH ENGINEERS, INC.—See Nutech, Inc., pg. 818
NUTECH, INC., pg. 817
NUTECH INTERNATIONAL, INC—See Nutech, Inc., pg. 818
NUTRI/SYSTEM INC., pg. 818
NUTRILITE PRODUCTS, INC.—See Amway Corporation, pg. 70
NUTRITION WORLD, pg. 818
NUTRIUS DAIRY FEED SUPPLEMENTS DIV.—See Bioproducts, Inc., pg. 152
NUTTALL EQUIPMENT CO. INC., pg. 818
NUTTALL GEAR CORPORATION, pg. 818
NUYENS LIQUOR IMPORTING, INC.—See White Rock Distilleries Inc., pg. 1186
NYACOL PRODUCTS, INC.—See PQ Corporation, pg. 837
NYLIFE FUNDING INC.—See New York Life Insurance Company, pg. 803
NYLIFE INC.—See New York Life Insurance Company, pg. 802
NYLIFE INSURANCE COMPANY OF ARIZONA—See New York Life Insurance Company, pg. 803
NYLON CORPORATION OF AMERICA, pg. 818

O

O/B LEASING COMPANY—See Budco Group Inc., pg. 186
OCTUS, pg. 818
ODI, pg. 818
ODI—See ODI, pg. 819
ODL INCORPORATED, pg. 819
O/E AUTOMATION, INC., pg. 819
OLT-I CORP.—See Fiklis Family Corporation, pg. 934
OMCO MOULD, INC., pg. 819
OPT INDUSTRIES, INC., pg. 819
OSC CORPORATION D/B/A OLYMPIC SALES CO., pg. 819
O'T.V. & O'SPACE—See Young & Rubicam Inc., pg. 1212
OAHU SUGAR COMPANY, LIMITED—See JMB Realty Corporation, pg. 585
OAHU WASTE ENERGY RECOVERY, INC.—See JMB Realty Corporation, pg. 585
OAK PRODUCTS, INC.—See ROC Properties Inc., pg. 908
THE OAK RIDGER—See Stauffer Communications, Inc., pg. 1042
OAK RUBBER COMPANY, pg. 819
OAK TECHNICAL, INC.—See Oak Rubber Company, pg. 819
OAKHURST DAIRY, pg. 819
OAKLAND TOOL & MANUFACTURING COMPANY, pg. 819
BRUCE OAKLEY, INC., pg. 819
BENJAMIN OBDYKE, INC., pg. 819
OBERDORFER INDUSTRIES, INC., pg. 819
OBERG ARIZONA—See Oberg Industries Co., pg. 819
OBERG CARBIDE PUNCH & DIE—See Oberg Industries Co., pg. 819
OBERG INDUSTRIES CO., pg. 819
OBERG MFG. CO.—See Oberg Industries Co., pg. 820
OBERWEIS DAIRY, INC., pg. 820
THE O'BRIEN CORPORATION, pg. 820
O'BRIEN DIVISION—See Heico Inc., pg. 525
O'BRIEN ENERGY SYSTEMS INC., pg. 820
O'BRIEN INTERNATIONAL, INC.—See MacAndrews & Forbes Holdings Inc., pg. 695
O'BRIEN MACHINERY COMPANY, pg. 820
O'BRIEN POWDER PRODUCTS, INC.—See The O'Brien Corporation, pg. 820
O'BRIEN POWDER PRODUCTS, INC.—See The O'Brien Corporation, pg. 820
ROY O'BRIEN INC., pg. 820
O'BRYAN BROTHERS INC., pg. 820
OCEAN CHEVROLET, INC., pg. 820
OCEAN PROPERTIES, LTD., pg. 820
OCEAN SPRAY CRANBERRIES, INC., pg. 820
OCEANA FOODS—See Lakeside Foods, Inc., pg. 651
OCEANIC SHIPPING CO.—See Strachan Shipping Co., pg. 1052
OCHOCO LUMBER COMPANY, pg. 821
O'CONNOR MACCIOLI, INC., pg. 821
OCTAGON PROCESS INC., pg. 821
OCTAVIO, INC.—See Superba, Inc., pg. 1063
OCTOBER FILMS, INC., pg. 821
O'DELL PRODUCTS, INC.—See AFG Industries, Inc., pg. 3
THE ODOM CORPORATION, pg. 821
ODOMASTER CANADA—See Surco Products, Inc., pg. 1065
ODYSSEY PARTNERS, pg. 821
OESTERREICHISCH HERAKLITH, A.G.—See Belmont Industries, Inc., pg. 137
OFFICE CONNECTION, INC., pg. 821
OFFICE ELECTRONICS, INC., pg. 821
OFFICE EQUIPMENT COMPANY OF CHICAGO, pg. 821
THE OFFICE OF LEE KENDRICK—See Dewberry & Davis, pg. 334
C.M. OFFRAY & SON INC., pg. 822
THE OGDEN UNION RAILWAY AND DEPOT CO.—See Anschutz Corporation, pg. 76
OGLETHORPE POWER CORP., pg. 822
OH BOY CORPORATION, pg. 822
OH! BRIAN'S RIP ROARIN' RIBS—See Investor's Management Corp., pg. 581
O'HALLORAN ADVERTISING, INC., pg. 822
OHAUS CORPORATION, pg. 822
OHIO AUTO AUCTION—See Cox Enterprises, Inc., pg. 293
OHIO GAS COMPANY, pg. 822
OHIO LOTTERY COMMISSION, pg. 822
OHIO MACHINERY CO., pg. 822
THE OHIO MATTRESS COMPANY LICENSING AND COMPONENTS GROUP—See Sealy Corporation, pg. 985
OHIO RIVER ASSOCIATES, INC., pg. 822
OHIO ROD PRODUCTS COMPANY, INC.—See Jupiter Industries, Inc., pg. 609
OHIO-SEALY MATTRESS MANUFACTURING CO.-FORT WORTH—See Sealy Corporation, pg. 985
OHIO-SEALY MATTRESS MANUFACTURING CO.-HOUSTON—See Sealy Corporation, pg. 985
OHIO TAR ASPHALT—See Central Allied Enterprises, pg. 232
OHIO TRANSMISSION CORPORATION, pg. 822
OHIO VALLEY ALUMINUM COMPANY—See Interlock Industries, Inc., pg. 575
OHIO VALLEY ELECTRIC CORPORATION, pg. 822
OHMITE MANUFACTURING COMPANY, pg. 823
OIL & GAS SUPPLY COMPANY, pg. 823
O'KEEFFE'S, INC., pg. 823
OKLAHOMA PUBLISHING COMPANY—See Gaylord Entertainment Co., pg. 446
OKLAHOMA STEEL CASTING CO.—See American Foundry Group, Inc., pg. 55
THE OKONITE COMPANY, pg. 823
OLATHE DAILY NEWS—See Harris Enterprises Inc., pg. 511
OLD AMERICAN POTTERY COMPANY, pg. 823
OLD BEN COAL CO.—See Ziegler Coal Holding Co., pg. 1218
OLD DOMINION LIFE INSURANCE CO.—See Shenandoah Life Insurance Company, pg. 997
OLD DUTCH FOODS, INC., pg. 823
OLD HOME FOODS, INC., pg. 823
OLD QUAKER PAINT CO., pg. 823
OLD STONE BANK OF CALIFORNIA—See Old Stone of California, Inc., pg. 823
OLD STONE OF CALIFORNIA, INC., pg. 823
OLD WISCONSIN CHEESE CO., INC.—See Carl Buddig & Company, pg. 186
OLD WISCONSIN SAUSAGE—See Carl Buddig & Company, pg. 186
OLD WORLD AUTOMOTIVE PRODUCTS—See Old World Industries, Inc., pg. 824
OLD WORLD INDUSTRIES, INC., pg. 823
THE OLDENBURG GROUP COMPANIES, pg. 824
THE OLDHAM ERA—See Landmark Communications, Inc., pg. 655
L. L. OLDS SEED COMPANY, pg. 824
OLEFINAS, S.A.—See McNeel International Corp., pg. 732
OLEN CORPORATION—See Kokosing Construction Company, Inc., pg. 641
VIC OLESEN & PARTNERS, INC., pg. 824
B. OLINDE & SONS COMPANY, INC., pg. 824
OLIVE ELECTRONICS—See RS Electronics, pg. 908
OLIVER OIL COMPANY, INC., pg. 824
OLIVER PRODUCTS COMPANY, pg. 824
OLOKELE SUGAR CO., LIMITED—See C. Brewer & Company, Limited, pg. 174
JOHN M. OLSON COMPANY, pg. 824
OLSON RUG COMPANY, pg. 824
OLSON-TRAVELWORLD LTD., pg. 824
OLSONITE CORPORATION, pg. 824
OLTMANS CONSTRUCTION COMPANY, pg. 824
OLYMPIC MANUFACTURING CO.—See Caldwell Manufacturing Company, pg. 209
OLYMPIC STEEL INC., pg. 825
OMAHA CREATIVE GROUP, pg. 825
OMAHA PROPERTY & CASUALTY—See Mutual of Omaha Insurance Company, pg. 779
OMAHA PROPERTY & CASUALTY CO.—See Mutual of Omaha Insurance Company, pg. 779
OMAHA PUBLIC POWER DISTRICT, pg. 825
OMAHA STEAKS INTERNATIONAL, pg. 825
O'MALIA FOOD MARKETS INC., pg. 825
OMAN CONSTRUCTION CO. INC., pg. 825
OMCO CAST METALS, INC.—See OMCO Mould, Inc., pg. 819
OMCO MACHINING CONCEPTS, INC.—See OMCO Mould, Inc., pg. 819
OMEGA LIST COMPANY—See Eberle Direct Marketing Group, Inc., pg. 365
OMEGA PERFORMANCE GROUP, pg. 826
OMEGA TRANSWORLD LTD.—See Burrell Group, pg. 195
OMEGA WORLD TRAVEL, INC., pg. 826
OMNI FLIGHT HELICOPTERS, INC., pg. 826
OMNI HOTELS, pg. 826
OMNI INDUSTRY—See Global Turnkey Systems Inc., pg. 463
OMNI LENS CORPORATION, pg. 826
OMNI PUBLICATIONS INTERNATIONAL LTD.—See General Media Publishing Group, pg. 450
OMNI SAVINGS BANK, FSB—See FirstFed Michigan Corporation, pg. 414
OMNI SOURCE CORPORATION, pg. 826
OMNI SUPERSTORES—See Dominick's Finer Foods, pg. 344
OMNICARE HEALTH PLAN, pg. 826
OMNIFLIGHT HELICOPTERS, INC.—See Omniflight, Inc., pg. 826
OMNIFLIGHT, INC., pg. 826
OMON, NEW YORK LTD., pg. 826
ON-COR FROZEN FOODS INC., pg. 826
ONDINE DIV.—See Interbath, Inc., pg. 574
ONE HOUR MARTINIZING DRY CLEANING FRANCHISE (SYSTEM), pg. 826
ONE STOP SUPPLY, pg. 827
O'NEAL & PRELLE, pg. 827
O'NEAL STEEL INC., pg. 827
O'NEIL DATA SYSTEMS, INC.—See William O'Neil & Co., Inc., pg. 827
O'NEIL GRIFFIN & ASSOCIATES, INC., pg. 827
O'NEIL INDUSTRIES INC., pg. 827
W. E. O'NEIL CONSTRUCTION COMPANY—See O'Neil Industries Inc., pg. 827
WILLIAM O'NEIL & CO., INC., pg. 827
ONLINE INFORMATION NETWORK—See American Business Information, Inc., pg. 50
OOMPHIES, INC., pg. 827
OPEN COURT PUBLISHING CO.-GENERAL BOOKS—See Carus Corporation, pg. 227
OPEN COURT PUBLISHING COMPANY—See Carus Corporation, pg. 227
OPEN SYSTEMS CONSULTING—See Effective Management Systems, pg. 371
OPEN SYSTEMS CONSULTING—See Effective Management Systems, pg. 371
OPERATING PLANT SERVICES—See Day & Zimmermann, Inc., pg. 320
OPERATIONS MANAGEMENT INTERNATIONAL, INC.—See CH2M Hill Companies, Ltd., pg. 202
OPINION-TRIBUNE—See Landmark Communications, Inc., pg. 655
OPPENHEIMER ASSET MANAGEMENT CORP.—See Massachusetts Mutual Life Insurance Co., pg. 719
OPPENHEIMER MANAGEMENT CORP.—See Massachusetts Mutual Life Insurance Co., pg. 719
OPRYLAND USA, INC.—See Gaylord Entertainment Co., pg. 446
OPTIC GRAPHICS, INC., pg. 827
OPTICAL CORP. OF AMERICA, pg. 827
THE OPTICAL SHOPS—See Tuckerman Optical Co., pg. 1118
OPTIONS CLEARING CORP.—See The American Stock Exchange, pg. 63
OPTIWORLD, pg. 828
OPTYL EYEWEAR FASHION INTERNATIONAL CORP., pg. 828
OPUS CORP., pg. 828
OPUS SOUTH CORPORATION, pg. 828
THE ORANGE COUNTY REGISTER—See Freedom Newspapers Inc., pg. 431
ORANGE GROVE CO-OPERATIVE, pg. 828
ORANGE HILL RESTAURANT CORP.—See Specialty Restaurants Corporation, pg. 1028
ORANGE MOTOR COMPANY INC., pg. 828
ORBEL CORPORATION, pg. 828
ORBIT VALVE INTERNATIONAL, INC., pg. 828
ORBITAIR INTERNATIONAL LTD., pg. 828
ORCAD L.P., pg. 828
ORCHARD SUPPLY HARDWARE, pg. 828
ORCHEM (PTY) LTD. (PLANT)—See Uniroyal Chemical Company, Inc., pg. 1130
THE ORCHID CENTER—See Sun Bulb Company, Inc., pg. 1058
ORCO BLOCK COMPANY, pg. 828
ORDERS DISTRIBUTING CO., pg. 829
OREGON FREEZE DRY, INC., pg. 829
OREGON PACIFIC STATES INSURANCE CO.—See Blue Cross & Blue Shield of Oregon, pg. 160
OREGON STATE LOTTERY, pg. 829
OREGON TURKEY GROWERS—See Norbest, Inc., pg. 809
O'REILLY AUTO INC., pg. 829
ORGANICALLY GROWN CORPORATION, pg. 829
ORGILL BROTHERS & COMPANY, INC.—See West Union Corp., pg. 1178
ORIEL CORPORATION, pg. 829
ORIENTAL SOURCE—See Dentsu, Young & Rubicam Partnerships, pg. 331
THE ORIGINAL A-1—See Lettuce Entertain You Enterprises, Inc., pg. 669
ORIGINAL CYLINDER CORPORATION—See Belgrave Industries, pg. 134
ORIGINS NATURAL RESOURCES INC.—See Estee Lauder, Inc., pg. 389
ORIX REAL ESTATE EQUITIES, INC., pg. 829
ORLANDO SUN RAYS—See Minnesota Twins Baseball Club, pg. 758
ORLEANS INTERNATIONAL, INC., pg. 829
ORLEANS MATERIALS & EQUIPMENT CO., INC., pg. 829
ORMET CORPORATION—See Ohio River Associates, Inc., pg. 822
THE ORMOND SHOPS, INC., pg. 830
OROAMERICA, INC., pg. 830
THE ORR FELT COMPANY, pg. 830
ORR SAFETY EQUIPMENT COMPANY, pg. 830
ORTEL CORPORATION, pg. 830
ORTHO-KINETICS, INC., pg. 830
ORTRONICS, INC., pg. 830
THE ORVIS COMPANY, INC., pg. 830
OSBORN & BARR COMMUNICATIONS, pg. 830
OSCO INDUSTRIES INC., pg. 830
OSHKOSH B'GOSH HOSIERY CO.—See Heyman Corporation, pg. 532

OSKAMP NOLTING CO., INC.—See Zale Corporation, pg. 1216
OSMOSE WOOD PRESERVING CO., pg. 830
OSTARR CORPORATION, pg. 831
OSTER DE VENEZUELA S.A.—See Sunbeam-Oster Company, Inc., pg. 1059
THE OSTERNECK CO. INC., pg. 831
OSTROW TEXTILE CO., INC., pg. 831
OTACO SEATING CO., LTD.—See American Seating Company, pg. 60
OTO-SONIC, INC.—See Beltone Electronics Corporation, pg. 138
OTT COMMUNICATIONS, INC., pg. 831
OTT FOOD PRODUCTS, pg. 831
OTTENHEIMER & COMPANY, INC., pg. 831
OUACHITA COCA-COLA BOTTLING COMPANY, pg. 831
OUIMET INDUSTRIES, pg. 831
OUIMET STAY & LEATHER CO.—See Ouimet Industries, pg. 831
OUR OWN HARDWARE COMPANY, pg. 832
OUR OWN IMPORT INC.—See Cardinal Inc., pg. 218
OUR SUNDAY VISITOR, INC., pg. 832
OURSO INVESTMENT CORPORATION, pg. 832
BUTCH OUSTALET FORD SAAB, INC., pg. 832
OUT OF HOME MEDIA SERVICES, INC., pg. 832
OUTDOOR MEDIA INC.—See Western International Media Corporation, pg. 1180
OUTDOOR SERVICES, INC.—See Western International Media Corporation, pg. 1180
OUTDOOR VENTURE CORP., pg. 832
THE OUTLOOK—See The Copley Press, Inc., pg. 284
OUTLOOK, INCORPORATED—See The Kiplinger Washington Editors, Inc., pg. 632
OUTREACH PUBLICATIONS—See David C. Cook Publishing Co., pg. 282
OVALSTRAPPING INC.—See Enterprises International Inc., pg. 383
OVATION MARKETING, INC., pg. 832
OVERHEAD CONVEYOR CO., pg. 832
OVERHILL MFG., INC.—See Huntco Inc., pg. 554
OVERLAND TRANSPORTATION SYSTEM, INC., pg. 832
OVERLY MANUFACTURING CO., pg. 833
OVERSEAS MILITARY SALES CORPORATION, pg. 833
OVERSEAS PARTNERS, INC., pg. 833
OVERSEAS SERVICE CORPORATION, pg. 833
OVERSTREET PAVING COMPANY, pg. 833
OVERTON MOORE & ASSOCIATES, pg. 833
OWATONNA CANNING COMPANY, pg. 833
OWEN-AMES-KIMBALL CO., pg. 833
OWEN-AMES-KIMBALL ENGINEERING, INC.—See Owen-Ames-Kimball Co., pg. 833
OWEN HEALTH CARE, pg. 833
OWEN INDUSTRIES, INC., pg. 834
OWEN PACIFIC, pg. 834
OWEN STEEL CO., INC., pg. 834
OWENS POLLICK & ASSOCIATES, PHOENIX, INC., pg. 834
R.S. OWENS, pg. 834
OWENSBORO GRAIN CO., INC., pg. 834
OWNERS INSURANCE CO.—See Auto-Owners Insurance, pg. 100
OWNERS MAINTENANCE CORP.—See Helmsley Enterprises, Inc., pg. 527
OWSLEY & SONS, INC., pg. 834
OX-LINE PAINT DIV.—See California Products Corp., pg. 210
OXBOW CORPORATION, pg. 834
OXFORD COMMUNITIES, INC.—See Oxford First Corporation, pg. 834
OXFORD FINANCE COMPANIES, INC.—See Oxford First Corporation, pg. 835
OXFORD FIRST CORPORATION, pg. 834
OXFORD LIFE INSURANCE CO.—See Amerco, A Nevada Corporation, pg. 48
OXFORD REALTY SERVICES CORP., pg. 835
OZARK MOTOR LINES, pg. 835

P

P M COMPANY, pg. 835
P/A INDUSTRIES, INC., pg. 835
PAC MANUFACTURING & DISTRIBUTING CO.—See Precision Tune, Inc., pg. 885
PBM OFFICE PRODUCTS, pg. 835
PBS BUILDING SYSTEMS OF AMERICA, pg. 835
PC COMPUTING—See Ziff Communications Company, pg. 1219
PC CONCEPTS—See Ziff Communications Company, pg. 1219
PC DISTRIBUTING INC., pg. 835
PC MAGAZINE—See Ziff Communications Company, pg. 1219
PC WEEK—See Ziff Communications Company, pg. 1219
PC WORLD—See International Data Group, pg. 576
PCI, pg. 836
PCI INVESTMENTS INC.—See Paschen Contractors, Inc., pg. 851
PCM CONSTRUCTION, INC.—See Henkels & McCoy, Inc., pg. 529
P.D. FASHIONS, pg. 836
PD NEWS—See PCI, pg. 836
PE SYSTEMS, pg. 836
P.F.D. SUPPLY CORP.—See Prairie Farms Dairy, Inc., pg. 884
PHB PARKER DIE CASTINGS, pg. 836
PHC HOLDINGS, INC.—See Pacific Holding Corporation, pg. 840
PIC REALTY CANADA LTD.—See The Prudential Insurance Company of America, pg. 897
PIC REALTY CORP.—See The Prudential Insurance Company of America, pg. 896
PIP CAPITAL INC.—See Kane-Miller Corp., pg. 616
PLP PRODUTOS PARA LINHAS PROFORMADOS LTDA.—See Preformed Line Products, pg. 886
P/M BEARING DIV.—See Keystone Carbon Company, pg. 628
PM GROUP LIFE INSURANCE COMPANY—See Pacific Mutual Life Insurance Company, pg. 841
P.M. HEALTH CARE DIV.—See P M Company, pg. 835
PM HOLDINGS, INC.—See Phoenix Home Life Mutual Insurance Company, pg. 868
P.M. PAPER PRODUCTS DIV.—See P M Company, pg. 835
PM PROPERTIES INC.—See Petroleum Marketers, Inc., pg. 865
P/M STRUCTURAL PARTS DIV.—See Keystone Carbon Company, pg. 628
PM TERMINALS, INC.—See Petroleum Marketers, Inc., pg. 865
PM TRANSPORT, INC.—See Petroleum Marketers, Inc., pg. 865
PMC PARTNERSHIP, LTD., pg. 836
PMC, INC., pg. 836
PMC INDUSTRIES INC., pg. 836
PMI—See Todd & Sargent, Inc., pg. 1100
PML SECURITIES CO.—See Provident Mutual Life Insurance Co., pg. 896
PMT OF THE SOUTHWEST, INC.—See Anschutz Corporation, pg. 75
PON HOLDING CORP.—See Metromedia Company, pg. 743
P/O/N PRODUCT CORP.—See Penny/Ohlmann/Neiman, Inc., pg. 858
P/O/N SERVICE CORP.—See Penny/Ohlmann/Neiman, Inc., pg. 858
PPA INDUSTRIES, INC., pg. 836
PQ AUSTRALIA PTY., LTD.—See PQ Corporation, pg. 837
PQ ZEOLITES B.V.—See PQ Corporation, pg. 837
PQ CORPORATION, pg. 836
PRC OF AMERICA CORP.—See Plastic Reel Corp. of America, pg. 875
PRC OF AMERICA SUPPLY CORP.—See Plastic Reel Corp. of America, pg. 875
PRUCO LIFE INSURANCE COMPANY—See The Prudential Insurance Company of America, pg. 896
PRUCO, INC.—See The Prudential Insurance Company of America, pg. 896
P. S. INTERNATIONAL INC., pg. 837
PSB CO.—See White Castle System, Inc., pg. 1185
PSC DISTRIBUTING, INC.—See Carquest Corporation, pg. 225
PSI FABRICATORS, INC.—See PSI Group of Companies, pg. 837
PSI GROUP OF COMPANIES, pg. 837
PST VANS, INC., pg. 837
PTA CORPORATION, pg. 837
PTC AEROSPACE—See The Pullman Company, pg. 899
PTC AEROSPACE, INC., pg. 837
PTC THERMISTOR DIV.—See Keystone Carbon Company, pg. 628
PTS ELECTRONICS CORPORATION, pg. 837
PVS CHEMICALS, INC., pg. 837
PVS CHEMICALS, INC.—See PVS Chemicals, Inc., pg. 838
PVS-NOLWOOD CHEMICALS, INC.—See PVS Chemicals, Inc., pg. 838
PVS TECHNOLOGIES, INC.—See PVS Chemicals, Inc., pg. 838
PW PIPE CO.—See Simpson Investment Co., pg. 1007
PABST BREWING CO./MILWAUKEE—See S & P Company, pg. 959
PABST BREWING CO./TUMWATER—See S & P Company, pg. 959
PACE—See Regional Transportation Authority (RTA), pg. 922
PACE COLLECTION, INC., pg. 838
PACE FOODS, INC., pg. 838
PACE INDUSTRIES, INC., pg. 838
PACE INTERNATIONAL CORPORATION, pg. 838
PACE OIL CO., INC., pg. 838
PACE PRESS, INC., pg. 838
PACE RESOURCES, INC., pg. 838
PACESETTER CORPORATION, pg. 839
PACESETTER STEEL SERVICE, INC., pg. 839
PACHMAYR GUN WORKS INC., pg. 839
PACIFIC CAPITAL BANCORP, pg. 839
PACIFIC CLAY PRODUCTS—See Pacific Holding Corporation, pg. 840
PACIFIC COAST BRUSH CO.—See Flo-Pac Corporation, pg. 419
PACIFIC COAST BUILDING PRODUCTS INC., pg. 839
PACIFIC COAST PRODUCERS, pg. 839
PACIFIC ECONOMY COMPANY—See Certified Grocers Of California, pg. 237
PACIFIC ELECTRICORD CO.—See Leviton Mfg. Co., Inc., pg. 671
PACIFIC ENTERPRISES OIL COMPANY (USA), pg. 840
PACIFIC ENVELOPE COMPANY, pg. 840
PACIFIC EQUITIES NETWORK—See Pacific Mutual Life Insurance Company, pg. 841
PACIFIC FINANCIAL ASSET MANAGEMENT CORPORATION—See Pacific Mutual Life Insurance Company, pg. 841
PACIFIC FOODS, INC., pg. 840
PACIFIC FORGE, INC.—See Avis Industrial Corporation, pg. 102
PACIFIC FRUIT EXPRESS CO.—See Anschutz Corporation, pg. 75
PACIFIC HAWAIIAN LTD., pg. 840
PACIFIC HEATER CORPORATION—See Watlow Electric Manufacturing Company, pg. 1167
PACIFIC HIDE & FUR DEPOT, pg. 840
PACIFIC HOLDING CORPORATION, pg. 840
PACIFIC INVESTMENT MANAGEMENT CO.—See Pacific Mutual Life Insurance Company, pg. 841
PACIFIC LUMBER & SHIPPING CO., pg. 840
PACIFIC METAL COMPANY, pg. 841
PACIFIC MOTOR TRANSPORT CO.—See Anschutz Corporation, pg. 75
PACIFIC MOTOR TRUCKING CO.—See Anschutz Corporation, pg. 75
PACIFIC MUTUAL LIFE INSURANCE COMPANY, pg. 841
PACIFIC NORTHERN OIL CORP., pg. 841
PACIFIC NUCLEAR SYSTEMS, INC.—See Nutech, Inc., pg. 818
PACIFIC OPTICAL DIVISION—See Recon/Optical, Inc., pg. 917
PACIFIC PAPERS UNLIMITED—See Bradner Central Company, pg. 171
PACIFIC SCENE INC., pg. 841
PACIFIC SHIPPER, INC.—See K-III Communications Corporation, pg. 611
PACIFIC SOUND RESOURCES, pg. 841
PACIFIC STATES CASUALTY CO., pg. 841
PACIFIC STEEL CASTING CO., pg. 841
PACIFIC WINE CO.—See Paterno Imports Limited, pg. 851
PACIFIC WOOD TREATING COPORATION, pg. 842
PACIFICA REAL ESTATE GROUP, pg. 842
PACIFICA SERVICES, INC., pg. 842
PACIFICARE HEALTH SYSTEMS, INC.—See UniHealth America, pg. 1127
PACIFICARE OF CALIFORNIA—See UniHealth America, pg. 1127
PACIFICARE OF OKLAHOMA INC.—See UniHealth America, pg. 1127
PACIFICARE OF OREGON, INC.—See UniHealth America, pg. 1127
PACKAGE SERVICE COMPANY, INC., pg. 842
PACKAGING PRODUCTS & DESIGN, pg. 842
PACKAGING RESOURCES, INC.—See H.P.H. Industries Ltd., pg. 497
PACKARD INSTRUMENT CO., INC.—See Canberra Industries, Inc., pg. 213
PACKERLAND PACKING CO.—See Gillett Holdings, Inc., pg. 459
PACO RABANNE PARFUMS, pg. 842
PACOR, INC., pg. 842
PACORD—See SPD Technologies, pg. 964
PADDOCK POOL CONSTRUCTION CO., pg. 842
PADDOCK PUBLICATIONS, INC., pg. 842
PADILLA SPEER BEARDSLEY INC., pg. 842
LOUIS PADNOS IRON & METAL CO., pg. 842
PADNOS-SUMMIT—See Louis Padnos Iron & Metal Co., pg. 843
PADOVA AYER—See N W Ayer Incorporated, pg. 104
PAECO INDUSTRIES, INC.—See Great American Industries, Inc., pg. 480
PAGANO, SCHENCK & KAY, INC., pg. 843
PAGE BOY COMPANY, INC., pg. 843
PAGES DRUGS—See Randall's Food Markets, Inc., pg. 912
PAINE FURNITURE CO., pg. 843
PAISANO PUBLICATIONS, INC., pg. 843
PAJAMA CRAFT, INC.—See Host Apparel, Inc., pg. 545
PAK-SHER CO.—See T C Manufacturing Company, Inc., pg. 1072
PAKULA & COMPANY, pg. 843
PALA GROUP, INC., pg. 843
PALA INTERSTATE—See Pala Group, Inc., pg. 843
PALLAS ADVERTISING, INC., pg. 843
PALLMARK INTERNATIONAL, INC.—See The Cherokee Group, pg. 243
PALM BEACH BEAUTY PRODUCTS CO., pg. 843
PALM BEACH NEWSPAPERS, INC.—See Cox Enterprises, Inc., pg. 292
PALM HARBOR HOMES, INC., pg. 843
PALM IRON & BRIDGE WORKS, INC., pg. 843
ARNOLD PALMER CADILLAC INC.—See Don Massey Cadillac Inc., pg. 719
R.M. PALMER COMPANY, pg. 843
PALMER ELECTRIC CO., pg. 843
R.J. PALMER, INC., pg. 844
PALMER INTERNATIONAL, INC., pg. 844
PALMER MANUFACTURING COMPANY, pg. 844
PALMER MOVING & STORAGE CO., pg. 844
PALMER WATER CO.—See Horsehead Industries, Inc., pg. 545
PALMETTO SPINNING CORP., pg. 844
PALMETTO WHOLESALE CO., INC., pg. 844
PALOMA PRODUCTION CO. INC.—See Pearce Industries Inc., pg. 853
PALTIER DIV.—See Lyon Metal Products, Inc., pg. 690
PAMCO ESPANA SOCIEDAD ANONIMA DE SEGUROS—See The Prudential Insurance Company of America, pg. 897
R. B. PAMPLIN CORP., pg. 844
PAN-AMERICAN LIFE INSURANCE COMPANY, pg. 845
PAN AMERICAN OCEAN RESORT HOTEL—See Hubbard Broadcasting, Inc., pg. 549
PAN-AMERICAN SEED CO.—See Geo. J. Ball, Inc., pg. 116
PAN AMERICAN TRADE DEVELOPMENT CORP., pg. 845
PAN HANDLE FRUIT CO.—See Ben E. Keith Company, pg. 620
PAN-O-GRAV, INC.—See Plastic Engineering Components Inc., pg. 875
PANAMERICANA DE AVALUOS, S.A.—See American Appraisal Associates, Inc., pg. 49
PANARCO, INC., pg. 845
PANCOM INTERNATIONAL CORP., pg. 845
PANDUIT AUST. PTY. LTD.—See Panduit Company, pg. 845
PANDUIT CANADA LTD.—See Panduit Company, pg. 845
PANDUIT COMPANY, pg. 845
PANDUIT CORP.—See Panduit Company, pg. 845
PANDUIT CORP. JAPAN BRANCH—See Panduit Company, pg. 846
PANDUIT GMBH—See Panduit Company, pg. 846
PANDUIT LIMITED—See Panduit Company, pg. 846
PANDUIT NEDERLAND—See Panduit Company, pg. 846
PANDUIT PHILIPPINES—See Panduit Company, pg. 846

PANDUIT S.A.S.—See Panduit Company, pg. 846
PANDUIT SINGAPORE PTE. LTD.—See Panduit Company, pg. 846
PANDUIT S.N.C.—See Panduit Company, pg. 845
PANDUIT TRADING PTE. LTD.—See Panduit Company, pg. 846
PANDUIT TRADING PTE. LTD.—See Panduit Company, pg. 846
PANEL PRINTS, INC., pg. 846
PANEL PROCESSING, INC., pg. 846
CHARLES PANKOW BUILDERS, LTD., pg. 846
PANNIER CORPORATION, pg. 846
PANORAMA PRESS, INC., pg. 846
PANTEX CISSELL—See The Dyson-Kissner-Moran Corporation, pg. 358
THE PANTRY, INC., pg. 846
PAOLI, INC., pg. 846
PAOLIN & SWEENEY, pg. 847
PAPER CALMENSON & CO., pg. 847
PAPER ENTERPRISES, INC., pg. 847
PAPER EXPRESS—See Graphisphere Holding Company, pg. 478
PAPERTRONICS, INCORPORATED—See American Tara Corporation, pg. 63
PAPOULIS GREEK TAVERNA—See Lettuce Entertain You Enterprises, Inc., pg. 669
PAR BEVERAGE CO.—See Grandpa Brands Company, pg. 476
PAR ENTERPRISES, INC., pg. 847
PAR INDUSTRIES, INC., pg. 847
PARA NATAL CARE SERVICES, INC.—See Phillips Plastics Corporation, pg. 867
PARA SYSTEMS INC.—See Components Corporation Of America, pg. 270
PARADATA COMPUTER NETWORKS, INC., pg. 847
PARADE PUBLICATIONS INC., pg. 847
PARADIES & CO. ATLANTA—See The Zamoiski Co., pg. 1216
PARADIGM COMMUNICATIONS, pg. 847
PARADISE FRUIT COMPANY, INC., pg. 847
PARAGON GROUP, INC., pg. 847
PARAGON LIFE INSURANCE CO.—See General American Life Insurance Co., pg. 448
PARAGON PAINT & VARNISH CORP., pg. 848
PARAGRAPHE/SUDLER & HENNESSEY—See Young & Rubicam Inc., pg. 1212
PARAGUS—See Lettuce Entertain You Enterprises, Inc., pg. 669
PARAMETRIC PORTFOLIO ASSOCIATES, INC.—See Pacific Mutual Life Insurance Company, pg. 841
PARAMOUNT CITRUS ASSOCIATION—See American Protection Industries, Inc., pg. 60
PARAMOUNT FARMING COMPANY—See American Protection Industries, Inc., pg. 60
PARAMOUNT FITNESS EQUIPMENT CORP., pg. 848
PARAMOUNT FOODS INC., pg. 848
PARAMOUNT PACKAGING CORP., pg. 848
PARAMOUNT PETROLEUM CORP., pg. 848
PARCPLACE SYSTEMS—See Gemini Consulting, pg. 448
PARIS PRESENTS, pg. 848
PARISH WATER COMPANY, INC.—See Baton Rouge Water Works Company, pg. 126
PARISI, INC., pg. 848
PARISIAN, INC., pg. 848
PARK BANK—See Bankmanagers Corp., pg. 118
THE PARK CIRCLE MOTOR CO., pg. 848
PARK CONSTRUCTION COMPANY, pg. 848
PARK CORPORATION, pg. 849
GEORGE W. PARK SEED CO., INC., pg. 849
PARK MOTOR SALES COMPANY, pg. 849
PARK PLACE MOTORCARS, pg. 849
PARK RIDGE CORPORATION, pg. 849
PARKDALE MILLS, pg. 849
PARKER FERTILIZER CO., INC., pg. 849
PARKER STEEL COMPANY, pg. 849
PARKLANE HOSIERY CO., INC., pg. 849
PARKMONT NURSING HOME—See Meritcare, Inc., pg. 740
PARKS CORPORATION, pg. 849
PARKS PRODUCTS, INC., pg. 850
PARKS SAUSAGE COMPANY, pg. 850
PARKWAY FABRICATORS, INC.—See Great American Industries, Inc., pg. 480
PARLIAMENT CO., pg. 850
THE PARMAN CORPORATION, pg. 850
PARMAN OIL CO.—See The Parman Corporation, pg. 850
PARMART STORES—See The Parman Corporation, pg. 850
PARNELL FOODS LTD.—See ARA Group, pg. 7
PARRISH TIRE COMPANY, INC., pg. 850
PARSEC—See Budco Group Inc., pg. 186
PARSEC/DOTSON, INC.—See Budco Group Inc., pg. 186
PARSONS BRINCKERHOFF CONSTRUCTION SERVICES, INC.—See Parsons Brinckerhoff Inc., pg. 850
PARSONS BRINCKERHOFF DEVELOPMENT CORP.—See Parsons Brinckerhoff Inc., pg. 850
PARSONS BRINCKERHOFF FACILITIES SERVICES, INC.—See Parsons Brinckerhoff Inc., pg. 850
PARSONS BRINCKERHOFF INC., pg. 850
PARSONS BRINCKERHOFF INTERNATIONAL, INC.—See Parsons Brinckerhoff Inc., pg. 850
PARSONS BRINCKERHOFF QUADE & DOUGLAS, INC.—See Parsons Brinckerhoff Inc., pg. 850
PARSONS & WHITTEMORE ENTERPRISES, pg. 850
PARTNERS MEANY, INC., pg. 850
PARTNERS & SHEVACK, INC., pg. 850
PARTS WHOLESALERS, INC.—See Carquest Corporation, pg. 225
PARTY PAC DIV.—See Gilster Mary Lee Corp., pg. 460
PASCHEN CONTRACTORS, INC., pg. 851
PASCOE BUILDING SYSTEMS, INC., pg. 851
PASOTEX CORPORATION, pg. 851
PATCH COMMUNICATIONS, pg. 851
PATERNO IMPORTS LIMITED, pg. 851
SID PATERSON ASSOC., INC., pg. 851
PATERSON STAMP WORKS—See American Marking Systems, pg. 58
PATHMARK—See Supermarkets General Corporation, pg. 1064
PATHMARK DEVELOPMENT GROUP—See Kroh Operating L.P., pg. 645
PATIENT CARE, INC., pg. 851
PATRICIAN ASSOCIATES, INC.—See The Principal Financial Group, pg. 891
THE PATRICIAN GROUP, pg. 851
C. H. PATRICK & CO., INC.—See Graniteville Co., pg. 477
PATRINI SHOE STORES—See The Kobacker Company & Affiliates, pg. 638
PATRIOT DIRECT DIAL SYSTEMS—See Western International Media Corporation, pg. 1180
PATRIOT GENERAL INSURANCE CO.—See Middlesex/ Patriot General Insurance Companies, pg. 751
PATRON COMERCIO E REPRESENTACOES LTDA.—See Panduit Company, pg. 846
PATSON'S PRESS, pg. 851
PATSY'S, INC., pg. 851
PATTEN-BEERS CONSTRUCTORS—See Beers Construction Company, pg. 132
GEORGE PATTERSON (BRISBANE) PTY LTD.—See Backer Spielvogel Bates Worldwide, Inc., pg. 112
PATTERSON DENTAL COMPANY, pg. 851
PATTERSON FROZEN FOODS, INC., pg. 851
GEORGE PATTERSON PTY. LIMITED—See Backer Spielvogel Bates Worldwide, Inc., pg. 112
PATTERSON LABORATORIES, INC., pg. 852
THE PATY COMPANY, pg. 852
PAVEY ENVELOPE & TAG CORP., pg. 852
PAVING STONE DIV.—See E.P. Henry Corporation, pg. 530
PAVION LTD., pg. 852
PAWLING CORPORATION, pg. 852
PAWNEE EXTRUSIONS—See Pawnee Industries, Inc., pg. 852
PAWNEE INDUSTRIES, INC., pg. 852
PAWNEE SPECIALTY PRODUCTS—See Pawnee Industries, Inc., pg. 852
PAWTUCKET FASTENERS INC., pg. 852
PAX COMPANY—See CENEX (Farmers Union Central Exchange, Inc.), pg. 231
PAXALL CIRCLE MACHINERY—See The Paxall Group, Inc., pg. 852
PAXALL CLYBOURN MACHINERY—See The Paxall Group, Inc., pg. 852
THE PAXALL GROUP, INC., pg. 852
PAXALL PAK-MASTER MACHINERY—See The Paxall Group, Inc., pg. 852
PAXALL PARSONS MACHINERY—See The Paxall Group, Inc., pg. 852
PAXTON BEAUTIFUL WOODS—See Jeld-Wen, Inc., pg. 592
PAXTON BEAUTIFUL WOODS—See Jeld-Wen, Inc., pg. 592
FRANK PAXTON COMPANY—See Jeld-Wen, Inc., pg. 592
PAXTON PROPERTIES, INC.—See Jeld-Wen, Inc., pg. 592
PAXTON & VIERLING—See Owen Industries, Inc., pg. 834
PAY LESS SUPER MARKETS, INC., pg. 852
PAYLESS CAR RENTAL SYSTEM, INC., pg. 853
PAYLESS CASHWAYS, INC., pg. 853
PAYSON BRONCO, INC.—See Payson Casters, Inc., pg. 853
PAYSON CASTERS, INC., pg. 853
PAYSON GEORGIA, INC.—See Payson Casters, Inc., pg. 853
PAYSON TEXAS, INC.—See Payson Casters, Inc., pg. 853
PBM PUBLISHING—See PBM Office Products, pg. 835
PEABODY ENGINEERING CORP.—See The Pullman Company, pg. 899
PEABODY FLOWAY, INC.—See The Pullman Company, pg. 899
PEABODY HOLMES LIMITED—See The Pullman Company, pg. 900
PEABODY MYERS CORP.—See The Pullman Company, pg. 900
PEABODY N.E., INC.—See The Pullman Company, pg. 900
PEABODY OFFICE FURNITURE CORPORATION, pg. 853
PEABODY TECTANK, INC.—See The Pullman Company, pg. 900
PEAKE PRINTERS, INC., pg. 853
PEARCE EQUIPMENT LEASING—See Pearce Industries Inc., pg. 853
PEARCE INDUSTRIES INC., pg. 853
PEARCE INTERNATIONAL INC.—See Pearce Industries Inc., pg. 853
PEARL CONTAINER CO.—See S & P Company, pg. 959
PEARL DRUM CENTER—See Gibson Guitar Corporation, Inc., pg. 457
PEARL-PRESSMAN-LIBERTY COMMUNICATIONS GROUP, pg. 853
PEARLOOM FABRICS—See N. Erlanger, Blumgart & Company, Inc., pg. 387
PEARLSTINE DISTRIBUTORS INC., pg. 853
PEASE INDUSTRIES, INC., pg. 854
PEAVEY ELECTRONIC CORP., pg. 854
PEBSCO INC.—See Nationwide Mutual Insurance Company, pg. 795
PECK IRON & METAL COMPANY, INC., pg. 854
PECK JONES CONSTRUCTION, pg. 854
PECK ROAD FORD TRUCK SALES, pg. 854
PECK SIMS MUELLER, INC., pg. 854
PECK SPRING COMPANY, pg. 854
PECKHAM INDUSTRIES, INC., pg. 854
PECO INC., pg. 854
PECO MFG. CO.—See Peco Inc., pg. 854
PEDONE & PARTNERS INC., pg. 854
PEDUS BUILDING SERVICES—See Pedus Services, Inc., pg. 855
PEDUS FOOD SERVICES—See Pedus Services, Inc., pg. 855
PEDUS OFFICE SERVICES—See Pedus Services, Inc., pg. 855
PEDUS SECURITY SERVICES—See Pedus Services, Inc., pg. 855
PEDUS SERVICES, INC., pg. 854
PEEBLES, INC., pg. 855
PEELERS RUG COMPANY, INC., pg. 855
PEERLESS CHAIN CO., pg. 855
PEERLESS CHAIN COMPANY—See Bridgewater Resources Corporation, pg. 175
PEERLESS CONFECTION COMPANY, pg. 855
PEERLESS DISTRIBUTING CO.—See Lakeside Refining Co. Inc., pg. 652
PEERLESS IMPORTERS, INC., pg. 855
PEERLESS INC.—See The Zamoiski Co., pg. 1216
PEERLESS LIGHTING CORP., pg. 855
PEERLESS POTTERY, INC., pg. 855
PEERLESS UMBRELLA CO., INC., pg. 855
PEET PACKING CO. INC., pg. 855
PEGASUS INTERNATIONAL CORPORATION, pg. 855
PEIRCE-PHELPS, INC., pg. 855
PEIRONE PRODUCE COMPANY—See U.R.M. Stores, Inc., pg. 1124
DAVID L. PEISTER CO., INC., pg. 856
PELICAN PRODUCTS, pg. 856
PELLA CORPORATION, pg. 856
PELOUZE SCALE CO., pg. 856
PEMCO DIE CASTING CORPORATION, pg. 856
PEMKO MANUFACTURING COMPANY, pg. 856
PEN HOLDINGS, INC., pg. 856
PEN SALES CORPORATION—See Atlas Pen & Pencil Corporation, pg. 96
PEN-TAB INDUSTRIES, INC., pg. 856
PENCO PRODUCTS, pg. 857
PENDA CORPORATION, pg. 857
PENDLETON WOOLEN MILLS, INC., pg. 857
PENETONE CORP.—See Wechco, Inc., pg. 1172
PENGUIN INDUSTRIES, INC., pg. 857
PENHALL INTERNATIONAL, pg. 857
PENN ALUMINUM INTERNATIONAL—See The Marmon Group, Inc., pg. 711
PENN COLOUR GRAPHICS, INC., pg. 857
PENN-DANIELS, INC., pg. 857
PENN EMBLEM CO., pg. 857
PENN ERIE DIV.—See Plastek Group, pg. 875
PENN INSURANCE & ANNUITY CO.—See The Penn Mutual Life Insurance Company, pg. 858
H.O. PENN MACHINERY CO. INC., pg. 857
PENN MEDICAL SERVICES, INC.—See Syracuse Supply Company, pg. 1070
PENN MUTUAL EQUITY SERVICES INC.—See The Penn Mutual Life Insurance Company, pg. 858
THE PENN MUTUAL LIFE INSURANCE COMPANY, pg. 858
PENN POCAHONTAS COAL COMPANY—See The Marmon Group, Inc., pg. 711
PENNEX PRODUCTS CO., INC., pg. 858
PENNINGTON CORPORATION—See Society for Savings Bancorp, Inc., pg. 1016
PENNINSULAR MEAT COMPANY, INC., pg. 858
PENNOCK, pg. 858
PENNSYLVANIA CRUSHER CORP., pg. 858
PENNSYLVANIA PARKING, INC.—See Allright Corporation, pg. 42
PENNSYLVANIA PETROLEUM PRODUCT COMPANY, pg. 858
PENNSYLVANIA SERVICES CORP.—See Cox Enterprises, Inc., pg. 293
PENNSYLVANIA SERVICES CORPORATION—See Cox Enterprises, Inc., pg. 293
PENNSYLVANIA STATE LOTTERY, pg. 858
PENNY/OHLMANN/NEIMAN, INC., pg. 858
PENNY PLATE, INC., pg. 858
PENNY & SPEIER INC., pg. 858
PENNYSAVER (HARTE-HANKS CALIFORNIA CDM, INC.)—See Harte-Hanks Communications, Inc., pg. 513
PENNYSAVER PUBLICATIONS, INC. (THE SHOPPER'S GUIDE)—See Harte-Hanks Communications, Inc., pg. 513
PENOBSCOT FROZEN FOODS, INC., pg. 858
PENROD DRILLING CORPORATION, pg. 859
PENROD DRILLING CORPORATION (UK)—See Penrod Drilling Corporation, pg. 859
PENROD INTERNATIONAL DRILLING COMPANY—See Penrod Drilling Corporation, pg. 859
PENROD INTERNATIONAL DRILLING COMPANY—See Penrod Drilling Corporation, pg. 859
PENSIONS & INVESTMENTS—See Crain Communications, Inc., pg. 295
PENSKE CORPORATION, pg. 859
PENSKE TRANSPORTATION INC.—See Penske Corporation, pg. 859
PENSKE TRUCK LEASING—See Penske Corporation, pg. 859
PENSKE TRUCK LEASING—See Penske Corporation, pg. 859
PENSKE TRUCK LEASING—See Penske Corporation, pg. 859
PENSKE TRUCK LEASING CORP.—See Penske Corporation, pg. 859
PENT ASSEMBLIES, INC.—See Group Dekko International Inc., pg. 490
PENT PLASTICS, INC.—See Group Dekko International Inc., pg. 490
PENT PRODUCTS, INC.—See Group Dekko International Inc., pg. 490
PENTAX PRECISION INSTRUMENTS CORP., pg. 859
PENTEK CORPORATION—See The Dyson-Kissner-Moran Corporation, pg. 357
PENTHOUSE KNITTING MILLS—See Reliable Knitting Works, pg. 925
PENTRON PRODUCTS, INC.—See Actron Manufacturing Company, pg. 15

PEOPLE AND COMPUTERS—See International Data Group, pg. 577
PEOPLEMARK, INC.—See Guardsmark, Inc., pg. 493
PEOPLES ELECTRIC COMPANY, INC., pg. 859
PEOPLES GAS SYSTEM, INC.—See Lykes Energy, Inc., pg. 689
HARRY PEPPER & ASSOCIATES, pg. 859
THE PEPPER COMPANIES, INC., pg. 859
PEPPER CONSTRUCTION CO.—See The Pepper Companies, Inc., pg. 860
PEPPER, HAMILTON & SCHEETZ—See Pepper, Hamilton & Scheetz, pg. 860
PEPPER, HAMILTON & SCHEETZ—See Pepper, Hamilton & Scheetz, pg. 860
PEPPER, HAMILTON & SCHEETZ, pg. 860
PEPPER-LAWSON—See The Pepper Companies, Inc., pg. 860
PEPPER WEST, INC.—See The Pepper Companies, Inc., pg. 860
PEPSI-COLA ALBANY BOTTLING CO., INC., pg. 860
PEPSI-COLA BOTTLING CO., pg. 860
PEPSI-COLA BOTTLING COMPANY OF CHARLOTTE INC., pg. 860
PERDOMO-TED BATES/PUBLICIDAD—See Backer Spielvogel Bates Worldwide, Inc., pg. 112
PERDUE FARMS INC., pg. 860
PERDUE FOODS INCORPORATED—See Perdue Farms Inc., pg. 860
PERDUE INCORPORATED—See Perdue Farms Inc., pg. 860
PERDUE TRANSPORTATION INC.—See Perdue Farms Inc., pg. 860
PEREZ TRADING CO. INC., pg. 860
PERFECT EQUIPMENT CORP.—See Berwind Corporation, pg. 145
PERFECT FIT INDUSTRIES, INC., pg. 861
PERFECT-HOFFMAN CO. LTD.—See Berwind Corporation, pg. 145
PERFECT PEARL COMPANY, INC., pg. 861
PERFECTION AUTOMOTIVE PRODUCTS CORPORATION, pg. 861
PERFECTION BAKERIES INC., pg. 861
PERFECTION HY-TEST COMPANY—See The Marmon Group, Inc., pg. 711
PERFECTION-SCHWANK INC., pg. 861
PERFORMANCE CONTRACTING GROUP, pg. 861
PERFORMANCE CONTRACTORS INC., pg. 861
PERFORMANCE FOOD GROUP, INC., pg. 861
PERGAMENT HOME CENTERS, INC., pg. 862
PERIODICAL PUBLISHERS' SERVICE BUREAU, INC.—See The Hearst Corporation, pg. 523
PERIPHONICS CORP., pg. 862
PERIPHONICS S.A. DE C.V.—See Periphonics Corp., pg. 862
PERIPHONICS VOICE PROCESSING SYSTEMS LTD.—See Periphonics Corp., pg. 862
PERKASIE INDUSTRIES CORPORATION, pg. 862
PERKINS/BUTLER DIRECT MARKETING—See Chiat/Day/Mojo Inc. Advertising, pg. 244
PERKINS FAMILY RESTAURANTS—See Tennessee Restaurant Corp., pg. 1088
PERLMUTER PRINTING COMPANY, pg. 862
PERMA-PIPE DIV.—See Midwesco Inc., pg. 751
PERMANENT GENERAL COMPANIES—See Ingram Industries Inc., pg. 569
PERPETUAL CORPORATION, pg. 862
PERRI SAUSAGE, INC.—See Johnsonville Foods, Inc., pg. 601
PERRY/BARABOO—See Journal Communications Inc., pg. 607
PERRY BROTHERS, INC., pg. 862
PERRY & DERRICK CO., pg. 863
PERRY EQUIPMENT CORPORATION, pg. 863
PERRY GROUP, INC., pg. 863
PERRY & HYLTON, INC.—See WRM, Inc., pg. 1156
PERRY/MILWAUKEE—See Journal Communications Inc., pg. 607
PERRY/NORWAY—See Journal Communications Inc., pg. 607
PERRY PRINTING CORP.—See Journal Communications Inc., pg. 607
PERRY'S ICE CREAM CO., INC., pg. 863
PERRYTON EQUITY, pg. 863
PERSIS CORPORATION, pg. 863
PERSONAL FINANCE CO.—See The Minnesota Mutual Life Insurance Company, pg. 758
PET AG INC.—See Milk Specialties Company, pg. 753
PET LIFE FOODS, INC., pg. 863
PET SPECIALTIES, INC.—See E-II Holdings, Inc., pg. 358
PETALS—See Corham, Inc., pg. 286
PETCARE PLUS, INC., pg. 863
PETER J. SCHMITT CO., INC.—See Peter J. Schmitt Holdings, pg. 977
PETER LUMBER COMPANY, pg. 864
PETER PAN BUS LINES, INC., pg. 864
PETER STRAATON—See Austin Sculpture, pg. 100
J. M. PETERS CO., pg. 864
PETERSEN ALUMINUM CORPORATION, pg. 864
PETERSEN DEVELOPMENT CORP.—See American Tool Companies, Inc., pg. 64
PETERSEN GRAPHICS GROUP, pg. 864
PETERSEN MANUFACTURING CO., INC.—See American Tool Companies, Inc., pg. 64
PETERSEN PUBLISHING COMPANY, pg. 864
PETERSON AMERICAN CORP., pg. 864
PETERSON BUILDERS, INC., pg. 864
PETERSON INDUSTRIES INC., pg. 864
PETERSON MOTOR COMPANY, pg. 865
PETERSON TRACTOR COMPANY, pg. 865
PETOSEED CO.—See Geo. J. Ball, Inc., pg. 116
PETRICCA INDUSTRIES, INC., pg. 865
PETRO CHEM DEVELOPMENT COMPANY, pg. 865
PETRO-HUNT CORPORATION, pg. 865
PETROLEUM INC., pg. 865
PETROLEUM, INC.—See Garvey Industries, Inc., pg. 444
PETROLEUM MARKETERS, INC., pg. 865
PETROLEUM PRODUCTS CORP., pg. 865
PETROLEUM SPECIALTIES—See Lakeside Refining Co. Inc., pg. 652
PETROLEUM TRADERS CORPORATION, pg. 865
PETROLEUM WORLD—See Colonial Petroleum Co., pg. 264
PETRON CORPORATION—See Wechco, Inc., pg. 1172
PETS-N-SUCH—See Van Leunens Inc., pg. 1144
PETTY COMPANY, INC., pg. 866
PETULA ASSOCIATES, LTD.—See The Principal Financial Group, pg. 891
PEVELY DAIRY COMPANY—See Prairie Farms Dairy, Inc., pg. 884
THE PFALTZGRAFF CO.—See Susquehanna Pfaltzgraff, pg. 1065
PFAUDLER-U.S., INC., pg. 866
PHAR-MOR, INC., pg. 866
PHARMACAPS INC., pg. 866
PHARMACISTS PUBLIC RELATIONS BUREAU—See Cullman Ventures, Inc., pg. 304
PHARMAVITE CORP., pg. 866
PHASE LINEAR—See International Jensen Inc., pg. 578
THE PHELPS GROUP, pg. 866
PHELPS TOINTON INC., pg. 866
THE PHILADELPHIA BOURSE, INC., pg. 866
PHILADELPHIA COCA-COLA BOTTLING CO., pg. 866
PHILADELPHIA GEAR CORP., pg. 866
PHILADELPHIA RESERVE SUPPLY COMPANY, pg. 867
PHILADELPHIA SIGN COMPANY, pg. 867
PHILIPP BROTHERS CHEMICALS, INC., pg. 867
THE PHILLIES-A LIMITED PARTNERSHIP, pg. 867
PHILLIES CIGAR COMPANY—See Havatampa Incorporated, pg. 517
THE PHILLIPS AGENCY, pg. 867
PHILLIPS FINE ART AUCTIONEERS, pg. 867
PHILLIPS, MILLER, SPEYER & FROST, INC., pg. 867
PHILLIPS PLASTICS CORPORATION, pg. 867
PHILLIPS PUBLISHING INC., pg. 868
PHOENIX AMERICAN ALARM AFFILIATES, INC.—See Phoenix American Incorporated, pg. 868
PHOENIX AMERICAN INCORPORATED, pg. 868
PHOENIX AMERICAN LIFE INS. CO.—See Phoenix Home Life Mutual Insurance Company, pg. 868
PHOENIX CABLE INCORPORATED—See Phoenix American Incorporated, pg. 868
PHOENIX CONCRETE CUTTING—See Penhall International, pg. 857
PHOENIX DATA INCORPORATED—See Kinetic Systems Corporation, pg. 630
PHOENIX ENTERPRISES INC., pg. 868
PHOENIX EQUITY PLANNING CORP.—See Phoenix Home Life Mutual Insurance Company, pg. 868
PHOENIX FIBER LINK INC.—See Phoenix American Incorporated, pg. 868
PHOENIX FOUNDERS, INC—See Phoenix Home Life Mutual Insurance Company, pg. 868
PHOENIX FUEL COMPANY, INC., pg. 868
PHOENIX GROWTH CAPITAL CORP.—See Phoenix American Incorporated, pg. 868
PHOENIX HOME LIFE MUTUAL INSURANCE COMPANY, pg. 868
PHOENIX INDUSTRIES—See Trinidad/Benham Corporation, pg. 1114
PHOENIX INTERNATIONAL, INC., pg. 868
PHOENIX INVESTMENT COUNSEL INC.—See Phoenix Home Life Mutual Insurance Company, pg. 868
PHOENIX LEASING INCORPORATED—See Phoenix American Incorporated, pg. 868
PHOENIX MAGAZINE—See Media America Corp., pg. 734
PHOENIX SECURITIES, INC.—See Phoenix American Incorporated, pg. 868
PHOENIX STEEL, INC., pg. 869
PHOENIX SYSTEMS EXCHANGE, INC.—See Phoenix American Incorporated, pg. 868
PHOENIX VENTURES, pg. 869
PHONEMATE, INC., pg. 869
PHONETICS, INC., pg. 869
PHOTO CENTRAL OFFICE—See Guardian Industries Corp., pg. 492
PHOTOGENIC MACHINE COMPANY, INC., pg. 869
PHOTOTYPE COLOR GRAPHICS, INC., pg. 869
PIAGET WATCH CORPORATION—See North American Watch Corporation, pg. 812
PIASA MOTOR FUELS INC., pg. 869
PIASA OIL TRANSPORT INC.—See Piasa Motor Fuels Inc., pg. 869
PIC'N PAY STORES, INC.—See CHB Corp., pg. 201
PIC N'PAY SUPERMARKETS, INC., pg. 869
PICK QUICK PAPERS, INC.—See Central Paper Company, pg. 234
PICKERING INDUSTRIES INC., pg. 869
PICK'S COVE MARINA—See Pickering Industries Inc., pg. 870
PICOMA INDUSTRIES—See Bitrek Corporation, pg. 153
PICOU BROTHERS CONSTRUCTION COMPANY, pg. 870
PICOU BROTHERS TRACTOR & RENTAL COMPANY OF GONZALES—See Picou Brothers Construction Company, pg. 870
PICWAY SHOE STORES—See The Kobacker Company & Affiliates, pg. 638
PIE PIPER PRODUCTS, LTD.—See Vienna Sausage Mfg. Co., pg. 1151
PIEDMONT AUTO EXCHANGE—See AEA, Inc., pg. 3
PIEDMONT MECHANICAL, INC., pg. 870
PIEDMONT MECHANICAL, INC.—See Piedmont Mechanical, Inc., pg. 870
PIEDMONT MINERALS—See Thiele Kaolin Co., pg. 1092
PIEDMONT-WHITE MOP CO.—See White Mop Wringer Company, pg. 1186
THE PIERCE CO., INC.—See Avis Industrial Corporation, pg. 102
PIERCE MANUFACTURING, INC., pg. 870
PIERCE YEE ASSOCIATES, LTD—See Harley Ellington Pierce Yee Associates, Inc., pg. 509
PIERCING PAGODA, INC., pg. 870
PIERRE CARDIN FORMAL WEAR—See West Mill Clothes, Inc., pg. 1177
PIERRE CARDIN KNITS—See Beldoch Industries Corporation, pg. 133
JOS. J. PIETRAFESA CO., INC., pg. 870
PIGGYBACK SERVICES, INC.—See Budco Group Inc., pg. 186
PIKE & FISCHER—See The Bureau of National Affairs, Inc., pg. 190
PIKNIK PRODUCTS COMPANY, INC., pg. 870
PIKROSE & CO., LTD.—See The Marmon Group, Inc., pg. 712
PILLOWTEX CORPORATION, pg. 870
PILOT AIR FREIGHT CORP., pg. 870
PINCKNEY MOLDED PLASTICS—See The ISI Manufacturing, Inc., pg. 560
PINCUS BROS., INC., pg. 870
PINE STATE BEVERAGE—See Pine State Tobacco & Candy Company, pg. 871
PINE STATE CREAMERY CO., pg. 871
PINE STATE TOBACCO & CANDY COMPANY, pg. 871
PINE STATE VENDING—See Pine State Tobacco & Candy Company, pg. 871
PINELLAS CRABCOOKER, INC.—See Specialty Restaurants Corporation, pg. 1028
PINELLAS FARMHOUSE, INC.—See Specialty Restaurants Corporation, pg. 1028
PINNACLE MEDIA—See Wyse Advertising, Inc., pg. 1206
PINNE/HERBERS ADVERTISING INC., pg. 871
PIONEER ALUMINUM, INC., pg. 871
PIONEER COMMUNICATIONS OF AMERICA, pg. 871
PIONEER/ECLIPSE CORP., pg. 871
PIONEER ENGINEERING & MANUFACTURING CO., pg. 871
PIONEER EXPRESS INC.—See Overland Transportation System, Inc., pg. 833
PIONEER INDUSTRIAL PRODUCTS CO., pg. 871
PIONEER MILL COMPANY, LTD.—See JMB Realty Corporation, pg. 585
PIONEER MUTUAL LIFE INSURANCE COMPANY, pg. 872
PIONEER NEWS—See Landmark Communications, Inc., pg. 655
PIONEER OIL COMPANY INC., pg. 872
PIONEER PAPER CORPORATION, pg. 872
PIONEER PLASTICS HOLDING, INC., pg. 872
PIONEER PRESS NEWSPAPERS INC.—See Adler & Shaykin, pg. 18
PIONEER SNACKS—See Melody Foods, Inc., pg. 738
PIONEER SUPERMARKETS, pg. 872
PIP PRINTING—See Kane-Miller Corp., pg. 616
PIPE FABRICATING & SUPPLY COMPANY, pg. 872
PIPECO, INC.—See Pasotex Corporation, pg. 851
N.V. PIPECO, S.A.—See Victaulic Company of America, pg. 1149
PIPER AIRCRAFT CORPORATION, pg. 872
PIPER INDUSTRIES, INC., pg. 872
PIPING RESOURCES—See Bovaird Supply Co., pg. 169
PIRELLA GOETTSCHE LOWE S.P.A.—See The Lowe Group, pg. 685
PIRELLA GOETTSCHE LOWE S.P.A.—See The Lowe Group, pg. 685
MALCOLM PIRNIE, INC., pg. 872
PISTOL PETE'S PIZZA, pg. 872
PITCO MASTERMATIC INC.—See G.S. Blodgett Corporation, pg. 157
HAROLD M. PITMAN CO., INC., pg. 872
PITTSBURG MORNING SUN—See Stauffer Communications, Inc., pg. 1042
PITTSBURGH BREWING COMPANY, pg. 873
PITTSBURGH GEAR COMPANY—See Brad Foote Gear Works, Inc., pg. 169
PITTSBURGH PIRATES PROFESSIONAL BASEBALL CLUB, pg. 873
PITTSBURGH STADIUM CONCESSIONS, INC.—See ARA Group, pg. 6
PITTSBURGH TUBE CO., pg. 873
PIZZA HAVEN INC., pg. 873
PIZZAGALLI CONSTRUCTION CO., pg. 873
PLACID OIL COMPANY, pg. 873
PLACID REFINING COMPANY—See Placid Oil Company, pg. 873
PLAID ENTERPRISES INC.—See The Dyson-Kissner-Moran Corporation, pg. 357
PLAID PANTRIES, INC., pg. 873
PLAINS CO-OP OIL MILL, pg. 873
PLAINS COTTON CO-OP ASSOCIATION, pg. 873
PLAINS ELECTRIC GENERATION TRANSMISSION CO-OP, INC., pg. 873
PLAINVIEW DAILY HERALD—See The Hearst Corporation, pg. 524
PLAINVILLE STOCK COMPANY, INC., pg. 874
PLAN INTERNATIONAL U.S.A., pg. 874
PLANES MOVING AND STORAGE, INC., pg. 874
PLANNING SYSTEMS INC., pg. 874
PLANO MOLDING CO., pg. 874
PLANT MAINTENANCE SERVICE CORPORATION, pg. 874
PLANTATION FOODS INC., pg. 874
PLASCAL CORPORATION, pg. 874
PLASKOLITE INC., pg. 874
PLASMA TECHNOLOGY, INC., pg. 874
PLASTECH CORPORATION, pg. 874
PLASTEK GROUP, pg. 874
PLASTEK INDUSTRIES, INC.—See Plastek Group, pg. 875
PLASTEK TOOL, INC.—See Plastek Group, pg. 875
PLASTI-KOTE CO., PACTRA HOBBY—See Plasti-Kote Company Inc., pg. 875
PLASTI-KOTE COMPANY INC., pg. 875
PLASTIC ENGINEERING COMPONENTS INC., pg. 875

PLASTIC ENGINEERING, INC.—See Plastic Engineering Components Inc., pg. 875
PLASTIC MOLDINGS CORP., pg. 875
PLASTIC PACKAGING, INC., pg. 875
PLASTIC PRODUCTS DIVISION—See Freudenberg-NOK (MI), pg. 432
PLASTIC PRODUCTS DIVISION—See Freudenberg-NOK (MI), pg. 432
PLASTIC PRODUCTS OF INDIANA—See Transilwrap Company, Inc., pg. 1107
PLASTIC REEL CORP. OF AMERICA, pg. 875
PLASTIC SUPPLIERS, INC., pg. 875
PLASTIC SUPPLIERS, INC.—See Plastic Suppliers, Inc., pg. 876
PLASTICS MANUFACTURING COMPANY, pg. 876
PLASTICS RESEARCH & DEVELOPMENT CO.—See Ebsco Industries, Inc., pg. 365
PLASTICS TECHNOLOGY—See Bill Communications, Inc., pg. 150
PLASTIGAGE CORPORATION, pg. 876
PLASTIPAK PACKAGING INC., pg. 876
PLASTOID CORPORATION, pg. 876
PLASTOMER CORP., pg. 876
PLASTRON—See Action Technology Company, pg. 15
PLASTRON DALTON—See Action Technology Company, pg. 15
PLATT SACO LOWELL CORPORATION, pg. 876
PLAYTEX APPAREL CANADA, LTD.—See Playtex Apparel Inc., pg. 876
PLAYTEX APPAREL CANADA, LTD., RENFREW—See Playtex Apparel Inc., pg. 876
PLAYTEX APPAREL INC., pg. 876
PLAYTEX BEAUTY CARE, INC.—See Playtex FP Group Incorporated, pg. 877
PLAYTEX ESPANA S.A.—See Playtex Apparel Inc., pg. 876
PLAYTEX ESPANA S.A.—See Playtex Apparel Inc., pg. 876
PLAYTEX FAMILY PRODUCTS CORP.—See Playtex FP Group Incorporated, pg. 877
PLAYTEX FP GROUP INCORPORATED, pg. 877
PLAYTEX FRANCE—See Playtex Apparel Inc., pg. 876
PLAYTEX FRANCE—See Playtex Apparel Inc., pg. 876
PLAYTEX INVESTMENT CORP.—See Playtex FP Group Incorporated, pg. 877
PLAYTEX, ITALIA S.P.A.—See Playtex Apparel Inc., pg. 876
PLAYTEX ITALIA S.P.A.—See Playtex Apparel Inc., pg. 876
PLAYTEX LIMITED—See Playtex Apparel Inc., pg. 876
PLAYTEX LIMITED—See Playtex Apparel Inc., pg. 877
PLAYTEX, LTD.—See Playtex Apparel Inc., pg. 876
PLAYTEX, LTD., ARNPRIOR—See Playtex Apparel Inc., pg. 876
PLAYTEX MARKETING CORPORATION—See Playtex FP Group Incorporated, pg. 877
PLAYTEX MEXICANA S.A. DE C.V.—See Playtex Apparel Inc., pg. 877
PLAYTEX MEXICANA S.A. DE C.V.—See Playtex Apparel Inc., pg. 877
PLAYTEX (PTY.) LTD.—See Playtex Apparel Inc., pg. 877
PLAZA INVESTMENT ASSOCIATES—See Rotterdam Ventures Inc., pg. 952
PLIBRICO CO., pg. 877
PLIBRICO SALES & SERVICE, INC.—See Plibrico Co., pg. 877
PLOOF TRUCK LINES, INC., pg. 877
PLOVER BLFC BRANCH—See W.A. Roosevelt Co., pg. 946
THE PLUMMER GROUP—See Warner, Bicking, Morris & Partners, Inc., pg. 1164
PLUNKETT-WEBSTER, INC., pg. 877
PLYMKRAFT INC.—See Columbian Rope Company, pg. 266
PLYMOUTH—See Plymouth Lamston Stores, Corp., pg. 877
PLYMOUTH CREAMERIES, INC., pg. 877
PLYMOUTH LAMSTON STORES, CORP., pg. 877
PLYMOUTH LOCOMOTIVE INTERNATIONAL, INC., pg. 877
PLYMOUTH TUBE COMPANY, pg. 877
PLYWOOD PANELS, INC., pg. 878
PLYWOOD PLASTICS INC., pg. 878
PMREALTY ADVISORS, INC.—See Pacific Mutual Life Insurance Company, pg. 841
PNEUMAFIL CORP., pg. 878
PNEUMATIC SCALE CORPORATION—See Barry-Wehmiller Company, pg. 122
PNEUMATIC SCALE EUROPE—See Barry-Wehmiller Company, pg. 122
POCAHONTAS FOODS, USA—See Performance Food Group, Inc., pg. 862
THE POCONO BANK—See High Point Financial Corp., pg. 534
POCONO KNITS, INC.—See Jack Young Associates, pg. 1209
POHLSCHRODER & CO. KG—See Steelcase Inc., pg. 1044
POINT BUILDERS—See Gosnell Builders, pg. 473
POINT COMMUNICATIONS, INC., pg. 878
POINT ELECTRIC—See Swivelier Co., Inc., pg. 1068
POIPU WASTE WATER CORPORATION—See JMB Realty Corporation, pg. 585
POLAR CORPORATION, pg. 878
POLAR WARE COMPANY, pg. 878
POLARIS POOL SYSTEMS, INC., pg. 878
POLAROME MFG. CO. INC., pg. 878
POLERA BUILDING CORP., pg. 878
POLHEMUS INC.—See Kaiser Aerospace & Electronics Corp., pg. 614
THE POLIZOS AGENCY, pg. 879
R. L. POLK & CO., pg. 879
POLK MOTOR VEHICLE REGISTRATIONS DIV.—See R. L. Polk & Co., pg. 879
POLKA DOT DAIRY, pg. 879
POLLACK CORPORATION, pg. 879
POLLAK LEVITT CHAIET, ADVERTISING, pg. 879
POLLENEX CORPORATION, pg. 879
POLLENEX CORPORATION—See Odyssey Partners, pg. 821
THE POLLOCK CORP., pg. 879
POLO/RALPH LAUREN CORPORATION, pg. 879
POLY PAK AMERICA, INC., pg. 880
POLY-SEAL CORPORATION, pg. 880
POLYCOAT SYSTEMS, INC., pg. 880
POLYKEN TECHNOLOGIES—See Kendall Healthcare Products Co., pg. 622
POLYMER DEVELOPMENT LABORATORIES, INC., pg. 880
POLYMER PLASTICS CORPORATION, pg. 880
POLYMER, S.A.—See McNeel International Corp., pg. 732
POLYMER TECHNOLOGIES—See Maclean-Fogg Co., pg. 697
POLYPLASTIC PRODUCTS—See Brooks Products, Inc., pg. 180
POLYURETHANE INTERNATIONAL DIVISION—See Flexible Products Company, pg. 419
POLYVINYL FILMS, INC., pg. 880
A. POMERANTZ & CO., pg. 880
POMPEIAN, INC., pg. 880
PONDEROSA FINANCIAL CORPORATION—See Metromedia Company, pg. 744
PONDEROSA, INC.—See Metromedia Company, pg. 743
PONDEROSA INSURANCE AGENCY—See Amerco, A Nevada Corporation, pg. 48
PONLUPA RESTAURANT FINANCING, INC.—See Metromedia Company, pg. 744
PONY EXPRESS COURIER CORP.—See Borg-Warner Corporation, pg. 166
PONY SPORTS & LEISURE INC., pg. 880
POOL COMMUNICATIONS - CHICAGO—See Pool Communications, pg. 880
POOL COMMUNICATIONS, pg. 880
POOL WORLD, INC.—See Ideal Pool Corp., pg. 562
POP TV—See MPO Videotronics, Inc., pg. 693
THE POPCORN FACTORY—See Foster & Gallagher Inc., pg. 426
POPOFSKY ADVERTISING, INC., pg. 880
POPPE TYSON, pg. 880
POPULAR MECHANICS—See The Hearst Corporation, pg. 523
PORCARO BLANKENSHIP ADVERTISING, pg. 881
PORCELAIN METALS CORP., pg. 881
PORT CITY PRESS, INC.—See Judd's Incorporated, pg. 608
PORT CLYDE FOODS CO.—See Connors Brunswick, Inc., pg. 276
PORT OF GALVESTON, pg. 881
PORT OF HOUSTON AUTHORITY, pg. 881
PORT OF OAKLAND, pg. 881
PORTAGE TOOL COMPANY—See Tempel Steel Company, pg. 1086
PORTEOUS—See The Dunlap Companies, pg. 353
ARTHUR PORTER CONSTRUCTION, pg. 881
PORTFOLIO HOMES—See The Hassinger Companies, pg. 516
PORTLAND AUTO AUCTION—See Cox Enterprises, Inc., pg. 293
PORTLAND BEAVERS—See Minnesota Twins Baseball Club, pg. 758
PORTLAND CHAIN MFG. CO.—See Webster Industries Inc., pg. 1172
PORTLAND FOOD PRODUCTS COMPANY, pg. 881
PORTLAND GLASS/AMERICAN MANAGEMENT GROUP—See American Management Group, pg. 58
PORTLAND NEWSPAPERS—See Guy Gannett Publishing Company, pg. 442
PORTLAND SERVICE DIVISION—See Altec Industries, Inc., pg. 45
PORTLAND TERMINAL RAILROAD CO.—See Anschutz Corporation, pg. 76
PORTLAND TRACTION CO.—See Anschutz Corporation, pg. 76
PORTS O'CALL RESTAURANT CORP.—See Specialty Restaurants Corporation, pg. 1028
PORTS OF CALL, INC.—See Amtran, Inc., pg. 70
POSITECH CORPORATION—See Columbus McKinnon Corp., pg. 267
POSITRONIC INDUSTRIES, INC., pg. 881
POST BUCKLEY SCHUH & JERNIGAN, pg. 881
POSTAL COMMEMORATIVE SOCIETY COLLECTION—See MBI Inc., pg. 691
POTAMKIN MANHATTAN, pg. 882
POTAMKIN TOYOTA, INC., pg. 882
POTATO SALES COMPANY, INC., pg. 882
POTPOURRI (HARTE-HANKS CALIFORNIA CDM, INC.)—See Harte-Hanks Communications, Inc., pg. 513
POTRAIT INDUSTRIES CORPORATION—See Lifetouch, Inc., pg. 675
POTTER HAZLEHURST INCORPORATED, pg. 882
LUKE POTTER DODGE INC., pg. 882
POTTER-SHACKELFORD CONSTRUCTION CO., pg. 882
POTTERS INDUSTRIES, INC.—See PQ Corporation, pg. 837
L. POWELL CO., INC., pg. 882
POWELL ELECTRONICS INC., pg. 882
POWELL LABORATORIES—See Carolina Biological Supply Co., pg. 223
ROBERT C. POWELL DEVELOPMENTS, INCORPORATED, pg. 882
THE WM. POWELL COMPANY, pg. 882
POWELL'S INC.—See Sathers Inc., pg. 972
J.D. POWER AND ASSOCIATES, pg. 883
POWER BASE—See Compuware Corporation, pg. 272
POWER CONTRACTING & ENGINEERING CORP., pg. 883
POWER CONVERSION, INC., pg. 883
POWER DISCS—See The Benson Music Group, pg. 140
POWER ENGINEERING CO. INC., pg. 883
POWER KING PRODUCTS CO., pg. 883
THE POWER LINE—See Publishers Clearing House, pg. 898
POWER-ONE, INC., pg. 883
POWER PIPING COMPANY—See Harlan Electric Co., pg. 509
POWER PLASTICS INC.—See Tiffany Extruders, Inc., pg. 1097
POWER PROCESS PIPING, INC., pg. 883
POWER SHRED DIVISION—See Fellowes Manufacturing Co., pg. 406
POWER & TELEPHONE SUPPLY COMPANY, pg. 883
POWER WHEELS, INC.—See Kransco, pg. 644
POWERFORCE COMPANY, INC.—See IDC Services, Inc., pg. 560
POWERFORCE COMPANY, INC.—See IDC Services, Inc., pg. 560
POWERINE OIL COMPANY—See Powerine Oil Company Holdings, pg. 883
POWERINE OIL COMPANY HOLDINGS, pg. 883
POWERS CONSTRUCTION CO., INC., pg. 883
ARTHUR A. POZZI CO., INC., pg. 883
PRACTICAL AUTOMATION, INC.—See Alinabal, Inc., pg. 34
PRACTICAL PERIPHERALS—See Hayes Microcomputer Products, Inc., pg. 519
PRACTICE DEVELOPMENT INSTITUTE—See Friedman, Eisenstein, Raemer & Schwartz, pg. 433
PRAIRIE FARMS DAIRY, INC., pg. 884
H. C. PRANGE COMPANY, pg. 884
PRANGE SPECIALTY STORES GROUP, INC.—See H. C. Prange Company, pg. 884
PRANGE WAY—See H. C. Prange Company, pg. 884
PRATT-READ CORPORATION, pg. 884
PRAXIS INTERNATIONAL INC., pg. 884
PREBOUND PERIODICALS, INC.—See The American Companies, Inc., pg. 51
PRECISE METALS & PLASTICS, INC.—See KDI Corporation, pg. 612
PRECISE TECHNOLOGY & ELECTRONICS, INC.—See Air Gage Company, pg. 27
PRECISION ARC CO.—See Smith Industries, Inc., pg. 1013
PRECISION ASBESTOS ABATEMENT COMPANY—See Hoffman Corporation, pg. 538
PRECISION CARBIDE TOOL COMPANY, INC., pg. 885
PRECISION CONSTRUCTION COMPAN Y—See Hoffman Corporation, pg. 538
PRECISION DISC CORP.—See North American Products Corp., pg. 811
PRECISION ECHO, INC., pg. 885
PRECISION INDUSTRIES, pg. 885
PRECISION METAL PRODS., INC.—See Phoenix International, Inc., pg. 869
PRECISION PARTS CORP., pg. 885
PRECISION PIPE & SUPPLY CO.—See Premarc Corporation, pg. 886
PRECISION PLASTICS—See Precision Plastics Inc., pg. 885
PRECISION PLASTICS INC., pg. 885
PRECISION POWER DIV.—See AEI Holding Co., Inc., pg. 3
PRECISION PRODUCTS BUSINESS—See American Optical Corp., pg. 59
PRECISION ROLL GRINDERS, INC., pg. 885
PRECISION SPECIALTY METALS, INC.—See Dubin-Clark & Company, pg. 350
PRECISION TUNE, INC., pg. 885
PRECISION TWIST DRILL CO., pg. 885
PRECISION VALVE CORPORATION, pg. 885
PRECISIONAIRE, INC., pg. 886
PREDCO, INC.—See Dixon Valve & Coupling Company, pg. 341
PREDICASTS—See Ziff Communications Company, pg. 1219
PREFERRED MILLWORK, INC.—See Marmac Corporation, pg. 710
PREFERRED PROPERTIES—See Tucson Realty & Trust Co., pg. 1118
PREFERRED RISK LIFE INSURANCE CO.—See Preferred Risk Mutual Insurance, pg. 886
PREFERRED RISK MUTUAL INSURANCE, pg. 886
PREFORMADOS DE MEXICO SA—See Preformed Line Products, pg. 886
PREFORMED LINE PRODUCTS, pg. 886
PREFORMED LINE PRODUCTS CANADA—See Preformed Line Products, pg. 886
PREFORMED LINE PRODUCTS(GREAT BRITAIN) LTD.—See Preformed Line Products, pg. 886
PREMARC CORPORATION, pg. 886
PREMIER BEVERAGES—See Dr Pepper/Seven-Up Companies, Inc., pg. 342
PREMIER CHEMICAL CO., LTD.—See Uniroyal Chemical Company, Inc., pg. 1129
PREMIER CHEMICAL PLANT—See Uniroyal Chemical Company, Inc., pg. 1129
PREMIER COATINGS, INC., pg. 886
PREMIER DENTAL PRODUCTS COMPANY, pg. 886
PREMIER INDUSTRIES, INC., pg. 887
PREMIER MILL CORP., pg. 887
PREMIER PUBLISHING CO.—See Pacific Envelope Company, pg. 840
PREMIER REFRACTORIES (CANADA) LTD.—See Premier Refractories & Chemicals Inc., pg. 887
PREMIER REFRACTORIES & CHEMICALS INC., pg. 887
PREMIERE MAGAZINE—See K-III Communications Corporation, pg. 611
PREMIUM ADVANCE COMPANY—See Robert F. Driver Co., Inc., pg. 349
PREMIUM PORK PROCESSORS—See Sunnyland Foods, Inc., pg. 1061
PREMIUM PRODUCTS DIVISION—See Consolidated Cigar Corporation, pg. 276
PREMIUMS INTL. LTD.—See Carlson Companies, Inc., pg. 221
PRE-MIX CONCRETE CO.—See H.G. Fenton Material Company, pg. 406

PRENTISS INCORPORATED, pg. 887
PREPCO, pg. 887
PREPLINK—See Great Lakes Lithograph Co., pg. 481
GEORGE W. PRESCOTT PUBLISHING CO., pg. 887
PRESERVATIVE PAINT COMPANY, pg. 887
THE PRESMET CORP., pg. 887
PRESQUE ISLE CORP.—See National Steel Corporation, pg. 794
PRESRAY CORP.—See Pawling Corporation, pg. 852
PRESS ASSOCIATION, INC.—See The Associated Press, pg. 92
PRESS ENTERPRISE COMPANY, pg. 887
PRESSED STEEL TANK CO., INC., pg. 887
PRESSMAN TOY CORP., pg. 887
PRESSURE PAK CONTAINER, INC.—See Amtrol Inc., pg. 70
PRESSURE PRODUCTS INDUSTRIES—See Cawsl Corporation, pg. 230
PRESSURE SYSTEMS, pg. 888
PREST RACK INC.—See Binkley Company, pg. 151
PRESTCON, INC.—See Cenvill Development Corp., pg. 236
PRESTIGE FRAGRANCE & COSMETICS, INC.—See MacAndrews & Forbes Holdings Inc., pg. 696
PRESTIGE FRAGRANCES, LTD.—See MacAndrews & Forbes Holdings Inc., pg. 696
PRESTIGE PERFUMES LTD.—See MacAndrews & Forbes Holdings Inc., pg. 696
PRESTIGE STAMPING, INC., pg. 888
PRESTO FOOD PRODUCTS, INC., pg. 888
PRESTO FOOD STORES, INC., pg. 888
PRESTO LOCK, INC., pg. 888
PRESTOLITE WIRE CORPORATION—See New Hampshire Oak, pg. 801
PRESTON ENERGY INC., pg. 888
PRESTON PROPERTIES OF ARIZONA, INC.—See Washington Mutual Savings Bank, pg. 1167
PRESTON PROPERTIES OF CALIFORNIA, INC.—See Washington Mutual Savings Bank, pg. 1167
PRESTON PROPERTIES TEXAS, INC.—See Washington Mutual Savings Bank, pg. 1167
PRESTON PROPERTY MANAGEMENT COMPANY—See Washington Mutual Savings Bank, pg. 1167
PRESTON RIDGE FINANCIAL SERVICES CORPORATION—See Washington Mutual Savings Bank, pg. 1167
PRESTONIA OFFICE PRODUCTS LTD.—See American Trading and Production Corporation, pg. 65
PRETEC PRECISIE TECHNIEK B.V.—See Bell & Howell Company, pg. 135
PRICE BROTHERS CO., pg. 888
PRICE BROTHERS COMPOSITE PIPE, INC.—See Price Brothers Co., pg. 888
PRICE CHOPPER—See Golub Corporation, pg. 469
PRICE/MCNABB, INC., pg. 888
PRICE WATERHOUSE - U.S., pg. 888
PRICE WEBER MARKETING COMMUNICATIONS, INC., pg. 889
PRICE WOODS, INC.—See Joe E. Woods, Inc., pg. 1200
PRIDE OIL CO., INC.—See Kelso Oil Company, pg. 622
PRIDE PRODUCTS, INC., pg. 889
PRIDGEON & CLAY, INC., pg. 889
BENJAMIN PRIEST LTD.—See International Marine Holdings, Inc., pg. 579
PRIMACARE HEALTH RESOURCES, INC.—See Syracuse Supply Company, pg. 1070
PRIMARY COAL INC.—See Primary Industries Corporation, pg. 889
PRIMARY INDUSTRIES CORPORATION, pg. 889
PRIMARY STEEL INC.—See Primary Industries Corporation, pg. 889
PRIME CONSTRUCTION CO.—See Prime Hospitality Corp., pg. 889
PRIME-FLORIDA, INC.—See Prime Hospitality Corp., pg. 889
PRIME HOSPITALITY CORP., pg. 889
PRIME HOSPITALITY CORP LIMITED PARTNERSHIP—See Prime Hospitality Corp., pg. 889
PRIME MANAGEMENT CO., INC.—See Prime Hospitality Corp., pg. 889
PRIME TANNING CO., INC., pg. 889
PRIME TECHNOLOGY, INC., pg. 889
PRIMEX PLASTICS CORP.—See ICC Industries, Inc., pg. 558
PRIMUS INC., pg. 890
PRINCE CORPORATION, pg. 890
PRINCE GARDNER INCORPORATED, pg. 890
PRINCE MANUFACTURING, INC., pg. 890
PRINCETON LANGUAGE CENTER—See Berlitz International, Inc., pg. 143
PRINCETON PARTNERS, INC., pg. 890
PRINCETON PARTNERS, INC.—See West Coast National Video, pg. 1177
PRINCEVILLE CANNING CO.—See Owatonna Canning Company, pg. 833
PRINCEVILLE CORPORATION, pg. 890
PRINCEVILLE HOTEL CORPORATION—See Princeville Corporation, pg. 890
PRINCEVILLE MANAGEMENT CORPORATION—See Princeville Corporation, pg. 890
PRINCEVILLE REALTY CORPORATION—See Princeville Corporation, pg. 890
PRINCEVILLE UTILITIES COMPANY, INC.—See Princeville Corporation, pg. 890
PRINCEVILLE WATER SYSTEMS, INC.—See Princeville Corporation, pg. 890
PRINCIPAL CASUALTY INSURANCE COMPANY—See The Principal Financial Group, pg. 891
PRINCIPAL DEVELOPMENT ASSOCIATES, INC.—See The Principal Financial Group, pg. 891
THE PRINCIPAL/EGT FINANCIAL CORPORATION—See The Principal Financial Group, pg. 891
THE PRINCIPAL FINANCIAL GROUP, pg. 890
PRINCIPAL HEALTH CARE, INC.—See The Principal Financial Group, pg. 891
PRINCIPAL LIFE INSURANCE COMPANY—See The Principal Financial Group, pg. 891
PRINCIPAL MANAGEMENT INC.—See The Principal Financial Group, pg. 891
PRINCIPAL MARKETING SERVICES, INC.—See The Principal Financial Group, pg. 891
PRINCIPAL MUTUAL LIFE INSURANCE CO.—See The Principal Financial Group, pg. 891
PRINCIPAL NATIONAL LIFE INSURANCE COMPANY—See The Principal Financial Group, pg. 891
PRINCIPAL RESIDENTIAL ADVISORS—See The Principal Financial Group, pg. 891
PRINCOR FINANCIAL SERVICES CORPORATION—See The Principal Financial Group, pg. 891
PRINS, MEIJER, STAMENKOVITS EN VAN WALBEEK/ YOUNG & RUBICAM B.V.—See Young & Rubicam Inc., pg. 1212
PRINT NORTHWEST, pg. 891
PRINT-O-STAT, INC.—See Pace Resources, Inc., pg. 839
PRINT-O-TAPE, pg. 891
PRINTCO, INC., pg. 891
PRINTED CIRCUIT CORPORATION, pg. 891
PRINTING DEVELOPMENTS, INC.—See New Hampshire Oak, pg. 801
PRINTING HOUSE, INC., pg. 891
PRIORITY FINISHING CORP.—See The Cherokee Group, pg. 243
PRISM INTEGRATED SANITATION MANAGEMENT, INC.—See S. C. Johnson & Son, Inc., pg. 599
PRISS PRINTS, INC.—See Educational Publishing Corporation, pg. 369
THE PRITCHARD CORPORATION—See Black & Veatch, pg. 155
PRO CLINICA INC., pg. 891
THE PRO CORPORATION, pg. 891
PRO HARDWARE, INC., pg. 891
PRO LINE—See Flexfab, Inc., pg. 418
PRO-LINE CORPORATION, pg. 892
PRO-LOG CORPORATION, pg. 892
PRO MEDIA, INC., pg. 892
THE PRO-QUIP CORPORATION, pg. 892
PRO-SELECT—See Northwestern Golf Company, pg. 815
PRO*PORTION INDUSTRIES, INC.—See Bresler's Industries, Inc., pg. 174
PROCESS COLOR PLATE—See Schawk, Inc., pg. 975
PROCESS MATERIALS—See Central National-Gottesman Inc., pg. 233
PROCESS SYSTEMS, INC. CONSTRUCTION CO.—See PSI Group of Companies, pg. 837
PROCESSED PLASTIC COMPANY, pg. 892
PROCOR ENGINEERING LTD.—See The Marmon Group, Inc., pg. 712
PROCOR LPG STORAGE DIVISION—See The Marmon Group, Inc., pg. 712
PROCOR RAIL CAR DIVISION—See The Marmon Group, Inc., pg. 712
PROCOR SULPHUR SERVICES DIVISION—See The Marmon Group, Inc., pg. 712
PROCOR TECHNOLOGIES—See Land O'Lakes, Inc., pg. 654
PROCRANE INC.—See The Marmon Group, Inc., pg. 712
PROCTOR & GARDNER ADVERTISING, INC., pg. 892
PRODUCERS CO-OP ASSOCIATION, INC., pg. 892
PRODUCERS LIVESTOCK, pg. 892
PRODUCERS RICE MILL INC., pg. 892
PRODUCTION MACHINERY CORPORATION, pg. 893
PRODUCTION MANAGEMENT COMPANIES, INC., pg. 893
PRODUCTION MANAGEMENT CONTROL SYSTEMS, INC.—See Production Management Companies, Inc., pg. 893
PRODUCTION MANAGEMENT CORPORATION—See Production Management Companies, Inc., pg. 893
PRODUCTION MANAGEMENT INDUSTRIES, INC.—See Production Management Companies, Inc., pg. 893
PRODUCTION MANAGEMENT STRUCTURAL SYSTEMS, INC.—See Production Management Companies, Inc., pg. 893
PRODUCTION PAYMENTS, INC.—See IDC Services, Inc., pg. 560
PRODUCTION TOOL SUPPLY CO., pg. 893
PRODUCTIVE BUSINESS INTERIORS—See Indiana Records Managers, pg. 565
PRODUCTO DIEMAKERS SUPPLIES LTD.—See The Producto Machine Co., pg. 893
PRODUCTO MACHINE CO. RING DIVISION—See The Producto Machine Co., pg. 893
THE PRODUCTO MACHINE CO., pg. 893
PRODUTEC HOUGHTON S.A.—See E. F. Houghton & Co., pg. 546
PROFESCO CORPORATION—See John Hancock Mutual Life Insurance Company, pg. 596
PROFESSIONAL APARTMENT MANAGEMENT, INC., pg. 893
PROFESSIONAL BOOK DISTRIBUTORS, INC., pg. 894
PROFESSIONAL COMMUNITY MANAGEMENT, INC.—See Affiliates Group Inc., pg. 24
PROFESSIONAL ECONOMIC SERVICES, INC.—See John Hancock Mutual Life Insurance Company, pg. 596
PROFESSIONAL HEALTHCARE SYSTEMS, INC., pg. 894
PROFESSIONAL INFORMATION MANAGMENT—See Seligman & Associates, Inc., pg. 988
PROFESSIONAL SECURITIES CORP.—See Huntco Inc., pg. 554
PROFESSIONAL TRAVEL, INC., pg. 894
PROFILE INTL. MICROCIRCUITS, LTD.—See International Microcircuits, Inc., pg. 579
PROFIT MANAGEMENT CORP.—See Family Inns of America, Inc., pg. 398
PROGLASS—See American Management Group, pg. 58
PROGRAMMES MARKETING ANNUAIRES (PMA)—See TMP Worldwide, Inc., pg. 1074
PROGRESS CASTING GROUP, INC., pg. 894
PROGRESS PAINT MFG. CO., pg. 894
PROGRESS PRINTING COMPANY, pg. 894
PROGRESS WEST, pg. 894
PROGRESSIVE DRIVER SERVICES, INC., pg. 894
PROGRESSIVE TOOL & INDUSTRIES CO., pg. 894
PROMOTION SERVICES, INC.—See Dairymen, Inc., pg. 311
PROPERTY MANAGEMENT SERVICES, INC., pg. 894
PROPERTY-OWNERS INSURANCE CO.—See Auto-Owners Insurance, pg. 100
PROPPER MANUFACTURING CO., INC., pg. 895
PROPRIETORY PRODUCTS GROUP—See Esco Corporation, pg. 388
PROSNIP CORPORATION—See American Tool Companies, Inc., pg. 64
PROSPECT FOUNDRY, INC., pg. 895
PROSPECT MOTORS, INC., pg. 895
PROSSER/ENPO INDUSTRIES—See Harbour Group Ltd., pg. 507
PROSTROLLO MOTOR COMPANY, pg. 895
PROSTROLLO MOTOR SALES, INC.—See Prostrollo Motor Company, pg. 895
PROTECTION TECHNOLOGY—See Day & Zimmermann, Inc., pg. 320
PROTECTO PLASTICS, INC.—See Penguin Industries, Inc., pg. 857
THE PROTECTOR CORPORATION, pg. 895
PROTIMEX CORPORATION, pg. 895
PROTO SYSTEMS OF ATLANTA, pg. 895
PROVIDENCE JOURNAL BROADCASTING CORP.—See Providence Journal Company, pg. 896
PROVIDENCE JOURNAL COMPANY, pg. 895
PROVIDENCE JOURNAL TELECOMMUNICATIONS, INC.—See Providence Journal Company, pg. 896
PROVIDENT MUTUAL LIFE & ANNUTIY COMPANY OF AMERICA—See Provident Mutual Life Insurance Co., pg. 896
PROVIDENT MUTUAL LIFE INSURANCE CO., pg. 896
PROVIMI VEAL CORPORATION, pg. 896
PROXIMA CORPORATION, pg. 896
PROXIMITY CONTROLS CORP.—See Dwyer Instruments Inc., pg. 356
PRUCAPITAL, INC.—See The Prudential Insurance Company of America, pg. 897
PRUCAPITAL MANAGEMENT, INC.—See The Prudential Insurance Company of America, pg. 897
PRUCAPITAL SECURITIES CO., INC.—See The Prudential Insurance Company of America, pg. 897
PRUCO LIFE INSURANCE COMPANY OF NEW JERSEY—See The Prudential Insurance Company of America, pg. 896
PRUCO SECURITIES CORP.—See The Prudential Insurance Company of America, pg. 896
PRUCO SERVICES, INC.—See The Prudential Insurance Company of America, pg. 896
PRUDENTIAL AGRICULTURAL CREDIT, INC.—See The Prudential Insurance Company of America, pg. 897
PRUDENTIAL ASIA CAPITAL LIMITED—See The Prudential Insurance Company of America, pg. 897
PRUDENTIAL ASIA INVESTMENTS LIMITED—See The Prudential Insurance Company of America, pg. 897
THE PRUDENTIAL ASSET MANAGEMENT CO., INC.—See The Prudential Insurance Company of America, pg. 897
PRUDENTIAL CAPITAL & INVESTMENT SERVICES, INC.—See The Prudential Insurance Company of America, pg. 897
PRUDENTIAL COMMERCIAL INSURANCE CO.—See The Prudential Insurance Company of America, pg. 897
PRUDENTIAL DEVELOPMENT & RETAIL DIV.—See The Prudential Insurance Company of America, pg. 897
PRUDENTIAL EASTERN HOME OFFICE—See The Prudential Insurance Company of America, pg. 897
PRUDENTIAL EQUITY INVESTMENT DIV.—See The Prudential Insurance Company of America, pg. 897
PRUDENTIAL FUND MANAGEMENT CANADA LTD.—See The Prudential Insurance Company of America, pg. 897
PRUDENTIAL FUNDING CORP.—See The Prudential Insurance Company of America, pg. 897
PRUDENTIAL GENERAL INSURANCE CO.—See The Prudential Insurance Company of America, pg. 897
PRUDENTIAL INSTITUTIONAL INVESTMENT MANAGEMENT DIV.—See The Prudential Insurance Company of America, pg. 897
THE PRUDENTIAL INSURANCE COMPANY OF AMERICA, pg. 896
PRUDENTIAL INTERFUNDING CORP.—See The Prudential Insurance Company of America, pg. 897
THE PRUDENTIAL INVESTMENT CORP.—See The Prudential Insurance Company of America, pg. 897
THE PRUDENTIAL LIFE INSURANCE COMPANY, LTD.—See The Prudential Insurance Company of America, pg. 897
PRUDENTIAL-LMI COMMERCIAL INSURANCE COMPANY—See The Prudential Insurance Company of America, pg. 897
PRUDENTIAL METAL SUPPLY CORP., pg. 898
PRUDENTIAL MORTGAGE CAPITAL—See The Prudential Insurance Company of America, pg. 897
PRUDENTIAL OF AMERICA GENERAL INSURANCE CO. (CANADA)—See The Prudential Insurance Company of America, pg. 897
PRUDENTIAL OVERSEAS FUNDING CORP. N.V.—See The Prudential Insurance Company of America, pg. 897
PRUDENTIAL PROPERTY & CASUALTY INSURANCE COMPANY—See The Prudential Insurance Company of America, pg. 897
THE PRUDENTIAL REALTY GROUP—See The Prudential Insurance Company of America, pg. 897
PRUDENTIAL REINSURANCE—See The Prudential Insurance Company of America, pg. 897
PRUDENTIAL REINSURANCE CO.—See The Prudential Insurance Company of America, pg. 897

PRUDENTIAL SECURITIES GROUP INC.—See The Prudential Insurance Company of America, pg. 897
PRUDENTIAL SECURITIES INC.—See The Prudential Insurance Company of America, pg. 897
PRUDENTIAL SUPPORT OPERATIONS, INC.—See The Prudential Insurance Company of America, pg. 897
PRUSERVICOS PARTICIPACOES, S.A., C/O PRUDENTIAL ATLANTIC COMPANHIA BRASILEIRA DE SEGUROS—See The Prudential Insurance Company of America, pg. 898
PRUSUPPLY, INC.—See The Prudential Insurance Company of America, pg. 897
PSOMAS & ASSOCIATES, pg. 898
P.T. S.C. JOHNSON & SON (INDONESIA) LTD.—See S. C. Johnson & Son, Inc., pg. 599
PTI TECHNOLOGIES—See Esco Corporation, pg. 388
PUBLIC MEDIA CENTER, pg. 898
PUBLIC RELATIONS PRODUCTIONS CO., INC.—See Ruder, Finn, Inc., pg. 954
PUBLIC STORAGE COMMERCIAL PROPERTIES GROUP, INC.—See Public Storage, Inc., pg. 898
PUBLIC STORAGE, INC., pg. 898
PUBLICACIONES EN COMPUTACION LTDA.—See International Data Group, pg. 577
PUBLIMERCA S.A.—See N W Ayer Incorporated, pg. 105
PUBLISHER RESOURCES INC.—See Ingram Industries Inc., pg. 569
PUBLISHERS CLEARING HOUSE, pg. 898
PUBLIX GROUP, pg. 898
PUBLIX SUPER MARKETS, INC.—See Publix Supermarkets Inc., pg. 899
PUBLIX SUPERMARKETS INC., pg. 898
THE PUCKETT GROUP, pg. 899
PUEBLO INTERNATIONAL, INC., pg. 899
PUEBLO INTERNATIONAL, INC.-P.R. DIV.—See Pueblo International, Inc., pg. 899
PUEBLO METALS CO.—See CF&I Steel Corporation, pg. 201
PUEBLO RAILROAD SERVICE COMPANY—See CF&I Steel Corporation, pg. 201
PUERTO RICO TOURISM COMPANY, pg. 899
PUGET SOUND PLYWOOD, INC., pg. 899
PUGH MARINA—See Pugh Oil Company, pg. 899
PUGH OIL COMPANY, pg. 899
PULASKI RUBBER CO.—See R.C.A. Rubber Company, pg. 906
PULLIAM MOTOR COMPANY, pg. 899
THE PULLMAN COMPANY, pg. 899
PULLMAN INDUSTRIES, INC., pg. 900
PULSE MAGAZINE—See MTS, Inc., pg. 694
PUMA MANUFACTURING LTD.—See O'Brien Energy Systems Inc., pg. 820
THE PUMP ROOM—See Lettuce Entertain You Enterprises, Inc., pg. 669
PUMPELLY OIL, INC., pg. 900
PUNA PLANTATION HAWAII LTD., pg. 900
PUNA SUGAR CO., LTD.—See JMB Realty Corporation, pg. 585
PURCELL CO., INC., pg. 900
PURCELL INTERNATIONAL GROUP, INC., pg. 900
PURE CARBON COMPANY—See The Stackpole Corporation, pg. 1034
PURITAN BAKERY, INC., pg. 900
PURITAN/CHURCHILL CHEMICAL COMPANY, pg. 900
PURITAN OIL COMPANY, INC.—See Warren Equities Inc., pg. 1165
PURITY DAIRIES INC., pg. 901
PURITY, INC., pg. 901
PURITY SUPREME, INC., pg. 901
LAT PURSER & ASSOCIATE, pg. 901
PUSKAR GIBBON CHAPIN, INC., pg. 901
PUTMAN PUBLISHING CO., pg. 901
PUTT PUTT GOLF COURSES OF AMERICA, INC., pg. 901
DR. PUTTNER & BSB WORLDWIDE WERBEGESELLSCHAFT M.B.H.—See Backer Spielvogel Bates Worldwide, Inc., pg. 111
PUTZMEISTER, INC., pg. 901
PVC COMPOUNDERS—See Group Dekko International Inc., pg. 490
PY-O-MY DIV.—See Gilster Mary Lee Corp., pg. 460
PYLE INC.—See LPL Technologies, Inc., pg. 648
PYRAMID CHEMICAL COMPANY, INC.—See Theochem Labs., Inc., pg. 1090
THE PYRAMID COMPANIES, pg. 901
PYRAMID HANDBAGS INC., pg. 901
PYRAMID MOUNTAIN LUMBER, pg. 901
PYRO CHEM, INC.—See Borg-Warner Corporation, pg. 166
PYROMET, INC., pg. 901
PYTTRONIC INDUSTRIES, INC., pg. 901

Q

QC, INC.—See Atlantic Dairy Cooperative, pg. 95
QEI, INC., pg. 902
QF, INC.—See Fishking Processors, Inc., pg. 415
QLM ASSOCIATES, INC., pg. 902
QPP QUALITY PIPING PRODUCTS—See Nibco, Inc., pg. 806
QSC, INC.—See Castle-Harlan, Inc., pg. 229
QST INDUSTRIES, INC., pg. 902
QDI, INC.—See Arizona Wholesale Supply Company, pg. 82
QISMET LTD.—See Milady Brassiere & Corset Co., Inc., pg. 753
Q.P. CORPORATION—See Kifuki U.S.A. Co., Inc., pg. 629
QUACKENBUSH CO. INC., pg. 902
QUAD/GRAPHICS, INC., pg. 902
QUAD SYSTEMS CORPORATION, pg. 902
QUAD/WEST PRE-PRESS—See Quad/Graphics, Inc., pg. 902
QUADION CORPORATION, pg. 902
QUADRANGLE DEVELOPMENT CORPORATION, pg. 902
QUADRANGLE MANAGEMENT COMPANY—See Quadrangle Development Corporation, pg. 902
QUADRANT ENGINEERING DIV.—See AEI Holding Co., Inc., pg. 3
QUADRASTAT CORP.—See Adams Rite Manufacturing Co., pg. 17
QUAEL CORP., pg. 902
QUAKER BRIDGE MALL—See R. H. Macy & Co., Inc., pg. 699
QUAKER CITY MOTOR PARTS COMPANY, pg. 903
QUAKER CITY STAMP CO.—See American Marking Systems, pg. 58
QUAKER FABRIC CORPORATION, pg. 903
QUAKER INDUSTRIES LIMITED, pg. 903
QUALITY BAKERS OF AMERICA COOPERATIVE, INC., pg. 903
QUALITY CHEKD DAIRY PRODUCTS ASSOCIATION, pg. 903
QUALITY COMPUTER FORMS, INC.—See Rotary Forms Press, Inc., pg. 951
QUALITY CONTROL CORPORATION, pg. 903
QUALITY FOOD OILS, INC., pg. 903
QUALITY FOODS INC., pg. 903
QUALITY HOTEL DOWNTOWN—See Taj International Hotels, pg. 1076
QUALITY KING DISTRIBUTORS, pg. 903
QUALITY LIGHTING, INC.—See Jac Jacobsen Industries, Inc., pg. 588
QUALITY MEDICAL ADJUDICATION, INC.—See Health Management Systems, Inc., pg. 521
QUALITY PACKAGING PRODUCTS, INC., pg. 903
QUALITY PETROLEUM CORP., pg. 903
QUALITY PONTIAC, INC., pg. 904
QUALITY STORES INC., pg. 904
QUALITY TECHNOLOGIES CORPORATION, pg. 904
QUANTA ADVERTISING CORPORATION—See Carrols Corporation, pg. 225
QUANTIC INDUSTRIES, INC., pg. 904
QUANTUM SPORTSWEAR, LTD.—See Milady Brassiere & Corset Co., Inc., pg. 753
QUEBEDEAUX PONTIAC, INC., pg. 904
QUEEN OXYGEN COMPANY, pg. 904
QUEENS GROUP DESIGN—See Queens Group, Inc., pg. 904
QUEENS GROUP, INC., pg. 904
QUEENS GROUP INDIANA, INC.—See Queens Group, Inc., pg. 904
QUEENSGATE PRESS—See The Nielsen Company, pg. 807
QUEROY S.A.—See American Standard Inc., pg. 62
THE QUEST BUSINESS AGENCY, INC., pg. 904
QUEST ELECTRONICS DIV.—See La Belle Industries, Inc., pg. 648
QUIK N TASTY FOODS—See QuikTrip Corporation, pg. 905
QUIK PARK INC.—See Quadrangle Development Corporation, pg. 902
QUIK PRINT INC., pg. 905
QUIK WOK CORPORATION, pg. 905
QUIKTRIP CORPORATION, pg. 905
QUILL CORP., pg. 905
QUILL TRADE PAPERBACKS—See The Hearst Corporation, pg. 522
QUIMICA S.C. JOHNSON & SON CHILENA S.A.C.I.—See S. C. Johnson & Son, Inc., pg. 600
QUINCY MUTUAL FIRE INSURANCE COMPANY, pg. 905
QUINCY SOYBEAN CO.—See Moorman Mfg. Company, pg. 769
QUINDAR PRODUCTS LTD.—See QEI, Inc., pg. 902
QUINLAN ADVERTISING, pg. 905
QUINTANA ENVIRONMENTAL SERVICES, INC.—See Quintana Petroleum Corp., pg. 905
QUINTANA PETROLEUM CORP., pg. 905
QUINTANA PETROLEUM SERVICES—See Quintana Petroleum Corp., pg. 905
QUINTRON SYSTEMS, INC., pg. 905
QUOIZEL INC., pg. 905
QUORUM HEALTH GROUP, INC., pg. 905

R

R & B MACHINE TOOL CO., pg. 906
R & R ADVERTISING, pg. 906
R & R PLASTICS—See Component Technology Corp., pg. 270
RAIL COMPANY, pg. 906
R.A. INDUSTRIES, INC., pg. 906
THE RAL CORPORATION—See The Dyson-Kissner-Moran Corporation, pg. 357
R.C.A. RUBBER COMPANY, pg. 906
RCI QUALITY SERVICES, INC.—See Resort Condominiums International, pg. 929
RCI TRAVEL—See Resort Condominiums International, pg. 929
RCM INDUSTRIES, pg. 906
RCR PUBLICATIONS—See Crain Communications, Inc., pg. 295
RDI, INC., pg. 906
RF DESIGN INC.—See Ruder, Finn, Inc., pg. 954
RFI CORP.—See KDI Corporation, pg. 612
RGA BYPRODUCTS—See Rice Growers Association of California, pg. 931
RHC/SPACEMASTER CORPORATION, pg. 906
RHM INGREDIENTS, LTD.—See Newly Weds Foods Inc., pg. 804
RHS, pg. 907
RI HOLDINGS, pg. 907
RII (RICARDS INTERNATIONAL INC.), pg. 907
RIM DEVELOPMENT CENTER—See The Chardon Rubber Co., pg. 239
RJO ENTERPRISES, INC., pg. 907
RK MECHANICAL, INC., pg. 907
RMI MARKETING & ADVERTISING, pg. 907
RMS TECHS, INC., pg. 907
RNF MEDIA CORPORATION INC., pg. 907
RNL DESIGN—See RNL Facilities Corporation, pg. 907
RNL FACILITIES CORPORATION, pg. 907
RNL/INTERPLAN—See RNL Facilities Corporation, pg. 908
RNL TECHNICAL SERVICES—See RNL Facilities Corporation, pg. 908
ROC PROPERTIES INC., pg. 908
RP & C—See Conbraco Industries Inc., pg. 272
R.P. PARTNERS SRL—See Ketchum Communications Inc., pg. 626
RPR & ASSOCIATES, INC., pg. 908
RS ELECTRONICS, pg. 908
RSI—See Wakefern Food Corporation, pg. 1158
RTA ADVERTISING, INC.—See Leo Burnett Company, Inc., pg. 193
RTKL ASSOCIATES INC., pg. 908
R.T.M. WINNERS, pg. 908
RTMX-UNIFLEX INC., pg. 908
RTS SYSTEMS—See Telex Communications, Inc., pg. 1085
RTW, ROGERS TOOL WORKS, INC., pg. 908
R.W. ELECTRONICS, pg. 908
RABCO HEALTH SERVICE, pg. 908
RABSON'S—See Mateco Electronics Corp., pg. 720
RACETRAC PETROLEUM, INC., pg. 909
RACINE FEDERATED, INC., pg. 909
RADEX INTERNATIONAL S.A.—See Belmont Industries, Inc., pg. 137
RADIATOR SPECIALTY COMPANY, pg. 909
THE RADIO GROUP—See LaMarca Group Inc., pg. 652
RADIO INDIANAPOLIS, INC.—See Susquehanna Pfaltzgraff, pg. 1065
RADIO METROPLEX INC.—See Susquehanna Pfaltzgraff, pg. 1065
RADIOMATIC INSTRUMENTS—See Canberra Industries, Inc., pg. 214
RADIONICS, INC., pg. 909
RADISSON HOTEL CORPORATION—See Carlson Companies, Inc., pg. 221
RADISSON HOTELS INTERNATIONAL INC.—See Carlson Companies, Inc., pg. 221
RADIUS ADVERTISING—See Leo Burnett Company, Inc., pg. 193
RADIUS ADVERTISING—See Leo Burnett Company, Inc., pg. 193
RADIX CORPORATION, pg. 909
RADIX WIRE COMPANY, pg. 909
RADO WATCH COMPANY, INC., pg. 909
RAFFI & SWANSON, INC., pg. 909
C. B. RAGLAND COMPANY, pg. 909
T.S. RAGSDALE COMPANY, INCORPORATED, pg. 910
RAIL CAR SERVICES LTD.—See The Marmon Group, Inc., pg. 712
RAIL EUROPE INC., pg. 910
RAILHEAD RESTAURANTS, INC.—See Victoria Station Incorporated, pg. 1150
RAILWAY EDUCATIONAL BUREAU—See Simmons-Boardman Publishing Corp., pg. 1005
RAIN BIRD SPRINKLER MFG. CORP., pg. 910
RAINBOW APPAREL DISTRIBUTION CENTER, pg. 910
RAINBOW HOME RENTALS, pg. 910
RAINFAIR, INC., pg. 910
RAINIER BREWING CO.—See G. Heileman Brewing Co., Inc., pg. 526
RAINSOFT WATER CONDITIONING CO., pg. 910
RALEIGH ENTERPRISES, INC., pg. 910
RALEY'S, pg. 910
RAM GOLF CORPORATION, pg. 910
RAM GOLF UK—See RAM Golf Corporation, pg. 910
RAM GRAPHICS, INC., pg. 910
RAMA GROUP OF COMPANIES, pg. 910
RAMADA INN DOWNTOWN—See Taj International Hotels, pg. 1076
RANCARE INC.—See Randolph Medical Inc., pg. 912
RANCHERS COTTON OIL, pg. 911
RANCHERS SUPPLY COMPANY—See Carder, Inc., pg. 217
RANCH-WAY, INC., pg. 911
RAND, pg. 911
RAND MCNALLEY & COMPANY, D/B/A CHAMPION MAP CORP.—See Rand McNally & Company, pg. 911
RAND MCNALLY BOOK MANUFACTURING CO.—See Rand McNally & Company, pg. 911
RAND MCNALLY BOOK & MEDIA SERVICES—See Rand McNally & Company, pg. 911
RAND MCNALLY & COMPANY, pg. 911
RAND MCNALLY DOCUSYSTEMS GROUP—See Rand McNally & Company, pg. 911
RAND MCNALLY INTERNATIONAL—See Rand McNally & Company, pg. 911
RAND MCNALLY MAP SERVICES CO.—See Rand McNally & Company, pg. 911
RAND MCNALLY MAP SERVICES COMPANY—See Rand McNally & Company, pg. 911
RAND MCNALLY PUBLISHING GROUP—See Rand McNally & Company, pg. 911
RAND MCNALLY PUBLISHING GROUP—See Rand McNally & Company, pg. 911
RAND MCNALLY PUBLISHING GROUP—See Rand McNally & Company, pg. 911
RAND MCNALLY-TDM, INC.—See Rand McNally & Company, pg. 911
RANDALL COUNTY FEED YARD—See Friona Industries, L.P., pg. 434
RANDALL STORES, INC., pg. 911
RANDALL'S FOOD MARKETS, INC., pg. 911
RANDALL'S WAREHOUSE CORPORATION—See Randall's Food Markets, Inc., pg. 912
RANDOLPH MEDICAL INC., pg. 912
RANDOM CORPORATION, pg. 912
RANDOM HOUSE—See Advance Publications Inc., pg. 19
RANDOM HOUSE, INC.—See Advance Publications Inc., pg. 19

RAND'S INC., pg. 912
RANGAIRE & COMPANY, pg. 912
RANGEN AQUACULTURE RESEARCH—See Rangen, Inc., pg. 912
RANGEN, INC., pg. 912
RANGING—See Crossman Corp., pg. 300
RANIR CORPORATION, pg. 912
RANSCO INDUSTRIES, INC.—See Despatch Industries, pg. 332
RANSOM & RANDOLPH DIV.—See Dentsply International Inc., pg. 330
RAO WHOLESALE TIRE CENTERS, INC., pg. 912
RAPID DISTRIBUTION SERVICE, INC.—See Riklis Family Corporation, pg. 934
RAPID ENGINEERING INC., pg. 913
RAPID INDUSTRIAL PLASTICS COMPANY, pg. 913
RAPID INDUSTRIES, INC., pg. 913
RAPID MOUNTING & FINISHING—See Rapid Mounting & Finishing Co., pg. 913
RAPID MOUNTING & FINISHING CO., pg. 913
RAPID POWER TECHNOLOGIES, INC., pg. 913
RAPID RAIL SYSTEMS—See The Heil Co., pg. 526
RAPTON HONDA-GMC, pg. 913
ANN RASKAS GOURMET CONFECTIONERS, pg. 913
RASON OIL & GAS CORP.—See The Benatty Corporation, pg. 138
RATH MANUFACTURING—See Dubin-Clark & Company, pg. 350
RAU FASTENERS, INC., pg. 913
RAUB SUPPLY COMPANY, pg. 913
RAUH, GOOD, DARLO & BARNES ADVERTISING ASSOCIATES, INC., pg. 914
RAULAND-BORG (CANADA) INC.—See Rauland-Borg Corporation, pg. 914
RAULAND-BORG CORPORATION, pg. 914
RAVENSWOOD ALUMINUM CORP., pg. 914
THE RAWLPLUG COMPANY, INC., pg. 914
RAY-CARROLL COUNTY GRAIN CO-OP, pg. 914
RAY COMMUNICATIONS, INC., pg. 914
RAY SATELLITE NETWORK—See Ray Communications, Inc., pg. 914
RAY SPORTS NETWORK—See Ray Communications, Inc., pg. 914
RAYCO, pg. 914
RAYMARK FRICTION COMPANY, pg. 914
RAYMOND AUTOMATION CO., INC., pg. 915
RAYMOND GRANITE CO.—See Cold Spring Granite Company, pg. 260
RAYNOR GARAGE DOOR COMPANY, pg. 915
RAYON VERT—See Young & Rubicam Inc., pg. 1212
RAYOVAC CORPORATION, pg. 915
RAYOVAC CORPORATION—See RAYOVAC Corporation, pg. 915
RAYOVAC LIMITED—See RAYOVAC Corporation, pg. 915
RAYOVAC UK LIMITED—See RAYOVAC Corporation, pg. 915
RAYOVAC/VIDOR LIMITED—See RAYOVAC Corporation, pg. 915
RCM CABOT—See Arnold Fortuna Lawner & Cabot, pg. 84
RE CAS—See Multi-Ad Services, Inc., pg. 775
RE/MAX INSURANCE DIV.—See RE/MAX International, Inc., pg. 915
RE/MAX INTERNATIONAL, INC., pg. 915
REA MAGNET WIRE COMPANY, INC., pg. 915
REACTIVE METALS & ALLOYS CORPORATION (REMACOR), pg. 916
THE READ CORPORATION, pg. 916
READING ANTHRACITE CO., pg. 916
READING BODY WORKS, INC., pg. 916
READING EAGLE COMPANY, pg. 916
READING TUBE CORP., pg. 916
READY METAL MANUFACTURING COMPANY, pg. 916
READY SYSTEMS, pg. 916
READY SYSTEMS, FRANCE—See Ready Systems, pg. 916
READY SYSTEMS, GERMANY—See Ready Systems, pg. 916
READY SYSTEMS, U.K.—See Ready Systems, pg. 916
REAGAN EQUIPMENT COMPANY, INC., pg. 917
REAL ESTATE AUCTIONS, INC.—See Sheldon Good & Co., Inc., pg. 470
REAL ESTATE CORP. OF FLORIDA, pg. 917
REAL HOLDING MANAGEMENT CORP., pg. 917
REALCOLD STORAGE—See Spiegel Meats, Inc., pg. 1031
REALTY ONE, pg. 917
RECKSON ASSOCIATES, pg. 917
RECLAIMERS, INC.—See Group Dekko International Inc., pg. 490
RECOLD, INC.—See The Marley Company, pg. 710
RECON/OPTICAL, INC., pg. 917
RECON SERVICES, INC.—See Computer Sales International Inc., pg. 271
THE RECORD-JOURNAL PUBLISHING COMPANY, pg. 917
RECORDING & STATISTICAL CORPORATION, pg. 917
RECREATIONAL EQUIPMENT, INC., pg. 917
RED APPLE COMPANIES, pg. 917
RED APPLE, INC., pg. 918
RED BALL CORPORATION, pg. 918
RED BALL FORWARDERS, INC.—See Red Ball Corporation, pg. 918
RED BALL LEASING, INC.—See Red Ball Corporation, pg. 918
RED BALL VAN & STORAGE, INC.—See Red Ball Corporation, pg. 918
RED CALLIOPE & ASSOCIATES, INC., pg. 918
RED CARPET REAL ESTATE SERVICES, INC., pg. 918
RED DEVIL INC., pg. 918
RED L FOODS—See Union Holdings, Inc., pg. 1128
RED OAK EXPRESS—See Landmark Communications, Inc., pg. 655
RED ROOF INNS, INC., pg. 918
RED SPOT PAINT & VARNISH CO., pg. 918
RED SPOT WESTLAND INC.—See Red Spot Paint & Varnish Co., pg. 919
RED T. PRODUCTS—See EVCON Holdings, pg. 391
RED WING PRODUCTS, INC., pg. 919
RED WING PUBLISHING COMPANY, pg. 919
RED WING SHOE CO., INC., pg. 919
RED WING SHOE VASQUE DIV.—See Red Wing Shoe Co., Inc., pg. 919
REDBOOK—See The Hearst Corporation, pg. 523
REDBURN TIRE COMPANY, pg. 919
REDCO FOODS, INC., pg. 919
REDECO INDUSTRIES—See West Central Co-op, pg. 1177
REDGATE COMMUNICATIONS CORP., pg. 919
REDI-SERVE FOODS—See On-Cor Frozen Foods Inc., pg. 826
REDIFFUSION—See Dentsu, Young & Rubicam Partnerships, pg. 331
REDKEN INTL. (PACIFIC), INC.—See Redken Laboratories, Inc., pg. 919
REDKEN LABORATORIES (DISC), INC.—See Redken Laboratories, Inc., pg. 919
REDKEN LABORATORIES, INC., pg. 919
REDMAN BUILDING PRODUCTS, INC.—See Redman Industries, Inc., pg. 919
REDMAN HOLDING CORP.—See Redman Industries, Inc., pg. 919
REDMAN HOMES, INC.—See Redman Industries, Inc., pg. 919
REDMAN INDUSTRIES, INC., pg. 919
W. C. REDMON CO., pg. 919
REDMOND PRODUCTS, INC., pg. 920
REDSTONE PROPERTIES, INC.—See National Life Insurance Company, pg. 791
REECE-CAMPBELL, INC., pg. 920
REED & BARTON CORPORATION, pg. 920
REED & BARTON GIFTSOURCES—See Reed & Barton Corporation, pg. 920
REED & BARTON HOUSEWARES—See Reed & Barton Corporation, pg. 920
REED & BARTON SILVERSMITHS—See Reed & Barton Corporation, pg. 920
REED EXHIBITION COMPANIES, pg. 920
GENE REED CHEVROLET, pg. 920
REED GRAIN & BEAN COMPANY, pg. 920
REED MOTORS, INC., pg. 920
REEDRILL INC.—See Zimmerman Holdings, Inc., pg. 1220
REEL-O-MATIC SYSTEMS, INC., pg. 920
REESE ENTERPRISES, INC., pg. 920
REESE FINER FOODS, INC., pg. 921
REEVE ALEUTIAN AIRWAYS, INC., pg. 921
THE REEVES AGENCY, INC., pg. 921
REEVES SOUTHEASTERN CORPORATION, pg. 921
REFCO GROUP LTD., pg. 921
REFCO INC.—See Refco Group Ltd., pg. 921
REFERENCE SOFTWARE INTERNATIONAL, pg. 921
REFRACTORIES CONSULTING & ENGINEERING GMBH—See Belmont Industries, Inc., pg. 137
REFRIGERATION SUPPLIES DISTRIBUTORS, pg. 921
REGAL MARINE INDUSTRIES INC., pg. 921
REGAL WARE, INC., pg. 921
REGAN HOLDING CORPORATION, pg. 921
REGENCY ASSOCIATES LIMITED PARTNERSHIP, pg. 922
REGENCY DODGE INC., pg. 922
REGENCY GROUP INC., pg. 922
REGENCY LINCOLN MERCURY, pg. 922
REGIAN ADVERTISING & PUBLIC RELATIONS, pg. 922
THE REGINA COMPANY, pg. 922
THE REGINA COMPANY—See The Regina Company, pg. 922
REGIONAL DEVELOPMENT CORP.—See Family Inns of America, Inc., pg. 398
REGIONAL TRANSPORTATION AUTHORITY (RTA), pg. 922
REHRIG PACIFIC COMPANY, pg. 922
THE REICH GROUP, INC., pg. 922
REICHEL & DREWS INC.—See RDI, Inc., pg. 906
REICHENSTEIN ADVERTISING AGENCY, pg. 922
REID & O'DONAHUE ADVERTISING, INC., pg. 923
RUSS REID COMPANY, INC., pg. 923
REIDBORD BROS., INC., pg. 923
REILLY CHEMICALS S.A.—See Reilly Industries, Inc., pg. 923
F/S REILLY, MEDIA +, pg. 923
REILLY INDUSTRIES, INC., pg. 923
REILLY-WHITEMAN INC.—See Carlyle Holding Corporation, pg. 222
REILY ELECTRIC SUPPLY, INC., pg. 923
WILLIAM B. REILY & CO., INC., pg. 923
THE JOEY REIMAN AGENCY, pg. 923
REIMEL CARTER ADVERTISING, INC., pg. 923
REINALT-THOMAS CORP., pg. 923
REINKE MANUFACTURING CO., INC., pg. 924
REITMAN INDUSTRIES, pg. 924
REITZ COAL COMPANY—See Berwind Corporation, pg. 145
RELA, INC., pg. 924
RELA MANUFACTURING DIVISION—See RELA, Inc., pg. 924
RELA MODEL AND MACHINE SHOP—See RELA, Inc., pg. 924
RELA PRODUCT DEVELOPMENT DIV. (PDD)—See RELA, Inc., pg. 924
RELCO—See Reliable Stores, Inc., pg. 925
RELIABLE AUTOMATIC SPRINKLER CO., INC., pg. 924
RELIABLE/BETHEA POWER PRODUCTS INC.—See Maclean-Fogg Co., pg. 698
RELIABLE CASTINGS CORPORATION, pg. 924
RELIABLE CHEVROLET, pg. 924
THE RELIABLE CORP., pg. 924
RELIABLE GRAPHICS—See Warrens Waller Press, pg. 1165
RELIABLE KNITTING WORKS, pg. 924
RELIABLE POWER PRODUCTS—See Maclean-Fogg Co., pg. 697
RELIABLE STORES, INC., pg. 925
RELIANCE ELEVATOR COMPANY, pg. 925
RELIANCE GRATING, INC.—See Belmont Industries, Inc., pg. 136
RELIANCE MEDICAL PRODUCTS, INC., pg. 925
RELIANCE STEEL & ALUMINUM CO., pg. 925
RELIEF PRINTING CORPORATION, pg. 925
REMARK ADVERTISING—See The Shidler Group, pg. 999
REMARKS, INC., pg. 925
REMCO BABY—See Remco Toys, pg. 926
REMCO ENTERPRISES, INC., pg. 926
REMCO TOYS, pg. 926
REMCOR PRODUCTS CO., pg. 926
REMINGTON APPAREL, INC., pg. 926
REMINGTON AUSTRALIA—See Remington Products Inc., pg. 926
REMINGTON CONSUMER PRODUCTS, LTD.—See Remington Products Inc., pg. 926
REMINGTON HILL VENTURES—See Rotterdam Ventures Inc., pg. 952
REMINGTON PRODUCTS (CANADA) INC.—See Remington Products Inc., pg. 926
REMINGTON PRODUCTS INC., pg. 926
REMMELE ENGINEERING, INC., pg. 926
REMPRO TRADING, LTD.—See Remington Products Inc., pg. 926
RENA ROWAN FOR SAVILLE—See Jones Apparel Group, Inc., pg. 602
RENA-WARE DISTRIBUTORS INC., pg. 926
RENA-WARE GMBH—See Rena-Ware Distributors Inc., pg. 926
RENAISSANCE CENTER MANAGEMENT CO.—See Orix Real Estate Equities, Inc., pg. 829
RENAISSANCE PUBLISHING CO., INC., pg. 926
RENCO GROUP, pg. 926
RENFRO CORP., pg. 926
RENKEN BOAT MANUFACTURING CO., pg. 927
RENNOC CORPORATION, pg. 927
RENOSOL CORP., pg. 927
THE RENOVATOR'S SUPPLY, INC., pg. 927
RENTAL AMERICA—See America Outdoors Ltd, pg. 48
RENTENBACH CONSTRUCTORS INCORPORATED—See Rentenbach Engineering Company, pg. 927
RENTENBACH ENGINEERING COMPANY, pg. 927
REP FORCE—See EvansGroup, pg. 391
REPCO BEARING COMPANY, DIV. OF REPCO LTD.—See The Pullman Company, pg. 900
REPCO INCORPORATED, pg. 927
REPLACEMENTS, LTD., pg. 927
REPLOGLE GLOBES, INC., pg. 927
REPORTER PUBLISHING COMPANY—See Harte-Hanks Communications, Inc., pg. 513
REPUBLIC ALLOYS, INC., pg. 927
REPUBLIC CHEMICAL COMPANY—See Harwick Chemical Corp., pg. 515
REPUBLIC CONTAINER CORP., pg. 927
REPUBLIC CONTRACTING CORP., pg. 928
REPUBLIC DIE & TOOL COMPANY, pg. 928
REPUBLIC ENGINEERED STEELS, INC., pg. 928
REPUBLIC FASTENER PRODUCTS CORP., pg. 928
REPUBLIC FRANKLIN INSURANCE CO.—See Utica Mutual Insurance Company, pg. 1141
REPUBLIC INDUSTRIES, INC., pg. 928
REPUBLIC NATIONAL BANK OF MIAMI, pg. 928
REPUBLIC SALES CO., INC.—See Lewis Homes Management Corp., pg. 673
REPUBLIC STORAGE SYSTEMS COMPANY INC., pg. 928
REPUBLIC SUPPLY COMPANY, pg. 928
REPUBLIC TELCOM SYSTEMS CORPORATION, pg. 928
REPUBLIC WESTERN INSURANCE CO.—See Amerco, A Nevada Corporation, pg. 48
RES-Q-TECH INC.—See Eastern Technologies Ltd, pg. 364
RESCO PRODUCTS, INC., pg. 928
RESEARCH & FORECASTS, INC.—See Ruder, Finn, Inc., pg. 954
RESEARCH PRODUCTS CORPORATION, pg. 928
RESEARCH SEEDS, INC.—See Land O'Lakes, Inc., pg. 654
RESERVATIONS SERVICES, INC.—See Best Western International, Inc., pg. 147
RESERVE MOTION CONTROL SYSTEMS—See Bodine Electric Company, pg. 162
RESIDENTIAL SUPPORT SERVICES, INC.—See John Wieland Homes Inc., pg. 1188
RESISTOR DIVISION—See Caddock Electronics, Inc., pg. 207
RESONEX, INC., pg. 929
RESORT CONDOMINIUMS INTERNATIONAL, pg. 929
RESORT QUALITY SERVICES, INC.—See Resort Condominiums International, pg. 929
RESOURCE, INC., pg. 929
RE:SOURCE MARKETING, pg. 929
RESOURCES FUNDING CORP.—See Integrated Resources, Inc., pg. 573
RESOURCES LIFE INSURANCE CO.—See Integrated Resources, Inc., pg. 573
RESOURCES PROPERTY MANAGEMENT CORP.—See Integrated Resources, Inc., pg. 573
RESOURCES REAL ESTATE FINANCE GROUP, INC.—See Integrated Resources, Inc., pg. 573
RESPONSE COMMUNICATIONS, INC.—See The Direct Marketing Group Inc., pg. 339
RESPONSE SYSTEMS, INC.—See Humiston-Keeling, Inc., pg. 553
RESPONSIVE MARKETING COMMUNICATIONS, INC., pg. 929
RESTAURANT BUSINESS—See Bill Communications, Inc., pg. 150
RESTAURANT COMPANY, INC., pg. 929
RESTAURANT DEVELOPERS CORP., pg. 929
RESTAURANT ENTERPRISES GROUP, INC., pg. 929

RESTAURANT/HOTEL DESIGN INTERNATIONAL—See Bill Communications, Inc., pg. 150
RESTAURANTS UNLIMITED, pg. 929
RESTONIC CORPORATION, pg. 929
RETAIL VENTURES, INC., pg. 929
RETEC USA, INC.—See Gaymar Industries, Inc., pg. 447
RETIREMENT ADVISORS, INC.—See The Hearst Corporation, pg. 522
RETIREMENT LIVING AFFILIATES, INC.—See Affiliates Group Inc., pg. 24
REULAND ELECTRIC COMPANY, pg. 930
REV-A-SHELF, pg. 930
REVCO SCIENTIFIC INC., pg. 930
REVCOR, INC., pg. 930
REVERE ELECTRIC SUPPLY CO., pg. 930
REVLON GROUP INC.—See MacAndrews & Forbes Holdings Inc., pg. 695
REVLON, INC.—See MacAndrews & Forbes Holdings Inc., pg. 696
REVLON INTERNATIONAL CORPORATION—See MacAndrews & Forbes Holdings Inc., pg. 696
REVLON-REALISTIC PROFESSIONAL PRODUCTS, INC.—See MacAndrews & Forbes Holdings Inc., pg. 696
REVLON RESEARCH CENTER, INC.—See MacAndrews & Forbes Holdings Inc., pg. 696
REVLON SERVICE, INC.—See MacAndrews & Forbes Holdings Inc., pg. 696
REVLON S.P.A.—See MacAndrews & Forbes Holdings Inc., pg. 696
CHARLES REVSON, INC.—See MacAndrews & Forbes Holdings Inc., pg. 696
REX LUMBER COMPANY, pg. 930
REX MARINE CENTER, INC., pg. 930
REX SUPPLY COMPANY—See Production Tool Supply Co., pg. 893
REXALL GROUP—See Sundown Vitamin Co., Inc., pg. 1060
REXALL INC. CONSUMER PRODUCTS DIV.—See Sundown Vitamin Co., Inc., pg. 1060
REYCO INDUSTRIES, INC., pg. 930
JOHN REYER COMPANY, pg. 930
REYNEN, BARDIS & WINN, pg. 930
F.T. REYNOLDS COMPANY, pg. 930
JOHN J. REYNOLDS, INC.—See Helmsley Enterprises, Inc., pg. 527
RHEA & KAISER ADVERTISING, INC., pg. 930
RHOADES DEVELOPMENT, pg. 931
RHODE ISLAND LOTTERY, pg. 931
RHODE ISLAND MONTHLY—See Communications International, pg. 269
RHODES, INC., pg. 931
M. H. RHODES, INC., pg. 931
RHODES INTERNATIONAL, INC., pg. 931
RIBBON NARROW FABRIC COMPANY, pg. 931
RICART FORD INC., pg. 931
RICCOBON & COMPANY, INC., pg. 931
RICE FOOD MARKETS INC., pg. 931
RICE GROWERS ASSOCIATION OF CALIFORNIA, pg. 931
RICE & RICE INC.—See Valentine-Radford, Inc., pg. 1143
GEORGE RICE & SONS, pg. 931
RICE/SPECTOR INC., pg. 931
RICELAND FOODS, INC., pg. 931
RICH FRUIT PAK CO.—See Rich Products Corp., pg. 932
RICH-MIX PRODUCTS—See Ritchie Corporation, pg. 936
RICH PRODUCTS CORP., pg. 932
RICH PRODUCTS DAYTON—See Rich Products Corp., pg. 932
THE RICHARD & DAVID JACOBS GROUP, pg. 932
RICHARDS BROTHERS OF MOUNTAIN GROVE, pg. 932
THE RICHARDS GROUP, INC., pg. 932
RICHARDSON BROTHERS CO., pg. 932
RICHARDSON INDUSTRIES, INC., pg. 932
RICHARDSON, MYERS & DONOFRIO, INC., pg. 933
RICHARDSON STRANG ASSOCIATES, pg. 933
RICHCO PLASTICS COMPANY, pg. 933
RICHDALE DAIRY STORES, INC.—See Scangas Brothers Holdings, Inc., pg. 974
RICHHEIMER FOOD—See Wechsler Coffee Corp., pg. 1172
RICHLAND SHOE CO.—See H.H. Brown Shoe Company, Inc., pg. 183
S.D. RICHMAN SONS, INC., pg. 933
RICHMOND FOUNDRY AND MANUFACTURING CO.—See Josam Company, pg. 607
RICHMOND MOTOR COMPANY, pg. 933
RICHMOND SCREW ANCHOR COMPANY, pg. 933
RICHMOND SERVICE CENTER—See Carolina Steel Corporation, pg. 223
RICHMOND TECHNOLOGY INC., pg. 933
RICHMONT CORPORATION—See Mary Kay Corporation, pg. 717
RICHTER & RATNER CONTRACTING CORPORATION, pg. 933
RICKEL HOME CENTERS—See Supermarkets General Corporation, pg. 1064
RICO MOTOR COMPANY, pg. 933
RIDDLEBERGER BROTHERS, INC., pg. 933
RIDG-U-RAK, INC., pg. 933
RIDGEVIEW MOTORS, INC., pg. 934
RIDGWAY'S, INC.—See YRJ Corporation, pg. 1207
RIECHELMANN, LOPES CARDOZO & VAN BERCUM B.V.—See Young & Rubicam Inc., pg. 1212
RIEMEIER LUMBER COMPANY, INC., pg. 934
RIETH-RILEY CONSTRUCTION CO. INC., pg. 934
RIGGS INDUSTRIES, INC., pg. 934
J. A. RIGGS TRACTOR CO., pg. 934
RIGHT AWAY FOODS CORPORATION—See The Wornick Company, pg. 1203
RIGOLI COMMUNICATIONS, pg. 934
RIHM MOTOR COMPANY, pg. 934
RIKLIS FAMILY CORPORATION, pg. 934
RILEY CREEK LUMBER COMPANY, pg. 935
HAL RINEY & PARTNERS, INC., pg. 935
RING SCREW WORKS, pg. 935
RING TECHNOLOGIES, INC., pg. 935
RINGLING BROS., BARNUM & BAILEY COMBINED SHOWS, INC., pg. 935
RINKE PONTIAC-GMC CO., pg. 935
THE RIO GRANDE INDUSTRIES INC.—See Anschutz Corporation, pg. 75
RIO GRANDE LAND CO.—See Anschutz Corporation, pg. 75
RIPON FOODS, INC., pg. 935
RIS PAPER COMPANY, pg. 935
JOHN RISDALL ADVERTISING, pg. 935
RISH EQUIPMENT COMPANY, pg. 935
RISING PAPER COMPANY—See Fox Valley Corporation, pg. 428
RISSER OIL CORP., pg. 936
RISSLER & MCMURRY COMPANY, pg. 936
RITA-ANN DISTRIBUTORS—See Alco Health Services Corporation, pg. 32
RITCHIE CORPORATION, pg. 936
RITCHIE INDUSTRIES, INC., pg. 936
RITCHIE PAVING, INC.—See Ritchie Corporation, pg. 936
RITCHIE SAND COMPANY, INC.—See Ritchie Corporation, pg. 936
RITE-HITE CORPORATION, pg. 936
RITE-WAY, INC., pg. 936
RITTENHOUSE INC., pg. 936
RITTENHOUSE PAPER CO.—See Rittenhouse Inc., pg. 936
RITTER BROS., INC., pg. 936
RITZ CORPORATION—See MacAndrews & Forbes Holdings Inc., pg. 696
RITZ-CARLTON HOTEL COMPANY—See W.B. Johnson Property, Inc., pg. 598
RIVER BEND, INC.—See Spatz & Co., pg. 1026
RIVER CITY PROTECTIVE WEAR, INC.—See Shelby Group International, Inc., pg. 996
RIVER OAKS COMMUNITIES, INC.—See ROC Properties Inc., pg. 908
RIVER OAKS DOUBLE-WIDE PLANT—See ROC Properties Inc., pg. 908
RIVER OAKS HOMES, INC.—See ROC Properties Inc., pg. 908
RIVER OAKS VANS, INC.—See ROC Properties Inc., pg. 908
RIVERDALE CHEMICAL CO., pg. 937
RIVERGATE PLANT—See Ash Grove Cement Company, pg. 88
RIVERHEAD SAVINGS BANK—See American Savings Bank, pg. 60
RIVERS TRAINOR DOYLE & WALSH, INC., pg. 937
RIVERSIDE CENTRAL SERVICES, INC., pg. 937
RIVERSIDE DEVELOPMENT CORP.—See Dugan & Meyers Interests, Inc., pg. 351
RIVERSIDE MANUFACTURING CO., pg. 937
RIVERSIDE MILLWORK COMPANY, INC., pg. 937
RIVERSIDE PRESS, INC., pg. 937
RIVERSIDE PRODUCTS DIV.—See Everett Smith Investment Co. of Delaware, pg. 1013
RIVERSONG RECORDS—See The Benson Music Group, pg. 140
RIVERTON TRUCKERS, INC.—See Gohmann Asphalt & Construction Inc., pg. 465
RIVES CARLBERG, pg. 937
RIVIANA FOODS INC., pg. 937
RLJC, INC.—See The Napier Company, pg. 783
ROAD MACHINERY COMPANY, pg. 937
ROAD MACHINERY & SUPPLIES CO., pg. 937
ROANE COUNTY NEWS—See Landmark Communications, Inc., pg. 655
ROBANNE CORP.—See Zale Corporation, pg. 1216
ROBBINS AUTO PARTS, INC., pg. 938
ROBBINS, INC., pg. 938
ROBBINS MANUFACTURING COMPANY, pg. 938
ROBBY LEN FASHIONS—See Apparel America, Inc., pg. 78
ROBERTSON-WHITEHOUSE—See The Marmon Group, Inc., pg. 713
CHAS ROBERTS AIR CONDITIONING, INC., pg. 938
F. L. ROBERTS & CO. INC., pg. 938
ROBERTS COMMUNICATIONS INC., pg. 938
JOHN ROBERTS COMPANY, pg. 938
ROBERTS CONSOLIDATED INDUSTRIES—See Dubin-Clark & Company, pg. 350
ROBERTS FOODS, INC., pg. 938
ROBERTS FOUNDRY CO., INC.—See Grede Foundries, Inc., pg. 483
J. H. ROBERTS INDUSTRIES INC., pg. 938
ROBERTS & RAYMOND ASSOC., INC., pg. 939
ROBERTS & SCHAEFER CO.—See Jupiter Industries, Inc., pg. 609
ROBERTS & SCHAEFFER COMPANY-SALT LAKE CITY—See Jupiter Industries, Inc., pg. 609
STANLEY ROBERTS, INC., pg. 939
ROBERTSON FACTORIES, INC., pg. 939
ROBERTSON MARKETING INC., pg. 939
ROBERTSONS AUTO BODY—See Robertson's Auto Salvage, pg. 939
ROBERTSON'S AUTO SALVAGE, pg. 939
ROBINHOOD HOMES, INC., pg. 939
ROBINS ENGINEERS & CONSTRUCTORS, INC., pg. 939
ROBINSON BUS SERVICE, pg. 939
C. H. ROBINSON CO. INC., pg. 939
SWAYNE ROBINSON & COMPANY, pg. 939
ROBINSON EXPORT-IMPORT CORPORATION—See Mico Inc., pg. 748
ROBINSON HELICOPTER COMPANY, INC., pg. 940
ROBINSON INDUSTRIES—See Schawk, Inc., pg. 975
ROBINSON LUMBER COMPANY—See Robinson Lumber & Export Company, pg. 940
ROBINSON LUMBER & EXPORT COMPANY, pg. 940
ROBINSON & MAITES, INC., pg. 940
ROBINSON & ST. JOHN ADVERTISING & PUBLIC RELATIONS, INC., pg. 940
ROBINSON, YESAWICH & PEPPERDINE, pg. 940
ROBSON, CAVIGNAC & ASSOCIATES—See Lawrence Group, Inc., pg. 662
ROCCO BUILDING SUPPLIES INC.—See Rocco Inc., pg. 940
ROCCO FARM FOODS, INC.—See Rocco Inc., pg. 940
ROCCO FARMS—See Rocco Inc., pg. 940
ROCCO FEEDS, INC.—See Rocco Inc., pg. 940
ROCCO FURTHER PROCESSING—See Rocco Inc., pg. 940
ROCCO INC., pg. 940
ROCCO TURKEYS, INC.—See Rocco Inc., pg. 940
ROCHE CONSTRUCTORS, INC., pg. 940
LE ROCHER, COMPAGNIE DE REASSURANCE, S.A.—See The Prudential Insurance Company of America, pg. 898
LE ROCHER UK, LTD.—See The Prudential Insurance Company of America, pg. 898
ROCHESTER GAUGES INC. OF TEXAS—See Gas Equipment Company, Inc., pg. 444
ROCHESTER INSTRUMENTS SYSTEMS, INC.—See The Marmon Group, Inc., pg. 712
ROCHESTER MIDLAND CORPORATION, pg. 940
ROCK HILL MATERIALS COMPANY, pg. 941
ROCK-TENN COMPANY, pg. 941
ROCK-TENN COMPANY, MILL DIVISION, INC.—See Rock-Tenn Company, pg. 941
ROCK-TENN CONVERTING CO.—See Rock-Tenn Company, pg. 941
THE ROCKBESTOS COMPANY—See The Marmon Group, Inc., pg. 711
ROCKET INDUSTRIES, INC./EXCEL, THE EXERCISE COMPANY, pg. 941
ROCKET SUPPLY CORP.—See Hicks Oil-Hicks Gas, Inc., pg. 533
ROCKETT, BURKHEAD, LEWIS & WINSLOW, pg. 941
ROCKFORD ACROMATIC PRODUCT CO., pg. 941
ROCKFORD-ECLIPSE—See Eclipse, Inc., pg. 366
ROCKFORD INTERNATIONAL GROUP—See Rockford Products Corp., pg. 942
ROCKFORD PRODUCTS CORP., pg. 941
ROCKINGHAM STAINLESS STEEL—See Stockham Valves & Fittings, Inc., pg. 1050
ROCKVILLE FABRICS CORPORATION, pg. 942
ROCKWOOD GARDENS, LTD.—See KNOX International Corp., pg. 638
ROCKWOOD RESEARCH—See Farm Journal, Inc., pg. 401
ROCKWOOD TIMES—See Landmark Communications, Inc., pg. 655
ROCKY MOUNTAIN BANK NOTE COMPANY, pg. 942
ROCKY MOUNTAIN COMPANY, pg. 942
ROCKY MOUNTAIN CONCEPTS—See Austin Sculpture, pg. 100
ROCKY MOUNTAIN MECHANICAL, INC., pg. 942
ROCKY POINT VILLAGE CORP.—See Specialty Restaurants Corporation, pg. 1028
ROCKY ROCOCO CORPORATION, pg. 942
ROCOR PROPERTIES, INC.—See Rocor Transportation Companies Inc., pg. 942
ROCOR TRANSPORTATION COMPANIES INC., pg. 942
RODALE PRESS, INC., pg. 942
W. B. RODDENBERY COMPANY, INC., pg. 942
RODEFELD CO., INC., pg. 942
RODGERS BUILDERS, INC., pg. 942
J.B. RODGERS MECHANICAL CONTRACTORS, pg. 943
ROESSING BRONZE CO., pg. 943
ROFFE, INC., pg. 943
ROGERS & ASSOCIATES ADVERTISING, INC., pg. 943
ROGERS GROUP INC., pg. 943
T. H. ROGERS LUMBER CO. INC., pg. 943
ROGERS, LUNT & BOWLEN CO., pg. 943
ROGERS MARKETS INC., pg. 943
ROGERS TOOL WORKS, INC.—See Harbour Group Ltd., pg. 507
ROGERSON ATS—See Rogerson Aircraft Corporation, pg. 943
ROGERSON AIRCRAFT CONTROLS—See Rogerson Aircraft Corporation, pg. 943
ROGERSON AIRCRAFT CORPORATION, pg. 943
ROGERSON AIRCRAFT SYSTEMS—See Rogerson Aircraft Corporation, pg. 944
ROGERSON HILLER CORPORATION—See Rogerson Aircraft Corporation, pg. 944
ROGERSON KRATOS—See Rogerson Aircraft Corporation, pg. 944
ROHRER CORPORATION, pg. 944
ROINOKE SERVICE CENTER—See Carolina Steel Corporation, pg. 223
I. ROKEACH & SONS, INC., pg. 944
ROKOP CORPORATION, pg. 944
ROLAND INTERNATIONAL CORPORATION, pg. 944
ROLANE CORPORATION—See Collins & Aikman Group Inc., pg. 263
ROLFS—See Amity Leather Products Company, pg. 67
ROLL FORMING CORPORATION, pg. 944
THE ROLL SEAL VALVE CO., INC.—See AEI Holding Co., Inc., pg. 3
ROLLED STEEL PRODUCTS CORPORATION, pg. 944
ROLLER DERBY SKATE COMPANY, pg. 944
ROLLERBLADE, INC., pg. 944
ROLLEX CORPORATION, pg. 944
ROLLING STONE MAGAZINE—See Straight Arrow Publishers, Inc., pg. 1052
ROLLMAN SUPPLY COMPANY—See The Sico Company, pg. 1001
ROLOCK, INC., pg. 944
ROLOCK OF CALIFORNIA—See Rolock, Inc., pg. 945
ROLODEX CORP.—See Insilco Corporation, pg. 571
ROMA HOLDINGS, pg. 945
ROMAC INDUSTRIES, INC., pg. 945
ROMAC INDUSTRIES, INC., HAYS DIVISION—See Romac Industries, Inc., pg. 945
ROMAN ELECTRIC COMPANY, INC., pg. 945
ROMAN, INC., pg. 945

ROMAN MEAL COMPANY, pg. 945
ROMANN & TANNENHOLZ ADVERTISING, INC., pg. 945
ROMANOFF INTERNATIONAL, INC., pg. 945
ROMANY CERAMICS INC.—See United States Ceramic Tile Co., pg. 1135
ROME CABLE CORPORATION, pg. 945
ROME MANUFACTURING CO., pg. 945
ROME SENTINEL CO., pg. 946
ROME STRIP STEEL CO., INC., pg. 946
RONALD JAMES DIRECT, pg. 946
RONCO COMMUNICATIONS & ELECTRONICS INC., pg. 946
RONEY & CO., pg. 946
ROOFING WHOLESALE CO., INC., pg. 946
W.A. ROOSEVELT CO., pg. 946
ROOSEVELT PAPER CO., pg. 946
A.I. ROOT COMPANY, pg. 946
ROOT CORPORATION, pg. 946
ROPA SULTANA, INC.—See Williamson-Dickie Mfg. Co., pg. 1192
ROPER BROS. LUMBER CO., INC., pg. 947
ROPPE CORP., pg. 947
ROPS TEXTILES INC.—See Arley Merchandise Corporation, pg. 83
ROSANIO, BAILETS & TALAMO, INC., pg. 947
ROSAUER'S SUPERMARKETS, INC., pg. 947
ROSCO LABORATORIES, INC., pg. 947
ROSCO MANUFACTURING CO., pg. 947
ROSE ACRE FARMS, pg. 947
ROSE ART INDUSTRIES, pg. 947
ROSE FUEL CORPORATION—See Bayside Fuel Oil Depot Corp., pg. 128
ROSE PACKING COMPANY, pg. 947
ROSE PRINTING COMPANY, INC., pg. 948
ROSEBURG FOREST PRODUCTS CO., pg. 948
ROSELLE PAPER CO., INC., pg. 948
ROSEN ASSOCIATES MANAGEMENT CORP., pg. 948
RAYMOND ROSEN CO., pg. 948
ROSENBERGERS DAIRIES, INC., pg. 948
ROSENDIN ELECTRIC, INC., pg. 948
ROSENFELD, SIROWITZ, HUMPHREY & STRAUSS, INC., pg. 948
ROSENFIELD/DENTINO, INC., pg. 948
ROSENS DIVERSIFIED, INC., pg. 948
ROSENS, INC.—See Rosens Diversified, Inc., pg. 948
ROSENSHEIN ASSOCIATES, pg. 948
ROSENTHAL AUTOMOTIVE ORGANIZATION, pg. 949
ROSENTHAL CHEVROLET CO., pg. 949
ROSEVILLE CHRYSLER PLYMOUTH INC., pg. 949
ROSEWOOD CORPORATION—See Caroline Hunt Trust Estate, pg. 553
ROSEWOOD PROPERTY COMPANY, pg. 949
ROSKA DIRECT MARKETING, INC., pg. 949
ROSS ADVERTISING, INC., pg. 949
ROSS BICYCLES USA LTD., pg. 949
FRANK B. ROSS CO. INC., pg. 949
ROSS ENGINEERING CO., INC., pg. 949
ROSS ISLAND SAND & GRAVEL CO., INC.—See R. B. Pamplin Corp., pg. 845
JACK ROSS MOTORS INC., pg. 949
ROSS ROY CANADA, LTD.—See Ross Roy Group, Inc., pg. 950
ROSS ROY COMMUNICATIONS—See Ross Roy Group, Inc., pg. 950
ROSS ROY COMMUNICATIONS CANADA, INC.—See Ross Roy Group, Inc., pg. 950
ROSS ROY COMMUNICATIONS/N.Y.—See Ross Roy Group, Inc., pg. 950
ROSS ROY DIRECT—See Ross Roy Group, Inc., pg. 950
ROSS ROY FRANCHISE—See Ross Roy Group, Inc., pg. 950
ROSS ROY GROUP, INC., pg. 949
ROSS ROY INC.—See Ross Roy Group, Inc., pg. 950
ROSS ROY RETAIL—See Ross Roy Group, Inc., pg. 950
ROSSER FABRAP INTERNATIONAL, pg. 950
ROSSIN GREENBERG SERONICK, pg. 950
BRUCE ROSSMEYER'S TOYOTALAND, pg. 950
ROSTONE CORPORATION, pg. 950
ROTA ADVERTISING LIMITED—See Backer Spielvogel Bates Worldwide, Inc., pg. 112
ROTANDO LERCH & IAFELIECE ADVERTISING, pg. 950
ROTARY FORMS PRESS, INC., pg. 950
ROTARY MULTIFORMS, INC., pg. 951
ROTARY PAPER MANIFOLD CO.—See Bradner Central Company, pg. 171
ROTHCHILD ASSET MANAGEMENT INC.—See Rothschild North America Inc., pg. 951
ROTHCHILD REALTY INC.—See Rothschild North America Inc., pg. 951
S. ROTHCHILD & CO., INC., pg. 951
ROTHSCHILD INC.—See Rothschild North America Inc., pg. 951
ROTHSCHILD NORTH AMERICA INC., pg. 951
ROTOR DYNAMICS PTY. LTD.—See Bently Nevada Corporation, pg. 141
THE ROTOR TOOL COMPANY, pg. 951
ROTT-KELLER SUPPLY CO., pg. 951
ROTTERDAM INDUSTRIAL PARK—See Rotterdam Ventures Inc., pg. 951
ROTTERDAM VENTURES INC., pg. 951
ROUBIN & JANEIRO, INC.—See Roubinco, Inc., pg. 952
ROUBINCO, INC., pg. 952
ROUGH BROTHERS, INC., pg. 952
ROUND HILL FOODS, INC., pg. 952
ROUNDTREE AUTOMOTIVE GROUP, pg. 952
ROUNDY'S, INC., pg. 952
ROUNDY'S INC., MILWAUKEE DIV.—See Roundy's, Inc., pg. 952
ROUNDY'S WAYCO FOODS—See Roundy's, Inc., pg. 952
ROUSH PRODUCTS CO., INC.—See Windmill Holdings Corp., pg. 1195
ROUX LABORATORIES, INC.—See MacAndrews & Forbes Holdings Inc., pg. 696
ROWE CORP., pg. 952
ROWE INTERNATIONAL, INC.—See RI Holdings, pg. 907
ROWMAN & LITTLEFIELD PUBLISHERS, INC., pg. 952
ROWOCO—See Wilton Industries, Inc., pg. 1195
ROWTRONICS COMPANY INC., pg. 953
ROXANNE SWIM SUITS CO., INC.—See Milady Brassiere & Corset Co., Inc., pg. 753
ROYAL CARIBBEAN CRUISES LTD., pg. 953
THE ROYAL CHINA & PORCELAIN COMPANIES INC., pg. 953
ROYAL CRUISE LINE INC., pg. 953
ROYAL GREENFIELD INC.—See F. L. Roberts & Co. Inc., pg. 938
ROYAL JEEP EAGLE CHRYSLER PLYMOUTH, INC., pg. 953
ROYAL MELROSE GRANITES—See Cold Spring Granite Company, pg. 260
ROYAL OAK ENTERPRISES, INC., pg. 953
ROYAL OAK FORD INC., pg. 953
ROYAL OLDSMOBILE MAZDA, INC., pg. 953
ROYAL PAPER BOX OF CALIFORNIA, pg. 953
ROYAL PLASTIC—See M.C. Gill Corporation, pg. 458
ROYAL VIKING LINE—See Norwegian Cruise Line, pg. 816
ROYAL WATERBEDS, pg. 953
ROYALE PAINT & BODY—See Regency Lincoln Mercury, pg. 922
ROYDON WEAR, INC.—See Coordinated Apparel, Inc., pg. 283
ROYLE SYSTEMS GROUP, pg. 953
ROYTEX, INC., pg. 953
RUBATEX CORPORATION—See Great American Industries, Inc., pg. 480
RUBBER PRODUCTS DIVISION—See Freudenberg-NOK (MI), pg. 433
RUBBER PRODUCTS DIVISION—See Freudenberg-NOK (MI), pg. 433
RUBBER PRODUCTS DIVISION—See Freudenberg-NOK (MI), pg. 433
RUBBER PRODUCTS DIVISION—See Freudenberg-NOK (MI), pg. 433
RUBICON INC.—See Uniroyal Chemical Company, Inc., pg. 1129
RUBIN EHRENTHAL & ASSOCIATES, pg. 953
LILLIE RUBIN AFFILIATES INC., pg. 954
RUBIN POSTAER & ASSOCIATES, pg. 954
RUBIN RESPONSE SERVICES, INC., pg. 954
M. RUBIN & SONS INC., pg. 954
ARTHUR RUBLOFF & CO. OF FLORIDA—See Orix Real Estate Equities, Inc., pg. 829
RUBLOFF CAPITAL INC.—See Orix Real Estate Equities, Inc., pg. 829
RUBLOFF CAPITAL INVESTMENTS INC.—See Orix Real Estate Equities, Inc., pg. 829
RUBLOFF-COLONIAL OAKS, INC.—See Orix Real Estate Equities, Inc., pg. 829
RUBLOFF CORPORATE SERVICES, INC.—See Orix Real Estate Equities, Inc., pg. 829
RUDEL MACHINERY COMPANY, INC., pg. 954
RUDER FINN HEALTH CARE—See Ruder, Finn, Inc., pg. 954
RUDER, FINN, INC., pg. 954
RUDER FINN JAPAN DESK—See Ruder, Finn, Inc., pg. 954
RUDER, FINN/RALEIGH (NC)—See Ruder, Finn, Inc., pg. 954
RUDER FINN/WASHINGTON—See Ruder, Finn, Inc., pg. 954
RUDOLPH FOODS COMPANY, pg. 954
RUDOLPH/LIBBE, INC., pg. 955
RUDOLPH & WEST—See Mico Inc., pg. 748
RUFFIN BUILDING SYSTEMS, INC., pg. 955
RUGBY-DARBY GROUP OF COS., pg. 955
RUGBY FARMERS UNION ELEVATOR COMPANY, pg. 955
RUGG MANUFACTURING COMPANY, pg. 955
RUHL COMPANIES, INC., pg. 955
THE RUHLIN COMPANY, pg. 955
CHUCK RUHR ADVERTISING, pg. 955
RUIZ FOOD PRODUCTS, INC., pg. 955
RUMRILL-HOYT, INC., pg. 955
RUMS OF PUERTO RICO, pg. 956
RUMSEY ELECTRIC CO., pg. 956
RUNDEL PRODUCTS, INC., pg. 956
RUNWAY TWO FIVE CORPORATION—See Specialty Restaurants Corporation, pg. 1028
RUPPMAN NATIONAL YELLOW PAGES SERVICE (RNYPS), pg. 956
RURAL ELECTRIC CO-OP, pg. 956
RURAL METRO CORPORATION, pg. 956
RUSCON CORP., pg. 956
RUSH COUNTY FARM BUREAU CO-OP, pg. 956
RUSH PRESS—See Continental Graphics Holdings, Inc., pg. 279
RUSKA INSTRUMENT CORPORATION, pg. 956
RUSKA LABORATORIES—See Ruska Instrument Corporation, pg. 956
RUSLANDER & SONS, INC., pg. 956
JOHN RUSLING LTD.—See Up-Right, Inc., pg. 1139
RUSSELL CHEVROLET COMPANY, pg. 957
H. J. RUSSELL CORP., pg. 957
RUSSELL INDUSTRIES, INC., pg. 957
RUSSELL PETROLEUM CORPORATION, pg. 957
RUSSELL-STANLEY CORPORATION, pg. 957
RUSSELL-STANLEY WEST, INC.—See Russell-Stanley Corporation, pg. 957
RUSSELL STOVER CANDIES, INC., pg. 957
RUSSETT FOODS—See Zemco Industries, Inc., pg. 1217
RUSSIAN TRAVEL BUREAU, INC.—See Orbitair International Ltd., pg. 828
RUSTCO PRODUCTS COMPANY, pg. 957
RUTHERFORD WAREHOUSE CORP.—See Stonecutter Mills Corp., pg. 1051
RUTHMAN PUMP & ENGINEERING CO., pg. 957
RUTT CUSTOM CABINETRY, pg. 957
RUXTON GROUP—See Chicago Reader, Inc., pg. 246
RYAN CONSTRUCTION COMPANY—See Ryan Properties Inc., pg. 958
RYAN CONSTRUCTION COMPANY OF MINNESOTA—See Ryan Properties Inc., pg. 958
RYAN HERCO PRODUCTS CORP., pg. 958
RYAN OLDSMOBILE, pg. 958
RYAN PROPERTIES INC., pg. 958
RYDELLE LABORATORIES—See S. C. Johnson & Son, Inc., pg. 599
RYDER & SCHILD, INC., pg. 958
RYNONE MANUFACTURING CORPORATION, pg. 958
RYSER BROS. OF WISCONSIN—See Ryser Brothers Inc., pg. 958
RYSER BROTHERS INC., pg. 958
RYSTAN COMPANY, INC.—See Carnrick Labs., Inc., pg. 222

S

S & W FINE FOODS, INC.—See Tri Valley Growers Inc., pg. 1111
S & A RESTAURANT CORP., pg. 958
S & C ELECTRIC CANADA LTD.—See S & C Electric Company, pg. 959
S & C ELECTRIC COMPANY, pg. 958
S & C MAINTENANCE CORP.—See Spatz & Co., pg. 1026
S&D COFFEE INC., pg. 959
S & J INDUSTRIES—See North American Products Corp., pg. 811
S&K PRODUCTS, INC.—See Armstrong International, Inc., pg. 83
S&N KATZ JEWELERS—See Reliable Stores, Inc., pg. 925
S & P COMPANY, pg. 959
S & S CAFETERIAS—See Smith & Sons Foods, Inc., pg. 1014
S & S DIVERSIFIED FOOD SERVICE, INC.—See Smith & Sons Foods, Inc., pg. 1014
S & S FOOD ADMINISTRATORS—See Smith & Sons Foods, Inc., pg. 1014
S & S GRAPHICS, INC., pg. 959
SAE ENGINEERING, INC., pg. 959
SAIC COMMERCIAL ENTERPRISES, INC.—See Science Applications International Corporation, pg. 982
SAIC UK LIMITED—See Science Applications International Corporation, pg. 982
SAS CONSULTING SERVICES, INC.—See SAS Institute Inc., pg. 959
SAS INSTITUTE AB—See SAS Institute Inc., pg. 960
SAS INSTITUTE A/S—See SAS Institute Inc., pg. 960
SAS INSTITUTE AUSTRALIA PTY. LTD.—See SAS Institute Inc., pg. 960
SAS INSTITUTE (CANADA) INC.—See SAS Institute Inc., pg. 960
SAS INSTITUTE GMBH—See SAS Institute Inc., pg. 960
SAS INSTITUTE INC., pg. 959
SAS INSTITUTE JAPAN LTD.—See SAS Institute Inc., pg. 960
SAS INSTITUTE LTD.—See SAS Institute Inc., pg. 960
SAS INSTITUTE LTD.—See SAS Institute Inc., pg. 960
SAS INSTITUTE LTD. (PHILIPPINES)—See SAS Institute Inc., pg. 960
SAS INSTITUTE NV/SA—See SAS Institute Inc., pg. 960
SAS INSTITUTE (NZ) LTD.—See SAS Institute Inc., pg. 960
SAS INSTITUTE OY—See SAS Institute Inc., pg. 960
SAS INSTITUTE PTE. LTD.—See SAS Institute Inc., pg. 960
SAS INSTITUTE S.A.—See SAS Institute Inc., pg. 960
SAS INSTITUTE S.A. (GENEVE)—See SAS Institute Inc., pg. 960
SAS INSTITUTE S.A. (MADRID)—See SAS Institute Inc., pg. 960
SAS INSTITUTE SDN. BHD.—See SAS Institute Inc., pg. 960
SAS INSTITUTE S.R.L.—See SAS Institute Inc., pg. 960
SAS SOFTWARE KOREA LTD.—See SAS Institute Inc., pg. 960
SAS SOFTWARE, LTD.—See SAS Institute Inc., pg. 960
SAS SOFTWARE TAIWAN LTD.—See SAS Institute Inc., pg. 960
SB ENTERTAINMENT INC., pg. 960
SBC ADVERTISING, pg. 960
SBN SYSTEM INC., pg. 960
SBS PRODUCTS, INC.—See Deb Holdings, Inc., pg. 323
SC COMPANIES, INC., pg. 960
SCC HOLDING CO., pg. 961
SCH HOLDING CORP.—See Riklis Family Corporation, pg. 934
SCR, INC., pg. 961
SCS ENGINEERS, pg. 961
SCT YARNS, INC., pg. 961
SD LEASING COMPANY—See Stephens, Inc., pg. 1046
SDTV, INC.—See News-Press & Gazette Company, pg. 804
SF SERVICES, pg. 961
SFA, INC., pg. 961
SFM MEDIA CORPORATION, pg. 962
S-G METALS INDUSTRIES, INC., pg. 962
SGD INTERNATIONAL CORP., pg. 962
SGI INC., pg. 962
SI HOLDINGS INC., pg. 962
SJL OF KANSAS CORP., pg. 962
S.K. TSOUMANIS REPRESENTATIONS—See Panduit Company, pg. 846
SK HAND TOOL CORP., pg. 963
SKR RESOURCES, INC., pg. 963
S L C GRAPHICS, INC., pg. 963
SLM ELECTRONICS—See St. Louis Music, Inc., pg. 967
SLM, INC., pg. 963
SOR EUROPE, LTD.—See SOR Inc., pg. 963
SOR INC., pg. 963
SP TELCOM CORPORATION—See Anschutz Corporation, pg. 75

SPC INTERNATIONAL CORP.—See System Planning Corp., pg. 1070
S.P.C. TRANSPORT, pg. 963
SPD TECHNOLOGIES, pg. 963
SPEC GROUP—See Sauer Industries, Inc., pg. 972
SPSS EUROPE B.V.—See SPSS Inc., pg. 964
SPSS INC., pg. 964
SRI DEVELOPMENT CORP.—See SRI International, pg. 964
SRI INTERNATIONAL, pg. 964
SRS TECHNOLOGIES, pg. 964
SS SERVICE CORPORATION—See Washington Mutual Savings Bank, pg. 1166
SSD&W INTEGRATED MARKETING COMMUNICATIONS, pg. 964
S-T INDUSTRIES, INC., pg. 964
S.T. RESEARCH, pg. 964
STG MARKETING COMMUNICATIONS, INC., pg. 964
STS CONSULTANTS, LTD.—See STS Holdings, Inc., pg. 965
STS HOLDINGS, INC., pg. 964
SUL CORPORATION—See Victory Financial Group, Inc., pg. 1150
S.W.B. & COMPANY—See I. Rokeach & Sons, Inc., pg. 944
S.W. JR. ENTERPRISES, INC., pg. 965
SYC-SELMEC, S.A. DE C.V.—See S & C Electric Company, pg. 959
SABBETH INDUSTRIES LTD, pg. 965
SABBETH INTERNATIONAL FOREST PRODUCTS—See Sabbeth Industries Ltd, pg. 965
SABBETH WORLD WIDE WOOD CORP.—See Sabbeth Industries Ltd, pg. 965
SABIN ROBBINS PAPER CO., pg. 965
SABINE TRUCKING, INC.—See Trinidad/Benham Corporation, pg. 1114
SABRELINER CORP., pg. 965
SACHNOWITZ & CO., pg. 965
SACHS ENERGY MANAGEMENT SYSTEMS—See Sachs Holding Company, pg. 965
SACHS HOLDING COMPANY, pg. 965
SACHS PROPERTIES—See Sachs Holding Company, pg. 965
ANN SACKS TILE & STONE, INC.—See Kohler Company, pg. 640
THE SACKS ELECTRICAL SUPPLY CO.—See UIS, Inc., pg. 1123
SACKS & ROSEN, INC. ADVERTISING, pg. 965
SACRAMENTO INDUSTRIAL SUPPLY—See DoAll Company, pg. 341
SACRAMENTO KINGS, pg. 965
SACRAMENTO MUNICIPAL UTILITY DISTRICT, pg. 965
SADCO LTD.—See Joffko International, pg. 595
SADLIER—See William H. Sadlier, Inc., pg. 966
WILLIAM H. SADLIER, INC., pg. 966
W.H. SADLIER OXFORD—See William H. Sadlier, Inc., pg. 966
SAE-PINKERTON & LAWS INC., pg. 966
SAFE HARBOR WATER POWER CORPORATION, pg. 966
SAFEGUARD BUSINESS SYSTEMS, INC., pg. 966
SAFEGUARD BUSINESS SYSTEMS LIMITED—See Safeguard Business Systems, Inc., pg. 966
SAFEGUARD EUROPE S.A.—See Safeguard Business Systems, Inc., pg. 966
SAFEGUARD FINANCIAL CORP.—See Safeguard Business Systems, Inc., pg. 966
SAFEGUARD SYSTEMS GB, LTD.—See Safeguard Business Systems, Inc., pg. 966
SAFELITE AUTOGLASS—See Lear Siegler Diversified Holdings Corp., pg. 664
SAFETY AND FIRE TECHNOLOGY, INC.—See O'Keeffe's, Inc., pg. 823
SAFETYMASTER CORPORATION—See Strategic Distribution Inc., pg. 1053
SAGE-ALLEN & CO., INC., pg. 966
SAGINAW MEAT & PRODUCE COMPANY—See United Stores, pg. 1137
SAHARA COAL CO., pg. 966
ST. ANNE CHEMICAL CO., LTD.—See Parsons & Whittemore Enterprises, pg. 850
ST. ANNE INDUSTRIES LTD.—See Parsons & Whittemore Enterprises, pg. 850
ST. ANNE - NACKAWIC PULP CO., LTD.—See Parsons & Whittemore Enterprises, pg. 850
ST. ANNE PULP SALES CO. LTD.—See Parsons & Whittemore Enterprises, pg. 850
ST. CLAIR MANUFACTURING CO.—See Stockham Valves & Fittings, Inc., pg. 1050
ST. CROIX PRESS, INC., pg. 966
THE ST. GEORGE GROUP, INC., pg. 966
ST. JOHNSBURY TRUCKING CO., INC., pg. 966
ST. LOUIS AUTO AUCTION—See Cox Enterprises, Inc., pg. 293
ST. LOUIS METALLIZING CO.—See Nooter Corporation, pg. 808
ST. LOUIS MUSIC, INC., pg. 967
ST. LOUIS SOUTHWESTERN RAILWAY CO.—See Anschutz Corporation, pg. 75
SAINT MARYS RAILROAD CO.—See Gilman Paper Co., pg. 459
SAINT PAUL BANK FOR COOPERATIVES—See Federal Farm Credit Banks Funding Corporation, pg. 405
ST. PAUL METALCRAFT, INC., pg. 967
ST. PETE AUTO AUCTION—See Cox Enterprises, Inc., pg. 293
SAKRETE, INC., pg. 967
BOB SAKS JEEP-EAGLE—See Farmington Hills Holding Company, pg. 402
BOB SAKS OLDSMOBILE INC.—See Farmington Hills Holding Company, pg. 402
BOB SAKS TOYOTA—See Farmington Hills Holding Company, pg. 402
SALADMASTER, pg. 967
SALEM CARRIERS. INC.—See Salem National Corporation, pg. 967
SALEM LEASING CORP.—See Salem National Corporation, pg. 967
SALEM NATIONAL CORPORATION, pg. 967
SALEM TECHNICAL SERVICES—See Day & Zimmermann, Inc., pg. 320
SALES AND MARKETING MANAGEMENT—See Bill Communications, Inc., pg. 150
SALINE INVESTMENT CO.—See R & B Machine Tool Co., pg. 906
SALL-ECLIPSE—See Eclipse, Inc., pg. 366
SALLY LOU FASHIONS CORPORATION, pg. 967
SALT RIVER PROJECT AGRICULTURAL IMPROVEMENT AND POWER DISTRICT, pg. 967
H. SALT SEAFOOD RESTAURANTS, pg. 967
SALVATI MONTGOMERY SAKODA, INC., pg. 967
SALWASSER MANUFACTURING COMPANY, INC., pg. 968
SALZ LEATHERS, INC., pg. 968
SAMELSON-LEON COMPANY, INC., pg. 968
SAMMONS COMMUNICATIONS, INC.—See Sammons Enterprises, Inc., pg. 968
SAMMONS ENTERPRISES, INC., pg. 968
SAMPLER PUBLICATIONS INC., pg. 968
SAMSILL CORPORATION, pg. 968
SAMSONITE CORPORATION—See E-II Holdings, Inc., pg. 358
SAMSTEEL, INC.—See Ferro Union, Inc., pg. 407
SAMTEC INC., pg. 968
MILTON SAMUELS ADVERTISING AGENCY, INC., pg. 968
ALLEN SAMUELS CHEVROLET GEO, pg. 969
SAN ANGELO ELECTRIC SERVICE COMPANY, pg. 969
SAN ANGELO STANDARD, INC.—See Harte-Hanks Communications, Inc., pg. 513
SAN ANTONIO AUTO AUCTION—See Cox Enterprises, Inc., pg. 293
SAN ANTONIO LIGHT—See The Hearst Corporation, pg. 524
SAN DIEGO CHARGERS, pg. 969
SAN DIEGO WILD ANIMAL PARK—See San Diego Zoo, pg. 969
SAN DIEGO ZOO, pg. 969
SAN FRANCISCO EXAMINER—See The Hearst Corporation, pg. 524
SAN FRANCISCO FRENCH BREAD COMPANY, pg. 969
SAN FRANCISCO GIANTS BASEBALL CLUB, pg. 969
SAN FRANCISCO KNITTING MILLS—See School Apparel, Inc., pg. 978
SAN FRANCISCO REALTIES—See The Hearst Corporation, pg. 524
SAN GABRIEL VALLEY MEDICAL CENTER—See UniHealth America, pg. 1127
SAN JOSE & ASSOCIATES, pg. 969
SAN MIGUEL (U.S.A.) INC., pg. 969
SANBORN MANUFACTURING COMPANY, pg. 969
SANCHEZ & LEVITAN, INC., pg. 970
SANDERSON PLUMBING PRODUCTS INC., pg. 970
SANDLER COMMUNICATIONS INC., pg. 970
SANDS INVESTMENTS, INC., pg. 970
SANDS MOTOR COMPANY, INC., pg. 970
SANDTEX—See Cooperheat, Inc., pg. 283
SANDUSKY PLASTICS, INC.—See Envirodyne Industries, Inc., pg. 383
SANEL AUTO PARTS, INC.—See Automotive Supply Assoc., Inc., pg. 101
SANFORD & HAWLEY, INC., pg. 970
SANGRE DE CRISTOS RANCHES INC.—See Forbes, Inc., pg. 423
SANI-MATIC SYSTEMS—See DEC International, Inc., pg. 309
SANISERV, pg. 970
SANITARIOS DOMINICANOS, S.A.—See American Standard Inc., pg. 62
SANITARY WARES MFG. CORP.—See American Standard Inc., pg. 62
SANITAS HEALTHCARE DIV.—See Dutton-Lainson Co., pg. 356
SANTA MONICA FORD COMPANY, pg. 970
SANTA MONICA HOSPITAL MEDICAL CENTER—See UniHealth America, pg. 1127
SANTA ROSA STEEL FORMING, INC., pg. 970
SANTANDER MET., S.A. MADRID—See Metropolitan Life Insurance Co., pg. 745
SANTEE DAIRIES—See Hughes Markets Inc., pg. 552
SANTEE PRINT WORKS, INC., pg. 970
SANUS CORP. HEALTH SYSTEMS—See New York Life Insurance Company, pg. 803
THE SANYMETAL PRODUCTS CO., INC., pg. 970
SAPROMA S.A.—See Carlson Companies, Inc., pg. 221
SARASOTA MOVING SYSTEMS INC.—See Cook Moving Systems, Inc., pg. 282
SARATOGA HARNESS RACING, INC., pg. 970
SARGENT-FLETCHER CO., pg. 970
SARGENT & GREENLEAF, INC., pg. 971
SARGENT & GREENLEAF INTERNATIONAL—See Sargent & Greenleaf, Inc., pg. 971
H. E. SARGENT, INC., pg. 971
SARGENT & LUNDY, pg. 971
SARGENT MANUFACTURING COMPANY—See ESSTAR Incorporated, pg. 361
SARGENT & POTRATZ, INC., pg. 971
THE SARGENT-SOWELL COMPANY, pg. 971
SARGENTO CHEESE CO.—See Sargento Incorporated, pg. 971
SARGENTO FOOD SERVICE CORP.—See Sargento Incorporated, pg. 971
SARGENTO INCORPORATED, pg. 971
C.G. SARGENTS SONS—See Aeroglide Corporation, pg. 22
DAVID SARNOFF RESEARCH CENTER—See SRI International, pg. 964
SAS INSTITUTE B.V.—See SAS Institute Inc., pg. 960
SASCO ELECTRIC—See Sasco Group, pg. 972
SASCO GROUP, pg. 971
SASCO/VALLEY ELECTRIC—See Sasco Group, pg. 972
SASS & ASSOCIATES, pg. 972
SASSON JEANS FOR MEN, pg. 972
SATELLITE DATA BROADCAST NETWORKS, INC. (SATNET)—See The Associated Press, pg. 92
SATHERS INC., pg. 972
THE SATURDAY EVENING POST SOCIETY—See Benjamin Franklin Literary & Medical Society, Inc., pg. 139
SATURDAY REVIEW MAGAZINE—See General Media Publishing Group, pg. 450
SATURN OF INDIANAPOLIS—See Lockhart Cadillac Inc., pg. 680
SATURN OF PLYMOUTH—See Don Massey Cadillac Inc., pg. 719
SAUDER MANUFACTURING CORPORATION, pg. 972
SAUDER WOODWORKING CO., pg. 972
SAUER HOLDINGS—See Sauer Industries, Inc., pg. 972
SAUER INDUSTRIES, INC., pg. 972
THE SAUGATUCK MARKETING GROUP, pg. 972
SAUL BROS. & COMPANY, INC., pg. 972
SAUNDERS BROTHERS, pg. 972
SAUNDERS INCORPORATED, pg. 972
SAUNDERS, LUBINSKI & WHITE, INC., pg. 973
SAV-RITE ADVERTISING, pg. 973
SAVAGE ARMS INC., pg. 973
SAVE MART SUPERMARKETS, pg. 973
SAVE MORE FOOD MART, INC., pg. 973
SAVEMART INC., pg. 973
SAVILLE—See Jones Apparel Group, Inc., pg. 602
SAVOGRAN OF CALIFORNIA—See The Savogran Company, pg. 973
MIKE SAVOIE CHEVROLET INC., pg. 973
THE SAVOGRAN COMPANY, pg. 973
SAVOY BAR AND GRILL—See Lettuce Entertain You Enterprises, Inc., pg. 669
SAVOY CONSTRUCTION CO. INC., pg. 973
SAVOY DRAPERY DIV.—See CC Industries, Inc., pg. 200
SAWYER RILEY COMPTON INC., pg. 973
SAXON PAINT & HOME CARE CENTERS INC., pg. 973
RON SAXON FORD, INC., pg. 973
SAXONY DISTILLERS ET CIE, INC.—See Charles Jacquin et Cie, Inc., pg. 588
CECIL SAYDAH COMPANY, pg. 973
S.B. FOOT TANNING CO.—See Red Wing Shoe Co., Inc., pg. 919
SBN SYSTEMS INC.-CANADIAN OPERATIONS—See SBN System Inc., pg. 960
SBN SYSTEMS INC.-CORPORATE—See SBN System Inc., pg. 960
SBN SYSTEMS INC.-IMPRINTER DIVISION—See SBN System Inc., pg. 960
SBN SYSTEMS INC.-MONTREAL—See SBN System Inc., pg. 960
SCAFA TORNABENE—See Goldmark Industries, Ltd., pg. 468
SCALAMANDRE, INC., pg. 974
SCAN GLOBE A/S—See Replogle Globes, Inc., pg. 927
SCANELO, YOUNG & RUBICAM AS—See Young & Rubicam Inc., pg. 1212
SCANGAS BROTHERS HOLDINGS, INC., pg. 974
SCHAAKE PACKING COMPANY, INC., pg. 974
SCHAD INDUSTRIES, INC., pg. 974
SCHAEDLER BROTHERS, INC., pg. 974
SCHAEPS ICE CREAM COMPANY, pg. 974
SCHAFER BAKERIES, INC.—See Perfection Bakeries Inc., pg. 861
S. SCHAFFER GROCERY CORPORATION, pg. 974
SCHARER ASSOCIATES, INC., pg. 974
SCHARFBERG & ASSOCIATES, LTD. ADV., pg. 974
SCHAWK, INC., pg. 974
SCHAWKGRAPHICS—See Schawk, Inc., pg. 975
SCHEDULING TECHNOLOGY CORPORATION, pg. 975
SCHEER ADVERTISING AGENCY, pg. 975
SCHEIN/BLATTSTEIN ADVERTISING, INC., pg. 975
HENRY SCHEIN, INC., pg. 975
SCHEIN PHARMACEUTICAL, INC.—See Henry Schein, Inc., pg. 975
SCHELL/MULLANEY, pg. 975
SCHENECTADY CHEMICALS AUSTRALIA PTY. LTD.—See Schenectady Chemicals, Inc., pg. 975
SCHENECTADY CHEMICALS CANADA LTD.—See Schenectady Chemicals, Inc., pg. 975
SCHENECTADY CHEMICALS, INC., pg. 975
SCHENECTADY DE FRANCE—See Schenectady Chemicals, Inc., pg. 975
SCHENECTADY IBERICA S.A.—See Schenectady Chemicals, Inc., pg. 975
SCHENECTADY MIDLAND, LTD.—See Schenectady Chemicals, Inc., pg. 975
SCHENECTADY QUIMICA DO BRASIL LIMITADA—See Schenectady Chemicals, Inc., pg. 975
THE JULIUS SCHEPPS CO., pg. 975
SCHERER BROS. LUMBER COMPANY, pg. 976
SCHERER SCIENTIFIC, LTD., pg. 976
SCHERING-PLOUGH HEALTHCARE PRODUCTS ADVERTISING CORP., pg. 976
SCHIAVONE CONSTRUCTION CO., pg. 976
SCHILLER-PFEIFFER, INC.—See Belmont Industries, Inc., pg. 136
SCHILLING ENTERPRISES—See Dealers Transport Company, Inc., pg. 322
SCHILLING MOTORS, INC.—See Dealers Transport Company, Inc., pg. 322
G. SCHIRMER, INC.—See Music Sales Corporation, pg. 777
SCHLOSSER FORGE COMPANY, pg. 976
SCHMIDT BAKING CO., INC., pg. 976
GEORGE T. SCHMIDT, pg. 976
H.W. SCHMIDT GMBH—See Haworth, Inc., pg. 518
THE SCHMIDT/WESTERDAHL GROUP LTD., pg. 976
SCHMIEDING ENTERPRISES INC., pg. 976

PAUL A. SCHMITT MUSIC COMPANY, pg. 976
PETER J. SCHMITT HOLDINGS, pg. 976
SCHNADIG CORPORATION, pg. 977
ALEXANDER SCHNEIDER LTD.—See Panduit Company, pg. 846
SCHNEIDER COMMERCIAL REAL ESTATE, pg. 977
SCHNEIDER MILLS, INC., pg. 977
SCHNEIDER NATIONAL, INC., pg. 977
SCHNELLER, INC., pg. 977
SCHNIEBER FINE FOODS, INC., pg. 977
SCHNITZER STEEL INDUSTRIES, INC., pg. 977
SCHNUCK MARKETS, INC., pg. 977
GUY SCHOENECKER, INC., pg. 977
SCHOENEMAN BROTHERS COMPANY, pg. 978
SCHOLASTIC BOOK FAIRS, INC.—See SI Holdings Inc., pg. 962
SCHOLASTIC-CANADA, LTD.—See SI Holdings Inc., pg. 962
SCHOLASTIC INC.—See SI Holdings Inc., pg. 962
SCHOLASTIC INC. INFORMATION CENTER—See SI Holdings Inc., pg. 962
SCHOLASTIC INC. NATIONAL DISTRIBUTION CENTER—See SI Holdings Inc., pg. 962
SCHOLASTIC PRODUCTIONS INC.—See SI Holdings Inc., pg. 962
SCHOLASTIC PUBLICATIONS LTD.—See SI Holdings Inc., pg. 962
SCHOLZ & FRIENDS DESIGN GMBH—See Backer Spielvogel Bates Worldwide, Inc., pg. 112
SCHOLZ & FRIENDS GMBH—See Backer Spielvogel Bates Worldwide, Inc., pg. 112
SCHOOL APPAREL, INC., pg. 978
SCHOTT BROTHERS, INC., pg. 978
SCHOTT CORPORATION, pg. 978
SCHOTTENSTEIN STORES CORPORATION, pg. 978
SCHREIBER FOODS, INC., pg. 978
SCHREIBER MILLING CO.—See Hubbard Milling Company, pg. 549
SCHREIER MALTING CO., pg. 978
SCHUCK & SONS CONSTRUCTION CO., pg. 979
SCHUFF STEEL CO., pg. 979
GEO. F. SCHULER, INC., pg. 979
SCHULTZ STEEL COMPANY, pg. 979
SCHULZE & BURCH BISCUIT COMPANY, pg. 979
SCHUMACHER-DUGAN CONSTRUCTION, pg. 979
SCHUMACHER ELECTRIC CORPORATION, pg. 979
F. SCHUMACHER & CO., pg. 979
SCHUMACHER & FORELLE, INC., pg. 979
SCHURZ COMMUNICATIONS, INC., pg. 979
SCHUTTE & COMPANY, pg. 979
SCHUTTE LUMBER COMPANY, pg. 980
SCHWAB CORP., pg. 980
S. SCHWAB COMPANY, pg. 980
SCHWAN'S SALES ENTERPRISES, pg. 980
BEN SCHWARTZ MARKET, INC., pg. 980
SCHWARTZ & BENJAMIN, INC., pg. 980
JACK SCHWARTZ SHOES, INC., pg. 980
SCHWARZ PAPER COMPANY, pg. 980
SCHWEGMANN GIANT SUPER MARKETS, pg. 980
SCHWEIZER AIRCRAFT CORPORATION, pg. 981
SCHWINN BICYCLE COMPANY, pg. 981
SCHWINN (USA)-CSEPEL LTD.—See Schwinn Bicycle Company, pg. 981
F.J. SCIAME CONSTRUCTION, pg. 981
SCICOM DATA SERVICES, LTD., pg. 981
SCIENCE APPLICATIONS INTERNATIONAL CORPORATION, pg. 981
SCIENCE APPLICATIONS INTERNATIONAL CORPORATION (SAIC VIRGIN ISLANDS)—See Science Applications International Corporation, pg. 982
SCIENCE APPLICATIONS INTERNATIONAL, EUROPE S.A.—See Science Applications International Corporation, pg. 982
SCIENCE & ENGINEERING ASSOCIATES, pg. 982
SCIENCE PRESS—See Mack Printing Company, pg. 697
SCIENTIFIC ADVANCES INC.—See Battelle Memorial Institute, pg. 126
SCIENTIFIC CORPORATION—See Hinderliter Industries, Inc., pg. 535
SCIENTIFIC DUST COLLECTORS—See Venturedyne, Ltd., pg. 1148
SCIPAR, pg. 982
L. M. SCOFIELD COMPANY, pg. 982
SCOOZI—See Lettuce Entertain You Enterprises, Inc., pg. 669
SCOTCHMAN INDUSTRIES, INC., pg. 982
SCOTIA INDUSTRIAL PARK, INC.—See Rotterdam Ventures Inc., pg. 952
THE SCOTSMAN GROUP, INC., pg. 982
SCOTSMAN GROUP, INC.—See The Scotsman Group, Inc., pg. 982
LOUIS SCOTT ASSOCIATES, INC., pg. 982
THE SCOTT COMPANY, pg. 982
SCOTT FARM SEED CO.—See Land O'Lakes, Inc., pg. 654
SCOTT JEWELERS—See Reliable Stores, Inc., pg. 925
SCOTT/LANCASTER/HERSHFIELD, pg. 982
SCOTT LUMBER COMPANY, pg. 983
SCOTT MOTOR TRANSPORT—See Dead River Company, pg. 322
SCOTT PRINTING CORPORATION, pg. 983
SCOTT SPECIALTY GASES, INC., pg. 983
SCOTT TOBACCO—See Conwood Company L.P., pg. 282
SCOTT U.S.A., pg. 983
SCOTTSDALE PUBLISHING, INC.—See Cowles Media Company, pg. 291
THE SCOULAR COMPANY, pg. 983
SCOULAR GRAIN COMPANY—See The Scoular Company, pg. 983
SCOVILLE PRESS, INC., pg. 983
SCRAP CORPORATION OF AMERICA—See Tang Industries Inc., pg. 1078
SCREEN PRODUCTS AUSTRALIAN PTY LTD—See Flexible Products Company, pg. 419
SCREW CONVEYOR CORP., pg. 983
SCRIPTO-TOKAI, INC., pg. 983
SCRUFARI CONSTRUCTION CO. INC., pg. 983
SCS ANALYTICAL LABORATORY—See SCS Engineers, pg. 961
SCS FIELD SERVICES—See SCS Engineers, pg. 961
SCUDDER, STEVENS & CLARK, INC., pg. 983
SEA ISLAND COMPANY, pg. 983
SEA ISLAND SERVICES, INC.—See Sea Island Company, pg. 983
SEA ISLAND PROPERTIES, INC.—See Sea Island Company, pg. 983
SEABEAM IND., INC.—See Channel Technologies, Inc., pg. 239
SEABOARD CORPORATION—See Seaboard Flour Corporation, pg. 984
SEABOARD CORPORATION, GRAIN DIVISION—See Seaboard Flour Corporation, pg. 984
SEABOARD ELECTRONICS CO., pg. 983
SEABOARD ELECTRONICS-EAST COAST BRANCH—See Seaboard Electronics Co., pg. 984
SEABOARD FARMS DIVISION—See Seaboard Flour Corporation, pg. 984
SEABOARD FLOUR CORPORATION, pg. 984
SEABROOK BROTHERS & SONS, INC., pg. 984
SEABROOK FOODS, INC., pg. 984
SEABROOK INC.—See Draper Corporation, pg. 348
SEABROOK WALLCOVERINGS, INC., pg. 984
SEACOAST ELECTRIC COMPANY—See Edwardstone & Company, Inc., pg. 370
SEACOR SERVICES, INC. (SSI)—See Day & Zimmermann, Inc., pg. 321
SEAFRESH INC.—See Wards Cove Packing Company, pg. 1163
SEALAND TECHNOLOGY—See Nelson A. Taylor Co., Inc., pg. 1081
SEALASKA CORPORATION, pg. 984
SEALASKA TIMBER CORPORATION—See Sealaska Corporation, pg. 984
SEALD-SWEET GROWERS, INC., pg. 984
SEALING DEVICES INC., pg. 984
SEALS DIVISION—See Freudenberg-NOK (MI), pg. 433
SEALS DIVISION—See Freudenberg-NOK (MI), pg. 433
SEALS DIVISION—See Freudenberg-NOK (MI), pg. 433
SEALTRON CORPORATION—See Transilwrap Company, Inc., pg. 1107
SEALTRON, INC.—See HCC Industries, pg. 496
SEALY CANADA, LTD.—See Sealy Corporation, pg. 986
SEALY CONNECTICUT, INC.—See Sealy Corporation, pg. 985
SEALY CORPORATION, pg. 985
SEALY, INC.—See Sealy Corporation, pg. 985
SEALY MATTRESS COMPANY, pg. 986
SEALY MATTRESS COMPANY OF ALBANY, INC.—See Sealy Corporation, pg. 985
SEALY MATTRESS COMPANY OF ILLINOIS—See Sealy Corporation, pg. 985
SEALY MATTRESS COMPANY OF KANSAS CITY, INC.—See Sealy Corporation, pg. 985
SEALY MATTRESS COMPANY OF MEMPHIS—See Sealy Corporation, pg. 985
SEALY MATTRESS COMPANY OF MICHIGAN, INC.—See Sealy Corporation, pg. 985
SEALY MATTRESS COMPANY OF PUERTO RICO—See Sealy Corporation, pg. 985
SEALY OF MARYLAND & VIRGINIA, INC.—See Sealy Corporation, pg. 985
SEALY OF MINNESOTA, INC.—See Sealy Corporation, pg. 985
SEAMAN FURNITURE CO., INC., pg. 986
SEAMAN-PATRICK PAPER COMPANY, pg. 986
SEAMAN TIMBER COMPANY, INC., pg. 986
KENNETH M. SEATON ENTERPRISES—See Family Inns of America, Inc., pg. 398
SEATS INCORPORATED—See Nordic Group of Companies, Ltd., pg. 810
SEATTLE CITY LIGHT, pg. 986
SEATTLE LIGHTING FIXTURE CO., pg. 986
SEATTLE PACIFIC INDUSTRIES, INC., pg. 986
SEATTLE PACKAGING CORPORATION, pg. 986
SEATTLE PLANT—See Ash Grove Cement Company, pg. 88
SEATTLE POST-INTELLIGENCER—See The Hearst Corporation, pg. 524
SEATTLE TIMES COMPANY, pg. 986
SEAWAY SHOPPING CENTERS, INC.—See Charan Industries, Inc., pg. 239
SEBASTIAN & COOKE, pg. 986
SEBASTIAN COTTON & GRAIN CORP., pg. 986
SECHRIST INDUSTRIES, INC., pg. 987
SECO WARWICK CORPORATION, pg. 987
SECURITY ALARMS & FIRE ENGINEERING INC., pg. 987
SECURITY EQUITY LIFE INSURANCE CO.—See Security Mutual Life Insurance Co. of New York, pg. 987
SECURITY INDUSTRIAL INSURANCE CO., INC.—See Ourso Investment Corporation, pg. 832
SECURITY MUTUAL LIFE INSURANCE CO. OF NEW YORK, pg. 987
SECURITY PLASTICS, INC., pg. 987
SECURITY PRODUCTS COMPANY—See Universal Cooperatives, Inc., pg. 1138
SECURITY PRODUCTS COMPANY OF DELAWARE, INC.—See Universal Cooperatives, Inc., pg. 1138
SECURITY TITLE & GUARANTY CO.—See Helmsley Enterprises, Inc., pg. 527
SECURITY VAN LINE, INC.—See Johnson Storage & Moving Company, pg. 600
SECURITY VAN LINES, INC., pg. 987
SEELY EQUIPMENT & SUPPLY CO., INC.—See Modern Group Ltd., pg. 763
SEESSEL HOLDINGS, INC., pg. 987
SEFTON ASSOCIATES INC., pg. 987
THE SEGERDAHL CORP., pg. 987
SEGUE PARTNERS—See Praxis International Inc., pg. 885
SEGUROS GENSIS, SA—See Metropolitan Life Insurance Co., pg. 745
SEGWAY PARTNERS—See Praxis International Inc., pg. 885
SEGWAY PARTNERS—See Praxis International Inc., pg. 885
SEIBEL & STERN CORP., pg. 987
SEIGLE'S HOME & BUILDING CENTERS, pg. 987
SEILER CORPORATION, pg. 987
SEKO-AIR FREIGHT, pg. 988
SELCO TRUCKING CO.—See Seton Company, pg. 993
SELECT SIRES, INC., pg. 988
SELECTO-FLASH, INC., pg. 988
SELECTONE CORPORATION, pg. 988
SELF—See Advance Publications Inc., pg. 19
SELIG MANUFACTURING COMPANY—See Cox Furniture, pg. 294
SELIGMAN & ASSOCIATES, INC., pg. 988
SELIGMAN & ASSOCS. OF MICHIGAN—See Seligman & Associates, Inc., pg. 988
SELLEN CONSTRUCTION COMPANY, pg. 988
DEAN SELLERS FORD INC., pg. 988
BOB SELLERS PONTIAC GMC TRUCK INC., pg. 988
SELLERSBURG STONE COMPANY, INC.—See Gohmann Asphalt & Construction Inc., pg. 465
SELLSTROM MANUFACTURING CO., pg. 988
THE SELMER CO.—See Integrated Resources, Inc., pg. 573
SELOVER BUICK, INC., pg. 988
SEMAC INDUSTRIES INC., pg. 989
SEMBLEX CORPORATION, pg. 989
SEMCO, INC., pg. 989
SEMCO INDUSTRIES, pg. 989
SEMEX, INC.—See Seton Company, pg. 993
SEMINOLE MANUFACTURING COMPANY, pg. 989
SENATE INSURANCE COMPANY—See Lawrence Group, Inc., pg. 662
SENATOR FORD, pg. 989
SENCO PRODUCTS, INC.—See SENCORP, pg. 989
SENCORE, INC., pg. 989
SENCORP, pg. 989
SENECA WIRE & MANUFACTURING CO., pg. 989
SENIOR WORLD (CALIFORNIA)—See Landmark Communications, Inc., pg. 656
SENNHEISER ELECTRONIC CORP., pg. 989
SENSENICH PROPELLER CO.—See The Philadelphia Bourse, Inc., pg. 866
SENSOR DEVELOPMENTS INC., pg. 990
SENTINEL ADMINISTRATIVE SERVICE CORPORATION—See National Life Insurance Company, pg. 791
SENTINEL ADVISORS, INC.—See National Life Insurance Company, pg. 791
SENTINEL COMPUTER SERVICES INC., pg. 990
SENTINEL CONSUMER PRODUCTS, INC., pg. 990
SENTINEL MANAGEMENT SERVICES, INC.—See Erin Group Administrators, Inc., pg. 387
THE SENTINEL-NEWS—See Landmark Communications, Inc., pg. 655
SENTROL EUROPE S.A.—See Berwind Corporation, pg. 145
SENTROL, INC.—See Berwind Corporation, pg. 145
SENTRON MEDICAL, INC.—See SENCORP, pg. 989
SENTRY GROUP, pg. 990
SENTRY INSURANCE, A MUTUAL COMPANY, pg. 990
SEPPALA & AHO CONSTRUCTION COMPANY, pg. 990
SEQUATCHIE HANDLE WORKS, INC.—See O.P. Link Handle Company, pg. 677
SEQUENTIA INC., pg. 990
SEREVCO & COMPANY LTD.—See National Steel Corporation, pg. 794
SERFILCO, LTD., pg. 990
SERIGRAPH, INC., pg. 991
SERINO COYNE INC., pg. 991
SERONO BAKER DIAGNOSTICS, pg. 991
SERTA, INC., pg. 991
SERTA MATTRESS COMPANY, pg. 991
SERVAAS, INC., pg. 991
SERVAAS INVESTMENTS, INC.—See Servaas, Inc., pg. 991
SERVAAS LABORATORIES INC.—See Servaas, Inc., pg. 991
SERVCO PACIFIC INC., pg. 991
SERVICE AMERICA CORPORATION, pg. 992
SERVICE ASSETS CORP.—See Bromar Inc., pg. 179
SERVICE MOTOR CO.—See Service Motor Company, pg. 992
SERVICE MOTOR COMPANY, pg. 992
SERVICE PACKING COMPANY, pg. 992
SERVICE SUPPLY CO. INC. OF INDIANA, pg. 992
SERVICE SUPPLY CORP.—See Seiler Corporation, pg. 988
SERVICE WEB OFFSET CORPORATION, pg. 992
SERVICERECORDER—See Sycon Corporation, pg. 1069
SERVICIOS EXPECIALES DE EDICION—See International Data Group, pg. 577
SERVISTAR CORPORATION, pg. 992
SERVITEX, INC.—See National Distributing Co., Inc., pg. 787
SERVO CORPORATION OF AMERICA, pg. 993
SERVO INTERNATIONAL, INC.—See Servo Corporation of America, pg. 993
SERVO PRODUCTS COMPANY—See Silicon Valley Development, pg. 1004
SERVUS FOOTWEAR COMPANY, pg. 993
SETCO SALES COMPANY, pg. 993
SETLOWEAR, INC.—See Williamson-Dickie Mfg. Co., pg. 1192
SETON COMPANY, pg. 993
SETZER FOREST PRODUCTS, pg. 993
SETZER FOREST PRODUCTS-OROVILLE PLANT—See Setzer Forest Products, pg. 993
SEVCO, INC.—See Ingrid-Sevko, Inc., pg. 569
SEVEN SEAS LEASING—See International Airline Support Group, Inc., pg. 575

SEVEN-UP BOTTLING CO. OF AKRON—See Brooks Beverage Management, Inc., pg. 179
SEVEN-UP BOTTLING CO. OF CLEVELAND—See Brooks Beverage Management, Inc., pg. 179
SEVEN-UP BOTTLING CO. OF DAYTON—See Brooks Beverage Management, Inc., pg. 179
SEVEN-UP BOTTLING CO. OF DETROIT—See Brooks Beverage Management, Inc., pg. 179
THE SEVEN-UP COMPANY—See Dr Pepper/Seven-Up Companies, Inc., pg. 342
7UP OF CORPUS CHRISTI—See Grant-Lydick Beverage Co., pg. 477
7UP OF VICTORIA—See Grant-Lydick Beverage Co., pg. 477
7UP/RC OF AUSTIN—See Grant-Lydick Beverage Co., pg. 477
7UP/RC OF HARLINGEN—See Grant-Lydick Beverage Co., pg. 477
SEVEN-UP ROYAL CROWN-CANADA DRY OF CINCINNATI—See Brooks Beverage Management, Inc., pg. 179
SEVEN-UP ROYAL CROWN CANADA DRY OF COLUMBUS—See Brooks Beverage Management, Inc., pg. 179
1740 VENTURES, INC.—See The Mutual Life Insurance Company of New York (MONY), pg. 778
SEVENTEEN MAGAZINE—See K-III Communications Corporation, pg. 611
SEWARD LUGGAGE COMPANY, pg. 993
SEWELL VILLAGE CADILLAC CO., pg. 993
J. A. SEXAUER—See The Dyson-Kissner-Moran Corporation, pg. 357
SEXTON CAN CO., INC., pg. 993
SEYBOLD LIMITED—See Ziff Communications Company, pg. 1219
SEYBOLD PUBLICATIONS—See Ziff Communications Company, pg. 1219
SEYBOLD SEMINARS—See Ziff Communications Company, pg. 1219
SEYMOUR MANUFACTURING COMPANY, pg. 994
SEYMOUR OF SYCAMORE, INC., pg. 994
SHADE COMPUTER FORMS CO., pg. 994
SHADE FOODS, INC.—See Norfoods, Inc., pg. 810
SHADE PASTA, INC.—See Norfoods, Inc., pg. 810
SHAFER COMMERCIAL SEATING INC., pg. 994
SHAKER ADVERTISING AGENCY, pg. 994
SHAKEY'S INCORPORATED, pg. 994
SHAKOPEE VALLEY PRINTING CO.—See Guy Gannett Publishing Company, pg. 442
MARK SHALE, pg. 994
SHAMROCK BROADCASTING, INC.—See Shamrock Holdings, Inc., pg. 994
SHAMROCK FOODS CO., pg. 994
SHAMROCK HOLDINGS, INC., pg. 994
THE SHANE GROUP INC., pg. 995
SHANNON & WILSON, INC., pg. 995
SHAPCO, INC., pg. 995
SHAPE INC., pg. 995
SHAPE SOUTH, INC.—See Shape Inc., pg. 995
SHAPELL INDUSTRIES, INC., pg. 995
SHAPERO STORES—See Quael Corp., pg. 903
SHAPSON GERO & SOMMERS, INC., pg. 995
SHARON CONCEPTS, INC., pg. 995
SHARON-JAY TOGS, INC., pg. 995
SHARON TUBE COMPANY, pg. 995
SHARP HARTWIG, INC., pg. 995
SHARP OIL COMPANY, pg. 995
SHARPE ENDOSURGICAL CORPORATION—See Phillips Plastics Corporation, pg. 867
SHAW CREATIONS, INC., pg. 996
SHAW-PERKINS INC.—See Reactive Metals & Alloys Corporation (REMACOR), pg. 916
SHAWNEE NEWS-STAR—See Stauffer Communications, Inc., pg. 1042
SHAWNEE PRESS, INC.—See Music Sales Corporation, pg. 777
SHAW'S CRAB HOUSE/CHICAGO—See Lettuce Entertain You Enterprises, Inc., pg. 669
SHAW'S DEERFIELD—See Lettuce Entertain You Enterprises, Inc., pg. 669
SHEA HOMES, pg. 996
SHEA HOMES NORTHERN CALIFORNIA—See Shea Homes, pg. 996
SHEA HOMES SAN DIEGO—See Shea Homes, pg. 996
SHEA HOMES SOUTHERN CALIFORNIA—See Shea Homes, pg. 996
SHEA HOMES SOUTHWEST—See Shea Homes, pg. 996
SHEALY ELECTRICAL WHOLESALERS, pg. 996
SHEARMAN CORPORATION, pg. 996
SHEEHY, KNOPF & SHAVER, INC., pg. 996
SHEER HOSIERY DIV.—See Collins & Aikman Group Inc., pg. 263
SHEFFIELD HARDWARE COMPANY, pg. 996
SHEFFIELD STEEL CORPORATION-JOLIET, pg. 996
THE SHELBURNE CORPORATION, pg. 996
SHELBURNE CYCLEBINDING DIVISION—See The Shelburne Corporation, pg. 996
SHELBURNE HUSKY DIV.—See The Shelburne Corporation, pg. 996
SHELBY GROUP INTERNATIONAL, INC., pg. 996
THE SHELBY INSURANCE GROUP—See The Associated Group, pg. 90
SHELBY & SHANE MARKETING COMMUNICATIONS, pg. 996
SHELDON GOOD & CO. OF CALIFORNIA—See Sheldon Good & Co., Inc., pg. 470
SHELDON GOOD & CO. OF CANADA—See Sheldon Good & Co., Inc., pg. 470
SHELDONS' INC., pg. 996
SHELF STABLE FOODS, INC.—See The Wornick Company, pg. 1203
SHELLY BROS., INC.—See Brock Candy Company, pg. 178
SHELLY DATA SYSTEMS—See National Reproductions Corporation, pg. 793
SHELTER MUTUAL INSURANCE COMPANY, pg. 997
SHENANDOAH LIFE INSURANCE COMPANY, pg. 997
SHENANDOAH MFG. CO. INC., pg. 997
SHENANDOAH PRODUCTS—See Perdue Farms Inc., pg. 860
SHENANDOAH VALLEY FARMS—See Perdue Farms Inc., pg. 860
SHENANDOAH VALLEY PRESS, INC.—See Judd's Incorporated, pg. 608
SHENANGO FURNACE COMPANY, pg. 997
SHEPARD CLOTHING COMPANY, pg. 997
SHEPARD NILES, INC., pg. 997
SHEPAUG CORPORATION, pg. 997
SHEPHERD CONSTRUCTION CO., INC., pg. 998
SHEPLERS, INC., pg. 998
SHERBORNE GROUP, INC., pg. 998
THE SHERIDAN GROUP, pg. 998
THE SHERIDAN PRESS, INC.—See The Sheridan Group, pg. 998
SHERLEY GRAIN COMPANY, pg. 998
SHERMAN & REILLY, INC., pg. 998
SHERMS THUNDERBIRD MARKET, pg. 998
SHERWOOD CO.—See Hypro Corporation, pg. 557
SHERWOOD CORPORATION—See Inkel Corp., pg. 570
SHERWOOD FOOD DISTRIBUTORS, pg. 998
SHERWOOD LUMBER CORPORATION, pg. 999
SHERWOOD & SCHNEIDER ADVERTISING, pg. 999
THE SHIDLER GROUP, pg. 999
SHIELD INSURANCE—See Spartan Stores Inc., pg. 1026
SHIELD SECURITY, INC., pg. 999
SHIELDALLOY METALLURGICAL CORPORTATION—See Metallurg, Inc., pg. 742
SHIFFMAN/FERGUSSON/STONE ADVERTISING INC., pg. 999
SHILLCRAFT, INC., pg. 999
SHIOCTON KRAUT CO.—See Bush Brothers & Company, pg. 196
SHIP ANALYTICS, INC., pg. 999
SHIPLEY OIL COMPANY, pg. 999
SHIVERS TRADING & OPERATING CO., pg. 999
SHMINA CONSTRUCTION, INC.—See Peter A. Basile Sons Inc., pg. 124
SHOE-TOWN, INC., pg. 999
THE SHOE WORKS SHOE STORES, INC.—See The Kobacker Company & Affiliates, pg. 638
R. M. SHOEMAKER CO., pg. 1000
SHOEMART EXPRESS—See Chernin's Shoes, pg. 243
SHOFAR KOSHER FOODS, INC., pg. 1000
SHOGYO INTERNATIONAL CORPORATION, pg. 1000
SHOKAI FAR EAST LTD., pg. 1000
SHONAC CORPORATION, pg. 1000
SHOOK, INC.—See Shook National Corporation, pg. 1000
SHOOK NATIONAL CORPORATION, pg. 1000
SHOP-RITE BEVERAGES, INC.—See Wakefern Food Corporation, pg. 1158
SHOP-RITE CIGARETTES (CT)—See Wakefern Food Corporation, pg. 1158
SHOP-RITE OF BENSALEM INC.—See Wakefern Food Corporation, pg. 1158
SHOP-RITE SUPERMARKETS, INC.—See Wakefern Food Corporation, pg. 1158
SHOPKO STORES, INC., pg. 1000
SHOPPER PUBLISHING GROUP—See Stauffer Communications, Inc., pg. 1042
SHOPPER'S GUIDE, INC. (TUCSON SHOPPER)—See Harte-Hanks Communications, Inc., pg. 513
SHOPRITE SUPERMARKETS—See Big V Supermarkets, Inc., pg. 149
SHORELINE PRODUCTS, INC., pg. 1000
SHOWELL FARMS, INC., pg. 1000
SHOWELL FARMS, INC.—See Showell Farms, Inc., pg. 1000
SHOWELL FARMS, INC.—See Showell Farms, Inc., pg. 1001
SHOWTIME SATELLITE NETWORKS, INC.—See National Amusements, Inc., pg. 785
SHUFORD MILLS, INC., pg. 1001
SHUGART CORPORATION, pg. 1001
SHURE BROTHERS INCORPORATED, pg. 1001
SHURE, GMBH—See Shure Brothers Incorporated, pg. 1001
SHURFINE-CENTRAL CORP., pg. 1001
SHUTTLECRAFT—See Sioux Steel Company, pg. 1008
SHUTTLELIFT, INC.—See Marine Travelift, Inc., pg. 707
THE SICO COMPANY, pg. 1001
SICO INC., pg. 1001
SICOLA MARTIN KOONS FRANK, INC., pg. 1001
SID TOOL CO. INC., pg. 1002
SIDDALL, MATUS & COUGHTER, INC. ADVERTISING & PUBLIC RELATIONS, pg. 1002
SIEBEL/MOHR, INC., pg. 1002
SIEG COMPANY, pg. 1002
SIEGEL CORP., pg. 1002
SIEGEL & GALE, pg. 1002
HENRY I. SIEGEL COMPANY, INC., pg. 1002
SIEGLE'S HOME & BUILDING CENTERS—See Seigle's Home & Building Centers, pg. 987
SIEMER MILLING COMPANY, pg. 1002
THE SIERRA CAPITAL COMPANIES, pg. 1002
SIERRA CAPITAL REALTY SERVICES—See The Sierra Capital Companies, pg. 1003
SIERRA PACIFIC INDUSTRIES, pg. 1003
SIERRA PACIFIC INDUSTRIES-ARCATA DIVISION—See Sierra Pacific Industries, pg. 1003
SIERRA PACIFIC INDUSTRIES-HAYFORK DIVISION—See Sierra Pacific Industries, pg. 1003
SIERRACIN CORPORATION, pg. 1003
SIERRACIN/SYLMAR CORPORATION—See Sierracin Corporation, pg. 1003
THE SIESEL COMPANY, pg. 1003
SIFTCO CANADA, INC.—See North American Salt Company, pg. 812
SIFTO CANADA, INC.—See North American Salt Company, pg. 812
SIGAL CONSTRUCTION, pg. 1003
SIGAL/ZUCKERMAN CO., pg. 1003
SIGALLO, LTD., pg. 1003
SIGLER & REEVES, pg. 1003
SIGMA—See Young & Rubicam Inc., pg. 1212
SIGMA GROUP—See Provident Mutual Life Insurance Co., pg. 896
SIGMA PLATING CO., LTD.—See Standun, Inc., pg. 1038
SIGMAN MEAT CO. INC., pg. 1003
SIGNAL TRANSFORMER CO., INC.—See Insilco Corporation, pg. 571
SIGNAL TRANSFORMER CO., INC.—See Insilco Corporation, pg. 571
THE SIGNATURE GROUP—See Montgomery Ward & Co., Inc., pg. 768
SIGNATURE TRAVEL, INC.—See Washington Mutual Savings Bank, pg. 1166
SIGNATURES—See Starcrest Products of California, pg. 1040
SIGNBOARD HILL PRODUCTIONS—See Hallmark Cards, Inc., pg. 502
SIGNET INDUSTRIES, pg. 1003
SIGNET SYSTEMS, INC.—See The Equion Corporation, pg. 385
SIGNIFICS, INC., pg. 1004
SILGAN CORPORATION, pg. 1004
SILICON POWER CUBE CORPORATION, pg. 1004
SILICON VALLEY DEVELOPMENT, pg. 1004
SILICONES, INC.—See Group Dekko International Inc., pg. 490
SILLCOCKS PLASTICS INTERNATIONAL, INC., pg. 1004
SILVER DOLLAR CITY, INC., pg. 1004
SILVER SPRINGS CITRUS CO-OP, pg. 1004
SILVER STATE DISPOSAL SERVICE, INC., pg. 1004
SILVERCREST WESTERN HOME INDUSTRIES CORPORATION, pg. 1004
SILVERMAN PRODUCTS & TEXTILES, pg. 1004
SILVER'S INC., pg. 1005
SILVERSTONE, ADKINS & BREIT, INC., pg. 1005
SILVESTRI CORP., pg. 1005
SIMCO/RAMIC CORPORATION—See Quantic Industries, Inc., pg. 904
SIMKINS CAROLINA FOLDING BOX DIV.—See Simkins Industries, Inc., pg. 1005
SIMKINS CARTON DIV.-CHICAGO—See Simkins Industries, Inc., pg. 1005
SIMKINS CARTON DIV.-CLEVELAND—See Simkins Industries, Inc., pg. 1005
SIMKINS CARTON DIV.-DALLAS—See Simkins Industries, Inc., pg. 1005
SIMKINS CARTON DIV.-MARIETTA—See Simkins Industries, Inc., pg. 1005
SIMKINS INDUSTRIES, INC., pg. 1005
SIMKINS MARYLAND BOARD—See Simkins Industries, Inc., pg. 1005
SIMKINS NEW HAVEN BOARD—See Simkins Industries, Inc., pg. 1005
SIMKINS NEW HAVEN CARTON—See Simkins Industries, Inc., pg. 1005
SIMMONS-BOARDMAN PUBLISHING CORP., pg. 1005
SIMMONS, DURHAM & ASSOCIATES, pg. 1005
SIMMONS OIL CORP., pg. 1005
SIMMONS OUTDOOR CORP., pg. 1005
SIMMONS UPHOLSTERED FURNITURE, INC., pg. 1005
SIMMS & MCIVOR MARKETING COMMUNICATIONS, pg. 1005
SIMON & ASSOCIATES, pg. 1006
SIMON MARKETING, INC., pg. 1006
MELVIN SIMON & ASSOCIATES, pg. 1006
JOSEPH SIMON & SONS, INC., pg. 1006
SIMONDS INDUSTRIES INC., pg. 1006
SIMONDS-SHIELDS-THEIS GRAIN CO., pg. 1006
SIMONIZ CANADA LTD.—See Blue Coral, Inc., pg. 159
SIMONS MICHELSON ZIEVE, INC., pg. 1006
SIMPLEX CONSTRUCTION CO. INC.—See Simplex Industries, Inc., pg. 1006
SIMPLEX INDUSTRIES, INC., pg. 1006
SIMPLEX INTL. TIME EQUIP. CO. LTD. (CANADA)—See Simplex Time Recorder Co., pg. 1006
SIMPLEX INTL. TIME EQUIP. PTY. LTD.—See Simplex Time Recorder Co., pg. 1006
SIMPLEX MANAGEMENT SERVICES, LTD.—See Simplex Time Recorder Co., pg. 1006
SIMPLEX TIME RECORDER CO., pg. 1006
SIMPLICITY MANUFACTURING, INC., pg. 1006
J.R. SIMPLOT CO. FOOD GROUP—See J.R. Simplot Company, pg. 1007
J.R. SIMPLOT COMPANY, pg. 1007
SIMPSON DURA-VENT CO., INC., pg. 1007
SIMPSON ELECTRIC CO., pg. 1007
SIMPSON INVESTMENT CO., pg. 1007
SIMPSON PAPER CO.—See Simpson Investment Co., pg. 1007
SIMPSON PASADENA PAPER CO.—See Simpson Investment Co., pg. 1007
SIMPSON PLAINWELL PAPER CO., INC.—See Simpson Investment Co., pg. 1007
SIMPSON TACOMA KRAFT CO.—See Simpson Investment Co., pg. 1007
SIMPSON TIMBER CO.—See Simpson Investment Co., pg. 1007
SIMUNICO, INC., pg. 1007
SINCLAIR OIL CORP., pg. 1008
SINCLAIR PAINT CO.—See Insilco Corporation, pg. 571
SINCLAIR PRINTING & LITHO, INC., pg. 1008
SINGERS SUPERMARKETS, INC., pg. 1008
SINGH INDUSTRIES, pg. 1008
SINTEL, INC., pg. 1008
SIOUX FALLS CONSTRUCTION COMPANY, pg. 1008
SIOUX HONEY ASSOCIATION, pg. 1008
SIOUX MANUFACTURING CORP., pg. 1008
SIOUX STEEL COMPANY, pg. 1008

SIOUX VALLEY EMPIRE ELECTRIC ASSOCIATION, pg. 1009
SIOUX VALLEY RURAL TELEVISION—See Sioux Valley Empire Electric Association, pg. 1009
SIPES SUPER MARKETS—See Hale-Halsell Company, pg. 501
SIPEX CORPORATION, pg. 1009
SIRTEX PRINTING COMPANY—See Dettra Flag Company, pg. 333
SISCO COMPANY—See First Mount Joy Corporation, pg. 413
SISTA'S PRIVATE LIMITED—See Backer Spielvogel Bates Worldwide, Inc., pg. 112
SISTI, ZINBARG & HOWARD, INC., pg. 1009
SITE OIL CO. OF MISSOURI, pg. 1009
SITHE ENERGIES, U.S.A., INC., pg. 1009
SIVALLS, INC., pg. 1009
SIVE/YOUNG & RUBICAM—See Young & Rubicam Inc., pg. 1211
SIVYER STEEL CORPORATION—See Everett Smith Investment Co. of Delaware, pg. 1013
SKEETER PRODUCTS, INC.—See MacAndrews & Forbes Holdings Inc., pg. 695
SKINNER CORP., pg. 1009
NANCY SKINNER & ASSOCIATES—See Biggs Gilmore Communications, pg. 149
SKOKIE VALLEY BEVERAGE CO., pg. 1009
SKYWAY FREIGHT SYSTEMS, INC., pg. 1009
SKYWAY LUGGAGE CO., pg. 1009
SKYWAY SYSTEMS, INC.—See Skyway Freight Systems, Inc., pg. 1009
SLANE HOSIERY MILLS, INC., pg. 1010
SLANT/FIN CORPORATION, pg. 1010
SLANT-FIN, LTD./LTEE—See Slant/Fin Corporation, pg. 1010
SLATER HANFT MARTIN, INC., pg. 1010
SLAUGHTER BROS., INC.—See Furman Lumber Company, pg. 436
SLEEPECK PRINTING COMPANY, pg. 1010
SLEEPY'S THE MATTRESS PROFESSIONALS, pg. 1010
SLICK AIRCRAFT PRODUCTS—See Unison Industries, pg. 1130
SLIP-X SAFETY TREADS, INC.—See Bissell Inc., pg. 153
SLOAN TECHNOLOGY—See Veeco Instrumentations, Inc., pg. 1146
SLOAN VALVE COMPANY, pg. 1010
R & G SLOANE MFG. CO., INC., pg. 1010
SLOANS SUPERMARKETS, INC., pg. 1010
J.T. SLOCOMB COMPANY, pg. 1010
SMALL PARTS, INC., pg. 1010
SMALL TUBE PRODUCTS CO., INC., pg. 1010
SMARTSTAR CORPORATION, pg. 1011
SMARTY PANTS N TOPS TOO, INC., pg. 1011
SMEAD MANUFACTURING COMPANY, pg. 1011
ANTON SMIT & CO., INC., pg. 1011
WILBUR SMITH ASSOCIATES, pg. 1011
SMITH, BADOFSKY & RAFFEL, INC. ADVERTISING, pg. 1011
SMITH BROTHERS FARMS, INC., pg. 1011
PETER W. SMITH & COMPANY, INC., pg. 1011
J. M. SMITH CORP., pg. 1012
EBERLE M. SMITH ASSOCIATES, INC.—See Ghafari Associates, Inc., pg. 455
SMITH-EDWARDS-DUNLAP COMPANY, pg. 1012
SMITH-EMERY COMPANY, pg. 1012
SMITH ENTERPRISES, pg. 1012
SMITH FARMS, INC., pg. 1012
KEITH SMITH FARMS, INC., pg. 1012
SMITH FROZEN FOODS, INC., pg. 1012
SMITH & GILLESPIE ENGINEERS, INC., pg. 1012
SMITH/GREENLAND, INCORPORATED, pg. 1012
THE SMITH GROUP, INC., pg. 1012
H. B. SMITH CO., INC., pg. 1013
SMITH HINCHMAN GRYLLS ASSOCIATES, INC.—See The Smith Group, Inc., pg. 1013
L. B. SMITH, INC., pg. 1013
SMITH INDUSTRIES, INC., pg. 1013
EVERETT SMITH INVESTMENT CO. OF DELAWARE, pg. 1013
SMITH JEWELERS & DISTRIBUTORS, INC.—See Zale Corporation, pg. 1216
SMITH, KAPLAN, ALLEN & REYNOLDS, INC., pg. 1013
L. J. SMITH, INC.—See Marmac Corporation, pg. 710
SMITH-LEE CO., INC., pg. 1013
J. RICHARD SMITH, LTD., pg. 1013
T. L. SMITH MACHINE, pg. 1013
SMITH MAILER—See California Manufacturing Enterprises, pg. 210
SMITH METAL ARTS COMPANY, INC., pg. 1013
SMITH MOTORS, INC., pg. 1014
OKLA HOMER SMITH FURNITURE CO.—See Century Products Co., pg. 235
SMITH PIPE & STEEL CO., pg. 1014
S. R. SMITH, INC.—See Aqua Fab Industries, Inc., pg. 79
SMITH-SHAFER OIL CO., pg. 1014
SMITH & SONS CATERING CO.—See Smith & Sons Foods, Inc., pg. 1014
SMITH & SONS FOODS, INC., pg. 1014
SMITH SYSTEM MANUFACTURING COMPANY, pg. 1014
SMITH TRACTOR & EQUIPMENT CO.—See Smith Brothers Farms, Inc., pg. 1011
SMITH VALVE CORPORATION, pg. 1014
SMITH WHOLESALE DRUG DIV.—See J. M. Smith Corp., pg. 1012
SMITH'S MOVING & STORAGE CORP.—See Mayflower Transit, Inc., pg. 724
SMITH'S PERSONNEL SERVICE, INC., pg. 1014
SMOKIE PRODUCTS, INC.—See Carl Buddig & Company, pg. 186
SMYTH, BAUER & LEWIS ADVERTISING INC., pg. 1014
H.M. SMYTH CO., pg. 1014
JOHN M. SMYTH CO., pg. 1014
SMYTH MANUFACTURING COMPANY—See Beacon Group, pg. 129
SNAP-TITE, INCORPORATED, pg. 1014
SNAP-TITE PONN—See Snap-Tite, Incorporated, pg. 1015
SNARK BOATS DIV.—See The Entwistle Company, pg. 383
SNAVELY FOREST PRODUCTS, INC., pg. 1015
SNOKIST GROWERS, pg. 1015
SNUGL MFG. CO. INC.—See Berwind Corporation, pg. 145
SNYDER BAKERY—See United States Bakery, pg. 1134
SNYDER BROTHERS, INC., pg. 1015
SNYDER-DIAMOND, pg. 1015
SNYDER INDUSTRIES, INC., pg. 1015
SNYDER POTATO CHIPS—See Agway, Inc., pg. 26
SNYDER TANK CORP., pg. 1015
SNYDERGENERAL CORPORATION, pg. 1015
SNYDER'S DRUG STORES, INC., pg. 1015
SNYDER'S OF HANOVER, INC., pg. 1015
SO-LO-FOOD, INC., pg. 1016
SOALCO—See Acorn Building Components Inc., pg. 14
SOAP OPERA DIGEST—See K-III Communications Corporation, pg. 611
SOCIETY COMMERCIAL PROPERTIES, INC.—See Society for Savings Bancorp, Inc., pg. 1016
SOCIETY MORTGAGE CORPORATION—See Society for Savings Bancorp, Inc., pg. 1016
SOCIETY FOR SAVINGS BANCORP, INC., pg. 1016
SOCKS DIVISION—See Collins & Aikman Group Inc., pg. 263
SOFCO-MEAD, INC., pg. 1016
SOFEDEM S.A.—See Sunbeam-Oster Company, Inc., pg. 1059
SOFT SHEEN PRODUCTS, INC., pg. 1016
SOFTOOL CORPORATION, pg. 1016
SOFTRANS INTERNATIONAL, LTD.—See Berlitz International, Inc., pg. 143
SOFTWARE VIDEO PRODUCTION—See PCI, pg. 836
SOKOL & COMPANY, pg. 1016
SOLAR PLASTICS-MINNEAPOLIS—See Upper Midwest Industries, Inc., pg. 1140
SOLAR PLASTICS-QUAD CITIES—See Upper Midwest Industries, Inc., pg. 1140
SOLAR PRESS, INC., pg. 1016
SOLAR SERVICES, INC.—See Society for Savings Bancorp, Inc., pg. 1016
SOLID STATE DEVICES, INC., pg. 1017
SOLIDSTATE CONTROLS, INC.—See The Marmon Group, Inc., pg. 712
GEORGE SOLLITT CONSTRUCTION, pg. 1017
SOLO CUP COMPANY—See SCC Holding Co., pg. 961
P.R. SOLO CUP, INC.—See SCC Holding Co., pg. 961
ROBERT SOLOMON & ASSOCIATES ADV. INC., pg. 1017
SOLON MANUFACTURING COMPANY, pg. 1017
SOLVAY PHARMACEUTICALS, INC., pg. 1017
SOMERSET PONTIAC GMC INC., pg. 1017
SOMERSET REFINERY INC., pg. 1017
SOMERSET TECHNOLOGIES, INC., pg. 1017
SOMERSET WELDING & STEEL, INC.—See Riggs Industries, Inc., pg. 934
SOMERVILLE LUMBER & SUPPLY CO.—See Payless Cashways, Inc., pg. 853
SOMMER & MACA INDUSTRIES, INC., pg. 1017
SOMMER METALCRAFT CORPORATION, pg. 1018
SON CHIEF ELECTRICS, INC., pg. 1018
SONATECH, INC.—See Channel Technologies, Inc., pg. 239
SONEE HEAT TREATING—See Karsten Manufacturing Corporation, pg. 617
SONIC MESSENGER SERVICE—See Sonicair, pg. 1018
SONICAIR, pg. 1018
SONIFORM, INC.—See MacAndrews & Forbes Holdings Inc., pg. 695
SONNEVELDT COMPANY, pg. 1018
SONOMA MISSION INN & SPA, pg. 1018
SOONER PIPE & SUPPLY CORP., pg. 1018
SOUND CREATION—See Venturedyne, Ltd., pg. 1148
SOUND WAREHOUSE, INC., pg. 1018
SOUND WAREHOUSE, INC.—See Shamrock Holdings, Inc., pg. 995
SOUNDESIGN CORP. HONG KONG LTD.—See Soundesign Corporation, pg. 1019
SOUNDESIGN CORP. JAPAN LTD.—See Soundesign Corporation, pg. 1019
SOUNDESIGN CORPORATION, pg. 1018
SOUTH ATLANTIC EQUIPMENT, INC.—See The Dickerson Group, Inc., pg. 336
SOUTH BAY GROWERS, INC.—See United States Sugar Corporation, pg. 1137
SOUTH BEND PLASTICS, INC., pg. 1019
SOUTH BEND SCRAP & PROCESSING—See Sturgis Iron & Metal Company, Inc., pg. 1055
SOUTH BEND STAMPING DIV.—See EWI, Inc., pg. 361
SOUTH CENTRAL CO-OP, pg. 1019
SOUTH CHESTER TUBE CO., pg. 1019
SOUTH COAST LIGHTING SYSTEMS—See Jac Jacobsen Industries, Inc., pg. 588
SOUTH DAKOTA LOTTERY, pg. 1019
SOUTH EAST COAL CO., pg. 1019
SOUTH-EAST COAL SALES CO.—See South East Coal Co., pg. 1019
SOUTH-EAST OHIO COAL CO.—See South East Coal Co., pg. 1019
SOUTH EASTERN BRUSH CO.—See Flo-Pac Corporation, pg. 419
SOUTH HAVEN COIL INC.—See Humphrey Products Company, pg. 553
SOUTH SEATTLE AUTO AUCTION—See Cox Enterprises, Inc., pg. 293
SOUTH SHORE MALL—See R. H. Macy & Co., Inc., pg. 699
SOUTH STATES INC.—See Distribution America, pg. 340
THE SOUTHAMPTON CORP.—See Washington Homes, Inc., pg. 1166
SOUTHAMPTON SAWMILLS, LTD.—See Parsons & Whittemore Enterprises, pg. 850
SOUTHCO DISTRIBUTING COMPANY, pg. 1019
SOUTHEAST CORRECT CRAFT, INC.—See Correct Craft, Inc., pg. 287
SOUTHEAST FIRE SPRINKLER COMPANY—See S. I. Goldman Co., pg. 468
SOUTHEASTERN CAPITAL CORPORATION, pg. 1019
SOUTHEASTERN CORP.—See Southeastern Steel Company, pg. 1020
SOUTHEASTERN EQUIPMENT COMPANY, INC., pg. 1019
SOUTHEASTERN FREIGHT LINES, INC., pg. 1019
SOUTHEASTERN INVESTMENT PROPERTIES INC., pg. 1019
SOUTHEASTERN MEDEQUIP, INC., pg. 1019
SOUTHEASTERN PENNSYLVANIA TRANSPORTATION AUTHORITY, pg. 1020
SOUTHEASTERN STEEL COMPANY, pg. 1020
SOUTHEASTERN TEXTILE CO. DIV.—See Best Manufacturing, Inc., pg. 146
SOUTHEASTERN TEXTILES HOTEL CO. DIV.—See Best Manufacturing, Inc., pg. 146
SOUTHERN AGRICULTURAL INSECTICIDES, pg. 1020
SOUTHERN APPAREL CORPORATION, pg. 1020
SOUTHERN BEAUTY ENTERPRISES—See Beauty Enterprises Inc., pg. 130
SOUTHERN BELLE DAIRY COMPANY, INC., pg. 1020
SOUTHERN BEVERAGE PACKERS, INC., pg. 1020
SOUTHERN CALIFORNIA AUTO AUCTION—See Cox Enterprises, Inc., pg. 293
SOUTHERN CALIFORNIA BANCORP, pg. 1020
SOUTHERN CASE, INC., pg. 1020
SOUTHERN COMBUSTION & CONTROLS, INC.—See Eclipse, Inc., pg. 366
SOUTHERN CONTAINER CORPORATION, pg. 1020
SOUTHERN ELECTRIC SUPPLY CO., INC., pg. 1020
SOUTHERN ELECTRIC SUPPLY CO., INC.—See Southern Electric Supply Co., Inc., pg. 1021
SOUTHERN ELECTRIC SUPPLY CO., INC.—See Southern Electric Supply Co., Inc., pg. 1021
SOUTHERN FARM BUREAU CASUALTY INSURANCE COMPANY, pg. 1021
SOUTHERN FOODS, INC., pg. 1021
SOUTHERN FROZEN FOODS—See Agway, Inc., pg. 26
SOUTHERN GOLF DISTRIBUTORS, INC.—See Putt Putt Golf Courses of America, Inc., pg. 901
SOUTHERN ILLINOIS AND MISSOURI BRIDGE CO.—See Anschutz Corporation, pg. 76
SOUTHERN LEATHER COMPANY, pg. 1021
SOUTHERN LIFE AND HEALTH INSURANCE COMPANY—See Geneve Corporation, pg. 452
SOUTHERN MILLS, INC., pg. 1021
SOUTHERN MINNESOTA BEET SUGAR COOPERATIVE, pg. 1022
SOUTHERN OHIO FABRICATORS, INC., pg. 1022
SOUTHERN OPTICAL—See Optical Corp. of America, pg. 828
SOUTHERN OUTDOORS MAGAZINE—See B.A.S.S., Inc., pg. 105
SOUTHERN PACIFIC LINES, pg. 1022
SOUTHERN PACIFIC TRANSPORTATION CO.—See Anschutz Corporation, pg. 75
SOUTHERN PACIFIC WAREHOUSE CO.—See Anschutz Corporation, pg. 76
SOUTHERN PAVING CO.—See LeGrand Johnson Construction Co., pg. 598
SOUTHERN PIPE & SUPPLY CO., INC., pg. 1022
SOUTHERN PRECISION DIV.—See Walter Industries, Inc., pg. 1162
SOUTHERN PUMP & TANK CO. INC., pg. 1022
SOUTHERN RADIO CORPORATION, pg. 1022
SOUTHERN REALTY CO.—See Zale Corporation, pg. 1216
SOUTHERN SALTWATER MAGAZINE—See B.A.S.S., Inc., pg. 106
SOUTHERN STATES COOPERATIVE, INC., pg. 1022
SOUTHERN STEEL COMPANY—See Phelps Tointon Inc., pg. 866
SOUTHERN UNITED CORPORATION—See Victory Financial Group, Inc., pg. 1150
SOUTHERN UNITED FIRE INSURANCE COMPANY—See Victory Financial Group, Inc., pg. 1150
SOUTHERN UNITED LIFE INSURANCE COMPANY—See Victory Financial Group, Inc., pg. 1150
SOUTHERN WHOLESALE—See AFG Industries, Inc., pg. 4
SOUTHGATE FORD INC., pg. 1023
SOUTHLAND FLOORING SUPPLIES OF LOUISVILLE, INC., pg. 1023
SOUTHLAND INDUSTRIES, pg. 1023
SOUTHSIDE FORD TRUCK SALES INC., pg. 1023
SOUTHTEC, INC.—See South Chester Tube Co., pg. 1019
SOUTHWARK METAL MANUFACTURING COMPANY, pg. 1023
SOUTHWEST DOALL INDUSTRIAL SUPPLY—See DoAll Company, pg. 342
SOUTHWEST FLOOR COVERING INC., pg. 1023
SOUTHWEST MARINE, INC., pg. 1023
SOUTHWEST RESEARCH INSTITUTE, pg. 1023
SOUTHWEST SAMPLE & MARKETING—See H & H Advertising, pg. 496
SOUTHWESTERN EQUIPMENT CO.—See Union Holdings, Inc., pg. 1128
SOUTHWESTERN EXPLOSIVES—See Austin Powder Co., pg. 99
SOUTHWESTERN FOUNDRIES—See Stockham Valves & Fittings, Inc., pg. 1050
SOUTHWESTERN/GREAT AMERICAN INC., pg. 1023
SOUTHWESTERN INDUSTRIES, INC., pg. 1023
SOUTHWESTERN PETROLEUM CANADA LTD.—See Southwestern Petroleum Corporation, pg. 1024
SOUTHWESTERN PETROLEUM CORPORATION, pg. 1024
N.V. SOUTHWESTERN PETROLEUM EUROPE S.A.—See Southwestern Petroleum Corporation, pg. 1024
SOUTHWESTERN WHOLESALE JEWELRY CO.—See Zale Corporation, pg. 1216
SOUTHWIDE, INC., pg. 1024
SOUTHWIRE COMPANY, INC., pg. 1024

THE SOUTHWOOD COMPANY—See Artesian Resources Corporation, pg. 87
SOVEREIGN GROUP INC., pg. 1024
SOVEX NATURAL FOODS—See McKee Foods Corporation, pg. 730
L.H. SOWLES COMPANY, INC., pg. 1024
SPACE CONTROL CORP.—See Stratmar Systems, Inc., pg. 1053
SPACE MANAGEMENT SYSTEMS—See RNL Facilities Corporation, pg. 908
SPACE MASTER INTERNATIONAL, pg. 1024
SPALDING—See Spalding & Evenflo Companies, Inc., pg. 1024
SPALDING AUSTRALIA PTY. LTD.—See Spalding & Evenflo Companies, Inc., pg. 1025
SPALDING CANADA—See Spalding & Evenflo Companies, Inc., pg. 1025
SPALDING & EVENFLO COMPANIES, INC., pg. 1024
SPALDING JAPAN INC.—See Spalding & Evenflo Companies, Inc., pg. 1025
SPANG & COMPANY, pg. 1025
SPANG & COMPANY-BOONEVILLE PLANT—See Spang & Company, pg. 1025
SPANG POWER CONTROL—See Spang & Company, pg. 1025
SPANG SPECIALTY METALS—See Spang & Company, pg. 1025
SPANGLER CANDY COMPANY, pg. 1025
SPANGLER, INC., pg. 1025
SPANGLES' FLOUR MILLS OF MT. JOY—See Wilkins-Rogers Incorporated, pg. 1190
SPANISH COMMUNICATIONS CORP.—See Western International Media Corporation, pg. 1180
SPANJERSBURG—See Hallmark Cards, Inc., pg. 502
A. G. SPANOS DEVELOPMENT, INC., pg. 1025
SPARKOMATIC CORPORATION, pg. 1025
SPARTA MOSAIC, INC.—See United States Ceramic Tile Co., pg. 1135
SPARTAN INTERNATIONAL, pg. 1026
SPARTAN MILLS, pg. 1026
SPARTAN OIL CORP., pg. 1026
SPARTAN PLASTICS CANADA—See Spartan International, pg. 1026
SPARTAN STORES INC., pg. 1026
SPARTYWOOD PRODUCTS, INC.—See Semac Industries Inc., pg. 989
SPATZ CENTERS, INC.—See Spatz & Co., pg. 1026
SPATZ & CO., pg. 1026
SPATZ & CO. DEVELOPMENT—See Spatz & Co., pg. 1026
SPAULDING & SLYE CONSTRUCTION—See Spaulding & Slye Company, pg. 1027
SPAULDING COMPANY, INC.—See Semco Industries, pg. 989
SPAULDING & SLYE COMPANY, pg. 1026
SPEAKMAN COMPANY, pg. 1027
SPECIAL ERECTION SERVICES, INC.—See Construction Specialties, Inc., pg. 277
SPECIALIZED MEDIA SERVICES, INC., pg. 1027
SPECIALTY CASTINGS—See The Johnson Corporation, pg. 598
SPECIALTY ENGINEERED DOORS-CLARK DOOR CO.—See Clark Door Co., Inc., pg. 252
SPECIALTY EQUIPMENT COMPANIES INC., pg. 1027
SPECIALTY FOODS GROUP—See Sargento Incorporated, pg. 971
SPECIALTY INDUSTRIES, INC., pg. 1027
SPECIALTY LIGHTING—See Jac Jacobsen Industries, Inc., pg. 588
SPECIALTY MANUFACTURING COMPANY, pg. 1027
SPECIALTY PAPERBOARD INC., pg. 1027
SPECIALTY RESTAURANTS CORPORATION, pg. 1027
SPECIALTY RETAILERS, INC., pg. 1029
SPECIALTY UNDERWRITERS, INC.—See American Financial Corporation, pg. 54
SPECTRA NATIONAL—See National Group, Inc., pg. 790
SPECTRADYNE INC.—See Davis Companies, pg. 318
SPECTROL ELECTRONICS—See The Dyson-Kissner-Moran Corporation, pg. 358
SPECTROL ELECTRONICS CORP.—See The Dyson-Kissner-Moran Corporation, pg. 357
SPECTRONICS CORPORATION, pg. 1029
SPECTRULITE CONSORTIUM, INC., pg. 1029
SPECTRUM COLOR CENTER, pg. 1029
SPECTRUM INDUSTRIES, INC., pg. 1029
SPECTRUM MOLDING—See Plastek Group, pg. 875
SPEEDFAM CO LTD.—See FamTec International, Inc., pg. 398
SPEEDFAM CORPORATION—See FamTec International, Inc., pg. 398
SPEEDFAM GMBH—See FamTec International, Inc., pg. 398
SPEEDFAM MACHINES CO. LTD.—See FamTec International, Inc., pg. 398
SPEEDLING INCORPORATED, pg. 1029
SPEEDRACK PRODUCTS GROUP, LTD., pg. 1029
SPEER HARDWARE—See Servistar Corporation, pg. 993
SPEER, YOUNG & HOLLANDER, INC., pg. 1030
SPELLING ENTERTAINMENT GROUP, INC.—See American Financial Corporation, pg. 54
SPENCER COMPANIES INC., pg. 1030
SPENCER INDUSTRIES, INC., pg. 1030
SPENCER MAGNET—See Landmark Communications, Inc., pg. 655
SPENCER OIL COMPANY—See Spencer Companies Inc., pg. 1030
SPENCER PRESS, INC., pg. 1030
THE SPENCER TURBINE CO., pg. 1030
SPENCER'S INC., pg. 1030
SPERLING, pg. 1030
SPHERICAL PRODUCTS CORP.—See PQ Corporation, pg. 837
SPIEGEL MEATS, INC., pg. 1030
FRANKLIN SPIER, INC., pg. 1031
I. SPIEWAK & SONS, INC., pg. 1031
SPINNAKER SOFTWARE CORPORATION, pg. 1031
SPINNERIN YARN CO., INC., pg. 1031
SPIRALKOTE—See Fleming Packaging Corp., pg. 418
SPIRES RESTAURANTS INC., pg. 1031
SPIRIT CRUISES, pg. 1031
SPIRITE INDUSTRIES, INC., pg. 1031
SPIROL IND. LTD.—See Spirol International Corp., pg. 1031
SPIROL INTERNATIONAL CORP., pg. 1031
SPIROL S.A.—See Spirol International Corp., pg. 1031
SPLENDOR FORM BRASSIERE, INC.—See Splendor Form International Inc., pg. 1032
SPLENDOR FORM INTERNATIONAL INC., pg. 1031
SPLITFIRE, INC.—See Old World Industries, Inc., pg. 824
THE SPOHN CORPORATION, pg. 1032
SPONSORED PUBLICATIONS—See The Hearst Corporation, pg. 522
SPORLAN VALVE COMPANY, pg. 1032
SPORTO CORP., pg. 1032
SPORTS AFIELD—See The Hearst Corporation, pg. 523
SPORTS CALL, INC.—See Western International Media Corporation, pg. 1180
SPORTS TRAVEL—See K-III Communications Corporation, pg. 611
SPORTSERVICE CORPORATION—See Delaware North Companies, Inc., pg. 326
THE SPORTSMAN'S GUIDE, INC., pg. 1032
SPORTSWEAR INTERNATIONAL—See K-III Communications Corporation, pg. 611
SPORTSYSTEMS CORPORATION—See Delaware North Companies, Inc., pg. 326
SPOTNAILS INC., pg. 1032
SPRAYING SYSTEMS CO., pg. 1032
SPRAYING SYSTEMS CO. FAR EAST—See Spraying Systems Co., pg. 1032
SPRAYING SYSTEMS DEUTSCHLAND GMBH—See Spraying Systems Co., pg. 1032
SPRAYWAY, INC.—See Carlyle Holding Corporation, pg. 222
SPRECKLES INDUSTRIES, INC., pg. 1032
THE SPRING AIR COMPANY, pg. 1032
SPRING ARBOR DISTRIBUTORS, pg. 1033
SPRING ENGINEERS, INC., pg. 1033
SPRING-GREEN LAWN CARE CORPORATION, pg. 1033
SPRING HILL NURSERIES CO.—See Foster & Gallagher Inc., pg. 426
SPRING LAKE FEED YARD—See Friona Industries, L.P., pg. 434
SPRING, O'BRIEN & CO. INC., pg. 1033
SPRINGBORN ENVIRONMENTAL SCIENCES DIVISION—See Springborn Laboratories, Inc., pg. 1033
SPRINGBORN LABORATORIES (EUROPE) AG—See Springborn Laboratories, Inc., pg. 1033
SPRINGBORN LABORATORIES (HONG KONG) LTD.—See Springborn Laboratories, Inc., pg. 1033
SPRINGBORN LABORATORIES, INC., pg. 1033
SPRINGBORN LABORATORIES-MATERIALS SCIENCE DIVISION—See Springborn Laboratories, Inc., pg. 1033
SPRINGBORN LABORATORIES-TESTING & QA DIVISION—See Springborn Laboratories, Inc., pg. 1033
SPRINGBORN (TAIWAN) LTD.—See Springborn Laboratories, Inc., pg. 1033
SPRINGER SCHMID GROUP, pg. 1033
SPRINGFIELD BANK FOR COOPERATIVES—See Federal Farm Credit Banks Funding Corporation, pg. 405
SPRINGFIELD INSTRUMENT COMPANY—See Sunbeam-Oster Company, Inc., pg. 1059
SPRINGFIELD MILLING CORP.—See Hubbard Milling Company, pg. 549
SPRINGFIELD NEWSPAPERS, INC.—See Cox Enterprises, Inc., pg. 292
SPRINGFIELD SUGAR & PROD. CO.—See Sweetlife Foods, Inc., pg. 1067
THE SPRINGFIELD SUN—See Landmark Communications, Inc., pg. 655
THE SPRINGWALL MATTRESS CO., pg. 1033
SPROTT OIL CO., INC., pg. 1034
SPURGEON MERCANTILE COMPANY, pg. 1034
SQUIRE-COGSWELL COMPANY, pg. 1034
SRIVATHSA ELECTRICAL CORP.—See Panduit Company, pg. 846
STABLER COMPANIES, INC., pg. 1034
STABLER CONSTRUCTION COMPANY—See Stabler Companies, Inc., pg. 1034
STACKIG, SANDERSON & WHITE, INC., pg. 1034
THE STACKPOLE CORPORATION, pg. 1034
STACKPOLE LIMITED—See The Stackpole Corporation, pg. 1034
STACKPOLE MAGNET DIVISION—See The Stackpole Corporation, pg. 1034
STACOENERGY PRODUCTS CO.—See Components Corporation Of America, pg. 270
STACOSWITCH, INC.—See Components Corporation Of America, pg. 270
STACY EQUIPMENT CO.—See Webster Industries Inc., pg. 1172
STADELMAN FRUIT INC., pg. 1034
RUSSELL STADELMAN & COMPANY, pg. 1034
STAFLEX CO.—See The Harodite Finishing Company Inc., pg. 510
STAFLEX/HAROTEX—See The Harodite Finishing Company Inc., pg. 510
STAHMANN FARMS, INC., pg. 1034
STAINLESS INCORPORATED, pg. 1035
STAINLESS STEEL PRODUCTS, INC.—See Zimmerman Holdings, Inc., pg. 1220
STAKMORE INC., pg. 1035
STAMCO INDUSTRIES INC., pg. 1035
STAMLER CORPORATION, pg. 1035
STAMPTECH—See Maclean-Fogg Co., pg. 697
STANBEE COMPANY, INC., pg. 1035
STANCHEM INC., pg. 1035
STANCO METAL PRODUCTS, INC., pg. 1035
STAND-COTE INDUSTRIAL COATINGS DIV.—See Standco Industries, Inc., pg. 1038
STANDARD ADVERTISING AGENCY, pg. 1035
STANDARD ALLOYS & MANUFACTURING—See Blue Tee Corporation, pg. 161
STANDARD BRANDS OF AMERICA, INC., pg. 1035
STANDARD CANDY CO., INC., pg. 1035
STANDARD CHLORINE CHEMICAL COMPANY, pg. 1035
STANDARD COFFEE SERVICE—See William B. Reily & Co., Inc., pg. 923
STANDARD COMMUNICATIONS CORPORATION, pg. 1036
STANDARD CONCRETE—See C B R Cement Corporation, pg. 199
STANDARD CORPORATION, pg. 1036
STANDARD DISTRIBUTING CO., INC.—See National Distributing Co., Inc., pg. 787
STANDARD DUPLICATING MACHINES CORP., pg. 1036
STANDARD ELECTRONICS, INC., pg. 1036
STANDARD FLOUR CO.—See Westco Products, Inc., pg. 1178
STANDARD GARMENT COMPANY, INC., pg. 1036
STANDARD GRAVURE CORP./SHEA COMMUNICATIONS, pg. 1036
STANDARD GRAVURE D/B/A OKLAHOMA GRAPHICS—See Standard Gravure Corp./Shea Communications, pg. 1036
STANDARD INDUSTRIES, INC., pg. 1036
STANDARD-KNAPP, INC., pg. 1036
STANDARD LAFARGE, pg. 1036
STANDARD LOCKNUT & LOCKWASHER, pg. 1037
STANDARD MANIFOLD COMPANY, INC., pg. 1037
STANDARD MANUFACTURING COMPANY, pg. 1037
STANDARD MEDICAL IMAGING, INC., pg. 1037
STANDARD PLYWOOD, INC., pg. 1037
STANDARD PROCESS & ENGRAVING CO.—See Crane & Co., Inc., pg. 296
STANDARD RESEARCH CONSULTANTS—See American Appraisal Associates, Inc., pg. 48
STANDARD RESTAURANT EQUIPMENT CO.—See Standard Industries, Inc., pg. 1036
STANDARD RESTAURANT EQUIPMENT CO.—See Standard Industries, Inc., pg. 1036
STANDARD RONEO—See Standard Duplicating Machines Corp., pg. 1036
STANDARD SECURITY LIFE INSURANCE COMPANY OF NEW YORK—See Geneve Corporation, pg. 452
STANDARD SHADE ROLLER DIV.—See CC Industries, Inc., pg. 200
STANDARD SHOE COMPANY, pg. 1037
STANDARD STEEL—See Freedom Forge Corporation, pg. 431
STANDARD SUPPLY & HARDWARE, pg. 1037
STANDARD TAG MFG. CO.—See Pavey Envelope & Tag Corp., pg. 852
STANDARD TEXTILE CO., INC., pg. 1037
STANDARD-THOMSON CORPORATION, pg. 1037
STANDARD TOOL & MANUFACTURING COMPANY, pg. 1037
STANDARD WELDERS SUPPLY CO., pg. 1038
STANDCO INDUSTRIES, INC., pg. 1038
STANDCO OILFIELD PRODUCTS DIV.—See Standco Industries, Inc., pg. 1038
STANDLEY BURRIDGE COLLINGS LTD.—See Backer Spielvogel Bates Worldwide, Inc., pg. 112
STANDUN, INC., pg. 1038
STANLEIGH INTERNATIONAL, INC.—See Kennington Ltd., Inc., pg. 623
STANLEY CONSULTANTS, INC.—See SC Companies, Inc., pg. 961
STANLEY DRYING COMPANY—See DEC International, Inc., pg. 309
STANLEY FASTENING SYSTEMS, pg. 1038
STANLEY KNIGHT CORPORATION, pg. 1038
STANLEY STEEMER INTERNATIONAL, INC., pg. 1038
STANLEY STORES INC., pg. 1038
STANTON COOPER—See Markwood Inc., pg. 710
STAPLE COTTON COOPERATIVE ASSOCIATION, pg. 1038
STAPLE COTTON DISCOUNT CORPORATION—See Staple Cotton Cooperative Association, pg. 1039
STAR BRONZE COMPANY, pg. 1039
STAR CHILDREN'S DRESS COMPANY, INC., pg. 1039
STAR CIRCUITS—See Daktronics, Inc., pg. 312
STAR CONTAINER, INC.—See The Tech Group, pg. 1082
STAR CONTAINER, INC.—See The Tech Group, pg. 1082
STAR CRANES—See Ederer Inc., pg. 368
STAR CUTTER CO., pg. 1039
STAR ENGRAVING CO.—See Zale Corporation, pg. 1216
STAR EXPANSION COMPANY, pg. 1039
STAR EXPANSION INDUSTRIES, LTD.—See Star Expansion Company, pg. 1039
STAR EXPANSION SHIELDS LTD.—See Star Expansion Company, pg. 1039
STAR FOOD PROCESSING, INC., pg. 1039
STAR FOOD PRODUCTS, INC., pg. 1039
STAR LIQUOR DEALERS, pg. 1039
STAR LUMBER & SUPPLY COMPANY, INC., pg. 1039
STAR MAGAZINE—See K-III Communications Corporation, pg. 611
STAR-PARTS INC., pg. 1039
STAR PUBLICATIONS—See Adler & Shaykin, pg. 18
STAR SALES CO., INC., pg. 1040
STAR SPORTSWEAR MANUFACTURING—See Londontown Holdings Corporation, pg. 682
STAR TRASNPORTATION, INC.—See Humboldt Express, Inc., pg. 552
STAR TRIBUNE, MINNEAPOLIS-ST. PAUL—See Cowles Media Company, pg. 291
STAR VIDEO ENTERTAINMENT, L.P., pg. 1040
STARCRAFT AUTOMOTIVE CORP., pg. 1040
STARCREST OF CALIFORNIA—See Starcrest Products of California, pg. 1040

STARCREST PRODUCTS OF CALIFORNIA, pg. 1040
THE STARFLO CORPORATION—See The Wm. Powell Company, pg. 883
THE STARFLO CORPORATION—See The Wm. Powell Company, pg. 883
STARK CANDY COMPANY—See UIS, Inc., pg. 1123
STARKEY LABORATORIES, INC., pg. 1040
STARMASTER—See Sycon Corporation, pg. 1069
J-STARR INDUSTRIES, INC., pg. 1040
STARR SEIGLE MCCOMBS, INC., pg. 1040
STARVING STUDENTS, INC., pg. 1040
STATE ELECTRIC SUPPLY CO., pg. 1040
STATE FARM COUNTY MUTUAL INSURANCE CO. OF TEXAS—See State Farm Mutual Automobile Insurance Company, pg. 1041
STATE FARM FIRE AND CASUALTY CO.—See State Farm Mutual Automobile Insurance Company, pg. 1041
STATE FARM GENERAL INSURANCE CO.—See State Farm Mutual Automobile Insurance Company, pg. 1041
STATE FARM LIFE AND ACCIDENT ASSURANCE CO.—See State Farm Mutual Automobile Insurance Company, pg. 1041
STATE FARM LIFE INSURANCE CO.—See State Farm Mutual Automobile Insurance Company, pg. 1041
STATE FARM LLOYDS, INC.—See State Farm Mutual Automobile Insurance Company, pg. 1041
STATE FARM MUTUAL AUTOMOBILE INSURANCE COMPANY, pg. 1041
STATE INDUSTRIES INC., pg. 1041
THE STATE JOURNAL-REGISTER—See The Copley Press, Inc., pg. 284
STATE MUTUAL LIFE ASSURANCE COMPANY OF AMERICA—See All America Financial, pg. 35
STATE STAMP WORKS—See American Marking Systems, pg. 58
STATE STREET RESEARCH & MANAGEMENT COMPANY—See Metropolitan Life Insurance Co., pg. 744
STATE VOLUNTEER MUTUAL INSURANCE CO. INC., pg. 1041
STATE-WIDE CAPITAL CORP., pg. 1041
STATES, INC., pg. 1041
STATLER INDUSTRIES, pg. 1041
STATTON FURNITURE MANUFACTURING COMPANY, pg. 1042
STAUCH VETROMILE & MITCHELL ADVERTISING, INC., pg. 1042
STAUFFER COMMUNICATIONS, INC., pg. 1042
STAUFFER MEDIA SYSTEMS, INC.—See Stauffer Communications, Inc., pg. 1043
STAVELEY SENSORS, INC., pg. 1043
STAWASZ PUBLIC RELATIONS—See Jordan, McGrath, Case & Taylor Inc., pg. 605
STEADLY COMPANY, pg. 1043
STEAK AND ALE RESTAURANTS—See S & A Restaurant Corp., pg. 958
STEAKLEY CHEVROLET SUBARU INC., pg. 1043
STEARNS ENTERPRISES, INC., pg. 1043
THE STEARNS & FOSTER BEDDING COMPANY—See Sealy Corporation, pg. 985
THE STEARNS & FOSTER UPHOLSTERY FURNITURE COMPANY—See Sealy Corporation, pg. 985
STEBBINS ENGINEERING & MFG. CO., pg. 1043
STEEL, INC., pg. 1044
STEEL PARTS CORP.—See Insilco Corporation, pg. 571
STEEL PROCESSORS DIV.—See Hutchens Industries Inc., pg. 555
STEELCASE CANADA LTD.—See Steelcase Inc., pg. 1044
STEELCASE FINANCIAL SERVICES, INC.—See Steelcase Inc., pg. 1044
STEELCASE INC., pg. 1044
STEELCASE, INC./ATHENS PLANT—See Steelcase Inc., pg. 1044
STEELCASE INC./INTERNATIONAL DIV.—See Steelcase Inc., pg. 1044
STEELCASE KUROGANE LTD.—See Steelcase Inc., pg. 1044
STEELCASE-STRAFOR S.A.—See Steelcase Inc., pg. 1044
STEELCASE STRAFOR (U.K.) LTD.—See Steelcase Inc., pg. 1044
STEELITE, INC., pg. 1044
STEELOX SYSTEMS, INC., pg. 1044
STEENBERG HOMES, INC., pg. 1045
STEFFEN DAIRY FOODS CO., INC.—See Prairie Farms Dairy, Inc., pg. 884
STEGNER FOOD PRODUCTS CO., pg. 1045
STEIBER DIV. DER BORG-WARNER GMBH—See Borg-Warner Corporation, pg. 166
STEIN, KILLPATRICK & ROGAN ADVERTISING, pg. 1045
STEIN ROBAIRE HELM, INC., pg. 1045
STEINBACH, pg. 1045
STEINER/BRESSLER ADVERTISING, pg. 1045
STEINER & COMPANY, pg. 1045
STEINER CORPORATION, pg. 1045
STEINER ELECTRIC CO., pg. 1045
STEINER FOREIGN LINEN DIVISION—See Steiner Corporation, pg. 1045
STEINER U.S. LINEN DIV.—See Steiner Corporation, pg. 1045
STEINERT & ASSOCIATES, INC., pg. 1045
STEINHEIL-LEAR SIEGLER AG—See Lear Siegler Diversified Holdings Corp., pg. 664
STEINWAY MUSICAL PROPERTIES, INC., pg. 1045
STEINWAY & SONS—See Steinway Musical Properties, Inc., pg. 1046
STEKETEE PAUL & SONS COMPANY, INC.—See The Dunlap Companies, pg. 353
THE STELLAR GROUP INC., pg. 1046
STENCILS USA—See Bucilla Corporation, pg. 185
STEPHAN & BRADY, INCORPORATED, pg. 1046
STEPHEN ASSOCIATES, INC., pg. 1046
STEPHENSON, INC., pg. 1046
STEPHENS HOLDING COMPANY, INC.—See Stephens, Inc., pg. 1046
STEPHENS, INC., pg. 1046
STEPHENS OVERSEAS SERVICES, INC.—See Stephens, Inc., pg. 1046
STEREO ADVERTISING CORP.—See Bose Corporation, pg. 167
STEREO CORP. OF AMERICA—See Mateco Electronics Corp., pg. 720
STEREO WAREHOUSE INC.—See Mateco Electronics Corp., pg. 720
STERIS LABORATORIES, INC.—See Henry Schein, Inc., pg. 975
STERLING BUILDERS, INC.—See Sterling Homes Corp., pg. 1047
STERLING COLOR PROCESS—See Kalamazoo Label Co., pg. 615
JOHN STERLING CORPORATION, pg. 1046
STERLING ELECTRIC, INC., pg. 1046
THE STERLING GROUP—See Kohler Company, pg. 640
STERLING HEIGHTS DODGE, INC., pg. 1046
STERLING HOMES CORP., pg. 1046
STERLING HOSIERY CO.—See Heyman Corporation, pg. 532
STERLING, INC., pg. 1047
STERLING JEWELRY & DISTRIBUTING CO., pg. 1047
STERLING LUMBER & INVESTMENT CO., pg. 1047
STERLING MACHINERY CO., INC.—See Montgomery Elevator Company, pg. 767
STERLING PAPER CO., pg. 1047
STERLING RUBBER & GASKET—See Standco Industries, Inc., pg. 1038
STERLING SAVINGS & LOAN—See Seligman & Associates, Inc., pg. 988
STERLING SAVINGS & LOAN—See Sterling Homes Corp., pg. 1047
STERLING STEEL BALL DIV.—See Frantz Manufacturing Co., pg. 430
STERLING SUPPLY COMPANY, INC., pg. 1047
STERLITE CORPORATION, pg. 1047
STERN ADVERTISING, INC., pg. 1047
M.L. STERN & COMPANY, INC., pg. 1047
JACOB STERN & SONS, INC., pg. 1047
STERN & STERN INDUSTRIES INC., pg. 1048
STERNHEIMER BROTHERS INC., pg. 1048
STERN'S MIRACLE-GRO PRODUCTS, INC., pg. 1048
STETSON-HARZA—See Harza Engineering Co., pg. 516
STEUART INVESTMENT CO., pg. 1048
STEUART PETROLEUM COMPANY—See Steuart Investment Co., pg. 1048
STEUART PETROLEUM COMPANY, pg. 1048
STEUART SEAFOODS—See Steuart Investment Co., pg. 1048
STEUART TRANSPORTATION CO.—See Steuart Investment Co., pg. 1048
STEVEDORING SERVICES OF AMERICA, pg. 1048
DAVID G. STEVEN, INC., pg. 1048
STEVENS AVIATION, INC.—See Farley Industries, pg. 400
STEVENS GRAPHICS, INC.—See Bell South Enterprises, pg. 136
STEVENS HOME FASHIONS—See Farley Industries, pg. 400
STEVENS-LEE COMPANY, pg. 1048
MICHAEL STEVENS LTD., pg. 1048
STEVES & SONS, pg. 1048
STEWART CONNECTOR SYSTEMS, INC.—See Insilco Corporation, pg. 571
STEWART DECATUR SECURITY SYSTEMS, INC.—See Folger Adam Company, pg. 422
STEWART STAMPING CORP.—See Insilco Corporation, pg. 571
STEWART'S ICE CREAM CO., INC., pg. 1048
STIEFEL LABORATORIES, INC., pg. 1048
STIEGLER, WELLS & BRUNSWICK, INC., pg. 1049
STEINY & COMPANY, INC., pg. 1049
THE STIFFEL COMPANY, pg. 1049
STIHL EASTERN CANADA LTD.—See Stihl Inc., pg. 1049
STIHL INC., pg. 1049
STIHL PARTS, INC.—See Stihl Inc., pg. 1049
STILES CORPORATION, pg. 1049
H. A. STILES CO.—See Saunders Brothers, pg. 972
STILLMAN & HOAG, INC., pg. 1049
STILLMAN SEAL, pg. 1049
EDWIN B. STIMPSON COMPANY, INC., pg. 1049
STINSON SEAFOOD COMPANY, pg. 1049
STINTA & TECHNICA S.A.—See International Data Group, pg. 577
STIRLING PROPERTIES, INC.—See The Maurin-Odgen Companies, pg. 722
STOCK YARDS PACKING CO., INC., pg. 1049
STOCKER & YALE, INC., pg. 1050
STOCKHAM VALVES & FITTINGS, INC., pg. 1050
STOCKTON CHILI PEPPER, INC.—See Specialty Restaurants Corporation, pg. 1028
STOCKTON RESTAURANT CORP.—See Specialty Restaurants Corporation, pg. 1028
STOCKTON WEST BURKHART INC., pg. 1050
THE STOGEL COMPANIES INC., pg. 1050
STOLPER-FABRALLOY CO., pg. 1050
STOLTZE-CONNER LUMBER CO.—See F.H. Stoltze Land & Lumber Company, pg. 1050
F.H. STOLTZE LAND & LUMBER COMPANY, pg. 1050
STONCO, pg. 1050
STONE ADVERTISING, pg. 1050
DON STONE ASSOCIATES INC., pg. 1050
STONE, AUGUST, BAKER COMMUNICATIONS COMPANIES, pg. 1050
STONE AUGUST BAKER PUBLIC RELATIONS—See Stone, August, Baker Communications Companies, pg. 1051
STONE FORT NATIONAL BANK—See Texas Commerce Bancshares, Inc., pg. 1089
STONE & HOOVER CONTRACTING, INC.—See W. B. Goode Company, Inc., pg. 470
STONE MANUFACTURING COMPANY, INC., pg. 1051
STONE & SIMONS ADVERTISING, INC., pg. 1051
STONE & THOMAS, pg. 1051
STONE & THOMAS ADVERTISING & VISUAL OFFICES—See Stone & Thomas, pg. 1051
STONE & THOMAS MERCHANDISING OFFICES—See Stone & Thomas, pg. 1051
STONECUTTER MILLS CORP., pg. 1051
STONECUTTER TRUCKING CO.—See Stonecutter Mills Corp., pg. 1051
STONES, INC., pg. 1051
STONEWALL INSURANCE CO.—See American Financial Corporation, pg. 54
STONHARD, EUROPE—See Stonhard, Inc., pg. 1051
STONHARD, INC., pg. 1051
STONHARD LATIN AMERICA—See Stonhard, Inc., pg. 1051
STONHARD, LTD.—See Stonhard, Inc., pg. 1052
STOOPS EXPRESS, INC.—See Burlington Motor Carriers Inc., pg. 191
STOP IN FOOD STORES—See Petroleum Marketers, Inc., pg. 865
STOP SHOP SAVE, pg. 1052
STORAGE SYSTEMS ENGINEERING—See Handling Systems Engineering, pg. 505
STORE DEVELOPMENT, INC.—See Affiliated of Florida Inc., pg. 23
STORM PRODUCTS COMPANY, INC., pg. 1052
STOW & DAVIS FURNITURE CO.—See Steelcase Inc., pg. 1044
STOWE-PHARR MILLS, INC., pg. 1052
G. A. STOWERS FURNITURE CO.—See Zale Corporation, pg. 1216
STRACHAN SHIPPING CO., pg. 1052
STRAFCO—See Carquest Corporation, pg. 225
STRAFCO, INC., pg. 1052
STRAHMAN VALVES, INC., pg. 1052
STRAIGHT ARROW PUBLISHERS, INC., pg. 1052
STRANG COMMUNICATIONS COMPANY, pg. 1052
STRATEGIC COMPENSATION ASSOCIATES—See Korn/Ferry International, pg. 642
STRATEGIC DISTRIBUTION INC., pg. 1053
STRATEGIC EVENTS GROUP—See The Highland Group, Inc., pg. 534
STRATEGIC IDENTITY CONSULTANTS—See Young & Rubicam Inc., pg. 1212
THE STRATEGY COMPANY—See Stone, August, Baker Communications Companies, pg. 1051
STRATEGY GAMES—See Monarch Avalon, Inc., pg. 765
STRATIS CORPORATION—See Phillips Plastics Corporation, pg. 867
STRATMAR RESEARCH CORP.—See Stratmar Systems, Inc., pg. 1053
STRATMAR RESOURCES, INC.—See Stratmar Systems, Inc., pg. 1053
STRATMAR SYSTEMS, INC., pg. 1053
STRATTON CORP., pg. 1053
STRATTON GROWTH FUND, INC.—See Stratton Management Company, pg. 1053
STRATTON MANAGEMENT COMPANY, pg. 1053
STRATTON MONTHLY DIVIDEND SHARES, INC.—See Stratton Management Company, pg. 1053
R & S STRAUSS, INC., pg. 1053
STRAW HAT COOPERATIVE CORP., pg. 1053
STREAMLIGHT INC., pg. 1053
STREATER STORE FIXTURES DIV.—See Joyce International, Inc., pg. 608
STREECH ELECTRIC COMPANY, pg. 1053
J. D. STREETT & CO., INC., pg. 1053
STRIKE RITE MATCHES LTD.—See D. D. Bean & Sons Co., pg. 129
STRINGER VERONI KETCHUM—See Ketchum Communications Inc., pg. 626
STRITE-ANDERSON DIE CASTINGS—See Kurt Manufacturing Co. Inc., pg. 646
O. J. STROBEL OIL & TIRE CO., INC., pg. 1053
THE STROH BREWERY COMPANY, pg. 1053
STROMBECKER CHEMTOY DIVISION—See Strombecker Corporation, pg. 1054
STROMBECKER CORPORATION, pg. 1054
STROMBECKER (HK) LTD.—See Strombecker Corporation, pg. 1054
STROMBERG-CONNORS COMMUNICATIONS, pg. 1054
STRONGHEART PRODUCTS, INC., pg. 1054
STROUDS, pg. 1054
THE STROUSE, ADLER COMPANY, pg. 1054
STROUSE GREENBERG & CO., INC., pg. 1054
STRUCTURAL FOAM PLASTICS—See Structural Foam Plastics, Inc., pg. 1054
STRUCTURAL FOAM PLASTICS—See Structural Foam Plastics, Inc., pg. 1054
STRUCTURAL FOAM PLASTICS, INC., pg. 1054
STRUCTURAL INDUSTRIES, INC., pg. 1054
STUART ANDERSON'S BLACK ANGUS/CATTLE COMPANY RESTAURANTS—See American Restaurant Group, Inc., pg. 60
STUART EDGAR LTD.—See Fort Howard Corporation, pg. 425
PAUL STUART, INC., pg. 1054
STUART-IRONSIDES, INC., pg. 1054
STUHR ENTERPRISES INC., pg. 1055
STURGEON ELECTRIC COMPANY—See Harlan Electric Co., pg. 509
STURGIS FOUNDRY CORP.—See Armstrong International, Inc., pg. 83
STURGIS IRON & METAL COMPANY, INC., pg. 1055
STURGIS METALS DIVISION, ELKHART—See Sturgis Iron & Metal Company, Inc., pg. 1055
THE STURM COMMUNICATIONS GROUP, INC., pg. 1055
STUSSER ELECTRIC COMPANY, pg. 1055
STYLE AUTO, pg. 1055
SUBURBAN COMMUNICATIONS CORP., pg. 1055
SUBWAY FRANCHISEE ADVERTISING FUND TRUST, pg. 1055
SUCCESS ADVERTISING, INC.—See The Cherenson Group, pg. 243

SUCCESSFUL MEETINGS—See Bill Communications, Inc., pg. 150
SUCCURSALE DE GENEVA—See CS First Boston Group, Inc., pg. 204
SUDCO DEVELOPMENT CO., INC.—See The Suddath Companies, pg. 1056
THE SUDDATH COMPANIES, pg. 1055
SUDDATH MOVING SYSTEMS, INC.—See The Suddath Companies, pg. 1056
SUDDATH TRANSPORTATION SERVICE—See The Suddath Companies, pg. 1056
SUDDATH VAN LINES—See The Suddath Companies, pg. 1056
SUDLER & HENNESSEY—See Young & Rubicam Inc., pg. 1211
SUDLER & HENNESSEY CANADA—See Young & Rubicam Inc., pg. 1213
SUDLER & HENNESSEY CONSUMER GROUP—See Young & Rubicam Inc., pg. 1211
SUDLER & HENNESSEY GMBH—See Young & Rubicam Inc., pg. 1212
SUDLER & HENNESSEY LIMITED—See Young & Rubicam Inc., pg. 1212
SUES, YOUNG & BROWN INC., pg. 1056
SUGAR CANE GROWERS COOPERATIVE OF FLORIDA, pg. 1056
SUGAR CREEK PACKING CO., pg. 1056
SUGARDALE FOODS INC.—See Fresh Mark, Inc., pg. 432
SUISSA/MILLER, pg. 1056
SUITT CONSTRUCTION COMPANY, INC., pg. 1056
SULA SUPPLY—See Vienna Sausage Mfg. Co., pg. 1151
SULLIVAN & BROWNELL, INC., pg. 1056
SULLIVAN & COZART INC., pg. 1056
SULLIVAN GRAPHICS—See Sullivan Holding Company, pg. 1057
SULLIVAN HAAS COYLE, pg. 1056
SULLIVAN HIGDON & SINK INCORPORATED, pg. 1056
SULLIVAN HOLDING COMPANY, pg. 1056
SULLIVAN LONG & HAGERTY, INC., pg. 1057
SULLIVAN OIL COMPANY, pg. 1057
SULLIVAN PAPER COMPANY, pg. 1057
SULPACO WEST—See Sullivan Paper Company, pg. 1057
SUMMA CORPORATION, pg. 1057
SUMMA FOUR, INC., pg. 1057
SUMMA FOUR LIMITED—See Summa Four, Inc., pg. 1057
SUMMERFIELD TRUCK CO. INC., pg. 1057
SUMMIT COMMERCIAL PROPERTY, INC.—See The Suddath Companies, pg. 1056
SUMMIT COMMUNICATIONS, INC., pg. 1057
SUMMIT CORPORATION OF AMERICA, pg. 1058
SUMMIT ENVIRONMENTAL GROUP, pg. 1058
SUMMIT-BEERS CONSTRUCTION COMPANY—See Beers Construction Company, pg. 132
SUMTER COUNTY TIMES—See Landmark Communications, Inc., pg. 655
SUN BULB COMPANY, INC., pg. 1058
SUN CHEMICAL COMPANY, INC.—See Sun Bulb Company, Inc., pg. 1058
SUN COMPUTERS, INC., pg. 1058
SUN DATA INC., pg. 1058
SUN DIAMOND GROWERS OF CALIFORNIA, pg. 1058
SUN FINANCIAL GROUP, INC., pg. 1058
SUN HILL INDUSTRIES, pg. 1059
SUN LAKES MARKETING, pg. 1059
SUN-LAND PRODUCTS OF CALIFORNIA—See Sun Diamond Growers of California, pg. 1058
SUN-LITHO—See Morris Newspaper Corporation, pg. 771
SUN PRINTING COMPANY—See Cox Enterprises, Inc., pg. 292
SUN PROCESS CONVERTING COMPANY, pg. 1059
SUNBEAM APPLIANCE COMPANY—See Sunbeam-Oster Company, Inc., pg. 1059
SUNBEAM CASUAL FURNITURE CO.—See Sunbeam-Oster Company, Inc., pg. 1059
SUNBEAM CONSUMER PRODUCTS FAR EAST, LTD.—See Sunbeam-Oster Company, Inc., pg. 1059
SUNBEAM CORPORATION (CANADA) LIMITED—See Sunbeam-Oster Company, Inc., pg. 1059
SUNBEAM DEL PERU S.A.—See Sunbeam-Oster Company, Inc., pg. 1059
SUNBEAM DIV.—See Sunbeam-Oster Company, Inc., pg. 1059
SUNBEAM HOME COMFORT—See Sunbeam-Oster Company, Inc., pg. 1059
SUNBEAM IBERICA S.A.—See Sunbeam-Oster Company, Inc., pg. 1059
SUNBEAM INTERCONTINENTAL LTD.—See Sunbeam-Oster Company, Inc., pg. 1059
SUNBEAM MEXICANA S.A. DE C.V.—See Sunbeam-Oster Company, Inc., pg. 1059
SUNBEAM-OSTER COMPANY, INC., pg. 1059
SUNBEAM-OSTER HOUSEHOLD PRODUCTS—See Sunbeam-Oster Company, Inc., pg. 1059
SUNBEAM OUTDOOR PRODUCTS CO.—See Sunbeam-Oster Company, Inc., pg. 1059
SUNBEAM VERTRIEBSGESELLSCHAFT MBH—See Sunbeam-Oster Company, Inc., pg. 1059
SUNBELT LODGING DEVELOPMENT CO.—See Investor's Management Corp., pg. 581
SUNBURST—See Farrar, Straus & Giroux, Inc., pg. 403
SUNCLIPSE, INC., pg. 1059
SUNCREST COMPANY OF CANADA—See The Monarch Company, Inc., pg. 765
SUNDAY MAGAZINE NETWORK—See Metropolitan Sunday Newspapers, Inc., pg. 745
SUNDAY RIVER SKIWAY CORPORATION, pg. 1059
SUNDOWN VITAMIN CO., INC., pg. 1060
SUNDT CORP., pg. 1060
SUNDT PRODUCTS, INC.—See Sundt Corp., pg. 1060
SUNFLOWER CARRIERS—See Crete Carrier Corp., pg. 299
SUNFLOWER ELECTRIC POWER CORPORATION, pg. 1060
THE SUNFLOWER GROUP, pg. 1060
SUNGLASS HUT CORPORATION, pg. 1060
SUNICAL LAND & LIVESTOCK DIVISION—See The Hearst Corporation, pg. 524
SUNKIST (EUROPE) S.A.—See Sunkist Growers, Inc., pg. 1061
SUNKIST (FAR EAST) PROMOTION, LTD.—See Sunkist Growers, Inc., pg. 1061
SUNKIST GROWERS, INC., pg. 1060
SUNKIST PACIFIC, LTD.—See Sunkist Growers, Inc., pg. 1061
SUNLINE COACH CO., INC., pg. 1061
SUNMAC HAWAII, LTD.—See Sunkist Growers, Inc., pg. 1061
SUNNE CONTROLS DIV.—See Peco Inc., pg. 854
SUNNEN PRODUCTS COMPANY, pg. 1061
SUNNILAND CORPORATION, pg. 1061
SUNNYLAND FOODS, INC., pg. 1061
SUNNYLAND REFINING CO., INC.—See Kane-Miller Corp., pg. 616
SUNNYVALE TOWNCENTER—See R. H. Macy & Co., Inc., pg. 699
SUNOLA FOOD CORP.—See Quality Food Oils, Inc., pg. 903
SUNOX, INC., pg. 1062
SUNRISE INDUSTRIAL AUTOMATION & DESIGN—See IBT, Inc., pg. 558
SUNRISE MALL ASSOCS.—See Shepaug Corporation, pg. 998
SUNRISE NISSAN OF ORANGE PARK, pg. 1062
SUNROC CORPORATION, pg. 1062
SUNSET RAILWAY CO.—See Anschutz Corporation, pg. 76
SUNSHINE BISCUITS, INC.—See GF Industries, Inc., pg. 439
SUNSHINE/SALERNO (IL)—See GF Industries, Inc., pg. 439
SUNSHINE SHIPPERS, INC.—See Hickory Farms, Inc., pg. 533
SUNSTATES PROPERTIES, INC.—See Sunstates Realty Group Inc., pg. 1062
SUNSTATES REALTY GROUP INC., pg. 1062
SUNSWEET GROWERS INC.—See Sun Diamond Growers of California, pg. 1058
SUNTEC INDUSTRIES INC., pg. 1062
SUNWEAVE LINEN CORPORATION, pg. 1062
SUOMEN LEVI STRAUSS OY—See Levi Strauss & Co., pg. 671
SUPER CLUB MUSIC CORP., pg. 1062
SUPER D DRUG STORES, pg. 1062
SUPER 8 MANAGEMENT, INC.—See Super 8 Motels, Inc., pg. 1063
SUPER 8 MOTELS, INC., pg. 1062
SUPERBA, INC., pg. 1063
SUPERIOR AUCTIONEERS & MARKETING, INC., pg. 1063
SUPERIOR COFFEE & FOODS/HAWAII—See C. Brewer & Company, Limited, pg. 174
SUPERIOR CONTAINER, INC., pg. 1063
SUPERIOR DAIRY, INC., pg. 1063
SUPERIOR DIE TOOL AND MACHINE COMPANY—See The Gerstenslager Company, pg. 455
SUPERIOR DIVISION OF KEY PLASTICS—See Key Plastics, Inc., pg. 627
SUPERIOR FAST FREIGHT, pg. 1063
SUPERIOR FEDERAL BANK, pg. 1063
SUPERIOR GRAPHITE COMPANY, pg. 1063
SUPERIOR INDUSTRIES OF NEBRASKA, INC., pg. 1063
SUPERIOR LABEL SYSTEMS, INC., pg. 1063
SUPERIOR LINEN & DRAPERY COMPANY, pg. 1064
SUPERIOR LINKAGE DIVISION—See Tuthill Corporation, pg. 1120
SUPERIOR MACHINE COMPANY OF SOUTH CAROLINA, INC., pg. 1064
SUPERIOR MACHINE SYSTEMS—See Superior Label Systems, Inc., pg. 1064
SUPERIOR OIL CO. INC., pg. 1064
SUPERIOR REPROGRAPHICS, pg. 1064
SUPERIOR TUBE COMPANY, pg. 1064
SUPERIOR'S BRAND MEATS—See Fresh Mark, Inc., pg. 432
SUPERMARKETS GENERAL CORPORATION, pg. 1064
SUPERNAIL—See Ardell International, Inc., pg. 81
SUPERSHUTTLE INTERNATIONAL, pg. 1064
SUPPORT SYSTEMS ASSOCIATES, INC., pg. 1064
SUPREME BEAUTY PRODUCTS—See Johnson Publishing Company, Inc., pg. 599
SUPREME CATTLE CO.—See Union Holdings, Inc., pg. 1128
SUPREME FEEDERS, INC.—See Union Holdings, Inc., pg. 1128
SUPREME MACHINE DIV.—See Frontier Foundries, Inc., pg. 434
SURCO PRODUCTS, INC., pg. 1065
SURGICAL APPLIANCE INDUSTRIES, INC., pg. 1065
SURGICAL SPECIALTIES, pg. 1065
SUSQUEHANNA PFALTZGRAFF, pg. 1065
SUSQUEHANNA RADIO CORP.—See Susquehanna Pfaltzgraff, pg. 1065
SUSSEN, INC.—See Carquest Corporation, pg. 225
THE SUSSMAN/ZICCARDI GROUP, pg. 1065
SUTTER HOME WINERY, INC., pg. 1065
SUTTER/MARTIN, INC., pg. 1065
SUZANNAH FARMS, pg. 1065
SVENSKA JOHNSON'S VAX AB—See S. C. Johnson & Son, Inc., pg. 600
SVERDRUP BUILDING CORPORATION—See Sverdrup Corporation, pg. 1066
SVERDRUP CORPORATION, pg. 1065
SVERDRUP ENVIRONMENTAL INC.—See Sverdrup Corporation, pg. 1066
SVERDRUP INVESTMENTS, INC.—See Sverdrup Corporation, pg. 1066
SVERDRUP SOUTHERN CONSTRUCTORS, INC.—See Sverdrup Corporation, pg. 1066
SVERDRUP TECHNOLOGY, INC.—See Sverdrup Corporation, pg. 1066
SWALLEN'S, INC., pg. 1066
SWANER HARDWOOD COMPANY, INC., pg. 1066
SWANSON RUSSELL ASSOCIATES, pg. 1066
THE SWANSON COMPANY MANUFACTURERS, pg. 1066
SWEDE SPORTSWEAR COMPANY, INC., pg. 1066
E.A. SWEEN COMPANY, pg. 1066
JAKE SWEENEY AUTO LEASING INC., pg. 1066
JAKE SWEENEY AUTOMOTIVE INC., pg. 1067
SWEENEY & COMPANY DIVISION—See GSC Enterprises, Inc., pg. 440
SWEETHEART CUP CO., INC., pg. 1067
SWEETHEART CUP CO., INC.—See Sweetheart Cup Co., Inc., pg. 1067
SWEETHEART CUP CORPORATION—See Sweetheart Cup Co., Inc., pg. 1067
SWEETHEART CUP CORPORATION—See Sweetheart Cup Co., Inc., pg. 1067
SWEETLIFE FOODS, INC., pg. 1067
SWELL-WEAR, INC., pg. 1067
SWEPCO TUBE CORPORATION, pg. 1067
SWIFT-COR TOOL ENGINEERING, pg. 1067
SWIFT DODGE ROLLS ROYCE INC., pg. 1067
SWIFT INSTRUMENTS, INC., pg. 1068
M. SWIFT & SONS CANADA INC.—See M. Swift & Sons Inc., pg. 1068
M. SWIFT & SONS INC., pg. 1068
SWINERTON & WALBERG CO., pg. 1068
SWINGSTER COMPANY—See American Marketing Industries, Inc., pg. 58
SWIRL, INC., pg. 1068
SWIRL SALES, INC.—See Swirl, Inc., pg. 1068
SWISHER COUNTRY CATTLE CO.—See Friona Industries, L.P., pg. 434
THE SWISS COLONY, pg. 1068
SWISS-M-TEX, L.P., pg. 1068
SWIVELIER CO., INC., pg. 1068
SWOPE AUTOMOTIVE GROUP, INC., pg. 1068
SYAR INDUSTRIES, INC., pg. 1068
SYBEX GROUP, pg. 1069
SYCAMORE SYSTEMS, INC.—See Lyon Metal Products, Inc., pg. 690
SYCON CORPORATION, pg. 1069
SYLVAN POOLS OF ARIZONA, INC.—See KDI Corporation, pg. 612
SYLVAN POOLS OF TEXAS, INC.—See KDI Corporation, pg. 612
SYMMONS INDUSTRIES INC., pg. 1069
SYMONS CORPORATION, pg. 1069
SYMPLEX COMMUNICATIONS CORP., pg. 1069
SYNCHRO-START PRODUCTS, INC.—See Knowles Electronics, Inc., pg. 638
SYNDET PRODUCTS, INC., pg. 1069
SYNDICATE SYSTEMS, INC., pg. 1069
SYNERGETICS, INC.—See Simms & McIvor Marketing Communications, pg. 1006
SYNERGISM, INC., pg. 1069
SYRACUSE CHINA CORP.—See Susquehanna Pfaltzgraff, pg. 1065
SYRACUSE SUPPLY COMPANY, pg. 1070
SYRACUSE SUPPLY CONSTRUCTION & EQUIPMENT DIVISION—See Syracuse Supply Company, pg. 1070
SYRACUSE SUPPLY INDUSTRIAL PRODUCTS DIVISION—See Syracuse Supply Company, pg. 1070
SYRACUSE SUPPLY LEASING CO., INC.—See Syracuse Supply Company, pg. 1070
SYRATECH CORPORATION, pg. 1070
SYSTEM PLANNING CORP., pg. 1070
SYSTEMS ENGINEERING ASSOCIATES CO. (SEACOR)—See Day & Zimmermann, Inc., pg. 320
SYSTEMS ENGINEERING & MANUFACTURING CORP., pg. 1071
SYSTEMS ENGINEERING & MFG. NEDERLANDS B.V.—See Systems Engineering & Manufacturing Corp., pg. 1071
SYSTEMS MANAGEMENT & DEVELOPMENT—See Technical Aid Corporation, pg. 1083
SYSTEMS PARKING, INC., pg. 1071
SYSTEMS RESEARCH AND APPLICATIONS CORPORATION, pg. 1071
SYSTECH COMPUTER CORPORATION, pg. 1071
DAVE SYVERSON TRUCK CENTER, INC.—See Dave Syverson Lincoln Mercury, pg. 1071
DAVE SYVERSON LINCOLN MERCURY, pg. 1071

T

T SHIRT GRAPHICS—See The Vernon Company, pg. 1148
T & R ELECTRIC SUPPLY COMPANY, INC., pg. 1071
T-R PRINTING & PUBLISHING—See Tribune Review Publishing Co., pg. 1113
TAC/MEDICAL SERVICES INC.—See Technical Aid Corporation, pg. 1083
TAC/TEMPS INC.—See Technical Aid Corporation, pg. 1083
TAD TECHNICAL SERVICES CORP., pg. 1071
TAI SERVICES, INC.—See Technology Applications, Inc., pg. 1084
TBV, INC.—See Victaulic Company of America, pg. 1149
TBWA—See TBWA Advertising, Inc., pg. 1072
TBWA ADVERTISING, INC., pg. 1071
TBWA DUSSELDORF GMBH—See TBWA Advertising, Inc., pg. 1072
TBWA ESPANA S.A.—See TBWA Advertising, Inc., pg. 1072
TBWA HAMBURG GMBH—See TBWA Advertising, Inc., pg. 1072
TBWA KERLICK SWITZER—See TBWA Advertising, Inc., pg. 1071
T C MANUFACTURING COMPANY, INC., pg. 1072
TCC, pg. 1072

TCG FIBERS, PHILIPPINES—See Columbian Rope Company, pg. 266
TCH INDUSTRIES INC., pg. 1072
TDA, pg. 1072
TD INDUSTRIES INC., pg. 1072
TDW BUILDING CORPORATION—See T.D. Williamson, Inc., pg. 1192
TDW DELAWARE, INC.—See T.D. Williamson, Inc., pg. 1192
TDW FOREIGN SALES CORP.—See T.D. Williamson, Inc., pg. 1192
TDW SERVICES, INC.—See T.D. Williamson, Inc., pg. 1192
TDW TRADING, INC.—See T.D. Williamson, Inc., pg. 1192
TFI (TAPE FILMS INC.)—See MPO Videotronics, Inc., pg. 693
T.G. & Y. HOLDINGS, INC.—See Riklis Family Corporation, pg. 934
T.G. & Y. STORES CO.—See Riklis Family Corporation, pg. 934
TGI FRIDAY'S, INC.—See Carlson Companies, Inc., pg. 221
TH&M ADVERTISING, INC., pg. 1073
TIC INVESTMENT CORP.—See TIC United Corporation, pg. 1073
TIC UNITED CORPORATION, pg. 1073
T. J. CINNAMONS LTD., pg. 1073
TLC BEATRICE INTERNATIONAL HOLDINGS INC., pg. 1073
TMP LTD.—See TMP Worldwide, Inc., pg. 1074
TMP/TELEPHONE MARKETING PROGRAMS, LTD.—See TMP Worldwide, Inc., pg. 1074
TMP WORLDWIDE, INC., pg. 1073
TMP WORLDWIDE, INC.—See TMP Worldwide, Inc., pg. 1074
TMP WORLDWIDE, INC.—See TMP Worldwide, Inc., pg. 1074
TMP WORLDWIDE, INC.—See TMP Worldwide, Inc., pg. 1074
TMP WORLDWIDE, INC.—See TMP Worldwide, Inc., pg. 1074
TMP WORLDWIDE, INC.—See TMP Worldwide, Inc., pg. 1074
TMP WORLDWIDE, INC.—See TMP Worldwide, Inc., pg. 1074
TNE FUNDING CORPORATION—See The New England, pg. 799
TNE INVESTMENT SERVICES CORP.—See The New England, pg. 799
T O PLASTICS, INC., pg. 1074
TOC RETAIL, INC.—See E-Z Serve Corp., pg. 362
TRR CARRIERS, INC.—See Wakefern Food Corporation, pg. 1158
TRW-KEYSTONE POWDER METAL PRODUCTS CO.—See Keystone Carbon Company, pg. 628
T & S BRASS & BRONZE WORKS, INC., pg. 1074
TS CAPITAL CORP.—See The Troy Savings Bank, pg. 1117
TSC CARBIDE CO.—See Precision Twist Drill Co., pg. 885
TSC INDUSTRIES, INC., pg. 1075
TSE LEASING CO.—See I. Spiewak & Sons, Inc., pg. 1031
TSI INDUSTRIES, INC., pg. 1075
TSR, INC., pg. 1075
TST/IMPRESO, INC., pg. 1075
TTA/NEWPORT, INC.—See Ted Thomas Associates Inc., Advertising, pg. 1092
TTX CO., pg. 1075
TV HOST CENTRAL, INC.—See TV Host Inc., pg. 1075
TV HOST INC., pg. 1075
TV HOST WEST, INC.—See TV Host Inc., pg. 1075
TV PREVIEW, INC.—See TV Host Inc., pg. 1075
TVESCO, INC., pg. 1075
TAB CHEMICALS, INC., pg. 1075
TABER METALS, INC.—See Tang Industries Inc., pg. 1078
TABOR MACHINE CO.—See Jupiter Industries, Inc., pg. 609
TABS ASSOCIATES, pg. 1076
TACA INTERNATIONAL AIRLINES, S. A., pg. 1076
TACO INC., pg. 1076
TACO JOHN'S INTERNATIONAL, INC., pg. 1076
TACONY CORPORATION, pg. 1076
TACT HOLDING, pg. 1076
TACTAIR ADVANCED TECHNOLOGY, INC.—See Phoenix International, Inc., pg. 869
TACTAIR FLUID CONTROLS CORP.—See Phoenix International, Inc., pg. 869
TAGSONS PAPERS, INC., pg. 1076
TAJ INTERNATIONAL HOTELS, pg. 1076
TAKATTA INC., pg. 1076
TAL INC., pg. 1077
TALENT & RESIDUALS, INC.—See IDC Services, Inc., pg. 560
TALENT & RESIDUALS, INC.—See IDC Services, Inc., pg. 560
OY TALENTUM AB—See International Data Group, pg. 577
TALK-A-PHONE CO., pg. 1077
TALLANT LAPOINTE & PARTNERS, INC., pg. 1077
TALLAPOOSA RIVER ELECTRIC CO-OP, pg. 1077
TALLGRASS TECHNOLOGIES CORP., pg. 1077
TALON, INC., pg. 1077
TAM O'SHANTER INN—See Lawry's Restaurants, Inc., pg. 663
TAMAQUA CABLE PRODUCTS CORPORATION, pg. 1077
TAMARKIN CO., INC.—See Giant Eagle, Inc., pg. 456
TAMAROFF BUICK INC., pg. 1077
TAMAROFF LEASING CO.—See Tamaroff Buick Inc., pg. 1077
TAMBOURINE BOOKS—See The Hearst Corporation, pg. 522
TAMPA BAY MOVING SYSTEMS INC.—See Cook Moving Systems, Inc., pg. 282
TAMPA VENTURES, INC.—See Rotterdam Ventures Inc., pg. 952
THE TANEY CORPORATION, pg. 1077
TANG INDUSTRIES INC., pg. 1078
TANK SERVICE, INC.—See The Heil Co., pg. 526
TANNER CO. INC., pg. 1078
TANNING RESEARCH LABS., INC., pg. 1078
TAPCO PRODUCTS COMPANY, pg. 1078
TAPE COAT DIVISION—See T C Manufacturing Company, Inc., pg. 1072
TAPE & LABEL ENGINEERING—See Weber Marking Systems, Inc., pg. 1171
TAPEMARK, pg. 1078
TAPETECH TOOL CO., INC.—See AXIA Incorporated, pg. 8
TAPSA AYER—See N W Ayer Incorporated, pg. 104
TARACORP EVANS, INC.—See Taracorp, Inc., pg. 1078
TARACORP IMACO, INC.—See Taracorp, Inc., pg. 1078
TARACORP, INC., pg. 1078
TARACORP INDUSTRIES, INC.—See Taracorp, Inc., pg. 1078
TARCO, pg. 1078
TARCO OF TEXAS, INC.—See Tarco, pg. 1078
TAREN HOLDINGS, INC., pg. 1078
TARGET ENTERPRISES LTD., pg. 1079
TARGET SPORTSWEAR, INC., pg. 1079
TARGET STAMPED PRODUCTS CORP., pg. 1079
TARGETCOM, INC., pg. 1079
TARGETS ADV.—See Leo Burnett Company, Inc., pg. 193
TARLOW ADVERTISING, pg. 1079
TARLTON CORPORATION, pg. 1079
TARRANT SERVICE AGENCY, INC., pg. 1079
SARKES TARZIAN, INCORPORATED, pg. 1079
TASA CORPORATION, pg. 1079
TASCO, pg. 1079
TASH, INC., pg. 1080
TASSANI COMMUNICATIONS, pg. 1080
TASTEE FREEZ INTL. INC.—See De Novo Corporation, pg. 321
TATE ACCESS FLOORS, INC., pg. 1080
TATUM FARMS, pg. 1080
TATUM TOOMEY & WHICKER, pg. 1080
TATUNG/CONAIR CORPORATION—See Conair Corporation, pg. 272
TAUBER OIL COMPANY, pg. 1080
TAUCHER, YOUNG & RUBICAM—See Young & Rubicam Inc., pg. 1212
TAUSCHE MARTIN LONSDORF, pg. 1080
TAWIL ASSOCIATES INC., pg. 1080
TAX FORMS PRINTING—See Taylor Corporation, pg. 1081
TAX MANAGEMENT, INC.—See The Bureau of National Affairs, Inc., pg. 190
TAYLOR ADVERTISING, INC., pg. 1080
TAYLOR ASSOCIATES—See Midcoast Industrial Services Corporation, pg. 751
TAYLOR BROS.—See Conwood Company L.P., pg. 282
TAYLOR COMPANY—See Specialty Equipment Companies Inc., pg. 1027
NELSON A. TAYLOR CO., INC., pg. 1080
TAYLOR CORPORATION, pg. 1081
D. C. TAYLOR CO.—See Midcoast Industrial Services Corporation, pg. 751
TAYLOR DRUG STORES, INC., pg. 1081
ED TAYLOR CONSTRUCTION CO., pg. 1081
TAYLOR-EVANS SEED CO., pg. 1081
TAYLOR-GORDON/WIDMANN & CO., INC., pg. 1081
TAYLOR HOME HEALTH INC.—See Taylor Medical Inc., pg. 1081
TAYLOR LUMBER & SUPPLY CORP.—See Devlin Lumber & Supply Corp., pg. 334
TAYLOR MACHINE WORKS, INC., pg. 1081
TAYLOR MEDICAL INC., pg. 1081
TAYLOR MEDICAL OF LA—See Taylor Medical Inc., pg. 1081
TAYLOR-MORLEY, INC., pg. 1081
TAYLOR OIL CO. INC., pg. 1082
TAYLOR PUBLISHING CO.—See Insilco Corporation, pg. 571
TAYLOR-SMITH GROUP, pg. 1082
TAYLOR WOODCRAFT—See Brodhead-Garrett Co., pg. 178
TAYLOR'S HITEK PRODUCT FINISHING, INC.—See Cowden Metal Specialties, Inc., pg. 291
T.D. WILLIAMSON (U.K.) LTD.—See T.D. Williamson, Inc., pg. 1192
TEACHERS INSURANCE AND ANNUITY ASSOCIATION-COLLEGE RETIREMENT EQUITIES FUND, pg. 1082
TEACHERS MANAGEMENT & INVESTMENT CORPORATION, pg. 1082
TEAM BANCSHARES, INC., pg. 1082
TEAM BANK—See Team Bancshares, Inc., pg. 1082
TEAM BANK/AMARILLO—See Team Bancshares, Inc., pg. 1082
TEAM BANK/DALLAS—See Team Bancshares, Inc., pg. 1082
TEBBAS SALES CORP.—See Sabbeth Industries Ltd, pg. 965
TECA CORPORATION, pg. 1082
TECH-AEROFOAM PRODUCTS, INC.—See Great American Industries, Inc., pg. 480
TECH/AID—See Technical Aid Corporation, pg. 1083
TECH CBI—See The Tech Group, pg. 1083
THE TECH GROUP, pg. 1082
TECH INDUSTRIES, INC., pg. 1083
TECH MEDICAL INC.—See The Tech Group, pg. 1083
TECH MOLD, INC.—See The Tech Group, pg. 1083
TECH PLASTICS—See The Tech Group, pg. 1083
TECH POULSON, INC.—See The Tech Group, pg. 1083
TECH SYSTEMS CORP.—See Datron Incorporated, pg. 317
TECHFORM LABORATORIES—See Gardiner Metal Company, pg. 443
TECHMEDIA—See International Data Group, pg. 577
TECHNIC INCORPORATED, pg. 1083
TECHNICAL AID CORPORATION, pg. 1083
TECHNICAL COATINGS CO.—See Benjamin Moore & Co., pg. 139
TECHNICAL PUBLISHING—See Nelson & Schmidt, Inc., pg. 797
TECHNICARBON COMPANY, INC., pg. 1083
TECHNICARE CLEANING SYSTEMS INC.—See EBSC Corporation, pg. 359
TECHNICOLOR PROFESSIONAL FILM DIV.—See MacAndrews & Forbes Holdings Inc., pg. 695
TECHNICOLOR VIDEOCASSETTE INC.—See MacAndrews & Forbes Holdings Inc., pg. 695
TECHNOGRAPHICS, INC., pg. 1083
TECHNOLOGY APPLICATIONS, INC., pg. 1083
TECHNOLOGY FOR ENERGY CORPORATION, pg. 1084
TECHNOLOGY FOR MEDICINE, INC.—See Medical Laboratory Automation, Inc., pg. 735
TECHNOLOGY INVESTMENT STRATEGIES CORP.—See International Data Group, pg. 578
TECHNOLOGY TRANSFER INSTITUTE, pg. 1084
TECHSTEEL, INC.—See W.C. Caye & Company, Inc., pg. 230
TECHWELD LTD.—See Eastern Technologies Ltd, pg. 364
TECKNIT, pg. 1084
TECNA LTDA.—See Panduit Company, pg. 846
TECON PACIFIC, pg. 1084
TECOT ELECTRIC SUPPLY COMPANY, pg. 1084
TEEPAK, INC.—See Hillside Capital, Inc., pg. 535
TEEPAK, INC., ZURICH BRANCH—See Hillside Capital, Inc., pg. 535
TEICHERT LAND CO.—See A. Teichert & Son, Inc., pg. 1084
A. TEICHERT & SON, INC., pg. 1084
TEKNI-PLEX, INC., pg. 1084
TEKNOR APEX COMPANY, pg. 1084
TEKO REALTY CORPORATION—See Thomas Engineering Inc., pg. 1093
TEKRA CORP., SOUTHEAST DIV.—See Tekra Corporation, pg. 1084
TEKRA CORPORATION, pg. 1084
TELCO CAPITAL CORP.—See Libco Corporation, pg. 674
TELE-COM PRODUCTS, INC., pg. 1084
TELE-TRIP CO.—See Mutual of Omaha Insurance Company, pg. 779
TELECHRON, INC., pg. 1085
TELEFLORA—See American Protection Industries, Inc., pg. 60
TELEGRAPHICS PRINTING—See Telescope Casual Furniture, Inc., pg. 1085
TELEPHONE DIRECTORY ADVERTISING, INC.-CINCINNATI—See TMP Worldwide, Inc., pg. 1074
TELEPHONE MARKETING PROGRAMS-SMET—See TMP Worldwide, Inc., pg. 1074
TELEREP, INCORPORATED—See Cox Enterprises, Inc., pg. 293
TELESCIENCE TRANSMISSION SYSTEMS, INC.—See Telesciences Co. Systems Inc., pg. 1085
TELESCIENCES CO. SYSTEMS INC., pg. 1085
TELESCOPE CASUAL FURNITURE, INC., pg. 1085
TELESENSORY, pg. 1085
TELEX COMMUNICATIONS, INC., pg. 1085
TELEX HY-GAIN DIV.—See Telex Communications, Inc., pg. 1085
TELL CITY CHAIR CO., pg. 1085
TELMARK, INC.—See Agway, Inc., pg. 25
TELONIC BERKELEY—See Berkeley Industries Inc., pg. 141
TELSCO INDUSTRIES, pg. 1085
TEMKIN & TEMKIN, pg. 1086
TEMP-CONTROL MECHANICAL CORP., pg. 1086
TEMPEL STEEL COMPANY, pg. 1086
TEMPERATURE EQUIPMENT CORPORATION, pg. 1086
TEMPLETON, KENLY & CO., INC., pg. 1086
TEMPORARIES, INCORPORATED, pg. 1086
TEMPS & COMPANY, pg. 1086
TENAX CORPORATION, pg. 1086
TENCARVA MACHINERY CO., INC., pg. 1086
TENCARVA MACHINERY CO.-ASHEVILLE—See Tencarva Machinery Co., Inc., pg. 1087
A. TENENBAUM CO. INC., pg. 1087
TENGEN—See Atari Games Corporation, pg. 93
TENNANAH LAKE GOLF & TENNIS CLUB, INC.—See Construction Counsellors, Inc., pg. 277
TENNELEC/NUCLEUS, INC., pg. 1087
TENNESSEE BOOK COMPANY—See Ingram Industries Inc., pg. 569
TENNESSEE DRESSED BEEF COMPANY, pg. 1087
TENNESSEE FARMERS CO-OP, pg. 1087
TENNESSEE INSURANCE CO.—See Ingram Industries Inc., pg. 569
TENNESSEE RESTAURANT CORP., pg. 1087
TENNESSEE TUBEBENDING INC.—See Morris Coupling Co., pg. 771
TENNESSEE VALLEY AUTHORITY, pg. 1088
TENNESSEE WHOLESALE DRUG COMPANY, pg. 1088
TENNSCO CORPORATION, pg. 1088
TENSION ENVELOPE CORP., pg. 1088
TERRAL-NORRIS SEED CO., INC., pg. 1088
TERMINAL GRAIN CORP., pg. 1088
TERMINAL RAILROAD ASSOCIATION OF ST. LOUIS—See Anschutz Corporation, pg. 76
TERMINIX SERVICE, INC., pg. 1088
TERRE HILL CONCRETE PRODUCTS, INC., pg. 1089
TERRY, BATH & KITCHEN PRODUCTS DIV.—See Farley Industries, pg. 400
SUSAN TERRY DIV.—See Masters, Inc., pg. 720
TERUYA BROS., LTD., pg. 1089
TESCO—See The Heil Co., pg. 526
TETKO, INC., pg. 1089
TEXAS AUTO AUCTION SERVICES, INC. D/B/A BIG H AUTO AUCTION—See Cox Enterprises, Inc., pg. 293
TEXAS COMMERCE BANCSHARES, INC., pg. 1089
TEXAS COMMERCE BANK-AMARILLO—See Texas Commerce Bancshares, Inc., pg. 1089
TEXAS COMMERCE BANK-AUSTIN—See Texas Commerce Bancshares, Inc., pg. 1089

TEXAS COMMERCE BANK-BEAUMONT—See Texas Commerce Bancshares, Inc., pg. 1089
TEXAS COMMERCE BANK-CORPUS CHRISTI—See Texas Commerce Bancshares, Inc., pg. 1089
TEXAS COMMERCE BANK-HOUSTON—See Texas Commerce Bancshares, Inc., pg. 1089
TEXAS COMMERCE BANK-LONGVIEW—See Texas Commerce Bancshares, Inc., pg. 1089
TEXAS COMMERCE BANK-LUBBOCK—See Texas Commerce Bancshares, Inc., pg. 1089
TEXAS COMMERCE BANK-NATIONAL ASSOCIATION—See Texas Commerce Bancshares, Inc., pg. 1089
TEXAS COMMERCE BANK-NEW BRAUNFELS—See Texas Commerce Bancshares, Inc., pg. 1089
TEXAS COMMERCE BANK-ODESSA—See Texas Commerce Bancshares, Inc., pg. 1089
TEXAS COMMERCE BANK-RIO GRANDE VALLEY—See Texas Commerce Bancshares, Inc., pg. 1089
TEXAS COMMERCE BANK-SAN ANGELO—See Texas Commerce Bancshares, Inc., pg. 1089
TEXAS COMMERCE BANK-SAN ANTONIO—See Texas Commerce Bancshares, Inc., pg. 1089
TEXAS DRUG REPS—See Eon Labs, Inc., pg. 384
TEXAS ELECTRIC COOPERATIVES, INC., pg. 1089
TEXAS GRANITE CORP.—See Cold Spring Granite Company, pg. 260
TEXAS HOBBY AUTO AUCTION—See Cox Enterprises, Inc., pg. 294
TEXAS HOMESTEAD MORTGAGE CO.—See Rayco, pg. 914
TEXAS IRON WORKS INC.—See Pearce Industries Inc., pg. 853
TEXAS LIFE INSURANCE COMPANY—See Metropolitan Life Insurance Co., pg. 745
TEXAS METAL WORKS, INC., pg. 1089
TEXAS MONTHLY, INC.—See Mediatex Communications Corporation, pg. 735
TEXAS OLEFINS CO., pg. 1089
TEXAS REFINERY CORP., pg. 1089
TEXAS RESIN—See Jones Blair Company, pg. 603
TEXAS STEEL CO., INC., pg. 1090
TEXAS TRANSPORTATION CO.—See S & P Company, pg. 959
TEXTILE RUBBER & CHEMICAL COMPANY, pg. 1090
TEXTILEASE CORPORATION, pg. 1090
THE TEXWIPE CO., INC., pg. 1090
THAW, INC.—See Recreational Equipment, Inc., pg. 917
THEOCHEM LABS., INC., pg. 1090
THERADYNE CORPORATION—See Surgical Appliance Industries, Inc., pg. 1065
THERAPEDIC ASSOCIATES, INC., pg. 1090
THERM, INC., pg. 1090
THERMA-TRU CORP., pg. 1090
THERMA-TRU INDIANA MFG. OPERS.—See Therma-Tru Corp., pg. 1091
THERMA-TRU WESTERN MFG. OPERS.—See Therma-Tru Corp., pg. 1091
THERMAL AMERICAN FUSED QUARTZ CO., pg. 1091
THERMAL-CARE DIV.—See Midwesco Inc., pg. 751
THERMAL COMPONENTS, INC.—See Insilco Corporation, pg. 571
THERMAL TECHNOLOGY INDUSTRIES, pg. 1091
THERMALLOY, INC., pg. 1091
THERMO DYNAMICS, INC.—See Dixson, Inc., pg. 341
THERMO ELECTRIC (CANADA) LTD.—See Thermo Electric Co., Inc., pg. 1091
THERMO ELECTRIC CO., INC., pg. 1091
THERMO ELECTRIC GMBH—See Thermo Electric Co., Inc., pg. 1091
THERMO ELECTRIC INTL. B.V.—See Thermo Electric Co., Inc., pg. 1091
THERMO ELECTRIC INTL. LTD.—See Thermo Electric Co., Inc., pg. 1091
THERMO ELECTRIC S.A.—See Thermo Electric Co., Inc., pg. 1091
THERMO ELECTRIC (SOUTHEAST REGION)—See Thermo Electric Co., Inc., pg. 1091
THERMO INDUSTRIES INC., pg. 1091
THERMOJET—See Cooperheat, Inc., pg. 283
THERMOJET—See Cooperheat, Inc., pg. 283
THERMON AUSTRALIA—See Thermon Manufacturing Company, pg. 1092
THERMON BENELUX—See Thermon Manufacturing Company, pg. 1092
THERMON CANADA—See Thermon Manufacturing Company, pg. 1092
THERMON FAR EAST—See Thermon Manufacturing Company, pg. 1092
THERMON FRANCE—See Thermon Manufacturing Company, pg. 1092
THERMON INTERNATIONAL SERVICES SA—See Thermon Manufacturing Company, pg. 1092
THERMON MANUFACTURING COMPANY, pg. 1091
THERMON U.K. (LTD.)—See Thermon Manufacturing Company, pg. 1092
THERMOTRON INDUSTRIES, INC.—See Venturedyne, Ltd., pg. 1148
THERMWELL PRODUCTS CO., INC., pg. 1092
THETFORD (AQUA) PRODUCTS, LTD.—See The Dyson-Kissner-Moran Corporation, pg. 358
THETFORD CORPORATION—See The Dyson-Kissner-Moran Corporation, pg. 357
THETFORD CORP. MFG. FACILITY—See The Dyson-Kissner-Moran Corporation, pg. 358
THETFORD SANITATION LTD.—See The Dyson-Kissner-Moran Corporation, pg. 358
THIELE KAOLIN CO., pg. 1092
THIMBLE COLLECTORS CLUB COLLECTIONS—See MBI Inc., pg. 691
THIMBLES SPECIALTY STORES, INC.—See H. C. Prange Company, pg. 884
THINGS REMEMBERED—See Cole National Corporation, pg. 260
THINKING MACHINES CORPORATION, pg. 1092
THOM THUMB FOOD MARKET INC.—See Polka Dot Dairy, pg. 879
TED THOMAS ASSOCIATES INC., ADVERTISING, pg. 1092
IRA THOMAS ASSOCIATES, INC., pg. 1092
BOB THOMAS & ASSOCIATES—See Chiat/Day/Mojo Inc. Advertising, pg. 244
CHARLIE THOMAS AUTO WORLD, pg. 1092
BOB THOMAS ASSOCIATES—See Chiat/Day/Mojo Inc. Advertising, pg. 244
BOB THOMAS & ASSOCIATES, INC. PUBLIC RELATIONS—See Chiat/Day/Mojo Inc. Advertising, pg. 244
THOMAS BUILT BUSES, INC., pg. 1092
THOMAS BUILT BUSES OF CANADA, LTD.—See Thomas Built Buses, Inc., pg. 1093
THOMAS CONVEYOR COMPANY, pg. 1093
THOMAS ENGINEERING INC., pg. 1093
THOMAS & HOWARD, pg. 1093
THOMAS & PERKINS, pg. 1093
THOMAS PIPE & STEEL, INC., pg. 1093
THOMAS PUBLISHING CO., pg. 1093
THOMAS & SKINNER, INC., pg. 1093
THOMAS STEEL STRIP CORP., pg. 1094
I. C. THOMASSON ASSOCIATES, INC., pg. 1094
THOMPSON ADVERTISING PRODUCTIONS, INC., pg. 1094
THOMPSON & COMPANY, pg. 1094
THOMPSON ENTERPRISES INC., pg. 1094
THE THOMPSON GROUP COMPANIES, pg. 1094
C.F. THOMPSON GROUP, INC., pg. 1094
THOMPSON/MARINCE ADVERTISING, pg. 1094
THOMPSON-MCCULLY ASPHALT PAVING CO.—See Thompson-McCully Co., pg. 1094
THOMPSON-MCCULLY CO., pg. 1094
THOMPSON MEDICAL COMPANY, INC., pg. 1094
THOMPSON NUTRITIONAL PRODUCTS—See Sundown Vitamin Co., Inc., pg. 1060
THOMPSON-STARRETT CONSTRUCTION COMPANY, INC.—See Jupiter Industries, Inc., pg. 609
THOMPSON STEEL CO., INC., pg. 1094
THOMPSON TRACTOR COMPANY, pg. 1095
THOMSON MACCONNELL CADILLAC, INC., pg. 1095
THORDARSON MEISSNER, INC.—See Components Corporation Of America, pg. 270
THORNTON OIL CORP., pg. 1095
THOROBRED CONTAINERS INCORPORATED—See Interlock Industries, Inc., pg. 575
THOROUGHBRED EUROPE LTD.—See Thoroughbred Software International, Inc., pg. 1095
THOROUGHBRED/QUARK—See Thoroughbred Software International, Inc., pg. 1095
THOROUGHBRED RD-COM GMBH—See Thoroughbred Software International, Inc., pg. 1095
THOROUGHBRED SOFTWARE INTERNATIONAL, INC., pg. 1095
G.C. THORSEN, INC.—See Jupiter Industries, Inc., pg. 609
THRALL CAR MFG. CO.—See Duchossois Industries, Inc., pg. 350
THRALL ENTERPRISES, INC., pg. 1095
THREE BEALL BROTHERS 3, INC.—See Specialty Retailers, Inc., pg. 1029
THREE RIVERS IRON & METAL—See Sturgis Iron & Metal Company, Inc., pg. 1055
THREE STATES SUPPLY CO., INC.—See UIS, Inc., pg. 1123
THRIFTWAY, INC., pg. 1095
THRIFTY CORPORATION—See Leonard Green & Partners, pg. 485
THRIFTY DRUG STORES, INC., pg. 1096
THRIFTY OIL COMPANY, pg. 1096
THRUWAY FASTENERS INC., pg. 1096
THUNDERBIRD STEEL CORPORATION, pg. 1096
THUNDERLINE CORPORATION, pg. 1096
THYBONY WALL COVERINGS CO., pg. 1096
TICKETMASTER CORPORATION, pg. 1096
TICOR TITLE GUARANTEE CO., pg. 1096
TIDELANDS OIL PRODUCTION CO., pg. 1096
TIDEWATER GRAIN CO.—See EDI International, Inc., pg. 359
TIDY CAR INTERNATIONAL, INC.—See Ziebart International Corporation, pg. 1217
TIERNAY METALS, INC., pg. 1096
TIFFANY EXTRUDERS, INC., pg. 1096
TIFFANY INDUSTRIES AMERICAS CORP.—See Tiffany Industries, Inc., pg. 1097
TIFFANY INDUSTRIES, INC., pg. 1097
TIFFANY STAND & FURNITURE COMPANY—See Tiffany Industries, Inc., pg. 1097
TIFFIN MOTOR HOMES, INC., pg. 1097
TIGER ELECTRONICS, INC., pg. 1097
TIGHE INDUSTRIES, INC., pg. 1097
TILCON, INC., pg. 1097
TILEWAYS INC.—See Dal-Tile Corp., pg. 312
TILLAMOOK COUNTY CREAMERY ASSN., pg. 1097
TILLBROOKS STUDIOS—See Backer Spielvogel Bates Worldwide, Inc., pg. 112
TIMBER PRODUCTS COMPANY, LP, pg. 1097
TIME INDEX, INC.—See Time Systems, Inc., pg. 1097
TIME OIL COMPANY, pg. 1097
TIME PRODUCTS, INC.—See Theochem Labs., Inc., pg. 1090
TIME SYSTEMS, INC., pg. 1097
TIMEC COMPANY, pg. 1097
TIMEMED LABELING SYSTEMS, INC., pg. 1098
TIMES BOOKS—See Advance Publications Inc., pg. 19
TIMES FIBER COMMUNICATIONS, INC.—See LPL Technologies, Inc., pg. 648
THE TIMES-PICAYUNE PUBLISHING CORP., pg. 1098
TIMES PRINTING COMPANY, INC., pg. 1098
TIMES PUBLISHING COMPANY OF WICHITA FALLS—See Harte-Hanks Communications, Inc., pg. 513
TIMES SUPER MARKET LTD.—See Teruya Bros., Ltd., pg. 1089
TIMES-WORLD CORPORATION—See Landmark Communications, Inc., pg. 656
TIMESAVERS INC., pg. 1098
TIMEX CORPORATION, pg. 1098
TIMPTE, INC.—See Timpte Industries, Inc., pg. 1098
TIMPTE INDUSTRIES, INC., pg. 1098
TINGLEY RUBBER CORPORATION, pg. 1098
TINIUS OLSEN TESTING MACHINE CO., INC., pg. 1098
TINSLEY ADVERTISING, pg. 1099
TINSLEY PUBLIC RELATIONS—See Tinsley Advertising, pg. 1099
TINSLEY SPORTS NETWORK—See Tinsley Advertising, pg. 1099
TINSLEY YELLOW PAGE SERVICES—See Tinsley Advertising, pg. 1099
TIPPINS INCORPORATED, pg. 1099
TIROLER MAGNESIT, A.G.—See Belmont Industries, Inc., pg. 137
TISHMAN REALTY & CONSTRUCTION CO., pg. 1099
TITAN INDUSTRIAL CORP., pg. 1099
TITAN PRT—See Construction Counsellors, Inc., pg. 277
TITANIUM METALS CORPORATION—See Tremont Corporation, pg. 1109
E. H. TITCHENER & COMPANY, pg. 1099
TOBACCO SUPPLY, pg. 1099
TOBER INDUSTRIES, INC., pg. 1099
TOBERMAN, pg. 1099
THE TOBIN CORPORATION—See Avis Industrial Corporation, pg. 102
TODAY'S KIDS—See Spang & Company, pg. 1025
THE TODD-AO CORPORATION, pg. 1099
TODD-AO/EAST—See The Todd-AO Corporation, pg. 1099
J. L. TODD AUCTION CO., pg. 1099
A.M. TODD COMPANY, pg. 1100
TODD PIPE & SUPPLY HAWTHORNE, pg. 1100
TODD & SARGENT, INC., pg. 1100
THE TOG SHOP, pg. 1100
TOLEDO STAMPING & MANUFACTURING CO.—See New Hampshire Oak, pg. 801
TOLLESON LUMBER COMPANY, INC., pg. 1100
TOLLMAN/HUNDLEY HOTELS, pg. 1100
TOLLYCRAFT YACHTS CORP., pg. 1100
TOM THUMB FOOD & DRUGS, INC.—See Randall's Food Markets, Inc., pg. 912
TOM THUMB STORES, INC.—See Randall's Food Markets, Inc., pg. 912
TOMAHAWK FARMS, INC.—See Lundy Packing Co. Inc., pg. 687
CHARLES TOMBRAS ADVERTISING, INC., pg. 1100
TOMCO AUTO PRODUCTS, INC., pg. 1100
JAY DEE TOMFOR TRANSPORTATION CO.—See American Protection Industries, Inc., pg. 60
TOM'S DISTRIBUTING INC.—See Tom's Foods, pg. 1101
TOM'S FOODS, pg. 1101
TOM'S SNAX CO.—See Tom's Foods, pg. 1101
TONE COMMANDER SYSTEMS, pg. 1101
TOOL KING, pg. 1101
TOOL SHOP—See Freudenberg-NOK (MI), pg. 433
TOOTSIETOY DIVISION—See Strombecker Corporation, pg. 1054
TOOTSIETOY PRESCHOOL PRODUCTS DIV.—See Strombecker Corporation, pg. 1054
TOP BILLING INC., pg. 1101
TOP FLIGHT, INC., pg. 1101
TOP-SEAL CORP.—See The Tech Group, pg. 1083
TOPA EQUITIES LTD, INC., pg. 1101
TOPAKA SCIENTIFIC SAFETY CO.—See Pioneer/Eclipse Corp., pg. 871
TOPCO ASSOCIATES, INC., pg. 1101
TOPCOR FINANCIAL CORPORATION, pg. 1101
THE TOPEKA CAPITAL-JOURNAL—See Stauffer Communications, Inc., pg. 1042
TOPEKA TELEVISION, CORP.—See SJL of Kansas Corp., pg. 963
TOPEXPRESS, LTD.—See Science Applications International Corporation, pg. 982
TOPFLIGHT CORP., pg. 1102
TOPLINE ADVERTISING, pg. 1102
TOPLINE IMPORTS, INC., pg. 1102
TOPSY'S INTERNATIONAL INC., pg. 1102
TORCO OIL, pg. 1102
TORCON, INC., pg. 1102
TORINO BAKING CO.—See Gonnella Baking Co., pg. 470
TORINO FASHIONS, INC., pg. 1102
TORK ELECTRO SISTEMAS S.A.—See Tork, Inc., pg. 1102
TORK, INC., pg. 1102
TORKE COFFEE COMPANY, INC., pg. 1102
TORNADO PRODUCTS, INC.—See Simplicity Manufacturing, Inc., pg. 1007
TORONTO AUTO AUCTION—See Cox Enterprises, Inc., pg. 294
TORRANCE NISSAN, INC., pg. 1102
TOTAL COMMUNICATIONS GROUP, pg. 1102
TOTAL EXPOSITION CONCEPTS—See Servistar Corporation, pg. 993
TOTAL MANAGEMENT SYSTEMS—See Effective Management Systems, pg. 370
TOTAL PLAN ALTERNATIVES, INC.—See Blue Cross & Blue Shield of Oregon, pg. 160
TOTAL REPRODUCTIONS, INC.—See Schawk, Inc., pg. 975
TOTEM RESOURCES CORPORATION, pg. 1103
TOTER INCORPORATED, pg. 1103
TOTES CANADA LTD.—See Totes Incorporated, pg. 1103
TOTES EUROPE—See Totes Incorporated, pg. 1103
TOTES INCORPORATED, pg. 1103
TOTES U.K. LIMITED—See Totes Incorporated, pg. 1103
TOTSY MANUFACTURING COMPANY, INC., pg. 1103
TOTTEN TUBES, INC., pg. 1103
TOULIN INC.—See GSC Enterprises, Inc., pg. 441
J.J. TOUREK CO.—See Tuthill Corporation, pg. 1120

TOURNEAU INC., pg. 1103
TOW WATER CO., INC.—See Rotterdam Ventures Inc., pg. 952
TOWER LOAN OF MISSISSIPPI, INC.—See Capitol Street Corp., pg. 216
TOWER METAL PRODUCTS—See Tang Industries Inc., pg. 1078
TOWER RECORDS—See MTS, Inc., pg. 694
TOWERS, PERRIN, FORSTER & CROSBY, INC., pg. 1103
ROBERT TOWERS ADVERTISING, INC., pg. 1103
TOWN & COUNTRY—See The Hearst Corporation, pg. 523
TOWN & COUNTRY FOOD MARKETS, INC., pg. 1103
TOWN & COUNTRY FORD INC., pg. 1103
TOWN & COUNTRY SUPERMARKET, pg. 1103
TOWN PUMP, INC., pg. 1104
TOWN SQUARE FURNITURE, INC., pg. 1104
TOWNE PROPERTIES, pg. 1104
TOWNE REALTY, INC.—See Zilber, Ltd., pg. 1219
TOWNE, SILVERSTEIN, ROTTER INC., pg. 1104
THE TOWNSEND AGENCY, LTD., pg. 1104
TOWNSEND & BOTTUM, INC., pg. 1104
TOWNSEND ENGINEERING CO., pg. 1104
TOWNSEND & O'LEARY, INC., pg. 1104
TOY BIZ, INC., pg. 1104
THE TOY FACTORY—See Pride Products, Inc., pg. 889
TRACE PRODUCTS, pg. 1104
TRACE U.K., LTD.—See Trace Products, pg. 1104
TRACO ADVERTISING, INC., pg. 1104
TRACOR AEROSPACE, INC.—See Tracor, Inc., pg. 1105
TRACOR AEROSPACE, INC. EXPENDABLES DIVISION—See Tracor, Inc., pg. 1105
TRACOR APPLIED SCIENCES, ANALYSIS & APPLIED RESEARCH DIV.—See Tracor, Inc., pg. 1105
TRACOR APPLIED SCIENCES, ELECTRONIC SYSTEMS DIV.—See Tracor, Inc., pg. 1105
TRACOR APPLIED SCIENCES, SYSTEMS TECHNOLOGY DIV.—See Tracor, Inc., pg. 1105
TRACOR ELSIN—See Tracor, Inc., pg. 1105
TRACOR FLIGHT SYSTEMS, INC.—See Tracor, Inc., pg. 1105
TRACOR GIE—See Tracor, Inc., pg. 1105
TRACOR, INC., pg. 1104
TRACOR TECHNOLOGY RESOURCES, INC.—See Tracor, Inc., pg. 1105
TRACOR ULTRON—See Tracor, Inc., pg. 1105
TRADE SHOW ENTERPRISES—See I. Spiewak & Sons, Inc., pg. 1031
TRADEHOME SHOE STORES, INC., pg. 1105
TRADEMARK PRESS, INC.—See Harte-Hanks Communications, Inc., pg. 513
TRADER JOES CO.—See TACT Holding, pg. 1076
TRADERS SUPERMARKETS, INC., pg. 1105
TRADING PORT, INC., pg. 1105
TRAFALGAR/GHURKA, pg. 1105
TRAHAN, BURDEN & CHARLES, INC., pg. 1105
TRAILER WHEEL & FRAME COMPANY, pg. 1105
TRAILMOBILE—See The Pullman Company, pg. 900
TRAINER WORTHAM & COMPANY INCORPORATED, pg. 1106
TRAINING DYNAMICS—See The Forum Corporation, pg. 426
TRAK INTERNATIONAL, INC., pg. 1106
TRAMMELL CROW COMPANY, pg. 1106
TRAMMELL CROW INTERESTS—See Trammell Crow Company, pg. 1106
TRAMMELL CROW RESIDENTIAL—See Trammell Crow Company, pg. 1106
TRANE DO BRAZIL—See American Standard Inc., pg. 62
TRANE COMMERCIAL SYSTEMS GROUP—See American Standard Inc., pg. 61
TRANE CO. OF CANADA—See American Standard Inc., pg. 62
TRANE EUROPE—See American Standard Inc., pg. 62
TRANE LTD.—See American Standard Inc., pg. 62
TRANS NATIONAL TRAVEL, pg. 1106
TRANS UNION CORP.—See The Marmon Group, Inc., pg. 712
TRANS UNITARY PRODUCTS GROUP-COMMERCIAL—See American Standard Inc., pg. 61
TRANS WORLD AIRLINES, INC.—See Icahn & Co., Inc., pg. 561
TRANSAMERICAN REFINING CORP.—See Transamerican Refining Corporation, pg. 1106
TRANSAMERICAN REFINING CORPORATION, pg. 1106
TRANSAMMONIA AG—See Transammonia Inc., pg. 1106
TRANSAMMONIA INC., pg. 1106
TRANSBULK, INC.—See National Engineering & Contracting Co., pg. 788
TRANSCO INC., pg. 1106
TRANSCO INC., pg. 1107
TRANSCO PRODUCTS INC.—See Transco Inc., pg. 1107
TRANSCO RAILWAY PRODUCTS INC.—See Transco Inc., pg. 1107
TRANSCO REALTY INC.—See Transco Inc., pg. 1107
TRANSCOASTAL MORTGAGE COMPANY, pg. 1107
TRANSFERTECH, INC.—See Castcraft Industries, Inc., pg. 228
TRANSILWRAP CO., INC.—See Transilwrap Company, Inc., pg. 1107
TRANSILWRAP CO., INC.—See Transilwrap Company, Inc., pg. 1107
TRANSILWRAP CO., INC.—See Transilwrap Company, Inc., pg. 1107
TRANSILWRAP CO., INC.—See Transilwrap Company, Inc., pg. 1107
TRANSILWRAP CO., INC.—See Transilwrap Company, Inc., pg. 1107
TRANSILWRAP COMPANY, INC., pg. 1107
TRANSILWRAP COMPANY, INC.—See Transilwrap Company, Inc., pg. 1107
TRANSILWRAP COMPANY, INC.—See Transilwrap Company, Inc., pg. 1107
TRANSILWRAP CO. OF PHILADELPHIA—See Transilwrap Company, Inc., pg. 1107
TRANSISTOR DEVICES, INC., pg. 1107
TRANSIT SYSTEMS INC.—See Eastern Technologies Ltd, pg. 364
TRANSMET CORPORATION, pg. 1107
TRANSMISSION DIV. BORG-WARNER AUTOMOTIVE GMBH—See Borg-Warner Corporation, pg. 166
TRANSNATIONAL MOTORS INC., pg. 1107
TRANSPO ELECTRONICS, INC., pg. 1108
TRANSPORT INSURANCE CO.—See American Financial Corporation, pg. 54
TRANSPORT SERVICE OF INDIANA, INC.—See Mayflower Transit, Inc., pg. 725
TRANSPORTATION & DISTRIBUTION ASSOCIATES—See Day & Zimmermann, Inc., pg. 320
TRANSUS INC., pg. 1108
TRAPP FAMILY LODGE, INC., pg. 1108
TRAPPINGS CO.—See I. Spiewak & Sons, Inc., pg. 1031
TRASE-MILLER—See MTI Vacations, Inc., pg. 694
TRAUTH DAIRY INC., pg. 1108
THE TRAVEL CHANNEL—See Landmark Communications, Inc., pg. 654
TRAVELING SOFTWARE INC., pg. 1108
TRAYCO OF S.C., INC.—See The Dyson-Kissner-Moran Corporation, pg. 358
TRAYER PRODUCTS, INC., pg. 1108
TRAYLOR BROTHERS, INC., pg. 1108
TRAYLOR CHEMICAL & SUPPLY CO., pg. 1108
TREADWELL CORPORATION, pg. 1108
TREASURE CHEST ADVERTISING CO., INC., pg. 1108
TREASURE ISLAND FOODMARTS INC., pg. 1109
TREATY CO., pg. 1109
TRECO COMMUNITIES, INC.—See Sunstates Realty Group Inc., pg. 1062
TRECO PROPERTY SERVICES, INC.—See Sunstates Realty Group Inc., pg. 1062
TRECO REALTY GROUP, INC.—See Sunstates Realty Group Inc., pg. 1062
TREE FRESH FOODS CORP.—See Home Juice Company, pg. 542
TREE TOP, INC., pg. 1109
J. TREFFILETTI & SONS, INC., pg. 1109
TREK BICYCLE CORPORATION—See Intrepid Corp., pg. 581
TREMONT CORPORATION, pg. 1109
TREMONT FOODS, pg. 1109
TREND LINE CORPORATION, pg. 1109
TREND OFFSET PRINTING SERVICES, pg. 1109
TRENDWAY CORPORATION, pg. 1109
TRENTON TIMES CORP.—See Perpetual Corporation, pg. 862
THE TRENTONIAN—See Journal Register Company, pg. 608
H.O. TRERICE COMPANY, pg. 1110
TRERICE DEVELOPMENT CO.—See Trerice Tosto International, pg. 1110
TRERICE MANAGEMENT CO.—See Trerice Tosto International, pg. 1110
TRERICE TOSTO INTERNATIONAL, pg. 1110
TRERICE/TOSTO INVESTMENT SERVICES CO.—See Trerice Tosto International, pg. 1110
TRESSA, INC., pg. 1110
TRI-CHEM, INC., pg. 1110
TRI-CITY ELECTRICAL CONTRACTORS INC., pg. 1110
TRI-CITY ELECTRICAL CONTRACTORS INC.—See Tri-City Electrical Contractors Inc., pg. 1110
TRI-CITY ELECTRICAL CONTRACTORS INC.—See Tri-City Electrical Contractors Inc., pg. 1110
TRI-CITY OLDSMOBILE INC., pg. 1110
TRI-DATA SYSTEMS—See Avatar Corporation, pg. 102
TRI-K INDUSTRIES, INC., pg. 1110
TRI-MANAGEMENT CORP.—See Family Inns of America, Inc., pg. 398
TRI-MARK INC.—See Hobart Brothers Co., pg. 537
TRI-MARK METAL CORP., pg. 1110
TRI-PAC DIV.—See Triangle Pacific Corporation, pg. 1112
TRI-PALM ESTATE—See GWP, Inc., pg. 441
TRI-STATE ARMATURE ELECTRIC WORKS, pg. 1110
TRI-STATE CONCRETE PRODUCTS CO., INC.—See Bristol Steel & Iron Works, Inc., pg. 177
TRI-STATE DEVELOPMENT CO.—See Invetech Co., pg. 582
TRI-STATE DIES, INC.—See Modern Drop Forge Co., pg. 762
TRI-STATE MACK DISTRIBUTORS, pg. 1111
TRI-STATE MOTOR TRANSIT CO., pg. 1111
TRI STATE STEEL CONSTRUCTION—See National Engineering & Contracting Co., pg. 788
TRI-STATE WHOLESALE ASSOCIATED GROCERS, pg. 1111
TRI VALLEY GROWERS INC., pg. 1111
THE TRIAD GROUP, INC.—See Altus Federal Savings Bank, pg. 46
TRIAN GROUP, pg. 1111
TRIANGLE AUTO SPRING COMPANY—See The Marmon Group, Inc., pg. 711
TRIANGLE DISTRIBUTING COMPANY, pg. 1111
TRIANGLE ELECTRIC COMPANY, pg. 1112
TRIANGLE MACHINE PRODUCT CO.—See Freeway Corporation, pg. 432
TRIANGLE MAINTENANCE CORPORATION, pg. 1112
TRIANGLE MARKETING CORP., pg. 1112
TRIANGLE METALS, INC.—See Thomas Engineering Inc., pg. 1093
TRIANGLE PACIFIC—See Dentsu, Young & Rubicam Partnerships, pg. 331
TRIANGLE PACIFIC CORPORATION, pg. 1112
TRIANGLE PARACHUTE—See The Entwistle Company, pg. 383
TRIANGLE PWC, INC.—See Trian Group, pg. 1111
TRIANGLE TOOL CO.—See Plastek Group, pg. 875
TRIBBLE & STEPHENS CO., pg. 1112
TRIBORO ELECTRIC CORP., pg. 1112
TRIBOROUGH BRIDGE & TUNNEL AUTHORITY—See Metropolitan Transportation Authority, pg. 745
TRIBUNE REVIEW PUBLISHING CO., pg. 1112
TRI-CITY ELECTRICAL CONTRACTORS INC.—See Tri-City Electrical Contractors Inc., pg. 1110
TRI-CITY ELECTRICAL CONTRACTORS INC.—See Tri-City Electrical Contractors Inc., pg. 1110
TRICO ELECTRIC CO-OP, pg. 1113
TRICON ELECTROMECHANICAL PLANT—See Tricon Industries, Inc., pg. 1113
TRICON INDUSTRIES, INC., pg. 1113
TRIDATA INC.—See System Planning Corp., pg. 1070
TRIDENT FINANCIAL CORPORATION, pg. 1113
TRIDENT SEAFOOD CORPORATION, pg. 1113
TRILAN SYSTEMS CORPORATION—See Dukane Corporation, pg. 352
THE TRIMBLE BANNER-DEMOCRAT—See Landmark Communications, Inc., pg. 656
WM. S. TRIMBLE COMPANY, INC., pg. 1113
TRIMFIT COMPANY LIMITED—See Trimfit, Inc., pg. 1113
TRIMFIT, INC., pg. 1113
TRIMTEX CO. INC., pg. 1113
TRINA, INC., pg. 1113
TRINIDAD BEAN & ELEVATOR CO.—See Trinidad/Benham Corporation, pg. 1114
TRINIDAD/BENHAM CORPORATION, pg. 1113
TRINKLE SALES, INC., pg. 1114
TRIO PRODUCTS INC., pg. 1114
TRIPLE A SPECIALTY COMPANY, pg. 1114
TRIPLE F, INC., pg. 1114
TRIPLE F LIMOUSIN CATTLE—See V.F. Energies, Inc., pg. 1141
TRIPLE F LIMOUSIN CATTLE—See V.F. Energies, Inc., pg. 1141
TRIPLE S PLASTICS, INC.—See Triple S Technologies, Inc., pg. 1114
TRIPLE S TECHNOLOGIES, INC., pg. 1114
TRIPLETT ELECTRICAL INSTRUMENT CORPORATION, pg. 1114
TRISTATE ELECTRICAL SUPPLY CO., INC., pg. 1114
TRITON INC., pg. 1114
TRITON INDUSTRIES, INC., pg. 1114
TRIUMPH*LOR, INC., pg. 1115
TRIUMPH-LOR, INC.—See Triumph*Lor, Inc., pg. 1115
TRIUMPH-LOR, INC.—See Triumph*Lor, Inc., pg. 1115
TRIUMPH-LOR, INC.—See Triumph*Lor, Inc., pg. 1115
TRIUMPH-LOR, INC.—See Triumph*Lor, Inc., pg. 1115
TRIUMPH-LOR, INC.—See Triumph*Lor, Inc., pg. 1115
TRIUMPH-LOR, INC.—See Triumph*Lor, Inc., pg. 1115
TRIUMPH/LOR OILFIELD SERVICES LTD.—See Triumph*Lor, Inc., pg. 1115
TRIUMPH MACHINE CO.—See Alamo Group, Inc., pg. 29
TRIUMPH PET INDUSTRIES, INC., pg. 1115
TRIUMPH TWIST DRILL CO.—See Precision Twist Drill Co., pg. 885
TRIZEC PROPERTIES, INC., pg. 1115
TROJAN SPECIALIZED LIVESTOCK EQUIP.—See Ritchie Industries, Inc., pg. 936
TROJAN STEEL CO., pg. 1115
TRONCALLI MOTORS, INC., pg. 1115
TRONE ADVERTISING, INC., pg. 1115
TROPAR MFG. CO., INC., pg. 1115
TROPIC ISLE—See Agway, Inc., pg. 26
TROPICAL GARMENT MANUFACTURING COMPANY, pg. 1116
TROPITONE FURNITURE CO. INC., pg. 1116
ALBERT TROSTEL PACKINGS, LTD., pg. 1116
ALBERT TROSTEL PACKINGS LTD.—See Albert Trostel & Sons Company, pg. 1116
ALBERT TROSTEL & SONS COMPANY, pg. 1116
TROUT INC., pg. 1116
TROY CORPORATION, pg. 1116
TROY MILLS, INC., pg. 1116
TROY SAVINGS BANK—See The Troy Savings Bank, pg. 1117
TROY SAVINGS BANK-CLIFTON PARK—See The Troy Savings Bank, pg. 1117
TROY SAVINGS BANK-EAST GREENBUSH—See The Troy Savings Bank, pg. 1117
TROY SAVINGS BANK-GLENS FALLS—See The Troy Savings Bank, pg. 1117
TROY SAVINGS BANK-HUDSON VALLEY PLAZA—See The Troy Savings Bank, pg. 1117
TROY SAVINGS BANK-LATHAM—See The Troy Savings Bank, pg. 1117
TROY SAVINGS BANK-SCHENECTADY—See The Troy Savings Bank, pg. 1117
THE TROY SAVINGS BANK, pg. 1116
TROY SAVINGS BANK-WHITEHALL—See The Troy Savings Bank, pg. 1117
TROY SB REAL ESTATE CO., INC.—See The Troy Savings Bank, pg. 1117
TROY/TRAK LIGHTING, INC.—See Jac Jacobsen Industries, Inc., pg. 588
TRU-FIT GLOVE & HEADWEAR DIV.—See Heyman Corporation, pg. 532
TRU-FIT PRODUCTS CORP., pg. 1117
TRU-TEST MFG. CO.—See Cotter & Company, pg. 288
TRU-WELD GRATING, INC., pg. 1117
TRUCCHIS MARKETS, pg. 1117
TRUCK WORLD INC., pg. 1117
TRUE COMPANIES, pg. 1117
TRUE DRILLING CO.—See True Companies, pg. 1117
TRUE OIL CO.—See True Companies, pg. 1117
TRUE RANCHES—See True Companies, pg. 1117
TRUMBULL CORPORATION, pg. 1117
TRUMBULL INVESTMENTS, INC.—See Trumbull Corporation, pg. 1117
THE TRUMP GROUP, pg. 1117
TRUMP ORGANIZATION, pg. 1118
TRUMP PLAZA OF THE PALM BEACHES—See Trump Organization, pg. 1118
TRUMP TOWERS—See Trump Organization, pg. 1118
TRUMPF INC., pg. 1118
TRUMP'S CASTLE CASINO RESORT—See Trump Organization, pg. 1118

TRUNK & ASSOCIATES, INC., pg. 1118
TRUSTCORP.—See D.A. Davidson & Co., pg. 318
TUBE TURNS DE MEXICO, S.A.—See Sunbeam-Oster Company, Inc., pg. 1059
TUBETEC—See Plymouth Tube Company, pg. 878
TUBULAR SERVICES, INC.—See Pasotex Corporation, pg. 851
TUBULAR STEEL INC., pg. 1118
TUCCI BENUCCH—See Lettuce Entertain You Enterprises, Inc., pg. 669
TUCCI MILAN—See Lettuce Entertain You Enterprises, Inc., pg. 669
TUCHETTI—See Lettuce Entertain You Enterprises, Inc., pg. 669
THE TUCKER GROUP—See Avrett, Free & Ginsberg, Inc., pg. 103
TUCKER ROCKY DISTRIBUTING, pg. 1118
TUCKER WAYNE/LUCKIE & COMPANY, pg. 1118
TUCKERMAN OPTICAL CO., pg. 1118
TUCKER-ROCKY DISTRIBUTING—See LDI, Ltd., pg. 647
TUCSON REALTY & TRUST CO., pg. 1118
TUDOR INC., pg. 1118
TUFFY ASSOCIATES CORP., pg. 1119
OY TULENKESTAVAAT TILIET, A.B.—See Belmont Industries, Inc., pg. 137
TULIP CORPORATION, pg. 1119
TULLEY BUICK-PONTIAC COMPANY, INC., pg. 1119
TULSA GAUGE & INSTRUMENT CO.—See Harley Industries, Inc., pg. 510
TUNMORE OLDSMOBILE INC., pg. 1119
TUPMAN THURLOW CO. INC., pg. 1119
TURBO REFRIGERATING—See Henry Vogt Machine Co., pg. 1154
TURNBULL ENTERPRISES, INC., pg. 1119
TURNER DAIRIES, INC., pg. 1119
TURNER, DAY & WOOLWORTH HANDLE CORP.—See O.P. Link Handle Company, pg. 677
TURNER MACHINE COMPANY—See Electric Furnace Co., pg. 373
THE TURNER & SEYMOUR MFG. COMPANY, pg. 1119
TURNER SUBSCRIPTION AGENCY—See The Faxon Company, Inc., pg. 404
TURNER SUPPLY COMPANY, pg. 1119
TURTLE & HUGHES, INC., pg. 1119
TURTLE WAX, INC., pg. 1120
TURTLE WAX MANUFACTURING LTD.—See Turtle Wax, Inc., pg. 1120
TURTLEDOVE CLEMENS, INC., pg. 1120
TUSCARORA YARNS INC., pg. 1120
TUTHILL CORPORATION, pg. 1120
TUTHILL PUMP—See Tuthill Corporation, pg. 1120
TUTHILL PUMP COMPANY OF CALIFORNIA—See Tuthill Corporation, pg. 1120
TUTOR-SALIBA CORPORATION, pg. 1120
R.C. TWAY COAL COMPANY, pg. 1120
TWEDDLE LITHO COMPANY, pg. 1120
TWENTIETH CENTURY COMPANIES, pg. 1121
TWENTIETH CENTURY INVESTORS, INC.—See Twentieth Century Companies, pg. 1121
TWENTIETH CENTURY SERVICES—See Twentieth Century Companies, pg. 1121
25 CORPORATION—See Lincoln Industries, pg. 676
THE "21" CLUB, INC.—See 21 International Holdings, Inc., pg. 1121
21 INTERNATIONAL HOLDINGS, INC., pg. 1121
TWIN CITY DIE CASTINGS CO., pg. 1121
TWIN CITY FOODS, INC., pg. 1122
TWIN COUNTY GROCERS, INC., pg. 1122
TWIN PALMS CARE CENTER—See Meritcare, Inc., pg. 740
TWIN Y CORPORATION—See Jeld-Wen, Inc., pg. 592
TWINCO SERVICES, INC.—See Twin County Grocers, Inc., pg. 1122
TWINCO TRUCKING CO., INC.—See Twin County Grocers, Inc., pg. 1122
TWINCRAFT, INC., pg. 1122
TYLAN GENERAL, INC., pg. 1122
TYLAN GMBH—See Tylan General, Inc., pg. 1122
TYLAN SARL—See Tylan General, Inc., pg. 1122
TYLAN (UK) LTD.—See Tylan General, Inc., pg. 1122
TYLER ELEVATOR PRODUCTS, INC., pg. 1122
TYLER LIMITED PARTNERSHIP, pg. 1122
TYLUS SDN BHD—See Panduit Company, pg. 846
TYNDALE HOUSE PUBLISHERS, INC., pg. 1122
TYPE FILMS OF CHICAGO CO.—See Castcraft Industries, Inc., pg. 228
TYPE FOUNDERS OF CHICAGO—See Castcraft Industries, Inc., pg. 228

U

U. A. HEALTH CARE CORPORATION—See OmniCare Health Plan, pg. 826
U-HAUL INTERNATIONAL, INC.—See Amerco, A Nevada Corporation, pg. 48
U-HAUL REAL ESTATE COMPANY—See Amerco, A Nevada Corporation, pg. 48
U-HAUL SALES & LEASING COMPANY—See Amerco, A Nevada Corporation, pg. 48
U PUMP 'EM—See Victory Markets Inc., pg. 1150
UC INDUSTRIES, INC., pg. 1122
UDT SENSORS, INC., pg. 1122
UES, INC., pg. 1122
UFE CAL TEC INC.—See UFE Incorporated, pg. 1123
UFE INCORPORATED, pg. 1123
UFE PTE LTD—See UFE Incorporated, pg. 1123
UFL FOODS, INC.—See Newly Weds Foods Inc., pg. 804
UIS EXPORT CORPORATION—See UIS, Inc., pg. 1123
UIS, INC., pg. 1123
ULLICO INC., pg. 1124
UMI DATA COURIER—See Bell & Howell Company, pg. 135
UNI-SERVICE OPERATIONS CORPORATION—See Utica Mutual Insurance Company, pg. 1141
UPS/ALIMONDO—See United Parcel Service of America, Inc., pg. 1133
U.R.M. DEVELOPMENT CORP.—See U.R.M. Stores, Inc., pg. 1124
U.R.M. STORES, INC., pg. 1124
U.S. RING BINDER CORP.—See Lane Industries, Inc., pg. 657
U.S. SLATE & MARBLE CO.—See Triangle Pacific Corporation, pg. 1112
U.S. TRANSPARTS—See Moran Industries, Inc., pg. 769
USA-GLAS, INC.—See Globe Glass & Mirror Co., pg. 464
USA NETWORK CONTROL CENTER—See USA Network, pg. 1124
USA PETROLEUM CORPORATION, pg. 1124
USAA BUYING SERVICE—See United Services Automobile Association (USAA), pg. 1134
USAA FEDERAL SAVINGS BANK—See United Services Automobile Association (USAA), pg. 1134
USAA INVESTMENT MANAGEMENT CO.—See United Services Automobile Association (USAA), pg. 1134
USAA LIFE INSURANCE CO.—See United Services Automobile Association (USAA), pg. 1134
USAA SATELLITE COMMUNICATIONS—See United Services Automobile Association (USAA), pg. 1134
USAA TRAVEL AGENCIES—See United Services Automobile Association (USAA), pg. 1134
USA NETWORK, pg. 1124
UTP (UNITED TECHNICAL PUBLICATIONS) DIVISION—See The Hearst Corporation, pg. 522
UVP, INC., pg. 1124
KEITH UDDENBERG, INC., pg. 1125
UFORMA SHELBY BUSINESS FORMS—See Miami Systems Corporation, pg. 746
UGLY DUCKLING RENT-A-CAR, pg. 1125
GEORGE UHE CO., INC., pg. 1125
THE UHLMANN CO., pg. 1125
ULBRICH STAINLESS STEELS & SPECIAL METALS, INC., pg. 1125
ULBRICH WIRE, INC.—See Ulbrich Stainless Steels & Special Metals, Inc., pg. 1125
ULLENBERG CORP., pg. 1125
ULTIMO LTD., pg. 1125
ULTRA DRUG—See Eon Labs, Inc., pg. 384
ULTRA INDUSTRIES, INC.—See Macklanburg-Duncan Co., pg. 697
ULTRA TOOL & PLASTICS, INC., pg. 1125
UN GRAND CAFE'—See Lettuce Entertain You Enterprises, Inc., pg. 669
UNCAS MANUFACTURING COMPANY, pg. 1125
UNCLE BEN'S, INC.—See Mars, Incorporated, pg. 713
UNDERGROUND CONSTRUCTION COMPANY, INC., pg. 1125
UNDERWRITERS NATIONAL ASSURANCE CO.—See The Chesapeake Life Insurance Co., pg. 243
UNDERWRITERS SERVICE AGENCY, INC.—See Integrated Resources, Inc., pg. 573
UNDERWRITERS SERVICE AGENCY, INC.—See Integrated Resources, Inc., pg. 573
UNECO INVESTOR SERVICES INC.—See Farmland Industries, Inc., pg. 402
UNEX CONVEYING SYSTEMS, INC., pg. 1126
UNGER COMPANY, pg. 1126
UNIBILT—See Jervis B. Webb Company, pg. 1170
UNIBIT CORP.—See American Tool Companies, Inc., pg. 64
UNICOVER CORPORATION, pg. 1126
UNIFAX, INC., pg. 1126
UNIFLEX, INC., pg. 1126
UNIFLOW MANUFACTURING CO., pg. 1126
UNIFOIL CORPORATION, pg. 1126
UNIGARD INDEMNITY CO.—See John Hancock Mutual Life Insurance Company, pg. 596
UNIGARD INSURANCE CO.—See John Hancock Mutual Life Insurance Company, pg. 596
UNIGARD SECURITY INSURANCE CO.—See John Hancock Mutual Life Insurance Company, pg. 596
UNIGARD SERVICE CORP.—See John Hancock Mutual Life Insurance Company, pg. 596
UNIGROUP, INC., pg. 1126
UNIHEALTH AMERICA, pg. 1126
UNIKOR CHEMICAL, INC.—See Uniroyal Chemical Company, Inc., pg. 1130
THE UNIMAX CORPORATION, pg. 1127
UNIMAX HOLDING CORP.—See Shepaug Corporation, pg. 998
THE UNION OF ARKANSAS CORP., pg. 1127
UNION BOILER CO.—See Concorp, Inc., pg. 273
THE UNION CENTRAL LIFE INSURANCE CO., pg. 1127
UNION CITY BODY COMPANY, INC., pg. 1128
UNION DRAWN STEEL CO., LTD.—See Nelsen Steel & Wire Co., pg. 797
UNION EQUITY—See Farmland Industries, Inc., pg. 402
UNION FORGING CO.—See UIS, Inc., pg. 1123
THE UNION FORK & HOE CO., pg. 1128
UNION HOLDINGS, INC., pg. 1128
UNION INDUSTRIES, INC., pg. 1128
THE UNION LABOR LIFE INSURANCE CO.—See ULLICO Inc., pg. 1124
UNION NATIONAL BANK OF ARKANSAS—See The Union of Arkansas Corp., pg. 1127
UNION NATIONAL BANK OF AUSTIN—See The Union of Arkansas Corp., pg. 1127
UNION NATIONAL BANK OF OKLAHOMA—See The Union of Arkansas Corp., pg. 1127
UNION PAPER CO.—See Union Industries, Inc., pg. 1128
UNION PEN COMPANY, pg. 1128
UNION PUMP (CANADA) LTD.—See Union Pump Company, pg. 1129
UNION PUMP COMPANY, pg. 1128
UNION QUARRIES, INC.—See Ash Grove Cement Company, pg. 88
UNION SEED CO.—See Land O'Lakes, Inc., pg. 654
UNION STEEL PRODUCTS, INCORPORATED, pg. 1129
UNION SWITCH & SIGNAL INC., pg. 1129
UNION TANK CAR COMPANY—See The Marmon Group, Inc., pg. 712
UNION-TRIBUNE PUBLISHING COMPANY—See The Copley Press, Inc., pg. 284
UNION UNDERWEAR CO., INC.—See Farley Industries, pg. 400
UNIONBAY DIVISION—See Seattle Pacific Industries, Inc., pg. 986
UNIPAS, INC.—See Taco Inc., pg. 1076
UNIPHASE CORPORATION, pg. 1129
UNIROYAL CHEMICAL CO., INC. (LEFFINGWELL)—See Uniroyal Chemical Company, Inc., pg. 1129
UNIROYAL CHEMICAL CO., INC. (SINGAPORE)—See Uniroyal Chemical Company, Inc., pg. 1129
UNIROYAL CHEMICAL COMPANY, INC., pg. 1129
UNIROYAL CHEMICAL COMPANY LIMITED—See Uniroyal Chemical Company, Inc., pg. 1129
UNIROYAL CHEMICAL JAPAN—See Uniroyal Chemical Company, Inc., pg. 1129
UNIROYAL CHEMICAL LTD.—See Uniroyal Chemical Company, Inc., pg. 1129
UNIROYAL CHEMICAL LTD.—See Uniroyal Chemical Company, Inc., pg. 1129
UNIROYAL CHIMICA, S.P.A.—See Uniroyal Chemical Company, Inc., pg. 1129
UNIROYAL QUIMICA, S.A.—See Uniroyal Chemical Company, Inc., pg. 1130
UNISEAL, INC.—See George Koch Sons, Inc., pg. 639
UNISON INDUSTRIES, pg. 1130
UNISON INDUSTRIES—See Unison Industries, pg. 1130
UNISON INSURANCE CO.—See Amerisure Companies, pg. 66
UNISTRUT CORPORATION, pg. 1130
UNISYSTEMS, INC., pg. 1130
UNITARY PRODUCTS GROUP-RESIDENTIAL—See American Standard Inc., pg. 61
UNITECH DIVISION—See The Marmon Group, Inc., pg. 712
UNITED ACQUISITION CORPORATION, pg. 1130
UNITED A G CO-OP, INC., pg. 1130
UNITED AIR SPECIALISTS, INC., pg. 1130
UNITED ALUMINUM CORPORATION, pg. 1130
UNITED AMERICAN HEALTHCARE CORP.—See OmniCare Health Plan, pg. 826
UNITED ARTISTS THEATRE CIRCUIT, INC., pg. 1130
UNITED BROADCASTING INC., pg. 1131
UNITED CAPITAL SERVICES, INC.—See Unigroup, Inc., pg. 1126
UNITED CHEMICAL PRODUCTS—See Mays Chemical Company, pg. 725
UNITED COATINGS, INC., pg. 1131
UNITED COMMUNITY INSURANCE CO.—See Lawrence Group, Inc., pg. 662
THE UNITED COMPANY, pg. 1131
UNITED DAIRY FARMERS, INC., pg. 1131
UNITED DAIRYMEN OF ARIZONA, pg. 1131
UNITED DESIGN, pg. 1131
UNITED ENERGY CORPORATION—See Alabama Electric Cooperative, Inc., pg. 28
UNITED ENGINE & MACHINE COMPANY, pg. 1131
UNITED ENGINES, INC., pg. 1131
UNITED ENVELOPE COMPANY, INC., pg. 1131
UNITED EXPOSITION SERVICE COMPANY—See Topcor Financial Corporation, pg. 1102
UNITED FARM BUREAU FAMILY LIFE INSURANCE CO., pg. 1131
UNITED FARM BUREAU LIFE INSURANCE CO.—See United Farm Bureau Family Life Insurance Co., pg. 1131
UNITED FARM TOOLS, INC., pg. 1131
UNITED FEEDS, INC., pg. 1132
UNITED FILTERS, INC.—See Perry Equipment Corporation, pg. 863
UNITED FINANCIAL RESOURCES—See United A G Co-op, Inc., pg. 1130
UNITED FINANCIAL SERVICES—See Altus Federal Savings Bank, pg. 46
UNITED FOAM PLASTICS CORPORATION, pg. 1132
UNITED FOOD SERVICE DISTRIBUTORS, INC., pg. 1132
UNITED FOODS SERVICE, INC.—See Shamrock Foods Co., pg. 994
UNITED-GENERAL PRODUCTS OF KNOXVILLE, INC.—See Zale Corporation, pg. 1216
UNITED GILSONITE LABORATORIES, pg. 1132
UNITED GRAPHICS, INC., pg. 1132
UNITED GROCERS INC., pg. 1132
UNITED-HAMILTON, INC.—See Zale Corporation, pg. 1216
UNITED HARDWARE DISTRIBUTING CO., pg. 1132
UNITED HEALTH PLAN, pg. 1133
UNITED JEWELERS & DISTRIBUTORS OF ARIZONA, INC.—See Zale Corporation, pg. 1216
UNITED JEWELERS & DISTRIBUTORS OF ARKANSAS, INC.—See Zale Corporation, pg. 1216
UNITED JEWELERS & DISTRIBUTORS OF LOUISIANA, INC.—See Zale Corporation, pg. 1216
UNITED JEWELERS & DISTRIBUTORS OF TEXAS, INC.—See Zale Corporation, pg. 1216
UNITED LABORATORIES, INC., pg. 1133
UNITED LEASING, INC.—See Unigroup, Inc., pg. 1126
UNITED MAILING, INC.—See The Instant Web Companies, pg. 571
UNITED MCGILL CORP., pg. 1133
UNITED METAL FABRICATORS, INC., pg. 1133
UNITED PARCEL SERVICE OF AMERICA, INC., pg. 1133
UNITED PARCEL SERVICE OF CANADA—See United Parcel Service of America, Inc., pg. 1133
UNITED PARKING, INC., pg. 1134
UNITED PIECE DYE WORKS, LP, pg. 1134
UNITED PLANNERS' GROUP, INC.—See Pacific Mutual Life Insurance Company, pg. 841
UNITED POWER ASSOCIATION, pg. 1134
UNITED PRODUCERS & CONSUMERS CO-OP, pg. 1134

V

VELOBIND, INC.—See Lane Industries, Inc., pg. 657
VELOBIND, INC.—See Lane Industries, Inc., pg. 657
VELOBIND, INC.—See Lane Industries, Inc., pg. 657
VELOBIND-RENO DIVISION—See Lane Industries, Inc., pg. 657
VELSICOL AUSTRALIA LIMITED—See Velsicol Chemical Corporation, pg. 1147
VELSICOL CHEMICAL CORPORATION, pg. 1147
VELSICOL CHEMICAL LIMITED—See Velsicol Chemical Corporation, pg. 1147
VELSICOL OVERSEAS CORPORATION—See Velsicol Chemical Corporation, pg. 1147
VENCHURS PACKAGING, INC., pg. 1147
VENEMAN—See Tropitone Furniture Co. Inc., pg. 1116
THE VENET COMPANIES, INC., pg. 1147
VENGROFF WILLIAMS & ASSOCIATES, INC., pg. 1147
VENGROFF WILLIAMS REALTY MANAGEMENT—See Vengroff Williams & Associates, Inc., pg. 1147
VENICE MAID CO., INC.—See Connelly Containers, Inc., pg. 275
VENTA INC., pg. 1147
VENTILATING SYSTEMS MANAGEMENT—See Savoy Construction Co. Inc., pg. 973
VENTRE PACKING COMPANY, INC., pg. 1147
VENTURA ASSOCIATES, INC., pg. 1147
VENTURA COASTAL CORPORATION, pg. 1147
VENTURA TRAVELWARE, INC., pg. 1147
VENTURA TRAVELWARE, INC.-INTERNATIONAL DIV.—See Ventura Travelware, Inc., pg. 1148
VENTUREDYNE, LTD., pg. 1148
VERDUGO RESTAURANT CORP.—See Specialty Restaurants Corporation, pg. 1028
VERMEER MANUFACTURING COMPANY, pg. 1148
VERMONT LIFE INSURANCE COMPANY—See National Life Insurance Company, pg. 791
VERMONT LOTTERY COMMISSION, pg. 1148
VERMONT TAP & DIE CO.—See Harbour Group Ltd., pg. 507
VERMONT USA MACHINE TOOL GROUP—See Goldman Financial Group, pg. 468
VERNAY LABORATORIES, INC., pg. 1148
VERNELL'S CANDY COMPANY, pg. 1148
THE VERNON COMPANY, pg. 1148
VERNON SASSOS MCGILL, INC., pg. 1148
VERSA SERVICES LTD.—See ARA Group, pg. 7
VERSABEC INC.—See ARA Group, pg. 7
VERSATECH ENGINEERING—See Mason Company, pg. 718
VERTIPILE—See Claremont Flock Corporation, pg. 251
VERYFINE PRODUCTS, INC., pg. 1148
VESCO OIL CORP., pg. 1149
VESS BEVERAGES, INC., pg. 1149
VESTAL MANUFACTURING—See Walter Industries, Inc., pg. 1162
VIACOM BROADCASTING INC.—See National Amusements, Inc., pg. 785
VIACOM CABLE—See National Amusements, Inc., pg. 785
VIACOM CANADA LTD.—See National Amusements, Inc., pg. 785
VIACOM ENTERPRISES—See National Amusements, Inc., pg. 785
VIACOM ENTERPRISES CANADA LTD.—See National Amusements, Inc., pg. 785
VIACOM INC.—See National Amusements, Inc., pg. 785
VIACOM INTERNATIONAL INC.—See National Amusements, Inc., pg. 785
VIACOM INTL. LTD.—See National Amusements, Inc., pg. 785
VIACOM INTL. PTY. LTD.—See National Amusements, Inc., pg. 786
VIACOM JAPAN, INC.—See National Amusements, Inc., pg. 786
VIACOM NETWORKS INC.—See National Amusements, Inc., pg. 785
VIACOM S.A.—See National Amusements, Inc., pg. 786
VIACOM SATELLITE NETWORKS INC.—See National Amusements, Inc., pg. 785
VIACOM VIDEO-AUDIO COMUNICACOES, LTDA.—See National Amusements, Inc., pg. 786
VIBRA SCREW INC., pg. 1149
VIBRAX/MCA INC.—See Normark Corporation, pg. 810
VIC MANUFACTURING, pg. 1149
VICTAULIC COMPANY OF AMERICA, pg. 1149
VICTAULIC COMPANY OF CANADA LIMITED—See Victaulic Company of America, pg. 1149
VICTAULIC INTERNATIONAL—See Victaulic Company of America, pg. 1149
VICTAULIC TOOL COMPANY—See Victaulic Company of America, pg. 1149
VICTOR CORPORATION, pg. 1149
VICTORIA—See The Hearst Corporation, pg. 523
VICTORIA PACKING CORPORATION, pg. 1149
VICTORIA STATION OF ARIZONA, INC.—See Victoria Station Incorporated, pg. 1150
VICTORIA STATION OF ATLANTA, INC.—See Victoria Station Incorporated, pg. 1150
VICTORIA STATION OF COLORADO, INC.—See Victoria Station Incorporated, pg. 1150
VICTORIA STATION INCORPORATED, pg. 1149
VICTORIA STATION INCORPORATED, A CALIFORNIA CORP.—See Victoria Station Incorporated, pg. 1150
VICTORIA STATION OF LOUISIANA, INC.—See Victoria Station Incorporated, pg. 1150
VICTORIA STATION OF TEXAS, INC.—See Victoria Station Incorporated, pg. 1150
VICTORIA STATION OF VIRGINIA, INC.—See Victoria Station Incorporated, pg. 1150
VICTORIA STATION OF WASHINGTON, INC.—See Victoria Station Incorporated, pg. 1150
VICTORIA STATION OF WISCONSIN, INC.—See Victoria Station Incorporated, pg. 1150
VICTORY DISCOUNT BEVERAGE CENTER—See Victory Markets Inc., pg. 1150
VICTORY ENVELOPE, INC.—See The Instant Web Companies, pg. 571
VICTORY FINANCIAL GROUP, INC., pg. 1150
VICTORY GAMES, INC.—See Monarch Avalon, Inc., pg. 765
VICTORY LIFE INSURANCE COMPANY—See Victory Financial Group, Inc., pg. 1150
VICTORY MARKETS INC., pg. 1150
VICTORY VIDEO INC.—See Victory Markets Inc., pg. 1150
VID AMERICA, INC.—See Andrews Group, Incorporated, pg. 74
VIDEO AIR EXPRESS—See City Postal, Inc., pg. 251
VIDEO PRODUCTS DISTRIBUTORS, INC., pg. 1150
VIDEO SERVICE COMPANY—See Cox Enterprises, Inc., pg. 294
VIDICOM, L.D. BEVAN COMPANY, INC., pg. 1151
VIENNA BEEF, LTD.—See Vienna Sausage Mfg. Co., pg. 1151
VIENNA BISCUIT CO.—See Hubbs Importing Corp., pg. 550
VIENNA SAUSAGE MFG. CO., pg. 1151
THE VIERA COMPANY—See A. Duda & Sons Inc., pg. 351
VIGORENA FEEDS, INC.—See Hubbard Milling Company, pg. 550
VIKING COLOR CORPORATION—See Viking Graphics, pg. 1151
VIKING GRAPHICS, pg. 1151
VIKING RANGE CORP., pg. 1151
VIKING YACHT CO., pg. 1151
VILE-GOLLER, FINE ART PRINTING & LITHOGRAPHY, pg. 1151
VILLA SOUTH INC.—See Thiele Kaolin Co., pg. 1092
VILLAGE CAR COMPANY, pg. 1151
VILLAGE FORD INC., pg. 1151
VILLAGE MARKETS—See Victory Markets Inc., pg. 1150
VILLARD BOOKS—See Advance Publications Inc., pg. 19
VILLAUME INDUSTRIES, INC., pg. 1151
VILLAZON COMPANY INC., pg. 1152
VILTER EXPORT CORP.—See Vilter Manufacturing Corporation, pg. 1152
VILTER MANUFACTURING CORPORATION, pg. 1152
VINCENNES STEEL CORP., pg. 1152
VINCENT FOOD INDUSTRIES, INC., pg. 1152
VINDICATOR CORPORATION, pg. 1152
VINSON SUPPLY CO.—See Sammons Enterprises, Inc., pg. 968
VINTNERS INTERNATIONAL COMPANY, INC., pg. 1152
VINYL THERM, INC., pg. 1152
HARRY VIOLA ADVERTISING, pg. 1152
VIRGINIA APPAREL MANUFACTURING CO., INC.—See Star Children's Dress Company, Inc., pg. 1039
VIRGINIA DEPARTMENT OF ECONOMIC DEVELOPMENT TOURISM DEVELOPMENT GROUP, pg. 1152
VIRGINIA HOT SPRINGS, INC., pg. 1152
VIRGINIA METAL INDUSTRIES, INC., pg. 1152
VIRGINIA STATE LOTTERY DEPARTMENT, pg. 1153
THE VIRGINIAN-PILOT AND THE LEDGER STAR—See Landmark Communications, Inc., pg. 656
THE VIRTUAL GROUP, pg. 1153
VISA U.S.A. INC., pg. 1153
VISALIA ELECTRIC RAILROAD CO.—See Anschutz Corporation, pg. 76
VISALIA OAKS BASEBALL CLUB—See Minnesota Twins Baseball Club, pg. 758
VISCOM ENTERPRISES—See Full Circle Media Corp., pg. 436
VISIBLE CHANGES, pg. 1153
VISIBLE CHANGES OF AUSTIN—See Visible Changes, pg. 1153
VISIBLE CHANGES OF TEXAS—See Visible Changes, pg. 1153
VISIRECORD SYSTEMS, INC., pg. 1153
VISKASE—See Envirodyne Industries, Inc., pg. 383
VISKASE CANADA INC.—See Envirodyne Industries, Inc., pg. 383
VISKASE CORPORATION—See Envirodyne Industries, Inc., pg. 383
VISTA MULTI METHOD—See Berlitz International, Inc., pg. 143
VISTA MULTI NATIONAL—See Berlitz International, Inc., pg. 143
VISUAL TECHNOLOGIES—See Ruder, Finn, Inc., pg. 954
VITA FOOD PRODUCTS, INC., pg. 1153
VITA-MILK DAIRY, INC., pg. 1153
VITAFREZE FROZEN CONFECTIONS—See Crystal Cream & Butter Company, pg. 303
VITARINE PHARMACEUTICALS, INC.—See Eon Labs, Inc., pg. 383
VITARINE PHARMACEUTICALS OF THE VIRGIN ISLANDS INC.—See Eon Labs, Inc., pg. 384
VITATECH INTERNATIONAL, INC., pg. 1153
C.J. VITNER & CO., INC., pg. 1153
VITRUVIO/LEO BURNETT—See Leo Burnett Company, Inc., pg. 193
VITT MEDIA INTERNATIONAL, INC., pg. 1153
VITT MEDIA INTERNATIONAL, INC. - LOS ANGELES—See Vitt Media International, Inc., pg. 1154
VITT/REYNOLDS MEDIA INTERNATIONAL LIMITED—See Vitt Media International, Inc., pg. 1154
VITUS ELECTRICAL SUPPLY COMPANY, pg. 1154
VITUVIO/LEO BURNETT—See Leo Burnett Company, Inc., pg. 193
VIVIAN MILLWORKS, pg. 1154
THE VOGEL COMMUNICATIONS GROUP, pg. 1154
VOGLER MOTOR COMPANY, INC., pg. 1154
HENRY VOGT MACHINE CO., pg. 1154
VOGUE & BODY SHOPS, INC., pg. 1154
VOGUE MAGAZINE—See Advance Publications Inc., pg. 19
VOIT CORP., pg. 1154
VOIT SPORTS, INC., pg. 1154
THE JOHN VOLK COMPANY, pg. 1154
THE VOLLRATH COMPANY INC., pg. 1154
VOLLRATH REFRIGERATION INC.—See The Vollrath Company Inc., pg. 1155
VOLTEC—See Sauer Industries, Inc., pg. 972
VOLUNTEER FABRICATORS, INC.—See The H. T. Hackney Co., pg. 498
VOLVO SALES & SERVICE CENTER, pg. 1155
G. VON HAMM TEXTILES, INC., pg. 1155
VON HOUSEN AUTO PARTS—See Von Housen Motors, pg. 1155
VON HOUSEN MOTORS, pg. 1155
VOORHEESVILLE VENTURES, INC.—See Rotterdam Ventures Inc., pg. 952
VORTEC CORPORATION—See Chicago West Pullman Corporation, pg. 246
VOSS INDUSTRIES, INC., pg. 1155
VOTAW PRECISION TECHNOLOGIES—See Kaiser Aerospace & Electronics Corp., pg. 614
VOUGHT AIRCRAFT CO.—See Carlyle Holding Corporation, pg. 222
VOYAGER EMBLEMS, INC., pg. 1155
VULCAN ASPHALT REFINING COMPANY—See United Acquisition Corporation, pg. 1130
VULCAN - ECLIPSE—See Eclipse, Inc., pg. 367
VULCAN IRON WORKS, INC., pg. 1155

W

W-B SUPPLY CO., pg. 1155
W&F MANUFACTURING CORPORATION, INC., pg. 1155
W-P MILLING CO., INC.—See Altair Corporation, pg. 45
WALA-TV—See Burnham Broadcasting Company, pg. 194
WARM BROADCASTING CO.—See Susquehanna Pfaltzgraff, pg. 1065
WBAL-AM—See The Hearst Corporation, pg. 522
WBAL DIVISION—See The Hearst Corporation, pg. 522
WBAL-TV—See The Hearst Corporation, pg. 522
WBBB—See Curtis Media Group Inc., pg. 306
THE WBDC GROUP, pg. 1155
WBH INDUSTRIES, INC., pg. 1155
W.C. COMMODITIES—See West Central Co-op, pg. 1177
WCKG, INC.—See Cox Enterprises, Inc., pg. 292
WCPS—See Curtis Media Group Inc., pg. 306
WCTU RAILWAY COMPANY—See The Marmon Group, Inc., pg. 712
WCVB DIVISION—See The Hearst Corporation, pg. 522
WCVB-TV—See The Hearst Corporation, pg. 522
WDIO-TV—See Hubbard Broadcasting, Inc., pg. 549
WDP, INC., pg. 1156
WDTN-TV—See The Hearst Corporation, pg. 522
WDTN DIV.—See The Hearst Corporation, pg. 522
WEN PRODUCTS, INC., pg. 1156
WEWO—See Curtis Media Group Inc., pg. 306
W F I, INC., pg. 1156
WFTV, INC.—See Cox Enterprises, Inc., pg. 292
WGBR—See Curtis Media Group Inc., pg. 306
WGGB-TV—See Guy Gannett Publishing Company, pg. 442
WGM/HYDRO, pg. 1156
WGME-TV—See Guy Gannett Publishing Company, pg. 442
WGM SAFETY CORPORATION, pg. 1156
WHIO, INC.—See Cox Enterprises, Inc., pg. 292
WHLT—See News-Press & Gazette Company, pg. 804
WHTX-FM—See The Hearst Corporation, pg. 522
WIBW-TV AM & FM—See Stauffer Communications, Inc., pg. 1043
WICO CORPORATION, pg. 1156
WIFC-FM—See Journal Communications Inc., pg. 608
WIOD, INC.—See Cox Enterprises, Inc., pg. 292
WISN-AM—See The Hearst Corporation, pg. 522
WISN DIVISION—See The Hearst Corporation, pg. 522
WISN-TV—See The Hearst Corporation, pg. 522
WIYY-FM—See The Hearst Corporation, pg. 522
WJCS-TV—See Guy Gannett Publishing Company, pg. 442
WJLA-TV—See Perpetual Corporation, pg. 862
WJPC RADIO STATION—See Johnson Publishing Company, Inc., pg. 599
WJTV—See News-Press & Gazette Company, pg. 804
WKBD, INC.—See Cox Enterprises, Inc., pg. 292
WKTC—See Curtis Media Group Inc., pg. 306
WLNR RADIO STATION—See Johnson Publishing Company, Inc., pg. 599
WLOU RADIO STATION—See Johnson Publishing Company, Inc., pg. 599
WLTQ-FM—See The Hearst Corporation, pg. 522
WLTY-FM—See Landmark Communications, Inc., pg. 655
WLUC, INC.—See Gillett Holdings, Inc., pg. 459
WLUK-TV—See Burnham Broadcasting Company, pg. 194
WM FINANCIAL, INC.—See Washington Mutual Savings Bank, pg. 1166
WM LIFE INSURANCE COMPANY—See Washington Mutual Savings Bank, pg. 1166
WM TRUST COMPANY—See Washington Mutual Savings Bank, pg. 1166
WMXF AM/FM—See Curtis Media Group Inc., pg. 306
WPCM—See Curtis Media Group Inc., pg. 306
WPRI-TV—See Narragansett Capital Inc., pg. 783
WPTF—See Curtis Media Group Inc., pg. 306
WPXI INC., D/B/A WPXI-TV—See Cox Enterprises, Inc., pg. 292
WQDR—See Curtis Media Group Inc., pg. 306
WRAL-TV—See Capitol Broadcasting Co., Inc., pg. 215
WRM, INC., pg. 1156
W S HOLDING COMPANY, pg. 1156
WS PUBLISHING COMPANY, INC.—See International Data Group, pg. 577
WSAU-AM—See Journal Communications Inc., pg. 608
WSB, INC.—See Cox Enterprises, Inc., pg. 292
WSB, INC. D/B/A KLRX (FM)—See Cox Enterprises, Inc., pg. 292
WSBA AM/FM—See Susquehanna Pfaltzgraff, pg. 1065
WSF INDUSTRIES, INC., pg. 1156
WSOC RADIO, INC.—See Cox Enterprises, Inc., pg. 293
WSOC TELEVISION, INC.—See Cox Enterprises, Inc., pg. 293

WSYM-TV—See Journal Communications Inc., pg. 608
WTAB—See Curtis Media Group Inc., pg. 306
WTAE-AM—See The Hearst Corporation, pg. 522
WTAE DIVISION—See The Hearst Corporation, pg. 522
WTAE-TV—See The Hearst Corporation, pg. 523
WTAR-AM—See Landmark Communications, Inc., pg. 655
WTKR-TV—See Narragansett Capital Inc., pg. 783
WTMJ, INC.—See Journal Communications Inc., pg. 608
WTOG-TV, INC.—See Hubbard Broadcasting, Inc., pg. 549
WTTW (CHANNEL 11), pg. 1156
WVUE-TV—See Burnham Broadcasting Company, pg. 194
WW ENGINEERING & SCIENCE INC.—See Summit Environmental Group, pg. 1058
WWF INTERNATIONAL LIMITED—See WWF Paper Corporation, pg. 1157
WWF NATIONAL—See WWF Paper Corporation, pg. 1157
WWF PAPER CORPORATION, pg. 1157
WWF PAPER SALES U.K., LTD.—See WWF Paper Corporation, pg. 1157
WWF/ROYAL PAPER COMPANY—See WWF Paper Corporation, pg. 1157
WWRM, INC.—See Cox Enterprises, Inc., pg. 293
WYNA—See Curtis Media Group Inc., pg. 306
WYO-BEN, INC., pg. 1157
WABASH ALLOYS DIVISION—See Connell Limited Partnership, pg. 275
WABASH FIBRE BOX CO.-CHICAGO PLANT—See Weston Paper & Manufacturing Co., pg. 1183
WABASH FIBRE BOX CO.-FORT WAYNE PLANT—See Weston Paper & Manufacturing Co., pg. 1183
WABASH FIBRE BOX CO.-LEXINGTON PLANT—See Weston Paper & Manufacturing Co., pg. 1183
WABASH FIBRE BOX CO.-SOUTH—See Weston Paper & Manufacturing Co., pg. 1183
WABASH FIBRE BOX CO.-SOUTH—See Weston Paper & Manufacturing Co., pg. 1183
WABASH FIBRE BOX CO.-TERRE HAUTE PLANT—See Weston Paper & Manufacturing Co., pg. 1183
WABASH MAGNETICS—See The Dyson-Kissner-Moran Corporation, pg. 357
WABASH PIONEER CONTAINER CORP.—See Weston Paper & Manufacturing Co., pg. 1183
WABCO FREINAGE DE VEHICULES S.A.—See American Standard Inc., pg. 62
WABCO STANDARD INC.—See American Standard Inc., pg. 62
WABCO WESTINGHOUSE—See American Standard Inc., pg. 62
WABCO WESTINGHOUSE AB—See American Standard Inc., pg. 62
WABCO WESTINGHOUSE B.V.—See American Standard Inc., pg. 62
WABCO WESTINGHOUSE COMPAGNIA FRENI S.P.A.—See American Standard Inc., pg. 62
WABCO WESTINGHOUSE EQUIPEMENTS FERROVIAIRES S.A.—See American Standard Inc., pg. 62
WABCO WESTINGHOUSE FAHRZEUGBREMSEN G.M.B.H.—See American Standard Inc., pg. 62
WABCO WESTINGHOUSE FRENI VEICOLI INDUSTRIALI S.P.A.—See American Standard Inc., pg. 62
WABCO WESTINGHOUSE G.M.B.H.—See American Standard Inc., pg. 62
WACCAMAW CORPORATION—See Georgetown Industries, Inc., pg. 453
WADDELL DIV. OF GHENT MFG. CO.—See Ghent Manufacturing, Inc., pg. 455
TOM WADE CO., pg. 1157
WADE GIN CO.—See Tom Wade Co., pg. 1157
WADE LAND CO.—See Tom Wade Co., pg. 1157
WAFFAI & ASSOCIATES—See International Data Group, pg. 577
WAFFLE HOUSE, INC., pg. 1157
WAGGONER CORP., pg. 1158
E.R. WAGNER MFG. CO. WAGNER PRODS. DIV., pg. 1158
WAGNER MILLS INC., pg. 1158
WAGNER SPRAY TECH CORP., pg. 1158
WAGSTAFF EASTERN—See Wagstaff Inc., pg. 1158
WAGSTAFF INC., pg. 1158
WAHL CLIPPER CORP., pg. 1158
WAHL INSTRUMENTS, pg. 1158
WAIAHOLE IRRIGATION CO., LTD.—See JMB Realty Corporation, pg. 585
WAILUKU AGRIBUSINESS CO., INC.—See C. Brewer & Company, Limited, pg. 175
WAKEFERN FINANCE CO.—See Wakefern Food Corporation, pg. 1158
WAKEFERN FOOD CORPORATION, pg. 1158
WAKELON AGRI-PRODUCTS, INC.—See Fred Webb Inc., pg. 1170
WALBRIDGE ALDINGER COMPANY, pg. 1158
WALCO-LINCK COMPANY, pg. 1159
WALD MOVING AND STORAGE SERVICES, INC.—See Mayflower Transit, Inc., pg. 725
WALDBILLIG & BESTEMAN, INC., pg. 1159
WALDES TRUARC, INC., pg. 1159
D. WALDNER COMPANY, INC., pg. 1159
WALDO BROS. COMPANY, pg. 1159
WALDORF CORPORATION, pg. 1159
WALDRICH COBURG INGERSOLL GMBH INC.—See Ingersoll International Inc., pg. 568
WALDRICH COBURG WERKZEUGMASCHINENFABRIK GMBH—See Ingersoll International Inc., pg. 568
WALDRICH SIEGEN INGERSOLL GMBH INC.—See Ingersoll International Inc., pg. 568
WALDRICH SIEGEN WERKZEUGMASCHINEN GMBH—See Ingersoll International Inc., pg. 568
WALES INDUSTRIES, INC.—See Citrus World Inc., pg. 251
WALK, HAYDEL & ASSOCIATES, INC., pg. 1159
WALK-OVER SHOES—See Geo. E. Keith Company, pg. 620
WALKER & ASSOCIATES, INC., pg. 1159
WALKER & ASSOCIATES, INC., pg. 1159
WALKER DIE CASTING, INC., pg. 1160
WALKER GLEN PROPERTIES, INC.—See Society for Savings Bancorp, Inc., pg. 1016
WALKER MAGNETICS GROUP, INC., pg. 1160
WALKER NATIONAL, INC.—See Walker Magnetics Group, Inc., pg. 1160
O. S. WALKER CO. INC., pg. 1160
WALKER-PIONEER MOSS, pg. 1160
M.S. WALKER, INC./SEACOAST, pg. 1160
WALKER WIRE & STEEL COMPANY, pg. 1160
WALL COLMONOY CORP., pg. 1160
WALLA WALLA GRAIN GROWERS, INC., pg. 1160
WALLA-WALLA UNION BULLETIN—See Seattle Times Company, pg. 986
WALLACE CO. INC., pg. 1160
WALLACE LEISURE PRODUCTS, INC., pg. 1160
WALLACE SILVERSMITHS—See Syratech Corporation, pg. 1070
WALLACE & WALLACE FUEL OIL, pg. 1160
WALLE CORPORATION, pg. 1161
WALLED LAKE DOOR COMPANY, pg. 1161
WALLICH LUMBER CO., pg. 1161
W.W. WALLWORK, INC., pg. 1161
WALMAN OPTICAL COMPANY, pg. 1161
WALNUT CREEK RESTAURANT CORP.—See Specialty Restaurants Corporation, pg. 1028
WALNUT GROVE-NUTRENA FEED DIV., CARGILL, INC.—See Cargill Inc., pg. 219
ED WALPERT & ASSOCIATES, pg. 1161
WALPOLE WOODWORKERS, INC., pg. 1161
WALSER AUTOMOTIVE CORPORATION, pg. 1161
WALSER FORD INC.—See Walser Automotive Corporation, pg. 1161
WALSER LEASING INC.—See Walser Automotive Corporation, pg. 1161
WALSH CONSTRUCTION CO. OF ILLINOIS, pg. 1161
WALSWORTH PUBLISHING COMPANY, INC., pg. 1161
JIM WALTER COMPUTER SERVICES, INC.—See Walter Industries, Inc., pg. 1162
JIM WALTER HOMES, INC.—See Walter Industries, Inc., pg. 1162
J. W. WALTER, INC.—See Walter Industries, Inc., pg. 1162
WALTER INDUSTRIES, INC., pg. 1161
WALTER-JONES CHEVROLET-BUICK-OLDSMOBILE—See Jones Company, Inc., pg. 603
WALTER LAND CO.—See Walter Industries, Inc., pg. 1162
WALTON MONROE MILLS, INC., pg. 1162
WALWORTH COMPANY, pg. 1162
WANG'S INTERNATIONAL, INC., pg. 1162
ASHLEY F. WARD, INC., pg. 1162
WARD LEONARD ELECTRIC COMPANY, INC.—See The Unimax Corporation, pg. 1127
THE WARD MACHINERY COMPANY, pg. 1162
WARD MANUFACTURING, INC., pg. 1163
WARD PRODUCTS CORPORATION, pg. 1163
WARD TRUCKING CORP., pg. 1163
WARDROP MURTAUGH TEMPLE, pg. 1163
WARD'S COMMUNICATIONS, INC.—See K-III Communications Corporation, pg. 611
WARDS COVE PACKING COMPANY, pg. 1163
WAREHOUSE HOME FURNISHINGS DISTRIBUTOR, pg. 1163
WAREHOUSE OUTLET STORES—See Schottenstein Stores Corporation, pg. 978
WAREMART INC., pg. 1163
WAREX PETROLEUM CORPORATION—See Warren Equities Inc., pg. 1165
WARING & LAROSA, INC., pg. 1163
WARM BROTHERS CONSTRUCTION COMPANY, pg. 1163
WARMINGTON HOMES, pg. 1164
WARN INDUSTRIES, INC., pg. 1164
WARNER, BICKING, MORRIS & PARTNERS, INC., pg. 1164
WARNER CANDY COMPANY, INC., pg. 1164
WARNER-ISHI CORPORATION—See Borg-Warner Corporation, pg. 166
WARNER PRESS, INC., pg. 1164
WARNER PRESS PUBLISHERS—See Warner Press, Inc., pg. 1164
WARNER VINEYARDS, pg. 1164
GEORGE E. WARREN CORP., pg. 1164
WARREN DISTRIBUTING CORP., pg. 1164
WARREN DISTRIBUTION, INC., pg. 1164
WARREN DIV.—See Graniteville Co., pg. 477
WARREN EQUITIES INC., pg. 1164
WARREN PROPERTIES, pg. 1165
WARREN TOOL GROUP, pg. 1165
WARREN/KREMER/CMP/ADVERTISING/INC., pg. 1165
WARREN OIL COMPANY—See Warren Equities Inc., pg. 1165
WARREN REFRIGERATOR COMPANY, INC.—See Great American Industries, Inc., pg. 480
WARRENS WALLER PRESS, pg. 1165
WARRICK CONTROLS, INC.—See Armstrong International, Inc., pg. 84
WARWICK BAKER & FIORE INC., pg. 1165
WASCO PRODUCTS, INC., pg. 1165
WASHERS, INC., pg. 1165
WASHINGTON AREA DISTRIBUTION CENTER—See Reliable Stores, Inc., pg. 925
WASHINGTON AVENUE VENTURES, INC.—See Rotterdam Ventures Inc., pg. 952
WASHINGTON BEEF COMPANY, pg. 1165
WASHINGTON CORPORATION, pg. 1165
WASHINGTON CRANES—See Ederer Inc., pg. 368
WASHINGTON HOMES FINANCIAL CORPORATION—See Washington Homes, Inc., pg. 1166
WASHINGTON HOMES, INC., pg. 1166
WASHINGTON HOMES, INC. OF VIRGINIA—See Washington Homes, Inc., pg. 1166
WASHINGTON LANGUAGE CENTER—See Berlitz International, Inc., pg. 143
WASHINGTON MUTUAL FEDERAL SAVINGS BANK—See Washington Mutual Savings Bank, pg. 1166
WASHINGTON MUTUAL LIFE INSURANCE SERVICES—See Washington Mutual Savings Bank, pg. 1166
WASHINGTON MUTUAL SAVINGS BANK, pg. 1166
WASHINGTON NATIONAL LIFE INSURANCE CO. OF NEW YORK—See Columbian Mutual Life Insurance Co., pg. 266
THE WASHINGTON SAVINGS BANK, FSB—See Washington Homes, Inc., pg. 1166
WASHINGTON STATE DAIRY PRODUCTS COMMISSION, pg. 1167
WASHINGTON TERMINAL COMPANY—See Amtrak-National Railroad Passenger Corp., pg. 69
WASSERSTROM COMPANY, pg. 1167
WATER CONTROL INTERNATIONAL INC.—See Sloan Valve Company, pg. 1010
WATERLOO SERVICE COMPANY, pg. 1167
WATEROUS COMPANY—See American Cast Iron Pipe Co., pg. 50
WATERS COAL COMPANY—See Alabama Electric Cooperative, Inc., pg. 28
WATKINS ASSOCIATED DEVELOPERS—See Watkins Associated Industries Inc., pg. 1167
WATKINS ASSOCIATED INDUSTRIES INC., pg. 1167
WATKINS ENGINEERS & CONSTRUCTORS, INC.—See Dillingham Construction Corporation, pg. 338
WATKINS INCORPORATED, pg. 1167
WATKINS SYSTEM INC., pg. 1167
WATLOW AOV, INC.—See Watlow Electric Manufacturing Company, pg. 1167
WATLOW BATAVIA, INC.—See Watlow Electric Manufacturing Company, pg. 1167
WATLOW COLUMBIA, INC.—See Watlow Electric Manufacturing Company, pg. 1167
WATLOW ELECTRIC COMPANY OF CALIFORNIA—See Watlow Electric Manufacturing Company, pg. 1168
WATLOW ELECTRIC FOREIGN SALES CORPORATION—See Watlow Electric Manufacturing Company, pg. 1168
WATLOW ELECTRIC MANUFACTURING COMPANY, pg. 1167
WATLOW ELECTRIC MFG. CO. GMBH—See Watlow Electric Manufacturing Company, pg. 1168
WATLOW FRANCE S.A.R.L.—See Watlow Electric Manufacturing Company, pg. 1168
WATLOW INDUSTRIES, INC.—See Watlow Electric Manufacturing Company, pg. 1168
WATLOW INFRARED COMPANY—See Watlow Electric Manufacturing Company, pg. 1168
WATLOW ITALY—See Watlow Electric Manufacturing Company, pg. 1168
WATLOW KOREA—See Watlow Electric Manufacturing Company, pg. 1168
WATLOW LIMITED—See Watlow Electric Manufacturing Company, pg. 1168
WATLOW PROCESS SYSTEMS, INC.—See Watlow Electric Manufacturing Company, pg. 1168
WATLOW SINGAPORE PTE. LTD.—See Watlow Electric Manufacturing Company, pg. 1168
WATLOW ST. LOUIS, INC.—See Watlow Electric Manufacturing Company, pg. 1168
WATLOW TAIWAN—See Watlow Electric Manufacturing Company, pg. 1168
WATLOW WINONA, INC.—See Watlow Electric Manufacturing Company, pg. 1167
WATSON BOWMAN ACME CORP.—See Berwind Corporation, pg. 145
WATSON BOWMAN ACME, INC.—See Berwind Corporation, pg. 145
WATSON ELECTRIC SUPPLY INC., pg. 1168
WATSON FOOD SERVICE INDUSTRIES—See W S Holding Company, pg. 1156
WATSON'S QUALITY TURKEY PRODUCTS, INC., pg. 1168
WATT INDUSTRIES, pg. 1168
WATT, ROOP & CO., pg. 1168
WAUKESHA FOUNDRY INC., pg. 1168
WAUKESHA-PEARCE INDUSTRIES—See Pearce Industries Inc., pg. 853
WAUSAU HOMES, INC., pg. 1168
WAUSAU INSURANCE COMPANY (U.K.), LTD.—See Employers Insurance of Wausau a Mutual Co., pg. 380
WAUSAU LIFE INSURANCE COMPANY—See Employers Insurance of Wausau a Mutual Co., pg. 380
WAUSAU UNDERWRITERS LIFE INSURANCE COMPANY—See Employers Insurance of Wausau a Mutual Co., pg. 380
WAVERLY FABRICS—See F. Schumacher & Co., pg. 979
WAVETEK CORPORATION, pg. 1168
WAVETEK DATRON—See Wavetek Corporation, pg. 1169
WAVETEK ELECTRONICS GMBH—See Wavetek Corporation, pg. 1169
WAVETEK ELECTRONICS LTD.—See Wavetek Corporation, pg. 1169
WAVETEK MICROWAVE, INC.—See Wavetek Corporation, pg. 1168
WAVETEK SAN DIEGO INC.—See Wavetek Corporation, pg. 1168
WAWA, INC., pg. 1169
WAY BAKERIES, INC.—See Perfection Bakeries Inc., pg. 861
WAYANDOT, INC.—See Wyandot Inc., pg. 1205
WAYN-TEX INC., pg. 1169
WAYNE CORPORATION, pg. 1169
WAYNE STEEL, INC., pg. 1169
WAYNE WIRE CLOTH PRODUCTS, INC., pg. 1169
W.C. CAYE & CO.—See W.C. Caye & Company, Inc., pg. 230
WALTER H. WEABER SONS, INC., pg. 1169
WEASLER ENGINEERING INC., pg. 1169
THE WEATHER CHANNEL—See Landmark Communications, Inc., pg. 654

THE WEATHER CHANNEL, INC.-ATLANTA SALES OFFICE—See Landmark Communications, Inc., pg. 654
THE WEATHER CHANNEL, INC.-CHICAGO SALES OFFICE—See Landmark Communications, Inc., pg. 654
THE WEATHER CHANNEL, INC.-DETROIT SALES OFFICE—See Landmark Communications, Inc., pg. 654
THE WEATHER CHANNEL, INC.-LOS ANGELES SALES OFFICE—See Landmark Communications, Inc., pg. 654
THE WEATHER CHANNEL, INC.-NEW YORK SALES OFFICE—See Landmark Communications, Inc., pg. 654
WEATHER-MATIC DIV.—See Telsco Industries, pg. 1086
WEATHERBY, INC., pg. 1169
WEATHERKING PRODUCTS, INC.—See Aqua Fab Industries, Inc., pg. 79
WEATHERLY CAPITAL CORP.—See Weatherly Financial Group, pg. 1169
WEATHERLY CONSUMER PRODUCTS, INC.—See Weatherly Financial Group, pg. 1169
WEATHERLY FINANCIAL GROUP, pg. 1169
WEATHERLY FROZEN FOODS GROUP, INC.—See Weatherly Financial Group, pg. 1169
WEATHERLY PRIVATE CAPITAL, INC.—See Weatherly Financial Group, pg. 1170
WEATHERLY SECURITIES CORP.—See Weatherly Financial Group, pg. 1170
C. WEAVER CHEVROLET, INC., pg. 1170
W.H. WEAVER CONSTRUCTION CO., pg. 1170
WEAVER POPCORN COMPANY, INC., pg. 1170
WEB FOOD PRODUCTS CORP., pg. 1170
WEB PROCESSING EQUIP. DIV.—See P/A Industries, Inc., pg. 835
JERVIS B. WEBB CO. OF CALIFORNIA—See Jervis B. Webb Company, pg. 1170
JERVIS B. WEBB CO. OF GEORGIA—See Jervis B. Webb Company, pg. 1170
JERVIS B. WEBB COMPANY OF CANADA LTD.—See Jervis B. Webb Company, pg. 1170
JERVIS B. WEBB COMPANY, pg. 1170
JERVIS B. WEBB COMPANY LTD.—See Jervis B. Webb Company, pg. 1170
WEBB ELECTRIC CO.—See Jervis B. Webb Company, pg. 1170
WEBB FORGING—See Jervis B. Webb Company, pg. 1170
FRED WEBB INC., pg. 1170
WEBB-MATERIALS HANDLING EQUIP.—See Jervis B. Webb Company, pg. 1170
WEBB, MURRAY & ASSOCIATES, pg. 1170
WEBB-NORFOLK CONVEYOR—See Jervis B. Webb Company, pg. 1170
WEBB-TRIAX COMPANY—See Jervis B. Webb Company, pg. 1170
DEL WEBB'S COVENTRY, pg. 1171
WEBCRAFT GAMES, INC.—See Webcraft Technologies, Inc., pg. 1171
WEBCRAFT TECHNOLOGIES, INC., pg. 1171
WEBER COHN & RILEY, INC., pg. 1171
MARTIN F. WEBER COMPANY—See Martin Universal Design, Inc., pg. 716
FRED WEBER INC., pg. 1171
WEBER MARKING SYSTEMS CANADA LTD.—See Weber Marking Systems, Inc., pg. 1171
WEBER MARKING SYSTEMS (FAR EAST) CO. LTD.—See Weber Marking Systems, Inc., pg. 1171
WEBER MARKING SYSTEMS, INC., pg. 1171
WEBER MARKING SYSTEMS LTD.—See Weber Marking Systems, Inc., pg. 1171
WEBER-STEPHEN PRODUCTS, pg. 1171
WEBSTER INDUSTRIES INC., pg. 1171
WEBSTER MFG. CO.—See Webster Industries Inc., pg. 1172
WEBSTER-PORTALLOY CHAINS, INC.—See Webster Industries Inc., pg. 1172
WECHCO, INC., pg. 1172
WECHSLER COFFEE CORP., pg. 1172
WEDLO, INC.—See Peter W. Smith & Company, Inc., pg. 1012
WEEKLY READER CORP.—See K-III Communications Corporation, pg. 611
WEGMANS FOOD MARKETS, INC., pg. 1172
WEHCO MEDIA, INC., pg. 1172
WEHCO VIDEO INC.—See Wehco Media, Inc., pg. 1172
WEHR CONSTRUCTORS INC., pg. 1172
WEHRUNG FAMILY HOME CENTER—See Modern Concrete Septic Tank Company, pg. 762
WEIBEL VINEYARDS, pg. 1173
WEICHERT COMPANY, pg. 1173
WEICHERT INSURANCE AGENCY, INC.—See Weichert Company, pg. 1173
WEICHERT REALTY CAREER DEVELOPMENT—See Weichert Company, pg. 1173
WEICHERT REALTY, INC.—See Weichert Company, pg. 1173
WEIDER HEALTH & FITNESS, pg. 1173
WEIGHTMAN ADVERTISING, INC.—See The Weightman Group, pg. 1173
THE WEIGHTMAN GROUP, pg. 1173
WEIGHTMAN PUBLIC RELATIONS—See The Weightman Group, pg. 1173
WEIGHTMAN RESEARCH—See The Weightman Group, pg. 1173
WEIL BROTHERS COTTON INC., pg. 1173
WEIL-MCLAIN—See The Marley Company, pg. 710
WEILWOOD INDUSTRIES, INC.—See Santee Print Works, Inc., pg. 970
WEINBERGER WERBEHAUS GES.M.B.H & CO. KG—See N W Ayer Incorporated, pg. 105
WEINBRENNER SHOE COMPANY, INC., pg. 1173
WEINERS ENTERPRISES, INC., pg. 1173
WEINERS STORES INC.—See Weiners Enterprises, Inc., pg. 1173
SJ WEINSTEIN ASSOCIATES INC., pg. 1173
WEINSTEIN INTERNATIONAL SEAFOOD—See American Foods Group, pg. 54
WEINSTEIN OTTERMAN & ASSOCIATES, pg. 1173
WEINSTOCK, WHITE & ASSOCIATES, pg. 1174
WEINSTOCK'S FLORIST INC.—See KNOX International Corp., pg. 638
WEINSTOCK'S FLOWERS & GIFTS—See KNOX International Corp., pg. 638
WEINTRAUB AND ASSOCIATES, INC., pg. 1174
WEISER MINKUS WALEK COMMUNICATIONS, INC., pg. 1174
WEISS JEWELERS—See Reliable Stores, Inc., pg. 925
WEISS PACKING CO., INC., pg. 1174
WEISS SHEET METAL COMPANY, pg. 1174
WEISS, WHITTEN, CARROLL, STAGLIANO INC., pg. 1174
CARL WEISSMAN & SONS, INC., pg. 1174
WEISZ GRAPHICS—See Fred B. Johnston Company, Inc., pg. 601
THE WEITZ-COHEN CONSTRUCTION CO., pg. 1174
THE WEITZ COMPANY, INC.—See The Weitz Corporation, pg. 1174
THE WEITZ CORPORATION, pg. 1174
WEITZMAN//LIVINGSTON, INC., pg. 1174
WEKSLER INSTRUMENTS CORP., pg. 1174
WELCH'S—See National Grape Co-Op Association, Inc., pg. 789
WELCH'S CARBONATED BEVERAGES—See Dr Pepper/Seven-Up Companies, Inc., pg. 342
WELCO LUMBER COMPANY, pg. 1175
WELDON, WILLIAMS & LICK, INC., pg. 1175
WELLBORN - DE CORP.—See Dunn-Edwards Corporation, pg. 354
WELLCO CARPET CORP.—See Mannington Mills, Inc., pg. 704
WELLCRAFT MARINE—See Minstar, Inc., pg. 759
WELLENS & CO., INC., pg. 1175
WELLER & O'SULLIVAN ADVERTISING, pg. 1175
WELLINGTON INDUSTRIES INC., pg. 1175
WELLMADE INDUSTRIES, INC., pg. 1175
WELLS ALUMINUM CORP., pg. 1175
WELLS FARGO ALARM SERVICES—See Borg-Warner Corporation, pg. 166
WELLS FARGO ARMORED SERVICE CORP.—See Borg-Warner Corporation, pg. 166
WELLS FARGO GUARD SERVICES—See Borg-Warner Corporation, pg. 166
WELLS LAMONT—See The Marmon Group, Inc., pg. 712
WELLS MANUFACTURERA DE MEXICO S.A. DE C.V.—See UIS, Inc., pg. 1124
WELLS MANUFACTURING CANADA LTD.—See UIS, Inc., pg. 1124
WELLS MFG. CORP.—See UIS, Inc., pg. 1123
WELLSVILLE FIRE BRICK COMPANY—See CFB Industries, Inc., pg. 201
WELSBACH ELECTRIC CORP., pg. 1175
J.W. WELSCH & ASSOCIATES—See Summit Environmental Group, pg. 1058
WELSCO INC., pg. 1175
WELSH COMPANY, pg. 1175
WELSH FARMS, INC., pg. 1175
WELSH GRAPHICS, pg. 1176
WEMCO, INC., pg. 1176
WENCZEL TILE CO., pg. 1176
WENCZEL TILE DISTRIBUTING COMPANY—See Wenczel Tile Co., pg. 1176
WENCZEL TILE DISTRIBUTING COMPANY—See Wenczel Tile Co., pg. 1176
WENDEL TOBACCO CO.—See A.C. Monk Co., Inc., pg. 766
WENDT ADVERTISING, INC., pg. 1176
WENGER CORPORATION, pg. 1176
WERTHAN PACKAGING, INC., pg. 1176
WESBAR CORPORATION, pg. 1176
WEST ADVERTISING/PUBLIC RELATIONS, INC.—See KOA Holdings, pg. 613
WEST CENTRAL CO-OP, pg. 1176
WEST CENTRAL TURKEYS—See Norbest, Inc., pg. 809
WEST CHEMICAL PRODUCTS, INC.—See Wechco, Inc., pg. 1172
WEST COAST CORRECT CRAFT, INC.—See Correct Craft, Inc., pg. 287
WEST COAST GROWERS & PACKERS, INC., pg. 1177
WEST COAST LIFE INSURANCE CO.—See Nationwide Mutual Insurance Company, pg. 795
WEST COAST NATIONAL VIDEO, pg. 1177
WEST & COMPANY MARKETING & ADVERTISING, pg. 1177
WEST DAIRIES, INC., pg. 1177
WEST LUMBER CO., pg. 1177
WEST LYNN CREAMERY, INC.—See Scangas Brothers Holdings, Inc., pg. 974
WEST MILL CLOTHES, H.M.C. DIV.—See West Mill Clothes, Inc., pg. 1177
WEST MILL CLOTHES, INC., pg. 1177
WEST MILL CLOTHES, TUXACCO ACCESSORIES DIV.—See West Mill Clothes, Inc., pg. 1177
WEST, PAUSBACK & VAUGHAN, INC., pg. 1177
WEST PENTONE INC.—See Wechco, Inc., pg. 1172
WEST POINT-PEPPEREL (U.K.) LTD.—See Farley Industries, pg. 401
WEST POINT-PEPPERELL, INC.—See Farley Industries, pg. 400
WEST PUBLISHING CO., pg. 1177
WEST SERVICES, INC.—See West Publishing Co., pg. 1177
WEST TEXAS WHOLESALE SUPPLY CO.—See Distribution America, pg. 340
WEST UNION CORP., pg. 1177
WEST VIRGINIA LOTTERY, pg. 1178
WESTAIR HOLDING INC., pg. 1178
WESTAT INC., pg. 1178
WESTCHESTER LACE, INC., pg. 1178
WESTCO FOOD SERVICE—See Westco Products, Inc., pg. 1178
WESTCO INDUSTRIAL CORPORATION—See The Gage Company, pg. 441
WESTCO PRODUCTS, INC., pg. 1178
WESTCO PRODUCTS/SEATTLE—See Westco Products, Inc., pg. 1178
WESTCON—See Sycon Corporation, pg. 1069
WESTECH GEAR GROUP—See Zimmerman Holdings, Inc., pg. 1220
NELSON WESTERBERG, INC., pg. 1178
WESTERN CO-OP ELECTRIC UTILITY ASSOCIATION, pg. 1178
WESTERN CONTROLS, pg. 1178
WESTERN DAIRYMEN COOPERATIVE, INC., pg. 1178
WESTERN DATA SYSTEMS, pg. 1178
WESTERN DEVELOPMENT CORPORATION, pg. 1179
WESTERN DIESEL SERVICES INC., pg. 1179
WESTERN EXTRUSIONS, pg. 1179
WESTERN FARM CREDIT BANK—See Federal Farm Credit Banks Funding Corporation, pg. 405
WESTERN FEDERAL SAVINGS & LOAN ASSOCIATION, pg. 1179
WESTERN GRAIN, INC., pg. 1179
THE WESTERN GROUP, pg. 1179
WESTERN HOMES CORPORATION—See Redman Industries, Inc., pg. 919
WESTERN INDUSTRIES, INC., pg. 1179
WESTERN INTERNATIONAL MEDIA CORPORATION, pg. 1179
WESTERN LAND PROPERTIES—See Lewis Homes Management Corp., pg. 673
WESTERN LINEN CORP., pg. 1180
WESTERN LUMBER COMPANY, INC.—See Georgetown Industries, Inc., pg. 453
WESTERN MEDICAL SERVICES DIV.—See Western Temporary Services, Inc., pg. 1182
WESTERN METAL FINISHING DIVISION—See TIC United Corporation, pg. 1073
WESTERN PACIFIC DATA SYSTEMS, pg. 1180
WESTERN PERMANENT SERVICES AGENCY, INC.—See Western Temporary Services, Inc., pg. 1182
WESTERN PERSONNEL SERVICES PTY. LTD.—See Western Temporary Services, Inc., pg. 1182
WESTERN PETROLEUM COMPANY, pg. 1181
WESTERN REGIONAL OFF TRACK BETTING, pg. 1181
WESTERN REINSURANCE BROKERS, INC., pg. 1181
WESTERN SERVICE A/S—See Western Temporary Services, Inc., pg. 1182
WESTERN SERVICE, INC.—See Western Temporary Services, Inc., pg. 1182
WESTERN SLOPE REFINING CO.—See The Gary-Williams Company, pg. 444
WESTERN & SOUTHERN LIFE INSURANCE CO., pg. 1181
WESTERN SPECIALTY CONTAINER—See Independent Can Company, pg. 565
WESTERN STAFF SERVICES (NZ) LTD.—See Western Temporary Services, Inc., pg. 1182
WESTERN STAFF SERVICES (U.K.) LTD.—See Western Temporary Services, Inc., pg. 1182
WESTERN STATES ENVELOPE CO., pg. 1181
WESTERN STATES MACHINE CO., pg. 1181
WESTERN STATES PETROLEUM INC., pg. 1181
WESTERN STORAGE INSURANCE CO.—See Public Storage, Inc., pg. 898
WESTERN SUPPLY CORP.—See Lewis Homes Management Corp., pg. 673
WESTERN TECHNICAL DIV.—See Western Temporary Services, Inc., pg. 1182
WESTERN TEMPORARY SERVICES, INC., pg. 1181
WESTERN TEMPORARY SERVICES OFFICE DIV.—See Western Temporary Services, Inc., pg. 1182
WESTERN TEMPORARY SERVICES (USA), INC.—See Western Temporary Services, Inc., pg. 1182
WESTERN TRAILER EQUIPMENT & MANUFACTURING CO., pg. 1182
WESTERN VIDEO IMAGES, INC.—See Western Temporary Services, Inc., pg. 1182
WESTERN WATERPROOFING COMPANY, INC.—See The Western Group, pg. 1179
WESTERN WATERPROOFING COMPANY OF AMERICA, INC.—See The Western Group, pg. 1179
WESTERVELT LAND CO.—See Gulf States Paper Corporation, pg. 494
WESTFALL GMC TRUCK INC., pg. 1182
WESTFIELD COMPANIES, pg. 1182
WESTFIELD RIVER PAPER CO.—See Simkins Industries, Inc., pg. 1005
WESTGATE FABRICS, INC., pg. 1182
WESTGATE INC., pg. 1182
WESTIN, INC., pg. 1183
WESTLAKE HARDWARE, INC., pg. 1183
WESTLAM FOODS—See Trinidad/Benham Corporation, pg. 1114
WESTLIE MOTOR COMPANY, pg. 1183
WESTON ENGRAVING—See Schawk, Inc., pg. 975
WESTON GALLERY—See Wilton Industries, Inc., pg. 1195
WESTON PAPER & MANUFACTURING CO., pg. 1183
WESTPEAK INVESTMENT ADVISORS, INC.—See The New England, pg. 799
WESTREET INDUSTRIES—See Specialty Industries, Inc., pg. 1027
WETSEL-OVIATT LUMBER COMPANY, pg. 1183
WETSEL SEED COMPANY—See Southern States Cooperative, Inc., pg. 1023
WEXNER & JACOBSON, INC., pg. 1183
WHALING INDUSTRIES, INC., pg. 1183
WHALING MANUFACTURING COMPANY, INC.—See Whaling Industries, Inc., pg. 1183
WHAM-O DIV. OF KRANSCO—See Kransco, pg. 644
WHARFSIDE RESTAURANTS, INC., pg. 1184
WHATABURGER, INC., pg. 1184
WHEAT, FIRST SECURITIES INC., pg. 1184
WHEATLAND TUBE COMPANY, pg. 1184
WHEATON CARTAGE—See Wheaton Inc., pg. 1184
WHEATON COATED PRODUCTS—See Wheaton Inc., pg. 1184

WHEATON DO BRAZIL—See Wheaton Inc., pg. 1184
WHEATON GLASS CO.—See Wheaton Inc., pg. 1184
WHEATON INC., pg. 1184
WHEATON INJECTION MOLDING—See Wheaton Inc., pg. 1184
WHEATON INSTRUMENTS—See Wheaton Inc., pg. 1184
WHEATON SAFETY CONTAINER CO.—See Wheaton Inc., pg. 1184
WHEATON SCIENTIFIC—See Wheaton Inc., pg. 1184
WHEATON VAN LINES, INC., pg. 1184
WHEELER BROTHERS GRAIN CO., pg. 1184
WHEELER MANUFACTURING CO.—See Cotter & Company, pg. 288
WHEELOCK INC., pg. 1185
BUFF WHELAN CHEVROLET & GEO, INC., pg. 1185
THE WHELAND FOUNDRY DIV.—See North American Royalties, Inc., pg. 812
WHIBCO, INC., pg. 1185
WHIPPS, pg. 1185
WHISPER SOFT MILLS INC., pg. 1185
WHITE CASTLE DISTRIBUTING, INC.—See White Castle System, Inc., pg. 1185
WHITE CASTLE SYSTEM, INC., pg. 1185
E. JAMES WHITE COMPANY, pg. 1185
WHITE COUNTY FARM BUREAU CO-OP ASSOCIATION, pg. 1185
WHITE DRUG ENTERPRISES, INC.—See Thrifty Drug Stores, Inc., pg. 1096
WHITE ELECTRICAL CONSTRUCTION CO., pg. 1185
WHITE FLASH OIL CO.—See Pugh Oil Company, pg. 899
WHITE, GOOD & CO., pg. 1185
WHITE HEN PANTRY, INC., pg. 1185
THE WHITE LILY FOODS CO., pg. 1186
WHITE/MIPRO RECEPTABLES—See White Mop Wringer Company, pg. 1186
WHITE MOP WRINGER COMPANY, pg. 1186
WHITE PIGEON PAPER COMPANY—See Artistic Carton Company, pg. 87
WHITE ROCK DISTILLERIES INC., pg. 1186
WHITE ROCK PRODUCTS CORP., pg. 1186
WHITE ROSE CORPORATION—See Di Giorgio Corporation, pg. 335
WHITE ROSE DAIRY—See Di Giorgio Corporation, pg. 335
WHITE ROSE FOOD—See Di Giorgio Corporation, pg. 335
WHITE STAG MANUFACTURING COMPANY, pg. 1186
WHITE STAR STEEL—See Nashville Steel Corp., pg. 784
WHITE STORAGE & RETRIEVAL SYSTEMS, INC., pg. 1186
WHITE SWAN, INC.—See W S Holding Company, pg. 1156
WHITEHALL EDUCATIONAL TOYS—See Educational Publishing Corporation, pg. 369
WHITEHAWK PARTNERSHIP, pg. 1186
WHITEMYER ADVERTISING, INC., pg. 1186
WHITESTAR GRAPHICS, INC., pg. 1186
WHITFIELD FOODS, INC., pg. 1187
WHITIN ROBERTS CO., pg. 1187
WHITIN ROBERTS MFG. DIV.—See Whitin Roberts Co., pg. 1187
WHITING CORPORATION, pg. 1187
WHITING EQUIPMENT CANADA, INC.—See Whiting Corporation, pg. 1187
WHITING MANUFACTURING CO., INC., pg. 1187
WHITING-TURNER CONTRACTING CO., pg. 1187
WHITLOCK, INC.—See Sterling, Inc., pg. 1047
WHITMIRE DISTRIBUTION, pg. 1187
WHITTAKER, CLARK & DANIELS, INC., pg. 1187
WHITTENBERG CONSTRUCTION CO., pg. 1187
WHIZ AUTOMOTIVE CHEMICALS DIV.—See Malco Products, Inc., pg. 702
WHOLESALE ELECTRONIC SUPPLY, pg. 1188
WICK BUILDING SYSTEMS, pg. 1188
WICKER PARK L.P., pg. 1188
WICKES BUMPER DIVISION—See Collins & Aikman Group Inc., pg. 262
WICKES ENGINEERING GROUP—See Collins & Aikman Group Inc., pg. 263
WICKES LUMBER CO., pg. 1188
WICKES MFG. CO.—See Collins & Aikman Group Inc., pg. 262
WICKLAND CORPORATION, pg. 1188
WICKLAND OIL COMPANY, INC.—See Wickland Corporation, pg. 1188
WIDE WORLD PHOTOS, INC.—See The Associated Press, pg. 92
WIEDEN & KENNEDY, INC., pg. 1188
E.M. WIEGMANN & COMPANY, INC., pg. 1188
WIELAND FINANCIAL SERVICES, INC.—See John Wieland Homes Inc., pg. 1188
JOHN WIELAND HOMES INC., pg. 1188
WIELAND REALTY ASSOCIATES, INC.—See John Wieland Homes Inc., pg. 1189
WIGAND CORPORATION, pg. 1189
WIGWAM MILLS, INC., pg. 1189
WIL-FREDS CONSTRUCTION, INC., pg. 1189
WIL-RICH NOBLE COMPANY—See TIC United Corporation, pg. 1073
WILBUR CHOCOLATE CO., INC.—See Cargill Inc., pg. 219
WILBUR-ELLIS COMPANY & CONNELL BROTHERS COMPANY, pg. 1189
WILBUR-ELLIS COMPANY OF CANADA—See Wilbur-Ellis Company & Connell Brothers Company, pg. 1189
WILCOM PRODUCTS, INC.—See North Atlantic Industries, Inc., pg. 812
WILCOX & FOLLETT CO.—See Follett Corporation, pg. 422
WILCOX-WALTER-FURLONG PAPER CO.—See WWF Paper Corporation, pg. 1157
WILCOX-WALTER-FURLONG PAPER CO. OF WASHINGTON—See WWF Paper Corporation, pg. 1157
WILDCAT LTD.—See International Airline Support Group, Inc., pg. 575
WILDCAT SPORTS NETWORK—See Stauffer Communications, Inc., pg. 1043
WILDER MANAGEMENT ASSOCIATES, pg. 1189
WILDERNESS FOODS—See Agway, Inc., pg. 26
WILD'S BAKING COMPANY, pg. 1189
WILEN MANUFACTURING COMPANY, INC., pg. 1189
F.A. WILHELM CONSTRUCTION CO., INC., pg. 1189
WILKATA PACKAGING CORPORATION, pg. 1189
WILKENS AYER—See N W Ayer Incorporated, pg. 104
WILKINS OUTDOOR NETWORK, INC., pg. 1189
WILKINS-ROGERS INCORPORATED, pg. 1190
WILKINSON COMPANY, INC.—See Electric Furnace Co., pg. 373
WILL & BAUMER INCORPORATED, pg. 1190
THE WILL-BURT COMPANY, pg. 1190
WILLAMETTE-WESTERN CORPORATION, pg. 1190
WILLAMINA LUMBER CO. INC.—See Hampton Resources Inc., pg. 504
WILLARD GRAIN & FEED, INC., pg. 1190
WILLERT HOME PRODUCTS, INC., pg. 1190
R.C. WILLEY HOME FURNISHINGS, pg. 1190
JOHN WILLIAMS & ASSOCIATES, LTD., pg. 1190
WILLIAM'S BAKERY—See United States Bakery, pg. 1134
DON E. WILLIAMS CO., pg. 1190
WILLIAMS & COMPANY, INC.—See Cawsl Corporation, pg. 230
WILLIAMS COMPANY OF ORLANDO, INC., pg. 1190
WILLIAMS CRANE & RIGGING, INC.—See Williams International Industries, Inc., pg. 1191
WILLIAMS DISTRIBUTING COMPANY, pg. 1190
WILLIAMS DRUGS DISTRIBUTORS—See Humiston-Keeling, Inc., pg. 553
WILLIAMS FASTENER & SUPPLY CO.—See Williams Steel & Hardware Company, pg. 1191
WILLIAMS FOODS INC., pg. 1191
WILLIAMS HOUSE OF METALS, INC.—See Cawsl Corporation, pg. 230
DAVID R. WILLIAMS, INC.—See Vitt Media International, Inc., pg. 1154
WILLIAMS INTERNATIONAL, pg. 1191
WILLIAMS INTERNATIONAL INDUSTRIES, INC., pg. 1191
MARTIN WILLIAMS ADVERTISING INC., pg. 1191
WILLIAMS PATENT CRUSHER AND PULVERIZER CO., pg. 1191
ROBERT WILLIAMS—See Flexel, Inc., pg. 418
WILLIAMS & ROCKWOOD, pg. 1191
WILLIAMS STEEL & HARDWARE COMPANY, pg. 1191
WILLIAMS STEEL & SUPPLY—See Williams Steel & Hardware Company, pg. 1191
WILLIAMS TELEVISION TIME, INC., pg. 1191
WILLIAMS, WHITE & COMPANY, pg. 1191
WILLIAMS WHITTLE ASSOCIATES, INC., pg. 1191
WILLIAMSON-DICKIE APPAREL MFG. CO.—See Williamson-Dickie Mfg. Co., pg. 1192
WILLIAMSON-DICKIE MFG. CO., pg. 1192
T.D. WILLIAMSON, INC., pg. 1192
WILLIAMSON INTERNATIONAL CORP.—See T.D. Williamson, Inc., pg. 1192
T.D. WILLIAMSON S.A.—See T.D. Williamson, Inc., pg. 1192
WILLIS CASE HARWOOD, INC., pg. 1192
WILLITTS DESIGN—See Hallmark Cards, Inc., pg. 502
WILLMAR MANUFACTURING, pg. 1193
WILLOUGHBY'S, pg. 1193
WILLS AND EVANS, pg. 1193
WILLS GROUP, INC., pg. 1193
WILLSON SAFETY PRODUCTS, pg. 1193
WILMOR WAREHOUSE & SHIPPING CO., INC.—See The Hearst Corporation, pg. 522
WILMORE COAL COMPANY—See Berwind Corporation, pg. 145
WILMORITE INC., pg. 1193
WILSEY BENNETT CO., pg. 1193
WILSEY BENNETT REAL ESTATE DIVISION—See Wilsey Bennett Co., pg. 1193
WILSEY FOODS, INC.—See Wilsey Bennett Co., pg. 1193
WILSHIRE NEWPORT INC., pg. 1193
JIM WILSON & ASSOCIATES, pg. 1193
THE H. W. WILSON CO., pg. 1193
WILSON, HORNE, MCCLELLAND & GRAY, INC., pg. 1193
WILSON INDUSTRIES INC., pg. 1193
KEMMONS WILSON COMPANIES, pg. 1194
WILSON MACHINE KNIFE CO., INC.—See Hyde Manufacturing Co., pg. 556
WILSON PRODUCTS CO., pg. 1194
WILSON PUGH INC., pg. 1194
RALPH C. WILSON ENTERPRISES, pg. 1194
WILSON SCULLEY ASSOCIATES, pg. 1194
WILSON SEEDS INC.—See Land O'Lakes, Inc., pg. 654
WILSON SERVICE CENTER—See Carolina Steel Corporation, pg. 223
WILSON STEEL & WIRE—See MCM Enterprises, Inc., pg. 691
WILSON SUPPLY INTERNATIONAL (U.K.) LTD.—See Wilson Industries Inc., pg. 1194
WILTEL COMMUNICATIONS SYSTEMS, INC., pg. 1194
WILTIC CHEMICAL MANUFACTURING—See Genova Products, Inc., pg. 452
WILTON CORPORATION, pg. 1194
WILTON INDUSTRIES, INC., pg. 1194
WINCHELL MARKETING, pg. 1195
WINCHESTER CARTON CORP.—See Rock-Tenn Company, pg. 941
WINCUP, pg. 1195
WINDART HOLDING INC., pg. 1195
WINDEMULLER ELECTRIC INC., pg. 1195
WINDERMERE COMMUNICATIONS, INC., pg. 1195
THE WINDHAM COMPANY, pg. 1195
WINDMILL CORP. D/B/A MARTHA WHITE FOODS, INC.—See Windmill Holdings Corp., pg. 1195
WINDMILL HOLDINGS CORP., pg. 1195
WINDSOR ART PRODUCTS, INC.—See Windart Holding Inc., pg. 1195
WINDSOR FASHIONS, pg. 1195
WINDSOR GROUP LIMITED—See New York Life Insurance Company, pg. 803
WINDSOR INDUSTRIES, INC., pg. 1195
WINDSOR PLASTICS, INC.—See Guardian Industries Corp., pg. 492
WINDSOR PUBLICATIONS, INC., pg. 1196
WINDSOR SERVICE, INC., pg. 1196
WINDSOR SHADE TOBACCO COMPANY, INC., pg. 1196
WINE & SCHULZ INC., pg. 1196
WING INDUSTRIES, INC., pg. 1196
WINGATE/TAYLOR MAID TRANSPORTATION INC.—See Burlington Motor Carriers Inc., pg. 191
WINGFOOT FILMS CORPORATION—See Huntsman Chemical Corporation, pg. 555
BILL WINK CHEVROLET & GEO, pg. 1196
WINKLER MCMANUS, pg. 1196
WINKO-MATIC SIGNAL CO./MULTISONICS CORP., pg. 1196
FRANK W. WINNE & SON, INC., pg. 1196
WINNEBAGO COLOR PRESS, INC.—See Gillett Holdings, Inc., pg. 459
WINNER COMMUNICATIONS, INC., pg. 1196
WINNER'S LADIES OFF-PRICE SPECIALTY STORE—See Schottenstein Stores Corporation, pg. 978
WINONA KNITS, pg. 1196
WINONA KNITTING MILLS, INC., pg. 1196
WINRIDGE AURORA VENTURES, INC.—See Rotterdam Ventures Inc., pg. 952
WINROCK ENTERPRISES, INC., pg. 1197
WINROS, INC.—See MacAndrews & Forbes Holdings Inc., pg. 694
WINSLOW TAYLOR PUBLIC RELATIONS—See EvansGroup, pg. 391
HARRY WINSTON, INC., pg. 1197
WINSTON STEEL PRODUCTS CO., pg. 1197
WINSTON TIRE COMPANY, pg. 1197
WINTER HAVEN NEWS CHIEF—See Stauffer Communications, Inc., pg. 1042
WINTER PARK LEASING, INC.—See Luke Potter Dodge Inc., pg. 882
WINTER VOLVO & LINCOLN MERCURY, pg. 1197
WINTERKORN LILLIS INC., pg. 1197
WINTERS WELDING WORKS, INC., pg. 1197
WINTHROP PRINTING COMPANY, INC., pg. 1197
WIPFLI, ULLRICH, BERTELSON—See Effective Management Systems, pg. 370
WIRE ROPE CORP. OF AMERICA, INC., pg. 1197
WIRE TECH, INC.—See Group Dekko International Inc., pg. 490
WIREGRASS CONTAINER, INC.—See Rock-Tenn Company, pg. 941
THE WIREMOLD COMPANY, pg. 1197
WISCONSIN & CALUMET RAILROAD COMPANY—See Chicago West Pullman Corporation, pg. 246
WISCONSIN DAIRIES COOPERATIVE, pg. 1197
WISCONSIN LABEL CORPORATION, pg. 1198
WISCONSIN SERVICES CORP.—See Cox Enterprises, Inc., pg. 294
WISDOM IMPORTS SALES CO. INC., pg. 1198
WISSOTA TRADER & B.A. MASON—See Mason Shoe Mfg. Co., pg. 718
WISSOTA TRADER LTD.—See Mason Shoe Mfg. Co., pg. 718
WITCHER CONSTRUCTION COMPANY, pg. 1198
WITHERS/SUDDATH VAN LINES, INC.—See The Suddath Companies, pg. 1056
WITT COMPANY, pg. 1198
WITT GALVANIZING DIVISION—See Witt Company, pg. 1198
WITT PRODUCTS DIVISION—See Witt Company, pg. 1198
WITTE HARDWARE CORP.—See Distribution America, pg. 340
BILL WOESTE DEALER GROUP, pg. 1198
WOHLERT CORP., pg. 1198
WOLCOTT & LINCOLN, INC., pg. 1198
LELAND A. WOLF & ASSOCIATES, pg. 1199
WOLF, BLOCK, SCHORR & SOLIS-COHEN, pg. 1199
WOLF BLUMBERG KRODY INC., pg. 1199
WOLF MANUFACTURING COMPANY, pg. 1199
WOLFBERG, ALVAREZ & ASSOCIATES INC., pg. 1199
WOLFER PRINTING COMPANY, pg. 1199
WOLFF ASSOCIATES, INC., pg. 1199
WOLFF & MUNIER, INC., pg. 1199
WOLFF & PARTNER—See Backer Spielvogel Bates Worldwide, Inc., pg. 112
WOLFINGTON BODY COMPANY, pg. 1199
WOLLARD AIRPORT EQUIPMENT CO.—See Hobart Brothers Co., pg. 537
WOLLIN PRODUCTS, INC., pg. 1199
WOLVERINE MASSACHUSETTS CORPORATION, pg. 1199
WOLVERINE PACKING CO., pg. 1199
THE WOMEN'S BANK, N.A.—See Equitable Bankshares of Colorado, Inc., pg. 385
WOMETCO ENTERPRISES, INC., pg. 1199
PETER WONG & ASSOCIATES, INC., pg. 1199
THE W.B. WOOD COMPANY, pg. 1199
WOOD KNAPP & CO., INC.—See Knapp Communications Corporation, pg. 636
WOOD TREATERS OF BUFFALO CO., INC.—See Frontier Lumber Company, Inc., pg. 435
WOODBRIDGE SANITARY POTTERY CORP.—See Gerber Plumbing Fixtures Corporation, pg. 454
WOODBURN FOODS CORP.—See Agripac Inc., pg. 25
WOODBURY BUSINESS FORMS, INC., pg. 1200
WOODCRAFT INDUSTRIES, INC., pg. 1200
WOODFIELD COUNTRY CLUB—See The Barbar Group, Inc., pg. 119
WOODFIN HOLDING CORPORATION, pg. 1200
WOODFIN HOTEL MANAGEMENT, INC.—See Woodfin Holding Corporation, pg. 1200
WOODFIN-SMITH PONTIAC, INC., pg. 1200
WOODFIN SUITES, INC.—See Woodfin Holding Corporation, pg. 1200
WOODHAVEN FOODS—See ARA Group, pg. 7
WOODHAVEN FOODS-MIDWEST—See ARA Group, pg. 7

WOODLAND MOLDED PLASTICS—See Freudenberg-NOK (MI), pg. 433
WOODLORE—See Allen-Edmonds Shoe Corp., pg. 36
WOODMARK ORIGINALS—See Markwood Inc., pg. 710
WOODMEN ACCIDENT & LIFE CO., pg. 1200
WOODRUFF ELECTRICAL CO-OP, pg. 1200
JOE E. WOODS, INC., pg. 1200
T.B. WOOD'S SONS COMPANY, pg. 1200
WOODSTUFF MANUFACTURING, INC.—See Sealy Corporation, pg. 986
WOODWARD-CLYDE GROUP, INC., pg. 1200
WOODWARD-CLYDE CONSULTANTS—See Woodward-Clyde Group, Inc., pg. 1201
WOODWARD-CLYDE FEDERAL SERVICES—See Woodward-Clyde Group, Inc., pg. 1201
WOODWARD-CLYDE INTERNATIONAL—See Woodward-Clyde Group, Inc., pg. 1201
WOODWARD DIRECT, INC., pg. 1201
WOODWARD & LOTHROP/JOHN WANAMAKER, pg. 1201
WOODWORK CORPORATION OF AMERICA, pg. 1201
WOOL FILTERS INTL.—See Farley Industries, pg. 401
WOOLCAN—See Woolrich, Inc., pg. 1201
WOOLKONG, LTD.—See Woolrich, Inc., pg. 1201
WOOLKONG LTD.—See Woolrich, Inc., pg. 1201
WOOLPERT CONSULTANTS, pg. 1201
WOOLRICH, INC., pg. 1201
WOOLRICH STORE DIV.—See Woolrich, Inc., pg. 1201
WOOLVERTON OLDSMOBILE-G.M.C. TRUCK, INC., pg. 1201
THE WOOSTER BRUSH COMPANY, pg. 1202
WOOSTER MAGIKOTER WEST DIVISION—See The Wooster Brush Company, pg. 1202
WORD-TECH BUSINESS SYSTEMS—See Effective Management Systems, pg. 370
WORDPERFECT CORPORATION, pg. 1202
WORDPERFECT MANUFACTURING—See WordPerfect Corporation, pg. 1202
WORLD AEROSPACE CORPORATION, pg. 1202
WORLD CARPETS, INC., pg. 1202
WORLD COMPUTER CORP., pg. 1202
WORLD COUNCIL OF CREDIT UNIONS—See Credit Union National Association, pg. 298
WORLD EXPO CORPORATION—See International Data Group, pg. 578
WORLD EXPO CORPORATION—See International Data Group, pg. 578
WORLD EXPO CORPORATION—See International Data Group, pg. 578
WORLD EXPO CORPORATION—See International Data Group, pg. 578
WORLD EXPO CORPORATION—See International Data Group, pg. 578
WORLD EXPO CORPORATION—See International Data Group, pg. 578
WORLD IMPORT CO.—See Tober Industries, Inc., pg. 1099
WORLD JAI-ALAI, pg. 1202
WORLD JAI-ALAI PLAYERS—See World Jai-alai, pg. 1203
WORLD LANGUAGES SRL—See Berlitz International, Inc., pg. 143
WORLD OIL COMPANY, pg. 1203
WORLD PUBLISHING COMPANY—See Century Publishing Company, pg. 235
WORLD PUBLISHING COMPANY, pg. 1203
WORLD REPORT VERLAG GMBH—See Berlitz International, Inc., pg. 143
WORLD SHIPPING, INC., pg. 1203
WORLD TITLE COMPANY, pg. 1203
WORLD'S FINEST CHOCOLATE AUSTRALIA PTY. LTD.—See World's Finest Chocolate, Inc., pg. 1203
WORLD'S FINEST CHOCOLATE CANADA LTD.—See World's Finest Chocolate, Inc., pg. 1203
WORLD'S FINEST CHOCOLATE, INC., pg. 1203
WORLDWIDE LEASING—See Hobart Brothers Co., pg. 537
WORLITE CORPORATION—See P.J. Keating Company, pg. 619
THE WORNICK COMPANY, pg. 1203
WORNICK PROPERTIES, INC.—See The Wornick Company, pg. 1203
WORRAD SERVICES INC.—See Henkels & McCoy, Inc., pg. 529
WORRELL ENTERPRISES, INC., pg. 1203
WORSLEY COMPANIES INC., pg. 1204
WORZALLA PUBLISHING CO., INC., pg. 1204
WOTCO INC., pg. 1204
WOZNIAK INDUSTRIES, INC., pg. 1204
WRAY-WARD-LASETER ADVERTISING, pg. 1204
CAROLE WREN, INC., pg. 1204
WRIGHT BRAND FOODS, INC., pg. 1204
CAROL WRIGHT SALES, INC.—See Peter W. Smith & Company, Inc., pg. 1011
F.B. WRIGHT CO., pg. 1204
WRIGHT-SCHUCHART, INC., pg. 1204
G.F. WRIGHT STEEL & WIRE COMPANY, pg. 1205
WRIGHT & WILHELMY CO.—See Distribution America, pg. 340
WM. E. WRIGHT LIMITED PARTNERSHIP, pg. 1205
WROUGHT WASHER MFG., INC., pg. 1205
WUNDA WEVE CARPET CO., pg. 1205
WUNDA WEVE CARPET YARN PLANT—See Wunda Weve Carpet Co., pg. 1205
WUNDERMAN—See Young & Rubicam Inc., pg. 1212
WUNDERMAN—See Dentsu, Young & Rubicam Partnerships, pg. 331
WUNDERMAN CATO JOHNSON—See Young & Rubicam Inc., pg. 1211
WUNDERMAN DO BRAZIL—See Young & Rubicam Inc., pg. 1213
WUNDERMAN TAUCHER TURKU OY—See Young & Rubicam Inc., pg. 1212
WUNDERMAN TENDER—See Young & Rubicam Inc., pg. 1212
WUNDERMAN WORLDWIDE—See Young & Rubicam Inc., pg. 1212
WUNDERMAN WORLDWIDE—See Young & Rubicam Inc., pg. 1211
WUNDERMAN WORLDWIDE AB—See Young & Rubicam Inc., pg. 1212
WUNDERMAN WORLDWIDE A/S—See Young & Rubicam Inc., pg. 1212
WUNDERMAN WORLDWIDE LIMITED—See Young & Rubicam Inc., pg. 1212
WUNDERMAN WORLDWIDE V.O.F.—See Young & Rubicam Inc., pg. 1212
WURZBURG, INC., pg. 1205
WYANDOT INC., pg. 1205
WYATT CAFETERIAS INC., pg. 1205
WYATT FIELD SERVICE CO.—See Nooter Corporation, pg. 808
WYATT INC., pg. 1205
THE WYCO TOOL CO.—See Racine Federated, Inc., pg. 909
JEFF WYLER CHEVROLET DEALERSHIP—See Jeff Wyler Dealer Group, Inc., pg. 1206
JEFF WYLER DEALER GROUP, INC., pg. 1206
JEFF WYLER NISSAN DEALERSHIP—See Jeff Wyler Dealer Group, Inc., pg. 1206
WYNMOOR HOMES, INC.—See Cenvill Development Corp., pg. 236
WYNMOOR LTD. PARTNERSHIP—See Cenvill Development Corp., pg. 236
WYNMOOR MANAGEMENT & CO., INC.—See Cenvill Development Corp., pg. 236
WYNVILLE REALTY—See Cenvill Development Corp., pg. 236
WYOMING MACHINE COMPANY, pg. 1206
WYSE ADVERTISING, INC., pg. 1206
WYSE ADVERTISING/CLEVELAND—See Wyse Advertising, Inc., pg. 1206
WYSE ADVERTISING/NEW YORK—See Wyse Advertising, Inc., pg. 1206
WYSE DIRECT—See Wyse Advertising, Inc., pg. 1206

X

X-A CABINET CORPORATION, pg. 1206
XA SYSTEMS CORPORATION—See Compuware Corporation, pg. 272
XALOY, INC.—See Peter W. Smith & Company, Inc., pg. 1012
XEBEC CORPORATION, pg. 1206
XERXES CORPORATION, pg. 1206
XPLORER MOTOR HOME DIV.—See Frank Industries, Inc., pg. 429
XTEK CANADA, LTD.—See Xtek, Inc., pg. 1206
XTEK, INC., pg. 1206
XTRA SUPER FOOD CENTERS, INC.—See Pueblo International, Inc., pg. 899

Y

YPMS/TMP WORLDWIDE, INC.—See TMP Worldwide, Inc., pg. 1074
Y&R CAPITAL IMAGE—See Young & Rubicam Inc., pg. 1212
Y&R/WUNDERMAN WORLDWIDE/DETROIT—See Young & Rubicam Inc., pg. 1211
YRJ CORPORATION, pg. 1206
YSD INDUSTRIES, pg. 1207
YSI INCORPORATED, pg. 1207
YAFFE & CO., pg. 1207
YALE INDUSTRIAL TRUCKS—See Yale Industrial Trucks Of Southern California, pg. 1207
YALE INDUSTRIAL TRUCKS OF SOUTHERN CALIFORNIA, pg. 1207
YALE UNIVERSITY PRESS, pg. 1207
YANKEE PUBLISHING INCORPORATED, pg. 1207
YANKEE WHALER COMPANY—See Specialty Restaurants Corporation, pg. 1028
THE YANKTON PRESS & DAKOTAN—See Stauffer Communications, Inc., pg. 1042
YARDLEY PRODUCTS CORPORATION—See Dixon Valve & Coupling Company, pg. 341
YARDNEY TECHNICAL PRODUCTS, INC., pg. 1207
YATES ENTERPRISES INC., pg. 1207
YAZOO INVESTMENT CORPORATION, pg. 1207
YELLO-BOLE—See S. M. Frank & Co., Inc., pg. 429
YELLOWSTONE TRANSPORTATION SERVICE, INC.—See Martrade Ltd., pg. 716
YENKIN-MAJESTIC PAINT CORPORATION, pg. 1208
YERGER BROS., INC., pg. 1208
YOAKUM PACKING COMPANY, pg. 1208
YODER OIL COMPANY INC., pg. 1208
H. L. YOH COMPANY—See Day & Zimmermann, Inc., pg. 320
YORK BARBELL CO., INC., pg. 1208
YORK BUILDING PRODUCTS CO., INC., pg. 1208
THE YORK NEWS-TIMES—See Stauffer Communications, Inc., pg. 1042
YORK WALLCOVERINGS INC., pg. 1208
YORKTOWN TOOL & DIE CORPORATION, pg. 1208
YORKTOWNE, INC., pg. 1208
YORKTOWNE PAPER MILLS, INC., pg. 1208
YORKTOWNE PAPER MILLS OF MAINE—See Yorktowne Paper Mills, Inc., pg. 1209
YORKTOWNE PAPER MILLS OF ME—See Yorktowne Paper Mills, Inc., pg. 1209
YOSEMITE EXPRESS CO.—See Save Mart Supermarkets, pg. 973
YOUNG AUTOMOTIVE GROUP, pg. 1209
YOUNG ELECTRIC SIGN COMPANY, pg. 1209
YOUNG ELECTRIC SIGN DENVER DIV.—See Young Electric Sign Company, pg. 1209
YOUNG ELECTRIC SIGN LAS VEGAS DIV.—See Young Electric Sign Company, pg. 1209
R.S. YOUNG ENVIRONMENTAL CLEAN UP—See R.S. Young Excavating, Inc., pg. 1209
R.S. YOUNG EXCAVATING, INC., pg. 1209
YOUNG & FRANKLIN, INC., pg. 1209
DANIEL F. YOUNG, INC., pg. 1209
JACK YOUNG ASSOCIATES, pg. 1209
YOUNG & LARAMORE, pg. 1209
YOUNG PECAN COMPANY WEST, INC.—See Young Pecan Shelling Co., Inc., pg. 1210
YOUNG PECAN SHELLING CO., INC., pg. 1209
YOUNG-PHILLIPS SALES CO., pg. 1210
YOUNG RADIATOR COMPANY, pg. 1210
YOUNG REFINING CORP., pg. 1210
RICHARD YOUNG OFFICE PRODUCTS, INC.—See Hillman Company, pg. 535
YOUNG & ROEHR, INC., pg. 1210
YOUNG & RUBICAM—See Young & Rubicam Inc., pg. 1213
YOUNG & RUBICAM BELGIUM S.A.—See Young & Rubicam Inc., pg. 1212
YOUNG & RUBICAM BRASIL—See Young & Rubicam Inc., pg. 1213
YOUNG & RUBICAM CHICAGO—See Young & Rubicam Inc., pg. 1211
YOUNG & RUBICAM COPENHAGEN—See Young & Rubicam Inc., pg. 1213
YOUNG & RUBICAM CZECHOSLOVAKIA—See Young & Rubicam Inc., pg. 1212
YOUNG & RUBICAM DETROIT—See Young & Rubicam Inc., pg. 1211
YOUNG & RUBICAM EST—See Young & Rubicam Inc., pg. 1212
YOUNG & RUBICAM GOTEBURG AB—See Young & Rubicam Inc., pg. 1213
YOUNG & RUBICAM HOLDINGS LTD.—See Young & Rubicam Inc., pg. 1213
YOUNG & RUBICAM INC., pg. 1210
YOUNG & RUBICAM ITALIA, S.P.A.—See Young & Rubicam Inc., pg. 1213
YOUNG & RUBICAM NEW YORK—See Young & Rubicam Inc., pg. 1211
YOUNG & RUBICAM & OGMIOS—See Young & Rubicam Inc., pg. 1213
YOUNG & RUBICAM OUEST—See Young & Rubicam Inc., pg. 1213
YOUNG & RUBICAM (PORTUGAL)—See Young & Rubicam Inc., pg. 1213
YOUNG & RUBICAM SAN FRANCISCO—See Young & Rubicam Inc., pg. 1211
YOUNG & RUBICAM SUD OUEST—See Young & Rubicam Inc., pg. 1213
YOUNG STUFF APPAREL GROUP, INC., pg. 1214
YOUNG SUPPLY CO.—See Meenan Oil Co. Limited Partnership, pg. 736
YOUNG SUPPLY COMPANY, pg. 1214
YOUNG'S MARKET COMPANY, pg. 1214
YOUNGSTOWN TIRE & SUPPLY COMPANY—See Ziegler Tire & Supply Company, Inc., pg. 1218
YOUR MAN TOURS, INC., pg. 1214
YPSI-ARBOR LANES—See Great Lakes Recreation Co., pg. 482
YUBA HEAT TRANSFER DIVISION—See Connell Limited Partnership, pg. 275
THE YUCAIPA COMPANIES, pg. 1214
YUKON ALASKA TRANSPORT LTD.—See Lynden Incorporated, pg. 690
YUM YUM DONUT SHOP, INC., pg. 1214

Z

Z. CAVARICCI INC., pg. 1215
ZBS INDUSTRIES, INC., pg. 1215
H.B. ZACHRY, pg. 1215
ZACK COMPANY, pg. 1215
ZACKY FARMS, INC., pg. 1215
ZALE CORPORATION, pg. 1215
ZALK JOSEPH FABRICATIONS, INC.—See Heico Inc., pg. 525
THE ZAMOISKI CO., pg. 1216
ZANDER'S CREAMERY INC., pg. 1216
THE ZANE GREY LIBRARY—See Walter J. Black, Inc., pg. 154
ZANTOP AIRCRAFT MAINTENANCE FACILITY—See Zantop International Airlines, Inc., pg. 1216
ZANTOP INTERNATIONAL AIRLINES, INC., pg. 1216
ZAPIECKI & PARTNERS INC., pg. 1216
ZAPPA PLASTICS, pg. 1216
ZAREMBA CORPORATION, pg. 1216
ZECHMAN & ASSOCIATES ADV. INC., pg. 1216
ZELLER CORP., pg. 1216
ZELLER WORLD TRADE CORPORATION—See Zeller Corp., pg. 1217
ZEMCO INDUSTRIES, INC., pg. 1217
ZENA JEANS, pg. 1217
ZENITH ADMINISTRATORS, INC.—See ULLICO Inc., pg. 1124
ZENITH ADMINISTRATORS OF TEXAS—See ULLICO Inc., pg. 1124
ZENITH INTL. INSURANCE LTD.—See Levi Strauss & Co., pg. 671
ZENITH LABORATORIES, INC., pg. 1217
ZENITH PRODUCTS CORP., pg. 1217
ZENITH WEST CORP.—See Zenith Products Corp., pg. 1217
ZEPHYR BASKETS & BALLOONS, pg. 1217
ZEPHYR INC., pg. 1217
ZEPHYR MFG. CO.—See Standun, Inc., pg. 1038
A. ZEREGAS SONS, INC., pg. 1217
ZETEC, INC., pg. 1217
ZIEBART CANADA, INC.—See Ziebart International Corporation, pg. 1218

ZIEBART CORP.—See Ziebart International Corporation, pg. 1217
ZIEBART (E.C.) LIMITED—See Ziebart International Corporation, pg. 1218
ZIEBART INTERNATIONAL CORPORATION, pg. 1217
ZIEBART JAPAN LIMITED—See Ziebart International Corporation, pg. 1218
ZIEBART PRODUCTS GROUP—See Ziebart International Corporation, pg. 1217
ZIEGLER CHEMICAL & MINERAL CORP., pg. 1218
R.L. ZIEGLER CO. INC., pg. 1218
ZIEGLER COAL HOLDING CO., pg. 1218
ZIEGLER INC., pg. 1218
ZIEGLER TIRE & SUPPLY COMPANY, INC., pg. 1218
ZIEMAN MANUFACTURING COMPANY, INC., pg. 1218
ZIFF COMMUNICATIONS COMPANY, pg. 1218
ZIFF-DAVIS FRANCE SARL—See Ziff Communications Company, pg. 1219
ZIFF-DAVIS GERMANY—See Ziff Communications Company, pg. 1219
ZIFF-DAVIS PRESS—See Ziff Communications Company, pg. 1219
ZIFF-DAVIS PUBLISHING COMPANY—See Ziff Communications Company, pg. 1219
ZIFF-DAVIS TAIWAN—See Ziff Communications Company, pg. 1219
ZIFF-DAVIS U.K.—See Ziff Communications Company, pg. 1219
ZIFF INFORMATION SERVICES—See Ziff Communications Company, pg. 1219
ZIFF TECHNOLOGIES—See Ziff Communications Company, pg. 1219
ZILBER, LTD., pg. 1219
AVEDIS ZILDJIAN COMPANY, pg. 1219
ZILKHA ENERGY COMPANY, pg. 1219
ZIM-AMERICAN ISRAELI SHIPPING CO., pg. 1219
ZIM CONTAINER SERVICE—See Zim-American Israeli Shipping Co., pg. 1219
ZIMA CORP., pg. 1219
ZIMDAR ENTERPRISES, pg. 1220
ZIMMER PAPER PRODUCTS INC., pg. 1220
ZIMMERMAN HOLDINGS, INC., pg. 1220
ZINC CORPORATION OF AMERICA—See Horsehead Industries, Inc., pg. 545
ZINIZ INC., pg. 1220
JOHN ZINK CO.—See Koch Industries, Incorporated, pg. 639
ZINK & TRIEST—See A.M. Todd Company, pg. 1100
ZION'S SECURITIES CORP.—See Deseret Management Corporation, pg. 332
THE ZIPPERTUBING CO., pg. 1220
ZIPPO MANUFACTURING COMPANY, pg. 1220
ZIPPO MANUFACTURING COMPANY OF CANADA LIMITED—See Zippo Manufacturing Company, pg. 1220
ZLOFIN OY—See J.M. Huber Corporation, pg. 550
ZMP, INC.—See Certified Holding Corp., pg. 237
ZOELLER CO., pg. 1220
ZOLLNER CORPORATION, pg. 1221
ZUBI ADVERTISING SERVICES, INC., pg. 1221
ZUCKERMAN-HONICKMAN INC., pg. 1221
C. W. ZUMBIEL COMPANY, pg. 1221
ZWEINIEDERLASSUNG ZURICH—See CS First Boston Group, Inc., pg. 204
ZYCON CORPORATION, pg. 1221
ZYLKE & ASSOCIATES, pg. 1221
ZYMARK CORPORATION, pg. 1221
ZYNTEC GMBH—See Zytec Corp., pg. 1221
ZYTEC CORP., pg. 1221

U.S. PRIVATE COMPANIES

A & A MANUFACTURING CO.
2300 S. Calhoun Rd.
New Berlin, WI 53151
Tel.: 414-786-1500
Fax: 414-786-3280
Approx.Sls.: $13,000,000
Emp.: 125
Bellows, Machinery Protectors, Cable Carriers
S.I.C.: 3069; 3199; 3499; 3545; 3599
Ruth E. O'Rourke *(Chm. & Treas.)*
Gerald J. O'Rourke *(Pres.)*
Thomas E. Schoenauer *(V.P.-Sls. & Adv. Mgr.)*
Lawrence M. Kean *(Sec.)*
Tim Brehm *(Pur. Agent)*
Ken Czyzewski *(Mgr.-Sls.)*
Principal(s):
Ruth E. O'Rourke
Gerald J. O'Rourke

Computer Systems/Hardware:
IBM System 36

Outside Service Firm(s):

Arthur Andersen & Co.*(Auditors)*
777 E. Wisconsin Ave., P.O. Box 1215
Milwaukee, WI 53202
Tel.: 414-271-5100
Fax: 414-283-3200

Godfrey & Kahn*(Legal Firm)*
780 N. Water St.
Milwaukee, WI 53202
Tel.: 414-273-3500
Fax: 414-273-5198

First Interstate Bank*(Major Banking Relationship)*
Milwaukee, WI

A-DEC, INC.
2601 Crestview Dr.
Newberg, OR 97132
Mailing Address:
P.O. Box 111
Newberg, OR 97132
Tel.: 503-538-9471
Fax: 503-538-0276
Year Founded: 1964
Approx.Sls.: $70,000,000
Emp.: 580
Export
Mfr. of Dental Equipment
S.I.C.: 3843
George K. Austin, Jr. *(Pres.)*
Joan D. Austin *(Exec. V.P. & Treas.)*
Gene Davis *(V.P. & G.M.)*
G. Kenneth Austin III *(Sec.)*
Alan Steiger *(Dir.-Fin.)*
Tom Eder *(Dir.-Personnel)*
Pat Ridenour *(Dir.-Engrng.)*
Hank Poertner *(Dir.-Mktg.)*
Charles Cook *(Dir.-Mfg.)*
Joe Plews *(Dir.-Intl. Mktg.)*

A & E Business Products
(Acquired by Taylor Corporation)

A & E STORES, INC.
1125 Pleasantview Terrace
Ridgefield, NJ 07657
Tel.: 201-941-9601 NY
Fax: 201-941-3645
Year Founded: 1973
Assets: $30,752,000
Liabilities: $15,015,000
Net Worth: $15,737,000
Sales Range: $60-79 Million
Emp.: 1,000
Fiscal Year-end: 12/31/90
Import
Operator of Women's Apparel Stores Featuring Junior & Misses Sportswear, Footwear, Jewelry, Hosiery & Accessories
S.I.C.: 5621; 5632
Corporate Giving Program: Basic 4 GPX 9520
Alan Ades *(Chm., Pres. & Chief Exec. Officer)*
Dennis Erani *(Exec. V.P. & G.M.)*
Albert Erani *(Exec. V.P. & Sec.)*
Philip Harrison *(V.P.-Fin. & Controller)*
Craig Ward *(V.P. Admin.-Human Resources)*
Jim Hamlin *(V.P.-Store Opers.)*
Ed Baran *(V.P.-Real Estate & Employee Benefits)*
Murry Setton *(V.P.-Opers.)*
Bruce Kleiman *(V.P.-Mdsg. & Mktg.)*
Walter Ziclinski *(Dir.-Data Processing)*
Al Cohen *(Sportswear Buyer)*
Maria Cosentino *(Shoe Buyer)*
Andrew Lee *(Mgr.-Imports)*
Leah Dwerle *(Mgr.-Personnel)*

Outside Service Firm(s):

Coopers & Lybrand*(Auditors)*
1301 Avenue of The Americas
New York, NY 10019
Tel.: 212-536-2000

Chemical Banking Corp.*(Major Banking Relationship)*
277 Park Ave.
New York, NY 10041
Tel.: 212-310-6407

A-MARK FINANCIAL
100 Wilshire Blvd., 3rd Fl.
Santa Monica, CA 90401
Tel.: 310-319-0200
Precious Metals Wholesaler
S.I.C.: 5094
Steven Markoff *(Pres.)*

A & S TRIBAL INDUSTRIES
P.O. Box 308
Poplar, MT 59255
Tel.: 406-768-5151
Fax: 406-768-3356
Year Founded: 1974
Emp.: 450
Manufactures Camouflage Netting & Fabricated Metal Products
S.I.C.: 2399; 3469; 3499
Norman Hollow *(Pres.)*
Pearl Hopkins *(Sec. & Treas.)*
Mark C. Stack *(Controller)*
Bill Neulman *(Dir.-Opers.)*
Patrick Beauchman *(Mgr.-Personnel)*

Outside Service Firm(s):

Childs & Smith*(Auditors)*
Sidney, MT

Trader State Bank*(Major Banking Relationship)*
Poplar, MT

A & W FOODS, INC.
4900 Crayton Ave.
Cleveland, OH 44104
Tel.: 216-431-8000 OH
Fax: 216-361-1844
Year Founded: 1932
Approx.Sls.: $175,000,000
Emp.: 910
Fiscal Year-end: 12/31/91
Import Export
Wholesale Poultry, Meat & Related Food Products
S.I.C.: 5144; 5147
Jeff Weisberg *(Pres.)*
Glenn Pollack *(Chief Exec. Officer)*
C. Thomas Kennedy *(Chief Fin. Officer)*

No. of Mfg. Plants/Facilities: 2
No. of U.S. Offices: 6

Computer Systems/Hardware:
Hewlett-Packard 3058

Outside Service Firm(s):

Bober, Markey & Company*(Auditors)*
Akron, OH

Blue Cross & Blue Shield of Northern Ohio*(Group Insurer)*
2060 E. 9th St.
Cleveland, OH 44115
Tel.: 216-687-7000

Hahn, Loeser & Parks*(Legal Firm)*
Natl. City E. 6 Bldg.
Cleveland, OH 44114
Tel.: 216-621-0150

Society National Bank*(Major Banking Relationship)*
Cleveland, OH

Division:

The Markey Company **(1)**
3316 W. 67th Pl.
Cleveland, OH 44102
Tel.: 216-631-8850
Portion Control Meat Processing
S.I.C.: 5144
George N. Stewart *(Chief Oper. Officer)*

A & W RESTAURANTS, INC.
(Sub. of Taubman Investments Co.)
17197 Laurel Park Dr., Ste. 500
Livonia, MI 48152
Tel.: 313-462-0029
Tel.: 800-222-2337
Fax: 313-462-1017
Year Founded: 1919
Approx.Sls.: $150,000,000
Emp.: 15,000
Fiscal Year-end: 12/31/91
Operator & Franchiser of Fast Food Restaurants
S.I.C.: 5812
George E. Michel *(Pres. & Chief Exec. Officer)*
Paul Nierzwicki *(V.P.-Opers., Franchise Sls. & Devel.)*
Kevin Bazner *(V.P.-Intl. Opers.)*
Mike Smith *(V.P.-Construction & Bus. Devel.)*
Mary Smith *(V.P.-Res., Devel. & Pur.)*
Kathryn A. Owens *(V.P.-Fin.)*
Wendy E. Becker *(Dir.-Mktg.)*
Patty O'Callahan *(Mgr.-Programmer)*
Sue Wildenhaus *(Mgr.-Personnel)*
George Kortlandt *(Mgr.-Personnel Training & Devel.)*
Mary Owens *(Mktg. Coord.)*
Larry Kohler *(Merger/Acquisition Contact)*
Mary-Ann Fody *(Corp. Travel Planner)*

A & Z HAYWARD, INC.
655 Waterman Ave.
East Providence, RI 02914
Tel.: 401-438-0550
Fax: 401-438-6970
Approx.Sls.: $10,000,000
Emp.: 250
Jewelry
S.I.C.: 3911; 5944
Jason Adelman *(Pres.)*
Michael Poissant *(Exec. V.P. & Gen. Mgr.)*

A A CATER TRUCK MANUFACTURING COMPANY, INC.
750 E. Slauson Ave.
Los Angeles, CA 90011
Tel.: 213-235-2191
Fax: 310-235-6656
Approx.Sls.: $10,000,000
Emp.: 75
Manufacture & Repair Catering Trucks
S.I.C.: 3713; 7538
Vahe Karapetian *(Pres.)*
Ed Pelenghian *(Gen. Mgr.)*

Outside Service Firm(s):

Sanwa Bank*(Major Banking Relationship)*
Bell Gardens, CA

A.B. DATA, LTD.
8050 N. Port Washington Rd.
Milwaukee, WI 53217
Tel.: 414-352-4404
Fax: 414-352-3994
Year Founded: 1976
Approx.Billings: $10,000,000
Emp.: 100
Direct Marketing
Bruce Arbit *(Co-Mng. Dir.)*
Robert Syut *(V.P., Data Processing Services)*
Steve Mullins *(Dir., Pub. Rels.)*
Richard Martin *(Res. Dir.)*
Alan Wichtoski *(Controller)*

A-B EMBLEM DIV. OF CONRAD INDUSTRIES, INC.
P. O. Box 695
Weaverville, NC 28787
Tel.: 704-645-3015
Tel.: 800-438-4285
Fax: 704-658-3581
Year Founded: 1962
Approx.Sls.: $14,000,000
Emp.: 300
Import Export
Mfrs. & Designers of Swiss Embroidered Emblems, Promotional Caps-Baseball & Golf Style
S.I.C.: 2395
E. Henry Conrad *(Chm. Bd.)*
Bernhard Conrad *(Pres.)*
Paul E. Gilsdorf *(V.P.-Sls. & Mktg.)*

ABB ENVIRONMENTAL SYSTEMS
(Formerly Environmental Systems Div., Flakt, Inc.)
1400 Centerpoint Blvd.
Knoxville, TN 37932-1966
Tel.: 615-693-7550
Approx.Sls.: $100,000,000
Emp.: 130
Air Systems Pollution Control
S.I.C.: 4953
William Scott *(V.P. & Gen. Mgr.)*
D.E. Boyd *(V.P.-Mktg. & Sls., Pre-contract)*
D. Stover *(Controller)*

A B C APPLIANCE INC.
(d/b/a Warehouse Group World)
One Silverdome Industrial Park
Pontiac, MI 48343
Tel.: 313-335-4222
Fax: 313-335-2568
Approx.Sls.: $140,000,000
Emp.: 500
Retail Household Appliances
S.I.C.: 5722
Gordon Hartunian *(Pres.)*
Frieda Hartunian *(Sec.)*
Martin Hartunian *(Treas.)*
Don Behrendt *(Controller)*
Principal(s):
Gordon Hartunian

Outside Service Firm(s):

Arthur Andersen & Co.*(Auditors)*
400 Renaissance Center
Detroit, MI 48243
Tel.: 313-259-8100

Comerica Bank*(Major Banking Relationship)*
211 W. Fort St.
Detroit, MI 48226
Tel.: 313-222-3300

ABC SUPPLY COMPANY, INC.
820 Broad St.
Beloit, WI 53511
Mailing Address:
P.O. Box 838,
Beloit, WI 53511
Tel.: 608-362-7777
Telex: 608-362-6215
Fax: 608-362-6529
Year Founded: 1982
Approx.Sls.: $279,000,000
Emp.: 1,000
Fiscal Year-end: 4/30/91
Export
Wholesale Roofing, Siding & Drywall Products, Windows
S.I.C.: 5039
Kenneth A. Hendricks *(Chm. Bd., Pres. & Chief Exec. Officer)*
Diane M. Hendricks *(V.P. & Sec.)*
Kendra A. Story *(Treas. & Controller)*
David G. Grisham *(Dir.-Personnel Training)*
Lisa Cullen *(Dir.-Employee Benefits)*
Kathy M. Murray *(Dir.-Data Processing)*
Tom Lasse *(Dir.-Plng.)*
Jeff Garrow *(Dir.-Adv.)*
Duane B. Blakely *(Credit Mgr.)*
Brent A. Fox *(Research Mgr.)*
Principal(s):
Kenneth A. Hendricks
Diane M. Hendricks
Kendra A. Story

No. of Mfg. Plants/Facilities: 2
No. of U.S. Offices: 93

Computer Systems/Hardware:
IBM 3600

Outside Service Firm(s):

Ernst & Young*(Auditors)*
Madison, WI

Thilman-Filippine*(Group Insurer)*
Chicago, IL

Bank of America NT&SA*(Investment Banker)*
335 Madison Ave.
New York, NY 10017
Tel.: 212-503-8337

First Chicago Bank*(Investment Banker)*
One First National Plaza
Chicago, IL 60670

A.B.P. MIDWEST, INC.
601 Atlas Ave.
Madison, WI 53714
Mailing Address:
P.O. Box 8678,
Madison, WI 53708-8678
Tel.: 608-222-6700
Fax: 608-222-4480
Approx.Sls.: $70,000,000
Emp.: 500
Fiscal Year-end: 7/31/90
Restaurants: Henrici's & Hoffman House
S.I.C.: 5812
Raymond Steck *(Pres.)*
Steve Murphy *(V.P. & Chief Fin. Officer)*

ACI FINANCIAL CORP.
10159 Wayzata Blvd.
Minnetonka, MN 55305
Tel.: 612-541-0444
Fax: 612-541-1572
Year Founded: 1971
Emp.: 50
Provides Insurance & Financial Services, Marketing & Adminstration
S.I.C.: 6411
Clifford Koltes *(Pres.)*
Don Waletzko *(Chief Fin. Officer)*
James McMahill *(Exec. V.P.)*
James M. Pederson *(V.P.)*

Outside Service Firm(s):

Larson, Allen, Weishair & Co.*(Auditors)*
Minneapolis, MN

Oppenheimer, Wolff & Donnelly*(Legal Firm)*
IDS Ctr., 45 S. Seventh St.
Minneapolis, MN 55402
Tel.: 612-344-9300
Fax: 612-344-9376

National City Bank*(Major Banking Relationship)*
75 S. Fifth St.
Minneapolis, MN 55402

ACL TECHNOLOGIES
1505 E. Warner Ave.
Santa Ana, CA 92705
Tel.: 714-979-5500 **CA**
Fax: 714-979-6353
Year Founded: 1954
Approx.Sls.: $15,000,000
Emp.: 145
Mfr. Automated & Dedicated Hydraulic, Pneumatic & Fuel Test Equipment for Servovalves, Actuators, Pumps, Motors, CSD/IDG, Engine Accessories; Fluid Power Supplies & Fluid Cooling Systems
S.I.C.: 3728; 3825; 3829
Tom Wurzel *(Chm. Bd., Pres. & Chief Exec. Officer)*
Stephen P. Abdo *(Exec. V.P.)*
Jim L. Bybee *(V.P.-Engrng.)*
Gregory Ward *(V.P.-Sls. & Mktg.)*
Peter Fox *(Controller)*
Robert Fetch *(Mgr.-Opers.)*
Henry Yoshimoto *(Mgr.-Mktg.)*
Judy Gamble *(Mgr.-Customer Service)*
Wes Schwery *(Mgr.-Personnel)*
Principal(s):
Tom Wurzel

No. of Mfg. Plants/Facilities: 1
No. of U.S. Offices: 1

Computer Systems/Hardware:
IBM System 36

Outside Service Firm(s):

Deloitte & Touche*(Auditors)*
1000 Wilshire Blvd.
Los Angeles, CA 90017-2472
Tel.: 213-688-0800
Fax: 213-688-0100

First Interstate Bank*(Major Banking Relationship)*
Santa Ana, CA

ACO INC.
23333 Commerce Dr.
Farmington Hills, MI 48335-2764
Tel.: 313-471-0100 **MI**
Fax: 313-474-9758
Year Founded: 1946
Approx.Sls.: $96,000,000
Emp.: 1,400
Fiscal Year-end: 2/28/91
Retail Hardware Stores
S.I.C.: 5251
William Aiken *(Chm. Bd. & Chief Exec. Officer)*
Heber L. Noseworthy *(Pres. & Chief Oper. Officer)*
Theodore N. Traskos *(Founder & Chm.-Exec. Committee)*
David Gronbach *(V.P.-Real Estate)*
J. LaBond *(V.P.-Data Processing)*
Mary Tutor *(V.P.)*
Theodore Zimbo *(Controller)*
Patti Rotta *(Dir.-Adv.)*
Wes Mewer *(Dir.-Personnel)*

Outside Service Firm(s):

Ernst & Young*(Auditors)*
One Detroit Center, 500 Woodward, Ste. 1700
Detroit, MI 48243
Tel.: 313-259-9600

Dickinson, Wright, Moon, VanDusen & Freeman*(Legal Firm)*
800 First National Bldg.
Detroit, MI 48226
Tel.: 313-223-3546

National Bank of Detroit*(Major Banking Relationship)*
Farmington Hills, MI

ACR INDUSTRIES INC.
15375 23 Mile Rd.
Mount Clemens, MI 48042-4000
Tel.: 313-781-2800 **MI**
Fax: 313-781-0152
Year Founded: 1976
Assets: $29,100,000
Liabilities: $20,400,000
Net Worth: $8,700,000
Approx.Sls.: $28,000,000
Emp.: 260
Fiscal Year-end: 3/31/91
Export
Manufacturer of Precision Gears & Gearboxes for Aircraft
S.I.C.: 3728
Roger Blanchard *(Chm. Bd.)*
Robert Kazmarek *(Vice Chm.)*
Michael J. Brzoska *(Pres.)*
Danial Hennen *(V.P.)*
Robert Kotz *(Sec.)*
Edward C. Kozlowski *(Treas.)*
David Zonsius *(Dir.-Mfg.)*
Principal(s):
Roger Blanchard
Robert Kazmarek

No. of Mfg. Plants/Facilities: 2
No. of U.S. Offices: 2

Computer Systems/Hardware:
Qantel-Main; IBM PC & CAD Stations

Outside Service Firm(s):

Arthur Andersen & Co.*(Auditors)*
400 Renaissance Center
Detroit, MI 48243
Tel.: 313-259-8100

Pearson, Nordstrom & Tanner*(Group Insurer)*
San Diego, CA

Comerica Bank*(Major Banking Relationship)*
211 W. Fort St.
Detroit, MI 48226
Tel.: 313-222-3300

ACR MECHANICAL CORPORATION
P.O. Box 5380
Orange, CA 92613
Tel.: 714-998-6320
Fax: 714-921-9763
Approx.Sls.: $19,000,000
Emp.: 150
Industrial & Commercial Contracting For Air Conditioning
S.I.C.: 1711; 1521; 1541
Erwine Solloway *(Chm. Bd. & Pres.)*
Wayne Graham *(V.P.)*
Steven W. Hopkins *(V.P.-Fin.)*

Outside Service Firm(s):

Gaugler, Wiegel & Szekel*(Auditors)*
Orange, CA

Barton, Klugman & Oetting*(Legal Firm)*
333 S. Grand
Los Angeles, CA 90071
Tel.: 213-621-4000
Fax: 213-625-1832

First Los Angeles Bank*(Major Banking Relationship)*
Los Angeles, CA

ADV MARKETING GROUP, INC.
408 Elm St.
Stamford, CT 06902
Tel.: 203-356-9621
Fax: 203-324-4680
Year Founded: 1982
Approx.Billings: $10,110,000
Emp.: 20
Business-to-Business & Consumer Advertising, Marketing, Promotion & Public Relations
Alexander Virvo *(Pres. & New Bus. Contact)*
Deirdre J.P. Virvo *(Exec. V.P.)*

Computer Systems/Hardware:
Macintosh

AEA, INC.
700 W. 28th St.
Charlotte, NC 28206
Mailing Address:
P.O. Box 32425
Charlotte, NC 28232
Tel.: 704-377-6991 **NC**
Fax: 704-377-6991, Ext. 124
Approx.Sls.: $40,000,000
Emp.: 255
Wholesale Auto Parts & Air-Cooled Engine Parts
S.I.C.: 5013; 5015
Lowrance Warry *(Chm. Bd. & Treas.)*
C.G. Rider *(Pres. & Chief Exec. Officer)*
William E. Underwood, Jr. *(Sec. & Gen. Counsel)*
Sherry Strickland *(Coord.-Adv.)*
Everett Crayton *(Dir.-Data Processing)*
Jack Graham *(Dir.-Pur.)*
Dick Stewart *(Dir.-Personnel)*
Principal(s):
Lowrance Warry
C.G. Rider

No. of Mfg. Plants/Facilities: 6

Computer Systems/Hardware:
Triad 90

Outside Service Firm(s):

Coopers & Lybrand*(Auditors)*
1850 Charlotte Plaza
Charlotte, NC 28244
Tel.: 704-375-8414
Fax: 704-347-1601

Vernon, Vernon, Wooten, Brown, Andrews, & Garrett, P.A.*(Legal Firm)*

First Union National Bank*(Major Banking Relationship)*
Two First Union Center CMG-5-1154
Charlotte, NC 28288-1154
Tel.: 704-374-6250

Subsidiaries:

AEA Inc./Auto Parts **(1)**
700 W. 28th St.
Charlotte, NC 28206
Tel.: 704-377-6991
S.I.C.: 5013

AEA of Columbia **(1)**
1825 Laurel St.
Columbia, SC 29282
Tel.: 803-765-0750
Auto & Engine Parts Distr.
S.I.C.: 5013

AEA of Raleigh **(1)**
1115 New Hope Rd.
Raleigh, NC 27610
Tel.: 919-231-6145
S.I.C.: 5013

Central All Pro **(1)**
1323 Central Ave.
Charlotte, NC 28206
Tel.: 704-334-1624
S.I.C.: 5013

Piedmont Auto Exchange **(1)**
406 W. 6th St.
Charlotte, NC 28206
Tel.: 704-332-5195

AEC
2022 N. Ferry St.
Anoka, MN 55303
Tel.: 612-323-2600
Fax: 612-421-1343
Year Founded: 1936
Approx.Sls.: $71,000,000
Emp.: 200
Electric Cooperative
S.I.C.: 4911
Arlo Peterson *(Pres.)*
Bert Wedell *(V.P.)*
Lyle Schleif *(Sec. & Treas.)*
Richard Newland *(Gen. Mgr.)*
Ron Olson *(Mgr.-Admin. & Fin.)*

Outside Service Firm(s):

Deloitte & Touche*(Auditors)*
900 Pillsbury Ctr.
Minneapolis, MN 55402
Tel.: 612-332-2301
Fax: 612-375-5418

Levander, Maun & Simon*(Legal Firm)*
South St. Paul, MN

Northern Bank of Anoka*(Major Banking Relationship)*
Anoka, MN

AEI HOLDING CO., INC.
1600 E. Valencia Dr.
Fullerton, CA 92631
Mailing Address:
P.O. Box 3070,
Fullerton, CA 92634
Tel.: 714-871-3020 **CA**
Fax: 714-871-1403
Year Founded: 1986
Holding Company
S.I.C.: 6719
Richard F. Holland *(Pres. & Chief Exec. Officer)*
D.J. Monaco *(V.P.-Fin.)*
William Holland *(V.P.-Sls.)*
Jean M. Roades *(Corp. Sec.)*

Outside Service Firm(s):

Kenneth Leventhal & Co.*(Auditors)*
Ste. 800, 660 Newport Center Dr.
Newport Beach, CA 92660
Tel.: 714-640-5000

Marsh & McLennan*(Commercial Insurance Carrier)*
4695 MacArthur Ct., Ste. 550
Newport Beach, CA 92660
Tel.: 714-253-5800
Fax: 714-833-3027

William M. Mercer Incorporated*(Group Insurer)*
Orange, CA

Davis & Killian*(Legal Firm)*
Newport Beach, CA

Security Pacific National Bank*(Major Banking Relationship)*
Costa Mesa, CA

Subsidiary:

American Electronics, Inc. **(1)**
1600 E. Valencia Dr.
Fullerton, CA 92631
Tel.: 714-871-3020 (100%)
Telex: 910-592-1256
Fax: 714-871-1403
Assets: $8,000,000
Earnings: $700,000
Liabilities: $4,500,000
Net Worth: $3,500,000
Approx.Sls.: $14,000,000
Emp.: 200
Fiscal Year-end: 12/31/90
Mfr. Precision Electromechanical Equip. Including Resolvers, Stepper Motors, Servo Motors, Motor Tachometers, Frequency Converters & Motor Generators; Mfr. Precision Machines, Intricate Hydraulic, Fuel & Liquid Oxygen Valves & Structural Components for Aircraft, Security Cameras & Power Supplies
S.I.C.: 3492; 3621; 3679; 3825
Richard F. Holland *(Pres. & Chief Exec. Officer)*
William Holland *(V.P.-Sls.)*
Dominick J. Monaco *(V.P.-Fin.)*
Mona Caple *(Pur. Agent)*
George Caple *(Production Mgr.)*
Ron Dalton *(Quality Control Mgr.)*
Jean Roades *(Sec.)*
Paul Lee *(Chief Engineer)*

Divisions:

D/B Cameras Microcheck Division **(2)**
1600 E. Valencia Dr.
Fullerton, CA 92631
Tel.: 714-871-3020
16mm & 35mm Film Surveillance Cameras
S.I.C.: 3861

Dressen-Barnes Electronics Div. **(2)**
1600 E. Valencia Dr.
Fullerton, CA 92631
Tel.: 714-871-3020
Standard & Specialized Electronic Power Supplies for Military & Commercial Applications
S.I.C.: 3679

Electro-Mechanical Instruments Div. **(2)**
1600 E. Valencia Dr.
Fullerton, CA 92631
Tel.: 714-871-3020
Manufacture of Miniature Horsepower Alternating Current & Direct Current Motors; Precision Resolvers, Stepper Motors, Servo Motors, Motor Tachometers & Motor Generators; Auxiliary Equipment
S.I.C.: 3621; 3679

Precision Power Div. **(2)**
1600 E. Valencia Dr.
Fullerton, CA 92634
Tel.: 714-871-3020
Manufacture of Rotating Electrical Power Equipment
S.I.C.: 3679

Quadrant Engineering Div. **(2)**
1600 E. Valencia Dr.
Fullerton, CA 92634
Tel.: 714-871-3020
Subcontractor for Aerospace Components Requiring Precision Machining
S.I.C.: 3764

Subsidiary:

The Roll Seal Valve Co., Inc. **(2)**
42024 Avenida Alvarado Unit B
Temecula, CA 92593
Tel.: 909-676-3900 (80%)
Fax: 909-676-3927
Emp.: 5
Manufacture of Valves Used in Liquid Flow Applications
S.I.C.: 3492

AFCG
(Name Changed to ASCG, Inc.)

AFG INDUSTRIES, INC.
301 Commerce St., Ste. 3300
Fort Worth, TX 76102
Tel.: 817-332-5006 **DE**
Fax: 817-870-2685
Year Founded: 1977
Emp.: 5,455
Fiscal Year-end: 12/31/90
Export
Mfrs. Clear & Colored Flat Glass, Insulated Units, Tempered Glass & Rolled Glass
S.I.C.: 3211; 3231
R.D. Hubbard *(Chm. Bd., Pres. & Chief Exec. Officer)*
D.L. Kirkland *(Pres.-Glass Group & Chief Oper. Officer)*
R.C. Cunningham *(Exec. V.P.)*
R.G. McMasters *(Exec. V.P.)*
G.G. Miller *(V.P.-Fin., Chief Fin. Officer & Treas.)*
J.W. Bradford *(V.P., Gen. Counsel & Sec.)*
L.C. Kaufman *(V.P.-Field Sls.)*
William Dankmyer *(Controller)*
Carter Shelton *(Dir.-Pur.)*
E.V. Harris *(Dir.-Human Resources)*
Dave Redd *(Dir.-Data Processing)*
Mark Montgomery *(Dir.-Adv.)*

Computer Systems/Hardware:
IBM ES/9000

Outside Service Firm(s):

KPMG Peat Marwick*(Auditors)*
1 Mellon Bank Ctr.
Pittsburgh, PA 15219
Tel.: 412-391-9710

Shook, Hardy & Bacon*(Legal Firm)*
One Kansas City Place
Kansas City, MO 64105
Tel.: 816-474-6550

Subsidiaries:

AFG International, Inc. **(1)**
P.O. Box 929,
Kingsport, TN 37662
Tel.: 615-229-7200 (100%)
Emp.: 4
Sale of Float Glass Prods./Rolled Glass Prods.e
S.I.C.: 5039
Randy Lantz *(V.P.)*

Fourco Glass Co. **(1)**
P.O. Box 890,
Bridgeport, WV 26330
Tel.: 304-842-6271 (100%)
Emp.: 288
Mfg. & Sale of Float Glass, Boxed Window Glass
S.I.C.: 3211; 5039
A. Slavich *(Plant Mgr.)*

Subsidiary:

Hamilton, Inc. **(2)**
2000 Chestnut St.
Vincennes, IN 47591
Tel.: 812-882-2680
Fax: 812-882-7679
Emp.: 250
Glass Tempering & Mirror Fabrication; Temper-Tuf, Leaded Glass
S.I.C.: 3231
Gary Kimsey *(Pres.)*
Chris Steininger *(Natl. Sls. Mgr.)*

Gemtron Corporation **(1)**
510 Hwy. 68 W.
Sweetwater, TN 37874
Tel.: 615-337-3522 (100%)
Fax: 615-337-7979
Approx.Sls.: $33,000,000
Emp.: 375
Fiscal Year-end: 9/30/92
Computer Systems/Hardware:
AS 400 IBM
Mfr. of Tempered & Decorative Glass For Uses Including Shower Doors, Ovens & Shelving
S.I.C.: 3211
Helmut Fahlbush *(Chm. Bd.)*
R.D. Hubbard *(Vice Chm.)*
Gary Kimsey *(Pres.)*
Tom Tallent *(V.P.-Fin.)*
P. Roberts *(V.P.-Mfg.)*
Mark Delp *(V.P.-Mktg. & Sls.)*
Gary Miller *(Treas.)*
Diane Allmon *(Controller)*
Mark Clinton *(Dir.-Personnel)*
John Canada *(Dir.-Human Resources)*
C. Kizer *(Product Mgr.)*
Keith Sitzler *(Pur. Agent)*
Dale Biehl *(Gen. Mgr.)*

Glass Products, Inc. **(1)**
Clindo Drive
Carbondale, PA 18407
Tel.: 717-282-6711 (100%)
Emp.: 102
Mfg. Laminated Glass
S.I.C.: 3231

New Jersey Float Glass, Inc. **(1)**
2600 River Road
Cinnaminson, NJ 08077
Tel.: 609-829-0400 (100%)
Emp.: 191
Mfg. & Sale of Float Glass
S.I.C.: 3211
Floyd Austin *(Plant Mgr.)*

AFG Industries, Inc.—(Continued)

O'Dell Products, Inc. **(1)**
Univeter Road
Canton, GA 30114
Tel.: 706-345-5566 (100%)
Emp.: 64
Glass Fabricator
S.I.C.: 3211
Ralph Armstrong *(Plant Mgr.)*

Southern Wholesale **(1)**
3200 Austell Road
Marietta, GA 30060
Tel.: 404-434-2041 (100%)
Emp.: 457
Glass Fabricator
S.I.C.: 3211
Steve Michael *(Pres.)*

Non-U.S. Holding:

AFG Glass Inc. **(1)**
101 Richmond St., West
Toronto, ON M5H 1V9, Canada
Tel.: 416-363-7561
Mfrs. Flat Glass
S.I.C.: 3211
D. Kirkland *(Pres.-Glass Group)*

A-G CO-OP CREAMERY
502 W. Main
Arcadia, WI 54612
Tel.: 608-323-2141 **WI**
Fax: 608-323-3081
Approx.Sls.: $75,000,000
Emp.: 340
Producers of Cheese: Natural & Processed; Chicken: Processed & Fresh; Fertilizer & Fertilizer Materials; Feed; Seeds: Field, Garden & Flower; Chicken Hatchery
S.I.C.: 2022; 2015; 5191; 0254
Russell Butman *(Pres.)*
Dave Schwarz *(V.P.)*
John Rud *(Treas.)*
Roger Filla *(Sec.)*
C.J. Smith *(Gen. Mgr.)*
Clareton Smitty *(Gen. Mgr.)*

AGCO INC.
2782 Simpson Circle
Norcross, GA 30071
Tel.: 404-447-6990
Mfr. & Sales of Farm Machinery
S.I.C.: 3523
Larry Pulliam *(Pres.)*

Subsidiary:

AGCO Corporation **(1)**
5295 Triangle Pkwy.
Norcross, GA 30092
Tel.: 404-447-5546 (100%)
Fax: 404-246-6158
Approx.Sls.: $300,000,000
Emp.: 1,000
Fiscal Year-end: 12/31/90
Import Export
Manufacturing & Sale of Farm Machinery: Tractors, Diesel Implements, Combines, Corn Heads, Grain Headers & Diesel Generator Systems; Planting Systems
S.I.C.: 3523
Larry Pulliam *(Pres.)*
Susan Hogan *(V.P.-Communications & Adv.)*

Division:

AGCO Manufacturing Group **(2)**
627 So. Cottage St.
Independence, MO 64051
Tel.: 816-836-0500 (100%)
Fax: 816-836-6393
Combines (Conventional & Rotary), Grain Headers for Harvesting Small Grains
S.I.C.: 3523
James M. Lucas *(V.P.)*

Hesston **(1)**
5295 Triangle Pkwy.
Norcross, GA 30092
Tel.: 404-447-5546
Fax: 404-246-6118
Approx.Sls.: $122,000,000
Fiscal Year-end: 12/31/90
Import Export
Mfr. of Windrowers, Hay Handling Equipment; Tillage, Balers & Mower Conditioners; Manure Spreaders; Skid Stter Loaders; Hay Rakes; Forage Boxes
S.I.C.: 3523
Robert J. Ratliff *(Pres. & Chief Exec. Officer)*
John M. Shumejoa *(Sr. V.P.-Opers.)*
Harold D. Dent *(V.P.-Mktg.)*
Susan Hogan *(V.P.-Communications)*
R.J. Hohlman *(V.P. & Controller)*
S.I. Oakford *(V.P. & Chief Fin. Officer)*
James M. Seaver *(V.P.-Parts Distr.)*
Edward R. Swingle *(V.P.-Sls.)*
Michael F. Swick *(Gen. Counsel)*
Art Hammerstrom *(Adv. Mgr.)*

Joint Venture:

Hay & Forage Industries **(2)**
420 W. Lincoln Blvd.
Hesston, KS 67062
Tel.: 316-327-6300
Fax: 316-327-6191
Approx.Sls.: $157,512,000
Emp.: 900
Mfr. of Self-Propelled Windrowers, Pull-Type Windrower, Windrower-Mounted Hay Conditioner, Pull-Type Forage Harvesters, Balers, Round Bale Movers
S.I.C.: 3523
Charles H. Miller *(Gen. Mgr.)*
Don Schmidt *(Controller)*
Gary Sneed *(Dir.-Matls.)*
Dave Fritz *(Dir.-Engrng.)*
Gary Van Dolah *(Dir.-Personnel)*
Tom Tryber *(Mgr.-Systems)*

AGI INC.
1950 N. Ruby St.
Melrose Park, IL 60160
Tel.: 708-344-9100
Fax: 708-344-9113
Approx.Sls.: $30,000,000
Emp.: 380
Printing For Folding Cartons
S.I.C.: 2759
Richard Block *(Pres.)*
David Underwood *(Chief Fin. Officer)*
Jim Oppenheimer *(V.P.-Sls.)*
Dennis McGuin *(Dir.-Personnel)*
Principal(s):
Donald K. Kosterka

Computer Systems/Hardware:
NCR

Outside Service Firm(s):

Arthur Andersen & Co.*(Auditors)*
33 W. Monroe St.
Chicago, IL 60603-4067
Tel.: 312-580-0033
Fax: 312-507-6748

AGR INTERNATIONAL, INC.
615 Whitestown Rd.
Butler, PA 16001
Mailing Address:
P.O. Box 149
Butler, PA 16003-0149
Tel.: 412-482-2163
Fax: 412-482-2767
Year Founded: 1957
Sales Range: $10-19 Million
Emp.: 235
Fiscal Year-end: 12/31/91
Export
Mfr. of Container Testing Equipment
S.I.C.: 3829
Henry M. Dimmick *(Chm. Bd. & Chief Exec. Officer)*
R.D. Southwick *(Pres.)*
D.A. Rugaber *(Sr. V.P.)*
W.J. Bellis *(Treas. & Controller)*
P.A. Chuba *(Sec.)*
R.J. Tait *(Mfg. Group Mgr.)*
R.W. Ryder *(Mgr.-Pur.)*
D.R. Byers *(Mgr.-Personnel)*
K.M. Link *(Corp. Librarian)*

No. of Mfg. Plants/Facilities: 1

Outside Service Firm(s):

Price Waterhouse*(Auditors)*
600 Grant St., Ste. 4400
Pittsburgh, PA 15219
Tel.: 412-355-6000
Fax: 412-391-0609

Buchanan, Ingersoll p.c.*(Legal Firm)*
600 Grant St., 57th Flr.
Pittsburgh, PA 15219
Tel.: 412-562-8800

Citizens National Bank of Evans City*(Major Banking Relationship)*
Evans City, PA

AGSCO, INC.
2600 Mill Rd.
Grand Forks, ND 58206
Mailing Address:
P.O. Box 458
Grand Forks, ND 58206
Tel.: 701-775-5325
Fax: 701-775-9587
Year Founded: 1935
Approx.Sls.: $18,000,000
Emp.: 75
Import
Agricultural Chemicals & Seeds
S.I.C.: 2879; 5191
Lawrence A. Brown *(Chm. Bd.)*
Russell Brown *(Pres.)*
Randy Brown *(V.P.-Sls. & Mktg.)*
Orville Swenson *(Dir.-Chemical Research)*

Outside Service Firm(s):

Brady, Martz & Associates*(Auditors)*
Grand Forks, ND

McConn, Fisher, Olsen & Daley Ltd.*(Legal Firm)*
Grand Forks, ND

Valley National Bank*(Major Banking Relationship)*
Grand Forks, ND

AJC INTERNATIONAL, INC.
5188 Roswell Rd., N.W.
Atlanta, GA 30342
Tel.: 404-252-6750 **GA**
Fax: 404-252-9340
Year Founded: 1972
Approx.Sls.: $203,000,000
Emp.: 105
Fiscal Year-end: 7/31/91
Import Export
Importers & Exporters of Meat, Poultry, Seafood, Canned, Frozen, Dry Fruits & Vegetables
S.I.C.: 4731; 5141; 5144; 5146; 5147; 5148; 5149
Eric J. Joiner *(Pres.)*
Gerald L. Allison *(Chief Exec. Officer)*
James Gillaspy *(Chief Information Officer)*
George Bell *(Treas.)*
John Partington *(Controller)*
Shirley J. Owen *(Sec.)*
Evan Davidman *(Dir.-Sls.)*
Stacy Stewart *(Dir.-Human Resources)*
Michael Wisniewski *(Dir.-Mktg.)*
Dale Brunton *(Prod. Mgr.-Poultry)*
H. Ray Contino *(Prod. Mgr.-Frozen Foods)*
Kurt Holdmeyer *(Prod. Mgr.-Pork)*
Jeanette P. Jeffrey *(Prod. Mgr.-Canned Foods)*

Computer Systems/Hardware:
Data General/IBM

Outside Service Firm(s):

Braver & Co.*(Auditors)*
Atlanta, GA

First National Bank of Atlanta*(Major Banking Relationship)*
2 Peachtree Street N.W.
Atlanta, GA 30383

Subsidiaries:

American Institutional Foods **(1)**
P.O. Box 367,
Chattanooga, TN 37401
Tel.: 615-266-7114
Emp.: 23
Food Distribution
S.I.C.: 5142
Leon Russell *(Gen. Mgr.)*

D'Jesco, Inc. **(1)**
P.O. Box S-1653,
Old San Juan, PR 00903
Tel.: 809-784-0520
Emp.: 25
Food Distribution
S.I.C.: 5142
Alfonso Civile *(Retail Food Distributor)*

Economy International Service Inc. **(1)**
P.O. Box 1247,
Hato Rey, PR 00920
Cold Storage/Warehouse
Manuel Espinosa, Jr. *(Gen. Mgr.)*

A J M PACKAGING CORPORATION
6910 Dix
Detroit, MI 48209
Tel.: 313-842-7530 **MI**
Fax: 313-842-7691
Approx.Sls.: $50,000,000
Emp.: 160
Mfr. of Paper Bags Made From Purchased Materials; Pails, Sanitary Food
S.I.C.: 2674; 2656
Abram Epstein *(Pres.)*
Robert Epstein *(V.P.)*
Lawrence Epstein *(Sec. & Treas.)*

Outside Service Firm(s):

Grant Thornton*(Auditors)*
Southfield, MI

Rubenstein, Isaacs, Lax & Bordman*(Legal Firm)*
Southfield, MI

Manufacturers National Bank N.A.*(Major Banking Relationship)*
38th Fl., 100 Renaissance Center
Detroit, MI 48243
Tel.: 313-222-4227

A K H COMPANY, INC.
(d/b/a Discount Tire)
6565 E. Washington Blvd.
Los Angeles, CA 90040
Tel.: 213-725-0099 **CA**
Fax: 213-725-0759
Year Founded: 1975
Assets: $21,415,028
Liabilities: $18,510,842
Net Worth: $2,904,186
Approx.Sls.: $115,071,939
Emp.: 750
Fiscal Year-end: 12/31/90
Wholesale Distribution & Retail Sales of Automotive Tires & Tubes; Automotive Brake Lining Installation; Wheel Alignment
S.I.C.: 5531; 5014; 7539
Andy K. Andonian *(Pres.)*
Hratch K. Andonian *(Exec. V.P., Sec. & Treas.)*
John Andonian *(Exec. V.P.)*
George Andonian *(V.P.)*
Principal(s):
Andy K. Andonian
Hratch K. Andonian
John Andonian
George Andonian

No. of U.S. Offices: 1

Computer Systems/Hardware:
IBM System 5380

Outside Service Firm(s):

Coopers & Lybrand*(Auditors)*
350 S. Grand Ave.
Los Angeles, CA 90071
Tel.: 213-481-1000
Fax: 213-482-6440

Tokai Bank of California*(Major Banking Relationship)*
Los Angeles, CA

ALP/FREDDY'S
90 Commerce Dr.
Rochester, NY 14623
Tel.: 716-334-2580
Approx.Sls.: $194,061,000
39 Discount Drug Stores
S.I.C.: 5912
William Edwards *(Pres.)*
John Mashaua *(Exec. V.P.)*
Richard McLean *(V.P.)*
Michael Miskell *(V.P.)*
Ken Koester *(Controller)*

AMD INDUSTRIES INC.
4620 W. 19th St.
Cicero, IL 60650
Tel.: 708-863-8900
Tel.: 800-367-9999
Fax: 708-863-2065
Year Founded: 1922
Approx.Sls.: $13,000,000
Emp.: 110
Fiscal Year-end: 12/31/91

Export
Designers & Mfrs. of Point-of-Purchase Merchandising Programs
S.I.C.: 3993
David Allen *(Chm., Pres. & Chief Exec. Officer)*
Tim Norton *(Exec. V.P.-Sls. & Mktg.)*
Robert W. Harris *(V.P.-Admin. & Opers.)*
Gerald Sweeney *(Controller)*
Jerry Dohse *(Dir.-Mfg.)*
Ranesh Gandhi *(Dir.-Pur.)*
Tom Miller *(Dir.-Engrng.)*

AMF BAKERY SYSTEMS
2115 W. Laburnum Ave.
Richmond, VA 23227
Mailing Address:
P.O. Box 9168,
Richmond, VA 23227
Tel.: 804-355-7961
Tel.: 800-225-3771
Fax: 804-355-1074
Approx.Sls.: $40,000,000
Emp.: 400

Export
Bakery Machinery
S.I.C.: 3599
Bill Goodwin *(Chm. Bd.)*
Harry Franze *(Pres.)*
Toby Steward *(V.P.-Sls. & Mktg.)*
Eamond Rowan *(Controller)*
Larry Gore *(Mgr.-Sls. Office)*
Dena Hembrick *(Mgr.-Human Resources)*

AMI INDUSTRIES, INC.
1275 North Newport Rd.
Colorado Springs, CO 80916-2779
Tel.: 719-380-0020
Fax: 719-380-0040
Year Founded: 1932
Approx.Sls.: $16,700,000
Emp.: 200
Fiscal Year-end: 12/31/91

Import Export
Manufactures Aircraft & Surface Transportation Seating, Aircraft Landing Gear & Components, & Specialized Precision Machined Assemblies
S.I.C.: 3728; 3499
Jim MacDougald *(Pres.)*
Edward Osborne *(V.P. & Dir.-Engrng.)*
Tom Ekle *(Chief Fin. Officer)*
Jay Ruic *(Controller)*
Thomas Green *(Dir.-Opers.)*
Frank Leon *(Dir.-Mktg.)*
Lana Yeakel *(Dir.-Personnel)*
Jeff Golik *(Mgr.-Data Processing)*

Computer Systems/Hardware:
Sanyo-Icon

AMSPEC CHEMICAL CORPORATION
Water St.
Gloucester City, NJ 08030
Tel.: 609-456-3930
Fax: 609-456-6704
Sales Range: $20-39 Million
Emp.: 68
Antimony Oxide, Sodium Alcholoates, Metal Acetyl Acetonates, Guar Gum
S.I.C.: 2861; 2869; 2899
J. Gustavsen *(Chief Exec. Officer)*
T.L. Jelinski *(V.P.-Mktg.)*
K.R. Stewart *(Plant Mgr.)*

Outside Service Firm(s):

Hass & Company*(Auditors)*
Philadelphia, PA

Norris, McLaughlin & Marcus*(Legal Firm)*
Philadelphia, PA

Chemical Banking Corp.*(Major Banking Relationship)*
277 Park Ave.
New York, NY 10041
Tel.: 212-310-6407
Fax: 212-310-4526

A-P-A TRANSPORT CORP.
2100 88th St.
North Bergen, NJ 07047
Tel.: 201-869-6600 **NJ**
Fax: 201-869-5470
Year Founded: 1947
Approx.Sls.: $145,000,000
Emp.: 1,800
National & Local Trucking
S.I.C.: 4212; 4213
Arthur E. Imperatore *(Chm. Bd.)*
Armand Pohan *(Pres.)*
Frederic C. Astle *(V.P.-Fin. & Treas.)*
Andrew Park *(V.P.-Opers.)*
Daniel Solazzo *(V.P.-Sls.)*
Burton Trebour *(V.P.-Labor & Admin.)*
Dominick Alesso *(Sec. & Gen. Counsel)*
William Bischoff *(Dir.-Data Processing)*
David O'Dowd *(Dir.-Insurance)*
Richard Santee *(Dir.-Mktg.)*
Joseph Whelan *(Dir.-Personnel)*
Bruce Zeman *(Dir.-Pur.)*

No. of Mfg. Plants/Facilities: 33
No. of U.S. Offices: 28
No. of Foreign Offices: 7

Computer Systems/Hardware:
Datapoint ARCNET

Outside Service Firm(s):

Deloitte & Touche*(Auditors)*
Newark, NJ

McCarter & English*(Legal Firm)*
550 Broad
Newark, NJ 07102
Tel.: 201-622-4444

First National Bank of Boston*(Major Banking Relationship)*
P.O. Box 644,
Boston, MA 02102-0644
Tel.: 617-575-2900
Fax: 617-575-2549

APG SECURITY, INC.
12000 E. 47th Ave., Ste. 105
Denver, CO 80239
Tel.: 303-373-5840 **CO**
Fax: 303-375-9534
Approx.Sls.: $10,000,000
Emp.: 650
Security Guard Service
S.I.C.: 7381
Anthony Pisani *(Pres.)*
Charles Marshall *(V.P.)*
Patricia Pisani *(Sec. & Treas.)*

Outside Service Firm(s):

United Bank*(Major Banking Relationship)*
NorthGlenn, CO

API GROUP INC.
2366 Rose Pl.
Saint Paul, MN 55113
Tel.: 612-636-4320 **MN**
Twx: 910-563-3703
Fax: 612-636-0312
Year Founded: 1924
Approx.Sls.: $112,000,000
Emp.: 500
Fiscal Year-end: 12/31/91
Holding Company; Industrial Insulation Contractor & Insulation Materials Distributors; Plumbing & Heating Contractor; Manufacture Flexible Air Ducts; Engineering Services; Bank Holding Company Operating 5 Banks
S.I.C.: 6719; 6712; 1799; 1731; 1711; 3444; 5039
Lee R. Anderson, Sr. *(Chm. Bd. & Chief Exec. Officer)*
Robert J. Koth *(Pres.)*
William M. Beadie *(Sec.)*
Loren Rachey *(Treas.)*

Outside Service Firm(s):

Wilkerson, Guthmann & Johnson*(Auditors)*
Hastings, MN

Moore, Costello & Hart*(Legal Firm)*
St. Paul, MN

First Bank Minneapolis*(Major Banking Relationship)*
P.O. Box A700, 120 S. Sixth St.
Minneapolis, MN 55480
Tel.: 612-370-4141

A.P.S., INC.
3000 Pawnee St.
Houston, TX 77054
Tel.: 713-741-2470
Year Founded: 1963
Approx.Sls.: $400,000,000
Emp.: 2,000
Fiscal Year-end: 1/31/91
Distributor of Automotive Parts
S.I.C.: 5013
Richard Spelleri *(Chm. Bd.)*
Mark Hoffman *(Pres.)*
Mike Preston *(Sr. V.P.)*
Chris Romeis *(V.P.-Big A Program)*
David Barbeau *(Chief Fin. Officer)*
Barbara Shinabery *(Dir.-Adv.)*
Ray Rarey *(Dir.-Personnel)*

Subsidiary:

A.P.S. Supply, Inc. **(1)**
3000 Pawnee St.
Houston, TX 77054
Tel.: 713-741-2470
S.I.C.: 5531
Jim McWilliams *(Gen. Mgr.)*

AQHI, INC.
87 Upton Rd.
Colchester, CT 06415
Tel.: 203-537-4681
Fax: 203-537-4332
Holding Company; Machine Shop Products
S.I.C.: 6719; 3599
Stephen Prout *(Pres. & Chief Exec. Officer)*

Outside Service Firm(s):

KPMG Peat Marwick*(Auditors)*
345 Park Ave.
New York, NY 10154
Tel.: 212-758-9700
Fax: 212-872-3308

Kirkland & Ellis*(Legal Firm)*
55 E. 52nd St., 16th Fl.
New York, NY 10055

Chemical Banking Corp.*(Major Banking Relationship)*
277 Park Ave.
New York, NY 10041
Tel.: 212-310-6407
Fax: 212-310-4526

Subsidiary:

Alpha Q, Inc. **(1)**
87 Upton Rd.
Colchester, CT 06415
Tel.: 203-537-4681
Approx.Sls.: $15,000,000
Emp.: 110
Machine Shop Products
S.I.C.: 3599
Paul V. Allegretto *(Pres. & Chief Exec. Officer)*
Ron Bonito *(V.P. & Gen. Mgr.)*
L. Steven Proat *(Chief Fin. Officer)*
Dominick Luppachino *(Pur. Agent.)*

ARA GROUP
ARA Tower, 1101 Market St.
Philadelphia, PA 19107
Tel.: 215-238-3000
Tel.: 800-999-8989 **DE**
Fax: 215-238-3333
Year Founded: 1959
Earnings: $64,223,000
Approx.Sls.: $4,774,356,000
Emp.: 135,000
Fiscal Year-end: 9/27/91
Holding Company for Food Service
S.I.C.: 5812; 6719
Joseph Neubauer *(Chm. Bd., Pres. & Chief Exec. Officer)*
Martin W. Spector *(Exec. V.P. & Gen. Counsel)*
James Ksansnak *(Exec. V.P.-Fin. & Personnel)*
L. Frederick Sutherland *(Sr. V.P.)*
Anthony J. Tanzola *(V.P., Controller & Admin. Officer)*
Harry Belinger *(V.P.-Pub. Affairs)*
Gene R. Remoff *(V.P.-Human Resources)*
John Kallelis *(V.P.)*
Melvin M. Mahoney *(Treas.)*
Elmer Shamwell *(Dir.-Real Estate)*
David Flaherty *(Dir.-Pub. Affairs)*
Noreen Duffy *(Media Adv. Specialist)*
Elizabeth B. Cartmell *(Asst. Treas.)*
Marie E. West *(Mgr.-Benefits Fin.)*

Computer Systems/Hardware:
IBM

Outside Service Firm(s):

Arthur Andersen & Co.*(Auditors)*
1601 Market St.
Philadelphia, PA 19103
Tel.: 215-241-7300

Chemical Banking Corp.*(Major Banking Relationship)*
277 Park Ave.
New York, NY 10041
Tel.: 212-310-6407
Fax: 212-310-4526

Subsidiaries:

ARA Services, Inc. **(1)**
ARA Tower, 1101 Market St.
Philadelphia, PA 19107
Tel.: 215-238-3000
Fax: 215-238-3333
Approx.Sls.: $4,800,100,000
Emp.: 120,000
Fiscal Year-end: 9/29/90
Diversified Service Management, Including Food & Refreshment Services; Management of Nursing Homes, Child Care Facilities & Hospital Emergency Departments; Magazine & Book Distributor; Building Maintenance Services; Textile Rental & Laundry Services
S.I.C.: 8741; 5994; 7011; 7213; 7218; 7349; 8051; 5812
Joseph Neubauer *(Chm. Bd. & Pres.)*
James Ksansnak *(Exec. V.P.-Fin. & Chief Fin. Officer)*
Martin W. Spector *(Sr. V.P., Gen. Counsel & Sec.)*
L. Frederick Sutherland *(V.P.-Fin. & Devel.)*
Thomas Fitzgerald *(V.P.-Mktg.)*
Gerald Van Duser *(Dir.-Property & Facilities)*
David Flaherty *(Dir.-Public Affairs)*

ARA Group—(Continued)

Manufacturing Division:

Aratex of Puerto Rico **(2)**
Free Trade Zone, P.O. Box B
Mayaguez, PR 00708
Tel.: 809-832-1868
Mfg. of Uniforms
S.I.C.: 2326; 2337

Subsidiaries:

ARA/Cory Refreshment Services, Inc. **(2)**
431 Lakeview Ct.
Mount Prospect, IL 60056
Tel.: 708-803-6800
Approx.Sls.: $50,000,000
Emp.: 800
Supplies Coffee & Related Prods. to Indus., Comml., Institutional & General Business Offices
S.I.C.: 5812
William Edmonson *(Pres.)*
Carrie McBride *(Dir.-Adv.)*
Carm J. Notaro *(Branch Mgr.)*

ARA Environmental Services, Inc. **(2)**
1101 Market St.
Philadelphia, PA 19107
Tel.: 215-238-3486
Waste Disposal Services
S.I.C.: 4953

ARA Healthcare Nutrition Services, Inc. **(2)**
2911 Ogletown Rd.
Newark, DE 19713
Tel.: 302-737-3200
Food Catering Services Mngmt.
S.I.C.: 5812

ARA Leisure Services, Inc. **(2)**
1101 Market Street
Philadelphia, PA 19107
Tel.: 215-238-3333
S.I.C.: 5812

Operations:

ARA Leisure Convention Services, Inc. **(3)**
1101 Market Street
Philadelphia, PA 19107
S.I.C.: 5812

ARA Leisure Services Group, Florida **(3)**
600 Ashley Drive
Tampa, FL 33602
Tel.: 813-223-7872
Handles Concessions for Curtis Hixon Convention Hall
S.I.C.: 5812
James Foreman *(Div. Mgr.)*

ARA Leisure Services, Hawthorne Race Course **(3)**
3501 Laramie
Cicero, IL 60650
Tel.: 708-780-0800
S.I.C.: 5812
Ed Becker *(Div. Mgr.)*

ARA Leisure Services, New Orleans Convention Center **(3)**
900 Convention Center Blvd.
New Orleans, LA 70130
Tel.: 504-582-3575
Concessions, Catering Service for New Orleans Convention Center
S.I.C.: 5812
James Pritchard *(Div. Mgr.)*

ARA Leisure Services of Texas, Inc. **(3)**
650 So. Griffin
Dallas, TX 75202
Tel.: 214-749-0283
Catering Services for the Dallas Convention Center
S.I.C.: 5812
Karen Whittig *(Div. Mgr.)*

ARA Leisure Services, Rivergate **(3)**
4 Canal St.
New Orleans, LA 70130
Tel.: 504-592-2000
Concessions, Catering Services for Rivergate Exhibition Hall Convention Center
S.I.C.: 5812
Katie Batchelor *(Div. Mgr.)*

ARA Leisure Services, Soldier Field **(3)**
425 E. McFetridge Dr.
Chicago, IL 60605
Tel.: 312-786-2142
Concessions & Catering Services
S.I.C.: 5812
Rich Roper *(Div. Mgr.)*

ARA Leisure Services, Wrigley Field **(3)**
1060 W. Addison
Chicago, IL 60613
Concessions & Catering Services
S.I.C.: 5812
John Doncrank *(Gen. Mgr.)*

ARA Services, John Hancock Center **(3)**
875 N. Michigan Ave.
Chicago, IL 60611
Fine Dining, Catering, Cafeteria Services
S.I.C.: 5812
Richard Roman *(Gen. Mgr.)*

ARA Services, Loyola University **(3)**
47 E. Pearson
Chicago, IL 60611
Catering Services
S.I.C.: 5812
Tim Siehl *(Gen. Mgr.)*

ARA Services, Rosemont Horizon **(3)**
6920 Mannheim Rd.
Rosemont, IL 60018
Tel.: 708-635-6680
Concession for the Rosemont Horizon Auditorium
S.I.C.: 5812
Rich Roper *(Div. Mgr.)*

Aero Enterprises, Inc. **(3)**
Philadelphia International Airport
Philadelphia, PA 19153
Tel.: 215-492-3250
Catering Services
S.I.C.: 5812; 5994

Mile High Enterprises, Inc. **(3)**
2800 W. 20th Ave.
Denver, CO 80211
Tel.: 303-455-6617
Handles Concessions for Mile High Stadium
S.I.C.: 5812
Albert Valdes *(Div. Mgr.)*

Pittsburgh Stadium Concessions, Inc. **(3)**
100 Stadium Circle
Pittsburgh, PA 15212
Tel.: 412-321-2800
Handles Concessions at Three Rivers Stadium
S.I.C.: 5812
Tim Lawler *(Div. Mgr.)*

ARA Magazine & Book Division, Inc. **(2)**
P.O. Box 25489, 7000 N. Robinson
Oklahoma City, OK 73125
Tel.: 405-843-9383
Distrs. Magazines, Books, Newspapers & Other Published Material
S.I.C.: 5199
Bob Anderson *(Mgr.)*

ARA Services of Texas, Inc. **(2)**
1101 Market St.
Philadelphia, PA 19107
Tel.: 215-574-5000

ARA Virginia Sky-Line Co., Inc. **(2)**
1101 Market St.
Philadelphia, PA 19106
Tel.: 215-574-5000
Food Concessions
S.I.C.: 5812

Aramont Properties, Inc.-Delaware **(2)**
2911 Ogletown Rd.
Newark, DE 19713
Tel.: 302-737-3200
Real Estate Mgmnt. Services
S.I.C.: 6531

ARAserve, Inc. **(2)**
2911 Ogletown Rd.
Newark, DE 19713
Tel.: 302-737-3200
Vending Company & Food Service
S.I.C.: 5812; 5962
Don Waters *(Div. Mgr.)*

Aratex Services, Inc. **(2)**
115 N. First St.
Burbank, CA 91502
Tel.: 818-973-3700
Uniform Rental
S.I.C.: 7218
William Leonard *(Pres.)*

Subsidiaries:

Araclean Services, Inc. **(3)**
Independence Sq. W., Sixth & Walnut Sts.
Philadelphia, PA 19106
S.I.C.: 7218; 7216

Aratex Services **(3)**
625B Old Norcross Rd.
Lawrenceville, GA 30245
Tel.: 404-822-1420
Mfg., Renting & Servicing Work Clothes, Supplying Protective & Consumable Cleansing Prods., Bldg. Maintenance
S.I.C.: 7213; 7218; 5169; 7349
Philip A. Lane *(Chm. Bd.)*
Mary Smallworth *(Area Pres.)*
Eric S. Cohen *(V.P.)*
Carl G. Coben *(V.P., Sec. & Legal)*
Corinne Burns *(Pur. Dir.)*
Daniel Boyle *(Data Processing Dir.)*
Philip D. Carnevale *(Dir.-Fin.)*

Aratex Services **(3)**
2315 25th St., N.
Birmingham, AL 35234
Tel.: 205-322-2453
Rental of Uniforms
S.I.C.: 7218
John Hargis *(Gen. Mgr.)*

Aratex Services **(3)**
2321 Wilkerson Blvd.
Charlotte, NC 28208
Tel.: 704-375-1705
Rental of Uniforms
S.I.C.: 7218
Steve Howard *(Gen. Mgr.)*

Aratex Services **(3)**
11200 Decimal Dr.
Louisville, KY 40299
Tel.: 502-267-5212
Rental of Uniforms
S.I.C.: 7218

Aratex Services **(3)**
919 Airport Blvd.
Columbia, SC 29205
Tel.: 803-799-1470
Rental of Uniforms
S.I.C.: 7218
Steven Howard *(Gen. Mgr.)*

Aratex Services **(3)**
509 Teague St.
Greensboro, NC 27406
Tel.: 919-275-3381
Rental of Uniforms
S.I.C.: 7218
Jim Brandt *(Gen. Mgr.)*

Aratex Services **(3)**
110 Glenn St.
Lawrence, MA 01843
Tel.: 508-685-1936
Rental of Uniforms
S.I.C.: 7218
Bob Crist *(Gen. Mgr.)*

Aratex Services **(3)**
379 W. Michigan St., Ste. 208
Orlando, FL 32806
Tel.: 407-841-1130
Rental of Uniforms
S.I.C.: 7218
Jeff Cahan *(Gen. Mgr.)*

Aratex Services **(3)**
103 Old Colony Ave.
East Taunton, MA 02718
Tel.: 508-824-7538
Rental of Uniforms
S.I.C.: 7218
David Graham *(Gen. Mgr.)*

Aratex Services **(3)**
958 28th St.
Oakland, CA 94608
Tel.: 510-832-3027
Rental of Uniforms
S.I.C.: 7218

Aratex Services **(3)**
401 Glen Iris Dr.
Atlanta, GA 30308
Tel.: 404-681-1731
Uniform Rental
S.I.C.: 7218
Dwight Miller *(Gen. Mgr.)*

Aratex Services **(3)**
740 Frelinghuisen Ave.
Newark, NJ 07114
Tel.: 201-824-1101
Rental of Uniforms
S.I.C.: 7218
Tonio O'Connor *(Gen. Mgr.)*

Aratex Services **(3)**
205 E. Morningside
Fort Worth, TX 76104
Tel.: 817-924-5489
Rental of Uniforms
S.I.C.: 7218
Robert Holmes *(Gen. Mgr.)*

Aratex Services **(3)**
1200 Webster
Dayton, OH 45404
Tel.: 513-223-6667
Rental of Uniforms
S.I.C.: 7218

Aratex Services **(3)**
2010 Martin Luther King Dr.
East Saint Louis, IL 62205
Tel.: 618-271-3232
Rental of Uniforms
S.I.C.: 7218
Carl Lammers *(Gen. Mgr.)*

Aratex Services **(3)**
2500 Delaware Ave.
Des Moines, IA 50317
Tel.: 515-265-8171
Rental of Uniforms
S.I.C.: 7218
Graham Duffield *(Gen. Mgr.)*

Aratex Services **(3)**
2928 Washington Blvd.
Baltimore, MD 21230
Tel.: 410-644-9330
Rental of Uniforms
S.I.C.: 7218
Thadd Cradwell *(Gen. Mgr.)*

Aratex Services **(3)**
2860 Rudder Rd.
Memphis, TN 38130
Tel.: 901-365-4561
Rental of Uniforms
S.I.C.: 7218
George Willis *(Gen. Mgr.)*

Aratex Services **(3)**
1900 Empire Central
Dallas, TX 75235
Tel.: 214-637-0970
Rental of Uniforms
S.I.C.: 7218
Lou Malloy *(Gen. Mgr.)*

Aratex Services **(3)**
10110 Cash Rd.
Stafford, TX 77477
Tel.: 713-499-4506
Rental of Uniforms
S.I.C.: 7218
Melanie Person *(Gen. Mgr.)*

Aratex Services **(3)**
357 E. 31st St.
Jacksonville, FL 32206
Tel.: 904-355-3528
Rental of Uniforms
S.I.C.: 7218

Aratex Services **(3)**
202 Cassidy Rd.
Thomasville, GA 31792
Tel.: 912-226-6242
Rental of Uniforms
S.I.C.: 7218
Jean Hicks *(Gen. Mgr.)*

Aratex Services **(3)**
2911 Ogletown Rd.
Newark, DE 19711
Tel.: 302-737-3200
S.I.C.: 5962
Don Weaters *(Supvr.)*

Aratex Services, Inc. **(3)**
1834 Walden Office Sq.
Schaumburg, IL 60173
Tel.: 708-397-9500
Approx.Sls.: $115,569,146
Emp.: 12,000
Textile Rental & Maintenance
S.I.C.: 7219
Fred Lenway *(Pres.)*

Aratex Services, Inc. **(3)**
1178 Marlkress
Cherry Hill, NJ 08003
Tel.: 609-424-9320
S.I.C.: 7213
Carl Philip *(Area Pres.)*

Aratex Textile Services, Inc. **(3)**
1834 Walden Office Sq., Ste. 45
Schaumburg, IL 60195
Tel.: 708-397-9500
S.I.C.: 7219
Fred Lenway *(Area Pres.)*

Woodhaven Foods **(2)**
11151 Roosevelt Blvd.
Philadelphia, PA 19154
Tel.: 215-698-1200
Distr. Wholesale Foods
S.I.C.: 5149
Henry Langknecht *(Pres.)*

Division:

Woodhaven Foods-Midwest **(3)**
1007 Geneva
Shorewood, IL 60436
Tel.: 815-744-4000
S.I.C.: 5149
Joe Ray *(V.P.-Midwest Div.)*

Children's World Learning Centers, Inc. **(1)**
573 Park Point Dr.
Golden, CO 80401
Tel.: 303-526-1600
Emp.: 10,000
Operates Child Care Centers for Preschool, Kindergarten & Elementary School Age Children
S.I.C.: 8351
Duane Larson *(Pres.)*
Jack H. Cook *(V.P.-Devel.)*
Mark R. Eaton *(V.P.-Fin.)*
Kenneth Riemer *(V.P.-Human Resources)*
Michael McGorrin *(V.P.-Mktg.)*
Delores J. Pearson *(V.P.)*
Judith E. Simpson *(V.P.)*
David L. Brenner *(Sec.)*

Non-U.S. Holdings:

ARA Belgium, S.A. **(1)**
Ave. Louise 326 B-1050
Brussels, Belgium
Tel.: 32-2-640-2325
Vending Machine Opers.
S.I.C.: 5962

ARA Europe Headquarters **(1)**
Glenthorne House, Glenthorne Road
London, W6 OLW, United Kingdom
Tel.: 071-741-5451
Vending Machine Opers.
S.I.C.: 5962

ARA Food Services, Ltd. **(1)**
ARA House, Honey End Lane Tilehurst
Reading, Berkshire RG3 4QI, United Kingdom
Tel.: 0734 596761
Telex: 848982 ararea g
Fax: 0734 5800939
Catering & Janitorial Services
S.I.C.: 5812; 7349

ARA N.V. **(1)**
Ave. Louise 326 B-1050
Brussels, Belgium
Tel.: 32-2-640-2325
Vending Machine Opers.
S.I.C.: 5962

ARA Services, GmbH **(1)**
Strahlenbergerstrasse 127 D-6050
Offenbach/Main, Germany
Tel.: 49-6-118-0971
Vending Machine Opers.
S.I.C.: 5962

ARA Services, Ltd. **(1)**
ARA House, Honey End Lane Tilehurst,
Reading, Berks RG3 4QL, United Kingdom
Tel.: 44-73-459-6761
Vending Machine Opers.
S.I.C.: 5962

ARA Services, S.A. **(1)**
Avenue Louise 326 B-1050
Brussels, Belgium
Tel.: 32-2-640-7200
Vending Machine Opers.
S.I.C.: 5962

ARA Vending Services Ltd. **(1)**
Glenthorne House, Glenthorne Road
London, W6 0LW, United Kingdom
Vending Machine Opers.
S.I.C.: 5962

Aim Services Co., Ltd. **(1)**
1-15 Nishishinbashi 1-chome
Tokyo, Japan
Tel.: 81-3-502-3731
Vending Machine Opers.
S.I.C.: 5962

La Societe VS Limitee **(1)**
4900 Fisher Street
Montreal, PQ H4T 1J6, Canada
Tel.: 514-341-7770
Vending Machine Opers.
S.I.C.: 5962
George Tavernier *(Exec. V.P.)*

Major Foods Ltd. **(1)**
41 Ilsley Ave.
Dartmouth, NS Canada B3B 1K9
Tel.: 902-468-8877
Food Service & Vending Machine Opers.
S.I.C.: 5812; 5962

Modern Building Cleaning Inc. **(1)**
1470 Triole St.
Ottawa, ON Canada K1B 3S6
Tel.: 613-745-9106
Contract Janitorial Services
S.I.C.: 7349

Parnell Foods Ltd. **(1)**
487 Newbold St.
London, ON Canada N6E 1K4
Tel.: 519-681-0110
Food Service Opers.
S.I.C.: 5812

Versa Services Ltd. **(1)**
811 Islington Ave.
Etobicoke, ON M8Z 5W8, Canada
Tel.: 416-255-1331 (56%)
Fax: 416-255-4706
Assets: $90,868,000
Liabilities: $33,393,000
Net Worth: $57,475,000
Approx.Rev.: $350,000,000
Emp.: 20,000
Fiscal Year-end: 9/30/92
Computer Systems/Hardware:
IBM 400
Service Management Company that Provides Dietary Food Service, Vending, Office Coffee Systems, Laundry, Housekeeping, Maintenance & Material Management to Clients in Health Care, Business, Education & Public Markets
S.I.C.: 5962; 5812; 7213; 7218; 7349
Dixon S. Chant *(Chm. Bd.)*
James Graham *(Pres. & Chief Exec. Officer)*
J. Mitchell *(Exec. V.P. & Chief Oper. Officer)*
R.E. Boone *(Sr. V.P.)*
H. MacDonald *(V.P. Fin. & Chief Fin. Officer)*
P. Glover *(V.P.-Mktg.)*
P. Coupey *(V.P.-Human Resources)*

Versabec Inc. **(1)**
4900 Rue Fisher
Montreal, PQ H4T 1J6, Canada
Tel.: 514-341-7770
Food Service Opers.; Vending Machine Opers.
S.I.C.: 5812; 5962

ASC INCORPORATED
One Sunroof Center
Southgate, MI 48195
Mailing Address:
P.O. Box 1186,
Southgate, MI 48195
Tel.: 313-285-4911 **MI**
Fax: 313-246-0500
Year Founded: 1965
Sales Range: $100-499 Million
Emp.: 3,000
Fiscal Year-end: 6/30/91

Import Export
Resource to the Worldwide Transportation Industry for Design, Engineering, Manufacturing, Marketing and Program Management of Specialty Vehicles Product Groups Includes: Convertibles; Sunroofs; Trim Systems and Composites; and Powertrain Enhancement
S.I.C.: 3714; 6719; 5013; 3716; 8711
Heinz C. Prechter *(Chm. & Chief Exec. Officer)*
Gerald Szpotek *(Vice Chm.)*
Karl H. Knoth *(Pres. & Chief Oper. Officer, Mfg. & Assembly)*
Mark S. Gebhard *(Exec. V.P.-Chief Opers. Officer, Technology & Systems)*
Bruce W. Clements *(Sr. V.P., Productivity & Organization)*
Tom W. Weber *(Sr. V.P., Business & Technology Devel.)*
Michael P. Alexander *(Sr. V.P., Prod. Devel.)*
Joseph D. Bator *(Sr. V.P., Bus. Devel. & Mktg.)*
G.E. Bryen *(V.P. & Controller)*
John D. Nechiporchik *(V.P. & Gen. Mgr.-Automobile Specialty Co.)*
Al W. Luke *(V.P.-Systems Supply)*
Richard F. Gorski *(V.P.-O.E. Sls.)*
Bruce C. Greening *(Treas.)*
L. Redmer *(Sec.)*
Steve Morello *(Gen. Counsel)*
Arthur L. MacNee *(Exec. Dir.-Business Plng.)*
David L. Treadwell *(Mng. Dir.-Real Estate)*
Patrick A. Doman *(Dir.-Mngmt. Information Systems)*
John Marcozzi *(Dir.-Direct Sls.)*
Ron Smith *(Dir.-Materials Mgmnt.)*
Kyle P. Chura *(Mgr.-Corp. Rels.)*
Marilyn Bannon *(Mgr.-Human Resourses)*
Ron Nalette *(Mgr.-Human Resources)*
Jack Burns *(Mgr.-Mktg. Plans)*

Outside Service Firm(s):

Ernst & Young*(Auditors)*
One Detroit Center, 500 Woodward, Ste. 1700
Detroit, MI 48243
Tel.: 313-259-9600

Comerica Bank*(International Bank Affiliate)*
211 W. Fort St.
Detroit, MI 48226
Tel.: 313-222-3300

Honigman, Miller, Schwartz & Cohn*(Legal Firm)*
2290 First National Bldg.
Detroit, MI 48226
Tel.: 313-256-7800

Manufacturers National Bank N.A.*(Major Banking Relationship)*
38th Fl., 100 Renaissance Center
Detroit, MI 48243
Tel.: 313-222-4227

Subsidiaries:

Aeromotive Systems Co. **(1)**
One Sunroof Center
Southgate, MI 48195
Tel.: 313-285-4911
Mfr. of Aftermarket Prods. for Automobiles
S.I.C.: 3714

Automobile Specialty Co. **(1)**
One Sunroof Center
Southgate, MI 48195
Tel.: 313-285-4911
Fax: 313-246-0500
Import Export
S.I.C.: 5013
John D. Nechiporchik *(V.P. & Gen. Mgr.)*

American Sunroof Company **(1)**
One Sunroof Center
Southgate, MI 48195
Tel.: 313-285-4911
Fax: 313-246-0500
Import Export
Mfr. of Sunroofs for Automobiles & Vans
S.I.C.: 3714; 5013
Allan W. Luke *(V.P.)*

ASC Trim **(1)**
1533 Alum Creek Dr.
Columbus, OH 43209
Tel.: 614-253-7263
Fax: 614-252-6266
Mfr. of Automotive Trim & Van Bodies
S.I.C.: 3714; 3711
Allan W. Luke *(V.P.)*

Non-U.S. Holdings:

ASC/Canada Incorporated **(1)**
5280 Creekbank Road
Mississauga, ON L4W 1N4, Canada
Tel.: 416-624-7414 (100%)
Fax: 416-624-2354
Distribution of Automotive Products; Sunroof Conversion
S.I.C.: 5013; 7532
Nick Rehmtulla *(Gen. Mgr.)*

ASC Weinsberg Karosseriewerke Weinsberg GmbH **(1)**
Lindichstrasse 11 Postfach 1169, 7102
Weinsberg, Germany
Tel.: 49-7134-506134
Fax: 49-7134-506103
Mfr. of Van Bodies
S.I.C.: 3711
Michael Runte *(Prokurist)*

Joint Ventures:

ASC Protocraft **(1)**
19335 S. Laurel Park
Rancho Dominguez, CA 90220
Tel.: 213-605-0110
Fax: 213-632-5409
Specialty Vehicle (Automotive) Manufacturer
S.I.C.: 3711
George Gaffoglio *(Gen. Mgr.)*

Hyosung ASC **(1)**
11-14 Yoido dong Youngdeung Po-Ku,
Seoul, Korea
Tel.: 82-2-784-8154
Fax: 82-2-784-4852
Mfr. of Automotive Sunroofs
S.I.C.: 3714
S.D. Park *(Gen. Mgr.)*

ASCG, INC.
(Formerly AFCG)
6600 Bldg., Ste. 21, 6600 SW 92nd Ave.
Portland, OR 97223
Tel.: 503-293-8902 **AK**
Fax: 503-293-7215
Year Founded: 1981
Sales Range: $20-39 Million
Emp.: 200
Fiscal Year-end: 6/30/92
Engineering Consultants
S.I.C.: 8711
Leland A. Johnson *(Pres.)*
Gary L. McNeil *(Sr. V.P.)*
Kent Grinage *(V.P.)*
Harley H. Hightower *(V.P.)*
Dale R. Merrell *(V.P.)*
Joellen Tenison *(Dir.-Fin.)*

ASCG, Inc.—(Continued)

Outside Service Firm(s):

Price Waterhouse*(Auditors)*
Anchorage, AK

Key Bank of Alaska*(Major Banking Relationship)*
P.O. Box 100420, 101 West Benson Blvd.
Anchorage, AK 95510
Tel.: 907-862-6100

THE ASCII GROUP, INC.
7475 Wisconsin Ave.
Bethesda, MD 20814
Tel.: 301-718-2600
Fax: 301-718-0435
Year Founded: 1984
Approx.Sls.: $2,500,000,000
Emp.: 15
Import Export
1500 Computer Retail Stores
S.I.C.: 5734
Alan D. Weinberger *(Chm., Pres. & Chief Exec. Officer)*
Jill Kerr *(Chief Oper. Officer & V.P.-Sls. & Mktg.)*
Lisa Leff *(Chief Fin. Officer)*
Barbara Rhodes *(Chief Info. Officer (MIS))*
Edward Smith *(Gen. Counsel)*
Laura Weinberger *(Sec.)*
Robert Brook *(Asst. Dir.-US Sls.)*
Hilda Maxim *(Asst. Dir.-US Sls.)*
Noel Abu-Ghazold *(Dir.-Sls.)*
Heidi Feldman *(Dir.-Admin. & Opers.)*
Ramsey Gazaler *(Dir.-Reseller Opers.)*

A S H, INC.
(d/b/a Auto Safety House)
2630 W. Buckeye Rd.
Phoenix, AZ 85009
Tel.: 602-269-9721 **AZ**
Fax: 602-269-9721
Year Founded: 1955
Approx.Sls.: $17,000,000
Emp.: 48
Retail Sales of School Buses & Heavy Equipment
S.I.C.: 5531; 5013; 7538
Harry S. Amster *(Pres.)*
Kirk Amster *(V.P., Treas. & Sec.)*

Outside Service Firm(s):

Arizona Bank*(Major Banking Relationship)*
Phoenix, AZ

ASICS TIGER CORPORATION
10540 Talbert Ave.
Fountain Valley, CA 92708
Tel.: 714-962-7654
Approx.Sls.: $250,000,000
Emp.: 160
Import
ASICS Sporting Goods Mfr.-Tiger, Athletic Footwear/Apparel/Accesories
S.I.C.: 2329; 2339; 3149
Shunji Nakajima *(Pres.)*
H. Peter Goehirig *(V.P. & Gen. Mgr.)*
Richard Bourne *(Dir.-Fin. & Admin.)*
Dennis DiDominicis *(Sr. Dir.-Footwear Div.)*
David Chandler *(Sr. Dir.-Apparel Div.)*
Kazuo Tsujino *(Dir.-New Business Devel.)*
John Hay *(Mgr.-Footwear Mktg.)*
Lauren Brooks *(Sr. Mgr.-Apparel Sls. & Mktg.)*
Linda Nielander *(Mgr.-Adv. & Promotion)*
Eileen Schaaf *(Mgr.-Personnel)*

ASM INTERNATIONAL
Materials Park, OH 44073
Tel.: 216-338-5151
Tel.: 800-336-5152
Telex: 98-0619
Fax: 216-338-4634
Year Founded: 1913
Approx.Sls.: $19,000,000
Emp.: 150
Fiscal Year-end: 12/31/90
Technical Society for Engineered Materials Executives & Engineers, Providing Periodicals, Handbooks, Tech. Engineering Textbooks, Expositions & Conferences, Seminars, Home Study Courses, Computerized Materials Databases, Engrng. Software
S.I.C.: 8621
Willaim P. Koster *(Pres.)*
Edward H. Kottcamp Jr. *(V.P.)*
Robert D. Halverstadt *(Treas.)*
Edward L. Langer *(Mng. Dir.)*
David L. Moffatt *(Membership Devel. & Mktg.)*
William W. Scott *(Technical Dir.)*
Pat Brooks *(Mgr.-Adv.)*
Robert M. Pavlik *(Mgr.-Mktg. Admin. & Production)*
Beverly Borak *(Mgr.-Institutional Mktg.)*
Sharon Harper *(Mgr.-Mktg. Communications)*
H. David Chafe *(Matls. Info. Dir.)*
Robert Uhl *(Reference Publication Dir.)*
Rod W. Allwood *(Education Dir.)*
J. Randy Cicen *(Member Activities Dir.)*

ATI INDUSTRIES
2425 Vineyard
Escondido, CA 92025
Tel.: 619-746-8301
Fax: 619-746-4295
Assets: $10,000,000
Earnings: $5,000,000
Net Worth: $10,000,000
Approx.Sls.: $15,000,000
Emp.: 250
Fiscal Year-end: 12/31/89
Aircraft Fabricating Tools; Specialty Communication Tools; Aircraft & Missile Components
S.I.C.: 3728; 3542; 3545; 3769
Duane Minard *(Chm. Bd.)*
Warren Johnson *(Pres. & Chief Exec. Officer)*
William Quirk *(V.P.-Fin. & Chief Fin. Officer)*
Biddy Humphrey *(Corp. Sec.)*

No. of Mfg. Plants/Facilities: 2

Computer Systems/Hardware:
Wang

Outside Service Firm(s):

White & Case*(Legal Firm)*
1155 Avenue of The Americas
New York, NY 10036

AVA-AUTOMATIC VENDORS OF AMERICA
2175 Parklake Dr., N.E., Ste. 200
Atlanta, GA 30345
Tel.: 404-934-0780 **DE**
Fax: 404-939-5973
Sales Range: $20-39 Million
Emp.: 250
Import Export
Product, Vending Machine and Equipment Sales; Vehicle Leasing
S.I.C.: 5962; 7513; 5044; 5046
Donald Dawe *(Pres.)*
Charles R. Bryan *(Exec. V.P., Sec. & Treas.)*
Leslie Scardaci *(Controller)*
Christopher W. Dyck *(Controller-Food Service & Vending Div.)*

Computer Systems/Hardware:
Data General

Outside Service Firm(s):

Deloitte & Touche*(Auditors)*
1 World Trade Center
New York, NY 10048
Tel.: 212-669-5000

Chadbourne & Parke*(Legal Firm)*
30 Rockefeller Plaza
New York, NY 10112
Tel.: 212-408-5100

Subsidiaries:

Automatic Service Co. **(1)**
1596 Catherine Lake Rd.
Jacksonville, NC 28540
Tel.: 919-324-2014 (100%)
Vending Machine Services
S.I.C.: 5962

Automatic Service Co. **(1)**
P.O. Box 114D, Hwy. 301 So.
Hope Mills, NC 28348
Tel.: 919-425-0700 (100%)
Vending Machine Services
S.I.C.: 5962

Automatic Service Co. of Virginia, Lynchburg Branch **(1)**
P.O. Box 10278, 3224 Odd Fellow Rd.
Lynchburg, VA 24506
Tel.: 804-845-7811 (100%)
Vending Machine Services
S.I.C.: 5962

Automatic Service Co. of Virginia, No. Virginia Branch **(1)**
P.O. Box 218,
Edinburg, VA 22824
Tel.: 703-984-4131 (100%)
Vending Machine Services
S.I.C.: 5962

AXIA INCORPORATED
2001 Spring Rd., Ste. 300
Oak Brook, IL 60521
Tel.: 708-571-3360 **DE**
Fax: 708-571-3360
Year Founded: 1891
Approx.Rev.: $163,000,000
Emp.: 1,200
Fiscal Year-end: 12/31/90
Import Export
Mfr. of Hardware & Metal Stampings; Manufacture & Sales of Tools & Equipment for Construction Industry
S.I.C.: 3496; 3559; 3423; 5961
Dennis W. Sheehan *(Chm. Bd., Pres. & Chief Exec. Officer)*
Robert J. Robinson *(Exec. V.P. & Chief Oper. Officer)*
Uma N. Aggarwal *(Sr. V.P.)*
Raymond J. Kulla *(V.P., Gen. Counsel & Sec.)*
H. John Vogt *(V.P.-Fin. & Treas.)*
Robert G. Zdravecky *(V.P.-Construction Tools Grp.)*
Lyle Feye *(Controller & Asst. Treas.)*

No. of Mfg. Plants/Facilities: 11
No. of U.S. Offices: 6
No. of Foreign Offices: 2

Outside Service Firm(s):

Arthur Andersen & Co.*(Auditors)*
33 W. Monroe St.
Chicago, IL 60603-4067
Tel.: 312-580-0033
Fax: 312-507-6748

Continental Bank N. A.*(Major Banking Relationship)*
231 S. LaSalle St.
Chicago, IL 60697
Tel.: 312-828-2345
Tel.: 800-426-5754
Telex: 312-828-1783

Sullivan & Cromwell*(Legal Firm)*
Chicago, IL

Divisions:

Ames Taping Tool Systems Co. **(1)**
6691 Owens Dr.
Pleasanton, CA 94588
Tel.: 510-847-8300
Fax: 510-847-9600
Emp.: 200
Mfr. & Sls. or Lease of Tools & Paper Tape for Finishing Gypsum Drywall Board Joints
S.I.C.: 3423; 2672; 5031; 7359
C. Robert MacKendree *(Pres. & Gen. Mgr.)*

Dave Fischbein Co. **(1)**
2700 30th Ave. S.
Minneapolis, MN 55406
Tel.: 612-721-4806
Telex: 29-0963
Fax: 612-721-4743
Emp.: 75
Mfr. & Sls. of Bag-Closing Equipment
S.I.C.: 3559; 5084
Donald J. Bachner *(Pres. & Gen. Mgr.)*

Nestaway Co. **(1)**
9501 Granger Rd.
Cleveland, OH 44125
Tel.: 216-587-1500 (100%)
Fax: 216-587-2833
Emp.: 300
Mfr. & Sls. of Material Handling Systems & Coated Wire Products for Automatic Dishwashers
S.I.C.: 3479
David H. Chesney *(Pres. & Gen. Mgr.)*

Subsidiaries:

TapeTech Tool Co., Inc. **(1)**
30009 Ahern Ave.
Union City, CA 94587
Tel.: 510-429-1666
Fax: 510-429-0423
Emp.: 12
Sales of Tools for Finishing Gypsum Drywall Board Joints
S.I.C.: 5049
C. Robert MacKendree *(Pres. & Gen. Mgr.)*

Non-U.S. Holdings:

Ames Taping Tools Co. of Canada Limited **(1)**
7779 Edmonds St.
Burnaby, BC V3N 1B9, Canada
Tel.: 604-525-1811 (100%)
Mfr. of Hand & Edge Tools
S.I.C.: 3423
W.A. Cassidy *(Reg. Mgr.-Canada)*

Andamios Atlas, S.A. **(1)**
Rio Lerma No. 5 Fracc. Industrial, San Nocolas Tlaxcoapa, 5430 Tlalnepant, Mexico
Tel.: 5-390-61-22 (49%)
Fax: 5-565-68-96
Mfr. of Scaffolding
S.I.C.: 3446
Antonio Larrea *(Pres.)*

Compagnie Fischbein, S.A. **(1)**
64 Rue Previnaire 1070
Brussels, Belgium
Tel.: 2-521.01.94 (100%)
Fax: 2-520-33-90
Mfr. of Bag-Closing Equipment
S.I.C.: 3559
Donald J. Bachner *(Gen. Mgr.)*

Fibelco S.A./N.V. **(1)**
64 bis rus Previnaire 1070
Brussels, Belgium
Tel.: 2-521-61-00 (100%)
Fax: 2-520-33-90
Mktg. & Sales of Bag-Closing Equipment
S.I.C.: 5084
Eddy Palstermans *(Operational Mgr.)*

Finelpac B.V. **(1)**
Edisonstraat 9A NL-2723 RS, Zoetermeer, Netherlands
Tel.: 79-424-854 (100%)
Fax: 79-424-643
Mktg. & Sales of Bag-Closing Equipment
S.I.C.: 5084
Eddy Palstermans *(Operational Mgr.)*

Ficomet S.A.R.L. **(1)**
BP 100 94123
Fontenay-sous-Bois, France
Tel.: 01-48-77-15-34 (100%)
Fax: 1-48-77-26-41
Mktg. & Sales of Bag-Closing Equipment
S.I.C.: 5084
Roland Beynel *(Area Mgr.)*

Finopac APS **(1)**
26, Industrivej. DK-2640
Hedehusene, Denmark
Tel.: 42-165-516 (100%)
Fax: 42-160-487

Mktg. & Sales of Bag-Closing Equipment
S.I.C.: 5084
Lauge Nielsen *(Area Mgr.)*

Fisax **(1)**
Unit E4, Northway Trading Estate
Tewkesbury, Gloucestershire GL2 08JH, United Kingdom
Tel.: 684-298-182 (100%)
Fax: 684-292-678
Mktg. & Sales of Bag-Closing Equipment
S.I.C.: 5084
David Greenfield *(Gen. Mgr.)*

M/S Fischbein Packaging (Singapore) Pte. Ltd. **(1)**
No. 37, Lorong 23 02-03 Yihi Industrial Bldg., Geylang,
Singapore, 1438, Singapore
Tel.: 745-0161
Telex: RS 38807
Fax: 745-1478
Marketing & Sales of Bag-Closing Equipment
S.I.C.: 5084
Ricky Tan *(Reg. Mgr.)*

Aaron's Office Furniture Co., Inc.
(See listing under AXIA Incorporated)

THE AARQUE COMPANIES
111 W. 2nd St.
Jamestown, NY 14701
Mailing Address:
P.O. Box 310,
Jamestown, NY 14702-0310
Tel.: 716-664-6014
Approx.Sls.: $400,000,000
Emp.: 3,000
Sheet Metal, Metal Stampings, Fabricated Metal Products, Steel Tubing & Miscellaneous Metal Work
S.I.C.: 3444; 3465; 3499; 3089; 3316; 3449; 3469; 3579; 6719
R. Quintus Anderson *(Chm. Bd. & Pres.)*
Wilber Berner *(Chief Fin. Officer)*
Arnold Swanson *(Dir.-Personnel)*

Outside Service Firm(s):

Cohen Swados Wright Hanifin Bradford & Brett*(Legal Firm)*
New York, NY

Subsidiaries:

Aarque Management Corp. **(1)**
111 W. 2nd St.
Jamestown, NY 14701
Tel.: 716-664-6014
Wilbur J. Berner *(Pres.)*

Aarque Steel Corporation **(1)**
111 W. 2nd St.
Jamestown, NY 14701
Tel.: 716-664-6014
Approx.Sls.: $20,000,000
Emp.: 250
Precision Sheet Metal, Wood & Plastic Laminates, Metal Stampings
S.I.C.: 3089; 3444; 3465; 3469
R. Quintus Anderson *(Pres.)*

Non-U.S. Holding:

Dahlstrom of Canada Ltd. **(1)**
7 Copeland St.
Toronto, ON M4G 3E7, Canada
Tel.: 416-421-5900
Approx.Sls.: $10,000,000
Emp.: 120
Precision Sheet Metal; Elevator Cars
S.I.C.: 3499; 3535
Jim Brown *(Pres.)*

ABBELL ASSOCIATES
332 S. Michigan Ave., Ste. 1260
Chicago, IL 60604
Tel.: 312-341-9000
Fax: 312-341-9012
Year Founded: 1971
Sales Range: $10-19 Million
Emp.: 8
Real Estate Developers
S.I.C.: 6552
Joseph J. Abbell *(Chm. Bd. & Pres.)*
Bruno Dalmaso *(Controller & Leasing Dir.)*
Jane Dickey *(Dir.-Mktg.)*
Principal(s):
Joseph J. Abbell

Outside Service Firm(s):

BDO Seidman*(Auditors)*
Detroit, MI

Continental Bank N. A.*(Major Banking Relationship)*
231 S. LaSalle St.
Chicago, IL 60697
Tel.: 312-828-2345
Tel.: 800-426-5754
Telex: 312-828-1783

ABBEY ETNA MACHINE COMPANY
11140 Avenue Rd.
Perrysburg, OH 43552
Mailing Address:
P.O. Box 408
Perrysburg, OH 43552-0408
Tel.: 419-874-4301 OH
Telex: 286476 ABBEYCOIN PEBG
Fax: 419-874-8200
Year Founded: 1901
Assets: $9,000,000
Liabilities: $4,000,000
Net Worth: $5,000,000
Approx.Sls.: $10,000,000
Emp.: 75
Fiscal Year-end: 9/30/91
Import Export
Manufactures Pipe & Tube Mills, Draw Benches, Tube Cut-Off Machines, Stationary Die & Rotary Swaging Machines, Slitters, Shear End Welders & Allied Equipment
S.I.C.: 3542; 3541; 3549
Corporate Giving Program: United Way
Nelson Dan Abbey, Jr. *(Chm. Bd. & Chief Exec. Officer)*
Nelson D. Abbey III *(Pres. & Chief Oper. Officer)*
John L. Young *(Exec. V.P.)*
Robert A. Abbey *(V.P.)*
Richard L. Dreier *(V.P.-Domestic Sls.)*
Ralph C. Girkins *(V.P.-Sales Mgr.)*
Charlie J. Jones *(V.P.-Electrical Engrng.)*
Branch J. Springer *(V.P., Chief Fin. Officer, Treas. & Sec.)*
H. Chappell *(Mgr.-Mfr.)*
Jim Ku *(Dir.-MIS)*
William J. Clark *(Pur. Agent)*

No. of Mfg. Plants/Facilities: 2
No. of U.S. Offices: 1
No. of Foreign Offices: 1

Computer Systems/Hardware:
Hewlett-Packard; IBM; Wyse

Outside Service Firm(s):

Ernst & Young*(Auditors)*
One Sea Gate
Toledo, OH 43604
Tel.: 419-244-8000

Hylant-MacLean*(Commercial Insurance Carrier)*
1505 Jefferson Ave., P.O. Box 1687
Toledo, OH 43603-1687
Tel.: 419-255-1020

Community Mutual*(Group Insurer)*
Cleveland, OH

Shumaker, Loop & Kendrick*(Legal Firm)*
1000 Jackson St.
Toledo, OH 43624
Tel.: 419-241-9000

Toledo Trust Co.*(Major Banking Relationship)*
Toledo, OH

Non-U.S. Holding:

Abbey Etna Machine Co. GmbH **(1)**
Bloetterweg 139 9330
Mulheim/Ruhr, 1, Germany
Tel.: 49-208-590831 (100%)
Telex: 856426 ABBEY D
Fax: 208-591522
Approx.Sls.: $5,000,000
Emp.: 50
Mfrs. of Pipe and Tube Mills and Associated Equipment
S.I.C.: 3542; 3549
A. K. Hofmeister *(Gen. Mgr.)*

ABBOTT BALL COMPANY
Railroad Place
West Hartford, CT 06110
Tel.: 203-236-5901 CT
Fax: 203-233-1069
Year Founded: 1909
Approx.Sls.: $15,000,000
Emp.: 100
Export
Mfr. Stainless Steel & Carbon Steel Balls, Steel Burnishing Media & Compounds
S.I.C.: 3399; 3312
Roger A. Bond *(Pres.)*
Emil H. Berges *(V.P.-Sls.)*
G. Glennon *(V.P.-Mfg.)*
Llyod Stevenson *(V.P.-Mktg. & Sls.)*
Marco Savona *(Treas.)*
W. LaPiore *(Mgr.-Quality Control)*

Outside Service Firm(s):

Arthur Andersen & Co.*(Auditors)*
One Financial Plaza
Hartford, CT 06103
Tel.: 203-280-0649
Fax: 203-280-0898

Robinson & Cole*(Legal Firm)*
Hartford, CT

Security Pacific National Bank*(Major Banking Relationship)*
40 East 52 St.
New York, NY 10022
Tel.: 212-836-5833

J.R. ABBOTT CONSTRUCTION, INC.
3512 Airport Way
Seattle, WA 98124
Mailing Address:
P.O. Box 84048,
Seattle, WA 98124-8448
Tel.: 206-467-8500
Fax: 206-447-1885
Approx.Sls.: $11,000,000
Emp.: 94
Commercial Building Construction
S.I.C.: 1521; 1542
John R. Abbott *(Pres.)*
Ken Blodgett *(V.P.)*
Art Solbakken *(V.P.)*

Outside Service Firm(s):

Puget Sound Bank*(Major Banking Relationship)*
Seattle, WA

ABBOTT ELECTRONICS, INC.
2727 So. La Cienega
Los Angeles, CA 90034
Tel.: 310-202-8820
Fax: 310-836-1027
Year Founded: 1961
Approx.Sls.: $18,000,000
Emp.: 220
Fiscal Year-end: 6/30/91
Export
Mfr. of Mil-Spec Power Supplies & Transformers
S.I.C.: 3612; 3679
F. Grant *(Chm. Bd.)*
Jerry Jeffers *(Pres.)*
D. Melendes *(Controller)*
Brooke Hartman *(Dir. Mktg.)*
D. Harris *(Mgr.-Mfg.)*
B. Standen *(Dir.-Pur.)*

ABBOTT GLASS CO., INC.
59-30 54th St.
Maspeth, NY 11378
Tel.: 718-381-8800
Telex: 718-417-1483
Telex: 718-386-0572
Year Founded: 1927
Approx.Sls.: $14,000,000
Emp.: 95
Fiscal Year-end: 12/31/89
Special Trade Contractors, Glass & Glazing Work, Architectural Metal Contractors, Wholesale Glass
S.I.C.: 1799; 1793; 5039
Alan R. Abrams *(Pres.)*
Enrico Daledda *(Sec.)*
Bernie Zuckerman *(Controller)*

ABBOTT GROUP LTD.
3129 W. 36th St.
Chicago, IL 60632
Tel.: 312-247-6555
Fax: 312-890-9626
Year Founded: 1978
Approx.Sls.: $21,500,000
Emp.: 160
Holding Company For Industrial Metal & Office Products Manufacturers
S.I.C.: 6719; 5051; 3499; 5112
Nelson Carlo *(Pres. & Treas.)*
Thomas Hacker *(V.P.)*

Outside Service Firm(s):

Rome & Associates*(Auditors)*
Chicago, IL

Matuszewich & Associates*(Legal Firm)*
Chicago, IL

American National Bank & Trust Company of Chicago*(Major Banking Relationship)*
33 N. LaSalle St.
Chicago, IL 60602
Tel.: 312-661-5000
Fax: 312-661-6417

First State Bank*(Major Banking Relationship)*
Chicago, IL

Subsidiaries:

Abbott Industrial Supply **(1)**
3159 W. 36th St.
Chicago, IL 60632
Tel.: 312-247-6555
Fax: 312-890-9482
Stocking Distributor of Valves & Fittings
S.I.C.: 5051
David Andalcio *(Pres.)*

Abbott Products Inc. **(1)**
3129 W. 36th St.
Chicago, IL 60632
Tel.: 312-247-6555
Manufacturer of Miscellaneous Steel Products
S.I.C.: 3499
Nelson Carlo *(Pres. & Treas.)*

ABBOTT LABORATORIES/ ASHLAND
(Formerly Faultless Rubber Company)
268 E. Fourth St.
Ashland, OH 44805
Tel.: 419-289-3555
Tel.: 800-544-9067
Fax: 419-281-3970
Approx.Sls.: $12,000,000
Emp.: 650
Import Export
Mfr. of Precision Molded Rubber, Dipped Latex, Molded & Extruded Plastic Products
S.I.C.: 3069; 3089
George White *(Gen. Mgr.)*
Ken Lynch *(Controller)*
Frank Niemi *(Dir.-Mktg.)*
Frank Katkaveck *(Dir.-Mfg.)*
C. Floyd *(Dir.-Plastic Opers.)*
R. Steiger *(Dir.-Engrng.)*

Abbott Laboratories/Ashland—(Continued)

Ben Sponseller *(Dir.-Personnel)*
E. Helal *(Dir.-Pur.)*
E. Sechrist *(Mgr.-Data Processing)*

ABBYLAND FOODS, INC.
(Formerly Abbyland Processing, Inc.)
502 E. Linden St.
Abbotsford, WI 54405
Mailing Address:
P.O. Box 69
Abbotsford, WI 54405
Tel.: 715-223-6386
Fax: 715-223-6388
Year Founded: 1977
Approx.Sls.: $53,000,000
Emp.: 150
Export
Wholesale Fresh Meats & Butchering
S.I.C.: 2011; 5147
Harland Schraufnagel *(Pres.)*
Tom Beczkiewicz *(Controller)*
Tim Schwecke *(Dir.-Quality Control)*
Ron Hinch *(Mgr.-Natl. Sls.)*
Principal(s):
Harland Schraufnagel

Outside Service Firm(s):

KPMG Peat Marwick*(Auditors)*
4200 Norwest Center, 90 S. 7th St.
Minneapolis, MN 55402
Tel.: 612-341-2222

Hartford Life Insurance Co.*(Commercial Insurance Carrier)*
Hartford, CT 06104-2999

SISCO*(Group Insurer)*
East Dubuque, IL

Ruder, Ware & Michler, S.C.*(Legal Firm)*
First American Center, 500 3rd St.
Wausau, WI 54402-8050
Tel.: 715-845-4336
Fax: 715-845-2718

Norwest Bank Minnesota, N.A.*(Major Banking Relationship)*
P.O. Box 738, 161 North Concord Exchange
St. Paul, MN 55075
Tel.: 612-450-4046

Subsidiary:

Abbyland Pork Rack **(1)**
539 N. Meridan St.
Curtis, WI 54422
Tel.: 715-223-4676
Emp.: 14
Wholesale Fresh Meats & Butchering
S.I.C.: 2011; 5147
Harland Schraufnagel *(Pres.)*

ABCO MARKETS, INC.
3001 W. Indian School Rd.
Phoenix, AZ 85017
Tel.: 602-222-1600 **AZ**
Fax: 602-222-1684
Approx.Sls.: $708,000,000
Emp.: 5,700
Import
Supermarket Chain
S.I.C.: 5411
Thomas W. Field *(Chm. Bd.)*
Edward G. Hill, Jr. *(Pres. & Chief Exec. Officer)*
Dave Walters *(Chief Fin. Officer)*
Edward A. Gast *(Sr. V.P. Fin.)*
Richard V. Jennings *(Sr. V.P.-Admin.)*
Leslie H. Knox *(Sr. V.P.-Sls. & Mktg.)*
Sal Sepulveda *(V.P.-Opers.)*
Dennis Williams *(Dir.-Personnel)*

Computer Systems/Hardware:
IBM 4680

Outside Service Firm(s):

Deloitte & Touche*(Auditors)*
One Cascade Plaza, Ste. 1600
Akron, OH 44303-1187
Tel.: 216-253-2022

Arizona Bank*(Major Banking Relationship)*
Phoenix, AZ

ABDALLA'S LAFAYETTE, INC.
900 E. St. Mary
Lafayette, LA 70503
Mailing Address:
P.O. Box 51348
Lafayette, LA 70505
Tel.: 318-261-2418 **LA**
Fax: 318-261-2499
Year Founded: 1895
Approx.Sls.: $18,000,000
Emp.: 300
Family Clothing Specialty Stores
S.I.C.: 5651
Herbert A. Abdalla *(Pres. & Chief Exec. Officer)*
Edward Abdalla IV *(Exec. V.P.)*
Harold C. Abdalla *(Exec. V.P.)*
Evelina Abdalla *(Sr. V.P.)*
Irma B. Abdalla *(Sr. V.P.)*
Barbara Abdalla Black *(V.P. & Treas.)*
Carolyn Abdalla *(Sec.)*
John McKnight *(Controller)*
Barbara Black *(Dir.-Sls. Promo.)*
M. Savage *(Dir.-Pub. Rels.)*

Outside Service Firm(s):

Gardes & Co.*(Auditors)*
Lafayette, LA

Subsidiaries:

Abform Company **(1)**
900 E. St. Mary
Lafayette, LA 70503
Tel.: 318-261-2418
Uniforms
S.I.C.: 5699
Herbert A. Abdalla *(Pres.)*

Abdalla Women's Shoe Salon **(1)**
900 E. St. Mary
Lafayette, LA 70503
Tel.: 318-261-2418
Women's Shoe Salon
S.I.C.: 5661
Herbert A. Abdalla *(Pres.)*

Brothers **(1)**
900 E. St. Mary
Lafayette, LA 70503
Tel.: 318-261-2418
Young Apparel Specialty Stores
S.I.C.: 5699
Herbert A. Abdalla *(Pres.)*

ABELSON-TAYLOR, INC.
35 E. Wacker Drive
Chicago, IL 60601
Tel.: 312-781-1700 **IL**
Fax: 312-781-1126
Year Founded: 1981
Approx.Billings: $46,500,000
Emp.: 50
Health Care Industry Advertising; Marketing & Consumer Franchise Services
S.I.C.: 7311
Marv Abelson *(Chm. Bd.)*
Dale Taylor *(Pres. & Chief Exec. Officer)*
Robert McCormick *(Exec. V.P.)*
Jay Carter *(V.P., Grp. Dir.)*
Jay Doniger *(V.P., Grp. Dir.)*
Angela Lustig *(V.P., Grp. Dir)*
Cindy Stone *(V.P., Grp. Dir.)*
John Reisdorf *(V.P., Fin.)*
Principal(s):
Marv Abelson
Dale Taylor
Robert McCormick

Computer Systems/Hardware:
NCR Tower

Outside Service Firm(s):

Popower & Company*(Auditors)*
Chicago, IL

Lake Shore National Bank*(Major Banking Relationship)*
605 N. Michigan Ave.
Chicago, IL 60611
Tel.: 312-787-1900

ABINGDON PRESS
(Div. of The United Methodist Publishing House)
201 8th Ave. South
Nashville, TN 37202
Mailing Address:
P.O. Box 801,
Nashville, TN 37202
Tel.: 615-749-6290
Fax: 615-749-6512
Approx.Sls.: $12,000,000
Emp.: 100
Religious Books, Church Resources, Video Cassettes
S.I.C.: 2731; 7812
Robert K. Feaster *(Pres.)*
Claude R. Young *(V.P.)*
Michael E. Lawrence *(Mng. Editor)*
Clarinda Bowman *(Publicity & Promo. Coord.)*
Carol C. Williams *(Sls. Dir.)*

ABRAMS PUBLISHING INC.
61 Mattatuck Heights
Waterbury, CT 06705
Tel.: 203-756-6562 **DE**
Fax: 203-756-2895
Year Founded: 1966
Publishing of Elementary School Texts
S.I.C.: 2731
Richard Abrams *(Pres.)*
Vesta Gray *(Fin. Officer)*
Patricia Abrams *(Sec.)*

Divisions:

Graphic Learning **(1)**
61 Mattatuck Heights
Waterbury, CT 06705
Tel.: 203-756-6562
S.I.C.: 2731

New Dimensions in Education **(1)**
61 Mattatuck Heights
Waterbury, CT 06705
Tel.: 203-756-3580
Publisher of Elementary School Texts
S.I.C.: 2731
Richard Abrams *(Pres.)*

ABRAMSON EHRLICH MANES, INC.
1275 K St., N.W.
Washington, DC 20005
Tel.: 202-289-6900
Fax: 202-789-2596
Year Founded: 1965
Approx.Billings: $44,000,000
Emp.: 65
Nella C. Manes *(Chm. Bd.)*
David B. Abramson *(Pres. & Chief Exec. Officer)*
Martin Moser *(Chief Fin. Officer)*
Michelle I. Galler *(V.P., Mktg.)*
Rana Matthes *(V.P.-Abramson Entertainment)*

THE ACACIA GROUP
51 Louisiana Ave. N.W.
Washington, DC 20001
Tel.: 202-628-4506 **DC**
Fax: 202-628-7424
Year Founded: 1869
Assets: $1,194,485,000
Earnings: $8,047,000
Liabilities: $1,108,000,000
Net Worth: $86,485,000
Approx.Premiums: $104,957,000
Emp.: 1,300
Fiscal Year-end: 12/31/90
Import Export
Mutual Life Insurance Co. Providing Life Insurance, Annuities, Banking, Investments, Financial Planning
S.I.C.: 6311
Corporate Giving Program: Company Funds the Acacia Charitable Trust
Charles T. Nason *(Chm. Bd., Pres. & Chief Exec. Officer)*
Paul L. Schneider *(Sr. V.P. & Chief Fin. Officer)*
Eugene S. Koster *(Sr. V.P.-Mktg.)*
Mary Todd Stocker *(V.P.-Fin. & Controller)*
Robert L. Dolan *(V.P. & Treas.)*
Robert-John H. Sands *(V.P. & Gen. Counsel)*
Haluk Ariturk *(V.P. & Chief Actuary)*
Richard D. Mayfield *(V.P.-Quality & Org. Analysis)*
James A. Andrepont *(V.P.-Mktg.)*
Michael J. Rensberger *(V.P.-Mktg. Support)*
Stephen B. Couch *(V.P. & Chief Investment Officer)*
R. Larry Mauzy *(V.P.-IMS)*
Stephen Volk *(V.P.-Mktg.)*
Andrew S. White *(V.P.-Securities)*
Rodney Hertz *(V.P.-Human Resources)*
Paul N. Jones *(2nd V.P.-IMS Opers.)*
Richard J. Fedalen *(Sec.)*
W. Nicholas Goetz *(Asst. Sec.)*
N. David Trosko *(Asst. Treas.)*
Arnold L. Rexroad *(Mgr.-Pur.)*
Christine Seheley *(Pub. Rels. Specialist)*

No. of U.S. Offices: 353

Computer Systems/Hardware:
IBM 3083 & 4341

Outside Service Firm(s):

Ernst & Young*(Auditors)*
1225 Connecticut Ave., NW
Washington, DC 20036

Morgan Guaranty Trust Company of New York*(Investment Banker)*
23 Wall St.
New York, NY 10015
Tel.: 212-483-2323

Reasoner, Davis & Fox*(Legal Firm)*
Washington, DC

First Chicago Shareholder Services Trust Co.*(Major Banking Relationship)*
153 West 51st St.
New York, NY 10019
Tel.: 212-791-6422
Fax: 212-385-9798

Riggs National Bank of Washington, D.C.*(Major Banking Relationship)*
P.O. Box 96206, 1120 Vermont Ave. N.W.
Washington, DC 20090-6206
Tel.: 202-835-4082

Subsidiaries:

Acacia Financial Corporation **(1)**
51 Louisiana Ave., N.W.
Washington, DC 20001
Tel.: 202-628-4506 (100%)
Business Credit
S.I.C.: 6153; 6159
Charles T. Nason *(Pres. & Chief Exec. Officer)*

Subsidiary:

Acacia Insurance Sales Corporation **(2)**
51 Louisiana Ave., N.W.
Washington, DC 20001
Tel.: 202-628-4506 (100%)
Inactive
Charles T. Nason *(Pres. & Chief Exec. Officer)*

Acacia Mortgage Corporation (1)
7023 Little River Turnpike
Annandale, VA 22003
Tel.: 703-642-3000
Tel.: 800-669-6671
Fax: 703-642-3016
Emp.: 18
Mortgage Lending
S.I.C.: 6163

Acacia National Life Ins. Co. (1)
51 Louisiana Ave., N.W.
Washington, DC 20001
Tel.: 202-628-4506 (100%)
Assets: $213,192,000
Earnings: $4,918,000
Liabilities: $189,984,000
Net Worth: $23,208,000
Approx.Sls.: $53,046,000
Annuities
S.I.C.: 6311
Charles T. Nason *(Pres. & Chief Exec. Officer)*

Calvert Group, Ltd. (1)
4550 Montgomery Ave., Ste. 1000 N
Bethesda, MD 20814
Tel.: 301-951-4800
Fax: 301-657-1982
Mutual Funds
S.I.C.: 6211

Subsidiary:

Calvert Securities Corporation (2)
51 Louisiana Ave, NW
Washington, DC 20001
Tel.: 202-783-0753
Fax: 202-737-5380

ACADEMY INSURANCE GROUP, INC.
6600 Peachtree Dunwoody Rd.
Atlanta, GA 30328
Tel.: 404-698-7000 **DE**
Fax: 404-393-1999
Assets: $362,349,002
Earnings: $4,093,000
Liabilities: $274,048,685
Net Worth: $88,300,317
Approx.Rev.: $108,731,928
Emp.: 220
Fiscal Year-end: 12/31/90
Insurance Holding Co.
S.I.C.: 6311; 6321; 6719
Hans Decker *(Chm. Bd.)*
Rodney L. Hale *(Pres. & Chief Exec. Officer)*
Gary E. Jenkins *(Chief Fin. Officer & Treas.)*
Terry D. Beall *(Exec. V.P.-Mktg.)*
Jerome J. Cwiok *(Exec. V.P. & Chief Oper. Officer)*
Frederick E. Raach *(Sr. V.P., Chief Actuary)*
Stephen A. Cohen *(V.P., Sec. & Gen. Counsel)*
Anthony Geyelin *(V.P., Asst. Sec. & Deputy Gen. Counsel)*
Joseph Gleason *(V.P.-Mktg.)*
Walter Jones *(V.P.-Admin. & Opers.)*
Terry Morrison *(V.P.-Information Systems)*
Nancy Coiter *(Dir.-Personnel)*
Robert Hines *(Dir.-Pur.)*

Outside Service Firm(s):

Coopers & Lybrand*(Auditors)*
1155 Peachtree St.
Atlanta, GA 30309
Tel.: 404-870-1309

Friedlander, Gaines, Cohen & Rosenberg*(Legal Firm)*
1140 Ave. of the Americas
New York, NY
Tel.: 212-575-9100

Subsidiaries:

Academy Life Insurance Co. (1)
600 Embassy Row, 6600 Peachtree-Dunwoody Rd.
Atlanta, GA 30328
Tel.: 404-698-7000 (100%)
Approx.Sls.: $83,000,000
Emp.: 275
Life, Accident & Health Insurance
S.I.C.: 6311; 6321
Rodney L. Hale *(Pres. & Chief Exec. Officer)*

Charter Investment Co. (1)
600 Embassy Row, 6600 Peachtree Dunwoody Rd.
Atlanta, GA 30328
Tel.: 404-698-7000 (100%)
Guarantee Premium Notes
S.I.C.: 6159
Rodney L. Hale *(Chm. Bd. & Pres)*

ACCRA PAC GROUP
2730 Middlebury St.
Elkhart, IN 46516
Mailing Address:
P. O. Box 878
Elkhart, IN 46515
Tel.: 219-295-0000
Tel.: 800-388-7472
Fax: 219-522-1468
Year Founded: 1967
Approx.Sls.: $100,000,000
Emp.: 500
Fiscal Year-end: 9/30/92
Export
Antiseptics; Pharmaceuticals; First Aid Kits, Drugs, Nutritionals & Cosmetics; Primarily Custom Contract Manufacturing of Consumer Products for the Pharmaceutical, Household, Personal Care & Automotive Industries. Aerosol, Liquid & Cream Products from Personal Care to Insecticides
S.I.C.: 2834
Satish Shah *(Pres. & Chief Exec. Officer)*
Rob Theroux *(V.P.-Mfg.)*
Anthony Brinkman *(Chief Fin. Officer)*

Computer Systems/Hardware:
IBM AS 400

Divisions:

General Generic Trucking Div. (1)
2020 Toledo Rd.
Elkhart, IN 46516
Tel.: 219-295-0000
Fax: 219-295-8443
Freight

Health Care, Inc. (1)
2835 Middlebury St.
Elkhart, IN 46516
Tel.: 219-295-0000
Tel.: 800-388-7472
Fax: 219-522-1468
Export
Health Care

Kem Krest Corp. (1)
2020 Toledo Rd.
Elkhart, IN 46516
Tel.: 219-295-0000
Fax: 219-295-8443
Export
Warehousing & Distr.

ACCU-SORT SYSTEMS, INC.
511 School House Rd.
Telford, PA 18969
Tel.: 215-723-0981
Tel.: 800-BAR-CODE **PA**
Fax: 215-723-1515
Year Founded: 1971
Approx.Sls.: $20,630,000
Emp.: 250
Fiscal Year-end: 9/30/91
Export
Manufacture Optical Scanners & Computer Systems For Scanners
S.I.C.: 3577
Albert Wurz *(Pres.)*
Steven Luscinski *(Exec. V.P. & Gen. Mgr.)*
Michael Hrabina *(V.P.-Sls. & Mktg.)*
John Schultz *(V.P.-Engrng.)*
Jane Wurz *(Sec. & Treas.)*
Richard Rusoff *(Pur. Agent)*
Sandra Shearer *(Pur. Agent)*
Carolyn Wolfer *(Coord.-Mktg.)*
John Rose *(Dir.-Bus. Devel.)*
Ralph Smoot *(Dir.-Mngmt. Information Systems)*
Lance Brosovich *(Mgr.-Intl. Sls.)*
Richard Cogossi *(Mgr.-Quality Assurance)*
Dona Cuppett *(Mgr.-Human Resources)*
David Wurz *(Mgr.-Research & Devel.)*
Principal(s):
Albert Wurz
Jane Wurz

No. of Mfg. Plants/Facilities: 1
No. of U.S. Offices: 12

Outside Service Firm(s):

Grant Thornton*(Auditors)*
2000 Market St.
Philadelphia, PA 19101

Chubb Group*(Commercial Insurance Carrier)*
New York, NY

Blue Cross & Blue Shield Association*(Group Insurer)*
Philadelphia, PA

Riley & DeFalice*(Legal Firm)*
Philadelphia, PA

Union National Bank*(Major Banking Relationship)*
10 W. Broad St.
Souderton, PA
Tel.: 215-721-2455

Union National Bank*(Pension Manager)*
10 W. Broad St.
Souderton, PA
Tel.: 215-721-2455

Affiliate:

Accu-Sort Time System (1)
P.O. Box 630
Ellington, CT 06029
Tel.: 203-870-5000
Emp.: 2
Design & Develop Time Keeping Systems
S.I.C.: 3579
Peter DiMaria *(Chief Oper. Officer)*
James Madsen *(Chief Tech. Officer)*

ACCURATE BOX CO., INC.
86 Fifth Ave.
Paterson, NJ 07509
Tel.: 201-345-2000
Fax: 201-345-8158
Approx.Sls.: $22,000,000
Emp.: 200
Paperboard Boxes, Folding Displays, Food Carton Specialties
S.I.C.: 2657; 2653; 2656
Charles Hirsh *(Pres.)*
Mark Schlossman *(V.P.-Sls.)*
Richard Koss *(Plant Mgr.)*

Outside Service Firm(s):

Isner & Tennenbaum*(Auditors)*
Woodbridge, NJ

First Fidelity Bank, N.A.*(Major Banking Relationship)*
Paterson, NJ

ACCURATE BUSHING CO., INC.
443 North Ave.
Garwood, NJ 07027
Tel.: 908-789-1121
Tel.: 800-932-0076 **NJ**
Fax: 201-789-9429
Year Founded: 1942
Sales Range: $10-19 Million
Emp.: 74
Fiscal Year-end: 10/31/90
Export
Aircraft Parts, Bushings, Roller Needle Bearings
S.I.C.: 3724; 3562; 3568
John J. McCormack, III *(Pres. & Chief Exec. Officer)*
Robert W. Leitner *(Exec. V.P.)*
Thomas J. Carew *(V.P.-Fin.)*
Alan M. Wolfers *(V.P. & Engrng. Dir.)*

No. of Mfg. Plants/Facilities: 1
No. of U.S. Offices: 1

Outside Service Firm(s):

Arthur Andersen & Co.*(Auditors)*
P.O. Box 221, 101 Eisenhower Pkwy.
Roseland, NJ 07068
Tel.: 201-403-6100
Fax: 201-403-0579

National State Bank*(Major Banking Relationship)*
Roseland, NJ

ACCURATE PERFORATING CO.
3636 S. Kedzie Ave.
Chicago, IL 60632
Tel.: 312-254-3232
Fax: 312-254-9453
Approx.Sls.: $10,000,000
Emp.: 65
Fiscal Year-end: 12/31/90
Mfr. Perforated Metal Stampings
S.I.C.: 3469
Ralph A. Cohen *(Pres.)*
Peter Barber *(V.P. & Sls. Dir.)*
Larry Cohen *(V.P.)*
Phillip Penner *(Adv. Mgr. & Pur. Agent)*

ACCURATE THREADED FASTENERS, INC.
3550 W. Pratt Ave.
Lincolnwood, IL 60645
Tel.: 708-677-1300
Fax: 708-677-9335
Emp.: 194
Screws, Bolts, Rivets, Metal Components Assemblies
S.I.C.: 3452; 3469
Don Surber *(Pres.)*
Porter McLean *(Exec. V.P.)*
Ruth Harding *(Controller)*
Ash Perti *(Dir.-MIS)*
Steve Noble *(Mgr.-Opers.)*
Kevin Brennan *(Mgr.-Sls.)*
Pat Christensen *(Mgr.-Human Resources)*
Ray Rafferty *(Mgr.-Quality Control)*
Jackie Roberti *(Pur. Agent)*

Outside Service Firm(s):

Ernst & Young*(Auditors)*
233 S. Wacker Dr.
Chicago, IL 60606
Tel.: 312-368-1800
Fax: 312-645-3095

Bank of Lincolnwood*(Major Banking Relationship)*
Lincolnwood, IL

ACE GLASS INCORPORATED
1430 N.W. Blvd.
Vineland, NJ 08360
Tel.: 609-692-3333
Fax: 609-692-8919
Approx.Sls.: $12,000,000
Emp.: 150
Export
Chemical & Laboratory Glassware & Supplies
S.I.C.: 3231
Paul E. Kramme, Jr. *(Pres.)*
Richard G. Kramme *(V.P. & Treas.)*
Harry F. Clouser *(Comptroller)*
Gerald A. Kramme *(Sec.)*
Matthew Tighe *(Mgr.-Sls.)*
Anthony Cesta *(Pur. Agent)*
Charles M. DeWoody *(Dir.-Research)*

Outside Service Firm(s):

KPMG Peat Marwick*(Auditors)*
1600 Market St.
Philadelphia, PA 19103
Tel.: 215-299-3100

Ace Glass Incorporated—(Continued)

Midlantic National Bank*(Major Banking Relationship)*
Mt. Laurel, NJ

Archer & Greiner*(Legal Firm)*
1 Centennial Sq.
Haddonfield, NJ 08033
Tel.: 609-795-2121

Division:

Ace Glass Incorporated-Midwest Div. (1)
P.O. Box 996
Louisville, KY 40201
Tel.: 502-584-8144
Manufacture Chemical & Laboratory Glassware & Supplies
S.I.C.: 3231
John Magara *(Gen. Mgr.)*

ACE HARDWARE CORPORATION
2200 Kensington Ct.
Oak Brook, IL 60521
Tel.: 708-990-6600 **IL**
Telex: 9106510186
Fax: 708-571-4512
Year Founded: 1924
Assets: $540,953,666
Earnings: $59,156,353
Liabilities: $376,543,513
Net Worth: $164,410,153
Approx.Sls.: $1,704,000,000
Emp.: 3,110
Fiscal Year-end: 12/31/91
Import Export
Dealer-Owned Hardware Cooperative
S.I.C.: 5072; 5251
Corporate Giving Program: Ace Hardware Foundation Consists of Donations From Employees, Dealers & Vendors to Support 2 Causes: Diaster Relief & Children's Miracle Network
Richard E. Laskowski *(Chm. Bd.)*
Roger E. Peterson *(Pres. & Chief Exec. Officer)*
David F. Hodnik *(Exec. V.P.)*
William A. Loftus *(Sr. V.P.)*
David League *(V.P., Gen. Counsel & Sec.)*
David F. Myer *(V.P.-Distr.)*
Fred J. Neer *(V.P.-Human Resources)*
Donald Schuman *(V.P.-Mngmt. Information Systems)*
Rita D. Kahle *(V.P. & Controller)*
Jerry Barton *(Dir.-Operational Support)*
John J. Cameron *(Dir.-Corp. Communications)*
Lee Johnson *(Dir.-Adv.)*
Jim Grywalski *(Mgr.-Grp. Retail Support)*
Dave Gusse *(Mgr.-Adv. Dept.)*
Bill Moore *(Mgr.-Grp. Retail Support)*
Ken Nichols *(Mgr.-Grp. Retail Support)*
Joel Stevens *(Mgr.-Grp. Retail Support)*
Dan Olsen *(Mgr.-Export)*
Earl Primm *(Mgr.-Real Estate & Devel.)*
Murray Armstrong *(Import Buyer)*

No. of Mfg. Plants/Facilities: 16
No. of U.S. Offices: 1

Computer Systems/Hardware:
IBM 3081K, IBM 8100; Texas Instruments

Outside Service Firm(s):

KPMG Peat Marwick*(Auditors)*
Peat Marwick Plaza, 303 E. Wacker Dr.
Chicago, IL 60601
Tel.: 312-938-1000

The Northern Trust Co.*(Major Banking Relationship)*
50 S. LaSalle St.
Chicago, IL 60675
Tel.: 312-630-6000
Fax: 312-630-6516

Prudential Insurance Co. of America*(Pension Manager)*
751 Broad St.
Newark, NJ 07102-3777
Tel.: 201-802-6000

ACE NOVELTY COMPANY, INC.
13434 N.E. 16th
Bellevue, WA 98005
Tel.: 206-644-1820 **WA**
Fax: 206-641-0195
Approx.Sls.: $60,000,000
Emp.: 500
Mfr. of Stuffed Toys & Animals
S.I.C.: 5092; 3942
Benjamin H. Mayers *(Pres.)*
Lois E. Mayers *(Sec. & Treas.)*

Outside Service Firm(s):

Deloitte & Touche*(Auditors)*
700 Fifth Ave., Suite 4500
Seattle, WA 98104-5044
Tel.: 206-292-1800

Martin B. Zells*(Legal Firm)*
Chicago, IL

Seattle First National Bank*(Major Banking Relationship)*
Seattle, WA 98154

Division:

Ace Novelty Fun Service Division (1)
13434 N.W. 16th
Bellevue, WA 98005
Tel.: 206-644-1820
Toys; Gifts & Novelties
S.I.C.: 3942; 5092
Benjamin H. Mayers *(Pres.)*

ACE OFFICE PRODUCTS
1100 Hicks Rd.
Rolling Meadows, IL 60008
Tel.: 708-259-1620
Tel.: 800-873-2239
Fax: 708-259-9236
Year Founded: 1940
Approx.Sls.: $14,000,000
Emp.: 108
Fiscal Year-end: 12/31/90
Import Export
Ace Stapling Machines & Knives
S.I.C.: 3579; 3421
Mark Wilson *(Pres. & Chief Exec. Officer)*
James Lee *(V.P.-Fin.)*
Joe Ksiaek *(V.P.-Mfg.)*
Lynnea Brown *(Exec. Asst.)*
Win Waterman *(Dir.-Sls.)*
Larry Allen *(Dir.-Sls.)*
Kay McGovern *(Mgr.-Pur.)*
Al Ramsey *(Mgr.-Data Processing)*
Mary Petke *(Export Mgr.)*

Computer Systems/Hardware:
IBM System 38, IBM PC

ACESS ENERGY CORPORATION
655 Metro Place, S.
Dublin, OH 43017
Tel.: 614-792-6060 **DE**
Fax: 614-792-6049
Approx.Sls.: $150,000,000
Emp.: 77
Gas Transmission & Distribution
S.I.C.: 4923
Lance W. Schneier *(Pres.)*
Scott W. Gebhardt *(Chief Oper. Officer)*
Toni Cialella *(Chief Fin. Officer)*
Steven B. Jaffee *(Exec. V.P.)*
Tim Battaglia *(Sr. V.P. & Gen. Counsel)*
Jon D. Ervin *(Sr. V.P.)*

Outside Service Firm(s):

KPMG Peat Marwick*(Auditors)*
Dublin, Ireland

Vorys, Sater, Seymour & Pease*(Legal Firm)*
52 E. Gay St.
Columbus, OH 43215
Tel.: 614-464-6400

Banque Paribas*(Major Banking Relationship)*
787 Seventh Ave.
New York, NY 10019

ACHESON INDUSTRIES, INC.
511 Fort St., Rm. 315
Port Huron, MI 48061-0489
Mailing Address:
P.O. Box 610489,
Port Huron, MI 48061-0489
Tel.: 313-984-5583
Fax: 313-984-5980
Approx.Sls.: $100,000,000
Emp.: 750
Specialty Lubricants & Chemicals & Spray Equipment
S.I.C.: 2992; 2851; 2899
James C. Acheson *(Chm. Bd.)*
Herbert A. Hoover *(Pres. & Chief Exec. Officer)*
Robert J. Zimmer *(V.P.-Fin. & Chief Fin. Officer & Sec.)*
Robert A. Culberson *(V.P.-Asian & South American Opers.)*
Michael D. Porter *(V.P.-European Opers.)*
Donald T. Walker *(V.P.-North American Opers.)*
Raymond L. Wine *(V.P.-Mfg.)*

Division:

Acheson Colloids Company (1)
1600 Washington Ave.
Port Huron, MI 48060
Tel.: 313-984-5581
Emp.: 225
Computer Systems/Hardware:
IBM Model 400
Speciality Lubricants & Coatings Containing Graphite, Molydisulfide, PTEE & Other Solids; Aerodag, Aquadag, Castordag, Dag, Electrodag Emralon, Gredag, Molydag, Oildag, Prodag
S.I.C.: 2992
D.T. Walker *(V.P. & Gen. Mgr.)*
R.J. Thompson *(Div. Business Mgr.)*
J.M. Bouwens *(Div. Business Mgr.)*
James A. McGuigan *(Adv. Mgr.)*
J.E. Anderson *(Mgr.-Dist. Services & Office Admin.)*

Non-U.S. Holdings:

Acheson A.N.Z. Pty. Ltd. (1)
63 Davies Road P.O. Box 48,
Padstow, N.S.W. Australia
Tel.: (612) 772-1588/1322
Mfr. & Sale of Lubricants
S.I.C.: 2992

Acheson Colloiden B.V. (1)
Postbus 1 9679ZG
Scheemda, Netherlands
Tel.: 5979-1303
Mfr. of Lubricants
S.I.C.: 2992

Acheson Colloiden B.V. (1)
Sucursal en Espana Gran Via Carlos III, 99, 08028
Barcelona, Spain
Tel.: 330-1600
Sales of Specialty Lubricants
S.I.C.: 5172

Acheson Colloids (Canada) Ltd. (1)
P.O. Box 665,
Brantford, ON N3T 5P9, Canada
Tel.: 519-752-5461
Mfr. of Specialty Lubricants
S.I.C.: 2992

Acheson Colloids Company (1)
Prince Rock
Plymouth, PL4 0SP, United Kingdom
Tel.: 0752-266351
Telex: 45549
Fax: 0752-222343
Mfg. of Lubricants
S.I.C.: 2992

Acheson do Brasil Ind. e Com Ltda. (1)
Rua Howard A. Acheson Jr. 279 Granja Vianna Cotia, 06700
Sao Paulo, S.P. Brazil
Tel.: 5511 492-4000
Mfr. & Sale of Lubricants
S.I.C.: 2992

Acheson France S.A. (1)
4, Passage Saint-Antoine 92500
Rueil-Malmaison, France
Tel.: 3314 708-4350
Sales of Lubricants
S.I.C.: 5172

Acheson Industries (Europe) Ltd. (1)
Sun LifeHouse 85 Queens Road,
Reading, Berkshire RG1 4PT, United Kingdom
Tel.: 0734-588844
Mfr. of Lubricants
S.I.C.: 2992

Acheson International S.A.-Equipment Div. (1)
Lerchenbergstrasse 23 P.O. Box 7, 7901
Darmstadt, Germany
Tel.: 07348-21044
Mfr. of Spray Equipment
S.I.C.: 3563

Acheson Italiana s.r.l. (1)
Via G. Frua 18 20146
Milan, Italy
Tel.: 392-434647
Sales of Lubricants
S.I.C.: 5172

Acheson (Japan) Ltd. (1)
P.O. Box 538,
Kobe, 651-01, Japan
Tel.: 078-332-3601
Mfr. of Lubricants
S.I.C.: 2992

Acheson Korea Ltd. (1)
1305-6 Seocho-Dong Kangnan-ku,
Seoul, 135, Korea
Tel.: (82 02) 554-3935/7
Mfr. of Lubricants
S.I.C.: 2992

Deutsche Acheson GmbH (1)
Karlstrasse 29 Postfach 1165, 7900
Ulm, Donau Germany
Tel.: 0731-66091
Mfg. Equipment & Products
S.I.C.: 2992; 3563

Graphoil S.A. (1)
La Gueroulde B.P. 36 27160
Breteuil-sur-Iton, France
Tel.: 32 29 8063
Mfr. of Lubricants
S.I.C.: 2992

ACKER DRILL CO. INC.
Shady Lane Rd.
Chinchilla, PA 18410
Mailing Address:
P. O. Box 830
Scranton, PA 18501
Tel.: 717-586-2061
Tel.: 800-75-ACKER
Telex: 244603 ACKR UR
Fax: 717-586-2659
Year Founded: 1919
Approx.Sls.: $10,000,000
Emp.: 130
Fiscal Year-end: 12/31/90
Import Export
Mfr. Core Drills & Core Drilling Equip., Diamond Bits, Thin Wall Bits, Grouting Equip. & Auger Drills
S.I.C.: 3545
William L. Acker III *(Pres.)*
W. Jones *(V.P.-Sls.)*
T.J. Heaney *(Treas.)*
John M. Wilk *(Pur. Agent)*

ACKERMAN AM McQUEEN

ACKERMAN MCQUEEN, INC.
1100 Equity Tower, 1601 NW Expressway
Oklahoma City, OK 73118
Tel.: 405-843-7777
Fax: 405-848-8034
Year Founded: 1939
Approx.Billings: $75,000,000
Emp.: 123
Angus McQueen *(Chm. Bd. & Chief Exec. Officer)*
Lee Allan Smith *(Pres. & Exec. Creative Dir.)*
William F. Winkler *(Chief Oper. Officer, Sec. & Treas.)*

ACME CANVAS CO., INC.
171 Medford St.
Malden, MA 02148
Tel.: 617-242-1850
Fax: 617-321-9471
Approx.Sls.: $12,000,000
Emp.: 175
Fiscal Year-end: 12/31/90
Mfr. of Canvas Covers & Tarpaulins
S.I.C.: 2394
Lewis M. Cohen *(Pres. & Chief Exec. Officer)*
Robert Cohen *(V.P.)*
Irving Cohen *(Treas. & Chief Fin. Officer)*
E. Parker *(Controller)*
Scott Holmes *(Gen. Mgr.)*

Principal(s):
Lewis M. Cohen

No. of Mfg. Plants/Facilities: 1

Computer Systems/Hardware:
Wang

Outside Service Firm(s):

Jason Goloboy*(Auditors)*
Boston, MA

Widett, Slater & Goldman*(Legal Firm)*
60 State St.
Boston, MA 02109

Subsidiary:

Century Products Inc. **(1)**
171 Medford St.
Malden, MA 02148
Tel.: 617-242-1850 (100%)
Swimming Pool Covers
S.I.C.: 2394
Lewis M. Cohen *(Pres. & Chief Exec. Officer)*

ACME CONTINENTAL FOODS, INC.
1255 W. Oakdale
Chicago, IL 60657
Tel.: 312-472-5400 **IL**
Fax: 312-472-8730
Year Founded: 1968
Approx.Sls.: $30,000,000
Emp.: 200
Poultry, Processed; Frozen; Luncheon Meat
S.I.C.: 2015
William Covitz *(Chief Exec. Officer)*
Jack Friedlander *(Pres.)*

Outside Service Firm(s):

Old Kent Bank*(Major Banking Relationship)*
Chicago, IL

ACME FOUNDRY, INC.
1502 Spruce
Coffeyville, KS 67337
Mailing Address:
P.O. Box 908,
Coffeyville, KS 67337
Tel.: 316-251-6800 **KS**
Fax: 316-251-4952
Assets: $12,400,000
Liabilities: $4,700,000
Net Worth: $7,700,000
Approx.Sls.: $18,000,000
Emp.: 275
Fiscal Year-end: 9/30/91
Export
Gray Iron Foundry
S.I.C.: 3321
Richard M. Tatman *(Chm. Bd. & Pres.)*
Robert L. Shepard *(Chief Fin. Officer, Dir.-Mngmt. Info. Systems, Sec. & Treas.)*
Thomas A. Tatman *(V.P.)*
Charles Gilchrist *(Dir.-Sls.)*
Jeanne Hartwig *(Dir.-Employee Benefits & Human Resources)*
Mike Northup *(Dir.-Quality Control)*
Thomas DeVore *(Legal Officer)*

Principal(s):
Richard M. Tatman

No. of Mfg. Plants/Facilities: 1
No. of U.S. Offices: 1

Computer Systems/Hardware:
NCR 10000

Outside Service Firm(s):

Kennedy & Coe*(Auditors)*
Salinas, KS

Coffeyville Insurance*(Commercial Insurance Carrier)*
Coffeyville, KS

Winston Insurance Agency*(Commercial Insurance Carrier)*
Coffeyville, KS

Hall, Levy, Lively, DeVore, Belot & Bell*(Legal Firm)*
Coffeyville, KS

Condon National Bank*(Major Banking Relationship)*
Coffeyville, KS

CPI Qualified Plan Consultants*(Pension Manager)*
Great Bend, KS

Division:

Magic Circle Manufacturing Div. **(1)**
1209 Buckey
Coffeyville, KS 67337
Tel.: 316-251-4920
Emp.: 35
Machine Shop
S.I.C.: 3321
Richard J. Tatman *(V.P.)*
Bill Seger *(Gen. Mgr.)*
Phil Mashburn *(Dir.-Pur.)*

ACME MILLS CO. INC.
5151 Loraine St.
Detroit, MI 48208
Tel.: 313-894-7110 **MI**
Fax: 313-894-2167
Year Founded: 1917
Approx.Sls.: $60,000,000
Emp.: 100
Fiscal Year-end: 12/31/91
Import Export
Automotive Industrial Textiles
S.I.C.: 2221; 2299
Beth E. Lowenstein *(Chm. Bd.)*
James A. Colman *(Pres. & Chief Exec. Officer)*
Neil G. Gross *(Sr. V.P.)*
Gregg Brumm *(Chief Fin. Officer)*
Francis Prainito *(Corp. Sec.)*
Sandra Michalski *(Controller)*

Outside Service Firm(s):

Deloitte & Touche*(Auditors)*
200 Renaissance Center, 16th Fl.
Detroit, MI 48243
Tel.: 313-396-3000
Fax: 313-259-8087

Silver, Gould, Eizelman, Zoller & Jackier*(Legal Firm)*
1533 N. Woodward
Bloomfield Hills, MI 48304

Comerica Bank*(Major Banking Relationship)*
211 W. Fort St.
Detroit, MI 48226
Tel.: 313-222-3300

Subsidiaries:

Acme Trim **(1)**
5501 Enterprise Dr.
Warren, MI 48092
Tel.: 313-573-7260
Design & Engineer Automotive Interiors
S.I.C.: 8711; 5012
Harry Esmont *(Gen. Mgr.)*

Great Lakes Filter **(1)**
5151 Loraine St.
Detroit, MI 48208
Tel.: 313-894-7110
Manufacturers all Types of Filters
S.I.C.: 3569
John Redfield *(V.P.)*

ACME POULTRY COMPANY, INC.
1024 S. King St.
Seattle, WA 98114
Tel.: 206-323-8411
Fax: 206-235-1910
Year Founded: 1933
Approx.Sls.: $35,000,000
Emp.: 190
Import Export
Process Poultry
S.I.C.: 2015
Employee Matching Gifts Program: United Way, Match Employee Contribution
Morris Polack *(Chm. Bd.)*
Jack Polack *(Pres.)*
James Polack *(Exec. V.P.)*
Valerie Polack *(Sr. V.P.)*
Wendell Luse *(V.P.-Pur. & Sls.)*
Toni Mataya *(Controller)*
Rita DePoule *(Dir.-Data Processing)*

Outside Service Firm(s):

Price Waterhouse*(Auditors)*
1001 Fourth Ave. Plaza
Seattle, WA 98154
Tel.: 206-622-1505

Seafirst Bank*(Major Banking Relationship)*
Seattle, WA

ACME REFRIGERATION OF BATON ROUGE INC.
11844 South Choctaw Dr.
Baton Rouge, LA 70815
Tel.: 504-273-1740 **LA**
Fax: 504-273-1763
Year Founded: 1946
Approx.Sls.: $16,000,000
Emp.: 65
Fiscal Year-end: 2/28/91
Air Conditioning, Refrigeration Equipment & Supplies
S.I.C.: 3585; 5078
A.E. Kaiser *(Pres.)*
J.L. Kaiser *(V.P.)*
C.S. Banquer *(Treas. & Controller)*
Adrian Kaiser III *(Mgr-Data Processing & Branch Opers. Mgr.)*

Computer Systems/Hardware:
IBM System 38

Outside Service Firm(s):

Shelby D. Salter & Company*(Auditors)*
Baton Rouge, LA

Kean, Miller, Hawthorne, D'Armond, McCowan & Jarman*(Legal Firm)*
Baton Rouge, LA

Hibernia National Bank*(Major Banking Relationship)*
New Orleans, LA

ACME TRUCK LINE, INC.
1105 Peters Rd.
Harvey, LA 70059
Tel.: 504-368-2510
Fax: 504-368-2510, Ext. 352
Approx.Sls.: $37,000,000
Emp.: 1,100
Oilfield Hauling
S.I.C.: 4213
Doyle Coatney *(Pres. & Chief Exec. Officer)*
Michael Coatney *(Sr. V.P.)*
Joe Binder *(Sec.)*

ACME VISIBLE RECORDS
1000 Allview Dr.
Crozet, VA 22932
Tel.: 804-823-4351
Tel.: 800-368-3275
Fax: 804-823-1625
Fax: 804-823-2469
Year Founded: 1953
Sales Range: $10-19 Million
Emp.: 130
Fiscal Year-end: 12/31/91
Export
Business Record Filing Systems, Mobile & Open Shelving, Printed Business Forms, Manifold Forms & Filing Supplies
S.I.C.: 2522
Massie E. Hughes *(Controller)*
Andrew Jiritano *(Tresurer)*
Krysten Smith *(Dir.-Sls. & Mktg.)*
Karen Landes *(Dir.-Personnel)*
Warren G. Lohr *(Mgr.-Quality Control)*

Outside Service Firm(s):

Hantzman Wiebel & Co.*(Auditors)*
Charlottesville, VA

McGuire, Woods, Battle & Boothe*(Legal Firm)*
Court Square Building, P.O. Box 1288
Charlottesville, VA 22901
Tel.: 804-977-2500

Sovran Bank*(Major Banking Relationship)*
Charlottesville, VA

ACORN BUILDING COMPONENTS INC.
12620 Westwood Ave.
Detroit, MI 48223
Tel.: 313-272-5700 **MI**
Fax: 313-272-6804
Approx.Sls.: $73,000,000
Emp.: 1,200
Fiscal Year-end: 1/31/91
Manufacture Aluminum Doors & Windows, Patio Doors, Steel Entry Doors
S.I.C.: 3442; 3231; 5039
Marlin H. Pemberton *(Chm. Bd., Pres. & Chief Exec. Officer)*
Keith Pietila *(Chief Oper. Officer)*
Edward Grigg *(Chief Fin. Officer)*
Henry Miarka *(V.P.-Fin.)*
Carlos Fernandez *(V.P.-Sls.)*
Joseph DiFazio *(V.P.-Engrng. & Res.)*

No. of Mfg. Plants/Facilities: 3
No. of U.S. Offices: 1

Computer Systems/Hardware:
IBM System 38

Outside Service Firm(s):

KPMG Peat Marwick*(Auditors)*
Suite 1200, 150 W. Jefferson
Detroit, MI 48226

Acorn Building Components Inc.—(Continued)

National Bank of Detroit*(Major Banking Relationship)*
611 Woodward Ave.
Detroit, MI 48226

Subsidiaries:

Acorn Distributing Co. **(1)**
12612 Westwood
Detroit, MI 48223
Tel.: 313-838-7380 (100%)
Emp.: 25
Distr. of Aluminum Doors & Windows
S.I.C.: 5039
Carlos Fernandez *(V.P.-Sls.)*

Acorn of Florida **(1)**
8305 Garden Rd.
Riviera Beach, FL 33404
Tel.: 407-845-1401 (100%)
Distr. of Aluminum Doors & Windows
S.I.C.: 5039
Marlin H. Pemberton *(Chm.)*

Acorn of Illinois **(1)**
7630 So. Madison
Willowbrook, IL 60521
Tel.: 708-655-1880 (100%)
Emp.: 25
Distr. of Aluminum Doors & Windows
S.I.C.: 5039
Ted Josefzak *(Gen. Mgr.)*

Acorn South **(1)**
500 Acorn Dr.
Oneonta, AL 35121
Tel.: 205-625-4600 (100%)
Distr. of Aluminum Doors & Windows
S.I.C.: 5039
Lynn Muckel *(Gen. Mgr.)*

Soalco **(1)**
1699 Sheffield Dr.
Monroeville, AL 36460
Tel.: 305-558-1770 (100%)
Emp.: 5
Mfr. Window & Door Screens
S.I.C.: 3442

ACORN ENGINEERING COMPANY
15125 Proctor Ave.
City of Industry, CA 91744
Mailing Address:
P.O. Box 3527
City of Industry, CA 91744
Tel.: 818-336-4561
Fax: 818-961-2200
Year Founded: 1955
Approx.Sls.: $20,000,000
Emp.: 400
Export
Stainless Steel Plumbing Fixtures, Multishower Units, Shower Equipment, Industrial & Institutional Wash Fountains, Hose Bibb Boxes, Liquid Soap Systems, & Stainless Steel Security Fixtures, Hospital I.C.C. & C.C.U. Care Toilet & Lavatory Units
S.I.C.: 3431; 3432; 3448; 3842; 3800
Earl L. Morris *(Chm. Bd. & Chief Exec. Officer)*
Donald E. Morris *(Pres.)*
Volker W. Hafner *(V.P.-Engrng.)*
Harold Hoover *(V.P.-Mfg.)*
W. Dennis Morris *(V.P.)*
Pat Ruga *(V.P.-Mktg.)*
Robert L. Stevenson *(V.P.-Fin.)*
Richard Uhlig *(V.P.)*
Kathryn L. Morris *(Sec. & Treas.)*
Fred Larson *(Dir.-Personnel)*
Kim Klutz *(Mgr.-Pur.)*

Outside Service Firm(s):

White, Nelson & Co.*(Auditors)*
Anaheim, CA

Bewley, Lassleben & Miller*(Legal Firm)*
Whittier, CA

Bank of America NT&SA*(Major Banking Relationship)*
City of Industry, CA

ACOUSTI ENGINEERING CO. OF FLORIDA
4656 34th St. S.W.
Orlando, FL 32811
Tel.: 407-425-3467 **FL**
Fax: 407-422-6502
Year Founded: 1944
Approx.Sls.: $65,000,000
Emp.: 1,100
Fiscal Year-end: 10/31/91
Acoustical Interior Contracting, Noise Control
S.I.C.: 1742; 1542; 1629
George C. Verner, Jr. *(Chief Exec. Officer)*
James R. Verner *(Pres. & Chief Oper. Officer)*
Richard Terranova *(V.P.)*
Alan Hursh *(Treas. & Sec.)*

Outside Service Firm(s):

Deloitte & Touche*(Auditors)*
200 S. Orange Ave., Ste. 1800
Orlando, FL 32801
Tel.: 407-246-8200
Fax: 407-422-0936

Drosdick & Reeves*(Legal Firm)*
Orlando, FL

First Union National Bank*(Major Banking Relationship)*
P.O. Box 2565,
Jacksonville, FL 32203

ACRISON, INC.
20 Empire Blvd.
Moonachie, NJ 07074
Tel.: 201-440-8300 **NJ**
Telex: 134395
Fax: 201-440-4939
Year Founded: 1963
Sales Range: $20-39 Million
Emp.: 210
Fiscal Year-end: 6/30/92
Export
Mfr. of Metering, Mixing & Blending Equipment; Hoppers, Feeders & Related Controls for Dry Solids
S.I.C.: 3532; 3556; 3559
Ronald Ricciardi *(V.P. & Gen. Mgr.)*
Frank Russo *(V.P.-Mktg.)*
Sam Carofalo *(Mgr.-Pur.)*

No. of Mfg. Plants/Facilities: 1
No. of U.S. Offices: 60

ACROMETAL COMPANIES, INC.
210 N.E. 10th Ave.
Brainerd, MN 56401
Mailing Address:
P.O. Box 408,
Brainerd, MN 56401
Tel.: 218-829-4719
Assets: $10,000,000
Liabilities: $4,500,000
Net Worth: $5,500,000
Approx.Sls.: $15,000,000
Emp.: 200
Fiscal Year-end: 12/31/90
Metal Wire Spools & Equipment
S.I.C.: 3499; 3569; 6719
Paul M. Lindbloom *(Pres.)*
William F. Bieber *(Chief Exec. Officer)*
Bob Silhacek *(Chief Fin. Officer)*
James Beckmann *(Dir.-Pur.)*
Gary Obele *(Dir.-Human Resources)*
Principal(s):
William F. Bieber

No. of Mfg. Plants/Facilities: 11
No. of U.S. Offices: 1

Computer Systems/Hardware:
Qantel

Outside Service Firm(s):

Coopers & Lybrand*(Auditors)*
1700 Benneficial Life Tower
Salt Lake City, UT 84111
Tel.: 801-531-9666

First National Bank of Minneapolis*(Major Banking Relationship)*
P.O. Box A799
Minneapolis, MN 55480
Tel.: 612-370-4606

Division:

Abrasive Engineering & Manufacturing Div. **(1)**
540 E. Hwy. 56
Olathe, KS 66061
Tel.: 913-764-6040
Approx.Sls.: $8,000,000
Emp.: 100
Mfr. Abrasive Belt Grinders
S.I.C.: 3291
Howard Grivna *(Chief Oper. Officer)*
Gary Eckland *(Pur. Dir.)*

Subsidiary:

Acrometal Companies, Inc. **(1)**
210 N.E. 10th Ave.
Brainerd, MN 56401
Tel.: 218-829-4719 (100%)
Approx.Sls.: $12,000,000
Emp.: 150
Mfr. Tape Reels & Door Mats
S.I.C.: 3499
Paul Lindbloom *(Chief Oper. Officer)*

ACTION EQUIPMENT
134 W. Broadway
Londonderry, NH 03053
Mailing Address:
P.O. Box 1217,
Londonderry, NH 03053
Tel.: 603-434-4900
Fax: 603-434-3294
Year Founded: 1980
Assets: $10,500,000
Earnings: $500,000
Liabilities: $9,000,000
Net Worth: $1,500,000
Approx.Sls.: $16,000,000
Emp.: 100
Fiscal Year-end: 12/31/88
Retail & Lease Construction Equipment
S.I.C.: 7353
Francis P. Rich, Jr. *(Chm. Bd. & Pres.)*
William C. Mears *(Chief Fin. Officer)*
Steven T. Platten *(Gen. Counsel)*
Steven Guerra *(Dir.-Mngmt. Information Systems)*
Michael T. Winston *(Dir.-Personnel)*
Principal(s):
Francis P. Rich, Jr.

Computer Systems/Hardware:
IBM System 38

Outside Service Firm(s):

Henderson, Tully & Sullivan*(Auditors)*
Manchester, NH

American Hardware Mutual*(Commercial Insurance Carrier)*
Atlanta, GA

Provident Life & Accident Insurance Co.*(Group Insurer)*
P.O. Box 12015
Chattanooga, TN 37401
Tel.: 615-755-7088

Larsen, Townsend*(Legal Firm)*
Londonderry, NH

Subsidiaries:

AC Leasing Corporation **(1)**
134 W. Broadway
Londonderry, NH 03053
Tel.: 603-434-4900
Emp.: 2

Action Supply **(1)**
134 W. Broadway
Londonderry, NH 03053
Tel.: 603-434-8533
Emp.: 9

Action Tire **(1)**
134 W. Broadway
Londonderry, NH 03053
Tel.: 603-434-4900
Emp.: 5

JJJ Realty Trust **(1)**
134 W. Broadway
Londonderry, NH 03053
Tel.: 603-434-4900
Emp.: 2

ACTION INSTRUMENTS, INC.
8601 Aero Dr.
San Diego, CA 92123
Tel.: 619-279-5726 **CA**
Telex: 910-335-2030
Fax: 619-279-6290
Year Founded: 1972
Assets: $16,000,000
Earnings: $1,500,000
Net Worth: $16,000,000
Approx.Sls.: $30,000,000
Emp.: 250
Fiscal Year-end: 10/31/91
Export
Electronic Instrumentation for Measurement & Control; Industrial Computers, Hardware & Software
S.I.C.: 3571; 3823; 3825; 7372
James J. Pinto *(Pres. & Chief Exec. Officer)*
Harry Sundblad *(Exec. V.P.)*
Stan Mintz *(V.P.-Engrng.)*
John Roth *(V.P.-Opers.)*
Frank Williams *(V.P.-Sls.)*
Stewart Austin *(Mgr.-Mktg.)*
Steve Cobb *(Mgr.-Data Processing)*
Joan Lovejoy *(Mgr.-Pur.)*
Jack Lucas *(Mgr.-Quality Assurance)*
Scott Wall *(Mgr.-Personnel)*

No. of Mfg. Plants/Facilities: 3
No. of U.S. Offices: 5
No. of Foreign Offices: 1

Computer Systems/Hardware:
Digital Equipment 1170

Outside Service Firm(s):

Price Waterhouse*(Auditors)*
750 B St.
San Diego, CA 92101
Tel.: 619-231-9830

Northwestern National Life*(Group Insurer)*
20 Washington Ave. S.
Minneapolis, MN 55401

Berkeley International*(Investment Banker)*
San Francisco, CA

Martin Benowitz*(Legal Firm)*
Carlsbad, CA

Silicon Valley Bank*(Major Banking Relationship)*
San Francisco, CA

Non-U.S. Holdings:

Action Controls Pty. Ltd. **(1)**
11/12-14 Miles St.
Mulgrave, Victoria 3170, Australia
Tel.: 560 7144
Fax: 562 1359
Assistance Integration; Assembling
S.I.C.: 3571; 3823

Action Industrie Computer, GmbH **(1)**
201-203 Pallaswiesenstrasse 6100
Darmstadt, Germany
Tel.: 6103 35188
Fax: 6103 31784
Distribution & Manufacturing
S.I.C.: 3571; 5065; 7372

Action Instruments (China) Ltd. **(1)**
9/F, Unit D, Gee Chang, Hog Centre, 65
Wong Chuck Hang Rd.,
Hong Kong, Hong Kong
Tel.: 555 2107
Telex: 76490 armti hx
Fax: 873 3417

Distributors for Action Instruments Products
S.I.C.: 5065; 5084

Action Instruments, Ltd. **(1)**
Barbot Hall Industrial Estate Mangham Rd.,
Rotherham, South Yorkshire S61 4RJ,
United Kingdom
Tel.: 709 820823
Telex: 548214 actins
Fax: 709 820834
Distributors for Action Instruments Products
S.I.C.: 5065; 5084

Action Instruments, S.A. **(1)**
Z.A. De Courtaboeuf, 9 Avenue du Canada,
Batiment Zenith 91966 Lot 6, Parc Hightec,
Les Ulis, Cedex France
Tel.: 69 28 68 50
Telex: 603511F action I
Fax: 69 28 83 89
Software Distributors
S.I.C.: 7372

ACTION MANUFACTURING CO.
100 E. Erie
Philadelphia, PA 19134
Tel.: 215-423-7749
Approx.Sls.: $47,000,000
Emp.: 700
Mfr. Ordnance Prods., Electro-Mechanical Assemblies, Aluminum & Zinc Die Castings
S.I.C.: 3489; 3369; 3679
James Markey *(Chm. Bd. & Pres.)*
Arthur Mattia *(V.P.-Engrng.)*
Michael Fagan *(Dir.-Pur.)*

Outside Service Firm(s):

KPMG Peat Marwick*(Auditors)*
1600 Market St.
Philadelphia, PA 19103
Tel.: 215-299-3100

Greenstein, Gorelick, Price, Silverman & Laveson*(Legal Firm)*
Philadelphia, PA

Provident National Bank*(Major Banking Relationship)*
1000 Westlakes Dr.
Berwyn, PA 19312

ACTION TECHNOLOGY COMPANY
18 Green Pond Rd.
Rockaway, NJ 07866
Tel.: 201-625-9400
Fax: 201-625-9409
Year Founded: 1957
Approx.Sls.: $31,000,000
Emp.: 100
Import Export
Mfr. of Plastic Tubing, Hose, Rubber Gaskets & Dispenser Tubing
S.I.C.: 3052; 3053
Leo Gans *(Pres.)*
Robert Schmitt *(V.P.-Fin.)*
Norbert Hodapp *(V.P.-Mfg.)*
Robert J. Dettmann *(V.P.-Sls. & Mktg.)*
Ken Kuter *(Sls. Mgr.)*

Subsidiaries:

Action Clinton **(1)**
Route 10 E., P.O. Box 111
Clinton, IL 61727
Tel.: 217-935-8311
Fax: 217-935-9132
Mfg. of Plastic Tubing, Hose, Rubber Gaskets & Dispenser Tubing
S.I.C.: 3052; 3053

Action Rockaway **(1)**
18-32 Green Pond Rd.
Rockaway, NJ 07866
Tel.: 201-625-9400
Fax: 201-625-9409
Mfg. of Plastic Tubing, Hose, Rubber Gaskets & Dispenser Tubing
S.I.C.: 3052; 3053

American Gasket & Rubber **(1)**
9509 Winona Ave.
Schiller Park, IL 60176
Tel.: 708-678-3550
Fax: 708-678-0147
Mfg. of Plastic Tubing, Hose, Rubber Gaskets & Dispenser Tubing
S.I.C.: 3052; 3053

Plastron **(1)**
19555 E. Arenth Ave.
City of Industry, CA 91748
Tel.: 909-594-3660
Fax: 909-594-2414
Mfr. of Plastic Tubing, Hose, Rubber Gaskets & Dispenser Tubing
S.I.C.: 3052; 3053

Plastron Dalton **(1)**
207 Brookhollow Industrial Blvd.
Dalton, GA 30720
Tel.: 706-277-3364
Fax: 706-277-9203
Mfr. of Plastic Tubing, Hose, Rubber Gaskets & Dispenser Tubing
S.I.C.: 3052; 3053

ACTIVE ELECTRICAL SUPPLY COMPANY
4240 W. Lawrence Ave.
Chicago, IL 60630
Tel.: 312-282-6300 **IL**
Fax: 312-282-5206
Year Founded: 1953
Approx.Sls.: $23,000,000
Emp.: 80
Fiscal Year-end: 12/31/91
Wholesale of Electrical Supplies
S.I.C.: 5065; 5063
Herbert C. Fox *(Chm. Bd., Pres., Chief Exec. Officer & Dir.-Pub. Rels.)*
Raymond A. Fox *(V.P., Chief Oper. Officer & Sec.)*
Donald F. Huebner *(Chief Fin. Officer, Treas. & Controller)*

No. of Mfg. Plants/Facilities: 1
No. of U.S. Offices: 1

Outside Service Firm(s):

Wolf & Grieco*(Auditors)*
Chicago, IL

Blue Cross & Blue Shield of Illinois*(Group Insurer)*
100 Tower Drive
Burr Ridge, IL 60521
Tel.: 708-323-3666

ACTIVE TOOL & MANUFACTURING CO., INC.
32901 Gratiot Ave.
Roseville, MI 48066
Mailing Address:
P.O. Box 0722,
Roseville, MI 48066
Tel.: 313-294-9220 **MI**
Fax: 313-294-9371
Year Founded: 1929
Assets: $70,000,000
Liabilities: $5,200,000
Net Worth: $64,800,000
Approx.Sls.: $160,000,000
Emp.: 1,600
Fiscal Year-end: 6/30/91
Import Export
Manufacture Sinks, Tools, Dies, Stampings, Modular Housing
S.I.C.: 3465; 2452; 3469; 3544
Henry Drettmann *(Chm. Bd., Chief Exec. Officer & Treas.)*
Jerry A. Blake *(Pres. & Chief Oper. Officer)*
Henry A. Drettmann *(V.P.-Real Estate)*
James Widlaski *(V.P.-Quality Assurance)*
Richard Zimmer *(Chief Fin. Officer & Dir.-Acctg.)*
Margarete Drettmann *(Sec.)*
John McCormack *(Controller)*
Phillip Forhan *(Dir.-Sls.)*
Richard Laidlaw *(Dir.-Human Resources)*
Glenn Miller *(Dir.-Special Projects)*
Dave Montri *(Dir.-Pur.)*
Jim Unis *(Dir.-Engrng.)*
Joseph Kwiatek *(Mgr.-Data Processing)*

No. of Mfg. Plants/Facilities: 6

Computer Systems/Hardware:
Unisys

Outside Service Firm(s):

Deloitte & Touche*(Auditors)*
200 Renaissance Center, 16th Fl.
Detroit, MI 48243
Tel.: 313-396-3000
Fax: 313-259-8087

Northern Group Services, Inc.*(Group Insurer)*
P.O. Box 7676,
St. Clair Shores, MI 48080
Tel.: 313-779-7676

Keller, Thoma, Schwarze, Schwarze, Dubay & Katz*(Legal Firm)*
Detroit, MI

Manufacturers National Bank N.A.*(Major Banking Relationship)*
38th Fl., 100 Renaissance Center
Detroit, MI 48243
Tel.: 313-222-4227

Divisions:

Active Homes Corp. **(1)**
888 Clairpoint
Detroit, MI 48215
Tel.: 517-635-3532
S.I.C.: 2452

Active Industries, Inc. **(1)**
888 Clairpoint
Detroit, MI 48215
Tel.: 517-375-2201

ACTRON MANUFACTURING COMPANY
9999 Walford Ave.
Cleveland, OH 44102
Tel.: 216-651-9200
Fax: 216-651-2388
Year Founded: 1964
Sales Range: $20-39 Million
Emp.: 175
Import Export
Automotive Test Equipment
S.I.C.: 3825
Thomas F. Slater *(Chm., Pres. & Chief Exec. Officer)*
J.D. Adams *(V.P. & Chief Oper. Officer)*
L.C. Banig *(V.P.-Fin. & Treas.)*
M.C. Nugent *(V.P.-Professional Div.)*
Glen Matejka *(Mgr.-Human Resources)*

Subsidiary:

Pentron Products, Inc. **(1)**
9999 Walford Ave.
Cleveland, OH 44102
Tel.: 216-651-9200
Manufacturers Of Automotive Aftermarket Parts
S.I.C.: 5531

ACUREX ENVIRONMENTAL CORPORATION
(Formerly Acurex Corporation)
(Wholly-owned subsidiary of Xeruca Holding Corporation)
P.O. Box 7042,
Mountain View, CA 94039
Mailing Address:
P.O. Box 7555,
Mountain View, CA 94039
Year Founded: 1965
Assets: $25,200,000
Liabilities: $13,200,000
Net Worth: $12,000,000
Approx.Sls.: $50,000,000
Emp.: 500
Fiscal Year-end: 12/31/90
Export
Environmental Control; Onsite Hazardous Waste Management Services
Corporate Giving Program: United Way
William C. Edwards *(Chm. Bd.)*
Gilbert F. Decker *(Pres. & Chief Exec. Officer)*
William R. Byars *(V.P. & Gen. Mgr.-Environmental)*
John H. Barnet *(Chief Fin. Officer)*
Amy Begley *(Mktg. Coodinator)*
Principal(s):
William C. Edwards

Computer Systems/Hardware:
DEC VAX 11/750, 8200, 8350; IBM PC; Compaq PC; Zenith PC; DEC Micro Vax; Sun Microsystems; Apple Macintosh

Outside Service Firm(s):

Arthur Andersen & Co.*(Auditors)*
River Tower, 333 W. San Carlos St., Ste. 1500
San Jose, CA 95113
Tel.: 408-998-2112

Heller, Ehrman, White & McAuliffe*(Legal Firm)*
525 University Ave.
Palo Alto, CA 94301
Tel.: 415-326-7600

Wells Fargo Bank*(Major Banking Relationship)*
420 Montgomery St.
San Francisco, CA 94104

Divisions:

Acurex Corp. Aerotherm Products Division **(1)**
111 North Armando St.
Anaheim, CA 92806
Tel.: 714-630-5150
Design & Mfr. of Airplane Galley Refrigeration Equipment
S.I.C.: 3585
Stephen Ehrick *(V.P. & Gen. Mgr.)*

Acurex Corp. Aerotherm Division **(1)**
555 Clyde Ave.
Mountain View, CA 94039
Tel.: 415-961-6100
Fax: 415-967-7271
Aerospace--Strategic and Tactical Missile Weapon Systems, Strategic and Tactical Counter Measures Systems, Aerospace Structures and Materials & Strategic System Survivability Engineering Services
S.I.C.: 3769
Duane L. Baker *(V.P.-Aerotherm Div.)*
Charles T. Nardo *(V.P.-Aerotherm Div.)*

Operating Divisions:

Acurex Corp., Dayton Operations **(2)**
Wright Point Office Bldg., 5100 Springfield Pike, Ste. 120
Dayton, OH 45431
Tel.: 513-253-0112
Aerospace-Strategic & Tactical Missile Weapon Systems
S.I.C.: 3769

Acurex Corp., Huntsville Operations **(2)**
1500 Perimeter Pkwy., Ste. 225
Huntsville, AL 35806
Tel.: 205-830-1230
Aerospace-Strategic & Tactical Missile Weapon Systems
S.I.C.: 3769

Acurex Corp., Los Angeles Operations **(2)**
12440 E. Firestone Blvd., Ste. 308
Norwalk, CA 90650
Tel.: 310-868-3893
Aerospace-Strategic & Tactical Missile Weapon Systems
S.I.C.: 3769

Acurex Corp., San Bernardino Operations **(2)**
1950 S. Sunwest Lane, Ste. 108
San Bernardino, CA 92408
Tel.: 909-888-4688

Acurex Environmental Corporation—(Continued)

Aerospace-Strategic & Tactical Missile Weapon Systems
S.I.C.: 3769

Acurex Corp. Aerotherm Products Division (1)
1111 N. Armando St.
Anaheim, CA 92806
Tel.: 714-630-5150
Aircraft Galley Refrigeration Equipment
S.I.C.: 3585; 3728
Stephen D. Ehrick *(V.P. & Gen. Mgr.)*

Acurex Corp. Autodata Division (1)
P.O. Box 7042, 555 Clyde Avenue
Mountain View, CA 94039
Tel.: 415-967-9100
Electronics--Microprocessor Based Data-Acquisition, Close Coupled Telemetry Equipment, and Measurement and Control Systems.
S.I.C.: 3825
Robert L. Barch *(V.P. & Gen. Mgr.)*

Acurex Environmental (1)
555 Clyde Ave.
Mountain View, CA 94043
Tel.: 415-961-5700
Combustion Energy Research, Alternate Fuel Analysis, Hot Gas Filtration Systems, Cogeneration Systems, Environmental Measurements & Analysis & Hazardous Waste Management
S.I.C.: 8711
William R. Byars *(V.P. & Gen. Mgr.)*
Stuart Whitelsey *(Controller)*
John Schaefer *(Sls. & Mktg. Dir.)*
Connie Monahan *(Dir.-Pur.)*
Amy Begley *(Mktg. Communications Coord.)*

Non-U.S. Holding:

Acurex Export Sales, Ltd. (1)
Bay Street P.O. Box 261,
Bridgetown, Barbados

THE AD TEAM OF FLORIDA INC.
15251 NE 18th Ave.
North Miami, FL 33162
Tel.: 305-949-8326
Year Founded: 1979
Approx.Billings: $37,000,000
Emp.: 45
Retail, Real Estate, Automotive Assns. & Dealerships
Russ Oasis *(Pres.)*
Zev Auerbach *(Exec. V.P., Creative)*
Minda Bernstein *(Controller)*
Neal Abramson *(Gen. Mgr.)*

AD-TECH COMMUNICATIONS
14361 Commerce Way
Miami Lakes, FL 33016
Tel.: 305-556-7261
Tel.: 800-541-2943
Fax: 305-821-7102
Year Founded: 1985
Approx.Billings: $12,000,000
Emp.: 15
Medical Devices, Diagnostics, Instrumentation, Pharmaceuticals & Health Care Delivery
William R. Quinlivan *(Mktg. Partner)*
Albert R. Buscaino *(Dir., Program Devel.)*
Sandi Mahynski *(Admin. Asst. & Acct. Services)*
Debra Iannaci *(Editor & Pub. Rels. Coord.)*
Deborah Chelimsky *(Fin. Admin. Asst.)*

Computer Systems/Hardware:
Macintosh, IBM

ADA BEEF, INC.
1010 Grand River Dr.
Ada, MI 49301
Tel.: 616-949-2350
Fax: 616--949-6617
Year Founded: 1948
Approx.Sls.: $66,000,000
Emp.: 125
Fiscal Year-end: 6/30/91
Export
Beef Products from Beef Slaughtered on Site
S.I.C.: 2011
Orie Vander Boon *(Pres.)*
Ronald Vander Boon *(V.P.)*
Randall Vander Boon *(V.P.)*
John Vander Boon *(Sec. & Treas.)*

Outside Service Firm(s):

Van Loozenoord & Bebbler*(Auditors)*
Grand Rapids, MI

Jack Holwerda*(Legal Firm)*
Grand Rapids, MI

FMB State Savings Bank*(Major Banking Relationship)*
Lowell, MI

ADAIR FEED & GRAIN COMPANY
110 Audubon
Adair, IA 50002-3855
Tel.: 515-742-3294 **IA**
Fax: 515-742-5083
Emp.: 26
Grains; Feed; Agricultural Chemicals; Fertilizer & Fertilizer Materials
S.I.C.: 5153; 5191
Charles Crawford *(Pres. & Treas.)*
Randy Crawford *(V.P. & Sec.)*

Outside Service Firm(s):

Fisher, Fisher & Fisher*(Auditors)*
Adair, IA

Kyhnn, Jarvis & Co.*(Legal Firm)*
Atlantic, IA

Packers Bank & Trust Co.*(Major Banking Relationship)*
Omah, NE

ADAIR GREENE ADVERTISING
2126 De Foors Ferry Rd., NW
Atlanta, GA 30318
Tel.: 404-351-8424
Fax: 404-351-1495
Year Founded: 1966
Approx.Billings: $11,000,000
Emp.: 18
Adv., Sales Promo., Motivation & Training
Warren E. Greene *(Pres.)*
Judye Greene *(Exec. V.P., Mktg. Dir.)*
Ray Schoenke *(V.P., Mgr.-Healthcare Communications)*
Lynne Greene *(V.P.)*

Computer Systems/Hardware:
IBM PC's, AST 286

ADAM MELDRUM & ANDERSON CO., INC.
389 Main St.
Buffalo, NY 14203
Mailing Address:
P.O. Box 976,
Buffalo, NY 14205
Tel.: 716-853-4020 **NY**
Fax: 716-854-3480
Year Founded: 1867
Approx.Sls.: $130,000,000
Emp.: 2,340
Fiscal Year-end: 1/30/92
Import
Department Stores
S.I.C.: 5311
Robert B. Adam *(Chm. Bd.)*
J. Keith Alford *(Pres. & Chief Exec. Officer)*
George Malesic *(Chief Info. Officer & Dir.-Mngmt. Information)*
Don M. Alexander *(V.P.-Publicity)*
John Ditch *(V.P.-Opers.)*
Robert Rutman *(V.P. & Controller)*
Carmelo A. Scaccia *(V.P. & Treas.)*
Trudy Mollenberg *(Sec.)*
Rita Proul *(Dir.-Training)*
Arthur Wypych *(Dir.-Plng. & Devel.)*
Sue Roetzer *(Mgr.-Human Resources)*

Computer Systems/Hardware:
IBM 4380

Outside Service Firm(s):

Ernst & Young*(Auditors)*
1400 Key Tower - 50 Fountain Plaza
Buffalo, NY
Tel.: 716-843-5000
Fax: 716-847-6949

Saperston & Day, P.C.*(Legal Firm)*
1500 Liberty Bank Bldg.
Buffalo, NY 14202
Tel.: 716-856-5400

Manufacturers & Traders Trust Company*(Major Banking Relationship)*
1 M & T Plaza
Buffalo, NY 14240
Tel.: 716-842-4200

ADAMS BUSINESS FORMS
200 SW Jackson
Topeka, KS 66603
Tel.: 913-233-4101
Tel.: 800-444-3508
Fax: 913-233-4291
Year Founded: 1889
Approx.Sls.: $34,000,000
Emp.: 367
Business Forms & Commercial Printers
S.I.C.: 2761; 2752
Pelham E. Adams *(Pres.)*
Richard S. Corwin *(Chief Fin. Officer & Exec. V.P.)*
Barry Conway *(Exec. V.P.-Sls. & Mktg.)*
Jeff Morgan *(V.P.-Opers.)*
Joe Nobk *(V.P.-Admin.)*
Dick Thornburg *(V.P.-Sls., Custom Forms)*
Glenn E. Vernon *(V.P.-Sls.)*
Craig Snyder *(Dir.-Pur.)*

Outside Service Firm(s):

Deloitte & Touche*(Auditors)*
1010 Grand Ave.
Kansas City, MO 64106-2232
Tel.: 816-474-6180

Stinson, Mag & Fizzell*(Legal Firm)*
Kansas City, KS

Bank IV*(Major Banking Relationship)*
P.O. Box 1122,
Wichita, KS 67201
Tel.: 316-261-4304

ADAMS COLWAY & ASSOCIATES
Corbett's Glenn, 412 Linden Ave.
Rochester, NY 14625
Tel.: 716-586-0222
Fax: 716-262-3006
Year Founded: 1987
Approx.Billings: $13,500,000
Emp.: 60
Advertising, Direct Marketing, Database Management, Co-Op Advertising
H. Mat Adams *(Chm. & Chief Exec. Officer)*
David E. Colway *(Pres. & Chief Fin. Officer)*
Margret Fess *(Exec. V.P., Chief Oper. Officer)*
Kevin Farmer *(V.P., Sales & Mktg.)*
Hazel Christian *(Telemarketing Mgr.)*
Ken Schleede *(Systems Engr.)*
Darlene Condidorio *(Acctg. Mgr.)*

R. P. ADAMS COMPANY, INC.
225 E. Park Dr.
Tonawanda, NY 14150
Mailing Address:
P.O. Box 963
Buffalo, NY 14240
Tel.: 716-877-2608
Fax: 716-877-9385
Year Founded: 1937
Approx.Sls.: $10,000,000
Emp.: 100
Fiscal Year-end: 12/31/90
Import Export
Mfr. Air, Water & Chemical Filters, Automatic Water Strainers, Aftercoolers, Cyclone Separators, Heat Exchangers, Shell & Tube Design
S.I.C.: 3564; 3569; 3494; 3443
Robert J. Adams *(Pres. & Chief Exec. Officer)*
Richard B. Adams *(Exec. V.P., Sec. & Treas.)*
David A. Henning *(V.P.-Personnel)*
Robert E. O'Kane *(V.P.-Mfg.)*
Richard B. Adams *(Gen. Sls. Mgr.)*

Computer Systems/Hardware:
Unisys

ADAMS EXTRACT CO., INC.
11206 IH-35 S.
Austin, TX 78747
Mailing Address:
P. O. Box 17008
Austin, TX 78760
Tel.: 512-282-1100
Year Founded: 1889
Approx.Sls.: $10,000,000
Emp.: 45
Adams Best Vanilla, Adams Butter Flavoring, Adams Spices; Adams Food Colors
S.I.C.: 2099
John G. Adams *(Pres. & Gen. Mgr.)*
Ralph Church *(Mgr.-Opers. & Prod.)*
Guy Duggan *(Mgr.-Mktg.)*
Jim McDonald *(Mgr.-Adv.)*
Tom McGaha *(Mgr.-Sls.)*
Paul Ondrias *(Mgr.-Personnel)*

ADAMS RITE MANUFACTURING CO.
4040 S. Capital Ave.
City of Industry, CA 91749
Mailing Address:
P.O. Box 1301
City of Industry, CA 91749
Tel.: 310-699-0511 **CA**
Fax: 310-699-5094
Year Founded: 1946
Assets: $12,300,000
Liabilities: $5,500,000
Net Worth: $6,800,000
Approx.Sls.: $23,500,000
Emp.: 200
Fiscal Year-end: 9/29/91
Import Export
Manufacture Maximum Security Locks
S.I.C.: 3429
Peter D. Adams *(Chm. & Pres.)*
Mark J. Kelly *(Exec. V.P.)*
Robert M. McManigal *(Sec. & Gen. Counsel)*
George Faludi *(Chief Engineer)*
David Orban *(Dir.-Sls.)*
Nicholas Rosier *(Dir.-Fin.)*
Jack Buzard *(Mgr.-Communications)*
Jennifer Grams *(Mgr.-Personnel)*
David Speers *(Supvr.-Pur.)*
Ichi Tagiku *(Supvr.-Data Processing)*

No. of Mfg. Plants/Facilities: 1
No. of U.S. Offices: 1
No. of Foreign Offices: 1

Computer Systems/Hardware:
Unisys

Outside Service Firm(s):

Kellogg & Andelson*(Auditors)*
Los Angeles, CA

Transamerica Occidental Insurance Co.*(Group Insurer)*
P.O. Box 30253,
Los Angeles, CA 90099

Robert M. McManigal*(Legal Firm)*
1701 Camden Pkwy.
South Pasedena, CA 91030
Tel.: 818-799-1571

First Interstate Bank*(Major Banking Relationship)*
Glendale, CA

National Associates, Inc.*(Pension Manager)*
3415 Sepulveda Blvd., #800
Los Angeles, CA 90034
Tel.: 213-390-8801

Subsidiary:

Quadrastat Corp. **(1)**
3860 S. Capitol Ave.
City of Industry, CA 91749
Tel.: 310-695-0531 (100%)
Manufacture Mechanical Controls; Motor Vehicle Controls
S.I.C.: 3714; 3492
Peter Adams *(Pres.)*

Non-U.S. Holding:

Adams Rite (Europe) Ltd. **(1)**
Unit 6, Moreton Industrial Estate Unit #6, London Rd.,
Swanley, Kent BR8 8TZ, United Kingdom
Tel.: 071 322 68024 (100%)
Fax: 071 322 60996
Approx.Sls.: $4,500,000
Emp.: 25
Distributor of Security Door & Window Hardware
S.I.C.: 5072
Iain MacKay *(Sls. Dir.)*

ADAMS WINE CO.
(d/b/a Monarch Wine Co. of GA)
451 Sawtell Ave., S. E.
Atlanta, GA 30315
Mailing Address:
P. O. Box 6047, Lakewood Sta.
Atlanta, GA 30315
Tel.: 404-622-4661
Fax: 404-622-5421
Year Founded: 1935
Approx.Sls.: $16,000,000
Emp.: 55
Fiscal Year-end: 12/31/91
Import Export
Mfr. & Distr. of Bulk Wine Sales, Fruit Juice Concentrates; Cooking Wines; Fruit Wines; Red Roosters 21, Longhorn, Rocket; Monogram-White Port, Muscatel, Sherry; Kosher Products-Mother Goldstein, Schapiro Wines
S.I.C.: 2084; 5182; 2037
Howard J. Weinstein *(Chm., Pres. & Chief Exec. Officer)*
David Paszamant *(Vice Chm., Exec. V.P. & Dir.-Mktg.)*
Brenda S. Brittelli *(Chief Fin. Officer, Sec.,Treas. & Controller)*
Gary Maxson *(Dir.-Quality Control)*
Jack Griffin *(Mgr.-Mfg.)*

Computer Systems/Hardware:
IBM Compatible 286

ADAMSON ADVERTISING, INC.
222 S. Central
Saint Louis, MO 63105
Tel.: 314-727-9500
Year Founded: 1981
Approx.Billings: $10,250,000
Emp.: 18
Business-to-Business, Consumer Products & Services
Richard D. Rubenstein *(Pres. & Creative Dir.)*
Irv Litvag *(Pres.-Pub. Rels.)*
Lon D. Zimmerman *(Exec. V.P., Treas. & New Bus. Contact)*
Kim Boyer *(V.P.)*
Dave De Pew *(V.P.)*

ADDISON STEEL INC.
7351 Overland Rd.
Orlando, FL 32810-3403
Tel.: 407-295-6434 **Fl**
Fax: 407-295-6434, Ext. 144
Year Founded: 1960
Assets: $20,194,585
Earnings: $970,566
Liabilities: $11,728,815
Net Worth: $8,465,770
Approx.Sls.: $50,000,000
Emp.: 200
Fiscal Year-end: 6/30/89
Design, Fabricate & Erect Structural Steel
S.I.C.: 3441; 1791
E. Christopher Addison *(Chm. Bd.)*
Glen Davis *(Pres.)*
T. M. Phagans *(Sec. & Treas.)*

No. of U.S. Offices: 2

Outside Service Firm(s):

Mauldin & Jenkins*(Auditors)*
Orlando, FL

D. A. Yergey*(Legal Firm)*
Orlando, FL

ADEC INTERNATIONAL AUTOMATION CORP.
1360 W. Ninth St., Suite 210
Cleveland, OH 44113
Tel.: 216-621-5115
Ordinance Design and Manufacturing
S.I.C.: 3484; 3482; 3483
Dominic F. Yen, Esq. *(Pres.)*

Division:

Adec Automation **(1)**
701 Ashland Center Three
Folcroft, PA 19032
Tel.: 215-586-6200
Emp.: 4,000
Mfr. of Aluminum & Brass Extrusions, Forgings & Castings; Aluminum Pistons, Bearings & Bushings
S.I.C.: 3334; 3354; 3356; 3365; 3463

ADELPHIA LAMP & SHADE INC.
5000 Paschall Ave.
Philadelphia, PA 19143
Tel.: 215-729-2600
Fax: 215-729-8077
Year Founded: 1935
Emp.: 85
Mfr. Lamp Shades & Lamps
S.I.C.: 3645
Alfred H. Denenberg *(Pres.)*
Robert Denenberg *(Chief Oper. Officer & V.P.)*
Chris Paffect *(Chief Fin. Officer)*
Anna Weaver *(Sec.)*

Outside Service Firm(s):

M. H. Ressman Associates*(Auditors)*
Philadelphia, PA

ADEPT TECHNOLOGY, INC.
150 Rose Orchard Way
San Jose, CA 95134
Tel.: 408-432-0888 **CA**
Twx: 171942
Fax: 408-432-8707
Approx.Sls.: $34,000,000
Emp.: 275
Fiscal Year-end: 6/30/90
Manufacture Robotics
S.I.C.: 3569
Brian Carlisle *(Chm. Bd. & Chief Exec. Officer)*
B.G. Mitchell *(V.P. & Chief Fin. Officer)*
Bruce Shimano *(V.P.-Res. & Devel.)*
Charles S. Duncheon *(V.P.-Mktg. & Sls.)*
David Baxter *(V.P.-Engrng.)*

No. of Mfg. Plants/Facilities: 1
No. of U.S. Offices: 2
No. of Foreign Offices: 2

Computer Systems/Hardware:
DEC

Outside Service Firm(s):

Ernst & Young*(Auditors)*
55 Almaden Blvd.
San Jose, CA 95115
Tel.: 408-947-5476
Fax: 408-294-2744

Wilson, Sonsini, Goodrich & Rosati*(Legal Firm)*
Two Palo Alto Square, Ste. 900
Palo Alto, CA 94306
Tel.: 415-493-9300

Silicon Valley Bank*(Major Banking Relationship)*
San Jose, CA

Adistra Corporation
(See listing under Adept Technology, Inc.)

ADLAND
The Company of First Choice
for Reaching Asian Americans

ADLAND ADVERTISING, INC.
(World Headquarters)
3000 Steiner-on-Union
San Francisco, CA 94123
Tel.: 415-928-1728
Fax: 415-928-1720
Year Founded: 1984
Approx.Billings: $12,800,000
Emp.: 350
Nationally Acclaimed Authority on the Asian American Market, Largest Asian Data Base in the Nation; Pioneers of Asian Segment Marketing, Segmentation Technique Identifying the Most Lucrative Segments & Subsegments Out of 29 Asian Ethnic Segments, Winning Coast to Coast National Campaigns, Award Winning Fortune 500 Art Department
S.Y. Chan *(Chm. Bd.)*
Eleanor N. Yu *(Pres.)*
William P. Lee *(Chief of Staff)*
Kenneth P. Yu *(Exec. V.P., Treas. & Res. Dir.)*
Thomas Chin *(V.P.)*
Douglas Wong *(V.P.)*
Dr. Kenneth Yu *(Gen. Mgr.-Chinese Div.)*
Jaqueline Noh *(Gen. Mgr.-Korean Div.)*
Thomas Ngo *(Gen. Mgr.-Vietnamese Div.)*
Seiji Horibuchi *(Gen. Mgr.-Japanese Div.)*

Computer Systems/Hardware:
IBM & MacIntosh

ADLER BOSCHETTO PEEBLES
& PARTNERS • INC

ADLER BOSCHETTO PEEBLES & PARTNERS, INC.
136 Madison Ave., 12th Fl.
New York, NY 10016
Tel.: 212-684-5220
Fax: 212-684-0469
Year Founded: 1916
Assets: $6,200,000
Liabilities: $4,650,000
Net Worth: $1,550,000
Approx.Billings: $65,000,000
Emp.: 60
Fiscal Year-end: 12/31/89
Advertising & Mktg. Communications Agency
S.I.C.: 7311
Corporate Giving Program: Company Gives to the United Way
Larry M. Adler *(Pres. & Chief Exec. Officer)*
Laurence J. Boschetto *(Exec. V.P., Dir. Acct. Mngmt.)*
Howard Gelman *(Exec. V.P., Chief Fin. Officer)*
Elizabeth K. Connelly *(Sr. V.P., Corp. Sec., Human Resources & Office Mngmt.)*
Patti Goldrick *(Sr. V.P., Bus. Devel.)*
Kelley Gipson *(V.P., Acct. Mngmt.)*
Joan Carlson *(V.P., Acct. Mngmt.)*

No. of U.S. Offices: 1

Computer Systems/Hardware:
IBM System 36, MacIntosh, IBM PC's & Local Area Network

Outside Service Firm(s):

Panneth, Haber, Zimmerman*(Auditors)*
New York, NY

John B. Buttine, Inc.*(Commercial Insurance Carrier)*
New York, NY

Hall, Dickler, Lawler, Kent & Friedman*(Legal Firm)*
460 Park Ave.
New York, NY 10017
Tel.: 212-838-4600

Chemical Bank*(Major Banking Relationship)*
450 West 33rd St.
New York, NY 10001
Tel.: 212-613-7197
Fax: 212-947-7628

C & B Consulting Group*(Pension Manager)*
Fifty Fremont St., 24th Fl.
San Francisco, CA 94105
Tel.: 415-979-0600
Fax: 415-979-0177

ADLER & SHAYKIN
375 Park Ave.
New York, NY 10152
Tel.: 212-319-2800
Fax: 212-319-2808
Year Founded: 1983
Emp.: 9
Fiscal Year-end: 12/31/91
Leveraged Buyout Firm
S.I.C.: 6799
Frederick R. Adler *(Mng. Partner)*
Alan H. Fishman *(Mng. Partner)*
Jerry E. Goldress *(Mng. Partner)*
Leonard Shaykin *(Mng. Partner)*
Andre J. McSherry *(Controller)*
Robert H. Shaykin *(Chief Fin. Officer)*

Subsidiaries:

Best Products Co., Inc. **(1)**
1400 Best Plaza
Richmond, VA 23227
Tel.: 804-261-2000
Telex: 827-395
Fax: 804-261-2250
Assets: $1,438,208,000
Earnings: $4,202,000
Liabilities: $1,366,974,000
Net Worth: $71,234,000
Approx.Sls.: $2,088,317,000
Emp.: 18,000
Fiscal Year-end: 2/ 2/91
Catalog/Showroom Mdsg.; 194 Showrooms Located in CA, NC, VA, PA, TX, OH, MI, MD, FL, WV, MO, CO, MT, AZ, ND, SD, WA, OR, MN, ID, NM, UT, KS, IL, NJ, DE, WY & TN
S.I.C.: 5944; 5722; 5731; 5719; 5948; 5251; 5399

Adler & Shaykin—(Continued)

Jerry E. Goldress *(Co-Chm.)*
Leonard P. Shaykin *(Co-Chm.)*
Alan H. Fishman *(Co-Chm.)*
Stewart M. Kasen *(Co-Chm., Pres. & Chief Exec. Officer)*
Daniel Hough *(V.P.-Mktg. & Adv.)*
Michelle H. Gluck *(Sec.)*

Subsidiary:

First Land & Development, Inc. **(2)**
P.O. Box 26303,
Richmond, VA 23260
Tel.: 804-261-2000 (100%)
Real Estate Developers
S.I.C.: 6552
Jerry E. Goldress *(Chm. & Chief Exec. Officer)*
Stewart M. Kasen *(Pres. & Chief Oper. Officer)*
Richard M. Cross *(V.P. & Treas.)*
Michelle H. Gluck *(Sec.)*

Chicago Sun Times **(1)**
401 N. Wabash Ave.
Chicago, IL 60611
Tel.: 312-321-3000
Sales Range: $100-499 Million
Emp.: 1,500
Fiscal Year-end: 6/30/91
Computer Systems/Hardware:
IBM 4341
Daily Newspaper
S.I.C.: 2711
Arthur W. Schultz *(Vice Chm.)*
Sam S. McKeel *(Pres., Chief Exec. Officer & Publr.)*
Dennis A. Britton *(Exec. V.P. & Editor)*
Joseph P. Gaynor *(Exec. V.P.)*
Michael J. Veitch *(Exec. V.P. & Gen. Mgr.)*
Charles F. Champion *(Sr. V.P.-Adv. Sls. & Mktg.)*
Ted Biedron *(V.P.-Classfied Adv.)*
Thomas Foster *(V.P.-Circulation)*
Roger Saunders *(V.P.-Display Adv.)*
Mary Holland *(Supv.-Employee Benefits)*
William Kijek *(Cash Mgr.)*

Subsidiaries:

Pioneer Press Newspapers Inc. **(2)**
1232 Central Ave.
Wilmette, IL 60091
Tel.: 708-251-4300 (100%)
Publr. of Weekly Community Newspapers Distributed Throughout Chicago Suburbs
S.I.C.: 2711
Richard W. Gilbert *(Pres. & Publr.)*
Michael Esses *(V.P.-Sls. & Mktg.)*
Drew Davis *(V.P.-Newspapers)*
Douglas Rector *(Controller)*

Star Publications **(2)**
1526 Otto Blvd.
Chicago Heights, IL 60411
Tel.: 708-755-6161 (100%)
Publr. of Daily Newspaper Distributed Throughout Chicago's South Side & South Suburbs
S.I.C.: 2711
Norman Rosinski *(Pres. & Publr.)*

The Folger Adam Company **(1)**
16300 W. 103rd St.
Lemont, IL 60439
Tel.: 708-739-3900
Fax: 708-739-6138
Mfr. of Security Devices
S.I.C.: 3669
Donald C. Stading *(Pres.)*

ADMARK, INC.
3630 S.W. Burlingame Rd.
Topeka, KS 66611
Tel.: 913-267-4712
Year Founded: 1982
Approx.Billings: $17,000,000
Emp.: 54
Sondra L. Busch *(Chief Exec. Officer)*
Barry L. Busch *(Pres.-Sls. Promo. Div.)*
Cindy Maude *(Pres.-Adv. Div.)*
Cheryl Creviston *(V.P., Controller)*

Computer Systems/Hardware:
IBM, Macintosh

ADMARKETING, INC.
1801 Century Park East, Ste. 2000
Los Angeles, CA 90067
Tel.: 310-203-8400
Telex: 910 321-2489
Fax: 310-277-7621
Year Founded: 1971
Approx.Billings: $277,500,000
Emp.: 135
Advertising Agency
S.I.C.: 7311
Robert Recht *(Chm. Bd.)*
Jack Roth *(Pres. & Chief Exec. Officer)*
Martin Cagan *(Exec. V.P.)*
Denis Kalscheur *(Exec. V.P.)*
George Abdell *(Sr. V.P.)*
Frank Farrell *(Sr. V.P.)*
Arlynn Whittaker *(Sr. V.P.)*
Tim Balzer *(V.P.-Fin.)*
Robert Roth *(V.P., Treas.)*
Stelios Touchtidis *(Dir. Data Processing)*

Computer Systems/Hardware:
DAX 8200

Outside Service Firm(s):

Alder Green & Hasson*(Auditors)*
Los Angeles, CA

ADMIRAL MAINTENANCE SERVICE L.P.
(Formerly Admiral Maintenance Service Company)
4343 W. Touhy Ave.
Lincolnwood, IL 60646
Tel.: 708-675-6000
Fax: 708-675-6033
Year Founded: 1958
Emp.: 2,100
Office Buildings & Institutional Janitorial Services & Personnel Supply Services
S.I.C.: 7349
Louis P. Fiedler *(Chm. Bd.)*
Richard K. Fiedler *(Pres.)*
Alice Sarmiento *(Controller)*
Sid Bearak *(Dir.-Pur.)*
John Csehill *(Mktg. Dir.)*

Outside Service Firm(s):

Goldberg & Geiser*(Auditors)*
Chicago, IL

Altheimer & Gray*(Legal Firm)*
10 S. Wacker Dr.
Chicago, IL 60606
Tel.: 312-715-4000

ADOLFSON & PETERSON, INC.
6701 W. 23rd St.
Minneapolis, MN 55426
Mailing Address:
P.O. Box 9377
Minneapolis, MN 55440
Tel.: 612-544-1561 **MN**
Fax: 612-525-2333
Year Founded: 1946
Approx.Sls.: $120,000,000
Emp.: 300
General Contractors & Construction Managers; Commercial, Industrial & Apartment Buildings
S.I.C.: 1522; 1541; 1542
David G. Adolfson *(Chm. Bd., Pres. & Chief Exec. Officer)*
Brook P. Adolfson *(V.P.)*
Richard A. Weicht *(V.P. & Sec.)*
Douglas E. Myhre *(Treas.)*
Howard Rekstad *(Dir.-Bus. Devel.)*

No. of U.S. Offices: 3

Subsidiary:

AP Technology Management Inc. **(1)**
600 W. County Rd. D
Saint Paul, MN 55112
Tel.: 612-628-0102
Emp.: 10
Construction of Clean Rooms & Related Facilities
S.I.C.: 1521
Mark Houge *(Pres.)*

ADPLAN ASSOCIATES
(House Agency)
P.O. Box 59
Evansville, IN 47701
Tel.: 812-468-5640
Year Founded: 1962
Approx.Billings: $13,000,000
Emp.: 15
Financial Adv.
Donald Tennenhouse *(V.P., Mktg. & Bus. Devel.)*
Patti Lodato *(Adv. Dir.)*
Greg Thomas *(Mktg. Services Mgr.)*

ADRA SYSTEMS, INC.
59 Technology Dr.
Lowell, MA 01851
Tel.: 508-937-3700 **DE**
Fax: 508-453-2462
Year Founded: 1983
Assets: $11,000,000
Liabilities: $5,000,000
Net Worth: $6,000,000
Approx.Sls.: $25,000,000
Emp.: 130
Fiscal Year-end: 6/30/91
Export
Electronic Computers; Computer Software Development
S.I.C.: 3571; 7371
William T. Mason *(Pres. & Chief Exec. Officer)*
William L. Fiedler *(V.P.-Fin. & Admin.)*
Alfred L. Simensen *(V.P.-Sls.)*
James C. Blaschke *(V.P.-Mktg.)*
Ralph J. Mayer *(V.P.-Devel.)*
Michael Segal *(V.P.-Customer Service)*
Patrick Brochu *(V.P.-Intl. Mktg.)*
Richard Livermore *(Controller)*
Eileen Demers *(Mgr.-Human Resources)*

No. of Mfg. Plants/Facilities: 1
No. of U.S. Offices: 14
No. of Foreign Offices: 6

Outside Service Firm(s):

Arthur Andersen & Co.*(Auditors)*
One Intl. Place, 100 Oliver St.
Boston, MA 02110
Tel.: 617-330-4000
Fax: 617-439-9731

Chubb Group*(Auditors)*
Boston, MA

Testa, Hurwitz & Thibeault*(Legal Firm)*
53 State St.
Boston, MA 02109
Tel.: 617-248-7000
Fax: 617-248-7100

Silicon Valley Bank*(Major Banking Relationship)*
Wellesley, MA

ADRAY APPLIANCE & PHOTO CENTER, INC.
(Formerly Adray Appliance & Photo)
20219 Carlysle
Dearborn, MI 48124
Tel.: 313-274-9500 **MI**
Fax: 313-274-6874
Year Founded: 1955
Approx.Sls.: $27,000,000
Emp.: 100
Fiscal Year-end: 12/31/91
Retail Household Appliances & Electronics, Cameras & Photographic Supplies, Luggage, Jewelry & Housewares
S.I.C.: 5722; 5731; 5946; 5948; 5944; 5719
Debra Adray Cziraky *(Pres. & Chief Exec. Officer)*
George Bendar *(V.P. & Gen. Mgr.)*
Violet Zennedjian *(Sec. & Treas.)*

Outside Service Firm(s):

Clement & Francis*(Auditors)*
Southfield, MI

Brown, McGlynn & Fortescue*(Legal Firm)*
Bloomfield Hills, MI

Dearborn Bank & Trust Co.*(Major Banking Relationship)*
Dearborn, MI

ADVANCE BUSINESS GRAPHICS
3810 Wabash Dr.
Mira Loma, CA 91752
Tel.: 909-685-7100
Fax: 909-685-4201
Approx.Sls.: $28,000,000
Emp.: 250
Printing Business Forms
S.I.C.: 2752
Nicholas Kosta *(Chm. Bd.)*
Thomas Steiner *(Pres.)*
William Paxton *(V.P. & Chief Fin. Officer)*
John Kosta *(V.P.-Sls.)*
Fred Pruitt *(V.P.-Mfg.)*
J. Raynow *(Dir.-Personnel)*
Charles Gruber *(Pur. Agent)*

No. of Mfg. Plants/Facilities: 1
No. of U.S. Offices: 5

Computer Systems/Hardware:
HP 3000

Outside Service Firm(s):

Ernst & Young*(Auditors)*
515 S. Flower St.
Los Angeles, CA 90071
Tel.: 213-621-1666

Blue Cross of California*(Group Insurer)*
21555 Oxnard St.
Woodland Hills, CA 91367
Tel.: 818-703-2345

Kaiser Permanente*(Group Insurer)*
One Kaiser Place
Oakland, CA 94612
Tel.: 510-596-1000

Goldenring & Goldenring*(Legal Firm)*
Los Angeles, CA

Union Bank*(Major Banking Relationship)*
445 S. Figueroa St.
Los Angeles, CA 90071
Tel.: 213-236-5076

ADVANCE MACHINE COMPANY
14600 21st Ave. North
Plymouth, MN 55447
Tel.: 612-473-2235 **MN**
Fax: 612-475-9718
Year Founded: 1929
Approx.Sls.: $90,000,000
Emp.: 650
Fiscal Year-end: 12/31/91
Mfr. Floor Care Equip.
S.I.C.: 2842; 3589
Edward Michalek *(Pres. & Chief Exec. Officer)*
Joseph Grewe *(V.P.-Oper. & Chief Fin. Officer)*
David Olmstead *(V.P.-Sls. & Mktg.)*
Ronald Murray *(Treas.)*
Ken Frideres *(Dir.-Personnel)*
Kenneth Klinck *(Dir.-Intl.)*

Greg Jodzio *(Mgr.-Mktg. Communications)*
Dave Maiers *(Mgr.-MIS)*
Gary Maiers *(Mgr.-Data Processing)*

Outside Service Firm(s):

McGladrey & Pullen*(Auditors)*
Minneapolis, MN

Dorsey & Whitney*(Legal Firm)*
2200 First Bank Place East
Minneapolis, MN 55402

First Bank Minneapolis*(Major Banking Relationship)*
Minneapolis, MN

ADVANCE MECHANICAL SYSTEMS, INC.
2001 Estes
Elk Grove Village, IL 60007
Tel.: 708-593-2510 **IL**
Fax: 708-593-2536
Sales Range: $40-59 Million
Emp.: 250
Fiscal Year-end: 3/28/91
Heating & Air Conditioning Contractor; Water, Sewer & Utility Lines; Plumbing
S.I.C.: 1711; 1623
Herbert Kreisman *(Chm. Bd. & Treas.)*
Robert S. Blumenthal *(Pres.)*
John Nowicki *(Exec. V.P.)*
Jack Keller *(V.P.)*
Daniel Krebsbach *(V.P.)*
Thomas Whalen *(V.P.)*
David Wiener *(V.P.)*
David Rojek *(Sec.)*
Joe Clark *(Pur. Agent)*

Outside Service Firm(s):

Arthur Andersen & Co.*(Auditors)*
33 W. Monroe St.
Chicago, IL 60603-4067
Tel.: 312-580-0033
Fax: 312-507-6748

D'Ancora & Pflaum*(Legal Firm)*
Chicago, IL

Continental Bank N. A.*(Major Banking Relationship)*
231 S. LaSalle St.
Chicago, IL 60697
Tel.: 312-828-2345
Tel.: 800-426-5754
Telex: 312-828-1783

ADVANCE PACKAGING CORPORATION
4450 36th St., S.E.
Grand Rapids, MI 49512
Mailing Address:
P.O. Box 888311,
Grand Rapids, MI 49588-8311
Tel.: 616-949-6611
Fax: 616-949-7972
Year Founded: 1966
Approx.Sls.: $32,000,000
Emp.: 200
Fiscal Year-end: 11/ 1/91
Corrugated Shipping Containers
S.I.C.: 2653
Richard H. Strauss *(Pres.)*
Carol A. Hoyt *(V.P.-Human Resources)*
Edward J. McLean *(V.P.-Sls.)*
Clinton E. Ripley *(V.P.-Customer Service)*
Donald C. Yondo *(V.P.)*
Robert P. Hasper *(Treas.)*
Sharon A. Clemen *(Mgr.-Sls.)*
Scott A. Galloway *(Dir.-Data Processing)*
William G. Mize *(Dir.-Quality Control)*
Principal(s):
Richard H. Strauss
Carol A. Hoyt
Donald C. Yondo
Donald W. Crossley

No. of Mfg. Plants/Facilities: 2

Computer Systems/Hardware:
WANG 7200

Outside Service Firm(s):

Ernst & Young*(Auditors)*
171 Monroe Ave. NW
Grand Rapids, MI 49503
Tel.: 616-774-0710
Fax: 616-774-0190

Old Kent Bank*(Major Banking Relationship)*
Grand Rapids, MI

Varnum, Riddering, Schmidt & Howlett*(Legal Firm)*
666 Old Kent Bldg.
Grand Rapids, MI 49502
Tel.: 616-459-4186

Subsidiary:

Central Michigan Container Corporation **(1)**
2400 E. High St.
Jackson, MI 49204
Tel.: 517-788-9800
Emp.: 38
Corrugated Shipping Containers
S.I.C.: 2653
Donald W. Crossley *(Chief Oper. Officer)*
David Harrington *(Mgr.-Sls.)*

ADVANCE PUBLICATIONS INC.
950 Fingerboard Rd.
Staten Island, NY 10305
Tel.: 718-981-1234
Fax: 718-981-1415
Year Founded: 1886
Approx.Sls.: $2,200,000,000
Emp.: 19,000
Fiscal Year-end: 12/31/90
Newspaper, Magazine & Book Publishing
S.I.C.: 2711; 2721; 2731
Samuel I. Newhouse, Jr. *(Chm. Bd. & Chief Exec. Officer)*
Richard Diamond *(Publisher)*
Arthur Silverstein *(Controller)*
Gary Cognetta *(Display Adv. Mgr.)*
Principal(s):
Samuel I. Newhouse, Jr.

No. of Mfg. Plants/Facilities: 35
No. of U.S. Offices: 16

Computer Systems/Hardware:
Hewlett-Packard 3000 Model 68, 150 PC, 3000 Model 37; Atex 7000

Subsidiaries:

The Conde Nast Publications Inc. **(1)**
350 Madison Ave.
New York, NY 10017
Tel.: 212-880-8800 (100%)
Emp.: 1,800
Magazine Publisher
S.I.C.: 2721
S.I. Newhouse, Jr. *(Chm. Bd.)*
Bernard H. Leser *(Pres.)*
Eric Anderson *(Exec. V.P. & Treas.)*
John Brunelle *(Exec. V.P.)*
Joseph L. Fuchs *(Exec. V.P.)*
Pamela van Zandt *(Exec. V.P.)*
Peter Armour *(V.P.-Circulation)*
Irving Herschbein *(V.P.-Mfg. & Distr.)*
Neil Jacobs *(V.P.-Conde Nast Package)*
G. Doug Johnson *(V.P.)*
Daniel Salem *(V.P.-Intl.)*
Fred Thormann *(V.P.-Corp. Resources)*
Michael Clinton *(Publr.-Gentlemen's Quarterly)*
Richard B. Barthelmes *(Publr.-Gourmet)*
Thomas Florio *(Publr.-Conde Nast Traveler)*
Mitchell Fox *(Publr.-Details)*
Anne Sutherland Fuchs *(Publr.-Vogue)*
Roland Galotti *(Publr.-Vanity Fair)*
Marianne Howatson *(Publr.-Self)*
Jack Kliger *(Publr.-Glamour)*
Kevin Madden *(Publr.-House & Garden)*
Roger M. Antin *(Publr.-Bride's)*
Richard Kinsler *(Publr.-Mademoiselle)*
Kathy Neisloss *(Publr.-Allure)*

Publications:

Allure **(2)**
350 Madison Ave.
New York, NY 10017
Tel.: 212-880-8800
Monthly Women's Magazine
S.I.C.: 2721
Kathy Neisloss *(Publisher)*
Diane Silberstein *(Dir.-Adv.)*

Bride's **(2)**
350 Madison Ave.
New York, NY 10017
Six-Times-Yearly Magazine for Brides
S.I.C.: 2721
Elliot Marion *(Publisher)*
Barbara Tober *(Editor-in-Chief)*
Susan Ludlow *(Dir.-Adv.)*

Conde Nast Traveler **(2)**
360 Madison Ave.
New York, NY 10017
Tel.: 212-880-8800
Fax: 212-286-9244
Approx.Sls.: $21,000,000
Fiscal Year-end: 12/31/90
Travel Magazine
S.I.C.: 2721
Thomas Florio *(Publisher)*
Richard Beckman *(Dir.-Adv.)*
Kaye Wisecup Ginsberg *(Dir.-Mktg.)*
Karen Alfirevic *(Mgr.-Midwest Adv.)*
Bernadette Murray *(Mgr.-Sls. Devel.)*
Patrick J. Matthews *(Mgr.-West Coast/ Asia/Pacific)*

Details Magazine **(2)**
632 Broadway, Penthouse
New York, NY 10012
Tel.: 212-598-3710
Young Men's Style Magazine
S.I.C.: 2721
Mitchell B. Fox *(Publisher)*
Julie McGowan *(Dir.-Adv.)*

Gentlemen's Quarterly **(2)**
350 Madison Ave.
New York, NY 10017
Tel.: 212-880-8800
Men's Magazine
S.I.C.: 2721
Michael Clinton *(Publisher)*
Alan Stiles *(Dir.-Adv.)*

Glamour **(2)**
350 Madison Ave.
New York, NY 10017
Women's Magazine
S.I.C.: 2721
Jack Kluger *(Publisher)*
William J. Abbott *(Assoc. Publr.-Mktg.)*
Susan K. Blank *(Dir.-Adv.)*

Gourmet **(2)**
560 Lexington Ave.
New York, NY 10022
Tel.: 212-880-2759
Fax: 212-355-2932
Emp.: 75
Fiscal Year-end: 12/31/91
Magazine Featuring Travel, Fine Food, Restaurants & Recipes
S.I.C.: 2721
Richard B. Barthelmes *(Publisher)*
Gail Zweigenthal *(Editor-in-Chief)*
Peter King Hunsinger *(Dir.-Adv.)*
Marvin Krauss *(Dir.-Mktg.)*
Alan P. Berman *(Mgr.-Adv.)*
Sandra L. Jackson *(Coord.-Adv.)*

House & Garden **(2)**
350 Madison Ave.
New York, NY 10017
Home Decorating & Design Magazine
S.I.C.: 2721
J. Kevin Madden *(Publisher)*
Susan Rerat *(Dir.-Adv.)*

Mademoiselle **(2)**
350 Madison Ave.
New York, NY 10017
Magazine for Young Career Women
S.I.C.: 2721
Julie Lewit-Nirenberg *(Publisher)*
Nancy Jenks Harding *(Mktg. Dir.)*
Elinore Carmody *(Dir.-Adv.)*

Self **(2)**
350 Madison Ave.
New York, NY 10017
Tel.: 212-880-8800
Beauty & Health Magazine
S.I.C.: 2721
Lawrence C. Burstein *(Publisher)*
Alexandra Penney *(Editor-in-Chief)*
Lisa Shelkin *(Mng. Editor)*
Alexander Liberman *(Dir.-Editorial)*
Victoria Lasdon *(Dir.-Adv.)*
Gretel M. Schneider *(Dir.-Mktg.)*
Lynn Hofher *(Asst. Managing Editor)*
Andrea Coda *(Mgr.-Production)*
Allison Adler Matz *(Mgr.-Adv.)*

Vanity Fair **(2)**
350 Madison Ave.
New York, NY 10017
Tel.: 212-880-8800
Special Interest Magazine
S.I.C.: 2721
Ronald A. Galotti *(Publisher)*
Stephen M. Jacoby *(Dir.-Mktg.)*
Frances Orner *(Dir.-Adv.)*
Helene Tricarico *(Dir.-Intl. Adv.)*

Vogue Magazine **(2)**
350 Madison Ave.
New York, NY 10017
Tel.: 212-880-6921
Fax: 212-880-6921
Women's Magazine
S.I.C.: 2721
Anne Sutherland Fuchs *(Publisher)*
Anna Wintour *(Editor-in-Chief)*
Norman Waterman *(Assoc. Publisher)*
Diane Oshin *(Dir.-Adv.)*
Sarah Chubb *(Mgr.-Adv.)*
Marcia Weinberg *(Creative Dir.)*

Newhouse Newspapers Metro-Suburbia, Inc. **(1)**
485 Lexington Ave.
New York, NY 10017
Tel.: 212-697-8020 (100%)
Fax: 212-972-3146
Newspaper Representative
S.I.C.: 7313
Edwin F. Russell *(Pres.)*
Robert N. Schoenbacher *(V.P.-Sls. & Mktg.)*
Dino Zografos *(Sls. Mgr.)*

Random House, Inc. **(1)**
201 E. 50th St.
New York, NY 10022
Tel.: 212-751-2600
Fax: 212-872-8244
Books; Modern Library Series & Vintage Books
S.I.C.: 2731
Alberto Vitale *(Chm., Pres. & Chief Exec. Officer)*
Howard Kaminsky *(Publisher)*
Marc Jaffe *(Exec. V.P. & Editor-In-Chief-Vallard)*
Alexander MacGregor *(Exec. V.P.-Admin.)*
Greg Euson *(V.P.-Mktg.)*
Dante V. Del Col *(V.P.-Adv. & Promo.)*
Sandra E. Stiles *(V.P. & Controller)*

Divisions:

Ballantine Books **(2)**
201 E. 50th St.
New York, NY 10022
Tel.: 212-751-2600
Mass Market Books, Trade Paperbacks
S.I.C.: 2731
Linda Grey *(Pres.)*
George Fisher *(V.P.-Distributor Sales)*

Fawcett Books **(2)**
1515 Broadway
New York, NY 10030
Tel.: 212-751-2600
Book Publishing
S.I.C.: 2731
Leona Nevler *(V.P. & Editor-in-Chief)*

Fodor's Travel Publications, Inc. **(2)**
201 E. 50th St.
New York, NY 10022
Tel.: 212-872-8254
Tel.: 800-327-4801
Fax: 212-572-2248
Emp.: 40
Publishers of Travel Guides
S.I.C.: 2731
Kristina Peterson *(V.P. & Publisher-Reference & Travel)*
Michael Spring *(V.P. & Editorial Dir.)*

Random House **(2)**
201 E. 50th St.
New York, NY 10022
Tel.: 212-751-2600
Approx.Sls.: $100,000,000
Harold Evans *(Publisher)*
Walter I. Weintz *(Assoc. Publisher)*

Times Books **(2)**
201 E. 50th St.
New York, NY 10022
Tel.: 212-751-2600
Adult Trade Books Publishing
S.I.C.: 2731

Advance Publications Inc.—(Continued)

Villard Books **(2)**
201 E. 50th St.
New York, NY 10022
Tel.: 212-751-2600
Book Publisher
S.I.C.: 2731
Harold Evans *(Publisher)*

Subsidiary:

Crown Publishers, Inc. **(2)**
201 E. 50th St.
New York, NY 10003
Tel.: 212-572-2600
Fax: 212-572-6192
Emp.: 400
Publishers
S.I.C.: 2741; 2731; 2721; 2711
A. Vitale *(Chm. Bd.)*
Michelle Sidrane *(Pres.)*
Andrew Martin *(Dir.-Publicity)*
Helen Zimmerman *(Supvr.-Adv.)*

Affiliate:

Alfred A. Knopf, Inc. **(2)**
201 E. 50th St.
New York, NY 10022
Tel.: 212-751-2600
Fax: 212-572-2593
Emp.: 75
Fiscal Year-end: 12/31/90
Publishers of Fiction, Nonfiction, Juvenile Books
S.I.C.: 2731
Alberto Vitale *(Pres.)*
Sonny Mehta *(Publisher & Editor-in-Chief)*
Jane Becker Friedman *(Exec. V.P.)*
Elizabeth Sifton *(Exec. V.P.)*
Victoria A. Wilson *(V.P. & Assoc. Publr.)*
Charles Elliott *(V.P. & Sr. Editor)*
Ashbel Green *(V.P. & Sr. Editor)*
Judith B. Jones *(V.P. & Sr. Editor)*
Carol B. Janeway *(V.P., Sr. Editor & Dir.-Intl. Rights)*
Nina Bourne *(V.P.-Adv.)*
William T. Loverd *(V.P. & Dir.-Publicity)*
Ellen McNeilly *(V.P.-Production)*
Carl Lennertz *(Dir.-Mktg.)*

ADVANCE STEEL CO.
9635 French Rd.
Detroit, MI 48213
Tel.: 313-571-6700 **MI**
Fax: 313-571-6707
Approx.Sls.: $33,000,000
Emp.: 26
Fiscal Year-end: 6/30/91
Steel Service Center
S.I.C.: 5051
Robert A. Stewart *(Owner & Chief Exec. Officer)*
Charmaine Porte *(Chief Fin. Officer & Sec.)*
Joel Zanville *(Pres.)*
Principal(s):
Robert A. Stewart

Outside Service Firm(s):

Manufacturers Hanover Trust Co.*(Major Banking Relationship)*
Rochester, NY

ADVANCED CIRCUIT TECHNOLOGY
118 N. Eastern Blvd.
Nashua, NH 03061
Mailing Address:
P.O. Box 547X,
Nashua, NH 03061
Tel.: 603-880-6000
Tel.: 800-234-3539 **NH**
Telex: 710-228-8961
Fax: 603-880-7785
Year Founded: 1976
Sales Range: $10-19 Million
Emp.: 130
Export
Custom Sculptured Flexible Circuitry, Custom Modular Flexible Assemblies, Custom & Standard Interconnecting Devices
S.I.C.: 3679
Joseph Roberts *(Chm. Bd. & Chief Exec. Officer)*
Paul Downey *(Pres., Treas. & Sec.)*
Dennis Bonnette *(Exec. V.P. & Chief Oper. Officer)*
George Lavoie *(Controller & Dir.-Mngmt. Information Systems)*
Jack Skryness *(Dir.-Contract Admin.)*
Ed Bisbing *(Dir.-Pur.)*
Linda Tisdale *(Mgr.-Personnel)*
Larry Dexter *(Mgr.-Quality Control)*

No. of Mfg. Plants/Facilities: 2

Computer Systems/Hardware:
Wang VS100

Outside Service Firm(s):

Coopers & Lybrand*(Auditors)*
1 Post Office Square
Boston, MA 02110
Tel.: 617-574-5000
Fax: 617-345-0398

Travelers Insurance Co.*(Group Insurer)*
Danvers, MA

Devine, Millimet & Branch*(Legal Firm)*
Manchester, NH

ADVANCED CONTROLS, INC.
16901 Jamboree Blvd.
Irvine, CA 92714
Tel.: 714-863-9300 **CA**
Fax: 714-863-3049
Year Founded: 1972
Sales Range: $20-39 Million
Emp.: 90
Export
Mfr. Electronic Control Equip.
S.I.C.: 3629
Corporate Giving Program: United Way
Robert W. Quest *(Pres.)*
William Glass *(Chief Fin. Officer)*
Arch Conway *(Dir.-Mfg.)*
Jim Malloy *(Dir.-Mktg. & Sls.)*

No. of Mfg. Plants/Facilities: 1
No. of U.S. Offices: 6
No. of Foreign Offices: 2

Outside Service Firm(s):

White, Nelson & Co.*(Auditors)*
Los Angeles, CA

Frank B. Hall*(Commercial Insurance Carrier)*
3200 Wilshire Blvd.
Los Angeles, CA 90010
Tel.: 213-386-8553
Fax: 213-736-7602

Prudential Insurance Co. of America*(Group Insurer)*
1400 Fashion Island Blvd.
San Mateo, CA
Tel.: 415-574-6815
Fax: 415-574-8427

O'Melveny & Myers*(Legal Firm)*
Newport Beach, CA

Bank of New England*(Pension Manager)*
28 State Street
Boston, MA 02109
Tel.: 617-742-4000

ADVANCED ENERGY INDUSTRY
1600 Prospect Pkwy.
Fort Collins, CO 80525
Tel.: 303-221-4670 **CO**
Fax: 303-221-5583
Approx.Sls.: $21,500,000
Emp.: 230
Fiscal Year-end: 12/31/89
Export
Manufacture Electronic Power Supplies & Controls
S.I.C.: 3679
Douglas S. Schatz *(Pres. & Chief Exec. Officer)*
G. Brent Backman *(V.P.)*
Sue Schell *(V.P.-Human Resources & Quality Services)*

No. of Mfg. Plants/Facilities: 1
No. of U.S. Offices: 3
No. of Foreign Offices: 2

Outside Service Firm(s):

United Bank*(Major Banking Relationship)*
Ft. Collins, CO

ADVANCED INPUT DEVICES, INC.
W. 250 A I D Dr.
Coeur D'Alene, ID 83814
Tel.: 208-765-8000 **ID**
Fax: 208-772-7613
Year Founded: 1988
Approx.Sls.: $20,000,000
Emp.: 250
Export
Mfr. of Computer Keyboards, Office Machine
S.I.C.: 3575
Leslie A. Larsen *(Pres.)*
R. Crawford Byxbee *(V.P.-Research & Devel.)*
Dene Geary *(V.P.-Mfg.)*
Kent Kimball *(V.P.-Sls.)*
Kevin Malone *(V.P.-Customer Service & Sls.)*

ADVANCED INSTRUMENTS, INC.
1000 Highland Ave.
Needham Heights, MA 02194
Tel.: 617-449-3000 **MA**
Fax: 617-455-8468
Sales Range: $10-19 Million
Emp.: 100
Scientific Instruments & Hospital Equipment
S.I.C.: 3826
Blanton C. Wiggin *(Chm. Bd.)*
Romano Micciche *(Pres.)*
Douglas Guerette *(V.P.-Opers.)*
Sharon Onigman *(Dir.-Mktg.)*
Erma N. Wiggin *(Treas.)*
Jack Hughes *(Dir.-Fin.)*

Outside Service Firm(s):

Wolf & Company*(Auditors)*
Boston, MA

Shawmut Bank*(Major Banking Relationship)*
One Federal St.
Boston, MA 02211
Tel.: 617-292-2969
Fax: 617-292-4417

ADVANCED MANUFACTURING & DEVELOPMENT
300 E. Hill Rd.
Willits, CA 95490
Tel.: 707-459-9451
Fax: 707-459-2046
Year Founded: 1958
Approx.Sls.: $15,000,000
Emp.: 140
Fiscal Year-end: 12/31/88
Precision Sheet Metal Shop for Electronics Indus.
S.I.C.: 3444
Gary Remos *(Chm. Bd., Pres. & Chief Exec. Officer)*
Jerry Colwell *(Treas. & Chief Fin. Officer)*
Principal(s):
Gary Remos

Computer Systems/Hardware:
MAI Basic 4; IBM PC

Outside Service Firm(s):

Frederick A. Steele CPA, Inc.*(Auditors)*
Willits, CA

First Farwest*(Group Insurer)*
San Francisco, CA

Bank of America, N.T. & S.A.*(Major Banking Relationship)*
P.O. Box 37002,
San Francisco, CA 94137

Commonwealth Funding*(Major Banking Relationship)*
San Francisco, CA

ADVANCED MARINE ENTERPRISES, INC.
1725 Jefferson Davis Hwy., Ste. 1300
Arlington, VA 22202
Tel.: 703-979-9200 **VA**
Fax: 703-553-0593
Year Founded: 1976
Assets: $7,700,000
Earnings: $328,000
Liabilities: $4,700,000
Net Worth: $3,000,000
Approx.Sls.: $17,600,000
Emp.: 225
Fiscal Year-end: 5/31/91
Naval Architecture; Marine Engineering; Management & Computer Sciences
S.I.C.: 8741; 8711
Simon Glatz *(Pres. & Chief Exec. Officer)*
John T. Drewry *(V.P., Chief Oper. & Chief Fin. Officer & Treas.)*
Otto P. Jons *(V.P.-Engrng.)*
Barbara S. Lamade *(Gen. Counsel)*
Principal(s):
Simon Glatz
John T. Drewry
Otto P. Jons

No. of U.S. Offices: 3

Computer Systems/Hardware:
DEC VAX 785; Microvax II (3)

Outside Service Firm(s):

Gelman, Rosenberg & Freedman*(Auditors)*
Chevy Chase, MD

Great American Insurance Co.*(Group Insurer)*
Cincinnati, OH

Wood, Lucksinger & Epstein*(Legal Firm)*
Washington, DC

Signet Bank*(Major Banking Relationship)*
McLean, VA

ADVANCED TECHNOLOGY, INC.
12005 Sunrise Valley Dr.
Reston, VA 22091
Tel.: 703-620-8000 **DE**
Fax: 703-620-2033
Year Founded: 1976
Assets: $78,224,000
Earnings: $4,311,000
Net Worth: $78,224,000
Approx.Sls.: $140,000,000
Emp.: 2,300
Fiscal Year-end: 12/30/87
Mngmt., Engrng. & Computer Services
S.I.C.: 8741; 8711
Scott Thompson *(Chm. Bd., Pres., Chief Exec. & Chief Oper. Officer)*
Anthony A. St. George *(Vice Chm. & Sr. V.P.)*
Ronald H. Hobbs *(Exec. V.P.)*
Ford Byrd *(Sr. V.P.-Real Estate & Legal Affairs)*
Girish K. Jindia *(Sr. V.P.-Fin., Treas. & Chief Fin. Officer)*
Tom Edgar *(V.P.-Human Resources)*
Bill Sabo *(V.P.-Mktg.)*
Anthony H. Blackstone *(Chief of Staff)*
Thomas Davis *(Exec. Dir. & Gen. Counsel)*
Mike DeBruhl *(Exec. Dir.-Employment)*

Terry McManus *(Exec. Dir.-Acctg. & Controller)*
Donna Franks *(Communications Mgr.)*
Francis J. Kelley *(Profit Sharing Plan Admin.)*
Mark Scheffel *(Dir.-Mngmt. Information Systems)*
Ronald J. Slusher *(Dir.-Facilities)*

Principal(s):
Scott Thompson

No. of U.S. Offices: 40

Computer Systems/Hardware:
Sperry Univac

Outside Service Firm(s):

Arthur Andersen & Co.*(Auditors)*
1666 K Street, N.W.
Washington, DC 20006

Travelers Insurance Co.*(Commercial Insurance Carrier)*
1 Tower Square
Hartford, CT 06183-2492
Tel.: 203-277-4542
Fax: 203-277-5038

Veatch & Cross*(Group Insurer)*
Falls Church, VA

Riggs National Bank of Washington, D.C.*(Investment Banker)*
P.O. Box 96206, 1120 Vermont Ave. N.W.
Washington, DC 20090-6206
Tel.: 202-835-4082

Riggs National Bank of Washington, D.C.*(Major Banking Relationship)*
P.O. Box 96206, 1120 Vermont Ave. N.W.
Washington, DC 20090-6206
Tel.: 202-835-4082

ADVANSTAR COMMUNICATIONS

7500 Old Oak Blvd.
Cleveland, OH 44130
Tel.: 218-723-9200
Fax: 216-891-2791
Year Founded: 1987
Approx.Sls.: $201,563,000
Emp.: 1,500
Fiscal Year-end: 12/31/90
Export
Business Magazine & Trade Journal Publishing; Exposition Production & Management; School Supplies Distribution
S.I.C.: 2721; 7389
Richard B. Swank *(Chm. Bd. & Chief Exec. Officer)*
Richard J. Moeller *(Pres.)*
James A. Adler *(V.P.-Human Resources)*
Arland E. Hirman *(V.P., Sec. & Treas.)*
Dave Mayer *(V.P.-Mfg.)*
Brian Nairm *(V.P.-Mktg.)*
Phillip Stocker *(V.P.-Personnel)*
Mary E. Abood *(Dir.-Pub. Rels.)*
Robert Brown *(Dir.-Mngmt. Information Systems)*

Principal(s):
Richard J. Moeller

No. of U.S. Offices: 12
No. of Foreign Offices: 1

Computer Systems/Hardware:
NCR, Data General

Outside Service Firm(s):

Insurance Service Agency*(Group Insurer)*
Lonsdale Bldg., Suite 400
Duluth, MN 55801-0137
Tel.: 218-722-7753

Kidder, Peabody & Co.*(Investment Banker)*
10 Hanover Square
New York, NY 10005
Tel.: 212-510-3000

Norwest Bank of Minnesota, N.A.*(Major Banking Relationship)*
Duluth, MN

Subsidiaries:

Beckley-Cardy, Inc. **(1)**
Five W. First St.
Duluth, MN 55802
Tel.: 218-725-2200
Tel.: 800-227-1178
Fax: 218-725-2222
Approx.Sls.: $82,000,000
Emp.: 350
Fiscal Year-end: 12/31/91
Export
Computer Systems/Hardware:
NCR 9800
Distr. School Supplies, Blackboards, Bulletin Boards, Erasers, Art Matls., Maps & Globes, Educational Aids, School Furniture & Equip.
S.I.C.: 5021; 5112; 2741; 3952; 3999; 2531
Corporate Giving Program: United Way
Richard B. Swank *(Chm. Bd.)*
O. Lars Fladmark *(Pres.)*
Joe Bilderbach *(V.P.-Opers.)*
Ed Gyenes *(V.P.-Sls. & Mktg.)*
Phil Stocker *(V.P.-Personnel)*
Patrick Flattery *(V.P.-Fin.)*
Paul Estep *(Dir.-Mktg.)*
John Dumais *(Dir.-Pur.)*
Robert Brown *(Mgr.-Data Processing)*

Davidson Printing Company **(1)**
4920 Ramsey St.
Duluth, MN 55807
Tel.: 218-628-1016
Jim Sigfrids *(Chief Oper. Officer)*

ADVENT INTERNATIONAL

101 Federal St.
Boston, MA 02110
Tel.: 617-951-9400
S.I.C.: 6799; 8732; 8741; 2211
Peter A. Brooke *(Chm. Bd & Chief Exec. Officer)*
Thomas R. Armstrong *(Chief Oper. Officer, Exec. V.P.)*

Subsidiary:

Forster Mfg. Co., Inc. **(1)**
Depot St.
Wilton, ME 04294
Tel.: 207-645-2574
Fax: 207-645-2541
Sales Range: $60-79 Million
Emp.: 700
Toothpicks, Clothes Pins, Wooden & Plastic Spoons & Other Wood Products
S.I.C.: 2499; 3089
Philip H. Behr *(Chm. Bd.)*
Richard J. Corbin *(Pres. & Chief Exec. Officer)*
Arthur Goldberg *(Chief Fin. Officer, V.P.-Fin & Treas.)*
Richard S. Campbell *(V.P.-Opers.)*
Bruce Coggeshall *(Sec.)*

ADVENTURE LANDS OF AMERICA, INC.

Interstate 80 & Hwy. 65
Des Moines, IA 50316
Mailing Address:
P.O. Box 3355
Des Moines, IA 50316
Tel.: 515-266-2121 **IA**
Fax: 515-266-9831
Year Founded: 1972
Approx.Sls.: $18,000,000
Emp.: 500
Fiscal Year-end: 12/31/91
Amusement Park
S.I.C.: 7996; 7033; 7011
John F. Krantz *(Chief Exec. Officer & Treas.)*
John M. Krantz *(Pres.)*
Mary Jan Krantz *(V.P. & Sec.)*
Dan A. Bohner *(Controller)*
Steve Anderson *(Dir.-Personnel)*
Courtenay Wolf *(Dir.-Adv.)*
Bill Fisher *(Dir.-Mktg.)*

Outside Service Firm(s):

KPMG Peat Marwick*(Auditors)*
2500 Ruan Center
Des Moines, IA 50309
Tel.: 515-288-7465

S. David Peshkin*(Legal Firm)*
Des Moines, IA

Benton National Bank*(Major Banking Relationship)*
Des Moines, IA

ADVENTURE TOURS USA, INC.

5459 Sherry Lane, Ste. 1900
Dallas, TX 75225
Tel.: 214-360-5050
Fax: 214-373-9108
Year Founded: 1975
Approx.Sls.: $39,000,000
Emp.: 130
Arrangement of Travel Tour Packages-Wholesale
S.I.C.: 4724
Charles Kairella *(Pres.)*
Calvin Ridgeway *(V.P.-Opers.)*
Jeff Gorman *(V.P. & Gen. Counsel)*
Dan Daniel *(V.P.)*
Les Deslauriers *(V.P.)*
George R. Ludwig *(V.P.)*
Robert Korba *(Sec.)*

ADVERTISING, BOELTER & LINCOLN

123 E. Doty St.
Madison, WI 53703
Tel.: 608-251-3381
Year Founded: 1974
Approx.Billings: $15,000,000
Emp.: 16
Consumer, Business Services & Products
Corporate Giving Program: Pro Bono Work for Selected Charitable Organizations & Contribute to Foundations of Agency's Non-Profit Clients
Robert Boelter *(Pres.)*
Terrie Treland *(V.P., Bus. Mgr.)*
Al Zins *(Pub. Rels.)*

Computer Systems/Hardware:
ADMAN, Word Perfect, Lotus 1-2-3, IBM, Novell Network, MacIntosh

ADVERTISING CHECKING BUREAU INCORPORATED

500 Fifth Avenue
New York, NY 10110
Tel.: 212-921-0080
Fax: 212-840-7638
Year Founded: 1917
Emp.: 1,200
Bus. Information & Fin. Services; Mktg. Decision Support Systems
S.I.C.: 7319; 7383; 8742
Warren Grieb *(Chm. & Chief Exec. Officer)*
Edward Davis *(Pres. & Chief Oper. Officer)*
Brian McShane *(Exec. V.P. & Dir.-Mktg.)*
William Panczak *(Sr. V.P.-Customer & Trade Rels.)*
Mike Bookman *(V.P.)*
Arthur R. Fiordaliso *(V.P.-Sls.)*
William Kowalsky *(V.P.-Fin. & Plng. & Chief Fin. Officer)*
Frank Payton *(V.P. & Dir.-Human Resources)*

No. of U.S. Offices: 7

Computer Systems/Hardware:
IBM 4381

Outside Service Firm(s):

Chemical Banking Corp.*(Major Banking Relationship)*
277 Park Ave.
New York, NY 10041
Tel.: 212-310-6407
Fax: 212-310-4526

Chemical Banking Corp.*(Pension Manager)*
277 Park Ave.
New York, NY 10041
Tel.: 212-310-6407
Fax: 212-310-4526

Advertising to Women, Inc.

ADVERTISING TO WOMEN, INC.

226 E. 54th St., Ste. 501
New York, NY 10022
Tel.: 212-750-4500
Fax: 212-750-6464
Year Founded: 1975
Approx.Billings: $32,000,000
Emp.: 28
Women's Market
Lois Geraci Ernst *(Chm. & Chief Exec. Officer)*
F. Phillip Geraci *(Pres.)*
David de Bello *(Chief Fin. Officer & Comptroller)*
Carl Maier *(Sr. V.P.)*
Joseph Sweeney *(Sr. V.P.)*
Adele Juressen *(Creative Services, Admin.)*
Angele Davis *(Admin. Asst.)*

ADVISERS CAPITAL MANAGEMENT INC.

58 Pine St.
New York, NY 10005
Tel.: 212-248-8989 **DE**
Fax: 212-248-8109
Year Founded: 1978
Emp.: 18
Minority Owned Independent Adviser Providing Portfolio Management Services to Domestic & Global Institutional Investors in Fixed Income Securities
S.I.C.: 6799
Patricia W. DeBlank Klink *(Pres. & Chief Exec. Officer)*

Outside Service Firm(s):

Debevoise & Plimpton*(Legal Firm)*
875 Third Ave.
New York, NY 10022
Tel.: 212-909-6000

ADVISORS ADVERTISING

8200 W. Sunrise Blvd., Ste. D-2
Fort Lauderdale, FL 33322
Tel.: 305-474-7800
Fax: 305-474-7808
Year Founded: 1981
Approx.Billings: $20,000,000
Emp.: 14
Bernard Weisblum *(Pres.)*
J. Paul Davis *(V.P.)*

ADWORKS, INC.

1025 Thomas Jefferson St., NW
Washington, DC 20007
Tel.: 202-342-5585
Year Founded: 1979
Approx.Billings: $30,125,000
Emp.: 32
Consumer & Business-to-Business Adv.
Richard J. Hindin *(Pres.)*
Bruce Levin *(Chief Fin. Officer & Controller)*
Dan Johnson *(MIS Dir.)*
Laurie Conley *(Illustrator)*

AERCO INTERNATIONAL INC.
159 Paris Ave.
Northvale, NJ 07647
Tel.: 201-768-2400 **NJ**
Fax: 201-768-7789
Year Founded: 1949
Approx.Sls.: $12,000,000
Emp.: 78
Manufacture Heat Exchangers, Control Valves, Hot Water Heaters, Steam Generators, Heat Recovery Systems and Gas-Fired Water Heaters & Boilers
S.I.C.: 3433; 3443; 3494; 3822; 3639
Tim Buhl *(Pres. & Chief Exec. Officer)*
Basem L. Hishmeh *(Chm. Bd. & Treas.)*
Kurt Syvertsen *(Pur. Dir.)*

Outside Service Firm(s):

Weber, Lipshie & Co.*(Auditors)*
1430 Broadway
New York, NY 10018
Tel.: 212-382-3400

Stern, Steiger, Croland, Tanenbaum & Schielke*(Legal Firm)*
One Mack Center Dr.
Paramus, NJ 07652
Tel.: 201-262-9400

AERO DATA METAL CRAFTERS
220 Knickerbocker Ave.
Bohemia, NY 11716
Tel.: 516-567-9600
Fax: 516-563-3345
Year Founded: 1978
Emp.: 45
Fiscal Year-end: 3/31/91
Precision Sheet Metal Parts
S.I.C.: 3444
Robert DeLuca *(Chm. Bd., Pres. & Chief Exec. Officer)*
Susan DeLuca *(Exec. V.P., Controller & Chief Fin. Officer)*
William Mabanta *(Corp. Sec.)*

Computer Systems/Hardware:
IBM

Outside Service Firm(s):

Colonial Life Insurance Co. of America*(Group Insurer)*
Parsippany, NJ

HIP Insurance Company*(Group Insurer)*
New York, NY

AERO PERU CORPORATION
8181 N.W. 36th St., Ste. 5
Miami, FL 33166
Mailing Address:
P.O. Box 523952,
Miami, FL 33152
Tel.: 305-591-9240
Tel.: 800-777-7717
Fax: 305-477-4226
Approx.Sls.: $22,000,000
Emp.: 200
Commercial Air Line
S.I.C.: 4512
Dante Matellini *(Chm. Bd. & Pres.)*
Manuel de la Pena *(Vice Chm.)*
Jean Marie Sertillange *(Chief Exec. Officer)*
Isabel de la Cruz *(Chief Fin. Officer)*
Victor Valenzuela *(Treasurer)*
Alfonso Kau *(Controller)*
Luis Cabrera *(Dir.-Telecommunications)*
Oscar Benavides *(Dir.-Plng. & Devel)*
Manuel Garcia *(Dir.-Admin./Opers.)*
Carlos Lopez *(Dir.-Mktg.)*
Marie A. Algre *(Gen. Mgr.-North America)*
Alicia Delgado *(Mgr.-Pub. Rels.)*
Rodolfo Perez *(Mgr.-Personnel)*

Division:

Aeroperu **(1)**
530 W. 6th St., Ste. 1200
Los Angeles, CA 90014
Tel.: 213-488-0515
Fax: 213-488-9895
S.I.C.: 4512
Johnnie Paxton *(District Sls. Mgr.-West Coast)*

AEROGLIDE CORPORATION
100 Aeroglide Dr.
Cary, NC 27511
Mailing Address:
P.O. Box 29505
Raleigh, NC 27626-0505
Tel.: 919-851-2000 **NC**
Telex: 579421
Fax: 919-851-6029
Year Founded: 1940
Approx.Sls.: $13,000,000
Emp.: 150
Fiscal Year-end: 12/31/90
Export
Mfr. Grain Driers, Process Driers/ Coolers, Dehydrators, Charcoal Briquet Machinery & Materials Handling Equip.
S.I.C.: 3556; 3559
J. Fredrick Kelly, Jr. *(Pres. & Chief Exec. Officer)*
Michael Williams *(V.P.-Fin.)*
Mike Williams *(Chief Fin. Officer)*
Russ Reed *(Dir.-Sls. & Mktg.)*
John M. Richardson *(Mgr.-Reg. Sls.)*

Computer Systems/Hardware:
IBM PC-AT

Outside Service Firm(s):

Arthur Andersen & Co.*(Auditors)*
Raleigh, NC

BB&T Bank*(Major Banking Relationship)*
Cary, NC

Hutchinson & Associates*(Pension Manager)*
Raleigh, NC

Division:

C.G. Sargents Sons **(1)**
100 Aeroglide Dr.
Cary, NC 27511
Tel.: 919-851-2000
Export
Mfg. of Conveyor Driers, Extrusion Equipment & Feeders
S.I.C.: 3523; 3542
Bill Moore *(Prod. Mgr.)*

Subsidiaries:

Aeroglide Americas International, Inc. **(1)**
P.O. Box 29505
Raleigh, NC 27626
Tel.: 919-851-2000 (100%)
Telex: 579421
Fax: 919-851-6029
Foreign Sales
S.I.C.: 5044; 5084
J. Fredrick Kelly, Jr. *(Pres. & Chief Exec. Officer)*
Emil Popa *(Mgr.-Sls.)*

American Machinery Corp. **(1)**
2730 Eunice Ave.
Orlando, FL 32808
Tel.: 407-295-2581
Fax: 407-290-5203
Approx.Sls.: $5,000,000
Emp.: 40
Fiscal Year-end: 12/31/90
Import Export
Pac Rite Fruit & Vegetable Packing, Canning Equipment & Industrial Fabrication
S.I.C.: 3556; 3565
J. Fredrick Kelly, Jr. *(Pres.)*
Thomas A. Gnesda *(Exec. V.P.)*
Dirk Story *(Controller)*

THE AEROSPACE CORPORATION
2350 E. El Segundo Blvd.
El Segundo, CA 90245-4691
Mailing Address:
P.O. Box 92957-MS: MI/448
Los Angeles, CA 90009
Tel.: 310-336-5000 **CA**
Fax: 310-336-7055
Year Founded: 1960
Assets: $147,000,000
Earnings: $8,700,000
Liabilities: $43,000,000
Net Worth: $104,000,000
Approx.Sls.: $390,000,000
Emp.: 3,800
Fiscal Year-end: 9/30/92
Engrng. & Scientific Services for U.S. Govt.
S.I.C.: 3761; 3764; 3769; 8711
James W. Plummer *(Chm. Bd.)*
Edward C. Aldridge, Jr. *(Pres. & Chief Exec. Officer)*
Marge Anderson *(Chief Fin. Officer & V.P.)*
Allan J. Boardman *(Grp. V.P.-Admin. & Treas.)*
Edward M. Lassiter *(Grp. V.P.-Devel.)*
Dr. George A. Paulikas *(Grp. V.P.-Programs)*
Dr. Arthur J. Schiewe *(Grp. V.P.-Engrng. & Tech.)*
Richard M. Allman *(V.P.-Space Program Opers.)*
Susan G. Lowenstam *(V.P., Gen. Counsel & Sec.)*
Wesley M. Mann, Jr. *(V.P.-Strategic Defense Opers.)*
William J. Aston *(Gen. Mgr.-Admin. Opers. Div.)*
Shirley McCarty *(Gen. Mgr.-Human Resources Div.)*
Thomas O'Connor *(Dir.-Pension Admin.)*
Patricia A. Downing *(Head-Gen. Services)*
Earl D. Flick *(Head-Office Pub. Affairs)*
Jack Pappa *(Head-Matl. Dept.)*
Richard Rodriguez *(Head-Acctg.)*

No. of U.S. Offices: 8

Computer Systems/Hardware:
Cray X-MP/18, IBM 3090-200, IBM 4381

Outside Service Firm(s):

KPMG Peat Marwick*(Auditors)*
725 S. Figueroa St.
Los Angeles, CA 90017
Tel.: 213-972-4000

William M. Mercer Incorporated*(Auditors)*
3303 Wilshire Blvd.
Los Angeles, CA 90076
Tel.: 213-480-6400

Bank of America*(Major Banking Relationship)*
701 S. Western Ave.
Los Angeles, CA 91201

Bank of America NT&SA*(Major Banking Relationship)*
555 So. Flower St., 5th Fl.
Los Angeles, CA 90071
Tel.: 213-228-3526
Fax: 213-228-4062

Union Bank*(Major Banking Relationship)*
445 S. Figueroa St.
Los Angeles, CA 90071
Tel.: 213-236-5076

BEA Associates, Inc.*(Pension Manager)*
One Citicorp Center, 153 East 53rd St.
New York, NY 10022
Tel.: 212-832-2626
Fax: 212-751-2470

Breau Capital*(Pension Manager)*
Waltham, MA

Equitable Real Estate Investment Managment Inc.*(Pension Manager)*
3414 Peachtree Rd. N.E.
Atlanta, GA 30326-1162

Grantham, Mayo, Van Otterloo*(Pension Manager)*
Boston, MA

Merganser Capital Management*(Pension Manager)*
One Cambridge Center,
Cambridge, MA 02142
Tel.: 617-494-1000

Neuberger & Berman Pension Management, Inc.*(Pension Manager)*
605 Third Ave.
New York, NY 10158-3698
Tel.: 212-476-9000
Fax: 212-476-5610

Quest Advisory Corp.*(Pension Manager)*
1414 Ave. of the Americas
New York, NY 10019
Tel.: 800-348-1414
Fax: 212-752-8875

RCM Capital Management*(Pension Manager)*
4 Embarcadero Center, Ste. 2900
San Francisco, CA 94111

W. H. Reaves & Co., Inc.*(Pension Manager)*
30 Montgomery St.
Jersey City, NJ 07302
Tel.: 201-332-4596
Fax: 201-332-8593

Trust Company of the West*(Pension Manager)*
400 S. Hope St.
Los Angeles, CA 90071
Tel.: 213-683-4000
Fax: 213-683-4142

Wells Fargo Nikko Investment Advisors*(Pension Manager)*
45 Fremont St., 16th Fl.
San Francisco, CA 94105
Tel.: 415-597-2000
Fax: 415-597-2199

AEROTRON, INC.
4901 Capital Blvd.
Raleigh, NC 27611
Mailing Address:
P.O. Box 27500
Raleigh, NC 27611
Tel.: 919-872-4400
Fax: 919-872-8751
Approx.Sls.: $18,000,000
Emp.: 138
Fiscal Year-end: 12/31/90
Mfr. of Two-Way Radios
S.I.C.: 3651
Ernest Schwabe *(Pres.)*
Bill Parr *(Sls. Mgr.)*

AEROVIRONMENT, INC.
222 E. Huntington Dr., Ste.200
Monrovia, CA 91016
Mailing Address:
P.O. Box 5031
Monrovia, CA 91017
Tel.: 818-357-9983 **CA**
Fax: 818-359-9628
Year Founded: 1971
Approx.Sls.: $18,000,000
Emp.: 230
Fiscal Year-end: 4/30/90
Export
Air Pollution & Energy Research
S.I.C.: 8731
Dr. Paul MacCready *(Chm. Bd. & Chief Exec. Officer)*
Tim Conver *(Pres.)*
Michael D. Wynn *(V.P.-Fin.)*
Cathy Cline *(Dir.-Human Resources)*
Don Gonzales *(Dir.-Data Processing)*
Principal(s):
Dr. Paul MacCready
General Motors

No. of Mfg. Plants/Facilities: 2

No. of U.S. Offices: 4

Computer Systems/Hardware:
VAX

Outside Service Firm(s):

Deloitte & Touche*(Auditors)*
21550 Oxnard St., Ste. 800
Woodland Hills, CA 91367-7100
Tel.: 818-593-4800
Fax: 818-347-4278

Alta Administrators*(Group Insurer)*
P.O. Box 160
Tustin, CA

Paul, Hastings, Janofsky & Walker*(Legal Firm)*
555 S. Flower, 22nd Fl.
Los Angeles, CA 90072
Tel.: 213-683-6299

Wells Fargo Bank*(Major Banking Relationship)*
Ontario, CA

AETNA BEARING COMPANY
4600 W. Schubert
Chicago, IL 60639
Tel.: 312-227-2410
Fax: 312-227-2640
Year Founded: 1916
Approx.Sls.: $12,000,000
Emp.: 150
Export
Mfr. Bearings & Related Products
S.I.C.: 3562
G.S.B. Gilbert *(Chm. Bd.)*
Patrick Balson *(Pres.)*
Richard N. Jenkins *(Dir.-Fin. & Plng.)*
Steve C. Shepherd *(Dir-Mfg.)*
Carson Eddy *(Dir.-Engrng.)*
Robert Milkie *(Dir.-Pur.)*
David Crook *(Mgr.-Mktg.)*
Principal(s):
Patrick Balson

No. of Mfg. Plants/Facilities: 1

Computer Systems/Hardware:
Micro Data Sequel

Outside Service Firm(s):

Ernst & Young*(Auditors)*
233 S. Wacker Dr.
Chicago, IL 60606
Tel.: 312-368-1800
Fax: 312-645-3095

Thomas H. Thorelli*(Legal Firm)*
Chicago, IL

American National Bank*(Major Banking Relationship)*
33 North LaSalle St.
Chicago, IL 60690
Tel.: 312-661-6967

AETNA HEALTH PLANS
(Formerly Bay Pacific Health Corporation)
1111 Bayhill Dr., Ste. 300
San Bruno, CA 94066
Tel.: 415-952-5000
Fax: 415-871-9144
Year Founded: 1978
Assets: $33,375,000
Earnings: $196,000
Liabilities: $23,533,000
Net Worth: $9,842,000
Approx.Sls.: $152,900,000
Emp.: 270
Fiscal Year-end: 12/31/89
Health Care Mngmt.
S.I.C.: 8099
Corporate Giving Program:
Healthcare in the Bay Area
James Howell *(Chm. Bd. & Dir.)*
Jay Gellert *(Pres., Chief Exec. Officer & Dir.)*
Paul Swenson *(Exec.V.P. & Chief Oper. Officer)*
Jay Harris *(Chief Fin. Officer & Treas.)*
Sam Leader *(V.P.-Mgmt. Info. Systems)*
Sue Myrick *(Controller)*
Hamilton Chaffee *(V.P.-Opers.)*
Denise Hanson *(V.P.-Admin. & Sec.)*
Pam Bouey *(Legal Counsel)*
Janice Wilborn *(Human Resources Mgr.)*

Computer Systems/Hardware:
Hewlett Packard

AETNA INDUSTRIES, INC.
24331 Sherwood
Center Line, MI 48015
Mailing Address:
P.O. Box 3067,
Center Line, MI 48015-0067
Tel.: 313-759-2200
Fax: 313-759-2209
Year Founded: 1940
Sales Range: $100-499 Million
Emp.: 1,000
Export
Manufacture & Assemble Automotive Stampings, Special Dies & Tools
S.I.C.: 3465; 3544
Jerome Singer *(Pres.)*
Tom Sweeney *(Treas. & Controller)*
Daniel Pierce *(Dir.-Personnel)*

Outside Service Firm(s):

Price Waterhouse*(Auditors)*
200 Renaissance Center, Ste. 3900
Detroit, MI 48243

Hale and Dorr*(Legal Firm)*
60 State St.
Boston, MA 02109-6098
Tel.: 617-526-6000

National Westminster Bank plc*(Major Banking Relationship)*
Astor Plaza, 1515 Broadway
New York, NY 10036

AETNA PLYWOOD, INC.
3233 N. Arlington Heights
Arlington Heights, IL 60004
Tel.: 708-577-8500 **DE**
Fax: 708-577-1793
Approx.Sls.: $55,000,000
Emp.: 95
Wholesale Distributor Of Interior & Exterior Building Materials; Rough, Dressed & Finished Plywood
S.I.C.: 5031
Jeffrey G. Davis *(Chm., Pres. & Chief Exec. Officer)*
John Francione *(V.P., Sec. & Treas.)*

Outside Service Firm(s):

Lake Shore National Bank*(Major Banking Relationship)*
605 N. Michigan Ave.
Chicago, IL 60611
Tel.: 312-787-1900

AFFILIATED COMPUTER SERVICES, INC.
(Formerly Affiliated Computer Systems)
2828 N. Haskell
Dallas, TX 75204
Tel.: 214-841-6111 **DE**
Fax: 214-823-1155
Year Founded: 1988
Approx.Sls.: $177,000,000
Emp.: 1,400
Fiscal Year-end: 6/30/92
Data Processing Service
S.I.C.: 7374
Darwin Deason *(Chm. Bd. & Chief Exec. Officer)*
Charles Young *(Pres. & Chief Oper. Officer)*
Jeff Rich *(Chief Fin. Officer & V.P.)*
Bill Deckelman *(Sec.)*
Christopher Jaeb *(Dir.-Communications)*

Computer Systems/Hardware:
IBM, Tandem, Amdane, DEC

Outside Service Firm(s):

NationsBank Texas*(Major Banking Relationship)*
One Dallas Center, 350 St. Paul St.
Dallas, TX 75201
Tel.: 808-836-0136

AFFILIATED OF FLORIDA INC.
1102 N. 28th St.
Tampa, FL 33605
Mailing Address:
P.O. Box 31667
Tampa, FL 33631-3667
Tel.: 813-248-5781
Fax: 813-248-5531
Year Founded: 1937
Approx.Sls.: $181,106,209
Emp.: 221
Fiscal Year-end: 4/25/92
Export
Wholesale Grocery Cooperative
S.I.C.: 5141
Robert Hitchcock *(Chm. Bd.)*
Arnold Stanaland *(Vice Chm.)*
Donald M. Kolvenbach *(Pres., Chief Exec. Officer & Chief Oper. Officer)*
Peter McGregor *(Chief Fin. Officer)*
Jerry Schuldt *(Sr. V.P.)*
John Trivento *(Exec. V.P.)*
Gary Rinehart *(V.P.-Retail Opers.)*
James Sapp *(Treas.)*
Jack Alge *(Sec.)*
Harry Britton *(Dir.-Personnel)*
Roger Cripe *(Dir.-Mngmt. Information Systems)*
John Stark *(Dir.-Pur. & Mdsg.)*
Don Brauneker *(Mgr.-Pension Admin.)*
Judy Korosck *(Mgr.-Adv.)*
Debbie Covington *(Admin. Asst.)*

No. of Mfg. Plants/Facilities: 1
No. of U.S. Offices: 1

Computer Systems/Hardware:
IBM

Outside Service Firm(s):

Daniel J. Bartz*(Auditors)*
Milwaukee, WI

Langford, Mooney & McDuffee, P.A.*(Legal Firm)*
Tampa, FL

First Florida Bank*(Major Banking Relationship)*
P.O. Box 31265,
Tampa, FL 33631-3265
Tel.: 813-224-1475

National Cooperative Bank*(Major Banking Relationship)*
Washington, DC

Subsidiary:

Store Development, Inc. **(1)**
1102 N. 28th St.
Tampa, FL 33605
Tel.: 813-248-5781
Emp.: 75
Warehousing
S.I.C.: 4225
Donald M. Kolvenbach *(Pres.)*
Gary Rinehart *(V.P.)*

AFFILIATED FOOD DISTRIBUTORS
1000 N. South Rd.
Scranton, PA 18508
Mailing Address:
P.O. Box 31
Scranton, PA 18501
Tel.: 717-343-4731 **PA**
Fax: 717-341-0232(Buying Dept)
Fax: 717-341-0230(Main Office)
Year Founded: 1951
Approx.Sls.: $169,000,000
Emp.: 330
Fiscal Year-end: 1/30/90
Co-op Agency; Wholesale Groceries, Meat & Produce
S.I.C.: 5141; 5147; 5148
William Bracey *(Chm. Bd.)*
Raymond Alunni *(Vice Chm.)*
Robert Schofield *(Pres. & Chief Exec. Officer)*
Joseph Kutsop *(Treas.)*
Elmer A. Thomas *(Comptroller)*
William Nish *(Dir.-Personnel)*

Computer Systems/Hardware:
IBM System 4361

Outside Service Firm(s):

Joseph H. Williams Co.*(Auditors)*
Wilkes-Barre, PA

Bialkowski & Savitsky*(Legal Firm)*
Scranton, PA

Northeastern Bank of Pennsylvania*(Major Banking Relationship)*
Scranton, PA

AFFILIATED FOOD STORES
100 Affiliated Drive
Keller, TX 76244
Mailing Address:
P.O. Box 1000
Keller, TX 76244
Tel.: 817-431-4417
Tel.: 800-388-0610
Fax: 817-431-6409
Year Founded: 1946
Assets: $85,411,000
Liabilities: $24,058,000
Net Worth: $61,353,000
Approx.Sls.: $346,085,000
Emp.: 495
Fiscal Year-end: 12/31/91
Grocery Distribution
S.I.C.: 5141
Richard Bransom *(Chm. Bd.)*
Gene Sharp *(Pres. & Chief Exec. Officer)*
Jackie W. Brewer *(V.P.-Fin. & Chief Fin. Officer)*
Rick Ruth *(V.P.-Opers.)*
Terry Skodack *(V.P-MIS)*
Don Smith *(V.P.-Mktg.)*
John Zachary *(V.P.-Sls. & Retail Opers.)*
Jim Zimcosky *(V.P.-Human Resources)*
Josephine Benedetto *(Sec.)*
Willis Reese *(Treas.)*
Ken Schilling *(Controller)*
David Boatwright *(Dir.-Adv.)*

No. of Mfg. Plants/Facilities: 1
No. of U.S. Offices: 1

Computer Systems/Hardware:
IBM 4300

Outside Service Firm(s):

Nelson & Nelson*(Auditors)*
Dallas, TX

Haynes & Boone*(Legal Firm)*
3100 Interfirst Plaza, 901 Main St.
Dallas, TX 75202
Tel.: 214-670-0550

First City National Bank*(Major Banking Relationship)*
Dallas, TX

Pension Administrators*(Pension Manager)*
Dallas, TX

Subsidiary:

Affiliated General Agency, Inc. **(1)**
100 Nat Gibbs Dr.
Keller, TX 76248
Tel.: 817-281-4417
S.I.C.: 5141

AFFILIATED FOODS COOPERATIVE INC.
13th St. & Omaha Ave.
Norfolk, NE 68701
Mailing Address:
P.O. Box 1067, Johnny Carson Blvd.
Norfolk, NE 68701
Tel.: 402-371-0555 **NE**
Fax: 402-371-1884
Year Founded: 1931
Approx.Sls.: $465,000,000
Emp.: 450
Fiscal Year-end: 6/29/92
Import
Distr. Center for Member-Owned Cooperative
S.I.C.: 5141; 5148; 5142; 5143; 5144; 5147
Harold Bates *(Chm. Bd.)*
Donrel Herbolsheimier *(Vice Chm.)*
Virgil Froehlich *(Pres. & Gen. Mgr.)*
Robert Crain *(V.P.-Special Projects)*
Martin T. Simon *(V.P.- Treas. & Asst. Gen. Mgr.)*
Tim Goetsch *(V.P.-Wholesale Opers.)*
Dave Engelhaupt *(V.P.-Data Processing)*
Charles W. Svoboda *(V.P.-Opers.)*
Jeannie Wesemann *(Sec.)*

Computer Systems/Hardware:
IBM 400 Series

Outside Service Firm(s):

Gerald L. Sobotka*(Auditors)*
Norfolk, NE
Tel.: 402-371-1410

Protection Mutual*(Commercial Insurance Carrier)*
Norfolk, NE

Affiliated Insurance Services, Inc.*(Group Insurance Broker/Consult)*
Norfolk, NE
Tel.: 402-371-0555

Domina Copple*(Legal Firm)*
P.O. Box 78
Norfolk, NE
Tel.: 402-371-4300

Norwest Bank Minnesota, N.A.*(Major Banking Relationship)*
Norfolk, NE

AFFILIATED FOODS, INC.
1401 W. Farmer's Ave.
Amarillo, TX 79118
Mailing Address:
P.O. Box 30300
Amarillo, TX 79120
Tel.: 806-372-3851 **TX**
Fax: 806-374-2655
Year Founded: 1946
Assets: $53,281,000
Liabilities: $33,760,000
Net Worth: $19,521,000
Approx.Sls.: $500,000,000
Emp.: 800
Fiscal Year-end: 9/30/91
Import Export
Wholesale Food Cooperative
S.I.C.: 5141; 5122; 5148; 5147; 5149
Roger Lowe *(Chm. Bd.)*
Benny Cooper *(Pres.)*
C.W. Millikin *(Chief Fin. Officer)*
George Lankford *(Exec. V.P.)*
Jess Claiborne *(Sec.)*
Don Barclay *(Dir.-Human Resources)*
Curtis Baty *(Dir.-Mktg.)*
James Hilliard *(Dir.-Warehouse)*
James Jolly *(Dir.-Trans.)*
Bob Mitchusson *(Dir.-Adv.)*
Charles Sanyour *(Dir.-Mngmt. Information Systems & Data Processing)*
Joe Self *(Dir.-Pur.)*
Carroll Wofford *(Dir.-HBC/Gen. Mgr.)*

Computer Systems/Hardware:
IBM

Outside Service Firm(s):

Ault & Associates*(Auditors)*
P.O. Box 9294,
Amarillo, TX 79105-9294
Tel.: 806-376-1555
Fax: 806-376-1554

Amarillo National Bank*(Major Banking Relationship)*
Amarillo, TX
Tel.: 806-378-8000

AFFILIATED FOODS SOUTHWEST
(Formerly Affiliated Food Stores, Inc.)
12103 Interstate 30
Little Rock, AR 72209
Mailing Address:
P.O. Box 3627
Little Rock, AR 72203
Tel.: 501-455-3590
Fax: 501-455-6556
Year Founded: 1952
Approx.Sls.: $425,000,000
Emp.: 785
Fiscal Year-end: 6/30/91
Wholesale Groceries, Food Distributor & Related Services
S.I.C.: 5141
C. E. Toland *(Chm. Bd. & Chief Exec. Officer)*
Jerry Davis *(Pres. & Chief Oper. Officer)*
Hubert D. Fugett *(Chief Fin. Officer)*
John Mills *(Controller)*
Charles Moore *(Corp. Sec.)*
Herston Ingle *(Dir.-Pur.)*
Alton Wayne Miller *(Dir.-Sls. & Mktg.)*
Ronald W. Rivers *(Dir.-Store Systems)*
Jimmy Simmon *(Dir.-Store Devel.)*
Robert E. Southern *(Dir.-Personnel)*
William Lind *(Mgr.-Produce)*
Lewis Sewell *(Mgr.-Meats)*
Wayne Loftin *(Chief Engineer)*

Outside Service Firm(s):

Deloitte & Touche*(Auditors)*
411 Hackensack Ave.
Hackensack, NJ 07601-6367
Tel.: 201-646-7700

Morgan, Keegan, Black, Latimore, Cain*(Investment Banker)*
Nashville, TN

House Wallace & Jewell*(Legal Firm)*
Little Rock, AR

First Commercial Bank*(Major Banking Relationship)*
P.O. Box 1331,
Little Rock, AR 72201

AFFILIATES GROUP INC.
4219 Hillsboro Rd., Ste. 306
Nashville, TN 37215
Tel.: 615-383-1211 **DE**
Fax: 615-292-6732
Year Founded: 1981
Assets: $33,000,000
Liabilities: $19,000,000
Net Worth: $14,000,000
Approx.Sls.: $45,000,000
Emp.: 1,225
Fiscal Year-end: 12/31/88
Construction & Operation of Retirement Centers
S.I.C.: 1522; 6513
Mark Burress *(Chm. Bd. & Pres.)*

Outside Service Firm(s):

KPMG Peat Marwick*(Auditors)*
1900 Nashville Center, 511 Union St.
Nashville, TN 37219

Subsidiaries:

Hospital Affiliates Development Corporation **(1)**
3401 W. End Ave.
Nashville, TN 37203
Tel.: 615-383-1211

Professional Community Management, Inc. **(1)**
23726 Birtcher Drive
El Toro, CA 92630
Tel.: 714-768-7261

Retirement Living Affiliates, Inc. **(1)**
6991 E. Camelback
Scottsdale, AZ 85251
Tel.: 602-947-8600

AFTER SIX, INCORPORATED
G. St. & Hunting Pk. Ave.
Philadelphia, PA 19124
Tel.: 215-289-6666
Tel.: 800-4 AFTER 6 **PA**
Fax: 215-289-7600
Year Founded: 1903
Approx.Sls.: $65,000,000
Emp.: 1,050
Manufacturer of Men's Formal Wear & Accessories
S.I.C.: 2311
Victor Ameye *(Chief Exec. Officer)*
Michael Mizenko *(Chief Fin. Officer)*
Jeff De Luca *(V.P. & Controller)*
Marilyn Spiegel *(V.P. & Dir.-Communications)*
Robert Maggetti *(V.P.-Sls.)*
Paul Tresca *(Dir.-Personnel)*

Computer Systems/Hardware:
IBM 4361

Outside Service Firm(s):

Ernst & Young*(Auditors)*
1300 Huntington Bldg.
Cleveland, OH 44115
Tel.: 216-861-5000
Fax: 303-291-6234

Dilworth, Paxson, Kalish & Kauffman*(Legal Firm)*
2600 Fidelity Bldg., 123 S. Broad St.
Philadelphia, PA 19109
Tel.: 215-875-7000

Philadelphia National Bank*(Major Banking Relationship)*
P.O. Box 13834, Broad & Chestnut Streets
Philadelphia, PA 19101-7618
Tel.: 215-973-8327

Division:

After Six Access **(1)**
22nd & Market Sts.
Philadelphia, PA 19103
Tel.: 215-561-6666 (100%)
Emp.: 100
Mfr. of Formal Wear Accessories
S.I.C.: 2311

AG PROCESSING INC A COOPERATIVE
P.O. Box 2047,
Omaha, NE 68103-2047
Tel.: 402-496-7809 **IA**
Telex: 438-074
Year Founded: 1943
Assets: $258,493,000
Earnings: $41,243,000
Liabilities: $85,042,000
Net Worth: $173,451,000
Approx.Sls.: $864,675,000
Emp.: 744
Fiscal Year-end: 8/31/91
Export
Soybean Processing; Refining of Vegetable Oil & Soy Flour; Grain Mdsg.; Truck Transportation Services
S.I.C.: 2075; 2048
Urban Knobbe *(Chm. Bd. & Pres.)*
James W. Lindsay *(Chief Exec. Officer)*
Gordon Dorff *(V.P.-Human Resources)*
Kenneth S. Grubbe *(V.P.-Fin.)*
William C. Lester *(V.P.-Member, Pub. Rels. & Security)*
Kenneth J. McQueen *(V.P.-Admin. & Asst. Sec.)*
Joseph Meyer *(V.P.-Vegetable Oil & Export Soybean Meal)*
James Yeates *(V.P.-Opers.)*
Lowell Wilson *(Treas. & Sec.)*
Tim Witty *(Controller)*
Gary Chestnut *(Mgr.-Pur.)*
Mike Reed *(Mgr.-Data Processing)*
J. Keith Spackler *(Mgr.-Bus. Analysis)*
Principal(s):
James W. Lindsay
Joseph Meyer

No. of Mfg. Plants/Facilities: 8
No. of U.S. Offices: 1

Computer Systems/Hardware:
NCR 9400

Outside Service Firm(s):

Deloitte & Touche*(Auditors)*
2000 First National Center
Omaha, NE 68102
Tel.: 402-346-7788

Arkwright Mutual Insurance*(Commercial Insurance Carrier)*
Kansas City, MO

Cigna*(Commercial Insurance Carrier)*
525 W. Monroe St., Ste. 1900
Chicago, IL 60606
Tel.: 312-648-3742

Nationwide Insurance*(Commercial Insurance Carrier)*
One Nationwide Plaza
Columbus, OH 43216
Tel.: 614-249-6488

Sedgwick James*(Commercial Insurance Carrier)*
Omaha, NE

Principal Mutual Life Insurance Co.*(Group Insurer)*
711 High St.
Des Moines, IA 50309

Omaha Bank for Co-ops*(Investment Banker)*
Omaha, NE

Davis, Hockenberg, Wine, Brown, Koehn & Shors*(Legal Firm)*
Des Moines, IA

FirsTier Bank*(Major Banking Relationship)*
Omaha, NE

Omaha Bank for Co-ops*(Major Banking Relationship)*
Omaha, NE

Omaha National Bank*(Major Banking Relationship)*
Omaha, NE

ABC Health Benefit Trust*(Pension Manager)*
Houston, TX

AGEMA INFRARED SYSTEMS, INC.
(Affil. of Pharos AB, Stockholm, Sweden)
550 County Ave.
Secaucus, NJ 07094
Tel.: 201-867-5390
Fax: 201-867-2191
Approx.Sls.: $12,000,000
Emp.: 25
Fiscal Year-end: 12/31/91
Import & Sell Thermovision Infrared Imaging Systems
S.I.C.: 3812
Philip Smith *(Pres.)*
P. Smith *(Chief Information Officer)*
M. Neilsen *(Chief Fin. Officer)*
Mark Nielsen *(V.P.-Fin.)*
Maria Capela *(Admin. Mgr.)*
Jay Levy *(Communications Mgr.)*

AGENCIAS USA
980 N. Michigan Ave.
Chicago, IL 60611
Tel.: 312-988-9490
Fax: 312-988-9854
Approx.Billings: $14,000,000
Emp.: 40
Hispanic Market Adv., Research, Promotions, Direct Response & Public Relations
Marta Miyares *(Pres.)*

AGRI-MARK, INC.
P.O. Box 5800,
Lawrence, MA 01842
Tel.: 800-225-0532
Fax: 800-225-0532 X214
Diary Co-Operatives
Carl Peterson *(Chm.)*
Paul Johnston *(Pres. & Gen. Mgr)*
Jane Conradsen *(Sec.)*

Subsidiary:

Cabot Creamery Co-Operative Inc. **(1)**
130 Main Hwy.
Cabot, VT 05647
Tel.: 802-563-2231
Fax: 802-563-2604
Assets: $35,000,000
Liabilities: $27,000,000
Net Worth: $8,000,000
Approx.Sls.: $70,000,000
Emp.: 225
Computer Systems/Hardware:
IBM
Cabot Brand Dairy Products: Wholesale Dairy Products, Mfr. Natural & Processed Cheese, Fluid Milk & Creamery Butter
S.I.C.: 2021; 2022; 2026; 5143
Paul Johnston *(Chm. Bd.)*
William Davis *(Pres. & Chief Exec. Officer)*
Roberta McDonald *(Exec. V.P. & Chief Oper. Officer)*
R. Steve Harper *(V.P.-Sls.)*
Roberta P. MacDonald *(V.P.-Mktg.)*
Bruce S. MacDonald *(Controller)*
Karen Saudek *(Dir.-Personnel)*

AGRINORTHWEST, INC.
2810 W. Clearwater Ave.
Kennewick, WA 99336
Mailing Address:
P.O. Box 2308,
Tri Cities, WA 99302
Tel.: 509-735-6461 **UT**
Fax: 509-735-6471
Approx.Sls.: $50,000,000
Emp.: 260
Producer & Distributor of Raw Farm Products
S.I.C.: 5148
Martin Wistisen *(Pres. & Chief Exec. Officer)*
R. Thomas Markay *(V.P.-Fin.)*

AGRIPAC INC.
325 Patterson N.W.
Salem, OR 97304
Mailing Address:
P.O. Box 5346
Salem, OR 97304
Tel.: 503-363-9255 **OR**
Fax: 503-371-5666
Year Founded: 1971
Assets: $106,000,000
Liabilities: $82,000,000
Net Worth: $24,000,000
Sales Range: $100-499 Million
Emp.: 320
Import Export
Agricultural Cooperative, Manufacturer of Food Specialties, Canned & Frozen Fruits & Vegetables
S.I.C.: 2037; 2033
Les Green *(Chm. Bd.)*
James Dishon *(Pres. & Chief Exec. Officer)*
Martin Myers *(Chief Fin. Officer & Treas.)*
James Rice *(Chief Information Officer (MIS))*
Robert Isaac *(Sr. V.P. & Chief Oper. Officer)*
Ned Roache *(Sr. V.P.-Sls. & Mktg.)*
George Crispin *(V.P.-Procurement & Co-pack)*
Dennis Spink *(V.P.-Quality Assurance, Research & Devel.)*
Charles Schaeffer *(Controller)*
Doug Fiengle *(Mgr.-Export)*
Dave Heniff *(Mgr.-Retail Sls.)*
Sue Johnson *(Mgr.-Pur.)*
James B. Scott *(Mgr.-Personnel)*
Ray Hoffmaster *(Distr. Mgr.)*

No. of Mfg. Plants/Facilities: 6

Computer Systems/Hardware:
Unisys

Outside Service Firm(s):

KPMG Peat Marwick*(Auditors)*
1211 S.W. Fifth Ave.
Portland, OR 97204

Harrang, Long, Watkinson & Laird*(Legal Firm)*
Eugene, OR

United States National Bank of Oregon*(Major Banking Relationship)*
Portland, OR

Subsidiary:

Woodburn Foods Corp. **(1)**
101 Birdseye Ave.
Woodburn, OR 97304
Tel.: 503-363-9255 (100%)
Emp.: 250
Frozen Fruits & Vegetables
S.I.C.: 2038

AGWAY, INC.
333 Butternut Dr.
De Witt, NY 13214
Mailing Address:
P. O. Box 4933
Syracuse, NY 13221
Tel.: 315-449-7061 **DE**
Fax: 315-449-6078
Year Founded: 1964
Assets: $1,837,220,000
Earnings: $8,102,000
Liabilities: $163,724,000
Net Worth: $1,673,496,000
Approx.Sls.: $3,489,788,000
Emp.: 7,500
Fiscal Year-end: 6/30/91
Import Export
Farm Supply Cooperative; Manufacture & Distribution of Farm Production Supplies; Wholesale Food, Farm & Petroleum Products
S.I.C.: 2096; 5172; 2033; 5143; 5153; 2022; 2037
Corporate Giving Program: United Way; Agway Foundation
Ralph H. Heffner *(Chm. Bd.)*
Charles L. Brosius *(Vice Chm.)*
Charles F. Saul *(Pres. & Chief Exec. Officer)*
A.J. Fogerty *(Sr. V.P.)*
R.G. Radey *(Sr. V.P.-Fin. & Controller)*
Courtney B. Burdette *(Sr. V.P.-Cooperative Rels.)*
Bruce D. Ruppert *(Sr. V.P.-Plng. & Opers.)*
Carleton E. Whittemore *(Sr. V.P.-Information Services)*
D.M. Hayes *(Sr. V.P., Sec. & Gen. Counsel)*
Peter J. O'Neill *(Grp. V.P.-Energy Grp.)*
John L. Norris *(Grp. V.P.-Consumer Grp.)*
Joel G. Newman *(Grp. V.P.-Agriculture Grp.)*
Stephen B. Burnett *(V.P.-Country Foods)*
Theodore J. Nakoski *(V.P.)*
Donald P. Cardarelli *(V.P. & Treas.)*
Robert T. Engfer *(V.P.-Human Resources)*
Darwin G. Braund *(Dir.-Res. & Applied Technology)*
Gene A. Freid *(Dir.-Training & Labor Rels.)*
Robert D. Sears *(Dir.-Member Rels.)*
Stephen H. Hoefer *(Dir.-Govt. Rels. & Transportation)*
John P. Ryan *(Dir.-Trust Investments)*
Richard A. Schlote *(Dir.-Compensation & Benefits)*
Donald A. Sibley *(Dir.-Real Estate & Property Devel.)*
Richard K. Arnold *(Mgr.-Corp. Communications)*
Lawrence J. Gessini *(Mgr.-Telecommunications)*
Francois LaChance *(Mgr.-Distr. Communications)*

No. of U.S. Offices: 1

Computer Systems/Hardware:
IBM

Outside Service Firm(s):

Coopers & Lybrand*(Auditors)*
1301 Avenue of The Americas
New York, NY 10019
Tel.: 212-536-2000

Chase Manhattan Bank, N.A.*(Major Banking Relationship)*
One Chase Manhattan Plaza
New York, NY 10081
Tel.: 212-552-2222
Tel.: 800-526-0801
Fax: 212-552-7175

Subsidiaries:

Agway Data Services, Inc. **(1)**
333 Butternut Dr.
De Witt, NY 13214
Tel.: 315-477-7061 (100%)
Computer & Communications Services for the Commercial Agriculture Market
S.I.C.: 7372; 7374
Dennis J. LaHood *(Pres.)*

Agway Financial Corporation **(1)**
333 Butternut Dr.
De Witt, NY 13214
Tel.: 315-477-7061 (100%)
Agricultural Credit Institution
S.I.C.: 6159
Stephen B. Burnett *(V.P.-Fin. Services)*

Agway Insurance Co. **(1)**
P.O. Box 4851
Syracuse, NY 13221
Tel.: 315-477-6253 (100%)
S.I.C.: 6411
Gerald R. Seeber *(Exec. V.P.)*

Subsidiaries:

Agway Indemnity Insurance Company **(2)**
P.O. Box 4851
Syracuse, NY 13221
Tel.: 315-477-6253
Property & Casualty Indemnity Company
S.I.C.: 6331

Agway General Agency **(2)**
P.O. Box 4851
Syracuse, NY 13221
Tel.: 315-477-6253
S.I.C.: 6411

Agway Petroleum Corp. **(1)**
333 Butternut Dr.
De Witt, NY 13214
Tel.: 315-449-7380 (100%)
Approx.Sls.: $1,880,000,000
Emp.: 7,700
Distribute Petroleum Products
S.I.C.: 5172
Courtney B. Burnette *(Pres.)*
Ralph Gaiss *(V.P.-Stores & Representative)*
Don Schalk *(Dir.-Mktg. & Sls.)*
Sallyann Cosmo *(Mgr.-Reg. Sls.)*

H. P. Hood Inc. **(1)**
500 Rutherford Ave.
Boston, MA 02129
Tel.: 617-242-0600 (99%)
Fax: 617-242-2625
Emp.: 2,300
Fiscal Year-end: 6/30/90
Dairy & Food Products
S.I.C.: 5143
Robert L. Keller *(Chief Exec. Officer)*
Robert Schaejbe *(Chief Fin. Officer)*
Peter F. Minasian *(Dir.-Pub. Rels.)*
Katherine L. Shepard *(Mgr.-Communications)*

Telmark, Inc. **(1)**
P.O. Box 4943
Syracuse, NY 13221
Tel.: 315-477-6294 (100%)
Leasing
S.I.C.: 7359
Daniel J. Edinger *(Pres. & Chief Oper. Officer)*

Affiliate:

Curtice-Burns Foods, Inc. **(1)**
90 Linden Place
Rochester, NY 14603
Tel.: 716-383-1850 (33%)
Fax: 716-383-1281
Earnings: $3,657,000
Approx.Sls.: $896,931,000
Emp.: 6,000
Fiscal Year-end: 6/26/92
Export
Food Mfg.
S.I.C.: 2033; 2099
Donald E. Pease *(Chm. Bd.)*
David J. McDonald *(Pres. & Chief Exec. Officer)*
J. William Petty *(Exec. V.P.)*
Roy Myers *(Exec. V.P.)*
William Rice *(Sr. V.P.-Finance Admin.)*
Darryl L. Canfield *(V.P. & Controller)*
Bea Slizewski *(Dir.-Corp. Communications)*

Divisions:

Comstock Foods **(2)**
1000 S. Main St.
Newark, NJ 07105
Tel.: 315-331-1800
Canning of Fruits & Vegetables
S.I.C.: 2033

Comstock Michigan Fruit **(2)**
90 Linden Place
Rochester, NY 14603
Tel.: 716-383-1070
Fax: 716-383-8689
Approx.Sls.: $350,000,000
Emp.: 1,500
Fiscal Year-end: 6/30/91
Export
Process Fresh Fruits & Vegetables
S.I.C.: 2033
William Petty *(Chief Exec. Officer)*
Richard Anderson *(Exec. V.P.-Retail Brands)*
D. Mullen *(Exec. V.P.-Food Service)*
H.J. Remington *(Sr. V.P.-Mfg.)*
Earl Powers *(V.P.-Fin.)*
J. Skwara *(V.P.-Technical Services & Devel.)*
Mary Pawloski *(Dir.-Pur.)*

Nalleys Fine Foods **(2)**
3303 S. 35th St.
Tacoma, WA 98411
Tel.: 206-383-1621
Fax: 206-272-2730
Approx.Sls.: $200,000,000
Emp.: 1,000
Fiscal Year-end: 6/30/91
Export
S.I.C.: 2033
Patrick Lindenbach *(Pres. & Chief Exec. Officer)*
Ron Sage *(V.P.-Custom Pack Sls.)*
Dennis A. Myers *(Exec. V.P.-Sls.)*
Richard McEntee *(V.P.-Opers.)*
Richard S. Meyer *(V.P.-Technical Services)*
James O'Brien *(V.P.-Mfg.)*
Kent L. Roberts *(Dir.-Human Resources)*

Divisions:

Lucca Packing Div., Nalley's Fine Foods **(3)**
360 Harbor Way
South San Francisco, CA 94080
Tel.: 415-589-0221
Fax: 415-589-6903
Approx.Sls.: $18,000,000
Emp.: 100
Fiscal Year-end: 6/31/91
Export
Frozen & Canned Food Packers
S.I.C.: 2099
Mary Jane Valby *(Dir.-Sls. & Mktg.)*

National Brands Beverage Div. **(3)**
882 Linden Ave.
Rochester, NY 14625
Tel.: 716-381-0820
Manufactures Soft Drinks
S.I.C.: 2086

Agway, Inc.—(Continued)

National Oats Co. **(2)**
1515 H Ave. N.E.
Cedar Rapids, IA 52402
Tel.: 319-364-9161
Fax: 319-364-0764
Emp.: 400
Manufactures Oats & Pop Corn; Elevator Buckets
S.I.C.: 2043; 2099; 3535
Nevin W. Meredith *(Pres. & Chief Exec. Officer)*
Douglas Tomney *(V.P.-Fin.)*
Claude Choate *(V.P.-Natl. Sls. & Consumer Prods.)*
Karel Zachar *(V.P.-Intl. Sls.)*
George Busha *(V.P.-Mfg.)*
Tony Cahill *(V.P.-Indus. Prods.)*
Scott Seibert *(V.P.- Research)*
J. Scanlan *(V.P.-Pur.)*
Kevin Courteau *(V.P.-Mktg.)*
Courtney Mayne *(Customer Service Dir.)*
Dee Struve *(Mgr.-Mktg. Services)*
Wayne Howes *(Personnel Dir.)*
Henry Hey *(MIS Dir.)*

Snyder Potato Chips **(2)**
1313 Stadium Dr.
Berlin, PA 15530
Tel.: 814-267-4641
Fax: 814-267-5648
Approx.Sls.: $40,000,000
Emp.: 350
Manufactures Potato Chips
S.I.C.: 2096
Tommy Murray *(Pres.)*
Michael Gaffney *(Chief Oper. Officer)*
John Blough *(V.P.-Pur.)*
John Hayes *(Dir.-Quality Control)*
Michele James *(Mktg. Coord.)*
Jim Bason *(Production Mgr.)*

Southern Frozen Foods **(2)**
P.O. Box 306
Montezuma, GA 31063
Tel.: 912-472-8101
Fax: 912-472-6351
Approx.Sls.: $110,000,000
Emp.: 1,100
Fiscal Year-end: 1/30/91
Import Export
Computer Systems/Hardware:
IBM
Frozen Fruits, Vegetables & Prepared Food Items
S.I.C.: 5142
Thomas A. Collins *(Pres.)*
Paden Avera *(V.P.-Opers.)*
Robert G. Downs *(V.P.-Fin. & Admin.)*
Jim Trask *(V.P.-Sls.)*
Mikel Cates *(Dir.-Quality Control)*
Glenn Dowlen *(Dir.-Mktg.)*
Mickey Head *(Dir.-Pur.)*
Max Wood *(Dir.-Data Processing)*

Subsidiaries:

Adams Natural Peanut Butter **(2)**
3303 35th St.
Tacoma, WA 98409
Tel.: 206-272-3261
Manufactures Peanut Butter
S.I.C.: 2099

Blevins Popcorn **(2)**
1515 H Ave. N.E.
Cedar Rapids, IA 52402
Tel.: 319-364-9161
Manufactures Popping Corn
S.I.C.: 2099

Brooks Foods **(2)**
P.O. Box 157,
Mt. Summit, IN 47361
Emp.: 150
Food Processing; Brooks, Diner, Tangy Ketchup & Tomato Juice, Boone County, Ritter Tomato Juice & Private Label, Canned Whole Tomatoes, Stewed Tomatoes, Chili Hot Beans, Light & Dark Kidney Beans in Sauce
S.I.C.: 2033
E.W. Hermenet *(Pres.)*
Doug Knott *(V.P.-Sls.)*
A. Leoni *(V.P.-Admin.)*
M. Berkshire *(Dir.-Quality Assurance & Technical Srvcs.)*
K. Baiers *(Opers. Mgr.)*
S. Keesling *(Field Mgr.)*
Dave Wells *(Personnel Mgr.)*
E. Battoe *(Pur. Mgr.)*
Kim Riley *(Exec. Sec.)*

Calypso Foods **(2)**
P.O. Box 306
Montezuma, GA 31063
Tel.: 912-472-8101
Manufactures Frozen Grated Coconut
S.I.C.: 2099

Curtice Burns Meat Snacks, Inc. **(2)**
208 So. Kalamath St.
Denver, CO 80223
Tel.: 303-722-5771
Manufactures Beef Snacks
S.I.C.: 2013
William Benowicz *(Pres.)*

Farman's Pickle Company **(2)**
5501 4th Ave. So., Ste. 207
Seattle, WA 98108
Tel.: 206-767-3961
Manufactures Pickles
S.I.C.: 2035
Richard Farman *(Pres.)*

Tropic Isle **(2)**
P.O. Box 306
Montezuma, GA 31063
Tel.: 912-472-8101
Manufactures Frozen Grated Coconut
S.I.C.: 2099

Wilderness Foods **(2)**
P.O. Box 68
Benton Harbor, MI 49022
Tel.: 616-927-4411
Manufactures Canned Fruit & Pie Fillings
S.I.C.: 2033

AHERN NEW YORK
(Formerly Ahern & Heussner Advertising)
322 Eighth Ave.
New York, NY 10001
Tel.: 212-633-6200
Fax: 212-633-9287
Year Founded: 1992
Approx.Billings: $18,000,000
Emp.: 18
Paul J. Ahern *(Pres.)*
Maria Vega *(V.P., Bus. Affairs)*

AID ASSOCIATION FOR LUTHERANS
4321 N. Ballard Rd.
Appleton, WI 54919
Tel.: 414-734-5721 **WI**
Fax: 414-730-4820
Year Founded: 1902
Assets: $9,373,176,000
Earnings: $80,300,000
Liabilities: $8,826,015,000
Net Worth: $547,161,000
Approx.Rev.: $2,272,543,000
Emp.: 3,900
Fiscal Year-end: 12/31/91
Life & Health Insurance; Fraternal Benefit Society
S.I.C.: 6311; 6321
Corporate Giving Program: Minimum Contribution $25.00 per Donor, Maximum Match Per Donor Per Calendar Year is $1,000.00 to Nonprofit & Nonproprietary Institutions on a Paid not Pledged Basis
Henry F. Schieg *(Chm. Bd.)*
Richard L. Gunderson *(Pres. & Chief Exec. Officer)*
Charles W. Dull *(Sr. V.P.-Corp. Staff Services & Chief Quality Officer)*
John O. Gilbert *(Sr. V.P.-Member Insurance Services)*
William R. Heerman *(Sr. V.P.-Law & Communications, Sec. & Gen. Counsel)*
Roger J. Johnson *(Sr. V.P.-Corp. Info. Services, Chief Fin. Officer & Treas.)*
John H. Pender *(Sr. V.P., Chief Invest. Officer & Member Invest. Services)*
James A. Richardson *(Sr. V.P.-Member Field Services)*
Carl J. Rudolph *(V.P. & Controller)*
Thomas R. Houston *(Asst. V.P.-Fin. & Tax Reporting)*
J. Phil Snyder *(Asst. V.P.-Communications Services)*

Computer Systems/Hardware:
IBM

Outside Service Firm(s):

Ernst & Young*(Auditors)*
111 E. Kilbourn Ave., Ste. 900
Milwaukee, WI 53202
Tel.: 414-273-5900

Harris Trust & Savings Bank*(Major Banking Relationship)*
111 W. Monroe St.
Chicago, IL 60690
Tel.: 312-461-2265
Tel.: 800-858-0840

Subsidiaries:

AAL Capital Management Corp. **(1)**
4321 N. Ballard Rd.
Appleton, WI 54919
Tel.: 414-734-5721
Manages Investments
S.I.C.: 6282
Rochelle Lamm Wallach *(Chief Oper. Officer)*

AAL Distributors Inc. **(1)**
4321 N. Ballard Rd.
Appleton, WI 54919
Tel.: 414-734-5721
Distributor of Funds
S.I.C.: 6211
Rochelle Lamm Wallach *(Chief Oper. Officer)*

AID AUTO STORES, INC.
275 Grand Blvd.
Westbury, NY 11590-0281
Tel.: 516-338-7889
Fax: 516-338-7803
Approx.Sls.: $20,000,000
Emp.: 75
Wholesale Auto Parts
S.I.C.: 5013
Phillip L. Stephen *(Pres. & Chief Oper. Officer)*
Michael A. Guaneri *(Dir.-Adv.)*

Computer Systems/Hardware:
IBM System 38

Outside Service Firm(s):

Lazar, Levine & Co.*(Auditors)*
350 Fifth Ave.
New York, NY 10118
Tel.: 212-736-8466

Cowan, Liebowitz & Latman*(Legal Firm)*
New York, NY

Standard Chartered Bank*(Major Banking Relationship)*
New York, NY

Subsidiary:

Ames Automotive Warehouse **(1)**
275 Grand Blvd.
Westbury, NY 11590
Tel.: 516-338-7229
Peter Chifolo *(Gen. Mgr.)*

AIKEN ELECTRIC COOPERATIVE INC.
P.O. Box 417
Aiken, SC 29802
Tel.: 803-649-6245
Fax: 803-648-9868
Year Founded: 1938
Assets: $41,114,000
Liabilities: $25,853,000
Net Worth: $15,261,000
Approx.Sls.: $21,500,000
Emp.: 133
Fiscal Year-end: 5/31/90
Distribute Electric Power
S.I.C.: 4911
Edward Swartz *(Pres.)*
Dewitt Livingston *(Treas.)*
Thomas Huff *(Gen. Counsel)*
Ann Robinson *(Data Processing Supvr.)*

Outside Service Firm(s):

Collins & Company*(Auditors)*
Walterboro, SC

Citizens & Southern National Bank*(Major Banking Relationship)*
Aiken, SC

ROBERT B. AIKENS & ASSOCIATES INC.
2690 Crooks Rd.
Troy, MI 48084
Tel.: 313-362-1370
Fax: 313-362-0614
Year Founded: 1971
Sales Range: $100-499 Million
Emp.: 250
Real Estate Developer & Broker
S.I.C.: 6552; 6531
Robert B. Aikens *(Chm. Bd.)*
Patrick Finerty *(Pres. & V.P.-Fin.)*
James Fielder *(V.P.-Opers. & Mktg.)*
Denny Moore *(V.P. & Leasing Dir.)*
Jeff Thompson *(V.P.-Construction)*

AIN PLASTICS, INC.
249 E. Sandford Blvd.
Mount Vernon, NY 10550
Mailing Address:
P.O. Box 151
Mount Vernon, NY 10550
Tel.: 914-668-6800
Tel.: 800-431-2451 **NY**
Fax: 914-668-8820
Year Founded: 1970
Approx.Sls.: $34,000,000
Emp.: 200
Fiscal Year-end: 12/31/91
Wholesale Distributor of Plastics
S.I.C.: 5162
Norman Drucker *(Pres.)*
Alex Gabay *(V.P.)*
Patricia McGowan *(Dir.-Data Processing)*
Lynda Wagner *(Dir.-Adv.)*
Adriane Bonfigio *(Mgr.-Personnel)*
Stan Williams *(Mgr.-Sls.)*
Jane Neumiester *(Pur. Agent)*
Principal(s):
Norman Drucker
Alex Gabay

No. of U.S. Offices: 10

Computer Systems/Hardware:
IBM System 36

Outside Service Firm(s):

Eisner & Lubin*(Auditors)*
New York, NY

Robert Swetnick, Esq.*(Legal Firm)*
New York, NY

Chase Manhattan Bank, N.A.*(Major Banking Relationship)*
One Chase Manhattan Plaza
New York, NY 10081
Tel.: 212-552-2222

AIR CONDITIONING CO., INC.
6265 San Fernando Rd.
Glendale, CA 91201
Tel.: 818-244-6571 **CA**
Fax: 818-247-6533
Year Founded: 1934
Approx.Sls.: $100,000,000
Emp.: 600
Fiscal Year-end: 9/30/90
Design, Manufacture, Install & Service Heating, Ventilating & Air Conditioning Systems
S.I.C.: 1711
Theodore M. Seidman *(Chm. Bd. & Pres.)*
John Aversano *(Chief Exec. Officer)*
William B. McNamara *(Chief Fin. Officer, Treas. & Asst. Sec.)*

Robert P. Vlick *(Sr. V.P.-Bldg. System Services Group)*
Robert A. Brown *(Controller)*
Muriel A. Winslow *(Sec.)*
Milton L. Goodman *(Dir.-Pur.)*
Roberta R. Kessler *(Dir.-Human Resources)*

Principal(s):
Theodore M. Seidman
Robert P. Vlick

No. of Mfg. Plants/Facilities: 1
No. of U.S. Offices: 4

Computer Systems/Hardware:
Prime; Radio Shack; IBM PC

Outside Service Firm(s):

KPMG Peat Marwick*(Auditors)*
725 S. Figueroa St.
Los Angeles, CA 90017
Tel.: 213-972-4000

Alexander & Alexander*(Group Insurer)*
One Constitution Plaza
New York, NY 10036
Tel.: 617-241-9800

Munns, Kofford, Hoffman, Hunt & Throckmorton*(Legal Firm)*
Pasadena, CA

First Interstate Bank of California, N.A.*(Major Banking Relationship)*
P.O. Box 3667,
Los Angeles, CA 90051
Tel.: 213-614-4000

Steven A. Noroian & Assoc.*(Pension Manager)*
San Francisco, CA

Branches:

Air Conditioning Co., Inc. **(1)**
6952 South 220th St.
Kent, WA 98032
Tel.: 206-395-7220
Steven R. Burns *(N.W. Reg. Mgr.)*

Air Conditioning Co., Inc. **(1)**
1700 Industrial Rd.
San Carlos, CA 94070
Tel.: 510-594-0182
Air Conditioning
S.I.C.: 1711
Carl H. Johnson *(Sr. V.P.)*

Air Conditioning Co., Inc. **(1)**
7179 Construction Ct., Ste. A
San Diego, CA 92121
Tel.: 619-695-3977
Air Conditioning
S.I.C.: 1711
Frank J. Falcone *(Regional Project Mgr.)*

AIR GAGE COMPANY
12170 Globe
Livonia, MI 48150
Tel.: 313-591-9220
Fax: 313-591-0434
Year Founded: 1965
Approx.Sls.: $25,000,000
Emp.: 265
Export
Manufacturer of Air, Electronic & Computer Gages
S.I.C.: 3545
Dominic Persichini *(Pres.)*
David E. Joslyn *(Exec. V.P.)*
Vince Zane *(V.P.-Mfg.)*
R.F. Lapiere *(Sec.)*
Don McNeill *(Mgr.-Sls.)*
Tom Barrell *(Pur. Agent)*

Outside Service Firm(s):

Comerica Bank*(Major Banking Relationship)*
211 W. Fort St.
Detroit, MI 48226
Tel.: 313-222-3300

Subsidiary:

Precise Technology & Electronics, Inc. **(1)**
24727 Gibson
Warren, MI 48089
Tel.: 313-758-7100
Design & Fabricate Electric Test Equipment
S.I.C.: 8711; 3825
Tom Fleming *(Gen. Mgr.)*

AIR INDUSTRIES CORPORATION
12570 Knott St.
Garden Grove, CA 92641
Tel.: 714-892-5571
Fax: 714-892-7904
Approx.Sls.: $40,000,000
Emp.: 500
Precision Fasteners-Bolts, Rivets, Screws, Special Tools, Screwdriver Bits & Punches
S.I.C.: 3452
S.L. Higgins *(Chm. Bd. & Pres.)*
Dan Arredondo *(V.P.-Sls.)*
Jean Hager *(Sec. & Treas.)*
Floyd Twede *(Controller)*

Outside Service Firm(s):

Stephen Hatch*(Auditors)*
Santa Ana, CA

Irell & Manella*(Legal Firm)*
1800 Ave. of the Stars
Los Angeles, CA 90067
Tel.: 310-277-1010

Security Pacific National Bank*(Major Banking Relationship)*
Santa Ana, CA

AIR JAMAICA LTD.
444 Brickell Ave.
Miami, FL 33131
Tel.: 305-358-3222
Approx.Sls.: $100,000,000
Emp.: 1,400
Fiscal Year-end: 12/31/90
Commercial Air Line
S.I.C.: 4512
Mike Sennell *(Pres. & Chief Exec. Officer)*
Marjorie Robinson *(Adv. Mgr.)*

AIR MASTER CORPORATION
1211 Ford Rd.
Bensalem, PA 19020
Tel.: 215-638-8600
Fax: 215-638-0268
Approx.Sls.: $15,000,000
Emp.: 6
Manufacture Aluminum Replacement Windows For Commercial Application
S.I.C.: 3442

AIR POWER, INC.
1430 Trinity Ave.
High Point, NC 27260
Tel.: 919-886-5081
Tel.: 800-334-1001 **NC**
Fax: 919-889-2745
Year Founded: 1967
Approx.Sls.: $14,000,000
Emp.: 67
Import Export
Wholesale Distribution of Industrial Machinery & Equipment
S.I.C.: 5084
William A. Ball, Sr. *(Pres.)*
Harvey S. McFatridge *(V.P.)*
Alice Ball *(Treas. & Sec.)*

Outside Service Firm(s):

High Point Bank & Trust Company*(Major Banking Relationship)*
High Point, NC

AIRCO MECHANICAL INC.
5720 Alder Ave.
Sacramento, CA 95828
Tel.: 916-381-4523
Fax: 916-386-0350
Year Founded: 1974
Approx.Sls.: $22,000,000
Emp.: 200
Fiscal Year-end: 6/30/91
Warm Air Heating & Air Conditioning, Ventilation & Duct Work & Plumbing Contractors
S.I.C.: 1711
James C. Jones *(Pres.)*
Georgene Anderson *(V.P.-Personnel)*
Larry Cook *(V.P.-Opers., P/P)*
Steve Humason *(V.P.-Engrng.)*
Don Jamarck *(V.P.-Fin.)*
Charles C. Jones *(V.P.)*
Garry Westover *(V.P.-Opers.,A/C)*
Marilyn Szulman-Jones *(Sec. & Treas.)*

Outside Service Firm(s):

Cinnamon, Casterton, Hage & Dorn*(Legal Firm)*
Sacramento, CA

River City Bank*(Major Banking Relationship)*
Sacramento, CA

Subsidiary:

Airco Commercial Services, Inc. **(1)**
324 Commercial St.
San Jose, CA 95112
Tel.: 408-286-5477
Fax: 408-286-5665
Emp.: 10
Air Conditioning & Heating Services
S.I.C.: 1711; 8711
James C. Jones *(Pres.)*

AIRCRAFT GEAR CORPORATION
6633 W. 65th
Chicago, IL 60638
Tel.: 708-594-2100
Fax: 708-594-8310
Approx.Sls.: $15,000,000
Emp.: 100
Fiscal Year-end: 3/31/91
Import Export
Aircraft Engine Gear Boxes
S.I.C.: 3728; 3769
Dean A. Olson *(Gen. Mgr.)*
Art T. O'Day *(Controller)*
John A. Davey *(Mgr.-Mfg.)*
Joseph J. Tokich *(Mgr.-Quality Assurance)*
Donald B. Brodt *(Mgr.-Materials)*
Thomas C. Purvin *(Mgr.-Mktg.)*

Computer Systems/Hardware:
Western Data Compass Contract

Outside Service Firm(s):

Coopers & Lybrand*(Auditors)*
6000 E. State St.
Rockford, IL 61108
Tel.: 815-394-0300

Illinois National Bank & Trust Co.*(Major Banking Relationship)*
Rockford, IL

Division:

Aircraft Gear Corporation-Arizona Division **(1)**
1800 So. Price Rd.
Chandler, AZ 85248
Tel.: 602-821-2434
Skip Stohlgren *(Gen. Mgr.)*
William Karpinski *(Business Mgr.)*

AIRGUARD INDUSTRIES INC.
3807 Bishop Lane
Louisville, KY 40218
Mailing Address:
P.O. Box 32578
Louisville, KY 40232
Tel.: 502-969-2304
Fax: 502-969-2759
Year Founded: 1963
Approx.Sls.: $15,000,000
Emp.: 300
Mfr. Air Filtration Prods.
S.I.C.: 3564
Robert F. Bender *(Chm. Bd., Pres. & Chief Exec. Officer)*
Frank Saving *(Chief Engineer)*
James French *(V.P.-Mktg.)*
William B. Walker, III *(V.P. & Gen. Mgr.)*
Rita M. Bender *(Treas.)*
Sharon Alteri *(Sec.)*
Ray A. Bender *(Comptroller)*
Joe Barber *(Mgr.-Mfg.)*
Harvey Goble *(Mgr.-Data Processing)*
Phillip McCluskey *(Mgr.-Pur.)*
James Tackett *(Plant Mgr.)*

Outside Service Firm(s):

Ernst & Young*(Auditors)*
1000 Brown & Williamson Tower
Louisville, KY 40202
Tel.: 502-585-1400

Ewen, McKenzie & Peden*(Legal Firm)*
650 Strauss Bldg.
Louisville, KY 40202
Tel.: 502-589-1110

First National Bank of Louisville*(Major Banking Relationship)*
P.O. Box 36000,
Louisville, KY 40233

AIRLINE HYDRAULICS CORPORATION
1-95 & Street Rd.
Bensalem, PA 19020
Mailing Address:
P.O. Box 8500
Bensalem, PA 19020
Tel.: 215-638-4700
Fax: 215-638-1707
Approx.Sls.: $18,000,000
Emp.: 86
Wholesale Distributor of Hydraulic & Pneumatic Electronic Components
S.I.C.: 5085
Joseph E. Loughran *(Pres.)*
J.R. Moorhead *(V.P.-Sls.)*
John J. Lombard, Jr. *(Sec.)*
R. Pickus *(Controller)*
Thomas Dobson *(Pur. Agent)*
John Wus *(Mgr.-Fabrication)*

Outside Service Firm(s):

Halbert, Katz & Company*(Auditors)*
Philadelphia, PA

Morgan, Lewis & Bockius*(Legal Firm)*
123 So. Broad St.
Philadelphia, PA 19109
Tel.: 215-875-2500

Philadelphia National Bank*(Major Banking Relationship)*
5th & Market Sts.
Philadelphia, PA 19101
Tel.: 215-629-3100
Fax: 215-834-2069

AIRLINE MANUFACTURING COMPANY, INC.
104 Williamson Rd.
Columbus, MS 39704
Tel.: 601-328-6355
Fax: 601-328-6355
Emp.: 350
Manufacture Furniture Parts, Hardwood Frames
S.I.C.: 2426
Ralph Williamson *(Pres.)*
Fred Williamson *(V.P.)*

Airline Manufacturing Company, Inc.—(Continued)

Daphne Williamson *(Sec. & Treas.)*

Outside Service Firm(s):

T.E. Lott & Company*(Auditors)*
Columbus, MS

National Bank of Commerce*(Major Banking Relationship)*
Columbus, MS

AIRMASTER FAN CO.
1300 Falahee Rd.
Michigan Center, MI 49203
Mailing Address:
P. O. Box 968
Jackson, MI 49204
Tel.: 517-764-2300
Year Founded: 1975
Approx.Sls.: $15,000,000
Emp.: 150
Import Export
Air Circulators, Exhaust Fans, Ceiling Fans, Roof Ventilators
S.I.C.: 3822
Robert LaZebnik *(Owner)*
Dan Gregorich *(Pres.)*
Ron Johnson *(Controller)*

Principal(s):
Robert LaZebnik

THE AIROLITE COMPANY
114 Westview Ave.
Marietta, OH 45750
Mailing Address:
P.O. Box 666
Marietta, OH 45750-0666
Tel.: 614-373-7676 **OH**
Fax: 614-373-6666
Year Founded: 1919
Assets: $4,500,000
Liabilities: $750,000
Net Worth: $3,750,000
Approx.Sls.: $10,000,000
Emp.: 130
Fiscal Year-end: 12/31/90
Mfr. Ventilating Louvers
S.I.C.: 3444
Norman J. Murray *(Chm. Bd.)*
N. Leight Murray *(Pres. & Chief Exec. Officer)*
A. Allen Brokaw *(V.P.-Mktg. & Sls.)*
Mark D. Roos *(V.P., Treas. & Chief Fin. Officer)*
George D. Sauer *(Sec.)*
William E. Ross *(Dir.-Matls. & Pur.)*
John R. Pitcher *(Mgr.-Data Processing)*

Principal(s):
Norman J. Murray
Mark D. Roos

No. of Mfg. Plants/Facilities: 2

Computer Systems/Hardware:
Burroughs B 8000; IBM PC

Outside Service Firm(s):

Arthur Andersen & Co.*(Auditors)*
Columbus, OH

Lincoln National Life Insurance Co.*(Group Insurer)*
Fort Wayne, IN

Theisen, Brock, Frye & Erb*(Legal Firm)*
424 2nd St.
Marietta, OH 45750
Tel.: 614-373-5455

Peoples Bank*(Major Banking Relationship)*
Marietta, OH

Peoples Bank*(Pension Manager)*
Marietta, OH

Subsidiary:

Louv-Aire, Inc. **(1)**
1655 N. 15th Ave.
Tucson, AZ 85705
Tel.: 602-622-3681 (100%)
Fax: 602-622-2777
Emp.: 25
Mfrs. Ventilating Louvers
S.I.C.: 3444
L. John Martin *(V.P.)*

AIRTROL, INC.
3960 North St.
Baton Rouge, LA 70806
Tel.: 504-383-2617
Fax: 504-343-7986
Year Founded: 1946
Approx.Sls.: $11,000,000
Emp.: 19
Heating & Air Conditioning Contractor
S.I.C.: 1711
Warren I. Pol *(Chm. Bd.)*
Steve W. Pol *(Pres.)*
Francis Jumonville *(Sec. & Treas.)*

Outside Service Firm(s):

Postlethwaite & Netterville*(Auditors)*
Baton Rouge, LA

Richard Nevills Legal Firm*(Legal Firm)*
Baton Rouge, LA

AJAX MANUFACTURING COMPANY, INC.
321 Valley Rd.
Hillsborough, NJ 08876
Tel.: 908-369-5544
Fax: 908-369-5415
Approx.Sls.: $10,000,000
Emp.: 100
Manufacture Truck Trailers
S.I.C.: 3715
Carl Massaro *(Pres.)*
Karl Massaro *(V.P.-Engrng.)*
Jerry Patt *(V.P.-Sls.)*

Outside Service Firm(s):

Irving Sturm*(Legal Firm)*
Fort Lee, NJ

National State Bank of New Jersey*(Major Banking Relationship)*
Springfield, NJ

AJAX PAVING INDUSTRIES INC.
One Ajax Dr.
Madison Heights, MI 48071
Mailing Address:
P.O. Box 317
Madison Heights, MI 48071
Tel.: 313-398-2300
Fax: 313-398-7695
Year Founded: 1951
Approx.Sls.: $44,000,000
Emp.: 200
Highway & Street Construction; Manufacture Asphalt Paving Mixtures
S.I.C.: 1611; 2951
Herbert H. Jacob *(Chm. Bd. & Chief Exec. Officer)*
James A. Jacob *(Pres.)*
Dale Haver *(V.P.-Sls. & Mktg.)*
James Friel *(Comptroller)*

Outside Service Firm(s):

National Bank of Detroit*(Major Banking Relationship)*
611 Woodward
Detroit, MI 48226
Tel.: 313-225-1000

AKERS PACKAGING SERVICE INC.
2820 Lefferson Rd.
Middletown, OH 45044
Mailing Address:
P.O. Box 610
Middletown, OH 45042
Tel.: 513-422-6313 **OH**
Fax: 513-422-2829
Year Founded: 1963
Approx.Sls.: $40,000,000
Emp.: 210
Manufacture of Corrugated Boxes
S.I.C.: 2653
William C. Akers *(Pres.)*
Joseph Lyons *(Gen. Mgr.)*
Larry Pratt *(Dir.-Personnel)*

Outside Service Firm(s):

Clark, Schaeffer & Hackett*(Auditors)*
Cincinnati, OH

Smith & Schnacke*(Legal Firm)*
2000 Courthouse Plz.
Dayton, OH 45401
Tel.: 513-226-6500

Bank One*(Major Banking Relationship)*
100 E. Broad St.
Columbus, OH 43216
Tel.: 614-248-5995

Bank One of Middletown*(Major Banking Relationship)*
Middletown, OH

ALABAMA ELECTRIC COOPERATIVE, INC.
Hwy. 29 N.
Andalusia, AL 36420
Mailing Address:
P.O. Box 550
Andalusia, AL 36420
Tel.: 205-222-2571 **AL**
Fax: 205-222-7785
Year Founded: 1941
Assets: $492,206,183
Liabilities: $465,437,606
Net Worth: $26,768,577
Approx.Sls.: $177,137,248
Emp.: 548
Fiscal Year-end: 12/31/91
Import Export
Electrical Power Distributor
S.I.C.: 4911
Jack Taylor *(Chm. Bd.)*
James A. Vann, Jr. *(Pres. & Chief Oper. Officer)*
A.G. Palmore *(V.P.-Fin. & Admin.)*
Larry Avery *(V.P.-Engrng. & Opers.)*
B.R. Clausen *(V.P.-Corp. Plng. & Mktg.)*
Jeff Parish *(V.P.-Bulk Power & Delivery)*
John Howard *(V.P.-Power Prod.)*
Elmer G. McDaniel *(Sec. & Treas.)*
James B. Lee *(Mgr.-Human Resources)*
Earl McBryde *(Mgr.-Admin. Services)*
David Brooks *(Mgr.-Data Processing)*
Gary Smith *(Dir.-Legal Affairs)*
B.W. Thompson, Jr. *(Dir.-Fuel Procurement)*
Phillip Burgess *(Dir.-Corp. Video Systems & Telecommunications)*

Computer Systems/Hardware:
Data General MU 2000; Microvax II & Harris-Scada System

Outside Service Firm(s):

Deloitte & Touche*(Auditors)*
Mobile, AL

Wausau Insurance*(Commercial Insurance Carrier)*
2000 Westwood Dr.
Wausau, WI 54401-7881
Tel.: 715-842-6902
Fax: 715-847-8534

National Rural Electric Cooperative Association*(Group Insurer)*
Washington, DC

Rushton, Stakely, Johnston & Garrett*(Legal Firm)*
P.O. Box 270
Montgomery, AL 36195
Tel.: 205-834-8480

South Trust Bank of Covington County*(Major Banking Relationship)*
Andalusia, AL

Subsidiaries:

Lakeside Coal Company **(1)**
P.O. Box 550,
Andalusia, AL 36420
Tel.: 205-222-2571

United Energy Corporation **(1)**
P.O. Box 550,
Andalusia, AL 36420
Tel.: 205-22-2571

Waters Coal Company **(1)**
P.O. Box 550,
Andalusia, AL 36420
Tel.: 205-222-2571

ALABAMA FARMERS CO-OP
121 Somerville Rd. N.E.
Decatur, AL 35609-2227
Mailing Address:
P.O. Box 2227
Decatur, AL 35609-2227
Tel.: 205-353-6843 **AL**
Fax: 205-350-1770
Year Founded: 1936
Assets: $99,408,255
Earnings: $4,130,619
Liabilities: $86,267,095
Net Worth: $13,141,160
Approx.Sls.: $211,860,908
Emp.: 300
Fiscal Year-end: 12/31/89
Wholesaler Fertilizer & Feed; Producer Vegetables; Horticultural Specialties; Wholesaler Farm Supplies; Grain & Fertilizer
S.I.C.: 0161; 5159; 5153; 5191
Gene Pickens *(Chm. Bd.)*
John Anderson *(Pres., Chief Exec. & Oper. Officer)*
Joseph Lovvorn *(Treas. & Controller)*
Karen Greenhaw *(Sec.)*
Wayne Holt *(Dir.-Data Processing)*
Robert Slate *(Dir.-Sls.)*
Tom Hill *(Mgr. Mktg.-Feeds)*

No. of Mfg. Plants/Facilities: 3

Outside Service Firm(s):

Coopers & Lybrand*(Auditors)*
1901 6th Ave. North, Ste. 1600
Birmingham, AL 35203-2602

Eyster, Eyster, Key & Tubb*(Legal Firm)*
Decatur, AL

ALABAMA METAL INDUSTRIES CORPORATION
3245 Fayette Ave.
Birmingham, AL 35208
Mailing Address:
P.O. Box 3928
Birmingham, AL 35208
Tel.: 205-787-2611
Fax: 205-780-3303
Year Founded: 1949
Emp.: 283
Import Export
Manufacture of Metal Laths & Accessories, Steel Studs & Steel Floor Joists, Expanded Metal Products, Bar Grating, Security Mesh, Stayform
S.I.C.: 3452; 3449; 3446
Charles B. Webb, Jr. *(Chm. Bd. & Chief Exec. Officer)*

William S. Baird *(Pres. & Chief Oper. Officer)*
Roland T. Short *(Exec. V.P. & Sec.)*
John Kidd *(V.P.-Opers.)*
Roger L. Lowery *(V.P.-Mktg.)*
Joan W. Moreno *(Mgr.-Adv.)*

Outside Service Firm(s):

Coopers & Lybrand*(Auditors)*
1901 6th Ave. North, Ste. 1600
Birmingham, AL 35203-2602

AmSouth Bank N.A.*(Major Banking Relationship)*
P.O. Box 11426
Birmingham, AL 35202
Tel.: 205-326-5321

Bradley, Arant, Rose & White*(Legal Firm)*
1400 Park Place Tower
Birmingham, AL 35203
Tel.: 205-521-8000

Divisions:

AMICO-Cincinnati Distr. Center **(1)**
5210 Duff Dr.
Cincinnati, OH 45246
Tel.: 513-874-9224
Polly Brewer *(Mgr.-Customer Service)*

AMICO-Dallas Distr. Center **(1)**
148 Fordyce
Dallas, TX 75207
Tel.: 214-653-1723
Jerry Bailey *(Mgr.-Customer Service)*

AMICO Greenville Distr. Center **(1)**
P.O. Box 26534
Greenville, SC 29616
Tel.: 803-458-7241
Maria McGaha *(Mgr.-Customer Service)*

AMICO-Houston Distr. Center **(1)**
415 A North Wayside Dr.
Houston, TX 77020
Tel.: 713-671-0621
Dan Robertson *(Mgr.-Customer Service)*

AMICO-Lakeland **(1)**
1033 Pine Chase Ave.
Lakeland, FL 33801
Tel.: 813-688-9256
Ken Baker *(Mgr.)*

AMICO-Riverside **(1)**
601 NW Business Park Lane
Riverside, MO 64150
Tel.: 816-587-8680
Nancy Forbes *(Mgr.-Customer Service)*

AMICO-West Distr. Center **(1)**
2651 Willow St.
Oakland, CA 94607
Tel.: 510-839-2251

AMICO-West Distr. Center **(1)**
11093 Beech Ave.
Fontana, CA 92335
Tel.: 714-350-9280
Jerry Bailey *(V.P. & Gen. Mgr.)*

ALACON
158 Commercial St.
Sunnyvale, CA 94086
Tel.: 408-720-1157 **CA**
Fax: 408-733-3461
Year Founded: 1964
Sales Range: $40-59 Million
Emp.: 90
Fiscal Year-end: 7/31/88
General Contractor
S.I.C.: 1541; 1542
Richard P. Arens *(Chm. Bd., Pres., Chief Exec. & Fin. Officer)*
Joel Arens *(Exec. V.P., Treas. & Sec.)*
Principal(s):
Richard P. Arens
Joel Arens

No. of U.S. Offices: 24

Computer Systems/Hardware:
Texas Instruments

Outside Service Firm(s):

Caruther & Gard*(Auditors)*
Palo Alto, CA

Western Cleverdon*(Group Insurer)*
San Francisco, CA

Wells Fargo Bank*(Major Banking Relationship)*
Palo Alto, CA

ALADDIN INDUSTRIES, INCORPORATED
703 Murfreesboro Rd.
Nashville, TN 37210
Tel.: 800-456-1233 **DE**
Fax: 615-748-3030
Approx.Sls.: $200,000,000
Emp.: 1,200
Fiscal Year-end: 4/30/91
Mfr. of Kerosene Lamps, Thermosware, Lunch Kits, Institutional Food Service Equipment & Insulated Jugs
S.I.C.: 3231; 3589; 3086; 3499
Frederick R. Meyer *(Chm. Bd. & Pres.)*
J.C. Crowley *(V.P.-Fin. & Chief Fin. Officer)*
John Parker *(V.P.-Sls. & Mktg.)*
Bill Cooper *(V.P.-Opers.)*
John Bridges *(V.P.-Res. & Devel.)*
Michael Schimmel *(Dir.-Mktg., Consumer Prods. Div.)*
Al Ragland *(Dir.-Pur.)*
Tom Bryant *(Dir.-Human Resources)*
Jim Viviano *(Dir.-Information Services)*

No. of Mfg. Plants/Facilities: 1
No. of U.S. Offices: 1
No. of Foreign Offices: 3

Computer Systems/Hardware:
IBM 4341

Outside Service Firm(s):

Arthur Andersen & Co.*(Auditors)*
Third Natl. Fin. Cntr., 424 Church St., Ste. 1100
Nashville, TN 37219

Third National Bank*(Major Banking Relationship)*
Nashville, TN

Division:

Consumer Products Division **(1)**
703 Murfreesboro Rd.
Nashville, TN 37210
Tel.: 615-748-3000
Mfr. of Thermosware, Kerosene Lamps, Lunch Kits
S.I.C.: 3645

Subsidiaries:

Aladdin Resources, Inc. **(1)**
703 Murfreesboro Rd.
Nashville, TN 37210
Tel.: 615-748-3000 (100%)
Metrocenter Land Developer
S.I.C.: 6552
F.R. Meyer *(Chm. Bd.)*

Aladdin Synergetics, Inc. **(1)**
555 Mariott Dr., Ste. 400
Nashville, TN 37210
Tel.: 615-748-3700
Tel.: 800-888-8018 (100%)
Fax: 615-748-3634
Emp.: 600
Fiscal Year-end: 4/30/92
Mfr. of Insulated Food Service Systems for Use by Hospitals, Correctional Facilities, Institutions
S.I.C.: 3589
R.K. Oakes *(Pres.)*
Richard Necorvo *(Controller)*
Martin Rothschild *(V.P.-Mktg.-Healthcare)*
Mike Allen *(Dir.-Sls. & Mktg.-C Stores, Airlines & New Business)*
Heiner Wischhusen *(Dir.-Intl.)*
Carol Koenig *(Mktg. Mgr.-Healthcare)*

Non-U.S. Holdings:

Aladdin Industries Pty. Ltd. **(1)**
P.O. Box 22
Westgate, N.S.W. 2048, Australia
Tel.: 61-2-51-2826
Mfr. of Thermos Ware, Lunch Kits, Food Service Equip.
S.I.C.: 3585
Graham Close *(Chief Oper. Officer)*

Aladdin International Corporation (UK) **(1)**
Unit 4, Polychrome Estate, Sandown Rd., Watford, Hertfordshire WD2 4XD, United Kingdom
Thermosware
S.I.C.: 3499
M. Willik *(Mng. Dir.)*

Aladdin International Corp. S.A.R.L. **(1)**
5 Rue de LaCroix Martre 91120
Palaiseau, France
Mfr. Thermosware
S.I.C.: 3499

ALADDIN MILLS INC.
2001 Antioch Rd.
Dalton, GA 30721
Tel.: 706-277-1100
Year Founded: 1958
Approx.Sls.: $211,000,000
Emp.: 1,670
Mfr. of Carpets & Rugs
S.I.C.: 2273
Alan S. Lorberbaum *(Pres.)*
Jack Sharp *(Treas.)*

ALADDIN PETROLEUM CORPORATION
221 S. Broadway, Ste. 809
Wichita, KS 67202
Tel.: 316-265-9602
Fax: 316-265-7014
Year Founded: 1927
Approx.Sls.: $10,000,000
Emp.: 25
Crude Oil Production & Operation
S.I.C.: 1311
Robert Bruce *(Pres.)*
Thomas Richardson *(V.P., Sec., Treas. & Controller)*

ALAMO GROUP, INC.
1502 E. Walnut
Seguin, TX 78155
Tel.: 210-379-1480 **DE**
Telex: 754674
Fax: 210-379-4363
Year Founded: 1965
Sales Range: $40-59 Million
Emp.: 400
Fiscal Year-end: 12/31/91
Manufacturer Industrial & Agricultural Mowing Equipment & Accessories
S.I.C.: 3523
Don Douglass *(Chm. Bd.)*
Oran Logan *(Pres. & Chief Oper. Officer)*
John Detter *(V.P.)*
John Fisher *(V.P.-Engrng.)*
Robert George *(V.P.-Admin.)*
Marvin Morris *(V.P.-Mktg.)*
George Murphy *(V.P.-Oper.)*
Joe Pryor *(Gen. Counsel & Tech. Affairs Dir.)*
Terry Stevens *(Dir.-Data Processing)*
Keith Vinyard *(Mgr.-Parts Distr.)*
Principal(s):
Don Douglass
Oran Logan

No. of Mfg. Plants/Facilities: 4
No. of U.S. Offices: 4

Computer Systems/Hardware:
Prime; IBM PC

Outside Service Firm(s):

Ernst & Young*(Auditors)*
1 Houston Ctr., 1200 McKinney
Houston, TX 77002
Tel.: 713-750-1500

First City Bank of Houston*(Major Banking Relationship)*
10001 Main St.
Houston, TX 77002
Tel.: 713-658-6011

Subsidiaries:

Alamo Group, Inc. **(1)**
500 Shawnut
La Grange, IL 60525
Tel.: 708-354-7220
Emp.: 80
Industrial Flail & Hammer Knife Mowers
S.I.C.: 3523
Marvin Morris *(V.P.-Mktg.)*
Edward Highley *(Sec.)*
Marie Stroud *(Acctg. Mgr.)*
Natt Ricker *(Trainer & Adv. Mgr.)*

BMB Company **(1)**
N. Vermont at 9th
Holton, KS 66436
Tel.: 913-364-2186
Emp.: 100
S.I.C.: 3523
Tim Gardner *(Plant Mgr.)*

Triumph Machine Co. **(1)**
P.O. Box 610
Hackettstown, NJ 07840
Tel.: 201-852-0222
Emp.: 40
S.I.C.: 3523
Doug Heel *(Opers. Mgr.)*

ALAMO INDUSTRIAL GROUP
P.O. Box 231
San Antonio, TX 78291-0231
Tel.: 210-223-6161
Tel.: 800-292-7817 **TX**
Fax: 210-978-8351
Year Founded: 1878
Approx.Sls.: $53,000,000
Emp.: 485
Import Export
Industrial Supplies, Fabricating & Contractors Equipment, Machinery; Steel Service Center, Foundry & Machine Shop, Fabricated Steel
S.I.C.: 5085; 3441; 3559; 3569; 5051; 5084
Anthony H. Koch *(Chm. Bd. & Pres.)*
Edward R. Lenz *(Sr. V.P.-Distr.)*
John Gaubatz *(V.P.-Fabrication)*
Steven R. Smith *(V.P.-Foundry)*
Mark Sobotik *(V.P. & Controller)*
Keith Barnett *(Dir.-Purch.)*
Greg English *(Dir.-Human Res.)*
Bill Long *(Dir.-Leasing)*
Teresa Ochoa *(Dir.-Data Proc.)*
Joe Riveria *(Dir.-Import)*
John Traeger *(Dir.-Qual. Control)*
Richard Ochoa *(Mgr.-Sls.)*
James Teat *(Mgr.-Mktg.)*

No. of Mfg. Plants/Facilities: 2
No. of U.S. Offices: 7

Outside Service Firm(s):

Mendez & Boysen*(Auditors)*
San Antonio, TX

Adams & Flake*(Legal Firm)*
San Antonio, TX

Barclays Business Credit, Inc.*(Major Banking Relationship)*
3811 Turtle Creek, Ste. 2100
Dallas, TX 75219

Subsidiary:

Alamo Iron Works **(1)**
P.O. Box 231
San Antonio, TX 78291
Tel.: 210-223-6161
Fax: 210-978-8351
Industrial Supplies, Fabricating & Contractors Equipment, Machinery; Steel Service Center, Foundry & Machine Shop, Fabricated Steel
S.I.C.: 3441; 3559; 3569; 5051; 5084; 5085
Anthony H. Koch *(Chm. Bd. & Pres.)*
Mark Sobotic *(V.P.-Fin.)*
Richard Ochoa *(Mgr.-Sls.)*
James Teat *(Mgr.-Mktg.)*

THE ALAMO LEARNING SYSTEMS, INC.
3160 Crow Canyon Rd., Ste. 250
San Ramon, CA 94583
Tel.: 510-277-1818
Fax: 510-277-1919
Year Founded: 1979
Sales Range: $10-19 Million
Emp.: 50
Export
Innovation & Rational Thinking Training Programs for Organization Development
S.I.C.: 8742; 7389
Guy A. Hale *(Chm. Bd., Pres. & Chief Exec. Officer)*
Brandt Brooksby *(Chief Fin. Officer)*
Judy Axtman *(Office Mgr.)*

No. of U.S. Offices: 7

Computer Systems/Hardware:
IBM

Outside Service Firm(s):

Arthur Andersen & Co.*(Auditors)*
Columbus, OH

Blanding, Boyer, Ryan*(Auditors)*
San Francisco, CA

First Farwest*(Group Insurer)*
San Francisco, CA

Sloss & Becker*(Legal Firm)*
San Francisco, CA

Bank of America*(Major Banking Relationship)*
3100 Crow Canyon Place
San Ramon, CA 94583

Security Pacific National Bank*(Major Banking Relationship)*
District Trust Office
San Francisco, CA 94108
Tel.: 415-445-4175

ALAMO RENT-A-CAR INC.
110 S.E. 6th St.
Fort Lauderdale, FL 33301
Mailing Address:
P.O. Box 22776
Ft. Lauderdale, FL 33335
Tel.: 305-522-0000
Fax: 305-527-4758
Year Founded: 1976
Approx.Sls.: $900,000,000
Emp.: 4,900
Automobile Rentals
S.I.C.: 7514
Michael S. Egan *(Chm. Bd. & Chief Exec. Officer)*
Charles Platt *(Pres. & Chief Oper. Officer)*
MacDonald Clark *(Exec. V.P.)*
Karen Beard *(V.P.-Sls.)*
Donald Moonjian *(V.P.-Mktg.)*
Candida H. Cremona *(Exec. Dir.-Adv.)*

Computer Systems/Hardware:
IBM System 36

Outside Service Firm(s):

KPMG Peat Marwick*(Auditors)*
P.O. Box 3031, 111 N. Orange Ave., Suite 1600
Orlando, FL 32802
Tel.: 407-423-3426

Sun Bank, N.A.*(Major Banking Relationship)*
200 S. Orange Ave.
Orlando, FL 32802
Tel.: 407-237-4899
Fax: 407-237-6704

ALAN LITHOGRAPH, INC.
550 N. Oak St.
Inglewood, CA 90302
Tel.: 310-330-3800 **CA**
Fax: 310-412-7134
Year Founded: 1958
Sales Range: $20-39 Million
Emp.: 130
Fiscal Year-end: 12/30/90
Export
Lithographic Printing
S.I.C.: 2752
Jerry Waxman *(Pres.)*
Steven Henry *(V.P.-Sls.)*
Harold Huttas *(V.P.)*
Irving Geller *(V.P.)*

No. of Mfg. Plants/Facilities: 1
No. of U.S. Offices: 1

Computer Systems/Hardware:
Hagen (NCR)

Outside Service Firm(s):

Martin & Algaze*(Auditors)*
Los Angeles, CA

ALARON INC.
185 Park St.
Troy, MI 48083
Mailing Address:
P.O. Box 550
Troy, MI 48099
Tel.: 313-585-8400 **MI**
Fax: 313-524-2668
Year Founded: 1959
Assets: $5,000,000
Liabilities: $2,500,000
Net Worth: $2,500,000
Approx.Sls.: $30,000,000
Emp.: 74
Import Export
Wholesale Distributor of Home Electronics, Televisions, Radios, Musical Instruments (Toytronics), Telephones, Quartz Clocks
S.I.C.: 5064
Bernard Klein *(Chm. Bd., Sec. & Treas.)*
Emery I. Klein *(Pres.)*
Thomas Bishop *(Exec. V.P.)*
Ronald A. Klein *(V.P.)*
Thomas Mandel *(V.P.-Opers.)*
Jerry Mikovich *(V.P.-Fin.)*
Terry Sexton *(V.P.-Sls.)*
Bob Stoewsand *(V.P.-Sls. Admin.)*
Principal(s):
Bernard Klein
Emery I. Klein
Thomas Bishop

No. of U.S. Offices: 1
No. of Foreign Offices: 2

Computer Systems/Hardware:
IBM System 36

Outside Service Firm(s):

BDO Seidman*(Auditors)*
Detroit, MI

First of America Bank*(International Bank Affiliate)*
Detroit, MI

Plotkin, Yolles, Siegel, Schultz & Polk*(Legal Firm)*
Detroit, MI

Subsidiary:

Alaron Electronics Far East Ltd., Hong Kong **(1)**
Silvercord Tower II, 30 Canton Rd., Suite 1402
Kowloon, Hong Kong
Tel.: 3-375-7448
Fax: 852-375-7445
Emp.: 13
Electronics Trading Co.
S.I.C.: 5064
H.K. Law *(Gen. Mgr.)*

ALASKA INDUSTRIAL HARDWARE INC.
2192 Viking Dr.
Anchorage, AK 99501
Tel.: 907-276-7201 **AK**
Fax: 907-258-3054
Year Founded: 1959
Assets: $15,889,000
Liabilities: $8,443,000
Net Worth: $7,446,000
Approx.Sls.: $24,000,000
Emp.: 130
Fiscal Year-end: 12/31/91
Wholesale & Retail of Hardware
S.I.C.: 5072; 5251
Josef F. Boehm *(Pres. & Chief Oper. Officer)*
Jeff C. Bartenstein *(Sec., Treas. & Controller)*
Principal(s):
Josef F. Boehm

Computer Systems/Hardware:
McDonnell Douglas Series 18/600

Outside Service Firm(s):

KPMG Peat Marwick*(Auditors)*
1600 Market St.
Philadelphia, PA 19103
Tel.: 215-299-3100

National Bank of Alaska*(Major Banking Relationship)*
P.O. Box 100600,
Anchorage, AK 99510-0600

Divisions:

Alaska Tool & Equipment Service **(1)**
3207 Arctic Blvd.
Anchorage, AK 99503
Tel.: 907-562-6151 (100%)
Repair of Tools & Equipment
S.I.C.: 7699

General Hardware Distributors **(1)**
2192 Viking Dr.
Anchorage, AK 99501
Tel.: 907-279-6691 (100%)
Wholesale of Hardware
S.I.C.: 5072
Josef F. Boehm *(Pres.)*

ALASKA PULP CORPORATION
(Sub. of Alaska Pulp Co., Ltd., Tokyo, Japan)
1301 Fifth Ave, Ste. 3000
Seattle, WA 98101
Tel.: 206-682-6400 **AK**
Fax: 206-625-9716
Year Founded: 1953
Approx.Sls.: $120,000,000
Emp.: 400
Mfr. of Pulp Produced From Wood Base
S.I.C.: 2611
George S. Ishlyama *(Pres., Located in Tokyo)*
Frank Roppel *(Exec. V.P.)*
Dennis Huse *(V.P.-Fin.)*

Outside Service Firm(s):

Security Pacific Bank Washington N.A.*(Major Banking Relationship)*
P.O. Box 3966,
Seattle, WA 98124

ALASKAN COPPER COMPANIES
3223 6th Ave., S.
Seattle, WA 98134
Tel.: 206-623-5800
Fax: 206-382-7335
Year Founded: 1913
Sales Range: $80-99 Million
Emp.: 450
Distributor Of Corrosion-Resisting Metals; Manufacture Of Stainless Steel & Copper Nickel Pipe & Fittings
S.I.C.: 5039; 3443; 5051
William M. Rosen *(Chm. Bd.)*
Kermit Rosen *(Pres.)*
Brian M. Lucarelli *(Comptroller)*
Alan J. Rosen *(Treas.)*
Douglas C. Rosen *(Sec.)*
H. Troeh *(Mgr.-Portland)*
Principal(s):
Rosen Family

Outside Service Firm(s):

Ernst & Young*(Auditors)*
999 Third Av., Ste. 3500
Seattle, WA 98104
Tel.: 206-621-1800
Fax: 206-682-1234

Bogle & Gates*(Legal Firm)*
Two Union Square, 601 Union St.
Seattle, WA 98101-2322
Tel.: 206-682-5151

Seattle First National Bank*(Major Banking Relationship)*
P.O. Box 24186
Seattle, WA 98124
Tel.: 206-583-7677

Division:

Alaskan Copper Companies **(1)**
P.O. Box 5067,
Portland, OR 97208

ALATEC PRODUCTS, INC.
12747 Saticoy St.
North Hollywood, CA 91605
Tel.: 818-764-5600
Fax: 818-503-0064
Year Founded: 1972
Approx.Sls.: $22,000,000
Emp.: 180
Industrial Fasteners
S.I.C.: 5085
Donald A. List *(Pres.)*
Stan Fitch *(V.P.)*
Ruth List *(Sec. & Treas.)*

Outside Service Firm(s):

Ostrow, Bowman & Firestone*(Auditors)*
Los Angeles, CA

Mitsui Manufacturers Bank*(Major Banking Relationship)*
Los Angeles, CA

ALBA FORWARDING CO., INC.
One Exchange Place, Ste. 501
Jersey City, NJ 07302
Tel.: 201-435-7050
Fax: 201-435-5650
Year Founded: 1949
Approx.Sls.: $70,000,000
Emp.: 40
International Freight Forwarder & Custom House Broker
S.I.C.: 4731
Stanford J. Lesser *(Pres.)*
Raymond I. Hasson *(Exec. V.P.)*
Robert A. Lesser *(V.P.-Imports)*

Outside Service Firm(s):

Bloom, Hochberg & Co.*(Auditors)*
New York, NY

Chemical Bank*(Major Banking Relationship)*
450 West 33rd St.
New York, NY 10001
Tel.: 212-613-7197
Fax: 212-947-7628

Subsidiaries:

Alba Forwarding Co., Inc. **(1)**
147-39 175th St.
Jamaica, NY 11434
Tel.: 718-656-7470
Fax: 718-917-6404
Emp.: 10
InternationalFreight forwarder & Custom House Broker
S.I.C.: 4731

Alba Forwarding Co., Inc. **(1)**
1801 N.W. 82nd Ave.
Miami, FL 33126
Tel.: 305-593-8322
Fax: 305-593-8175
Emp.: 3
International Freight Forwarder & Custom House Broker
S.I.C.: 4731

ALBAN TRACTOR CO. INC.
8531 Pulaski Hwy.
Baltimore, MD 21237
Mailing Address:
P.O. Box 9595
Baltimore, MD 21237
Tel.: 301-686-7777
Fax: 301-686-3729
Sales Range: $80-99 Million
Emp.: 400
Tractor Sls. & Service
S.I.C.: 5082; 5084; 7699
James C. Alban, III *(Pres.)*
Linda Church *(V.P.-Pur.)*
M.K. Mudge *(V.P.-Sls.)*
Mary Walsh *(V.P.-Mktg.)*
C.P. Witmer *(V.P.-Parts & Service)*
George Wolbert *(V.P.-Fin.)*
Principal(s):
James C. Alban, III

Computer Systems/Hardware:
Sperry 1100-71/E1

Outside Service Firm(s):

C. W. Amos & Co.*(Auditors)*
2 N. Charles St.
Baltimore, MD 21201
Tel.: 410-727-5341

Venable, Baetjer & Howard*(Legal Firm)*
1800 Mercantile Bank Bldg., 2 Hopkins Plaza
Baltimore, MD 21201
Tel.: 410-244-7400

First National Bank of Maryland*(Major Banking Relationship)*
25 S. Charles St.
Baltimore, MD 21201
Tel.: 410-244-4025

J. S. ALBERICI CONSTRUCTION CO., INC.
(Sub. of Alberici Corp.-A Holding Co.)
2150 Kienlen Ave.
Saint Louis, MO 63121-5592
Tel.: 314-261-2611 **MO**
Telex: 44-2438
Fax: 314-261-4225
Year Founded: 1946
Assets: $100,000,000
Liabilities: $75,000,000
Net Worth: $25,000,000
Approx.Sls.: $350,000,000
Emp.: 1,000
Fiscal Year-end: 12/31/91
General Building & Heavy Construction
S.I.C.: 1541; 1542
Gabriel J. Alberici *(Chm. Bd. & Treas.)*
Edward L. Calcaterra *(Pres.)*
John S. Alberici *(Chief Fin. Officer, Sr. V.P. & Sec.)*
John C. Bartnett *(V.P.-Human Resources)*
Guy E. Jester *(V.P.-Corp. Plng.)*
Herman Woodcock *(Controller)*
Frank Kropiunik *(Dir.-Mngmt. Info. Systems)*
Robert McCoole *(Dir.-Mktg. & Adv.)*
Steven Stawizynski *(Dir.-Pur.)*
George VanHoogstraat *(Office Mgr.)*
Principal(s):
Gabriel J. Alberici
Edward L. Calcaterra
John S. Alberici

No. of Mfg. Plants/Facilities: 1
No. of U.S. Offices: 1

Computer Systems/Hardware:
Prime 6350, IBM AS-400

Outside Service Firm(s):

Wolfe Nilges Nahorski*(Auditors)*
St. Louis, MO

Aetna Surety & Casualty*(Group Insurer)*
St. Louis, MO

Metropolitan Life Insurance Co.*(Group Insurer)*
One Madison Ave.
New York, NY 10010-3690
Tel.: 215-578-9292

Millar, Schaefer & Hoffmann*(Legal Firm)*
St. Louis, MO

Boatmen's National Bank*(Major Banking Relationship)*
800 Market St.
St. Louis, MO 63166
Tel.: 314-554-6000

Subsidiaries:

General Installation Co. **(1)**
2500 Drilling Dr.
Maryland Heights, MO 63043
Tel.: 314-291-5330

Gunther Nash Mining Constr. **(1)**
2150 Kienlen
Saint Louis, MO 63121
Tel.: 314-261-4111

J. H. Hudson Construction Co. **(1)**
P.O. Box 1983
Greenville, NC 27834
Tel.: 919-758-2138

MIKE ALBERT LEASING, INC.
10340 Evendale Dr.
Cincinnati, OH 45241
Tel.: 513-563-1400 **OH**
Fax: 513-563-9316
Year Founded: 1957
Sales Range: $100-499 Million
Emp.: 200
Automobile Leasing
S.I.C.: 7515
Robert Betagole *(Pres.)*
John Betagole *(V.P.)*
Stuart Lowitz *(V.P.)*
Donald Miller *(V.P.)*
Robert E. Ryan, Jr. *(V.P.-Mktg.)*
Patrick Stull *(V.P.)*
Principal(s):
Robert Betagole

Computer Systems/Hardware:
IBM

Outside Service Firm(s):

Aronowitz, Chaiken & Hardesty*(Auditors)*
Cincinnati, OH

Arthur Andersen & Co.*(Auditors)*
425 Walnut St.
Cincinnati, OH 45202
Tel.: 513-381-6900

Katz, Teller, Brant & Hild*(Legal Firm)*
Cincinnati, OH

Fifth Third Bank*(Major Banking Relationship)*
Corporate Trust Services, 38 Fountain Square Plaza
Cincinnati, OH 45263

R.L. ALBERT & SON, INC.
19 W. Elm St.
Greenwich, CT 06830
Tel.: 203-622-8655
Fax: 203-622-7454
Year Founded: 1915
Approx.Sls.: $25,000,000
Emp.: 23
Fiscal Year-end: 3/31/90
Importer & Distributor of Confections
S.I.C.: 5145; 5149
Larry Albert *(Pres.)*
Robert Katz *(Gen. Mgr.)*
Insulinde Albert *(Treas. & Sec.)*

Outside Service Firm(s):

Connecticut Bank & Trust*(Major Banking Relationship)*
One Constitution Plaza,
Hartford, CT 06115

THE FRED W. ALBRECHT GROCERY CO.
2700 Gilchrist Rd.
Akron, OH 44305
Mailing Address:
P.O. Box 1910
Akron, OH 44309
Tel.: 216-733-2861
Fax: 216-733-8782
Year Founded: 1891
Assets: $77,740,500
Liabilities: $52,382,700
Net Worth: $25,357,800
Approx.Sls.: $384,000,000
Emp.: 3,200
Wholesale Food & Drugs
S.I.C.: 5411; 5141; 5912; 5122; 5331
Fred I. Albrecht *(Chm. Bd.)*
Steven Albrecht *(Pres. & Chief Exec. Officer)*
James P. Nilsen *(Chief Fin. Officer & Treas.)*
David A. Stanek *(V.P.-Mngmt. Info. Systems)*
Samuel H. Stites *(V.P.-Pur.)*
William Selle *(Controller)*
Ivan Albrecht *(Dir.-Gilcrest Storage)*
Joe Parsons *(Dir.- Real Estate)*
Principal(s):
Fred I. Albrecht

No. of Mfg. Plants/Facilities: 32

Computer Systems/Hardware:
IBM 4381

Outside Service Firm(s):

Deloitte & Touche*(Auditors)*
One Cascade Plaza, Ste. 1600
Akron, OH 44303-1187
Tel.: 216-253-2022

Brouse & McDowell*(Legal Firm)*
500 First National Tower
Akron, OH 4308
Tel.: 216-535-5711

Bank One*(Major Banking Relationship)*
Akron, OH

Subsidiary:

Gilcrest Storage **(1)**
2700 Gilcrest Rd.
Akron, OH 44305
Tel.: 216-733-2861 (100%)
Emp.: 3,130
Ivan Albrecht *(Pres.)*

ALCO HEALTH SERVICES CORPORATION
300 Chester Field Pkwy.
Malvern, PA 19355
Mailing Address:
P.O. Box 959
Valley Forge, PA 19482
Tel.: 215-296-4480 **DE**
Fax: 215-647-0141
Year Founded: 1985
Assets: $782,357,000
Earnings: ($14,532,000)
Liabilities: $753,843,000
Net Worth: $28,514,000
Approx.Rev.: $2,827,161,000
Emp.: 2,323
Fiscal Year-end: 9/30/91
Distribution of Pharmaceutical Products; Health & Beauty Aids, Cosmetics & Fragrances; Durable Medical Equipment & Home Health Care Supplies; Medical & Surgical Products, Sundries & General Merchandise to Drugstores, Hospitals, Mass Merchandisers, Nursing Homes, Physicians, Clinics & Other Commercial Customers
S.I.C.: 5122; 5100
John F. McNamara *(Chm. Bd., Pres. & Chief Exec. Officer)*
Kenneth M. Zoeller *(V.P. & Treas.)*
Teresa T. Ciccotelli *(V.P., Legal Counsel & Sec.)*
Robert D. Gregory *(V.P.-Human Resources)*
John A. Kurcik, Jr. *(V.P. & Controller)*
Robert E. McHugh *(V.P.-Mktg.)*
David M. Flowers *(Grp. Pres.-Eastern Region)*
R. David Yost *(Grp. Pres.-Central Region)*
M. Curtis Young *(Mgr.-Corp. Assets)*
Kathleen K. Rittenhouse *(Mgr.-Corp. Risk & Benefits)*

Outside Service Firm(s):

Ernst & Young*(Auditors)*
1800 John F. Kennedy Blvd.
Philadelphia, PA 19103-7499
Tel.: 215-864-3300

Dechert, Price & Rhoads*(Legal Firm)*
477 Madison Ave.
New York, NY 10022
Tel.: 212-326-2041
Fax: 212-308-2041

Philadelphia National Bank*(Major Banking Relationship)*
Philadelphia, PA

Divisions:

Alco Health Services Corp.-Joplin Div. **(1)**
5th St. & Grand Ave.
Joplin, MO 64801
Tel.: 417-623-2302
Fax: 417-623-4136
Wholesale Distribution of Pharmaceutical Products
S.I.C.: 5122; 5100
B. Larry Hall *(Gen. Mgr.)*

Alco Health Services Corp.-Minneapolis **(1)**
6810 Shady Oak Rd.
Eden Prairie, MN 55344
Tel.: 612-941-9550
Fax: 612-941-9556
Wholesale Distribution of Pharmaceutical Products
S.I.C.: 5122; 5100
Richard Koppen *(Gen. Mgr.)*

Alco Health Services Corp.-Paducah Div. **(1)**
322 N. Third St.
Paducah, KY 42001-0028
Tel.: 502-444-7300
Fax: 502-444-7047
Wholesale Distribution of Pharmaceutical Products
S.I.C.: 5122; 5100
Gary M. Davis *(Reg. V.P. & Gen. Mgr.)*
Terry Haas *(Mgr.-Pur.)*

Alco Health Services Corp.-Sioux Falls Div. **(1)**
1414 "M" Ave.
Sioux Falls, SD 57104
Tel.: 605-336-3150
Fax: 605-335-7857
Wholesale Distr. of Pharmaceutical Products
S.I.C.: 5122; 5100
Dennis Lindell *(Gen. Mgr.)*

Alco Health Services Corporation-Chattanooga Div. **(1)**
200 N. Holly St.
Chattanooga, TN 34704
Tel.: 615-698-4426
Fax: 615-698-0519
Emp.: 120
Wholesale Distribution of Pharmaceutical & Health Care Products
S.I.C.: 5122; 5100
Frank F. Duff, Jr. *(V.P. & Gen. Mgr.)*

Alco Health Services Corporation-Columbus Div. **(1)**
1200 E. 5th Ave.
Columbus, OH 43219
Tel.: 614-253-2721
Fax: 614-253-5124
Emp.: 415
Wholesale Distribution of Pharmaceutical Products
S.I.C.: 5122; 5100
Gregory J. Zurlage *(Reg. V.P. & Gen. Mgr.)*

Alco Health Services Corporation—(Continued)

Alco Health Services Corporation-Council Bluffs Div. **(1)**
3319 Nebraska Ave.
Council Bluffs, IA 51501
Tel.: 712-323-7511
Fax: 712-323-0019
Wholesale Distribution of Pharmaceutical Products
S.I.C.: 5122; 5100

Alco Health Services Corporation-Johnson City Div. **(1)**
410 Princeton Rd.
Johnson City, TN 37602
Tel.: 615-282-1271
Fax: 615-283-4339
Wholesale Distribution of Pharmaceutical Products
S.I.C.: 5122; 5100
Kathy Gage *(Gen. Mgr.)*

Alco Health Services Corporation-Louisville Div. **(1)**
244 E. Woodlawn Ave.
Louisville, KY 40214
Tel.: 502-363-2631
Fax: 502-368-0441
Wholesale Distr. of Pharmaceutical Products
S.I.C.: 5122; 5100
Joe Meiman *(Gen. Mgr.)*

Alco Health Services Corporation-Lynchburg Div. **(1)**
9221 Timberland Rd.
Lynchburg, VA 24506
Tel.: 804-230-6971
Fax: 804-582-4755
Emp.: 200
Wholesale Distribution of Pharmaceutical & Health Care Products
S.I.C.: 5122; 5100
Phil Gibson *(Reg. V.P.)*

Alco Health Services Corporation-Mishawaka Div. **(1)**
1655 E. 12th St.
Mishawaka, IN 46544
Tel.: 219-259-3784
Fax: 219-255-7699
Wholesale Distribution of Pharmaceutical Products
S.I.C.: 5122; 5100
Daniel Wilhelm *(Pres.)*

Alco Health Services Corporation-Tiffin Div. **(1)**
Airport Industry Pk., 1780 S. County Rd. One
Tiffin, OH 44883
Tel.: 419-447-7252
Fax: 419-447-6673
Wholesale Distribution of Pharmaceutical Products
S.I.C.: 5122; 5100
Robert W. Meyer *(Reg. V.P.)*
Carol Smith *(Dir.-Human Resources)*

Alco Health Services Corporation-Toledo Div. **(1)**
3145 Nebraska Ave.
Toledo, OH 43607
Tel.: 419-531-2881
Fax: 419-531-7694
Wholesale Distribution of Pharmaceutical Products
S.I.C.: 5122; 5100
Thomas P. Connolly *(V.P.)*

Alco Health Services Corporation-Valdosta Div. **(1)**
311 W. Central Ave.
Valdosta, GA 31601
Tel.: 912-245-6900
Fax: 912-245-6907
Wholesale Distribution of Pharmaceutical Products
S.I.C.: 5122; 5100
David Farley *(V.P. & Gen. Mgr.)*

Alco Health Services Northeast-Harrisburg **(1)**
600 S. 17th St.
Harrisburg, PA 17104
Tel.: 717-236-9071
Fax: 717-236-5296
Wholesale Distribution of Pharmaceutical Products
S.I.C.: 5122; 5100

Alco Health Services Northeast-Philadelphia **(1)**
1011 W. Butler St.
Philadelphia, PA 19140
Tel.: 215-223-9000
Fax: 215-229-6425
Emp.: 400
Wholesale Distribution of Pharmaceutical Products
S.I.C.: 5122; 5100
Donald E. Steinbacher *(Reg. V.P.)*

Alco Health Services Northeast-Thorofare **(1)**
100 Friars Ln.
Thorofare, NJ 08086
Tel.: 609-848-3400
Fax: 609-848-1884
Wholesale Distribution of Pharmaceutical Products
S.I.C.: 5122; 5100

Family Pharmacy General Office **(1)**
3220 Cleveland Ave.
Columbus, OH 43224
Tel.: 614-261-7347
Fax: 614-261-7630
Voluntary Organization Providing Member Drugstores With Services Encompassing All Aspects of Their Operations: Advertising, Shipping & Other Services
S.I.C.: 8742; 7389; 5122
Warren Howe *(V.P. & Gen. Mgr.)*
Timothy Doyle *(Dir.-Mktg. Services)*

Rita-Ann Distributors **(1)**
901 Curtain Ave.
Baltimore, MD 21218
Tel.: 410-876-2506
Distribution of Cosmetics & Personal Care Products
S.I.C.: 5122
David C. Carter *(Sr. V.P. & Gen. Mgr.)*

Subsidiary:

Health Services Plus, Inc. **(1)**
5080 Sinclair Rd., Ste. 305
Columbus, OH 43229
Tel.: 614-433-9997
Fax: 614-433-7188
Administrative Services: Claims Processing, Electronic Claims Networking, Drug Utilization Reporting Services & TPA In the Area of Managed Care, Including HMOs & PPOs
S.I.C.: 8742; 7389
Charles F. Schmidt *(Pres.)*

ALCO INDUSTRIES, INC.
P.O. Box 937
Valley Forge, PA 19482
Tel.: 215-666-0930
Fax: 215-666-0752
Year Founded: 1983
Approx.Sls.: $225,000,000
Emp.: 2,173
Fiscal Year-end: 9/30/91
Mfrs. Chemical, Rubber, Plastic & Metal Products
S.I.C.: 2899; 3069; 3089; 3499; 3469
George E. Smith *(Pres. & Chief Exec. Officer)*
Thomas E. Betscher *(V.P.-Opers.)*
Bette J. Walters *(V.P. & Gen. Counsel)*
John E. Young *(V.P.-Fin. & Chief Fin. Officer)*

Computer Systems/Hardware:
IBM 3081

Outside Service Firm(s):

Ernst & Young*(Auditors)*
1800 John F. Kennedy Blvd.
Philadelphia, PA 19103-7499
Tel.: 215-864-3300

Bank One*(Major Banking Relationship)*
Columbus, OH

Division:

Miether Bearing Products, Inc. **(1)**
8720 W. County Rd.
Odessa, TX 79764
Tel.: 915-366-3838
Tel.: 800-643-8437
Fax: 915-683-6608
Approx.Sls.: $10,000,000
Emp.: 110
Fiscal Year-end: 9/30/91
Export
Computer Systems/Hardware:
IBM
Mfr. Pillowblock Housings & Accessories, Repair Large Machinery in the Oil Field & Power Generating Industries
S.I.C.: 3562
Robert W. Espen *(Pres.)*
David Tredinnick *(Natl. Sls. Mgr.)*

Subsidiaries:

McDowell Mfg. Co. **(1)**
P.O. Box 665,
Du Bois, PA 15801
Tel.: 814-371-6550
Fax: 814-371-7110
Approx.Sls.: $14,000,000
Emp.: 250
Export
Deep Draw Stamping & Tubular Thread Protectors, Pressure Cylinders, Fuse Liners
S.I.C.: 3469
James Onoratti *(Pres.)*
Robert Morse *(Controller)*
Ned Brewer *(Gen. Sls. Mgr.)*
Paul Aiken *(Pur. Agent)*

Miller Chemical & Fertilizer Corp. **(1)**
Radio Road
Hanover, PA 17331
Tel.: 717-632-8921
Tel.: 800-233-2040
Fax: 717-632-4581
Approx.Sls.: $18,000,000
Emp.: 62
Fiscal Year-end: 9/30/92
Import Export
Computer Systems/Hardware:
IBM System 36
Fertilizers, Pesticides
S.I.C.: 2873; 2874; 2879
D.E. Fiery *(Pres.)*
C.H. Svec *(Exec. V.P.)*
T.L. Way *(V.P.-Fin.)*
A.D. Vidyarthi *(V.P.-Mfg.)*
W.S. Felix *(Dir.-Pur.)*

Modern Equipment Co., Inc. **(1)**
P.O. Box 266
Port Washington, WI 53074
Approx.Sls.: $10,000,000
Emp.: 100
Fiscal Year-end: 9/30/90
Mfr. of Foundry Melting & Hot Metal Handling Equip.
S.I.C.: 3443; 3536; 3559; 3569
R.N. Olmstead *(Chm. Bd. & Pres.)*
C.G. Buenger *(Exec. V.P.)*
R.T. Dudek *(V.P. & Pur. Mgr.)*
L.L. Socks *(V.P.-Engrng. Products)*
Christy Mohr *(Personnel Dir.)*
D.A. Donner *(Gen. Sls. Mgr. & Adv. Mgr.)*

ALCOM PRINTING GROUP, INC.
2285 Ave. A
Bethlehem, PA 18017
Tel.: 215-691-5050 **PA**
Fax: 215-861-0565
Approx.Sls.: $15,000,000
Emp.: 250
Commercial Lithograph & Web Printing Computerized Typesetting
S.I.C.: 2752; 2791
Frank Eichman *(Chm. Bd. & Pres.)*
William Coale *(Chief Oper. Officer)*
George Onimus *(V.P.)*
Roland Grietzer *(Controller & Treas.)*
Bob Dugan *(Dir.-Purch.)*
Bob Stefanowski *(Dir.-Quality Control)*
James Lowrie *(Sec.)*

Outside Service Firm(s):

Harold A. Eisenhauer*(Auditors)*
Bethlehem, PA

First Valley Bank*(Major Banking Relationship)*
Bethlehem, PA

ALDAN RUBBER CO.
2701 E. Tioga St.
Philadelphia, PA 19134-6184
Tel.: 215-739-6500
Fax: 215-426-1750
Year Founded: 1909
Approx.Sls.: $22,000,000
Emp.: 200
Export
Mfr. Rubber, Synthetic Rubber & Synthetic Resin Coated Fabrics
S.I.C.: 3069; 2295; 2822
Alan J. Hirsch *(Pres.)*
Donald K. Klumpp *(Exec. V.P.)*
Barry Fleischer *(V.P.-Sls. & Mktg.)*
Jerry Spade *(Dir.-Fin.)*
Dick Hanes *(Dir.-Pur.)*

Outside Service Firm(s):

Margolis & Co.*(Auditors)*
Bala Cynwyd, PA

Fox, Rothschild, O'Brien & Frankel*(Legal Firm)*
2000 Market St., 10th Flr.
Philadelphia, PA 19103
Tel.: 215-299-2012

First Valley Bank*(Major Banking Relationship)*
Bethlehem, PA

ALDEN AUTO PARTS WHOLESALE, INC.
535 Grand Army Hwy.
Somerset, MA 02725
Tel.: 508-673-4233 **MA**
Fax: 508-674-4468
Year Founded: 1955
Approx.Sls.: $17,000,000
Emp.: 100
Wholesale Distributor of Automotive Supplies & Parts
S.I.C.: 5013
Louis Nulman *(Pres. & Chief Exec. Officer)*
Paul Kachapis *(V.P.)*

Outside Service Firm(s):

First Bristol National Bank*(Major Banking Relationship)*
Taunton, MA

THE ALDEN GROUP LTD.
52 Vanderbilt Ave.
New York, NY 10017
Tel.: 212-867-6400 **NY**
Fax: 212-986-5988
Year Founded: 1956
Approx.Billings: $30,000,000
Emp.: 26
Advertising Agency
S.I.C.: 7311
Jack H. Casper *(Chm. Bd., Chief Exec. Officer)*
Sy Ripka *(Pres., Chief Fin. Officer)*
Mary Apesa *(Controller)*
Laura Baddish *(Dir.-Pub. Rels.)*
Gail Huttner *(Dir.-Mktg. Services)*

No. of U.S. Offices: 1

Outside Service Firm(s):

Chase Manhattan Bank, N.A.*(Major Banking Relationship)*
One Chase Manhattan Plaza
New York, NY 10081
Tel.: 212-552-2222
Tel.: 800-526-0801
Fax: 212-552-7175

Subsidiaries:

Alden Advertising Agency, Inc. **(1)**
52 Vanderbilt Ave.
New York, NY 10017
Tel.: 212-867-6400
Fax: 212-986-5988

J.S. Alden Public Relations, Inc. **(1)**
52 Vanderbilt Ave.
New York, NY 10017
Tel.: 212-867-6400
Fax: 212-986-4784

JOHN ALDEN FINANCIAL CORPORATION
7300 Corporate Center Dr.
Miami, FL 33126
Mailing Address:
P.O. Box 020270
Miami, FL 33102
Tel.: 305-470-3100 DE
Fax: 305-470-3009
Year Founded: 1987
Assets: $4,653,323,000
Liabilities: $4,515,262,000
Net Worth: $138,061,000
Sales Range: $1 Billion +
Emp.: 2,494
Fiscal Year-end: 12/31/91
Holding Co.
S.I.C.: 6719
Glendon E. Johnson *(Chm. Bd., Pres. & Chief Exec. Officer)*
Bruce L. Caldwell *(Exec. V.P.-Bus. Devel.)*
Marvin H. Assofsky *(Sr. V.P. & Chief Investment Officer)*
Lloyd E. Gearhart *(Sr. V.P.)*
David A. Olson *(Sr. V.P. & Gen. Counsel)*
Roger L. Rosenberger *(Sr. V.P.-Telemarketing)*
J. Calvin Winter *(Sr. V.P.-Fin. & Corp. Services)*
Lonnie R. Wright *(Sr. V.P.-Fin. Institutions)*
William S. Wilkins *(Sr. V.P.-Information Systems)*
Kerry D. Clemmons *(Sr. V.P.)*
William G. Piel *(V.P. & Treas.)*

Outside Service Firm(s):

Price Waterhouse*(Auditors)*
Southeast Financial Ctr., Ste. 3000
Miami, FL 33131-2330

NationsBank Carolinas*(Major Banking Relationship)*
Henderson, NC

Subsidiary:

John Alden Life Insurance Company **(1)**
7300 Corporate Center Dr.
Miami, FL 33126
Tel.: 305-470-3100
Fax: 305-470-3220
Emp.: 1907
Life & Health Insurance & Annuities
S.I.C.: 6311; 6321
Glendon E. Johnson *(Pres. & Chief Exec. Officer)*

ALDEN SHOE CO., INC.
Taunton St.
Middleboro, MA 02346
Tel.: 508-947-3926
Fax: 508-947-7753
Year Founded: 1884
Emp.: 150
Export
Mfr. of Alden Pedic, Alden New England Shoes
S.I.C.: 3143
Arthur S. Tarlow, Sr. *(Chm. Bd.)*
Arthur S. Tarlow, Jr. *(Pres.)*
Richard Hajjar *(V.P.)*
Thelma H. Tarlow *(Asst. Treas.)*

Outside Service Firm(s):

Grant Thornton*(Auditors)*
53 State St.
Boston, MA 02109
Tel.: 617-723-7900

Fleet National Bank*(Major Banking Relationship)*
Middleboro, MA

ALDI INC.
1200 N. Kirk
Batavia, IL 60510
Tel.: 708-879-8100
Fax: 708-879-8152
Retail Grocery at Warehouse Prices
S.I.C.: 5411
Philip Neally *(Chm. Bd. & Chief Exec. Officer)*
Tim LaBeau *(Pres.)*
Rebecca Chrzanowski *(Sec. & Treas.)*

Computer Systems/Hardware:
IBM-XT

Outside Service Firm(s):

Coopers & Lybrand*(Auditors)*
Aurora, IL

Gardner, Carton & Douglas*(Legal Firm)*
321 N. Clark St., Ste. 3400
Chicago, IL 60610
Tel.: 312-644-3000

The Northern Trust Co.*(Major Banking Relationship)*
50 S. LaSalle St.
Chicago, IL 60675
Tel.: 312-630-6000
Fax: 312-630-6516

ALDINE TECHNOLOGIES
585 Industrial Rd.
Carlstadt, NJ 07072-1611
Tel.: 201-935-5695
Tel.: 800-524-1058 DE
Fax: 201-641-8043
Year Founded: 1921
Sales Range: $10-19 Million
Emp.: 215
Export
Manufacturer & Converter of Non-Woven Material
S.I.C.: 2297
Peter J. Gould *(Pres. & Chief Exec. Officer)*
G.B. Wheeler, III *(Exec. V.P.)*
Charles Noselli *(V.P.-Fin.)*
Liz Fader *(Mgr.-Pub. Rels. & Adv.)*

Principal(s):
Peter J. Gould

No. of Mfg. Plants/Facilities: 1
No. of U.S. Offices: 2
No. of Foreign Offices: 1

Computer Systems/Hardware:
IBM 36

Outside Service Firm(s):

National Westminster Bank plc*(Major Banking Relationship)*
Astor Plaza, 1515 Broadway
New York, NY 10036

Subsidiary:

Lensclean, Inc. **(1)**
585 Industrial Rd.
Carlstadt, NJ 07072-1611
Tel.: 201-932-0044
Fax: 201-641-8043
Assets: $1,000,000
Net Worth: $1,000,000
Approx.Sls.: $10,000,000
Emp.: 25
Fiscal Year-end: 12/31/90
Import Export
Computer Systems/Hardware:
IBM 3X
Mfr. of Lens Tissue & Cleaning Liquids
S.I.C.: 2676; 2834; 2844
Peter J. Gould *(Pres. & Chief Exec. Officer)*
G.B. Wheeler *(Exec. V.P.)*
Charles Noselli *(Chief Fin. Officer)*
B. Blumberg *(Gen. Counsel)*
L. Wilner *(Sec.)*
M. Crane *(Dir.-Engrng.)*
L. Fader *(Dir.-Sls. Promo.)*
D. Gordon *(Dir.-Import & Export)*
D. Isakson *(Dir.-Telecommunications)*
R. McCabe *(Dir.-Sls.)*
S. Scogland *(Dir.-Personnel Training & Devel.)*
K. Shobrun *(Dir.-Quality Control)*
Liz Fader *(Mgr.-Pub. Rels. & Adv.)*
R. Leiber *(Corp. Travel Planner)*

ALEX FOODS, INC.
PO Box 3129, 2125 E. Orangewood
Anaheim, CA 92803
Mailing Address:
P.O. Box 3129,
Anaheim, CA 92803
Tel.: 714-634-8441 CA
Fax: 714-978-3743
Year Founded: 1908
Emp.: 300
Fiscal Year-end: 11/14/92
Mfr. Mexican Food Products: Pinata, Don Miguel, Zippie
S.I.C.: 2099
Steve Charton *(Chm. Bd., Pres & Chief Exec. Officer)*
Mark Brown *(V.P. & Gen. Mgr.)*
Sarlyn Brown *(V.P. & Controller)*
Mike Elliot *(V.P.-Sls.)*
Skip Johnson *(V.P.-Mfr.)*
Don Kimball *(V.P.-Sls. & Mktg.)*
Joyce Hammond *(Dir.-Data Processing)*

No. of Mfg. Plants/Facilities: 2
No. of U.S. Offices: 2

Computer Systems/Hardware:
IBM

Outside Service Firm(s):

Deloitte & Touche*(Auditors)*
695 Town Center Dr.
Costa Mesa, CA 92626
Tel.: 714-436-7100

Wells Fargo Bank*(Major Banking Relationship)*
420 Montgomery St.
San Francisco, CA 94104

ALEX LEE, INC.
120 4th St., S.W.
Hickory, NC 28601
Mailing Address:
P.O. Box 800,
Hickory, NC 28603-0800
Tel.: 704-323-4424
Fax: 704-323-4424
Approx.Sls.: $936,000,000
Emp.: 4,000
Fiscal Year-end: 9/29/91
Holding Company
S.I.C.: 6719; 5141
Boyd George *(Chm. & Chief Exec. Officer)*
Ronald Knedlik *(Chief Fin. Officer, Treas. & Sec.)*
Glenn Debiasi *(V.P.-Human Resources)*
Cal Sihilling *(V.P.-Information Services)*
Lyndon Byrum *(Controller)*
Tom Haye *(Dir.-Real Estate)*
Don Ottomeyer *(Dir.-Compensation & Benefits)*

Subsidiary:

Merchants Distributors, Inc. **(1)**
120 4th St., S.W.
Hickory, NC 28601
Tel.: 704-323-4424
Fax: 704-323-4435
Approx.Sls.: $936,000,000
Emp.: 4,000
Fiscal Year-end: 9/29/91
Computer Systems/Hardware:
IBM
Wholesale Groceries
S.I.C.: 5141
Gerald Davis *(Pres.)*
Frank Sherman *(Dir.-Corp. Plng.)*

Subsidiaries:

Capital Resources **(2)**
120 4th St., S.E.
Hickory, NC 28602
Tel.: 704-323-4424 (100%)
Fax: 704-323-4435
Finance Company
S.I.C.: 6799

Institution Food House, Inc. **(2)**
700 12th St., N.W.
Hickory, NC 28601
Tel.: 704-323-4424
Emp.: 450
Foodservice Distributor
S.I.C.: 5141
Robert Donaldson *(Pres.)*

Lowe's Food Stores, Inc. **(2)**
1381 Old Mill Circle, Ste. 200
Winston-Salem, NC 27114-4908
Tel.: 919-659-0180 (100%)
Fax: 919-768-4702
Approx.Sls.: $300,000,000
Emp.: 2,200
52 Supermarkets & 23 Convenience Stores in Virginia & North Carolina
S.I.C.: 5411
Boyd George *(Chm. Bd.)*
Dennis Hatchell *(Pres.)*
Herbert Privette *(Controller)*
Neil Davis *(Dir.-Adv.)*
Mike Lebo *(Dir.-Human Resources)*
Greg Caldwell *(Facility Engrng. Dir.)*

Merchants Transport of Hickory **(2)**
543 12th St., N.W.
Hickory, NC 28601
Tel.: 704-323-4100 (100%)
Common Carrier
S.I.C.: 4212

ALEXANDER DOLL CO., INC.
615 W. 131st St.
New York, NY 10027
Tel.: 212-283-5900
Fax: 212-283-4263
Approx.Sls.: $20,000,000
Emp.: 300
Mfr. Dolls
S.I.C.: 3942
William Birnaum *(Pres.)*
Beau James *(V.P.-Sls.)*
Mildred Birnbaum *(V.P.-Res. & Devel.)*

ALEXANDER MARKETING SERVICES, INC.
277 Crahen Ave., NE
Grand Rapids, MI 49516
Tel.: 616-957-2000
Fax: 616-957-3514
Year Founded: 1965
Approx.Billings: $27,000,000
Emp.: 48
Advertising Agency
S.I.C.: 7311
Robert C. Milroy *(Pres.)*
Richard H. Hill *(Exec. V.P.)*
Howard H. Rice *(V.P.-Pub. Rels.)*
Mary Cody *(V.P., Controller)*
Richard H. Hopperton *(Dir.-Pub. Rels.)*

Branches:

Alexander Marketing Services/ Chicago **(1)**
1700 W. Central Rd.
Arlington Heights, IL 60005
Tel.: 708-296-3300
Emp.: 6
Susan Lowry *(V.P. & Gen. Mgr.)*

Alexander Marketing Services/Detroit **(1)**
3271 Five Points Dr.
Auburn Hills, MI 48326
Tel.: 313-340-0800
Emp.: 7
Rick Hedden *(V.P., Gen. Mgr.)*

ALFORD INDUSTRIES, INC.
Industrial Ave.
Ridgefield Park, NJ 07660
Tel.: 201-440-3000
Fax: 201-440-8556
Sales Range: $100-499 Million
Emp.: 650
Fiscal Year-end: 12/31/91
Export
Packaging Company
S.I.C.: 2672; 3089
Raymond P. Kane *(Chm. Bd.)*

Alford Industries, Inc.—(Continued)

Jess Ball *(Pres. & Chief Exec. Officer)*
Donald Kane *(V.P.-Sls.)*
Horst O. Sieben *(V.P.-Fin. & Controller)*

No. of Mfg. Plants/Facilities: 3

Outside Service Firm(s):

KPMG Peat Marwick*(Auditors)*
345 Park Ave.
New York, NY 10154
Tel.: 212-758-9700
Fax: 212-872-3308

Chemical Bank*(Major Banking Relationship)*
450 West 33rd St.
New York, NY 10001
Tel.: 212-613-7197
Fax: 212-947-7628

Subsidiary:

Alford Packaging **(1)**
2631 Merchant Dr.
Baltimore, MD 21230
Tel.: 410-644-3000

ALFORD REFRIGERATED WAREHOUSE, INC.
318 Cadiz St.
Dallas, TX 75207
Tel.: 214-426-5151
Fax: 214-426-0245
Approx.Sls.: $10,000,000
Emp.: 315
Dry & Cold Storage Warehousing
S.I.C.: 4225; 4222
Olita M. Alford *(Chm. Bd.)*
B.W. Alford, II *(Pres.)*
Ahmad Azari *(V.P.-Engrng.)*
Donald L. Murphy *(V.P.-Opers.)*
Fred F. Alford, Jr. *(Treas.)*
Clayton Alexander *(Controller)*
Dorothy William *(Asst. Controller)*

Outside Service Firm(s):

Ernst & Young*(Auditors)*
2121 San Jacinto, Ste. 500
Dallas, TX 75201
Tel.: 214-969-8000

Carrington, Coleman*(Legal Firm)*
2500 So. Tower, Plz. of the America
Dallas, TX 75201
Tel.: 214-698-8000

Bank One Texas*(Major Banking Relationship)*
1717 Main St.
Dallas, TX 75201
Tel.: 214-290-2367

ALGOOD FOOD COMPANY
2440 S. Floyd St.
Louisville, KY 40217
Mailing Address:
P.O. Box 17554
Louisville, KY 40217
Tel.: 502-637-3631 **KY**
Fax: 502-637-1502
Year Founded: 1985
Approx.Sls.: $50,000,000
Emp.: 130
Fiscal Year-end: 12/31/91
Export
Manufacturer of Specialty Items: Algood Peanut Butter, Algood Old Fashioned Peanut Butter, Algood Peanut Oil & Cap'N Kid Peanut Butter
S.I.C.: 2033; 2099
Cecil C. Barnett *(Chm. Bd., Pres., Chief Exec. Officer & Treas.)*
Robert M. Blais *(Exec. V.P.)*
Gillian H. Barnett *(V.P. & Sec.)*
Kathleen Smith *(Controller)*
Dave Frantz *(Mgr.-Pur.)*
Judy Kahn *(Mgr.-Indus. Sls.)*
James P. Melhuish *(Mgr.-Retail Sls.)*
Nicolas B. Melhuish *(Mgr.-Export & Food Svc. Sls.)*
Dick Schulhafer *(Mgr.-Plant)*
Keith Weatherholt *(Mgr.-Quality Control)*

Principal(s):
Cecil C. Barnett

No. of Mfg. Plants/Facilities: 1
No. of U.S. Offices: 1

Computer Systems/Hardware:
IBM AS/400

Outside Service Firm(s):

Coopers & Lybrand*(Auditors)*
Louisville, KY 46201

Dickie McCamey Chilcote*(Legal Firm)*
Pittsburgh, PA

Wyatt, Tarrant, Combs, Gilbert & Milom*(Legal Firm)*
28th Fl., Citizens Plaza
Louisville, KY 40202
Tel.: 502-589-5235

Citizens Fidelity Bank & Trust Co.*(Major Banking Relationship)*
Citizens Plaza, P.O. Box 3300
Louisville, KY 40232
Tel.: 502-581-3389

ALIMAK ELEVATOR COMPANY
1100 Boston Ave.
Bridgeport, CT 06610
Mailing Address:
P.O. Box 1950,
Bridgeport, CT 06601
Tel.: 203-367-7400
Fax: 203-367-9251
Year Founded: 1948
Approx.Sls.: $19,000,000
Emp.: 80
Fiscal Year-end: 8/31/92
Import Export
Manufactures Rack & Pinion Personnel/Material Industrial Elevators & Passenger/Service/Freight Elevators; Mining Equipment
S.I.C.: 3534; 3532
Ulf Lundell *(Pres.)*
Allan McQuilkin *(Natl. Sls. Mgr.)*
Pamela Murray *(Mktg. & Adv. Mgr.)*
William King *(Treas.)*
Bill Ayles *(Personnel Dir.)*
Albert Marchant *(Chief Engr.)*

Divisions:

Alimak Elevator Company **(1)**
P.O. Box 997
Media, PA 19063
Tel.: 215-565-0610
S.I.C.: 3534
Tom Flynn *(Regional Mgr.)*

Alimak Elevator Company **(1)**
157 Fairground St. S.E.
Marietta, GA 30060
Tel.: 404-499-9902
Fax: 404-499-0115
S.I.C.: 3534
Tim Isbell *(Regional Mgr.)*

Alimak Elevator Company **(1)**
2101 John's Court
Glenview, IL 60025
Tel.: 708-998-4646
Fax: 708-998-4660
S.I.C.: 3534
John Dreyezhner *(Regional Mgr.)*

Alimak Elevator Company **(1)**
11912 Rivera Rd.
Santa Fe Springs, CA 90670
Tel.: 310-698-2571
Fax: 310-696-5513
S.I.C.: 3534
Bill Thorn *(Regional Mgr.)*

Alimak Elevator Company **(1)**
P.O. Box 57117, 16920 Texas Ave., Ste. C13
Webster, TX 77598
Tel.: 713-338-1114
Fax: 713-338-0019
S.I.C.: 3534
Jose Olguin *(Mgr.-Regional)*

ALIMED, INC.
297 High St.
Dedham, MA 02026
Tel.: 617-329-2900
Tel.: 800-225-2610
Year Founded: 1968
Approx.Sls.: $15,000,000
Emp.: 40
Fiscal Year-end: 12/31/89
Rehabilitation Prods., X-Ray Accessories & Other Accessories
S.I.C.: 3842
Julian Cherubini *(Pres.)*
Jonathon Bretz *(V.P.-Gen. Mgr..)*
Alice Shafer *(V.P.-Sls. & Mktg.)*
Fred Smith *(Dir.-Art)*
Susan Jones *(Editro)*
Larry Wiener *(Pur. Mgr.)*
Carol Welch *(Mgr.-Customer Service & Telemarketing)*

ALINABAL, INC.
28 Woodmont Rd.
Milford, CT 06460
Tel.: 203-877-3241
Fax: 203-874-5063
Approx.Sls.: $28,000,000
Emp.: 250
Metal Stamping, Ball & Roller Bearings, Primary Metal Products
S.I.C.: 3469; 3399; 3562
S.G. Cerri *(Chm. Bd.)*
Samuel Bergami *(Pres.)*
K.M. Conlisk *(Chief Fin. Officer)*
S.S. Bergami *(V.P.-Mfg.)*
John M. Robertson *(V.P.-Sls.)*
B.M. Bickley *(Dir.-Human & Matl. Resources)*

Outside Service Firm(s):

Arthur Andersen & Co.*(Auditors)*
400 Atlantic St.
Stamford, CT 06901
Tel.: 203-327-6100

Debevoise & Plimpton*(Legal Firm)*
875 Third Ave.
New York, NY 10022
Tel.: 212-909-6000

Subsidiary:

Practical Automation, Inc. **(1)**
2 Research Dr.
Shelton, CT 06484
Tel.: 203-929-5381
Fax: 203-929-9941
Sales Range: $10-19 Million
Emp.: 150
Dot Matrix & 20 to 132 Columns Printers
S.I.C.: 3577
Samuel S. Bergami, Jr. *(Pres.)*
George Hoag *(Gen. Mgr.)*
R. Banzaca *(Sls. Mgr.)*
R. Krasko *(Chief Engr.)*

ALKOTA CLEANING SYSTEMS, INC.
110 Iowa St.
Alcester, SD 57001
Mailing Address:
P.O. Box 288,
Alcester, SD 57001
Tel.: 605-934-2222 **SD**
Fax: 605-934-1808
Year Founded: 1983
Approx.Sls.: $11,000,000
Emp.: 73
Import Export
Mfr. of High Pressure Cleaning Equipment
S.I.C.: 3589
Charles Amant *(Chm. Bd.)*
Joseph R. Bjorkman *(Pres.)*
Gene H. Bowling *(V.P.-Mktg. & Sls.)*
Gary L. Scott *(V.P.-Natl. Sls. Mgr. & Corp. Sec.)*
Ron Swanson *(Controller)*
Sami Boulas *(Mgr.-Export)*
Kevin Johnson *(Mgr.-Matls.)*
Gary Mount *(Mgr.-Production)*
James A. Scott *(Mgr.-Adv.)*
Principal(s):
Charles Amant
Joseph R. Bjorkman
Gene H. Bowling
Gary L. Scott
Gary Mount
James A. Scott
Woody Woodward

No. of Mfg. Plants/Facilities: 2
No. of U.S. Offices: 2

Computer Systems/Hardware:
IBM 3600

Outside Service Firm(s):

Pederson & Carlson*(Auditors)*
Alcester, SD

Culbert - Davis*(Commercial Insurance Carrier)*
Sioux Falls, SD

Mutual of Omaha Insurance Company*(Group Insurer)*
Mutual of Omaha Plaza,
Omaha, NE 68175
Tel.: 800-228-7775

Woods, Fuller, Schultz*(Legal Firm)*
Sioux Falls, SD

State Bank of Alcester*(Major Banking Relationship)*
Alcester, SD

ALL AMERICA FINANCIAL
440 Lincoln St.
Worcester, MA 01605
Tel.: 508-855-1000
Insurance Services, Investment Services
S.I.C.: 6311; 6331; 6726
John F. O'Brien *(Pres. & Chief Exec. Officer)*
John F. Kelly *(Sr. V.P.-Gen. Counsel)*
Henry P. St. Cyr *(V.P. & Treas.)*
Sharon Dagnello *(Sec.)*

Subsidiaries:

All American Financial **(1)**
440 Lincoln St.
Worcester, MA 01605
Tel.: 508-855-1000
Management Investment Services
S.I.C.: 6726
John F. O'Brien *(Pres. & Chief Exec. Officer)*

The Hanover Insurance Company **(1)**
100 N. Parkway
Worcester, MA 01605
Tel.: 508-855-7200
Fax: 508-856-9092
Assets: $3,241,209,000
Liabilities: $2,468,836,000
Net Worth: $772,373,000
Approx.Rev.: $53,208,000
Emp.: 5,540
Fiscal Year-end: 12/31/90
Automobile, Fire & Allied Lines, General Casualty, Marine & Aircraft, Fidelity & Surety Insurance
S.I.C.: 6331; 6351
John F. O'Brien *(Chm. Bd. & Pres.)*
Joseph C. Henry *(V.P., Treas. & Chief Fin. Officer)*
John Kittel *(V.P.-Mktg.)*
John Hogan *(V.P.-Information Systems)*
Patrick G. Finckler *(V.P.)*
Thomas J. Grimes *(V.P.)*
James M. Mahoney *(V.P.)*
James F. Richardson *(V.P.)*
Joseph C. Rovito *(V.P.)*
John S. Gillis *(2nd V.P.)*
Barnett D. Ovrut *(Assoc. Gen. Counsel & Sec.)*
Lyn Kunde *(Dir.-Cash Mngmt.)*

Subsidiaries:

AMGRO, Inc. **(2)**
472 Lincoln St.
Worcester, MA 01605
Tel.: 508-853-7200 (80%)
Approx.Sls.: $3,569,445
Emp.: 55
Premium Financing
S.I.C.: 6141
Eleanor R. Raye *(Pres.)*

Beacon Insurance Co. of America **(2)**
774 Park Meadow Rd.
Westerville, OH 43081
Tel.: 614-890-3500 (95%)
Approx.Sls.: $49,040,000
Emp.: 182
Insurance; Property & Casualty
S.I.C.: 6331
Phillip E. Frakes *(Pres.)*

Subsidiary:

American Select Insurance Co. **(3)**
774 Park Meadow Rd.
Westerville, OH 43081
Tel.: 614-890-3500 (100%)
Approx.Sls.: $25,311,000
Insurance; Property & Casualty
S.I.C.: 6331
Phillip E. Frakes *(Pres.)*

(2)
Tel.: 517-546-2160 (100%)
Approx.Sls.: $539,465,000
Emp.: 1,500
Insurance; Property & Casualty
S.I.C.: 6331
John R. Wintermute *(Pres.)*
Frederic W. Richter *(V.P.-Underwriting)*
Richard J. Marencic *(V.P.-Admin.)*
D. Joseph Olson *(V.P., Gen. Counsel & Sec.)*
James K. Coville *(V.P.-Field Opers.)*
Patrick Coffey *(V.P.-Mktg.)*
Roger H. Gardner *(V.P.-Claims)*
William J. Lohr *(Treas.)*
Duane Ramsey *(Mgr.-Adv.)*
Sheila Wright *(Mgr.-Mktg. Communications)*

Hanover Lloyd's Insurance Company **(2)**
801 E. Campbell Rd., Ste. 500
Richardson, TX 75081
Tel.: 214-680-3399 (100%)
Approx.Sls.: $3,317,000
Fire & Casualty Insurance
S.I.C.: 6331

State Mutual Life Assurance Company of America **(1)**
440 Lincoln St.
Worcester, MA 01605
Tel.: 508-855-1000
John F. O'Brien *(Pres. & Chief Exec. Officer)*
John F. Kelly *(Sr. V.P. & Gen. Counsel)*
Eric A. Simonsen *(V.P. & Chief Fin. Officer)*
James R. McAuliffe *(V.P. & Chief Investment Officer)*
Bruce C. Anderson *(V.P.-Human Resources)*
Richard J. Baker *(V.P.-Govt. Affairs)*
Henry P. St. Cyr *(V.P. & Treas.)*

ALL AMERICAN BOTTLING CORP.
15 N. Robinson, Ste. 700
Oklahoma City, OK 73102
Tel.: 405-232-1158 **DE**
Fax: 405-232-1523
Year Founded: 1982
Approx.Sls.: $205,000,000
Emp.: 1,100
Fiscal Year-end: 12/31/91
Bottling & Distribution of Soft Drinks & Related Products
S.I.C.: 2086; 5149
Steven B. Browne *(Chm. Bd., Pres. & Chief Exec. Officer)*
Dan Perry *(V.P. & Chief Oper. Officer)*
Stephen R. Kerr *(V.P. & Chief Fin. Officer)*
Norma Lessmann *(Plan Admin.)*

No. of Mfg. Plants/Facilities: 20
No. of U.S. Offices: 1

Computer Systems/Hardware:
IBM AT, IBM Systems 34 & 36

Outside Service Firm(s):

Price Waterhouse*(Auditors)*
Colcord Bldg., 15 N. Robinson, Ste. 400
Oklahoma City, OK 73102
Tel.: 405-272-9251

ALL AMERICAN HOME CENTER
7201 E. Firestone Blvd.
Downey, CA 90241
Tel.: 310-927-8666 **CA**
Fax: 310-928-0633
Year Founded: 1959
Approx.Sls.: $32,000,000
Emp.: 295
Retail Sales of Hardware
S.I.C.: 5251
Irving Gerter *(Chm. Bd.)*
Leonard Gertier *(Pres.)*
Tamar Gertier *(V.P. & Sec.)*
D.A. Fraser *(Treas.)*

Outside Service Firm(s):

Fink & Company*(Auditors)*
Downey, CA

Gibson, Dunn & Crutcher*(Legal Firm)*
333 S. Grand Ave.
Los Angeles, CA 90071
Tel.: 213-229-7000

ALL-LUMINUM PRODUCTS, INC.
10981 Decatur Rd.
Philadelphia, PA 19154-3297
Tel.: 215-632-2800
Fax: 215-824-1172
Approx.Sls.: $20,000,000
Emp.: 250
Fiscal Year-end: 12/31/91
Import Export
Aluminum & Steel Folding Tables & Chairs, Leisure Loungers, Outdoor Furniture, Folding Beds
S.I.C.: 2514; 2519
Boris Cohen *(Chm. Bd.)*
Warren Cohen *(Pres.)*
Ira Cohen *(Chief Fin. Officer & V.P.-Opers.)*
Art Blank *(V.P.-Pur. & Mfg.)*
Mark J. Cohen *(V.P.-Sls. & Mktg.)*
David Hunter *(Controller)*
Jerry Brown *(Mgr.-Sls.)*
Rich Gillece *(Mgr.-Natl. Sls.)*
Charlotte Goldberg *(Mgr.-Export)*
Jay Lazar *(Mgr.-Mfg.)*
Principal(s):
Boris Cohen
Warren Cohen

Computer Systems/Hardware:
DEC

Outside Service Firm(s):

Margolis & Associates*(Auditors)*
Philadelphia, PA

Meltzer & Schiffrin*(Legal Firm)*
Philadelphia, PA

Philadelphia National Bank*(Major Banking Relationship)*
P.O. Box 13834, Broad & Chestnut Streets
Philadelphia, PA 19101-7618
Tel.: 215-973-8327

Division:

Fanta Furniture **(1)**
10981 Decatur Rd.
Philadelphia, PA 19154-3297
Tel.: 215-289-3400
Tel.: 215-824-1172
Import Export
S.I.C.: 2514; 2519
Warren Cohen *(Pres.)*

ALL NATION INSURANCE CO.
155 Aurora Ave.
Saint Paul, MN 55164
Mailing Address:
P.O. Box 64697
St. Paul, MN 55164
Tel.: 612-224-5765 **MN**
Fax: 612-224-4918
Assets: $17,000,000
Liabilities: $11,500,000
Net Worth: $5,500,000
Approx.Rev.: $19,000,000
Emp.: 70
Automobile & Mobile Home Insurance
S.I.C.: 6331
John A. Mayerle *(Chm. Bd.)*
Daryl E. Durum *(Pres.)*
John L. Ivancie *(V.P.)*
Al J. Bier *(V.P.)*
Thomas West *(V.P.-Adv.)*
Judith Youngren *(Sec.)*
Charlotte Kwosniewski *(Treas.)*
Edward Willman *(Claims Mgr.)*

ALL-PHASE ELECTRIC SUPPLY CO. INC.
875 Riverview Dr.
Benton Harbor, MI 49022
Tel.: 616-926-6194
Fax: 616-926-0077
Year Founded: 1959
Approx.Sls.: $450,000,000
Emp.: 1,800
Fiscal Year-end: 2/28/89
Whlslr. Electrical Supplies
S.I.C.: 5063
Ronald F. Kinney *(Chm. Bd. & Pres.)*
Bill Vector *(V.P.-Fin.)*
Patrick J. Kinney *(Gen. Counsel)*

No. of U.S. Offices: 102

Computer Systems/Hardware:
Unisys

Outside Service Firm(s):

Crowe, Chizek & Co.*(Auditors)*
South Bend, IN

National Bank of Detroit*(Major Banking Relationship)*
611 Woodward
Detroit, MI 48226
Tel.: 313-225-1000

ALL SEASONS SERVICES, INC.
100 Grandview Rd.
Braintree, MA 02184-2624
Tel.: 617-849-3750 **DE**
Fax: 617-849-3760
Year Founded: 1986
Assets: $21,500,000
Liabilities: $17,500,000
Net Worth: $4,000,000
Approx.Sls.: $70,000,000
Emp.: 1100
Fiscal Year-end: 7/31/92
Institutional Food Service
S.I.C.: 5812
Donald G. Friedl *(Chm. Bd., Pres. & Chief Exec. Officer)*
Robert L. Ashton *(V.P., Chief Fin. Officer & Controller)*
Richard Boucher *(V.P.)*
Mark Bruno *(V.P. & Reg. Mgr.)*
Priscilla Hall *(Corp. Sec.)*
Justin P. Morreale *(Gen. Counsel)*
Paula Tobias *(Pur. Agent)*
Mark L. Seeley *(Dir.-Data Processing)*
Patricia M. Hanrahan *(Admin.-Employee Benefits)*
Jan E. LaBelle *(Corp. Travel Planner)*

No. of U.S. Offices: 12

Computer Systems/Hardware:
Digital

Outside Service Firm(s):

Arthur Andersen & Co.*(Auditors)*
One Intl. Place, 100 Oliver St.
Boston, MA 02110
Tel.: 617-330-4000
Fax: 617-439-9731

Corroon & Black*(Commercial Insurance Carrier)*
One Exeter Plaza
Boston, MA 02116
Tel.: 617-437-6900

Metropolitan Life Insurance Co.*(Group Insurer)*
Warwick, RI

Bingham, Dana & Gould*(Legal Firm)*
150 Federal St.
Boston, MA 02110
Tel.: 617-951-8000
Fax: 617-951-8736

First National Bank of Boston*(Major Banking Relationship)*
P.O. Box 644,
Boston, MA 02102-0644
Tel.: 617-575-2900
Fax: 617-575-2549

ALLECO INC.
Allegheny Circle
Cheverly, MD 20781
Tel.: 301-341-6000 **MD**
Fax: 301-341-6018
Year Founded: 1960
Assets: $250,024,000
Earnings: $865,000
Liabilities: $236,392,000
Net Worth: $13,632,000
Approx.Rev.: $19,000,000
Emp.: 315
Fiscal Year-end: 9/30/90
Textile Printing; Manufacturer of Rivets; Financial Services
S.I.C.: 3452; 6719; 2759
Morton M. Lapides *(Chm. Bd., Pres. & Chief Exec. Officer)*
Mark A. Garfinkle *(V.P., Gen. Counsel & Sec.)*
Joan L. Nickel *(V.P.)*

Outside Service Firm(s):

Bank of Maryland*(Major Banking Relationship)*
Cheverly, MD

ALLEN CANNING COMPANY
305 E. Main St.
Siloam Springs, AR 72761
Mailing Address:
P.O. Box 250
Siloam Springs, AR 72761
Tel.: 501-524-6431
Fax: 501-524-3291
Year Founded: 1926
Approx.Sls.: $150,000,000
Emp.: 900
Fiscal Year-end: 2/28/91
Export
Vegetable Packers: Sweet Potatoes, Whole Sliced & Diced White Potatoes, Fresh Lima Beans, Okra & Squash, Green Beans, Spinach, Fresh Southern Peas, Dry Beans
S.I.C.: 2033
Roderick Allen *(Chm. Bd. & Chief Exec. Officer)*
Delbert E. Allen, Jr. *(Pres.)*
Bill Allison *(V.P.-Retail Sls.)*
Jim Robason *(V.P.-Production)*
Melinda Davis *(Treas.)*
Charlotte D. Allen *(Sec.)*

Computer Systems/Hardware:
IBM 3800

Outside Service Firm(s):

Arkansas Blue Cross & Blue Shield, Inc.*(Group Insurer)*
Little Rock, AR

ALLEN & COMPANY INCORPORATED
711 Fifth Ave.
New York, NY 10022
Tel.: 212-832-8000 **NY**
Fax: 212-832-7050
Year Founded: 1964
Assets: $282,085,000
Liabilities: $108,679,000
Net Worth: $173,406,000
Emp.: 160
Fiscal Year-end: 11/30/90
Investment Banking
S.I.C.: 6211
Herbert A. Allen *(Pres. & Mng. Dir.)*
James W. Quinn *(Chief Fin. Officer)*
Robert H. Coseriff *(Mng. Dir.)*

Allen & Company Incorporated—(Continued)

Paul A. Gould *(Mng. Dir.)*
Irwin H. Kramer *(Mng. Dir.)*
Walter T. O'Hara, Jr. *(Mng. Dir.)*
Philip Scaturro *(Mng. Dir.)*
John A. Schneiorr *(Mng. Dir.)*
Enrique F. Senior *(Mng. Dir.)*
Stanley S. Shuman *(Mng. Dir.)*
John M. Simon *(Mng. Dir.)*
Harold M. Wit *(Mng. Dir.)*

Outside Service Firm(s):

Coopers & Lybrand*(Auditors)*
1301 Avenue of The Americas
New York, NY 10019
Tel.: 212-536-2000

Chemical Banking Corp.*(Major Banking Relationship)*
277 Park Ave.
New York, NY 10041
Tel.: 212-310-6407
Fax: 212-310-4526

ALLEN-EDMONDS SHOE CORP.
201 E. Seven Hills Rd.
Port Washington, WI 53074
Mailing Address:
P.O. Box 998,
Port Washington, WI 53074
Tel.: 414-284-3461
Fax: 414-284-1265
Approx.Sls.: $35,000,000
Emp.: 400
Fiscal Year-end: 12/31/90
Export
Mfr., Importer & Exporter Men's Shoes
S.I.C.: 3131; 3143; 5139
John J. Stollenwerk *(Pres.)*
Ronald W. Neuman *(Treas. & Controller)*
Mark Lustig *(Dir.-Matls. Mngmt.)*
Robert Melvin *(Dir.-Mktg.)*
Virginia Riddle *(Dir.-Pub. Rels.)*
Louis J. Ripple *(Dir.-Sls.)*
Charles Thimm *(Dir.-Mngmt. Information Systems)*
Principal(s):
John J. Stollenwerk

No. of Mfg. Plants/Facilities: 2
No. of U.S. Offices: 1
No. of Foreign Offices: 1

Computer Systems/Hardware:
IBM AS/400

Outside Service Firm(s):

Ernst & Young*(Auditors)*
111 E. Kilbourn Ave., Ste. 900
Milwaukee, WI 53202
Tel.: 414-273-5900

First Wisconsin South West of Sheboygan*(Major Banking Relationship)*
Box 816, 1450 S. 12th St.
Sheboygan, WI 53081
Tel.: 414-457-7795

Subsidiary:

Woodlore **(1)**
3820 Highway KW
Port Washington, WI 53074
Tel.: 414-284-5047
Fax: 414-284-5047
Mfr. of Cedar Products
S.I.C.: 2511
Jay Wilcox *(Chief Oper. Officer)*

ALLEN FOODS, INC.
8543 Page
Saint Louis, MO 63114
Tel.: 314-426-4100
Fax: 314-426-4201
Emp.: 300
Manufacture Speciality Foods
S.I.C.: 2035; 2087; 5141
Benjamin F. Allen *(Chm. Bd.)*
Stanley Allen *(Pres.)*
Joel Allen *(V.P.-Sls., Mktg. & Adv.)*
Richard Allen *(V.P.-Sls.)*
Louis D. Cohen *(V.P.-Mktg.)*
Angelo J. Nebuloni *(V.P.-Fin.)*

Outside Service Firm(s):

Grant Thornton*(Auditors)*
St. Louis, MO

Susman, Schermer, Rimmel, Shifrin*(Legal Firm)*
St. Louis, MO

Boatmen's Trust Company*(Major Banking Relationship)*
100 North Broadway
St. Louis, MO 63102
Tel.: 314-466-2469

ALLEN & HOSHALL, INC.
2430 Poplar Ave.
Memphis, TN 38182
Mailing Address:
P.O. Box 12788,
Memphis, TN 38182
Tel.: 901-327-8222 **TN**
Fax: 901-324-7154
Year Founded: 1915
Assets: $3,500,000
Earnings: $300,000
Liabilities: $2,000,000
Net Worth: $1,500,000
Approx.Sls.: $16,300,000
Emp.: 208
Fiscal Year-end: 12/31/90
Architectural, Engineering & Consulting Services
S.I.C.: 8711
Tom Needham *(Chm., Pres. & Chief Exec. Officer)*
A. Robert Kelley *(Sr. V.P.)*
Michael R. Young *(V.P.-Intl. Div.)*
Jesse G. Thomas *(Treas., Sec., Chief Fin. & Chief Information Officer)*
Thomas R. Needham *(Dir.-Plng. & Devel.)*
David L. Nicholson *(Dir.-Mktg.)*
George Flew *(Mgr.-Computer Applications)*
M. Lewis Wood, Jr. *(Mgr.-Adv.)*
Principal(s):
Tom Needham

No. of Mfg. Plants/Facilities: 5
No. of U.S. Offices: 5

Computer Systems/Hardware:
DEC VAX 11/750

Outside Service Firm(s):

Rhea & Ivy*(Auditors)*
Memphis, TN

Pilot Life*(Group Insurer)*
Greensboro, NC

Morgan Keegan & Company, Inc.*(Investment Banker)*
Morgan Keegan Tower, 50 Front St.
Memphis, TN 38103
Tel.: 901-524-4100

First American Bank, N.A.*(Major Banking Relationship)*
Memphis, TN

Armstrong, Allen, Prewitt, Gentry, Johnson & Holmes*(Pension Manager)*
1900 One Commerce Sq.
Memphis, TN 38103
Tel.: 901-523-8211

Morgan Keegan & Company, Inc.*(Pension Manager)*
Morgan Keegan Tower, 50 Front St.
Memphis, TN 38103
Tel.: 901-524-4100

Divisions:

Allen & Hoshall **(1)**
9041 Executive Park Dr.
Knoxville, TN 37990
Tel.: 615-693-7881 (100%)
Fax: 615-693-7824
Architectural, Engineering & Consulting Services
S.I.C.: 8711
Christopher Soro *(Gen. Mgr.)*

Allen & Hoshall **(1)**
50 Century Blvd., Ste. 100
Nashville, TN 37228
Tel.: 615-889-0370 (100%)
Fax: 615-889-0439
Architectural, Engineering & Consulting Services
S.I.C.: 8711
Bobby McKinney *(Gen. Mgr.)*

Allen & Hoshall **(1)**
612 N. State St.
Jackson, MS 39201
Tel.: 601-355-3675 (97%)
Fax: 601-354-5755
Architectural, Engineering & Consulting Services
S.I.C.: 8711
John Almond *(Gen. Mgr.)*

IVAN ALLEN COMPANY, INC.
221 Peachtree Center Ave. N.E.
Atlanta, GA 30303
Mailing Address:
P.O. Box 1712
Atlanta, GA 30301
Tel.: 404-332-3000 **GA**
Year Founded: 1900
Approx.Sls.: $116,000,000
Emp.: 700
Fiscal Year-end: 6/30/90
Dealer of Office Prods. Including Office Furniture; Design & Printing of Business Forms, Stationery Prods.; Office Design Services; Distr. Drafting & Engrng. Supplies
S.I.C.: 5021; 5049; 8712; 2759; 2752; 5112
Ivan Allen, Jr. *(Chm. Bd.)*
Thomas L. Bolton *(Pres.)*
M. Wayne Smith *(Exec. V.P.-Sls. & Mktg.)*
Marie Walters Dodd *(V.P.-Adv.)*
O. Gene Ownby *(V.P.-Supplies)*
Rick Plunkett *(V.P., Sec. & Treas.)*
Nathan Tieman *(V.P.-Opers.)*

Computer Systems/Hardware:
IBM System 38

Outside Service Firm(s):

Windham, Brannon & Co.*(Auditors)*
Atlanta, GA

Jones, Day, Reavis & Pogue*(Legal Firm)*
3300 First Atlanta Tower
Atlanta, GA 30383
Tel.: 404-581-8000

First National Bank of Atlanta*(Major Banking Relationship)*
2 Peachtree Street N.W.
Atlanta, GA 30383

J.W. ALLEN & COMPANY
555 Allendale Dr.
Wheeling, IL 60090
Tel.: 708-459-5400 **IL**
Fax: 708-459-0314
Year Founded: 1881
Approx.Sls.: $60,000,000
Emp.: 230
Fiscal Year-end: 12/31/91
Export
Prepared Flour Mixes & Doughs; Dessert Mixes & Fillings; Bakery Equipment & Supplies
S.I.C.: 2045; 2099; 5046
John W. Allen *(Chm. Bd.)*
J. William Allen, Jr. *(Pres.)*
Allan Foster *(V.P.-Div. I)*
Mark Richard *(V.P.-Div. II)*
Douglas Allen *(Pur. Agent)*
Diane Baker *(Mgr.-Human Resources)*

No. of Mfg. Plants/Facilities: 2
No. of U.S. Offices: 8

Outside Service Firm(s):

Crowe, Chizek & Co.*(Auditors)*
P.O. Box 3687,
Oak Brook, IL 60822
Tel.: 708-954-7408
Fax: 708-799-1299

Wildman, Harrold, Allen & Dixon*(Legal Firm)*
225 W. Wacker Dr.
Chicago, IL 60606
Tel.: 312-222-0400

Harris Trust & Savings Bank*(Major Banking Relationship)*
111 W. Monroe St.
Chicago, IL 60690
Tel.: 312-461-2265
Tel.: 800-858-0840

ALLEN & OHARA, INC.
3385 Airways Blvd.
Memphis, TN 38116
Tel.: 901-345-7620 **TN**
Fax: 901-346-2914
Year Founded: 1984
Approx.Sls.: $17,000,000
Management Consulting Service
S.I.C.: 8742; 8748
Harry S. Hays *(Pres.)*
Paul Bower *(Sr. V.P.)*
Clyde Porter *(Sr. V.P.)*
Leyton E. Wright *(Treas.)*
Barbara Sue Hays *(Sec.)*

Outside Service Firm(s):

Price Waterhouse*(Auditors)*
One Commerce Square,
Memphis, TN 38103

Martin, Tate, Morrow & Marston, P.C.*(Legal Firm)*
Union Planters Natl. Bank Bldg.
Memphis, TN 38103
Tel.: 901-525-5881

First Tennessee Bank, N.A.*(Major Banking Relationship)*
P.O. Box 84
Memphis, TN 38101-0034
Tel.: 901-523-4541

ALLEN STEEL CO.
1340 S. 200 West
Salt Lake City, UT 84115
Tel.: 801-484-8591 **UT**
Year Founded: 1947
Approx.Sls.: $11,000,000
Emp.: 25
Structural Steel Fabrication
S.I.C.: 1791
Robert B. Allen, Sr. *(Chm. Bd.)*
Robert Allen, Jr. *(Pres.)*
Lynn Anderson *(Controller)*
Principal(s):
Robert B. Allen, Sr.

No. of Mfg. Plants/Facilities: 1
No. of U.S. Offices: 1

Outside Service Firm(s):

Tebbs, Smith*(Auditors)*
Salt Lake City, UT

Moyle & Draper*(Legal Firm)*
Salt Lake City, UT

First Security Bank of Utah*(Major Banking Relationship)*
Salt Lake City, UT

ALLENS OF HASTINGS, INC.
1115 W. Second St.
Hastings, NE 68901
Tel.: 402-463-5633
Fax: 402-463-5730
Approx.Sls.: $21,000,000
Emp.: 170
Independent Supermarkets; Non-Discount Department Stores
S.I.C.: 5411; 5311
Robert M. Allen *(Pres.)*
Bryant Allen *(V.P.)*
Georgene Allen *(V.P.)*

Christine M. Guest *(Treas.)*
Erik Allen *(Mgr.-Grocery)*

Outside Service Firm(s):

Hancock & Dana*(Auditors)*
Omaha, NE

William Connolly*(Legal Firm)*
Hastings, NE

Norwest Bank Minnesota, N.A.*(Major Banking Relationship)*
Hastings, MN

ALLESON OF ROCHESTER, INC.
2921 Brighton-Henrietta T.L. Rd.
Rochester, NY 14623
Tel.: 716-272-0606
Fax: 716-272-9639
Approx.Sls.: $15,000,000
Emp.: 300
Fiscal Year-end: 6/30/91
Mfr. of Don Alleson Athletic Sportswear for Men & Boys
S.I.C.: 2329
Richard Levine *(Pres. & Chief Exec. Officer)*
Michael Dodge *(V.P.-Mktg. & Sls.)*
Elena Oliveri *(V.P., Sec. & Treas.)*
Steven Schwarz *(V.P.-Mfg. & New Products)*
Michael Kretovic *(Controller)*
Jay Fedorchuk *(Mgr.-Data Processing)*

Computer Systems/Hardware:
IBM System 36

Outside Service Firm(s):

Chase Lincoln First Bank, N.A.*(Major Banking Relationship)*
One Lincoln First Sq.
Rochester, NY 14643
Tel.: 716-385-3200

ALLEY-CASSETTY COAL CO.
N. #2 Oldham St.
Nashville, TN 37213
Mailing Address:
P.O. Box 23305
Nashville, TN 37202
Tel.: 615-244-7077
Fax: 615-254-4280
Year Founded: 1964
Assets: $15,100,000
Earnings: $475,000
Liabilities: $12,900,000
Net Worth: $2,200,000
Approx.Sls.: $40,000,000
Emp.: 150
Coal Brokerage; Building Supply; Concrete Blocks; Truck Sales & Repair; Trucking
S.I.C.: 5989; 5052
Fred Cassetty *(Chm. Bd., Pres. & Chief Exec. Officer)*
G. W. West *(Chief Fin. Officer, Corp. Sec. & Treas.)*
Jeffrey L. Oliver *(Controller)*

No. of Mfg. Plants/Facilities: 1
No. of U.S. Offices: 5

Computer Systems/Hardware:
Basic 4; Ultimate

Outside Service Firm(s):

Burton, Henderson & Co.*(Auditors)*
Nashville, TN

CNA Insurance*(Group Insurer)*
CNA Plaza,
Chicago, IL 60685
Tel.: 312-822-5000

Gilbert & Milon*(Legal Firm)*
Nashville, TN

First American National Bank*(Major Banking Relationship)*
First American Center
Nashville, TN 37237
Tel.: 615-748-2000

ALLFAST FASTENING SYSTEMS, INC.
15200 E. Don Julian Rd.
City of Industry, CA 91745
Tel.: 818-968-9388
Fax: 818-968-9393
Year Founded: 1965
Approx.Sls.: $21,000,000
Emp.: 230
Export
Mfr. of Aerospace Solid & Blind Rivets
S.I.C.: 3452
James H. Randall *(Pres.)*
Don Hawes *(V.P. & Chief Fin. Officer)*
Ralph Luhm *(V.P.-Engrng.)*
Glenn Willey *(V.P.-Mktg.)*

Outside Service Firm(s):

BDO Seidman*(Auditors)*
1900 Avenue of the Stars, 11th Fl.
Los Angeles, CA 90067-6008
Tel.: 310-557-0300

Paul, Hastings & Janofsky*(Legal Firm)*
23rd Floor, 555 S. Flower St.
Los Angeles, CA 90071
Tel.: 213-683-6000

Sumitomo Bank*(Major Banking Relationship)*
Los Angeles, CA

Subsidiary:

Allfast Facility **(1)**
15200 E. Don Julian Rd.
City of Industry, CA 91745
Tel.: 818-968-9388
Fax: 818-968-9393

ALLIANCE AMERICA
4888 S. Old Peachtree Rd.
Norcross, GA 30071
Mailing Address:
P.O. Box 920488
Norcross, GA 30092
Tel.: 404-447-5043 **GA**
Twx: 810-766-0436
Fax: 404-446-5951
Year Founded: 1963
Approx.Sls.: $24,000,000
Emp.: 160
Fiscal Year-end: 12/31/90
Export
Porcelain Enameling of Steel Exterior Architectural & Interior Panels, Industrial, Transportation, Chalkboard, Whiteboard
S.I.C.: 3469; 3479
Phillip W. Unger *(Chm. Bd. & Pres.)*
Paul S. Mullock *(Sr. V.P.-Sls.)*
Tommy R. Watkins *(Sr. V.P.-Mfg.)*
David Seem *(Chief Fin. Officer)*
Mardy Shepherd *(Controller)*
Gerald H. Weinstein *(Legal Officer)*
Duane Bennett *(Dir.-Personnel)*
Susan Courier *(Mgr.-Data Processing)*
Jill Robertson *(Mgr.-Adv. & Sls. Admin.)*

No. of Mfg. Plants/Facilities: 2
No. of U.S. Offices: 1

Computer Systems/Hardware:
IBM System 36

Outside Service Firm(s):

Ernst & Young*(Auditors)*
600 Peachtree St. N.E.
Atlanta, GA 30308
Tel.: 404-874-8300

Bank of New England*(International Bank Affiliate)*
New York, NY

Paul, Weiss, Rifkind, Wharton & Garrison*(Legal Firm)*
345 Park Ave.
New York, NY 10022
Tel.: 212-644-8000

Fleet National Bank*(Major Banking Relationship)*
28 State St.
Boston, MA 02109

ALLIANCE
AUTOMATION SYSTEMS
AN AMBAC AUTOMATION COMPANY

ALLIANCE AUTOMATION SYSTEMS
(Div. Ambac Automation Corp., Dallas, TX)
400 Trabold Rd.
Rochester, NY 14624
Tel.: 716-426-2700
Fax: 716-426-3788
Year Founded: 1947
Approx.Sls.: $20,000,000
Emp.: 120
Engineered Manufacturing Systems, Plastic Molding Systems
S.I.C.: 3559
Stuart Rodman *(Chief Exec. Officer)*
Chris Edwall *(V.P. & Gen. Mgr.)*
Bill Querney *(V.P.-Opers.)*
Jim Baker *(Dir.-Sls.)*
Eugene Blazey *(Dir.-Tech.)*
Ann Clark *(Dir.-Fin. & Admin.)*
Tim West *(Mgr.-Applications)*

ALLIANCE MANAGEMENT, INC.
701 Dexter Ave., N., Ste. 407
Seattle, WA 98109
Tel.: 206-281-7300
Fax: 206-283-1554
Year Founded: 1986
Sales Range: $10-19 Million
Emp.: 205
Fiscal Year-end: 11/ 7/88
Real Estate Investor & Broker; Property Mngmt.
S.I.C.: 6531; 6798
Robert Kellum *(Pres.)*
Linden Larson *(V.P.)*
Michael J. Roeter *(V.P.)*
Colleen Casey *(Dir.-Pur. & Office Mgr.)*

Outside Service Firm(s):

King County Medical Blue Shield*(Group Insurer)*
P.O. Box 21267
Seattle, WA 98111
Tel.: 206-464-3958
Fax: 206-622-7959

Steven Ricor*(Legal Firm)*
Bellevue, WA

ALLIED ADVERTISING AGENCY
141 Tremont St., 12th Fl.
Boston, MA 02111
Tel.: 617-482-4100
Fax: 617-695-9837
Approx.Billings: $59,520,000
Advertising Agency
S.I.C.: 7311
Gerald Feldman *(Pres. & Chief Exec. Officer)*
Matthew Newell *(V.P. & Controller)*
Jane Lanouette *(Dir.-Pub. Rels.)*
Jane Clysdale *(Mgr.-Office & Bus. Admin.)*

Computer Systems/Hardware:
DEC

Outside Service Firm(s):

Blue Shield of Massachusetts, Inc.*(Group Insurer)*
Boston, MA

First National Bank of Boston*(Pension Manager)*
P.O. Box 644,
Boston, MA 02102-0644
Tel.: 617-575-2900
Fax: 617-575-2549

Branches:

Allied Advertising Agency **(1)**
2218 Race St.
Philadelphia, PA 19103
Tel.: 215-496-0675
Fax: 215-496-9255
Bob Arnold *(Gen. Mgr.)*

Allied Advertising Agency **(1)**
6311 Fly Rd., Ste. E
Syracuse, NY 13057
Tel.: 315-437-2223
Fax: 315-437-5920
Nat Tobin *(Gen. Mgr.)*

Allied Advertising **(1)**
9403 Kenwood Rd., Suite D-105
Cincinnati, OH 45242
Tel.: 513-891-5562
Erie Hiles *(Gen. Mgr.)*

AM Entertainment **(1)**
1500 Broadway, Ste. 1915
New York, NY 10036
Tel.: 212-944-1990
Fax: 212-944-6185
Reggie Morrison *(Gen. Mgr.)*

ALLIED BUILDING PRODUCTS CORPORATION
15 E. Union Ave.
East Rutherford, NJ 07073
Tel.: 201-507-8400
Fax: 201-507-3855
Approx.Sls.: $298,500,000
Emp.: 1,000
Roofing, Siding, Insulation, Sheet Metal & Waterproofing
S.I.C.: 5033; 5051
Herbert Smilowitz *(Chm. Bd.)*
Robert Feury *(Pres.)*
George Jones *(V.P.)*
Bernard Smilowitz *(Sec. & Treas.)*
Kevin Koons *(Comptroller)*

Outside Service Firm(s):

Handler & Burnstein*(Auditors)*
Jersey City, NJ

Ruskin Kors Meltzer & Rubin, Starr & Hoberman*(Legal Firm)*
Jersey City, NJ

United Jersey City*(Major Banking Relationship)*
Jersey City, NJ

ALLIED CHUCKER & ENGINEERING COMPANY
3529 Scheele Dr.
Jackson, MI 49202
Tel.: 517-787-1370 **MI**
Fax: 517-787-2878
Year Founded: 1948
Approx.Sls.: $15,500,000
Emp.: 190
Export
Production Machinery of Castings, Forgings & Bar Stocks
S.I.C.: 3499; 3489
Melvin A. Schalhamer *(Pres. & Treas.)*
William P. Schomer *(Exec. V.P.)*
Albert F. Thorrez *(V.P.)*
Henry C. Thorrez *(V.P.)*
Michael Betz *(Controller)*
Morris C. Thorrez *(Sec.)*
Roger Cook *(Mgr.-Quality Control)*
James B. Lovely *(Mgr.-Pur.)*

Outside Service Firm(s):

Rehmann Robson & Co.*(Auditors)*
Jackson, MI

Allied Chucker & Engineering Company—(Continued)

Dykema, Gossett*(Legal Firm)*
400 Renaissance Ctr., 35th Fl.
Detroit, MI 48243
Tel.: 313-568-6800

Comerica Bank*(Major Banking Relationship)*
245 W. Michigan
Jackson, MI 49201

ALLIED FOODS, INC.
1450 Hills Place NW
Atlanta, GA 30318
Mailing Address:
Box 93326
Atlanta, GA 30318
Tel.: 404-351-2400 **DE**
Fax: 404-355-9299
Sales Range: $40-59 Million
Emp.: 150
Fiscal Year-end: 12/31/90
Manufacturer of Canned Dog & Cat Foods; Metal Cans
S.I.C.: 2047; 3411
Fred H. Pinkerton, Jr. *(Pres. & Chief Exec. Officer)*
Bruce Shealy *(Exec. V.P.-Sls. & Mktg.)*
Andrew Lasky *(Sr. V.P.-Opers.)*
Sasson Bechor *(V.P.-Fin. & Sec.)*
W.C. Pearson *(V.P.-Mfg.)*
Kevin Ritter *(Dir.-Pur.)*
Michael Zimmerman *(Dir.-Data Processing)*
Tina Brewer *(Mgr.-Personnel)*

No. of Mfg. Plants/Facilities: 2
No. of U.S. Offices: 1

Computer Systems/Hardware:
NCR Tower System

Outside Service Firm(s):

Ernst & Young*(Auditors)*
600 Peachtree St. N.E.
Atlanta, GA 30308
Tel.: 404-874-8300

Liberty Mutual*(Commercial Insurance Carrier)*
175 Berkeley St.
Boston, MA

General American Life Insurance Co.*(Group Insurer)*
700 Market
Saint Louis, MO 63101
Tel.: 314-525-5458
Fax: 314-525-3677

King & Spalding*(Legal Firm)*
25 Park Place N.E.
Atlanta, GA 30303
Tel.: 404-572-4600

Bank South, N.A.*(Major Banking Relationship)*
P.O. Box 4387
Atlanta, GA 30302
Tel.: 404-529-4111

ALLIED MERCANTILE COMPANY
1627 Meadow St.
Philadelphia, PA 19124
Tel.: 215-831-0550
Fax: 215-831-0246
Approx.Sls.: $10,000,000
Emp.: 160
Retail of Beauty Aids
S.I.C.: 5912
Joseph Kieseman *(Pres. & Chief Exec. Officer)*
John Kieseman *(Asst. Sec. & Asst. Treas.)*

Outside Service Firm(s):

Kopple & Gottlieb*(Auditors)*
Philadelphia, PA

Frankford Trust Company*(Major Banking Relationship)*
Philadelphia, PA

ALLIED MINERAL PRODUCTS, INC.
2700 Scioto Pkwy.
Columbus, OH 43221
Tel.: 614-876-0244 **OH**
Twx: 241232
Fax: 614-876-0981
Year Founded: 1961
Approx.Sls.: $34,000,000
Emp.: 160

Import Export
Manufacture Nonclay Monolithic Refractories
S.I.C.: 3297
Jon K. Tabor *(Chm. Bd., Pres. & Chief Exec. Officer)*
John L. Turner *(Exec. V.P. & Gen. Mgr.)*
Rodney B. Clark *(V.P.)*
Suzanne Tabor Deffet *(Controller)*
Vincent D. Restivo *(Gen. Sls. Mgr.)*
Joseph H. Casey *(Intl. Sls. Mgr.)*
William M. Carmean *(Mgr.-Opers.)*
Robert K. Burke *(Mgr.-Pur.)*
C. Eugene Dew *(Mgr.-Human Resources)*
James D. Parmelee *(Dir.-Research & Devel.)*

Principal(s):
Employee-owned

Outside Service Firm(s):

Deloitte & Touche*(Auditors)*
155 E. Broad St.
Columbus, OH 43215
Tel.: 614-221-1000
Fax: 614-229-4647

Porter, Wright, Morris & Arthur*(Legal Firm)*
Huntington Center, 41 S. High St.
Columbus, OH 43215-3406
Tel.: 614-227-2000

BancOhio National Bank*(Major Banking Relationship)*
155 E. Broad St.
Columbus, OH 43251

ALLIED MUTUAL INSURANCE COMPANY
701 Fifth Ave.
Des Moines, IA 50304
Mailing Address:
P.O. Box 974, Fifth Ave.
Des Moines, IA 50304
Tel.: 515-280-4211 **IA**
Year Founded: 1929
Assets: $769,072,225
Liabilities: $548,809,933
Net Worth: $220,262,292
Sales Range: $100-499 Million
Emp.: 1,950
Fiscal Year-end: 12/31/91
Property/Casualty & Life Insurance & Data Procewssing Excess & Surplus Lines Insurance; Investment Management & Broker Dealer Operations
S.I.C.: 6331; 6311
John E. Evans *(Chm. Bd. & Chief Exec. Officer)*
James Kirkpatrick *(Pres.)*
Douglas Andersen *(V.P.-Adv., Pub. Rels. & Mktg.)*
Charles H. McDonald *(V.P.-Human Resources)*
Jim Shaffer *(Treas. & Dir.-Investor Rels.)*
Michael G. Kean *(Asst. Treas.)*
George T. Oleson *(Legal Officer)*
Bob O. Myers *(Dir.-Data Processing)*

Principal(s):
Employee-Owned

No. of Mfg. Plants/Facilities: 6
No. of U.S. Offices: 6

Computer Systems/Hardware:
IBM

Outside Service Firm(s):

KPMG Peat Marwick*(Auditors)*
2500 Ruan Center
Des Moines, IA 50309
Tel.: 515-288-7465

Davis, Hockenberg, Wine, Brown, Koehn & Shors*(Legal Firm)*
Des Moines, IA

Norwest Bank Iowa N.A.*(Major Banking Relationship)*
666 Walnut
Des Moines, IA

Subsidiary:

Allied Group Inc. **(1)**
701 Fifth Ave.
Des Moines, IA 50304
Tel.: 515-280-4211
Earnings: $12,217,000
Emp.: 1,400
Fiscal Year-end: 12/31/89
Insurance & Financial Services
S.I.C.: 6311; 6331
John E. Evans *(Pres.)*

Allied Of Chicago, Inc.
(Name Changed To Paris Presents)

ALLIED OIL & SUPPLY, INC.
2209 S. 24th
Omaha, NE 68108
Tel.: 402-344-4343
Tel.: 800-33-3717 **NE**
Fax: 402-344-4360
Approx.Sls.: $40,000,000
Emp.: 150
Lubricating Oils & Greases; Tires & Tubes
S.I.C.: 5172; 5014
R. Conrad Heinson *(Pres.)*
Tamara Heinson Fowler *(V.P.)*
Ann Heinson *(Sec.)*
Debra Heinson Thiesfeld *(Treas.)*
Tony Mudd *(Controller)*

Outside Service Firm(s):

FirsTier Bank*(Major Banking Relationship)*
Omaha, NE

Division:

Allied Tire Co. **(1)**
2209 S. 24th St.
Omaha, NE 68108
Tel.: 402-344-4343
Fax: 402-344-4360
R. Conrad Heinson *(Pres.)*

ALLIED OLD ENGLISH, INC.
100 Markley St.
Port Reading, NJ 07064-1897
Tel.: 908-636-2060 **NJ**
Fax: 908-636-2538
Approx.Sls.: $20,000,000
Emp.: 85

Import Export
Prepared Foods, Chinese Condiments, Molasses & Fruit Conserves
S.I.C.: 2099; 2032
Harold M. Ross *(Chm. Bd.)*
Fred C. Ross *(Vice Chm., Pres. & Chief Exec. Officer)*
Carol Pressman *(Exec. V.P.-Sls. & Mktg.)*
Richard H. Owens *(V.P.-Fin.)*
Judy Pavlovich *(Pur. Agent)*
Josie Alves *(Dir.-Quality Control)*
Anne Fallon *(Dir.-Natl. Pur.)*

Outside Service Firm(s):

J. H. Cohn & Co.*(Auditors)*
75 Eisenhower Pkwy.
Roseland, NJ 07068-1697
Tel.: 201-228-3500

Orloff, Lowenbach, Stifelman & Siegel*(Legal Firm)*
Roseland, NJ

ALLIED PAPER INCORPORATED
P.O. Box 125
Dayton, OH 45449
Tel.: 513-866-7421 **DE**
Fax: 513-865-8513
Year Founded: 1893
Approx.Sls.: $130,000,000
Emp.: 490
Fiscal Year-end: 9/30/91
Continuous Business Forms, Allset Cabron Interleaved Forms, Computer Forms
S.I.C.: 2761
William Ames *(Pres.)*
Gregory A. Waddell *(Chief Fin. Officer & V.P. Fin.)*
Joel Horne *(V.P.-Mfg.)*
Robert Lytle *(V.P.-Sls. & Mktg.)*
Alan DeAngulo *(Mgr.-Mktg.)*
R.L. Schoenberger *(Mgr.-Adv., Sls., & Promo.)*
Roger Walker *(Mgr.-Natl. Sls.)*

No. of Mfg. Plants/Facilities: 8
No. of U.S. Offices: 27

Outside Service Firm(s):

Ernst & Young*(Auditors)*
1300 Chiquita Center, 250 E. Fifth St.
Cincinnati, OH 45202
Tel.: 513-621-6454

Security Pacific National Bank*(Major Banking Relationship)*
San Francisco, CA

ALLIED PLYWOOD CORP.
4740 Eisenhower Ave.
Alexandria, VA 22304
Mailing Address:
P.O. Box 9645,
Alexandria, VA 22304
Tel.: 703-922-2804
Fax: 703-922-3450
Year Founded: 1951
Approx.Sls.: $32,000,000
Emp.: 80
Fiscal Year-end: 9/30/91
Plywood & Related Prods.
S.I.C.: 5031
Robert A. Shaw *(Chm. Bd. & Pres.)*
Randy Best *(Chief Fin. Officer)*
Gene Scales *(Treas. & Sec.)*
Paul Morgan *(Dir.-Pur.)*
Wendi Cook *(Dir.-Data Processing)*
Larry Richards *(Mgr.-Human Resources)*
Jane Clark *(Mgr.-Personnel Training & Dev.)*

Computer Systems/Hardware:
NCR

ALLIED PRINTING SERVICES, INC.
579 Middle Turnpike W.
Manchester, CT 06040
Tel.: 203-643-1101
Fax: 203-646-7954
Emp.: 275
Fiscal Year-end: 12/31/91
Commercial Printing
S.I.C.: 2759
Joseph F. Sommers *(Chm. Bd.)*
John G. Sommers *(Pres.)*
Bettina Sommers *(Exec. V.P.)*
Gerald Sommers *(Exec. V.P.)*
Heather Sommers *(Exec. V.P.)*
Norris Drummond, Jr. *(V.P.)*
Peter Swan *(V.P. & Controller)*
Thomas Turner, Jr. *(V.P.)*

Outside Service Firm(s):

Arthur Andersen & Co.*(Auditors)*
One Financial Plaza
Hartford, CT 06103
Tel.: 203-280-0649
Fax: 203-280-0898

Reid & Riege*(Legal Firm)*
Hartford, CT

Connecticut Bank & Trust*(Major Banking Relationship)*
Bridgeport, CT

ALLIED SECURITY, INC.
2840 Library Rd.
Pittsburgh, PA 15234
Tel.: 412-884-2636
Tel.: 800-334-2038 **PA**
Year Founded: 1957
Approx.Rev.: $117,728,838
Emp.: 6,600
Fiscal Year-end: 6/30/91
Provides Security Personnel, Investigative Services, Facility Management Services, Loss Prevention, Consulting Services
S.I.C.: 7381
Neal H. Holmes *(Chm. Bd.)*
Steven B. Stein *(Pres. & Chief Oper. Officer)*
Vincent J. Papi *(V.P.-Mktg.)*
Kenneth B. Slutzky *(V.P.-Opers.)*
Glenn A. Pifer *(Treas. & Sec.)*
Richard W. Welsh *(Controller)*
Andrew Hvostal *(Mgr.-Data Processing)*

Computer Systems/Hardware:
IBM AS/400

Outside Service Firm(s):

Deloitte & Touche*(Auditors)*
2400 One PPG Place
Pittsburgh, PA 15222
Tel.: 412-281-2232

Meyer, Darragh, Buckler, Bebenek, Eck & Hall*(Legal Firm)*
2000 Frick Bldg.
Pittsburgh, PA 15219
Tel.: 412-261-6600

Pittsburgh National Bank*(Major Banking Relationship)*
Stock Transfer Dept., Fifth & Wood Streets
Pittsburgh, PA 15265

Security Pacific Corporation*(Major Banking Relationship)*
Two North Lake Ave.
Pasadena, CA 91101
Tel.: 818-397-1833

Subsidiaries:

Allied Security Inc. **(1)**
6825 Jimmy Carter Blvd., Ste. 1860
Norcross, GA 30071
Tel.: 404-441-2200 (100%)
Approx.Sls.: $3,340,000
Emp.: 199
Detective Agencies & Guard Services
S.I.C.: 7381

Allied Security Inc. **(1)**
41 Third Ave.
Burlington, MA 01803
Tel.: 617-273-3840 (100%)
Approx.Sls.: $6,813,000
Emp.: 330
Detective Agencies & Protective Services
S.I.C.: 7381

Allied Security Inc. **(1)**
1222 Leone Lane
Dunbar, WV 25064
Tel.: 304-768-1064 (100%)
Approx.Sls.: $2,115,000
Emp.: 106
Dectective Agencies & Guard Services
S.I.C.: 7381

Allied Security Inc. **(1)**
10001 W. Roosevelt Rd., Ste. 300
Westchester, IL 60154
Tel.: 708-681-3700 (100%)
Approx.Sls.: $3,646,000
Emp.: 200
Detective Agencies & Guard Services
S.I.C.: 7381

Allied Security Inc. **(1)**
1313 East Kemper Road, Ste. 154
Cincinnati, OH 45246
Tel.: 513-671-1255 (100%)
Approx.Sls.: $2,970,000
Emp.: 170
Detective Agencies & Guard Services
S.I.C.: 7381

Allied Security Inc. **(1)**
7123 Pearl Rd., Ste. 309
Middleburg Heights, OH 44130
Tel.: 216-888-5500 (100%)
Approx.Sls.: $3,086,000
Emp.: 175
Detective Agencies & Protective Services
S.I.C.: 7381

Allied Security Inc. **(1)**
1515 W. Mockingbird, Ste. 105
Dallas, TX 75235
Tel.: 214-631-6928 (100%)
Approx.Sls.: $2,250,000
Emp.: 160
Detective Agencies & Protective Services
S.I.C.: 7381

Allied Security Inc. **(1)**
1675 Carr St., Ste. 210N
Lakewood, CO 80215
Tel.: 303-239-6319 (100%)
Approx.Sls.: $1,527,000
Emp.: 94
Detective Agencies & Guard Services
S.I.C.: 7381

Allied Security Inc. **(1)**
Crossroads Centre, 16250 Northland Dr., Ste. 315
Southfield, MI 48075
Tel.: 313-559-9860 (100%)
Emp.: 30
Detective Agencies & Guard Services
S.I.C.: 7381

Allied Security Inc. **(1)**
6666 Harwin, Ste. 440
Houston, TX 77036
Tel.: 713-781-6565 (100%)
Approx.Sls.: $4,155,000
Emp.: 240
Detective Agencies & Guard Services
S.I.C.: 7381

Allied Security Inc. **(1)**
3515 Broadway, Ste. 203
Kansas City, MO 64111
Tel.: 816-561-3201 (100%)
Approx.Sls.: $2,476,000
Emp.: 200
Detective Agencies & Guard Services
S.I.C.: 7381

Allied Security Inc. **(1)**
2147 University Ave., Ste. 206
Saint Paul, MN 55114
Tel.: 612-645-2295 (100%)
Approx.Sls.: $1,383,000
Emp.: 125
Detective Agencies & Guard Services
S.I.C.: 7381
Steven B. Stein *(Chief Oper. Officer)*

Allied Security Inc. **(1)**
7900 Bustleton Ave.
Philadelphia, PA 19152
Tel.: 215-745-3010 (100%)
Approx.Sls.: $4,865,000
Emp.: 220
Detective Agencies & Guard Services
S.I.C.: 7381

Branches:

Allied Security Inc. **(2)**
214 Center St.
Oil City, PA 16301
Tel.: 814-676-2946 (100%)
Detective Agencies & Guard Services
S.I.C.: 7381

Allied Security Inc. **(2)**
2840 Library Road
Pittsburgh, PA 15234
Tel.: 412-884-2636 (100%)
Approx.Sls.: $12,000,000
Emp.: 820
Detective Agencies & Guard Services
S.I.C.: 7381

Allied Security Inc. **(1)**
4467 Old Branch Ave., Ste. 104
Temple Hills, MD 20748
Tel.: 410-423-7100 (100%)
Approx.Rev.: $5,821,000
Emp.: 240
Detective Agencies & Guard Services
S.I.C.: 7381

Allied Security Inc. **(1)**
1550 Old Henderson Rd., Ste. N160
Columbus, OH 43220
Tel.: 614-538-0500 (100%)
Approx.Sls.: $1,943,000
Emp.: 145
Detective Agencies & Guard Services
S.I.C.: 7381

Allied Security Inc. **(1)**
1825 Woodlawn Dr., Ste. 105
Baltimore, MD 21207
Tel.: 410-281-7781 (100%)
Approx.Sls.: $1,457,000
Emp.: 95
Detective Agencies & Guard Services
S.I.C.: 7381

Allied Security Inc. **(1)**
8546 Broadway, Ste. 212
San Antonio, TX 78217
Tel.: 210-829-1711 (100%)
Emp.: 70
Detective Agencies & Protective Services
S.I.C.: 7381

Allied Security Inc. **(1)**
221 W. 41st St., 23rd Fl.
New York, NY 10036
Tel.: 212-768-4320 (100%)
Approx.Sls.: $5,063,000
Emp.: 315
Detective Agencies & Guard Services
S.I.C.: 7381

Allied Security Inc. **(1)**
901 S. Highland St.
Arlington, VA 22204
Tel.: 703-521-3600
Approx.Sls.: $5,592,000
Emp.: 270
Detective Agencies & Guard Services
S.I.C.: 7381

Allied Security Inc. **(1)**
363 Lincoln St.
Manchester, NH 03103
Tel.: 603-623-7212
Approx.Sls.: $1,984,000
Emp.: 105
Detective Agencies & Guard Services
S.I.C.: 7381

Allied Security Inc. **(1)**
4232 Forest Park Blvd.
St. Louis, MO 63108
Tel.: 314-535-9444
Approx.Sls.: $4,185,000
Emp.: 275
Detective Agencies & Guard Services
S.I.C.: 7381

Allied Security Inc. **(1)**
475 Metroplex Dr., Ste. 204
Nashville, TN 37211
Tel.: 615-781-8594
Approx.Sls.: $1,000,000
Emp.: 90
Detective Agencies & Guard Services
S.I.C.: 7381

Allied Security Inc. **(1)**
Essex Towers, 55 Washington St., Ste. 308
East Orange, NJ 07017
Tel.: 201-673-3240 (100%)
Approx.Sls.: $1,789,000
Emp.: 77
Detective Agencies & Guard Services
S.I.C.: 7381

Branch:

Allied Security Inc. **(2)**
501 Hose Lane, Ste. 105
Piscataway, NJ 08854
Tel.: 908-699-0341
Approx.Sls.: $2,267,000
Emp.: 110
S.I.C.: 7382

Allied Security Inc. **(1)**
3948 Browning Pl., Ste. 200
Raleigh, NC 27609
Tel.: 919-781-8822 (100%)
Approx.Sls.: $2,044,000
Emp.: 140
Detective Agencies & Guard Services
S.I.C.: 7381

Allied Security Inc. **(1)**
6151 Fairmont Ave., Ste. 207
San Diego, CA 92120
Tel.: 619-280-3200 (100%)
Approx.Sls.: $2,075,000
Emp.: 135
Detective Agencies & Guard Services
S.I.C.: 7381

Allied Security Inc. **(1)**
50 First Street Bldg., Ste. 511
San Francisco, CA 94105
Tel.: 415-512-0366 (100%)
Approx.Sls.: $1,450,000
Emp.: 90
Detective Agencies & Guard Services
S.I.C.: 7381

Allied Security Inc. **(1)**
1900 McCarthy Blvd., Ste. 302
Milpitas, CA 95035
Tel.: 408-954-8274 (100%)
Approx.Sls.: $5,300,000
Emp.: 241
Detective Agencies & Guard Services
S.I.C.: 7381

Allied Security Inc. **(1)**
Horizen Bldg., 4511 N. Himes Ave., Ste. 191
Tampa, FL 33614
Tel.: 813-878-2911 (100%)
Approx.Sls.: $1,648,000
Emp.: 125
Detective Agencies & Guard Services
S.I.C.: 7381

Allied Security Inc. **(1)**
3150 N. 24th St., Ste. 203
Phoenix, AZ 85016
Tel.: 602-381-1795
Approx.Sls.: $4,835,000
Emp.: 340
Detective Agencies & Guard Services
S.I.C.: 7381

Allied Security Inc. **(1)**
One Idlewild Office Park, 6101 Idlewild Rd., Ste. 117
Charlotte, NC 28212
Tel.: 704-535-7484 (100%)
Detective Agencies & Guard Services; Inactive-Office Closed
S.I.C.: 7381

Allied Security Inc. **(1)**
2880 W. Oakland Park Blvd., Ste. 111
Fort Lauderdale, FL 33311
Tel.: 305-486-5608
Approx.Sls.: $1,125,000
Emp.: 70
Detective Agencies & Guard Services
S.I.C.: 7381

Allied Security Inc. **(1)**
The Nolon Bldg., 320 E. Charleston, Ste. E
Las Vegas, NV 89104
Tel.: 702-598-0598
Approx.Sls.: $2,000,000
Emp.: 125
Detective Agencies & Guard Services
S.I.C.: 7381

Allied Security Inc. **(1)**
5151 Adanson St., Ste. 98
Orlando, FL 32804
Tel.: 407-629-6064
Approx.Sls.: $1,210,000
Emp.: 120
Detective Agencies & Guard Services
S.I.C.: 7381

Allied Security Inc. **(1)**
228 New Haven Ave.
Milford, CT 06460
Tel.: 203-874-4717
Approx.Sls.: $2,449,000
Emp.: 125
Detective Agencies & Guard Services
S.I.C.: 7381

Allied Security Inc. **(1)**
1844 Atlantic Blvd.
Jacksonville, FL 32207
Tel.: 904-399-1813
Emp.: 50
Detective Agencies & Guard Services
S.I.C.: 7381

Allied Printing Services, Inc.—(Continued)

Allied Security Inc. **(1)**
3901 N. Meridian St., Ste. 15
Indianapolis, IN 46208
Tel.: 317-920-0402
Emp.: 70
Detective Agencies & Guard Services
S.I.C.: 7381

Allied Security Inc. **(1)**
Wilshire Center Bldg., 3727 W. 6th St., Ste. 612
Los Angeles, CA 90020
Tel.: 213-383-2596
Emp.: 70
Detective Agencies & Guard Services
S.I.C.: 7381

Allied Security Inc. **(1)**
2713 Lancaster Ave., Ste. B2
Wilmington, DE 19805
Tel.: 302-428-1213 (100%)
Approx.Sls.: $1,416,000
Emp.: 75
Detective Agencies & Guard Services
S.I.C.: 7381

Allied Security Inc. (CA) **(1)**
519 17th St., Ste. 410
Oakland, CA 94612
Tel.: 510-839-4041 (100%)
Approx.Sls.: $2,748,000
Emp.: 160
Detective Agencies & Guard Services
S.I.C.: 7381

Allied Security Inc. (NY) **(1)**
63 Washington St., Ste. 9
Rensselaer, NY 12144
Tel.: 518-462-2500 (100%)
Approx.Sls.: $1,110,000
Emp.: 70
Detective Agencies & Guard Services
S.I.C.: 7381

Allied Security Inc. (OH) **(1)**
200 N. Defiance St.
Archbold, OH 43502
Tel.: 419-445-8181 (100%)
Emp.: 75
Detective Agencies & Protective Services
S.I.C.: 7381

Allied Security Inc. (Westchester Operation) **(1)**
110-122 Mamaronek Ave., Ste. 6
White Plains, NY 10601
Tel.: 914-681-0170
Emp.: 25
Detective Agencies & Guard Services
S.I.C.: 7381

Allsafe Security Inc. **(1)**
Crossroads Centre, 16250 Northland Dr., Ste. 317
Southfield, MI 48075
Tel.: 313-559-9862 (100%)
Approx.Sls.: $2,600,000
Emp.: 140
Detective Agencies & Guard Services
S.I.C.: 7381

ALLIED SECURITY, INTERNATIONAL
W. 425 2nd Ave.
Spokane, WA 99204
Tel.: 509-624-3152
Fax: 509-624-6909
Approx.Sls.: $25,000,000
Emp.: 45
Manufacture & Retail Service Security
S.I.C.: 3499; 5999; 7699
Terrill E. Hunt *(Pres.)*
Dwayne Harney *(Chief Fin. Officer)*
Robin R. Hunt *(Exec. V.P.)*
Max F. Kirklin *(Sr. V.P.)*
Linda K. Blevins *(V.P.)*

ALLIED SPORTING GOODS INC.
3030 Northwestern Pkwy.
Louisville, KY 40212
Mailing Address:
P.O. Box 11200
Louisville, KY 40211
Tel.: 502-778-3321 **KY**
Fax: 502-774-2400
Approx.Sls.: $27,000,000
Emp.: 425
Retail Sporting Goods
S.I.C.: 5941
Armand J. Essig *(Chm. Bd. & Chief Exec. Officer)*
John A. Tichenor *(Chief Fin. Officer, Treas. & Sec.)*
Samuel L. Marks *(Pres.)*
Ronnie Goldstein *(Exec. V.P.-Opers.)*
Greg Marks *(Exec. V.P.)*
Harry Marks *(Exec. V.P.)*
Michael Marks *(Exec. V.P.)*
Alan Simon *(Exec. V.P.)*
Jim F. Gill *(V.P.)*
Robert Rayome *(V.P.)*

Outside Service Firm(s):

Welenken, Himmelfarb & Co.*(Auditors)*
Louisville, KY

Lynch, Cox, Gilman & Mahan, P.S.C.*(Legal Firm)*
Louisville, KY

First National Bank of Louisville*(Major Banking Relationship)*
P.O. Box 36000,
Louisville, KY 40233

ALLIED SYSTEMS, LTD.
(A Georgia Limited Partnership)
160 Clairmont Ave., Ste. 600
Decatur, GA 30030
Tel.: 404-371-0379
Fax: 404-377-9687
Year Founded: 1934
Sales Range: $100-499 Million
Emp.: 2,300
Fiscal Year-end: 12/31/90
Common Motor Carrier
S.I.C.: 4213
Robert J. Rutland *(Chm. Bd. & Chief Exec. Officer)*
Guy W. Rutland, III *(Vice Chm.)*
Jack Nelson *(Pres. & Chief Oper. Officer)*
Joseph W. Collier *(Exec. V.P.)*
William J. Berberich *(Sr. V.P.)*
Joe Collier *(Sr. V.P.)*
Kelvin Khadan *(Controller)*

Principal(s):
Robert J. Rutland
Guy W. Rutland, III

Outside Service Firm(s):

Arthur Andersen & Co.*(Auditors)*
133 Peachtree St., N.E.
Atlanta, GA 30303
Tel.: 404-658-1776

Bank of Boston*(Major Banking Relationship)*
Atlanta, GA

ALLIED TIRE SALES
3320 Maggie Blvd., Ste. A
Orlando, FL 32811
Tel.: 407-648-1555
Fax: 407-839-0318
Year Founded: 1989
Approx.Sls.: $40,000,000
Emp.: 375
Retail Auto Tires; Truck & Auto Batteries; Auto Accessories
S.I.C.: 5331
Glen Bynum *(Pres.)*
Stanley Hanin *(V.P.)*
Francine Hanin *(Treas. & Sec.)*

ALLING & CORY COMPANY
25 Verona St.
Rochester, NY 14608
Mailing Address:
P.O. Box 20403,
Rochester, NY 14602-0403
Tel.: 716-454-1880 **NY**
Fax: 716-454-6169
Year Founded: 1819
Approx.Sls.: $515,000,000
Emp.: 1,200
Fiscal Year-end: 12/31/90
Distribute Printing & Writing Paper, Industrial Packaging & Computer Products
S.I.C.: 5111; 5113; 5112
Richard M. Harris, Jr. *(Chm. Bd.)*
Samuel T. Hubbard *(Pres. & Chief Exec. Officer)*
James W. Stenger *(Treas.)*
Kevin J. Monacelli *(Controller)*
R. Macy Harris III *(Sec.)*
Arthur E. Chester *(Dir.-Data Processing)*
Margaret P. Supinski *(Mgr.-Pension Admin.)*

No. of Mfg. Plants/Facilities: 18

Computer Systems/Hardware:
IBM 3800

Outside Service Firm(s):

Arthur Andersen & Co.*(Auditors)*
Ste. 1500, One Marine Midland Plaza
Rochester, NY 14604

Allyn, Small, Gosling*(Group Insurer)*
Rochester, NY

Goldstein, Goldman, Kessler & Underberg*(Legal Firm)*
Rochester, NY

Chase Lincoln First Bank, N.A.*(Major Banking Relationship)*
P.O. Box 1250,
Rochester, NY 14603
Tel.: 716-232-5000

Chase Lincoln First Bank, N.A.*(Pension Manager)*
P.O. Box 1250,
Rochester, NY 14603
Tel.: 716-232-5000

Subsidiary:

The Alan & Gray Co. **(1)**
27-17 Jackson Ave.
Long Island City, NY 11101
Printing Papers
S.I.C.: 5111
Elwyn Lieberman *(Gen. Mgr.)*

Alcor Envelope Co. **(1)**
25 Verona St.
Rochester, NY 14608
Tel.: 716-454-1880 (100%)
S.I.C.: 5111
Charlie Gerber *(Pres.)*

ALLISON CORPORATION
630 W. Mt. Pleasant Ave.
Livingston, NJ 07039
Tel.: 201-992-3800
Fax: 201-992-3095
Year Founded: 1960
Approx.Sls.: $20,000,000
Emp.: 40
Import Export
Auto Accessories
S.I.C.: 3714
Samuel M. Seltzer *(Chm. Bd. & Pres.)*
Saul Dennison *(V.P.)*
John Gage *(Mgr.-Engrng.)*
Floyd Griffith *(Mgr.-Pur.)*

Outside Service Firm(s):

Gaines Fox & Co.*(Auditors)*
New York, NY

Blodnick, Pomeranz, Schultz & Abramowitz, P.C.*(Legal Firm)*
New York, NY

United Jersey Bank*(Major Banking Relationship)*
Hackensack, NJ

Plant:

Allison Corporation **(1)**
630 W. Mt. Pleasant Ave.
Livingston, NJ 07039
Tel.: 201-992-3800
Manufacture Fabricated Textile Products, Broad Woven Fabrics, Woven Carpets & Rugs
S.I.C.: 2211; 2399
Tommy Williams *(Gen. Mgr.)*

ALLISON-ERWIN CO. INC.
2920 N. Tryon St.
Charlotte, NC 28206
Mailing Address:
P.O. Box 32308
Charlotte, NC 28232
Tel.: 704-334-8621 **NC**
Fax: 704-334-8381
Year Founded: 1893
Approx.Sls.: $76,000,000
Emp.: 310
Wholesale Electronics, Home Furnishings Floor Coverings, Heating & Air Conditioning Equipment, Small Business Computers, Window Treatment Products & Outdoor Power Equipment
S.I.C.: 5064; 5023; 5075; 5065; 5045; 5046; 5261
James R. Allison, Sr. *(Chm. Bd. & Chief Exec. Officer)*
H. J. Allison, Jr. *(Vice Chm.)*
Douglas McMillan *(Pres. & Chief Oper. Officer)*
Ken Causey *(Sr. V.P.-Opers.)*
J.E. Griffin *(Sr. V.P.-Window Treatment Prods.)*
H.A. Smith *(Sr. V.P. & Sec.)*
J.G. Wolfe, Jr. *(Sr. V.P.-Zenith Div.)*
H.P. McClure *(V.P.-Parts & Services Div.)*
H.E. Pennell *(V.P.-Data Processing)*
M.M. Scanlon *(V.P.-Floor Coverings)*
L.B. Griffin *(Treas.)*
A. James Thornhill *(Dir.-Personnel)*

No. of U.S. Offices: 3

Outside Service Firm(s):

Coopers & Lybrand*(Auditors)*
1850 Charlotte Plaza
Charlotte, NC 28244
Tel.: 704-375-8414
Fax: 704-347-1601

Johnston, Taylor, & Allison*(Legal Firm)*
Charlotte, NC

NationsBank Carolinas*(Major Banking Relationship)*
One NCNB Plaza T18-7
Charlotte, NC 28255

ALLMETAL SCREW PRODUCTS CORP.
200 Executive Dr.
Edgewood, NY 11717
Tel.: 516-243-5200 **DE**
Fax: 516-243-5307
Year Founded: 1929
Sales Range: $10-19 Million
Emp.: 65
Fiscal Year-end: 6/30/91
Import Export
Stainless Steel Fasteners; Screw Machine Parts; Electronic Hardware
S.I.C.: 3452; 3541; 3679; 5072
William Campbell *(Pres.)*
Lester Serulneck *(V.P.-Admin. & Sls.)*
Rodney Stanger *(V.P., Controller & Chief Fin. Officer)*

No. of U.S. Offices: 8

Computer Systems/Hardware:
IBM Main Frame & PC; Lotus

Outside Service Firm(s):

United States Life Insurance Co.*(Group Insurer)*
New York, NY

ALLOWAY MANUFACTURING
1330 43rd. St., N.W.
Fargo, ND 58102
Mailing Address:
P.O. Box 2825
Fargo, ND 58108
Tel.: 701-282-7014
Tel.: 800-284-3067
Fax: 701-282-5865
Year Founded: 1946
Approx.Sls.: $12,000,000
Emp.: 74
Fiscal Year-end: 9/30/91
Import Export
Mfr. of Farm Equipment
S.I.C.: 3523
Horst Rapp *(Chm. Bd. & Pres.)*
Peter Silbernagel *(V.P. & G.M.)*
Ron Werner *(Mgr.-Fin. & Admin.)*
Lynn Anderson *(Mktg. Mgr.)*
Glen Austin *(Sls. Mgr.)*
Fred Burbidge *(Production Mgr.)*
Dave Soderstrom *(Data Processing Dir.)*
Ron Berger *(Pur. Agent)*

Computer Systems/Hardware:
IBM

ALLOY PRODUCTS CORPORATION
P.O. Box 529
Waukesha, WI 53187
Approx.Sls.: $13,000,000
Emp.: 165
Fiscal Year-end: 12/31/91
Export
Food Products Machinery & Industrial Process Vessels
S.I.C.: 3556
John J. Trotter *(Pres.)*
Stanley J. Piza *(Exec. V.P.)*
Conrad Nelson *(V.P.-Fin. & Chief Fin. Officer)*
Mike Reister *(V.P.-Mfg.)*
Craig Bear *(Mgr.-Mktg. & Sls.)*
Duke Granger *(Mgr.-Adv. & Sls. Promo.)*
Kap Paquette *(Mgr.-Human Resources)*
Robert Lombardi *(Pur. Agent)*

Outside Service Firm(s):

Reilly, Penner & Benton*(Auditors)*
Milwaukee, WI

Bank One*(Major Banking Relationship)*
Waukesha, WI

ALLOY TECHNOLOGY INTERNATIONAL INC.
169 Western Hwy.
West Nyack, NY 10994
Tel.: 914-358-5900
Tel.: 800-431-1854
Fax: 914-358-5925
Approx.Sls.: $10,000,000
Emp.: 80
Export
Manufactures Alloy/TIC Composites, Thermal Spray Coatings, Bonded Carbides
S.I.C.: 3499; 3398; 3399
Gary Bowker *(Pres.)*
Gene Harzenski *(Exec. V.P.)*
P.M. Siagle *(Mktg. Mgr.)*

ALLRIGHT CORPORATION
1111 Fannin, Ste. 1300
Houston, TX 77002
Tel.: 713-222-2505 DE
Telex: 775918
Fax: 713-222-6833
Year Founded: 1926
Earnings: $9,622,000
Approx.Sls.: $161,000,000
Emp.: 2,800
Fiscal Year-end: 6/30/92
Parking & Garage Operators-Parking Consultants
S.I.C.: 7521
A.J. Layden *(Chm. Bd. & Chief Exec. Officer)*
Bernard Meyer *(Pres. & Chief Oper. Officer)*
Richard Sawka *(Pres.-Planning Div.)*
Peter Dane *(Sr. V.P.)*
Richard Dane *(Sr. V.P.)*
Harold Matthews *(Sr. V.P.)*
Monty Stone *(Sr. V.P.)*
Keith Wise *(Sr. V.P. & Controller)*
T.C. Chang *(V.P.-Property Div.)*
Andrew D. Travis *(V.P. & Legal Counsel)*
Terry Chen *(Chief Fin. Officer & Sr. V.P.)*
H.M. Sinclair *(Dir.-Pub. Rels.)*
Larry A. Page *(Treas.)*
Jean Brocksher *(Sec. & Asst. Treas.)*
Cathy Willis *(Asst. to the Pres.)*

No. of U.S. Offices: 68
No. of Foreign Offices: 4

Computer Systems/Hardware:
IBM System 36

Outside Service Firm(s):

Ernst & Young*(Auditors)*
1 Houston Ctr., 1200 McKinney
Houston, TX 77002
Tel.: 713-750-1500

Confederation Life Insurance Co.*(Group Insurer)*
P.O. Box 105103, 260 Interstate North
Atlanta, GA 30348
Tel.: 404-859-3300
Fax: 404-955-6170

Fulbright & Jaworski*(Legal Firm)*
1301 McKinney St.
Houston, TX 77010
Tel.: 713-651-5151

Skadden, Arps, Slate, Meagher & Flom*(Legal Firm)*
Los Angeles, CA

Texas Commerce Bank*(Major Banking Relationship)*
600 Travis Street, Suite 1150
Houston, TX 77002
Tel.: 713-236-4865

Texas Commerce Bank*(Pension Manager)*
717 Travis St.
Houston, TX 77002
Tel.: 713-236-4636
Fax: 713-236-5476

Subsidiaries:

Allright Baltimore, Inc. **(1)**
5 No. Liberty St.
Baltimore, MD 21201
Tel.: 410-685-2700 (100%)
Fax: 410-837-3111
Emp.: 85
Parking
S.I.C.: 7521
John W. Gann *(Chief Oper. Officer)*

Allright Baton Rouge, Inc. **(1)**
218 Laurel
Baton Rouge, LA 70801
Tel.: 504-344-4142 (100%)
Emp.: 7
Parking
S.I.C.: 7521
Charles I. Sutton *(Chief Oper. Officer)*

Allright Beaumont Co. **(1)**
227 Main
Beaumont, TX 77704
Tel.: 713-835-1865 (100%)
Emp.: 4
Parking
S.I.C.: 7521
David Lee *(Chief Oper. Officer)*

Allright Birmingham Inc. **(1)**
101 N. Royal St.
Mobile, AL 36602
Tel.: 205-433-4524
Emp.: 9
Parking
S.I.C.: 7521
Jim Floyd, Jr. *(Chief Oper. Officer)*

Allright Birmingham, Inc. **(1)**
1919 Morris Ave., Suite 555
Birmingham, AL 35203
Tel.: 205-322-0671 (100%)
Emp.: 35
Parking
S.I.C.: 7521
Robert P. Sparks *(Chief Oper. Officer)*

Allright Boston Parking, Inc. **(1)**
31 Milk Street, Ste. 402
Boston, MA 02111
Tel.: 617-426-6748 (100%)
Fax: 617-350-5044
Emp.: 132
Parking
S.I.C.: 7521
Charles Lane *(Chief Oper. Officer)*

Allright Cal. Inc. **(1)**
631 S. Olive, Ste. 210
Los Angeles, CA 90014
Tel.: 213-627-5481 (100%)
Fax: 213-627-2546
Emp.: 231
Parking
S.I.C.: 7521
Roger Schneider *(Chief Oper. Officer)*

Subsidiary:

Allright Long Beach Parking, Inc. **(2)**
107 B W. Broadway
Long Beach, CA 90802
Tel.: 310-437-2368 (100%)
Fax: 310-436-6464
Emp.: 8
Parking
S.I.C.: 7521
Tom Schneider *(Chief Oper. Officer)*

Allright Carolina, Inc. **(1)**
102 N. Elm St., Ste. 626
Greensboro, NC 27402
Tel.: 919-272-2769 (100%)
Emp.: 5
Parking
S.I.C.: 7521
Fred Hayes *(Co-Chief Oper. Officer)*
Roscoe Nelson *(Co-Chief Oper. Officer)*

Allright Carpark, Inc. **(1)**
1221 Baltimore-Suite 300
Kansas City, MO 64105
Tel.: 816-471-3289 (100%)
Emp.: 42
Parking
S.I.C.: 7521
Larry Bergen *(Chief Oper. Officer)*

Allright Cincinnati, Inc. **(1)**
435 Elm St., Room 530
Cincinnati, OH 45202
Tel.: 513-241-4920 (100%)
Fax: 513-241-8133
Emp.: 136
Parking
S.I.C.: 7521
John Winchester *(Chief Oper. Officer)*

Allright Colorado, Inc. **(1)**
1616 Glenarm Pl., Suite 1910
Denver, CO 80202
Tel.: 303-893-9402 (100%)
Fax: 303-893-5312
Emp.: 146
Parking
S.I.C.: 7521
Daniel L. McKee *(Chief Oper. Officer)*

Allright Columbus Parking, Inc. **(1)**
145 N. High St.
Columbus, OH 43215
Tel.: 614-224-1320 (100%)
Fax: 614-224-1304
Emp.: 62
Parking
S.I.C.: 7521
James Kniep *(Chief Oper. Officer)*

Allright Corporation **(1)**
603 N. Main
Wichita, KS 67203
Tel.: 316-264-0585
Parking
S.I.C.: 7521
Robert Livingston *(Chief Oper. Officer)*

Allright Corporation **(1)**
202 N. 19th St.
Omaha, NE 68102
Tel.: 402-345-7122
Vince Smith *(Chief Oper. Officer)*

Allright Corporation of Delaware **(1)**
3101 N. Central Ave., Ste. 970
Phoenix, AZ 85012
Tel.: 602-248-0850
Fax: 602-264-3319
Parking
S.I.C.: 7521
Billy D. Scott *(Chief Oper. Officer)*

Allright Corpus Christi, Inc. **(1)**
One Shoreline Plaza, #733
Corpus Christi, TX 78403
Tel.: 512-880-5866 (100%)
Emp.: 1
Parking
S.I.C.: 7521
George Culver *(Chief Oper. Officer)*

Allright Dayton Parking, Inc. **(1)**
100 No. Jefferson
Dayton, OH 45402
Tel.: 513-222-7123 (100%)
Emp.: 4
Parking
S.I.C.: 7521
Charles Burton *(Chief Oper. Officer)*

Allright Florida, Inc. **(1)**
P.O. Box 1404
Tampa, FL 83601
Tel.: 813-229-0325 (100%)
Emp.: 10
Parking
S.I.C.: 7521
Sidney Rose *(Chief Oper. Officer)*

Allright Jacksonville, Inc. **(1)**
218 W. Adams St., Suite 505
Jacksonville, FL 32202
Tel.: 904-359-0349 (100%)
Emp.: 18
Parking
S.I.C.: 7521
James R. Bagwell *(Chief Oper. Officer)*

Allright Little Rock, Inc. **(1)**
209 W. 6th
Little Rock, AR 72201
Tel.: 501-374-2259 (100%)
Emp.: 22
Parking
S.I.C.: 7521
Jeff Duncan *(Chief Oper. Officer)*

Allright Louisville Co., Inc. **(1)**
321 W. Chestnut St.
Louisville, KY 40202
Tel.: 502-582-1693 (100%)
Emp.: 4
Parking
S.I.C.: 7521
James A. Dixon *(Chief Oper. Officer)*

Allright Miami, Inc. **(1)**
150 S.E. Second Ave., Ste. 900
Miami, FL 33131
Tel.: 305-374-1767 (100%)
Fax: 305-358-4308
Emp.: 40
Parking
S.I.C.: 7521
Larry Massey *(Chief Oper. Officer)*

Allright Missouri, Inc. **(1)**
915 Olive St., Ste. 953C
Saint Louis, MO 63101
Tel.: 314-241-0528 (100%)
Fax: 314-241-6424
Emp.: 27
Parking
S.I.C.: 7521
Steve Blakeney *(Chief Oper. Officer)*

Allright Corporation—(Continued)

Allright Nashville Parking, Inc. (1)
541 Broadway
Nashville, TN 37203
Tel.: 615-256-0823 (100%)
Fax: 615-244-3856
Emp.: 34
Parking
S.I.C.: 7521
W.H. Clem *(Chief Oper. Officer)*

Allright New Orleans, Inc. (1)
150 Barrone St., Ste. 301
New Orleans, LA 70112
Tel.: 504-522-9434 (100%)
Fax: 504-522-4142
Emp.: 48
Parking
S.I.C.: 7521
Jules C. Morales, Jr. *(Chief Oper. Officer)*

Allright New York Parking, Inc. (1)
P.O. Box 40310 Midtown, Lincoln First Tower
Rochester, NY 14604
Tel.: 716-232-3411 (100%)
Fax: 716-454-4119
Emp.: 29
Parking
S.I.C.: 7521
David L. Ernisse *(Chief Oper. Officer)*

Allright Parking Charlotte, Inc. (1)
129 W. Trade St., Suite 720
Charlotte, NC 28202
Tel.: 704-333-5411 (100%)
Emp.: 28
Parking
S.I.C.: 7521
Arthur Jones *(Chief Oper. Officer)*

Allright Parking Chicago, Inc. (1)
216 N. Jefferson, 2nd Fl.
Chicago, IL 60661
Tel.: 312-648-0998 (100%)
Fax: 312-648-0149
Emp.: 100
Parking
S.I.C.: 7521
James Prendergast *(Chief Oper. Officer)*

Allright Parking Corporation (1)
210 W. 6th St., Ste. 1101
Fort Worth, TX 76102
Tel.: 817-332-3719 (100%)
Fax: 817-332-8016
Emp.: 41
Parking
S.I.C.: 7521
Elmer Grammer *(Chief Oper. Officer)*

Allright Parking El Paso, Inc. (1)
601 Magoffin Ave.
El Paso, TX 79901
Tel.: 915-532-7681 (100%)
Fax: 915-532-1268
Emp.: 18
Parking
S.I.C.: 7521
Gabriel Maito *(Chief Oper. Officer)*

Allright Parking Minnesota, Inc. (1)
320 Young-Quinlan Bldg., 81 S. Ninth St.
Minneapolis, MN 55402
Tel.: 612-340-9025 (100%)
Emp.: 55
Parking
S.I.C.: 7521
Steve Meyer *(Chief Oper. Officer)*

Allright Parking of Austin, Inc. (1)
720 Brazos T., Suite S-14
Austin, TX 78701
Tel.: 512-474-1132 (100%)
Fax: 512-474-5819
Emp.: 15
Parking
S.I.C.: 7521
John Schmid *(Chief Oper. Officer)*

Allright Parking of Cleveland, Inc. (1)
1276 W. 3rd, Suite 400
Cleveland, OH 44113
Tel.: 216-781-1356 (100%)
Emp.: 13
Parking
S.I.C.: 7521
Eugene T. Killeen *(Chief Oper. Officer)*

Allright Parking of Georgia (1)
100 Luckie NW
Atlanta, GA 30301
Tel.: 404-524-8005 (100%)
Fax: 404-523-8270
Emp.: 52
Parking
S.I.C.: 7521
Ed Wynn, Jr. *(Chief Oper. Officer)*

Allright Parking of Georgia, Inc. (1)
401 W. Bay St.
Savannah, GA 31401
Tel.: 912-232-8903
John Scott *(Chief Oper. Officer)*

Allright Parking of Indianapolis, Inc. (1)
312 Massachusetts Ave.
Indianapolis, IN 46204
Tel.: 317-635-3473 (100%)
Emp.: 8
Parking
S.I.C.: 7521
Earl Barrett *(Chief Oper. Officer)*

Allright Parking of Milwaukee, Inc. (1)
710 N. Plankington Ave., Ste. 726
Milwaukee, WI 53202
Tel.: 414-272-3265 (100%)
Emp.: 53
Parking
S.I.C.: 7521
Daniel G. Schmidt *(Chief Oper. Officer)*

Allright Parking of Texas, Inc. (1)
815 Walker St., Ste. 1047
Houston, TX 77002
Tel.: 713-237-1668 (100%)
Fax: 713-237-8530
Emp.: 163
Parking
S.I.C.: 7521
A.J. Layden, Jr. *(Chief Oper. Officer)*

Allright Parking System, Inc. (1)
1700 Commerce Pl., Ste. 732
Dallas, TX 75201
Tel.: 214-748-2491 (100%)
Fax: 214-748-4860
Emp.: 28
Parking
S.I.C.: 7521
Wayne Boyce *(Chief Oper. Officer)*

Allright Parking Virginia, Inc. (1)
P.O. Box 742, 10th & Commerce Key Bldg.
Lynchburg, VA 24505
Tel.: 804-846-5029 (100%)
Emp.: 13
Parking
S.I.C.: 7521
Tom Webb *(Chief Oper. Officer)*

Allright Parking Virginia, Inc. (1)
100 Virginia St.
Richmond, VA 23219
Tel.: 804-225-7340
Parking
S.I.C.: 7521
Michael Sanchez *(Chief Oper. Officer)*

Allright Parking Virginia, Inc. (1)
2501 Washington Ave., Ste. 300
Newport News, VA 23607
Tel.: 804-244-3291
Emp.: 9
Parking
S.I.C.: 7521
Deborah Marston *(Chief Oper. Officer)*

Allright Parking Washington, Inc. (1)
104 Irving St., N.W.
Washington, DC 20010
Tel.: 202-726-0142 (100%)
Fax: 202-882-9417
Emp.: 28
Parking
S.I.C.: 7521
Stephano Du Buc *(Chief Oper. Officer)*

Allright Pensacola Parking (1)
134 W. Government St.
Pensacola, FL 32501
Tel.: 904-432-6262
Emp.: 6
Parking
S.I.C.: 7521
Keith East *(Chief Oper. Officer)*

Allright Roanoke Parking, Inc. (1)
Shenandoah Bldg., Ste. 719, 305 1st S.W.
Roanoke, VA 24011
Tel.: 703-343-5560 (100%)
Fax: 703-343-6172
Emp.: 20
Parking
S.I.C.: 7521
John Wynn *(Chief Oper. Officer)*

Allright Sacramento (1)
708 10th St., Ste. 140
Sacramento, CA 95814
Tel.: 916-441-1074 (100%)
Fax: 916-441-1309
Emp.: 25
Parking
S.I.C.: 7521
Roy Jeske *(Chief Oper. Officer)*

Allright San Antonio Parking, Inc. (1)
405 No. St. Marys, Suite 920
San Antonio, TX 78295
Tel.: 210-226-2623 (100%)
Fax: 210-226-6930
Emp.: 28
Parking
S.I.C.: 7521
George Culver *(Chief Oper. Officer)*

Allright San Diego Parking, Inc. (1)
3740 Fifth Ave
San Diego, CA 92103
Tel.: 619-298-6944 (100%)
Fax: 619-298-7001
Emp.: 22
Parking
S.I.C.: 7521
Bill Lehtonen *(Chief Oper. Officer)*

Allright San Francisco Parking, Inc. (1)
655 Fourth St.
San Francisco, CA 94107
Tel.: 415-495-3770 (100%)
Fax: 415-495-6344
Emp.: 8
Parking
S.I.C.: 7521
Chuck Cid *(Chief Oper. Officer)*

Allright Shreveport, Inc. (1)
729 Travis St.
Shreveport, LA 71162
Tel.: 318-424-3686 (100%)
Emp.: 20
Parking
S.I.C.: 7521
J.R. Walker *(Chief Oper. Officer)*

Allright Sierra Parking, Inc. (1)
220 S. Center
Reno, NV 89501
Tel.: 702-329-5344 (100%)
Fax: 702-329-6690
Parking
S.I.C.: 7521
Jim Black *(Chief Oper. Officer)*

Allright Sierra Parking Inc. (1)
222 East Carson Av.
Las Vegas, NV 89101
Tel.: 702-385-6944
Parking
S.I.C.: 7521
Billy Scott *(Pres.)*

Allright Springfield (1)
4 Columbus Tower, 150 Bridge St.
Springfield, MA 01103
Tel.: 413-732-0872
Richard Coughlin *(Chief Oper. Officer)*

Allright System Parking, Inc. (1)
8 South Third St, Concourse Level
Memphis, TN 38103
Tel.: 901-525-0436 (100%)
Emp.: 94
Parking
S.I.C.: 7521
Van Carter *(Chief Oper. Officer)*

Allright Tenn. Inc. (1)
701 Broad St., Ste. LL2
Chattanooga, TN 37402
Tel.: 615-267-5629 (100%)
Emp.: 4
Parking
S.I.C.: 7521
James A. Hall *(Chief Oper. Officer)*

Allright Toledo, Inc. (1)
332 N. Michigan Ave.
Toledo, OH 43624
Tel.: 419-255-1626 (100%)
Emp.: 19
Parking
S.I.C.: 7521
Kevin Donnelly *(Chief Oper. Officer,*

Allright West Palm Beach, Inc. (1)
335 Clematis St.
West Palm Beach, FL 33402
Tel.: 407-655-8640 (100%)
Emp.: 13
Parking
S.I.C.: 7521
Douglas G. Fanshawe *(Chief Oper. Officer)*

Bay Park, Inc. (1)
1624 Franklin St., Rm. 722
Oakland, CA 94612
Tel.: 510-832-7227 (100%)
Fax: 510-832-3001
Emp.: 17
Parking
S.I.C.: 7521
Ken Moffett *(Chief Oper. Officer)*

Dutch Parking Inc. (1)
Centerway Parking Facility, 1 Centerway Square
Corning, NY 14830
Tel.: 607-962-4018
Parking
S.I.C.: 7521
George Lewis *(Chief Oper. Officer)*

Dutch Parking Inc. (1)
Clemens Square, 1 West Gray St.
Elmira, NY 14901
Tel.: 607-734-4104
Parking
S.I.C.: 7521
Allen Caldwell *(Chief Oper. Officer)*

Dutch Parking, Inc. (1)
345 So. Warren St.
Syracuse, NY 13202
Tel.: 315-471-5863 (100%)
Fax: 315-478-5251
Emp.: 84
Parking
S.I.C.: 7521
Thomas MacLachlan *(Chief Oper. Officer)*

Knox Allright, Inc. (1)
517 W. Clinch Ave.
Knoxville, TN 37901
Tel.: 615-525-6152 (100%)
Fax: 615-974-9243
Emp.: 33
Parking
S.I.C.: 7521
Jim Cox *(Chief Oper. Officer)*

Multiple Parking Services, Inc. (1)
335 Statler Tower, 107 Delaware Ave.
Buffalo, NY 14202
Tel.: 716-849-5811 (100%)
Fax: 716-849-0652
Emp.: 209
Parking
S.I.C.: 7521
Rick Serra *(Chief Oper. Officer)*

Multiple Parking Services, Inc. (1)
Collier Street Ramp Garage, P.O. Box 1569
Binghamton, NY 13902
Tel.: 607-772-7151
Parking
S.I.C.: 7521
Thomas Parrotti *(Chief Oper. Officer)*

Northwest Parking Services Inc. (1)
721 First Ave.
Seattle, WA 98104
Tel.: 206-624-0882
Fax: 206-682-6796
Parking Services
S.I.C.: 7521
William Beattie *(Chief Oper. Officer)*

Pennsylvania Parking, Inc. (1)
1201 Walnut St., 2nd Fl.
Philadelphia, PA 19107
Tel.: 215-925-4883 (100%)
Fax: 215-925-2248
Emp.: 106
Parking
S.I.C.: 7521
Marco Paredes, Jr. *(Chief Oper. Officer)*

Non-U.S. Holding:

Ideal Parking, Inc. **(1)**
5 Complexe, Place Desjardins
Montreal, PQ H5B 1B5, Canada
Tel.: 514-288-2727 (100%)
Telex: 775918
Fax: 713-288-3735
Auto Park
S.I.C.: 7521

ALLSOP, INC.
4201 Meridian
Bellingham, WA 98226
Mailing Address:
P.O. Box 23
Bellingham, WA 98227
Tel.: 206-734-9090 **WA**
Fax: 206-734-9858
Year Founded: 1964
Assets: $11,000,000
Liabilities: $7,000,000
Net Worth: $4,000,000
Approx.Sls.: $16,000,000
Emp.: 140
Import Export
Mfr. of Ski & Recreation Products; Merchandise Display Systems; Electronic Audio, Video & Computer Accessories; Bicycle Suspension Accessories; Office Care Products
S.I.C.: 2541; 2542; 3679; 3949
Jeff Heininger *(Chief Exec. Officer)*
Ivor J. Allsop *(Pres.)*
Michael G. Allsop *(V.P.-Opers.)*
James D. Allsop *(V.P.-Sls., Product Div.)*
Kevin Moore *(Sec. & Treas.)*
Dennis Williams *(Gen. Counsel)*
Karn Patteson *(Dir.-Exports)*
Mitch Rydholm *(Dir.-Adv. & Special Projects)*
Susan Dickenson *(Mgr.-Human Resources)*
Elvind Clausen *(Res. & Devel. Chief)*
Ken Partlow *(Pur. Agent)*

Outside Service Firm(s):

Moss Adams*(Auditors)*
Bellingham, WA

West One Bank*(Major Banking Relationship)*
101 S. Capitol Blvd.
Boise, ID 83701
Tel.: 208-383-7947
Fax: 208-383-3870

ALLSTATE CAN CORPORATION
40 Isabella St.
Clifton, NJ 07012
Tel.: 201-773-0100
Fax: 201-779-8475
Approx.Sls.: $15,000,000
Emp.: 80
Manufacture Tin Cans
S.I.C.: 3411
Joseph R. Papera *(Pres.)*
Joseph F. Papera *(V.P.-Mfg.)*
Richard D. Papera *(V.P.-Sls. & Mktg.)*
Michael F. Papera *(Sec.)*
Gabriel Papera *(Treas.)*

Outside Service Firm(s):

Savastano, Kaufman & Co.*(Auditors)*
Hackensack, NJ

Valley National Bank*(Major Banking Relationship)*
Passaic, NJ

ALLSUPS CONVENIENCE STORES INC.
2112 Thornton
Clovis, NM 88101
Mailing Address:
P.O. Box 1907
Clovis, NM 88101
Tel.: 505-769-2311 **NM**
Fax: 505-762-7573
Year Founded: 1956
Assets: $43,553,017
Liabilities: $35,101,070
Net Worth: $8,451,947
Approx.Sls.: $110,000,000
Emp.: 2,000
Fiscal Year-end: 3/31/88
Retail Convenience Stores; Gasoline Service Stations; Wholesale Commercial Machines & Equipment
S.I.C.: 5411; 5541; 5046
Lonnie D. Allsup *(Chm. Bd. & Pres.)*
Mark A. Allsup *(V.P.)*
Barbara J. Allsup *(V.P., Sec. & Treas.)*
RoGene Chaddick *(Controller)*
Jerry Harlow *(Dir.-Data Processing)*
Vern Johnston *(Dir.-Personnel)*
Principal(s):
Lonnie D. Allsup
Mark A. Allsup
Barbara J. Allsup

No. of Mfg. Plants/Facilities: 315

Computer Systems/Hardware:
IBM Sys 38, AS-400

Outside Service Firm(s):

Ernst & Young*(Auditors)*
P.O. Box 1836,
Roswell, NM 88202

Ted Hartley*(Legal Firm)*
Cloris, NM

ALMA INDUSTRIES
1300 Prospect St.
High Point, NC 27260
Mailing Address:
P.O. Box 2250
High Point, NC 27260
Tel.: 919-885-4101
Fax: 919-885-4110
Year Founded: 1932
Sales Range: $80-99 Million
Manufacture Wood Office, Library & Institutional Furniture, Open-Plan Furniture Systems
S.I.C.: 2521; 2531; 2541
Don Mumford *(Pres.)*
Jerry Dixon *(V.P.-Sls. & Mktg.)*

Outside Service Firm(s):

Ernst & Young*(Auditors)*
Wachovia Bldg., 301 N. Main, Ste. 200
Winston-Salem, NC 27111
Tel.: 919-725-0611
Fax: 919-725-4327

NationsBank Carolinas*(Major Banking Relationship)*
Winston-Salem, NC

Womble, Carlyle, Sandridge & Rice*(Legal Firm)*
High Point, NC

ALMO CORP.
9815 Roosevelt Blvd.
Philadelphia, PA 19114
Tel.: 215-698-4000
Fax: 215-698-8831
Wholesale Distributor of Consumer Prods. & Industrial Electronics
S.I.C.: 5065
Eugene B. Chaiken *(Chm., Pres. & Chief Exec. Officer)*
Roslyn Chaiken *(Exec. V.P.)*
Leonard J. Lobel *(Exec. V.P., Sec. & Treas.)*
Frank J. Sucharski *(V.P.-Systems Div.)*

Outside Service Firm(s):

Rudney, Rudney & Co.*(Auditors)*
Philadelphia, PA

White & Williams*(Legal Firm)*
Philadelphia, PA

Meridian Bank*(Major Banking Relationship)*
One Meridian Plaza, 36th Fl.
Philadelphia, PA
Tel.: 215-854-3900

ALOHA AIRGROUP, INC.
371 Aokea Place
Honolulu, HI 96819
Mailing Address:
P.O. Box 30028,
Honolulu, HI 96820
Tel.: 808-836-4101 **HI**
Telex: 743-0125
Fax: 808-836-0303
Year Founded: 1946
Approx.Rev.: $233,350,000
Emp.: 2,065
Fiscal Year-end: 12/31/91
Holding Co. for Aloha Airlines & Aloha IslandAir
S.I.C.: 4512; 6719
Sheridan C.F. Ing *(Chm. Bd.)*
Hung Wo Ching *(Vice Chm.)*
Han H. Ching *(Vice Chm. & Sec.)*
A. Maurice Myers *(Pres., Chief Exec. Officer & Dir.)*
Thomas Derieg *(Sr. V.P.-Opers.)*
John L. Garibaldi *(Sr. V.P.-Fin., Chief Fin. Officer & Treas.)*
Brenda Cutright *(V.P-Finance & Controller)*
Kenneth G. Best *(V.P.-Cargo, Sls. & Services of Aloha)*
Albert J. Pattison *(V.P.-Human Resources)*
Neil M. Takekawa *(V.P.-Customer Service)*
Stephanie C. Ackerman *(Dir.-Corp. Communications of Aloha)*

Subsidiaries:

Aloha Airlines, Inc. **(1)**
Honolulu Intl. Airport
Honolulu, HI 96820
Tel.: 808-836-4101 (100%)
Fax: 808-839-7620
Air Carrier; Aircraft Leasing & Services; Equip. Maintenance, Ground Services & Cargo Systems
S.I.C.: 4512; 4581; 7359
Sheridan C.F. Ing *(Chm. Bd. & Dir.)*
Hung Wo Ching *(Vice Chm. & Dir.)*
Han H. Ching *(Vice Chm., Corp. Sec. & Dir.)*
A. Maurice Myers *(Pres., Chief Exec. Officer & Dir.)*
John L. Garibaldi *(Sr. V.P.-Fin., Chief Fin. Officer & Treas.)*
Thomas F. Derieg *(Sr. V.P.-Opers.)*
Daniel S. Gleason *(V.P.-Sls.)*
Neil Takekawa *(V.P.-Customer Service)*
Albert J. Pattison *(V.P.-Human Resources)*
Kenneth G. Best *(V.P.-Cargo Sls. & Service)*
Stephanie C. Ackerman *(Dir.-Corp. Communications)*

Aloha IslandAir **(1)**
Intl. Airport, 99 Kapalulu Place
Honolulu, HI 96819
Tel.: 808-836-7693 (100%)
Fax: 808-833-5498
Emp.: 217
S.I.C.: 4512
Lawrence Cabrihna *(Pres.)*
Richard K.C. Hee *(V.P.-Mktg. & Services)*
Larry Zimmerman *(V.P.-Opers.)*

ALPHA ASSOCIATES, INC.
2 Amboy Ave.
Woodbridge, NJ 07095
Mailing Address:
P.O. Box 128
Woodbridge, NJ 07095
Tel.: 908-634-5700 **NJ**
Fax: 908-634-1430
Sales Range: $10-19 Million
Emp.: 68
Resin Coated & Laminated Fabrics
S.I.C.: 2295
A. Louis Avallone *(Pres.)*
Al Raggi *(V.P.-Opers.)*
John T. Baxter *(V.P.-Sls. & Mktg.)*
Richard C. DePrimo *(Controller)*
Robert Orecchio *(Mgr.-Mtls.)*
Pamela Avallone *(Sec.)*

THE ALPHA CORPORATION OF TENNESSEE
P.O. 670
Collierville, TN 38027-0670
Approx.Sls.: $117,000,000
Emp.: 620
Manufacturer Polyester Resins, Architectural Sheet, Copper Laminates For The Circuit Board Industry; Insulators For The Electrical Industry
S.I.C.: 2821; 3644
William D. Watkins *(Chm. Bd. & Chief Exec. Officer)*
R.L. Holtzendorf *(Vice Chm.)*
J.D. Burris *(Pres. & Chief Oper. Officer)*
Gerald P. Griffith *(Exec. V.P.)*
George W. Carey, Jr. *(V.P.-Opers.)*
Jack W. Riggleman *(V.P.-Tech. Resources)*
Joe B. Simpson, Jr. *(V.P.-Fin., Chief Fin. Officer & Treas.)*
Jerry Stauffer *(V.P., Gen. Counsel & Sec.)*
Mike Kelly *(Dir.-Mktg. & Tech. Resources)*
Gene Harris *(Mgr.-Sls.)*

Outside Service Firm(s):

Ernst & Young*(Auditors)*
1400 One Commerce Sq.
Memphis, TN 38103

NationsBank Carolinas*(Major Banking Relationship)*
Memphis, TN

Alpha Distributors Ltd.
(See listing under The Alpha Corporation Of Tennessee)

ALPHA ELECTRONIC SIGNAL TECHNOLOGIES, INC.
(Formerly Alpha Wire Corporation)
711 Lidgerwood Ave.
Elizabeth, NJ 07207
Tel.: 908-925-8000
Fax: 908-925-7429
Emp.: 350
Wire, Cable & Tubing
S.I.C.: 5063
Philip R. Cowen *(Chm. Bd. & Chief Exec. Officer)*
Grant McLennan *(Pres.)*
Linda Smith *(V.P.-Sls.)*
Charles Wiggins *(Controller)*
David Beisswanger *(Dir.-Mktg.)*

Outside Service Firm(s):

Arthur Andersen & Co.*(Auditors)*
Elizabeth, NJ

Lowenstein, Sandler, Kohl, Fisher & Boylan*(Legal Firm)*
65 Livingston Ave.
Roseland, NJ 07068
Tel.: 908-992-8700

First National Bank of Boston*(Major Banking Relationship)*
P.O. Box 644,
Boston, MA 02102-0644
Tel.: 617-575-2900
Fax: 617-575-2549

ALPHA MILLS CORP.
122 Margaretta St.
Schuylkill Haven, PA 17972
Tel.: 717-385-0511
Year Founded: 1936
Approx.Sls.: $20,000,000
Emp.: 174
Knitwear, Underwear, Sportswear
S.I.C.: 2329; 2339; 2341
Barton R. Biever, Jr. *(Pres.)*
Richard D. Biever *(V.P.)*

Computer Systems/Hardware:
IBM AS400

ALPHA ONE EXCHANGE
121 Chanlon Rd.
New Providence, NJ 07974
Tel.: 908-933-3320
Year Founded: 1989
Assets: $7,000,000
Earnings: $455,000
Liabilities: $4,000,000
Net Worth: $3,000,000
Approx.Rev.: $22,000,000
Emp.: 21
Fiscal Year-end: 3/31/91
Data Processing Services
S.I.C.: 7374
George Cowley *(Chm. Bd. & Chief Exec. Officer)*
Kerrie Beckner *(Pres. & Chief Oper. Officer)*
Signe Hovde *(V.P.-Fin. & Treas.)*
Sam Beckett *(V.P.-Mngmt. Information Systems)*
Cullen Murphy *(V.P.-Bus. Devel.)*

ALPHA SHIRT CO.
4309 G St.
Philadelphia, PA 19124
Tel.: 215-533-2000
Fax: 215-533-9682
Year Founded: 1933
Approx.Sls.: $17,000,000
Emp.: 53
Wholesale Men's & Boys' Clothing
S.I.C.: 5136
Ronald Berg *(Pres.)*
Adolph Berg *(Chief Fin. Officer)*
Principal(s):
Ronald Berg
Adolph Berg

Outside Service Firm(s):

Henry Frank & Co.*(Auditors)*
Philadelphia, PA

Nelson Pomisher*(Legal Firm)*
Philadelphia, PA

Philadelphia National Bank*(Major Banking Relationship)*
P.O. Box 13834, Broad & Chestnut Streets
Philadelphia, PA 19101-7618
Tel.: 215-973-8327

ALRA LABORATORIES, INC.
3850 Clearview Ct.
Gurnee, IL 60031
Tel.: 708-244-9440
Tel.: 800-248-2672 IL
Fax: 708-244-9464
Year Founded: 1978
Emp.: 60
Mfr. of Generic Pharmaceutical Products
S.I.C.: 2833; 2834
Dr. Raj Bhutani *(Pres. & Chief Exec. Officer)*
Neelam Bhutani *(Exec. V.P.)*
George Mocoghi *(Controller)*
Robert Vocker *(Dir.-Mktg.)*
Stanley Mitchell *(Dir.-Quality Control)*
Kathy Gunderson *(Mgr.-Human Resources)*
Jane Manarik *(Section Head-Adv. & Creative Arts)*

ALRO GROUP
(Formerly Alro Steel Corporation)
3100 E. High St.
Jackson, MI 49204
Mailing Address:
P.O. Box 927
Jackson, MI 49204
Tel.: 517-787-5500
Fax: 517-787-6393
Approx.Sls.: $14,000,000
Emp.: 900
Wholesaler; Steel Service Center; Industrial Supplies; Safety Equipment
S.I.C.: 5051; 2819; 3569; 3089
Alvin Glick *(Chm. Bd.)*
G. Mark Alyea *(Pres. & Chief Oper. Officer)*
Albert Binger *(V.P.)*
Barry Glick *(V.P. & Pres.-Alro Metals Service Center)*
Carlton Glick *(V.P.)*
Robert Glick *(V.P.)*
Richard Hoogerwerf *(V.P.-Corp. Sls.)*
Stanley Lockhart *(V.P. & Pres.-Alro Industrial)*
David Riley *(V.P.-Pur.)*
Dave Mahon *(Sec. & Treas.)*

Outside Service Firm(s):

Arthur Andersen & Co.*(Auditors)*
400 Renaissance Center
Detroit, MI 48243
Tel.: 313-259-8100

Marcoux, Allen, Abbott & McQuillan, P.C.*(Legal Firm)*
Jackson, MI

Citibank N.A.*(Major Banking Relationship)*
Jackson, MI

Branches:

Alro Group, Alpena **(1)**
815 W. Miller St.
Alpena, MI 49707
Tel.: 517-354-4188
Tel.: 800-456-8716
Fax: 517-354-4801
Distributor of Steel
S.I.C.: 5051
Dan Hunter *(Gen. Mgr.)*

Arlo Group, Battle Creek **(1)**
P.O. Box 20, 801 N. 20th St.
Battle Creek, MI 49016-0020
Tel.: 616-968-0234
Tel.: 800-442-5401
Fax: 616-968-3865
Distributor of Steel
S.I.C.: 5051
Albert Binger *(Gen. Mgr.)*

Alro Group, Benton Harbor **(1)**
1860 Yore Ave.
Benton Harbor, MI 49022-9610
Tel.: 616-925-2117
Tel.: 800-442-0777
Fax: 616-925-7553
Distributor of Steel
S.I.C.: 5051
Tom Gear *(Gen. Mgr.)*

Alro Group, Dayton **(1)**
821 Springfield St.
Dayton, OH 45403
Tel.: 513-253-6121
Tel.: 800-762-3447
Fax: 513-253-6126
Distributor of Steel
S.I.C.: 5051
Terry Welihan *(Gen. Mgr.)*

Alro Group, Detroit **(1)**
18695 Sherwood Ave.
Detroit, MI 48234
Tel.: 313-366-8000
Tel.: 800-482-3224
Fax: 313-366-8039
Distributor of Steel
S.I.C.: 5051
John Simons *(Gen. Mgr.)*

Alro Group, Flint **(1)**
P.O. Box 496, 3501 Western Rd.
Flint, MI 48501-0496
Tel.: 313-736-1234
Tel.: 800-482-6970
Fax 313-736-6949
Distributor of Steel
S.I.C.: 5051
Ron Allard *(Gen. Mgr.)*

Alro Group, Fort Wayne **(1)**
P.O. Box 10360, 2211 Freeman St.
Fort Wayne, IN 46851-0360
Tel.: 219-432-3524
Tel.: 800-348-3622
Fax: 219-436-0883
Distributor of Steel
S.I.C.: 5051
Steve Horne *(Gen. Mgr.)*

Alro Group, Grand Rapids **(1)**
P.O. Box 1846, 1033 Freeman S.W.
Grand Rapids, MI 49501-1846
Tel.: 616-452-5111
Tel.: 800-633-0013
Fax: 616-452-2779
Distributor of Steel
S.I.C.: 5051
Randy Maitland *(Gen. Mgr.)*

Alro Group, Indianapolis **(1)**
5620 Churchman Ave.
Indianapolis, IN 46203
Tel.: 317-781-3800
Tel.: 800-677-ALRO
Fax: 317-781-3810
Distributor of Steel
S.I.C.: 5051
Mark Timberlake *(Gen. Mgr.)*

Alro Group, Jackson **(1)**
P.O. Box 927, 3100 E. High St.
Jackson, MI 49204-0927
Tel.: 517-787-5500
Tel.: 800-877-ALRO
Fax: 517-787-6390
Distributor of Steel
S.I.C.: 5051; 3569
David Zantek *(Gen. Mgr.)*

Alro Group, Jackson Plastics **(1)**
903 Baldan Rd.
Jackson, MI 49203
Tel.: 517-787-5500
Tel.: 800-877-ALRO
Fax: 517-787-6380
Plastics
S.I.C.: 3089
Randy Glick *(Gen. Mgr.)*

Alro Group, Jackson Tool-Pac **(1)**
1410 W. Ganson St.
Jackson, MI 49202
Tel.: 517-787-5500
Tel.: 800-877-ALRO
Fax: 517-788-3329
Jim Sexton *(Gen. Mgr.)*

Alro Group, Lansing **(1)**
1800 W. Willow St.
Lansing, MI 48915
Tel.: 517-371-9600
Tel.: 800-456-ALRO
Fax: 517-371-9640
Emp.: 85
Distributor of Steel
S.I.C.: 5051
David Forquer *(Gen. Mgr.)*

Alro Group, Louisville **(1)**
P.O. Box 17349, 310 Baxley Ave.
Louisville, KY 40217-0349
Tel.: 502-635-7481
Tel.: 800-722-5054 (KY only)
Fax: 502-637-4290
Distributor of Steel
S.I.C.: 5051
Tom Guy *(Gen. Mgr.)*

Alro Group, Muncie **(1)**
2301 S. Walnut St.
Muncie, IN 47302
Tel.: 317-282-5335
Tel.: 800-234-ALRO
Fax: 317-289-3083
Distributor of Steel
S.I.C.: 5051
Steve Horne *(Gen. Mgr.)*

Alro Group, South Bend **(1)**
P.O. Box 2319, 2025 S. Main St.
South Bend, IN 46680-2319
Tel.: 219-288-9181
Tel.: 800-342-5520
Fax: 219-288-3816
Distributor of Steel
S.I.C.: 5051
Paul Hubbard *(Gen. Mgr.)*

Alro Group, Perrysburg **(1)**
361 D St.
Perrysburg, OH 43551
Tel.: 419-666-4899
Tel.: 800-537-1333
Fax: 419-666-4507
Distributor of Steel
S.I.C.: 5051
Terry Medley *(Gen. Mgr.)*

Specialty Metal Group:

Alro Specialty Metals, Charlotte **(1)**
2300 Distribution St.
Charlotte, NC 28203
Tel.: 704-372-9300
Tel.: 800-438-2992
Fax: 704-376-2522
Specialty Metals
S.I.C.: 2819
Todd Hicks *(Gen. Mgr.)*

Alro Specialty Metals, Menomonee Falls **(1)**
N49 W13545 Campbell Dr.
Menomonee Falls, WI 53051
Tel.: 414-781-5616
Tel.: 800-365-4140
Fax: 414-781-1020
Specialty Metals
S.I.C.: 2819
Irving Rowen *(Gen. Mgr.)*

Alro Specialty Metals, Nashville **(1)**
143 Park S. Ct.
Nashville, TN 37210
Tel.: 615-242-1288
Tel.: 800-342-8328 (TN only)
Fax: 615-244-4657
Specialty Metals
S.I.C.: 2819
Ralph Hanna *(Gen. Mgr.)*

Alro Specialty Metals, Redford **(1)**
24800 Plymouth Rd.
Redford Township, MI 48239
Tel.: 313-534-1300
Tel.: 800-322-ALRO
Telex: 313-534-3836
Specialty Metals
S.I.C.: 2819
Bill Konyvka *(Gen. Mgr.)*

Alro Specialty Metals, Tallmadge **(1)**
184 South Ave.
Tallmadge, OH 44278
Tel.: 216-633-0350
Tel.: 800-345-6847
Fax: 216-633-2541
Specialty Metals
S.I.C.: 2819
Joe Prioli *(Gen. Mgr.)*

Alro Specialty Metals, Tonawanda **(1)**
50 Ensminger Rd.
Tonawanda, NY 14150-6793
Tel.: 716-877-6342
Tel.: 800-441-7366
Fax: 716-877-6851
Specialty Metals
S.I.C.: 2819
Dennis Areangel *(Gen. Mgr.)*

Alro Specialty Metals, Villa Park **(1)**
236 E. Sidney Ct.
Villa Park, IL 60181-1198
Tel.: 708-530-4220
Tel.: 800-942-0191
Fax: 708-530-4245
Specialty Metals
S.I.C.: 2819
Eugene Sartore *(Gen. Mgr.)*

Industrial Supply Group:

Alro Group, Boca Raton **(1)**
P.O. Box 3031, 6200 Park of Commerce Blvd.
Boca Raton, FL 33431-0931
Tel.: 407-997-6766
Tel.: 800-432-0458 (FL only)
Fax: 407-994-6261
Industrial Supplies
S.I.C.: 3569; 5051

Arlo Group, Clearwater **(1)**
12490 49th St.
Clearwater, FL 34622
Tel.: 813-572-4344
Tel.: 800-282-8815 (FL only)
Fax: 813-572-6812
Industrial Supplies
S.I.C.: 3569; 5051
Dick Harding *(Gen. Mgr.)*

Arlo Group, Kalamazoo **(1)**
5139 Wynn Rd.
Kalamazoo, MI 49003-3537
Tel.: 616-343-9575
Tel.: 800-643-4649
Fax: 616-343-0480
Industrial Supplies
S.I.C.: 3569
Brian Campbell *(Gen. Mgr.)*

Arlo Group, Orlando **(1)**
2505 Forsyth Rd.
Orlando, FL 32807
Tel.: 407-678-2576
Tel.: 800-432-5101 (FL only)
Fax: 407-679-0495
Industrial Supplies
S.I.C.: 3569; 5051

ALSTIN ADVERTISING, INC.
The Drexel Bldg., 1435 Walnut St.
Philadelphia, PA 19102
Tel.: 215-568-3200
Fax: 215-568-4744
Year Founded: 1968
Approx.Billings: $10,000,000
Emp.: 25
Recruitment Adv., Brochures, & Other Printed Materials
Michael V. Schluth *(Pres.)*
Mike Tedesco *(Gen. Mgr.)*

ALTAIR CORPORATION
350 Barclay Blvd.
Lincolnshire, IL 60069
Tel.: 708-634-9540 **DE**
Fax: 708-634-2627
Assets: $24,000,000
Liabilities: $6,000,000
Net Worth: $18,000,000
Approx.Sls.: $43,500,000
Emp.: 300
Mfr. of Process Control Equipment; Automated Control Systems; Animal Feed & Feed Supplements
S.I.C.: 3559; 3625; 3679; 2047; 2048
Garry Brainin *(Chm. Bd. & Pres.)*
John F. Guy *(V.P.-Fin. & Chief Fin. Officer)*
Robert J. Bond, Jr. *(Sec.)*
J. W. Philbin *(Dir.-Mktg. & Sls.)*

Outside Service Firm(s):

Deloitte & Touche*(Auditors)*
Two Prudential Plaza, 180 N. Stetson
Chicago, IL 60601
Tel.: 312-946-2039

American National Bank & Trust Company of Chicago*(Major Banking Relationship)*
33 N. LaSalle St.
Chicago, IL 60602
Tel.: 312-661-5000
Fax: 312-661-6417

Subsidiaries:

Harvest Industries, Inc. **(1)**
350 Barclay Blvd.
Lincolnshire, IL 60069
Tel.: 708-634-1870
Animal Feeds & Feed Supplements
S.I.C.: 2047; 2048
G. Brainin *(Chm. Bd. & Pres.)*

Operating Companies:

Agri-Graphics, Inc. **(2)**
Box 46
Pittsburg, KS 66762
Tel.: 316-231-6700
Marketing & Advertising
S.I.C.: 7311
John W. Philbin *(G.M. & Dir. Mktg.)*

Harvest Brands, Inc. **(2)**
Box 46
Pittsburg, KS 66762
Tel.: 316-231-6700
Animal Feed Supplements
S.I.C.: 2048
Paul Lemert *(Asst. Gen. Mgr.)*

Kern Livestock Supplement Co., Inc. **(2)**
130 Industrial St.
Bakersfield, CA 93307
Tel.: 805-327-0246
Animal Feed Supplements
S.I.C.: 2047; 2048
Don Bower *(Gen. Mgr.)*

W-P Milling Co., Inc. **(2)**
1119 So. Cherokee
Muskogee, OK 74402
Tel.: 918-682-3388
Formulated Animal Feeds
S.I.C.: 2047; 2048
Bill Fuller *(Asst. Gen. Mgr.)*

Hurletron Inc. **(1)**
1938 E. Fairchild St.
Danville, IL 61834
Tel.: 217-446-6500 (100%)
Printing & Packaging Control Systems
S.I.C.: 3625; 3679
David W. Wilson *(Gen. Mgr.)*

Vacudyne Inc. **(1)**
375 E. Joe Orr Rd.
Chicago Heights, IL 60411
Tel.: 708-757-5200 (100%)
Approx.Sls.: $6,000,000
Emp.: 60
Controlled Atmosphere Processing Equip.
S.I.C.: 3559
Russell Skocypec *(V.P. & Gen. Mgr.)*
Edward Radwin *(Controller)*
Richard Cimaroli *(Mgr.-Engrng.)*
Richard Mathews *(Mgr.-Mktg. & Sls.)*

ALTAMA DELTA CORP.
Hwy. 251
Darien, GA 31305
Mailing Address:
P.O. Box 727
Darien, GA 31305
Tel.: 912-437-4107
Fax: 912-437-2194
Approx.Sls.: $20,000,000
Emp.: 420
Men's Shoe Manufacturer
S.I.C.: 3143
W. Whitlow Wyatt *(Chm. Bd.)*
Robert C. Rose, III *(Pres. & Chief Exec. Officer)*
Douglas M. Horsley *(Chief Fin. Officer)*
Parviz Maleki *(Gen. Mgr.)*
Steven Neifeld *(Mgr.-Sls.)*

No. of Mfg. Plants/Facilities: 2
No. of U.S. Offices: 2

ALTEC INDUSTRIES, INC.
210 Inverness Center Dr.
Birmingham, AL 35242
Mailing Address:
P.O. Box 10264,
Birmingham, AL 35202
Tel.: 205-991-7733 **AL**
Telex: 78-2089
Fax: 205-991-9993
Year Founded: 1929
Approx.Sls.: $180,000,000
Emp.: 1,500
Fiscal Year-end: 12/31/91
Export
Mfr. of Mobile Utility Bodies, Hydraulic Digger Derricks & Aerial Devices
S.I.C.: 3713
Lee J. Styslinger, Jr. *(Chm. Bd.)*
Thomas L. Merrill *(Pres. & Chief Exec. Officer)*
Dan Cox *(Sr. V.P. & Gen. Mgr.-Southern Div.)*
Frank Fruedenthal *(Sr. V.P. & Gen. Mgr.-Midwest Div.)*
Mike Bryant *(Sr. V.P.-Sls.)*
Howard A. Marshall *(Sr. V.P.-Mktg.)*
Lee J. Styslinger III *(Sr. V.P.-Corp. Group)*
Jerry Eisenhart *(V.P. & Gen. Mgr.-Northern Div.)*
Hank Malitsky *(V.P. & Gen. Mgr.-Eastern Div.)*
Mark Mason *(V.P. & Gen. Mgr.-Creedmoor Mfg. Div.)*
James Pitts *(V.P. & Gen. Mgr.-Western Div.)*
Jon C. Styslinger *(V.P.-Opers., Southern Div.)*
James A. Sytsma *(V.P.-Engrng., Res. & Devel.-Midwest Div.)*
J. Don Williams *(V.P.-Fin. & Admin.)*
Harry House *(Dir.-Meeting Plans)*
Marc Miles *(Dir.-Sls.-Southern Div.)*
J. William Riley *(Dir.-Human Resources)*
Danny Sheppard *(Dir.-Information Systems)*
Principal(s):
Lee J. Styslinger, Jr.

No. of Mfg. Plants/Facilities: 7
No. of U.S. Offices: 6
No. of Foreign Offices: 1

Computer Systems/Hardware:
IBM ES9000 Model 190

Outside Service Firm(s):

Deloitte & Touche*(Auditors)*
417 No. 20th St., Ste. 1000
Birmingham, AL 35203-3289
Tel.: 205-322-0534

Lange, Simpson, Robinson & Somerville*(Legal Firm)*
1700 1st Alabama Bk. Bldg., 417 N. 20th
Birmingham, AL 35203
Tel.: 205-252-7000

First Alabama Bank*(Major Banking Relationship)*
Birmingham, AL

Divisions:

Altec Industries Eastern Division **(1)**
250 Laird St.
Plains, PA 18705
Tel.: 717-822-3104 (100%)
Mfr. of Mobile Utility Bodies, Hydraulic Digger Derricks & Aerial Devices
S.I.C.: 3713
Tom Merrill *(Chief Exec. Officer)*

Creedmoor Manufacturing Division **(1)**
Creedmoor, NC
S.I.C.: 3713

Portland Service Division **(1)**
13817 N.E. Sandy Blvd.
Portland, OR 97220
Tel.: 503-253-3900
Service & Installation of Truck Bodies
S.I.C.: 1541
Hank Malitsky *(V.P. & Gen. Mgr.)*

Non-U.S. Holding:

Altec Industries, Ltd. **(1)**
831 Nipissing Rd.
Milton, ON L9T 4Z4, Canada
Tel.: 416-875-2000 (100%)
Fax: 416-875-2009
Mfr. of Automobile Parts & Accessories
S.I.C.: 3714
L. Lipsett *(Mng. Dir.)*

THE HARRY ALTER COMPANY
5940 N. Northwest Highway
Chicago, IL 60631
Tel.: 312-775-5552
Fax: 708-775-7082
Year Founded: 1933
Assets: $8,000,000
Liabilities: $6,200,000
Net Worth: $1,800,000
Approx.Sls.: $22,000,000
Emp.: 105
Fiscal Year-end: 10/31/88
Whlse. Air Conditioning & Refrigeration Systems, Parts & Supplies; Warm Air Heating
S.I.C.: 5075; 5078
James M. Alter *(Chm. Bd. & Chief Exec. Officer)*
R. Todd Allen *(Pres. & Chief Oper. Officer)*
David Blons *(Opers. Mgr.)*
Larry Fall *(Data Processing Mgr.)*
Greg Liadis *(Data Processing Mgr.)*
Principal(s):
James M. Alter

No. of U.S. Offices: 13

Computer Systems/Hardware:
NCR I9050; IBM PC

Outside Service Firm(s):

Blackman Kallick Bartelstein*(Auditors)*
300 Riverside Plaza
Chicago, IL 60606
Tel.: 312-207-1040

Adams, Fox, Adelstein & Rosen*(Legal Firm)*
208 So. LaSalle St.
Chicago, IL 60604
Tel.: 312-368-1900

The Northern Trust Co.*(Major Banking Relationship)*
50 S. LaSalle St.
Chicago, IL 60675
Tel.: 312-630-6000
Fax: 312-630-6516

Connecticut General Life Insurance Co.*(Pension Manager)*
P.O. Box 2975,
Hartford, CT 06104
Tel.: 203-726-6000

ALTERMAN TRANSPORT LINES, INC.
12805 N.W. 42nd Ave.
Opa Locka, FL 33054
Tel.: 305-688-3571
Fax: 305-688-0423
Approx.Sls.: $46,000,000
Emp.: 1,200
Motor Common Carrier
S.I.C.: 4213
Sidney Alterman *(Pres.)*
Richard Alterman *(V.P.)*
Roy Livigni *(Controller)*
Joe Alterman *(Dir.-Pur.)*
Principal(s):
Sidney Alterman
Richard Alterman

Outside Service Firm(s):

Deloitte & Touche*(Auditors)*
100 S.E. 2nd St.
Miami, FL 33131-2135
Tel.: 305-538-4141

Florida Union National Bank*(Major Banking Relationship)*
Miami, FL

ALTIER & SONS SHOES INC.
164 Mushroom Blvd.
Rochester, NY 14623
Tel.: 716-424-5650 **NY**
Fax: 716-424-3965
Year Founded: 1921
Approx.Sls.: $18,000,000
Emp.: 275
Retail Shoes & Accessories
S.I.C.: 5661
Richard L. Altier *(Chm. Bd.)*
Richard J. Altier *(Pres. & Chief Oper. Officer)*
James Salzano *(Chief Fin. Officer, Sec. & Treas.)*
Myron S. Lewis *(Gen. Counsel)*
Chris Connor *(Mgr.-Gen. Accounting)*
Paul Havens *(Mgr.-Data Processing)*
Principal(s):
Richard L. Altier
Richard J. Altier
Theodore J. Altier

Outside Service Firm(s):

Price Waterhouse*(Auditors)*
1900 Lincoln First Tower
Rochester, NY 14604
Tel.: 716-232-4000

Central Trust Co.*(Major Banking Relationship)*
Rochester, NY

ALTO DAIRY COOPERATIVE
N. 3545 County EE
Waupun, WI 53963
Tel.: 414-346-2215 **WI**
Fax: 414-346-2377
Year Founded: 1943
Approx.Sls.: $100,000,000

Alto Dairy Cooperative—(Continued)

Emp.: 225
Manufacture & Distribute Cheese & Milk Products
S.I.C.: 5143; 2022; 2023; 2026
Courtland Sperger *(Chm. Bd.)*
John Prince *(Pres. & Gen. Mgr.)*
Adam Doro *(V.P.)*
Don Desjarlais *(Comptroller)*
Wesley Greenfield *(Sec.)*
Larry Lemmenes *(Mgr.-Field Service)*

Outside Service Firm(s):

Schenk & Associates*(Auditors)*
Appleton, WI

First Interstate Bank*(Major Banking Relationship)*
Milwaukee, WI

Employers Health Insurance*(Group Insurer)*
La Crosse, WI

ALTO SHAAM INC.
W164 N9221 Water St.
Menomonee Falls, WI 53052
Mailing Address:
P.O. Box 450
Menomonee Falls, WI 53052
Tel.: 414-251-3800
Tel.: 800-558-8744 WI
Telex: 4311070
Fax: 414-251-7067
Year Founded: 1965
Sales Range: $20-39 Million
Emp.: 225
Import Export
Mfr. of Foodservice Equipment; Low Temperature Cooking & Holding Ovens; Food Holding Cabinets; Hot Food Buffet & Deli Systems; Combitherm/Oven
S.I.C.: 3589
Jerry D. Maahs *(Pres.)*
Tom Kanas *(V.P.-Sls. & Mktg.)*
L. Kerski *(V.P.-Fin.)*
Patrick Willis *(V.P.-Intl.)*
Milada Moucka *(Dir.-Pur.)*

Computer Systems/Hardware:
IBM, MacIntosh Quantell

Outside Service Firm(s):

Bank One Milwaukee, N.A.*(Major Banking Relationship)*
111 E. Wisconsin Ave.
Milwaukee, WI
Tel.: 414-765-3000

First Bank, N.A.*(Major Banking Relationship)*
201 W. Wisconsin Ave.
Milwaukee, WI 53259-1000
Tel.: 414-227-5474

ALTUS FEDERAL SAVINGS BANK
(Company in Receivership, Manage by RTC)
851 S. Beltline Hwy.
Mobile, AL 36606
Mailing Address:
P.O. Box 16267,
Mobile, AL 36616
Tel.: 205-473-0500 AL
Fax: 205-473-0554
Year Founded: 1991
Emp.: 490
Fiscal Year-end: 12/31/90
Federal Savings Bank
S.I.C.: 6035
Jack R. Crigger *(Mng. Agent)*
Doug McCaffrey *(Sr. V.P. & Controller)*
Verna E. Ledlow *(V.P. & Sec.)*
B. Rodrick Marlow *(Dir.-Opers.)*
John M. McQueen *(Dir.-Credit)*
Thomas R. Bandy *(Credit Specialist)*
Lee Ann Corrigan *(Dir.-Human Resources)*

Subsidiaries:

Altus Mortgage Corporation **(1)**
851 S. Beltline Hwy.
Mobile, AL 36606
Tel.: 205-473-0500 (100%)
Mortgage Banking Company
S.I.C.: 6162
Harry M. Barnes, Jr. *(Pres.)*

Altus Real Estate Services, Inc. **(1)**
851 S. Beltline Hwy.
Mobile, AL 36606
Tel.: 205-473-0500 (100%)
Real Estate Services
S.I.C.: 6531
William L. Watson III *(Pres.)*

Altus Services, Inc. **(1)**
851 S. Beltline Hwy.
Mobile, AL 36606
Tel.: 205-473-0500 (100%)
Property, Casualty, & Life Insurance; Securities Brokerage; Accounting Services to Service Corporations; Manage Real Estate
S.I.C.: 6311; 8721; 6211; 6531

The Triad Group, Inc. **(1)**
851 S. Beltline Hwy.
Mobile, AL 36606
Tel.: 205-473-0738 (100%)
Manage & Market Real Estate Projects
S.I.C.: 6531

United Financial Services **(1)**
851 S. Beltline Hwy.
Mobile, AL 36606
Tel.: 205-473-0500 (100%)
Land Acquisition & Development
S.I.C.: 6552

ALUMA SHIELD INDUSTRIES, INC.
405 Fentress Blvd.
Daytona Beach, FL 32114
Tel.: 904-255-5391 FL
Fax: 904-258-1693
Approx.Sls.: $38,700,000
Emp.: 234
Mfr. of Refrigeration Equipment
S.I.C.: 3585
M.S. Sastri *(Pres.)*
Carlo Vezza *(V.P. & Sec.)*
Murphey Bates *(V.P.)*
Al Rockafellow *(V.P.-Mktg.)*

Outside Service Firm(s):

Sun Bank, N.A.*(Major Banking Relationship)*
200 S. Orange Ave.
Orlando, FL 32802
Tel.: 407-237-4899
Fax: 407-237-6704

ALUMINUM SHAPES, INC.
9000 River Rd.
Delair, NJ 08110
Mailing Address:
P.O. Box 397
Delair, NJ 08110
Tel.: 609-662-5500
Fax: 609-662-5605
Year Founded: 1953
Sales Range: $100-499 Million
Emp.: 900
Manufacture Aluminum Products
S.I.C.: 3354; 3365
Stephen F. Kendall *(Pres. & Chief Exec. Officer)*
I. Ressler *(V.P. & Sec.)*
J. Collins *(V.P.-Mfg.)*
P. Antinoff *(V.P.-Sls.)*

Outside Service Firm(s):

Ostroff & Fair*(Auditors)*
Philadelphia, PA

Kleinbard, Bell & Brecker*(Legal Firm)*
30 S. 17th St.
Philadelphia, PA 19103
Tel.: 215-568-2000

Mellon Bank, N.A.*(Major Banking Relationship)*
P.O. Box 444,
Pittsburgh, PA 15230
Tel.: 412-236-8000
Tel.: 1-800-451-7392
Fax: 412-236-8157

Subsidiary:

Delair Group, Inc. **(1)**
8600 River Rd.
Delair, NJ 08110
Tel.: 609-662-5500
Approx.Sls.: $26,000,000
Emp.: 75
Swimming Pools, Not Plastic; Hot Tubs
S.I.C.: 3949; 3999
Frank Kessler *(Pres.)*
Fred Schall *(Sec. & Treas.)*

ALVA/AMCO PHARMACAL COMPANIES, INC.
6625 N. Avondale Ave.
Chicago, IL 60631
Tel.: 312-792-0200 IL
Fax: 312-792-0798
Year Founded: 1904
Export
Distr. of Proprietary Drugs; Nutritional & Dietary Supplements
S.I.C.: 5122; 5100; 2834
Emile H. Gerchenson *(Chm. Bd. & Chief Exec. Officer)*
Jeffery H. Gerchenson *(Pres. & Chief Oper. Officer)*
Donald J. Karper *(V.P.-Sls. & Mktg.)*
N.A. Dahlstrom *(V.P.-Admin. & Pur.)*
Louis Tabano *(V.P.-Acctng.)*
M. Moore *(Dir.-Opers.)*
K. O'Kelly *(Dir.-Adv.)*
D. Taus *(Mgr.-Sls. Admin.)*

No. of U.S. Offices: 1

Computer Systems/Hardware:
MDS-Qantel; IBM

ALVEY INC.
9301 Olive Blvd.
Saint Louis, MO 63132
Tel.: 314-993-4700
Tel.: 800-325-1596
Fax: 314-993-8998
Year Founded: 1911
Approx.Sls.: $100,000,000
Emp.: 700
Fiscal Year-end: 12/31/90
Export
Package Handling Conveyors, Palletizers, Pallet Handling Conveyors
S.I.C.: 3535
William Michaels *(Pres.)*
Stephen O'Neill *(Sr. V.P.-Mktg.)*
Michael Tilton *(Sr. V.P.)*
Armen Oumedian *(Sr. V.P.)*
Richard Sampson *(Sr. V.P.-St. Louis Opers.)*
W.J. Burke *(V.P.-Mktg.)*
Roger Alderink *(V.P.-Engrng.)*
James Cahill *(V.P.)*
J.A. Sharp *(Treas.)*
Steve Williams *(Mgr.-Mktg. & Adv.)*

AMALLOY
202 Route #207
Goshen, NY 10924
Mailing Address:
P.O. Box 90
Goshen, NY 10924
Tel.: 914-294-1600
Approx.Sls.: $60,000,000
Emp.: 600
Fiscal Year-end: 12/31/90
Mfr. Hardfacing Welding Products, Specialized Cast Metal Products for Wear Control
S.I.C.: 3548; 2899; 5084; 3356
Arthur A. Borin *(Pres.)*
Allen J. Underwood *(V.P. & Treas.)*
R. Daniel Galadding *(V.P.-Mktg., Technical & Sourcing)*
Richard B. Cooper *(V.P.-Sls. Worldwide)*
Charles V. Linfante *(Chief Fin. Officer)*

AMANA SOCIETY
P.O. Box 189
Amana, IA 52203
Tel.: 319-622-3051 IA
Fax: 319-622-3119
Year Founded: 1855
Approx.Sls.: $25,000,000
Emp.: 300
Import Export
Diversified; General Farms & Stores; Manufacture Woolen, Wood, Household Furniture; Prepared Meat Products; Bakery Products
S.I.C.: 2231; 2511; 5131; 7999; 1522; 2051
Glenn Wendler *(Chm. Bd. & Pres.)*
Arthur Selzer *(Vice Chm.)*
John Ruth *(Chief Exec. Officer)*
Don Shoup *(Exec. V.P. & Sec.)*
Janet Boresi *(V.P. & Chief Fin. Officer)*
Shirley Reihman *(Treas.)*
Allyn Neubauer *(Dir.-Mktg. & Adv.)*
John Arthaud *(Dir.-Sls.)*
Caroline Ertz *(Mgr.-Human Resources)*
Reynold Moessner *(Admin. Asst.)*

No. of Mfg. Plants/Facilities: 3
No. of U.S. Offices: 1

Computer Systems/Hardware:
NCR 9300

Outside Service Firm(s):

McGladrey & Pullen*(Auditors)*
221 3rd Ave., Ste. 300
Cedar Rapids, IA 52401
Tel.: 319-366-2791

Amana Society Insurance Co.*(Group Insurer)*
Amana, IA

Blue Shield of Iowa*(Group Insurer)*
Des Moines, IA

Simmons Perrine*(Legal Firm)*
Cedar Rapids, IA

Shuttleworth & Ingersoll*(Legal Firm)*
P.O. Box 2107,
Cedar Rapids, IA 52406-2107
Tel.: 319-365-9461

The Merchants National Bank of Cedar Rapids*(Major Banking Relationship)*
Amana, IA

Subsidiaries:

Amana Farms, Inc. **(1)**
P.O. Box 189
Amana, IA 52203
Tel.: 319-622-3148 (100%)
Emp.: 45
Farming
S.I.C.: 0291; 0191
Roy Moser *(Chief Oper. Officer-Crop)*
Michael Shoup *(Chief Oper. Officer-Livestock)*

Amana-Nordstrom Motel Co. **(1)**
P.O. Box 189
Amana, IA 52203
Tel.: 319-622-3051 (50%)
Emp.: 100
Motel Operation
S.I.C.: 7011
Don Shoup *(Pres.)*
Tim Trieschmann *(Chief Oper. Officer)*
William Nordstrom *(Chief Fin. Officer & Sec.)*

Amana Society Service Co. **(1)**
Second St.
Amana, IA 52203
Tel.: 319-622-3052 (100%)
Emp.: 10
Electric, Water & Telephone Utilities
S.I.C.: 4911; 4941; 4813
Terry Herschberger *(Chief Oper. Officer)*

AMANO CINCINNATI, INC.
(Formerly Cincinnati Time, Inc.)
1733 Central Ave.
Cincinnati, OH 45214
Tel.: 513-241-5500
Tel.: 800-551-PARK (7275)
Fax: 513-241-9549
Year Founded: 1896
Approx.Sls.: $20,000,000
Emp.: 330
Fiscal Year-end: 3/31/92
Export
Complete Parking & Access Control Systems
S.I.C.: 3559
Thomas W. Frey *(Pres. & Chief Exec. Officer)*
Ray Greis *(V.P.-Human Resources)*
Brent Mitchell *(V.P.-Mfg.)*
Thomas Reif *(V.P.-Fin.)*
Michael Hanney *(Dir.-Parking Sls.-Cincinnati Brand)*
Tony Hiraoka *(Dir.-Parking Sls.-Amano Brand)*
Sally J. Fredrecks *(Mktg. Communications Specialist)*

No. of Mfg. Plants/Facilities: 2
No. of U.S. Offices: 150

Computer Systems/Hardware:
IBM System 38

Outside Service Firm(s):

Arthur Andersen & Co.*(Auditors)*
425 Walnut St.
Cincinnati, OH 45202
Tel.: 513-381-6900

Cors & Bassett*(Legal Firm)*
Cincinnati, OH

AMARLITE ARCHITECTURAL PRODUCTS
3765 Atlanta Industrial Dr.
Atlanta, GA 30331
Tel.: 404-691-5750
Tel.: 800-969-2586
Fax: 404-696-8994
Approx.Sls.: $20,000,000
Emp.: 115
Export
Aluminum Doors, Entrances, Storefronts, Curtin Walls & Windows & Framing Systems
S.I.C.: 3442; 3446
Marc Werner *(Pres. & Chief Exec. Officer)*
Robert A. Boyer *(V.P.-Sls. & Mktg.)*
Terry Vick *(V.P.-Mktg.)*

Computer Systems/Hardware:
ADP

AMBAC INTERNATIONAL

AMBAC INTERNATIONAL CORP.
I-77 at Killian Rd.
Columbia, SC 29203
Mailing Address:
P.O. Box 85
Columbia, SC 29202
Tel.: 803-735-1400
Fax: 803-735-2163
Year Founded: 1987
Approx.Sls.: $50,000,000
Emp.: 425
Fiscal Year-end: 9/30/90
Mfr. of Fuel Injection Equipment; Electric Governors
S.I.C.: 3714
Robert Isherwood *(Chm. Bd. & Pres.)*
Richard Webb *(Chief Fin. Officer)*
Dave Berner *(V.P.-Matls.)*
Eric Brisbon *(V.P.-Mktg.)*
Rick Willbrant *(V.P. & Treas.)*
Laurence Hurwitz *(Gen. Counsel)*
Laurie Regan *(Product Promo. Admin.)*

Computer Systems/Hardware:
IBM 4031

Outside Service Firm(s):

Harris Trust & Savings Bank*(Major Banking Relationship)*
111 W. Monroe St.
Chicago, IL 60690
Tel.: 312-461-2265
Tel.: 800-858-0840

AMBASSADOR STEEL CO.
1469 E. Atwater
Detroit, MI 48207
Tel.: 313-259-6600 **MI**
Fax: 313-259-0671
Year Founded: 1951
Approx.Sls.: $15,000,000
Emp.: 50
Fiscal Year-end: 12/31/91
Steel Warehouse & Service Center
S.I.C.: 5051
Hymen Freedland *(Pres.)*
Michael Freedland *(Treas. & Sec.)*
Renana Wolff *(Controller)*
Ron Pochinco *(Gen. Mgr.)*
Principal(s):
Hymen Freedland
Michael Freedland

No. of Mfg. Plants/Facilities: 1
No. of U.S. Offices: 1

Computer Systems/Hardware:
Data General Point 4

Outside Service Firm(s):

Lee & Klein*(Auditors)*
Southfield, MI

Michigan National Bank*(Major Banking Relationship)*
22595 W. 8 Mile Rd.
Detroit, MI 48219
Tel.: 313-255-6148

AMBULATORY ONE AMERICA INC.
(Formerly American Medical Buildings, Inc.)
325 E. Chicago
Milwaukee, WI 53202
Tel.: 414-291-4420 **DE**
Fax: 414-291-4432
Year Founded: 1965
Assets: $2,304,000
Earnings: $150,000
Liabilities: $2,047,000
Net Worth: $257,000
Approx.Rev.: $20,000,000
Emp.: 14
Fiscal Year-end: 12/31/90
Designs, Develops & Constructs Medical Office Bldgs., Clinics, Ambulatory Care Centers & Parking Structures
S.I.C.: 1542; 8711; 8712

AMCELL CORPORATION
1 Galen St.
Watertown, MA 02172
Tel.: 617-924-0800
Approx.Sls.: $52,000,000
Emp.: 25
Manufacture Polyethylene Bags
S.I.C.: 2673
Lloyd Gordon *(Pres. & Treas.)*
Michael Milich *(V.P.)*
Gary M. Olem *(V.P.)*
Robert Connor *(V.P.)*

AMCLYDE ENGINEERED PRODUCTS, INC.
240 E. Plato Blvd.
Saint Paul, MN 55107
Tel.: 612-293-4646 **DE**
Telex: 203037
Fax: 612-293-4648
Year Founded: 1882
Approx.Rev.: $66,000,000
Emp.: 251
Fiscal Year-end: 12/31/91
Export
Construction & Material Handling Equip., Heavy Duty Cranes, Derricks, Hoists, Car Pullers, Capstans, Barge Movers, Hydraulic Linear Winches; Services, & Parts
S.I.C.: 3531; 3536; 8711
Corporate Giving Program: United Way Matching
Wallace K. Fisk *(Pres. & Chief Exec. Officer)*
Richard J. Juelich *(Exec. V.P. & Chief Oper. Officer)*
Roger Baumhober *(V.P. & Chief Fin. Officer)*
Terrie J. Thompson *(Sr. V.P.)*
John T. Perron *(V.P.-Admin.)*
Dale DeBoth *(Controller)*
Pierre C. Delago *(Dir.-Engrng.)*

Outside Service Firm(s):

Simma Flottemesch & Orenstein*(Auditors)*
2200 Foshay Tower, 821 Marquette Ave.
Minneapolis, MN 55402

Subsidiary:

Sauerman **(1)**
1953 N. 15th Ave.
Melrose Park, IL 60160
Tel.: 708-544-4892
Fax: 708-547-7718
Approx.Sls.: $5,000,000
Emp.: 20
Mfr. of Drag Scrapers, Cableways, Crescent Scrapers & Durolite Blocks & Sheaves
S.I.C.: 3531
Dan Murphy *(V.P. & Gen. Mgr.)*

AMCO FOLDING CARTONS, INC.
2 Como Ct.
Towaco, NJ 07082
Tel.: 201-334-3030
Fax: 201-334-6982
Year Founded: 1950
Sales Range: $20-39 Million
Emp.: 135
Folding Paperboard Boxes, Containers & Displays
S.I.C.: 2657; 3993
John Como, Sr. *(Pres.)*
Lee Alexander *(V.P.-Sls.)*
John Como, Jr. *(V.P., Sec. & Treas.)*
Dennis Falduto *(V.P.-Sls.)*
Principal(s):
John Como, Sr.
John Como, Jr.

Outside Service Firm(s):

United Jersey Bank*(Major Banking Relationship)*
Lincoln Park, NJ

AMELCO CORPORATION
19208 S. Vermont Ave.
Gardena, CA 90248
Tel.: 310-327-3070
Fax: 310-538-3417
Assets: $31,600,000
Liabilities: $19,300,000
Net Worth: $12,300,000
Approx.Sls.: $90,000,000
Emp.: 500
Fiscal Year-end: 9/30/91
Electrical, Air Conditioning & Special Trade Contracting; Mfr. Concrete & Concrete Prods.
S.I.C.: 1731; 1711
Samuel M. Angelich *(Chm., Pres. & Chief Exec. Officer)*
Mark Angelich *(Exec. V.P.)*
Patrick T. Miike *(Treas.)*
John M. Carmack *(Sec.)*

Subsidiaries:

Air Engineering Co., Inc. **(1)**
2308 Pahounui Dr.
Honolulu, HI 96819
Tel.: 808-848-1040 (100%)
Emp.: 50
Mechanical Construction
S.I.C.: 1711
William Hulick *(Pres.)*

Amelco, Inc. **(1)**
2308 Pahounui Dr.
Honolulu, HI 96819
Tel.: 808-848-1040
William Hulick *(Pres.)*

Amelco Industries **(1)**
19208 S. Vermont
Gardena, CA 90248
Tel.: 310-327-3070 (100%)
Emp.: 250
Electrical Construction
S.I.C.: 1711; 1731
Mark S. Angelich *(Pres.)*

American Electric Co., Ltd. **(1)**
2308 Pahounui Dr.
Honolulu, HI 96819
Tel.: 808-848-0751 (100%)
Emp.: 100
Electrical Construction
S.I.C.: 1731
Raymond Awakuni *(Pres.)*

AMERBELLE CORPORATION
104 E. Main St.
Rockville, CT 06066
Tel.: 203-875-3325
Fax: 203-875-2238
Emp.: 300
Dyeing, Finishing & Coating of Synthetic & Blend Fabrics
S.I.C.: 2262; 2231; 2261; 2295
Nat N. Schwedel *(Chm. Bd.)*
Irving Horowitz *(Vice Chm., Exec. V.P.-Opers. & Engrng.)*
Alan R. Schwedel *(Pres. & Chief Exec. Officer)*
William R. Horowitz *(Sr. V.P. & Asst. Sec.)*

Outside Service Firm(s):

Kostin, Ruffkess & Co.*(Auditors)*
345 N. Main
West Hartford, CT
Tel.: 203-236-1975
Tel.: 203-236-0847

Murtha, Cullina, Richter & Pinney*(Legal Firm)*
City Place 1 185 Asylum St.
Hartford, CT 06103-3469
Tel.: 203-240-6000
Fax: 2032406150

Connecticut Bank & Trust*(Major Banking Relationship)*
One Constitution Plaza,
Hartford, CT 06115

AMERCO, A NEVADA CORPORATION
1325 Airmotive Way, Ste. 100
Reno, NV 89502
Mailing Address:
c/o U-Haul International, Inc.,
2727 N. Central Ave.
Phoenix, AZ 85004
Tel.: 702-688-6300 **NV**
Fax: 702-688-6338
Year Founded: 1945
Assets: $1,099,482,000
Earnings: $13,479,000
Liabilities: $713,262,000
Net Worth: $386,220,000
Approx.Sls.: $776,902,000
Approx.Rev.:$794,889,000
Emp.: 11,995
Fiscal Year-end: 3/31/90

Amerco, A Nevada Corporation—(Continued)

Holding Company of U-Haul Systems; Diversified Transportation Services; Insurance
S.I.C.: 6411; 7311; 8721; 4214; 7513; 7519
E.J. Shoen *(Chm. Bd. & Pres.)*
Gary B. Horton *(Treas.)*
Deborah Adams *(Controller)*
Gary V. Klinefelter *(Sec. & Gen. Counsel)*

No. of Foreign Offices: 7

Computer Systems/Hardware:
IBM NAS 9000; Burroughs Microcomputer

Outside Service Firm(s):

Price Waterhouse*(Auditors)*
3300 North Central
Phoenix, AZ 85012
Tel.: 602-274-0550

Lionel, Sawyer & Collins*(Legal Firm)*
Las Vegas, NV

Mariscal, Weeks, McIntyre & Friedlander, P.A.*(Legal Firm)*
Phoenix, AZ

U.S. National Bank*(Major Banking Relationship)*
Phoenix, AZ

Valley National Bank*(Major Banking Relationship)*
241 North Central Ave., 11th Floor
Phoenix, AZ 85001

Wells Fargo Bank*(Major Banking Relationship)*
420 Montgomery St.
San Francisco, CA 94104

Valley National Bank*(Pension Manager)*
3636 N. Central Av.
Phoenix, AZ 85038
Tel.: 602-261-1313

Subsidiaries:

Amerco Leasing Company **(1)**
2727 No. Central Ave.
Phoenix, AZ 85004
Tel.: 602-263-6011 (100%)
Trailer Rental
S.I.C.: 7519

Oxford Life Insurance Co. **(1)**
2721 No. Central Ave.
Phoenix, AZ 85004
Tel.: 602-263-6536 (100%)
Approx.Sls.: $50,000,000
Insurance
S.I.C.: 6411
Henry E. Martin *(Pres.)*

Ponderosa Insurance Agency **(1)**
2721 No. Central Ave.
Phoenix, AZ 85004
Tel.: 602-263-6536 (100%)
Emp.: 80
Insurance
S.I.C.: 6411
Henry E. Martin *(Pres. & Chief Exec. Officer)*

Subsidiary:

Nationwide Commercial Co. **(2)**
2721 No. Central Ave.
Phoenix, AZ 85004
Tel.: 602-263-6536 (100%)
Insurance
S.I.C.: 6411
Gary Horton *(Pres.)*

Republic Western Insurance Co. **(1)**
2721 No. Central Ave.
Phoenix, AZ 85004
Tel.: 602-263-6536 (100%)
Approx.Sls.: $90,000,000
Insurance
S.I.C.: 6411
Henry E. Martin *(Pres.)*

U-Haul International, Inc. **(1)**
2727 No. Central Ave.
Phoenix, AZ 85004
Tel.: 602-263-6011 (100%)
Fax: 602-277-5203
Approx.Sls.: $800,000,000
Emp.: 1,800
Fiscal Year-end: 4/30/91
Marketing, Advertising, Customer Relations, Accounting, Data Processing, Finance, Legal, Engineering, Communications and Personnel Services
S.I.C.: 6141; 7311; 7374; 8741; 8111; 8621; 8721; 9641; 4213; 7514; 7519; 7359
Paul Schoen *(Pres.)*
John M. Dodds *(Exec. V.P.)*
Richard Renckley *(V.P.-Human Resources)*
Tim Carty *(V.P.-Pur.)*
Gary Horton *(Treas.)*
Jack A. Lorentz *(Gen. Counsel)*
Mark Shoen *(Mktg. Dir.)*
Paul J. Kelley *(Dir.-Govt. & Pub. Rels.)*
Duane Swanson *(Adv. Mgr.)*
Sam Briggs *(Asst. to Pres.)*

Subsidiary:

A & M Associates, Inc. **(2)**
2727 No. Central Ave.
Phoenix, AZ 85004
Tel.: 602-263-6505 (100%)
Approx.Sls.: $36,000,000
Emp.: 32
Advertising & Public Relations
S.I.C.: 8721; 7311
Duane Swanson *(Pres. & Chief Exec. Officer)*

U-Haul Real Estate Company **(1)**
2727 No. Central Ave.
Phoenix, AZ 85004
Tel.: 602-263-6011 (100%)
Real Estate Services
S.I.C.: 6512

U-Haul Sales & Leasing Company **(1)**
2727 No. Central Ave.
Phoenix, AZ 85004
Tel.: 602-263-6011 (100%)
Sales & Leasing of Trailers
S.I.C.: 7519; 5012

AMERICA OUTDOORS LTD
501 N. Main St.
Thiensville, WI 53092
Tel.: 414-242-3900
Fax: 414-242-4281
Year Founded: 1868
Approx.Sls.: $14,000,000
Emp.: 25
Wholesale & Retail Building Materials & Garden Supplies; Distribute Farm & Outdoor Power Equipment
S.I.C.: 5083; 5191
Dick Vogel *(Pres.)*

Computer Systems/Hardware:
Scientific Computer Instruments

Outside Service Firm(s):

Aetna Life & Casualty*(Group Insurer)*
151 Farmington Avenue
Hartford, CT 06156
Tel.: 203-273-2128
Fax: 203-729-4295

CNA Insurance*(Group Insurer)*
CNA Plaza,
Chicago, IL 60685
Tel.: 312-822-5000

M & I Marshall & Ilsley Bank*(Major Banking Relationship)*
770 N. Water St.
Milwaukee, WI 53202
Tel.: 414-765-8700

Subsidiary:

Rental America **(1)**
505 N. Main St.
Thiensville, WI 53092
Tel.: 414-242-3900
Rental Equipment for Homes & Offices
S.I.C.: 7359
Jeff Koehn *(Rental Mgr.)*

AMERICAN AIRCRAFT PARTS MANUFACTURING CO.
25331 Trowbridge
Dearborn, MI 48124
Mailing Address:
P.O. Box 2188
Dearborn, MI 48123
Tel.: 313-565-6700 **MI**
Fax: 313-565-9220
Year Founded: 1952
Approx.Sls.: $25,000,000
Emp.: 100
Manufacture Aircraft Precision Parts
S.I.C.: 3728
Harry Lipton *(Pres. & Chief Exec. Officer)*
Maxine Lipton *(V.P.)*
Edgar Claeys *(Dir.-Pur.)*
Michael Thomas *(Dir.-Production)*

Principal(s):
Harry Lipton

Outside Service Firm(s):

Rosen, Feinberg, Coppola*(Auditors)*
Southfield, MI

Manufacturers National Bank N.A.*(Major Banking Relationship)*
38th Fl., 100 Renaissance Center
Detroit, MI 48243
Tel.: 313-222-4227

AMERICAN APPRAISAL ASSOCIATES, INC.
(Sub. of RLM Investments, Inc., Milwaukee, WI)
100 E. Wisconsin Ave., Ste. 2100
Milwaukee, WI 53202
Mailing Address:
P.O. Box 664,
Milwaukee, WI 53201
Tel.: 414-271-7240
Tel.: 800-228-4888 **DE**
Telex: 43-11114
Year Founded: 1896
Emp.: 531
Fairness Opinion in Mergers/ Acquisitions; Valuation Consulting Services
S.I.C.: 8741; 8748
Corporate Giving Program: Contact Company for Further Information on Corporate Giving Program
Employee Matching Gifts Program: Contact Company for Further Information On Employee Matching Gifts Program
Richard A. Giesen *(Chm. Bd., Pres. & Chief Exec. Officer)*
Michael S. Megna *(Sr. V.P.)*
Lee P. Hackett *(V.P.-U.S. Opers.)*
Ronald M. Goergen *(V.P.-International, Sec.)*
Paul H. Gross *(V.P.)*
Edward W. Raether *(V.P.)*
Alfiero Vita *(V.P.)*
Scott Frederick *(Chief Fin. Officer & Treas.)*
Edmond V. Russ *(Dir.-Mktg.)*
William L. Summers *(Dir.-Data Processing)*
Laurie Giesen *(Mgr.-Pub. Rels.)*

Computer Systems/Hardware:
IBM

Outside Service Firm(s):

Price Waterhouse*(Auditors)*
1500 Bank One Plaza, 100 E. Wisconsin Ave.
Milwaukee, WI 53202

Michael, Best & Friedrich*(Legal Firm)*
100 East Wisconsin Avenue
Milwaukee, WI 53202
Tel.: 414-271-6560

Winston & Strawn*(Legal Firm)*
One 1st Natl. Plaza, No. 5000
Chicago, IL 60603
Tel.: 312-558-5600

John Hancock Mutual Life Insurance Co.*(Pension Manager)*
John Hancock Place, P.O. Box 111
Boston, MA 02117

Marine Trust Co.*(Pension Manager)*
Milwaukee, WI

Divisions:

The American Appraisal Co. **(1)**
525 E. Michigan St.
Milwaukee, WI 53201
Tel.: 414-271-7240

E. H. Boeckh Co. **(1)**
525 E. Michigan St.
Milwaukee, WI 53202
Tel.: 414-271-5544
Professional Valuation Service
S.I.C.: 8999
Daniel W. Rosien *(Mng. Dir.)*

Standard Research Consultants **(1)**
26 Broadway
New York, NY 10004
Tel.: 212-558-6660

Subsidiary:

American Appraisal Capital Services, Inc. **(1)**
525 E. Michigan St.
Milwaukee, WI 53202
Tel.: 414-271-7240 (100%)
Finders Services, Mergers, Acquisitions Fairness Opinions
S.I.C.: 8741
R.M. Goergen *(Pres.)*

Non-U.S. Holdings:

AA Japan Co. **(1)**
Kabutocho Yachiyo Bldg., 20-5 Nihonbashi Kubatocho Chuo-ku,
Tokyo, 103, Japan
Tel.: 3-3-661-2661
Fax: 3-3-639-5927
Hatasa Hiroyuki *(Mgr.)*

American Appraisal Canada, Inc. **(1)**
310 Front St. W., Suite 800
Toronto, ON M5V 3B5, Canada
Tel.: 416-593-4050 (100%)
Emp.: 28
Also Located in Montreal, PQ, Vancouver, BC, Canada
S.I.C.: 8741
Russell J. Sheppard *(Pres.)*

American Appraisal Espana, S.A. **(1)**
Colon De Larreategui, 26-3H 48009
Bilbao, Spain
Tel.: 424-39-12 (98.2%)
Telex: 34265
Professional Valuation Services
S.I.C.: 8741

American Appraisal Espana, S.A. **(1)**
Principe de Vergara, 9 28001
Madrid, Spain
Tel.: 1-276-5600 (98.2%)
Telex: 45973
Emp.: 45
Professional Valuation Services
S.I.C.: 8741
Andres Carrasco *(Mng. Dir.)*

American Appraisal Espana, S.A. **(1)**
Diputacion, 238 -Atico 2 08007
Barcelona, Spain
Tel.: 302-21-16 (98.2%)
Telex: 542 38
Emp.: 6
S.I.C.: 8742

American Appraisal Espana, S.A. **(1)**
Calle Luis de Morales, 32-1 Modulo 34 - Edificio FORUM, 41005
Seville, Spain
Tel.: 5-458-1706
Fax: 5-457-5548
Juan Marquez *(Mgr.)*

American Appraisal France **(1)**
32, Rue Notre Dame des Victoires 75002
Paris, France (100%)
Professional Valuation Services
S.I.C.: 8742
Robin Edme *(Mgr.)*

American Appraisal Hong Kong Ltd. (1)
1301 Bond Centre, East Tower
Queensway, Hong Kong
Tel.: 801-5555 (100%)
Telex: 780-83201
Emp.: 35
Professional Valuation Services
S.I.C.: 8741
George Liu *(Mng. Dir.)*

American Appraisal Hungary Co. Ltd. (1)
Ganz U.16, 3rd Fl., 304 PF.18 (1277) H.-1027,
Budapest, II, Hungary
Tel.: 1-202-0415 (100%)
Telex: 722-23525
Emp.: 13
Professional Valuation Services
S.I.C.: 8742
Ferenc Tordai *(Mng. Dir.)*

American Appraisal Italia S.r.l. (1)
Centro Direzionale Colleoni Viale Colleoni 21, 20041 Edificio Pegaso 1,
Agrate Brianza, Milan Italy
Tel.: 39 654432 (100%)
Emp.: 12
Professional Valuation Services
S.I.C.: 8741
Dino Georgescu *(Mng. Dir.)*

American Appraisal Italia S.r.l. (1)
Piazza Salvemini, 4 35131
Padova, Italy
Tel.: 2-49-656533 (100%)
Emp.: 9
Professional Valuation Services
S.I.C.: 8742
Mauro Pasquali *(Mgr.)*

American Appraisal Italia S.r.l. (1)
Galleria Passarella, 2 20121
Milan, Italy
Tel.: 2-798-724 (100%)
Emp.: 68
Professional Valuation Services
S.I.C.: 8742
Dino Georgescu *(Mng. Dir.)*

American Appraisal Italia S.r.l. (1)
Via Cavour, 1 10123
Turin, Italy
Tel.: 11 540 556 (100%)
Emp.: 4
S.I.C.: 8742

American Appraisal Italia, S.r.l. (1)
Via Flavio Domiziano, 10 00145
Rome, Italy
Tel.: 6-513--7697
Fax: 6-512-8994
Emp.: 16
Lucio Cammarano *(Mgr.)*

American Appraisal Poland Sp. z.o.o. (1)
ul. Filtrowa 43 02-057,
Warsaw, Poland
Tel.: 48-22-25-60 (100%)
Emp.: 3
Professional Valuation Services
S.I.C.: 8742
Miroslaw Miernik *(Mng. Dir.)*

American Appraisal Portugal Consultores de. Avaliacao S.A. (1)
Av. da Boavista, 1015-6.0 Office No. 601, 4100
Porto, Portugal
Tel.: 2-600-4107
Fax: 2-600-4108
Frederico Borges de Castro *(Mgr.)*

American Appraisal (Portugal) Ltd. (1)
Av. Miguel Bombarda, 36-11 1000
Lisbon, Portugal (100%)
Emp.: 15
S.I.C.: 8742
Miguel Dias Costa *(Mng. Dir.)*

American Appraisal Thailand Ltd. (1)
12th Fl., American Intl. Tower 181/19
Suriwongse Rd.,
Bangkok, 10500, Thailand
Tel.: 2-238-4251 (50.5%)
Emp.: 85
Professional Valuation Services
S.I.C.: 8742
Rodolfo L. Vergara *(Mng. Dir.)*

American Appraisal (U.K.) Ltd. (1)
49 Whitehall
London, SWIA 2BX, United Kingdom
Tel.: 071-839-1776 (100%)
Telex: 851-8950118
Emp.: 4
Professional Valuation Services
S.I.C.: 8741
John Lawton *(Mgr.)*

American Appraisal (U.K.) Ltd. (1)
Ship Canal House, King Street
Manchester, M2 4WU, United Kingdom (100%)
Emp.: 9
S.I.C.: 8742
John Lawton *(Mng. Dir.)*

Panamericana de Avaluos, S.A. (1)
Colonia del Valle, Moras No. 850 01300
Mexico, D.F. Mexico
Tel.: 5-669-4707 (19%)
Telex: 383-01771154
Emp.: 42
Professional Valuation Services
S.I.C.: 8742
Thomas Voticky *(Mng. Dir.)*

AMERICAN ARBITRATION ASSOCIATION
140 W. 51st St.
New York, NY 10020
Tel.: 212-484-4000 **NY**
Fax: 212-765-4874
Year Founded: 1926
Assets: $26,000,000
Liabilities: $25,000,000
Net Worth: $1,000,000
Approx.Sls.: $42,000,000
Emp.: 650
Fiscal Year-end: 12/31/91
Arbitration & Concillation Service; Book Publishing; Periodicals
S.I.C.: 7389; 2731; 2721
Robert Coulson *(Pres. & Chief Exec. Officer)*
Mildred York *(V.P.-Personnel)*
Susan Klein *(V.P.-Publishing)*
Robert E. Meade *(V.P.)*
Elvira Robbins *(V.P.)*
Allan Silberman *(V.P.)*
Jan Williamson Wagner *(V.P.)*
Michael F. Hoellering *(Gen. Counsel)*

Outside Service Firm(s):

KPMG Peat Marwick*(Auditors)*
345 Park Ave.
New York, NY 10154
Tel.: 212-758-9700
Fax: 212-872-3308

Manufacturers Hanover Trust Co.*(Major Banking Relationship)*
4 New York Plaza
New York, NY 10015
Tel.: 212-633-7938

AMERICAN AUTOMOBILE ASSOCIATION, NATIONAL TRAVEL DEPARTMENT
1000 AAA Dr.
Heathrow, FL 32746
Tel.: 407-444-8280
Fax: 407-222-6790
Year Founded: 1902
Approx.Sls.: $25,000,000
Emp.: 200
Travel Publications Provided to AAA Members in the U.S. & Canada
S.I.C.: 2741
Paul R. Verkuil *(Pres.)*
Harold Yankelevitz *(Dir.-Mktg. & Opers.)*
Barbara Coenson *(Mktg. Coord.)*
Glenn Cooper *(Sls. Dir.)*

THE AMERICAN BANKERS ASSOCIATION
1120 Connecticut Ave., N.W.
Washington, DC 20036
Tel.: 202-663-5000
Fax: 202-828-4532
Year Founded: 1883
Assets: $77,286,000
Liabilities: $32,818,000
Net Worth: $44,468,000
Approx.Sls.: $66,121,000
Emp.: 500
Fiscal Year-end: 8/31/90
Trade & Professional Association for Commercial Banks
S.I.C.: 8611
Corporate Giving Program: UGF
William H. Brandon Jr. *(Pres.)*
Donald Ogilvie *(Exec. V.P. & Chief Oper. Officer)*
John J. Gill *(Gen. Counsel)*
Gail McGowan *(Corp. Sec.)*
L. Leon Patterson *(Treas.)*
Joanne Wharton *(Controller)*
J. Douglas Adamson *(Exec. Dir.-Bank Programs & Prof. Devel.)*
James E. Lodge *(Exec. Dir.-Communications & Corp. American Banking)*
Jeffrey S. Owen *(Exec. Dir.-Banking Organizations & American Financial Skylink)*
Robert A. Wallgren *(Exec. Dir.-Opers. & Fin.)*
Edward L. Yingling *(Exec. Dir.-Govt. Rels.)*
George Collett *(Dir.-Fin. Services)*
Carl Jacobs *(Dir.-Personnel)*
Gerry Peterson *(Dir.-Human Resources)*
Ray Wills *(Dir.-Mgmt. Info. Systems)*
Paul Rossi *(Mgr.-Meetings Planning)*
Joan Gervino *(Corp. Librarian)*

Outside Service Firm(s):

Arthur Andersen & Co.*(Auditors)*
1666 K Street, N.W.
Washington, DC 20006

American Security Bank, N.A.*(Pension Manager)*
1501 Pennsylvania Ave. N.W.
Washington, DC 20013
Tel.: 202-624-4000

United States Trust Company of New York*(Pension Manager)*
45 Wall Street
New York, NY 10005

Affiliate:

Bank Marketing Association (1)
309 W. Washington St.
Chicago, IL 60606
Tel.: 312-782-1442
S.I.C.: 8611
J. Douglas Adamson *(Exec. V.P.)*

AMERICAN BARMAG CO.
1101 Westinghouse Blvd.
Charlotte, NC 28241
Tel.: 704-588-0072
Telex: 810-621-0485
Fax: 704-588-2047
Year Founded: 1965
Approx.Sls.: $65,000,000
Emp.: 100
Fiscal Year-end: 12/31/90
Import Export
Textile Machinery, Extrusion Equip., Hydraulic Valves, Barmag
S.I.C.: 3552; 3542; 3492
Jochen Becker *(Chm. Bd)*
Dr. Michael Haniseh *(Pres.)*
Kay E. Schnaidt *(Exec. V.P.)*
Norbert Baron *(Chief Fin. Officer)*
Klans Fuefing *(Sec. & Treas.)*
Laurie Hanen *(Dir.-Pub. Rels.)*

American Beauty Homes
(See First Financial Group, Inc. Listing)

AMERICAN BIBLE SOCIETY
1865 Broadway
New York, NY 10023
Tel.: 212-408-1200
Fax: 212-408-1512
Year Founded: 1816
Emp.: 290
Translating, Publishing & Distributing The Scriptures
S.I.C.: 2731; 7389
James Wood *(Chm. Bd.)*
Ruth Peale *(Vice Chm.)*
Eugene B. Habecker *(Pres. & Chief Exec. Officer)*
Maria I. Martinez *(V.P)*
Daniel K. Scarberry *(Treas.)*
Gary R. Ruth *(Dir.-Prod.)*

AMERICAN BREAD COMPANY - SUNBEAM BAKERY
702 Murfreesboro Rd.
Nashville, TN 37210
Mailing Address:
P.O. Box 100390
Nashville, TN 37224
Tel.: 615-254-1161 **TN**
Fax: 615-244-6243
Year Founded: 1889
Approx.Sls.: $25,000,000
Emp.: 520
Bread, Rolls & Doughnuts
S.I.C.: 2051
Charles K. Evers *(Chm. Bd., Pres. & Chief Exec. Officer)*
Tim Wiell *(V.P., Treas. & Controller)*
Jack James *(V.P.-Sls.)*
Linda Evers *(Sec. & Asst. Treas.)*
John Florida *(Dir.-Data Processing)*
James W. Phillips *(Dir.-Personnel & Investor Rels.)*
Richard Kirk *(Mgr.-Traffic & Pur. Agent)*
George Grubbs *(Chief Engineer)*
Principal(s):
Charles K. Evers

No. of Mfg. Plants/Facilities: 3
No. of U.S. Offices: 3

Computer Systems/Hardware:
IBM AS 400-Model 45

Outside Service Firm(s):

Kraft Bros., Esstman, Patton & Harrell*(Auditors)*
Nashville, TN

First American National Bank*(Major Banking Relationship)*
Nashville, TN

Subsidiary:

American Bread Co. of Alabama Inc. (1)
7200 Governors West
Huntsville, AL 35807
Tel.: 205-837-1511 (100%)
Wholesale Bakery
S.I.C.: 5149
Jack Halbrook *(Gen. Mgr.)*

AMERICAN BUILDINGS CO.
State Docks Rd.
Eufaula, AL 36027
Mailing Address:
P.O. Box 800,
Eufaula, AL 36027
Tel.: 205-687-2032 **DE**
Fax: 205-687-8315
Year Founded: 1967
Approx.Sls.: $176,000,000
Emp.: 1,200
Mfr. Steel Buildings
S.I.C.: 3448
Len George *(Pres.)*
L.L. Wilson *(Sr. V.P.-Engrng.)*
Ron Buchholz *(V.P.-Mfg.)*
R.L. Pritts *(V.P.-Fin.)*
Alvan E. Richey, Jr. *(V.P.-Mktg.)*
Joel Voelkert *(V.P.-Sls.)*
P.S. Woodham *(V.P.-Admin.)*
W.P. Cole *(Treas.)*
Judy McCullan *(Mgr.-Mktg.)*

Outside Service Firm(s):

Arthur Andersen & Co.*(Auditors)*
Avenue des Arts 56 1040
Brussels, Belgium

American Buildings Co.—(Continued)

Arthur Andersen & Co.*(Auditors)*
133 Peachtree St., N.E.
Atlanta, GA 30303
Tel.: 404-658-1776

Merritt & McClain*(Legal Firm)*
Eufaula, AL

Eufaula Bank & Trust Co.*(Major Banking Relationship)*
Eufaula, AL

Subsidiary:

ABC Transportation Co. (1)
State Docks Rd.
Eufaula, AL 36027
Tel.: 205-687-2032 (100%)
Contract Carrier
S.I.C.: 4213
James D. Murphy *(Chief Oper. Officer)*

AMERICAN BUREAU OF SHIPPING

Two World Trade Center-106th Fl.
New York, NY 10048
Mailing Address:
P.O. Box 910,
Paramus, NJ 07653-0910
Tel.: 212-839-5000 **NY**
Fax: 212-839-5130
Year Founded: 1862
Sales Range: $100-499 Million
Emp.: 1,475
Classification Society
S.I.C.: 8611; 4499; 4493
Frank J. Iarossi *(Chm. Bd. & Pres.)*
James L. Dolan *(Sr. V.P.-Opers.)*
Donald Liu *(Sr. V.P.-Tech. Services)*
Donald M. Birney *(V.P.-Personnel)*
Allan E. Johnson *(V.P. & Controller)*
Frank M. Meyler *(V.P., Sec. & Gen. Counsel)*
Thomas J. Tucker *(V.P.-Corp. Services)*

No. of U.S. Offices: 36
No. of Foreign Offices: 195

Computer Systems/Hardware:
IBM

Outside Service Firm(s):

KPMG Peat Marwick*(Auditors)*
345 Park Ave.
New York, NY 10154
Tel.: 212-758-9700
Fax: 212-872-3308

United Jersey Bank*(Major Banking Relationship)*
Hackensack, NJ

Subsidiary:

ABS Industrial Verification, Inc. (1)
16855 N. Chase Dr.
Houston, TX 77060-6008
Tel.: 713-873-5200
Emp.: 100
Provides Inspection, Certification, Quality Assurance & Analysis Services to Diverse Businesses
S.I.C.: 8711; 8999
A.V. DeStena *(Pres.)*

AMERICAN BUSINESS INFORMATION, INC.

5711 S. 86th Circle
Omaha, NE 68127
Mailing Address:
P.O. Box 27347
Omaha, NE 68127
Tel.: 402-593-4500 **NV**
Fax: 402-331-1505
Year Founded: 1972
Assets: $36,000,000
Liabilities: $14,000,000
Net Worth: $22,000,000
Approx.Sls.: $50,000,000
Emp.: 685
Fiscal Year-end: 12/31/90
Export
Publisher of Business Lists; Directories & On-Line Information Service
S.I.C.: 7331; 2741; 7375
Vinod Gupta *(Chm., Pres., Chief Exec. Officer)*
Jon Hoffmaster *(Exec. V.P. & Chief Oper. Officer)*
Jack Betts *(V.P.-Oper.)*
Tom Lingelbach *(V.P.-Sls.)*
Monica Messer *(V.P.-Data Processing)*
Jim Pflug *(V.P.-Fin.)*
Glenn C. Prettyman *(V.P. Adv.)*

Computer Systems/Hardware:
IBM AS400

Outside Service Firm(s):

Coopers & Lybrand*(Auditors)*
1 Post Office Square
Boston, MA 02110
Tel.: 617-574-5000
Fax: 617-345-0398

Chemical Banking Corp.*(Major Banking Relationship)*
277 Park Ave.
New York, NY 10041
Tel.: 212-310-6407
Fax: 212-310-4526

Divisions:

American Business Directories (1)
5707 S. 86th Circle
Omaha, NE 68127
Tel.: 402-331-7169
Andy Bock *(Mgr.)*

American Directory Publishing (1)
5707 S. 86th Circle
Omaha, NE 68127
Tel.: 402-331-7169
Jim Nichols *(Mgr.)*

Marketing Research Group (1)
5711 S. 86th Circle
Omaha, NE 68127
Tel.: 402-593-4545
Jeff Ferris *(Mgr.)*

Online Information Network (1)
5707 S. 86th Circle
Omaha, NE 68127
Tel.: 402-593-4593
Bill Chasse *(Mgr.)*

Subsidiaries:

ABI National Accounts (1)
466 Main St.
New Rochelle, NY 10801

ABI National Accounts (1)
8120 Penn Ave., South #151-0
Bloomington, MN 55431

ABI National Accounts (1)
657 E. Golf Rd., Suite 312
Arlington Heights, IL 60005
Tel.: 708-228-0905

ABI National Accounts (1)
1 World Trade Center, #7967
New York, NY 10048

ABI National Accounts (1)
70 Mausell Ct., Suite 100
Rosewell, CA 30076

Compilers Plus (1)
466 Main St.
New Rochelle, NY 10801
Tel.: 914-633-5240
Information Publishers
S.I.C.: 2741; 7375
Ed Mallin *(Pres.)*

AMERICAN CAPITAL MANAGEMENT & RESEARCH, INC.

2800 Post Oak Blvd.
Houston, TX 77056
Mailing Address:
P.O. Box 3121,
Houston, TX 77253
Tel.: 713-993-0500 **MD**
Closed End Investment Co.
S.I.C.: 6726
Don G. Powell *(Chm. Bd. & Pres.)*
Curtis W. Morell *(V.P. & Treas.)*
Lawrence A. Rogers *(V.P. & Gen. Counsel)*

Outside Service Firm(s):

Ernst & Young*(Auditors)*
1 Houston Ctr., 1200 McKinney
Houston, TX 77002
Tel.: 713-750-1500

State Street Bank & Trust Co.*(Registrar)*
P.O. Box 5003
Boston, MA 02107
Tel.: 617-786-6316

AMERICAN CAST IRON PIPE CO.

1501 31st Ave., N.
Birmingham, AL 35207
Mailing Address:
P.O. Box 2727
Birmingham, AL 35202
Tel.: 205-325-7701
Telex: 5-9736 ACIPCO B-ham
Fax: 205-325-8014
Year Founded: 1905
Approx.Sls.: $400,000,000
Emp.: 2,600
Fiscal Year-end: 12/31/90
Mfr. & Wholesaler of Primary Metals & Fabricated Metal Products
S.I.C.: 3321; 3069; 3325; 3494; 3317
Van L. Richey *(Pres. & Chief Exec. Officer)*
H. Arthur Edge *(Chief Oper. Officer)*
J. Michael O'Brien *(V.P.-Sls. & Sec.)*
R.M. Bragdon *(V.P.-Engrng.)*
J.M. Cook *(V.P., Chief Fin. Officer & Treas.)*
L. Barr *(Dir.-Personnel)*
G. Bailey *(Dir.-Data Processing)*
Cynthia Lovoy *(Publicity Mgr.)*
B.W. Erwin *(Pur. Agent.)*

No. of Mfg. Plants/Facilities: 1
No. of U.S. Offices: 11

Computer Systems/Hardware:
IBM

Outside Service Firm(s):

KPMG Peat Marwick*(Auditors)*
1200 Financial Center
Birmingham, AL 35203
Tel.: 205-324-2495

Blue Cross & Blue Shield of Alabama*(Group Insurer)*
450 Riverchase Pkwy. East
Birmingham, AL 35298
Tel.: 205-988-2245

Burr & Forman*(Legal Firm)*
3000 SouthTrust Towers
Birmingham, AL 35203
Tel.: 205-251-3000
Fax: 205-328-2950

Subsidiary:

Waterous Company (1)
300 John E. Carroll Ave. E
South Saint Paul, MN 55075
Tel.: 612-450-5000 (100%)
Fax: 612-450-5090
Approx.Sls.: $51,056,000
Emp.: 300
Fiscal Year-end: 12/31/90
Mfrs. Fire Hydrants, Fire Pumps, Valves
S.I.C.: 3321; 3492; 3561
Robert Nassau *(Chm. Bd.)*
Jerome M. Mandel *(Pres.)*
Donald Haugen *(V.P.)*
Heinz Otte *(V.P.)*
James Nauer *(V.P.)*
Richard Lloyd *(Treas.)*
Edward O. Pagel *(Sec.)*
Michael Anderson *(Sls. Mgr.)*
Michael Waldoch *(Sls. Mgr.)*
Gabe Madrinich *(Dir.-Pur.)*
Colleen Leahy *(Personnel Asst.)*

AMERICAN CHEMICAL SOCIETY

1155 16th St. N.W.
Washington, DC 20036
Tel.: 202-872-4600 **DC**
Telex: 202-872-4615
Year Founded: 1876
Assets: $244,000,000
Earnings: $10,841,000
Liabilities: $133,000,000
Net Worth: $111,000,000
Approx.Sls.: $190,000,000
Emp.: 1,922
Fiscal Year-end: 12/31/91
Publisher Scientific Journals
S.I.C.: 2721
Dr. Joseph A. Dixon *(Chm. Bd.)*
Dr. Ernest L. Eliel *(Pres.)*
Dr. John K. Crum *(Chief Exec. Officer)*
Brian A. Bernstein *(Chief Fin. Officer & Treas.)*
Frank Young *(Controller)*
Dr. Justin W. Collat *(Sec.)*
Ross M. Wilson, III *(Asst. Treas.)*
Michael Phillippe *(Dir.-Mngmt. Information Systems)*
David A. Daniel *(Asst. to Exec. Dir.)*

Computer Systems/Hardware:
NRC Tower

Outside Service Firm(s):

Deloitte & Touche*(Auditors)*
1900 M St. N.W., 4th Fl.
Washington, DC 20036

Goldman, Sachs & Co.*(Investment Banker)*
85 Broad St.
New York, NY 10004
Tel.: 212-902-1000
Fax: 212-902-4451

O'Brien, Birney & Butler*(Legal Firm)*
888 17th St. N.W.
Washington, DC

American Security Bank, N.A.*(Major Banking Relationship)*
1501 Pennsylvania Ave. N.W.
Washington, DC 20013
Tel.: 202-624-4000

First National Bank of Maryland*(Major Banking Relationship)*
Washington, DC

Sanford C. Bernstein & Co., Inc.*(Pension Manager)*
767 Fifth Ave.
New York, NY 10153
Tel.: 212-756-4383
Fax: 212-756-4405

Pacific Investment Management*(Pension Manager)*
P.O. Box 9000, 840 Newport Center Dr.
Newport Beach, CA 92660
Tel.: 714-640-3347

Wells Fargo Nikko Investment Advisors*(Pension Manager)*
45 Fremont St., 16th Fl.
San Francisco, CA 94105
Tel.: 415-597-2000
Fax: 415-597-2199

THE AMERICAN COMPANIES, INC.

2101 N. Topeka
Topeka, KS 66608
Mailing Address:
P.O. Box 1777,
Topeka, KS 66601
Tel.: 913-233-4252
Fax: 913-233-3129
Year Founded: 1968
Approx.Sls.: $20,000,000

Emp.: 450
Fiscal Year-end: 1/31/91
Export
Prebound Paperback Books; Library Binding
S.I.C.: 2789
Dana D. Bram *(V.P.- Fin. & Controller)*
Joseph E. Gigous *(V.P. & Gen. Mgr.- American Bindery, Mid-West)*
Richard Tinder *(V.P. & Gen. Mgr.- Econo-Clad Books)*
Fred Schilling *(V.P.-Sls.)*
Donna M. Crawford *(Sec.)*

No. of Mfg. Plants/Facilities: 4

Computer Systems/Hardware:
IBM System 36; IBM PC; Digital PDP 1184 & 1124

Outside Service Firm(s):

Mize Houser Mehlinger & Kimes*(Auditors)*
Topeka, KS

George Erickson*(Legal Firm)*
Topeka, KS

First National Bank of Topeka*(Major Banking Relationship)*
Topeka, KS

Division:

American Bindry-East **(1)**
801 Ivey
Colonial Hills, VA 23834
Tel.: 804-526-8970

American Bindry-Midwest **(1)**
914 Jefferson
Topeka, KS 66607
Tel.: 913-233-4252

Econo-Clad Books **(1)**
P.O. Box 1777
Topeka, KS 66601
Tel.: 913-233-4252
Book Bindery; Wholesaler
S.I.C.: 2789

Subsidiary:

Prebound Periodicals, Inc. **(1)**
914 Jefferson
Topeka, KS 66607
Tel.: 913-233-4252
S.I.C.: 2789

AMERICAN CRANE & EQUIPMENT CORP.
531 Old Swede Rd.
Douglassville, PA 19518
Tel.: 215-385-6061 **PA**
Fax: 215-385-3191
Year Founded: 1972
Sales Range: $10-19 Million
Emp.: 90
Fiscal Year-end: 3/31/91
Export
Manufacturer of Overhead Electric Cranes & Hoists
S.I.C.: 3536
Oddvar Norheim *(Chm. Bd. & Pres.)*
David G. Schaeffer *(V.P.-Sls.)*
D. Weber *(Chief Engnr.)*
S. Hoffman *(Pur. Agent)*

Computer Systems/Hardware:
IBM 386

AMERICAN CRYSTAL SUGAR COMPANY
101 N. Third St.
Moorhead, MN 56560
Tel.: 218-236-4400 **MN**
Year Founded: 1898
Assets: $256,738,000
Liabilities: $150,032,000
Net Worth: $106,706,000
Approx.Sls.: $489,007,000
Emp.: 1,100
Fiscal Year-end: 8/31/91
Import Export
Beet Sugar Cooperative
S.I.C.: 2063; 2062
Fred Born *(Chm. Bd.)*
Joseph Famalette *(Pres. & Chief Exec. Officer)*
James J. Horvath *(V.P.-Fin.)*
Jack G. Lackman *(V.P.-Mktg.)*
Larry L. Mathias *(V.P.-Human Resources & Pub. Rels.)*
Mark Richardson *(V.P.-Opers.)*
C.A. Nordhougen *(Sec. & Gen. Counsel)*
Richard Saylor *(Controller)*
Sam Wai *(Treas.)*
Eugene DeMinck *(Mgr.-Purch.)*
Ed Janzen *(Mgr.-Mngmt. Information Systems)*

No. of Mfg. Plants/Facilities: 5

Computer Systems/Hardware:
IBM 4381

Outside Service Firm(s):

Eide, Helmeke & Co.*(Auditors)*
Fargo, ND

Dosland, Nordhougen, Lillehaug, Johnson & Saande, P.A.*(Legal Firm)*
American Bank Bldg.
Moorhead, MN 56560
Tel.: 218-233-2744

Bank for Co-ops*(Major Banking Relationship)*
St. Paul, MN

Norwest Bank Minnesota, N.A.*(Major Banking Relationship)*
Fargo, ND

Sales & Distribution Offices:

American Crystal Sugar Co. **(1)**
P.O. Box 65,
Chaska, MN 55318
Sls. & Distr.
S.I.C.: 5149
La Var Varney *(Distr. Facility Mgr.)*

American Crystal Sugar Co. **(1)**
Box 1098,
Mason City, IA 50401
Tel.: 515-423-1214
Sls. & Distr.
S.I.C.: 5149
Dale Borchardt *(Distr. Facility Supt.)*

Research Center:

American Crystal Sugar Co. **(1)**
Box 1227,
Moorhead, MN 56560
Tel.: 218-236-4340
Research Center
S.I.C.: 8731
J. Gary Fox *(V.P.-Research & Devel.)*

AMERICAN DECAL & MFG. CO.
4100 W. Fullerton Ave.
Chicago, IL 60639
Tel.: 312-489-4700
Fax: 312-489-2361
Year Founded: 1919
Approx.Sls.: $17,000,000
Emp.: 230
Mfr. of Decals & Related Products
S.I.C.: 2752; 2759
Thomas O'Brian *(Pres.)*
James Murphy *(V.P.-Chemistry)*
Jim Marousis *(Treas.)*

Outside Service Firm(s):

Weiss Simon & Company*(Auditors)*
Chicago, IL

Continental Bank N. A.*(Major Banking Relationship)*
231 S. LaSalle St.
Chicago, IL 60697
Tel.: 312-828-2345
Tel.: 800-426-5754
Telex: 312-828-1783

AMERICAN DEVELOPMENT CORPORATION
1930 Hanahan Rd.
North Charleston, SC 29406
Tel.: 803-572-0010
Fax: 803-797-7519
Emp.: 300
Metal Fabrication; Systems Integration
S.I.C.: 3469; 7373
W. Melvin Brown, Jr. *(Pres.)*
Carl S. Holland *(V.P.)*
Frank W. Price *(Treas.)*
Gerald Kaynard *(Sec. & Legal Counsel)*

Outside Service Firm(s):

Gamble Givens & Moody*(Auditors)*
Charleston, SC

Nationsbank South Carolina*(Major Banking Relationship)*
Charleston, SC

AMERICAN EAGLE AIRLINES
900 N. Franklin, Ste. 800
Chicago, IL 60610
Tel.: 312-280-8222
Fax: 312-280-2219
Assets: $82,648,000
Earnings: $1,372,000
Net Worth: $82,648,000
Approx.Sls.: $90,000,000
Emp.: 1,300
Fiscal Year-end: 1/ 3/91
Regional Air Carrier
S.I.C.: 4512
Peter A. Piper *(Pres. & Chief Oper. Officer)*
John Boyd *(V.P.-Fin. & Treas.)*
Tricia Frank *(V.P.-Sls. & Mktg.)*
Sally Ruecking *(Dir.-Personnel)*

Outside Service Firm(s):

The Northern Trust Co.*(Major Banking Relationship)*
50 S. LaSalle St.
Chicago, IL 60675
Tel.: 312-630-6000
Fax: 312-630-6516

Metropolitan Life Insurance Co.*(Group Insurer)*
Detroit, MI

AMERICAN ENTERPRISE INSTITUTE FOR PUBLIC POLICY RESEARCH
1150 17th St. N.W.
Washington, DC 20036
Tel.: 202-862-5800
Fax: 202-862-7177
Year Founded: 1943
Emp.: 100
Fiscal Year-end: 12/31/90
Nonprofit, Nonpartisan, Publicly Supported Educational Research Organization
S.I.C.: 8733
Paul Oreffice *(Chm. Bd.)*
Christopher DeMuth *(Pres.)*
David Gerson *(Exec. V.P.)*
Chris Myers *(Dir.-Mktg.)*

AMERICAN EXCELSIOR COMPANY
850 Ave. H. East
Arlington, TX 76011
Mailing Address:
P.O. Box 5067,
Arlington, TX 76005
Tel.: 817-640-1555
Fax: 817-649-7816
Year Founded: 1888
Approx.Sls.: $55,000,000
Emp.: 700
Import Export
Mfr. & Distributor of Urethane Foam, Polyethylene, Polystyrene, Carpet Underlay, Excelsior for Packaging
S.I.C.: 3086; 2679; 3069; 3089; 5078; 5162
W.E. Johnson *(Chm. Bd.)*
R.L. Gregerson *(Pres.)*
K.E. Starrett *(V.P.-Mktg.)*
L.A. Myren *(Reg. V.P.-Central)*
D.H. Offerman *(Reg. V.P.-West)*
R.A. Vesey *(Reg. V.P.-East)*
M. Heil *(Sec. & Treas.)*
Sharon Trowbridge *(Dir.-Data Processing)*
J.M. Morris *(Mgr.-Intl. Sls.)*
John Tengvall *(Mgr.-Adv.)*
Principal(s):
Employee-Owned

No. of U.S. Offices: 30

Outside Service Firm(s):

KPMG Peat Marwick*(Auditors)*
1601 Elm St., Ste. 1600
Dallas, TX 75201
Tel.: 214-754-2000
Fax: 214-754-2297

Johnson & Swanson*(Legal Firm)*
100 Founders Sq., 900 Jackson St.
Dallas, TX 75202
Tel.: 214-977-9000

AMERICAN FABRICS COMPANY
29th St. & 36th
New York, NY 10018
Tel.: 212-868-0100
Fax: 212-714-9385
Emp.: 550
Laces, Embroideries, Fancy Linens & Trimmings & Knited Fabrics
S.I.C.: 2258; 2241; 2257
Harvey Ostrover *(Chm. Bd. & Chief Exec. Officer)*
Julian Ostrover *(Pres.)*
Robert Ostrover *(V.P.)*
Walter Brennan *(Sec. & Treas.)*

Outside Service Firm(s):

Edward Isaacs & Co.*(Auditors)*
New York, NY

Goldstein & Peck, P.C.*(Legal Firm)*
Bridgeport, CT

Connecticut Bank & Trust*(Major Banking Relationship)*
Bridgeport, CT

Plant:

American Fabrics Co. **(1)**
1069 Connecticut Ave.
Bridgeport, CT 06609
Tel.: 203-366-5481
Gerhart Geiser *(Mgr.)*

AMERICAN FAMILY MUTUAL INSURANCE CO.
3099 E. Washington Ave.
Madison, WI 53783
Mailing Address:
P.O. Box 7430
Madison, WI 53783
Tel.: 608-249-2111 **WI**
Fax: 608-249-0100
Assets: $4,228,000,000
Liabilities: $3,256,000,000
Net Worth: $972,000,000
Approx.Rev.: $2,450,000,000
Emp.: 6,200
Fiscal Year-end: 12/31/90
Property, Casualty & Life Insurance, Business, Health, Farm/Ranch; Small Consumer Loans
S.I.C.: 6311; 6321; 6331; 6399
Dale F. Mathwich *(Chm. Bd. & Chief Exec. Officer)*
Harvey Pierce *(Pres. & Chief Oper. Officer)*
James F. Eldridge *(Exec. V.P.-Legal & Sec.)*

American Family Mutual Insurance Co.—(Continued)

Paul L. King *(Exec. V.P.-Fin. & Treas.)*
James R. Klokner *(Exec. V.P.-Admin.)*
Clayton M. Nelson *(Exec. V.P.-Bus. Opers.)*
Rodney Christenson *(V.P.-Mngmt. Information Systems)*
Jack L. Chopp *(V.P.-Mktg.)*
Vicki Chvala *(V.P.-Human Resources)*
Darnell Moore *(V.P.-Claims)*
Bradley J. Gleason *(V.P.-Actuarial)*
Richard J. Haas *(V.P.-Office Admin.)*
Alan F. Hunter *(V.P.-Underwriting)*
J. Brent Johnson *(V.P. & Controller)*
Joe Tisserand *(V.P.-WI Region)*
Thomas S. King *(V.P.-Investments)*
David Krueger *(V.P.-Northwest Region)*
Russell Lemons *(V.P.-Midland Region)*
Annette S. Knapstein *(Dir.-Adv.)*
Patti Barchus *(Corp. Communications Dir.)*
Keith Koppemolle *(Pur. & Supply Dir.)*
Cary R. Pierce *(Mgr.-Telecommunications)*

No. of U.S. Offices: 46

Outside Service Firm(s):

Coopers & Lybrand*(Auditors)*
Madison, WI

Foley & Lardner*(Legal Firm)*
777 E. Wisconsin Ave.
Milwaukee, WI 53202
Tel.: 414-271-2400

First Wisconsin National Bank*(Major Banking Relationship)*
Madison, WI

Subsidiaries:

American Family Financial Services, Inc. **(1)**
3099 E. Washington Ave.
Madison, WI 53783
Tel.: 608-249-2111 (100%)
Finance Company
S.I.C.: 6141
Dale F. Mathwich *(Chm. Bd. & Chief Exec. Officer)*

American Family Life Insurance Co. **(1)**
3099 E. Washington Ave.
Madison, WI 53783
Tel.: 608-249-2111 (100%)
Emp.: 197
Life Insurance
S.I.C.: 6311
Peter Walton *(V.P.-Life)*

American Family Mutual Insurance Co. **(1)**
3099 E. Washington Ave.
Madison, WI 53783
Tel.: 608-249-2111 (100%)
Insurance
S.I.C.: 6331
Dale F. Mathwich *(Chm. Bd. & Chief Exec Officer)*

American Standard Insurance Company of Wisconsin **(1)**
P.O. Box 7430, 3099 E. Washington Ave.
Madison, WI 53783
Tel.: 608-249-2111 (100%)
Insurance
S.I.C.: 6331
Dale Mathwich *(Chm. Bd. & Chief Exec. Officer)*

AmFam, Inc. **(1)**
3099 E. Washington Ave.
Madison, WI 53783
Tel.: 608-249-2111 (100%)
Insurance
S.I.C.: 6331
Dale F. Mathwich *(Chm. Bd. & Chief Exec. Officer)*

AMERICAN FAST PRINT, LIMITED
I-85 & Bryant Rd.
Spartanburg, SC 29303
Mailing Address:
P.O. Box 5765,
Spartanburg, SC 29304
Tel.: 803-578-2020
Fax: 803-578-8593
Year Founded: 1968
Sales Range: $40-59 Million
Emp.: 540
Fiscal Year-end: 12/31/90
Material Designs, Sheeting & Upholstery, Drapery Nonwovens, Yarn
S.I.C.: 2261; 2396
J.S. Fryml *(Pres. & Chief Exec. Officer)*
Martin Fryml *(V.P.-Mfg.)*
William W. Hodge *(V.P.-Fin. & Chief Fin. Officer)*
Ann Thompson *(Comptroller)*
Glenn Cash *(Dir.-Personnel)*
Junior Johnson *(Pur. Agent)*

No. of Mfg. Plants/Facilities: 2
No. of U.S. Offices: 1

Computer Systems/Hardware:
Data General

Outside Service Firm(s):

Ernst & Young*(Auditors)*
905 E. Main St., Ste. G
Spartanburg, SC 29302
Tel.: 803-573-7801

South Carolina National Bank*(Major Banking Relationship)*
700 Main St.
Columbia, SC 29201

Division:

U.S. Finishing **(1)**
3335 Old Buncombe Rd.
Greenville, SC 29602
Tel.: 803-242-6400

Non-U.S. Affiliate:

Montreal Fast Print **(1)**
9500 Blvd. St. Laurant
Montreal, PQ Canada H2N 1P5
Tel.: 514-384-5900

AMERICAN FELT & FILTER
311 First St.
Newburgh, NY 12550
Mailing Address:
P.O. Box 951
Newburgh, NY 12550
Tel.: 914-561-3560
Fax: 914-561-4008
Approx.Sls.: $32,000,000
Emp.: 250
Fiscal Year-end: 12/31/90
Mfrs. & Fabricators of Natural & Synthetic Felts & Felt Filter Prods
S.I.C.: 5199
Cornelius E. Hubner *(Pres. & Chief Exec. Officer)*
Robert Sweeney *(Treas.)*
Richard Price *(Dir.-Personnel)*
R. Bartolozzi *(Dir.-Pur.)*
Jerry C. Peill *(Mgr.-Mktg.)*

AMERICAN FENCE COMPANY
2525 N. 27th Ave.,
Phoenix, AZ 85009
Tel.: 602-272-2333
Fax: 602-278-6068
Sales Range: $60-79 Million
Emp.: 900
Special Trade Contractors & Wholesalers Construction Materials
S.I.C.: 1799; 5039
John P. Van Denburgh, Jr. *(Chm. Bd., Pres. & Chief Exec. Officer)*
Gary Javitch *(V.P.-Fin.)*
David S. Van Denburgh *(V.P.)*
John Van Denburgh III *(Treas.)*
Lois J. Maurin *(Sec.)*

Computer Systems/Hardware:
IBM System 36

Outside Service Firm(s):

James Ryan*(Legal Firm)*
Phoenix, AZ

Security Pacific Bank Arizona*(Major Banking Relationship)*
Phoenix, AZ

Subsidiaries:

American Fence Co. AZ **(1)**
2525 N. 27th Ave.,
Phoenix, AZ 85005
Tel.: 602-272-2335
Emp.: 150
Fence Contractor
S.I.C.: 1799
J. Van Denburgh, III *(Pres.)*

American Fence Co. Ltd. **(1)**
2525 N. 27th Ave.,
Phoenix, AZ 85005
Tel.: 602-272-2335
Emp.: 60
Special Trade Contractors
S.I.C.: 1799
John P. Van Denburgh, Jr. *(Pres.)*

American Fence Co. of Midwest **(1)**
2525 N. 27th Ave.,
Phoenix, AZ 85005
Tel.: 602-272-2335
Emp.: 40
Fencing Contractor
S.I.C.: 1799
Frank Van Denburgh *(Pres.)*

AMERICAN FIDELITY CORP.
2000 Classon Blvd.
Oklahoma City, OK 73106
Tel.: 405-523-200
S.I.C.: 6311; 6321; 6351
William E. Durrett *(Chm. Bd., Pres. & Chief Exec. Officer)*

Subsidiary:

Cimarron American Fidelity **(1)**
101 No. Main
Cimarron, KS 67835
Tel.: 316-855-3456
Fax: 316-855-7756
Approx.Rev.: $36,000,000
Emp.: 171
Fiscal Year-end: 12/31/90
Holding Co.; Fire & Casualty Insurance & Computer Services
S.I.C.: 6331; 6321
William Durrett *(Pres.)*
Irvin Pfannenstiel *(Reg. Pres.)*
Steven Garrett *(Sec.)*

AMERICAN FINANCE GROUP
Exchange Place
Boston, MA 02109
Tel.: 617-542-1200
Fax: 617-523-1410
Approx.Sls.: $20,000,000
Emp.: 120
Heavy Equipment, Aircraft & Construction Leasing
S.I.C.: 7359; 7513
William J. Montgomery *(Chm. Bd. & Chief Exec. Officer)*
Geoffrey MacDonald *(Pres.)*
Robert J. Bukala *(Chief Fin. Officer)*
John L. Lee *(Exec. V.P. & Gen. Counsel)*
Daniel J. Roggemann *(Exec. V.P.)*
James Skiles *(Sr. V.P.)*
Jeffery Zerrer *(Sr. V.P.)*
John Paine *(V.P.)*
Donald Tyler *(V.P.)*
Robert Hallier *(Controller)*

No. of U.S. Offices: 11

Computer Systems/Hardware:
Wang

Outside Service Firm(s):

Bingham, Dana & Gould*(Legal Firm)*
150 Federal St.
Boston, MA 02110
Tel.: 617-951-8000
Fax: 617-951-8736

Subsidiary:

American Financial Security **(1)**
Exchange Place
Boston, MA 02109
Tel.: 617-542-1200
Fax: 617-523-1410
Security Company
S.I.C.: 7381
Robert Hallier *(V.P.)*
Donald Tyler *(V.P.)*

AMERICAN FINANCIAL CORPORATION
One E. 4th St.
Cincinnati, OH 45202
Tel.: 513-579-2121 **OH**
Fax: 513-579-2580
Year Founded: 1959
Assets: $12,057,261,000
Earnings: $72,350,000
Liabilities: $11,713,623,000
Net Worth: $343,638,000
Approx.Income: $2,860,695,000
Emp.: 65,000
Fiscal Year-end: 12/31/91
Holding Company; Insurance; Annuities; Securities & Investments; Filmed Entertainment Production and Distribution;Systems Engineering and Industrial Manufacturing
S.I.C.: 6331; 6719; 7822; 6311; 8711
Carl H. Lindner *(Chm. Bd. & Chief Exec. Officer)*
Ronald F. Walker *(Pres. & Chief Oper. Officer)*
Carl H. Linder, III *(Pres.-The Penn Central Corp. & Pres.-Great American Insurance Co.)*
Keith E. Linder *(Pres. & Chief Oper. Officer-Chiquita Brands Intl., Inc.)*
S. Craig Linder *(Chief Exec. Officer-Spelling Entertainment Inc.)*
Fred J. Runk *(V.P. & Treas.)*
James E. Evans *(V.P. & Gen. Counsel)*
Robert C. Lintz *(V.P.)*
Thomas E. Mischell *(V.P.)*
Sandra W. Heimann *(V.P.)*
Kathleen Brown *(Asst. V.P.)*
James C. Kennedy *(Sec. & Dep. General Counsel)*
Robert H. Ruffing *(Controller)*
Lawrence J. Otto *(Mgr.-Human Resources)*

Computer Systems/Hardware:
IBM

Outside Service Firm(s):

Ernst & Young*(Auditors)*
1300 Chiquita Center, 250 E. Fifth St.
Cincinnati, OH 45202
Tel.: 513-621-6454

Keating, Muething & Klekamp*(Legal Firm)*
1 E. Fourth St.
Cincinnati, OH 45202
Tel.: 513-579-6400

Continental Bank N. A.*(Major Banking Relationship)*
231 S. LaSalle St.
Chicago, IL 60697
Tel.: 312-828-2345
Tel.: 800-426-5754
Telex: 312-828-1783

Division:

Great American Broadcasting Company **(1)**
1 E. 4th St., 6th Fl.
Cincinnati, OH 45202
Tel.: 513-562-8000
Fax: 513-721-8413
Assets: $1,540,037,000
Liabilities: $336,942,000
Net Worth: $1,203,095,000
Approx.Sls.: $499,774,000
Emp.: 1,600

Fiscal Year-end: 12/31/90
18 Radio & 5 TV Stations; Production of TV Programs & Motion Pictures; Distr. of TV Programs
S.I.C.: 4832; 7812; 4833
John P. Zanotti *(Pres. & Chief Oper. Officer)*
David H. Crowl *(Pres-Radio Grp.)*
Ron Bergamo *(Pres. & Gen. Mgr.-KTSP-TV)*
Perry Frey *(Pres. & Gen. Mgr.-WTVN-AM)*
Herndon Hasty *(Pres. & Gen. Mgr.-KYYS-FM)*
Steve Mauldin *(Pres. & Gen. Mgr.-WTSP-TV)*
Dave Milner *(Pres. & Gen. Mgr.-KEX-AM)*
William Moll *(Pres. & Gen. Mgr.-WKRC-TV)*
Edward Piette *(Pres. & Gen. Mgr.-WDAF-TV)*
Dave Pugh *(Pres. & Gen. Mgr.-WLZR-AM-FM)*
Gregory Thomas *(Exec. V.P. & Chief Fin. Officer)*
Bill Bauman *(Exec. V.P.)*
Craig Millar *(V.P.-Broadcasting Sls.; Pres. & Gen. Mgr.-WBRC-TV)*
Jim Bryant *(V.P. & Gen. Mgr.-WKRQ-FM)*
Tom Connolly *(V.P. & Gen. Mgr.-WKLS-FM)*
Dan DiLoreto *(V.P. & Gen. Mgr.)*
Tom Schurr *(V.P. & Gen. Mgr.-KSEG-FM)*
Robert D. Schutt *(V.P. & Gen. Mgr.-WRIF-FM)*
Clint Sly *(V.P. & Gen. Mgr.-KBPI-FM)*
Thomas Thon *(V.P. & Gen. Mgr.-WLVQ-FM)*
Marcie Ersoff *(V.P.-T.V. News)*
Jerome L. Kersting *(V.P.-Broadcast Business Affairs)*
Nick Miller *(V.P.-Mktg. Radio Grp.)*
Anita Wallgren *(V.P.-Admin. & Corp. Rels.)*
Bill Ashenden *(Gen. Mgr.-KKRZ-FM)*
Dennis Logsdon *(Gen. Mgr.-WKEC-AM)*
Sam Simon *(Gen. Counsel & Sec.)*
Gretlyn Z. Thomas *(Mgr.-Pub. Rels.)*

Subsidiaries:

ABI Management, Inc. **(1)**
160 Spear St., Ste. 1540
San Francisco, CA 94105
Tel.: 415-541-0404 (100%)
Approx.Rev.: $17,500,000
Emp.: 280
Fiscal Year-end: 12/31/86
Insurance Agency
S.I.C.: 6411
Bernard H. Mizel *(Chm. Bd. & Pres.)*

Agricultural Insurance Company **(1)**
515 Main St.
Cincinnati, OH 45202
Tel.: 513-369-5881 (100%)
Agricultural Insurance
S.I.C.: 6331
Carl H. Lindner *(Pres.)*

American Empire Surplus Lines Insurance Company **(1)**
910 Dixie Terminal Bldg., 49 East Fourth St.
Cincinnati, OH 45202
Tel.: 513-369-5000 (100%)
Approx.Rev.: $34,709,000
Emp.: 90
Fiscal Year-end: 12/31/91
Property & Casualty Insurer
S.I.C.: 6331
Walter E. Snyder *(Pres.)*

American Financial Enterprises, Inc. **(1)**
One E. Fourth St.
Cincinnati, OH 45202
Tel.: 513-579-2172 (82%)
Approx.Assets: $414,783,000
Fiscal Year-end: 12/31/91
Holding Company; Successor to The New York, New Haven & Hartford Railroad Companies
S.I.C.: 6719
S. Craig Lindner *(Exec. V.P.)*

American Money Management Corporation **(1)**
One E. Fourth St.
Cincinnati, OH 45202
Tel.: 513-579-2121 (100%)
Approx.Assets: $6,836,000
Emp.: 40
Fiscal Year-end: 12/31/91
Securities Management for AFC & Affiliates
S. Craig Lindner *(Sr. Exec. V.P.)*

American National Fire Insurance Company **(1)**
580 Walnut St.
Cincinnati, OH 45202
Tel.: 513-369-5000 (100%)
Approx.Rev.: $37,338,000
Emp.: 10
Fiscal Year-end: 12/31/91
Property & Casualty Insurer
S.I.C.: 6331
Carl H. Lindner, III *(Pres.)*

Atlanta Casualty Company **(1)**
3169 Holcomb Ridge Rd.
Norcross, GA 30071
Tel.: 404-447-8930 (100%)
Property & Casualty Insurance
S.I.C.: 6331
Robert L. Lowe *(Pres.)*

Chiquita Brands, Inc. **(1)**
250 East Fifth St.
Cincinnati, OH 45202
Tel.: 513-784-8000 (100%)
Fax: 513-784-8030
Approx.Rev.: $1,895,657,000
Emp.: 38,540
Fiscal Year-end: 12/31/90
Producer & Distributor of Bananas & Other Fresh Fruits
S.I.C.: 5148
Keith E. Lindner *(Pres. & Chief Oper. Officer)*
Robert F. Kistinger *(Exec. V.P.)*
Anthony D. Battaglia *(Sr. V.P.)*
Dennis M. Doyle *(Sr. V.P.)*
Jos P. Stalenhoef *(Sr. V.P.)*
Charles R. Morgan *(V.P. & Gen. Counsel)*
Michael O'Brien *(V.P.-Mktg.)*

Chiquita Brands International, Inc. **(1)**
250 E. Fifth St.
Cincinnati, OH 45202
Tel.: 513-784-8011 (48%)
Fax: 513-784-8030
Assets: $3,142,500,000
Earnings: $128,495,000
Liabilities: $2,174,600,000
Net Worth: $967,900,000
Approx.Rev.: $4,627,397,000
Emp.: 44,000
Fiscal Year-end: 12/31/91
Producer, Processor and Distributor of Food Products
S.I.C.: 2099; 5148; 0179
Carl H. Lindner *(Chm. Bd. & Chief Exec. Officer)*
Keith E. Lindner *(Pres. & Chief Oper. Officer)*
Peter Shea *(Chief Oper. Officer-Meat Grp.)*
Anthony Battaglia *(Grp. Exec. V.P.-Mktg.-Chiquita Brands, Inc.)*
Robert A. Dearth Jr. *(Sr. V.P.-Chiquita Tropical Products Grp.)*
Jos P. Stalenhoef *(Sr. V.P.-North America, Chiquita Tropical Products Grp.)*
Fred J. Runk *(V.P. & Chief Fin. Officer)*
Gerald R. Kondritzer *(V.P. & Treas.)*
Peter P. Fay *(V.P.-Human Resources)*
Joseph W. Hagin II *(V.P.-Corp. Affairs)*
C. Richard Keener *(V.P.-Mngmt. Information Systems)*
William A. Tsacalis *(V.P. & Controller)*
Steve G. Warshaw *(V.P. & Chief Admin. Officer)*
Wilfred W. White *(V.P.-Internal Audit)*
Robert E. Crowe *(V.P.)*
Thomas E. Mischell *(V.P.)*
Michael O'Brien *(Dir.-Adv.)*

Dempsey & Siders Insurance Agency **(1)**
7840 Montgomery Rd.
Cincinnati, OH 45236
Tel.: 513-891-4400 (100%)
Approx.Rev.: $1,000,000
Emp.: 10
Fiscal Year-end: 12/31/86
Insurance Agency
S.I.C.: 6411
Wagner L. Voorhees *(Pres. & Treas.)*

Dinner Bell Foods, Inc. **(1)**
250 E. 5th St.
Cincinnati, OH 45202
Tel.: 419-782-9015
Fax: 419-782-3530
Approx.Sls.: $250,000,000
Emp.: 1,500
Fiscal Year-end: 12/31/90
Meat & Meat Products
S.I.C.: 2011; 2013
Eric Wallin *(Chm. Bd.)*
Austin McNamara *(Pres. & Chief Exec. Officer)*
Terry S. Elberson *(V.P.-Natl. Accts.)*
Barbara Wagner *(V.P.-Legal)*
Marline Koop *(Sls. Office Mgr.)*
Theresa Stafford *(Sec.)*
Gene Schnegg *(Dir.-Pur.)*
B. A. Cole *(Mgr.-Gen. Sls.)*
Dave Beck *(Mgr.-Data Processing)*
Mary Beth Baker *(Special Asst.to Pres.)*

Dinner Bell Foods, Inc. **(1)**
2401 Wilco Blvd.
Wilson, NC 27893
Tel.: 919-237-2141
Mfr. of Meat & Meat Products
S.I.C.: 2011

Dinner Bell Foods, Inc. **(1)**
P.O. Box 388
Troy, OH 45373
Tel.: 513-339-7511
Mfr. of Meat & Meat Products
S.I.C.: 2011

Dinner Bell Foods, Inc. **(1)**
Archbold, OH 43502
Tel.: 419-446-2556
Mfr. of Meat & Meat Products
S.I.C.: 2011

Dixie Insurance Company **(1)**
2204 Lakeshore Dr.
Birmingham, AL 35209
Tel.: 205-870-4000 (100%)
Property & Casualty Insurance
S.I.C.: 6331
James C. Sullivan *(Pres.)*

FMI Properties Corp. **(1)**
One E. 4th St.
Cincinnati, OH 45202
Tel.: 513-579-2177 (100%)
S.I.C.: 6531
H. Sibley, Jr. *(Chief Oper. Officer)*

GACC Holding Company **(1)**
One E. Fourth St.
Cincinnati, OH 45202
Tel.: 513-579-2177 (100%)
Approx.Rev.: $295,000,000
Emp.: 1,600
Fiscal Year-end: 12/31/90
Broadcasting; Holding Company
S.I.C.: 4832; 4833; 6719
George E. Castrucci *(Pres.)*

Great American Broadcasting Company **(1)**
One E. Fourth St.
Cincinnati, OH 45202
Tel.: 513-579-2177 (100%)
Emp.: 1,600
Fiscal Year-end: 12/31/90
Television & Radio Broadcasting
S.I.C.: 4832; 4833
George E. Castrucci *(Pres. & Chief Oper. Officer)*
William T. Baumann *(Sr. V.P.-Plng. & Corp. Devel.)*
Greg Thomas *(Sr. V.P.-Fin. & Chief Fin. Officer)*
William E. Kelley *(V.P.-Information Services)*
Verna Meyer *(Treas.)*

Great American Communications Company **(1)**
One E. Fourth St., 6th Fl.
Cincinnati, OH 45202
Tel.: 513-562-8000 (40%)
Fax: 513-721-8413
Assets: $2,144,628,000
Earnings: $91,986,000
Liabilities: $1,892,840,000
Net Worth: $251,788,000
Approx.Rev.: $211,538,000
Emp.: 1,500
Fiscal Year-end: 12/31/91
Diversified Financial Holding Company For Broadcasting, Insurance, Real Estate & Other Investments
S.I.C.: 6719
Carl H. Lindner *(Chm. & Chief Exec. Officer)*
John P. Zanotti *(Exec. V.P.)*
Gregory C. Thomas *(Exec. V.P. & Chief Fin. Officer)*
William T. Baumann *(Exec. V.P.)*
Anita L. Wallgren *(V.P.)*
Samuel J. Simon *(Gen. Counsel & Sec.)*
Gretlyn Z. Thomas *(Mgr.-Public Rels.)*

The Great American Entertainment Company **(1)**
3330 Cahuenga Blvd
Los Angeles, CA 90068
Tel.: 213-851-5000
Animation and Live-Action Production Activities
S.I.C.: 7922

Great American Holding Corporation **(1)**
580 Walnut St.
Cincinnati, OH 45202
Tel.: 513-369-5000 (100%)
Approx.Rev.: $2,042,000,000
Emp.: 4
Fiscal Year-end: 12/31/91
Insurance Holding Company
S.I.C.: 6331; 6719; 6311
Carl H. Lindner III *(Pres.)*

Great American Insurance Company **(1)**
580 Walnut St.
Cincinnati, OH 45202
Tel.: 513-369-5000 (100%)
Approx.Rev.: $1,670,835,000
Emp.: 3,500
Fiscal Year-end: 12/31/91
Property & Casualty Insurer
S.I.C.: 6331
Carl H. Lindner III *(Pres.)*

Great American Management Services, Inc. **(1)**
One E. Fourth St.
Cincinnati, OH 45202
Tel.: 513-369-5602 (100%)
Approx.Rev.: $10,665,000
Emp.: 5
Fiscal Year-end: 12/31/91
Data Processing & Equipment Leasing
S.I.C.: 7379; 7359
Robert C. Lintz *(Pres.)*

Great American Television & Radio Company, Inc. **(1)**
One E. Fourth St.
Cincinnati, OH 45202
Tel.: 513-579-2177 (100%)
Approx.Rev.: $200,000,000
Emp.: 1,380
Fiscal Year-end: 12/31/90
Television & Radio Broadcasting
S.I.C.: 4832; 4833
George E. Castrucci *(Pres. & Chief Oper. Officer)*

Hanna-Barbera Productions, Inc. **(1)**
3400 Cahuenga Blvd.
Los Angeles, CA 90068
Tel.: 213-851-5000
Approx.Sls.: $45,000,000
Emp.: 600
Producer of Animated Shows
S.I.C.: 7812
David Kirschner *(Chm.)*
Fred Seibert *(Pres.)*
Martyn Weinberg *(Exec. V.P. & Chief Oper. Officer)*
Sheldon B. Rabinowitz *(Sr. V.P. & Chief Fin. Officer)*
Mark Young *(Sr. V.P.-Animation Devel.)*
Richard Sigler *(V.P.-Admin.)*
Don Mirisch *(V.P.-Bus. Affairs)*
Jeff Segal *(V.P.-Creative Affairs)*
Bruce Johnson *(V.P.-Special Projects)*
Sam Ewing *(V.P.-Program Devel.)*
Sarah Baisley *(Dir.-Publicity & Pub. Rels.)*

Kings Island Company **(1)**
One E. Fourth St.
Cincinnati, OH 45202
Tel.: 513-579-2121 (100%)
Approx.Rev.: $79,607,000
Emp.: 210
Fiscal Year-end: 12/31/91
Theme Park Operations
S.I.C.: 7996
Carl H. Lindner *(Chm. Bd.)*
Richard P. Belmont *(Pres.)*
Dean Nahrup *(Gen. Mgr.)*

Mid-Continent Casualty Co. **(1)**
1646 So. Boulder
Tulsa, OK 74101
Tel.: 918-587-7221 (100%)
Emp.: 240
Property & Casualty Insurance
S.I.C.: 6331; 6399
Perry Inhofe *(Chm. Bd. & Pres.)*

Mid-Continent Casualty Co. **(1)**
1646 S. Boulder
Tulsa, OK 74101
Tel.: 918-587-7221 (100%)
Approx.Rev.: $92,364,000
Emp.: 260
Fiscal Year-end: 12/31/91
Property & Casualty Insurance
S.I.C.: 6331
Jim L. Pierce *(Pres.)*

American Financial Corporation—(Continued)

Mid-Continent Casualty Company **(1)**
1646 S. Boulder
Tulsa, OK 74101
Tel.: 918-587-7221 (100%)
Approx.Rev.: $94,190,000
Approx.Assets: $173,217,000
Emp.: 250
Fiscal Year-end: 12/31/88
Property & Casualty Insurer
S.I.C.: 6331
Jim L. Pierce *(Pres. & Chief Oper. Officer)*

John Morrell & Co. **(1)**
Chiquita Center, 250 E. 5th St.
Cincinnati, OH 45202
Tel.: 513-852-3500 (100%)
Fax: 513-852-7427
Approx.Rev.: $1,882,094,000
Approx.Assets: $226,348,000
Emp.: 5,380
Fiscal Year-end: 12/31/91
Export
Slaughtering, Processing & Distribution of Meat in Fresh, Frozen & Processed Forms
S.I.C.: 2011
Peter Shea *(Chief Oper. Officer)*
Thomas Davis *(Sr. V.P.)*
Don Breen *(V.P.-Sls. & Mktg.)*
Austin McNamara *(V.P.-John Morrell Mktg.)*
Jim Ruehlmann *(V.P.-Brand Mktg.)*
Ron Eliason *(V.P.-Engrng.)*
Gary Junso *(V.P.-Human Resources)*

New England Petroleum Corporation **(1)**
4655 Salisbury Rd., Ste. 220
Jacksonville, FL 32256
Tel.: 904-281-4400 (100%)
Fax: 904-281-0051
Approx.Rev.: $346,596,000
Approx.Assets: $59,914,000
Emp.: 170
Fiscal Year-end: 12/31/91
Sale of Residual Fuel Oil to Utilities
S.I.C.: 5171

Specialty Underwriters, Inc. **(1)**
122 Main St.
Cincinnati, OH 45242
Tel.: 513-831-7475 (100%)
Property & Casualty Insurance
S.I.C.: 6331

Spelling Entertainment Group, Inc. **(1)**
One E. Fourth St.
Cincinnati, OH 45202
Tel.: 513-579-2482 (53%)
Fax: 513-579-2580
Approx.Rev.: $122,748,000
Emp.: 600
Fiscal Year-end: 12/31/91
Holding Company: Petroleum & Petroleum Products; Filmed Entertainment Production & Distribution
S.I.C.: 6719; 5172; 7822
Carl H. Lindner *(Chm. Bd. & Chief Exec. Officer)*
S. Craig Lindner *(Pres. & Chief Oper. Officer)*
Rodger M. Miller *(Exec. V.P.)*
Fred J. Runk *(V.P., Treas. & Chief Fin. Officer)*
James C. Kennedy *(V.P. & Gen. Counsel)*
Robert H. Ruffing *(V.P.)*
Don Cacchiotti *(Controller)*
John E. Ross *(Sec.)*
Larry Otto *(Dir.-Personnel)*

Stonewall Insurance Co. **(1)**
P.O. Box 1688, 2204 Lakeshore Dr.
Birmingham, AL 35201-1688
Tel.: 205-870-5357 (100%)
Approx.Rev.: $23,250,000
Emp.: 320
Fiscal Year-end: 12/31/91
Property & Casualty Insurer
S.I.C.: 6331
Ronald F. Johnson *(Pres.)*

Transport Insurance Co. **(1)**
4100 Harry Hines Blvd.
Dallas, TX 75219
Tel.: 214-526-3876 (100%)
Approx.Rev.: $54,454,000
Approx.Assets: $114,679,000
Emp.: 125
Fiscal Year-end: 12/31/91
Property & Casualty Insurer
S.I.C.: 6331
Gene S. Yerant *(Chm. & Pres.)*
John Urankar *(Sr. V.P.-Claims)*
Cynthia Campbell *(V.P., Gen. Counsel & Sec.)*
Donna Smith *(V.P. & Treas.)*
Kurt Fisher *(V.P.-Mktg.)*
Gordon Larson *(V.P.-Underwriting)*
Tommy Stone *(V.P.-Mngmt. Information Systems)*
Ken Utz *(V.P.-Loss Prevention)*
Greg Hayden *(V.P.-Sls.)*

Worldvision Enterprises **(1)**
1700 Broadway
New York, NY 10019-5992
Tel.: 212-261-2700
Telex: 62401 WOR UW
Fax: 212-261-2788
Emp.: 91
Distribution of Television Shows
S.I.C.: 7822; 4841
John D. Ryan *(Pres. & Chief Exec. Officer)*
Bert Cohen *(Exec. V.P. & Chief Oper. Officer)*
Lawrence Gottlieb *(Exec. V.P.-Fin. & Admin.)*
John T. Brady *(Exec. V.P. & Treas.)*
Ronald Lightstone *(Exec. V.P. & Sec.)*
Lawrence Gottlieb *(Exec. V.P.-Fin.)*
Linda Tobin *(Dir.-Intl. Sls. Admin.)*

AMERICAN FLUORESCENT CORPORATION
3821 Hawthorne Ct.
Waukegan, IL 60087
Mailing Address:
P.O. Box 119
Waukegan, IL 60087
Tel.: 708-249-5970
Fax: 708-249-2618
Year Founded: 1938
Approx.Sls.: $24,000,000
Emp.: 180
Fiscal Year-end: 12/31/91
Export
Mfr. Fluorescent Lighting Products
S.I.C.: 3645; 3646
Jerry L. Solomon *(Chm. Bd.)*
William R. Solomon *(Pres.)*
James D. Fiffer *(Legal Officer)*
Don Clark *(Dir.-Opers.)*
Tom Dicks *(Dir.-Mktg. & Sls. Promo)*
Pat Koons *(Dir.-Personnel)*
Gene Kough *(Dir.-Pur.)*
Mary Palmer *(Dir.-Fin. & Controller)*
Naomi Price *(Dir.-Data Processing)*
Lew Russakov *(Natl. Sls. Mgr.)*
Jan Smith *(Office Mgr.)*
Principal(s):
Jerry L. Solomon
William R. Solomon

No. of Mfg. Plants/Facilities: 1

Computer Systems/Hardware:
Qantel

Outside Service Firm(s):

M. J. Robinson & Co., Ltd.*(Auditors)*
Lincolnwood, IL

NBD Park Ridge*(Major Banking Relationship)*
Park Ridge, IL

Wildman, Harrold, Allen & Dixon*(Legal Firm)*
225 W. Wacker Dr.
Chicago, IL 60606
Tel.: 312-222-0400

AMERICAN FOODS GROUP
P.O. Box 8547, 544 Acme St.
Green Bay, WI 54308
Tel.: 414-437-6330
Fax: 414-437-4311
Year Founded: 1971
Emp.: 2,200
Slaughtering And Processing of Beef & Pork
S.I.C.: 2011; 2092
Carl Kuehne *(Chief Exec. Officer)*
James Coulombe *(V.P.-Fin.)*

Subsidiaries:

Dakota Pork Industries **(1)**
5738 Olson Memorial Hwy.
Minneapolis, MN 55422
Tel.: 612-546-4471
Pork Processing & Slaughtering
S.I.C.: 2011
Rick Denzel *(Pres.)*

Green Bay Dressed Beef Company **(1)**
544 Acme
Green Bay, WI 54308
Tel.: 414-437-6330
Meat Slaughtering And Processing
S.I.C.: 2011
Donald Garsow *(Pres.)*

Weinstein International Seafood **(1)**
5738 Olson Memorial Hwy.
Minneapolis, MN 55422
Tel.: 612-546-4471
Beef Processing & Slaughtering; Seafood
S.I.C.: 2011; 2013
Louis Lipshultz *(Pres.)*

AMERICAN FOODS GROUP, INC.
5738 Olson Memorial Hwy.
Minneapolis, MN 55422
Tel.: 612-546-4471
Year Founded: 1953
Approx.Sls.: $585,000,000
Emp.: 1,300
Fiscal Year-end: 6/00/89
Import Export
Seafood, Pork & Meat Prods.
S.I.C.: 5146; 2013; 2011
Carl W. Kuehne *(Pres. & Chief Exec. Officer)*
Elliot Weinstein *(V.P.)*
James D. Coulonbe *(Chief Fin. Officer& Treas.)*
Doug Hagen *(Treas.)*
Ron Bouche *(Dir.-Pur.)*
Cindy Notch *(Mgr.-Data Processing)*
Jean Mayberry *(Coord.-Benefit)*

Computer Systems/Hardware:
IBM AS/400

Outside Service Firm(s):

Deloitte & Touche*(Auditors)*
900 Pillsbury Ctr.
Minneapolis, MN 55402
Tel.: 612-332-2301
Fax: 612-375-5418

Connecticut General Life Insurance Co.*(Group Insurer)*
P.O. Box 2975,
Hartford, CT 06104
Tel.: 203-726-6000

Smith Barney, Harris Upham & Company, Inc.*(Investment Banker)*
Minneapolis, MN

Grossman, Karlins, Siegel, Brill, Gruetner & Duffy*(Legal Firm)*
Minneapolis, MN

First National Bank of Minneapolis*(Major Banking Relationship)*
Minneapolis, MN

AMERICAN FOODSERVICE CORP.
400 Drew Ct.
King of Prussia, PA 19406
Tel.: 215-277-5010
Fax: 215-277-8474
Approx.Sls.: $125,000,000
Emp.: 185
Meat Products, Prepared Meats
S.I.C.: 2013
John F. Ireton *(Chm. Bd.)*
Donald F. Blackburn *(Pres.)*
Ronald Allen *(V.P. & Sec.)*
Richard S. Downs *(V.P. & Treas.)*
Ed McGroarty *(Comptroller)*
Principal(s):
John F. Ireton
Donald F. Blackburn

Outside Service Firm(s):

Elko, Fischer, McCabe & Rudman*(Auditors)*
999 West Chester Rd.
West Chester, PA
Tel.: 215-431-1003

Duane, Morris & Heckscher*(Legal Firm)*
One Liberty Place
Philadelphia, PA 19103
Tel.: 215-979-1800

CoreStates First Pennsylvania Bank, N.A.*(Major Banking Relationship)*
Center Sq. West Tower, 15th & Market Streets
Philadelphia, PA 19101

AMERICAN FOUNDRY GROUP, INC.
14602 S. Grant
Bixby, OK 74008
Tel.: 918-366-4401 **OK**
Fax: 918-366-4802
Year Founded: 1966
Approx.Sls.: $29,000,000
Emp.: 485
Fiscal Year-end: 6/30/90
Export
Casting Foundries; Steel, High & Low Alloy Sand Castings; Brass, Bronze, Aluminum Sand Castings; Ferrous & Non-Ferrous Investment Castings; Lost Foam Castings; DUP-LI-CAST Process Forgings
S.I.C.: 3366; 3364; 3324; 3325; 3299
Madan P. Makhani *(Chm. Bd., Pres., Chief Oper. Officer & Chief Fin. Officer)*
L. Neff *(Chief Exec. Officer)*
Robert Bell *(Treas.)*
H. Crowe *(Gen. Counsel)*
Jack Gibson *(Controller)*
Evelyn Graham *(Dir.-Pur.)*
J. McGouldrick *(Dir.-Mktg.)*
C. Seritchfield *(Dir.-Personnel)*
Principal(s):
Madan P. Makhani

No. of Mfg. Plants/Facilities: 5
No. of U.S. Offices: 6

Computer Systems/Hardware:
Microdata, IBM & Apple

Outside Service Firm(s):

Coopers & Lybrand*(Auditors)*
1400 Mid-Continent Tower
Tulsa, OK 74103
Tel.: 918-596-8200
Fax: 918-596-8300

Sturtevant Insurance Agency*(Group Insurer)*
Tulsa, OK

Crawford, Growe, Bainbridge*(Legal Firm)*
Tulsa, OK

Bank of Oklahoma*(Major Banking Relationship)*
One Williams Center
Tulsa, OK 74012
Tel.: 918-588-5100

Bank of Oklahoma*(Pension Manager)*
One Williams Center
Tulsa, OK 74012
Tel.: 918-588-5100

Subsidiaries:

American Alloy Castings Company **(1)**
14602 S. Grant
Bixby, OK 74008
Tel.: 918-366-4401 (100%)
Fax: 918-366-4802
S.I.C.: 3369
L. O'Brien *(Gen. Mgr.)*

American Bar & Bushing Stock **(1)**
14602 S. Grant
Bixby, OK 74008
Tel.: 918-366-4401 (100%)
S.I.C.: 3299

American Castings Co. **(1)**
14602 S. Grant
Bixby, OK 74008
Tel.: 918-366-4401 (100%)
Fax: 918-366-4802
S.I.C.: 3325

American Investment Casting Co. (1)
14602 S. Grant
Bixby, OK 74008
Tel.: 918-366-4401 (100%)
S.I.C.: 4212; 4213

Oklahoma Steel Casting Co. (1)
14602 S. Grant
Bixby, OK 74008
Tel.: 918-366-4401 (100%)
Fax: 918-366-4802
S.I.C.: 3325

AMERICAN FROZEN FOODS, INC.
355 Benton St.
Stratford, CT 06497
Tel.: 203-378-7900 **CT**
Fax: 203-386-8676
Approx.Sls.: $82,000,000
Emp.: 1,200
General Line Of Groceries & Meats; Food & Freezer Plans; Purchasers Of Accounts Receivable & Commercial Paper; Water Purification Equipment
S.I.C.: 5421; 5142
Norman Rapport *(Chm. Bd.)*
Kenneth Cherry *(Chief Exec. Officer)*
Donald Monjello *(Pres.)*
Calvin Hurt *(V.P.-Sls.)*
Bert Zahner *(V.P.-Opers.)*
William Corey *(Sec.)*

Outside Service Firm(s):

Deloitte & Touche*(Auditors)*
1600 Summer St.
Stamford, CT 06905-5121
Tel.: 203-351-4600

City Trust*(Major Banking Relationship)*
961 Main St.
Bridgeport, CT 06601
Tel.: 203-384-5402

AMERICAN FUEL CELL & COATED FABRICS CO. (AMFUEL)
601 Firestone Dr.
Magnolia, AR 71753
Mailing Address:
P.O. Box 887
Magnolia, AR 71753
Tel.: 501-234-3381 **AR**
Fax: 501-235-7270
Year Founded: 1983
Assets: $15,007,540
Liabilities: $4,541,848
Net Worth: $10,465,692
Approx.Sls.: $40,000,000
Emp.: 600
Fiscal Year-end: 9/30/92
Export
Mfr. Rubber Coated Fabric Containers, Fuel Cells, Airholding Devices
S.I.C.: 3728; 3764; 3069
Joe D. Woodward *(Chm. Bd.)*
Edward J. Mara, Jr. *(Pres. & Chief Exec. Officer)*
T. Halyburton *(Chief Oper. Officer)*
Ray Uhrich *(Exec. V.P.)*
Martin Cain *(V.P.-Human Resources)*
Paul Considine *(V.P.-Sls. & Mktg.)*
Herbert G. Frost, Jr. *(V.P.-Opers.)*
H.G. Hesser *(V.P.-Personnel)*
Anthony A. Hilliard *(Controller)*
M. Mike Kinard *(Sec.)*
Donald L. Byerley *(Dir.-Res. & Devel.)*
J. Barry Johnson *(Dir.-Quality Control)*
Ronald Rasberry *(Dir.-Telecommunications)*
Ken Rawls *(Dir.-Pur.)*
James B. Wallace *(Dir.-Data Processing)*
H.G. Hasser *(Mgr.-Aerospace Products)*
A. Delwyn Wiley *(Mgr.-Factory)*

No. of Mfg. Plants/Facilities: 3
No. of Foreign Offices: 1

Computer Systems/Hardware:
Digital

Outside Service Firm(s):

KPMG Peat Marwick*(Auditors)*
Tower Bldg., 11th Fl.,
Little Rock, AR 72201
Tel.: 501-375-3275

The Travelers*(Group Insurer)*
P.O. Box 2911,
Overland Park, KS 66201-1311

Friday, Eldridge & Clark*(Legal Firm)*
2000 First Commercial Bldg.
Little Rock, AR 72201
Tel.: 501-376-2011

First National Bank of Magnolia*(Major Banking Relationship)*
Magnolia, AR

Howard Simon Assoc.*(Pension Manager)*
425 Huehl Rd., Bldg. 20
Northbrook, IL 60062

AMERICAN FUNDS ADVISOR INC.
(Formerly AFA Funds, Inc.)
1415 Kellum Pl.
Garden City, NJ 11530
Tel.: 516-739-1017 **MD**
Investment Services; Deals Only With Private Clients
S.I.C.: 6211
Howard Buhse *(Chm. Bd.)*
Barry J. Gordon *(Pres.)*
Marc H. Klee *(Sr. V.P.)*
Alan J. Loewenstein *(V.P.)*
Lawrence E. Errera *(Sec. & Treas.)*

Computer Systems/Hardware:
IBM Compatibles

Outside Service Firm(s):

KPMG Peat Marwick*(Auditors)*
345 Park Ave.
New York, NY 10154
Tel.: 212-758-9700
Fax: 212-872-3308

Leboeuf, Lamb, Leiby, MacRae*(Legal Firm)*
260 Franklin Street
Boston, MA 02110
Tel.: 617-439-9500

AMERICAN FURNITURE COMPANY
P.O. BOx 3685
Albuquerque, NM 87190
Tel.: 505-883-2015
Sales Range: $60-79 Million
Fiscal Year-end: 12/31/91
Import
Furniture Stores, Electric Household Appliances, Household Furniture & Home Furnishings
S.I.C.: 5712; 5722; 5021; 5023
Lee S. Blaugrund *(Pres.)*
Clifford Blaugrund *(Pres.- American Business Interiors)*
Flo Gallegos *(V.P.-Opers.)*
Harris Klein *(V.P.-Home Prods.)*
Lim Cheng Ten *(Controller)*
Linda Alongi *(Sec. & Treas.)*
Tracy Blaugrund *(Dir.-Personnel)*

Outside Service Firm(s):

KPMG Peat Marwick*(Auditors)*
Two Park Square, 6565 Americas Pkwy., N.E., Ste. 700
Albuquerque, NM 87110
Tel.: 505-884-3939
Fax: 505-884-8348

Sun West Bank of Albuquerque*(Major Banking Relationship)*
P.O. Box 25500
Albuquerque, NM 87125-0500
Tel.: 505-765-2698
Fax: 505-842-6661

AMERICAN GILSONITE CO.
136 E. South Temple St., Ste. 1460
Salt Lake City, UT 84111
Tel.: 801-524-7900
Telex: 910-925-5658
Fax: 801-328-9116
Approx.Sls.: $20,000,000
Emp.: 75
Producer of Gilsonite Used in Manufacturing of Industrial Products
S.I.C.: 1499
Robert A. Franden *(Chief Exec. Officer)*
Loren S. Campbell *(Pres.)*
Harry D. Lewis *(V.P.-Mktg.)*
Cliff Doner *(Chief Fin. Officer)*
K.C. Christensen *(Opers. Mgr.-Bonanza)*
J.E. Baldassare *(Mgr.-Export Mktg.)*
Julie Densley *(Mngmt. Sec.)*

AMERICAN GRAIN & RELATED INDUSTRIES
2829 Westown Pkwy. Ste. 100
West Des Moines, IA 50265
Tel.: 515-223-3700 **IA**
Fax: 515-223-7770
Approx.Sls.: $1,030,000,000
Emp.: 6
Agri Grain Marketing
S.I.C.: 5153
Jerry Van Der Kamp *(Chief Exec. Officer & Exec. V.P.)*
Gene O. Peters *(Fin. Consultant)*
Principal(s):
Farmer Owned Co-Operative

Outside Service Firm(s):

KPMG Peat Marwick*(Auditors)*
2500 Ruan Center
Des Moines, IA 50309
Tel.: 515-288-7465

Nyemaster, Goode, McLaughlin, Emery & O'Brien*(Legal Firm)*
1900 Hubtower
Des Moines, IA 50309

First Interstate Bank*(Major Banking Relationship)*
Locust at Sixth
Des Moines, IA 50304
Tel.: 515-245-7047
Fax: 515-245-7225

Associated Benefits Corp.*(Pension Manager)*
2929 Westown Pkwy.
Des Moines, IA 50265

AMERICAN HARDWARE MUTUAL INSURANCE CO.
5995 Opus Pkwy.
Minnetonka, MN 55343
Mailing Address:
P. O. Box 435
Minneapolis, MN 55440
Tel.: 612-935-1400
Fax: 612-935-7695
Year Founded: 1899
Approx.Sls.: $130,000,000
Emp.: 605
Fiscal Year-end: 12/31/92
Property and Liability Insurance
S.I.C.: 6331
Corporate Giving Program: Company donates to the United Way Organization
Robert J. Odegard *(Chm. Bd.)*
Richard W. Tongen *(Pres. & Chief Exec. Officer)*
Leon Smith *(Sr. V.P. & Chief Fin. Officer)*
Marvin D. Alpern *(Sr. V.P. & Chief Info. Officer)*
Richard J. Downham *(Sr. V.P.-Claims)*
David W. Lemon *(Exec. V.P.)*
Gopal Khanna *(V.P.-Computer Opers.)*
Patricia Iverson *(V.P.-Human Resources)*
Paul R. Holmquist *(Gen. Counsel & Sec.)*
Paul Markey *(Dir.-Mktg.)*
Larry w. Borgen *(Mgr.-Adv.)*

Computer Systems/Hardware:
IBM

Subsidiary:

American Merchants Life Insurance Co. (1)
5995 Opus Pkwy.
Minnetonka, MN 55343
Tel.: 612-935-1400
S.I.C.: 6311
Richard W. Tongen *(Pres. & Chief Exec. Officer)*
Paul R. Holmquist *(Sr. V.P. & Gen. Mgr.)*
Leon P. Smith *(Sr. V.P.)*

AMERICAN HEALTH COMPANIES, INC.
921 Penn Ave., 9th Fl.
Pittsburgh, PA 15222
Tel.: 412-338-8700 **ID**
Fax: 412-338-8743
Year Founded: 1972
Sales Range: $40-59 Million
Emp.: 150
Fiscal Year-end: 3/31/91
Holding Company, Diet Services
S.I.C.: 6719; 8999
Dennis Brown *(Pres.)*
Billy DuPree *(Sr. V.P., Gen. Counsel & Sec.)*
Frank Strangis *(V.P.-Mktg.)*

Computer Systems/Hardware:
IBM

Subsidiary:

Diet Center, Inc. (1)
921 Penn Ave., 9th Fl.
Pittsburgh, PA 15222
Tel.: 412-338-8700
Tel.: 800-333-2581 (100%)
Fax: 412-338-8743
Emp.: 39
Fiscal Year-end: 3/31/91
Diet Center Franchises & Wholesale Distr. of Vitamins & Food Products
S.I.C.: 8099; 8999; 5122; 5100; 5149
Thomas R. Shepherd *(Chm. Bd.)*
Dennis Brown *(Pres. & Chief Exec. Officer)*
Jay Gilmer *(Gen. Counsel & Sec.)*
Frank Strangis *(V.P.-Mktg.)*
Matt Miller *(V.P.-Plng. & Support Services)*
Dr. Claire Boasi *(V.P.-Scientific Affairs)*

AMERICAN INDUSTRIES INC.
4033 N.W. Yeon Ave.
Portland, OR 97210
Mailing Address:
P.O. Box 10086,
Portland, OR 97210
Tel.: 503-226-1511 **OR**
Fax: 503-225-0211
Year Founded: 1944
Approx.Sls.: $115,000,000
Emp.: 400
Fiscal Year-end: 12/31/91
Import
Wholesale Metal Products
S.I.C.: 5051
Corporate Giving Program: Corporate *Contribution to UGN & Other Local* Charities
Howard Hedinger *(Chm. Bd. & Treas.)*
Neil Thornton *(Pres. & Chief Exec. Officer)*
Robert E. Duffy *(V.P.-Fin., Sec. & Chief Fin. Officer)*
Keith Erickson *(Controller)*
Russ Hada *(Dir.-Pur.)*
Carol Nicolai *(Dir.-Cash Mgmt.)*
Sheri Lynch *(Dir.-Human Resources)*
Larry Potter *(Dir.-Data Processing)*
Principal(s):
Howard Hedinger

No. of Mfg. Plants/Facilities: 7
No. of U.S. Offices: 5
No. of Foreign Offices: 1

American Industries Inc.—(Continued)

Computer Systems/Hardware:
IBM 4341

Outside Service Firm(s):

Deloitte & Touche*(Auditors)*
3900 U.S. Bancorp Tower
Portland, OR 97204
Tel.: 503-222-1341
Fax: 503-224-2172

Rollins Burdick Hunter*(Commercial Insurance Carrier)*
1211 S.W. Fifth, Ste. 600
Portland, OR 97204-3799

Principal Mutual Life Insurance Co.*(Group Insurer)*
Des Moines, IA

Standard Life Insurance Co.*(Group Insurer)*
P.O. Box 209,
Portland, OR 97207-0209

Tonkon, Torp, Galen, Marmaduke & Booth*(Legal Firm)*
1600 Pioneer Tower, 888 S.W. Fifth Ave.
Portland, OR 97204
Tel.: 503-221-1440

United States National Bank of Oregon*(Major Banking Relationship)*
Portland, OR

Principal Mutual Life Insurance Co.*(Pension Manager)*
Des Moines, IA

Division:

Diversified Steel **(1)**
1223 Dervent Way New Westminster,
Vancouver, British Columbia Canada
Tel.: 604-524-8000
Steel Service Center
S.I.C.: 5051
Dennis Butchart *(Gen. Mgr.)*

AMERICAN INKS & COATINGS CORP.
Pawling Rd.
Valley Forge, PA 19482
Mailing Address:
P.O. Box 803
Valley Forge, PA 19482
Tel.: 215-272-8866
Fax: 215-933-2173
Year Founded: 1927
Approx.Sls.: $14,000,000
Emp.: 120
Import Export
Mfr. of Coatings & Inks for the Printing Trade
S.I.C.: 2893
R.W. Shaw *(Chm. Bd.)*
Eugene H. Buttle *(Pres. & Chief Exec. Officer)*
M.J. Wagner *(Sec. & Treas.)*
William P. Rimel *(Dir.-Sls.)*
D. Smith *(Dir.-Data Processing)*
D. Kucharik *(Pur. Agent)*
Principal(s):
R.W. Shaw

No. of Mfg. Plants/Facilities: 4
No. of U.S. Offices: 4

Computer Systems/Hardware:
Unisys; IBM

Outside Service Firm(s):

Dreslin & Co.*(Auditors)*
Norristown, PA

Philadelphia National Bank*(Major Banking Relationship)*
P.O. Box 13834, Broad & Chestnut Streets
Philadelphia, PA 19101-7618
Tel.: 215-973-8327

Divisions:

American Inks & Coatings Corp., Ink Division **(1)**
1540 Wrightwood Ct.
Addison, IL 60101
Tel.: 708-543-6050
Fax: 708-543-4263
Manufacturers Ink for the Printing Trade
S.I.C.: 2893
Robert Kirby *(Gen. Mgr.)*

American Inks & Coatings Corp., Ink Division **(1)**
111 Agency Ave.
Richmond, VA 23225
Tel.: 804-232-5565
Fax: 804-232-3077
Sales & Distribution; Warehousing
S.I.C.: 5085
E.H. Buttle *(Pres.)*

American Inks & Coatings Corp., Ink Division **(1)**
3755 Kimwell Dr.
Winston-Salem, NC 27103
Tel.: 919-765-4950
Fax: 919-768-3490
Manufacturing & Distribution of Inks for the Printing Trades
S.I.C.: 5085; 2893
E.H. Buttle *(Pres.)*
R.C. Oppenheimer *(Gen. Mgr.)*

AMERICAN INSTITUTE FOR FOREIGN STUDY
102 Greenwich Ave.
Greenwich, CT 06830
Tel.: 203-869-9090
Year Founded: 1964
Earnings: $2,000,000
Approx.Sls.: $135,000,000
Emp.: 750
Fiscal Year-end: 12/31/91
Designs, Markets, and Operates Educational Programs Worldwide
S.I.C.: 8299
Cyril J.H. Taylor *(Chm. Bd.)*
Robert J. Brennan *(Vice Chm. & Chief Oper. Officer)*
Henry C. Kahn *(Pres.)*
William Gertz *(Sr. V.P.-Mktg.)*
Ronald M. Koehn *(Sr. V.P.-College Program Devel.)*
Peter Lasalandra *(Sr. V.P.-Fin.)*
John S. Linakis *(Sr. V.P.-Transporation & Pur.)*
C. Thomas Whitehouse *(Chief Info. Officer)*

Divisions:

Au Pair in America **(1)**
102 Greenwich Ave.
Greenwich, CT 06830
Tel.: 203-869-9090
Approx.Sls.: $7,633,000
Childcare & Cultural Exchange Program That Enables Young Adults to Live With an American Family & Take Care of Their Young Children
S.I.C.: 8299
Lauren Kratovil *(Dir.)*

Camp America **(1)**
102 Greenwich Ave.
Greenwich, CT 06830
Tel.: 203-869-4040
Approx.Sls.: $7,142,000
Exchange Program For Foreign Students Interested in Working as Camp Counselors in the US
S.I.C.: 8299
Henry C. Kahn *(Pres.)*

College Division **(1)**
102 Greenwich Ave.
Greenwich, CT 06830
Tel.: 203-869-9090
Provides Overseas Educational Programs for US Students at Richmond College in the UK & Other European Institutions
S.I.C.: 8299
Edward S. Blankenship *(Exec. V.P.)*
Gerry Thompson *(Sr. V.P.)*

Subsidiaries:

American Council for International Studies **(1)**
19 Bay State Rd.
Boston, MA 02215
Tel.: 617-236-2051
Approx.Rev.: $28,339,000
Operates High School Programs That Take High School Students Abroad to Study
S.I.C.: 8299
Michael I. Eizenberg *(Pres.)*

Division:

High School Division **(2)**
19Bay State Rd.
Boston, MA 02215
Tel.: 6176-236-2051
Approx.Sls.: $28,339,000
Travel Programs For U.S High School Students & Teachers
S.I.C.: 8299
Michael I. Eizenberg *(Pres. & Chief Exec. Officer)*
Thomas C. Jones *(Sr. V.P.)*

ELS Educational Services **(1)**
5761 Buckingham Pkwy.
Culver City, CA 90230
Tel.: 213-642-0982
Provides English Language Study & Educational Exchange Programs for Foreign Students
S.I.C.: 8299
Perry S. Akins *(Pres. & Chief Exec. Officer)*
Rochelle Wechter *(Sr. V.P.)*
William K. Brown *(V.P. & Treas.)*
Nancy Morrin *(V.P. & Asst. Sec.)*

ELS Educational Services **(1)**
3661 Buchanan St.
San Francisco, CA 34123
Tel.: 415-563-2500
Overseas Educational Programs For College Students
S.I.C.: 8299

Non-U.S. Holding:

American Institute for Foreign Study **(1)**
37 Queen's Gate
London, SW7 5HR, United Kingdom
Tel.: 71-581 2733
Educational Exchange Program
S.I.C.: 8299
Cyril J.H. Taylor *(Chm. & Chief Exec. Officer)*
Robert J. Brennan *(Pres. & Chief Oper. Officer)*
Peter Lasalandra *(Sr. V.P.-Fin.)*
John S. Linakis *(Sr. V.P.-Transportation & Pur.)*
C. Thomas Whitehouse *(Chief Information Officer)*
Anthony J. Taylor *(Dir.-Fin.)*

AMERICAN INSTITUTE OF C.P.A.'S INC.
1211 Ave. of the Americas
New York, NY 10036
Tel.: 212-575-6200 **DC**
Fax: 212-575-3846
Year Founded: 1887
Assets: $52,269,000
Earnings: ($2,933,000)
Liabilities: $32,736,000
Net Worth: $19,533,000
Approx.Sls.: $107,530,000
Emp.: 828
Fiscal Year-end: 7/31/91
Provides Professional Membership Services to Certified Public Accountants
S.I.C.: 8621
Gerald A. Polansky *(Chm. Bd.)*
Philip B. Chenok *(Pres. & Chief Exec. Officer)*
Edward W. Niemiec *(Grp. V.P.-Opers. & Chief Oper. Officer)*
Donald L. Adams *(V.P.-Fin. & Admin. & Chief Fin. Officer)*
Richard E. Piluso *(Treas.)*
Donald J. Schneeman *(Gen. Counsel & Sec.)*
Robert V. Boos *(Controller)*
Joseph Davis *(Dir.-Data Processing)*
Francine Gallo *(Dir.-Office Admin.)*
Leonard I. Green *(Dir.-Fin. Mngmt.)*
Frank J. Katusak *(Dir.-Planning & Research)*
John Lewison *(Dir.-Human Resources)*
Marilyn Stoddard *(Dir.-Meetings & Corp. Travel Plng.)*
Joanne Lindstrom *(Mgr.-Employee Benefits)*
Karen Neloms *(Librarian)*
Joe Ciccone *(Telecommunications Admin.)*

No. of U.S. Offices: 3

Computer Systems/Hardware:
IBM

Outside Service Firm(s):

J. H. Cohn & Co.*(Auditors)*
New York, NY

Rollins Burdick Hunter*(Commercial Insurance Carrier)*
New York, NY

Prudential Insurance Co. of America*(Group Insurer)*
Roseland, NJ

BEA Associates, Inc.*(Investment Banker)*
One Citicorp Center, 153 East 53rd St.
New York, NY 10022
Tel.: 212-832-2626
Fax: 212-751-2470

Capital Guardian Trust*(Investment Banker)*
333 South Hope Street
Los Angeles, CA 90071
Tel.: 213-486-9334

Skadden, Arps, Slate, Meagher, & Flom*(Legal Firm)*
New York, NY

Bankers Trust Co.*(Major Banking Relationship)*
P.O. Box 318, Church St. Station
New York, NY 10008
Tel.: 212-454-2212
Fax: 212-454-2783

Citibank N.A.*(Major Banking Relationship)*
Corporate Trust Services, 399 Park Ave.
New York, NY 10043
Tel.: 212-559-1605

Buck Pension Fund Services*(Pension Manager)*
Two Pennsylvania Plaza
New York, NY 10121

AMERICAN INTERNATIONAL CONTAINER, INC.
3724 N.W. 73rd St.
Miami, FL 33147
Tel.: 305-836-8650
Fax: 305-696-7458
Year Founded: 1977
Sales Range: $80-99 Million
Emp.: 167
Fiscal Year-end: 12/31/91
Import Export
Distribute Glass, Plastics & Metal Containers and Closures; Containers & Plastic & Metal Caps For Toiletries, Cosmetics, Food, Pharmaceutical, Beverage, Paint & Allied Industries
S.I.C.: 3089; 3466; 5085
Gary Carpender *(Exec. V.P.)*
Gladys Canals *(Controller)*
Irma Bermudez *(Dir.-Pur.)*
Rosa M. Flores *(Dir.-Communications)*
Garry Steinbert *(Dir.-Mktg.)*
Linda Tangolics *(Dir.-Personnel)*
Maria E. Navarro *(Mgr.-Admin.)*
Jesus Chinique *(Bookkeeper)*
Principal(s):
Gary Carpender

No. of U.S. Offices: 3
No. of Foreign Offices: 12

Computer Systems/Hardware:
IBM

Outside Service Firm(s):

Arthur Andersen & Co.*(Auditors)*
2100 One Biscayne Tower
Miami, FL 33131
Tel.: 305-374-3700

Paul, Landy, Bailey*(Legal Firm)*
Miami, FL

Ocean Bank*(Major Banking Relationship)*
Miami, FL

Total Bank*(Major Banking Relationship)*
Miami, FL

AMERICAN JOURNAL OF NURSING COMPANY
555 W. 57th St.
New York, NY 10019-2961
Tel.: 212-582-8820
Fax: 212-586-5462
Year Founded: 1900
Approx.Sls.: $13,000,000
Emp.: 65
Fiscal Year-end: 11/30/91
American Journal of Nursing; Nursing Research; AJN Intl. Nursing Index; MCN, The American Journal of Maternal/Child Nursing; The AJN Guide
S.I.C.: 2721
Howard Clutterbuck *(Pres.)*
Gerald Meyerson *(Prod. Dir.)*
James Nagle *(Natl. Sls. Mgr.)*
Kelli Steinkamp *(Sls. Rep.)*
Gregory Willinger *(Sls. Rep.)*
Doug Mitchell *(Sls. Rep.)*
JoBeth Mitchell *(Sls. Rep.)*

Computer Systems/Hardware:
PC/LAN

AMERICAN KENNEL CLUB, INC.
51 Madison Ave.
New York, NY 10010
Tel.: 212-696-8200
Fax: 212-696-8299
Approx.Sls.: $30,000,000
Emp.: 390
Publishing & Printing Of Books
S.I.C.: 2731
John S. Ward *(Chm. Bd.)*
Robert G. Maxwell *(Pres.)*
John Mandeville *(V.P.)*
Robert H. McKowen *(V.P.)*
Samuel Perry *(V.P.)*
Frederick G. Sheppard *(V.P.)*
W. Terry Stacy *(V.P.)*
A. Nelson Sills *(Treas.)*
Thomas G. Murphy *(Controller)*
James E. Dearinger *(Sec.)*

Outside Service Firm(s):

Deloitte & Touche*(Auditors)*
1 World Trade Center
New York, NY 10048
Tel.: 212-669-5000

AMERICAN LAUBSCHER CORP.
80 Finn Court
Farmingdale, NY 11735
Tel.: 516-694-5900
Fax: 516-293-0935
Year Founded: 1950
Approx.Sls.: $18,000,000
Emp.: 56
Import Export
Mfr. of Precision Components; Screw Machine Products; Jewel Bearings; Wire Guides; Ground Shafts
S.I.C.: 3451
Heinz R. Lehmann *(Pres.)*
Lloyd Miller *(Exec. V.P.)*
Robert K. Kunz *(V.P.)*
Antoine O. Welti *(V.P.)*
Richard Fox *(Treas.)*

AMERICAN LAUNDRY MACHINERY INC.
5050 Section Ave.
Cincinnati, OH 45212
Tel.: 513-731-5500 **DE**
Telex: 21-4428
Fax: 513-731-5513
Year Founded: 1868
Approx.Sls.: $34,000,000
Emp.: 325
Fiscal Year-end: 12/31/91
Import Export
Mfr. Commercial Laundry, Dry Cleaning & Textile Processing Machinery
S.I.C.: 3582
Corporate Giving Program:
Contributes to Established Charities
George L. Strike *(Chm. Bd.)*
Paul J. Gerling *(Pres. & Chief Oper. Officer)*
Alan Karam *(Exec. V.P.)*
Stephen J. Crank *(V.P.-Fin.)*
Ted Hyle, Jr. *(V.P.-Human Resources)*
Al Kammer *(V.P.-Fin., Controller & Chief Fin. Officer)*
George Williamson *(V.P.-Engrng.)*
Richard Herbert *(Dir.-Data Processing)*
Timothy Nymberg *(Dir.-Intl. Sls.)*
Ron Randolph *(Dir.-Mktg.)*
Gil Trepal *(Dir.-Adv. & Pub. Rel.)*
Jim Stautberg *(Mgr.-Matls.)*
Principal(s):
George L. Strike

No. of Mfg. Plants/Facilities: 1
No. of U.S. Offices: 1
No. of Foreign Offices: 1

Computer Systems/Hardware:
IBM

Outside Service Firm(s):

Coopers & Lybrand*(Auditors)*
Canton, OH

Santen & Hughes*(Legal Firm)*
Cincinnati, OH

Star Bank*(Major Banking Relationship)*
425 Walnut Street
Cincinnati, OH 45202
Tel.: 513-632-4000

AMERICAN LEGEND CORPORATE
400 Strander Blvd.
Seattle, WA 98138
Mailing Address:
P.O. Box 58308,
Seattle, WA 98138
Tel.: 206-244-1303
Fax: 206-244-4945
Year Founded: 1985
Approx.Sls.: $60,000,000
Emp.: 10
Processor of Mink Skins
S.I.C.: 5159
Ted Jacob *(Chm. Bd.)*
Thomas Haass *(Chief Exec. Officer)*
Edward Brennan *(V.P.-Mktg.)*
Patricia Fortune *(Sec.)*

AMERICAN LIBERTY FINANCIAL CORP.
4962 Florida Blvd.
Baton Rouge, LA 70806
Mailing Address:
P.O. Box 64626
Baton Rouge, LA 70896
Tel.: 504-927-9630
Fax: 504-925-2715
Sales Range: $100-499 Million
Emp.: 22
Insurance, Oil & Gas Partnerships
S.I.C.: 6211; 6311; 6321; 6792
James I. Dunham *(Chm. Bd. & Pres.)*
N.H. Deckle *(Treas.)*
W.P. Duplesis *(Sec.)*

Principal(s):
James I. Dunham

Computer Systems/Hardware:
IBM System 36

Outside Service Firm(s):

Amend Smith & Co.*(Auditors)*
Oklahoma City, OK

Montgomery, Barnett, Brown & Read*(Legal Firm)*
New Orleans, LA

Sunburst Bank*(Major Banking Relationship)*
Baton Rouge, LA

AMERICAN LIBRARY ASSOCIATION
50 E. Huron St.
Chicago, IL 60611
Tel.: 312-944-6780
Fax: 312-440-9374
Year Founded: 1876
Approx.Sls.: $10,000,000
Emp.: 260
Fiscal Year-end: 8/31/91
Import Export
Publishers
S.I.C.: 2731
Roger Parent *(Deputy Exec. Dir.)*
Linda Crismond *(Exec. Dir.)*
Ed McLarin *(Assoc. Exec. Dir.-Publishing)*
Peggy Barber *(Assoc. Exec. Dir.-Communications)*
Marcia Kuszmaul *(Dir.-Mktg. Communications & Graphics)*
Evelyn Shaevel *(Dir.-Mktg.)*
Kathy Repholz *(Mgr. Adv.)*
Robert Hershman *(Mgr. Sls.)*
Danea Rush *(Mgr.-Adv. Sls. & Circulation)*
Charles Harmon *(Librarian)*

AMERICAN LINEN SUPPLY COMPANY
47 S. 9th St.
Minneapolis, MN 55402
Tel.: 612-371-4200
Fax: 612-371-4252
Year Founded: 1889
Approx.Sls.: $14,000,000
Emp.: 6,000
Fiscal Year-end: 12/31/91
Rental of Linens
S.I.C.: 7213; 7218
Lawrence G. Steiner *(Pres. & Chief Exec. Officer)*
John A. Hilliard *(V.P.-Fin., Treas. & Chief Fin. Officer)*
J. Norman Hove *(V.P. & Controller)*

Computer Systems/Hardware:
Data Point

Outside Service Firm(s):

KPMG Peat Marwick*(Auditors)*
Peat Marwick Plaza, 303 E. Wacker Dr.
Chicago, IL 60601
Tel.: 312-938-1000

First National Bank of Chicago*(Major Banking Relationship)*
One First National Plaza
Chicago, IL 60670
Tel.: 312-732-9781
Tel.: 312-732-4050
Fax: 312-732-4840
Fax: 312-732-3055

AMERICAN LOCK & SUPPLY INC.
4411 E. La Palma Ave.
Anaheim, CA 92807
Tel.: 714-996-8882
Tel.: 800-854-8775
Year Founded: 1963
Approx.Sls.: $75,000,000
Emp.: 250
Fiscal Year-end: 11/30/92
Distr. of Locks & Locksmith Equipment
S.I.C.: 5072
James R. De Forrest *(Chm. Bd.)*
Sean B. De Forrest *(Pres.)*
Jane A. Chapek *(V.P.-Fin. & Sec.)*
William Power *(V.P.-Sls.)*
Richard Schwarzstein *(Gen. Counsel)*

Computer Systems/Hardware:
IBM AS400 Model E70

AMERICAN LOUVER CO.
7700 Austin Ave.
Skokie, IL 60077
Mailing Address:
P.O. Box 206
Skokie, IL 60077
Tel.: 708-470-3300
Fax: 708-470-0420
Approx.Sls.: $15,000,000
Emp.: 125
Louvers & Lenses for Fluorescent Lighting
S.I.C.: 3648
Walter Glass *(Chm. Bd. & Pres.)*
Robert Oblak, Jr. *(Exec. V.P.)*
Thomas Friedl *(Controller)*
Carol Brandenburg *(Mktg. Mgr.)*

AMERICAN MACHINE & TOOL COMPANY
4th Ave. & Spring St.
Royersford, PA 19468
Tel.: 215-948-3800
Year Founded: 1928
Approx.Sls.: $22,000,000
Emp.: 85
Import
Mfr. of Power Tools & Centrifugal Pumps
S.I.C.: 3569; 3546
H.M. Pollak *(Pres.)*
Chau Chang *(V.P.-Admin.)*
Alex Cushman *(V.P.-Mfg.)*
Edwin A. Hartz *(V.P.-Engrng.)*
Samuel Marcus *(V.P.)*
Mark Furlong *(Mgr.-Mktg.)*
Keith Bearde *(Mgr.-Opers.)*
Scott Yeagley *(Mgr.-Catalog)*

Outside Service Firm(s):

O'Donnell, Weiss & Matteis*(Legal Firm)*
Royersford, PA

AMERICAN MANAGEMENT GROUP
(d/b/a Portland Glass/Proglass)
865 Spring St.
Westbrook, ME 04092
Mailing Address:
P.O. Box 558
Westbrook, ME 04092
Tel.: 207-775-3703 **ME**
Fax: 207-775-4367
Year Founded: 1947
Sales Range: $40-59 Million
Emp.: 542
Holding Company
S.I.C.: 6719
Weston Bonney *(Chm. Bd.)*
Richard M. Bakke *(Pres. & Chief Exec. Officer)*
Kathleen Flanagan *(V.P.-Sls. & Mktg.)*
Dana Mather *(V.P.-Opers.)*
Douglas Norton *(V.P.-Distribution & Mfg.)*
James R. Phillips *(Treas.)*
Charles Miller *(Corp. Sec.)*
Katherine Davis *(Dir.-Human Resources)*

Outside Service Firm(s):

Morse, Payson, Noyes*(Commercial Insurance Carrier)*
100 Middle St. Plaza
Portland, ME

American Management Group—(Continued)

Marine Midland Bank*(Major Banking Relationship)*
Portland, ME

Divisions:

Portland Glass/American Management Group **(1)**
865 Spring St.
Westbrook, ME 04098
Tel.: 207-775-3703
Tel.: 800-777-3703
Sales Range: $40-59 Million
Emp.: 470
Computer Systems/Hardware:
Digital Equipment Corp., VAX
Storm Products, Garage Doors, Sunroofs (Autos), Windshield Repair & Replacement, Tub & Shower Doors, Vinyl Replacement Windows, Manufacturing & Sales (Wholesale/Retail)
S.I.C.: 1793
Richard Bakke *(Pres. & Chief Exec. Officer)*
Kathleen Flanagan *(V.P. Sls.)*
Dana Mather *(V.P.-Store Opers.)*
Douglas Norton *(V.P.-Mfg. & Distr.)*
Randy Phillips *(Treas.)*
Hank Gale *(Dir.-Adv.)*
Frank Levesque *(Dir.-Training & Safety)*
Kathy Peterson *(Dir.-Human Resources)*
Doug Noble *(Mgr.-Mngmt. Information Systems)*

Proglass **(1)**
865 Spring St.
Westbrook, ME 04092
Tel.: 207-775-3703
Marketing & Sales
S.I.C.: 5039

AMERICAN MANUFACTURING CO. (TN)
3600 N. Hawthorne St.
Chattanooga, TN 37406
Tel.: 615-624-1191
Tel.: 800-264-9473
Fax: 615-629-4852
Year Founded: 1898
Approx.Sls.: $11,000,000
Emp.: 200
Export
Wire Products & Stampings, Display Racks, Hardware, Floral Wire Products, Wreaths, Easels, Wire Shelving
S.I.C.: 3469; 7319
James B. Robinson *(Chm. Bd. & Pres.)*
D.L. Lamsey *(V.P.-Fin.)*
Robert Snyder *(V.P.-Mfg. & Engrng.)*
William M. Hewgley Jr. *(V.P.-Sls. & Mktg.)*
J. Northcut *(Dir.-Personnel)*
John Edwards *(Pur. Mgr.)*

AMERICAN MANUFACTURING COMPANY, INC. (LA)
200 Southpark Rd.
Lafayette, LA 70508
Mailing Address:
P.O. Box 88000
Lafayette, LA 70598-8000
Tel.: 318-837-9241
Telex: 831889
Fax: 318-837-9246
Approx.Sls.: $25,000,000
Emp.: 500
Import Export
American Brand & Amco Rope & Twine
S.I.C.: 3552
Walter Juodis *(Pres. & Chief Exec. Officer)*
George Berger *(V.P.-Mfg.)*
Joseph A. Berthelot *(V.P.)*
Glenda Jones *(Pur. Agent)*

AMERICAN MARKETING INDUSTRIES, INC.
10450 Holmes Rd., Ste. 501
Kansas City, MO 64131
Tel.: 816-943-5180 **DE**
Fax: 816-943-5199
Year Founded: 1985
Approx.Sls.: $180,000,000
Emp.: 2,500
Holding Company; Mfr. of T-Shirts, Sweat Shirts, Children's Knit Pajamas, Jackets & Athletic Uniforms
S.I.C.: 6719; 2321; 2322; 2329
Alan Kosloff *(Chm. Bd., Chief Exec. Officer & Pres.)*
Everett L. Midkiff *(Chief Fin. Officer)*

Subsidiary:

Swingster Company **(1)**
10450 Holmes Rd.
Kansas City, MO 64131
Tel.: 816-943-5000
Emp.: 400
Swingster Premium Marketing; Jackets, Caps, Ad Specialty Items, Shirts; Swingster Athletic Team Uniforms, Caps, Warm-ups, Leisure Apparel Swingster Sport Graphic Active Wear, Licensed Apparel for MLB, NHL, Garfield, College NHL
S.I.C.: 5199
Alan Kosloff *(Pres.)*
Roger Henry *(Sr. V.P.)*
Howard Trilling *(V.P.-Adv.)*
Stan Morrison *(V.P.-Athletic Apparel Div.)*
John Vallejo *(Dir.-Adv.)*

AMERICAN MARKETING WORKS & INTERNATIONAL CORPORATION
14501 S. Figueroa
Gardena, CA 90248
Tel.: 310-715-6118
Fax: 310-715-1507
Fax: 800-775-7529
Year Founded: 1989
Screen Printing on Sport Shirts
S.I.C.: 2261
Marvin Winkler *(Chm. Bd.)*
Sheri Winkler *(Pres.)*

Outside Service Firm(s):

Goldfarb Whitman Cohen*(Auditors)*
Los Angeles, CA

Mitsui Manufacturers Bank*(Major Banking Relationship)*
Los Angeles, CA

AMERICAN MARKING SYSTEMS
1015 Paulson Ave.
Clifton, NJ 07015
Mailing Address:
P.O. Box 1677
Clifton, NJ 07015
Tel.: 201-478-5600
Fax: 201-478-0039
Approx.Sls.: $10,000,000
Emp.: 130
Marking Devices, Rubber Stamps, Steel Stamps, Printing Plates Stencils, Special Inks, Numbering Machines
S.I.C.: 3953; 5112
John A. Collins III *(Pres.)*
John Newburger *(Controller)*
Jack Collins *(Dir.-Adv.)*

Affiliates:

Baumgarten Stamp Co. **(1)**
342 N. Charles St.
Baltimore, MD 21203
Tel.: 410-727-3733

CCW Stamp Co. **(1)**
2324 W. Rt. 70
Cherry Hill, NJ 08002
Tel.: 609-665-8665

Dilks Stamp Co. **(1)**
1613 Sansom St.
Philadelphia, PA 19103
Tel.: 215-564-1775

Harrisburg Stamp Co. **(1)**
2741 Paxton St.
Harrisburg, PA 17111
Tel.: 717-236-9000

Krengel Mfg. Co. **(1)**
545 8th Ave.
New York, NY 10018
Tel.: 212-564-8850

Paterson Stamp Works **(1)**
1015 Paulson Ave.
Clifton, NJ 07015
Tel.: 201-478-5600

Quaker City Stamp Co. **(1)**
4234 Macalester Ave.
Philadelphia, PA 19124
Tel.: 215-457-7910

State Stamp Works **(1)**
226 South St.
Hartford, CT 06110
Tel.: 203-246-5601

AMERICAN MATHEMATICAL SOCIETY, INC.
201 Charles St.
Providence, RI 02904
Mailing Address:
P.O. Box 6248
Providence, RI 02940
Tel.: 401-455-4000
Tel.: 800-321-4AMS
Telex: 797192
Fax: 401-331-3842
Year Founded: 1888
Approx.Sls.: $20,000,000
Emp.: 225
Fiscal Year-end: 12/31/90
Export
Books & Journals Publisher, Meetings, Symposia, Seminar Sponsor, such as CD-Rom and Tex Software
S.I.C.: 2731
Paul J. Sally, Jr. *(Chm. Bd.)*
Michael Artin *(Pres.)*
William H. Jaco *(Exec. Dir.)*
Ronald L. Graham *(Pres.-Elect)*
Steve Armentrout *(Assoc. Treas.)*
Bob Blanchette *(Controller)*
Gary Brownell *(Fin. Exec.)*
Jacques Hopkins *(Gen. Counsel)*
Franklin Peterson *(Treas.)*
Robert Fossom *(Sec.)*
Jeremy Soldevilla *(Dir.-Mktg.)*
William B. Woolf *(Assoc. Exec. Dir.)*
H. Hope Daly *(Meetings Plng. Dir.)*
Tim Goggins *(Dir.-Plng. & Devel.)*
Carol-Ann Blackwood *(Membership Mgr.)*
Lynda Bonclarek *(Mgr.-Personnel)*
Mary Ellen Griffiths *(Pur. Agent)*
Lisa Madigan *(Mktg. Asst.)*

Division:

Mathematical Reviews **(1)**
416 4th St.
Ann Arbor, MI 48107
Tel.: 313-996-5250
Export

AMERICAN METAL & PLASTICS
450 32nd St. SW
Grand Rapids, MI 49518
Tel.: 616-452-6061
Fax: 616-452-3835
Approx.Sls.: $24,000,000
Emp.: 250
Automotive Stampings; Injection Molding Of Plastics
S.I.C.: 3465; 3089
Martin Cook *(Chm. Bd.)*
Thomas Cook *(Pres.)*
Michael Cook *(V.P.-Sls.)*
David Haadsma *(V.P.-Mfg.)*
Dale Van Allsburg *(Sec.)*
Clay Cough *(Dir.-Engrng.)*
David Westover *(Dir.-Pur.)*

Outside Service Firm(s):

Ernst & Young*(Auditors)*
171 Monroe Ave. NW
Grand Rapids, MI 49503
Tel.: 616-774-0710
Fax: 616-774-0190

AMERICAN MILITARY ARMS CORPORATION
2202 Redmond Rd.
Jacksonville, AR 72076
Tel.: 501-982-1633
Fax: 501-982-8075
Approx.Sls.: $13,000,000
Emp.: 100
Firearms & Accessories
S.I.C.: 5099
Louis Imperato *(Pres. & Chief Exec. Officer)*
Nena Duncan *(Controller)*
Bert Emmitt *(Production Mgr.)*

Division:

Arkansas Investment Casting **(1)**
2202 Redmond Rd.
Jacksonville, AR 72076
Tel.: 501-982-9491

AMERICAN MITAC CORPORATION
48571 Milmont Dr.
Fremont, CA 94538
Tel.: 510-623-5300
Fax: 510-623-5390
Year Founded: 1984
Emp.: 45
Wholesalers For Micro Computers
S.I.C.: 5065
Francis Tsai *(Pres.)*
C.K. Cheng *(V.P.)*
Kelly Yang *(Dir.-Mngmt. Information Systems)*

Outside Service Firm(s):

Price Waterhouse*(Auditors)*
150 Almaden Blvd.
San Jose, CA 95113
Tel.: 408-282-1200

AMERICAN MUTUAL LIFE INSURANCE COMPANY
418 Sixth Ave.
Des Moines, IA 50309
Tel.: 515-280-1331
Fax: 515-280-3908
Year Founded: 1897
Approx.Sls.: $1,424,912,000
Emp.: 200
Fiscal Year-end: 12/31/90
Life Insurance
S.I.C.: 6311
S.C. Kalainov *(Chm. Bd. & Chief Exec. Officer)*
W.R. Engel *(Pres. & Treas.)*
James J. Streck *(Sr. V.P.-Ins. Opers. & Sec.)*
W.E. McGrath *(Sr. V.P.-Mktg.)*
James W. Agnew *(V.P.-Mktg.)*
Richard Lozier *(Gen. Counsel)*
Linda Knodle *(Publications Editor & Sls. Promo. Mgr.)*

AMERICAN OFFICE EQUIPMENT
405 E. Shawmut
La Grange, IL 60525
Tel.: 708-354-1100
Fax: 708-354-6823
Year Founded: 1978
Assets: $15,500,000
Earnings: $610,000
Liabilities: $13,800,000
Net Worth: $1,700,000
Approx.Sls.: $30,000,000
Emp.: 375
Fiscal Year-end: 2/28/90
Distributor of Office Equipment
S.I.C.: 5111; 5044
John L. Leinweber *(Pres. & Chief Exec. Officer)*
Victor Althoff *(V.P.-Internal Sls.)*
Robert J. Coldwell *(V.P.-Admin.)*
Debie Constantini *(V.P.-Field Opers.)*
Jim Hynes *(V.P.-Field Opers.)*

Phil Lampugnano *(V.P.-Fin. & Chief Fin. Officer)*
Robert Marcantonio *(V.P.-Mktg.)*
John Specht *(V.P.-Field Opers.)*
John Tait *(V.P.-Service)*
W. F. Tschanen *(V.P.-Opers.)*
Jim Vitiello *(V.P.-Field Opers.)*
Edward Litke *(Controller)*
Stephen Bauer *(Dir.-Data Processing)*
Patricia Lindsey *(Dir.-Personnel)*

Principal(s):
John L. Leinweber
Carl R. Davis

No. of Mfg. Plants/Facilities: 14
No. of U.S. Offices: 14

Computer Systems/Hardware:
Texas Instruments 1500

Outside Service Firm(s):

Rome & Associates*(Auditors)*
Chicago, IL

Mack & Paker*(Commercial Insurance Carrier)*
Chicago, IL

Blue Cross & Blue Shield of Illinois*(Group Insurer)*
100 Tower Drive
Burr Ridge, IL 60521
Tel.: 708-323-3666

Laser, Schostok, Kolman & Frank*(Legal Firm)*
Chicago, IL

American National Bank & Trust Company of Chicago*(Major Banking Relationship)*
33 N. LaSalle St.
Chicago, IL 60602
Tel.: 312-661-5000
Fax: 312-661-6417

Subsidiaries:

American Office Equipment Distributing, Inc. **(1)**
405 E. Shawmut
La Grange, IL 60525
Tel.: 708-354-1100
Wholesaler of Office Equipment
S.I.C.: 5044

Funding Services Inc. **(1)**
405 E. Shawmut
La Grange, IL 60525
Tel.: 708-354-1100 (100%)
Emp.: 330
Retail Copiers, Duplicators, Electronic Typing Systems, Facsimile, Computers, Word Processors & Related Supplies
S.I.C.: 5044; 5111
John L. Leinweber *(Pres. & Chief Oper. Officer)*

AMERICAN OPTICAL CORP.
80 Field Point Rd.
Greenwich, CT 06830
Tel.: 203-622-6600 **DE**
Fax: 203-622-1292
Year Founded: 1833
Approx.Sls.: $275,000,000
Emp.: 5,000
Fiscal Year-end: 3/31/91
Worldwide Mfr. & Distr. of Ophthalmic Lenses & Frames, Occupational Safety Products, Infrared Instruments, Precision Molding & Precision Optical Products, Industrial Abrasives & Grinding Wheels
S.I.C.: 3559; 3851; 3842
Maurice J. Cunniffe *(Chm. Bd. & Chief Exec. Officer)*
Ernest A. Du Quette *(V.P.-Human Res. & Admin.)*
William Cotter *(V.P. & Gen. Counsel)*
Steven J. Beckett *(Treas.)*
George Meir *(Natl. Sls. Mgr.)*

No. of Mfg. Plants/Facilities: 12
No. of Foreign Offices: 15

Computer Systems/Hardware:
Hewlett-Packard; IBM

Outside Service Firm(s):

Cahill, Gordon & Reindel*(Legal Firm)*
80 Pine St.
New York, NY 10005
Tel.: 212-701-3000
Fax: 212-269-5420

Shawmut Bank*(Major Banking Relationship)*
Worcester, MA

Divisions:

American Optical Corp. **(1)**
14 Mechanic St.
Southbridge, MA 01550
Tel.: 508-765-9711
Mktg. & Sales of Optical Products
S.I.C.: 5048
Gordon Terry *(Gen. Mgr.)*

Precision Products Business **(1)**
14 Mechanic
Southbridge, MA 01550
Tel.: 508-765-9711

AMERICAN PACKAGING CORPORATION
Grant Ave. & Ashton Rd.
Philadelphia, PA 19114
Tel.: 215-698-4800
Fax: 215-698-5499
Approx.Sls.: $100,000,000
Emp.: 1,000
Bags, Cartons, Papers-Printed & Unprinted
S.I.C.: 2657; 5113
S.A. Schottland *(Chm. Bd.)*
S.B. Schottland *(Pres.)*
R.L. Coleman *(V.P.-Mfg.)*
David J. Howley *(V.P. & Gen. Mgr.-Coating Laminated Prods. Div.)*
Larry Manaugh *(V.P. & Gen. Mgr.-Bag Div.)*
J. Mossholder *(Treas.)*
Mary Lou McCanlis *(Dir.-Adv.)*

Principal(s):
S.B. Schottland

Computer Systems/Hardware:
IBM System 34

Outside Service Firm(s):

Deloitte & Touche*(Auditors)*
One Cascade Plaza, Ste. 1600
Akron, OH 44303-1187
Tel.: 216-253-2022

Philadelphia National Bank*(Major Banking Relationship)*
P.O. Box 13834, Broad & Chestnut Streets
Philadelphia, PA 19101-7618
Tel.: 215-973-8327

Divisions:

American Packaging Corporation **(1)**
777 Driving Park Ave.
Rochester, NY 14613
Tel.: 716-254-9500
S.I.C.: 2657; 5113
Peter Schottland *(V.P. & Gen. Mgr.)*

American Packaging Corporation **(1)**
W. James St.
Columbus, WI 53925
Tel.: 414-623-2291
S.I.C.: 2657; 5113
Mike Duroche *(Gen. Mgr.)*

American Packaging Corporation **(1)**
300 S. Verity Pkwy.
Middletown, OH 45043
Tel.: 513-422-5434
S.I.C.: 2657; 5113
George Petzelt *(Gen. Mgr.)*

American Packaging Corporation **(1)**
200 Continental Dr.
Columbus, WI 53925
Tel.: 414-623-4534
S.I.C.: 2657; 5113
Tom Ringelstetter *(Mgr.-Plant)*

American Packaging Corporation **(1)**
P.O. Box 240, 125 W. Broad St.
Story City, IA 50248
Tel.: 515-733-5136
Art Curkstorf *(Gen. Mgr.)*

AMERICAN PAPER PRODUCTS GROUP, LTD.
8401 Southern Blvd.
Youngstown, OH 44512
Tel.: 216-758-4545
Fax: 216-758-8235
Year Founded: 1916
Approx.Sls.: $40,000,000
Emp.: 450
Fiscal Year-end: 12/31/91
Mfr. Appco Envelopes
S.I.C.: 2677
Hilary B. Miller *(Chm. Bd.)*
C. Preston Miller *(Pres.)*
Jim Jakubovic *(V.P.-Mfg.)*
John E. Gill *(V.P.-Sls. & Mktg.)*
Barbara J. Kolesar *(V.P.-Fin.)*
W. Arthur Marion *(Mgr.-Matls.)*

Computer Systems/Hardware:
Datapoint & Wyse

AMERICAN PASSAGE MEDIA CORPORATION
215 W. Harrison
Seattle, WA 98119
Tel.: 206-282-8111
Tel.: 800-426-5537 **WA**
Fax: 206-282-1280
Year Founded: 1976
Earnings: $83,000
Sales Range: $20-39 Million
Emp.: 100
Fiscal Year-end: 9/30/92
College Media Marketing; Mail Order
S.I.C.: 7319
Gilbert Scherer *(Pres.)*
Mitchell Hymonitz *(Chief Fin. Officer)*
Linda Naismith *(Exec. V.P.)*
Carlton Bryant *(V.P.-Mktg.)*
Loren Ray *(Dir.-Data Processing)*
Heidi Finn *(Mgr.-Personnel)*

No. of U.S. Offices: 5

Computer Systems/Hardware:
Sanyo/ICON

Outside Service Firm(s):

Ernst & Young*(Auditors)*
999 Third Av., Ste. 3500
Seattle, WA 98104
Tel.: 206-621-1800
Fax: 206-682-1234

Bankers Life & Casualty*(Group Insurer)*
Chicago, IL

Blue Cross of Washington & Alaska*(Group Insurer)*
Seattle, WA

Stoel, Rives, Boley, Jones & Grey*(Legal Firm)*
One Union Sq. Bldg.
Seattle, WA 98101
Tel.: 206-624-0900

Commerce Bank*(Major Banking Relationship)*
Seattle, WA

AMERICAN PLASTIC TOYS INC.
799 Ladd Rd.
Walled Lake, MI 48390
Mailing Address:
P.O. Box 100
Walled Lake, MI 48390
Tel.: 313-624-4881
Fax: 313-624-4918
Year Founded: 1961
Approx.Sls.: $33,000,000
Emp.: 500
Toy Manufacturer
S.I.C.: 3944
David B. Littleton *(Pres.)*
John Beeskow *(V.P.-Sls.)*
Robert Fischer *(V.P. & Chief Engineer)*
D.A. Rice *(V.P. & Treas.)*
Patrick Hebert *(Pur. Agent)*
Marcia Schelter *(Pur. Agent)*

Outside Service Firm(s):

Doeren & Mayhew*(Auditors)*
Troy, MI

Butzel Long*(Legal Firm)*
Madden Bldg., 150 W. Jefferson, Ste. 900
Detroit, MI 48226-4430
Tel.: 313-225-7000
Fax: 313-225-7080

Michigan National Bank*(Major Banking Relationship)*
Troy, MI

AMERICAN PRINTERS & LITHOGRAPHERS
6701 W. Oakton St.
Chicago, IL 60714
Tel.: 708-966-6500
Tel.: 312-267-6500
Fax: 312-267-6553
Year Founded: 1911
Sales Range: $40-59 Million
Commercial Sheeted Lithographers
S.I.C.: 2752
Robert Lifton *(Chm. Bd.)*
Leon S. Jaffee *(Pres.)*
John Wittstock *(Chief Fin. Officer)*
William Wahl *(Dir.-Pur.)*

Principal(s):
Robert Lifton
Leon S. Jaffee

No. of Mfg. Plants/Facilities: 1
No. of U.S. Offices: 1

Computer Systems/Hardware:
Digital Equipment

Outside Service Firm(s):

Phillip Rootberg*(Auditors)*
Chicago, IL

AMERICAN PRODUCE & VEGETABLE CO.
4721 Simonton Rd.
Dallas, TX 75244
Mailing Address:
P.O. Box 802332
Dallas, TX 75380-2332
Tel.: 214-233-5750 **TX**
Fax: 214-233-6909
Fax: 214-239-2820
Year Founded: 1917
Approx.Sls.: $110,000,000
Emp.: 650
Fiscal Year-end: 6/30/91
Wholesale Imported & Domestic Wine, Fresh & Frozen Fruits & Vegetables, Canned & Frozen Poultry
S.I.C.: 5182; 5148; 5142; 5149; 5144
Lucian M. LaBarba *(Pres. & Chief Exec. Officer)*
Mack Standlee *(Chief Oper. Officer)*
James E. LaBarba *(V.P.)*
Roger D. LaBarba *(V.P.)*
James A. LaBarba *(Treas.)*
James F. LaBarba *(Sec.)*
Rick Regan *(Controller, & Dir.-Data Processing)*

Outside Service Firm(s):

KPMG Peat Marwick*(Auditors)*
1601 Elm St., Ste. 1600
Dallas, TX 75201
Tel.: 214-754-2000
Fax: 214-754-2297

Strasburger & Price*(Legal Firm)*
Dallas, TX

American Produce & Vegetable Co.—(Continued)

Hibernia National Bank *(Major Banking Relationship)*
1601 Elm St., Third Fl.
Dallas, TX 75201
Tel.: 214-969-6369

Division:

American FoodService **(1)**
4721 Simonton Rd.
Dallas, TX 75244
Tel.: 214-233-5750
Fax: 214-239-2820
Wholesale Food Distribution To Hotels, Restaurants, Clubs
S.I.C.: 5142
James F. LaBarba *(Pres.)*
J. Mack Standlee *(Chief Oper. Officer)*
Hank Weinstein *(Mgr.-Sls.)*
Karen Krebs *(Mktg. Coord.)*

AMERICAN PROTECTION INDUSTRIES, INC.
12233 W. Olympic Blvd., Ste. 380
Los Angeles, CA 90064
Tel.: 310-442-5700 DE
Fax: 310-207-1557
Year Founded: 1957
Approx.Sls.: $600,000,000
Emp.: 5,500
Fiscal Year-end: 12/31/90
Holding Company; Manufacturing & Direct Marketing of Collectibles, Home Decor & Jewelry; Florist Wire Services; Agribusiness; School Transportation
S.I.C.: 3911; 3469; 7389; 0191; 4151; 6719
Stewart Resnick *(Chm. Bd.)*
Loren R. Rothschild *(Pres.)*
Neil R. Bersch *(Sr. V.P. & Chief Fin. Officer)*
Richard S. Kolodny *(V.P. & Gen. Counsel)*
Peter R. Gurney *(V.P.-Fin.)*
R. Jane Westrich *(Treas.)*
Principal(s):
Stewart Resnick

Outside Service Firm(s):

Arthur Andersen & Co. *(Auditors)*
1500 Commerce Tower, 911 Main St.
Kansas City, MO 64105
Tel.: 816-221-4200
Fax: 816-221-7693

First National Bank of Boston *(Major Banking Relationship)*
P.O. Box 644,
Boston, MA 02102-0644
Tel.: 617-575-2900
Fax: 617-575-2549

Wells Fargo Bank *(Major Banking Relationship)*
333 S. Grand
Los Angeles, CA 90071
Tel.: 213-253-6836

Divisions:

Bundy Properties **(1)**
Teleflora Plaza, 12233 W. Olympic Blvd.
Los Angeles, CA 90064
Tel.: 213-442-5700
Opers. Office Bldgs. in CA & PA
S.I.C.: 6512
Bea Martin *(Bldg. Mgr.)*

The Franklin Mint **(1)**
U.S. Rte. 1
Franklin Center, PA 19091
Tel.: 215-459-6000
Fax: 215-459-6880
Emp.: 4,700
Manufacturing & Direct Marketing of Heirloom Quality Collectibles, Sculptures, Dolls, Jewelry, Library, Die-Cast Model Cars, Home Decor Items & Historic Weapons Replicas
S.I.C.: 3999; 3911; 2752; 5961
Stewart Resnick *(Chm. Bd. & Chief Exec. Officer)*
Lynda R. Resnick *(Vice Chm.)*
Thomas E. Durovsik *(Pres.)*
Pat Gonnelli *(V.P. & Treas.)*
Martin A. Breisblatt *(V.P.-Sls.)*
Jack Wilkie *(V.P.-Corp. Communications)*
Jerry Russ *(V.P.-Prod. Design & Adv.)*

Paramount Citrus Association **(1)**
P.O. Box 8599
Mission Hills, CA 91346
Tel.: 818-361-1171
Orange Growing, Juice Processing, Packing
S.I.C.: 0174; 3556; 2033; 0723
Ali Carbalai *(Plant Mgr.)*

Paramount Farming Company **(1)**
P.O. Box 1107
Bakersfield, CA 93308
Tel.: 805-399-4456
Production of Pistachios, Almonds, Grapes & Olives
S.I.C.: 0175; 0174
Joe MacIlvaine *(Pres.)*

Teleflora **(1)**
12233 W. Olympic Blvd.
Los Angeles, CA 90064
Tel.: 310-826-5253
Approx.Sls.: $100,000,000
Emp.: 350
Flowers by Wire Service, Floral Prods.
S.I.C.: 7389; 5992
Lynda Resnick *(Chm. Bd.)*
Greg Coccari *(Pres.)*
Nan Joesten *(Dir.-Mktg.)*

Jay Dee Tomfor Transportation Co. **(1)**
43 Debevoise Ave., P.O. Box E
Roosevelt, NY 11575
Tel.: 516-623-6200
Transportation of Handicapped Children
S.I.C.: 4111
Charles Tomeo *(Pres.)*

AMERICAN REPUBLIC INSURANCE CO.
601 Sixth Ave.
Des Moines, IA 50309
Mailing Address:
P.O. Box 1
Des Moines, IA 50334
Tel.: 515-245-2000
Fax: 515-245-2252
Approx.Sls.: $92,000,000
Emp.: 475
Fiscal Year-end: 12/31/90
Accident, Health & Life Insurance
S.I.C.: 6311; 6321
Watson Powell, Jr. *(Chm. Bd.)*
Watson Powell III *(Chief Exec. Officer)*
Michael Abbott *(Pres.)*
Burdette N. Heikens *(Exec. V.P. & Chief Oper. Officer)*
Ronald P. Morden *(Sr. V.P. & Treas.)*
Mary K. Durand *(Sec.)*

AMERICAN RESTAURANT GROUP, INC.
450 Newport Center Dr., Ste. 600
Newport Beach, CA 92660
Tel.: 714-721-8000
Fax: 714-721-8941
Emp.: 60
Oper. of Restaurants throughout U.S.; Spoons, Velvet Turtles, Spectrum, Black Angus
S.I.C.: 5812
Anwar Soliman *(Pres. & Chief Exec. Officer)*
William McCaffrey *(Chief Fin. Officer)*

Subsidiary:

Stuart Anderson's Black Angus/ Cattle Company Restaurants **(1)**
4410 El Camino Real, Ste. 201
Los Altos, CA 94022
Tel.: 415-949-6400
Fax: 415-949-3587
Emp.: 8,000
Steak House Restaurants
S.I.C.: 5812
Ralph Robert *(Pres.)*
Julia Stewart *(V.P.-Mktg.)*
Meredith Taylor *(V.P.-Fin. & Admin.)*
Rosemary McGinnis *(Mktg. Asst.)*

AMERICAN RUG CRAFTSMEN INC.
3090 Sugar Valley Rd. N.W.
Sugar Valley, GA 30746
Mailing Address:
P.O. Box 130,
Sugar Valley, GA 30746
Tel.: 706-629-7916
Tel.: 800-843-4473
Fax: 706-625-3544
Year Founded: 1984
Approx.Sls.: $37,000,000
Emp.: 300
Mfr. of Rugs & Mats
S.I.C.: 2273
John C. Thornton *(Pres.)*
James Collins *(Controller)*

AMERICAN SAVINGS BANK
99 Church St.
White Plains, NY 10601
Tel.: 914-287-2600
Tel.: 800-367-2721
Year Founded: 1848
Emp.: 800
Fiscal Year-end: 12/31/91
State-Chartered Savings Institutions
S.I.C.: 6022
Corporate Giving Program: Grant Support from $250 to $1,500, One Grant Yearly Per Group, to Tax-Exempt, Non-Profit Organizations Located Primarily in New York City Area; Also New York Chapters of National Organizations
Employee Matching Gifts Program: American Savings Bank Matches Amounts up to $300 to Eligible Tax-Exempt Organizations
W.R. Dietz *(Chm. Bd., Pres. & Chief Exec. Officer)*
C.J. Buchta *(Sr. Exec. V.P.)*
Joseph LaMagna *(Exec. V.P. & Chief Fin. Officer)*
Jeffrey S. Tallackson *(Exec. V.P., Sec. & Gen. Counsel)*
Phillip Blumenfeld *(Exec. V.P.)*
Ellen Rose *(Sr. V.P. & Auditor)*
John J. DeMita *(Sr. V.P.-Mngmt. Information Systems)*
Edward W. Philipps *(Sr. V.P.)*
Diane F. Sherry *(V.P. & Reg. Mgr.)*
Claudia Dumitrescu *(V.P.)*
Gary Zimbalatti *(Controller)*
Christina Darville *(Asst. Controller)*
Robert Stemper *(Dir.-Mktg.)*

Outside Service Firm(s):

Ernst & Young *(Auditors)*
277 Park Avenue
New York, NY 10172
Tel.: 212-773-3000
Telex: 177704
Fax: 212-773-1996/7

Riverhead Savings Bank **(1)**
7 W. Main Street
Riverhead, NY 11901
Tel.: 516-369-8500
Fax: 516-369-8527
S.I.C.: 6022

AMERICAN SAW & MANUFACTURING CO.
301 Chestnut St.
East Longmeadow, MA 01028
Tel.: 413-525-3961
Fax: 413-525-8224
Approx.Sls.: $45,000,000
Emp.: 500
Manufacturer & Marketer of Saw Blades for Consumer & Industrial Use
S.I.C.: 3425
John H. Davis *(Pres. & Treas.)*
Donald B. Rooke *(Exec. V.P.-Mktg. & Sls.)*
Suresh Samant *(V.P.-Mfg.)*

AMERICAN SEATING COMPANY
901 Broadway NW
Grand Rapids, MI 49504
Tel.: 616-732-6600
Tel.: 1-800-748-0268 DE
Fax: 616-732-6401
Year Founded: 1886
Approx.Sls.: $125,000,000
Emp.: 1,000
Fiscal Year-end: 10/ 3/92
Export
Furniture For Offices, Education, Amusement, Transportation, Contract Furniture For Laboratories & Industrial Markets
S.I.C.: 2531
Edward Clark *(Chm. Bd.)*
David J. Kuyers *(Exec. V.P.-Fin., Admin., Sec. & Treas.)*
Larry Miller *(Pres.-Interior Systems Group)*
Dave McLaughlin *(Pres.-Transportation Product Grp.)*
Al Meyer *(Pres.-Architectural Product Grp.)*
James R. Wittig *(V.P.-Human Resources)*
Principal(s):
Edward Clark

No. of Mfg. Plants/Facilities: 4
No. of U.S. Offices: 13
No. of Foreign Offices: 1

Outside Service Firm(s):

Ernst & Young *(Auditors)*
171 Monroe Ave. NW
Grand Rapids, MI 49503
Tel.: 616-774-0710
Fax: 616-774-0190

Frank B. Hall *(Commercial Insurance Carrier)*
Grand Rapids, MI

Travelers Insurance Co. *(Group Insurer)*
Grand Rapids, MI

Tolley, Fisher & VerWys *(Legal Firm)*
Grand Rapids, MI

Old Kent Bank *(Major Banking Relationship)*
Grand Rapids, MI

LVM Capital Management *(Pension Manager)*
Kalamazoo, MI

Scutter, Stevens & Clark *(Pension Manager)*
New York, NY

Non-U.S. Affiliate:

Otaco Seating Co., Ltd. **(1)**
Harvie Settlement Rd. P.O. Box 2310,
Orillia, ON L3V 6S2, Canada
Tel.: 705-325-7052
Emp.: 43
Manufacturer of Seats for Buses

AMERICAN SELFCARE CORPORATION
233 12th St., Ste. 910
Columbus, GA 31901
Mailing Address:
233 12th St., Ste. 910
Columbus, GA 31901
Tel.: 706-324-1170
Tel.: 800-241-2025
Fax: 706-323-8174
Approx.Sls.: $38,000,000
Emp.: 120
Fiscal Year-end: 12/31/90
Administrator of Health Care Plans
S.I.C.: 6324
Leonard J. Jagoda *(Chm., Pres. & Chief Exec. Officer)*
J. Allen Holladay *(Exec. V.P. & Chief Oper. Officer)*
Ronald D. Grant *(V.P.-Data Processing Services)*

Howard Huneke *(V.P.-Sls.)*
Kathy Warner *(V.P.-Chief Fin. Officer)*
N. Ann Safford *(Asst. V.P.-Midwest Opers.)*
Kathy C. Wakner *(Asst. V.P.-Controller)*
Peter Bowden *(Dir.-Mktg. & Adv. Mgr.)*
Stephen Stell *(Dir.-Data Processing)*
Victoria Wilson *(Dir.-Pub. Rels. & Personnel)*
Jo Ann King *(Gen. Mgr.)*

Outside Service Firm(s):

Ernst & Young*(Auditors)*
600 Peachtree St. N.E.
Atlanta, GA 30308
Tel.: 404-874-8300

Smith, Gambrell & Russell*(Legal Firm)*
2400 First Atlanta Tower
Atlanta, GA 30383
Tel.: 404-656-1800
Fax: 404-264-2652

Subsidiaries:

American Health & Security Insurance Co., Inc. **(1)**
233 12th St.
Columbus, GA 31901
Tel.: 706-324-5840
Fax: 706-328-8174
Life Insurance Company
S.I.C.: 6311
Allen Holladay *(Chief Oper. Officer)*
Kathy Warner *(Chief Fin. Officer)*
Syble Farmer *(Mgr. Opers.)*
Howard Huneke *(Sls. Dir.)*

American Selfcare Corporation **(1)**
800 Roosevelt Rd., Bldg. E., Ste. 200
Glen Ellyn, IL 60137
Tel.: 708-469-6466
Fax: 708-469-0348
Administrator of Health Care Plans
S.I.C.: 6324
N. Ann Safford *(Asst. V.P.-Midwest Opers.)*
Howard H. Huneke *(Acct. Exec.)*

ANS Insurance Agency **(1)**
233 12th St.
Columbus, GA 31901
Tel.: 706-324-1170
Fax: 706-323-8174
Insurance Agency
S.I.C.: 6411

AMERICAN SIGN & MARKETING SERVICES, INC.
7430 Industrial Rd.
Florence, KY 41042
Mailing Address:
P.O. Box 247
Florence, KY 41042
Tel.: 606-371-2880
Approx.Sls.: $18,000,000
Emp.: 200
Fiscal Year-end: 12/31/91
Designers & Producers of Outdoor & Indoor Illuminated Signs & Clocks; Permanent Displays; Illuminated Indoor & Outdoor Menuboards
S.I.C.: 3993; 3873
Rick Jordan *(Pres.)*
Jim McCormick *(Dir.-Fin.)*
Dennis Wheeler *(Dir.-Customer Service)*
Minda Matthews *(Dir.-Mktg.)*
David Flynn *(Dir.-Opers.)*

AMERICAN SNACKS, INC.
400 Eastern Ave.
Chelsea, MA 02150
Tel.: 617-884-6660 **DE**
Year Founded: 1961
Approx.Sls.: $19,000,000
Emp.: 1,200
Fiscal Year-end: 1/27/91
Donut Shops: Amy Joy, The Fatted Calf; Company Operated Coffee Shops in Discount Dept. Stores
S.I.C.: 5812
David Casty *(Chm. Bd.)*
Philip L. Segal *(Pres.)*
Norman Dunn *(V.P.)*
Ronald Casty *(Treas.)*
Robert C. Osiecki *(Controller)*
Robert Walker *(Sec.)*
Stuart Goldstein *(Dir.-Opers.)*

No. of U.S. Offices: 1

Computer Systems/Hardware:
IBM 3400

Outside Service Firm(s):

Blue Cross of Massachusetts, Inc.*(Group Insurer)*
Boston, MA

Lane & Altman*(Legal Firm)*
201 Devonshire
Boston, MA 02110
Tel.: 617-345-9800

First National Bank of Boston*(Major Banking Relationship)*
P.O. Box 644,
Boston, MA 02102-0644
Tel.: 617-575-2900
Fax: 617-575-2549

Divisions:

Fast Food Div. **(1)**
400 Eastern Ave.
Chelsea, MA 02150
Tel.: 617-884-2400
Approx.Sls.: $2,400,000
Emp.: 120
Food Service
S.I.C.: 5812
P. Segal *(Chief Oper. Officer)*

Snack Bar Div. **(1)**
400 Eastern Ave.
Chelsea, MA 02150
Tel.: 617-884-2400
Approx.Sls.: $14,600,000
Emp.: 1,100
Food Service
S.I.C.: 5812
P. Segal *(Chief Oper. Officer)*

AMERICAN SPECIALTIES INC.
441 Saw Mill River Rd.
Yonkers, NY 10701
Tel.: 914-476-9000
Fax: 914-476-0688
Year Founded: 1961
Sales Range: $10-19 Million
Emp.: 200
Fiscal Year-end: 12/31/91
Mfr. of Washroom Soap Dispensing Equip. & Washroom Accessories; Telephone Enclosures, Hospital Accessories
S.I.C.: 3469; 3999; 3431; 2542
Peter M. Rolla *(Exec. V.P.)*
Charles V. LaBarbera *(V.P.-Opers.)*
Gilbert Pesavento *(V.P.-Sls. & Mktg.)*
Gary Drossman *(Controller)*
Heather Rafael *(Janitorial Sls. Mgr.)*
Principal(s):

No. of Mfg. Plants/Facilities: 1
No. of U.S. Offices: 1

Outside Service Firm(s):

Ronayne, Hackeling & Rolla*(Legal Firm)*
New York, NY

AMERICAN SPEEDY PRINTING CENTERS, INC.
2555 S. Telegraph Rd.
Bloomfield Hills, MI 48302
Tel.: 313-335-6200
Tel.: 1-800-726-9050
Fax: 313-335-0267
Year Founded: 1976
Assets: $27,122,344
Earnings: $3,046,703
Liabilities: $21,084,793
Net Worth: $6,037,551
Approx.Sls.: $141,000,000
Emp.: 50
Fiscal Year-end: 12/31/90
Quick Printing Franchisor
S.I.C.: 2759
Vern Buchanan *(Chm. Bd.)*
William D. McIntyre *(Chief Oper. Officer)*
Gerald Bergler *(Exec. V.P.)*
Gary Shovlin *(Sr. V.P. & Chief Fin. Officer)*
Glynn Culver *(Sr. V.P.-Devel.)*
John Tosch *(V.P. & Corp. Counsel)*
Mark Crowley *(Controller)*
Kristin Brender *(Dir.-Pub. Rels.)*
Marcy Goldstein *(Dir.-Mktg.)*
Yvonne Buchanan *(Special Events Planner)*

Computer Systems/Hardware:
IBM System 36; Personal Computers

AMERICAN STABILIS, INC.
60 Lexington St.
Lewiston, ME 04240
Tel.: 207-784-9389
Fax: 207-782-4797
Sales Range: $10-19 Million
Emp.: 200
Mfr. of Electric Base Board Heaters, Electronic Controls & Components
S.I.C.: 3634; 3822; 3823
Roger P. Michaud *(Pres.)*
David Rowe *(Controller)*

Outside Service Firm(s):

Berry, Dunn & McNeill*(Auditors)*
Portland, ME

Skelton, Taintor & Abbott*(Legal Firm)*
Lewiston, ME

AMERICAN STANDARD INC.
1114 Ave. of the Americas
New York, NY 10036
Tel.: 212-703-5100 **DE**
Fax: 212-703-5284
Assets: $2,208,436,000
Earnings: $22,051,000
Liabilities: $1,367,478,000
Net Worth: $840,958,000
Approx.Sls.: $3,595,267,000
Emp.: 32,900
Fiscal Year-end: 12/31/91
Import Export
Air Conditioning Products, Building Products, Transportation & Fluid Power Products
S.I.C.: 3261; 3585; 3432; 3714; 3492; 3564; 3431; 3593; 3699; 3724; 3743; 3822
Emmanuel A. Kampouris *(Chm. Bd, Pres. & Chief Exec. Officer)*
Horst Hinrichs *(Sr. V.P.-Transportation Prods.)*
John J. Griffin *(Grp. V.P.-Intl. & Export)*
Fred A. Allardyce *(V.P. & Chief Fin. Officer)*
Thomas S. Battaglia *(V.P. & Treas.)*
Frederick W. Jaqua *(V.P., Gen. Counsel & Sec.)*
Daniel Kenney *(V.P. & Tax Counsel)*
William A. Klug *(V.P. & Grp. Exec.-Unitary Prods. Grp.)*
James E. Schultz *(V.P.-Indus. Rels.)*
Gary J. Biddle *(Staff V.P.)*
Joseph P. Seidel *(Staff V.P.)*
Herbert F. Hadley *(Dir.-Benefits Plan)*
Gene Tannen *(Dir.-Real Estate Services)*

Outside Service Firm(s):

Ernst & Young*(Auditors)*
787 Seventh Ave.
New York, NY 10019
Tel.: 212-773-1243

Aetna Life & Casualty*(Commercial Insurance Carrier)*
151 Farmington Avenue
Hartford, CT 06156
Tel.: 203-273-2128
Fax: 203-729-4295

Sullivan & Cromwell*(Legal Firm)*
125 Broad St.
New York, NY 10004
Tel.: 212-558-4000

The Northern Trust Co.*(Major Banking Relationship)*
50 S. LaSalle St.
Chicago, IL 60675
Tel.: 312-630-6000
Fax: 312-630-6516

Delaware Investment Advisors*(Pension Manager)*
One Commerce Square
Philadelphia, PA 19103

First Chicago Shareholder Services Trust Co.*(Pension Manager)*
153 West 51st St.
New York, NY 10019
Tel.: 212-791-6422
Fax: 212-385-9798

Groups:

American Standard Air Conditioning Products **(1)**
1114 Ave. of the Americas
New York, NY 10036
Tel.: 212-703-5100
Approx.Sls.: $1,910,000,000
Emp.: 14,700
Devel., Mfg. & Sls. of Air Conditioning, Heating & Refrigeration Equipment
S.I.C.: 3433; 3564; 3585
Emmanuel Kampouris *(Pres.)*

Group:

Unitary Products Group-Residential **(2)**
6200 Troup Hwy.
Tyler, TX 75711
Tel.: 903-581-3200
Residential & Small Comml. Air Conditioning
S.I.C.: 3585
H. Thompson Smith *(Pres.)*

Groups:

Trane Commercial Systems Group **(3)**
3600 Pammel Creek Rd.
La Crosse, WI 54601
Tel.: 608-787-2000
Large Comml. Air Conditioning
S.I.C.: 3585
James Schultz *(V.P.)*

Trans Unitary Products Group-Commercial **(3)**
2701 Guthrie Highway
Clarksville, TN 37040
Tel.: 615-645-6471
Fax: 615-648-5939
Mfr. of Heating, Ventilating, Air Conditioning & Building Management Equipment & Systems
S.I.C.: 3585

American-Standard, Fluid Power Group **(1)**
5800 Corporate Dr.
Pittsburgh, PA 15237
Tel.: 412-366-2400
S.I.C.: 3492
Arthur H. Tichnor *(Grp. V.P.)*

American Standard Inc., Railway Brake Prods. **(1)**
100 Airbrake Ave.
Wilmerding, PA 15148
Tel.: 412-825-1070
S.I.C.: 3743
William E. Kassling *(Grp. V.P.)*

American Standard Plumbing Products **(1)**
One Centennial Ave.
Piscataway, NJ 08855
Tel.: 908-980-3000
Tel.: 800-442-1902
Plumbing Fixtures & Fittings, Steel Frames & Doors
S.I.C.: 3261; 3431; 3432
Emmanuel A. Kampouris *(Sr. V.P.)*

American Standard Signaling Products Group **(1)**
5800 Corporate Dr.
Pittsburgh, PA 15237
Tel.: 412-366-2400
S.I.C.: 3743

American Standard Inc.—(Continued)

American Standard Transportation Products **(1)**
1114 Ave. of the Americas
New York, NY 10036
Tel.: 212-703-5100
Approx.Sls.: $686,000,000
Emp.: 5,500
Mfr. of Pneumatic, Hydraulic & Electronic Braking Systems & Components for Heavy Vehicles
S.I.C.: 3714

International & Export Group **(1)**
One Centennial Ave.
Piscataway, NJ 08855
Tel.: 908-885-1900
Mfr. Plumbing Fixtures & Fittings
S.I.C.: 3432
John Griffin *(Grp. V.P.)*

Steelcraft **(1)**
9017 Blue Ash Rd.
Cincinnati, OH 45242
Tel.: 513-745-6400
Steel Frames & Doors, Movable Walls & Partitions, Pre-fabricated Fireplaces
S.I.C.: 3442
William P. Moore *(Grp. V.P.)*

The Trane Company **(1)**
3600 Pammel Creek Rd.
La Crosse, WI 54601
Tel.: 608-787-2000 (100%)
Fax: 608-787-2552
Approx.Sls.: $1,700,000,000
Emp.: 14,000
Fiscal Year-end: 12/31/90
Export
Devel., Mfg. & Sale of Air Conditioning Heating & Refrigeration
S.I.C.: 3585; 3433; 3564
H.T. Smith *(Pres.)*
James Schultz *(Exec. V.P.)*
Jerry Arndt *(V.P. & G.M.-Compressor BU)*
Pat Spencer *(V.P. & G.M.-Centrifugal/Absorption Systems BU)*
Dave Eber *(V.P.-Engrng.)*
Bruce Lenio *(V.P.-Human Resources)*
Tom Mikulina *(V.P.-Mktg. & Sls.)*
Ronald Simon *(V.P.-Controller)*
Arthur Scheskie *(Mgr.-Communications)*
Cristi Johnson *(Assoc. Editor-Publicity & Publications)*

The Trane Company **(1)**
P.O. Box 1008
Tyler, TX 75711
Tel.: 903-581-3200
S.I.C.: 3585
H. Thompson Smith *(Grp. V.P.)*

The Trane Company **(1)**
P.O. Box 1008
Clarksville, TN 37040
Tel.: 615-648-6471
David R. Farris *(Grp. V.P.)*

Tyler Refrigeration Corp. **(1)**
1329 Lake St.
Niles, MI 49120
Tel.: 616-683-2000
Fax: 616-684-9802
Approx.Sls.: $120,000,000
Emp.: 1,000
Mfr. of Commercial Refrigerated Cases Used in Supermarkets
S.I.C.: 3585; 5078
James E. Mack *(Pres.)*
Charles Bloome *(V.P.-Fin.)*
Albert Bragenberg *(V.P.-Human Resources)*
Richard Dittoe *(V.P.-Mktg.)*
Joseph Humphrey *(V.P.-Engrng.)*
Greg Osterman *(V.P.-Intl. Opers.)*

United States Plumbing Prods. Group **(1)**
P.O. Box 2003
New Brunswick, NJ 08903
Tel.: 908-980-5000
Mfr. Plumbing Fixtures & Fittings
S.I.C.: 3431
John W. Clarke *(Grp. V.P.)*

Non-U.S. Holdings:

American Standard Sanitaryware (Thailand) Ltd. **(1)**
392 Piyatanee Bldg., Sukhumvit Rd., SCI 1
Bangkok, 11, Thailand
Tel.: 391-7314 (49.9%)
Vitreous China Fixtures
S.I.C.: 3261

Automotive Products Group **(1)**
Tour Albertler 65, Av. de Colmer F-92507
Rueil-Malmaison, France
Tel.: 749-0927
Holding Co.
S.I.C.: 6719

European Plumbing Prods. Group **(1)**
Blvd. du Souverain 348 B-1160
Brussels, Belgium
Tel.: 02-673-60-70
Holding Co.
S.I.C.: 6719

Fresinbra Indus. S.A. **(1)**
Caixa Postal 24.065 01000
Sao Paulo, Brazil
Tel.: (011) 260-3122 (60%)
Sls. Office Truck Braking Systems
S.I.C.: 3714

Ideal-Standard **(1)**
Dohlenweg 28 8050
Zurich, Switzerland
Tel.: 1-3025520
Sales of Plumbing Supplies
S.I.C.: 5074

Ideal-Standard **(1)**
Pasettistrasse 32-35 1200
Vienna, Austria
Tel.: 222 355117/8
Mfr. Plumbing Supplies
S.I.C.: 3431

Ideal-Standard **(1)**
Lange Herenstraat 45-47
Haarlem, Netherlands
Tel.: 23 319149
Sales of Plumbing Supplies
S.I.C.: 5074

Ideal-Standard **(1)**
Chaussee Paul Houtart, 88
Houdeng-Goegnies, B-7070, Belgium
Tel.: 064-22-21-85
Sales of Plumbing Supplies
S.I.C.: 5074

Ideal-Standard Brazil **(1)**
Al. Jauaperi 299 04523
Sao Paulo, 91454, Brazil
Tel.: 544-0010
Mfr. Plumbing Products
S.I.C.: 3261

Ideal-Standard GmbH **(1)**
Euskirchener Str. 80 P.O. Box 549, 5300
Bonn, Germany
Tel.: 228-5211
Mfr. Plumbing Equip. & Fixtures
S.I.C.: 3261; 3432

Ideal-Standard Ltd. **(1)**
P.O. Box 60, National Ave.
Kingston-upon-Hull, HU5-4JE, United Kingdom
Tel.: 482-46461
Mfr. Sanitary Equip. & Fixtures
S.I.C.: 3261

Ideal-Standard, S.A. de C.V. **(1)**
Apartado Postal 291
Mexico, D.F. 1, Mexico
Tel.: 905-557-6066
Mfr. Plumbing Fixtures
S.I.C.: 3261; 3432

Ideal-Standard S.A.I. **(1)**
23 Alexandroupoleos St.
Athens, 610, Greece
Tel.: 770.35.16/9
Mfr. Plumbing Equip.
S.I.C.: 3261; 3432; 3089

Ideal-Standard S.p.A. **(1)**
Via A.M. Ampere 102 20131
Milan, Italy
Tel.: 2-2888
Mfr. Plumbing Fixtures
S.I.C.: 3261

Ideal-Standard Wabco Ind. E Com. Ltda **(1)**
Rua Honorato Spiandorim 189
Jundiai, Sao Paulo Brazil
Tel.: 544-0010
Mfr. Plumbing Equip.
S.I.C.: 3494

Industria Centroamericana de Sanitarios, S.A. **(1)**
P.O. Box 2533
Guatemala City, 1, Guatemala
Tel.: 61841 (50%)
Mfr. Plumbing Supplies
S.I.C.: 3261

Industria Ceramica Centroamericana, S.A. **(1)**
Apartado Postal 2551
Managua, Nicaragua
Tel.: 4756 (80%)
Mfr. Plumbing Supplies
S.I.C.: 3261

Industria Ceramica Costarricense, S.A. **(1)**
Apartado Postal 4120
San Jose, Costa Rica
Tel.: 506-32.52.66 (50%)
Mfr. Plumbing Supplies
S.I.C.: 3261

Mosler Canada **(1)**
280 Britannia Rd. E.
Mississauga, ON L4Z 1S6, Canada
Tel.: 416-890-2451
Sls. Office-Security Systems
S.I.C.: 5063

Queroy S.A. **(1)**
Breuil le Sec (Oise),Domaine de Bailly 60480
Clermont, France
Mfr. of Plumbing Prods., Sanitary Wares
S.I.C.: 3679; 3261; 3432

Sanitarios Dominicanos, S.A. **(1)**
P.O. Box 910
Santiago de los Caballeros, Dominican Republic
Tel.: 809-583-1823 (34%)
Mfr. Plumbing Fixtures & Vitreous Sanitary Wares
S.I.C.: 3261

Sanitary Wares Mfg. Corp. **(1)**
P.O. Box 499MCC, Makati,
Metro Manila, Philippines
Tel.: 887101 (40%)
Mfr. of Vitreous Plumbing Prods., Sanitary Wares
S.I.C.: 3261

Trane Co. of Canada **(1)**
401 Horner Ave.
Toronto, ON M8W 2A5, Canada
Tel.: 416-259-8221 (100%)
Emp.: 380
Mfg. & Selling of Refrigeration & Air Handling Equip.
S.I.C.: 3585
E. Schellenberg *(Pres.)*

Trane do Brazil **(1)**
Caixa Postal 362 Diaema
Sao Paulo, 09900, Brazil
Tel.: 011-445-2255 (100%)
Mfr. of Refrigeration & Air Handling Equip.
S.I.C.: 3585

Trane Europe **(1)**
B. P. 127 88004
Epinal, Cedex France
Tel.: (29) 82.98.21 (100%)
Emp.: 1,262
Mfg. & Selling Unitary Air Conditioners
S.I.C.: 3585; 5064
D. Hilger *(Pres.)*

Trane Ltd. **(1)**
Gastons Wood Reading Rd.
Basingstoke, Hants United Kingdom
Tel.: (0256) 79-4731 (100%)
S.I.C.: 5064; 3585

WABCO Freinage de Vehicules S.A. **(1)**
124 Avenue Aristide Briand F-77410
Claye-Souilly, France
Tel.: 026-88-06
Mfr. Truck Braking Equip.
S.I.C.: 3714

WABCO Standard Inc. **(1)**
80 Ward St.
Toronto, ON Canada
Tel.: 416-534-3521
Administrative Offices
S.I.C.: 8742

WABCO Westinghouse **(1)**
Ave. Van Volxem 164-166
Brussels, B-1190, Belgium
Tel.: 344.49.38
Div. of Wabco Standard S.A.
S.I.C.: 3714

WABCO Westinghouse AB **(1)**
Industriegatan S-540 70
Hova, Sweden
Tel.: 50-306-10
Mfr. Truck Braking Equip.
S.I.C.: 3714

WABCO Westinghouse B.V. **(1)**
Mient 12-16, Postbus 26 Postbus 26, NL-2900
Capelle aan den Ijssel, Netherlands
Tel.: 50.49.66
Mfr. Truck Braking Equip.
S.I.C.: 3714

WABCO Westinghouse Compagnia Freni S.p.A. **(1)**
Via Pier Carlo Boggio n. 20 I-10138
Turin, Italy
Tel.: 39 55-831
Mfr. Truck Braking Equip.
S.I.C.: 3743

WABCO Westinghouse Fahrzeugbremsen G.m.b.H. **(1)**
Postfach 91 12 80 D-3000
Hanover, 91, Germany
Tel.: 511-44-471 (99.9%)
Mfr. Truck Braking Equip.
S.I.C.: 3714

WABCO Westinghouse Freni Veicoli Industriali S.p.A. **(1)**
Via Volvera 51 I-10045
Piossasco, Torino Italy
Tel.: 906-54-44
Mfr. Truck Braking Equip.
S.I.C.: 3714

WABCO Westinghouse Equipements Ferroviaires S.A. **(1)**
2 Blvd. Westinghouse
Sevran, Seine-St. Denis France
Mfr. Truck Braking Equip.
S.I.C.: 3714

WABCO Westinghouse G.m.b.H. **(1)**
Hochstadtplatz 4, Postfach 49
Vienna, A-1205, Austria
Tel.: 33.15.11
Mfr. Truck Braking Equip.
S.I.C.: 3714

THE AMERICAN STOCK EXCHANGE
86 Trinity Place
New York, NY 10006
Tel.: 212-306-1000
Fax: 212-306-1644
Approx.Sls.: $114,000,000
Emp.: 769
Fiscal Year-end: 12/31/90
International Securities Exchange
S.I.C.: 6231
James Jones *(Chm. Bd. & Chief Exec. Officer)*
Joel Lovett *(Vice Chm.)*
Ivers W. Riley *(Sr. Exec. V.P.-Derivative Properties)*
Gordon L. Nash *(Sr. Exec. V.P.-Legal & Regulatory Affairs)*
Sarah P. Boehmler *(Exec. V.P.-Market Devel.)*
Christopher Finn *(Exec. V.P.-External Opers.)*
Philip T. Steele *(Exec. V.P.-Strategic Plng./Total Quality)*
William D. Strauss *(Exec. V.P.-Admin. & Fin.)*
Patrick F. Conroy *(Sr. V.P.-Fin.)*
James F. Duffy *(Sr. V.P. & Gen. Counsel)*
Carrie Dwyer *(Sr. V.P. & Gen. Counsel)*
Warren L. Kaiser *(Sr. V.P.-Information Technology)*
Delia McQuade Emmons *(Sr. V.P.-Corp. Services)*

Nathan Most *(Sr. V.P.-New Products Plng)*
Sarah C. Mullen Luke *(Sr. V.P.-Communications)*
Lee Murray *(Sr. V.P.-Personnel)*
Steven M. Bloom *(V.P.-New Prods. Devel.)*
Robert E. McKiernan *(V.P.-Human Resources)*
Ralph R. Rafaniello *(V.P.-Floor Opers.)*
George E. Stokes *(V.P.-Information Technology)*

Subsidiaries:

American Stock Exchange Clearing Corp. **(1)**
86 Trinity Place
New York, NY 10006
Tel.: 212-306-1000
S.I.C.: 6231
Barry Appel *(Pres.)*

American Stock Exchange Realty Associates Inc. **(1)**
86 Trinity Place
New York, NY 10006
Tel.: 212-306-1000
S.I.C.: 6231
Alan L. Streusand *(Chm. Bd.)*

Amex Commodities Corporation **(1)**
86 Trinity Place
New York, NY 10006
Tel.: 212-306-1000
S.I.C.: 6231
Nathan Most *(Pres.)*

Affiliates:

National Securities Clearing Corp. **(1)**
55 Water St.
New York, NY 10041
Tel.: 212-412-8400
S.I.C.: 6231
David Kelly *(Pres.)*

Options Clearing Corp. **(1)**
440 S. LaSalle St.
Chicago, IL 60605
Tel.: 312-322-6200
Clears & Regulates Options Trade
S.I.C.: 6289; 6231
Wayne Luthringshausen *(Chm. Bd.)*

AMERICAN STONE-MIX, INC.
8320 Bellona Ave.
Towson, MD 21204
Tel.: 410-296-6770
Fax: 410-494-0897
Approx.Sls.: $40,000,000
Emp.: 450
Fiscal Year-end: 2/28/91
Supplier of Package Cement & Blacktop Products
S.I.C.: 5032
Donald J. Peters *(Pres. & Chief Oper. Officer)*
David L. Mehtlan *(V.P.-Sls. & Mktg.)*
Mark E. Goldstrom *(Mgr.-Adv.)*

AMERICAN STRIP STEEL INC.
55 Passaic Ave.
Kearny, NJ 07032
Tel.: 201-991-1500 **NY**
Fax: 201-955-2222
Year Founded: 1951
Approx.Sls.: $70,000,000
Emp.: 300
Steel Service Center; Manufacturer of Metal Stud & Track
S.I.C.: 5051; 3429
Leroy Schecter *(Chm. Bd. & Chief Exec. Officer)*
James Daniell *(Pres.)*
Craig Eisenberg *(Chief Fin. Officer & Treas.)*
Stan Altscher *(Controller)*
Barry Rosenthal *(V.P.-Opers.)*
Cal Semel *(V.P.)*
Principal(s):
Leroy Schecter

No. of Mfg. Plants/Facilities: 2

Computer Systems/Hardware:
Data General

Outside Service Firm(s):

Goldstein, Golub, Kessler & Co.*(Auditors)*
New York, NY

Republic National Bank*(Major Banking Relationship)*
355 Lexington Ave.
New York, NY 10017
Tel.: 212-573-5514

AMERICAN SYSTEMS CORPORATION
14200 Park Meadow Dr.
Chantilly, VA 22021
Tel.: 703-968-6300
Tel.: 800-733-2721 **VA**
Fax: 703-968-5151
Year Founded: 1975
Assets: $18,500,000
Liabilities: $11,900,000
Net Worth: $6,600,000
Approx.Sls.: $45,000,000
Emp.: 1,000
Fiscal Year-end: 12/31/91
Export
Professional Technical Services; Systems & Facilities Engineering; Production of Electronic Hardware & Systems; Fabrication of Precision Sheet Metal Products; Development Of Computer Based Trainer Systems; Installation of LANs; System Integration & Cable Plant Design
S.I.C.: 3499; 3679; 1731; 8711; 3799
Forrest G. Ramsey, Jr. *(Chm. Bd.)*
H. Thomas Curran *(Pres.)*
William R. Roberts *(Sr. V.P.)*
Kenneth R. Boehs *(V.P.-Mktg.)*
Thomas G. Jennings *(V.P.-Applied Technology)*
Joseph Kopfman *(V.P.-Contracts)*
Donald A. Kirk *(V.P.-American Communications)*
Charles E. Sampson *(V.P.-Technical Services)*
Mark J. Schuler *(V.P.-Fin. & Sec.)*
William M. Valentine *(V.P.-Engrng. Services)*
Mark Danisewicz *(Treas.)*
Robert M. Cambridge *(Gen. Counsel)*
Theresa J. Walker *(Dir.-Personnel)*
Thomas S. Raup *(Mgr.-Pur.)*

No. of Mfg. Plants/Facilities: 3
No. of U.S. Offices: 18
No. of Foreign Offices: 1

Outside Service Firm(s):

Deloitte & Touche*(Auditors)*
Ste. 700, 8201 Greensboro Dr.
McLean, VA 22102
Tel.: 202-955-4000

Travelers Insurance Co.*(Commercial Insurance Carrier)*
Fairfax, VA

Prudential Insurance Co. of America*(Group Insurer)*
Fairfax, VA

NationsBank*(Investment Banker)*
4th Fl. Pavilion, 1111 E. Main St.
Richmond, VA
Tel.: 804-788-2551

Elliot, Bray & Riley*(Legal Firm)*
Washington, DC

NationsBank*(Major Banking Relationship)*
35 Broad St.
Atlanta, GA 30303
Tel.: 404-581-2121
Tel.: 800-848-8198

MONY*(Pension Manager)*
Fairfax, VA

AMERICAN TANK & FABRICATING CO.
12314 Elmwood Ave.
Cleveland, OH 44111
Tel.: 216-252-1500
Tel.: 800-544-5316
Fax: 216-252-4871
Year Founded: 1940
Approx.Sls.: $20,000,000
Emp.: 100
Steel Plate Fabrication & Warehousing
S.I.C.: 3443; 3449; 3499; 5051
Lawrence Ripich *(Chief Exec. Officer)*
Terry Ripich *(Pres.)*
John R. Ripich *(Exec. V.P.)*
Stanley Youtt *(V.P.-Mfg.)*

AMERICAN TAPE CORPORATION
(Formerly Devon Tape Corporation)
1511 Tonnelle Ave.
North Bergen, NJ 07047
Tel.: 201-866-2777
Fax: 201-866-0469
Approx.Sls.: $30,000,000
Emp.: 216
Pressure Sensitive Adhesive Tapes
S.I.C.: 2672
I.J. Choy *(Pres.)*

Outside Service Firm(s):

Coopers & Lybrand*(Auditors)*
Morristown, NJ

Chemical Bank*(Major Banking Relationship)*
Morristown, NJ

AMERICAN TARA CORPORATION
Bldg. 6, 750 Hammond Dr., Ste. 200
Atlanta, GA 30328
Tel.: 404-257-5544 **IL**
Fax: 404-257-5522
Year Founded: 1943
Approx.Sls.: $20,000,000
Emp.: 100
Paper Converter
S.I.C.: 2678; 2679
Robert J. Bridell *(Chm. Bd. & Chief Exec. Officer)*
Alex L. Sartini *(Exec. V.P.)*
Susan Brown *(Chief Fin. Officer & Treas.)*
Marcelene F. Fulton *(Sec.)*
Rhonda W. Barker *(Controller)*

No. of Mfg. Plants/Facilities: 3

Outside Service Firm(s):

Ernst & Young*(Auditors)*
600 Peachtree St. N.E.
Atlanta, GA 30308
Tel.: 404-874-8300

Powell, Goldstein, Frazer & Murphy*(Legal Firm)*
191 Peachtree St. NE, 16th Fl.
Atlanta, GA 30303
Tel.: 404-572-6700
Fax: 404-572-5958

Wachovia Bank of Georgia, N.A.*(Major Banking Relationship)*
P.O. Box 4148,
Atlanta, GA 30302

Subsidiaries:

B & J Supply, Inc. **(1)**
1117 West Washington Street
Appleton, WI 54913
Tel.: 414-739-9491
Fax: 414-739-6777
Emp.: 60
Paper Converter; School Supplies
S.I.C.: 2678
Alex L. Sartini *(Pres.)*

Papertronics, Incorporated **(1)**
3636D 7th Ave. N
Birmingham, AL 35222
Tel.: 205-591-1980
Fax: 205-595-4117
Paper Converter; Small Roll Products
S.I.C.: 2679
William A. Bridell *(Pres.)*

AMERICAN TECHNICAL PUBLISHERS, INC.
1155 W. 175th St.
Homewood, IL 60430
Tel.: 708-957-1100
Tel.: 800-323-3471 **IL**
Fax: 708-957-1137
Year Founded: 1898
Emp.: 30
Fiscal Year-end: 12/31/92
Export
Publisher of Vocational & Technical Textbooks
S.I.C.: 2731
Thomas E. Proctor *(Pres.)*
Robert Deisinger *(Sr. V.P.)*
David Holloway *(V.P.-Mktg.)*
J. David Holloway *(Sec.)*
Brigid Ryan *(Mgr.-Mfg. & Pur.)*

No. of U.S. Offices: 1

Computer Systems/Hardware:
IBM Compatible Systems; AST

Outside Service Firm(s):

Arthur Andersen & Co.*(Auditors)*
33 W. Monroe St.
Chicago, IL 60603-4067
Tel.: 312-580-0033
Fax: 312-507-6748

Schiff, Hardin & Waite*(Legal Firm)*
7200 Sears Tower, 233 S. Wacker Dr.
Chicago, IL 60606
Tel.: 312-876-1000

Boulevard Bank*(Major Banking Relationship)*
410 N. Michigan Ave.
Chicago, IL 60611
Tel.: 312-836-6500

AMERICAN TECHNICAL SERVICES GROUP, INC.
5680 Oakbrook Pkwy, Ste. 165
Norcross, GA 30093-1841
Mailing Address:
P.O. Box 1047,
Tucker, GA 30085
Tel.: 404-447-9444 **GA**
Fax: 404-447-0015
Year Founded: 1975
Approx.Sls.: $26,000,000
Emp.: 375
Fiscal Year-end: 3/31/90
Engineering, Construction & Technical Services of Instrument Process Control Systems
S.I.C.: 7629; 1731; 1799
J. Neil Smith *(Chm. Bd., Pres. & Chief Exec. Officer)*
Robert S. Russo *(V.P.)*
Ellen W. Smith *(Sec.)*
Principal(s):
J. Neil Smith
Robert S. Russo

No. of U.S. Offices: 7

Computer Systems/Hardware:
IBM System 36

Outside Service Firm(s):

Crum & Forster*(Commercial Insurance Carrier)*
Atlanta, GA

Northwestern National Life*(Group Insurer)*
20 Washington Ave. S.
Minneapolis, MN 55401

Roberts & Isaf*(Legal Firm)*
Atlanta, GA

American Technical Services Group, Inc.—(Continued)

First American Bank, N.A.*(Major Banking Relationship)*
Atlanta, GA

Robinson Humphrey Company, Inc.*(Pension Manager)*
Atlanta, GA

Subsidiaries:

American Technical Services **(1)**
5680 Oakbrook Pkwy., Ste. 165
Norcross, GA 30093-1841
Tel.: 404-447-9444
Fax: 404-447-0015
Emp.: 173
S.I.C.: 7629
J. Neil Smith *(Pres.)*

National Technical Services **(1)**
5680 Oakbrook Pkwy., Ste. 165
Norcross, GA 30093-1841
Tel.: 404-447-9444
Fax: 404-447-0015
S.I.C.: 7629
J. Neil Smith *(Pres.)*

AMERICAN TOOL COMPANIES, INC.
301 S. 13th St., Ste. 600
Lincoln, NE 68508
Tel.: 402-435-3300 **NE**
Telex: 910-622-0018
Fax: 402-435-3619
Year Founded: 1924
Assets: $69,805,588
Liabilities: $35,036,595
Net Worth: $34,768,993
Approx.Sls.: $57,000,000
Emp.: 648
Fiscal Year-end: 10/26/90
Import Export
Mfr. Hand Tools
S.I.C.: 3423
Allen D. Petersen *(Chm. Bd., Pres. & Chief Exec. Officer)*
Flemming Andresen *(Pres.-Intl.)*
Kenneth L. Cheloha *(Chief Oper. Officer)*
Robert W. Brady *(Exec. V.P.-Sls. & Mktg.)*
Thomas Hearn *(V.P.-Sls. U.S. Domestic)*
Gary Eckhardt *(V.P.-Human Resources)*
William L. Kiburz *(V.P. & Treas.)*
Charles A. Poremba *(V.P.-Mfg.)*
John J. Robert *(V.P.-Sls. Natl. Accts.)*
Clark T. Chandler *(V.P. & Controller)*
Douglas R. Custer *(Dir.-Procurement)*
Betty P. Talley *(Mgr.-Mktg. Services)*
Tom Chervenak *(Dir.-Engrng. Programs & Standards)*

No. of Mfg. Plants/Facilities: 3
No. of U.S. Offices: 2
No. of Foreign Offices: 6

Computer Systems/Hardware:
IBM & Compatibles

Outside Service Firm(s):

Deloitte & Touche*(Auditors)*
1040 NBC Center
Lincoln, NE 68508

Massachusetts Mutual Life Insurance Co.*(Group Insurer)*
1295 State St.
Springfield, MA 01111
Tel.: 413-788-8411
Fax: 413-730-6144

Woodmen Accident & Life Co.*(Group Insurer)*
Lincoln, NE

Prudential-Bache*(Investment Banker)*
Virginia Beach, VA

Rembolt Luedtke Parker et al*(Legal Firm)*
Lincoln, NE

DeWitt State Bank*(Major Banking Relationship)*
DeWitt, NE

First National Bank*(Major Banking Relationship)*
Lincoln, NE

Bankers Life & Casualty*(Pension Manager)*
Des Moines, IA

The Principal Financial Group*(Pension Manager)*
711 High St.
Des Moines, IA 50309
Tel.: 515-247-4593
Tel.: 800-543-4015

Subsidiaries:

ATC Air, Inc. **(1)**
301 S. 13th St., Ste. 600
Lincoln, NE 68508
Tel.: 402-435-3300 (100%)
Emp.: 2
Contract Passenger Air Carrier
S.I.C.: 4512

Bergman Tool Mfg. Co., Inc. **(1)**
1573 Niagara
Buffalo, NY 14213
Tel.: 716-885-5974
Fax: 716-885-5636
Emp.: 20
Blue Bird Tools
S.I.C.: 3423
Alan Peterson *(Pres.)*

Chesco Products, Inc. **(1)**
P.O. Box 686,
Beatrice, NE 68310
Tel.: 402-223-7430
Emp.: 65
Mfr. of Hand Tools
S.I.C.: 3546
Steve Tracey *(Controller)*

Cobra Tool, Inc. **(1)**
P.O. Box 356,
De Witt, NE 68341
Tel.: 402-683-2315
Emp.: 7
Sls. & Mktg. of Tools
S.I.C.: 5072
Connie Blackstock *(Mktg. Mgr.)*

Petersen Development Corp. **(1)**
P.O. Box 337,
De Witt, NE 68341
Tel.: 402-683-2315
Lessor-Real Estate
S.I.C.: 6531

Petersen Manufacturing Co., Inc. **(1)**
P.O. Box 337
De Witt, NE 68341
Tel.: 402-683-2315

Prosnip Corporation **(1)**
P.O. Box 337,
De Witt, NE 68341
Tel.: 402-683-2315
Emp.: 65
Mfr. of Hand Tools
S.I.C.: 3546

Unibit Corp. **(1)**
P.O. Box 337,
De Witt, NE 68341
Tel.: 402-683-2315
Emp.: 20
Mfr. of Hand Tools
S.I.C.: 3546

Non-U.S. Holding:

ATC AG **(1)**
Weinmanngasse 24 P.O. Box 1416, CH-8700
Kusnacht, Switzerland
Tel.: 01 910 1002 (100%)
Telex: 825763
Mktg. of Hand Tools, Step Drills, Snips, Tool Chests
S.I.C.: 5072
Robert K. Grootes *(Mng. Dir.)*

AMERICAN TRADING AND PRODUCTION CORPORATION
1 N. Charles St.
Baltimore, MD 21201
Mailing Address:
P.O. Box 238,
Baltimore, MD 21203
Tel.: 410-347-7000 **MD**
Fax: 410-659-0552
Year Founded: 1931
Sales Range: $500-999 Million
Emp.: 4,000
Fiscal Year-end: 12/31/90
Import Export
Oil & Gas Extraction; Fabricated Metal Products; Electric & Electronic Equipment; Real Estate; Office Products; Mfr. & Marketer; Security & Communications Equipment
S.I.C.: 1311; 2675; 2678; 2761; 2782; 3651; 3663; 3669; 6512; 6519
Employee Matching Gifts Program: Contact Company for Information
Louis B. Thalheimer *(Chief Exec. Officer & Chm. Bd.)*
Hans Fristedt *(Pres. & Chief Oper. Officer)*
I.M. Zimet *(Sr. V.P.)*
Phillip W. Taff *(Sr. V.P. & Chief Fin. Officer)*
Sanford Schmidt *(V.P. & Chief Admin. Officer)*
Stephen A. Morris *(V.P. & Controller)*
A.G. Choate *(Sec. & Gen. Counsel)*
Donald W. Rahmlow *(Dir.-Computer Information Systems)*

Computer Systems/Hardware:
IBM AS 400

Outside Service Firm(s):

Ernst & Young*(Auditors)*
1 N. Charles St.
Baltimore, MD 21201
Tel.: 410-539-7940
Fax: 410-783-3832

Connecticut General Life Insurance Co.*(Group Insurer)*
P.O. Box 2975,
Hartford, CT 06104
Tel.: 203-726-6000

Cable, McDaniel, Bowie & Bond*(Legal Firm)*
One N. Charles St.
Baltimore, MD 21201
Tel.: 410-752-3650

Union Trust*(Major Banking Relationship)*
P.O. Box 17034
Baltimore, MD 21203
Tel.: 410-332-5857

Union Trust*(Pension Manager)*
P.O. Box 17034
Baltimore, MD 21203
Tel.: 410-332-5857

Groups:

ATAPCO Office Products Group **(1)**
12312 Olive Blvd., Ste. 400
Saint Louis, MO 63141
Tel.: 314-542-5400
Fax: 314-469-8963
Approx.Sls.: $70,000,000
Emp.: 1,000
Fiscal Year-end: 12/31/89
Mfr. of Paper & Fiberboard Office Supplies, Indexing Prods., Filing Systems, Polyethylene Binders & Related Items, Desk Accessories, Expanding Prods. & Filing Cabinets
S.I.C.: 2782; 2675; 2678; 2542; 5112
I.M. Zimet *(Pres.)*
Jim Burrow *(V.P.-Mfg. & Opers.)*
Fred E. McCown *(V.P.-Sls. & Mktg.)*
John R. McCune *(V.P.-Opers.)*
Michael Maschmann *(Controller)*
Robert E. Snell *(Dir.-Mktg. Services)*
Reagan Holm *(Dir.-Sls. & Mktg.)*
Andrew Roth *(Dir.-Mktg.)*
Steve Tomasi *(Dir.-Prod. Mngmt.-Globe-Weis)*
Jim Miller *(Dir.-Prod. Mngmt.-Hazel/Cardinal)*
K. McKenna *(Mgr.-Natls. Sls.)*
Debbie Monzyk *(Mgr.-Mktg. Opers.)*
David Sentivany *(Mgr.-Engrng.)*
Juanita Kizor *(Sls. Mgr.-West)*
Jim Ciccone *(Sls. Mgr.-East)*
Gary Zucker *(Sls. Mgr.-Midwest)*
H.W. Craycraft *(Sls. Mgr.-South)*
Susan Czerwonka *(Prod. Mgr.-Cardinal Brand)*
Luke Harris *(Prod. Mgr.-Globe-Weis Brand)*
Mike McNamara *(Prod. Mgr.-Globe-Weis Brand)*
Leo Klimaszewski *(Prod. Mgr.-Hazel Brand)*

Divisions:

ATAPCO Globe-Weis/Bristol **(2)**
P.O. Box 11,
Bristol, PA 19007
Tel.: 215-785-1531
Mfrs. Office Products
S.I.C.: 2782; 2675; 2678
Frank Carpino *(Plant Mgr.)*

ATAPCO Globe-Weis/Fresno **(2)**
2851 E. Florence St.
Fresno, CA 93721
Tel.: 209-441-1413
Mfrs. Office Supplies
S.I.C.: 2782; 2675; 2678
Marvin Nofziger *(Gen. Mgr.)*

ATAPCO Globe-Weis/Kosciusko **(2)**
No. 1 Superior Dr.
Kosciusko, MS 39090
Tel.: 601-289-7215
Mfr. Office Products
S.I.C.: 2782; 2675; 2678
Ed Heidorn *(Mgr.-Mfg.)*
John McCoy *(District Mgr.)*

Crawford Industries **(2)**
1414 Crawford Dr.
Crawfordsville, IN 47933
Tel.: 317-362-6733
Mfr. Plastic Book Binders
S.I.C.: 2678
Samuel Hildebrand *(Exec. V.P.)*

Atlas/Soundolier **(1)**
1859 Intertech Dr.
Fenton, MO 63026
Tel.: 314-349-3110
Tel.: 800-876-7337
Telex: 910-760-1650
Fax: 314-349-1251
Loudspeakers, Microphone Stands & Accessories,Communications Equipment, Electro Acoustic Signaling Devices, Equipment Cabinets, Metal Enclosures
S.I.C.: 3651; 3669; 3679; 5065
Kenneth L. Cation *(Grp. Pres.)*
Charles Gushwa *(V.P.-Mktg. & Sls.)*
Keith Walters *(V.P.-Mfg.)*
Charles J. Fink *(V.P. & Controller)*
Colleen Sullivan *(Mgr.-Adv.)*
Bud Waters *(Mgr.-Natl. Sls.)*
Jim Edwards *(Mgr.-Mktg. Services)*

American Trading & Production Corporation, Oil & Gas Div. **(1)**
1221 Lamar, Ste. 1000
Houston, TX 77010
Tel.: 713-658-0445
Headquarters
S.I.C.: 8741
C.E. Payton *(V.P. & Gen. Mgr.)*
H.M. Johnson *(Controller)*
Beth Garrett *(Mgr.-Personnel)*
J.W. Wilson *(Mgr.-Land & Contracts)*

American Trading and Production Corporation, Oil & Gas Div. **(1)**
Attrium Center Bldg., Ste. 300, 110 West Louisiana Ave.
Midland, TX 79701
Tel.: 915-684-4463

American Trading and Production Corporation, Oil & Gas Div. **(1)**
2000 Liberty Tower,
Oklahoma City, OK 73102
Tel.: 405-232-6321
S.J. Carlson *(V.P.)*

Javelin Electronics **(1)**
19831 Magellan Dr.
Torrance, CA 90502-1188
Tel.: 310-327-7440
Graham Wallis *(Pres.)*
Raymond Payne *(V.P.)*
Terry Muldowney *(Controller)*

Subsidiaries:

American Trading Real Estate Properties, Inc. **(1)**
P.O. Box 238
Baltimore, MD 21203
Tel.: 410-347-7000
S.I.C.: 6552
Samuel R. Wells *(Pres.)*
Alan E. Kerry *(Sr. V.P.)*
Robert D. Alewine *(V.P.-Eastern Reg.)*
Ralph Murphy *(V.P.-Western Reg.)*

American Trading Real Estate Properties, Inc. **(1)**
Research Blvd. Ctr., Ste. 304, 1803 Research Blvd.
Rockville, MD 20850
Tel.: 301-762-1840
S.I.C.: 6531

American Trading Real Estate Properties, Inc. **(1)**
Trefoil Park, 35 Corporate Dr.
Trumbull, CT 06611
Tel.: 203-261-3700
S.I.C.: 6531
George Walker *(Site Mgr.)*

American Trading Real Estate Properties, Inc. **(1)**
Wilshire-Bixel Bldg., Ste.1504, 1055 Wilshire Blvd.
Los Angeles, CA 90017
Tel.: 213-481-2600
S.I.C.: 6531

American Trading Transportation Co., Inc. **(1)**
555 Fifth Ave.
New York, NY 10017
Tel.: 212-682-7722
Marine Transportation, Tankers
S.I.C.: 4412; 4424; 4449
S.V. Schmidt *(Pres.)*
V.C. Rasole *(Treas.)*
Victor Goldberg *(V.P.)*
Michael Murphy *(V.P.-Opers.)*

Northern Computers Inc. **(1)**
5007 S. Howell Ave.
Milwaukee, WI 53207
Tel.: 414-769-5980
Manufacture of Electronic Access Control
S.I.C.: 3577
Joel Konicek *(Pres.)*
Dave James *(V.P.)*

Non-U.S. Holdings:

American Trading & Production Corp., Canadian Oil & Gas Operations **(1)**
1405-500 4th Avenue, S.W.
Calgary, AB T2P 3N4, Canada
Tel.: 403-266-2036
S.I.C.: 1311
Stewart J. Carlson *(V.P.-Opers.)*
E.L. Varty *(Mgr.-Prod.)*
M. Croteau *(Mgr.-Land)*

Atapco Azteca, S.A. de C.V. **(1)**
Calle 21 Este No. 305 Cuernavaca, Morelos, Mexico
Tel.: 7319-0899

John Heath & Co. Limited **(1)**
230 Bradford St.
Birmingham, B12 0RJ, United Kingdom
Tel.: 021-766-6363 (100%)
Telex: 8954667
Fax: 021-766-6027
Wholesale of Office Supplies
S.I.C.: 5112

Millbank Electronics Group Ltd. **(1)**
Bellbrook Industrial Estate, Uckfield, East Sussex TN22 1QL, United Kingdom
Tel.: 0825-761620
Telex: 95505 MILBNK G
Wholesale of Stationery
S.I.C.: 5112

Prestonia Office Products Ltd. **(1)**
163 King St.,
Stratford, ON N5A 6T1, Canada
Tel.: 519-271-1470
Wholesale of Office Supplies
S.I.C.: 5112

AMERICAN TV & APPLIANCE OF MADISON, INC.
2404 W. Beltline Hwy.
Madison, WI 53713
Tel.: 608-271-1000 **WI**
Fax: 608-275-7439
Year Founded: 1954
Assets: $78,000,000
Earnings: $7,000,000
Liabilities: $56,000,000
Net Worth: $22,000,000
Approx.Sls.: $225,000,000
Emp.: 1,400
Fiscal Year-end: 6/30/91
Retail Furniture & Electrical Appliances
S.I.C.: 5712; 5722
Leonard S. Mattioli *(Chm. Bd.)*
Douglas G. Reuhl *(Pres.)*
Steven B. Mixtacki *(V.P. & Chief Fin. Officer)*
Terri McNamara *(Mgr.-Personnel)*

No. of Mfg. Plants/Facilities: 8

Computer Systems/Hardware:
Data General System S280; F140

Outside Service Firm(s):

Grant Thornton*(Auditors)*
Madison, WI

M & I Marshall & Ilsley Bank*(Major Banking Relationship)*
Madison, WI

Central Life*(Group Insurer)*
Madison, WI

Stroud, Stroud, Willink, Thompson & Howard*(Legal Firm)*
Madison, WI

AMERICAN UNITED LIFE INSURANCE COMPANY
One American Square
Indianapolis, IN 46204
Mailing Address:
P.O. Box 368,
Indianapolis, IN 46206-0368
Tel.: 317-263-1877 **IN**
Year Founded: 1877
Assets: $4,523,082,754
Earnings: $30,805,430
Liabilities: $4,327,096,394
Net Worth: $195,986,360
Approx.Rev.: $1,003,189,585
Emp.: 900
Fiscal Year-end: 12/31/91
Mutual Life Insurance
S.I.C.: 6311
Jerry D. Semler *(Chm. Bd., Pres. & Chief Exec. Officer)*
John H. Barbre *(Sr. V.P.-Individual Div.)*
Charles D. Lineback *(Sr. V.P.-Reinsurance Div.)*
James W. Murphy *(Sr. V.P.-Corp. Fin.)*
R. Stephen Radcliffe *(Sr. V.P. & Chief Actuary)*
G. David Sapp *(Sr. V.P.-Investments)*
James P. Shanahan *(Sr. V.P.-Pension Div.)*
Gerald T. Walker *(Sr. V.P.-Grp. Div.)*
Kent R. Adams *(V.P.-Fixed Income Securities)*
James H. Akins, Jr. *(V.P.-Pension Contracts & Compliance)*
William M. Andria *(V.P.-Retirement Plan Services)*
Keith L. Bennett *(V.P.-Information Systems)*
Drew C. Boggs *(V.P.-Mortgage Loans)*
Lewis F. Born *(V.P.-Reinsurance Mktg.)*
Doyle D. Champion *(V.P.-Admin.)*
Lee H. Christenson *(V.P. & Reinsurance Actuary)*
H. Eugene Cramer *(V.P.-Reinsurance Underwriting)*
Edmund W. Genier *(V.P.-Real Estate)*
Philip E. Glassley *(V.P.-Underwriting & Policy Issue)*
James C. Harris *(V.P. & Reinsurance Medical Dir.)*
James R. Hetherington *(V.P.-Corp. Communications)*
Catherine B. Husman *(V.P. & Corp. Actuary)*
Michael O. Khalil *(V.P. & Pension Actuary)*
John W. Lauter *(V.P.-Annuity Services)*
James L. Leslie *(V.P.-Grp. Reinsurance Mktg. Services)*
Richard J. Lorenz *(V.P.-Grp. Underwriting)*
Bruce A. Miller *(V.P.-Grp. Mktg.)*
Dayton H. Molendorp *(V.P.-Individual Mktg.)*
Terry A. Nicodemus *(V.P. & Individual Actuary)*
Jerry L. Plummer *(V.P.-Human Resources)*
Paula J. Ringler *(V.P.-Policy Contract Services)*
Maurice E. Rougraff, M.D. *(V.P. & Medical Dir.)*
N. Sam Stone *(V.P.-MAAS Project)*
James A. Suiter *(V.P.-Grp. Claims)*
C. Dewayne Wilson *(V.P.-Grp. Pension Mktg.)*
Daniel L. Wolak *(V.P. & Grp. Actuary)*
Jack E. Hufford *(Treas.)*
William R. Brown *(Gen. Counsel & Sec.)*
Larry Sweany *(Controller)*
Earl E. Coleman *(Pur. Agent)*
Nancy A. Piercy *(Librarian)*

No. of U.S. Offices: 8

Computer Systems/Hardware:
IBM 3083 JX

Outside Service Firm(s):

Coopers & Lybrand*(Auditors)*
2900 One American Square, Box 82002
Indianapolis, IN 46282
Tel.: 317-639-4161

Ice, Miller, Donadio & Ryan*(Legal Firm)*
One American Square, Box 82001
Indianapolis, IN 46282
Tel.: 317-236-2219

American Federal National Bank*(Major Banking Relationship)*
Indianapolis, IN

Bank One, Indianapolis, N.A.*(Major Banking Relationship)*
111 Monument Circle, Ste. 1611
Indianapolis, IN 46204-1611
Tel.: 317-321-8110

American United Life*(Pension Manager)*
One American Square
Indianapolis, IN 46204
Tel.: 317-263-1877

AMERICAN VISION CENTERS, INC.
90 John St.
New York, NY 10038
Tel.: 212-385-1000
Tel.: 800-232-5558 **NY**
Fax: 212-385-1149
Year Founded: 1977
Approx.Sls.: $25,000,000
Emp.: 15
Fiscal Year-end: 12/31/91
Franchises Retail Optical Stores Specializing in Sale of Eyeglasses, Contact Lenses & Related Ophthalmic Accessories
S.I.C.: 5995; 6794
Seth Poppel *(Chm. Bd. & Pres.)*
Scott M. Schecter *(Sr. V.P., Chief Fin. Officer & Treas.)*
Lee Barkan *(Sr. V.P, Sec. & Gen. Counsel)*
Leon Bailey *(V.P.-Opers.)*
Don Baasch *(V.P.-Mktg.)*

AMERICAN WATER WORKS ASSOCIATION
6666 W. Quincy Ave.
Denver, CO 80235
Tel.: 303-794-7711
Tel.: 800-926-7337
Telex: 45-0895 AWWA DVR
Fax: 303-794-7310
Year Founded: 1881
Earnings: $57,088,000
Approx.Rev.: $14,000,000
Emp.: 130
Fiscal Year-end: 12/31/91

Export
Non-Profit Scientific & Educational Society for Quality Drinking Water; Books, Manuals, Standards & Periodicals
S.I.C.: 8699
Corporate Giving Program: United Way, Christmas for the Needy
John B. Mannion *(Exec. Dir.)*
Jack Hoffbuhr *(Deputy Exec. Dir.)*
Mark Abusamra *(Mktg. Dir.)*
Beverly Gipson *(Mktg. Sls. Mgr.)*
John Kayser *(Mktg. Promo. Mgr.)*
Lynn Laskey *(Dir.-Fin.)*
Joan Dent *(Dir.-Pub. Rels. Info.)*
John DeBoer *(Dir.-Tech. & Professional)*
Al Griggs *(Dir.-Human Resources)*
Jean Lowry *(Dir.-Computer Services)*
Darlene Daley *(Dir.-Meetings)*
Kurt Keely *(Info. Services Dir.)*
Lucy Hayes *(Sls. Mgr.)*
JoAnne Smith *(Sls. Mgr.)*

AMERICAN WELDING & MANUFACTURING CO.
250 Dietz Rd.
Warren, OH 44483
Tel.: 216-393-2531
Fax: 216-394-3131
Year Founded: 1918
Approx.Sls.: $70,000,000
Emp.: 350
Fiscal Year-end: 12/31/91

Import Export
Mfr. Rings, Flash Welded & Seamless
S.I.C.: 3724
Paul E. Emmerling *(V.P.-Sls. & Mktg.)*
C. Wheeler *(Controller)*
Frank Judge *(Sr. Buyer)*
Gary Coupland *(Dir.-Mfg.)*
Mark Hertzog *(Dir.-Pur.)*
L. Weller *(Dir.-Quality Control)*
D. Bevilagua *(Mgr.-Indus. Rels.)*
Thomas Laird *(Plant Mgr.)*

Computer Systems/Hardware:
IBM Anvil 5000

AMERICAN WHITE CROSS LABORATORIES, INC.
40 Nardozzi Pl.
New Rochelle, NY 10801
Tel.: 914-632-3045
Approx.Sls.: $35,000,000
Emp.: 350
Mfr. of Adhesive Tapes, Medicated Plasters, Absorbent Cotton, Gauze Bandages, First Aid Kits, Plastic Strips
S.I.C.: 3842
J. Orentzel *(Chief Exec. Officer)*
Richard Orentzel *(Pres.)*
Kaare Numme *(Treas. & Controller)*
B. Orentzel *(Sec.)*
B. Novick *(Gen. Counsel)*
Lawrence B. Wallerstein *(Dir.-Engrng.)*

AMERICAN WYOTT CORPORATION
1938 Wyott Dr.
Cheyenne, WY 82007
Mailing Address:
P.O. Box 1829,
Cheyenne, WY 82003
Tel.: 307-634-5801
Approx.Sls.: $15,000,000
Emp.: 150
Fiscal Year-end: 12/30/90
Mfr. Food Service Equip.; Lowerator, Hot Rod, Titan, Speedster & P.O.P.
S.I.C.: 3589
Logan Bernie *(V.P.-Mfg.)*
Lynn Weeberg *(Controller)*
Sue Hickman *(Dir.-Personnel & Indus. Rels.)*
David Yanchek *(Customer Service Mgr.)*

AMERICO MANUFACTURING CO., INC.
6224 No. Main St.
Acworth, GA 30101
Mailing Address:
P.O. Box 10000
Acworth, GA 30101
Tel.: 404-974-7000
Tel.: 800-241-9902
Fax: 404-974-0614
Approx.Sls.: $10,000,000
Emp.: 100
Fiscal Year-end: 6/30/91

Import Export
Mfr. & Distr. Janitorial Supplies
S.I.C.: 2842; 5169
James Rones *(Chm. Bd.)*
Henry Murphy *(Pres.)*
Ben Weisman *(Exec. V.P.)*
Allan Tanner *(V.P.-Sls.)*
Gail Rones *(Sec. & Treas.)*
Douglas Evenson *(Dir.-Adv.)*
Jane Hasty *(Dir.-Personnel)*

Principal(s):
James Rones

AMERIDATA, INC.
10200-51st Ave. North
Minneapolis, MN 55442
Tel.: 612-557-2500 **MN**
Fax: 612-557-6946
Year Founded: 1968
Assets: $28,362,000
Earnings: $596,000
Liabilities: $23,831,000
Net Worth: $4,531,000
Approx.Sls.: $102,571,000
Emp.: 275
Fiscal Year-end: 3/31/92

Import Export
Computers, Micro-Computers, Data Terminals, Maintenance Systems, Software
S.I.C.: 5046; 3575; 7372
Corporate Giving Program:
Computers To Non-Profit Organizations Benefiting Handicapped and Less Privileged
James K. McCleary *(Chief Exec. Officer)*
Dave Buck *(V.P.)*
John Harvatine *(V.P.-Fin. & Treas.)*
Harry Kaminsky *(V.P.)*
Jared Sour *(V.P.-Opers.)*
John Stanton *(V.P.)*
Harry Maher *(Controller)*
Louis B. Oberhauser *(Corp. Sec.)*
Sharon Berglund *(Mgr.-Personnel)*
Jean Green *(Mgr.-Personnel Training & Devel.)*

Principal(s):
James K. McCleary

No. of U.S. Offices: 10

Computer Systems/Hardware:
Compaq System Pro

Outside Service Firm(s):

Ernst & Young*(Auditors)*
1400 Pillsbury Center
Minneapolis, MN 55402
Tel.: 612-343-1000

Oberhauser & Associates*(Legal Firm)*
Minneapolis, MN

NBD Business Finance, Inc.*(Major Banking Relationship)*
1190 First National Bldg.
Detroit, MI 48226
Tel.: 313-962-8600

Minnesota Mutual Life Insurance Co.*(Pension Manager)*
400 N. Robert St.
St. Paul, MN 55101
Tel.: 612-298-3826

AMERISERV FOOD COMPANY
13335 Noel Rd., Ste. 2225
Dallas, TX 75240
Tel.: 214-385-8595
Fax: 214-702-7391
Year Founded: 1989
Emp.: 1,150
Fiscal Year-end: 12/31/91
Wholesale Food Distributor
S.I.C.: 5141
John Lewis *(Chm. Bd. & Chief Exec. Officer)*
Bill Burgess *(Pres. & Chief Oper. Officer)*
Wes Mayland *(Chief Fin. Officer)*
Scott Letier *(V.P. & Controller)*

No. of Mfg. Plants/Facilities: 16
No. of U.S. Offices: 17

Outside Service Firm(s):

Ernst & Young*(Auditors)*
1300 Huntington Bldg.
Cleveland, OH 44115
Tel.: 216-861-5000
Fax: 303-291-6234

Jackson & Walker*(Legal Firm)*
901 Main St., Ste. 6000
Dallas, TX 75202
Tel.: 214-953-6000

Division:

Alpha Distributors Ltd. **(1)**
1849 Wright St.
Madison, WI 53704
Tel.: 608-241-2107
Fax: 608-241-9212
Wholesale Groceries & Fresh Meats
S.I.C.: 5141
Mark Prowell *(Sr. V.P.)*
Mike McHugh *(Controller)*

AMERISURE COMPANIES
28 W. Adams Ave.
Detroit, MI 48226
Tel.: 313-965-8600
Tel.: 800-845-6063
Fax: 313-965-7787
Year Founded: 1912
Approx.Sls.: $525,000,000
Emp.: 2,100
Fiscal Year-end: 12/31/90
Casualty & PropertyInsurance
S.I.C.: 6331; 6531
Employee Matching Gifts Program:
$1 for $1 Contributions are Matched up to $500
J. John Wortman *(Pres. & Chief Exec. Officer)*
Charles Angell *(V.P.-Underwriting, Actuarial & Reinsurance)*
Roger Loughran *(V.P.-Personnel)*
Richard Lutenski *(V.P.-Fin.)*
Francis W. McMillan II *(V.P.-Mktg.)*
Susan Vincent *(Sec.)*
Kay Solsbury *(Mgr.-Personnel Training)*
Judith J. Willis *(Mgr.-Adv.)*
Paula Leon *(Pur. Agent)*
Jeffrey C. Paige *(Data Processing)*

Computer Systems/Hardware:
IBM

Division:

Unison Insurance Co. **(1)**
P.O. Box 31190,
Charleston, SC 29417-1190
Tel.: 803-571-0510
Fire Insurance Company
S.I.C.: 6331
Richard Russell *(Pres.)*

AMERITAS LIFE INSURANCE CORP.
5900 O St.
Lincoln, NE 68510
Mailing Address:
P.O. Box 81889
Lincoln, NE 68501
Tel.: 402-467-1122
Fax: 402-467-7956
Year Founded: 1887
Assets: $1,170,687,000
Net Worth: $1,170,687,000
Approx.Premiums: $426,500,000
Emp.: 1,000
Fiscal Year-end: 12/31/90
Mutual Insurance Co.; Life, Disability, Pensions, Dental, Annuities Insurance; Variable Life Products
S.I.C.: 6311; 6321; 6371; 6211; 6221; 6324
Neal E. Tyner *(Chm. & Chief Exec. Officer)*
Lawrence J. Arth *(Pres. & Chief Oper. Officer)*
Richard P. Day *(Exec. V.P.-Business Devel.)*
Judge Norman M. Krivosha *(Exec. V.P.-Admin. & Gen. Counsel)*
David Moore *(Sr. V.P.-Grp. Ins.)*
David R. Moore *(Sr. V.P.-Admin.)*
Kenneth C. Louis *(Sr. V.P.-Individual Markets)*
Jon C. Headrick *(Sr. V.P.)*
James R. Haire *(Sr. V.P.)*
Kenneth R. Jones *(2nd V.P.-Group Claims)*
Jack L. Took *(2nd V.P.-Grp. Sls. & Mktg.)*
Richard D. Brandt *(V.P.-Underwriting)*
Roxanne Brennfoerder *(V.P.-Pensions)*
Gerry Dimon *(V.P.-Corp. Resources)*
JoAnn Martin *(V.P. & Comptroller)*
Bruce R. McMullen *(V.P. & Medical Dir.)*
Gordon G. Pejsar *(V.P.-Dental Sciences)*
Barry C. Ritter *(V.P.-Information Services)*
Richard W. Vautravers *(V.P.)*
D. Doc Chaves *(Asst. V.P.-Corp. Communications)*
Gayle Burr *(Mgr.-Office Services)*

Computer Systems/Hardware:
IBM, Apple

Outside Service Firm(s):

Deloitte & Touche*(Auditors)*
1040 NBC Center
Lincoln, NE 68508

Bankers Life Insurance Co. of Nebraska*(Group Insurer)*
Lincoln, NE

FirsTier Bank*(Major Banking Relationship)*
Lincoln, NE

AMES SAFETY ENVELOPE COMPANY, INC.
21 Properzi Way
Somerville, MA 02143
Tel.: 617-776-3360
Fax: 617-623-7347
Approx.Sls.: $30,000,000
Emp.: 500
Wholesale & Manufacture Envelopes & Filing Systems
S.I.C.: 5112; 2522
Robert H. Arnold *(Chm. Bd.)*
William E. Shea *(Pres.)*
Neil Fitzgerald *(V.P.-Mfg.)*
Edward Lynch *(V.P.-Sls. & Intl. Mktg.)*
Charles Benoit *(Mgr.-Data Processing)*
Ted Dolan *(Pur. Agent)*

Outside Service Firm(s):

Coopers & Lybrand*(Auditors)*
1 Post Office Square
Boston, MA 02110
Tel.: 617-574-5000
Fax: 617-345-0398

Gilman, McLaughlin & Hanrahan*(Legal Firm)*
Boston, MA

State Street Bank & Trust Co.*(Major Banking Relationship)*
P.O. Box 5003
Boston, MA 02107
Tel.: 617-786-6316
Fax: 617-654-4266

Division:

Ames Color File Division **(1)**
21 Properzi Way
Somerville, MA 02143
Tel.: 617-776-3360
Fax: 617-623-7347
S.I.C.: 5112; 2522
William E. Shea *(Pres.)*

AMICA MUTUAL INSURANCE CO.
10 Weybosset St.
Providence, RI 02940
Tel.: 401-521-9100
Fax: 401-751-1464
Year Founded: 1907
Approx.Premiums: $600,000,000
Emp.: 2,926
Automobile Insurance Underwriters
S.I.C.: 6331
Joel N. Tobey *(Pres. & Chief Exec. Officer)*
Clayton T. Koelb *(Sr. Exec. V.P.)*
Donald R. Goodby *(Exec. V.P.)*
Kenneth M. Moffat *(Sr. V.P.-Personnel)*
Davies W. Bisset, Jr. *(Sr. V.P.-Underwriting)*
Harold Hitchen, Jr. *(Sr. V.P. & Treas.)*
Alfred C. Toegemann *(Sr. V.P.-Legal)*
Earl D. Chambers *(Sr. V.P.-Fin.)*
Thomas A. Taylor *(Sr. V.P.-Claims)*
Richard W. Pearce, Jr. *(Sr. V.P. & Sec.)*
Charles E. Horne III *(V.P.-Adv. & Communications)*

AMICALE INDUSTRIES, INC.
1375 Broadway
New York, NY 10018
Tel.: 212-398-0300
Fax: 212-398-0306
Approx.Sls.: $30,000,000
Emp.: 450
Import Export
Manufacture Woolen Spun Yarn & Knitted Cloth
S.I.C.: 2281
Boris Shlomm *(Pres. & Chief Exec. Officer)*
Walter D. Marx *(V.P.-Import/Export)*
George Bass *(V.P.-Cloth Prod.)*
Jerry Kaplan *(V.P.-Yarn Sls.)*
Art Shatz *(Treas.)*
Paul Aberasturi *(Controller & Mgr.-Traffic)*

Outside Service Firm(s):

Anchin, Block & Anchin*(Auditors)*
1375 Broadway
New York, NY 10018

Stroock & Stroock & Lavan*(Legal Firm)*
7 Hanover Square
New York, NY 10004
Tel.: 212-425-5200

Bankers Trust Co.*(Major Banking Relationship)*
One Bankers Trust Plaza
New York, NY 10006

Tel.: 212-250-6902

AMICK CONSTRUCTION LTD.
401 N. Ferguson Dr.
Orlando, FL 32805
Mailing Address:
P.O. Box 568492
Orlando, FL 32856
Tel.: 407-293-6562
Fax: 407-291-2815
Approx.Sls.: $14,000,000
Emp.: 105
Fiscal Year-end: 12/31/90
Highway & Heavy Construction
S.I.C.: 1611; 1629
Jeffrey B. Fuqua *(Pres.)*
James J. Smeenge *(Sec., Treas. & Comptroller)*
Walter Bohannon *(Gen. Supvr.)*

Outside Service Firm(s):

Kane & Shuck*(Auditors)*
Altamonte Springs, FL

A. Wayne Rich*(Legal Firm)*
Orlando, FL

Sun Bank, N.A.*(Major Banking Relationship)*
200 S. Orange Ave.
Orlando, FL 32802
Tel.: 407-237-4899
Fax: 407-237-6704

AMINCO, INC.
64 Ross Rd.
Savannah, GA 31405
Mailing Address:
P.O. Box 22307
Savannah, GA 31405
Tel.: 912-651-3400 **GA**
Fax: 912-651-3489
Year Founded: 1985
Approx.Sls.: $47,000,000
Emp.: 210
Mfr. of Toilet Preparations
S.I.C.: 2844
David Young *(Chm. Bd. & Chief Exec. Officer)*
Mario DeLaguardia *(Pres.)*

Outside Service Firm(s):

Price Waterhouse*(Auditors)*
Savannah, GA

Subsidiary:

Carson Products Company **(1)**
64 Ross Rd.
Savannah, GA 31405
Tel.: 912-651-3400
Approx.Sls.: $37,000,000
Emp.: 160
Mfr. of Cosmetic, Toilet, Shaving & Hair Coloring Preparations; Hair Dressing For The Trade
S.I.C.: 2844; 3999
Donald A. Young *(Chm. Bd. & Chief Exec. Officer)*
Mike DeLaguardia *(Pres.)*
Louis F. Parent *(Exec. V.P.-Sls.)*
H.L. Cornish, Jr. *(Sr. V.P., Treas. & Sec.)*
Henry H. Minis *(V.P.-Sls.)*
Kenneth D. Hall *(V.P.-Mktg.)*
Kaye Ginn *(V.P.-Personnel)*

AMITY LEATHER PRODUCTS COMPANY
735 S. Main St.
West Bend, WI 53095
Tel.: 414-335-1000
Fax: 414-335-1010
Year Founded: 1915
Approx.Sls.: $30,000,000
Emp.: 1,100
Import Export
Billfolds, Key Cases, Letter Cases, Travel Access.; Rolfs, Amity
S.I.C.: 3172
John F. Rozek *(Pres.)*
Dick Gagan *(Exec. V.P.)*
Joel Kirsch *(Sr. V.P.-Amity)*
John M. Pendergast *(V.P.-Fin.)*
Richard Kirwin *(Adv. Mgr.-Amity)*
Sue Olsen *(Adv. Mgr.-Rolfs)*
William Schecshel *(Pur. Mgr.)*

Computer Systems/Hardware:
Unisys

Division:

Rolfs **(1)**
735 S. Main St.
West Bend, WI 53095
Tel.: 414-338-6601
Leather Accessories
S.I.C.: 3172
Dennis Gajewski *(Sls. Promo Mgr.)*

AMKOR ELECTRONICS, INC.
1345 Enterprise Dr.
West Chester, PA 19380
Tel.: 215-431-9600 **PA**
Fax: 215-431-5881
Year Founded: 1970
Approx.Sls.: $150,000,000
Emp.: 100
Contract Assembly of Semiconductor Devices
S.I.C.: 3674
James J. Kim *(Chm. & Chief Exec. Officer)*
John Boruch *(Pres.)*
Frank J. Marcucci *(V.P.-Fin. & Admin.)*
Harry S. Kim *(V.P.-Worldwide Info. Systems)*
Memma S. Kilgannon *(Sec. & Treas.)*
Daniel Balkit *(Controller)*
Principal(s):
James J. Kim

No. of U.S. Offices: 4

Outside Service Firm(s):

Siana Deegan Carr & O'Connor*(Auditors)*
Paoli, PA

Siana & Shields*(Legal Firm)*
Exton, PA

Korea Exchange Bank*(Major Banking Relationship)*
New York, NY

AMLINGS FLOWERLAND
540 W. Ogden Ave.
Hinsdale, IL 60521
Tel.: 708-654-8820 **IL**
Fax: 708-654-8051
Year Founded: 1890
Approx.Sls.: $22,000,000
Emp.: 600
Fiscal Year-end: 12/31/91
Retail Flowers, Garden Products & Gifts; Landscaping; Commercial Plant Rentals
S.I.C.: 5992; 0781; 5261
Carl R. Hayes *(Pres.)*
Douglas F. Aniballi *(Sr. V.P.-Stores & Sls.)*
Scott Graunke *(Sr. V.P. & Treas.)*
Karl R. Grupp *(V.P.-Opers.)*
Darrell Fringer *(Dir.-Adv.)*
Principal(s):
Carl R. Hayes

Outside Service Firm(s):

Crowe, Chizek & Co.*(Auditors)*
P.O. Box 3687,
Oak Brook, IL 60822
Tel.: 708-954-7408
Fax: 708-799-1299

Altheimer & Gray*(Legal Firm)*
10 S. Wacker Dr.
Chicago, IL 60606
Tel.: 312-715-4000

Pathway Financial*(Major Banking Relationship)*
99 W. Washington St.
Chicago, IL 60602
Tel.: 312-346-4200

Subsidiary:

Amlings Landscape Co. **(1)**
540 W. Ogden Ave.
Hinsdale, IL 60521
Tel.: 708-789-6400
Fax: 708-654-8051
S.I.C.: 0781
Carl R. Hayes *(Pres.)*

AMLOID CORPORATION
81 5th St.
Saddle Brook, NJ 07662
Mailing Address:
P.O. Box 557
Saddle Brook, NJ 07662
Tel.: 201-368-1000
Fax: 201-587-0767
Approx.Sls.: $14,000,000
Emp.: 180
Plastic Toys
S.I.C.: 3944
Michael Albarelli, Jr. *(Chm. Bd. & Pres.)*
Joseph Albarelli *(Exec. V.P. & Treas.)*
Anthony Barberia *(Exec. V.P. & Sec.)*

Outside Service Firm(s):

Arthur Andersen & Co.*(Auditors)*
P.O. Box 221, 101 Eisenhower Pkwy.
Roseland, NJ 07068
Tel.: 201-403-6100
Fax: 201-403-0579

First Bank, N.A.*(Major Banking Relationship)*
Hasbrouck Heights, NJ

AMMIRATI & PURIS INC.
100 Fifth Avenue, New York, NY 10011
Tel.: 212-206-0500
Telefax: 212-337-9481

AMMIRATI & PURIS INC.
100 Fifth Ave.
New York, NY 10011
Tel.: 212-206-0500
Fax: 212-337-9481
Year Founded: 1974
Approx.Billings: $400,000,000
Emp.: 280
Advertising Agency
S.I.C.: 7311
Ralph Ammirati *(Chm. & Creative Dir.)*
Martin Puris *(Pres. & Chief Exec. Officer)*
Stephen Gardner *(Exec. V.P.)*
Mary Herrmann *(Exec. V.P.)*
Phil Palazzo *(Exec. V.P., Chief Fin. Officer)*
Duncan Pollock *(Exec. V.P.)*
Vivian Young *(Exec. V.P., Dir. Strategic Services)*
Jan Boyle *(Sr. V.P., Grp. Dir.)*
Alan Causey *(Sr. V.P., Dir. Social Analysis & Forecasts)*
Alyson B. Henning *(Sr. V.P., Dir. Bus. Devel.)*
Rule Johnson-Morris *(Sr. V.P., Dir.-MIS)*
Louis Killeffer *(Sr. V.P., Grp. Dir.)*
Steven Lanzano *(Sr. V.P., Group Media Dir.)*
Howard Lesman *(Sr. V.P., Grp. Dir.)*
Joseph Pessolano *(Sr. V.P., Fin.)*
Andrea Sessler *(Sr. V.P., Dir. Human Resources & Pub. Rels.)*
LeRoy Brown *(V.P., Dir. Office Services)*
Wendy Day *(V.P.; Personnel Mgr.)*
Nancy Stricko *(V.P., Controller)*
Ron Taguba *(V.P., Dir. MIS)*
Principal(s):
Ralph Ammirati
Martin Puris

No. of U.S. Offices: 1

Computer Systems/Hardware:
MacIntosh, Compaq

Outside Service Firm(s):

KPMG Peat Marwick*(Auditors)*
345 Park Ave.
New York, NY 10154
Tel.: 212-758-9700
Fax: 212-872-3308

Davis & Gilbert*(Legal Firm)*
850 Third Ave.
New York, NY 10022
Tel.: 212-326-1300

Chemical Banking Corp.*(Major Banking Relationship)*
277 Park Ave.
New York, NY 10041
Tel.: 212-310-6407
Fax: 212-310-4526

AMPACET CORPORATION
660 White Plains Rd.
Tarrytown, NY 10591
Tel.: 914-631-6600 **NY**
Telex: 62588
Fax: 914-631-7197
Year Founded: 1937
Approx.Sls.: $250,000,000
Emp.: 510
Fiscal Year-end: 12/31/90
Import Export
Mfr. of Plastic Color Concentrates
S.I.C.: 2821
Norman E. Alexander *(Chm. Bd.)*
David S. Weil *(Pres., Chief Exec. & Chief Oper. Officer)*
Martin J. Fernandi *(V.P.-Mktg.)*
Donald Fleischman *(V.P.-Fin., Treas. & Chief Fin. Officer)*

No. of Mfg. Plants/Facilities: 4
No. of U.S. Offices: 3
No. of Foreign Offices: 1

Computer Systems/Hardware:
DEC; ADDS 5700

Outside Service Firm(s):

Grant Thornton*(Auditors)*
605 Third Ave.
New York, NY 10158
Tel.: 212-599-0100
Fax: 212-370-4520

Rich, Krinsly, Katz & Lillienstein, P.C.*(Legal Firm)*
99 Park Ave.
New York, NY 10016
Tel.: 212-867-7200

Chase Manhattan Bank, N.A.*(Major Banking Relationship)*
One Chase Manhattan Plaza
New York, NY 10081
Tel.: 212-552-2222
Tel.: 800-526-0801
Fax: 212-552-7175

Chemical Bank*(Major Banking Relationship)*
450 West 33rd St.
New York, NY 10001
Tel.: 212-613-7197
Fax: 212-947-7628

Max Weil Associates*(Pension Manager)*
New York, NY

AMPCO METAL INCORPORATED
1745 S. 38th St.
Milwaukee, WI 53215
Mailing Address:
P.O. Box 2004,
Milwaukee, WI 53201
Tel.: 414-645-3750
Fax: 414-645-3225
Year Founded: 1914
Approx.Sls.: $40,000,000
Emp.: 285
Fiscal Year-end: 12/31/90
Import Export

Ampco Metal Incorporated—(Continued)

Custom Cast, Wrought & Machined, Aluminum Bronzes, Nickel-Aluminum Bronzes, High Copper Alloys in Extruded & Continuous Cast Rounds & Rectangular Bar, Tube, Rolled Sheet & Plate; Safety Tools; Bronze Weldrod
S.I.C.: 3366; 3548; 3351; 3423
F.J. Happel *(Pres.)*
R.M. Darling *(Chief Exec. Officer)*
M.L. Nicholson *(V.P.-Fin.)*
G.L. Nelson *(V.P.-Sls. & Mktg.)*
R.A. Lustig *(Adv. Mgr.)*
J.G. Darling *(Mgr.-Admin.)*
C.R. Bell *(Pur. Agent)*

Outside Service Firm(s):

Ernst & Young*(Auditors)*
111 E. Kilbourn Ave., Ste. 900
Milwaukee, WI 53202
Tel.: 414-273-5900

Division:

Ampco Metal Inc., Dallas Div. **(1)**
204 Barnes Dr.
Garland, TX 75042
Tel.: 214-276-6181
Fax: 214-276-5815
Emp.: 25
Export
Non-Ferrous Metal Products
S.I.C.: 3366
K.J. Norman *(Pres.)*

Non-U.S. Holdings:

Ampco Metal Ltd. **(1)**
17, Binns Cl, Torrington Av
Coventry, CV4 9TB, United Kingdom
Tel.: 0203-467011
Telex: 311415 AMPCOV G
Produces Copper Alloys
S.I.C.: 3366

Ampco Metal Nederlands B.V. **(1)**
P.O. Box 56, 3340AB
Woerden, Netherlands
Produces Copper Alloys
S.I.C.: 3366

Ampco Metal Nordiska AB **(1)**
Mockelv 38 Box 61, 121 22
Johanneshov, Sweden
Tel.: 81 84 20
Telex: 11735 Ampco S
Produces Copper Alloys
S.I.C.: 3366

Ampco Metal S.A. **(1)**
9 Route de Chesalles
Fribourg, Switzerland
Produces Copper Alloys
S.I.C.: 3366
C. Guenther *(Pres.)*

AMPERIF CORPORATION
9232 Eton Ave.
Chatsworth, CA 91311
Tel.: 818-998-7666 **CA**
Fax: 818-998-8129
Year Founded: 1971
Assets: $35,000,000
Earnings: $3,000,000
Liabilities: $15,000,000
Net Worth: $20,000,000
Approx.Sls.: $55,000,000
Emp.: 270
Fiscal Year-end: 12/31/90
Export
Mfr. of Memory System Products
S.I.C.: 3674
Keith Tattersall *(Chm. Bd., Pres. & Chief Exec. Officer)*
Donald Orr *(Exec. V.P., Chief Oper. Officer & Gen. Mgr.)*
Alex Beickovsky *(Sr. V.P.-Research & Technology)*
Bruce Hooker *(Sr. V.P. & Chief Fin. Officer)*
Webster Scroggin *(Sr. V.P.-Opers.)*
Walter Tuchman *(Sr. V.P.-Engrng.)*
Frank Vukmanic *(Sr. V.P.-Sls. & Mktg.)*
Thomas Bates *(V.P.-Human Resources)*
Stephen Fox *(V.P., Gen. Counsel & Sec.)*
Anthony Williams *(Dir.-Mngmt. Information Systems)*
Principal(s):
Keith Tattersall

No. of Mfg. Plants/Facilities: 2
No. of U.S. Offices: 5
No. of Foreign Offices: 18

Computer Systems/Hardware:
Hewlett-Packard 3000; Sperry-Univac 1100; IBM 4341 & 4381; CDC Cyber; Burroughs 32900; A-3; A-5

Outside Service Firm(s):

KPMG Peat Marwick*(Auditors)*
Woodland Hills, CA

Gendel, Raskoff, Shapiro & Quittner*(Legal Firm)*
Los Angeles, CA

Barclays Bank plc*(Major Banking Relationship)*
Sherman Oaks, CA

AMRAY, INC.
160 Middlesex Turnpike
Bedford, MA 01730
Tel.: 617-275-1400
Fax: 617-275-0740
Approx.Sls.: $18,000,000
Emp.: 185
Manufacture Electron Optical Scanners & X-Ray Equipment
S.I.C.: 3844; 3826
Gerald T. Cameron, Sr. *(Chm. Bd. & Chief Exec. Officer)*
Gerald T. Cameron, Jr. *(Pres.)*
Dr. Sheldon H. Moll *(Sr. V.P.-Tech.)*
Manfred A. Schippert *(Sr. V.P.-Engrng.)*
Laurence P. Harrington *(Treas.)*
Daniel Lynch *(Dir.-Data Processing)*

Outside Service Firm(s):

Ernst & Young*(Auditors)*
200 Clarendon St., 46th Fl.
Boston, MA 02116
Tel.: 617-266-2000

Nutter, McClennen & Fish*(Legal Firm)*
One International Place
Boston, MA 02210-2699
Tel.: 617-439-2000

State Street Bank & Trust Co.*(Major Banking Relationship)*
P.O. Box 366,
Boston, MA 02101
Tel.: 617-426-5523

AMRECORP REALTY INC.
(d/b/a Univesco)
16415 Addison Rd., Ste. 200-LB6
Dallas, TX 75248
Tel.: 214-380-8000 **DE**
Fax: 214-931-8015
Assets: $54,612,757
Liabilities: $47,870,133
Net Worth: $6,742,624
Sales Range: $10-19 Million
Emp.: 70
Real Estate Investment & Syndication
S.I.C.: 6798; 6552
Robert Werra *(Chm., Pres. & Chief Exec. Officer)*
David M. Kalnes *(Legal Officer)*
Paul M. Ivanoff *(Dir.-Data Processing)*
Principal(s):
Robert Werra

No. of U.S. Offices: 3

Computer Systems/Hardware:
IBM

Outside Service Firm(s):

Deloitte & Touche*(Auditors)*
1400 Lincoln Plaza, LB-4
Dallas, TX 75201-3302
Tel.: 214-220-8000

Aetna Life & Casualty*(Commercial Insurance Carrier)*
151 Farmington Avenue
Hartford, CT 06156
Tel.: 203-273-2128
Fax: 203-729-4295

National Union Fire Insurance Co. of Pittsburgh*(Commercial Insurance Carrier)*
70 Pine Street
New York, NY
Tel.: 212-837-0832

Reliance Insurance Co.*(Commercial Insurance Carrier)*
Philadelphia, PA

ALTA Health Strategies*(Group Insurer)*
Phoenix, AZ

First Bank Milwaukee*(Major Banking Relationship)*
201 W. Wisconsin Ave.
Milwaukee, WI 53259
Tel.: 414-278-6000

Williamson, Johnson, Gruber*(Pension Manager)*
Dallas, TX

AMSCO SCHOOL PUBLICATIONS, INC.
315 Hudson St.
New York, NY 10013
Tel.: 212-675-7000 **NY**
Fax: 212-675-7010
Year Founded: 1935
Approx.Sls.: $13,000,000
Emp.: 120
Publishing & Printing of Books
S.I.C.: 2731
Albert Beller *(Pres.)*
Patrick T. Kirby *(V.P.-Pur.)*
Jack Willig *(V.P.-Sls.)*
Laurence Beller *(Treas.)*

Outside Service Firm(s):

David Berdon & Co.*(Auditors)*
415 Madison Ave.
New York, NY 10017
Tel.: 212-832-0400

Chase Manhattan Bank, N.A.*(Major Banking Relationship)*
One Chase Manhattan Plaza
New York, NY 10081
Tel.: 212-552-2222
Tel.: 800-526-0801
Fax: 212-552-7175

AMSTED INDUSTRIES INCORPORATED
205 N. Michigan Ave.
Chicago, IL 60601
Tel.: 312-645-1700 **DE**
Fax: 312-819-8494
Year Founded: 1902
Assets: $501,174,000
Earnings: $17,800,000
Liabilities: $281,840,000
Net Worth: $219,334,000
Approx.Sls.: $817,215,000
Emp.: 7,600
Fiscal Year-end: 9/30/91
Export
Diversified Industrial Parts Manufacturer
S.I.C.: 3315; 3479; 3493; 3499; 3519; 3568; 3569; 3585; 3592; 3321; 3325
Employee Matching Gifts Program:
One-to-One Match Limited to Active ESOP Participants
Gordon R. Lohman *(Pres. & Chief Exec. Officer)*
Gerald K. Walter *(V.P. & Chief Fin. Officer)*
Thomas C. Berg *(V.P., Gen. Counsel & Sec.)*
O.J. Sopranos *(V.P.-Personnel)*
Warren W. Rasmussen *(V.P.)*
David B. Whitehurst *(V.P.)*
Howard R. Murray *(Treas.)*
Gary B. Montgomery *(Controller)*
Arthur M. Meske *(Dir.-Personnel)*
Jerry Gura *(Dir.-Pub. Affairs)*
Ronald J. Nalepa *(Dir.-Data Processing)*
Gary Marsch *(Asst. Treas.)*
Donald Tinsley *(Dir.)*

No. of Mfg. Plants/Facilities: 34
No. of Foreign Offices: 8

Computer Systems/Hardware:
IBM; Burroughs

Outside Service Firm(s):

Price Waterhouse*(Auditors)*
200 E. Randolph
Chicago, IL 60601
Tel.: 312-565-1500

Marsh & McLennan*(Commercial Insurance Carrier)*
222 S. Riverside Plaza
Chicago, IL 60606
Tel.: 312-648-6652

Aetna Life & Casualty*(Group Insurer)*
151 Farmington Avenue
Hartford, CT 06156
Tel.: 203-273-2128
Fax: 203-729-4295

Goldman, Sachs & Co.*(Investment Banker)*
85 Broad St.
New York, NY 10004
Tel.: 212-902-1000
Fax: 212-902-4451

Continental Bank N. A.*(Major Banking Relationship)*
231 S. LaSalle St.
Chicago, IL 60697
Tel.: 312-828-2345
Tel.: 800-426-5754
Telex: 312-828-1783

First National Bank of Chicago*(Major Banking Relationship)*
One First National Plaza
Chicago, IL 60670
Tel.: 312-732-9781
Tel.: 312-732-4050
Fax: 312-732-4840
Fax: 312-732-3055

Harris Trust & Savings Bank*(Major Banking Relationship)*
111 W. Monroe St.
Chicago, IL 60690
Tel.: 312-461-2265
Tel.: 800-858-0840

Harris Trust & Savings Bank*(Pension Manager)*
111 W. Monroe St.
Chicago, IL 60690
Tel.: 312-461-2265
Tel.: 800-858-0840

JMB Institutional Realty Corp.*(Pension Manager)*
900 N. Michigan Ave., Ste. 1800
Chicago, IL 60611-1585
Tel.: 312-915-1900
Fax: 312-915-1852

Kemper Financial Services*(Pension Manager)*
Chicago, IL

LaSalle National Bank*(Pension Manager)*
135 S. LaSalle St., Rm.260
Chicago, IL 60603

Lincoln Capital Management*(Pension Manager)*
200 South Wacker Dr.
Chicago, IL 60606
Tel.: 312-559-2880
Fax: 312-559-1837

Mathers & Co.*(Pension Manager)*
Chicago, IL

Subsidiaries:

AMSTED Industries International **(1)**
200 W. Monroe St.
Chicago, IL 60606
Tel.: 312-372-5384
Export
Negotiates, Licenses & Sells Amsted's Railroad Components & Industrial Castings Abroad
S.I.C.: 5088
O.J. Sopranos *(Pres.)*

American Steel Foundries **(1)**
10 S. Riverside Plaza
Chicago, IL 60606
Tel.: 312-938-4000
Export
Mfr. of Cast Steel Freight Car Components, Steel Springs & Fifth Wheels
S.I.C.: 3325; 3493
N.A. Berg *(Pres.)*
R.A. Bernard *(Dir.-Indus. Rels.)*

Baltimore Aircoil Company **(1)**
7595 Montevideo Rd.
Jessup, MD 20794
Tel.: 410-799-6200
Hot-Dip Galvanized Steel Cooling Towers, Evaporative Condensers, Closed Circuit Fluid Coolers, Heat Exchangers, Ice Chiller Thermal Storage Units, Filters
S.I.C.: 3569
M.J. McKenna *(Pres.)*
W.D. McCloskey *(Exec. V.P.)*
E. Schinner *(Sr. V.P.)*
B.D. Speice *(V.P.-Opers.)*
J.F. Carroll *(V.P.-Mktg.)*
Charles B. McCurley *(Mgr.-Adv. & Sls. Promo.)*

Subsidiaries:

BAC-Pritchard, Inc. **(2)**
P.O. Box 7322
Baltimore, MD 21227
Tel.: 410-799-6200
Mfr. of Field Erected Cooling Towers
S.I.C.: 3443

Ceramic Cooling Tower Co. **(2)**
1100 Northway Dr.
Ft. Worth, TX 76131
Tel.: 817-232-4661 (100%)
Fax: 817-232-4703
Mfr. of Water Cooling Systems
S.I.C.: 3585; 1799; 5084
Charles Bardo *(Pres.)*
Fred Griffith *(V.P. & Controller)*
Jess Seawell *(V.P.-Engrng.)*
Toby Daley *(V.P.-Engrng. Design)*
M.A. Dew *(Dir.-Data Processing)*

Burgess-Norton Mfg. Co. **(1)**
737 Peyton St.
Geneva, IL 60134
Tel.: 708-232-4100
Fax: 708-232-3634
Emp.: 800
Fiscal Year-end: 9/00/92
Export
Mfr. of Piston Pins & Powder Metal Parts
S.I.C.: 3519; 3592
C. James Brewer *(Pres.)*
Matthew J. Hower *(Controller)*
S.E. Kelm *(Dir.-Indus. Rels.)*
Ralph A. Cushna *(Dir.-Sales & Mktg.)*

Diamond Chain Company **(1)**
402 Kentucky Ave.
Indianapolis, IN 46207
Tel.: 317-638-6431
Fax: 317-633-2243
Approx.Sls.: $20,000,000
Emp.: 545
Fiscal Year-end: 9/30/90
Import Export
Mfr. of Roller Chains, Conveyor Chains
S.I.C.: 3535; 3568; 3499
J.R. Milby *(Pres.)*
Gary B. Pennell *(V.P.-Mktg.)*
G.E. Bachman *(Controller)*
E.G. Flaningham *(Personnel Dir.)*

Griffin Pipe Products Co. **(1)**
1400 Opus Pl., Ste. 700
Downers Grove, IL 60515
Tel.: 708-719-6500
Mfr. of Gray Iron & Ductile Iron Pressure Pipe for Water, Cast Iron Soil Pipe
S.I.C.: 3321
T.C. Fitzgerald *(Pres.)*
R.L. Hendrix *(Indus. Rels. Dir.)*

Griffin Wheel Co. **(1)**
200 W. Monroe St.
Chicago, IL 60606
Tel.: 312-346-3300
Export
Mfr. of Steel Railroad Wheels; Composition Brake Shoes
S.I.C.: 3325
Arthur W. Goetschel *(Pres.)*
M.J. White *(Dir.-Employee Rels.)*

Macwhyte Co. **(1)**
2906 14th Ave.
Kenosha, WI 53141
Tel.: 414-654-5381
Fax: 414-654-5384
Approx.Sls.: $28,000,000
Emp.: 625
Fiscal Year-end: 9/30/90
Wire Rope Prods.
S.I.C.: 3315
Robert W. Plaskett *(Pres.)*
L.O. Farley *(V.P.-Mfg.)*
Richard J. Connor *(V.P.-Mktg.)*
D.A. Pawlowski *(Controller)*
R.B. Hoganson *(Dir.-Engrng.)*
Greg Ladzinski *(Dir.-Personnel & Indus. Rels.)*
Chas. E. Alisauskas *(Pur. Agent)*

Non-U.S. Holding:

Griffin Canada Inc. **(1)**
1375 Brouillette St.
Saint Hyacinthe, PQ J25 7B6, Canada
Tel.: 514-774-5311
Steel Railroad Wheels; Composition Brake Shoes; Plants Located at Winnipeg, MB & St. Hyacinthe, PQ
S.I.C.: 3325
Arthur W. Goetschel *(Pres.)*

AMSTORE CORPORATION
1221 E. Keating
Muskegon, MI 49442
Mailing Address:
P.O. Box 6
Muskegon, MI 49443
Tel.: 616-722-6681
Fax: 616-726-2504
Approx.Sls.: $28,000,000
Emp.: 225
Store Fixtures, Wood Showcases
S.I.C.: 2541
Richard F. Kaufman *(Pres. & Chief Exec. Officer)*
Robert Kuieies *(V.P.-Opers. & Treas.)*
Ronald F. Kittle *(Mgr.-Pur.)*

Outside Service Firm(s):

Old Kent Bank*(Major Banking Relationship)*
Grand Rapids, MI

AMTRAK-NATIONAL RAILROAD PASSENGER CORP.
60 Massachusetts Ave, N.E.
Washington, DC 20002
Tel.: 202-906-3000 **DC**
Telex: 892418
Fax: 202-906-3560
Year Founded: 1971
Assets: $4,077,237,000
Liabilities: $803,669,000
Net Worth: $3,273,568,000
Approx.Rev.: $1,358,950,000
Emp.: 23,000
Fiscal Year-end: 9/30/91
Provides Rail Passenger Service to Approximately 500 Cities Across the U.S.
S.I.C.: 4011
W. Graham Claytor, Jr. *(Chm. Bd., Pres. & Chief Exec. Officer)*
William S. Norman *(Exec. V.P.)*
Dennis F. Sullivan *(Exec. V.P. & Chief Oper. Officer)*
Peter A. Cannito *(V.P.-Engrng.)*
Anthony DeAngelo *(V.P.-Real Estate & Oper. Devel.)*
Eugene N. Eden *(V.P.-Passenger Services)*
Robert E. Gall *(V.P.-Sls. & Mktg.)*
Charles W. Hayward *(V.P.-Fin. & Admin. & Chief Fin. Officer)*
Norris W. Overton *(V.P.-Information Systems)*
Robert C. VanderClute *(V.P.-Transportation)*
Elyse G. Wander *(V.P.-Plng. & Devel. & Sec.)*
Thomas J. Gillespie, Jr. *(Asst. V.P.-Govt. & Pub. Affairs)*
John P. Lange *(Asst. V.P.-Labor Rels.)*
Neil David Mann *(Asst. V.P.-Personnel)*
Robert L. Lewis III *(Controller)*
Richard I. Klein *(Treas.)*
Stephen C. Rogers *(Gen. Counsel)*
Floyd L. Kemerer *(Dir.-Pur.)*
Joan E. Wheatley *(Dir.-Adv. & Sls. Promo.)*

Computer Systems/Hardware:
IBM

Outside Service Firm(s):

Arthur Andersen & Co.*(Auditors)*
1666 K Street, N.W.
Washington, DC 20006

Arkwright Mutual Insurance*(Commercial Insurance Carrier)*
225 Wyman St.
Waltham, MA 02254-9198
Tel.: 617-890-9300
Fax: 617-890-0075

Railroad Association Insurance, Ltd.*(Commercial Insurance Carrier)*
Hamilton, Bermuda

Connecticut General Life Insurance Co.*(Group Insurer)*
195 Broadway, 12th floor
New York, NY 10017
Tel.: 212-618-5500

American Security Bank, N.A.*(Major Banking Relationship)*
1501 Pennsylvania Ave. N.W.
Washington, DC 20013
Tel.: 202-624-4000

Chemical Bank*(Major Banking Relationship)*
450 West 33rd St.
New York, NY 10001
Tel.: 212-613-7197
Fax: 212-947-7628

Capitoline Investment Services*(Pension Manager)*
Richmond, VA

Investment Counselors of Maryland, Inc.*(Pension Manager)*
Baltimore, MD

Subsidiaries:

Chicago Union Station Company **(1)**
400 N. Capitol St., N.W.
Washington, DC 20001
Tel.: 202-906-4700 (100%)
Fax: 202-906-4704
Railroad Passenger Terminal
S.I.C.: 4011
Charles W. Hayward *(Pres. & Chief Oper. Officer)*
Jack L. Pearson *(Gen. Mgr.)*
Robert L. Lewis *(Controller)*

Washington Terminal Company **(1)**
400 N. Capitol St., N.W.
Washington, DC 20001
Tel.: 202-906-3000
Railroad Passenger Terminal
S.I.C.: 4011
Robert C. Vanderclute *(Pres.)*

AMTRAN CORPORATION
(Formerly American Transportation Corporation)
Hwy. 65 S.
Conway, AR 72032
Mailing Address:
P.O. Box 6000,
Conway, AR 72032
Tel.: 501-327-7761 **AR**
Fax: 501-327-9147
Year Founded: 1933
Approx.Sls.: $75,000,000
Emp.: 850
Fiscal Year-end: 10/31/91
Export
Manufacturer of Bus Bodies & Component Parts; Military Sales of Parts; Assembly of Bus Chassis
S.I.C.: 3713
Corporate Giving Program: Local & State Education Employee Assist Programs
Employee Matching Gifts Program: United Way
William S. Bankston *(Pres. & Chief Exec. Officer)*
Edward L. Raniszeski *(Exec. V.P.-Sls. & Mktg.)*
Wilbur Bennett *(V.P.-Engineering)*
Debbie Isaacs *(V.P.-Fin. & Controller)*
Charles Koger *(V.P.-Pur.)*
Dan Allen *(Dir.-Engrng.)*
John Mattox *(Dir.-Human Resources)*

Outside Service Firm(s):

KPMG Peat Marwick*(Auditors)*
Tower Bldg., 11th Fl.,
Little Rock, AR 72201
Tel.: 501-375-3275

Wright, Lindsey, & Jennings*(Legal Firm)*
2200 Worthen Bank Bldg.
Little Rock, AR 72201
Tel.: 501-371-0808
Fax: 501-375-1617

First Commercial Bank*(Major Banking Relationship)*
P.O. Box 1331,
Little Rock, AR 72201

AMTRAN, INC.
7337 W. Washington St.
Indianapolis, IN 46231
Mailing Address:
P.O. Box 51609, Ind. Airport
Indianapolis, IN 46251
Tel.: 317-247-4000 **IN**
Fax: 317-243-4165
Year Founded: 1984
Approx.Sls.: $450,000,000
Emp.: 2,600
Fiscal Year-end: 12/31/90
Holding Company
S.I.C.: 6719; 4512
J. George Mikelsons *(Chm. Bd., Pres. & Chief Exec. Officer)*
James H. Hlavacek *(Exec. V.P.)*
Kenneth K. Wolff *(Exec. V.P. & Chief Fin. Officer)*
John Tague *(Sr. V.P.-Mktg. & Sls.)*
Michael Barnard *(V.P. & Treas.)*
Bruce Baun *(V.P.-Admin.)*
William L. Culkin *(V.P.-Sls.)*
Richard Meyer *(V.P.-Human Resources)*
Rick Leoff *(V.P.-Tour Opers.)*
Ed Wright *(V.P.-Information Services)*
Brian Hunt *(Gen. Counsel & Sec.)*
Tom Bericopes *(Controller)*
Mary M. Cochran *(Dir.-Corp. Communications)*
Jeffrey Bair *(Mgr.-Treasury)*

Outside Service Firm(s):

Blue & Co.*(Auditors)*
Indianapolis, IN

First of America Bank*(Major Banking Relationship)*
Kalamazoo, MI

Subsidiaries:

Ambassadair Travel Club, Inc. **(1)**
7337 W. Washington St.
Indianapolis, IN 46231
Tel.: 313-247-4000
Membership Travel Club
S.I.C.: 4724
Jack Richards *(V.P.-Tour Opers.)*

Amber Tours, Inc. **(1)**
7337 W. Washington St.
Indianapolis, IN 46231
Tel.: 317-247-4000

Amtran, Inc.—(Continued)

Tour Operations
S.I.C.: 4725
Jack Richards *(V.P.-Tour Opers.)*

Amber Travel, Inc. **(1)**
7337 W. Washington St.
Indianapolis, IN 46231
Tel.: 317-247-4000
Full Service Travel Agency
S.I.C.: 4724
Jack Richards *(V.P.-Tour Opers.)*

American Trans Air Execujet, Inc. **(1)**
7337 W. Washington St.
Indianapolis, IN 46231
Tel.: 317-247-4000
Corporate Aircraft Charter Operation
S.I.C.: 4512
Gordon Moebius *(Dir.-Corp. Devel.)*

American Trans Air, Inc. **(1)**
7337 W. Washington St.
Indianapolis, IN 46231
Tel.: 317-247-4000
Tel.: 800-225-9920
Passenger Charter Airlines
S.I.C.: 4512
J. George Mickelsons *(Pres. & Chief Exec. Officer)*
John Tague *(Chief Mktg. Officer)*

American Trans Air Training Corp. **(1)**
7337 W. Washington St.
Indianapolis, IN 46231
Tel.: 317-247-4000
Flight Crew Training Company
Jim Hlavacek *(Pres.)*
Donald Miller *(V.P.-Training Corp.)*

Ports of Call, Inc. **(1)**
2121 Valencia St.
Denver, CO 80220
Tel.: 303-321-6767
Travel Club & Charter-Certified Air Trans.
S.I.C.: 4512; 4522
J. George Mikelsons *(Chm. Bd., Pres. & Chief Exec. Officer)*

AMTROL INC.
1400 Division Rd.
West Warwick, RI 02893
Tel.: 401-884-6300
Fax: 401-885-2567
Year Founded: 1946
Approx.Sls.: $125,000,000
Emp.: 1,200
Manufacturing Components & Accessories For Heating Systems, Water Well Systems, Refrigeration & Air Conditioning
S.I.C.: 3469; 3494; 3567; 3585
Chester H. Kirk *(Chm. Bd. & Chief Exec. Officer)*
David Beretta *(Pres.)*
Edward Cooney *(Sr. V.P. & Treas.)*
Michael J. Regan *(V.P. & Sec.)*

Outside Service Firm(s):

Arthur Andersen & Co.*(Auditors)*
One Intl. Place, 100 Oliver St.
Boston, MA 02110
Tel.: 617-330-4000
Fax: 617-439-9731

Hinkley, Allen, Snyder & Comen*(Legal Firm)*
1500 Fleet Ctr.
Providence, RI 02903
Tel.: 401-274-2000

Fleet National Bank*(Major Banking Relationship)*
125 Dupont Dr.
Providence, RI 02907-3178
Tel.: 401-278-5335

Subsidiaries:

American Granby, Inc. **(1)**
1111 Vine St.
Liverpool, NY 13088
Tel.: 315-451-1100
Sam Daniels *(Gen. Mgr.)*

Automatic Metal Blanking, Inc. **(1)**
1440 Grays Rd.
Sparrows Point, MD 21219
Tel.: 301-477-3200
Norm Dubicki *(Plant Supervisor)*

Clayton Mark **(1)**
1203 N. 6th St.
Rogers, AR 72756
Tel.: 501-636-1800
Sam Daniels *(Gen. Mgr.)*

Pressure Pak Container, Inc. **(1)**
3200 Bullard St.
Paducah, KY 42001
Tel.: 502-442-9678
Bruce Farris *(Gen. Mgr.)*

AMURCON CORPORATION
26555 Evergreen, Ste. 1300
Southfield, MI 48076
Tel.: 313-352-0202
Telex: 352-0725
Fax: 313-352-0202, Ext. 254
Year Founded: 1971
Sales Range: $40-59 Million
Emp.: 350
Real Estate Developer & Syndicator
S.I.C.: 6531; 6552
Barton M. Berman *(Chm. Bd., Pres. & Chief Exec. Officer)*
Willie Martin *(V.P. & Treas.)*
Sally Friday *(Dir.-Mktg.)*

Computer Systems/Hardware:
Texas Instruments

Outside Service Firm(s):

Coopers & Lybrand*(Auditors)*
400 Renaissance Center
Detroit, MI 48243
Tel.: 313-446-7100
Fax: 313-446-7117

Jaffe, Snider, Raitt & Heuer*(Legal Firm)*
1800 First Natl. Bldg.
Detroit, MI 48226
Tel.: 313-761-8380

Manufacturers National Bank N.A.*(Major Banking Relationship)*
38th Fl., 100 Renaissance Center
Detroit, MI 48243
Tel.: 313-222-4227

Subsidiaries:

Amurcon Equities **(1)**
26555 Evergreen, Ste. 1118
Southfield, MI 48076
Tel.: 313-352-0202
Kathryn J. Morris *(Dir.)*

Amurcon Management **(1)**
26555 Evergreen, Ste. 1118
Southfield, MI 48076
Tel.: 313-352-0202
Scott Allen *(Pres.)*

Amurcon Securities Corp. **(1)**
26555 Evergreen, Ste. 1118
Southfield, MI 48076
Tel.: 313-352-0202
Kathryn J. Morris *(Pres.)*

AMWAY CORPORATION
7575 Fulton St. E.
Ada, MI 49355-0001
Tel.: 616-676-6000 **MI**
Fax: 616-676-8140
Year Founded: 1959
Approx.Sls.: $3,900,000,000
Emp.: 10,000
Fiscal Year-end: 8/31/92
Import Export
Household Cleaning Products, Home & Personal Care Items, Health, Beauty & Nutrition Products, Housewares, Catalog & Commercial Products; Auto, Realty, Communications, Travel, Legal Services; Catalog Services
S.I.C.: 2842; 2841; 2844; 5199; 2741; 8621; 6531; 4813; 8111; 2731; 5961; 3743; 2023
Corporate Giving Program: The Amway Environmental Foundation, Easter Seals
Jay Van Andel *(Chm. Bd.)*
Richard DeVos *(Pres.)*
David Braun *(Chief Info. Officer (MIS))*
Roger E. Beutner *(Sr. V.P.-Opers.)*
Gregory Grochoski *(Sr. V.P.-Res. & Devel.)*
Thomas W. Eggleston *(Exec. V.P. & Gen. Counsel)*
David H. Brenner *(Sr. V.P.-Mktg.)*
Lawrence M. Call *(V.P., Chief Fin. Officer)*
Dan DeVos *(V.P.-Pacific Liason)*
Donald MacDonald *(V.P.-Pur. & Engrng.)*
James Rosloniec *(V.P.-Audit & Contol)*
Dwight A. Sawyer *(V.P.-Human Resources)*
Barb Van Andel-Gaby *(V.P.-Amway Properties)*
Nan Van Andel *(V.P.-Catalog & Communications)*
Steve Van Andel *(V.P.-Americas)*
Doug Devos *(Dir.-Europe)*
Dan Shuster *(Dir.-Intl. Admin.)*
Frank Miceli *(Asst. Treas.)*
Ken J. McDonald *(Dir.-Communications)*
Dave Van Andel *(Dir.-Mfg. Opers.)*
R.E. Wayman *(Dir.-Global Fin. Reporting Devel.)*
Kimberly Bruyn *(Mgr.-Pub. Rels.)*
Allan Engel *(Sr. Mgr.-Fin. Projects)*
Susan Wilcox *(Mgr.-Meetings Planning)*
Robert Bogacy *(Mgr.-Adv.)*
Jean Westrop *(Corp. Librarian)*

No. of Foreign Offices: 18

Computer Systems/Hardware:
IBM 3081 H, 3081 K; Digital 1170

Outside Service Firm(s):

BDO Seidman*(Auditors)*
99 Monroe Ave. NW, Ste. 800
Grand Rapids, MI 49503
Tel.: 616-774-7000
Fax: 616-451-2096

Michigan National Bank*(Investment Banker)*
77 Monroe Center
Grand Rapids, MI 49501
Tel.: 616-451-7600

Michigan National Bank*(Major Banking Relationship)*
77 Monroe Center
Grand Rapids, MI 49501
Tel.: 616-451-7600

Subsidiaries:

Amway Hotel Corporation **(1)**
Pearl Northwest at Monroe
Grand Rapids, MI 49503
Tel.: 616-774-2000
S.I.C.: 7011
Richard M. DeVos *(Pres.)*

NutriLite Products, Inc. **(1)**
5600 Beach Blvd.
Buena Park, CA 90620
Tel.: 714-521-3900
Mfr. of Food Supplements
S.I.C.: 2099
Sam Rehnborg *(Pres.)*

Non-U.S.-Holdings:

Amway Argentina, Inc. **(1)**
Maipu 939-P.B. 1006,
Buenos Aires, Argentina
Steve Robbins *(Gen. Mgr.)*

Amway Belgium Co. **(1)**
Ikaroslaan 4 B-1930,
Zaventem, Belgium
Tel.: 32-2-720-5935
Telex: 84440879
Fax: 32-2-720-5938
Emp.: 5
Distribution of Amway Products
S.I.C.: 5963
Arie Van Vugt *(Mgr.)*
Chris Bolsover *(Reg. Mgr.)*

Amway de Espana, S.A. **(1)**
C/Industria, 101-115, Poligono Gran Via, Zona 22A 08908 Hospitalet De Llobregat, Barcelona, Spain
Tel.: 34-3-263-31-88
Fax: 34-3-263-25-88
Emp.: 12
Distribution of Amway Products
S.I.C.: 5963
Patric Sullivan *(Gen. Mgr.)*
Stewart McArthur *(Mng. Dir.)*

Amway de Guatemala, S.A. **(1)**
7A Avenida 6-69 Zona 9,
Guatemala City, Guatemala
Tel.: 502-2-32-6948
Fax: 502-2-34-4390
Emp.: 15
Distribution of Amway Products
S.I.C.: 5963
Alvaro Martinez *(Gen. Mgr.)*

Amway de Mexico, S.A. de C.V. **(1)**
Washington #539 Ote piso 10
Monterrey, N.L., Mexico C.P. 64000
Tel.: 52-83-19-80-00
Fax: 52-83-19-80-98
Distribution of Amway Products
S.I.C.: 5963
Russ Hall *(Gen. Mgr.)*

Amway de Panama S.A. **(1)**
Apartado 6-4200
El Dorado, Panama Panama
Tel.: 507-61-7661 (100%)
Fax: 507-61-3535
Emp.: 19
Distribution of Amway Products
S.I.C.: 5963
Steve Robbins *(Gen. Mgr.)*
Diogenes Duenas *(Affiliate Mgr.)*

Amway de Portugal, Inc. **(1)**
Av. do Forte, 10 Carnaxide, 2795 Linda-A-Velha, Portugal
Tel.: 351-1-417-2890
Fax: 351-1-418-6814
Luis Delgado *(Gen. Mgr.)*

Amway Do Brasil LTDA. **(1)**
Av. Eng. Eusebio Stevaux 1257 04696-000
Sao Paulo, SP Brazil
Tel.: 55-11-548-2188
Fax: 55-11-246-6080
Ken Smith *(Gen. Mgr.)*

Amway (Europe) Ltd. **(1)**
Bank House - 1st Fl., 171 Midsummer Blvd.
Central Milton Keynes, MK9 1ED, United Kingdom
Tel.: 44-908-691118
Fax: 44-908-694360
Distribution of Amway Products
S.I.C.: 5963
Stewart McArthur *(Mng. Dir.)*

Amway France **(1)**
14, Avenue Francois-Sommer F-92185
Antony, CEDEX France
Tel.: 46-68-04-25 (100%)
Telex: 201228
Fax: 33-1-42-37-08-11
Emp.: 80
Distribution of Amway Products
S.I.C.: 5963
Nicolas Lefranc *(Gen. Mgr.)*
Ian Morgan *(Reg. Mgr.)*

Amway Gesellschaft M.B.H. **(1)**
Wienerstrasse 720 A-2203,
Grossebersdorf, Austria
Tel.: 43-2245-5202
Fax: 43-2245-3770
Emp.: 23
Distribution of Amway Products
S.I.C.: 5963
Klaus Tremmel *(Gen. Mgr.)*

Amway GmbH **(1)**
Benzstrasse 11 a-c W-8039
Puchheim, Germany
Tel.: 49-89-800 940 (100%)
Telex: 5213072
Fax: 49-89-808739
Emp.: 75
Distribution of Amway Products
S.I.C.: 5963
Stewart McArthur *(Mng. Dir.)*
Jim Payne *(Gen. Mgr.)*

Amway Hungaria Marketing KFT. (1)
1089 Budapest Kalvaria ter 7, Hungary
Tel.: 36-1-114-1836
Fax: 36-1-269-9176
Klaus Tremmel *(Reg. Mgr.)*

Amway Indonesia (1)
Wisma SSK - 3rd Fl., Jl. Daan Mogot Km 11
Jakarta, 11460, Indonesia
Tel.: 62-21-540-2160
Fax: 62-21-540-2170
Peter Beaumont *(Gen. Mgr.)*

Amway International, Inc.-Hong Kong Branch (1)
26/F Citicorp centre, 18 Whitfield Rd., Causeway Bay
Hong Kong, Hong Kong
Tel.: 852-5-662-239 (100%)
Telex: 780-81496
Fax: 852-5-8073920
Emp.: 73
Distribution of Amway Products
S.I.C.: 5963
Eva Cheng *(Chief Exec.)*

Amway Italia s.r.l. (1)
Via G. di Vittorio 10 1-20094
Corsico, Italy
Tel.: 39-2-451951 (100%)
Fax: 39-2-44-75-873
Emp.: 30
Distribution of Products
S.I.C.: 5963
Martine Heines *(Gen. Mgr.)*
Stewart McArthur *(Mng. Dir.)*

Amway (Japan) Limited (1)
Arco Tower, 1-8-1 Shimomeguro Meguro-Ku
Tokyo, 153, Japan
Tel.: 81-3-5434-8484 (100%)
Telex: 781-28267
Fax: 81-3-5434-4897
Emp.: 342
Distribution of Amway Products
S.I.C.: 5963
William Hemmer *(Chm. Bd. & Pres.)*
Dick Johnson *(Pres. & Representative Dir.)*

Amway Korea, Ltd. (1)
Dong Sung Bldg., 12th Fl., 158-24
Samsung-dong Kangnam-ku,
Seoul, Korea
Tel.: 82-2-556-6577
Fax: 82-2-569-3111
Distribution of Amway Products
S.I.C.: 5963
Dave Ussery *(Pres. & Representative Dir.)*

Amway (Malaysia) Sdn. Bhd. (1)
P.O. Box 84, Jalan Sultan 46710 Petaling Jaya,
Selangor, Malaysia
Tel.: 60-3-775-5222 (100%)
Telex: 78437469
Fax: 60-3-755-5007
Emp.: 210
Distribution of Amway Products
S.I.C.: 5963
L.H. Choong *(Mng. Dir.)*

Amway Nederland Ltd. (1)
Edisonstraat 18 Postbus 278, 4000 AG
Tiel, Netherlands
Tel.: 313 440 18344 (100%)
Fax: 31-34-4015337
Emp.: 31
Distribution of Amway Products
S.I.C.: 5963
Chris Bolsover *(Reg. Mgr.)*
Stewart McArthur *(Mng. Dir.)*
Arie Van Vugt *(Mgr.)*

Amway of Australia Pty. Ltd. (1)
46 Carrington Rd., P.O. Box 202
Castle Hill, N.S.W. 2154, Australia
Tel.: 612-680-2222 (100%)
Telex: 79025413
Fax: 61-2-680-2868
Emp.: 177
Distribution of Amway Products
S.I.C.: 5963
Bruce Shankland *(Mng. Dir.)*

Amway of Canada, Ltd. (1)
3897 Exeter Rd.
London, ON Canada N6A 4S5
Tel.: 519-685-7700 (100%)
Fax: 519-685-4421
Emp.: 185
Distribution of Amway Products
S.I.C.: 5963
Brian Chalmers *(Opers. Mgr.)*

Amway of New Zealand Limited (1)
Private Bag 94401, Greenmount
Auckland, New Zealand
Tel.: 64-9-274-9494 (100%)
Fax: 64-9-274-8844
Emp.: 36
Distribution of Amway Products
S.I.C.: 5963
Don Sutton *(Gen. Mgr.)*
Bruce Shankland *(Mng. Dir.)*

Amway (Schweiz) AG (1)
IndustrieStrasse 444 4703
Kestenholz, Switzerland
Tel.: 41-62-63 2525 (100%)
Telex: 982878
Fax: 41-62-632378
Emp.: 15
Distribution of Amway Products
S.I.C.: 5963
Stewart McArthur *(Mng. Dir.)*
Jim Payne *(Reg. Mgr.)*

Amway Taiwan, Ltd. (1)
8/F, No. 18, Section 4, Nan-King East Road
Taipei, Taiwan
Tel.: 886-2-741-7566 (100%)
Telex: 78524337
Fax: 886-741-9791
Emp.: 73
Distribution of Amway Products
S.I.C.: 5963
Audie Wong *(Gen. Mgr.)*
Eva Cheng *(Mng. Dir.)*

Amway (Thailand) Limited (1)
52/193 Ramkhamhaeng Rd. (Sukhapibal 3), Huamark, Bangapi,
Bangkok, 10240, Thailand
Tel.: 66-2-374-8000
Fax: 66-2-374-2918
Emp.: 53
Distribution of Amway Products
S.I.C.: 5963
Preecha Prakobkit *(Gen. Mgr.)*
L.H. Choong *(Mng. Dir.)*

Amway (U.K.) Limited (1)
Snowdon Dr., Winterhill
Milton Keynes, Buckinghamshire MK6 1AR, United Kingdom
Tel.: 44-908-679888 (100%)
Telex: 826817
Fax: 44-908-679811
Emp.: 63
Distribution of Amway Products
S.I.C.: 5963
Martin Williams *(Gen. Mgr.)*

ANAHEIM MANUFACTURING COMPANY
(Div. of Frigidaire Company)
4240 E. LaPalma
Anaheim, CA 92807
Mailing Address:
P. O. Box 4146
Anaheim, CA 92803
Tel.: 714-524-7770
Tel.: 800-854-3229
Fax: 714-996-7073
Year Founded: 1953
Approx.Sls.: $30,000,000
Emp.: 150
Fiscal Year-end: 1/31/91
Export
Mfr. Food Waste Disposers; Whirlaway, Sinkmaster, O.E.M. Brands & Private Label
S.I.C.: 3639
Thomas Dugan *(V.P. & Gen. Mgr.)*
John Alseth *(Controller)*
Kim Dyke *(Mgr.-Mktg. Services)*
Susanna Perosio *(Personnel Mgr.)*
Walter Kovacs *(Mgr.-Opers.)*

ANCHOR CONTINENTAL INCORPORATED
2000 S. Beltline Blvd.
Columbia, SC 29205
Tel.: 803-799-8800
Fax: 803-254-3367
Approx.Sls.: $70,000,000
Emp.: 800
Pressure Sensitive Tapes; Stone Culting Stencil
S.I.C.: 2672; 3559
Lacy Hayes *(Pres.)*
Dick Butcher *(Exec. V.P.)*
Mike Briggs *(V.P.-Mktg. & Human Resources)*
Bernie Lipka *(V.P.-Res. & Devel.)*
Grover Pilot *(V.P.-Engrng.)*
Ken Burton *(Comptroller)*
Merle Norris *(Mgr.-Sls.)*
Marion Francis *(Pur. Agent)*

Outside Service Firm(s):

Whaley, McCutchen, Blanton & Rhodes*(Legal Firm)*
Columbia, SC

ANCHOR FINANCIAL CORPORATION
2002 Oak St.
Myrtle Beach, SC 29577-3145
Mailing Address:
P.O. Box 2428
Myrtle Beach, SC 29578
Tel.: 803-448-1411
Fax: 803-946-3169
Year Founded: 1985
Assets: $155,009,403
Earnings: $1,000,391
Liabilities: $140,210,719
Net Worth: $14,798,684
Approx.Sls.: $13,102,827
Emp.: 84
Fiscal Year-end: 12/31/91
Bank Holding Company
S.I.C.: 6712; 6022
Stephen L. Chryst *(Pres. & Chief Exec. Officer)*
Tommy E. Looper *(Exec. V.P., Chief Fin. Officer & Sec.)*
John J. Moran *(V.P. & Asst. Controller)*
James H. Dusenbury *(Gen. Counsel)*

Outside Service Firm(s):

Price Waterhouse*(Auditors)*
Columbia, SC

Dusenbury, Hendrix & Little*(Legal Firm)*
602 27th Ave. N.
Myrtle Beach, SC 29577
Tel.: 803-448-7137

The Lourie Law Firm*(Legal Firm)*
1224 Pickens St.
Columbia, SC 29201
Tel.: 803-799-9805

ANCHOR GASOLINE CORPORATION
114 E. 5th Street
Tulsa, OK 74103
Tel.: 918-584-5291
Fax: 918-584-0595
Year Founded: 1940
Approx.Sls.: $110,000,000
Emp.: 20
Extraction & Manufacturing of Petroleum Products
S.I.C.: 1321; 1311
B.A. Mockley *(Chm. Bd. & Pres.)*
Michael E. Mockley *(Exec. V.P. & Chief Oper. Officer)*
Cooke Newman *(V.P.-Fin.)*
Ruth Harrison *(Sec.)*

No. of Mfg. Plants/Facilities: 1

Computer Systems/Hardware:
IBM PC; Digital

Outside Service Firm(s):

Ernst & Young*(Auditors)*
4300 One Williams Ctr.
Tulsa, OK 74142
Tel.: 918-560-3600
Fax: 918-560-3691

Moyers, Martin, Conway, Sante & Imel*(Legal Firm)*
Tulsa, OK

Bank of Oklahoma*(Major Banking Relationship)*
One Williams Center
Tulsa, OK 74012
Tel.: 918-588-5100

First Tulsa Bank*(Major Banking Relationship)*
15 East Fifth Street
Tulsa, OK 74103
Tel.: 918-586-5563

Subsidiaries:

Canal Refining Co. (1)
114 E. 5th St.
Tulsa, OK 74103
Tel.: 918-584-5291
B.A. Mockley *(Pres.)*

Cove Petroleum (1)
114 E. 5th St.
Tulsa, OK 74103
Tel.: 918-584-5291
B.A. Mockley *(Pres.)*

ANCHOR INDUSTRIES INC.
1100 Burch Dr.
Evansville, IN 47711
Mailing Address:
P.O. Box 3477
Evansville, IN 47733-3477
Tel.: 812-867-2421
Tel.: 800-544-4445
Fax: 812-867-1429
Year Founded: 1892
Approx.Sls.: $20,000,000
Emp.: 400
Fiscal Year-end: 9/30/92
Export
Canvas Awnings, Fabric & Vinyl-Laminated Tents, Trailer & Patio Awnings & Tarpaulins, Safety Pool Covers, Custom Canvas & Synthetic Fabric Industrial Covers, Private Label Bags
S.I.C.: 2394; 5039
John Daus, Jr. *(Pres. & Chief Exec. Officer)*
John Weber *(V.P.-Govt. Contract Sls.)*
Louis R. Brown *(V.P.-Tent Sls.)*
Pete Mogavero *(V.P.-Sls.)*
Robecca Phipps *(Treas.)*
Stella Stephens *(Dir.-Adv. & Mktg.)*
Earl Wells *(Dir.-Personnel)*
Glen Seger *(Dir.-Intl. Tent Sls.)*

ANCHOR TOOL & DIE COMPANY
11830 Brookpark Rd.
Cleveland, OH 44130
Tel.: 216-362-1850
Fax: 216-362-7442
Approx.Sls.: $28,000,000
Emp.: 225
Export
Manufacture Tools, Dies, Jigs, Fixtures & Metal Stampings; Machining & Welding Services& Assembly
S.I.C.: 3544; 3465; 3469; 7692; 3599
Edward Pfaff *(Chm. Bd.)*
Frederick A. Pfaff *(Pres.)*
D. Hrach *(V.P.-Sls.)*
Ronald R. Kozak *(V.P.-Fin.)*
Amelia Pfaff *(Sec.)*
Bonnie Dunlap *(Dir.-Human Resources)*
Dallas Griffith *(Dir.-Quality Control)*
Joseph J. Krish, Sr. *(Mgr.-Opers.)*
Principal(s):
Edward Pfaff

No. of Mfg. Plants/Facilities: 2

Outside Service Firm(s):

Society National Bank*(Major Banking Relationship)*
900 Euclid Ave., P.O. Box 6477
Cleveland, OH 44101-6477
Tel.: 216-737-5000
Fax: 216-566-8947

Anchor Tool & Die Company—(Continued)

Affiliate:

Condor Tool & Die, Inc. **(1)**
4541 Industrial Pkwy.
Cleveland, OH 44135
Tel.: 216-671-6000
Emp.: 25
Tool & Die Construction; Machining
S.I.C.: 3544; 3465; 3469
Dale Wagner *(Pres.)*
Jeff Pfaff *(V.P.)*

ANCO INSULATIONS, INC.
15981 Airline Hwy.
Baton Rouge, LA 70817
Tel.: 504-752-2000
Fax: 504-752-7686
Year Founded: 1962
Approx.Sls.: $95,000,000
Emp.: 2,000
Insulation Contractor & Wholesale Construction Materials
S.I.C.: 1742; 5039
Ruel L. Anderson, Jr. *(Pres. & Chief Exec. Officer)*
Ronald Bourgeois *(Exec. V.P.)*
William Devillier *(V.P.-Contracting)*
Harold F. Johnson *(V.P.-Construction)*
Thomas L. Virgets *(V.P.-Customer Rels.)*
John D. Walker *(Sec. & Treas.)*

Outside Service Firm(s):

H. J. Lowe*(Auditors)*
Baton Rouge, LA

Kean, Miller, Hawthorne, D'Armond, McCowan & Jarman*(Legal Firm)*
Baton Rouge, LA

Hibernia National Bank*(Major Banking Relationship)*
Baton Rouge, LA

ANCRA CORPORATION
4880 W. Rosecrans Ave.
Hawthorne, CA 90250
Tel.: 213-973-5000
Fax: 213-973-1138
Year Founded: 1969
Approx.Sls.: $70,000,000
Emp.: 450
Import Export
Winches, Fasteners, Cargo Nets
S.I.C.: 3531; 3965; 2298
Paul S. Brenia *(Chm., Pres. & Chief Exec. Officer)*
Joe McKeon *(Chief Oper. Officer & Group Pres.)*
Richard Chambliss *(Chief Fin. Officer)*
Ed Milhausen *(V.P.-Corp. Devel.)*
Victor Vaughn *(Controller)*
Ed Gokata *(Mgr.-Adv.)*
Al Coleman *(Mgr.-Pur.)*
Dan Rinkin *(Mgr.-Human Resources)*

Outside Service Firm(s):

Arthur Andersen & Co.*(Auditors)*
Torrance, CA

Caditz & Grant*(Legal Firm)*
Beverly Hills, CA

Barclays Bank plc*(Major Banking Relationship)*
Los Angeles, CA

Division:

Ancra Cincinatti **(1)**
3300 Turfway Rd., Suite 110
Erlanger, KY 41018
Tel.: 606-371-7272

Non-U.S. Holding:

Elfin Industries, Ltd. **(1)**
174 Maura Rd. P.O. Box 12675,
Auckland, 6, New Zealand
Winches, Fasteners & Cargo Nets
S.I.C.: 2298; 3531; 3965
Warren McIvor *(Chief Oper. Officer)*

ARTHUR ANDERSEN & CO., S.C.
1345 Avenue of the Americas
New York, NY 10019
Tel.: 212-708-4000 **IL**
Year Founded: 1913
Approx.Rev.: $5,600,000,000
Emp.: 60,100
Fiscal Year-end: 8/31/91
Certified Public Accountants; Tax Business Advisory & Information Technology Consulting
S.I.C.: 7389; 8721
Lawrence A. Weinbach *(Mng. Partner & Chief Exec. Officer)*
John D. Lewis *(Mng. Partner & Chief Fin. Officer)*
Stanley Cornelison *(Mng. Partner & Consultant)*
Jon N. Ekdahl *(Sec. & Gen. Counsel)*
Michael Grabish *(Dir.-Creative)*
Theresa Jaffe *(Dir.-Mktg.)*

No. of U.S. Offices: 75
No. of Foreign Offices: 150

Computer Systems/Hardware:
IBM System 4381; Wang VS 100

Outside Service Firm(s):

Chase Manhattan Bank, N.A.*(Investment Banker)*
One Chase Manhattan Plaza
New York, NY 10081
Tel.: 212-552-2222
Tel.: 800-526-0801
Fax: 212-552-7175

Sidley & Austin*(Legal Firm)*
One First National Plaza, 42nd Fl.
Chicago, IL 60603
Tel.: 312-853-7000
Fax: 312-853-7036

Divisions:

Arthur Andersen **(1)**
69 W. Washington
Chicago, IL 60602
Tel.: 312-580-0069
Approx.Rev.: $2,682,000,000
Emp.: 33,000
Audit, Advisory & Tax Services
S.I.C.: 8721
Richard L. Measelle *(Mng. Partner)*
Jose Luis Vazquez *(Chief Fin. Officer)*

Andersen Consulting **(1)**
69 W. Washington St.
Chicago, IL 60602
Tel.: 312-580-0069
Fax: 312-507-2548
Approx.Rev.: $2,299,000,000
Emp.: 25,000
Fiscal Year-end: 8/31/91
Business Consulting
S.I.C.: 8748
George T. Shaheen *(Mng. Partner)*
A. George Battle *(Mng. Partner-Mktg. Devel.)*
Doug G. Scrivner *(Mng. Partner-Litigation)*
Michael O. Hill *(Chief Fin. Officer)*
Rene Ordogne *(Controller)*
Jon N. Ekdahl *(Sec.)*
Gip Bonar *(Dir.-Res. & Devel.)*
Al Burgess *(Dir.-Telecommunications)*
Tom Fiske *(Dir.-Meetings Plng.)*
John Gullo *(Dir.-Mergers/Acquisitions)*
Bob Burton *(Dir.-Pur.)*
W. James Fischer *(Dir.-Tech. Services)*
Charles Paulk *(Dir.-Personnel Training & Devel.)*
Teresa Poggenpohl *(Dir.-Mkt. Res.)*
J. Robert Prince *(Mgr.-Personnel)*
Dan F. Collins *(Mgr.-Pub. Rels.)*
Marilyn Murray *(Librarian)*

Non-U.S. Holding:

Arthur Andersen & Co. **(1)**
1 Surrey St.
London, WC2R 2PS, United Kingdom
Tel.: 071-836 1200
Fax: 071-831 1133
Auditing, Tax & Management Information Counseling
S.I.C.: 8721
J.D. Hanson *(Mng. Partner)*

ANDERSEN WINDOWS INC.
(Formerly Andersen Corporation)
100 Fourth Ave. No.
Bayport, MN 55003-1096
Tel.: 612-439-5150
Fax: 612-430-7246
Year Founded: 1903
Approx.Sls.: $1,000,000,000
Emp.: 3,900
Fiscal Year-end: 12/31/90
Import Export
Mfr. Wood Windows, Patio Doors & Related Accessories
S.I.C.: 2431
Corporate Giving Program: Corporate Foundation
W. Arvid Wellman *(Chm. Bd.)*
Harold C. Meissner *(Vice Chm.)*
Jerold W. Wulf *(Pres. & Chief Exec. Officer)*
Len W. Kedrowski *(Chief Fin. Officer, Treas. & Controller)*
Alan Johnson *(V.P.-Opers.)*
Terry Anderson *(Mgr.-Personnel)*
Joseph E. Arndt *(Mgr.-Mktg. Communications)*
Ross A. Dahlin *(Mgr.-Export Sls.)*
Donald Garofalo *(Mgr.-Research & Product Devel.)*
John Jensen *(Mgr.-Employee Benefits)*
Paul S. Linduska *(Mgr.-Sls. & Mktg.)*
Laurence Sutten *(Mgr.-Pur.)*
Principal(s):
Harold C. Meissner

No. of Mfg. Plants/Facilities: 1
No. of U.S. Offices: 1

Computer Systems/Hardware:
Sperry-Univac

Outside Service Firm(s):

Ernst & Young*(Auditors)*
111 E. Kilbourn Ave., Ste. 900
Milwaukee, WI 53202
Tel.: 414-273-5900

Travelers Insurance Co.*(Group Insurer)*
1 Tower Square
Hartford, CT 06183-2492
Tel.: 203-277-4542
Fax: 203-277-5038

First Bank of St. Paul*(Investment Banker)*
St. Paul, MN

First National Bank of St. Paul*(Investment Banker)*
St. Paul, MN

Oppenheimer, Wolff & Donnelly*(Legal Firm)*
IDS Ctr., 45 S. Seventh St.
Minneapolis, MN 55402
Tel.: 612-344-9300
Fax: 612-344-9376

First Bank of St. Paul*(Major Banking Relationship)*
St. Paul, MN

First National Bank of Minneapolis*(Major Banking Relationship)*
Minneapolis, MN

First National Bank of Minneapolis*(Pension Manager)*
Minneapolis, MN

First National Bank of Minneapolis*(Pension Manager)*
Minneapolis, MN

First Trust Company, Inc.*(Pension Manager)*
332 Minnesota St.
St. Paul, MN 55113
Tel.: 612-223-7577

William M. Mercer Incorporated*(Pension Manager)*
1800 Piper Jaffray Tower
Minneapolis, MN 55402
Tel.: 612-338-5440

ANDERSON ADVERTISING, INC.
Anderson Exec. Center, 1017 N. Main, Ste. 300
San Antonio, TX 78212
Tel.: 210-223-6233
Fax: 210-223-9692
Year Founded: 1970
Approx.Billings: $24,000,000
Emp.: 49
James F. Anderson *(Chm. Bd.)*
Charles J. Anderson *(Pres.)*
Julius Germano *(Exec. V.P.)*
Allen J. Barrett *(V.P.)*
Brad Elmhorst *(V.P., Dir., Foodservice)*
Florence J. Anderson *(Treas.)*
Ken Clegg *(Controller)*
Lynn Nowak *(Mktg. Mgr.-Foodservice)*

ANDERSON BROTHERS CONSTRUCTION BRAINERD
1500 Highway 210 E.
Brainerd, MN 56401
Mailing Address:
P.O. Box 421
Brainerd, MN 56401
Tel.: 218-829-1768 **MN**
Year Founded: 1966
Approx.Sls.: $19,000,000
Emp.: 27
Road Construction Contractor
S.I.C.: 1611
James Anderson *(Chm. Bd. & Chief Exec. Officer)*
John T. Erickson *(Pres.)*
Linnea Anderson *(Sec.)*
Terrence M. Johnson *(Dir.-Fin.)*
Alan Jensen *(Dir.-Adv.)*
Donald C. Anderson *(Mgr.-Mktg. Opers. & Engrng.)*

Outside Service Firm(s):

John A. Knutson & Co.*(Auditors)*
Minneapolis, MN

First American Bank, N.A.*(Major Banking Relationship)*
Minneapolis, MN

ANDERSON DIE CASTINGS, INC.
1720 S. Wolf Rd.
Wheeling, IL 60090
Tel.: 708-541-3030
Fax: 708-541-4017
Year Founded: 1926
Approx.Sls.: $19,000,000
Emp.: 62
Zinc & Aluminum Die Castings
S.I.C.: 3363; 3364
Patrick Tang *(Pres.)*
Principal(s):
Patrick Tang

ANDERSON, DUSENBURY & ALBAN
3343 Peachtree Rd., N.E., Ste. M-50
Atlanta, GA 30326
Tel.: 404-364-2255
Fax: 404-364-2250
Year Founded: 1990
Approx.Billings: $10,000,000
Emp.: 7
Corporate Giving Program: United Way
Ernest R. Anderson *(Pres.)*
Leo Blumberg *(V.P., Mktg. Services)*
Kathy Stuntebeck *(Office Mgr.)*
Carolyn Fuller *(Acctg. Mgr.)*

ANDERSON INDUSTRIES, INC.
13601 Preston Rd., Ste. 307 West
Dallas, TX 75240
Tel.: 214-233-1805

Fax: 214-233-6332
Assets: $20,562,420
Liabilities: $11,990,624
Net Worth: $8,571,796
Approx.Sls.: $27,197,397
Emp.: 350
Diversified Holding Company; Mfr. of Metal Buildings, Boat Trailers & Athletic Goods
S.I.C.: 3448; 2329; 2339; 3792; 6719
Thomas L. Anderson *(Chm. Bd. & Pres.)*
John T. Eubanks *(V.P. & Treas.)*
Charles W. Anderson *(V.P. & Asst. Treas.)*
Shirley Calvert *(Sec.)*

Divisions:

Fab-Knit Manufacturing Co. **(1)**
1415 N. 4th St.
Waco, TX 76703
Tel.: 817-752-2511
Manufacture Athletic Clothing & Uniforms
S.I.C.: 2329; 2339
Robert K. Landon *(Pres.)*

Mesco Metal Buildings Corp. **(1)**
P.O. Box 20
Grapevine, TX 76051
Tel.: 817-488-8511
Emp.: 125
Pre-Engineered Metal Buildings
S.I.C.: 3448
Gary Heithecker *(Pres.)*

ANDERSON INDUSTRIES INC.
803 N. Church St.
Rockford, IL 61103
Tel.: 815-987-9070
Fax: 815-962-0660
Year Founded: 1917
Approx.Sls.: $140,800,000
Emp.: 1,300
Fiscal Year-end: 12/31/90
Holding Co.: Recreational Vehicle Hardware, Contract Pkg. & Venture Capital
S.I.C.: 3465; 3429; 6799; 7389; 6719
John R. Anderson *(Chm. Bd. & Pres.)*
R. Steven Holdeman *(Exec. V.P.)*
Principal(s):
John R. Anderson
Harry Conn
Jimmy Hall

Computer Systems/Hardware:
IBM PC

Outside Service Firm(s):

Coopers & Lybrand*(Auditors)*
6000 E. State St.
Rockford, IL 61108
Tel.: 815-394-0300

Amcore Bank*(Major Banking Relationship)*
Rockford, IL

ANDERSON & LEMBKE INC.
79 5th Ave., 17th Fl.
New York, NY 10003
Tel.: 212-886-2100
Year Founded: 1982
Approx.Billings: $68,000,000
Emp.: 66
Business to Business
Steve Trygg *(Chm. Bd. & New Bus. Contact)*
Hana Ullmark *(Pres.)*
Larry McNaughton *(Exec. V.P., Gen Mgr. & New Bus. Contact)*
Harald Bugge *(V.P., Intl.)*
Donald Hov *(Treas.)*

ANDERSON LITHOGRAPH COMPANY
3217 S. Garfield Ave.
Los Angeles, CA 90040
Tel.: 213-727-7767
Fax: 213-722-2328
Year Founded: 1951
Approx.Sls.: $110,000,000
Emp.: 400
Lithographic Commercial Printing, Annual Reports,Automotive Brochures, Offset
S.I.C.: 2752
Gene T. Parana *(Pres. & Chief Exec. Officer)*
John Fosmire *(Exec. V.P.-Mfg.)*
Arlyn Stanford *(Exec. V.P.)*
Garry D. Pearson *(V.P.-Sls., Los Angeles, CA)*
Alan Pemberton *(V.P. & Treas.)*
Fred J. Salazar *(V.P.-Sls., San Francisco, CA)*

Outside Service Firm(s):

Ernst & Young*(Auditors)*
515 S. Flower St.
Los Angeles, CA 90071
Tel.: 213-621-1666

Donnelly, Clark, Chase & Smiland*(Legal Firm)*
One Bunker Hill, 601 W. 5th St. 12th FL.
Los Angeles, CA 90071
Tel.: 213-891-1010

Security Pacific Corporation*(Major Banking Relationship)*
Security Pacific Plaza
Los Angeles, CA 90071
Tel.: 213-345-6211
Fax: 213-625-0809

ANDERSON LUMBER COMPANY
4700 S. Harrison Blvd.
Ogden, UT 84403
Tel.: 801-479-3400 **UT**
Fax: 801-476-1953
Year Founded: 1890
Approx.Sls.: $104,000,000
Emp.: 530
Wholesale Distribution of Rough, Dressed & Finished Lumber, Wallboard & Plywood; Home Centers
S.I.C.: 5031; 5211
James C. Beardall *(Chm. Bd., Pres. & Chief Exec. Officer)*
Guy Nickerson *(V.P.-Fin. & Treas.)*
William G. Zickgraf *(V.P.)*

Outside Service Firm(s):

First Security Bank of Utah*(Major Banking Relationship)*
Salt Lake City, UT

MARK ANDERSON ASSOCIATES, INC.
9 N. Vail
Arlington Heights, IL 60005
Tel.: 708-577-8505
Fax: 708-577-3618
Year Founded: 1977
Approx.Billings: $17,000,000
Emp.: 26
Business-to-Business Advertising Agency Specializing in Marketing Communications & Public Relations
S.I.C.: 7311
Mark R. Anderson *(Pres. & Chief Exec. Officer)*
Steven E. Bork *(Exec. V.P.)*
Marlene Lambert *(Dir.-Pub. Rels.)*
Rita DeCastello *(Mgr.-Admin. & Fin.)*

No. of Mfg. Plants/Facilities: 4
No. of U.S. Offices: 3

Computer Systems/Hardware:
MacIntosh, Apple

Outside Service Firm(s):

Miller-Cooper & Co., Ltd.*(Auditors)*
Chicago, IL

George T. Drost & Assoc. Ltd.*(Legal Firm)*
Arlington Heights, IL

Howard Simon Assocs.*(Pension Manager)*
Arlington Heights, IL

Branch:

Mark Anderson Associates, Inc. **(1)**
8335 Allison Pointe Trail, Ste. 340
Indianapolis, IN 46250
Tel.: 317-579-6030
Fax: 317-579-6031
Steven E. Bork *(Exec. V.P. & Mng. Dir.)*

Subsidiary:

Mark Anderson Associates, Inc. **(1)**
8700 Via De Ventura, Ste. 235
Scottsdale, AZ 85258
Tel.: 602-483-0133
Fax: 602-443-1071
James A. Layne *(Mng. Dir.)*
Gary Delude *(Pub. Rels. & Acct. Exec.)*

ANDERSON, ROTHSTEIN & FIQUA
28 Geary St., 7th Fl.
San Francisco, CA 94108
Tel.: 415-394-8000
Fax: 415-394-5588
Year Founded: 1977
Approx.Billings: $16,600,000
Emp.: 28
Food & Food Related Accounts
Norm Anderson *(Pres., Chief Exec. Officer)*
Jim Fiqua *(Exec. V.P.)*
Pearl Gee *(Controller)*

ANDERSON TRUCKING SERVICE INC.
203 Cooper Ave. N.
Saint Cloud, MN 56302
Mailing Address:
P.O. Box 1377
St. Cloud, MN 56301
Tel.: 612-255-7400
Tel.: 800-328-2316 **MN**
Fax: 612-255-7432
Year Founded: 1955
Approx.Sls.: $100,000,000
Emp.: 500
Import Export
Trucking Common Carrier
S.I.C.: 4213
Corporate Giving Program: United Way-Annual Fund Drive
Harold E. Anderson *(Pres.)*
Rollie Anderson *(V.P.)*
Daniel Bishop *(V.P.-Sls.-Flat Bed)*
Jim DeBroux *(V.P.-Mktg.-Vans)*
Oscar D. Kleman, Jr. *(V.P.-Human Resources)*
Jon C. Beaulieu *(Treas.)*
Principal(s):
Harold E. Anderson

Outside Service Firm(s):

R. J. McKinley*(Auditors)*
Eagan, MN

Hall, Byers, Hanson, Still & Weinberger*(Legal Firm)*
St. Cloud, MN

First American National Bank*(Major Banking Relationship)*
Saint Cloud, MN

Subsidiary:

K & W Transportation **(1)**
P.O. Box 1377,
Saint Cloud, MN 56302
Tel.: 612-255-7474
Tel.: 800-328-8524
Emp.: 50
Transportation
S.I.C.: 4213

ANDERSON-TULLY CO.
1242 N. 2nd St.
Memphis, TN 38107
Mailing Address:
P.O. Box 28
Memphis, TN 38101
Tel.: 901-576-1400
Fax: 901-526-8842
Year Founded: 1889
Approx.Sls.: $34,400,000
Emp.: 900
Fiscal Year-end: 12/31/91

Export
Kiln-Dried Hardwood, Industrial Floor Blocks & Laminated Truck Flooring
S.I.C.: 2426
John M. Tully *(Pres.)*
P. Lewis Jr. *(1st V.P.)*
E.D. Coombs, Jr. *(V.P. & Treas.)*
Bruce Nesmith *(V.P.-Vix Opers.)*
Tony R. Parks *(V.P.-Land Mngmt.)*
John O. Schaffhauser *(V.P.-Lumber Sls.)*
V.L. Tucker *(Pur. Agent)*

Principal(s):
John M. Tully

Computer Systems/Hardware:
Data General

Outside Service Firm(s):

Deloitte & Touche*(Auditors)*
Memphis, TN

Martin, Tate, Morrow & Marston, P.C.*(Legal Firm)*
Union Planters Natl. Bank Bldg.
Memphis, TN 38103
Tel.: 901-525-5881

Union Planters National Bank*(Major Banking Relationship)*
Memphis, TN

ANDERSON WHOLESALE COMPANY
2211 W. Shawnee
Muskogee, OK 74401
Mailing Address:
P.O. Box 69
Muskogee, OK 74402
Tel.: 918-682-5568 **OK**
Fax: 918-687-9567
Year Founded: 1949
Assets: $7,934,067
Liabilities: $5,812,458
Net Worth: $2,121,609
Approx.Sls.: $27,000,000
Emp.: 200
Fiscal Year-end: 6/30/90
Distribute Health & Beauty Aids, Housewares, School Supplies, Toys, Stationery, Soft Goods, Notions, Electrical Items, Candy, Pet Needs, Ammunition & Automotive
S.I.C.: 5063; 5023; 5091; 5092; 5112; 5131; 5145; 5013
James T. Anderson *(Chm.)*
John F. Anderson *(Vice Chm.)*
John Gilliam *(Pres.)*
Brent Anderson *(V.P. & Chief Information Officer)*
Mike Anderson *(V.P. & Chief Fin. Officer)*
James W. Thomas *(Sec. & Gen. Mgr.)*
Mark Anderson *(Dir.-Opers.)*
Jerry Frazier *(Dir.-Pur. & Mdsg.)*
Tom Shelton *(Dir.-Data Processing)*
Victor Buie *(Warehouse Mgr.)*
Charles Frazier *(Buyer)*
Ray Orman *(Buyer)*
Alan Dismukes *(Buyer)*

Principal(s):
James T. Anderson

Outside Service Firm(s):

Moffitt, Parker & Co.*(Auditors)*
Muskogee, OK

Grober & Shumacher*(Legal Firm)*
Muskogee, OK

Commercial Bank & Trust Co.*(Major Banking Relationship)*
Muskogee, OK

THE ANDERSONS
1200 Dussel Dr.
Maumee, OH 43537
Mailing Address:
P.O. Box 119,
Maumee, OH 43537
Tel.: 419-893-5050
Fax: 419-891-6513
Year Founded: 1947
Assets: $293,000,532
Earnings: $3,860,788
Liabilities: $247,139,909
Net Worth: $45,860,623
Approx.Sls.: $656,824,165
Emp.: 2,300
Fiscal Year-end: 12/31/91

Import Export
Grain Merchandising, Handling & Related Products; Retail Stores; Agricultural & Lawn Fertilizer Products; Corn Cob Milling
S.I.C.: 5153; 5399
Corporate Giving Program: Anderson Foundation
Employee Matching Gifts Program: Maximum of $2,000 Per Full Time Employee
Tom Anderson *(Chm. Bd.)*
Richard P. Anderson *(Pres. & Chief Exec. Officer)*
Dale Fallat *(Exec. V.P.-Govt. Affairs)*
Mike Anderson *(V.P.-Grain Group)*
Joseph Broker *(V.P.-Agricultural Prods.)*
Terry Rigel *(V.P.-Retail Group)*
Gary Smith *(Treas.)*
Beverly McBride *(Gen. Counsel & Corp. Sec.)*
Chuck Gallagher *(Dir.-Personnel)*
Bill Schmoekle *(Dir.-Telecommunications)*
Merl Thomas *(Dir.-Mngmt. Information Systems)*
Richard George *(Controller)*
Chris Anderson *(Gen. Mgr.-Venture & Bus. Devel.)*
Rick Anderson *(Gen. Mgr.-Ind. Prods.)*
Peter Machin *(Gen. Mgr.-Farm Prods.)*
Jennifer Perry *(Mgr.-Employee Benefits)*
Nick Conrad *(Cash Mgr.)*

Computer Systems/Hardware:
Hewlett-Packard

Outside Service Firm(s):

Ernst & Young*(Auditors)*
One Sea Gate
Toledo, OH 43604
Tel.: 419-244-8000

Ohio Co.*(Investment Banker)*
Toledo, OH

Toledo Trust Co.*(Major Banking Relationship)*
Toledo, OH

Society National Bank*(Pension Manager)*
900 Euclid Ave., P.O. Box 6477
Cleveland, OH 44101-6477
Tel.: 216-737-5000
Fax: 216-566-8947

Subsidiaries:

The Andersons Investment Services Corp. **(1)**
1200 Dussel Dr.
Maumee, OH 43537
Tel.: 419-891-2750
Fax: 419-891-6516

The Andersons White Pigeon Terminal **(1)**
13600 Anderson Rd.
White Pigeon, MI 49099
Tel.: 616-483-7691
Grain Elevator
S.I.C.: 4221

B & R Pet Supplies, Inc. **(1)**
1142 Ave. South
Grand Prairie, TX 75050
Tel.: 214-641-3859
Wholesale Put Supplier
S.I.C.: 5199

ANDIAMO, INC.
P.O. Box 8415,
Fountain Valley, CA 92728
Mailing Address:
P.O. Box 8415,
Fountain Valley, CA 92728
Year Founded: 1976
Approx.Sls.: $10,000,000
Emp.: 140
Fiscal Year-end: 12/31/90
Mfr. Luggage
S.I.C.: 3161
Jay Myers *(Pres. & Dir.-Adv.)*

ANDIS COMPANY
1718 Layard Ave.
Racine, WI 53404
Tel.: 414-634-3356
Fax: 414-634-1641
Year Founded: 1922
Approx.Sls.: $12,000,000
Emp.: 140
Fiscal Year-end: 12/31/91
Mfr. of Andis Clippers & Blow Dryers for the Professional Market; Hair Curlers; Home Market Products; Pet Grooming Clippers, Razors, Trimmers; Personal Care Appliances
S.I.C.: 3523; 3999
M. L. Andis *(Chm. Bd. & Pres.)*
Robert Gesinski *(V.P.-Fin. & Chief Fin. Officer)*
Fred Koeller *(V.P.-Mktg.)*
Denton Richards *(V.P.-Retail Sls.)*
Norman Hermann *(Pur. Mgr.)*
Chris Ritzman *(Dir.-Adv.)*
Elaine Severson *(Dir.-Data Processing)*

Computer Systems/Hardware:
IBM System 36

Outside Service Firm(s):

CNA Insurance*(Group Insurer)*
CNA Plaza,
Chicago, IL 60685
Tel.: 312-822-5000

Thompson & Coates*(Legal Firm)*
Racine, WI

M & I Bank of Racine*(Major Banking Relationship)*
Racine, WI

ANDMORE SPORTSWEAR CORPORATION
21 Minisink Ave.
Port Jervis, NY 12771 **NY**
Tel.: 914-856-5291
Fax: 914-858-8645
Year Founded: 1949
Assets: $5,827,307
Liabilities: $3,243,407
Net Worth: $2,583,900
Approx.Sls.: $17,000,000
Emp.: 300
Fiscal Year-end: 12/31/90
Mfr. Sportswear; Team Apparel Supplier; Bathing Suits
S.I.C.: 2253; 5961; 2329; 2339
Philip Platania *(Pres., Chief Exec. & Chief Fin. Officer)*
Andrew Platania *(V.P.)*
John Platania *(Sec.)*
Betty Wilcox *(Controller & Dir.-Mngmt. Information Systems)*
Steve Seis *(Mgr.-Sls.-Mystic Bay)*

Computer Systems/Hardware:
IBM 5291 Model 2

Outside Service Firm(s):

Kipnis & Karchmer*(Auditors)*
386 Park Ave. S.
New York, NY 10016
Tel.: 212-447-5588

Bondy & Schloss*(Legal Firm)*
6 East 43rd St.
New York, NY 10017
Tel.: 212-661-3535

Chemical Bank*(Major Banking Relationship)*
450 West 33rd St.
New York, NY 10001
Tel.: 212-613-7197
Fax: 212-947-7628

National Community Bank*(Major Banking Relationship)*
Maywood, NJ

Subsidiary:

The Finals, Ltd. **(1)**
21 Minisink Ave.
Port Jervis, NY 12771
Tel.: 914-856-5291
Mfr. Competitive Swimwear & Active Wear
S.I.C.: 2329; 2339; 2253
Philip Platania *(Pres.)*

ANDREWS GROUP, INCORPORATED
21 E. 63rd St.
New York, NY 10021
Tel.: 212-593-4300 **CA**
Fax: 212-421-1617
Assets: $270,017,000
Earnings: $107,000
Liabilities: $241,538,000
Net Worth: $28,479,000
Approx.Rev.: $155,689,000
Emp.: 6,150
Fiscal Year-end: 12/31/90
Holding Co.
S.I.C.: 5122; 6719; 5912; 7384; 7819; 7822
Ronald O. Perelman *(Chm. Bd. & Chief Exec. Officer)*
Howard Gittis *(Vice Chm.)*
Bruce Slovin *(Pres.)*
Fred L. Tepperman *(Sr. Exec. V.P. & Chief Fin. Officer)*

Outside Service Firm(s):

KPMG Peat Marwick*(Auditors)*
725 S. Figueroa St.
Los Angeles, CA 90017
Tel.: 213-972-4000

Gibson, Dunn & Crutcher*(Legal Firm)*
333 S. Grand Ave.
Los Angeles, CA 90067
Tel.: 310-552-8500
Fax: 310-277-5827

Bank of America NT&SA*(Major Banking Relationship)*
555 So. Flower St., 5th Fl.
Los Angeles, CA 90071
Tel.: 213-228-3526
Fax: 213-228-4062

Continental Bank N. A.*(Major Banking Relationship)*
231 S. LaSalle St.
Chicago, IL 60697
Tel.: 312-828-2345
Tel.: 800-426-5754
Telex: 312-828-1783

Division:

Compact Sound Services **(1)**
2813 W. Alameda Ave.
Burbank, CA 91505
Tel.: 818-840-7000
Film & Videotape
John Donlon *(Pres.)*

Subsidiaries:

Compact Video Services, Inc. **(1)**
2813 W. Alameda
Burbank, CA 91505
Tel.: 818-840-7000
Emp.: 148
Videotape & Film Post Production Services
S.I.C.: 7384; 7819
John Donlon *(Pres.)*

Four Star Holdings Corp. **(1)**
1440 So. Sepulveda Blvd.
Los Angeles, CA 90025
Tel.: 213-444-8100 (100%)
Emp.: 17
Television & Motion Picture Production
S.I.C.: 7812; 7822

Image Transform **(1)**
4142 Lankershim Blvd.
North Hollywood, CA 91602
Tel.: 818-985-7566
Emp.: 85
Telecine, Standards Conversion, Tape to Film, Film Processing, Duplication
S.I.C.: 7384; 7819
Richard Lebre *(Pres.)*

Plant:

Image Transform Lab **(2)**
3611 San Fernando Road
Burbank, CA 91506
Tel.: 818-841-3832
Telecine, Standards Conversion, Tape to Film, Film Processing, Duplication
S.I.C.: 7384; 7819
Dick Lebre *(Pres.)*

New World Entertainment, Inc. **(1)**
1440 S. Sepulveda Blvd.
Los Angeles, CA 90025
Tel.: 310-444-8100
Fax: 310-444-8540
Earnings: ($4,659,000)
Approx.Rev.: $279,373,000
Emp.: 100
Import Export
Motion Picture & Television Production & Distribution
S.I.C.: 7812
James McNamara *(Pres. & Chief Exec. Officer)*
Robert C. Peters *(Pres. & Chief Oper. Officer)*
Brian Frons *(Exec. V.P.-New World Televison)*
Larry Levin *(Sr. V.P.-Special Projects)*
Jerry Zanitsch *(V.P.-Mktg.)*
Joan Mazzarella *(V.P.-Finance)*
Paul A. Birmingham *(V.P.-Admin.)*
Ray Donahue *(V.P.-Intl.)*
Thea Diserio *(V.P.-Intl.)*
Sidney R. Mandell *(V.P.-Post Production)*
John Janisch *(V.P.-Production Acctg.)*
Emmet G. Lavery, Jr. *(V.P.-Bus. Affairs)*

Vid America, Inc. **(1)**
231 E. 55 St.
New York, NY 10022
Tel.: 212-355-1600
Emp.: 7
Motion Picture Film Exchanges
S.I.C.: 7822
Alfred Markim *(Pres.)*

ANDREWS/MAUTNER, INC.
600 N. Broadway
Milwaukee, WI 53202
Tel.: 414-272-4482
Fax: 414-272-2669
Year Founded: 1943
Approx.Billings: $13,107,000
Emp.: 25
Business-to-Business, Financial & Healthcare
Christopher M. Vernon *(Chm. Bd.)*
Kenneth W. Snyder *(Pres.)*
Stephen F. Johnstone *(Sr. V.P., Pub. Rels. Dir.)*
Terry Thomas *(V.P., Adv.)*
William W. Sheahan *(V.P., Adv. & Pub. Rels.)*

ANGELO BROTHERS CO.
12401 McNulty Rd.
Philadelphia, PA 19154
Tel.: 215-671-2000
Tel.: 800-289-8359
Fax: 215-464-4115
Year Founded: 1943
Approx.Sls.: $70,000,000
Emp.: 525
Wholesale Decorative Electrical Products & Lamp Parts
S.I.C.: 5063
Stanley Angelo, Jr. *(Chm. Bd.)*
Ray Angelo *(Pres.)*

John Angelo *(Exec. V.P.-Opers.)*
Ed Dean *(V.P.-Sls.)*
Lou DiLossi *(V.P.-Fin.)*
Leonard Dubas *(V.P.-Mktg.)*
Pat Fleming *(V.P.-Adv.)*
Louis Kuchler *(V.P.-Pur.)*
Kathy Lane *(V.P.-Personnel)*
Frank Schiavo *(V.P.-Lighting/ Electrical Sls.)*
Fred Tomlin *(V.P.-Opers.)*
Vicki Boyer *(Sec.)*
Pat Kerwin *(Dir.-Creative)*
Owen Forrest *(Mgr.-MIS)*

Outside Service Firm(s):

Margolis & Co.*(Auditors)*
Bala Cynwyd, PA

Continental Bank N. A.*(Major Banking Relationship)*
231 S. LaSalle St.
Chicago, IL 60697
Tel.: 312-828-2345
Tel.: 800-426-5754
Telex: 312-828-1783

ANGLERS ROSLYN GROUP LTD.
45-25 162nd St.
Flushing, NY 11358
Tel.: 718-961-7744
Fax: 718-445-1384
Approx.Sls.: $12,000,000
Emp.: 280
Mfr. of Vinyl School Stationery & Art Items, High Frequency Welded And/ Or Sewn
S.I.C.: 3089
Gerrson Strassberg *(Pres.)*
Stuart Schrager *(V.P.-Opers.)*
Roslyn Strassberg *(Sec.)*

Outside Service Firm(s):

Buchbinder, Stein, Tunick & Platkin*(Auditors)*
One Pennsylvania Plaza
New York, NY 10119-0219

Bank of New York*(Major Banking Relationship)*
90 Washington St.
New York, NY 10015

ANGLO FABRICS COMPANY, INC.
561 Seventh Ave., 16th Fl.
New York, NY 10018
Tel.: 212-736-2230
Fax: 212-391-6698
Year Founded: 1940
Approx.Sls.: $25,000,000
Emp.: 400
Fiscal Year-end: 12/31/90
Woolens & Worsteds
S.I.C.: 2299
John Honig *(Pres.)*
Fred Natkin *(V.P.)*
David Siegel *(V.P.-Sls.)*
Leonard Siegel *(V.P. & Treas.)*
Peter Asplen *(Dir.-Adv.)*

ANGUS CHEMICAL COMPANY
1500 East Lake Cook Rd.
Buffalo Grove, IL 60089
Tel.: 708-215-8600
Tel.: 800-362-2580
Telex: 275422 ANGUS UR
Fax: 708-215-8626
Year Founded: 1982
Approx.Sls.: $125,000,000
Emp.: 330
Export
Manufacturer & Marketer of Nitroparaffins & Derivatives
S.I.C.: 2869; 2899
Roger E. Secrist *(Chm. & Chief Exec. Officer)*
O. Wayne Chandler *(Vice Chm.)*
Gary W. Granzon *(Pres. & Chief Oper. Officer)*
Robert J. Frederick *(V.P.-Admin.)*
Janet E. Mann *(V.P.-Mktg.)*
James E. Morrison *(V.P.-Fin. & Chief Fin. Officer)*
Kenton E. Gulledge *(V.P.-Opers.)*
Alan T. Radcliffe *(V.P.-Europe)*
Kent S. Strong *(V.P.-Sls. & Tech. Services)*
Lowell D. Pals *(V.P.-Intl.)*
Robert L. Klein *(V.P.-Res. & Devel.)*
Cindi Maher *(Communications Supvr.)*

Non-U.S. Holdings:

ANGUS Chemie GmbH **(1)**
Essen, Germany (100%)
Manufacturer of Fine Chemicals
S.I.C.: 2869; 2899

ANGUS Fine Chemicals Ltd. **(1)**
Ringaskiddy, County Cork Ireland (100%)
Manufacturer of Fine Chemicals
S.I.C.: 2869; 2899

Alberta National Gas Company Ltd. **(1)**
240 Fourth Ave. S.W. P.O. Box 2900,
Calgary, AB T2P 4L7, Canada
Tel.: 403-691-7777
S.I.C.: 1311

ANNABELLE CANDY COMPANY
27211 Industrial Blvd.
Hayward, CA 94545
Mailing Address:
P.O. Box 3665
Hayward, CA 94540
Tel.: 510-783-2900 **CA**
Fax: 510-785-7675
Year Founded: 1954
Sales Range: $10-19 Million
Emp.: 85
Fiscal Year-end: 12/31/90
Export
Mfr. Candy & Chocolate
S.I.C.: 2064; 2066
Annabelle Block *(Chm. Bd.)*
Gary J. Gogol *(Pres. & Chief Exec. Officer)*
Colleen J. Peters *(V.P. & Fin. Administrator)*
Susan Gamson Karl *(V.P. & Chief Fin. Officer)*
Principal(s):
Annabelle Block

No. of Mfg. Plants/Facilities: 1
No. of U.S. Offices: 1

Computer Systems/Hardware:
IBM 36

Division:

Concord Division **(1)**
1221 Franquette Ave.
Concord, CA 94520
Tel.: 510-685-8130
Mfr. of Abba-Zaba, U-No Bar, U-No Mint Bar
S.I.C.: 2064; 2066

ANNIN & COMPANY
One Annin Dr.
Roseland, NJ 07068
Tel.: 201-228-9400
Fax: 201-228-1633
Year Founded: 1847
Sales Range: $20-39 Million
Emp.: 450
Fiscal Year-end: 12/31/88
Export
Manufacture Flags, Banners, Pennants & Flagpoles
S.I.C.: 2399; 2499; 3446
C. Randolph Beard, Jr. *(Pres.)*
C.L. Beard *(V.P. & Sec.)*
John N. Dennis *(V.P.-Sls. Dept.)*
Henry P. Hibo *(V.P. & Controller)*

No. of Mfg. Plants/Facilities: 6
No. of U.S. Offices: 1

Computer Systems/Hardware:
Qantel

Outside Service Firm(s):

Arthur Andersen & Co.*(Auditors)*
P.O. Box 221, 101 Eisenhower Pkwy.
Roseland, NJ 07068
Tel.: 201-403-6100
Fax: 201-403-0579

Chubb Group*(Commercial Insurance Carrier)*
Warren, NJ

Booth, Bate & Greico*(Legal Firm)*
Montclair, NJ

Chemical Bank*(Major Banking Relationship)*
Morristown, NJ

The Anniston Star
(See Consolidated Publishing Company Listing)

ANO-COIL CORPORATION
60 E. Main St.
Rockville, CT 06066
Tel.: 203-871-1200
Fax: 203-872-0534
Approx.Sls.: $20,000,000
Anodized Aluminum & Lithographic
S.I.C.: 3471; 3555
Howard A. Fromson *(Pres.)*
Michael Fromson *(V.P.-Fin.)*
C.G. Knorr *(V.P.-Sls.)*

Outside Service Firm(s):

Deloitte & Touche*(Auditors)*
Hartford, CT

Jackson & Nash*(Legal Firm)*
Rockville, CT

Connecticut Bank & Trust*(Major Banking Relationship)*
New Haven, CT

ANSCHUTZ CORPORATION
2400 Anaconda Tower, 555 17th St.
Denver, CO 80202
Tel.: 303-298-1000
Fax: 303-298-8881
Sales Range: $1 Billion +
Holding Company; Oil & Gas Extraction; General Building Contractors; Real Estate; Railroad Operations
S.I.C.: 1382; 1311; 1381; 6719
Philip Anschutz *(Pres.)*
Miles A. Williams *(Exec. V.P.)*
D.L. Polson *(V.P.-Fin.)*
Richard Jones *(V.P. & Gen. Counsel)*
Thomas G. Kundert *(Treas.)*
Craig Slater *(Sec.)*
Jim Bane *(Dir.-Adv.)*
Doug Lindsey *(Mgr.-Intl.)*

Outside Service Firm(s):

KPMG Peat Marwick*(Auditors)*
707 17th St.
Denver, CO 80202
Tel.: 303-296-2323
Fax: 303-295-8829

Great-West Life Assurance Co.*(Group Insurer)*
8505 East Orchard Rd.
Englewood, CO 8011
Tel.: 800-537-2033

Holme Roberts & Owen*(Legal Firm)*
1701 Lincoln St., Ste. 4100
Denver, CO 80202
Tel.: 303-861-7000

Subsidiaries:

The Rio Grande Industries Inc. **(1)**
P.O. Box 5482
Denver, CO 80217
Tel.: 303-629-5533 (100%)
Holding Company: Real Estate Investors & Operators of Non-Residential Buildings
S.I.C.: 6512; 6719; 4011
W.J. Holtman *(Chm., Pres. & Chief Exec. Officer)*
Kenneth Sanford *(V.P. & Gen. Counsel)*

Subsidiary:

Denver & Rio Grande Western Railroad Co. **(2)**
P.O. Box 5482
Denver, CO 80217
Tel.: 303-629-5533 (100%)
Transportation by Rail
S.I.C.: 4011; 4119
W.J. Holtman *(Pres.)*
L.R. Parsons *(V.P.-Opers.)*

Subsidiary:

Rio Grande Land Co. **(3)**
1515 Arapahoe St.
Denver, CO 80202
Tel.: 303-629-5533 (100%)
Developers of Industrial Land
S.I.C.: 6552
H.A. Phillips *(Pres.)*

Southern Pacific Transportation Co. **(1)**
One Market Plaza, Southern Pacific Bldg.
San Francisco, CA 94105
Tel.: 415-541-1000 (100%)
Earnings: $219,417,000
Approx.Rev.: $2,412,111,000
Fiscal Year-end: 12/31/89
Railroad
S.I.C.: 4011; 4213
D.M. Mohan *(Pres. & Chief Exec. Officer)*

Subsidiaries:

Los Angeles Union Terminal, Inc. **(2)**
746 S. Central Ave., Rm. 250
Los Angeles, CA 90021
Tel.: 213-627-9767 (100%)
Manages Properties
S.I.C.: 6531

Northwestern Pacific Railroad Co. **(2)**
One Market Plaza, Southern Pacific Bldg.
San Francisco, CA 94105
Tel.: 415-541-1000 (100%)
Railroad
S.I.C.: 4011
D.M. Mohan *(Pres.)*

Pacific Fruit Express Co. **(2)**
100 Valley Dr.
Brisbane, CA 94005
Tel.: 415-541-1000 (100%)
Refrigerator Car Service; Sub. of Southern Pacific Transportation Co., Dormant
S.I.C.: 4741
D.M. Mohan *(Pres.)*

Pacific Motor Transport Co. **(2)**
1766 El Camino Real
Burlingame, CA 94010
Tel.: 415-692-1300 (100%)
Trucking; Sub. of Southern Pacific Transportation Co.
S.I.C.: 4213
E.P. Ahern *(Chmn.)*

Pacific Motor Trucking Co. **(2)**
1766 El Camino Real
Burlingame, CA 94010
Tel.: 415-692-1300 (100%)
Trucking; Sub. of Southern Pacific Transportation Co.
S.I.C.: 4213
R.J. O'Leary *(Chm. Bd. & Pres.)*

Subsidiary:

PMT of the Southwest, Inc. **(3)**
1766 El Camino Real
Burlingame, CA 94010
Tel.: 415-692-1300 (100%)
Trucking
S.I.C.: 4213
R.J. O'Leary *(Chmn. & Pres.)*

SP Telcom Corporation **(2)**
One Market Plaza
San Francisco, CA 94105
Tel.: 415-541-1000 (100%)
Lease-Out Freight Cars; Sub. of Southern Pacific Transportation Co.
S.I.C.: 4741
Stephen Hanson *(Exec. V.P.)*

St. Louis Southwestern Railway Co. **(2)**
One Market Plaza, Southern Pacific Bldg.
San Francisco, CA 94105
Tel.: 415-541-1000 (99.83%)

Anschutz Corporation—(Continued)

Railroad
S.I.C.: 4011
D.M. Mohan *(Pres.)*

Subsidiary:

Dallas Terminal Railway and Union Depot Co. **(3)**
One Market Plaza, Southern Pacific Bldg.
San Francisco, CA 94105
Tel.: 415-541-1000 (100%)
Railroad
S.I.C.: 4013
K.A. Moore *(Pres.)*

Affiliates:

The Alton & Southern Railway Co. **(3)**
210 N. 13th St.
Saint Louis, MO 63103
Tel.: 314-622-2022 (50%)
Railroad
S.I.C.: 4013
D.M. Mohan *(Pres.)*

Arkansas & Memphis Railway Bridge and Terminal Co. **(3)**
Southern Pacific Bldg., One Market Plaza
San Francisco, CA 94105
Tel.: 415-541-1000 (66.6%)
Operation of Railroad Bridge
S.I.C.: 4789
L.G. Simpson *(Pres.)*

Kansas City Terminal Railway Co. **(3)**
3435 Broadway
Kansas City, MO 64111
Tel.: 816-753-8411 (8.33%)
Railroad
S.I.C.: 4013
G.W. Thompson *(Pres. & Gen. Mgr.)*

Southern Illinois and Missouri Bridge Co. **(3)**
210 N. 13th St.
Saint Louis, MO 63103
Tel.: 314-622-2022 (40%)
Operation of Railroad Bridge
S.I.C.: 4789
R.K. Davidson *(Pres.)*

Terminal Railroad Association of St. Louis **(3)**
2016 Madison Ave.
Granite City, IL 62040
Tel.: 618-451-8443 (12.5%)
Railroad Terminal Facilities
S.I.C.: 4013
B.C. Davidson *(Pres.)*

Southern Pacific Warehouse Co. **(2)**
One Market Plaza, Southern Pacific Bldg.
San Francisco, CA 94105
Tel.: 415-541-1000 (100%)
Warehousing
S.I.C.: 4225
R.E. Mesick *(Pres.)*

Sunset Railway Co. **(2)**
One Market Plaza, Southern Pacific Bldg.
San Francisco, CA 94105
Tel.: 415-541-1000 (50%)
Railroad
S.I.C.: 4011
R.E. Welk *(Pres.)*

Visalia Electric Railroad Co. **(2)**
One Market Plaza, Southern Pacific Bldg.
San Francisco, CA 94105
Tel.: 415-541-1000 (100%)
Railroad
S.I.C.: 4011
K.A. Moore *(Pres.)*

Affiliates:

Central California Traction Co. **(2)**
One Market Plaza
San Francisco, CA 94105
Tel.: 415-541-1000 (33.33%)
Railroad; 33.3 Owned by The Atchison, Topeka & Santa Fe Railway Co.
S.I.C.: 4011
A.W. Rees *(Pres.)*

The Ogden Union Railway and Depot Co. **(2)**
198 W. 28th St.
Ogden, UT 84401
Tel.: 801-626-8321 (50%)
Depot Co.; Affiliate of Southern Pacific Transportation Co.
S.I.C.: 4789
K.A. Moore *(Pres.)*

Portland Terminal Railroad Co. **(2)**
Union Station, Rm. 209, 800 N.W. 6th
Portland, OR 97209
Tel.: 503-228-2630 (20%)
Terminal Facilities; Sub. of Southern Pacific Transportation Co.
S.I.C.: 4013
G.A. Greblo *(Pres.)*

Portland Traction Co. **(2)**
1640 S.E. Water Ave.
Portland, OR 97214
Tel.: 503-233-5481 (50%)
Railroad; Sub. of Southern Pacific Transportation Co.
S.I.C.: 4013
K.A. Moore *(Pres.)*

ANSCO PHOTO-OPTICAL PRODUCTS CORP.
(Sub. of Haking Intl.)
1801 Touhy Ave.
Elk Grove Village, IL 60007
Tel.: 708-593-7404
Tel.: 800-323-6697
Fax: 708-981-0108
Approx.Sls.: $16,000,000
Emp.: 35
Fiscal Year-end: 12/31/91
Import Export
Wholesale Cameras
S.I.C.: 5043
Fred Wong *(Exec. V.P.)*
Earl Moss *(Prod. Mgr.-Cameras)*
Betsy Skibinski *(Midwest Reg. Mgr.)*

BENJAMIN ANSEHL COMPANY
1555 Page Industrial Blvd.
Saint Louis, MO 63132
Tel.: 314-429-4300
Fax: 314-429-5459
Approx.Sls.: $23,000,000
Emp.: 120
Mfr. Personal Care Products
S.I.C.: 2844
W. Linton Edwards III *(Pres.)*
Robert Ballard *(V.P.-Fin.)*
Sol Benkendorf *(V.P.-Res. & Devel.)*
William Bond *(V.P.-Sls.)*
Kip Bowers *(Mgr.-Prod. Devel.)*

ANSER (ANALYTIC SERVICES INC.)
1215 Jeff Davis Hwy., Ste. 800
Arlington, VA 22202
Tel.: 703-685-1000 **CA**
Fax: 703-685-3225
Year Founded: 1958
Assets: $17,150,000
Liabilities: $3,350,000
Net Worth: $13,800,000
Approx.Sls.: $43,400,000
Emp.: 450
Fiscal Year-end: 9/30/91
Not-for-profit Research Corp.; Studies & Analysis For Government Agencies
S.I.C.: 8733
John M. Fabian *(Pres. & Chief Exec. Officer)*
A.R. Deshmukh *(Sr. V.P.-Advanced Programs)*
E.M. Mignogna *(Sr. V.P.-AF Acquisition Programs)*
J. R. Murtaugh *(V.P.-Fin., Sec. & Treas.)*
E.B. Payson *(V.P.-Human Resources & Admin)*
Robert E. Brofft *(V.P.-Information Systems)*
P.A. Adler *(V.P.-Space & Strategic Defense Systems)*
J.R. Hilliard *(V.P.-Space & SDI Programs)*
J.W. Seelig *(V.P.-Strategic/SOF/Airlift Systems)*
C.A. Marino *(V.P.-Systems & Operations Analysis)*

No. of U.S. Offices: 4

Outside Service Firm(s):

Ernst & Young*(Auditors)*
1225 Connecticut Ave., NW
Washington, DC 20036

Volpe, Boskey & Lyons*(Legal Firm)*
Washington, DC

Riggs National Bank of Washington, D.C.*(Major Banking Relationship)*
P.O. Box 96206, 1120 Vermont Ave. N.W.
Washington, DC 20090-6206
Tel.: 202-835-4082

MOSES ANSHELL, INC.
234 N. Central Ave., Ste. 900
Phoenix, AZ 85004
Tel.: 602-254-7312
Fax: 602-252-0904
Year Founded: 1981
Approx.Billings: $15,300,000
Emp.: 20
J.G. Anshell *(Chm. Bd. & Chief Exec. Officer)*
Louis S. Moses *(Pres. & Creative Dir.)*
Jan Walters *(Controller)*
Karen Culver *(Mktg. Coord.)*
Beth Brooks *(Admin. Asst.)*

ANSON INDUSTRIES, INC.
1959 Anson Dr.
Melrose Park, IL 60160
Tel.: 708-681-1300
Fax: 708-681-1310
Year Founded: 1940
Approx.Sls.: $90,000,000
Emp.: 700
Fiscal Year-end: 12/31/91
Plastering Drywall Acoustical Insulation Roofing & Sheet Metal Work; Special Trade Contractors
S.I.C.: 1742; 1761; 1799
Edward R. Simonson *(Chm. Bd.)*
Gene A. Warren *(Pres. & Chief Exec. Officer)*
David V. Brueggen *(V.P.-Fin.)*

Outside Service Firm(s):

Arthur Andersen & Co.*(Auditors)*
33 W. Monroe St.
Chicago, IL 60603-4067
Tel.: 312-580-0033
Fax: 312-507-6748

Keck, Mahin, Cate & Koehler*(Legal Firm)*
8300 Sears Tower, 233 S. Wacker Dr.
Chicago, IL 60606
Tel.: 312-876-3400

Subsidiary:

Anning-Johnson Company **(1)**
1959 Anson Dr.
Melrose Park, IL 60160
Tel.: 708-681-1300
Approx.Sls.: $70,000,000
Emp.: 500
Plastering Drywall; Acustical Insulation Roofing Sheet Metal & Special Trade Contractors
S.I.C.: 1742; 1761; 1799
Edward R. Simonson *(Chm.)*
Gene A. Warren *(Pres.)*

ANSON-STONER, INC.
111 E. Fairbanks Ave.
Winter Park, FL 32789
Tel.: 407-629-9484 **FL**
Fax: 407-629-1616
Year Founded: 1983
Approx.Billings: $19,000,000
Emp.: 32
Advertising Agency
S.I.C.: 7311
Joe Anson *(Pres.)*
Mike Stoner *(Exec. V.P.)*
Jeff Sternberg *(Sr. V.P., Mngmt. Supvr.)*
Teresa Scinto *(Comptroller)*

No. of Mfg. Plants/Facilities: 1
No. of U.S. Offices: 1

Computer Systems/Hardware:
Data General; Macintosh; IBM

Outside Service Firm(s):

Hilliard, Ennis & Taylor*(Auditors)*
Jacksonville, FL

Jamerson-Mc Lean*(Commercial Insurance Carrier)*
Oviedo, FL

Aetna Life & Casualty*(Group Insurer)*
3541 Winchester Road
Allentown, PA 18195-0501

Higley & Barfield*(Legal Firm)*
Maitland, FL

Bank First*(Major Banking Relationship)*
Winter Park, FL

First Union National Bank*(Pension Manager)*
P.O. Box 2565,
Jacksonville, FL 32203

ANTARES GROUP INC.
4950 Harvard Ave.
Cleveland, OH 44105
Tel.: 216-441-4050 **OH**
Telex: 297607-SOSUR
Fax: 216-441-1627
Year Founded: 1974
Assets: $3,500,000
Earnings: $400,000
Liabilities: $3,200,000
Net Worth: $300,000
Approx.Sls.: $20,000,000
Emp.: 4,000
Fiscal Year-end: 6/30/88
Building Maintenance, Security Guards; Energy Management Products; Asbestos Removal
S.I.C.: 7349; 7382
Patrick J. Cassese *(Chm. Bd., Pres. & Chief Exec. Officer)*
John Regala *(Treas. & Chief Fin. Officer)*
Mary A. Kowalski *(Controller)*
Mary J. Knapik *(Dir.-Data Processing)*
Principal(s):
Patrick J. Cassese

No. of U.S. Offices: 6

Computer Systems/Hardware:
IBM

Outside Service Firm(s):

Lytkowski & Co., Inc.*(Auditors)*
Cleveland, OH

Home Life Insurance*(Commercial Insurance Carrier)*
Cleveland, OH

New York Life*(Group Insurer)*
New York, NY

McDonald & Co.*(Investment Banker)*
2100 Society Bldg.
Cleveland, OH 44114

Arter & Hadden*(Legal Firm)*
1144 Union Commerce Bldg.,
Cleveland, OH 44115
Tel.: 216-696-1144

The Huntington National Bank*(Major Banking Relationship)*
41 S. High St.
Columbus, OH 43216

Society National Bank*(Major Banking Relationship)*
800 Superior Ave.
Cleveland, OH 44114
Tel.: 216-689-3696

ANTENNA PRODUCTS CORP.
101 S.E. 25th Ave.
Mineral Wells, TX 76067
Mailing Address:
P.O. Box 520
Mineral Wells, TX 76067
Tel.: 817-325-3301
Telex: 882-163
Fax: 817-325-0716
Approx.Sls.: $10,000,000
Emp.: 120
Fiscal Year-end: 5/31/91
Export
Military & Airport Antennas, Towers, Telescopic Masts, Accessories
S.I.C.: 3679; 3663; 3669
Gary Havener *(Chm. Bd.)*
Gary Skaggs *(Pres.)*
Ron Chandler *(V.P.-Sls.)*
Phil Litzel *(V.P.-Engrng.)*
Clark Wraight *(V.P.-Opers.)*
Ken Whitley *(Pur. Agent)*

C. R. ANTHONY COMPANY
701 N. Broadway
Oklahoma City, OK 73102
Mailing Address:
P.O. Box 25725
Oklahoma City, OK 73125-0725
Tel.: 405-278-7649 **OK**
Fax: 405-278-7500
Year Founded: 1922
Assets: $162,814,000
Earnings: ($2,305,000)
Liabilities: $159,618,000
Net Worth: $3,196,000
Approx.Sls.: $378,000,000
Emp.: 4,600
Fiscal Year-end: 1/31/92
Import
Retail Clothing for Family; Junior Department Store
S.I.C.: 5651
John J. Wiesner *(Chm. Bd. & Chief Exec. Officer)*
William A. North *(Exec. V.P.)*
Mike McCreery *(Exec. V.P. & Chief Fin. Officer)*
Jim Dailey *(Sr. V.P.-Opers.)*
Mark Clasby *(Sr. V.P.-Admin.)*
Glenn Smith *(sr. V.P.-Mktg.)*
Roger Coe *(Controller)*
John Guida *(Dir.-Mngmt. Information Systems)*
Gary Nugent *(Dir.-Real Estate)*
Charlie Martin *(Dir.-Adv.)*
Karis Eulich *(Mgr.-Pub. Rels.)*

Computer Systems/Hardware:
NCR 8635, 8565 Group 2

Outside Service Firm(s):

Deloitte & Touche*(Auditors)*
101 N. Robinson
Oklahoma City, OK 73102
Tel.: 405-239-6891

Liberty National Bank & Trust Co.*(Investment Banker)*
P.O. Box 25848,
Oklahoma City, OK 73125-0848
Tel.: 800-395-2662

Crowe & Dunlevy*(Legal Firm)*
20 N. Broadway
Oklahoma City, OK 73102
Tel.: 405-232-0661
Tel.: 405-235-7700

Liberty National Bank & Trust Co.*(Major Banking Relationship)*
P.O. Box 25848,
Oklahoma City, OK 73125-0848
Tel.: 800-395-2662

Liberty National Bank & Trust Co.*(Pension Manager)*
P.O. Box 25848,
Oklahoma City, OK 73125-0848
Tel.: 800-395-2662

Travelers Insurance Co.*(Pension Manager)*
1 Tower Square
Hartford, CT 06183
Tel.: 203-222-7821
Fax: 203-222-7813

Subsidiaries:

Anco Transportation Service, Inc. **(1)**
701 No. Broadway
Oklahoma City, OK 73102
Tel.: 405-235-3711
Emp.: 5,500
Retail
S.I.C.: 4213

C. R. Anthony International, Ltd. **(1)**
701 No. Broadway
Oklahoma City, OK 73103
Tel.: 405-278-7400
Fax: 405-278-7500
S.I.C.: 5651

Anthony's of Sandpoint, Inc. **(1)**
701 No. Broadway
Oklahoma City, OK 73102
Tel.: 405-235-3711
S.I.C.: 5651

Anthony's of Sleepy Eye, Inc. **(1)**
701 No. Broadway
Oklahoma City, OK 73102
Tel.: 405-235-3711
S.I.C.: 5651

Anthony's of Spring Valley, Inc. **(1)**
701 No. Broadway
Oklahoma City, OK 73102
Tel.: 405-235-3711
S.I.C.: 5651

ANTHONY FOREST PRODUCTS CO., INC.
P.O. Box 1877
El Dorado, AR 71730
Tel.: 501-862-3414 **DE**
Fax: 501-862-4296
Year Founded: 1966
Assets: $20,000,000
Earnings: $2,000,000
Net Worth: $20,000,000
Approx.Sls.: $30,000,000
Emp.: 250
Fiscal Year-end: 4/30/91
Manufacture of Lumber & Wood Products
S.I.C.: 2421; 2493; 2431; 5031
Beryl Anthony, Sr. *(Chm. Bd.)*
Clary Anthony, Sr. *(Pres.)*
Aubra Anthony, Sr. *(V.P.-Mfg.)*
Aubra Anthony, Jr. *(Treas., Sec. & Counsel)*
Priscilla Smith *(Controller)*
Carlyn Drake *(Dir.-Adv.)*
Lynda Anthony *(Mgr.-Human Resources)*
E.J. Langley *(Mgr.-Sls.)*
Richard Lawrence *(Mgr.-Sls.)*
Principal(s):
Beryl Anthony, Sr.
Clary Anthony, Sr.

No. of Mfg. Plants/Facilities: 4
No. of U.S. Offices: 4

Computer Systems/Hardware:
IBM

Outside Service Firm(s):

Findley & Jenkins*(Auditors)*
Little Rock, AR

Protection Mutual*(Commercial Insurance Carrier)*
El Dorado, AR

Massachusetts Mutual Life Insurance Co.*(Group Insurer)*
1295 State St.
Springfield, MA 01111
Tel.: 413-788-8411
Fax: 413-730-6144

Tri-State Underwriters*(Group Insurer)*
Springhill, LA

McConnell & Harris*(Legal Firm)*
Springhill, LA

National Bank of Commerce*(Major Banking Relationship)*
El Dorado, AR

Divisions:

Anthony Forest Div. **(1)**
South Louis St.
Atlanta, TX 75551
Tel.: 903-796-4464
Wholesale of Lumber & Wood Products
S.I.C.: 5031
Clary Anthony, Jr. *(Gen. Mgr.)*

Anthony Forest Div. **(1)**
1236 Urbana Rd.
Urbana, AR 71768
Tel.: 501-862-3825
Wholesale of Lumber & Wood Products
S.I.C.: 5031
Ross Anthony *(Gen. Mgr.)*

Engineered Wood Div. **(1)**
P.O. Box 1877
El Dorado, AR 71730
Tel.: 501-862-5594
Fax: 501-862-6502
Mfr. of Laminated Wood Products
S.I.C.: 2491
John Anthony *(V.P.)*

Laminated Beam Div. **(1)**
High Way 3 North
Plain Dealing, LA 71604
Tel.: 318-326-5811
Mfr. of Chip Products
S.I.C.: 2421

Subsidiary:

Anthony International **(1)**
P.O. Box 1877
El Dorado, AR 71730
Tel.: 501-862-3414
Fax: 501-863-4296
Emp.: 250
Mfr. of Lumber Products
S.I.C.: 5031

ANTWERP DIAMOND DISTRIBUTORS INC.
587 Fifth Ave.
New York, NY 10017
Tel.: 212-319-3300
Tel.: 800-223-0444 **NY**
Fax: 212-207-8168
Year Founded: 1950
Approx.Sls.: $20,000,000
Emp.: 22
Wholesale Diamonds, Loose & Mounted
S.I.C.: 5094
Phyllis Lisker *(Pres.)*
Lawrence Lisker *(Chief Exec. Officer & Treas.)*
Harvey Lisker *(V.P.-Pur.)*
M. Gottesman *(Legal Officer)*
Meshulam Lisker *(Sec. & Mktg. Dir.)*
Irwin Schor *(Controller)*

No. of Mfg. Plants/Facilities: 1
No. of U.S. Offices: 2

Computer Systems/Hardware:
Data General

Outside Service Firm(s):

Schwartz, Thaler*(Auditors)*
New York, NY

Subsidiary:

Antwerp Diamond Distributors Inc. **(1)**
643 So. Olive, Ste. 400
Los Angeles, CA 90014
Tel.: 213-623-7000
Wholesale Diamonds, Loose & Mounted
S.I.C.: 5094
Marty Lisker *(Gen. Mgr.)*

APACHE HOSE & BELTING COMPANY
2515 18th St., S.W.
Cedar Rapids, IA 52404
Mailing Address:
P.O. Box 1719
Cedar Rapids, IA 52406
Tel.: 319-365-0471 **IA**
Fax: 319-365-2252
Year Founded: 1989
Approx.Sls.: $27,000,000
Emp.: 148
Mfr. & Wholesale Distribution of Hose, Belting & Packing; Industrial Fittings; Conveyor Belts
S.I.C.: 5085; 3496
William Nissen *(Chm. Bd. & Pres.)*
Richard Heacock *(V.P.-Fin., Treas., Sec. & Controller)*
Mike Galligar *(V.P.-Opers.)*
Phil Giglis *(V.P.-Mktg.)*
Jack Sweet *(V.P.-Pur.)*

Outside Service Firm(s):

Norwest Bank of Iowa*(Major Banking Relationship)*
Cedar Rapids, IA

APACHE PLASTICS, L.P.
2050 E. Fremont
Stockton, CA 95205
Tel.: 209-466-4356
Fax: 209-466-1730
Approx.Sls.: $50,000,000
Emp.: 200
Plastic Pipe & Fittings
S.I.C.: 3084; 3089
Lawrence H. Beasley *(Pres.)*
William Werner *(Comptroller)*
David Fisher *(Mgr.-Data Processing)*
Francis John Welsh *(Mgr.-Sls.)*
Daniel Crownover *(Chief Engr.)*

Outside Service Firm(s):

Coopers & Lybrand*(Auditors)*
333 Market Street, 21st Fl.
San Francisco, CA 94105

Neumiller & Beardslee*(Legal Firm)*
Stockton, CA

Bank Of Duluth*(Major Banking Relationship)*
Duluth, MN

APCO ARGENTINA INC.
(A Cayman Islands Corporation)
P.O. Box 2400,
Tulsa, OK 74102
Tel.: 918-588-2164
Year Founded: 1979
Assets: $23,330,829
Earnings: $10,334,509
Liabilities: $4,736,771
Net Worth: $18,594,058
Approx.Rev.: $17,170,011
Fiscal Year-end: 12/31/90
Production & Devel. of Oil & Gas Resources in Argentina
S.I.C.: 1311
Vernon T. Jones *(Chm. Bd. & Chief Exec. Officer)*
Ronald D. Jeffris *(V.P. & Chief Fin. Officer)*
David M. Higbee *(Sec.)*

APEX BROACH & MACHINE CO.
6401 E. Seven Mile Rd.
Detroit, MI 48234
Tel.: 313-891-8600
Fax: 313-891-5083
Approx.Sls.: $10,000,000
Emp.: 100
Fiscal Year-end: 6/30/90
Export
Broaching Machines, Tools, Holders, Fixtures
S.I.C.: 3541; 3544; 3545; 3549; 3559
Gust Headbloom, Jr. *(Pres.)*

Apex Broach & Machine Co.—(Continued)

H.E. Heinrich *(Exec. V.P.)*
Thomas P. Heinrich *(Mgr.-Sls.)*

APEX CORPORATION
2060 Yandes
Indianapolis, IN 46202
Tel.: 317-925-5363
Fax: 317-927-7847
Year Founded: 1951
Approx.Sls.: $10,000,000
Emp.: 50
Fiscal Year-end: 1/31/90
Manufacture Aircraft Engine Components & Transmission Parts
S.I.C.: 3728
Robert Oswald *(Pres.)*
James Shelton *(Sec. & Treas.)*
Brian Clagg *(Sr. Sls. Engr.)*
Karl Illg *(Sls. Engr.)*
Rick Picone *(Sls. Engr.)*

Outside Service Firm(s):

Ernst & Young*(Auditors)*
One Indiana Square, Ste. 3400
Indianapolis, IN 46204
Tel.: 317-236-1100

Merchants National Bank & Trust Company of Indianapolis*(Major Banking Relationship)*
One Merchants Plaza, Ste. 901E
Indianapolis, IN 46255
Tel.: 317-267-7109

APEX MILLS CORPORATION
168 Doughty Blvd.
Inwood, NY 11696
Tel.: 516-239-4400
Fax: 516-239-4951
Approx.Sls.: $16,000,000
Emp.: 26
Export
Mfg. of Manmade Broadwoven Fabrics & Knitted Netting Solid Fabrics
S.I.C.: 2221; 2258
Milton Kurz *(Chief Exec. Officer)*
Edward Schlussel *(Pres.)*
David Kurz *(V.P.)*
Jonathan Kurz *(V.P.)*

Outside Service Firm(s):

Summit, Solomon & Feldesman*(Legal Firm)*
445 Park Ave.
New York, NY 10022
Tel.: 212-702-2200

The Bank Of New York*(Major Banking Relationship)*
Hewlett, NY

APEX OIL COMPANY, INC.
8182 Maryland Ave.
Saint Louis, MO 63105
Tel.: 314-889-9600
Fax: 314-854-8539
Year Founded: 1930
Approx.Sls.: $1,000,000,000
Emp.: 800
Fiscal Year-end: 9/30/89
Wholesale Oil Distributor
S.I.C.: 5172
Samuel R. Goldstein *(Chm. Bd. & Treas.)*
Paul A. Novelly *(Pres. & Chief Exec. Officer)*
Neil Miller *(Gen. Counsel)*
Jody McMahon *(Dir.-Personnel)*

Computer Systems/Hardware:
Digital

Outside Service Firm(s):

Arthur Andersen & Co.*(Auditors)*
1010 Market St.
St. Louis, MO 63101

APEX SUPPLY CO. INC.
2500 Button Gwinnett Dr.
Atlanta, GA 30340
Tel.: 404-449-7000
Fax: 404-263-4834
Year Founded: 1955
Sales Range: $100-499 Million
Emp.: 327
Fiscal Year-end: 4/25/92
Wholesale Distributor Plumbing, Air Conditioning, Heating, Pipe Valves & Fittings, Builder Products & Cabinets
S.I.C.: 3498; 5074; 5075; 5084
Clyde A. Rodbell *(Pres.)*
Paul N. Rodbell *(V.P. & Treas.)*
Sidney P. Rodbell *(V.P. & Sec.)*
Principal(s):
Clyde A. Rodbell

No. of U.S. Offices: 16

Computer Systems/Hardware:
Burroughs A-9

Outside Service Firm(s):

A. Sheiffer & Co.*(Auditors)*
Westbury, NY

Smith, Gambrell & Russell*(Legal Firm)*
2400 First Atlanta Tower
Atlanta, GA 30383
Tel.: 404-656-1800
Fax: 404-264-2652

Bank South, N.A.*(Major Banking Relationship)*
P.O. Box 4387
Atlanta, GA 30302
Tel.: 404-529-4111

APOLLO COLORS, INC.
3000 Dundee Rd. , Suite 415
Northbrook, IL 60062
Tel.: 708-564-9190 **IL**
Fax: 708-564-9296
Approx.Sls.: $30,000,000
Emp.: 150
Mfr. of Organic Color Pigments
S.I.C.: 2865
Norman Rumpf *(Pres.)*
Larry Bykerk *(V.P.-Sls.)*
Jesse M. Wilson, Sr. *(Treas.)*
Robert J. Ley *(Sec.)*

Outside Service Firm(s):

Harris Trust & Savings Bank*(Major Banking Relationship)*
111 W. Monroe St.
Chicago, IL 60690
Tel.: 312-461-2265
Tel.: 800-858-0840

APPAREL AMERICA, INC.
1175 State St.
New Haven, CT 06511
Tel.: 203-777-5531 **DE**
Year Founded: 1968
Approx.Rev.: $72,000,000
Emp.: 900
Fiscal Year-end: 1/31/92
Women's Swimwear & Imprinted Casual Sportswear
S.I.C.: 2339
Burton I. Koffman *(Chm. Bd.)*
Richard E. Koffman *(Vice Chm., Exec. V.P. & Sec.)*
Charles C. Murray *(Pres., Chief Exec. Officer)*
Jacob I. Feigenbaum *(Exec. V.P.)*
David M. Golden *(V.P.-Fin & Admin., Chief Fin. Officer)*
David L. Koffman *(V.P. & Asst. Sec.)*
Jeffrey Koffman *(V.P. & Asst. Treas.)*

Subsidiaries:

Mayfair Industries, Inc. **(1)**
1407 Broadway
New York, NY 10018
Tel.: 212-921-1717
Fax: 212-827-0647
Approx.Sls.: $58,000,000
Emp.: 235
Fiscal Year-end: 12/31/90
Design & Mktg of Women's & Children's Clothing
S.I.C.: 2331; 2361
Steven Chernick *(Pres.)*
Frederick D'Amato *(V.P.-Fin. & Admin.)*

Robby Len Fashions **(1)**
1411 Broadway
New York, NY 10018
Tel.: 212-391-2525
Emp.: 450
Design, Manufacture & Distribution of Women's Swimwear
S.I.C.: 2339
Jacob I. Feigenbaum *(Pres.)*
Mark D. Greenburg *(V.P.-Fin. & Admin.)*
Eric I. Weitz *(V.P.-Mktg. & Sls.)*
Murray Merl *(V.P.-Mfg.)*
Sandy Sharpentier *(Pur. Dir.)*

THE APPAREL GROUP, LTD.
1370 Ave. of the Americas
New York, NY 10019
Tel.: 212-399-3500
Tel.: 800-535-4162 **NY**
Fax: 212-408-8332
Year Founded: 1988
Assets: $59,340,551
Earnings: ($10,705,127)
Liabilities: $52,018,640
Net Worth: $7,321,911
Approx.Sls.: $81,000,000
Emp.: 1,100
Fiscal Year-end: 3/31/91
Import Export
Mfr. Men's Shirts, Neckwear, Sportswear, Sweaters; Ladieswear
S.I.C.: 2321; 2323; 2329; 2331
Corporate Giving Program:
Merchandise
Dr. Richard Lee *(Chm. Bd.)*
V. Jerome Kaplan *(Chief Exec. Officer)*
Walter Bearden *(Exec. V.P.-Foxcroft)*
Lawrence Smith *(Exec. V.P.-Opers.)*
Arthur Penn *(Sr. V.P.-Sls.)*
Donald Yeung *(V.P. & Chief Fin. Officer)*
Angelo Fusaro *(V.P.-Corp. Affairs)*
Jimmy Mak *(V.P.-Admin.)*
Eubert Troutt *(V.P.-Wholesale & Distr.)*
Wayne King *(V.P.-Mfg.)*
William Clapp *(Mgr.-Quality Control)*
Brenda Fink *(Mgr.-Acct.)*
Nancy Parks Roy *(Mgr.-Human Resources)*
Al Schoch *(Mgr.-Mngmt. Information Systems)*
Gil Pedigo *(Mgr.-Pur.)*
Rommel Redito *(Import Admin.)*

Computer Systems/Hardware:
Honeywell

Outside Service Firm(s):

Ernst & Young*(Auditors)*
1000 Brown & Williamson Tower
Louisville, KY 40202
Tel.: 502-585-1400

Coudert Brothers*(Legal Firm)*
200 Park Ave.
New York, NY 10166
Tel.: 212-880-4400

Division:

The Enro Shirt Company, Inc. **(1)**
4300 Leghorn Dr.
Louisville, KY 40218
Tel.: 502-473-6300
Tel.: 800-626-2884
Fax: 502-473-6118
Approx.Sls.: $45,000,000
Emp.: 850
Import Export
Computer Systems/Hardware:
Honeywell DPS 7
Mfr. Men's Dress Shirts, Sport Shirts
S.I.C.: 2321; 2311
V. Jerome Kaplan *(Pres.)*
Lawrence Smith *(Exec. V.P.-Opers.)*
Arthur Penn *(V.P.-Sls.)*
Robert Browne *(V.P.-Credit)*
Nancy Roy *(Personnel Dir.)*
Gil Pedigo *(Pur.& Traffic, Mgr.)*
Al Schoch *(Mgr.-Data Processing)*

APPAREL INDUSTRIES, INC.
1407 Broadway
New York, NY 10018
Tel.: 212-869-1400
Fax: 212-398-0462
Approx.Sls.: $70,000,000
Emp.: 275
Mfr. Women's Apparel
S.I.C.: 2339; 2253; 2329
Seymour Bag *(Pres.)*
Richard Bag *(Exec. V.P. & Adv. Mgr.)*
Daniel Jaffee *(V.P. & Sec.)*
Ira Krampf *(V.P. & Controller)*

APPAREL VENTURES, INC.
204 W. Rosecrans
Gardena, CA 90248
Tel.: 310-538-4980
Fax: 310-538-0515
Year Founded: 1977
Approx.Sls.: $48,000,000
Emp.: 500
Mfr. of Cha Cha Cha, Citrus & La Blanca Women's, Misses & Juniors Bathing Suits; Citrus Surfwear Athletic Clothing & Women's Sportswear
S.I.C.: 2339
Marvin Goodman *(Pres.)*
David Goodman *(V.P.)*
Lucy Brockmann *(Mgr.-Personnel)*

Outside Service Firm(s):

Stonefield & Josephson*(Auditors)*
Los Angeles, CA

Bank of America NT&SA*(Major Banking Relationship)*
555 So. Flower St., 5th Fl.
Los Angeles, CA 90071
Tel.: 213-228-3526
Fax: 213-228-4062

I. APPEL CORPORATION
136 Madison Ave., 11th Flr.
New York, NY 10016
Tel.: 212-685-3900
Approx.Sls.: $90,000,000
Emp.: 1,750
Mfr. Robes, Gowns & Lingerie, Bras & Girdles
S.I.C.: 2384; 2341
H. Feinberg *(Chm. Bd.)*
N. Katz *(Pres. & Chief Exec. Officer)*
Larry Herz *(Exec. V.P.)*
Stephen Katz *(V.P.-Opers.)*

Divisions:

Formfit Rogers **(1)**
136 Madison Ave.
New York, NY 10016
Tel.: 212-685-3900
Fax: 212-481-6017
Emp.: 10
Ladies' Intimate Apparel Bras, Girdle, Foundationwear, Daywear, Leisurewear, Loungewear
S.I.C.: 2342
Max Carmon *(V.P.-Mfg.)*
Cathy Priore *(Dir.-Customer Service)*
Nilda Hernandez *(Admin. Asst.)*

Jones New York Intimates **(1)**
136 Madison Ave.
New York, NY 10016
Tel.: 212-685-3900
Fax: 212-481-6017
Emp.: 10
Mfr. Ladies' Intimate Apparel, Bras, Girdles, Foundation Wear, Daywear, Leisurewear, Loungewear
S.I.C.: 2342
Max Carmon *(V.P.-Mfg.)*
Cathy Priore *(Dir.-Customer Service)*

Loralyn Fashion **(1)**
463 7th Ave
New York, NY 10010
Tel.: 212-391-1146

Myonne Panties **(1)**
180 Madison Ave.
New York, NY 10016
Tel.: 212-684-0840

APPERSON BUSINESS FORMS, INC.
6855 E. Gage Ave.
Los Angeles, CA 90040
Mailing Address:
P.O. Box 60666, Terminal Annex,
Los Angelos, CA 90040
Tel.: 310-927-4718 CA
Fax: 310-927-2169
Year Founded: 1955
Approx.Sls.: $24,000,000
Emp.: 325
Mfr. Business Forms
S.I.C.: 2761
R.P. Apperson *(Chm. Bd. & Pres.)*
C.A. Apperson *(Exec. V.P.-Sls.)*
Doug Gabriel *(V.P., Treas. & Controller)*
Z.H. Astor *(Sec.)*
Principal(s):
R.P. Apperson

No. of Mfg. Plants/Facilities: 2
No. of U.S. Offices: 20

Outside Service Firm(s):

Ernst & Young*(Auditors)*
515 S. Flower St.
Los Angeles, CA 90071
Tel.: 213-621-1666

Astor & Phillips*(Legal Firm)*
Los Angeles, CA

Union Bank*(Major Banking Relationship)*
City of Commerce, CA

APPLE LINES, INC.
212 S.W. Second St.
Madison, SD 57042
Tel.: 605-256-6661
Fax: 605-256-6798
Year Founded: 1957
Approx.Sls.: $16,000,000
Emp.: 46
Contract Hauler; Refrigerated Products
S.I.C.: 4213
Robert A. Appelwick *(Chm. Bd. & Chief Exec. Officer)*
D. Pixler *(Pres.)*
Karen K. Appelwick *(Sec. & Treas.)*

Outside Service Firm(s):

McGladrey & Pullen*(Auditors)*
Sioux Falls, SD

Norwest Bank Minneosta, N.A.*(Major Banking Relationship)*
Sioux Falls, SD

APPLE VACATIONS WEST INC.
(d/b/a Thomson Vacations)
25 Northwest Point Blvd.
Elk Grove Village, IL 60007
Tel.: 708-640-1150
Fax: 708-640-1940
Approx.Sls.: $100,000,000
Emp.: 135
Package Tours & Travel Retailing
S.I.C.: 4724
J.J. Mullen *(Pres.)*
D. Domek *(Chief Oper. Officer)*
A. McNish *(V.P.-Contracting)*
Colleen Caponi *(Mgr.-Adv. & Mktg.)*
Mary Zinngrabe *(Mgr.-Communications)*

APPLETREE MARKETS
4301 Windfern
Houston, TX 77041
Mailing Address:
P.O. Box 40524,
Houston, TX 77240-0524
Tel.: 713-460-5000
Fax: 713-460-8262
Approx.Sls.: $823,000,000
Emp.: 8,462
Fiscal Year-end: 12/31/89
Grocery Stores
S.I.C.: 5411
Fred Lummis *(Chm. Bd., Pres. & Chief Exec. Officer)*
Arthur Patch *(Pres. & Chief Exec. Officer)*
R.T. Kubicek *(Sr. V.P. & Chief Fin. Officer)*
Thomas Kees *(Sr. V.P.-Mktg.)*
Ray DelFranco *(Sr. V.P.-Retail Opers.)*
Richard A. Goeggel *(Treas.)*
James Y'Barbo *(Controller)*
Principal(s):
AST General Corp.

Outside Service Firm(s):

Arthur Andersen & Co.*(Auditors)*
711 Louisiana, Ste. 1300
Houston, TX 77002-2323
Tel.: 713-237-2793

Long-Term Credit Bank of Japan, Ltd.*(Major Banking Relationship)*
New York, NY

APPLIED INDUSTRIAL MATERIALS CORPORATION
1 Parkway North, Ste. 400
Deerfield, IL 60015
Tel.: 708-940-7800 DE
Fax: 708-940-0811
Year Founded: 1986
Assets: $155,000,000
Liabilities: $98,000,000
Net Worth: $57,000,000
Approx.Sls.: $360,000,000
Emp.: 550
Fiscal Year-end: 9/30/91
Import Export
Wholesale Distributor of Petroleum & Calcined Coke; Manufacturer & Distributor of Ferroalloys; Miner of Minerals Including Clay & Sands
S.I.C.: 5052; 3313; 3295; 1459
Charles P. Gallagher *(Chm. Bd. & Chief Exec. Officer)*
Wayne C. Kocourek *(Vice Chm. & Pres.)*
Peter Scott-Hansen *(Pres.-Carbon Grp.)*
Charles W. Kopec *(Pres.-Metals/ Minerals Grp.)*
James B. Ehren *(Chief Fin. Officer & Sr. V.P.)*
Jon M. Burns *(V.P.-Human Resources)*
James A. Cebulski *(Asst. Controller)*

Outside Service Firm(s):

Arthur Andersen & Co.*(Auditors)*
777 E. Wisconsin Ave., P.O. Box 1215
Milwaukee, WI 53202
Tel.: 414-271-5100
Fax: 414-283-3200

Altheimer & Gray*(Legal Firm)*
10 S. Wacker Dr.
Chicago, IL 60606
Tel.: 312-715-4000

Harris Trust & Savings Bank*(Major Banking Relationship)*
P.O. Box 755, 111 W. Monroe
Chicago, IL 60603
Tel.: 312-461-2121

APPLIED MICROSYSTEMS CORPORATION
5020 148th Ave., N.E.
Redmond, WA 98052
Mailing Address:
P.O. Box 97002
Redmond, WA 98073-9702
Tel.: 206-882-2000
Tel.: 800-426-3925 WA
Telex: 185196
Fax: 206-883-3049
Year Founded: 1979
Sales Range: $20-39 Million
Emp.: 246
Fiscal Year-end: 12/31/90
Export
Mfr. & Mktr. of In-Circuit Emulators & Integrated Development Systems
S.I.C.: 3825; 7372
Robert L. Deinhammer *(Pres.)*
Jay Caldwell *(V.P.-Fin. & Admin.)*
Steve Dearden *(V.P. & Gen. Mgr.-Microcontroller Div.)*
David L. Eitelbach *(V.P. & Gen. Mgr.-Microprocessor Div.)*
Kenneth Jenkins *(V.P.-Mfg.)*
Richard Jensen *(V.P.-New Bus. Dev.)*
Karen K. Edwards *(Dir.-Mktg, Sls. Promo., Mdse. & Communications)*
Clark Keller *(Dir.-Domestic Sls.)*
Irene Pasternack *(Dir.-Mktg. Communications)*
Will Smith *(Dir.-Mngmt. Information Systems)*
Gale Mowrer *(Mgr.-Human Resources)*
Betty Soward *(Mgr.-Office Services)*

No. of Mfg. Plants/Facilities: 1
No. of U.S. Offices: 5
No. of Foreign Offices: 3

Computer Systems/Hardware:
Honeywell Ultimate; DEC VAX; IBM PC; Compaq PC

Outside Service Firm(s):

Ernst & Young*(Auditors)*
999 Third Av., Ste. 3500
Seattle, WA 98104
Tel.: 206-621-1800
Fax: 206-682-1234

Stoel, Rives, Boley, Jones & Grey*(Legal Firm)*
3600 One Union Sq., 600 University
Seattle, WA 98101
Tel.: 206-624-0900
Fax: 206-386-7500

APPLIED SOLAR ENERGY CORPORATION
(73%-Owned Affiliated Company of American Cyanamid Company)
15251 E. Don Julian Rd.
City of Industry, CA 91746
Mailing Address:
P.O. Box 1212
City of Industry, CA 91749-1212
Tel.: 818-968-6581 CA
Fax: 818-336-8694
Year Founded: 1955
Approx.Rev.: $30,000,000
Emp.: 285
Fiscal Year-end: 10/31/91
Import Export
Design, Develop, Manufacture & Marketing of Silicon & Compound Semiconductor Photovoltaic Products; Mfrs. of Electronic Military Training Systems
S.I.C.: 3674; 3669
Charles A. Ruibal *(Chm. Bd.)*
David Van Buren *(Pres. & Chief Exec. Officer)*
Steve Cohen *(V.P.-Mfg.)*
Frank F. Ho *(V.P.-Solar Engrng.)*
Dr. John Tracy *(V.P.-Optoelectronic Prods.)*
Brian Sullivan *(Controller & Sec.)*
Maureen Adkins *(Pur. Agent)*
Jeff Bloom *(Dir.-Quality Assurance)*
Joe Capitano *(Dir.-Solar Cell Mktg.)*
Earl Hackman *(Dir.-Program Mngmt. & Information Systems)*
Nancy Hughey *(Dir.-Human Resources)*
R. Hutchinson *(Dir.-Contracts & Pur.)*
Erik Monsen *(Dir.-Pub. Rels. & Safety)*
David Snelson *(Mgr.-Mngmt. Information Services)*
Jill Vincent *(Admin. Specialist)*

Computer Systems/Hardware:
Mainframe; Ultimate 3040

AQUA FAB INDUSTRIES, INC.
1485 S. County Trail
East Greenwich, RI 02818
Tel.: 401-884-3700 DE
Fax: 401-885-5322
Approx.Assets: $95,000,000
Emp.: 200
Fiscal Year-end: 10/31/89
Manufacturer & Distributor Diving Boards, Slides, Vinyl Liner Pools, Spas & Related Products
S.I.C.: 5091
Peter Briukerhoff *(Chm. Bd., Pres. & Chief Exec. Officer)*

No. of Mfg. Plants/Facilities: 23
No. of U.S. Offices: 21

Outside Service Firm(s):

Ernst & Young*(Auditors)*
One Old Stone Square
Providence, RI 02903
Tel.: 401-331-7000

Bangser & Weiss*(Legal Firm)*
230 Park Ave.
New York, NY 10169
Tel.: 212-856-5800

Subsidiaries:

Custom Distributors, Inc. **(1)**
21150 Rogers Dr.
Rogers, MN 55374
Tel.: 612-428-4315
Emp.: 50
Wholesale Swimming Pools & Related Products
S.I.C.: 5091
Harold Grotte *(Exec. V.P.)*

E-Z Clor/Kratz **(1)**
1920 Belt Way Dr.
Saint Louis, MO 63114
Tel.: 314-426-4533
Pkgs. Swimming Pool and Spa Chemicals
S.I.C.: 5169
Robert F. Kennedy *(Chief Oper. Officer)*

S. R. Smith, Inc. **(1)**
P.O. Box 400, 1017 S.W. Berg Pkwy.
Canby, OR 97013
Tel.: 503-266-2231
Emp.: 100
Mfr. Diving Boards, Pool Slides & Pool Rails
S.I.C.: 3949
Robert Sigler *(Pres.)*

Weatherking Products, Inc. **(1)**
1485 S. County Trail
East Greenwich, RI 02818
Tel.: 401-884-3700
Emp.: 75
Manufacture & Wholesale Swimming Pools & Related Products
S.I.C.: 3949; 5099; 7999
Frank Pimental *(Exec. V.P.-Sls. & Mktg.)*
Robert M. Petrin *(Chief Fin. Officer)*

ARANDELL-SCHMIDT CORPORATION
N82 W. 13118 Leon Rd.
Menomonee Falls, WI 53051
Tel.: 414-255-4400
Fax: 414-253-3162
Approx.Sls.: $91,000,000,000
Emp.: 410
Lithography & Printer Of Catalogs
S.I.C.: 2741; 2752
Edward F. Treis *(Chm Bd. & Chief Exec. Officer)*
Donald J. Treis *(Pres. & Chief Oper. Officer)*
Donald F. Balchunas *(V.P. & Controller)*
Jan Memmel *(Sec.)*

Outside Service Firm(s):

Vrakas Blum & Co. SC*(Auditors)*
Milwaukee, WI

ARBURG, INC.
(Formerly Polymer Machinery Corp.)
154 Woodlawn Rd.
Berlin, CT 06037
Mailing Address:
P.O. Box 7358,
Kenington, CT 06037
Tel.: 203-828-0501
Fax: 203-828-8330
Approx.Sls.: $20,000,000
Emp.: 50
Fiscal Year-end: 12/31/90
Import Export
Mfr. Plastic Processing Equip.; Arburg Injection Molding Machines
S.I.C.: 3599
Hans E. Gompf *(Pres.)*
Lawrence R. Bauer *(Exec. V.P.)*
Louis Camerota *(Chief Fin. Officer)*
Bruce H. Bowman *(Dir.-Sls.)*

Division:

Granulator Div. **(1)**
168 Woodlawn Rd.
Berlin, CT 06037
Tel.: 203-828-0541
S.I.C.: 3599

ARCADE INC.
1815 E. Main St.
Chattanooga, TN 37404
Tel.: 615-624-3301
Year Founded: 1902
Approx.Sls.: $30,000,000
Emp.: 150
Fiscal Year-end: 6/30/91
Import Export
Direct Response Printers; Lithographic & Commercial Printing, Scented/Unscented Magazine Inserts, Envelopes, Statement Enclosures, Catalog Inserts, Tabloid Attached Scented Devices, Micro-Encapsulated Products, Controlled Release, Sustained Release
S.I.C.: 2752
Corporate Giving Program: United Way
Elliott Mitchell *(Chm. Bd., Pres. & Chief Exec. Officer)*
Gordon Jones *(V.P. & Chief Fin. Officer)*
Donnie Thompson *(Sec.)*

ARCADIA FRYERS
(Formerly A-G Co-Operative Creamery, Inc.)
502 W. Main St.
Arcadia, WI 54612
Mailing Address:
P.O. Box 190,
Arcadia, WI 54612
Tel.: 608-323-2141
Fax: 608-323-2036
Fax: 608-323-3081
Year Founded: 1924
Approx.Sls.: $74,000,000
Emp.: 370
Produces Cheeses & Arcadia Fryers
S.I.C.: 2015; 2022
Mark Page *(Plant Mgr.)*
Gretchen Witte *(Office Mgr.)*
John Rud *(Treas.)*
Roger Fille *(Sec.)*

Outside Service Firm(s):

Reilly, Penner & Benton*(Auditors)*
Milwaukee, WI

State Bank of Arcadia*(Major Banking Relationship)*
Arcadia, WI

ARCADIAN POWER CORP.
(Formerly Fayette Energy Corporation)
(d/b/a Fayette Energy Corp.)
5990 Stone Ridge Dr., Ste. 119
Pleasanton, CA 94588-3234
Mailing Address:
P.O. Box 1149
Tracy, CA 95378-1149
Tel.: 510-416-0600
Fax: 209-836-5714
Year Founded: 1977
Sales Range: $60-79 Million
Emp.: 120
Producers of Wind Energy
S.I.C.: 3621
John D. Kuhns *(Chm. Bd.)*
Dwight Kuhns *(Pres.)*

No. of U.S. Offices: 2

Computer Systems/Hardware:
Sperry-Univac IT; IBM System 36

Outside Service Firm(s):

Bank of Stockton*(Major Banking Relationship)*
Stockton, CA

ARCATA CORPORATION
601 California St., Ste. 1800
San Francisco, CA 94108
Tel.: 415-781-4200 **CA**
Fax: 415-989-2413
Year Founded: 1939
Approx.Sls.: $550,000,000
Emp.: 6,750
Fiscal Year-end: 12/31/91
Book & Magazine Printing
S.I.C.: 2732; 2759; 2752; 2731
Edward Scarff *(Chm. Bd.)*
Jack Fowler *(Pres.)*
C.G. Mumford *(Exec. V.P., Treas. & Chief Fin. Officer)*
John A. Barrett *(V.P.-Plng.)*
Shelley A. Lorenzen *(V.P., Sec. & Gen. Counsel)*
Jane M. Downs *(Dir.-Human Resources)*
Linda Langland *(Cash Mgr.)*

No. of Mfg. Plants/Facilities: 12

Computer Systems/Hardware:
IBM 3083; Prime

Outside Service Firm(s):

Arthur Andersen & Co.*(Auditors)*
Spear Street Tower, One Market Plaza, Ste. 3500
San Francisco, CA 94105
Tel.: 415-546-8200

Mutual of New York*(Group Insurer)*
New York, NY

The Bank of New York*(Major Banking Relationship)*
One Wall Street
New York, NY 10286
Tel.: 212-635-6805
Fax: 212-635-3201

Barclays Bank plc*(Major Banking Relationship)*
75 Wall St.
New York, NY 10265
Tel.: 212-412-4000

Mutual of New York*(Pension Manager)*
New York, NY

Third National Bank*(Pension Manager)*
Nashville, TN

Reich & Tang*(Pension Manager)*
100 Park Ave.
New York, NY 10017
Tel.: 212-270-1110

Subsidiary:

Arcata Graphics Company **(1)**
201 N. Charles St., Ste. 2100
Baltimore, MD 21201
Tel.: 410-783-5200
Fax: 410-685-9065
Approx.Sls.: $550,000,000
Emp.: 7,000
Fiscal Year-end: 12/31/90
Book & Commercial Printing
S.I.C.: 2732; 2759
Jack W. Fowler *(Pres. & Chief Exec. Officer)*
Burgess Hildreth *(V.P.-Admin.)*
Herbert S. Cohen *(Controller)*
Jane Downs *(Dir.-Human Resouces)*
David Bremer *(Dir.-MIS)*

Subsidiaries:

Arcata Graphics Baird Ward, Inc. **(2)**
P.O. Box 305127
Nashville, TN 37230
Tel.: 615-385-0460
Tel.: 615-553-4400 (100%)
Emp.: 1,250
Printing
S.I.C.: 2759
Robert Wilcox *(V.P. & Div. Mgr.-Clarksville)*
Gary R. Hamacher *(V.P. & Div. Mgr.-Nashville)*

Arcata Graphics Buffalo, Inc. **(2)**
TC Indus. Pk.
Depew, NY 14043
Tel.: 716-686-2500 (100%)
Emp.: 1,400
Printing
S.I.C.: 2759
Michael D. Harris *(V.P. & Div. Mgr.)*

Arcata Graphics Fairfield Inc. **(2)**
P. O. Drawer AN
Fairfield, PA 17320
Tel.: 717-642-5871
Tel.: 304-267-3600 (100%)
Fax: 717-642-8485
Emp.: 930
Book Mfrs.
S.I.C.: 2759
Gary Daum *(V.P. & Div. Mgr.)*
Joe Topley *(V.P.-Opers.)*
Dan Hill *(Sls.-Service Mgr.)*
Wayne Teague *(Controller)*

Arcata Graphics Halliday **(2)**
Circuit St.
West Hanover, MA 02339
Tel.: 617-826-8385 (100%)
Fax: 617-826-6653
Emp.: 500
Mfr. of Books
S.I.C.: 2731
Gary Brusseau *(V.P. & Div. Mgr.)*

Arcata Graphics Kingsport **(2)**
P.O. Box 711
Kingsport, TN 37662
Tel.: 615-378-1000
Tel.: 615-357-2000 (100%)
Fax: 615-378-1052
Emp.: 2,150
Mfr. of Books
S.I.C.: 2732; 2782
Luther Odom *(V.P. & Div. Mgr.-Kingsport Plant)*
Paul R. Hollinger, Jr. *(V.P. & Div. Mgr.-Hawkins County Plant)*
Don Solt *(Div. Sls. Mgr.)*
Ron McAiley *(Mgr.-Customer Service)*
Terry Medukas *(Contr.)*

Arcata Graphics Sherwood **(2)**
P.O. Box 3948,
Kingsport, TN 37664
Tel.: 615-378-1202
Fax: 615-378-1075
Deluxe Book Binding
S.I.C.: 2789
Jerry Townsed *(V.P. & Gen. Mgr.)*

Subsidiary:

Karl M. Harrop Co., Inc. **(3)**
307 9th St.
Bristol, TN 37620
Tel.: 615-764-5152
Wholesale Printing Paper
S.I.C.: 5111
Ira Luster *(Div. Mgr.)*

ARCHER/MALMO ADV., INC.
65 Union Ave., Ste. 500
Memphis, TN 38103
Mailing Address:
P.O. Box 3300,
Memphis, TN 38173
Tel.: 901-523-2000
Fax: 901-523-7654
Year Founded: 1952
Sales Range: $20-39 Million
Emp.: 63
Fiscal Year-end: 12/31/91
Advertising Agency
S.I.C.: 7311
John Malmo *(Chm. Bd.)*
Ward Archer, Jr. *(Pres. & Chief Exec. Officer)*
Bob Michie *(Chief Fin. Officer, Treas. & Sec.)*
Marsha Cameron *(Exec. V.P.-Pub. Rels.)*
Greer Simonton *(Exec. V.P.-Mktg.)*

Computer Systems/Hardware:
Media Management Plus, Lightspeed Graphic Design, IBM System 36, NEC Word Processing

Division:

Archer/Malmo Public Relations Div. **(1)**
65 Union at Front
Memphis, TN 38103
Tel.: 901-523-2000
Marsha Cameron *(Exec. V.P., Pub. Rels. Dir.)*

THE ARCHITECTS COLLABORATIVE, INC. (TAC)
46 Brattle St.
Cambridge, MA 02138
Tel.: 617-868-4200
Telex: 200165 TACCAM UR
Fax: 617-868-4226
Year Founded: 1945
Approx.Sls.: $24,000,000
Emp.: 125
Export
Architecture, Planning, Landscape Architecture, Interiors & Graphic Design
S.I.C.: 8712
John P. Sheehy *(Chm. Bd.)*
John Hayes *(Pres.)*
Principal(s):
John Hayes
Richard Brooker
James E. Burlage
Sherry T. Caplan
Gregory Downes
Norman C. Fletcher
John C. Harkness
John Hayes
William J. Higgins
Leonard Notkin
John P. Sheehy
David G. Sheffield
H. Malcolm Ticknor

No. of U.S. Offices: 2
No. of Foreign Offices: 1

Outside Service Firm(s):

Deloitte & Touche*(Auditors)*
125 Summer St.
Boston, MA 02110
Tel.: 617-261-8000
Fax: 617-261-8111

Hill & Barlow*(Legal Firm)*
One International Place
Boston, MA 02110
Tel.: 617-439-3555

Cambridge Trust Co.*(Major Banking Relationship)*
Cambridge, MA

Branch:

The Architects Collaborative, Inc. **(1)**
649 Front St.
San Francisco, CA 94111
Tel.: 415-392-4200
Telex: 200165 TACCAMUR
Fax: 415-392-4429
Architecture, Planning, Landscape Architecture, Interiors & Graphic Design
S.I.C.: 8712
John Hayes *(Pres.)*

ARCHWAY COOKIES, INC.
5451 W. Dickman Rd.
Battle Creek, MI 49015
Mailing Address:
P.O. Box 762
Battle Creek, MI 49016
Tel.: 616-962-6205
Fax: 616-962-8149
Approx.Sls.: $45,000,000
Emp.: 40
Mfr. Archway Cookies
S.I.C.: 2052
Thomas F. Olin *(Chm. Bd.)*
Eugene H. McKay, Jr. *(Pres.)*
Clara L. McKelvey *(V.P.-Admin.)*
Donald Keaton *(V.P.-Adv.)*
Eugene McKay III *(V.P.-Natl. Opers.)*
Thomas F. Olin, Jr. *(V.P.-Sls.)*
Chris T. Christ *(Sec.)*
Judith M. Reynolds *(Adv. Coord.)*

Computer Systems/Hardware:
IBM

Outside Service Firm(s):

Price Waterhouse*(Auditors)*
67 W. Michigan Mall
Battle Creek, MI 49017

Lewis, Overbeck & Furman*(Legal Firm)*
Chicago, IL

Michigan National Bank*(Major Banking Relationship)*
Battle Creek, MI

ARCINCO, INC.
(House Agency)
22 Lincoln Place
Garfield, NJ 07026
Tel.: 201-471-4300
Approx.Billings: $10,100,000
Direct Mail Adv.
A. Cinader *(Chm. Bd.)*
J. Grabowski *(Pres.)*
Craig Krasin *(V.P., Mktg.)*
Doreen Cavallo *(Mgr., Mktg. Services)*

ARCOLA WIRE COMPANY
(Formerly Durable Wire Company)
13 Beaver Rd.
Branford, CT 06405
Tel.: 203-481-5381
Fax: 203-488-0285
Year Founded: 1947
Approx.Sls.: $20,000,000
Emp.: 65
Fiscal Year-end: 6/30/90
Mfr. Aluminum & Shaped Wire; Copper Based Alloy Wire; Bandoliered Electronic Connector Pins
S.I.C.: 3351; 3355; 3357; 3678
Bradway B. Adams *(Pres.)*
Fred Prekosovich *(V.P. & Gen. Mgr.)*
Paul Morris *(V.P.-Human Resources & Controller)*

Outside Service Firm(s):

Friedber, Smith & Company*(Auditors)*
Bridgeport, CT

Union Trust*(Major Banking Relationship)*
New Haven, CT

Mason, Drew & Merscrean*(Legal Firm)*
New Haven, CT

ARCON CONSTRUCTION CO., INC.
903 E. Forest
Mora, MN 55051
Tel.: 612-679-2244
Fax: 612-679-2332
Approx.Sls.: $22,000,000
Emp.: 40
Street, Bridge, Concrete Curb Paving, Sewer & Water Line Construction
S.I.C.: 1611; 1623
Dean C. Johnson *(Pres.)*
David Baum *(Exec. V.P.)*
Michael Denker *(Sec. & Treas.)*

Outside Service Firm(s):

John A. Knutson & Co.*(Auditors)*
Minneapolis, MN

Robert Lindig*(Legal Firm)*
Mora, MN

Kanabec State Bank*(Major Banking Relationship)*
Mora, MN

Divisions:

Arcon Bridge Div. **(1)**
903 E. Forest
Mora, MN 55051
Tel.: 612-679-2244
Bridge Construction
S.I.C.: 1622
Terry Johnson *(V.P.)*

Arcon Municipal Div. **(1)**
903 E. Forest
Mora, MN 55051
Tel.: 612-679-2244
Sewer & Water Line Construction
S.I.C.: 1623
David Baum *(V.P.)*

Arcon Street Construction Div. **(1)**
903 E. Forest
Mora, MN 55051
Tel.: 612-679-2244
Street Construction
S.I.C.: 1611
Curt Radeke *(V.P.)*

ARDCO, INC.
12400 S. Laramie Ave.
Alsip, IL 60658
Tel.: 708-388-4300
Fax: 708-388-0952
Approx.Sls.: $100,000,000
Emp.: 1,000
Glass Refrigeration Equipment, Heat Transfer Equipment & Bent Glass
S.I.C.: 3231; 3443; 3585; 5078
Henry M. Buchbiner *(Chm. Bd. & Treas.)*
Larry Spang *(Pres.)*
Andrew G. Menke *(V.P.-Mfg.)*
Jack L. Etka *(V.P.-Prod. Service)*
J. Michael Barton *(V.P.-Mktg.)*
Paul Artwohl *(V.P.-Engrng.)*
Chester P. Lempicki *(Sec. & Comptroller)*

Outside Service Firm(s):

KPMG Peat Marwick*(Auditors)*
Peat Marwick Plaza, 303 E. Wacker Dr.
Chicago, IL 60601
Tel.: 312-938-1000

Katten, Muchin & Zavis*(Legal Firm)*
525 W. Monroe St., Ste. 1600
Chicago, IL 60661-3693
Tel.: 312-902-5200

Harris Trust & Savings Bank*(Major Banking Relationship)*
111 W. Monroe St.
Chicago, IL 60690
Tel.: 312-461-2265
Tel.: 800-858-0840

Divisions:

Ardco Door Div. **(1)**
P.O. Box 457
Elkton, KY 42220-0457
Tel.: 502-265-2581
Larry Spang *(Pres.-Glass Prods. Grp.)*
P. Artwohl *(V.P.-Engrng.)*
M. Barton *(V.P.-Mktg.)*
J. Etka *(V.P.-Mfg. & Product Service)*
A. Menke *(V.P.-Mfg. & Glass Technology)*

Buchbinder Div. **(1)**
12400 S. Laramie Ave.
Alsip, IL 60658
Tel.: 708-388-4300
M. Britigan *(Gen. Mgr.)*

Cold Zone+Filco **(1)**
221 S. Berry St.
Brea, CA 92622
Tel.: 714-529-4461
Will Wilson *(Pres. & Chief Exec. Officer-Heat Transfer Prod. Grp.)*
R. Echols *(Mgr.-Natl. Sls.)*

Kramer Div. **(1)**
1230 Parkway Ave., Ste. 104
West Trenton, NJ 08628
Tel.: 609-771-4096
G. Mahler *(Gen. Mgr.)*
Z. Piet *(Mgr.-Natl. Sls.)*

Russell Div. **(1)**
221 S. Berry St.
Brea, CA 92622
Tel.: 714-529-4461

Russell Div. **(1)**
3860 Arizona Ave.
Yuma, AZ 85365
Tel.: 602-726-6937
R. Neff *(V.P.-Mfg.)*
R. Davis *(Controller)*
W. Clark *(Mgr.-Mktg.)*
J. Fyne *(Mgr.-Natl. Sls.)*
K. Vogel *(Mfg.-Engrng.)*

Witt Div. **(1)**
435 Washington St.
Collierville, TN 38027
Tel.: 901-853-2770
D. Boulden *(Pres.)*
D. Peterson *(V.P.-Engrng.)*
M. Saxton *(Controller)*
M. Pitoniak *(Mgr.-Natl. Sls.)*

Ardell Industries Inc.
(Acquired by Jordan Company)

ARDELL INTERNATIONAL, INC.
2220 Gaspar Ave.
City of Commerce, CA 90040
Tel.: 213-728-2999
Year Founded: 1971
Emp.: 25
Import Export
Toilet Requisites; Hair Care Products; Cosmetics; Cosmetic Accessories
S.I.C.: 2844
Terri Cooper *(Vice Chm. & Chief Oper. Officer)*
Zvi Ryzman *(Pres.)*
David Woolf *(Exec. V.P.-Sls.)*

Computer Systems/Hardware:
Digital

Outside Service Firm(s):

Morey, Fischer*(Legal Firm)*
Beverly Hills, CA

Union Bank*(Major Banking Relationship)*
Beverly Hills, CA

Divisions:

Andrea International **(1)**
2220 Gaspar Ave.
City of Commerce, CA 90040
Tel.: 213-728-2999
Manufacturer of Eye Care Products
S.I.C.: 2844

Clubman **(1)**
2220 Gaspar Ave.
City of Commerce, CA 90040
Tel.: 213-728-2999
Manufacturer of Toiletries
S.I.C.: 2844

Delore **(1)**
2220 Gaspar Ave.
City of Commerce, CA 90040
Tel.: 213-728-2999
Manufacturer of Organic Nail Care Products
S.I.C.: 2844

GiGi **(1)**
2220 Gaspar Ave.
City of Commerce, CA 90040
Tel.: 213-728-2999
Manufacturer of Depilatory Wax Products
S.I.C.: 2844

SuperNail **(1)**
2220 Gaspar Ave.
City of Commerce, CA 90040
Tel.: 213-728-2999
Manufacturer of Professional Nail Care Products
S.I.C.: 2844

DONALD L. ARENDS INC.
1000 Jorie Blvd.
Oak Brook, IL 60521
Tel.: 708-990-0220
Year Founded: 1958
Approx.Billings: $10,600,000
Emp.: 19
Robert K. Erickson *(Pres.)*
Donald L. Arends *(Chief Exec. Officer)*
Gary E. Everhart *(V.P.)*
John C. Arends *(V.P.)*
Kathleen M. Hill *(Sec.)*
Martha O. Arends *(Treas.)*
Pauline Babusis *(Bookkeeper)*

ARGILAND COMPANY
(Formerly Byron Elevator Company)
302 Byron Ave. N.
Byron, MN 55920
Mailing Address:
P.O. Box 127,
Byron, MN 55920
Tel.: 507-775-2323
Fax: 507-775-2905
Approx.Sls.: $18,000,000
Emp.: 24
Wholesale & Retail Grain & Farm Supplies; Manufacture Livestock Feed
S.I.C.: 2048; 5153; 5191
Lyle S. Kuhlman *(Pres.)*
Nancy Kuhlman *(V.P.)*
Mike Kuhlman *(Treas.)*
Lou B. Kuhlman *(Sec.)*

Outside Service Firm(s):

Schuetzle & Carlson*(Auditors)*
New Ulm, MN

Michaels, Seeger, Rosenblad & Arnold*(Legal Firm)*
Rochester, MN

First Bank Rochester*(Major Banking Relationship)*
Rochester, MN

ARGO INTERNATIONAL CORP.
140 Franklin St.
New York, NY 10013
Tel.: 212-431-1700
Fax: 212-226-0694
Year Founded: 1954
Approx.Sls.: $114,191,000
Emp.: 330
Fiscal Year-end: 12/31/90
Distr. of Mechanical & Electrical Components, Renewal Parts & General Supplies for Marine & Industrial Use
S.I.C.: 5084; 5063
John Calicchio *(Chm. Bd.)*
S. Benincasa *(Pres.)*
Thomas J. Calicchio *(V.P.)*
John Santacroce *(Controller)*
Milton Rubin *(Sec. & Gen. Counsel)*
Ann Lackowitz *(Dir.-Adv.)*
John Stuart *(Mgr.-Mktg.)*

ARGO-TECH CORPORATION
23555 Euclid Ave.
Cleveland, OH 44117
Tel.: 216-692-6000 **DE**
Fax: 216-692-5011
Year Founded: 1986
Approx.Sls.: $80,000,000
Emp.: 850
Fiscal Year-end: 10/31/91
Export
Mfr. Products for the Aerospace & Defense Industry
S.I.C.: 3728
Michael S. Lipscomb *(Pres. & Chief Exec. Officer)*
Robert Schroeder *(Exec. V.P.)*
David L. Chrenick *(V.P.-Opers.)*
James M. Cunnigham *(V.P.-Human Resources)*
Steve Graettinger *(V.P.-Quality Control)*
Francis St. Clair *(V.P.-Fin.)*
Yoichi Fujiki *(Treas.)*
Paul R. Keen *(Gen. Counsel & Sec.)*
Ronald C. Barlow *(Dir.-Data Processing)*
Richard C. Cottrell *(Dir.-Real Estate)*
Robert E. Eichhorn *(Dir.-Pur.)*
Ken Hicks *(Dir.-Mktg.)*
Pat Totedo *(Mgr.-Customer Service)*

No. of U.S. Offices: 2

Outside Service Firm(s):

Deloitte & Touche*(Auditors)*
1717 East Ninth St.
Cleveland, OH 44114
Tel.: 216-589-1300

ARGOSY ELECTRONICS, INC.
10300 W. 70th St.
Eden Prairie, MN 55344
Tel.: 612-942-9232 **DE**
Fax: 612-942-0503
Emp.: 155
Mfr. of Hearing Aids
S.I.C.: 3842
Ronald J. Regan *(Pres.)*
Michael Hoke *(V.P. & Treas.)*
Jeffery Ringer *(V.P.-Fin.)*
Paul Hinker *(Sec.)*

Outside Service Firm(s):

Marquette Bank*(Major Banking Relationship)*
777 Marquette Ave.
Minneapolis, MN 55402
Tel.: 612-370-2182

ARIAN, LOWE, TRAVIS & GUSICK, INC.
343 W. Erie St., Ste. 520
Chicago, IL 60610
Tel.: 312-787-3300
Fax: 312-787-3599
Year Founded: 1982
Approx.Billings: $31,323,269
Emp.: 50
David M. Lowe *(Chm.)*
Daryl Travis *(Pres.)*
Bob Jaeschke *(Chief Fin. Officer)*
R. Powell Johns, Jr. *(Exec. V.P.)*
Jewell Lowe *(V.P.)*
Donnita Meredith *(V.P.)*
Robert E. Davies *(V.P., Acct. Dir.)*

ARINC INC.
2551 Riva Rd.
Annapolis, MD 21401
Tel.: 410-266-4000 **DE**
Fax: 301-266-4049
Year Founded: 1929
Assets: $109,684,000
Liabilities: $75,348,000
Net Worth: $34,336,000
Approx.Sls.: $26,118,000
Emp.: 220
Fiscal Year-end: 12/31/91
Holding Co.
S.I.C.: 6719
Andrew T. Hospodor *(Chm. Bd. & Chief Exec. Officer)*
Richard F. Jones *(V.P.-Fin. & Chief Fin. Officer)*
Daniel E. Sassi *(V.P.-Human Resources & Admin.)*
Michael P. Yacisin *(Treas.)*
A. James Sadler *(Controller)*
John L. Bartlett *(Corp. Sec. & Gen. Counsel)*
John Panagopulos *(Dir.-Pur.)*
Lenard Kotz *(Dir.-Personnel)*
William Jawish *(Dir.-Data Processing)*

Computer Systems/Hardware:
IBM 4381

Outside Service Firm(s):

Price Waterhouse*(Auditors)*
1801 K. Street, N.W.
Washington, DC 20006
Tel.: 202-296-0800

Alexander & Alexander*(Group Insurer)*
P.O. Box 73223
Baltimore, MD 21273
Tel.: 310-547-2800

Connecticut General Life Insurance Co.*(Group Insurer)*
P.O. Box 2975,
Hartford, CT 06104
Tel.: 203-726-6000

Wiley, Rein & Fielding*(Legal Firm)*
Baltimore, MD

Bank of America NT&SA*(Major Banking Relationship)*
555 So. Flower St., 5th Fl.
Los Angeles, CA 90071
Tel.: 213-228-3526
Fax: 213-228-4062

First National Bank of Maryland*(Major Banking Relationship)*
25 S. Charles St.
Baltimore, MD 21201
Tel.: 410-244-4025

Connecticut General Life Insurance Co.*(Pension Manager)*
P.O. Box 2975,
Hartford, CT 06104
Tel.: 203-726-6000

Subsidiaries:

ARINC Research Corp. **(1)**
2551 Riva Rd.
Annapolis, MD 21401
Tel.: 410-266-4000 (100%)
Approx.Sls.: $123,752,000
Emp.: 1,700
Fiscal Year-end: 12/31/91
Management & Engineering Co.
S.I.C.: 8711; 8741
Andrew T. Hospodor *(Chm. & Chief Exec. Officer)*
James L. Pierce *(Chief Oper. Officer)*
Richard F. Jones *(V.P.-Fin. & Chief Fin. Officer)*
Frederick J. Jacoby *(V.P.-Aerospace Systems)*
Robert F. Jeffonsor *(V.P.-Mktg.)*
Fred J. Jacoby *(V.P. & Gen. Mgr.)*
John L. Bartlett *(Sec. & Gen. Counsel)*

Aeronautical Radio, Inc. **(1)**
2551 Riva Rd.
Annapolis, MD 21401
Tel.: 410-226-4000
Approx.Rev.: $77,429,000
Emp.: 650
Provides Telecommunication Services To Air Transport Industry
S.I.C.: 4813
Andrew T. Hospodor *(Chm. Bd. & Chief Exec. Officer)*
Richard F. Jones *(V.P.-Fin. & Chief Fin. Officer)*
Edward R. Adelson *(V.P.-IA)*
Calvin E. Barfield *(V.P.-Opers.)*
Jeffrey L. McKnight *(V.P.-Mktg. & Strategic Plng.)*
John J. Sullivan *(V.P.- Quality)*
Chris A. Wargo *(V.P.-Engrng.)*
John L. Bartlett *(Sec. & Gen. Counsel)*

ARIZONA GRAINS INC.
601 E. Main Ave
Casa Grande, AZ 85222
Mailing Address:
P.O. Box T
Casa Grande, AZ 85222
Tel.: 602-836-8228
Fax: 602-421-0832
Year Founded: 1972
Assets: $28,000,000
Liabilities: $25,000,000
Net Worth: $3,000,000
Emp.: 80
Fiscal Year-end: 3/31/89
Farmer Owned Co-operative
S.I.C.: 8611
Greg Wuertz *(Chm. Bd.)*
John Skelley *(Pres.)*

Outside Service Firm(s):

Arthur Andersen & Co.*(Auditors)*
Phoenix, AZ

Arthur Andersen & Co.*(Auditors)*
Phoenix, AZ

Stanfield & McCarville*(Legal Firm)*
Casa Grande, AZ

Valley National Bank*(Major Banking Relationship)*
Casa Crande, AZ

Subsidiary:

Valley Seed Co. **(1)**
601 E. Main Ave.
Casa Grande, AZ 85222
Tel.: 602-836-8228
Wholesale & Retail Seeds & Grain
S.I.C.: 5191; 5261; 5153; 5199
Robert Huntington *(Pres.)*

ARIZONA LOTTERY
4740 E. University Dr.
Phoenix, AZ 85034
Tel.: 602-921-4400
Fax: 602-921-4512
Year Founded: 1981
Approx.Sls.: $287,900,000
Emp.: 130
Fiscal Year-end: 6/30/90
State Lottery
S.I.C.: 7999
Robert Lightfoot *(Acting Exec. Dir.)*
Ben Nova *(Asst. Dir.-Mktg.)*
Bill Forney *(Mgr.-Adv.)*

ARIZONA SUPERMARKETS, INC.
2452 W. Lincoln St.
Phoenix, AZ 85009
Tel.: 602-252-5185 **AZ**
Fax: 602-252-6914
Year Founded: 1989
Approx.Sls.: $50,000,000
Emp.: 400
Fiscal Year-end: 12/31/90
Import
6 Supermarkets Located in Arizona
S.I.C.: 5411
Tom Zaricki *(Pres. & Chief Exec. Officer)*
J. Paul Quinn *(Controller)*
Bill Spear *(Dir.-Sls. & Mktg.)*
David Miller *(Div. Mgr.-Sls.)*

No. of Mfg. Plants/Facilities: 48

Outside Service Firm(s):

Coopers & Lybrand*(Auditors)*
2901 N. Central
Phoenix, AZ 85012

Arizona Television, KTVK Channel 3
(See Arizona Supermarkets, Inc.)

ARIZONA WHOLESALE SUPPLY COMPANY
2020 E. University Dr.
Phoenix, AZ 85036
Mailing Address:
P.O. Box 2979,
Phoenix, AZ 85062
Tel.: 602-258-7901
Fax: 602-258-8335
Year Founded: 1944
Approx.Sls.: $40,000,000
Emp.: 115
Export
Distributor of Electrical Products & Consumer Appliances; Carpet; Air Conditioning Equipment
S.I.C.: 5023; 5064; 5075
Terence W. Thomas *(Chm. Bd. & Pres.)*
Floyd Slasor *(Sr. V.P.-Sls.)*
Ned Dryer *(Sec.)*
Jim Smith *(Sls. Mgr.-Dealer Sls.)*
Bob Markham *(Sls. Mgr.-RCA/GE Video)*
William Parks *(Sls. Mgr.-Carpet)*
Jim Smith *(Mgr.-Dlr. Appliance Div.)*

Principal(s):
Terence W. Thomas

Computer Systems/Hardware:
IBM

Outside Service Firm(s):

Ernst & Young*(Auditors)*
40 North Central, Ste. 900
Phoenix, AZ 85004
Tel.: 602-258-3366

Snell & Wilmer*(Legal Firm)*
3100 Valley Ctr.
Phoenix, AZ 85073
Tel.: 602-257-7211

First Interstate Bank*(Major Banking Relationship)*
P.O. Box 53441,
Phoenix, AZ 85072-3441
Tel.: 602-229-4049

Division:

QDI, Inc. **(1)**
11585 E. 53rd Ave., Unit G
Denver, CO 80239
Tel.: 303-371-1996
Jim Taylor *(Pres.)*

ARK-LES CORPORATION
51 Water St.
Watertown, MA 02172
Tel.: 617-924-2330
Fax: 617-924-5460
Approx.Sls.: $31,900,000
Emp.: 500
Electric Switches & Interconnect Devices, Terminals
S.I.C.: 3643; 3575
Norman E. MacNeil *(Chm. Bd. & Treas.)*
Bruce M. MacNeil *(Pres.)*
Thomas Hooper *(V.P.-Fin.)*
Joseph Paraboschi *(V.P.-Mfg.)*
Peter Pignone *(V.P.-Tech. Service)*
Thomas F. Prince *(V.P.-Engrng.)*
Ellen T. Maguire *(V.P.)*

Outside Service Firm(s):

Deloitte & Touche*(Auditors)*
125 Summer St.
Boston, MA 02110
Tel.: 617-261-8000
Fax: 617-261-8111

Hutchins & Wheeler*(Legal Firm)*
101 Federal St.
Boston, MA 02110
Tel.: 617-725-1500

Bay Bank*(Major Banking Relationship)*
Burlington, MA

ARKANSAS ELECTRIC COOPERATIVES INC.
8000 Scott Hamilton Dr.
Little Rock, AR 72209
Mailing Address:
P.O. Box 194208
Little Rock, AR 72219
Tel.: 501-570-2200 **AR**
Fax: 501-570-2337
Year Founded: 1942
Assets: $12,066
Liabilities: $9,689
Net Worth: $2,377
Approx.Sls.: $33,276,000
Emp.: 223
Fiscal Year-end: 12/31/91
Mfg. & Wholesale Distribute Electrical Equipment; Printing; Electrical Construction Management & Maintenance
S.I.C.: 5063; 3612; 1731; 2741
George Williams *(Chm. Bd.)*
Wayne Whitaker *(Vice Chm.)*
Carl S. Whillock *(Pres.)*
David Sain *(V.P.-Systems Services)*
Bill Welch *(V.P.-Sls. Services)*
Gene Sweat *(Treas.)*
William Beck *(Sec.)*
Bob Lyford *(Gen. Counsel)*
Bobby L. Daniel *(Acting V.P.-Fin. & Admin.)*
Janna H. Winchester *(Chief Accountant)*
Jim Hughes *(Pur. Agent)*
Don Parish *(Dir.-Personnel)*
Gary Stone *(Data Processing Dir.)*
Derwood Brett *(Corp. Communications)*

No. of Mfg. Plants/Facilities: 1
No. of U.S. Offices: 1

Computer Systems/Hardware:
IBM AS 400 Model B45

Outside Service Firm(s):

Baird, Kurtz & Dobson*(Auditors)*
Little Rock, AR

Federated Rural Electric Insurance Corp.*(Commercial Insurance Carrier)*
Kansas City, KS

National Rural Electric Cooperative Association*(Group Insurer)*
Washington, DC

The McMath Law Firm*(Legal Firm)*
Little Rock, AR

Worthen National Bank of Arkansas*(Major Banking Relationship)*
P.O. Box 1681, 200 W. Capitol
Little Rock, AR 72201
Tel.: 501-378-1209
Fax: 501-378-1062

Subsidiary:

Electric Research and Manufacturing Cooperative, Inc. (ERMCO) **(1)**
2225 Industrial Rd.
Dyersburg, TN 38024
Tel.: 901-285-9121
Emp.: 262
Manufacture Transformers
S.I.C.: 3612
W.F. McClain *(Exec. V.P. & Gen. Mgr.)*

ARKANSAS FARM BUREAU FEDERATION
10720 Kanis Rd.
Little Rock, AR 72211
Mailing Address:
P.O. Box 31,
Little Rock, AR 72203-0031
Tel.: 501-224-4400
Fax: 501-228-1557
Year Founded: 1935
Approx.Sls.: $160,500,000
Emp.: 325
Fire, Marine & Casualty Insurance Companies
S.I.C.: 6331
Andrew Whisenhunt *(Pres. & Chief Exec. Officer)*
Pat Baldridge *(Dir.-Defense Services)*

Subsidiaries:

Farm Bureau Casualty Insurance Co. **(1)**
10720 Kanis Rd.
Little Rock, AR 72203
Tel.: 501-224-4400
S.I.C.: 6331
Sam Cooper *(V.P. & Gen. Mgr.)*

Farm Bureau Mutual Insurance Co. of Arkansas **(1)**
10720 Kanis Road
Little Rock, AR 72203
Tel.: 501-224-4400
S.I.C.: 6331
Sam Cooper *(V.P. & Gen. Mgr.)*

ARKANSAS INDUSTRIAL DEVELOPMENT COMMISSION
One State Capitol Mall
Little Rock, AR 72201
Tel.: 501-682-1121
Fax: 501-682-7691
Year Founded: 1953
Approx.Sls.: $695,300,000
Emp.: 115
State Industrial Development Agency
S.I.C.: 7389
David Harrington *(Exec. Dir.)*
Cherry Duckett *(Deputy Dir.)*
Charles Sloan *(Dir.-Mktg.)*
Rob Middleton *(Dir.-Community Devel.)*
Jim Blakely *(Dir.-Established Industries)*
Mark Day *(Dir.-Fin.)*
Kym Patterson *(Mgr.-Res.)*
Windell Adams *(Special Asst.-Dir.)*
Melissa Thomas *(Mgr.-Communications)*

ARKANSAS OAK FLOORING
2200 W. 5th St.
Pine Bluff, AR 71601
Tel.: 501-534-3110
Fax: 501-534-3110, ext. 24
Approx.Sls.: $17,000,000
Emp.: 300
Hardwood Flooring; Lumber
S.I.C.: 2426
John E. Fox, Sr. *(Chm. Bd.)*
John E. Fox, Jr. *(Pres.)*
Fred T. Fox *(V.P.)*
Joe S. Fox *(V.P.)*
William H. Fox, Jr. *(V.P.)*
Mary E. Jehlen *(Sec. & Treas.)*
Frederick Fox *(Mgr.-Sls.)*
Joseph Fox *(Pur. Agent)*

Outside Service Firm(s):

Ramsey, Bridgforth, Harrelson & Starling*(Legal Firm)*
Pine Bluff, AR

Simmons First National Bank of Pine Bluff*(Major Banking Relationship)*
Pine Bluff, AR

ARKAY PACKAGING CORPORATION
22 Arkay Dr.
Hauppauge, NY 11788
Tel.: 516-273-2000
Fax: 516-273-2478
Approx.Sls.: $25,000,000
Emp.: 250
Custom Packaging
S.I.C.: 2657
Howard T. Kaneff *(Pres.)*
Walter Shiels *(V.P.-Mfg.)*
Keith Simmons *(Dir.-Fin.)*

Outside Service Firm(s):

Nussbaum, Yates & Walpow*(Auditors)*
Hauppauge, NY

Esterman & Reich*(Legal Firm)*
New York, NY

Marine Midland Bank*(Major Banking Relationship)*
140 Broadway
New York, NY 10015

ARLEN
ADVERTISING

ARLEN ADVERTISING
1516 S. Bundy Dr.
Los Angeles, CA 90025
Tel.: 310-820-3433
Year Founded: 1982
Approx.Billings: $14,760,000
Emp.: 14
High Tech, Pharmaceuticals, Food, Real Estate, Financial, Entertainment, Recruitment Adv. & Legal Mktg.
Michael Arlen *(Pres. & Creative Dir.)*
Phebe Arlen *(V.P., Opers.)*
Pauline Adams-Mizelle *(V.P. & Branch Mgr.-Irvine Facility)*
Mary Arlen *(Controller)*
Linda Nishimoto *(Acct. Exec. & Branch Mgr.-San Jose Office)*

ARLEY MERCHANDISE CORPORATION
540 Miles Standish Blvd.
Taunton, MA 02780
Tel.: 508-823-1400
Fax: 508-823-7387
Approx.Sls.: $140,000,000
Emp.: 2,200
Manufacture Domestics & Specialty Household Items; Curtains, Draperies & Kitchen Textiles
S.I.C.: 2391; 2392
David Riemer *(Chm. Bd., Pres. & Chief Exec. Officer)*
Michael Costa *(Chief Fin. Officer)*
Paul O'Reilly *(Exec. V.P. & Chief Oper. Officer)*
Kenneth Santos *(Exec. V.P.-Mfg.)*

Outside Service Firm(s):

Arthur Andersen & Co.*(Auditors)*
One Intl. Place, 100 Oliver St.
Boston, MA 02110
Tel.: 617-330-4000
Fax: 617-439-9731

Bank Of New England*(Major Banking Relationship)*
Taunton, MA

Subsidiary:

Rops Textiles Inc. **(1)**
540 Myles Standish Blvd.
Taunton, MA 02780
Tel.: 508-823-1400
Fax: 508-823-7387
Home Furnishings
S.I.C.: 2392
David I. Riemer *(Chm. Bd., Pres. & Chief Exec. Officer)*

ARMSTRONG INTERNATIONAL, INC.
900 Maple
Three Rivers, MI 49093
Tel.: 616-273-1415 **MI**
Fax: 616-278-6555
Year Founded: 1907
Sales Range: $60-79 Million
Emp.: 517
Fiscal Year-end: 6/29/92
Import Export
Manufacture Steam Traps, Steam Humidifiers, Purgers for Refrigeration, Pipe Line Strainers, Air Vents, Fishing & Marine Equipment
S.I.C.: 6719; 3494; 3585; 3949; 3429; 3613; 3443
L.F. Armstrong *(Chm. Bd.)*
M.H. Armstrong *(Pres. & Chief Exec. Officer)*
S.P. Gibson *(Chief Fin. Officer)*
Edgar A. Carter, Jr. *(Sr. V.P.-Fin.)*
R.T. Dewhirst *(V.P.-Mktg.)*
L.R. O'Dell *(V.P.)*
T. Morris *(Gen. Counsel)*
R.E. Imgrund *(Dir.-Data Processing)*
G.N. Phelps *(Dir.-Pur.)*
C.F. Roberts *(Dir.-Mktg. Services)*
H. Greene *(Mgr.-Personnel)*
Principal(s):
L.F. Armstrong
M.H. Armstrong

No. of Mfg. Plants/Facilities: 9
No. of U.S. Offices: 7
No. of Foreign Offices: 2

Computer Systems/Hardware:
Honeywell-DP S7

Outside Service Firm(s):

BDO Seidman*(Auditors)*
700 Commercial Bldg.
Kalamazoo, MI 49007-4758

Butzbaugh & Ryan*(Legal Firm)*
St. Joseph, MI

First National Bank of Three Rivers*(Major Banking Relationship)*
Three Rivers, MI

Division:

Armstrong Machine Works **(1)**
816 Maple
Three Rivers, MI 49093
Tel.: 616-273-1415 (100%)
Steam Traps, Steam Humidifiers, Purgers for Refrigeration, Pipe Line Strainers, Air Vents
S.I.C.: 3494; 3559
Gerald J. Gilchrist Jr. *(Gen. Mgr.)*

Subsidiaries:

Armstrong-Hunt, Inc. **(1)**
1 Armstrong Rd.
Milton, FL 32583
Tel.: 904-626-0051 (100%)
Manufacture Industrial Heat Exchangers
S.I.C.: 3443
David Boykin *(Pres.)*

Everlasting Valve Co. **(1)**
108 Somogyi Court
South Plainfield, NJ 07080
Tel.: 201-769-0700 (100%)
Emp.: 40
Manufacture Service Specialty Valves
S.I.C.: 3494
Robert Bunting *(Pres.)*

Computrol, Inc. **(1)**
499 E. Corporate Dr.
Meridian, ID 83642
Tel.: 208-376-0500 (96%)
Manufacture Fishing Equipment
S.I.C.: 3949
David A. Keech *(Pres.)*

S&K Products, Inc. **(1)**
4999 E. Corporate Dr.
Meridian, ID 83642
Tel.: 208-887-1000 (100%)
Emp.: 45
Manufacture Fishing Equipment
S.I.C.: 3949

Armstrong International, Inc.—(Continued)

Sturgis Foundry Corp. **(1)**
1000 W. West
Sturgis, MI 49091
Tel.: 616-651-8544 (100%)
Gray Iron Foundry
S.I.C.: 3321
James Goethals *(Pres.)*

Warrick Controls, Inc. **(1)**
4237 Normandy Ct.
Royal Oak, MI 48073
Tel.: 313-545-2512 (100%)
Emp.: 55
Manufacture Electrical Relays
S.I.C.: 3625
Ted J. Wrona *(Pres.)*

Joint Venture:

Armstrong-Yoshitake, Inc. **(1)**
816 Maple St.
Three Rivers, MI 49093
Tel.: 616-273-1415
Industrial Water Heaters & Valves
S.I.C.: 3494
David M. Armstrong *(Pres.)*

Non-U.S. Holding:

Armstrong Machine Works, S.A. **(1)**
Parc Industrial Des Hauts-Sarts B 4040
Herstal,
Liege, Belgium
Tel.: 480152
Mfrs. Steam Traps
S.I.C.: 3494
Roger Closset *(Plant Mgr.)*

ARMSTRONG PRODUCE LTD.
651 Ilalo St.
Honolulu, HI 96813
Tel.: 808-538-7051
Fax: 808-538-1401
Approx.Sls.: $24,000,000
Emp.: 65
Fresh Fruits & Vegetables
S.I.C.: 5148
Harold S. Teruya *(Chm. Bd.)*
Mark Teruya *(Pres.)*
Margaret S. Yamauchi *(Treas.)*
Calvin Shigemura *(V.P.)*
Wayne Teruya *(V.P.)*
Ethel Teruya *(Sec.)*

Outside Service Firm(s):

First Hawaiian Bank*(Major Banking Relationship)*
165 South King St.
Honolulu, HI 96813
Tel.: 808-525-5876
Fax: 808-525-5791

ARNAV INDUSTRIES, INC.
31 W. 27th St.
New York, NY 10001
Tel.: 212-532-6268 **DE**
Fax: 212-532-6265
Year Founded: 1967
Approx.Sls.: $40,000,000
Emp.: 20
Mfr. of Women's Jackets & Vests, Except Fur & Leather; Women's, Misses' & Juniors Suits; Men's & Boys Tailored Suit-type Suits Made From Purchased Materials
S.I.C.: 2337; 2311
Leonard Wassner *(Pres.)*
Joseph Wassner *(V.P.-Fin.)*
Judah Wassner *(Controller)*

Outside Service Firm(s):

Otterbourg, Steindler, Houston & Rosen*(Legal Firm)*
230 Park Ave.
New York, NY 10017
Tel.: 212-661-9100

National Westminster Bank plc*(Major Banking Relationship)*
175 Water St.
New York, NY 10038-4924
Tel.: 212-602-3364

ARNHOLD AND S. BLEICHROEDER, INC.
45 Broadway
New York, NY 10006
Tel.: 212-943-9200
Fax: 212-248-8861
Year Founded: 1937
Assets: $2,076,102,908
Liabilities: $1,969,952,258
Net Worth: $106,150,650
Sales Range: $60-79 Million
Emp.: 200
Fiscal Year-end: 9/30/91
Investment Banker; Security Broker
S.I.C.: 6211
Henry H. Arnhold *(Chm. Bd.)*
Stanford S. Warshawsky *(Vice Chm. & Legal Officer)*
Stephen M. Kellen *(Pres.)*
James Lever *(Sr. V.P. & Dir.-Mngmt. Info. Systems)*
Charles Rodriguez *(Sr. V.P.-Opers. & Personnel Dir.)*
Ronald A. Bendelius *(Sr. V.P. & Controller)*
Allen Langman *(Sr. V.P. & Treas.)*
Principal(s):
Henry H. Arnhold
Stephen M. Kellen

Computer Systems/Hardware:
IBM AS/400 Model B-50

Outside Service Firm(s):

Joel E. Sammett & Co.*(Auditors)*
New York, NY

Shearman & Sterling*(Legal Firm)*
599 Lexington Ave.
New York, NY 10022
Tel.: 212-848-4000

BEN ARNOLD CO., INC.
300 Plaza Dr.
Binghamton, NY 13903
Tel.: 607-729-9331
Fax: 607-797-7103
Approx.Sls.: $100,000,000
Emp.: 190
Holding Co.; Wholesale Liquor
S.I.C.: 6719; 5182
Burton Koffman *(Pres. & Treas.)*
Richard Koffman *(Sec.)*

Division:

Ben Arnold Co., Inc. **(1)**
700 Gervais St.
Columbia, SC 29201
Tel.: 803-251-3456
Fax: 803-251-3406
Wholesale Liquor
S.I.C.: 5182
Norman J. Arnold *(Pres.)*

TRUMAN ARNOLD COMPANIES
701 S. Robison Rd.
Texarkana, TX 75501
Mailing Address:
P.O. Box 1481
Texarkana, TX 75501
Tel.: 903-794-3835 **TX**
Fax: 903-832-7226
Year Founded: 1969
Approx.Sls.: $150,000,000
Emp.: 250
Retail Service Stations & Road Runner Convenience Stores; Wholesale Petroleum Prods.; Patent Owners; Wholesale Petroleum Marketer; Bulk Storage & Terminal Operator; Aviation-Fixed Base Operator
S.I.C.: 5541; 5411; 6794; 5171
Truman Arnold *(Chm. Bd., Pres. & Chief Exec. Officer)*
Greg Arnold *(Chief Oper. Officer & V.P.)*
Larry Fincher *(Exec. V.P., Sec. & Treas.)*
James H. Day *(Sec. & Dir.-Admin.)*

Outside Service Firm(s):

Holliday, Lemons, Thomas & Cox*(Auditors)*
Texarkana, TX

Skaggs & Farnell*(Auditors)*
Texarkana, TX

State First National Bank*(Major Banking Relationship)*
Texarkana, TX

ARNOLD FORTUNA LAWNER & CABOT

ARNOLD FORTUNA LAWNER & CABOT
(Formerly Arnold Fortuna Lane & Cabot, Inc.)
(Arnold Fortuna Lane & Cabot, Inc. Merged with Lawner Reingold Britton & Partners)
101 Arch St.
Boston, MA 02110
Tel.: 617-737-6400
Fax: 617-737-6658
Year Founded: 1946
Assets: $19,873,000
Liabilities: $18,693,000
Net Worth: $1,180,000
Approx.Billings: $225,000,000
Emp.: 360
Fiscal Year-end: 12/31/91
Advertising Agency
S.I.C.: 7311
Ed Eskandarian *(Chm. & Chief Exec. Officer)*
John C. Verret *(Vice Chm.)*
Michael H. Reingold *(Vice Chm.)*
Ron Lawner *(Vice Chm., Chief Creative Officer)*
Richard L. Britton *(Exec. V.P., Gen Mgr.)*
Richard B. Emerson *(Exec. V.P., Gen. Mgr. & Div. Oper.)*
Charles Kiefer III *(Exec. V.P., Chief Fin. Officer)*
William Monaghan *(Exec. V.P., Dir., Creative Services)*
Joseph Teixeira *(Exec. V.P., Chief Admin. Officer)*
Michael B. Fortuna *(Exec. V.P., Creative Dir.)*
Keith Lane *(Exec. V.P., Creative Dir.)*
Charles J. Matzell *(Exec. V.P., Assoc. Creative Dir.)*
Karen Driscoll *(Exec. V.P., Acct. Dir.)*
Carolyn Smith *(Exec. V.P., Acct. Dir.)*
Timothy Brenton *(Sr. V.P., Mngmt. Supvr.)*
Ernest Pagliese *(Sr. V.P., Mngmt. Supvr.)*
Lyn Rosoff *(Sr. V.P., Mngmt. Supvr.)*
William J. Boch *(Sr. V.P., Assoc. Creative Dir.)*
Robert Minihan *(Sr. V.P., Assoc. Creative Dir.)*
John Welsh *(Sr. V.P., Assoc. Creative Dir.)*
Maureen McNamara *(Sr. V.P., Dir. Strategic Plng. & Media Services)*
John Gaffney *(Sr. V.P., Natl. Media Dir.)*
Peter Crowell *(Sr. V.P., Grp. Media Dir.)*
Jean Hudson *(Sr. V.P., Media Dir.-Retail)*
Peter Bergstrom *(V.P., Assoc. Media Dir.)*
James Conley *(V.P., Dir. Pub. Rels.)*
Ann Gary *(V.P., Mngmt. Supvr.)*
Jean Manasian *(V.P., Mngmt. Supvr.)*
George Rogers *(V.P., Mngmt. Supvr.)*
Sharon McCabe *(V.P., Mngmt. Supvr.)*
Adam Sholley *(V.P., Mngmt. Supvr.)*
John Newton *(V.P., Mngmt. Supvr.)*
Carol Bengis *(V.P., Mngmt. Supvr.)*
Laura Murphy *(V.P., Mngmt. Supvr.)*
Kristin Volk *(V.P., Consumer Insight Dir.)*
Steve Connelly *(V.P., Assoc. Creative Dir.)*
Kevin Kearns *(V.P., Assoc. Creative Dir.)*
Robert Pye *(V.P., Assoc. Creative Dir.)*
Bruce Patteson *(V.P., Copy Chief)*
David Abend *(V.P., Copy Supvr.)*
Rod Smith *(V.P., Art Supvr.)*
Marge Sullivan-Kaplan *(V.P., Dir., Brdcst. Production)*
William Goodell *(V.P., Assoc. Dir, Brdcst. Production)*
Betsy Wheeler *(V.P., Dir., Pritn Production & Traffic)*
Gaspar Marsala *(V.P., Production Mgr.)*
John Miller *(V.P., Print Production)*

No. of U.S. Offices: 8

Branches:

Arnold Fortuna Lawner & Cabot **(1)**
600 Southborough Dr.
Portland, ME 04106
Tel.: 207-773-7233
Fax: 207-774-7437
Alison Dodson *(Agency Dir., Acct. Supvr.)*
Beryl Velverde *(Pub. Rels. Acct. Supvr.)*
Denise Beck *(Pub. Rels. Mgr.)*

Arnold Fortuna Lawner & Cabot **(1)**
241 Main St.
Hartford, CT 06106
Tel.: 203-278-1500
Fax: 203-278-1506
Janet Riccio *(Sr. V.P., Agency Dir.)*
E.J. Conlin *(Acct. Supvr., Pub. Rels.)*

Arnold Fortuna Lawner & Cabot **(1)**
One Columbia Circle
Albany, NY 12203
Tel.: 518-456-4200
Fax: 518-456-5539
Lauren Mancuso *(V.P., Agency Dir.)*

Arnold Fortuna Lawner & Cabot **(1)**
Southview Commons, 100 Whitespruce Blvd.
Rochester, NY 14623
Tel.: 716-424-1373
Fax: 716-424-1375
Jerrie VanGelder *(Sr. V.P., Dir. NY State Opers.)*

Arnold Fortuna Lawner & Cabot **(1)**
5788 Widewaters Parkway
De Witt, NY 13214
Tel.: 315-446-0037
Fax: 315-446-0379
Sam Catalano *(V.P., Agency Dir.)*

Arnold Fortuna Lawner & Cabot **(1)**
280051 Charlesvoix Drive, S.E.
Grand Rapids, MI 49546
Kathy Koepnick *(Supvsr.)*

Arnold Fortuna Lawner & Cabot **(1)**
9881 Broken Land Pkwy.
Columbia, MD
Jasson Bellushi *(V.P.)*

Divisions:

Cipriani Kremer Design **(1)**
2 Copley Place
Boston, MA 02116
Tel.: 617-236-1422
Fax: 617-262-1385
Robert Cipriani *(Pres., Creative Dir.)*
Murray Kremer *(Exec. V.P.)*

RCM Cabot **(1)**
40 Broad St.
Boston, MA 02109
Tel.: 617-482-7300
Direct Marketing & Database Marketing

ARNOLD MACHINERY CO.
2975 W. 21st So.
Salt Lake City, UT 84119
Mailing Address:
P.O. Box 30020
Salt Lake City, UT 84130
Tel.: 801-972-4000
Year Founded: 1929
Approx.Sls.: $70,000,000
Emp.: 250
Fiscal Year-end: 9/30/91
Import
Distr. of Construction & Material Handling Equip., Implements; Indus. Equip.; Concrete Aggregate Equip.; Mining Large Bucket Shovels, Loaders
S.I.C.: 3531
Alvin Richer *(Chm., Pres. & Chief Exec. Officer)*
Kayden Bell *(V.P., Sec. & Treas.)*
Ken Koehler *(Adv. Mgr.)*

Computer Systems/Hardware:
IBM System 36, IBM RISC 6000

Divisions:

Construction & Mining Div. **(1)**
2975 W. 21st So.
Salt Lake City, UT 84119
Tel.: 801-972-4000
Fax: 801-975-9749
Frank Hammond *(Pres.)*

General Implement Distributors **(1)**
2955 W. 21st So.
Salt Lake City, UT 84119
Tel.: 801-972-4321
Fax: 801-975-9749
Wendell Nelson *(V.P. & Gen. Mgr.)*

Material Handling Div. **(1)**
2921 W. 21st So.
Salt Lake City, UT 84119
Tel.: 801-972-4000
Fax: 801-975-9749
Rex Mecham *(V.P. & Gen. Mgr.)*

Subsidiary:

Arnold Machinery Company of Arizona **(1)**
6024 W. Southern Ave.
Laveen, AZ 85339
Tel.: 602-237-3755
Terence Cunningham *(Pres.)*

ARNOLD STEEL COMPANY, INC.
P.O. Box 739
Lakewood, NJ 08701
Tel.: 908-363-1079
Fax: 908-905-7460
Sales Range: $10-19 Million
Emp.: 60
Structural Steel
S.I.C.: 3441
Felix Pflaster *(Pres.)*
Ernest Olsen *(Exec. V.P.)*
Tina Pflaster *(Sec.)*

Outside Service Firm(s):

Mohel, Vogel & Elliott*(Auditors)*
Lakewood, NJ

Brenner, Wallock & Hill*(Legal Firm)*
Princeton, NJ

National Westminster Bank plc*(Major Banking Relationship)*
2 Montgomery St.
Jersey City, NJ 07302
Tel.: 201-547-7000

ARNOLDS INTERIORS, INC.
9740 Scranton, Ste. 300
San Diego, CA 92121
Tel.: 619-625-0128 **CA**
Fax: 619-625-3202
Year Founded: 1966
Approx.Sls.: $35,000,000
Emp.: 250
Furniture Stores
S.I.C.: 5712
Fred Comrie *(Owner)*
Rick Huffman *(Pres. & Dir.-Stores)*
Lawrence Belinsky *(Dir.-Stores)*

Outside Service Firm(s):

Kramer & Zucker*(Auditors)*
San Diego, CA

Union Bank*(Major Banking Relationship)*
Trust Dept., 8155 Mercury Ct.
San Diego, CA 92112
Tel.: 619-230-4487

PAUL ARPIN VANLINES, INC.
Box 1302
East Greenwich, RI 02818
Tel.: 401-828-8111
Tel.: 800-343-3500 **RI**
Year Founded: 1900
Approx.Sls.: $67,900,000
Emp.: 348
Fiscal Year-end: 12/31/91
Local & Long Distance Trucking
S.I.C.: 4212; 4213
Paul G. Arpin *(Chief Exec. Officer)*
David Arpin *(Pres.)*
Robert F. Caldwell *(V.P.-Admin.)*
John C. Cottier *(V.P.-Sls.)*
John P. Leistritz *(V.P.-Mktg.)*
Michael F. Killoran *(Controller)*
Principal(s):
Paul G. Arpin
David Arpin

No. of Mfg. Plants/Facilities: 9
No. of U.S. Offices: 9

Outside Service Firm(s):

Sansiveri, Ryan & Sullivan*(Auditors)*
Providence, RI

Pucci & Goldin*(Legal Firm)*
123 Dyer St.
Providence, RI 02909
Tel.: 401-861-7400

Fleet National Bank*(Major Banking Relationship)*
125 Dupont Dr.
Providence, RI 02907-3178
Tel.: 401-278-5335

ARRINGTON TRAVEL CENTER INC.
55 W. Monroe St.
Chicago, IL 60603
Tel.: 312-726-4900
Tel.: 800-621-9226
Fax: 312-726-1447
Year Founded: 1969
Approx.Sls.: $100,000,000
Emp.: 200
Fiscal Year-end: 12/31/91
Corporate Travel Agency
S.I.C.: 4724
Michael B. Arrington *(Pres. & Chief Exec. Officer)*
Gayle Bisso *(Gen. Mgr.)*
Mark Walton *(Dir.-Mktg. & Sls.)*
Kelly L. Kuhn *(Mgr.-Pub. Rels.)*
Principal(s):
Michael B. Arrington

Non-U.S. Holding:

Arrington-Hillgate International **(1)**
Shropshire House, 2-10 Capper St., London, WC1E 6JA, United Kingdom
Tel.: 011-44-71-753-8811
Business Travel Management
S.I.C.: 8741
Michael B. Arrington *(Chief Oper. Officer)*
Jeremy Bull *(Chief Fin. Officer)*

ARROW CHEVROLET, INC.
14640 Cicero Ave.
Midlothian, IL 60445
Tel.: 708-389-0600 **IL**
Fax: 708-389-7354
Approx.Sls.: $93,000,000
Emp.: 215
New & Used Automobiles
S.I.C.: 5511
Cary Frank *(Pres.)*
Gary Dunn *(V.P. & Treas.)*

Outside Service Firm(s):

Southwest Financial Bank*(Major Banking Relationship)*
Chicago, IL

ARROW FASTENER CO., INC.
271 Mayhill St.
Saddle Brook, NJ 07662
Tel.: 201-843-6900 **NJ**
Fax: 201-843-3911
Year Founded: 1929
Emp.: 600
Import Export
Stapling Machines & Pliers, Gun Tackers, Staples, Glue Guns, Glues Rivet Tools & Rivets
S.I.C.: 3579; 2899; 3315; 3423; 3452; 3542
Allan Abrams *(Chm. Bd. & Pres.)*
Barry Knispel *(Exec. V.P.)*
Robert Hand *(V.P.-Sls.)*
Isabel Knispel *(Treas. & Sec.)*
Fred Davidson *(Mgr.-Adv.)*
Jerry Fitzsimmons *(Pur. Agent)*

No. of Mfg. Plants/Facilities: 1
No. of U.S. Offices: 2

Outside Service Firm(s):

Stoopler & Stoopler*(Auditors)*
Great Neck, NY

First Fidelity Bank, N.A.*(Major Banking Relationship)*
Rochelle Park, NJ

ARROW INDUSTRIES, INC.
(Sub. of ConAgra Inc.)
2625 Belt Line Rd.
Carrollton, TX 75006
Mailing Address:
P.O. Box 810489,
Dallas, TX 75381
Tel.: 214-416-6500
Year Founded: 1951
Approx.Sls.: $180,000,000
Emp.: 1,100
Process, Package & Distribute Dried Beans & Peas, Rice, Popcorn, Pepper, Household Aluminum Foil, Polyethylene Packaging Materials, Charcoal Lighter Fluid
S.I.C.: 2034; 2099; 2673; 2861; 2899; 5149; 5199
Steven Rosenberg *(Pres.)*
Michael M. Conway *(V.P.-Fin. & Chief Fin. Officer)*
Randall Gathright *(V.P.-Mngmt. Information Systems)*
Ronnie E. Rothwell *(Controller)*
David Swanson *(Mgr.-Personnel)*

Computer Systems/Hardware:
IBM AS/400

Outside Service Firm(s):

Coopers & Lybrand*(Auditors)*
1999 Bryan St., Ste. 3000
Dallas, TX 75201
Tel.: 214-754-5000

NationsBank Texas*(Major Banking Relationship)*
901 Main St., 16th Fl.
Dallas, TX 75202
Tel.: 214-922-5000

ARROW METAL PRODUCTS CORPORATION
1200 Mt. Elliott Ave.
Detroit, MI 48207
Tel.: 313-567-6112
Fax: 313-567-8459
Approx.Sls.: $13,000,000
Emp.: 95
Automobile Body Parts, Stamped Metal
S.I.C.: 3465
Philip K. Mebus, Jr. *(Pres. & Treas.)*
J. Howard Kay *(V.P.)*
Christopher Mebus *(Controller)*
Clara Mebus Kay *(Sec.)*

Outside Service Firm(s):

Manufacturers National Bank N.A.*(Major Banking Relationship)*
38th Fl., 100 Renaissance Center
Detroit, MI 48243
Tel.: 313-222-4227

ARROW PNEUMATICS CO. INC.
500 N. Oakwood Rd.
Lake Zurich, IL 60047
Tel.: 708-438-9100
Fax: 708-438-7110
Year Founded: 1914
Approx.Sls.: $16,000,000
Emp.: 100
Import Export
Manufacture Compressed Air Dryer For Heating & Air Conditioning
S.I.C.: 3569; 3585
Jerry Brown *(Pres.)*
Robert Shulick *(V.P.-Opers.)*
Philip Pick *(Controller)*
Pauline Brown *(Mgr.-Pub. Rels. & Adv.)*
Kendall P. Hayes *(Mgr.-Adv. & Mktg. Consultant)*
Jules Scaglione *(Mgr.-Mktg.)*
Martin Fiedler *(Chief Engr.)*
Jean Bourke *(Pur. Agent)*

Computer Systems/Hardware:
IBM System 36

Outside Service Firm(s):

Price Waterhouse*(Auditors)*
200 E. Randolph
Chicago, IL 60601
Tel.: 312-565-1500

The Northern Trust Co.*(Major Banking Relationship)*
50 S. LaSalle St.
Chicago, IL 60675
Tel.: 312-630-6000
Fax: 312-444-7028

Divisions:

Arrow Fluid Power **(1)**
2111 W. 21st. St.
Broadview, IL 60153
Tel.: 708-343-6176
Fax: 708-343-1907
Import Export
Computer Systems/Hardware:
IBM System 36
Manufacture of Fluid Power Accessories; Air Filters, Regulators
S.I.C.: 3585
Robert Shulick *(V.P.-Oper.)*
Philip Pick *(Controller)*
Jules Seaglione *(Mgr.-Mktg.)*
Walt Lukitsh *(Mgr.-Sls.)*
Pauline Brown *(Mgr.-Adv.)*
Joe Magnano *(Pur. Agent)*
James Loughran *(Chief Engineer)*
Joe Magnano *(Pur. Agent)*

Arrow Sintered Products **(1)**
7650 Industrial Dr.
Forest Park, IL 60130
Tel.: 708-771-5010

J.R. Technical **(1)**
500 Oakwood Rd.
Lake Zurich, IL 60047
Tel.: 708-438-6229
Fax: 708-438-7110
Import
Computer Systems/Hardware:
IBM Sys. 36
Rick Hege *(V.P.-Mktg.)*

ARROW TANK & ENGINEERING CO.
8950 Evergreen Blvd.
Minneapolis, MN 55433
Tel.: 612-786-9510

Arrow Tank & Engineering Co.—(Continued)

Fax: 612-786-2104
Approx.Sls.: $20,000,000
Emp.: 150
Fiscal Year-end: 6/30/92

Export
Pressure Vessels, Steel Plate Fabrication
S.I.C.: 3443
John H. Haskins *(Pres.)*
Betty Haskins *(Sec.)*
Gary Anderson *(Dir.-Pur.)*

Outside Service Firm(s):

Copeland, Buhl & Co.*(Auditors)*
Minneapolis, MN

Richfield Bank & Trust Co.*(Major Banking Relationship)*
Minneapolis, MN

ARROWHEAD MILLS, INC.
110 S. Lawton
Hereford, TX 79045
Mailing Address:
P.O. Box 2059
Hereford, TX 79045
Tel.: 806-364-0730 **TX**
Fax: 806-364-8242
Year Founded: 1960
Approx.Sls.: $10,000,000
Emp.: 68

Import Export
Mfr. Flour, Grain Mill Products, Unrefined Vegetable Salad & Cooking Oil
S.I.C.: 2041; 2079
J. Frank Ford *(Chm. Bd.)*
Boyd Foster *(Pres. & Chief Exec. Officer)*
Hubert Holcombe, Jr. *(Exec. V.P.-Sls. & Chief Oper. Officer)*
Vance A. Devareaux *(Exec. V.P., Sec., Treas. & Chief Fin. Officer)*
W. Joe Hacker *(V.P.-Pur.)*
Larry R. Hendershot *(V.P.-Quality Control)*
Armando Torres *(V.P.-Opers.)*
Oscar L. Williams *(V.P.)*

Outside Service Firm(s):

Amarillo National Bank*(Major Banking Relationship)*
Amarillo, TX
Tel.: 806-378-8000

ART IRON, INC.
860 Curtis St.
Toledo, OH 43607-0964
Mailing Address:
P.O. Box 964
Toledo, OH 43697-0964
Tel.: 419-241-1261 **OH**
Fax: 419-242-9768
Year Founded: 1905
Approx.Sls.: $24,000,000
Emp.: 300
Fiscal Year-end: 12/31/91
Fabricates Structural Steel, Stairs & Railings for Buildings; Distribute Steel, Aluminum, Stainless Steel & Tool Steel
S.I.C.: 3441; 3446; 5051
H.H. Schlatter *(Chm. Bd.)*
Donald A. Schlatter *(Pres., Chief Exec. Officer & Gen. Counsel)*
M.F. Retcher *(Chief Fin. Officer & Treas.)*
J. A. Arquette *(Mgr.-Benefits Insurance)*

Principal(s):
H.H. Schlatter
Donald A. Schlatter

No. of Mfg. Plants/Facilities: 8

Computer Systems/Hardware:
Bull 6000

Outside Service Firm(s):

KPMG Peat Marwick*(Auditors)*
Toledo, OH

Metropolitan Life Insurance Co.*(Group Insurer)*
One Madison Ave.
New York, NY 10010-3690
Tel.: 215-578-9292

Eastman & Smith*(Legal Firm)*
240 N. Huron St.
Toledo, OH 43604
Tel.: 419-241-6152

Society National Bank*(Major Banking Relationship)*
Toledo, OH

The Principal Financial Group*(Pension Manager)*
Des Moines, IA

Subsidiaries:

Abros, Inc. **(1)**
860 Curtis St., P.O. Box 940
Toledo, OH 43697
Tel.: 419-241-1261 (100%)
S.I.C.: 3441; 3446
D.A. Schlatter *(Chief Oper. Officer)*

E.K. Morris & Co., Inc. **(1)**
10270 Wayne Ave.
Cincinnati, OH 45215
Tel.: 513-771-4494
Steel Service Center
S.I.C.: 5051
Jeff Enia *(Gen. Mgr.)*

ART VAN FURNITURE INC.
6500 E. Fourteen Mile Rd.
Warren, MI 48092
Tel.: 313-939-0800
Fax: 313-959-3055
Approx.Sls.: $175,000,000
Emp.: 1,250
Retail Home Furnishings
S.I.C.: 5712
Art Van Elsander *(Chm. Bd.)*
Ray Plummer *(V.P.)*
Cathy DiSante *(Dir.-Adv.)*

Outside Service Firm(s):

Manufacturers National Bank N.A.*(Major Banking Relationship)*
38th Fl., 100 Renaissance Center
Detroit, MI 48243
Tel.: 313-222-4227

ARTCO-BELL CORPORATION
1302 Industrial Blvd.
Temple, TX 76503
Mailing Address:
P.O. Box 608
Temple, TX 76503
Tel.: 817-778-1811 **TX**
Fax: 817-771-0827
Year Founded: 1961
Approx.Sls.: $30,000,000
Emp.: 500

Import Export
Mfr. School Furniture, Tables, Desks, Computer & Furniture
S.I.C.: 2531; 2521; 2522
Noble Oldham *(Pres. & Chief Exec. Officer)*
Russell Wilson *(Exec. V.P.)*
Robert D. Agee *(V.P.-Sls.)*
Louis Vittek *(V.P.-Mfg.)*
Pat Beard *(Gen. Counsel)*
David Hardwick *(Dir.-Data Processing)*
Robert Ranly *(Dir.-Pur.)*
Larry Tomlin *(Dir.-Human Resources)*

Principal(s):
Noble Oldham
Robert D. Agee
Louis Vittek

No. of Mfg. Plants/Facilities: 2

Computer Systems/Hardware:
IBM

Outside Service Firm(s):

Jaynes, Reitmeier, Boyd & Therrell, P.C.*(Auditors)*
Waco, TX
Tel.: 817-776-4190

Beard & Kultgen*(Legal Firm)*
Waco, TX

NationsBank Texas*(Major Banking Relationship)*
P.O. Box 831000
Dallas, TX 75283-1000
Tel.: 214-508-0972

Subsidiary:

Artco-Bell Steel Corp. **(1)**
3601 Eberhardt Rd.
Temple, TX 76503
Tel.: 817-771-2253
Tel.: 800-933-2252
Emp.: 30
Manufacture of Coils & Tubing
S.I.C.: 3312
Doyle Clement *(Gen. Mgr.)*

ARTEC DISTRIBUTING, INC.
One Pine Haven Shore Rd.
Shelburne, VT 05482
Mailing Address:
P.O. Box 309
Shelburne, VT 05482
Tel.: 802-985-9411 **VT**
Fax: 802-985-3403
Year Founded: 1970
Sales Range: $100-499 Million
Emp.: 251
Fiscal Year-end: 12/31/91

Import Export
Distributor Of Prerecorded Home Video, CD's & Audio Cassettes
S.I.C.: 5099
Martin F. Gold *(Pres. & Chief Exec. Officer)*
Howard D. Goldberg *(Corp. Sec.)*
Frederick Ames *(V.P. & Controller)*
Bill Boyle *(V.P.-Mktg.)*
John Le Claire *(V.P.-Opers.)*
Ken Miller *(V.P.-Sls.)*
Jay Austin *(Mgr.-Pur. & Video)*
Ed Nenert *(Mgr.-Mkgt.)*
Joe Snee *(Mgr.-Human Resources)*
Vinnie Spagnolo *(Mgr.-Telecommunications)*

Principal(s):
Martin F. Gold
Howard D. Goldberg

Computer Systems/Hardware:
VAX/VMS 6330

Outside Service Firm(s):

Price Waterhouse*(Auditors)*
160 Federal St.
Boston, MA 02110
Tel.: 617-439-3308
Fax: 617-439-3308

Pomperleau Insurers, Inc., *(Commercial Insurance Carrier)*
Burlington, VT

Blue Cross & Blue Shield Association*(Group Insurer)*
Montpelier, VT

Paul, Frank & Collins Inc.*(Legal Firm)*
1 Church St.
Burlington, VT 05402
Tel.: 802-658-2311

Barclays Bank PLC*(Major Banking Relationship)*
15 Colmore Row
Birmingham, B3 2BY, United Kingdom

Subsidiary:

Academy Entertainment Inc. **(1)**
9250 Wilshire Blvd., Ste. 404
Beverly Hills, CA 90212
Tel.: 310-275-2170
Fax: 310-275-1098
Emp.: 30
Manufacture Prerecorded Home Video Cassettes
S.I.C.: 3651
Trisha Robinson *(Pres.)*
Jules Abramson *(V.P.-Sls.)*
M.J. Pectros *(V.P.-Mktg.)*

Branch:

Academy Entertainment, Inc. **(2)**
One Pine Haven Shore Rd.
Shelburne, VT 05482
Tel.: 802-985-2060
Emp.: 2
Manufacture Prerecorded Home Video Cassettes
S.I.C.: 3651
Don Chatham *(Pres.)*

ARTESIAN RESOURCES CORPORATION
664 Churchmans Rd.
Newark, DE 19702
Mailing Address:
P.O. Box 15004,
Wilmington, DE 19850
Tel.: 302-453-6900 **DE**
Fax: 302-453-6957
Year Founded: 1905
Assets: $73,500,000
Liabilities: $61,500,000
Net Worth: $12,000,000
Approx.Sls.: $18,000,000
Emp.: 124
Fiscal Year-end: 12/31/91
Utilities, Land Devel., Commercial, Laboratory Research & Data Processing
S.I.C.: 4941; 7389; 8731; 6552
Employee Matching Gifts Progra
John R. Eisenbrey *(Chm. Bd., Pres. & Chief Exec. Officer)*
Dian C. Taylor *(Exec. V.P.)*
Peter N. Johnson *(Sr. V.P.-Chief Oper. Officer)*
Ernest L. Rector *(V.P.-Opers.)*
David B. Spacht *(Chief Fin. Officer & Asst. Treas.)*
Joseph A. DiNinzio *(Asst. Sec.)*
Marvin E. Harding *(Sec. & Treas.)*
Albert W. Marvel *(Mgr.-Chief Information Officer & Data Processing)*
Patti L. Riale *(Mgr.-Corp. Stock Registar)*
Lynn A. Joos *(Personnel Mgr.)*
Nancy W. Parker *(Dir.-Pub. Rels.)*

Computer Systems/Hardware:
IBM

Subsidiaries:

Artesian Development Corporation **(1)**
664 Churchmans Rd.
Newark, DE 19702
Tel.: 302-453-6900 (100%)
Fax: 302-453-6957
Land Development
S.I.C.: 6552
John R. Eisenbrey *(Pres.)*
Marvin E. Harding *(V.P., Chief Fin. Officer, Treas. & Sec.)*

Artesian Laboratories, Inc. **(1)**
630 Churchmans Rd.
Newark, DE 19702
Tel.: 302-453-6920 (100%)
Fax: 302-453-6957
Commercial Laboratory
S.I.C.: 8731
Ellis D. Taylor *(Pres.)*
Robin T. Thurlow *(V.P., Chief Fin. Officer, Treas. & Sec.)*
Marlene O. Frey *(V.P.-Mktg.)*
Marvin E. Harding *(Asst. Sec. & Asst. Treas.)*

Artesian Water Company, Inc. **(1)**
664 Churchmans Rd.
Newark, DE 19702
Tel.: 302-453-6900 (100%)
Fax: 302-453-6957
Approx.Sls.: $18,000,000
Emp.: 104
Fiscal Year-end: 12/31/91
Public Water Utility
S.I.C.: 4941
John R. Eisenbrey *(Chm. Bd., Pres. & Chief Exec. Officer)*
Dian C. Taylor *(Exec. V.P.)*

Peter N. Johnson *(Sr. V.P.-Chief Oper. Officer)*
Ernest L. Rector, Jr. *(V.P.-Opers.)*
David B. Spacht *(Chief Fin. Officer & Asst. Treas.)*
Joseph A. DiNinzio *(Asst. Sec.)*
Marvin E. Harding *(Sec. & Treas.)*
Albert W. Marvel *(Chief Information Officer & Data Processing Mgr.)*
Patti L. Riale *(Corp. Stock Registar)*
Lynn A. Joos *(Personnel Mgr.)*
Nancy W. Parker *(Dir.-Pub. Rels.)*

Subsidiary:

The Southwood Company **(2)**
664 Churchmans Rd.
Newark, DE 19702
Tel.: 302-453-6900 (100%)
Fax: 302-453-6957
Utility Company
S.I.C.: 4941
John R. Eisenbrey *(Pres.)*
Peter N. Johnson *(Sr. V.P.)*
Marvin E. Harding *(Sec. & Treas.)*

Churchmans Road Associates, L.P. **(1)**
664 Churchmans Rd.
Newark, DE 19702
Tel.: 302-453-6900 (100%)
Fax: 302-453-6957
Land Devel.
S.I.C.: 6552
John R. Eisenbrey *(Pres.)*
Marvin E. Harding *(Sec. & Treas.)*

ARTHUR CHEESE COMPANY
320 E. Second St.
Arthur, IL 61911
Tel.: 217-543-2166
Year Founded: 1971
Approx.Sls.: $10,700,000
Emp.: 22
Import
Mfr. of Natural & Processed Cheese
S.I.C.: 2022
Erland Kondrup *(Pres.)*

ARTHUR TREACHER'S, INC.
5121 Mahoning Ave.
Youngstown, OH 44515
Tel.: 216-792-2252
Fax: 216-792-4225
Year Founded: 1969
Approx.Sls.: $32,000,000
Emp.: 225
Fiscal Year-end: 6/30/90
Operate & License 250 Specialty Restaurants
S.I.C.: 5182
James R. Cataland *(Pres. & Chief Exec. Officer)*
William F. Saculla *(Sec.)*
Amy L. Plowden *(Dir.-Mktg.)*
Linda Paskey *(Graphic Designer)*

Computer Systems/Hardware:
Hewlett-Packard 386

ARTICHOKE INDUSTRIES, INC.
11599 Walsh St.
Castroville, CA 95012
Tel.: 408-633-2423
Fax: 408-633-2301
Sales Range: $10-19 Million
Emp.: 350
Canned & Frozen Artichoke Products, Marinated Mushrooms
S.I.C.: 2033; 2037
Tony Leonardini, Jr. *(Pres.)*
Albert Pieri *(V.P., Sec. & Treas.)*

Outside Service Firm(s):

Kasavan & Pope*(Auditors)*
Salinas, CA

Abramson, Church & Stave*(Legal Firm)*
Salinas, CA

Wells Fargo Bank*(Major Banking Relationship)*
Castroville, CA

ARTISTIC CARTON COMPANY
1975 Big Timber Rd.
Elgin, IL 60123
Tel.: 708-741-0247
Fax: 708-741-8529
Approx.Sls.: $40,000,000
Emp.: 400
Setup Paperboard Boxes
S.I.C.: 2652
John E. Traeger *(Chm. Bd.)*
Peter Traeger *(Pres.)*
Steven Traeger *(V.P.)*
Kurt Stromberg *(Treas.)*

Outside Service Firm(s):

Mayer, Brown & Platt*(Legal Firm)*
190 S. LaSalle St., Ste. 3900
Chicago, IL 60603
Tel.: 312-782-0600

Associated Bank*(Major Banking Relationship)*
Chicago, IL

Boulevard Bank*(Major Banking Relationship)*
410 N. Michigan Ave.
Chicago, IL 60611
Tel.: 312-836-6500

Subsidiary:

White Pigeon Paper Company **(1)**
River St.
White Pigeon, MI 49099
Tel.: 616-483-7601
Fax: 616-483-9989
Approx.Sls.: $22,000,000
Emp.: 108
Boxboard
S.I.C.: 2631
James V. La Marre *(Chm. Bd.)*
William Schmidt *(Pres.)*
John A. Oakes *(V.P.)*
Kenneth A. Shane *(Controller)*
Kurt Stromberg *(Treas.)*
Dwight J. Fawcett *(Sec.)*

ASAHI/AMERICA, INC.
19 Green St., P.O. Box 653
Malden, MA 02148
Approx.Sls.: $20,000,000
Emp.: 115
Fiscal Year-end: 12/31/89
Manufacture Thermoplastic Valves, Actuation & Piping Systems
S.I.C.: 5075; 5084
Leslie B. Lewis *(Chm. & Pres.)*
Timothy R. Robinson *(Exec. V.P.)*
Douglas N. Place *(V.P.-Fin. & Chief Fin. Officer)*

Outside Service Firm(s):

Arthur Andersen & Co.*(Auditors)*
One Intl. Place, 100 Oliver St.
Boston, MA 02110
Tel.: 617-330-4000
Fax: 617-439-9731

Gadsby & Hannah*(Legal Firm)*
140 Federal St.
Boston, MA 02110
Tel.: 617-482-1700

U.S. Trust Co.*(Major Banking Relationship)*
40 Court St.
Boston, MA 02108
Tel.: 617-726-7371
Fax: 617-726-7380

ASBURY CARBONS, INC.
Main St. & RD #1
Asbury, NJ 08802
Tel.: 908-537-2155
Fax: 908-537-2908
Approx.Sls.: $40,000,000
Emp.: 350
Holding Company, Manufacture & Wholesale Graphite Petroleum Coke & Coal Products
S.I.C.: 2999; 5051; 6719
H. Marvin Riddle, III *(Pres.)*
Stephen Riddle *(Exec. V.P.)*
Jean C. Mayberry *(Treas. & Data Processing Mgr.)*

William T. Meglaughlin, Jr. *(Controller)*

Outside Service Firm(s):

KPMG Peat Marwick*(Auditors)*
Bethlehem, PA

First Fidelity Bank, N.A.*(Major Banking Relationship)*
Flemington, NJ

Subsidiaries:

Asbury Ferst, Inc. **(1)**
3550 Zip Industrial Blvd.
Atlanta, GA 30354
Tel.: 404-768-8868
Fax: 404-768-0336
Approx.Sls.: $4,000,000
Emp.: 107
Manufacture Pencil Lead & Erasers
S.I.C.: 3069; 3952
Sydney Anderson *(Pres.)*
T.H. Childress *(V.P.-Sls. & Opers.)*
W.R. Conn *(Prod. Opers. Mgr.)*
Arthur L. Martin *(Controller)*

Asbury Graphite Mills, Inc. **(1)**
Main St. & RD #1
Asbury, NJ 08802
Tel.: 908-537-2155
Fax: 908-537-2908
Approx.Sls.: $22,000,000
Emp.: 125
Ground & Treated Minerals
S.I.C.: 3295
H. Marvin Riddle, III *(Pres.)*
Leonard C. Ziegler *(V.P.)*
William T. Meglaughlin, Jr. *(Sec. & Treas.)*

ASH GROVE CEMENT COMPANY
8900 Indian Creek Pkwy.
Overland Park, KS 66210
Mailing Address:
P.O. Box 25900,
Overland Park, KS 66225
Tel.: 913-451-8900 **DE**
Fax: 913-451-8324
Year Founded: 1882
Approx.Sls.: $188,000,000
Emp.: 1,450
Fiscal Year-end: 12/31/89
Export
Mfr. of Cement & Lime; Quarry Limestone
S.I.C.: 3241; 3274; 1422
Robert Sunderland *(Chm. Bd.)*
James P. Sunderland *(Chm. Bd.)*
George M. Wells *(Pres.)*
John F. Woodfill *(V.P.-Fin. & Chief Fin. Officer)*
Richard E. Cooke *(V.P.-Opers., Western Reg.)*
Ronald V. Deleenheer *(V.P.-Mktg.)*
Walter L. Greer *(V.P.-Environmental Affairs)*
Eric R. Hansen *(V.P.-Technical Dir.)*
Graham D. Jones *(V.P.-Opers.)*
William R. Mahorney *(V.P.-Sls., Western Reg.)*
James W. Post *(V.P.-Tech. Service, Western Reg.)*
John H. Ross III *(V.P. & Gen. Counsel)*
Stephen E. Sheridan *(V.P.-Prod., Western Reg.)*
Joe W. Sisk *(V.P.-Sls.)*
Donald R. Young *(V.P.-Production)*
George J. McCausland *(Treas. & Controller)*
Charles T. Sunderland *(V.P.-Corp. Devel.)*
Kent W. Sunderland *(Sec.)*
Gene P. Billings *(Dir.-Personnel)*
Robert L. Phillips *(Dir.-Pur.)*
James L. Weaver *(Mgr.-Data Processing)*

No. of Mfg. Plants/Facilities: 8
No. of U.S. Offices: 4

Computer Systems/Hardware:
IBM AS/400

Outside Service Firm(s):

Arthur Andersen & Co.*(Auditors)*
1500 Commerce Tower, 911 Main St.
Kansas City, MO 64105
Tel.: 816-221-4200
Fax: 816-221-7693

KPMG Peat Marwick*(Auditors)*
1000 Walnut St.
Kansas City, MO 64106

Mutual of Omaha Insurance Company*(Group Insurer)*
Mutual of Omaha Plaza,
Omaha, NE 68175
Tel.: 800-228-7775

Stinson, Mag & Fizzell*(Legal Firm)*
2100 Charter Bank Ctr.
Kansas City, MO 64105

First National Bank of Kansas City*(Major Banking Relationship)*
10th & Baltimore
Kansas City, MO 64105
Tel.: 816-221-2800

The Principal Financial Group*(Pension Manager)*
711 High St.
Des Moines, IA 50309
Tel.: 515-247-4593
Tel.: 800-543-4015

Equitable Real Estate Investment Managment Inc.*(Pension Manager)*
3414 Peachtree Rd. N.E.
Atlanta, GA 30326-1162

First National Bank of Kansas City*(Pension Manager)*
10th & Baltimore
Kansas City, MO 64105
Tel.: 816-221-2800

Plants:

Ash Grove Cement **(1)**
P.O. Box 519,
Chanute, KS 66720
Tel.: 316-431-4500
Mfr. of Cement
S.I.C.: 3241
James Shea *(Plant Mgr.)*

Ash Grove Cement **(1)**
P.O. Box 130,
Foreman, AR 71836
Tel.: 501-542-6217
Mfr. of Cement
S.I.C.: 3241
James Gordon *(Plant Mgr.)*

Ash Grove Cement **(1)**
P.O. Box 323, Rte. 3
Springfield, MO 65803
Tel.: 417-881-3545
Mfr. of Lime
S.I.C.: 3274
Charles D. Newton *(Plant Mgr.)*

Ash Grove Cement **(1)**
P.O. Box 609,
Louisville, NE 68037
Tel.: 402-234-2415
Mfr. of Cement
S.I.C.: 3241
Ed Parker *(Plant Mgr.)*

Ash Grove Cement Co. **(1)**
10025 W. Markham
Little Rock, AR 72205
Tel.: 501-225-9424 (100%)
Wholesale of Cement
S.I.C.: 5211
Charles Puckett *(Reg. Sls. Mgr.)*

Ash Grove Cement Co., Durkee Plant **(1)**
P.O. Box 5,
Durkee, OR 97905
Tel.: 503-877-2411 (100%)
Mfr. of Limestone, Shale Quarry & Cement
S.I.C.: 3274; 3241
Michael Hrizuk *(Plant Mgr.)*

Inkom, Idaho Plant **(1)**
230 Cement Rd.
Inkom, ID 83245
Tel.: 208-775-3351 (100%)
Mfr. & Sale of Portland Cement
S.I.C.: 3241; 5039
Henrik Voldbaek *(Plant Mgr.)*

Ash Grove Cement Company—(Continued)

Leamington Plant **(1)**
A6 West
Leamington, UT 84648
Tel.: 801-857-2380
S.I.C.: 3241
George Crutchfield *(Plant Mgr.)*

Montana City Plant **(1)**
100 Montana Hwy. 518
Clancy, MT 59634
Tel.: 406-442-8850
Mfr. of Cement
S.I.C.: 3241
Charles D. Peterson *(Plant Mgr.)*

Rivergate Plant **(1)**
13939 N. Rivergate Blvd.
Portland, OR 97203
Tel.: 503-286-1677
Mfr. of Lime
S.I.C.: 3274
William A. Kistler *(Plant Mgr.)*

Seattle Plant **(1)**
3801 E. Marginal Way So.
Seattle, WA 98134
Tel.: 206-623-5596 (100%)
Storage & Shipping Operations
S.I.C.: 3241
Ken Rone *(Plant Mgr.)*

Subsidiaries:

Cedar Creek Properties Inc. **(1)**
8900 Indian Creek Pkwy.
Shawnee Mission, KS 66225
Tel.: 913-451-8900
Real Estate Devel.
S.I.C.: 6552
Charles T. Sunderland *(Pres.)*

Cedar Creek Realty Co., Inc. **(1)**
8900 Indian Creek Pkwy.
Shawnee Mission, KS 66225
Tel.: 913-451-8900
Real Estate Devel.
S.I.C.: 6552

Century Concrete, Inc. **(1)**
8858 Woodend Rd.
Kansas City, KS 66113
Tel.: 913-441-8050
Mfr. Ready-Mixed Concrete
S.I.C.: 3273

Fordyce Concrete Co., Inc. **(1)**
8900 Indian Creek Pkwy.
Shawnee Mission, KS 66225
Tel.: 913-345-2030
Mfr. Ready-Mixed Concrete
S.I.C.: 3273
John Novak *(Pres.)*

Union Quarries, Inc. **(1)**
P.O. Box 25348,
Shawnee Mission, KS 66225
Tel.: 913-345-2030
Rock Quarry
S.I.C.: 1422
John Novak *(Pres.)*

Divisions:

Batesco Quarries Div. **(2)**
Buffalo, MO 65622
Tel.: 417-345-8216
Rock Quarry
S.I.C.: 1422
John M. Lutz *(Mgr.)*

Batesco Quarries Div. **(2)**
Hwy. 52
Butler, MO 64730
Tel.: 816-679-4128
Rock Quarry
S.I.C.: 1422
John M. Lutz *(Mgr.)*

Subsidiary:

Material Transport Co. **(2)**
8900 Indian Creek Pkwy.
Shawnee Mission, KS 66225
Tel.: 913-345-2030
Local Trucking
S.I.C.: 4212

ASHER/GOULD ADVERTISING, INC.
5900 Wilshire Blvd., 16th Fl.
Los Angeles, CA 90036
Tel.: 213-931-4151 **CA**
Fax: 213-931-4548
Year Founded: 1961
Approx.Billings: $81,000,000
Emp.: 80
Fiscal Year-end: 12/31/91
Advertising Agency
S.I.C.: 7311
Harold Asher *(Chm.-Exec. Committee)*
Morley Gould *(Chm. Bd.)*
Bruce Silverman *(Pres. & New Bus. Contact)*
John Auwaerter *(Sr. V.P., Chief Fin. Officer)*
Lee Leibman *(Sr. V.P., Promo.)*
Susan Retherford *(Dir., Spot Brdcst.)*
Peter Nicholson *(Controller)*
Nancy Baker *(Dir., Human Resources)*
Peter Chan *(Mgr., Data Processing)*
Carlos Bailey *(Mgr., Office Services)*

No. of U.S. Offices: 1

Computer Systems/Hardware:
IMS/Adserve; Hewlett-Packard

Outside Service Firm(s):

Solursh, Kimmel & Co.*(Auditors)*
16030 Ventura Blvd., #605
Encino, CA 91436
Tel.: 818-905-8030

Jefferson Pilot*(Group Insurer)*
Ste. 210, 3450 Wilshire Blvd.
Los Angeles, CA 90010

Heller, Ehrman, White & McAuliffe*(Legal Firm)*
601 S. Figueroa St.
Los Angeles, CA 90017
Tel.: 213-689-0200

City National Bank*(Major Banking Relationship)*
120 S. Spalding Dr.
Beverly Hills, CA 90213
Tel.: 310-550-5821

CIGNA*(Pension Manager)*
Los Angeles, CA

Trust Services of America, Inc.*(Pension Manager)*
700 Wilshire Blvd.
Los Angeles, CA 90017
Tel.: 213-614-7241

Subsidiary:

Media Buyers, Inc. **(1)**
5900 Wilshire Blvd., 16th Fl.
Los Angeles, CA 90036
Tel.: 213-931-4151
Fax: 213-931-4548
Emp.: 5
Advertising Media Buying Service
S.I.C.: 7319
Bruce Silverman *(Pres. & New Business Contact)*

THE ASHER WINER COMPANY
307 Airport Rd.
Fitchburg, MA 01420
Tel.: 508-342-8771
Fax: 508-342-9353
Year Founded: 1900
Approx.Sls.: $15,000,000
Emp.: 300
Fiscal Year-end: 12/31/90
Manufacturer Men's Trousers & Sportcoats
S.I.C.: 2325
Harry Henry *(Chm. Bd.)*
Jerry LaFond *(Chief Exec. Officer)*
James Arsenault *(Treas. & Controller)*
Mark Comeau *(Dir.-Mfg.)*

Principal(s):
Jerry LaFond

Computer Systems/Hardware:
IBM System 36

Outside Service Firm(s):

Joseph B. Cohan & Associates*(Auditors)*
Worcester, MA

Hale and Dorr*(Legal Firm)*
60 State St.
Boston, MA 02109-6098
Tel.: 617-526-6000

First American National Bank*(Major Banking Relationship)*
First American Center
Nashville, TN 37237
Tel.: 615-748-2000

ASHMAN ENTERPRISES, INC.
10100 Brecksville Rd.
Brecksville, OH 44141
Mailing Address:
P.O. Box 477951,
Brecksville, OH 44147
Tel.: 216-526-1600
Tel.: 1-800-468-3749
Fax: 216-526-3158
Sales Range: $20-39 Million
Emp.: 200
Manufacture of Drop Forged Fittings for Wire Rope & Structural Clevises, Turnbuckles, Eye, Coupling & Sleeve Nuts; Piping Systems; Construction Attachments for Excavators, Cranes & Loaders
S.I.C.: 3462; 3498; 3531
Raymond D. Ashman, Jr. *(Chm. Bd. & Pres.)*
Martin J. Eble *(Chief Fin. Officer)*
R. Couch *(V.P.-Engrng.-Mechanical Systems)*
Harold Weitzel *(V.P. & Gen. Mgr.)*

No. of Mfg. Plants/Facilities: 4

Computer Systems/Hardware:
IBM

Outside Service Firm(s):

Deloitte & Touche*(Auditors)*
1717 East Ninth St.
Cleveland, OH 44114
Tel.: 216-589-1300

Subsidiary:

Intergy, Inc. **(1)**
10100 Brecksville Rd.
Brecksville, OH 44141
Tel.: 216-526-1600
Manufacture Drop Forged Fittings For Wire Rope & Structural Clevises
S.I.C.: 3462
Raymond D. Ashman, Jr. *(Pres.)*

ASHWORTH BROS., INC.
89 Globe Mills Ave.
Fall River, MA 02724
Tel.: 508-674-4693 **MA**
Fax: 508-675-9622
Year Founded: 1894
Approx.Sls.: $35,000,000
Emp.: 450
Export
Mfr. of Flexible & Metallic Card Clothing; Woven Wire & Flat Wire Conveyor Belts; Conveyors & Conveying Equipment; Reinforced Fiberglass Platic Products
S.I.C.: 3535; 3552; 2221
David J. Daylor *(Chm. Bd.)*
Rick Ritchie *(Pres.)*
R.C. Ashworth III *(Exec. V.P.)*
John P. Sullivan *(Treas.)*
Virginia Murray *(Sec.)*
W. Karzeniawski *(Mgr.-Opers.)*

Outside Service Firm(s):

Ernst & Young*(Auditors)*
One Old Stone Square
Providence, RI 02903
Tel.: 401-331-7000

Durfee Attleboro Bank*(Major Banking Relationship)*
Fall River, MA

Divisions:

Card Clothing Division **(1)**
P.O. BOx 5029
Greenville, SC 29606
Tel.: 803-233-3631
Mfr. of Flexible & Metallic Card Clothing
S.I.C.: 3552
Ron Johnson *(Gen. Mgr.)*

Plastics Division **(1)**
P.O. Box 670
Fall River, MA 02722
Tel.: 508-674-4693
Mfr. of Reinforced Fiberglas Plastic Products
S.I.C.: 2221
Stephen Buckley *(Gen. Mgr.)*

ASKO, INC
501 W. 7th Ave.
Homestead, PA 15120
Mailing Address:
P.O. Box 355
Homestead, PA 15120
Tel.: 412-461-4110
Fax: 412-461-5400
Sales Range: $20-39 Million
Emp.: 350
Mfr. of Steel Shear Knives, Slitter & Chipper Knives, Wearing Plates, Processing Rolls, Tungsten Carbide Rolls & Knives
S.I.C.: 3914; 3423
S.R. Rackoff *(Chm. Bd.)*
W.H. Rackoff *(Pres.)*
Harold Levy *(Sr. V.P.-Sls.)*
S.A. Jacoby *(V.P.)*
J.M. Racoff *(V.P.)*
S.L. Marlowe *(Treas.)*
Seymour Schafer *(Sec.)*
Jay Griffin *(Mgr.-Pur.)*

Outside Service Firm(s):

Horovitz, Rudoy & Roteman*(Auditors)*
Pittsburgh, PA

Markel, Schafer & Means*(Legal Firm)*
Pittsburgh, PA

Union National Bank*(Major Banking Relationship)*
Pittsburgh, PA

Division:

American Shear Knive Co. **(1)**
501 W. 7th Ave.
Homestead, PA 15120
Tel.: 412-461-4110
Mfr. of Steel Shear Knives, Slitter & Chipper Knives, Wearing Plates, Processing Rolls, Tungsten Carbide Rolls & Knives
S.I.C.: 3914; 3356
W.H. Rackoff *(Pres.)*

ASPLUNDH TREE EXPERT CO.
708 Blair Mill Rd.
Willow Grove, PA 19090-1784
Tel.: 215-784-4200
Fax: 215-784-4493
Year Founded: 1928
Approx.Sls.: $400,000,000
Emp.: 11,300
Tree Trimming for Electrical Utilities
S.I.C.: 0781
Robert Asplundh *(Chm. Bd.)*
Christopher Asplundh *(Pres.)*
Carl Asplundh, Jr. *(Exec. V.P.-Equip.)*
Paul Asplundh *(Sr. V.P.)*
Dave Kosek *(Treas. & Sec.)*

Outside Service Firm(s):

Coopers & Lybrand*(Auditors)*
2400 Eleven Penn Center
Philadelphia, PA 19103-2962
Tel.: 215-963-8000

Blue Cross of Greater Philadelphia*(Group Insurer)*
Philadelphia, PA

CoreStates First Pennsylvania Bank, N.A.*(Major Banking Relationship)*
Center Sq. West Tower, 15th & Market Streets
Philadelphia, PA 19101

ASSOCIATED ADVERTISING AGENCY, INC.
4601 E. Douglas
Wichita, KS 67218
Tel.: 316-683-4691
Fax: 316-683-1990
Year Founded: 1946
Approx.Billings: $15,000,000
Emp.: 34
Preston D. Huston *(Chm. Bd. & Chief Exec. Officer)*
Kerry Gray *(Pres.)*
Kathy Wiebe *(Exec. V.P.)*
Susan Leasure *(Sec. & Dir. Admin. Services)*
Rudea Lupton *(Treas.)*
Marilyn Potts *(Pub. Rels. Dir.)*

ASSOCIATED AIR FREIGHT, INC.
3333 New Hyde Park Rd.
New Hyde Park, NY 11042
Tel.: 516-627-8910
Fax: 516-627-8851
Year Founded: 1958
Approx.Sls.: $48,000,000
Emp.: 325
Import Export
Air Freight Forwarding
S.I.C.: 4731
Norman Freeman *(Pres.)*
James Tucci *(Exec. V.P.)*
Edward Blakely *(V.P.-Intl.)*
Louis Santangelo *(V.P.-Admin.)*
Michael J. Occicone *(Controller)*

Outside Service Firm(s):

Gassman, Rebhun & Co., P.C.*(Auditors)*
New York, NY

Chemical Banking Corp.*(Major Banking Relationship)*
277 Park Ave.
New York, NY 10041
Tel.: 212-310-6407
Fax: 212-310-4526

ASSOCIATED AIRCRAFT SUPPLY COMPANY
5021 W. Jefferson
Dallas, TX 75211
Tel.: 214-331-4381
Fax: 214-339-9840
Approx.Sls.: $14,000,000
Emp.: 29
Electronic Parts
S.I.C.: 5065
John L. Mann *(Pres.)*
Tommy DeRossett *(Exec. V.P.)*
Johnny Mann *(Exec. V.P.)*
Wally Clyce *(V.P.)*

Outside Service Firm(s):

Chistopher M. Weil*(Legal Firm)*
Dallas, TX

Bank One*(Major Banking Relationship)*
Akron, OH

ASSOCIATED COMPANY, INC.
1441 S. McLean Blvd.
Wichita, KS 67213
Tel.: 316-265-9451 KS
Fax: 316-265-0355
Year Founded: 1947
Approx.Sls.: $11,000,000
Emp.: 165
Aircraft Assemblies, Subassemblies & Parts
S.I.C.: 3728
William F. Bowman *(Pres.)*
Harry Hiskett *(V.P.-Mfg.)*
Terrence R. Lindsey *(V.P.-Sls.)*
Craig Leonard *(Treas. & Sec.)*
Don Davis *(Gen. Mgr.)*
Fred Stewart *(Mgr.-Pur.)*

Outside Service Firm(s):

F.B. Kubick & Co.*(Auditors)*
Wichita, KS

Morris, Loing, Evans, Brock & Kennedy*(Legal Firm)*
Wichita, KS

First National Bank*(Major Banking Relationship)*
Wichita, KS

ASSOCIATED DIESEL SERVICE & EQUIPMENT COMPANY
1741 Colon St.
Wilmington, CA 90744
Tel.: 310-835-3161
Fax: 310-518-3019
Approx.Sls.: $10,000,000
Emp.: 65
Wholesale & Repair Diesel Engines; Wholesale Heavy Construction Equipment
S.I.C.: 5084; 7538; 5082
Robert F. Kafka *(Pres.)*
Marvin L. Johnson *(V.P.)*
Jack M. Devine *(Sec. & Treas.)*

Outside Service Firm(s):

Sanwa Bank*(Major Banking Relationship)*
601 S. Figueroa St.
Los Angeles, CA 90017
Tel.: 213-896-7817
Fax: 213-489-1977

ASSOCIATED ELECTRIC CO-OP INC.
2814 S. Golden
Springfield, MO 65801
Tel.: 417-881-1204 MO
Year Founded: 1961
Assets: $1,261,000,000
Liabilities: $1,162,000,000
Net Worth: $99,000,000
Approx.Sls.: $408,000,000
Emp.: 1,074
Fiscal Year-end: 12/31/91
Electric Power Supplier
S.I.C.: 4911
O.B. Clark *(Pres.)*
James Jura *(Chief Exec. Officer)*
Maurice L. Happel *(V.P.)*
Arthur Carrier *(Sec. & Treas.)*
Eugene Andereck *(Gen. Counsel)*
William W. Bretall *(Dir.-Pur.)*
Max Cates *(Dir.-Mtkg. Communications)*
James McNabb *(Dir.-Sls. & Mktg.)*
Wesley Ohrenberg *(Dir.-Fin. & Acctg.)*
Bruce Stone *(Dir.-Power Production Opers.)*
David Stump *(Dir.-Personnel)*
Michael Yallez *(Dir.-Coal Mining Opers.)*

No. of Mfg. Plants/Facilities: 2
No. of U.S. Offices: 1

Computer Systems/Hardware:
Prime

Outside Service Firm(s):

Coopers & Lybrand*(Auditors)*
Kansas City, MO

Shearson Lehman Brothers, Inc.*(Investment Banker)*
Tower C, World Financial Center
New York, NY 10285
Tel.: 212-298-2000

Stockard, Andereck, Hauck, Sharp & Evan*(Legal Firm)*
Jefferson City, MO

Boatmen's Trust Company*(Major Banking Relationship)*
100 North Broadway
St. Louis, MO 63102
Tel.: 314-466-2469

National Rural Electric Cooperative Association*(Pension Manager)*
Washington, DC

ASSOCIATED EQUIPMENT COMPANY, INC.
1230 N. Beltline Hwy.
Mobile, AL 36607
Mailing Address:
P.O. Box 7157
Mobile, AL 36607
Tel.: 205-476-1082 DE
Fax: 205-471-2597
Year Founded: 1955
Assets: $5,145,618
Liabilities: $4,201,111
Net Worth: $944,507
Approx.Sls.: $10,000,000
Emp.: 30
Fiscal Year-end: 12/31/91
Distribute Heating & Air Conditioning Equipment
S.I.C.: 5075; 5074
Frank P. Ellis, IV *(Chm. Bd.)*
Luther F. Clemons *(Pres.)*
O. Malcolm Sumrall *(Chief Fin. Officer, Sec. & Treas.)*
Principal(s):
Frank P. Ellis, IV

No. of Mfg. Plants/Facilities: 6
No. of U.S. Offices: 6

Computer Systems/Hardware:
IBM System 36

Outside Service Firm(s):

Dudley, Rutland & Chateau*(Auditors)*
Mobile, AL

Vickers, Riis, Murray & Curran*(Legal Firm)*
Mobile, AL

Central Bank of the South*(Major Banking Relationship)*
Mobile, AL

ASSOCIATED FOOD STORES INC.
1812 S. Empire Rd.
Salt Lake City, UT 84104
Mailing Address:
P.O. Box 30430
Salt Lake City, UT 84130
Tel.: 801-973-4400 UT
Year Founded: 1940
Assets: $159,748,764
Earnings: $21,809,000
Liabilities: $91,931,168
Net Worth: $67,817,596
Approx.Sls.: $766,034,910
Emp.: 1,200
Fiscal Year-end: 3/28/92
Wholesale Grocery Distributor
S.I.C.: 5141; 5149; 5399
Gerald Day *(Chm. Bd.)*
D. Gill Warner *(Pres., Chief Exec. Officer & Gen Mgr.)*
Richard Parkinson *(Exec. V.P. & Asst. Gen Mgr.)*
Stan Brewer *(V.P.-Opers., Sec. & Treas.)*
Larry Rowe *(V.P.-Human Resources)*
Ron Christensen *(Dir.-Pur.)*
Neal Berube *(Comptroller)*
Frank M. Romney *(Asst. Sec. & Treas.)*

No. of Mfg. Plants/Facilities: 5

Computer Systems/Hardware:
Burroughs A 12

Outside Service Firm(s):

Coopers & Lybrand*(Auditors)*
1700 Benneficial Life Tower
Salt Lake City, UT 84111
Tel.: 801-531-9666

Kirton, McConkie & Poelman*(Legal Firm)*
Salt Lake City, UT

First Bank Billings*(Major Banking Relationship)*
P. O. Box 30678, 303 N. Broadway
Billings, MT 59101
Tel.: 406-657-8000
Fax: 406-657-8035

First National Bank Helena*(Major Banking Relationship)*
Helena, MT

Key Bank*(Major Banking Relationship)*
Pocatello, ID

West One Bank*(Major Banking Relationship)*
101 S. Capitol Blvd.
Boise, ID 83701
Tel.: 208-383-7947
Fax: 208-383-3870

Zions First National Bank*(Major Banking Relationship)*
P.O. Box 30880
Salt Lake City, UT 84130
Tel.: 801-524-4624
Fax: 801-533-0464

Zions First National Bank*(Pension Manager)*
One South Main St.
Salt Lake City, UT 84111
Tel.: 801-582-4812

Subsidiary:

AFS Insurance Services, Inc. **(1)**
1812 S. Empire Rd.
Salt Lake City, UT 84130
Tel.: 801-973-4400
Insurance Services
S.I.C.: 6321
Gene Denning *(Mgr.)*

ASSOCIATED GROCERS, INC.
8686 Anselmo Ln.
Baton Rouge, LA 70810
Mailing Address:
P.O. Box 1748
Baton Rouge, LA 70821
Tel.: 504-769-2020 LA
Year Founded: 1950
Assets: $47,200,000
Liabilities: $31,981,000
Net Worth: $15,219,000
Sales Range: $100-499 Million
Emp.: 400
Fiscal Year-end: 5/29/92
Retail Owned Grocery Cooperative
S.I.C.: 5411
Anthony Rouse *(Chm. Bd.)*
Hillar C. Moore, Jr. *(Pres. & Chief Exec. Officer)*
J.H. Campbell, Jr. *(Chief Fin. Officer, Treas. & Legal Counsel)*
Richard Price *(Controller)*
Mitch Hele *(Dir.-Retail Services)*
John P. Schittone, Jr. *(Dir.-Human Resources)*
Clayton F. Lester *(Dir.-Adv.)*
Ralph P. Kelleher *(Mgr.-Data Processing)*

No. of U.S. Offices: 1

Computer Systems/Hardware:
IBM 4381 Group 2

Outside Service Firm(s):

Postlethwaite & Netterville*(Auditors)*
Baton Rouge, LA

Associated Grocers, Inc.—(Continued)

Allendale Mutual Insurance Co.*(Commercial Insurance Carrier)*
New Orleans, LA

Delta Insurance Services Corp.*(Commercial Insurance Carrier)*
P.O. Box 1748,
Baton Rouge, LA 70821

Hibernia National Bank*(Major Banking Relationship)*
New Orleans, LA

Premier Bank*(Major Banking Relationship)*
P.O. Box 1511
Baton Rouge, LA 70821

ASSOCIATED GROCERS, INC.
3301 S. Norfolk St.
Seattle, WA 98118
Mailing Address:
P.O. Box 3763,
Seattle, WA 98124
Tel.: 206-762-2100
Fax: 206-764-7731
Year Founded: 1923
Approx.Sls.: $1,000,000,000
Emp.: 1,300
Wholesale Grocery Products
S.I.C.: 5141
Corporate Giving Program: Company Gives to the United Way
Robert L. Mead *(Chm. Bd.)*
Donald W. Benson *(Pres. & Chief Exec. Officer)*
Christopher Bounds *(Sr. V.P.-Support Service)*
Frank M. Johnson *(Sr. V.P.-Retail Mktg.)*
Arthur L. Jones *(Sr. V.P.-Retail Devel.)*
Dennis Stalder *(Sr. V.P.-Wholesale Opers.)*
Angelo Bruscas *(V.P.-Human Resources)*
Richard Lester *(V.P.-Information Services)*
William Young *(V.P.-Retail Programs)*
Annette Otis *(Dir.-Business Rels.)*

Computer Systems/Hardware:
IBM

Outside Service Firm(s):

Deloitte & Touche*(Auditors)*
700 Fifth Ave., Suite 4500
Seattle, WA 98104-5044
Tel.: 206-292-1800

Washington Grocery Benefits*(Group Insurer)*
Seattle, WA

Betts, Patterson & Mines*(Legal Firm)*
Seattle, WA

Security Pacific National Bank*(Major Banking Relationship)*
1301 Fifth Ave.
Seattle, WA 98101
Tel.: 206-621-4530

ASSOCIATED GROCERS OF ALABAMA, INC.
3600 Vanderbilt Rd.
Birmingham, AL 35217
Mailing Address:
P.O. Box 11044
Birmingham, AL 35202
Tel.: 205-841-6781 **AL**
Fax: 205-849-4920
Year Founded: 1927
Assets: $26,167,000
Earnings: $2,100,000
Liabilities: $18,539,000
Net Worth: $7,628,000
Approx.Sls.: $160,000,000
Emp.: 320
Wholesale Grocery Warehouse
S.I.C.: 5141
Dewey Thornton *(Chm. Bd.)*
Billy Barnes *(Vice Chm.)*
Paul Siebenthal *(Pres.)*
Mary F. Plott *(V.P.-Fin.)*
Becky Mitchell *(Dir.-Personnel)*
Hank Shields *(Dir.-Buying/Mktg.)*
Mike Higgins *(Mgr.-Data Processing)*

No. of U.S. Offices: 1

Computer Systems/Hardware:
IBM

Outside Service Firm(s):

Dent, Baker & McDowell*(Auditors)*
Birmingham, AL

Bradley, Arant, Rose & White*(Legal Firm)*
1400 Park Place Tower
Birmingham, AL 35203
Tel.: 205-521-8000

SouthTrust Bank*(Major Banking Relationship)*
Birmingham, AL
Tel.: 205-254-5068

ASSOCIATED GROCERS OF NEW ENGLAND, INC.
725 Gold St.
Manchester, NH 03108
Mailing Address:
P.O. Box 5200,
Manchester, NH 03108
Tel.: 603-669-3250
Year Founded: 1946
Approx.Sls.: $179,131,353
Emp.: 290
Fiscal Year-end: 3/28/92
Wholesale & Distribution of Grocery
S.I.C.: 5141
Robert E. Heath *(Chm. Bd.)*
Norman J. Turcotte *(Pres. & Chief Exec. Officer)*
Keith H. Thye *(Exec. V.P.)*
Marcel O. Chalifour *(V.P.-Sls. & Mktg.)*
Richard A. Ennis *(V.P.-Fin. & Admin. & Treas.)*
Thomas Manter *(Controller)*
Donald Dickson *(Mgr.-Information Services)*
Clement Deschenes *(Head Buyer)*

No. of Mfg. Plants/Facilities: 1

Computer Systems/Hardware:
IBM 4381

Outside Service Firm(s):

Bigelow & Co.*(Auditors)*
Manchester, NH

Wiggin & Nourie*(Legal Firm)*
Manchester, NH

Bay Bank*(Major Banking Relationship)*
Burlington, MA

Hartford Life Insurance Co.*(Pension Manager)*
Hartford, CT 06104-2999

Subsidiaries:

Associated Foods Inc. **(1)**
P.O. Box 5200
Manchester, NH 03108
Tel.: 603-669-3250 (100%)
S.I.C.: 5141

Associated Lease Corp. **(1)**
P.O. Box 5200
Manchester, NH 03108
Tel.: 603-669-3250 (100%)

Certified Wholesalers Inc. **(1)**
P.O. Box 5200
Manchester, NH 03108
Tel.: 603-669-3250 (100%)
S.I.C.: 5141

French & Bean **(1)**
P.O. Box 5200
Manchester, NH 03108
Tel.: 603-669-3250 (100%)
S.I.C.: 5141

THE ASSOCIATED GROUP
(Formerly Associated Insurance Companies, Inc.)
120 Monument Circle
Indianapolis, IN 46204
Tel.: 317-263-8000
Approx.Rev.: $1,850,000,000
Emp.: 6,000
Insurance Services, Financial Services
S.I.C.: 6324; 6311; 6371; 6289; 6321; 6411
L. Ben Lytle *(Pres. & Chief Exec. Officer)*
Patrick M. Sheridan *(Exec. V.P. & Chief Fin. Officer)*
Richard C. Huber, Jr. *(Exec. V.P.)*
Chester E. Burrell *(Exec. V.P.)*
Ronald E. Rosenberg *(Exec. V.P.)*
Donald C. Trigg *(Sr. V.P.-Sec. & Gen. Counsel)*
George D. Martin *(V.P. & Treas.)*
Matthew Kennedy *(Dir.-Personnel)*

Outside Service Firm(s):

Ernst & Young*(Auditors)*
One Indiana Square, Ste. 3400
Indianapolis, IN 46204
Tel.: 317-236-1100

Subsidiary:

Associated Group Inc. **(1)**
120 Monument Circle
Indianapolis, IN 46204
Tel.: 317-263-8000 (100%)
Insurance Services, Financial Services
S.I.C.: 6324; 6311; 6321; 6411; 6289

Subsidiaries:

The Acordia, Inc. **(2)**
120 Monument Circle
Indianapolis, IN 46204
Tel.: 317-263-8000
Health Plans
S.I.C.: 6324

Anthem Companies, Inc. **(2)**
5451 Lakeview Parkway South Dr.
Indianapolis, IN 46268
Tel.: 317-290-5600
Fax: 317-290-5690
Preferred Provider Organization
S.I.C.: 6324
Michael O. Bell *(Pres.)*

Anthem Health Plans of Florida Inc. **(2)**
P.O. Box 48000
Jacksonville, FL 32247-8000
Tel.: 904-348-3824
Fax: 904-348-2815
Health Maintenance Organization
S.I.C.: 6324
John D. Cuny *(Pres.)*

Anthem Life Insurance Companies, Inc. **(2)**
3988 N. Central Expwy.
Dallas, TX 75204
Tel.: 214-841-1000
Life Insurance
S.I.C.: 6311
George Walken *(Actg. Pres.)*

Key Health Plan **(2)**
333 N. Alabama
Indianapolis, IN 46204
Tel.: 317-262-4557
Fax: 317-262-4697
Health Plan
S.I.C.: 6324

The Shelby Insurance Group **(2)**
175 Mansfield Ave.
Shelby, OH 44875
Tel.: 419-347-1880 (100%)
Insurance Services
S.I.C.: 6311; 6351
Dan R. Carmichael *(Pres.)*

ASSOCIATED INDUSTRIAL SUPPLY, INC.
1207 Lincoln St., Suite 200
Columbia, SC 29201
Mailing Address:
P.O. Box 208,
Columbia, SC 29202
Tel.: 803-765-0990 **SC**
Fax: 803-779-0649, Ext. 136
Year Founded: 1902
Approx.Sls.: $45,000,000
Emp.: 275
Fiscal Year-end: 12/31/89
Wholesale Industrial Supplies & Equipment
S.I.C.: 5084; 5085
Robert D. McBeth *(Chm. Bd., Pres. & Chief Exec. Officer)*
Philip L. Holson *(Sr. V.P. & Chief Fin. Officer)*
Jerry R. Brock *(V.P.)*
Jack Lee *(V.P.)*
Gayle Stevens *(Sec.)*

No. of U.S. Offices: 10

Outside Service Firm(s):

Arthur Andersen & Co.*(Auditors)*
Columbia, SC

Robinson, McFadden & Moore*(Legal Firm)*
Columbia, SC

Bank of Boston*(Major Banking Relationship)*
Atlanta, GA

ASSOCIATED OF LOS ANGELES
2585 E. Olympic Blvd.
Los Angeles, CA 90023
Mailing Address:
P.O. Box 23950
Los Angeles, CA 90023
Tel.: 213-268-8411
Fax: 213-264-2244
Year Founded: 1928
Approx.Sls.: $14,500,000
Emp.: 55
Distributes Electrical Equipment & Supplies
S.I.C.: 5063
Chester D. Russell, Jr. *(Pres.)*
Barry Ericksen *(V.P.)*
Robert Mirolla *(V.P.)*

Outside Service Firm(s):

McCalla & Associates*(Auditors)*
Anaheim, CA

Sanwa Bank*(Major Banking Relationship)*
601 S. Figueroa St.
Los Angeles, CA 90017
Tel.: 213-896-7817
Fax: 213-489-1977

ASSOCIATED MACHINECRAFT CORPORATION
637 E. Slauson Ave.
Los Angeles, CA 90011
Tel.: 213-235-2114
Fax: 213-235-3031
Year Founded: 1956
Approx.Sls.: $24,800,000
Emp.: 55
Fiscal Year-end: 6/30/89
Metal Stamping
S.I.C.: 3469; 3462
Martin Epstein *(Pres., Chief Exec. & Chief Fin. Officer)*
Larry Fagan *(Gen. Mgr., Corp. Sec. & Treas.)*
Paul Conley *(Controller)*

Computer Systems/Hardware:
IBM PC

Outside Service Firm(s):

Haley & Therian*(Auditors)*
Los Angeles, CA

Kaiser Insurance*(Group Insurer)*
Los Angeles, CA

Kaiser Insurance*(Group Insurer)*
Oakland, CA

Maxicare*(Group Insurer)*
Los Angeles, CA

Wells Fargo Bank*(Major Banking Relationship)*
420 Montgomery St.
San Francisco, CA 94104

Pacific Mutual*(Pension Manager)*
Los Angeles, CA

ASSOCIATED MATERIALS INC.
2200 Ross Ave., Ste. 4100 East
Dallas, TX 75201
Tel.: 214-220-4600 **DE**
Fax: 214-220-4607
Year Founded: 1983
Assets: $165,000,000
Liabilities: $115,000,000
Net Worth: $50,000,000
Approx.Sls.: $320,000,000
Emp.: 2,300
Fiscal Year-end: 12/31/89
Manufacture Steel, Aluminum & Vinyl Siding, Steel Wire & Electric Cable
S.I.C.: 3444; 3089; 3315
William W. Winspear *(Pres.)*
C. Glen Beattie *(Pres. & Dir.-Sls., Amercable Div.)*
Donald L. Kaufman *(Pres. & Dir.-Sls. & Mktg., Alside Div.)*
Robert F. Hogan, Jr. *(V.P. & Treas.)*
Principal(s):
William W. Winspear
Donald L. Kaufman

Computer Systems/Hardware:
IBM PC

Outside Service Firm(s):

Jones, Day, Reavis & Pogue*(Legal Firm)*
2300 Trammell Crow Center, 2001 Ross Avenue
Dallas, TX 75201

ASSOCIATED MERCHANDISING CORP.
1440 Broadway
New York, NY 10018
Tel.: 212-536-4000 **NY**
Fax: 212-536-4014
Year Founded: 1918
Emp.: 1,330
Marketing & Merchandising Consultants to Retail Store Operations
S.I.C.: 8741
Lee Abraham *(Chm. Bd. & Chief Exec. Officer)*
Zachary Solomon *(Pres. & Chief Oper. Officer)*
Phyllis Albertson *(Exec. V.P.-Intl. Opers.)*
Richard Mancuso *(Sr. V.P. & Chief Fin. Officer)*
Douglas Bertsch *(Sr. V.P. & Mdsg.)*
Bill L. Lucas *(Sr. V.P.-Human Resources)*
Kim Roy *(V.P. & Gen. Mgr.-Ready-to-Wear)*
Franco Franchi *(V.P.-Europe & South America, Africa)*
Kris Reid *(V.P.& Gen. Mdse. Mgr.-Home & Export)*
Cleo Ryan *(V.P.-Quality Control, Sourcing & Production)*
Sharon Wax *(V.P.-Gen. Mdse. Mgr.-O.M.S.)*
Joanne Kaye *(Deputy V.P.-Accessories, Intimate Apparel, Women's Shoes)*

No. of U.S. Offices: 1
No. of Foreign Offices: 28

Computer Systems/Hardware:
IBM PC

Outside Service Firm(s):

Deloitte & Touche*(Auditors)*
1 World Trade Center
New York, NY 10048
Tel.: 212-669-5000

Weil, Gotshal & Manges*(Legal Firm)*
767 Fifth Ave.
New York, NY 10153

Citibank N.A.*(Major Banking Relationship)*
Corporate Trust Services, 399 Park Ave.
New York, NY 10043
Tel.: 212-559-1605

Non-U.S. Holdings:

AMC **(1)**
Bleichstrasse, 2-4 D-6000
Frankfurt/Main, 1, Germany (100%)
Emp.: 8
Retail Consulting Services
S.I.C.: 8742

Associated Merchandising Corp. (France) S.A. **(1)**
14 Rue de Castiglione F-75001
Paris, France
Tel.: 260-3403 (100%)
Emp.: 27
Retail Consulting Services
S.I.C.: 8742
Amirest Florence *(Continental V.P., Europe & South America)*

ASSOCIATED METALS & MINERALS CORP.
3 N. Corporate Park Dr.
White Plains, NY 10604
Tel.: 914-251-5400 **NY**
Telex: MCI 232268
Telex: WU420721
Fax: 914-251-1073
Fax: 914-251-1074
Approx.Sls.: $650,000,000
Emp.: 150
Fiscal Year-end: 12/31/91
Import Export
Carbon Steel, Stainless Steel, Pig Iron, Ferrous & Non-Ferrous Metals
S.I.C.: 5051
Colin Benjamin *(Chm., Pres. & Chief Exec. Officer)*
Donald P. Wefer *(Sr. V.P., Gen. Counsel & Sec.)*
Salvatore Purpura *(Chief Fin. Officer & Controller)*
Joanne Waxman *(Treas.)*
Nancy Kovar *(Personnel Dir.)*

No. of Mfg. Plants/Facilities: 1

Computer Systems/Hardware:
IBM System 36; Hewlett-Packard 3000

Outside Service Firm(s):

Eisner & Lubin*(Auditors)*
New York, NY

Empire Blue Cross & Blue Shield*(Group Insurer)*
New York, NY

Paskus, Gordon & Mandel*(Legal Firm)*
New York, NY

Chase Manhattan Bank, N.A.*(Major Banking Relationship)*
One Chase Manhattan Plaza
New York, NY 10081
Tel.: 212-552-2222
Tel.: 800-526-0801
Fax: 212-552-7175

Non-U.S. Holding:

Metall Und Rohstoff AG **(1)**
Bahnfostrasse 10 6301
Zug, Switzerland
Tel.: 042/23 44 11
Telex: 868 787
Telecopier: 042/21 66 84
International Trade in Steel and Raw Materials
S.I.C.: 5039

ASSOCIATED MILK PRODUCERS, INC.
6609 Blanco Rd.
San Antonio, TX 78216
Mailing Address:
P.O. Box 790287
San Antonio, TX 78279
Tel.: 210-340-9100 **KS**
Fax: 210-340-9158
Year Founded: 1969
Assets: $562,400,000
Earnings: $698,000
Liabilities: $432,600,000
Net Worth: $129,800,000
Approx.Sls.: $2,720,006,000
Emp.: 4,320
Fiscal Year-end: 12/31/91
Dairy Marketing Cooperative
S.I.C.: 5143
Irvin Elkin *(Pres.)*
Noble Anderson *(Chief Exec. Officer & Gen. Mgr.)*
Terry Krueger *(Chief Fin. Officer & Controller)*
William Lenschow *(Treas.)*
Joe Bavido *(Sec.)*
Jim Wilson *(Mgr.-Data Processing)*

Computer Systems/Hardware:
IBM; Hewlett Packard

Outside Service Firm(s):

Deloitte & Touche*(Auditors)*
700 N. St. Mary's, Suite 1100
San Antonio, TX 78205-3589
Tel.: 210-224-1041

Robert Halvorson*(Legal Firm)*
P.O. Box 458,
New Ulm, MN 56673
Tel.: 507-354-3111

First National Bank of Chicago*(Major Banking Relationship)*
One First National Plaza
Chicago, IL 60670
Tel.: 312-732-9781
Tel.: 312-732-4050
Fax: 312-732-4840
Fax: 312-732-3055

InterFirst Bank Dallas*(Major Banking Relationship)*
Dallas, TX

Texas Commerce Bank*(Major Banking Relationship)*
600 Travis Street, Suite 1150
Houston, TX 77002
Tel.: 713-236-4865

American Funds Group*(Pension Manager)*
Brea, CA 92622-2205
Tel.: 800-325-3590

Fidelity Investments*(Pension Manager)*
400 East Las Colinas Blvd.
Dallas, TX 75265-0078
Tel.: 214-830-7179

Westcore*(Pension Manager)*
600 17th St., Ste. 1605 S.
Denver, CO 80202
Tel.: 303-595-9156

Regional Offices:

Associated Milk Producers North Central Region **(1)**
P.O. Box 455,
New Ulm, MN 56073
Tel.: 507-354-8295
Fax: 507-259-8695
Approx.Sls.: $400,000,000
Emp.: 80
S.I.C.: 5143
Donald F. Gregg *(Reg. Mgr.)*
Irv Elkin *(Pres.)*
Ira Rutherford *(Gen. Mgr.)*
Mark Furth *(Reg. Mgr.)*
Bob Eisenberg *(Dir.-Adv.)*
Kenneth Rock Vam *(Sls. Mgr.-Dehydrated Dairy Prods. Div.)*
James Walsh *(Sls. Mgr.-Butter Div.)*

Morning Glory Farms Region **(1)**
116 N. Main St.
Shawano, WI 54166
Tel.: 715-526-2131
S.I.C.: 5143
James Kasten *(Reg. Mgr.)*

Southern Region **(1)**
P.O. Box 5040,
Arlington, TX 76011
Tel.: 817-461-2674
S.I.C.: 5143
Noble Anderson *(Reg. Mgr.)*

Subsidiaries:

AMPI Investment Corp. **(1)**
6609 Blanco Rd.
San Antonio, TX 78216
Tel.: 210-340-9100

AMPI Research Corp. **(1)**
6609 Blanco Rd.
San Antonio, TX 78284
Tel.: 210-340-9100

AMPI Venture, Inc. **(1)**
6609 Blanco Rd.
San Antonio, TX 78284
Tel.: 210-340-9100

ASSOCIATED PETROLEUM CARRIERS
1746 Union Rd.
Spartanburg, SC 29302
Mailing Address:
P.O. Box 2808
Spartanburg, SC 29304
Tel.: 803-573-9301 **SC**
Year Founded: 1950
Approx.Sls.: $34,000,000
Emp.: 15
Trucking Company; Bulk Transportation
S.I.C.: 4213
O'Neil Sanders *(Chm. Bd., Pres., Chief Exec. & Chief Oper. Officer)*
Russell E. Stone *(Gen. Mgr.)*
Rogers Weed *(Dir.-Data Processing)*

Outside Service Firm(s):

Citizens & Southern Trust Company, Inc.*(Major Banking Relationship)*
Spartanburg, SC

THE ASSOCIATED PRESS
50 Rockefeller Plaza
New York, NY 10020
Tel.: 212-621-1500 **NY**
Fax: 212-621-1519
Year Founded: 1848
Approx.Sls.: $363,500,000
Emp.: 3,108
Fiscal Year-end: 12/31/91
Collection & Distr. of News, Photos & Feature Service for Newspapers & Broadcast Stations
S.I.C.: 7383
William J. Keating *(Chm. Bd.)*
Louis D. Boccardi *(Pres. & Chief Exec. Officer)*
Patrick O'Brien *(V.P., Treas. & Dir.-Strategic Plng.)*
Wick Temple *(V.P. & Dir.-Newspaper Membership)*
Walter R. Mears *(V.P.-Washington)*
James F. Tomlinson *(V.P., Sec. & Asst. to the Pres.)*
Claude E. Erbsen *(V.P. & Dir.-World Services)*
John W. Reid *(V.P. & Dir.-Communications & Tech.)*
William E. Ahearn *(V.P. & Exec. Editor)*
Paul H. Jenssen *(Controller)*

The Associated Press—(Continued)

Lawrence G. Blasko *(Dir.-Admin. Services)*
Wendell Wood Collins *(Dir.-Corp. Communications)*
Byron Yake *(Dir.-Human Resources)*
Vincent Alabiso *(Exec. Photo Editor)*

No. of U.S. Offices: 142
No. of Foreign Offices: 84

Outside Service Firm(s):

Aetna Life & Casualty*(Pension Manager)*
151 Farmington Avenue
Hartford, CT 06156
Tel.: 203-273-2128
Fax: 203-729-4295

First Chicago Shareholder Services Trust Co.*(Pension Manager)*
153 West 51st St.
New York, NY 10019
Tel.: 212-791-6422
Fax: 212-385-9798

Subsidiaries:

La Prensa Asociada, Inc. **(1)**
207 Second Ave.
San Mateo, CA 94401
Tel.: 415-342-6222 (100%)
Publr. La Prensa Spanish Newspaper
S.I.C.: 2711
Dante Beteo *(Mng. Editor)*

Press Association, Inc. **(1)**
50 Rockefeller Plaza
New York, NY 10020
Tel.: 212-621-1500 (100%)
News Syndicate
S.I.C.: 7383

SaTellite Data Broadcast Networks, Inc. (SATNET) **(1)**
50 Rockefeller Plaza
New York, NY 10020
Tel.: 212-621-1500 (100%)
News Syndicate
S.I.C.: 7383

Wide World Photos, Inc. **(1)**
50 Rockefeller Plaza
New York, NY 10020
Tel.: 212-621-1930 (100%)
Photo Syndication
S.I.C.: 7383
Louis D. Boccards *(Pres. & Chief Exec. Officer)*
Patrick O'Brien *(V.P., Treas. & Dir.-Strategic Planning)*
Vincent Alabiso *(Exec. Photo Editor)*

Non-U.S. Holdings:

The Associated Press A/S **(1)**
Fridtiof Mansens Plass 5
Oslo, Norway
News Syndicate
S.I.C.: 7383

The Associated Press A/S **(1)**
55 Road Rup Lad Ser DK-1550
Copenhagen, Denmark
News Syndicate
S.I.C.: 7383

The Associated Press AB **(1)**
Vattugatten 12
Stockholm, Sweden
Tel.: 31 11 12 80
Telex: 19195 appress s red
News Syndicate
S.I.C.: 7383

The Associated Press (Belgium) S.A. **(1)**
Boulevard Charlemagne B-1040
Brussels, Belgium
Tel.: 2-230-58-31
News Syndicate
S.I.C.: 7383

The Associated Press GmbH **(1)**
27 Mosel Strasse D-6000
Frankfurt/Main, Germany
Tel.: 25-31-90
Telex: 25-12-89
News Syndicate
S.I.C.: 7383

The Associated Press, Ltd. **(1)**
12 Norwich St.
London, EC4, United Kingdom
Tel.: 071-353-6323
News Syndicate
S.I.C.: 7383

The Associated Press, Ltd. **(1)**
36 King St., E.
Toronto, ON M5C 2L9, Canada
Tel.: 416-368-1388 (100%)
News Syndicate
S.I.C.: 7383
Jeffrey Ulbrich *(Chief of Bureau)*

The Associated Press de Venezuela, S.A. **(1)**
Apartado A de Correo 1015-A,
Caracas, Venezuela
Tel.: 2 42 53 62 (100%)
S.I.C.: 7383
Harold Olmos *(Chief of Bureau)*

ASSOCIATED PROCESS CONTROLS
7150 Koll Center Pkwy.
Pleasanton, CA 94566
Tel.: 510-846-9000 CA
Fax: 510-846-0396
Year Founded: 1962
Assets: $4,000,000
Liabilities: $2,000,000
Net Worth: $2,000,000
Approx.Sls.: $20,000,000
Emp.: 60
Technical Sales; Systems Engineering/Integration, Distribution For Process Instrumentation & Controls
S.I.C.: 3829
Michael A. McCoy *(Pres.)*
Michael Kitchens *(Controller)*
Jim Noel *(Dir.-Process Instrumentation)*
Rich Ash *(Mgr.-Inside Sls.)*
Jim Carson *(Mgr.-Outside Sls.)*
Jing Firmeza *(Mgr.-Data Processing)*
Wayne Harbert *(Mgr.-Quality Control)*
W. Glenn Redden *(Mgr.-Fin. & Opers.)*
Principal(s):
Michael A. McCoy

No. of Mfg. Plants/Facilities: 1
No. of U.S. Offices: 1

Computer Systems/Hardware:
IBM System 36

Outside Service Firm(s):

Elwood And Espina*(Auditors)*
Foster City, CA

Liberty Mutual*(Group Insurer)*
Pleasanton, CA

Wells Fargo Bank*(Investment Banker)*
Palo Alto, CA

Carr, McClellan, Ingersol, Thompson & Horn*(Legal Firm)*
Burlingame, CA

Wells Fargo Bank*(Major Banking Relationship)*
Palo Alto, CA

ASSOCIATED WHOLESALE GROCERS, INC.
5000 Kansas Ave.
Kansas City, KS 66106
Mailing Address:
P.O. Box 2932,
Kansas City, KS 66110-0932
Tel.: 913-321-1313
Fax: 913-573-1592
Year Founded: 1926
Approx.Sls.: $2,114,000,000
Emp.: 1,100
Fiscal Year-end: 12/31/90
Co-Operative Grocery Distributor
S.I.C.: 5141
Fred Ball *(Chm. Bd.)*
Jim Baska *(Pres. & Chief Exec. Officer)*
Douglas Carolan *(Exec. V.P.-Mdsg. & Mktg.)*
Mike DeFabis *(Exec. V.P. & Chief Oper. Officer)*
Tom Williams *(Sr. V.P.-Kansas City Div.)*
Gary Phillips *(Sr. V.P.-Springfield Div.)*
Joseph Campbell *(V.P. & Treas.)*
Bill Lancaster *(V.P.-Sls.)*
Doug Boehmer *(Controller)*
Frances Pellegrino Puhl *(Gen. Counsel)*
Steve Dillard *(Exec. Dir.-Mdsg. & Mktg., Kansas City Div.)*
Jon Spies *(Dir.-Human Resources-Kansas City Div.)*
Tom Nelson *(Dir.-Human Resources-Springfield Div.)*
Lew Cort *(Mgr.-Adv. & Sls. Promo., Springfield Div.)*
Bob Roberts *(Mgr.-Adv., Kansas City Div.)*

ASTER NUT PRODUCTS INC.
(Filed Bankruptcy Chapter 11-July 6, 1992)
1455 McCarter Hwy.
Newark, NJ 07104
Tel.: 201-483-8680
Tel.: 800-899-NUTS
Fax: 201-483-2756
Year Founded: 1888
Approx.Sls.: $16,000,000
Emp.: 125
Fiscal Year-end: 12/31/90
Import Export
Nut & Snack Food Mfg.
S.I.C.: 2068; 2096
Ewing Smith *(Pres.)*
Larry Oberman *(Exec. V.P. & Chief Oper. Officer)*
Lou Inzillo *(V.P.-Sls.)*
Sean Horan *(V.P.-Pur.)*
Doug Lieb *(Controller)*
Sigmund Oberman *(Treas.)*
Al Jaffe *(Chief Engineer)*

ASTON MARTIN LAGONDA OF NORTH AMERICA, INC.
1290 E. Main St.
Stamford, CT 06902
Tel.: 203-359-2259
Fax: 203-323-2558
Approx.Sls.: $11,000,000
Emp.: 2
Fiscal Year-end: 12/31/91
Import
Importer & Distributor for Aston Martin & Lagonda Automobiles & Parts
S.I.C.: 5015; 5012
Walter Hayes *(Chm., Pres. & Chief Exec. Officer)*
M.R. Haysey *(Sr. V.P. & Mktg. Dir.)*
Kathy Johnson *(Corp. Sec.)*
David Graham *(Treas.)*
S.T. Rodd *(US Tech. Rep.)*

ASTRE CORPORATE GROUP
809 Princess St.
Alexandria, VA 22314
Tel.: 703-739-0397
Tel.: 800-83-ASTRE DE
Fax: 703-684-3767
Year Founded: 1967
Assets: $1,273,296
Earnings: $237,125
Liabilities: $171,253
Net Worth: $1,102,043
Approx.Sls.: $10,750,000
Emp.: 113
Fiscal Year-end: 12/31/91
Export
Research & Development; Product Design & Process Development
S.I.C.: 8731; 2834; 3841
Roy A. Ackerman *(Chm. Bd. & Chief Exec. Officer)*
Samuel C. Crosby *(Chief Oper. Officer)*
Frank Hyman *(Gen. Counsel)*
James F. Tobey *(Mgr.-Research & Devel.)*
Scott Mahler *(Dir.-Mngmt. Information Systems)*
John Brace *(Controller)*
Principal(s):
Roy A. Ackerman
Samuel C. Crosby

No. of U.S. Offices: 3
No. of Foreign Offices: 1

Computer Systems/Hardware:
IBM System 36; Novell Network

Outside Service Firm(s):

Hartford Life Insurance Co.*(Commercial Insurance Carrier)*
Hartford, CT 06104-2999

MedMark*(Commercial Insurance Carrier)*
Washington, DC

New York Life*(Group Insurer)*
Chicago, IL

Richmond & Fishburne, PC*(Legal Firm)*
Charlottesville, VA

Wendell Wynn, Esq.*(Legal Firm)*
Charlottesville, VA

Central Fidelity Bank*(Major Banking Relationship)*
Charlottesville, VA

Subsidiaries:

Astre Consulting Corp. **(1)**
1610 Quail Run
Charlottesville, VA 22901
Tel.: 804-973-2355 (100%)
Fax: 703-684-3767
Roy A. Ackerman *(Chief Oper. Officer)*

Industrial Design Associates **(1)**
1610 Quail Run
Charlottesville, VA 22901
Tel.: 804-973-7380 (100%)
Samuel C. Crosby *(Chief Oper. Officer)*

Industrial Microgenics **(1)**
809 Princess St.
Alexandria, VA 22314
Tel.: 703-739-0536 (100%)
James F. Tobey, Jr. *(Chief Oper. Officer)*

ASTRO WIRE & CABLE CORPORATION
50 Gardner St.
Worcester, MA 01613
Mailing Address:
P.O. Box 246
Worcester, MA 01613
Tel.: 508-754-3281
Fax: 508-755-5189
Year Founded: 1976
Assets: $10,000,000
Liabilities: $7,000,000
Net Worth: $3,000,000
Approx.Sls.: $16,000,000
Emp.: 125
Fiscal Year-end: 9/31/88
Mfr. Electrical Wires & Cables
S.I.C.: 3643
Sam Perlman *(Pres.)*
Bernard L. Pemstein *(Chief Fin. Officer)*
Joseph Hussar *(Chief Exec. Officer)*
Al Iacobucci *(Controller)*
M. Fitzsimmons *(Dir.-Data Processing)*
Paul Cummings *(Dir.-Pur.)*

No. of Mfg. Plants/Facilities: 1
No. of U.S. Offices: 1

Computer Systems/Hardware:
DEC VAX 750

Outside Service Firm(s):

Martin Braver & Assoc.*(Auditors)*
Boston, MA

Guardian Life Insurance Co.*(Group Insurer)*
New York, NY

Mechanics Bank*(Major Banking Relationship)*
Worcester, MA

Finegold Assoc.*(Pension Manager)*
Worcester, MA

ASTRONAUTICS CORP. OF AMERICA
4115 N. Teutonia Ave.
Milwaukee, WI 53209
Mailing Address:
P.O. Box 523
Milwaukee, WI 53201
Tel.: 414-447-8200 **WI**
Telex: 687-8037
Fax: 414-447-8231
Year Founded: 1959
Approx.Sls.: $650,000,000
Emp.: 5,600

Export
Mfr. of Aircraft Instruments, Flight Control Systems, Guidance & Navigation Systems, Robotics, Mini Supercomputers, Thermal Magnetic Refrigeration, Secure Communication Systems, Avionic Displays & Display Processors, Systems Integrators
S.I.C.: 3728; 3812; 3571; 3569; 3669; 3829
Norma Paige *(Chm. Bd.)*
N.K. Zelazo *(Chief Exec. Officer)*
Dr. R.E. Zelazo *(Pres.)*
M. Russek *(V.P. & Gen. Mgr.)*
M. Sargent *(V.P.-Fin.)*
R.D. Seinfeld *(V.P.-Mktg.)*
J. Potts *(Dir.-Pur.)*
Patricia Zingen *(Mktg. Coord.)*
D. Broadhead *(Mgr.-Personnel)*

Outside Service Firm(s):

Deloitte & Touche*(Auditors)*
250 E. Wisconsin Ave.
Milwaukee, WI 53202-4283
Tel.: 414-271-3000

Paige & Paige*(Legal Firm)*
Milwaukee, WI

First Wisconsin National Bank*(Major Banking Relationship)*
777 E. Wisconsin Ave.
Milwaukee, WI 53202
Tel.: 414-765-4321
Fax: 414-355-6903

Subsidiary:

Kearfott Guidance & Navigation Corp. **(1)**
150 Totowa Road
Wayne, NJ 07474-0595
Tel.: 201-785-6000
Telex: 133440
Fax: 201-785-6025
Approx.Sls.: $300,000,000
Emp.: 3,600
Fiscal Year-end: 5/31/91
Import Export
Mfr. of Ring Laser Gyro & Tuned Rotor Gyro Inertial Navigation Systems, Stellar Inertial Navigation Systems, Land Navigation Systems, Attitude Reference Systems, Inertial Measurement Units, Accelerometers, Gyroscopes, Automatic Ground Support Systems, Precision Rotary Components & Ships' Integration Equipment
S.I.C.: 3812
Dr. R.E. Zelazo *(Pres. & Chief Exec. Officer)*
R. Acker *(V.P.-Engrng.)*
C.H. Hevert *(V.P.-Opers. Mfg.)*
Harvey Truppi *(V.P.-Programs/Logistics)*
John Krawczuk *(V.P.-Bus. Devel. & Plng.)*
Blaise Russo *(V.P.-Human Resources)*
Stephen Givant *(Gen. Counsel)*
Les Seelig *(Comptroller)*
J.C. Stiles *(Dir.-Res.)*
R.A. Kunzier *(Dir.-Bus. Devel.)*
Walter Geib *(Dir.-Procurement)*

Non-U.S. Holdings:

Astronautics C.A. Ltd. **(1)**
23 Hayerarkon Street P.O. Box 882, Bnei-Brak, Israel
Tel.: 972-35791555 (100%)
Telex: 922341294
Fax: 972-35794404
Mfr. of Aircraft Instruments & Controls, Avionics Dispalys & DisplayProcessors, Guidance & Navigation Systems
S.I.C.: 3571; 3728; 3812
Dr. Shlomo Karniel *(Gen. Mgr.)*

D. Chaklin, Dir. European Operations **(1)**
28 Tekels Ave.
Camberley, Surrey GU15 2LB, United Kingdom
Tel.: 4989-484072 (100%)
Telex 84117898041
Fax: 4989484074
Mfr. of Aircraft Instruments & Controls, Avionics, Guidance & Navigation Systems
S.I.C.: 3571; 3728; 3812
Dave Chalklin *(Gen. Mgr.)*

ASTRUP DRUGS, INC.
1417 S.W. First Ave.
Austin, MN 55912
Tel.: 507-433-7447
Year Founded: 1952
Approx.Sls.: $18,000,000
Emp.: 245
Retail Drugs, Sundries & General Merchandise
S.I.C.: 5912; 5399
Leonard Astrup *(Pres.)*
Chris Astrup *(V.P.)*
Corrine Astrup *(Treas. & Sec.)*

ATARI GAMES CORPORATION
675 Sycamore Dr.
Milpitas, CA 95035
Tel.: 408-434-3700 **CA**
Fax: 408-434-3776
Year Founded: 1985
Approx.Sls.: $38,478,705
Emp.: 250
Fiscal Year-end: 3/31/91
Mfr. Coin-Operated Video Games
S.I.C.: 3999
Hide Nakajima *(Pres.)*
Dennis Wood *(Sr. V.P., Gen. Counsel & Personnel)*
Mike Taylor *(V.P.-Intl. Sls.)*
Richard Moore *(V.P.-Engrng.)*

Outside Service Firm(s):

Arthur Andersen & Co.*(Auditors)*
Milpitas, CA

Union Bank*(Major Banking Relationship)*
Sunnyvale, CA

Subsidiary:

Tengen **(1)**
675 Sycamore Dr.
Milpitas, CA 95035
Tel.: 408-473-9400
Software Company
S.I.C.: 7371
Dan Van Elderen *(Chief Oper. Officer)*

ATCHISON COUNTY CO-OP ASSOCIATION
812 Main St.
Atchison, KS 66002
Mailing Address:
P.O. Drawer B,
Atchison, KS 66002
Tel.: 913-367-0318
Year Founded: 1917
Assets: $12,264,700
Liabilities: $7,215,627
Net Worth: $5,049,073
Approx.Sls.: $31,192,000
Emp.: 40
Fiscal Year-end: 12/31/90
Agricultural Production & Services; Wholesale Trade-Nondurable Goods; Membership Organizations
S.I.C.: 5153; 5191
Milton Hines *(Chm. & Pres.)*
William Nienstedt *(Exec. V.P. & Chief Exec. Officer & Gen. Mgr.)*
Mark Shields *(Controller & Dir.-Data Processing)*
Thomas Morrill *(Dir.-Sls. & Mktg.)*
Jay Nower *(Sec.)*

Computer Systems/Hardware:
IBM Series I

Outside Service Firm(s):

Lindburg & Vogel*(Auditors)*
Topeka, KS

Kansas Farmers Service Assoc.*(Commercial Insurance Carrier)*
Hutchinson, KS

Kansas Farmers Service Assoc.*(Group Insurance Broker/ Consult)*
Hutchinson, KS

National Bank for Cooperatives*(Major Banking Relationship)*
Wichita, KS

Farmland Industries, Inc.*(Pension Manager)*
Kansas City, MO

ATCOM, INC.
4920 Alston Ave.
Research Triangle Park, NC 27709
Mailing Address:
P.O. Box 13476
Research Triangle Park, NC 27709
Tel.: 919-544-5751 **NC**
Year Founded: 1979
Assets: $2,630,848
Earnings: $186,846
Liabilities: $867,142
Net Worth: $1,763,706
Sales Range: $10-19 Million
Emp.: 65
Fiscal Year-end: 10/31/91
Telecommunication Sales, Design & Service
S.I.C.: 4813
James H. Watkins *(Chief Exec. & Oper. Officer)*
Kenneth M. Munsch *(Pres.)*
David B. Finch *(V.P.-Sls.)*
J. Sheldon Yarborough *(V.P.-Fin.)*

No. of U.S. Offices: 3

Computer Systems/Hardware:
IBM PCs, Altos, COMPAQ

Outside Service Firm(s):

Deloitte & Touche*(Auditors)*
One Triangle Exec. Park, Ste. 600, P.O. Box 13866
Research Triangle Park, NC 27709-3866

First Union National Bank*(Major Banking Relationship)*
Durham, NC

Parker, Poe, Adams & Bernstein*(Legal Firm)*
Raleigh, NC

ATERON CORP.
(Formerly Giordano Associates, Inc.)
5 Century Dr.
Parsippany, NJ 07054
Mailing Address:
P.O. Box 868
Pine Brook, NJ 07058
Tel.: 201-292-0079
Fax: 201-292-9416
Year Founded: 1976
Approx.Sls.: $13,000,000
Emp.: 115
Export
Manufacture Automatic Electronic Test Equipment & System Engineering
S.I.C.: 3825
Philip C. Jackson *(Chm. Bd., Pres. & Chief Exec. Officer)*
Paul Biegel *(Chief Fin. Officer)*

Outside Service Firm(s):

KPMG Peat Marwick*(Auditors)*
Stamford Square, 3001 Summer St.
Stamford, CT 06905
Tel.: 203-356-9800

de Mare & Harvey*(Legal Firm)*
Sparta, NJ

Midlantic National Bank*(Major Banking Relationship)*
Sparta, NJ

ATEX OIL CO. OF TEXAS, INC.
2740 Southwest 45th
Amarillo, TX 79110
Tel.: 505-622-4800
Approx.Sls.: $36,000,000
Emp.: 55
Wholesale Trade-Nondurable Goods; Automotive Dealer & Svc. Station
S.I.C.: 5171; 5541
Ray Bell *(Chm. Bd., Pres. & Chief Exec. Officer)*
Eugene Bell *(V.P.)*
Tom Lancaster *(Treas. & Sec.)*
Bobbie Merchant *(Data Processing Mgr.)*

Computer Systems/Hardware:
IBM System 34

Outside Service Firm(s):

May-Taylor Inc.*(Auditors)*
Roswell, NM

Liberty Mutual*(Group Insurer)*
175 Berkeley St.
Boston, MA

Atwood, Malone, Mann & Cooter*(Legal Firm)*
Roswell, NM

First Interstate Bank*(Major Banking Relationship)*
Roswell, NM

ATHENS PAPER CO. INC.
1898 Elmtree Dr.
Nashville, TN 37210
Mailing Address:
P.O. Box 100835
Nashville, TN 37210
Tel.: 615-889-7900
Fax: 615-889-5477
Approx.Sls.: $63,000,000
Emp.: 150
Paper Distributor
S.I.C.: 5111
Milton Chamberlain *(Chm. Bd.)*
Don Jenkins, Jr. *(Pres. & Treas.)*

Computer Systems/Hardware:
IBM System 36

Outside Service Firm(s):

Ernst & Young*(Auditors)*
200 One Commerce Place
Nashville, TN 37239

Willis Corroon*(Commercial Insurance Carrier)*
7 Hanover Square
New York, NY
Tel.: 212-837-0823
Fax: 212-344-8290

Willis Corroon*(Group Insurer)*
7 Hanover Square
New York, NY
Tel.: 212-837-0823
Fax: 212-344-8290

Sovran Bank*(Major Banking Relationship)*
One Commerce Place M-B
Nashville, TN 37219

Athens Paper Co. Inc.—(Continued)

Tel.: 615-749-4113

THE ATHLETE'S FOOT GROUP, INC.
1950 Vaughn Rd.
Kennesaw, GA 30144
Tel.: 404-514-4500
Fax: 404-514-4903
Approx.Sls.: $210,000,000
Emp.: 325
Fiscal Year-end: 1/31/91
Franchisers & Operators of Retail Specialty Stores; Athletic Shoes & Related Soft Goods
S.I.C.: 5941; 5661
Gene Kash *(V.P.-Store Opers.)*
Bob Wabler *(V.P. & Chief Fin. Officer)*
James Hutchinson *(Dir.-Adv.)*
Joe Demarco *(Dir.-Franchise Sls.)*

ATHLETIC ATTIC PROPERTIES INC.
18 NW 33rd Ct.
Gainesville, FL 32607
Tel.: 904-377-5289 **FL**
Fax: 904-377-7169
Year Founded: 1972
Approx.Sls.: $20,000,000
Emp.: 360
Fiscal Year-end: 8/31/91
Retail Athletic Shoes & Apparel; Patent Owners & Lessors
S.I.C.: 5599; 5661; 6794
Gerald D. Shackow *(Chm. Bd.)*
Jack B. Thompson *(Chief Exec. Officer)*
Marty Liquori *(Pres.)*
Vivian Boza *(Controller)*
Dave Dover *(Gen. Mgr.-Corp. Div.)*
Rob Luetjen *(Mgr.-Personnel Training & Dev.)*
Alex Vergara *(Mgr.-Adv.)*
Principal(s):
Gerald D. Shackow
Martin Liquori
James Carnes

Outside Service Firm(s):

Davis, Monk, Farnsworth & Company*(Auditors)*
Gainesville, FL

Southeast Bank, N.A.*(Major Banking Relationship)*
Gainesville, FL

THE ATKINS AGENCY
1777 NE Loop 410, Ste. 1100
San Antonio, TX 78217
Tel.: 210-826-5500
Fax: 210-826-1247
Year Founded: 1963
Approx.Billings: $24,185,420
Emp.: 44
Tourism, Healthcare, Consumer Prod. Services, Auto Aftermarket, Financial & International
Chip Atkins *(Chm. Bd.)*
Steve Atkins *(Pres. & New Bus. Contact)*
Doug Brown *(Pres., Dir.-Intl. Mktg.)*
Calhoun Allen *(Sr. V.P., Dir.-Mktg. Services/Opers.)*
Mary Rose Brown *(V.P., Pub. Rels. Services)*
Denise Geiger *(V.P., Chief Fin. Officer & Controller)*
Misty Krohn *(V.P. Admin. Services)*
Pat Atkins *(Corp. Sec., Treas.)*

Computer Systems/Hardware:
Wang, Macintosh

ATLANTA BEVERAGE CO.
5000 Fulton Industrial Blvd. SW
Atlanta, GA 30336
Tel.: 404-699-6700
Fax: 404-699-6778
Year Founded: 1930
Sales Range: $100-499 Million
Emp.: 420
Wholesale Beer Distributor
S.I.C.: 5181
John Economos *(Pres.)*
Charles Hardy *(Exec. V.P.)*
Mark Pirrung *(Chief Oper. Offcier)*
Elaine Slocumbe *(Coord.-Personnel)*

Outside Service Firm(s):

Atlanta HMO*(Group Insurer)*
Atlanta, GA

ATLANTA MARKET CENTER
240 Peachtree St. N.W., Ste. 2200
Atlanta, GA 30303
Tel.: 404-220-3000
Fax: 404-220-3030
Year Founded: 1961
Sales Range: $60-79 Million
Emp.: 375
Fiscal Year-end: 12/31/90
Trade Centers
S.I.C.: 7389; 8744
Sam A. Williams *(Pres.)*
John C. Portman, Jr. *(Chief Oper. Officer)*
Rob Hollis *(Chief Fin. Officer & V.P.)*
Ralph Jones *(Exec. V.P.-Opers. & Admin.)*
Tom Fulghum *(Exec. V.P. & Gen. Mgr.-Mdse.)*
Jim Kranzusch *(Exec. V.P. & Gen. Mgr.-Inforum)*
Jack Sasser *(Exec. V.P. & Gen. Mgr.-Apparel Mart)*
Bill Bryant *(V.P.-Mktg.-Atlanta Apparel Ctr.)*
Peg Canter *(V.P.-Leasing Atlanta Gift Mart)*
Diana Getz *(V.P.-Trade Shows East)*
Susie Longino *(V.P.-Mktg.-Atlanta Mdsg. & Gift Mkt.)*
Rich Mauro *(V.P.-Mktg.-Inforum)*
Tom Mitchell *(V.P. & Gen. Mgr.-San Francisco Fashion Ctr.)*
Joliene Price *(V.P.-Communications)*
Jeff Portman *(V.P. & Gen. Mgr.-Atlanta Decorative Arts Ctr.)*
Tina Malthie *(Exec. Dir.-Human Resources & Admin.)*
Betsy Longino *(Dir.-Tech.)*
Jack Chalden *(Gen. Mgr.-AMC Trade Shows Ltd.)*

No. of Mfg. Plants/Facilities: 5
No. of U.S. Offices: 5

Computer Systems/Hardware:
IBM

ATLANTA MOTOR LINES, INC.
1622 Cedar Grove Rd., S.E.
Conley, GA 30027
Tel.: 404-363-0010 **GA**
Fax: 404-366-8578
Approx.Sls.: $21,000,000
Emp.: 400
Carlton E. Kline *(Pres.)*
Ed Copenhaver *(Exec. V.P.)*

Outside Service Firm(s):

Howard & Smith*(Auditors)*
Atlanta, GA

NationsBank*(Major Banking Relationship)*
35 Broad St.
Atlanta, GA 30303
Tel.: 404-581-2121
Tel.: 800-848-8198

ATLANTA WIRE WORKS, INC.
1117 Battle Creek Rd.
Jonesboro, GA 30236
Tel.: 404-471-0660
Fax: 404-471-1365
Approx.Sls.: $23,000,000
Emp.: 320
Mfr. of Fourdrinier Forming Fabrics
S.I.C.: 3554
G.E. Kirby *(Chm. & Pres.)*
Malcolm H. Miller *(Asst. to Pres.)*
J.B. McCann *(Natl. Mktg. Dir.)*
Wayne F. Kuhne *(Pur. Agent)*
Robert Johnston *(Personnel Dir)*

ATLANTIC AVIATION CORP.
153 N. DuPont Hwy.
New Castle, DE 19720-5000
Mailing Address:
P.O. Box 15000
Wilmington, DE 19850
Tel.: 302-322-7000 **DE**
Fax: 302-322-7227
Year Founded: 1947
Approx.Sls.: $100,000,000
Emp.: 581
Fiscal Year-end: 12/31/91
Aircraft Maintenance; Paint; Interior Refurbishment; Component Overhaul; Fuel Sales; Charters; Aircraft Parts & Headsets; Aviation Insurance
S.I.C.: 5088; 3699; 3728; 4522; 5172
Stockton N. Smith *(Chm. Bd. & Chief Exec. Officer)*
Malcolm S. Graham *(Pres.)*
Frank C. Zirnkilton, Jr. *(Chief Fin. Officer & Sr. V.P.)*
Franklin S. Eyster II *(Sr. V.P., Sec. & Gen. Counsel)*
Michael D. Langston *(Sr. V.P.-Opers. & Mktg.)*
Joseph McShulkis *(Sr. V.P.)*
Donald H. Willhite *(V.P. & Comptroller)*

Outside Service Firm(s):

KPMG Peat Marwick*(Auditors)*
1600 Market St.
Philadelphia, PA 19103
Tel.: 215-299-3100

Bank of Delaware*(Major Banking Relationship)*
Wilmington, DE

ATLANTIC BUILDERS GROUP INC.
23 Fontana Lane
Baltimore, MD 21237
Mailing Address:
P.O. Box 70239
Baltimore, MD 21237
Tel.: 410-682-8900
Fax: 410-682-8950
Year Founded: 1982
Assets: $11,563,000
Earnings: $175,000
Liabilities: $6,438,000
Net Worth: $5,125,000
Approx.Sls.: $36,000,000
Emp.: 88
Fiscal Year-end: 11/30/91
Design & Construction of Properties to Meet Industrial & Office Needs
S.I.C.: 1541; 1542
Donald R. Clark *(Chm. Bd.)*
Weldon A. Lee *(Pres., Chief Exec. Officer)*
Alexander Chicknoski *(V.P.-Pur.)*
John C. Pomory *(V.P.-Interior Group)*
D. Gary Dohler *(Chief Fin. Officer)*
Arthur Trump *(Sec. & Gen. Counsel)*
James Sanford *(Asst. Controller)*
Eric G. Regelin *(Sr. Project Mgr.)*
Joseph J. Welkie *(Sr. Project Mgr.)*
John Sadler *(Dir.-Sls.)*
Richard Stor *(Dir.-Mktg., Sls. & Adv.)*
Juanita Drass *(Mgr.-Human Resources)*
Juanita Wilson *(Corp. Librarian)*

No. of Mfg. Plants/Facilities: 1
No. of U.S. Offices: 1

Computer Systems/Hardware:
IBM 36 CMAS

Outside Service Firm(s):

C. W. Amos & Co.*(Auditors)*
2 N. Charles St.
Baltimore, MD 21201
Tel.: 410-727-5341

The PMA Group*(Commercial Insurance Carrier)*
Charlotte, NC

Lincoln National Life Insurance Co.*(Group Insurer)*
Baltimore, MD

Merrill Lynch*(Investment Banker)*
Baltimore, MD

Whiteford, Taylor & Preston*(Legal Firm)*
Baltimore, MD

First National Bank of Maryland*(Major Banking Relationship)*
25 S. Charles St.
Baltimore, MD 21201
Tel.: 410-244-4025

ATLANTIC CONCRETE PRODUCTS, INC.
8900 Old Rte. 13
Tullytown, PA 19007-0098
Mailing Address:
P.O. Box 129
Tullytown, PA 19007-0098
Tel.: 215-945-5600 **PA**
Fax: 215-946-3102
Year Founded: 1969
Approx.Sls.: $10,000,000
Emp.: 145
Mfr. of Pre-cast Concrete Products
S.I.C.: 3272
Joseph J. Westhoff *(Pres.)*
John Ditcher *(V.P. & Sec.)*
Joseph A. Westhoff *(Controller)*
Jerry Donahue *(Mgr.-Sls.)*

No. of Mfg. Plants/Facilities: 3

Outside Service Firm(s):

Holmes & Holmes*(Auditors)*
Colmar, PA

Begley, Carlin & Mandio*(Legal Firm)*
Bristol, PA

Meridian Bank*(Major Banking Relationship)*
One Meridian Plaza, 36th Fl.
Philadelphia, PA
Tel.: 215-854-3900

ATLANTIC DAIRY COOPERATIVE
1225 Industrial Hwy.
Southampton, PA 18966
Mailing Address:
P.O. Box 127
Southampton, PA 18966
Tel.: 215-322-0200
Fax: 215-322-8790
Year Founded: 1917
Assets: $67,203,548
Earnings: $2,307,898
Liabilities: $51,318,805
Net Worth: $15,884,743
Approx.Sls.: $524,371,031
Emp.: 340
Fiscal Year-end: 7/31/91
Farmers Dairy Co-operative
S.I.C.: 5143
Robert B. McSparran *(Chm. Bd. & Pres.)*
Paul E. Hand *(Chief Exec. Officer)*
Evan L. Fineman *(Treas. & Chief Fin. Officer)*
Donald F. Copeland *(Gen. Counsel)*
Barry Loss *(Dir.-Telecommunications)*
Don Bryner *(Mgr.-Quality Control)*
Johnie Christiance *(Mgr.-Data Processing)*
Laura E. England *(Mgr.-Pub. Rels.)*
Henry Heerlyn *(Mgr.-Sls.)*

Sally Trotman *(Mgr.-Acctg.)*
Robert M. Dever *(Asst. Gen. Mgr.)*
Terri Milinovich *(Corp. Travel Planner)*

No. of Mfg. Plants/Facilities: 3
No. of U.S. Offices: 3

Computer Systems/Hardware:
IBM AS 400

Outside Service Firm(s):

KPMG Peat Marwick*(Auditors)*
1600 Market St.
Philadelphia, PA 19103
Tel.: 215-299-3100

Alexander & Alexander*(Commercial Insurance Carrier)*
One Constitution Plaza
New York, NY 10036
Tel.: 617-241-9800

Alexander & Alexander*(Group Insurer)*
One Constitution Plaza
New York, NY 10036
Tel.: 617-241-9800

Donald Copeland*(Legal Firm)*
Philadelphia, PA

Provident National Bank*(Major Banking Relationship)*
1000 Westlakes Dr.
Berwyn, PA 19312

Subsidiaries:

Holly Milk Plant **(1)**
405 Park Dr.
Carlisle, PA 17013
Tel.: 717-486-7000
Emp.: 120
Mfrs. of Condensed & Dry Milk Products & Butter
S.I.C.: 0241
Bill Schreiber *(Chief Oper. Officer)*

QC, Inc. **(1)**
1205 Industrial Hwy.
Southampton, PA 18966
Tel.: 215-355-3900
Emp.: 160
Computer Systems/Hardware:
IBM AS/400
Commercial Testing & Environmental Laboratory
S.I.C.: 8734
Allen Schopback *(Chief Oper. Officer)*

ATLANTIC GULF COMMUNITIES CORPORATION
(Formerly General Development Corporation)
2601 S. Bayshore Dr.
Miami, FL 33133
Tel.: 305-859-4000
Fax: 305-859-4360
Year Founded: 1955
Approx.Sls.: $250,000,000
Emp.: 4,000
Community Devel., Home Bldg. & Commercial Property Resorts
S.I.C.: 6552; 6531
James W. Apthorp *(Chm. Bd.)*
J. Larry Rutherford *(Pres. & Chief Exec. Officer)*
Gordon J. Pfersich *(Exec. V.P.)*
Michael Moore *(Sr. V.P.)*
Mack Wilcox *(Sr. V.P.)*
Harold Fenno *(Sr. V.P.)*
Michael Garretson *(Sr. V.P.)*
Jack O'Neal *(Sr. V.P.)*
Thomas W. Jeffrey *(Sr. V.P., Gen. Counsel & Corp. Sec.)*
Margaret A. Graff *(Sr. V.P. & Treas.)*
Joseph P. Zdon, Jr. *(Sr. V.P. & Controller)*
James Watts *(Sr. V.P. & Dir.-Mktg.)*
Susan Kinsey *(V.P.-Human Resources)*
Karen Boren *(Mgr.-Pub. Rels. & Media)*

Subsidiaries:

Cumberland Cove **(1)**
Rte. 2, Box 362
Monterey, TN 38574
Tel.: 615-839-2246
S.I.C.: 6552
David Osterman *(Reg. Mgr.)*
Marvin Badger *(Dir.-Community Opers.)*

Five Star Homes **(1)**
1111 S. Bayshore Dr.
Miami, FL 33131
Tel.: 305-350-1409
S.I.C.: 6552

Florida Home Finders **(1)**
1111 S. Bayshore Dr.
Miami, FL 33131
Tel.: 305-350-1266
S.I.C.: 6552

Port Charlotte **(1)**
1649 N.W. Tamiami Trail
Port Charlotte, FL 33952
Tel.: 813-625-8282
S.I.C.: 6552
Mack R. Wilcox *(Reg. Mgr.)*
Charles W. Telfair *(Dir.-Community Opers.)*
Gerry Gilbert *(Mgr.-Sls.)*

Port Malabar **(1)**
1120 S. E. Port Malabar Blvd.
Palm Bay, FL 32905
Tel.: 407-724-2000
S.I.C.: 6552
Michael Moore *(Reg. Mgr.)*
George Kulczycki *(Dir.-Community Opers.)*
Larry Slay *(Dir.-Sls.)*

Port La Belle **(1)**
Welcome Center Hwy., 80 E.
La Belle, FL 33935
Tel.: 813-675-1151
S.I.C.: 6552
Mack Wilcox *(Reg. Mgr.)*
Jim Coddington *(Dir.-Community Opers.)*
B.J. Smith *(Mgr.-Sls.)*

Port Saint Lucie **(1)**
11111 S. U.S. #1
Port Saint Lucie, FL 33452
Tel.: 305-878-2000
S.I.C.: 6552
Michael Moore *(Reg. Mgr.)*
Preston Hix *(Dir.-Community Opers.)*
Chris Dalfo *(Mgr.-Sls.)*

Sebastian Highlands **(1)**
U.S. #1, Box 305
Sebastian, FL 32958
Tel.: 407-562-4889
S.I.C.: 6552
Michael Moore *(Reg. Mgr.)*
George Kulczycki *(Dir.-Community Opers.)*

Silver Springs Shores **(1)**
504 Emerald Rd.
Ocala, FL 33672
Tel.: 904-288-8556
S.I.C.: 6552
Mack Wilcox *(Reg. Mgr.)*
John J. Palumbo *(Dir.-Community Opers.)*
Jack Ratkovic *(Mgr.-Sls.)*

Vero Beach Highlands **(1)**
2055 S.E. U.S. #1
Vero Beach, FL 32960
S.I.C.: 6552
Michael Moore *(Reg. Mgr.)*
George Kulczycki *(Dir.-Community Opers.)*

ATLANTIC METALS CORPORATION
Orthodox St. at Delaware River
Philadelphia, PA 19137
Tel.: 215-744-9400
Fax: 215-744-9406
Approx.Sls.: $10,000,000
Emp.: 100
Mfr. of Chemicals For Steel Industry
S.I.C.: 2819; 2869
Maurice Sall *(Chm. Bd.)*
Hyman L. Sall *(Pres.)*
M.K. Koul *(V.P. & Gen. Mgr.)*
George Gallagher *(Pur. Agent)*

Outside Service Firm(s):

Freedman & Adelman*(Auditors)*
Huntington Valley, PA

Fox, Rothschild, O'Brien & Frankel*(Legal Firm)*
2000 Market St., 10th Flr.
Philadelphia, PA 19103
Tel.: 215-299-2012

Fidelity Bank*(Major Banking Relationship)*
Broad & Walnut St.
Philadelphia, PA 19109

THE ATLANTIC MONTHLY MAGAZINE
745 Boylston St.
Boston, MA 02116
Tel.: 617-536-9500
Fax: 212-326-5566
Year Founded: 1857
Approx.Sls.: $11,900,000
Emp.: 55
Fiscal Year-end: 12/31/91
The Atlantic Monthly Magazine
S.I.C.: 2721
Mortimer Zuckerman *(Chm. Bd.)*
Fred Drasner *(Vice Chm. & Chief Exec. Officer)*
Ira Ellenthal *(Pres. & Publisher)*
Jayne Young *(Assoc. Publisher)*
Meredith Welch *(Dir.-Mktg.)*
Kimberly J. Smith Jenson *(Gen. Mgr.)*

Affiliate:

The Atlantic Advertising Sales **(1)**
599 Lexington Ave.
New York, NY 10022
Tel.: 212-326-5350
Fax: 212-326-5566
S.I.C.: 7313
Jayne Young *(V.P. & Assoc. Publisher)*
Frances Broudy *(Dir.-Adv.)*
Meredith Welch *(Dir.-Mktg.)*

ATLANTIC MUTUAL COMPANIES
45 Wall St.
New York, NY 10005
Tel.: 212-943-1800
Year Founded: 1842
Approx.Sls.: $655,000,000
Emp.: 1,850
Fiscal Year-end: 12/31/90
Property, Liability & Marine Insurance
S.I.C.: 6331; 6411
Edward K. Trowbridge *(Chm. & Chief Exec. Officer)*
Kenneth J. Gorman *(Pres. & Chief Oper. Officer)*
Klaus G. Dorf *(Exec. V.P.-Insurance Opers.)*
William Murphy *(Dir.-Corp. Communications)*

Subsidiaries:
Atlantic Mutual Insurance Co. **(1)**
45 Wall St.
New York, NY 10005
Tel.: 212-943-1800

Centennial Insurance Co. **(1)**
45 Wall St.
New York, NY 10005
Tel.: 212-943-1800

ATLANTIC PLUMBING SUPPLY COMPANY
807 V St., N.W.
Washington, DC 20001
Tel.: 202-667-6500 **DC**
Fax: 202-387-1331
Approx.Sls.: $13,000,000
Emp.: 35
Wholesale Distribution of Hydronic Heating Equipment
S.I.C.: 5074
Gilbert Needle *(Chm. Bd.)*
Edward G. Needle *(Pres.)*
William C. Gary *(Exec. V.P.)*
Ruth C. Needle *(V.P.)*
Malcolm Jacobs *(Treas.)*

Outside Service Firm(s):

Donald M. Caplan*(Legal Firm)*
Bethesda, MD

American Security Bank, N.A.*(Major Banking Relationship)*
1501 Pennsylvania Ave. N.W.
Washington, DC 20013
Tel.: 202-624-4000

ATLANTIC STEEL COMPANY
1300 Mecaslin St., N. W.
Atlanta, GA 30318
Mailing Address:
P.O. Box 1714
Atlanta, GA 30301
Tel.: 404-897-4500
Fax: 404-897-4623
Year Founded: 1901
Approx.Sls.: $250,000,000
Emp.: 900
Fiscal Year-end: 12/31/91
Export
Steel Bars Wire Rods & Wire Prods.
S.I.C.: 3312
J.J. Webb *(Pres. & Chief Exec. Officer)*
R.B. Webb *(V.P.-Sls.)*
K.P. Thurston *(V.P.-Fin.)*
R.J. Dervales *(V.P.-Indus. Rels.)*
R.S. Melum *(Gen. Mgr.-Mktg.)*

ATLANTIC SUGAR ASSOCIATION, INC.
26400 State Rd. 80
Belle Glade, FL 33430
Mailing Address:
P.O. Box 1570
Belle Glade, FL 33430
Tel.: 407-996-6541 **FL**
Fax: 407-996-8021
Year Founded: 1964
Approx.Sls.: $52,000,000
Emp.: 250
Manufacture Cane Sugar
S.I.C.: 2061
Francisco Pons *(Chm. Bd. & Pres.)*
David L. Young *(V.P.)*
Otto Larsens *(Sec.)*
Val F. Galan *(Controller)*
Surbando Diego *(Mgr.-Opers.)*
Adalberto Pacheco *(Dir.-Engrng.)*
Ernesto Priede *(Dir.-Personnel)*

Outside Service Firm(s):

KPMG Peat Marwick*(Auditors)*
One Biscayne Tower, 2 South Biscayne Blvd., Ste.2900
Miami, FL 33131

James Gann*(Legal Firm)*
Belle Glade, FL

Southeast Bank, N.A.*(Major Banking Relationship)*
One Southeast Financial Center
Miami, FL 33131

ATLANTIC TO PACIFIC BEDDING CORP.
700 Havemeyer Ave.
Bronx, NY 10473
Tel.: 718-597-3300 **NY**
Fax: 718-597-6616
Year Founded: 1974
Assets: $4,300,000
Liabilities: $3,100,000
Net Worth: $1,200,000
Approx.Sls.: $30,000,000
Emp.: 90
Fiscal Year-end: 6/30/90
Franchised Retail Bedding Chain
S.I.C.: 5712
Robert Martire *(Chm. Bd. & Pres.)*
Morton Swirsky *(Chief Oper. Officer & Controller)*
Mary Martife *(Sec.)*
Betty Muscarrella *(Dir.-Personnel)*

Atlantic to Pacific Bedding Corp.—(Continued)

Frank Profe *(Dir.-Franchise Opers.)*
Rohan Wallace *(Dir.-Data Processing)*
Louis DeGrazzio *(Mgr.-Trucking)*
John Garland *(Mgr.-Warehouse)*
Phillip P. Sherman *(Mgr.-Sls.)*

Principal(s):
Robert Martire

No. of Mfg. Plants/Facilities: 1
No. of U.S. Offices: 2

Computer Systems/Hardware:
Ultimate

Outside Service Firm(s):

Seidel, Kessler, Blum & Co., P.C.*(Auditors)*
Great Neck, NY

Aetna Life & Casualty*(Commercial Insurance Carrier)*
100 N. Riverside Plaza
Chicago, IL 60606

Hartford Life Insurance Co.*(Group Insurer)*
Hartford, CT 06104-2999

Josephthal's Co.*(Investment Banker)*
New York, NY

Brownstein, Zeidman & Schomer*(Legal Firm)*
Washington, DC

Josephthal's Co.*(Pension Manager)*
New York, NY

ATLAS CITRON HALIGMAN & BEDECARRE
855 Front St.
San Francisco, CA 94111
Tel.: 415-393-9400
Fax: 415-705-0150
Year Founded: 1990
Approx.Billings: $25,000,000
Emp.: 18
Jeff Atlas *(Chm.)*
Kirk Citron *(Pres.)*
Tom Bedecarre *(Gen. Mgr. & New Bus. Contact)*
Bob Mischak, Jr. *(Controller)*
Lisa Sandberg *(Office Mgr.)*

THE ATLAS CONSTRUCTION CO.
110 Lenox Ave.
Stamford, CT 06906
Mailing Address:
P.O. Box 2099,
Stamford, CT 06906
Tel.: 203-327-0330 **CT**
Fax: 203-323-1295
Year Founded: 1959
Assets: $18,374,130
Liabilities: $15,371,831
Net Worth: $3,002,299
Approx.Sls.: $71,800,000
Emp.: 90
Fiscal Year-end: 10/31/90
Construction Managers & General Contractors for Industrial & Residential Property
S.I.C.: 8741; 1541
Joseph L. Gambino *(Pres. & Chief Exec. Officer)*
Joseph M. Constantino *(Exec. V.P.)*
Ralph Cerreta *(Sr. V.P. & Chief Oper. Officer)*
Robert N. Jacobson *(V.P.-Fin., Treas., Sec. & Chief Fin. Officer)*
Robert S. Carlson *(V.P.)*
John J. McGowan *(V.P.)*
Laura M. Lopez *(Controller)*

Principal(s):
Joseph L. Gambino
Joseph M. Constantino
Robert N. Jacobson
Robert S. Carlson

No. of U.S. Offices: 2

Computer Systems/Hardware:
MAI Basic Four; IBM PC, XT; KAYPRO

Outside Service Firm(s):

Jaffe, Haft, Shalik & Co.*(Auditors)*
Great Neck, NY

ITT Hartford Insurance Group*(Group Insurer)*
Hartford Plaza
Hartford, CT 06115
Tel.: 203-547-5000

Sanford C. Bernstein & Co., Inc.*(Investment Banker)*
767 Fifth Ave.
New York, NY 10153
Tel.: 212-756-4383
Fax: 212-756-4405

Michael D. Bromley*(Legal Firm)*
Stamford, CT

Fidelity Trust Co.*(Major Banking Relationship)*
Stamford, CT

Hooker & Holcombe, Inc.*(Pension Manager)*
Hartford, CT

Subsidiary:

A.D. Herman Construction Co. **(1)**
532 Broad Hallow Rd.
Melville, NY 11747
Tel.: 516-752-8700
Emp.: 30
General Contractors
S.I.C.: 1541

ATLAS HOTELS, INC.
500 Hotel Circle
San Diego, CA 92186
Mailing Address:
P.O. Box 85098,
San Diego, CA 92186
Tel.: 619-291-2232
Tel.: 619-298-1281 **DE**
Fax: 619-291-4097
Fax: 619-298-1281
Year Founded: 1953
Approx.Sls.: $60,000,000
Emp.: 2,200
Fiscal Year-end: 9/30/91
Hotels; Restaurants
S.I.C.: 7011; 5812
Employee Matching Gifts Program: Contributes to United Way
C. Terry Brown *(Chm. Bd., Pres., Chief Exec. Officer & Chief Oper. Officer)*
Mike Cagalj *(Chief Fin. Officer, V.P. & Controller)*
Robert Dubaghian *(Chief Information Officer & Dir.-Data Processing)*
Jim Oddo *(V.P.-Mktg.)*
Henry Hoxie *(Sec. & Dir.-Human Resources)*
Ruben Munos *(Dir.-Adv.)*
Jim Schrieks *(Dir.-Pur.)*
Alecia Buncher *(Adv. Coord.)*

Computer Systems/Hardware:
Basic Four

Outside Service Firm(s):

Pannell, Kerr, Forster*(Auditors)*
San Diego, CA

William M. Mercer Incorporated*(Group Insurance Broker/Consult)*
3303 Wilshire Blvd.
Los Angeles, CA 90076
Tel.: 213-480-6400

Duke, Gerstel, Shearer & Bregante*(Legal Firm)*
101 West Broadway
San Diego, CA
Tel.: 619-232-0816

Wells Fargo Bank*(Major Banking Relationship)*
420 Montgomery St.
San Francisco, CA 94104

ATLAS LIFT TRUCK RENTALS & SALES, INC.
5050 N. River Rd.
Schiller Park, IL 60176
Tel.: 708-678-3450 **IL**
Fax: 708-678-1750
Year Founded: 1951
Approx.Sls.: $36,000,000
Emp.: 100
Import Export
Distribution of Material Handling Equipment & Fork Lift Trucks
S.I.C.: 5084
Howard Bernstein *(Chm. Bd.)*
Harold Birndorf *(Pres.)*
Jon Hagenson *(Dir.-Export)*

No. of Mfg. Plants/Facilities: 5
No. of U.S. Offices: 3

Computer Systems/Hardware:
IBM

Outside Service Firm(s):

Michael Silver & Company*(Auditors)*
Skokie, IL

NBD Bank, N.A.*(Major Banking Relationship)*
Woodfield, IL

ATLAS PEN & PENCIL CORPORATION
3040 N. 29th Ave.
Hollywood, FL 33022
Mailing Address:
P.O. Box 600,
Hollywood, FL 33022
Tel.: 305-920-4444
Fax: 305-920-8899
Year Founded: 1948
Emp.: 20
Direct Mail Advertising
S.I.C.: 7319; 2796; 7331
Heather Brooks *(Pres.)*
Eric Schneider *(V.P.)*
Robert Schneider *(V.P.)*
Howard Schwamenfeld *(Adv. Mgr.)*
Henrietta Schneider *(Treas.)*

Subsidiary:

Pen Sales Corporation **(1)**
3040 N. 29th Ave.
Hollywood, FL 33022
Tel.: 305-920-4444
Mfr. Pens
Howard Schwamenfeld *(Adv. Mgr.)*

ATLAS POWER EQUIPMENT COMPANY
201 E. Brink
Harvard, IL 60033
Tel.: 815-943-7411
Fax: 815-943-7888
Approx.Sls.: $12,500,000
Emp.: 275
Export
Power Mowers, Tillers, Snow Throwers
S.I.C.: 3524
Robert Simmons *(Pres.)*
Theodore R. Behle *(V.P.-Mktg.)*
Nevin Gage *(Sls. Mgr.)*

ATLAS REFINERY
142 Lockwood St.
Newark, NJ 07105
Tel.: 201-589-2002
Telex: 138425 ATLASOIL
Fax: 201-589-7377
Year Founded: 1887
Approx.Sls.: $12,000,000
Emp.: 37
Import Export
Mfg. of Specialty Chemicals: Lubricants; Emulsifiers; Wetting Agents & Surfactants Serving the Leather Tanning & Textile Industries
S.I.C.: 2843
Steven B. Schroeder *(Pres.)*
David L. Schroeder *(Exec. V.P.)*
Thomas V. Jardine *(V.P.-Legal & Treas.)*
James K. Koeniger *(V.P.-Sls. & Mktg.)*
Barbara A. Nagengast *(Controller)*

ATLAS SUPPLY COMPANY
2625 Cumberland Pkwy., Ste. 300
Atlanta, GA 30339
Tel.: 404-431-3880 **DE**
Fax: 404-481-3893
Year Founded: 1929
Emp.: 45
Fiscal Year-end: 12/31/91
Trademark Licensing of Automotive Tires Batteries, Accessories & Service Equipment, Contract Services & Testing of Automotive Products & Service Equipment
S.I.C.: 5013; 5014
H.D. Hanna *(Pres.)*
J.R. Small *(Sec. & Treas.)*
Dave Pierce *(Dir.-Adv.)*

Computer Systems/Hardware:
NCR

Outside Service Firm(s):

KPMG Peat Marwick*(Auditors)*
Newark, NJ

Crum & Forster*(Commercial Insurance Carrier)*
Morristown, NJ

Prudential Insurance Co. of America*(Group Insurer)*
751 Broad St.
Newark, NJ 07102-3777
Tel.: 201-802-6000

Wachovia Bank of Georgia, N.A.*(Major Banking Relationship)*
P.O. Box 4148,
Atlanta, GA 30302

Metropolitan Life Insurance Co.*(Pension Manager)*
One Madison Ave.
New York, NY 10010-3690
Tel.: 215-578-9292

ATLAS TOOL INC.
29880 Groesbeck Hwy.
Roseville, MI 48066
Tel.: 313-778-3570 **MI**
Fax: 313-778-3931
Year Founded: 1962
Approx.Sls.: $33,000,000
Emp.: 260
Mfr. Special Dies, Tools, Jigs & Fixtures
S.I.C.: 3544
Marcus Schmidt *(Pres. & Chief Exec. Officer)*
Elizabeth Schmidt *(V.P.)*

Outside Service Firm(s):

First America Bank*(Major Banking Relationship)*
Detroit, MI

ATLAS VAN LINES, INC.
1212 St. George Rd.
Evansville, IN 47711
Mailing Address:
P.O. Box 509,
Evansville, IN 47703-0509
Tel.: 812-424-2222
Tel.: 800-638-9797 **DE**
Fax: 812-421-7125
Year Founded: 1948
Assets: $117,000,000
Liabilities: $115,000,000

Net Worth: $2,000,000
Approx.Sls.: $267,000,000
Emp.: 418
Fiscal Year-end: 12/31/91
Domestic & International Transportation of Household Goods & Sensitive Shipments; Long Distance Moving & Storage
S.I.C.: 4213
Norman D. Gee *(Chm. Bd. & Chief Exec. Officer)*
Michael L. Shaffer *(Pres.-U.S. Van Lines Transportation Group)*
James A. Stamm *(Pres.-Specialized Transportation Group)*
Michael L. Harvey *(Sr. V.P.-Law, Gen. Counsel & Sec.)*
J.S. Mumma *(Sr.-V.P.-Mktg. & Pub. Rels.)*
Howard E. Parker *(Sr. V.P.-Fin. & Admin. & Chief Fin. Officer)*
J.R. Patterson *(Sr. V.P.-Customer Service)*
Tony Jenkins *(V.P. & Gen. Mgr., Atlas Van Lines Intl.)*
Richard Arneson *(V.P.-Mngmt. Information Services)*
Glen Dunkerson *(V.P.-Claims Admin.)*
Carol Garrett *(V.P.-Revenue Acctg.)*
Dennie Lynn *(V.P.-Household Goods Opers.)*
Stephen McBride *(V.P.-Admin. Services & Terminal Co.)*
Michael Scavuzzo *(V.P.-Agency Services & Devel.)*
R.J. Olson *(Treas.)*
Ben Sloan *(Asst. V.P. & Controller, Atlas Van Lines)*
Stephen Hollingsworth *(Asst. V.P.-Govt. Bussiness)*
Gene Wagner *(Asst. V.P.-Pricing)*
Patricia Walter *(Asst. V.P.-Human Resources)*
Kathy Godsey *(Dir. & Gen. Mgr.-Travel)*
William Cooper *(Dir.-Sls. & Mktg.)*
Ronald Herrenbruck *(Dir.-Pur. & Terminal Services)*
James E. Huth *(Dir.-Corp. Communications)*
Melynda Morrow *(Dir.-Sls.)*
Jo Mary Gray *(Mgr.-Communications)*
Bill Cooper *(Dir.-Mktg. Programs)*
Stephanie Gerbig *(Corp. Communications Coord.)*

Computer Systems/Hardware:
IBM 4381

Outside Service Firm(s):

Ernst & Young*(Auditors)*
One Indiana Square, Ste. 3400
Indianapolis, IN 46204
Tel.: 317-236-1100

Coates & Davenport*(Legal Firm)*
McLean, VA

Fifth Third Bank*(Major Banking Relationship)*
Corporate Trust Services, 38 Fountain Square Plaza
Cincinnati, OH 45263

Travelers Insurance Co.*(Pension Manager)*
1 Tower Square
Hartford, CT 06183
Tel.: 203-222-7821
Fax: 203-222-7813

Division:

Atlas Specialized Transportation **(1)**
1212 St. George Rd.
Evansville, IN 47711
Tel.: 812-424-2222
Fax: 800-638-9797 ext. 7130
Atlas Specialized Transportation
S.I.C.: 4213
James Stamm *(Pres.-Specialized Transportation Grp.)*
Robert Jeske *(Sr. V.P.-Specialized Transportation Grp.)*
Richard Gorbett *(V.P.-Mktg., Special Tran. Grp.)*
David Coulter *(Mgr.-Sls., Special Tran. Grp.)*
Frank Corbett *(Mgr.-Sls., Special Tran. Grp.)*

Subsidiaries:

ATL Terminal Corp. **(1)**
1212 St. George Rd.
Evansville, IN 47711
Tel.: 812-424-2222 (100%)
S.I.C.: 4213

Atlas Van Lines Intl. **(1)**
1212 St. George Rd.
Evansville, IN 47711
Tel.: 812-424-2222 (100%)
Fax: 812-423-5193
International Freight Forwarder
S.I.C.: 4213
Anthony Jenkins *(V.P. & Gen. Mgr.-Atlas Van Lines Intl.)*

Atlas Van Lines of Texas **(1)**
55 I.H. 35
Austin, TX 78769
Tel.: 512-480-8500
Fax: 512-834-0523
Trucking
S.I.C.: 4213
Larry Huff *(V.P. & Gen. Mgr.-Atlas Van Lines of Texas)*
Sharon White *(Dir.-Admin. Services)*

Atlas World-Class Travel **(1)**
1212 St. George Rd.
Evansville, IN 47711
Tel.: 812-421-7168
Tel.: 800-446-2077
Kathy Godsey *(Dir. & Gen. Mngr.-Travel)*

ATLAS WIRE CORPORATION
9525 W. River St.
Schiller Park, IL 60176
Tel.: 708-678-1210
Fax: 708-678-1281
Approx.Sls.: $15,000,000
Emp.: 25
Nonferrous Rolling & Drawing Wire
S.I.C.: 3356
John R. Herley *(Chm. Bd.)*
John W. Herley *(Pres.)*
Harvey Featherly *(V.P.)*
Virlyn Herley *(Treas.)*
Virlyn Leitner *(Sec.)*

Outside Service Firm(s):

Phillip Rich*(Auditors)*
Chicago, IL

The Northern Trust Co.*(Major Banking Relationship)*
50 S. LaSalle St.
Chicago, IL 60675
Tel.: 312-630-6000
Fax: 312-444-7028

ATLITE LIGHTING EQUIP, INC.
5747 47th St.
Maspeth, NY 11378
Tel.: 718-497-0394 NY
Fax: 718-821-9316
Year Founded: 1945
Approx.Sls.: $10,000,000
Emp.: 110
Mfr. of Commercial, Industrial & Institutional Electric Lighting Fixtures; Signs
S.I.C.: 3646; 3993
Jack Pearlman *(Pres.)*
Ted Pearlman *(V.P., Sec. & Treas.)*

Outside Service Firm(s):

Chemical Bank*(Major Banking Relationship)*
450 W. 33rd St., 15th Fl.
New York, NY 10001
Tel.: 212-613-7202
Tel.: 800-647-4273

ATOLS TOOL AND MOLD CORP.
3828 N. River Rd.
Schiller Park, IL 60176
Tel.: 708-671-4420
Fax: 708-671-4777
Year Founded: 1935
Approx.Sls.: $13,000,000
Emp.: 150
Fiscal Year-end: 4/30/91
Molds for Die Castings & Plastics
S.I.C.: 3544
John M. Atols *(Chm. Bd. & Chief Exec. Officer)*
Robert M. Atols *(Pres.)*
James L. Atols *(Exec. V.P.)*
Chuck Collar *(V.P.-Fin.)*

ATTORNEY'S TITLE INSURANCE FUND
5955 T. G. Lee Blvd., Ste. 500
Orlando, FL 32822
Mailing Address:
P.O. Box 628600
Orlando, FL 32862-8600
Tel.: 407-240-3863
Fax: 407-240-1106
Approx.Sls.: $74,000,000
Emp.: 800
Title Insurance & Title Information
S.I.C.: 6361
Daniel Adams *(Chm. Bd.)*
Charles J. Kovaleski *(Pres.)*

Outside Service Firm(s):

Pan American Bank*(Major Banking Relationship)*
Orlando, FL

Sun Bank, N.A.*(Major Banking Relationship)*
222 E. Robinson St., Ste. 350
Orlando, FL 32801

ATWOOD DISTRIBUTING, INC.
2717 N. Van Buren
Enid, OK 73703
Tel.: 405-233-3702 OK
Fax: 405-234-4332
Approx.Sls.: $20,000,000
Emp.: 150
Country General Stores; Hardware & Automotive Supplies
S.I.C.: 5399; 5072; 5013
Gary A. Atwood *(Pres.)*
Johnnie Atwood *(Sec.)*
Fern Atwood *(Asst. Sec. & Treas.)*

Outside Service Firm(s):

Bank of Woodward*(Major Banking Relationship)*
Woodward, OK

ATWOOD INDUSTRIES, INC.
1400 Eddy Ave.
Rockford, IL 61103
Tel.: 815-877-5771 IL
Fax: 815-877-4844
Year Founded: 1909
Approx.Sls.: $200,000,000
Emp.: 2,200
Fiscal Year-end: 12/31/91
Import Export
Transportation Equipment
S.I.C.: 3714; 3429; 3999
John R. Anderson *(Chm. Bd.)*
James H. Rilott *(Pres.)*
D. Kraig Pierceson *(Pres.-Automotive Div.)*
Robert A. Pickering *(Pres.-Mobile Products Div.)*
Richard J. Augustine *(V.P.-Fin. & Chief Fin. Officer)*
Rick Holm *(V.P.-Human Resources)*
R. Steven Holdeman *(Sec.)*
Steven L. Boyle *(Controller)*
M.O. O'Brien *(Dir.-Pur.)*
David Sterna *(Dir.-Data Processing)*
Roberta Runberg *(Dir.-Meetings Plng.)*

No. of Mfg. Plants/Facilities: 11
No. of U.S. Offices: 1

Computer Systems/Hardware:
IBM 4341

Outside Service Firm(s):

Coopers & Lybrand*(Auditors)*
6000 E. State St.
Rockford, IL 61108
Tel.: 815-394-0300

Williams & McCarthy*(Legal Firm)*
321 West State St.
Rockford, IL 61101

Harris Trust & Savings Bank*(Major Banking Relationship)*
111 W. Monroe St.
Chicago, IL 60690
Tel.: 312-461-2265
Tel.: 800-858-0840

First Wisconsin National Bank*(Pension Manager)*
Madison, WI

Harris Trust & Savings Bank*(Pension Manager)*
111 W. Monroe St.
Chicago, IL 60690
Tel.: 312-461-2265
Tel.: 800-858-0840

Divisions:

Atwood Automotive Inc. **(1)**
5701 W. Dickman Rd.
Battle Creek, MI 49015
Tel.: 616-962-5473
Fax: 616-962-8179
D. Kraig Pierceson *(Pres.)*

Mark I Molded Plastics, Inc. **(1)**
P.O. Box 35, U.S. 12 East
Jonesville, MI 49250
Tel.: 517-849-9911
Fax: 517-849-9740
Emp.: 390
Plastic Injection Molding
S.I.C.: 3089

W.E. AUBUCHON CO., INC.
95 Aubuchon Dr.
Westminster, MA 01473
Tel.: 508-874-0521
Year Founded: 1908
Approx.Sls.: $75,000,000
Emp.: 950
Hardware, Plumbing, Housewares, Paint, Garden, Hand & Power Tools and Equipment
S.I.C.: 5251; 5261; 5719
William E. Aubuchon, Jr. *(Pres.)*
M. Marcus Moran, Sr. *(V.P.-Devel. & Real Estate)*
Peter J. Aubuchon, Sr. *(V.P.-Pur.)*
Bernard W. Aubuchon, Sr. *(V.P.-Adv.)*
M. Marcus Moran, Jr. *(Treas. & Dir.-Personnel)*
William E. Aubuchon III *(Mgr.-Mktg.)*

AUBURN FAITH COMMUNITY HOSPITAL
(A Sutter Health Systems Hospital)
11815 Education St.
Auburn, CA 95604
Tel.: 916-885-7201
Fax: 916-888-4561
Year Founded: 1966
Sales Range: $40-59 Million
Emp.: 650
Acute Care Hospital
S.I.C.: 8062
William Kirby *(Chm. Bd.)*
Joel Grey *(Administrator)*
James Deiser *(Controller)*
Gerald Baseman *(Dir.-Personnel)*
James Eichman *(Dir.-Pur.)*

Outside Service Firm(s):

St. Paul Insurance Companies*(Commercial Insurance Carrier)*
Sacramento, CA

The Bank of California, N.A.*(Major Banking Relationship)*
400 California
San Francisco, CA 94104
Tel.: 415-765-0400

GEORGE W. AUCH CO.
735 S. Paddock
Pontiac, MI 48341
Mailing Address:
P.O. Box 430719,
Pontiac, MI 48343
Tel.: 313-334-2000 **MI**
Fax: 313-334-3404
Year Founded: 1908
Assets: $13,462,012
Liabilities: $9,057,374
Net Worth: $4,404,638
Approx.Sls.: $45,763,037
Emp.: 97
Fiscal Year-end: 3/31/92
General Contractors; Commercial & Institutional Construction; Construction Management
S.I.C.: 8741; 1542
Frederick J. Auch, Jr. *(Chm. Bd. & Chief Exec. Officer)*
John K. Hagen, Jr. *(Pres.)*
G. William Auch, III *(Chief Oper. Officer & V.P.)*
Belton R. Williams *(Chief Fin. Officer, Treas. & Sec.)*
Alan L. Whiting *(V.P.)*
L. Whithing *(V.P.)*
Janet L. Glascock *(Controller)*
Principal(s):
Frederick J. Auch, Jr.
G. William Auch, III

No. of Mfg. Plants/Facilities: 1
No. of U.S. Offices: 1

Computer Systems/Hardware:
IBM System 36

Outside Service Firm(s):

McEndarffer, Hoke & Bernard, P.C.*(Auditors)*
Bloomfield Hills, MI

Aetna Life & Casualty*(Commercial Insurance Carrier)*
151 Farmington Avenue
Hartford, CT 06156
Tel.: 203-273-2128
Fax: 203-729-4295

UNUM Life Insurance Company*(Group Insurer)*
P.O. Box 9500,
Portland, ME 04104
Tel.: 800-521-9750

Miller, Canfield, Paddock & Stone*(Legal Firm)*
Bloomfield Hills, MI

Comerica Bank*(Major Banking Relationship)*
211 W. Fort St.
Detroit, MI 48226
Tel.: 313-222-3300

Arnold & Company*(Pension Manager)*
Troy, MI

Subsidiary:

GenCon Services, Inc. **(1)**
735 South Paddock St.
Pontiac, MI 48341
Tel.: 313-334-6565
Emp.: 15
General Contractors and Construction Managers
S.I.C.: 8741; 8611
J. Gary Whiteman *(Pres.)*
Belton R. Williams *(Sec. & Treas.)*

THE AUCHTER COMPANY
1021 Oak St.
Jacksonville, FL 32204
Tel.: 904-355-3536
Fax: 904-353-0234
Year Founded: 1929
Approx.Sls.: $50,000,000
Emp.: 100
General Contractors Commercial & Industrial Buildings
S.I.C.: 1541; 1542
Wilbur H. Glass, Jr. *(Pres.)*
Thomas Starnes *(Chief Exec. Officer)*
B. Glynn Stevens *(Comptroller)*

No. of U.S. Offices: 1

Outside Service Firm(s):

Meek & McLeod*(Auditors)*
Jacksonville, FL

First Union National Bank*(Major Banking Relationship)*
P.O. Box 2565,
Jacksonville, FL 32203

AUDIO SPECIALIST, INC.
(Formerly Sound Playground)
2230 Berlin Turnpike
Newington, CT 06111
Tel.: 203-667-4401
Cable: 22
Fax: 203-667-2597
Approx.Sls.: $60,000,000
Emp.: 200
Fiscal Year-end: 12/31/90
Retailer Audio & Video Equipment
S.I.C.: 5731
Robert Fagan *(Chm. Bd. & Pres.)*
Robert Johnson *(Exec. V.P.)*
Larry Annello *(V.P.-Fin.)*

Computer Systems/Hardware:
Qantel 45

Outside Service Firm(s):

Coopers & Lybrand*(Auditors)*
280 Trumbull St.
Hartford, CT 06103

Cummings & Lockwood*(Legal Firm)*
P.O. Box 120, City Place I - 36th Fl.
Hartford, CT 06103
Tel.: 203-275-6700

AUGSBURG FORTRESS, PUBLISHERS
426 S. 5th St.
Minneapolis, MN 55415
Mailing Address:
Box 1209
Minneapolis, MN 55440
Tel.: 612-330-3300
Tel.: 800-328-4648
Fax: 612-330-3455
Year Founded: 1891
Approx.Sls.: $65,000,000
Emp.: 660
Fiscal Year-end: 12/31/90
Import Export
Publisher of Religious Books: Augsburg (Book Line), Fortress Press (Book Line), Augsburg Vacation Bible School; Periodicals: The Lutheran, Lutheran Woman Today, Lutheran Partners, Parish Teacher
S.I.C.: 2741; 2389; 8299
Gaery N.J. Aamodt *(Pres. & Chief Exec. Officer)*
Leonard Flackman *(Asst. to the Pres.)*
Marvin Roloff *(V.P.-Mktg.)*
Alice Peppler *(Dir.-Mktg. Services)*
Robert Hanson *(Pur. Dir.)*

AUNT NELLIE'S FARM KITCHENS, INC.
640 Caughlin Rd.
Clyman, WI 53016
Mailing Address:
P.O. Box 250,
Clyman, WI 53016
Tel.: 414-696-3331
Fax: 414-696-3566
Approx.Sls.: $67,000,000
Emp.: 2,000
Mfr. Aunt Nellie's Glass Pack Vegetables & Specialties, Aunt Nellie's Tin Packed Drinks, Spaghetti Sauce, Sandwich Sauce, Copacked Sauce, Juices, Ripe Olives, Maraschino Cherries & Glace Fruit
S.I.C.: 2033
David C. Lau *(Pres.)*
Tom Andringa *(V.P.-Opers.)*
Nancy Poellman *(V.P.-Res. & Devel., Quality Control Dir.)*
Richard Ward *(V.P.-Sls.)*
Steve Zickert *(V.P.-Mktg.)*
Dave Yeager *(Controller)*
Sharon Henrioet *(Pur. Agent)*

Outside Service Firm(s):

First Bank Minneapolis*(Major Banking Relationship)*
Minneapolis, MN

AURORA CASKET COMPANY
U.S. 50 West
Aurora, IN 47001
Mailing Address:
P.O. Box 29
Aurora, IN 47001
Tel.: 812-926-1111
Fax: 812-926-4837
Year Founded: 1890
Approx.Sls.: $68,000,000
Emp.: 650
Export
Mfr. Metal Burial Caskets
S.I.C.: 3995
William D. Backman, Jr. *(Pres. & Chief Exec. Officer)*
Patrick Brady *(Exec. V.P.)*
William D. Backman III *(V.P.-Special Mkts.)*
William E. Barrott III *(V.P.-Mktg.)*
William G. Robinson *(V.P.-Pre-Need Devel.)*
E.L. Yoe *(V.P.-Fin.)*
John C. Barrott *(Sec. & Asst. Treas.)*
Gary Schmidt *(Pur. Agent)*

Outside Service Firm(s):

Arthur Andersen & Co.*(Auditors)*
425 Walnut St.
Cincinnati, OH 45202
Tel.: 513-381-6900

Frost & Jacobs*(Legal Firm)*
2500 Central Trust Ctr.
Cincinnati, OH 45202
Tel.: 513-651-6800

Star Bank*(Major Banking Relationship)*
425 Walnut Street
Cincinnati, OH 45202
Tel.: 513-632-4000

AURORA PACKING CO., INC.
125 Grant St.
North Aurora, IL 60542
Mailing Address:
P.O. Box 209
North Aurora, IL 60542
Tel.: 708-897-0551
Fax: 708-897-0647
Emp.: 275
Fiscal Year-end: 10/26/91
Meat Packing
S.I.C.: 2011
Harold Fagel *(Pres. & Chief Exec. Officer)*
Marvin Fagel *(V.P.-Investor Rels. & Sec.)*
Nicholas Venneman *(Comptroller)*

No. of Mfg. Plants/Facilities: 1

Computer Systems/Hardware:
MAI Basic 4

Outside Service Firm(s):

Ostrow, Reisin, Berk, & Abrams, Ltd.*(Auditors)*
Chicago, IL

First National Bank of Chicago*(Major Banking Relationship)*
One First National Plaza
Chicago, IL 60670
Tel.: 312-732-9781
Tel.: 312-732-4050
Fax: 312-732-4840
Fax: 312-732-3055

The Merchants National Bank of Aurora*(Major Banking Relationship)*
Aurora, IL

AUSHERMAN CONSTRUCTION COMPANY
8031 Reichs Ford Rd.
Frederick, MD 21701
Tel.: 301-663-6104 **MD**
Fax: 301-663-3929
Approx.Sls.: $22,000,000
Emp.: 90
New Contruction Of Single Family Homes & Townhouses
S.I.C.: 1521; 1542
Ernest W. Ausherman *(Chm. Bd.)*
Marvin E. Ausherman *(Pres.)*
Robert A. Garvey *(Chief Fin. Officer)*
Kenneth W. Abrecht *(V.P.-Tech. Services)*
Joseph F. Devibiss *(V.P.-Construction Services)*
James B. MacGillivray *(V.P.-Land Development)*
Raymond E. Venema *(V.P.-Plng. & Admin.)*
Mark Butterfield *(Sec. & Treas.)*

Outside Service Firm(s):

Fredericktown Bank & Trust Co.*(Major Banking Relationship)*
Frederick, MD

Miles & Stockbridge*(Legal Firm)*
10 Light St.
Baltimore, MD 21202
Tel.: 410-727-6464

THE AUSTAD COMPANY
4500 E. 10th St.
Sioux Falls, SD 57101
Tel.: 605-336-3135
Fax: 605-339-0362
Year Founded: 1963
Approx.Sls.: $60,000,000
Emp.: 430
Fiscal Year-end: 12/31/89
Import Export
Direct Marketers of Recreational & Leisure Equipment
S.I.C.: 5091
Oscar Austad *(Chm. Bd.)*
Dave Austad *(Pres. & Chief Exec. Officer)*
Randall Austad *(Exec. V.P.)*
Wayne Steinhauer *(V.P.-Mktg. Devel.)*
Sharon Stahl *(Treas.)*
Vance Goldammer *(Gen. Counsel)*
Mike Wagner *(Mgr.-Oper.)*
Kathy Bacon *(Dir.-Personnel)*
Brian Carmichael *(Dir.-Retail)*
Principal(s):
Oscar Austad
Dave Austad

No. of Mfg. Plants/Facilities: 1
No. of U.S. Offices: 5

Computer Systems/Hardware:
Stratus

Outside Service Firm(s):

Stuart, Noonan & Co.*(Auditors)*
Sioux Falls, SD

First Bank of South Dakota*(Major Banking Relationship)*
Sioux Falls, SD

AUSTIN ASSOCIATES, INC.
2055 Gateway Place, Ste. 600
San Jose, CA 95110
Tel.: 408-453-7776
Year Founded: 1982
Approx.Billings: $16,200,000
Emp.: 20
Business-to-Business Adv.
Mike Austin *(Chm. Bd. & Pres.)*
Georgette LaChance *(Controller)*

AUSTIN CO., INC.
Hall & Cutler Sts.
Greeneville, TN 37743
Mailing Address:
P.O. Box 1360,
Greenville, TN 37744-1360
Tel.: 615-638-4124 **TN**
Telex: 55-3433
Fax: 615-638-1601
Year Founded: 1919
Approx.Sls.: $200,000,000
Emp.: 1,000
Fiscal Year-end: 6/30/91
Export
Tobacco Processors
S.I.C.: 2131
Sam J. Calvert Jr. *(Chm. Bd.)*
Clyde B. Austin, III *(Vice Chm.)*
Larry R. Corbett *(Pres.)*
James H. Felts *(Exec. V.P.-Opers.)*
R. B. Barnes, Jr. *(Sec. & Treas.)*
Howard Bailey *(Dir.-Data Processing)*
Eugene Murray *(Dir.-Personnel)*
Terry Koonce *(Dir.-Pur.)*

No. of Mfg. Plants/Facilities: 3
No. of U.S. Offices: 4
No. of Foreign Offices: 6

Computer Systems/Hardware:
IBM System 36

Outside Service Firm(s):

Deloitte & Touche*(Auditors)*
424 Church St., Ste. 2400
Nashville, TN 37219-2396

Sovran Bank*(Major Banking Relationship)*
One Commerce Place M-B
Nashville, TN 37219
Tel.: 615-749-4113

Arkwright Mutual Insurance*(Commercial Insurance Carrier)*
Atlanta, GA

Milligan, Coleman, Fletcher & Gaby*(Legal Firm)*
Nashville, TN

Subsidiaries:

Austin Carolina Co. **(1)**
Hall & Cutler Sts.
Greeneville, TN 37743
Tel.: 615-638-4124 (100%)
S.I.C.: 2131

Cigar Supply Co. **(1)**
Hall & Cutler Sts.
Greeneville, TN 37743
Tel.: 615-638-4124 (100%)
S.I.C.: 2131

Mullins Leaf Tobacco Co. **(1)**
Hall & Cutler Sts.
Greeneville, TN 37743
Tel.: 615-638-4124 (100%)
S.I.C.: 2131

AUSTIN INDUSTRIES, INC.
3535 Travis Ste. 300
Dallas, TX 75204
Mailing Address:
P.O. Box 1590
Dallas, TX 75221
Tel.: 214-443-5500 **DE**
Fax: 214-951-9514
Year Founded: 1918
Approx.Sls.: $456,000,000
Emp.: 6,000
Fiscal Year-end: 12/31/88
Construction & Related Products
S.I.C.: 1542; 1622
William T. Solomon *(Chm. Bd., Pres. & Chief Exec. Officer)*
J. P. Olsson *(Sr. V.P.-Fin. & Chief Fin. Officer)*
Ray Washburne *(V.P.-Real Estate)*
George Dawkins *(Treas. & Sec.)*
Elaine Nelson *(Gen. Counsel)*
James Schranz *(Controller)*
Tony J. Jackson *(Asst. Treas.)*
Tom Dilly *(Dir.-Data Processing)*
David Vance *(Dir.-Corp. Mktg. & Communications)*
Rob Brewer *(Mgr.-Human Resources)*

No. of U.S. Offices: 8

Computer Systems/Hardware:
IBM

Outside Service Firm(s):

Ernst & Young*(Auditors)*
2121 San Jacinto, Ste. 500
Dallas, TX 75201
Tel.: 214-969-8000

Jackson, Walker, Winstead, Cantwell & Miller*(Legal Firm)*
1401 Elm St.
Dallas, TX 15202
Tel.: 214-655-2911

First City National Bank*(Major Banking Relationship)*
Houston, TX

First Republic Bank Ft. Worth*(Major Banking Relationship)*
Ft. Worth, TX

NationsBank Texas*(Major Banking Relationship)*
901 Main St., 16th Fl.
Dallas, TX 75202
Tel.: 214-922-5000

Texas Commerce Bank*(Major Banking Relationship)*
Beaumont, TX

NationsBank Texas*(Pension Manager)*
Dallas, TX

Southland Trust*(Pension Manager)*
Dallas, TX

Subsidiaries:

Austin Bridge & Rd. Co.-Asphalt Div. **(1)**
P.O. Box 185130, 2301 Austin Rd.
Fort Worth, TX 76181
Tel.: 817-589-1929 (100%)
Robert Millwee *(Pres.)*

Austin Bridge & Rd.-Concrete Div. **(1)**
2949 Spemmons Freeway
Dallas, TX 75247
Tel.: 214-630-6110 (100%)

Austin Bridge & Rd.-Highway Div. **(1)**
3535 Travis St.
Dallas, TX 75204
Tel.: 214-443-5500 (100%)
Fax: 214-630-5441

JAMES AUSTIN CO.
P.O. Box 827
Mars, PA 16046
Tel.: 412-625-1535 **PA**
Fax: 412-625-3288
Year Founded: 1889
Approx.Sls.: $21,400,000
Emp.: 171
Fiscal Year-end: 5/31/92
Mfr. of Household Cleaning Products
S.I.C.: 2841; 2842
Harry G. Austin, Jr. *(Chm. Bd.)*
John T. Austin, Sr. *(Pres.)*
Robert Downie *(V.P. & Chief Fin. Officer)*
Lisa Henderson *(V.P. & Sec.)*
John T. Austin, Jr. *(V.P.-Mktg.)*
Harry G. Austin, III *(V.P.-Sls.)*
Karen Collins *(Mgr.-Personnel)*
Beverly Ray *(Mgr.-Data Processing)*
Frank A. Bjalobok, Jr. *(Pur. Agent)*

No. of Mfg. Plants/Facilities: 3
No. of U.S. Offices: 3

Computer Systems/Hardware:
IBM

Outside Service Firm(s):

Marshall & Kroll*(Auditors)*
Pittsburgh, PA

Henderson Brothers*(Commercial Insurance Carrier)*
Pittsburgh, PA

Yauger & Austin*(Legal Firm)*
Mars, PA

Mars Bank*(Major Banking Relationship)*
Pittsburgh, PA

Austin Kelley Advertising, Inc.

AUSTIN KELLEY ADVERTISING, INC.
The Palisades, 5901 Peachtree Dunwoody Rd., NE
Atlanta, GA 30328
Tel.: 404-396-6666
Fax: 404-396-0301
Year Founded: 1975
Approx.Billings: $50,000,000
Emp.: 75
Corporate Giving Program: United Way, ORFUN
Austin P. Kelley *(Chm. & Chief Exec. Officer)*
Geoffrey R. Nixon *(Pres. & Chief Oper. Officer)*
H. Jay Shields *(Sr. V.P., Bus. Devel.)*
Rob Arnold *(V.P.)*
Margaret Gearing *(V.P.)*
Dean Lukehart *(V.P.)*
Linda Pechman *(V.P.)*
Keri Palmer *(V.P., Fin.)*
Maria Beasley *(Admin. Dir.)*
Anita Thomas *(Telecommunications)*

J. AUSTIN OIL CO.
2300 Austin Pky.
Flint, MI 48507
Tel.: 313-232-9141
Fax: 313-232-0021
Year Founded: 1931
Assets: $12,098,000
Liabilities: $6,934,000
Net Worth: $5,164,000
Approx.Sls.: $56,650,000
Emp.: 125
Fiscal Year-end: 12/31/88
Own & Lease Gasoline Stations
S.I.C.: 5013; 5014; 5172; 5531; 5541
J. E. Truesdell, Jr. *(Pres. & Sec.)*
J. E. Truesdell III *(Treas.)*
Robert Beavais *(Chief Fin. Officer)*
Stanley Langdon *(Dir.-Pur.)*
Principal(s):
J. E. Truesdell, Jr.
J. E. Truesdell III

No. of Mfg. Plants/Facilities: 1

Computer Systems/Hardware:
Honeywell DPS 4

Outside Service Firm(s):

Du Puis & Ryden, P.C.*(Auditors)*
Flint, MI

Citizens Bank & Trust*(Investment Banker)*
Flint, MI

Bruce Newman*(Legal Firm)*
Flint, MI

Citizens Bank & Trust*(Major Banking Relationship)*
Flint, MI

AUSTIN POWDER CO.
25800 Science Park Dr.
Cleveland, OH 44122
Tel.: 216-464-2400
Fax: 216-464-4418
Year Founded: 1833
Sales Range: $100-499 Million
Emp.: 750
Fiscal Year-end: 1/31/91
Manufacture & Distributor Industrial Explosives
S.I.C.: 2892; 5082; 5099
W. Jack Davis *(Chm. Bd.)*
David M. Gleason *(Pres.)*
Jeff R. Steinhilber *(Treas., Fin. Mgr. & Chief Fin. Officer)*
Michael Leppla *(Mgr.-Computer Information Systems)*
Principal(s):
W. Jack Davis

No. of Mfg. Plants/Facilities: 21

Computer Systems/Hardware:
IBM System 38

Outside Service Firm(s):

Arthur Andersen & Co.*(Auditors)*
River Tower, 333 W. San Carlos St., Ste. 1500
San Jose, CA 95113
Tel.: 408-998-2112

Insurance Company of North America*(Commercial Insurance Carrier)*
Indianapolis, IN

Northwestern National Life*(Group Insurer)*
20 Washington Ave. S.
Minneapolis, MN 55401

Jones, Day, Reavis & Pogue*(Legal Firm)*
901 Lakeside Ave.
Cleveland, OH 44114
Tel.: 216-586-3939
Fax: 216-579-0212

Society National Bank*(Major Banking Relationship)*
800 Superior Ave.
Cleveland, OH 44114
Tel.: 216-689-3696

Towers, Perrin, Forster & Crosby*(Pension Manager)*
1100 Superior Ave.
Cleveland, OH 44114
Tel.: 216-696-8400
Fax: 216-696-5023

Subsidiary:

Southwestern Explosives **(1)**
P.O. Box 1558
Gonzales, TX 78629
Tel.: 210-672-9545
Mfr. Explosives
S.I.C.: 2892
Rex McNew *(Gen. Mgr.)*

AUSTIN SCULPTURE
815 Grundy Ave.
Holbrook, NY 11741
Tel.: 516-981-7300
Tel.: 800-645-7303
Fax: 516-467-8823
Year Founded: 1952
Approx.Sls.: $20,000,000
Emp.: 700
Fiscal Year-end: 8/31/91
Export
Sculpture; Cast Paper Art; Pedestals; Outdoor Sculpture; Bronze Sculpture
S.I.C.: 3299
Peter Strugatz *(Chief Exec. Officer)*
Pamela Pierce *(Pres.)*
Andrew Cymrot *(V.P.-Sls.)*
Larry Dobroff *(Chief Fin. Officer)*
Leonard Lauffer *(Dir.-Mfg.)*
Phil Okonom *(Dir.-MIS)*
Robert Weiss *(Dir.-Personnel & Pur.)*
Selena Batsilas *(Mgr.-Pub. Rels. & Mktg.)*
Jeriann Bradley *(Mgr.-Adv.)*

Divisions:

Austin-New York **(1)**
225 Fifth Ave.
New York, NY 10010
Tel.: 212-725-8379
Fax: 212-689-4631

Austin Sculpture—(Continued)

Austin Productions (1)
Hamilton Wing, Space #445
High Point, NC 27261
Tel.: 919-887-8118
Lee Harrison *(Showroom Mgr.)*

Austin Productions (1)
224 World Trade Ctr.
Dallas, TX 75207
Tel.: 214-748-8782
Leanne Reiter *(Chief Oper. Officer)*

Danzig/Rosenberg (1)
L. A. Mart, 1933 So. Broadway
Los Angeles, CA 90007
Tel.: 213-748-8324
Scott Rosenberg *(Chief Oper. Officer)*

Dick Carlson Associates (1)
Upper Midwest Trade Ctr., Space 229
Minnetonka, MN 55343
Tel.: 602-894-1755
Dick Carlson *(Chief Oper. Officer)*

Giftreps Northwest (1)
6100 4th Ave. S.
Seattle, WA 98108
Tel.: 206-767-5949
Fax: 206-764-4784
Rob Brown *(Chief Oper. Officer)*

Peter Straaton (1)
Merchandise Mart
Chicago, IL 60654
Tel.: 312-649-1539
Fax: 312-649-9006
Mike Straaton *(Chief Oper. Officer)*

Rocky Mountain Concepts (1)
451 E. 58th Ave., Ste. 1025
Denver, CO 80216
Tel.: 303-298-0649
Fax: 303-972-9069
Dennis Greer *(Chief Oper. Officer)*

AUSTRIAN AIRLINES
17-20 White Stone Expy.
White Stone, NY 11357
Tel.: 718-670-8600
Year Founded: 1957
Approx.Sls.: $15,000,000
Emp.: 90
Fiscal Year-end: 12/31/90
Serving Major Air Routes of Europe, North Africa, Middle East
S.I.C.: 4512
Jorgen Jensen *(Gen. Mgr.-North America)*
Hans Schneider *(Mgr.-North America & Mgr.-Mktg.)*

AUTO CRANE COMPANY
4707 N. Mingo Rd.
Tulsa, OK 74117
Mailing Address:
P.O. Box 581510
Tulsa, OK 74158
Tel.: 918-438-2760
Telex: 158108
Fax: 918-438-6688
Approx.Sls.: $15,000,000
Emp.: 100
Fiscal Year-end: 9/30/90
Export
Truck Mounted Electric Cranes & Hydraulic Cranes Model: 8005H, 6006H, 5005H, 5004, 3203, 2703 2003, Econo-Ton II, Econo-Miser; Service Crane Bodies: 50K, 36K; Air Compressors; Articulating Crane Model: A50, A72, A95 & A125
S.I.C.: 3531
William Ramsey *(Chm. Bd.)*
Joe E. Henry *(Pres.)*
Doyle Powell *(Gen. Mgr.)*
Steve Sibole *(Natl. Sls. Mgr.)*
Patrick Duffy *(Mktg. Mgr.)*
Sharon Blessing *(Adv. Coord.)*
Larry Lyster *(Controller)*

AUTO DRIVEAWAY CO.
310 S. Michigan Ave.
Chicago, IL 60604
Tel.: 312-341-1900
Year Founded: 1952
Approx.Sls.: $12,000,000
Emp.: 100
Fiscal Year-end: 9/30/90
Export
Vehicle Transporters, Chauffeur Service of Automobiles, Trucks & RV's
S.I.C.: 7389
John F. Sohl *(Chm. Bd.)*
Brandon A. Sohl *(Pres.)*
Ronald I. Fredriksen *(V.P.)*
Perry L. Barcroft *(V.P.)*

Computer Systems/Hardware:
IBM 400

Division:

Driveaway Service (1)
310 S. Michigan Ave.
Chicago, IL 60604
Tel.: 312-341-1900

AUTO GLASS SPECIALISTS
2814 Syene Rd.
Madison, WI 53713
Mailing Address:
P.O. Box 9500,
Madison, WI 53715
Tel.: 608-271-5484
Tel.: 800-558-1000 WI
Fax: 608-271-4847
Year Founded: 1961
Assets: $11,900,000
Liabilities: $8,100,000
Net Worth: $3,800,000
Approx.Sls.: $26,000,000
Emp.: 400
Fiscal Year-end: 12/31/91
Import Export
Sales & Installation of Auto & Truck Glass, Sunroofs & Pickup Truck Sliding Back Windows
S.I.C.: 7536; 7539; 5531
Corporate Giving Program:
Percentage of Earnings
Robert R. Birkhauser *(Chm.)*
Robert R. Birkhauser III *(Pres.)*
Thomas J. Greenhalgh *(Exec. V.P.-Admin.)*
Lonn R. Schwartz *(Exec. V.P.-Fin.)*
Jerald C. Remy *(V.P.-Pur.)*
Peter Winne *(V.P.-AEGIS Div.)*
David Gaspar *(Dir.-Human Resources)*
Steve Pierick *(Dir.-Sls. & Opers.)*
Gerald L. Sphatt *(Dir.-Mngmt. Information Systems)*
Kristopher D. Hampton *(Sr. Mgr.-Pur.)*
Perry Nealis *(Mgr.-Natl. Mktg.)*
Guy N. Webster *(Mgr.-Corp. Communication)*
Principal(s):
Robert R. Birkhauser

No. of Mfg. Plants/Facilities: 46
No. of U.S. Offices: 46

Computer Systems/Hardware:
Honeywell DPS 7000

Outside Service Firm(s):

Grant Thornton*(Auditors)*
Madison, WI

First Wisconsin National Bank*(Investment Banker)*
Madison, WI

First Wisconsin National Bank*(International Bank Affiliate)*
Madison, WI

Lathrop & Clark*(Legal Firm)*
Madison, WI

First Wisconsin National Bank*(Major Banking Relationship)*
Madison, WI

AUTO-OWNERS INSURANCE
6101 Anacapri Blvd.
Lansing, MI 48917
Mailing Address:
P.O. Box 30660
Lansing, MI 48909
Tel.: 517-323-1200 MI
Fax: 517-323-8796
Year Founded: 1916
Assets: $3,116,981,794
Liabilities: $2,136,927,984
Net Worth: $980,053,810
Approx.Sls.: $1,257,270,154
Emp.: 1,775
Fiscal Year-end: 12/31/91
Insurance Company
S.I.C.: 6331
Richard E. Otto *(Chm. Bd. & Chief Exec. Officer)*
H.J. Arends *(Pres.)*
B.E. Smith *(Exec. V.P.)*
S.R. Birn *(Sr. V.P. & Assoc. Gen. Counsel)*
T.J. Buda *(Sr. V.P., Sec. & Gen. Counsel)*
J.W. Fisher *(Sr. V.P.-Underwriting)*
R.L. Looyenga *(Sr. V.P.-Mktg.)*
D.P. Marsh *(Sr. V.P.-Life Mktg.)*
J.D. Peterson *(Sr. V.P. & Personnel Dir.)*
E.A. Ploor *(Sr. V.P.-Data Services)*
H.E. Powell *(Sr. V.P.-Claims)*
G.L. Cornell *(V.P.-Acctng. & Real Estate & Treas.)*
Neva Jean Fizzell *(Adv. Admin.)*
W.C. Pamerleau *(Mgr.-Communications)*
G.W. Wakulsky *(Mgr.-Forms Mngmt.)*

Outside Service Firm(s):

Coopers & Lybrand*(Auditors)*
400 Renaissance Center
Detroit, MI 48243
Tel.: 313-446-7100
Fax: 313-446-7117

Michigan National Bank*(Major Banking Relationship)*
Lansing, MI

Subsidiaries:

Auto-Owners Life Insurance Co. (1)
6101 Anacapri Blvd.
Lansing, MI 48917
Tel.: 517-323-1200
Insurance
S.I.C.: 6311

Home-Owners Insurance Co. (1)
6101 Anacapri Blvd.
Lansing, MI 48917
Tel.: 517-323-1200
S.I.C.: 6361
R.E. Otto *(Chm. Bd.)*
H.J. Arends *(Pres.)*

Owners Insurance Co. (1)
2325 N. Cole St.
Lima, OH 45801
Tel.: 517-323-1200
Insurance
S.I.C.: 6361
H. Max Tanner *(Chm. Bd.)*
Richard E. Otto *(Pres.)*

Property-Owners Insurance Co. (1)
3950 W. Delphi Pike
Marion, IN 46952
Tel.: 517-323-1200
Insurance
S.I.C.: 6361
R.E. Otto *(Chm. Bd.)*
H.J. Arends *(Pres.)*

Auto Safety House
(See A S H, Inc. Listing)

AUTOMANAGE
5449 Dixie Highway
Fairfield, OH 45014
Tel.: 513-421-0737
Fax: 513-870-0520
Approx.Sls.: $325,000,000
Emp.: 1,054
Auto Dealership
S.I.C.: 5511
Michael L. Dever *(Pres.)*

Outside Service Firm(s):

The Huntington National Bank*(Major Banking Relationship)*
17 S. High St.
Columbus, OH 43215
Tel.: 614-476-8303

AUTOMATED MARKETING SYSTEMS, INC.
225 W. Wacker Dr., Ste. 2275
Chicago, IL 60606
Tel.: 312-346-9097 DE
Fax: 312-346-9097
Emp.: 20
Provides a Full Range of Communication Products & Services to Businesses & Organizations
S.I.C.: 8741; 2741
John C. Bachman *(Chm. Bd., Pres., Chief Exec. & Oper. Officer)*
Edward G. Panschar *(V.P., Treas. & Chief Fin. Officer)*

Computer Systems/Hardware:
IBM PC

Outside Service Firm(s):

Canada Life Assurance*(Group Insurer)*
San Francisco, CA

Walsh, Case, Coale, Brown & Burke*(Legal Firm)*
Chicago, IL

Divisions:

Automated Marketing Systems, Inc. (1)
Travellers Tower II, 26533 Evergreen
Southfield, MI 48076
Tel.: 313-352-5900
Specialized Marketing Services
S.I.C.: 8741

National Research Bureau (1)
424 No. Third St.
Burlington, IA 52601
Tel.: 319-752-5415
Business Directories, Advertising Services; Special Audience Services
S.I.C.: 2741

AUTOMATIC LIQUID PACKAGING, INC.
2200 W. Lake Shore Dr.
Woodstock, IL 60098
Tel.: 815-338-9500
Fax: 815-338-5504
Approx.Sls.: $28,000,000
Emp.: 255
Export
Contract Mfr. of Pharmaceutical Products; Private Label Manufacturing; Packaging Machinery Sales; Manufacturing & Sales of Respiratory Care Products; Packaging & Labeling Services
S.I.C.: 7389; 5084; 2752; 5122; 5047; 3845
Gerhard Weiler *(Pres. & Chief Exec. Officer)*
Frank N. Leo *(V.P.-New Prods.)*
Siegfried Weller *(V.P.)*
John Feltes *(Sec. & Treas.)*

Outside Service Firm(s):

American National Bank*(Major Banking Relationship)*
33 North LaSalle St.
Chicago, IL 60690
Tel.: 312-661-6967

AUTOMATIC MACHINE PRODUCTS COMPANY
17 Wall St.
Attleboro, MA 02703
Tel.: 508-222-2300
Fax: 508-222-2307
Approx.Sls.: $11,000,000
Emp.: 260
Manufacture Steel & Brass Valves
S.I.C.: 3494
John S. Holden, Jr. *(Pres.)*
Richard N. Cronon *(Treas. & Pur. Agent)*

Outside Service Firm(s):

Ward, Fisher & Co.*(Auditors)*
Providence, RI

Shawmut Bank*(Major Banking Relationship)*
Taunton, MA

Automatic Timing & Controls, Inc.
(See listing under Automatic Machine Products Company)

AUTOMATION INTELLIGENCE, INC.
850 Trafalgar Ct.
Maitland, FL 32751-4153
Tel.: 407-661-7000
Tel.: 800-343-2851 **DE**
Fax: 407-661-6966
Year Founded: 1983
Assets: $11,391,396
Earnings: ($1,284,590)
Liabilities: $8,375,141
Net Worth: $3,016,255
Approx.Sls.: $18,021,052
Emp.: 173
Fiscal Year-end: 9/30/90
Import Export
Computer Programming Services; Manufacture Industrial Controls, Numerical Control Software, Field Engineering Services & Manufacturing Sub-Contracts
S.I.C.: 7372; 7379; 3625; 7378; 7373
Chris Hudson *(Chm. Bd., Pres. & Chief Exec. Officer)*
Leah B. Yeager *(Chief Fin. Officer, Treas. & Controller)*
Thomas J. Weber *(Exec. V.P.-Sls. & Mktg.)*
Selim J. Ayoub *(V.P.-Mfg.)*
John H. Birmingham *(V.P.-Customer Supports)*
Robert Gold *(V.P. & Gen. Mgr.-Numeridex Cam Div.)*
Christopher Hudson *(V.P.-Bus. Devel.)*
Charles Robins *(Corp. Sec.)*
Phyllis Bender *(Dir.-Pur.)*
Ernie Worley *(Dir.-Human Resources)*
Joe Labrunda *(Mgr.-Customer Support)*
Mark Potter *(Mgr.-Software Devel.)*
Bob Samson *(Mgr.-Intl. Sales)*
Principal(s):
Chris Hudson
Christopher Hudson

No. of Mfg. Plants/Facilities: 1
No. of U.S. Offices: 15
No. of Foreign Offices: 1

Outside Service Firm(s):

Deloitte & Touche*(Auditors)*
200 S. Orange Ave., Ste. 1800
Orlando, FL 32801
Tel.: 407-246-8200
Fax: 407-422-0936

Best Insurors*(Commercial Insurance Carrier)*
1500 N. Dale Mabry
Tampa, FL 33631-3601
Tel.: 813-871-4671
Fax: 813-871-4099

Lloyds Bank Plc*(International Bank Affiliate)*
London, United Kingdom

Hutchins & Wheeler*(Legal Firm)*
100 Federal Street
Boston, MA 02110
Tel.: 617-951-6600
Fax: 617-951-1295

Sun Bank, N.A.*(Major Banking Relationship)*
200 S. Orange Ave.
Orlando, FL 32802
Tel.: 407-237-4899
Fax: 407-237-6704

Non-U.S. Holding:

Automation Intelligence UK Ltd. **(1)**
Crastlands Court, St. Peters Rd.
Rugby, Warwickshire CV21 30P, United Kingdom
Tel.: 011-44-788541331
Fax: 44-908-564841
Emp.: 6
Sales & Service Office Of US Products
S.I.C.: 3625; 7372; 7379
Michael Etherington *(Gen. Mgr.)*

AUTOMOTIVE MOULDING COMPANY
23751 Amber
Warren, MI 48089
Tel.: 313-757-7800
Fax: 313-757-8329
Year Founded: 1948
Approx.Sls.: $70,000,000
Emp.: 850
Import Export
Mfr. Automotive Moldings
S.I.C.: 3714
Frank P. Peslar *(Chm. Bd.)*
Drew Peslar *(Vice Chm.)*
Norman Peslar *(Pres.)*
Soc Souyias *(V.P.-Sls.)*
Richard Abbey *(Sec. & Treas.)*
Rita Carswell *(Pur. Agent)*

Outside Service Firm(s):

Deloitte & Touche*(Auditors)*
200 Renaissance Center, 16th Fl.
Detroit, MI 48243
Tel.: 313-396-3000
Fax: 313-259-8087

Comerica Bank*(Major Banking Relationship)*
211 W. Fort St.
Detroit, MI 48226
Tel.: 313-222-3300

AUTOMOTIVE NEWS
1400 Woodbridge Ave.
Detroit, MI 48207-3187
Tel.: 313-446-6000 (Editorial)
Tel.: 313-446-1680 (Sales)
Fax: 313-446-0383
Year Founded: 1925
Approx.Sls.: $19,000,000
Emp.: 60
Fiscal Year-end: 12/31/90
Publish Automotive News
S.I.C.: 2721; 2731; 2711
Keith E. Crain *(Publr. & Editorial Dir.)*
Peter Brown *(Assoc. Publr. & Editor)*
Edward Lapham *(Mng. Editor)*
Bob Adams *(V.P. & Dir.-Production)*
Bill Strong *(V.P. & Dir.-Circulation)*
M. Reid MacGuidwin *(V.P.-Mktg.)*
Edward Fisher *(Dir.-Adv.)*
Dutch Mandel *(Adv. Rep.)*
Tony Merpi *(Adv. Rep.)*
James R. Farnan *(Adv. Rep.)*
Thomas J. Collins *(Adv. Rep.)*
Edward J. Noonan *(Adv. Rep.)*
Colleen Kettenhofen *(Adv. Rep.)*
Richard Taw *(Adv. Rep.)*
Howard E. Bradley *(Eastern Adv. Mgr.)*
K. Michael Foss *(Western Adv. Mgr.)*
Michelle Minor *(Sls. Promo. Mgr.)*
Marie Hingst *(Classified Adv. Mgr.)*
Diane Carver *(Adv. Production Mgr.)*
Deanne Barry *(Asst. Mgr.-Sls. Promo.)*

AUTOMOTIVE PLASTIC TECHNOLOGIES, INC.
6600 E. Fifteen Mile Rd.
Sterling Heights, MI 48312
Tel.: 313-979-5000 **MI**
Fax: 313-979-0499
Approx.Sls.: $150,000,000
Emp.: 2,500
Plastic Injection Molding & Finishing for the Automotive Indus.
S.I.C.: 3083; 3089
Charles Beeker *(Pres.)*
Bruce Beeker *(V.P. & Dir.-Fin.)*

Computer Systems/Hardware:
IBM

AUTOMOTIVE RENTALS, INC.
9000 Midlantic Dr.
Mount Laurel, NJ 08054
Tel.: 609-663-5200
Fax: 609-234-9245
Year Founded: 1948
Approx.Sls.: $250,000,000
Emp.: 400
Vehicle Leasing & Fleet Management Programs
S.I.C.: 7519
John W. Kolb *(Chm. Bd.)*
Michael Laporta *(Pres.)*
Kenneth Baittinger *(Sr. V.P.-Sls. & Mktg.)*
Howard Wodack *(Sr. V.P.-Opers.)*
Jack Bier *(Sr. V.P.-Fin.)*
Stanley Shaeffer *(Treas.)*
Jim Zerbe *(Dir.-Mktg. Communications & Adv. Mgr.)*
Audre Wanzler *(Dir.-Support Services & Personnel Mgr.)*

AUTOMOTIVE SUPPLY ASSOC., INC.
(Formerly Sanel Auto Supply Associates)
129 Manchester St.
Concord, NH 03301
Tel.: 603-225-4000 **NH**
Fax: 603-225-2484
Year Founded: 1989
Approx.Sls.: $30,000,000
Emp.: 260
Wholesale Distribution of Automotive Parts & Supplies & Industrial Supplies
S.I.C.: 5531; 5013
George Segal *(Pres.)*
Henry Sanel *(Chm. Bd.)*
Robert Schadee *(V.P.-Fin.)*

Outside Service Firm(s):

Fleet Bank-NH*(Major Banking Relationship)*
Indian Head Plaza
Nashua, NH 03060
Tel.: 603-594-5000

Subsidiary:

Sanel Auto Parts, Inc. **(1)**
219 S. Main St.
Concord, NH 03301
Tel.: 603-225-4100
Wholesale Distribution of Automotive Parts & Supplies & Industrial Supplies
S.I.C.: 5531; 5013

AUTOROLL MACHINE CORP.
11 River St.
Middleton, MA 01949
Tel.: 508-777-2160
Fax: 508-777-9453
Approx.Sls.: $10,000,000
Emp.: 90
Silk Screen Printing Equip. for Plastic Containers & Circuit Board Indus. & Pad Transfer Printing; Rotary Offset Printers
S.I.C.: 3555
William M. Karlyn *(Pres.)*
John Huston *(Controller)*
Ben Adner *(Prod. Mgr.)*
Jeff Marini *(Natl. Sls. Mgr.)*

AUTOSWAGE PRODUCTS, INC.
726 River Rd.
Shelton, CT 06484
Tel.: 203-929-1401 **CT**
Fax: 203-929-6187
Year Founded: 1946
Approx.Sls.: $12,000,000
Emp.: 100
Import Export
Beaded Chain & Tubular Metal Parts, Wrappost Wire Wrap Terminals
S.I.C.: 3679; 3999; 3496
Donald L. Brenton *(Pres. & Chief Oper. Officer)*
Brian N. Collings *(Chief Fin. Officer)*
Evelyn Brenton *(Sec.)*
Arthur DeFabbio *(Mgr.-Sls.)*
David Brenton *(Pur. Agent)*

No. of Mfg. Plants/Facilities: 1

Outside Service Firm(s):

Arthur Andersen & Co.*(Auditors)*
One Financial Plaza
Hartford, CT 06103
Tel.: 203-280-0649
Fax: 203-280-0898

Massachusetts Mutual Life Insurance Co.*(Group Insurer)*
Boston, MA

Dice, Maloney, Lenz, & Malloy*(Legal Firm)*
Cheshire, CT

Connecticut Bank & Trust*(Major Banking Relationship)*
111 Founders Plaza
E. Hartford, CT 06108

AVADYNE, INC.
2801 Salinas Highway, Bldg. F
Monterey, CA 93940
Tel.: 408-624-5452
Fax: 408-373-7167
Year Founded: 1981
Approx.Sls.: $10,000,000
Emp.: 50
Fiscal Year-end: 12/31/90
Mfr. Diet & Nutrition Powdered Formulas
S.I.C.: 2023
Vaughn Feathers *(Chm. Bd. & Chief Exec. Officer)*
Spencer Chapple *(Pres. & Chief Oper. Officer)*
James Coover *(Sr. V.P.)*
Robert Nesheim *(Sr. V.P.-Science & Technology)*
Beverly Walter *(V.P. & Gen. Mgr.-CPI Div.)*
Robert Forlizzo *(Gen. Mgr.-Retail Div.)*
Stephen Schultz *(Gen. Mgr.-Advance Healthcare Div.)*
Yvonne Simons *(Sr. Buyer)*
Cary Brown *(Dir.-MIS)*
Mike Dowling *(Dir.-Matls. Mngmt.)*
Nancy Pasch *(Natl. Sls. Mgr.-Paragon Div.)*

AVATAR CORPORATION
65 South St.
Hopkinton, MA 01748
Tel.: 508-435-3000
Tel.: 800-282-3270 **MA**
Fax: 508-435-2470
Year Founded: 1981
Sales Range: $10-19 Million
Emp.: 75
Export
Mfr. PC Networks
S.I.C.: 3577
Thomas F. Bogan *(Pres.)*
Fred Schlaffer *(V.P.-Devel.)*
Art Garafalo *(V.P.-Sls.)*
Mark Lynch *(V.P.-Mfg.)*
Richard Sterry *(V.P.-Mktg.)*
Tracey K. Poulin *(Chief Fin. Officer)*
Anita Bloom *(Mgr.-Pur.)*
Joyce Enos *(Mgr.-Intl. Sls.)*

Avatar Corporation—(Continued)

Heidi Palmer *(Mgr.-Pub. Rels.)*
Mark Frazier *(Mgr.-Matls. Control)*
Charles E. Coppa *(Mgr.-General Acctg.)*
William Suarez *(Mgr.-Opers.)*
Heidi P. Sylvia *(Mgr.-Mktg. Communications)*
Tom Pincines *(Mgr.-Product, Micro-to-mainframe)*

No. of Mfg. Plants/Facilities: 1
No. of U.S. Offices: 2

Computer Systems/Hardware:
Hewlett-Packard 3000 Series 37; IBM System 36

Outside Service Firm(s):

Republic Hogg Robinson*(Commercial Insurance Carrier)*
Boston, MA

BHR Life & Group*(Group Insurer)*
Gardner, MA

Testa, Hurwitz & Thibeault*(Legal Firm)*
53 State St.
Boston, MA 02109
Tel.: 617-248-7000
Fax: 617-248-7100

U.S. Trust Co.*(Major Banking Relationship)*
40 Court St.
Boston, MA 02108
Tel.: 617-726-7371
Fax: 617-726-7380

Subsidiary:

Tri-Data Systems (1)
3270 Scott Blvd.
Santa Clara, CA 95054
Tel.: 408-727-3270
Mfr. of Electronic Gateways
S.I.C.: 3577
Tom Bogan *(Pres.)*

AVES ADVERTISING, INC.
800 Exhibitors Plaza
Grand Rapids, MI 49503
Tel.: 616-459-3351
Fax: 616-459-9075
Year Founded: 1943
Approx.Billings: $12,000,000
Emp.: 35
Print Adv., Direct Response, Pub. Rels. & Inquiry Mngmt. Publishing
John C. Aves *(Chm., Pres. & Chief Exec. Officer)*
Robert Spaman *(Chief Fin. Officer & Treas.)*
Derek Hanson *(V.P.)*
Bill Austin *(Gen. Mgr.-Aves/Direct)*

AVIBANK MFG., INC.
210 S. Victory Blvd.
Burbank, CA 91502
Tel.: 818-843-4330 DE
Fax: 818-846-1872
Year Founded: 1945
Approx.Sls.: $35,000,000
Emp.: 480
Mfr. of Bale Lock Quick Release Pin; Self Retaining Bolts, Electronic Latching Devices, Nut-sert Blind Threaded Fasteners, Quick-connect & Die-connect Metal Fabricated Specialty Fasteners & Fastening System
S.I.C.: 3429; 3452
Milton I. Berman *(Chm. Bd., Pres. & Treas.)*
Dennis P. Arnold *(V.P.-Sls.)*
John A. Duran *(V.P.-Engrng.)*
Terry Boyer *(Controller)*
Linda Fogelsong *(Sec.)*

AVIS FORD INC.
29200 Telegraph Rd.
Southfield, MI 48034
Tel.: 313-355-7500 MI
Fax: 313-358-2455
Year Founded: 1946
Assets: $12,000,000
Liabilities: $10,000,000
Net Worth: $2,000,000
Approx.Sls.: $55,000,000
Emp.: 111
Fiscal Year-end: 12/31/90
Car Dealership
S.I.C.: 5511
Walter E. Douglas *(Chm. Bd. & Pres.)*
James Witmer *(Chief Fin. Officer)*
Principal(s):
Walter E. Douglas
James Witmer
Edward C. Brown

No. of U.S. Offices: 1

Outside Service Firm(s):

Coopers & Lybrand*(Auditors)*
400 Renaissance Center
Detroit, MI 48243
Tel.: 313-446-7100
Fax: 313-446-7117

Manufacturers National Bank N.A.*(Major Banking Relationship)*
38th Fl., 100 Renaissance Center
Detroit, MI 48243
Tel.: 313-222-4227

AVIS, INC.
900 Old Country Rd.
Garden City, NY 11530
Tel.: 516-222-3000 DE
Fax: 516-222-4381
Year Founded: 1946
Approx.Sls.: $1,220,000,000
Emp.: 12,500
Fiscal Year-end: 2/28/92
Passenger Car Rental & Leasing
S.I.C.: 7514
Joseph V. Vittoria *(Chm. Bd. & Chief Exec. Officer)*
Lawrence Ferenzy *(Exec. V.P. & Chief Fin. Officer)*
David P. McNicholas *(Exec. V.P.-Systems Mktg.)*
James E. Collins *(Exec. V.P.)*
Donald L. Korn *(Sr. V.P.-Human Resources)*
Gerald Kennell *(V.P. & Treas.)*
John J. Lynch *(V.P. & Gen. Counsel)*
Thomas Byrnes *(V.P.-Sls.)*
Robert Cardillo *(V.P.-Sls. & Mktg.)*
Michael Collins *(V.P.-Intl.)*
James Fitzsimmons *(V.P.-Properties & Facilities)*
John Forsythe *(V.P.-Opers.)*
W. Ross Hislop *(V.P.-Mktg. Programs)*
Allen J. Kurzman *(V.P.-Mktg. Services)*
Vincent Manago *(V.P.-Acctg.)*
Michael Caton *(Dir.-Quality of Service)*
Demetria Mudar *(Dir.-Pub. Rels.)*
Raymond Noble *(Mgr.-Pub. Rels.)*
Don Simon *(Mgr.-Adv.)*

Computer Systems/Hardware:
IBM

Outside Service Firm(s):

KPMG Peat Marwick*(Auditors)*
345 Park Ave.
New York, NY 10154
Tel.: 212-758-9700
Fax: 212-872-3308

Connecticut General Life Insurance Co.*(Group Insurer)*
P.O. Box 2975,
Hartford, CT 06104
Tel.: 203-726-6000

AVIS INDUSTRIAL CORPORATION
1909 So. Main St.
Upland, IN 46989
Mailing Address:
P.O. Box 548
Upland, IN 46989
Tel.: 317-998-8100 IN
Fax: 317-998-8111
Year Founded: 1959
Assets: $67,756,138
Liabilities: $41,864,874
Net Worth: $25,891,264
Approx.Sls.: $132,178,947
Emp.: 1688
Fiscal Year-end: 12/31/91
Import Export
Manufacture Industrial & Automotive Locks, Standby Electrical Generators, Industrial Steel Tubing, Machine Tools, Miscellaneous Automotive Parts, Forgings
S.I.C.: 3317; 3429; 3452; 3462; 3463; 3496; 3531; 3536; 3541; 3545; 3569; 3593; 3599; 3621; 3643; 3714
Leland E. Boren *(Chm. Bd., Pres. & Chief Exec. Officer)*
Richard T. Doermer *(Vice Chm.)*
Carol J. Mineart *(Chief Fin. Officer & Treasurer)*
Judith E. Owen *(V.P. & Sec.)*
LaRita R. Bowen *(V.P.-Pub. Rels.)*
Leland K. Crist *(V.P.-Employee Benefits)*
David B. Ashby *(V.P.-Strategic Planning)*
Ron D. Richardson *(Asst. to Pres.& Dir.-Oper.)*
William Maki *(Controller)*
Principal(s):
Leland E. Boren
Richard T. Doermer

No. of Mfg. Plants/Facilities: 12
No. of U.S. Offices: 12

Outside Service Firm(s):

KPMG Peat Marwick*(Auditors)*
135 N. Pennsylvania St.
Indianapolis, IN 46204
Tel.: 317-636-5592
Fax: 317-635-3314

Bank One, Indianapolis, N.A.*(Major Banking Relationship)*
111 Monument Circle, Ste. 1611
Indianapolis, IN 46204-1611
Tel.: 317-321-8110

Subsidiaries:

American Baler Co. (1)
200 Hickory St., P.O. Box 29
Bellevue, OH 44811
Tel.: 419-483-5790
Fax: 419-483-3815
Emp.: 55
Export
Manufactures Baling Equipment for the Recycling Industry
S.I.C.: 3569
Jerry W. Johnson *(Pres.)*
Richard L. Harris *(V.P.-Sls.)*
David L. Kowaleski *(Treas.)*

Badger Equipment Company (1)
Airport Industrial Park, P.O. Box 798
Winona, MN 55987
Tel.: 507-454-1563
Fax: 507-545-3326
Emp.: 126
Export
Manufacturer of Excavators & Cranes for the Construction & Mining Industries
S.I.C.: 3531; 3535
Frank W. Norris, Jr. *(Pres.)*
Delwin Tschumper *(Treas.)*
Clarence Craven *(Mgr.-Mfg.)*

Crankshaft Machine Company (1)
314 N. Jackson St., P.O. Box 1127
Jackson, MI 49204
Tel.: 517-787-3791
Fax: 517-787-6326
Emp.: 49
Export
Designs & Builds Special Purpose Machine Tools; Designs & Installs Flexible Turn-Key Systems
S.I.C.: 7373; 3541; 3545
J. Mykala *(V.P. & Gen. Mgr.)*
Ron DuBois *(V.P.-Sls.)*
S. Kallio *(Controller)*

Edgerton Forge, Inc. (1)
257 E. Morrison St., R.R. 2, Box 12
Edgerton, OH 43517
Tel.: 419-298-2333
Fax: 419-298-3487
Emp.: 78
Manufacturer of Wheel Wrenches, Auto & Truck Suspension Parts
S.I.C.: 3462; 3714
Richard B. Horton *(Pres.)*
Michelle Burkey *(Controller & Treas.)*

Hurd Lock & Manufacturing Co. (1)
603 Bohannon Ave., P.O. Box 1450
Greeneville, TN 37744
Tel.: 615-639-4101
Fax: 615-639-0266
Emp.: 771
Manufacturer of Locks for Original Equipment Manufacturers in Industry: Switch Locks, Ratchet Locks, Padlocks, Side Bar Locks, Furniture & Specialty Locks
S.I.C.: 3429; 3714
J.S. Duggan *(Pres.)*
Steve Bone *(Chief Fin. Officer)*
Brenda G. Wallace *(Pur. Agent)*

James Steel & Tube Company (1)
29774 Stephenson Hwy., P.O. Box 545
Madison Heights, MI 48071
Tel.: 313-547-4200
Fax: 313-547-0430
Emp.: 52
Cold Formed Welded Structural Tubing
S.I.C.: 3317
Robert C. Becker *(Pres.)*
James LaDouceur *(Controller)*
Dennis Ashby *(Gen. Sls. Mgr.)*
James Burzynski *(Pur. Agent)*

Melling Forging Company (1)
1709 Thompson St.
Lansing, MI 48906
Tel.: 517-482-0791
Fax: 517-482-0085
Emp.: 150
Producer of Carbon & Low Alloy Closed Die Forgings for Auto, Trucking & Other Industries
S.I.C.: 3462
Richard B. Horton *(Pres.)*
William Slade *(Controller)*
Norman Nolff *(Sls. Mgr.)*

Pacific Forge, Inc. (1)
10641 Etiwanda Ave.
Fontana, CA 92335
Tel.: 909-986-6701
Fax: 909-986-3490
Emp.: 49
Producer of High Quality Forgings for the Aircraft, Chemical, Nuclear, Ordnance, Orthopedic Implant & Petroleum Industries
S.I.C.: 3463; 3462
Michael Hann *(Pres.)*
Ron Brown *(Controller)*
Ron Browne *(Sls. Mgr.)*

The Pierce Co., Inc. (1)
201 N. 8th St.
Upland, IN 46989
Tel.: 317-998-2712
Fax: 317-998-2540
Approx.Sls.: $20,000,000
Emp.: 143
Fiscal Year-end: 12/31/91
Export
Produces a Variety of Engineered Assemblies for Auto Industry; Formed Wire Products, Engine Speed Controls, Water Pumps, Aftermarket Fuel Pumps & Castings
S.I.C.: 3496; 3621; 3714
Gene L. Hainen *(Pres.)*
Lucy A. Davis *(Treas.)*
Thomas Graham *(Dir.-Sls.)*
Terry McDaniel *(Pur. Mgr.)*
Edwina Dumpert *(Mgr.-Personnel)*
John E. Cantwell *(Dir.-Engrng.)*

The Tobin Corporation (1)
35544 Lorain Rd.
North Ridgeville, OH 44939
Tel.: 216-327-4244
Fax: 216-327-6129
Emp.: 46
Producer of Specialty Fasteners: Anchor Bolts, U-Bolts, Heating Element Pins, Electrode Rods, Hinge Pins & Various Connecting Rods
S.I.C.: 3452; 3429; 3643
Richard Collins *(Pres. & Gen. Mgr.)*
Jacqueline Dangelo *(Controller & Treas.)*

U.S. Broach & Machine Company (1)
Bypass 378 Frontage Rd., P.O. Box 1649
Sumter, SC 29150
Tel.: 803-775-2357
Fax: 803-481-3155
Emp.: 27
Manufacturer of Vertical Broaching Machines; Broach Tooling
S.I.C.: 3541
Mark Sari *(Gen. Mgr.)*

Jackie Motley *(Controller)*

Universal Vise & Tool Co. **(1)**
8500 E. Michigan Ave.
Parma, MI 49269
Tel.: 517-531-4401
Fax: 517-531-4989
Approx.Sls.: $3,000,000
Emp.: 28
Fiscal Year-end: 12/31/92
Export
Computer Systems/Hardware:
Open Systems-Accounting, Auto CAD-Engineering
Manufacturer of Hydraulic/Pneumatic Cylinders, Portable Milling/Drilling Machines
S.I.C.: 3541; 3593; 3599; 3545
Ron Richardson *(Pres.)*
Matt Hurt *(Controller)*
Roger Smith *(Gen. Mgr.)*
Vianna Hutchinson *(Quality Control Mgr.)*

AVONDALE MILLS, INC.
(Sub. of A M Acquisition Co.)
900 Avondale Ave.
Sylacauga, AL 35150
Tel.: 205-249-1200 **AL**
Fax: 205-249-1546
Year Founded: 1897
Assets: $193,571,000
Liabilities: $91,273,000
Net Worth: $102,298,000
Approx.Sls.: $450,000,000
Emp.: 4,000
Fiscal Year-end: 8/28/92
Export
Textile Manufacturer
S.I.C.: 2211; 2281; 5131
G. Stephen Felker *(Chm. Bd. & Chief Exec. Officer)*
Richard H. Monk, Jr. *(Pres. & Chief Oper. Officer)*
Jack R. Altherr, Jr. *(Chief Fin. Officer, V.P. & Sec.)*
C. Michael Billingsley *(V.P.)*
Craig S. Crockard *(V.P.-Plng. & Devel.)*
Bill W. Henry *(V.P.-Raw Matls. Pur.)*
Keith M. Hull *(V.P.)*
Lorton S. Livingston *(V.P. & Treas.)*
T. Wayne Spraggins *(V.P.-Mfg. Services)*
Michael Delen Boyd *(Controller)*
John Dragonetti *(Dir.-Intl. Sls.)*
L. Stephen Lipham *(Dir.-Mgmt. Information Systems)*
Kelley Sawyer *(Dir.-Asst. Pub. Rels.)*
Tim Stansell *(Dir.-Pur.)*

No. of Mfg. Plants/Facilities: 12
No. of U.S. Offices: 10

Computer Systems/Hardware:
IBM

Outside Service Firm(s):

Ernst & Young*(Auditors)*
Harbert Plaza, 1900 AmSouth
Birmingham, AL 35243

Travelers Insurance Co.*(Commercial Insurance Carrier)*
One Tower Square
Hartford, CT 06183-6130
Tel.: 203-277-4542
Fax: 203-277-5038

United Medical Resources Inc.*(Group Insurer)*
2343 Auburn Ave.
Cincinnati, OH 45219

King & Spalding*(Legal Firm)*
Trust Co. Tower
Atlanta, GA 30303
Tel.: 404-572-4600

First Wachovia Bank & Trust Co.*(Major Banking Relationship)*
2 Peachtree St., NW
Atlanta, GA 30383
Tel.: 404-332-4000

Trust Company Bank*(Major Banking Relationship)*
Stock Trans. Dept. P.O.B. 4625, Trust Company of Georgia Bldg.
Atlanta, GA 30302
Tel.: 404-588-7831

Divisions:

Avondale Mills Fabric Div. **(1)**
900 Avondale Ave.
Sylacauga, AL 35150
Tel.: 205-249-1200
Fax: 205-249-1472
Textile Manufacturer
S.I.C.: 2211; 5131
Keith M. Hull *(Pres. & V.P.)*

Avondale Mills Yarn Div. **(1)**
900 Avondale Ave.
Sylacauga, AL 35150
Tel.: 205-249-1200
Fax: 205-249-1417
Mfg. of Yarn & Thread Mills
S.I.C.: 2281
C. Michael Billingsley *(Pres. & V.P.)*

Subsidiary:

Avondale Foreign Sales Corporation **(1)**
900 Avondale Ave.
Sylacauga, AL 35150
Tel.: 205-249-1200
Exporter Textiles
S.I.C.: 2211; 2281
Richard H. Monk, Jr. *(Pres. & Chief Oper. Officer)*

AF&G
AVRETT, FREE & GINSBERG, INC.

AVRETT, FREE & GINSBERG, INC.
800 Third Ave.
New York, NY 10022
Tel.: 212-832-3800 **NY**
Fax: 212-826-7143
Fax: 212-759-9603
Fax: 212-593-2849
Year Founded: 1970
Approx.Billings: $260,000,000
Emp.: 150
Advertising Agency
S.I.C.: 7311
Corporate Giving Program: United Fund
Employee Matching Gifts Program: 401K
John G. Avrett *(Chm. & Chief Exec. Officer)*
Frank Ginsberg *(Pres. & Creative Dir.)*
Manny DeMagistris *(Sr. Exec. V.P., Creative Dir. on Ralston Cereals)*
Lynne Kluger *(Exec. V.P., Brdcst. Production)*
Jim Symon *(Exec. V.P., Assoc. Creative Dir.)*
Tom James *(Sr. Exec. V.P., Dir. Client Services)*
Donald Bandman *(Exec. V.P., Grp. Acct. Dir.)*
Larry Riegel *(Exec. V.P., Grp. Acct. Dir.)*
Bill Tucker *(Exec. V.P., Grp. Acct. Dir.)*
William Lahr *(Sr. V.P., Chief Fin. Officer)*
Gary Cunningham *(Sr. V.P., Dir. Print Services)*
Mark Gershman *(Sr. V.P., Assoc. Creative Dir.)*
Jamie Rhind *(Sr. V.P., Assoc. Media Dir.)*
Toby Dunn *(Sr. V.P., Mngmt. Supvr.)*
Gunar Skillins *(Sr. V.P., Assoc. Creative Dir.)*
Stuart Grau *(V.P., Strategic Planning)*
Mitch Krevat *(Sr. V.P., Mngmt Supvr. & Bus. Devel. Dir.)*
Cherie Dunn *(V.P., Admin. Services)*
Principal(s):
John G. Avrett
Frank Ginsberg

No. of U.S. Offices: 1

Computer Systems/Hardware:
Macintosh, MicrofotWord, Pagemaker, Cricket, Graph, Wingz, IBM System 36, Phase X Software, Persuasion, Excel

Outside Service Firm(s):

Robert A. Goodman & Co.*(Auditors)*
230 Park Ave.
New York, NY 10169

The Kooper Group*(Group Insurer)*
New York, NY

Davis & Gilbert*(Legal Firm)*
850 Third Ave.
New York, NY 10022
Tel.: 212-326-1300

Marine Midland Bank*(Major Banking Relationship)*
140 Broadway
New York, NY 10015
Tel.: 212-658-1620

Branch:

The Tucker Group **(1)**
800 Third Ave.
New York, NY 10022
Tel.: 212-832-3800
Fax: 212-759-9568
William W. Tucker *(Mng. Dir.)*

AWREY BAKERIES, INC.
12301 Farmington Rd.
Livonia, MI 48150
Tel.: 313-522-1100
Fax: 313-522-1453
Year Founded: 1910
Approx.Sls.: $54,000,000
Emp.: 540
Wholesale & Retail Bakery Goods
S.I.C.: 5461; 5149
Robert C. Awrey *(Chm. Bd.)*
Howard Hollister *(V.P.-Food Services Sls. & Mktg.)*
John Adams *(Dir.-Plant Opers.)*
Shawn Walker *(Dir.-Pur.)*

Outside Service Firm(s):

Plante & Moran*(Auditors)*
Detroit, MI

AXELBAND & BROWN & ASSOCIATES INC.
24100 Chagrin Blvd.
Cleveland, OH 44122
Tel.: 216-831-0440
Year Founded: 1948
Approx.Billings: $15,400,000
Emp.: 19
Retail Advertising
Corporate Giving Program: Profit Sharing Plan, Defined Benefit Program; After One Year of Employment 100% Vester After Ten Years
Irving Brown *(Pres.)*
Leonard Axelband *(Exec. V.P., Sec.)*
Wayne Schakel *(V.P., Pub. Rels. Dir.)*
Priscilla Hobbs *(Office Mgr.)*

Computer Systems/Hardware:
Macintosh, IBM, Compugraphics

AXELSON, INC.
110 Industrial Blvd.
Longview, TX 75602
Mailing Address:
P.O. Box 2427,
Longview, TX 75606
Tel.: 903-757-6650
Fax: 903-753-8479
Year Founded: 1892
Approx.Sls.: $47,000,000
Emp.: 450
Fiscal Year-end: 12/31/90
Export
Mfr. Equipment for Oil & Gas Production, Pipeline & Processing
S.I.C.: 3533; 3559; 3569
Glen H. Denison *(Chm. Bd.)*
Jim McMichael *(Pres.)*
Lance Poulsen *(V.P.-Sls. & Mktg.)*
Robert Hardwick *(Sec., Controller & Treas.)*
Luis R. Celerier *(Mgr.-Mktg. Admin.)*
Emil Preiss *(Pur. Mgr.)*

AYDLOTTE & CARTWRIGHT, INC.
6 Concourse Pkwy., Ste. 2800
Atlanta, GA 30339
Tel.: 404-551-5000
Fax: 404-551-5001
Year Founded: 1985
Approx.Billings: $24,000,000
Emp.: 50
Healthcare, Business-to-Business & Service Business
William Y. Aydlotte *(Pres. & Creative Dir.)*
Jeane H. Cartwright *(Exec. V.P., New Bus. Contact)*
Kathryn Slagle *(Controller)*
Jill Kampfe *(Dir., Pub. Rels.)*

Computer Systems/Hardware:
MacIntosh, IBM, Novell Network

Ayer

N W AYER INCORPORATED
Worldwide Plaza, 825 Eighth Ave.
New York, NY 10019-7498
Tel.: 212-474-5000
Telex: 177307
Fax: 212-474-5400
Year Founded: 1869
Approx.Billings: $754,400,000
Approx.Billings:$1,361,000,000
Emp.: 2,900
International Advertising Agency
S.I.C.: 7311
Jerry J. Siano *(Chm. & Chief Exec. Officer)*
Thomas F. Maxey *(Vice Chm. & Chief Oper. Officer)*
Patrick J. Cunningham *(Vice Chm. & Chief Creative Officer-Ayer WW)*
Dominick F. Rossi, Jr. *(Pres.-Ayer USA)*
Richard Hedger *(Chm. & Dir.-Europe)*
Glenn E. Corlett *(Exec. V.P., Chief Fin. Officer)*
Fred I. Posner *(Exec. V.P., Research & Mktg. Dir.)*
Warren E. Albright *(Exec. V.P. Dir.)*
David Gantman *(Exec. V.P., Dir.)*
Keith B. Gould *(Exec. V.P., Dir. Creative Services-NY)*
Arthur W. Meranus *(Exec. V.P., Dir.)*
Marcella Rosen *(Exec. V.P., Mng. Dir. Media Services)*
Fernando Ocana *(Dir. & Chm.-TAPSA AYER)*
Michael J. Kelly *(Sr. V.P. & Treas.)*
Walter C. Lance *(Sr. V.P., Controller & Asst. Sec.)*
Bertrand M. Lanchner *(Sr. V.P., Legal & Sec.)*
Joseph M. Harte *(Sr. V.P., Dir. Human Resources)*
Janet Petkus *(Pur. Agent)*

No. of U.S. Offices: 3
No. of Foreign Offices: 14

Computer Systems/Hardware:
AT & T 3B5

Outside Service Firm(s):

Price Waterhouse*(Auditors)*
153 E. 53rd St., 44th Fl.
New York, NY 10022
Tel.: 212-371-2000

N W Ayer Incorporated—(Continued)

Aetna Life & Casualty*(Group Insurer)*
151 Farmington Avenue
Hartford, CT 06156
Tel.: 203-273-2128
Fax: 203-729-4295

Continental Bank N. A.*(Investment Banker)*
231 S. LaSalle St.
Chicago, IL 60697
Tel.: 312-828-2345
Tel.: 800-426-5754
Telex: 312-828-1783

Scudder, Stevens & Clark*(Investment Banker)*
New York, NY

Wood, Struthers & Winthrop*(Investment Banker)*
New York, NY

Chemical Banking Corp.*(Major Banking Relationship)*
277 Park Ave.
New York, NY 10041
Tel.: 212-310-6407
Fax: 212-310-4526

Aetna Life & Casualty*(Pension Manager)*
151 Farmington Avenue
Hartford, CT 06156
Tel.: 203-273-2128
Fax: 203-729-4295

CoreStates First Pennsylvania Bank, N.A.*(Pension Manager)*
Philadelphia, PA

Lazard Freres & Co.*(Pension Manager)*
One Rockefeller Plaza
New York, NY 10020
Tel.: 212-632-6442
Fax: 212-373-4430

Divisions:

N W Ayer Inc. **(1)**
Worldwide Plaza-35th Fl., 825 Eighth Ave.
New York, NY 10019-7498
Tel.: 212-474-5000
Jerry J. Siano *(Chm. & Chief Exec. Officer)*
Thomas F. Maxey *(Vice Chm. & Chief Oper. Officer)*
Patrick J. Cunningham *(Vice Chm. & Chief Creative Officer-Ayer WW)*
Dominick F. Rossi, Jr. *(Pres.-Ayer USA)*
Warren E. Albright *(Exec. V.P., Dir.)*
Beverly Beaudoin *(Exec. V.P., Gen. Mgr.-Ayer Direct)*
Glenn E. Corlett *(Exec. V.P., Chief Fin. Officer)*
Arthur B. Meranus *(Exec. V.P., Assoc. Dir., Creative Services)*
Fred I. Posner, Jr. *(Exec. V.P., Mng. Dir., Mktg. Plng. & Res.)*
Joseph Abruzzo *(Sr. V.P., Dir. Mktg. Plng.)*
Julie Cascio *(Sr. V.P., Dir. Info. Systems)*
Aaron Cohen *(Sr. V.P., Dir. Natl. Brdcst. & Programming)*
Richard I. Golden *(Sr. V.P., Dir. Devel. Labs)*
Len Goldenberg *(Sr. V.P., Mng. Dir., WW Communications)*
Ephraim Goldstein *(Sr. V.P., Asst. Dir. Mktg. Plng.)*
Joseph M. Harte *(Sr. V.P., Dir. Human Resources & Devel.-WW)*
Rosemary E. Hartigan *(Sr. V.P., Admin.)*
Sally I. Kandle *(Sr. V.P., Casting Dir.)*
Michael Kelly *(Sr. V.P., Treas.)*
Walter C. Lance *(Sr. V.P., Controller & Asst. Sec.)*
Bertrand M. Lanchner *(Sr. V.P., Legal & Corp. Sec.)*
Stephen J. Magee *(Sr. V.P., Creative Supvr.)*
Peter Varvara *(Sr. V.P., Exec. Acct. Dir.)*
John D. Carlucci *(V.P., Asst. Treas.)*
James F. Murphy *(V.P., Asst. Treas.)*
Lennox Purcell *(V.P., Tax Mgr.)*
Susan Acero *(V.P., Admin. Commercial Production)*
John Bowman *(V.P., Asst. Dir. Devel. Labs)*
Sally Bruner *(V.P., Mgr. Admin./Intl. & USA)*
Jack Lynch *(V.P., Dir. Client Fin. Mngmt.)*
Janet Petkus *(V.P., Pur. Dir.)*
Rachel Treitelman *(V.P., Mfr. Rels. Supvr.)*
Elliot Lawrence *(Music Consultant)*

Ayer Public Relations **(1)**
Worldwide Plaza, 825 Eighth Ave.
New York, NY 10019
Tel.: 212-474-5000
Fax: 212-474-5400
Approx.Billings: $1,859,800
Emp.: 16
Fashion & Beauty Products, Diamond Jewelry, Footwear & Pharmaceuticals
Joan Parker *(Sr. V.P., Pub. Rels.)*
Patricia Kenney *(V.P., Deputy Dir.)*
Lynn Ramsey *(V.P., Mgr.-DIC)*

AyerDirect, Direct Response **(1)**
Worldwide Plaza, 825 Eighth Ave.
New York, NY 10019
Tel.: 212-474-5000
Beverly A. Beaudoin *(Exec. V.P. & Gen. Mgr.-Ayer Direct)*
Robert Sanchez *(Sr. V.P., Dir. New Business)*

Subsidiaries:

Ayer Chicago **(1)**
515 N. State St., Ste. 2100
Chicago, IL 60610
Tel.: 312-644-2937
Approx.Billings: $20,000,000
Emp.: 28
S.I.C.: 7311
Frank Maher *(Sr. V.P., Gen. Mgr.)*
Tim Prosch *(Sr. V.P., Mng. Dir., Client Services)*
John Trusk *(Sr. V.P., Mng. Dir., Creative Services)*
Rich Prowse *(Controller)*

N W Ayer Inc. **(1)**
2000 Fisher Bldg.
Detroit, MI 48202
Tel.: 313-874-8500
Dannielle Colliver *(Pres.-Detroit/Ayer & Sr. V.P., Mng. Dir.)*
R.C. Morrison *(Sr. V.P. & Deputy Dir.)*

GBF/Ayer **(1)**
5900 Wilshire Blvd., Ste. 2750
Los Angeles, CA 90036
Tel.: 213-931-6301
Fax: 213-931-6301
Approx.Billings: $24,500,000
Emp.: 30
Advertising Agency
S.I.C.: 7311
Richard Fried *(Pres. & Mngmt. Supvr.)*
Jerry Wright *(Sr. V.P., Acct. Services)*
Robert A. Berry *(V.P., Fin. & Admin.)*
Kathy Richards *(V.P.)*
Gwynne Lehr *(V.P.)*
Robert Monfrini *(V.P.)*

Partner Agencies:

Ayer Europe **(1)**
Metropolis House 22 Percy St.,
London, W1F 9FF, United Kingdom
Tel.: 071-8958890
Telex: 265-871 REFCBY 029
Fax: 071-8958889
Advertising
S.I.C.: 7311
Richard Hedger *(Dir. & Chm.-Europe)*
Andrew Stewart *(Sr. V.P., European Fin. Dir.)*
David Wilkinson *(Sr. V.P., Deputy Mng. Dir., Europe)*

Ayer Frankfurt **(1)**
Hedderichstr. 108-110 6000
Frankfurt/Main, 70, Germany
Tel.: 69-6050950
Telex: 403 2077
Fax: 69-6059513
Advertising
S.I.C.: 7311
Ernst ten Hoevel *(Mng. Dir.)*

Ayer Ltd. **(1)**
Metropolis House, 22 Percy St.
London, W1P 9FF, United Kingdom
Tel.: 071-5288888
Telex: 263 135
Fax: 071-6361119
Approx.Billings: $70,000,000
Emp.: 60
Advertising
S.I.C.: 7311
Dick Hedger *(Chm.)*
Stephen Woodward *(Chief Exec. Officer)*
Jonathan Taylor *(Mng. Dir.)*
Harriet Vogt *(Dir.-Research & Plng.)*

Ayer Milano **(1)**
Via Cerva 24 20122
Milan, Italy
Tel.: 2-76005312
Telex: 334150
Fax: 2-781180
Advertising
S.I.C.: 7311
Fausto Gardini *(Chm.)*
Fausto Rebuffat *(Chief Exec. Officer)*
Giuseppe Pizzinato *(Mng. Dir.)*

Ayer/Nederland B.V. **(1)**
Keulenstraat 1 7418 ET
Deventer, Netherlands
Tel.: 5-70079898
Fax: 5-70037720
Approx.Billings: $19,700,000
Emp.: 27
Advertising
S.I.C.: 7311
Ton Kamp *(Mng. Dir.)*
Stan Horsthuis *(Fin. Dir.)*

Ayer Portugal **(1)**
Av da Liberdade, 229-3 Andar
Lisbon, 1200, Portugal
Tel.: 11-3524700
Fax: 11-3524279
Advertising
S.I.C.: 7311
Edite Duque *(Chief Exec. Officer)*

Ayer Roma **(1)**
Via Salaria 290 00199
Rome, Italy
Tel.: 6-866051
Telex: 623-245
Fax: 6-866051
Advertising
S.I.C.: 7311
Gabriele Foschini *(Mng. Dir.)*

Ayer Vazquez S.A. de Publicidad **(1)**
Av. Callao 1046, 3 Piso C.P. 1023,
Buenos Aires, Argentina
Tel.: 1-415773
Telex: 23802
Fax: 1-8140494
Approx.Billings: $6,000,000
Emp.: 62
Advertising
S.I.C.: 7311
Jorge Vazquez *(Mng. Dir.)*
Juan Luis Posse Molina *(V.P.)*
Diego Leon *(Oper. Mgr.)*
Gonzalo Machado *(Client Svcs. Dir.)*
Gustavo Razzetti *(Mktg. Svcs. Dir.)*
Bernadette Giannuzzi *(Press & Public Rels. Dir.)*
Charlie Mei *(Fin. Dir.)*

Lee Davis Ayer **(1)**
8F, C.C. Wu Bldg., 302-308 Hennessy Rd.
Hong Kong, Hong Kong
Tel.: 5-8332033
Telex: 83242
Fax: 5-8345877
Approx.Billings: $14,000,000
Emp.: 52
Computer Systems/Hardware:
DOS/APPLE
Brand Direct Graphic Design
S.I.C.: 7311
Michael K. Davis *(Chm. Bd. & Chief Oper. Officer)*
Andrew Lee *(Chief Exec. Officer)*
Simon Au *(Chief Fin. Officer)*

MGTB Ayer **(1)**
2 rue du Pont Neuf 75001
Paris, France
Tel.: 1-42369036
Telex: 214885 F
Fax: 1-42339216
Approx.Billings: $120,000,000
Emp.: 100
Full Service Advertising
S.I.C.: 7311
Jean-Paul Treguer *(Pres.)*

TAPSA Ayer **(1)**
Jenner 3 28010
Madrid, Spain
Tel.: 1-3190462
Telex: 48631 TAP E
Fax: 1-4102620
Approx.Billings: $15,000,000
Emp.: 97
Advertising
S.I.C.: 7311
Fernando Ocana *(Chm. Bd.)*
Juan Carlos de Prada *(Gen. Mgr.)*
Jose Luis Sandin *(Fin. Mgr.)*

TAPSA Ayer **(1)**
Numancia 187, 70-A
Barcelona, Spain
Tel.: 3-3083261
Fax: 3-2803518
Advertising
S.I.C.: 7311
Santiago Jordan Avila *(Mng. Dir.)*

Wilkens Ayer **(1)**
An der Alster 42 2000
Hamburg, 1, Germany
Tel.: 40-28810
Telex: 17 403 496
Fax: 40-2881270
Emp.: 202
Advertising
S.I.C.: 7311
Niels Grothgar *(Chm. Bd. & Chief Exec. Officer)*
Joerg Lathwesen *(Mng. Partner)*
Dr. Gerhild Werner *(Mng. Dir.)*
Gabriele Kant *(Sec.)*

Non-U.S. Holdings:

Chuo Senko Advertising Co., Ltd. **(1)**
2-6-1 Ginza, Chuo-ku
Tokyo, 104, Japan
Tel.: 03-3562-0151
Telex: j 28210
Twx: J28210
Fax: 03-3535-3576
Approx.Billings: $376,500,000
Emp.: 408
Advertising
S.I.C.: 7311
Takashi Ohsawa *(Chm.)*
Kuniko Osawa *(Chairwoman)*
Shoji Koshizawa *(Pres., Chief Exec. Officer)*
Yoshinobu Teraoka *(Sr. Exec. Mng. Dir.)*
Shogo Sakurai *(Exec. Mng. Dir.)*
Yoshito Kikuchi *(Exec. Mng. Dir.)*
Yutaka Ohsawa *(Exec. Sr. V.P.)*
Mikio Yuzawa *(Exec. V.P., Domestic)*
Masatoshi Matsubara *(Exec. Counselor Intl.)*
Katsuhiko Matsunaga *(V.P., Intl. Div.)*
Sean F. Mooney *(Mgr., Intl. Devel.)*

Dolriis, Gorm Larsen & Partner **(1)**
Hammershusgade 9 2100
Copenhagen, Denmark
Tel.: 39-270277
Fax: 39-271114
Approx.Billings: $7,000,000
Emp.: 16
Advertising
S.I.C.: 7311
Soren Dolriis *(Mng. Dir.)*

ICW Copartner **(1)**
An der Alster 42 2000
Hamburg, 1, Germany
Tel.: 40-2801430
Telex: 17 403 496
Fax: 40-2804360
Advertising
S.I.C.: 7311
Joachim Kossert *(Mng. Dir.)*

J & C Advertising **(1)**
Keskustatu 4B 00100
Helsinki, Finland
Tel.: 0-170099
Fax: 0-175840
Advertising
S.I.C.: 7311
Alpo Collanus *(Pres.)*

Lebrija Rubio Publicidad S.A. **(1)**
Sierra Santa Rosa 99-30, Col. Lomas de Barrilaco Sec. Vertientes, 11010
Mexico, D.F. Mexico
Tel.: 5-2592323
Telex: 176-3436
Fax: 5-2024507
Approx.Billings: $10,000,000
Emp.: 51
Advertising
S.I.C.: 7311
Jose Antonio Lebrija *(Pres.)*
Gonzalo Martinez Del Rio *(Fin. Dir.)*

Matari Advertising **(1)**
J1 HR Rasuna Said Kav, H 1-2 Kuningan
Jakarta, Indonesia
Tel.: 21-515160
Telex: 62920
Fax: 21-516440
Advertising
S.I.C.: 7311
Ken T. Sudarto *(Pres., Chief Exec. Officer)*
Paul W. Karmadi *(Exec. V.P., Dir. Opers. & Mktg. Services)*

Padova Ayer **(1)**
Piazza Garibaldi 8 35122
Padova, Italy
Tel.: 49-664722
Telex: 430054
Fax: 49-8751452
Advertising
S.I.C.: 7311
Annibale Pagliarin *(Mng. Dir.)*

Publimerca S.A. **(1)**
4A Av. A 7-64, Zona 10
Guatemala City, Guatemala
Tel.: 22-315518
Fax: 22-324670
Approx.Billings: $1,500,000
Emp.: 25
Advertising
S.I.C.: 7311
Luis R. Bollat S. *(Pres.)*
Yolanda Bollat *(Admin. & Fin. Dir.)*

Weinberger Werbehaus Ges.m.b.H & Co. KG **(1)**
Kaulbachstrasse 22 A-1120
Vienna, Austria
Tel.: 431-8048511
Fax: 431-804851137
Approx.Billings: $8,200,000
Emp.: 15
Advertising
S.I.C.: 7311
Lutz Nowotny *(Pres.)*
Ludwig Nowotny *(Mng. Dir.)*
S. Weinberger *(Exec. V.P.)*
E. Nothnagel *(Sec.)*

AZON CORPORATION
720 Azon Rd.
Johnson City, NY 13790
Mailing Address:
P.O. Box 290
Johnson City, NY 13790
Tel.: 607-797-2368
Fax: 607-797-4506
Year Founded: 1949
Sales Range: $100-499 Million
Emp.: 299
Mfr. Reprographic Paper & Films Used Primarily in the Drafting & Engineering Industries
S.I.C.: 3089; 3861
William Bordages *(Pres.)*
Mark Rapp *(Sr. V.P.)*
Darrell Gauby *(V.P.-Adv.)*
James Donovan *(Controller)*
Arthur Markey *(Dir.-Human Resources)*
Kathi Muggeo *(Mgr.-Data Processing)*

Computer Systems/Hardware:
IBM

Outside Service Firm(s):

Coopers & Lybrand*(Auditors)*
One Lincoln Center
Syracuse, NY 13202
Tel.: 315-474-8541
Fax: 315-474-0259

Chase Lincoln First Bank, N.A.*(Major Banking Relationship)*
Syracuse, NY

Subsidiary:

Keuffel & Esser **(1)**
P.O. Box 800
Rockaway, NJ 07866
Tel.: 201-625-9005 (100%)
Fax: 201-625-0539
Emp.: 263
Mfr. Engrng. Documentation Supplies: Drafting Media, Photographic Imaging Prods. & Microfilm Supplies
S.I.C.: 3826; 3861; 3952; 5049
William Bordages *(Pres.)*
Mark A. Rapp *(V.P.)*
Paul Parzanese *(Treas.)*
Walter Damian *(Sec.)*
Jerry Gaube *(Dir.-Mktg.)*

AZTECA FOODS, INCORPORATED
5005 So. Nagle
Chicago, IL 60638
Tel.: 708-563-6600 IL
Fax: 708-563-0331
Approx.Sls.: $20,000,000
Emp.: 125
Mfr. of Tortillas, Taco Shells & Tortilla Chips
S.I.C.: 2099; 2096; 2038
Arthur R. Velasquez *(Pres. & Chief Exec. Officer)*
Joanne Velasquez *(V.P.)*
Joseph Klomes *(Controller)*
James J. DeCoste *(Mgr.-Opers.)*
Gary Senter *(Mgr.-Gen. Sls.)*
David Sty *(Mgr.-Mfg.)*
Renee Togher *(Mgr.-Mktg.)*

B & B CASH GROCERY STORE
9330 Adamo Dr.
Tampa, FL 33619
Mailing Address:
P.O. Box 1808
Tampa, FL 33601
Tel.: 813-621-6411
Fax: 813-622-8163
Year Founded: 1923
Approx.Sls.: $166,500,000
Emp.: 1,200
Fiscal Year-end: 12/31/90
Retail Groceries
S.I.C.: 5411
C.C. Bever, Jr. *(Chm. Bd., Pres. & Chief Oper. Officer)*
J. Andrew Bever *(Vice Chm. & Dir.-Real Estate)*
Sam Posey *(Chief Exec. Officer)*
Dave Easterman *(Chief Fin. Officer & Controller)*
Doug Davis *(Asst. Chief Exec. Officer & Dir.-Mktg.)*
Ron Emerson *(Dir.-Adv.)*
Gordon Goodyear *(Dir.-Data Processing & Opers.)*
Mark Popovich *(Dir.-Warehousing)*
W.H. Tidwell *(Dir.-Pur.)*
Principal(s):
C.C. Bever, Jr.
J. Andrew Bever

No. of Mfg. Plants/Facilities: 1
No. of U.S. Offices: 1

Computer Systems/Hardware:
IBM Series 1

Outside Service Firm(s):

Smith Barney, Inc.*(Investment Banker)*
Tampa, FL

First National Bank of Florida*(Major Banking Relationship)*
Tampa, FL

B & B HOMES CORPORATION
(d/b/a Teton International)
3283 N. Nine Mile Rd.
Casper, WY 82604
Mailing Address:
P.O. Box 2349,
Mills, WY 82644
Tel.: 307-235-1525 IN
Fax: 307-577-6027
Approx.Sls.: $16,000,000
Emp.: 195
Travel Trailer Chasis; Fifth Wheels
S.I.C.: 3792; 2451
Tony Ingram *(Pres.)*
Betty Ingram *(Sec. & Treas.)*

Outside Service Firm(s):

Hilltop National Bank*(Major Banking Relationship)*
Casper, WY

B & B MOTOR & CONTROL CORPORATION
39-40 Crescent St.
Long Island City, NY 11101
Tel.: 718-784-1313
Tel.: 800-638-7808
Year Founded: 1921
Approx.Sls.: $10,000,000
Emp.: 70
Export
Motors, Variable Speed Drives, Clutches, Counters, Photoelectric Controls, Gear Reducers, Programmable Controls, Servo Systems, Stepping Motors, Controls
S.I.C.: 3621
Paul A. Berson *(Pres.)*
Steve Israel *(Chief Exec. Officer)*
Ralph Seidenfeld *(V.P.-Finance)*
Tom Miceli *(V.P.-Mktg.)*
Paul Martin *(Mgr.-Mktg.)*
Selma Berson *(Sec. & Treas.)*

B & K STEEL & SUPPLY, INC.
2393 S. 1900 W.
Ogden, UT 84401
Tel.: 801-731-0615 UT
Fax: 801-731-5785
Approx.Sls.: $19,000,000
Emp.: 95
Holding Company; Fabricated Structural Metal
S.I.C.: 6719; 5051; 3441
Melvin T. Kemp *(Chief Exec. Officer)*
Lael P. Boman *(Pres.)*
Lloyd Grantham *(V.P.-Engrng.)*

Outside Service Firm(s):

Tanners Place*(Auditors)*
Salt Lake City, UT

Zions National Bank*(Major Banking Relationship)*
Ogden, UT

Subsidiary:

Boman & Kemp Steel & Supply Company **(1)**
2393 S. 1900 W.
Ogden, UT 84401
Tel.: 801-731-0615
Fabricated Structural Metal; Steel
S.I.C.: 3441; 5051
Lael P. Boman *(Pres.)*

BA ADVERTISING
6500 Greenville Ave., Ste. 665
Dallas, TX 75206
Tel.: 214-691-1304
Fax: 214-691-1315
Year Founded: 1983
Approx.Billings: $15,000,000
Emp.: 29
Automotive/Automotive Dealer Assns.
A. Chris Bryan, II *(Pres., Chief Exec. Officer, Sec. & Treas.)*
Don Eubank *(Chief Fin. Officer)*
Debbie Romine *(Controller)*
Donna Rucker *(Mktg. Dir.)*

B.A.S.S., INC.
5845 Carmichael Rd.
Montgomery, AL 36117
Mailing Address:
P.O. Box 17900
Montgomery, AL 36141
Tel.: 205-272-9530
Tel.: 800-477-2277
Fax: 205-279-7148
Year Founded: 1968
Assets: $17,467,000
Liabilities: $7,755,000
Net Worth: $9,712,000
Approx.Sls.: $28,000,000
Emp.: 150
Fiscal Year-end: 11/30/90
Import
Publisher; Service Organization
S.I.C.: 2721; 8641
Helen Sevier *(Chm. Bd., Pres., Chief Exec. & Chief Oper. Officer)*
Raney Grayson *(Chief Info. Officer)*
Robert D. Cobb *(V.P.-Communications)*
Karl Dabbs *(V.P.-Fin., Treas. & Sec.)*
Jim Davis *(Group V.P.)*
Faye Hood *(Controller)*
Delisa Boswell *(Dir.-Human Resources)*
Anita Capauno *(Dir.-Circulation & Mktg.)*
Bob Cobbs *(Dir.-Broadcast Production)*
Wayne Goble *(Dir.-Res. & Devel., Mkt. Res. & Librarian)*
Al Mills *(Dir.-Environmental)*
Jane Rea *(Dir.-Pur. & Corp. Travel Planner)*
Jose Valenti *(Dir.-Data Processing)*
Ken Woodard *(Dir.-Group Adv.)*
Principal(s):
Helen Sevier
Karl Dabbs
Jim Davis
Jemison Investments

No. of U.S. Offices: 1

Computer Systems/Hardware:
IBM, MAC, NCR & Basic IV

Outside Service Firm(s):

Deloitte & Touche*(Auditors)*
417 No. 20th St., Ste. 1000
Birmingham, AL 35203-3289
Tel.: 205-322-0534

Great American Insurance Co.*(Commercial Insurance Carrier)*
Montgomery, AL

The Travelers Insurance Co.*(Group Insurance Broker/Consult)*
Brentwood, TN

Jemison Investment, Inc.*(Investment Banker)*
Birmingham, AL

Berkowicz, Lefkowicz, Isom & Kurshner*(Legal Firm)*
Birmingham, AL
Tel.: 205-328-0480

SouthTrust Bank*(Major Banking Relationship)*
Birmingham, AL
Tel.: 205-254-5068

The Principal Group*(Pension Manager)*
Demoines, IA

Subsidiaries:

Bassmaster Magazine **(1)**
P.O. Box 17116
Montgomery, AL 36141
Tel.: 205-272-9530
Tel.: 800-477-2277
Fax: 205-279-7148
Emp.: 15
Consumer Magazine Publishing
S.I.C.: 2741; 2721; 8641
Dave Precht *(Editor)*
Helen Sevier *(Chief Oper. Officer)*
Karl Dabbs *(Chief Fin. Officer)*
Ken Woodard *(Dir.-Sls.)*
Jane Rea *(Dir.-Pur.)*
Hunter Cole *(Mgr.-Adv.)*

Fishing Tackle Retailer **(1)**
P.O. Box 17151
Montgomery, AL 36141
Tel.: 205-272-9530
Fax: 205-279-7148
Emp.: 3
Publishing- Trade Magazine
S.I.C.: 2741; 2721
Dave Ellison *(Editor)*
Helen Sevier *(Chief Oper. Officer)*
Karl Dabbs *(Chief Fin. Officer)*
Clem Dippel *(Dir.-Sls. & Adv.)*

B.A.S.S., Inc.—(Continued)

Southern Outdoors Magazine **(1)**
P.O. Box 17915
Montgomery, AL 36141
Tel.: 205-272-3940
Fax: 205-279-7148
Emp.: 10
Consumer Magazine
S.I.C.: 2741; 2721
Larry Teague *(Editor)*
Helen Sevier *(Chief Oper. Officer)*
Karl Dabbs *(Chief Fin. Officer)*
Ken Woodard *(Dir.-Sls.)*
Mike Swain *(Dir.-Adv.)*

Southern Saltwater Magazine **(1)**
P.O. Box 17055
Montgomery, AL 36141
Tel.: 205-272-9530
Fax: 205-279-7148
Emp.: 5
Magazine
S.I.C.: 2741; 2721
Colin Moore *(Editor)*
Helen Sevier *(Chief Oper. Officer)*
Karl Dabbs *(Chief Fin. Officer)*
Ken Woodard *(Dir.-Sls.)*
Gordon Andrews *(Dir.-Mktg.)*

BCM ENGINEERS INC.
One Plymouth Meeting Mall
Plymouth Meeting, PA 19462
Tel.: 215-825-3800
Tel.: 800-221-1226 **DE**
Fax: 215-828-3347
Year Founded: 1890
Assets: $30,700,000
Liabilities: $18,300,000
Net Worth: $12,400,000
Approx.Sls.: $80,000,000
Emp.: 1,000
Fiscal Year-end: 12/31/91
Consulting Engineering & Design Services Including Plant Facilities, Environmental Services & Laboratory Services
S.I.C.: 8711; 8731; 8741
H.E. Myers, Jr. *(Chm. Bd.)*
Mark Z. Hanlon *(Pres.)*
James J. Jablonski *(Chief Fin. Officer & Sec.)*
Robert Ouellette *(Sr. V.P.-Mktg.)*
Thomas J. Baker *(Treas.)*
Darwin N. Roseberry *(Gen. Counsel)*
Norbert Kubilus *(Dir.-Data Processing)*
Brian Case *(Mgr.-Pub. Rels.)*
Joan M. Hylinski *(Mgr.-Employee Benefits)*
Richard Romejko *(Mgr.-Corp. Recruiting)*
Principal(s):
Employee-Owned

No. of U.S. Offices: 22

Outside Service Firm(s):

Ernst & Young*(Auditors)*
1800 John F. Kennedy Blvd.
Philadelphia, PA 19103-7499
Tel.: 215-864-3300

Philadelphia National Bank*(Major Banking Relationship)*
P.O. Box 13834, Broad & Chestnut Streets
Philadelphia, PA 19101-7618
Tel.: 215-973-8327

Fidelity Institutional Retirement Services Co.*(Pension Manager)*
Boston, MA

BCP TECHNICAL SERVICE, INC.
401 Whitney Ave., Ste. 314
Gretna, LA 70056
Tel.: 504-361-4236 **FLA**
Fax: 504-362-8601
Year Founded: 1981
Approx.Sls.: $10,000,000
Emp.: 80
Fiscal Year-end: 6/30/92
Export
Nuclear Engineering Service & Technical Support; Oil Refineries
S.I.C.: 8711; 8712
Ronald L. Rowley *(Pres.)*
Chris Staubus *(V.P.)*

Outside Service Firm(s):

Kushner, LaGraize & Moore*(Auditors)*
New Orleans, LA

Hibernia National Bank*(Major Banking Relationship)*
New Orleans, LA

BEC ADVERTISING
(House Agency)
5701 N. Tripp
Chicago, IL 60646
Tel.: 312-583-3600
Tel.: 800-621-1275
Fax: 312-583-1955
Year Founded: 1975
Approx.Billings: $10,000,000
Emp.: 25
Direct Response
Dennis Roy *(Chief Oper. Officer & Dir., Mktg. Services)*
Cindy Lieberman *(Dir., Corp. Communications)*
Jean Snyder *(Mgr., Direct Response & Media)*
Joyce Sherry *(Adv. Mgr. & Creative Dir.)*
Les Winiarczyk *(Studio Supvr.)*

Computer Systems/Hardware:
IBM, MacIntosh

BEC INC.
37601 Logg Rd.
Richmond, MI 48062
Tel.: 313-365-4300 **MI**
Fax: 313-365-4739
Year Founded: 1962
Assets: $5,392,461
Liabilities: $3,959,743
Net Worth: $1,432,718
Approx.Sls.: $26,900,000
Emp.: 175
Fiscal Year-end: 9/30/88
Holding Co.; General Contractor Industrial & Commercial Buildings
S.I.C.: 6719; 1541; 1542
Mary L. Brickel *(Chm. Bd.)*
Jack W. Brickel *(Pres., Chief Exec. & Chief Oper. Officer & Dir.-Personnel)*
Principal(s):
Mary L. Brickel
Jack W. Brickel

No. of U.S. Offices: 1

Computer Systems/Hardware:
Burroughs

Outside Service Firm(s):

Jan Chapski*(Auditors)*
Livonia, MI

Security Bank & Trust*(Major Banking Relationship)*
Richmond, MI

Sterling Ferguson Associates*(Commercial Insurance Carrier)*
Rochester, MI

Harold McDonald*(Legal Firm)*
Southfield, MI

Subsidiary:

Brencal Contractors Inc. **(1)**
6686 E. McNichols Rd.
Detroit, MI 48212
Tel.: 313-365-4300
Gen. Contractor
S.I.C.: 1541; 1542
Jack W. Brickel *(Pres. & Treas.)*
Ann Colo *(Personnel Dir.)*
Jerry Kopjo *(Engrng. Dir.)*
Karen Lassiter *(Data Processing Dir.)*
Shirley Rhein *(Pur. Dir.)*

B-E HOLDINGS INC.
1100 Milwaukee Ave.
South Milwaukee, WI 53172
Mailing Address:
P.O. Box 56
South Milwaukee, WI 53172
Tel.: 414-768-4000
Fax: 414-768-5060
Approx.Sls.: $191,030,000
Emp.: 763
Fiscal Year-end: 12/31/90
Mfr. of Energy Products; Mining Machinery, Walking Draglines, Electric Mining Shovel & Blast Hole Drills
S.I.C.: 3531; 3532
W.B. Winter *(Chm. & Chief Exec. Officer)*
R.G. Olander *(Vice Chm.)*
P.W. Mork *(Pres.)*
J.H. Westerman *(V.P.-Mktg.)*
N.J. Verville *(V.P., Treas. & Controller)*
R.D. Vitale *(V.P.)*
Jim Rossle *(Dir.-Adv.)*
D.M. Goelzer *(Sec. & Gen. Counsel)*

BE & K, INC.
2000 International Park Dr.
Birmingham, AL 35243
Mailing Address:
P.O. Box 2332,
Birmingham, AL 35201
Tel.: 205-972-6000 **DE**
Fax: 205-972-6300
Year Founded: 1972
Sales Range: $500-999 Million
Emp.: 2,800
Fiscal Year-end: 3/31/90
Industrial Engineering & Construction, Construction Management, Consulting & Commercial Developer
S.I.C.: 1541; 8711; 6552
T.C. Kennedy *(Chm. Bd.)*
T.M. Goodrich *(Pres.)*
C.M. Smith *(V.P. & Chief Fin. Officer)*
Frank Hull *(Dir.-Pur.)*
W.H. Rubar *(Asst. Controller)*
Principal(s):
T.C. Kennedy
T.M. Goodrich

No. of U.S. Offices: 13
No. of Foreign Offices: 1

Computer Systems/Hardware:
Hewlett Packard 58

Outside Service Firm(s):

Bradley, Arant, Rose & White*(Legal Firm)*
1400 Park Place Tower
Birmingham, AL 35203
Tel.: 205-521-8000

AmSouth Bank N.A.*(Major Banking Relationship)*
P.O. Box 11426
Birmingham, AL 35202
Tel.: 205-326-5321

B & G WHOLESALERS, INC.
337 28th Ave., N.
Nashville, TN 37209
Tel.: 615-320-7292 **TN**
Fax: 615-321-4173
Approx.Sls.: $27,000,000
Emp.: 80
Wine & Distilled Beverages
S.I.C.: 5182
Thomas E. Bernard *(Pres.)*
Ann Bernard *(Treas.)*
Kim Conard *(Controller)*
James Armstrong *(Mgr.-Sls.)*
Henry McKinnon *(Mgr.-Opers.)*
Austin White *(Sls. Advisor)*

Outside Service Firm(s):

R. Edward Demars & Associates*(Auditors)*
Nashville, TN

First American National Bank*(Major Banking Relationship)*
Nashville, TN

BGW SYSTEMS, INC.
13130 Yukon Ave.
Hawthorne, CA 90250
Tel.: 310-973-8090 **CA**
Fax: 310-676-6713
Year Founded: 1971
Sales Range: $10-19 Million
Emp.: 100
Import Export
Professional Audio Equipment
S.I.C.: 3651
Brian Gary Wachner *(Chm. Bd. & Pres.)*
Barbara Jo Wachner *(Exec. V.P.-Mktg., Personnel & Sec.)*
Donald Carson *(Controller)*

Computer Systems/Hardware:
IBM System 34

Outside Service Firm(s):

Bank of America NT&SA*(Major Banking Relationship)*
555 So. Flower St., 5th Fl.
Los Angeles, CA 90071
Tel.: 213-228-3526
Fax: 213-228-4062

B. H. AIRCRAFT CO., INC.
441 Eastern Parkway
Farmingdale, NY 11735
Tel.: 516-249-5000
Fax: 516-249-5009
Sales Range: $10-19 Million
Emp.: 150
Mfr. of Aircraft Engine Parts
S.I.C.: 3724
Vincent E. Kearns *(Pres.)*
Robert F. Kearns *(Exec. V.P.)*
Joseph A. Scafidi *(V.P.-Engrng.)*
Leonard Grant *(Pur. Agent)*

Outside Service Firm(s):

KPMG Peat Marwick*(Auditors)*
1 Jericho Plaza
Jericho, NY 11753
Tel.: 516-822-9100

Marine Midland Bank*(Major Banking Relationship)*
250 Park Ave.
New York, NY 10017
Tel.: 212-503-6642

BIW CABLE SYSTEMS, INC.
22 Joseph E. Warner Blvd.
North Dighton, MA 02764
Tel.: 508-822-6600 **MA**
Fax: 508-822-1944
Year Founded: 1905
Assets: $31,416,916
Liabilities: $6,487,559
Net Worth: $24,929,357
Approx.Sls.: $44,888,301
Emp.: 230
Fiscal Year-end: 12/31/90
Export
Manufacturer of Electrical Wire, Cable & Connectors
S.I.C.: 3357; 3643
S.J. van Kesteren *(Chm. Bd.)*
J. Pirrong *(Pres. & Chief Exec. Officer)*
Donald N. Leef *(V.P., Chief Fin. Officer & Treas.)*
Stephen M. Adams *(V.P.)*
Frederick Schwelm *(V.P.-Mfg.)*
Norman A. Bikales *(Sec. & Clerk)*
Shirley O'Neill *(Personnel Dir.)*
John Manning *(Pur. Dir.)*
Mary Dolbec *(Adv. Coord.)*

Outside Service Firm(s):

KPMG Peat Marwick*(Auditors)*
One Boston Place
Boston, MA 02108
Tel.: 617-723-7700

Sullivan & Worcester*(Legal Firm)*
One Post Office Square, 100 Federal St.
Boston, MA 02110
Tel.: 617-338-2800

Bay Bank Harvard Trust Company*(Major Banking Relationship)*
Boston, MA

Subsidiary:

BIW Cable Systems-Connector Systems Div. **(1)**
500 Tesconi Circle
Santa Rosa, CA 95401
Tel.: 707-523-2300
Mfr. of Electrical Wire, Cable & Connectors
S.I.C.: 3643; 3357
E.G. Barss *(Pres.)*

Non-U.S. Holding:

Boston Insulated Wire & Cable Co. Ltd. **(1)**
1800 Ironstone Dr.
Burlington, ON L7L 5V3, Canada
Tel.: 416-336-3800 (100%)
Emp.: 57
Electrical Wire & Cable
S.I.C.: 3357
Ron Whitelock *(Mgr.-Mktg.)*

BJ ACQUISITION CORP.
9600 H. Southern Pine Blvd.
Charlotte, NC 28273
Mailing Address:
P.O. Box 24039,
Charlotte, NC 28224
Tel.: 704-527-2675
Fax: 704-523-6803
Year Founded: 1990
Assets: $30,088,000
Liabilities: $27,340,000
Net Worth: $2,748,000
Approx.Sls.: $31,646,000
Emp.: 1,850
Fiscal Year-end: 12/31/91
Franchised Fast Food Restaurants
S.I.C.: 5812
Tom Turpin *(Chm. Bd.)*
Dick Campbell *(Pres. & Chief Exec. Officer)*
Kurt Kenkel *(V.P. Fin.)*
Jim Elkin *(V.P.-Plng. & Devel.)*
Dave Maisel *(V.P.-Opers.)*
Eric H. Newman *(V.P. & Legal Counsel)*
Randy Poindexter *(V.P.-Mktg.)*
Dave Rush *(V.P.-Controller)*
Joe Santaniello *(V.P.-Pur. System & Admin.)*
Dick Winters *(V.P.-Human Resources)*
Victor Webber *(V.P.-Real Estate)*
Karen Braswell *(Mktg. Mgr.)*

Computer Systems/Hardware:
Novell Network

BKM ENTERPRISES, INC.
222 Pitkin St.
East Hartford, CT 06108
Tel.: 203-528-9981
Fax: 203-528-1843
Approx.Sls.: $62,000,000
Emp.: 122
Wholesale Office Furniture & Carpets; Retail Office Furniture & Supplies
S.I.C.: 5021; 5023; 5712
Donald Griesdorn *(Chief Exec. Officer)*
Donald Northrup *(Pres.)*
Peter J. Murgio *(Exec. V.P.)*
Dan Sabia *(V.P.-Fin.)*

Division:

BKM Total Office Today, Inc. **(1)**
222 Pitkin St.
East Hartford, CT 06108
Tel.: 203-528-9981
Wholesale Office Furniture & Carpets; Retail Office Furniture & Supplies
S.I.C.: 5021; 5023; 5712
Donald Griesdorn *(Pres.)*

BLH ELECTRONICS
75 Shawmut
Canton, MA 02021
Tel.: 617-821-2000
Telex: 172116
Fax: 617-828-1451
Approx.Sls.: $20,000,000
Emp.: 200
Import Export
Mfrs. Strain Gages, Transducers, Process Control Instruments & Systems
S.I.C.: 3674; 3679
T. Selig *(Pres.)*
J. Szostek *(V.P.-Mktg.)*
Martin Rosen *(Controller)*
R. Dennis Windsor *(Supvr.-Mktg. Services)*
Gregory Davis *(Pur. Agent)*

BSA ADVERTISING, INC.
360 Lexington Ave.
New York, NY 10017
Tel.: 212-599-6600
Tel.: 800-272-4237
Fax: 212-599-6609
Year Founded: 1946
Approx.Billings: $40,000,000
Emp.: 200
Recruitment Adv.
Bernard H. Kaplan *(Pres.)*
Wendy Surkis *(Dir., Opers.)*

B.T.F. CORPORATION
450 Murray Hill Pkwy.
East Rutherford, NJ 07073
Tel.: 201-935-4611
Fax: 201-935-1432
Approx.Sls.: $20,000,000
Emp.: 200
Manufacture Knit Fabrics
S.I.C.: 2259
Ben Fried *(Pres.)*
Eda Sorokoff *(V.P.)*
Stephen Sorokoff *(V.P.)*
Tamara Fried *(Sec.)*

Outside Service Firm(s):

Konigberg, Wolf & Co.*(Auditors)*
New York, NY

National Westminster Bank plc*(Major Banking Relationship)*
Astor Plaza, 1515 Broadway
New York, NY 10036

BTG, INC.
1945 Old Gallows Rd.
Vienna, VA 22182
Tel.: 703-556-6518 **VA**
Fax: 703-556-9290
Year Founded: 1982
Approx.Sls.: $27,500,000
Emp.: 300
Data Telephone Communications
S.I.C.: 4813
Dr. Edward H. Bersoff *(Pres.)*
Harry P. Ridenour, Jr. *(V.P.-Fin.)*
Marilyn Bersoff *(Sec. & Treas.)*

Outside Service Firm(s):

C&S Sovran Bank*(Major Banking Relationship)*
P.O. Box 26904,
Richmond, VA 23261
Tel.: 804-344-1359

B-W ADVERTISING AGENCY

P.O. Box 10203
Phoenix, AZ 85064-0203
Tel.: 602-957-5728
Fax: 602-957-5942
Year Founded: 1971
Approx.Billings: $11,114,000
Emp.: 15
Lodging & Travel Adv.
Troy W. Davis *(Chm. Bd.-Best Western Intl.)*
John P. McCoy *(Vice Chm.-Best Western Intl.)*
Ronald Evans *(Pres. & Chief Exec. Officer-Best Western Intl.)*
Robert Fitzgerald *(Chief Oper. Officer-Best Western Intl.)*
William Watson *(Sr. V.P.-Mktg., Best Western Intl.)*
Vicki Cabianca *(Dir.)*

B&W CO-OP, INC.
216 Eastman
Breckenridge, MI 48615
Mailing Address:
P.O. Box 518
Breckenridge, MI 48615
Tel.: 517-842-3104
Tel.: 1-800-968-2068 **MI**
Fax: 517-842-3104
Year Founded: 1957
Assets: $22,546,466
Liabilities: $12,027,157
Net Worth: $10,519,309
Approx.Sls.: $64,716,341
Emp.: 90
Fiscal Year-end: 6/31/92
Export
Cooperative; Dry Edible Beans, Grain, Farm Supplies
S.I.C.: 0119; 5153; 5191
Michael Trees *(Chief Exec. Officer)*
Phil Barlett *(V.P.-Plant Opers.)*
Cynthia Gulick *(Controller)*
Larry Schmitz *(Corp. Admin.)*
Don Beard *(Mgr.-Fertilizer Sls.)*
Barry Marlow *(Mgr.-Farm Service)*
Bob Zimmerman *(Mgr.-Seed & Chemical Sls.)*

No. of Mfg. Plants/Facilities: 7
No. of U.S. Offices: 1

Computer Systems/Hardware:
Datapoint

Outside Service Firm(s):

McCartney & McIntyre*(Auditors)*
Lansing, MI

American Community Mutual Insurance Co.*(Commercial Insurance Carrier)*
Livonia, MI

Michigan Mill Mutual*(Group Insurer)*
Lansing, MI

Masuad Associates*(Legal Firm)*
Saginaw, MI

Saint Paul Bank for Cooperatives*(Major Banking Relationship)*
Saint Paul, MN

Subsidiary:

B & W Farm Center **(1)**
7581 E. Monroe
Breckenridge, MI 48615
Tel.: 517-842-3141
Emp.: 35
Distribute Farm Machinery
S.I.C.: 5083
Jim Zimmerman *(Mgr.)*

BAAR & BEARDS
15 W. 37th
New York, NY 10018-6201
Tel.: 212-391-6606
Fax: 212-391-8174
Year Founded: 1937
Approx.Sls.: $14,000,000
Emp.: 500
Ladies Scarves & Accessories
S.I.C.: 2339; 2389
Ted Markson *(Pres.)*
Irwin Perlow *(Exec. V.P.)*
Amelia Alfonto *(Dir.-Pub. Rels.)*

BABCOCK LUMBER COMPANY
2220 Palmer St.
Pittsburgh, PA 15218
Tel.: 412-351-3515
Fax: 412-351-1522
Year Founded: 1887
Sales Range: $100-499 Million
Emp.: 400
Wholesale Lumber & Building Supplies; Manufacture & Process Domestic & Foreign Hardwoods
S.I.C.: 2426; 5031
Fred C. Babcock *(Chm. Bd.)*
Carl P. Stilitano *(Pres.)*

No. of Mfg. Plants/Facilities: 13

Computer Systems/Hardware:
IBM

Outside Service Firm(s):

Price Waterhouse*(Auditors)*
600 Grant St., Ste. 4400
Pittsburgh, PA 15219
Tel.: 412-355-6000
Fax: 412-391-0609

Kirkpatrick & Lockhart*(Legal Firm)*
1500 Oliver Bldg., 535 Smithfield St.
Pittsburgh, PA 15222
Tel.: 412-355-6500
Fax: 412-355-6501

THE BABCOCK & WILCOX COMPANY
1010 Common St.
New Orleans, LA 70161
Tel.: 504-587-5700
Fax: 504-587-6153
Year Founded: 1867
Approx.Rev.: $1,600,000,000
Emp.: 12,000
Fiscal Year-end: 3/31/91
Import Export
Mfr. of Power Generation Products, Systems & Services
S.I.C.: 3621; 1629; 3255; 3312; 3443; 3492; 3542
Robert E. Howson *(Chm. & Chief Exec. Officer)*
John P. Eckert *(Pres. & Chief Oper. Officer)*
Robert W. Page *(Exec. V.P. & Grp. Exec.)*
Joseph J. Stewart *(Exec. V.P. & Grp. Exec.)*
Brock A. Hattox *(Sr. V.P. & Chief Fin. Officer)*
Richard E. Woolbert *(Sr. V.P. & Chief Admin. Officer)*
Frank C. Allen *(V.P., Sec. & Gen. Counsel)*
George J. Clessuras *(V.P. & Gen. Mgr.)*
Marion Edward Eagles *(V.P.-Mktg.)*
William M. Farrell *(V.P. & Gen. Mgr.)*
Thomas A. Henzler *(V.P.-Tax)*
Elbert O. Hooker *(V.P. & Gen. Mgr.)*
Paul P. Koenderman *(V.P. & Gen. Mgr.)*
George A. Stoddart *(V.P.-Corp. Communications)*
John R. Woolsey *(V.P. & Gen. Mgr.)*
John E. Pollock *(V.P.)*
Edgar A. Womack *(V.P.-Res. & Devel.)*
Robert A. Joliff *(Treas.)*
D.R. Ganbert *(V.P. & Controller)*

BABY TOGS, INC.
460 W. 34th St.
New York, NY 10001
Tel.: 212-868-2100 **NY**
Year Founded: 1942
Approx.Sls.: $50,000,000
Emp.: 150
Mfr. of Girls', Children's & Infants Shirts & Playsuits; Girls' & Children's Slacks
S.I.C.: 2361; 2369
Celia Sitt *(Chm. Bd.)*
Eddie Sitt *(Pres.)*

Baby Togs, Inc.—(Continued)

Herbert Missry *(V.P.-Mktg.)*
Jack Sitt *(V.P.)*

Outside Service Firm(s):

Chase Manhattan Bank, N.A.*(Major Banking Relationship)*
One Chase Manhattan Plaza
New York, NY 10081
Tel.: 212-552-2222
Tel.: 800-526-0801
Fax: 212-552-7175

BACARDI IMPORTS, INC.
2100 Biscayne Blvd.
Miami, FL 33137
Tel.: 305-573-8511
Fax: 305-573-0756
Year Founded: 1944
Approx.Sls.: $580,000,000
Emp.: 288
Fiscal Year-end: 12/31/91
Import
Wholesale Wine, Liquor & Soft Drinks
S.I.C.: 5182; 5149; 5142
Corporate Giving Program: Contact Company for Further Information On Corporate Giving Program
Juan Grau *(Chm. Bd., Pres. & Chief Exec. Officer)*
Eduardo M. Sardina *(Exec. V.P. & Chief Oper. Officer)*
Steven Naclerio *(Sr. V.P. & Gen. Counsel)*
Jose Aragon *(V.P.-Human Resources)*
Rodolfo Ruiz *(V.P.-Fin. & Chief Fin. Officer)*
W.W. Tovell *(V.P.-Mktg.)*
T.A. Valdes *(V.P.-Sls.)*
William P. Anderson *(Asst. V.P.-Corp. Plng./MIS)*
Jorge Larrieu *(Asst. V.P.-Admin./ Oper.)*
Alfredo Piedra *(Asst. V.P.-Mktg.)*
Ibrahim Rosell *(Asst. V.P. & Controller)*
K.C. Smith *(Asst. V.P.-Mktg.)*
Gail Matthews *(Dir.-Pub. Rels.)*
Michael Shea *(Mgr.-Personnel Training & Devel.)*
Victoria Ascione *(Supvr.-Employee Benefits)*
Jose Argamasilla *(Corporate Travel Planner)*

Computer Systems/Hardware:
IBM System 36

Outside Service Firm(s):

Deloitte & Touche*(Auditors)*
100 S.E. 2nd St.
Miami, FL 33131-2135
Tel.: 305-538-4141

Insurance Company of North America*(Commercial Insurance Carrier)*
1600 Arch St.
Philadelphia, PA 19103
Tel.: 215-523-4000

Travelers Insurance Co.*(Group Insurer)*
1 Tower Square
Hartford, CT 06183-2492
Tel.: 203-277-4542
Fax: 203-277-5038

Kelley Drye & Warren*(Legal Firm)*
350 Park Ave.
New York, NY 10022
Tel.: 212-752-5800
Fax: 212-808-7800

Citibank N.A.*(Major Banking Relationship)*
Corporate Trust Services, 399 Park Ave.
New York, NY 10043
Tel.: 212-559-1605

Southeast Bank, N.A.*(Major Banking Relationship)*
1 Southeast Financial Center
Miami, FL 33131
Tel.: 305-666-5656

BACCO CONSTRUCTION CO.
P.O. Box 458
Iron Mountain, MI 49801
Tel.: 906-774-2616
Fax: 906-774-1160
Approx.Sls.: $15,000,000
Emp.: 175
Highway Construction, Industrial Site Preparation, Concrete Supply, Bituminous Concrete Paving
S.I.C.: 1611; 1771; 3273
Joseph J. Rigoni *(Chm. Bd.)*
John A. Fortier *(Pres.)*
Robert J. Rigoni *(Exec. V.P.)*
John A. Fortier, Jr. *(V.P.)*
Patricia L. Arnold *(Sec.)*
John Mouw *(Gen. Counsel)*
Douglas R. Rigoni *(Treas.)*
Charles D. Erickson *(Mgr.-Equipment)*

Outside Service Firm(s):

Fleury, Singer & Co.*(Auditors)*
Iron Mountain, MI

Mouw & Celello, P.C.*(Legal Firm)*
Iron Mountain, MI

First National Bank*(Major Banking Relationship)*
Iron Mountain, MI

BACHARACH INC.
625 Alpha Dr.
Pittsburgh, PA 15238
Tel.: 412-963-2000
Fax: 412-963-2091
Year Founded: 1909
Approx.Sls.: $40,000,000
Emp.: 321
Fiscal Year-end: 12/31/90
Export
Manufacturer of Mechanical, Chemical & Electrical Measuring Instruments; Fyrite, Monoxor, Tempscribe, Draftrite & Tempoint, Diesel Service Equipment, Gas Detection Instruments
S.I.C.: 3825
Paul M. Zito *(Pres. & Chief Exec. Officer)*
Edward Startari *(Sr. V.P.-Opers.)*
William Raible *(V.P. & Controller)*
Daniel Strafalace *(V.P.-Sls.)*
J. Wolf *(V.P.-Engrng.)*
John Figan *(Sls. Mgr.-Testing & Measurement Prods.)*

Outside Service Firm(s):

Blue Cross of Western Pennsylvania*(Group Insurer)*
One Smithfield St.
Pittsburgh, PA 15222
Tel.: 1-800-242-6425

BACHMAN COMPANY
50 N. 4th St.
Reading, PA 19601
Mailing Address:
P.O. Box 15053
Reading, PA 19612-5053
Tel.: 215-320-7800
Tel.: 800-523-8253
Fax: 215-320-7897
Year Founded: 1884
Approx.Sls.: $75,000,000
Emp.: 530
Fiscal Year-end: 12/31/91
Export
Mfr. Snack Foods: Pretzels, Potato Chips, Popcorn, Cheese Twists, Corn Chips, Tortilla Chips, Pellet Snacks
S.I.C.: 2096; 2099
Joseph F. Welch *(Chm., Pres. & Chief Exec. Officer)*
John Mastromarino *(Vice Chm.)*
Lou Trager *(V.P.-Admin.)*
Ronald G. Meacham *(V.P.-Sls. & Mktg.)*
Cyril Banko *(V.P.-Pur.)*
Rory Emery *(V.P.-Acctg.)*
John George *(V.P.-Personnel)*
Karen Fidler *(Dir.-Mktg.)*
Steven Peck *(Dir.-Mktg.)*

Computer Systems/Hardware:
IBM AS400

BACHMANN INDUSTRIES, INC.
1400 E. Erie Ave.
Philadelphia, PA 19124
Tel.: 215-533-1600
Fax: 215-744-4699
Approx.Sls.: $25,000,000
Emp.: 70
Fiscal Year-end: 12/31/91
Import Export
Plastic Articles By Injection, Plasticville U.S.A. Toys, Scaled Model Train Sets & Access. in 'HO', 'N', & 'G' Scales
S.I.C.: 3612; 5162
Kenneth Ting *(Chm. Bd.)*
Shirley Chow *(V.P.-Fin. & Sec.)*
Richard Maddox *(V.P.-Sls. & Mktg.)*
George Haggerty *(Plant Mgr.)*
Manohar Hattangadi *(Adv. Mgr.)*
Frank Lippincott *(Mgr.-Pur.)*

Computer Systems/Hardware:
VMS/VAX Digital

BACHMAN'S, INC.
6010 Lyndale Ave. S.
Minneapolis, MN 55419 **MN.**
Tel.: 612-861-7600
Fax: 612-861-7730
Year Founded: 1885
Approx.Sls.: $173,000,000
Emp.: 1,000
Fiscal Year-end: 1/31/92
Import
Floral, Nursery, Garden, Gift Merchandise
S.I.C.: 5261; 5331
Corporate Giving Program: Require Written Submission To Contribution Committee
Stanley F. Bachman *(Chm. Bd.)*
Dale L. Bachman *(Pres.)*
Richard Herberg *(Chief Oper. Officer & V.P.-Mktg.)*
Lee W. Bachman *(V.P.-Fin. & Treas.)*
Michael Bonk *(V.P. & Controller)*
Alan Bachman *(V.P. & Sec.)*
Paul Bachman *(V.P.)*
Judy Paul *(Dir.-Human Resources)*

No. of Mfg. Plants/Facilities: 4
No. of U.S. Offices: 3
No. of Foreign Offices: 1

Computer Systems/Hardware:
IBM AS/400

Outside Service Firm(s):

Coopers & Lybrand*(Auditors)*
1000 TCF Bldg.
Minneapolis, MN 55402
Tel.: 612-293-2929
Fax: 612-370-9395

Ernest Lindstrom, Ltd.*(Legal Firm)*
Minneapolis, MN

First National Bank of Minneapolis*(Major Banking Relationship)*
P.O. Box A799
Minneapolis, MN 55480
Tel.: 612-370-4606

BACKER SPIELVOGEL BATES WORLDWIDE, INC.
The Chrysler Bldg., 405 Lexington Ave.
New York, NY 10174
Tel.: 212-297-7000
Telex: 423171
Fax: 212-986-0270
Year Founded: 1940
Approx.Billings: $5,400,000,000
Advertising Agencies
S.I.C.: 7311
Carl Spielvogel *(Chm. & Chief Exec. Officer)*
Alvin A. Achenbaum *(Vice Chm.-Professional Services)*
William M. Backer *(Pres. & Exec. Creative Dir.)*
John N. Citron *(Exec. V.P., Fin. & Admin.)*
Anne M. Melanson *(Exec. V.P., Dir. Human Resources)*
Judy Torello *(Sr. V.P., Dir. Corp. Communications)*
Kim Walker *(Sr. V.P.-Multinatl. Bus. Devel.)*

Subsidiaries:

Backer Spielvogel Bates, Inc. **(1)**
The Chrysler Bldg., 405 Lexington Ave.
New York, NY 10174
Tel.: 212-297-7000
Telex: 423171
Fax: 212-986-0270
Advertising
S.I.C.: 7311
Kenneth R. Rogers *(Pres. & Chief Oper. Officer)*
Norman Bierman *(Exec. V.P., Acct. Mngmt.)*
Edward G. Bonsaing *(Exec. V.P., Dir. Local Brdcst. & Field Opers.)*
Larry Chiagouris *(Exec. V.P., Dir. Strategic Plng. & Research)*
William Chororos *(Exec. V.P., Grp. Creative Dir.)*
Mel Epstein *(Exec. V.P., Chief Fin. Officer)*
Gordon Fenton *(Exec. V.P., Intl. Creative Dir.)*
Robert L. Froelich *(Exec. V.P., Grp. Creative Dir.)*
Jerry Gottlieb *(Exec. V.P., Acct. Mngmt.)*
Randall W. Hackett *(Exec. V.P., Acct. Mngmt.)*
Anne M. Melanson *(Exec. V.P., Dir. Human Resources & Opers.)*
Ann Meschery *(Exec. V.P., Grp. Media Dir.)*
Mark R. Morris *(Exec. V.P., Acct. Mngmt.)*
Peter Murphy *(Exec. V.P., Grp. Creative Dir.)*
John Noble *(Exec. V.P., Creative Dir.)*
Charles Rutman *(Exec. V.P., Grp. Media Dir.)*
Jay B. Schoenfeld *(Exec. V.P., Media Dir.)*
Robert Silberberg *(Exec. V.P., Dir. Natl. Brdcst. & Programming)*
Jim White *(Exec. V.P., Creative Dir.)*
Rick Wysocki *(Exec. V.P., Dir. Creative Services)*
Bernard P. Dolan *(Sr. V.P., Treas.)*
Judith Feinerman *(Sr. V.P., Dir. Brdcst. Services)*
Craig Gugel *(Sr. V.P., Dir. Media Res. & Tech.)*
Tino Pelino *(Sr. V.P., Dir. Print Services)*
Merle Schell *(Sr. V.P., Dir. Bus. Devel.)*
Judy Torello *(Sr. V.P., Dir. Corp. Communications)*

Divisions:

BSB/Leff & Squicciarini **(2)**
94 N. High St., Ste. 300
Dublin, OH 43017
Tel.: 614-792-0555
Fax: 614-792-3301
Advertising
S.I.C.: 7311
Myron J. Leff *(Pres. & Gen. Mgr.)*
Robert Gale *(V.P., Mngmt. Rep.)*
Robbi White *(Office Supvr.)*

Backer Spielvogel Bates, Inc. **(2)**
2010 Main St., Ste. 700
Irvine, CA 92714
Tel.: 714-261-0330
Fax: 714-261-0548
Advertising
S.I.C.: 7311
E. Michael Roche *(Exec. V.P, Dir.-Western Region)*
John Noble *(Exec. V.P., Creative Dir.)*
James A. Sanfilippo *(Exec. V.P., Mngmt. Supvr.)*
Kevin Coyne *(Sr. V.P., Media Dir.)*
Susan Bock *(V.P., Admin.)*
Marilyn Rowe *(V.P., Bus. Affairs Dir.)*

Backer Spielvogel Bates, Inc. **(2)**
Eight Piedmont Ctr., Ste. 420
Atlanta, GA 30305
Tel.: 404-233-1613
Fax: 404-233-0579
Advertising
S.I.C.: 7311
Dan Craig *(V.P., Field Supvr.)*

Backer Spielvogel Bates, Inc. (2)
500 N. Michigan Ave., Ste. 2010
Chicago, IL 60611
Tel.: 312-464-0900
Fax: 312-464-0291
Advertising
S.I.C.: 7311
Kurt Kostur *(Field Acct. Exec.)*

Backer Spielvogel Bates, Inc. (2)
4322 N. Beltline Rd., Ste. B212
Irving, TX 75038
Tel.: 214-258-1742
Fax: 214-258-5932
Advertising
S.I.C.: 7311
Maynard Baker *(V.P., Field Supvr.)*

Backer Spielvogel Bates, Inc. (2)
384 Inverness Dr., South, Ste. 202
Englewood, CO 80112
Tel.: 303-799-9415
Fax: 303-799-9468
Advertising
S.I.C.: 7311
Doug Ochsner *(Field Acct. Exec.)*

Backer Spielvogel Bates, Inc. (2)
Vanguard Ctr., 23800 Ten Mile Rd., Ste. 228
Southfield, MI 48034
Tel.: 313-353-8990
Fax: 313-353-8193
Advertising
S.I.C.: 7311
Thomas Obradovic *(V.P., Field Supvr.)*

Backer Spielvogel Bates, Inc. (2)
2400 Veterans Memorial Blvd., Ste. 430
Kenner, LA 70062
Tel.: 504-468-5441
Fax: 504-468-5498
Advertising
S.I.C.: 7311
Earl Galle *(V.P., Sr. Field Acct. Exec.)*

Backer Spielvogel Bates, Inc. (2)
100 Spear St., Ste. 940
San Francisco, CA 94105
Tel.: 415-957-1034
Fax: 415-957-9288
Advertising
S.I.C.: 7311
Craig Alexander *(Field Acct. Exec.)*

Backer Spielvogel Bates, Inc. (2)
701 Emerson Rd., Ste. 290
Saint Louis, MO 63141
Tel.: 314-993-2266
Fax: 314-993-2144
Advertising
S.I.C.: 7311
Eric Gutberlet *(Field Acct. Exec.)*

Backer Spielvogel Bates, Inc. (2)
112 W. Pennsylvania Ave., Ste. 101
Bel Air, MD 21014
Tel.: 410-879-5280
Fax: 410-838-5751
Advertising
S.I.C.: 7311
Lee Nicholson *(Sr. V.P., Dir. Field Service Grp.)*

Backer Spielvogel Bates, Inc. (2)
650 Hampshire Rd., Ste. 210
Westlake Village, CA 91361
Tel.: 805-497-2006
Fax: 805-379-0344
Advertising
S.I.C.: 7311
Gerald M. Ross *(Sr. Field Acct. Exec.)*

Custom Event Marketing, Inc. (1)
633 Third Ave., 20th Fl.
New York, NY 10017
Tel.: 212-692-4080
Fax: 212-692-4095
Direct Marketing
S.I.C.: 7331
Elizabeth Phillips *(Pres.)*

Kobs & Draft Advertising, Inc. (1)
142 E. Ontario
Chicago, IL 60611
Tel.: 312-944-3500
Fax: 312-944-3566
Approx.Billings: $357,000,000
Emp.: 438
Direct Marketing Advertising
S.I.C.: 7331
Howard Draft *(Chm. Bd. & Chief Exec. Officer)*
Dan Ginsburg *(Pres.-K&D Worldwide)*
Sid Liebenson *(Exec. V.P., Dir. Mktg.)*
Richard Meyers *(Exec. V.P., Dir. Fin. & Treas.)*
David Florence *(Exec. V.P., Dir.-European Oper.)*
Ian Kennedy *(Exec. V.P., Dir.-Pacific Rim Region)*
Deb Coulson *(Sr. V.P., Reg. Dir.-K&D Asia)*
Yvonne Furth *(Exec. V.P., Gen. Mgr.)*
Sanford Moltz *(Exec. V.P., Exec. Creative Dir.)*
Thomas Brady *(Exec. V.P.)*
Sandra Toback *(Sr. V.P., Dir., Strategic Plng.)*

Non-U.S. Holdings:

Adshop (1)
Erottajankatu 11 SF 00130
Helsinki, Finland
Tel.: 0-644501
Fax: 0-641054
Advertising
S.I.C.: 7311
Teini Palo *(Mng. Dir.)*

Alas/D.P.P. (1)
Orense 12, 1st Fl., Office 10 28020
Madrid, Spain
Tel.: 1-5973108
Fax: 1-5971606
Advertising
S.I.C.: 7311
Juan Antonio Guerrero *(Mng. Dir.)*

Alas/DPP Barcelona S.A. (1)
Avda. Diagonal 615, 4A 08028
Barcelona, Spain
Tel.: 3-4192244
Fax: 3-4192607
Advertising
S.I.C.: 7311
Conrado Salas *(Dir.)*

Alas/DPP Valencia S.A. (1)
San Vicente 53-1 46002
Valencia, Spain
Tel.: 6-3521369
Fax: 6-3522425
Advertising
S.I.C.: 7311
Conrado Salas *(Dir.)*

Arellano/BSB Publicidad (1)
Goldsmith 225
Mexico, D.F. 5, Mexico
Tel.: 5-2501000
Telex: 383 176 3464
Fax: 5-5311460
Advertising
S.I.C.: 7311
Ignacio Arellano *(Pres.)*

Asset Marketing, Ltd. (1)
3 Park St.
Windsor, Berkshire SL4 1LU, United Kingdom
Tel.: 081-830267
Fax: 081-842129
S.I.C.: 7311
Jim Tattersall *(Mng. Dir.)*

Av-Kontakt A/S (1)
Munkedamsveien 35 P.O. Box 2464, 0202 Solli, Vika,
Oslo, 2, Norway
Tel.: 2-832626
Telex: 856-76151
Fax: 2-832170
Advertising
S.I.C.: 7311
Lasse Hovd *(Mgr.)*

BSB/Adaptus AB (1)
Kungsgatan 66 S-111 22
Stockholm, Sweden
Tel.: 8-230230
Fax: 8-110677
Advertising
S.I.C.: 7311
Ake Borgudd *(Mng. Dir.)*

BSB Amsterdam (1)
President Kennedylaan 1 1079 MB
Amsterdam, Netherlands
Tel.: 20-6448933
Telex: 844-16081
Fax: 20-6422545
Approx.Billings: $40,000,000
Emp.: 54
Full Service Advertising, Direct Marketing, Sales Promotion, Retail Advertising
S.I.C.: 7311
Boudewijn Hoogeweegen *(Chm. & Chief Exec. Officer)*
S. Bergsma *(Chief Fin. Officer)*

BSB Athens Advertising S.A. (1)
11b Konitsis St. 151 25 Maroussi,
Athens, Greece
Tel.: 1-8062208
Tel.: 1-8065704
Telex: 863-219802
Fax: 1-8053064
Approx.Billings: $6,300,000
Emp.: 45
Full Service Advertising
S.I.C.: 7311
Costas Papagiannacopoulos *(Chm., Mng. Dir. & Chief Exec. Officer)*

BSB Bates-Gruppen A/S (1)
Munkedamsveien 35, Solli P.O. Box 2464, 0202 Vika,
Oslo, 2, Norway
Tel.: 02-629700
Telex: 856-76151
Fax: 02-629770
Approx.Billings: $4,000,000
Emp.: 180
Full Service Advertising
S.I.C.: 7311
Anders Eckhoff *(Chm. Bd.)*
Arne A. Jensen *(Chief Exec. Officer)*
Jan-Erik Naess *(Exec. V.P.)*
Jan Hogebol *(Exec. V.P.)*
Hilmar Lunde *(Exec. V.P.)*
Mille Alstad *(Mgr., Personnel Dept.)*
Aage Eylertsen *(Fin. Dir.)*

BSB Brussels SA/NV (1)
26 Boulevard General Jacques 1050
Brussels, Belgium
Tel.: 2-6274711
Telex: 846-26335 COERTN-B
Fax: 2-6274779
Approx.Billings: $50,000,000
Emp.: 98
Full Service Advertising
S.I.C.: 7311
Andre Vrydagh *(Mng. Dir.)*

BSB/Canada Inc. (1)
2 St. Clair Ave. W.
Toronto, ON M4V 1L5, Canada
Tel.: 416-925-8835
Fax: 416-925-1206
Approx.Billings: $135,000,000
Emp.: 163
S.I.C.: 7311
Stan D. Buda *(Chm.)*
William J. Whitehead *(Chief Exec. Officer)*
Jai Narine *(V.P., Fin.)*

BSB/Canada Inc. (1)
1425 Blvd. Rene-Levesque Ouest Suite 300E,
Montreal, PQ H3G 1T7, Canada
Tel.: 514-861-5721
Fax: 514-861-0480
Approx.Billings: $15,000,000
Emp.: 17
S.I.C.: 7311
Ross MacKay *(Exec. V.P., Gen. Mgr.)*

BSB Chile Publicidad (1)
Galvarino Gallardo 1536
Santiago, Chile
Tel.: 2-2236077
Fax: 2-2231693
S.I.C.: 7311
Luis Mackenna *(Exec. Dir.)*

BSB City (1)
Lapinlahdenkatu 3A SF 00180
Helsinki, Finland
Tel.: 0-1344344
Fax: 0-6947758
Advertising
S.I.C.: 7311
Pekka Sillfors *(Mng. Dir.)*

BSB Dinfo (1)
Mikonkatu 8A SF 00100
Helsinki, Finland
Tel.: 0-134431
Fax: 0-13443334
Advertising
S.I.C.: 7311
Krister Kronlof *(Mng. Dir.)*

BSB Dorland Limited (1)
121-141 Westbourne Terrace
London, W2 6JR, United Kingdom
Tel.: 071-2625077
Telex: 851-27778
Fax: 071-2583757
Approx.Billings: $514,000,000
Emp.: 376
Full Service Advertising
S.I.C.: 7311
Michael Bungey *(Chm. & Chief Exec. Officer)*
Andrew Cracknell *(Vice Chm. & Exec. Creative Dir.)*
Neil Kennedy *(Exec. V.P.-BSB Europe)*
Les Stern *(Exec. Plng. Dir.)*
Roy Powell *(Fin. Dir.)*

BSB Europe (1)
121-141 Westbourne Terrace
London, W2 6JR, United Kingdom
Tel.: 071-2625077
Fax: 071-2583757
Advertising
S.I.C.: 7311
David Beecroft *(Regional Dir.)*

BSB Europe/The Eurocentre (1)
3 rue Bellini 92806
Puteaux, La Defense France
Tel.: 1-47764121
Telex: 842-6204446
Fax: 1-49010423
Advertising
S.I.C.: 7311
Tim Corrigan *(Exec. V.P., European Bus. Dir.)*

BSB Finnad Oy (1)
Mikonkatu 8 A SF 00100
Helsinki, Finland
Tel.: 0-134431
Telex: 857-126199 FINNBAT
Cable: Finnadco
Fax: 0-626566
Full Service Advertising
S.I.C.: 7311
Carl-Eric Holm *(Chm. & Chief Exec. Officer)*

BSB Finnad West (1)
Yliopistonkatu 33A SF 20100
Turku, Finland
Tel.: 21-336322
Fax: 21-331060
Advertising
S.I.C.: 7311
Hakan Nordstrom *(Mng. Dir.)*

BSB France (1)
3 rue Bellini 92806
Puteaux, La Defense France
Tel.: 1-47764121
Telex: 842-620446
Fax: 1-47730248
Approx.Billings: $6,816,300
Emp.: 80
Consumer Advertising, Sales Promotion & Public Relations
S.I.C.: 7311
Jean-Loup le Forestier *(Mng. Dir.)*
Jacques Masquelier *(Treas)*

BSB Frankfurt Werbeagentur GmbH (1)
Hanauer Landstrasse 287-289 Postfach 11 17 41, D-6000
Frankfurt/Main, 1, Germany
Tel.: 69-405 72 00
Telex: 411969
Fax: 69-405 72-359
Approx.Billings: $115,701,750
Emp.: 104
Advertising
S.I.C.: 7311
Albert Loschengruber *(Mng. Dir.)*
Gerd Wionski *(Fin. Dir.)*
Gerd Wionski *(Client Services Dir.)*

BSB/Ghersy-Quintero, C.A. Publicidad (1)
Av. La Estancia Centro, Banaven, Torre B, Piso 3 Chuao,
Caracas, Venezuela
Tel.: 2-924322
Telex: 395-28241/Ghersy Quintero
Fax: 2-919239
Advertising
S.I.C.: 7311
Gustavo Ghersy *(Pres.)*

Backer Spielvogel Bates Worldwide, Inc.—(Continued)

BSB Goteborg AB (1)
Jarntorget 413 04
Goteborg, Sweden
Tel.: 31-420770
Fax: 31-146958
Advertising
S.I.C.: 7311
Carl-Erik Mossberg *(Mng. Dir.)*

BSB Graffix Limited (1)
1201 Kam Chung Bldg., 52-54 Jaffee Rd.
Wanchai, Hong Kong
Tel.: 5-5272766
Fax: 5-8611216
Advertising
S.I.C.: 7311
Jerry Green *(Gen. Mgr.)*

BSB Helsingborg AB (1)
Kullagatan 30 Box 802, 251 08
Helsingborg, Sweden
Tel.: 42-127830
Fax: 42-123562
Advertising
S.I.C.: 7311
Jan Hedlund *(Dir.)*

BSB Hong Kong (1)
2/F Asian House, 1 Hennessy Rd.
Hong Kong, Hong Kong
Tel.: 852 823 0111
Telex: HX65321 BATES
Fax: 852 861 3935
Approx.Billings: $51,000,000
Emp.: 125
Computer Systems/Hardware:
IBM AS400
Full Service: Creative, Media, Direct Marketing
S.I.C.: 7311
Chris Jaques *(Chief Exec. Officer)*
Jeffrey Yu *(Mng. Dir.)*
Lawren Yuen *(Fin. Dir. & Sec.)*

BSB Hunter Advertising (1)
9/10 Upper Pembroke St.
Dublin, 2, Ireland
Tel.: 760221
Telex: 852-90111
Fax: 765201
Approx.Billings: $20,000,000
Emp.: 40
Advertising
S.I.C.: 7311
Gareth J. Oldham *(Chm. & Chief Exec. Officer)*

BSB Indonesia (1)
3rd Fl., Wisma Sejahtera, J1 S. Parman Kav. 75 Slipi,
Jakarta, 11410, Indonesia
Tel.: 21-5485105
Telex: 796-62017 BATES JA
Fax: 21-5480242
Approx.Billings: $9,000,000
Emp.: 50
Consumer Products Advertising
S.I.C.: 7311
Amri Noor *(Gen. Mgr.)*
Timotheus Suherman *(Controller)*

BSB Italia (1)
Via Paleocapa 7 20121
Milan, Italy
Tel.: 2-722231
Fax: 2-867469
Approx.Billings: $83,149,000
Emp.: 68
Full Service Advertising
S.I.C.: 7311
Giorgio Lodi *(Mng. Dir.)*
Ezio Castiglioni *(Chief Fin. Officer)*
Margherita Venturelli *(Pub. Rels. Dir., New Bus. Contact & External Rels. Dir.)*
Sergio Baratelli *(Client Services Dir.)*

BSB Italia (1)
Via Romagnosi, 18/A 00196
Rome, Italy
Tel.: 6-3222581
Fax: 6-3222588
Advertising
S.I.C.: 7311
Roberto Onofri *(Creative Dir.)*

BSB Japan Ltd. (1)
Shibaura Square Bldg., 4-9-25, Shibaura, Minato-ku
Tokyo, 108, Japan
Tel.: 3-34554123
Telex: 781-2223644
Cable: ADORIKOMI, TOKYO
Fax: 3-34539633
Approx.Billings: $56,000,000
Emp.: 59
Advertising
S.I.C.: 7311
Carl Spielvogel *(Chm. & Chief Exec. Officer (BSB Worldwide Inc.))*
David Meredith *(Pres. & New Business Contact)*
Kazuo Watanabe *(Pres.-ORIKOMI Ltd.)*
Alex Snyder *(Chief Fin. Officer)*
Yoshi Kawashima *(Exec. V.P.)*
Yuko Kuriyama *(Corp. Sec)*
Yuzo Umemoto *(Admin./Opers.)*

BSB Madco (1)
P.O. Box 161, Deira,
Dubai, United Arab Emirates
Tel.: 4-694550
Telex: 47158 click em
Fax: 4-694783
Approx.Billings: $17,500,000
Emp.: 35
Full Service Advertising
S.I.C.: 7311
Burhan S. Beidas *(Chief Exec. Officer & Mng. Partner)*

BSB Malaysia Sdn. Bhd. (1)
11th Fl., Pernas Intl., Jalan Sultan Ismail 50250
Kuala Lumpur, Malaysia
Tel.: 3-2610290
Telex: 784-31056
Fax: 3-2610327
Advertising
S.I.C.: 7311
Stephen Brown *(Mng. Dir.)*
Gerald Miranda *(Dir. & Corp. Sec.)*

BSB Media & Research (1)
Mikonkatu 8A 8F 00100
Helsinki, Finland
Tel.: 0-134431
Fax: 0-626566
Advertising
S.I.C.: 7311
Pirjo Paavolainen *(Mng. Dir.)*

BSB Medical (1)
Via Paleocapa 7 20121
Milan, Italy
Tel.: 2-72223 1
Telex: 843-311155
Fax: 2-867469
Emp.: 20
Advertising
S.I.C.: 7311
Leonardo Vinci *(Mng. Dir.)*

BSB/Meza, Ltda. (1)
Calle 97 A, #9 A-18 P.O. Box 29960,
Bogota, Colombia
Tel.: 6111634
Tel.: 1-2578117
Telex: 396-45242
Fax: 1-2180627
Approx.Billings: $10,700,000
Emp.: 54
Marketing & Advertising
S.I.C.: 7311
Gonzalo Meza *(Chm. & Pres.)*
Catalina Meza *(Chief Oper. Officer, Mng. Dir. & Chief Fin. Officer)*
Juan Carlos Mejia *(Exec. V.P.-Client Services/Special Projects & New Bus. Contact)*
Fernando Valencia *(V.P., Client Services)*
America Villabona *(Sec.)*

BSB Naess & Morch A/S (1)
Parkveien 60 P.O. Box 2464 Solli, 0202
Oslo, 2, Norway
Tel.: 2-558550
Fax: 2-562078
Advertising
S.I.C.: 7311
Svein Lang *(Mng. Dir.)*

BSB New Zealand (1)
10th Fl., 17 Albert St. P.O. Box 991,
Auckland, New Zealand
Tel.: 9-3033549
Telex: 791-21662
Fax: 9-3089085
Advertising
S.I.C.: 7311
Bob Vines *(Chief Exec Officer & Chm.)*

BSB New Zealand Limited (1)
43 Kent Terrace P.O. Box 1491,
Wellington, New Zealand
Tel.: 4-843629
Fax: 4-852667
Approx.Billings: $57,000,000
Full Service Advertising
S.I.C.: 7311
Andrew Mazey *(Mng. Dir.)*

BSB Portugal (1)
Avenida 5 de Outubro 35, 8th Fl. 1000
Lisbon, Portugal
Tel.: 1-3523132
Telex: 42709 BOOM P
Fax: 1-543441
Approx.Billings: $19,660,000
Emp.: 31
Marketing & Advertising
S.I.C.: 7311
Victor Lopes Centeno *(Chm. & Chief Exec. Officer)*
Nelson Santos *(Fin. Dir.)*
Fatima Amaral *(Liason Officer)*
Teresa Neto *(Acctg. Chief)*
Madalena Frade *(Acctg. Asst.)*
Luis Moreira *(Visualizer)*
Pedro Rosa *(Visualizer)*

BSB Publicidad S.A. (1)
Goya 8, 2nd Fl. 28001
Madrid, Spain
Tel.: 1-5771848
Fax: 1-5774549
Advertising
S.I.C.: 7311
Mena Benatar *(Mng. Dir.)*

BSB Publicidad S.A. (1)
Avda. Diagonal, 615-4o-A 08028
Barcelona, Spain
Tel.: 3-4192244
Fax: 3-4192607
Advertising
S.I.C.: 7311
Ignasi Puig *(Mng. Dir.)*

BSB Publicidad S.A. (1)
Plaza Espana 4 48001
Bilbao, Spain
Tel.: 3-4239300
Fax: 3-4234433
Advertising
S.I.C.: 7311
German Imaz *(Deputy Office Mgr.)*

BSB Publicidad S.A. (1)
Acera del Darro 72,3o 18005
Granada, Spain
Tel.: 58-257662
Fax: 58-258164
Advertising
S.I.C.: 7311
Jose Ignacio Romero *(Office Mgr.)*

BSB Publicidad S.A. (1)
San Lorenzo, 2, 2do 29001
Malaga, Spain
Tel.: 52-214671
Fax: 52-212092
Advertising
S.I.C.: 7311
Ignacio Fernandez de Bobadilla *(Office Mgr.)*

BSB Publicidad S.A. (1)
Santa Susana, 43 33007
Oviedo, Spain
Tel.: 85-232012
Fax: 85-250750
Advertising
S.I.C.: 7311
Julian Moreno *(Office Mgr.)*

BSB Publicidad S.A. (1)
Av. Baranain 2 31001
Pamplona, Spain
Tel.: 48-263700
Fax: 48-266968
Advertising
S.I.C.: 7311
Carlos Ciganda *(Joint Office Mgr.)*
Fernando Garcia Mina *(Joint Office Mgr.)*

BSB Publicidad S.A. (1)
Juan Florez, 28 15004
La Coruna, Spain
Tel.: 81-264433
Fax: 81-264556
Advertising
S.I.C.: 7311
Miguel Conde *(Office Mgr.)*

BSB Publicidad S.A. (1)
Plaza de la Feria, 40 35003
Las Palmas, de Gran Canaria Spain
Tel.: 28-231600
Fax: 28-242337
Advertising
S.I.C.: 7311
Felipe Hernandez Ravina *(Office Mgr.)*

BSB Publicidad S.A. (1)
Castilla 19, Esc. B 6toC. 39009
Santander, Spain
Tel.: 42-212067
Fax: 42-223665
Advertising
S.I.C.: 7311
Julian Moreno *(Office Mgr.)*

BSB Publicidad S.A. (1)
Plaza Nueva 8, duplicado 41001
Seville, Spain
Tel.: 54-225357
Fax: 54-214866
Advertising
S.I.C.: 7311
Juan Gonzalez *(Office Mgr.)*

BSB September AB (1)
Jarnvagsgatan 14 P.O. Box 1043, 251 10
Helsingborg, Sweden
Tel.: 42-189300
Fax: 42-139700
Advertising
S.I.C.: 7311
Bengt Liljedahl *(Mng. Dir.)*

BSB Singapore (1)
100 Beach Rd., #30-06 Shaw Towers
Singapore, 0718, Singapore
Tel.: 65-2953301
Telex: 786-26190
Fax: 65-2967525
Approx.Billings: $23,000,000
Emp.: 45
Advertising
S.I.C.: 7311
Michael Ang *(Dir., Fin. & Admin.)*
Robert Gibralter *(Mng. Dir.)*
Michael Jordan *(Dir., Plng. & Multi-Natl. Bus.)*

BSB Stockholm AB (1)
Klara Norra Kyrkogata 29 111 22
Stockholm, Sweden
Tel.: 8-6767500
Fax: 8-241321
Advertising
S.I.C.: 7311
Thomas Olsson *(Mng. Dir.)*

BSB Sweden (1)
Klara Norra Kyrkogata 29 111 22
Stockholm, Sweden
Tel.: 8-6767500
Telex: 854-10813
Fax: 8-241321
Advertising
S.I.C.: 7311
Ake Borgudd *(Chief Exec. Officer)*

BSB/Taiwan Company Limited (1)
6th Fl., Chant Bldg., 120 Chien Kou N. Rd., Sec. 2
Taipei, Taiwan R.O.C.
Tel.: 2-5055305
Fax: 2-5055332
Approx.Billings: $5,555,662
Emp.: 32
Advertising
S.I.C.: 7311
Georg Janssen *(Mng. Dir.)*
Donald Chiang *(Fin. Dir.)*

BSB Thailand (1)
164 Sukhumvit Soi 20
Bangkok, 10110, Thailand
Tel.: 2-2596730
Telex: 788-87472
Fax: 2-2581454
Advertising
S.I.C.: 7311
David Bell *(Mng. Dir.)*

Bates Advertising A/S (1)
Parkveien 60 P.O. Box 2604, 0203 Solli,
Oslo, Norway
Tel.: 02-447070
Fax: 02-556730
Advertising
S.I.C.: 7311
Jarle Jodnes *(Mng. Dir.)*

Ted Bates A/S (1)
Landemaerket 29 DK-1119
Copenhagen, K, Denmark
Tel.: 33-137913
Telex: 855-16679
Fax: 33-157126
Advertising
S.I.C.: 7311
Hans-Ulrik Longhi *(Mng. Dir.)*

Bates Backer & Spielvogel A/S (1)
Munkedamsveien 35 P.O. Box 2464, 0202
Solli, Vika,
Oslo, 2, Norway
Tel.: 02-629700
Telex: 856-76151
Fax: 02-629655
Emp.: 18
Advertising
S.I.C.: 7311
Magne Friestad *(Mng. Dir.)*

Bates Benjamin A/S (1)
Cort Adelersgt. 16 P.O. Box 2464 Solli,
0202
Oslo, 2, Norway
Tel.: 02-629780
Fax: 02-559202
Emp.: 22
Advertising
S.I.C.: 7311
Tor Bertheussen *(Mng. Dir.)*

Bates Bergen A/S (1)
Hellandgarden 2 P.O. Box 811, 5001
Bergen, Norway
Tel.: 05-234600
Fax: 05-231160
Advertising
S.I.C.: 7311
Halle Kvassheim *(Mng. Dir.)*

Bates Film (1)
Munkedamsveien 35,V Box 2464 Solli,
0202
Oslo, 2, Norway
Tel.: 2-837500
Telex: 856-76151
Fax: 2-831851
Advertising
S.I.C.: 7311
Birger Libell *(Mgr.)*

Ted Bates Greenhouse (1)
Cort Adelersgt, 16 0254
Oslo, 2, Norway
Tel.: 2-837400
Fax: 2-443225
Advertising
S.I.C.: 7311
Hilmar Lunde *(Mng. Dir.)*

Bates Stavanger A/S (1)
Hillevagsveien 85 4000
Stavanger, Norway
Tel.: 04-581050
Telex: 856-33224
Fax: 04-588088
Advertising
S.I.C.: 7311
Nils Naley *(Mng. Dir.)*

Bates Telemarketing (1)
Cort Adelersgt. 16 P.O. Box 2464 Solli,
0202
Oslo, 2, Norway
Tel.: 2-442366
Telex: 856-76151
Fax: 2-438574
Advertising
S.I.C.: 7311
Per Morten Olafsen *(Mgr.)*

Ted Bates-Vestfold (1)
Stavernsveien 15 P.O. Box 154, 3251
Larvik, Norway
Tel.: 34-85490
Fax: 34-81082
Advertising
S.I.C.: 7311
Rolf Greger Stroem *(Mgr.)*

Bungey Medical (1)
30 Eastbourne Terrace
London, W2 6LG, United Kingdom
Tel.: 071-2622266
Fax: 071-7238899
Approx.Billings: $25,000,000
Emp.: 14
Computer Systems/Hardware:
Donovan
Healthcare Advertising
S.I.C.: 7311
Phil Welch *(Mng. Dir.)*
Roy Powell *(Fin. Dir.)*

The Campaign Palace (1)
20 Burton St.
Darlinghurst, N.S.W. 2010, Australia
Tel.: 2-3324999
Telex: 790-70275
Fax: 2-3321627
Advertising
S.I.C.: 7311
Des Speakman *(Mng. Dir.)*

The Campaign Palace (1)
409 St. Kilda Rd.
Melbourne, Victoria 3004, Australia
Tel.: 03 867 7877
Telex: 790-36559
Fax: 03 867 5307
Approx.Billings: $52,000,000
Emp.: 50
Advertising
S.I.C.: 7311
L. Hunt *(Chm.)*
D. Speakman *(Mng. Dir.)*
G. Moran *(Sec.)*

Central Media, S.A. (1)
Plaza Colegio del Patriarca 4 46002
Valencia, Spain
Tel.: 6-3525456
Fax: 6-3517000
Advertising
S.I.C.: 7311
Jose Maria Casero *(Mng. Dir.)*

Central Media, S.A. (1)
Conde de Penalver 38-4o 28006
Madrid, Spain
Tel.: 1-4021061
Telex: 831-45320
Fax: 1-4029237
Advertising
S.I.C.: 7311
Jose Maria Casero *(Mng. Dir.)*

Central Media, S.A. (1)
Traversera de Gracia 18-20 08021
Barcelona, Spain
Tel.: 3-2097311
Fax: 3-2098001
Advertising
S.I.C.: 7311
Jose Maria Casero *(Mng. Dir.)*

Cerca GmbH (1)
Bettinastrasse 53/55 6000
Frankfurt/Main, 1, Germany
Tel.: 69-743505
Telex: 841-4189191
Fax: 69-7435459
Advertising
S.I.C.: 7311
Veit Emschermann *(Mng. Dir.)*

Cicero/BSB Publicidad S.A. (1)
Paraguay 610, Piso 23 1350
Buenos Aires, Argentina
Tel.: 1-3129633/3868/6616
Telex: 390-9900/CICERO TED BATES
Fax: 1-3114086
Approx.Billings: $3,760,000
Emp.: 31
Computer Systems/Hardware:
Epson (AT 386 System), IBM PS 2
Full Service Advertising
S.I.C.: 7311
Carlos M. Mosquera *(Chm. Bd., Pres. & Chief Exec. Officer)*
Maria C. Lafiandra *(Vice Chm.,Chief Oper. Officer & Brdcst. Production)*
Maria Ines Bo *(Chief Fin. Officer)*

Consensus Research Pty., Ltd. (1)
107 Mount St., 3rd Fl.
North Sydney, N.S.W. 2060, Australia
Tel.: 2-9577388
Fax: 2-9549787
Advertising
S.I.C.: 7311
Keith Sentis *(Mng. Dir.)*

Creative Communications Werbegesellshaft, m.b.H. (1)
Gymnasiumstr. 81 1190
Vienna, Austria
Tel.: 1-3199560/63
Fax: 1-34916033
Approx.Billings: $7,500,000
Emp.: 9
Advertising
S.I.C.: 7311
Hermann-Paul Butzi *(Mng. Dir.)*

Darby & Associates (1)
99-101 Victoria St. P.O. Box 25053,
Christchurch, New Zealand
Tel.: 3-661077
Fax: 3-663905
Advertising
S.I.C.: 7311
John J. Darby *(Mng. Dir.)*

The Decision Shop (1)
106 Westbourne Terrace
London, W2 6QE, United Kingdom
Tel.: 071-7064535
Telex: 851-918865
Fax: 071-7248690
S.I.C.: 7311
Bernard Walsh *(Mng. Dir.)*

Delvico/Bates, S.A. (1)
Hermosilla 30 28001
Madrid, Spain
Tel.: 1-4354244
Telex: 831-43280 DELVIE
Fax: 1-5764887
Approx.Billings: $115,700,000
Emp.: 39
Full Service Advertising
S.I.C.: 7311
Julio Sierra *(Gen. Mgr.)*
Vicente Hernandez *(Fin. Dir.)*

Delvico/Bates, S.A. (1)
Plaza Porta de la Mar, 6-12 46004
Valencia, Spain
Tel.: 6-3523835
Fax: 6-3525678
Advertising
S.I.C.: 7311
Joan Puig *(Gen. Mgr.)*

Delvico/Bates, S.A. (1)
Escuelas Pias 118 08017
Barcelona, Spain
Tel.: 3-4171937
Telex: 831-97035 DLVE
Fax: 3-2113012
Emp.: 31
Full Service Advertising
S.I.C.: 7311
Luis Cuesta *(Mng. Dir.)*
Andreu Martin *(Gen. Mgr.)*
Vicente Hernandez *(Fin. Dir.)*

Denison/BSB (1)
Av. Brigadeiro Luiz Antonio 2050
Sao Paulo, CEP 01318, Brazil
Tel.: 11-2892633
Telex: 391-1123325
Fax: 11-2852667
S.I.C.: 7311
Raul Cruz Lima *(Chm.)*

Diamond Ad Ltd. (1)
Hyundai Bldg., 5th Fl., 178 Sejong-ro,
Chongro-ku P.O. Box Kwanghwamun 1087,
Seoul, Korea
Tel.: 2-7392611
Fax: 2-7250896
Approx.Billings: $107,260,000
Emp.: 196
Advertising
S.I.C.: 7311
Il-hae Hong *(Pres.)*
Samuel Kim *(Sr. V.P., Intl.)*
Chae Kap-byung *(V.P.-Gen. Services)*
Jay S. Kim *(Intl. Dir.)*
Thomas Song *(Intl. Credit Dir.)*
Chae Kwang-Chul *(Domestic Credit Dir.)*
Kim Young-sun *(Mktg. Dir.)*

Dr. Puttner & BSB Worldwide Werbegesellschaft m.b.H. (1)
Wambachergasse 2 A-1130
Vienna, Austria
Tel.: 1-80103
Telex: 847-134249 CONEX
Fax: 1-8010337
Approx.Billings: $43,000,000
Emp.: 39
Advertising
S.I.C.: 7311
Dr. Gerhard Puttner *(Chm. & Pres.)*
Hans Naszada *(Chief Oper. Officer)*
Axel Kadenbach *(Chief Fin. Officer)*
Erich Schonberg *(Mng. Dir.)*

Dorland Business Communications (1)
27-29 Cursitor St.
London, EC4A 1LT, United Kingdom
Tel.: 071-4045804
Telex: 851-262644
Fax: 071-4044756
Business to Business
S.I.C.: 7311
Michael Fredman *(Chm.)*

Ethical Communications (1)
30 Eastbourne Terrace
London, W2 6LG, United Kingdom
Tel.: 071-2624189
Telex: 851-918865
Fax: 071-7248690
Advertising
S.I.C.: 7311
Michael L. Lees *(Chief Exec. Officer)*

Final Art (1)
Rosario Pino 12 28020
Madrid, Spain
Tel.: 1-5710586
Telex: 831-49094 TBEW-E
Cable: Dibates, Madrid
Fax: 1-5715877
Approx.Billings: $2,000,000,000
Emp.: 40
Full Service Advertising
S.I.C.: 7311
Juan Antonio Guerraro *(Mng. Dir.)*

Finnad Communications (1)
Mikonkatu 8A SF 00100
Helsinki, Finland
Tel.: 0-134431
Telex: 857-126199
Fax: 0-13443334
Advertising
S.I.C.: 7311
Tepa Wallin *(Dir.)*

Geindre Marketing Services (1)
Tours Suresnes 2000, 9 rue Benoit Malon
92150
Suresnes, France
Tel.: 1-47288384
Telex: 842-620639
Fax: 1-47044843
Advertising
S.I.C.: 7311
Patrick Geindre *(Mgr.)*

Geomedia S.A. (1)
Rue de Geneve 6 1140
Brussels, Belgium
Tel.: 2-2444740
Fax: 2-2444653
S.I.C.: 7311
Michele Vandekerctchove *(Mng. Dir.)*

Gestro Horne (1)
The Terrace, 1st Floor, Level 8, 203 Willis
St. P.O. Box 10106,
Wellington, New Zealand
Tel.: 4-732705
Fax: 4-732709
Advertising
S.I.C.: 7311
Phil Hartley *(Dir.)*

Gestro Horne (1)
Level 7, 110 Symonds St. P.O. Box 1262,
Auckland, New Zealand
Tel.: 9-792370
Fax: 9-396656
Advertising
S.I.C.: 7311
Colin Gestro *(Dir.)*
Graeme Horne *(Dir.)*

Grupo BSB SA (1)
Goya 8, 1st Fl. 28001
Madrid, Spain
Tel.: 1-5771848
Fax: 1-5774299
Advertising
S.I.C.: 7311
Stanley Bendelac *(Chm. & Chief Exec. Officer)*
Ramon Roses *(Vice Chm.)*
Carlos Usandizaga *(Exec. V.P.)*

Insight Communications Ltd. (1)
Plot 58, Akanbi Onitiri Close, Off Eric
Moore Rd. P.O. Box 2588, Surulere,
Lagos, Nigeria
Tel.: 1-830209/802470
Telex: 22612 BECENT NG
Fax: 1-832819
Approx.Billings: $5,460,000
Emp.: 127
Television, Print & Radio Advertising
S.I.C.: 7311
Abiodun O. Shobanjo *(Mng. Dir.)*
Funmi Onabolu *(Gen. Mgr.)*
Kola Ogunde *(Head of Fin.)*
Crislaw Nominees *(Corp. Sec.)*
Osar Emokpae *(Head of Strategic Plng.)*

Backer Spielvogel Bates Worldwide, Inc.—(Continued)

K&B DBM Marketing Oy (1)
Iso Roobertinkatu #43A SF-00120
Helsinki, Finland
Tel.: 358-060-5900
Fax: 358-060-7042
Direct Marketing
S.I.C.: 7331
Anssi Jarvinen *(Mng. Dir.)*

K&D Adaptus Direct (1)
Kungsgatan 66 11122
Stockholm, Sweden
Tel.: 8-230230
Fax: 8-110677
Direct Marketing
S.I.C.: 7331
Mats Netterwall *(Mng. Dir.)*

K&D Asia-Hong Kong (1)
2nd Fl., Asian House, 1 Hennessy Rd.
Wanchai, Hong Kong
Tel.: 852-8230310
Fax: 852-8661605
Approx.Billings: $20,000,000
Emp.: 25
Computer Systems/Hardware:
MAC Graphics, IBM Wordstar 5.1, Lotus
Response Advertising & Promotions Across All media
Deborah Coulson *(Reg. Dir.-K&D Asia)*
Ana Lee *(Gen. Mgr.)*
Catherine Howley *(Mng. Dir. & Creative Dir.)*

K&D Bond Direct (1)
3rd. Fl., 8-24 Kippax St.
Surrey Hills, N.S.W. 2010, Australia
Tel.: 2-2889000
Fax: 2-2816121
Emp.: 54
Direct Marketing
S.I.C.: 7331
Ian Kennedy *(Chm. Bd.)*

K&D Bond Direct (1)
10th Fl., West Tower, 608 St. Kilda Rd.
Melbourne, Victoria 3004, Australia
Tel.: 3-5252688
Fax: 3-5252818
Direct Marketing
S.I.C.: 7331
Stephen Bennett *(Gen. Mgr.)*

K&D Hellas (1)
264 Kifisias Ave. & 1 Kodrou St. 152 32
Halandei,
Athens, Greece
Tel.: 1-6850846
Fax: 1-6850839
Advertising
S.I.C.: 7311
Antigoni Dimitriadi *(Mng. Dir.)*

K&D Italia (1)
Via Ariosto 23 20145
Milan, Italy
Tel.: 2-48019480
Fax: 2-48019836
Advertising
S.I.C.: 7311
Francesca Sorge *(Mng. Dir.)*

K&D Werbeagentur (1)
Hudwalckerstrasse 11 2000
Hamburg, 60, Germany
Tel.: 40-471050
Fax: 40-47105105
Advertising
S.I.C.: 7311
Lars Brustad *(Mng. Dir.)*

Kobs & Draft (1)
177 rue Armand Silvestre 92400
Courbevoie, France
Tel.: 1-47689880
Fax: 1-47880778
Approx.Billings: $21,573,000
Emp.: 25
Direct Marketing
Florence Cotel *(Mng. Dir.)*

Kobs & Draft (1)
Munkedamsveien 35 P.O. Box 2464, 0202
Solli,
Oslo, 2, Norway
Tel.: 2-837500
Fax: 2-832417
Advertising
S.I.C.: 7311
Arne Eggen *(Mng. Dir., Dir. os Scandinavian Opers.)*

Kobs & Draft (1)
141 Westbourne Terrace
London, W2 6JR, United Kingdom
Tel.: 071-2620708
Fax: 071-4020020
Approx.Billings: $11,000,000
Emp.: 20
Full Service Direct Marketing Agency
S.I.C.: 7331
Peter Middleton *(Mng. Dir.)*

Kobs & Draft Advertising (1)
2 St. Clair Ave. W., 21st Fl.
Toronto, ON M4V 1L5, Canada
Tel.: 416-925-0759
Fax: 416-925-1206
Advertising
S.I.C.: 7311
Sue Hipp *(Gen. Mgr.)*

Kobs & Draft Asia-Malaysia (1)
270 Jalan Ampang P.O. Box 11876, 50450
Kuala Lumpur, Malaysia
Tel.: 3-4573654
Fax: 3-4573429
Advertising
S.I.C.: 7311
Lea Long *(Mng. Dir.)*

Kobs & Draft Asia-Thailand (1)
166/1 Sukhumvit 20 Rd.
Bangkok, Thailand
Tel.: 2-2581564/66
Fax: 2-2606789
Advertising
S.I.C.: 7311
John Padorr *(Mng. Dir. & Creative Dir.)*

Kobs & Draft Belgium (1)
Rue de Geneve 6 1140
Brussels, Belgium
Tel.: 2-2444611
Fax: 2-2444679
Advertising
S.I.C.: 7311
Henk DeDoncker *(Acct. Dir.)*

Kobs & Draft Europe (1)
83-89 Whitfield St.
London, W1A 4XA, United Kingdom
Tel.: 071-6363650
Fax: 071-6363649
Advertising
S.I.C.: 7311
David Florence *(Exec. V.P., Dir.-European Opers.)*
Denise Henshaw *(Fin. Dir.)*

Kobs & Draft bv (1)
Amsteldijk 166 1079 LH
Amsterdam, Netherlands
Tel.: 20-6464205
Fax: 20-6464592
Advertising
S.I.C.: 7311
Bart Leusink *(Mng. Dir.)*

Kobs & Draft S.A. (1)
Rosario Pino, 12 28020
Madrid, Spain
Tel.: 1-5711900
Fax: 1-5715877
Emp.: 17
Advertising
S.I.C.: 7311
Juan Antonio Guerrero *(Gen. Mgr.)*

Mann Hughes Gerrish (1)
30 Eastbourne Terrace
London, W2 6LG, United Kingdom
Tel.: 071-7062306
Fax: 071-2620756
Advertising
S.I.C.: 7311
Robert Gerrish *(Mng. Dir.)*

Marketforce Australia (1)
1314 Hay St.
West Perth, 6005, Australia
Tel.: 9-3221655
Fax: 9-4813240
Approx.Billings: $72,500,000
Emp.: 107
Advertising, Marketing, TV Production
S.I.C.: 7311
Ian Tassell *(Mng. Dir.)*
Howard Read *(Chm.)*

Marketforce Australia (1)
4th Fl., 168 Walker St.
North Sydney, 2060, Australia
Tel.: 2-9573244
Fax: 2-9595578
Advertising
S.I.C.: 7311
Stephen Kulmar *(Joint Mng. Dir.)*

Marketforce Australia (1)
125-127 Ferrars St.
South Melbourne, 3205, Australia
Tel.: 3-6993899
Fax: 3-6907971
Advertising
S.I.C.: 7311
Vic Hopkins *(Chief Exec. Officer)*

Media Decisions (1)
107 Mount St.
North Sydney, N.S.W. 2060, Australia
Tel.: 2-9577700
Fax: 2-9290633
Advertising
S.I.C.: 7311
Daryl Paterson *(Mng. Dir.)*

Media Decisions (1)
409 St. Kilda Rd.
Melbourne, Victoria 3004, Australia
Tel.: 3-2674833
Fax: 3-8203254
Advertising
S.I.C.: 7311
Peter Davy *(Mng. Dir.)*

Media Marketing Research (1)
Munkedamsveien 35 P.O. Box 2464, 0202
Solli, Vika,
Oslo, 2, Norway
Tel.: 2-837500
Telex: 856-76151
Fax: 2-838052
Advertising
S.I.C.: 7311
Kjell Nilsen *(Mng. Dir.)*

Norgard Mikkelsen Reklamebureau A/S (1)
Vandvaerksvej 18 DK-5100
Odense, C, Denmark
Tel.: 66-141480
Fax: 66-141943
Advertising
S.I.C.: 7311
Ove Norgard Mikkelsen *(Mng. Dir.)*

George Patterson (Brisbane) Pty Ltd. (1)
459/461 Adelaide St.
Brisbane, Queensland 4000, Australia
Tel.: 7-8318122
Telex: 790-40152
Fax: 7-8325693
Advertising
S.I.C.: 7311
Bil Hawley *(Mng. Dir.-Brisbane)*

George Patterson Pty. Limited (1)
107 Mount St.
North Sydney, N.S.W. 2060, Australia
Tel.: 02-9577100
Telex: 790-20449
Fax: 02-9593478
Approx.Billings: $457,408,000
Emp.: 430
Advertising
S.I.C.: 7311
G.A. Cousins *(Chm.)*
John Fawcett *(Chief Exec. Officer)*

George Patterson Pty. Limited (1)
394 La Trobe St.
Melbourne, Victoria 3000, Australia
Tel.: 3-2871200
Telex: 790-30375
Fax: 3-3283157
S.I.C.: 7311
Noel Browne *(Mng. Dir.-Melbourne)*

George Patterson Pty. Limited (1)
82 East Terrace
Adelaide, S.A. 5000, Australia
Tel.: 8-2237122
Telex: 790-82103
Fax: 8-2240387
Advertising
S.I.C.: 7311
Simon O'Brien *(Mng. Dir.-Adelaide)*

Perdomo-Ted Bates/Publicidad (1)
Prolongacion Av., Primavera 120A, Oficinas 209-210-217 Chacarilla del-Estanque,
Santiago de Surco,
Lima, 33, Peru
Tel.: 14-367657
Fax: 14-352574
Approx.Billings: $500,000
Emp.: 9
Full Service Advertising
S.I.C.: 7311
Luis A. Perdomo *(Chm. Bd., Pres. & Chief Exec. Officer)*
Alejandra Arana *(Chief Oper. Officer & Acct. Supvr.)*
Luis Orbegozo *(Chief Fin. Officer)*
Lou Perdomo *(Gen. Mgr., Acct. Dir. & New Bus. Contact)*

Rota Advertising Limited (1)
Nisantasi, Poyracik Sok 32-80200
Istanbul, Turkey
Tel.: 1-1314002
Telex: 821-23528
Fax: 1-1601128
Advertising
S.I.C.: 7311
Cinar Kilic *(Chm. & Chief Exec. Officer)*

Scholz & Friends Design GmbH (1)
Steinhoft 9 P.O. Box 110393, 2000
Hamburg, 11, Germany
Tel.: 40-376810
Telex: 841-2161625
Fax: 40-366869
Advertising
S.I.C.: 7311
Renate Scholz *(Mng. Dir.)*

Scholz & Friends GmbH (1)
Steinhoft 9 P.O. Box 110393, 2000
Hamburg, 11, Germany
Tel.: 40-376810
Telex: 841-2161 625
Fax: 40-366869
Advertising
S.I.C.: 7311
Jurgen Scholz *(Chm.)*
Gunther Gahren *(Mng. Dir.)*

Sista's Private Limited (1)
Poonam Chambers, B Block, Shivsager Estate, Dr. Annie Besant Rd. Worli, P.B. No. 9931,
Bombay, 400018, India
Tel.: 22-4920926
Telex: 953-1173680
Fax: 22-4947375
Emp.: 262
Advertising
S.I.C.: 7311
Shambhu V. Sista *(Mng. Dir.)*

Standley Burridge Collings Ltd. (1)
121-141 Westbourne Terrace
London, W2 6JR, United Kingdom
Tel.: 071-7063155
Fax: 071-7244028
Approx.Billings: $17,000,000
Emp.: 15
Healthcare Advertising (Intl. & UK)
S.I.C.: 7311
Martin Standley *(Mng. Dir.)*
Roy Powell *(Chief. Fin. Officer)*

Tillbrooks Studios (1)
Bridge House, 63-65 N. Wharf Rd.
London, W2 1LA, United Kingdom
Tel.: 071-7243073
Telex: 851-918865
Fax: 071-7244371
Advertising
S.I.C.: 7311
Martin Tillbrook *(Mng. Dir.)*

VIP Publicidad (1)
Whimper 777 P.O. Box 4568-A,
Quito, Ecuador
Tel.: 2-502024
Fax: 2-563901
Advertising
S.I.C.: 7311
Gustavo Vallejo *(Gen. Mgr.)*

Wolff & Partner (1)
Birkenwald Str. 200 7000
Stuttgart, Germany
Tel.: 11-2573050
Fax: 11-2579240
Advertising
S.I.C.: 7311
Eike Wolff *(Mng. Dir.)*

BACKUS TURNER & PARTNERS, INC.
Advertising Marketing Communications

BACKUS TURNER & PARTNERS, INC.
1001 S. Bayshore Dr., Ste. 2506
Miami, FL 33131
Tel.: 305-371-2525
Fax: 305-371-2126
Year Founded: 1978
Approx.Billings: $19,500,000
Emp.: 20
Retail, Travel, Healthcare, Real Estate & Financial
Roberta Backus *(Chm. Bd., Chief Exec. Officer & New Bus. Contact)*
Lawrence O. Turner, Jr. *(Pres.)*
Faye Barton *(Chief Fin. Officer)*

Computer Systems/Hardware:
IBM

HENRY BACON BUILDING MATERIALS, INC.
5210 E. Lake Sammamish Pkwy. S.E.
Issaquah, WA 98027-7012
Mailing Address:
P.O. Box 7012
Issaquah, WA 98027-7012
Tel.: 206-391-2075
Fax: 206-391-2060
Year Founded: 1945
Sales Range: $40-59 Million
Emp.: 300
Fiscal Year-end: 12/31/91
Wholesale & Retail Lumber & Construction Materials
S.I.C.: 5211; 5031; 5039
James B. Curran *(Chm. Bd. & Chief Exec. Officer)*
Richard L. Carson *(Pres.)*
Ken Plass *(V.P. & Gen Mgr.)*
Curt Le Master *(V.P.-Mdsg.)*
Robert Frederick *(Sec.)*
Hal Roys *(Treas.)*

Outside Service Firm(s):

Deloitte & Touche*(Auditors)*
700 Fifth Ave., Suite 4500
Seattle, WA 98104-5044
Tel.: 206-292-1800

U.S. Bank of Washington*(Major Banking Relationship)*
1414 Fourth Ave.
Seattle, WA 98101
Tel.: 206-344-2300

W.S. BADCOCK CORPORATION
200 Phosphate Boulevard N.W.
Mulberry, FL 33860
Mailing Address:
P.O. Box 497,
Mulberry, FL 33860
Tel.: 813-425-4921 **FL**
Year Founded: 1904
Approx.Sls.: $275,000,000
Emp.: 900
Fiscal Year-end: 6/30/91
Home Furnishings, Appliance, Electronics & Floor Covering Retailer
S.I.C.: 5712; 5021; 2515; 5722; 5731; 5713
Wogan S. Badcock, Jr. *(Chm. Bd. & Pres.)*
William K. Pou, Sr. *(Exec. V.P. & Asst. Sec. & Treas.)*
Mary R. Badcock *(Exec. V.P.)*
William L. Girtman *(V.P.-Fin. & Treas.)*
James R. Meyer *(V.P. & Gen. Counsel)*
Richard P. Barnes, Sr. *(V.P.-Opers.)*
William D. Seigler, Sr. *(V.P.-Dealer Opers.)*
Carl M. Ellis, Jr. *(V.P.-Dealer Opers.)*
W. Frank Lunsford *(V.P.-Warehouse Opers.)*
Luther N. Pipkin, Jr. *(V.P.-Appliance & Electronics)*
Harry J. Barnhart *(V.P.-Dealer Audit)*
Ben M. Badcock *(V.P.-Dir.-Mktg. & Mdsg.)*
Henry C. Badcock *(Exec. V.P.-Dealer Opers. & Sec.)*
Wogan S. Badcock, III *(Exec. V.P.-Admin.)*
Randy R. Wilkerson *(V.P. & Gen. Mgr.-Cullman Opers.)*
Douglas D. Wineland *(V.P.-Personnel Services)*
Mitchell P. Stiles *(V.P. Pub. Rels. Dir.)*
Richard E. Wendel *(V.P.-Data Processing)*
Leslie M. Hurley *(V.P.-Mngmt. Information Systems)*
William E. Sparkman *(V.P.-Customer Dealer Rels.)*
William T. Daughtrey *(V.P. & Asst. to the Pres.)*
J. Timothy Birge *(V.P.)*
Evelyn Susan Pou *(Asst. Sec.)*
Evelyn Badcock Bader *(Asst. Sec.)*
Malda Badcock Pou *(Asst. Sec.)*
Lavada M. Chiodo *(Exec. Asst. to the V.P. Fin. & Treas.)*

No. of Mfg. Plants/Facilities: 289
No. of U.S. Offices: 4

Computer Systems/Hardware:
NCR

Outside Service Firm(s):

Peat Marwick Main & Co.*(Auditors)*
Orlando, FL

Atlantic National Bank*(Major Banking Relationship)*
Jacksonville, FL

American Heritage Life Insurance Co.*(Group Insurer)*
Jacksonville, FL

Trenam, Simmons, Kemker, Scharf, Barkin, Frye & O'Neil*(Legal Firm)*
2700 Barnett Plaza
Tampa, FL 33602
Tel.: 813-223-7474

BADER & CO.
P.O. Box 19
Ipava, IL 61441
Tel.: 309-753-8511
Tel.: 800-752-2969 **IL**
Year Founded: 1917
Assets: $1,182,400
Earnings: ($47,000)
Liabilities: $567,800
Net Worth: $614,600
Approx.Sls.: $26,400,000
Emp.: 20
Fiscal Year-end: 4/30/92
Wholesale Grain & Related Farm Products & Equipment
S.I.C.: 5153
Burke B. Bader *(Pres.)*
Harold D. Lindsey *(Chief Oper. Officer, Chief Fin. Officer, & V.P.)*
Rick L. Harris *(Treas.& Controller)*

No. of Mfg. Plants/Facilities: 10

Outside Service Firm(s):

McGladrey & Pullen*(Auditors)*
Peoria, IL

Miller's Mutual Insurance*(Commercial Insurance Carrier)*
Alton, IL

Pekin Insurance*(Group Insurer)*
Pekin, IL

Kost & Kost*(Legal Firm)*
Lewistown, IL

Farmers State Bank of Fulton County*(Major Banking Relationship)*
Lewiston, IL

Table Grove State Bank*(Major Banking Relationship)*
Table Grove, IL

Vermont State Bank*(Major Banking Relationship)*
Vermont, IL

BADER RUTTER & ASSOC., INC.
Bishop's Woods Centre, 13555 Bishop's Court
Brookfield, WI 53005
Tel.: 414-784-7200 **WI**
Fax: 414-784-8682
Year Founded: 1973
Approx.Billings: $62,310,000
Emp.: 115
Fiscal Year-end: 12/31/91
Advertising & Public Relations Agency
S.I.C.: 7311; 8743
Ronald L. Bader *(Pres. & Chief Exec. Officer)*
Richard S. Jensen *(Exec. V.P., Chief Oper. Officer)*
Greg Nickerson *(V.P., Pub. Rels.)*
Miller Hogan *(V.P., Grp. Supvr.)*
Steve King *(V.P., Grp. Supvr.)*
Bobbi Kuter *(V.P., Acctg. & Data Processing Dir.)*
Jim Palmer *(V.P., Grp. Supvr.)*
Frank Siebrecht *(V.P., Client Mktg. Plng.)*
Jeff Wedeward *(V.P., Indus. Grp.)*

No. of Mfg. Plants/Facilities: 1
No. of U.S. Offices: 2

Computer Systems/Hardware:
IBM

Outside Service Firm(s):

Coopers & Lybrand*(Auditors)*
411 East Wisconsin Bldg.
Milwaukee, WI 53202

CNA Insurance*(Commercial Insurance Carrier)*
CNA Plaza,
Chicago, IL 60685
Tel.: 312-822-5000

Blue Cross & Blue Shield of Wisconsin*(Group Insurer)*
Madison, WI

M & I Marshall & Isley Bank*(Investment Banker)*
Milwaukee, WI

Fox, Carpenter, O'Neil & Shannon*(Legal Firm)*
Milwaukee, WI

M & I Marshall & Isley Bank*(Major Banking Relationship)*
Milwaukee, WI

M & I Marshall & Isley Bank*(Pension Manager)*
Milwaukee, WI

BADGER AIR BRUSH COMPANY
9128 W. Belmont Ave.
Franklin Park, IL 60131
Tel.: 708-678-3104
Tel.: 800-222-7553
Fax: 708-671-4352
Year Founded: 1963
Approx.Sls.: $13,175,703
Emp.: 85
Fiscal Year-end: 6/30/91
Import Export
Mfr. of Lead Pencils & Art Goods
S.I.C.: 3952
Walter Schlotfeldt *(Pres. & Chief Exec. Officer)*
Ken Schlotfeldt *(V.P. & Chief Oper. Officer)*
John Fennell *(V.P., Sec. & Dir.-Mktg.)*
Candace Carnes *(Treas.)*

BADGER CONSTRUCTION EQUIPMENT CO., INSLEY DIV.
Airport Industrial Park
Winona, MN 55987
Mailing Address:
P.O. Box 168
Winona, MN 55987
Tel.: 507-454-1563
Fax: 507-454-3326
Year Founded: 1945
Approx.Sls.: $20,000,000
Emp.: 200
Fiscal Year-end: 12/31/90
Export
Distr. of Excavating Equipment & Hydraulic R.T. Cranes
S.I.C.: 5082
Frank W. Norris Jr. *(Pres.)*
L.E. Boren *(Chm. Bd. & Chief Exec. Officer)*
D.F. Tschumper *(Controller)*
R.T. Doermer *(V.P.)*
V.C. Schueler *(Mgr.-Mktg. Services)*
J.E. Christopherson *(Factory-Service Mgr.)*
M.N. Cloutier *(Factory Sls. Admin.)*

Computer Systems/Hardware:
IBM

Division:

Burro Crane Co. **(1)**
Airport Industrial Park
Winona, MN 55987
Tel.: 507-454-1563
Frank W. Norris Jr. *(Pres.)*

BADGER NORTHLAND INC.
1215 Hyland Ave.
Kaukauna, WI 54130
Mailing Address:
P.O. Box 1215
Kaukauna, WI 54130
Tel.: 414-766-4603 **DE**
Telex: 26-3431
Fax: 414-766-5011
Year Founded: 1946
Approx.Sls.: $28,000,000
Emp.: 250
Fiscal Year-end: 12/31/90
Export
Mfr. Farm Equipment
S.I.C.: 3523
Gail Janssen *(Chm. Bd.)*
Kenneth B. Myers *(Pres.)*
James Poskie *(V.P.-Mfg.)*
Travis Unterzuber *(V.P.-Engrng.)*
Richard Andres *(Mgr.-Personnel)*
Robert School *(Mgr.-Mktg.)*
James Radant *(Mgr.-Pur.)*
Dean Zamzow *(Mgr.-Quality Control)*
Principal(s):
Employee-Owned

No. of Mfg. Plants/Facilities: 1
No. of U.S. Offices: 1

Computer Systems/Hardware:
IBM System 400

Outside Service Firm(s):

Schenck & Associates*(Auditors)*
Appleton, WI

McCarty, Curry, Wydeven, Peeters & Riester*(Legal Firm)*
Milwaukee, WI

First Wisconsin National Bank*(Major Banking Relationship)*
Sheboygan, WI

BADGER TRUCK CENTER, INC.
2326 W. St. Paul Ave.
Milwaukee, WI 53233
Tel.: 414-344-9500 **WI**
Fax: 414-344-4323
Approx.Sls.: $30,000,000
Emp.: 80

Badger Truck Center, Inc.—(Continued)

Commercial Trucks; Motor Vehicle Supplies & New Parts
S.I.C.: 5012; 5013
Edward B. Schlagenhauf *(Pres.)*
Paul Schlagenhauf *(V.P.)*
Richard O. Theisfeldt *(V.P.)*
John Schlagenhauf *(Treas.)*
June A. Schlagenhauf *(Sec.)*

Outside Service Firm(s):

Bank One Milwaukee, N.A.*(Major Banking Relationship)*
111 E. Wisconsin Ave.
Milwaukee, WI
Tel.: 414-765-3000

BAHLSEN INC.
One Quality Lane
Cary, NC 27513
Tel.: 919-677-3400 **DE**
Fax: 919-677-3247
Year Founded: 1980
Sales Range: $100-499 Million
Emp.: 830
Fiscal Year-end: 12/31/92
Import Export
Cracker & Cookie Vending Snacks, Grocery Products
S.I.C.: 2052; 5149
William C. Burkhardt *(Pres. & Chief Exec. Officer)*
Steve Grissom *(Sr. V.P.-Fin. & Admin.)*
Bill Sauls *(Sr. V.P.-Opers.)*
R.R. Eavey *(V.P.-Vending Sls.)*
Michael Ganey *(V.P.-Mktg.)*
William E. Hickman *(V.P.-Bus. Devel.)*
Ray Murphy *(V.P.-Contract Bus. Devel.)*
David Metzler *(V.P.-Human Resources)*
Jeffrey Odom *(V.P. & Chief Information Officer)*

Computer Systems/Hardware:
IBM; Hewlett-Packard

Outside Service Firm(s):

Blue Cross & Blue Shield of North Carolina*(Group Insurer)*
Durham, NC

GORDON BAILEY & ASSOCIATES, INC.
675 Village Square Dr.
Stone Mountain, GA 30083
Tel.: 404-296-2777 **GA**
Fax: 404-299-5538
Year Founded: 1973
Approx.Billings: $33,000,000
Emp.: 39
Fiscal Year-end: 12/31/91
Advertising Agency Specializing in Foodservice & Industrial Advertising
S.I.C.: 7311
Corporate Giving Program: 401 K
Gordon Bailey *(Pres. & Treas.)*
Ron Strauss *(Exec. V.P.)*
Jeri Christopher *(V.P.- Human Resources)*
Tom Bailey *(Chief Fin. Officer)*
David Doiron *(Controller)*
Clayton R. Jones *(Dir.- Opers.)*
Lisa W. Peters *(Mgr.-Office)*
C.J. Thompson *(Mgr.-Computer Graphics)*
Cindy Balte *(Coord.-Pub. Rels.)*

No. of U.S. Offices: 1

Computer Systems/Hardware:
Macintosh; UNISYS

Outside Service Firm(s):

Arnall, Golden & Gregory*(Legal Firm)*
55 Park Place
Atlanta, GA 30335
Tel.: 404-577-5100

NationsBank*(Major Banking Relationship)*
35 Broad St.
Atlanta, GA 30303
Tel.: 404-581-2121
Tel.: 800-848-8198

BAILEY, KLEPINGER & MEDRICH, INC.
130 S. First St.
Ann Arbor, MI 48104
Tel.: 313-769-6771
Fax: 313-769-3713
Year Founded: 1969
Approx.Billings: $19,830,000
Emp.: 27
Employee Matching Gifts Program: 401K Program
Harvey A. Bailey *(Chm.)*
Mel Medrich *(Vice Chm.)*
Robert Klepinger *(Pres.)*
Mark Paris *(V.P., Dir. Plng.)*
Susan Lewis-Phillips *(Pub. Rels. Dir.)*
Kathleen Mahoney *(Controller)*

Computer Systems/Hardware:
Heavy Weight WordPerfect

BAILEY LAUERMAN & ASSOCIATES, INC.
900 NBC Center
Lincoln, NE 68508
Tel.: 402-475-2800
Tel.: 402-342-5651 (Omaha)
Fax: 402-475-5115
Year Founded: 1970
Approx.Billings: $13,627,728
Emp.: 35
Richard W. Bailey *(Chm. & Chief Exec. Officer)*
James M. Lauerman *(Pres. & Chief Oper. Officer)*
Ronald Plageman *(Exec. V.P., Chief Fin. Officer)*

BAIRD, PATRICK & CO., INC.
20 Exchange Pl.
New York, NY 10005
Tel.: 212-493-6600 **DE**
Year Founded: 1950
Assets: $9,265,350
Liabilities: $4,923,268
Net Worth: $4,342,082
Sales Range: $10-19 Million
Emp.: 90
Fiscal Year-end: 12/31/91
Distributors, Dealers & Underwriters in Corporate & Municipal Securities, Stocks, Bonds & Mutual Fund Shares
S.I.C.: 6211
Joseph A. Patrick *(Chm. Bd.)*
Stuart K. Patrick *(Pres. & Chief Exec. Officer)*
David G. Baird, Jr. *(V.P.)*
Christian G. Keller *(V.P.)*
John J. Glynn *(Sec. & Treas.)*

No. of U.S. Offices: 2

Outside Service Firm(s):

Lieberman & Lieberman*(Auditors)*
Wantagh, NY

Polleck & Kaminsky*(Legal Firm)*
New York, NY

The Bank of New York*(Major Banking Relationship)*
One Wall Street
New York, NY 10286
Tel.: 212-635-6805
Fax: 212-635-3201

BAIRD RAY NISSAN, INC.
2724 N. Hwy. 1792
Longwood, FL 32750
Mailing Address:
P.O. Box 521400,
Longwood, FL 32752-1400
Tel.: 407-831-1318 **FL**
Fax: 407-834-3177
Approx.Sls.: $25,000,000
Emp.: 70
New & Used Automobile Sales & Service
S.I.C.: 5511
Yvonne Baird *(Pres.)*
William D. Ray, Jr. *(Exec. V.P.)*
David Ray *(V.P.-Mktg. & Pur.)*
William D. Ray, III *(V.P.)*
F. King *(Sec. & Treas.)*

Outside Service Firm(s):

Colley, Trumbower & Howell*(Auditors)*
Orlando, FL

Lubet & Woodard*(Legal Firm)*
Orlando, FL

Barnett Banks Trust Company, N.A.*(Major Banking Relationship)*
Winter Park, FL

THE U.S. BAIRD CORPORATION
1700 Stratford Ave.
Stratford, CT 06497
Tel.: 203-375-3361
Fax: 203-378-6006
Year Founded: 1846
Approx.Sls.: $10,000,000
Emp.: 200
Export
Mfr. of Multiple Transfer Presses, Tumbling Equipment, Chucking Machines, Multi-Slide & Four-Slide Machines, Springenerator Spring Machines, Automatic Press Room Equipment, Multi Slide Machines, U.S. Baird Four Slides, Nilson Wire & Strip Forming Machines, Finzer-U.S. Baird Strip & Forming Machines, Henderson Barrel Finishing Equipment, Globe Multi-Purpose Machines
S.I.C.: 3541; 3545; 3549
Charles N. Warner *(Pres.)*
Deborah Blaisdell *(Exec. V.P.)*
John Crisanti *(Treas.)*
C.J. Gomez *(Dir.-Pur.)*
Edward Dunbar *(Gen. Sls. Mgr.)*
John Varga *(Plant Mgr.)*
Claire Lavendar *(Mgr.-Benefits)*
Principal(s):
Charles N. Warner

Computer Systems/Hardware:
NCR Tower

Outside Service Firm(s):

Milton H. Friedberg, Smith & Co.*(Auditors)*
855 Main St., 4th Fl.
Bridgeport, CT 06604
Tel.: 203-366-5876

Subsidiary:

The A. H. Nilson Machine Co. **(1)**
1700 Stratford Ave.
Stratford, CT 06497
Tel.: 203-375-3361
Fax: 203-378-6006
Approx.Sls.: $10,000,000
Emp.: 200
Export
Mfr. Wire & Metal Forming Machinery, Fourslide Machines, Wire Reels, Wire Straighteners
S.I.C.: 3542; 3549
Charles N. Warner *(Pres.)*
Deborah A. Blaisdell *(Exec. V.P.)*
John Crisanti *(Treas.)*
C.J. Gomez *(Dir.-Pur.)*
Edward Dunbar *(Sls. Mgr.)*
John Varga *(Plant Mgr.)*

BAIRD & WARNER INC.
200 W. Madison St.
Chicago, IL 60606
Tel.: 312-368-1855 **IL**
Fax: 312-368-1490
Year Founded: 1855
Approx.Sls.: $59,500,000
Emp.: 1,150
Fiscal Year-end: 12/31/91
Real Estate Co.
S.I.C.: 6531
John W. Baird *(Chm. Bd.)*
Stephen W. Baird *(Pres.)*
James L. Mann *(V.P. & Controller)*
Norbert Michalak *(V.P. & Dir.-Human Resources)*
Principal(s):
John W. Baird

No. of U.S. Offices: 36

Computer Systems/Hardware:
AS 400 & System 36

Outside Service Firm(s):

KPMG Peat Marwick*(Auditors)*
Peat Marwick Plaza, 303 E. Wacker Dr.
Chicago, IL 60601
Tel.: 312-938-1000

General American Life Insurance Co.*(Group Insurer)*
Chicago, IL

Stein, Roe & Farnham*(Investment Banker)*
One S. Wacker Dr.
Chicago, IL 60606
Tel.: 312-368-7700

Sidley & Austin*(Legal Firm)*
One First National Plaza, 42nd Fl.
Chicago, IL 60603
Tel.: 312-853-7000
Fax: 312-853-7036

American National Bank & Trust Company of Chicago*(Major Banking Relationship)*
33 N. LaSalle St.
Chicago, IL 60602
Tel.: 312-661-5000
Fax: 312-661-6417

Stein, Roe & Farnham*(Pension Manager)*
One S. Wacker Dr.
Chicago, IL 60606
Tel.: 312-368-7700

BAKE-LINE PRODUCTS, INC.
One Bake-Line Plaza
Des Plaines, IL 60016
Tel.: 708-699-1000 **IL**
Fax: 708-699-0789
Year Founded: 1959
Approx.Sls.: $75,000,000
Emp.: 700
Fiscal Year-end: 6/30/92
Export
Cookie Baking
S.I.C.: 2052
Thomas E. Kallen *(Chm. Bd. & Treas.)*
Howard S. Stone *(Pres. & Sec.)*

No. of Mfg. Plants/Facilities: 1
No. of U.S. Offices: 1

Outside Service Firm(s):

Ostrow, Reisin, Berk, & Abrams, Ltd.*(Auditors)*
Chicago, IL

American National Bank & Trust Company of Chicago*(Major Banking Relationship)*
33 N. LaSalle St.
Chicago, IL 60602
Tel.: 312-661-5000
Fax: 312-661-6417

H.J. BAKER & BRO., INC.
100 E. 42nd St.
New York, NY 10017
Tel.: 212-867-0200
Fax: 212-370-1639
Emp.: 135
Fertilizers, Vegetable & Animal Oils, Industrial Chemicals, Feeds, Soil Conditioners, Sulphur, Canned Meat, Fish & Fruits
S.I.C.: 2873; 1479; 2032; 2033; 2048; 2076; 2077; 2091; 2819; 2874; 5169
J. Morse Smith *(Chm. Bd. & Pres.)*
Christopher Smith *(Exec. V.P.)*

David Smith *(Exec. V.P.)*
Aaron L. Mathis *(V.P.-Fertilizers)*
Patrick F. Porzio *(V.P. & Chief Fin. Officer)*
Edward F. Reheuser *(V.P.)*
Thomas J. Starkey *(V.P.)*
Joseph A. Entrono *(Treas.)*
Mary Deegan *(Sec.)*

Outside Service Firm(s):

BDO Seidman*(Auditors)*
1430 Broadway
New York, NY
Tel.: 212-765-7500

Proskauer, Rose, Goetz & Mendelsohn*(Legal Firm)*
1585 Broadway
New York, NY 10036
Tel.: 212-969-3000

BAKER COMMODITIES, INC.
4020 Bandini Blvd.
Los Angeles, CA 90023
Tel.: 213-268-2801
Fax: 213-268-5166
Year Founded: 1956
Approx.Sls.: $100,000,000
Emp.: 600
Fiscal Year-end: 12/31/91
Producer & Distributor of Animal Fats & Oils, Tallow, Feed Fat, Blood Meal, Meat & Bone Meal
S.I.C.: 2077; 2011; 2048; 5159; 5191
James M. Andreoli *(Pres. & Chief Exec. Officer)*
Raymond F. Kelly *(Exec. V.P. & Chief Oper. Officer)*
George L. Congleton *(V.P.-Mktg.)*
Larry Friend *(V.P.-Information Systems)*
Dennis N. Luckey *(V.P. & Controller)*
Edward S. Murakami *(V.P.-Research & Quality Assurance)*
James K. Reynolds *(V.P.-Fin. & Chief Fin. Officer)*
William Sikes *(V.P.-Production)*
Charles Varteresian *(V.P.-Procurement)*
M. A. Ebright *(Sec.)*
Tom Vaughan *(Chief Engineer)*

No. of Mfg. Plants/Facilities: 8

Outside Service Firm(s):

Price Waterhouse*(Auditors)*
400 S. Hope St.
Los Angeles, CA 90071-2889
Tel.: 213-236-3000

Bank of America NT&SA*(Major Banking Relationship)*
555 So. Flower St., 5th Fl.
Los Angeles, CA 90071
Tel.: 213-228-3526
Fax: 213-228-4062

BAKER CONCRETE CONSTRUCTION, INC.
900 N. Garver Rd.
Monroe, OH 45050
Tel.: 513-539-4000 **OH**
Fax: 513-539-4380
Approx.Sls.: $141,000,000
Emp.: 1,500
Concrete Construction Contractor
S.I.C.: 1771
Daniel L. Baker *(Chm. Bd. & Pres.)*
Edward L. Mueller *(Sr. V.P.-Estimating)*
Cynthia Baker *(V.P. & Adv. Dir.)*
Stephen E. Martin *(V.P.-Estimating)*
Dennis W. Phillips *(V.P.-Opers.)*
Michael J. Schneider *(V.P.-Bus. Devel.)*
John F. Groth *(Treas.)*
Louis J. Schwartz *(Sec.)*
Jeff Arnold *(Dir.-Data Processing)*
Mike Ward *(Dir.-Pur.)*

Computer Systems/Hardware:
IBM

Outside Service Firm(s):

Grant Thornton*(Auditors)*
1600 Atrium One
Cincinnati, OH 45202
Tel.: 513-762-5000

Schwartz, Manes & Ruby*(Legal Firm)*
Cincinnati, OH

The Central Trust Company, N.A.*(Major Banking Relationship)*
Cincinnati, OH
Tel.: 513-651-8896

BAKER MATERIAL HANDLING CORP.
2450 W. 5th North St.
Summerville, SC 29484
Mailing Address:
P.O. Box 2400,
Summerville, SC 29484
Tel.: 803-875-8000
Fax: 803-875-8329
Approx.Sls.: $50,000,000
Emp.: 150
Import Export
Industrial Trucks (Fork Lift, Narrow-Aisle & Utility Vehicles)
S.I.C.: 3537
Mitch Milovich *(Pres.)*
Robert Crandell *(V.P.-Sls. & Mktg.)*
Manfred Baumann *(V.P.-Engrng.)*
Herman Kling *(V.P.-Fin.)*

BAKER & MCKENZIE INTERNATIONAL
130 E. Randolph Dr., Ste. 3900
Chicago, IL 60601
Tel.: 312-861-8800
Fax: 312-861-8823
Sales Range: $10-19 Million
Insurance Consultants
S.I.C.: 6282
Mr. McGuinan *(Chm.)*
Principal(s):
Mr. McGuinan

No. of U.S. Offices: 9
No. of Foreign Offices: 36

THE BAKERSFIELD CALIFORNIAN
1707 Eye St.
Bakersfield, CA 93302-0440
Mailing Address:
P.O. Box 440
Bakersfield, CA 93302
Tel.: 805-395-7500 **CA**
Fax: 805-395-7288
Year Founded: 1866
Emp.: 480
Fiscal Year-end: 12/31/91
Newspaper Publishing, Commercial Printing
S.I.C.: 2711
Virginia F. Moorhouse *(Chm. Bd. & Publr.)*
Michael J. Fisch *(Pres. & Cheif Exec. Officer)*
Daniel A. Lacey *(Chief Fin. Officer & Dir.-Admin.)*
Alfred T. Fritts *(V.P.-Special Projects)*
Harold S. Clifton *(Sec.)*
Jolene D. Selby *(Controller)*
Bob Johnson *(Dir.-Communications)*
John Wells *(Dir.-Sls. & Mktg.)*
Robert Bently *(Exec. Editor & Dir.-News Editing Div.)*

Outside Service Firm(s):

Price Waterhouse*(Auditors)*
Bakersfield, CA

Zinser & Domina*(Legal Firm)*
Nashville, TN
Tel.: 615-244-9700

Union Bank*(Major Banking Relationship)*
3810 Wilshire Blvd.
Los Angeles, CA 90010
Tel.: 213-480-6566

BALCO, INC. (MA)
306 Northern Ave., Bldg. 53
Boston, MA 02205
Tel.: 617-482-0100
Fax: 617-951-2991
Year Founded: 1941
Approx.Sls.: $28,000,000
Emp.: 175
Fiscal Year-end: 12/31/90
Plumbing, Fire Protection, Facility Automation, Heating, Ventilation & Air Conditioning Service, Design, Repair & Construction, Cogeneration, Energy Services
S.I.C.: 1711; 1796; 1799; 8711
Anthony I. Shaker *(Pres.)*
Michael J. Kotubey *(V.P.-Construction Sls.)*
Wayne Webber *(V.P.-Construction Opers.)*
Howard McKew *(V.P.-Engrng.)*
Gus Pesaturo *(V.P.-Service Sls.)*
Walter Mahoney *(V.P.-Service Opers.)*

BALDI, BLOOM & WHELAN ADVERTISING
41 Madison Ave.
New York, NY 10010
Tel.: 212-679-1400
Fax: 212-213-0112
Year Founded: 1982
Approx.Billings: $41,240,000
Emp.: 43
Jack Bloom *(Pres.)*
Joseph Baldi, Jr. *(Exec. V.P.)*
Nancy Whelan *(Exec. V.P.)*

BALDT, INC.
P.O. Box 350
Chester, PA 19016
Tel.: 215-447-5200
Fax: 215-874-8599
Sales Range: $10-19 Million
Emp.: 75
Fiscal Year-end: 12/31/90
Import Export
Mooring, Anchoring & Rigging Systems For Offshore Construction & Commerical Shipping; Acoustic Release Systems
S.I.C.: 3296; 3462
P.J. Carcara *(Pres. & Chief Exec. Officer)*
G.S. Supplee *(Pres. & Owner)*
Robert McCauley *(Chief Fin. Officer)*
Principal(s):
P.J. Carcara
G.S. Supplee

No. of Mfg. Plants/Facilities: 1
No. of U.S. Offices: 1

Outside Service Firm(s):

Price Waterhouse*(Auditors)*
30 S. 17th St.
Philadelphia, PA 19103
Tel.: 215-665-9500

Morgan, Lewis & Bockius*(Legal Firm)*
2000 One Logan Square
Philadelphia, PA 19103
Tel.: 215-963-5000

BALDWIN CONSTRUCTION, INC.
301 E. Lincoln Ave.
Fort Collins, CO 80524
Tel.: 303-482-7722 **CO**
Fax: 303-484-7428
Year Founded: 1982
Assets: $1,273,000
Liabilities: $490,000
Net Worth: $783,000
Approx.Sls.: $23,500,000
Emp.: 25
Fiscal Year-end: 2/28/91
Construction Managers, General Contractor, Commercial Construction
S.I.C.: 1542; 8741
Corporate Giving Program: United Way; Mercy Medical Center; Colorado State University Foundation
Ed F. Baldwin *(Chm. Bd., Pres. & Treas.)*
William J. Griffith *(Chief Fin. Officer & Controller)*
Bill Carpenter *(V.P.)*
Steve Ferguson *(V.P.)*
Fred J. Sauer *(V.P.)*
Cherlynn S. Baldwin *(Sec.)*
Principal(s):
Ed F. Baldwin

No. of U.S. Offices: 2

Computer Systems/Hardware:
IBM Software Shop

Outside Service Firm(s):

T. F. Bauerie & Company*(Auditors)*
Denver, CO

Talbert Corp.*(Commercial Insurance Carrier)*
Denver, CO

Hospital Services, Inc.*(Group Insurer)*
Ft. Collins, CO

Boettcher & Co.*(Investment Banker)*
Denver, CO

Fischer, Brown, Huddleston & Gunn*(Legal Firm)*
Fort Collins, CO

Norwest Bank*(Major Banking Relationship)*
Ft. Collins, CO

Norwest Bank*(Pension Manager)*
Ft. Collins, CO

BALE OF KENTUCKY, INC.
1288 E. Main St.
Horse Cave, KY 42749
Mailing Address:
P.O. Box 316
Horse Cave, KY 42749
Tel.: 502-786-2124 **KY**
Fax: 502-786-2120
Year Founded: 1984
Approx.Sls.: $83,000,000
Emp.: 200
Tobacco Auctioning & Warehousing; Petroleum Bulk Stations; Bituminous Coal & Lignite-Surface; Ground Limestones; Wholesale Distribution of Tires, Tubes, Supplies & Parts
S.I.C.: 5159; 5171; 1221; 1422; 5014; 5013
James K. Bale *(Pres.)*
David Denton *(Treas. & Sec.)*

Outside Service Firm(s):

First National Bank*(Major Banking Relationship)*
Florence, AL

Subsidiary:

Farmers Investment Company, Inc. (1)
1288 E. Main St.
Horse Cave, KY 42749
Tel.: 502-786-2124
Approx.Sls.: $54,000,000
Emp.: 150
Tobacco Auctioning & Warehousing; Motels; Commercial & Industrial Building Operation
S.I.C.: 5159; 7011; 6512
James K. Bale *(Pres.)*
David Denton *(Controller)*
Ruth Dale Scharden *(Sec.)*

GEO. J. BALL, INC.
622 Town Rd.
West Chicago, IL 60185-2698
Tel.: 708-231-3600 **IL**

Geo. J. Ball, Inc.—(Continued)

Fax: 708-231-3507
Sales Range: $60-79 Million
Emp.: 400
Fiscal Year-end: 6/30/91
Import Export
Wholesale of Suppliers to Flower & Vegetable Growing Industry; Super Seedlings, Flower & Vegetable Seeds, Plant Containers & Growing Supplies
S.I.C.: 0181; 5191; 5193
G. Carl Ball *(Chm. Bd.)*
Victor Ball *(Vice Chm.)*
Anna C. Ball *(Pres.)*
John S. Guenther *(Sr. V.P.)*
Barrie Ricketts *(V.P.-Fin. & Treas.)*
Nickolas Kaskovich *(Controller)*
John A. Harrington *(Sec. & Asst. Treas.)*

Computer Systems/Hardware:
IBM System AS 400

Outside Service Firm(s):

Arthur Andersen & Co.*(Auditors)*
33 W. Monroe St.
Chicago, IL 60603-4067
Tel.: 312-580-0033
Fax: 312-507-6748

Liberty Mutual*(Commercial Insurance Carrier)*
Boston, MA

Metropolitan Life Insurance Co.*(Group Insurer)*
One Madison Ave.
New York, NY 10010-3690
Tel.: 215-578-9292

Bank of America NT&SA*(Major Banking Relationship)*
200 W. Adams, 28th Fl.
Chicago, IL 60606
Tel.: 312-269-4600

LaSalle National Bank*(Major Banking Relationship)*
135 S. LaSalle St., Rm.260
Chicago, IL 60603

The Northern Trust Co.*(Major Banking Relationship)*
50 S. LaSalle St.
Chicago, IL 60675
Tel.: 312-630-6000
Fax: 312-630-6516

Divisions:

Ball Seed Co. **(1)**
622 Town Rd.
West Chicago, IL 60185-2698
Tel.: 708-231-3500
Fax: 708-231-3605
Distribution of Horticultural Products to Greenhouse Growers
S.I.C.: 5191; 5193
James Huggins *(Pres.)*
John Bourke *(V.P.-Fin.)*
D.T. Thomas *(V.P.-Sls. & Mktg.)*

Pan-American Seed Co. **(1)**
728 Town Rd.
West Chicago, IL 60185
Tel.: 708-231-1400
Fax: 708-231-1419
Emp.: 35
Flower Seed Breeders & Producers
S.I.C.: 0181
George Ball, Jr. *(Pres.)*
Hans Miller *(V.P.-Fin.)*
Ben Walraven *(V.P.-Sls.)*
Ben Lacson *(V.P.-Opers.)*
Francis Kwong *(V.P.-Res. & Devel.)*
Sten Larsson *(Dir.-European Sls.)*

Subsidiaries:

W. Atlee Burpee Co. **(1)**
300 Park Ave.
Warminster, PA 18974
Tel.: 215-674-4900
Fax: 215-674-4170
Sales Range: $40-59 Million
Emp.: 215
Fiscal Year-end: 6/30/92
Import Export
Computer Systems/Hardware:
IBM 4341
Mail Order Seeds, Bulbs, Nursery Stock, Gen. Mdse.
S.I.C.: 0181; 5961
George Ball *(Pres.)*
Christian M. Troll *(Exec. V.P.)*
Scott Phillips *(V.P.-Mktg.)*
James DeLash *(Dir.-Direct Mktg.)*

Petoseed Co. **(1)**
1905 Lirio
Saticoy, CA 93003
Tel.: 805-647-1188 (100%)
Fax: 805-656-5012
Import Export
Vegetable Seed Production
S.I.C.: 0181
Dietrich Schmidt *(Pres.)*
James Larkin *(V.P.-Fin.)*
David Atkinson *(V.P.-Mktg.)*
Allen Stevens *(V.P.-Res.)*
Richard Edsall *(V.P.-Production)*
C. Edward Green *(V.P.-New Sciences)*

Non-U.S. Holding:

Ball Superior Ltd. **(1)**
1155 Birchview Dr.
Mississauga, ON L5H 3E1, Canada
Tel.: 416-278-5204
Wholesale Horticultural Products
S.I.C.: 5193
Brian Tregunno *(Gen. Mgr.)*

BALLENGER PAVING COMPANY, INC.
900 W. Lee Rd.
Taylors, SC 29687
Mailing Address:
P.O. Box 127
Greenville, SC 29602
Tel.: 803-292-9550 **SC**
Fax: 803-244-9310
Year Founded: 1988
Assets: $8,000,000
Liabilities: $5,500,000
Net Worth: $2,500,000
Approx.Sls.: $22,700,000
Emp.: 155
Fiscal Year-end: 12/31/91
Concrete Paving of Airports & Highways
S.I.C.: 1611
M. Lee Powell, III *(Pres.)*
Stewart H. Johnson *(V.P. & Sec.)*
George D. Johnson *(V.P. & Treas.)*
R.C. Ashmore *(V.P. & Asst. Sec.)*
Mike E. Mace *(V.P. & Asst. Sec.)*
C. Scott Childers *(Controller)*
Grady Ballenger *(Mgr.)*
Olif Ellison *(Pur. Agent)*
Principal(s):
M. Lee Powell, III
Stewart H. Johnson
George D. Johnson
R.C. Ashmore
Mike E. Mace

Computer Systems/Hardware:
IBM RT-125

Outside Service Firm(s):

Ernst & Young*(Auditors)*
C & S Bank Tower, Two Shelter Centre, Ste. 800
Greenville, SC 29603

Aetna Life & Casualty*(Commercial Insurance Carrier)*
Greenville, SC 29602

Benefit Planning Services, Inc. (TPA)*(Commercial Insurance Carrier)*
Spartanburg, SC

Smith & Fleming*(Legal Firm)*
Atlanta, GA

Carolina First Bank*(Major Banking Relationship)*
P.O. Box 1029, 102 Main St.
Greenville, SC 29602

Edgar Norris & Co., Inc.*(Pension Manager)*
Greenville, SC

Y.C. BALLENGER ELECTRICAL CONTRACTORS
2627 N. Pine St.
Spartanburg, SC 29304
Tel.: 803-599-4747
Fax: 803-578-7702
Approx.Sls.: $20,000,000
Emp.: 350
Fiscal Year-end: 9/30/92
Pole Line Construction & Electrical Contractor
S.I.C.: 1623; 1731
W. David Poole, Jr. *(Pres.)*
Tim L. Moore *(V.P.)*
Jane Ballenger May *(Sec. & Treas.)*

Outside Service Firm(s):

Smith, Kessler & Co.*(Auditors)*
Gaffeney, SC

Johnson Smith Hibbard & Cleveland*(Legal Firm)*
Spartanburg, SC

NationsBank Carolinas*(Major Banking Relationship)*
One NCNB Plaza T18-7
Charlotte, NC 28255

BALLET MAKERS, INC.
One Campus Rd.
Totowa, NJ 07512
Tel.: 201-595-9000
Fax: 201-595-1767
Year Founded: 1887
Sales Range: $40-59 Million
Emp.: 500
Mfr. of Dance Shoes, Garments & Accessories
S.I.C.: 2389; 2339; 2369; 3149
Nick Terlizzi, Jr. *(Chm. Bd.)*
Alfred Terlizzi *(Pres.)*
Anthony Giacoio *(Chief Exec. Officer)*
Donald Terlizzi *(Exec. V.P.)*
Bert Robinson *(Sr. V.P.)*
Janine Misdom *(Mgr.-Communications)*

Outside Service Firm(s):

Lutz & Carr*(Auditors)*
New York, NY

Koenig, Rotner & Mott*(Legal Firm)*
New York, NY

First Fidelity Bank, N.A.*(Major Banking Relationship)*
Totowa, NJ

Subsidiary:

Capezio Ballet Makers, Inc. **(1)**
1411 Broadway
New York, NY 10018
Tel.: 212-354-1887
S.I.C.: 3149
Alfred Terlizzi *(Pres.)*

B.A. BALLOU & CO. INC.
800 Waterman Ave.
East Providence, RI 02914
Tel.: 401-438-7000
Fax: 401-434-3336
Approx.Sls.: $25,000,000
Jewelry Findings; Jewelry
S.I.C.: 3911; 3915
F. Remington Ballou *(Pres.)*
E. L. Caldwell *(V.P.)*
Ken Delisle *(Treas.)*
John J. Alves *(Mgr.-Findings Sls.)*
J. Douglas McDowell *(Mgr.-Jewelry Sls.)*
Arthur J. Mott *(Mgr.-Intl. Sls.)*
Rene Yates *(Pur. Agent)*

Outside Service Firm(s):

Sansiveri, Ryan & Sullivan*(Auditors)*
Providence, RI

Hinkley, Allen, Snyder & Comen*(Legal Firm)*
1500 Fleet Ctr.
Providence, RI 02903
Tel.: 401-274-2000

Rhode Island Hospital Trust National Bank*(Major Banking Relationship)*
Hospital Trust Tower
Providence, RI

BALTIC LINEN COMPANY, INC.
260 W. Sunrise Hwy.
Valley Stream, NY 11582
Tel.: 516-791-4500
Fax: 516-792-2124
Year Founded: 1936
Approx.Sls.: $70,000,000
Emp.: 100
Wholesale Institutional Textiles
S.I.C.: 5023
Marvin Greenberg *(Chm. Bd.)*
Frank Greenberg *(Pres.)*
Mark Lichter *(V.P. & Sec.)*

Outside Service Firm(s):

Marine Midland Bank*(Major Banking Relationship)*
250 Park Ave.
New York, NY 10177
Tel.: 212-949-6527

BALTIMORE LUGGAGE COMPANY
1919 Anapolis Rd.
Baltimore, MD 21230
Tel.: 410-539-1100
Fax: 410-752-3108
Approx.Sls.: $20,000,000
Emp.: 200
Luggage; Amelia Earhart, Wallstreeter by Earhart, Airlite by Earhart, Lady Baltimore, Lord Baltimore, Tweeds by Earhart & Nonstop by Earhart, British Tweeds, Dynamite by Earhart
S.I.C.: 3161
Harvey Bones *(Pres.)*

BALTIMORE ORIOLES, INC.
Memorial Stadium
Baltimore, MD 21218
Mailing Address:
333 W. Camden St.
Baltimore, MD 21201
Tel.: 410-685-9800
Fax: 410-467-5333
Year Founded: 1954
Approx.Sls.: $30,000,000
Emp.: 80
Fiscal Year-end: 12/31/90
Import
Baseball Team
S.I.C.: 3949
Eli S. Jacobs *(Chm. Bd.)*
Lawrence Lucchino *(Pres.)*
Bob Aylward *(V.P.-Bus. Affairs)*
Martin B. Conway *(V.P.-Mktg.)*
Roland Hemond *(V.P. & Gen. Mgr.)*
Aric Holsinger *(V.P.-Fin.)*
Robert Crisafulli, Jr. *(Treas.)*
M. Schein *(Sec.)*
Robert W. Brown *(Dir.-Pub. Rels.)*
David Cope *(Dir.-Adv. & Mktg.)*

BALTIMORE STATIONERY CO.
2524 Kirk Ave.
Baltimore, MD 21218
Mailing Address:
P.O. Box 16010,
Baltimore, MD 21218
Tel.: 410-366-6000 **MD**
Fax: 410-366-7012
Year Founded: 1930
Approx.Sls.: $35,000,000
Emp.: 165
Fiscal Year-end: 5/31/92
Sales & Service of Office Furniture & Equipment; Interior Design, Layout, Space Planning, Office Supplies, Printing & School Furniture
S.I.C.: 2522; 2531; 7389; 2759; 5044; 5049; 5112

Barbara R. Jones *(Chm. Bd.)*
William W. Jones, Jr. *(Pres. & Chief Exec. Officer)*
John S. Sharff *(Exec. V.P. & Chief Oper. Officer)*
Clyde H. Shaffer *(Sr. V.P.-Sls. & Mktg.)*
Warren Smith *(Sr. V.P.-Admin.)*
Michael Haas *(V.P.-Stationery)*
Ted Wasielewski *(V.P.-Personnel)*
Richard M. Klein *(Sec.)*
Alan L. McCracken *(Comptroller & Treas.)*
Don Akehurst *(Mgr.-Computer Services)*
John R. Franklin *(Mgr.-Mktg. & Adv.)*

Principal(s):
Barbara R. Jones
William W. Jones, Jr.

No. of Mfg. Plants/Facilities: 3
No. of U.S. Offices: 3

Computer Systems/Hardware:
IBM RISC 6000

Outside Service Firm(s):

Deloitte & Touche*(Auditors)*
1100 Mercantile Bank Bldg., 2 Hopkins Plaza
Baltimore, MD 21201
Tel.: 410-576-6700

V. B. & Howard*(Legal Firm)*
Mercantile Building, 2 Hopkins Plaza
Baltimore, MD 21201

Maryland National Bank*(Major Banking Relationship)*
2 N. Charles St.
Baltimore, MD 21202

Signet Bank*(Major Banking Relationship)*
P.O. Box 1077, 7 St. Paul St.
Baltimore, MD 21203

BAM PUBLICATIONS, INC.
3470 Buskirk Ave.
Pleasant Hill, CA 94523
Tel.: 510-934-3700
Fax: 510-934-3958
Year Founded: 1976
Sales Range: $10-19 Million
Emp.: 70
Export
Magazine Publisher
S.I.C.: 2721
Dennis Erokan *(Pres. & Editor-in-Chief)*
Art Magnus *(Chief Fin. Officer)*
Joe Amadeo *(Publr.-Bam)*
Mike Calamusa *(Publr.-Drive Magazine)*
Chuck Stanley *(Publr.-Micro Times)*
Steven Gellman *(Adv. Dir.-Southern California)*

Principal(s):
Dennis Erokan

No. of U.S. Offices: 6

Computer Systems/Hardware:
Apple Macintosh; Compaq; Zenith

Outside Service Firm(s):

Travelers Insurance Co.*(Group Insurer)*
1 Tower Square
Hartford, CT 06183-2492
Tel.: 203-277-4542
Fax: 203-277-5038

Arthur Sohcat*(Legal Firm)*
San Francisco, CA

Bank of America NT&SA*(Major Banking Relationship)*
Oakland, CA

BANANA SERVICES INC.
2100 Salzedo St., Ste. 303
Coral Gables, FL 33134
Tel.: 305-441-9036
Fax: 305-446-4291
Approx.Sls.: $43,000,000
Emp.: 120
Import & Distribute Bananas & Fruits
S.I.C.: 5148
Luis Guillermo Velasquez *(Pres.)*
Rosie Elton *(V.P.)*
Luis Laya *(V.P.)*
Hernan Mesa *(Dir.-Sls.)*

Computer Systems/Hardware:
IBM

BANDINI FERTILIZER COMPANY
4139 Bandini Blvd.
Los Angeles, CA 90023
Tel.: 213-263-7391
Fax: 213-268-3274
Emp.: 95
Mfr. Plant Foods, Fertilizers & Soil Products
S.I.C.: 2873; 2874; 2879
Byron Reynolds, Jr. *(Chief Exec. Officer)*
James Joseph *(Pres.)*
Don McKenna *(Controller)*
Jim Story *(Mgr.-Sls.)*
Don Knipp *(Mgr.-Mktg.)*

Outside Service Firm(s):

Bank of America*(Major Banking Relationship)*
701 S. Western Ave.
Los Angeles, CA 91201

BANDY CARROLL HELLIGE ADVERTISING
239 S. Fifth St., Ste. 18
Louisville, KY 40202
Tel.: 502-589-7711
Fax: 502-589-0390
Year Founded: 1972
Approx.Billings: $11,495,000
Emp.: 25
Food & Business-to-Business Adv.
Tim Hellige *(Chm.)*
Mark Carroll *(Co-Chm.)*
Susan Bandy *(Pres.)*

Computer Systems/Hardware:
MacIntosh

BANK M F & COMPANY, INC.
615 First Ave., N.E.
Minneapolis, MN 55413
Tel.: 612-379-2810 **MN**
Fax: 612-379-0415
Year Founded: 1978
Approx.Sls.: $22,000,000
Emp.: 250
Appraisal Service & Miscellaneous Retail Stores; Commercial & Office Buildings Renovation & Repair
S.I.C.: 7389; 5999
Marvin F. Bank *(Chm. Bd.)*
Morton B. Bank *(Pres. & Chief Exec. Officer)*
Christian C. Hafstead *(Chief Fin. Officer)*
David L. Bank *(Exec. V.P.)*
Richard C. Lien *(Exec. V.P.)*
Michael F. Bank *(V.P.)*

Outside Service Firm(s):

Norwest Bank Minnesota, N.A.*(Major Banking Relationship)*
P.O. Box 2900, Loop Station
Minneapolis, MN 55402
Tel.: 612-372-8114

BANK OF NORTH DAKOTA
700 E. Main St.
Bismarck, ND 58502
Tel.: 701-224-5600
Fax: 701-224-5632
Year Founded: 1919
Assets: $956,758,548
Liabilities: $863,840,828
Net Worth: $92,917,720
Approx.Sls.: $16,413,783
Emp.: 165
Fiscal Year-end: 12/31/91
Bank
S.I.C.: 6022
Joseph S. Lamb *(Pres. & Chief Exec. Officer)*
John Malmberg *(Chief Oper. Officer & Exec. V.P.)*
Dale Eberle *(Sr. V.P.-Retail & Bank Opers.)*
Robert Gruman *(Sr. V.P.-Lending)*
Edward B. Sather *(Sr. V.P.-Investments & Trust)*
Timothy Moore *(V.P.)*
Kirby Martz *(Controller)*
Carl Arndt *(Mgr.-Opers.)*

No. of U.S. Offices: 1

Computer Systems/Hardware:
IBM

Outside Service Firm(s):

Brady, Martz & Associates*(Auditors)*
Grand Forks, ND

BANK SHARES, INC.
P.O. Box 1467
Minneapolis, MN 55480
Tel.: 612-341-5757
Fax: 612-341-5680
Assets: $2,467,262,000
Liabilities: $2,326,037,000
Net Worth: $141,225,000
Approx.Rev.: $204,284,000
Emp.: 1,067
Fiscal Year-end: 12/31/90
Bank Holding Company
S.I.C.: 6719; 6021
Carl R. Pohlad *(Pres.)*
Donald E. Benson *(Exec. V.P.)*
Thomas A. Herbst *(Exec. V.P.)*
Jann Ozzello Wilcox *(V.P. & Chief Fin. Officer)*
William McKnight *(V.P.-Human Resources)*
Paige Winebarger *(V.P. & Counsel)*
Bruce W. Gilmore *(V.P. & Sec.)*
Robert T. Lund *(V.P. & Assoc. Counsel)*
Nadine E. Schissel *(V.P.-Staffing & Compensation)*
James O. Pohlad *(V.P.)*
Albert J. Colianni, Jr. *(V.P.)*
Charles A. Martin *(Controller)*

Outside Service Firm(s):

Arthur Andersen & Co.*(Auditors)*
45 S. 7th St.
Minneapolis, MN 55402

Briggs & Morgan*(Legal Firm)*
Minneapolis, MN

Subsidiaries:

Marquette Bank Minneapolis, National Association **(1)**
Sixth & Marquette
Minneapolis, MN 55480
Tel.: 612-341-5600
Fax: 612-341-5680
Emp.: 833
Carl R. Pohlad *(Pres.)*
Albert J. Colianni, Jr. *(Exec. V.P. & Chief Oper. Officer)*
Thomas A. Herbst *(Exec. V.P.)*
Thomas H. Jenkins *(Sr. V.P.-Bus. Banking)*
Jerry W. Hayes *(Sr. V.P.-Opers. & Instituional Sls.)*
W. Douglas Hile *(Sr. V.P.-Consumer Banking)*
Jann Ozzello Wilcox *(Sr. V.P. & Chief Fin. Officer)*
Paige Winebarger *(V.P. & Corp. Sec.)*
Jane Warrelmann *(Chief Quality Officer)*

Marquette Bank Rochester **(1)**
P.O. BOx 4800
Rochester, MN 55903
Tel.: 507-285-2600
Fax: 507-285-2639
Emp.: 105
Bank
S.I.C.: 6022
Dennis Williams *(Pres.)*
J. Van Sickle *(Sr. V.P.)*
C.L. Jossart *(Sr. V.P. & Controller)*
A. Freiborg *(Sr. V.P.)*
T.J. Shea *(V.P.)*
I.J. Lewison *(V.P.)*
W.J. Nigbur *(V.P.)*
G. Brinkman *(V.P.)*
Jon Adams *(V.P.)*
Stephen Knox *(V.P.)*
C. Bedney *(V.P.)*
J. Olson *(V.P.)*
J. Siegel *(V.P.)*
B. Pawlik *(Cashier)*

BANKCRAFTERS, INC.
12 Oregon Ave.
Philadelphia, PA 19148
Tel.: 215-467-3700 **PA**
Fax: 215-463-7870
Year Founded: 1963
Approx.Sls.: $11,000,000
Emp.: 200
Mfr. Wooden & Metal Store Fixtures & Refrigeration Fixtures
S.I.C.: 2542; 2541; 3499; 3089
Daniel S. Bernheim, Jr. *(Pres.)*
Herbert Dickler *(Treas. & Sec.)*
Carmen Taradorelli *(Dir.-Adv.)*

Computer Systems/Hardware:
IBM

Outside Service Firm(s):

Goldenberg & Rosenthal*(Auditors)*
Philadelphia, PA

Provident National Bank*(Major Banking Relationship)*
1000 Westlakes Dr.
Berwyn, PA 19312

BANKERS SYSTEMS INC.
6815 Sauk View Dr.
Saint Cloud, MN 56303
Mailing Address:
P.O. Box 1457
St. Cloud, MN 56302
Tel.: 612-251-3060
Tel.: 800-397-2341 **MN**
Fax: 612-251-8110
Year Founded: 1952
Approx.Sls.: $68,000,000
Emp.: 850
Print Legal, Technical & Financial Forms, Brochures & Promotional Material
S.I.C.: 2752
William E. Clemens *(Chm. Bd. & Chief Exec. Officer)*
John P. Weitzel *(Pres. & Chief Oper. Officer)*
John P. Clemens *(Sr. Exec. V.P.)*
Randy Potter *(Exec. V.P.)*
Mary Sue Poiter *(Exec. V.P.)*
Jack Lochner *(Sr. V.P.-Sls. & Mktg.)*
John Swift *(V.P.)*
Ronald Johnson *(Sec. & Gen. Counsel)*
Raymond L. Bernardy *(Treas.)*

BANKHEAD ENTERPRISES INC.
1080 Bankhead Ave.
Atlanta, GA 30318
Tel.: 404-894-7900
Fax: 404-894-7963
Approx.Sls.: $40,000,000
Emp.: 500
Manufacture Automobile Carrier Trailers; Asphalt & Paving
S.I.C.: 1771; 2951; 3715
G. Frank Felder *(Pres.)*
D. Perry Kinard *(V.P.)*
Edward Thompson *(V.P.)*
Beatrice V. Taylor *(Treas.)*
Glenda Cole *(Corp. Sec.)*
Everette Barker *(Asst. Sec.)*
Thomas Gresham *(Asst. Sec.)*

Outside Service Firm(s):

Hopkins & Gresham*(Legal Firm)*
120 Ralph McGill Blvd.
Atlanta, GA 30308
Tel.: 404-892-3100

Bankhead Enterprises Inc.—(Continued)

Trust Company Bank*(Major Banking Relationship)*
Trust Co. Tower
Atlanta, GA 30303
Tel.: 404-588-7963

BANKMANAGERS CORP.
7540 W. Capitol Dr.
Milwaukee, WI 53216
Tel.: 414-466-1940 **WI**
Fax: 414-466-7773
Year Founded: 1970
Assets: $21,295,861
Liabilities: $1,135,738
Net Worth: $20,160,123
Emp.: 115
Fiscal Year-end: 12/31/91
Bank Holding Company
S.I.C.: 6022; 6719
P. Michael Mahoney *(Pres.)*
Michael J. Kelly *(V.P.)*
James W. Wright *(V.P. & Sec.)*
Cynthia K. Rutkowski *(Treas.)*

No. of U.S. Offices: 2

Outside Service Firm(s):

Deloitte & Touche*(Auditors)*
250 E. Wisconsin Ave.
Milwaukee, WI 53202-4283
Tel.: 414-271-3000

Chubb Group*(Commercial Insurance Carrier)*
330 E. Kilbourn Ave.
Milwaukee, WI 53202

Wausau Insurance*(Group Insurer)*
11270 W. Park Pl.
Milwaukee, WI

Foley & Lardner*(Legal Firm)*
777 E. Wisconsin Ave.
Milwaukee, WI 53202
Tel.: 414-271-2400

Park Bank*(Major Banking Relationship)*
Milwaukee, WI

First Wisconsin Trust Company*(Pension Manager)*
777 E. Wisconsin Ave.
Milwaukee, WI

Subsidiary:

Park Bank **(1)**
330 E. Kilbourn Ave.
Milwaukee, WI 53202
Tel.: 414-466-8000
Fax: 414-223-3077
Emp.: 115
Bank
S.I.C.: 6022
P. Michael Mahoney *(Chm. Bd. & Pres.)*
James W. Wright *(Sr. V.P. & Cashier)*
Andrew T. Sawyer Jr. *(Exec. V.P.)*
Robert E. Long *(Sr. V.P. & Admin.)*

W. O. BANKSTON ENTERPRISES INC.
4755 McEwen Rd.
Dallas, TX 75244
Tel.: 214-788-5400 **TX**
Year Founded: 1971
Approx.Sls.: $172,000,000
Emp.: 420
Fiscal Year-end: 3/31/90
Holding Company; Automobile Dealerships
S.I.C.: 6719; 5511
William O. Bankston *(Chm. Bd.)*
James G. Bankston *(Pres.)*
Edward B. Stone *(V.P. & Sec.)*
Christopher L. Price *(Treas.)*
Principal(s):
William O. Bankston
James G. Bankston

Outside Service Firm(s):

Ernst & Young*(Auditors)*
2121 San Jacinto, Ste. 500
Dallas, TX 75201
Tel.: 214-969-8000

Marvin Thomas*(Legal Firm)*
Dallas, TX

Texas Commerce Bank*(Major Banking Relationship)*
2200 Ross Ave.
Dallas, TX 75266

Subsidiaries:

Bankston Nissan in Irving, Inc. **(1)**
1580 East Airport Fwy.
Irving, TX 75062
Tel.: 214-438-4300
Automobile Dealership
S.I.C.: 5511
Bob Swanson *(Pres.)*

W. O. Bankston Leasing Inc. **(1)**
4747 LBJ Fwy.
Dallas, TX 75234
Tel.: 214-233-1441
Automobile Rental & Leasing
S.I.C.: 7514
William O. Bankston *(Pres.)*

W. O. Bankston Lincoln Mercury **(1)**
4747 LBJ Fwy.
Dallas, TX 75240
Tel.: 214-233-1441
Automobile Dealership
S.I.C.: 5511
William O. Bankston *(Chm. Bd. & Pres.)*

W. O. Bankston Nissan Inc. **(1)**
13130 Preston Rd.
Dallas, TX 75240
Tel.: 214-450-2400
Automobile Dealership
S.I.C.: 5511
Don Miller *(Pres.)*

BANNER ASSOCIATES INC.
620 Plaza Ct.
Laramie, WY 82070
Mailing Address:
P.O. Box 550
Laramie, WY 82070
Tel.: 307-745-7366 **WY**
Fax: 307-721-2152
Year Founded: 1947
Assets: $11,983,464
Liabilities: $8,710,357
Net Worth: $3,273,107
Sales Range: $10-19 Million
Emp.: 120
Fiscal Year-end: 10/31/91
Consulting Engineers & Architects
S.I.C.: 8711; 8712
James O. Edwards *(Chm. Bd.)*
Forrest M. Kepler, Jr. *(Pres.)*
Kenneth J. Brotsky *(V.P.)*
Jim I. Cavalli *(V.P.)*
Timothy R. Conner *(V.P.)*
Kenneth G. Moore *(V.P. & Sec.)*
Fred J. Rittershaus *(V.P. & Treas.)*
Christian H. Gunther *(Comptroller)*

No. of U.S. Offices: 4

Computer Systems/Hardware:
DEC VAX 3400 & 3100

Outside Service Firm(s):

McGladrey & Pullen*(Auditors)*
320 W. 25th
Cheyenne, WY
Tel.: 307-634-2151

Jones, Jones, Vines, Hunkins*(Legal Firm)*
Wheatland, WY

First Interstate Bank*(Major Banking Relationship)*
Laramie, WY

BANNER ENGINEERING CORP.
9714 10th Ave. N.
Minneapolis, MN 55441
Tel.: 612-544-3164 **MN**
Fax: 612-544-3213
Industrial Controls Manufacturing
S.I.C.: 3625
Robert Fayfield *(Pres., Chief Exec. Officer & Chm. Bd.)*

Outside Service Firm(s):

Peat Marwick Main & Co.*(Auditors)*
St. Paul, MN

Lindquist & Vennum*(Legal Firm)*
Minneapolis, MN

Norwest Bank Calhoun-Isles, N.A.*(Major Banking Relationship)*
1455 W. Lake St.
Minneapolis, MN 55408
Tel.: 612-827-8700

BANNER WHOLESALE GROCERS, INC.
115 S. Water Market
Chicago, IL 60608
Tel.: 312-421-2650 **IL**
Fax: 312-421-1257
Approx.Sls.: $35,000,000
Emp.: 55
General Line Of Groceries
S.I.C.: 5141
Albert Friedman *(Pres.)*
Irving Saltzman *(Treas.)*
Shirley Saltzman *(Sec.)*
Irwin Friedman *(Asst. Sec.)*
Richard Saltzman *(Asst. Treas.)*
Principal(s):
Albert Friedman
Irving Saltzman
Shirley Saltzman
Irwin Friedman
Richard Saltzman

Outside Service Firm(s):

Irving Nathan & Associates*(Auditors)*
Chicago, IL

Colman Ginsparg*(Legal Firm)*
Chicago, IL

BAR-S FOODS CO.
4041 N. Central, Ste. 1300
Phoenix, AZ 85012
Mailing Address:
P.O. Box 29049
Phoenix, AZ 85038
Tel.: 602-264-7272 **DE**
Fax: 602-285-5252
Year Founded: 1981
Assets: $42,000,000
Earnings: $6,000,000
Liabilities: $21,000,000
Net Worth: $21,000,000
Approx.Sls.: $300,000,000
Emp.: 800
Fiscal Year-end: 8/30/91
Processor & Distributor Meat & Poultry Products
S.I.C.: 2011; 2013; 2015
Timothy T. Day *(Pres. & Chief Exec. Officer)*
Morris Kinne *(V.P. & Gen. Counsel)*
Mike Paquette *(V.P.-Opers.)*
John Sirridge *(V.P.-Sls. & Mktg.)*
R.W. Uhl *(V.P.-Fin.)*
James S. Kuykendall *(Controller)*
Thomas F. Weinman *(Treas.)*
Joe Stewart *(Dir.-Mktg.)*
Bob Choronzuk *(Mgr.-Pur.)*
Principal(s):
Timothy T. Day
Morris Kinne
R.W. Uhl

No. of Mfg. Plants/Facilities: 2
No. of U.S. Offices: 10

Computer Systems/Hardware:
Honeywell Ultimate; IBM 9375

Outside Service Firm(s):

KPMG Peat Marwick*(Auditors)*
2020 No. Central Ave.
Phoenix, AZ 85004
Tel.: 602-253-2000

First Interstate Bank*(Major Banking Relationship)*
P.O. Box 53441,
Phoenix, AZ 85072-3441
Tel.: 602-229-4049

The Northern Trust Co.*(Pension Manager)*
50 S. LaSalle St.
Chicago, IL 60675
Tel.: 312-630-6000
Fax: 312-630-6516

BARANCORP
Northern Cross Ranch, Rte. 1
Lecompton, KS 66050
Tel.: 913-887-6010 **KS**
Sales Range: $10-19 Million
Emp.: 25
Import Export
Holding Company: Energy; Advertising & Public Relations; Investment Counseling; Investment Brokers; Publishing; Manufacturing
S.I.C.: 7311; 2741; 7389; 6719; 6531; 1382
Dennis A. Baranski *(Chm. Bd., Pres. & Chief Exec. Officer)*
Principal(s):
Dennis A. Baranski

No. of Mfg. Plants/Facilities: 1
No. of U.S. Offices: 2

Computer Systems/Hardware:
IBM

Divisions:

Baranski & Associates **(1)**
Northern Cross Ranch, Rte. 1
Lecompton, KS 66050
Tel.: 913-887-6010 (100%)
Approx.Sls.: $200,000
Emp.: 10
Commercial Advertising, Public & Market Research Relations, Legal-Arbitration, Mediation & Jury Selection Consulting Services
S.I.C.: 7311

Baranski Publishing Company **(1)**
Northern Cross Ranch, Rte. 1
Lecompton, KS 66050
Tel.: 913-887-6010 (100%)
Emp.: 4
Trade Book Publishers
S.I.C.: 2731

D. A. Baranski & Co. **(1)**
Northern Cross Ranch
Lecompton, KS 66050
Tel.: 913-887-6010 (100%)
Approx.Sls.: $750,000
Emp.: 10
Investment Brokerage: Real Estate, Art & Antiquities Appraisal Services, Commodities & Precious Metals
S.I.C.: 6531

Baranski Energy Company **(1)**
Northern Cross Ranch
Lecompton, KS 66050
Tel.: 913-887-6010 (100%)
Energy Research, Exploration & Development; Oil, Gas, Solar & Other Alternative Energy Sources
S.I.C.: 1382

Joseph A. Baranski Literary Agency **(1)**
Northern Cross Ranch, Rte. 1
Lecompton, KS 66050
Tel.: 913-887-6010 (100%)
Approx.Sls.: $125,000
Emp.: 5
Authors' Representatives, Foreign & Domestic
S.I.C.: 7389

Northern Cross, Ltd. **(1)**
Northern Cross Ranch, Rte. 1
Lecompton, KS 66050
Tel.: 913-887-6010 (100%)
Sales Range: $10-19 Million
Computer Systems/Hardware:
IBM

Mfr. of Survival Equipment for Motorists, Pilots, Backpackers, Hunters; Road Emergency Kit, Pocket Survival Kit, Road Survival Pak, Storm Survaval Pak, Campus Survival Pak
S.I.C.: 3999; 7389
Dennis A. Baranski *(Pres.)*

THE BARBAR GROUP, INC.
150 E. Palmetto Park Rd., Ste. 645
Boca Raton, FL 33432
Tel.: 407-368-0818
Fax: 407-395-2410
Year Founded: 1974
Sales Range: $40-59 Million
Emp.: 140
Land Developers
S.I.C.: 1629
George E. Barbar *(Chm. Bd. & Pres.)*
Anthony K.G. Barbar *(Exec. V.P.)*
Stephen Haskins *(V.P.-Fin., Treas. & Admin. Mgr.)*
Philip G. Barbar *(V.P.-Mktg.)*
Principal(s):
George E. Barbar
Anthony K.G. Barbar

No. of U.S. Offices: 4

Computer Systems/Hardware:
IBM, Macintosh, Digital Equip. Corp.

Outside Service Firm(s):

Ernst & Young*(Auditors)*
Boca Raton, FL

Blue Cross & Blue Shield Association*(Group Insurer)*
Boca Raton, FL

Moore, Farmer, Menkhaus & Juran*(Legal Firm)*
Boca Raton, FL

Steel, Hector & Davis*(Legal Firm)*
Boca Raton, FL

NationsBank Flordia*(Major Banking Relationship)*
Boca Raton, FL

Mutual Benefit Life Insurance*(Pension Manager)*
Boca Raton, FL

Subsidiaries:

Barbar Realty, Inc. **(1)**
150 E. Palmetto Park Rd., Ste. 101
Boca Raton, FL 33432
Tel.: 407-368-0818
Anthony K.G. Barbar *(Pres.)*

Boca Raton Financial Center **(1)**
150 E. Palmetto Park Rd.
Boca Raton, FL 33432
Tel.: 407-368-0818
Anthony K.G. Barbar *(Pres.)*

Woodfield Country Club **(1)**
3600 Club Place
Boca Raton, FL 33431
Tel.: 407-994-1000
Anthony K.G. Barbar *(Pres.)*

BARBER BROTHERS CONTRACTING COMPANY
2636 Dougherty Dr.
Baton Rouge, LA 70805
Tel.: 504-355-5611 **LA**
Fax: 504-355-5615
Year Founded: 1928
Approx.Sls.: $36,000,000
Emp.: 200
General Contractor; Highway & Street Construction & Maintenance
S.I.C.: 1611
Aubrey L. Barber, Jr. *(Pres.)*
Paul T. Barber *(V.P.)*

Outside Service Firm(s):

Hibernia National Bank*(Major Banking Relationship)*
New Orleans, LA

BARBER DAIRIES, INC.
36 Barber Court
Birmingham, AL 35209
Tel.: 205-942-2351
Fax: 205-942-8993
Year Founded: 1925
Sales Range: $100-499 Million
Emp.: 800
Fiscal Year-end: 12/31/91
Produces Milk & Milk Products
S.I.C.: 2026
George W. Barber, Jr. *(Chm. Bd., Chief Fin. Officer & Treas.)*
W.P. Langston *(Pres.)*
Vernon H. Hydorn *(Exec. V.P.)*
Ralph Lindsey *(V.P.-Mktg.)*
B. Austin Cunningham *(Asst. V.P., Mgr.-Real Estate & Risk Mngmt.)*
Phillip G. Mishalanie *(Controller)*
Carlyn Mcfall *(Dir.-Personnel)*
M.O. Tank *(Dir.-Pur.)*

No. of Mfg. Plants/Facilities: 6

Computer Systems/Hardware:
IBM System 34

Outside Service Firm(s):

Coopers & Lybrand*(Auditors)*
1901 6th Ave. North, Ste. 1600
Birmingham, AL 35203-2602

Liberty Mutual*(Commercial Insurance Carrier)*
Birmingham, AL

Blue Cross & Blue Shield of Alabama*(Group Insurer)*
450 Riverchase Pkwy. East
Birmingham, AL 35298
Tel.: 205-988-2245

Bradley, Arant, Rose & White*(Legal Firm)*
1400 Park Place Tower
Birmingham, AL 35203
Tel.: 205-521-8000

Division:

Barber Ice Cream Company **(1)**
36 Barber Court
Birmingham, AL 35209
Tel.: 205-942-2351
Fax: 205-942-8993
Approx.Sls.: $20,000,000
Emp.: 120
Fiscal Year-end: 12/31/90
Ice Cream Processor
S.I.C.: 2024
W. P. Langston *(Pres. & Chief Exec. Officer)*
Joseph Knott *(V.P.)*
Ralph Lindsey *(Mktg. Dir.)*
Carlyn McFall *(Personnel Dir.)*

BARCLAY WHITE INCORPORATED
22 Cassatt Ave.
Berwyn, PA 19312
Tel.: 215-296-3700 **PA**
Fax: 215-640-4489
Year Founded: 1913
Approx.Sls.: $90,000,000
Emp.: 65
Construction Management Services
S.I.C.: 1522; 1541; 1542; 6552
Robert B. Hemphill *(Chm., Pres. & Chief Exec. & Chief Oper. Officer)*
Robert J. Hyland *(Chief Fin. Officer & Treas.)*
Edwin W. Jorden *(Exec. V.P.)*
W. Wayne Dunlop *(Sr. V.P.)*
John J. Quigley *(V.P.-Construction)*
William H. Surgner *(V.P.-Mktg.)*
Nadene R. Cole *(Sec.)*

Computer Systems/Hardware:
Maxwell System

Outside Service Firm(s):

Rainer & Co.*(Auditors)*
Newton Square, PA

Duane, Morris & Heckscher*(Legal Firm)*
One Liberty Place
Philadelphia, PA 19103
Tel.: 215-979-1800

CoreStates First Pennsylvania Bank, N.A.*(Major Banking Relationship)*
Center Sq. West Tower, 15th & Market Streets
Philadelphia, PA 19101

BARD MFG. CO.
1914 Randolph Dr.
Bryan, OH 43506
Mailing Address:
P.O. Box 607,
Bryan, OH 43506
Tel.: 419-636-1194
Fax: 419-636-2640
Year Founded: 1914
Emp.: 350
Export
Mfr. of Gas-Oil Heating Equipment, Air to Air & Water to Air Heat Pumps & Air Conditioning Equipment
S.I.C.: 3567; 3699
Richard O. Bard *(Chm. Bd.)*
James R. Bard *(Pres.)*
John V. Briggs *(V.P.-Matls.)*
Ron Wenger *(V.P.-Mfg.)*
Thomas A. Williams *(V.P.-Sls.)*
Stephen R. Rieman *(Sec. & Treas.)*
Mike Lehman *(Dir.-Mktg.)*
Pam Bard Steel *(Prod. Mgr.-Residential)*
Bill Steel *(Mgr.-Human Resources)*

Outside Service Firm(s):

Baden, Conrad, Gage & Schroeder*(Auditors)*
Ft. Wayne, IN

BARDEN & ROBESON CORPORATION
103 Kelly Ave.
Middleport, NY 14105
Tel.: 716-735-3732
Fax: 716-735-3752
Emp.: 150
Prefabricated Homes
S.I.C.: 2452
G. Richard Barden *(Chm. Bd.)*
Robert Gelder *(Pres. & Treas.)*
Thomas Barden *(Exec. V.P. & Chief Exec. Officer)*
Mark Barden *(V.P.-Mktg.)*

Outside Service Firm(s):

J.D. Elliott & Co.*(Auditors)*
Buffalo, NY

Fleet Bank*(Major Banking Relationship)*
Deer Park, NY 14202

BARDES CORP.
4730 Madison Rd.
Cincinnati, OH 45227
Tel.: 513-871-4000 **OH**
Fax: 513-871-4084
Year Founded: 1908
Sales Range: $60-79 Million
Emp.: 650
Fiscal Year-end: 12/31/89
Export
Holding Co.; Manufacturer Electrical Connectors, Screw Machine Products, Tool & Die & Specialty Machines
S.I.C.: 6719; 3451; 3544; 3643
Brittain B. Cudlip *(Co-Chm. Bd.)*
Merrilyn Reynolds *(Co-Chm. Bd.)*
David A. FitzGibbon *(V.P. & Chief Oper. Officer)*
Marilyn Stoeckle *(V.P. & Sec.)*
James Valenting *(V.P.-Fin.)*

No. of Mfg. Plants/Facilities: 8
No. of U.S. Offices: 6
No. of Foreign Offices: 2

Outside Service Firm(s):

Arthur Andersen & Co.*(Auditors)*
425 Walnut St.
Cincinnati, OH 45202
Tel.: 513-381-6900

Taft, Stettinius & Hollister*(Legal Firm)*
First Natl. Bank Center
Cincinnati, OH 45202
Tel.: 513-381-2838

Star Bank*(Major Banking Relationship)*
425 Walnut Street
Cincinnati, OH 45202
Tel.: 513-632-4000

Subsidiary:

FTZ Industries, Inc. **(1)**
515 Palmetto Dr.
Simpsonville, SC 29681
Tel.: 803-963-5000
Manufacturer of Connectors
S.I.C.: 3643
Richard Feeny *(Gen. Mgr.)*

BARDONS & OLIVER, INC.
1133 West 9th
Cleveland, OH 44113
Tel.: 216-621-0195
Telex: 71201992
Fax: 216-621-3238
Year Founded: 1892
Approx.Sls.: $10,000,000
Emp.: 120
Fiscal Year-end: 11/30/90
Turret Lathes & Cutting Off Lathes & Special Machinery
S.I.C.: 3545
Lockwood Oliver *(Chm. Bd.)*
Heath Oliver *(Pres.)*
James S. Dalton *(V.P.-Sls.)*
Thomas W. Walker *(Pur. Agent)*

BARGE-WAGENER, INC.
1815 The Exchange
Atlanta, GA 30339
Tel.: 404-951-0324 **GA**
Fax: 404-951-0135
Year Founded: 1921
Sales Range: $100-499 Million
Emp.: 600
Fiscal Year-end: 12/31/89
General Contractor; Commercial, Industrial & Public Utilities
Alvin Barge *(Chm. Bd.)*
John M. Barge *(Chief Exec. Officer)*
John H. Wagener *(Pres.)*
Mary Ellen Getsay *(Controller)*
Joseph G. Ondras *(Mktg. Dir.)*
Principal(s):
John M. Barge
John H. Wagener

No. of U.S. Offices: 1

Computer Systems/Hardware:
IBM System 36

BARGER BUILDER & DEVELOPERS
300 First Ave. South
Saint Petersburg, FL 33701
Mailing Address:
P.O. Box 2244
St. Petersburg, FL 33731
Tel.: 813-821-5421 **FL**
Fax: 813-822-5262
Year Founded: 1951
Sales Range: $20-39 Million
Emp.: 10
Industrial & Commercial Developer
S.I.C.: 1542
Michael E. Barger *(Chief Exec. Officer)*
Principal(s):
Michael E. Barger
John W. Barger, Sr.
John W. Barger, Jr.

No. of U.S. Offices: 1

BARIS SHOE COMPANY, INC.
47 W. 34th St.
New York, NY 10001
Tel.: 212-594-9750 **NY**
Year Founded: 1946
Approx.Sls.: $14,000,000
Emp.: 19
Wholesale Distribution of Footwear
S.I.C.: 5139
Seth Gaffin *(Pres. & Chief Exec. Officer)*
Melvin Graf *(V.P.)*
Sylvia Baris *(Treas.)*
Helen Gaffin *(Sec.)*

Outside Service Firm(s):

Citrin Cooperman & Company*(Auditors)*
New York, NY

BARKER CAMPBELL & FARLEY
240 Business Park Dr.
Virginia Beach, VA 23462
Tel.: 804-497-4811
Year Founded: 1980
Approx.Billings: $30,000,000
Emp.: 45
Healthcare, Banking, Agri-Business, Travel & Cable Mktg.
Robert A. Barker *(Pres.)*
William T. Campbell *(Exec. V.P., Sec.)*
A. Palmer Farley *(Exec. V.P., Treas.)*
Cathy L'Heureux *(V.P., Acctg. Mgr.)*
Joan Prescott *(V.P., Pub. Rels. Mgr.)*

BARKLEY & EVERGREEN ADVERTISING, INC.
4350 Shawnee Mission Pkwy.
Shawnee Mission, KS 66205
Tel.: 913-432-2600
Fax: 913-432-2198
Year Founded: 1964
Approx.Billings: $60,000,000
Emp.: 96
Automotive Aftermarket, Business-to-Business, Retail & Franchising Adv.
William M. Fromm *(Pres.)*
Ron Dickson *(Exec. V.P., Pres.-Direct Mktg.r)*
Mike Swenson *(Pres., Pub. Rels.)*
Mike Gaston *(V.P., Bus. Devel.)*
Wayne Hart *(V.P., Chief Fin. Officer)*
Mark Pelofsky *(V.P., Internal Mktg. Mgr.)*
Wendy Kuhn *(Mktg. Services Mgr.)*
Kay Moore *(Opers. Mgr.)*
Perry Hunter *(Desktop Publ. Mgr.)*

A. BARLETTA & SONS
P.O. Box 40
Hazleton, PA 18201
Tel.: 717-455-1511
Fax: 717-455-7767
Sales Range: $20-39 Million
Emp.: 230
Highway Construction, Ready Mixed Concrete, Asphalt, Sand & Stone
S.I.C.: 2951; 3273
Frank Barletta *(Pres.)*
Principal(s):
Frank Barletta
Fred Barletta
James Barletta
John Barletta
Rocco Barletta

Outside Service Firm(s):

Hazleton National Bank*(Major Banking Relationship)*
Hazleton, PA

JOHN S. BARNES CORP.
2222 15th St.
Rockford, IL 61104
Mailing Address:
P.O. Box 6166
Rockford, IL 61125
Tel.: 815-398-4400
Fax: 815-398-5977
Year Founded: 1929
Approx.Sls.: $38,000,000
Emp.: 300
Fiscal Year-end: 12/31/90
Hydraulic Pumps & Power Units, Hydraulic Equip.
S.I.C.: 3594
John M. Pepe *(Pres.)*
Dennis Schaer *(V.P.-Fin.)*
Art Smith *(V.P.-Mktg.)*
Paul Hoffman *(Mgr.-Matls.)*

BARNES & NOBLE BOOKSTORES, INC.
122 5th Ave.
New York, NY 10011
Tel.: 212-633-3300
Fax: 212-675-0413
Approx.Sls.: $295,000,000
Emp.: 4,500
Fiscal Year-end: 2/28/91
Operates the Largest Separate Book Store in the US, Plus 166 Outlets for College & Trade Books in Universities
S.I.C.: 5942
Leonard Riggio *(Chm. Bd., Pres. & Chief Exec. Officer)*
Carl Rosendorf *(Exec. V.P.-Mdse. & Mktg., College)*
William Maloney *(Sr. V.P.-Mktg., College)*
Ron Marshall *(V.P. & Controller)*
Janine von Juergenson *(V.P.-Mktg., College)*
Gail Gittleson *(V.P.-Human Resources)*
Katherine A. McDonough *(V.P.-Pub. Affairs)*
Steve Murri *(Dir.-Adv., Retail)*

Outside Service Firm(s):

KPMG Peat Marwick*(Auditors)*
345 Park Ave.
New York, NY 10154
Tel.: 212-758-9700
Fax: 212-872-3308

Subsidiaries:

Bookstop, Inc. **(1)**
6106 Baldwin Dr.
Austin, TX 78724
Tel.: 512-926-7001
Bookstores
S.I.C.: 5942
Thomas Christopher *(Pres.)*

B. Dalton Bookseller, Inc. **(1)**
122 5th Ave.
New York, NY 10011
Tel.: 212-633-3300 (100%)
Fax: 212-675-0413
Approx.Sls.: $850,000,000
Emp.: 14,000
Fiscal Year-end: 10/31/90
Joint Venture Between Vendex International NV & Barnes & Noble; 738 Bookstores in 48 States
S.I.C.: 5942
R. Richard Fontaine *(Pres. & Chief Oper. Officer)*
Stephen Riggio *(Exec. V.P. & Chief Oper. Officer)*
Mitchell Klipper *(Exec. V.P. & Chief Fin. Officer)*
Dorinda Freeman *(Dir.-Adv.)*

Doubleday Book Shops, Inc. **(1)**
673 Fifth Ave.
New York, NY 10022
Tel.: 212-223-6550
Book Stores
S.I.C.: 5942
Gary DelVecchio *(Chief Exec. Officer)*

Marboro Books Inc. **(1)**
120 Fifth Ave., 4th Floor
New York, NY 10011
Tel.: 212-633-3300
Fax: 212-645-9461
Emp.: 100
Mail Order & Wholesaler of Books
S.I.C.: 5192; 5961
Steve Riggio *(Exec. V.P. & Chief Oper. Officer)*
Jerry D'Aquino *(V.P.)*
John Kelly *(V.P.-Opers.)*
Neil Boyle *(Dir.-Mktg.)*

BARNETT MILLWORKS, INC.
4915 Hamilton Blvd.
Theodore, AL 36590
Mailing Address:
P.O. Box 389
Theodore, AL 36590
Tel.: 205-443-7710 **AL**
Fax: 205-653-6376
Assets: $7,664,000
Liabilities: $2,483,000
Net Worth: $5,181,000
Approx.Sls.: $20,000,000
Emp.: 140
Millwork Mfg.
S.I.C.: 2431
Charles E. Barnett *(Chm. Bd.)*
Paul S. Barnett *(Pres.)*
Dan Barber *(Sec. & Treas.)*
Principal(s):
Charles E. Barnett
Paul S. Barnett

No. of Mfg. Plants/Facilities: 1
No. of U.S. Offices: 1

Computer Systems/Hardware:
DEC; IBM PC

Outside Service Firm(s):

Wood, Singleton & Mackey*(Auditors)*
Mobile, AL

Kemper Insurance*(Group Insurer)*
Long Grove, IL 60049-0001

E.F. Hutton*(Investment Banker)*
Mobile, AL

Lattoff & Gardner*(Legal Firm)*
Mobile, AL

First Alabama Bank*(Major Banking Relationship)*
Mobile, AL

First Alabama Bank*(Pension Manager)*
Mobile, AL

BARNEYS NEW YORK
106 Seventh Ave.
New York, NY 10011
Tel.: 212-929-9000
Fax: 212-463-8215
Approx.Sls.: $200,000,000
Emp.: 1,000
Retailers of Men's, Boy's & Women's Clothing
S.I.C.: 5611; 5621
Fred Pressman *(Pres.)*
Gene Pressman *(V.P. & Chief Exec. Officer)*
Robert Pressman *(V.P. & Chief Oper. Officer)*
Mallory Andrews *(V.P.-Publicity)*
Irv Rosenthal *(Chief Fin. Officer)*
John Antaman *(Treas.)*
Marc Perlowitz *(Legal Counsel)*
Joe Seccarelli *(Controller)*
Principal(s):
Fred Pressman
Gene Pressman
Robert Pressman

Outside Service Firm(s):

Eisner & Lubin*(Auditors)*
New York, NY

Citibank N.A.*(Major Banking Relationship)*
Corporate Trust Services, 399 Park Ave.
New York, NY 10043
Tel.: 212-559-1605

BARNHARDT MANUFACTURING CO.
1100 Hawthorne Ln.
Charlotte, NC 28205
Mailing Address:
P.O. Box 34276
Charlotte, NC 28234
Tel.: 704-376-0380 **NC**
Fax: 704-342-1892
Year Founded: 1900
Sales Range: $40-59 Million
Emp.: 340
Export
Mfr. of Polyester Batting, Polyurethane Foam & Absorbent Cotton Products
S.I.C.: 2299; 3843
James H. Barnhardt, Sr. *(Chm. Bd.)*
T.M. Barnhardt III *(Pres. & Chief Exec. Officer)*
T.L. Barnhardt *(V.P.-Human Resources)*
George Hargrove *(V.P.-Mfg.)*
John E. Smith *(V.P.-Sls.)*
James H. Barnhardt, Jr. *(V.P.)*
Dan C. Ragan *(V.P.)*
Sadler H. Barnhardt *(Sec. & Treas.)*
Joseph Mitchell *(Personnel Dir.)*
John Smith *(Dir.-Adv.)*
Principal(s):
James H. Barnhardt, Sr.

No. of Mfg. Plants/Facilities: 6
No. of U.S. Offices: 1

Computer Systems/Hardware:
IBM System 36

Outside Service Firm(s):

Owen H. Whitfield*(Auditors)*
Charlotte, NC

North Carolina National Bank*(Major Banking Relationship)*
Charlotte, NC

Parker, Poe, Adams & Bernstein*(Legal Firm)*
Charlotte, NC

Division:

Carolina Absorbent Cotton Co. **(1)**
1100 Hawthorne Ave.
Charlotte, NC 28205
Tel.: 704-376-0380 (100%)
Fax: 704-342-1892
Emp.: 400
Surgical Dressings & Hospital Textiles
S.I.C.: 2211
J.H. Barnhardt *(Chm. Bd.)*
T.M. Barnhardt III *(Pres. & Chief Oper. Officer)*
James H. Barnhardt, Jr. *(V.P.)*
Sadler H. Barnhardt *(Sec.)*
James Edwards *(Gen. Mgr.)*
E.C. Aycack *(Natl. Sls. Mgr.)*
Bill Brewer *(Pur. Agent)*

Subsidiary:

North Carolina Foam Industries, Inc. **(1)**
P.O. Box 1528,
Mount Airy, NC 27030
Tel.: 919-789-9161 (100%)
Plastic Materials; Flexible Urethane Foam
S.I.C.: 3089
J.C. Barnhardt, Jr. *(Pres.)*

BARNHART ADVERTISING, MARKETING & PUBLIC RELATIONS, INC.
455 Sherman, Ste. 500
Denver, CO 80203
Tel.: 303-698-3200 **CO**
Fax: 303-777-8712
Fax: 303-744-7273
Year Founded: 1974
Approx.Billings: $28,000,000
Emp.: 44
Fiscal Year-end: 6/30/91
Advertising & Public Relations Agency
S.I.C.: 7311
Terry L. Barnhart *(Pres. & Chief Oper. Officer)*
Mary Hacking *(Exec. V.P., Gen. Mgr.)*
Robert E. Mazerov *(V.P., Dir. of Acct. Service & Plng.)*
Angela Sanders *(Controller)*

Computer Systems/Hardware:
Novell Network

Outside Service Firm(s):

Bank Western*(Major Banking Relationship)*
1675 Broadway, Ste. 1600
Denver, CO 80202
Tel.: 303-571-1313

Blue Cross & Blue Shield of Colorado*(Group Insurer)*
Denver, CO

BARNHILL CONTRACTING COMPANY
2311 N. Main St.
Tarboro, NC 27886
Mailing Address:
P.O.Box 1529,
Tarboro, NC 27886
Tel.: 919-823-1021 **NC**
Approx.Sls.: $100,000,000
Emp.: 650
Fiscal Year-end: 3/31/91
General Contractor for Industrial, Highway & Commercial Construction
S.I.C.: 1611; 1541; 1542
R.E. Barnhill *(Chm. Bd.)*
R.E. Barnhill, Jr. *(Pres.)*
William F. Davis *(Chief Fin. Officer)*
William L. Cooper *(Exec. V.P.)*
Allen Barnhill *(V.P.)*
Jean Berry *(V.P.)*
Kyle Cave *(V.P.)*
Kermit Moser *(V.P.)*
Sophia Hardy *(Sec. & Treas.)*
Scott G. Fisher *(Dir.-Data Processing)*
James Hughes *(Dir.-Personnel)*

Principal(s):
R.E. Barnhill
R.E. Barnhill, Jr.

No. of Mfg. Plants/Facilities: 8
No. of U.S. Offices: 4

Computer Systems/Hardware:
IBM System 36

Outside Service Firm(s):

Pittard, Perry & Crone*(Auditors)*
LaGrange, NC

Ward & Smith*(Legal Firm)*
P.O. Box 867,
New Bern, NC 28560
Tel.: 919-633-1000

BARON-ABRAMSON, INC.
4000 Mystic Valley Pkwy.
Medford, MA 02155
Tel.: 617-396-2000 **MA**
Fax: 617-391-1421
Year Founded: 1941
Approx.Sls.: $12,000,000
Emp.: 65
Mfr. of Women's Sportswear
S.I.C.: 5137
Howard J. Abramson *(Pres.)*
Donald Baron *(Exec. V.P.-Personnel)*
Lawrence Abramson *(V.P.)*

Outside Service Firm(s):

Harry Ferngold Company*(Auditors)*
Boston, MA

Brown, Rudnick, Freed & Gesmer*(Legal Firm)*
One Financial Center
Boston, MA 02111
Tel.: 617-330-9000

State Street Bank & Trust Co.*(Major Banking Relationship)*
P.O. Box 5003
Boston, MA 02107
Tel.: 617-786-6316

BARON ADVERTISING, INC.
645 Hanna Bldg., 1422 Euclid Ave., Ste. 645
Cleveland, OH 44115
Tel.: 216-621-6800
Fax: 216-621-6806
Year Founded: 1953
Approx.Billings: $13,000,000
Emp.: 25
Selma Baron *(Pres.)*
Michael Baron *(V.P.)*

BARON & ZARETSKY ADVERTISING, INC.
928 BROADWAY, N.Y., N.Y.10010,(212)677-1747

BARON & ZARETSKY ADVERTISING, INC.
928 Broadway
New York, NY 10010
Tel.: 212-677-1747
Fax: 212-982-2735
Year Founded: 1981
Approx.Billings: $21,500,000
Emp.: 25
Ken Baron *(Pres. & Creative Dir.)*
Burton Zaretsky *(Exec. V.P., Opers. Dir.)*
Myrna Baron *(V.P., Pub. Rels. Dir.)*

BAROUM EATON ALLEN CORPORATION
67 Kent Ave.
Brooklyn, NY 11211
Tel.: 718-782-2601
Sales Range: $20-39 Million
Emp.: 200
Fiscal Year-end: 12/31/91
Mfr. of Inked Ribbons, Typewriter Correction Materials, Carbon Paper
S.I.C.: 3955
Victor Barouh *(Chm. Bd.)*
Rich Barouh *(Pres.)*
Barbara Glover *(Exec. V.P.)*
Seth Dinsky *(V.P.-Mfg.)*
Richard Burrell *(Controller)*

Outside Service Firm(s):

Manufacturers Hanover Trust Co.*(Major Banking Relationship)*
Brooklyn, NY

Division:

Korectype Div. **(1)**
67 Kent Ave.
Brooklyn, NY 11211
Tel.: 718-782-2601
Mfr. of Correction Materials
S.I.C.: 2899
Rich Barouh *(Pres.)*

Subsidiary:

Ko-Rec-Type **(1)**
67 Kent Ave.
Brooklyn, NY 11211
Tel.: 718-782-2601
Fax: 718-486-6340
Approx.Sls.: $50,000,000
Emp.: 500
Fiscal Year-end: 12/31/90
Import Export
Copy Film, Carbon Paper; Ko Rec Type & Ko Rec Copy for Typewriter Corrections; Word Processing Supplies, Ribbons, Computer Ribbons; KO-RECT'BLE Film Ribbons, Facsimile Paper, Thermal Transfer Ribbons for Bar Coding & Plain Paper Facsimile
S.I.C.: 3955
Victor Barouh *(Chm. & Chief Exec. Officer)*
Barbara Gibbs *(Exec. V.P.)*
Gabriel S. Carlin *(Sr. V.P.)*
Seth Dinsky *(V.P.-Mfg.)*
Lee Abrahamson *(V.P.-Sls.-OEM)*

BARQ'S, INC.
601 Poydras St., Ste. 1925
New Orleans, LA 70130
Tel.: 504-524-5142
Fax: 504-524-3861
Year Founded: 1898
Sales Range: $20-39 Million
Emp.: 50
Fiscal Year-end: 12/31/91
Export
Soft Drink Franchisor
S.I.C.: 2086
John Oudt *(Chm. Bd.)*
John Koerner *(Pres.)*
Richard Hill *(V.P.-Natl. Mktg.)*
Joseph Corizzo *(V.P.-Sls.)*
Ralph Lehmann *(Treas. & Controller)*
Fred C. Walters *(Dir.-Mktg.)*
E. Barq IV *(Dir.-Quality Control)*
Principal(s):
John Oudt
John Koerner

No. of Mfg. Plants/Facilities: 1

Computer Systems/Hardware:
UNIX

Outside Service Firm(s):

Whitney National Bank of New Orleans*(Major Banking Relationship)*
P.O. Box 61260,
New Orleans, LA 70161

Subsidiary:

Delaware Punch Co. **(1)**
601 Poydras St., Ste. 1925
New Orleans, LA 70130
Tel.: 504-524-5142
Fax: 504-524-3861
Approx.Sls.: $10,000,000
Emp.: 10
Fiscal Year-end: 9/30/90
Export
Beverage Concentrate
S.I.C.: 2087; 2086
John Oudt *(Chm. Bd.)*
John Koerner *(Pres.)*
Joseph Corizzo *(V.P.-Sls.)*
Richard Hill *(V.P.-Mktg.)*
Don Woods *(Dir.-Sls.)*
Fred C. Walters *(Dir.-Mktg.)*

BARR & BARR, INC.
330 W. 42nd St.
New York, NY 10036
Tel.: 212-563-2330
Fax: 212-967-2297
Year Founded: 1927
Emp.: 275
General Contractors & Institutional Builders; Hospitals & Universities
S.I.C.: 1542
Thomas A. Barr *(Chm. Bd.)*
Donald M. Barr *(Pres.)*
Michael Barr *(V.P.)*
Thomas D. Barr *(Treas.)*
Gregory Hess *(Legal Counsel & Sec.)*

Computer Systems/Hardware:
Wang VS 45

Outside Service Firm(s):

Christy & Veiner*(Legal Firm)*
620 5th Ave.
New York, NY 10020
Tel.: 212-632-5500

The Bank of New York*(Major Banking Relationship)*
One Wall Street
New York, NY 10286
Tel.: 212-635-6805
Fax: 212-635-3201

BARR BROTHERS & CO., INC.
90 Washington St.
New York, NY 10006
Tel.: 212-269-4500 **DE**
Fax: 212-269-7637
Year Founded: 1913
Assets: $26,000,000
Liabilities: $19,000,000
Net Worth: $7,000,000
Emp.: 20
Fiscal Year-end: 6/30/91
Bond Dealer
S.I.C.: 6211
Robert F. Derrey *(Pres. & Chief Exec. Officer)*
Joseph A. Mangin *(V.P., Chief Oper. & Chief Fin. Officer)*
John V. Kick *(Treas. & Sec.)*

No. of U.S. Offices: 1

Outside Service Firm(s):

Price Waterhouse*(Auditors)*
1251 Ave. of the Americas
New York, NY 10020
Tel.: 212-819-5000
Telex: 12-6798

The Principal Financial Group*(Group Insurer)*
New York, NY

Chemical Bank*(Major Banking Relationship)*
450 West 33rd St.
New York, NY 10001
Tel.: 212-613-7197
Fax: 212-947-7628

W. M. BARR & CO., INC.
2105 Channel Ave.
Memphis, TN 38113
Mailing Address:
P.O. Box 1879
Memphis, TN 38101
Tel.: 901-775-0100 **TN**
Fax: 901-942-2029
Year Founded: 1946
Assets: $50,000,000
Liabilities: $10,000,000
Net Worth: $40,000,000
Sales Range: $100-499 Million
Emp.: 360
Fiscal Year-end: 5/31/91
Liquid & Aerosol Chemicals; Custom Packaging; Private Labeling; Contract Packaging
S.I.C.: 2816; 7389
Corporate Giving Program: United Way
A. Vernon Richmond *(Pres.)*
Ron Riley *(Sr. V.P.)*
Bruce Doan *(Sr. V.P.)*
Charles Glover *(V.P.-Gen. Mfg. Sls.)*
Brad Sharpe *(V.P.-Klean Strip Sls.)*
Robert McMillan *(Pur. Agent-Accessories)*
Angie Hudgins *(Pur. Agent-Raw. Matls.)*

No. of Mfg. Plants/Facilities: 3

W. M. Barr & Co., Inc.—(Continued)

Computer Systems/Hardware:
IBM AS 400

Outside Service Firm(s):

Price Waterhouse*(Auditors)*
One Commerce Square,
Memphis, TN 38103

Boone, Wellford, Clark, Langschmidt & Apperson*(Legal Firm)*
One Commerce Sq.
Memphis, TN 38103
Tel.: 901-523-0311

First Tennessee Bank, N.A.*(Major Banking Relationship)*
P.O. Box 101
Memphis, TN 38101
Tel.: 901-523-4555

BARR ELECTRIC CORPORATION
300 W. Holbrook Dr.
Wheeling, IL 60090
Tel.: 708-520-4474 **IL**
Fax: 708-520-4479
Emp.: 90
Electrical Work; Mechanical Contractor
S.I.C.: 1731; 1711
Michael Barr *(Pres. & Treas.)*
Emil Widitz *(V.P.)*
Marie Barr *(Sec.)*

Outside Service Firm(s):

Seyfarth, Shaw, Fairweather & Geraldson*(Legal Firm)*
55 E. Monroe
Chicago, IL 60606
Tel.: 312-346-8000

Harris Trust & Savings Bank*(Major Banking Relationship)*
111 W. Monroe St.
Chicago, IL 60690
Tel.: 312-461-2265
Tel.: 800-858-0840

BARREL O'FUN SNACK FOODS CO.
800 4th St. N.W.
Perham, MN 56573
Mailing Address:
P.O. Box L
Perham, MN 56573
Tel.: 218-346-7000
Tel.: 800-346-4910 **MN**
Fax: 218-346-7003
Year Founded: 1973
Approx.Sls.: $32,000,000
Emp.: 300
Fiscal Year-end: 12/31/90
Export
Mfr. of Potato Chips & Snacks
S.I.C.: 2096
Ken Nelson *(Pres.)*
Mike Holper *(V.P. & Gen. Mgr.)*
Terry Nelson *(V.P.-Sls.)*
Duane Dorow *(Dir.-Mktg. & Adv.)*
Dennis Iverson *(Mgr.-Prod.)*

Outside Service Firm(s):

First Bank of North Dakota*(Major Banking Relationship)*
Fargo, ND

THEODORE BARRY & ASSOCIATES
1520 Wilshire Blvd.
Los Angeles, CA 90017
Tel.: 213-413-6080
Fax: 213-413-2983
Year Founded: 1985
Approx.Sls.: $18,000,000
Emp.: 100
Management Consulting
S.I.C.: 8742
Jasse Cheema *(Chm. Bd. & Pres.)*
John Wilson *(V.P. & Chief Fin. Officer)*
William J. Kaffer *(V.P.-Mktg.)*

Outside Service Firm(s):

Price Waterhouse*(Auditors)*
400 S. Hope St.
Los Angeles, CA 90071-2889
Tel.: 213-236-3000

BankAmerica Corp.*(Major Banking Relationship)*
Anaheim, CA

Bank of New York*(Major Banking Relationship)*
90 Washington St.
New York, NY 10015

BARRY-WEHMILLER COMPANY
8020 Forsyth Blvd.
Saint Louis, MO 63105
Tel.: 314-862-8000
Cable: 22
Fax: 314-862-8858
Year Founded: 1885
Approx.Sls.: $65,000,000
Emp.: 250
Machinery & Processing Equipment
S.I.C.: 3556
Robert H. Chapman *(Chm. & Pres.)*
Phil Ostapowicz *(V.P.-Mktg. & Sls.)*
Gary F. Pluth *(V.P.-Fin.)*

Outside Service Firm(s):

Price Waterhouse*(Auditors)*
One Boatmen's Plaza
St. Louis, MO 63101
Tel.: 314-425-0500

Thompson & Mitchell*(Legal Firm)*
One Mercantile Center
Saint Louis, MO 63101

Mark Twain St. Louis Bank*(Major Banking Relationship)*
1630 S. Lindbergh Blvd.
St. Louis, MO 63131

Subsidiaries:

Barry-Wehmiller Packaging Systems **(1)**
13325 U.S. Hwy. 19N.
Clearwater, FL 34624

Barry-Wehmiller Packaging Systems **(1)**
11316 N. 46th St., Suite 2
Tampa, FL 33617
Tel.: 813-972-2447

Holmatic, Inc. **(1)**
1750 Corporate Dr.
Norcross, GA 30093
Tel.: 404-925-2004
Fax: 404-925-0939
Mfr. of Food Packaging Equip.
S.I.C.: 3556; 3565
Brian F. Holman *(Pres. & Chief Exec. Officer)*
Donald A. Vestrand *(Sec. & Treas.)*
Derek Baxter *(Asst. Sec.)*

Inex Vision Systems **(1)**
13327 U.S. Hwy. 19N
Clearwater, FL 34624
Tel.: 813-535-5502 (100%)
Fax: 813-535-8380
Mfr. of Inspection Systems
S.I.C.: 3829
James Schemenaur *(Chief Exec.)*

Jetstream Systems **(1)**
6105 W. 55th Ave.
Arvada, CO 80002
Tel.: 303-425-1454

Jetstream Systems **(1)**
3795 S. Sanford Ave.
Sanford, FL 32773
Tel.: 407-322-2725

Jetstream Systems **(1)**
3486 Investment Blvd.
Hayward, CA 94545
Tel.: 510-785-9360
Fax: 510-786-9316
Approx.Sls.: $8,000,000
Emp.: 58
Fiscal Year-end: 12/31/90
Custom Engineered Air Conveying & Processing Equip.
S.I.C.: 3535; 3559
Stan Lenox *(Pres.)*
Eugene S. Batter *(V.P.-Opers.)*
James B. Webb *(V.P.-Mktg.)*
Carol F. Wright *(Mgr.-Mktg. Services)*

Kartridg Pak Co. **(1)**
807 W. Kimberly Road
Davenport, IA 52806
Tel.: 319-391-1100
Tel.: 800-257-5622 (100%)
Fax: 319-391-4951
Approx.Sls.: $25,000,000
Emp.: 170
Fiscal Year-end: 7/31/92
Export
Manufacturer of Packaging Machinery, Fillers; Fat Analysis Instruments; Process Generators, Dairy, Fish; Deboning Machinery & Separators; Metal Fabricators, Electropolishers, Tortilla Folders, Air Crafter Polishing
S.I.C.: 3565; 3823; 3556; 3599
Brian F. Holman *(Chm.)*
Barry W. Shoulders *(Pres.)*
Kim P. Tack *(Sec. & Treas.)*
Jerry D. Douthitt *(Pur. Agent)*
Linda L. Bewley *(Asst. Sec.)*

Pneumatic Scale Corporation **(1)**
65 Newport Ave.
Quincy, MA 02171
Tel.: 617-328-6100
Telex: 940169
Fax: 617-770-3845
Assets: $24,669,196
Earnings: $63,000
Liabilities: $9,819,398
Net Worth: $14,849,798
Approx.Sls.: $33,141,312
Emp.: 350
Fiscal Year-end: 7/31/92
Import Export
Bottling & Packaging Machinery & Parts
S.I.C.: 3565; 3556
R.N. Chapman *(Chm. Bd., Pres. & Chief Exec. Officer)*
Bill Morgan *(Dir.-Sls. Admin.)*
Dale Barnard *(V.P.-Mfg.)*
Wallace MacDonald *(Dir.-Engrng.)*
Jay Corbett *(Dir.-Human Resources)*
Jim Lawson *(Controller)*

Non-U.S. Holdings:

Inex Vision Systems **(1)**
P.O. Box 95, Atlantic St.,
Ahringham, Cheshire WA 14 5EW, United Kingdom
Tel.: 61-928-6344

Pneumatic Scale Europe **(1)**
Hemel Hempstead, Hertfordshire 2-HP2 7BJ, United Kingdom
Tel.: 442-212-871 (100%)
Emp.: 10
Packaging & Bottling Machinery
S.I.C.: 3565

THE BARTELL DRUG COMPANY
4727 Denver Ave. S.
Seattle, WA 98134
Tel.: 206-763-2626 **WA**
Fax: 206-763-2062
Year Founded: 1890
Sales Range: $80-99 Million
Emp.: 750
Fiscal Year-end: 12/31/91
Chain of 38 Drug Stores
S.I.C.: 5912
George D. Bartell *(Pres.)*
Val B. Storrs *(Sr. V.P.-Opers.)*
George Bartell, Jr. *(Chief Exec. Officer)*
Walter Stephen Nash *(Controller)*
Karl Wilkinson *(Dir.-Personnel)*
David Barber *(Dir.-Real Estate & Devel.)*
Paul Lofgren *(Buyer)*
Lisa Scott *(Buyer)*
John Weith *(Buyer)*
Gary W. Trahan *(Mgr.-Adv.)*
Principal(s):
Bartell Family

Outside Service Firm(s):

Ernst & Young*(Auditors)*
999 Third Av., Ste. 3500
Seattle, WA 98104
Tel.: 206-621-1800
Fax: 206-682-1234

Gordon, Thomas, Honeywell, Malanca, Peterson & Daheim*(Legal Firm)*
One Union Square
Seattle, WA

Seattle First National Bank*(Major Banking Relationship)*
701 Fifth Avenue
Seattle, WA 98104
Tel.: 206-358-3035

E.J. BARTELLS CO.
700 Powell Ave., S.W.
Renton, WA 98055
Tel.: 206-228-4111
Fax: 206-228-8807
Emp.: 300
Refractories, Industrial Insulations
S.I.C.: 3296; 3297
Michael R. Helton *(Chm. Bd.)*
Gary D. Pratte *(Pres. & Treas.)*
Harold R. Farnsworth *(V.P.-Sls.)*
Erik A. Jensen *(V.P.-Contracts)*
Gail Slater *(Pur. Agent)*

Outside Service Firm(s):

Seafirst Bank*(Major Banking Relationship)*
Columbia-SeaFirst Center, 701 5th Ave., 11th Flr.
Seattle, WA 98124
Tel.: 206-358-3039
Fax: 206-358-3113

BARTLETT BRAINARD & EACOTT, INC.
30 Tobey Rd.
Bloomfield, CT 06002
Tel.: 203-242-5565 **CT**
Fax: 203-243-8929
Year Founded: 1921
Approx.Sls.: $40,000,000
Emp.: 150
Fiscal Year-end: 12/31/89
Commercial & Industrial Building Construction
S.I.C.: 1542; 1541
James H. Eacott, Jr. *(Chm. Bd.)*
James H. Eacott, III *(Pres. & Treas.)*
Thomas E. Anderson *(V.P.)*
Susan H. Eacott *(Sec.)*
Douglas M. Lewanda *(Controller)*

Outside Service Firm(s):

Coopers & Lybrand*(Auditors)*
280 Trumbull St.
Hartford, CT 06103

Reide & Riege*(Legal Firm)*
Hartford, CT

Connecticut Bank & Trust*(Major Banking Relationship)*
Bloomfield, CT

BARTLETT AND COMPANY
4800 Main St., Ste. 600
Kansas City, MO 64112
Tel.: 816-753-6300 **MO**
Fax: 816-753-0062
Year Founded: 1907
Assets: $181,000,000
Liabilities: $58,000,000
Net Worth: $123,000,000
Approx.Sls.: $50,000,000
Emp.: 550
Fiscal Year-end: 12/31/91
Export
Grain Merchandising & Storage; Cattle, Milling
S.I.C.: 0211; 2041; 5153

Paul D. Bartlett, Jr. *(Chm. Bd.)*
James B. Hebenstreit *(Pres.)*
W. Robert Berg *(Vice Chm., Treas. & Sec.)*
Robert P. Erwin *(Gen. Counsel)*
Arnold F. Wheeler *(Controller)*
Principal(s):
Paul D. Bartlett, Jr.

No. of Mfg. Plants/Facilities: 27

Computer Systems/Hardware:
IBM Systems 36 & 38; IBM PC

Outside Service Firm(s):

Ernst & Young*(Auditors)*
Kansas City, KS

Stinson, Mag & Fizzell*(Legal Firm)*
1201 Walnut, Ste. 2800
Kansas City, MO 64152
Tel.: 816-842-8600

United Missouri Bank*(Major Banking Relationship)*
10th & Grand
Kansas City, MO 64106
Tel.: 816-860-7000
Fax: 800-892-2944

United Missouri Bank*(Pension Manager)*
10th & Grand
Kansas City, MO 64106
Tel.: 816-860-7000
Fax: 800-892-2944

THE F.A. BARTLETT TREE EXPERT CO.
1290 E. Main St.
Stamford, CT 06902
Mailing Address:
P. O. Box 3067
Stamford, CT 06905
Tel.: 203-323-1131
Fax: 203-323-1129
Year Founded: 1907
Approx.Sls.: $58,000,000
Emp.: 1,500
Fiscal Year-end: 10/ 3/92
Scientific Shade Tree Care & Public Utility Line Clearance; Mfr. Boost Fertilizer
S.I.C.: 0783; 2879
Robert A. Bartlett *(Chm. & Chief Exec. Officer)*
Robert A. Bartlett, Jr. *(Pres. & Chief Oper. Officer)*
J.E. Signorini *(Exec. V.P., Treas. & Chief Fin. Officer)*
J.J. Bedosky *(Sr. V.P.)*
V.B. Fleck *(V.P.-Human Resources)*
David C. Andry *(V.P.-Mngmt. Information Systems)*
Dr. Bruce R. Fraedrich *(V.P.-Res.)*
Anne Ferrucci *(Asst. V.P.-Mktg.)*
N.J. Cirillo *(Asst. V.P. & Controller)*
Howard F. Acker *(Sec.)*
W.E. Dages *(Dir.-Pub. Rels.)*
S. Malin *(Dir.-Pur.)*

Computer Systems/Hardware:
Data General

Division:

Utility Tree Service **(1)**
104 W. Street
Eureka, CA 95501
Tel.: 707-443-9794
Public Utility Line Clearance
Carl N. Center *(Pres.)*
Richard A. Shaw *(V.P.)*

BARTON BRANDS, LTD.
55 E. Monroe St., Ste. 1700
Chicago, IL 60603
Tel.: 312-346-9200 **IL**
Fax: 312-855-1220
Year Founded: 1944
Approx.Sls.: $300,000,000
Emp.: 436
Fiscal Year-end: 3/31/91
Distilling; Importing & Exporting Spirits & Beers
S.I.C.: 2085; 5182
Ellis M. Goodman *(Chm. Bd.)*
Fred R. Mardell *(Vice Chm., Exec. V.P. & Sec.)*
Alexander Berk *(Pres.)*
Edward L. Golden *(Pres.-Barton Brands)*
Raymond Powers *(Exec. V.P.-Fin.)*
William F. Hackett *(Exec. V.P.)*
Charles L. Kinzer *(Sr. V.P.-Opers.)*
Norman R. Goldstein *(V.P., Treas. & Asst. Sec.)*
Joel A. Robbins *(V.P. & Western Div. Mgr.)*
Harry Mekow *(V.P. & Midwest Div. Mgr.)*
Marvin Weisenfeld *(V.P. & Sls. Mgr.-Eastern Div.)*
Richard Renkens *(V.P.-Control States)*
John Kent *(V.P.-Natl. Sls. Admin.)*
Donald S. Hirsch *(V.P.)*
Fred V. McMillen *(V.P.)*
Philip L. Lapin *(Asst. Sec. & Asst. Treas.)*
Gary Kunath *(Mgr.-Mngmt. Information Systems)*
Jack Kavanagh *(Dir.-Adv. & Mktg. Mgr.)*
Sharon Jaenel *(Dir.-Human Resources)*
Robert J. Egan *(Mgr.-Office Services)*

No. of Mfg. Plants/Facilities: 3

Computer Systems/Hardware:
Burroughs 4925

Outside Service Firm(s):

Arthur Andersen & Co.*(Auditors)*
33 W. Monroe St.
Chicago, IL 60603-4067
Tel.: 312-580-0033
Fax: 312-507-6748

American National Bank & Trust Company of Chicago*(Major Banking Relationship)*
33 N. LaSalle St.
Chicago, IL 60602
Tel.: 312-661-5000
Fax: 312-661-6417

Subsidiaries:

Barton Beers, Ltd. **(1)**
55 E. Monroe St., Ste. 1710
Chicago, IL 60603
Tel.: 312-346-9200
Fax: 312-855-1220
Approx.Sls.: $120,000,000
Emp.: 42
Fiscal Year-end: 3/31/91
Import
Imported Beer; Corona Extra, Corona Light, Modelo Especial, Negra Modelo, Peroni
S.I.C.: 5181
Ellis M. Goodman *(Chm. Bd.)*
Fred R. Mardell *(Vice Chm., V.P. & Sec.)*
Willian F. Hackett *(Exec. V.P. & Natl. Sls. Mgr.)*
Thomas A. McNichols *(Sr. V.P.-Mktg.)*
James P. Ryan *(Sr. V.P.-Admin.)*
Ralph D. Silver *(V.P. & Treas.)*
Richard B. Barron *(V.P.)*
Donald S. Hirsch *(V.P.)*
Eddie Merideth *(V.P.)*
Norman R. Goldstein *(Asst. Sec. & Asst. Treas.)*
Philip L. Lapin *(Asst. Sec. & Asst. Treas.)*

Barton Brands of California, Inc. **(1)**
2202 E. Del Amo Blvd.
Carson, CA 90749
Tel.: 310-604-0017
S.I.C.: 5182
Ellis M. Goodman *(Pres.)*
William C. Groman *(Div. Mgr.)*

Barton Brands of Georgia, Inc. **(1)**
650 Fairburn Rd., S.W.
Atlanta, GA 30331
Tel.: 404-691-5470
Alcohol Distillery
S.I.C.: 5182
Ellis Goodman *(Pres.)*
Thomas Medley *(Plant Mgr.)*

BUZZ BARTON & ASSOCIATES, INC.
900 Jorie Blvd.
Oak Brook, IL 60521
Tel.: 708-990-0330
Year Founded: 1966
Approx.Billings: $11,250,000
Emp.: 24
Automotive, Real Estate, Financial, Healthcare & Business-to-Business
L.G. Barton *(Chm. Bd.)*
Mark Lundeen *(Pres. & Chief Exec. Officer)*
Edward A. Sakoff *(Sr. V.P.)*
R. Alin Michaels *(V.P., Mktg.)*
Barbara Magna *(Comptroller)*

E.C. BARTON & CO.
2929 Brown's Lane
Jonesboro, AR 72401
Mailing Address:
P.O. Box 4040
Jonesboro, AR 72403-4040
Tel.: 501-932-6673 **DE**
Fax: 501-972-1304
Year Founded: 1885
Assets: $28,133,242
Liabilities: $6,607,176
Net Worth: $21,526,066
Approx.Sls.: $58,848,948
Emp.: 375
Fiscal Year-end: 10/31/91
Retail & Wholesale Lumber & Building Materials
S.I.C.: 5211; 5039; 5031
Allen Nixon *(Chm. Bd.)*
Roy H. Jolly *(Pres. & Chief Exec. Officer)*
Ed Wiseman *(Exec. V.P.)*
Doyle Roach *(V.P.)*
Harold Bouland *(V.P. & Treas.)*
Doyle Gilliam *(V.P.-Sls. & Mktg.)*
Niel Crowson *(Asst. V.P.)*
Tony Futrell *(Sec.)*
David Cameron *(Dir.-Data Processing)*

No. of U.S. Offices: 41

Computer Systems/Hardware:
Data General

Outside Service Firm(s):

Jones, Clayton & Worlow*(Auditors)*
Jonesboro, AR

Protective Life Insurance*(Group Insurer)*
Box 11407,
Birmingham, AL 35246

Barrett, Wheatley, Smith & Deacon*(Legal Firm)*
Jonesboro, AR

Citizens Bank*(Major Banking Relationship)*
Jonesboro, AR

Simmons First Bank of Jonesboro*(Major Banking Relationship)*
Jonesboro, AR

Simmons First Bank of Jonesboro*(Pension Manager)*
Jonesboro, AR

BARTON-MALOW ENTERPRISES, INC.
American Center Bldg., 27777
Franklin Rd., Ste. 800
Southfield, MI 48034
Tel.: 313-351-4500 **MI**
Fax: 313-351-4629
Year Founded: 1924
Assets: $99,400,000
Liabilities: $88,780,000
Net Worth: $10,620,000
Approx.Sls.: $723,129,000
Fiscal Year-end: 3/31/91
Construction Management, General Contracting, Facilities Services, Rigging & Machinery Installation
S.I.C.: 1522; 1541; 1542; 1796; 8744
Benjamin C. Maibach, Jr. *(Chm. Bd.)*
Benjamin C. Maibach, III *(Pres.)*
Mark A. Bahr *(Exec. V.P. & Sec.)*
Thomas M. Brady *(Sr. V.P.)*
Donald Shalibo *(Sr. V.P.)*
Edward R. Jarchow *(V.P. & Treas.)*
Martin C.P. McElroy *(Dir.-Corp. Devel.)*

No. of U.S. Offices: 4

Computer Systems/Hardware:
IBM & MacIntosh

Outside Service Firm(s):

Collins, Buri & McConkey*(Auditors)*
Birmingham, MI

Grant Thornton*(Auditors)*
Southfield, MI

Amerisure*(Commercial Insurance Carrier)*
28 W. Adams
Detroit, MI 48226
Tel.: 313-965-8600

Dykema, Gossett*(Legal Firm)*
400 Renaissance Ctr., 35th Fl.
Detroit, MI 48243
Tel.: 313-568-6800

Manufacturers National Bank N.A.*(Major Banking Relationship)*
38th Fl., 100 Renaissance Center
Detroit, MI 48243
Tel.: 313-222-4227

NationsBank Carolinas*(Major Banking Relationship)*
One NCNB Plaza,
Charlotte, NC 28255
Tel.: 704-374-5000

Subsidiaries:

The ARGOS Group **(1)**
American Center Bldg., Ste 675, 27777 Franklin Rd.
Southfield, MI 48034
Tel.: 313-353-3535
Emp.: 60
Facility Planning, Engineering, Construction & Management
S.I.C.: 8744
John M. Czarnecki *(Pres.)*

Barton-Malow Company **(1)**
P.O. Box 5200
Detroit, MI 48235
Tel.: 313-351-4500
Emp.: 900
Construction Management, Program Management, General Contracting for Health Care, Educational, Government, Industrial & Special Event Facilities
S.I.C.: 8742; 8741
Benjamin C. Maibach, III *(Pres.)*
Mark Bahr *(Exec. V.P.)*
Thomas M. Brady *(Sr. V.P.)*
Donald L. Shalibo *(Sr. V.P.)*
Edward R. Jarchon *(V.P. & Treas.)*
E. Twitchell *(Sec.)*
Martin C.P. McElroy *(Dir.-Corp. Devel.)*

Barton-Malow Rigging Co. **(1)**
21090 Fern Ave.
Oak Park, MI 48237
Tel.: 313-548-5000
Emp.: 50
Heavy Machinery Rigging & Erection
S.I.C.: 1799
John Wozniak *(Sr. V.P.)*

BARTON PRESS, INC.
55 Lakeside Ave.
West Orange, NJ 07052
Tel.: 201-736-4700 **NJ**
Fax: 201-736-7929
Year Founded: 1922
Approx.Sls.: $21,000,000
Emp.: 165
Fiscal Year-end: 3/31/92
Commercial Printing; Lithographic Letterpress & Web
S.I.C.: 2752; 2754
Stanley M. Denburg *(Pres.)*

Barton Press, Inc.—(Continued)

Edmund Denburg *(V.P.-Sls.)*
Paul Denburg *(V.P.)*
Robert Denburg *(V.P.-Admin.)*
Sheldon Denburg *(V.P. & Treas.)*
Robert Rosenfeld *(Controller)*
Paul Kissin *(Gen. Mgr.)*
Joseph Fernandez *(Plant Mgr.)*

Principal(s):
Denburg Family

No. of Mfg. Plants/Facilities: 1

Outside Service Firm(s):

Levin, Clancy, Foster & Arena*(Legal Firm)*
Livingston, NJ

First Fidelity Bank, N.A.*(Major Banking Relationship)*
Totowa, NJ

Affiliates:

Barton Associates **(1)**
55 Lakeside Ave.
West Orange, NJ 07052
Tel.: 201-736-4700

Lakeside Enterprises, Inc. **(1)**
55 Lakeside Ave.
West Orange, NJ 07052
Tel.: 201-736-4700

THE BASES GROUP

(Formerly Bases Burke Institute, Inc.)
50 E. River Center Blvd., Ste. 1000
Covington, KY 41011
Tel.: 606-655-6000 **DE**
Fax: 606-655-6100
Sales Range: $20-39 Million
Emp.: 180
Fiscal Year-end: 6/30/92
Marketing Research
S.I.C.: 8732
Corporate Giving Program: Corporate United Way campaign-strictly voluntary
Jack E. Brown *(Chm. & Chief Exec. Officer)*
Steven A. Wilson *(Pres. & Chief Oper. Officer)*
David F. Bieber *(Sr. V.P.-Natl. Client Service & Mktg. Mgr.)*
Michael J. Huber *(Chief Fin. Officer)*
Mary C. Messman *(Controller)*
Dana Pogorzelski *(Dir.-Mktg.)*
E.T. Wilson *(Dir.-Systems)*
Susan Most Armstrong *(Acct. Mgr.)*

Divisions:

The Bases Group **(1)**
50 E. River Center Blvd., Suite 1000
Covington, KY 41011
Tel.: 606-655-6000
Fax: 606-655-1600
Emp.: 175
Marketing Research
S.I.C.: 8741
Steven A. Wilson *(Pres.)*

Bases International **(1)**
50 E. River Center Blvd., Suite 1000
Covington, KY 41011
Tel.: 606-655-6000
Fax: 606-655-1600
Emp.: 5
Marketing Services
S.I.C.: 8741
Steve Wilson *(Pres. & Chief Oper. Officer)*

The Burke Institute **(1)**
50 E. River Center Blvd., Suite 1000
Covington, KY 41011
Tel.: 606-655-6000
Fax: 606-655-1600
Emp.: 6
Marketing Services
S.I.C.: 8741
S. Venkatesh *(Pres.)*

BASHAS

P.O. Box 488
Chandler, AZ 85244
Tel.: 602-895-9350 **AZ**
Fax: 602-895-1206
Approx.Sls.: $200,000,000
Emp.: 2,500
Retail Grocery Stores
S.I.C.: 5411
Edward N. Basha, Jr. *(Chm. Bd.)*
Wayne Manning *(Pres.)*
Edward R. Felix *(V.P.-Warehouse Distr.)*

Principal(s):
Edward N. Basha, Jr.

Computer Systems/Hardware:
IBM

Outside Service Firm(s):

Valley National Bank*(Major Banking Relationship)*
241 North Central Ave., 11th Floor
Phoenix, AZ 85001

BASIC AMERICAN FOODS

550 Kearny, Ste. 1000
San Francisco, CA 94108
Tel.: 415-981-5590
Fax: 415-421-6618
Earnings: $10,000,000
Approx.Sls.: $130,000,000
Emp.: 3,400
Mfr. & Distributor Dehydrated Potatoes, Onions, Garlic, Refried Beans
S.I.C.: 2034; 5141
William J. Hume *(Chm. Bd.)*
George H. Hume *(Pres.)*
John W. Argent *(V.P.-Fin.)*
Joseph Behrendt *(V.P.-Mngmt. Information Systems)*

Computer Systems/Hardware:
Digital

Outside Service Firm(s):

Arthur Andersen & Co.*(Auditors)*
Spear Street Tower, One Market Plaza, Ste. 3500
San Francisco, CA 94105
Tel.: 415-546-8200

Aetna Life & Casualty*(Group Insurer)*
Boston, MA

Wyatt Co.*(Pension Manager)*
345 California St.
San Francisco, CA 94104
Tel.: 415-986-6568

BASIC COMPUTER

1585 Frederick Blvd.
Akron, OH 44320
Tel.: 216-873-1000
Tel.: 800-227-4286 **DE**
Fax: 216-873-1010
Year Founded: 1977
Sales Range: $100-499 Million
Emp.: 300
Fiscal Year-end: 1/31/92
Retail Computer Chain; Microcomputer
S.I.C.: 5734
Robert F. Meyerson *(Chm. Bd.)*
Frank E. Brick *(Pres. & Chief Exec. Officer)*
David Porter *(V.P.-Oper.)*
Michael Riemenschneider *(V.P.-Mdsg. & Plng.)*
Al Schmeiderer *(V.P.-Finance)*
John Blackburn *(Area V.P.-Northeast Ohio)*
Kenneth Haver *(Treas.)*
Jan Hammond *(Asst. Comptroller)*
Bettyann Hale *(Admin. Asst. to Pres.)*
Michael V. Wise *(Client Services & Field Service Oper.)*
Barb Duey *(Dir.-Personnel)*
Dan Aslip *(Mgr.-Mktg.)*
Robert Nebiker *(Mgr.-Communications)*

Principal(s):
Frank E. Brick

No. of U.S. Offices: 6

Computer Systems/Hardware:
Wang VS-100

Outside Service Firm(s):

D H & S*(Auditors)*
Cleveland, OH

Alexander & Alexander*(Commercial Insurance Carrier)*
Cleveland, OH

Prudential Insurance Co. of America*(Group Insurer)*
751 Broad St.
Newark, NJ 07102-3777
Tel.: 201-802-6000

Goodman Weiss & Freedman*(Legal Firm)*
100 Erieview Plaza, 27th Fl.
Cleveland, OH 44114
Tel.: 216-696-3366

Society National Bank*(Major Banking Relationship)*
127 Public Square
Cleveland, OH 44114
Tel.: 216-689-3000

BASIC CONSTRUCTION COMPANY

538 Oyster Point Rd.
Newport News, VA 23602
Mailing Address:
P.O.Box 2719,
Newport News, VA 23609-0719
Tel.: 804-249-3789 **VA**
Fax: 804-249-2229
Year Founded: 1915
Assets: $28,000,000
Net Worth: $28,000,000
Approx.Sls.: $10,000,000
Emp.: 100
Fiscal Year-end: 12/31/90
Construction of Highways & Utilities
S.I.C.: 1611; 1623
L.U. Noland, Jr. *(Chm. Bd.)*
John E. Poindexter *(Pres.)*
Malcolm R. Wade *(V.P.-Fin. & Chief Fin. Officer)*
George E. Lemon *(V.P.-Opers.)*
Walter Vinson *(Pur. Dir. & Asst. Treas.)*
Michael N. Derreberry *(Mgr.-Utility Dept.)*

Principal(s):
L.U. Noland, Jr.
John E. Poindexter

No. of Mfg. Plants/Facilities: 1
No. of U.S. Offices: 1

Computer Systems/Hardware:
Point Four

Outside Service Firm(s):

Coopers & Lybrand*(Auditors)*
P.O. Box 538, 800 Akron Centre Plaza
Akron, OH 44308

Blue Cross & Blue Shield of Virginia*(Group Insurer)*
2015 Staples Mill Rd.
Richmond, VA 23230
Tel.: 804-359-7000
Fax: 804-354-7397

Hunton & Williams*(Legal Firm)*
100 Park Ave.
New York, NY 10017
Tel.: 213-309-1000

Crestar Bank*(Major Banking Relationship)*
Bank-Newport News, V

BASIC FOOD INTERNATIONAL INC.

1300 S.E. 17th St., Ste. 300
Fort Lauderdale, FL 33335
Tel.: 305-467-1700 **FL**
Fax: 305-764-5110
Year Founded: 1976
Approx.Sls.: $75,000,000
Emp.: 63
Import Export
Wholesale, Import & Export Fresh Fruits & Vegetables, Canned & Packaged Groceries, Frozen Meats, Poultry & Seafood & Cosmetics
S.I.C.: 5148; 5149; 5142; 5122
John P. Bauer *(Pres.)*
Dr. Oscar Berg *(V.P.)*
Mimi Bauer *(Treas. & Sec.)*
Thomas Morgan *(Controller)*

Outside Service Firm(s):

Ernst & Young*(Auditors)*
Fort Lauderdale, FL

Bank Leumi le-Israel B.M.*(International Bank Affiliate)*
Miami, FL

Deutsch Sued Amerikanische*(International Bank Affiliate)*
Miami, FL

Subsidiary:

Global Food Corporation **(1)**
1300 S.E. 17th St., Ste. 300
Fort Lauderdale, FL 33335
Tel.: 305-467-1700
Food Wholesalers; Frozen Meats, Poultry & Seafood
S.I.C.: 5142; 5148; 5149
John P. Bauer *(Pres.)*

PETER A. BASILE SONS INC.

13000 Newburgh Rd.
Livonia, MI 48151
Mailing Address:
P.O. Box 2666
Livonia, MI 48151
Tel.: 313-591-4200 **MI**
Fax: 313-464-1644
Year Founded: 1958
Approx.Sls.: $12,500,000
Emp.: 87
Concrete Paving, Site Utilities Contractor
S.I.C.: 4939
Peter A. Basile *(Pres.)*
Michael Bileti *(V.P.-Estimating)*
Peter Messina *(V.P.-Opers.)*
Thomas J. Cicotte *(V.P.)*

Outside Service Firm(s):

Michael Woodgate*(Auditors)*
Livonia, MI

Willis Corroon*(Commercial Insurance Carrier)*
38777 W. 6 Mile Rd.
Livonia, MI 48151

Driggers, Schultz, Herbest & Patterson*(Legal Firm)*
Troy, MI

National Bank of Detroit*(Major Banking Relationship)*
Livonia, MI

Subsidiary:

Metropolitan Asphalt, Inc. **(1)**
13000 Newburgh Rd.
Livonia, MI 48151
Tel.: 313-425-7730
Emp.: 25
Asphalt Paving
S.I.C.: 1611
Peter A. Basile *(Pres.)*
Thomas Cicotte *(V.P.)*
Peter Messina *(V.P.)*
Soraya Nowland *(Gen. Mgr.)*

Affiliate:

Shmina Construction, Inc. **(1)**
13000 Newburgh Rd.
Livonia, MI 48151
Tel.: 313-464-1600
Emp.: 15

General Contractor
S.I.C.: 4939
Peter A. Basile *(Chief Exec. Officer)*
Arthur Shmina *(Pres.)*
Thomas Cicotte *(Sec. & Treas.)*

BASIN ELECTRIC POWER CO-OP
1717 E. Interstate Ave.
Bismarck, ND 58501
Tel.: 701-223-0441 **ND**
Fax: 701-224-5336
Year Founded: 1961
Approx.Sls.: $750,000,000
Emp.: 1,900
Electric Power Generation, Transmission & Distribution; Coal Gastifcation; Bituminous Coal & Lignite Surface
S.I.C.: 4911; 1311; 1221
Robert L. McPhail *(Gen. Mgr.)*
Michael Hinman *(Gen. Counsel)*
Clifton Hudgins *(Mgr.-Fin. Services)*
Rod Kuhn *(Mgr.-Tax, Audit & Insurance)*
Kenneth Ziegler *(Mgr.-Govt. Rels.)*
Howard Easton *(Asst. Gen. Mgr.-Mktg. & Member Services)*
Richard Fockler *(Asst. Gen. Mgr.-Opers. & Engrng.)*
Richard Weber *(Asst. Gen. Mgr.-Mngmt. Services)*

Outside Service Firm(s):

Coopers & Lybrand*(Auditors)*
1000 TCF Bldg.
Minneapolis, MN 55402
Tel.: 612-293-2929
Fax: 612-370-9395

BASLER ELECTRIC COMPANY
Rte. 143
Highland, IL 62249
Mailing Address:
P.O. Box 269
Highland, IL 62249
Tel.: 618-654-2341 **IL**
Fax: 618-654-2351
Year Founded: 1942
Assets: $33,670,000
Liabilities: $12,290,000
Net Worth: $21,380,000
Approx.Sls.: $80,300,000
Emp.: 1,700
Fiscal Year-end: 9/30/91
Export
Mfr. Custom Engineering Magnetic Components & Electric Power Control Systems, Double Sided Printed Circuit Boards, Switching Power Supplies
S.I.C.: 3625
William L. Basler *(Chm. Bd., Chief Exec. Officer & Treas.)*
Floyd J. Basler *(Vice Chm.)*
Arthur E. Johnson *(Pres., Chief Oper. Officer & Gen. Mgr.)*
Richard Mathy *(Chief Information Officer)*
Allan Beyer *(V.P.-Fin. & Sec.)*
Herbert Roach *(V.P.-Admin.)*
Marilyn Frey *(Dir.-Personnel)*
Ben Paige *(Dir.-Central Pur.)*
Dale Rutz *(Dir.-Pur. Magnetics)*
Jake Hinterser *(Supvr.-Sls. Promo. & Adv.)*
Principal(s):
William L. Basler

No. of Mfg. Plants/Facilities: 8

Computer Systems/Hardware:
IBM 9375 Model 60

Outside Service Firm(s):

Boyd, Franz, Stevens*(Auditors)*
St. Louis, MO

Daniel & Henry Co.*(Group Insurer)*
St. Louis, MO

Kappel, Neill & Staed*(Legal Firm)*
St. Louis, MO

Boatmen's Trust Company*(Major Banking Relationship)*
100 North Broadway
St. Louis, MO 63102
Tel.: 314-466-2469

Division:

Basler Electric Circuits, Inc. **(1)**
P.O.Box 1165
Taylor, TX 76574
Tel.: 512-352-7683
Twx: 510-100-3841
Emp.: 47
Mfr. Printed Circuit Boards
S.I.C.: 3672
Warwick Tobias *(Pres.)*

BASS ENTERPRISES PRODUCTION COMPANY
First City Bank Tower, 201 Main St.
Fort Worth, TX 76102
Tel.: 817-390-8400
Fax: 817-390-8893
Year Founded: 1932
Sales Range: $100-499 Million
Emp.: 1,000
Holding Company; Investor Group
S.I.C.: 6719
Sid R. Bass *(Chm. Bd.)*
William Medary *(Pres. & Chief Exec. Officer)*
Cheryl Barekman *(Dir.-Pur.)*
Principal(s):
Sid R. Bass
William Medary

No. of U.S. Offices: 4

Computer Systems/Hardware:
IBM System 38

Outside Service Firm(s):

KPMG Peat Marwick*(Auditors)*
301 Commerce, Ste. 2500
Ft. Worth, TX 76102
Tel.: 817-335-2655

Kelly, Hart & Hallman*(Legal Firm)*
2500 First City Bank Tower
Ft. Worth, TX 76102
Tel.: 817-332-2500

First City Bank Texas*(Major Banking Relationship)*
Fort Worth, TX

BASS PRO SHOPS, INC.
1935 S. Campbell
Springfield, MO 65898
Tel.: 417-887-1915 **MO**
Fax: 417-887-1807
Year Founded: 1971
Approx.Sls.: $700,000,000
Emp.: 4,000
Mail Order Retail Sales of Fishing, Hunting & Camping Equipment & Supplies, Wholesale Distribution of Sporting Goods; Bicycle Shops
S.I.C.: 5961; 5941; 5091
John L. Morris *(Pres.)*
Vergil Collins *(V.P.-Admin.)*

Outside Service Firm(s):

Commercial Bank of Springfield*(Major Banking Relationship)*
Springfield, MO

THE W.E. BASSETT COMPANY
100 Trap Falls Rd. Ext.
Shelton, CT 06484
Tel.: 203-929-8483 **CT**
Fax: 203-929-8963
Year Founded: 1939
Emp.: 190
Manufacture Manicure Implements, Gift Sets & Advertising Specialties
S.I.C.: 3421; 3999
H.W. Bassett *(Chm. Bd.)*
William C. Bassett *(Pres.)*
David M. Bassett *(Sec. & Project Mgr.)*

No. of Mfg. Plants/Facilities: 2

Computer Systems/Hardware:
IBM System 36

BASSO & ASSOCIATES INC. ADV. & PUBLIC RELATIONS
3158 Redhill Ave., Ste. 200
Costa Mesa, CA 92626
Mailing Address:
P.O. Box 8030,
Newport Beach, CA 92658
Tel.: 714-641-0111
Fax: 714-641-0274
Year Founded: 1972
Approx.Billings: $24,000,000
Emp.: 27
Joseph Basso *(Pres.)*
Pola Duncan *(Chief Fin. Officer)*

BAST CHEVROLET INC.
3660 Sunrise Hwy.
Seaford, NY 11783
Tel.: 516-785-4100 **NY**
Fax: 516-785-4107
Year Founded: 1955
Approx.Sls.: $128,000,000
Emp.: 80
Retail Sales of New & Used Automobiles; Car Leasing; Auto Repair Shops
S.I.C.: 5511; 7538
Charles W. Bast *(Pres. & Treas.)*
Bonnie R. Bast *(V.P. & Sec.)*

Outside Service Firm(s):

Chemical Bank*(Major Banking Relationship)*
3875 Merrick Rd.
Seaford, NY 11783

BATEMAN BROTHERS LUMBER CO., INC.
89 Sand Rd.
New Britain, PA 18901
Mailing Address:
P.O. Box 1039
Doylestown, PA 18901
Tel.: 215-345-7331 **DE**
Fax: 215-345-4238
Year Founded: 1946
Approx.Sls.: $10,000,000
Emp.: 35
Fiscal Year-end: 12/31/90
Import
Wholesale Imported & Domestic Lumber
S.I.C.: 5031
Edward D. Bateman *(Chm. Bd.)*
Howard F. Bateman *(Pres.)*
John R. Bateman *(V.P.)*
Kevin P. Bateman *(Treas.)*
George W. Bateman *(Sec.)*

No. of Mfg. Plants/Facilities: 3

Computer Systems/Hardware:
Digital

Outside Service Firm(s):

McCarthy, Hoffman & Sowers*(Auditors)*
Philadelphia, PA

Bucks County Bank & Trust Company*(Major Banking Relationship)*
Perkasie, PA

Subsidiaries:

Bateman Bros. Lumber Co., Inc. **(1)**
P.O. Box 1039
New Britain, PA 18901
Tel.: 215-345-7331
Wholesale Distributor Of Forest Products
S.I.C.: 0851
Jack Bateman *(V.P.)*

E.D. Collier & Son **(1)**
Reid & Namoni Sts.
Woodbury, NJ 08096
Tel.: 609-845-8100
Wholesale Distributor Of Forest Products
S.I.C.: 0851
Bill Collier, Jr. *(Gen. Mgr.)*

BATES CONTAINER, INC.
6433 Davis Blvd.
North Richland Hills, TX 76180
Mailing Address:
P.O. Box 822028,
North Richland Hills, TX 76180
Tel.: 817-498-3200
Fax: 817-581-8802
Approx.Sls.: $30,000,000
Emp.: 190
Manufacture Corrugated Boxes; Coated, Glazed & Varnished Paper; Miscellaneous Bags
S.I.C.: 2653
Warren H. Bates *(Chm. Bd.)*
Allen H. Sanders *(Pres.)*
Merle Boyd *(V.P.-Mfg.)*
Maxine Bates *(Treas.)*
Linda Timmons *(Sec.)*
Ron Johnson *(Controller)*
Sally Hackfeld *(Mgr.-Personnel)*
J. Barrett Scott *(Mgr.-Mktg.)*
Charles Welch *(Mgr.-Sls.)*
Ron Welch *(Pur. Agent)*

Outside Service Firm(s):

Vink, Pier & Teague*(Auditors)*
Dallas, TX

Simon, Anisman, Doby, Wilson & Skirn*(Legal Firm)*
Dallas, TX

NationsBank Texas*(Major Banking Relationship)*
NCNB Plaza, 16th Fl., P.O. Box 830501
Dallas, TX 75283-1402
Tel.: 214-508-1729

BATES FABRICS, INC.
33 Canal St.
Lewiston, ME 04243
Tel.: 207-784-7311
Fax: 207-784-2598
Approx.Sls.: $18,000,000
Emp.: 115
Bedspreads, Drapes & Tablecovers
S.I.C.: 2391; 2392
Alfred J. Lebel *(Pres. & Chief Exec. Officer)*

Outside Service Firm(s):

Albin, Randall & Bennett*(Auditors)*
Portland, ME

Skelton, Taintor & Abbott*(Legal Firm)*
Lewiston, ME

THE BATES MFG. CO.
36 Newburgh Rd.
Hackettstown, NJ 07840
Tel.: 908-852-9300
Fax: 908-852-7837
Approx.Sls.: $25,000,000
Emp.: 240
Fiscal Year-end: 12/31/90
Mfr. Numbering Machines, Office Products; Information Processing Supplies; Computer Care Products
S.I.C.: 3578; 3579
C.E. Williams *(Chm. Bd.)*
Thomas M. Williams *(Pres. & Chief Exec. Officer)*
Paul Keane *(Exec. V.P. & Gen. Mgr.)*
Peter S. Williams *(Exec. V.P.-Devel.)*
Harry Van Gorp *(Sr. V.P.-Devel.)*

Computer Systems/Hardware:
IBM 38

Outside Service Firm(s):

J. H. Cohn & Co.*(Auditors)*
75 Eisenhower Pkwy.
Roseland, NJ 07068-1697

The Bates Mfg. Co.—(Continued)

Tel.: 201-228-3500

Pitney, Hardin, Kipp & Szuch*(Legal Firm)*
163 Madison Ave.
Morristown, NJ 07960
Tel.: 201-267-3333

Midlantic National Bank*(Major Banking Relationship)*
Bloomfield, NJ

BATEY/POINDEXTER
3780 Wilshire Blvd., Ste. 210
Los Angeles, CA 90010
Tel.: 213-738-8078
Fax: 213-384-1248
Year Founded: 1980
Approx.Billings: $20,000,000
Emp.: 16
Larry Poindexter *(Pres.)*
Tony Preece *(Chief Exec. Officer)*
Arthur Nissman *(Sr. V.P.)*
Andy Carmichael *(V.P.)*

BATH IRON WORKS
700 Washington St.
Bath, ME 04530
Tel.: 207-443-3311
Fax: 207-442-1567
Year Founded: 1884
Approx.Sls.: $700,000,000
Emp.: 11,500
Ship Building & Repairs
S.I.C.: 3731
Duane D. Fitzgerald *(Pres. & Chief Exec. Officer)*

Computer Systems/Hardware:
IBM System 3090; 2005

Outside Service Firm(s):

Arthur Andersen & Co.*(Auditors)*
One Intl. Place, 100 Oliver St.
Boston, MA 02110
Tel.: 617-330-4000
Fax: 617-439-9731

Gibbons, Goodwin & Van Amerongen*(Investment Banker)*
600 Madison Ave.
New York, NY 10022-1615
Tel.: 212-832-2400

Chemical Bank*(Major Banking Relationship)*
450 West 33rd St.
New York, NY 10001
Tel.: 212-613-7197
Fax: 212-947-7628

BATON ROUGE WATER WORKS COMPANY
8755 Goodwood
Baton Rouge, LA 70806
Mailing Address:
P.O. Box 96016,
Baton Rouge, LA 70896-9016
Tel.: 504-928-1000 **LA**
Fax: 504-231-0311
Approx.Sls.: $23,000,000
Emp.: 206
Fiscal Year-end: 12/31/91
Water Supply Distributor
S.I.C.: 4941
Corporate Giving Program: Gives to recognized charities
J. Luther Jordan, Jr. *(Chm. Bd.)*
E.H. Owen *(Pres.)*
Edward D. Roberts, Jr. *(Sr. V.P. & Treas.)*
J.W. Dellsperger, Jr. *(Sr. V.P.-Opers.)*
R.E. Johnson *(V.P. & Sec.)*

Principal(s):
J. Luther Jordan, Jr.
E.H. Owen

No. of Mfg. Plants/Facilities: 1
No. of U.S. Offices: 1

Outside Service Firm(s):

Arthur Andersen & Co.*(Auditors)*
201 St. Charles Ave., Ste. 4500
New Orleans, LA 70170

Louisiana Companies*(Commercial Insurance Carrier)*
801 North Blvd.
Baton Rouge, LA 70821-0991

Taylor, Porter, Brooks & Phillips*(Legal Firm)*
Baton Rouge, LA

Whitney National Bank of New Orleans*(Major Banking Relationship)*
P.O. Box 61260
New Orleans, LA 70161
Tel.: 504-586-7422

William M. Mercer Incorporated*(Pension Manager)*
One Perimeter Park South, Ste. 130-S
Birmingham, AL 35243

Subsidiary:

Parish Water Company, Inc. **(1)**
9232 Joor Rd.
Baton Rouge, LA 70816
Tel.: 504-261-0100
Emp.: 33
Water Utility
S.I.C.: 4941
E.H. Owen *(Pres.)*
E.D. Roberts, Jr. *(Sr. V.P. & Treas.)*

BATSON-COOK COMPANY
817 Fourth Ave.
West Point, GA 31833
Mailing Address:
P.O. Box 151
West Point, GA 31833
Tel.: 706-643-2101
Fax: 706-643-2199
Year Founded: 1915
Approx.Sls.: $160,000,000
Emp.: 600
Export
Construction; Manufacture Textile Machinery; Building Materials Dealer
S.I.C.: 1542; 3552; 5211
Cliff C. Glover *(Chm. Bd. & Chief Exec. Officer)*
W.H. Huguley III *(Asst. Chm.)*
Edmund C. Glover *(Pres.)*
William H. Huguley IV *(Exec. V.P. & Treas.)*
Raymond L. Moody, Jr. *(Exec. V.P.)*
J.L. Glover, Sr. *(V.P.)*
J.L. Glover, Jr. *(V.P.)*
Cecil G. Hood *(Sec. & Controller)*
Ron Smith *(Dir.-Personnel)*
Ben N. Myers *(Pur. Agent)*

Outside Service Firm(s):

Grant Thornton*(Auditors)*
Atlanta, GA

Glover & Davis*(Legal Firm)*
Atlanta, GA

Trust Company Bank*(Major Banking Relationship)*
P.O. Box 4655,
Atlanta, GA 30302

BATTEAST CONSTRUCTION COMPANY, INC.
430 E. LaSalle Ave.
South Bend, IN 46617
Tel.: 219-234-3539
Fax: 219-289-2270
Approx.Sls.: $26,000,000
Emp.: 35
Fiscal Year-end: 12/31/91
Industrial, Commercial, Institutional & Municipal Construction
S.I.C.: 1541; 1542
Robert V. Batteast *(Chm. Bd. & Pres.)*
Robert V. Batteast, Jr. *(V.P.)*
T. Clifford Fleming *(Treas.)*

Computer Systems/Hardware:
IBM

Outside Service Firm(s):

Price Waterhouse*(Auditors)*
202 S. Michigan
South Bend, IN 46624

Walker, Fleming, Corbin & Greenberg*(Legal Firm)*
Merrillville, IN

St. Joseph Bank & Trust*(Major Banking Relationship)*
South Bend, IN

BATTELLE MEMORIAL INSTITUTE
505 King Ave.
Columbus, OH 43201
Tel.: 614-424-6424 **OH**
Telex: 24-5454 BATTELLE COL
Fax: 614-424-5263
Year Founded: 1929
Approx.Sls.: $775,000,000
Emp.: 8,000
Fiscal Year-end: 12/31/91
Contract Technology Development, Commercialization & Management
S.I.C.: 8731; 7375
Willis S. White, Jr. *(Chm. Bd.)*
Dr. Douglas E. Oleson *(Pres. & Chief Exec. Officer)*
Dr. William J. Madia *(Sr. V.P.)*
Dr. William R. Wiley *(Sr. V.P.)*
Maurice G. Stark *(V.P.-Fin.)*
John J. Christie *(V.P.-Corp. Devel.)*
Paul T. Santilli *(V.P. & Gen. Counsel)*
Robert W. Smith, Jr. *(V.P.-Human Resources)*
William L. Evans *(Dir.-Computing & Information Systems)*
Thomas E. McClain *(Dir.-Communications)*
Harry R. Templeton *(Mgr.-Mktg. Communications & Publications)*

Principal(s):
Dr. Douglas E. Oleson

No. of Mfg. Plants/Facilities: 8
No. of U.S. Offices: 19
No. of Foreign Offices: 9

Computer Systems/Hardware:
CDC; DEC VAX; IBM

Outside Service Firm(s):

KPMG Peat Marwick*(Auditors)*
4905 Tildgman St.
Allentown, PA 18104
Tel.: 215-391-6380

The Huntington National Bank*(Major Banking Relationship)*
41 S. High St.
Columbus, OH 43216

Division:

Battelle Pacific Northwest Div. **(1)**
Battelle Blvd.
Richland, WA 99352
Tel.: 509-375-2121
Emp.: 3,450
Contract Research
S.I.C.: 8731
William R. Wiley *(Pres.)*

Subsidiaries:

Battelle Development Corp. **(1)**
505 King Ave.
Columbus, OH 43201
Tel.: 614-424-7950 (100%)
Emp.: 2
Invention, Development & Licensing
S.I.C.: 8731
Thomas J. Atterbury *(Pres.)*

Geosafe Corporation **(1)**
Battelle Blvd.
Richland, WA 99352
Tel.: 509-375-2121
Emp.: 12
Environmental Services
S.I.C.: 8731
Bruce W. Johnson *(Pres.)*

Information Dimensions, Inc. **(1)**
655 Metro Place South
Dublin, OH 43017
Tel.: 614-761-8083
Emp.: 225
Computer Programming and Other Software Services
S.I.C.: 7372
William G. Griffith *(Pres.)*

Scientific Advances Inc. **(1)**
601 W. 5th Ave.
Columbus, OH 43201
Tel.: 614-424-7005 (100%)
Emp.: 7
Venture Capital; Technical Products & Services
S.I.C.: 6799
Paul T. Santilli *(Pres.)*

Non-U.S. Holdings:

Battelle-Institut E.V. **(1)**
Am Romerhof 35 6000
Frankfurt/Main, 90, Germany
Tel.: 69-79080 (100%)
Telex: 411966
Fax: 069/7908-80
Earnings: $60,000,000
Emp.: 500
Fiscal Year-end: 12/31/90
Contract Research & Development
S.I.C.: 8731
Dr. Gert Hewig *(Gen. Mgr.)*
Thomas Gaitzsch *(Chief Fin. Officer)*
Edeast Waller *(Dir.-Human Resources)*
Gunter Gutmann *(Dir.-Public Rels.)*
Jutta Hornes *(Dir.-Travel Plng.)*
Heinz Herweling *(Dir.-Quality Control)*
Werner Beberich *(Dir.-Pension Admin.)*
Kurt Wiedemann *(Dir.-Real Estate & Engrng.)*
Dr. Heinrich Klefert *(Dir.-Envrnmt. & Natural Resources)*
Dr. Ralf Dornhaus *(Dir.-Electronics & Matls. Technology)*
Dr. Hans Spenke *(Dir.-Nuclear Engrng. & Process Technology)*
Dr. Klaus Melzer *(Dir.-Engine & Vehicle Technology)*
Dr. Heinrich Ulefenz *(Dir.-Envrnmtl. Technology & Biotechnology)*
Dr. Thomas Sabourin *(Dir.-Product Registration)*
Dr. Emilio Biamonte *(Dir.-Technology Assesment)*

Battelle Institute, Limited **(1)**
15, Hanover Square
London, WIR 9AJ, United Kingdom
Tel.: 071-493-0184 (100%)
Emp.: 12
Contract Research & Development Services
S.I.C.: 8731
Dr. Douglas E. Olesen *(Chm.)*

BATTENBERG, FILLHARDT & WRIGHT, INC.
70 N. Second St.
San Jose, CA 95113
Tel.: 408-287-8500
Fax: 408-971-2494
Year Founded: 1969
Approx.Billings: $20,000,000
Emp.: 18
Curtis Wright *(Pres.)*

BATTENFELD GLOUCESTER ENGINEERING CO. INC.
P.O. Box 900, Blackburn Industrial Park
Gloucester, MA 01930
Tel.: 508-281-1800
Telex: 940-333
Fax: 508-283-9206
Year Founded: 1961
Approx.Sls.: $60,000,000
Emp.: 450
Fiscal Year-end: 6/31/91
Export
Mfr. Plastics Processing & Converting Machinery
S.I.C.: 3559
Harold Wrede *(Pres.)*
Robert Weeks *(V.P.-Sls. & Mktg.)*
Brian Marvelley *(V.P.-Fin.)*
Ron Ross *(V.P.-Personnel & Corp. Grants Contact)*

D. Smith *(V.P.-Engrng.)*
J. Nicholes *(Dir.-Pur.)*
Ron Townsend *(Mgr.-Data Processing)*
James Wade *(Mgr.-Export & Intl. Mktg.)*
Robert C. Bell *(Mgr.-Communications & Dir.-Internal Art, Meetings Plng. & Video)*
Karl Keim *(Mgr.-Res. & Devel.)*
Doug Opie *(Serv. Mgr.)*
Don Shade *(Govt. Affairs)*

Computer Systems/Hardware:
IBM

BATTEY MACHINERY COMPANY
2960 New Calhoun Hwy., N.E.
Rome, GA 30161
Tel.: 706-291-4141
Fax: 706-291-4141, Ext. 270
Approx.Sls.: $18,800,000
Emp.: 77
Fiscal Year-end: 12/31/91
Distribute Industrial, Electric & Plumbing Supplies
S.I.C.: 5074; 5063; 5085
Jack Cummings, Jr. *(Chm. Bd.)*
Edmund L. Yeargan, Jr. *(Pres.)*
Don Hyde *(Dir.-Opers. & Personnel)*
Victor B. Yeargan, Jr. *(Sec. & Treas.)*

Computer Systems/Hardware:
IBM

Outside Service Firm(s):

Read, Martin & Slickman*(Auditors)*
Rome, GA

NationsBank*(Major Banking Relationship)*
35 Broad St.
Atlanta, GA 30303
Tel.: 404-581-2121
Tel.: 800-848-8198

Garner & Glover*(Commercial Insurance Carrier)*
Rome, GA

Blue Cross & Blue Shield of Georgia, Inc.*(Group Insurer)*
Atlanta, GA

Smith, Shaw, Maddox, Davidson & Graham*(Legal Firm)*
Atlanta, GA

BAUERLEIN INC.
Poydras Center, 650 Poydras St., Ste. 1100
New Orleans, LA 70130
Tel.: 504-522-5461
Fax: 504-522-5518
Year Founded: 1922
Approx.Billings: $21,700,000
Emp.: 40
John Green *(Pres. & Chief Exec. Officer)*
Ray Littell *(Chief Fin. Officer)*
Eugene Barnes *(Sr. Counsellor)*
Kenneth Gormin *(Sr. Counsellor)*

BAUGH CONSTRUCTION COMPANY
900 Poplar Place So.
Seattle, WA 98114
Tel.: 206-726-8000
Fax: 206-328-9235
Year Founded: 1952
Approx.Sls.: $132,000,000
Emp.: 100
Commercial & Industrial Construction Contracting Services
S.I.C.: 1542; 1522; 1541
Robert H. Baugh *(Chm. Bd. & Pres.)*
Lloyd Wiebe *(V.P., Sec. & Treas.)*
William P. Dorsey *(V.P.)*
Robert Good *(V.P.)*
Tom Hansler *(V.P.)*
Larry Persinger *(V.P.)*
Mike Finney *(Controller)*

Albert Rogalski *(Mgr.-Data Processing)*

Computer Systems/Hardware:
NCR

Outside Service Firm(s):

Benson & McLaughlin*(Auditors)*
Seattle, WA

Sylvester, Rundo, Petrie & Cruzen*(Legal Firm)*
Seattle, WA

Seattle First National Bank*(Major Banking Relationship)*
701 Fifth Avenue
Seattle, WA 98104
Tel.: 206-358-3035

BAUGHER CHEVROLET-BUICK-GEO, INC.
2551 W. Main
Waynesboro, VA 22980
Mailing Address:
P.O. Box 1188
Waynesboro, VA 22980
Tel.: 703-949-8311
Tel.: 800-955-0342 **VA**
Year Founded: 1946
Approx.Sls.: $15,000,000
Emp.: 42
Fiscal Year-end: 12/31/91
New & Used Autos & Trucks, Parts, Service
S.I.C.: 5511; 5531; 7532
Claude O. Baugher *(Chm. Bd.)*
John O. Baugher *(Pres. & Treas.)*
Sandy H. Baugher *(Mgr.-Opers.)*
Susie E. Baugher *(Sec.)*
Scott Powell *(Mgr.-New Cars)*
Tammie Rodgers *(Mgr.-Bus.)*
Principal(s):
Claude O. Baugher
John O. Baugher

Outside Service Firm(s):

Beers & Cutler*(Auditors)*
Washington, DC

Travelers Insurance Co.*(Commercial Insurance Carrier)*
One Tower Square
Hartford, CT 06183-6130
Tel.: 203-277-4542
Fax: 203-277-5038

Blue Cross & Blue Shield of Virginia*(Group Insurer)*
2015 Staples Mill Rd.
Richmond, VA 23230
Tel.: 804-359-7000
Fax: 804-354-7397

Allen, Dalton & Watkins*(Legal Firm)*
Washington, DC

NationsBank of Virginia, N.A.*(Major Banking Relationship)*
P.O. Box 26904
Richmond, VA 23261
Tel.: 804-344-1300

W. A. BAUM COMPANY, INC.
620 Oak St.
Copiague, NY 11726
Tel.: 516-226-3940
Fax: 516-226-3969
Approx.Sls.: $10,000,000
Emp.: 150
Mfr. of Blood Pressure Instruments
S.I.C.: 3841
W.A. Baum, Jr. *(Chm. Bd.)*
John C. Baum *(Pres.)*
W.A. Baum *(Sec. & Treas.)*

Outside Service Firm(s):

Chase Manhattan Bank, N.A.*(Major Banking Relationship)*
One Chase Manhattan Plaza
New York, NY 10081
Tel.: 212-552-2222

BAWDEN CORPORATION
400 S. 14th Ave.
Eldridge, IA 52748
Tel.: 319-323-4610 **IA**
Fax: 319-285-4828
Approx.Sls.: $44,000,000
Emp.: 300
Holding Company For Bawden Printing
S.I.C.: 6719; 2752
John D. Bawden *(Pres.)*
Clancy Wright *(Exec. V.P.)*
Joyce Bawden *(V.P.)*
Duane Schipall *(Sec. & Treas.)*

Outside Service Firm(s):

McGladrey & Pullen*(Auditors)*
Davenport, IA

Subsidiaries:

Bawden Printing, Inc. **(1)**
400 S. 14th Ave.
Eldridge, IA 52748
Tel.: 319-285-4800
Commercail Printing, Offset
S.I.C.: 2752
John D. Bawden *(Chief Exec. Officer)*
Mark Bawden *(Pres.)*
Clancy Wright *(Exec. V.P., Treas. & Sec.)*
Terry Sarver *(V.P.-Mfg.)*
Ted Ewing *(V.P.-Sls.)*

Bawden, Torrey & Associates **(1)**
400 Executive Sq., 400 Main St.
Davenport, IA 52801
Tel.: 319-326-1224
Fax: 319-326-3353
Approx.Billings: $3,500,000
Emp.: 12
Computer Systems/Hardware:
Adman; Media Mngmt. Plus; MacIntosh Design System Network
Integrated Communications Services
Mike Bawden *(Pres.)*
Tom Torrey *(Exec. V.P.)*

BAXTER ADVERTISING, INC.
Interchange Tower, 600 S. Highway 169, Ste. 1950
Minneapolis, MN 55426
Tel.: 612-593-2500
Fax: 612-593-8338
Year Founded: 1948
Approx.Billings: $10,000,000
Emp.: 25
Richard Hatch *(Pres.)*
Terrence Keegan *(Exec. V.P.)*
Lori Kern *(Bookkeeper)*

J.H. BAXTER & COMPANY
1700 S. El Camino Real
San Mateo, CA 94402
Tel.: 415-349-0201
Fax: 415-570-6878
Approx.Sls.: $29,000,000
Emp.: 275
Mfr. of Pressure Treated Poles, Piling & Lumber
S.I.C.: 2491
Alfred X. Baxter *(Chm. & Chief Exec. Officer)*
Robert A. Boyd *(Pres. & Chief Oper. Officer)*
J. Morgan III *(V.P.-Tech.)*
N.V. Poletika *(V.P.-Special Prods.)*
William Yuen *(V.P.-Fin., Sec. & Treas.)*
Sandy Lavino *(Gen. Sls. Mgr.)*

BAXTER HODELL DONNELLY PRESTON INC.
3500 Red Bank Rd.
Cincinnati, OH 45227-4188
Tel.: 513-271-1634
Fax: 513-271-7017
Year Founded: 1960
Emp.: 56
Architectural Firm
S.I.C.: 8712
James Donnelly *(Pres. & Chief Exec. Officer)*
Darrell Wolff *(V.P.-Design)*
Russ Couch *(V.P.)*
Robert Habel *(V.P.)*
Jerry Willging *(Sec. & Treas.)*
T. Patrick Donnelly *(Mgr.-Bus. Devel.)*
Cynthia A. Jackson *(Mktg. Coordinator)*

Outside Service Firm(s):

Fifth Third Bank*(Major Banking Relationship)*
Corporate Trust Services, 38 Fountain Square Plaza
Cincinnati, OH 45263

Subsidiaries:

Baxter/Peas **(1)**
4460 Carver Woods Rd.
Cincinnati, OH 45242
Tel.: 513-792-7600
Fax: 513-792-7610
Architectural Services to Corporate Clients
S.I.C.: 8712

Baxter Shirk Design Collaborative **(1)**
319 W. Fourth St., Ste. 200
Cincinnati, OH 45202
Tel.: 513-287-6700
Fax: 513-287-6708
Architectural Services & Planning with Emphasis on Retail
S.I.C.: 8712

Bay City Milling & Grocery Co.
(Name Changed To United Stores)

BAY INDUSTRIES INC.
Mailing Address:
1330 Elizabeth St.
Greenbay, WI 54302
Sub-Contractors
S.I.C.: 2431; 3442; 5031
Arnold Schmidt *(Pres.)*

Subsidiary:

Brower Company **(1)**
7043 S. 190th St.
Kent, WA 98032
Tel.: 206-251-6750
Fax: 206-251-6225
Approx.Sls.: $11,000,000
Emp.: 100
Sub-contractors
S.I.C.: 1542; 1541; 5031
Barbara Peters *(Controller)*

BAY STATE MILLING CO.
100 Congress St.
Quincy, MA 02169
Tel.: 617-328-4400
Fax: 617-479-8910
Year Founded: 1899
Approx.Sls.: $230,000,000
Emp.: 380
Fiscal Year-end: 6/30/91
Miller & Distributor of Flour
S.I.C.: 5149; 2041
Bernard J. Rothwell, III *(Chm. Bd.)*
Brian G. Rothwell *(Pres. & Chief Exec. Officer)*
William Quigley *(V.P.-Fin.)*
John Hillman *(Sr. V.P.-Opers.)*
Roger Hipwell *(Sr. V.P.-Sls. & Mktg.)*
Steven Bromwell *(V.P.-Sls.)*
Richard Schefer *(V.P.-Human Resources)*
Antonio Scippa *(V.P.-Production)*
Alyce M. Brommels *(Corp. Sec.)*
Leo O'Brien *(Controller)*
Principal(s):
Bernard J. Rothwell, III
Brian G. Rothwell

No. of Mfg. Plants/Facilities: 7

Computer Systems/Hardware:
NCR; Digital

Outside Service Firm(s):

Deloitte & Touche*(Auditors)*
125 Summer St.
Boston, MA 02110
Tel.: 617-261-8000
Fax: 617-261-8111

Bay State Milling Co.—(Continued)

KPMG Peat Marwick*(Auditors)*
One Boston Place
Boston, MA 02108
Tel.: 617-723-7700

Mutual of Omaha Insurance Company*(Group Insurer)*
Mutual of Omaha Plaza,
Omaha, NE 68175
Tel.: 800-228-7775

Goodwin, Procter & Hoar*(Legal Firm)*
Exchange Place
Boston, MA 02109-2881
Tel.: 617-570-1000

State Street Bank & Trust Co.*(Major Banking Relationship)*
P.O. Box 366,
Boston, MA 02101
Tel.: 617-426-5523

State Street Bank & Trust Co.*(Pension Manager)*
225 Franklin St.
Boston, MA 02101
Tel.: 617-654-3652

Bayer Bess Vanderwarker

BAYER BESS VANDERWARKER INC.
225 N. Michigan Ave., Ste. 1900
Chicago, IL 60601
Tel.: 312-861-3800 **IL**
Fax: 312-856-9044
Year Founded: 1969
Approx.Billings: $125,312,407
Emp.: 220
Advertising Agency
S.I.C.: 7311
Gary R. Bayer *(Chm. & Chief Exec. Officer)*
Ron Bess *(Pres. & Chief Oper. Officer)*
Bernard McLean *(Chief Fin. Officer)*
Richard Corelitz *(Exec. V.P. & Mng. Dir.)*
G. Brian Goodall *(Exec. V.P. & Mng. Dir.)*
Robert Irvine *(Exec. V.P. & Mng. Dir.)*
Ellen Plusker *(Sr. V.P., Dir. Strategic Plng.)*
Liane Adduci *(V.P. & Dir.-Corp. Communications)*
Scott Brewer *(V.P., Dir. Admin.)*
Principal(s):
Gary R. Bayer
Ron Bess

Computer Systems/Hardware:
Panasonic

Outside Service Firm(s):

Altschuler, Melvoin & Glasser*(Auditors)*
30 S. Wecker Dr.
Chicago, IL 60606
Tel.: 312-207-2800

First Chicago Trust Co. of New York*(Major Banking Relationship)*
One First Natl. Plaza, Ste. 123
Chicago, IL 60670
Tel.: 312-407-4660

ROBERT E. BAYLEY CONSTRUCTION
205 Columbia St.
Seattle, WA 98104
Mailing Address:
P.O. Box 4567,
Seattle, WA 98104
Tel.: 206-621-8884
Fax: 206-343-7728
Year Founded: 1963
Approx.Sls.: $132,000,000
Emp.: 450
Fiscal Year-end: 9/30/91
General Building Contractor; Commercial Construction
S.I.C.: 1522
Robert E. Bayley *(Chm. Bd. & Chief Exec. Officer)*
Ronald Bayley *(Pres.)*
James Lansciardi *(Exec. V.P.)*
Linda Simpson *(V.P.-Admin.)*
Joanne Bayley *(Treas. & Sec.)*
Richard Eliason *(Mgr.-Acctg.)*
Principal(s):
Robert E. Bayley

Computer Systems/Hardware:
Wang

Outside Service Firm(s):

KPMG Peat Marwick*(Auditors)*
3100 Two Union Square, 601 Union St., Ste. 3100
Seattle, WA 98101
Tel.: 206-292-1500

Davis, Wright, Tremaine*(Legal Firm)*
2200 One Union Square
Seattle, WA 98101-1688
Tel.: 206-622-3150

Seattle First National Bank*(Major Banking Relationship)*
701 Fifth Avenue
Seattle, WA 98104
Tel.: 206-358-3035

Subsidiaries:

Images Woodworking, Inc. **(1)**
1601 One Union Sq.
Seattle, WA 98101
Tel.: 206-621-8884
Commercial Construction Co.
S.I.C.: 1542

Programmed Maintenance Services, Inc. **(1)**
13221 NE 126th Place
Kirkland, WA 98034
Tel.: 206-820-2032
Approx.Sls.: $2,500,000
Emp.: 13
Total Facility Maintenance
S.I.C.: 2842; 7213; 7218; 7389; 7349
Robert E. Bayley *(Pres.)*
James Lansciardi *(Exec. V.P.)*
Ronald E. Bayley *(Treas.)*
Bill Freeburg *(Project Mgr.)*

THE WILLIAM BAYLEY CO.
1200 Warder St.
Springfield, OH 45503
Mailing Address:
P.O. Box 1287
Springfield, OH 45501
Tel.: 513-325-7301
Fax: 513-325-7305
Fax: 513-325-9607
Year Founded: 1881
Approx.Sls.: $12,000,000
Emp.: 148
Fiscal Year-end: 3/31/91
Manufacture Steel Windows; Steel Security Screens
S.I.C.: 3442; 3443; 3496
Donald C. Stading *(Chm. Bd.)*
James K. Ramsey *(Pres.)*
Joseph Gorecki *(Corp. Sec.)*
I.E. Veidemanis *(Natl. Sls. Mgr.)*
Walter Bauer *(Res. & Devel. Mgr.)*
E.L. Dougherty *(Mfr. Mgr.)*
Don Yeagle *(Pur. Mgr.)*
Glenda Robertson *(Asst. to Pres.)*

BAYOU STATE OIL CORPORATION
1115 Hawn Ave.
Shreveport, LA 71107
Mailing Address:
P.O. Drawer 2147,
Shreveport, LA 71166
Tel.: 318-222-0739
Emp.: 43
Fiscal Year-end: 4/30/92
Crude Oil Extraction
S.I.C.: 1311
Charles Brown *(Chm. Bd., Pres. & Chief Exec. Officer)*
Vicki Cromer *(Chief Fin. Officer)*
Julia Reeves *(Sec.)*

Computer Systems/Hardware:
IBM System 36

Outside Service Firm(s):

Commercial National Bank*(Major Banking Relationship)*
Shreveport, LA

BAYSIDE FUEL OIL DEPOT CORP.
1776 Shore Pkwy.
Brooklyn, NY 11214
Tel.: 718-372-9800 **NY**
Fax: 718-266-3744
Year Founded: 1965
Assets: $27,424,016
Liabilities: $15,333,010
Net Worth: $12,091,006
Approx.Sls.: $100,000,000
Emp.: 21
Wholesale Fuel Oil
S.I.C.: 5171
Alfred Allegretti *(Pres.)*
Victor Allegretti *(V.P.)*
Principal(s):
Alfred Allegretti
Victor Allegretti

Outside Service Firm(s):

Charles L. Ciaccio*(Auditors)*
Middle Village, NY

Coudert Brothers*(Legal Firm)*
200 Park Ave.
New York, NY 10166
Tel.: 212-880-4400

National Bank of North America*(Major Banking Relationship)*
80 Pine St.
New York, NY 10005
Tel.: 212-623-4000

National Westminster Bank plc*(Major Banking Relationship)*
175 Water St.
New York, NY 10038-4924
Tel.: 212-602-3364

Division:

Rose Fuel Corporation **(1)**
8301 Third Ave.
Brooklyn, NY 11209
Tel.: 718-7487-1117
Retail Petroleum
S.I.C.: 2911
Robert Rose *(Pres.)*

Subsidiary:

Bayside Fuel Oil Corp. **(1)**
1810 Shore Pkwy.
Brooklyn, NY 11214
Tel.: 718-946-4000
Retail Fuel Oil; Plumbing, Heating & Air Conditioning Contractor
S.I.C.: 5983; 1711
Victor Allegretti *(Pres.)*

BEACH CITY CHEVROLET CO.
3001 E. Pacific Coast Hwy.
Long Beach, CA 90804
Tel.: 310-597-6633 **CA**
Fax: 310-597-6440
Year Founded: 1947
Approx.Sls.: $26,000,000
Emp.: 75
Retail Sales of New & Used Automobiles & Pickups; Automotive Parts; General Automotive Repair Shops; Automotive Body Shops
S.I.C.: 5511; 5531; 7538; 7532
Bill Saul *(Pres.)*
James Crooker *(V.P.)*
Les Saul *(Treas. & Sec.)*

BEACH MOLD & TOOL INC.
999 Progress Blvd.
New Albany, IN 47150
Mailing Address:
P.O. Box 227
New Albany, IN 47150
Tel.: 812-945-2688 **KY**
Fax: 812-944-3705
Year Founded: 1972
Assets: $14,000,000
Liabilities: $5,000,000
Net Worth: $9,000,000
Approx.Sls.: $46,500,000
Emp.: 300
Fiscal Year-end: 5/31/91
Plastic Injection Molders & Assemblers
S.I.C.: 3544
William H. Beach *(Chm. Bd., Pres., Chief Exec. & Oper. Officer)*
Juanita Beach *(Sec. & Treas.)*
Nelson Wolfe *(Controller)*
Gil Rake *(Gen. Mgr.)*
Doug Batliner *(Dir.-Production & Pur.)*
Ben Blackman *(Dir.-Data Processing)*
Keith Masoud *(Dir.-Personnel)*
Max Petry *(Dir.-Pur. & Traffic Mgr.)*
Tim Becht *(Mgr.-Quality Control)*
Charles Miller *(Mgr.-Sls.)*
Linda Bamforth *(Admin. Asst.)*

No. of Mfg. Plants/Facilities: 1
No. of U.S. Offices: 1

Computer Systems/Hardware:
IBM Network

Outside Service Firm(s):

Melhizer, Endess & Tucker*(Auditors)*
New Albany, IN

Midwestern Insurance Alliance*(Commercial Insurance Carrier)*
Louisville, KY

Citizens Fidelity Bank & Trust of Indiana*(Major Banking Relationship)*
New Albany, IN
Tel.: 812-945-2265

William H. Beach*(Pension Manager)*
New Albany, IN

BEACON GROUP
85 Granby St.
Bloomfield, CT 06002
Tel.: 203-242-3659
Fax: 203-242-2204
Approx.Sls.: $13,000,000
Emp.: 8
Holding Company; Bookbinding Machinery, Aircraft Component Parts
S.I.C.: 6719; 3555
Norman Sarkisian *(Owner, Pres. & Chief Exec. Officer)*
Kerry B. Sarkisian *(V.P.)*
Donald Lopardo *(V.P.)*
Pamela Rose Sarkisian *(Treas.)*
Kerry Bouthot *(Sec.)*
Principal(s):
Norman Sarkisian

Outside Service Firm(s):

Kostin, Ruffkess & Co.*(Auditors)*
345 N. Main
West Hartford, CT
Tel.: 203-236-1975
Tel.: 203-236-0847

Reid & Reige*(Legal Firm)*
Terryville, CT

Connecticut Bank & Trust*(Major Banking Relationship)*
One Constitution Plaza,
Hartford, CT 06115

Subsidiaries:

Beacon Industries, Inc. **(1)**
85 Granby St.
Bloomfield, CT 06002
Tel.: 203-243-1616
Approx.Sls.: $6,000,000

Emp.: 60
Aircraft Engines & Engine Parts
S.I.C.: 3724
Norman Sarkisian *(Pres.)*

Beacon Winch Company **(1)**
85 Granby St.
Bloomfield, CT 06002
Tel.: 203-243-3264
Approx.Sls.: $2,000,000
Emp.: 16
Winches
S.I.C.: 3531
Norman Sarkisian *(Pres.)*

Smyth Manufacturing Company **(1)**
85 Granby St.
Bloomfield, CT 06002
Tel.: 203-242-2201
Approx.Sls.: $2,000,000
Emp.: 5
Bookbinding Machinery
S.I.C.: 3555
Norman Sarkisian *(Pres.)*

BEACON MFG. CO.
P.O. Box 395
Swannanoa, NC 28778
Tel.: 704-686-3861
Year Founded: 1904
Approx.Sls.: $100,000,000
Emp.: 1,400
Fiscal Year-end: 12/31/91
Institutional Bed Prods., Infant Prods., Bedspreads, Adult Blankets, Wools, Cottons & Manmade Fibers, Blanket Throws, Lap Blankets
S.I.C.: 2221; 2211; 2231; 2269; 2281; 2297
E. Randall Chestnut *(Pres.)*
John Hill *(Sr. V.P.-Mktg. & Mfg. Services)*
Tedd Smith *(Sr. V.P.-Sls.)*
John Pierce *(V.P. & Chief Fin. Officer)*
David Hollowell *(Dir.-Mktg.)*
Joe Chandler *(Dir.-Human Resources)*

Computer Systems/Hardware:
IBM

BEACON SALES CORPORATION
(d/b/a Commercial Roof Decks)
5905 Macy Ave.
Jacksonville, FL 32211
Mailing Address:
P.O. Box 8664
Jacksonville, FL 32239
Tel.: 904-743-9770 **FL**
Fax: 904-743-9775
Year Founded: 1959
Approx.Sls.: $14,000,000
Emp.: 200
Fiscal Year-end: 9/30/91
Roofing Subcontractors
S.I.C.: 1761
Roy L. Mullins, Jr. *(Pres. & Chief Exec. Officer)*
Michael D. Mullins *(V.P.)*
Marlene Haddock *(Comptroller)*
Principal(s):
Roy L. Mullins, Jr.

No. of Mfg. Plants/Facilities: 1
No. of U.S. Offices: 1

Computer Systems/Hardware:
Burroughs

Outside Service Firm(s):

Morrison & Delarbre*(Auditors)*
Tampa, FL

Barnett Banks Trust Company, N.A.*(Investment Banker)*
9000 Southside Blvd., P.O. Box 40200
Jacksonville, FL 32202-0200
Tel.: 904-464-2802

Foley & Lardner*(Legal Firm)*
Jacksonville, FL

Barnett Banks Trust Company, N.A.*(Major Banking Relationship)*
9000 Southside Blvd., P.O. Box 40200
Jacksonville, FL 32202-0200
Tel.: 904-464-2802

First Union National Bank*(Major Banking Relationship)*
P.O. Box 2565,
Jacksonville, FL 32203

BEAD INDUSTRIES INC.
110 Mountain Grove
Bridgeport, CT 06605
Mailing Address:
P.O. Box K,
Bridgeport, CT 06605
Tel.: 203-334-4124
Fax: 203-367-9957
Year Founded: 1914
Approx.Sls.: $10,000,000
Emp.: 175
Export
Bead Chain & Attachments; Radio Contact Prongs & Electronic Parts, Terminal Fishing Tackle
S.I.C.: 3949; 3678; 3999
W. Dexter Bryant *(Chm. Bd.)*
Robert Barnes *(Pres.)*
K. Thwing *(V.P.-Chief Oper. Officer)*
J. Vaccarella *(V.P.-Chief Fin. Officer)*
J. Lasko *(Prod. Mgr.-Chain Div.)*
K. Lebo *(Prod. Mgr.-Electronics)*

Computer Systems/Hardware:
Symix

BEADLES LUMBER COMPANY, INC.
900 6th St., N.E.
Moultrie, GA 31768
Mailing Address:
P.O. Box 987
Moultrie, GA 31768
Tel.: 912-985-6996 **DE**
Fax: 912-985-0344
Year Founded: 1961
Approx.Sls.: $10,000,000
Emp.: 75
Fiscal Year-end: 12/31/91
General Sawmills & Planing Mills; Pulpwood
S.I.C.: 2421; 5099
C. Victor Beadles, III *(Pres.)*
Tony Brock *(Exec. V.P. & Treas.)*
Vernon W. Horne *(V.P.)*

Outside Service Firm(s):
Lanigan & Associates*(Auditors)*
Thomasville, GA

BEALL'S, INC.
1806 38th Ave. E.
Bradenton, FL 31283
Mailing Address:
P.O. Box N,
Bradenton, FL 34206
Tel.: 813-747-2355
Fax: 813-746-1171
Approx.Sls.: $120,000,000
Emp.: 1,700
Fiscal Year-end: 8/ 3/91
38 Department Stores in Central & W. Florida
S.I.C.: 5311
E.R. Beall *(Chm. Bd.)*
Robert M. Beall II *(Pres.)*
Chuck Driscoll *(Sr. V.P.-Opers.)*
George Hiskes *(V.P.-Data Processing)*
Stephen M. Knopik *(V.P.-Fin.)*

Outside Service Firm(s):

Christopher, Smith & Gentile*(Auditors)*
Bradenton, FL

Blalock, Landers, Walters & Vogler*(Legal Firm)*
Bradenton, FL

NationsBank Florida*(Major Banking Relationship)*
Bradenton, FL

Bean & Conquest
(See Village Car Company Listing)

D. D. BEAN & SONS CO.
Peterborough Rd.
Jaffrey, NH 03452
Mailing Address:
P.O. Box 348
Jaffrey, NH 03452
Tel.: 603-532-8311 **NH**
Fax: 603-532-7361
Year Founded: 1938
Assets: $11,500,000
Liabilities: $700,000
Net Worth: $10,800,000
Approx.Sls.: $22,000,000
Emp.: 450
Paper Book Matches
S.I.C.: 3999
Vernon J. Bean *(Chm. Bd.)*
Delcie D. Bean *(Pres., Treas. & Chief Exec. Officer)*
William E. Bean *(V.P.-Mfg.)*
Robert Bennett *(Exec. V.P.)*
Mark C. Bean *(V.P.-Sls.)*
Peter Leach *(Mgr.-Sls.)*
Susan Peterson *(Mgr.-Personnel)*
B. Leonard Krause *(V.P.-Pur.)*
Stephen H. Krause *(Sec.)*
Christopher V. Bean *(Gen. Counsel)*
Peter A. Rivard *(Comptroller)*
Principal(s):
Bean Family

No. of Mfg. Plants/Facilities: 4
No. of U.S. Offices: 5
No. of Foreign Offices: 2

Computer Systems/Hardware:
IBM

Outside Service Firm(s):

Bridgman, Valiante, & Villard, PC*(Auditors)*
Lebanon, NH

Wausau Insurance*(Commercial Insurance Carrier)*
2000 Westwood Dr.
Wausau, WI 54401-7881
Tel.: 715-842-6902
Fax: 715-847-8534

Blue Cross & Blue Shield of New Hampshire-Vermont*(Group Insurer)*
Concord, NH

Fleet National Bank*(Investment Banker)*
Nashua, NH

Upton, Sander & Smith*(Legal Firm)*
Concord, NH

Fleet National Bank*(Major Banking Relationship)*
Nashua, NH

Fleet National Bank*(Pension Manager)*
Nashua, NH

Subsidiaries:

D. D. Bean & Sons (N.C.) Inc. **(1)**
P.O. Box N93
Winston-Salem, NC 27115
Tel.: 919-767-1187
Bookmatches
S.I.C.: 3999

W.W. Cross, Inc. **(1)**
77 Webster St.
Jaffrey, NH 03452
Tel.: 603-532-8332
Precision Fastening Products
S.I.C.: 3999
Delcie D. Bean *(Pres.)*

Jaffrey Fire Protection Co. **(1)**
Peterborough Rd., P.O. Box 348
Jaffrey, NH 03452
Tel.: 603-532-8311
Fire Hose & Fittings
S.I.C.: 3052

Non-U.S. Holdings:

D. D. Bean & Sons (Canada) Ltd. **(1)**
P.O. Box 180 Union St.,
Saint Cesaire, PQ JOL 1T0, Canada
Bookmatches
S.I.C.: 3999

Strike Rite Matches Ltd. **(1)**
P.O. Box 4367,
London, ON N5W 5J2, Canada
Bookmatches
S.I.C.: 3999

THE LEWIS BEAR COMPANY
4150 W. Blount St.
Pensacola, FL 32505
Mailing Address:
P.O. Box 17209,
Pensacola, FL 32522
Tel.: 904-438-9651
Fax: 904-434-3016
Year Founded: 1876
Approx.Sls.: $300,000,000
Emp.: 375
Wholesale Groceries, Beer, Drugs, Frozen Foods & Meats
S.I.C.: 5141; 5122; 5142; 5147; 5100
Robert H. Kahn, Jr. *(Chm. Bd.)*
Lewis Bear, Jr. *(Pres.)*
Lewis B. Pollak, Sr. *(Exec. V.P.)*
Harry Huelsbeck *(V.P.-Data Processing & Opers.)*
Arthur C. Lynch, Sr. *(V.P.)*
Robert K. Boyle *(Sec. & Treas.)*
Principal(s):
Lewis Bear, Jr.

No. of Mfg. Plants/Facilities: 6

Outside Service Firm(s):

KPMG Peat Marwick*(Auditors)*
277 Lakeshore Road East
Oakville, ON Canada
Tel.: 416-842-4722

Arnall, Golden & Gregory*(Legal Firm)*
55 Park Place
Atlanta, GA 30335
Tel.: 404-577-5100

First Wachovia Bank & Trust Co.*(Major Banking Relationship)*
Atlanta, GA

BEARDEN LUMBER COMPANY, INC.
111 N. Plum St.
Bearden, AR 71720
Mailing Address:
P.O. Box 137
Bearden, AR 71720
Tel.: 501-687-2246 **AR**
Fax: 501-687-3712
Assets: $18,300,000
Liabilities: $13,460,000
Net Worth: $4,840,000
Approx.Sls.: $25,000,000
Emp.: 170
Fiscal Year-end: 3/31/92
Export
Rough, Sawed Or Planed Lumber
S.I.C.: 2421
John E. Anthony *(Chm. Bd. & Pres.)*
James Norman Anthony *(Exec. V.P.)*
James R. Green *(Chief Fin. Officer)*
O.D. Cathey *(Sec. & Treas.)*
Ronnie D. Thompson *(Controller)*
Steven M. Anthony *(Gen. Counsel)*
John Clark *(Dir.-Mktg.)*
Terry Clark *(Dir.-Mktg.)*
Kenneth Shinn *(Dir.-Human Resources)*
Jeff Turpin *(Dir.-Sls.)*
Bud Walthal *(Dir.-Pur.)*
Jerry Crutcher *(Mgr.-Mill)*

Bearden Lumber Company, Inc.—(Continued)

Principal(s):
John E. Anthony
James Norman Anthony

No. of Mfg. Plants/Facilities: 1
No. of U.S. Offices: 1

Outside Service Firm(s):

Findley & Jenkins*(Auditors)*
Little Rock, AR

Bridges, Young, Matthews, Holmes & Drake*(Legal Firm)*
Little Rock, AR

Worthen National Bank of Arkansas*(Major Banking Relationship)*
P.O. Box 1681, 200 W. Capitol
Little Rock, AR 72201
Tel.: 501-378-1209
Fax: 501-378-1062

BEARING DISTRIBUTORS, INC.
930 S. Stadium Rd.
Columbia, SC 29202
Tel.: 803-799-0834 **SC**
Fax: 803-256-3824
Year Founded: 1939
Approx.Sls.: $17,000,000
Emp.: 142
Fiscal Year-end: 1/31/92
Wholesale Distribution of Bearings, Power Transmission Equipment & Apparatus
S.I.C.: 5085
Shelby J. Deborde, Sr. *(Chm. Bd.)*
Shelby J. Deborde, Jr. *(Pres.)*
W. Paul Deborde, Sr. *(V.P. & Treas.)*

Outside Service Firm(s):

National Bank of South Carolina*(Major Banking Relationship)*
Columbia, SC

BEARING SERVICE COMPANY
500 Dargan St.
Pittsburgh, PA 15224
Tel.: 412-621-7300
Fax: 412-621-7125
Year Founded: 1934
Approx.Sls.: $27,000,000
Emp.: 125
Fiscal Year-end: 12/31/91
Import Export
Manufacture & Distribute Ball & Roller Bearings
S.I.C.: 3562
Jacob W. Banks *(Chm. Bd. & Pres.)*
Franklin Blackstone, Jr. *(Gen. Counsel & Sec.)*
Meredith Rose *(Controller)*
Wm. J. Banks *(Gen. Mgr.)*
Robert A. Banks *(Dir.-Quality Control)*
Michael Barcheski *(Plant Superintendant)*
Principal(s):
Jacob W. Banks & Family

No. of Mfg. Plants/Facilities: 6
No. of U.S. Offices: 6

Computer Systems/Hardware:
Ultimate

Outside Service Firm(s):

Hinds, Lind & Miller*(Auditors)*
Pittsburgh, PA

Pittsburgh National Bank*(Major Banking Relationship)*
Stock Transfer Dept., Fifth & Wood Streets
Pittsburgh, PA 15265

Bearings Headquarters Co.
(See Headco Industries, Inc. Listing)

BEAUCHAMP DISTRIBUTING COMPANY
1911 S. Santa Fe Ave.
Compton, CA 90221
Tel.: 310-639-5320 **CA**
Fax: 310-537-8641
Year Founded: 1971
Approx.Sls.: $30,000,000
Emp.: 106
Import
Wholesale Distributor of Beer & Wine
S.I.C.: 5182; 5181
Patrick L. Beauchamp *(Chm. Bd., Pres. & Treas.)*
Peter Gumpert *(Controller)*
Victor Fiss *(Mgr.-Gen. Sls.)*

Outside Service Firm(s):

Hallstein & Warner*(Auditors)*
Long Beach, CA

Lagerlof, Senecal, Drescher & Swift*(Legal Firm)*
Pasadena, CA

The Bank of California, N.A.*(Major Banking Relationship)*
550 So. Flower St.
Los Angeles, CA 90071

BEAUDRY FORD, INC.
141 Piedmont Ave., N.E.
Atlanta, GA 30303
Tel.: 404-659-3673 **GA**
Fax: 404-659-1939
Approx.Sls.: $91,000,000
Emp.: 156
New & Used Automobiles; Truck Leasing Without Drivers, Rent-A-Car Service
S.I.C.: 5511; 7513; 7514
Harmon M. Born *(Pres.)*
J. Ivan Born *(V.P., Sec. & Treas.)*

BEAUTY ENTERPRISES INC.
150 Meadow St.
Hartford, CT 06114
Tel.: 203-296-9303 **CT**
Fax: 203-296-0421
Year Founded: 1969
Assets: $10,295,000
Liabilities: $5,964,190
Net Worth: $4,330,810
Approx.Sls.: $48,000,000
Emp.: 190
Fiscal Year-end: 9/30/91
Import Export
Wholesale Distribute Black Hair Care & Skin Products
S.I.C.: 5122
Robert H. Cohen *(Chm. Bd. & Pres.)*
Rocco Piccirillo *(V.P.-Opers. & Sec.)*
George Tyrrell *(V.P.-Sls.)*
John Carabetta *(Comptroller & Dir.-Personnel & Investor Rels.)*
Jim Normandin *(Pur. Agent)*
Richard Bailey *(Dir.-Exports)*
Michael Chareste *(Mgr.-Adv.)*
Fabian Pineros *(Mgr.-Warehouse)*
Stella Wilkos *(Mgr.-Data Processing)*

No. of Mfg. Plants/Facilities: 2
No. of U.S. Offices: 2

Computer Systems/Hardware:
Basic Four

Outside Service Firm(s):

Schaffman, Sussman & Co.*(Auditors)*
West Hartford, CT

Aetna Life & Casualty*(Commercial Insurance Carrier)*
Glastonbury, CT

Greene & Bloom*(Legal Firm)*
Hartford, CT

Fleet National Bank*(Major Banking Relationship)*
One Constitution Plaza
Hartford, CT 06115
Tel.: 203-244-5000

Pension Planning Designs*(Pension Manager)*
West Hartford, CT

Subsidiary:

Southern Beauty Enterprises **(1)**
2904 Commerce Sq. South
Irondale, AL 35210
Tel.: 205-956-2333
Fax: 205-956-2399
Emp.: 18
Ethnic Hair & Skin Care Distributors
S.I.C.: 5122
Mike Gable *(Chief Oper. Officer)*

BEAUTY HANDBOOK CORPORATION
10100 Santa Monica Blvd.
Los Angeles, CA 90067
Tel.: 310-286-0988
Fax: 212-557-5258
Approx.Sls.: $12,500,000
Emp.: 760
Communications, Publishing; Beauty Handbook, Beauty Traveler Kit
S.I.C.: 2731
John McAuliffe *(Chm. Bd. & Pres.)*
Joan McAuliffe *(Sr. V.P. & Gen. Counsel)*
Juanita Holder *(V.P.-Mktg.)*
Brenda Nicholls *(V.P.-Sls.)*
Joe Pecorino *(Editor)*
Hawley Hilton McAuliffe *(Editor)*
Grace Scura *(Editor)*

BEAVER STREET FISHERIES, INC.
1741 W. Beaver St.
Jacksonville, FL 32209
Mailing Address:
P.O. Box 41430,
Jacksonville, FL 32203
Tel.: 904-354-5661 **FL**
Fax: 904-354-2607
Year Founded: 1955
Approx.Sls.: $150,000,000
Emp.: 320
Fiscal Year-end: 5/30/90
Import Export
Frozen Foods; Groceries; Processed Seafood
S.I.C.: 5141; 5142; 5146
Alfred Frisch *(Pres.)*
Hans Frisch *(Exec. V.P.)*
Benjamin P. Frisch *(V.P., Sec. & Treas.)*
E. Karl Frisch *(V.P.)*
Jeff Edwards *(Comptroller)*
Harry Salisbury *(Mgr.-Sls., Frozen Seafood)*
Ben Strickland *(Mgr.-Sls., Food Service)*
Charles Bowman *(Dir.-Data Processing)*

Outside Service Firm(s):

Ernst & Young*(Auditors)*
1800 Independent Square
Jacksonville, FL 32202
Tel.: 904-358-2000

Ulmer, Murchison, Ashby, Taylor & Corrigan*(Legal Firm)*
1600 Atlantic Bank Bldg.
Jacksonville, FL 32202
Tel.: 904-354-5652

NationsBank*(Major Banking Relationship)*
35 Broad St.
Atlanta, GA 30303
Tel.: 404-581-2121
Tel.: 800-848-8198

BEBER SILVERSTEIN & PARTNERS, INC.
3361 SW Third Ave.
Miami, FL 33145
Tel.: 305-856-9800
Fax: 305-854-1932
Year Founded: 1971
Approx.Billings: $44,000,000
Emp.: 56
Advertising Agency
S.I.C.: 7311
Joyce Beber *(Chm. Bd.)*
Elaine Silverstein *(Pres.)*
Jennifer Beber *(Exec. V.P.)*
Ivor Bamberger *(V.P., Fin.)*

Computer Systems/Hardware:
IBM System 34

Branches:

Beber Silverstein & Partners, Inc. **(1)**
1500 Broadway, Ste. 902
New York, NY 10036
Tel.: 212-764-4600
Fax: 212-764-7064
George Klas *(V.P.)*

Beber Silverstein & Partners, Inc. **(1)**
1211 Connecticut Ave.
Washington, DC 20036
Tel.: 202-822-9491
Francis O'Brien *(Dir.)*

BECHTEL GROUP, INC.
50 Beale St.
San Francisco, CA 94105
Mailing Address:
P.O. Box 193965,
San Francisco, CA 94119
Tel.: 415-768-1234 **DE**
Telex: 34783 (Domestic)
Fax: 415-768-9038
Year Founded: 1898
Approx.Sls.: $5,100,000,000
Emp.: 27,800
Fiscal Year-end: 12/31/90
Engrng., Construction, Procurement, Mngmt., Financing, Opers. & Maintenance Services for the Following Industries: Electricity Generation, Transmission & Distr.; Nuclear Fuel; Advanced Systems; Metals & Minerals; Oil & Gas; Chemical; Synthetic Fuel; Industrial Manufacturing; Transportation; Water Use & Conservation; Pollution Control; Waste Cleanup; Non-Residential Building; Defense & Communications
S.I.C.: 1522; 1541; 1542; 1611; 1622; 1623; 1629; 8731; 8711; 8742; 8999
Riley Bechtel *(Pres.)*
Cordell W. Hull *(Exec. V.P. & Dir.)*
John Neerhout, Jr. *(Exec. V.P. & Dir.)*
J.L. Moore, Jr. *(Sr. V.P. & Dir.)*
T.G. Flynn *(Sr. V.P. & Mgr.-Pub. Rels.)*
John Carter *(Sr. V.P., Bechtel Group, Inc.)*
John W. Weiser *(Sr. V.P. & Gen. Counsel)*
J.C. Stromberg *(Sr. V.P.)*
D.M. Slavich *(Sr. V.P. & Dir.)*
V. Paul Unruh *(V.P. & Controller)*
Matthew Cooke *(Mgr.-Internal Audit)*
J.M. Geary *(Mgr.-Treasury)*
David L. Redo *(Mgr.-Trust & Thrift)*

No. of U.S. Offices: 13
No. of Foreign Offices: 17

Outside Service Firm(s):

Coopers & Lybrand*(Auditors)*
333 Market Street, 21st Fl.
San Francisco, CA 94105

Thelen, Marrin, Johnson & Bridges*(Legal Firm)*
Two Embarcadero Center
San Francisco, CA 94111
Tel.: 415-392-6320

Prudential Insurance Co. of America*(Pension Manager)*
751 Broad St.
Newark, NJ 07102-3777
Tel.: 201-802-6000

Rosenberg Capital Management*(Pension Manager)*
4 Embarcadero Center, Ste. 2900
San Francisco, CA 94111

Sit Investments*(Pension Manager)*
4600 Norwest Center
Minneapolis, MN 55402

Wellington Management*(Pension Manager)*
75 State St.
Boston, MA 02109
Tel.: 617-951-5463

Wells Fargo Bank*(Pension Manager)*
45 Fremont St.
San Francisco, CA 94105

Operating Companies:

Bechtel Civil, Inc. **(1)**
50 Beale St.
San Francisco, CA 94105
Tel.: 415-768-1234 (100%)
Emp.: 3,841
Engrng., Construction, Procurement, Mngmt., Opers. & Maintenance Services for the Following Industries: Defense, Transportation, Communications, Water & Waste, Non-Residential Bldg. & Industrial Mfg.
S.I.C.: 1522; 1541; 1542; 1611; 1623; 1629; 8711; 8742; 8999
A. P. Yates *(Chm. Bd.)*
John Neerhout, Jr. *(Vice Chm.)*
R. L. Polvi *(Pres.)*

Bechtel Eastern Power Corporation **(1)**
15740 Shady Grove Rd.
Gaithersburg, MD 20877
Tel.: 301-258-3000 (100%)
Emp.: 5,012
Engrng., Construction, Procurement, Mngmt., Opers. & Maintenance Services for the Electricity Generation, Transmission & Distribution Industry
S.I.C.: 1623; 1629; 8711; 8742; 8999
A. P. Yates *(Chm.)*
C. W. Hull *(Vice Chm.)*
Adrian Baccaria *(Gen. Mgr.)*

Bechtel, Inc. **(1)**
3000 Post Oak Blvd.
Houston, TX 77056
Tel.: 713-235-2000
Emp.: 1,901
Engrng., Construction, Procurement, Mngmt., Opers. & Maintenance Services for the Following Industries: Oil & Gas, Chemical, Synthetic Fuels, Indus. Mfg.
S.I.C.: 1541; 1623; 1629; 8711; 8742; 8999
A. P. Yates *(Chm.)*
John Neerhout, Jr. *(Vice Chm.)*
D. J. Gunther *(Pres.)*

Bechtel, Inc. Mining & Metals Special Operation **(1)**
50 Beale St.
San Francisco, CA 94105
Tel.: 415-768-1234
Emp.: 490
Engrng., Construction, Procurement, Mngmt., Opers. & Maintenance Services for the Metals & Minerals Industry
S.I.C.: 1541; 1629; 8711; 8742; 8999
A. P. Yates *(Chm.)*
John Neerhout, Jr. *(Vice Chm.)*
D. J. Gunther *(Pres.)*

Bechtel National, Inc. **(1)**
50 Beale St.
San Francisco, CA 94105
Tel.: 415-768-1234
Emp.: 1,448
Engrng. & Startup, Opers. & Major Maintenance of Industrial Mfg. Facilities, Electronics Plants, Nuclear Fuel Cycle Facilities, Hazardous Waste & Other Non-Nuclear Facilities
S.I.C.: 1541; 1629; 8731; 8711; 8742; 8999
A. P. Yates *(Chm. Bd.)*
W. L. Friend *(Pres.)*

Bechtel Power Corporation **(1)**
50 Beale St.
San Francisco, CA 94105
Tel.: 414-768-1234 (100%)
Emp.: 12,120
Engrng., Construction, Procurement, Mngmt., Opers. & Maintenance Services for the Electricity Generation, Transmission & Distribution Industry
S.I.C.: 1623; 1629; 8711; 8742; 8999
Cordell W. Hull *(Pres.)*
Howard W. Wahl *(Mng. Dir.)*
Loren G. Hinkelman *(Mng. Dir.)*

Branch Office:

Bechtel Power Corporation **(2)**
15740 Shady Grove Rd.
Gaithersburg, MD 20877
Tel.: 301-258-3000
Consulting Engineers
S.I.C.: 8711; 8742; 8999
Cordell W. Hull *(Pres.)*

Becon Construction Company, Inc. **(1)**
650 N. Belt Dr. E.
Houston, TX 77060
Tel.: 713-878-1500
Full Range of Construction Services in the U.S. & Canada for the Industrial Market
S.I.C.: 1522; 1541; 1542; 1611; 1622; 1623; 1629; 8742
J. M. Komes *(Pres.)*
George Loizou *(Exec. V.P.)*

Non-U.S. Holding:

Bechtel Great Britain Ltd. **(1)**
Bechtel House, 245 Hammersmith Rd. P.O. Box 739,
London, W6 8DP, United Kingdom
Tel.: 071 846-5111 (100%)
Telex: 934151
Emp.: 794
Engrng., Construction, Procurement, Mngmt., Opers. & Maintenance Services for the Following Industries: Oil & Gas, Synthetic Fuel, Chemical & Industrial Mfg.
S.I.C.: 1541; 1623; 1629; 8711; 8742; 8999
John Neerhout, Jr. *(Chm. & Exec. Sponsor)*
Sir Gordon Booth *(Vice Chm. & Dir.)*
K. Turnbull *(Mng. Dir.)*

R. W. BECK & ASSOCIATES, INC.
Fourth & Blanchard Bldg.,
2101 Fourth Ave., Ste. 600
Seattle, WA 98121
Tel.: 206-441-7500
Telex: 4990402 Beck SEA
Fax: 206-441-4962
Year Founded: 1942
Sales Range: $20-39 Million
Emp.: 690
Engineering & Consulting Services Specializing in Utilities
S.I.C.: 8711; 8742
Steve A. Windell *(Mng. Partner & Chief Fin. Officer)*
William R. Mayben *(Exec. Partner)*

No. of U.S. Offices: 12

Computer Systems/Hardware:
Honeywell DPS 8/49; Hewlett-Packard 3000 Series 68

Outside Service Firm(s):

Arthur Andersen & Co.*(Auditors)*
Norton Building, 801 2nd Ave.
Seattle, WA 98104
Tel.: 206-623-8023
Fax: 206-386-8675

Carney, Stephenson, Bradley, Smith & Mueller*(Legal Firm)*
Seattle, WA

Rainier National Bank*(Major Banking Relationship)*
Seattle, WA

BECKWITH ELEVATOR CO.
274 Southampton St.
Boston, MA 02118
Tel.: 617-427-5525
Fax: 617-427-1494
Year Founded: 1889
Approx.Sls.: $12,000,000
Emp.: 100
Import
Mfr. of Elevators & Dumbwaiters
S.I.C.: 3534
N. Clark Bedford *(Pres.)*
Sally Bedford *(V.P.)*
Norman C. Bedford *(Treas.)*
Hilda L. Bedford *(Sec.)*

Outside Service Firm(s):

Frederick H. Boynton*(Auditors)*
Boston, MA

Corwin & Corwin*(Legal Firm)*
Boston, MA

First National Bank of Boston*(Major Banking Relationship)*
150 Royall St.
Canton, MA 02021
Tel.: 617-575-2900
Tel.: 800-442-2001

BECKWITH MACHINERY COMPANY
U.S. Route 22 East
Murrysville, PA 15668
Mailing Address:
P.O. Box 8718
Pittsburgh, PA 15221
Tel.: 412-327-1300
Fax: 412-327-9318
Year Founded: 1915
Sales Range: $100-499 Million
Emp.: 725
Wholesale Non-Electrical Machinery
S.I.C.: 5085; 5084
James S. Beckwith III *(Chm. Bd.)*
G. Nicholas Beckwith III *(Pres. & Chief Exec. Officer)*
Fred A. Holcomb *(Chief Fin. Officer)*
Thomas J. Fleury *(Treas.)*
John E. Trabbuco *(Sec. & Gen. Counsel)*
E. Anthony Dills *(Controller)*
Robert M. McDonald *(Dir.-Pur.)*
Charles Israel *(Mgr.-Systems)*
Hank Murawski *(Mgr.-Human Resources)*
Principal(s):
James S. Beckwith III

No. of Mfg. Plants/Facilities: 9

Computer Systems/Hardware:
IBM 4341

Outside Service Firm(s):

Price Waterhouse*(Auditors)*
600 Grant St., Ste. 4400
Pittsburgh, PA 15219
Tel.: 412-355-6000
Fax: 412-391-0609

Reed, Smith, Shaw & McClay*(Legal Firm)*
Mellon Square, P.O. Box 2009
Pittsburgh, PA 15230
Tel.: 412-288-3131
Fax: 412-288-3063

Dillon, Read & Co.*(Pension Manager)*
New York, NY

The Principal Financial Group*(Pension Manager)*
711 High St.
Des Moines, IA 50309
Tel.: 515-247-4593
Tel.: 800-543-4015

Rothschild Asset Management*(Pension Manager)*
Baltimore, MD

Thompson, Siegel & Walmsley*(Pension Manager)*
P.O. Box 6883,
Richmond, VA 23230-0883

BEDFORD INDUSTRIES, INC.
1659 Rowe Ave.
Worthington, MN 56187
Tel.: 507-376-4136
Fax: 507-376-6742
Approx.Sls.: $15,000,000
Emp.: 150
Fiscal Year-end: 12/31/91
Manufacture Twist-Ties
S.I.C.: 3089
Robert B. Ludlow *(Pres.)*
Robert Boushek *(V.P.-Opers.)*
Ted Ludlow *(V.P.-Sls. & Mktg.)*
Patricia Ludlow *(Sec.)*
David Reker *(Controller)*
Darrold Peck *(Pur. Agent)*

Outside Service Firm(s):

Grant Thornton*(Auditors)*
500 Pillsbury Center
Minneapolis, MN 55402-1459

Norwest Bank Minnesota, N.A.*(Major Banking Relationship)*
Marshall, MN

BEECH HOLDINGS CORP.
200 N. Michigan Ave.
Chicago, IL 60601
Tel.: 312-580-5000
Fax: 312-726-0039
Holding Company
S.I.C.: 6719
Clifton Haley *(Chm. Bd., Pres. & Chief Exec. Officer)*
William Plamondon *(Exec. V.P. & Chief Oper. Officer)*
Robert L. Aprati *(Sr. V.P. & Gen. Counsel)*
Kevin McShea *(Sr. V.P. & Chief Fin. Officer)*
Herbert Luckwaldt *(Sr. V.P.-Oper.)*
David Sparks *(Sr. V.P.-Mrktg & Sls.)*
John Beaulieu *(Sr. V.P.-Human Resources)*
Thomas Hawkes *(Sr. V.P.-Gen. Counsel)*
Dirk Beadleston *(V.P.-Quality)*
Michael MacDonald *(V.P.-Sls.)*
Joel Himpelmann *(Mgr.-Pur.)*
Timothy Hermeling *(Mgr.-Public Rel.)*

Outside Service Firm(s):

KPMG Peat Marwick*(Auditors)*
Peat Marwick Plaza, 303 E. Wacker Dr.
Chicago, IL 60601
Tel.: 312-938-1000

Subsidiary:

Budget Rent A Car Corporation **(1)**
4225 Naperville Rd.
Lisle, IL 60532
Tel.: 708-955-7628 (100%)
Earnings: $12,300,000
Approx.Rev.: $982,700,000
Emp.: 6,000
Fiscal Year-end: 12/31/90
Computer Systems/Hardware:
IBM; DEC
Car Rental System; Franchising
S.I.C.: 7514; 6794
Clifton Haley *(Chm.Bd., Pres. & Chief Exec. Officer)*
Martin Smircich *(Pres.-North American Group (Beech Holding Corp.))*
William Plamondon *(Pres. & Chief Oper. Officer (Budget Corp.))*
Kevin McShea *(Exec. V.P. & Chief Fin. Officer)*
Robert L. Aprati *(Sr. V.P. & Gen. Counsel)*
David J. Sparks *(Sr. V.P.-Sls. & Mktg.)*
Thomas Hawkes *(Sr. V.P.-Fleet Oper.)*
Herbert Luckwaldt *(Sr. V.P.-Oper.)*
L. Eugene Williams *(Sr. V.P.-Human Resources)*
Tim Hermeling *(Mgr.-Pub. Rels.)*

Subsidiary:

BRAC Credit Corp. **(2)**
3414 Midcourt Rd., Bldg. 2
Carrollton, TX 75006
Tel.: 214-385-7622 (100%)
Emp.: 50
Financial Services
S.I.C.: 6159

BEEFAMERICA OPERATING CO., INC.
5600 Harry Andersen Ave.
Omaha, NE 68137
Tel.: 402-896-2400 **IA**
Fax: 402-896-9074
Year Founded: 1931
Assets: $92,497,000
Liabilities: $62,597,000
Net Worth: $29,900,000
Approx.Sls.: $1,500,000,000
Emp.: 1,850
Fiscal Year-end: 10/31/91

BeefAmerica Operating Co., Inc.—(Continued)

Beef Slaughtering & Packaging; Pigskin Gelatin; Processed Meats
S.I.C.: 2011; 2013
Joe Amore *(Chm. Bd., Pres. & Chief Exec. Officer)*
William Hughes *(Exec. V.P. & Sec.)*
Robert R. Norton, Jr. *(Exec. V.P., Chief Oper. & Fin. Officer)*
Rich Grover *(Sr. V.P. & Treas.)*
Mike Rubach *(Sr. V.P.)*
Dean A. Miller *(V.P.-Industrial Rels.)*
Roger McConnell *(Controller)*
Jerry Eilers *(Mgr.-Pur.)*
B.J. Svajgl *(Indus. Engr.)*

Principal(s):
Joe Amore

No. of Mfg. Plants/Facilities: 8
No. of U.S. Offices: 1
No. of Foreign Offices: 1

Computer Systems/Hardware:
IBM Systems 34 & 4331; ADDS Mentor

Outside Service Firm(s):

Arthur Andersen & Co.*(Auditors)*
1700 Farnam
Omaha, NE 68102
Tel.: 402-348-0123

Connecticut General Life Insurance Co.*(Group Insurer)*
P.O. Box 2975,
Hartford, CT 06104
Tel.: 203-726-6000

Norwest Bank Minnesota, N.A.*(Investment Banker)*
Omaha, NE

Dow, Lohnes & Albertson*(Legal Firm)*
1225 Connecticut Ave.
Washington, DC 20036
Tel.: 202-862-8000

Fraser, Stryker, Veach, Vaughn, Meusey, Olson, Boyer*(Legal Firm)*
409 S. 17th
Omaha, NE

Citibank N.A.*(Major Banking Relationship)*
Corporate Trust Services, 399 Park Ave.
New York, NY 10043
Tel.: 212-559-1605

Norwest Bank Minnesota, N.A.*(Major Banking Relationship)*
Omaha, NE

Subsidiary:

BeefAmerica **(1)**
1500 S. Logan
Norfolk, NE 68701
Tel.: 402-371-5700
Emp.: 114
Slaughter Facility
S.I.C.: 2011
Joe Amore *(Pres.)*

BEER NUTS, INC.
103 N. Robinson St.
Bloomington, IL 61702
Mailing Address:
P.O. Box 1327
Bloomington, IL 61702
Tel.: 309-827-8580 **DE**
Fax: 309-827-0914
Year Founded: 1955
Emp.: 80
Mfr. Beer Nuts Products
S.I.C.: 5145
Russell O. Shirk *(Chm. Bd.)*
James A. Shirk *(Pres.)*
Betty J. Shirk *(Treas. & Sec.)*
Lynn Ammerman *(Plant Mgr.)*
Jerry Morris *(Mgr.-Sls.)*
William K. Rader *(Office Mgr.)*

Computer Systems/Hardware:
IBM AS 400

Outside Service Firm(s):

Dunbar, Breitweiser & Co.*(Auditors)*
202 No. Center St.
Bloomington, IL 61701
Tel.: 309-827-0348

Hayes, Schneider, Hammer & Miles*(Legal Firm)*
Bloomington, IL

McLean County Bank*(Major Banking Relationship)*
Bloomington, IL

BEERS CONSTRUCTION COMPANY
70 Ellis St., N.E.
Atlanta, GA 30303
Tel.: 404-659-1970 **GA**
Fax: 404-656-1665
Year Founded: 1935
Assets: $89,744,029
Liabilities: $70,635,425
Net Worth: $19,108,604
Approx.Sls.: $369,044,299
Emp.: 600
Fiscal Year-end: 9/30/91
Holding Company, Commercial Contractors
S.I.C.: 1542; 6719
Corporate Giving Program: United Way
L.L. Gellerstedt, Jr. *(Chm. Bd.)*
L.L. Gellerstedt, III *(Pres. & Chief Exec. Officer)*
Frank E. Fralick *(Grp. Pres.)*
Elmon Henry *(Grp. Pres.)*
William K. Millkey, A.I.A. *(Grp. Pres.)*
Craig A. Mitchell, P.E. *(Grp. Pres.)*
Ted Hudgins *(Exec. V.P.-Opers.)*
Chris Williams *(Chief Fin. Officer)*

No. of U.S. Offices: 3

Computer Systems/Hardware:
IBM System 36

Outside Service Firm(s):

Ernst & Young*(Auditors)*
600 Peachtree St. N.E.
Atlanta, GA 30308
Tel.: 404-874-8300

Federal Insurance Co.*(Commercial Insurance Carrier)*
Atlanta, GA

The Benefits Group*(Group Insurer)*
Atlanta, GA

Alston & Bird*(Legal Firm)*
One Atlantic Center, 1201 West Peachtree St.
Atlanta, GA 30309-3424
Tel.: 404-881-7000

NationsBank*(Major Banking Relationship)*
35 Broad St.
Atlanta, GA 30303
Tel.: 404-581-2121
Tel.: 800-848-8198

Subsidiaries:

Patten-Beers Constructors **(1)**
1901 21st Ave. South
Nashville, TN 37212
Tel.: 615-329-3353
Emp.: 800
General Contractors
S.I.C.: 1542
Tom Patten *(Pres.)*
Janice Goodwin *(Chief Fin. Officer)*

Summit-Beers Construction Company **(1)**
P.O. Box 866,
Scottdale, GA 30079
Tel.: 404-298-0915
Waste Water Treatment Plant Builders
S.I.C.: 1629
Al Fisher *(Pres.)*

BEHLEN MFG. CO.
4025 E. 23rd St.
Columbus, NE 68601
Mailing Address:
P. O. Box 569
Columbus, NE 68602-0569
Tel.: 402-564-3111 **NE**
Telex: 6875051
Fax: 402-563-7405
Year Founded: 1936
Approx.Sls.: $70,000,000
Emp.: 800
Fiscal Year-end: 4/27/91
Export
Grain Handling & Manufacture of Storage Systems, Corn Cribs, Grain Bins, Crop Dryers, Metal Building Systems, all Steel Bucket Elevators, Roof Systems, Fencing, Strip Joining Presses Dubl-Panl Stressed-Skin Building Systems, Farmaster Ranchmaster Ag Building, Ironwood Pole Building, Big Bin Grain Storage Tanks, F-Series Crop Dryers
S.I.C.: 3448; 3523
A.F. Raimondo *(Pres. & Chief Exec. Officer)*
Richard Anderson *(V.P. & Gen. Mgr.-Farmaster/Indus. Prods.)*
Richard F. Casey *(V.P. & Gen. Mgr.-Agriculture)*
John Underwood *(V.P. & Gen. Mgr.-Bldg. Systems)*
Larry Costello *(Dir.-Opers.)*
Bruce Juhnke *(Dir.-Intl. Mktg. & Sls.)*
Russel Ferris *(Mgr.-Adv./Graphics)*
Jim McElfresh *(Mgr.-Personnel)*

Outside Service Firm(s):

Washington Square*(Major Banking Relationship)*
Chicago, IL

Division:

Farmaster/Big Valley Div. **(1)**
P.O. Box 569,
Columbus, NE 68602-0569
Export

JOSEPH BEHR & SONS INC.
1100-1200 Seminary St.
Rockford, IL 61104
Mailing Address:
P.O. Box 740,
Rockford, IL 61104
Tel.: 815-987-2600
Fax: 815-968-4560
Approx.Sls.: $90,000,000
Emp.: 150
Fiscal Year-end: 7/31/89
Dealers & Brokers in Scrap Iron & Steel; Smelters of Secondary Aluminum Ingot; Wholesale Industrial Machinery
S.I.C.: 5093; 5084; 3341
Richard Behr *(Pres. & Chief Exec. Officer)*
William H. Day *(Chief Fin. Officer)*
Leland R. Foecking *(Treas., Controller & Sec.)*

No. of Mfg. Plants/Facilities: 1

Computer Systems/Hardware:
IBM System 36

Outside Service Firm(s):

McGladrey & Pullen*(Auditors)*
Drawer G-2, 230 N. Elm St.
Greensboro, NC 27402
Tel.: 919-273-4461

Katten, Muchin & Zavis*(Legal Firm)*
525 W. Monroe St., Ste. 1600
Chicago, IL 60661-3693
Tel.: 312-902-5200

American National Bank & Trust Company of Chicago*(Major Banking Relationship)*
33 N. LaSalle St.
Chicago, IL 60602
Tel.: 312-661-5000
Fax: 312-661-6417

MSF Associates*(Pension Manager)*
Los Angeles, CA

BEHR STORES INC.
1713 Cobalt Dr.
Louisville, KY 40299
Mailing Address:
P.O. Box 99605,
Louisville, KY 40299
Tel.: 502-267-4411 **KY**
Fax: 502-267-4411
Year Founded: 1940
Approx.Sls.: $25,000,000
Emp.: 400
Import
Women's Specialty Stores
S.I.C.: 5632
Claus Behr *(Pres. & Chief Exec. Officer)*
Nick Eve *(V.P.-Property Mngmt.)*
Joel Lerner *(V.P.)*
Millie Fralick *(Sec. & Asst. Treas.)*
Angela Foos *(Mgr.-Adv.)*
Sondra Haynes *(Mgr.-Data Processing)*

Outside Service Firm(s):

Youngblood, Burton & Dicken*(Auditors)*
Louisville, KY

Morris, Garlove, Waterman & Johnson*(Legal Firm)*
Louisville, KY

First National Bank of Louisville*(Major Banking Relationship)*
P.O. Box 36000,
Louisville, KY 40233

THE BEKINS COMPANY
777 Flower St.
Glendale, CA 91201
Tel.: 818-507-1200 **CA**
Fax: 818-545-3193
Year Founded: 1891
Approx.Sls.: $327,000,000
Emp.: 2,000
Fiscal Year-end: 3/31/90
Holding Co.; Intrastate Transportation & Storage of Household Goods, Business Records, Industrial & Electronic Equipment, Interstate Transportation of Household & Commercial Goods
S.I.C.: 4213; 4214; 4731; 4225; 6719
Robert E. Wheaton *(Chm. Bd., Pres., Chief Exec. & Chief Fin. Officer)*
David R. Elliott *(V.P. & Chief Admin. Officer)*
Larry Marzullo *(V.P. & Chief Information Officer)*
Principal(s):
Robert E. Wheaton

No. of U.S. Offices: 40

Computer Systems/Hardware:
IBM 3090-200

Outside Service Firm(s):

KPMG Peat Marwick*(Auditors)*
725 S. Figueroa St.
Los Angeles, CA 90017
Tel.: 213-972-4000

Latham & Watkins*(Legal Firm)*
633 West Fifth St.
Los Angeles, CA 90071
Tel.: 213-485-1234
Fax: 213-643-9086

Security Pacific Corporation*(Major Banking Relationship)*
Security Pacific Plaza
Los Angeles, CA 90071
Tel.: 213-345-6211

Fax: 213-625-0809

Security Pacific Corporation *(Pension Manager)*
Security Pacific Plaza
Los Angeles, CA 90071
Tel.: 213-345-6211
Fax: 213-625-0809

Subsidiaries:

Bekins BoxStores **(1)**
777 Flower St.
Glendale, CA 91201
Tel.: 818-545-3191
Fax: 818-545-3193
Susan Marshall *(V.P. & Gen. Mgr.)*

Bekins Moving & Storage Co. **(1)**
777 Flower St.
Glendale, CA 91201
Tel.: 818-507-1200 (100%)
S.I.C.: 4214; 4213; 4212; 4226; 4225
Vern Fruehling *(Pres.)*

Bekins Van Lines Co. **(1)**
330 S. Mannheim Rd.
Hillside, IL 60162
Tel.: 708-547-2000 (100%)
Approx.Sls.: $200,000,000
Emp.: 450
Motor Carrier of Household Goods
S.I.C.: 4213; 4212
James Bender *(Pres.)*
Louhon Tucker *(V.P.-Fin. & Chief Fin. Officer)*
Ed Pianki *(Controller)*

Data Transportation Company **(1)**
2801 E. 46th St.
Los Angeles, CA 90058
Tel.: 213-581-3282 (100%)
Business Records
S.I.C.: 7379

BEKINS DISTRIBUTION SERVICES CO.
111 West Port Plaza, Ste. 800
Saint Louis, MO 63146
Tel.: 314-434-3400
Sales Range: $10-19 Million
Commercial Warehousing & Storage
S.I.C.: 4225
Michael Sconnell *(Pres.)*

BEL AIR MARKETS
1901 Royal Oaks Dr.
Sacramento, CA 95815
Mailing Address:
P.O. Box 13778,
Sacramento, CA 95853
Tel.: 916-929-6342 **CA**
Fax: 916-920-3808
Year Founded: 1955
Approx.Sls.: $333,000,000
Emp.: 2,500
Fiscal Year-end: 7/25/92
Import Export
Retail Grocery; Wholesale Produce & Flowers; Crafted Bakery Products; Seafood Shop, Delicatessen, Hot Foods Take Out, Pharmacy, Video Shop
S.I.C.: 5411; 5148; 5461; 5421; 5912; 7389
George R. Wong *(Pres.)*
Gene Wong *(Controller)*
Rodger M. Bottel *(V.P.-Fin. & Admin.)*
Nancy Beach *(V.P.-Human Resources)*
Gary Wong *(V.P.-Real Estate)*
Albert Wong *(Treas.)*
Terrance Tremelling *(Comptroller)*
Gordon Wong *(Mgr.-Mngmt. Information Systems)*
Dave Daly *(Adv. Dir.)*
Principal(s):
George R. Wong
Gene Wong
Albert Wong
Bill Wong
Paul Wong
Lillie Wong

No. of Mfg. Plants/Facilities: 14

Computer Systems/Hardware:
AT&T/NCR Tower/386 Novell Network

Outside Service Firm(s):

Rooney, Ida, Nolt & Ahern *(Auditors)*
Oakland, CA

Blair & Sons Insurance *(Commercial Insurance Carrier)*
433 J. St.
Sacramento, CA 95813

Foundation Health *(Group Insurer)*
Sacramento, CA

Boutin, Lassner, Gibson & Delehant *(Legal Firm)*
Sacramento, CA

Wells Fargo Bank *(Major Banking Relationship)*
Sacramento, CA

BEL-ART PRODUCTS
6 Industrial Rd.
Pequannock, NJ 07440-1992
Tel.: 201-694-0500 **NJ**
Telex: 219359
Fax: 201-694-7199
Year Founded: 1946
Approx.Sls.: $20,000,000
Emp.: 200
Fiscal Year-end: 12/31/90
Import Export
Mfr. of Molded & Fabricated Plastics for Science & Industry
S.I.C.: 5049
Kurt Landsberger *(Chm. Bd.)*
David Landsberger *(Pres.)*
George McClure *(Sr. V.P.-Engrng.)*
Herb Ginsberg *(V.P.-Sls.)*
Steve Levine *(V.P.-Mktg.)*
Stan Spass *(V.P.-Admin.)*
Anny Landsberger *(Sec.)*
Jon Blume *(Controller)*
Bernadette Zitelli *(Dir.-Human Resources)*
Peter Sutherland *(Mgr.-Intl. Sls.)*
M. Timoney *(Mgr.-Data Processing)*

No. of Mfg. Plants/Facilities: 5
No. of U.S. Offices: 1

Computer Systems/Hardware:
MAI

Outside Service Firm(s):

Lowenstein, Sandler, Kohl, Fisher & Boylan *(Legal Firm)*
65 Livingston Ave.
Roseland, NJ 07108
Tel.: 908-992-8700

Chemical Bank *(Major Banking Relationship)*
East Brunswick, NJ

Subsidiaries:

Applied Coatings **(1)**
661 Rt. 23
Wayne, NJ 07470
Tel.: 201-628-8600
Fax: 201-305-0841
Metal Coatings Using Teflon, Epoxy, Nylon, Vinyl
S.I.C.: 3479
H. Kirchheimer *(Plant Mgr.)*

D & S Marketing **(1)**
6 Industrial Rd.
Pequannock, NJ 07440-1992
Tel.: 201-694-0500
In-House Advertising Agency
S.I.C.: 7311
B. Loibl *(Mgr.Adv.)*

Maddak Inc. **(1)**
6 Industrial Rd.
Pequannock, NJ 07440
Tel.: 201-628-8600
Tel.: 800-443-4926
Fax: 201-305-0841
Import Export
Mfr. & Distr. of Handicap Aids
S.I.C.: 3842; 3800
Kurt Landsberger *(Chm. Bd.)*
David Landsberger *(Pres.)*
Bridie DeLime *(Dir.-Mktg.)*
Jim Nasalroad *(Dir.-Sls.)*

BEL PAESE SALES COMPANY, INC.
1935 Swarthmore Ave.
Lakewood, NJ 08701
Tel.: 908-363-3800
Tel.: 800-524-2713
Fax: 908-363-1019
Year Founded: 1917
Approx.Sls.: $20,000,000
Emp.: 15
Fiscal Year-end: 12/31/90
Import
Bel Paese Domestic & Imported Cheese, Galbani Prods.; Salami, Mortadella & Prosciutto
S.I.C.: 2022; 2013
A.M. Dominioni *(Pres.)*
Valerie Dominioni *(Sec. & Treas.)*

Computer Systems/Hardware:
ADP

BEL-RAY COMPANY, INC.
Bowman Ave.
Farmingdale, NJ 07727
Mailing Address:
P.O. Box 526
Farmingdale, NJ 07727
Tel.: 908-938-2421 **NJ**
Fax: 908-938-4232
Year Founded: 1946
Approx.Sls.: $30,000,000
Emp.: 210
Export
Manufacture of Special Lubricants
S.I.C.: 2992
William C. Kiefer *(Chm. Bd. & Pres.)*
Daryl Brosnan *(Exec. V.P.)*
Evelyn D. Kiefer *(Sec.)*
Charles E. Husko *(Mgr.-Indus. Div.)*
Steve Petti *(Mgr.-Fin.)*
Jane Verdoni *(Mgr.-Personnel)*

Outside Service Firm(s):

Kane & Fiamingo *(Legal Firm)*
Farmingdale, NJ

Midlantic National Bank *(Major Banking Relationship)*
Farmingdale, NJ

BELCAN CORPORATION
10200 Anderson Way
Cincinnati, OH 45242
Tel.: 513-891-0972 **OH**
Fax: 513-793-8618
Year Founded: 1958
Approx.Sls.: $201,000,000
Fiscal Year-end: 12/31/91
Engineering, Consulting & Design Services
S.I.C.: 8711
Ralph Anderson *(Chm Bd., Pres., & Chief Exec. Officer)*
Paul Riordan *(V.P.-Fin.)*

Outside Service Firm(s):

Cors & Bassett *(Legal Firm)*
Cincinnati, OH

Society National Bank *(Major Banking Relationship)*
900 Euclid Ave., P.O. Box 6477
Cleveland, OH 44101-6477
Tel.: 216-737-5000
Fax: 216-566-8947

BELDOCH INDUSTRIES CORPORATION
44 Cherry Valley Ave.
West Hempstead, NY 11552
Tel.: 516-485-4400 **DE**
Fax: 516-485-6014
Year Founded: 1939
Approx.Sls.: $60,000,000
Emp.: 300
Fiscal Year-end: 3/31/91
Import Export
Ladies Knitwear & Sportswear
S.I.C.: 5137
J. Gene Hochfelder *(Chm. & Chief Exec. Officer)*
James Lawrence Hochfelder *(Pres.)*
Thomas G. Hochfelder *(Sr. V.P. & Treas.)*
Ronald B. Norris *(V.P.-Fin., Admin. & Plng.)*
Principal(s):
J. Gene Hochfelder
James Lawrence Hochfelder
Thomas G. Hochfelder

No. of Mfg. Plants/Facilities: 2
No. of U.S. Offices: 6

Computer Systems/Hardware:
IBM System 38

Outside Service Firm(s):

BDO Seidman *(Auditors)*
1430 Broadway
New York, NY
Tel.: 212-765-7500

Chemical Banking Corp. *(Major Banking Relationship)*
277 Park Ave.
New York, NY 10041
Tel.: 212-310-6407
Fax: 212-310-4526

Divisions:

Alberoy Division **(1)**
1411 Broadway
New York, NY 10018
Tel.: 212-869-9000
Jr.'s Knitwear
S.I.C.: 5137

Beldoch Popper Division **(1)**
1411 Broadway
New York, NY 10018
Tel.: 212-869-9000
Contemporary Missy Knitwear
S.I.C.: 5137
Carol Spinelli *(Pres.)*

Knitmaker Division **(1)**
1411 Broadway
New York, NY 10018
Tel.: 212-869-9000
S.I.C.: 5137
Thomas G. Hochfelder *(Pres.)*

Pierre Cardin Knits **(1)**
1411 Broadway
New York, NY 10018
Tel.: 212-354-9760
Ladies Sportswear
S.I.C.: 5137
James L. Hochfelder *(Pres.)*

BELGRAVE INDUSTRIES
3320 W. MacArthur
Santa Ana, CA 92704
Tel.: 714-540-5120
Approx.Sls.: $25,000,000
Emp.: 250
Fiscal Year-end: 12/31/89
Holding Company
S.I.C.: 6719
Ronald J. Klammer *(Chm. Bd.)*
H. Van Forsythe *(Pres.)*
Casey Rasmussen *(Controller)*
Jo Ann Dodson *(Dir.-Personnel)*

Outside Service Firm(s):

Arthur Andersen & Co. *(Auditors)*
633 W. Fifth St.
Los Angeles, CA 90071
Tel.: 213-614-6500

Divisions:

Benmar **(1)**
3320 W. MacArthur Blvd.
Santa Ana, CA 92704
Tel.: 714-540-5120 (100%)
Telex: 678-338
Approx.Sls.: $5,000,000
Emp.: 30
Fiscal Year-end: 12/31/91

Belgrave Industries—(Continued)

Marine Autopilot Systems
S.I.C.: 3625
Darrel Stucky *(Gen. Mgr.)*
Robert Crick *(Mktg. Mgr.)*

Original Cylinder Corporation **(1)**
652 W. 18th St.
Los Angeles, CA 90015
Tel.: 213-747-9487 (100%)
Remanufacture Power Brake Units for Passenger Automobiles
S.I.C.: 3714
Tommy Lee *(G.M.)*

BELK STORES SERVICES INC.
2801 W. Tyvola Rd.
Charlotte, NC 28217-4500
Tel.: 704-357-1000
Fax: 704-357-1883
Year Founded: 1888
Approx.Sls.: $1,680,000,000
Emp.: 1,200
Fiscal Year-end: 12/31/90
Department Stores
S.I.C.: 5311
John M. Belk *(Chm. Bd. & Chief Exec. Officer)*
Thomas M. Belk *(Pres.)*
Richard Cox *(Exec. V.P.-Systems & Control)*
Ray A. Killian, Sr. *(Exec. V.P.-Human Resources & Pub. Rels.)*
Thomas Nipper *(Exec. V.P.-Belk Dept. Store Grp./Wilmington)*
Russell E. Solt *(Exec. V.P.-Fin.)*
William Wilson *(Exec. V.P.-Real Estate)*
Johnny Belk *(Sr. V.P.-Systems & Control)*
Dixie Brock Helms *(V.P.-Systems Support)*
John Lassiter *(V.P. & Gen. Counsel)*
William McGill *(V.P. & Treas.)*
Allen Williams *(V.P.-Mngmt. Information Systems)*
Bill R. Walton *(Controller)*
Leroy Robinson *(Gen. Counsel & Consultant)*
Principal(s):
John M. Belk

No. of Mfg. Plants/Facilities: 350

Computer Systems/Hardware:
IBM

Outside Service Firm(s):

KPMG Peat Marwick*(Auditors)*
345 Park Ave.
New York, NY 10154
Tel.: 212-758-9700
Fax: 212-872-3308

Prudential Insurance Co. of America*(Group Insurer)*
751 Broad St.
Newark, NJ 07102-3777
Tel.: 201-802-6000

First Union National Bank*(Major Banking Relationship)*
CMG-5, Two First Union Center
Charlotte, NC 28288-1154
Tel.: 704-374-2698
Fax: 704-374-6987

Wachovia Bank & Trust Co.*(Major Banking Relationship)*
P.O. Box 3001,
Winston-Salem, NC 27102
Tel.: 800-633-4236

Equitable Life*(Pension Manager)*
1221 Ave. of the Americas
New York, NY 10022
Tel.: 212-382-8038
Fax: 212-382-8089

Fayez Sarofim & Co.*(Pension Manager)*
Two Houston Center, Suite 2907
Houston, TX 77010
Tel.: 713-654-4484
Fax: 713-654-8184

IDS Advisory Group*(Pension Manager)*
Minneapolis, MN

NationsBank Carolinas*(Pension Manager)*
One NCNB Plaza T18-7
Charlotte, NC 28255

BELL-CARTER FOODS, INC.
3742 Mt. Diablo Blvd.
Lafayette, CA 94549
Tel.: 510-284-5933
Fax: 510-284-1289
Year Founded: 1930
Assets: $35,000,000
Net Worth: $35,000,000
Approx.Sls.: $65,000,000
Emp.: 325
Fiscal Year-end: 7/31/91
Olive Processor
S.I.C.: 2033
Tim Carter *(Chm. Bd. & Chief Exec. Officer)*
Jud Carter *(Pres.)*
Mike Hoversen *(V.P.-Fin. & Chief Oper. Officer)*
Ken Wienholz *(V.P.-Sls & Mktg.)*
Barry Borsaglia *(Dir.-Pur.)*
Principal(s):
Tim Carter
Jud Carter
Mary Bell Floyd

No. of Mfg. Plants/Facilities: 2
No. of U.S. Offices: 5
No. of Foreign Offices: 1

Computer Systems/Hardware:
IBM System 36; Wang

Outside Service Firm(s):

Ernst & Young*(Auditors)*
2175 N. California Blvd., Ste. 400
Walnut Creek, CA 94596

Atlantic Mutual Insurance*(Commercial Insurance Carrier)*
New York, NY

New York Life*(Group Insurer)*
New York, NY

Rankin & O'Shea*(Legal Firm)*
Oakland, CA

Security Pacific National Bank*(Major Banking Relationship)*
50 California, 13th Fl.
San Francisco, CA 94111

Subsidiary:

Bell Carter Distributing **(1)**
806 Kiernan Ave.
Modesto, CA 95356
Tel.: 209-545-5561
Distribution of Bell-Carter Foods
S.I.C.: 5141

BELL CHEMICAL COMPANY
411-415 N. Wolcott Ave.
Chicago, IL 60622
Tel.: 312-733-5960
Fax: 312-666-5525
Approx.Sls.: $15,000,000
Emp.: 100
Automotive Maintenance Chemicals
S.I.C.: 2899; 2869; 2992
Sam Paget *(Pres.)*
D. Lingle *(Mgr.-Opers.)*
T.P. Stitt *(Mgr.-Sls.)*
J.A. Costello *(Pur. Agent)*

Outside Service Firm(s):

American National Bank*(Major Banking Relationship)*
33 North LaSalle St.
Chicago, IL 60690
Tel.: 312-661-6967

BELL CONSTRUCTION CO. INC.
255 Wilson Pike Circle
Brentwood, TN 37027
Mailing Address:
P.O. Box 363,
Brentwood, TN 37024
Tel.: 615-373-4343 **TN**
Fax: 615-373-9224
Year Founded: 1969
Approx.Sls.: $75,000,000
Emp.: 300
Fiscal Year-end: 12/31/89
General Contractor
S.I.C.: 1541; 1542; 1522; 1622
Ray Bell *(Pres.)*
Randy Brent *(V.P.)*
Donald Estes *(V.P.)*
Thomas Robbins *(V.P.)*
Jody Evans *(Sec. & Treas.)*
Rosemary Gregory *(Dir.-Data Processing)*
Principal(s):
Ray Bell

Computer Systems/Hardware:
IBM System 36

Outside Service Firm(s):

Winnetts & Associates*(Auditors)*
Nashville, TN

Frank E. Neal & Co.*(Commercial Insurance Carrier)*
2223 8th Ave. South
Nashville, TN 37204

Blue Cross & Blue Shield of Tennessee*(Group Insurer)*
Chattanooga, TN

Manier, Herod, Hollabaugh & Smith*(Legal Firm)*
2200 One Nashville Pl., 150 4th Ave. N
Nashville, TN 37219

The Bank of Nashville*(Major Banking Relationship)*
401 Church St.
Nashville, TN 37219
Tel.: 615-271-2000

Turner P. Williams & Assoc.*(Pension Manager)*
111 28th Ave. South
Nashville, TN 37212

BELL FLAVORS & FRAGRANCES
500 Academy Dr.
Northbrook, IL 60062
Tel.: 708-291-8300
Tel.: 800-323-4387
Fax: 708-291-1217
Emp.: 350
Export
Marketing of Flavors, Fragrances & Aromatics
S.I.C.: 5169
Edward Heinz *(Chm. Bd.)*
Raymond J. Heinz *(Vice Chm.)*
James H. Heinz *(Pres.)*
Joanne Anderson *(Controller)*

Plant:

Bell Flavors & Fragrances **(1)**
33 Lake Ave.
Monticello, NY 12701
Tel.: 914-794-4444
Mfr. of Flavors, Fragrances & Aromatics
S.I.C.: 2869
Mike Amidei *(Plant Mgr.)*

Affiliate:

American Bio Synthetics **(1)**
710 W. National Ave.
Milwaukee, WI 53204
Tel.: 414-384-7017
Manufacturer of Flavors, Fragrances & Aromatics
S.I.C.: 2869
Jerry Nueser *(Gen. Mgr.)*

BELL GARDENS BICYCLE CLUB
7301 Eastern Ave
Bell Gardens, CA 90201
Tel.: 310-806-4646
Fax: 310-806-1075
Year Founded: 1984
Assets: $36,500,000
Liabilities: $23,000,000
Net Worth: $13,500,000
Approx.Sls.: $98,000,000
Emp.: 1,990
Fiscal Year-end: 12/31/91
Card Rooms; Coffee Shop
S.I.C.: 7999; 5812
George Hardie *(Mng. Gen. Partner)*
Gary Amundson *(Controller)*
George G. Hardie *(Gen. Mgr.)*

Outside Service Firm(s):

Sanwa Bank*(Major Banking Relationship)*
Bell Gardens, CA

BELL GAS, INC.
1811 S.E. Main
Roswell, NM 88201
Tel.: 505-622-4800 **NM**
Fax: 505-622-4710
Year Founded: 1950
Approx.Sls.: $35,000,000
Emp.: 250
Petroleum Bulk Stations; Filling Stations; Automobile Tires & Tubes
S.I.C.: 5171; 5541; 5014
Ray L. Bell *(Pres. & Chief Exec. Officer)*
Eugene Bell *(V.P.)*
Tom Lancaster *(Treas. & Sec.)*
Keith Bell *(Mgr.-Adv.)*
Richard Brown *(Mgr.-Sls.)*

Outside Service Firm(s):

May-Taylor Inc.*(Auditors)*
Roswell, NM

Atwood, Malone, Mann & Cooter*(Legal Firm)*
Roswell, NM

United New Mexico Bank*(Major Banking Relationship)*
Roswell, NM

HARRY H. BELL & SONS, INC.
756 28th St., South
Saint Petersburg, FL 33712
Mailing Address:
P.O. Box 15406,
St. Petersburg, FL 33733
Tel.: 813-327-3474
Tel.: 800-289-5010
Fax: 813-321-9599
Year Founded: 1922
Approx.Sls.: $15,000,000
Emp.: 75
Fiscal Year-end: 12/31/90
Import Export
Processor & Distr. of Fresh & Frozen Seafood
S.I.C.: 2092
Harry H. Bell, Jr. *(Pres. & Chief Exec. Officer)*
Robert P. Bell *(Exec. V.P., Sec. & Treas.)*
Terry W. Riggs *(V.P.-Pur.)*
Kenneth Moroz *(Controller)*
John S. Wilber *(Natl. Sls. Mgr.)*
Karen Wilfong *(Dir.-Personnel & Data Processing)*

BELL & HOWELL COMPANY
5215 Old Orchard Rd.
Skokie, IL 60077-1076
Tel.: 708-470-7100 **DE**
Telex: 650-1248258 MCI
Fax: 708-470-9825
Year Founded: 1907
Assets: $736,153,000
Liabilities: $664,916,000

Net Worth: $71,237,000
Approx.Rev.: $624,961,000,000
Emp.: 5,700
Fiscal Year-end: 12/31/91
Import Export
Publishing & Information Services
S.I.C.: 3579; 3861; 2731; 2741; 3577; 3695
William J. White *(Chm. Bd., Pres. & Chief Exec. Officer)*
Nils A. Johansson *(Sr. V.P. & Chief Fin. Officer)*
Eugene F. Sikorovsky *(Sr. V.P., Gen. Counsel & Sec.)*
Stuart T. Lieberman *(V.P., Controller & Chief Acctg. Officer)*
Henry A. D'Ambrosio *(V.P.-Admin.)*
Joseph J. Fitzsimmons *(V.P.)*
David F. Gump *(V.P.)*
Robert T. Stirling *(V.P.)*
Dieter E.A. Tannenberg *(V.P.)*
Patrick J. Graver *(Treas.)*
Stephen R. Myers *(Asst. Controller)*
Gary S. Salit *(Asst. Sec.)*
Thomas H. Jones *(Dir.-Information Systems Div.)*
J.J. Puetz *(Dir.-Compensation & Ben.)*

Outside Service Firm(s):

KPMG Peat Marwick*(Auditors)*
Peat Marwick Plaza, 303 E. Wacker Dr.
Chicago, IL 60601
Tel.: 312-938-1000

Allendale Mutual Insurance Co.*(Commercial Insurance Carrier)*
Chicago, IL

Travelers Insurance Co.*(Group Insurer)*
1 Tower Square
Hartford, CT 06183
Tel.: 203-222-7821
Fax: 203-222-7813

National Westminster Bank plc*(International Bank Affiliate)*
25 Old Broad St. EC2N1HQ
London, England

McDermott, Will & Emery*(Legal Firm)*
227 W. Monroe St.
Chicago, IL 60606-5096
Tel.: 312-372-2000

Wells Fargo Bank*(Major Banking Relationship)*
333 S. Grand
Los Angeles, CA 90071
Tel.: 213-253-6836

Harris Trust & Savings Bank*(Major Banking Relationship)*
111 W. Monroe St.
Chicago, IL 60690
Tel.: 312-461-2265
Tel.: 800-858-0840

BEA Associates, Inc.*(Pension Manager)*
One Citicorp Center, 153 East 53rd St.
New York, NY 10022
Tel.: 212-832-2626
Fax: 212-751-2470

Dreyfus Management Inc.*(Pension Manager)*
767 Fifth Av.
New York, NY 10022

Divisions:

Bell & Howell Information Systems Division **(1)**
2231 W. Howard
Evanston, IL 60202
Tel.: 708-570-4600
Sorters for the U.S. Postal Service & Sorters & Letter Openers for Commercial Use
S.I.C.: 3579
Thomas H. Jones *(Gen. Mgr.)*

DocuMail Systems Division **(1)**
2300 Brummel Pl.
Evanston, IL 60202
Tel.: 708-475-6100
Sorters for the U.S. Postal Service; Sorters & Letter Openers for Commercial Use
S.I.C.: 3579
Jerry Loftis *(Gen. Mgr.)*

Subsidiaries:

Bell & Howell Acceptance Corporation **(1)**
5215 Old Orchard Rd.
Skokie, IL 60077
Tel.: 708-470-7100 (100%)
Financial Services
S.I.C.: 6159
Nicholas Dennis *(Pres.)*

Bell & Howell Document Management Products Company **(1)**
6800 McCormick Rd.
Chicago, IL 60645
Tel.: 312-675-7600 (100%)
Export
Optical Disk-Based Computer Assisted Retrieval Systems & Networks; Microfilm-Based Computer Assisted Retrieval Systems & Networks; Digital Image Scanners; Document Management Software; Bar Code Systems; Microfilm Capture & Retrieval Systems; Image Conversion Services; Document Management Supplies; National Direct Sales & Service Networks; National Customer Service & Product Support
S.I.C.: 8741; 7384
Dieter E.A. Tannenberg *(Pres. & Chief Exec. Officer)*
Frank L. Rocks *(V.P.-Sls. & Service)*

Division:

N.B. Jackets Division **(2)**
1899 Powers Ferry Rd., Ste. 400
Marietta, GA 30067
Tel.: 809-744-9397 (100%)
Export
Microfilm Jackets
S.I.C.: 3861
Michael Bauer *(V.P. & Gen. Mgr.)*
George Wrabel *(V.P.-Sls. & Mktg.)*

Bell & Howell Mailmobile Co. **(1)**
411 E. Roosevelt St.
Zeeland, MI 49464
Tel.: 616-772-1000 (100%)
Mailmobile Unmanned Delivery Vehicles
S.I.C.: 3579
David E. Michaud *(Gen. Mgr.)*

Bell & Howell Phillipsburg Company **(1)**
P.O. Box 7950,
Lehigh Valley, PA 18001
Tel.: 215-264-4510 (100%)
Export
Mfr. of High-Volume Mail & Document Processing Machines
S.I.C.: 3579
James R. Stirling *(Pres.)*

Bell & Howell Publication Systems Company **(1)**
Old Mansfield Rd.
Wooster, OH 44691
Tel.: 216-264-6666 (100%)
Export
Microfilm & Microfiches Publisher of Information Products Including Newspapers, Periodicals, Indexes, Directories, Career Guidance; Production Facilities also in NJ & Puerto Rico; Publish Proprietary Databases & Technical Information for Large Industrial Companies; Electronic Catalog Systems
S.I.C.: 2741
David F. Gump *(Pres.)*

University Microfilms Inc. **(1)**
300 N. Zeeb Rd.
Ann Arbor, MI 48106
Tel.: 313-761-4700 (100%)
Republish & Market Public Information Products in Microform, Print-on Paper & Electronic Formats
S.I.C.: 2741
Joe Fitzsimmons *(Pres.)*

Operating Unit:

UMI Data Courier **(1)**
620 S. Third St.
Louisville, KY 40202
Tel.: 502-583-4111
Data Base Retrieval Service
S.I.C.: 7375
Joe Fitzsimmons *(Gen. Mgr.)*
Bonnie Maxwell *(V.P.)*
Naomi Diaz *(Mgr.-Personnel)*

Non-U.S. Holdings:

Bell & Howell France S.A. **(1)**
32-34, rue Fernand-Pelloutier 92112
Clichy, Cedex France
Tel.: 331-4270-9480
Telex: 842-620992 BEHOW CLICHY
Fax: 331 4270 9480
Mail Handling & Visual Communications
S.I.C.: 5043

Bell & Howell GmbH **(1)**
Gruener Weg 8 P.O. Box 100154, D-6360
Friedberg, Germany
Tel.: 496-031-871
Telex: 841-415914 BEHOW D
Fax: 496-031-87308
Phillipsburg Systems & Electronic Devices
S.I.C.: 4822; 3579

Bell & Howell Japan Co. K.K. **(1)**
Ando Fukuyoshi Bldg., 8th Fl., 11-28
Akaska 1-chome Minato-ku,
Tokyo, 107, Japan
Tel.: 03-3582-4691
Telex: 781-22734 BHFE
Cable: BHFEJMTM
Fax: 81-3-582-1748
Visual Communications, Mail Handling & Microimagery

Bell & Howell Ltd. **(1)**
230 Barmac Drive
Weston, ON Canada M9L 2X5
Tel.: 416-746-2200
Telex: 369-06527166 BEHOWTOR CAN
Fax: 416-746-0026
Visual Communications, Mail Handling & Microimagery
S.I.C.: 5043; 5065; 5192
Ray Patterson *(Pres.)*

Bell & Howell Ltd., (UK) Mailhandling Div. **(1)**
33-35 Woodthorpe Rd.
Ashford, Middlesex TW15 2RZ, United Kingdom
Tel.: 447-842-51234
Tel.: 441-751-0921
Telex: 851-266119 BEHOW G
Fax: 447-842-54833
Electronic Document & Mail Sorting Systems for Postal Operations
S.I.C.: 3579; 4822; 7221

Bell & Howell Ltd. England, Dansk Filial **(1)**
Fabriksparken 22 DK-2600
Glostrup, Denmark
Tel.: 452-96-7711
Telex: 855-21096 BEHOW DK
Fax: 452-96-7677
Visual Communications
S.I.C.: 7221

Bell & Howell Nederland B.V. **(1)**
Nijverheidsstraat 22 Postbus 2, 6987 ZG
Giesbeek, Netherlands
Tel.: 31-08-336-1841
Telex: 844-35418 BEHOW NL
Fax: 318-336-2052
Visual Communications

Micromedia Limited **(1)**
Units 7-8, Telford Rd., Launton Indust. Estate
Bicester, Oxon United Kingdom
Tel.: 44-869-45711
Fax: 447-842-54833
Micropublishing Prods. & Microfilm Jackets
S.I.C.: 3861

Pretec Precisie Techniek B.V. **(1)**
Kuyperlan 28 Postbus 2, 6987 ZG
Giesbeek, Netherlands
Tel.: 31-08-336-1841
Telex: 844-35418 BEHOW NL
Fax: 318-336-2052
Mail Handling Prods. & Microimagery
S.I.C.: 3861; 3579

BELL PACKAGING CORPORATION
3102 S. Boots St.
Marion, IN 46953
Mailing Address:
P.O. Box 3333
Marion, IN 46953
Tel.: 317-664-1261 **IN**
Fax: 317-664-7693
Year Founded: 1913

Approx.Sls.: $240,000,000
Emp.: 1,550
Manufacturer of Packaging & Paperboard, Corrugated Containers & Flexible Packaging
S.I.C.: 2653; 2657; 2672
John Bell, Jr. *(Chm. Bd. & Chief Exec. Officer)*
F. Howard East *(Pres., Chief Oper. & Chief Fin. Officer)*
V.E. Chrismer *(V.P.-Container Div.)*
R.W. McMullen *(V.P.-Human Resources)*
Hubert Tucker *(Treas.)*
H.D. Sills *(Controller)*
Vern Tinkle *(Mgr.-Data Processing)*
Principal(s):
John Bell, Jr.

No. of Mfg. Plants/Facilities: 7
No. of Foreign Offices: 1

Computer Systems/Hardware:
Data General

Outside Service Firm(s):

Ernst & Young*(Auditors)*
One Indiana Square, Ste. 3400
Indianapolis, IN 46204
Tel.: 317-236-1100

Arkwright Mutual Insurance*(Commercial Insurance Carrier)*
225 Wyman St.
Waltham, MA 02254-9198
Tel.: 617-890-9300
Fax: 617-890-0075

Prudential Insurance Co. of America*(Group Insurer)*
751 Broad St.
Newark, NJ 07102-3777
Tel.: 201-802-6000

Krieg DeVault Alexander & Capehart*(Legal Firm)*
One Indiana Square
Indianapolis, IN 46204
Tel.: 317-636-4341

INB National Bank*(Major Banking Relationship)*
One Indiana Sq.
Indianapolis, IN 46266
Tel.: 317-266-6000

Summit Bank*(Major Banking Relationship)*
Marion, IN

Subsidiaries:

Bell Fibre Products **(1)**
3102 So. Boots St.
Marion, IN 46953
Tel.: 317-664-1261
Manufacturer of Corrugated Shipping Containers, Flexible Packaging, Liner Board & Wax Paper
S.I.C.: 2621; 2631; 2653
F. Howard East *(Pres.)*

Dixico, Inc. **(1)**
1415 So. Vernon St.
Dallas, TX 75224
Tel.: 214-943-7521 (100%)
Fax: 214-943-4046
Emp.: 500
Manufacturer of Flexible Packaging & Plastic Film
S.I.C.: 2671; 2673
John Bell *(Pres. & Chief Exec. Officer)*
Mike Flannigan *(V.P.-Sls.)*
Stan Lee *(V.P.-Opers.)*
L. DeWayne Fant *(V.P.-Res. & Devel.)*
Gary Reighling *(V.P.-Fin.)*
Robert A. Adler *(Dir.-Mktg.)*

Plants:

Dixico Division (Plant) **(2)**
276 So. Pkwy., W.
Memphis, TN 38109
Tel.: 901-948-5687
S.I.C.: 2671

Flexible Packaging Division (Plant) **(2)**
1300 So. Polk St.
Dallas, TX 75224
Tel.: 214-943-7521
S.I.C.: 2671

Bell Packaging Corporation—(Continued)

Menominee Paper Co. (1)
P.O. Box 300
Menominee, MI 49858
Tel.: 906-863-5595 (100%)
S.I.C.: 2653; 2672; 2657
M. Schneider *(V.P. & Gen. Mgr.)*

BELL SOUTH ENTERPRISES
(Formerly Graphics Holding Company)
713 Ralph David Abernathy St. S.W.
Atlanta, GA 30310
Tel.: 404-249-4050
Approx.Sls.: $165,000,000
Emp.: 1,000
Publishing & Printing Of Catalogs, Directories & Business Forms; Lithographed
S.I.C.: 2741; 2752
Hugh Inman *(Pres.)*
William Davidson *(Division Pres.)*
Thomas Stubbs *(Treas.)*

Outside Service Firm(s):

Coopers & Lybrand*(Auditors)*
1155 Peachtree St.
Atlanta, GA 30309
Tel.: 404-870-1309

The First National Bank of Atlanta*(Major Banking Relationship)*
2 Peachtree St., N.W. P.O. Box 3260
Atlanta, GA 30302
Tel.: 404-588-6656

Divisions:

Bell South Advertising & Publishing Division (1)
1100 Peak St.
Atlanta, GA 30309
Tel.: 404-753-1121
Management Services
Larry A. Taylor *(Pres.)*

Bell South Business Product Division (1)
880 Great S.W. Pky.
Atlanta, GA 30336
Tel.: 404-753-1121
William Davidson *(Pres.)*
Thomas Stubs *(Treas.)*

Stevens Graphics, Inc. (1)
713 Ralph David Abernathy S.W.
Atlanta, GA 30310
Tel.: 404-753-1121
Directory Printing
S.I.C.: 2752
Hugh M. Inman *(Pres.)*
William J. Davidson *(V.P., Sec. & Controller)*
Thomas H. Stubbs *(Treas.)*

BELLACICCO & SONS
217-44 98th Ave.
Queens Village, NY 11429
Tel.: 718-479-5100
Fax: 718-776-8173
Year Founded: 1934
Approx.Sls.: $20,000,000
Emp.: 175
Fiscal Year-end: 12/31/91
Mfr. of Fresh & Frozen Bread & Rolls & Bread Crumbs
S.I.C.: 2051; 2052
Vincent Bellacicco *(Chm. Bd.)*
Robert Ronzoni *(Chief Exec. Officer)*
Joseph Bellacicco *(Pres.)*

Outside Service Firm(s):

Joseph Albanese*(Legal Firm)*
New York, NY

City Bank*(Major Banking Relationship)*
Queens Village, NY

BELLAMY BROTHERS, INC.
Fairview Rd. at Panola Rd.
Ellenwood, GA 30049
Tel.: 404-474-8726
Emp.: 175
Bridge & Dam Construction
S.I.C.: 1622; 1629
Otis Bellamy *(Pres.)*
Wesley E. Allen *(V.P.)*
John Vansant *(Treas.)*

Outside Service Firm(s):

Patrick & Warner*(Legal Firm)*
Atlanta, GA

Subsidiary:

Bellamy Brothers Constructing Company (1)
16 Fairview Rd.
Ellenwood, GA 30049
Tel.: 404-474-8724
Emp.: 2
Heavy Construction Equipment Rental
S.I.C.: 7353
Clifford Bellamy *(Partner)*
Otis Bellamy *(Partner)*

BELLE TIRE DISTRIBUTOR INC.
3500 Enterprise Dr.
Allen Park, MI 48101
Tel.: 313-271-9400 **MI**
Fax: 313-271-7946
Approx.Sls.: $44,000,000
Emp.: 350
Wholesale & Retail Tires & Accessories
S.I.C.: 5014; 5531
Donald Barnes, Jr. *(Pres.)*
Robert Barnes *(Chief Exec. Officer)*
John Babinski *(V.P.-Mktg.)*
Daniel T. Light *(Sec. & Treas.)*

Outside Service Firm(s):

Gross, Bornstein, Grey & Co.*(Auditors)*
Southfield, MI

Comerica Bank*(Major Banking Relationship)*
211 W. Fort St.
Detroit, MI 48226
Tel.: 313-222-3300

BELLOFRAM CORP.
State Rte. 2, Box 305
Newell, WV 26050
Tel.: 304-387-1200 **OH**
Fax: 304-387-1212
Year Founded: 1952
Sales Range: $20-39 Million
Emp.: 300
Fiscal Year-end: 12/31/90
Export
Manufactures Fabric Reinforced Elastomer Diaphragms, Air Cylinders & Actuators, Liquid Dispensing Pumps, Pneumatic Regulators & Relays, Valve Positioners Gage Protectors, I/P Transducers, Hydraulic Actuators
S.I.C.: 3561; 3593; 3494
Al Siemer *(Pres.)*
Dennis Rutledge *(V.P. & Gen. Mgr.)*
David Lewis *(Mgr.-Natl. Sls.)*
M. Standish *(Mgr.-Opers.)*

No. of Mfg. Plants/Facilities: 1
No. of U.S. Offices: 1

Outside Service Firm(s):

Ernst & Young*(Auditors)*
1300 Huntington Bldg.
Cleveland, OH 44115
Tel.: 216-861-5000
Fax: 303-291-6234

BELLWETHER TECHNOLOGY CORPORATION
(d/b/a Computerland)
203 Carondelet St., Ste. 250
New Orleans, LA 70130
Tel.: 504-525-2258
Fax: 504-525-2344
Approx.Sls.: $23,000,000
Emp.: 52
Wholesale Computer Hardware Software & Peripherals
S.I.C.: 7372
Edgar A. Bright, Jr. *(Owner)*
Lynes Sloss *(Pres. & Chief Exec. Officer)*
Glenn Benton *(V.P.)*
Charles Stewart *(V.P.-Fin.)*

BELMONT INDUSTRIES, INC.
1900 Rittenhouse Sq.
Philadelphia, PA 19103
Tel.: 215-732-2500 **PA**
Fax: 215-666-7006
Approx.Sls.: $250,000,000
Emp.: 3,000
Fiscal Year-end: 12/31/90
Holding Company for Manufacturing of Machined Products, Residential Heating Equipment, Lawn & Garden Equipment, Bridge Floors & Grating & Dental Equipment & Supplies
S.I.C.: 3555; 3441; 1791; 3524; 6719; 3295; 3843
Raymond G. Perelman *(Chm. Bd. & Chief Exec. Officer)*
Jeffrey Perelman *(Pres.)*
Irving M. Moses *(V.P.-Fin.)*
Grace Lite *(Sec.)*
Principal(s):
Raymond G. Perelman

No. of Mfg. Plants/Facilities: 6
No. of U.S. Offices: 6

Outside Service Firm(s):

Fishbein & Co.*(Auditors)*
Philadelphia, PA

Blue Cross of Greater Philadelphia*(Group Insurer)*
Philadelphia, PA

CoreStates First Pennsylvania Bank, N.A.*(Major Banking Relationship)*
Philadelphia, PA

Division:

General Refractories Co., U. S. Refractories Div. (1)
600 Grant St.
Pittsburgh, PA 15219
Tel.: 412-562-6000
Telex: 710-664-4480
Fax: 412-562-6174
Emp.: 750
Mfr. of Refractory Prods.
S.I.C.: 3255; 3297
Joseph L. Stein *(Pres.)*
Russell Pickus *(V.P. & Controller)*
William P. Phelan *(Dir.-Dealers)*
Allen R. Wipf *(Midwest Reg Sls. Mgr.)*
Earle W. McLean *(Southeast Reg. Sls. Mgr.)*
Robert F. Mattox *(Western Reg. Sls. Mgr.)*
Mark Becker *(Pittsburgh Reg. Sls. Mgr.)*
Leon J. Kazmierczak *(Mgr.-Export Sls.)*
Glen Jones *(Buyer)*

Subsidiaries:

American Refractories Co. (1)
1250 Clarion St.
Reading, PA 19601
Tel.: 215-375-4422 (100%)
Emp.: 41
Refractory Repair & Installation
S.I.C.: 1629
Glenn R. Fehr *(V.P. & Gen. Mgr.)*

Chemrock Corporation (1)
1101 Kermit Dr., Ste. 503
Nashville, TN 37217
Tel.: 615-360-7911 (100%)
Emp.: 4
Installation of Cryogenic Perlite
S.I.C.: 3295
Whitney Waugh *(V.P. & Gen. Mgr.)*

Dicalite Corporation (1)
Rte. 1, Box 600
Burney, CA 96013
Tel.: 916-335-5451 (100%)
Emp.: 35
Diatomite Filter Aids & Fillers
S.I.C.: 3295
Daniel Froning *(Mgr.)*

GREFCO, Inc. (1)
3435 W. Lomita Blvd.
Torrance, CA 90509
Tel.: 310-517-0700 (100%)
Emp.: 333
Indus. Filteraids, Fillers, Perlite & Diatomite
S.I.C.: 3295; 1499
Jeffrey F. Lang *(Pres.)*

Mapleton Development, Inc. (1)
P.O. Box 240
Minerva, OH 44657
Tel.: 216-868-4142 (100%)
Emp.: 9
Mfr. Specialty Refractory Prods.
S.I.C.: 3255
Kenneth D. Smith *(Gen. Mgr.)*

Reliance Grating, Inc. (1)
P.O. Box 20
Cottondale, AL 35453
Tel.: 205-553-3111
Gratings
S.I.C.: 3446

Schiller-Pfeiffer, Inc. (1)
Street Rd.
Southampton, PA 18966
Tel.: 215-357-5110 (100%)
Little Wonder Garden Equip. & Precision Machine Components
S.I.C.: 3524
Norman Pfeiffer *(Pres.)*

Plants:

Belmont Industries, U.S. Refractories Div. (1)
1000 N. Clark Rd.
Gary, IN 46406
Tel.: 219-949-1546 (100%)
Emp.: 8
Clay & Non-Clay Refractories
S.I.C.: 3255; 3297
J. D. Clark *(Chief Oper. Officer)*

Belmont Industries, U.S. Refractories Div. (1)
Denton Rd.
Hitchins, KY 41146
Tel.: 606-474-5131 (100%)
Emp.: 75
Clay Refractories
S.I.C.: 3255
J. D. Clark *(Chief Oper. Officer)*

Belmont Industries, U.S. Refractories Div. (1)
2200 N. 1100 West
Lehi, UT 84043
Tel.: 801-768-3591 (100%)
Emp.: 60
Clay & Non-Clay Refractories
S.I.C.: 3255; 3297
Bob Maddox *(Pres.)*

Belmont Industries, U.S. Refractories Div. (1)
Joliet, IL 60436
Tel.: 815-725-5300 (100%)
Emp.: 56
Non-Clay Refractories
S.I.C.: 3297
J. D. Clark *(Chief Oper. Officer)*

Belmont Industries, U.S. Refractories Div. (1)
Sproul, PA 16682
Tel.: 814-239-2111 (100%)
Emp.: 47
Clay & Non-Clay Refractories
S.I.C.: 3255; 3297
Joseph L. Stein *(Pres.)*

Belmont Industries, U.S. Refractories Div. (1)
Troup, TX 75789
Tel.: 214-842-3084 (100%)
Emp.: 13
Non-Clay Refractories
S.I.C.: 3297
Sam Brewer *(Plant Mgr.)*

Belmont Industries, U.S. Refractories Div. **(1)**
400 Refractory Dr., N.W.
Warren, OH 44483
Tel.: 216-847-0536 (100%)
Emp.: 94
Non-Clay Refractories
S.I.C.: 3297
Frank Orris *(Plant Mgr.)*

Belmont Industries, U.S. Refractories Div. **(1)**
1410 Albert St.
Youngstown, OH 44505
Tel.: 216-747-9391
Emp.: 27
Precast Refractory Linings
S.I.C.: 3297
J. D. Clark *(Chief Operating Officer)*

Chemrock Corporation **(1)**
Osage St.
Nashville, TN 37210
Tel.: 615-320-1787
Emp.: 13
Perlite Aggregates & Filter Aids
S.I.C.: 3295
H. Martin Sharp *(Chief Oper. Officer)*

Chemrock Corporation **(1)**
Jacksonville, FL 32208
Tel.: 904-355-0096 (100%)
Emp.: 11
Perlite Aggregates & Filter Aids
S.I.C.: 3295
H. Martin Sharp *(Chief Oper. Officer)*

Chemrock Corporation **(1)**
Lafayette, IN 47902
Tel.: 317-474-8413 (100%)
Emp.: 16
Perlite Aggregates & Fillers
S.I.C.: 3295
H. Martin Sharp *(Chief Oper. Officer)*

Chemrock Corporation **(1)**
Thomaston, ME 04861
Tel.: 207-594-8225 (100%)
Emp.: 7
Perlite Filter Aids
S.I.C.: 3295
H. Martin Sharp *(Chief Oper. Officer)*

GREFCO, Inc. **(1)**
1489 Concord Rd.
Crawfordsville, IN 47933
Tel.: 317-362-6000 (100%)
Emp.: 22
Perlite Filter Aids
S.I.C.: 3295
James R. Meske *(Gen. Mgr.)*

GREFCO, Inc. **(1)**
P.O. Box 1436
Socorro, NM 87801
Tel.: 505-835-2892 (100%)
Emp.: 27
Perlite Mining
S.I.C.: 1499
Norman Richardson *(Gen. Mgr.)*

GREFCO, Inc. **(1)**
Basalt, NV 89422 (100%)
Emp.: 9
Diatomite Fillers
S.I.C.: 3295

GREFCO, Inc. **(1)**
Hwy 1 & 246
Lompoc, CA 93436
Tel.: 805-736-4501 (100%)
Emp.: 92
Diatomite Filter Aids
S.I.C.: 3295
Lewis Zemanek *(Plant Mgr.)*

GREFCO, Inc. **(1)**
P.O. Box 308
Antonito, CO 81120
Tel.: 303-376-5475 (100%)
Emp.: 65
Perlite Filter Aids & Perlite Mining
S.I.C.: 3295; 1499
Norman Richardson *(Gen. Mgr.)*

Non-U.S. Holdings:

Amol Dicalite Ltd. **(1)**
Ahmedabad, India (30%)
Filteraids & Filler Prods.; Sub. of Grefco, Inc. 3435 West Lomita Blvd. Torrance, CA 90509 (213) 517-0700
S.I.C.: 3295
A.P. Sheth *(Chief Oper. Officer)*

Anglo-Austrian Magnesite, Ltd. **(1)**
Dale House, London Rd.
Sunningdale, Berkshire S15 0HB, United Kingdom (100%)
Refractory Sales
S.I.C.: 5085
J. Howe *(Gen. Mgr.)*

Deutsche Heraklith A.G. **(1)**
D-8346
Simbach, Germany
Tel.: 08571-40-100 (100%)
Construction Prods., Insulating Prods. & Bldg. Board
S.I.C.: 2899
Kurt Klein *(Mng. Dir.)*

Dicaser S.A. de C.V. **(1)**
Lafayette #121 11590
Mexico, D.F. Mexico
Tel.: (905) 511-17-37 (49%)
Filteraids & Filler Prods.; Sub. of Grefco, Inc.
S.I.C.: 3295
Rolf Rauh-Hain *(Mng. Dir.)*

Dicalite Europe Nord, S.A. **(1)**
Av. Louise 430-Bte. 2 B-1050
Brussels, Belgium
Tel.: (32) 02-649-20-46 (100%)
Fillers & Filteraids; Sub. of Grefco, Inc.
S.I.C.: 3295
Louis P. Jansen *(Gen. Mgr.)*

Dicalite France, S.A. **(1)**
Bvld. de Creteil,163 94100
Saint-Maur-des-Fosses, France (100%)
Subsidiary of Grefco; Minerals Sls.
S.I.C.: 5085
G. Prevost *(Gen. Mgr.)*

Dicalite Holding B.V. **(1)**
Rotterdam, Netherlands (100%)
Subsidiary of Grefco Inc.

Dicalite Orient Co. Ltd. **(1)**
Tachibana Bldg. 5, 4-Chome Kojimachi Chiyodaku,
Tokyo, 102, Japan
Tel.: 03-3261-8677 (50%)
Filteraids & Filler Prods.; Sub. of Grefco, Inc.
S.I.C.: 3295
Shunichi Nagano *(Gen. Mgr.)*

Dicalite Scandinavia **(1)**
Rysensteensgade, 1 1564
Copenhagen, Denmark
Tel.: (01) 153 570 (100%)
Subsidiary of Grefco; Mineral Sls.
S.I.C.: 5085
L.P. Jansen *(Mng. Dir.)*

Dicalite Trading, S.A. **(1)**
Av. Louise, 430-BTE 2 B-1500
Brussels, Belgium
Tel.: (32) 02-649-20-46 (100%)
Subsidiary of Grefco, Inc. Mineral Sls.
S.I.C.: 5085
L.P. Jansen *(Mng. Dir.)*

Empresa de Refractarios Colombianos S.A. **(1)**
Apartado Aereo 865
Medellin, Colombia
Tel.: (57) 32-26-00 (49%)
Mfg. Refractory Prods.
S.I.C.: 3255
Dario Fernandez *(Gen. Mgr.)*

General Refractories Co. of Canada, Ltd. **(1)**
P.O. Box 160
Smithville, ON Canada L0R 2A0
Tel.: 416-957-3311 (100%)
Mfr. of Refractories
S.I.C.: 3255
G. Ross Tollstam *(Gen. Mgr.)*

Hector & Co. A.B. **(1)**
Drottninggatan 25 S-111 51
Stockholm, Sweden
Tel.: 46-823419S (100%)
Refractory Sales
S.I.C.: 5085
F. Zauner *(Gen. Mgr.)*

Induplex, Inc. **(1)**
Legaspi, Philippines (40%)
Filteraids & Filler Prods.; Sub. of Grefco, Inc.
S.I.C.: 3295
Pablito S. del Villar, Jr. *(Chief Oper. Officer)*

Maerz Ofenbau AG **(1)**
Richard Wagnerstrasse 28 CH-8027
Zurich, Switzerland
Tel.: (41) 1-202-53-96 (50%)
Engrng. Design
S.I.C.: 8711
P.R. Schurmann *(Gen. Mgr.)*

Maerz Ofenbau G.m.b.H. **(1)**
Corneliusstrasse 36 D-4000
Dusseldorf, Germany
Tel.: (49) 211-320048 (50%)
Furnace Design & Construction
S.I.C.: 8711
Paul Lerche *(Gen. Mgr.)*

Magnomin-General Mining S.A. **(1)**
17 Agia Sophia St. 54110
Thessaloniki, Greece
Tel.: 30-31-225443 (100%)
Construction Prods.; Building Prods.; Insulating Prods. & Building Board
S.I.C.: 2899
Wolfgang Pohl *(Gen. Mgr.)*

Materiales Industriales S.A. **(1)**
Apartado Aereo 80046
Bogota, Colombia
Tel.: (57) 44-62-04 (48%)
Refractory Sales
S.I.C.: 5085
Dario Fernandez *(G.M.)*

Oesterreichisch Heraklith, A.G. **(1)**
A-9545
Radenthein, Carinthia Austria
Tel.: (43) 04-246-2100 (100%)
Construction Prods., Insulating Prods. & Bldg. Board
S.I.C.: 2899
Rudolph Kanzi *(Gen. Mgr.)*

Radex Austria, A.G. **(1)**
A-9545
Radenthein, Carinthia Austria
Tel.: (43) 04246-2100
Refractory Prods.
S.I.C.: 3255
Helmut Pichl *(Gen. Dir.)*

Radex Deutschland, A.G. **(1)**
5401
Urmitz, Germany
Tel.: 2630-89-0
Mfr. of Refractories
S.I.C.: 3297

Radex-Heraklith Industriebeteiligungs, A.G. **(1)**
Opernring 1 A-1010
Vienna, Austria
Tel.: 43-222-587-7671
European Headquarters
S.I.C.: 5085
Hellmut Longin *(Gen. Mgr.)*

Radex International S.A. **(1)**
109 Rue du Faubourg St. Honore F-75008
Paris, France
Tel.: 33-12603308 (100%)
Refractory Sales
S.I.C.: 5085
Wilhelm Kuchinka *(Gen. Mgr.)*

Refractories Consulting & Engineering GmbH **(1)**
c/o Opernring 1 A-1010
Vienna, Austria
Tel.: (43) 222-587-7671
Engrng. Design
S.I.C.: 8711
Gunther Jungmeier *(Gen. Mgr.)*

Tiroler Magnesit, A.G. **(1)**
6395
Hochfilzen, Austria
Tel.: (43) 5359-281 (100%)
Mine & Sinter Magnesite
S.I.C.: 1061

Oy Tulenkestavaat Tiliet, A.B. **(1)**
Bolevardo 17C14 SF-00120
Helsinki, 12, Finland
Tel.: 358-0645342 (100%)
Refractory Sales
S.I.C.: 5085
Armas O. Nikkanen *(Gen. Mgr.)*

BELMONT METALS, INC.
314-30 Belmont Ave.
Brooklyn, NY 11207
Tel.: 718-342-4900 **NY**
Fax: 718-342-0175
Year Founded: 1896
Approx.Sls.: $17,000,000
Emp.: 110
Fiscal Year-end: 12/31/91

Import Export
Mfr. of Refiners & Alloyes of Non-ferrous Metals & Alloys For Casting, Joining & Chemical Purpose
S.I.C.: 3341
Robert V. Henning *(Pres.)*
Theodore W. Wenning *(V.P. & Treas.)*
Bruce M. Reed *(V.P.)*
Robert V. Henning, Jr. *(Sec.)*

Outside Service Firm(s):

Coopers & Lybrand*(Auditors)*
1301 Avenue of The Americas
New York, NY 10019
Tel.: 212-536-2000

European American Bank*(Major Banking Relationship)*
New York, NY

BELTONE ELECTRONICS CORPORATION
4201 W. Victoria
Chicago, IL 60646
Tel.: 312-583-3600
Tel.: 800-621-1275
Fax: 312-583-3980
Fax: 312-583-1955(Mktg. Dept.)
Year Founded: 1940
Sales Range: $40-59 Million
Emp.: 1,100
Fiscal Year-end: 10/31/91

Import Export
Mfr. of Hearing Aids
S.I.C.: 3842; 3800; 3679
L.M. Posen *(Pres.)*
E. Weiss *(V.P. & Chief Oper. Officer)*
Rita Whalen *(Chief Fin. Officer)*
Fay Posen *(Sec.)*
Cindy S. Lieberman *(Dir.-Corp. Communications)*
Bill Lucas *(Dir.-Sls.)*
Donald Malaker *(Dir.-Opers.)*
Laura Michard *(Dir.-Sls. & Mktg.)*
Miles Posen *(Dir.-Research & Devel.)*
Robert Riefke *(Dir.-Personnel)*
Dennis S. Roy *(Dir.-Mktg. Services)*
Pete Ciocci *(Mgr.-Data Processing)*
Ed Braun *(Mgr.-Sls.)*
Jean Snyder *(Mgr.-Direct Response)*
Mike Jordan *(Mgr.-Export)*
Joyce Sherry *(Mgr.-Adv.)*
Henry Pielach *(Mgr.-Pur.)*
Roberta Miller *(Disperser Relations/ Meeting)*
George Markham *(A/V & Training Dir.)*

Computer Systems/Hardware:
IBM System 38; IBM 4341, Macintosh

Outside Service Firm(s):

Ernst & Young*(Auditors)*
233 S. Wacker Dr.
Chicago, IL 60606
Tel.: 312-368-1800
Fax: 312-645-3095

Signa Insurance*(Group Insurer)*
Des Plaines, IL

Beltone Electronics Corporation—(Continued)

Subsidiaries:

Oto-Sonic, Inc. **(1)**
4200 W. Bryn Mawr
Chicago, IL 60646
Tel.: 312-463-9173
Import Export
Mfr. of Beltone Hearing Aids, Otosonic Hearing Aids, Audiometers, Impedence Analyzers, Components, Batteries & Accessories
S.I.C.: 3842; 3679
Steve Hannibal *(Gen. Mgr.)*
John Cariola *(Dir.-Mktg.)*

Special Instruments **(1)**
4201 W. Victoria
Chicago, IL 60646
Tel.: 312-583-3600
Mfr. of Beltone Hearing Aids, Otosonic Hearing Aids, Audiometers, Impedence Analyzers, Components, Batteries & Accessories
S.I.C.: 3842; 3679; 3800
Grace DeFilippis *(Mgr.)*

BELVEDERE COMPANY
(Div. of Smith Investment Co.)
One Belvedere Blvd.
Belvidere, IL 61008
Tel.: 815-544-3131
Fax: 815-544-6747
Year Founded: 1927
Approx.Sls.: $25,000,000
Emp.: 250
Fiscal Year-end: 12/31/90
Export
Mfg. Beauty & Barber Shop Furniture & Equip., Kitchen Cabinets, Belvedere, First Lady, Rockford
S.I.C.: 3999; 2521; 2522; 2599
Martin Holmes *(Pres.)*
Peter G. Crosby *(Sr. V.P.-Mktg. & Sls.)*
Ron Britt *(Sr. V.P.-Mfg.)*
Stuart Smith *(V.P.-Sls.)*
Mark Waldron *(V.P. & Controller)*
Larry Handel *(V.P.-Mfg. Systems)*

Computer Systems/Hardware:
Unisys

Subsidiary:

Central Beauty Equipment **(1)**
One Belvedere Blvd.
Belvidere, IL 61008
Tel.: 815-544-3131
Mfr. Hair Dryers, Bowls & Chairs for Salon Industry
S.I.C.: 3999

BELZ ENTERPRISES
530 Oak Court Dr.
Memphis, TN 38117
Mailing Address:
P.O. Box 171199
Memphis, TN 38117
Tel.: 901-767-4780
Fax: 901-762-7203
Year Founded: 1940
Approx.Sls.: $100,000,000
Emp.: 100
Real Estate Development & Management
S.I.C.: 6552
Philip Belz *(Chm. Bd.)*
Jack A. Belz *(Pres. & Chief Exec. Officer)*
Martin S. Belz *(Exec. V.P. & Chief Oper. Officer)*
Jimmie D. Williams *(Exec. V.P., Chief Fin. Officer, Treas. & Sec.)*
Ronald A. Belz *(Exec. V.P.-Special Projects)*
Jerome A. Hanover *(Sr. V.P.)*
Andrew Groveman *(V.P.)*
Irvin Skopp *(V.P.)*
Earl Williams *(Controller)*
Principal(s):
Jack A. Belz
Jimmie D. Williams

Outside Service Firm(s):

Arthur Andersen & Co.*(Auditors)*
165 Madison Ave., Ste. 165
Memphis, TN 38103
Tel.: 901-525-4451

Johnson & Higgins*(Group Insurer)*
25 Park Place, N.E.
Atlanta, GA 30303
Tel.: 404-658-9877

BEMCO INC.
2255 Union Pl.
Simi Valley, CA 93065
Tel.: 805-583-4970 **CA**
Fax: 805-583-5033
Year Founded: 1951
Emp.: 40
Fiscal Year-end: 2/28/91
Export
Mfr. of Environmental Test Equipment, Space Simulation Systems, Electronic Burn-in & Temperature Cycling Chambers
S.I.C.: 9511
W.R. Bruskrud *(Pres. & Treas.)*
Barry Bruskrud *(Exec. V.P.)*
Randy Bruskrud *(Sec.)*
Glen Elliott *(Adv. Mgr.)*
Melinda Brunskrud *(Pur. Agent)*

No. of Mfg. Plants/Facilities: 1
No. of U.S. Offices: 1

Computer Systems/Hardware:
IBM PC-XT

Outside Service Firm(s):

Take Care Corporation*(Group Insurer)*
Oakland, CA

Jennings & Engstrom*(Legal Firm)*
North Hollywood, CA

Union Bank*(Major Banking Relationship)*
North Hollywood, CA

BEN VENUE LABORATORIES, INC.
270 Northfield Rd.
Bedford, OH 44146
Tel.: 216-232-3320 **PA**
Fax: 216-232-2772
Year Founded: 1938
Approx.Sls.: $45,000,000
Emp.: 320
Mfr. of Pharmaceuticals
S.I.C.: 2834
Edward C. Smith *(Chm. Bd. & Chief Exec. Officer)*
Thomas R. Russillo *(Pres. & Chief Oper. Officer)*
Mary R. Smith *(V.P. & Sec.)*
Charles F. Grosel *(V.P.-Admin. & Engrng.)*
Charles Insalaco *(V.P.-Opers.)*
Gary L. Price *(Treas. & Comptroller)*

THE BENATTY CORPORATION
61234 Southgate Rd.
Cambridge, OH 43725
Mailing Address:
P.O. Box 75,
Cambridge, OH 43725
Tel.: 614-439-5506
Fax: 614-439-3409
Assets: $7,440,000
Earnings: $1,968,000
Net Worth: $7,440,000
Approx.Sls.: $12,000,000
Emp.: 30
Fiscal Year-end: 12/31/89
Exploration & Production of Oil & Natural Gas
S.I.C.: 1311; 1382
Gerald Benson *(Chm. Bd., Pres. & Chief Exec. Officer)*
Susan Bates *(Controller, Chief Fin. Officer & Sec.)*
Joseph Ezratty *(Treas.)*

No. of U.S. Offices: 1

Computer Systems/Hardware:
IBM

Outside Service Firm(s):

Thomas Flynn, CPA*(Auditors)*
Columbus, OH

Central Reserve Life Insurance Co.*(Group Insurer)*
Durham, NC

Emens, Kegler, Brown, Hill & Ritter*(Legal Firm)*
65 E. State St.
Columbus, OH 43215
Tel.: 614-462-5400

BancOhio National Bank*(Major Banking Relationship)*
Columbus, OH

Peoples Bank*(Major Banking Relationship)*
Martins Ferry, OH

Subsidiary:

Rason Oil & Gas Corp. **(1)**
61234 Southgate Pkwy.
Cambridge, OH 43725
Tel.: 614-439-5506 (100%)
S.I.C.: 1311; 1382

BENCHMARK HOMES, INC.
630 Hay Ave.
Brookville, OH 45309
Tel.: 513-833-4091
Fax: 513-833-5268
Approx.Sls.: $20,000,000
Emp.: 100
Mfr. of Pre-Fab Manufactured Housing
S.I.C.: 2952
George Kirby *(Pres.)*
Dan Riedel *(Chief Exec. Officer & Pres.-Benchmark Communities Inc.)*
Todd Bailey *(Adv. Dir.)*

BENCO INDUSTRIES, INC.
One Benco Industrial Dr.
Fort Deposit, AL 36032
Tel.: 205-227-4333 **TN**
Fax: 205-227-8718
Approx.Sls.: $14,000,000
Emp.: 200
Fiscal Year-end: 6/30/90
Mfr. of Illuminated & Non-Illuminated Indoor & Outdoor Signs & Displays Using Industrial Plastics
S.I.C.: 3993
Jerry Schweiner *(Chm. Bd., Pres. & Chief Exec. Officer)*
T.L. Hollingsworth *(V.P.)*
Ron McSpadden *(V.P. & Controller)*
Leo Fritch *(Asst. V.P.-Sls.-S.W. Reg.)*
Bill Janner *(Mktg. Mgr.)*

Computer Systems/Hardware:
DEC

Outside Service Firm(s):

Pugh & Co.*(Auditors)*
Knoxville, TN

Lincoln National Insurance Co.*(Group Insurer)*
Knoxville, TN

Whitesell, Morrow & Romine*(Legal Firm)*
Montgomery, AL

First Tennessee Bank, N.A.*(Major Banking Relationship)*
Knoxville, TN

BENDER SHIPBUILDING & REPAIR COMPANY
265 S. Water St.
Mobile, AL 36603
Tel.: 205-431-8000 **AL**
Fax: 205-432-2260
Approx.Sls.: $60,000,000
Emp.: 600
Shipbuilding & Reapir
S.I.C.: 3731
Thomas B. Bender, Jr. *(Chm. Bd. & Pres.)*
Robert A. Beckman *(V.P.-Ship Repair)*
Bruce J. Croushore *(V.P., Sec. & Gen. Counsel)*
Danny R. Irby *(V.P.-New Construction)*
Danny C. Sellers *(V.P.-Mfg. Support)*
Dina B. Middlekauff *(Treas.)*

Outside Service Firm(s):

Deloitte & Touche*(Auditors)*
417 No. 20th St., Ste. 1000
Birmingham, AL 35203-3289
Tel.: 205-322-0534

AmSouth Bank N.A.*(Major Banking Relationship)*
P.O. Box 11426
Birmingham, AL 35202
Tel.: 205-326-5321

BENDERSON DEVELOPMENT CO., INC.
570 Delaware Ave.
Buffalo, NY 14202
Tel.: 716-886-0211
Fax: 716-886-2269
Year Founded: 1957
Assets: $173,000,000
Liabilities: $136,000,000
Net Worth: $37,000,000
Approx.Sls.: $90,000,000
Emp.: 150
Fiscal Year-end: 3/31/92
Real Estate Development & Management
S.I.C.: 6552; 6531
Nathan Benderson *(Pres.)*
Alan Wolfson *(Chief Fin. Officer)*
David Baldauf *(V.P. & Sec.)*
Randall Benderson *(V.P.-Opers. & Chief Exec. Officer)*
Rex Burgher *(V.P.-Mktg.)*
Robert Kearney *(V.P.-MIS)*
David Baldave *(Gen. Counsel)*
Anthony Battista *(Mgr.-Property)*
Mike Yeomans *(Mgr.-Construction & Engrng.)*

Outside Service Firm(s):

Brock, Schechter & Polakoff*(Auditors)*
Buffalo, NY

Borins, Setel, Snitzer & Brownstein*(Legal Firm)*
Buffalo, NY

Chase Lincoln First Bank, N.A.*(Major Banking Relationship)*
295 Main St.
Buffalo, NY 14203
Tel.: 716-849-8531

THE BENHAM GROUP
One Benham Place, 9400 N. Broadway
Oklahoma City, OK 73114-0400
Mailing Address:
P.O. Box 20400
Oklahoma City, OK 73156-0400
Tel.: 405-478-5353
Fax: 405-478-1238
Year Founded: 1909
Approx.Sls.: $32,000,000
Emp.: 461
Engineering & Architectural Services
S.I.C.: 8711; 8712; 8742
John F. Benham *(Vice Chm.)*
Donald L. Wickens *(Chm. & Pres.)*
Allen Smith *(Chief Fin. Officer, Treas. & Sec.)*
William E. Allison *(Sr. V.P.-Structural)*
Webster Lance Benham, III *(Sr. V.P.-Mechanical)*
Joe R. Moody *(Sr. V.P.-Electrical)*
Larry Roach *(Sr. V.P.-Civil)*
N. Ross Bell *(V.P.-Architecture)*

William N. Holway *(V.P. & Grp. Exec.-Water & Power)*
Harry A. Koenig, Jr. *(V.P.-Architecture)*
Kenneth A. Nelson *(V.P.-Electrical & Asst. Sec.)*
Allen G. Poppino *(V.P. & Grp. Exec.-Transportation)*
Richard D. Prahl *(V.P.-Industrial & Asst. Sec.)*

No. of U.S. Offices: 8

Computer Systems/Hardware:
Prime

Outside Service Firm(s):

Deloitte & Touche*(Auditors)*
101 N. Robinson
Oklahoma City, OK 73102
Tel.: 405-239-6891

Ledbetter Insurance*(Commercial Insurance Carrier)*
Oklahoma City, OK

Prudential Insurance Co. of America*(Group Insurer)*
Oklahoma City, OK

Bank of Oklahoma*(Major Banking Relationship)*
201 Robert S. Kerr Ave.
Oklahoma City, OK 73102
Tel.: 918-588-6000

Bank of Oklahoma*(Pension Manager)*
One Williams Center
Tulsa, OK 74012
Tel.: 918-588-5100

BENJAMIN FRANKLIN LITERARY & MEDICAL SOCIETY, INC.
1100 Waterway Blvd.
Indianapolis, IN 46202
Mailing Address:
P.O. Box 567
Indianapolis, IN 46206
Tel.: 317-636-8881
Fax: 317-637-0126
Year Founded: 1976
Approx.Sls.: $12,500,000
Emp.: 80
Fiscal Year-end: 12/31/91
Publishers of Health, Medical & Literary Magazines: Turtle Magazine; Humpty Dumpty's Magazine; Children's Playmate; Jack & Jill; Child Life; Children's Digest; Medical Update; The Saturday Evening Post
S.I.C.: 2721
Cory SerVaas, M.D. *(Chm. Bd., Pres. & Chief Exec. Officer)*
Robert Silvers *(Sr. V.P., Assoc. Publisher & Sec.)*
Terry Clark *(Controller)*
Dwight Lamb, Jr. *(V.P., Treas. & Production Mgr.-Post)*
Donald R. Sutton *(Dir.-Mktg.)*
Ted Kreiter *(Exec. Editor)*
Greg Joray *(Circulation Mgr.)*

Divisions:

The Saturday Evening Post Society **(1)**
1100 Waterway Blvd.
Indianapolis, IN 46202
Tel.: 317-636-8881
Fax: 317-637-0126
Publisher of The Saturday Evening Post
S.I.C.: 2721
Cory SerVaas, M.D. *(Pres. & Chief Exec. Officer)*
Donald R. Sutton *(Dir.-Mktg.)*

Children's Better Health Institute **(1)**
1100 Waterway Blvd.
Indianapolis, IN 46202
Tel.: 317-636-8881
Jeff Richardson *(Dir.-Mktg.)*

BENJAMIN METALS COMPANY
14400 S. Figueroa St.
Gardena, CA 90248
Mailing Address:
P.O. Box 59906
Los Angeles, CA 90059
Tel.: 213-321-1700
Fax: 213-770-0102
Approx.Sls.: $40,000,000
Emp.: 90
Import Export
Aluminum Bars, Rods, Sheets & Plates
S.I.C.: 5051
Mark E. Benjamin *(Pres.)*
Ed Purvis *(Exec. V.P.)*
Doug Hopper *(Gen. Sls. Mgr.)*

No. of Mfg. Plants/Facilities: 1
No. of U.S. Offices: 1

Outside Service Firm(s):

Vineberg & Brown*(Auditors)*
Los Angeles, CA

BENJAMIN MOORE & CO.
51 Chestnut Ridge Rd.
Montvale, NJ 07645
Tel.: 201-573-9600
Year Founded: 1883
Approx.Sls.: $438,000,000
Emp.: 1,500
Export
Mfr. of Paints, Stains & Enamels
S.I.C.: 2851
R. Roob *(Chm. Bd.)*
M.C. Workman *(Pres.)*
M.C. Quaid *(Exec. V.P.)*
B.M. Belcher, Jr. *(V.P.-Planning & Sec.)*
W.C. Belcher *(V.P.-Opers.)*
Y. Dupuy *(V.P.-Mktg.)*
W.J. Fritz *(V.P.-Fin. & Treas.)*
R H. Delventhal *(Controller)*
R.T. Knauer *(Dir.-Pur.)*
S. Langner *(Dir.-Pub. Rels.)*
C.R. Arnau *(Mgr.-Sls.)*
S.J. Rozzi *(Mgr.-Corp. Mktg.)*
D. Wilson *(Corp. Export)*
Principal(s):
R. Roob
M.C. Workman

Computer Systems/Hardware:
IBM System 4341

Outside Service Firm(s):

Deloitte & Touche*(Auditors)*
411 Hackensack Ave.
Hackensack, NJ 07601-6367
Tel.: 201-646-7700

Chemical Banking Corporation*(Major Banking Relationship)*
450 W. 33rd. St.
New York, NY 10001
Tel.: 212-613-7147

Divisions:

Benjamin Moore & Co. **(1)**
North & 25th Aves.
Melrose Park, IL 60160
Tel.: 708-343-3100
Export
Mfg. Paint, Stains & Clear Finishes
S.I.C.: 2851
J.S. May *(V.P.)*

Benjamin Moore & Co. **(1)**
4400 E. 71st St.
Cleveland, OH 44105
Tel.: 216-341-1611
S.I.C.: 2851

Subsidiary:

Technical Coatings Co. **(1)**
57 E. Centre St
Nutley, NJ 07110
Tel.: 201-667-8400
S.I.C.: 2851
R.J. Hodgson *(Gen. Mgr.)*

BENNETT BROTHERS, INC.
30 E. Adams St.
Chicago, IL 60603
Tel.: 312-263-4800 **IL**
Fax: 312-621-1669
Emp.: 100
Catalog & Showroom Sales of Watches & Parts, Diamonds; Home Furnishings; Electrical Appliances; Television & Radio; Photographic Cameras & Projectors Equipment & Supplies; Sporting & Recreation Goods; Gifts & Novelties
S.I.C.: 5094; 5023; 5064; 5043; 5091; 5399
Gail Kirk Bennett, Sr. *(Pres.)*
G. Kirk Bennett, Jr. *(V.P. & Treas.)*
George O. Bennett *(V.P. & Sec.)*
Shirley O. Bennett *(Asst. Sec.)*

Outside Service Firm(s):

Coopers & Lybrand*(Auditors)*
203 N. LaSalle St.
Chicago, IL 60601
Tel.: 312-701-5500

BENNETT KUHN VARNER, INC.
3490 Piedmont Rd., Ste. 1450
Atlanta, GA 30305
Tel.: 404-233-0332
Fax: 404-233-0302
Year Founded: 1989
Approx.Billings: $14,500,000
Emp.: 34
Direct Response
Dick Bennett *(Chm. Bd. & Production Dir.)*
Brent Kuhn *(Pres., New Bus. Contact & Media Dir.)*
Maribett Varner *(Exec. V.P., Client Services)*
Perry Mitchell *(Exec. V.P., Creative Dir.)*

BENNETT RINGROSE WOLSFELD JARVIS, INC.
(Formerly Bennett Ringrose Wolsfeld)
700 Third St., S.
Minneapolis, MN 55415
Tel.: 612-370-0700 **MN**
Fax: 612-370-1378
Year Founded: 1964
Approx.Sls.: $23,000,000
Emp.: 370
Fiscal Year-end: 12/31/92
Civil & Highway Engineering
S.I.C.: 8711
Donald Hunt *(Pres.)*
David J. Bennett *(V.P.)*
Richard P. Wolsfeld, Jr. *(V.P.)*
Donald W. Ringrose *(Dir.-Urban Infrastructure)*

Walter Bennett Communications

WALTER BENNETT COMMUNICATIONS
7111 Valley Green Rd., Ste. 220
Fort Washington, PA 19034
Tel.: 215-836-2727
Fax: 215-836-2726
Year Founded: 1950
Approx.Billings: $27,200,000
Emp.: 32
Fred Dienert *(Chm.)*
Robert Straton *(Sr. V.P., Mktg.)*
Louise Tabasso *(Office Mgr.)*

BENNINGTON IRON WORKS, INC.
Harmon Rd.
Bennington, VT 05201
Mailing Address:
P.O. Box 798
Bennington, VT 05201
Tel.: 802-442-3145 **DE**
Fax: 802-447-3440
Approx.Sls.: $11,435,000
Emp.: 85
Fiscal Year-end: 12/31/91
Structural Steel & Miscellaneous Iron Products
S.I.C.: 3321; 3441
Curtis L. Morin *(Pres. & Treas.)*
Thomas Flood *(V.P.-Engrng.)*
Gerald Provost *(V.P.-Sls.)*
John Williams *(Gen. Counsel)*
Susan Campbell *(Pur. Agent)*

Outside Service Firm(s):

Coopers & Lybrand*(Auditors)*
Bennington, VT

McSoley McCoy & Co.*(Auditors)*
Burlington, VT

John H. Williams*(Legal Firm)*
Bennington, VT

First Vermont Bank & Trust Company*(Major Banking Relationship)*
Bennington, VT

BENO'S
1620 S. Los Angeles St.
Los Angeles, CA 90015
Tel.: 213-748-2222 **CA**
Fax: 213-741-2329
Year Founded: 1938
Approx.Sls.: $33,000,000
Emp.: 550
Chain of Retail Stores Carring Women's, Men's & Children's Clothing & Sport Shoes
S.I.C.: 5311
Maxwell H. Salter *(Chm. Bd.)*
Michael Salter *(Pres. & Chief Oper. Officer)*
James A. Caron *(Exec. V.P.)*
Robert Kaufman *(V.P.)*
Larry Johnson *(V.P.-Field Opers.)*

Outside Service Firm(s):

Deloitte & Touche*(Auditors)*
1000 Wilshire Blvd.
Los Angeles, CA 90017-2472
Tel.: 213-688-0800
Fax: 213-688-0100

Capital Bank of California*(Major Banking Relationship)*
Los Angeles, CA

W.L.M. BENSDORP COMPANY
1800 W. Park Dr.
Westborough, MA 01581
Tel.: 508-366-9910
Year Founded: 1840
Approx.Sls.: $12,000,000
Emp.: 4
Fiscal Year-end: 12/31/90
Royal Dutch Cocoa & Chocolate Products
S.I.C.: 2066
Maureen Lussier *(Gen. Mgr.)*

BENSON INDUSTRIES, INC.
1650 N.W. Front #250
Portland, OR 97209
Tel.: 503-226-7611 **OR**
Fax: 503-226-0070
Approx.Sls.: $60,000,000
Emp.: 300
Import Export
Glass & Storefront Contractor; Wholesale Construction Materials & Hardware
S.I.C.: 1793; 5039; 5072

Benson Industries, Inc.—(Continued)

Claris Poppert *(Chm. Bd. & Chief Exec. Officer)*
Lou Niles *(Pres.)*
Mark Beasley *(V.P.)*
Peter V. Potwin *(Treas.)*

Principal(s):
Claris Poppert

No. of Mfg. Plants/Facilities: 3
No. of U.S. Offices: 4
No. of Foreign Offices: 1

Computer Systems/Hardware:
DEC 1134

Outside Service Firm(s):

Price Waterhouse*(Auditors)*
1221 S.W. Morrison, Suite 1800
Portland, OR 97204
Tel.: 503-224-9040

Capital Trust*(Pension Manager)*
Portland, OR

BENSON MANAGEMENT COMPANY
16414 San Pedro Ave., Ste. 9100
San Antonio, TX 78216
Mailing Address:
P.O. Box 34147
San Antonio, TX 78215-5738
Tel.: 210-308-8881 **TX**
Fax: 210-340-5738
Year Founded: 1956
Approx.Sls.: $490,000,000
Emp.: 1,500
Manages Automobile Dealerships
S.I.C.: 8741; 5511
Tom Benson, Jr. *(Chm. Bd. & Pres.)*
Jerome Benson *(V.P.)*
Jack Smith *(Sec.)*
Arnold Gold *(Gen. Sls. Mgr.)*

Principal(s):
Tom Benson, Jr.
Jerome Benson

No. of U.S. Offices: 10

Outside Service Firm(s):

Groos Bank*(Major Banking Relationship)*
San Antonio, TX

THE BENSON MUSIC GROUP
365 Great Circle Rd.
Nashville, TN 37228
Tel.: 615-742-6800
Fax: 615-742-6911
Fax: 615-742-6915
Approx.Sls.: $14,000,000
Emp.: 85
Records, Printed Music, Video Prods.
S.I.C.: 3652; 5099; 7389; 7812
Jerry Park *(Pres.)*
Dan Lynch *(V.P.-Mktg.)*
Sheron Sherman *(Controller)*
Allan Hardin *(Reg. Sls. Mgr.)*
Mike Gay *(Reg. Sls. Mgr.)*

Divisions:

Benson Records **(1)**
365 Great Circle Rd.
Nashville, TN 37228
Tel.: 615-742-6844
Dan Cleary *(Gen. Mgr.)*

Greentree Records **(1)**
365 Great Circle Rd.
Nashville, TN 37228
Tel.: 615-742-6800

Power Discs **(1)**
365 Great Circle Dr.
Nashville, TN 37228
Tel.: 615-742-6873
Ken Pennell *(Label Mgr.)*

Riversong Records **(1)**
365 Great Circle Rd.
Nashville, TN 37228
Tel.: 615-742-6868
Norman Holland *(Label Mgr.)*

BENSON'S, INC.
Elder St.
Bogart, GA 30622
Mailing Address:
P.O. Box 429,
Bogart, GA 30622
Tel.: 706-725-5711
Fax: 706-725-5888
Approx.Sls.: $20,000,000
Emp.: 350
Fiscal Year-end: 6/30/90
Bakeries; Benson's Old Home Kitchens Fruit Cake & Candy; Golden Acres Variety Breads and Rolls; Operates Holiday Inn in Athens, GA
S.I.C.: 2051; 7011
H. E. Benson *(Chm. Bd.)*
Larry R. Benson *(Pres.)*
David R. Ellisor *(V.P.-Fin. & Admin.)*

Divisions:

Benson's of South Carolina **(1)**
1505 Buncombe Rd.
Greenville, SC 29609
Tel.: 803-235-3415
Fax: 803-242-5082
Robert Painter *(Gen. Mgr.)*

Benson's Old Home Kitchens **(1)**
P.O. Box 429
Bogart, GA 30622
Tel.: 706-725-5711
Fax: 706-725-5888
Larry Benson *(Pres.)*

Holiday Inn **(1)**
P.O. Box 1666, Broad & Lumpkin Sts.
Athens, GA 30602
Tel.: 706-549-4433
Fax: 706-548-3031
Hotel
S.I.C.: 7011
Lewis Schropshire *(Gen. Mgr.)*

S. BENT & BROTHERS, INC.
85 Winter St.
Gardner, MA 01440
Tel.: 508-632-4300
Fax: 508-632-3657
Approx.Sls.: $15,000,000
Emp.: 200
Manufacture Wooden Chairs, Tables & Case Goods
S.I.C.: 2511
Gardner L. Bent *(Chm. Bd. & Pres.)*
Roger Leblanc *(Mgr.-Personnel)*
Charles Putnum *(Pur. Agent)*

Outside Service Firm(s):

Arthur Andersen & Co.*(Auditors)*
Manchester, NH

Bowditch & Dewey*(Legal Firm)*
Main St.
Worcester, MA 01608

First Safety Fund National Bank*(Major Banking Relationship)*
Fitchburg, MA

BENT TUBE, INC.
9649 W. Van Buren Rd.
Fowlerville, MI 48836
Mailing Address:
PO Box 709,
Fowler, MI 48836
Tel.: 517-223-9151 **MI**
Year Founded: 1961
Approx.Sls.: $12,000,000
Emp.: 180
Tube Fabricating; Automotive Stampings
S.I.C.: 3498; 3465
William R. Doak *(Pres.)*
Steven Hudson *(V.P.)*
Allen Harper *(Mgr.-Plant)*

Outside Service Firm(s):

First of America Bank*(Major Banking Relationship)*
Howell, MI

BENTEX KIDDIE CORPORATION
112 W. 34th St.
New York, NY 10120
Tel.: 212-594-4250
Fax: 212-967-9328
Approx.Sls.: $25,000,000
Fiscal Year-end: 3/31/92
Girls Dresses; Childrens & Infants Shirts, Slacks, T-Shirts & Outerwear
S.I.C.: 2361; 2369
Ronald Benun *(Pres.)*
Joseph Benun *(V.P.)*
Fred Goldstein *(Controller)*
Eli Benun *(Mgr.-Sls.)*

Outside Service Firm(s):

Ernst & Young*(Auditors)*
787 Seventh Ave.
New York, NY 10019
Tel.: 212-773-1243

Chase Manhattan Bank, N.A.*(Major Banking Relationship)*
One Chase Manhattan Plaza
New York, NY 10081
Tel.: 212-552-2222

BENTLEY, BARNES & LYNN, INC.
420 N. Wabash
Chicago, IL 60611
Tel.: 312-467-9350
Fax: 312-321-5893
Year Founded: 1955
Approx.Billings: $55,000,000
Emp.: 120
Advertising Agency
S.I.C.: 7311
Merrill Litow *(Chm. Bd.)*
Paul K. Oleff *(Pres.)*
Paul Austermuehle *(V.P.)*
Arthur Koff *(V.P.)*
Gary Young *(V.P.)*
Sam Conforti *(Sec. & Treas.)*
Neil O'Sullivan *(Dir.-Data Processing)*
Diane Zdeb *(Dir.-Personnel)*

Computer Systems/Hardware:
Epson Equity One

Outside Service Firm(s):

Aetna Life & Casualty*(Group Insurer)*
151 Farmington Avenue
Hartford, CT 06156
Tel.: 203-273-2128
Fax: 203-729-4295

Boulevard Bank*(Major Banking Relationship)*
410 N. Michigan Ave.
Chicago, IL 60611
Tel.: 312-836-6500

BENTLEY-HARRIS MANUFACTURING CO.
241 Welsh Pool Rd.
Lionville, PA 19353
Tel.: 215-363-2600
Fax: 215-524-9086
Year Founded: 1922
Approx.Sls.: $30,000,000
Emp.: 265
Fiscal Year-end: 12/31/91
Export
Mfr. of Thermal Gasketing, Wrapping Products, Electrical Sleeving, Wire Harnessing Materials
S.I.C.: 3644; 2241
Richard A. Barlow *(Pres. & Chief Exec. Officer)*
Thomas Conaghan *(V.P.-Opers.)*
Ben Treptow *(Mgr.-Sls.)*
Mark Drewicz *(Mgr.-Personnel)*

BENTLEY MILLS, INC.
14641 E. Don Julian Rd.
City of Industry, CA 91746
Tel.: 818-333-4585 **CA**
Fax: 818-333-3103
Year Founded: 1988
Approx.Sls.: $132,000,000
Emp.: 625
Mfr. of Textile Fiber Carpets
S.I.C.: 2273
Royce Renfroe *(Pres. & Chief Exec. Officer)*
Osby Borchardt *(V.P.-Style & Design)*
Randall Drummond *(V.P.-Opers.)*
Jim Harley *(V.P.-Mfg.)*
George Maibach *(V.P.-Sls.)*

Outside Service Firm(s):

Ernst & Young*(Auditors)*
Pasadena, CA

Security Pacific National Bank*(Major Banking Relationship)*
Pasadena, CA

BENTLY NEVADA CORPORATION
P.O. Box 157
Minden, NV 89423
Tel.: 702-782-3611
Telex: 1561105
Fax: 702-782-9253
Year Founded: 1961
Sales Range: $100-499 Million
Emp.: 970
Fiscal Year-end: 12/31/91
Manufacture of Electronic Monitoring Equipment
S.I.C.: 3699; 3612; 3823
Donald E. Bently *(Chm. Bd. & Chief Exec. Officer)*
Roger Harker *(Pres. & Chief Oper. Officer)*
Raymond J. Case *(V.P.-Fin. & Human Resources)*
David H. Biggs *(V.P.-Mfg. & Prod. Devel.)*
Steven Riggs *(V.P.-Sls. & Service)*
William J. Shaw *(Co. Sec.)*
James Schmid *(Dir.-Personnel)*
Michael Hardman *(Mgr.-Data Processing)*
Robert Shaver *(Quality Assurance)*

No. of Mfg. Plants/Facilities: 1
No. of U.S. Offices: 17
No. of Foreign Offices: 36

Computer Systems/Hardware:
IBM System 38

Outside Service Firm(s):

Coopers & Lybrand*(Auditors)*
333 Market Street, 21st Fl.
San Francisco, CA 94105

Bankers Life & Casualty*(Group Insurer)*
Chicago, IL

Bank of America, N.T. & S.A.*(Major Banking Relationship)*
P.O. Box 37002,
San Francisco, CA 94137

Subsidiaries:

Bently Nevada Corporation - Alignment Service **(1)**
7651 Airport Blvd.
Houston, TX 77061
Tel.: 713-640-1111

Bently Rotor Dynamics Research Corp. **(1)**
P.O. Box 2529
Minden, NV 89423
Tel.: 702-782-3611

Non-U.S. Holdings:

Bently Nevada Canada Ltd. (1)
1906 4th St.
Nisku, AB T0C 2G0, Canada
Tel.: 403-955-8922 (100%)
Mktg. & Sales of Electronic Monitoring Systems
S.I.C.: 5063
Ray Lariviere *(Mng. Dir.)*

Branch:

Bently Nevada Canada ltd. (2)
70 Gibson Dr., Unit 4
Markham, ON L3R 2Z3, Canada
Tel.: 416-475-2240
Mktg. & Sales of Electronic Monitoring Systems
S.I.C.: 5063
Brian Leahy *(Branch Mgr.)*

Bently Nevada Europa B.V. (1)
Weterinweg 14 2641 KM
Pijnacker, Netherlands
Tel.: 1736 5240 (100%)
Mktg. & Sales of Vibration Monitoring Equipment
S.I.C.: 5063

Bently Nevada France S.A.R.L. (1)
30 Ave. de L'Admiral Lemonnier F-78160
Marly-le-Roi, France
Tel.: 139 585 001 (100%)
Mktg. & Sales of Electronic Monitoring Devices
S.I.C.: 5063

Bently Nevada GmbH (1)
Werner-von-Braun Str. 8-10 Postfach 60, D-6078
Neu-Isenburg, Germany
Tel.: 06102/3 40 39 (100%)
Telex: 417 632 BENEV D
Fax: 06102/3 12 50
Mfr. of Vibration Measuring & Analysing Machines
S.I.C.: 3829

Bently Nevada Sales & Service Singapore Pte. Ltd. (1)
101 Thomson Road, Ste. 07-04A
Singapore, Singapore
Tel.: 253 4488 (100%)
Sales & Service of Electronic Monitoring Systems
S.I.C.: 5063

Bently Nevada (UK) Ltd. (1)
2 Kelvin Close Science Park North, Birchwood,
Warrington, Cheshire WA3 7PB, United Kingdom
Tel.: 0925 818 504 (100%)
Telex: 629 831 BENNEV G
Fax: 0925 817819
Mfr. of Vibration Monitoring Equipment & Vibration Proximity Transducers
S.I.C.: 3829

Rotor Dynamics Pty. Ltd. (1)
1 Millers Road
Altona, Victoria 3018, Australia
Tel.: 03 398 5155
Mfr. of Vibration Measuring Equipment
S.I.C.: 3829

BEPCO, INC.
2475 S. Stratford Rd.
Winston-Salem, NC 27103
Mailing Address:
P.O. Box 24159
Winston-Salem, NC 27114-4159
Tel.: 919-760-0740
Fax: 919-768-3756
Emp.: 120
Remanufacturing of Air Brake Components for Heavy Duty Equipment
S.I.C.: 3714
Norman Moore *(Chm. Bd.)*
Steve D. Winters *(Pres. & Chief Exec. Officer)*
B. A. Moore *(Treas.)*
Yvonne Winters *(Sec.)*

Computer Systems/Hardware:
Data General MV 2000

Outside Service Firm(s):

Price Waterhouse*(Auditors)*
1800 One Triad Plaza
Winston-Salem, NC 27101
Tel.: 919-725-0691
Fax: 919-725-5022

Pilot Life*(Group Insurer)*
Greensboro, NC

Greeson & Grace*(Legal Firm)*
Winston-Salem, NC

Triad Bank*(Major Banking Relationship)*
Winston-Salem, NC

First Union National Bank*(Pension Manager)*
Raleigh, NC

Berenson, Isham & Partners, Inc.

BERENSON, ISHAM & PARTNERS, INC.
31 Milk St.
Boston, MA 02109
Tel.: 617-423-1120
Fax: 617-423-4597
Year Founded: 1971
Approx.Billings: $30,100,000
Emp.: 19
Direct Response Marketing
S.I.C.: 7311
Paul S. Berenson *(Chm., Pres. & Dir.-Creative)*
Carolynn C. Isham *(Exec. V.P.)*
James Rosenberg *(Exec. V.P. & Dir.-Mktg.)*
Debra Isenberg *(V.P.)*
Pat DesRoches *(Mgr.-Opers.)*
Dotty Zukoff *(Dir.-Media & Res.)*

BERENTER GREENHOUSE & WEBSTER

BERENTER GREENHOUSE & WEBSTER, INC.
233 Park Ave., South
New York, NY 10003
Tel.: 212-995-9500
Year Founded: 1981
Approx.Billings: $68,500,000
Emp.: 65
Advertising Agency
S.I.C.: 7311
Bill Berenter *(Chm. Bd. & Co-Creative Dir.)*
Martin Greenhouse *(Pres. & Co-Creative Dir.)*
Sandy Frank *(Sr. V.P., Chief Fin. Officer)*
Walter Yablonsky *(Mgr.-Studio)*
Principal(s):
Bill Berenter

LB/A
Lou Beres & Associates, Inc.
Advertising

LOU BERES & ASSOCIATES, INC.
410 N. Michigan Ave.
Chicago, IL 60611
Tel.: 312-670-0470
Fax: 312-670-2586
Year Founded: 1982
Approx.Billings: $15,500,000
Emp.: 25
Louis H. Beres *(Pres. & Chief Exec. Officer)*

Earl Weingarden *(Sr. V.P., Exec. Creative Dir.)*
Ann J. York *(Sr. V.P., Dir. Opers./Services)*
Louis B. Tishler *(Gen. Counsel)*
Sandra Bogunia *(Pub. Rels. Dir.)*
Shannon Clack *(Admin. Asst.)*

Computer Systems/Hardware:
MacIntosh; Microsoft Word; Excel; Pagemaker

BERGELECTRIC CORPORATION
5650 Centinela Blvd.
Los Angeles, CA 90045
Tel.: 310-337-1377 **CA**
Fax: 310-337-2663
Year Founded: 1948
Assets: $37,648,788
Liabilities: $6,466,450
Net Worth: $31,182,338
Approx.Sls.: $63,730,500
Emp.: 460
Fiscal Year-end: 1/31/92
General Electrical Contractor
S.I.C.: 1731
John R. Briscoe *(Pres. & Chief Exec. Officer)*
Robert Drinkward *(Exec. V.P. & Sec.)*
Thomas Anderson *(V.P.-Construction-San Diego)*
Ed Billig *(V.P.-Construction-L.A.)*
Don L. Briscoe *(V.P.-Sls.)*
Paul Crossland *(Dir.-Pur.)*

Outside Service Firm(s):

Union Bank*(Major Banking Relationship)*
3810 Wilshire Blvd.
Los Angeles, CA 90010
Tel.: 213-480-6566

BERGER TRANSFER & STORAGE, INC.
2950 Long Lake Rd.
Saint Paul, MN 55113
Tel.: 612-639-2260
Fax: 612-639-2277
Approx.Sls.: $30,000,000
Emp.: 300
Long Distance & Local Specialized Trucking, Commercial Office & Household Goods Moving & Warehousing
S.I.C.: 4213; 4214; 4225
R.D. Dircks *(Chm. Bd. & Chief Exec. Officer)*
W.R. Dircks *(Pres.)*
R.J. Dircks *(Exec. V.P.-Mktg., Sls. & Adv.)*
Tom Boehme *(V.P.-Fin.)*
Paul Luxem *(Pur. Agent)*
Bill Dircks *(Mgr.-Opers.)*
Thomas Miller *(Mgr.-Personnel)*

Outside Service Firm(s):

Deloitte & Touche*(Auditors)*
900 Pillsbury Ctr.
Minneapolis, MN 55402
Tel.: 612-332-2301
Fax: 612-375-5418

Mackall, Crounse & Moore*(Legal Firm)*
1600 TCF Tower
Minneapolis, MN 55402
Tel.: 612-333-1341

First National Bank of Minneapolis*(Major Banking Relationship)*
120 S. Sixth St.
Minneapolis, MN 55402
Tel.: 612-370-4141

BERGQUIST COMPANY, INC.
5300 Edina Industrial Blvd.
Minneapolis, MN 55439
Tel.: 612-835-2322
Tel.: 800-347-4572 **MN**
Fax: 612-835-4156
Year Founded: 1964

Approx.Sls.: $36,000,000
Emp.: 255
Import Export
Wholesale & Manufacture Electrical & Electronic Devices
S.I.C.: 3679; 3644; 5065
Corporate Giving Program: Company Gives 5% of Net Profits (5% Club) To Various Charities
C.R. Bergquist *(Chm. Bd., Pres. & Chief Exec. Officer)*
Paul Grant *(Chief Fin. Officer & Controller)*
D. Dungey *(Sr. V.P.)*
R. Savage *(Sr. V.P.-Sls. & Mktg.)*
M. Green *(V.P.-Mfg.)*
Bonnie Lyles *(V.P.-Admin. & Mngmt. Information Services)*
Owen Nelson *(Gen. Counsel & Sec.)*

No. of Mfg. Plants/Facilities: 5
No. of U.S. Offices: 5
No. of Foreign Offices: 3

Computer Systems/Hardware:
IBM System 36

Outside Service Firm(s):

Ernst & Young*(Auditors)*
1400 Pillsbury Center
Minneapolis, MN 55402
Tel.: 612-343-1000

Lommen, Nelson, Sullivan*(Legal Firm)*
Minneapolis, MN

First Bank Minneapolis*(Major Banking Relationship)*
P.O. Box A700, 120 S. Sixth St.
Minneapolis, MN 55480
Tel.: 612-370-4141

BERKELEY INDUSTRIES INC.
2825 Laguna Canyon Rd.
Laguna Beach, CA 92652
Mailing Address:
P.O. Box 277
Laguna Beach, CA 92652
Tel.: 714-494-9401
Fax: 714-497-7331
Approx.Sls.: $20,000,000
Emp.: 150
Electronics Mfr.; Avionics Distr.
S.I.C.: 3679; 5065
Edward M. Zimmer, Jr. *(Chm. Bd. & Chief Exec. Officer)*
Richard J. Aaron *(Pres. & Chief Oper. Officer)*
Barbara Barda *(V.P.-Fin. & Admin.)*
Steve Hilbert *(Controller)*
Jeri Mahood *(Acctg. Mgr.)*

Subsidiary:

Telonic Berkeley (1)
2825 Laguna Canyon Rd.
Laguna Beach, CA 92652
Tel.: 714-494-9401
Fax: 714-497-7331
Electronics Mfr.; Avionics Distr.
S.I.C.: 3679; 5065
Richard Aaron *(Pres.)*

BERKLEY, INC.
One Berkley Dr.
Spirit Lake, IA 51360
Tel.: 712-336-1520
Tel.: 800-237-5539
Fax: 712-336-5183
Year Founded: 1937
Approx.Sls.: $50,000,000
Emp.: 450
Fiscal Year-end: 8/31/91
Import Export
Berkley Trilene & Berkley Trimax Fishing Line, Fishing Rods & Lightning Rods; Berkley Steelon Leaders, Ski Tow Ropes, Power Baits, Packaged Rope, Marine & Cordage Items & Outdoor Acces
S.I.C.: 3949
Thomas Bedell *(Pres.)*
Dennis Stulc *(Exec. V.P.)*
Mike Brenny *(Dir.-Sls.)*

Berkley, Inc.—(Continued)

Ben Alspach *(Mgr.-Mktg. Services)*
Linda Rubis *(Mgr.-Adv. Services)*
Charles Skogerboe *(Dir.-Personnel)*
Steve Smith *(Dir.-Pur.)*

Computer Systems/Hardware:
Hewlett Packard

BERKLIFF CORPORATION
180 Madison Ave.
New York, NY 10016
Tel.: 212-683-9880
Fax: 212-683-9887
Sales Range: $20-39 Million
Emp.: 1,000
Mfr. of Women's Underwear & Nightwear
S.I.C.: 2341
Allen Berkley *(Pres.)*
Herbert R. Berkley *(Sec. & Treas.)*
Ariel Medel *(Controller)*

Outside Service Firm(s):

Martin M. Rubin*(Auditors)*
New York, NY

Proskauer, Rose, Goetz & Mendelsohn*(Legal Firm)*
New York, NY

Manufacturers Hanover Trust Co.*(Major Banking Relationship)*
4 New York Plaza
New York, NY 10015
Tel.: 212-633-7938

J.E. BERKOWITZ, LP
Delsea Dr. & Harvard Ave.
Westville, NJ 08093
Tel.: 609-456-7800
Fax: 609-456-1032
Approx.Sls.: $20,000,000
Emp.: 175
Mfr. of Flat Glass Products, Mirrors, Insulating & Tempered Glass
S.I.C.: 3211; 3231
A.M. Berkowitz *(Pres.)*
D.B. Byruch *(V.P. & Controller)*
Jim Carroll *(Mgr.-Plant)*
Robert Price *(Mgr.-Sls.)*
Roger Thomas *(Pur. Agent)*

Outside Service Firm(s):

CoreStates First Pennsylvania Bank, N.A.*(Major Banking Relationship)*
Philadelphia, PA

BERKS PRODUCTS CORPORATION
726 Spring St.
Reading, PA 19604
Tel.: 215-374-5131
Fax: 215-375-1469
Emp.: 250
Wholesale Building Material; Retail Fuel Oil Quarry Products; Manufacture Prefabricated Wooden Buildings & Ready-Mixed Concrete, Plumbing, Heating & Air Conditioning Contractor
S.I.C.: 1442; 1711; 2452; 3273; 5039; 5983
William H. Fehr *(Chm. Bd. & Chief Exec. Officer)*
John Hanon *(Pres.)*
Richard Dodson *(Treas.)*
Samuel Mauger *(Sec.)*
Gary Reidenhour *(Pur. Agent)*

Outside Service Firm(s):

Beard & Company*(Auditors)*
Reading, PA

Meridian Bank*(Major Banking Relationship)*
Reading, PA

Bingaman, Hess, Coblentz & Bell*(Legal Firm)*
601 Penn St.
Reading, PA 19603

Tel.: 215-374-8377

BERKSHIRE INDUSTRIES, INC.
109 Apremont Way
Westfield, MA 01085
Tel.: 413-568-8676
Fax: 413-562-0061
Approx.Sls.: $17,000,000
Emp.: 140
Aircraft Components & Precision Machining
S.I.C.: 3728
Otto Essig *(Chm. Bd.)*
John T. Williams *(Pres.)*
Charles Green *(V.P.-Opers.)*
Henry A. Moran, Jr. *(Sec.)*
Stanley Gelina *(Mgr.-Sls.)*
Steven Swayger *(Mgr.-Quality Control)*

Outside Service Firm(s):

Coopers & Lybrand*(Auditors)*
2300 Bay Bank Tower, 1500 Main St.
Springfield, MA 01101
Tel.: 413-781-7200

Shawmut Bank*(Major Banking Relationship)*
Springfield, MA

THE BERKSHIRE LIFE INSURANCE COMPANY
700 South St.
Pittsfield, MA 01201
Tel.: 413-499-4321
Fax: 413-499-4831
Year Founded: 1851
Approx.Sls.: $55,000,000
Emp.: 778
Life Insurance, Disability Income Insurance, Pensions, Annuities & Mutual Funds
S.I.C.: 6311; 6371
Richard L. Whitehead *(Chm. Bd. & Chief Admin. Officer)*
Albert C. Cornelio *(Pres. & Chief Exec. Officer)*
Richard L. Olewnik *(V.P.-Mktg. Services)*
Thomas S. Franco *(V.P.-Corp. Communications)*
Christopher W. Daly *(Pur. Agent)*

BERLIN STEEL CONSTRUCTION CO.
76 Depot Rd.
Berlin, CT 06037
Mailing Address:
P.O. Box 428
Berlin, CT 06037
Tel.: 203-828-3531 **CT**
Fax: 203-828-5489
Year Founded: 1990
Approx.Sls.: $26,000,000
Emp.: 210
Structural & Miscellaneous Fabricators & Erectors
S.I.C.: 3441; 1791
Carl A. Johnson *(Pres., Chief Exec. & Chief Oper. Officer)*
Kenneth Beaulieu *(Exec. V.P.-Opers.)*
John T. Holcomb *(1st V.P.-Sls.)*
Norman A. Jacques *(V.P.-Fin.)*
Ben Padilla *(Chief Engr.)*
Robert Smith *(Asst. Treas.)*

Outside Service Firm(s):

KPMG Peat Marwick*(Auditors)*
City Place II
Hartford, CT 06103-4103
Tel.: 203-522-3200
Fax: 203-297-5555

Fleet National Bank*(Major Banking Relationship)*
New Britain, CT

THE BERLINE GROUP INC.
31600 Telegraph, Ste. 100
Bingham Farms, MI 48025
Tel.: 313-540-7557
Fax: 313-540-7710
Year Founded: 1982
Approx.Billings: $33,000,000
Emp.: 30
Full Service Advertising, Public Relations & Marketing
Jim Berline *(Pres. & New Bus. Contact)*
Angela Fok *(Treas.)*

BERLITZ INTERNATIONAL, INC.
(d/b/a The Berlitz Language Centers)
293 Wall St.
Princeton, NJ 08540-1555
Tel.: 609-497-9911
Tel.: 800-257-9449 **NY**
Fax: 609-683-9138
Year Founded: 1878
Earnings: ($171,947,000)
Approx.Sls.: $259,771,000
Emp.: 3,630
Fiscal Year-end: 12/31/91
Language Instruction
S.I.C.: 8299
Joe M. Rodgers *(Chm. & Acting Chief Exec. Officer)*
Elio Boccitto *(Pres. & Chief Oper. Officer)*
Manuel Fernandez *(Exec. V.P.)*
Michael Mulligan *(Exec. V.P.)*
Jose Alvarino *(V.P.)*
Paul Gendler *(V.P.)*
Rob Hendon *(V.P.-Corp. Counsel)*
Henry D. James *(V.P. & Worldwide Controller)*
Robert Minsky *(V.P. & Chief Fin. Officer)*
Nancy Nugent *(V.P.- Human Resources)*
Kim Sonne *(V.P.)*
Anthony F. Tedesco *(V.P.)*
Wolfgang Wiedeler *(V.P.)*
Robert C. Hendon, Jr. *(Gen. Counsel & Sec.)*
William Mueller *(Treas.)*
Deidre O. Aubuchon *(Dir.-Fin. Plng. & Analysis)*
Robert Long *(Dir.-Mngmt. Information System)*
Maryanne Reside *(Dir.-Telecommunications)*
Art Sims *(Dir. Real Estate)*
Patricia M. Sze *(Dir.-Mktg.)*

Computer Systems/Hardware:
Hewlett Packard

Language Institute for English (L.I.F.E.) **(1)**
C/O FDU, Kingsland House
Rutherford, NJ 07070
Tel.: 201-460-0070
Fax: 201-460-0131
Language Training
S.I.C.: 8299
Dr. Paul Gendler *(Pres.)*
Alexandra Zilovic *(Exec. V.P.)*

Divisions:

Berlitz Translation Services, Inc. **(1)**
257 Park Ave. So.
New York, NY 10010
Tel.: 212-777-7878
Translation Services
S.I.C.: 7389
Michael J. Mulligan *(Exec. V.P.)*

Non-U.S. Divisions:

Able Translations Limited **(1)**
Meeting House Lane
Baldock, Herts. SG7 5BP, United Kingdom
Translation Services
S.I.C.: 7389
B. Tyler, Esq. *(Mng. Dir.)*

Alpine Center, s.r.l. (Berlitz) **(1)**
Via Mercadante, 17 20124
Milan, Italy
Tel.: 39-2 670-5884 (100%)
Language Instruction
S.I.C.: 8299
Manuel Fernandez *(Mgr.)*
Ferdinando Mantero *(Dir.)*
Elena Ligabue *(Regional Dir.)*
Giulio Turconi *(District Dir.)*

Alps Institute s.r.l. (Berlitz) **(1)**
Via P.L. da Palestrina 19
Rome, 00189, Italy
Tel.: 39-6-320-4624 (100%)
Language Services
S.I.C.: 8299
Elena Ligabue *(Regional Dir.)*
Manuel Fernandez *(Mgr.)*
Antonio Grassi *(Dir.)*

Alps Institute **(1)**
Via P.L. da Palestrina, 19 00189
Rome, Italy
Tel.: 39-6-320-4624 (100%)
Language Services
S.I.C.: 8299
Antonio Grassi *(Dir.)*

Oy Berlitz AB **(1)**
Kaivokatu 10 A 8. Krs. 00100
Helsinki, Finland
Tel.: 358-0-17-64-31 (100%)
Language Instruction
S.I.C.: 8299
Andre-Yves Recorbet *(Dir.)*
Kim Sonne *(Country Mgr.)*

Berlitz Escola de Idiomas Ltda. **(1)**
Praca Charles Miller 16 CEP 01234,
Sao Paulo, S.P. Brazil
Tel.: 55-11-263-1423 (100%)
Language Instruction
S.I.C.: 8299
Daniel Olaso Braga *(Country Mgr.)*
Ademir Baldao *(Country Mgr.)*
Keiji Narazaki *(Controller)*
Lincoln Pow *(Sls. Mgr.)*

Berlitz Escuelas de Idiomas Ltda. **(1)**
Padre Mariano No. 305
Santiago, Chile
Tel.: 56-2-223-0307 (100%)
Language Instruction
S.I.C.: 8299
Gerd Luders *(Country Mgr.)*
Eduardo Morello *(Controller)*

Berlitz International Danmark A/S **(1)**
Vimmelskaftet 42A 1161
Copenhagen, Denmark
Tel.: 12-25-66 (100%)
Language Instruction
S.I.C.: 8299
Kim Sonne *(V.P. & Country Mgr.)*
Ella Frantzen *(Controller)*

Berlitz Language Centers of Canada Ltd. **(1)**
130 Bloor St. W., Ste. 603
Toronto, ON M5S 1N5, Canada
Tel.: 416-924-5167 (100%)
Language Instruction
S.I.C.: 8299
Sandro d'Addario *(Country Mgr.)*

Berlitz Language Centers, S.R.L. **(1)**
Via Cavour 256 00184
Rome, Italy
Tel.: 39-6-481-5294
Language Instruction
S.I.C.: 8299
Elena Ligabue *(Regional Dir.)*
Roberto Minella *(Controller)*

Berlitz de Mexico, S.A. de C.V. **(1)**
530 Ejercito Nacional 11550 Polanco,
Mexico, D.F. Mexico
Tel.: 52-5-255-2987 (100%)
Language Instruction
S.I.C.: 8299
Jose Alvarino *(V.P.)*
Juan Tamez *(Country Mgr.)*
Marcelino Martinez *(Controller)*
Anthony Wilkes *(Dir. Sls.)*

Berlitz A/S **(1)**
Lille Grensen 5 N-0159
Oslo, Norway
Tel.: 47-2-33-10-30 (100%)
Language Services
S.I.C.: 8299
Yvonne Cagnol Hveem *(Dir.)*

Berlitz KFT **(1)**
Sommelweis Utca 2 1052,
Budapest, Hungary
Tel.: 36-11-370-014 (100%)
Language Services
S.I.C.: 8299
Eva Baumgartner *(Dir.)*

Berlitz Publishing Company Inc. **(1)**
257 Park Ave. So.
New York, NY 10010
Tel.: 212-777-7878 (100%)
Fax: 212-505-9975
Emp.: 250
Self-Teaching Language Programs
S.I.C.: 2731
Michael J. Mulligan *(Exec. V.P.)*
Elio Boccitto *(Pres.)*
Robert Minsky *(V.P. & Chief Fin. Officer)*
Robert Miller *(V.P.-Self-Teaching)*
Ellen Mastromica *(Dir.)*
Joseph McLaughlin *(Dir.-Sales)*
Patricia M. Sze *(Dir.-Mktg.)*

Berlitz Schools of Languages AB **(1)**
Vasgatan 52 111 20
Stockholm, Sweden
Tel.: 14-18-80 (100%)
Language Instruction
S.I.C.: 8299
Kim Sonne *(Country Mgr.)*
Andre-Yves Recorbet *(District Dir.)*

Berlitz Schools of Languages Czechsolovakia Spol.sr.o **(1)**
Na Porici 12
Prague, 1-110.00, Czechoslovakia
Tel.: 42-2-287-2052 (100%)
Language Services
S.I.C.: 8299
Hanna Navotna *(Dir.)*

Berlitz Schools of Languages GmbH **(1)**
Kaiser Str. 66 Postfach 160 164, 6000
Frankfurt/Main, 1, Germany
Tel.: 49-69-271-0000 (100%)
Language Instruction
S.I.C.: 8299
Wolfgang Wiedeler *(V.P. & Country Mgr.)*
Inge Haesser *(Controller)*
Gerhard Bertges *(Sls. Dir.)*
Hans-Jurgen Hess *(Personnel Dir.)*

Berlitz Schools of Languages B.V. **(1)**
Robin 87-89 1012 KL,
Amsterdam, Netherlands
Tel.: 31-20-622-1375 (100%)
Language Instruction
S.I.C.: 8299
Constant Reinders *(Country Mgr.)*
Hedwig Baetens *(Controller)*
Lidy Bosken *(Sls. Dir.)*

The Berlitz Schools of Languages (Japan) Inc. **(1)**
Kowa Bldg. No. 1, 5F, 1-11-41 Akasaka
Minato-ku,
Tokyo, 107, Japan
Tel.: 81-3-3589-3525 (80%)
Language Instruction
S.I.C.: 8299
Jacques Meon *(V.P. & Country Mgr.)*
Kazumi Kitamura *(Controller)*
Michiko Vakayama *(Mgr. Admin.)*

Berlitz Schools of Languages Ltd. **(1)**
Wells House, 79 Wells St.
London, W1A 3BZ, United Kingdom
Tel.: 44-71-637-0330 (100%)
Telex: 27653
Fax: 071-323-2880
Language Instruction
S.I.C.: 8299
Rosalie Read *(Country Mgr.)*
Richard Freeman *(Controller)*

Berlitz Schools of Languages of Argentina S.A. **(1)**
Avenida Santa Fe 1605
Buenos Aires, 1060 Argentina
Tel.: 54-1-41-78-76 (100%)
Language Instruction
S.I.C.: 8299
Paul Manen *(Country Mgr.)*
Carlos Bassetti *(Country Mgr.)*
Carlos Cuesta *(Fin. Controller)*

Berlitz Schools of Languages of Benelux S.A. **(1)**
306-310 Avenue Louise Boite 3 or 7, 1050
Brussels, Belgium
Tel.: 649-5676 (100%)
Language Instruction
S.I.C.: 8299
Constant Reinders *(Country Mgr.)*
Hedwig Baetens *(Controller)*
Eric Werbrouck *(Sls. Dir.)*

Berlitz France S.A. **(1)**
29 rue de la Michodiere 75002
Paris, France
Tel.: 47-42-46-54 (100%)
Language Instruction
S.I.C.: 8299
Patrick Morel *(Country Mgr.)*
Guy Simon *(Controller)*

Berlitz Schools of Languages AG **(1)**
1, Carrefour de Rive CH 1207
Geneva, Switzerland
Tel.: 21-52-83
Language Instruction
S.I.C.: 8299
Wolfgang Wiedeler *(V.P. & Country Mgr.)*
Elizabeth Schuster *(Dir. Sls. & Mktg.)*
Suzanne Uremery *(District Dir.)*

Berlitz Sprachschulen GmbH **(1)**
Graben 13 A-1010
Vienna, Austria
Tel.: 43-222-586-1286 (100%)
Language Instruction
S.I.C.: 8299
Wolfgang Wiedeler *(V.P. & Country Mgr.)*
Inge Haesser *(Controller)*
Hans-Juergen Hess *(Personnel Dir.)*

Berlitz Thailand Ltd. **(1)**
Cathay House, 10th Fl., 8 North Sathorn Rd. 10500
Bangkok, Thailand
Tel.: 66-2-235-3853 (100%)
Language Instruction
S.I.C.: 8299
Hans-Martin Peters *(Country Mgr.)*

Centro de Idiomas Berlitz de Venezuela **(1)**
Av. Fca De Miranda, Piso 1, Torre Oeste
1062 Los Palos Grandes,
Caracas, Venezuela
Tel.: 58-2-284-2065 (100%)
Language Instruction
S.I.C.: 8299
John Carter *(Country Mgr.)*
Sylvia Mesado *(Controller)*

Europe Language Center SrL **(1)**
V. le Giulio Cesare, 207 00192
Rome, Italy
Tel.: 39-6-591-6645 (100%)
Language Services
S.I.C.: 8299
Daniela Allesandri *(Dir.)*

Escuelas de Idiomas Berlitz de Espana, S.A. **(1)**
Gran Via 80-4 28013
Madrid, Spain
Tel.: 34-1-541-6215 (100%)
Language Instruction
S.I.C.: 8299
Jose Sanchez *(Country Mgr.)*
Armando Garcia *(Controller)*

International Learning Systems (Japan) Ltd. **(1)**
1-7-1 Nishi-Shinjuku, Shinjuku-ku
Tokyo, 160, Japan
Tel.: 03-3343-2311 (65%)
Fax: 91-3-344 3405
Distr. of Language Cassettes
S.I.C.: 5099
Mamoru Ofuku *(Pres.)*

Instituto de Idiomas Colombia, S.A. **(1)**
Avenida 13, No. 88-20
Bogota, D.E. Colombia (100%)
Language Instruction
S.I.C.: 8299
Ofelia Diaz *(Country Mgr.)*
Luis Forero *(Controller)*

Kayser Coll. Technische Ubersetzer **(1)**
Postfach 449, D-7032
Sindelfingen, Germany
Translation, Interpretation Services to Commercial Customers
S.I.C.: 7389
Alfred H. Kayser *(Mng. Dir.)*

New York Language Center **(1)**
Via delle Asole, 2 20123
Milan, Italy
Tel.: 39-2-864-50974 (100%)
Language Services
S.I.C.: 8299
Anna Abe *(Dir.)*

Princeton Language Center **(1)**
Via Pascoli, 9
San Donato Milanese, Italy
Tel.: 39-2-523-0537 (100%)
Language Services
S.I.C.: 8299
Patrizia Marasca *(Acting Dir.)*

World Languages SrL **(1)**
V. le Giulio Cesare, 207 00192
Rome, Italy
Tel.: 39-6-3972-6139 (100%)
Language Services
S.I.C.: 8299
Stefania Ruspi *(Acting Dir.)*

Multi Language Center SrL **(1)**
Via Larga, 8 20100
Milan, Italy
Tel.: 39-2-896-0814 (100%)
Language Services
S.I.C.: 8299
Oscar Zannini *(Acting Dir.)*

Vista Multi Method **(1)**
Via di Torre Argentina, 21 00185
Rome, Italy
Tel.: 39-6-654-0951 (100%)
Language Services
S.I.C.: 8299
Umberto Manassei *(Acting Dir.)*

Vista Multi National **(1)**
Via C. Battisti, 2 40123
Bologna, Italy
Tel.: 39-51-264-034 (100%)
Language Services
S.I.C.: 8299
Paola Forni *(Dir.)*

Washington Language Center **(1)**
Via Lagrange, 7 10100
Torino, Italy
Tel.: 39-2-561-1462 (100%)
Language Services
S.I.C.: 8299
Elizabetta Rizzini *(Acting Dir.)*

Joint Ventures:

Berlitz-Cyztelnik Language School **(1)**
UL. Wiejska 12A
Warsaw, 00-490, Poland
Tel.: 48-2-628-3870 (54%)
Language Services
S.I.C.: 8299
Grazyna Slowikowska *(Dir.)*

Berlitz Sovincenter **(1)**
12, Krasnopresenskaya NAB 123610,
Moscow, Russia
Tel.: 7-095-253-8223 (60%)
Language Services
S.I.C.: 8299
Natalija V. Uvarova *(Dir.)*

Softrans International, Ltd. **(1)**
14, Carysfort Ave. Blackrock, Co.,
Dublin, Ireland
Tel.: 353-12-83-13-89 (51%)
Language Services (translations)
S.I.C.: 7389
Brian Kelly *(Managing Dir.)*

World Report Verlag Gmbh **(1)**
W-6242, Minnholzweg 2,
Kronberg, 1, Germany
Tel.: 49-61-73-709168 (51%)
Language Publishing
S.I.C.: 2731
Bernd Munzenmaier *(Gen. Mgr.)*
Hans W. Schneider *(Managing Editor)*

BERMO, INC.
4501 Ball Rd., N.E.
Circle Pines, MN 55014 **MN**
Tel.: 612-786-7676
Fax: 612-785-2159
Approx.Sls.: $18,000,000
Emp.: 140
Stamping Metal For The Trade; Injection Molded Finished Plastic Products
S.I.C.: 3469
Fred P. Berdass *(Chm. Bd.)*
Daniel M. Berdass *(Pres.)*
Margo Berdass *(V.P. & Treas.)*
Linda Heltemes *(Controller)*

Outside Service Firm(s):

McGladrey & Pullen*(Auditors)*
Minneapolis, MN

Richfield Bank & Trust Co.*(Major Banking Relationship)*
Minneapolis, MN

BERNARDS BROTHERS, INC.
610 Ilex St.
San Fernando, CA 91340 **CA**
Tel.: 818-365-9573
Fax: 818-361-9208
Year Founded: 1974
Approx.Sls.: $90,000,000
Emp.: 150
New Construction of Industrial, Commercial & Office Buildings
S.I.C.: 1541; 1542
Douglas Bernards *(Pres.)*
Gregory Bernards *(V.P.)*
Jeffrey Bernards *(V.P. & Sec.)*
Robert H. Hampton *(V.P.)*
Gary Wadsworth *(V.P. & Chief Fin. Officer)*

Outside Service Firm(s):

Leatly Hood & Co.*(Auditors)*
Los Angeles, CA

Kestler & Walsh*(Legal Firm)*
Lancaster, CA

BERNEA FOOD SERVICE, INC.
557 Lincoln Rd.
Otsego, MI 49078
Mailing Address:
P.O. Box 234
Otsego, MI 49078 **MI**
Tel.: 616-694-9478
Fax: 616-694-6052
Year Founded: 1974
Assets: $3,573,009
Liabilities: $2,480,196
Net Worth: $1,092,813
Approx.Sls.: $27,000,000
Emp.: 71
Fiscal Year-end: 9/30/91
Distributor of Dairy Products
S.I.C.: 5143; 5149
Philip Berner *(Pres.)*
Mike Summers *(V.P.-Mktg.)*
John Winters *(Treas.)*
Bill Clock *(Dir.-Pur.)*

Principal(s):
Philip Berner

No. of Mfg. Plants/Facilities: 1

Computer Systems/Hardware:
IBM

Outside Service Firm(s):

K. William Gidris*(Auditors)*
Grand Rapids, MI

ASR*(Group Insurer)*
Grand Rapids, MI

Old Kent Bank*(Investment Banker)*
Kalamazoo, MI

Warner, Norcross and Judd*(Legal Firm)*
900 Old Kent Bldg.
Grand Rapids, MI 49503
Tel.: 616-459-6121

Old Kent Bank*(Major Banking Relationship)*
Kalamazoo, MI

BERNHARD MECHANICAL CONTRACTOR, INC.
10321 Airline Hwy.
Baton Rouge, LA 70816
Mailing Address:
P.O. Box 15687,
Baton Rouge, LA 70895
Tel.: 504-293-2791

Bernhard Mechanical Contractor, Inc.—(Continued)

Fax: 504-296-0931
Year Founded: 1908
Approx.Sls.: $12,771,000
Emp.: 85
Mechanical Contractor
S.I.C.: 1711
Charles R. Bernhard *(Pres.)*
James M. Bernhard *(V.P.)*
Alice B. McCraine *(Sec. & Treas.)*

Outside Service Firm(s):

Hannis T. Bourgois*(Auditors)*
Baton Rouge, LA

Hibernia National Bank*(Major Banking Relationship)*
New Orleans, LA

BERNHARDT FURNITURE CO.
1839 Morganton Blvd., S.W.
Lenoir, NC 28645
Tel.: 704-758-9811
Fax: 704-754-0321
Sales Range: $100-499 Million
Emp.: 2,400
Fiscal Year-end: 11/30/92
Manufacturer of Wood & Upholstered Dining Room, Living Room & Bedroom Furniture
S.I.C.: 2511; 2512
John C. Bernhardt *(Chm. Bd.)*
George A. Bernhardt *(Pres.)*
Lewis G. Norman, III *(Exec. V.P.)*
Rountree Collett *(V.P., Sec. & Treas.)*
William M. Deal *(V.P.)*
Dan B. Wortman *(V.P.-Human Resources)*

Outside Service Firm(s):

Deloitte & Touche*(Auditors)*
Lenoir, NC

First Union National Bank*(Major Banking Relationship)*
Lenoir, NC

SANFORD C. BERNSTEIN & CO., INC.
767 Fifth Ave.
New York, NY 10153
Tel.: 212-486-5800 **NY**
Fax: 212-756-4574
Year Founded: 1967
Assets: $435,783,000
Liabilities: $393,184,000
Net Worth: $42,599,000
Emp.: 491
Fiscal Year-end: 12/31/91
Investment Advising, Investment Banking & Research, Pension Managers
S.I.C.: 6211; 6282; 6371
Zalman C. Bernstein *(Chm. & Chief Exec. Officer)*
Lewis A. Sanders *(Pres.)*
Roger Hertog *(Exec. V.P.)*
Andrew S. Adelson *(Sr. V.P.)*
Kevin R. Brine *(Sr. V.P.)*
Charles C. Cahn, Jr. *(Sr. V.P.)*
Peter Carmen *(Sr. V.P.)*
Joseph B. Greeley *(Sr. V.P.-Opers.)*
Stuart K. Nelson *(Sr. V.P. & Gen. Counsel)*
Francis H. Trainer Jr. *(Sr. V.P.)*
George Reid *(Dir.-Computer Opers.)*

No. of U.S. Offices: 3

Computer Systems/Hardware:
IBM System 4381

Outside Service Firm(s):

BDO Seidman*(Auditors)*
1430 Broadway
New York, NY
Tel.: 212-765-7500

Coopers & Lybrand*(Auditors)*
1301 Avenue of The Americas
New York, NY 10019
Tel.: 212-536-2000

Price Waterhouse*(Auditors)*
153 E. 53rd St., 44th Fl.
New York, NY 10022
Tel.: 212-371-2000

Shereff, Friedman, Hoffman & Goodman*(Legal Firm)*
919 Third Ave.
New York, NY 10022
Tel.: 212-758-9500

BR
BERNSTEIN REIN

BERNSTEIN-REIN ADVERTISING, INC.
4600 Madison
Kansas City, MO 64112
Tel.: 816-756-0640
Fax: 816-756-1753
Year Founded: 1964
Approx.Billings: $135,000,000
Emp.: 200
Corporate Giving Program: United Way
Robert Bernstein *(Chm. Bd., Pres. & Chief Exec. Officer)*
Irwin "Skip" Rein *(Exec. V.P.)*
Stan Seligson *(V.P., Chief Fin. Officer)*
Phil Spell *(V.P., Dir. Yellow Pages)*
Thomas Peacock *(Chief Information Officer & Information System Mgr.)*
Herbert Kohn *(Treas. & Gen. Counsel)*
Rose Messick *(Corp. Sec. & Dir., Acctg. Services)*
Irene Pasternak *(Dir., Community Affairs)*
Dan Willinsky *(Mgr., Pub. Rels.)*

Computer Systems/Hardware:
Honeywell

THE BERNUTH CORPORATION
1405 S.W. 107th Ave.
Miami, FL 33176
Tel.: 305-225-9194
Fax: 305-598-9197
Approx.Sls.: $30,000,000
Emp.: 50
Import & Export Creosote, Lumber, Chemicals
S.I.C.: 5169; 5031; 5085
Peter K. Bernuth *(Chm. Bd., Pres. & Treas.)*
Dorothy Kohler *(Sec.)*
Thomas Gary *(Gen. Counsel)*

Outside Service Firm(s):

Post Oak Bank*(Major Banking Relationship)*
Miami, FL

BERRY BEARING CO.
4242 S. 1st Ave.
Lyons, IL 60534
Tel.: 708-442-1200
Fax: 708-442-0147
Year Founded: 1920
Approx.Sls.: $330,000,000
Emp.: 1,300
Fiscal Year-end: 9/30/92
Distributor of Bearings & Power Transmission Equipment
S.I.C.: 5085
Gardner Larned *(Chm. Bd., Pres., & Chief Exec. Officer)*
Ross Andersen *(V.P. & Chief Fin. Officer)*
James McWethy *(V.P.)*
Richard Curtin *(Corp. Sec. & Gen. Counsel)*
James Hopper *(Dir.-Information Systems)*

Principal(s):
Gardner Larned

No. of Mfg. Plants/Facilities: 75

Computer Systems/Hardware:
IBM System 3090

Outside Service Firm(s):

Ernst & Young*(Auditors)*
233 S. Wacker Dr.
Chicago, IL 60606
Tel.: 312-368-1800
Fax: 312-645-3095

Curtin & Tryzna*(Legal Firm)*
Chicago, IL

Continental Bank N. A.*(Major Banking Relationship)*
231 S. LaSalle St.
Chicago, IL 60697
Tel.: 312-828-2345
Tel.: 800-426-5754
Telex: 312-828-1783

John Hancock Mutual Life Insurance Co.*(Pension Manager)*
John Hancock Place, P.O. Box 111
Boston, MA 02117

BERRY-BROWN ADVERTISING, INC.
2602 McKinney Ave., Ste. 300
Dallas, TX 75204
Tel.: 214-871-1001
Fax: 214-871-1137
Year Founded: 1972
Approx.Billings: $28,200,000
Emp.: 51
Fiscal Year-end: 12/31/91
Advertising Agency
S.I.C.: 7311
Robert E. Berry *(Chm. Bd.)*
Robert D. Brown *(Pres.)*
Phil Schieber *(Chief Fin. Officer)*
Gary Bradbury *(V.P.)*
Carol Irwin *(V.P.)*
Elias Lucero *(V.P.)*
Tricia Magel *(V.P.)*
Tom Prikryl *(V.P.-Berry Brown Bus. Grp.)*

Computer Systems/Hardware:
IBM

Outside Service Firm(s):

Travis & Associates*(Auditors)*
Dallas, TX

Kroney, Silverman*(Legal Firm)*
Dallas, TX

BERRY COMPANIES, INC.
3223 N. Hydraulic
Wichita, KS 67219
Mailing Address:
P.O. Box 829,
Wichita, KS 67201
Tel.: 316-832-0171 **KS**
Fax: 316-832-1375
Year Founded: 1957
Approx.Sls.: $49,000,000
Emp.: 220
Fiscal Year-end: 3/31/92
Lease & Wholesale Construction & Industrial Equipment
S.I.C.: 5082; 5084
Fred F. Berry, Jr. *(Pres.)*
Jerry Edwards *(Sr. V.P, Sec. & Treas.)*

Outside Service Firm(s):

Allen, Gibbs, Houlik*(Auditors)*
301 N. Main, Ste. 1700
Wichita, KS 67202
Tel.: 316-267-7231

Foulston & Siefkin*(Legal Firm)*
700 Fourth Financial Center
Wichita, KS 67202
Tel.: 316-267-6371

Bank IV*(Major Banking Relationship)*
P.O. Box 1122,
Wichita, KS 67201
Tel.: 316-261-4304

BERRYMAN PRODUCTS, INC.
3800 E. Randol Mill Rd.
Arlington, TX 76011
Tel.: 817-640-2376
Tel.: 800-433-1704
Fax: 817-640-4850
Year Founded: 1918
Approx.Sls.: $20,000,000
Emp.: 52
Fiscal Year-end: 9/31/92
Export
Mfr. Lubricating Oils & Greases; Specialty Cleaning, Polishing & Sanitation Preparations; Automotive Chemicals, Fuel Conditioners, Carburator Cleaner, Parts Cleaners, Degreasers, Aerosol Lubricants, Tire Sealers
S.I.C.: 2842; 2911
Truman Blankenship *(Pres.)*
Charles F. Hillman *(V.P.-Sls.)*
Jim Sanderson *(Dir.-Pur.)*
Lisa Young *(Co-op Adv.)*

BERTRAND ADVERTISING AGENCY, INC.
1680 N. Vine St., Ste. 406
Hollywood, CA 90028
Tel.: 213-464-8181
Year Founded: 1950
Approx.Billings: $18,000,000
Emp.: 24
Employment Recruitment Adv.
Leona C. Bertrand *(Owner & Pres.)*
Dr. Stephanie Stolarz-Fantino *(Exec. V.P., Sec.)*
Diane Andre *(Comptroller)*
Lily Edwards *(Treas. & Office Mgr.)*
Maxine Kellem *(Billing Supvr.)*

BERWICK BAY OIL CO. INC.
1020 David Dr.
Morgan City, LA 70380
Mailing Address:
P.O. Box 2708
Morgan City, LA 70381
Tel.: 504-384-1610 **LA**
Fax: 504-384-1611
Year Founded: 1957
Assets: $22,300,000
Liabilities: $18,900,000
Net Worth: $3,400,000
Approx.Sls.: $137,000,000
Emp.: 75
Fiscal Year-end: 2/29/88
Water Transportation; Marine Petroleum Distributor; Boat & Barge Rentals; Convenience Store Owner
S.I.C.: 4499; 5172; 5399
W. McKerall O'Neill, Jr. *(Chm. Bd.)*
John O'Neill *(Pres.)*

Principal(s):
W. McKerall O'Neill, Jr.
John O'Neill

Computer Systems/Hardware:
IBM System 38

Outside Service Firm(s):

Coopers & Lybrand*(Auditors)*
New Orleans, LA

Continental Insurance*(Commercial Insurance Carrier)*
180 Maiden Lane
New York, NY

Louisiana Oil Marketers Association*(Group Insurer)*
Shreveport, LA

McGlinchey, Stafford, Cellini & Lang*(Legal Firm)*
643 Magazine St.
New Orleans, LA 70130

First National Bank of Commerce*(Major Banking Relationship)*
New Orleans, LA

St. Mary's Bank*(Major Banking Relationship)*
Franklin, LA

BERWIND CORPORATION
3000 W. Tower, Centre Square, 1500 Market St.
Philadelphia, PA 19102
Tel.: 215-563-2800 **PA**
Fax: 215-563-8347
Year Founded: 1886
Approx.Sls.: $395,000,000
Emp.: 3,300
Fiscal Year-end: 12/31/90
Mines Bituminous Coal; Leases Coal Lands; Manufactures Auto Parts; Repairs Railroad Cars; Real Estate Services; Chemical Specialties; Security Systems & Alarm Products; Highway & Bridge Expansion Segments; Electronic Pressure Transducers & Power Supplies
S.I.C.: 1221; 3822; 3559; 6531; 6519; 2819; 2865; 3714; 6399; 1222
Employee Matching Gifts Program: Matches Employee Gifts up to $1, 000 to Educational Institutions
C. Graham Berwind, Jr. *(Chm. Bd., Pres., Chief Exec. & Chief Oper. Officer)*
Dennis P. Conlon *(V.P.-Devel.)*
W.J. Eckenrode *(V.P.-Fin. & Admin.)*
William W. Heilig *(V.P. & Treas.)*
Bruce J. McKenney *(V.P.-Tax & Fin. Plng.)*
Richard D. Rivers *(V.P., Gen. Counsel & Asst. Sec.)*
Mary La Rue *(Sec.)*
J.N. Sicks *(Asst. Sec.)*
June Beal *(Mgr.-Employee Benefits)*

No. of Mfg. Plants/Facilities: 12
No. of U.S. Offices: 9
No. of Foreign Offices: 16

Computer Systems/Hardware:
IBM PC

Outside Service Firm(s):

Alexander & Alexander*(Auditors)*
Public Ledger Bldg.
Philadelphia, PA 19106
Tel.: 215-923-5300
Fax: 215-923-5024

Metropolitan Life Insurance Co.*(Group Insurer)*
One Madison Ave.
New York, NY 10010-3690
Tel.: 215-578-9292

Dechert, Price & Rhoads*(Legal Firm)*
4000 Bell Atlantic Tower, 1717 Arch St.
Philadelphia, PA 19103
Tel.: 215-994-4000
Tel.: 2000

Subsidiaries:

Berwind Coal Sales Company **(1)**
3000 Centre Square West
Philadelphia, PA 19102
Tel.: 215-563-2800
Coal Sales Agent
S.I.C.: 5052
Harry M. Easton *(Pres.)*

Berwind Natural Resources Corporation **(1)**
1500 Market St.
Philadelphia, PA 19102
Tel.: 215-563-2800
Emp.: 23
Management of Mining & Coal Lands Leasing
S.I.C.: 1221; 1222
T. V. Falkie *(Pres.)*

Berwind Property Group, Inc. **(1)**
3000 Centre Square West
Philadelphia, PA 19102
Tel.: 215-941-0100
Emp.: 23
Real Estate
S.I.C.: 6531
D.M. Dilella *(Pres.)*

Berwind Railway Service Company **(1)**
3400 West Marshall, Ste. 316
Longview, TX 75604
Tel.: 903-759-9778
Railroad Repair Services; Shop Locations Include Neodesha, KS, Hollidaysburg, PA & Marshall, TX
S.I.C.: 4011
D.R. Turner *(Pres.)*

Bindicator Company **(1)**
1915 Dove St., P.O. Box 9
Port Huron, MI 48060
Tel.: 313-987-2700
Emp.: 94
Mfr. Special Instruments
S.I.C.: 3823
N.F. Marsh *(Pres.)*

CRC Industries Inc. **(1)**
885 Louis Dr.
Warminster, PA 18974
Tel.: 215-674-4300
Emp.: 80
Mfr. Chemical Specialties, Lubricants, Rust Preventives, Cleaners, Degreasers
S.I.C.: 2992; 2899; 2842
W.T. Clements *(Pres.)*
E. Fleishman *(Pres.-Americas)*

Dynisco, Inc. **(1)**
Four Commercial St.
Sharon, MA 02067
Tel.: 617-784-8400
Mfr. of Electronic Pressure Transducers
S.I.C.: 3629
Roger E. Brooks *(Pres.)*

Subsidiaries:

Kayeness, Inc. **(2)**
115 Thousand Oaks Blvd., Ste. 101
Morgantown, PA 19543
Tel.: 215-286-7555
Mfr. of Physical Property & Testing Equipment
S.I.C.: 3629
Richard J. Pavero *(Pres.)*

Normag Corporation **(2)**
P.O. Box 6010, Bethlehem Station
Hickory, NC 28603
Tel.: 704-495-4613
Mfr. of Gear Pump Systems for Plastic Extrusion Lines
S.I.C.: 3423
Steve A. Fox *(Pres.)*

Electronic Measurements, Inc. **(1)**
405 Essex Rd.
Neptune, NJ 07753
Tel.: 908-922-9300
Approx.Sls.: $20,000,000
Emp.: 275
Mfr. of Power Supplies
S.I.C.: 3559
Gerald D. Posner *(Pres.)*
G.J. Lehmann *(Mgr.-Sls. & Mktg.)*
Bob Ward *(Pur. Mgr.)*

Subsidiary:

A.L E. Systems, Inc. **(2)**
150 Homer Ave.
Ashland, MA 01721
Tel.: 508-881-5252
Mfr. of High Voltage Power Supplies for Laser & Industrial Applications
S.I.C.: 3679
George L. Bees *(Pres.)*

Kentucky Berwind Land Company **(1)**
1150 One Valley Sq.
Charleston, WV 25301
Tel.: 304-346-0569
Emp.: 10
Leasing Coal Lands
S.I.C.: 6519
R.C. Brainard *(Pres.)*

Kyber Coal Co. **(1)**
8259 Upper Johns Creek Rd.
Kimper, KY 41539
Tel.: 606-432-0084
Steam Coal
S.I.C.: 1221
Jimmy L. Walker *(Pres.)*

Jesse Branch Coal Co. **(1)**
8259 Upper Johns Creek Rd.
Kimper, KY 41539
Tel.: 606-835-4345
Steam Coal
S.I.C.: 1221
Jimmy L. Walker *(Pres.)*

Perfect Equipment Corp. **(1)**
1435 Heil Quaker Blvd., Box 600
La Vergne, TN 37086
Tel.: 615-641-1950
Emp.: 140
Mfr. of Auto Wheel Balance Weights, Tire Repair Materials
S.I.C.: 3559; 3011; 3824; 3714
T.K. Willingham *(Pres.)*

Manufacturing Plant:

Perfect Equipment Corp. **(2)**
855 Scott St., Box 942
Murfreesboro, TN 37130
Tel.: 615-893-0643
Mfr. of Auto Wheel Balance Weights, Tire Repair Equipment
S.I.C.: 3714; 3559; 3011

Subsidiaries:

Kex Products, Inc. **(2)**
1435 Heil Quaker Blvd.
La Vergne, TN 37086
Tel.: 615-641-1950
Telex: 810-381-4383 PFT-MFEC
Fax: 615-641-3969
Approx.Sls.: $10,000,000
Emp.: 150
Fiscal Year-end: 12/31/90
Export
Mfr. of Tire Repair Plugs, Patches, Tubeless Tire Repair Products, Tubeless Tire Valves, Gauges, Chemicals
S.I.C.: 3011; 3824
Thomas K. Willingham *(Pres.)*
John M. Burns *(V.P.-Fin. & Opers.)*
Michael Astorino *(V.P.-Mktg. & Sls.)*
Ann Ness *(Assoc. Product Mgr.)*

Snugl Mfg. Co. Inc. **(2)**
12468 E. Lambert Rd.
Whittier, CA 90608
Tel.: 213-945-2355 (100%)
Mfr. of Wheel Weight Equipment
S.I.C.: 3714; 3559

Reitz Coal Company **(1)**
509 15th St.
Windber, PA 15963
Tel.: 814-467-4519
Emp.: 185
Mines Bituminous Coal
S.I.C.: 1221
A.T. Sossong *(Pres.)*

Sentrol, Inc. **(1)**
10831 S.W. Cascade Blvd.
Portland, OR 97223
Tel.: 503-684-9230
Mfr. of Security Alarm Systems
S.I.C.: 3669; 7382
K.L. Boyda *(Pres.)*

Watson Bowman Acme Corp. **(1)**
95 Pineview Drive
Amherst, NY 14228
Tel.: 716-691-7566
Mfr. of Expansion Joints
S.I.C.: 3441
Barry K. Heckman *(Pres.)*

Wilmore Coal Company **(1)**
509 15th St.
Windber, PA 15963
Tel.: 814-467-4557
Emp.: 9
Leases Coal Lands
S.I.C.: 6519
A.T. Sossong *(Pres.)*

Affiliate:

Berwind Pharmaceuticals Services, Inc. **(1)**
610 Freedom Bus. Center, Ste. 204
King of Prussia, PA 19406
Tel.: 215-962-0300
Approx.Sls.: $60,000,000
Emp.: 399
Mfr. of Pharmaceutical Products; Medical Equipment Rental
S.I.C.: 2834; 7352
C. Graham Berwind *(Chm. Bd.)*
J.J. Byrne, Jr. *(Pres.)*
William R. Motzer *(V.P., Chief Fin. Officer & Sec.)*

Division:

Colorcon **(2)**
Moyer Blvd.
West Point, PA 19486
Tel.: 215-699-7733
Emp.: 170
Mfr. of Dispersed Edible Color Systems
S.I.C.: 2865
T.D. Boehning *(Pres.)*

Subsidiaries:

GPS Healthcare **(2)**
1515 Mount Hope Ave.
Pottsville, PA 17901
Tel.: 717-622-3558
Sales of Durable Medical Equipment & Supplies & Health Care Services
S.I.C.: 5047; 8011
Charles DiTrapano *(Pres.)*

Joint Venture:

Elton Coal Co. **(1)**
509 15th St.
Windber, PA 15963
Tel.: 814-467-4510 (50%)
Coal Mining
S.I.C.: 1221
A T. Sossong *(Chief Oper. Officer)*

Non-U.S. Holdings:

Colorcon Ltd. **(1)**
Murray Road St. Paul's Cray,
Orpington, Kent BR5 3QY, United Kingdom
Tel.: 689-38301
Sales Dispersed Edible Color Systems; Chemicals, Sub. of Colorcon, West Point, PA
S.I.C.: 5169
T.W.D. Blaney *(Mng. Dir.)*

Dynisco Gerate G.m.b.H. **(1)**
Ind. Geb. Bollinger Hofe, Postfach 1547 D-7100
Heilbronn, Germany
Tel.: 07131 2 97 0
Telex: 728 430
Fax: 07131 2 32 60
Mfr. & Sales of Measurement Instruments
S.I.C.: 3825; 5084
Hans G. Kranzler *(Mng. Dir.)*

Dynisco Instrument Sarl. **(1)**
Paris, France
Mfr. of Specialty Equipment
S.I.C.: 3825

Dynisco (U.K.) Limited **(1)**
8, The Windmills, Turk St.
Alton, GU34 1EF, United Kingdom
Tel.: 0420 80111
Fax: 0420 80128
Mfr. of Pressure Transducers
S.I.C.: 3825

Perfect-Hoffman Co. Ltd. **(1)**
39 Dussek St.
Belleville, ON K8N 2R9, Canada
Tel.: 613-962-9130 (50%)
Mfr. of Automotive Products; Joint Venture of Perfect Equip. Corp., TN
S.I.C.: 2396
Gerhard Rossteuscher *(Pres.)*

Sentrol Europe S.A. **(1)**
6 rue d'Estienne d'Arves B.P. 60, 92250
La Garenne-Colombes, France
Tel.: 1 47 82 76 10
Mfr. of Specialty Equipment
S.I.C.: 3825
Patrick Wolf *(Mng. Dir.)*

Watson Bowman Acme, Inc. **(1)**
4205 Fairview St.
Burlington, ON L7L 2A4, Canada
Tel.: 416-639-1691
Mfrs., Sls. & Mktg. Expansion Joints
S.I.C.: 3441; 5051
Timothy Pace *(Gen. Mgr. & Plant Opers. Mgr.)*

BESCHE OIL COMPANY, INC.
Old Washington Rd.
Waldorf, MD 20604
Mailing Address:
P.O. Box 277
Waldorf, MD 20604
Tel.: 301-645-7061 **MD**
Fax: 301-843-8582
Year Founded: 1948
Approx.Sls.: $49,000,000
Emp.: 225
Petroleum Bulk Stations; Fuel Oil Dealers, Filling Stations; Convenience Stores
S.I.C.: 5171; 5983; 5541; 5411
Michael Besche *(Pres.)*
Norman Norris *(Exec. V.P.)*
John Hartline *(V.P.-Admin.)*
Jack Miller *(V.P.-Opers.)*
Melvin Williams *(Sec. & Treas.)*

Outside Service Firm(s):

Stegman & Associates*(Auditors)*
Baltimore, MD

First National Bank of Maryland*(Major Banking Relationship)*
25 S. Charles St.
Baltimore, MD 21201
Tel.: 410-244-4025

BESS EATON DONUT FLOUR CO., INC.
79 Tom Harvey Rd.
Westerly, RI 02891
Tel.: 401-596-0171
Fax: 401-596-0114
Approx.Sls.: $23,000,000
Emp.: 575
Fiscal Year-end: 8/31/92
Retail Donut Shops
S.I.C.: 5461
Louis A. Gencarelli, Sr. *(Pres.)*
Eugene Aiello *(V.P.-Opers.)*
Angelo Gencarelli *(Chief Fin. Officer & Sec.)*

Outside Service Firm(s):

Peat Marwick*(Auditors)*
Providence, RI

Fleet National Bank*(Major Banking Relationship)*
125 Dupont Dr.
Providence, RI 02907-3178
Tel.: 401-278-5335

BESSER COMPANY
801 Johnson St.
Alpena, MI 49707
Mailing Address:
P.O. Box 336,
Alpena, MI 49707-1870
Tel.: 517-354-4111 **MI**
Fax: 517-354-3190
Fax: 517-356-1432
Fax: 517-354-3120
Year Founded: 1904
Sales Range: $40-59 Million
Emp.: 550
Fiscal Year-end: 6/30/90
Export
Mfr. of Concrete Block Machinery & Product Handling Equipment
S.I.C.: 3531; 3559; 3533
James C. Park *(Chm. Bd. & Chief Exec. Officer)*
James E. Arbuckle *(Pres. & Chief Oper. Officer)*
Kevin L. Curtis *(V.P.-Sls. & Mktg.)*
Mike Kelly *(V.P.-Mfg.)*
Jere M. Doyle *(Dir.-Human Resources)*
Stanley J. Mazany II *(Mgr.-Matl. Control, Dir.-Pur.)*
Thomas L. O'Neil *(Mgr.-Mngmt. Information Systems)*
Terri Rondeau *(Mgr.-Adv.)*

No. of Mfg. Plants/Facilities: 1
No. of U.S. Offices: 3
No. of Foreign Offices: 3

Computer Systems/Hardware:
Unisys

Outside Service Firm(s):

Price Waterhouse*(Auditors)*
200 Renaissance Center, Ste. 3900
Detroit, MI 48243

Travelers Insurance Co.*(Group Insurer)*
1 Tower Square
Hartford, CT 06183-2492
Tel.: 203-277-4542
Fax: 203-277-5038

Subsidiary:

Besser/APPCO **(1)**
442 N. W.W. White Rd.
San Antonio, TX 78219
Tel.: 210-333-1111
Fax: 210-333-1508
Emp.: 115
Mfr. of Special Machinery
S.I.C.: 3559
Raymond L. Kinsel *(Pres.)*
L. Garcia *(V.P.-Engrng. & Sls.)*
S. Willeford *(Mgr.-Pur.)*

Non-U.S. Holding:

Besser Canada, Ltd. **(1)**
387 Orenda Rd.
Bramalea, ON L6T 1G4, Canada
Tel.: 416-791-1654 (100%)
Fax: 416-791-7952
Approx.Sls.: $3,000,000
Emp.: 60
Mfr. of Special Machinery
S.I.C.: 3559
Robert Conway *(Pres.)*

BESSIN CORPORATION
207 W. South Water Market
Chicago, IL 60608
Tel.: 312-738-2100
Fax: 312-738-2888
Holding Company; Manufacturer of Sausages & Other Prepared Meat Products
S.I.C.: 6719; 2011; 2013
Sheldon Sternberg *(Pres.)*
Jane Horberg *(Controller)*
Michael Hahn *(V.P.-Sls.)*
Sandy Imyak *(Dir.-Personnel)*
Robert Saternus *(Dir.-Personnel)*
Marc Simon *(Dir.-Mktg.)*

Outside Service Firm(s):

Altschuler, Melvoin & Glasser*(Auditors)*
Chicago, IL

Associated Agencies*(Commercial Insurance Carrier)*
Chicago, IL

Zurich American Insurance Co.*(Group Insurer)*
Schaumberg, IL

LaSalle National Bank*(Major Banking Relationship)*
120 S. LaSalle St.
Chicago, IL 60603
Tel.: 312-781-8000

Subsidiaries:

Best Kosher Sausage Co. **(1)**
207 W. South Water Market
Chicago, IL 60608
Tel.: 312-738-2100
Fax: 312-738-2888
Emp.: 275
Computer Systems/Hardware:
IBM System 36
Kosher Sausage, Prepared & Smoked Meats
S.I.C.: 2013
Sheldon Sternberg *(Chm. Bd. & Pres.)*
Jerry Oscherwitz *(V.P., Asst. Treas. & Sec.)*
Robert A. Mann *(V.P.)*
Michael W. Sternberg *(V.P.)*
Jane Horberg *(Controller)*
Sandy Abramowitz *(Pur. Dir.)*
Robert Olesczkiewicz *(Data Processing Dir.)*
Robert Saternus *(Dir.-Personnel)*
Mark Simon *(Adv. Dir.)*
Willie T. Fisher *(Plant Mgr.)*

Sinai 48 Kosher Foods Corp. **(1)**
1000 W. Pershing Rd.
Chicago, IL 60609
Tel.: 312-650-6330
Fax: 312-650-9046
Emp.: 275
Manufacturer of Sausages & Cured and Smoked Meats
S.I.C.: 2011
Sheldon Oscherwitz *(Pres.)*
J. Oscherwitz *(Exec. V.P.)*
Irving Walchirk *(Gen. Sls. Mgr.)*

BEST BRANDS
1765 Yankee Doodle Rd.
St. Paul, MN 55121
Tel.: 612-454-5850
Fax: 612-454-0062
Emp.: 485
Food Processing & Distribution
S.I.C.: 2051
Kenneth Malecha *(Pres.)*
Wayne Mosey *(V.P.)*
Rick Sundal *(Chief Fin. Officer)*

Outside Service Firm(s):

Crowe, Chizek & Co.*(Auditors)*
P.O. Box 3687,
Oak Brook, IL 60822
Tel.: 708-954-7408
Fax: 708-799-1299

Subsidiary:

Michigan Bakery Supply Co. **(1)**
32680 Capital St.
Detroit, MI 48207
Tel.: 313-427-3520
Fax: 313-571-1920
Wholesale Bakery Supplies & Equipment
S.I.C.: 5046
Mike Maurine *(Gen. Mgr.)*

BEST MANUFACTURING, INC.
1633 Broadway, 18th Fl.
New York, NY 10019
Tel.: 212-974-1100 **NY**
Fax: 212-245-0385
Year Founded: 1914
Approx.Sls.: $130,000,000
Emp.: 1,020
Fiscal Year-end: 12/31/90
Import
Manufacturer of Washable Service Apparel & Distributor of Textile Products to the Institutional Trade
S.I.C.: 7213
Lester Maslow *(Chm. Bd. & Pres.)*
Henry Broccoli *(Exec. V.P.)*
Michael Cooper *(Exec. V.P.)*
Sol Corenthal *(Sr. V.P.-Sls. & Pur.)*
Murray Dennenberg *(V.P.-Apparel Div.)*
John Johnson *(V.P.-Mfg.)*
Irving Miles *(V.P.-Fin.)*
James Decker *(Dir.-Data Processing)*

No. of Mfg. Plants/Facilities: 5
No. of U.S. Offices: 8

Computer Systems/Hardware:
IBM System 38

Outside Service Firm(s):

Kraft, Fischman & Assoc.*(Auditors)*
New York, NY

Phillips, Nizer, Benjamin, Krim & Ballon*(Legal Firm)*
40 W. 57th St.
New York, NY 10019
Tel.: 212-977-9700

Chemical Bank*(Major Banking Relationship)*
450 West 33rd St.
New York, NY 10001
Tel.: 212-613-7197
Fax: 212-947-7628

Divisions:

Best Hospital Supply Div. **(1)**
1633 Broadway
New York, NY 10019
Tel.: 212-974-1100
Whlse. Mens & Boys Washable Service Apparel & Textiles

Best Textile Co. Div. **(1)**
1633 Broadway
New York, NY 10019
Tel.: 212-974-1100
Whlse. Textile Prods.

New England Co. Div. **(1)**
150 Maple St.
Stoughton, MA 02062
Tel.: 617-821-1650
Whlse. Washable Service Apparel & Textiles

Southeastern Textile Co. Div. **(1)**
222 E. Solomon St.
Griffin, GA 30223
Tel.: 706-227-5561
Whlse. Washable Service Apparel & Textile

Southeastern Textiles Hotel Co. Div. **(1)**
222 E. Solomon St.
Griffin, GA 30223
Tel.: 706-227-5561
Whlse. Mens & Boys Washable Service Apparel & Textiles

BEST PROVISION CO., INC.
144 Avon Ave.
Newark, NJ 07108
Tel.: 201-242-5000
Tel.: 800-631-4466 **NJ**
Fax: 201-648-0041
Year Founded: 1943
Sales Range: $20-39 Million
Emp.: 115
Fiscal Year-end: 12/31/91
Beef Frankfurters, Meat & Deli Products
S.I.C.: 2013
Paul Dolinko *(Pres.)*
Leonard Karp *(V.P., Chief Exec. Officer & Treas.)*
Floyd Jason *(V.P. & Sec.)*
Morris Dolinko *(V.P.)*
Bernard Karp *(V.P.)*

Outside Service Firm(s):

Zeller, Weiss & Kohn*(Auditors)*
Newark, NJ

BEST WESTERN INTERNATIONAL, INC.
6201 N. 24th Pkwy.
Phoenix, AZ 85016-2023
Mailing Address:
P.O. Box 10203,
Phoenix, AZ 85064-0203
Tel.: 602-957-4200
Tel.: 800-528-1234-Reservations **AZ**
Telex: 165743 Best West Phx
Fax: 602-957-5695 Sales Prom.
Fax: 602-957-5505 Corp. Comm.
Year Founded: 1946
Sales Range: $1 Billion +
Emp.: 1,150
Fiscal Year-end: 11/30/91
Lodging Chain Association: Independently Owned Hotels, Motor Inns & Resorts
S.I.C.: 7011; 7389
Troy Davis *(Chm. Bd.)*
John McCoy *(Vice. Chm.)*
Ronald A. Evans *(Pres. & Chief Exec. Officer)*
Robert Fitzgerald *(Chief Oper. Officer)*
William S. Watson *(Sr. V.P.-Worldwide Mktg.)*
Clay Carpenter *(V.P.-Fin. & Chief Fin. Officer)*
Keith Barlow *(V.P.-Reservations & Systems Devel.)*
Stan Dyck *(V.P.-Intl. Opers.)*
Brian Murcott *(V.P.-Membership Devel. & Quality Assurance)*
Judy Nelson *(V.P.-Membership & Staff Admin.)*

Doug Zimmerman *(Legal Officer)*
Terry Solomon *(Controller)*
Carol Alverson *(Dir.-Human Resources Mngmt.)*
Werner Braum *(Dir.-Intl. Devel.)*
John Goertz *(Dir.-Reservations)*
Tom Bogart *(Dir.-Intl. Mktg.)*
Richard Howles *(Dir.-Systems Devel.)*
Jim Longwell *(Dir.-Data Processing)*
Vicki Meyers *(Dir.-Adv.)*
Jim Ritenour *(Dir.-Pur.)*
Charles Ryder *(Dir.-Mktg. Services)*
Joe Striss *(Dir.-Quality Assurance)*
Cosimo Tripodi *(Dir.-Education & Training)*
Paul Verhaak *(Dir.-European Sls.)*
Alice Weis *(Dir.-Membership Devel. Admin.)*
Debi Wesson *(Dir.-Membership Admin.)*
Ken Whitley *(Dir.-Insurance)*
Steve Tripp *(Mgr.-Media Relations)*
Michelle Poisson *(Meeting Planner)*
Elaine DeWitt *(Benefits Specialist)*
Steve Tripp *(Mgr.-Media Rels.)*

No. of U.S. Offices: 10
No. of Foreign Offices: 3

Computer Systems/Hardware:
IBM 4381 & 4341

Outside Service Firm(s):

KPMG Peat Marwick*(Auditors)*
2020 No. Central Ave.
Phoenix, AZ 85004
Tel.: 602-253-2000

Lincoln National Life Insurance Co.*(Major Banking Relationship)*
116 E. Berry
Ft. Wayne, IN 46802
Tel.: 219-423-6111

Blue Cross & Blue Shield of Arizona, Inc.*(Group Insurer)*
Phoenix, AZ

Evans, Kitchel & Jenckes*(Legal Firm)*
Phoenix, AZ

Black, Gould & Associates*(Pension Manager)*
Phoenix, AZ

Subsidiaries:

B-W Advertising Agency **(1)**
P.O. Box 10203
Phoenix, AZ 85064
Tel.: 602-957-5728 (100%)
Fax: 602-957-5942
Emp.: 18
Adv. Agency
S.I.C.: 7311
Vicki Meyers *(Dir.-Adv.)*

B-W Insurance Agency **(1)**
6201 N. 24th Pkwy.
Phoenix, AZ 85064
Tel.: 602-957-5784
Tel.: 800-528-3616 (100%)
Fax: 602-957-5910
Emp.: 7
Insurance Agency
S.I.C.: 6411
Ken Whitley *(Dir.)*

B-W Supply, Inc. **(1)**
6201 N. 24th Pkwy.
Phoenix, AZ 85064
Tel.: 602-957-5856
Tel.: 800-528-3601 (100%)
Fax: 602-957-5729
Emp.: 35
Wholesale Lodging Supplies
S.I.C.: 5087
Jim Ritenour *(Dir.)*

Reservations Services, Inc. **(1)**
P.O. Box 10203,
Phoenix, AZ 85064
Tel.: 602-780-6000
Tel.: 800-528-1234 (100%)
Fax: 602-780-6099
Emp.: 720
Toll-Free Reservations System
S.I.C.: 7389
Keith Barlow *(V.P.)*

BESTEEL INDUSTRIES
15279 Alton Pkwy.
Irvine, CA 92718
Mailing Address:
P.O. Box 19715
Irvine, CA 19715
Tel.: 714-727-4155
Tel.: 800-BESTEEL **CA**
Fax: 714-727-4254
Year Founded: 1956
Sales Range: $40-59 Million
Emp.: 350
Export
Prefabricated Metal Buildings
S.I.C.: 3448
Preston R. Lee *(Chm. Bd. & Pres.)*
Gary L. Woodward *(Chief Fin. Officer)*
Karena Lang *(Mgr.-Mktg.)*

No. of Mfg. Plants/Facilities: 4
No. of U.S. Offices: 10

Outside Service Firm(s):

KPMG Peat Marwick*(Auditors)*
Irvine, CA

Union Bank*(Major Banking Relationship)*
City of Industry, CA

BESTFORM FOUNDATIONS, INC.
38-01 47th Ave.
Long Island City, NY 11101
Tel.: 718-392-2200
Fax: 718-392-2224
Approx.Sls.: $50,000,000
Emp.: 2,200
Mfr. Brassieres, Girdles, Corsets, Sleepwear
S.I.C.: 2342; 2341
Gertrude Goldberg *(Chm. Bd.)*
Marvin Bienenfeld *(Pres.)*
Julius Bienenfeld *(Exec. V.P.)*
Jerry Pinsky *(Exec. V.P.)*
Marty Weiss *(Sr. V.P.-Natl. Sls.)*
Stanley Bienenfeld *(V.P.)*
Stanley Rothstein *(V.P.-Fin., Treas. & Asst. Sec.)*
Max Wagner *(V.P.-Pur.)*
Richard Mezan *(Sec.)*
Bernard Dolgin *(Mgr.-Sls.)*
Henry N. Rouder *(Mgr.-Adv. & Sls. Promo.)*
Harvey Toback *(Dir.-Adv.)*

Outside Service Firm(s):

Grant Thornton*(Auditors)*
605 Third Ave.
New York, NY 10158
Tel.: 212-599-0100
Fax: 212-370-4520

Pollner Mezan Stolzberg & Frechtman*(Legal Firm)*
New York, NY

National Westminster Bank plc*(Major Banking Relationship)*
Long Island, NY

Subsidiaries:

Lily of France, Inc. **(1)**
136 Madison Ave.
New York, NY 10016
Tel.: 212-696-1110
Fax: 212-481-7815
Emp.: 80
Computer Systems/Hardware:
IBM
Mfr. Foundations, Lingerie & Sleepwear
S.I.C.: 2342
Gertrude Goldberg *(Chm. Bd.)*
Marvin Bienenfeld *(Pres.)*
Kingsley McAlpine *(Sr. V.P.)*
Harvey Toback *(Dir.-Adv.)*

Poirette Corsets, Inc. **(1)**
136 Madison Ave.
New York, NY 10016
Tel.: 212-696-1110
Fax: 212-481-7815
Approx.Sls.: $10,000,000
Emp.: 250
Mfr. Foundation Garments, Fashion Undergarments
S.I.C.: 2342
Gertrude Goldberg *(Chm. Bd.)*
Marvin Bienenfeld *(Pres.)*
Harvey Toback *(Dir.-Adv.)*

BESTOP, INC.
2100 W. Midway Blvd.
Broomfield, CO 80038
Mailing Address:
P.O. Box 307
Broomfield, CO 80010
Tel.: 303-465-1755
Fax: 303-466-3436
Emp.: 475
Fiscal Year-end: 12/31/90
Import Export
Mfr. of Soft Tops for Jeep, Suzuki and Other Vehicles
S.I.C.: 2399; 3714
Rick Sabourin *(Pres. & Treas.)*
Ron Fox *(V.P.)*
Dallas Vernon *(Adv. Mgr.)*

Computer Systems/Hardware:
IBM System 36

Outside Service Firm(s):

United Bank of Denver*(Major Banking Relationship)*
P.O. Box 5247
Denver, CO 80217
Tel.: 303-861-8811

BETAC INTERNATIONAL CORPORATION
2001 N. Beauregard St.
Alexandria, VA 22311
Tel.: 703-824-3100 **DE**
Year Founded: 1977
Assets: $6,700,000
Liabilities: $5,300,000
Net Worth: $1,400,000
Approx.Sls.: $20,000,000
Emp.: 200
Fiscal Year-end: 9/30/91
Holding Company; Conducts Systems Design & Analysis & Management Consulting for Government Departments, Federal Agencies & Private Industry
S.I.C.: 8731
Earl F. Lockwood *(Pres. & Chief Exec. Officer)*
Bradford M. Chalk *(Chief Fin. Officer)*
Peter F. Bahnsen *(Sr. V.P.-Bus. & Tech. Devel.)*
Harley Hughes *(Sr. V.P.-Air Force Opers.)*
Owen Greenblatt *(V.P.-Intelligence Architectures)*
Robert Haley *(V.P.-Southwest Engrng. Div.)*
Malcolm MacNichol *(Dir.-Personnel)*
Sandra Morrow *(Dir.-Contracts Admin.)*
Douglas Potter *(Dir.-Procurement & Facilities)*
Charles Skinner *(Dir.-Air Force Opers.)*
Mattie Couples *(Security Officer)*
Principal(s):
Earl F. Lockwood

No. of U.S. Offices: 13
No. of Foreign Offices: 3

Computer Systems/Hardware:
IntelliMac 7000M; PDP-11/23; HP3000; PRIME Minicomputers

Outside Service Firm(s):

KPMG Peat Marwick*(Auditors)*
8150 Leesburg Pike
Vienna, VA 22180

Aetna Life & Casualty*(Commercial Insurance Carrier)*
151 Farmington Avenue
Hartford, CT 06156
Tel.: 203-273-2128
Fax: 203-729-4295

Blue Cross & Blue Shield of the National Capital Area*(Group Insurer)*
Washington, DC

Connecticut General Life Insurance Co.*(Group Insurer)*
P.O. Box 2975,
Hartford, CT 06104
Tel.: 203-726-6000

Arent, Fox, Kintner, Plotkin & Kahn*(Legal Firm)*
1815 H St. N.W.
Washington, DC 20006
Tel.: 202-857-6000

Crestar Bank*(Major Banking Relationship)*
Arlington, VA

Subsidiary:

Betac Corporation **(1)**
2001 N. Beauregard St.
Alexandria, VA 22311
Tel.: 703-824-3192 (100%)
Conducts Systems Design & Analysis & Mngmt. Consulting for Govt. Depts., Fed. Agencies & Private Industry
S.I.C.: 7372; 8731; 7373
Earl F. Lockwood *(Pres. & Chief Exec. Officer)*

CHANNING L. BETE CO., INC.
200 State Rd.
South Deerfield, MA 01373
Tel.: 413-665-7611
Fax: 413-665-2671
Sales Range: $20-39 Million
Emp.: 200
Publishing & Printing of Scriptographic Informational & Educational Booklets & Related Materials
S.I.C.: 2721; 2731; 2741; 2752; 7331
Channing L. Bete, Jr. *(Pres.)*
Robert L. Underhill *(Chief Oper. Officer & Sr. V.P.)*
J. Michael Cahill *(Exec. V.P. & Treas.)*
Carol W. Tyman *(V.P.-Prod. Testing/ Publishing)*

Principal(s):
Channing L. Bete, Jr.

Outside Service Firm(s):

Arthur Andersen & Co.*(Auditors)*
One Financial Plaza
Hartford, CT 06103
Tel.: 203-280-0649
Fax: 203-280-0898

Trudel, Bartlett, Barry, Wilson & MacNicol*(Legal Firm)*
Deerfield, MA

THE BETHAM CORPORATION
Lincoln Blvd. & River Rd.
Middlesex, NJ 08846
Tel.: 908-356-2870 **DE**
Fax: 908-356-8720
Year Founded: 1968
Approx.Sls.: $14,000,000
Emp.: 85
Import Export
Mfr. of Coated & Laminated Paper, Adhesive Tapes, Custom Adhesive Coating, Medical Adhesives
S.I.C.: 2671; 2672; 3842
G. Laurence Liedel *(Pres.)*
M.A. Natale *(V.P.)*
Richard Balazs *(Mgr.-Quality Control)*
Jim Deming *(Plant Mgr.)*
Valerie Franco *(Mgr.-Strategic Plng.)*
Ray Frank *(Mgr.-Matls.)*
Don Haurey *(Mgr.-Tech. Services)*

Principal(s):
G. Laurence Liedel
M.A. Natale

No. of Mfg. Plants/Facilities: 1
No. of U.S. Offices: 1

The Betham Corporation—(Continued)

Outside Service Firm(s):

United Jersey Bank*(Major Banking Relationship)*
Franklin Park, NJ

BETHEL MILLS, INC.
1 N. Main St.
Bethel, VT 05032
Mailing Address:
P.O. Box 61
Bethel, VT 05032
Tel.: 802-234-9300
Tel.: 800-234-9951 VT
Fax: 802-234-5631
Year Founded: 1781
Approx.Sls.: $11,000,000
Emp.: 30
Import
Retail Sales of Lumber & Other Building Materials
S.I.C.: 5211
John Durfee *(Pres.)*
J. Eric Durfee *(V.P.)*
J. Lang Durfee *(V.P.)*
Barbara Durfee *(Treas. & Sec.)*

Outside Service Firm(s):

Smith, Batchelder & Rugg*(Auditors)*
Bethel, VT

Randolph National Bank*(Major Banking Relationship)*
Randolph, VT

BETTCHER MANUFACTURING CORP.
16000 Commerce Park Dr.
Cleveland, OH 44142
Tel.: 216-267-0850
Fax: 216-267-7654
Approx.Sls.: $13,000,000
Emp.: 100
Manufacture Metal Stampings & Fabricated Metal Prods.
S.I.C.: 3469; 3499
John Ling *(Pres. & Chief Exec. Officer)*
Barry Webne *(Controller)*

Computer Systems/Hardware:
H.P.

Outside Service Firm(s):

Ernst & Young*(Auditors)*
1300 Huntington Bldg.
Cleveland, OH 44115
Tel.: 216-861-5000

Arter & Hadden*(Legal Firm)*
1144 Union Commerce Bldg.,
Cleveland, OH 44115
Tel.: 216-696-1144

Society National Bank*(Major Banking Relationship)*
800 Superior Ave.
Cleveland, OH 44114
Tel.: 216-689-3696

BETTER BAKED FOODS, INC.
56 Smedley St.
North East, PA 16428
Mailing Address:
P.O. Box 432
North East, PA 16428
Tel.: 814-725-8778 DE
Fax: 814-725-8785
Year Founded: 1970
Approx.Sls.: $32,000,000
Emp.: 350
Fiscal Year-end: 12/31/91
Frozen Pizza & Garlic Bread
S.I.C.: 2051
Robert S. Miller *(Chm. Bd. & Chief Exec. Officer)*
Robert Mikytuck, Jr. *(Pres.)*
Sandra Vetter *(Sec. & Treas.)*
Jerry DelBalso *(Dir.-Sls. & Technical Services)*
William Miller *(Dir.-Opers.)*
Michael J. Williams *(Dir.-Fin. & Admin.)*
Frank Casciere *(Mgr.-Pur.)*
Yvonne Curtis *(Mgr.-Mngmt. Information Systems)*
Principal(s):
Robert S. Miller

No. of Mfg. Plants/Facilities: 2
No. of U.S. Offices: 2

Computer Systems/Hardware:
Hewlett Packard

Outside Service Firm(s):

Ernst & Young*(Auditors)*
1400 Key Tower - 50 Fountain Plaza
Buffalo, NY
Tel.: 716-843-5000
Fax: 716-847-6949

Hodgson, Russ, Andrews, Woods & Goodyear*(Legal Firm)*
1800 One M & T Plaza
Buffalo, NY 14203
Tel.: 716-856-4000

Mellon Bank (North) N.A.*(Major Banking Relationship)*
Erie, PA

BETTER BRANDS OF ATLANTA, INC.
755 Jefferson St. NW
Atlanta, GA 30377
Tel.: 404-872-4731
Fax: 404-892-7916
Approx.Sls.: $65,000,000
Emp.: 245
Wholesale Beer Wines
S.I.C.: 5181; 5182
Robert H. Hogg, III *(Chief Exec. Officer & Pres.)*
Bob Bailey *(Exec. V.P. & Gen. Mgr.)*
Jack B. Hogg *(Sr. V.P.)*
G. Scott Hogg *(Sec. & Treas.)*
Dexter Manning *(V.P.-Fin.)*
Tilden Martin *(V.P.-Sls.)*
Bill Maynard *(V.P.-Opers.)*
Betty Jordan *(Dir.-Personnel)*

Outside Service Firm(s):

Grant Thornton*(Auditors)*
Atlanta, GA

Weiner Dwyer & Yancy*(Legal Firm)*
Atlanta, GA

NationsBank*(Major Banking Relationship)*
35 Broad St.
Atlanta, GA 30303
Tel.: 404-581-2121
Tel.: 800-848-8198

BETTER LIVING INC.
Rte. 29 N.
Charlottesville, VA 22906
Mailing Address:
P.O. Box 7627
Charlottesville, VA 22906
Tel.: 804-973-4333
Fax: 804-973-1141
Year Founded: 1893
Approx.Sls.: $13,500,000
Emp.: 95
Retail Building Materials; Household Furnishings
S.I.C.: 5211; 5719
Richard L. Nunley *(Chm. Bd., Pres. & Treas.)*
Charles E. Haney *(V.P.)*
John Nunley *(V.P.)*
Lloyd S. Walker *(V.P.)*
James E. Bowen *(Sec. & Comptroller)*
Principal(s):
Richard L. Nunley

Computer Systems/Hardware:
Enterprise

Outside Service Firm(s):

Hantzmon & Wiebel Inc.*(Auditors)*
Charlottesville, VA

Sovran Bank*(Major Banking Relationship)*
Charlottesville, VA

BEUTLER HEATING & AIR CONDITIONING INC.
9605 Oates Dr.
Sacramento, CA 95827
Tel.: 916-369-2222
Fax: 916-369-6340
Year Founded: 1947
Sales Range: $20-39 Million
Emp.: 303
Heating, Ventilating, Air Conditioning & Sheet Metal For Residential Tract Homes & Apartments
S.I.C.: 1711; 3585
Gary Beutler *(Chm. Bd.)*
Rick Wylie *(Pres.)*
Ed Terkoskie *(V.P.)*
Tom Beutler *(Sec., Treas. & Controller)*
Mark Radcliff *(Dir.-Pur.)*
Bill Poff *(Dir.-Personnel)*
Principal(s):
Gary Beutler

No. of Mfg. Plants/Facilities: 2

Computer Systems/Hardware:
Tandy 6000, ALR Flexcache

Outside Service Firm(s):

Shea & Smith*(Legal Firm)*
Sacramento, CA

Sacramento Commercial Bank*(Major Banking Relationship)*
Sacramento, CA

L.D. Bevan Company, Inc./ Vidicom
(Name Changed To Vidicom, L.D. Bevan Company, Inc.)

BEVERAGE CANNERS INTERNATIONAL CORP.
3550 N.W. 110th St.
Miami, FL 33167
Tel.: 305-685-5061 FL
Fax: 305-769-1466
Approx.Sls.: $60,000,000
Emp.: 225
Export
Carbonated Beverages & Water
S.I.C.: 2086
Ben Bezalel *(Vice Chm.)*
John Shurman *(Pres.)*
J. Roy Corrie *(Exec. V.P.-Fin.)*
Paul Kirkman *(Exec. V.P.-Mktg. & Sls.)*
John D. Slocum *(Exec. V.P.-Admin. & Mfg.)*
Paul Forney *(V.P.-Sls.)*
Anthony Tucci *(V.P.-Sls., Juice Prods.)*
Doug Dunman *(Dir.-Mngmt. Information Systems)*

No. of Mfg. Plants/Facilities: 3
No. of U.S. Offices: 2

Computer Systems/Hardware:
IBM System 36

Outside Service Firm(s):

Berkowitz, Dick & Kaplan*(Auditors)*
Miami, FL

Humana Insurance*(Group Insurer)*
Miami, FL

McGill & Lewis*(Legal Firm)*
Miami, FL

Southeast First National Bank of Miami*(Major Banking Relationship)*
One Biscayne Tower, 34th Flr.
Miami, FL 33131
Tel.: 305-577-3235

Division:

Beverage Canners Div. **(1)**
3550 N.W. 110th St.
Miami, FL 33167
Tel.: 305-685-5061
S.I.C.: 2086
John Shurman *(Pres.)*

THE BEVERLY HILLS HOTEL
9641 Sunset Blvd.
Beverly Hills, CA 90210
Tel.: 310-276-2251
Tel.: 800-283-8885 Reservations
Telex: 188586
Fax: 310-271-0319
Year Founded: 1912
Approx.Sls.: $30,000,000
Emp.: 500
Fiscal Year-end: 12/31/90
Hotels
S.I.C.: 7011
Kerman Beriker *(Chief Exec. Officer & Gen. Mgr.)*
Bakir Jaluddin *(Owner's Representative)*
Marc Gerard *(Controller)*
Chuck Cartier *(Dir.-Sls. & Mktg.)*
Atill Kumar *(Dir.-Pur.)*
Barbara Wardell *(Dir.-Personnel)*
Principal(s):
Sajatera, Inc.

Outside Service Firm(s):

KPMG Peat Marwick*(Auditors)*
725 S. Figueroa St.
Los Angeles, CA 90017
Tel.: 213-972-4000

O'Melveny & Myers*(Legal Firm)*
400 S. Hope St.
Los Angeles, CA 90071
Tel.: 213-669-6000

BIBLER BROTHERS, INC.
P.O. Box 490
Russellville, AR 72801
Tel.: 501-968-4986 AR
Fax: 501-968-5281
Year Founded: 1972
Approx.Sls.: $15,000,000
Emp.: 125
Rough, Sawed or Planed Lumber
S.I.C.: 2421
James Bibler *(Pres.)*
Laurie Bibler *(Treas. & Sec.)*
Terry Freeman *(V.P. & Gen. Mgr.)*
Bud Wait *(Dir.-Sls.)*

Outside Service Firm(s):

Shoptaw, Labahn & Co.*(Auditors)*
Russellville, AR

Worthen National Bank*(Major Banking Relationship)*
Russellvile, AR

BIDDLE INSTRUMENTS
510 Township Line Rd.
Blue Bell, PA 19422
Tel.: 215-646-9200
Fax: 215-643-2670
Year Founded: 1895
Approx.Sls.: $20,000,000
Emp.: 250
Fiscal Year-end: 3/31/91
Electrical Testing & Precision Measuring Instruments & Systems
S.I.C.: 3825; 3829
P. F. Pearce *(Pres.)*
J.R. Rounce *(V.P.-Mktg.)*

BIDDLE SAWYER CORPORATION
2 Penn Plaza
New York, NY 10121
Tel.: 212-736-1580
Fax: 212-239-1089

Emp.: 100
Distributor Chemicals, Oils & Enzymes
S.I.C.: 5169; 5199
Wallace Chavkin *(Chm. Bd. & Chief Exec. Officer)*
Robert Chavkin *(Pres.)*

Outside Service Firm(s):

Deloitte & Touche*(Auditors)*
1 World Trade Center
New York, NY 10048
Tel.: 212-669-5000

MONY*(Group Insurer)*
New York, NY

Emmet, Marvin, Martin*(Legal Firm)*
New York, NY

The Bank of New York*(Major Banking Relationship)*
One Wall Street
New York, NY 10286
Tel.: 212-635-6805
Fax: 212-635-3201

BIDDULPH OLDSMOBILE
4611 W. Glendale
Glendale, AZ 85301
Tel.: 602-934-5211 **AZ**
Fax: 602-842-0712
Year Founded: 1964
Emp.: 200
Retail New & Used Automobiles, RV's; Parts & Service
S.I.C.: 5012; 5511
Kemp Biddulph *(Pres.)*
C.E. Hermonson *(V.P.-Sls.)*
Mike Fellenstein *(Sec., Treas. & Comptroller)*

Outside Service Firm(s):

Murray & Murray*(Auditors)*
Phoenix, AZ

Valley National Bank*(Major Banking Relationship)*
3636 N. Central Av.
Phoenix, AZ 85038
Tel.: 602-261-1313

Biederman, Kelly & Shaffer
475 Park Ave. South,
15th Flr.
New York, NY 10016

Tel.: 212-213-5500 **DE**
Fax: 212-213-4775
Year Founded: 1984
Approx.Billings: $40,000,000
Emp.: 40
Advertising Agency
S.I.C.: 7311
Barry Biederman *(Chm. Bd. & Creative Dir.)*
John Kelly *(Pres. & Chief Oper. Officer)*
Philip Carlson *(Sr. V.P., Chief Fin. Officer)*
Principal(s):
Barry Biederman

BIG BEAR SUPERMARKETS NO. 3
5075 Federal Blvd.
San Diego, CA 92102
Tel.: 619-263-3161 **CA**
Fax: 619-263-4421
Year Founded: 1944
Approx.Sls.: $175,000,000
Emp.: 1,100
Retail Groceries, Meat, Liquor; Gen. Bldg. Contractors
S.I.C.: 5411; 5921; 5431; 1542
John C. Mabee *(Chm. Bd.)*
Larry Mabee *(Pres.)*
Betty L. Mabee *(Sr. V.P.)*
Gerald Homes *(Sec. & Treas.)*
Joe Lucia *(Adv. Mgr.)*
Principal(s):
John C. Mabee
Larry Mabee
Betty L. Mabee

Outside Service Firm(s):

Deloitte & Touche*(Auditors)*
701 "B" St., Ste. 1900
San Diego, CA 92101-8198

Wells Fargo Bank*(Major Banking Relationship)*
420 Montgomery St.
San Francisco, CA 94104

BIG HORN CO-OP MARKETING ASSOCIATION
346 S. 6th
Greybull, WY 82426
Tel.: 307-765-2079
Fax: 307-765-2562
Approx.Sls.: $14,000,000
Emp.: 45
Fiscal Year-end: 12/31/91
Agricultural Chemicals; Feed; Fertilizer & Fertilizer Materials; Garden, Field & Flower Seeds; Dry Beans; Petroleum Bulk Stations
S.I.C.: 5191; 5153; 5171; 5541
Louis Pistulka *(Gen. Mgr.)*
David Ramberg *(Controller)*

Outside Service Firm(s):

Scott McCoullgh*(Legal Firm)*
Greybull, WY

First National Bank*(Major Banking Relationship)*
Lovell, WY

BIG JOE MANUFACTURING CO.
7225 N. Kostner
Lincolnwood, IL 60646
Tel.: 708-675-8700
Fax: 708-675-7204
Approx.Sls.: $10,000,000
Emp.: 30
Fiscal Year-end: 12/31/90
Big Joe Hydraulic Lift Trucks
S.I.C.: 3537
Jerry Kiefus *(Pres.)*
Ed Horwich *(Exec. V.P.)*
Tom Fisher *(Pur. Mgr.)*

BIG V SUPERMARKETS, INC.
176 N. Main St.
Florida, NY 10921
Tel.: 914-651-4411 **NY**
Fax: 914-651-7048
Assets: $110,121,244
Earnings: $110,000,000
Liabilities: $67,366,669
Net Worth: $42,754,575
Approx.Sls.: $588,000,000
Emp.: 1,450
Fiscal Year-end: 12/26/89
Supermarket Chain Located Throughout NY State
S.I.C.: 5411; 5912
William Rosenberg *(Chm. Exec. Committee)*
David G. Bronstein *(Pres. & Chief Exec. Officer)*
Gary S. Koppele *(Sr. V.P.)*
Cornelius J.J. Madera, Jr. *(Sr. V.P., Gen. Counsel & Corp. Devel.)*
John W. Beisel, Jr. *(V.P.-Opers.)*
Erwin J. Fox *(V.P.-Indus. Rels.)*
James Krbec *(V.P.-Human Resources)*
John Mench *(V.P.-Constr. Engrng.)*
Dennis Melville *(V.P.-Information Services)*
Dwayne Wilkes *(Controller)*

Outside Service Firm(s):

Deloitte & Touche*(Auditors)*
1 World Trade Center
New York, NY 10048
Tel.: 212-669-5000

Kronish, Lieb, Weiner & Hellman*(Legal Firm)*
1345 Ave. of the Americas
New York, NY 10105
Tel.: 212-841-6246

Subsidiary:

ShopRite Supermarkets **(1)**
176 No. Main St.
Florida, NY 10921
Tel.: 914-651-4411 (100%)
32 Supermarkets Located in NY; 1 located in NJ; 1 located in PA
S.I.C.: 5411

BIG Y FOODS INC.
280 Chestnut St.
Springfield, MA 01102-7840
Mailing Address:
P.O. Box 7840,
Springfield, MA 01102-7840
Tel.: 413-784-0600 **MA**
Fax: 413-732-8475
Year Founded: 1936
Assets: $120,000,000
Liabilities: $80,000,000
Net Worth: $40,000,000
Approx.Sls.: $450,000,000
Emp.: 4,000
Fiscal Year-end: 6/28/92
Import
Grocery Stores; Holding Co.
S.I.C.: 5411; 5921; 6512; 6719
Gerald E. D'Amour *(Chm. Bd. & Pres.)*
Charles L. D'Amour *(Sr. V.P. & Gen. Counsel)*
Donald H. D'Amour *(Sr. V.P. & Chief Exec. Officer)*
Joseph H. Fisher *(Chief Fin. Officer & V.P.)*
David Brunelle *(V.P.-Oper.)*
Claire M. D'Amour *(V.P.-Corp. Affairs)*
Tony Gomes *(V.P.-Plng. & Devel.)*
Daniel Lescoe *(V.P.-Sls. & Mktg.)*
William Murray *(V.P.-Real Estate)*
John Sarno *(V.P.-Info. Systems)*
Steve Hurwitz *(Dir.-Real Estate)*
David Marti *(Dir.-Adv.)*
Donald Trella *(Dir.-Human Resources)*

No. of Mfg. Plants/Facilities: 30

Computer Systems/Hardware:
IBM AS 400

Outside Service Firm(s):

KPMG Peat Marwick*(Auditors)*
City Place II
Hartford, CT 06103-4103
Tel.: 203-522-3200
Fax: 203-297-5555

Bank of New England*(Major Banking Relationship)*
Springfield, MA

Fleet National Bank*(Major Banking Relationship)*
28 State St.
Boston, MA 02109

First National Bank of Boston*(Major Banking Relationship)*
P.O. Box 644,
Boston, MA 02102-0644
Tel.: 617-575-2900
Fax: 617-575-2549

Cooley, Shrair P.C.*(Legal Firm)*
Springfield, MA

BIGGS GILMORE COMMUNICATIONS

BIGGS GILMORE COMMUNICATIONS
100 W. Michigan Ave., Suite 300
Kalamazoo, MI 49007
Tel.: 616-349-7711 **MI**
Fax: 616-349-3051
Year Founded: 1973
Assets: $6,200,000
Liabilities: $3,999,407
Net Worth: $2,200,593
Approx.Billings: $47,101,000
Emp.: 85
Fiscal Year-end: 12/31/89
Advertising Agency
S.I.C.: 7311
Ronald J. Davis *(Pres. & Chief Exec. Officer)*
Don DeGroot *(Chief Fin. Officer & Sr. V.P.)*
David A. Hunt *(Exec. V.P.)*
Phil Long *(Exec. V.P.)*
Stan Felder *(Sr. V.P.)*
Bill Hooe *(Sr. V.P.)*
Jeff White *(Sr. V.P.)*
Paul Wilson *(Sr. V.P.)*
Wendy Allen *(V.P.)*
Jim Cope *(V.P.)*
Ed Corey *(V.P.)*
Debbie Dedo *(V.P.)*
Paul Hermberg *(V.P.)*
Joyce Peterman *(V.P.-Human Resources)*
Steve Salzman *(V.P.)*
Nancy Skinner *(V.P. & Dir.-Training)*

No. of U.S. Offices: 6
No. of Foreign Offices: 1

Computer Systems/Hardware:
Wang

Outside Service Firm(s):

Ernst & Young*(Auditors)*
1100 Old Kent Bank Bldg.
Kalamazoo, MI 49007
Tel.: 616-349-6671

John Keyser Agency*(Commercial Insurance Carrier)*
Kalamazoo, MI

Varnum, Riddering, Schmidt & Howlett*(Legal Firm)*
666 Old Kent Bldg.
Grand Rapids, MI 49502
Tel.: 616-459-4186

PrimeBank Savings & Loan*(Major Banking Relationship)*
Grand Rapids, MI

Subsidiaries:

Harrington Market Research **(1)**
100 W. Michigan Ave.
Kalamazoo, MI 49007
Emp.: 29
Market Research/Telemarketing
S.I.C.: 7389; 8732

Nancy Skinner & Associates **(1)**
111 Pearl St.
Grand Rapids, MI 49503
Tel.: 616-942-8280
Emp.: 11
Communications/Sales Training
S.I.C.: 5065
Nancy Skinner *(V.P.)*

Branches:

William R. Biggs/Gilmore Associates, Inc. **(1)**
100 W. Michigan Ave.
Kalamazoo, MI 49007
Tel.: 616-349-7711
Carolyn Barton *(V.P., Gen. Mgr.)*

Biggs Gilmore Communications—(Continued)

Biggs Gilmore Communications (1)
111 Pearl St.
Grand Rapids, MI 49503
Tel.: 616-459-1200
Stan Felder *(Sr. V.P.)*

Biggs Gilmore Communications (1)
501 Monroe, Ste. 200
South Bend, IN 46601
Tel.: 219-233-7364
Jim Cope *(V.P., Gen. Mgr.)*

Biggs Gilmore Communications (1)
100 Country Pine Lane, Ste. 5
Battle Creek, MI 49015
Tel.: 616-979-1776

BIGG'S HYPER SHOPPES, INC.
25 Whitney Dr., Ste. 122
Milford, OH 45150
Tel.: 513-248-9300
Fax: 513-248-9731
Year Founded: 1984
Approx.Sls.: $400,000,000
Emp.: 1,500
General Merchandise & Food Retailing
S.I.C.: 5411; 5311
Gilbert Weil *(Pres.)*
Pierre Wevers *(Exec. V.P. & Chief Oper. Officer)*

Outside Service Firm(s):

Deloitte & Touche*(Auditors)*
Chiquita Center, 250 E. 5th St., Ste. 1900
Cincinnati, OH 45202
Tel.: 513-784-7100

Subsidiary:

Bigg's Hyper Shoppes Ohio, Inc. (1)
25 Whitney Dr., Ste. 122
Milford, OH 45150
Tel.: 513-248-9300
Fax: 513-248-9731
General Merchandise & Food Retailing
S.I.C.: 5411; 5311
Gilbert Weil *(Pres.)*

BIGSBY & KRUTHERS, INC.
1750 N. Clark
Chicago, IL 60614
Tel.: 312-440-1700 **IL**
Fax: 312-440-9843
Approx.Sls.: $19,000,000
Emp.: 195
Men's & Boys Clothing Stores
S.I.C.: 5611
Joe Silverberg *(Chm. Bd.)*
H. Gene Silverberg *(Pres.)*
Michael Karpik *(Chief Oper. Officer-Mdse.)*
David Marshall *(Chief Oper. Officer & V.P.-Fin.)*

Outside Service Firm(s):

Deloitte & Touche*(Auditors)*
Two Prudential Plaza, 180 N. Stetson
Chicago, IL 60601
Tel.: 312-946-2039

Continental Bank N. A.*(Major Banking Relationship)*
231 S. LaSalle St.
Chicago, IL 60697
Tel.: 312-828-2345
Tel.: 800-426-5754
Telex: 312-828-1783

BIJUR LUBRICATING CORPORATION
50 Kocher Dr.
Bennington, VT 05201
Tel.: 802-442-6381
Fax: 802-447-1365
Sales Range: $20-39 Million
Emp.: 225
Fiscal Year-end: 12/31/91
Automatic Lubricating Pumps & Deep Hole Drilling Equipment
S.I.C.: 3569; 3532; 3561
Donald Preston *(Pres. & Chief Exec. Officer)*
Samy Karuppana *(V.P.-Oper.)*
Roger Yamamoto *(V.P.-Fin. & Admin.)*
Chrystal Harrington *(Pur. Agent)*

Outside Service Firm(s):

Deloitte & Touche*(Auditors)*
1 World Trade Center
New York, NY 10048
Tel.: 212-669-5000

Gibson, Dunn & Crutcher*(Legal Firm)*
Bennington, VT

First Vermont Bank & Trust Company*(Major Banking Relationship)*
Bennington, VT

BIKE ATHLETIC CO.
2801 Red Dog Dr.
Knoxville, TN 37914
Mailing Address:
P.O. Box 666,
Knoxville, TN 37901
Tel.: 615-546-4703
Fax: 615-525-2471
Approx.Sls.: $50,000,000
Emp.: 600
Fiscal Year-end: 12/31/90
Mfr. of Athletic Equipment
S.I.C.: 3949
James R. Corbett *(Pres.)*
Randy Black *(V.P.-Sls. & Mktg.)*
Joe Black *(Dir.-Mfg.)*
Cecil Jackson *(Dir.-Personnel)*
David Patterson *(Controller)*

BILL COMMUNICATIONS, INC.
355 Park Avenue South
New York, NY 10010
Tel.: 212-592-6200 **NY**
Fax: 212-818-1159
Approx.Sls.: $66,000,000
Emp.: 312
Fiscal Year-end: 12/31/91
Business Magazine Publication
S.I.C.: 2721
Corporate Giving Program: To Education & Cultural Organizations in the U.S. & it's Possessions; Matching Donations of $25 & Above, not to Exceed $1,000 to any Organization in any Year & will Match Employee Donations up to $500 in any Year
John Wickersham *(Pres. & Chief Exec. Officer)*
Daniel O'Shea *(Chief Oper. Officer)*
Jeffrey Berlind *(V.P.)*
M.J. Madigan *(V.P.)*
Howard Neibart *(V.P.)*
Richard O'Connor *(V.P.)*
Russell Piersons *(V.P.)*
Malcolm Riley *(V.P.)*
Stanley Romaine *(V.P.)*
Greg Smith *(V.P.)*
Joseph Furey *(Controller)*
John Mulvey *(Dir.-Human Resources)*
Thomas Tzoucalis *(Dir.-Mfg.)*
Marlene Weisler *(Mgr.-Office Facilities)*

No. of U.S. Offices: 5

Computer Systems/Hardware:
IBM Systems 36, AS 400 & 4361

Outside Service Firm(s):

Deloitte & Touche*(Auditors)*
1 World Trade Center
New York, NY 10048
Tel.: 212-669-5000

Choate, Hall & Stewart*(Legal Firm)*
Exchange Place, 53 State St.
Boston, MA 02109
Tel.: 617-227-5020

First National Bank of Boston*(Major Banking Relationship)*
150 Royall St.
Canton, MA 02021
Tel.: 617-575-2900
Tel.: 800-442-2001

Divisions:

BillCom Automotive (1)
341 White Pond Rd.
Akron, OH 44313
Tel.: 216-867-4401
Fax: 216-867-0019
Emp.: 45
Publishes JOBBER RETAILER & MODERN TIRE DEALER
S.I.C.: 2721
Russell Piersons *(Publr.)*

Billcom Exposition & Conference (1)
P.O. Box 17413, Dulles International Airport
Washington, DC 20041
Tel.: 703-741-5761
Exhibit & Conference Management
S.I.C.: 7999; 8741
Don Vaughn *(Pres.)*
Fred Hofnagel *(Exec. V.P.)*

BillCom Exposition & Conference Group (1)
P.O. Box 17413, Washington-Dulles Intl. Airport
Washington, DC 20041
Tel.: 703-318-0300
S.I.C.: 2721
Fred Hufnagel *(Pres.)*

Contemporary Long Term Care (1)
341 White Pond Rd.
Akron, OH 44313
Tel.: 216-867-4401
Fax: 216-867-0019
Nursing Home Care Publication
S.I.C.: 2721
Russell Piersons *(Publr.)*

Datacomm (1)
438 Camino del Rio So., Ste. 201
San Diego, CA 92198
Tel.: 619-298-2421
Research for Succcessful Meetings Magazine; Research for the Meeting & Convention Industry
S.I.C.: 8732
Phillip R. Mogle *(Pres.)*

Foodservice Director (1)
633 Third Ave.
New York, NY 10017
Tel.: 212-986-4800
Publishes Foodservice Director
S.I.C.: 2721
Jeffrey Berlind *(Publr.)*
Walter Schruntek *(Editor)*

Incentive (1)
633 Third Ave.
New York, NY 10017
Tel.: 212-986-4800
Fax: 212-867-4395
Marketing Facts Featuring Case Studies, Special Survey Material & Market Studies
S.I.C.: 2721
Bruce Bolger *(Co-Publr.)*
Peter Edmunds *(Co-Publr.)*
Joann DePalma *(Prod.)*

Institutional Distribution (1)
633 Third Ave.
New York, NY 10017
Tel.: 212-986-4800
Fax: 212-983-3198
Approx.Sls.: $6,000,000
Emp.: 25
Fiscal Year-end: 12/31/90
Publications Focusing on Foodservice Market; Annual Handbook of Foodservice Distributors; Magazine
S.I.C.: 2721; 2741
Niles D. Crum *(Publisher)*
Robert Civin *(Assoc. Publisher & Editor)*
Ed Tashjian *(V.P.-Mktg.)*
Thomas Tzoucalis *(V.P. & Dir.-Mfg.)*

Jobber Retailer (1)
341 White Pond Rd.
Akron, OH 44313
Tel.: 216-867-4401
Fax: 216-867-0019
Features "How-To" Articles on Business Practices, Mdsg., Display, Adv. & Other Articles Dealing with the Wholesaling & Retailing of Auto Parts
S.I.C.: 2721
M. Mavrigian *(Editor)*

Market Statistics (1)
355 Park Avenue South
New York, NY 10010
Tel.: 212-986-4800
Fax: 212-983-1588
Demographic Data & Market Analysis Publication
S.I.C.: 8742; 2721
Edward Spar *(Pres.)*
Robert Katz *(V.P.)*

Modern Tire Dealer (1)
341 White Pond Rd.
Akron, OH 44313
Tel.: 216-867-4401
Telex: 07
Fax: 216-867-0019
Edited for Independent Tire Dealers in wholesale/Retail Tire Sls. & Automotive Repair Featuring Articles on Indus. News & Auto Services; Wheel Alignment, Suspension Work, Tune-Ups, Etc.
S.I.C.: 2721
Greg Smith *(Publr.)*
Lloyd Stoyer *(Editor)*

Plastics Technology (1)
633 Third Ave.
New York, NY 10017
Tel.: 212-986-4800
Features New Devel. & Trends in Plastic Machinery & Equip., Chemicals & Additives, Resin & Molding Compounds & Indus. News
S.I.C.: 2721
Malcolm W. Riley *(Publisher Editorial Dir.)*
Matthew Naitove *(Editor)*

Publications Division (1)
633 Third Ave.
New York, NY 10017
Tel.: 212-986-4800
Publish Magazines
S.I.C.: 2721
Jeffrey Berlind *(Pres. & Publr.)*
Thomas Lenberg *(V.P. & Assoc. Publr.)*

Restaurant Business (1)
633 Third Ave.
New York, NY 10017
Tel.: 212-986-4800
Fax: 212-983-3198
Information on all Types & Uses of Food, Equip., Supplies & Services Required to Operate a Business
S.I.C.: 2721
Jeffrey P. Berlind *(Publisher)*
Peter R. Berlinski *(Editor & Assoc. Publisher)*

Restaurant/Hotel Design International (1)
633 Third Ave.
New York, NY 10017
Tel.: 212-986-4800
Features Problem Solving Articles on the Interior Design & Architectural Devel. in Hotels & Restaurants
S.I.C.: 2721
Mary Jean Madigan *(Publr. & Editor)*

Sales and Marketing Management (1)
633 Third Ave.
New York, NY 10017
Tel.: 212-986-4800
Sls. & Mktg. Information
S.I.C.: 2721
Howard Neibart *(Publr.)*
Howard Kern *(Editor)*

Successful Meetings (1)
633 Third Ave.
New York, NY 10017
Tel.: 212-986-4800
Fax: 212-986-3727
Featuring Articles on Techniques for Preparing Various Business Meetings & Exhibits
S.I.C.: 2721
Charles Wrye *(Publr.)*
Richard O'Connor *(Editor)*

BILL'S DOLLAR STORES, INC.
3800 I-55 North
Jackson, MS 39211
Mailing Address:
P.O. Box 9407,
Jackson, MS 39286
Tel.: 601-981-7171
Fax: 601-366-4823
Year Founded: 1919

Sales Range: $100-499 Million
Emp.: 2,500
General Merchandise Stores
S.I.C.: 5331
Francis Rooney *(Chm. Bd.)*
Charles Acklen *(Pres. & Chief Exec. Officer)*
Paul Barrett *(Sr. V.P.-Fin., Treas., & Chief Fin. Officer)*
James Lander *(V.P.-Admin.)*
Paul Long *(V.P.-Devel.)*
Merill Sizemore *(V.P.-Opers.)*
A.R. Williams *(V.P.-Controller)*
Jess Waddell *(Dir.-Mngmt. Information Systems)*
Ken Peacock *(Mgr.-Adv. & Sls. Promo.)*

Computer Systems/Hardware:
IBM 4143

Outside Service Firm(s):

KPMG Peat Marwick*(Auditors)*
One Jackson Place,
Jackson, MS 39201
Tel.: 601-354-3701
Fax: 601-354-3745

Brundini, Granthem, Grower, & Hughes*(Legal Firm)*
Jackson, MS

Deposit Guaranty National Bank*(Major Banking Relationship)*
One Deposit Guaranty Plaza,
Jackson, MS 39201

THE BILTRITE CORPORATION
51 Sawyer Rd.
Waltham, MA 02254-9045
Mailing Address:
P.O. Box 9045
Waltham, MA 02254-9045
Tel.: 617-647-1700 DE
Fax: 617-647-0919
Year Founded: 1982
Approx.Sls.: $83,000,000
Emp.: 525
Fiscal Year-end: 12/31/91
Export
Rubber Shoe-Bottoming Materials; Rubber Floor Tiles; Rubber & Vinyl Matting; Rubber Industrial Goods
S.I.C.: 3069; 3089
S.J. Bernstein *(Chm. Bd. & Chief Exec. Officer)*
S.A. Fine *(Pres. & Chief Oper. Officer)*
E.A. Beaulieu *(V.P.-Fin.)*
W.F. Foshage, Jr. *(V.P.)*
G. Konvalinka *(V.P.)*
W. Matfess *(V.P.)*
H.F. McKeon, Jr. *(V.P. & Treas.)*
G. Weinstein *(V.P. & Sec.)*
J.T. Mooney *(V.P.)*
Principal(s):
S.J. Bernstein
S.A. Fine

No. of Mfg. Plants/Facilities: 2
No. of U.S. Offices: 2

Computer Systems/Hardware:
IBM System 38

Outside Service Firm(s):

Ernst & Young*(Auditors)*
200 Clarendon St., 46th Fl.
Boston, MA 02116
Tel.: 617-266-2000

Paul, Weiss, Rifkind, Wharton & Garrison*(Legal Firm)*
1285 Ave. of the Americas
New York, NY 10154
Tel.: 212-373-3000

Ropes & Gray*(Legal Firm)*
One International Place
Boston, MA 02110
Tel.: 617-951-7000

Fleet National Bank*(Major Banking Relationship)*
Corporate Trust Dept., 125 Dupont Dr.
Providence, RI 02907
Tel.: 617-426-9555

BING STEEL INC.
1130 W. Grand Blvd.
Detroit, MI 48208
Tel.: 313-895-3400 DE
Fax: 313-895-7565
Approx.Sls.: $64,900,000
Emp.: 34
Fiscal Year-end: 6/30/92
Steel Service Center
S.I.C.: 5051
Dave Bing *(Chm. Bd.)*
Valerie Woods *(Dir.-Human Resources)*

Computer Systems/Hardware:
IBM

Outside Service Firm(s):

N.B.D. Bank, N.A.*(Major Banking Relationship)*
611 Woodward Ave.
Detroit, MI 48226
Tel.: 313-225-1122
Fax: 313-225-3420

BINGHAM
479 Business Center Dr., Ste. 109
Mt. Prospect, IL 60056
Tel.: 708-298-6777 DE
Year Founded: 1826
Sales Range: $20-39 Million
Emp.: 400
Export
Rubber & Polyurethane Covered Rollers; Pressroom Chemicals
S.I.C.: 2822; 2899; 3069; 3089
R.E. Jenkins *(Chm. Bd.)*
L.W. Ekstrom *(Pres.)*
T. Muzyczko *(Exec. V.P.)*
JoAnn Barrett *(Treas.)*
Principal(s):
R.E. Jenkins
L.W. Ekstrom
T. Muzyczko

No. of Mfg. Plants/Facilities: 22
No. of U.S. Offices: 20

Computer Systems/Hardware:
IBM System 36

Outside Service Firm(s):

Ernst & Young*(Auditors)*
233 S. Wacker Dr.
Chicago, IL 60606
Tel.: 312-368-1800
Fax: 312-645-3095

Alexander & Alexander*(Commercial Insurance Carrier)*
225 N. Michigan Av.
Chicago, IL 60611
Tel.: 312-565-6221

Allstate Insurance*(Group Insurer)*
Northbrook, IL

Richard Crane*(Legal Firm)*
Northbrook, IL

BINKLEY COMPANY
(Wholly-Owned Sub. of Holland Hitch Co., Holland, MI)
Main & Elm Sts.
Warrenton, MO 63383
Mailing Address:
P.O. Box 370,
Warrenton, MO 63383-0370
Tel.: 314-456-3455
Fax: 314-456-7900
Year Founded: 1933
Approx.Sls.: $54,000,000
Emp.: 450
Fiscal Year-end: 10/31/91
Export
Fabricates & Manufactures Steel Products, Proprietary & Custom Products to the Truck/Trailer Industry, Landing Gears, Tandem Sliders & Rollform Structural Components; Produces Steel Curved Wall System to Commercial & Industrial Building Products
S.I.C.: 3714; 3743; 3441
Richard W. Muzzy, Jr. *(Chm. Bd. & Chief Exec. Officer)*
Thomas E. DeBlase *(Pres. & Chief Oper. Officer)*
Samuel A. Martin *(Exec. V.P.)*
Raymond A. Behrens *(V.P.-Northside Opers.)*
Jeffrey E. Ditto *(V.P.-Southside & Dumas Opers.)*
Joseph Gallo *(V.P.-Sls.)*
Wayne Larson *(V.P.-Human Resources)*
James S. MacLellan *(V.P.-Materials)*
Gerald J. Otten *(Treas.)*
Kenneth Haveman *(Sec. & Asst. Treas.)*
Darrel Mishler *(Dir.-Mngmt. Information Systems)*

Computer Systems/Hardware:
IBM System 38

Outside Service Firm(s):

Deloitte & Touche*(Auditors)*
One City Centre
St. Louis, MO 63101
Tel.: 314-342-4900
Fax: 314-342-1100

Rollins Burdick Hunter*(Commercial Insurance Carrier)*
50 Monroe Place
Grand Rapids, MI

Great-West Life Assurance Co.*(Group Insurer)*
8505 East Orchard Rd.
Englewood, CO 8011
Tel.: 800-537-2033

Boatmen's National Bank of St. Louis*(Investment Banker)*
One Boatmen's Plaza, 800 Market St.
St. Louis, MO 63101
Tel.: 314-466-6000

Boatmen's Trust Company*(Investment Banker)*
100 North Broadway
St. Louis, MO 63102
Tel.: 314-466-2469

Plant:

The Binkley Co., Dumas Plant **(1)**
P.O. Box 825
Dumas, AR 71639
Tel.: 501-382-2299
Fax: 501-382-2434
Emp.: 50
W.D. Newsom *(Mgr.)*

Subsidiary:

Prest Rack Inc. **(1)**
Main & Elm Sts.
Warrenton, MO 63383
Tel.: 314-456-1100 (100%)
Fax: 314-456-1101
Emp.: 49
Mfr. Racks For Warehousing
S.I.C.: 3496
Tom DeBlase *(Pres.)*
Geo Prest *(Mgr.-Mktg.)*

BINNING'S BUILDING PRODUCTS, INC.
Walser Rd.
Lexington, NC 27292
Mailing Address:
P.O. Box 868
Lexington, NC 27292
Tel.: 704-249-9193 DE
Year Founded: 1958
Sales Range: $40-59 Million
Emp.: 760
Fiscal Year-end: 12/31/90
Export
Mfr. of Aluminum Building Products, Storm Windows & Doors, Primary Aluminum & Vinyl Windows
S.I.C.: 3442; 3089
Dugald Fletcher *(Chm. Bd.)*
Bill F. Ray *(Pres., Chief Exec. Officer & Chief Oper. Officer)*
Sam Bamman *(V.P.-Sls.)*
Gerry H. Ferguson *(V.P.-Mktg. & Sls.)*
Robbie Watson *(Controller)*
William E. Mitchell *(Sec.)*
Marlene Cannon *(Dir.-Data Processing)*
Tom Lamb *(Dir.-Materials Mngmt.)*
T. Rackard *(Dir.-Prod. Planning & Devel.)*
Carl Sharpe *(Dir.-Human Resources)*
Lamar Clark *(Mgr.-Sls.)*
Jo Siceloff *(Corp. Travel Planner)*

No. of Mfg. Plants/Facilities: 2
No. of U.S. Offices: 11

Computer Systems/Hardware:
Unisys

Outside Service Firm(s):

Arthur Andersen & Co.*(Auditors)*
901 Main St., Ste. 5600
Dallas, TX 75202
Tel.: 214-741-8300

Kemper Insurance*(Commercial Insurance Carrier)*
Charlotte, NC

Brinkley, Walser, McGirt, Miller, Smith & Coles*(Legal Firm)*
Lexington, NC
Tel.: 704-249-2101

THE BINSWANGER COMPANY
Seven Penn Center, 1635 Market St.
Philadelphia, PA 19103
Tel.: 215-448-6000 PA
Fax: 215-448-6238
Year Founded: 1931
Approx.Sls.: $600,000,000
Emp.: 325
Fiscal Year-end: 12/31/90
Commercial & Industrial Real Estate Brokers, Managers, Appraisers, Investments Counseling & Project Development, Tenant Consulting
S.I.C.: 6531; 6552
Frank G. Binswanger, Jr. *(Chm. Bd.)*
John K. Binswanger *(Pres.)*
Malcolm P. Brown *(Sr. V.P.-Mktg. & Communications)*
Michael J. Brennan *(V.P. & Chief Fin. Officer)*
David E. Thurston *(V.P. & Gen. Counsel)*
James J. Dunleavy *(Controller)*
Cheryl Fortunato *(Dir.-Human Resources & Office Admin.)*
George McGeehan *(Dir.-Pub. Rels.)*
Bud DuPlessius *(Mgr.-Mngmt. Info. Systems)*

Computer Systems/Hardware:
MAI Basic 4

Outside Service Firm(s):

Wolf, Block, Schorr & Solis-Cohen*(Legal Firm)*
111 S. 15th
Philadelphia, PA 19102
Tel.: 215-569-4000

Provident National Bank*(Major Banking Relationship)*
1000 Westlakes Dr.
Berwyn, PA 19312

Divisions:

Binswanger Advisory Services **(1)**
Seven Penn Center, 1635 Market St.
Philadelphia, PA 19103
Tel.: 215-448-6000
S.I.C.: 6531
David R. Binswanger *(Pres.)*
Clive G. Mendelow *(Chief Oper. Officer)*

Binswanger Chicago **(1)**
1111 W. 22nd St., Ste. 520
Oak Brook, IL 60521
Tel.: 708-575-9500
Fax: 708-575-9510
S.I.C.: 6531

The Binswanger Company—(Continued)

Lawrence M. Spinelli *(Pres.)*

Binswanger Development **(1)**
Seven Penn Center, 1635 Market St.
Philadelphia, PA 19103
Tel.: 215-448-6000
S.I.C.: 6552
John K. Binswanger *(Pres.)*

Binswanger Industrial **(1)**
Seven Penn Center, 1635 Market St.
Philadelphia, PA 19103
Tel.: 215-448-6000
S.I.C.: 6531
Frank G. Binswanger, Jr. *(Chm.)*

Binswanger Investment **(1)**
Seven Penn Center, 1635 Market St.
Philadelphia, PA 19103
Tel.: 215-448-6000
S.I.C.: 6531
Robert M. Brasler *(Pres.)*

Binswanger Management Corp. **(1)**
Seven Penn Center, 1635 Market St.
Philadelphia, PA 19103
Tel.: 215-448-6000
S.I.C.: 6512
Jerry Castafero *(Pres.)*

Binswanger Realty **(1)**
Seven Penn Center, 1635 Market St.
Philadelphia, PA 19103
Frank G. Binswanger III *(Pres.)*

Branches:

Binswanger **(2)**
1175 Peachtree St., N.E., Ste. 408
Atlanta, GA 30361
Tel.: 404-892-4100
S.I.C.: 6531

Binswanger **(2)**
904 N. Lamar Ave.
Oxford, MS 38655
Tel.: 601-234-6500
S.I.C.: 6531

Binswanger **(2)**
1 Triad Center, Ste. 110, 7736 McCloud Rd.
Greensboro, NC 27409
Tel.: 919-668-0017
S.I.C.: 6531

Binswanger **(2)**
One Exchange Plaza, Ste. 708
Raleigh, NC 27601
Tel.: 919-833-6445
S.I.C.: 6531

Binswanger **(2)**
NCNB Plaza, Ste. 300
Winston-Salem, NC 27101
Tel.: 919-722-0883
S.I.C.: 6531

Binswanger **(2)**
NCNB Tower, 1301 Gervais St., Ste. 908
Columbia, SC 29201
Tel.: 803-799-9452
S.I.C.: 6531

Binswanger Southern **(1)**
230 S. Tryon St., Ste. 930
Charlotte, NC 28202
Tel.: 704-377-0801
S.I.C.: 6531
J. Holmes Davis, III *(Pres.-Indus. Div.)*
David J. Goode *(Pres.-Comml. Div.)*

Binswanger West **(1)**
First Bank Bldg., Ste. 200, 5105 DTC Pkwy.
Englewood, CO 80111
Tel.: 303-779-4345
S.I.C.: 6531

BIO MEDIC CORPORATION
255 W. Spring Valley Ave.
Maywood, NJ 07607
Tel.: 201-587-8300
Fax: 201-843-8816
Approx.Sls.: $14,000,000
Emp.: 320
Wire Products For Animal Cages
S.I.C.: 3496
George S. Gabriel *(Chm. Bd.)*
Neil Campbell *(Pres.)*
Frank Marinaccio *(V.P.)*
Edmond Silverberg *(V.P.)*

Outside Service Firm(s):

Pargot & Popok *(Auditors)*
Perth Amboy, NJ

Miles & Stockbridge *(Legal Firm)*
10 Light St.
Baltimore, MD 21202
Tel.: 410-727-6464

Equitable Bank, N.A. *(Major Banking Relationship)*
100 S. Charles St.
Baltimore, MD 21201
Tel.: 410-547-4000

Subsidiaries:

Harford Systems, Inc. **(1)**
P.O. Box 700
Aberdeen, MD 21001
Tel.: 301-272-3400
Approx.Sls.: $17,000,000
Emp.: 300
Research Animal Cage Systems; Design Consultants; Manufacture & Leasing of Contract Special Metals, Walk-In Coolers & Freezers
S.I.C.: 1541; 3496; 3499; 3585
Alan Penrod *(Pres.)*
Arley Mead *(V.P. & Gen. Mgr.)*
Dominic Slezak *(Controller)*
Ed Lodanski *(Dir.-Sls., Caging Systems)*
Frank McDonald *(Dir.-Sls., Bioclean Systems)*
Henry Pabst, Jr. *(Dir.-Sls., Walk-In Collers & Freezers)*
Clarence Ely *(Mgr.-Production, Duracol)*
Robert Colaianni *(Mgr.-Production, Metals)*
Richard Lemen *(Mgr.-Materials)*

Lab Products, Inc. **(1)**
255 W. Spring Valley Ave.
Maywood, NJ 07607
Tel.: 201-843-4600
Fax: 201-843-6040
Lab Equipment
S.I.C.: 3496
Douglas J. Anderson *(Pres.)*

Maryland Plastics, Inc. **(1)**
251 E. Central Ave.
Federalsburg, MD 21632
Tel.: 410-754-5566
Fax: 410-754-8882
Approx.Sls.: $25,000,000
Emp.: 325
Custom Molded Products, Plastic Cutlery & Plastic Laboratory Equipment
S.I.C.: 3089
Allen Penrod *(Pres.)*
George Nicoletos *(Sls. Mgr.-Cutlery & Scientific)*
Charles Butler *(Sls. Mgr.-Custom)*
George E. Weeks *(Mgr.-Personnel)*

BIO-TEK INSTRUMENTS, INC.
Highland Park, Box 998
Winooski, VT 05404
Tel.: 802-655-4044 **VT**
Fax: 802-655-7941
Year Founded: 1968
Approx.Sls.: $20,500,000
Emp.: 175
Fiscal Year-end: 3/31/91
Mfr. & Researchers of Diagnostic Testing Equipment
S.I.C.: 3841; 8731
Norman R. Alpert *(Chm. Bd., Pres. & Chief Exec. Officer)*
Klaus Deutcher *(Chief Fin. Officer & Controller)*
Kathleen Gilpin *(Dir.-Personnel & Mngmt. Information Systems)*
Eric Perron *(Gen. Mgr.-Plng. & Devel.)*
Principal(s):
Norman R. Alpert

No. of Mfg. Plants/Facilities: 1
No. of U.S. Offices: 1

Computer Systems/Hardware:
DEC VAX 8200

Outside Service Firm(s):

P.F. Jurgs *(Auditors)*
1 Church St.
Burlington, VT 05402
Tel.: 802-864-7491

Smith, Bell, Thompson *(Commercial Insurance Carrier)*
Burlington, VT

Connecticut General Life Insurance Co. *(Group Insurer)*
P.O. Box 2975,
Hartford, CT 06104
Tel.: 203-726-6000

Paul, Frank & Collins Inc. *(Legal Firm)*
1 Church St.
Burlington, VT 05402
Tel.: 802-658-2311

Chase Lincoln First Bank, N.A. *(Major Banking Relationship)*
P.O. Box 1250,
Rochester, NY 14603
Tel.: 716-232-5000

BIOPRODUCTS, INC.
8221 Brecksville Rd., Bldg. #2
Brecksville, OH 44141
Tel.: 216-526-5522
Fax: 216-526-7077
Year Founded: 1981
Approx.Sls.: $85,000,000
Emp.: 250
Import Export
Mfr. Feed Additives, Petfood Palatibilty Enhancers
S.I.C.: 2048; 2879; 2047
R. Michael Hickey *(Pres. & Chief Exec. Officer)*
Stephen C. Latta *(Sr. V.P.-Mktg.)*
John W. Orendorff *(Sr. V.P.-Quality Assurance)*
Bruce B. Buckmaster *(V.P. & Gen. Mgr.-Fish Feeds Div.)*
John W. Kennedy *(V.P.-Devel.)*
Steve E. Koenig *(V.P. & Gen Mgr.-Dairy Feed Supplements)*
Donald Vondriska *(Treas. & Controller)*
Thomas E. Ball *(Dir.-Mfg.)*
Patrick J. Lynn *(Dir.-Human Resources)*

Divisions:

Bioproducts, Inc. **(1)**
117 N. Morgan St.
Aurora, MO 65605
Tel.: 417-678-5988
Fax: 417-678-2056
S.I.C.: 2048; 2879
Stephen C. Latta *(Sr. V.P.)*

Bioproducts, Inc. **(1)**
8221 Brecksville Rd., Bldg. #2
Cleveland, OH 44141
Tel.: 216-526-5522
Tel.: 800-722-7242
Telecopier: 216-526-7077
S.I.C.: 2048; 2879
R. Michael Hickey *(Pres.)*

Bioproducts, Inc. **(1)**
5421 Philo St.
Cypress, CA 90630
Tel.: 714-826-5125
Tel.: 213-865-9595
Fax: 714-826-5710
S.I.C.: 2048; 2879
Steve E. Koenig *(V.P. & Gen. Mgr.)*

Bioproducts, Inc. **(1)**
P.O. Box 2425, 1246 Loyce Lane
Douglas, GA 31533
Tel.: 912-384-7515
Tel.: 800-633-9785
Fax: 912-384-7517
S.I.C.: 2048; 2879
Stephen C. Latta *(Sr. V.P.)*

Bioproducts, Inc. **(1)**
830 W. Lexington Ave., P.O. Box 316
Lititz, PA 17543
Tel.: 717-626-6005
Fax: 717-626-6061
S.I.C.: 2048; 2879
Stephen C. Latta *(Sr. V.P.)*

Bioproducts, Inc. **(1)**
4820 Jennings Lane
Louisville, KY 40218
Tel.: 502-968-3321
Tel.: 800-225-4519
Fax: 502-962-0720
S.I.C.: 2048; 2879
Stephen C. Latta *(Sr. V.P.)*

Bioproducts, Inc. **(1)**
#1 Industrial Rd.
Manson, IA 50563
Tel.: 712-469-3348
Tel.: 800-321-0533
Fax: 712-469-3015
S.I.C.: 2048; 2879
Stephen C. Latta *(Sr. V.P.)*

Bioproducts, Inc. **(1)**
4221 E. Mariposa Rd., P.O. Box 30416
Stockton, CA 95213-0416
Tel.: 209-467-1070
Fax: 209-467-4097
S.I.C.: 2048; 2879
Stephen C. Latta *(Sr. V.P.)*

Bioproducts, Inc. **(1)**
1935 N.W. Warrenton Dr., P.O. Box 429
Warrenton, OR 97146
Tel.: 503-861-2256
Tel.: 800-962-2001
Fax: 503-861-3701
S.I.C.: 2048; 2879
Bruce B. Buckmaster *(V.P. & Gen. Mgr.)*

Nutrius Dairy Feed Supplements Div. **(1)**
39494 Clarkson Drive
Kingsburg, CA 93631
Tel.: 209-897-5862
Tel.: 800-523-7746
Fax: 209-897-3371
S.I.C.: 2048; 2879
Steve Koenig *(V.P. & Gen. Mgr.)*

WILLIAM M. BIRD & CO., INC.
1142 Morrison Dr.
Charleston, SC 29403
Mailing Address:
P.O. Box 20040
Charleston, SC 29413
Tel.: 803-722-5930 **SC**
Fax: 803-723-5179
Year Founded: 1865
Approx.Sls.: $36,000,000
Emp.: 130
Fiscal Year-end: 12/31/90
Import
Wholesale Floor Coverings, Hardwood Floors, Carpets; Retail Paint
S.I.C.: 5023; 5198; 5039
Benjamin A. Hagood *(Pres.)*
John Apple *(V.P.-Floor Covering)*
D. Maybank Hagood *(V.P. & Treas.)*
Larry Laval *(V.P.-Carpets)*
Pat Sullivan *(V.P.-Specialty Prods.)*
Derrill M. Hagood *(Sec.)*

No. of Mfg. Plants/Facilities: 5

Computer Systems/Hardware:
IBM AS 400

Outside Service Firm(s):

Arthur Andersen & Co. *(Auditors)*
Columbia, SC

Freemont Financial Corporation *(Major Banking Relationship)*
Atlanta, GA

BIRDSALL VOSS & KLOPPENBURG, INC.
1355 W. Towne Square Rd.
Mequon, WI 53092
Tel.: 414-241-4890
Fax: 414-241-8729
Year Founded: 1984
Approx.Billings: $31,650,000
Emp.: 43
Consumer & Business-to-Business Adv.
Don R. Birdsall *(Chm. & Chief Exec. Officer)*

Michael P. Voss *(Pres.)*
Jerry Kloppenburg *(Grp. Exec. V.P.)*
Larry Kabins *(Grp. Exec. V.P.)*
Mary Louise Shaver *(Grp. Exec. V.P.)*
Karen Naumann *(V.P., Administrator)*

BIRDSONG CORPORATION
612 Madison Ave.
Sulfolk, VA 23434
Tel.: 804-539-3456 **VA**
Year Founded: 1947
Approx.Sls.: $255,000,000
Emp.: 300
Export
Marketing of Nuts & Nut By-Products; Bulk Unroasted Peanuts; Oil Nuts; Kernels, Seeds
S.I.C.: 5159
T.H. Birdsong, III *(Chm. Bd.)*
W.J. Spain, Jr. *(Pres. & Chief Exec. Officer)*
George Y. Birdsong *(V.P.)*
McLenore Birdsong, Jr. *(V.P.)*
William M. Birdsong, Jr. *(V.P.)*
D. Presley Duke, Jr. *(V.P.)*
G. Max Grice *(V.P.)*
J.B. Johnson, Jr. *(V.P.)*
Warren L. Birdsong *(Asst. V.P.)*
F. Ray Johns *(Controller)*
Terry D. Motley *(Mgr.-Data Processing)*
Everett B. Birdsong *(Asst. Mgr.-Data Processing)*

No. of Mfg. Plants/Facilities: 8
No. of U.S. Offices: 3

Computer Systems/Hardware:
IBM

Outside Service Firm(s):

Frank, Edward, Sheffer & Co.*(Auditors)*
Richmond, VA

Crestar Bank*(Major Banking Relationship)*
P.O. Box 26665,
Richmond, VA 23261
Tel.: 804-782-5995

Division:

Birdsong Peanuts **(1)**
612 Madison Ave.
Sulfolk, VA 23434
Tel.: 504-539-3456
Warehousing, Cold Storage or Refrigerated
S.I.C.: 4222
W.J. Spain, Jr. *(Pres.)*
J.B. Johnson *(Dir.-sls.)*

DAMIAN
BISCH
& PARTNERS, INC.
ADVERTISING

DAMIAN BISCH & PARTNERS, INC. ADVERTISING
841 Broadway
New York, NY 10003
Tel.: 212-353-1010
Fax: 212-353-1979
Year Founded: 1975
Approx.Billings: $28,000,000
Emp.: 20
Damian Bisch *(Pres. & Chief Exec. Officer)*
Amy Diamond *(V.P.-Devel.)*
Eileen Eck *(V.P.-Communications)*

BISCO INDUSTRIES
1620 S. Clementine Ave.
Anaheim, CA 92802
Tel.: 714-635-3980
Fax: 714-635-1406
Approx.Sls.: $20,000,000
Emp.: 110
Fiscal Year-end: 12/31/91
Electronic Parts
S.I.C.: 5065
Glen Ceiley *(Pres.)*
Linda Hamm *(V.P.)*

Outside Service Firm(s):

Security National Bank*(Major Banking Relationship)*
Los Angeles, CA

BISSELL INC.
2345 Walker N.W.
Grand Rapids, MI 49504
Mailing Address:
P.O. Box 1888,
Grand Rapids, MI 49501
Tel.: 616-453-4451
Fax: 616-784-5880
Approx.Sls.: $85,000,000
Emp.: 1,400
Fiscal Year-end: 12/31/91
Mfr. Carpet Sweepers, Vacuum Cleaners, Home Care Devices & Chemicals Floor Scrubbers, Rug Shampooers, Home Cleaning Chemical Specialties
S.I.C.: 3589; 3635; 2842
John M. Bissell *(Pres.)*
Mark J. Bissell *(Pres.-Home Care)*
T.L. Aldrich *(V.P.-Healthcare Grp.)*
Matt L. Bissell *(V.P.-Graphics Div.)*
J.D. Burggraaf *(V.P.-Mfg.)*
N.W. Fleury *(V.P.-European Div.)*
John S. Hughes, Jr. *(V.P.-Sls.)*
D.E. McDowell *(V.P.-Prod. Devel.)*
S.R. Kretschman *(Sec.)*
June Emperor *(Buyer)*
Dave Kagan *(Dir.-Adv.)*
Gary Bylsma *(Mgr.-Personnel)*
Hugh Vander Woude *(Pur. Agent)*
Principal(s):
John M. Bissell

Outside Service Firm(s):

BDO Seidman*(Auditors)*
99 Monroe Ave. NW, Ste. 800
Grand Rapids, MI 49503
Tel.: 616-774-7000
Fax: 616-451-2096

Warner, Norcross & Judd*(Legal Firm)*
Grand Rapids, MI

Old Kent Bank & Trust Co.*(Major Banking Relationship)*
One Vandenberg Center
Grand Rapids, MI 49503
Tel.: 616-774-5000

Subsidiaries:

Atlas Tag & Label Inc. **(1)**
P.O. Box 638
Neenah, WI 54957
Tel.: 414-722-1557
Approx.Sls.: $4,000,000
Emp.: 80
Mfr. Paper & Cloth Tags, Multiple Forms, Continuous Pinfeed
S.I.C.: 2679
H. J. Bloem *(Chm.)*
James Drechsel *(Pres.)*
John M. Bissell *(Pres.)*
J. W. Conway *(Sec. & Treas.)*
Calvin Hober *(Comptroller)*

Barcolene Penn Champ **(1)**
Lincoln & Railroad St.
East Butler, PA 16029
Tel.: 412-287-8771
Fax: 412-287-3544
Emp.: 90
Mfr. Health & Beauty Aids, Homecare Prods. & Automotive Specialty Chemicals
S.I.C.: 2844; 2842; 2992
E.S. Ivnik *(V.P.-Opers.)*
Roger A. Hitchcock *(Natl. Sls. Mgr.)*
Peg Selfridge *(Admin. Asst.)*
Paul Simitoski *(Mfg. Dir.)*

Bissell Ltd. **(1)**
Box 1003, 6934 Kinsmen Court
Niagara Falls, ON L2E 2W2, Canada (100%)
Tel.: 416-356-1531
Fax: 416-356-0625
Mktg. of Carpet Sweepers, Rug & Upholstery Shampoo, Vacuum Cleaners
S.I.C.: 5064; 5122
William A. Calisina *(V.P. & Gen. Mgr.)*

Camp International **(1)**
744 W. Michigan
Jackson, MI 49201
Tel.: 517-787-1600
Fax: 517-789-3299
Emp.: 350
Camp Supports, Braces, Binders, Patient Aids; Naturalwear Mastectomy Prods.; Sea Scamp Swimwear; Cadenza Elastic Supports, Cadence & Cadet Men's Elastic Supports, Sports Medicine
S.I.C.: 3842; 2329; 2339; 2389
John Bissell *(Chm. Bd.)*
Thomas L. Aldrich *(Pres. & Chief Exec. Officer)*
William J. Donahue *(V.P. & Gen. Mgr.)*
Fred G. Foster *(V.P.-Opers.)*
James Duncan *(Acting V.P.-Mktg.)*
George Caston *(Chief Fin. Officer)*
Charles A. Berhang *(Dir.-Sls.)*
Cindy Chrisman *(Adv. Coord.)*

Slip-X Safety Treads, Inc. **(1)**
P. O. Box 1888
Grand Rapids, MI 49501
Peter M. Sears *(Gen. Mgr.)*

BITREK CORPORATION
East 9th St.
Waynesboro, PA 17268
Mailing Address:
P.O. Box 510
Waynesboro, PA 17268
Tel.: 717-762-5313
Fax: 717-762-9153
Emp.: 450
Holding Company
S.I.C.: 6719
J. Edward Beck, Jr. *(Pres.)*
Stephen Beck *(V.P. & Sec.)*
Thomas E. Beck *(V.P. & Treas.)*

Outside Service Firm(s):

Grant Thornton*(Auditors)*
Two Hopkins Plaza
Baltimore, MD 21201
Tel.: 410-685-4000

Patterson, Komensli, Keller & Kiers*(Legal Firm)*
Waynesboro, PA

First National Bank & Trust Co.*(Major Banking Relationship)*
Waynesboro, PA

Subsidiaries:

Beck Manufacturing, Inc. **(1)**
East 9th St.
Waynesboro, PA 17268
Approx.Sls.: $8,000,000
Emp.: 50
Mfr. Steel Pipe Couplings
S.I.C.: 3494
Stephen Beck *(Pres.)*
Thomas E. Beck *(V.P. & Treas.)*
J. Edward Beck, Jr. *(Sec.)*
Rosina Novak *(Controller)*

Picoma Industries **(1)**
3800 Picoma Dr.
Texarkana, TX 75501
Tel.: 903-832-3562

BITUMINOUS ROADWAYS, INC.
2825 Cedar Ave. S.
Minneapolis, MN 55407
Tel.: 612-721-2451 **MN**
Fax: 612-721-6875
Year Founded: 1946
Approx.Sls.: $10,000,000
Emp.: 20
General Contractors, Highway & Street Contruction; Manufacture Asphalt
S.I.C.: 1611; 2951
Palmer G. Peterson *(Pres.)*
Edward Otremba *(Treas.)*

No. of Mfg. Plants/Facilities: 2

Outside Service Firm(s):

Popham, Haik, Schnobrich Ltd.*(Legal Firm)*
Minneapolis, MN

American National Bank & Trust of St. Paul*(Major Banking Relationship)*
Fifth & Minnesota Streets
St. Paul, MN 55101
Tel.: 612-298-6000

BIXBY INTERNATIONAL CORP.
One Preble Rd.
Newburyport, MA 01950
Tel.: 508-462-4100
Fax: 508-465-5184
Approx.Sls.: $18,000,000
Emp.: 100
Manufacture Box Toes & Counter Materials, Adhesives, Extruded Plastic Sheeting
S.I.C.: 3131; 2891; 3083; 3089
B.C. Bixby *(Chm. Bd.)*
Robert S. McLellan *(Pres.)*
Principal(s):
B.C. Bixby

Outside Service Firm(s):

BayBank Merrimack Valley, N.A.*(Major Banking Relationship)*
23 Main St.
Andover, MA 01810
Tel.: 617-475-3620
Fax: 617-475-3620 Ext. 6114

BIZZACK INC.
(Formerly Bizzack Brothers Construction Corp.)
2265 Executive Dr.
Lexington, KY 40505
Mailing Address:
P.O. Box 12530,
Lexington, KY 40583
Tel.: 606-299-8001
Approx.Sls.: $25,000,000
Emp.: 300
Highway Construction
S.I.C.: 1611
Gary Howard *(Pres.)*
Stan Bray *(Controller)*
Principal(s):
Stan Bray

Computer Systems/Hardware:
IBM

Outside Service Firm(s):

Charles T. Mitchell Co.*(Auditors)*
Frankfort, KY

Stoll, Keenon & Park*(Legal Firm)*
Lexington, KY

First National Bank*(Major Banking Relationship)*
Louisville, KY

BLACK CADILLAC OLDS, INC.
601 E. Bessemer Ave.
Greensboro, NC 27405
Tel.: 919-275-9641
Fax: 919-275-0528
Approx.Sls.: $43,000,000
Emp.: 125
Cadillac-Oldsmobile Dealer
S.I.C.: 5511
William H. Black, II *(Chm. Bd.)*
William H. Black, III *(Pres.)*
Nancy U. Cusimono *(Office Mgr.)*
Ronald E. McKinney *(Bus. Mgr.)*
Principal(s):
William H. Black, II
William H. Black, III

Computer Systems/Hardware:
IBM

Outside Service Firm(s):

Deloitte & Touche*(Auditors)*
Greensboro, NC

Black Cadillac Olds, Inc.—(Continued)

Brooks, Pierce, McLendon, Humphrey & Leonard*(Legal Firm)*
2000 Renaissance Plaza
Greensboro, NC 27402
Tel.: 919-373-8850

Wachovia Bank & Trust Co.*(Major Banking Relationship)*
P.O. Box 21048,
Greensboro, NC 27402

THE BLACK CLAWSON CO.
405 Lexington Ave
New York, NY 10174
Mailing Address:
605 Clark St.
Middletown, OH 45042
Tel.: 212-916-8000
Tel.: 513-424-7400
Approx.Sls.: $30,000,000
Emp.: 1,900
Fiscal Year-end: 3/31/90
Mfrs. of Machinery for Pulp & Paper; Converting, Plastics & Concrete Pipe
S.I.C.: 3599
C.C. Landegger *(Chm. Bd.)*
R.D. Agronin *(Grp. V.P.)*
D.E. Parker *(Chief Fin. Officer)*
S.T. Temple *(Corp. Communications Mgr.)*

Divisions:

The Black Clawson Company **(1)**
Fulton, NY 13069
Tel.: 315-598-7121
S.I.C.: 3599
J.S. Simcox *(Pres. & Gen. Mgr.)*

The Black Clawson Company **(1)**
605 Clark St.
Middletown, OH 45042
Tel.: 513-424-7400
S.I.C.: 3599
W.J. Fondow *(Pres. & Gen. Mgr.)*

Subsidiary:

BC Hydrotile Machinery Co. **(1)**
Nashua, IA 50658
Tel.: 515-435-4141
S.I.C.: 3599
Michael Knight *(V.P. & Gen. Mgr.)*

BLACK & CO.
1717 E. Garfield Ave.
Decatur, IL 62526
Mailing Address:
P.O. Box 1170
Decatur, IL 62525
Tel.: 217-428-4424
Fax: 217-428-1439
Approx.Sls.: $19,000,000
Emp.: 300
Distribute Hardware, Machine Tools, Industrial Supplies, Paint & Contractor's Supplies
S.I.C.: 5072; 5039; 5084; 5085; 5251
Stuart M. Black *(Chm. Bd.)*
Jeff Black *(Pres. & Treas.)*
Bradley Kent *(V.P.)*
Donna Thorpe *(Sec.)*
Principal(s):
Stuart M. Black

Computer Systems/Hardware:
Burroughs B-28

Outside Service Firm(s):

KPMG Peat Marwick*(Auditors)*
Decatur, IL

Citizens National Bank*(Major Banking Relationship)*
Decatur, IL

BLACK FIN YACHT CORPORATION
3391 S.E. 14th Ave.
Fort Lauderdale, FL 33316
Mailing Address:
P.O. Box 22982
Ft. Lauderdale, FL 33335
Tel.: 305-525-6314 **FL**
Fax: 305-523-7728
Sales Range: $10-19 Million
Emp.: 225
Manufacture Sportfishing Boats
S.I.C.: 3732
Robert L. Ross *(Chm. Bd.)*
Carl M. Herndon *(Pres.)*
Mark Sweeney *(V.P.-Sls., Mktg. & Pub. Rels.)*
Robert Sherman *(Cntroller)*
Principal(s):
Robert L. Ross
Carl M. Herndon
Wesmar Partners

No. of Mfg. Plants/Facilities: 1
No. of U.S. Offices: 1

Outside Service Firm(s):

Deloitte & Touche*(Auditors)*
Fort Lauderdale, FL 33394

Alexander & Alexander*(Commercial Insurance Carrier)*
Pittsburgh, PA

Equicor*(Group Insurer)*
Pittsburgh, PA

Citizens & Southern National Bank*(Major Banking Relationship)*
Dalton, GA

Willis Corroon*(Major Banking Relationship)*
301 Plus Park Blvd.
Nashville, TN 37217
Tel.: 615-367-9702

BLACK GILLOCK & LANGBERG

BLACK GILLOCK & LANGBERG
5851 San Felipe, Ste. 100
Houston, TX 77057
Tel.: 713-781-6666
Year Founded: 1982
Approx.Billings: $55,000,000
Emp.: 76
Scott Black *(Pres.)*
Stephen Rogers *(Sr. Exec. V.P.)*
Eric Herbst *(Exec. V.P., Dir. Media & Strategic Planning)*
Dana Worley *(Sr. V.P., Chief Fin. Officer)*
Bonnie Davidson *(Dir. Admin.)*

WALTER J. BLACK, INC.
99 Seaview Blvd.
Port Washington, NY 11050
Tel.: 516-484-4445 **NY**
Fax: 516-484-4709
Year Founded: 1923
Approx.Sls.: $1,500,000
Emp.: 25
Fiscal Year-end: 12/31/90
Export
Book Publishers
S.I.C.: 2731
T.M. Black, Sr. *(Chm. Bd. & Editor-in-Chief)*
W.J. Black II *(Pres., Chief Exec. Officer & Treas.)*
B. Ward *(Assoc. Editor)*
E.D. Falk *(V.P.-Fin.)*
R.T. McManus *(V.P.-Distr. & Warehousing, Gen. Mgr. & Dir.-Personnel)*
Francis C. Pavlak *(V.P.-Production)*
T.M. Black, Jr. *(Sec. & Dir.-Research)*
J. Reszko *(Dir.-Mktg.)*
L.S. Holler *(Dir.-Computer Opers.)*
L.H. Brockmann *(Asst. Gen. Mgr.)*

No. of U.S. Offices: 1
No. of Foreign Offices: 1

Computer Systems/Hardware:
Datapoint

Outside Service Firm(s):

Theodore Present*(Auditors)*
New York, NY

Hults & Steuer, Inc.*(Commercial Insurance Carrier)*
Old Northern Blvd.
Roslyn, NY 11576

Empire Blue Cross & Blue Shield*(Group Insurer)*
New York, NY

Forman, Arweiler & Schaeffer*(Legal Firm)*
Mineola, NY

Divisions:

Walter J. Black, Inc. Fulfillment Services **(1)**
99 Seaview Blvd.
Port Washington, NY 11050
Tel.: 516-484-4445
Mail-Order Fulfillment; Problem Jobs, Small-to-Medium Quantities; Storage, Select, Pack, Affix Labels/Invoices/Postage; Arrangements for Carrier Pick-up
S.I.C.: 5961

Black's Readers Service **(1)**
99 Seaview Blvd.
Port Washington, NY 11050
Tel.: 516-484-4445
S.I.C.: 2731

The Classics Club **(1)**
99 Seaview Blvd.
Port Washington, NY 11050
Tel.: 516-484-4445
S.I.C.: 2731

The Detective Book Club **(1)**
99 Seaview Blvd.
Port Washington, NY 11050
Tel.: 516-484-4445
S.I.C.: 2731

The (Erle Stanley) Gardner Mystery Library **(1)**
99 Seaview Blvd.
Port Washington, NY 11050
Tel.: 516-484-4445
S.I.C.: 2731

The Giants of Literature Series **(1)**
99 Seaview Blvd.
Port Washington, NY 11050
Tel.: 516-484-4445
S.I.C.: 2731

The Golden Giants Series **(1)**
99 Seaview Blvd.
Port Washington, NY 11050
Tel.: 516-484-4445
S.I.C.: 2731

The Zane Grey Library **(1)**
99 Seaview Blvd.
Port Washington, NY 11050
Tel.: 516-484-4445
S.I.C.: 2731

BLACK MILLWORK CO., INC.
230 W. Crescent Ave.
Allendale, NJ 07401
Tel.: 201-934-0100
Fax: 201-934-9358
Sales Range: $80-99 Million
Emp.: 140
Distributor Of Windows & Doors
S.I.C.: 3442; 2431
T. Councilor *(Pres. & Treas.)*
Rob Councilor *(V.P.-Opers.)*
Ed Vanderbeck, Jr. *(V.P.-Sls.)*

Outside Service Firm(s):

Ludwig, Balmer, Seifert & Lane*(Auditors)*
Hackensack, NJ

Kelley Drye & Warren*(Legal Firm)*
6 Stamford Forum
Stamford, CT 06901

Citizens First National Bank*(Major Banking Relationship)*
Allendale, NJ

BLACK & VEATCH
8400 Ward Pkwy.
Kansas City, MO 64114
Mailing Address:
P.O. Box 8405
Kansas City, MO 64114
Tel.: 913-339-2000
Fax: 913-339-3511
Year Founded: 1915
Approx.Sls.: $220,700,000
Emp.: 4,300
Engineering & Management Services for Power, Water & Wastewater Utilities, Municipalities, Industry & Federal Agencies
S.I.C.: 8711; 8712
John H. Robinson *(Mng. Partner)*
P.J. Adam *(Asst. Mng. Partner)*
A M. Acheson *(Exec. Partner)*
R.D. Hardten *(Exec. Partner)*
J.L. Patton *(Exec. Partner)*
J.H. Robinson, Jr. *(Exec. Partner)*
R.G. Ruisch *(Exec. Partner)*
G.F. Cockrell *(Controller)*
F.E. Schoenlaub *(Legal Officer)*
D.E. Disbrow *(Dir.-Pur.)*
F.B. Groover *(Dir.-Telecommunications)*
D.M. Lanter *(Dir.-Communications)*
D.H. Lillard *(Dir.-Personnel)*
M.L. Cortner *(Mgr.-Data Processing)*
Principal(s):
John H. Robinson
P.J. Adam
A M. Acheson
R.D. Hardten
J.L. Patton
J.H. Robinson, Jr.
R.G. Ruisch

No. of U.S. Offices: 35
No. of Foreign Offices: 3

Computer Systems/Hardware:
IBM 4361; DEC VAX; Sperry 1100

Outside Service Firm(s):

Blackwell, Sanders, Matheny, Weary & Lombardi*(Legal Firm)*
2300 Main Street
Kansas City, MO 64108
Tel.: 816-474-5700

Commerce Bank of Kansas City*(Major Banking Relationship)*
10th & Walnut
Kansas City, MO 64141
Tel.: 816-234-2000
Fax: 816-234-2548

Subsidiaries:

B & V Waste Science & Technology Corp. **(1)**
4717 Grand
Kansas City, MO 64112
Tel.: 913-339-2900
Fax: 913-339-6645
Engineering Firm
S.I.C.: 8711
P.B. MacRoberts *(Chief Oper. Officer)*

Black & Veatch Architects, Inc. **(1)**
4717 Grand
Kansas City, MO 64112
Tel.: 913-339-8700
Fax: 913-339-3626
Architectural Firm
S.I.C.: 8712
Joe Brown *(Pres.)*

Black & Veatch International **(1)**
6601 College Blvd.
Overland Park, MO 66211
Tel.: 913-339-8700
Fax: 913-339-8711
Engineering, Architectural & Surveying Service
S.I.C.: 8711; 8712

R. Stamm *(Pres.)*

The Pritchard Corporation **(1)**
10950 Grandview Dr.
Overland Park, KS 66210
Tel.: 913-661-6000
Fax: 913-661-6030
Engineering Firm
S.I.C.: 8711
John Nobles *(Chief Oper. Officer)*

STANLEY BLACKER, INC.
1801 Courtland St.
Philadelphia, PA 19140
Tel.: 215-455-9868
Fax: 215-445-9497
Approx.Sls.: $65,000,000
Emp.: 500
Manufacture Men's & Women's Tailored Clothing & Sportswear
S.I.C.: 2311; 2329; 2325; 2331; 2337
Stanley Blacker *(Chm. Bd. & Pres.)*

Principal(s):
Stanley Blacker

Outside Service Firm(s):

NatWest Bank U.S.A.*(Major Banking Relationship)*
New York, NY

BLACKSTONE PARTNERSHIP (NYC)
345 Park Ave.
New York, NY 10154
Tel.: 212-935-2626
Holding Co.
S.I.C.: 6719

BLADE COMMUNICATIONS, INC.
541 Superior St.
Toledo, OH 43660
Tel.: 419-245-6000
Year Founded: 1835
Sales Range: $100-499 Million
Emp.: 1,500
Fiscal Year-end: 12/31/91
Newspaper Publisher; Cablevision, Television & Mobile Broadcasting; Advertising Distribution
S.I.C.: 2711; 4841; 4833; 7331
Corporate Giving Program: The United Way
William Block *(Chm. Bd.)*
Allan Block *(Vice Chm.)*
William Block, Jr. *(Pres.)*
John Block *(Exec. V.P., Co-Publr. & Editor-in Chief)*
Gary J. Blair *(V.P.-Admin. & Treas.)*
Joseph Restivo *(Asst. Treas.)*
Malcolm Edge *(Dir.-Mngmt. Information Systems)*
Leroy Gagle *(Dir.-Telecommunications)*
Jo Kerns *(Dir.-Human Resources)*
Joe Fredrickson *(Dir.-Mktg.)*
Jacqueline Porter *(Mgr.-Fleet Leasing)*

No. of Mfg. Plants/Facilities: 15

Outside Service Firm(s):

Ernst & Young*(Auditors)*
One Sea Gate
Toledo, OH 43604
Tel.: 419-244-8000

Hylant-MacLean*(Group Insurer)*
1505 Jefferson Ave., P.O. Box 1687
Toledo, OH 43603-1687
Tel.: 419-255-1020

Fritz Byers*(Legal Firm)*
501 Spitzer Bldg.
Toledo, OH 43604
Tel.: 419-241-8013

The Huntington National Bank*(Major Banking Relationship)*
Toledo, OH

Subsidiaries:

The Herald **(1)**
8 Upper Ragsdale Dr.
Monterey, CA 93940
Tel.: 408-372-3311
Newspaper Publishing
S.I.C.: 2711
Christopher S. Dix *(Gen. Mgr.)*
Ken Kraft *(Controller)*
Alice Burton *(Dir.-Adv.)*

Toledo Blade Co. **(1)**
541 Superior St.
Toledo, OH 43660
Tel.: 419-245-6000
Emp.: 650
The Blade Newspaper
S.I.C.: 2711
William Block Sr. *(Chm. Bd.)*
Allan Block *(Vice Chm.)*
William Block, Jr. *(Pres. & Co-Publr.)*
John Block *(Co-Publr. & Editor-in-Chief)*
Gary J. Blair *(V.P.-Admin. & Treas.)*
Robert Higdon *(V.P. & Gen. Mgr.)*
Linda Hoyt *(Controller)*
Tom Walton *(Editor)*
Jo K. Adams *(Dir.-Human Resources)*
Joseph Frederickson *(Dir.-Mktg.)*
Lee Gagle *(Dir.-Systems)*
Michael McCaffrey *(Dir.-Circulation)*
Joseph Restivo *(Dir.-Fin.)*
Edward Schultz *(Dir.-Adv.)*
David Smith *(Dir.-Pur.)*
L. Hank Baker *(Mgr.-Natl. Adv.)*
Hope Nofziger *(Mgr.-Credit)*
Kevin O'Connell *(Mgr.-Retail Adv.)*
Charles Stroh *(Mgr.-Prod.)*
Mary Maczum *(Librarian)*

TIM & DIANE BLAGGE INC.
(d/b/a Blagge Enterprises)
2590 Mercantile Dr., Suite K
Rancho Cordova, CA 95742
Tel.: 916-638-7013
Fax: 916-638-0626
Year Founded: 1977
Assets: $4,266,000
Earnings: $113,014
Net Worth: $4,266,000
Approx.Sls.: $20,785,000
Emp.: 70
Fiscal Year-end: 6/30/91
Distribute Blank Audio & Video Tapes, Electronics, Small Appliances
S.I.C.: 5064; 5065
Timothy J. Blagge *(Pres. & Chief Exec. Officer)*
Diane L. Blagge *(V.P. & Treas.)*
Denise Watts *(Dir.-Pur.)*

ALGERNON BLAIR INTERNATIONAL
One Algernon Blair Pl.
Montgomery, AL 36116
Mailing Address:
P.O. Box 749,
Montgomery, AL 36101
Tel.: 205-279-7300
Fax: 205-279-7304
Year Founded: 1896
Sales Range: $100-499 Million
Emp.: 100
Fiscal Year-end: 9/30/89
Holding Company; Construction Contractors
S.I.C.: 1629; 6719
C. B. Shewmake *(Chm. Bd. & Chief Exec. Officer)*
C. B. Shewmake, Jr. *(Pres.)*
Larry Caterbury *(Comptroller)*

No. of U.S. Offices: 4

Computer Systems/Hardware:
IBM System 36

Outside Service Firm(s):

Jackson Thornton*(Auditors)*
Montgomery, AL

Bankers Life & Casualty*(Group Insurer)*
Des Moines, IA

Blue Cross & Blue Shield of Alabama*(Group Insurer)*
450 Riverchase Pkwy. East
Birmingham, AL 35298
Tel.: 205-988-2245

New England Mutual Life Insurance Co.*(Group Insurer)*
Boston, MA

Union Bank*(Major Banking Relationship)*
Montgomery, AL

JOHN BLAIR COMMUNICATIONS, INC.
1290 Ave. of the Americas
New York, NY 10104
Tel.: 212-603-5000 **DE**
Twx: 710-581-4351
Fax: 212-603-5003
Approx.Billings: $800,000,000
Emp.: 560
Television Program Production, Distribution & Syndication
S.I.C.: 7313
James Rosenfield *(Chm. Bd.)*
Timothy M. McAuliff *(Pres. & Chief Exec. Officer)*
Sanford S. Ackerman *(Sr. V.P. & Chief Fin. Officer)*
Kenneth P. Donnellon *(V.P.-Adv. & Communications)*
Ronald J. Brooks *(Gen. Counsel)*
Lynne Welbrock *(Dir.-Human Resources)*

Outside Service Firm(s):

KPMG Peat Marwick*(Auditors)*
345 Park Ave.
New York, NY 10154
Tel.: 212-758-9700
Fax: 212-872-3308

Roseman, Colin, Freund, Lewis & Cohen*(Legal Firm)*
575 Madison Ave.
New York, NY 10022
Tel.: 212-644-7000

The Bank of New York*(Major Banking Relationship)*
One Wall Street
New York, NY 10286
Tel.: 212-635-6805
Fax: 212-635-3201

Division:

Blair Television **(1)**
1290 Ave. of the Americas
New York, NY 10104
Tel.: 212-603-5000
Twx: 710-581-4351
Fax: 212-603-5501
Television Station Sales Representative
S.I.C.: 7313
James H. Rosenfield *(Chm. Bd.)*
Timothy M. McAuliff *(Pres. & Chief Exec. Officer)*
Sanford S. Ackerman *(Sr. V.P.-Fin. & Admin. & Chief Fin. Officer)*
William E. Breda, Jr. *(Sr. V.P. & Gen. Sls. Mgr.)*
Floyd J. Gelini *(Sr. V.P. & Dir.-Reg. Sls.)*
Kenneth P. Donnellon *(V.P.-Adv. & Communications)*
Donald K. Williams *(V.P. & Dir.-Mktg.)*
Ronald J. Brooks *(Gen. Counsel)*
Lynne Wellbrock *(Dir.-Human Resources)*
Mary Jane Berkowitz *(Mgr.-Human Resources)*
Barry Murley *(Mgr.-Mngmt. Information Systems)*

WILLIAM BLAIR & COMPANY
135 S. LaSalle St.
Chicago, IL 60603
Tel.: 312-236-1600
Telex: 02-53013
Year Founded: 1934
Assets: $138,000,000
Liabilities: $88,000,000
Net Worth: $50,000,000
Sales Range: $100-499 Million
Emp.: 435
Fiscal Year-end: 12/31/90
Underwriting, Investment Management
S.I.C.: 6211; 6282
Edgar D. Jannotta *(Mng. Partner)*
Edward McCormick Blair *(Sr. Partner)*
Bowen Blair *(Sr. Partner)*
John P. Kayser *(Chief Fin. Partner & Mgr.)*
Steven J. Ashby *(Cashier & Partner)*
Patricia M. Aylward *(Dir.-Personnel)*
W. Newton Burdick, III *(Dir.-Computer Systems)*
Kathleen Wieland *(Dir.-Compliance)*
Dana McMullen *(Dir.-Gen. Office)*
Stephen Campbell *(Mgr.-Financial Control)*

No. of U.S. Offices: 2
No. of Foreign Offices: 2

Computer Systems/Hardware:
IBM PC

Outside Service Firm(s):

Arthur Andersen & Co.*(Auditors)*
33 W. Monroe St.
Chicago, IL 60603-4067
Tel.: 312-580-0033
Fax: 312-507-6748

WHITNEY BLAKE COMPANY OF VERMONT, INC.
Industrial Dr.
Bellows Falls, VT 05101
Mailing Address:
P.O. Box 579,
Bellows Falls, VT 05101
Tel.: 802-463-9541
Fax: 802-463-3926
Year Founded: 1985
Approx.Sls.: $10,000,000
Emp.: 230
Fiscal Year-end: 12/31/90
Import Export
Rubber & Plastic Insulated Retractile Cords, Communications Cable
S.I.C.: 3357
Roland Scott *(Pres.)*
Keith Zimmermann *(Exec. V.P.)*
Lawrence McAuliffe *(Controller)*
Carl Hill *(V.P.-Engrng. & Tech.)*
Keith Zimmermann, Jr. *(Mgr.-Natl. Sls.)*
Betsy Bascom *(Personnel Admin.)*

WM. BLANCHARD CO.
199 Mountain Ave.
Springfield, NJ 07081
Mailing Address:
P.O. Box 298,
Springfield, NJ 07081
Tel.: 201-376-9100 **NJ**
Fax: 201-376-9154
Year Founded: 1860
Approx.Sls.: $35,000,000
Emp.: 100
Hospital & Office Building Construction
S.I.C.: 1542; 1541
Richard F. Blanchard *(Pres.)*
Charles Samenfeld *(V.P.)*
William C. Blanchard *(Sec. & Treas.)*
Principal(s):
Richard F. Blanchard
William C. Blanchard

Outside Service Firm(s):

Saul A. Cohn Co.*(Auditors)*
Union, NJ

Horizon Bank*(Major Banking Relationship)*
Morristown, NJ

BLAND CADILLAC COMPANY
2100 Bagby
Houston, TX 77002
Mailing Address:
P.O. Box 2147
Houston, TX 77252
Tel.: 713-527-6600

Bland Cadillac Company—(Continued)

Fax: 713-527-0290
Approx.Rev.: $70,000,000
Emp.: 150
Cadillac Dealership
S.I.C.: 5511
William W. Bland *(Chm. Bd. & Pres.)*
Marva N. Reese *(Sec.)*
Richard H. Fedson *(Gen. Mgr.)*
Bill Ford *(Mgr.-Sls.)*
Principal(s):
William W. Bland

Outside Service Firm(s):

McGee, Wheeler & Co.*(Auditors)*
Houston, TX

Baker & Botts*(Legal Firm)*
3000 One Shell Plaza
Houston, TX 77002
Tel.: 713-229-1789

Texas Commerce Bank*(Major Banking Relationship)*
600 Travis Street, Suite 1150
Houston, TX 77002
Tel.: 713-236-4865

Blattner/Brunner INC.
ADVERTISING, MARKETING & PUBLIC RELATIONS

BLATTNER/BRUNNER INC.
814 Penn Ave.
Pittsburgh, PA 15222
Tel.: 412-263-2979
Fax: 412-263-2126
Year Founded: 1975
Approx.Billings: $21,000,000
Emp.: 43
Joseph R. Blattner *(Chm. & Chief Exec. Officer)*
Michael J. Brunner *(Pres. & Chief Oper. Officer)*
Katie Bicknell *(V.P., Dir. Mktg. Services)*
David Fleeger *(Dir. Pub. Rels.)*

D.H. BLATTNER & SONS, INC.
P.O. Box 37
Avon, MN 56310
Tel.: 612-356-7351
Fax: 612-356-7392
Approx.Sls.: $45,000,000
Emp.: 350
Fiscal Year-end: 2/28/92
Grading & Bridge Contractors, Contract Mining
S.I.C.: 1389; 1611; 1622
William H. Blattner, Jr. *(Pres.)*
Christopher J. Blattner *(Exec. V.P.)*
Stephen C. Blattner *(Sec., Treas. & Chief Fin. Officer)*
James S. Kampa *(Mgr.-Equip.)*

Outside Service Firm(s):

Grant Thornton*(Auditors)*
500 Pillsbury Center
Minneapolis, MN 55402-1459

Moore, Costello & Hart*(Legal Firm)*
St. Paul, MN

First Bank Minneapolis*(Major Banking Relationship)*
P.O. Box A700, 120 S. Sixth St.
Minneapolis, MN 55480
Tel.: 612-370-4141

BARRY BLAU & PARTNERS, INC.
1960 Bronson Rd.
Fairfield, CT 06430
Tel.: 203-254-3700
Tel.: 718-584-1220
Fax: 203-255-2807
Year Founded: 1979
Earnings: ($271,256)
Approx.Billings: $127,048,000
Emp.: 132
Fiscal Year-end: 6/30/90
Direct Response Marketing
Barry Blau *(Chm. Bd. & Chief Exec. Officer)*
Dennis Eastman *(Pres., Chief Oper. Officer)*
Ron Friedman *(Vice Chm.)*
David Finkel *(Exec. V.P., Gen. Mgr.)*
Fred Kaseff *(Sr. V.P., Chief Fin. Officer)*
Michelle Beyman *(V.P., Dir. Mktg.)*

BLAUER MANUFACTURING CO., INC.
20 Aberdeen St.
Boston, MA 02215
Tel.: 617-536-6606
Fax: 617-536-6948
Year Founded: 1936
Approx.Sls.: $16,000,000
Emp.: 450
Fiscal Year-end: 12/31/90
Mfr. of Men's & Women's Uniform Outerwear
S.I.C.: 2339; 2326
Charles Blauer *(Pres.)*
Stephen Blauer *(V.P.-Mktg.)*
Michael Blauer *(V.P.-Engrng.)*
Thomas Seaman *(Controller & Dir.-Personnel)*
Joseph Stacy *(Dir.-Data Processing)*

Outside Service Firm(s):

Goldstein, Burkin, Wennett & Carter*(Legal Firm)*
Boston, MA

Shawmut Bank*(Major Banking Relationship)*
Boston, MA

BLAW KNOX CORP.
One Oliver Plaza
Pittsburgh, PA 15222
Tel.: 412-263-2300 **DE**
Fax: 412-263-2308
Approx.Sls.: $80,000,000
Emp.: 800
Fiscal Year-end: 9/30/91
Export
Mfr. of Steel Mill Machinery & Equipment, Food & Chemical Equipment, Material Handling Equipment & Construction Products; Ferrous & Metal Alloy Castings; Engineering Services; Iron & Steel Base Rolls
S.I.C.: 3535; 3321; 3363; 3531; 3537; 3556; 8711; 3644; 3541; 3542; 3545; 3547; 3549; 3559; 3324; 3325
Dean G. Wilson *(Chm. Bd., Pres. & Chief Exec. Officer)*
Richard A. McIntyre *(V.P.-Fin., Treas. & Sec.)*
Carol M. Selznick *(Mgr.-Admin.)*

No. of Mfg. Plants/Facilities: 4

Computer Systems/Hardware:
Zenith PC

Outside Service Firm(s):

Grant Thornton*(Auditors)*
One Oxford Centre
Pittsburgh, PA 15219-6402
Tel.: 412-232-3100

Meyer, Unkovic, & Scott*(Legal Firm)*
Oliver Bldg.
Pittsburgh, PA 15222
Tel.: 412-456-2833

Society National Bank*(Major Banking Relationship)*
900 Euclid Ave., P.O. Box 6477
Cleveland, OH 44101-6477
Tel.: 216-737-5000
Fax: 216-566-8947

Divisions:

Blaw Knox - Duraloy Division **(1)**
P.O. Box 81, Bridge St.
Scottdale, PA 15683
Tel.: 412-887-5100
Fax: 412-887-5224
Specialty Foundry; Heat Resistant & Corrosion Resistant Castings & Fabrications
S.I.C.: 3325
Larry D. Wright *(Pres.)*
S. Clarke *(V.P.-Sales)*
M. Rodnar *(Chief Fin. Officer)*

Blaw Knox Food & Chemical Equipment Company **(1)**
750 E. Ferry St.
Buffalo, NY 14211
Tel.: 716-895-2100
Tel.: 800-332-2419
Telex: 62932507
Fax: 716-895-8263
Emp.: 200
Export
Dryers, Evaporators, Flakers, Reactors, Agglomerators, Coffee, Nut & Cocoa Bean Roasters, Volumetric Feeders, Sifters, Screens, Granulizers
S.I.C.: 3556
John M. Gentner *(Pres.)*
D.L. Hemink *(V.P.-Fin.)*
Daryl T. Zurawski *(V.P.-Buflovak Sls. & Engrng.)*
R. Trzecki *(Mgr.-Production Control)*
H.H. Roberts *(Mgr.-Personnel)*
J.S. Wasik *(Mgr.-Quality Assurance)*
J. Gregory Cannon *(Mgr.-Pur.)*
E.B. Pinkel *(Dir.-Laboratory Services)*

Blaw Knox Rolls Division **(1)**
98 Peninsula St.
Wheeling, WV 26003
Tel.: 304-234-9600
Fax: 304-234-9595
Rolls for Steel & Aluminum Industry
S.I.C.: 3325
R.A. Kusner *(Pres.)*
Sam Hague *(V.P.-Sls.)*

BLUE GRASS CHRYSLER-PLYMOUTH
1651 N. Broadway
Lexington, KY 40505
Tel.: 606-299-1231
Fax: 606-299-1231, Ext. 430
Approx.Sls.: $40,000,000
Emp.: 85
New & Used Car Dealer
S.I.C.: 5511
Rodney B. Hatfield *(Pres.)*
Betty Hinton *(Sec. & Treas.)*

Outside Service Firm(s):

Central Bank & Trust Co.*(Major Banking Relationship)*
Lexington, KY

BLEVINS CONCESSION SUPPLY CO.
P.O. Box 79136
Tampa, FL 33619
Tel.: 813-247-7116 **FL**
Fax: 813-248-2604
Year Founded: 1945
Assets: $15,000,000
Liabilities: $9,000,000
Net Worth: $6,000,000
Approx.Sls.: $50,000,000
Emp.: 175
Fiscal Year-end: 12/31/90
Export
Distributor: Popcorn, Oil & Seasonings; Candy; Paper Cups; Concession Supplies & Equipment; Janitorial Supplies
S.I.C.: 2099; 5046; 5441; 5087; 5145
Randy Greene *(Chm. Bd. & Pres.)*
Marvin Lowry *(V.P.-Oper.)*
Principal(s):
Randy Greene
Pam Rush

No. of Mfg. Plants/Facilities: 18
No. of U.S. Offices: 20

Computer Systems/Hardware:
IBM RISC 6000

Outside Service Firm(s):

Deloitte & Touche*(Auditors)*
Tampa, FL

Poe & Associates, Inc.*(Commercial Insurance Carrier)*
Tampa, FL

MacFarlane, Ferguson, Allison & Kelly*(Legal Firm)*
512 No. Florida Ave.
Tampa, FL 33602
Tel.: 813-223-2411

Bank of Boston*(Major Banking Relationship)*
Atlanta, GA

Division:

Iroquois Popcorn **(1)**
1370 Lively Blvd.
Elk Grove Village, IL 6007
Tel.: 708-439-9000
Processors of Popcorn
S.I.C.: 2099
Jay Marshall *(Chief Oper. Officer)*

BLEVINS INC.
421 Hart Ln.
Nashville, TN 37206
Mailing Address:
P.O. Box 160387
Nashville, TN 37216
Tel.: 615-226-6453 **TN**
Fax: 615-228-1301
Year Founded: 1971
Approx.Sls.: $30,000,000
Emp.: 140
Fiscal Year-end: 12/31/91
Import
Wholesale Distributor of Mobile Homes, RVs, Parts & Accessories
S.I.C.: 5099
James W. Blevins *(Pres. & Chief Exec Officer)*
C.A. Hayes *(Dir.-Pur., Adv. & Mktg.)*
R.L. Nobles *(Controller & Dir.-Data Processing)*
Principal(s):
James W. Blevins

Computer Systems/Hardware:
DEC Prophet 21

Outside Service Firm(s):

Deloitte & Touche*(Auditors)*
424 Church St., Ste. 2400
Nashville, TN 37219-2396

Aetna Life & Casualty*(Group Insurer)*
Nashville, TN

Third National Bank*(Major Banking Relationship)*
Nashville, TN

Subsidiary:

The Marble Company **(1)**
421 Hart Lane
Nashville, TN 37216
Tel.: 615-227-7772
Tel.: 800-759-5905
Emp.: 5
Wholesale Theatre Supplies
S.I.C.: 5043
J. William Blevins *(Pres.)*
Ron Purtee *(Gen. Mgr.)*

Blinn Wholesale Drug Co., Inc.
(Acquired by Commons Bros., Inc., name changed to Commons Metro Inc.)

BLISS-SALEM, INC.
530 S. Ellsworth
Salem, OH 44460
Tel.: 216-337-3444
Fax: 216-337-7067
Year Founded: 1857
Approx.Sls.: $45,000,000
Emp.: 340
Fiscal Year-end: 6/30/91
Rolling Mills & Allied Equip. for Ferrous & Nonferrous Metals, Continuous Casting Systems, Hot Strip Downcoilers, Computerized

Hydraulic Mill Automatic Gauge Control Systems, Mill Modernization of Existing Facilities & Contract Machining Services
S.I.C.: 3547; 3549; 3823; 1799; 3599
Michael J. Zugay *(Pres.)*
C. William Paxton *(Sr. V.P.-Engineered Prods.)*
L.H. Lutz *(V.P.-Engrng.)*
Ted Boop *(V.P.-Sls.)*
Jack Spencer *(Gen. Mgr.-Mfg.)*

Division:

Atlas Car Div., Bliss-Salem Inc. **(1)**
530 S. Ellsworth
Salem, OH 44460
Tel.: 216-337-3444
Approx.Sls.: $10,000,000
Emp.: 250
Manufacture & Installation of Rail Transfer Car Systems Used in Steel Mills for Transportation of Coke & Other Raw Materials
S.I.C.: 1799; 3559; 3599
Michael Zugay *(Pres.)*
Ted Boop *(V.P.-Sls.)*
Jack Spencer *(Gen. Mgr.)*

BLISSFIELD MANUFACTURING COMPANY
626 Depot St.
Blissfield, MI 49228
Tel.: 517-486-2121
Fax: 517-486-2128
Approx.Sls.: $15,000,000
Emp.: 300
Refrigeration System for Vending & Display Equipment; Belt Driven Refrigeration Compressors & Condensing Units, Evaporators, Finned Tube, Oil & Transmission Coolers for Mobile Power Equipment
S.I.C.: 3585
Herb Farver *(Chm. Bd. & Pres.)*
Donald L. Ball *(V.P. & Treas.)*
Pat Farver *(V.P.-Sls.)*
Doug Miller *(V.P.-Mfg.)*
John D. Bobo *(Controller)*
Troy Smith *(Mgr.-Pur.)*
Fred Morrison *(Chief Engr.)*

Outside Service Firm(s):

KPMG Peat Marwick*(Auditors)*
Toledo, OH

Walker, Watts & Jackson*(Legal Firm)*
Adrian, MI

Adrian State Bank*(Major Banking Relationship)*
Adrian, MI

BLISTEX, INC.
1800 Swift Dr.
Oak Brook, IL 60521
Tel.: 708-571-2870
Fax: 708-571-3437
Year Founded: 1949
Emp.: 125
Export
Mfr. of Topical Analgesics & Ointments; Blistex Ointment; Blistik Lip Balm, Dentrue-Eze Denture Liner; Dyprotex Diaper Rash Ointment; Foille First Aid & Burn Products; Ivarest Poison Ivy Cream; Kanka Formula for Canker/Mouth Sores
S.I.C.: 2834
D.C. Arch *(Chm. Bd. & Chief Exec. Officer)*
Richard K. Green *(Pres. & Chief Oper. Officer)*
Bradley F. Dubas *(V.P.-Fin.)*
Ronald H. Kovich *(V.P.-Sls.)*
Mike Wojcik *(V.P.-Opers.)*
Michael Donnantuono *(Dir.-Mktg.)*

Non-U.S. Holding:

Blistex Limited **(1)**
2395 Drew Rd.
Mississauga, ON L5S 1A1, Canada
Tel.: 416-678-2521 (100%)
Fax: 416-762-1186
Mktg. & Sales of Ointments, Lotions, Lip Balms
S.I.C.: 5122; 5100

Michael Sloan *(Dir.-Sls. & Mktg.)*

BLITZ USA
(Formerly U.S. Metal Container Company)
404 26nd Ave. N.W.
Miami, OK 74354
Tel.: 918-540-1515
Tel.: 800-331-3795
Fax: 918-542-1380
Year Founded: 1960
Approx.Sls.: $10,000,000
Emp.: 250
Fiscal Year-end: 6/30/90
Mfr. Fuel Containers & Accessories, Haircombs, BBQ, Styrofoam
S.I.C.: 3411
John R. Elmburg *(Pres.)*
Larry Chrisco *(V.P.-Admin.)*
Rocky Flick *(V.P.-Sls. & Mktg.)*
George Foster *(V.P.-Mfg.)*
Tom Jackson *(Controller)*
Linda T. Elmburg *(Sec.)*
Art Robertson *(Dir.-Pur.)*

Principal(s):
John R. Elmburg
Linda T. Elmburg

Computer Systems/Hardware:
Digital & TDT 1137

Outside Service Firm(s):

Gage & Tucker*(Legal Firm)*
2345 Grand Ave., 28th Fl.
Kansas City, MO 64108
Tel.: 816-292-2000

Security National Bank*(Major Banking Relationship)*
Miami, OK

Subsidiary:

Blitz U.S.A., Inc. **(1)**
404 26th Ave., N.W.
Miami, OK 74354
Tel.: 918-540-1515
Tel.: 800-331-3795
Fax: 918-542-1380
Emp.: 150
Fiscal Year-end: 6/30/90
Export
Skotch Koolers, Jugs, Chests, Foam & Plastic
S.I.C.: 3086
John R. Elmburg *(Pres.)*
George Foster *(V.P.-Mfg.)*
Rocky Flick *(V.P.-Mktg., Sls., Adv. & Export)*
Larry Chrisco *(V.P.-Govt. Affairs, Tech. Services, Res. & Devel.)*
Tom Jackson *(Chief Fin. Officer & Controller)*

BLOCK DISTRIBUTING COMPANY
827-829 Coliseum Rd.
San Antonio, TX 78219
Tel.: 210-224-7531 **TX**
Fax: 210-227-7810
Approx.Sls.: $78,000,000
Emp.: 270
Liquor; Wine
S.I.C.: 5182
Edward L. Block *(Pres. & Chief Exec. Officer)*
Alan Dreeben *(Exec. V.P.)*
Phil Boeck *(Sr. V.P.)*
Raleigh Lair *(Treas.)*

Outside Service Firm(s):

Cundiff, Rogers, Soit & Walker*(Auditors)*
San Antonio, TX

Frost National Bank*(Major Banking Relationship)*
P.O. Box 1600
San Antonio, TX 78296

BLOCK INDUSTRIES, INC.
(Formerly Block Industries)
525 N. College Rd.
Wilmington, NC 28405
Tel.: 919-392-2100
Fax: 919-791-6691
Approx.Sls.: $41,000,000
Emp.: 950
Mfr. Popular Priced Men's Dress & Sport Shirts, Jackets & Sweaters
S.I.C.: 2321; 2329
Andrew Traub *(Pres.)*
Richard P. Thrush *(Chief Exec. Officer)*

BLOCK & NARDIZZI
One Stamford Landing
Stamford, CT 06902
Tel.: 203-969-1311
Fax: 203-969-1309
Year Founded: 1987
Approx.Billings: $12,500,000
Emp.: 47
Promotion, Mktg. Consulting, Public Relations & Graphic Design
Joseph Block *(Pres.)*
Chuck Nardizzi *(Chief Exec. Officer)*
Harry Squasoni *(Exec. V.P., Mktg.)*
Norman Sylvester *(Exec. V.P.)*
Frank Wainwright *(Exec. V.P.)*
John Eccleston *(Sr. V.P., Pub. Rels.)*

BLOCKHOUSE CO., INC.
121 First Ave.
Red Lion, PA 17356
Tel.: 717-246-3031
Fax: 717-246-1506
Sales Range: $10-19 Million
Emp.: 47
Mfr. of Institutional Furniture
S.I.C.: 2531
William Laird *(Pres.)*
Stephen Perko *(V.P.)*
Marg E. Laird *(Sec. & Treas.)*

Outside Service Firm(s):

Bernard Friedrich*(Auditors)*
Rosemont, PA

Kassab, Cherry, Archbold, Ferrara*(Legal Firm)*
Red Lion, PA

Mellon Bank, N.A.*(Major Banking Relationship)*
Red Lion, PA

G.S. BLODGETT CORPORATION
50 Lakeside Ave.
Burlington, VT 05401
Mailing Address:
P.O. Box 586
Burlington, VT 05402
Tel.: 802-658-6600
Fax: 802-864-0183
Emp.: 600
Mfr. of Ovens & other Equipment for the Food Industry
S.I.C.: 3589
J.D. Johnson *(Co-Chm. Bd., Pres. & Chief Exec. Officer)*
Samuel A. Hartwell *(Co-Chm. Bd. & Chief Fin. Officer)*
Christopher R. Gannon *(Gen. Counsel & Sec.)*

Outside Service Firm(s):

Deloitte & Touche*(Auditors)*
Hartford, CT

Division:

The Blodgett Oven Co., Inc. **(1)**
50 Lakeside Ave.
Burlington, VT 05402
Tel.: 802-658-6600
Emp.: 200
Blodgett Baking & Roasting Ovens
S.I.C.: 3589
Gerald F. Veino *(Pres.)*
Steve Amos *(V.P.-Sls. & Mktg.)*

Subsidiaries:

Magikitch'n, Inc. **(1)**
P.O. Box 729
Quakertown, PA 18951
Tel.: 215-536-8140
Allan P. Marshall *(V.P.)*

Pitco Frialator Inc. **(1)**
P.O. Box 501
Concord, NH 03301
Tel.: 603-225-6684
Tel.: 800-258-3708
Fax: 603-224-6930
Approx.Sls.: $15,000,000
Emp.: 200
Fiscal Year-end: 12/31/91
Export
Computer Systems/Hardware:
DEC #8350
Manufactures Pitco Frialators, Commercial Deep Fat Fryers
S.I.C.: 3589
Robert A. Nerbonne *(Pres.)*
Thomas C. Cassin *(V.P.-Mktg.)*
Robert Granger *(Controller)*
Frederick M. Reed *(Gen. Counsel)*
George McMahon *(Dir.-Engrng.)*
Terri Miller *(Dir.-Pur.)*
Joseph Wirtz *(Mgr.-Personnel)*
David Delude *(Export Mgr.)*
Philip Dei Dolori *(Natl. Sls. Mgr.)*

Pitco Mastermatic Inc. **(1)**
P.O. Box 2272
Concord, NH 03301
Tel.: 603-225-5190

BLOMMER CHOCOLATE CO.
600 W. Kinzie St.
Chicago, IL 60610
Tel.: 312-226-7700
Fax: 312-226-4141
Emp.: 100
Fiscal Year-end: 12/31/90
Mfr. Chocolate Coating, Cocoa Powder, Cocoa Butter, Chocolate Bars
S.I.C.: 2066
Henry Blommer, Jr. *(Pres.)*
M. Krueger *(V.P.)*
James Meagher *(V.P.)*
Rita Ranallo *(V.P.)*
Joseph Blommer *(Treas.)*

Outside Service Firm(s):

Ernst & Young*(Auditors)*
233 S. Wacker Dr.
Chicago, IL 60606
Tel.: 312-368-1800
Fax: 312-645-3095

Cosmopolitan Bank*(Major Banking Relationship)*
Chicago, IL

BLONDER-TONGUE LABORATORIES, INC.
One Jake Brown Rd.
Old Bridge, NJ 08857
Tel.: 908-679-4000
Fax: 908-679-4353
Approx.Sls.: $14,000,000
Emp.: 500
Fiscal Year-end: 3/31/91
Export
Manufactures TV Signal Distribution Equipment: Indoor & Outdoor Amplifiers, Antennas, MATV Systems, CATV Systems, & Accessory Items; Earth Station, Antennas, Components & Amplifiers
S.I.C.: 3663
James A. Luksch *(Pres.)*
Robert J. Palle, Jr. *(Exec. V.P.)*
Daniel J. Altiere *(Exec. V.P.)*
Peter Pugiello *(Controller)*
John Mayeski *(Mgr.-Adv.)*
A. Horvath *(Mgr.-Quality Assurance)*
Richard Colasurdo *(Pur. Agent)*

BLOOM ELECTRIC SERVICES, INC.
P.O. Box 271200
Oklahoma City, OK 73137
Tel.: 405-495-7500

Bloom Electric Services, Inc.—(Continued)

Emp.: 12
Design, Build & Service Electric Systems for Industrial & Commercial Buildings
S.I.C.: 1731
Donald Bloom *(Pres. & Chief Exec. Officer)*
David B. Bloom *(Chief Fin. Officer & Treas.)*
Betty J. Bloom *(V.P.)*
Richard A. Bloom *(Gen. Mgr.-Sls. & Mktg.)*

Computer Systems/Hardware:
Data General 13

BLOOMHORST STORY O'HARA INC.
200 S. Meridian St., Ste. 510
Indianapolis, IN 46225
Tel.: 317-639-4436
Fax: 317-639-5134
Year Founded: 1967
Approx.Billings: $11,000,000
Emp.: 19
Kenneth F. Bloomhorst *(Chm. Bd. & Art Dir.)*
Tom F. Hirschauer *(Pres. & Chief Exec. Officer)*
John C. O'Hara *(Exec. V.P., Creative Dir.)*

BLOOMSBURG MILLS INC.
1460 Broadway
New York, NY 10036
Tel.: 212-221-6114 **PA**
Fax: 212-354-9375
Year Founded: 1890
Approx.Sls.: $110,000,000
Emp.: 500
Fiscal Year-end: 3/31/91
Mfr. Textiles
S.I.C.: 2211; 2221
James P. Marion, Jr. *(Chm. Bd.)*
James P. Marion, III *(Pres. & Chief Exec. Officer)*
Frederick J. Shaw *(Exec. V.P.-Sls.)*
Michael Spruyt *(V.P., Treas. & Chief Fin. Officer)*
Edward Cole *(Dir.-Data Processing)*
Principal(s):
James P. Marion, Jr.

No. of Mfg. Plants/Facilities: 3
No. of U.S. Offices: 4

Computer Systems/Hardware:
IBM System 38

Outside Service Firm(s):

KPMG Peat Marwick*(Auditors)*
345 Park Ave.
New York, NY 10154
Tel.: 212-758-9700
Fax: 212-872-3308

Philadelphia Manufacturers Mutual Insurance Co.*(Commercial Insurance Carrier)*
Valley Forge, PA

Blue Cross & Blue Shield of North Carolina*(Auditors)*
Durham, NC

Hahn & Hessen*(Legal Firm)*
350 Fifth Ave., Ste. 3700
New York, NY 10118
Tel.: 212-736-1000

Chase Manhattan Bank, N.A.*(Major Banking Relationship)*
One Chase Manhattan Plaza
New York, NY 10081
Tel.: 212-552-2222
Tel.: 800-526-0801
Fax: 212-552-7175

BLOUNT LUMBER COMPANY
P.O. Box 220
Lacona, NY 13083
Tel.: 315-387-3451
Fax: 315-387-6358
Year Founded: 1897
Sales Range: $20-39 Million
Emp.: 225
Wholesale Distributor of Flush Doors & Millwork; Manufactures Wood Flush Doors
S.I.C.: 2431; 2434; 3442; 5031
David J. Parker *(Chm. Bd. & Chief Exec. Officer)*
Clarence H. Yahn *(Pres. & Chief Oper. Officer)*
H. Peter Blount II *(V.P.)*
Nathan Foote *(V.P.-Sls. & Mktg.)*
Joseph Rocco *(Controller)*

Outside Service Firm(s):

Price Waterhouse*(Auditors)*
One Mony Plaza
Syracuse, NY 13202

BLUE ANCHOR, INC.
730 Howe Ave.
Sacramento, CA 95825
Mailing Address:
P.O. Box 15498,
Sacramento, CA 95825
Tel.: 916-929-3050 **CA**
Fax: 916-921-9362
Year Founded: 1901
Assets: $14,186,440
Liabilities: $11,293,776
Net Worth: $2,892,664
Approx.Sls.: $58,758,388
Emp.: 75
Fiscal Year-end: 3/31/91
Export
Fresh Fruit Marketing Cooperative
S.I.C.: 5431
Howard Nakae *(Chm. Bd.)*
Pat Sanguinetti *(Pres. & Chief Exec. Officer)*
John C. Dibb *(V.P.-Opers.)*
Barry T. Powell *(V.P.-Fin.)*
John Rast *(V.P.-Sls.)*
Kenta Duffey *(Gen. Counsel)*
Jan Lederer *(Corp. Sec.)*
James Llano *(Dir.-Export)*
Marilyn Watkins *(Dir.-Adv. & Pub. Rels.)*
Gary Alsup *(Mgr.-Pur.)*
Principal(s):
750 Co-op Owners

No. of Mfg. Plants/Facilities: 4
No. of U.S. Offices: 5

Computer Systems/Hardware:
IBM System 36

Outside Service Firm(s):

Peat Marwick*(Auditors)*
Sacramento, CA

Union Bank*(Major Banking Relationship)*
Sacramento, CA

Rollins Burdick Hunter*(Group Insurer)*
7801 Folsom Blvd., Ste. 210
Sacramento, CA

The New England*(Investment Banker)*
Boston, MA

McCutchen, Doyle, Brown & Enersen*(Legal Firm)*
3 Embacadero Ctr.
San Francisco, CA 94111
Tel.: 415-393-2000

New England Mutual Life Insurance Co.*(Pension Manager)*
Boston, MA

BLUE BELL CREAMERIES, INC.
1000 Horton Loop, #577
Brenham, TX 77833
Mailing Address:
P.O. Box 1807
Brenham, TX 77833
Tel.: 409-836-7977
Fax: 409-830-2198
Approx.Sls.: $100,000,000
Emp.: 950
Fiscal Year-end: 12/30/90
Manufacturer & Distributor of Ice Cream
S.I.C.: 2024
Ed F. Kruse *(Chm. & Chief Exec. Officer)*
Howard W. Kruse *(Pres.)*
John W. Barnhill, Jr. *(Exec. V.P. & Gen. Sls. Mgr.)*

Divisions:

Central Texas District Office **(1)**
P.O. Box 1807, Loop 577
Brenham, TX 77833
Tel.: 409-836-7977
Steve James *(District Mgr.)*

Dallas/Ft. Worth District Office **(1)**
1123 Military Parkway
Mesquite, TX 75149
Tel.: 214-285-0241
Melvin Ziegenbein, Jr. *(District Mgr.)*

Houston District Office **(1)**
2211 Karbach
Houston, TX 77092
Tel.: 713-686-3468
Larry Ainsworth *(District Mgr.)*

BLUE BELL/KING KOIL, INC.
770 Bloomfield Ave.
Windsor, CT 06095
Mailing Address:
P.O. Box 546,
Windsor, CT 06095
Tel.: 203-688-6496
Fax: 203-688-9341
Approx.Sls.: $10,000,000
Emp.: 65
Mattress, Box Springs, Headboards, King Koil Bedding
S.I.C.: 2515
Frank Stavis *(Pres.)*
Mark Kolovson *(V.P. & Treas.)*

BLUE BIRD COACH LINES INC.
One Blue Bird Sq.
Olean, NY 14760
Tel.: 716-372-5500
Year Founded: 1919
Approx.Sls.: $16,000,000
Emp.: 450
Bus Tours & Charter Services
S.I.C.: 4141; 4142
Louis A. Magnano *(Pres. & Chief Exec. Officer)*
Steven Sellberg *(Chief Fin. Officer)*
B.J. Covert *(V.P.-Maintenance)*
Richard Crowther *(V.P.-Rochester Div.)*
Elaine Kwiatkowski *(V.P.-Sls.)*
Louis M. Magnano *(V.P.-Buffalo Div.)*
Vince Pacifico *(V.P.-Erie Div.)*
Dave Rugg *(V.P.-Opers.)*
Joe Keller *(Treas.)*
Charles Corcoran *(Comptroller)*
Principal(s):
Louis A. Magnano

No. of U.S. Offices: 7

Computer Systems/Hardware:
IBM

Outside Service Firm(s):

Ernst & Young*(Auditors)*
1400 Key Tower - 50 Fountain Plaza
Buffalo, NY
Tel.: 716-843-5000
Fax: 716-847-6949

Marine Midland Bank*(Major Banking Relationship)*
P.O. Box 803, 1 Marine Midland Center, 23rd Floor
Buffalo, NY 14203
Tel.: 716-841-2582

BLUE BIRD CORPORATION
(Formerly Blue Bird Body Co., Inc.)
N. Camellia Blvd.
Fort Valley, GA 31030
Mailing Address:
P.O. Box 937,
Fort Valley, GA 31030
Tel.: 912-825-2021 **GA**
Fax: 912-825-0330
Year Founded: 1927
Assets: $235,000,000
Net Worth: $235,000,000
Approx.Sls.: $428,000,000
Emp.: 2,500
Fiscal Year-end: 10/ 3/91
Export
Mfr. Buses & Motor Homes
S.I.C.: 3713; 3714; 3792; 3711
Paul E. Glaske *(Pres. & Chief Exec. Officer)*
James Granthan *(V.P.-Mfg.)*
Richard Maddox *(V.P.-Sls.)*
Bob Wallace *(V.P.-Fin. & Admin.)*
Verna Borders *(Mgr.-Mktg. Communications)*
David S. Bumpus *(Mgr.-Leasing)*

Computer Systems/Hardware:
IBM 4381; IBM 3083

Outside Service Firm(s):

George A. Pennington & Co.*(Auditors)*
Atlanta, GA

Smith, Gambrell & Russell*(Legal Firm)*
2400 First Atlanta Tower
Atlanta, GA 30383
Tel.: 404-656-1800
Fax: 404-264-2652

Bank of America, N.T. & S.A.*(Major Banking Relationship)*
P.O. Box 37002,
San Francisco, CA 94137

Bankers Trust Co.*(Major Banking Relationship)*
P.O. Box 318, Church St. Station
New York, NY 10008
Tel.: 212-454-2212
Fax: 212-454-2783

First National Bank of Atlanta*(Major Banking Relationship)*
2 Peachtree Street N.W.
Atlanta, GA 30383

Bank South, N.A.*(Major Banking Relationship)*
P.O. Box 4387
Atlanta, GA 30302
Tel.: 404-529-4111

BLUE BOAR CAFETERIA CO.
1725 Dixie Hwy.
Louisville, KY 40256-9001
Mailing Address:
P.O. Box 169001
Louisville, KY 40216
Tel.: 502-776-2481 **KY**
Fax: 502-776-2486
Approx.Sls.: $15,000,000
Emp.: 700
Cafeterias
S.I.C.: 5812
Wesley S. Johnson *(Chm. Bd. & Pres.)*
Wesley Johnson, Jr. *(Chief Oper. Officer)*
L. Eugene Johnson, Jr. *(Sr. V.P.)*
N. W. Lubbers *(V.P.-Opers.)*
Paul Mullett *(Treas.)*
Sharon Hutchens *(Comptroller)*

No. of Mfg. Plants/Facilities: 5

Outside Service Firm(s):

Cotton & Allen*(Auditors)*
Louisville, KY

First National Bank of Louisville*(Major Banking Relationship)*
P.O. Box 36000,
Louisville, KY 40233

BLUE CORAL, INC.
1215 Valley Belt Rd.
Cleveland, OH 44131-1451
Tel.: 216-351-3000
Tel.: 800-321-8577
Fax: 216-351-0270
Year Founded: 1978
Sales Range: $100-499 Million
Emp.: 148
Fiscal Year-end: 10/31/91
Export
Auto Polish; Car Wax; Rug, Carpet & Upholstery Cleaner
S.I.C.: 2842; 2891
Sheldon G. Adelman *(Chm. Bd. & Chief Exec. Officer)*
Norton S. Rose *(Vice Chm.)*
Michael Moshontz *(Pres.)*
Nicholas Federico, Sr. *(Sr. V.P.-Mktg.)*
Michael Turk *(Sr. V.P. & Chief Fin. Officer)*
Ken Herrmann *(V.P.-Sls.)*
Lawrence Minich *(V.P. & Treas.)*
Graham Reed *(V.P.-Res. & Devel.)*
Robert G. Markey *(Corp. Sec.)*
Paul Angart *(Controller)*
Rachelle Arnold *(Dir.-Mktg.)*
David Lupyan *(Dir.-Res. & Devel.)*
Christopher Norris *(Dir.-Mngmt. Information Systems)*
Sharon Walker *(Dir.-Admin.)*
Joel Adelman *(Mgr.-Sls.)*
Sherman Brown *(Mgr.-Quality Control)*
Margaret Kicey *(Mgr.-Export)*
Paul Sydorenko *(Plant Mgr.)*
Paul Russo *(Mgr.-Govt. Affairs)*
Bob Varda *(Mgr.-Pur.)*
Kelly Musarra *(Meetings Planner)*

Principal(s):
Sheldon G. Adelman
Michael Moshontz

No. of Mfg. Plants/Facilities: 5
No. of U.S. Offices: 6
No. of Foreign Offices: 1

Computer Systems/Hardware:
IBM AS400; IBM PC XT

Outside Service Firm(s):

Arthur Andersen & Co.*(Auditors)*
1717 E. 9th St.
Cleveland, OH 44114
Tel.: 216-781-2140
Fax: 216-781-3683

Republic Hogg Robinson*(Commercial Insurance Carrier)*
Pepper Pike, OH

Prudential Insurance Co. of America*(Group Insurer)*
1228 Euclid Ave.
Cleveland, OH

National City Bank*(Investment Banker)*
P.O. Box 92301, Ninth & Euclid Avenues
Cleveland, OH 44193

Baker & Hostetler*(Legal Firm)*
3200 National City Center
Cleveland, OH 44114
Tel.: 216-621-0200
Fax: 216-696-0740

National City Bank*(Major Banking Relationship)*
P.O. Box 92301, Corp. Trust Dept.
Cleveland, OH 44101
Tel.: 216-575-2000

Principal Mutual Life Insurance Co.*(Pension Manager)*
711 High St.
Des Moines, IA 50309

Division:

Trewax Company **(1)**
13707 Marquardt Ave.
Santa Fe Springs, CA 90670
Tel.: 310-926-9948
Tel.: 800-443-9978
Tel.: 800-677-4769
Telex: 194996
Fax: 310-243-6329
Approx.Sls.: $10,000,000
Emp.: 24
Fiscal Year-end: 10/31/92
Export
Household Waxes, Polishes & Cleaners; Carpet Cleaning Chemicals
S.I.C.: 2841; 2842; 2851
Thomas Each *(Pres.)*
Robert A. Elert *(V.P.-Sls.)*

Subsidiaries:

Blue Coral International **(1)**
High Street
Newport, Saffron Walden, Essex United Kingdom CB11 3PQ
Tel.: 0-11-44-799-41936
Fax: 0-11-44-799-41940
Emp.: 4
Specialty Cleaning, Polishing & Sanitation Preparations
S.I.C.: 2842
John Kegg *(Mng. Dir.)*
Nina Marriott *(Dir.-Mktg.)*
Jane Readman *(Dir.-Opers.)*

Chemifax **(1)**
6423 Bandini Blvd.
City of Commerce, CA 90040
Tel.: 213-926-9948
Tel.: 800-243-6329
Fax: 213-404-3449
Emp.: 62
Soap, Cleaners & Toilet Goods
S.I.C.: 2842
Sheldon G. Adelman *(Chm. Bd. & Chief Exec. Officer)*
Tom Each *(Pres.)*
Michael G. Turk *(Chief Fin. Officer)*
Mike Meller *(Mgr.-Sls.)*
Morgan Lawrence *(Mgr.-Pur.)*
Mohammad Nilchian *(Mgr.-Opers.)*

McKay Chemical Co. **(1)**
1920 Randolph St.
Los Angeles, CA 90001
Tel.: 213-582-7477
Tel.: 800-446-2529
Fax: 213-582-7527
Approx.Sls.: $8,000,000
Emp.: 50
Fiscal Year-end: 12/31/90
Mfr. of Automotive Chemicals
S.I.C.: 2842
Sheldon G. Adelman *(Chm. Bd. & Chief Exec. Officer)*
James McDowell *(Pres.)*
Alfred Gaspar *(Exec. V.P.-Mktg.)*
Gerald E. Martin *(V.P.-Opers.)*
Thomas Fleming *(Controller)*
Calvin Lane *(Mgr.-Pur.)*
Rick Skelton *(Mgr.-Sls.)*

Nic Sand **(1)**
1215 Valley Belt Rd.
Cleveland, OH 44131
Tel.: 216-351-3333
Fax: 216-351-6646
Emp.: 42
Sand Paper Products
S.I.C.: 3291
Sheldon G. Adelman *(Chm. Bd. & Chief Exec. Officer)*
James Sandusky *(Pres.)*
Michael G. Turk *(Chief Fin. Officer)*
Debbie Doedoerlein *(Dir.-Pur.)*
Mike Armagno *(Mgr.-Sls.)*
Roger Williams *(Plant Mgr.)*

Simoniz Canada Ltd. **(1)**
1215 Valley Belt Rd.
Cleveland, OH 44131-1415
Tel.: 216-351-3000
Tel.: 800-321-8577
Fax: 216-351-0270
Emp.: 15
Manufacturer of Auto Polish
S.I.C.: 2842
Sheldon G. Adelman *(Chm. Bd. & Chief Exec. Officer)*
Michael G. Turk *(Chief Fin. Officer)*
Margaret Kicey *(Mgr.-Simoniz Canada)*
Rachelle Arnold *(Dir.-Mktg.)*
Robert P. Varda *(Dir.-Pur.)*

BLUE CROSS AND BLUE SHIELD OF OKLAHOMA
1215 S. Boulder Ave.
Tulsa, OK 74119
Mailing Address:
P.O. Box 3283
Tulsa, OK 74102
Tel.: 918-560-3500 **OK**
Fax: 918-560-2112
Year Founded: 1940
Assets: $142,737,790
Liabilities: $107,474,728
Net Worth: $35,263,062
Approx.Sls.: $360,820,904
Emp.: 718
Fiscal Year-end: 12/31/90
Health Insurance
S.I.C.: 6324
Kenneth W. Townsend *(Chm. Bd.)*
Robert D. McCullough, III, D.O. *(Vice Chm.)*
Ralph S. Rhoades *(Pres. & Chief Exec. Officer)*
Tom Bowser *(Sr. V.P.-Benefits Admin.)*
Thomas H. Gudgel *(Sr. V.P. & Gen. Counsel)*
Ronald F. King *(Sr. V.P.-Information Services)*
Richard D. McCutchen *(Sr. V.P.-Mktg.)*
Michael A. Rhoads *(Sr. V.P.-Fin.)*
Larry L. Smith *(Sr. V.P.-Health Indus. Rels.)*
Bruce C. Burns *(V.P.-Mktg. Support)*
Carl O. Cabbiness *(V.P.-Specialized Benefits Admin.)*
Miles R. Call *(V.P.-Information Facilities)*
Steven Coulter *(V.P. & Medical Dir.)*
James M. Goodwin *(V.P.-Grp. Mktg., East)*
Nequita Hanna *(V.P.-Standard Benefits Admin.)*
Dick Howard *(V.P.-Pub. Affairs)*
James Kerlin *(V.P.-Facilities Mngmt.)*
Ann Metcalf *(V.P.-Adv. & Pub. Communications)*
Joseph Michalcik *(V.P.-Actuarial)*
Phil Myles *(V.P.-Underwriting)*
Robert Pearcy *(V.P.-Health Indus. Rels.)*
Peggy Risinger *(V.P.-Govt. Programs)*
Rick Rinehart *(V.P.-Grp. Mktg. Sls., West)*
David Ruttman *(V.P.-Human Resources)*
Delmas D. Sharp *(V.P.-Information Systems & Programming)*
Phillip C. Sloan *(V.P.-Plan 65/FEP)*
John Thomas *(V.P. & Controller)*
Mary Susan Robb *(Corp. Sec. & Treas.)*

Computer Systems/Hardware:
IBM; Data General; Amdahl

Outside Service Firm(s):

Deloitte & Touche*(Auditors)*
One Williams Center, Ste. 2400
Tulsa, OK
Tel.: 918-586-8800

Blue Cross & Blue Shield of Oklahoma*(Group Insurer)*
Tulsa, OK

Chapel, Wilkinson, Riggs, Abney & Henson*(Legal Firm)*
Tulsa, OK

Subsidiaries:

BlueLines HMO **(1)**
1437 S. Boulder Ave.
Tulsa, OK 74119
Tel.: 918-561-9900
Prepaid Health Service
S.I.C.: 6324
Larry Smith *(Chief Oper. Officer)*

Member Service Life Insurance Co. **(1)**
2727 E. 21st St.
Tulsa, OK 74114
Tel.: 918-747-9700
Emp.: 46
S.I.C.: 6311
Ron King *(Chief Oper. Officer)*

BLUE CROSS AND BLUE SHIELD ASSOCIATION
676 N. St. Clair St.
Chicago, IL 60611
Tel.: 312-440-6000 **IL**
Fax: 312-440-6609
Sales Range: $1 Billion +
Emp.: 700
Fiscal Year-end: 12/31/90
Membership Assn.: Health Care
S.I.C.: 6324
Bernard R. Tresnowski *(Pres.)*
Thomas Kinser *(Exec. V.P. & Chief Oper. Officer)*
Frederick C. Cue *(Sr. V.P.-Fin. & Mngmt. Services)*
Harry P. Cain, II *(Sr. V.P.-Federal Programs)*
Preston Jordon *(Sr. V.P.-Business Support)*
Douglas S. Peters *(Sr. V.P.-Representation & Public Affairs)*
Leonard E. Wood *(Sr. V.P.-Mktg.)*
Duane R. Carlson *(V.P.-Communications)*
James N. Gillman *(V.P.-Federal Employee Program)*
Mary Nell Lehnhard *(V.P.-Office of Govt. Rels.)*
Roger Wilson *(Gen. Counsel)*
Phil Petrilli *(Exec. Dir.-Human Resources & Admin.)*
Gere Collosky *(Mgr.-Adv. Services)*

No. of U.S. Offices: 77

Computer Systems/Hardware:
IBM; Wang

Outside Service Firm(s):

Ernst & Young*(Auditors)*
233 S. Wacker Dr.
Chicago, IL 60606
Tel.: 312-368-1800
Fax: 312-645-3095

First National Bank of Chicago*(Major Banking Relationship)*
One First National Plaza
Chicago, IL 60670
Tel.: 312-732-9781
Tel.: 312-732-4050
Fax: 312-732-4840
Fax: 312-732-3055

Regional Offices:

Blue Cross and Blue Shield Assn. Government Relations **(1)**
Metropolitan Square Building, 655 Fifteenth St., N.W., Ste. 350
Washington, DC 20005
Tel.: 202-626-4780
Mary Nell Lehnhard *(V.P.-Office Govt. Rels.)*

Blue Cross and Blue Shield Northeast Marketing Region **(1)**
1055 Washington Blvd.
Stamford, CT 06901
Tel.: 203-328-0358
Health Care Financing
S.I.C.: 6324
Bryon G. Dearborn *(Dir.)*

BLUE CROSS AND BLUE SHIELD OF MASSACHUSETTS
100 Summer St.
Boston, MA 02110
Tel.: 617-956-2000
Emp.: 6,600
Health Insurance
S.I.C.: 6321
William Van Faasen *(Pres.)*
John Larkin Thompson *(Chief Exec. Officer)*
Joseph Fermano *(Chief Fin. Officer)*
Fay Donohue-Rolfe *(Sr. V.P.-Mktg.)*
Martin Joyce *(V.P.-Information Mngmt. Services)*
Carol Nashe *(V.P.-Community Rels.)*
Steven Tringale *(V.P.-Pub. Affairs)*
Arlene Saffron *(Dir.-Adv.)*

Blue Cross and Blue Shield of Massachusetts—(Continued)

Outside Service Firm(s):

Shawmut Bank*(Major Banking Relationship)*
Boston, MA

BLUE CROSS & BLUE SHIELD OF ILLINOIS
233 N. Michigan Ave.
Chicago, IL 60601
Tel.: 312-938-6000 **IL**
Fax: 312-819-1220
Year Founded: 1936
Assets: $959,466,000
Liabilities: $524,374,000
Net Worth: $435,092,000
Approx.Rev.: $2,600,000,000
Emp.: 4,000
Fiscal Year-end: 12/31/91
Health Care Insurance
S.I.C.: 6321
Corporate Giving Program: Health-related Organizations
S. Martin Hickman *(Chm. Bd. & Chief Exec. Officer)*
Raymond F. McCaskey *(Pres. & Chief Oper. Officer)*
Tom J. Denham *(Sr. V.P.-Sls.)*
Theodore E. Desch *(Sr. V.P.-Law & Corp. Affairs)*
John F. Nutting *(Sr. V.P.-Govt. Contracts)*
Joanne M. Rounds *(Sr. V.P.-SSD)*
C. Jonathan Shattuck *(Sr. V.P.-Health Care Affairs)*
Michael F. Seibold *(Sr. V.P.-Mktg.)*
James F. Walsh *(Sr. V.P.-Direct Mkts. Div. & Corp. Opers. Services)*
Sherman M. Wolff *(Sr. V.P.-Fin.)*
Claudia J. Alt *(V.P.-State Sls.)*
Ray A. Angeli *(V.P.-SSD)*
Denise A. Bujak *(V.P.-Fin.)*
Katherine H. Cardulla *(V.P.-Corp. Plng. & Devel.)*
Karen A. Chesrown *(V.P.-SSD)*
Mary A. Deskovich *(V.P. & Chief Underwriter)*
William J. Gowen *(V.P.-Medicare B)*
Lawrence A. Hough *(V.P.-Admin. Services)*
Roxanne M. Ivey *(V.P.-Metropolitan Sls.)*
J. Kenneth Jansson *(V.P.-Audit & Performance Review)*
Brian A. Kennedy *(V.P. & Treas.)*
Arthur C. King, Jr. *(V.P.-SSD)*
Cecilia M. Krull *(V.P.-Medicare A)*
Paul J. Lacny *(V.P.-State Sls.)*
Richard G. Malcolm *(V.P.-Direct Mkts. Div.)*
Charles A. Meyers *(V.P.-Human Resources)*
Frank E.E. Nicholson *(V.P.-Provider Contracts & Reimbursement)*
Richard F. O'Connell *(V.P.-Pub. Affairs)*
Carl F. Ricciardelli *(V.P. & Chief Actuary)*
Raymond E. Santi *(V.P.-SSD)*
Richard L. Schleier *(V.P.-Group Mkts. Specialty Prods.)*
James G. Schoebel *(V.P.-Systems Opers. & Telecommunications)*
Ann J. Shannon *(V.P.-Govt. Contract Support)*
Cleveland A. Tyson *(V.P.-Municipal Accts.)*
Brian R. Van Vlierbergen *(V.P., Gen. Counsel & Sec.)*
Arnold L. Widen, M.D. *(V.P. & Medical Dir.)*
Carl A. Zimmerman *(V.P.-Hospital & Institutional Services)*

BLUE CROSS & BLUE SHIELD OF OREGON
100 S.W. Market St.
Portland, OR 97201
Mailing Address:
P.O. Box 1271
Portland, OR 97207
Tel.: 503-225-5221
Fax: 503-225-5274
Assets: $250,465,000
Liabilities: $142,966,000
Net Worth: $107,499,000
Approx.Rev.: $617,300,000
Emp.: 1,783
Fiscal Year-end: 12/31/90
Health Insurance
S.I.C.: 6411
Richard Woolworth *(Chm. Bd. & Pres.)*
Richard Larsen *(Exec. V.P.-External Affairs)*
Roderick Bunnell *(Sr. V.P., Sec. & Gen. Counsel)*
Joseph Martincic *(Sr. V.P.-Admin.)*
Arnold Holloway, Sr. *(V.P.-Benefit Services)*
Steven Hooker *(V.P.-Fin.)*
William Hoveke *(V.P.-Actuarial & Underwriting)*
Barney Speight *(V.P.-Health Care Services)*
Gerry Thompson *(V.P.-Mktg.)*
James Verdick *(V.P.-Govt. Programs)*

Computer Systems/Hardware:
IBM

Outside Service Firm(s):

Coopers & Lybrand*(Auditors)*
2700 First Interstate Tower, 1300 SW 5th Ave.
Portland, OR 97201

Blue Cross & Blue Shield of Oregon*(Group Insurer)*
Portland, OR

Bullivant, Houser, Bailey, Pendergrass & Hoffman*(Legal Firm)*
Portland, OR

Hanna, Murphy, Jensen & Holloway*(Legal Firm)*
Portland, OR

First Interstate Bank*(Major Banking Relationship)*
P.O. Box 3131,
Portland, OR 97208
Tel.: 503-220-4855
Fax: 503-225-7153

United States National Bank of Oregon*(Major Banking Relationship)*
P.O. Box 3850,
Portland, OR 97208
Tel.: 503-275-6111

Subsidiaries:

Health Maintenance Oregon **(1)**
1800 S.W. First, Ste. 505
Portland, OR 97201
Tel.: 503-274-0755
S.I.C.: 6324

Oregon Pacific States Insurance Co. **(1)**
P.O. Box 1271
Portland, OR 97207
Tel.: 503-225-4957
Life Insurance
S.I.C.: 6311

Total Plan Alternatives, Inc. **(1)**
P.O. Box 2580
Portland, OR 97208-2580
Tel.: 503-220-5879
Third Party Administrator
S.I.C.: 6324

BLUE CROSS & BLUE SHIELD OF TEXAS, INC.
901 S. Central Expwy.
Richardson, TX 75080
Mailing Address:
P.O. Box 225730
Dallas, TX 75265
Tel.: 214-669-6900 **TX**
Year Founded: 1939
Approx.Sls.: $800,000,000
Emp.: 3,100
Health Insurance
S.I.C.: 6324
Rogers K. Coleman *(Pres.)*
Raymond L. Hunter, Jr. *(Sr. V.P. & Chief Information Officer)*
Jeffrey P. Langmead *(Sr. V.P. & Chief Oper. Officer)*
Jan R. Newsom *(Sr. V.P., Gen. Counsel & Sec.)*
Ross B. Snyder *(Sr. V.P. & Chief Fin. Officer)*
James E.H. Ward *(Sr. V.P. & Chief Mktg. Officer)*
Charles E. Baxter *(V.P.-Govt. Rels.)*
James R. Crawford *(V.P.)*
Jim Cunningham *(V.P.-Customer Service)*
Eunice C. Manes *(V.P.-Human Resources)*
Vernon W. Walker *(V.P. & Comptroller)*
Jean A. Perkins *(Sec.)*

Computer Systems/Hardware:
IBM

Outside Service Firm(s):

KPMG Peat Marwick*(Auditors)*
1601 Elm St., Ste. 1600
Dallas, TX 75201
Tel.: 214-754-2000
Fax: 214-754-2297

Blue Cross & Blue Shield of Texas, Inc.*(Group Insurer)*
Dallas, TX

NationsBank Texas*(Major Banking Relationship)*
P.O. Box 831402,
Dallas, TX 75283-1402
Tel.: 214-508-0877
Tel.: 800-583-6877

Subsidiary:

Group Life & Health Insurance Company **(1)**
901 S. Central Expwy.
Richardson, TX 75080
Tel.: 214-669-6900
S.I.C.: 6311; 6324

BLUE CROSS & BLUE SHIELD OF VIRGINIA
2015 Staples Mill Rd.
Richmond, VA 23279
Mailing Address:
P.O. Box 27401
Richmond, VA 23279
Tel.: 804-354-7000
Fax: 804-342-2065
Approx.Sls.: $860,000,000
Emp.: 2,090
Prepaid Hospital & Medical Services
S.I.C.: 6324
Norwood Davis *(Chm. Bd. & Chief Exec. Officer)*
Phyllis C. Marstiller *(Pres. & Chief Oper. Officer)*
Raymond Sisk *(Chief Fin. Officer)*
Wyndham Kidd *(Sr. V.P.-Mktg.)*
Raymond M. Slabaugh, III *(Sr. V.P.)*
Thomas E. Martenstein *(V.P.-Legal Affairs)*
Ronald M. Nash *(V.P.-Corp. Services)*
Tom Snead *(V.P.-Fin.)*

Computer Systems/Hardware:
IBM

Outside Service Firm(s):

Blue Cross & Blue Shield of Virginia*(Group Insurer)*
2015 Staples Mill Rd.
Richmond, VA 23230
Tel.: 804-359-7000
Fax: 804-354-7397

BLUE CROSS LABORATORIES
26411 N. Golden Valley Rd.
Saugus, CA 91350
Tel.: 805-255-0955
Fax: 805-255-3628
Year Founded: 1951
Approx.Sls.: $18,000,000
Emp.: 150
Fiscal Year-end: 12/31/91
Export
Mfr. Pan Pal, Royal Flush, Glass More & Glass Brite, Sensation, Admire, Blue Too
S.I.C.: 5169; 2841; 2842; 2843
Darrell Mahler *(Pres., Gen. Mgr., Adv. & Sls. Promo. Mgr.)*
Glenn Mahler *(V.P., Sec. & Treas.)*

Outside Service Firm(s):

Union Bank*(Major Banking Relationship)*
Sherman Oaks, CA

BLUE DIAMOND GROWERS
1802 C St.
Sacramento, CA 95814
Mailing Address:
P.O. Box 1768
Sacramento, CA 95812-1768
Tel.: 916-442-0771 **CA**
Telex: 377449
Fax: 916-446-8620
Year Founded: 1910
Assets: $240,732,000
Earnings: $77,655,000
Liabilities: $163,077,000
Net Worth: $77,655,000
Approx.Sls.: $424,440,000
Emp.: 2,300
Fiscal Year-end: 6/30/91
Export
Almond Growers Cooperative; Wholesaler of Almonds
S.I.C.: 5159
W. Howard Isom *(Chm. Bd.)*
Clinton Shick *(Vice Chm.)*
Walter F. Payne *(Pres. & Chief Exec. Officer)*
Alfred D. DeGregory *(V.P.-Fin., Treas. & Chief Fin. Officer)*
Steven Easter *(V.P.-Govt. Member Rels. & Sec.)*
Ian Erridge *(V.P.-Sls. & Mktg.)*
Steve Huffman *(V.P.-Admin.)*
Raymond Linzy *(V.P.-Plant Opers.)*
Walter C. McDaniel *(Chief Information Officer)*
Lee Spratt *(Controller)*
Christine L. McGlasson *(Dir.-Mktg.)*
Phil Sellar *(Dir.-Human Resources)*
Algernon F. Greenlee *(Mgr.-Adv.)*
Don Rose *(Mgr.-Fin. Services)*
Richard Wetmore *(Pur. Agent)*

Outside Service Firm(s):

KPMG Peat Marwick*(Auditors)*
2495 Natomas Park Dr., Ste. 600
Sacramento, CA 95833-2936

BLUE GRASS FOODS, INC.
2645 Commerce Dr.
Crescent Springs, KY 41017
Tel.: 606-331-7100
Year Founded: 1867
Approx.Sls.: $24,000,000
Emp.: 100
Wholesale Distribution & Retail Sales of Meat Processing
S.I.C.: 5147; 2013
William B. Rice *(Chm. Bd.)*
Sam Finch *(Pres.)*
Glen E. Rice *(Exec. V.P.)*
David Kelgey *(V.P.-Sls.)*

Bernard J. Rice, Jr. *(Sec. & Treas.)*
Pamela J. West *(Mgr.-Acctng.)*
Principal(s):
The Rice Family

BLUE RIDGE TRANSFER CO.
1814 Hollins Rd., N.E.
Roanoke, VA 24012
Mailing Address:
P.O. Box 13447,
Roanoke, VA 24034
Tel.: 703-342-1835
Fax: 703-343-0839
Approx.Sls.: $29,000,000
Emp.: 500
Trucking Transport; Furniture
S.I.C.: 4213; 5021
John W. Stanley *(Chm. Bd.)*
John W. Stanley, Jr. *(Pres., Chief Exec. Officer & Sec.)*
Ronald E. DaShiell *(V.P. & Gen. Mgr.)*

Outside Service Firm(s):

Foti, Flynn & Co.*(Auditors)*
Roanoke, VA

Crestar Bank*(Major Banking Relationship)*
Roanoke, VA

BLUE SHIELD OF CALIFORNIA
Blue Shield Plaza, 2 N. Point
San Francisco, CA 94133
Mailing Address:
P.O. Box 7168
San Francisco, CA 94120
Tel.: 415-445-5000
Fax: 415-296-0697
Approx.Sls.: $950,000,000
Emp.: 2,300
Fiscal Year-end: 12/31/90
Health Care Service Plan, Calif. Physicians' Service
S.I.C.: 6321
Thomas C. Paton *(Chm. Bd. & Chief Exec. Officer)*
Charles W. Stewart *(Pres. & Chief Oper. Offier)*
Joseph Tyszkiewizz *(Sr. V.P.-Mktg.)*

Subsidiary:

California Physicians Insurance Corp. **(1)**
Two North Point
San Francisco, CA 94133
Tel.: 415-445-5668
Robert Donohoe *(Sr. V.P.)*

BLUE TEE CORPORATION
250 Park Avenue So.
New York, NY 10003
Tel.: 212-598-0880
Fax: 212-598-0896
Year Founded: 1986
Approx.Sls.: $210,000,000
Fiscal Year-end: 12/31/90
Manufacture Water Well Rigs & Related Equipment
S.I.C.: 3532
Richard Secrist *(Chm. Bd., Pres. & Chief Exec. Officer)*
William M. Kelly *(Exec. V.P.-Oper.)*
David Alldian *(V.P. & Controller)*
Bert Pollan *(V.P.)*
Glenn A. Smith *(V.P. & Treas.)*
Principal(s):
Richard Secrist

Outside Service Firm(s):

Deloitte & Touche*(Auditors)*
1 World Trade Center
New York, NY 10048
Tel.: 212-669-5000

Divisions:

Azcon Corp. **(1)**
224 S. Michigan Ave., Ste. 425
Chicago, IL 60604
Tel.: 312-362-0066
Fax: 312-362-0094
Burt Pollan *(Pres.)*

Brown-Strauss Steel, Inc. **(1)**
20400 E. 26th Ave.
Aurora, CO 80011
Tel.: 303-371-2200
Fax: 303-344-2227
Sales Range: $40-59 Million
Emp.: 60
Distributor Of Pipe & Steel
S.I.C.: 3317
Michael Rolnick *(Pres.)*
Michael Calvert *(Sr. V.P. & Chief Fin. Officer)*
Bill Singer *(Mgr.-Data Processing)*

Standard Alloys & Manufacturing **(1)**
KCS & 4th Ave.
Port Arthur, TX 77640
Tel.: 409-983-3201
Approx.Sls.: $10,000,000
Emp.: 150
Replacement Pump Parts; Manufacture Castings
S.I.C.: 3561; 3432; 5051; 5084
L.M. Paul *(Pres.)*
R.H. Fisher *(Controller)*
N. Ray Berrsard *(Gen. Counsel)*
Jay Sims *(Sls. Mgr. & Prod. Engr.)*

Subsidiary:

The George E. Failing Company **(1)**
2215 S. Van Buren
Enid, OK 73701
Tel.: 405-234-4141
Fax: 405-233-6807
Approx.Sls.: $50,000,000
Emp.: 350
Fiscal Year-end: 12/31/90
Portable Rotary Drilling Rigs
S.I.C.: 3532; 3533
Don Appleby *(Pres.)*
John McMahan *(V.P.-Sls.)*
James Kvasnicka *(V.P.-Mfg.)*
Don McAfee *(Personnel Dir.)*
Montia A. Rice *(Gen. Mgr.-Domestic Sls.)*
David Gannon *(Pur. Agent)*

BLUEWATER MARINE
811 E. Maple
Mora, MN 55051
Tel.: 612-679-3811
Fax: 612-679-3820
Year Founded: 1954
Approx.Sls.: $15,000,000
Emp.: 130
Fiscal Year-end: 7/31/92
Mfr. Motor Yachts, Yachts & Cruisers
S.I.C.: 3732
James E. Klapmeier *(Pres.)*
Lowell Larson *(Exec. V.P.)*
Al Hagen *(Sr. V.P.)*
Tom Major *(Controller)*
Connie Nordlander *(Dir.-Mktg.)*

Division:

Bluewater **(1)**
811 E. Maple
Mora, MN 55051
Tel.: 612-679-3811
Fax: 612-679-3820
Paul Harrington *(Dir.-Dealer Devel.)*

BLUFF CITY DISTRIBUTING CO., INC.
(d/b/a Bluff City Electronics)
3339 Fontaine Rd.
Memphis, TN 38116
Mailing Address:
P.O. Box 418
Memphis, TN 38101
Tel.: 901-345-9500
Fax: 901-398-4973
Approx.Sls.: $18,600,000
Emp.: 83
Fiscal Year-end: 4/30/90
Wholesale Electronic Parts & Entertainment Products
S.I.C.: 5064
Alfred Cowles, Jr. *(Pres. & Chief Exec. Officer)*
H.B. Cowles *(Chief Fin. Officer, Treas. & Controller)*
Glen Cowles *(V.P.-Pur.)*
Principal(s):
Alfred Cowles, Jr.
Glen Cowles

No. of U.S. Offices: 5

Computer Systems/Hardware:
IBM System 36

Outside Service Firm(s):

Rhea & Ivy*(Auditors)*
Memphis, TN

Treadwell & Harry*(Commercial Insurance Carrier)*
Memphis, TN

State Mutual Life Assurance Co. of America*(Group Insurer)*
440 Lincoln St.
Worcester, MA 01605
Tel.: 508-852-1000

Evans, Petree, Cobb, Edwards*(Legal Firm)*
Memphis, TN

Union Planters National Bank*(Major Banking Relationship)*
Memphis, TN

BLUMENTHAL PRINT WORKS, INC.
905 S. Broad Ave.
New Orleans, LA 70125
Tel.: 504-822-4620
Fax: 504-822-2147
Emp.: 300
Manufacture Textiles
S.I.C.: 2221; 2262; 5131
Harry J. Blumenthal, Jr. *(Pres.)*
Al Barnhill *(Exec. V.P.-Mfg.)*
Edward Heller *(Sec.)*
Alan Horwitz *(Treas.)*

Outside Service Firm(s):

Malcolm M. Dienes & Company*(Auditors)*
New Orleans, LA

Bronfin, Heller, Steinberg & Berins*(Legal Firm)*
New Orleans, LA

Whitney National Bank of New Orleans*(Major Banking Relationship)*
P.O. Box 61260
New Orleans, LA 70161
Tel.: 504-586-7422

BOBIT PUBLISHING COMPANY
2512 Artesia Blvd.
Redondo Beach, CA 90278
Tel.: 310-376-8788 DE
Fax: 310-376-9043
Year Founded: 1961
Approx.Sls.: $20,000,000
Emp.: 110
Magazine Publishing
S.I.C.: 2721
Edward J. Bobit *(Chm. Bd. & Chief Exec. Officer)*
Ty Bobit *(Pres.)*
Michael Dornhecker *(V.P.)*
Robert McAdams *(Controller)*
John Denniston *(Sec.)*

Outside Service Firm(s):

First Business Bank*(Major Banking Relationship)*
Los Angeles, CA

BOBST GROUP INC.
146 Harrison Ave.
Roseland, NJ 07068
Tel.: 201-226-8000
Fax: 201-226-8625
Approx.Sls.: $125,000,000
Emp.: 450
Fiscal Year-end: 12/31/90
Design, Manufacture & Distribute Printing & Converting Equipment for the Packaging Industry
S.I.C.: 3555; 3565; 3556; 5084
Harvey Share *(Pres. & Chief Exec. Officer)*
Josef Fuchs *(V.P.-Service Opers.)*
Michael Hurd *(V.P.-Fin. & Admin.)*
J.J. L'Eplattenier *(V.P.-Mfg.)*
Patricia Bonn *(Mgr.-Admin. & Employee Rels.)*
Laurence Tillis *(Mgr.-Corp. Communications)*

Computer Systems/Hardware:
Data General MV 8000

Outside Service Firm(s):

Equitable Life*(Group Insurer)*
1221 Ave. of the Americas
New York, NY 10022
Tel.: 212-382-8038
Fax: 212-382-8089

Carter & English*(Legal Firm)*
Newark, NJ

BODDIE-NOELL ENTERPRISES INC.
1021 Noell Lane
Rocky Mount, NC 27801
Mailing Address:
P.O. Box 1908
Rocky Mount, NC 27802
Tel.: 919-937-2000 NC
Fax: 919-937-2978
Year Founded: 1962
Approx.Sls.: $305,000,000
Emp.: 14,000
Fiscal Year-end: 9/30/90
Franchisee Hardee's Restaurants; Residential & Commercial Real Estate
S.I.C.: 5812; 6552
Ben Mayo Boddie *(Chm. Bd. & Chief Exec. Officer)*
Nick B. Boddie *(Vice Chm.)*
William L. Boddie *(Pres.)*
W. Craig Worthy *(Chief Fin. Officer & Sr. V.P.)*
Douglas E. Anderson *(Exec. V.P. & Sec.)*
Michael Hancock *(Exec. V.P.-Restaurant Devel.)*
Richard P. Jenkins, Sr. *(Exec. V.P. & Pres.-Hardee's Opers. Grp.)*
Bob Crumley *(Sr. V.P.-Personnel)*
Alton Oakley *(Sr. V.P.-Opers.)*
Principal(s):
Ben Mayo Boddie
Nick B. Boddie

Computer Systems/Hardware:
IBM 4381

Outside Service Firm(s):

Arthur Andersen & Co.*(Auditors)*
Raleigh, NC

Moore & Van Allen*(Legal Firm)*
P.O. Box 65045,
Charlotte, NC 28265

First Union National Bank*(Major Banking Relationship)*
CMG-5, Two First Union Center
Charlotte, NC 28288-1154
Tel.: 704-374-2698
Fax: 704-374-6987

Subsidiary:

BNE Land & Development Co. **(1)**
P.O. Box 1908
Rocky Mount, NC 27802-1908
Tel.: 919-937-2000
Acquisition & Development of Residential & Commercial Real Estate
S.I.C.: 6552
Douglas E. Anderson *(Pres.)*

THE BODINE CORP.
317 Mountain Grove
Bridgeport, CT 06605
Mailing Address:
P.O. Box 3245
Bridgeport, CT 06605
Tel.: 203-334-3107 **CT**
Fax: 203-334-4007
Year Founded: 1933
Approx.Sls.: $24,000,000
Emp.: 185
Fiscal Year-end: 6/30/91
Export
Mfr. Synchronous Assembly Machine Tool Systems, Tapping & Screw Inserting Machinery; Model 64 Assembly, Model 40-10 Tapping
S.I.C.: 3541
Corporate Giving Program: Through a Private Foundation Funded from Corporate Profits
Edward F. Bodine *(Chm. Bd. & Treas.)*
Richard P. Bodine *(Pres.)*
Joseph R. Farkas *(Sr. V.P.)*
David Bodine *(V.P.-Admin. & Sec.)*
Richard P. Bodine, Jr. *(V.P.)*
William E. Bodine *(V.P.)*
K. Thompson *(Pur. Agent)*

Outside Service Firm(s):

Milton H. Friedberg, Smith & Co.*(Auditors)*
855 Main St., 4th Fl.
Bridgeport, CT 06604
Tel.: 203-366-5876

BODINE ELECTRIC COMPANY
2500 W. Bradley Pl.
Chicago, IL 60618
Tel.: 312-478-3515
Tel.: 800-7BODINE **IL**
Fax: 312-478-3232
Year Founded: 1905
Assets: $31,000,000
Liabilities: $5,000,000
Net Worth: $26,000,000
Approx.Sls.: $47,000,000
Emp.: 620
Fiscal Year-end: 12/31/90
Import Export
Mfr. Electric FHP Motors & Gear Motors, Motion Control Systems
S.I.C.: 3621
Paul J. Bodine *(Chm. Bd.)*
John R. Bodine *(Pres. & Chief Exec. Officer)*
Jeffrey P. Bodine *(Chief Oper. Officer & Exec. V.P.)*
David J. Doll *(Chief Fin. Officer & Sr. V.P.)*
Gary L. Esterling *(V.P.-Mktg.)*
James E. Koncel *(V.P.-Engrng. & Devel.)*
T.J. Provencher *(V.P.-Intl. Mktg.)*
James Stormont *(V.P.-Sls.)*
William F. Nelson *(Controller)*
D.C. McClenahan *(Dir.-Human Resources)*
Joseph J. Kester *(Mgr.-Adv.)*
Principal(s):
Paul J. Bodine

No. of Mfg. Plants/Facilities: 1
No. of U.S. Offices: 2
No. of Foreign Offices: 1

Computer Systems/Hardware:
IBM 4300

Outside Service Firm(s):

Grant Thornton*(Auditors)*
700 One Prudential Plaza, 130 East Randolph St.
Chicago, IL 60601
Tel.: 312-856-0200
Fax: 312-565-4719

Continental Bank N. A.*(Major Banking Relationship)*
231 S. LaSalle St.
Chicago, IL 60697
Tel.: 312-828-2345
Tel.: 800-426-5754
Telex: 312-828-1783

Subsidiary:

Reserve Motion Control Systems **(1)**
6908 Engle Rd.
Middleburg Heights, OH 44130
Tel.: 216-826-0290
Emp.: 6
Industrial Distribution
S.I.C.: 5065
David Witwer *(Chief Oper. Officer)*

BOGUE ELECTRIC MANUFACTURING CO.
100 Pennsylvania Ave.
Paterson, NJ 07509-3027
Tel.: 201-523-2200 **NJ**
Fax: 201-278-8468
Year Founded: 1892
Assets: $6,000,000
Liabilities: $5,000,000
Net Worth: $1,000,000
Sales Range: $10-19 Million
Emp.: 60
Fiscal Year-end: 12/31/90
Import Export
Electrical Rotating Machinery & Equipment: Motor Generators, Diesel Generators, Turbine Generators, Fly Wheel Motor Generators, Uninterruptible Power Supplies, Static DC Power Supplies, Voltage & Frequency Regulators & Frequency Changers, Aircraft Ground Support Equipment, Transformers, Load Banks Fractional Horsepower
S.I.C.: 3621; 3612; 3629; 3694
H.L. Schinman *(Chm. Bd., Treas., Sec. & Gen. Counsel)*
Anthony Sabbatino *(Pres., Chief Oper. & Chief Exec. Officer)*
M. Krantzow *(Opers. Mgr.)*
Frederick Lavinthal *(Gen. Counsel)*

No. of Mfg. Plants/Facilities: 2
No. of U.S. Offices: 2

Computer Systems/Hardware:
IBM PC

Outside Service Firm(s):

Chubb Group*(Commercial Insurance Carrier)*
Boston, MA

Equitable Life*(Group Insurer)*
1221 Ave. of the Americas
New York, NY 10022
Tel.: 212-382-8038
Fax: 212-382-8089

Broadway Bank*(Investment Banker)*
Paterson, NJ

Stern, Lavinthal, Ackerman & Day*(Legal Firm)*
Livingston, NJ

Broadway Bank*(Major Banking Relationship)*
Paterson, NJ

BOH CORPORATION
730 S. Tonti St.
New Orleans, LA 70153
Mailing Address:
Box 53266
New Orleans, LA 70153
Tel.: 504-821-2400 **LA**
Fax: 504-821-0714
Year Founded: 1909
Assets: $107,000,000
Liabilities: $50,000,000
Net Worth: $57,000,000
Sales Range: $100-499 Million
Emp.: 1,500
Fiscal Year-end: 12/31/91
Holding Company; Heavy Construction Contractors
S.I.C.: 6719; 1629; 1711
Robert H. Boh *(Chm. Bd., Pres. & Chief Exec. Officer)*
Bingham C. Stewart *(Vice Chm.)*
Robert S. Boh *(V.P.)*
A.E. Holmes, Jr. *(V.P.-Indus. Devel.)*
James S. Hotard *(V.P.)*
Ralph W. Junius *(V.P.)*
John F. Lipani *(V.P. & Gen. Counsel)*
G.A. Seaver, III *(V.P.)*
Stephen H. Boh *(Treas.)*
Principal(s):
Robert H. Boh

No. of U.S. Offices: 3

Computer Systems/Hardware:
IBM AS 400

Outside Service Firm(s):

Ernst & Young*(Auditors)*
4200 One Shell Square, 701 Poydras St.
New Orleans, LA 70139
Tel.: 504-581-4200

AIG (American International Group)*(Commercial Insurance Carrier)*
70 Pine St.
New York, NY 10270
Tel.: 212-770-7000

Deutsch, Kerrigon & Stiles*(Legal Firm)*
New Orleans, LA

Hibernia National Bank*(Major Banking Relationship)*
New Orleans, LA

Subsidiary:

Boh Brothers Construction Company, Inc. **(1)**
730 S. Tonti St.
New Orleans, LA 70119
Tel.: 504-821-2400
Computer Systems/Hardware:
IBM System 38
Nonmetallic Minerals; General Building; Heavy Construction; Special Construction & Special Trade Contractors; Fabricated Metal Products
S.I.C.: 1611; 1622; 1623; 1629; 1541; 1794
Robert H. Boh *(Chm. Bd. & Pres.)*
Bingham C. Stewart *(Vice Chm.)*
Edwin L. Boehm, Jr. *(V.P.-Pipe Div.)*
Robert S. Boh *(V.P.)*
Archie E. Holmes, Jr. *(V.P.-Indus. Devel.)*
James S. Hotard *(V.P.-Paving Div.)*
Ralph W. Junius *(V.P.-Indus.)*
John F. Lipani *(V.P. & Gen. Counsel)*
G. Arthur Seaver, III *(V.P. & Mgr.-Heavy Construction Div.)*
Stephen H. Boh *(Treas.)*

Nobody Talks To Kids Like Bohbot.™

BOHBOT COMMUNICATIONS, INC.
41 Madison Ave., 26th Fl.
New York, NY 10010
Tel.: 212-213-2700
Fax: 212-889-3766
Year Founded: 1985
Approx.Billings: $350,000,000
Emp.: 120
Intergrated Marketing Services include: Broadcast Media Planning & Buying, TV Programming & Distribution, Public Relations, Promotion & Marketing Services
Allen J. Bohbot *(Pres. & Chief Exec. Officer)*
Dennis Fogarty *(Exec. V.P., Acct. Mngmt. & Strategic Plng.)*
Robin Silverman *(Exec. V.P., Opers.)*
Dennis Fogarty *(Exec. V.P., Acct. Mngmt. & Strategic Planning)*
Steven Kuperberg *(V.P., Acct. Supvr.-Bus. Devel.)*
Jennifer D'Addio *(Acct. Planner)*
Noreen Ryan *(Acct. Planner)*
Steve Kuperberg *(V.P., Acct. Supvr. Bus. Devel.)*
Robin Silverman *(Exec. V.P., Opers.)*
Linda Minucci *(V.P., Dir. M.I.S.)*
Robert Milligan *(Programmer Supvr.)*
Helen Lam *(Sr. Programmer/Analyst)*
Steve Kiernan *(Sr. Programmer/Analyst)*
Patrick Sullivan *(Programmer-Analyst)*
Tim Christian *(Jr. Programmer)*
Ralph Sorrentino *(Exec. V.P., Chief Fin. & Admin. Officer)*
Joanne Staikopoulos *(Sr. V.P., Fin. & Admin.)*
Ed Lyons *(Controller)*
Maureen Berger *(Billing Dir.)*
Grace Collins *(Asst. Controller)*
Peter Blunnie *(Staff Acct.)*
Patrick Haynes *(Sr. Biller)*
Sylvia Margaritas *(A/R - A/P)*
Cindy Forman *(Human Resources Mgr.)*
Steve Morello *(Office Mgr.)*
Denis Fogarty *(Exec. V.P., Acct. Mngmt./Strategic Plng.)*
Adrien Seixas *(Sr. V.P., Prgram Sales)*
Adrien Seixas *(Sr. V.P., Programming & Sls.)*
Jan Teich *(V.P. & Dir., Program Devel.)*
Christine Muhlbach *(Program Coord.)*
Marc Rosenberg *(Dir., Pub. Rels., Promo. & Affiliate Rels.)*
Paula Rockowitz *(Research Analyst)*

Computer Systems/Hardware:
IBM AS/400

DAVID BOLAND, INC.
3050 S. Hopkins Ave.
Titusville, FL 32871
Mailing Address:
P.O. Box 1870
Titusville, FL 32781-1870
Tel.: 407-269-1345 **FL**
Fax: 407-268-0577
Year Founded: 1976
Assets: $7,000,000
Earnings: $100,000
Net Worth: $7,000,000
Approx.Sls.: $16,000,000
Emp.: 85
General Contractor; Commercial Contractor
S.I.C.: 1522
David Boland *(Chm. Bd., Pres. & Chief Exec. Officer)*
Donna Brockelmeyer *(V.P. & Controller)*
Michael Boland *(Sec. & Treas.)*
Principal(s):
David Boland

No. of U.S. Offices: 1

Computer Systems/Hardware:
Bidtek

Outside Service Firm(s):

Osborne Henning & Co.*(Auditors)*
Orlando, FL

CNA Insurance*(Commercial Insurance Carrier)*
CNA Plaza,
Chicago, IL 60685
Tel.: 312-822-5000

Baker & Hostetler*(Legal Firm)*
3200 National City Center
Cleveland, OH 44114
Tel.: 216-621-0200
Fax: 216-696-0740

Sovran Bank*(Major Banking Relationship)*
Roanoke, VA

Pension Investors Corp.*(Pension Manager)*
Altamonte Springs, FL

M. R. BOLIN INC.
2318 Park Ave. S.
Minneapolis, MN 55404
Tel.: 612-872-1200

Fax: 612-872-7056
Year Founded: 1950
Approx.Billings: $13,000,000
Emp.: 24
M.R. Bolin *(Chm. Bd. & Chief Exec. Officer)*
Scott Bolin *(Chm. & Chief Creative Officer)*
Todd Bolin *(Pres. & Chief Oper. Officer)*
Larry Shear *(Exec. V.P.)*
Ruth Lood *(V.P., Fin.)*

BOLLIGER, INC.
One Bolliger Place
Stamford, CT 06907
Mailing Address:
P.O. Box 4444,
Stamford, CT 06907
Tel.: 203-324-5999
Tel.: 800-243-9517 **CT**
Telex: 691-9001
Fax: 203-324-2672
Year Founded: 1975
Assets: $5,512,765
Earnings: $176,529
Liabilities: $4,837,642
Net Worth: $675,123
Approx.Sls.: $16,288,434
Emp.: 82
Fiscal Year-end: 12/31/90
Import Export
Moving & Storage Co.; Travel Agency
S.I.C.: 4729; 4731
Corporate Giving Program:
Contributes $10,000 per Year
Richard Bolliger *(Chm. Bd.)*
Stephen Gerard *(Pres., Chief Exec. Officer & Treas.)*
Antonia Gerard *(Exec. V.P., Chief Fin. & Oper. Officer, Sec. & Controller)*
Gerry Delzio *(V.P.-Sls. & Mktg.)*
Jack McAuliffe *(V.P.)*
Gerry Lynch *(Mgr.-International Fin.)*
Liz Maroc *(Mgr.-Import)*
Principal(s):
Stephen Gerard
Antonia Gerard

No. of Mfg. Plants/Facilities: 4
No. of U.S. Offices: 3
No. of Foreign Offices: 4

Computer Systems/Hardware:
AT&T 3B2500

Outside Service Firm(s):

Walter J. McKeever & Co.*(Auditors)*
Greenwich, CT

Marsh & McLennan*(Commercial Insurance Carrier)*
1600 Summer St.
Stamford, CT 06904
Tel.: 203-964-5436
Fax: 203-964-5475

Aetna Life & Casualty*(Group Insurer)*
151 Farmington Avenue
Hartford, CT 06156
Tel.: 203-273-2128
Fax: 203-729-4295

Curtis, Brinckerhoff & Barrett*(Legal Firm)*
666 Summer St.
Stamford, CT 06901
Tel.: 203-324-6777

Chase Manhattan Bank of Connecticut, N.A.*(Major Banking Relationship)*
961 Main St.
Bridgeport, CT 06601
Tel.: 203-384-5402

Subsidiary:

Crown Lance, Inc. **(1)**
370 W. Main St.
Stamford, CT 06902
Tel.: 203-357-1400
Holding Co. for a CFC
S.I.C.: 6719
S. Gerard *(Pres. & Chief Exec. Officer)*

Non U.S. Holding:

Crown Lance Italia Srl **(1)**
Via dei Buonvisi, 61 00148
Rome, Italy
Moving & Storage Co.
S.I.C.: 4214
S. Gerard *(Pres. & Chief Exec. Officer)*

BOLLINGER INDUSTRIES INC.
222 W. Airport Fwy.
Irving, TX 75026
Tel.: 214-445-0386
Fax: 214-438-8471
Year Founded: 1974
Approx.Sls.: $35,000,000
Emp.: 190
Fiscal Year-end: 3/31/91
Import Export
Manufactures Sporting Goods
S.I.C.: 3949
Glenn D. Bollinger *(Chm. Bd. & Pres.)*
Bob Bollinger *(Chief Exec. Officer)*
Ed Dmytryk *(Chief Oper. Officer)*
Mike Beck *(Chief Fin. Officer)*
Franklin Ross *(V.P.-Mktg.)*
Principal(s):
Glenn D. Bollinger
Bob Bollinger

No. of Mfg. Plants/Facilities: 3
No. of U.S. Offices: 4

Computer Systems/Hardware:
IBM

Outside Service Firm(s):

Naman, Howell, Smith & Lee*(Legal Firm)*
Austin, TX

Subsidiaries:

Bollinger Health Care **(1)**
1020 S.E. Loop 289
Lubbock, TX 79404
Tel.: 806-795-7027
Import Export
Computer Systems/Hardware:
IBM
Weights, Neoprene Athletic & Rehabilitation Supports
Ed Dmytryk *(Pres.)*
Nancy Rosales *(V.P.-Mfg.)*
Pam Compton *(V.P.-Sls.)*
Angelia Ponath *(Controller)*

California-Gym Equipment Co. **(1)**
3140 S. Pico Blvd.
Los Angeles, CA 90023
Tel.: 213-263-2255
Import Export
Computer Systems/Hardware:
IBM
Manufacture Exercise Equipment
S.I.C.: 3949
John Swete *(Pres.)*
Ed Dmytryk *(Chief Oper. Officer)*
Ike Kelly *(Controller)*
Michelle Scolaro *(Dir.-Sls. & Mktg.)*

Elmer's Weights **(1)**
1020 S.E. Loop 289
Lubbock, TX 79404
Tel.: 806-745-6724
Manufacturer of Athletic Products
S.I.C.: 3949

BOLLINGER MACHINE SHOP AND SHIPYARD, INC.
P.O. Box 250, Highway 308
Lockport, LA 70374
Tel.: 504-532-2554
Twx: 584127
Fax: 504-532-5546
Year Founded: 1946
Assets: $35,000,000
Net Worth: $35,000,000
Approx.Sls.: $58,000,000
Emp.: 510
Fiscal Year-end: 11/30/91
Export
Ship & Boat Builders; Marine Repairs; Machine Shop
S.I.C.: 3731; 3732; 3599
Corporate Giving Program: Company gives to The United Way, Payroll deductions for Savings Bonds, Local Schools, Churches & Civic Centers
Employee Matching Gifts Program: Contributions of 10% up to 3% of Salary
Donald T. Bollinger *(Chm. Bd., Chief Exec. Officer & Dir.-Fin.)*
Richard Bollinger *(Pres.)*
Walter Berry *(V.P.-Admin.)*
Tilman Esteve *(V.P.)*
Michael Toups *(V.P.-Algiers Iron Works & Dry Dock, Inc.)*
Charlotte B. Troups *(Treas. & Dir.-Mdsg. & Adv.)*
Aubrey Orgeron *(Controller)*
Andrea Bollinger Suard *(Sec.)*
L.C. Dickerson, III *(Gen. Counsel)*
Boysie Bollinger *(Dir.-Mergers/ Acquisitions)*
George Bronsdard *(Dir.-Human Resources)*
Freddie Delaune *(Dir.-Fin.)*
Dennis Fanguy *(Dir.-Tech., Res. & Devel.)*
Ron Grisnick *(Dir.-Quality Control)*
Charles Hardy *(Dir.-Mktg. & Sls.)*
Flo Matherne *(Dir.-Pur.)*
Clarence Orgeron *(Dir.-Mfg.)*
Scott Ronesell *(Dir.-Data Processing)*
Scott Treriot *(Dir.-Sls.)*
Marc Stanley *(Gen. Mgr. & Dir.-Govt. Affairs)*
Patti Callais *(Corp. Librarian)*
Kathy Vaughn *(Corp. Travel Planner)*
Principal(s):
Donald T. Bollinger
Andrea Bollinger Suard
Charlotte B. Lonk

No. of Mfg. Plants/Facilities: 5
No. of U.S. Offices: 1

Computer Systems/Hardware:
DEC-Word Perfect; CINCOM System

Outside Service Firm(s):

Warren J. Arcement*(Auditors)*
Lockport, LA

Corroon & Black*(Auditors)*
New Orleans, LA

Great American Life Insurance Co.*(Group Insurer)*
New Orleans, LA

Premier Bank*(Investment Banker)*
Lockport, LA

Raceland Bank & Trust Company*(Major Banking Relationship)*
Raceland, LA

Delaware Charter*(Pension Manager)*
New Orleans, LA

Subsidiary:

Algiers Iron Works & Dry Dock, Inc. **(1)**
434 Powder St.
New Orleans, LA 70114
Tel.: 504-362-7960
Emp.: 30
Ship & Boat Builders, Marine Repairs, Machine Shop
S.I.C.: 3731; 3732; 3599
Mike Toupe *(Chief Oper. Officer, V.P. & Gen. Mgr.)*
Walter Berry *(Chief Fin. Officer)*
Scott Theriot *(Dir.-Sls. & Mktg.)*
T. Walter Berry *(V.P.)*

BOLTON-EMERSON, INC.
(Undergoing Reorganization)
9 Osgood St.
Lawrence, MA 01843
Tel.: 508-686-3961 **MA**
Fax: 508-688-8225
Year Founded: 1905
Approx.Sls.: $12,000,000
Emp.: 90
Fiscal Year-end: 12/31/90
Industry Processing Equipment, Paper Machinery, Size Reduction Equipment, Coating & Laminating Equipment
S.I.C.: 3554; 3559
John W. Fitzgerald *(Pres.)*
Gordon Driscoll *(V.P.-Fin.)*
G.I. Urquhart *(V.P.-Mktg. & Sls.)*
Regina C. Dombrowski *(V.P.-Personnel & Admin.)*
Joe Hanley *(Pur. Agent)*
Principal(s):
John W. Fitzgerald
Gordon Driscoll

No. of Mfg. Plants/Facilities: 4

Computer Systems/Hardware:
IBM 3400

Outside Service Firm(s):

Price Waterhouse*(Auditors)*
160 Federal St.
Boston, MA 02110
Tel.: 617-439-3308
Fax: 617-439-3308

Hale and Dorr*(Legal Firm)*
60 State St.
Boston, MA 02109-6098
Tel.: 617-526-6000

Divisions:

Bolton-Emerson Machine Knife Div. **(1)**
9 Osgood St.
Lawrence, MA 01843
Tel.: 508-686-3961
Fax: 508-688-8225
Mfrs. Paper Knives, Machine Knives & Knives for the Plastics Industry
S.I.C.: 3423
Fred Haselton *(Sr. Sls. Admin.)*

Bolton-Emerson Paper Machinery Div. **(1)**
9 Osgood St.
Lawrence, MA 01843
Tel.: 508-686-3961
Fax: 508-688-8225
Mfrs.Stock Preparation Equip. & Replacement Parts for the Paper Mill Industry
S.I.C.: 3554

Converting Machinery Div. **(1)**
9 Osgood St.
Lawrence, MA 01843
Tel.: 508-686-3961
Fax: 508-688-8225
Special Machinery
S.I.C.: 3559
Glenn I. Urquhart *(V.P.-Mktg. & Sls.)*

Subsidiaries:

Bolton-Emerson-McNiece, Inc. **(1)**
1215 Unity St.
Philadelphia, PA 19142
Tel.: 215-743-1113 (100%)
Emp.: 9
Repair & Resell Industrial Knives & Saws
S.I.C.: 7699
Thomas Donahue *(Mgr.)*

Bolton-Emerson-Southern, Inc. **(1)**
P.O. Box 769-Alton Hall Rd.,
Cairo, GA 31728
Tel.: 912-377-9001 (100%)
Fax: 912-377-6006
Emp.: 30
Attrition Plates for Disc Refiners
S.I.C.: 3554

Non-U.S. Holdings:

Bolton-Emerson Equipmentos Industrias Ltda. **(1)**
Sao Paulo, Brazil (100%)

Bolton-Emerson S.A. **(1)**
Case Ville 2333
Lausanne, Switzerland
Tel.: 206451 (100%)
Emp.: 25
Paper Machinery; Coating Equip.
S.I.C.: 3554; 3479
John Mladota *(Pres. & Mng. Dir.)*

Bolton-Emerson, Inc.—(Continued)

Bolton-Emerson Talamac Maquinas e Equipamentos Ltda. **(1)**
Sao Paulo, Brazil (100%)

BOMMER INDUSTRIES, INC.
Hwy. 176
Landrum, SC 29356
Mailing Address:
P.O. Box 187
Landrum, SC 29356
Tel.: 803-457-3301 **SC**
Year Founded: 1876
Sales Range: $10-19 Million
Emp.: 250
Manufacturer of Lavatory Hardware, Spring Hinges & Mail Receptacles
S.I.C.: 3429; 3469; 3431
Marie Bommer Frohlich *(Chm. Bd.)*
Peter E. Frohlich *(Pres.)*
Charles A. Martin *(Chief Fin. Officer)*
James Dunigan *(Dir.-Pur.)*
Marlene Fisher *(Dir.-Data Processing)*
W.J. Laughridge III *(Mgr.-Natl. Sls.)*
Robert Jutzi *(Asst. Mgr.-Sls.)*

Computer Systems/Hardware:
IBM System 38

Outside Service Firm(s):

McAbee Halliday & Co.*(Auditors)*
Spartanburg, SC

Blue Cross & Blue Shield of South Carolina*(Group Insurer)*
1517 Laurel St.
Columbia, SC 29201

NationsBank Carolinas*(Major Banking Relationship)*
Tryon, NC

THE BOMSTEIN AGENCY
2201 Wisconsin Ave., NW, Ste. C-150
Washington, DC 20007
Tel.: 202-965-6470
Fax: 202-338-8835
Year Founded: 1976
Approx.Billings: $38,000,000
Emp.: 44
Real Estate, Retail & Corp.
Howard Bomstein *(Chm. Bd., Pres. & Chief Exec. Officer)*
Joanne King Williams *(Exec. V.P., Chief Oper. Officer)*
Jenny Morrell *(V.P., Chief Fin. Officer)*
Maureen Kennedy *(Mktg. Dir.)*

BON JOUR INTERNATIONAL LTD.
1411 Broadway
New York, NY 10018
Tel.: 212-398-1000
Fax: 212-819-1454
Approx.Sls.: $150,000,000
Emp.: 200
Garment Mfr.; Bon Jour Sportwear, Jeans, Pants, Activewear Shirts & Accessories
S.I.C.: 2329; 2321; 2325; 2389
Ari Dayan *(Chm. Bd.)*
Mark Shulman *(Pres.)*
Charles Dayan *(Chief Exec. Officer)*

Division:

Licensing Div. **(1)**
1411 Broadway
New York, NY 10018
Tel.: 212-398-1000
Ari Dayan *(Chm.)*
Mark Shulman *(Pres.)*
Charles Dayan *(Chief Exec. Officer)*
Robert Golinger *(Chief Fin. Officer)*

BON TON FOODS, INC.
1120 Zinns Quarry Rd.
York, PA 17405
Tel.: 717-843-0026
Approx.Sls.: $20,000,000
Emp.: 1180
Mfr. of Potato Chips & Other Snacks
S.I.C.: 2096
Jack P. Cook *(Chm. Bd. & Pres.)*
Steve Shind *(V.P.-Sls. & Mktg.)*
Richard G. Vance *(V.P.-Sls. & Mktg.)*
William Reese *(Dir.-Engrng.)*

BONANZA BUS LINES, INC.
1 Bonanza Way
Providence, RI 02904
Tel.: 401-331-7500
Approx.Sls.: $14,000,000
Emp.: 200
Bus Transportation
S.I.C.: 4131
George Sage *(Pres.)*
George J. Hunter *(Exec. V.P.)*

BONGARDS CREAMERIES INC.
13-200 County Rd. 51
Norwood, MN 55368
Tel.: 612-466-5521 **MN**
Fax: 612-466-5556
Year Founded: 1908
Assets: $73,000,000
Liabilities: $10,000,000
Net Worth: $63,000,000
Approx.Sls.: $105,000,000
Emp.: 85
Fiscal Year-end: 12/31/91
Import Export
Dairy Products Cooperative
S.I.C.: 2022; 2021; 2023
Curtis Walter *(Pres.)*
Edwin W. Bruddgemeier *(V.P.)*
Duane Heuer *(Sec. & Treas.)*
Tom Simmons *(Controller)*
Matt Quade *(Gen. Mgr.)*
Ted Jacoby *(Dir.-Mktg.)*
Stu Kringen *(Dir.-Sls. & Purch.)*
Brent Jewitt *(Mgr.-Cheese Proc. Plant)*
Marvin Jewitt *(Mgr.-Cheese Plant)*
Clint Mueller *(Mgr.-Drying Plant)*

No. of Mfg. Plants/Facilities: 1
No. of U.S. Offices: 1

Outside Service Firm(s):

Maiser*(Auditors)*
Waconia, MN

Gray, Plant, Mooty, Mooty & Bennett*(Legal Firm)*
3400 City Center, 33 So. 6th St.
Minneapolis, MN 55402
Tel.: 612-343-2800
Fax: 612-830-0270

First National Bank of Minneapolis*(Major Banking Relationship)*
P.O. Box A799
Minneapolis, MN 55480
Tel.: 612-370-4606

BONHOMME SHIRTMAKERS, LTD.
350 Fifth Ave.
New York, NY 10118
Tel.: 212-947-8600 **NY**
Fax: 212-947-8613
Year Founded: 1971
Approx.Sls.: $14,000,000
Emp.: 300
Mfr. of Men's Woven & Knit Shirts
S.I.C.: 2321; 2253
Alvin Goodman *(Pres.)*
Marshall Goodman *(V.P.)*
Rhea Goodman *(Sec. & Treas.)*

Outside Service Firm(s):

Edwin K. Sperling*(Auditors)*
New York, NY

Paradise & Alberts*(Legal Firm)*
New York, NY

Bank of New York*(Major Banking Relationship)*
90 Washington St.
New York, NY 10015

BONLAND INDUSTRIES, INC.
50 Newark Pompton Turnpike
Wayne, NJ 07470
Tel.: 201-694-3211
Fax: 201-628-1120
Approx.Sls.: $15,000,000
Emp.: 250
Designing, Metal & HVAC Systems
S.I.C.: 3444; 3585; 3822
Ernest Boniface *(Chm. Bd.)*
William Boniface *(Pres.)*
Andrew Boniface *(Exec. V.P.)*
Kenneth Hauser *(V.P.-Opers.)*
Edward Rebenack *(V.P-Sls.)*
Nicolas Scheidel *(V.P.)*
Carol O'Keefe *(Controller)*

Outside Service Firm(s):

National Westminster Bank plc*(Major Banking Relationship)*
2 Montgomery St.
Jersey City, NJ 07302
Tel.: 201-547-7000

F.H. BONN COMPANY
111 N. Hickory
Arlington Heights, IL 60004
Tel.: 708-255-4656 **IL**
Fax: 708-255-4735
Year Founded: 1946
Approx.Sls.: $19,000,000
Emp.: 240
Export
Mfr. of Plushes & Piles, Broadwoven Cotton; Pads & Covers For Laundry & Dry Cleaning Pressing Equipment
S.I.C.: 2211; 2299; 2394
Neal F. Bonn *(Pres. & Chief Exec. Officer)*
James Garbrecht *(V.P. & Gen. Mgr.)*
Allan Bonn *(Treas. & Sec.)*

Outside Service Firm(s):

Clark, Schaeffer & Hackett*(Auditors)*
Springfield, IL

First National Bank*(Major Banking Relationship)*
Des Plaines, IL

Subsidiary:

International Steel Wool Corporation **(1)**
P.O. Box 1767
Springfield, OH 45501
Tel.: 513-323-4651
Mfr. of Steel Wool, Special Metal Wools
S.I.C.: 3291
Neal F. Bonn *(Pres. & Chief Exec. Officer)*

BONNEVILLE COMMUNICATIONS
130 Social Hall Ave.
Salt Lake City, UT 84111
Tel.: 801-237-2600
Fax: 801-237-2460
Year Founded: 1967
Approx.Billings: $33,000,000
Emp.: 52
Heart Sell-Strategic, Emotional Advertising that Stimulates Response
Corporate Giving Program: Salvation Army
Richard D. Alsop *(Pres.)*
Ellen Richardson *(V.P., Human Resources)*
Delon W. Williams *(V.P., Controller, Chief Fin. Officer)*

BONNEY FORGE CORPORATION
Cedar & Meadow Sts.
Allentown, PA 18105
Tel.: 215-435-9611
Tel.: 800-345-7546
Fax: 215-435-6973
Sales Range: $20-39 Million
Emp.: 300
Fiscal Year-end: 6/30/91
Export
Pipe Fittings & Valves
S.I.C.: 3494
John A. Leone *(Pres. & Chief Exec. Officer)*
Patrick R. Benavides *(V.P.-Engrng.)*
Keith J. Winterson *(V.P.-Fin.)*
Rick Leone *(Mgr.-Sls.)*
Principal(s):
John A. Leone
Keith J. Winterson
Patrick R. Benavides
M.W. Leone
J. Rosener

No. of Mfg. Plants/Facilities: 2
No. of U.S. Offices: 6

Outside Service Firm(s):

Ernst & Young*(Auditors)*
Wyomissing Professional Center, 875 Berkshire Blvd.
Reading, PA 19610

Pepper, Hamilton & Scheetz*(Legal Firm)*
123 S. Broad
Philadelphia, PA 19109
Tel.: 215-893-3000

Fidelity Bank*(Major Banking Relationship)*
Broad & Walnut St.
Philadelphia, PA 19109

B

BONSIB INC. *Marketing Services*

BONSIB INC.
The Bonsib Building, 927 S. Harrison St.
Fort Wayne, IN 46802
Tel.: 219-422-4661
Fax: 219-422-9497
Year Founded: 1923
Approx.Billings: $17,000,000
Emp.: 26
Richard E. Bonsib *(Chm. Bd. & Pres.)*
Gretchen A. Bonsib *(Sr. V.P., Sec. & Treas.)*
Joseph D. Brown, Ph.D. *(Mktg. Research Dir.)*
Amy S. Ahlersmeyer *(Pub. Rels. Mgr.)*
Cindy Link *(Office Mgr.)*

BOOKAZINE COMPANY, INC.
75 Hook Dr.
Bayonne, NJ 07002
Tel.: 201-339-7777 **NY**
Fax: 212-633-9731
Year Founded: 1946
Approx.Sls.: $35,000,000
Emp.: 150
Book & Catalog Publishers, Not Printed on Site
S.I.C.: 5192; 2741
Irwin Kallman *(Pres.)*
Gray Simone *(Controller)*

Outside Service Firm(s):

Ernst & Young*(Auditors)*
787 Seventh Ave.
New York, NY 10019
Tel.: 212-773-1243

Manufacturers Hanover Trust Co.*(Major Banking Relationship)*
4 New York Plaza
New York, NY 10015
Tel.: 212-623-3232

JOHN BOOS & COMPANY
315 S. 1st St.
Effingham, IL 62401
Mailing Address:
P.O. Box 609
Effingham, IL 62401
Tel.: 217-347-7701
Fax: 217-347-7705
Year Founded: 1887
Approx.Sls.: $10,000,000
Emp.: 100
Export
Meat & Produce Wood Blocks & Cutting Tables, Stainless Steel & Plastic Tables for Industry; Butcher Block Furniture
S.I.C.: 2499
Ted Gravenhorst, Jr. *(Pres.)*
Eric Johnson *(V.P.-Sls.)*
Randy Moore *(Natl. Sls. Mgr.)*

BOOTH AMERICAN
333 W. Fort St.
Detroit, MI 48226
Tel.: 313-965-3360
Fax: 313-965-1160
Approx.Sls.: $70,000,000
Emp.: 475
Broadcasting & Cable Television
S.I.C.: 4832; 4899
John L. Booth, Sr. *(Chm. Bd. & Chief Exec. Officer)*
John L. Booth II *(Pres. & Chief Fin. Officer)*
Ralph H. Booth II *(Pres. & Treas.)*
Louise Booth *(Sr. V.P.)*

Outside Service Firm(s):

Price Waterhouse*(Auditors)*
200 Renaissance Center, Ste. 3900
Detroit, MI 48243

Clark, Klein & Beaumont*(Legal Firm)*
1600 First Federal Bldg.
Detroit, MI 48226
Tel.: 313-965-8300

Cohn and Marks*(Legal Firm)*
Washington, DC

Manufacturers National Bank N.A.*(Major Banking Relationship)*
38th Fl., 100 Renaissance Center
Detroit, MI 48243
Tel.: 313-222-4227

BOOTH NEWSPAPERS, INC.
155 Michigan N.W.
Grand Rapids, MI 49503
Mailing Address:
P.O. Box 2168
Grand Rapids, MI 49501
Tel.: 616-459-3824 **NJ**
Fax: 616-459-1542
Approx.Sls.: $200,000,000
Emp.: 2,400
Fiscal Year-end: 12/31/90
Newspaper Publishing
S.I.C.: 2711
Werner Veit *(Pres.)*
Roger C. Schoemaker *(V.P.-Employee & Labor Rels.)*
Monica L. Benedict *(Dir.-Sls. & Mktg.)*

Outside Service Firm(s):

Paul Scherer & Co.*(Auditors)*
New York, NY

Bodman, Longley & Dahling*(Legal Firm)*
100 Renaissance Center
Detroit, MI 48243
Tel.: 313-259-7777

Old Kent Bank*(Major Banking Relationship)*
Grand Rapids, MI

BOOZ ALLEN & HAMILTON INC.
101 Park Ave.
New York, NY 10178
Tel.: 212-697-1900 **DE**
Fax: 212-880-9732
Year Founded: 1914
Sales Range: $500-999 Million
Emp.: 4,000
Management & Technology Consultants
S.I.C.: 8742; 8711; 8732; 8748; 4899; 7372; 8734
William F. Stasior *(Chm. Bd. & Chief Exec. Officer)*
Cyrus F. Freidheim *(Vice Chm.)*
Martin Waldenstrom *(Pres.-Worldwide Commercial Consulting)*
Gary D. Mather *(Pres.-Worldwide Technology Consulting)*
Daniel R. Idzik *(Sr. V.P. & Gen. Counsel)*
Edward H. Schwallie *(Sr. V.P. & Chief Fin. Officer)*
R. Michael McCullough *(Sr. Partner)*

Principal(s):
William F. Stasior
R. Michael McCullough

No. of Foreign Offices: 13

Computer Systems/Hardware:
IBM System 38

Outside Service Firm(s):

Grant Thornton*(Auditors)*
700 One Prudential Plaza, 130 East Randolph St.
Chicago, IL 60601
Tel.: 312-856-0200
Fax: 312-565-4719

Non-U.S. Holding:

Booz, Allen & Hamilton International (UK) Ltd. **(1)**
100 Piccadilly May Fair
London, WIV 9HA, United Kingdom
Tel.: 011-4471-493-9595 (100%)
Intl. Headquarters, Mngmt. Consulting
S.I.C.: 8742
Keith Oliver *(Mng. Partner)*

BORCHERS BROS.
550 Sunol St.
San Jose, CA 95126
Mailing Address:
P.O. Box 510
San Jose, CA 95103
Tel.: 408-297-3404 **CA**
Fax: 408-297-0331
Year Founded: 1896
Assets: $4,900,000
Liabilities: $3,750,000
Net Worth: $1,150,000
Approx.Sls.: $11,500,000
Emp.: 41
Fiscal Year-end: 3/31/91
Wholesale Building Materials Distribution; Hardware, Steel Products, Fireplaces, Woodburning Stoves, Masonry, Plastering & Lathing
S.I.C.: 5031; 5039; 5072; 5074; 5211; 5032; 5033
John D. Caldwell *(Chm. Bd., Pres. & Chief Exec. Officer)*
Benjamin D. Painter *(Sec. & Treas.)*
B.D. Painter *(Dir.-Data Processing)*
William Glennon *(Gen. Counsel)*
James Christman *(Mgr.-Division)*
Peter De Snoo *(Mgr.-Credit)*
Fred Holm *(Mgr.-Division)*
Ray Otis *(Mgr.-Division)*

Principal(s):
John D. Caldwell

No. of U.S. Offices: 3

Computer Systems/Hardware:
Alpha Micro 2000-10

Outside Service Firm(s):

Ruzzo, Scholl & Murphy*(Auditors)*
San Jose, CA

Winn Insurance Co.*(Commercial Insurance Carrier)*
Hollister, CA

Glennon & Burrows*(Legal Firm)*
San Jose, CA

Plaza Bank of Commerce*(Major Banking Relationship)*
San Jose, CA

Cupertino National Bank*(Pension Manager)*
San Jose, CA

BORDER STATES INDUSTRIES, INC.
105 25th St. N.
Fargo, ND 58108
Mailing Address:
P.O. Box 2767
Fargo, ND 58108
Tel.: 701-293-5833
Fax: 701-232-7673
Year Founded: 1953
Sales Range: $100-499 Million
Emp.: 350
Export
Wholesale Electrical Supplies
S.I.C.: 5063; 5065
Robert Gill *(Pres.)*
Paul C. Madson *(Chief Exec. Officer)*
Greg Hoffelt *(V.P.-Mktg.)*
Brad Thrau *(V.P.-Sls.)*

No. of U.S. Offices: 11

Computer Systems/Hardware:
IBM AS 400

Outside Service Firm(s):

Charles Bailly & Co.*(Auditors)*
406 Main Ave., Ste. 3000
Fargo, ND 58126-0001
Tel.: 701-239-8500

Conmy, Feste, Bossart, Hubbard & Corwin, Ltd.*(Legal Firm)*
Fargo, ND

Norwest Bank Fargo, N.A.*(Major Banking Relationship)*
Fargo, ND

BORDER STATES PAVING, INC.
Cass County Rd. 20
Fargo, ND 58102
Tel.: 701-237-4860
Fax: 701-237-0233
Approx.Sls.: $24,000,000
Emp.: 25
Asphalt Paving & Concrete Construction
S.I.C.: 1611
Lloyd Thompson *(Chm. Bd.)*
Dan Thompson *(Pres.)*
Nancy Slotten *(Exec. V.P. & Treas.)*
Don Carlson *(V.P.)*
Thomas H. Lee *(Sec.)*
Glen Bjerk *(Mgr.-Estimating & Employee Opers.)*

Outside Service Firm(s):

Eide Helmeke & Co.*(Auditors)*
500 Dakota Bank Building
Fargo, ND 58102

Kermit Bye*(Legal Firm)*
Fargo, ND

Norwest Bank Minnesota, N.A.*(Major Banking Relationship)*
Fargo, ND

BP&N
BORDERS PERRIN AND NORRANDER INC.

BORDERS, PERRIN & NORRANDER, INC.
222 S.W. Yamhill St., 7th Fl.
Portland, OR 97204
Tel.: 503-227-2506
Fax: 503-227-4827
Year Founded: 1977
Approx.Billings: $54,000,000
Emp.: 86
Advertising Agency
S.I.C.: 7311
Peter M. Hatt *(Chm. & Chief Exec. Officer)*
Bill Borders *(Pres. & Dir.-Creative Services)*
Michael O'Rourke *(Exec. V.P., Gen. Mgr.)*
Vicki Baker *(V.P., Controller)*
Donna Fitzpatrick *(V.P., Mktg. Dir.)*
Judy Wren Hamilton *(V.P.)*
Karen Coster *(Sr. Broadcast Producer)*
Carolyn Shefler *(Office Mgr.)*

Computer Systems/Hardware:
Basic Computer "The Heavyweight"

Outside Service Firm(s):

Bogumil & Associates*(Auditors)*
Portland, OR

Heestand & Co.*(Group Insurer)*
Portland, OR

Kell, Alterman & Runstein*(Legal Firm)*
Portland, OR

Prescott & Co.*(Legal Firm)*
Seattle, WA

Branch:

Borders, Perrin & Norrander **(1)**
1115 First Ave. S.
Seattle, WA 98101
Tel.: 206-343-7741
Fax: 206-343-7735
Emp.: 30
Peter M. Hatt *(Chm. & Chief Exec. Officer)*
Mike Jaglois *(V.P., Gen. Mgr.)*

BORG-WARNER CORPORATION
200 S. Michigan Ave.
Chicago, IL 60604
Tel.: 312-322-8500 **DE**
Fax: 312-322-8398
Year Founded: 1928
Approx.Sls.: $2,575,000,000
Emp.: 85,400
Fiscal Year-end: 12/31/92
Import Export
Manufacturer of Automotive Components; Protective Services
S.I.C.: 3714; 7382; 3585; 2821; 6153; 2869
Corporate Giving Program:
Foundation is Being Wound Down
Employee Matching Gifts Program: 2 For 1 to Universities
Donald C. Trauscht *(Pres. & Chief Exec. Officer)*
Neal F. Farrell *(Mng. Partner, V.P., Gen. Counsel & Chief Fin. Officer)*
John D. O'Brien *(Mng. Partner, V.P.-Human Resources)*
Timothy M. Wood *(V.P. & Controller)*
Jack L. Wentz *(Assoc. Gen. Counsel & Corp. Sec.)*
Joseph Allen *(Dir.-Communications)*
Angela D'Aversa *(Dir.-Human Resources & Office Admin.)*
Eloise Hirschey *(Dir.-Retirement Plans, Pensions & Benefit Systems)*
Robin Adams *(Asst. Treas.)*

Borg-Warner Corporation—(Continued)

Outside Service Firm(s):

KPMG Peat Marwick*(Auditors)*
Peat Marwick Plaza, 303 E. Wacker Dr.
Chicago, IL 60601
Tel.: 312-938-1000

Continental Bank N. A.*(Major Banking Relationship)*
231 S. LaSalle St.
Chicago, IL 60697
Tel.: 312-828-2345
Tel.: 800-426-5754
Telex: 312-828-1783

Automotive Group:

Borg Warner Automotive, Inc. **(1)**
P.O Box 8002, 6700 18 1/2 Mile Rd.
Sterling Heights, MI 48311
Tel.: 313-726-4400
Approx.Sls.: $1,000,000,000
Emp.: 10,000
Mfr. of Automotive Components and Systems
S.I.C.: 8741; 5013
Siegfried P. Adler *(Pres.)*

Divisions:

Borg-Warner Automotive Control Systems-Blytheville **(2)**
P.O. Box 1529, Blytheville Industrial Park
Blytheville, AR 72315
Tel.: 501-763-0830
Mfr. of Electronic Components for Automobiles
S.I.C.: 3694; 3714
Gary Burger *(Plant Mgr.)*

Borg-Warner Automotive Control Systems-Dixon **(2)**
1700 Franklin Grove Rd.
Dixon, IL 61021
Tel.: 815-288-1462
Mfr. of Electronic Components for Automobiles
S.I.C.: 3694; 3714
G. A. Burger *(Plant Mgr.)*

Borg-Warner Automotive Electronic Sensors-Cary **(2)**
P.O. Box 580, 406 Gregson Drive
Cary, NC 27511
Tel.: 919-469-2900
Mfr. of Electronic Sensors for Automotive Applications
S.I.C.: 3694; 3714
W. Leaver *(Plant Mgr.)*

Borg-Warner Automotive, Inc. **(2)**
12000 Tech Center Dr.
Livonia, MI 48150
Tel.: 313-458-1000
Fax: 313-458-1089
Approx.Sls.: $1,000,000,000
Emp.: 10,000
Wholesale Distr. of Automotive Components; Torque Converters, Torsional Dampers, Manual Transmissions, 4-Wheel Drive Systems, Chain, Engine, Emission & Suspension Controls, Turbochargers
S.I.C.: 5013
T.K. Lindquist *(V.P.-Tech.)*
W.H. Hernandez *(V.P.-Fin.)*
J.D. Davis *(Dir.-Communications & Pub. Rels.)*

Borg-Warner Automotive, Inc., Control Systems **(2)**
6700 18 1/2 Mile Rd.
Sterling Heights, MI 48314
Tel.: 313-726-1000
Emp.: 1,000
Mfr. of Electronic Components for Automobiles; Solenoids, Fuel Shut-Off Devices for Gasoline & LPG, Fuel Strainers, Custom-Design Automotive Control Devices, Automotive Emission Valves & Switches
S.I.C.: 3714; 3694
G.E. Hullinger *(V.P. & Gen. Mgr.)*
Doug Davis *(Adv. Mgr.)*
A.L. Edwards *(Dir.-Mktg. & Sls.)*

Borg-Warner Automotive, Inc., Transmission Systems **(2)**
P.O. Box 2688, 47302,
Muncie, IN 47302
Mfr. of Automotive, Truck, Indus., Off-Road & Marine Transmissions; Synchronizers; Conventional & Spin-Resistant Differentials; Spur & Bevel Gears; Gearboxes; Four-Wheel-Drive System Components
S.I.C.: 3714
A. Straub *(V.P.-Opers.)*
S. Zirke *(Dir.-Sls.)*

Borg-Warner Automotive-Michigan Powdered Metal Products, Inc. **(2)**
32059 Schoolcraft
Livonia, MI 48150
Tel.: 313-261-5322
Conventional & Forged Powdered Metal Products, Primarily for the Automotive Mkt.
S.I.C.: 3399; 3714
B. Moorehouse *(Plant Mgr.)*

Borg-Warner Transmission & Engine Components **(2)**
770 Warren Road
Ithaca, NY 14850
Tel.: 607-257-1800
Worldwide Supervision of Devel., Prod. & Mktg. of Transmission Components to Original Equip. Mfrs. & Authorized Distributors
S.I.C.: 3714
R. Ruzic *(Pres.)*

Borg-Warner-Spring/Brummer Division **(2)**
700 So. 25th Ave.
Bellwood, IL 60104
Tel.: 708-547-2600
Precision Stampings & Assemblies, One-Way Clutches, Friction Clutch Plates, Brake Bands, Water Pump & Oil Seals for Automotive, Aircraft & Indus. Equip.
S.I.C.: 3714; 3728; 3569; 3053
G. Fukiyama *(V.P.-Mfg. Oper.)*
Norman W. Burk *(Matls. Mgr.)*

Plant:

Borg-Warner Automotive, Inc. **(3)**
300 So. Maple Ave.
Frankfort, IL 60423
Tel.: 815-469-2721
Mfr. of Transmission Bands
S.I.C.: 3714
R. Welding *(Plant Mgr.)*

Morse Automotive Products **(2)**
800 Warren Rd.
Ithaca, NY 14850
Tel.: 607-257-6700
Mfr. of Engine Components for Internal Combustion Engines; Timing Chains, Timing Chain Tensioners, Hy-Vo Transmission Chain, Marine Bearings & Rubber Dock Fendering
S.I.C.: 3714; 3069
R. Ruzic *(V.P. & Gen. Mgr.)*

Warner-Ishi Corporation **(2)**
P.O. Box 583, Rt. #6,
Shelbyville, IL 62565
Tel.: 217-428-4631
Mfr. of Turbochargers
S.I.C.: 3714
Golden E. Hullinger *(Pres.)*
John Dennis *(Gen. Mgr.)*
Bruce Renton *(Mgr.-Sls.)*

Protective Services Subsidiaries:

Baker Industries, Inc. **(1)**
1633 Littleton Rd.
Parsippany, NJ 07054
Tel.: 201-267-5300 (100%)
Fax: 201-397-2014
Approx.Sls.: $1,400,000,000
Emp.: 80,000
Headquarters for Protective Services Offered throughout U.S., Canada, Puerto Rico, United Kingdom & Columbia
S.I.C.: 7382; 7381
Charles R. Schneider *(Pres. & Chief Exec. Officer)*
Paul Rathblott *(V.P., Sec. & Gen Counsel)*
Kenneth W. Oringer *(V.P.-Fin.)*
Joseph C. Allen *(Dir.-Pub. Rels.)*

Subsidiaries:

E. J. Burke Security Systems, Inc. **(2)**
520 N. Delaware, Ste. 201
Philadelphia, PA 19123
Tel.: 215-592-9205
Provides Guard Services, Investigative Services, Polygraph & Security Services, Undercover Services
S.I.C.: 7381
Paul Schmitt *(District Mgr.)*

Burns International Security Services, Inc. **(2)**
2 Campus Dr.
Parsippany, NJ 07054
Tel.: 201-397-2000 (100%)
Fax: 201-397-2493
Approx.Sls.: $670,000,000
Emp.: 40,000
Headquarters for Security Guard Service, Investigative & Consulting Services to Indus. & Institutional Clients Throughout the U.S., Canada, the United Kingdom & Columbia
S.I.C.: 7382; 7381
Rodger H. Comstock *(Pres.)*
Edwin Lewis *(V.P.-Law)*
Michael Geisler *(Controller)*
Joseph Arwady *(Dir.-Sls. & Mktg.)*

Globe Security Systems, Inc. **(2)**
520 No. Delaware, Ste. 201
Philadelphia, PA 19123
Tel.: 215-592-9205
Guard, Investigative, Polygraph, Security & Undercover Srvcs.
S.I.C.: 7381

Pony Express Courier Corp. **(2)**
5550 77 Centre Dr., Ste. 320
Charlotte, NC 28217
Tel.: 704-527-7121 (100%)
Fax: 704-521-8917
Approx.Sls.: $125,000,000
Emp.: 4,500
Transportation of Non-Negotiable, Time-Sensitive Financial Materials and Small Packages
S.I.C.: 4513; 4215
B.E. Moree *(Pres.)*
Drew Naber *(Exec. V.P.)*
Jerry Hess *(V.P. & Legal Counsel)*
Pete Bennett *(V.P.-Sls.)*
George Nero *(V.P.-Opers.)*
Edd Morrison *(V.P.-Controller)*
Tom Roth *(V.P.-Human Resources)*

Pyro Chem, Inc. **(2)**
301 Division St., P.O. Box 37
Boonton, NJ 07005
Tel.: 201-335-9750 (100%)
Fax: 201-335-0253
Emp.: 50
Mfr. of Fire Extinguishing Chemicals
S.I.C.: 2899
Neal Y. Lewis *(Gen. Mgr.)*
Edward A. Balogh *(Mgr.-Mktg. & Sls.)*

Wells Fargo Alarm Services **(2)**
780 Fifth Ave.
King of Prussia, PA 19406
Tel.: 215-337-3855 (100%)
Fax: 215-337-7322
Approx.Sls.: $200,000,000
Emp.: 2,500
Mfr. of Automatic Fire and/or Burglar Alarm Systems & Pre-Designed Proprietary Security Systems; Central Station Alarm Monitoring
S.I.C.: 3669; 7382
Philip R. Harper *(Pres.)*
William Urban *(V.P. & Controller)*
William C. Walsh *(V.P.-Sls.)*
Les McCoun *(Dir.-Adv. & Mktg.)*

Wells Fargo Armored Service Corp. **(2)**
6165 Barfield Rd.
Atlanta, GA 30328
Tel.: 404-256-0540 (100%)
Fax: 404-847-3144
Approx.Sls.: $150,000,000
Emp.: 4,000
Armored Transportation Services; ATM Servicing; Cash Services
S.I.C.: 7381
Hugh E. Sawyer *(Exec. V.P. & Chief Oper. Officer)*

Wells Fargo Guard Services **(1)**
2 Campus Dr.
Parsippany, NJ 07054
Tel.: 201-267-5800 (100%)
Fax: 201-267-8730
Approx.Sls.: $250,000,000
Emp.: 20,000
Security Guard Service & Investigative Service to Industrial, Institutional & Residential Clients
S.I.C.: 7381
Joseph Augustine *(Pres.)*

Non-U.S. Holdings:

Borg-Warner Automotive (Canada) Limited **(1)**
385 Second Ave.
Simcoe, ON N3Y 4L5, Canada
Tel.: 519-426-4960 (100%)
Transmission Components; Timing Chains; Bearings; Speed Reducers
S.I.C.: 3566; 3612; 3621; 3714
Roger Archibald *(Plant Mgr.)*

Borg-Warner Automotive Korea, Inc. **(1)**
65-4 Samjung-Ri, Daeso-Myun Eumsung-Kun,
Choongbuk, 369-820, Korea
Tel.: 446-78-8591 (77%)
Fax: 446-78-8600
Friction Plates; One-Way Clutches
S.I.C.: 3714
Mal S. Williams *(G.M.)*

Borg-Warner de Mexico, S.A. **(1)**
Av. las Granjas 473-C, Col. Jardin Azpeitia
Deleg. Atzcapotzalco,
Mexico, D.F. 02530, Mexico
Distr. of Automotive Parts
S.I.C.: 5013
Alejandro Galindo M. *(Mng. Dir.)*

B. W. Componentes Mexicanos De Transmissiones, S.A. de C.V. **(1)**
Calzada Lazardo CArdenas No. 4135-201
Fraccionamiento Camino Real,
Guadalajara, Jalisco 45040, Mexico
Mfg. of Timing Chains & Tensioners; Aluminum Sprockets
Gerardo Meiners *(Gen. Dir.)*

NSK-Warner K.K. **(1)**
2345 Aino
Fukuroi, Shizuoka 437, Japan
Tel.: 81-538-43-1121 (50%)
Fax: 81-538-43-1595
One-Way, Overrunning Roller & Spray Clutches; Indus. One-Way Clutch Assemblies; Steel & Friction Clutch Plates; Brake Bands; Seat Belt Assemblies
S.I.C.: 2399; 3714
Reijirou Hosokawa *(Pres.)*

Steiber Div. der Borg-Warner GmbH **(1)**
Kurpfalzring Postfach 101360, D-6900
Heidelberg, 1, Germany
Tel.: 06221-708-1
Precision Stampings & Assemblies; One-Way Clutches; Steel & Friction Plates & Brake Bands for Automotive & Aircraft Equip.
S.I.C.: 3714; 3724
Siegfried P. Adler *(Chm.)*
Guenter Lanzerath *(Exec. V.P.-Europe)*

Transmission Div. Borg-Warner Automotive GmbH **(1)**
Kenfig Industrial Estate, Margam
Port Talbot, West Glamorgan SA13 2PG,
United Kingdom
Tel.: 0656 741001 (100%)
Telex: 851-498613
Automatic Transmissions for Cars & Light Trucks; Precision Stampings; Torque Converters; Clutches
S.I.C.: 3714
Diederik Berghauser-Pont *(Dir.-Opers.)*

HUGO BOSCA CO., INC.
1905 W. Jefferson
Springfield, OH 45501
Mailing Address:
P.O. Box 777
Springfield, OH 45501
Tel.: 513-323-5523
Fax: 513-323-7063
Year Founded: 1910
Approx.Sls.: $15,000,000
Emp.: 140
Fiscal Year-end: 12/31/90
Mfr. Leather Billfolds, Leather Accessories
S.I.C.: 3172; 3199
C.B. Bosca *(Pres.)*
D.H. Bosca *(V.P.)*
Robert Breen *(Asst. Sls. Mgr.)*
Principal(s):
M.E. Bosca

Computer Systems/Hardware:
Modcomp Classic 7840

Outside Service Firm(s):

Sander, Shifman & Brannick*(Auditors)*
Springfield, OH

Bank One*(Major Banking Relationship)*
Kettering Tower
Dayton, OH 45401
Tel.: 513-449-8600

BOSCOV'S DEPARTMENT STORES, INC.
4500 Perkiomen Ave.
Reading, PA 19606
Tel.: 215-779-2000
Fax: 215-370-3495
Approx.Sls.: $500,000,000
Emp.: 4,500
Fiscal Year-end: 1/31/92
Department Store
S.I.C.: 5311
Albert Boscov *(Chm. Bd.)*
Edwin A. Lakin *(Pres.)*
Erwin Rosner *(Treas. & Sec.)*
Frank Krandel *(Dir.-Adv.)*

Outside Service Firm(s):

Coopers & Lybrand*(Auditors)*
2400 Eleven Penn Center
Philadelphia, PA 19103-2962
Tel.: 215-963-8000

American Bank*(Major Banking Relationship)*
Reading, PA

BOSE CORPORATION
The Mountain
Framingham, MA 01701-9168
Tel.: 508-879-7330 **MA**
Fax: 508-872-6541
Year Founded: 1964
Approx.Sls.: $424,642,000
Emp.: 2,900
Fiscal Year-end: 3/28/92

Import Export
Loudspeakers & Electronics
S.I.C.: 3651
Dr. Amar G. Bose *(Chm. Bd. & Chief Exec. Officer)*
Sherwin Greenblatt *(Pres. & Chief Oper. Officer)*
Daniel A. Grady *(Chief Fin. Officer)*
Thomas Beeson *(V.P.-Mfg.)*
John J. Geheran *(V.P.-Sls.)*
Joseph Vevanth *(V.P.-Engrng.)*
Mark Sullivan *(Gen. Counsel)*
William Swanson *(Treas.)*
Herbert W. Batchelder *(Controller)*
Lance Dixon *(Dir.-Pur.)*
Thomas Froeschle *(Dir.-Res. & Devel.)*
Warren Harkness *(Dir.-Information Systems)*
Joan Vasilopoulos *(Dir.-Human Resources)*
Nic Merks *(Gen. Mgr.-Component Audio Div.)*

No. of Mfg. Plants/Facilities: 6

Computer Systems/Hardware:
Hewlett-Packard; Prime; DEC; Data General

Outside Service Firm(s):

Price Waterhouse*(Auditors)*
160 Federal St.
Boston, MA 02110
Tel.: 617-439-3308
Fax: 617-439-3308

Hale and Dorr*(Legal Firm)*
60 State St.
Boston, MA 02109-6098
Tel.: 617-526-6000

Subsidiary:

Stereo Advertising Corp. **(1)**
The Mountain
Framingham, MA 01701
Tel.: 617-235-6640 (100%)
Emp.: 4
Sales Promotions
S.I.C.: 8742

Non-U.S. Holdings:

Bose AG **(1)**
Runenbergerstrasse 13 CH-4460
Gelterkinden, Switzerland
Tel.: 061-995544
Sales of Loudspeakers & Accessories
S.I.C.: 5064
Weiner Saegesser *(Mng. Dir.)*

Bose A/S **(1)**
Industriazej 7 2605
Brondby, Denmark
Tel.: 011-45-43-7777

Bose Australia **(1)**
11 Muriel Ave.
Rydalmere, N.S.W. 2116, Australia
Bob Schenk *(Gen. Mgr.)*

Bose B.V. **(1)**
Nijuerheidstratt 1135 GE
Edam, Netherlands
Paul Olean *(Gen. Mgr.)*

Bose Canada, Inc. **(1)**
Parc Industrial
Sainte Marie-Beauce, PQ G6E 3C2, Canada
Tel.: 418-387-7546
Mfr. Wood Cabinets
S.I.C.: 2517
Ed Lemieux *(Gen. Mgr.)*

Bose GmbH **(1)**
Postfach 1125 6382
Friedrichsdorf, Germany
Toni Schalkamp *(Mng. Dir.)*

Bose K.K. **(1)**
Harajuka-R, Bldg. 2F 6-7-10 Jingumae, Shibuya-K,
Tokyo, 150, Japan
Sumioshi Sakura *(Gen. Mgr.)*

Bose Ltd. **(1)**
8-35 E. Beaver Creek Rd.
Richmond Hill, ON L4K 1K6, Canada
Tel.: 416-886-9123
S.I.C.: 5064

Bose N.V. **(1)**
Essenestraat 15 B-1740
Ternat, Brabant Belgium
Tel.: 427-99-53
Jan van Alten *(Mng. Dir.)*

Bose Products B.V. Sucuvsal en Espana **(1)**
Avda. de Avagon 334 Poligono Las Mercedes, 28022
Madrid, Spain

Branch:

Bose Ireland **(2)**
Castleblaney Rd.
Carrickmacross, County Monaghan Ireland
Tel.: 042-61988
Telex: 33890
Loudspeakers & Electronics
S.I.C.: 3651
John Coleman *(Plant Mgr.)*

Bose S.A. de C.V. **(1)**
Plan de Alberque San Luis, Juarez No. 728
San Luis Potosi, Rio Colorado, Sonora, Mexico
Gerry Donovan *(Plant Mgr.)*

Bose S.A.R.L. **(1)**
6 Rue St. Vincent 78100
Saint-Germain-en-Laye, France
Andy Smaga *(Mng. Dir.)*

Bose S.P.A. **(1)**
Via Luigi Capucci, 1Z 00147
Rome, Italy
L. Franco Calo *(Mng. Dir.)*

Bose U.K., Ltd. **(1)**
Trinity Trading Estate
Sittingbourne, Kent ME10 2PD, United Kingdom
Tel.: 0795-75341
Telex: 965559
High Fidelity Equipment Importers
S.I.C.: 5064
Colin Cartwright *(Mng. Dir.)*

BOSTON CHICKEN, INC.
1804 Center Point Dr.
Naperville, IL 60563
Tel.: 708-955-6100 **MA**
Fax: 708-955-6132
Year Founded: 1986
Restaurant Franchise
S.I.C.: 5812
Scott Beck *(Chm. & Chief Exec. Officer)*
Saad J. Jadhir *(Vice Chm.)*
Jeff Shearer *(Pres. & Chief Oper. Officer)*
John Morlock *(Sr. V.P.-Opers.)*
David G. Stanchak *(Sr. V.P.-Real Estate)*
Donald J. Bingle *(V.P., Gen. Counsel & Clerk)*
Jeff Butler *(V.P.-Human Resources)*
F. Warren Ellish *(V.P.-Mktg.)*
Stuart Fullinwider *(V.P.-Fin. & Systems)*
Mark X. Hayden *(V.P.-Construction)*
Gerard Lewis *(V.P.-Res. & Prod. Devel.)*
Alan Palmeri *(V.P.-Franchise)*
Joren Peterson *(V.P.-Corp. Real Estate)*

BOSTON DISTRIBUTORS, INC.
5700 S. Lee Rd. at Rockside Rd.
Maple Heights, OH 44137
Tel.: 216-663-8252 **OH**
Fax: 216-663-1695
Year Founded: 1984
Assets: $37,728,954
Liabilities: $37,993,938
Net Worth: $264,984
Approx.Sls.: $204,000,000
Emp.: 800
Fiscal Year-end: 12/30/90
Merchandising & Distribution Services to Discount, Drug & Food Industries
S.I.C.: 4225
M. Raymond Prendergast *(Chm. Bd. & Chief Exec. Officer)*
Charles C. Bowlus *(Pres.)*
James G. Few *(Sr. V.P.-Fin. & Admin.)*
Gregory Low *(V.P.-Information Systems)*
Raymond Sizemore *(V.P.-Warehouse Opers.)*
Gregory D. Seeley *(Sec.)*
Martin Seekely *(Controller)*
Theresa Savelli *(Mgr.-Human Resources)*

Principal(s):
M. Raymond Prendergast
Charles C. Bowlus

No. of Mfg. Plants/Facilities: 1
No. of U.S. Offices: 1

Computer Systems/Hardware:
Wang VS-7310, IBM AS/400

Outside Service Firm(s):

Arthur Andersen & Co.*(Auditors)*
1717 E. 9th St.
Cleveland, OH 44114
Tel.: 216-781-2140
Fax: 216-781-3683

Nationwide Business Insurance*(Group Insurer)*
Cleveland, OH

Seeley, Savage, Aussem*(Legal Firm)*
Cleveland, OH

The Bank of New York*(Major Banking Relationship)*
One Wall Street
New York, NY 10286
Tel.: 212-635-6805
Fax: 212-635-3201

Subsidiary:

H.B.A. King Inc. **(1)**
Headquarters, 5700 Lee Rd.
Maple Heights, OH 44137
Tel.: 216-663-8252
Emp.: 25
5 Discount Stores Located in Detroit, Michigan; Candy, Chemicals, Stationery & School Supplies, Health And Beauty Aids
S.I.C.: 5311
Gary Reneau *(Gen. Mgr.)*
Scott Sweress *(Acct. Mgr.)*

BOSTON MUTUAL LIFE INSURANCE CO.
120 Royall St.
Canton, MA 02021
Tel.: 617-828-7000 **MA**
Fax: 617-821-4976
Year Founded: 1891
Assets: $218,990,909
Liabilities: $188,969,435
Net Worth: $30,021,474
Sales Range: $100-499 Million
Emp.: 670
Mass Marketer of Life Insurance
S.I.C.: 6311
Lawrence J. Finnegan *(Chm., Pres., Chief Exec. & Chief Oper. Officer)*
William M. Bresnahan *(V.P.-Grp. Insurance)*
Roy G. Daniels *(V.P. & Dir.-Dist. Agencies)*
David F. Devine *(V.P. & Sec.)*
Daniel B. Goggin *(V.P. & Controller)*
Everett B. Horn, Jr. *(V.P. & Gen. Counsel)*
Howard V. Neff, Jr. *(V.P.-Real Estate)*
Robert P. Ryan *(V.P. & Actuary)*
Edward J. Thompson *(V.P.-Gen. Agency)*
David A. Cullen *(2nd V.P.-Customer Service)*
Vincent J. Lioce *(2nd V.P.-Data Processing)*
James F. Sarcia *(Treas.)*
Joseph E. Lampert *(Dir.-Pur. & Mgr. Gen. Services)*
James I. Peters *(Medical Dir.)*

Principal(s):
Lawrence J. Finnegan

Computer Systems/Hardware:
IBM Systems 43 & 41

Outside Service Firm(s):

Ernst & Young*(Auditors)*
200 Clarendon St., 46th Fl.
Boston, MA 02116
Tel.: 617-266-2000

State Street Bank & Trust Co.*(Major Banking Relationship)*
P.O. Box 366,
Boston, MA 02101
Tel.: 617-426-5523

BOSTON SCIENTIFIC CORP.
480 Pleasant St.
Watertown, MA 02172
Tel.: 617-923-1720 **DE**
Fax: 617-923-0728
Year Founded: 1979
Approx.Sls.: $220,000,000
Emp.: 1,500
Fiscal Year-end: 12/31/91

Import Export
Holding Company; Medical Devices
S.I.C.: 3841; 6719
Peter M. Nicholas *(Pres.)*
Robert G. Anderson *(V.P., Sec. & Gen. Counsel)*
John Chiricotti *(V.P.-Fin.)*
Mike Mabrey *(V.P.-Opers.)*

Boston Scientific Corp.—(Continued)

Outside Service Firm(s):

Ernst & Young*(Auditors)*
200 Clarendon St., 46th Fl.
Boston, MA 02116
Tel.: 617-266-2000

Bingham, Dana & Gould*(Legal Firm)*
150 Federal St.
Boston, MA 02110
Tel.: 617-951-8000
Fax: 617-951-8736

First National Bank of Boston*(Major Banking Relationship)*
150 Royall St.
Canton, MA 02021
Tel.: 617-575-2900
Tel.: 800-442-2001

BOSTON TRADING LTD. INC.
315 Washington St.
Lynn, MA 01902
Tel.: 617-592-4603 **MA**
Fax: 617-595-9937
Year Founded: 1977
Assets: $13,000,000
Liabilities: $9,500,000
Net Worth: $3,500,000
Approx.Sls.: $35,000,000
Emp.: 125
Fiscal Year-end: 10/31/90
Import Export
Wholesale Distribution of Casual Apparel
S.I.C.: 6794; 5137; 5136
Arnold W. Kline *(Chm. Bd., Pres. & Chief Oper. Officer)*
Joseph E. Lynch *(Exec. V.P., Chief Exec. & Fin. Officer)*
Jack Stahl *(Treas.)*
Jim Rudolph *(Sec.)*
Gary Cohen *(Dir.-Sls.)*
Karen Fuller *(Mgr.-Leasing)*
Susan Stahl *(Mgr.-Adv.)*
Principal(s):
Arnold W. Kline
Jack Stahl

No. of Mfg. Plants/Facilities: 1
No. of U.S. Offices: 1
No. of Foreign Offices: 2

Computer Systems/Hardware:
IBM Systems 36 & 38

Outside Service Firm(s):

The Hong Kong & Shanghai Bank*(International Bank Affiliate)*
1, Des Voeux Rd.
Central, Hong Kong
Tel.: 822-1111

Chartered Bank H. K.*(International Bank Affiliate)*
Hong Kong, Hong Kong

Rudolph, Gargill & Sassoan*(Legal Firm)*
Boston, MA

Bank of New England*(Major Banking Relationship)*
28 State Street
Boston, MA 02109
Tel.: 617-742-4000

Division:

Boston Traders Div. **(1)**
315 Washington St.
Lynn, MA 01902
Tel.: 617-592-4603
Approx.Sls.: $30,000,000
Emp.: 120
Wholesale of Sweaters, Shirts, Pants, Shorts, Jackets, Rainwear & Ski Wear
S.I.C.: 5136; 5137
Joe Lynch *(V.P. & Chief Fin. Officer)*
Jack Stahl *(V.P.-Pur.)*

BOSTROM SEATING, INC.
Vigo Rd., P.O. Box 566
Piedmont, AL 36272
Tel.: 205-447-9051 **DE**
Fax: 205-447-2038
Year Founded: 1935
Assets: $20,000,000
Net Worth: $20,000,000
Approx.Sls.: $50,000,000
Emp.: 300
Fiscal Year-end: 9/30/92
Manufacture Truck Suspension Seats
S.I.C.: 2531
Harrison R. Horan *(Pres.)*
Charles E. Hird *(V.P.-Sls. & Mktg.)*
Daniel O'Connor *(V.P.-Fin.)*
Gene Albert *(Mgr.-Sls. Admin.)*

No. of Mfg. Plants/Facilities: 4
No. of U.S. Offices: 5

Computer Systems/Hardware:
IBM

Outside Service Firm(s):

Price Waterhouse*(Auditors)*
1500 Bank One Plaza, 100 E. Wisconsin Ave.
Milwaukee, WI 53202

Johnson & Higgins*(Commercial Insurance Carrier)*
500 W. Madison
Chicago, IL 60606
Tel.: 312-648-4200

DnC America Banking Corp.*(International Bank Affiliate)*
600 Fifth Ave
New York, NY 10020
Tel.: 212-315-6500
Telex: 23 66 56
Fax: 212-307-1589

Johnson & Higgins*(Group Insurer)*
500 W. Madison
Chicago, IL 60606
Tel.: 312-648-4200

Godfrey & Kahn*(Legal Firm)*
780 N. Water St.
Milwaukee, WI 53202
Tel.: 414-273-3500
Fax: 414-273-5198

Bank One Milwaukee, N.A.*(Major Banking Relationship)*
111 E. Wisconsin Ave.
Milwaukee, WI
Tel.: 414-765-3000

Bank One Milwaukee, N.A.*(Pension Manager)*
111 E. Wisconsin Ave.
Milwaukee, WI
Tel.: 414-765-3000

Subsidiary:

Bostrom Distribution Center **(1)**
2201 Hangar Pl.
Allentown, PA 18103
Tel.: 215-264-0102
S.I.C.: 5013

JOHN BOUCHARD & SONS COMPANY
1024 Harrison St.
Nashville, TN 37203
Tel.: 615-256-0112
Fax: 615-256-2427
Year Founded: 1913
Approx.Sls.: $11,000,000
Emp.: 150
Mechanical Contractor; Cast Iron Pipe & Fittings, Gray Iron Castings, Metal Manhole Covers, Machine Shop, Industrial Fittings, Valves & Fittings, Mill Supplies
S.I.C.: 1711; 3321; 3599; 5085
John E. Bouchard, III *(Chm. Bd. & Pres.)*
William T. Hall *(Treas.)*
William D. Margan *(Sec.)*
John Boyd *(Pur. Agent)*

Outside Service Firm(s):

Coomer Wells & Co.*(Auditors)*
Nashville, TN

Third National Bank*(Major Banking Relationship)*
201 4th Ave. No., Uptown Sta., Box 2844
Nashville, TN 37167
Tel.: 615-748-4742

Subsidiary:

Bouchard Fire Protection **(1)**
1024 Harrison St.
Nashville, TN 37203
Tel.: 615-256-0112 (100%)

BOURNS, INC.
1200 Columbia Ave.
Riverside, CA 92507-2114
Tel.: 909-781-5690 **CA**
Fax: 909-781-5273
Year Founded: 1947
Approx.Sls.: $325,000,000
Emp.: 4,000
Fiscal Year-end: 12/31/91
Mfr. of Electronic Components
S.I.C.: 3676
Gordon L. Bourns *(Chm. Bd.)*
Jim Booth *(V.P.-Pur.)*
Neal C. Weaver *(V.P. & Treas.)*
William P. McKenna *(V.P.-Fin.)*
Robert L. Reneau *(V.P.-Intl. Trade & MIS)*
Mary Chatham *(Communications Specialist)*
Principal(s):
Gordon L. Bourns

No. of Mfg. Plants/Facilities: 15
No. of U.S. Offices: 10

Computer Systems/Hardware:
Hewlett-Packard

Outside Service Firm(s):

KPMG Peat Marwick*(Auditors)*
Newport Beach, CA

National Farmers Union*(Group Insurer)*
Denver, CO

Kindel & Anderson*(Legal Firm)*
555 S. Flower, Ste. 2600
Los Angeles, CA 90071
Tel.: 213-680-2222

Chase Manhattan Bank, N.A.*(Major Banking Relationship)*
One Chase Manhattan Plaza
New York, NY 10081
Tel.: 212-552-2222
Tel.: 800-526-0801
Fax: 212-552-7175

Wells Fargo Bank*(Major Banking Relationship)*
420 Montgomery St.
San Francisco, CA 94104

Siebel Capital Management Co.*(Pension Manager)*
Larkspur, CA

Wells Fargo Bank*(Pension Manager)*
420 Montgomery St.
San Francisco, CA 94104

Subsidiary:

Bourns Instruments Inc. **(1)**
1200 Columbia Ave.
Riverside, CA 92507
Tel.: 909-781-5148
Fax: 909-781-5178
Mfrs. Pressure Transducers
S.I.C.: 3823
Robert L. Bell *(Pres.)*

Non-U.S. Holdings:

Bourns AG & Bourns (Schweiz) AG **(1)**
Zugerstrasse 74 CH-6340
Baar, Switzerland
Tel.: 042-33.33.33 (100%)
Sales/European Distributor
S.I.C.: 5065
Manfred Roehrig *(Pres. & Gen. Mgr.-European Sls. Opers.)*

Bourns Benelux B.V. **(1)**
Van Tuyl Van Serooskerkestraat 81-85
Postbus 37, 2270 AA
Voorburg, Netherlands
Tel.: 070 387-4400 (100%)
Sales of Electronic Parts
S.I.C.: 5065
Dietmar Schauer *(V.P.-European Sls. Opers.)*
Cor Blankendaal *(Area Sls. Mgr.-Benelux & France)*

Bourns Electronics, Ltd. **(1)**
90 Park St.
Camberley, Surrey GU15 3NY, United Kingdom
Tel.: 01-276-692392 (100%)
Sales of Electronic Parts
S.I.C.: 5065
Dietmar Schauer *(V.P.-Sls.)*
Phillip Bullus *(Area Sls. Mgr.)*

Bourns Electronics, Ltd. **(1)**
Hillend Industrial Estate
Dunfermline, KY11 5JO, United Kingdom
Tel.: 383-823221 (100%)
Sales of Electronic Parts
S.I.C.: 5065

Bourns, GmbH **(1)**
Breite Strasse 2 7000
Stuttgart, 10, Germany
Tel.: 711-22930 (100%)
Sales of Electronic Parts
S.I.C.: 5065
Dietmar Schauer *(V.P.-Sls.)*
Peter Leuther *(Area Sls. Mgr.)*

Bourns-Ohmic S.A. **(1)**
21/23 Rue des Ardennes F-75019
Paris, France
Tel.: 1-40033604 (100%)
Sales of Electronics
S.I.C.: 5065
Dietmar Schauer *(V.P.-Sls.)*
Cor Blankendaal *(Area Sls. Mgr.)*

BOURY INCORPORATED
1311 Main St.
Wheeling, WV 26003
Tel.: 304-233-5000
Fax: 304-233-5000, Ext. 555
Year Founded: 1912
Sales Range: $20-39 Million
Emp.: 4,800
Holding Co.; Restaurants; Wholesale Prepared Foods
S.I.C.: 6719; 5812; 5149
George Boury *(Chm. Bd. & Pres.)*
Michael Boury *(Vice Chm.)*
Michael Carney *(V.P. & Chief Oper. Officer)*
William Maxwell *(Dir.-Mktg.)*
Edwin Ehni *(Controller)*
Lorette Zanders *(Sec.)*
Principal(s):
George Boury
Michael Boury

Outside Service Firm(s):

Coopers & Lybrand*(Auditors)*
Wheeling, WV

BOVAIRD SUPPLY CO.
823 S. Detroit
Tulsa, OK 74102
Mailing Address:
P.O. Box 2590
Tulsa, OK 74102
Tel.: 918-587-7271
Tel.: 800-999-2724
Telex: 49 7534
Fax: 918-587-3086
Year Founded: 1871
Approx.Sls.: $250,000,000
Emp.: 280
Export
Sale & Distribution of Oil Field Equipment
S.I.C.: 5084
W.J. Bovaird *(Pres. & Chief Exec. Officer)*
J.R. Bovaird *(Exec. V.P.)*
Jeff A. Smyth *(V.P. & Chief Fin. Officer)*

W.G. Toelkes *(V.P.-Opers.)*
Rebbeca C. Tucker *(Corp. Sec.)*
Russel E. McNew *(Controller)*
B.H. Bovaird *(Mgr.-Sls. & Quality Assurance)*
Charles Gibson, Jr. *(Mgr.-Admin. Services)*
Mike Hedrick *(Mgr.-Credit Dept.)*
Hugh Moore *(Mgr.-Info. Systems Operations)*
Roger Price *(Mgr.-Data Processing)*

Principal(s):
W.J. Bovaird

No. of Mfg. Plants/Facilities: 44
No. of U.S. Offices: 6

Computer Systems/Hardware:
Hewlett-Packard Series 68, 44 & 3

Outside Service Firm(s):

Coopers & Lybrand*(Auditors)*
1400 Mid-Continent Tower
Tulsa, OK 74103
Tel.: 918-596-8200
Fax: 918-596-8300

Metropolitan Life Insurance Co.*(Group Insurer)*
One Madison Ave.
New York, NY 10010-3690
Tel.: 215-578-9292

Boesche, McDermott & Eskridge*(Legal Firm)*
800 Oneok Plaza
Tulsa, OK 74103

First National Bank of Tulsa*(Major Banking Relationship)*
P.O. Box One
Tulsa, OK 74193

NationsBank Texas*(Major Banking Relationship)*
P.O. Box 831000
Dallas, TX 75283-1000
Tel.: 214-508-0972

Fayez Sarofim & Co.*(Pension Manager)*
Two Houston Center, Suite 2907
Houston, TX 77010
Tel.: 713-654-4484
Fax: 713-654-8184

Subsidiary:

Piping Resources (1)
8011 Blankenship
Houston, TX 77055
Tel.: 713-681-5115
Distr. of Valve Actuators
S.I.C.: 5085
Pat Murphy *(V.P.)*
Bill Murphy *(Mgr.-Sls.)*

BOVAY
(Formerly Bovay/McGinty, Inc.)
1300 Post Oak Blvd. #300
Houston, TX 77056
Tel.: 713-439-0800 **TX**
Fax: 713-964-2860
Year Founded: 1946
Approx.Sls.: $10,000,000
Emp.: 160
Engineering & Architectural Services Including Aviation Facilities, Industrial, Commercial & Institutional Buildings; Advanced Manufacturing Facilities, Public Works & Transportation; Mechanical, Electrical & Energy Systems
S.I.C.: 8711; 8712
Vic Maloos *(Pres. & Chief Exec. Officer)*
M.J. Stegner *(Sr. V.P.)*
F.E. Flesch *(V.P.)*
R.J. Maguire *(V.P.)*
Milton McGinty *(V.P.)*
Dave G. Nicholas *(V.P.)*
C.R. Thomas *(V.P.)*

No. of U.S. Offices: 4

BOWEN BROTHERS FRUIT CO., INC.
(Formerly Bowen Brothers, Inc.)
305 Ave. E, SW
Winter Haven, FL 33880
Tel.: 813-299-1183
Fax: 813-293-1889
Approx.Sls.: $92,000,000
Emp.: 15
Fiscal Year-end: 8/31/92
Wholesale & Produce Citrus Fruit
S.I.C.: 0174; 5148
Jim Shuford *(Pres.)*
Arlene Shuford *(Sec. & Treas.)*

Outside Service Firm(s):

Carter, Belcourd & Atkinson*(Auditors)*
8th Flr., 500 Florida Ave.
Lakeland, FL 33801
Tel.: 813-687-4010

Allan Casey*(Legal Firm)*
P.O. Box 7146, 395 Ave. C. N.W.
Winter Haven, FL 33883-7146
Tel.: 813-294-4468

Southeast Bank, N.A.*(Major Banking Relationship)*
Tampa, FL

BOYD, TAMNEY & CROSS ADVERTISING/MARKETING
440 E. Swedesford Rd., St. 3040
Wayne, PA 19087
Tel.: 215-293-0500
Fax: 215-687-8199
Year Founded: 1980
Approx.Billings: $15,000,000
Emp.: 24
Automotive, Hospitality & Healthcare Adv.
Melvin C. Boyd *(Pres.)*
Joseph P. Tamney *(Exec. V.P.)*
Raymond C. Cross *(V.P.)*
Karl H. Klingelhoeffer *(V.P.-Hospitality)*
Louis D. Methfessel *(Dir.-Mktg.)*
Nancy Sakaduski *(Dir.-Healthcare Mktg.)*
Betsy Dru Tecco *(Dir.-Pub. Rels.)*
Patricia C. Mash *(Office Mgr.)*

BOYER BROS. INC.
(Sub. of Consolidated Brands Inc.)
821 17th St.
Altoona, PA 16602
Mailing Address:
P.O. Box 1232
Altoona, PA 16603
Tel.: 814-944-9401
Fax: 814-944-4923
Year Founded: 1936
Approx.Sls.: $20,000,000
Emp.: 250
Fiscal Year-end: 12/31/90
Export
Confectionery Mfg. Mallo Cup, Smoothie, Peanut Butter Cup
S.I.C.: 2064
Anthony Forgione *(Chm. Bd. & Pres.)*
H. E. Wood *(V.P. & Gen. Mgr.)*
Richard Peo *(Chief Fin. Officer & Controller)*
Dennis Forgione *(Corp. Sec.)*
Deborah Forgione *(Dir.-Mktg.)*
Loretta Brown *(Sls. & Mktg.)*
David A. Koelle *(Dir.-Pur.)*
Heather Young *(Personnel Mgr.)*
Connie Altimus *(Data Processing)*
Jennie Brubaker *(Quality Control)*

BOYLE ENGINEERING CORP.
1501 Quail St.
Newport Beach, CA 92660
Mailing Address:
P.O. Box 7350
Newport Beach, CA 92658
Tel.: 714-476-3400 **CA**
Fax: 714-721-7141
Year Founded: 1945
Approx.Sls.: $54,000,000
Emp.: 650
Engineering & Architectural Services
S.I.C.: 8711; 8712
Thomas S. Maddock *(Chm. Bd.)*
Henry W. Haeseker *(Pres. & Chief Exec. Officer)*
James A. Barton *(V.P.-Fin. & Admin.)*
Kimberly Stauffer *(V.P. & Sec.)*
Dennis Boyd *(Reg. V.P.)*
David L. Hardan *(Reg. V.P.)*
John J. Kincaid *(Reg. V.P.)*
Kermit Prime *(Reg. V.P.)*
Robert S. Poteraj *(Controller)*
Principal(s):
Employee-Owned

No. of U.S. Offices: 22
No. of Foreign Offices: 1

Outside Service Firm(s):

Ernst & Young*(Auditors)*
Newport Beach, CA

BOZOF DINETTES, INC.
6235 S. Cockrum St.
Olive Branch, MS 38654
Tel.: 601-895-7224 **TN**
Fax: 601-895-7225
Approx.Sls.: $10,000,000
Emp.: 180
Metal Dinette Sets
S.I.C.: 2514
Albert Bozof *(Pres.)*
Danny Bozof *(V.P.-Sls.)*
Dorothy Bozof *(V.P.)*
Michael Bozof *(V.P.)*
Steve Bozof *(Sec.)*

Outside Service Firm(s):

Union Planters National Bank*(Major Banking Relationship)*
P.O. Box 387,
Memphis, TN 38147
Tel.: 901-523-6865
Fax: 901-523-6490

E.J. BRACH CORPORATION
(Formerly E.J. Brach, Inc.)
One Tower Lane
Oakbrook Terrace, IL 60181
Tel.: 708-572-1600
Tel.: 800-343-2100
Fax: 708-572-0172
Year Founded: 1907
Approx.Sls.: $560,000,000
Emp.: 3500
Fiscal Year-end: 8/31/91
Export
Manufacturer of Candy
S.I.C.: 2064; 2066; 5145
K.J. Jacobs *(Chm. Bd.)*
Richard Condie *(Pres. & Chief Exec. Officer)*
Larry Dicke *(Chief Fin. Officer)*
Robert P. Magrann *(Exec. V.P.)*
Mike Coltart *(Sr. V.P.-Mfg.)*
Henry Wells *(Sr. V.P.-Human Resources)*
A. Brown *(V.P.-Sls.)*
John Flanyak *(V.P.-Quality Assurance & Process Improvement)*
J. Calcagno *(Treas.)*
J. Norton *(Gen. Counsel)*
T. Kaminski *(Mgr.-Pub. Rels.)*
Principal(s):
K.J. Jacobs

Computer Systems/Hardware:
IBM

Divisions:

E.J. Brach, Inc. (1)
811 S. Hamilton
Sullivan, IL 61951
Tel.: 217-728-7302
Fax: 217-728-8811
Mfr. of Candy
S.I.C.: 2064; 2066
Ken Uhlarik *(Plant Mgr.)*

E.J. Brach, Inc. (1)
4371 Boies Ave.
Davenport, IA 52808
Tel.: 319-324-9154
Fax: 319-322-5121
Manufacturer of Candy
S.I.C.: 2064; 2066
Rich Harper *(Plant Mgr.)*

E.J. Brach, Inc. (1)
1260 Southern Rd.
Morrow, GA 30260
Tel.: 404-961-5201
Distr. Center & Warehouse For Candy
S.I.C.: 5145
Joel Schultz *(Distr. Ctr. Mgr.)*

E.J. Brach, Inc. (1)
4656 W. Kinzie St.
Chicago, IL 60644
Tel.: 312-626-1200
Warehouse & National Distr. Ctr.
S.I.C.: 5154
George Reardon *(V.P.-Warehouse/Distr.)*

Subsidiary:

Andes Candies, Inc. (1)
1400 E. Wisconsin St.
Delavan, WI 53115
Tel.: 414-728-9121
Tel.: 800-538-8682
Telex: 910 278 2472
Fax: 414-728-6794
Approx.Sls.: $50,000,000
Emp.: 270
Fiscal Year-end: 8/31/92
Export
Computer Systems/Hardware:
IBM AS/400
Manufacturer of Candy
S.I.C.: 2066; 2064
Donna Elton *(Pres. & Chief Exec. Officer)*
Pietro Fenu *(Chief Oper. Officer & Chief Fin. Officer)*
Mike Smith *(V.P.-Sls.)*
Bob Oilschlager *(Controller)*
Don Vitullo *(Plant Mgr.)*
Jon Brew *(Dir.-Mktg.)*
Dr. Frank Finch *(Dir.-Res. & Devel.)*
Pete Mealus *(Dir.-Opers.)*
Tom Rupkey *(Dir.-Information Systems)*
Marilyn Hahn *(Mgr.-Personnel)*
Art Kanelos *(Pur. Agent)*
Marge Klade *(Quality Assurance Supvr.)*
Martin Rackow *(Maintenance Engr.)*
Julie Rupkey *(Sls./Mktg. Analyst)*

BRAD FOOTE GEAR WORKS, INC.
1309 S. Cicero Ave.
Cicero, IL 60650
Tel.: 312-242-1070
Tel.: 708-652-7700
Fax: 708-652-4140
Year Founded: 1924
Emp.: 190
Manufacture Gears & Speed Reducers
S.I.C.: 3566
Stewart R. Ward *(Pres. & Gen. Mgr.)*
Paul E. Seipel *(V.P.-Sls. & Mktg.)*
Michael J. Iglar *(Treas.)*
Victor Z. Rychlinski *(Dir.-Engrng.)*

Computer Systems/Hardware:
IBM System 36

Outside Service Firm(s):

Metropolitan Life Insurance Co.*(Group Insurer)*
Chicago, IL

Subsidiary:

Pittsburgh Gear Company (1)
Neville Island
Pittsburgh, PA 15255
Tel.: 412-771-4600
S.I.C.: 3566

BRADBURY COMPANY, INC.
Air Industrial Pk.
Moundridge, KS 67107
Mailing Address:
P.O. Box 667
Moundridge, KS 67107
Tel.: 316-345-6394 **KS**

Bradbury Company, Inc.—(Continued)

Fax: 316-345-6381
Year Founded: 1959
Approx.Sls.: $20,000,000
Emp.: 188

Export
Reforming Equipment & Tooling; Cut-to-length Euipment & Tooling; Slitting Equipment & Tooling; Flexible Cabinet Manufacturing Systems
S.I.C.: 3547; 3353
David Bradbury *(Chm. Bd. & Pres.)*
Donald L. Koehn *(Exec. V.P., Treas. & Sec.)*
Karl E. Voth *(V.P.)*
Phil E. Bradbury *(Mgr.-Mktg.)*
Al Strecker *(Mgr.-Sls.)*

Outside Service Firm(s):

Grant Thornton*(Auditors)*
800 Fourth Financial Center
Wichita, KS 67202

Union National Bank*(Major Banking Relationship)*
Wichita, KS

BRADFORD COMPANY
13500 Quincy St.
Holland, MI 49424
Tel.: 616-399-3000 **MI**
Fax: 616-399-3939
Year Founded: 1924
Approx.Sls.: $10,000,000
Emp.: 95

Import Export
Mfr. of Solid Fibre, Slotted & Assembled Partitions & Pads For Boxes, Plastic Partitions & Totes For Reusable Material Handling Applications; Electro Static Discharge Package Products
S.I.C.: 2679; 2653; 3086; 3089
Judson T. Bradford *(Chm. Bd. & Pres.)*
Donald D. Vander Zwaag *(Sr. V.P. & Treas.)*
Robert W. Kimber *(V.P.)*
David W. Mauger *(V.P.-Mfg. & Engrng.)*
John R. Nichols *(Sec.)*

Outside Service Firm(s):

Ferris, Busscher & Zwiers*(Auditors)*
Holland, MI

Law, Weathers & Richardson*(Legal Firm)*
Grand Rapids, MI

Old Kent Bank*(Major Banking Relationship)*
Holland, MI

BRADFORD EXCHANGE LTD.
9333 Milwaukee Ave. N.
Niles, IL 60714
Tel.: 708-966-2770
Fax: 708-966-3121
Approx.Sls.: $180,000,000
Emp.: 600
Direct Mail Retail Marketing of China
S.I.C.: 7331
Richard W. Tinberg *(Pres. & Chief Exec. Officer)*
David Bradford *(V.P.-Legal)*
Robert Del Ciella *(V.P.-Opers.)*
Shay Gallagher *(V.P.-Mktg.)*
Jack Hollander *(V.P.-Information Services)*
Tom Knaggs *(V.P.-New Bus.)*
Gina Camardo *(Controller)*
Al Ksiazk *(Gen. Mgr.-Norman Rockwell Fdtn.)*

Computer Systems/Hardware:
IBM 3081

Outside Service Firm(s):

Altschuler, Melvoin & Glasser*(Auditors)*
30 S. Wecker Dr.
Chicago, IL 60606
Tel.: 312-207-2800

Allstate Insurance*(Commercial Insurance Carrier)*
Northbrook, IL

Allstate Insurance*(Group Insurer)*
Northbrook, IL

J. C. BRADFORD & CO.
330 Commerce St.
Nashville, TN 37201
Tel.: 615-748-9000
Fax: 615-748-9614
Approx.Sls.: $120,000,000
Emp.: 1,000
Security Broker & Investment Banker
S.I.C.: 6211
James C. Bradford, Jr. *(Sr. Partner)*
W. Lucas Simons *(Mng. Partner)*
Robert S. Doolittle *(Partner & Dir.-Corp. Fin.)*
John Felber *(Partner & Dir.-Options)*
James F. Gallivan *(Partner & Acct. Exec.)*
R. Ray Harnass *(Partner & Chief Fin. Officer)*
Edward D. Hill *(Partner & Dir.-Sls. & Mktg.)*
Glenn W. Jones, Jr. *(Partner)*
Douglas O. Kitchen *(Partner & Dir.-Futures)*
Charles T. Malott *(Partner & Dir.-Admin.)*
James R. Scott *(Partner & Dir.-Municipal Bonds)*
Michael Shea *(Partner & Dir.-Corp. & Govt. Bonds)*
Jim McCoy *(Limited Investment Partner)*
Luanne T. Walkmath *(Limited Investment Partner & Dir.-Human Resources)*
Bruce Weathers *(Investment Limited Partner & Mktg. Dir.)*
Robert B. Sloan *(V.P. & Dir.-Human Rels.)*
Principal(s):
James C. Bradford, Jr.
W. Lucas Simons
Robert S. Doolittle
John Felber
James F. Gallivan
Edward D. Hill
Glenn W. Jones, Jr.
Douglas O. Kitchen
Charles T. Malott
James R. Scott
Michael Shea

Computer Systems/Hardware:
DEC VAX

Outside Service Firm(s):

Blue Cross & Blue Shield of Tennessee*(Group Insurer)*
Chattanooga, TN

NationsBank*(Major Banking Relationship)*
35 Broad St.
Atlanta, GA 30303
Tel.: 404-581-2121
Tel.: 800-848-8198

BRADFORD OIL COMPANY, INC.
Jcts. Rts. 5 & 25
Bradford, VT 05033
Tel.: 802-222-5252
Fax: 802-222-5100
Year Founded: 1969
Approx.Sls.: $35,000,000
Emp.: 250
Wholesale & Retail Petroleum Products & Service Station
S.I.C.: 5172; 5541; 5983
R. George Pratt, Jr. *(Pres. & Treas.)*
John Pratt *(V.P.)*
Hazel Pratt *(Sec.)*

Outside Service Firm(s):

Barrett & Genovese*(Auditors)*
White River Junction, VT

Christopher Dye Legal Firm*(Legal Firm)*
Bradford, VT

Bradford National Bank*(Major Banking Relationship)*
White River Junction, VT

W. C. BRADLEY CO.
1017 Front Ave.
Columbus, GA 31901
Mailing Address:
P.O. Box 140
Columbus, GA 31993
Tel.: 706-571-6040 **GA**
Fax: 706-571-6075
Year Founded: 1885
Assets: $105,230,613
Liabilities: $81,767,548
Net Worth: $23,463,065
Sales Range: $100-499 Million
Emp.: 1,100
Char-Broil Barbecue Grills, Universal-Fit Parts & Accessories
S.I.C.: 3631
Stephan T. Butler *(Chm. Bd. & Chief Exec. Officer)*
W.B. Turner, Jr. *(Pres. & Chief Oper. Officer)*
Timothy B. Horne *(Chief Exec. Officer-Charbroil Div.)*
James Morrow *(V.P.-Mktg.)*
Robert Wright *(Sec. & Treas.)*

Outside Service Firm(s):

KPMG Peat Marwick*(Auditors)*
277 Lakeshore Road East
Oakville, ON Canada
Tel.: 416-842-4722

Liberty Mutual*(Commercial Insurance Carrier)*
Columbus, GA

Provident Life & Accident Insurance co.*(Group Insurer)*
One Fountain Square
Chattanooga, TN 37402
Tel.: 615-755-1661

Davidson & Kruse*(Legal Firm)*
Nashville, TN

Columbus Bank & Trust Company*(Major Banking Relationship)*
Trust Dept., P.O. Box 120
Columbus, GA 31902
Tel.: 706-649-2311

Subsidiaries:

Bradley Specialty Retailing, Inc. (1)
1017 Front Ave.
Columbus, GA 31993
Tel.: 706-571-6060
Retail Stores
S.I.C.: 6512
Edwin S. Poole *(Pres.)*

Developers Investors, Inc. (1)
1017 Front Ave.
Columbus, GA 31993
Tel.: 706-571-6040
Real Estate Development
S.I.C.: 6798
Mathew D. Swift *(Pres.)*

BRADLEY COMMUNICATIONS, INC.
1840 S. Bragaw, Ste. 200
Anchorage, AK 99508
Tel.: 907-276-6353
Fax: 907-276-1042
Year Founded: 1968
Approx.Billings: $18,000,000
Emp.: 33
Rodney C. Bradley *(Chm. & Chief Exec. Officer)*
Connie Reid *(Pres. & Chief Oper. Officer)*
David K. Moran *(V.P., Chief Fin. Officer)*
Debi Florey *(V.P., Mktg., Adv. & New Bus. Contact)*

BRADLEY CORPORATION
W. 142 N. 9101 Fountain Blvd.
Menomonee Falls, WI 53051
Mailing Address:
P.O. Box 309,
Menomonee Falls, WI 53051
Tel.: 414-251-6000 **WI**
Fax: 414-251-5817
Year Founded: 1921
Sales Range: $60-79 Million
Emp.: 450
Fiscal Year-end: 12/31/91
Import Export
Washfountains, Faucets, Safety Fixtures, Showers, Security Prison/Jail Plumbing Fixtures & other Bathroom Accessories
S.I.C.: 3431; 3432
D.H. Mullett *(Pres.)*
James E. Carroll *(Exec. V.P. & Chief Oper. Officer)*
John Kleczka *(Sr. V.P.-Fin. & Treas.)*
T.G. Barnum *(V.P.-Res. & Devel.)*
Paul Clarkson *(V.P.-Div. Sls.)*
Bruce Kessler *(V.P.-Opers.)*
D.E. Kiefert *(V.P.-Mfg. Services)*
Larry Stover *(V.P.-Sls.)*
Robert Tremlett *(V.P.-Mngmt. Information System)*
J.F. Wandschneider *(V.P.-Corp. & Indus. Rels.)*
P.B. York *(V.P.-Mktg.)*
Carol McInerney *(Controller)*
Bob Falconer *(Dir.-Pur.)*

No. of Mfg. Plants/Facilities: 4
No. of U.S. Offices: 3
No. of Foreign Offices: 1

Computer Systems/Hardware:
IBM 4381 Model 2

Outside Service Firm(s):

Ernst & Young*(Auditors)*
111 E. Kilbourn Ave., Ste. 900
Milwaukee, WI 53202
Tel.: 414-273-5900

Foley & Lardner*(Legal Firm)*
777 E. Wisconsin Ave.
Milwaukee, WI 53202
Tel.: 414-271-2400

M & I Marshall & Ilsley Bank*(Major Banking Relationship)*
770 N. Water St.
Milwaukee, WI 53202
Tel.: 414-765-8700

Division:

Bradley Washroom Accessories Div. (1)
7020 Parkland Ct.
Milwaukee, WI 53223
Tel.: 414-354-0100
Manufacture Plumbing Accessories for Washrooms
S.I.C.: 3431; 3432

BRADNER CENTRAL COMPANY
333 S. Desplaines St.
Chicago, IL 60661-5596
Tel.: 312-454-1852
Fax: 312-454-0783
Year Founded: 1852
Assets: $36,746,000
Earnings: $1,454,000
Net Worth: $36,746,000
Approx.Rev.: $261,000,000
Emp.: 175
Fiscal Year-end: 10/31/90
Wholesale Paper Products
S.I.C.: 5111
Terence J. Shea *(Chm. Bd. & Chief Exec. Officer)*
Robert G. Van Dyck *(Pres.)*

Bernard J. Tarte, Jr. *(V.P. & Treas.)*
P. G. Tribby *(V.P. & Controller)*
Principal(s):
Bernard J. Tarte, Jr.

No. of Mfg. Plants/Facilities: 6
No. of U.S. Offices: 7

Computer Systems/Hardware:
Prime 250

Outside Service Firm(s):

Ernst & Young*(Auditors)*
233 S. Wacker Dr.
Chicago, IL 60606
Tel.: 312-368-1800
Fax: 312-645-3095

Blue Cross & Blue Shield of Illinois*(Group Insurer)*
100 Tower Drive
Burr Ridge, IL 60521
Tel.: 708-323-3666

Harris Trust & Savings Bank*(Investment Banker)*
111 W. Monroe St.
Chicago, IL 60690
Tel.: 312-461-2265
Tel.: 800-858-0840

Tenney & Bentley*(Legal Firm)*
111 W. Washington, Ste. 1900
Chicago, IL 60602
Tel.: 312-407-7800

First National Bank of Chicago*(Major Banking Relationship)*
One First National Plaza
Chicago, IL 60670
Tel.: 312-732-9781
Tel.: 312-732-4050
Fax: 312-732-4840
Fax: 312-732-3055

Massachusetts Mutual Life Insurance Co.*(Pension Manager)*
1295 State Street
Springfield, MA 01111
Tel.: 413-788-8411

Subsidiaries:

ALTO Papers **(1)**
2425 Camp Dr., Ste. 150
Carrollton, TX 75006
Tel.: 214-446-2586
Fax: 214-245-2326
S.I.C.: 5111
A. V. Collins *(Pres.)*

Bradner Smith & Co. **(1)**
333 S. DesPlaines St.
Chicago, IL 60606
Tel.: 312-454-1852
Fax: 312-454-0783
S.I.C.: 5111
Timothy F. Shannon *(Pres.)*

Diameter Paper Co. **(1)**
6200-B Purdue Dr., P.O. Box 43509
Atlanta, GA 30336
Tel.: 404-644-5007
Fax: 800-666-9752
S.I.C.: 5111
B. W. Browne *(Pres.)*

Pacific Papers Unlimited **(1)**
4550 Maywood Ave.
Vernon, CA 90058
Tel.: 213-587-5811
Fax: 213-587-3424
S.I.C.: 5111
W. B. Mangold *(Pres.)*

Rotary Paper Manifold Co. **(1)**
4250 United Pkwy.
Schiller Park, IL 60176
Tel.: 708-678-9095
Fax: 312-992-2137
S.I.C.: 5111
Richard S. Bull, III *(Pres.)*

BRADSHAW ASSOCIATES IN ADVERTISING, INC.
550 St. Louis St.
Springfield, MO 65806
Tel.: 417-866-2779
Fax: 417-866-3892
Year Founded: 1969
Approx.Billings: $20,000,000
Emp.: 15
Business-to-Business & Food Service
Raymond D. Bradshaw *(Pres. & Creative Dir.)*
Bob Bryant *(Exec. V.P.)*

THE BRADY COMPANY
N80 W12878 Fond du Lac Ave.
Menomonee Falls, WI 53051
Mailing Address:
P.O. Box 878
Menomonee Falls, WI 53051
Tel.: 414-255-0100
Fax: 414-255-3388
Year Founded: 1946
Approx.Billings: $15,000,000
Emp.: 52
Agricultural, Medical, Research, Technology & Business-to-Business
Karl F. Ohm *(Chm.)*
John B. Liebenstein *(Pres.)*
Jerry Langenecker *(V.P., Fin.)*
Steve Czarnecki *(Mgr., Intl. Mktg.)*
Paul Mamerow *(Mgr., Dir. Mail Services)*
Tim Riesterer *(Dir., Pub. Rels.)*

BRADY ENTERPRISES, INC.
167 Moore Rd.
East Weymouth, MA 02189
Mailing Address:
P. O. Box 99, E.
Weymouth, MA 02189
Tel.: 617-337-5000
Fax: 617-337-9338
Approx.Sls.: $13,500,000
Emp.: 150
Fiscal Year-end: 12/31/90
Food Mfr.; Bar Tender's Cocktail Mixes; Bell's Seasonings & Stuffings; Funny Face Children's Drink Mix
S.I.C.: 2087
John Brady *(Pres.)*
William Brady *(Treas.)*
William Gould *(Sls. Mgr.)*

Division:

The William G. Bell Company **(1)**
167 Moore Rd.
East Weymouth, MA 02189
Tel.: 617-337-5000
Fax: 617-337-9338
Emp.: 150
Bell's Seasoning, Ready-Mixed Stuffing, Meat Loaf Mix, Chicken Flavor Stuffing Mix, Rice Spicer, Premium Blend Stuffing Mix
S.I.C.: 2099
Desmond Gould *(Brand Mgr.)*

THE BRADY MARKETING COMPANY
80 Berry Dr.
Pacheco, CA 94553
Tel.: 510-676-1300
Fax: 510-676-3082
Emp.: 20
Manufacture Representatives
S.I.C.: 5149; 8611
Frank Brady *(Pres. & Chief Exec. Officer)*
Stuart Burge *(V.P.-Sls.)*
Ray Anne Freeman *(Controller)*

Computer Systems/Hardware:
IBM PC

Outside Service Firm(s):

Jones & Marzluft*(Auditors)*
Danville, CA

Bank of America NT&SA*(Major Banking Relationship)*
P.O. Box 27128, 1850 Gateway Blvd.
Concord, CA 94520
Tel.: 510-675-7479

BRAID ELECTRIC COMPANY
299 Cowan St.
Nashville, TN 37202
Mailing Address:
P.O. Box 23710,
Nashville, TN 37202
Tel.: 615-242-6511
Fax: 615-242-9684
Year Founded: 1879
Sales Range: $20-39 Million
Emp.: 150
Distribute Electrical, Lighting & Electronic Equipment
S.I.C.: 5063
Ben S. Gambill, Jr. *(Pres.)*
Thomas K. Gambill *(Exec. V.P.)*
Harold K. Duncan *(V.P.-Electrical Supplies)*
Bill Fitts *(Sec.)*
Bob Schmitt *(Dir.-Sls.)*

Computer Systems/Hardware:
Ultimate

Outside Service Firm(s):

Aetna Life & Casualty*(Commercial Insurance Carrier)*
100 N. Riverside Plaza
Chicago, IL 60606

American General Group Insurance Co.*(Group Insurer)*
Dallas, TX

BRAINARD STRAPPING
2250 Larchmont Ave. N.E.
Warren, OH 44483-2893
Mailing Address:
P.O. Box 1040
Rock Hill, SC 79731-1040
Tel.: 216-372-8200
Tel.: 800-321-7773
Fax: 216-372-8234
Year Founded: 1916
Approx.Sls.: $35,000,000
Emp.: 55
Fiscal Year-end: 12/31/90
Import Export
Mfr. of Steel & Plastic Products; Strapping Hand & Power Tools, Automatic Strapping Machines
S.I.C.: 3499
Corporate Giving Program: United Way
G.B. Thomasson *(V.P. & Gen. Mgr.)*
Charles R. Lucy *(Mgr.-Adv.)*

BRAINSTORM ADVERTISING & SALES PROMOTIONS
228 S. Wabash Ave.
Chicago, IL 60604
Tel.: 312-922-9797
Year Founded: 1981
Approx.Billings: $10,000,000
Emp.: 25
African-American Consumer Adv.
Terri Gardner *(Pres.)*
Gladyse Taylor *(V.P., Fin.)*

BRAMAN WORLD CAR CENTER
2044 Biscayne Blvd.
Miami, FL 33137
Tel.: 305-576-6900
Fax: 305-573-3293
Approx.Sls.: $520,000,000
Emp.: 900
Retail New & Used Automobiles & Trucks
S.I.C.: 5511
Norman Braman *(Pres.)*
Richard Hellawell *(Dir.-Store Opers.)*

No. of U.S. Offices: 8

DAVID A. BRAMBLE, INC.
705 Morgnel Rd.
Chestertown, MD 21620
Mailing Address:
P.O. Box 419,
Chestertown, MD 21620
Tel.: 301-778-3023 **MD**
Fax: 301-778-3427
Year Founded: 1964
Approx.Sls.: $21,000,000
Emp.: 200
Fiscal Year-end: 3/31/92
Excavation, Bituminous Concrete Paving
S.I.C.: 1611; 1794
David A. Bramble *(Chm. Bd. & Chief Exec. Officer)*
David C. Bramble *(Pres. & Chief Oper. Officer)*
Calvin C. Smith *(Exec. V.P.)*
David K. Sharretts *(Sr. V.P.)*
R. Preston Jacquette *(Treas.)*
Ellen R. Baldwin *(Sec.)*
Ernest S. Cookerly *(Gen. Counsel)*

No. of Mfg. Plants/Facilities: 3

Outside Service Firm(s):

Hartford Life Insurance Co.*(Commercial Insurance Carrier)*
Baltimore, MD

Chestertown Bank of Maryland*(Major Banking Relationship)*
Baltimore, MD

BRAMMER MANUFACTURING COMPANY
1701 Rockingham Rd.
Davenport, IA 52802
Mailing Address:
P.O. Box 3547,
Davenport, IA 52808
Tel.: 319-326-2585 **IA**
Fax: 800-334-7230
Year Founded: 1908
Approx.Sls.: $26,000,000
Emp.: 250
Mfr. of Wood Kitchen Cabinets
S.I.C.: 2434
H.P. Braunlich, Jr. *(Chm. Bd., Pres. & Chief Exec. Officer)*
Mike Moes *(V.P.-Fin.)*
Dale Schrad *(V.P.-Mfg.)*
Leonard VanBesien *(Pur. Agent)*

Outside Service Firm(s):

McGladrey & Pullen*(Auditors)*
Davenport, IA

Davenport Bank & Trust Co.*(Major Banking Relationship)*
Davenport, IA

BRANCE KRACHY COMPANY, INC.
4411 Navigation Blvd.
Houston, TX 77011
Mailing Address:
P.O. Box 1724,
Houston, TX 77251-1724
Tel.: 713-225-6661
Fax: 713-225-5044
Year Founded: 1932
Approx.Sls.: $12,000,000
Emp.: 75
Import Export
Power Transmission Equipment, Electric Generators & Transformers
S.I.C.: 5063
Durwood C. Lehmann *(Pres.)*
Ralph Babineaux *(V.P.)*
Milton G. LaPorte *(V.P. & Treas.)*
Clark Lehmann *(V.P.)*
Leslie Lehmann *(V.P.)*
Bennie L. Schiro *(V.P.)*
B. Glen Warburton *(V.P.)*
Greg Warburton *(V.P.)*
Roger Richards *(Sec.)*

Brance Krachy Company, Inc.—(Continued)

Outside Service Firm(s):

Winograd & Sparks*(Auditors)*
Houston, TX

Hoover, Bax & Shearer*(Legal Firm)*
Houston, TX

BRAND, SHICK & WESLEY
(A Joint Venture Between Brand & Shick, Inc. & Wesley & Assoc., Inc.)
1250 Old River Rd.
Cleveland, OH 44113
Tel.: 216-696-4550
Fax: 216-696-5368
Year Founded: 1962
Approx.Billings: $12,000,000
Emp.: 10
Juvenile Products, Medical, Financial & Industrial Adv.
David R. Brand *(Pres.)*
Susan Phillips *(Mgr., Acctg. & Fin., Controller)*
Eileen Petridis *(Acct. Mgr., Pub. Rels., New Bus. Contact)*

Computer Systems/Hardware:
IBM 36, Macintosh

BRANDYWINE SPORTS, INC.
2200 Concord Pike
Wilmington, DE 19803
Mailing Address:
P.O. Box 7009,
Wilmington, DE 19803
Tel.: 302-426-3197 **DE**
Fax: 302-478-8392
Sales Range: $10-19 Million
Harness Racing; Real Estate Mgmt.
S.I.C.: 7948; 6552; 6531
W.E. Hansen *(Chm. Bd. & Pres.)*

Outside Service Firm(s):

Price Waterhouse*(Auditors)*
30 S. 17th St.
Philadelphia, PA 19103
Tel.: 215-665-9500

Morris, Nichols, Arsht & Tunnell*(Legal Firm)*
1201 N. Market St.
Wilmington, DE 19801
Tel.: 302-658-9200

Delaware Trust*(Major Banking Relationship)*
Wilmington, DE

Subsidiaries:

Brandywine Raceway Assn., Inc. **(1)**
2200 Concord Pike
Wilmington, DE 19803
Tel.: 302-426-3197 (100%)
Racetrack
S.I.C.: 7948
W.E. Hansen *(Pres.)*

Brandywine Realty & Development, Inc. **(1)**
2200 Concord Pike
Wilmington, DE 19803
Tel.: 302-426-3197
Approx.Sls.: $100,000
Fiscal Year-end: 9/30/90
Subdividers & Developers; Real Estate Mgmt.
S.I.C.: 6552; 6531
W.E. Hansen *(Pres.)*

BRANT ALLEN INDUSTRIES, INC.
80 Field Point
Greenwich, CT 06830
Mailing Address:
P.O. Box 3443
Greenwich, CT 06830
Tel.: 203-661-3344
Fax: 203-661-3349
Approx.Sls.: $240,000,000
Paper Mills
S.I.C.: 2611; 2621
Murray Brant *(Chm. Bd.)*
Peter Brant *(Pres.)*
Joseph Allen *(Exec. V.P., Treas. & Sec.)*
Thomas E. Armstrong *(V.P.-Sls.)*
Principal(s):
Murray Brant
Peter Brant

No. of Mfg. Plants/Facilities: 2

Computer Systems/Hardware:
IBM System 38

Outside Service Firm(s):

Arthur Andersen & Co.*(Auditors)*
400 Atlantic St.
Stamford, CT 06901
Tel.: 203-327-6100

Carter, Ledyard & Milburn*(Legal Firm)*
2 Wall St.
New York, NY 10005
Tel.: 212-732-3200

Citibank N.A.*(Major Banking Relationship)*
Corporate Trust Services, 399 Park Ave.
New York, NY 10043
Tel.: 212-559-1605

BRAUM ICE CREAM STORES INC.
3000 N.E. 63rd St.
Oklahoma City, OK 73121
Mailing Address:
P.O. Box 25429
Oklahoma City, OK 73125
Tel.: 405-478-1656 **OK**
Fax: 405-478-8483
Approx.Sls.: $125,000,000
Emp.: 5,000
Manufacturer & Retailer of Ice Cream; Dairy & Restaurant
S.I.C.: 5451; 2024; 5812
William H. Braum *(Pres. & Chief Exec. Officer)*
Tony Bostwick *(V.P. & Treas.)*
Becky Hersh *(V.P.-Real Estate)*
Mary Braum *(Sec.)*
Armando Carro *(Comptroller)*

Computer Systems/Hardware:
IBM

Outside Service Firm(s):

Ernst & Young*(Auditors)*
1700 Liberty Tower
Oklahoma City, OK 73102
Tel.: 405-278-6823

David Walker*(Legal Firm)*
Oklahoma City, OK

Bank of Oklahoma*(Major Banking Relationship)*
One Williams Center
Tulsa, OK 74012
Tel.: 918-588-5100

W. BRAUN COMPANY
300 N. Canal St.
Chicago, IL 60606
Tel.: 312-346-6500
Fax: 312-346-9643
Year Founded: 1909
Sales Range: $40-59 Million
Fiscal Year-end: 12/31/90
Import Export
Designs & Supplies Decorative & Designer Glass, Plastic Bottles, Caps & Jars for the Cosmetic & Personal Care Industry
S.I.C.: 5085
Ethan M. Erenberg *(Chm. Bd. & Chief Exec. Officer)*
Edward Rappaport *(Pres.)*
Morris Braun *(V.P.)*
Al Cohen *(V.P.-Admin.)*
Leonard Perlman *(V.P., Chief Fin. Officer & Controller)*
Ralph P. Rettke *(V.P.-New Prod. Devel.)*
Craig Sawicki *(V.P. & Gen. Mgr. Sls.-Midwest)*
Gerald Briick *(Dir.-Mfg. & Customer Services-Midwest)*
Joan Corman *(Dir.-Human Resources)*
Sally Mason *(Dir.-Mktg.)*

Computer Systems/Hardware:
CAD/CAM & MacIntosh

Outside Service Firm(s):

Altschuler, Melvoin & Glasser*(Auditors)*
30 S. Wecker Dr.
Chicago, IL 60606
Tel.: 312-207-2800

Gilbert W. Gordon*(Legal Firm)*
Chicago, IL

Harris Trust & Savings Bank*(Major Banking Relationship)*
111 W. Monroe St.
Chicago, IL 60690
Tel.: 312-461-2265
Tel.: 800-858-0840

Divisions:

W. Braun Co. **(1)**
1050 Wall St., W.
Lyndhurst, NJ 07071
Tel.: 201-896-1700
Fax: 201-896-1809
Supplier of Decorative Plastic & Glass Bottles, Caps & Jars
S.I.C.: 5085
Frank Cornacchiulo *(V.P.)*
Edwin Lane *(Mgr. Sls.-Eastern Reg.)*
Scott Danheiser *(Mgr.-Mfg. Service-Eastern Reg.)*

W. Braun Co. **(1)**
24700 Center Ridge Rd., #210
Westlake, OH 44145
Tel.: 216-899-0121
Fax: 216-899-0219
Suppliers of Decorative of Plastic & Glass Bottles, Jars & Caps
S.I.C.: 5085
Neil Doren *(Mgr.-District)*
Mary Ziff *(Dir.-Customer Service)*

W. Braun Co. **(1)**
50 Washington St.
Norwalk, CT 06854
Tel.: 203-853-3660
Fax: 203-853-6616
Suppliers of Decorative Plastic & Glass Bottles, Jars & Caps
S.I.C.: 5085
Larry Taylor *(V.P., Gen. Mgr.-Southeast Reg.)*
Howard Stephens *(Mgr.-District)*

W. Braun Co. **(1)**
9455 Chivers Ave., Shadow Mountain Industrial Pk.
Sun Valley, CA 91352
Tel.: 818-504-0110
Fax: 818-504-0348
Suppliers of Decorative Plastic & Glass Bottles, Jars & Caps
S.I.C.: 5085
Ronald Peterson *(V.P.-Western Reg.)*

W. Braun Co. **(1)**
1 W. Water St.
Saint Paul, MN 55107
Tel.: 612-228-0966
Fax: 612-228-1721
Suppliers of Decorative Plastic & Glass Bottles, Jars & Caps
S.I.C.: 5085
David Kirch *(Gen. Mgr.)*

W. Braun Co. **(1)**
10480 Shady Trail Ste. 102
Dallas, TX 75220
Tel.: 214-351-2327
Fax: 214-350-7826
Suppliers of Decorative Plastic & Glass Bottles, Jars & Caps
S.I.C.: 5085
Steven Dykgraaf *(Gen. Mgr.)*

W. Braun Distribution Center **(1)**
7224 W. 60th St.
Summit, IL 60501
Tel.: 708-458-7808
Distribution Center of Decorative Glass & Plastic Bottles
S.I.C.: 5085
Ethan Frenberg *(Chief Oper. Officer)*
R.P. Rettke *(V.P.)*
Craig Sawicki *(V.P. & Mgr.-Midwest Region)*
Jack Leitman *(Dir.-Mktg.)*
Joan Corman *(Mgr.-Personnel)*
Sally Mason *(Mgr.-Adv.)*

W. Braun International **(1)**
13165 N.W. 45th Ave.
Opa Locka, FL 33054
Tel.: 305-681-3551
Fax: 305-685-0043
Suppliers of Decorative Plastic & Glass Bottles, Caps & Jars
S.I.C.: 5085
Lawrence Taylor *(V.P.)*

Non-U.S. Holdings:

W. Braun Packaging, Canada Ltd. **(1)**
215 Shields Court
Markham, ON L3R 8V2, Canada
Tel.: 416-475-7200
Fax: 416-497-1308
Mfrs. Bottle & Caps
S.I.C.: 3089; 3221
Jack Leitman *(Pres., Braun Canada)*

W. Braun Packaging, Canada Ltd. **(1)**
100 Alexis Nikon Blvd., #567
Montreal, PQ H4M 2P1, Canada
Tel.: 514-747-3507
Fax: 514-747-7391
Mfrs. Bottles & Caps
S.I.C.: 3089; 3221

BRAUNS FASHIONS, INC.
10000 Valley View Rd.
Minneapolis, MN 55344
Tel.: 612-941-9590
Fax: 612-941-9590, Ext. 61
Earnings: $1,502,000
Approx.Sls.: $70,755,000
Emp.: 1,200
Fiscal Year-end: 2/29/92
Import
Retail Women Apparel
S.I.C.: 5621
Nicholas H. Cook *(Pres. & Chief Exec. Officer)*
Herb Froemming *(Sr. V.P. & Chief Fin. Officer)*
Phil Lindley *(V.P.)*
Jerry Schramm *(V.P.-Stores)*
Rosemary C. Wolf *(Controller)*
Joanne Colvin *(Fashion Coord.)*
Debbie Jensen *(Dir.-Adv.)*
Lori Leonard *(Dir.-Personnel Training & Devel.)*
Phil Lindley *(Dir.-Data Processing)*

Outside Service Firm(s):

Ernst & Young*(Auditors)*
1400 Pillsbury Center
Minneapolis, MN 55402
Tel.: 612-343-1000

John Rice*(Legal Firm)*
Minneapolis, MN

First Bank Minneapolis*(Major Banking Relationship)*
P.O. Box A700, 120 S. Sixth St.
Minneapolis, MN 55480
Tel.: 612-370-4141

BRAZIER FOREST INDUSTRIES, INC.
4500 Columbia Center, 701 5th Ave.
Seattle, WA 98104
Tel.: 206-386-5800
Fax: 206-386-5846
Year Founded: 1965
Emp.: 225
Export
Rough, Dressed, Finished, Sawed & Planed Lumber
S.I.C.: 5031; 2421
John M. Brazier *(Pres. & Chief Exec. Officer)*
Kent C. Johnson *(V.P.-Fin.)*

Outside Service Firm(s):

Knight, Vale & Gregory*(Auditors)*
Tacoma, WA

Cairncross, Regan & Hempelman*(Legal Firm)*
Seattle, WA

U.S. Bank*(Major Banking Relationship)*
Wilmington, DE

Subsidiary:

Brazier Forest Products Of Oregon **(1)**
Hwy. 211
Molalla, OR 97038
Tel.: 503-829-9121
Emp.: 154
Rough, Sawed & Planed Lumber
S.I.C.: 2421
John Brazier *(Pres.)*
Luther Steinhauer *(Plant Mgr.)*

BRECKENRIDGE MATERIAL COMPANY
2829 Breckenridge Industrial Ct.
Saint Louis, MO 63144
Mailing Address:
P.O. Box 19918
St. Louis, MO 63144
Tel.: 314-962-1234
Approx.Sls.: $20,000,000
Emp.: 225
Fiscal Year-end: 3/31/92
Mfr. & Distr. Ready-Mix Concrete, Masonry Building Materials
S.I.C.: 5039; 3273; 5211
Gilbert R. McKean *(Pres.)*
Evelyn C. McKean *(Exec. V.P.)*
James G. Hudson *(V.P.)*
Bob Kintz *(Treas.)*

Computer Systems/Hardware:
IBM

Outside Service Firm(s):

Deloitte & Touche*(Auditors)*
One City Centre
St. Louis, MO 63101
Tel.: 314-342-4900
Fax: 314-342-1100

Dubail, Judge, Kilker, O'Leary & Smith*(Legal Firm)*
St. Louis, MO

Commerce Bank of Kansas City*(Major Banking Relationship)*
10th & Walnut
Kansas City, MO 64141
Tel.: 816-234-2000
Fax: 816-234-2548

BREGG DATA FORMS, INC.
75 Adams Ave.
Hauppauge, NY 11788
Tel.: 516-273-8383
Tel.: 800-645-1416
Fax: 516-273-8406
Approx.Sls.: $17,000,000
Emp.: 126
Business Forms Lithographed
S.I.C.: 2761
Irving Bressler *(Pres.)*
Morton Goldberg *(V.P.-Sls.)*
James Robertson *(V.P.-Mfg. & Dir.-Personnel)*
Henry Ehrlich *(Sec. & Treas.)*
James Keenan *(Mgr.-Sls.)*
Roni Roland *(Mgr.-Production)*

Outside Service Firm(s):

Coopers & Lybrand*(Auditors)*
225 Broad Hollow Dr.
Melville, NY 11747
Tel.: 516-753-2700

Wrenn & Schmid*(Legal Firm)*
East Islip, NY

Bank of New York*(Major Banking Relationship)*
Hicksville, NY

BREMER FINANCIAL CORPORATION
455 Minnesota St., Ste. 2000
Saint Paul, MN 55101
Tel.: 612-227-7621
Assets: $2,052,292,000
Earnings: $18,589,000
Liabilities: $1,888,889,000
Net Worth: $163,403,000
Approx.Rev.: $207,788,000
Fiscal Year-end: 12/31/91
Bank Holding Co.
S.I.C.: 6022; 6719
Robert J. Reardon *(Chm. Bd.)*
Terry M. Cummings *(Pres. & Chief Exec. Officer)*
Duaine C. Espegard *(V.P.)*
William H. Lipschultz *(V.P. & Treas.)*
Kenneth P. Nelson *(V.P.)*
Gene H. Sipe *(V.P.)*
Janice A. Aus *(Sec.)*

Regional Banks:

First American Bank **(1)**
P.O. Box 511,
International Falls, MN 56649
Tel.: 218-283-9411
Approx.Assets: $57,679,018
Bank
S.I.C.: 6029
Gary W. Bigler *(Pres.)*

First American Bank Southwest **(1)**
208 College Dr.
Marshall, MN 56258
Tel.: 507-537-0222
Approx.Assets: $120,198,209
Bank
S.I.C.: 6029
Gary L. Wickre *(Pres.)*

First American Bank Metro **(1)**
633 S. Concord St.
South Saint Paul, MN 55075
Tel.: 612-451-6822
Approx.Assets: $173,628,408
Bank
S.I.C.: 6029
Bruce G. Ruecker *(Pres.)*

First American Bank of Apostle Islands **(1)**
P.O. Box 278,
Washburn, WI 54891
Tel.: 715-373-5601
Approx.Assets: $42,183,408
Bank
S.I.C.: 6029
Michael R. Ginter *(Pres.)*

First American Bank **(1)**
301 Territorial St. E.
Watertown, MN 55388
Tel.: 612-955-1916
Approx.Assets: $23,542,528
Bank
S.I.C.: 6029
John A. Carlson *(Pres.)*

First American Bank **(1)**
720 Broadway
Alexandria, MN 56308
Tel.: 612-763-6622
Approx.Assets: $119,833,049
Bank
S.I.C.: 6029
John T. Wosepka *(Pres.)*

First American Bank **(1)**
321 S. Seventh St.
Brainerd, MN 56401
Tel.: 218-829-8781
Approx.Assets: $124,202,007
Bank
S.I.C.: 6029
Warren L. Williams *(Pres.)*

First American Bank **(1)**
225 N. Fifth St.
Breckenridge, MN 56520
Tel.: 218-643-8721
Approx.Assets: $54,808,121
Bank
S.I.C.: 6029
Donald R. Hass *(Pres.)*

First American Bank **(1)**
11 Langer Ave. N.
Casselton, ND 58012
Tel.: 701-347-4483
Approx.Assets: $35,401,645
Bank
S.I.C.: 6029
R.J. Klinkhammer *(Pres.)*

First American National Bank **(1)**
P.O. Box 613,
Crookston, MN 56716
Tel.: 218-281-4182
Approx.Assets: $146,002,504
Bank
S.I.C.: 6029
Rodney R. Nelson *(Pres.)*

First American Bank **(1)**
P.O. Box 827,
Detroit Lakes, MN 56502
Tel.: 218-847-9292
Approx.Assets: $102,938,086
Bank
S.I.C.: 6029
C. Leroy Larson *(Pres.)*

First American Bank & Trust **(1)**
P.O. Box 511,
Grafton, ND 58237
Tel.: 701-352-2410
Approx.Assets: $96,866,834
Bank
S.I.C.: 6029
Peter L. Keeley *(Pres.)*

First American Bank **(1)**
P.O. Box 599,
Larimore, ND 58251
Tel.: 701-343-2324
Approx.Assets: $28,408,431
Bank
S.I.C.: 6029
Robert R. Sobolik *(Pres.)*

First American Bank **(1)**
P.O. Box 273,
Lisbon, ND 58054
Tel.: 701-683-5233
Approx.Assets: $47,774,253
Bank
S.I.C.: 6029
Bruce D. Iserman *(Pres.)*

First American National Bank **(1)**
1100 W. St. Germain St.
Saint Cloud, MN 56301
Tel.: 612-251-3300
Approx.Assets: $272,399,207
Bank
S.I.C.: 6029
James H. Anderl *(Pres.)*

First American Bank **(1)**
202 W. Johnson Ave.
Warren, MN 56762
Tel.: 218-745-4411
Approx.Assets: $39,635,925
Bank
S.I.C.: 6029
Gary J. Lochow *(Pres.)*

First American Bank & Trust **(1)**
302 S.W. Fifth St.
Willmar, MN 56201
Tel.: 612-235-1111
Approx.Assets: $128,011,483
Bank
S.I.C.: 6029
Alan D. Marcyes *(Pres.)*

First American Bank & Trust **(1)**
P.O. Box 108,
Carrington, ND 58421
Tel.: 701-652-3127
Approx.Assets: $57,277,873
Bank
S.I.C.: 6029
Steven M. Skow *(Pres.)*

First American Bank & Trust **(1)**
21st S.W.
Minot, ND 58701
Tel.: 701-852-3361
Approx.Assets: $301,550,980
Bank
S.I.C.: 6029
Duaine C. Espegard *(Pres.)*

Subsidiaries:

Bremer Financial Services, Inc. **(1)**
445 Minnesota St., Ste. 2000
St. Paul, MN 55101
Tel.: 612-227-7621
Banks
S.I.C.: 6029
Terry M. Cummings *(Pres., Chief Exec. Officer & Sec.)*
Duaine C. Espegard *(Reg. Pres.)*
Kenneth P. Nelson *(Reg. Pres.)*
Gene H. Sipe *(Reg. Pres.)*
Brent J. Gray *(Sr. V.P. & Chief Fin. Officer)*

First American Information Services, Inc. **(1)**
633 S. Concord, Ste. 210
South Saint Paul, MN 55075
Tel.: 612-450-8200 (100%)
Automated Financial Services for Banks
S.I.C.: 7379
Robert J. Hall *(Pres.)*

First American Insurance Agencies, Inc. **(1)**
633 S. Concord, Ste. 225
South Saint Paul, MN 55075
Tel.: 612-451-1701
Personal, Business & Agricultural Insurance Products
S.I.C.: 6411
Charles D. Hendrickson *(Pres.)*

First American Trust Company of Minnesota **(1)**
Cold Spring Ctr., 4150 Second St. S.
Saint Cloud, MN 56302
Tel.: 612-255-7174
Corporate & Personal Trust Services
S.I.C.: 6091

BREMS EASTMAN GLADE, INC.
3131 Elliott Ave., Ste. 280
Seattle, WA 98121
Tel.: 206-284-9400
Fax: 206-284-9409
Year Founded: 1981
Approx.Billings: $14,000,000
Emp.: 24
Consumer, Business-to-Business & Medical Adv.
Christian Brems *(Pres.)*
Sue Eastman *(V.P.)*
Steve Glade *(V.P.)*
Diane Torrance *(V.P.)*
Gail Hannah *(Pub. Rels. Dir., Acct. Exec.)*
Luanne Short *(Office Mgr.)*

BRENDAMOUR'S SPORTING GOODS CO.
4831 Spring Grove Ave.
Cincinnati, OH 45232
Tel.: 513-542-5820
Fax: 513-542-6003
Year Founded: 1902
Approx.Sls.: $20,000,000
Emp.: 400
Retail Sporting Goods Stores
S.I.C.: 5941
Jerome A. Gordon *(Pres.)*
Darwin Grener *(Chief Fin. Officer)*
Bill Freppon *(V.P.-Store Opers.)*

THE BRENLIN GROUP
670 W. Market St.
Akron, OH 44303
Tel.: 216-762-2420
Telex: 216-762-4604
Fax: 216-762-4604
Year Founded: 1975
Assets: $405,000,000
Liabilities: $265,000,000
Net Worth: $140,000,000
Approx.Sls.: $700,000,000
Emp.: 4,200
Fiscal Year-end: 10/31/91

Import Export

The Brenlin Group—(Continued)

Holding Company; Subsidiaries Manufacture & Distribute Stampings, Containers, Axles & Other Metal Products Primarily for the Transportation Industry & Operate an Integrated Steel Mill
S.I.C.: 6719; 5013; 3714; 3312
David L. Brennan *(Chm. Bd. & Chief Exec. Officer)*
Richard M. Hamlin *(Vice Chm.)*
James P. McCready *(Pres. & Chief Oper. Officer)*
James D. Van Tiem *(Chief Fin. Officer & Treas.)*
James F. Gaul *(V.P.-Opers.)*
R. Mark Hamlin *(V.P.)*
Samuel C. Lehmann *(V.P.-Admin. & Mngmt. Information Services)*
Stephen J. Tomasko *(V.P.-Human Resources)*
John S. Steinhauer *(Sec.)*
Principal(s):
David L. Brennan

No. of Mfg. Plants/Facilities: 20

Outside Service Firm(s):

Amer, Cunningham & Brennan*(Legal Firm)*
Akron, OH

Bank One Texas*(Major Banking Relationship)*
1717 Main St.
Dallas, TX 75201
Tel.: 214-290-2367

BRESLER'S INDUSTRIES, INC.
999 E. Touhy Ave., Ste. 333
Des Plaines, IL 60018
Tel.: 708-298-1100
Tel.: 800-535-3333
Fax: 708-298-0697
Approx.Sls.: $55,000,000
Emp.: 30
Fiscal Year-end: 9/30/91
National Franchisor of Bresler's Ice Cream & Yogurt Shops; Distribution of Pro*Portion Cake
S.I.C.: 5812; 6794; 5143
David Lasky *(Pres.)*
Alan Marti *(V.P.-Opers.)*
Michael Rapaport *(Dir.-Mktg.)*
Dennis Rissman *(Controller)*
L. Matjko *(Admin. Asst.)*

Outside Service Firm(s):

LaSalle National Bank*(Major Banking Relationship)*
120 S. LaSalle St.
Chicago, IL 60603
Tel.: 312-781-8000

Subsidiaries:

Larry's Industries, Inc. **(1)**
999 E. Touhy Ave.
Des Plaines, IL 60018
Tel.: 708-298-1135
Mfr. of Ice Cream & Frozen Yogurt
S.I.C.: 2024
David Lasky *(Pres.)*
Michael Rapaport *(Dir.-Mktg.)*

Pro*Portion Industries, Inc. **(1)**
999 E. Touhy Ave.
Des Plaines, IL 60018
Tel.: 708-298-1135
Quick Service Restaurant
S.I.C.: 5812
David Lasky *(Pres.)*
Michael E. Rapaport *(Dir.-Mktg.)*

BRETON CONSTRUCTION, INC.
Two Corporate Park, Ste. 200
Irvine, CA 92714
Tel.: 714-660-9400 **CA**
Fax: 714-975-1690
Year Founded: 1972
Approx.Sls.: $60,000,000
Emp.: 52
Fiscal Year-end: 9/30/91
Industrial Buildings, New Construction
S.I.C.: 1541
Angus MacPherson *(Pres. & Chief Exec. Officer)*
Robert Harding *(Exec. V.P.-Opers.)*
Jerrold Pellizzon *(Exec. V.P. & Chief Fin. Officer)*
Randy P. Wages *(Sr. V.P.)*
Rick Atherton *(Dir.-Mktg.)*

No. of U.S. Offices: 1

Outside Service Firm(s):

Cummins & White*(Legal Firm)*
Santa Ana Heights, CA

City National Bank*(Major Banking Relationship)*
Newport Beach, CA

DAVID BRETT, INC.
35 Eastman St.
Easton, MA 02334
Tel.: 508-238-5330
Fax: 508-238-2972
Approx.Sls.: $30,000,000
Emp.: 65
Mfr. Ladies Knit Sweaters & Sportswear
S.I.C.: 2253; 2339
Benjamin P. Swartz *(Pres.)*
Bennett Adelman *(Exec. V.P.-Mktg.)*
Steve Adelman *(V.P.-Sls.)*
Sadie Swartz *(Sec.)*
James Hayes *(Controller)*
Allen Stepner *(Mgr.-Pur.)*

Outside Service Firm(s):

Aronson, Broner, Swartz, Aronson & Brookline*(Auditors)*
Easton, MA

Nutter, McClennen & Fish*(Legal Firm)*
One International Place
Boston, MA 02110
Tel.: 617-575-2900

First National Bank of Boston*(Major Banking Relationship)*
150 Royall St.
Canton, MA 02021
Tel.: 617-575-2900
Tel.: 800-442-2001

BREUER ELECTRIC MFG. CO.
7401 W. Lawrence Ave.
Chicago, IL 60656
Tel.: 708-867-5100
Tel.: 800-822-8867
Fax: 708-867-6968
Year Founded: 1927
Approx.Sls.: $20,000,000
Emp.: 140
Fiscal Year-end: 12/31/90
Import Export
Tornado Carpet Care Machines & Industrial Vacuum Cleaners, Portable Blowers, Floor Machines & Combination Scrub-Vacuum-Dry Machines
S.I.C.: 3589
Adam A. Breuer *(Chm. Bd.)*
Linda Breuer-Murray *(Pres.)*
Michael Schaffer *(Mgr.-Natl. Sls.)*
Gary V. Cirone *(V.P.-Fin.)*
James O'Leary *(V.P.-Mfg.)*
Maurice Moloney *(Pur. Agent)*

Outside Service Firm(s):

Price Waterhouse*(Auditors)*
200 E. Randolph
Chicago, IL 60601
Tel.: 312-565-1500

Vedder, Price, Kaufman & Kammholz*(Legal Firm)*
115 S. LaSalle St.
Chicago, IL 60603
Tel.: 312-781-2200

Boulevard Bank*(Major Banking Relationship)*
410 N. Michigan Ave.
Chicago, IL 60611
Tel.: 312-836-6500

C. BREWER & COMPANY, LIMITED
(Sub. of Buyco, Inc.)
827 Fort St. Mall
Honolulu, HI 96813
Mailing Address:
P.O. Box 1826,
Honolulu, HI 96805
Tel.: 808-536-4461 **HI**
Fax: 808-544-6182
Year Founded: 1826
Earnings: $8,000,000
Approx.Sls.: $253,000,000
Emp.: 5,000
Fiscal Year-end: 12/29/90
Agricultural Production & Marketing, Land Sales & Development, Stevedoring & Trucking, Chemicals
S.I.C.: 0133; 2061; 5191; 8731; 5169; 2068; 5149; 5148
John W.A. Buyers *(Chm. Bd.)*
James S. Andrasick *(Exec. V.P.)*
Terris H. Inglett *(Exec. V.P.)*
J. Alan Kugle *(Exec. V.P. & Gen. Counsel)*
Kent T. Lucien *(Exec. V.P., Chief Fin. Officer & Treas.)*
Mark W. Melidosian *(V.P.)*
Kim Peterson *(V.P.-Human Resources)*
D.S. Dymond *(Controller)*
Teresa Freticelli *(Corp. Sec.)*
Deane Wentworth *(Asst. Treas. & Asst. Sec.)*
Elizabeth Gamundoy *(Dir.-Employee Benefits)*
Paul Matsushima *(Dir.-MIS)*
Davis K. Yogi *(Dir.-Govt. & Employee Rels.)*

Outside Service Firm(s):

Coopers & Lybrand*(Auditors)*
Pacific Tower, 1001 Bishop St., Ste. 2500
Honolulu, HI 96813-3668
Tel.: 808-531-3400

Goodsill, Anderson, Quinn & Stifel*(Legal Firm)*
P.O. Box 3196
Honolulu, HI 96801
Tel.: 808-547-5600
Fax: 808-547-5880

Bank of Hawaii*(Major Banking Relationship)*
Honolulu, HI

First Hawaiian Bank*(Major Banking Relationship)*
165 South King St.
Honolulu, HI 96813
Tel.: 808-525-5876
Fax: 808-525-5791

Subsidiaries:

Brewer Environmental Industries, Inc. **(1)**
P.O. Box 48
Honolulu, HI 96810
Tel.: 808-533-4411 (100%)
Fax: 808-531-9078
Mfrs. Liquid Detergents
S.I.C.: 2841; 5169
James Andrasick *(Chm. Bd.)*
Terris H. Inglett *(Pres.)*

C. Brewer Properties, Inc. **(1)**
827 Fort St.
Honolulu, HI 96813
Tel.: 808-536-4461
Fax: 808-544-6182
B.G. Moynahan *(Pres. & Chief Oper. Officer)*

HT&T Company, Inc. **(1)**
P.O. Box 4190
Hilo, HI 96720
Tel.: 808-935-3301 (100%)
Fax: 808-935-4345
Trucking & Storage
S.I.C.: 4213; 4221
J. Alan Kugle *(V.P.)*
James D. Andrasick *(Chm. Bd.)*
Richard T. Hill *(Pres.)*
Herbert T. Takahashi *(V.P.-Fin. & Admin.)*
Kent T. Lucien *(V.P. & Treas.)*
James S. Andrasick *(V.P.)*
Kathleen F. Oshiro *(Sec.)*

Ka'u Agribusiness Co., Inc. **(1)**
P.O. Box 130
Pahala, HI 96777
Tel.: 808-928-8311 (100%)
Fax: 808-928-8434
Sugar Cane Grower & Processor of Sugar & Molasses
S.I.C.: 0133; 2061
James S. Andrasick *(Chm. Bd.)*
Richard Cushnie *(Pres.)*
Kent T. Lucien *(Sr. V.P. & Treas.)*
B.G. Moynahan *(V.P.)*
Kathleen F. Oshiro *(Sec.)*

Kilauea Agronomics, Inc. **(1)**
P.O. Box 80
Kilauea, HI 96754
Tel.: 808-828-1761 (100%)
Fax: 808-828-1880
Guava Producer
S.I.C.: 0179; 8731
J. Alan Kugle *(Chm. Bd.)*
James A. Frazier *(Pres.)*
Kent T. Lucien *(V.P. & Treas.)*
Bruce M. Rosen *(V.P.-Fin.)*
James S. Andrasick *(V.P.)*
Kathleen F. Oshiro *(Sec.)*

Mauna Kea Agribusiness Co., Inc. **(1)**
P.O. Box 68
Papaikou, HI 96781
Tel.: 808-964-5755 (100%)
Fax: 808-964-5703
Sugar Cane Production & Macadamia Nuts
S.I.C.: 2068; 0179
James S. Andrasick *(Chm. Bd.)*
Donald B. Cataluna *(Pres.)*
Kent T. Lucien *(V.P. & Treas.)*
B.G. Moynahan *(V.P.)*
Raymond S. Kuruhara *(V.P. & Controller)*
Kathleen F. Oshiro *(Sec.)*

Mauna Loa Macadamia Nut Corporation **(1)**
HC/01 Box 3
Hilo, HI 96720
Tel.: 808-966-9301 (100%)
Fax: 808-966-8410
Approx.Sls.: $72,000,000
Emp.: 500
Fiscal Year-end: 12/31/90
Processes & Markets Macadamia Nuts, Candy
S.I.C.: 2068; 2064
Terris Inglett *(Chm. Bd. & Pres.)*
Alan H. Witcher *(V.P.)*
Kent T. Lucien *(V.P. & Treas.)*
Gerald T. Nagata *(V.P. & Controller)*
James S. Andrasick *(V.P.)*
Albert K.F. Kam, Jr. *(V.P.)*
James S. Kendrick *(V.P.)*
Kathleen F. Oshiro *(Sec.)*

Subsidiary:

Mauna Loa Resources Inc. **(2)**
P.O. Box 1826, 827 Fort Street
Honolulu, HI 96813
Tel.: 808-544-6112 (100%)
Fax: 808-544-6182
Managing General Partner of Mauna Loa Macadamia Partners, L.P. (See Separate Listing)
S.I.C.: 6719
J.W.A. Buyers *(Chm. & Chief Exec. Officer)*
J. Alan Kugle *(Pres.)*
D.S. Dymond *(V.P. & Chief Fin. Officer)*
Kent T. Lucien *(V.P. & Treas.)*
Kathleen F. Oshiro *(Sec.)*

Olokele Sugar Co., Limited **(1)**
P.O. Box 156,
Kaumakani, HI 96747
Tel.: 808-335-3133 (84.88%)
Fax: 808-335-6424
Sugar Plantation
S.I.C.: 0133
James S. Andrasick *(Chm. Bd.)*
E. Alan Kennett *(Pres.)*
Kent T. Lucien *(V.P. & Treas.)*
Kathleen F. Oshiro *(Sec.)*

Superior Coffee & Foods/Hawaii **(1)**
99-910 Iwaena St.
Aiea, HI 96701
Tel.: 808-488-0923
Fax: 808-487-8603
Coffee Processor & Marketer
S.I.C.: 2095; 0179
J. Alan Kugle *(Chm. Bd.)*
Albert K.F. Kam, Jr. *(Pres. & Gen. Mgr.)*
Stanley D. Sollenbarger *(V.P.)*
James S. Andrasick *(V.P.)*
Albert K.F. Kam *(V.P.)*

Kent T. Lucien *(V.P. & Treas.)*

Wailuku Agribusiness Co., Inc. **(1)**
P.O. Box 520,
Wailuku, HI 96793
Tel.: 808-244-9570 (87.70%)
Fax: 808-242-7068
Pineapple & Macadamia Nuts
S.I.C.: 2068; 5148
J. Alan Kugle *(Chm. Bd.)*
Stephen W. Knox *(Pres.)*
Kent T. Lucien *(V.P. & Treas.)*
James S. Andrasick *(V.P.)*
B.G. Moynahan *(V.P.)*
Kathleen F. Oshiro *(Sec.)*

BRIAN CENTER MANAGEMENT CORPORATION
1331 4th St. Dr., N.W.
Hickory, NC 28601
Mailing Address:
P.O. Drawer 1148,
Hickory, NC 28603
Tel.: 704-322-3362 **NC**
Fax: 704-322-1474
Year Founded: 1972
Approx.Sls.: $10,000,000
Emp.: 250
Fiscal Year-end: 3/31/91
Management & Accounting Services
S.I.C.: 8721
Donald C. Beaver *(Pres., Chief Exec. Officer & Treas.)*
Tom I. Davis III *(Exec. V.P.)*
William Filippone *(Sr. V.P.-Opers.)*
Luther R. Beaver *(V.P.-Retirement Project Devel.)*
Rebecca Branan *(V.P.-Mktg.)*
Evans W. Fisher *(V.P. & Gen. Counsel)*
Anne Hall *(V.P.-Quality Assurance)*
Steve Merek *(V.P.-Human Resources)*
Patricia Beaver *(Treas.)*
James L. Martin, Jr. *(Controller)*
Nick Pollack *(Pur. Agent)*
John Kiser *(Dir.-Data Processing)*

Principal(s):
Donald C. Beaver

Outside Service Firm(s):

Durham, Martin, Jenkins & Co.*(Auditors)*
Raleigh, NC

Tate Young*(Legal Firm)*
Hickory, NC

NationsBank Carolinas*(Major Banking Relationship)*
Hickory, NC

BRIAN UNLIMITED DISTRIBUTION COMPANY, INC.
13131 Lyndon
Detroit, MI 48227
Tel.: 313-933-5100
Fax: 313-933-7990
Approx.Sls.: $10,000,000
Emp.: 206
Direct Mail Advertisers
S.I.C.: 2752; 7331; 7374
William A. Brian *(Pres.)*
John C. Galleher *(V.P.)*
Marie Buerger *(Sec.)*
William R. Yordy *(Controller & Treas.)*

Outside Service Firm(s):

Post, Smythe, Lutz & Zeil*(Auditors)*
Detroit, MI

Kemp, Klein, Humphrey, Edelman & Beer*(Legal Firm)*
Birmingham, MI

Manufacturers National Bank N.A.*(Major Banking Relationship)*
38th Fl., 100 Renaissance Center
Detroit, MI 48243
Tel.: 313-222-4227

BRIDAL ORIGINALS, INC.
1700 St. Louis Rd.
Collinsville, IL 62234
Mailing Address:
P.O. Box 749,
Collinsville, IL 62234
Tel.: 618-345-4499
Fax: 618-345-9768
Approx.Sls.: $50,000,000
Emp.: 900
Fiscal Year-end: 6/30/90
Bridal Gowns, Bridesmaids Dresses, Mother Of The Bride Dresses & Formals
S.I.C.: 2335
Richard L. Freundlich *(Chm. & Chief Exec. Officer)*
Jack Adler *(Sec. & Treas.)*

BRIDGEMAN'S RESTAURANTS INC.
6009 Wayzata Blvd.
Minneapolis, MN 55416
Tel.: 612-593-1455
Approx.Sls.: $20,000,000
Emp.: 1,000
Fiscal Year-end: 3/31/91
Ice Cream Parlors & Family Restaurants
S.I.C.: 5812
Steve Lampi *(Pres.)*
Doug Coy *(Chief Exec. Officer)*
Tom Hoblett *(Chief Fin. Officer)*
Joanne Gunderson *(Controller)*

BRIDGEPORT FITTINGS, INC.
705 Lordship Blvd.
Stratford, CT 06497
Mailing Address:
P.O. Box 619,
Bridgeport, CT 06601
Tel.: 203-377-5944 **CT**
Fax: 203-381-3488
Sales Range: $10-19 Million
Emp.: 400
Import Export
Die Cast Couplings & Connectors, Conduit & Cable Electrical Fittings
S.I.C.: 3644; 3494; 3643
Delbert L. Auray *(Pres. & Treas.)*
Richard J. Reidy *(V.P.-Sls.)*
Kirk Whiteman *(Dir.-Admin.)*
Charles Pigaty *(Mgr.-Pur.)*
Marta Testa *(Mgr.-Personnel)*
Garritt Van Dyke *(Mgr.-Engrng.)*
John Ferreira *(Plant Mgr.)*

Principal(s):
Delbert L. Auray

No. of Mfg. Plants/Facilities: 1
No. of U.S. Offices: 1

Computer Systems/Hardware:
NCR

Outside Service Firm(s):

Milton H. Friedberg, Smith & Co.*(Auditors)*
Bridgeport, CT

Cohen & Wolf*(Legal Firm)*
Bridgeport, CT

City Trust*(Major Banking Relationship)*
961 Main St.
Bridgeport, CT 06601
Tel.: 203-384-5402

BRIDGEPORT MACHINES, INC.
500 Lindley St.
Bridgeport, CT 06606
Tel.: 203-367-3651 **DE**
Fax: 203-335-0151
Year Founded: 1939
Sales Range: $100-499 Million
Emp.: 500
Fiscal Year-end: 3/31/92
Import Export
Manufacture of Milling Machines, Grinders, Machining Centers
S.I.C.: 3541; 3545; 3549; 7373
Joseph E. Clancy *(Chm. Bd., Pres. & Chief Oper. Officer)*
Dan L. Griffith *(Chief Fin. Officer & Exec. V.P.)*
Phillip Archard *(V.P. & Controller)*
Yvonne Hanson *(V.P. & Treas.)*
Michael LaMonica *(V.P.-Sls. & Mktg.)*
Ralph J. LoStocco *(V.P.-Admin.)*
Jack Benard *(Dir.-Mngmt. Information Systems)*
Thomas Corrigan *(Dir.-Pur.)*
Saul Estreicher *(Mgr.-Mktg. Support & Admin.)*
Denise Masulli *(Coord.-Personnel)*

Principal(s):
Joseph E. Clancy
Dan L. Griffith
Phillip Archard
Michael LaMonica
Ralph J. LoStocco

No. of Mfg. Plants/Facilities: 2
No. of U.S. Offices: 7
No. of Foreign Offices: 3

Outside Service Firm(s):

Arthur Andersen & Co.*(Auditors)*
400 Atlantic St.
Stamford, CT 06901
Tel.: 203-327-6100

Connecticut National Bank*(Major Banking Relationship)*
Bridgeport, CT

Travelers Insurance Co.*(Commercial Insurance Carrier)*
One Tower Square
Hartford, CT 06183-6130
Tel.: 203-277-4542
Fax: 203-277-5038

Aetna Life & Casualty*(Group Insurer)*
151 Farmington Avenue
Hartford, CT 06156
Tel.: 203-273-2128
Fax: 203-729-4295

Physicians Health Services*(Group Insurer)*
Trumbull, CT

Durant, Sabanosh, Nichols & Houston*(Legal Firm)*
Bridgeport, CT
Tel.: 203-366-3438

Subsidiaries:

Harig Grinders **(1)**
1875 Big Timber Rd.
Elgin, IL 60123
Tel.: 708-695-1000
Manufacture Industrial Steel Grinders
S.I.C.: 3541

Harig Products **(1)**
1875 Big Timber Rd.
Elgin, IL 60123
Tel.: 708-695-1000
Fax: 708-695-1043
Emp.: 100
Fiscal Year-end: 12/31/90
Export
Machine Tool Mfr.; Harig Precision Hand Feed & Power Feed Surface Grinders, Hogger, Slicer, CNC & Miscellaneous Tool Grinding Fixtures, Air-Flo, Model S, Presto-Dress
S.I.C.: 5084
Wayne Stastny *(Gen. Mgr.)*
David Sabin *(Customer Services Mgr.)*
Jim Simpson *(Pur. Agent)*

BRIDGES & COMPANY, INC.
1300 Brighton
Pittsburgh, PA 15233
Tel.: 412-321-5400
Fax: 412-321-9823
Approx.Sls.: $24,000,000
Emp.: 150
Commercial Construction
S.I.C.: 1542
Paul Bridges *(Pres.)*
M. Robert Mistick *(V.P.)*
D. Thomas Mistick *(Sec.)*
William Schwartz *(Dir.-Mktg.)*

Principal(s):
Mark A. Davis
Glenn A. Gates

Outside Service Firm(s):

Deloitte & Touche*(Auditors)*
2400 One PPG Place
Pittsburgh, PA 15222
Tel.: 412-281-2232

BRIDGEWATER RESOURCES CORPORATION
9701 Wilshire Blvd., Ste. 1200
Beverly Hills, CA 90212
Tel.: 310-859-7400 **TX**
Fax: 310-859-7445
Year Founded: 1982
Sales Range: $60-79 Million
Emp.: 600
Holding Company: Lumber, Logs, Flooring Hardwood
S.I.C.: 6719; 2411; 2426; 2435; 2499; 3496; 5031
Neil Sunderland *(Chm. Bd.)*
H.A. Thornburg *(Chief Exec. Officer)*
Lori J. Poulos *(V.P., Treas., Controller & Sec.)*

No. of Mfg. Plants/Facilities: 5
No. of U.S. Offices: 3

Outside Service Firm(s):

Coopers & Lybrand*(Auditors)*
1000 TCF Bldg.
Minneapolis, MN 55402
Tel.: 612-293-2929
Fax: 612-370-9395

Union Bank of Switzerland*(Major Banking Relationship)*
444 S. Flower, Ste. 4600
Los Angeles, CA 90071
Tel.: 213-489-0600
Fax: 213-489-0637

Divisions:

Connor Forest Industries, Inc. **(1)**
601 Sunday Lake St.
Wakefield, MI 49968
Tel.: 906-299-5135
Emp.: 300
Logging & Sawmills
S.I.C.: 2411; 2421
Dave Covington *(Chief Oper. Officer)*

Peerless Chain Company **(1)**
1416 E. Sanborn St.
Winona, MN 55987
Tel.: 507-457-9100
Emp.: 300
Mfr. of Tire Chains
S.I.C.: 3499
Lynn Graybill *(Chief Exec. Officer)*

BRIERLEY & PARTNERS
P.O. Box 50708,
Dallas, TX 75250
Tel.: 214-760-8700
Year Founded: 1985
Approx.Billings: $47,000,000
Emp.: 55
Relationship Marketing & Advertising
S.I.C.: 7311
Harold M. Brierley *(Chm. Bd. & Pres.)*
R.H. Metzner *(Sr. V.P.)*
S.A. Myers *(V.P.)*
C.L. Cheatham *(Treas.)*

Branches:

Brierley & Partners **(1)**
5900 Wilshire Blvd., Ste. 550
Los Angeles, CA 90036
Tel.: 213-932-7272
S.I.C.: 7311

Brierley & Partners **(1)**
8420 W. Bryn Mawr, #1120
Chicago, IL 60631
Tel.: 312-693-9900
S.I.C.: 7311

BRIGGS INDUSTRIES, INC.
4350 W. Cypress St., Ste. 800
Tampa, FL 33607
Tel.: 813-878-0178
Fax: 813-874-0627
Approx.Sls.: $100,000,000
Emp.: 950
Porcelain-on-Steel & Vitreous China Plumbing Fixtures, Brassware, Acrylic Tubs & Showers
S.I.C.: 3261; 3088; 3431; 3432
Jack Huss *(Pres. & Chief Exec. Officer)*
Charles Park *(Chief Fin. Officer & V.P.-Fin.)*
William G. Durocher *(V.P.-Sls. & Dir.-Mktg. & Intl. Sls.)*
Dennis Lamond *(V.P.-Sls.)*
Peter Porpora *(V.P. & Controller)*
Sterling Brown *(Mgr.-Adv. & Mktg. Support)*

Outside Service Firm(s):

Deloitte & Touche*(Auditors)*
Tampa, FL

BRIM, INC.
305 N.E. 102nd Ave.
Portland, OR 97220
Tel.: 503-256-2070 **OR**
Fax: 503-254-7619
Year Founded: 1971
Assets: $26,400,000
Liabilities: $21,600,000
Net Worth: $4,800,000
Approx.Sls.: $70,500,000
Emp.: 175
Fiscal Year-end: 12/31/91
Hospital & Health Care Facilities Management Services; Retirement Housing Development
S.I.C.: 8741; 8744; 6552
Corporate Giving Program: Allied with the Needs of Affiliated Health Care Organizations & Institutions
A. Eugene Brim *(Chm. Bd. & Pres.)*
James Williams, Jr. *(Pres.-Brim Senior Living)*
Steve Taylor *(Pres.-Brim Health Care)*
Craig VanValkenberg *(Pres.-Brim Services Group)*
Charles I. Gustafson *(Sr. V.P.-Corp. Devel.)*
John Miller *(V.P. & Chief Fin. Officer)*
K. David McAllister *(Chief Fin. Officer)*
Gary Elings *(Controller)*
Christine Craft *(Dir.-Pub. Rels.)*
Toni J. Grabler *(Dir.-Personnel)*
Jim McKinnery *(Dir.-Pur.)*

No. of U.S. Offices: 4
No. of Foreign Offices: 1

Outside Service Firm(s):

Coopers & Lybrand*(Auditors)*
2700 First Interstate Tower, 1300 SW 5th Ave.
Portland, OR 97201

Sedgwick James*(Commercial Insurance Carrier)*
Portland, ME

Vantage Group*(Group Insurer)*
Portland, OR

Tonkon, Torp, Galen, Marmaduke & Booth*(Legal Firm)*
1600 Pioneer Tower, 888 S.W. Fifth Ave.
Portland, OR 97204
Tel.: 503-221-1440

United States National Bank of Oregon*(Major Banking Relationship)*
P.O. Box 3850,
Portland, OR 97208
Tel.: 503-275-6111

William M. Mercer Incorporated*(Pension Manager)*
Portland, OR

Subsidiaries:

Brim Services Group **(1)**
305 N.E. 102nd Ave.
Portland, OR 97220
Tel.: 503-256-2070

Fifth Avenue Hospital **(1)**
10560 5th Ave., N.E.
Seattle, WA 98125
Tel.: 206-364-2050

Fort Morgan Community Hospital **(1)**
1000 Lincoln St.
Fort Morgan, CO 80701
Tel.: 303-867-3391
Emp.: 125
Health Care Industry, Mngmt., Consultation and Senior Living Activities
S.I.C.: 4729; 8741; 8742

General Hospital **(1)**
2200 Harrison Ave.
Eureka, CA 95501
Tel.: 707-445-5111
Emp.: 125
Health Care Industry, Mngmt., Consultation and Senior Living Activities
S.I.C.: 4729; 8741; 8742

BRIMMS INC.
425 Fillmore Ave.
Tonawanda, NY 14150
Tel.: 716-694-7100
Tel.: 800-828-7669
Fax: 716-694-0462
Year Founded: 1945
Approx.Sls.: $10,000,000
Emp.: 100
Fiscal Year-end: 12/31/91
Import Export
Brimms Plasti-Liner, Cushiony Denture Strips, Denture Customfit Denture Cushions, Quik-Fix Emergency Denture Repair Kit, Brimms Denture Bath, Curve-Clean Denture Brush, Ban-A-Stain Denture Cleanser, NFL Guardian Mouth Guards & Guardian Eye Glass Holders, Carry Clean Travel Toothbrush, Metal & Plastic Kazoos, Pertussin Cough & Cold Remedy, Nutra-Soothe Medicine Bath
S.I.C.: 2844; 2834; 3999; 3949; 3931
Robert Berghash *(Chief Exec. Officer)*
David Berghash *(Pres.)*
Robert N. Sarrasin *(Exec. V.P.)*
Mark Berghash *(Exec. V.P.)*
Karl Kuechler *(Controller)*
James Geraci *(Dir.-Sls.)*
Elizabeth Wing *(Intl. Sls. Admin.)*
Peter Baumgartner *(Mgr.-Quality Control)*
Roslyn Sciascia *(Mgr.-Pur.)*

Computer Systems/Hardware:
Rexon Basic IV

BRINK ELECTRIC CONSTRUCTION COMPANY
2950 N. Plaza Dr.
Rapid City, SD 57702
Tel.: 605-342-6966
Approx.Sls.: $11,000,000
Emp.: 140
Fiscal Year-end: 4/30/92
Transmission Power Lines & Substation Contractors & Industrial Electrical Contractors
S.I.C.: 1623; 1629
Jay Brink *(Chief Exec. Officer)*
Douglas Brink *(Pres.)*
Duane Brink *(Chief Fin. Officer)*
Howard Sutterfield *(Treas.)*
Wayne Bordewyk *(V.P.-Opers.)*
Lyle Brink *(V.P.-Mktg.)*

Outside Service Firm(s):

Melvin Wedmore*(Legal Firm)*
Rapid City, SD

First Bank of South Dakota*(Major Banking Relationship)*
Rapid City, SD

Division:

Brink Equipment & Supply Company **(1)**
2230 Rand Rd.
Rapid City, SD 57709
Tel.: 605-342-6966
Construction Material & Equipment Supplier
S.I.C.: 5063
Duane Brink *(Pres.)*

FRANK BRISCOE CO. INC.
Briscoe Building
Roseland, NJ 07068
Mailing Address:
3 ADP Boulevard
Roseland, NJ 07068
Tel.: 201-533-1000 **NJ**
Year Founded: 1920
Sales Range: $20-39 Million
Emp.: 25
Fiscal Year-end: 12/31/90
Building, Stadium, Race Track & Sewage Treatment Plants Construction
S.I.C.: 1541; 1542; 1623; 1629
Gabriel R. Calafati *(Chm. Bd., Pres. & Treas.)*
John Parrinello, Jr. *(Exec. V.P.)*
Peter G. Calafati *(V.P.)*
Robert D. Muccino *(Controller & Sec.)*

Principal(s):
Gabriel R. Calafati

No. of U.S. Offices: 2

Computer Systems/Hardware:
IBM System 36

Outside Service Firm(s):

KPMG Peat Marwick*(Auditors)*
150 John F. Kennedy Pkwy.
Short Hills, NJ 07078
Tel.: 201-467-9650

Blue Cross of New Jersey*(Group Insurer)*
Newark, NJ

Greenberg, Margolis, Ziegler, Schwartz, Dratch, Franzblau & Falkin*(Legal Firm)*
Roseland, NJ

Levy, Schlessinger & Briteman*(Legal Firm)*
Roseland, NJ

United Jersey Bank*(Major Banking Relationship)*
Newark, NJ

Prudential Insurance Co. of America*(Pension Manager)*
751 Broad St.
Newark, NJ 07102-3777
Tel.: 201-802-6000

BRISTOL INDUSTRIES
630 E. Lambert Rd.
Brea, CA 92621
Tel.: 714-990-4121 **CA**
Fax: 714-529-6726
Year Founded: 1978
Approx.Sls.: $25,000,000
Emp.: 300
Export
Mfr. Aerospace Fasteners
S.I.C.: 3452
Frank A. Klaus *(Pres.)*
Myron E. Harpole *(V.P.)*
James Mineo *(V.P. & Gen. Mgr.)*
Gerald Katzman *(Sec.)*
Wendy Guertz *(Mgr.-Fin.)*

Outside Service Firm(s):

Robert P. McDaniel*(Auditors)*
Brea, CA

Bank of America NT&SA*(Major Banking Relationship)*
Brea, CA

BRISTOL PRODUCTS, L.P.
(Formerly Bristol Corporation)
P.O. Box 1900,
Bristol, IN 46507
Tel.: 219-848-7681 **IN**
Fax: 219-848-7878
Year Founded: 1947
Approx.Sls.: $105,000,000
Emp.: 450
Fiscal Year-end: 11/30/92
Import
Mfr. of & Distr. of Plumbing Products
S.I.C.: 3089; 5074
John F. Turben *(Chm. Bd.)*
William J. Schmuhl, Jr. *(Pres. & Treas.)*
John G. Nestor *(Sec.)*
Kevin Hochstedler *(Controller & Asst. Treas.)*

No. of Mfg. Plants/Facilities: 4
No. of U.S. Offices: 13
No. of Foreign Offices: 1

Computer Systems/Hardware:
IBM System 36

Outside Service Firm(s):

Ernst & Young*(Auditors)*
2300 Fort Wayne Natl. Bank Bldg.
Fort Wayne, IN 46802

Metropolitan Life Insurance Co.*(Group Insurer)*
One Madison Ave.
New York, NY 10010-3690
Tel.: 215-578-9292

Barnes & Thornburg*(Legal Firm)*
100 N. Michigan., Ste. 600
South Bend, IN 46601
Tel.: 219-233-1171

Jones, Day, Reavis & Pogue*(Legal Firm)*
901 Lakeside Ave.
Cleveland, OH 44114
Tel.: 216-586-3939
Fax: 216-579-0212

Continental Bank N. A.*(Major Banking Relationship)*
231 S. LaSalle St.
Chicago, IL 60697
Tel.: 312-828-2345
Tel.: 800-426-5754
Telex: 312-828-1783

Divisions:

BPC Division **(1)**
State Rd. 15 South
Bristol, IN 46507
Tel.: 219-848-7681 (100%)
Emp.: 275
Manufacture & Distribute Plumbing Supplies to Manufactured Housing & Recreational Vehicle Industry; Miscellaneous Plastic Products
S.I.C.: 3089; 5074
William Kuehne *(Pres.)*

Bristolipe Division **(1)**
503 Vistula St.
Bristol, IN 46507
Tel.: 219-848-4402 (100%)
Emp.: 100
Extruder of Plastic Pipe & Tubing
S.I.C.: 3089
John Minelli *(Pres.)*

J & B Products **(1)**
461 N. Niles Ave.
South Bend, IN 46617
Tel.: 219-288-0607
Emp.: 50
Import
Mfrs. a Complete Line of Plastic Tubular Products Sold Primarily to the Conventional Housing Industry
S.I.C.: 3089
Patrick Delahanty *(Gen. Mgr.)*

BRISTOL STEEL & IRON WORKS, INC.
300 Piedmont St.
Bristol, VA 24201
Mailing Address:
P.O. Box 2147
Bristol, VA 24203
Tel.: 703-466-2241 VA
Fax: 703-645-9469
Year Founded: 1908
Assets: $65,000,000
Net Worth: $65,000,000
Approx.Sls.: $75,000,000
Emp.: 20
Fiscal Year-end: 9/30/90
Fabricates Structural Steel & Mfr. Concrete Prods. & Steel Erection
S.I.C.: 1791; 3441; 3271
Kenneth H. Cullum *(Pres. & Chief Exec. Officer)*
C. Farnham Jarrard, Jr. *(Sr. V.P.)*
Ned W. Shaw *(V.P.-Fin., Treas. & Chief Fin. Officer)*
Otis L. Hurt *(Consultant)*

No. of Mfg. Plants/Facilities: 6
No. of U.S. Offices: 5

Computer Systems/Hardware:
IBM 3800

Outside Service Firm(s):

Dent K. Burk*(Auditors)*
Bristol, VA
Tel.: 703-669-6171

Liberty Mutual*(Commercial Insurance Carrier)*
Boston, MA

Aetna Life & Casualty*(Group Insurer)*
151 Farmington Avenue
Hartford, CT 06156
Tel.: 203-273-2128
Fax: 203-729-4295

Penn, Stuart & Eskridge*(Legal Firm)*
Bristol, VA

Division:

Atlanta Structural Concrete Div. **(1)**
P.O. Box 5,
Powder Springs, GA 30073
Tel.: 404-943-5951
Approx.Sls.: $3,000,000
Emp.: 45
Prestressed Concrete
S.I.C.: 3272
Clyde E. Poovey *(Gen. Mgr.)*

Subsidiary:

Bristol Concrete Prods. Corp. **(1)**
111 E. Mary St.
Bristol, VA 24201
Tel.: 703-669-7112 (100%)
Approx.Sls.: $2,000,000
Emp.: 55
Mfrs. Concrete Block
S.I.C.: 3271
Freddie W. Hayter *(Pres.)*

Subsidiary:

Tri-State Concrete Products Co., Inc. **(2)**
Hwy. 11 West
Kingsport, TN 37665
Tel.: 615-288-2131 (100%)
Approx.Sls.: $2,000,000
Emp.: 25
Mfr. Concrete Masonry Prods.
S.I.C.: 3271
Fred W. Hayter *(Pres.)*

BRITTANY CORPORATION
1770 Huntington Bldg.
Cleveland, OH 44115
Tel.: 216-589-4977 OH
Fax: 216-589-0544
Year Founded: 1978
Approx.Sls.: $160,000,000
Emp.: 1,520
Fiscal Year-end: 12/31/91
Metal Stampings; Gray Iron Castings; Thermoformed Finished Plastic Products; Stoneware Pottery Products; Bedroom & Dining Room Wooden Furniture; Unassembled Or Unfinished Wooden Household Furniture
S.I.C.: 3469; 3321; 3089; 3269; 2511
Charles P. Bolton *(Chm. Bd.)*
Forrest Hayes *(Pres.)*
Kent Frisley *(V.P.)*
Jerome R. Gratry *(V.P.)*
Janet M. Tilton *(Controller)*

No. of Mfg. Plants/Facilities: 15
No. of U.S. Offices: 16

Outside Service Firm(s):

Hausser & Taylor*(Auditors)*
Cleveland, OH

Jones, Day, Reavis & Pogue*(Legal Firm)*
901 Lakeside Ave.
Cleveland, OH 44114
Tel.: 216-586-3939
Fax: 216-579-0212

BRITTANY DYEING & PRINTING CORPORATION
1357 E. Rodney French Blvd.
New Bedford, MA 02744
Tel.: 508-999-3281 MA
Year Founded: 1959
Approx.Sls.: $18,000,000
Emp.: 300
Dyeing Cotton Broadwoven Fabrics; Printing of Cotton Broadwoven Fabrics; Dyeing & Finishing Circular Knit Fabrics
S.I.C.: 2261; 2257
Kenneth Joblon *(Pres.)*
Jack Edreich *(Treas. & Sec.)*

Outside Service Firm(s):

Shawmut Arlington Bank*(Major Banking Relationship)*
Lawrence, MA

BRIX MARITIME CO.
9030 N.W. St. Helen's Rd.
Portland, OR 97231
Mailing Address:
P.O. Box 83018,
Portland, OR 97283-0018
Tel.: 503-286-0631
Tel.: 800-882-4143 DE
Fax: 503-286-1775
Year Founded: 1937
Assets: $50,001,142
Earnings: $907,594
Liabilities: $40,558,107
Net Worth: $9,443,035
Approx.Rev.: $46,094,000
Emp.: 296
Fiscal Year-end: 12/31/90
River & Ocean Transportation
S.I.C.: 4449; 4492; 4491
Peter J. Brix *(Chm. Bd. & Chief Exec. Officer)*
Edward S. Beall *(Pres. & Chief Oper. Officer)*
Robert A. Hindman *(Sr. V.P.-Fin., Treas. & Sec.)*
Laury L. Cooper *(Controller)*
E. Whitney Olson *(V.P.-Mktg.)*
Wendy M. McMorine *(Mgr.-Human Resources)*

Computer Systems/Hardware:
IBM AS-400

Outside Service Firm(s):

Coopers & Lybrand*(Auditors)*
2700 First Interstate Tower, 1300 SW 5th Ave.
Portland, OR 97201

Schwabe, Williamson, Wyatt, Moore & Roberts*(Legal Firm)*
Portland, OR

Subsidiaries:

Brix Maritime Barging, Inc. **(1)**
9030 N.W. St. Helens Rd.
Portland, OR 97231
Tel.: 503-286-0631 (100%)
Approx.Sls.: $10,730,000
Emp.: 90
Marine Cargo, Towing & Tugboat
S.I.C.: 4449; 4492; 4491
Edwin R. Haglund *(V.P. & Gen. Mgr.)*
Robert A. Hindman *(Chief Fin. Officer)*

Brix Maritime Towing, Inc. **(1)**
Blackwell Island
Coeur D'Alene, ID 83814
Tel.: 208-664-8215
Towing & Tugboat Services
S.I.C.: 4492

BROAD VOGT & CONANT INC.
195 Campbell St.
River Rouge, MI 48218
Tel.: 313-841-8100 MI
Fax: 313-841-5241
Year Founded: 1943
Approx.Sls.: $48,000,000
Emp.: 525
Fiscal Year-end: 12/31/90
Structural Steel Construction; Structural Renovation
S.I.C.: 1791
John W. Broad *(Chm. Bd., Pres. & Chief Exec. Officer)*
William H. Treharne *(Exec. V.P.)*
B.R. Fair *(V.P. & Controller)*
Robert Piro *(Gen. Mgr. & V.P.-Proposals)*
R. Lewandowski *(Dir.-Pur.)*
Thomas Schultz *(Dir.-Data Processing)*
Christine Accetta *(Dir.-Corp. Mktg.)*

No. of U.S. Offices: 4
No. of Foreign Offices: 1

Outside Service Firm(s):

Arthur Andersen & Co.*(Auditors)*
400 Renaissance Center
Detroit, MI 48243
Tel.: 313-259-8100

Comerica Bank*(Major Banking Relationship)*
211 W. Fort St.
Detroit, MI 48226
Tel.: 313-222-3300

BROADCAST ELECTRONICS, INC.
4100 N. 24th St.
Quincy, IL 62301
Mailing Address:
P.O. Box 3606
Quincy, IL 62305
Tel.: 217-224-9600
Fax: 217-224-9607
Year Founded: 1959
Approx.Sls.: $16,000,000
Emp.: 150
Fiscal Year-end: 3/31/92
Export
Mfr. of Tape Cartridge Machines, Turntables & Audio Consoles; FM Broadcast Transmitters
S.I.C.: 3663
Howard M. Crow, Jr. *(Chm. Bd.)*
John J. Nevin *(Pres. & Chief Exec. Officer)*
Howard M. Crow *(Exec. V.P.)*
W.T. Ash *(V.P.-Opers.)*
G.N. Mendenhall *(V.P.-Engrng.)*
William A. Harland *(Dir.-Domestic Sls.)*
Tim A. Bealor *(Dir.-Mktg.)*
Don Rust *(Mgr.-Mfg.)*
Steve F. Wall *(Mgr.-Pub. Rels.)*
Elizabeth K. Keck *(Controller)*
Charles W. Kelly *(Intl. Bus. Contact)*
Edwin L. Miller *(Sec.)*
Kim Winking *(Mktg. Svc. Admin.)*

Computer Systems/Hardware:
IBM

BROADCAST SUPPLY WEST
7012 27th St., W.
Tacoma, WA 98466
Tel.: 206-565-2301
Tel.: 800-426-8434
Fax: 206-565-8114
Sales Range: $10-19 Million
Emp.: 31
Communication Equipment
S.I.C.: 5065
Irving D. Law, Jr. *(Chm. Bd. & Chief Fin. Officer)*
Bernice McCullough *(Pres.)*
Betty J. Law *(V.P.-Treas. & Sec.)*
Pat Medved *(V.P.-Sls.)*
Tim Schwieger *(V.P.-Mktg.)*

Outside Service Firm(s):

First Interstate Bank*(Major Banking Relationship)*
Tacoma, WA

BROADCAST TIME, INC.
1044 Northern Blvd.
Roslyn, NY 11576
Tel.: 516-484-9306
Fax: 516-484-9404
Year Founded: 1981
Approx.Billings: $24,800,000
Emp.: 15
Media Planning & Buying; Media Buying Service
Bruce Kuperschmid *(Pres.)*
Peter Kuperschmid *(Exec. V.P.)*
Frank Howlett *(V.P., Radio)*

BROADMOOR HOTEL, INC.
One Lake Ave. at Lake Circle
Colorado Springs, CO 80906
Mailing Address:
P.O. Box 1439
Colorado Springs, CO 80901
Tel.: 719-634-7711
Fax: 719-577-5700
Year Founded: 1917
Approx.Sls.: $35,000,000
Emp.: 1,500
Resort Accomodations, Sports Facilities, Etc.
S.I.C.: 7011
Edward L. Gaylord *(Chm. & Pres.)*
Karl E. Eitel *(Vice Chm.)*
William B. Tutt *(Sr. V.P.)*
G. Russell Freymuth *(V.P.)*
R. Thayer Tutt, Jr. *(V.P. & Treas.)*
Siegfried Faller *(Sls. Catering & Conferences Dir.)*
Richard Cotton *(Personnel Dir.)*
Juli Jamison *(Art. Dir.)*
Ed Pralle *(Pur. Agent)*

R.F. BROADUS & ASSOCIATES, INC.
3400 Peachtree Rd. NE, Ste. 1239
Atlanta, GA 30326
Tel.: 404-237-1503
Fax: 404-262-7052
Year Founded: 1980
Approx.Billings: $11,000,000
Emp.: 19
Direct Response Adv.: Real Estate, Resorts, Health Care, Business to Business
Jennifer M. Broadus *(Vice Chm. & Creative Dir.)*
Robert F. Broadus *(Chief Exec. Officer)*
Larry Weltin *(Pres.)*
Lauren Fuller *(Admin./Opers. & Pur.)*
Janet Morse *(Controller)*

Computer Systems/Hardware:
MacIntosh-Graphics, IBM-Network (Adman Software)

BROCK CANDY COMPANY
4120 Jersey Pike
Chattanooga, TN 37422
Mailing Address:
P.O. Box 22427
Chattanooga, TN 37422
Tel.: 615-899-1100 **TN**
Fax: 615-899-3223
Year Founded: 1906
Assets: $39,000,000
Liabilities: $19,000,000
Net Worth: $20,000,000
Approx.Sls.: $81,000,000
Emp.: 600
Fiscal Year-end: 6/30/91
Manufacture Candy
S.I.C.: 2064; 2066
Paul K. Brock *(Pres. & Chief Exec. Officer)*
Harry J. Cynkas *(V.P.-Fin.)*
David Brock *(V.P.-Mktg.)*
David Britain *(V.P. & Dir.-Plng.)*
Paul Brock, Jr. *(V.P.-Mfg.)*
Bob Davis *(V.P.-Engrng.)*
Harold D. Gilbert *(V.P.-Pur.)*
Mel Warnecke *(V.P.-Tech. Services)*
Gordon Fleming *(Sec. & Treas.)*
Randall Tussey *(Dir.-Personnel)*
Ward Crimmins *(Mgr.-Data Processing)*
Principal(s):
Paul K. Brock

No. of Mfg. Plants/Facilities: 3
No. of U.S. Offices: 1

Outside Service Firm(s):

Joseph Decosomio & Co.*(Auditors)*
Chattanooga, TN

Corroon & Black*(Commercial Insurance Carrier)*
Chattanooga, TN

Provident Life & Accident Insurance Co.*(Group Insurer)*
P.O. Box 12015
Chattanooga, TN 37401
Tel.: 615-755-7088

Miller & Martin*(Legal Firm)*
Chattanooga, TN

American National Bank & Trust Company of Chattanooga*(Major Banking Relationship)*
736 Market St.
Chattanooga, TN 37402
Tel.: 615-757-3011

Subsidiaries:

Brock Candy Co. (MN) **(1)**
1000 W. 5th St.
Winona, MN 55987
Tel.: 507-452-3433
Emp.: 120
Chocolates
S.I.C.: 2066
Ed Lindborg *(Pres.)*

Shelly Bros., Inc. **(1)**
P.O. Box 115
Souderton, PA 18964
Tel.: 215-723-8111
Manufacturer of Hard Candies
S.I.C.: 2064
Donald Pritchard *(Plant Mgr.)*

BROCK CONTROL SYSTEMS, INC.
2859 Paces Ferry Rd., Ste. 1000
Atlanta, GA 30339
Tel.: 404-431-1200
Tel.: 800-221-0775 **GA**
Fax: 404-431-1201
Year Founded: 1984
Approx.Sls.: $12,700,000
Emp.: 117
Fiscal Year-end: 12/31/91
Export
Multi-user Sales, Marketing & Service Information Management Systems
S.I.C.: 7389
Corporate Giving Program: World Vision Sponsor A Child
Employee Matching Gifts Program: 401k
Richard T. Brock *(Chm. Bd. & Chief Exec. Officer)*
Rodger L. Johnson *(Pres. & Chief Oper. Officer)*
Anthony J. Palermo *(Exec. V.P.-Services)*
Tom Clements *(V.P.-Sls.)*
Bud Pass *(V.P.-Devel.)*
Mark R. Noyd *(Chief Fin. Officer)*
Judi A. Vitale *(Controller)*
Mary Niman *(Dir.-Mktg.)*
Wayne Webb *(Intl. Bus. Mgr.)*
Elizabeth Stevenson *(Pub. Rels. Dir.)*
Donna Eckman *(Corp. Travel Planner)*

No. of U.S. Offices: 2

Outside Service Firm(s):

Price Waterhouse*(Auditors)*
100 Cumberland Circle, Ste. 1400
Atlanta, GA 30339

Davis & Neal*(Legal Firm)*
Altanta, GA

C & S National Bank*(Major Banking Relationship)*
Atlanta, GA
Tel.: 404-392-2984

J. C. BROCK CORP.
25 Hardwood Pl.
Buffalo, NY 14210
Mailing Address:
P.O. Box 832
Buffalo, NY 14240
Tel.: 617-229-5751 **NY**
Fax: 716-827-5823
Year Founded: 1947
Approx.Sls.: $18,000,000
Emp.: 200
Fiscal Year-end: 3/31/91
Process, Package & Retail Fresh Fruits & Vegetables
S.I.C.: 5148; 5431
Joseph C. Brock *(Chief Exec. Officer)*
David Schwartz *(Pres.)*
Joseph Patti *(V.P.-Sls. & Admin.)*
Mark W. Crotty *(Controller & Sec.)*
David Paluch *(Dir.-Opers.)*
Jerry Queen *(Dir.-Pur.)*
Kathleen Toolen *(Dir.-Personnel)*

Computer Systems/Hardware:
Quantel

Outside Service Firm(s):

Freed, Maxick, Sachs & Murphy*(Auditors)*
Buffalo, NY
Tel.: 716-847-2651

Fleet Bank*(Major Banking Relationship)*
Deer Park, NY 14202

Subsidiary:

J. C. Brock Canada, Ltd **(1)**
HollandSt.
Bradford, ON L3Z 2A9, Canada
Tel.: 416-775-3367
Emp.: 30
Packaging Fresh Produce, Carrots
S.I.C.: 0723
Stefan Zurawski *(Plant Mgr.)*

M. J. BROCK & SONS, INC.
6767 Forest Lawn Dr.
Los Angeles, CA 90068
Tel.: 213-851-6767
Fax: 213-969-0529
Approx.Sls.: $150,000,000
Emp.: 200
General Contracting; Land Development; Commercial & Industrial Construction
S.I.C.: 1521; 1541; 6552
John D. Napolitan *(Pres.)*
Les Thomas *(V.P.)*

Outside Service Firm(s):

Ernst & Young*(Auditors)*
515 S. Flower St.
Los Angeles, CA 90071
Tel.: 213-621-1666

Irsfeld, Irsfeld & Younger*(Legal Firm)*
Glendale, CA

Security Pacific Corporation*(Major Banking Relationship)*
Security Pacific Plaza
Los Angeles, CA 90071
Tel.: 213-345-6211
Fax: 213-625-0809

GEORGE F. BROCKE & SONS, INC.
Second St. & Brown
Kendrick, ID 83537
Mailing Address:
P.O. Box 159
Kendrick, ID 83537
Tel.: 208-289-4231
Fax: 208-289-4242
Emp.: 35
Dehydrated Fruits, Vegetables, Soups; Fertilizer & Fertilizer Materials; Chemicals, Agricultural, Seeds
S.I.C.: 2034; 5191
George F. Brocke, Jr. *(Pres.)*
Darrel Brocke *(V.P.)*
Dean Brocke *(Treas.)*
Eugene Brocke *(Sec.)*

Outside Service Firm(s):

Clements, Clements & Brown*(Legal Firm)*
Lewiston, ID

BRODBECK ENTERPRISES, INC.
1035 E. Hwy. 151
Platteville, WI 53818
Mailing Address:
P.O. Box 656
Platteville, WI 53818
Tel.: 608-348-2345 **WI**
Fax: 608-348-3345
Year Founded: 1950
Sales Range: $60-79 Million
Emp.: 750
Supermarkets; Restaurants; Bakeries; Floral Shops, Video Rental, Book & Liquor Stores
S.I.C.: 5411; 5461; 5812; 5992; 5735; 5921; 5942
Corporate Giving Program: Brodbeck Foundation
William J. Brodbeck *(Pres. & Chief Exec. Officer)*
Robert J. Brodbeck *(Sr. V.P. & Chief Oper. Officer)*
Richard Taggart *(V.P.-Fin. & Chief Fin. Officer)*
Barry Brodbeck *(V.P.-Human Resources)*
Gary Fritz *(V.P.-Mktg.)*

Outside Service Firm(s):

Ernst & Young*(Auditors)*
111 E. Kilbourn Ave., Ste. 900
Milwaukee, WI 53202
Tel.: 414-273-5900

First National Bank of Platteville*(Major Banking Relationship)*
Platteville, WI

BRODER BROS. CO.
45555 Port St.
Plymouth, MI 48170
Tel.: 313-454-4800
Tel.: 800-543-4200 **MI**
Fax: 313-454-8971
Year Founded: 1919
Assets: $16,725,718
Liabilities: $12,858,556
Net Worth: $3,867,162
Approx.Sls.: $64,077,000
Emp.: 130
Fiscal Year-end: 12/31/90
Import
Distribution of Imprintable Sportswear
S.I.C.: 5136; 5137
Harold Brode *(Pres. & Chief Exec. Officer)*
David Margolis *(Chief Fin. Officer)*
Barry Zagerman *(Exec. V.P.)*
Michael Brode *(V.P. & Treas.)*
Todd Turkin *(V.P., Sec. & Dir.-Telecommunications)*
Robert Heidrich *(Dir.-Personnel)*
Mark Brode *(Mgr.-Warehouse & Asst. V.P.)*
Principal(s):
Harold Brode

No. of Mfg. Plants/Facilities: 2

Computer Systems/Hardware:
Honeywell

Outside Service Firm(s):

Morof, Sheplow, Weinstein & Co.*(Auditors)*
Detroit, MI

Meadowbrook Insurance Group*(Commercial Insurance Carrier)*
Southfield, MI

The Enterprise Group*(Group Insurer)*
Southfield, MI

Lionel Margolick*(Investment Banker)*
Southfield, MI

Maddin, Hauser, Wartell, Roth, Heller & Pesses*(Legal Firm)*
Southfield, MI

Comerica Bank*(Major Banking Relationship)*
211 W. Fort St.
Detroit, MI 48226
Tel.: 313-222-3300

Pension Consultants, Inc.*(Pension Manager)*
Farmington Hills, MI

Affiliate:

Broder Bros. Co. Of Florida, Inc. **(1)**
1255 LaQuinta Dr., Bldg. 130
Orlando, FL 32809
Tel.: 407-240-5590
Tel.: 800-521-0850
Wholesale Distributor Of Imprintable Sportswear
S.I.C.: 5136; 5137
Harold Brode *(Pres. & Chief Exec. Officer)*
Barry Zagerman *(Exec. V.P.)*
Todd Turkin *(V.P.)*
David Margolis *(Controller)*
Mark Rosenberg *(Mgr.)*

BRODHEAD-GARRETT CO.
223 S. Illinois Ave.
Mansfield, OH 44905
Tel.: 419-589-8222
Fax: 419-589-1517
Approx.Sls.: $40,000,000
Emp.: 300
Mfr. & Sale Educational Equip. & Programs for Schools; Brodhead Garrett & Taylor Woodcraft
S.I.C.: 5021; 5199
James Miller *(Pres.)*
Doug Dever *(Controller)*
Garrett Reid *(Mktg. Dir.)*
Craig Garfield *(Sls. & Mktg. Mgr.)*

Division:

Taylor Woodcraft **(1)**
Box 245, S. River Rd.
Malta, OH 43750
Tel.: 614-962-3741
S.I.C.: 5021

BROGAN & PARTNERS ADVERTISING/PUBLIC RELATIONS INC
2000 Fisher Bldg.
Detroit, MI 48202
Tel.: 313-874-8555
Fax: 313-874-8565
Year Founded: 1984
Approx.Billings: $18,000,000
Emp.: 20
Service, Retail, Healthcare, Automotive, Business-to-Business Adv., Public Relations & Promotions
Thomas B. Adams *(Chm.-Advisory Bd.)*
Marcia Brogan *(Mng. Partner)*
Barbara Palazzolo *(Partner & Pub. Rels.)*
Maria Marcotte *(Partner/Bus. Mgr.)*

WILLIAM BROJACK LUMBER COMPANY
Sales Range: $20-39 Million
Emp.: 35
Import Export
Sawmill & Planing Mill, Dimensional Lumber & Plywood
S.I.C.: 2421; 2426; 2435
William Brojack *(Pres.)*
Robert Cordaro *(Gen. Counsel)*
David Brojack *(Gen. Mgr.)*
Principal(s):
William Brojack

Outside Service Firm(s):

Jeffrey C. Webb*(Auditors)*
Olyphant, PA

First National Bank of Lake Ariel*(Major Banking Relationship)*
Eynon, PA

BROMAR INC.
15 Corporate Plaza
Newport Beach, CA 92660
Mailing Address:
P.O. Box 7908,
Newport Beach, CA 92658
Tel.: 714-640-6221 **CA**
Fax: 714-640-5813
Year Founded: 1892
Assets: $24,400,000
Liabilities: $17,100,000
Net Worth: $7,300,000
Approx.Sls.: $45,700,000
Emp.: 850
Fiscal Year-end: 12/31/90
Food Brokers & Importers
S.I.C.: 6221
W.N. Tahan *(Chm. & Chief Exec. Officer)*
Steve Parten *(Pres. & Chief Oper. Officer)*
D.J. Gaidano *(Chief Fin. Officer & Exec. V.P.)*
James Smith *(Sr. V.P.)*
Leo Shepherd *(V.P.)*
Thomas Oneto *(Treas.)*
Matthew Ketsdever *(Controller)*
John Hill *(Dir.-Mngmt. Information Services)*

No. of U.S. Offices: 15

Computer Systems/Hardware:
Hewlett Packard 3000, Model 937

Outside Service Firm(s):

Ernst & Young*(Auditors)*
3200 Park Center Dr., Ste. 900
Costa Mesa, CA 92626
Tel.: 714-850-9500
Fax: 714-850-9441

Johnson & Higgins*(Commercial Insurance Carrier)*
Costa Mesa, CA

McCutchen, Doyle, Brown & Enersen*(Legal Firm)*
3 Embacadero Ctr.
San Francisco, CA 94111
Tel.: 415-393-2000

Wells Fargo Bank*(Major Banking Relationship)*
Newport Beach, CA

Subsidiary:

Service Assets Corp. **(1)**
15 Corporate Plaza
Newport Beach, CA 92660
Tel.: 714-640-6221
Emp.: 3
Auto Leasing
S.I.C.: 7514
James T. Smith, Jr. *(Pres.)*
Matthew Ketsdever *(Treas.)*
Don J. Gaidano *(Sec.)*

BRONNER SLOSBERG HUMPHREY
695 Atlantic Ave.
Boston, MA 02111
Tel.: 617-737-2020
Fax: 617-951-2979
Year Founded: 1980
Approx.Billings: $310,000,000
Emp.: 400
Direct Response Adv.
Stephen Humphrey *(Pres.)*
Michael Bronner *(Chief Exec. Officer & New Bus. Contact)*
Robert Stoloff *(Sr. V.P., Chief Fin. Officer)*

BRONSON LEIGH WEEKS
5331 SW Macadam, Ste. 283
Portland, OR 97201
Tel.: 503-222-3546
Fax: 503-227-2369
Year Founded: 1972
Approx.Billings: $10,000,000
Emp.: 13
Dave Bronson *(Pres.)*
Todd Underwood *(Opers. Mgr.)*

BROOKFIELD ENGINEERING LABORATORIES, INC.
240 Cushing St.
Stoughton, MA 02072
Tel.: 617-344-4310
Tel.: 800-628-8139
Fax: 617-344-7141
Approx.Sls.: $11,000,000
Emp.: 130
Export
Mfr. of Viscosity Measuring Instruments
S.I.C.: 3821; 3829
Donald W. Brookfield *(Chm. Bd.)*
Louis A. DiCorpo *(Pres.)*
David A. Brookfield *(V.P.-Engrng.)*
Rob McGregor *(V.P.-Sls. & Adv.)*
James Owen *(Controller)*
William L. Paull *(Sls. Engineer)*

Outside Service Firm(s):

First National Bank*(Major Banking Relationship)*
Boston, MA

BROOKHURST, INC.
107 W. Carob
Compton, CA 90220
Tel.: 310-631-3500
Fax: 310-763-3846
Emp.: 300
Manufacture Mens & Womens Uniforms
S.I.C.: 2311; 2337
Fred Halpam *(Chm. Bd.)*
William Ott *(Pres.)*

Outside Service Firm(s):

Price Waterhouse*(Auditors)*
400 S. Hope St.
Los Angeles, CA 90071-2889
Tel.: 213-236-3000

BROOKLYN BOTTLING CO.
(Formerly Hudson Valley Apple Products Company)
P.O. Box 808
Milton, NY 12547
Tel.: 914-795-2171
Fax: 914-795-2589
Approx.Sls.: $25,000,000
Emp.: 80
Juices, Flavored Bottled Drinks & Spring Water
S.I.C.: 5149; 5148
Eric Miller *(Pres.)*
William F. Schneible *(Sec. & Treas.)*

Outside Service Firm(s):

Murray, Wilson & Hunter*(Auditors)*
Longhorne, PA

Atlantic Financial Federal*(Major Banking Relationship)*
Philadelphia, PA

BROOKS BEVERAGE MANAGEMENT, INC.
777 Brooks Ave.
Holland, MI 49423
Tel.: 616-396-1281 **MI**
Fax: 616-392-3291
Year Founded: 1934
Assets: $95,000,000
Net Worth: $95,000,000
Approx.Sls.: $350,000,000
Emp.: 1,500
Fiscal Year-end: 12/31/90
Soft Drinks & Beverages
S.I.C.: 2086
James W. Brooks *(Chm. & Chief Exec. Officer)*
George P. Julius, Jr. *(Pres. & Chief Oper. Officer)*
Michael R. Mucciolo *(Chief Fin. Officer & Sr. V.P.)*
James E. Sanderson *(V.P., Gen. Counsel & Sec.)*
Jim Sanderson *(V.P.-Real Estate)*
Tom Schippers *(V.P. & Treas.)*
Mike Nelson *(V.P.-Pension Admin.)*
Ken Stump *(Controller)*
Teresa Beagle *(Admin. Asst.)*

No. of Mfg. Plants/Facilities: 4
No. of U.S. Offices: 9

Computer Systems/Hardware:
Hewlett-Packard; Honeywell

Outside Service Firm(s):

Coopers & Lybrand*(Auditors)*
161 Ottawa Ave., N.W.
Grand Rapids, MI 49503
Tel.: 616-458-7700

Johnson & Higgins*(Commercial Insurance Carrier)*
600 Renaissance Center, Ste. 2100
Detroit, MI 48243

Employee Benefit Administrators*(Group Insurer)*
Grand Rapids, MI

James E. Sanderson*(Legal Firm)*
Grand Rapids, MI

First Michigan Bank*(Major Banking Relationship)*
Holland, MI

First Michigan Bank*(Pension Manager)*
Holland, MI

Subsidiaries:

Brooks Beverages Inc. **(1)**
1900 E. Dublin-Granville Rd., Ste. 200-D
Columbus, OH 43229
Tel.: 614-895-6880
Emp.: 950
Soft Drink Bottling
S.I.C.: 2086
Michael J. Coughlin *(Exec. V.P.)*
W. Mike Nelson *(V.P.-Human Resources & Legal)*
Peter P. Sullivan *(V.P.-Fin.)*
W. Michael Sullivan *(Gen. Counsel)*
Jerome Henderson *(Controller)*
Tom Levenick *(Dir.-Mktg. & Sls.)*

Beverage Management, Inc. **(1)**
777 Brooks Ave.
Holland, MI 49423
Tel.: 616-393-5800
Fax: 616-396-9770
Emp.: 500
Soft Drinks
S.I.C.: 2086
Dean L. Aukeman *(V.P.)*
Dennis H. Eade *(V.P.-Human Resources)*

Seven-Up Bottling Co. of Akron **(1)**
1477 Industrial Pkwy.
Akron, OH 44310
Tel.: 216-633-6677
Manufacture of Soft Drinks
S.I.C.: 2086
B.D. Smith *(Gen. Mgr.)*

Seven-Up Bottling Co. of Cleveland **(1)**
14301 Industrial Ave. N.
Maple Heights, OH 44137
Tel.: 216-475-4477
Manufacture of Soft Drinks
S.I.C.: 2086
Rodger L. Collins *(V.P.)*

Seven-Up Bottling Co. of Dayton **(1)**
3131 Transportation Rd.
Dayton, OH 45404
Tel.: 513-236-0333
Manufacture of Soft Drinks
S.I.C.: 2086
Michael A. Beekman *(V.P.)*

Seven-Up Bottling Co. of Detroit **(1)**
12201 Beech Daly Rd.
Detroit, MI 48239
Tel.: 313-937-3500
Fax: 313-937-3591
Manufacture of Soft Drinks
S.I.C.: 2086
James E. Miller *(Gen. Mgr.)*

Seven-Up Royal Crown-Canada Dry of Cincinnati **(1)**
5151 Fischer Ave.
Cincinnati, OH 45217
Tel.: 513-242-5151
Manufacture of Soft Drinks
S.I.C.: 2086
Mark Wendling *(Gen. Mgr.)*

Seven-Up Royal Crown Canada Dry of Columbus **(1)**
950 Stelzer Rd.
Columbus, OH 43219
Tel.: 614-237-4201
Manufacture of Soft Drinks
S.I.C.: 2086
Michael T. Strall *(V.P.)*

E. J. BROOKS COMPANY
164-192 N. 13th St.
Newark, NJ 07107
Tel.: 201-483-0335
Tel.: 800-458-7325
Telex: 132-026
Fax: 201-483-1936
Year Founded: 1873
Approx.Sls.: $30,000,000
Emp.: 350
Import Export
Mfr. Plastic, Lead & Metal Security Seals & Sealing Devices
S.I.C.: 3089; 3356; 3399
John K. Roessner III *(Chm. Bd. & Pres.)*
Albert Dreisbach *(Exec. V.P.)*
Michael Abatemarco *(V.P. & Gen. Mgr.)*
Frank Agnelli *(Plant Mgr.)*
Paul Dietlin *(Mgr.-Sls.)*
George Kozimor *(Mgr.-Mktg.)*
George Weber *(Pur. Agent)*

Outside Service Firm(s):

Berger & Bornstein*(Legal Firm)*
Newark, NJ

E. J. Brooks Company—(Continued)

Subsidiary:

Ekstrom Industries, Inc. **(1)**
23850 Freeway Park Dr.
Farmington Hills, MI 48335
Tel.: 313-477-0040
Fax: 313-477-2583
Emp.: 55
Import Export
Mfr. Meter Socket Adapters & Test Devices for Utility Companies
S.I.C.: 3825; 3829; 3621
John K. Roessner III *(Pres.)*
Albert J. Dreisbach *(Treas.)*
Sharon Dees *(Dir.-Admin.)*
Michael E. Lewis *(Mgr.-Sls. & Mktg.)*

JOHN W. BROOKS INC.
(d/b/a Rocky Shoes and Boots)
294 Harper St.
Nelsonville, OH 45764
Tel.: 614-753-1951
Fax: 614-753-4024
Approx.Sls.: $12,000,000
Emp.: 250
Manufacture Men's & Women's Shoes
S.I.C.: 3143; 3144; 3149
John W. Brooks *(Chm. Bd.)*
John M. Brooks *(Pres.)*
Gloria J. Brooks *(V.P.)*
David S. Fraedrich *(V.P., Sec. & Treas.)*
Robert Holenbaugh *(V.P.-Sls.)*
Michael Nolan *(Gen. Counsel)*
Jim McCumber *(Mgr.-Data Processing Systems)*
Principal(s):
John W. Brooks
John M. Brooks
Gloria J. Brooks

Computer Systems/Hardware:
IBM System 36

Outside Service Firm(s):

Norman, Jones, Enlow & Co.*(Auditors)*
Lancaster, OH

Manufacturers National Bank N.A.*(Major Banking Relationship)*
38th Fl., 100 Renaissance Center
Detroit, MI 48243
Tel.: 313-222-4227

BROOKS PRODUCTS, INC.
10141 Olney St.
El Monte, CA 91734
Mailing Address:
P.O. Box 4488
El Monte, CA 91731
Tel.: 818-443-5650 **CA**
Fax: 818-443-5538
Year Founded: 1910
Assets: $30,000,000
Liabilities: $18,500,000
Net Worth: $11,500,000
Approx.Sls.: $48,000,000
Emp.: 500
Fiscal Year-end: 12/31/90
Export
Manufacture Precast Concrete & Plastic Structures for Underground Utilities
S.I.C.: 3271; 3089; 3272
Frederick C. Heitman *(Pres.)*
Dean Mills *(Chief Fin. Officer & Treas.)*
Fred Crane *(Controller)*
Principal(s):
Frederick C. Heitman

No. of Mfg. Plants/Facilities: 16
No. of U.S. Offices: 18

Computer Systems/Hardware:
PC Local Area Networks

Outside Service Firm(s):

Deloitte & Touche*(Auditors)*
Newport Beach, CA

CNA Insurance*(Commercial Insurance Carrier)*
CNA Plaza,
Chicago, IL 60685
Tel.: 312-822-5000

Troy & Casden*(Legal Firm)*
Century City, CA

Security Pacific Corporation*(Major Banking Relationship)*
Security Pacific Plaza
Los Angeles, CA 90071
Tel.: 213-345-6211
Fax: 213-625-0809

Divisions:

Brooks Products, Arlington **(1)**
2001 W. Mayfield Rd.
Arlington, TX 76015
Tel.: 817-465-0080
Manufacture Precast Concrete & Plastic Structures for Underground Utilities
S.I.C.: 3089; 3271; 3272

Brooks Products, Orlando **(1)**
690 Taft-Vineland Rd.
Orlando, FL 32824
Tel.: 407-855-7580
Manufacture Precast Concrete & Plastic Structures for Underground Utilities
S.I.C.: 3089; 3271; 3272

Brooks Products, Stockton **(1)**
2441 Charter Way
Stockton, CA 95206
Tel.: 209-464-7696
Gary Leapic *(Div. Mgr.)*

Polyplastic Products **(1)**
10220 4th St.
Rancho Cucamonga, CA 91730
Tel.: 909-987-8966
Manufacture Plastic Structures
S.I.C.: 3089; 3271; 3272
Bob Soulerin *(Div. Mgr.)*

BROOKS PROVISIONS INC.
3445 S. Front St.
Philadelphia, PA 19148
Tel.: 215-465-3100 **PA**
Fax: 215-465-3259
Approx.Sls.: $120,000,000
Emp.: 80
Wholesale Meat & Meat Products
S.I.C.: 5147
Biagio De Mento, Sr. *(Pres. & Chief Exec. Officer)*
Albert Brody *(V.P.)*
Marty Brody *(V.P.)*
Robert De Mento *(Sec. & Treas.)*
Principal(s):
Biagio De Mento, Sr.

Computer Systems/Hardware:
IBM

Outside Service Firm(s):

Philadelphia National Bank*(Major Banking Relationship)*
P.O. Box 13834, Broad & Chestnut Streets
Philadelphia, PA 19101-7618
Tel.: 215-973-8327

BROOKS RESOURCES CORPORATION
416 N.E. Greenwood
Bend, OR 97701
Tel.: 503-382-1662
Fax: 503-385-3285
Emp.: 12
Real Estate Development
S.I.C.: 6552
Michael P. Hollern *(Chm. Bd. & Pres.)*
Paul H. Buchanan *(V.P. & Broker)*

Outside Service Firm(s):

KPMG Peat Marwick*(Auditors)*
1211 S.W. Fifth Ave.
Portland, OR 97204

Miller, Nash, Wiener, Hager & Carlsen*(Legal Firm)*
900 S.W. Fifth Ave.
Portland, OR 97204
Tel.: 503-224-5858

U.S. National Bank*(Major Banking Relationship)*
309 S.W. Sixth Ave.
Portland, OR 97208
Tel.: 503-275-4942

Subsidiary:

Mount Bachelor Village Corp. **(1)**
19717 Mt. Bachelor Dr.
Bend, OR 97705
Tel.: 503-389-5900
Real Estate Development
S.I.C.: 6552
Sue Cailliet *(Gen. Mgr.)*

BROOKSHIRE BROS., INC.
1201 Ellen Trout Dr.
Lufkin, TX 75901
Mailing Address:
P.O. Box 1688
Lufkin, TX 75901
Tel.: 409-634-8155
Fax: 409-634-9198
Approx.Sls.: $390,000,000
Emp.: 3,500
Retail Groceries
S.I.C.: 5141; 5411
Eugene Brookshire *(Chm. Bd.)*
R. A. Brookshire *(Pres.)*
Gene H. Nerren *(Exec. V.P. & Treas.)*
Owen Ray Campbell *(V.P.)*
Jim Roper *(V.P.)*
Buddy Colmer *(Dir.-Pur.)*
Wayne Wilkerson *(Sec.)*

Outside Service Firm(s):

Alexander, Longford & Heirs*(Auditors)*
Lufkin, TX

Zeleskey, Cornelius, Rogers, Hallmark & Borgfeld*(Legal Firm)*
Lufkin, TX

First City National Bank of Lufkin*(Major Banking Relationship)*
Lufkin, TX

BROOKSHIRE GROCERY
P.O. Box 1411, 1600 W.S.W. Coop 323
Tyler, TX 75701
Tel.: 903-534-3000
Fax: 214-903-3272
Emp.: 7,700
Retail Grocery Business, Supermarkets
S.I.C.: 5411
Bruce G. Brookshire *(Chm. & Chief Exec. Officer)*
Harvey King *(Vice Chm., Fin. & Sec.)*
James Hardin *(Pres.)*
Brad Brookshire *(Exec. V.P.-Corp. Devel.)*
Tim Brookshire *(Exec. V.P.-Human Resources)*
Charles Davis *(Exec. V.P.-Retail Opers.)*
Dale Whitton *(Sr. V.P.-Grocery Pur.)*
James Womack *(Sr. V.P.-Meat Opers.)*
Jim Powell *(V.P. & Dir.-Adv.)*
Preston Triplett *(V.P. & Controller)*
Jim Muckleroy *(Dir.-Public Rels.)*
Principal(s):
Bruce G. Brookshire

Outside Service Firm(s):

Squyres, Johnson, Squyres & Co.*(Auditors)*
Tyler, TX

Lawrence & Lawrence*(Legal Firm)*
Tyler, TX

First City National Bank of Tyler*(Major Banking Relationship)*
Tyler, TX

BROOKSTONE COMPANY, INC.
Vose Farm Rd.
Peterborough, NH 03458
Tel.: 603-924-7181 **NH**
Fax: 603-924-3989
Year Founded: 1965
Sales Range: $80-99 Million
Emp.: 1,400
Fiscal Year-end: 2/ 1/91
Import
Specialty Retailer Marketing Through Retail Stores & Mail Order Catalogs
S.I.C.: 5947; 5961
Merwin F. Kaminstein *(Chm. Bd., Pres. & Chief Exec. Officer)*
Thomas Carroll *(V.P.-Opers., Real Estate & Construction)*
Jo-Ann B. Karalus *(V.P.-Human Resources)*
Donald O'Brien *(V.P.-Mktg.)*
T. Jeffrey Temple *(V.P.-Fin. Systems)*
Alexander Winiecki *(V.P.-Stores)*
R. Wayne Roland *(Controller)*
Edward A. Stanley *(Dir.-Mngmt. Information Systems)*

No. of Mfg. Plants/Facilities: 95
No. of U.S. Offices: 2

Computer Systems/Hardware:
IP/AS 400

Outside Service Firm(s):

Price Waterhouse*(Auditors)*
160 Federal St.
Boston, MA 02110
Tel.: 617-439-3308
Fax: 617-439-3308

Marsh & McLennan*(Group Insurer)*
200 Clarendon Street
Boston, MA
Tel.: 617-421-0200
Fax: 617-421-0344

Ropes & Gray*(Legal Firm)*
One International Place
Boston, MA 02110
Tel.: 617-951-7000

Texas Commerce Bank*(Major Banking Relationship)*
717 Travis St.
Houston, TX 77002
Tel.: 713-236-4636
Fax: 713-236-5476

BROUGHTON FOODS COMPANY
210 N. 7th St.
Marietta, OH 45750
Mailing Address:
P.O. Box 656,
Marietta, OH 45750
Tel.: 614-373-4121 **OH**
Fax: 614-373-4771
Year Founded: 1910
Approx.Sls.: $58,000,000
Emp.: 350
Fiscal Year-end: 12/31/90
Holding Co.; Processing & Distribution of Dairy & Non-Dairy Foods
S.I.C.: 2026; 2021; 2024; 5451
Samuel R. Cook *(Chm. Bd. & Chief Exec. Officer)*
R.M. Collier *(Pres.)*
George W. Broughton *(Exec. V.P. & Dir.-Mktg.)*
Gary Cowell *(V.P.-Production)*
Richard K. Hoff *(V.P.-Sls.)*
Samuel Lipscomb *(V.P.-Milk Procurement)*
Lloyd T. Westbrook *(Controller)*
John R. Broughton *(Treas.)*
Helen L. Hinton *(Sec.)*
Principal(s):
Samuel R. Cook

No. of Mfg. Plants/Facilities: 2

No. of U.S. Offices: 8

Computer Systems/Hardware:
IBM System 36

Division:

Charleston Food Div. **(1)**
114 Virginia St. W.
Charleston, WV 25302
Tel.: 304-342-2176
Tel.: 800-624-8253
Computer Systems/Hardware:
IBM
Processing & Distribution of Pasteurized Dairy & Non-Dairy Foods
S.I.C.: 2026; 2021; 2024
Ronald Arthur *(Gen. Mgr.)*

Branches:

Broughton Foods Company **(1)**
I-70 & S.R. 285
Old Washington, OH 43768
Tel.: 614-489-5198
S.I.C.: 5451
Jeff Gebhart *(Branch Mgr.)*

Broughton Foods Company **(1)**
114 Virginia
Charleston, WV 25302
Tel.: 304-342-4131
S.I.C.: 5451
Earl Lenhart *(Branch Mgr.)*

Broughton Foods Company **(1)**
Rte. 2
Clarksburg, WV 26301
Tel.: 304-624-5487
S.I.C.: 5451
Joseph Null *(Branch Mgr.)*

BROWERPEASE, INC.
900 Laurel Ave.
Hamilton, OH 45023
Tel.: 513-867-3333
Fax: 513-867-3398
Year Founded: 1991
Approx.Sls.: $15,000,000
Emp.: 140
Fiscal Year-end: 12/31/91
Building Products Distributor; Manufacturer of Sink Tops and Custom Case Goods
William R. Brower *(Pres.)*
Dan R. Brower *(V.P.)*
Mark E. Fredricks *(V.P.)*
Vincent J. Gilday *(V.P.)*
John T. Anderson *(Mgr.-Sls.)*
Principal(s):
William R. Brower

No. of Mfg. Plants/Facilities: 1
No. of U.S. Offices: 4

Computer Systems/Hardware:
Data General/Data Point

Outside Service Firm(s):

Ernst & Young*(Auditors)*
1300 Chiquita Center, 250 E. Fifth St.
Cincinnati, OH 45202
Tel.: 513-621-6454

United of Omaha*(Group Insurer)*
Cincinnati, OH

Clark & Eyrich*(Legal Firm)*
Hamilton, OH

First National Bank Hamilton*(Major Banking Relationship)*
Hamilton, OH

Star Bank*(Major Banking Relationship)*
425 Walnut Street
Cincinnati, OH 45202
Tel.: 513-632-4000

First National Bank Hamilton*(Pension Manager)*
Hamilton, OH

E.H. BROWN ADVERTISING, INC.
20 N. Wacker Dr., Ste. 1865
Chicago, IL 60606-2996
Tel.: 312-372-9494
Fax: 312-372-2323
Year Founded: 1926
Approx.Billings: $21,000,000
Emp.: 25
Advertising Agency
S.I.C.: 7311
E.H. Brown, Jr. *(Chm. Bd., Chief Exec. Officer & Partner)*
R.L. McCullough *(Pres., Chief Oper. Officer & Partner)*
J.A. Grant *(Sr. V.P.-Admin.)*
S.J. Reshkin *(Sr. V.P.)*
A.H. Schullman *(Sr. V.P.)*
M.A. Phillips *(Controller)*

Computer Systems/Hardware:
IBM PC; CPT

Outside Service Firm(s):

The Principal Financial Group*(Group Insurer)*
Des Moines, IA

American National Bank & Trust Company of Chicago*(Major Banking Relationship)*
33 N. LaSalle St.
Chicago, IL 60602
Tel.: 312-661-5000
Fax: 312-661-6417

BROWN & BIGELOW, INC.
345 Plato Blvd. E.
Saint Paul, MN 55107
Tel.: 612-293-7000
Fax: 612-293-7277
Year Founded: 1896
Approx.Sls.: $60,000,000
Emp.: 1,000
Fiscal Year-end: 12/31/90
Import Export
Mfr. Calendars, Playing Cards & Advertising Specialties
S.I.C.: 2759
William D. Smith *(Pres. & Chief Exec. Officer)*
Philip R. Jungwirth *(Chief Fin. Officer)*
R.L. Petschke *(V.P.-Mfg.)*
William Smith, Jr. *(V.P.-Admin.)*

Computer Systems/Hardware:
IBM AS/400

Outside Service Firm(s):

Midway National Bank*(Major Banking Relationship)*
St. Paul, MN

Division:

Hoyle Products **(1)**
345 Plato Blvd., E.
Saint Paul, MN 55107
Tel.: 612-293-7000
Mfr. Calendars & Playing Cards
S.I.C.: 2759
Rick Farrell *(Pres.)*

BROWN BROTHERS, HARRIMAN & CO.
59 Wall St.
New York, NY 10005
Tel.: 212-483-1818
Telex: 12236
Fax: 212-493-8526
Year Founded: 1818
Approx.Assets: $1,390,852,169
Emp.: 1,500
Fiscal Year-end: 12/31/91
Private Bank
S.I.C.: 6029; 6081; 6211; 6531; 6099
T.M. Farley *(Mng. Partner & Chief Exec. Officer)*
Brian A. Berris *(Partner & Mktg. Dir.)*
Laurence F. Whittemore *(Partner)*
Richard H. Witmer Jr. *(Partner)*
Gerald Gold *(Sr. Mgr.)*
George E. Gage *(Mgr. & Controller)*
Edward J. Williams *(Mgr. & Treas.)*
Robert B. Davies *(Mgr. & Data Processing Dir.)*
Allan B. Wechsler *(Mgr. & Dir.-Personnel)*

No. of U.S. Offices: 8
No. of Foreign Offices: 6

Computer Systems/Hardware:
IBM; Hitachi

Outside Service Firm(s):

Coopers & Lybrand*(Auditors)*
1301 Avenue of The Americas
New York, NY 10019
Tel.: 212-536-2000

Davis, Polk & Wardwell*(Legal Firm)*
450 Lexington Ave.
New York, NY 10017
Tel.: 212-530-4000

Non-U.S. Holdings:

Brown Brothers, Harriman & Co., Tokyo **(1)**
Daimatsu Bldg., 4th Fl., 8-14 Nihonbashi, 3-chome Chu-ku,
Tokyo, 103, Japan
Tel.: 3278 1411
Fax: 3278 1416
Brokerage & Financial Advisory Services
S.I.C.: 6211
Kyosuke Hashimoto *(Partner)*
Kaikuzo Murata *(Mgr.)*

Brown Brothers, Harriman (Hong Kong) Ltd. **(1)**
Gloucester Tower, 22nd Fl., Landmark Centre
Central, Hong Kong
Tel.: 877 3222 (100%)
Fax: 877 2677
Brokerage & Financial Advisory Services
S.I.C.: 6211
Maria J. Pereira *(Mng. Dir.)*

Brown Brothers Harriman Trust Co. (Cayman) Ltd. **(1)**
Butterfield House, P.O. Box 705, Georgetown, Grand Cayman Cayman Islands
Tel.: 809-949-4719 (100%)
Fax: 809-949-9657
Intl. Banking
S.I.C.: 6081
Robert A. Sanford *(Mng. Dir.)*

Brown Brothers Harriman Limited **(1)**
Garden House, 18 Finsbury Circus
London, EC2M 7BP, United Kingdom
Tel.: 071-588 6166
Fax: 071-256 8055
Investment Brokerage & Advisory Financial Services
S.I.C.: 6211
J. Angus Ivory *(Mng. Dir.)*

Brown Harriman Corporation **(1)**
12-14 Rond Point des Champs Elysees 75008
Paris, France
Tel.: 4359 8904
Fax: 4563 6663
Investment Brokerage & Financial Advisory Services
S.I.C.: 6211
Frank J. Prissert *(Mng. Dir.)*

Brown Brothers Harriman Services AG **(1)**
Stockerstr. 38 8002
Zurich, Switzerland
Tel.: 201 1421
Fax: 201 3175
Investment Brokerage & Financial Advisory Services
S.I.C.: 6211
Nicolas K. Wyss *(Mng. Dir.)*

Brown Brothers Harriman (Luxembourg) S.A. **(1)**
33, Blvd. Prince Henri L-2014
Luxembourg, Luxembourg
Tel.: 474066 1 (100%)
Fax: 470580 1
International Banking
S.I.C.: 6081
John A. Gehret *(Mng. Dir.)*

Subsidiaries:

Brown Brothers Harriman Trust Co. of New York **(1)**
63 Wall St.
New York, NY 10005
Tel.: 212-493-8000 (100%)
Fax: 212-493-8206
Trust Company
S.I.C.: 6021
John F. King *(Pres.)*

Brown Brothers Harriman Trust Co. of Texas **(1)**
4900 Trammell Crow Ctr., 2001 Ross Ave.
Dallas, TX 75201
Tel.: 214-979-0034
Fax: 214-220-2897
Trust Company
S.I.C.: 6021
Robert J. McKenzie *(Exec. V.P.)*

Brown Brothers Harriman Trust Co. of Florida **(1)**
Collier Financial Center, 4501 Tamiami Trail North
Naples, FL 33940
Tel.: 813-263-4133 (100%)
Fax: 813-263-6107
Trust Company
S.I.C.: 6021
M. Bruce Miner *(Chief Oper. Officer)*

BROWN & CALDWELL CONSULTING ENGINEERS
3480 Buskirk Ave.
Pleasant Hill, CA 94523
Mailing Address:
P.O. Box 8045
Walnut Creek, CA 94596
Tel.: 510-937-9010
Fax: 510-937-9026
Year Founded: 1947
Approx.Sls.: $58,000,000
Emp.: 737
Provides Consulting, Engineering & Analytical Laboratory Services on Hazardous Waste, Wastewater, Water, Solid Waste Management, Energy, Storm Drainage & Flood Control & Resource Recovery
S.I.C.: 8711; 1629; 4953; 8731
Steven A. Fisher *(Chm. Bd. & Chief Exec. Officer)*
J. Lynn Hartford *(Pres.)*
George Cutler *(Chief Fin. Officer & V.P.)*
Garr M. Jones *(Sr. V.P.-Engrng. Design)*
Eric F. Mische *(Sr. V.P.)*
Denny S. Parker *(Sr. V.P.-Process Engrng.)*
Paul L. Armstrong *(V.P. & Gen. Counsel)*
Ray M. Graves *(V.P.-Construction Mngmt. Div.)*
James G. Smith *(V.P.)*
Principal(s):
Employee-Owned

No. of U.S. Offices: 18

Outside Service Firm(s):

Ernst & Young*(Auditors)*
2175 N. California Blvd., Ste. 400
Walnut Creek, CA 94596

First Interstate Bank*(Major Banking Relationship)*
Oakland, CA

BROWN DERBY, INC.
7850 Northfield Rd.
Cleveland, OH 44146
Tel.: 216-439-8200
Year Founded: 1941
Approx.Sls.: $148,000,000
Emp.: 2,000
Restaurant Chain; Inns; Wholesale Frozen Foods & Meats; Franchisor
S.I.C.: 5812; 5147; 5142; 7011; 6794
Parris Girves *(Pres. & Chief Exec. Officer)*
Mary Ann Siciarz *(Dir.-Mktg.)*

EARLE PALMER BROWN

EARLE PALMER BROWN
6935 Arlington St.
Bethesda, MD 20814
Tel.: 301-986-0510
Fax: 301-657-2590
Year Founded: 1952
Approx.Billings: $435,000,000
Emp.: 500
Advertising, Public Relations, Graphic Design, Sales Promotion & Direct Marketing
S.I.C.: 7335; 7336; 8743
Earle Palmer Brown *(Chm. Bd. & Founder)*
Jeremy E. Brown *(Chief Exec. Officer)*
Gary F. Jonas *(Pres. & Chief Oper. Officer)*
Mark Goldstein *(Pres.-Earle Palmer Brown Adv.)*
Mitch Kozikowski *(Pres.-Earle Palmer Brown Pub. Rels.)*
Russ Richmond *(Pres.-Earle Palmer Brown Direct)*
Chuck Walsh *(Exec. V.P., Chief Fin. Officer)*
Ann Eggers *(Sr. V.P., Opers.)*
Connie Whittington *(Sr. V.P., Corp. Communications)*
Rene Cunningham *(V.P., Human Resources)*
Gary Dancy *(V.P., MIS)*

Branches:

Earle Palmer Brown/Atlanta (1)
100 Colony Sq.
Atlanta, GA 30361
Tel.: 404-881-8585
Bill Garoutte *(Exec. V.P., Gen. Mgr.)*

Earle Palmer Brown/Bethesda (1)
6935 Arlington Rd.
Bethesda, MD 20814
Tel.: 301-657-6000
Fax: 301-657-2590
Tim Elliott *(Pres.)*
Claire Geier *(Exec. V.P., Gen. Mgr.)*
Jeff Schur *(Exec. V.P.)*

Earle Palmer Brown/Kalamazoo (1)
259 E. Michigan Ave.
Kalamazoo, MI 49007
Tel.: 616-344-5046
Fax: 616-344-0432
James R. Rohrback *(Pres.)*

Earle Palmer Brown/New York (1)
345 Hudson St.
New York, NY 10014
Tel.: 212-463-6900
Fax: 212-463-6964
Linda J. Srere *(Chm.)*
Bill Southard *(Pres.)*
Cary Lemkowitz *(Vice Chm. & Chief Creative Officer)*
John Fraoli *(Exec. V.P.)*
Richard Sawyer *(Exec. V.P.)*
Steve Cody *(Sr. V.P., Pub. Rels. Dir.)*

Earle Palmer Brown/Norfolk (1)
248 W. Bute St.
Norfolk, VA 23510
Tel.: 804-627-0261
Fax: 804-627-4050
Bruce Mansfield *(Exec. V.P., Creative Dir.)*
Michael C. Knaisch *(Exec. V.P., Dir. Client Services)*

Earle Palmer Brown/Richmond (1)
1710 E. Franklin St.
Richmond, VA 23219
Tel.: 804-775-0700
Fax: 804-775-0795
Brad Armstrong *(Chm.)*
Mark Raper *(Pres., Gen. Mgr., Pub. Rels.)*

Earle Palmer Brown/Tampa Bay (1)
260 1st Ave. S., Ste. 300
Saint Petersburg, FL 33701
Tel.: 813-821-5155
Craig Davis *(Pres.)*
Jeffrey Tucker *(Pres.-Pub. Rels.)*

Earle Palmer Brown & Spiro (1)
One Liberty Place, 1650 Market St.
Philadelphia, PA 19103
Tel.: 215-851-9600
Lonny Strum *(Pres.)*
Walter A. Spiro *(Chm.)*
Herbert Smith *(Exec. V.P., Gen. Mgr.)*
Paul Jacobson *(Sr. V.P., Dir. New Bus. Devel., Mngmt. Supvr.)*
Joyce Rivas *(Sr. V.P., Mngmt. Supvr.)*
Stephen Albertini *(Sr. V.P., Gen. Mgr., Pub. Rel.)*
Allen Liss *(Pres, SAI/EPB Promotions)*
Mike Colistra *(Pres.-Earle Palmer Brown Yellow Pages)*

BROWN EVANS COMPANY
(Formerly R.R. & R.R. Evans Company)
306 S. Country Club Dr.
Mesa, AZ 85202
Tel.: 602-962-6111 **AZ**
Fax: 602-890-8247
Approx.Sls.: $42,000,000
Emp.: 50
Wholesaler Petroleum & Petroleum Products
S.I.C.: 5172
Wayne J. Brown *(Pres.)*
Kathy Brown *(Dir.-Fin.)*
Dave Workman *(Gen. Mgr.)*
Principal(s):
Wayne J. Brown

Computer Systems/Hardware:
Point 4

Outside Service Firm(s):

Arthur Andersen & Co.*(Auditors)*
Phoenix, AZ

Lewis & Roca*(Legal Firm)*
Phoenix, AZ

BILL BROWN FORD INC.
32222 Plymouth Rd.
Livonia, MI 48150
Tel.: 313-421-7000 **MI**
Fax: 313-421-0221
Approx.Sls.: $62,300,000
Emp.: 115
Car Dealership
S.I.C.: 5511
Edward C. Brown *(Pres. & Treas.)*
Mike Schreiber *(Mgr.-Sls.)*
Bob Gunnigle *(Gen. Mgr.)*

Outside Service Firm(s):

Mathews, Nightingdale, Reich & Scott, P.C.*(Auditors)*
Birmingham, MI

Columbo & Columbo*(Legal Firm)*
Birmingham, MI

National Bank of Detroit*(Major Banking Relationship)*
611 Woodward
Detroit, MI 48226
Tel.: 313-225-1000

BROWN & HADLEY & PARTNERS
600 Market Place Tower, 2025 1st Ave.
Seattle, WA 98121
Tel.: 206-728-8300
Year Founded: 1976
Approx.Billings: $10,400,000
Emp.: 18
John Brown *(Chm. Bd. & Creative Dir.)*
Dick Hadley *(Pres.)*
Jan Benson *(Controller)*

BROWN & HALEY
1940 E. 11th St.
Tacoma, WA 98421
Mailing Address:
P.O. Box 1596
Tacoma, WA 98401
Tel.: 206-593-3000
Tel.: 800-426-8400 **WA**
Fax: 206-272-6742
Year Founded: 1914
Approx.Sls.: $36,000,000
Emp.: 225
Fiscal Year-end: 6/30/92
Import Export
Confection Manufacturing & Importing
S.I.C.: 2064; 2066
F.T. Haley *(Chm. Bd. & Chief Exec. Officer)*
Mark T. Haley *(Pres. & Gen. Mgr.)*
Clarence Guimond *(Exec. V.P.-Internal Affairs)*
Neil Booth *(V.P.-Sls. & Mktg.)*
Chas. Mellinger *(V.P.-Opers.)*
Al Hlas *(Controller)*
Steve Headley *(Mng. Dir.-Export)*
Larry Anderson *(Dir.-Data Processing)*
Bill Dube *(Mgr.-Natl. Sls.)*
Connie Klien *(Mgr.-Mktg. Services)*
Francis Lau *(Mgr.-Quality Control)*
Raj Patel *(Mgr.-Pur.)*
Paula Jacobson *(Corp. Travel Planner)*
Debbie Shrader *(Admin.-Personnel)*

Computer Systems/Hardware:
AS400

Outside Service Firm(s):

First Interstate Bank*(Major Banking Relationship)*
Tacoma, WA

Subsidiary:

Almond Roca International (1)
1940 E. 11th St., P.O. Box 1596
Tacoma, WA 98401
Tel.: 206-593-3000
Fax: 206-272-6742
Mark Haley *(Pres.)*
Steve Headley *(Mng. Dir.)*

BROWN-MINNEAPOLIS TANK & FABRICATING CO.
2875 Highway #55
Eagan, MN 55121
Mailing Address:
P.O. Box 64670
St. Paul, MN 55164
Tel.: 612-454-6750
Fax: 612-454-1987
Approx.Sls.: $22,000,000
Manufacture Steel Storage Tanks & Pressure Vessels For Petroleum, Ammonia, Water, Grain, Air & Water Treatment, Alcohol, Beer, Coal, Cement, Chemicals Pulp & Paper & Power Industries
S.I.C.: 1791; 3441; 3443
John Wirt *(Pres.)*
William F. Jennrich *(V.P. & Controller)*
Mike Peterson *(Pur. Agent)*
Ty Hagen *(Chief Engr.)*

Outside Service Firm(s):

Deloitte & Touche*(Auditors)*
900 Pillsbury Ctr.
Minneapolis, MN 55402
Tel.: 612-332-2301
Fax: 612-375-5418

Lindquist & Vennum*(Legal Firm)*
4200 IDS Center, 80 South 8th St.
Minneapolis, MN 55402
Tel.: 612-371-3211

First National Bank of Minneapolis*(Major Banking Relationship)*
P.O. Box A799
Minneapolis, MN 55480
Tel.: 612-370-4606

BROWN MOTORS
5625 W. Central Ave.
Toledo, OH 43615
Tel.: 419-531-0151 **OH**
Fax: 419-536-1318
Approx.Sls.: $53,000,000
Emp.: 122
New & Used Automobiles
S.I.C.: 5511
Willis E. Brown, Jr. *(Pres.)*
Robert W. Brown, Jr. *(Exec. V.P., Gen. Mgr. & Sec.)*
Thomas L. Halm *(V.P. & Controller)*
Principal(s):
Willis E. Brown, Jr.

Outside Service Firm(s):

KPMG Peat Marwick*(Auditors)*
Toledo, OH

Eastman & Smith*(Legal Firm)*
240 N. Huron St.
Toledo, OH 43604
Tel.: 419-241-6152

Huntington National Bank*(Major Banking Relationship)*
Toledo, OH 43604

H.H. BROWN SHOE COMPANY, INC.
124 W. Putnam Ave.
Greenwich, CT 06830
Tel.: 203-661-2424
Twx: 236213
Emp.: 1,400
Mfr. Men's & Boys' Shoes
S.I.C.: 3143
Francis C. Rooney Jr. *(Chm. Bd. & Chief Exec. Officer)*
Otto H. Woerner *(Vice Chm. & Treas.)*
James E. Issler *(Pres. & Chief Oper. Officer)*
William C. Keaton, Jr. *(Exec. V.P.)*
John Hefferman *(V.P.)*
R. Thomas Henderson *(V.P.)*
Charles Horton *(V.P.)*
Paul Isenberg *(V.P.)*
Norman W. Lavole *(V.P.-Fin. & Controller)*
Herb Lemoyne *(V.P.-Sls. & Mktg.)*
D. Wayne Miller *(V.P.)*
Avi Schour *(V.P.-Import Div.)*

Outside Service Firm(s):

Robert Finnegan & Lynan*(Auditors)*
Boston, MA

Bank of New England*(Major Banking Relationship)*
28 State Street
Boston, MA 02109
Tel.: 617-742-4000

Divisions:

Carolina Shoe Company (1)
P.O. Box 1079
Morganton, NC 28655
Tel.: 704-437-7755
Men's Shoes
S.I.C.: 3143
Otto Worner *(V.P. & Gen. Mgr.)*

Cove Shoe Company (1)
107 Highland St.
Martinsburg, PA 16662
Tel.: 814-793-3786
Men's Shoes
S.I.C.: 3143
Thomas Neal, Jr. *(Gen. Mgr.)*

Double H West Shoe Wholesale (1)
2300 S. Garfield Ave.
City of Commerce, CA 90040
Tel.: 213-726-4088

Warehousing
S.I.C.: 4225

Richland Shoe Co. **(1)**
30 N. Third St.
Womelsdorf, PA 19567
Tel.: 215-589-4586
Men's Dress Shoes
S.I.C.: 3143
Ted Dessinger *(Gen. Mgr.)*

F.M. BROWN SONS, INC.
205 Woodrew Ave.
Sinking Spring, PA 19608
Tel.: 215-582-2741
Sales Range: $20-39 Million
Emp.: 120
Flour Mill & Feed Supplies
S.I.C.: 2041; 2048
Franklin Brown, Sr. *(Pres.)*
Morris E. Brown, Jr. *(V.P.)*
C. Merrill Brown *(Treas.)*
Harvey J. Brown *(Sec.)*

Outside Service Firm(s):

Reinsel & Co.*(Auditors)*
Reading, PA

Miller & Murray*(Legal Firm)*
540 Court St.
Reading, PA 19601
Tel.: 215-376-6651

Bank of Pennsylvania*(Major Banking Relationship)*
Reading, PA

BROWN WOOD PRESERVING COMPANY
5200 Crittenden Dr.
Louisville, KY 40213
Tel.: 502-367-0179
Fax: 502-363-3994
Approx.Sls.: $13,000,000
Emp.: 110
Utility Poles, Treated Wood, Structural Lumber & Timber
S.I.C.: 2491
Lowell Stanley *(Pres.)*
Ray Bobo *(V.P.)*
Frederick G. Heath *(V.P., Sec. & Treas.)*

Outside Service Firm(s):

First National Bank*(Major Banking Relationship)*
Louisville, KY

E.T. BROWNE DRUG CO., INC.
140 Sylvan Ave.
Englewood Cliffs, NJ 07632
Tel.: 201-947-3050
Fax: 201-947-9276
Approx.Sls.: $40,000,000
Emp.: 102
Export
Mfr. of Perfumes, Cosmetics, Lotions & Toiletries
S.I.C.: 2844
Arnold Hayward Neis *(Pres.)*
David Stern *(V.P.-Sls.)*
Dan Wienecke *(V.P.-Opers.)*

Outside Service Firm(s):

Isadore B. Mirsky & Co.*(Auditors)*
Wayne, NJ

NatWest Bank*(Major Banking Relationship)*
Harrison, NJ

BROWNING CHEMICAL CORPORATION
707 Westchester Ave.
White Plains, NY 10604
Tel.: 914-686-0300 **NY**
Fax: 914-686-0310
Year Founded: 1948
Approx.Sls.: $15,000,000
Emp.: 20
Import Export
Wholesale Distribution of Industrial & Heavy Chemicals; Pharmaceuticals
S.I.C.: 5169; 5122
Frederick M. Browning *(Pres.)*
Joseph Golinowski *(V.P.)*
Debarah Hardesty *(V.P.)*
Irwin Pontell *(V.P.-Sls.)*
Jean Browning *(Treas. & Sec.)*

Outside Service Firm(s):

Joel E. Sammett & Co.*(Auditors)*
New York, NY

Manufacturers Hanover Trust Co.*(Major Banking Relationship)*
4 New York Plaza
New York, NY 10015
Tel.: 212-623-3232

BROWNS LUMBER & SUPPLY COMPANY
P.O. Box 1589,
Fairmont, WV 26554
Year Founded: 1951
Approx.Sls.: $25,000,000
Emp.: 160
Home Centers; New Construction of Industrial Buildings
S.I.C.: 5211; 1541
Charles T. Brown *(Chm. Bd.)*
David C. Brown *(Pres. & Chief Exec. Officer)*

THE BROWNSTEIN GROUP
215 S. Broad St.
Philadelphia, PA 19107
Tel.: 215-735-3470
Fax: 215-735-6298
Year Founded: 1964
Approx.Billings: $16,000,000
Emp.: 15
Retail & Business-to-Business Adv.
Berny Brownstein *(Pres.)*
Beverly Brownstein *(Exec. V.P., Pub. Rels. Dir.)*
Suzanne McElroy *(Controller)*

Computer Systems/Hardware:
MacIntosh Desktop Publishing Systems

BROYLES, ALLEBAUGH & DAVIS, INC.
Denver Technological Center,
8231 E. Prentice Ave.
Englewood, CO 80111
Tel.: 303-770-2000
Fax: 303-770-2009
Year Founded: 1933
Approx.Billings: $12,000,000
Emp.: 24
Kathleen K. Brock *(Pres.)*
James P. House *(Pub. Rels. Dir.)*
Jay G. Marks *(Acct. Services Dir., Corp. Sec.)*

BRUBAKER TOOL CORP.
Front & Center
Millersburg, PA 17061
Tel.: 717-692-2113 **NY**
Fax: 717-692-4995
Year Founded: 1881
Approx.Sls.: $25,000,000
Emp.: 350
Fiscal Year-end: 2/29/92
Export
Manufacture of Taps, Reamers, Milling Cutters, End Mills, Dies, Standard & Specialty Jig & Fixture Components
S.I.C.: 3545; 3544
Timothy E. Wyman *(Chm.)*
Raymond E. Putnam *(Pres.)*
Cliff Hanner *(V.P.-Engrng.)*
Bernard J. Kelly *(V.P.-Fin.)*

Outside Service Firm(s):

KPMG Peat Marwick*(Auditors)*
P.O. Box 1190, 225 Market St., Ste. 300
Harrisburg, PA 17108-1190
Tel.: 717-238-7131

McNee's, Wallace, & Nurick*(Legal Firm)*
100 Pine St.
Harrisburg, PA 17108-1166

Subsidiaries:

Fastcut Tool Corporation **(1)**
1830 Stephenson Hgwy.
Troy, MI 48083
Tel.: 313-689-3153 (100%)
Emp.: 15
Marketing Office for Milling Cutters, End Mills, Taps & Reamers, Jig & Fixture Components
S.I.C.: 5084
Raymond E. Putnam *(Pres.)*
Jack R. Hilt *(Mgr.-Sls.)*
Paul R. Frazho *(Mgr.-Sls. & Admin.)*

New England Tap Corporation (NETCO) **(1)**
15 Perry Dr.
Foxboro, MA 02035
Tel.: 508-543-6316
Sales & Marketing of Chromclad Taps
S.I.C.: 5084
John H. Webb *(Pres.)*
Leon L. Janik *(V.P.-Sls.)*

BRUCE-ANDERSEN COMPANY, INC.
642 Gallatin Field Rd.
Belgrade, MT 59714
Tel.: 406-388-7689
Fax: 406-388-1887
Approx.Sls.: $18,000,000
Emp.: 35
General Contractors; New Construction, Renovation & Repair Of Commercial & Office Buildings
S.I.C.: 1542
David F. Bruce *(Chm. Bd. & Chief Exec. Officer)*
Elmer Lee Johnson *(Pres.)*

Outside Service Firm(s):

Browning & Kaleczyc*(Legal Firm)*
Helena, MT

First National Bank*(Major Banking Relationship)*
Bozeman, MT

BRUCE FOODS CORP.
1653 Old Spanishtrail
Saint Martinville, LA 70582
Mailing Address:
P.O. Drawer 1030
New Iberia, LA 70561
Tel.: 318-365-8101 **LA**
Telex: 78-4855
Fax: 318-364-3742
Year Founded: 1928
Approx.Sls.: $60,000,000
Emp.: 780
Fiscal Year-end: 4/30/90
Import Export
Manufacturer & Wholesaler of Canned Vegetables, Seasonings, Mexican Food
S.I.C.: 2091; 2035; 5149
J.S. Brown III *(Pres.)*
Norman S. Brown *(V.P.)*
Gordon S. Brown *(Sec. & Treas.)*
B.J. Lovell *(Comptroller)*
Principal(s):
J.S. Brown III
Norman S. Brown

Computer Systems/Hardware:
IBM

Outside Service Firm(s):

Quirk & Co.*(Auditors)*
Lake Charles, LA

Mestayer & Simon*(Legal Firm)*
Lake Charles, LA

Hibernia National Bank*(Major Banking Relationship)*
New Orleans, LA

BRUCE INDUSTRIES, INC.
P.O. Box 1700
Dayton, NV 89403
Tel.: 702-246-0101 **NV**
Fax: 702-246-0451
Year Founded: 1956
Approx.Sls.: $25,000,000
Emp.: 410
Export
Lighting for Aircraft & Military Shelters
S.I.C.: 3641; 3647; 3499
Frank B. Bruce *(Chm. Bd.)*
Tom B. Bruce *(Pres.)*
Jim Bradshaw *(Controller)*
Diane Ashe *(Sec.)*
C. Sanders *(Dir.-Personnel)*
Ruth Hand *(Mgr.-Pur.)*
Principal(s):
Frank B. Bruce
Tom B. Bruce

No. of Mfg. Plants/Facilities: 1
No. of U.S. Offices: 2
No. of Foreign Offices: 1

Computer Systems/Hardware:
Macintosh; IBM

T. BRUCE SALES, INC.
Carbough St.
West Middlesex, PA 16159
Mailing Address:
P.O. Box 607
West Middlesex, PA 16159
Tel.: 412-528-9961 **PA**
Fax: 412-528-2050
Year Founded: 1964
Approx.Sls.: $11,000,000
Emp.: 80
Manufacture Foundry Flasks, Oil Field Fabrications & Steel Mill Fabrications
S.I.C.: 3441; 3443
T. Scott Campbell *(Pres.)*
Robert E. Campbell *(Exec. V.P.)*
Arthur Hoover *(Sec. & Prod. Mgr.)*
Richard L. McBride *(Mgr.-Sls.)*
John Baumgartner *(Chief Engineer)*
Principal(s):
T. Scott Campbell
Robert E. Campbell

No. of Mfg. Plants/Facilities: 2
No. of U.S. Offices: 3

Computer Systems/Hardware:
Point Four

Outside Service Firm(s):

Black, Bashor & Porsch*(Auditors)*
Sharon, PA

Routman, Moore, Goldstone & Valentino*(Legal Firm)*
West Middlesex, PA

First National Bank of Mercer County*(Major Banking Relationship)*
West Middlesex, PA

BRUCKNER MACHINE & TOOL CORP.
36 Harbor Park Dr.
Port Washington, NY 11050
Tel.: 516-484-6070
Fax: 516-484-1255
Approx.Sls.: $26,000,000
Emp.: 30
Fiscal Year-end: 12/31/90
Manufacture Hand Cutting, Machine & Precision Tools; Industrial Supplies
S.I.C.: 5085; 5084
Eli Rosenbaum *(Pres.)*
Robert Rosenbaum *(Exec. V.P.)*
Marlon Rosenbaum *(Treas.)*
Principal(s):
Eli Rosenbaum
Robert Rosenbaum
Marlon Rosenbaum

Bruckner Machine & Tool Corp.—(Continued)

Outside Service Firm(s):

Broman & Duerr*(Auditors)*
New York, NY

Alder & Blass*(Legal Firm)*
New York, NY

Bankers Trust Co.*(Major Banking Relationship)*
P.O. Box 9050, Church St. Station
New York, NY 10008
Tel.: 212-250-6037

M. A. BRUDER & SONS, INC.
600 Reed Rd.
Broomall, PA 19008
Tel.: 215-353-5100
Fax: 215-353-8189
Year Founded: 1899
Emp.: 1,000
Mfr. of Paint; Retail Paint Stores
S.I.C.: 5198; 5231; 2851
Thomas A. Bruder, Jr. *(Pres.)*
James J. Bruder *(Exec. V.P.)*
Michael A. Bruder *(V.P.-Florida Opers.)*
James J. Kelly *(V.P.-Mfg. & Research)*
David R. Winters *(V.P.-Fin. & Controller)*
Thomas A. Bruder III *(Mgr.-Mktg.)*
Bart Lorenzo *(Pur. Agent)*

Computer Systems/Hardware:
Burroughs 5920

Outside Service Firm(s):

Price Waterhouse*(Auditors)*
30 S. 17th St.
Philadelphia, PA 19103
Tel.: 215-665-9500

Sentry Insurance*(Group Insurer)*
1800 N. Point Dr.
Stevens Point, WI 54481

Subsidiaries:

M.A.B. Paints **(1)**
630 N. 3rd St.
Terre Haute, IN 47808
Tel.: 812-234-6621
Emp.: 400
Fiscal Year-end: 12/30/90
Computer Systems/Hardware:
IBM
Mfr. & Distribution of Paint
S.I.C.: 2851; 5198
Tom Bruder *(Chm. Bd.)*
Lee Roads *(Pres.)*
Merrill Bonebrake *(Treas.)*
Larry Fischer *(Adv. Dir.)*
Dan Williams *(Personnel & Pur. Dir.)*
Dave Bussing *(Gen. Sls. Mgr.)*

M.A.B. Paints **(1)**
52nd & Grays Ave.
Philadelphia, PA 19143
Tel.: 215-727-5112
Mfr. & Distribution of Paint
S.I.C.: 2851; 5198

M.A.B. Paints **(1)**
720 Central Florida Hwy.
Orlando, FL 32824
Tel.: 407-851-6160
Mfr. & Distribution of Paint
S.I.C.: 2851; 5198

M. BRUENGER & CO., INC.
6250 N. Broadway
Wichita, KS 67219
Tel.: 316-744-0494
Tel.: 800-876-7623 **KS**
Fax: 316-744-2671
Year Founded: 1936
Assets: $4,455,249
Liabilities: $946,724
Net Worth: $3,508,525
Approx.Sls.: $13,000,000
Emp.: 70
Fiscal Year-end: 12/31/90
Local & Interstate Trucking; Regulated & Exempt Commodities
S.I.C.: 4212; 4213
Leona Bruenger *(Chm. Bd.)*
M.W. Bruenger *(Pres.)*
Lonnie E. Collins *(V.P.-Personnel)*
Joseph Diekemper *(Controller)*
Principal(s):
Leona Bruenger
M.W. Bruenger

Computer Systems/Hardware:
NCR-Tower

Outside Service Firm(s):

Chesser & Company*(Auditors)*
Wichita, KS

Arvin & Arvin*(Legal Firm)*
Wichita, KS

Kansas State Bank & Trust Co.*(Major Banking Relationship)*
Wichita, KS
Tel.: 316-266-6600

DICK BRUHN INC.
300 Main St.
Salinas, CA 93901
Mailing Address:
P.O. Box 81600
Salinas, CA 93912-1600
Tel.: 408-758-4684
Fax: 408-422-2620
Year Founded: 1950
Assets: $16,860,000
Liabilities: $13,450,000
Net Worth: $3,410,000
Approx.Sls.: $24,500,000
Emp.: 500
Fiscal Year-end: 2/28/92
Retailer Men's, Boys' & Ladies' Wear; Formal Wear Sales & Rental Uniforms
S.I.C.: 5611; 5621; 5632
Richard L. Bruhn *(Chm. Bd.)*
John D. Maness *(Pres.)*
Evelyn Yolcomico *(Comptroller)*
Gary Kilbourn *(Mgr.-Sls.)*

Computer Systems/Hardware:
IBM System 36

Outside Service Firm(s):

Tomei & Chin*(Auditors)*
San Francisco, CA

James Reid, Esq.*(Legal Firm)*
Oakland, CA

Wells Fargo Bank*(Major Banking Relationship)*
420 Montgomery St.
San Francisco, CA 94104

THE BRULIN CORPORATION
2920 Dr. Andrew J. Brown Ave.
Indianapolis, IN 46205
Mailing Address:
P.O. Box 270
Indianapolis, IN 46206
Tel.: 317-923-3211
Tel.: 800-776-7149 **IN**
Fax: 317-925-4596
Year Founded: 1935
Sales Range: $10-19 Million
Emp.: 300
Fiscal Year-end: 12/31/89
Export
Specialty Cleaning, Polishing & Sanitation Preparations
S.I.C.: 2842; 2833; 2841; 2851
Charles Pollnow *(Chm. Bd., Chief Exec. & Oper. Officer)*
Michael Falkowski *(Pres.)*
Jolee Plaggenburg *(V.P.)*
Kim Essenburg *(Treas.)*
Ken Halcomb *(Controller)*
Richard Ott *(Dir.-Pur.)*
Jane Weichert *(Dir.-Data Processing)*
Principal(s):
Charles Pollnow
Michael Falkowski

No. of Mfg. Plants/Facilities: 3
No. of U.S. Offices: 3

Computer Systems/Hardware:
Burroughs

Outside Service Firm(s):

INB National Bank*(Investment Banker)*
One Indiana Sq.
Indianapolis, IN 46266
Tel.: 317-266-6000

Graham & Peat*(Legal Firm)*
St. Louis, IL

Bank of New England*(Major Banking Relationship)*
St. Louis, MO

BRUNER CORPORATION
500W. Oklahoma Ave.
Milwaukee, WI 53207
Mailing Address:
P.O. Box 07500
Milwaukee, WI 53207
Tel.: 414-747-3700
Fax: 414-747-3812
Approx.Sls.: $25,000,000
Emp.: 115
Import Export
Design & Manufacturing of Commercial & Residential Water Treatment Equipment
S.I.C.: 3589; 5087
David Nancarrow *(Chm. Bd.)*
Terry Daniels *(Chief Exec. Officer)*
J.B. Prochot *(Pres.)*
Thomas M. Cooksey *(V.P.-Mktg. & Sls.)*
William Koranda *(V.P.-Fin.)*
George O. Zach *(V.P.-Opers.)*
William Baxter *(Mgr.-Sls. Devel.)*
Gerold Block *(Mgr.-Mktg.)*
Rich Carlson *(Mgr.-Quality Assurance)*
Dan Dollison *(Mgr.-Pur.)*
Bob Kohlmann *(Mgr.-Intl. Sls.)*
Gary Matusin *(Mgr.-Engrng.)*
Gary Smith *(Coord.-Adv./Literature)*
Jim Hanson *(Systems Coord.)*

Computer Systems/Hardware:
EMS System

BRUNING PAINT COMPANY
601 South Haven St.
Baltimore, MD 21224
Tel.: 410-342-3636
Tel.: 800-852-3636
Fax: 410-675-0368
Year Founded: 1923
Approx.Sls.: $35,000,000
Emp.: 200
Fiscal Year-end: 12/31/90
Export
Mfr. Paint & Varnishes
S.I.C.: 2851
Claiborne Rankin *(Pres. & Chief Exec. Officer)*
Michael Gadbois *(V.P.-Opers.)*
K. Knudsen *(V.P.-Mktg.)*
David Quinn *(V.P.-Fin.)*
Donna Rossbach *(Mgr.-Personnel)*
S. Hepner *(Pur. Agent)*

Computer Systems/Hardware:
IBM 36

BRUNNER & LAY, INC.
9300 King
Franklin Park, IL 60131
Mailing Address:
P.O. Box 1329
Franklin Park, IL 60131
Tel.: 708-678-3232 **DE**
Fax: 708-678-0642
Year Founded: 1882
Emp.: 200
Export
Rock Drilling & Pneumatic Tool Accessories
S.I.C.: 3533; 3599; 3559; 5084
M.F. Brunner *(Pres.)*
R.B. Wolf *(Sec.)*
Larry McKissick *(Mgr.-Natl. Sls.)*
Donald Fortney *(Pur. Agent)*

No. of Mfg. Plants/Facilities: 3
No. of U.S. Offices: 11

Outside Service Firm(s):

Suburban Trust & Savings*(Major Banking Relationship)*
Franklin Park, IL

BRUNSCHWIG & FILS, INC.
75 Virginia Rd. N.
White Plains, NY 10603
Tel.: 914-684-5800 **NY**
Year Founded: 1925
Approx.Sls.: $70,000,000
Emp.: 325
Piece Goods & Other Fabrics; Woven Textiles; Wallcoverings; Furniture
S.I.C.: 5131; 5198; 5021
Thomas Peardon *(Pres. & Chief Exec. Officer)*
Murray Douglas *(Sr. V.P.)*
Francis J. Hand *(Treas.)*

Outside Service Firm(s):

Murphy O'Connor & Co.*(Auditors)*
New York, NY

BRUSH RESEARCH MANUFACTURING COMPANY
4642 E. Floral Dr.
Los Angeles, CA 90022
Tel.: 213-261-2193
Fax: 213-268-6587
Year Founded: 1964
Approx.Sls.: $10,000,000
Emp.: 100
Fiscal Year-end: 12/30/91
Import Export
Manufacture Industrial Brushes
S.I.C.: 3991
Tara Rands *(Pres.)*
Robert G. Fowlie *(V.P.-Opers.)*
Mary Rands *(Sec. & Treas.)*
Teri Lira *(Dir.-Pur.)*
Glorian Kunioka *(Mgr.-Export)*
Jay Tarlo *(Mgr.-Sls.)*
Principal(s):
Tara Rands
Robert G. Fowlie
Mary Rands

No. of Mfg. Plants/Facilities: 2
No. of U.S. Offices: 2

Computer Systems/Hardware:
IBM

Outside Service Firm(s):

Finocchiaro & Hill*(Auditors)*
Pasadena, CA

First Interstate Bank*(Major Banking Relationship)*
Pasadena, CA

BRUSS COMPANY
3548 N. Kostner Ave.
Chicago, IL 60641
Tel.: 312-282-2900 **IL**
Fax: 312-282-6966
Year Founded: 1989
Approx.Sls.: $55,000,000
Emp.: 110
Export
Wholesale Distribution of Fresh Meats
S.I.C.: 5147
Ellard Pfaelzer, Jr. *(Chm. Bd.)*
Robert Anderson *(Pres.)*
April Baynee *(Controller)*

Outside Service Firm(s):

BDO Seidman*(Auditors)*
111 E. Wacker Dr.
Chicago, IL 60601

BRUTGER EQUITIES, INC.
One Sunwood Plaza
Saint Cloud, MN 56301
Mailing Address:
P.O. Box 399
St. Cloud, MN 56302
Tel.: 612-252-6262 **MN**
Fax: 612-252-6268
Year Founded: 1988
Sales Range: $10-19 Million
Emp.: 250
Fiscal Year-end: 12/31/91
Operation of Apartments & Hotels
S.I.C.: 6513; 7011
Larry Brutger *(Chm. Bd. & Pres.)*
Sandra J. Lang *(Chief Fin. Officer)*
Ken Shane *(Dir.-Opers.)*

Principal(s):
Larry Brutger

Outside Service Firm(s):

Christoffel, Elliott & Holper, P.A.*(Legal Firm)*
805 Capital Centre, 386 North Wabasha St.
St. Paul, MN 55102

BRYANT ELECTRIC COMPANY, INC.
1901 English Rd.
High Point, NC 27262
Mailing Address:
P.O. Box 1430
High Point, NC 27261
Tel.: 919-884-1800
Fax: 919-882-2342
Approx.Sls.: $43,000,000
Emp.: 375
Electrical Contractor Specializing in Industrial, Utilities & Water & Sewer Construction
S.I.C.: 1731
John Linden Wall *(Chm. Bd. & Pres.)*
Kay D. Wall *(Sec. & Treas.)*

Computer Systems/Hardware:
NCR

Outside Service Firm(s):

Dixon, Odom & Co.*(Auditors)*
Concord, NC

Kruthers & Roth*(Legal Firm)*
High Point, NC

First Citizens Bank & Trust Co.*(Major Banking Relationship)*
High Point, NC

BRYANT SUPPLY COMPANY, INC.
605 E. Franklin Blvd.
Gastonia, NC 28054
Mailing Address:
P.O. Box 1277
Gastonia, NC 28053
Tel.: 704-866-6000
Fax: 704-853-1802
Year Founded: 1931
Sales Range: $60-79 Million
Emp.: 250
Import Export
Distribute Electrical, Industrial & Power Transmission Supplies & Controls
S.I.C.: 5063; 5065; 5085
Harry M. Bryant, Sr. *(Pres.)*
Harry M. Bryant, Jr. *(Exec. V.P.)*
Harvey L. Foy *(V.P.)*
Donald S. Lanier *(V.P.-Pur.)*
Richard J. Bryant *(Sec. & Treas.)*
Thomas L. Bryant *(Mgr.-Power Transmission)*

No. of U.S. Offices: 13

Outside Service Firm(s):

Cherry, Bekaert & Holland*(Auditors)*
Charlotte, NC

Branch Banking & Trust Co.*(Major Banking Relationship)*
Gastonia, NC

BRYANT UNIVERSAL ROOFERS INC.
3311 N. 44th St., Ste. 100
Phoenix, AZ 85018
Mailing Address:
P.O. Box 80649,
Phoenix, AZ 85060
Tel.: 602-952-5070 **AZ**
Fax: 602-840-2918
Year Founded: 1969
Sales Range: $60-79 Million
Emp.: 600
Installation & Repair Industrial & Commercial Roofing Systems
S.I.C.: 1761
Wayne Mullis *(Chm. Bd.)*
Richard Ransbottom *(Pres.)*
Kenneth R. Zinser *(Chief Fin. Officer)*
John Toolis *(Dir.-Equip. Assets)*

Principal(s):
Wayne Mullis

No. of Mfg. Plants/Facilities: 5
No. of U.S. Offices: 5

Computer Systems/Hardware:
MAI Basic 4

Outside Service Firm(s):

McGladrey & Pullen*(Auditors)*
Mesa, AZ

Emmett & Chandler*(Commercial Insurance Carrier)*
Chandler, AZ

Arizona Roofers Health & Welfare Trust Fund*(Group Insurer)*
Phoenix, AZ

Meyer, Vucichevich & Cinala*(Legal Firm)*
Phoenix, AZ

Security Pacific Bank Arizona*(Major Banking Relationship)*
Phoenix, AZ

Subsidiaries:

Universal Roofers, Inc. **(1)**
3430 S. Valley View Blvd.
Las Vegas, NV 89102
Tel.: 702-876-1777
Installation & Repair Industrial & Commercial Roofing Systems
S.I.C.: 1761
Scott Howard *(V.P. & Gen. Mgr.)*

Universal Roofers, Inc. **(1)**
2819 W. Ruthrauff
Tucson, AZ 85705
Tel.: 602-293-1891
Installation & Repair Industrial & Commercial Roofing Systems
S.I.C.: 1761
Jerry Bourdeau *(Gen. Mgr.)*

Universal Roofers, Inc. **(1)**
1245 S. 7th St.
Phoenix, AZ 85036
Tel.: 602-258-7941
Fax: 602-252-7195
Installation & Repair Industrial & Commercial Roofing Systems
S.I.C.: 1761
John Plescia *(Gen. Mgr.)*

BRYCE CORPORATION
4505 Old Lamar
Memphis, TN 38118
Tel.: 901-369-4400 **TN**
Fax: 901-367-1572
Year Founded: 1969
Approx.Sls.: $76,000,000
Emp.: 500
Coated Or Laminated Plastic Film For Packaging; Metal Foil & Leaf For Packaging
S.I.C.: 2671; 3497
William M. Riegel *(Chm. Bd.)*
William H. Bryce, Jr. *(Pres.)*
William H. Bryce, III *(V.P. & Sec.)*

Outside Service Firm(s):

Rhea & Ivy*(Auditors)*
Memphis, TN

BUCILLA CORPORATION
1 Oak Ridge Rd.
Hazleton, PA 18201-9764
Tel.: 717-384-2525
Tel.: 800-233-3239
Fax: 717-384-2555
Year Founded: 1867
Approx.Sls.: $30,000,000
Emp.: 300
Fiscal Year-end: 12/31/91
Import Export
Bucilla Needlecraft & Yarns, Gallery of Stitches, Special Edition, Stencils USA, Legacy Gifts
S.I.C.: 2299; 2395
Corporate Giving Program: Gifts to United Way
Robert P. Denise *(Chm., Pres., Chief Exec. Officer & Chief Fin. Officer)*
Glenn Nicholson *(Exec. V.P. & Vice Chm.)*
Jeffrey D. Steele *(Exec. V.P.)*

Computer Systems/Hardware:
IBM AS 400

Outside Service Firm(s):

Deloitte & Touche*(Auditors)*
Ste. 200, Two Windsor Dr., 7540 Windsor Dr.
Allentown, PA 18195
Tel.: 215-366-5100

Kirkland & Ellis*(Legal Firm)*
1776 "K" St. N.W.
Washington, DC 20006
Tel.: 202-857-5000

United Jersey Bank*(Major Banking Relationship)*
Hackensack, NJ

Subsidiaries:

Legacy Gifts **(1)**
1 Oak Ridge Rd.
Hazleton, PA 10201-9847
Tel.: 717-384-2525
Import Export

Stencils USA **(1)**
1 Oak Ridge Rd.
Hazleton, PA 18201-9847
Tel.: 717-384-2525
Import Export
Finished Needlecraft Kits
S.I.C.: 2395

BUCK KNIVES, INC.
1900 Weld Blvd.
El Cajon, CA 92020
Mailing Address:
P.O. Box 1267,
El Cajon, CA 92022
Tel.: 619-449-1100 **CA**
Telex: 910-331-1182 BUCK ELCJ
Fax: 619-449-2869
Year Founded: 1961
Approx.Sls.: $50,000,000
Emp.: 400
Fiscal Year-end: 12/31/91
Import Export
Manufacture Sportsman's Cutlery, Household Cutlery & Darts
S.I.C.: 3421
Charles T. Buck *(Chm. Bd., Pres. & Chief Exec. Officer)*
Gary Schwertly *(Sr. V.P.-Fin.)*
C.B. Buck *(Exec. V.P.)*
Al Evans *(V.P.-Mfg.)*
Charlie Gregory *(V.P.-Mktg. & Sls.)*
Candace Kilburn *(Dir.-Human Rels.)*
John Ranzi *(Dir.-Resource Devel.)*
Lisa Sanderson *(Corp. Counsel)*
Jan Drew *(Mgr.-Special Sls.)*
Greg Mooney *(Mgr.-Sls.)*

No. of Mfg. Plants/Facilities: 2
No. of U.S. Offices: 1

Computer Systems/Hardware:
DEC

Outside Service Firm(s):

Peterson & Co.*(Auditors)*
San Diego, CA

Luce Farward*(Legal Firm)*
San Diego, CA

Wells Fargo Bank*(Major Banking Relationship)*
San Diego, CA

Subsidiary:

County Tool & Abrasive **(1)**
9263 Abraham Way
Santee, CA 92071
Tel.: 619-449-0600
Emp.: 3
Abrasives Distributor
S.I.C.: 5085
Charles B. Buck *(Pres.)*
Gary Schwartz *(Dir.-Fin.)*

BUCK & PULLEYN, INC.
500 Helendale Rd.
Rochester, NY 14609
Tel.: 716-288-6900
Fax: 716-288-4474
Year Founded: 1982
Approx.Billings: $28,000,000
Emp.: 61
Fiscal Year-end: 10/31/91
Import Export
Advertising, Public Relations, Sales Promotions, Publications, High Technology
S.I.C.: 7311
Chris Pulleyn *(Partner & Mng. Dir.)*
Roxanne Bernardo *(Dir.-Fin.)*
Daisy Collinsworth *(Dir.-Pub. Rels.)*
Richard Vangaasbeck *(Dir.-Technical)*
Jane Lavery *(Mgr.-Personnel)*

Outside Service Firm(s):

Davie, Kaplan, Braverman*(Auditors)*
Rochester, NY

Allyn, Small, Gosling*(Commercial Insurance Carrier)*
Rochester, NY

Benefits Planning Services*(Group Insurer)*
Rochester, NY

Woods, Oviatt, Gilman, Sturman & Clarke*(Legal Firm)*
44 Exchange St.
Rochester, NY 14614
Tel.: 716-454-5370

Columbia Banking Federal Savings & Loan Association*(Major Banking Relationship)*
Rochester, NY

BUCKMAN LABORATORIES
1256 N. McLean Blvd.
Memphis, TN 38108
Tel.: 901-278-0330
Fax: 901-276-5343
Emp.: 715
Fiscal Year-end: 12/31/91
Mfr. of Specialty Chemicals For Use In Industrial, Agricultural & Human Environments
S.I.C.: 2836; 2899
R.H. Buckman *(Chm. Bd. & Chief Exec. Officer)*
S.B. Buckman *(Pres.)*
G.E. Baldwin *(V.P. & Gen Mgr.-USA & Canada)*
C.P. Barnaud *(V.P.-Opers.)*
Dennis Dalton *(V.P.-Intl. Mktg.)*

Buckman Laboratories—(Continued)

L.E. Dibble *(Treas.)*
C.G. Hollis *(V.P.-Res. & Devel.)*
M.D. Karve *(V.P.-Japan & Korean Mktg.)*
G.A. Ronidez *(V.P.-Mktg.)*
J.B. Sladen *(Sec.)*

Outside Service Firm(s):

Ernst & Young*(Auditors)*
1400 One Commerce Sq.
Memphis, TN 38103

Burch, Porter & Johnson*(Legal Firm)*
Memphis, TN

First Tennessee Bank, N.A.*(Major Banking Relationship)*
Memphis, TN

BUCYRUS-ERIE COMPANY
1100 Milwaukee Ave.
South Milwaukee, WI 53172
Mailing Address:
P.O. Box 500,
South Milwaukee, WI 53172
Tel.: 414-768-4000 DE
Telex: 3797360 BUCYRUS SMIL
Fax: 414-768-5060
Year Founded: 1927
Assets: $200,467,000
Earnings: ($16,498,000)
Liabilities: $201,634,000
Net Worth: $1,167,000
Approx.Sls.: $213,577,000
Emp.: 879
Fiscal Year-end: 12/31/90
Import Export
Designs, Manufactures & Sells Product for Surface Mining Industry
S.I.C.: 3532
Corporate Giving Program: Corp. Giving is Done Though Contributions at Irregular Intervals to Bucyrus-Erie Foundation, Inc., a Wisconsin Non-Member Not-for-Profit Corp. with no Corp. Affiliation to Bucyrus-Erie Co.
Employee Matching Gifts Program: Bucyrus-Erie Foundation, Inc. Matches Certain Employee Gifts to Qualifying Educational, Health, Welfare or Arts Organizations
W.B. Winter *(Chm. Bd. & Chief Exec. Officer)*
R.G. Olander *(Vice Chm. & Legal Officer)*
Phillip Mork *(Pres.)*
R.D. Vitale *(V.P.-Mfg.)*
E.F. Schweitzer *(V.P.-Engrng.)*
J.H. Westerman *(V.P.-Mktg.)*
David M. Goelzer *(Sec. & Gen. Counsel)*
N.J. Verville *(Chief Fin. Officer & Treas.)*
C.R. Mackus *(Controller)*
T.W. Sullivan *(Dir.-Parts Sls. & Opers.)*

Outside Service Firm(s):

Deloitte & Touche*(Auditors)*
250 E. Wisconsin Ave.
Milwaukee, WI 53202-4283
Tel.: 414-271-3000

Goldman, Sachs & Co.*(Investment Banker)*
85 Broad St.
New York, NY 10004
Tel.: 212-902-1000
Fax: 212-902-4451

Paine Webber*(Investment Banker)*
1285 Ave. of the Americas
New York, NY 10019
Tel.: 212-713-2000
Fax: 212-713-3010

Milbank, Tweed, Hadley & McCloy*(Legal Firm)*
One Chase Plaza
New York, NY 10005
Tel.: 212-530-5000

Chemical Bank*(Major Banking Relationship)*
450 West 33rd St.
New York, NY 10001
Tel.: 212-613-7197
Fax: 212-947-7628

Wyatt Co.*(Pension Manager)*
Milwaukee, WI

Subsidiaries:

Boonville Mining Services, Inc. (1)
110 W. Division St.
Boonville, IN 47601
Tel.: 812-897-2512
Fax: 812-897-5236
Mfr. & Repair of Mining Equipment
S.I.C.: 3532
R. Neil Massey *(Gen. Mgr.)*

Minserco, Inc. (1)
1100 Milwaukee Ave.
South Milwaukee, WI 53172
Tel.: 414-768-5160
Fax: 414-768-5165
Repair of Mining Equipment
S.I.C.: 3532
Kenneth C. Wachowski *(Gen. Mgr.)*

Non-U.S. Holdings:

Bucyrus (Africa) Proprietary Ltd. (1)
415 Wrench Rd.
Johannesburg, Isando 1600, South Africa
Tel.: 36-2391 (100%)
Mfr. Mining & Constr. Equip.
S.I.C.: 3532

Bucyrus (Australia) Proprietary Ltd. (1)
9th Floor G.W.A. House, 10 Market Street
Brisbane, QLD 4000, Australia
Tel.: 920-1221
Mfr. Mining & Constr. Equip.
S.I.C.: 3532

Bucyrus (Brasil) Ltda. (1)
Avenida Professor Magalhaes Penido, 439
Belo Horizonte, Bairro Aeroport CEP 30.000, Brazil
Tel.: 441-2399
Mfr. Mining & Constr. Equip.
S.I.C.: 3532

Bucyrus Chile Ltda. (1)
Casilla 16846-Providencia, Avda 11 de Sepiembre 2055 Torre C-OP, 1201, Santiago, Chile
Tel.: 571-468
Mfr. Mining & Constr. Equip.
S.I.C.: 3532

Bucyrus-Erie Co. of Canada Ltd. (1)
1310 8th Street
Nisku, AB T0C 2G0, Canada
Tel.: 604-273-4446
Mfg. Mining & Constr. Equip.
S.I.C.: 3532

Bucyrus-Europe Ltd. (1)
Becor House, Green Lane
Lincoln, LN6 7DJ, United Kingdom
Tel.: 522-513425 (100%)
Mfr. Mining & Constr. Equip.
S.I.C.: 3532

Equipment Assurance Ltd. (1)
P.O. Box 694
Georgetown, Grand Cayman Cayman Islands
Emp.: 2
Captive Insurance Company
S.I.C.: 6411

BUD INDUSTRIES, INC.
4605 E. 355th
Willoughby, OH 44094
Tel.: 216-946-3200
Fax: 216-951-4015
Year Founded: 1928
Approx.Sls.: $15,000,000
Emp.: 200
Import Export
Electronic Enclosures & Accessories
S.I.C.: 3679
Alvin N. Haas *(Chm. Bd.)*
B.K. Haas *(Pres.)*
G.E. Grove *(V.P.-Fin. & Controller)*
S.H. Haas *(V.P.-Personnel)*
Dan Lucas *(Dir.-Mfg.)*
William Deroche *(Dir.-Sls.)*
G. A. Haas *(Mgr.-Pur.)*

Subsidiary:

Bud West, Inc. (1)
7733 West Olive Ave.
Peoria, AZ 85345
Tel.: 602-979-0300
S.I.C.: 3679
B.K. Haas *(Pres.)*

BUDCO GROUP INC.
1100 Gest St.
Cincinnati, OH 45203
Tel.: 513-621-6111 OH
Fax: 513-621-4330
Year Founded: 1949
Assets: $27,000,000
Liabilities: $18,000,000
Net Worth: $9,000,000
Approx.Sls.: $24,000,000
Emp.: 800
Convention Decorating Services; Piggyback Ramping Services; Equipment Leasing; Real Estate Development
S.I.C.: 7389; 7359; 6552
Otto M. Budig, Jr. *(Pres.)*
George J. Budig *(V.P., Sec. & Treas.)*
Principal(s):
Otto M. Budig, Jr.
George J. Budig

No. of Mfg. Plants/Facilities: 29
No. of U.S. Offices: 29

Computer Systems/Hardware:
IBM System 38 ALS 400

Outside Service Firm(s):

McDott & Mellott*(Auditors)*
Cincinnati, OH

Marsh & McLennan*(Commercial Insurance Carrier)*
1400 Central Trust Center
Cincinnati, OH 45202-4191
Tel.: 513-721-5557

Principal Mutual Life Insurance Co.*(Group Insurer)*
711 High St.
Des Moines, IA 50309

Frost & Jacobs*(Legal Firm)*
2500 Central Trust Ctr.
Cincinnati, OH 45202
Tel.: 513-651-6800

The Central Trust Company, N.A.*(Major Banking Relationship)*
Cincinnati, OH
Tel.: 513-651-8896

H. J. Larmonn & Assoc.*(Pension Manager)*
Cincinnati, OH

Divisions:

George E. Fern Company (1)
1100 Gest St.
Cincinnati, OH 45203
Tel.: 513-621-6111
George J. Budig *(Pres.)*

O/B Leasing Company (1)
1100 Gest St.
Cincinnati, OH 45203
Tel.: 513-621-6111
S.I.C.: 7359
Otto M. Budig Jr. *(Pres.)*

Parsec/Dotson, Inc. (1)
1100 Gest St.
Cincinnati, OH 45203
Tel.: 513-621-6111

Parsec (1)
1100 Gest St.
Cincinnati, OH 45203
Tel.: 513-621-6111
Otto M. Budig Jr. *(Pres.)*

Piggyback Services, Inc. (1)
1100 Gest St.
Cincinnati, OH 45203
Tel.: 513-621-6111
Otto M. Budig Jr. *(Pres.)*

CARL BUDDIG & COMPANY
950 W. 175th St.
Homewood, IL 60430
Tel.: 708-798-0900
Tel.: 800-621-0868
Fax: 708-798-3178
Emp.: 400
Export
Processor Smoked Sliced Beef & Other Meat Prods.
S.I.C.: 2013
William C. Buddig *(Pres.)*
Thomas R. Buddig *(V.P.-Sls. & Mktg.)*
Eugene J. Donaghey *(V.P.-Fin.)*
Robert J. Buddig *(V.P.)*
John C. Buddig *(Treas.)*
Torrey Foster *(Dir.-Mktg.)*
Eleanor Honan *(Mktg. Admin.)*

Computer Systems/Hardware:
IBM System AS400

Subsidiaries:

Old Wisconsin Cheese Co., Inc. (1)
1085 E. Mineral St.
Platteville, WI 53818
Tel.: 608-348-9706
Mfr. Swiss Cheese
S.I.C.: 2022

Old Wisconsin Sausage (1)
2107 S. 17th St.
Sheboygan, WI 53081
Tel.: 414-458-4304
Specialty Sausage Mfr.
S.I.C.: 2013

Smokie Products, Inc. (1)
2107 17th St.
Sheboygan, WI 53037
Tel.: 414-458-4304
Mfr. Beef Sticks; Pepper Sticks
S.I.C.: 2013

BUDGET MARKETING, INC.
1171 W. 7th St.
Des Moines, IA 50306
Tel.: 515-243-7000 IA
Approx.Sls.: $29,000,000
Emp.: 450
Telemarketing Services
S.I.C.: 7389
Dennis H. Gougion *(Chief Exec. Officer)*
Jo Ann Butler *(Pres.)*
Ralph Kuhn *(V.P.)*
Phyllis Parr *(V.P. & Sec.)*
Joseph A. Pirillo *(V.P. & Treas.)*
Michael DeVourzi *(Chief Fin. Officer)*

Outside Service Firm(s):

Hawkeye Bancorporation*(Major Banking Relationship)*
7th & Locust Sts.
Des Moines, IA 50307
Tel.: 515-284-1930

BUERKLE BUICK-HONDA CO.
3350 Hwy. #61 N.
Saint Paul, MN 55110
Tel.: 612-484-0231
Fax: 612-484-9463
Approx.Sls.: $43,000,000
Emp.: 190
Fiscal Year-end: 12/31/91
Retail New & Used Automobiles; Leasing
S.I.C.: 5511; 7514
W.W. Buerkle *(Pres.)*
Jerome Fischer *(Sec. & Treas.)*

Outside Service Firm(s):

Sands, Lee & DeWald*(Auditors)*
St. Paul, MN

Briggs & Morgan*(Legal Firm)*
Minneapolis, MN

Norwest Bank Minnesota, N.A.*(Major Banking Relationship)*
6th St. & Marquette Av.
Minneapolis, MN 55479
Tel.: 612-667-1234

BUFFALO COLOR CORPORATION
959 Rt. 46 E., Ste. 403
Parsippany, NJ 07054
Tel.: 201-316-5600
Fax: 201-316-5828
Year Founded: 1977
Approx.Sls.: $50,000,000
Manufacture Dyes for Fabrics
S.I.C.: 2865
Kenneth W. McCourt *(Pres. & Chief Exec. Officer)*
W.O. Fields *(Controller)*
G. W. Collins *(Dir.-Personnel)*
William Smith *(Dir.-Data Processing)*

No. of Mfg. Plants/Facilities: 1
No. of U.S. Offices: 2

Computer Systems/Hardware:
IBM System 36

Outside Service Firm(s):

Coopers & Lybrand*(Auditors)*
Buffalo, NY

Empire Blue Cross & Blue Shield*(Group Insurer)*
New York, NY

Chemical Banking Corp.*(Major Banking Relationship)*
277 Park Ave.
New York, NY 10041
Tel.: 212-310-6407
Fax: 212-310-4526

Subsidiary:

Buffalo Color Corporation **(1)**
100 Lee St.
Buffalo, NY 14210
Tel.: 716-827-4500
K.W. McCourt *(Pres.)*

BUFFALO HOSPITAL SUPPLY CO., INC.
130 Pineview Dr.
Amherst, NY 14228
Tel.: 716-691-9400 **NY**
Fax: 716-691-7244
Year Founded: 1977
Approx.Sls.: $21,000,000
Emp.: 55
Fiscal Year-end: 8/31/92
Wholesale Medical & Surgical Supplies
S.I.C.: 5047
Michael J. Burke *(Pres.)*
Stephen Corroran *(V.P.-Opers.)*
Alan Wick *(V.P.-Mktg.)*
Margaret Kapanek *(Controller)*
James Casselman *(Dir.-Data Processing)*
Gary Skura *(Mgr.-Sls.)*

Outside Service Firm(s):

Leonard A. Dopkins & Company*(Auditors)*
Buffalo, NY

Gross & Shuman*(Legal Firm)*
Buffalo, NY

Key Bank*(Major Banking Relationship)*
Buffalo, NY

BUFFALO ROCK COMPANY
111 Oxmoor Rd.
Birmingham, AL 35209
Mailing Address:
P.O. Box 10048
Birmingham, AL 35202
Tel.: 205-942-3435
Fax: 205-942-2601
Approx.Sls.: $250,000,000
Emp.: 1,350
Fiscal Year-end: 12/31/91
Soft Drinks
S.I.C.: 2086
James C. Lee, Jr. *(Chm. Bd.)*
James C. Lee, III *(Pres.)*
James M. Reddinger *(Exec. V.P.-Admin.)*
Roger Barker *(V.P. & Treas.)*
Larry Dutton *(Controller)*
Mary B. Allums *(Sec.)*
Principal(s):
James C. Lee, Jr.
James C. Lee, III

Computer Systems/Hardware:
Hewlett Packard

Outside Service Firm(s):

Dudley, Hopton-Jones, Sims & Freeman*(Auditors)*
Huntsville, AL

Central Bank of the South*(Major Banking Relationship)*
Birmingham, AL

BUFFALO WHITE GMC, INC.
271 Dingens St.
Buffalo, NY 14206
Tel.: 716-821-9911
Fax: 716-821-9951
Year Founded: 1968
Assets: $3,500,000
Liabilities: $2,800,000
Net Worth: $700,000
Sales Range: $10-19 Million
Emp.: 65
Fiscal Year-end: 3/31/89
Heavy Truck Sales & Service
S.I.C.: 5084
Michael Graber *(Pres. & Chief Exec. Officer)*

No. of Mfg. Plants/Facilities: 2

Computer Systems/Hardware:
IBM; Honeywell; DEC

BUFFELEN WOODWORKING COMPANY
1901 Taylor Way
Tacoma, WA 98421
Tel.: 206-627-1191
Fax: 206-383-2060
Approx.Sls.: $38,000,000
Emp.: 400
Stile & Rail Doors
S.I.C.: 2431
Joseph Guizzetti *(Chief Exec. Officer & Gen. Mgr.)*
Tom Cobb *(Controller)*
Mike Krause *(Mgr.-Sls.)*
Marlene Rosier *(Mgr.-Human Resources)*
Cheryl Jorgensen *(Sec.)*

Computer Systems/Hardware:
IBM

Outside Service Firm(s):

Knight, Vale & Gregory*(Auditors)*
Tacoma, WA

Kane, Vandeberg, Hartinger & Walker*(Legal Firm)*
Tacoma, WA

Seafirst Bank*(Major Banking Relationship)*
Columbia-SeaFirst Center, 701 5th Ave., 11th Flr.
Seattle, WA 98124
Tel.: 206-358-3039
Fax: 206-358-3113

BUFKOR, INC.
13100 56th Court N., Ste. 710
Clearwater, FL 34620
Tel.: 813-572-9991 **NY**
Fax: 813-572-0746
Year Founded: 1900
Approx.Sls.: $20,000,000
Emp.: 100
Manufacture Jewelry Boxes, Displays & Packaging
S.I.C.: 2657; 3993
Nassin Yarhi *(Chm. Bd.)*
Les Unger *(Pres. & Chief Exec. Officer)*
Reg Martin *(V.P.-Mfg.)*

No. of Mfg. Plants/Facilities: 2
No. of U.S. Offices: 2

Computer Systems/Hardware:
IBM System 38

Outside Service Firm(s):

Freed, Maxick, Sachs & Murphy*(Auditors)*
Buffalo, NY
Tel.: 716-847-2651

Hartman & Craven*(Legal Firm)*
460 Park Ave.
New York, NY 10022
Tel.: 212-753-7500

BUGLE BOY INDUSTRIES, INC.
2900 Madera Rd.
Simi Valley, CA 93065
Tel.: 805-582-1010
Fax: 805-522-1212
Approx.Sls.: $150,000,000
Emp.: 400
Fiscal Year-end: 12/31/90
Import
Distribute Men's & Junior's Sportswear
S.I.C.: 5136
William Mow *(Chm. Bd.)*
Vincent Nesi *(Pres.)*
Phillip Molinari *(Exec. V.P.-Sls.)*
Rosa Wang *(Sr. V.P.)*
Ron Margolis *(Controller)*
Genevieve Squires *(Dir.-Adv. & Mktg.)*
Suzi Scheimann *(Mgr.-Adv.)*

Computer Systems/Hardware:
IBM System 32

Outside Service Firm(s):

Blue Cross of California*(Group Insurer)*
2101 Western St.
Oakland, CA 94659
Tel.: 800-645-3000

Subsidiary:

Dragon International **(1)**
2900 Madera Rd.
Simi Valley, CA 93065
Tel.: 805-582-1010
Fax: 818-709-8951
Import Company
S.I.C.: 5136

BUHLER INC.
1100 Xenium Ln.
Minneapolis, MN 55441
Mailing Address:
P.O. Box 9497
Minneapolis, MN 55440
Tel.: 612-545-1401 **MN**
Fax: 612-540-9246
Year Founded: 1957
Approx.Sls.: $40,000,000
Emp.: 287
Manufacture & Wholesale Industrial Food Processing Machinery & Equipment; Manufacture Bulk Conveying & Dust Control Systems & Machinery
S.I.C.: 3535; 3564; 3559; 5084
Anthony P. Beer *(Pres.)*
Hans Wanzenried *(Grp. V.P.)*
Willi Zogg *(Grp. V.P.)*
Bill Berger *(V.P.-Mgr. Waste Processing)*
Ursula Stephan *(Adv. Coord.)*

Outside Service Firm(s):

Deloitte & Touche*(Auditors)*
Memphis, TN

BUHRMAN-PHARR HARDWARE COMPANY
212-222 Laurel St.
Texarkana, AR 75502
Tel.: 501-773-3122 **AR**
Year Founded: 1879
Approx.Sls.: $13,000,000
Emp.: 105
Fiscal Year-end: 12/31/91
Wholesale Distribution & Retail Sales of Builders' Hardware, Hand Garden Tools & Plumbing Fittings & Supplies
S.I.C.: 5072; 5074; 5063; 5251
Stanley Jones *(Pres., Chief Exec. Officer & Gen. Mgr.)*
Les Smith *(Treas. & Sec.)*

Outside Service Firm(s):

Grier, Reeves & Lawley*(Auditors)*
Texarkana, TX

State First National Bank*(Major Banking Relationship)*
Texarkana, TX

BUILDER MARTS OF AMERICA
1 Independence Pointe
Greenville, SC 29615
Mailing Address:
P.O. Box 47,
Greenville, SC 29602
Tel.: 803-297-6101
Fax: 803-281-3381
Year Founded: 1966
Approx.Sls.: $289,000,000
Emp.: 180
Fiscal Year-end: 12/31/91
Import
Mfr. & Distribute Lumber & Wood Products; Building Materials
S.I.C.: 5039; 5031; 5063; 5074; 5198
Richard E. Ingram *(Chm. Bd., Chief Exec. & Chief Fin. Officer)*
Nellie G. Harvey *(Vice Chm.)*
Brian S. MacKenzie *(Pres. & Chief Oper. Officer)*
R. Steven Robins *(Sec., Treas., Controller & Cash Mgr.)*
Delores Brandon *(Dir.-Administrative Services)*
Lucy T. Tinsley *(Mgr.-Human Resources)*
Teresa G. Watson *(Mgr.-Meetings Planning)*
Principal(s):
Richard E. Ingram

No. of U.S. Offices: 4

Computer Systems/Hardware:
IBM System AS400

Outside Service Firm(s):

Ernst & Young*(Auditors)*
C & S Bank Tower, Two Shelter Centre, Ste. 800
Greenville, SC 29603

Carolina First Bank*(Major Banking Relationship)*
P.O. Box 1029, 102 Main St.
Greenville, SC 29602

Builder Marts of America—(Continued)

Barclays Business Credit*(Major Banking Relationship)*
Charlotte, NC

First American National Bank*(Major Banking Relationship)*
First American Center
Nashville, TN 37237
Tel.: 615-748-2000

Wyche, Burgess, Freeman & Parham, P.A.*(Legal Firm)*
44 E. Camperdown Way
Greenville, SC 29602
Tel.: 803-242-3131

BUILDING PLASTICS, INC.
3263 Sharpe Ave.
Memphis, TN 38111
Tel.: 901-744-6200
Fax: 901-744-7622
Approx.Sls.: $34,000,000
Emp.: 150
Wholesale Building Materials
S.I.C.: 5039
Alexander R. Hill *(Pres.)*
James H. Frazier *(Exec. V.P.-Sls.)*

Outside Service Firm(s):

Zoccola*(Auditors)*
Memphis, TN

Thomason, Crawford & Hendre*(Legal Firm)*
Memphis, TN

First Tennessee Bank, N.A.*(Major Banking Relationship)*
P.O. Box 84
Memphis, TN 38101-0034
Tel.: 901-523-4541

BUILDING PRODUCTS INC.
405 First Ave., N.E.
Watertown, SD 57201
Mailing Address:
P.O. Box 1413
Watertown, SD 57201
Tel.: 605-886-3495 **SD**
Fax: 605-886-3495 Ext. 3495
Year Founded: 1957
Approx.Sls.: $21,800,000
Emp.: 60
Distribute Building Materials
S.I.C.: 5039
Lee Schull *(Pres.)*
Lester Schull *(Exec. V.P.)*
Johanna Schull *(Sec. & Treas.)*
Earl Benson *(Dir.-Personnel)*

Principal(s):
Lee Schull
Lester Schull
Johanna Schull

No. of Mfg. Plants/Facilities: 3

Computer Systems/Hardware:
IBM System 36

Outside Service Firm(s):

Charles Bailly & Co.*(Auditors)*
100 N. Phillips Ave., 8th Flr.
Sioux Falls, SD 57102
Tel.: 605-339-1999

Farmers & Merchants Bank & Trust*(Major Banking Relationship)*
Watertown, SD

Subsidiary:

Building Products Inc. of S.D. **(1)**
2200 E. Rice St.
Sioux Falls, SD 57103
Tel.: 605-336-3460
Emp.: 18
Wholesale Building Materials
S.I.C.: 5039
Chris Fischer *(Branch Mgr.)*

Building Technologies Corporation
(Name Changed to Steelox Systems, Inc.)

BULAB HOLDINGS, INC.
1256 N. McLean Blvd.
Memphis, TN 38108
Tel.: 901-278-0330 **TN**
Fax: 901-276-5343
Year Founded: 1963
Approx.Sls.: $148,000,000
Emp.: 1,000
Export
Mfr. of Industrial Organic & Inorganic Chemicals
S.I.C.: 2869; 2819
M.W. Buckman *(Chm. Bd. & Pres.)*
Mary R. Goodloe *(Sec.)*
M.W. Buckman *(Treas. & Asst. Sec.)*
L.E. Dibble *(Treas. & Asst. Sec.)*

Outside Service Firm(s):

Ernst & Young*(Auditors)*
1400 One Commerce Sq.
Memphis, TN 38103

First Tennessee Bank, N.A.*(Major Banking Relationship)*
P.O. Box 101
Memphis, TN 38101
Tel.: 901-523-4555

Subsidiaries:

Bulab Realty Of Missouri, Inc. **(1)**
1256 N. McLean Blvd.
Memphis, TN 38108
Tel.: 901-278-0330
Approx.Sls.: $2,000,000
Emp.: 2
Equipment Rental & Leasing; Nonresidential Building Operators
S.I.C.: 7359; 6512
L.E. Diddle *(Pres.)*
Mary R. Goodloe *(Sec.)*

Bulab Realty Of Tennessee, Inc. **(1)**
1256 N. McLean Blvd.
Memphis, TN 38108
Tel.: 901-278-0330
Equipment Rental & Leasing; Nonresidential Building Operators
S.I.C.: 7359; 6512
L.E. Diddle *(Pres.)*

Buckman Laboratories, Inc. **(1)**
1256 N. McLean Blvd.
Memphis, TN 38108
Tel.: 901-278-0330
Approx.Sls.: $86,000,000
Emp.: 450
Mfr. of Industrial Organic & Inorganic Chemicals
S.I.C.: 2869; 2819
Steven B. Buckman *(Chm. Bd.)*
Gary E. Baldwin *(Pres.)*

Buckman Laboratories, International **(1)**
1256 N. McLean Blvd.
Memphis, TN 38108
Tel.: 901-278-0330
Approx.Sls.: $6,000,000
Emp.: 160
Management Services; Commercial Physical Research
S.I.C.: 8741; 8731
Steven B. Buckman *(Pres. & Chief Oper. Officer)*
Robert H. Buckman *(Chm Bd. & Chief Exec. Officer)*

E. D. BULLARD COMPANY
Rt. 7, Box 596
Cynthiana, KY 41031
Tel.: 606-234-6611
Tel.: 800-827-0423
Fax: 606-234-6858
Year Founded: 1898
Sales Range: $20-39 Million
Emp.: 240
Import Export
Mfr. of Industrial Head & Industrial Respiratory Protection Equipment & Safety Hoist Hooks
S.I.C.: 3842
Edward D. Bullard *(Pres.)*
James H. Beckstead *(V.P.-Sls.)*
John H. King *(V.P.-Engrng.)*
Rick Miller *(V.P.-Mktg.)*
William R. Emanuel, Jr. *(Dir.-Oper.)*
Mike Bross *(Mgr.-Prod.)*

Outside Service Firm(s):

Price Waterhouse*(Auditors)*
Oakland, CA

Wells Fargo Bank*(Major Banking Relationship)*
420 Montgomery St.
San Francisco, CA 94104

Cooley, Godward, Castro, Huddleson & Tatum*(Legal Firm)*
One Maritime Plaza, 20th Fl.
San Francisco, CA 94111-3580
Tel.: 415-981-5252

CURT BULLOCK BUILDERS, INC.
720 S. Gilbert St.
Danville, IL 61832
Mailing Address:
P. O. Box 1250
Danville, IL 61832
Tel.: 217-431-6400
Approx.Sls.: $25,000,000
Emp.: 400
Garage & Modular Home Mfr.; Bullock
S.I.C.: 3448; 2431; 3442; 5211
R.C. Bullock *(Chm. Bd. & Pres.)*
Jerry Bullock *(V.P.)*
Jim Bullock *(V.P.)*
Larry Messmore *(Sec. & Treas.)*

Divisions:

Alabama Div. **(1)**
P.O. Box 150
Florence, AL 35630
Tel.: 205-767-2300
S.I.C.: 3448
Charles Holt *(Div. Mgr.)*

East Div. **(1)**
P. O. Box 1925
Springfield, OH 45501
Tel.: 513-325-8760
S.I.C.: 3448
Jerry Bullock *(V.P. & Div. Mgr.)*

Northwest Div. **(1)**
2401 40th Ave.
Moline, IL 61265
Tel.: 309-764-6311
S.I.C.: 3448
Paul Peacock Taylor *(V.P. & Div. Mgr.)*

BUNN-O-MATIC CORPORATION
1400 Stevenson Dr.
Springfield, IL 62703
Mailing Address:
P.O. Box 3227,
Springfield, IL 62708
Tel.: 217-529-6601
Fax: 217-529-6644
Emp.: 150
Bunn-O-Matic Coffee Brewing Equipment; Iced Tea Brewers, Coffee Grinders, Hot Water Machines; Coffee & Tea Filters
S.I.C.: 3589
George R. Bunn *(Chm. Bd.)*
James E. Brown *(Vice Chm.)*
Arthur H. Bunn *(Pres. & Chief Exec. Officer)*
James W. Bolt *(V.P. & Natl. Sls. Mgr.)*
Ed McNamara *(V.P.)*
D.R. Sand *(V.P.-Customer Rels.)*
Larry E. Staley *(Treas.)*
Jacob Bunn *(Mgr.-Sls.)*
Jack Schleyhahn *(Mgr.-Export)*

Computer Systems/Hardware:
IBM System 38

Outside Service Firm(s):

Aetna Life & Casualty*(Group Insurer)*
151 Farmington Avenue
Hartford, CT 06156
Tel.: 203-273-2128
Fax: 203-729-4295

Non-U.S. Holding:

Bunn-O-Matic Corp. of Canada Ltd. **(1)**
280 Industrial Parkway S.
Aurora, ON L4G 3T9, Canada
Tel.: 416-841-2866 (100%)
Fax: 416-841-2775
Coffee Makers
S.I.C.: 3634
H.W. Cheatley *(Pres.)*

Buntin Advertising, Inc.

BUNTIN ADVERTISING, INC.
1001 Hawkins St.
Nashville, TN 37203
Tel.: 615-244-5720
Twx: 810-371-1046
Fax: 615-244-6511
Year Founded: 1972
Approx.Billings: $50,009,000
Emp.: 90
Advertising, Marketing, Media & Public Relations
Corporate Giving Program: United Way
Jeffrey W. Buntin *(Pres. & Creative Dir.)*
Roy Vaughn *(Pres.-Buntin Pub. Rels. Co.)*
John Sharpe *(Sr. V.P. & Dir.-Client Services)*
William R. Stejskal *(Sr. V.P. & Dir.-Mktg.)*
Debbie Goodwyn *(V.P. & Mgr.-Office & Opers.)*
Art Johnsen *(V.P. & Suprvr.-Mgmt.)*
Lucinda T. Trabue *(V.P.-Pub. Affairs)*
Don Wright *(V.P.- Out-of-Home Media Services Grp.)*
David Meredith *(Dir.-Fin. Services)*
Kathy Canady *(Mgr.-Research)*

BUNTON COMPANY
4601 E. Indian Trail
Louisville, KY 40213
Mailing Address:
P.O. Box 33247,
Louisville, KY 40232
Tel.: 502-966-0550
Fax: 502-966-0564
Year Founded: 1948
Sales Range: $10-19 Million
Emp.: 100
Fiscal Year-end: 7/31/92
Import Export
Mfr. of Commercial Lawnmowers, Golf Course Cutting Machines
S.I.C.: 3524
L.E. O'Connell *(Chm. Bd. & Chief Exec. Officer)*
Stan J. Byers *(Pres. & Chief Oper. Officer)*
David E. Bartley *(Exec. V.P.)*
James Butchart *(V.P.-Mfg.)*
James Gatewood *(Mgr.-Pur.)*
Robin Gaynor *(Mgr.-Engrng.)*
Joyce Hicks *(Mgr.-Office)*
Doug Korthals *(Mgr.-Natl. Sls. & Service)*

Outside Service Firm(s):

Christen, Brown & Rufer*(Auditors)*
Louisville, KY

Citizens Fidelity Bank & Trust Co.*(Major Banking Relationship)*
P.O. Box 33000-Citizens Plaza
Louisville, KY 40232
Tel.: 502-581-3381

BUQUET & LE BLANC INC.
18145 Petroleum Dr.
Baton Rouge, LA 70809
Mailing Address:
P.O. Box 549,
Baton Rouge, LA 70821
Tel.: 504-753-4150 **LA**
Fax: 504-751-1922
Year Founded: 1945
Approx.Sls.: $19,678,000
Emp.: 87
Commercial Buildings General Contractor
S.I.C.: 1542
Al Pickett, III *(Pres.)*
William T. Firesheets, II *(V.P.-Mktg.)*
Christopher N. Stuart *(V.P.-Projects)*
Robert Bogan *(Treas.)*

Outside Service Firm(s):

Postlethwaite & Netterville*(Auditors)*
Baton Rouge, LA

BURD & FLETCHER COMPANY
321 W. 7th St.
Kansas City, MO 64105
Tel.: 816-842-1122 **KS**
Fax: 816-234-9139
Emp.: 200
Manufacture Folding Cartons
S.I.C.: 2657
John A. Young, Sr. *(Chm. Bd.)*
John A. Young, Jr. *(Pres.)*
John A. Young, III *(Exec. V.P.)*
Peter A. Young *(Sec. & Treas.)*

Outside Service Firm(s):

Ernst & Young*(Auditors)*
One Kansas City Place, 1200 Main St.
Kansas City, MO 64105

Spencer, Fane, Britt & Browne*(Legal Firm)*
106 W. 14th St.
Kansas City, MO 64105
Tel.: 816-474-8100

United Missouri Bank*(Major Banking Relationship)*
P.O. Box 226
Kansas City, MO 64141
Tel.: 816-556-7000

BUREAU OF ENGRAVING
500 S. Fourth St.
Minneapolis, MN 55415
Tel.: 612-339-8721
Fax: 612-339-6647
Year Founded: 1906
Approx.Sls.: $70,000,000
Emp.: 1,000
Fiscal Year-end: 12/31/91
Printing; Graphic Arts; Printed Circuits; Art Instruction Schools
S.I.C.: 2759; 2752; 2754; 2796; 3672; 8249; 8299
Thomas Stuart *(Chm. Bd. & Chief Exec. Officer)*
Gerald K. Carlson *(Pres., Treas. & Chief Fin. Officer)*
Tom Bauer *(Exec. V.P.-Comml. Div.)*
John C. Buckbee, III *(V.P.)*
Michael Farr *(V.P.-Production)*
Judy Turner *(Corp. Sec.)*

Computer Systems/Hardware:
NCR

Outside Service Firm(s):

KPMG Peat Marwick*(Auditors)*
4200 Norwest Center, 90 S. 7th St.
Minneapolis, MN 55402
Tel.: 612-341-2222

Gray, Plant, Mooty, Mooty & Bennett*(Legal Firm)*
3400 City Center, 33 So. 6th St.
Minneapolis, MN 55402
Tel.: 612-343-2800
Fax: 612-830-0270

Norwest Bank of Minneapolis N.A.*(Major Banking Relationship)*
P.O. Box 738, 161 N. Concord Exchange
So. St. Paul, MN 55075-0738
Tel.: 612-450-4064
Fax: 612-450-4078

THE BUREAU OF NATIONAL AFFAIRS, INC.
1231 25th St., N.W.
Washington, DC 20037
Tel.: 202-452-4200
Tel.: 800-372-1033 **DE**
Fax: 202-822-8092
Year Founded: 1929
Emp.: 1,800
Fiscal Year-end: 12/31/90
Reports, Specialized Business, Legislative, Judicial & Regulatory Information Services, Books & On Line Services, Databases & Training Films
S.I.C.: 9199; 7375; 2721; 7812; 2731
John D. Stewart *(Chm. Bd.)*
William A. Beltz *(Pres., Chief Exec. Officer & Editor-in-Chief)*
Hugh J. Yarrington *(Sr. V.P. & Exec. Editor)*
George J. Korphage *(V.P. & Chief Fin. Officer)*
Paul N. Wojcik *(V.P., Gen. Counsel & Sec.)*
John J. Boylan, Jr. *(V.P.-Admin.)*
Bob Brooks *(V.P.-Sls. & Mktg.)*
John V. Schappi *(V.P.-Human Resources)*
John E. Jenc *(Treas.)*
Dorothy L. Shekarian *(Dir.-Admin. Services)*
James Larson *(Gen. Sls. Mgr.)*
Roger Miller *(Mgr.-Mktg.)*
John F. Downer, Jr. *(Mgr.-Pur.)*
Emily Pilk *(Mgr.-Communications)*
Gary C. Seltzer *(Mgr.-Circulation Systems)*
Kamla K. Hedges *(Corp. Librarian)*

Outside Service Firm(s):

KPMG Peat Marwick*(Auditors)*
2001 M St., N.W.
Washington, DC 20036
Tel.: 202-467-3800

First American Bank, N.A.*(Major Banking Relationship)*
Washington, DC

Hunton & Williams*(Legal Firm)*
Washington, DC

Divisions:

BNA Books Div. **(1)**
1250 23rd St., N.W., 3rd Fl.
Washington, DC 20037
Tel.: 202-833-7470
Fax: 202-833-7490
Publisher of Books on Law & Legal, Taxation & Finance, Management, Arbitration, Labor & Industrial Relations, Environment
S.I.C.: 2731
William A. Beltz *(Pres. & Editor-in-Chief)*
Randy P. Auerbach *(Mng. Editor)*
Richard H. Cornfield *(Assoc. Editor)*
Camille D. Christie *(Mgr.-Acquisitions, Labor Rels. & Arbitration)*
Timothy J. Darby *(Mgr.-Acquisitions, Labor & Business Law)*
James F. Fattibene *(Mgr.-Acquisitions, Environment & Saftey)*
Bertram Cotine *(Mgr.-Acquisitions, Intellectual Property & Legal Practice)*
Susan W. Garms *(Mgr.-Mktg.)*
Hill Slowinski *(Mgr.-Business & Reprints Editor)*

BNA PLUS **(1)**
1231 25th St. N.W.
Washington, DC 20037
Tel.: 202-452-4323
Tel.: 800-452-7773
Fax: 202-822-8092
Custom Research & Document Delivery Online Services; Book Publishing; Conferences & Seminars on Current Aspects of Labor Relations, Various Areas of Legal Practice, Business & Government
S.I.C.: 7375; 2731
Rebecca R. Karnes *(Assoc. Editor)*
Barbara J. Armentrout *(Product Design & Development Mgr.)*
Sally B. Coulton *(Mgr.-Sls. & Mktg.)*
Charlotte R. Endter *(Mgr.-Admin. Services)*
Mary E. Kelly *(Mgr.-Info. Services)*
Patricia K. Strongin *(Mgr.-Info. Services)*
Laura L. Fox *(Asst. Information Services Mgr.)*

BNA Software **(1)**
1231 25th St. N.W.
Washington, DC 20037
Tel.: 202-452-4453
Tel.: 800-424-2938
Fax: 202-452-7547
Publisher of Personal Computer Software Products for Financial Professionals
S.I.C.: 7372
David P. McFarland *(Gen. Mgr.)*
Lisa B. Kotzker *(Mgr.-Opers.)*
Diana M. Elkin *(Mgr.-User Support)*
Susan S. Jones *(Mgr.-Communications)*
Lorraine B. Moolchan *(Supvr.-Tax Software Support)*

BNA Business & Human Resources Div. **(1)**
1231 25th St., N.W.
Washington, DC 20037
Tel.: 202-452-4638
Fax: 202-822-8092
Reports, Specialized Business & Human Resources Information Services
S.I.C.: 2721
Kathleen D. Gill *(Assoc. Editor)*
William Bank *(Mng. Editor)*
Linda Botsford *(Mng. Editor)*
Mike Cavanagh *(Mng. Editor)*
Mary Davis *(Mng. Editor)*
Mary P. Dunn *(Mng. Editor)*
Roberto Federigan *(Mng. Editor)*
Anthony A. Harris *(Mng. Editor)*
Bill L. Manville *(Mng. Editor)*
Paul Massey *(Mng. Editor)*
Deanne E. Neuman *(Mng. Editor)*
Rebecca Pearl McCracken *(Mng. Editor)*
Susan Sala *(Mng. Editor)*
David A. Sayre *(Mng. Editor)*
Nancy Sedmak *(Mng. Editor)*

BNA Editorial Support Div. **(1)**
1231 25th St., N.W.
Washington, DC 20037
Tel.: 202-452-4555
Fax: 202-822-8092
Periodical Publishing
S.I.C.: 2731
Suzanne L. Geigle *(Mng. Dir.)*
Lucinda J. Davey *(Mgr.-New Systems Devel.)*
Larry E. Evans *(Chief of Correspondents)*
Jeffrey S. Day *(Asst. Chief of Correspondents)*
Enid I. Zafran *(Mgr.-Indexing Services)*
Inara Z. Apinis *(Mgr.-Chemical, Environmental & Safety Indexing Unit)*
Marjorie F. Cohen *(Mgr.-Business & Tax Indexing Unit)*
Kimberly W. Hunter *(Mgr.-Indexing Training)*
Jose R. Recinto, Jr. *(Mgr.-Legal Indexing Unit)*
Emil Z. Toth *(Mgr.-Indexing Admin.)*
Jane F. Sanchez *(Mgr.-Judicial Opinions Unit)*
Judith M. Springberg *(Mgr.-State Database/ Reprints)*
Ophelia K. Thomas *(Mgr.-Library Support Services)*
J. Michael Reidy *(Mgr.-Surveys Graphics Unit)*
Kamla King Hedges *(Corp. Librarian)*

BNA Electronic Media Div. **(1)**
1231 25th St., N.W.
Washington, DC 20037
Tel.: 202-452-4132 (BNA Online)
Tel.: 800-862-4636
Fax: 202-452-4062
On-line Electronic Information Services
S.I.C.: 7375
John A. Jenkins *(Gen. Mgr.)*
Donna Whalen Robinson *(Dir.-Mktg.)*
Charles F. Piontkowski *(Editorial Dir.)*
Charlotte A. Kuenen *(Dir.-Electronic Database Devel. & Opers.)*
Karyn S. Bowie *(Opers. Mgr.)*
JoAnn L. Pippin *(Mgr.-Product Devel. & Support)*
Jennifer Q. Ryan *(Mgr.-Online Product Devel.)*
Charlotte A. Garrison *(Product Mgr.)*

BNA Environment & Safety Services Div. **(1)**
1231 25th St., N.W.
Washington, DC 20037
Tel.: 202-452-4421
Fax: 202-452-4250
Reports, Environment & Safety Information Services
S.I.C.: 2721
Patricia R. Westlein *(Assoc. Editor)*
Marlon Allen *(Mng. Editor)*
Inara Z. Apinis *(Mng. Editor)*
Bernard S. Chabel *(Mng. Editor)*
William Harris Frank *(Mng. Editor)*
Eileen Joseph *(Mng. Editor)*
Wallis E. McClain Jr. *(Mng. Editor)*
Stanley S. Pond *(Mng. Editor)*
Glenn Totten *(Mng. Editor)*

BNA Legal Services Div. **(1)**
1231 25th St., N.W.
Washington, DC 20037
Tel.: 202-728-5201
Fax: 202-728-5203
Reports, Legal & Regulatory Information Services
S.I.C.: 2721
Sanford M. Morse *(Assoc. Editor)*
Randy P. Auerbach *(Mng. Editor)*
Cynthia J. Bolbach *(Mng. Editor)*
Melanie I. Dooley *(Mng. Editor)*
Robert L. Goebes *(Mng. Editor)*
Susan Raleigh Jenkins *(Mng. Editor)*
Larry Lempert *(Mng. Editor)*
Judith C. Mroczka *(Mng. Editor)*
Gregory R. Pease *(Mng. Editor)*
Sheldon B. Richman *(Mng. Editor)*
Larry Ritchie *(Mng. Editor)*
Robert A. Robbins *(Mng. Editor)*
Jeffrey M. Samuels *(Mng. Editor)*
Susan Webster *(Mng. Editor)*
Wendell Yee *(Mng. Editor)*

Subsidiaries:

BNA Communications, Inc. **(1)**
9439 Key West Ave.
Rockville, MD 20850
Tel.: 301-948-0540
Fax: 301-948-2085
Audio-Visual Training Materials for Human Resource Professionals, EEO Specialists, Safety Trainers or Personnel Officers
S.I.C.: 7812
Robert L. Velte *(Pres.)*
George A. Stillman *(V.P.)*
Brigitte E. Powell *(Dir.-Intl. Sls. & Exports)*
Clifton R. Witt *(Dir.-Film & Video Communications)*
William L. Flowers *(Mgr.-Sls.)*
Jackson D. Rains *(Mgr.-Product Acquisition & Training)*
Linda Waldron *(Mgr.-Opers.)*
Shirley J. Quinn *(Admin. Asst.)*
William R. Shores *(Asst. Supvr.-Opers.)*

Executive Telecom Systems, Inc. **(1)**
College Park North, 9585 Valpariso Ct.
Indianapolis, IN 46268
Tel.: 317-872-2045
Fax: 317-872-2059
Computer-Readable College Recruitment Data Base, Human Resource Information Network
S.I.C.: 7375
John W. Hawkins *(Pres.)*
Gregory A. Wells *(Treas. & Controller)*
Peter D. Blainey *(Dir.-Natl. Sls.)*
Judith A. Hashem *(Dir.-Mngmt. Information Systems)*
Ruth E. Eckstein *(Sr. Mgr.-Account)*
Ramsey L. Cooper *(Mgr.-Acctg.)*
Cheryl E. Nicholson *(Mgr.-Service & Training)*
Timothy W. Bryant *(Mgr.-Applications Systems Devel.)*
Gregory S. Hayes *(Mgr.-Opers. Support)*
Lisa D. Keltner *(Mgr.-Processing Support)*
David R. Clark *(Mgr.-Systems Opers.)*
Brian E. Holzer *(Mgr.-Project)*
Leslie A. Burns *(Mgr.-Mktg.)*

McArdle Printing Co., Inc. **(1)**
800 Commerce Dr.
Upper Marlboro, MD 20772
Tel.: 301-390-8500
Fax: 301-390-8525
Commercial Printing; Miscellaneous Publishing
S.I.C.: 2741
Joseph J. Fantozzi *(Pres.)*
Virgil W. Wright *(Sr. V.P.)*

The Bureau of National Affairs, Inc.—(Continued)

Frank M. Heneghan *(V.P.-Sls. & Mktg.)*
George A. Payne, Sr. *(V.P.-Opers. & Plant Mgr.)*
Paul D. Stout, Jr. *(V.P., Chief Fin. Officer & Treas.)*
John R. Fleishell *(Controller)*
Howard M. Callahan *(Mgr.-Communications)*

Pike & Fischer **(1)**
4550 Montgomery Ave.
Bethesda, MD 20814
Tel.: 301-654-6262
Fax: 301-961-6544
Emp.: 30
Publr. of Looseleaf Legal Reference Services in Communications Law, Administrative Law & Shipping Regulation
S.I.C.: 2731
John Sukenik *(Chm. Bd.)*
U. Joseph Hecker *(V.P. & G.M.)*
Robert E. Emeritz *(V.P.)*
John W. Willis *(Editor-in-Chief)*
Quintin M. Chatman *(Managing Editor)*
David B. Fialkoff *(Managing Editor)*
James A. Rauen *(Managing Editor)*
Ronnie E. Schulman *(Managing Editor)*
Doreen A. Strothman *(Managing Editor)*
Jeffrey Tobias *(Assoc. Editor)*
Christopher H. Hoving *(Assoc. Editor)*
Ruth Eisenstadt *(Treas. & Office Mgr.)*
Rosalie N.H. Nguyen *(Controller)*
Arleen N. Holmes *(Supervisor-Production & Distribution)*
Michael M. Eisenstadt *(Mgr.-Rules Database)*
Zachary Wheat *(Mktg. Mgr.)*

Tax Management, Inc. **(1)**
1250 23rd St., N.W., 2nd Fl.
Washington, DC 20037
Tel.: 202-833-7240
Fax: 202-833-7297
Publishes Info. Services on Legalities of Tax System
S.I.C.: 2731; 2721
Sandra C. Degler *(Pres.)*
Leonard L. Silverstein *(V.P.)*
Glenn B. Davis *(Assoc. Editor)*
Virginia A. Shew *(Asst. Mng. Editor)*
Michael G. Kushner *(Tax Law & Reprints Editor)*
Gerald F. Egan *(Mgr.-Plng. & Devel.)*
Ellen Hench *(Mgr.-Mktg. Support)*
Daniel M. Ranhart *(Mgr.-Communications)*
Barbara A. Patrick *(Asst. Mgr.-Communications)*

Non U.S. Holding:

BNA International Inc. **(1)**
17 Dartmouth Street
London, SW1H 9BL, United Kingdom
Tel.: 071-222-8831 (100%)
Telex: 262570 BNA LDN
Fax: 071-222-0294
Financial Publishing
S.I.C.: 2721; 2731
Alan M. Edmunds *(Sr. Mgr.)*
Robert Beattie *(Production Mgr.)*

C.F. BURGER CREAMERY COMPANY
8101 Greenfield
Detroit, MI 48228
Tel.: 313-584-4040
Fax: 313-584-9870
Emp.: 210
Processes Milk; Dairy Products
S.I.C.: 2026; 5451; 5143
Lawrence Angott *(Pres.)*

BURGESS & NIPLE, LIMITED
5085 Reed Road
Columbus, OH 43220
Tel.: 614-459-2050
Fax: 614-451-1385
Year Founded: 1912
Approx.Sls.: $38,446,000
Emp.: 520
Fiscal Year-end: 12/31/91
Engineering & Architectural Services
S.I.C.: 8711; 8712
Francis C. Smith *(Chm. Bd.)*
Frank Agin *(Exec. Dir.)*
Peggy Garrison *(Dir.-Admin. Services)*
Owen March *(Dir.-Engrng. Services)*
Terrence Sack *(Dir.-Reg. Opers.)*
Paul Shepard, Jr. *(Dir.-Architectural & Support Services)*
Principal(s):
Francis C. Smith
Frank Agin
Kenneth Davis
Dale DeCarlo
James Edwards
Jerry Keltch
Owen March
Richard Nolan
Richard Riethmiller
Walter Roehrs
Mark Rowland
Terrence Sack
Paul Shepard, Jr.
David Williams
David Zimmer

No. of U.S. Offices: 9

Outside Service Firm(s):

Arthur Andersen & Co.*(Auditors)*
Columbus, OH

Porter, Wright, Morris & Arthur*(Legal Firm)*
Huntington Center, 41 S. High St.
Columbus, OH 43215-3406
Tel.: 614-227-2000

BancOhio National Bank*(Major Banking Relationship)*
Columbus, OH

Subsidiaries:

Burgess & Niple, Inc. **(1)**
5025 E. Washington St., Ste. 212
Phoenix, AZ 85034
Tel.: 602-244-8100
Engineers & Architects
S.I.C.: 8711; 8712
Terrence Sack *(Pres.)*

Burgess & Niple, Inc. **(1)**
1106 N. Beeline Hwy.
Payson, AZ 85541
Tel.: 602-474-5313
Engineers & Architects
S.I.C.: 8711; 8712
Terrence Sack *(Pres.)*

BURGESS PIGMENT CO.
Box 349
Sandersville, GA 31082
Tel.: 912-552-2544 GA
Fax: 912-552-1772
Year Founded: 1948
Sales Range: $20-39 Million
Emp.: 141
Fiscal Year-end: 12/31/89
Kaolin Processing
S.I.C.: 3295
Malcolm S. Burgess, Jr. *(Chm. Bd. & Pres.)*
Dan Adrien *(Exec. V.P.)*
Polly Tompkins *(Sec. & Treas.)*
Marcus Sack *(Chief Engineer)*
DeWitt Avant *(Pur. Agent)*
Roy Avant *(Dir.-Personnel)*
Horace Mathis, Jr. *(Mgr.-Plant)*
Principal(s):
Malcolm S. Burgess, Jr.

No. of Mfg. Plants/Facilities: 1
No. of U.S. Offices: 2

Computer Systems/Hardware:
IBM System 34

Outside Service Firm(s):

Clifton, Lipford & Taylor*(Auditors)*
Macon, GA

Murphy, Taylor & Ellis*(Group Insurer)*
Macon, GA

Sell & Melton*(Legal Firm)*
Sandersville, GA

Citizens & Southern National Bank*(Major Banking Relationship)*
Sandersville, GA

Murphy, Taylor & Ellis*(Pension Manager)*
Macon, GA

BURGOYNE, INC.
2030 E. Byberry Rd.,
Philadelphia, PA 19116
Tel.: 215-677-8000 PA
Fax: 215-673-0828
Year Founded: 1907
Sales Range: $20-39 Million
Emp.: 90
Stationery & Greeting Cards
S.I.C.: 2771; 2754
James F. Burgoyne *(Pres.)*
Paul J. Scott *(V.P.-Fin. Admin.)*
Mary Louise Burgoyne *(Sec. & Treas.)*

No. of Mfg. Plants/Facilities: 2

Computer Systems/Hardware:
Wang VS 15

Outside Service Firm(s):

Coopers & Lybrand*(Auditors)*
2400 Eleven Penn Center
Philadelphia, PA 19103-2962
Tel.: 215-963-8000

Morgan, Lewis & Bockius*(Legal Firm)*
2000 One Logan Square
Philadelphia, PA 19103
Tel.: 215-963-5000

Mellon Bank, N.A.*(Major Banking Relationship)*
P.O. Box 444,
Pittsburgh, PA 15230
Tel.: 412-236-8000
Tel.: 1-800-451-7392
Fax: 412-236-8157

Subsidiary:

Curtis Swann **(1)**
50 Dorman St.
San Francisco, CA 94124-1845
Tel.: 415-550-7700
Greeting Card Publisher
S.I.C.: 5112
William J. QurGoyne *(Gen Mgr.)*

BURK ROYALTY CO.
1000 Petroleum Bldg.
Wichita Falls, TX 76301-2623
Mailing Address:
P.O. Box BRC
Wichita Falls, TX 76307-7507
Tel.: 817-322-5421 TX
Fax: 817-322-1934
Year Founded: 1934
Sales Range: $20-39 Million
Emp.: 115
Oil Production
S.I.C.: 1311
David A. Kimbell *(Chm. Bd. & Pres.)*
Jon H. Bear *(V.P.-Engrng.)*
Mike Elyea *(V.P. & Treas.)*
David Kimbell, Jr. *(V.P.-Exploration)*
G.T. Kimbell, II *(V.P.-S. Texas)*
Al Norris *(V.P.-Land)*
Stephen R. Stults *(V.P.-Production)*
Pat Hensley *(Sec.)*
Fred M. Lynch *(Petroleum Engr.)*

Computer Systems/Hardware:
Texas Instruments 990

Outside Service Firm(s):

Hupp, Thompson & Co.*(Auditors)*
Wichita Falls, TX

Sanders, Masters, Watson & Brown*(Legal Firm)*
Wichita Falls, TX

NationsBank Texas*(Major Banking Relationship)*
Wichita Falls, TX

BURKE COMMUNICATION INDUSTRIES, INC.
1165 N. Clark St.
Chicago, IL 60610
Tel.: 312-951-0500
Fax: 312-664-5397
Year Founded: 1930
Approx.Sls.: $21,000,000
Emp.: 300
Sls. Promo., Point-of-Purchase Adv. Displays; Wood, Metal & Plastic Fixtures
S.I.C.: 3993; 2541; 2542; 2759; 2752; 3089; 7319
Robert L. Burke *(Chm. Bd.)*
Lawrence J. Burke II *(Pres. & Chief Exec. Officer)*
Dennis Heinol *(Pres.-Display Mfg.)*
Rex Ryan *(Exec. V.P.)*

No. of U.S. Offices: 6

Computer Systems/Hardware:
MAI Basic 4 Mini-Computer

Outside Service Firm(s):

Ernst & Young*(Auditors)*
233 S. Wacker Dr.
Chicago, IL 60606
Tel.: 312-368-1800
Fax: 312-645-3095

Kirkland & Ellis*(Legal Firm)*
200 E. Randolph Dr.
Chicago, IL 60601
Tel.: 312-861-2000
Fax: 312-861-2200

Unibank*(Major Banking Relationship)*
Chicago, IL

BURKE ENGINEERING COMPANY
9700 Factorial Way
South El Monte, CA 91733
Tel.: 818-579-6763
Fax: 818-579-1156
Year Founded: 1949
Approx.Sls.: $28,000,000
Emp.: 126
Distributor of Automatic Controls For Heating, Air Conditioning & Refrigeration For Residential, Commercial & Industrial Applications
S.I.C.: 5075; 5078
Pauline E. Burke *(Chm. Bd.)*
Gary W. Burke *(Pres. & Chief Exec. Officer)*
Kelly M. Burke *(V.P.-Fin.)*
Michael Burke *(V.P.-Opers.)*
Kenneth F. Gleed *(V.P.-Admin.)*
E. Brian Wolf *(V.P.-Natl. Sls.)*
Andre A. Boucher *(Treas.)*
Cherri Conan *(Mgr.-Data Processing)*
Robert Pedersen *(Mgr.-Sls. Promotion Prod.)*

Outside Service Firm(s):

Biller, Frith-Smith & Archibald*(Auditors)*
Santa Monica, CA

Wells Fargo Bank*(Major Banking Relationship)*
9000 Flair
El Monte, CA

BURKE INDUSTRIES, INC.
2250 So. 10th
San Jose, CA 95112
Mailing Address:
P. O. Box 190
San Jose, CA 95103

Tel.: 408-297-3500
Tel.: 800-669-7010
Fax: 408-280-0699
Year Founded: 1942
Approx.Sls.: $38,000,000
Emp.: 500
Fiscal Year-end: 12/31/90
Rubber Floor Tile, Rubber Cove & Carpet Base, Stair Treads, Custom Molded Rubber Products, Flexible Membranes for Liners & Covers, Single-Ply Roofing Systems
S.I.C.: 3069
Gary Filler *(Chm Bd. & Chief Exec. Officer)*
Rocco C. Genovese *(Pres. & Chief Oper. Officer)*
Ray Brown *(V.P.-Burke Rubber Co.)*
Robert Engle *(V.P.-Mfg.)*
Rick Hoskins *(V.P.-Mktg.)*
Reed Wolthawen *(Chief Fin. Officer)*
Anne Howe *(Dir.-Human Resources)*
Fred Page *(Dir.-Engrng.)*
Robert Pitman *(Dir.-Technical Opers.)*
Douglas L. Bartlett *(V.P. & Gen. Mgr.-Liners, Covers & Roofing)*
Larry Sims *(V.P. & Gen. Mgr.-Burke Flooring Prods.)*
Rick Hoskins *(V.P.-Strategic Plng., Research & Devel.)*

No. of Mfg. Plants/Facilities: 2

Computer Systems/Hardware:
IBM System 38

Outside Service Firm(s):

Ernst & Young*(Auditors)*
55 Almaden Blvd.
San Jose, CA 95115
Tel.: 408-947-5476
Fax: 408-294-2744

Morrison & Foerster*(Legal Firm)*
345 California St.
San Francisco, CA 94104
Tel.: 415-677-7000

Wells Fargo Bank*(Major Banking Relationship)*
420 Montgomery St.
San Francisco, CA 94104

Divisions:

Burke Flooring Products Div. **(1)**
2250 S. 10th St.
San Jose, CA 95112
Tel.: 408-297-3500
Fax: 408-280-0699
Rocco C. Genovese *(Sr. V.P. & Chief Oper. Officer)*

Burke Rubber Co. **(1)**
2250 S. 10th St.
San Jose, CA 95112
Tel.: 408-297-3500
Fax: 408-280-0699

BURKHARDT & CHRISTY ADVERTISING, INC.
Penthouse Terrace, 304 East 45th St.
New York, NY 10017
Tel.: 212-661-2221
Fax: 212-661-0331
Year Founded: 1986
Approx.Billings: $33,000,000
Emp.: 32
High Profile Consumer Advertising; All Media
Ron Burkhardt *(Chief Exec. Officer & Exec. Creative Dir.)*
Ralph Doran, III *(Pres.)*
Judy Christy *(Chief Oper. Officer & Mng. Dir.)*
Maurice Michelson *(Sr. V.P., Chief Fin. Officer, & Dir.-Admin. & Pur.)*
Russ Barmmer *(V.P.-Pub. Rels.)*
Tony Ranazzissi *(V.P., Chief Info. Officer & Controller)*
Anne Brenninkmeyer *(Mgr.-Library & Office)*
Marianna Casissi *(Word Processing Coord.)*
Charito Rial *(Fin. & Bookeeper)*

Computer Systems/Hardware:
NEC, Apple MacIntosh

BURLINGTON BASKET CO.
922 Bluff Rd.
Burlington, IA 52601
Mailing Address:
P.O. Box 808
Burlington, IA 52601
Tel.: 319-754-6508
Fax: 319-754-5991
Year Founded: 1888
Approx.Sls.: $11,000,000
Emp.: 200
Fiscal Year-end: 11/30/91
Mfr. of Fiber Products & Household Accessories
S.I.C.: 2392; 2499; 2519
J.F. Thompson *(Chm. Bd.)*
C.H. Thompson, Jr. *(Pres. & Treas.)*
Dave Thompson *(V.P. & Sec.)*
Rick Thompson *(V.P.-Mktg.)*
Steve Thompson *(V.P., Gen. Mgr. & Treas.)*
Delbert H. Moeller *(Controller)*

Computer Systems/Hardware:
DEC

Outside Service Firm(s):

Walker Egerton*(Auditors)*
Burlington, IA

First National Bank*(Major Banking Relationship)*
Burlington, IA

BURLINGTON MOTOR CARRIERS INC.
14611 W. Commerce Rd.
Daleville, IN 47334
Mailing Address:
P.O. Box 287,
Anderson, IN 46015
Tel.: 317-378-0261
Tel.: 800-428-0461 **DE**
Fax: 317-378-4198
Year Founded: 1985
Approx.Rev.: $249,521,000
Emp.: 3,300
Fiscal Year-end: 12/31/91
Common Carrier Trucking & Contract Carrier Trucking
S.I.C.: 4213
Richard M. Rogan *(Pres. & Chief Exec. Officer)*
Ralph S. Nelson *(Exec. V.P., Sec. & Gen. Counsel)*
Ralph W. Arthur *(Sr. V.P.-Mktg. & Sls.)*
Michael T. Hodson *(Sr. V.P.-Opers.)*
Michael D. Kandris *(Sr. V.P.-Fin. & Treas.)*
Mark S. Macklin *(Sr. V.P.-Opers.)*
Robert Fox *(V.P. & Controller)*
J. Harold Fambro *(V.P.-Natl. Accts.)*
Robert LaMere *(V.P.-Mngmt. Information Systems)*
Debra Redden *(Mgr.-Employee Benefits)*
Elaine Cash *(Mktg. Services Coord.)*
Kevin Craig *(Systems Admin.)*

Computer Systems/Hardware:
AS/400

Outside Service Firm(s):

Deloitte & Touche*(Auditors)*
801 Cherry St., Ste. 2340
Fort Worth, TX 76102
Tel.: 817-336-2531
Fax: 817-336-2013

Chase Manhattan Bank, N.A.*(Major Banking Relationship)*
One Chase Manhattan Plaza
New York, NY 10081
Tel.: 212-552-2222
Tel.: 800-526-0801
Fax: 212-552-7175

Subsidiaries:

Burlington Motor Carriers **(1)**
P.O.Box 1919,
West Monroe, LA 71291
Tel.: 318-388-0201
Fax: 318-387-6902
Motor Carrier
S.I.C.: 4213

Monkem Company, Inc. **(1)**
P.O.Box 1196,
Joplin, MO 64802
Tel.: 417-624-5634
Fax: 417-624-2550
Motor Carries
S.I.C.: 4213

Stoops Express, Inc. **(1)**
P.O. Box 287,
Anderson, IN 46015
Tel.: 317-378-0261
Fax: 317-378-5992
Motor Carrier
S.I.C.: 4213

Wingate/Taylor Maid Transportation Inc. **(1)**
P.O. Box 1268,
Albany, GA 31703
Tel.: 912-439-8888
Fax: 912-883-5771
Motor Carrier
S.I.C.: 4213

DAVID K. BURNAP ADVERTISING AGENCY, INC.
7106 Corporate Way
Dayton, OH 45459
Tel.: 513-439-4800
Fax: 513-434-1260
Year Founded: 1959
Approx.Billings: $16,000,000
Emp.: 24
Advertising Agency
S.I.C.: 7311
David K. Burnap *(Pres.)*
D. Cummins *(Dir.-Bookeeping Dept.)*
Dorothy A. Smith *(Dir.-Admin. Services)*

Computer Systems/Hardware:
IBM 36

Outside Service Firm(s):

Ernst & Young*(Auditors)*
1300 Chiquita Center, 250 E. Fifth St.
Cincinnati, OH 45202
Tel.: 513-621-6454

First National Bank*(Major Banking Relationship)*
Dayton, OH

WM. T. BURNETT & CO., INC.
1500 Bush St.
Baltimore, MD 21230
Tel.: 410-837-3000
Fax: 410-837-4528
Approx.Sls.: $20,000,000
Emp.: 250
Polyurethane Foam, Cotton & Synthetic Battings
S.I.C.: 2821; 2299
Richard B.C. Tucker *(Chm. Bd. & Pres.)*
Joseph S. Sollers *(Exec. V.P. & Pres. Unifoam Div.)*
David D. Townsend *(Exec. V.P. & Pres. Fibers Div.)*
C. Kenneth Myers *(V.P.)*
Gregory C. Havlik *(Controller)*

Outside Service Firm(s):

Coyne & McClean*(Auditors)*
Baltimore, MD

Prem & Dumler*(Legal Firm)*
Baltimore, MD

First National Bank of Maryland*(Major Banking Relationship)*
25 S. Charles St.
Baltimore, MD 21201
Tel.: 410-244-4025

LEO BURNETT COMPANY, INC.

LEO BURNETT COMPANY, INC.
35 W. Wacker Dr.
Chicago, IL 60601
Tel.: 312-220-5959 **IL**
Telex: 414-674
Fax: 312-220-5959
Year Founded: 1935
Approx.Billings: $2,040,000,000
Approx.Billings:$1,850,000,000
Emp.: 2,440
Advertising Agency
S.I.C.: 7311
Corporate Giving Program: Supports Programs in the Chicago Metropolitan Area which Aid & Improve Lives of the Disadvantaged
Employee Matching Gifts Program: Supports Education, Health & Welfare, Art & Cultural, Environmental & Special Interest Not-For-Profit Groups
Richard B. Fizdale *(Chm. & Chief Exec. & Creative Officer)*
James G. Oates *(Chm. & Reg. Mng. Dir.-Leo Burnett USA)*
Stan May *(Chm. & Chief Creative Officer-Leo Burnett International)*
Kerry M. Rubie *(Chm.-Leo Burnett International)*
Henry J. Feeley *(Vice Chm. & Dir.-Client Services)*
Roger A. Haupt *(Vice Chm. & Chief Fin. Officer)*
Robert D. Nolan *(Vice Chm. & Dir.-Creative Services-Leo Burnett USA)*
John J. Smith *(Vice Chm. & Deputy Chief Creative Officer)*
Sergio Suarez-Solis *(Vice Chm.-Agency Opers.-Leo Burnett International)*
Albert C.M. Winninghoff *(Vice Chm. & Dir.-Corp. Plng.)*
Theodore A. Bell *(Pres. & Chief Creative Officer-Leo Burnett USA)*
Michael B. Conrad *(Pres. & Chief Creative Officer-Leo Burnett International)*
William T. Lynch *(Pres.)*
Michael Breslin *(Exec. V.P. & Gen. Counsel)*
Jerry Reitman *(Exec. V.P. & Dir.-Integrated Communications)*
Ella Strubel *(Exec. V.P. & Dir.-Corp. Affairs & Client Pub. Relations)*

No. of U.S. Offices: 4

Computer Systems/Hardware:
IBM 4341

Outside Service Firm(s):

Arthur Andersen & Co.*(Auditors)*
33 W. Monroe St.
Chicago, IL 60603-4067
Tel.: 312-580-0033
Fax: 312-507-6748

Allstate Insurance*(Group Insurer)*
Northbrook, IL

Leo Burnett Company, Inc.—(Continued)

Altschuler, Melvoin & Glasser *(Group Insurer)*
30 S. Wecker Dr.
Chicago, IL 60606
Tel.: 312-207-2800

Baker & McKenzie *(Legal Firm)*
One Prudential Plaza, 130 E. Randolph
Chicago, IL 60601-7026
Tel.: 312-861-8000

Continental Bank N. A. *(Major Banking Relationship)*
231 S. LaSalle St.
Chicago, IL 60697
Tel.: 312-828-2345
Tel.: 800-426-5754
Telex: 312-828-1783

Continental Bank N. A. *(Pension Manager)*
231 S. LaSalle St.
Chicago, IL 60697
Tel.: 312-828-2345
Tel.: 800-426-5754
Telex: 312-828-1783

Subsidiaries:

Leo Burnett Company **(1)**
3801 Barham Blvd.
Los Angeles, CA 90068
Tel.: 213-876-5959
Telex: 674238
Fax: 213-851-6180
Marsha Kabb *(V.P., Mgr.-TV Services)*

Leo Burnett Company **(1)**
950 Third Ave.
New York, NY 10022
Tel.: 212-759-5959
Telex: 126273
Fax: 212-755-0281
Joan Gilhooley *(V.P., Office Services Mgr.)*

Leo Burnett Company **(1)**
26555 Evergreen Rd.
Southfield, MI 48076
Tel.: 313-948-5959
Telex: 235231
Fax: 313-948-5800
Ted Jordan *(Sr. V.P. & Gen. Mgr.)*

Leo Burnett International, Latin American Hdqtrs. **(1)**
550 Biltmore, Ste. 870
Coral Gables, FL 33134
Tel.: 305-448-5959
Telex: 52-2739
Fax: 305-443-6834
S.I.C.: 8741
Daniel Moure *(Reg. Mng. Dir., Latin America)*

Non-U.S. Holdings:

AIM Communications **(1)**
Price Centre Bldg., 15th Fl., Jalan Jenderal Sudirman 3-4
Jakarta, 10220, Indonesia
Tel.: 021-5700415
Fax: 021-5703255
Approx.Billings: $8,700,000
Emp.: 52
Full Service Advertising
Juzar Junin *(Mng. Dir. & Mngmt. Supvr.)*

AMA Leo Burnett **(1)**
El Nahda Tower, 7th Fl., 21 Ahmed Orabi St. Post Code 11511, Al Sahafeyeen, Giza, Egypt
Tel.: 2-3462201/3474377
Telex: 21421 AMALB UN
Fax: 2-3460662
Approx.Sls.: $2,850,000
Emp.: 21
Agency Specializes in Consumer Packaged Goods
S.I.C.: 7311
Roger Darouny *(Mng. Dir.)*
George Grace *(Dir.-Fin.)*

Black Pencil S.A.R.L. **(1)**
Escape Clichy, 6 allee Jean Prouve 925787
Clichy, CEDEX, France
Tel.: 1-4968-7300
Fax: 1-4737-6664
Ad Agency
S.I.C.: 7311
Robert Schoenbeck *(Gen. Mgr.)*

Bordelais, Lemeunier & Leo Burnett **(1)**
Espace Clichy, 6 Allee Jean Prouve 925787
Clichy, Cedex France
Tel.: 1-49687300
Fax: 1-47376664
Full Service Agency
S.I.C.: 7311
Anny-Claude Lemeunier *(Pres.)*
Jacques Bordelais *(Chief Exec. Officer)*
Philip Purdon *(Chief Oper. Officer)*
Didier Rigaud *(Chief Fin. Officer)*
Michel Ferton *(Sec.)*
Kristel Adriaenssens *(Pub. Rels. Dir.)*

Causa Publicidad **(1)**
Tarata 269, Officina 210, 2nd Fl. Miraflores, Lima, 18, Peru
Tel.: 14-440505
Telex: 21505
Fax: 478335
Ad Agency
S.I.C.: 7311
Fernando Florez-Estrada *(Mng. Dir.)*

Chaitra Leo Burnett Advertising Private Ltd. **(1)**
9/11, N.S. Patkar Marg., Ardeshir B. Godrej Chowk
Bombay, 400 036, India
Tel.: 22-363-0373
Telex: 95311 75072
Fax: 22-2622027
Approx.Billings: $11,700,000
Emp.: 258
Agency Specializes in Industrial, Consumer, Corporate & Financial Advertising
S.I.C.: 7311
Walter Saldanha *(Chm. & Mng. Dir.)*
Julien Almeida *(Deputy Mng. Dir.)*
Arvind Sharma *(Dir.)*
H.S. Ayrton *(Dir.)*
N.R. Khire *(Controller)*
Joseph Cordo *(Audio-Visual Controller)*
J.W. Gonsalves *(Studio Controller)*

Comunica Leo Burnett **(1)**
5TA Avenida 6-39, Zone 14, Colonia El Campo
Guatemala City, Guatemala
Tel.: 2-373142/46
Telex: 5036
Fax: 2-373150
S.I.C.: 7311
Clemente Gonzalez *(Gen. Mgr.)*
Isadoro Serrano *(Gen Mgr.)*

Comunica Leo Burnett-Costa Rica **(1)**
De Pollos Kentucky, en San Pedro, 100 Metros Al Este and 250, Metros Al Sur, Barrio Francisco,
Peralta, Costa Rica
Tel.: 506-340606
Telex: 3677
Fax: 506-342424
S.I.C.: 7311
Mauricio Barriga *(Mng. Dir.)*

Comunica Leo Burnett Publicidad **(1)**
Calle Venezuela No.5 Bella Vista Apartado 2181,
Panama, Panama
Tel.: 507-23-15-60
Fax: 507-23-16-09
Fernando Moya *(Chief Oper. Officer)*

Michael Conrad & Leo Burnett GmbH & Co. KG **(1)**
Alexanderstr. 65 6000
Frankfurt/Main, 90, Germany
Tel.: 69-780770
Telex: 414618
Fax: 69-78077700
Approx.Billings: $289,711,000
Emp.: 391
Full Service Agency
S.I.C.: 7311
Reiner Erfert *(Chm.)*
Michael Conrad *(Partner)*
Hubert Bernadet *(Chief Fin. Officer)*
Helmut Konig *(Public Rels.)*

H & C, Leo Burnett **(1)**
Sofil Center, 5th Fl. P.O. Box 55369, Achrafiel,
Beirut, Lebanon
Tel.: 1450204
Telex: 44194/43643
Fax: 1450204
Approx.Billings: $15,000,000
Emp.: 90
Agency Specializes in Consumer Goods Advertising
S.I.C.: 7311
Maher Achi *(Mng. Dir.)*

Hemisphere-Leo Burnett, Inc. **(1)**
Planters Products Inc. Bldg., 2nd Fl., Esteban St. Legaspi Village, Makati, Metro Manila, Philippines
Tel.: 2-8186056
Telex: 45075
Fax: 2-8153629
Approx.Billings: $11,700,000
Emp.: 128
Full Service Agency
S.I.C.: 7311
Virgilio A. Yuzon *(Chm.)*
Gregorio D. Garcia III *(Mng. Dir., Exec. Creative Dir.)*
Eduardo R. Custodio *(Sr. V.P.)*
Amador P. Moriles *(Public Rels. Dir.)*
Antonina H. Joaquin *(Fin. Officer)*

Kastner & Partner GmbH Werbeagentur **(1)**
Kennedyallee 94 D-6000
Frankfurt/Main, 70, Germany
Tel.: 69-639011
Telex: 414782
Fax: 69-639016
Approx.Billings: $10,000,000
Emp.: 18
S.I.C.: 7311
Johannes Kastner *(Mng. Dir.)*

Leo Burnett Chile **(1)**
Eliodoro Yanez 2376 Providencia,
Santiago, Chile
Tel.: 2-2239649
Telex: 645488
Fax: 2-2049436
Approx.Billings: $12,187,000
Emp.: 77
S.I.C.: 7311
Jorge Cassis *(Mng. Dir.)*
Horacio Alarcon *(Exec. V.P.)*
Juanita Fuentes *(Fin. Dir.)*

Leo Burnett Co., Inc. Sucursal Argentina **(1)**
Carlos Pellegrini 1363, 12th Fl. 1011
Buenos Aires, Argentina
Tel.: 1-394-5033
Telex: 24504
Fax: 1-112049
Ad Agency
S.I.C.: 7311
Hardwood Campbell Hull *(Mng. Dir.)*
Patricia Brown *(Financial Dir.)*

Leo Burnett Co., S.R.L. **(1)**
Via Fatebenefratelli 14 20121
Milan, Italy
Tel.: 02-63541
Telex: 311161
Fax: 02-20-00-5229
Emp.: 70
Full Service Agency
S.I.C.: 7311
Alessio Fronzoni *(Mng. Dir.)*

Leo Burnett Colombia, S.A. **(1)**
Carrera 13 No. 89-59
Bogota, D.E. Colombia
Tel.: 1-2186900
Telex: 44854
Fax: 1-2189073
Approx.Billings: $16,500,000
Emp.: 118
S.I.C.: 7311
Juan Manuel Hernandez *(Mng. Dir.)*

Leo Burnett Company, Ltd.-Taiwan Branch **(1)**
7th Fl., Chung Hsin Textile Bldg. 123 Chung Hsiao East Rd., Section 2,
Taipei, Taiwan
Tel.: 2-3961222
Telex: 23504
Fax: 2-3973046
Emp.: 95
Full Service
Roland Janisse *(Gen. Dir.)*
Grace Ku *(Fin. Dir.)*

Leo Burnett Company Ltd. **(1)**
North Tower, 175 Bloor St. E.
Toronto, ON M4W 3R9, Canada
Tel.: 416-9255997
Telex: 06-219587
Fax: 416-925-3447
Approx.Billings: $150,000,000
Emp.: 185
S.I.C.: 7311
Tony Houghton *(Chm., Chief Exec. Officer)*
James McKenzie *(Pres.)*
T. Cook *(Chief Fin. Officer)*
T. Altilia *(Exec. V.P.)*
D. Chalmers *(Exec. V.P.)*
B. Hutchins *(Sr. V.P., Acct. Dir.)*
L. Williamson *(Sr. V.P., Corp. Devel.)*
G. Frascione *(Sr. V.P., Acct. Dir.)*

Leo Burnett Connaghan & May Pty. Ltd. **(1)**
Leo Burnett House, Levels 3&4, 73 Miller St.
North Sydney, N.S.W. 2060, Australia
Tel.: 2-9253555
Telex: 21565
Fax: 2-9572152
Approx.Billings: $100,000,000
S.I.C.: 8741
Stan May *(Chm. & Chief Creative Officer & Chief Exec. Officer)*
Selwyn Shapiro *(Reg. Fin. Dir.)*
Cam Carter *(Grp. Mng. Dir.)*
John Lambert *(Natl. Media Dir.)*

Leo Burnett/Conaghan & May S.a. Pty. Ltd. **(1)**
225 Greenhill Rd., 2nd Fl.
Dulwich, South Australia 5065, Australia
Tel.: 8-3640066
Telex: 82522
Fax: 8-3640054
S.I.C.: 7311
David Lester *(Mng. Dir.)*

Leo Burnett/Conaghan & May (Vic.) Pty. Ltd. **(1)**
464 St. Kilda Rd., 5th Fl.
Melbourne, Victoria 3004, Australia
Tel.: 3-8671166
Telex: 31788
Fax: 3-8674952
S.I.C.: 7311
Russell Alford *(Mng. Dir.)*

Leo Burnett/Conaghan & May (Qld.) Pty. Ltd. **(1)**
33 Park Rd.
Milton, Queensland 4064, Australia
Tel.: 7-3681222
Telex: 145318
Fax: 7-3697260
S.I.C.: 7311
Eddy Odden *(Mng. Dir.)*

Leo Burnett Denmark **(1)**
Vesterbrogade 2B 1620
Copenhagen, V, Denmark
Tel.: 33-149966
Telex: 22439
Fax: 33-141155
Emp.: 32
Full Service
S.I.C.: 7311
Ulrich Boesen *(Mng. Dir.)*

Leo Burnett Inc. **(1)**
Prolongacion Arabia No. 13 Arroyo Hondo, Santo Domingo, Dominican Republic
Tel.: 809-5650558
Fax: 809-5666634
Approx.Billings: $3,652,000
Emp.: 35
Ad Agency
S.I.C.: 7311
Aldo Martinez *(Admin./Opers.)*

Leo Burnett, Inc. **(1)**
Banco de Ponce Bldg., Ste. 2200
San Juan, PR 00918
Tel.: 809-754-7760
Telex: 345-3089
Fax: 809-766-1765
S.I.C.: 7311
Efran Pagan *(Mng. Dir.)*

Leo Burnett Intl., Asia Hdqtrs. **(1)**
City Plaza 3, 6th Fl., 14 Taiko Wan Rd.
Hong Kong, Hong Kong
Tel.: 6743333
Telex: 75468
Fax: 885-3209
S.I.C.: 8741
Malcolm Glenn *(Regional Mng. Dir.-Asia Region)*
Bruce Marsden *(Regional Fin. Dir.)*

Leo Burnett-Kyodo Co. Ltd. **(1)**
Akasaka Twin Tower, 17-22, Akasake 2-chome Minato-ku,
Tokyo, 107, Japan
Tel.: 3-35842331
Telex: 28410
Fax: 3-35842330
Approx.Billings: $222,198,000
Emp.: 270
Full Service Agency
S.I.C.: 7311
William Smith *(Pres. & Representative Dir.)*

Takayuki Okamoto *(Dir.-Mktg. Services & Gen. Affairs)*

Leo Burnett Limited **(1)**
Level 4, 100 Symonds St.
Auckland, New Zealand
Tel.: 9-798170
Fax: 9-371531
Approx.Billings: $13,500,000
Emp.: 18
Specializes in Consumer Advertising
S.I.C.: 7311
Jim Curry *(Mng. Dir.)*
Wayne Silver *(Fin. Dir.)*

Leo Burnett Limited **(1)**
Level 5, Barclays House, 36 Customhouse Quay P.O. Box 10-430,
Wellington, New Zealand
Tel.: 4-4993488
Fax: 4-4993509
S.I.C.: 7311
Chris Sharp *(Mng. Dir.)*

Leo Burnett Limited **(1)**
48 St. Martin's Lane
London, WC2N 4EJ, United Kingdom
Tel.: 071-8362424
Telex: 24243
Fax: 071-8297143
Approx.Billings: $261,300,000
Emp.: 270
Full Service Agency
S.I.C.: 7311
Richard Wheatly *(Chm.)*
Kerry Rubie *(Chief Exec. Officer)*

Leo Burnett Ltd. **(1)**
City Plaza 3, 6th Fl., 14 Taikoo Wan Rd.
Quarry Bay, Hong Kong
Tel.: 852-567-4333
Telex: 75468
Fax: 8853209
Approx.Billings: $68,400,000
Emp.: 200
Full Service Agency
S.I.C.: 7311
Vincent Swift *(Mng. Dir. & New Bus. Contact)*
Cecil Yow *(Deputy Mng. Dir. & New Bus. Contact)*
Malcolm Glenn *(Reg. Mng. Dir.-Asia Region)*
Andy Lai *(Gen. Mgr.-Leo Burnett China)*
Allan Chan *(Comml. Dir.)*
Bruce Marsden *(Reg. Fin. Dir.)*
Catherine Guthrie *(Integrated Communications Dir.)*
Peter Tong *(Fin. & Admin. Mgr.)*

Leo Burnett Ltd., Europe/Middle East Hdqtrs. **(1)**
48 St. Martin's Lane
London, WC2N 4EJ, United Kingdom
Tel.: 071-8362424
Telex: 24243
Fax: 071-8297143
Approx.Billings: $1,059,000,000
Emp.: 1,465
S.I.C.: 8741
Richard Zobel *(Reg. Mng. Dir.)*

Leo Burnett Ltd. Thailand **(1)**
2nd Fl. USOM Bldg., 37 Soi Somprasong 3 Petchburi Rd.,
Bangkok, 10400, Thailand
Tel.: 2-2552356
Fax: 2-2539189/2541743
Approx.Billings: $44,736,700
Emp.: 206
Full Service Agency
S.I.C.: 7311
Vince Swift *(Chm.)*
Bruce Martin *(Mng. Dir.)*
Daranee Charoen-Rajapark *(Mktg. Services Dir.)*
Wasuntara Kritpracha *(Fin. Dir.)*

Leo Burnett Prague **(1)**
Rep. Office Prague CSFR, Ceskomalinska 41,
Prague, CS-160 00 Praha, Czechoslovakia
Tel.: 42-2-323-029
Fax: 42-2-322-981
Josef Havelka *(Chief Oper. Officer)*

Leo Burnett Pte. Ltd. **(1)**
#03-01/04-01, Robinson Towers, 30 Robinson Rd.
Singapore, 0104, Singapore
Tel.: 2207022
Telex: RS 5139
Fax: 2207011
Approx.Billings: $20,000,000
Emp.: 80
Full Service Agency
S.I.C.: 7311
Jim Patterson *(Mng. Dir.)*
Lim Tian Soo *(Fin. Dir.)*
Lian Ai Lee *(Sec.)*

Leo Burnett Pty. Ltd. **(1)**
Leo Burnett House Level 3&4, 73 Miller St.
North Sydney, N.S.W. 2060, Australia
Tel.: 2-9253555
Telex: 21565
Fax: 2-9572152
S.I.C.: 7311
Cam Carter *(Mng. Dir.)*
Stan May *(Mng. Dir.)*

Leo Burnett Publicidade, Ltda. **(1)**
400 40th Ave. Cidade Jardim
Sao Paulo, 01454, Brazil
Tel.: 11-8153611
Telex: 1122884
Fax: 11-2119037
Approx.Billings: $60,000,000
Emp.: 112
Computer Systems/Hardware:
Sicap/Lotus/Clipper/HG/Windows/WS
S.I.C.: 7311
Jan Hommes *(Pres.)*
Francisco Costa *(Chief Fin. Officer)*
Steve Longley *(Exec. V.P.)*

Leo Burnett S.A. **(1)**
371 Sygrou Ave. 175 64
Athens, Greece
Tel.: 01-9412-365/9413-966-8
Telex: 218605
Fax: 1-9430432
Approx.Billings: $24,000,000
Emp.: 100
Specializes in Consumer Advertising
S.I.C.: 7311
Petros Venetis *(Chm.)*
Olga Koukouma *(Sec.)*
Alecos Psaropoulos *(Fin. Dir.)*
Dimitri Batayas *(Exec. V.P.-Media & Res.)*
Dina Galanou *(Public Rels. Dir.)*

Leo Burnett S.A. de C.V. **(1)**
Bosque de Duraznos 65-8P Bosques de las Lomas, 11700
Mexico, D.F. Mexico
Tel.: 525-596-61-88
Telex: 01774278
Fax: 525-596-6248
Approx.Billings: $53,000,000
Emp.: 190
Full Service Advertising
S.I.C.: 7311
Francisco Cardenas *(Chm., Pres. & Mng. Dir.)*
Walter Esteves *(V.P., Fin. & Admin.)*
Chris Robinson *(Integrated Communications Dir.)*

Leo Burnett Sdn. Bhd. **(1)**
8th Fl., Wisma Damansara, Damansara Heights Jalan Semantan,
Kuala Lumpur, Malaysia
Tel.: 603-2545777
Telex: 30423
Fax: 603-2550560
Full Service Ad Agency
S.I.C.: 7311
Phil Fiebig *(Mng. Dir.)*

Leo Burnett Sonyon, Inc. **(1)**
9th fl.-Youone Bldg., 75-95, Seosomun-dong Chung-ku,
Seoul, 100-110, Korea
Tel.: 82-2-774-8222
Fax: 82-2-774-2226
David Miller *(Chief Oper. officer)*

Leo Burnett Sp. z.o.o., ul. **(1)**
Zwyciezcow 18 P-03-933 Warszawa, Poland
Tel.: 48-22-172413
Fax: 48-39-121027
Tom Gresk *(Chief Oper. Officer)*

Leo Burnett Sweden A.B. **(1)**
Kunggatan 38 11135 .
Stockholm, Sweden
Tel.: 46-08-200-940
Telex: 46-08-203-707

Leo Bunett Turin **(1)**
Corso Vittorio Emanuele II 10121, 100,
Torino, Italy
Tel.: 39-11-562-0201
Fax: 39-11-561-7566

Leo Burnett Venezuela, C.A. **(1)**
Centro Plaza, Torre B, Niveles 7 y 8
Avenida Francisco de Miranda, Los Palos Grandes,
Caracas, Venezuela
Tel.: 2-2837066
Telex: 23339
Fax: 2-2838764
Approx.Billings: $45,000,000
Emp.: 190
Full Service Agency
S.I.C.: 7311
Jutus O'Brien *(Mng. Dir.)*
Clemencia Granados *(Admin. Dir.)*

Leo Burnett Worldwide Inc. **(1)**
Chaussee de Wavre 1789 Box 16, B-1160
Brussels, Belgium
Tel.: 32-2-675-49-00
Telex: 62517
Fax: 32-2-675-20-46
Approx.Billings: $55,000,000
Emp.: 70
Computer Systems/Hardware:
Hewlett Packard
Full Service Agency
S.I.C.: 7311
Michel Ducamp *(Mng. Dir.)*

Markom/Leo Burnett A.S. **(1)**
Perlhan Sokak No. 126, Sisli
Istanbul, Turkey
Tel.: 1-2463698
Telex: 927572
Fax: 1-2460842
Emp.: 60
Full Service Agency
S.I.C.: 7311
Haluk Mesci *(Chief Exec. Officer & Creative Dir.)*
Paolo Volpara *(Chief Oper. Officer, Mng. Dir.)*
Murat Bebiroglu *(Fin. Dir.)*

Matter Galbucci Leo Burnett, Werbeagentur **(1)**
Ausstellungs Strasse 80 8005
Zurich, Switzerland
Tel.: 01-3414680
Telex: 822670
Fax: 01-3412829
Approx.Billings: $28,000,000
Emp.: 30
S.I.C.: 7311
David Marsden *(Partner)*
Erich Hartmann *(Partner)*
Roland Lacher *(Partner)*

Noordervliet & Winninghoff/Leo Burnett B.V. **(1)**
Drentestraat 5 1083 HK
Amsterdam, Netherlands
Tel.: 20-6442445
Telex: 11674
Fax: 20-6448680
Approx.Billings: $73,000,000
Emp.: 90
S.I.C.: 7311
Albert Winninghoff *(Chm.)*
Philip Noordervliet *(Dir.)*
Wim Sturkenboom *(Fin. Dir.)*

Nordskar & Thorkildsen Leo Burnett A/S **(1)**
0277, Drammensveien 130,
Oslo, Norway
Tel.: 47-2-44-21-50
Fax: 47-2-926999
Terje Thorkildsen *(Chief Oper. Officer)*

N&T Leo Burnett A/S **(1)**
Drammensveien 130 0277
Oslo, Norway
Tel.: 2-442150
Fax: 2-926999
Emp.: 40
Full Service Agency
S.I.C.: 7311
Terje Thorkildsen *(Mng. Dir.)*
Bjorg Borgen *(Fin. Dir.)*

RTA Advertising, Inc. **(1)**
2050 Mountain St., 3rd Fl.
Montreal, PQ H3G 1Z7, Canada
Tel.: 514-849-9936
Fax: 514-849-6143
Approx.Billings: $13,415,239
Emp.: 17
Computer Systems/Hardware:
Macintosh
Advertising, Public Relations & Promotion
S.I.C.: 7311
Raymonde Lavoie *(Partner)*
Tina Schiefelbein *(Partner & Client Services)*
Lina Frattasio *(Fin. Dir.)*
Joy Berger *(Pub. Rels. Dir.)*

Radius Advertising **(1)**
Al Khaleejia Bldg., 12 Fl., Al Sharg P.O. Box 26100,
Safat, 13121, Kuwait
Tel.: 240-4967
Telex: 30983
S.I.C.: 7311
Roger Darouny *(Mng. Dir.)*

Radius Advertising **(1)**
The Blue Bldg., 2nd fl., Sharjah Rd.
Dubai, U.A.E.

Radius Leo Burnett U.A.E **(1)**
The Blue Bldg., 2nd Fl., Sharjah Rd.
Dubai, United Arab Emirates
Tel.: 4-620431
Telex: 49436 Radad EM
Fax: 4-696109
Approx.Billings: $22,000,000
Emp.: 42
Full Service Advertising
S.I.C.: 7311
Farid Chehab *(Chm. Bd.)*
Raja Trad *(Chief Exec. Officer)*

Targets Adv. **(1)**
Shinkar Commercial Center, 2nd Fl., Medina Rd. P.O. Box 6093,
Jeddah, 21442, Saudi Arabia
Tel.: 966 2 651 1272
Tel.: 966 2 651 5168
Telex: 601898 UNITED SJ
Fax: 2-6513166
Approx.Billings: $10,000,000
Emp.: 27
Full Service Advertising Agency
S.I.C.: 7311
Karim Tabet *(Mng. Dir.)*

Vitruvio/Leo Burnett **(1)**
Planta 27, Plaza de Pablo Ruiz, Torre Picasso S/N 28020
Madrid, Spain
Tel.: 1-5561120
Fax: 1-5565705
Approx.Billings: $75,000,000
Emp.: 80
Full Service Agency
S.I.C.: 7311
Miguel A. Furones *(Pres.)*
Roberto Forero *(V.P.)*

Vituvio/Leo Burnett **(1)**
08014, Diagonal 593,
Barcelona, Spain
Tel.: 34-3-419-3277
Telex: 34-3-419-5680

BURNHAM BROADCASTING COMPANY
980 N. Michigan Ave., Ste. 1200
Chicago, IL 60611
Tel.: 312-787-9800 **DE**
Fax: 312-787-3964
Year Founded: 1983
Assets: $133,000,000
Liabilities: $190,000,000
Net Worth: $57,000,000
Approx.Sls.: $67,000,000
Emp.: 538
Fiscal Year-end: 12/31/91
Owns & Operates TV Stations; Production Companies
S.I.C.: 4833; 7812
Peter B. Desnoes *(Mng. Gen. Partner)*
Tyler W. Sheffield *(Chief Fin. Officer & Treas.)*
Penny Lashner *(Controller)*
Janet Thelan *(Admin. Asst.)*

Principal(s):
Peter B. Desnoes

No. of U.S. Offices: 6

Computer Systems/Hardware:
IBM 34s & 36s

Outside Service Firm(s):

Coopers & Lybrand *(Auditors)*
203 N. LaSalle St.
Chicago, IL 60601
Tel.: 312-701-5500

Burnham Broadcasting Company—(Continued)

Hartford Life Insurance Co.*(Group Insurer)*
Hartford, CT 06104-2999

Shearson Lehman Brothers, Inc.*(Investment Banker)*
Tower C, World Financial Center
New York, NY 10285
Tel.: 212-298-2000

Pedersen & Houpt*(Legal Firm)*
180 N. LaSalle, Ste. 3400
Chicago, IL 60601

Massachusetts Mutual Life Insurance Co.*(Pension Manager)*
Chicago, IL

Units:

KBAK-TV **(1)**
19th & Westwind Dr.
Bakersfield, CA 93303
Tel.: 805-327-7955
Television Station
S.I.C.: 4833
Wayne Lansche *(Pres. & Gen. Mgr.)*

KHON-TV **(1)**
1116 Auahi St.
Honolulu, HI 96814
Tel.: 808-531-8585
Television Station
S.I.C.: 4833
Mike Rosenberg *(Pres. & Gen. Mgr.)*
Steve Hiramoto *(Sls. Mgr.)*

WALA-TV **(1)**
210 Government St.
Mobile, AL 36602
Tel.: 205-433-3754
Television Station
S.I.C.: 4833
Joseph W. Cook *(Pres. & Gen. Mgr.)*
John Dawson *(Gen. Sls. Mgr.)*
Larry Pate *(Program Dir.)*

WLUK-TV **(1)**
787 Lombardi Ave.
Green Bay, WI 54307
Tel.: 414-494-8711
Television Station
S.I.C.: 4833
Bill Fyffe *(Pres. & Gen. Mgr.)*
Mark Jollie *(Gen. Sls. Mgr.)*

WVUE-TV **(1)**
1025 S. Jefferson Davis Pkwy.
New Orleans, LA 70125
Tel.: 504-486-6161
Television Station
S.I.C.: 4833
Phil Nye *(Pres. & Gen. Mgr.)*
Jim Goodlad *(Sls. Mgr.)*

JOHN BURNHAM & CO.
610 W. Ash
San Diego, CA 92101
Mailing Address:
P.O. Box 2910
San Diego, CA 92112
Tel.: 619-236-1555 **CA**
Fax: 619-238-4118
Year Founded: 1891
Sales Range: $1 Billion +
Emp.: 350
Real Estate Investor & Broker; Insurance Company
S.I.C.: 6531; 6411
Malin Burnham *(Chm. Bd.)*
Robert Lichter *(Pres. & Chief Exec. Officer)*
Joanne Pastula *(Exec. V.P.)*
Tim Proudy *(Sr. V.P.-Real Estate Div.)*
Ron Hensley *(V.P.)*
Jonathan Wale *(V.P.)*
Antoinette West *(V.P.-Admin.)*
Kevin C. Kinslow *(Chief Fin. Officer)*
Ronald Hrusoff *(Gen. Counsel)*
Elsa Ford *(Corp. Sec.)*
Christopher Sparks *(Controller)*
Shari Laughlin *(Mgr.-Human Resources)*

No. of U.S. Offices: 4
No. of Foreign Offices: 1

Computer Systems/Hardware:
IBM PC-XT; XENIX/COMPAQ

Outside Service Firm(s):

Deloitte & Touche*(Auditors)*
701 "B" St., Ste. 1900
San Diego, CA 92101-8198

ALTA Health Strategies*(Group Insurer)*
Phoenix, AZ

BURNS & MCDONNELL ENGINEERS-ARCHITECTS-CONSULTANTS
4800 E. 63rd St.
Kansas City, MO 64141
Mailing Address:
P.O. Box 419173
Kansas City, MO 64141
Tel.: 816-333-4375
Fax: 816-333-3690
Year Founded: 1898
Approx.Sls.: $90,000,000
Emp.: 1,150
Fiscal Year-end: 12/31/91
Export
Engineering, Architecture & Construction Management Specializing in Industrial & Commercial Facilities, Electric Power Generation & Transmission, Aviation, Wastewater Treatment, Water Supply, Solid & Hazardous Waste Management, Gas Desulfurization & Environmental Analysis
S.I.C.: 8711; 8712; 8741; 4941; 4952; 4953; 4911
Newton A. Campbell *(Chm. Bd. & Treas.)*
Dave G. Ruf, Jr. *(Pres.)*
Darrell M. Hosler *(Exec. V.P. & Sec.)*
Joel A. Cerwick *(V.P. & Gen. Mgr.-Environmental/Civil)*
Douglas E. Criner *(V.P.-Mktg.)*
Daniel A. Froelich *(V.P. & Gen. Mgr. Air Quality, Plng. & Environ. Analysis)*
John R. Riley *(V.P. & Gen. Mgr.-Power)*
John B. Williams *(V.P. & Gen. Mgr.-Special Projects)*
Ed Wolfrom *(Controller)*
Gerry Bukowski *(Gen. Counsel)*
David E. Christianson *(Dir.-Human Resources)*
C. William Brisson *(Mgr.-Systems Dept.)*
Kady Hommel *(Mgr.-Mktg.)*
Joel Blobaum *(Editor)*
Kerry Maher *(Corp. Librarian)*
Principal(s):
Employee-Owned

No. of U.S. Offices: 7
No. of Foreign Offices: 2

Outside Service Firm(s):

Arthur Andersen & Co.*(Auditors)*
1500 Commerce Tower, 911 Main St.
Kansas City, MO 64105
Tel.: 816-221-4200
Fax: 816-221-7693

United Missouri Bank*(Major Banking Relationship)*
P.O. Box 226
Kansas City, MO 64141
Tel.: 816-556-7000

Subsidiaries:

Burns & McDonnell Waste Consultants, Inc. **(1)**
4800 E. 63rd St.
Kansas City, MO 64141
Waste Management & Environmental Consultants
S.I.C.: 4953
Paul Hustad *(Pres.)*

The C. W. Nofsinger Company **(1)**
4700 E. 63rd St.
Kansas City, MO 64141
Tel.: 816-361-7999
Fax: 816-822-3416
Emp.: 60
Engrng. Services for Petroleum, Chemical, Petrochemical & Food Processing Plants
S.I.C.: 8711; 8712; 1542; 8741
William M. Nofsinger *(Pres.)*
Rowland Nofsinger *(V.P.)*

BURNS & ROE ENTERPRISES, INC.
800 Kinderkamack Rd.
Oradell, NJ 07649
Tel.: 201-265-2000
Fax: 201-599-2958
Year Founded: 1932
Sales Range: $500-999 Million
Emp.: 1,800
Fiscal Year-end: 12/31/90
Engineering, Design, Construction & Construction Management
S.I.C.: 8711; 1542
K. Keith Roe *(Chm. Bd., Pres., Chief Exec. & Chief Oper. Officer)*
C.A. Doyle *(V.P., Sec. & Gen. Counsel)*
Gerald B. Pisani *(V.P.-Human Resources)*
Hollace L. Roe *(V.P.-Real Estate)*
George H. Schnitzer *(V.P.-Mktg.)*
Vincent J. Mackin *(Asst. V.P.-Fin.)*
A.T. Dajani *(Chief Fin. Officer)*
H.E. Bartoli *(Gen. Mgr.)*
Robert C. Baumbach *(Dir.-Quality Control)*
Steve Gertz *(Dir.-Environment)*
Carlos R. Guerra *(Dir.-Res. & Devel.)*
John A. Tesoro *(Dir.-Information Services)*
S. Achtner *(Mgr.-Sls.)*
Juliet F. Botwick *(Mgr.-Pension Admin.)*
R.F. Sabia *(Mgr.-Sls.)*
Patricia Bernstein *(Librarian)*

No. of U.S. Offices: 10

Computer Systems/Hardware:
Harris

Outside Service Firm(s):

KPMG Peat Marwick*(Auditors)*
Oradell, NJ

Aetna Life & Casualty*(Group Insurer)*
100 N. Riverside Plaza
Chicago, IL 60606

Ennis, Knupp & Associates*(Pension Manager)*
10 S. Riverside Plaza
Chicago, IL 60606
Tel.: 312-715-1700
Fax: 312-715-1952

United States Trust Company of New York*(Pension Manager)*
45 Wall Street
New York, NY 10005

Subsidiaries:

Burns & Roe Enterprises, Inc. **(1)**
1400 'K' St., N.W.
Washington, DC 20005
Tel.: 202-898-1500
Fax: 202-898-1561
Construction & Engineering Services
S.I.C.: 1541; 1542; 1629; 8711

Burns & Roe Environmental Services **(1)**
601 S. Henderson Rd., Ste. 250
King of Prussia, PA 19406
Tel.: 215-354-0500
Fax: 215-354-9347
Construction & Engineering Services
S.I.C.: 1541; 1542; 1629; 8711

Burns & Roe Industrial Services Company **(1)**
2812 Old Lee Hwy., Ste. 120
Fairfax, VA 22116
Tel.: 703-207-0800
Fax: 703-207-8538
Construction & Engineering Services
S.I.C.: 1541; 1542; 1629; 8711
A.T. Dahani *(Gen. Mgr.)*

Burns & Roe Pacific Company **(1)**
10805 Holder St., Ste.250
Cypress, CA 90630-5144
Tel.: 714-828-2200
Fax: 714-828-7007
Construction & Engineering Services
S.I.C.: 1541; 1542; 1629; 8711

Burns & Roe Southeast **(1)**
Southland Executive Park, 7800 Southland Blvd., Ste. 260
Orlando, FL 32809
Tel.: 407-857-0008
Fax: 407-855-3991
Construction & Engineering Services
S.I.C.: 1541; 1542; 1629; 8711

Non U.S. Holdings:

Burmot Australia Pty., Ltd. **(1)**
1 Chandos St., St. Leonards
Sydney, N.S.W. 2065, Australia
Tel.: 61 2 439 1288 (50%)
Emp.: 30
Engineering & Construction
S.I.C.: 8711; 1542; 1541; 1629

Lin & Roe Company **(1)**
Taiping & First Bldg., 550 Chung Hsiao East Rd., Section 4
Taipei, Taiwan
Tel.: 02 707 8777 (49%)
Telex: 25334
Construction & Engineering Services
S.I.C.: 8711; 1542; 1541; 1629

BURNSIDE CONSTRUCTION CO.
2400 Wisconsin Ave.
Downers Grove, WI 60515
Tel.: 708-515-9999 **IL**
Fax: 708-515-9555
Year Founded: 1911
Approx.Sls.: $17,000,000
Emp.: 250
Construction, Operative Builders
S.I.C.: 1521; 1531; 1542; 1522
George Arquilla, Jr. *(Chm. Bd.)*
George Arquilla, III *(Pres.)*
John Carlborg, Jr. *(Treas.)*
Lorraine Anderson *(Sec.)*
Principal(s):
George Arquilla, Jr.
George Arquilla, III

Outside Service Firm(s):

McGrane, Perozzi, Stelter, Gerardi, Brauer & Ross*(Legal Firm)*
Chicago Heights, IL

Heritage Bank*(Major Banking Relationship)*
Chicago Heights, IL

BURNSTAD BROTHERS, INC.
Hwy. 12 & 16 E.
Tomah, WI 54660
Mailing Address:
P.O. Box 768
Tomah, WI 54660
Tel.: 608-372-6335
Fax: 608-372-4062
Year Founded: 1969
Approx.Sls.: $72,000,000
Emp.: 750
Retail Groceries; Family Clothing; Garden Equipment & Supplies; Operates Management Service
S.I.C.: 0181; 5411; 5651
Victor Burnstad *(Pres.)*
Kirk Burnstad *(Chief Oper. Officer)*
Rita Burnstad *(V.P. & Sec.)*
Kent Burnstad *(Chief Fin. Officer)*

Outside Service Firm(s):

Farmers & Merchants Bank*(Major Banking Relationship)*
Tomah, WI

BURNSTEAD CONSTRUCTION COMPANY
1215 120th Ave., N.E., Ste. 201
Bellevue, WA 98005
Tel.: 206-454-1900 **WA**
Fax: 206-454-4543
Approx.Sls.: $25,000,000
Emp.: 30
New Construction; Speculative Builder Of Single-family Houses
S.I.C.: 1531; 1521
Frederick H. Burnstead *(Pres.)*
Joan Burnstead *(Sec. & Treas.)*

Outside Service Firm(s):

Seafirst Bank*(Major Banking Relationship)*
Columbia-SeaFirst Center, 701 5th Ave., 11th Flr.
Seattle, WA 98124
Tel.: 206-358-3039
Fax: 206-358-3113

W. Atlee Burpee Co.
(See listing under Burnstead Construction Company)

BURRELL COMMUNICATIONS GROUP INC.
20 N. Michigan Ave.
Chicago, IL 60602
Tel.: 312-443-8600
Year Founded: 1971
Approx.Billings: $70,068,300
Emp.: 115
African-American Advertising: Coca-Cola USA
S.I.C.: 7311
Thomas J. Burrell *(Chm.)*
Charles H. Curry *(Pres. & Chief Oper. Officer)*
Anna K. Morris *(Exec. V.P. & Chief Creative Officer)*
John G. Stanek *(Sr. V.P. & Chief Fin. Officer)*
Ronald Sampson *(Sr. V.P.)*
Amy Hilliard-Jones *(Sr. V.P. & Dir. Integrated Mktg. Services)*
Leslie Cole *(V.P. & Dir. Info. Services)*
Robert LeBeau *(V.P.-Admin.)*

Computer Systems/Hardware:
IBM

BURRELL GROUP
2400 Leechburg Rd.
New Kensington, PA 15068
Mailing Address:
P.O. Box 440,
New Kensington, PA 15068
Tel.: 412-339-2220
Tel.: 800-545-1575
Fax: 412-339-9880
Year Founded: 1935
Assets: $9,811,000
Liabilities: $3,075,000
Net Worth: $6,736,000
Approx.Sls.: $11,750,000
Emp.: 50
Fiscal Year-end: 12/31/90
Export
Land Development & Insurance; Blocks for Mining Industry
S.I.C.: 6411; 6552; 3532
Charles H. Booth, Jr. *(Chm. Bd., Pres. & Chief Exec. Officer)*
Thomas J. Phillis *(V.P.-Fin. & Treas.)*
William L. Harbaugh *(V.P.-Mktg. & Sls.)*
Shirley Trefelner *(Controller)*
No. of Mfg. Plants/Facilities: 2

Computer Systems/Hardware:
IBM

Outside Service Firm(s):

Ernst & Young*(Auditors)*
2000 Pittsburgh Natl. Bldg.
Pittsburgh, PA 15222
Tel.: 412-644-7800
Fax: 412-644-7419

Pittsburgh National Bank*(Major Banking Relationship)*
Stock Transfer Dept., Fifth & Wood Streets
Pittsburgh, PA 15265

CNA Insurance*(Commercial Insurance Carrier)*
CNA Plaza,
Chicago, IL 60685
Tel.: 312-822-5000

Phoenix Mutual Life Insurance Co.*(Group Insurer)*
Hartford, CT

Reed, Smith, Shaw & McClay*(Legal Firm)*
Mellon Square, P.O. Box 2009
Pittsburgh, PA 15230
Tel.: 412-288-3131
Fax: 412-288-3063

Subsidiaries:

Continental Development Company **(1)**
2400 Leechburg Rd.
New Kensington, PA 15068
Tel.: 412-339-2220
Tel.: 800-541-1575
Fax: 412-339-9880
Emp.: 15
Land Developer & Insurance Agency
S.I.C.: 6411; 6552
Charles H. Booth *(Pres.)*
T.J. Phillis *(V.P.-Fin.)*

Omega Transworld Ltd. **(1)**
2400 Leechburg Rd.
New Kensington, PA 15068
Tel.: 412-339-2220
Tel.: 800-541-1575
Fax: 412-339-9880
Emp.: 7
Produces Blocks for the Mining Industry
S.I.C.: 3532
Charles H. Booth *(Pres.)*
T.J. Phillis *(V.P.-Fin.)*
W.L. Harbaugh *(V.P.-Mktg.)*

Omega Transworld, Inc, Utah **(1)**
2400 Leechburg Rd.
New Kensington, PA 15068
Tel.: 412-339-2220
Emp.: 8
Produces Blockd for the Mining Industry
S.I.C.: 3532
Charles H. Booth *(Pres.)*
T.J. Phillis *(V.P. & Chief Fin. Officer)*
W.L. Harbaugh *(V.P.-Mktg.)*

THE BURRIS AGENCY, INC.
1208 Eastchester Dr., Ste. 130
High Point, NC 27265
Tel.: 919-884-4249
Fax: 919-882-4897
Year Founded: 1985
Approx.Billings: $10,985,000
Emp.: 20
J. Mark Burris *(Pres. & Chief Exec. Officer)*
Julie Bales *(Exec. V.P., Opers.)*

BURRIS CHEMICAL INC.
4210 Azalea Dr.
Charleston, SC 29415
Mailing Address:
P.O. Box 70788,
Charleston, SC 29415
Tel.: 803-554-7511
Telex: 576439
Fax: 803-554-3926
Approx.Sls.: $45,000,000
Emp.: 130
Wholesale Distributor of Chemicals
S.I.C.: 5169
A.A. Burris, III *(Chm. Bd. & Pres.)*
Bruce M. Burris *(V.P.-Pur. & Traffic)*
Steven Y. Burris *(Sec. & Treas.)*

Outside Service Firm(s):

Ernst & Young*(Auditors)*
1100 Independence Center
Charlotte, NC 28246
Tel.: 704-372-6300

Womble Carlyle Sandridge & Rice*(Legal Firm)*
Charleston, SC

South Carolina National Bank*(Major Banking Relationship)*
Charleston, SC

BURRIS FOODS, INC.
5th & McColley Sts.
Milford, DE 19963
Tel.: 302-422-4531 **DE**
Fax: 302-422-7588
Year Founded: 1939
Approx.Sls.: $200,000,000
Emp.: 350
Fiscal Year-end: 5/31/92
Packaged Frozen Goods; Storage, Frozen or Refrigerated Goods; Truck Tires & Tubes; Automotive Tires; Tire Recapping
S.I.C.: 5142; 4222; 5014; 5531; 7534
John E. Burris *(Chm. Bd.)*
Robert D. Burris *(Pres. & Chief Oper. Officer)*
John Cross *(Chief Fin. Officer & V.P.)*
Howard W. Burris *(V.P. & Asst. Sec.)*
L. Elizabeth Hoopman *(Sec.)*

Outside Service Firm(s):

Philadelphia National Bank*(Major Banking Relationship)*
Philadelphia, PA

Subsidiary:

Kent Sussex Tire Service **(1)**
5th & McColley St.
Milford, DE 19963
Tel.: 302-422-4531
Automobile Tires & Tubes; Rebuilding & Retreading Tires
S.I.C.: 5014

B. BURRISS COMPANIES
1011 Kinley Rd.
Columbia, SC 29212
Mailing Address:
P.O. Box 55,
Columbia, SC 29202
Tel.: 803-781-4300 **SC**
Fax: 803-781-7020
Approx.Sls.: $19,000,000
Emp.: 125
General Contractor Apartments, Condominiums, Motels; Commercial Construction
S.I.C.: 1522; 1542
John H. Burriss *(Pres.)*

Outside Service Firm(s):

Robert W. Sanders*(Auditors)*
Columbia, SC

Citizens & Southern National Bank*(Major Banking Relationship)*
Columbia, SC

Subsidiary:

Burriss Building Systems **(1)**
4186 Fernandina Rd.
Columbia, SC 29212
Tel.: 803-781-6800
General Contractors
S.I.C.: 1522; 1542
T. Moffatt Burriss, Jr. *(Pres.)*

BURROWS PAPER CORPORATION
501 W. Main St.
Little Falls, NY 13365
Tel.: 315-823-2300
Fax: 315-823-2417
Specialty Tissue Paper
S.I.C.: 2621
R.W. Burrows, Jr. *(Chm. Bd. & Pres.)*
Howard Davidson *(V.P.-Sls.)*
Paul A. Schwonke *(V.P. & Gen. Mgr.)*
S.A. Keyser *(Chief Fin. Officer)*

Outside Service Firm(s):

Coopers & Lybrand*(Auditors)*
One Lincoln Center
Syracuse, NY 13202
Tel.: 315-474-8541
Fax: 315-474-0259

Norstar Bank, N.A.*(Major Banking Relationship)*
Syracuse, NY

F.N. BURT COMPANY, INC.
2345 Walden Ave.
Buffalo, NY 14225
Tel.: 716-684-2345
Fax: 716-684-4789
Approx.Sls.: $26,000,000
Emp.: 400
Set Up Boxes, Folding Cartons & Other Paper & Plastic Container Products
S.I.C.: 2652; 2657
W. Russell Hurd *(Pres. & Chief Exec. Officer)*
Joseph GaNun *(V.P.-Sls. (Folding Carton Div.))*
Richard L. Ward *(V.P. & Controller)*
Donald Hanson *(Mgr.-Sls. (Rigid Box Div.))*

BURT EQUIPMENT COMPANY, INC.
Conn River Bridge Rd.
Westminster Station, VT 05159
Tel.: 802-722-3358
Fax: 802-722-9088
Emp.: 75
Steel Pipe & Tubes, Fabricated Structural Metal, Pipe, Extruded Aluminum
S.I.C.: 3317; 3441; 3354
Roland E. Scott *(Pres. & Treas.)*
Harlow Bates *(V.P.)*
Wendell S. Brown *(V.P.)*

Outside Service Firm(s):

Svendsen & Puls*(Auditors)*
Bellows Falls, VT

Salmon & Nostrand*(Legal Firm)*
Bellows Falls, VT

First Vermont Bank & Trust Company*(Major Banking Relationship)*
Bellows Falls, VT

Subsidiary:

Burtco Metal Systems **(1)**
Conn River Bridge Rd.
Westminster Station, VT 05159
S.I.C.: 3441

BURTMAN IRON WORKS, INC.
31 Industrial Dr.
Boston, MA 02137
Tel.: 617-364-1200 **MA**
Fax: 617-364-7643
Approx.Sls.: $11,000,000
Emp.: 85
Export
Merchandise Display Or Storage Racks; Hand Or Power Truck Dollies; Metal Plate Trash Racks
S.I.C.: 2542; 3537; 3443
Charles Burtman *(Pres. & Chief Exec. Officer)*
Phillip Goodman *(Treas.)*
Mark Goodman *(Sec.)*
Luther Kinman *(Dir.-Engrng.)*

No. of Mfg. Plants/Facilities: 3

Burtman Iron Works, Inc.—(Continued)

Outside Service Firm(s):

Gorsey & Wall*(Auditors)*
Boston, MA

Liberty Mutual*(Group Insurer)*
175 Berkeley St.
Boston, MA

Ropes & Gray*(Legal Firm)*
One International Place
Boston, MA 02110
Tel.: 617-423-6100

Fleet National Bank*(Major Banking Relationship)*
Corporate Trust Dept., 125 Dupont Dr.
Providence, RI 02907
Tel.: 617-426-9555

Division:

Dynabilt Products **(1)**
31 Industrial Dr.
Boston, MA 02136
Tel.: 617-364-1200
Industrial Trucks; Dumpsters; Plate Work; Pallet Racks; Mezzanine Systems; Pallet Machines; Recycling Containers; Refuse Containers; Floor Trucks
S.I.C.: 3443; 2542; 3537
Charles Burtman *(Pres.)*
Philip Goodman *(Chief Fin. Officer)*

THE BUSCHMAN CO.
10045 International Blvd.
Cincinnati, OH 45246
Tel.: 513-874-0788
Fax: 513-874-5625
Year Founded: 1932
Approx.Sls.: $30,000,000
Emp.: 450
Design, Manufacture & Installation of Turnkey Conveyor Systems
S.I.C.: 3533
William Michaels *(Chm. Bd. & Pres.)*
John G. Slater *(Exec. V.P.-Fin.)*
Lawrence D. Frey *(V.P.-Sls.)*
Gerald A. Fulkerson *(V.P.-Mktg.)*
Pat Burke *(Dir.-Pur.)*
Ed Varney *(Dir.-Data Processing)*
Ann Nicholson *(Mgr.-Personnel)*

Outside Service Firm(s):

Deloitte & Touche*(Auditors)*
Chiquita Center, 250 E. 5th St., Ste. 1900
Cincinnati, OH 45202
Tel.: 513-784-7100

Dinsmore & Shohl*(Legal Firm)*
2100 Fountain Square Plaza
Cincinnati, OH 45202-3172
Tel.: 513-977-8200

Fifth Third Bank*(Major Banking Relationship)*
Corporate Trust Services, 38 Fountain Square Plaza
Cincinnati, OH 45263

BUSH BROTHERS & COMPANY
3885 Hwy. 411
Dandridge, TN 37725
Mailing Address:
P.O. Box 52330,
Knoxville, TN 37950-2330
Tel.: 615-623-2361 **TN**
Fax: 615-625-3743
Year Founded: 1908
Approx.Sls.: $150,000,000
Emp.: 800
Fiscal Year-end: 4/30/91
Import
Canned Vegetables & Dog Food
S.I.C.: 2033; 2047
Condon Bush *(Chm. & Chief Exec. Officer)*
James B. Ethier *(Pres. & Chief Oper. Officer)*
Tom Rugotzke *(Sr. V.P. & Dir.-Mfg.)*
Ron Dix *(Sr. V.P.-Mktg. & Sls.)*
Barry Gray *(V.P. & Dir.-Acctg. Fin.)*
Ron Wheeler *(V.P. & Dir.-Retail Sls.)*
Paula Blankenship *(Sec.)*
Kenneth Hobbs *(Gen. Counsel)*
Ronald Maples *(Controller)*
T.M. Byar *(Dir.-Information)*
Jerry Baugh *(Mgr.-Sls. Service)*
James A. Everett *(Mgr.-Employee Benefits)*
Dan Dougherty *(Pur. Agent)*

No. of Mfg. Plants/Facilities: 6

Outside Service Firm(s):

Breazeale & Associates*(Auditors)*
Knoxville, TN

Egerton, McAfee, Armistead, & Davis*(Legal Firm)*
Knoxville, TN

First American National Bank*(Major Banking Relationship)*
Knoxville, TN

Subsidiaries:

Blytheville Canning Company, Inc. **(1)**
P.O. Box 167
Blytheville, AR 72316
Tel.: 501-763-4450
Fax: 501-762-8226
S.I.C.: 2033
James B. Ethier *(Pres.)*

Blytheville Canning Company, Inc. **(1)**
1900 North St.
Muskogee, OK 74402
Tel.: 918-682-5545
Fax: 918-682-8216
S.I.C.: 2033
James B. Ethier *(Pres.)*

Bush Brothers & Company **(1)**
600 S. Highway St.
Augusta, WI 54727
Tel.: 715-286-2211
Fax: 715-286-1179
S.I.C.: 2033
James B. Ethier *(Pres.)*

Shiocton Kraut Co. **(1)**
P.O. Box 27
Shiocton, WI 54170
Tel.: 414-986-3816
Fax: 414-986-3476
Canned Sauerkraut
S.I.C.: 2033
James B. Ethier *(Pres.)*

Valley Canning Co., Inc. **(1)**
P.O. Box D,
Ville Platte, LA 70586
Tel.: 318-363-1343
Fax: 318-363-7003
S.I.C.: 2033
James B. Ethier *(Pres.)*

BUSH DEVELOPMENT CORP.
4029 Ironbound Rd., Ste. 200
Williamsburg, VA 23188
Tel.: 804-220-2874
Fax: 804-229-2542
Year Founded: 1952
Assets: $22,250,199
Liabilities: $19,854,276
Net Worth: $2,395,923
Approx.Sls.: $8,500,000
Emp.: 51
Fiscal Year-end: 12/31/91
Construction & Real Estate Development
S.I.C.: 1522; 1531; 1542; 6552
M.B. Sharp *(Pres.)*
J.J. Digges *(Exec. V.P.)*
M.Z. Ball *(Treas.)*
V.G. West *(Sec.)*

Computer Systems/Hardware:
Hewlett Packard

Outside Service Firm(s):

Frederick B. Hill*(Auditors)*
Norfolk, VA

NationsBank*(Major Banking Relationship)*
One Commercial Pl.
Norfolk, VA 23510
Tel.: 804-441-4700

BUSINESS INFORMATION TECHNOLOGY
1011 Centre Rd., 7th Fl., Ste. 400
Wilmington, DE 19805
Tel.: 302-996-0720
Fax: 302-996-0729
Emp.: 78
Computer Software Consulting Service
S.I.C.: 7379
Paul J. Piper *(Chm. Bd.)*
John B. Maitland *(Pres.)*

Outside Service Firm(s):

Rudolph, Palitz & Co.*(Auditors)*
Philadelphia, PA

Fidelity Bank*(Major Banking Relationship)*
Broad & Walnut St.
Philadelphia, PA 19109

BUSINESS MENS INSURANCE CORPORATION
2620 SW 27th Ave.
Miami, FL 33133
Tel.: 305-443-2898 **FL**
Fax: 305-442-8486
Year Founded: 1973
Approx.Sls.: $17,000,000
Emp.: 50
Life Insurance Agents
S.I.C.: 6411
Antonio M. Sierra *(Pres.)*
Eloy R. DeArmas *(V.P.)*
Maria Becka *(Dir.-Personnel)*
Brent Bush *(Dir.-Sls.)*
Leonardo Macerias *(Dir.-Mktg.)*

Outside Service Firm(s):

KPMG Peat Marwick*(Auditors)*
One Biscayne Tower, 2 South Biscayne Blvd., Ste.2900
Miami, FL 33131

Rosario Duncan*(Legal Firm)*
Miami, FL

First Union National Bank*(Major Banking Relationship)*
1 S.E. Financial Ctr.
Miami, FL 33131
Tel.: 305-666-5656

BUTCHER & CO., INC.
211 S. Broad St.
Philadelphia, PA 19107
Tel.: 215-985-5000 **PA**
Fax: 215-985-5088
Year Founded: 1910
Emp.: 80
Holding Co.; Merchant Banking
S.I.C.: 6719; 6211; 6351; 6799
Jonathan Butcher *(Chm. Bd. & Pres.)*

Outside Service Firm(s):

Price Waterhouse*(Auditors)*
30 S. 17th St.
Philadelphia, PA 19103
Tel.: 215-665-9500

Saul, Ewing, Remick & Saul*(Legal Firm)*
Philadelphia, PA

Fidelity Bank*(Major Banking Relationship)*
Broad & Walnut St.
Philadelphia, PA 19109

THE BUTCHER CO.
120 Bartlett St.
Marlborough, MA 01752-3013
Tel.: 508-481-5700
Fax: 508-485-9998
Approx.Sls.: $50,000,000
Emp.: 100
Floor Waxes, Wax Removers, Cleaning Or Polishing Preparations, Janitor Supplies
S.I.C.: 2842; 5087
Charles Butcher *(Chm. Bd.)*
James Nelson *(Owner & Pres.)*
Dena Caradimitropoulo *(V.P.-Opers.)*
Chris Gray *(V.P.-Adv.)*
Roy Jorstad *(V.P.-Sls.)*
Bill Reinhart *(V.P.-Research & Devel.)*
Alan Sadler *(V.P.-Sls. & Mktg., Europe)*
Bill Taylor *(V.P.-Mktg.)*
Principal(s):
James Nelson

Outside Service Firm(s):

KPMG Peat Marwick*(Auditors)*
One Boston Place
Boston, MA 02108
Tel.: 617-723-7700

Gadsby & Hannah*(Legal Firm)*
One Post Office Square,
Boston, MA 02109
Tel.: 617-357-8700

Bank of New England*(Major Banking Relationship)*
28 State Street
Boston, MA 02109
Tel.: 617-742-4000

M. BUTEN & SONS INC.
5000 Ridge Ave.
Philadelphia, PA 19128
Tel.: 215-483-7500 **PA**
Fax: 215-487-2396
Year Founded: 1897
Approx.Sls.: $20,000,000
Emp.: 200
Fiscal Year-end: 12/31/90
Wholesale & Retail Paint, Wallpaper & Related Products
S.I.C.: 5999
S. Ty Steinberg *(Pres. & Chief Exec. Officer)*
Max Buten *(V.P.-Fin. & Treas.)*
Michael Steinberg *(V.P.-Opers.)*
Gary Steinberg *(V.P.-Mktg.)*
Herbert Picus *(Sec.)*
Joseph Gosse *(Dir.-Data Processing)*
John Olson *(Dir.-Pur.)*
Principal(s):
S. Ty Steinberg

No. of Mfg. Plants/Facilities: 30

Computer Systems/Hardware:
Hewlett-Packard 3000 Series 44

Outside Service Firm(s):

Voyow Bayard & Co.*(Auditors)*
Philadelphia, PA

Blue Cross of Greater Philadelphia*(Group Insurer)*
Philadelphia, PA

Wolf, Block, Schorr & Solis-Cohen*(Legal Firm)*
Packard Bldg.,
Philadelphia, PA 19102

Meridian Bank*(Major Banking Relationship)*
Philadelphia, PA

Savitt & Associates*(Pension Manager)*
Philadelphia, PA

BUTERA FINER FOODS INC.
1 Clock Tower Plaza
Elgin, IL 60120
Tel.: 708-741-1010 **IL**
Fax: 708-741-9610
Year Founded: 1965
Approx.Sls.: $100,000,000
Emp.: 700
Fiscal Year-end: 4/30/91
Grocery Stores
S.I.C.: 5411
Paul Butera *(Pres.)*
Sandro Milano *(Sec. & Treas.)*

Joseph Butera *(Mgr.-Admin.)*
Barbara Dugo *(Mgr.-Adv.)*
Principal(s):
Paul Butera

No. of U.S. Offices: 1

Outside Service Firm(s):

American Hardware Mutual*(Commercial Insurance Carrier)*
Chicago, IL

Midwest Health Insurance Benefit Fund*(Group Insurer)*
Chicago, IL

American National Bank & Trust Company of Chicago*(Major Banking Relationship)*
33 N. LaSalle St.
Chicago, IL 60602
Tel.: 312-661-5000
Fax: 312-661-6417

BUTLER AUTOMATIC, INC.
480 Neponset St.
Canton, MA 02021
Tel.: 617-828-5450
Tel.: 800-544-0070 DE
Fax: 617-828-2715
Year Founded: 1956
Approx.Sls.: $36,000,000
Emp.: 255
Import Export
Mfr. of Machinery for the Printing & Packaging Industries
S.I.C.: 3555; 3554
Richard A. Butler, Jr. *(Chm. Bd. & Chief Exec. Officer)*
Clint Holland *(V.P.-Mfg.)*
Carl E. Miller *(V.P.-Sls. & Mktg.)*
Paul Cleary *(Controller)*
Andrew Butler *(Dir.-Sls.)*

Outside Service Firm(s):

Deloitte & Touche*(Auditors)*
125 Summer St.
Boston, MA 02110
Tel.: 617-261-8000
Fax: 617-261-8111

Powers & Hall*(Legal Firm)*
100 Federal St.
Boston, MA 02110
Tel.: 617-357-1500

Shawmut Bank*(Major Banking Relationship)*
1 Federal St.
Boston, MA 02110

BUTLER FOODS, INC.
2300 E. Butler
Philadelphia, PA 19137
Tel.: 215-288-9920
Fax: 215-533-9050
Approx.Sls.: $78,000,000
Emp.: 400
Fiscal Year-end: 4/31/92
Processing & Sale of Meat & Pork
S.I.C.: 2011; 5147
Steven Lipoff *(Pres., Treas. & Chief Fin. Officer)*
Lawrence Lipoff *(Office Mgr. & Treas.)*

Outside Service Firm(s):

Ostroff & Fair*(Auditors)*
Philadelphia, PA

Schnader, Harrison, Segal & Lewis*(Legal Firm)*
1600 Market Street
Philadelphia, PA 19103
Tel.: 215-751-2000

Fidelity Bank*(Major Banking Relationship)*
Broad & Walnut St.
Philadelphia, PA 19109

BUTLER INTERNATIONAL
(Formerly North American Ventures, Inc.)
110 Summit Ave.
Montvale, NJ 07645
Mailing Address:
P.O. Box 460
Montvale, NJ 07645
Tel.: 201-573-8000 MD
Fax: 201-573-9723
Year Founded: 1985
Assets: $82,234,000
Earnings: ($4,547,000)
Liabilities: $40,950,000
Net Worth: $41,284,000
Approx.Sls.: $250,533,000
Emp.: 5,500
Fiscal Year-end: 12/29/91
Holding Company
S.I.C.: 6719
Edward M. Kopko *(Chm. Bd., Pres., Chief Exec. & Chief Oper. Officer)*
Warren F. Brecht *(V.P., Treas. & Sec.)*
Robert F. Murphy *(Controller)*
Cathy D. Shea *(Asst. Sec.)*

Subsidiary:

Butler Service Group, Inc. **(1)**
110 Summit Ave.
Montvale, NJ 07645
Tel.: 201-573-8000 (100%)
Approx.Sls.: $302,995,000
Emp.: 5,500
Contract Technical Services
S.I.C.: 8711
Edward M. Kopko *(Pres. & Chief Exec. Officer)*
Marc D. Freedman *(Sr. V.P., Gen. Counsel & Sec.)*
Raymond J. Lacroix *(Sr. V.P.-Fin. & Chief Fin. Officer)*
Michael C. Hellreigel *(V.P., Controller & Asst. Sec.)*
Marie L. Tornaquindici *(Asst. V.P.-Opers. Liaison)*
Richard S. Paras *(Asst. Sec.)*

Subsidiaries:

Butler Telecommunications Group **(2)**
3836 Dekalb Technology Pkwy.
Atlanta, GA 30340
Tel.: 404-451-0880 (100%)
Telecommunications Services
S.I.C.: 4899
Gary P. McGuire *(Pres.)*
Richard W. Savona *(V.P.-Branch Opers.)*

Subsidiaries:

Butler Installation Services, Inc. **(3)**
5304 Roseville Rd.
North Highlands, CA 95660
Tel.: 916-331-8101 (100%)
S.I.C.: 4899
Ebert J. Vellejos *(Project Mgr.)*

Butler Telecommunications Services **(3)**
110 Summit Ave.
Montvale, NJ 07645
Tel.: 201-573-8000 (100%)
S.I.C.: 4899
Gary P. McGuire *(Pres.)*
Richard W. Savona *(V.P.-Branch Opers.)*

Subsidiary:

Butler Fleet Maintenance Services **(4)**
5304 Roseville Rd., Ste. B
North Highlands, CA 95660
Tel.: 916-331-8101
Provides Maintenance for Vehicles in the Telecommunications Industry
S.I.C.: 4899
Robert L. Bogozzi *(V.P. & Gen. Mgr.)*

Butler Utilities Services, Inc. **(3)**
7201 20th Avenue
Brooklyn, NY 11214 (100%)
S.I.C.: 4899
John D'Angelo *(Acct. Rep.)*

Butler Design Services, Inc. **(3)**
110 Summit Ave.
Montvale, NJ 07458
Tel.: 201-573-8000 (100%)
Off-site Design & Drafting Services
S.I.C.: 8711
John A. Cimmarusti *(Pres.)*

Butler Quality Services, Inc. **(2)**
110 Summit Ave.
Montvale, NJ 07645
Tel.: 201-573-8000 (100%)
S.I.C.: 4899
Pat C. Arace *(Sr. V.P. & Gen. Mgr.)*
Robert M. Lyon *(V.P.)*

LBAI

Lawrence Butner Advertising, Inc.

LAWRENCE BUTNER ADVERTISING, INC.
228 East 45th St.
New York, NY 10017
Tel.: 212-682-3200
Year Founded: 1979
Approx.Billings: $29,100,000
Emp.: 36
Broadcast Direct Response
Lawrence Butner *(Pres.)*
Eleanor Butner *(Exec. V.P.)*
Robin Butner *(Sr. V.P., Gen. Mgr.)*
Pamela T. Weinberg *(Sr. V.P., Human Resources)*
Pamela Bennett-Jones *(V.P., Admin. Services)*
David Weber *(V.P., Telemarketing Services)*

H. E. BUTT GROCERY CO.
646 S. Main St.
San Antonio, TX 78204
Mailing Address:
P.O. Box 83999
San Antonio, TX 78283
Tel.: 210-246-8592
Fax: 210-246-8063
Year Founded: 1905
Approx.Sls.: $2,300,000,000
Emp.: 40,000
Retail Groceries & Video Rental Stores
S.I.C.: 5411; 7841
Charles C. Butt *(Pres. & Chief Exec. Officer)*
Jack Brouillard *(Chief Fin. Officer & Chief Admin. Officer)*
Wesley Nelson *(V.P. & Sec.)*
Dan E. Butt *(Treas.)*
Dean Deckard *(Asst. Treas.)*

Principal(s):
Charles C. Butt

No. of Mfg. Plants/Facilities: 260
No. of U.S. Offices: 1

Computer Systems/Hardware:
IBM 3083

Outside Service Firm(s):

Delaware Investment Advisors*(Pension Manager)*
One Commerce Square
Philadelphia, PA 19103

BUTTERICK COMPANY, INC.
161 6th Ave.
New York, NY 10013
Tel.: 212-620-2500
Tel.: 800-766-2670
Fax: 212-620-2736
Year Founded: 1863
Approx.Sls.: $120,000,000
Emp.: 1,000
Fiscal Year-end: 6/30/91
Export
Publishers of Vogue Patterns Magazine, Butterick Home Catalog & Vogue Knitting, Weddings & Special Occasions
S.I.C.: 2721; 2741
John Lehmann *(Chm. Bd., Pres. & Chief Exec. Officer)*
Allan Feller *(Pres.-Sls.)*
Jay Stein *(Chief Fin. Officer)*
Sidney Escowitz *(V.P.-Creative Services)*
William Fisher *(V.P.-Admin.)*
Steve Burke *(Controller)*
Dwight Wassong *(Gen Counsel & Dir. Taxes & Legal Services)*
Shirley Asper *(Dir.-Opers. & Data Processing)*
Janice Lewis *(Dir.-Pur.)*
Ed Parody *(Dir.-Telecommunications)*
Sheila Wahlers *(Dir.-Employee Benefits)*
Nora O'Hare *(Mgr.-Adv. Promo.)*

Computer Systems/Hardware:
Scitex

Outside Service Firm(s):

Aetna Life & Casualty*(Group Insurer)*
151 Farmington Avenue
Hartford, CT 06156
Tel.: 203-273-2128
Fax: 203-729-4295

BUXTON COMPANY
(Co. of DHP Partnership)
45 Plainfield
Chicopee, MA 01013
Mailing Address:
P.O. Box 1650
Springfield, MA 01102-1650
Tel.: 413-734-5900
Fax: 413-785-1367
Year Founded: 1898
Approx.Sls.: $30,000,000
Emp.: 1000
Fiscal Year-end: 12/31/90
Import Export
Mfr. & Distr. of Leather Goods & Accessories
S.I.C.: 3172; 3199
Russell E. Whiteford *(Pres. & Chief Exec. Officer)*
Alan L. Haberman *(Exec. V.P. & Chief Fin. Officer)*
Debra B. Jones *(Sr. V.P.-Mktg.)*
Paul Kleinheider *(V.P.-Sls.)*
Paul Vaillancourt *(V.P.-Pur.)*
Joanne Berwald *(Mgr.-Personnel)*

BUYER ADVERTISING, INC.
85 Wells Ave.
Newton, MA 02159
Tel.: 617-969-4646
Fax: 617-969-6807
Year Founded: 1966
Approx.Billings: $10,000,000
Recruitment & Adv.
Betty R. Buyer *(Pres.)*
Charles G. Buyer *(Exec. V.P., Gen. Mgr.)*
Marion B. Buyer *(V.P.)*
Beverly Eastman *(V.P.)*
Ann Toll *(V.P. & Mgr. Sls.)*
Elbert Taitz *(Dir.-Mktg.)*

BYER CALIFORNIA
66 Potrero Avenue
San Francisco, CA 94103
Tel.: 415-626-7844 CA
Fax: 415-626-7865
Year Founded: 1964
Approx.Sls.: $150,000,000
Emp.: 1,000
Fiscal Year-end: 11/30/91
Export
Manufacture of Women's & Girl's Apparel
S.I.C.: 2331; 2339; 2335
Allan G. Byer *(Chm. Bd., Pres. & Chief Exec. Officer)*
Joel D. Feldman *(Exec. V.P. & Chief Oper. Officer)*

Byer California—(Continued)

Gary A. Schwartz *(Chief Fin. Officer)*
Barbara Berling *(V.P.)*
Richard Bickett *(V.P. & Pres.-Brannan Apparel Grp. Division)*
Janis L. Byer *(V.P.)*
Philip J. Byer *(V.P.)*
Max Curry *(V.P.)*
Monte M. Hermann *(V.P. & Pres.-Alfred Paquette Mfg. Division)*
Mark Schatzberg *(V.P.)*
Jeffrey Zukerberg *(V.P.)*
Marian Byer *(Treas. & Sec.)*
Meyer Scher *(Gen. Counsel)*
Merrill Komai *(Mgr.-Data Processing)*
Principal(s):
Allan G. Byer
Marian Byer

No. of Mfg. Plants/Facilities: 2
No. of U.S. Offices: 10

Computer Systems/Hardware:
Sequent

Outside Service Firm(s):

Grant Thornton*(Auditors)*
San Francisco, CA

Home Life Insurance Co.*(Commercial Insurance Carrier)*
New York, NY

Connecticut General Life Insurance Co.*(Group Insurer)*
Visalia, CA

Scher & Bassett*(Legal Firm)*
Sunnyvale, CA

Bank of America, N.T. & S.A.*(Major Banking Relationship)*
P.O. Box 37002,
San Francisco, CA 94137

Tukman Capital Management*(Pension Manager)*
Larkspur, CA

BYERLY FORD-NISSAN INC.
4041 Dixie Hwy.
Louisville, KY 40216
Tel.: 502-448-1661 **KY**
Fax: 502-448-0819
Year Founded: 1944
Sales Range: $20-39 Million
Emp.: 140
Fiscal Year-end: 12/31/91
New & Used Automobile Dealerships, Parts & Service, Leasing
S.I.C.: 5511; 7538; 7515
John R. Daunhauer, Jr. *(Chm. Bd. & Pres.)*
Gregory Daunhauer *(Exec. V.P.)*
John Paul Daunhauer *(Sec.)*
Alice Butler *(Controller)*
Principal(s):
John R. Daunhauer, Jr.
Alice J. Daunhauer

No. of U.S. Offices: 1

Computer Systems/Hardware:
Reynolds & Reynolds

Outside Service Firm(s):

Cotton & Allen*(Auditors)*
Louisville, KY

Liberty National Bank & Trust Co.*(Major Banking Relationship)*
416 W. Jefferson St.
Louisville, KY 40202
Tel.: 502-566-2000

BYERLY'S INC.
7171 France Ave. So.
Edina, MN 55435
Tel.: 612-831-3601
Fax: 612-831-0751
Year Founded: 1968
Approx.Sls.: $215,000,000
Emp.: 3,000
Fiscal Year-end: 9/30/89
Grocery, Bakeries & Liquor Stores
S.I.C.: 5411; 5461; 5921
Thomas W. Harberts *(Pres. & Chief Exec. Officer)*
Douglas G. Clock *(Exec. V.P. & Chief Fin. Officer)*
Keith D. Kersten *(V.P.-Sls. & Food Processing)*
Dale Riley *(V.P.-Retail Opers.)*

JACK BYRNE FORD & MERCURY, INC.
S. Main St.
Mechanicville, NY 12118
Tel.: 518-664-9841
Fax: 518-664-8719
Approx.Sls.: $35,500,000
Emp.: 61
Fiscal Year-end: 3/31/92
Retail Automobiles
S.I.C.: 5511
John F. Byrne, Sr. *(Pres.)*
John Byrne, Jr. *(Gen. Mgr.)*
Principal(s):
John F. Byrne, Sr.

Outside Service Firm(s):

Budd & Carioto*(Auditors)*
Albany, NY

R.J. Carignan & Company*(Commercial Insurance Carrier)*
595 Fifth Ave.
Troy, NY 12180

Marine Midland Bank*(Major Banking Relationship)*
Troy, NY

Charles Boechel Associates*(Pension Manager)*
Albany, NY

Subsidiary:

Jack Byrne Minuteman Lube **(1)**
1768 Rte. 9
Clifton Park, NY 12065
Tel.: 518-371-3087 (100%)
Emp.: 8
Lubrication Services
S.I.C.: 7549

BYRNES & KIEFER COMPANY
131 Kline Ave.
Callery, PA 16024
Tel.: 412-538-9200
Fax: 412-538-9292
Year Founded: 1902
Approx.Sls.: $18,000,000
Emp.: 85
Wholesale Groceries; Manufacture Bread Baked Goods, Candy & Confectionery Products, Flavoring Extracts & Syrups
S.I.C.: 2051; 2087; 5149
Edward G. Brynes, Jr. *(Pres. & Chief Exec. Officer)*
Thomas Byrnes *(V.P., Sec. & Pur. Agent)*
Jay Thier *(V.P.-Fin.)*
Leo Hedderman *(Mgr.-Opers.)*

Outside Service Firm(s):

McLaughlin & Courson Company*(Auditors)*
Pittsburgh, PA

Reed, Smith, Shaw & McClay*(Legal Firm)*
Mellon Square, P.O. Box 2009
Pittsburgh, PA 15230
Tel.: 412-288-3131
Fax: 412-288-3063

C & K MARKETS, INC.
615 5th St.
Brookings, OR 97415
Tel.: 503-469-3113 **OR**
Fax: 503-469-6717
Year Founded: 1968
Approx.Sls.: $97,000,000
Emp.: 750
Supermarket Chain
S.I.C.: 5411
Ray L. Nidiffer *(Pres.)*
Douglas Nidiffer *(V.P.)*
Rex R. Scoggins *(Controller)*
M. June Nidiffer *(Treas. & Sec.)*

Outside Service Firm(s):

West One Bank*(Major Banking Relationship)*
Portland, OR

C-LINE PRODUCTS, INC.
1530 Birchwood Ave.
Des Plaines, IL 60018
Tel.: 708-827-6661 **IL**
Fax: 708-827-3329
Approx.Sls.: $35,000,000
Emp.: 280
Plastic Coated Office Products
S.I.C.: 3089
Robert Krumwiede *(Chm. Bd. & Pres.)*
James Krumwiede *(V.P.-Sls. & Mktg.)*
Norman Lukens *(V.P. & Treas.)*
Thomas E. Robertson *(V.P.-Services)*
Ronald Spears *(V.P.-Mfg.)*
Susan Travis *(Controller)*
Gerald Krumwiede *(Sec.)*

No. of Mfg. Plants/Facilities: 2

Outside Service Firm(s):

Arthur Andersen & Co.*(Auditors)*
33 W. Monroe St.
Chicago, IL 60603-4067
Tel.: 312-580-0033
Fax: 312-507-6748

NBD Park Ridge*(Major Banking Relationship)*
Park Ridge, IL

C & M CORPORATION
51 S. Walnut St.
Wauregan, CT 06387
Tel.: 203-774-4812
Fax: 203-774-7330
Sales Range: $20-39 Million
Emp.: 400
Manufacture Plastic Insulated Wire & Cable
S.I.C.: 3357
Warren A. Mueller *(Chm. Bd. & Treas.)*
Mark G. Andrews *(Pres.)*
Jack Fitzgibbons *(V.P.-Materials)*
Joe Lindley *(V.P.-Opers.)*
Ray Helie *(Controller)*

No. of Mfg. Plants/Facilities: 2

Outside Service Firm(s):

Joseph B. Cohan & Associates*(Auditors)*
Worcester, MA

Connecticut National Bank*(Major Banking Relationship)*
Central Village, CT

C & S WHOLESALE GROCERY INC.
Old Ferry Rd.
Brattleboro, VT 05301
Tel.: 802-257-4371
Fax: 802-257-6727
Year Founded: 1931
Approx.Sls.: $461,000,000
Emp.: 1,300
Grocery Wholesaler; Frozen Food, Dairy, Meat, Candy & Cigarettes
S.I.C.: 5141; 5142; 5143; 5145; 5194
Richard Cohen *(Pres.)*
Mitch Davis *(V.P.-Pub. Rels.)*
Perry Johns *(V.P.)*
Larry Newton *(V.P.-Sls.)*
Walter Pong *(V.P.-Mngmt. Information Systems)*
Joe Koziara *(Dir.-Data Processing)*
Janice Martin *(Benefits Admin.)*

Computer Systems/Hardware:
IBM 4381

Outside Service Firm(s):

Greenberg, Rosenblatt, Kull & Bitsoli*(Auditors)*
306 Main St.
Worcester, MA 01608
Tel.: 508-791-0901

Fleet National Bank*(Major Banking Relationship)*
Corporate Trust Dept., 125 Dupont Dr.
Providence, RI 02907
Tel.: 617-426-9555

CAC MICROCIRCUITS, INC.
2 Southgate Drive
Mount Carmel, IL 62863
Tel.: 618-263-4343
Fax: 618-263-4295
Approx.Sls.: $12,000,000
Emp.: 117
Fiscal Year-end: 12/31/88
Mfr. of Custom Thick Film Hybrids
S.I.C.: 3699
Lloyd Dustman *(Chm. & Pres.)*
Angela Lahr *(Treas, Controller, Chief Exec. & Fin. Officer)*
Jerry Hart *(Gen. Mgr.)*

CAE LINK ALLEN DIVISION
209 Madison St.
Alexandria, VA 22314
Tel.: 703-578-5800
Year Founded: 1975
Sales Range: $20-39 Million
Emp.: 700
Training Systems
S.I.C.: 7389
G.W. Menzer *(Chief Exec. Officer)*
H.L. DeCastro *(Pres.)*
J.L. Cross *(Exec. V.P.)*
B.E. Rutherford *(V.P.-Eastern Cpers.)*
D.S. Disler *(Chief Fin. Officer)*
Mario R. Mannarino *(Controller)*
Luis Parga *(Gen. Counsel)*
Ron Beaver *(Dir.-Mngmt. Information Systems)*
Sandy Bradshaw *(Dir.-Human Resources)*
Irene Byrne *(Dir.-Leasing)*
J. A. Doyle *(Dir.-Logistics Opers.)*
Tana Lambert *(Dir.-Employee Benefits)*
C. L. Plunkett *(Dir.-Engrng. Opers.)*
James Taylor *(Dir.-Plng. & Devel.)*
Doug Williams *(Dir.-Pur.)*
Leonard Steinbach *(Mgr.-Admin.)*

No. of U.S. Offices: 33

Computer Systems/Hardware:
Wang Word Processor; DEC Vax 11/750

Outside Service Firm(s):

KPMG Peat Marwick*(Auditors)*
Stamford Square, 3001 Summer St.
Stamford, CT 06905
Tel.: 203-356-9800

Bank of Virginia*(Major Banking Relationship)*
Alexandria, VA

Bank of Virginia*(Pension Manager)*
Alexandria, VA

C-B CORPORATION
1531 Tarhill Rd.
Charlotte, NC 28201
Tel.: 704-394-1140
Fax: 704-391-9920
Sales Range: $60-79 Million
Emp.: 450
Distribute Health & Beauty Aids & General Merchandise to Food Stores
S.I.C.: 5122

Bill Wootton *(Pres.)*
John Gioiofo *(Chief Fin. Officer)*
Roger Smith *(V.P.-Distr.)*
Walter Hamel *(Comptroller)*

Outside Service Firm(s):

Arthur Andersen & Co.*(Auditors)*
400 Renaissance Center
Detroit, MI 48243
Tel.: 313-259-8100

Walker, Palmer & Miller*(Legal Firm)*
Charlotte, NC

NationsBank Carolinas*(Major Banking Relationship)*
One NCNB Plaza T18-7
Charlotte, NC 28255

CB NORTH AMERICA, INC.
One Apollo Dr.
Glens Falls, NY 12801
Tel.: 518-792-2121
Fax: 518-792-6984
Approx.Sls.: $30,000,000
Emp.: 400
Mfr. of Ski Apparel
S.I.C.: 2329
David Rosen *(Pres. & Chief Exec. Officer)*
Butch Reilly *(Exec. V.P.)*
Ken Leccesse *(V.P. & Controller)*
Bill Post *(V.P.-Sls.)*
John Lemery *(Gen. Counsel)*
Kim Hinman *(Dir.-Adv. & Promo.)*
Craig Welcome *(Dir.-Pur.)*

Subsidiary:

CB Sports Inc. **(1)**
76 Lawrence St.
Glens Falls, NY 12801
Tel.: 518-792-2121
Fax: 518-792-4111
Approx.Sls.: $22,000,000
Emp.: 40
Fiscal Year-end: 12/31/91
Import
Computer Systems/Hardware:
IBM System 38
Mfr. Skiwear & Sportswear
S.I.C.: 2329; 2339
David Rosen *(Pres.)*

C B J ENTERPRISES, INC.
2802 Dow Ave.
Tustin, CA 92680
Tel.: 714-669-1800
Fax: 714-669-0555
Approx.Sls.: $10,000,000
Emp.: 105
Manufacture Diskettes & Magnetic Tapes
S.I.C.: 3679
Edward A. Conti *(Pres.)*
Chloe E. Conti *(V.P.-Admin.)*

Outside Service Firm(s):

Union Bank*(Major Banking Relationship)*
18300 Von Karman Ave.
Irvine, CA 92715

CBM AMERICA CORP.
2020 Santa Monica Blvd., Ste. 410
Santa Monica, CA 90404
Tel.: 310-828-8245
Fax: 310-828-8046
Approx.Sls.: $60,000,000
Emp.: 21
Fiscal Year-end: 3/31/91
Mfr. & Distr. of Office Machines, Citizen Dot Matrix Printer, Transfer Printer & Cash Register
S.I.C.: 3577
S. Takahashi *(Sr. V.P.)*
Lee Chin *(V.P. & Gen. Mgr.)*

CBM INDUSTRIES, INC.
13220 Co. Rd. #6
Minneapolis, MN 55441
Tel.: 612-559-4456 **MN**
Fax: 612-557-2198
Year Founded: 1967
Assets: $8,000,000
Liabilities: $4,000,000
Net Worth: $4,000,000
Approx.Sls.: $32,000,000
Emp.: 3000
Fiscal Year-end: 12/31/91
Non-Residential Building Operators; Building Service Contractor; Hospitals & Airports Building Maintenance Consultants
S.I.C.: 7349; 8742; 6512
Robert J. Wood *(Pres.)*
Mark Levenson *(V.P.-Admin., Personnel & Adv.)*
Kurt Wood *(Treas.)*

Outside Service Firm(s):

J.M. Barry Co., Ltd.*(Auditors)*
Minneapolis, MN

Peterson, Enberg & Peterson*(Legal Firm)*
Minneapolis, MN

Norwest Bank Minnesota, N.A.*(Major Banking Relationship)*
P.O. Box 2900, Loop Station
Minneapolis, MN 55402
Tel.: 612-372-8114

CBP RESOURCES, INC.
2410 Randolph Ave.
Greensboro, NC 27406
Mailing Address:
P.O. Drawer 20687,
Greensboro, NC 27420
Tel.: 919-333-3000 **DE**
Fax: 919-378-0435
Sales Range: $60-79 Million
Emp.: 500
Holding Company; Manufacture Chemicals, Animal Feed Supplements, Animal Fats & Proteins
S.I.C.: 2077; 2834; 2843; 6719
David S. Evans *(Pres.)*
Larry T. Fowler *(V.P. & Admin.)*
David Rosenstein *(V.P.-Fin.)*

Outside Service Firm(s):

Deloitte & Touche*(Auditors)*
Greensboro, NC

North Carolina National Bank*(Major Banking Relationship)*
Charlotte, NC 28255
Tel.: 704-374-5735

Subsidiary:

Carolina By-Products Co. **(1)**
2410 Randolph Ave.
Greensboro, NC 27420
Tel.: 919-272-3121
David Evans *(Pres.)*

C B R CEMENT CORPORATION
1875 S. Grant, Ste. 1000
San Mateo, CA 94402
Tel.: 415-572-8900
Fax: 415-572-9231
Sales Range: $500-999 Million
Natural Cement
S.I.C.: 3241
Richard Kline *(Pres.)*
Roger J. Bye *(Controller)*
Lesley Yarborough *(Mgr.-Communications)*

Subsidiaries:

The Cadman Companies **(1)**
P.O. Box 538
Redmond, WA 98073
Tel.: 206-868-1234
Redi-Mix Cement Producers; Sand & Gravel Distributor
S.I.C.: 3531; 1442

Calaveras Cement Corporation **(1)**
2033 N. Main St., Ste. 500
Walnut Creek, CA 94596
Tel.: 510-256-8837
Masonry & Pozzolana Cement
S.I.C.: 3241

Standard Concrete **(1)**
117 W. Fourth St.
Santa Ana, CA 92701
Tel.: 714-835-2931
Redi-Mix Concrete
S.I.C.: 3241

CC INDUSTRIES, INC.
222 N. LaSalle St.
Chicago, IL 60601
Tel.: 312-855-4000
Fax: 312-236-7074
Year Founded: 1948
Sales Range: $100-499 Million
Emp.: 6,400
Fiscal Year-end: 12/31/90
Import Export
Holding Co.: Home Furnishings; Paper Products; Outdoor & Casual Furniture; Provides Cellular Telephone Service; Owns, Develops & Manages Real Estate
S.I.C.: 2391; 2392; 2514; 3261; 6552; 6719; 2591; 2295; 3999; 2211; 2677
Lester Crown *(Chm. Bd.)*
Neele E. Stearns, Jr. *(Pres. & Chief Exec. Officer)*
Richard J. Nassau *(Pres.-Real Estate)*
D. Scott Bradley *(Treas.)*
David M. Rubin *(Sec. & Gen. Counsel)*
John J. Sobota *(Controller)*
George W. Mabey *(Mgr.-Admin.)*
William Stauffer *(Dir.-Mngmt. Information Systems)*

Principal(s):
Neele E. Stearns, Jr.

Computer Systems/Hardware:
IBM System As 400

Outside Service Firm(s):

Arthur Andersen & Co.*(Auditors)*
33 W. Monroe St.
Chicago, IL 60603-4067
Tel.: 312-580-0033
Fax: 312-507-6748

CNA Insurance*(Group Insurer)*
CNA Plaza,
Chicago, IL 60685
Tel.: 312-822-5000

Kemper Insurance*(Group Insurer)*
500 W. Madison St., Ste. 1100
Chicago, IL

Gould & Ratner*(Legal Firm)*
222 N. LaSalle St.
Chicago, IL 60601
Tel.: 312-236-3003

Continental Bank N. A.*(Major Banking Relationship)*
231 S. LaSalle St.
Chicago, IL 60697
Tel.: 312-828-2345
Tel.: 800-426-5754
Telex: 312-828-1783

First National Bank of Chicago*(Major Banking Relationship)*
One First National Plaza
Chicago, IL 60670
Tel.: 312-732-9781
Tel.: 312-732-4050
Fax: 312-732-4840
Fax: 312-732-3055

Subsidiaries:

American Envelope Company **(1)**
222 North LaSalle St.
Chicago, IL 60601
Tel.: 312-899-4900
Tel.: 800-232-6861
Fax: 312-236-4310
Approx.Sls.: $182,000,000
Emp.: 1,800
Fiscal Year-end: 12/31/91
Export
Computer Systems/Hardware:
IBM, AS400 & Sys36
Full Service Envelope Manufacturer; Specialize in Direct Mail
S.I.C.: 2677
John D. Weil *(Pres. & Chief Exec. Officer)*
Ben A. Renda *(V.P. & Controller)*
Michael M. Maloney *(V.P.-Sls. & Mktg.)*
David M. Rubin *(Gen. Counsel & Sec.)*
Scott Bradley *(Treas.)*
Michael R. Fox *(Mgr.-Mfg. Services)*

Divisions:

American Envelope Company-Kruysman Div. **(2)**
160 Varick St.
New York, NY 10013
Tel.: 212-255-1144
S.I.C.: 2677
Oliver Lednicer *(Pres.)*

American Envelope of Buffalo **(2)**
100 Centre Dr.
Orchard Park, NY 14127
Tel.: 716-662-2800
S.I.C.: 2677
Robert A. Fitzgerald *(Pres.)*

American Envelope of Chicago-Die Cut Div. **(2)**
4400 W. Ohio St.
Chicago, IL 60624
Tel.: 312-267-3600
S.I.C.: 2677
Stan Dvorak *(Pres.)*

American Envelope of Chicago-Web Div. **(2)**
3001 N. Rockwell St.
Chicago, IL
Tel.: 312-267-3600
S.I.C.: 2677
Stan Dvorak *(Pres.)*

American Envelope of Dallas **(2)**
14001 Inwood Rd.
Dallas, TX 75240
Tel.: 214-233-5711
S.I.C.: 2677
Duane Bennett *(Pres.)*

American Envelope of Denver **(2)**
5000 Kingston St.
Denver, CO 80239
Tel.: 303-373-5900
S.I.C.: 2677
Jon Murray *(Pres.)*

American Envelope of Los Angeles **(2)**
13341 Cambridge St.
Santa Fe Springs, CA 90670
Tel.: 310-802-1305
S.I.C.: 2677
David Junkin *(Pres.)*

American Envelope of Nashville **(2)**
820 7th Ave. N.
Nashville, TN 37219
Tel.: 615-244-2330
S.I.C.: 2677
Joe Shelton *(Pres.)*

American Envelope of Omaha **(2)**
915 N. 43rd Ave.
Omaha, NE 68131
Tel.: 402-553-1234
S.I.C.: 2677
Dan Boten *(Pres.)*

American Envelope of Philadelphia **(2)**
Fifth & Bristol
Philadelphia, PA 19140
Tel.: 215-324-9200
Fax: 215-457-0919
Approx.Sls.: $40,000,000
Emp.: 350
Computer Systems/Hardware:
IBM
Envelope Manufacturer
S.I.C.: 2677
Alan Gelman *(Pres. & Gen. Mgr.)*
Donald Alleback *(Pur. Agent)*
George Gallagher *(Technical Supvr.)*
V. Levitt *(Personnel Admin.)*

American Envelope of St. Louis **(2)**
601 Cannonball Lane
O'Fallon, MO 63366
Tel.: 314-272-2500
S.I.C.: 2677
Jack Smith *(Pres.)*

CC Industries, Inc.—(Continued)

American Envelope of San Antonio (2)
232 Iowa St.
San Antonio, TX 78210
Tel.: 210-533-5156
S.I.C.: 2677
David Hester *(Pres.)*

American Envelope of Seattle (2)
401 Andover Park East
Seattle, WA 98188
Tel.: 206-575-1400
S.I.C.: 2677
Larry Mead *(Pres.)*

CHF Industries, Inc. (1)
1 Park Ave., 9th Fl.
New York, NY 10016
Tel.: 212-951-7800 (100%)
Fax: 212-951-7801
Approx.Sls.: $100,000,000
Emp.: 1,950
Computer Systems/Hardware:
IBM 4341
Holding Company
S.I.C.: 6719
Charles Reifer *(Pres.)*
Mike Schwartzkoff *(Comptroller)*
Barbara Koller *(Mktg. Dir.)*
Fara Abramson *(Personnel Mgr.)*
Claire Coleman *(Pub. Rels. Asst.)*

Divisions:

Aberdeen Mfg. Corporation (2)
16 E. 34th St.
New York, NY 10016
Tel.: 212-889-8380
Manufacture Curtain, Draperies, Bedspreads & Comforters
S.I.C.: 2391; 2211; 2392
Charles Reifer *(Pres.)*
Murray Endick *(Dir.-Pur.)*
George Simmons *(Dir.-Personnel)*

Plants:

Aberdeen Mfg. Corp. Conway Plant (3)
16th Ave.
Conway, SC 29526
Tel.: 803-248-2291
Manufacture Draperies & Bedspreads
S.I.C.: 2391; 2392

Aberdeen Mfg. Corp. Kaufman Plant (3)
P.O. Box 70,
Kaufman, TX 74142
Tel.: 214-932-2173
Manufacture Curtains
S.I.C.: 2392

Aberdeen Mfg. Corp. Louis Hand Plant (3)
847 Pleasant St.
Fall River, MA 02722
Tel.: 617-679-8141
Manufacture Curtains & Shower Curtains
S.I.C.: 2392

Aberdeen Mfg. Corp. Savoy Plant (3)
8th & Wall St.
Tabor City, NC 28463
Tel.: 919-653-4096
Manufacture Bedspreads & Comforters
S.I.C.: 2391; 2392

Divisions:

Louis Hand Div. (3)
16 E. 34th St.
New York, NY 10016
Tel.: 212-889-8380
Manufacture Kitchen Curtains & Shower Curtains
S.I.C.: 2392
Charles Reifer *(Pres.)*

Savoy Drapery Div. (3)
16 E. 34th St.
New York, NY 10016
Tel.: 212-889-8380
Manufacture Draperies, Bedspreads & Comforters
S.I.C.: 2211
Charles Reifer *(Pres.)*

Cameo Curtains (2)
One Park Ave.
New York, NY 10016
Tel.: 212-679-3040
Emp.: 25
Mfr. of Curtains, Draperies, Bedspread & Comforters
S.I.C.: 2391; 2392
Jerry Pittman *(Pres.)*
Tom Murphy *(Natl. Sls. Mgr.)*

Finkel Outdoor Products, Inc. (2)
141 Lanza Ave.
Garfield, NJ 07026
Tel.: 201-772-7700 (100%)
Outdoor Furniture
S.I.C.: 2514; 3999
Frank Cucci *(Mgr.)*

Subsidiaries:

Finkel Outdoor Products of California (3)
3155 Bandini Blvd.
Vernon, CA 90023
Tel.: 213-268-2851 (100%)
Outdoor Furniture
S.I.C.: 2514; 3999

Finkel Outdoor Products of Florida (3)
740 King St.
Jacksonville, FL 32204
Tel.: 904-387-0421 (100%)
Outdoor Furniture
S.I.C.: 2511

Joanna (2)
8701 Red Oak Blvd.
Charlotte, NC 28217
Tel.: 704-522-5300
Tel.: 800-800-7878
Approx.Sls.: $120,000,000
Emp.: 1,200
Import Export
Manufacture Window Treatments
S.I.C.: 2591; 2211; 2295; 2431
Corporate Giving Program: United Way
Frederick Nichols *(Pres.)*
Vincent Paul *(V.P.-Mktg.)*
Ray Shaw *(Dir.-Distributor/Fabricator Sls.)*
Robert Tracy *(Dir.-Sls.)*
Phil Wolff *(Dir.-Imports)*

Divisions:

CC Industries, Kaywood Div. (3)
P.O. Box 307,
Benton Harbor, MI 49022
Tel.: 616-927-3561
Wood Shutters & Doors
S.I.C.: 2591

CC Industries, Kaywood-Southern Div. (3)
200 Pickens St.
Joanna, SC 29351
Tel.: 803-697-6706
Wood Shutters & Doors
S.I.C.: 2591

E. L. Mansure Div. (3)
P.O. Box 502,
Clinton, SC 29325
Tel.: 808-833-3953
S.I.C.: 2591
S.J. Deretchin *(Mgr.)*

Standard Shade Roller Div. (3)
P.O. Box 578,
Ogdensburg, NY 13669
Tel.: 315-393-3380
Shade Rollers, Woven Wood & Hinged Blinds
S.I.C.: 2431; 2591

Jakson-A CHF Company (2)
One Park Ave.
New York, NY 10016
Tel.: 212-951-7800
Fax: 212-779-8207
Emp.: 400
Mfr. of Shower Curtains & Bath Accessories
S.I.C.: 2392
Walter Wynkoop *(Pres.)*
Carol Frink *(Production Mgr.)*

Subsidiary:

Burton-Dixie of Blacksburg Inc. (2)
P.O. Box 608,
Blacksburg, SC 29702
Tel.: 803-839-6353 (100%)
Inactive
S.I.C.: 3086; 2519; 2299
David McDermott *(Pres.)*
Norman LaPeters *(Treas.)*

Divisions:

CC Industries Estia Div. (3)
P.O. Box 608,
Blacksburg, SC 29702
Manufacture Polyurethane Foam Furniture
S.I.C.: 3089

Crown Leisure Products (1)
317 S. Elm St.
Owosso, MI 48867
Tel.: 517-723-7881
Approx.Sls.: $60,000,000
Emp.: 400
Wrought Iron, Aluminum & Steel Furniture
S.I.C.: 2514
Alan Becker *(Pres.)*
Thomas Keating *(V.P.-Sls.)*
Ronda Marr *(Matls. Mgr.)*

Independent Cellular Network, Inc. (1)
2100 Electronics Lane
Fort Myers, FL 33912
Tel.: 813-489-1600
James Dwyer *(Pres.)*

CCI CORPORATION
P.O. Box 582800
Tulsa, OK 74158
Tel.: 918-836-0151 **DE**
Year Founded: 1959
Earnings: $2,000,000
Approx.Sls.: $40,000,000
Emp.: 450
Distribute Medium & Heavy-Duty Truck Parts
S.I.C.: 5013; 5531
Joseph M. Klein *(Pres.)*
Donald M. Hardin *(V.P. & Chief Fin. Officer)*
Henry Alcouloumre *(Dir.-Pub. Rels.)*
Jack Weakley *(Dir.-Insurance, Risk Mngmt. & Emp. Benefits)*
Karl Segner *(Mgr.-Acctg.)*

No. of U.S. Offices: 28

Outside Service Firm(s):

Coopers & Lybrand*(Auditors)*
1400 Mid-Continent Tower
Tulsa, OK 74103
Tel.: 918-596-8200
Fax: 918-596-8300

Rosenstein, Fist & Ringold*(Legal Firm)*
525 So. Main
Tulsa, OK 74103
Tel.: 918-585-9211

Bank of Oklahoma*(Major Banking Relationship)*
One Williams Center
Tulsa, OK 74012
Tel.: 918-588-5100

Aetna Life & Casualty*(Pension Manager)*
151 Farmington Avenue
Hartford, CT 06156
Tel.: 203-273-2128
Fax: 203-729-4295

CDA/TURK GROUP
90 North Broadway
Irvington-on-Hudson, NY 10533
Tel.: 914-591-9191
Fax: 914-591-4060
Year Founded: 1988
Approx.Billings: $10,000,000
Consumer Prods., Retail, New Product Devel. & Introduction
Stanley M. Turk *(Pres. & New Bus. Contact)*

CEI CONSTRUCTION, INC.
7500 Old Georgetown Road
Bethesda, MD 20814
Tel.: 301-657-7100
Approx.Sls.: $600,000,000
Emp.: 4,000
Gen. Bldg. & Heavy Construction Contractors; Stone, Clay & Glass Prods.; Misc. Svcs.
S.I.C.: 1541; 1542; 1611; 1629
A. James Clark *(Chm., Pres. & Chief Exec. Officer)*
Lawrence Nussdorf *(Chief Fin. Officer & Treas.)*
John Kezer *(Controller)*
Sandy Garchik *(Asst. Treas.)*
Martin Kerns *(Dir.-Employee Benefits)*
Kathy Taub *(Gen. Counsel)*

CF INDUSTRIES, INC.
One Salem Lake Dr.
Long Grove, IL 60047
Tel.: 708-438-9500 **IL**
Telex: 5106017095
Fax: 708-438-0211
Year Founded: 1946
Assets: $8,374,290,000
Earnings: $7,289,000
Liabilities: $333,731,000
Net Worth: $8,040,559,000
Approx.Rev.: $803,089,000
Emp.: 1,500
Fiscal Year-end: 12/31/91
Import Export
Manufacturer & Wholesaler of Chemical Fertilizers; Owned by 12 Regional Farm Supply Cooperatives in U.S. & Canada
S.I.C.: 2873; 2874; 1475
Gene A. James *(Chm. Bd.)*
R.C. Liuzzi *(Pres. & Chief Exec. Officer)*
Stephen R. Wilson *(Sr. V.P. & Chief Fin. Officer)*
C.E. Lynn *(V.P.-Human Resources)*
Paul R. Obert *(V.P., Gen. Counsel & Sec.)*
John H. Sultenfuss *(V.P.-Mktg.)*
Robert D. Webb *(V.P.-Plng. & Control)*
Dennis W. Baker *(Treas.)*
Eric B. Bergstrom *(Dir.-Cash Mngmt.)*
Wayne E. Brown *(Dir.-Mngmt. Information Systems)*
Ronald R. Landry *(Dir.-Employee Benefits)*
Daniel R. VanTassel *(Dir.-Corp. Communications)*
R.J. Erkman *(Mgr.-Corp. Fin.)*

No. of Mfg. Plants/Facilities: 61
No. of U.S. Offices: 1

Computer Systems/Hardware:
IBM Systems 34 & 36

Outside Service Firm(s):

KPMG Peat Marwick*(Auditors)*
Peat Marwick Plaza, 303 E. Wacker Dr.
Chicago, IL 60601
Tel.: 312-938-1000

Prudential Insurance Co. of America*(Commercial Insurance Carrier)*
751 Broad St.
Newark, NJ 07102-3777
Tel.: 201-802-6000

Prudential Insurance Co. of America*(Group Insurer)*
751 Broad St.
Newark, NJ 07102-3777
Tel.: 201-802-6000

Kirkland & Ellis*(Legal Firm)*
200 E. Randolph Dr.
Chicago, IL 60601
Tel.: 312-861-2000
Fax: 312-861-2200

Chase Manhattan Bank, N.A.*(Major Banking Relationship)*
One Chase Manhattan Plaza
New York, NY 10081
Tel.: 212-552-2222

Tel.: 800-526-0801
Fax: 212-552-7175

First National Bank of Chicago*(Major Banking Relationship)*
One First National Plaza
Chicago, IL 60670
Tel.: 312-732-9781
Tel.: 312-732-4050
Fax: 312-732-4840
Fax: 312-732-3055

CFB INDUSTRIES, INC.
1467 N. Elston
Chicago, IL 60622
Tel.: 312-278-8000 **IL**
Fax: 312-489-5461
Year Founded: 1989
Assets: $11,900,000
Liabilities: $4,846,000
Net Worth: $7,054,000
Approx.Sls.: $24,703,000
Emp.: 60
Fiscal Year-end: 9/30/91
Import Export
Fire Brick & Refractories; Mo Flint, Banner, Mohite, Duralite-60, Duralite-70, Dura-Tab, Hi-Al-Ram-G, C-W 85-HS Ram, Oxal-95-R, Kastite, Ladle-Kast, Lite-Kastite-2000, Super-Carbon Patch, Brickmix, P.S. Super
S.I.C.: 3255
George Taylor *(Pres.)*
Curtis Helwig *(Treas.)*

Outside Service Firm(s):

KPMG Peat Marwick*(Auditors)*
Peat Marwick Plaza, 303 E. Wacker Dr.
Chicago, IL 60601
Tel.: 312-938-1000

Ross & Hardies*(Legal Firm)*
1 IBM Plaza
Chicago, IL 60611
Tel.: 312-467-9300

National Security Bank of Chicago*(Major Banking Relationship)*
Chicago, IL

Subsidiaries:

Chicago Boat Yard, Inc. **(1)**
1269 W. Lemoyne St.
Chicago, IL 60622
Tel.: 312-276-2628
Boat Storage
S.I.C.: 4491
Richard Monastra *(Chief Oper. Officer)*

Chicago Fire Brick Company **(1)**
1467 N. Elston Ave.
Chicago, IL 60622
Tel.: 312-278-8000
Fax: 312-489-5461
Importer & Exporter of Fire Bricks & Clays
S.I.C.: 5211
Ralph J. Schindiun Jr. *(Chief Oper. Officer)*
Lido J. Schindler *(Sales Mgr.)*

Chicago Fire Brick of Delaware, Inc. **(1)**
1467 N. Elston Ave.
Chicago, IL 60622
Tel.: 312-278-8000
S.I.C.: 3255
Ralph J. Schindler Jr. *(Chief Oper. Officer)*

Wellsville Fire Brick Company **(1)**
P.O. Box 71, West Hwy. 19
Wellsville, MO 63384
Tel.: 314-684-2222
Fax: 314-684-2946
Import Export
Mfr. and Importer & Exporter of Refractory Products
S.I.C.: 3255
George H. Taylor *(Chief Oper. Officer)*
Lido J. Forassiepi *(Sales Mgr.)*

Non-U.S. Holding:

C&W Refractories, Ltd. **(1)**
191 Victoria Ave. So.
Hamilton, ON L8N 3C8, Canada
Tel.: 416-527-1145
Approx.Sls.: $1,000,000
Emp.: 2
Mktg. & Sls. of Refractory Brick
S.I.C.: 5085; 3255

William Cureton *(Pres.)*

CF&I STEEL CORPORATION
(Filed for Chapter 11 Bankruptcy, November 7, 1990)
225 Canal St.
Pueblo, CO 81004
Mailing Address:
P.O. Box 316,
Pueblo, CO 81002
Tel.: 719-561-6000
Tel.: 800-992-9900 **CO**
Fax: 719-561-7256
Year Founded: 1936
Assets: $241,557,575
Earnings: ($15,761,076)
Liabilities: $343,957,004
Net Worth: $102,399,429
Approx.Sls.: $249,679,000
Emp.: 1,500
Fiscal Year-end: 12/31/91
Export
Mfr. & Producer Steel Rails, Wire, Bars & Seamless Tubular Products
S.I.C.: 3312; 3315; 3317
Crocker Nevin *(Chm. Bd.)*
Frank J. Yaklich, Jr. *(Pres. & Chief Exec. Officer)*
Ronald K. Craft *(V.P.-Fin., Treas. & Controller)*
Richard L. Head *(V.P.-Comml.)*
J. David Houghton *(V.P.-Opers.)*
Michael W. Coriden *(Corp. Attorney & Sec.)*
Earl Emery *(Dir.-Pur. & Traffic)*
Robert Lloyd *(Mgr.-Mngmt. Information Systems)*

Subsidiaries:

Albuquerque Metals Co. **(1)**
3339 Second St.
Albuquerque, NM 87103
Tel.: 505-877-6110 (100%)
Emp.: 13
Wholesale Scrap Metals
S.I.C.: 5093
A. B. Borkowitz *(Chief Oper. Officer)*

C & W Railway Co. **(1)**
225 Canal St.
Pueblo, CO 81004
Tel.: 719-561-6358 (100%)
Emp.: 66
Railroad Plant
S.I.C.: 4011
F. J. Villa, Jr. *(Pres.)*

CF & I Fabricators of Colorado **(1)**
9002 N. Moore Rd.
Littleton, CO 80120
Tel.: 303-791-1022
Emp.: 36
Steel Fabrication
S.I.C.: 3441
Allen Moore *(Gen. Mgr.)*

CF & I Fabricators of Utah **(1)**
P.O. Box 25305
Salt Lake City, UT 84125
Tel.: 801-364-8421 (100%)
Emp.: 21
Steel Fabrication
S.I.C.: 3441
Walter E. McCullough *(V.P. & Gen. Mgr.)*

Denver Metals Co. **(1)**
2100 W. Oxford Ave.
Englewood, CO 80110
Tel.: 303-761-0281 (100%)
Emp.: 12
Scrap Steel Processing
S.I.C.: 5093
A. B. Borkowitz *(Chief Oper. Officer)*

Fountain Sand & Gravel Co. **(1)**
P.O. Box 535
Pueblo, CO 81002
Tel.: 719-561-6752 (100%)
Emp.: 22
Paving Mixtures
S.I.C.: 3273

Kansas Metals Co. **(1)**
225 Canal St.
Pueblo, CO 81002
Tel.: 316-832-1167 (100%)
Emp.: 12
Wholesale Scrap Metals
S.I.C.: 5093
A. B. Borkowitz *(Chief Oper. Officer)*

Pueblo Metals Co. **(1)**
728 Harlem
Pueblo, CO 81004
Tel.: 719-545-0263 (100%)
Emp.: 25
Scrap Metal
S.I.C.: 5093
A. B. Borkowitz *(Chief Oper. Officer)*

Pueblo Railroad Service Company **(1)**
P.O. Box 5104, 2621 Line Rd.
Pueblo, CO 81002
Tel.: 719-544-2411 (100%)
Emp.: 25
Rail Welding & Rail Services
S.I.C.: 7389
Gerald M. Bloder *(V.P. & Gen. Mgr.)*

CGF INDUSTRIES
800 Bank IV Tower
Topeka, KS 66603
Tel.: 913-233-0541
Fax: 913-233-3902
Approx.Sls.: $104,000,000
Emp.: 1,330
Fiscal Year-end: 3/31/92
Holding Co.; Manufacturers Electric Signs, Operates Apartments, Provides Commercial Lithographic Printing & Direct Mail Services; Mfrs. Hydraulic Cylinders, Pumps, Valves & Hoists; Mfrs. Mirrored Sliding Doors, Steel Bifold Doors & Steel & Aluminium Frames; Mfrs. Wood & Metal Threshhold & Astragals; Produce & Process Farm-raised Catfish; Provides Full-line Graphic Production & Printing Services
S.I.C.: 1311; 2752; 3561; 0921; 2092; 3442; 3993; 3566; 3593; 3594; 7331; 3492
H. Bernerd Fink *(Chm. Bd.)*
Ruth G. Fink *(Pres.)*
Jack H. Hamilton *(Chief Exec. Officer)*
Kenneth Swadley *(Chief Information Officer)*
Terry W. Wages *(Chief Oper. Officer)*
David L. Henriksen *(V.P. & Dir. Corp. Devel.)*
Larry D. Riggins *(Sec.)*
Richard Martinez *(Dir.-Benefits Admin.)*

Outside Service Firm(s):

Deloitte & Touche*(Auditors)*
Topeka, KS

Ed Learned*(Legal Firm)*
Wichita, KS

Bank IV*(Major Banking Relationship)*
P.O. Box 1122,
Wichita, KS 67201
Tel.: 316-261-4304

CGRW ADVERTISING, INC.
5750 Wilshire Blvd., Ste. 480
Los Angeles, CA 90036
Tel.: 213-938-9220
Fax: 213-938-9495
Year Founded: 1991
Approx.Billings: $15,000,000
Emp.: 11
Don Cunningham *(Pres., New Bus. Contact)*
Bob Holmes *(V.P., Admin.)*

CGS INDUSTRIES, INC.
34-09 Queens Blvd.
Long Island City, NY 11101
Tel.: 718-482-0700
Fax: 718-482-1385
Approx.Sls.: $35,000,000
Emp.: 50
Fiscal Year-end: 12/30/90
Mfr. Sportswear For Men & Boys
S.I.C.: 2329
Ashok Sani *(Pres.)*
Sunil Sani *(V.P.-Opers. & Adv.)*
Alan Katz *(V.P.-Sls.)*

Leonard Braun *(Treas.)*

CHB CORP.
1250 Brass Mill
Belcamp, MD 21017
Mailing Address:
P.O. Box 10,
Belcamp, MD 21017
Tel.: 410-272-1446 **DE**
Year Founded: 1980
Approx.Sls.: $245,000,000
Emp.: 3,400
Holding Company
S.I.C.: 6719; 3131; 3069; 5661
T.G. Bata *(Chm. Bd.)*
H.J. Meyer *(Pres.)*
A. Kelly *(V.P.-Fin.)*

Outside Service Firm(s):

Ernst & Young*(Auditors)*
1 N. Charles St.
Baltimore, MD 21201
Tel.: 410-539-7940
Fax: 410-783-3832

Ernst & Young*(Auditors)*
2175 N. California Blvd., Ste. 400
Walnut Creek, CA 94596

NationsBank Carolinas*(Major Banking Relationship)*
One NCNB Plaza T18-7
Charlotte, NC 28255

Prudential Insurance Co. of America*(Group Insurance Broker/ Consult)*
751 Broad St.
Newark, NJ 07102-3777
Tel.: 201-802-6000

Sullivan & Cromwell*(Legal Firm)*
125 Broad St.
New York, NY 10004
Tel.: 212-558-4000

Weinstein & Sturges*(Legal Firm)*
810 Baxter St.
Charlotte, NC 28202
Tel.: 704-372-4800

Subsidiaries:

Bata Shoe Co., Inc. **(1)**
Route 40
Belcamp, MD 21017
Tel.: 410-272-2000
Tel.: 800-365-2282
Fax: 410-272-3346
Emp.: 219
Import Export
Manufacture Waterproof Protective Footwear & Clothing; Commercial Compounding of Rubber
S.I.C.: 3131; 3069
Martin O'Neill *(Chm. Bd.)*
J. Tillie *(Pres.)*
Brian Letten *(Grp. V.P.-Mktg. & Sls.)*
William E. Hielke *(Controller, Admin. Sec. & Chief Fin. Officer)*
Barbara Higgins *(Personnel Trng. & Devel.)*
Michael Travers *(Mgr.-Admin.)*

Pic'n Pay Stores, Inc. **(1)**
10301 Old Monroe Rd.
Charlotte, NC 28261
Tel.: 704-847-8871
Fax: 704-841-6203
Assets: $89,385,000
Liabilities: $52,899,000
Net Worth: $36,486,000
Sales Range: $100-499 Million
Emp.: 3,000
Fiscal Year-end: 1/ 2/91
Import
Computer Systems/Hardware:
IBM 4381
717 Retail Stores in AL, DE, GA, IN, NC, OH, SC, PA, KY, MD, TN, VA, WV, FL, DC, TX, NJ, AR, LA, OK
S.I.C.: 5661
Jeff Sheperd *(Pres. & Chief Exec. Officer)*
Richard Garner *(Sr. V.P.-Human Resources)*
Talmage Tyler *(V.P.-Real Estate & Devel.)*
Art Raqosta *(V.P.-Budgets)*
Roger Osborne *(V.P.-Opers.)*
Betty Horton *(Controller)*
Martin Voss *(Chief Fin. Officer)*
Tom Moore *(General Counsel)*
Dewey Lowder *(Dir.-Pur.)*
Eugene T. Foley *(Dir.-Mktg.)*

CHC
ADVERTISING

CHC ADVERTISING
1480 Rt. 9 N.
Woodbridge, NJ 07095
Tel.: 908-636-7080
Fax: 908-750-8765
Year Founded: 1987
Approx.Billings: $45,500,000
Emp.: 38
Consumer Goods & Services
Robert Portman, Ph.D. *(Chm.)*
William W. Bishop *(Chief Exec. Officer)*
William H. Schmermund *(Pres.)*
Tom Donovan *(Controller)*

CH2M HILL COMPANIES, LTD.
6060 So. Willow Dr.
Englewood, CO 80111
Mailing Address:
P.O. Box 22508,
Denver, CO 80222
Tel.: 303-771-0900
Fax: 303-220-5106
Year Founded: 1946
Approx.Sls.: $525,000,000
Emp.: 5,336
Fiscal Year-end: 12/31/91
Engineering, Planning, Economics, Operations & Management Services
S.I.C.: 8711
James W. Poirot *(Chm. Bd.)*
Philip G. Hall *(Vice Chm.)*
Ralph R. Peterson *(Pres. & Chief Exec. Officer)*
McLane Fisher *(Exec. V.P., Sec. & Chief Fin. Officer)*
Richard L. Corrigan *(V.P.-Govt. Affairs)*
Robert H. Bullock *(Chief Information Officer)*
Douglas A. Bevis *(Treas.)*
Virginia Mares *(Sec.)*
L.L. Nelson *(Controller)*
S. Wyatt McCallie *(Gen. Counsel)*
S.C. DeAutremont *(Dir.-Admin.)*
E. Rudd Little *(Dir.-Pension Admin.)*
Donald V. Roberts *(Dir.-Mktg.)*
Craig T. Zeien *(Dir.-Tech.)*
Andre Armstrong *(Mgr.-Corp.)*
F.K. Berry *(Mgr.-Human Resources)*
Bob Latham *(Mgr.-Tax)*

Principal(s):
Employee Stockholders

No. of U.S. Offices: 60
No. of Foreign Offices: 11

Computer Systems/Hardware:
DEC 10; VAX 8600

Outside Service Firm(s):

Arthur Andersen & Co.*(Auditors)*
111 S.W. Columbia, Ste. 1400
Portland, OR 97201
Tel.: 503-226-1331

Aetna Life & Casualty*(Group Insurer)*
151 Farmington Avenue
Hartford, CT 06156
Tel.: 203-273-2128
Fax: 203-729-4295

P.E. Becker, Inc.*(Pension Manager)*
Portland, OR

New York Life*(Pension Manager)*
51 Madison Ave.
New York, NY 10010
Tel.: 212-576-6367
Fax: 212-576-6630

Subsidiaries:

CH2M Hill, Inc. **(1)**
6060 S. Willow Dr.
Greenwood Village, CO 80111
Tel.: 303-771-0900
Emp.: 4,146
Full Service Engineering Consultant
S.I.C.: 8711
Lyle G. Hassebroek *(Pres.)*

CH2M Hill Industrial Design Corp. **(1)**
Parkside Plaza, 2020 S.W. 4th, 3rd Fl.
Portland, OR 97201
Tel.: 503-224-6040
Emp.: 537
Industrial Engrng. Design Consultant
S.I.C.: 8711
Kenneth F. Durant *(Pres.)*
E. Wayne Hanson *(V.P.)*

CH2M Hill International, Ltd. **(1)**
6060 S. Willow Dr.
Greenwood Village, CO 80111
Tel.: 303-796-9001
Full Service Engrng. Consultant
S.I.C.: 8711
Howard A. Schirmer *(Pres.)*

Operations Management International, Inc. **(1)**
P.O. Box 5169
Kingwood, TX 77325-5169
Tel.: 800-950-4664
Emp.: 682
Utility Management Services
S.I.C.: 8748
Don S. Evans *(Pres.)*
Robert W. Monette *(Dir.-Mktg.)*

CJC HOLDINGS, INC.
7211 Circle S. Rd.
Austin, TX 78745
Tel.: 512-444-2596
Fax: 512-444-3040
Approx.Sls.: $130,000,000
Emp.: 1,220
Mfr. of Artcarved High School & College Rings; Artcarved Bridal Sets
S.I.C.: 3911
John T. Waugh *(Chm. Bd. & Chief Exec. Officer)*
C. Cook *(Pres.-Mfg. Div.)*
Park Davis *(Pres.-College Div.)*
Gary Epporly *(Pres.-Highschool Div.)*
Barry Sullivan *(Pres.-Bridal Div.)*
Mickey Gray *(Dir.-Mngmt. Information Systems)*

Division:

Manufacturing Div. **(1)**
7211 Circle S Rd.
Austin, TX 78745
Tel.: 512-444-2596
Mfr. of Artcarved Rings & Bridal Sets
S.I.C.: 3911
Charlyn Cook *(Pres.)*

Groups:

Bridal Group **(1)**
7211 Circle S. Rd.
Austin, TX 78745
Tel.: 512-444-2596
Mfr. of Artcarved Bridal Sets
S.I.C.: 3911
Barry Sullivan *(Pres.)*

College & New Products Group **(1)**
7211 Circle S Rd.
Austin, TX 78745
Tel.: 512-444-2596
Mfr. of Artcarved College Rings
S.I.C.: 3911
Park Davis *(Pres.)*

Highschool Group **(1)**
7211 Circle S Rd.
Austin, TX 78745
Tel.: 512-444-2596
Mfr. of Artcarved Highschool Rings
S.I.C.: 3911
Gary Epperly *(Pres.)*

CKS PARTNERS
(Cleary Kvamme & Suiter, Inc.)
345 Spear St., Ste. 500
San Francisco, CA 94105
Tel.: 415-905-1655
Year Founded: 1986
Approx.Billings: $36,000,000
Emp.: 33
High-Tech., Corp. I.D., Packaging, Sales Promotion & Adv.
William T. Cleary *(Pres.)*
Mark D. Kvamme *(Pres., New Bus. Contact)*
David Siskin *(Partner)*

CME•KHBB
ADVERTISING

CME-KHBB ADVERTISING
(Formerly Campbell-Mithun-Esty)
222 S. Ninth St.
Minneapolis, MN 55402
Tel.: 612-347-1000
Fax: 612-347-1515
Year Founded: 1932
Approx.Billings: $1,000,000,000
Emp.: 1,062
Creative, Media, Communications, Marketing, Promotions & Advertising
William D. Dunlap *(Worldwide Chief Exec. Officer)*
David C. Welch *(Chm.)*
Gene H. Zaske *(Chief Fin. Officer)*
A.L. (Bill) Powell *(Exec. V.P., Corp. Devel.)*

CMI INDUSTRIES, INC.
P.O. Box 11589,
Columbia, SC 29211
Tel.: 803-771-4434
Mfr. Fabrics & Textile Mill Products
S.I.C.: 2211; 2258; 2281
G.T. Williams *(Chief Exec. Officer)*
James A. Ovenden *(Chief Fin. Officer)*

Subsidiary:

Clinton Mills Inc. **(1)**
600 Academy St.
Clinton, SC 29325
Tel.: 803-833-5500
Fax: 803-833-5130
Approx.Sls.: $210,000,000
Emp.: 2,600
Fiscal Year-end: 12/31/89
Computer Systems/Hardware:
IBM 4331-2
Textile Mill Products; Fabric Manufacturer
S.I.C.: 2211; 2258; 2281
Robert M. Vance *(Chm. Bd.)*
George T. Williams *(Pres. & Chief Exec. Officer)*
J.A. Ovenden *(Chief Fin. Officer & Treas.)*
W.T. Chaffin *(V.P.-Human Resources)*
William E. Stanton *(Dir.-Pur.)*
Paul D. Tyson *(Dir.-Data Processing)*

Divisions:

Chatham Manufacturing Company **(2)**
304 E. Main St.,
Elkin, NC 28621
Tel.: 919-835-2211
Earnings: $3,199,000
Approx.Sls.: $125,899,000
Emp.: 2,345
Fiscal Year-end: 12/31/90
Blankets, Upholstery, Apparel & Yarn
S.I.C.: 2231
A.J. Raffo *(Pres.)*

Subsidiary:

Chatham Smith Corp. **(3)**
East Main St.
Elkin, NC 28621
Tel.: 919-835-2211 (50%)
Fabric Weaving
S.I.C.: 2231

Clinton Mills **(2)**
P.O. Box 699,
Geneva, AL 36340
Tel.: 205-684-2211
Fabrics
S.I.C.: 2211; 2258; 2281
Josh Hamilton *(Pres.)*

Clinton Mills Sales Co. **(2)**
111 W. 40th St., 22nd Fl.
New York, NY 10018
Tel.: 212-391-0550
Fabrics
S.I.C.: 2211; 2258; 2281
W.J. Raleigh *(Pres.)*

Elastic Fabrics of America **(2)**
P.O. Box 21986,
Greensboro, NC 27406
Tel.: 919-275-9401
Fabrics
S.I.C.: 2211; 2258; 2281
Joseph L. Gorga *(Pres.)*

CMI INTERNATIONAL INC.
30333 Southfield Rd.
Southfield, MI 48076
Tel.: 313-642-9450 **MI**
Fax: 313-642-4955
Year Founded: 1957
Assets: $147,000,000
Liabilities: $55,000,000
Net Worth: $92,000,000
Approx.Sls.: $245,000,000
Emp.: 2,500
Fiscal Year-end: 5/31/91
Import Export
Holding Company; Foundries; Manufacturer of Machined Metal Castings For the Auto Industry
S.I.C.: 6719; 3321; 3322; 3324; 3325; 3363
Ray H. Witt *(Pres.)*
Gary F. Ruff *(Exec. V.P.)*
Malcolm Engleby *(V.P.-Mfg.)*
Richard A. Nawrocki *(V.P.-Fin.)*

No. of Mfg. Plants/Facilities: 16

Outside Service Firm(s):

Moore, Smith & Dale*(Auditors)*
23800 W. Ten Mile Rd.
Southfield, MI 48034

Dean & Fulkerson*(Legal Firm)*
Detroit, MI

Comerica Bank*(Major Banking Relationship)*
211 W. Fort St.
Detroit, MI 48226
Tel.: 313-222-3300

Subsidiary:

CMI Schneible Co. **(1)**
P.O. BOx 100
Holly, MI 48442
Tel.: 313-634-8211
Emp.: 25
Air Polution Equipment, Wet Type Fume Scrubbers; Multi-Wash Collector, Conveyor & Recirculating Tools, Uni-Flo Hoods, DW Collector, Conveyor & Recirculating Tools
S.I.C.: 3564
Ken McKibben *(V.P.-Opers.)*

C M P PUBLICATIONS, INC.
600 Community Dr.
Manhasset, NY 11030
Tel.: 516-562-5000 **NY**
Year Founded: 1971
Approx.Sls.: $178,000,000
Emp.: 1100
Fiscal Year-end: 12/31/91
High Technology & Travel Industry
S.I.C.: 2721; 2741
Corporate Giving Program: C M P Foundation Distributes Money to Community Organizations upon Evaluation by an Employee Committee(P-5)
Gerard G. Leeds *(Co-Chm. Bd.)*
Lilo J. Leeds *(Co-Chm. Bd.)*
Michael S. Leeds *(Pres. & Chief Exec. Officer)*

Joseph E. Sichler *(Chief Fin. Officer)*
Kenneth Cron *(Exec. V.P.)*
Grace Monahan *(Exec. V.P.)*
Jack Dolce *(Sr. V.P. & Grp. Publr.)*
Jerry Landress *(V.P. & Grp. Publr.)*
Daniel H. Leeds *(V.P.)*
Pearl Turner *(V.P. & Treas.)*
Don Tydeman *(V.P. & Grp. Publr.)*
Robert Marafioti *(Gen. Counsel)*
Kathy Bernhard *(Dir.-Human Resources)*
Georgette Ross *(Mgr.-Customer Service)*

Principal(s):
Gerard G. Leeds
Lilo J. Leeds
Michael S. Leeds
Daniel H. Leeds

No. of Mfg. Plants/Facilities: 1
No. of U.S. Offices: 16
No. of Foreign Offices: 4

Outside Service Firm(s):

Miller Ellin & Co.*(Auditors)*
New York, NY

Chemical Bank*(Major Banking Relationship)*
450 West 33rd St.
New York, NY 10001
Tel.: 212-613-7197
Fax: 212-947-7628

Subsidiary:

C M P Printing Company **(1)**
551 Mid Atlantic Pkwy.
Thorofare, NJ 08086
Tel.: 609-848-0091
Commercial Publication Printers
S.I.C.: 2752; 2721
Dave Robinson *(V.P.)*

CORS
One Pierce Place, Ste. 300 E.
Itasca, IL 60143
Tel.: 708-250-8677
Tel.: 800-323-1352
Fax: 708-250-7362
Year Founded: 1974
Emp.: 60
Fiscal Year-end: 9/30/92
Corporate Organizing & Research Services
S.I.C.: 7363
David T. Hoppe *(Chm. Bd. & Pres.)*
David Geron *(Dir.-Client Services Dept.)*
Janna Guild *(Dir.-Acctg.)*
Tracy Foxen *(Dir.-Opers. & Sls.)*
William Marineau *(Dir.-Mngmt. Info. Services)*
Michael R. Khadivar *(Mgr.-Human Resources)*

No. of U.S. Offices: 1

Computer Systems/Hardware:
NOVELL

Outside Service Firm(s):

Ernst & Young*(Auditors)*
233 S. Wacker Dr.
Chicago, IL 60606
Tel.: 312-368-1800
Fax: 312-645-3095

Blue Cross of Illinois*(Commercial Insurance Carrier)*
233 N. Michigan Ave.
Chicago, IL 60601

Delta Dental*(Group Insurer)*
Chicago, IL

C P CONVERTERS, INC.
15 Grumbacher Rd.
York, PA 17402
Tel.: 717-764-1193
Fax: 717-764-2039
Year Founded: 1959
Sales Range: $20-39 Million
Emp.: 100
Flexible Packaging Products
S.I.C.: 2671
Ed D. England *(Pres.)*
Ronald Leech *(V.P.-Sls.)*
Mark R. Paules *(V.P.-Fin. & Mfg.)*

CPM MEDIA MANAGEMENT

CPM, INC.
515 N. State St., Ste. 2200
Chicago, IL 60610-4320
Tel.: 312-527-2100 DE
Fax: 312-527-1506
Fax: 312-527-1507
Year Founded: 1969
Sales Range: $100-499 Million
Emp.: 50
Media Planning and Buying Service
S.I.C.: 7319
Norman M. Goldring *(Pres. & Chief Exec. Officer)*
L. Roger Casty *(Exec. V. P.)*
Michael Willner *(Exec. V.P. & Chief Oper. Officer)*
Margaret Navolio *(Sr. V.P. & Gen. Mgr.)*
Cynthia Romine *(Controller)*
Fran Corn *(Mgr.-Office Services)*
William Strejc *(Mgr.-Computer Services)*
Jennifer White *(Mgr.-Plng.)*

Computer Systems/Hardware:
IBM System 36

Outside Service Firm(s):

Arthur Andersen & Co.*(Auditors)*
33 W. Monroe St.
Chicago, IL 60603-4067
Tel.: 312-580-0033
Fax: 312-507-6748

Tishler & Wald*(Legal Firm)*
Chicago, IL

American National Bank & Trust Company of Chicago*(Major Banking Relationship)*
33 N. LaSalle St.
Chicago, IL 60602
Tel.: 312-661-5000
Fax: 312-661-6417

CRE, INC.
400 Victoria Centre, 22 E. Washington
Indianapolis, IN 46204-3529
Tel.: 317-631-0260
Fax: 317-632-0272
Year Founded: 1971
Approx.Billings: $12,000,000
Emp.: 24
Mktg. Communications, Research & Pub. Rels.
Les Boyle *(Chm. Bd., Pres. & Chief Exec. Officer)*
Jerry Woolsey *(Exec. V.P., Sec.)*
Juri Tults *(V.P., New Bus. Contact & Devel.)*
Glenda Fink *(Dir.-Admin.)*
Ann Woolman *(Dir.-Pub. Rels.)*
Sandra Boyle *(Treas. & Acct. Mgr.)*

Computer Systems/Hardware:
NCR, Apple, MacIntosh, Wordperfect, Media Management Plus

CRK ADVERTISING

205 West 39th St., 14th Fl.
New York, NY 10018
Tel.: 212-719-2600
Fax: 212-221-4541
Year Founded: 1980
Approx.Billings: $21,950,000
Emp.: 10
Fashion Adv.
Barry Schwartz *(Chm.)*
Calvin Klein *(Pres.)*
Neil Kraft *(Sr. V.P., Dir.-Adv. & Creative Services)*
Kim Vernon *(Dir.- Adv. Admin.)*
Christine Clarke *(Asst. to Dir.-Adv. & Creative Services)*
Elizabeth Hussey *(Dir.-Retail Adv.)*
Tina Olson *(Dir.-Personnel)*

Computer Systems/Hardware:
MacIntosh

CRL, INC.
2200 E. Devon Ave.
Des Plaines, IL 60018
Tel.: 708-297-0808 DE
Fax: 708-299-7679
Assets: $147,835,000
Liabilities: $61,545,000
Net Worth: $86,290,000
Approx.Sls.: $201,000,000
Emp.: 2,300
Holding Company
S.I.C.: 6719; 3563; 3569; 3823; 5088
Thomas Carroll *(Chm. Bd. & Pres.)*
Morrow Garrison *(Vice Chm.)*
Barry J. Carroll *(V.P.)*
Carlos Tiernon *(V.P.)*
Joseph S. Haas *(Treas. & Controller)*

Outside Service Firm(s):

Deloitte & Touche*(Auditors)*
Two Prudential Plaza, 180 N. Stetson
Chicago, IL 60601
Tel.: 312-946-2039

Holleb & Coff, Ltd.*(Legal Firm)*
55 E. Monroe, Suite 4100
Chicago, IL 60603
Tel.: 312-807-4600

The Northern Trust Co.*(Major Banking Relationship)*
50 S. LaSalle St.
Chicago, IL 60675
Tel.: 312-630-6000
Fax: 312-630-6516

Subsidiary:

International Metals & Machines, Inc. **(1)**
2200 E. Devon Ave.
Des Plaines, IL 60018
Tel.: 708-297-0808
Approx.Sls.: $152,000,000
Emp.: 2,300
Mfr. Industrial Machinery & Equip., Measuring Devices; Wholesale Transportation Equip.
S.I.C.: 3563; 3569; 3823; 5088
George McKewen *(Chm. Bd. & Pres.)*
Morrow Garrison *(Vice Chm.)*
Barry J. Carroll *(V.P.)*
Denis Carroll *(V.P.)*
Carlos Tiernon *(V.P.)*

CRN INTERNATIONAL, INC.
One Circular Ave.
Hamden, CT 06514
Tel.: 203-288-2002 CT
Fax: 203-281-3291
Year Founded: 1973
Assets: $3,000,000
Liabilities: $2,500,000
Net Worth: $500,000
Sales Range: $10-19 Million
Emp.: 75
Fiscal Year-end: 6/30/90
Radio, TV Consumer & Trade Promotions
S.I.C.: 8742; 7319
Barry H. Berman *(Chm. Bd. & Pres.)*
S. Richard Kalt *(Exec. V.P.)*
Pat Kane *(Sr. V.P., Corp. Devel. & New Bus. Contact)*
Richard Burman *(V.P., Chief Fin. Officer)*
Steve Kotchko *(V.P.)*
Gary Zenobia *(Dir., Network Opers.)*
Paul Orio *(Dir.-Affilliate Rels.)*
Principal(s):
Barry H. Berman
S. Richard Kalt

No. of U.S. Offices: 2

Computer Systems/Hardware:
IBM

Outside Service Firm(s):

Capposella & Cohen*(Auditors)*
Southport, CT

Travelers Insurance Co.*(Group Insurer)*
New Haven, CT

Cantor, Floman, Russell & Johnson*(Legal Firm)*
Orange, CT

Bank of New Haven*(Major Banking Relationship)*
New Haven, CT

Conry Financial Services*(Pension Manager)*
Newington, CT

CS FIRST BOSTON GROUP, INC.
(55% Owned by CS Holding (Netherlands) N.V.)
Park Avenue Plaza
New York, NY 10055
Tel.: 212-909-2000 DE
Telex: 420950
Fax: 212-318-1187
Year Founded: 1988
Assets: $36,877,117,000
Liabilities: $36,018,801,000
Net Worth: $858,316,000
Emp.: 5,426
Engages in Investment Banking Activities that Facilitate the Flow of Capital from Investors in the United States & Abroad to Domestic & Foreign Corporations, Governments & to International Agencies
S.I.C.: 6211; 6719
Corporate Giving Program: Majority of Contributions made to Graduate Schools from which We recruit and Social Service, Art and Cultural Programs in New York City and Cities in which We Have Branch Offices
Employee Matching Gifts Program: Maximum of $2,500 Per Calendar Year per Employee to Educational Institutions Only
Rainer E. Gut *(Chm. Bd.)*
John M. Hennessy *(Pres. & Chief Exec. Officer)*
Jay T. Roelof *(V.P. & Sec.)*
Ruedi Stalder *(Chief Fin. & Admin. Officer)*
Thomas J. Carroll *(Mng. Dir. & Grp. Intl. Auditor)*
Anthony J. Cetta *(Mng. Dir. & Grp. Controller)*
John F. Cowell III *(Mng. Dir. & Grp. Comm. Officer)*
Michael G. Zeiss *(Mng. Dir. & Gen. Counsel)*

Subsidiaries:

The First Boston Corporation **(1)**
55 E. 52nd St.
New York, NY 10055
Tel.: 212-909-2000 (100%)
Fax: 212-308-1187
Emp.: 4,000
Investment Securities
S.I.C.: 6211
John M. Hennessy *(Chm. Bd.)*
Robert M. Baylis *(Vice Chm.)*
Archibald Cox, Jr. *(Pres. & Chief Exec. Officer)*
John F. Cowell *(Mng. Dir. & Dir.-Mktg.)*
David C. O'Leary *(Mng. Dir.-Human Resources)*
Benjamin H. Cohen *(Treas.)*
Jay T. Roelof *(Sec.)*
Michael G. Zeiss *(Gen. Counsel)*
Lori M. Russo *(Asst. Sec.)*
Linda H. Hanauer *(Asst. Treas.)*
Raymond Carli *(Asst. Treas.)*
Thomas A. DeGennaro *(Dir.-Taxes)*
Raymond Baumkirchner *(Controller)*

CS First Boston Group, Inc.—(Continued)

Subsidiary:

First Boston (Puerto Rico), Inc. **(2)**
1020 Banco Popular Center
Hato Rey, PR 00918
Tel.: 809-756-6400 (100%)
Investment Banking
S.I.C.: 6211
Archibald Cox, Jr. *(Chm. Bd.)*
Jose R. Gonzalez *(Pres.)*
Thomas Sexton *(Chief Exec. Officer)*

First Boston Asset Management Corporation **(1)**
12 E. 49th St.
New York, NY 10017
Tel.: 212-909-4522 (100%)
Asset Management
S.I.C.: 6282
John J. Cook, Jr. *(Chm. Bd. & Chief Exec. Officer)*
Edward McMillan *(Pres.)*

CS First Boston Financiere, Inc. **(1)**
Park Avenue Plaza
New York, NY 10055
Tel.: 212-909-2000 (100%)
Security Brokerage
S.I.C.: 6211
Hans-Jorg Rudloff *(Pres. & Chm. Bd.)*
Philip Colebatch *(Sec. & Treas.)*

CS First Boston USA, Inc. **(1)**
Park Avenue Plaza
New York, NY 10055
Tel.: 212-909-2000 (100%)
Security Brokerage
S.I.C.: 6211
Archibald Cox, Jr. *(Chm Bd.)*
Anthony Dub *(Pres.)*

Subsidiary:

First Boston International Limited **(2)**
Park Ave. Plaza
New York, NY 10055
Tel.: 212-909-2000 (100%)
Emp.: 78
Holding Co.
S.I.C.: 6712

CS First Boston Pacific, Inc. **(1)**
Park Aveune Plaza
New York, NY 10055 (100%)
Security Brokerage
S.I.C.: 6211
Robert E. Diamond, Jr. *(Chm., Pres. & Chief Exec. Officer)*
James R. Powers *(Chief Oper. Officer)*

First Boston Securities Corporation **(1)**
Park Ave. Plaza
New York, NY 10055
Tel.: 212-909-2000
Security Brokerage
S.I.C.: 6211
Archibald Cox, Jr. *(Pres.)*
Robert M. Raziano *(V.P.)*

Non-U.S. Holdings:

Financiere Credit Suisse-First Boston **(1)**
Alpenstrasse 15 6304
Zug, Switzerland
Tel.: 42 23 21 51
Telex: 868 900
Holding Company
S.I.C.: 6712; 6081
Hans-Joerg Rudloff *(Chm. Bd., Pres. & Chief Exec. Officer)*
Agnes T. Reicke *(Sr. V.P. & Sec.)*

First Boston (Japan) Limited **(2)**
Asahi Seimei Hibiya Bldg.5-1, Yurakucho 1-chome, Chiyoda-ku,
Tokyo, 100, Japan
Tel.: 03-3508-4200
Investment Banking
S.I.C.: 6081; 6211
Robert E. Diamond, Jr. *(Chm..)*
Maynard Toll *(Pres.)*

CS First Boston Australia (Holdings) Limited **(2)**
367 Collins St., Level 23
Melbourne, Victoria 3000, Australia
Tel.: 613-280-1666
Holding Bank
S.I.C.: 6081; 6712
Robert Diamond *(Chm.)*
Peter Thomas *(Chief Exec. Officer)*

First Boston Canada Limited **(2)**
121 King St., Ste. 2500
Toronto, ON M5H 3T9, Canada
Tel.: 416 947-2600 (100%)
Investment Banking
S.I.C.: 6081
John A. Wilcox *(Chm. Bd. & Chief Exec. Officer, Pres.)*

CS First Boston (Hong Kong) Limited **(2)**
9th Fl. One Exchange Square Central,
Hong Kong, Hong Kong
Tel.: 5-847-0333
International Banking
S.I.C.: 6081
Robert E. Diamond, Jr. *(Chm.)*
David P. Walker *(Mng. Dir.)*

CS First Boston (Singapore) Limited **(2)**
50 Raffles Place Shell Tower #36-05,
Singapore, 0104, Singapore
Tel.: 65-225-3088
International Banking
S.I.C.: 6081
David Walker *(Chm.)*

CS First Boston New Zealand Holdings Limited **(2)**
10th Floor, Caltex Tower 282 Lambton Quay,
Wellington, New Zealand
Tel.: 644-474-4000
Fax: 644-474-4412
S.I.C.: 6712
Paul Edward Alex Baines *(Chief Exec. Officer)*

Credit Suisse Financial Products **(1)**
2A Great Titchfield St.
London, W1P 7AA, United Kingdom
Tel.: 011-4471-322-3740
Derivative Product Trading
Allen Wheat *(Chief Exec. Officer)*
Ernst Schneider *(Chm.)*

Subsidiary:

Credit Suisse First Boston AG **(2)**
Alpenstrasse 15 P.O. Box 4263, 6304
Zug, Switzerland
Tel.: 42 23 21 51
Fax: 42 21 11 60
International Banking
S.I.C.: 6081

Branch:

Succursale de Geneva **(3)**
1, Quari du Mont-Blane 1211
Geneva, Switzerland
Tel.: 22 732 50 54
Fax: 22 732 68 63
International Banking
S.I.C.: 6081

Zweiniederlassung Zurich **(3)**
Eisengasse 16 8034
Zurich, Switzerland
Tel.: 1 252 44 77
Fax: 1 251 94 11
Stefan Imboden *(Chm.)*

Non-U.S. Holdings:

CSFB-Effectenbank Aktiengesellschaft **(2)**
Grueneburgweg 102, 6000
Frankfurt/Main, Germany
Tel.: 069 15340 (100%)
Telex: 410141
Investment Banking
S.I.C.: 6211
Hans-Joerg Rudloff *(Chm. Bd.)*

Credit Suisse First Boston Budapest Rt **(2)**
Ybl Miklos Ter 8 1013
Budapest, Hungary
Tel.: 01 175 9002
Corporate Finance, Advisory Services
S.I.C.: 6211
Hans-Joerg Rudloff *(Chm. Bd.)*

Credit Suisse First Boston Czechoslovakia a.s. **(2)**
Staromestske nam. 15
Prague, 1, Czechoslovakia
Tel.: 422-231-70-05
Fax: 422-231-74-56
Hans-Jorg Rudloff *(Chm.)*

Credit Suisse First Boston Espana S.A. **(2)**
Edificio "Alfredo Mahou", Plaza Manuel Gomez Moreno, s/n Centro Comercial AZCA, 28020
Madrid, Spain
Tel.: 01 555 0796
Corporate Finance, Advisory Services
S.I.C.: 6211
Hans-Joerg Rudloff *(Chm. Bd.)*

Credit Suisse First Boston France S.A. **(2)**
34 rue de Lisbonne 75008
Paris, France
Tel.: 1 4076 8888
Sales & Trading, Corporate Finance
S.I.C.: 6211
Hans-Joerg Rudloff *(Chm. Bd.)*

Credit Suisse First Boston Italia (Compagnia Mobiliare) SpA **(2)**
21 via Bigli 20121
Milan, Italy
Tel.: 02 7601 2482
Sales & Trading, Corporate Finance
S.I.C.: 6211
Hans-Joerg Rudloff *(Chm. Bd.)*

Credit Suisse First Boston UK Limited **(2)**
2A Great Titchfield St.
London, W1P 7AA, United Kingdom
Tel.: 071 322 4000
Fax: 071 580 2541
International Banking
S.I.C.: 6081
Sir John Riddell *(Chm.)*

Non-U.S. Indirect Subsidiaries:

CS First Boston Singapore Ltd. **(2)**
50 Raffles Place 28-05 Shell Tower
Singapore, 0104, Singapore
Tel.: 651225 30 88 (100%)
Telex: 254 10
Investment Banking
S.I.C.: 6211

CS First Boston Asset Management Limited **(2)**
2A Great Titchfield St.
London, W1P 7AA, United Kingdom
Tel.: 071 322 4000
Fax: 071 580 2541
Asset Management
S.I.C.: 8741
John J. Cook, Jr. *(Chm.)*

CSFB (Gilts) Limited **(2)**
2A Great Titchfield St.
London, W1P 7AA, United Kingdom
Tel.: 071 322 4000
Fax: 071 580 2541
Financial Services
S.I.C.: 6159
Sir John Riddell *(Chm.)*

CSFB Finance B.V. **(2)**
Herengracht 478 1017 CB
Amsterdam, Netherlands
Tel.: 31-20-556-7222
Fax: 31-20-556-7272
Johan T. van Marle *(Chm.)*

CSFB Fund Management Limited **(2)**
Level 2, Albert House St. Peter Port,
Guernsey, Channel Islands
Tel.: 44-481-713-996
Fax: 44-481-713-994
John Langlois *(Chm.)*

CSFB Investment Management Limited **(2)**
2A Great Titchfield St.
London, W1P 7AA, United Kingdom
Tel.: 071 322 4000 (100%)
Telex: 89 21 31
Asset Management
S.I.C.: 6211

Credit Suisse First Boston Ltd. **(2)**
2A Great Titchfield St.
London, EC2N 4BQ, United Kingdom
Tel.: 071 322 4000 (100%)
Telex: 892 131
Investment Banking
S.I.C.: 6211
Hans-Joerg Rudloff *(Chm. Bd. & Chief Exec. Officer)*

Credit Suisse First Boston Nederland N.V. **(2)**
Herengracht 478 P.O. Box 10589, NL-1000 EN
Amsterdam, Netherlands
Tel.: 020 556 72 22
Telex: 14517
Hans-Jorg Rudloff *(Chm.)*

CSA, INC.
107 Oakwood Dr.
Glastonbury, CT 06033
Tel.: 203-633-2254
Fax: 203-659-0323
Year Founded: 1974
Approx.Billings: $30,000,000
Emp.: 20
Robert D. Charnas *(Pres.)*
Claudia Vinueza *(Pub. Rels.)*
Lisa A. Pustis *(Opers. Mgr.)*

Computer Systems/Hardware:
MacIntosh, IBM

CSE CORPORATION
(Sub. of La Garantie Mutuelle des Fonctionnaires (GMF), Paris, France)
989 Market St.
San Francisco, CA 94103
Mailing Address:
P.O. Box 567,
San Francisco, CA 94101
Tel.: 415-495-6800
Tel.: 800-282-6848 **DE**
Fax: 415-974-1095
Year Founded: 1951
Assets: $143,937,386
Earnings: $345,592
Liabilities: $109,548,061
Net Worth: $34,389,325
Approx.Sls.: $138,793,530
Emp.: 249
Fiscal Year-end: 12/31/91
Insurance Holding Company
S.I.C.: 6411; 6311; 6331; 6719
Jean-Louis Petriat *(Chm. Bd.)*
Eugene F. Cronin, Jr. *(Pres. & Chief Exec. Officer)*
Richard Miles *(Exec. V.P.)*
Mary Williams *(Sr. V.P., Sec. & Corp. Librarian)*
Steve Balodimas *(V.P.-Mktg.)*
Gardner Gray, Jr. *(V.P. & Chief Fin. Officer)*
Larry Magna *(V.P. & Dir.-Mngmt. Information Systems)*
Rita Jo Jennerjahn *(Asst V.P.-Human Resources)*
Jay Gray *(Controller)*
Corinne Morrison *(Asst. Sec.)*
Joyce Amburger *(Mgr.-Pur.)*
Dorothy Bush *(Admin. Asst.)*
Berisha Allen *(Admin. Asst.)*

No. of U.S. Offices: 12

Computer Systems/Hardware:
IBM 4341

Outside Service Firm(s):

Coopers & Lybrand*(Auditors)*
333 Market Street, 21st Fl.
San Francisco, CA 94105

Pettit & Martin*(Legal Firm)*
600 Montgomery
San Francisco, CA 94111
Tel.: 415-495-6800

Wells Fargo Bank*(Major Banking Relationship)*
420 Montgomery St.
San Francisco, CA 94104

First Interstate Bank*(Major Banking Relationship)*
345 California St., 8th Flr.
San Francisco, CA 94104
Tel.: 415-773-7801

Aetna Capital Management*(Pension Manager)*
201 N. Civic Dr.
Walnut, CA 94596

Subsidiaries:

CSE Services Insurance Brokerage **(1)**
989 Market St.
San Francisco, CA 94103
Tel.: 415-495-6800
Tel.: 800-282-6848
Fax: 415-974-1095
S.I.C.: 6411
Eugene F. Cronin, Jr. *(Pres.)*

Civil Service Employees Insurance Co. **(1)**
989 Market St.
San Francisco, CA 94103
Tel.: 415-495-6800
Tel.: 800-0282-6848 (100%)
Approx.Sls.: $138,793,530
Emp.: 249
Property/Casualty Insurance
S.I.C.: 6411
Eugene F. Cronin, Jr. *(Pres.)*
Mary Williams *(Sr. V.P.-Admin.)*
Gardner Gray, Jr. *(V.P. & Chief Fin. Officer)*
Steven Balodimas *(V.P.-Mktg.)*

Subsidiary:

Civil Service Employees Life Insurance Co. **(2)**
989 Market St.
San Francisco, CA 94103
Tel.: 415-495-6800
Tel.: 800-282-6848 (100%)
Fax: 415-974-1095
Approx.Sls.: $5,000,000
Emp.: 7
Life Insurance
S.I.C.: 6311
Eugene F. Cronin, Jr. *(Pres.)*
Gardner Gray, Jr. *(V.P. & Chief Fin. Officer)*
Gary Adkins *(Mgr.-Mktg.)*

CSI ADVERTISING INC.
(Formerly Creative Services Inc.)
3925 Peachtree Road N.E.
Atlanta, GA 30317
Tel.: 404-262-7424
Fax: 404-365-9616
Year Founded: 1969
Approx.Billings: $12,000,000
Emp.: 20
Consumer/Business-to-Business (High Tech)
Thomas L. Wood *(Pres.)*
Charles R. Munhall, Jr. *(Exec. V.P., Mktg. & Client Services)*
Robert F. Scott *(Exec. V.P., Media & Bus. Devel., New Bus. Contact)*
Karen McCraney *(Sec.)*

CSI INTERNATIONAL CORPORATION
800 Second Ave.
New York, NY 10017
Tel.: 212-687-5600
Fax: 212-867-6113
Year Founded: 1979
Approx.Billings: $85,000,000
Emp.: 50
Barter & Reciprocal Trades
Stephen L. Geller *(Chm. & Chief Exec. Officer)*
June E. Brody *(Vice Chm. & Chief Oper. Officer)*
Wm. Schachter *(Pres.)*
Harry Rosner *(Sr. V.P., Opers.)*
Don Chevalier *(V.P., Travel Services)*

CTB INC.
P.O. Box 2000,
Milford, IN 46542
Tel.: 219-658-4101 **IN**
Fax: 219-658-4171
Year Founded: 1952
Emp.: 750
Export
Manufacture Feeding, Ventilation & Storage Equipment
S.I.C.: 3523
Howard S. Brembeck *(Chm. Bd. & Chief Exec. Officer)*
James C. Evans *(Pres.)*
John C. Frieden *(V.P. & Treas.)*
Tom T. Hamilton *(V.P. & Gen. Mgr.-CTB Adv.)*
Raymond Marttila *(V.P.-Engrng.)*
Carmon R. Wenger *(Sec.)*
Richard S. Gentry *(Dir.-Mfg. & Pur.)*
Sam Pfahler *(Mgr.-Personnel)*

No. of Mfg. Plants/Facilities: 4
No. of U.S. Offices: 5

Outside Service Firm(s):

Price Waterhouse*(Auditors)*
202 S. Michigan
South Bend, IN 46624

First National Bank Elkhart*(Major Banking Relationship)*
Elkhart, IN

Subsidiaries:

Brock Manufacturing **(1)**
P.O. Box 2000,
Milford, IN 46542
Tel.: 219-658-4191
Manufacture Industrial Flexible Auger Conveying Systems, Bulk Storage Silos, Farm Storage Silos for Feed & Grain, Plastic Fencing Systems for Horses, Livestock & Residential Use & Plastic Marine Docks & Piers
S.I.C.: 3535; 3448; 3089

Chore-Time/Brock International **(1)**
P.O. Box 2000,
Milford, IN 46542
Tel.: 219-658-9323 (100%)
Telex: 232488 Choretimebrock
Telex: 4973655 Choretimebrock
Fax: 219-658-9296
International Marketing
S.I.C.: 8742
Carmon R. Wenger *(Pres.)*

Chore-Time Cage Systems **(1)**
P.O. Box 2000,
Milford, IN 46542
Tel.: 219-658-4101 (100%)
Fax: 219-658-9564
Fax: 205-350-4130 (Decatur, AL Fax: office)
Manufacture Poultry Cage Rearing Systems, Egg Collection Systems, Feeding, Ventilation, Watering & Storage Equipment
S.I.C.: 3523

Chore-Time Equipment **(1)**
P.O. Box 2000,
Milford, IN 46542
Tel.: 219-658-4101 (100%)
Fax: 219-658-4171
Manufacture Feeding, Ventilation, Watering & Storage Equipment
S.I.C.: 3523

CUNA MUTUAL INSURANCE SOCIETY
5910 Mineral Point Rd.
Madison, WI 53705
Mailing Address:
P.O. Box 391,
Madison, WI 53701
Tel.: 608-238-5851 **WI**
Fax: 608-238-0830
Year Founded: 1935
Assets: $961,987,000
Earnings: $1,834,000
Liabilities: $760,977,000
Net Worth: $201,010,000
Approx.Rev.: $606,876,000
Emp.: 3,370
Fiscal Year-end: 12/31/90
Holding Co.; Subs. Provide Insurance for Credit Unions & Credit Union Members
S.I.C.: 6719; 6311; 6321
Richard M. Heins *(Pres. & Chief Exec. Officer)*
Richard L. Ensweiler *(Sr. V.P.-Corp. & Public Rels.)*
L.J. Rupp *(Sr. V.P. & Chief Actuary)*
John Waggoner *(Sr. V.P. & Gen. Counsel)*
Robert W. Story *(Sr. V.P.-Field Operations)*
John B. Tate *(V.P.-Fin.)*
Richard T. Keintz *(V.P.-Res. & Devel., Operations)*
Thomas O. Olson *(V.P.-Corp. Devel.)*
Donna Blankenheim *(Asst. V.P.-Corp. Services)*
R.C. Radtke *(V.P.-Pub. Rels.)*
Robert L. Guerin *(V.P.-Info. Systems Div.)*
Richard F. Kadera *(Comptroller)*
Dell Dockter *(Mgr.-Pub. Rels.)*
Charles Conklin *(Mgr.-Mkt. Promo. Services)*

No. of Mfg. Plants/Facilities: 5
No. of U.S. Offices: 2
No. of Foreign Offices: 3

Computer Systems/Hardware:
IBM

Outside Service Firm(s):

Ernst & Young*(Auditors)*
233 S. Wacker Dr.
Chicago, IL 60606
Tel.: 312-368-1800
Fax: 312-645-3095

Boardman, Suhr, Curry & Field*(Legal Firm)*
Madison, WI

Subsidiaries:

CMCI Corp. **(1)**
5910 Mineral Point Rd.
Madison, WI 53701
Tel.: 608-238-5851
Emp.: 53
Insurance Broker; Specializes in Pilot Consumer Programs
S.I.C.: 6321
Richard M. Heins *(Chief Exec. Officer)*

CUDIS Insurance Society, Inc. **(1)**
5910 Mineral Point Rd.
Madison, WI 53701
Tel.: 608-538-5851
Emp.: 187
Specializing in Credit Disability Ins. Protection
S.I.C.: 6321
Richard M. Heins *(Chief Exec. Officer)*

CUMIS Insurance Society, Inc. **(1)**
5910 Mineral Point Rd.
Madison, WI 53701
Tel.: 608-538-5851
Emp.: 479
Stock Insurance Co. Specializing in Property & Casualty Insurance Protection
S.I.C.: 6331
Richard M. Heins *(Chief Exec. Officer)*
John E. Heiser *(Exec. V.P.)*

CUNA Mutual Financial Services Corp. **(1)**
5910 Mineral Point Rd.
Madison, WI 53701
Tel.: 608-238-5851 (100%)
Individual Coverage Marketing Co.
S.I.C.: 8742
Richard M. Heins *(Chief Exec. Officer)*

CUNA Mutual Investment Corp. **(1)**
5910 Mineral Point Rd.
Madison, WI 53701
Tel.: 608-238-5851
Holding Co.
S.I.C.: 6719
Richard M. Heins *(Pres. & Chief Exec. Officer)*

League General Insurance Co. **(1)**
P.O. Box 33430,
Detroit, MI 48232-5430
Tel.: 313-357-8100 (100%)
Property & Casualty Insurance
S.I.C.: 6331
Richard M. Heins *(Chief Exec. Officer)*
Robert E. Vanderbeek *(Pres.)*
Andrew S. Markell *(Sr. V.P.)*
Patrick H. Young *(V.P.-Fin. & Admin.)*

League Life Insurance Co. **(1)**
P.O. Box 430,
Southfield, MI 48232
Tel.: 313-557-1300 (100%)
Life, Health & Disability Insurance
S.I.C.: 6311; 6321
Richard M. Heins *(Chief Exec. Officer)*
Robert E. Vanderbeek *(Pres.)*

District Offices:

Central Region:

CUNA North Central District **(1)**
2780 East 82nd St.
Bloomington, MN 55420
Tel.: 612-854-6633
S.I.C.: 6411
Robert O. Brokaw *(District V.P.)*
Donald J. Clinkert *(V.P.-Central Region)*

CUNA Central District **(1)**
15600 Providence Drive
Southfield, MI 48075
Tel.: 313-559-6291
S.I.C.: 6411
Dennis J. Cotter *(District V.P.)*
Donald J. Clinkert *(V.P.-Central Region)*

CUNA Lake Central District **(1)**
5670 Caito Drive, Suite 172
Indianapolis, IN 46226
Tel.: 317-545-4520
S.I.C.: 6411
Allan R. Oxley *(District V.P.)*
Donald J. Clinkert *(V.P.-Central Region)*

Eastern Region:

CUNA North East District **(1)**
Lynnfield Office Park, 40 Salem St.
Lynnfield, MA 01940
Tel.: 617-595-2433
S.I.C.: 6411
Richard Allen *(District V.P.)*
Russell M. Braun *(V.P.-Eastern Region)*

CUNA East Central District **(1)**
8501 LaSalle Road, Suite 104
Towson, MD 21204
S.I.C.: 6411
William J. McKeown *(District V.P.)*
Russell M. Braun *(V.P.-Eastern Region)*

CUNA Mid East District **(1)**
Two Wall Street
Albany, NY 12205
Tel.: 518-869-1748
S.I.C.: 6411
Douglas R. Wright *(District V.P.)*
Russell M. Braun *(V.P.-Eastern Region)*

CUNA Eastern District Office **(1)**
4309 N. Front St.
Harrisburg, PA 17110
Tel.: 215-232-1594
S.I.C.: 6411
John A. Gibson *(District V.P.)*
Russell M. Braun *(V.P.-Eastern Region)*

Southern Region:

CUNA South West District **(1)**
4455 LBJ Freeway, Suite 812
Dallas, TX 75244
Tel.: 214-661-8485
S.I.C.: 6411
David W. Cry *(District V.P.)*
Price L. Legg *(V.P.-Southern Region)*

CUNA South Central District **(1)**
5140 Galaxie Dr., Rm. 206
Jackson, MS 39206
Tel.: 601-981-1630
S.I.C.: 6411
John D. Davis Jr. *(District V.P.)*
Price L. Legg *(V.P.-Southern Region)*

CUNA Mutual Insurance Society—(Continued)

CUNA South East District (1)
2945 Flowers Rd. So., Ste. 101
Atlanta, GA 30341
Tel.: 404-497-1000
S.I.C.: 6411
J. E. Gene Kimbrell *(District V.P.)*
Price L. Legg *(V.P.-Southern Region)*

CUNA Southern District (1)
Eastgate Shopping Center, 6100 Bldg., Ste. 3900, P.O. Box 8397
Chattanooga, TN 37411
Tel.: 615-892-2507
S.I.C.: 6411
John R. Ackerman *(District V.P.)*
Price L. Legg *(V.P.-Southern Region)*

Western Region:

CUNA North West District (1)
P.O. Box 1457,
Bellevue, WA 98009
Tel.: 206-885-4200
S.I.C.: 6411
Fred A. Keller *(District V.P.)*
William F. Allison *(V.P.-Western Region)*

CUNA West Central District (1)
P.O. Box 27288,
Salt Lake City, UT 84127
Tel.: 801-973-8000
S.I.C.: 6411
LeRoy Kay *(District V.P.)*
William F. Allison *(V.P.-Western Region)*

CUNA Western District (1)
2350 S. Garey Ave.
Pomona, CA 91766
Tel.: 909-591-0393
S.I.C.: 6411
Julian E. Geiger *(District V.P.)*
William F. Allison *(V.P.-Western Region)*

Puerto Rico:

CUNA Mutual Insurance Society-Puerto Rico (1)
G.P.O. Box 2219,
San Juan, PR 00936-2219
Tel.: 809-753-1350
S.I.C.: 6411
Neftali Adames *(General Agent)*

Non-U.S. Holdings:

Cuibs Pty. Ltd. (1)
P.O. Box 1418,
North Sydney, NSW 2060, Australia

CUNA Mutual Insurance Soc. (1)
P.O. Box 1418
North Sydney, NSW 2060, Australia
Tel.: 922-5933
Insurance
S.I.C.: 6411
John P. Granata *(V.P. & Gen. Mgr.)*

The Cumis Group Ltd. (1)
151 North Service Rd.
Burlington, ON L7R 4C2, Canada
Tel.: 416-632-1221
S.I.C.: 6311; 6321
Michael B. Kitchen *(Pres.)*

Subsidiaries:

Canadian Northern Shield (2)
555 W. Hasting, Rm. 1900 P.O. Box 12133,
Vancouver, ON V6B 4N6, Canada
Tel.: 604-622-2911
General Insurance
S.I.C.: 6331
S. D. Corocoran *(Chief Oper. Officer)*

Cumis General Insurance Co. (2)
151 North Service Rd.
Burlington, ON L7R 4C2, Canada
Tel.: 416-632-1221
S.I.C.: 6411
J.L.H. Lanctot *(Chief Oper. Officer)*

Cumis Life Insurance Co. (2)
151 North Service Rd.
Burlington, ON L7R 4C2, Canada
S.I.C.: 6311
J.L.H. Lanctot *(Chief Oper. Officer)*

Cumis Group Insurance (1)
1700-555 W. Hastings St. P.O. Box 12069,
Vancouver, BC V6B 4N5, Canada
Tel.: 604-662-5620
Fax: 604-662-5680
Credit Union Insurance
S.I.C.: 6311; 6321
James Craig *(Chief Oper. Officer)*

CUNA Mutual Insurance Co. (1)
P.O. Box 5065
Burlington, ON Canada L7R 4C2
Tel.: 416-632-1221
Insurance
S.I.C.: 6411

CUNA Mutual Insurance Soc. (1)
2 Rust St., Cor Maraval Rd. P.O. Box 193,
Port of Spain, Trinidad & Tobago
Tel.: 62-80827
Insurance
S.I.C.: 6411
Thomas Rampersad *(Asst. V.P.-Caribbean Opers.)*

Cuna Caribbean Insurance Society Ltd. (1)
2 Rust St., Cor Maraval Rd. P.O. Box 193,
Port of Spain, Trinidad & Tobago
Tel.: 62-80827

Offices:

CUNA Mutual Insurance Soc. (2)
2A Manhattan Rd. P.O. Box 396,
Kingston, 5, Jamaica
Mktg. Individual Products, Credit Union
S.I.C.: 6321
Chris Robinson *(Principal Officer)*

CUNA Mutual Insurance Soc. (2)
Calle Anibal de Espinosa No. 358 Apartado Postal 386,
Santo Domingo, Dominican Republic
S.I.C.: 6411
Luis Cubillette *(Representative)*

CUNA Mutual Insurance Soc. (1)
Curacaostaat 50
Willemstad, Curacao Netherlands Antilles
Insurance
S.I.C.: 6411
Carlos Gerardina *(Representative)*

CUNA Mutual Insurance Soc. (1)
Calle 19 No. 13A-12, Piso 4
Bogota, D.E. Colombia
Tel.: 283-5936
Insurance
S.I.C.: 6411
Carlos Duque *(Intl. V.P.-Latin America)*

CUNA Mutual Insurance Soc. (1)
185-191 Sai Yee St. Flat A, Eliza Bldg., 12th Fl.,
Kowloon, Hong Kong
Tel.: 3-802-195
Insurance
S.I.C.: 6411
Andrew So *(Intl. V.P.-Asia & Africa)*

CUNA Mutual Insurance Soc. (1)
Calle Camilo Carrillo 114 Jesus Maria
Lima, 11, Peru
Tel.: 31-1925
Insurance
S.I.C.: 6411
Eddie Chavez *(Representative)*

CVC PRODUCTS, INC.
525 Lee Rd.
Rochester, NY 14606
Mailing Address:
P.O. Box 1886
Rochester, NY 14603
Tel.: 716-458-2550
Tel.: 800-448-5900
Year Founded: 1973
Approx.Sls.: $15,000,000
Emp.: 100
Export
Mfr. Deposition Systems & Vacuum Components
S.I.C.: 3821
Christine Whitman *(Pres.)*
Scott Armstrong *(V.P.-Fin.)*
Paul Ballentine *(V.P.-Res. & Devel.)*
Christopher Mann *(V.P.-Sls. & Mktg.)*
Larry Marowski *(Pur. Agent)*

CABANA FOODS, INC.
14245 Birwood St.
Detroit, MI 48238
Tel.: 313-834-0800
Fax: 313-834-0443
Year Founded: 1961
Assets: $6,954,722
Liabilities: $5,270,765
Net Worth: $1,683,957
Approx.Sls.: $24,000,000
Emp.: 120
Fiscal Year-end: 12/31/90
Processor of Snack Foods & Potato Chips
S.I.C.: 2096
Raymond H. Jenkins *(Pres. & Treas.)*
Mario Apruzzese *(V.P.-Fin.)*
John Oldani *(Dir.-Sls.)*

No. of Mfg. Plants/Facilities: 2
No. of U.S. Offices: 1

Computer Systems/Hardware:
IBM System 37

Outside Service Firm(s):

Doeren & Mayhew*(Auditors)*
Troy, MI

Donald Harms*(Legal Firm)*
Detroit, MI

Bank of New England*(Major Banking Relationship)*
28 State Street
Boston, MA 02109
Tel.: 617-742-4000

Jenkins & Qualis*(Pension Manager)*
Detroit, MI

Cabledata
(See U.S. Computer Systems Listing)

CABLEVISION INDUSTRIES CORP.
Cablevision Center
Liberty, NY 12754
Tel.: 914-292-7550
Fax: 914-292-2180
Year Founded: 1956
Assets: $1,259,200,000
Earnings: ($103,381,000)
Liabilities: $1,453,169,000
Net Worth: $193,969,000
Approx.Sls.: $258,799,000
Emp.: 1,400
Fiscal Year-end: 12/31/91
Cable TV services
S.I.C.: 4841
Alan Gerry *(Chm. & Chief Exec. Officer)*
Fred Cornelius *(Vice Chm.)*
Rocco Commisso *(Exec. V.P. & Chief Fin. Officer)*
Fred Schulte *(Chief Oper. Officer)*
Bill Doten *(V.P.-Mktg.)*
Mike Egan *(V.P.-Programming)*
Darlene Fedun *(V.P.-Customer Service)*
Mark Halpin *(V.P.)*
Joe Van Loan *(V.P.-Engrng.)*
George O'Leary *(V.P.-Audit)*
Keith Suehvholz *(V.P.-Fin.)*
Darrell Supak *(V.P.)*
Dave Testa *(V.P.-Govt. Rels.)*
Nickolas Speranza *(V.P.-Human Resources)*
Philip Dropkin *(Sec. & Gen. Counsel)*
Robert M. Jones *(Controller)*
George Kwoka *(Dir.-Mngmt. Information Systems)*
Joseph Rupert *(Dir.-Pur.)*

Computer Systems/Hardware:
IBM/400

CABLEWAVE SYSTEMS, INC.
60 Dodge Ave.
North Haven, CT 06473
Tel.: 203-239-3311
Fax: 203-234-7718
Approx.Sls.: $24,000,000
Emp.: 160
Import
Mfr. of Semi-Flexible Coaxial Cables, Eliptical Waveguides, Microwave Antennas & FM Antenna Subsystems
S.I.C.: 3679; 3357; 3678
George Gigas *(Pres.)*
Werner Mordarski *(Controller)*
William Bayne, Jr. *(Dir.-Mfg.)*
Udo Bode *(Dir.-Engrng.)*
Pat Caswell *(Mgr.-Personnel)*
Chuck Rafter *(Pur. Agent)*
Elizabeth Gaal *(Admin. Asst.)*

SAMUEL CABOT, INC.
100 Hale St.
Newburyport, MA 01950
Tel.: 508-465-1900
Tel.: 800-US-STAIN
Fax: 508-462-0511
Year Founded: 1877
Approx.Sls.: $28,000,000
Emp.: 100
Fiscal Year-end: 9/30/90
Export
Manufacturer of Stains & Wood Preservatives
S.I.C.: 2851
Samuel Cabot III *(Pres.)*
Anthony J. Faria *(V.P.-Mktg. & Sls.)*
Robert L. Marini *(V.P.-Western Div.)*
W. McGonigle *(Treas.)*
Jean-Yves Gourlay *(Dir.-Technical)*
Deborah Bertges *(Mgr.-Mktg. Services)*
Ken Fitzgerald *(Mgr.-Data Processing)*
John Gihlstorf *(Mgr.-Mfg.)*
Belinda Suntap *(Asst. Mgr.-Mtkg.)*
Principal(s):
Samuel Cabot III

Computer Systems/Hardware:
IBM System 36

Outside Service Firm(s):

Ernst & Young*(Auditors)*
200 Clarendon St., 46th Fl.
Boston, MA 02116
Tel.: 617-266-2000

Widett, Slater & Goldman*(Legal Firm)*
60 State St.
Boston, MA 02109

Fleet National Bank*(Major Banking Relationship)*
125 Dupont Dr.
Providence, RI 02907-3178
Tel.: 401-278-5335

State Street Bank & Trust Co.*(Major Banking Relationship)*
P.O. Box 366,
Boston, MA 02101
Tel.: 617-426-5523

Subsidiary:

Samuel Cabot, Inc. (1)
23284 Eichler St.
Hayward, CA 94545
Tel.: 510-786-2086

CACIQUE CHEESE CO., INC.
14940 Proctor Ave.
City of Industry, CA 91744
Tel.: 818-961-3399 **CA**
Fax: 818-961-4676
Year Founded: 1973
Approx.Sls.: $25,000,000
Emp.: 160
Fresh & Processed Natural Cheese
S.I.C.: 2022
Gilbert DeCardenas *(Pres.)*
Jennie DeCardenas *(Exec. V.P.)*
Charles Aedo *(V.P.)*

Frank Gutierrez *(V.P.)*

Outside Service Firm(s):

BankAmerica Corp.*(Major Banking Relationship)*
Anaheim, CA

CACTUS FEEDERS, INC.
2209 W. 7th St.
Amarillo, TX 79106
Mailing Address:
P.O. Box 3050,
Amarillo, TX 79116-3050
Tel.: 806-373-2333 **TX**
Fax: 806-371-4767
Year Founded: 1975
Approx.Sls.: $371,000,000
Emp.: 325
Fiscal Year-end: 10/31/91
Import Export
Cattle Feedlots, Farming, Ranching
S.I.C.: 0211; 0212
Paul F. Engler *(Chm. Bd. & Pres.)*
David Owen *(Exec. V.P.)*
Steve Denny *(V.P.-Feedyard Opers.)*
Terry K. Manz *(V.P., Sec. & Treas.)*

Outside Service Firm(s):

Wilson & Haag*(Auditors)*
Amarillo, TX

Gibson, Ochsner & Adkins*(Legal Firm)*
Amarillo, TX

First National Bank of Amarillo*(Major Banking Relationship)*
Amarillo, TX

CADDOCK ELECTRONICS, INC.
1717 Chicago Ave.
Riverside, CA 92507
Tel.: 909-788-1700 **CA**
Twx: 910-332-6108
Fax: 909-369-1151
Year Founded: 1962
Approx.Sls.: $14,000,000
Emp.: 225
Fiscal Year-end: 3/31/91
Export
Manufacture High Performance Resistor Networks
S.I.C.: 3679
Corporate Giving Program:
Evangelical Christian Organizations
Richard E. Caddock, Sr. *(Pres.)*
Sue E. Brinkman *(V.P. & Comptroller)*
Anne M. Caddock *(V.P.)*
Richard E. Caddock, Jr. *(V.P.-Engrng.)*
Milton J. Strief *(V.P.-Corp. Devel.)*
Gary R. Whited *(V.P.-Opers.)*
Marvin R. Kidd *(Dir.-Admin. Services)*
Vance Oligny *(Dir.-Mktg.)*
James Skelton *(Dir.-Corp. Sls.)*
Cindy Imel *(Mgr.-Pur.)*

No. of Mfg. Plants/Facilities: 4
No. of U.S. Offices: 4
No. of Foreign Offices: 2

Outside Service Firm(s):

Ross-Landis & Pauw*(Auditors)*
Riverside, CA

Johnson & Higgins*(Commercial Insurance Carrier)*
Riverside, CA

Best, Best & Krieger*(Legal Firm)*
P.O. Box 1028
Riverside, CA 92502
Tel.: 909-686-1450

Bank of America NT&SA*(Major Banking Relationship)*
Riverside, CA

Divisions:

Applied Sciences Division **(1)**
17271 N. Umpqua Highway
Roseburg, OR 97470
Tel.: 503-496-0700
Product Development
S.I.C.: 3679; 3676
John M. Caddock *(Dir.)*

Caddock Network Division **(1)**
1717 Chicago Ave.
Riverside, CA 92507
Tel.: 909-788-1700
High Performance Resistor Networks
S.I.C.: 3679

Resistor Division **(1)**
1717 Chicago Ave.
Riverside, CA 92507
Tel.: 909-788-1700
Discrete Resistors
S.I.C.: 3676

CADET MANUFACTURING COMPANY
2500 W. 4th Plain Blvd.
Vancouver, WA 98660
Mailing Address:
P.O. Box 1675
Vancouver, WA 98668-1675
Tel.: 206-693-2505
Tel.: 800-442-2338 **OR**
Fax: 206-694-6939
Year Founded: 1957
Approx.Sls.: $11,000,000
Emp.: 106
Import Export
Manufacturer Of Electric Heaters; Wholesale Warm Air Heating Equipment
S.I.C.: 3634; 5075
Richard E. Anderson *(Chm. Bd. & Pres.)*
Bruce W. Farnsworth *(Chief Oper. Officer)*
James Pomplun *(V.P.-Sls. & Mktg.)*
Vance C. Mosher *(Treas.)*
Thomas V. Crowley *(Dir.-Mktg. & Sec.)*

Outside Service Firm(s):

Moss Adams*(Auditors)*
Vancouver, WA

First Independent Bank*(Major Banking Relationship)*
Vancouver, WA

CADILLAC PRODUCTS, INC.
530 Stephenson Hwy.
Troy, MI 48083
Tel.: 313-583-1525 **MI**
Year Founded: 1942
Approx.Sls.: $75,000,000
Emp.: 650
Fiscal Year-end: 12/31/90
Import Export
Manufacturer Flexible Paper & Plastic Packaging, Automotive Trim & Thermo Formed Products & Plastic Pallets
S.I.C.: 3089; 2671; 2672; 2673; 2674; 2396
Robert J. Williams, Sr. *(Chm. Bd. & Chief Exec. Officer)*
Robert D. Hoien *(Chief Oper. Officer)*
Roger K. Williams *(Treas.)*
Robert J. Williams, Jr. *(Chief Fin. Officer)*
Michael P. Williams, II *(Chief Tech. Officer)*

No. of Mfg. Plants/Facilities: 7
No. of U.S. Offices: 1

Outside Service Firm(s):

McEndarffer, Hoke & Bernard, P.C.*(Auditors)*
Bloomfield Hills, MI

NBD Bank, N.A.*(Major Banking Relationship)*
Security Transfer Services, P.O. Box 330751
Detroit, MI 48232

THE CAFARO CO.
2445 Belmont Ave.
Youngstown, OH 44504
Tel.: 216-747-2661
Fax: 216-743-2902
Year Founded: 1945
Emp.: 700
Real Estate Developers & Brokers
S.I.C.: 6552; 6531
William M. Cafaro *(Chm. Bd.)*
Anthony M. Cafaro *(Pres. & Chief Exec. Officer)*
Anthony J. Ross *(Exec. V.P.)*
Flora M. Cafaro *(V.P. & Asst. Treas.)*
Joseph S. Nohra *(V.P. & Treas.)*
Augustas C. Rigas *(V.P.-Construction)*
J. Phillip Richley *(V.P.-Devel., Dir.-Pub. Rels. & Media Dir.)*
Benjamin J. Viloski *(V.P.)*
Vincent Morgione *(Controller)*
Ronald J. Ross *(Chief Real Estate Counsel)*
James Dobran *(Chief Litigation & Devel. Counsel)*
Joseph J. Natoli *(Chief Consulting Architect)*
Mark Klockner *(Specialty Leasing Dir.)*
Peter J. Debenedictis *(Dir.-Real Estate Plng.)*
Dan Mancuso *(Dir.-Mngmt. Training)*
Patrick O'Brien *(Dir.-Mngmt. Information Systems)*
Robert Piotter *(Dir.-Personnel)*
John P. Richley *(Dir.-Opers.)*
George W. Roth *(Dir.-Construction)*
Carolyn Kopp *(Corp. Travel Planner)*
Sandra Visser *(Corp. Mktg. Mgr.)*
Bruce Riley *(Sr. Property Admin.)*

No. of U.S. Offices: 2

CAIN & BULTMAN, INC.
2145 Dennis Street
Jacksonville, FL 32204
Mailing Address:
P.O. Box 2815
Jacksonville, FL 32203
Tel.: 904-356-4812 **FL**
Fax: 904-356-4812, Ext. 1947
Year Founded: 1924
Approx.Sls.: $250,000,000
Emp.: 650
Wholesaler of Large Appliances & Floor Coverings
S.I.C.: 5064; 5023
Norwood H. Sandifer *(Chm. Bd.)*
Thomas N. Sandifer *(Pres. & Chief Exec. Officer)*
Arthur Cahoon *(Chief Fin. Officer)*
Al Derrick *(Exec. V.P., Chief Fin. Officer & Controller)*
Mike Sandifer *(V.P.-Asset Mngmt.)*
Beatrice B. Tyler *(Treas.)*
Kathy Ingram *(Dir.-Personnel)*
Alan Kimball *(Dir.-Data Processing)*
Larry Blue *(Adv. Auditor)*

Computer Systems/Hardware:
DPS 7

Outside Service Firm(s):

Coopers & Lybrand*(Auditors)*
Jacksonville, FL

American Heritage Life Insurance Co.*(Group Insurer)*
Jacksonville, FL

Rogers, Bailey & Jones*(Legal Firm)*
Jacksonville, FL

Barclays Bank plc*(Major Banking Relationship)*
Jericho, NY

Barnett Banks Trust Company, N.A.*(Major Banking Relationship)*
9000 Southside Blvd., P.O. Box 40200
Jacksonville, FL 32202-0200
Tel.: 904-464-2802

Division:

Cain & Bultman **(1)**
501 S. 12th St.
Birmingham, AL 35233
Tel.: 205-323-1694
Fax: 205-326-3378
Emp.: 45
Wholesale Floor Coverings
S.I.C.: 5023
Therman Campbell *(Mgr.-Opers.)*

CAIRNS & BROTHER, INC.
60 Webro Rd.
Clifton, NJ 07012
Mailing Address:
P.O. Box 4076
Clifton, NJ 07012
Tel.: 201-473-5867
Fax: 201-473-1357
Year Founded: 1836
Approx.Sls.: $13,000,000
Emp.: 190
Export
Mfr. of Protective Clothing & Helmets for Firefighters
S.I.C.: 3069; 3089; 3842
Christopher E. Coombs *(Pres.)*
William McCutheon, Jr. *(V.P.-Sls.)*
K.J. Vidal *(Controller)*
R. Richter *(Dir.-Engrng.)*
Kerry Gordon *(Dir.-Adv., Helmets)*
Mark Sciacca *(Dir.-Adv., Clothing)*
W. McGehan *(Mgr.-Opers.)*
C. Mawhinney *(Mgr.-Pur.)*

CAJUN ELECTRIC POWER CO-OP
10719 Airline Hwy.
Baton Rouge, LA 70816
Mailing Address:
P.O. Box 15540
Baton Rouge, LA 70895-5540
Tel.: 504-291-3060 **LA**
Fax: 504-291-3076
Year Founded: 1962
Assets: $2,353,230,168
Liabilities: $3,527,277,117
Net Worth: $1,174,046,949
Approx.Sls.: $386,816,508
Emp.: 616
Fiscal Year-end: 12/31/91
Electric Power Generation
S.I.C.: 4911
Al Ewing *(Pres.)*
David L. Mohre *(Chief Exec. Officer & Exec. V.P.)*
Daniel E. MacLeod *(Chief Oper. Officer & Asst. Gen. Mgr.)*
D. Jack Harpole *(Chief Admin. Officer & Sr. V.P.)*
Philip G. Harris *(Chief Systems Officer & V.P.)*
Clark T. Colvin *(V.P.-External Affairs)*
Kevin Dolan *(V.P.-Fin. & Treas.)*
Gary F. Hall *(V.P. & Controller)*
Gerald W. Pellar *(V.P.-Admin.)*
Richard Stitman *(V.P.)*
Jerry D. Williams *(Treas. & Sec.)*
Philip E. Adams *(Corp. Counsel)*
James Daily *(Dir.-Human Resources)*
Dennis Johnson *(Dir.-Special Projects)*
Emile Poche *(Dir.-Information Services)*
James J. Weaver *(Dir.-Quality Assurances)*
Delores Wheat *(Dir.-Benefits)*
Resal Craven *(Mgr.-Power System Plng.)*
Gary Ellender *(Mgr.-Environmental Affairs)*
Ron McCabe *(Mgr.-Pur.)*
Randy Pierce *(Mgr.-Mktg. & Member Services)*
Manuel F. Gan *(Tax & Lease Analyst)*
Principal(s):

Cajun Electric Power Co-op—(Continued)

Member Owned Co-Operative

No. of Mfg. Plants/Facilities: 2
No. of U.S. Offices: 2

Computer Systems/Hardware:
IBM 4381; Prime 9955; Prime 750

Outside Service Firm(s):

Ernst & Young*(Auditors)*
Baton Rouge, LA

United States Fidelity & Guaranty Co.*(Commercial Insurance Carrier)*
Baltimore, MD

National Rural Electric Cooperative Association*(Group Insurer)*
Washington, DC

John Schwab*(Legal Firm)*
Baton Rouge, LA

Wachovia Bank of Georgia, N.A.*(Major Banking Relationship)*
191 Peachtree St. N.E.
Atlanta, GA 30303

National Rural Electric Cooperative Association*(Pension Manager)*
Washington, DC

CAL-AIR INC.
12484 E. Whittier Blvd.
Whittier, CA 90602
Tel.: 310-698-8301 CA
Fax: 310-698-4396
Year Founded: 1953
Approx.Sls.: $51,000,000
Emp.: 375
Warm Air Heating & Air Conditioning Contractor; Air Conditioning Repair
S.I.C.: 1711; 7623
Charles S. Middleton *(Chm. Bd., Pres. & Chief Exec. Officer)*
O.J. Clayton *(V.P.)*
Gerald Hill *(V.P.)*
Kenneth Petro *(V.P.)*
Harold Stenfort *(V.P.)*

Outside Service Firm(s):

King, King & Aleman*(Auditors)*
Burbank, CA

City National Bank*(Major Banking Relationship)*
LaMirada, CA

Subsidiary:

Cal-Air Construction **(1)**
12484 E. Whittier Blvd.
Whittier, CA 90602
Tel.: 310-698-8301
Nonresidential Construction
S.I.C.: 1542
Charles S. Middleton *(Pres.)*

CAL/EMBLEM LABELS, INC.
4790 W. Jacquelyn Ave.
Fresno, CA 93722
Mailing Address:
P.O. Box 9758,
Fresno, CA 93794
Tel.: 209-276-6300 CA
Fax: 209-277-0636
Emp.: 62
Manufacture Custom Pressure Sensitive Labels
S.I.C.: 2672
John Bailey *(Chm. Bd., Pres., Chief Exec. & Fin. Officer & Treas.)*
Jay Hunceker *(V.P.-Fin.)*
Robert Cain *(Controller)*
James Haun *(Mgr.-Sls.)*

Computer Systems/Hardware:
Alpha Micro 1072

Outside Service Firm(s):

Baird, Kurtz & Dobson*(Auditors)*
Commerce Tower, 911 Main, Ste. 1900
Kansas City, MO
Tel.: 816-221-7544

Husch, Eppenberger, Donohue, Dobson & Cornfeld*(Legal Firm)*
Kansas City, MO

Husch, Eppenberger, Donohue, Elson & Cornfield*(Legal Firm)*
100 N. Broadway
St. Louis, MO 63102
Tel.: 314-421-4800

First Interstate Bank*(Major Banking Relationship)*
Fresno, CA

CAL-MAINE FOODS, INC.
3320 Woodrow Wilson Blvd.
Jackson, MS 39209
Mailing Address:
P.O. Box 2960,
Jackson, MS 39207
Tel.: 601-948-6813 DE
Telex: 585-401
Fax: 601-969-0905
Year Founded: 1969
Sales Range: $100-499 Million
Emp.: 850
Fiscal Year-end: 5/31/90
Egg Production, Egg Products & Plants
S.I.C.: 0252; 0254; 2015
Fred Adams *(Chief Exec. Officer)*
R.K. Looper *(Pres. & Chief Oper. Officer)*
Bobby J. Raines *(V.P. & Treas.)*
Charles Collins *(Controller)*
Robert Russell *(Dir.-Personnel)*

Outside Service Firm(s):

Deloitte & Touche*(Auditors)*
Jackson, MS

First National Bank of Jackson*(Major Banking Relationship)*
Jackson, MS

Divisions:

Cal-Maine Egg Products Inc. **(1)**
3330 Woodrow Wilson Blvd.
Jackson, MS 39209
Tel.: 601-352-9462
Egg Distributor & Production
S.I.C.: 0252

Cal-Maine Farms **(1)**
3320 Woodrow Wilson Blvd.
Jackson, MS 39209
Tel.: 601-948-6813
Chicken Eggs
S.I.C.: 0252

CALAVO GROWERS OF CALIFORNIA
15661 Red Hill Ave.
Tustin, CA 92680
Mailing Address:
P.O. Box 26081
Santa Ana, CA 92799-6081
Tel.: 714-259-1166 CA
Telex: 674938
Fax: 714-259-4810
Year Founded: 1924
Assets: $43,533,000
Liabilities: $29,647,000
Net Worth: $13,886,000
Approx.Sls.: $132,500,000
Emp.: 108
Fiscal Year-end: 10/31/91
Import Export
Marketing Cooperative for Farmers; Packaging & Sales
S.I.C.: 5148; 4783; 5142; 5149
Lee Cole *(Chm. Bd.)*
Allen J. Vangelos *(Pres. & Chief Exec. Officer)*
Fred Ferrazzano *(Vice Chm.)*
Gene Carbone *(V.P.-Fin., Chief Fin. Officer & Sec.)*
Steve Davis *(V.P.-Sls. & Mktg.)*
Scott Runge *(Treas.)*
Randy Rozatti *(Dir.-Data Processing)*
Bruce Spurrell *(Dir.-Pur.)*
Rob Wedin *(Dir.-Avocado Opers. & Intl. Mktg.)*

No. of Mfg. Plants/Facilities: 3
No. of U.S. Offices: 7

Computer Systems/Hardware:
IBM System 38; AS 400

Outside Service Firm(s):

Deloitte & Touche*(Auditors)*
21550 Oxnard St., Ste. 800
Woodland Hills, CA 91367-7100
Tel.: 818-593-4800
Fax: 818-347-4278

Equitable Real Estate Investment Managment Inc.*(Group Insurer)*
3414 Peachtree Rd. N.E.
Atlanta, GA 30326-1162

Tuttle & Taylor Inc.*(Legal Firm)*
355 S. Grand Ave.
Los Angeles, CA 90071
Tel.: 213-683-0600

Bank of America NT&SA*(Major Banking Relationship)*
555 So. Flower St., 5th Fl.
Los Angeles, CA 90071
Tel.: 213-228-3526
Fax: 213-228-4062

Subsidiary:

Calavo Foods, Inc. **(1)**
15661 Red Hill Ave.
Tustin, CA 92680
Tel.: 714-259-1166
Fax: 714-259-7631
Avocado Processor
S.I.C.: 2032
Chuck Redman *(Pres.)*

CALCASIEU LUMBER COMPANY
4501 Burleson Rd.
Austin, TX 78744
Mailing Address:
P.O. Box 17097
Austin, TX 78744
Tel.: 512-444-3172
Fax: 512-462-2344
Year Founded: 1883
Assets: $17,000,000
Liabilities: $10,500,000
Net Worth: $6,500,000
Approx.Sls.: $32,000,000
Emp.: 160
Fiscal Year-end: 9/27/91
Lumber & Building Materials Sales; Building Contractors
S.I.C.: 2439; 2452; 5031; 5211; 5074; 5078
T.N. Morris, Jr. *(Chm., Pres. & Chief Exec. Officer)*
Larry Foust *(Exec. V.P. & Gen. Mgr.-Consolidated Wholesale Lumber Co.)*
Dixie Fromberg *(V.P. & Personnel Dir.)*
Ron Maupin *(Mgr.-Data Processing)*

Outside Service Firm(s):

Deloitte & Touche*(Auditors)*
919 Congress Ave., Ste. 700
Austin, TX 78701
Tel.: 512-476-7661

Maxwell Locke & Ritter*(Auditors)*
Austin, TX

Nieman Hanks*(Commercial Insurance Carrier)*
Austin, TX

Porter, Rogers & Dahlman*(Legal Firm)*
Corpus Christi, TX

First City National Bank*(Major Banking Relationship)*
Stock Transfer Div., P.O. Box 2127
Austin, TX 78768

Subsidiary:

Consolidated Wholesale Lumber Co. **(1)**
4501 Burleson Rd.
Austin, TX 78744
Tel.: 512-444-3172
Wholesale Lumber
S.I.C.: 5031
Larry Foust *(Gen. Mgr.)*

CALCOR SPACE FACILITY, INC.
12031 E. Philadelphia St.
Whittier, CA 90601
Tel.: 310-945-1661
Fax: 310-696-6961
Year Founded: 1896
Sales Range: $10-19 Million
Emp.: 370
Sheet Metal & Machined Assemblies; Electronic Racks; Ground Handling Equipment & Aircraft Components
S.I.C.: 3444; 3679; 3728
Andy F. Brown *(Chm. Bd.)*
Ronald A. Brown *(Pres. & Chief Exec. Officer)*
Robert H. Feltham *(V.P.)*
Peter Webber *(V.P. & Gen. Mgr.)*
Robert S. McCoy *(Controller)*
Art Andrade *(Pur. Agent)*

Outside Service Firm(s):

Price Waterhouse*(Auditors)*
400 S. Hope St.
Los Angeles, CA 90071-2889
Tel.: 213-236-3000

Union Bank*(Major Banking Relationship)*
4201 Wilshire Blvd.
Los Angeles, CA 90051
Tel.: 310-578-7534

CALCOT, LTD.
1601 E. Brundage
Bakersfield, CA 93307
Mailing Address:
P.O. Box 259,
Bakersfield, CA 93302
Tel.: 805-327-5961
Year Founded: 1927
Sales Range: $1 Billion +
Emp.: 200
Export
Raw Cotton Marketing, Compression & Storage
S.I.C.: 0724; 5159
John Pucheu, Jr. *(Chm. Bd.)*
T.W. Smith *(Pres.)*
Robert Norris *(Sr. V.P.-Fin. & Admin.)*
Bruce Groefsema *(Sr. V.P.-Sls.)*
Gene A. Lundquist *(V.P. & Corp. Sec.)*
Steve Newman *(V.P.-Data Processing)*
Joe Bruce *(V.P.-Merchant Sls.)*
Lon Emerson *(V.P.-Opers., Southern California)*
Larry Nichols *(Treas.)*
Claud Acker *(Asst. V.P.-Domestic Sls.)*
Mary Joe Pasek *(Asst. V.P.-Admin. & Personnel)*

Principal(s):
John Pucheu, Jr.
T.W. Smith

Computer Systems/Hardware:
IBM 373031

Outside Service Firm(s):

Eadie & Payne*(Auditors)*
San Bernardino, CA

Bank of America NT&SA*(Investment Banker)*
Bakersfield, CA

Griswold, La Salle, Cobb, Dowd & Gin*(Legal Firm)*
Hanford, CA

CALDWELL MANUFACTURING COMPANY
2605 Manitour Rd.
Rochester, NY 14624
Mailing Address:
P.O. Box 92891
Rochester, NY 14692
Tel.: 716-352-3790 NY
Fax: 716-352-3729
Year Founded: 1888
Approx.Sls.: $10,000,000
Emp.: 200
Export
Mfr. of Clock Spring & Spiral Type Sash Balances & Aluminum Weatherstrip Products
S.I.C.: 3495; 3442
Allen C. Boucher *(Chm. Bd.)*
Victor Cypher *(Pres. & Chief Exec. Officer)*
John Coughlin *(V.P.-Fin. & Treas.)*
Joyce J. Boucher *(Sec.)*
William Cochrane *(Mgr.-Sls.)*

Outside Service Firm(s):

Arthur Andersen & Co.*(Auditors)*
Ste. 1500, One Marine Midland Plaza
Rochester, NY 14604

Harris, Beach, Wilcox, Rubin & Levy*(Legal Firm)*
2 State St.
Rochester, NY 14614
Tel.: 716-232-4440

Central Trust Co.*(Major Banking Relationship)*
Rochester, NY

Subsidiary:

Olympic Manufacturing Co. **(1)**
Wilkesboro, NC
Walter Stroud *(Pres.)*

CALDWELL TANKS, INC.
4000 Tower Rd.
Louisville, KY 40219
Tel.: 502-964-3361
Fax: 502-966-8732
Emp.: 100
Steel Tanks & Towers
S.I.C.: 3443
James W. Robinson *(Chm. Bd.)*
Bernard S. Fineman *(Pres. & Treas.)*
David L. Dues *(V.P.-Sls.)*
C.P. Fineman *(Sec.)*

Outside Service Firm(s):

Monroe, Shine & Co.*(Auditors)*
Louisville, KY

Stites & Harbison*(Legal Firm)*
600 West Main St.
Louisville, KY 40202
Tel.: 502-587-3400

First National Bank of Louisville*(Major Banking Relationship)*
Louisville, KY

Caldwell VanRiper Marketing& Advertising

CALDWELL VANRIPER INC.
1314 N. Meridian
Indianapolis, IN 46202
Mailing Address:
P.O. Box 7046,
Indianapolis, IN 46207
Tel.: 317-632-6501
Year Founded: 1910
Sales Range: $10-19 Million
Emp.: 40
Advertising, Public Relations & Media Relations Marketing
James R. Roudebush *(Chm. Bd.)*
Paula R. MacVittie *(Pres. & Chief Exec. Officer)*
Darlene Muncy *(V.P., Dir. Acctg., Sec. & Treas.)*
Bobbi Simmons *(V.P., Dir. Pub. Rels.)*
Julie Muncy *(Dir.-Human Res.)*

Computer Systems/Hardware:
MacIntosh, Media Management Plus

CALICO CAT PRESS, INC.
121 Chanlon Rd.
New Providence, NJ 07974
Tel.: 908-464-6800
Fax: 908-771-7704
Year Founded: 1990
Assets: $3,872,000
Earnings: $430,776
Liabilities: $2,459,000
Net Worth: $1,413,000
Approx.Sls.: $47,889,340
Emp.: 37
Fiscal Year-end: 3/31/91
Publisher of Children's Books
S.I.C.: 2731
Thomas M. Bachmann *(Chm. Bd., Pres. & Chief Exec. Officer)*
Jill Zacharczyk *(V.P.-Contracts & Gen. Counsel)*
Megan Ciamillo *(V.P.-Support Services)*
Ralph J. Lennon *(Dir.-Mngmt. Information Systems)*

Computer Systems/Hardware:
Apple MacIntosh

CALICO CORNERS
(Div. of Everfast Inc.)
203 Gale Ln.
Kennett Square, PA 19348
Tel.: 215-444-9700
Fax: 215-444-1221
Approx.Sls.: $80,000,000
Emp.: 1,200
Retail Sale of Decorative Fabrics
S.I.C.: 5714
Roy Simpson *(Chm. Bd.)*
Bert Kerstetter *(Pres.)*
Harry Walsh *(Chief Fin. Officer)*
Stuart Brooks *(Dir.-Stores)*

CALIFORNIA APRICOT ADVISORY BOARD
1280 Boulevard Way
Walnut Creek, CA 94595
Tel.: 510-937-3660
Approx.Sls.: $26,000,000
Emp.: 2
Advertising & Promotion of Apricots
S.I.C.: 8611
Stan Lester *(Chm. Bd.)*
Raymond Benech *(Vice Chm.)*
Ray Grove *(Sec.)*
Gene Stokes *(Gen. Mgr., Adv. & Sls. Promo. Mgr.)*

CALIFORNIA ARTICHOKE & VEGETABLE GROWERS CORP.
11500 Del Monte Ave.
Castroville, CA 95012
Mailing Address:
P.O. Box 1247
Castroville, CA 95012
Tel.: 408-633-2144 CA
Fax: 408-633-4363
Year Founded: 1924
Approx.Sls.: $45,000,000
Emp.: 115
Fiscal Year-end: 6/30/92
Export
Growers, Packers & Shippers of Artichokes, Broccoli, Sprouts, Anise, Romaine, Lettuce, Peas, Mixed Vegetables & Califlower
S.I.C.: 0161; 0119; 5148
Albert Pieri *(Pres.)*
Tom Bengard *(V.P.)*
Les Tottino *(Treas. & Asst. Sec.)*
Stephen Collins *(Controller)*
Edward Boutonnet *(Gen. Mgr. & Sec.)*
Pat Hopper *(Dir.-Mktg.)*
LeRoy Miller *(Mgr.-Sls.)*
Principal(s):
Albert Pieri

Computer Systems/Hardware:
Micro 486 Network

Outside Service Firm(s):

Kasavan & Pope*(Auditors)*
Salinas, CA

Noland, Hamerly, Etienne & Hoss*(Legal Firm)*
Salinas, CA

Wells Fargo Bank*(Major Banking Relationship)*
420 Montgomery St.
San Francisco, CA 94104

Creative Capital Asset Managers*(Pension Manager)*
San Jose, CA

Subsidiaries:

Mr. Artichoke Packing Co., Inc. **(1)**
11500 Blackie Rd.
Castroville, CA 95012
Tel.: 408-633-2480
Artichoke Packing
S.I.C.: 0723
Les Tottino *(Mgr.-Opers.)*

CALIFORNIA AVOCADO COMMISSION
1251 E. Dyer Rd., Ste. 200
Santa Ana, CA 92705
Tel.: 714-558-6761
Fax: 714-641-7024
Year Founded: 1961
Approx.Sls.: $11,500,000
Emp.: 15
Fiscal Year-end: 10/31/92
California Avocados
S.I.C.: 8611
Bob Tobias *(Chm. Bd.)*
Al Vangelos *(Vice Chm.)*
Mark Affleck *(Pres.)*
Val Weaver *(V.P.-Fin. & Admin.)*
Betty Bohrk *(Intl. Mktg. Mgr.)*

Computer Systems/Hardware:
Novell Network, IBM Compatibles

CALIFORNIA CEDAR PRODUCTS, INC.
400 Fresno Ave.
Stockton, CA 95203
Tel.: 209-944-5800
Fax: 209-944-9072
Year Founded: 1929
Sales Range: $40-59 Million
Emp.: 500
Manufactures Cedar Pencil Slats, Wood/Wax Fire Logs
S.I.C.: 2411; 2499
Philip Berolzheimer *(Pres.)*
Susan MacIntyre *(Chief Fin. Officer)*
Lee Thomas *(Dir.-Personnel)*
Robert Baldwin *(Mgr.-Data Processing)*
Principal(s):
Philip Berolzheimer

Computer Systems/Hardware:
IBM 1138

Outside Service Firm(s):

Grant Thornton*(Auditors)*
Stockton, CA

Atherton & Dozier*(Legal Firm)*
Stockton, CA

The Bank of California, N.A.*(Major Banking Relationship)*
Stockton, CA

Division:

Duraflame, Inc. **(1)**
2005 W. Washington St.
Stockton, CA 95203
Tel.: 209-948-2515
Fax: 209-948-2862
Emp.: 500
Marketer & Distributor of Processed Logs
S.I.C.: 2499
Philip Berolzheimer *(Pres.)*
Pete Hermes *(V.P.-Sls.)*
Paula Sullivan *(Adv.)*

CALIFORNIA ELECTRIC SERVICE
1143 East 12th St.
Oakland, CA 94606
Tel.: 510-834-8563 CA
Fax: 510-836-1125
Year Founded: 1872
Emp.: 110
Fiscal Year-end: 3/31/92
Portable Appliance Service
S.I.C.: 5064; 5722; 7629
Jack McAboy *(Chm. Bd.)*
Bill Oddy *(Pres. & Chief Exec. Officer)*
Dale Chamblin *(Exec. V.P. & Sec.)*
Jack Whitaker *(V.P.)*

No. of U.S. Offices: 19

Computer Systems/Hardware:
Qantel; ALR

Outside Service Firm(s):

Ron Rockwood*(Auditors)*
Burlingame, CA

Nationwide Insurance*(Group Insurer)*
Columbus, OH

Stark, Wells, Rahl, Field & Schwartz*(Legal Firm)*
Oakland, CA

Bank of America NT&SA*(Major Banking Relationship)*
Oakland, CA

CALIFORNIA HARDWARE CO.
13085 E. Temple Ave.
City of Industry, CA 91746
Mailing Address:
P.O. Box 760,
La Puente, CA 91747
Tel.: 818-369-9411
Approx.Sls.: $100,000,000
Emp.: 380
Fiscal Year-end: 12/31/90
Wholesale Distribute Hardware & Industrial Supplies
S.I.C.: 5072; 5085
Terrence L. Smith *(Chm. Bd., Pres. & Chief Exec. Officer)*
Nina Dragoo *(V.P., Treas. & Chief Fin. Officer)*
Wes Fitzpatrick *(V.P.-Mngmt. Information Systems)*
Kelly Hoskins *(V.P.-Pur.)*
C. C. Snyder *(V.P.-Mktg., Sls. & Adv.)*
Gary Thompson *(V.P.-Opers.)*
Virginia Kerr *(Sec.)*
Rhonda Mata *(Personnel Admin.)*

Computer Systems/Hardware:
NCR Criterion V8555 M; Honeywell DPS 6; Ultimate 7200

Outside Service Firm(s):

Price Waterhouse*(Auditors)*
400 S. Hope St.
Los Angeles, CA 90071-2889
Tel.: 213-236-3000

Northwestern Mutual*(Group Insurer)*
Milwaukee, WI

Parker Milliken-Clarke & O'Hara*(Legal Firm)*
Los Angeles, CA

California Hardware Co.—(Continued)

Wells Fargo Bank*(Major Banking Relationship)*
9000 Flair
El Monte, CA

Pacific Mutual*(Pension Manager)*
700 Newport Center Dr.
Newport Beach, CA 92660
Tel.: 714-640-3011
Fax: 714-759-3372

CALIFORNIA & HAWAIIAN SUGAR COMPANY
1390 Willow Pass Rd.
Concord, CA 94520
Mailing Address:
P.O. Box 4126
Concord, CA 94524
Tel.: 510-356-6000
Fax: 510-356-6037
Year Founded: 1906
Assets: $225,000,000
Net Worth: $225,000,000
Approx.Sls.: $454,000,000
Emp.: 1000
Fiscal Year-end: 12/31/91
Grow, Refine & Distribute Cane Sugar
S.I.C.: 2061; 2062; 5159
H.R. Somerset *(Pres. & Chief Exec. Officer)*
David G. Koncelik *(Exec. V.P. & Chief Oper. Officer)*
T.W. Rowland *(Sr. V.P., Sec. & Gen. Counsel)*
William H. Stewart *(Sr. V.P.-Cooperative Opers.)*
M.L. Carnahan *(V.P.-Human Resources)*
R.A. DeTata *(V.P.-Indus. Prod. Sls.)*
R.L. Knecht *(V.P.-Refinery Opers.)*
T.J. Wilson *(V.P.-Grocery Prod. Sls.)*
P.G. Gibbons *(Dir.-Information Svcs.)*
F.M. Sammis *(Dir.-Mktg.)*
D.A. Bina *(Mgr.-Adv. & Sls. Promo.)*

Computer Systems/Hardware:
IBM 9370

Outside Service Firm(s):

Deloitte & Touche*(Auditors)*
50 Fremont St.
San Francisco, CA 94105-2230
Tel.: 415-393-4300
Fax: 415-227-0452

Aetna Life & Casualty*(Group Insurer)*
151 Farmington Avenue
Hartford, CT 06156
Tel.: 203-273-2128
Fax: 203-729-4295

Manhattan Life*(Group Insurer)*
New York, NY

Brobeck, Phleger & Harrison*(Legal Firm)*
Spear St. Tower, One Market Plaza
San Francisco, CA 94105
Tel.: 415-442-0900

McCutchen, Doyle, Brown & Enersen*(Legal Firm)*
3 Embarcadero
San Francisco, CA 94111

Bank of America, N.T. & S.A.*(Major Banking Relationship)*
P.O. Box 37002,
San Francisco, CA 94137

J. P. Morgan Investment Management, Inc.*(Pension Manager)*
522 Fifth Ave.
New York, NY 10036
Tel.: 212-837-2300
Fax: 212-819-1871

CALIFORNIA MANUFACTURING ENTERPRISES
19481 San Jose Ave.
City of Industry, CA 91748
Tel.: 909-595-2382
Fax: 909-594-8534
Approx.Sls.: $15,000,000
Emp.: 200
Aircraft Parts & Equipment, Coating of Metals & Formed Products, Stamping Metal for the Trade, Aircraft Engines & Engine Parts, Anodizing of Metals for Formed Products
S.I.C.: 3728; 3479; 3469; 3724; 3471
Stephen Braunheim *(Pres.)*
David Janes *(V.P. & Sec.)*
Gene Hersh *(Treas.)*
Principal(s):
Stephen Braunheim
Barry Altman

Outside Service Firm(s):

Grobstein, Blankstein & Goldman*(Auditors)*
Los Angeles, CA

Argue, Pearson, Harbison & Myers*(Legal Firm)*
801 So. Flower St.
Los Angeles, CA 90017
Tel.: 213-622-3100

Division:

Smith Mailer **(1)**
19481 San Jose Ave.
City of Industry, CA 91748
Tel.: 909-595-6444
Emp.: 40
Metal Stampings
S.I.C.: 3469
Barry Altman *(Pres.)*

CALIFORNIA MICRO DEVICES
2000 W. 14th St.
Tempe, AZ 85281
Tel.: 602-968-4431
Fax: 602-921-6598
Earnings: $1,173,000
Approx.Rev.: $32,286,000
Emp.: 250
Fiscal Year-end: 6/30/90
Mfr. Integrated Circuits
S.I.C.: 3674
Chan Desaigoudar *(Chm. Bd.)*
Kiamil Giontzeneli *(V.P.-Semiconductor Div.)*
Scott McNeese *(V.P.-Mktg.)*
Blayne Arnold *(Mktg. Mgr.)*

CALIFORNIA MILK PRODUCERS
11709 E. Artesia Blvd.
Artesia, CA 90701
Tel.: 310-865-1291 **CA**
Year Founded: 1974
Approx.Sls.: $460,000,000
Emp.: 250
Wholesale Distribution of Milk
S.I.C.: 5143
Gary Korsmeier *(Chief Exec. Officer)*
Lewis Aukeman *(Pres.)*
Arie VanRyan *(V.P.)*
John Bos *(Treas.)*

Outside Service Firm(s):

Deloitte & Touche*(Auditors)*
1000 Wilshire Blvd.
Los Angeles, CA 90017-2472
Tel.: 213-688-0800
Fax: 213-688-0100

Bank of America NT&SA*(Major Banking Relationship)*
Downey, CA

CALIFORNIA OFFSET PRINTERS, INC.
620 W. Elk Ave.
Glendale, CA 91204
Tel.: 213-245-6446
Fax: 213-245-2123
Year Founded: 1962
Approx.Sls.: $20,000,000
Emp.: 140
Import
Commercial Printers: Tabloids, Magazines, Directories
S.I.C.: 2721; 2759
J.C. Hedlund *(Chm. Bd. & Pres.)*
Robert Hughes *(Exec. V.P. & Chief Oper. Officer)*
William Jacot *(V.P.-Mfg.)*
Robert Marshall *(V.P.-Fin. & Credit)*
Cliff Shaw *(Dir.-Cust. Services)*

CALIFORNIA PACIFIC RESEARCH, INC.
1055 W. Moana
Reno, NV 89509
Tel.: 702-829-5600
Fax: 702-825-3907
Approx.Sls.: $10,000,000
Emp.: 14
Fiscal Year-end: 12/31/90
Hair Care Products
Robert E. Murphy *(Pres.)*
Karen Murphy *(V.P., Sec. & Treas.)*
Robert Hlade *(Controller)*

CALIFORNIA PANEL & VENEER COMPANY
14055 Artesia Blvd.
Cerritos, CA 90701
Tel.: 310-926-5834
Tel.: 800-451-1745 **CA**
Fax: 310-926-3139
Year Founded: 1923
Assets: $4,877,234
Liabilities: $2,252,735
Net Worth: $2,624,499
Approx.Sls.: $21,000,000
Emp.: 55
Fiscal Year-end: 12/31/91
Import Export
Wholesale Distributor of Plywood; Veneer; Interior Building Materials
S.I.C.: 5031
John C. Fahs *(Pres.)*
Gary Harker *(Exec. V.P.-Sls.)*
Carl Racavich *(Controller)*
Kathleen Allen *(Sec.)*
Principal(s):
John C. Fahs
Kathleen Allen

Computer Systems/Hardware:
IBM 36

Outside Service Firm(s):

Kellogg & Andelson*(Auditors)*
825 No. San Vicente Blvd.
West Hollywood, CA 90069
Tel.: 213-659-4477

Lincoln National Life Insurance Co.*(Group Insurance Broker/Consult)*
Los Angeles, CA

Allen, Matkins, Leck, Gamble & Mallory*(Legal Firm)*
515 So. Figueroa
Los Angeles, CA 90071

Wells Fargo Bank*(Major Banking Relationship)*
Buena Park, CA

Wells Fargo Bank*(Pension Manager)*
333 S. Grand
Los Angeles, CA 90071
Tel.: 213-253-6836

CALIFORNIA PRODUCTS CORP.
169 Waverly
Cambridge, MA 02139
Mailing Address:
P.O. Box 569
Cambridge, MA 02139
Tel.: 617-547-5300
Fax: 617-547-6934
Approx.Sls.: $35,000,000
Emp.: 150
Fiscal Year-end: 11/30/90
Paints, Tennis Court & Track Coating, Wood Stains
S.I.C.: 2851
J.S. Junkin *(Pres.)*
D.G. Lohr *(V.P. & Dir.-Mktg. & Sls.-Paints)*
A.F. Tucker *(V.P. & Dir.-Mktg. & Sls.-Sports Surfaces)*

Divisions:

California Paint Div. **(1)**
169 Waverly
Cambridge, MA 02139
Tel.: 617-547-5300
Fax: 617-547-6934
S.I.C.: 2851

Colorizer Paint Div. **(1)**
169 Waverly
Cambridge, MA 02139
Tel.: 617-547-5300
Fax: 617-547-6934
S.I.C.: 2851

Ox-Line Paint Div. **(1)**
169 Waverly
Cambridge, MA 02139
Tel.: 617-547-5300
Fax: 617-547-6934
S.I.C.: 2851

Recreational Products Div. **(1)**
169 Waverly
Cambridge, MA 02139
Tel.: 617-547-5300
Fax: 617-547-6934
S.I.C.: 2851

CALIFORNIA STATE LOTTERY
600 N. 10th St.
Sacramento, CA 95814
Tel.: 916-324-2025
Tel.: 916-324-2111
Year Founded: 1985
Approx.Sls.: $1,900,000,000
Emp.: 900
Fiscal Year-end: 6/30/91
State Lottery Tickets; Scratchers, Lotto, Little Lotto, Decco, Topper
S.I.C.: 7999
Dennis Malody *(Commission Chm.)*
James Barnett *(Chief Deputy Dir.)*
Sharon Sharp *(Exec. Dir.)*
Joanne Khimura-Hoffmann *(Dir.-Information Mngmt. System)*
Michael Kilpatrick *(Dir.-Sls.)*
Susan Kossack *(Dir.-Mktg.)*
Joanne McNabb *(Dir.-Pub. Affairs)*
Lew Ritter *(Dir.-Security)*
Dennis Sequeira *(Dir.-Fin. & Admin.)*
Roland Bowns *(Gen. Counsel)*
Susan S. Kossack *(Mgr.-Adv.)*
Elaine Chiao *(Mgr.-Personnel)*
Wayne Appleman *(Mgr.-Personnel Training & Devel.)*
Allen Edel *(Mgr.-Res. & Devel.)*
Diana Bosley *(Analyst)*

CALIFORNIA STRAWBERRY ADVISORY BOARD
41 Hangar Way
Watsonville, CA 95076
Mailing Address:
P.O. Box 269
Watsonville, CA 95077
Tel.: 408-724-1301
Fax: 408-724-5973
Approx.Sls.: $285,000,000
Emp.: 14
Fiscal Year-end: 1/31/91
Marketing of Fresh & Frozen Strawberries
S.I.C.: 8611
Dave Riggs *(Pres.)*
Cindy Butler *(Mktg. Coord.)*
Steve Tredi *(Dir.-Mktg.)*

THE CALKINS MANUFACTURING COMPANY
Spokane Industrial Park, Building 15
Spokane, WA 99216
Mailing Address:
P.O. Box 14527
Spokane, WA 99214
Tel.: 509-928-7420

Fax: 509-922-3268
Approx.Sls.: $24,000,000
Manufacture Farm Machinery, Boat Trailers; Wholesale & Retail Hydraulic Components
S.I.C.: 3523; 3799; 5085
James E. Calkins *(Chm. Bd. & Pres.)*
Charles C. Calkins *(V.P. & Sec.)*
Dwight L. Calkins, Jr. *(V.P.)*

Outside Service Firm(s):

Albert A. Stadmueller & Co.*(Auditors)*
Spokane, WA

Washington Trust Bank*(Major Banking Relationship)*
Spokane, WA

CALMARK INVESTMENT COMPANY
10866 Wilshire Blvd., 4th Fl.
Los Angeles, CA 90024
Tel.: 310-475-0505
Assets: $110,000,000
Liabilities: $95,000,000
Net Worth: $15,000,000
Approx.Sls.: $50,000,000
Emp.: 250
Fiscal Year-end: 1/31/91
Real Estate Development & Syndication; Investment Management Services
S.I.C.: 6512; 6513; 6552; 6282
Uri Sheinbaum *(Chm. Bd. & Pres.)*
John M. Huskey *(Pres.-Calmark Devel.)*
John L. Scott *(Sr. V.P. & Chief Fin. Officer)*
Principal(s):
Uri Sheinbaum
John M. Huskey

No. of U.S. Offices: 6

Computer Systems/Hardware:
MAI Basic 4; DEC; IBM PC

Outside Service Firm(s):

Arthur Dunn Co.*(Auditors)*
Los Angeles, CA

New York Life*(Group Insurer)*
New York, NY

Shearson Lehman Brothers, Inc.*(Investment Banker)*
Los Angeles, CA

Thompson McKinnon Securities*(Investment Banker)*
New York, NY

Troy & Gould*(Legal Firm)*
1801 Century Park East
Los Angeles, CA 90067
Tel.: 310-553-4441

Olympic National Bank*(Major Banking Relationship)*
Los Angeles, CA

Subsidiaries:

Calmark Asset Management Co. **(1)**
10866 Wilshire Blvd.
Los Angeles, CA 90024
Tel.: 310-475-0505 (100%)
Richard D. Gee *(V.P.)*
Matthew W. Smith *(V.P.)*
Michel Ward *(V.P.)*

Calmark Communities, Inc. **(1)**
11100 Santa Monica Blvd.
Los Angeles, CA 90025
Tel.: 310-312-1111
J.L. Michel *(Pres.)*

Calmark Development Corp. **(1)**
10866 Wilshire Blvd., 4th Fl.
Los Angeles, CA 90024
Tel.: 310-475-0505 (100%)
John M. Huskey *(Pres.)*
Michael A. Costa *(Sr. V.P.)*
John H. Kuhl *(Sr. V.P.-Construction & Engrng.)*
Judith C. Hansen *(V.P.)*
H. Scott Howell *(V.P.)*

Calmark Hospitality Systems **(1)**
5405 Morehouse Dr., #200
San Diego, CA 92121-4724
Tel.: 619-455-1800
Fax: 619-535-0396
Emp.: 60
Jeffrey Carlstead *(Pres.)*
James Johnson *(Exec. V.P.)*
Les Biggins *(V.P.-Fin.)*
MaryLou Drohr *(Dir.-Adv.)*

Calmark Properties, Inc. **(1)**
10866 Wilshire Blvd., 4th Fl.
Los Angeles, CA 90024
Tel.: 310-475-0505
S.I.C.: 6512; 6513; 6552; 6282
John M. Huskey *(Pres.)*

Calmark Realty Management, Inc. **(1)**
10866 Wilshire Blvd., 4th Fl.
Los Angeles, CA 90024
Tel.: 310-475-0505 (100%)
Joe E. Freeman *(Pres.)*
V. Tom Crockett *(V.P. & Eastern Reg. Mgr.)*

CALTEX PETROLEUM CORPORATION
125 E. John Carpenter Fwy.
Irving, TX 75062
Mailing Address:
P.O. Box 619500,
Dallas, TX 75261-9500
Tel.: 214-830-1000
Fax: 214-830-1078
Year Founded: 1937
Sales Range: $100-499 Million
Emp.: 9,100
Fiscal Year-end: 7/31/91
Oil Company with Operations Overseas
S.I.C.: 1389
Patrick J. Ward *(Chm. Bd., Pres. & Chief Exec. Officer)*
David J. Law-Smith *(Comptroller)*
A.W. Horan *(Mgr.-Benefits)*

Outside Service Firm(s):

KPMG Peat Marwick*(Auditors)*
1601 Elm St., Ste. 1600
Dallas, TX 75201
Tel.: 214-754-2000
Fax: 214-754-2297

Chemical Banking Corp.*(Pension Manager)*
277 Park Ave.
New York, NY 10041
Tel.: 212-310-6407
Fax: 212-310-4526

Equitable Life*(Pension Manager)*
1221 Ave. of the Americas
New York, NY 10022
Tel.: 212-382-8038
Fax: 212-382-8089

CALTROL, INC.
2011 E. Financial Way
Glendora, CA 91740
Tel.: 818-963-1010 **CA**
Fax: 818-914-8018
Year Founded: 1985
Wholesale Distributor For Controlling Instruments & Accessories
S.I.C.: 5084
Ben K. Rector *(Pres.)*
George Haslam *(Treas. & Sec.)*

Outside Service Firm(s):

Wells Fargo Bank*(Major Banking Relationship)*
Glendora, CA

CALUMET CONSTRUCTION CORPORATION
1247 169th St.
Hammond, IN 46324
Tel.: 219-844-9420 **IN**
Fax: 219-844-1022
Year Founded: 1946
Approx.Sls.: $70,000,000
Emp.: 450
Fiscal Year-end: 1/31/92
General Industrial, Commercial & Institutional Contractors, Construction Management, Design & Building Services
S.I.C.: 1542; 1622; 1623; 1629; 1771; 1791; 1794; 1796; 8741
Corporate Giving Program:
Solicitations Must Be Received in Writing via the U.S. Mails & They WillBe Acted On by the Board of Directors
Richard W. Gardner *(Chm. Bd.)*
Richard E. Gardner *(Pres.)*
J. Michael Schaum *(V.P., Sec. & Treas.)*
Joseph A. Simonetto *(V.P.-Mktg.)*

No. of U.S. Offices: 2

Computer Systems/Hardware:
Unix Lan Token Ring (IBM Compatable)

Outside Service Firm(s):

Geo. S. Olive & Company*(Auditors)*
Indianapolis, IN

Galvin, Galvin & Leeney*(Legal Firm)*
Hammond, IN

Mercantile National Bank of Indiana*(Major Banking Relationship)*
Hammond, IN

Subsidiary:

Calumet Contruction Corporation-Indianapolis Division **(1)**
5827 W. 74th St.
Indianapolis, IN 46278-1757
Tel.: 317-324-4300
Fax: 317-328-4301
General Industrial, Commerical & Institutional Management, Design & Building Services
S.I.C.: 1541; 1622; 1623; 1629; 1771; 1791; 1794; 1796; 8741
Albert B. Kabella *(Mgr.-Indianapolis Division)*

CALUMET PHOTOGRAPHIC, INC.
890 Supreme Dr.
Bensenville, IL 60106
Tel.: 708-860-7447
Fax: 708-860-7105
Approx.Sls.: $18,000,000
Emp.: 50
Fiscal Year-end: 12/31/90
Professional Cameras, Lenses & Accessories; Studio Lighting Equip.; Darkroom & Processing Equip.; Film, Paper & Chemicals
S.I.C.: 3827
K. Houde *(Pres.)*
David Gremp *(Dir.-Adv.)*

CAMALLOY, INC.
1960 N. Main St.
Washington, PA 15301
Tel.: 412-222-2022
Fax: 412-222-0336
Approx.Sls.: $30,000,000
Emp.: 75
Wholesale Metals, Stainless Steel, Coils, Sheets, Bars Plates, Construction Materials & Industrial Supplies
S.I.C.: 5051; 5039
W. Arthur Campbell *(Chm. Bd.)*
William M. Campbell *(Pres.)*
Edward J. Scier *(Treas. & Controller)*

Outside Service Firm(s):

Louis Plung & Co.*(Auditors)*
Pittsburgh, PA

Thorp, Reed & Armstrong*(Legal Firm)*
2900 Grant Bldg.
Pittsburgh, PA 15219
Tel.: 412-288-7711

Philadelphia National Bank*(Major Banking Relationship)*
P.O. Box 13834, Broad & Chestnut Streets
Philadelphia, PA 19101-7618
Tel.: 215-973-8327

CAMBIO EQUITIES CORP.
310 N. Harbor Blvd.
Fullerton, CA 92632
Tel.: 714-992-4620
Fax: 714-871-2715
Emp.: 206
Real Estate Investment & Syndication, Property Management & Commercial Real Estate Broker
S.I.C.: 6798; 6531; 6552
Allen Boerner *(Chm. Bd. & Pres.)*

No. of U.S. Offices: 2

CAMBRIDGE STREET METAL CO., INC.
500 Lincoln St.
Allston, MA 02134
Tel.: 617-254-7580
Cable: 06
Fax: 617-783-3100
Year Founded: 1963
Approx.Sls.: $215,000,000
Emp.: 550
Fiscal Year-end: 3/31/88
Wholesale Metals
S.I.C.: 5051
Harry Indursky *(Chm. Bd. & Pres.)*
Randy Raymond *(V.P.-Mktg.)*
Vincent P. Robinson *(V.P.)*
Donald E. Farquharson *(Treas.)*

No. of Mfg. Plants/Facilities: 25

Computer Systems/Hardware:
DEC VAX

Outside Service Firm(s):

Arthur Andersen & Co.*(Auditors)*
One Intl. Place, 100 Oliver St.
Boston, MA 02110
Tel.: 617-330-4000
Fax: 617-439-9731

Nathan Sallop*(Legal Firm)*
Boston, MA

State Street Bank & Trust Co.*(Major Banking Relationship)*
P.O. Box 366,
Boston, MA 02101
Tel.: 617-426-5523

CAMBRO MANUFACTURING COMPANY
7601 Clay Ave.
Huntington Beach, CA 92648
Mailing Address:
P.O. Box 2000
Huntington Beach, CA 92647-2000
Tel.: 714-848-1555
Tel.: 800-854-7631
Fax: 714-842-3430
Year Founded: 1949
Sales Range: $10-19 Million
Emp.: 500
Fiberglass & Plastic Serving Trays, Busboxes, Salad Bowls, Ice Caddies, Food Warmers, Banquet Covers, Food Storage Containers, Booster Seats, Plastic Dinnerware & Related Items
S.I.C.: 3083; 2656; 3089; 3229
Argyle Campbell *(Chm. Bd. & Pres.)*

Outside Service Firm(s):

Vilmure, Peeler & Boucher*(Auditors)*
Whittier, CA

Sanwa Bank*(Major Banking Relationship)*
Huntington Beach, CA

CAMELLIA FOOD STORES CO-OP INC.
1157 Production Rd.
Norfolk, VA 23502
Mailing Address:
P.O. Box 2320
Norfolk, VA 23501
Tel.: 804-855-3371 **VA**
Twx: 510-100-5155
Fax: 804-853-7405
Year Founded: 1938
Approx.Sls.: $195,000,000
Emp.: 400
Fiscal Year-end: 8/ 1/92
Wholesale Groceries, Dairy Products, Confectionery Products
S.I.C.: 5141; 5149; 5142; 5148; 5143; 5145
Manuel Saunders *(Chm. Bd.)*
Walter L. Grant *(Pres. & Chief Exec. Officer)*
Rick Bennett *(V.P.-Fin.)*
Jay Bhatt *(V.P.-Fin.)*
Jack Scott *(V.P.-Retail)*
Russell Chandler *(Dir.-Personnel)*
Mitch Moss *(Dir.-Data Processing)*
Bill Mull Jr. *(Dir.-Store Devel.)*
Douglas Parker *(Dir.-Pur. & Mktg.)*

Outside Service Firm(s):

KPMG Peat Marwick*(Auditors)*
2100 Dominion Tower, 999 Waterside Dr.
Norfolk, VA 23510
Tel.: 804-622-6533

Shuttleworth, Ruloff, Giordano & Kahle*(Legal Firm)*
Virginia Beach, VA

Subsidiary:

Be-Lo Markets Inc. **(1)**
4603 Cape Henry Ave.
Norfolk, VA 23513
Tel.: 804-855-1021
Fax: 804-855-3423
Approx.Sls.: $210,000,000
Emp.: 1,500
Fiscal Year-end: 8/ 1/92
Computer Systems/Hardware:
IBM
Retail Grocery Stores
S.I.C.: 5411
Manuel Saunders *(Chm. Bd.)*
Walter Grant *(Pres. & Chief Exec. Officer)*
Jay Bhatt *(V.P.-Misc. & Acctg.)*
James L. Harrel III *(V.P.)*
Mitch Moss *(Dir.-Data Processing)*
George Fisher *(Mgr.-Adv.)*
Dan Lazar *(Mgr.-Human Resources)*
David Roscoe *(Mgr.-Data Processing)*
Neil Phillips *(Mgr.-Retail)*

Camelot Communications Incorporated

CAMELOT COMMUNICATIONS, INC.
8140 Walnut Hill, Ste. 700
Dallas, TX 75231
Tel.: 214-373-6999
Fax: 214-373-6854
Year Founded: 1983
Approx.Billings: $80,000,000
Emp.: 31
Marketing & Media Services
T.L. Kalahar *(Chief Exec. Officer)*
J.S. Drake *(Exec. V.P.)*
B.J. Wurst *(Exec. V.P.)*
D.E. Judd *(Sr. V.P.)*
T.M. Hooke *(Sr. V.P.)*
D.E. Valentine *(Sr. V.P.)*
C.L. Smith *(V.P., Fin.)*
M.K. Massey *(V.P., Research)*

CAMELOT MUSIC, INC.
8000 Freedom Ave., NW
North Canton, OH 44720
Tel.: 216-494-2282
Fax: 216-494-0394
Approx.Sls.: $195,000,000
Emp.: 3,190
Wholesale Prerecorded Music, Sound Video & Audio Tapes, Records & Associated Accessory Items
S.I.C.: 5099
Paul David *(Pres. & Chief Exec. Officer)*
Jack Rogers *(Chief Fin. Officer)*
James E. Bonk *(Exec. V.P. & Chief Oper. Officer)*
Joseph R. Bressi *(Sr. V.P.-Pur. & Mktg.)*
Vern V. Benke *(V.P.-Southern Div. Opers.)*
Daniel A. Denino *(V.P.-Admin.)*
Lewis Garrett *(V.P.-Pur.)*
Gerry M. Gladieux *(V.P.-Adv.)*
Larry J. Hodgson *(V.P.-Northern Div. Opers.)*
William T. Rees *(V.P.-Opers.)*
James L. Sage *(V.P.-Data Processing)*

Outside Service Firm(s):

Ernst & Young*(Auditors)*
One Cascade Plaza
Akron, OH 44308

Stark & Knoll*(Legal Firm)*
Akron, OH

AmeriTrust Company, N.A.*(Major Banking Relationship)*
P.O. Box 5937, 900 Euclid Ave.
Cleveland, OH 44101-0937

WALTER F. CAMERON ADVERTISING INC.
275 Broad Hollow Rd.
Melville, NY 11747
Tel.: 516-752-1515
Fax: 516-752-1525
Year Founded: 1977
Approx.Billings: $43,000,000
Emp.: 40
Industrial, Financial, Real Estate, Automotive & Retail
Walter F. Cameron *(Pres.)*
Joseph J. Cameron, III *(V.P.)*
Mark Preiser *(V.P.)*

CAMERON & BARKLEY COMPANY, INC.
2864 Azalea Dr.
Charleston Heights, SC 29411
Mailing Address:
P.O. Box 10067
Charleston Heights, SC 29411
Tel.: 803-745-2400
Fax: 803-745-2490
Approx.Sls.: $190,000,000
Emp.: 950
Industrial Supplies; Electrical Apparatus & Equipment
S.I.C.: 5085; 5063
Rufus C. Barkley, Jr. *(Chm. Bd.)*
M. Joel Bateman *(Chief Exec. Officer)*
James R. Warren *(Pres.)*
William T. Tamsburg *(V.P.)*
Robert L. Weaver *(V.P. & Controller)*
J. Randall Bishop *(Sec. & Treas.)*

Outside Service Firm(s):

Ernst & Young*(Auditors)*
C & S Bank Tower, Two Shelter Centre, Ste. 800
Greenville, SC 29603

Sinkler & Boyd*(Legal Firm)*
P.O. Box 1889,
Columbia, SC 29211

South Carolina National Bank*(Major Banking Relationship)*
1426 Main St.
Columbia, SC 29226
Tel.: 803-765-3000
Fax: 803-765-4333

CAMERON-NEWELL ADVERTISING, INC.
15025 Oxnard St., Ste. 200
Van Nuys, CA 91411-2623
Tel.: 818-780-0194
Tel.: 800-443-0817
Fax: 818-780-1342
Year Founded: 1986
Approx.Billings: $23,000,000
Emp.: 45
Recruitment Adv.
Byron B. Newell *(Pres.)*
William C. Newell *(Exec. V.P.)*
Jeffrey Levin *(Dir., Bus. Devel.)*

CAMILLUS CUTLERY CO.
54 Main St.
Camillus, NY 13031
Tel.: 315-672-8111
Fax: 315-672-8832
Year Founded: 1876
Approx.Sls.: $12,000,000
Emp.: 241
Fiscal Year-end: 5/31/91

Export
Pocket Knives, Hunting & Kitchen Knives
S.I.C.: 3421
James W. Furgal *(Pres.)*
Angie C. Williams *(V.P. & Sec.)*
Paul A. Cappon *(V.P. & Treas.)*
Robert Stumpf *(Mktg. Mgr.)*
Toni Zona *(Mktg. Asst.)*

CAMINO REAL CHEVROLET
2401 S. Atlantic Blvd.
Monterey Park, CA 91754
Tel.: 213-264-3050 **CA**
Fax: 213-266-3803
Year Founded: 1976
Approx.Sls.: $26,000,000
Emp.: 97
Retail Sales of New & Used Automobiles
S.I.C.: 5511
Michael Hernandez, Jr. *(V.P.)*
Helen Thomas *(Treas. & Sec.)*

CAMOSY, INC.
Rt. 41 & Stateline Rd.
Russell, IL 60075
Mailing Address:
P.O. Box 1070
Waukegan, IL 60079
Tel.: 708-395-6800 **WI**
Fax: 708-395-6891
Year Founded: 1910
Assets: $18,900,000
Liabilities: $15,600,000
Net Worth: $3,300,000
Approx.Sls.: $50,000,000
Emp.: 150
Fiscal Year-end: 9/30/91
Nonresidential Construction
S.I.C.: 1542
Raymond J. Camosy *(Pres. & Chief Exec. Officer)*
Michael Rankin *(Sr. V.P.)*
Lyle Ehlers *(Sr. V.P.)*
John P. Camosy *(V.P.)*
Gary Ladovsa *(V.P.)*
Joseph W. Decono *(V.P.)*
Joseph E. Ferrano, Jr. *(V.P.)*

Outside Service Firm(s):

Clifton Gunderson*(Auditors)*
Racine, WI

First National Bank*(Major Banking Relationship)*
Kenosha, WI

CAMP DRESSER & MCKEE INC.
One Cambridge Center
Cambridge, MA 02142
Tel.: 617-621-8181 **MA**
Telex: 211967
Fax: 617-577-7501
Year Founded: 1947
Approx.Sls.: $220,000,000
Emp.: 2,000
Water Supply Transmission, Treatment & Distribution; Wastewater & Stormwater Collection, Treatment & Disposal; Solid & Hazardous Waste Management; Drainage, Flood Control & Irrigation; Water Resource Planning; Air Pollution Control; Surface Water & Groundwater Hydrology; Industrial Environmental Systems
S.I.C.: 8711
Robert C. Marini *(Chm. Bd. & Chief Exec. Officer)*
Thomas D. Furman, Jr. *(Pres. & Chief Oper. Officer)*
Paul G. Camell *(Sr. V.P.-Fin. & Dir.-Investor Rels.)*
Peter F. Palmisano *(V.P., Computer & Info. Resources)*
F. Peter Fairchild *(V.P.-Human Resources)*
Bruce J. Purdy *(V.P.)*
Richard M. Doherty *(Gen. Counsel)*
Paul Sorensen *(Dir.-Corp. Communications)*

No. of U.S. Offices: 50
No. of Foreign Offices: 10

Outside Service Firm(s):

Coopers & Lybrand*(Auditors)*
1 Post Office Square
Boston, MA 02110
Tel.: 617-574-5000
Fax: 617-345-0398

Bingham, Dana & Gould*(Legal Firm)*
150 Federal St.
Boston, MA 02110
Tel.: 617-951-8000
Fax: 617-951-8736

Shawmut Bank*(Major Banking Relationship)*
1 Federal St.
Boston, MA 02110
Tel.: 617-292-3715

Subsidiaries:

CDM Federal Programs Corporation **(1)**
13135 Lee Jackson Memorial Hwy. Ste. 200
Fairfax, VA 22033
Tel.: 703-968-0900
Emp.: 250
FPC Provides Environmental Program Management Services to Agencies and Entities of the Federal Government.
S.I.C.: 8711
Jonathan G. Curtis *(Pres.)*

Camp Dresser & McKee International Inc. **(1)**
One Cambridge Center
Cambridge, MA 02142
Tel.: 617-621-8181
Fax: 617-577-7504
Environmental Engineering and Related Services to International Clients in Public and Private Sector
S.I.C.: 8711
W. Dennis Moran *(Pres.)*

JOHN J. CAMPBELL CO., INC.
6012 Resources Dr.
Memphis, TN 38134
Tel.: 901-372-8400 **TN**
Fax: 901-372-8404
Year Founded: 1971
Approx.Sls.: $10,000,000
Emp.: 150
Roofing Contractor
S.I.C.: 1761
John J. Campbell, III *(Chm. Bd. & Pres.)*

Randy Fisher *(V.P.-Sls.)*
Jack Scholl *(V.P.)*
Carl Drennan *(V.P.)*
Lynda Brandon *(Sec. & Treas.)*

Outside Service Firm(s):

Richard R. Callcott*(Auditors)*
Memphis, TN

CAMPBELL CONSTRUCTION CO.
2120 20th St.
Sacramento, CA 95818
Tel.: 916-454-5454
Fax: 916-456-2881
Year Founded: 1906
Approx.Sls.: $60,000,000
Emp.: 200
Building Construction; General Contractor
S.I.C.: 1542
William A. Campbell *(Chm. Bd.)*
Robert C. McLean *(Pres.)*
Herbert J. Mittler *(V.P.-Estimating)*
Thomas E. Worth *(V.P.-Construction)*
John C. Lenk *(Sec. & Treas.)*

Outside Service Firm(s):

Diepenbrock, Wulff, Plant & Hannegan*(Legal Firm)*
Sacramento, CA

Wells Fargo Bank*(Major Banking Relationship)*
420 Montgomery St.
San Francisco, CA 94104

THE CAMPBELL GROUP
ADVERTISING

THE CAMPBELL GROUP
326 N. Charles St., 2nd Floor
Baltimore, MD 21201
Tel.: 301-547-0600
Year Founded: 1984
Approx.Billings: $19,225,000
Emp.: 24
Hotel/Travel Industry
Robert M. Campbell *(Chm. Bd. & Pres.)*
Lisa M. Schuler *(V.P., Production)*
Mark Liebowitz *(Controller)*

CAMPBELL OIL CO.
611 S. Erie
Massillon, OH 44646
Mailing Address:
P.O. Box 558
Massillon, OH 44648
Tel.: 216-833-8555 **OH**
Fax: 216-833-1043
Year Founded: 1939
Assets: $13,266,088
Earnings: $468,808
Liabilities: $5,911,245
Net Worth: $7,354,843
Approx.Sls.: $63,540,776
Emp.: 64
Fiscal Year-end: 12/31/90
Wholesale/Retail of All Petroleum Products, Including Home Heating Oil; Distributor for Tires & Other Auto Accessories
S.I.C.: 5171; 5172; 5014; 7538
Chester K. Campbell *(Chm. Bd.)*
Jack E. Decker *(Pres. & Chief Exec. Officer)*
Doug Donavan *(Chief Fin. & Info. Officer, Treas., Controller & Sec.)*
Delmar Phillips *(V.P. & Chief Oper. Officer)*
Principal(s):
Chester K. Campbell
No. of Mfg. Plants/Facilities: 3
No. of U.S. Offices: 3

Computer Systems/Hardware:
NCR Tower 32/700

Outside Service Firm(s):

Swallen, Lawhun, Hubbard, Abraham, Inc.*(Auditors)*
Massillon, OH

Federated Mutual Insurance Co.*(Commercial Insurance Carrier)*
Owatonna, MN

Blue Cross & Blue Shield of Northern Ohio*(Group Insurer)*
2060 E. 9th St.
Cleveland, OH 44115
Tel.: 216-687-7000

Society National Bank*(Investment Banker)*
900 Euclid Ave., P.O. Box 6477
Cleveland, OH 44101-6477
Tel.: 216-737-5000
Fax: 216-566-8947

Richard F. Maier*(Legal Firm)*
Massillon, OH

Society National Bank*(Major Banking Relationship)*
900 Euclid Ave., P.O. Box 6477
Cleveland, OH 44101-6477
Tel.: 216-737-5000
Fax: 216-566-8947

The Central Trust Company, N.A.*(Major Banking Relationship)*
Canton, OH

Metropolitan Life Insurance Co.*(Pension Manager)*
One Madison Ave.
New York, NY 10010-3690
Tel.: 215-578-9292

CAMPBELL AND WAGMAN
10960 Wilshire Blvd., Ste. 2300
Los Angeles, CA 90024
Tel.: 310-444-3200
Fax: 310-444-3244
Year Founded: 1986
Approx.Billings: $28,300,000
Emp.: 29
Michael Wagman *(Chm. Bd. & Creative Dir.)*
Craig Campbell *(Pres. & New Bus. Contact)*
Frank Wisinski *(Exec. V.P., Chief Fin. Officer)*

CAMPING WORLD HOLDINGS, INC.
3 Springs Rd.
Bowling Green, KY 42102
Mailing Address:
P.O. Box 90018
Bowling Green, KY 42102
Tel.: 502-781-2718 **KY**
Fax: 502-781-2775
Year Founded: 1968
Emp.: 475
Holding Company; Camping Equipment & Supplies
S.I.C.: 5941; 5091
David Garvin *(Chm. Bd.)*
Thomas Donnally *(Pres.)*
William Johnson *(Exec. V.P. & Chief Fin. Officer)*
Murray Coker *(V.P.)*
Rick Matar *(V.P.)*
James Schumn *(V.P.)*
Steve Snodgrass *(V.P.)*
Cathy Beard *(Adv. Mgr.)*

Outside Service Firm(s):

Deloitte & Touche*(Auditors)*
Bowling Green, KY

First Interstate Bank*(Major Banking Relationship)*
P.O. Box 53441,
Phoenix, AZ 85072-3441
Tel.: 602-229-4049

Subsidiary:

Camping World, Inc. **(1)**
3 Springs Rd.
Bowling Green, KY 42101
Tel.: 502-781-2718
Fax: 502-781-3968
Camping Equipment & Supplies
S.I.C.: 5941; 5091
Thomas Donnally *(Pres.)*

CAMPMOR INC.
810 St. Hwy. Route #17 N.
Paramus, NJ 07653
Mailing Address:
P.O. Box 999
Paramus, NJ 07653
Tel.: 201-445-5000
Year Founded: 1977
Approx.Sls.: $165,000,000
Emp.: 100
Fiscal Year-end: 7/31/89
Retail & Mail Order Equipment for Camping, Back-Packing, Bike Touring, Running & Mountain Climbing
S.I.C.: 5961; 5941
Morton Jay *(Chm. Bd.)*
Dan Jay *(Pres., Chief Exec. & Chief Fin. Officer)*

Computer Systems/Hardware:
Prime 2650

Outside Service Firm(s):

Hartford Life Insurance Co.*(Commercial Insurance Carrier)*
Hartford, CT 06104-2999

Equitable Real Estate Investment Managment Inc.*(Group Insurer)*
3414 Peachtree Rd. N.E.
Atlanta, GA 30326-1162

First Fidelity Bank, N.A.*(Major Banking Relationship)*
Oradell, NJ

CANAL INSURANCE CO.
417 E. North St.
Greenville, SC 29601
Mailing Address:
P.O. Box 7,
Greenville, SC 29602
Tel.: 803-242-5365
Year Founded: 1939
Assets: $307,452,335
Liabilities: $197,879,972
Net Worth: $109,572,363
Sales Range: $100-499 Million
Emp.: 150
Fiscal Year-end: 3/31/92
Property & Casualty Insurance
S.I.C.: 6331
T.J. Mims *(Pres., Chief Exec. & Chief Oper. Officer)*
Gordon K. Rodgers *(Sr. V.P.-Agency)*
William R. Timmons, Jr. *(Grp. V.P. & Treas.)*
Sr. C. Dunn *(V.P.-Legal Service)*
Doris W. Hunt *(V.P.-Underwriting)*
Betty J. Sheppard *(V.P.-Admin. & Dir.-Personnel)*
F.M. Timmons, Jr. *(V.P.-Claims)*
Charles M. Timmons *(V.P. & Treas.)*
William R. Timmons III *(V.P.-Investments)*
B.J. McMurry *(Controller)*

No. of U.S. Offices: 1

Outside Service Firm(s):

Harris, McMillan, Hudgins & Co.*(Auditors)*
Greenville, SC

Leatherwood, Walker, Todd & Mann*(Legal Firm)*
P.O. Box 2248
Greenville, SC 29602
Tel.: 803-242-6440

South Carolina National Bank*(Major Banking Relationship)*
7515 Northside Dr.
Greenville, SC
Tel.: 803-577-8280

Subsidiary:

Canal Indemnity Company **(1)**
P.O. Box 7
Greenville, SC 29602
Tel.: 803-242-5365
Emp.: 150
Auto Insurance
S.I.C.: 6331
T.J. Mims *(Pres.)*

D. CANALE FOOD SERVICES, INC.
7 W. George Ave.
Memphis, TN 38101
Tel.: 901-525-6811
Fax: 901-526-6923
Sales Range: $20-39 Million
Emp.: 160
Wholesale Frozen & Dry Foods for Restaurant & Institutional Use; Supplier & Distributor of Specialty Chemicals Pertaining to Food Industry
S.I.C.: 5142
John D. Canale *(Pres.)*
Chris W. Canale *(Treas.)*

Outside Service Firm(s):

Ernst & Young*(Auditors)*
1400 One Commerce Sq.
Memphis, TN 38103

CANBERRA INDUSTRIES, INC.
One State St.
Meriden, CT 06450
Tel.: 203-238-2351
Fax: 203-235-1347 (Intl.)
Sales Range: $100-499 Million
Emp.: 1,100
Fiscal Year-end: 12/31/91
Import Export
Mfr. of Nuclear Instruments
S.I.C.: 3571
Emery G. Olcott *(Pres. & Chief Exec. Officer)*
Richard McKernan *(Sr. V.P.)*
Robert Kane *(V.P. & Treas.)*
George Serrano *(V.P. & Sec.)*
Benjamin Campagnuolo *(V.P.-Intl.)*
Jerome E. Grader *(V.P.)*
Gerhard H. Kremer *(V.P.)*
Francoise Laveissiere *(V.P.)*
Orren K. Tench *(V.P.)*
Kim Rockwell *(Asst. To Pres.)*

Outside Service Firm(s):

Arthur Andersen & Co.*(Auditors)*
One Financial Plaza
Hartford, CT 06103
Tel.: 203-280-0649
Fax: 203-280-0898

Day, Berry & Howard*(Legal Firm)*
185 Asylum St.
Hartford, CT 06103-3499
Tel.: 203-275-0100
Fax: 203-275-0343

Units:

Nuclear Data Systems **(1)**
150 Spring Lake Dr.
Itasca, IL 60143-2096
Tel.: 708-285-3000
Telex: 687-1441
Fax: 708-884-4783
Computer-Based Multichannel Analyzers Used in Nuclear Physics, Nuclear Power & Medical Instrumentation
S.I.C.: 3672; 3699; 3845; 3829
Gerald W. Gaughran *(Exec. V.P. & Gen. Mgr.)*

Packard Instrument Co., Inc. **(1)**
One State St.
Meriden, CT 06450
Tel.: 203-238-2351
Tel.: 800-323-1891
Telex: 643251
Fax: 203-235-1347

Canberra Industries, Inc.—(Continued)

Approx.Sls.: $60,000,000
Emp.: 500
Fiscal Year-end: 12/31/91
Export
Mfr. of Nuclear Instruments, Chemicals & Supplies; Photon Detection Systems
S.I.C.: 3829
R.T. McKernan *(Pres.)*
S. van Cauter *(Dir.-Mktg.)*
R. Tyska *(Personnel Mgr.)*
Betsy A. Walsh *(Mgr.-Mktg. Support)*

Subsidiary:

Radiomatic Instruments **(1)**
One State St.
Meriden, CT 06450
Tel.: 203-238-2351

CANDLE CORPORATION
2425 Olympic Blvd.
Santa Monica, CA 90404
Tel.: 310-207-1400 **CA**
Fax: 310-442-4048
Year Founded: 1977
Approx.Sls.: $169,000,000
Emp.: 950
Export
Performance-Monitoring Software for IBM Mainframes
S.I.C.: 7372
Aubrey G. Chernick *(Chm. Bd. & Chief Exec. Officer)*
Merritt Lutz *(Pres. & Chief Oper. Officer)*
Donald Mellert *(Chief Fin. Officer)*
Lynn Anderson *(V.P.-Admin/Human Resources)*
Alex Kuli *(V.P.-Worldwide Sls.)*
Eric Duistermars *(Mgr.-Mktg. Communications)*
Jan Gruenwald *(Mgr.-Pub. Rels.)*
Mary Lewis *(Mgr.-Pur.)*
Paul Longstreet *(Mgr.-Compensation & Benefits)*
Linda Beunett *(Dir.-Management Information Systems)*
Kathy Cross *(Dir.-Telecommunications)*
Debra Danko *(Dir.-Sls & Bus. Support)*
Bonnie MacNeil *(Dir.-Corp. H.R.)*
Kathy Taylor *(Dir.-Mktg. Services)*
Art Weber *(Dir.-Mergers & Aquisitions)*
Douglas Weir *(Dir.-Res. & Devel.)*
Bobbie Johnson *(Corp. Librarian & Dir.-Mktg. Res.)*
Principal(s):
Aubrey G. Chernick

No. of U.S. Offices: 14
No. of Foreign Offices: 18

Outside Service Firm(s):

Union Bank*(Major Banking Relationship)*
3810 Wilshire Blvd.
Los Angeles, CA 90010
Tel.: 213-480-6566

CANDLE CORPORATION OF AMERICA
627 Bay Shore Dr.
Oshkosh, WI 54901
Tel.: 414-231-9620
Mfr. of Candles & Religious Goods
S.I.C.: 3999
Robert Goergen *(Chm. Bd.)*
Thomas K. Kreilick *(Pres.)*
Howard Rose *(V.P.-Fin.)*
James Friese *(V.P.)*
Larry Powell *(V.P.-Mfg.)*
Laurie A. Schmitt *(V.P.-Consumer Mktg.)*
Joseph Kelleher *(Treas.)*
Deloris Claycomb *(Mgr.-Human Resources)*

A. J. CANFIELD CO.
50 E. 89th Place
Chicago, IL 60619
Tel.: 312-483-7000
Fax: 312-483-9312
Year Founded: 1924
Approx.Sls.: $50,000,000
Emp.: 300
Fiscal Year-end: 12/31/90
Export
Mfr. of Canfield Beverages
S.I.C.: 2086
Arthur Canfield, Sr. *(Chm. Bd.)*
Arthur J. Canfield III *(Pres.)*
Frank G. Westerman *(Exec. V.P.)*
Alan B. Canfield *(Sr. V.P.)*
Art Kolk *(V.P.-Production)*
Manny Wesber *(V.P.-Res. & Devel.)*
Terry Glynn *(Treas. & Sec.)*
Bill Zilligen *(Mgr.-Mktg.)*
Jolan Young *(Office Mgr.)*
Principal(s):
Arthur Canfield, Sr.

Computer Systems/Hardware:
DEC VAX 11750

Outside Service Firm(s):

Connecticut General Life Insurance Co.*(Group Insurer)*
P.O. Box 2975,
Hartford, CT 06104
Tel.: 203-726-6000

The Northern Trust Co.*(Major Banking Relationship)*
50 S. LaSalle St.
Chicago, IL 60675
Tel.: 312-630-6000
Fax: 312-630-6516

CANNON
2170 Whitehaven Rd.
Grand Island, NY 14072
Tel.: 716-773-6800 **NY**
Fax: 716-773-5909
Year Founded: 1945
Sales Range: $20-39 Million
Emp.: 300
Engineering & Architectural Services, Interior Design, Construction Management
S.I.C.: 8711; 8712; 8741
John D. Cannon *(Chm.)*
Mark R. Mendell *(Pres.)*
Gary R. Miller *(Chief Exec. Officer)*
Paul F. Fritton *(Dir.-Personnel)*

No. of U.S. Offices: 5

Outside Service Firm(s):

Falk & Seimer*(Legal Firm)*
Buffalo, NY

Manufacturers & Traders Trust Company*(Major Banking Relationship)*
1 M & T Plaza
Buffalo, NY 14240
Tel.: 716-842-4200

CANTON DROP FORGE
4575 Southway St. S.W.
Canton, OH 44706
Mailing Address:
P.O. Box 6902
Canton, OH 44706
Tel.: 216-477-4511
Telex: 98-3428
Twx: 810-432-9084
Fax: 216-477-2046
Approx.Sls.: $40,000,000
Emp.: 450
Fiscal Year-end: 12/31/90
Export
Design, Manufacture & Sell Closed Die Forgings
S.I.C.: 3462; 3463
William K. Cordier *(Chm. Bd.)*
Jerome P. Bressanelli *(Pres.)*
John M. Motsay *(V.P.-Sls. & Mktg.)*
Larry Stalnaker *(V.P.-Mfg. & Engrng.)*
Paul V. Schario *(Controller)*

Computer Systems/Hardware:
IBM System 36

Outside Service Firm(s):

Ernst & Young*(Auditors)*
One Cascade Plaza
Akron, OH 44308

National City Bank*(Major Banking Relationship)*
Akron, OH

CAPELETTI BROS., INC.
16401 NW 58 Ave.
Miami Lakes, FL 33014
Tel.: 305-823-9500
Fax: 305-823-9500, Ext. 2211
Approx.Sls.: $55,500,000
Emp.: 400
Fiscal Year-end: 8/31/88
Heavy Construction Contractor
S.I.C.: 1622
Joe Capeletti *(Pres.)*
Dottie C. Meador *(V.P.)*
Orman L. Kitchens *(Treas. & Controller)*
Walter R. Greenwell *(Sec.)*

Outside Service Firm(s):

Coopers & Lybrand*(Auditors)*
5959 Blue Lagoon Dr.
Miami, FL 33126
Tel.: 305-263-8200

Barnett Bank of South Florida*(Major Banking Relationship)*
Miami, FL

CAPENER, MATTHEWS & WALCHER

CAPENER, MATTHEWS & WALCHER
620 C St., 6th Fl.
San Diego, CA 92101
Tel.: 619-238-8500
Fax: 619-238-8505
Year Founded: 1977
Approx.Billings: $15,500,000
Emp.: 30
Leonard S. Matthews *(Chm., Exec. Comm.)*
James Matthews *(Chm. Bd. & Chief Exec. Officer)*
Don R. Capener *(Pres., Adv.)*
Laura Walcher *(Pres., Pub. Rels. Div.)*
Janeen Jensen *(Controller)*

CAPITAL BANCORP
1221 Brickell Ave.
Miami, FL 33131
Tel.: 305-536-1500 **FL**
Year Founded: 1982
Assets: $1,135,335,000
Earnings: $1,983,000
Liabilities: $1,073,294,000
Net Worth: $62,041,000
Approx.Income: $120,012,000
Fiscal Year-end: 12/31/90
Bank Holding Company; Financial Services
S.I.C.: 6712
Corporate Giving Program: Proposals *to be Submitted in Writing to the* Marketing Director
Abel Holtz *(Chm. Bd. & Pres.)*
Simon Portnoy *(Exec. V.P.)*
Alex Halberstein *(Exec. V.P.-Intl.)*
Joann Makris *(Sr. V.P.-Mktg.)*
Michael Paul *(Sr. V.P.-Real Estate)*
Thomas J. Flood *(Sr. V.P.)*
John W. Kiefer *(Sr. V.P.)*
Daniel M. Holtz *(Sr. V.P.)*
David Promoff *(Sr. V.P.)*
Rebecca Hope Fisher *(V.P. & Corp. Counsel)*
Deborah Rocco *(V.P. & Asst. Sec.)*
James Stanton *(V.P. & Human Resources)*
Patricia Carroll *(V.P.-Personnel Training & Devel.)*
Richard Granger *(V.P.-Data Processing)*
William J. Brosnan *(V.P.)*
Charles F. Koehler *(V.P.)*
Javier J. Holtz *(V.P.)*
Stephen N. Ashman *(Treas.)*
Fana Holtz *(Sec.)*
Lucious T. Harris *(Asst. Treas.)*
Ralph Saxe *(Dir.-Telecommunications)*

Banking Subsidiary:

Capital Bank **(1)**
1221 Brickell Ave
Miami, FL 33131
Tel.: 305-536-1500 (100%)
Fax: 305-374-0409
Approx.Sls.: $120,224,000
Emp.: 700
S.I.C.: 6022
Abel Holtz *(Chm. & Pres.)*
Alex Halberstein *(Vice Chm.)*
Stephen Ashman *(Exec. V.P. & Chief Fin. Officer)*
Joann Makris *(Sr. V.P.-Mktg.)*
David DiBella *(Asst. Cashier)*

Non-Banking Subsidiary:

Capital Factors, Inc. **(1)**
1799 W. Oakland Park Blvd.
Fort Lauderdale, FL 33311
Tel.: 305-730-2900 (100%)
Telex: 264245 (CAPBK UR)
Fax: 305-480-9025
Telecopier: (305) 245-0195
Approx.Sls.: $461,740,000
Emp.: 46
Factoring
S.I.C.: 1541
Abel Holtz *(Chm. Bd.)*
John Kiefer *(Pres.)*

Affiliated Banks:

Capital Bank of California **(1)**
1875 Century Park E.
Los Angeles, CA 90067
Tel.: 310-550-0444 (4.9%)
Telex: 216548 (CAPBK CA)
Fax: 310-278-3250
Approx.Assets: $272,871,282
Emp.: 188
Fiscal Year-end: 12/31/90
Main Office
S.I.C.: 6022
Daniel M. Holtz *(Pres.)*
Michael D. Moore *(Exec. V.P. & Chief Oper. Officer)*
Charles Boyce *(Sr. V.P. & Chief Fin. Officer)*
Lonnie K. Umbenhower *(Sr. V.P.-Sls.)*
Debra-Lynne Solis *(V.P. & Mktg. Dir.)*

Capital Bank, N.A. **(1)**
815 Connecticut Ave., N.W.
Washington, DC 20006
Tel.: 202-872-1470 (4.9%)
Fax: 202-296-1077
Approx.Assets: $97,710,378
Emp.: 44
Main Office
S.I.C.: 6021
Abel Holtz *(Chm. Bd.)*
Richard B. Stone *(Vice Chm.)*
Howard G. Dymond *(Pres.)*
Richard B. Stone *(Chief Oper. Officer)*
Charles F. Koehler *(Exec. V.P.-Opers.)*
Manuel Sanchez *(V.P. & Chief Fin. Officer)*
Owen Frisby *(V.P.-Mktg.)*

CAPITAL CITY PRESS, INC.
Airport Rd.
Montpelier, VT 05602
Tel.: 802-223-5207
Fax: 802-223-1194
Approx.Sls.: $14,000,000
Emp.: 175
Commercial Lithographic Printing
S.I.C.: 2752
Richard E. Hearn *(Chm. Bd.)*
Christopher R. Johnson *(Pres.)*
William Parker *(Sls. Admin.)*
Wilbur Bliss *(Dir.-Pur.)*
Ron Craig *(Dir.-Engrng.)*
Chet Moulton *(Plant Mgr.)*

Outside Service Firm(s):

Bank Of Vermont*(Major Banking Relationship)*
Montpelier, VT

CAPITAL CONTROLS COMPANY INC.
(Sub. of Severn Trent, Birmingham, UK)
3000 Advance Lane
Colmar, PA 18915
Mailing Address:
P.O. Box 211,
Colmar, PA 18915
Tel.: 215-822-2901
Tel.: 800-523-2553 **PA**
Telex: 6851074 CAPCO UW
Fax: 215-822-8640
Year Founded: 1960
Assets: $23,322,000
Liabilities: $18,059,000
Net Worth: $5,263,000
Approx.Sls.: $26,892,000
Emp.: 131
Fiscal Year-end: 3/31/92
Export
Manufacture Water Disinfection Equipment
S.I.C.: 3824
Charles Reading *(Pres.)*
Dean Hertert *(V.P.-Mktg.)*
John Krieble *(V.P.-Opers. & Sec.)*
Joe Mellody *(Treas.)*
S. Oliver *(Dir.-Data Processing)*
Scott Biondi *(Mgr.-Sls. U.S.)*
Louis D'Agostino *(Mgr.-Mktg.)*
Bob Ekelbury *(Mgr.-Quality Control)*
H. Gupfinger *(Mgr.-Intl.)*
B. Jones *(Mgr.-Res. & Devel.)*
R. Mitman *(Mgr.-Plng. (Meetings))*
P.L. Spencer *(Mgr.-Adv.)*
C. Weidmann *(Mgr.-Pur.)*

No. of Mfg. Plants/Facilities: 2
No. of U.S. Offices: 3
No. of Foreign Offices: 1

Computer Systems/Hardware:
IBM AS/400

Outside Service Firm(s):

Coopers & Lybrand*(Auditors)*
2400 Eleven Penn Center
Philadelphia, PA 19103-2962
Tel.: 215-963-8000

Meridian Bank*(Commercial Insurance Carrier)*
Malvern, PA

Montgomery, McCracken, Walker & Rhoads*(Legal Firm)*
3 Parkway
Philadelphia, PA 19103
Tel.: 215-563-0650

Subsidiary:

Capital Controls Ltd. **(1)**
Sittingbourne Indus. Park, Crown Quay Lane
Sittingbourne, Kent ME10 3JG, United Kingdom
Tel.: 0795 476241
Telex: 965636 CAPCO G
Fax: 0795 479052
S.I.C.: 3824

CAPITAL DEVELOPMENT CO.
691 Sleater-Kinney Rd. S.E., Ste. 100
Lacey, WA 98503
Tel.: 206-491-6850
Fax: 206-459-8747
Approx.Sls.: $35,000,000
Emp.: 200
Commercial Construction; Leasing Property Management; General Contracting & Heavy Construction; Timber Operations
S.I.C.: 1541; 0811; 1542; 1629; 6531
William A. Ehlers *(Chm. Bd.)*
Robert L. Blume *(Pres. & Chief Exec. Officer)*
Gary A. Blume *(Exec. V.P.)*
Burdette Chapel *(Sr. V.P.)*
John Donaldson *(Sr. V.P.)*
G. Melvin Hastings *(Sr. V.P. & Controller)*

Computer Systems/Hardware:
IBM

Outside Service Firm(s):

Vadman, Dimon & Briggs*(Auditors)*
Olympia, WA

Security Pacific National Bank*(Major Banking Relationship)*
Lacey, WA

CAPITAL ELECTRIC GROUP, INC.
P.O. Box 16248,
Phoenix, AZ 85011
Tel.: 602-264-6177 **AZ**
Fax: 602-366-5342
Year Founded: 1961
Assets: $6,924,054
Liabilities: $4,075,308
Net Worth: $2,848,746
Approx.Sls.: $24,000,000
Emp.: 80
Fiscal Year-end: 11/30/91
Distributor of Wire, Pipe, Boxes, Fixtures & Lamps
S.I.C.: 5063
Joann K. Jones *(Chm. Bd.)*
Michael E. Jones *(Pres. & Chief Oper. Officer)*
Tim Collins *(Chief Fin. Officer, Treas. & Controller)*
Terry D. Rogers *(Exec. V.P.)*
Craig Caldwell *(Dir.-Data Processing)*
Jeff Crosby *(Mgr.-Sls.)*
Chuck Hearns *(Mgr.-Pur.)*
John Godson *(Gen. Counsel)*
Principal(s):
Joann K. Jones
Michael E. Jones

No. of U.S. Offices: 6

Outside Service Firm(s):

Collins & Collins*(Auditors)*
Phoenix, AZ

Security Pacific National Bank*(Major Banking Relationship)*
Phoenix, AZ

Affiliate:

Vegas Electric Supply **(1)**
P.O. Box 27108
Las Vegas, NV 89126
Tel.: 702-367-0980
Wholesale Electrical Appliances To Contractors
S.I.C.: 5063
Terry Rogers *(V.P.)*
Michael E. Jones *(Pres.)*
Gary Mudge *(Dir.-Pur.)*

CAPITAL INDUSTRIES, INC.
5801 3rd Ave. S.
Seattle, WA 98108
Tel.: 206-762-8585 **WA**
Fax: 206-762-5455
Year Founded: 1952
Assets: $15,500,000
Liabilities: $3,000,000
Net Worth: $12,500,000
Approx.Sls.: $15,000,000
Emp.: 125
Fiscal Year-end: 12/31/89
Metal Fabrication
S.I.C.: 3449
Ronald S. Taylor *(Pres.)*
David P. Taylor Jr. *(V.P.-Mktg.)*
William E. Garrity *(Treas. & Dir.-Data Processing)*
George Box *(Dir.-Engrng.)*
Steve Irish *(Dir.-Pur.)*
Bruce Stanley *(Dir.-Personnel)*
Jay Johnson *(Plant Prod. Mgr.)*
Principal(s):
Ronald S. Taylor
David P. Taylor Jr.

Outside Service Firm(s):

U.S. Bank Of Washington*(Major Banking Relationship)*
Seattle, WA

CAPITAL PANTS CO.
700 E. Erie Ave.
Philadelphia, PA 19134
Tel.: 215-291-9300
Fax: 215-291-9323
Approx.Sls.: $20,000,000
Emp.: 400
Mfr. of Women's Jeans, Skirts & Shorts
S.I.C.: 2339
Walter S. Marine *(Pres.)*
Shelly Sherry *(Exec. V.P.-Sls. & Mktg.)*
Jack J. Marine *(Sr. V.P.)*
Fred DeSabatino *(Treas. & Sec.)*

Outside Service Firm(s):

Kopple & Gottlieb*(Auditors)*
Philadelphia, PA

Steinberg, Greenstein, Goerlick, Price & Silverman*(Legal Firm)*
818 Widener Bldg., 1339 Chestnut St.
Philadelphia, PA 19107
Tel.: 215-LO4-3880

Meridian Bank*(Major Banking Relationship)*
One Meridian Plaza, 36th Fl.
Philadelphia, PA
Tel.: 215-854-3900

CAPITAL TIRE, INC.
1001-17 Cherry St.
Toledo, OH 43608
Tel.: 419-241-5111 **OH**
Fax: 419-241-7902
Approx.Sls.: $44,000,000
Emp.: 200
Automobile & Truck Tires & Tubes
S.I.C.: 5014
Thomas B. Geiger *(Chm. Bd.)*
Thomas B. Geiger, Jr. *(Pres.)*
Carl J. Eby *(Exec. V.P.)*
Robert J. Scheick *(V.P.)*
Richard D. Stichter *(Sec.)*

Outside Service Firm(s):

First National Bank of Toledo*(Major Banking Relationship)*
Toledo, OH

CAPITOL BROADCASTING CO., INC.
711 Hillsborough St.
Raleigh, NC 27605
Mailing Address:
P.O. Box 12000
Raleigh, NC 27605
Tel.: 919-890-6000
Fax: 919-821-8544
Approx.Sls.: $98,000,000
Emp.: 665
TV & Radio Broadcasting; Satellite Services
S.I.C.: 4833; 4832; 4841
James F. Goodman *(Pres. & Chief Exec. Officer)*
Fred Barber *(Sr. V.P.-TV)*
John M. Brennan *(Sr. V.P. & Treas.)*
David H. Witherspoon *(V.P.)*
Raymond S. Wilkinson *(V.P.)*
Stephen D. Grissom *(V.P.)*
W. Ben Waters *(V.P.-Admin.)*
Louise S. Stephenson *(Sec.)*
Paul Quinn *(Station Mgr.-WRAL-TV)*

Subsidiary:

WRAL-TV **(1)**
2619 Western Blvd.
Raleigh, NC 27605
Tel.: 919-821-8500
Paul Quinn *(Station Mgr.)*

CAPITOL CHEVROLET CADILLAC GEO, INC.
2711 Mission St. S.E.
Salem, OR 97309
Mailing Address:
P.O. Box 12456
Salem, OR 97309
Tel.: 503-585-4141
Year Founded: 1927
Approx.Sls.: $24,000,000
Emp.: 100
Automobile Sales, Service & Leasing
S.I.C.: 5511; 7515; 7538; 5541
Lester Green *(Chief Exec. Officer)*
Robert Myers *(Chief Fin. Officer)*
Scott Casebeer *(Pres.)*
Dan Green *(Dir.-Adv.)*
Marvin Dukes *(Gen. Mgr.-Sls.)*

Outside Service Firm(s):

KPMG Peat Marwick*(Auditors)*
1211 S.W. Fifth Ave.
Portland, OR 97204

Churchill, Leonard, Brown & Donaldson*(Legal Firm)*
Salem, OR

Commercial Bank*(Major Banking Relationship)*
Salem, OR 97309
Tel.: 503-399-2900

CAPITOL CONSTRUCTION GROUP, INC.
1000 Capitol Dr., Ste. 200
Wheeling, IL 60090
Tel.: 708-215-2500 **IL**
Fax: 708-215-5331
Approx.Sls.: $64,000,000
Emp.: 300
Nonresidential & Industrial Construction; Manufacture Wood Partitions & Fixtures
S.I.C.: 1541; 1542; 2541
Joseph Freed *(Chm. Bd. & Chief Exec. Officer)*
Marvin Goldblatt *(Pres.)*
Michael Brown *(Sr. V.P.)*
Arthur Paullin *(V.P. & Treas.)*
Jerry Van Ness *(V.P.-Mngmt. Information Systems)*

Computer Systems/Hardware:
IBM System 38

Outside Service Firm(s):

Warady & Davis*(Auditors)*
Chicago, IL

First National Bank of Chicago*(Major Banking Relationship)*
One First National Plaza
Chicago, IL 60670
Tel.: 312-732-9781
Tel.: 312-732-4050
Fax: 312-732-4840
Fax: 312-732-3055

CAPITOL GROUP
1900 S. 8th St.
Springfield, IL 62703
Mailing Address:
P.O. Box 1627
Springfield, IL 62705
Tel.: 217-753-6900
Fax: 217-753-6910
Approx.Sls.: $24,000,000
Emp.: 130
Wholesale Distributor Steel, Plumbing Wares, Air Conditioning Equipment
S.I.C.: 5074; 5075
Lee S. Drendel *(Chm. Bd.)*
Gene Drendel *(Pres.)*
Tom Lonson *(Exec. V.P.)*
Tim Birch *(V.P. & Gen. Mgr., Residential Kitchen & Bath Div.)*
Edward Brady *(V.P. & Gen. Mgr., MMI Div.)*
Warren Creyet *(V.P. & Gen. Mgr., HVAC Div.)*
Dan Mason *(V.P.-Opers. & Dir.-Personnel)*

Capitol Group—(Continued)

Janet Smith *(Controller)*
Tom Finn *(Mgr-Adv.)*
Gary Sullivan *(Mgr.-Pur.)*

Principal(s):
Lee S. Drendel

Computer Systems/Hardware:
Hewlett Packard

Outside Service Firm(s):

Patterson, Cameron & Londrigan*(Auditors)*
Springfield, IL

Springfield Marine Bank*(Major Banking Relationship)*
Springfield, IL

CAPITOL INDUSTRIES-EMI INC.
(Sub. of Thorn EMI Plc., London, United Kingdom)
1750 N. Vine St.
Hollywood, CA 90028
Tel.: 213-462-6252
Fax: 213-467-6550
Emp.: 2,000
Prerecorded Records & Tapes
S.I.C.: 3652; 2741; 7361; 5099
V.B. Menon *(Chm. Bd.)*
Joe Smith *(Pres. & Chief Exec. Officer)*
Ralph E. Cousino *(V.P.-Technology Dept.)*
Bob Brown *(V.P.-Human Resources & Admin.)*
Fred Willims *(V.P.-Fin.)*
Lee Simpson *(V.P.- Mfg. & Opers.)*
Robert B. O'Neill *(V.P., Gen. Counsel & Sec.)*

Subsidiaries:

C & L Marketing Inc. **(1)**
1750 No. Vine St.
Hollywood, CA 90028
Tel.: 213-462-6252 (100%)
Motion Pictures
S.I.C.: 7819
C. P. Fitzgerald *(Pres.)*

Capitol Records, Inc. **(1)**
1750 N. Vine St.
Hollywood, CA 90028
Tel.: 213-462-6252 (100%)
Record Company
S.I.C.: 3652
Hale Milgrim *(Pres. & Chief Exec. Officer)*
John Fagot *(V.P.-Promotions)*
Lou Mann *(V.P.-Sls.)*
Jeremy Hammond *(V.P.-Mktg.)*
Rayna Brown *(V.P.-Human Resources)*

Division:

EMI-Manhattan Records **(2)**
810 Seventh Ave.
New York, NY 10019
Tel.: 212-603-8600 (100%%)
Phonograph Records & Pre-Recorded Magnetic Tape
S.I.C.: 3651
Sal Licata *(Pres.)*

Plant:

Capitol Records, Inc. **(2)**
No. 1 Capitol Way
Jacksonville, IL 62650
Tel.: 217-245-9631
Mfg. Plant
S.I.C.: 3652
Lee Simpson *(V.P.-Mfg. & Opers.)*

EMI Music Publishing North America **(1)**
6920 Sunset Blvd.
Hollywood, CA 90028
Tel.: 213-469-8371 (100%)
Music Publishing
S.I.C.: 2741
V. B. Menon *(Chm. Bd.)*
Ira Jaffe *(Pres.)*

CAPITOL METALS PROCESSING, INC.
20000 S. Western Ave.
Torrance, CA 90501
Tel.: 213-775-7744
Fax: 301-212-7473
Approx.Sls.: $80,000,000
Emp.: 80
Steel Processing Plant
S.I.C.: 3312
John Crowley *(Pres.)*
Eileen Parr *(Dir.-Personnel & Office Mgr.)*
Leslie Roberts *(Mgr.-Sls.)*
Lee Slater *(Mgr.-Opers.)*

Computer Systems/Hardware:
IBM

Outside Service Firm(s):

Aetna Life & Casualty*(Group Insurer)*
151 Farmington Avenue
Hartford, CT 06156
Tel.: 203-273-2128
Fax: 203-729-4295

Care America*(Group Insurer)*
Chatsworth, CA

Bank of America NT&SA*(Major Banking Relationship)*
555 So. Flower St., 5th Fl.
Los Angeles, CA 90071
Tel.: 213-228-3526
Fax: 213-228-4062

CAPITOL STREET CORP.
(Formerly Lamar Life Corporation)
711 W. Capitol St.
Jackson, MS 39203
Tel.: 601-961-6936 **MS**
Fax: 601-961-6368
Approx.Sls.: $30,000,000
Fiscal Year-end: 12/31/91
Investment Company
S.I.C.: 6211
Matt Holleman *(Chm. Bd.)*

Subsidiaries:

Lamar Investment Management Company **(1)**
P.O. Box 880, 317 E. Capitol St.
Jackson, MS 39205
Tel.: 601-949-3103 (100%)
Approx.Sls.: $313,000
Investments
S.I.C.: 6722
Michael T. McRee *(Pres.)*

Lamar Leasing Co., Inc. **(1)**
P. O. Box 880, 317 E. Capitol St.
Jackson, MS 39205
Tel.: 601-949-3100 (100%)
Approx.Sls.: $4,000
Real Estate & Equipment Leasing
S.I.C.: 6531; 7359
Jack P. Dean *(Pres.)*

Tower Loan of Mississippi, Inc. **(1)**
P.O. Box 6482, 131 Channel 16 Way
Jackson, MS 39212
Tel.: 601-922-2229 (62%)
Approx.Sls.: $8,843,000
Emp.: 98
Small Loans
S.I.C.: 6061
Jack R. Lee *(Pres.)*

Affiliate:

Lamar Life Investors **(1)**
P.O. Box 880, 317 E. Capitol St.
Jackson, MS 39205
Tel.: 601-949-3103 (50%)
Investments-(A General Partnership)
S.I.C.: 6722
Michael T. McRee *(Mng. Gen. Partner)*

Subsidiary:

Lamar Financial Services Insurance Company **(2)**
P.O. Box 880, 317 E. Capitol St.
Jackson, MS 39205
Tel.: 601-949-3100 (100%)
Approx.Sls.: $1,044,000
Life Insurance
S.I.C.: 6311
Wm. Lynn Townsend, FSA *(Pres.)*

CAPP, INC.
6117-6135 Market St.
Philadelphia, PA 19138
Tel.: 215-472-7700 **PA**
Fax: 215-472-9740
Year Founded: 1954
Approx.Sls.: $25,000,000
Emp.: 120
Manufacture & Distribute Automatic Controls & Valves for Temperature Pressure, Flow & Humidity
S.I.C.: 5065; 3823; 3829
James A. Caplan *(Chm. Bd., Pres., Treas., Prod. Mgr. & Chief Engr.)*
Charles S. Yudis *(Exec. V.P.-Sls. & Mktg.)*

Principal(s):
James A. Caplan

No. of Mfg. Plants/Facilities: 3
No. of U.S. Offices: 41

Computer Systems/Hardware:
Ultimate

Outside Service Firm(s):

Dilworth, Paxson, Kalish & Kauffman*(Legal Firm)*
2600 Fidelity Bldg., 123 S. Broad St.
Philadelphia, PA 19109
Tel.: 215-875-7000

Philadelphia National Bank*(Major Banking Relationship)*
P.O. Box 13834, Broad & Chestnut Streets
Philadelphia, PA 19101-7618
Tel.: 215-973-8327

CAPPELLI MILES WILTZ & KELLY
101 S.W. Main, Ste. 1450
Portland, OR 97204
Tel.: 503-241-1515
Fax: 503-241-1511
Year Founded: 1969
Approx.Billings: $10,000,000
Emp.: 17
Rod Miles *(Chief Fin. Officer)*
Kathy Wiltz *(Dir., Client Services & Acct. Supvr.)*
Tom Kelly *(Art Dir.)*
Anne McCutchan *(Pub. Rels. Dir.)*

CAPSONIC GROUP, INC.
460 S. Second St.
Elgin, IL 60123
Tel.: 708-888-7300
Fax: 708-888-7514
Year Founded: 1968
Approx.Sls.: $25,000,000
Emp.: 180
Fiscal Year-end: 12/31/91
Export
High Volume Custom Composite Molding
S.I.C.: 3089
James P. Liautaud *(Chm. Bd. & Chief Exec. Officer)*
Pat Patel *(Pres.)*
Tom Bumsted *(V.P.-Mfg.)*
Robert Ladecky *(Chief Fin. Officer)*
Kirit Shah *(Dir.-Quality Control)*
Jason Brown *(Natl. Sls. Mgr.)*
Linda Leach *(Mgr.-Personnel)*
Craig Leitner *(Quality Assurance Mgr.)*
Ellie Shallcross *(Acct. Mgr.)*

Affiliate:

American Antenna Corp **(1)**
1500 Executive Dr.
Elgin, IL 60120
Tel.: 708-888-7200
Fax: 708-888-7094
Peggy Finley *(Pres.)*
Rita Lovejoy *(V.P.-Sls.)*
Debbie Grex *(Controller)*
Peggy Jensen *(Dir.-Pur.)*

CAPTIVE-AIRE SYSTEMS, INC.
120 Wheaton Dr.
Youngsville, NC 27596
Mailing Address:
PO Box 41903,
Raleigh, NC 27629
Tel.: 919-554-2410 **NC**
Fax: 919-554-1227
Year Founded: 1980
Emp.: 110
Fiscal Year-end: 12/31/89
Manufacture Stainless Steel Ventilation & Fire Protection Systems for Restaurants
S.I.C.: 3564; 3569
Robert Luddy *(Pres. & Chief Exec. Officer)*
William Francis *(Treas., Controller & Chief Fin. Officer)*

Computer Systems/Hardware:
Micro Specialist

Outside Service Firm(s):

Nassif & Whitley*(Auditors)*
Raleigh, NC

Pilot Life*(Group Insurer)*
Greensboro, NC

First Union National Bank*(Major Banking Relationship)*
Raleigh, NC

Southern National Bank*(Major Banking Relationship)*
Raleigh, NC

CAPTIVE PLASTICS
251 Circle Dr., N.
Piscataway, NJ 08854
Mailing Address:
P.O. Box 27
Piscataway, NJ 08855
Tel.: 908-469-7900 **NJ**
Fax: 908-356-9487
Year Founded: 1969
Sales Range: $40-59 Million
Emp.: 500
Fiscal Year-end: 6/30/91
Mfr. of Plastic Containers, Molds & Molded Plastics
S.I.C.: 3089; 3544
John M. Raymonds *(Chm. Bd. & Chief Exec. Officer)*
John Bungert, III *(Pres.)*
David L. Smith *(V.P.-Fin.)*
John Bungert, IV *(V.P.-Mfg.)*
Catherine Raymonds *(Treas.)*
Joyce Vivian *(Mgr.-Sls.)*
Jerry Jinks *(Mgr.-Engrng.)*

No. of Mfg. Plants/Facilities: 4
No. of U.S. Offices: 4

Computer Systems/Hardware:
Hewlett Packard

Outside Service Firm(s):

KPMG Peat Marwick*(Auditors)*
150 John F. Kennedy Pkwy.
Short Hills, NJ 07078
Tel.: 201-467-9650

Epstein, Epstein, Brown & Bosek*(Legal Firm)*
Piscataway, NJ

Mellon Bank, N.A.*(Major Banking Relationship)*
Piscataway, NJ

CAPUCCI CREATIONS INTERNATIONAL, INC.
9565 Santa Monica Blvd.
Beverly Hills, CA 90210
Tel.: 310-275-0700 **CA**
Year Founded: 1975
Approx.Sls.: $343,000,000
Emp.: 550
Mfr. of Sportswear & Leather Goods
S.I.C.: 2329; 2386

Albert J. Fenster *(Pres.)*
Eleanor Fenster *(V.P.)*
Fred A. Fenster *(Treas. & Sec.)*

Outside Service Firm(s):

Jeff Page & Associates*(Auditors)*
Los Angeles, CA

Richards, Watson, Dreyson & Gershan*(Legal Firm)*
Los Angeles, CA

Bank of America NT&SA*(Major Banking Relationship)*
555 So. Flower St.
Los Angeles, CA 90071
Tel.: 213-683-3868

CARAUSTAR INDUSTRIES, INC.
3100 Washington St.
Austell, GA 30001
Tel.: 404-948-3100
Fax: 404-732-3401
Approx.Sls.: $275,000,000
Emp.: 2,500
Holding Company; Management Services
S.I.C.: 6719
James G. Dalton *(Chm. Bd.)*
Harry M. Dalton, Sr. *(Vice Chm.)*
Thomas V. Brown *(Pres. & Chief Exec. Officer)*
Bob M. Prillman *(Sr. V.P.)*
Richard E. France *(V.P.-Human Resources)*
H. Lee Thrash, III. *(V.P.-Planning & Devel. & Chief Fin. Officer)*
Ann F. Strickland *(V.P.-Admin. Services)*
Claudia H. Pease *(Treas.)*

Outside Service Firm(s):

Arthur Andersen & Co.*(Auditors)*
133 Peachtree St., N.E.
Atlanta, GA 30303
Tel.: 404-658-1776

NationsBank Carolinas*(Major Banking Relationship)*
One NCNB Plaza T18-7
Charlotte, NC 28255

CARAVAN PRODUCTS COMPANY, INC.
100 Adams Dr.
Totowa, NJ 07511
Tel.: 201-256-8886
Fax: 201-256-8395
Approx.Sls.: $30,000,000
Emp.: 120
Suppliers & Manufacturers of Baking Products & Ingredients to Bakeries; Bread & Butter Type Roll Mixes from Purchased Flour, Blended Flour, Colorings, Jams & Jellies Both Imitation, Packaged & Jarred
S.I.C.: 2045; 2087; 2033
Alex Weber *(Pres.)*
Madalyn Ulino *(V.P.-Fin.)*
Frank Johnson *(V.P.-Strategic Plng.)*
J. Murray Grob *(V.P.)*
Doris J. Weber *(V.P.)*

Outside Service Firm(s):

Ross Lane & Company*(Auditors)*
Atlanta, GA

Valley National Bank*(Major Banking Relationship)*
Passaic, NJ

Subsidiary:

Carpro, Inc. **(1)**
100 Adams Dr.
Totowa, NJ 07512
Tel.: 201-256-8886
Fax: 201-256-8395
Approx.Sls.: $60,000,000
Emp.: 300
Fiscal Year-end: 12/31/90
Real Estate Corporation, Rent Properties
S.I.C.: 6512
Alex Weber *(Pres.)*
Madalyn Ulino *(V.P.-Fin.)*
Herbert Chernin *(Sec.)*

Subsidiary:

Brokay Products, Inc. **(2)**
9999 Gantry Rd.
Philadelphia, PA 19115
Tel.: 215-676-4800
Fax: 215-677-1973
Approx.Sls.: $8,000,000
Emp.: 50
Fiscal Year-end: 12/31/90
Manufacture Food Products & Specialty Items
S.I.C.: 2045; 2087
James A. Quinn *(Pres.)*
Thomas E. Keogh *(Gen. Mgr.)*
Dorothy Caprio *(Pur. Dir.)*
Emma Kilian *(Mktg.)*

THE CARBIDE/GRAPHITE GROUP, INC.
One Gateway Center-19th Fl.
Pittsburgh, PA 15222
Tel.: 412-562-3700 **DE**
Fax: 412-562-3739
Year Founded: 1899
Approx.Sls.: $245,000,000
Emp.: 1,530
Fiscal Year-end: 7/31/92
Export
Mfr. of Multiflex Brushes
S.I.C.: 3624
James G. Baldwin *(Chm. Bd.)*
Nicholas T. Kaiser *(Pres. & Chief Oper. Officer)*
Stephen D. Weaver *(Chief Fin. Officer & V.P. Fin.)*
Donald S. Masyada *(V.P.-Electrode Sls.)*

Computer Systems/Hardware:
IBM, PRIME

Outside Service Firm(s):

Coopers & Lybrand*(Auditors)*
600 Grant St., 35th Fl.
Pittsburgh, PA 15219
Tel.: 412-355-8000
Fax: 412-355-8089

Dickie McCamey Chilcote*(Legal Firm)*
Pittsburgh, PA

Pittsburgh National Bank*(Major Banking Relationship)*
Stock Transfer Dept., Fifth & Wood Streets
Pittsburgh, PA 15265

Divisions:

Carbide Products **(1)**
P.O. Box 3727
Louisville, KY 40201
Tel.: 502-423-4400
Fax: 502-775-4199
Export
Manufacture Calcium Carbide, Desulfurization Reagents, Acetylene, Hydrated Lime, Electrically Calcined Anthracite Coal & Soderberg Electrode Paste
S.I.C.: 3624; 2819; 2813; 3274; 2899
Ronald N. Clawson *(V.P. & Gen. Mgr., Carbide Prods.)*

Electrodes **(1)**
19th floor, One Gateway Center
Pittsburgh, PA 15222
Tel.: 412-562-3700
Fax: 412-562-3739
Export
Manufacture Graphite Electrodes, Graphite Anodes, Graphite Molds & Graphite Specialties
S.I.C.: 3624
Thomas L. Parks *(V.P. & Gen. Mgr., Electrodes)*

Graphite Specialites **(1)**
800 Theresia St.
Saint Marys, PA 15857
Tel.: 814-834-2801
Fax: 814-781-2664
Export
Manufacture Brushes for Motors & Generators, Electronic Tube Anodes, Carbon & Graphite Specialties
S.I.C.: 3624
Walter B. Fowler *(V.P. & Gen. Mgr., Graphite Products)*

MTC Corporation **(1)**
9224 King Arthur Dr.
Dallas, TX 75247
Tel.: 214-637-4190
Allen McCullough *(Gen. Mgr.)*

CARCO ELECTRONICS
195 Constitution Dr.
Menlo Park, CA 94025
Tel.: 415-321-8174 **CA**
Fax: 415-321-1890
Year Founded: 1961
Approx.Sls.: $10,000,000
Emp.: 85
Research, Devel. & Manufacture of Testing Equipment & Flight Simulators
S.I.C.: 3699
John M. Carter *(Chm. Bd., & Chief Exec. Officer)*
Paul J. Roberts *(Pres. & Chief Oper. Officer)*
Rudy L. Schneider *(V.P.-Engrng.)*
William M. Schultz *(V.P. & Admin.)*
Hugh D. Carter *(V.P.-Mfg.)*
William R. Meckfessel *(Chief Fin. Officer)*
Helen D. Carter *(Sec.)*
Ellen Evans *(Mgr.-Personnel & Admin.)*
Merle Spade *(Mgr.-Pur.)*

CARCO INTERNATIONAL, INC.
2721 Midland Blvd.
Fort Smith, AR 72904
Tel.: 501-441-3200
Fax: 501-783-1020
Emp.: 42
Truck Tractors, Agricultural Machinery & Equipment
S.I.C.: 5012; 5083
Carl M. Corley *(Chm. Bd.)*
Carl D. Corley *(Vice Chm.)*
Dan Greenfield *(Pres.)*
Ruby Reding *(Office Mgr.)*

Outside Service Firm(s):

First National Bank*(Major Banking Relationship)*
Fort Smith, AR

CARDEN & CHERRY, INC.

CARDEN & CHERRY, INC.
1220 McGavock St.
Nashville, TN 37203
Mailing Address:
P.O. Box 24267,
Nashville, TN 37202
Tel.: 615-255-6694
Tel.: 800-272-3225
Fax: 615-255-9302
Year Founded: 1953
Approx.Billings: $36,000,000
Emp.: 37
Advertising Agency
S.I.C.: 7311
Gerald T. Carden *(Pres.)*
John R. Cherry III *(Exec. V.P.)*
Roy Lightner *(V.P. & Dir.-Mktg. Services)*
Erma Clement *(Sec. & Controller)*
Stacy Haas *(Mgr.-Mktg. Services)*
Janice Gowen *(Acctg. & Ins. Coord.)*

Computer Systems/Hardware:
IBM System 36

CARDER, INC.
E. Crystal St.
Lamar, CO 81052
Mailing Address:
P.O. Box 721
Lamar, CO 81052
Tel.: 719-336-3479 **CO**
Fax: 719-336-5952
Year Founded: 1961
Emp.: 36
Highway & Street Paving Contractor; Excavation & Grading; Building Construction; Builders Hardware; Farm Supplies
S.I.C.: 1611; 1794; 5072; 5191
John Carder *(Pres.)*
Robert E. Carder *(V.P.)*
Bill Nordyke *(Gen. Mgr.)*
Ira J. Paulin *(Sec.)*

Outside Service Firm(s):

Valley State Bank*(Major Banking Relationship)*
Lamar, CO

Subsidiary:

Ranchers Supply Company **(1)**
P.O. Box 721
Lamar, CO 81052
Tel.: 719-336-3479
Wholesale Distributor of Lumber & Other Building Supplies; Farm Supplies
S.I.C.: 5072; 5191

CARDINAL ALUMINUM CO.
6910 Preston Hwy.
Louisville, KY 40219
Tel.: 502-969-9302 **KY**
Fax: 502-968-4269
Approx.Sls.: $15,000,000
Emp.: 290
Manufacture Fabricated & Finished Aluminum Extrusions
S.I.C.: 3354
William E. Edwards, Jr. *(Chm. Bd. & Chief Exec. Officer)*
William E. Edwards III *(Pres. & Chief Oper. Officer)*
Dalton Riley *(V.P.-Pur.)*
Mike Mueller *(Controller)*
Frank Bock *(Dir.-Production & Engrng.)*
William H. Seelbach *(Dir.-Mktg.)*

No. of U.S. Offices: 2

Outside Service Firm(s):

Chilton & Medley*(Auditors)*
Louisville, KY

Middleton & Reutlinger*(Legal Firm)*
2500 Brown & Williamson Tower
Louisville, KY 40202
Tel.: 502-584-1135

First National Bank of Louisville*(Major Banking Relationship)*
P.O. Box 36000,
Louisville, KY 40233

CARDINAL INC.
400 Markley St.
Port Reading, NJ 07064
Mailing Address:
P.O. Box 99
Port Reading, NJ 07064
Tel.: 908-636-6160
Tel.: 800-888-0936
Fax: 908-636-0017
Year Founded: 1946
Approx.Sls.: $18,000,000
Emp.: 65
Fiscal Year-end: 6/30/90
Import Export
Importers of Ceramic Giftwares, Doll House Furniture & Accessories, Porcelain Collector Dolls
S.I.C.: 5092
Sidney Darwin *(Pres.)*
Allen Darwin *(V.P. & Treas.)*
Gary Darwin *(V.P.-Sls.)*

Cardinal Inc.—(Continued)

Natalie Darwin *(Sec.)*
Mike Arlea *(Controller & Mgr.-Personnel)*
John Bellanicit *(Mgr.-Import & Export)*
Dennis Seeds *(Mgr.-Data Processing)*
Frank Fahey *(Mgr.-Admin. Sls.)*

Computer Systems/Hardware:
AS 400 Model 20

Affiliates:

Concord Miniatures **(1)**
P.O. Box 99
Port Reading, NJ 07064
Tel.: 908-636-6160
Import Export

Dynasty Dolls **(1)**
P.O. Box 99
Port Reading, NJ 07064
Tel.: 908-636-6160

Our Own Import Inc. **(1)**
P.O. Box 99
Port Reading, NJ 07064
Tel.: 908-636-6160

CARDINAL REALTY SERVICES INC.
(Formerly Cardinal Industries, Inc.)
6954 Americana Pkwy.
Reynoldsburg, OH 43068
Tel.: 614-755-6400 **OH**
Fax: 614-755-3845
Year Founded: 1954
Management of Residential Property, Cardinal Apartments
S.I.C.: 6513; 6531; 7011; 5211; 5251; 6162; 1521; 1522
Frank McDowell *(Pres. & Chief Exec. Officer)*
David Blackmore *(V.P. & Treas.)*
Robert E. Pausch *(V.P.-Partnership Fin.)*
Thomas Trubiana *(V.P.-Investor & Admin. Svcs.)*
David Williams *(V.P.-Apt. Opers.)*
Jim Bownas *(V.P. & Gen. Counsel)*
Michael F. Carbone *(V.P. & Chief Fin. Officer)*

No. of U.S. Offices: 4

Computer Systems/Hardware:
IBM System 4300

Outside Service Firm(s):

Coopers & Lybrand*(Auditors)*
100 E. Broad St.
Columbus, OH 43215

The Huntington National Bank*(Major Banking Relationship)*
41 S. High St.
Columbus, OH 43216

William F. Brown*(Legal Firm)*
Columbus, OH

Midland Mutual Insurance*(Pension Manager)*
Columbus, OH

CAREER BLAZERS INC.
590 Fifth Ave., 7th Fl.
New York, NY 10036
Tel.: 212-719-3232
Tel.: 800-284-3232 **NY**
Year Founded: 1949
Approx.Sls.: $25,200,000
Emp.: 150
Fiscal Year-end: 12/31/90
Full Service Personnel Firm
S.I.C.: 7361; 7363
William Lewis *(Chm. Bd., Pres. & Chief Exec. Officer)*
Arlene Covney *(Exec. V.P.)*
Nancy Schuman *(V.P.-Mktg. & Opers.)*
Kathy Klein *(V.P.)*
Linda Crochet *(Dir.-Acctg.)*
Susan Demuro *(Dir.-Special Projects)*
Principal(s):
William Lewis

No. of U.S. Offices: 12
No. of Foreign Offices: 1

Computer Systems/Hardware:
DEC

Outside Service Firm(s):

Price Waterhouse*(Auditors)*
153 E. 53rd St., 44th Fl.
New York, NY 10022
Tel.: 212-371-2000

Blue Cross & Blue Shield of New York*(Group Insurer)*
New York, NY

Fulbright Jaworski & Reavis McGrath*(Legal Firm)*
345 Park Ave.
New York, NY 10022
Tel.: 212-752-6830

Republic Bank Inc.*(Major Banking Relationship)*
New York, NY

Subsidiaries:

Career Blazers Agency, Inc. **(1)**
590 Fifth Ave.
New York, NY 10036
Tel.: 212-719-3232
Tel.: 800-284-3232
Fax: 212-921-1827
Emp.: 160
Full Service Employment Organization
S.I.C.: 7361
William Lewis *(Pres.)*

Career Blazers Service Company, Inc. **(1)**
590 Fifth Ave.
New York, NY 10036
Tel.: 212-719-3232
Fax: 212-921-0053
Franchising
S.I.C.: 6794
William Lewis *(Pres.)*

Career Blazers Learning Center **(1)**
230 Park Ave.
New York, NY 10169
Tel.: 212-661-7700
Training Center
S.I.C.: 7363
William Lewis *(Pres.)*
Paul Viboch *(V.P.-Training)*

Career Blazers Temporary Personnel **(1)**
590 Fifth Ave.
New York, NY 10036
Tel.: 212-719-3232
S.I.C.: 7363
William Lewis *(Pres.)*

Career Blazers of White Plains, Inc. **(1)**
202 Mamaroneck Ave.
White Plains, NY 10605
Tel.: 914-949-1166
S.I.C.: 7361
Robert Miller *(Pres.)*

CAREERS USA INC.
1825 JFK Blvd.
Philadelphia, PA 19103
Tel.: 215-561-3800
Tel.: 800-822-8300 **PA**
Fax: 215-977-8335
Year Founded: 1981
Assets: $2,993,216
Liabilities: $1,928,935
Net Worth: $1,064,281
Approx.Sls.: $15,000,000
Emp.: 70
Fiscal Year-end: 12/31/91
Temporary Employment Agency
S.I.C.: 7361
Marilyn J. Ounjian *(Chm. Bd. & Chief Exec. Officer)*
George E. Ounjian *(Pres.)*
Morris E. Berger *(Chief Fin. Officer)*
Walter Cantwell *(Chief Information Officer)*
Trudy Feldman *(Exec. V.P.)*
Frances Johnston *(Group V.P.)*
Christine Lafferty *(Group V.P.)*
Sandi Brown *(Dir.-Personnel Training & Devel.)*
Marnie Mathis *(Dir.-Human Resources)*
Ken Ranaldi *(Dir.-Sls. Promo. & Adv.)*
Principal(s):
Marilyn J. Ounjian

No. of U.S. Offices: 15

Outside Service Firm(s):

Coopers & Lybrand*(Auditors)*
2400 Eleven Penn Center
Philadelphia, PA 19103

Ernst & Young*(Auditors)*
1800 John F. Kennedy Blvd.
Philadelphia, PA 19103-7499
Tel.: 215-864-3300

Continental Bank, N.A.*(Major Banking Relationship)*
1500 Market St.
Philadelphia, PA 19102
Tel.: 215-564-7475

First National Bank of Chicago*(Major Banking Relationship)*
One First National Plaza
Chicago, IL 60670
Tel.: 312-732-9781
Tel.: 312-732-4050
Fax: 312-732-4840
Fax: 312-732-3055

CAREERTRACK INC.
3080 Center Green Dr.
Boulder, CO 80301
Tel.: 303-447-2323
Fax: 303-447-1696
Year Founded: 1982
Approx.Sls.: $66,500,000
Emp.: 425
Export
Audio Video Casette Programs, Tapes & One Day Seminars
S.I.C.: 2741; 5942; 5961; 5999
Corporate Giving Program: Donations *to Charity Organizations Limited to* Boulder County, Colorado
James C. Calano *(Pres. & Chief Exec. Officer)*
Jeff Salzman *(V.P. & Sec.)*
Jeffrey A. Hildebrandt *(Mgr.-Corp. Communications)*
Principal(s):
James C. Calano
Jeff Salzman

No. of U.S. Offices: 1
No. of Foreign Offices: 1

Outside Service Firm(s):

National Bank of The Rockies*(Major Banking Relationship)*
Boulder, CO

CARELLI, GLYNN & WARD
1250 Route 23
Butler, NJ 07405
Tel.: 201-838-2242
Fax: 201-838-0331
Year Founded: 1969
Approx.Billings: $15,700,000
Emp.: 28
Robert A. Ward, Jr. *(Chm. Bd., Pres., Dir. Client Services)*
Gloria A. Carelli *(Exec. V.P., Dir. Creative Services & Treas.)*
John Carelli *(V.P.)*
Nancy Ward *(Sec.)*
Eleanor Napoli *(Asst. Treas. & Controller)*
Larry Feld *(Pub. Rels.)*

W. P. CAREY & CO., INC.
620 Fifth Ave., Fourth Floor
New York, NY 10020
Tel.: 212-492-1100
Tel.: 800-972-2739 **NY**
Fax: 212-977-3022
Year Founded: 1972
Assets: $1,245,000,000
Liabilities: $484,000,000
Net Worth: $761,000,000
Sales Range: $100-499 Million
Emp.: 180
Fiscal Year-end: 12/31/91
Corporate Financing & Real Estate Investment Banking
S.I.C.: 6159; 8741
William P. Carey *(Chm. Bd. & Mng. Dir.)*
Francis J. Carey *(Pres. & Mng. Dir.)*
Madelon De Voe Talley *(Vice Chm. Bd.)*
Raymond S. Clark *(Chm. Exec. Committee)*
Dr. Lawrence R. Klein *(Chm. Economic Policy Committee)*
George E. Stoddard *(Chm. Investment Committee)*
Frank J. Hoenemeyer *(Vice Chm. Investment Committee)*
Barclay G. Jones III *(Exec. V.P. & Mng. Dir.)*
H. Cabot Lodge III *(Exec. V.P. & Mng. Dir.)*
Claude Fernandez *(Chief Fin. Officer, V.P. & Mng. Dir.)*
H. Augustus Carey *(1st V.P. & Natl. Mktg. Coordinator)*
Michael B. Pollack *(1st V.P. & Sec.)*
Michael D. Roberts *(1st V.P., Controller & Asst. Treas.)*
Debra E. Bigler *(V.P., Dir.-Mktg. & Asst. Sec.)*
Gordon F. DuGan *(V.P. & Asst. Sec.)*
Louis R. Hernandez *(V.P., Treas. & Asst. Sec.)*
Anthony S. Mohl *(V.P. & Asst. Sec.)*
George F. Norwine *(V.P.)*
John J. Park *(V.P., Dir.-Res. & Asst. Treas.)*
Howard J. Altmann *(2nd V.P. & Asst. Sec.)*
Eve E. Goldberg *(2nd V.P. & Asst. Sec.)*
Robert C. Kehoe *(2nd V.P. & Asst. Sec.)*
Debra E. Jordan *(Asst. to Chm. Bd. & Asst. Sec.)*
Ann Marie Luongo *(Exec. Asst. & Asst. Sec.)*
Sheila E. Murphy *(Asst. to Pres., Office Mgr. & Asst. Sec.)*
Sara S. Perkins *(Sr. Mktg. Asst. & Asst. Sec.)*
David G. Termine *(Mgr.-Acct. & Asst. Treas)*
David C. Auten *(Asst. Sec.)*
Stephen M. Lyons, III *(Asst. Sec.)*
Ruth S. Perfido *(Asst. Sec.)*
Principal(s):
William P. Carey

No. of U.S. Offices: 1

Computer Systems/Hardware:
IBM Novell SFT Netware 286

Outside Service Firm(s):

Coopers & Lybrand*(Auditors)*
1301 Avenue of The Americas
New York, NY 10019
Tel.: 212-536-2000

Reed, Smith, Shaw & McClay*(Legal Firm)*
Philadelphia, PA

The Bank of New York*(Major Banking Relationship)*
One Wall Street
New York, NY 10286
Tel.: 212-635-6805
Fax: 212-635-3201

CAREY MACHINERY & SUPPLY COMPANY
3501 Brehms Lane
Baltimore, MD 21213
Tel.: 301-485-2323 **MD**
Fax: 301-410-2914
Year Founded: 1887
Approx.Sls.: $10,000,000

Emp.: 42
Fiscal Year-end: 12/31/90
Power Transmission Equipment Abrasives; Tools, Materials Handling Machinery; Safety Equipment; Air Compressors/Vacuum Pumps
S.I.C.: 5085; 5084
G. Cheston Carey, Jr. *(Pres.)*
Christopher Lanahan *(V.P.-Sls. & Mktg., MRO)*
M.L. Mottley *(V.P.-Sls. & Mktg., Compressors)*
Josephine Zahner *(Sec. & Treas.)*

Outside Service Firm(s):

Coopers & Lybrand*(Auditors)*
217 E. Redwood St.
Baltimore, MD 21202

Semmes, Bowen, Semmes*(Legal Firm)*
10 Light Equitable Bldg.
Baltimore, MD 21204
Tel.: 410-296-4400

Maryland National Bank*(Major Banking Relationship)*
10 Light St.
Baltimore, MD 21203
Tel.: 410-244-5000

CARGILL DETROIT CORP.

1250 N. Crooks Rd.
Clawson, MI 48017
Tel.: 313-435-3500
Fax: 313-435-3525
Approx.Sls.: $35,000,000
Emp.: 300
Manufacture Machine Tools
S.I.C.: 3559; 3531; 3829
John S. Cargill *(Chm.)*
Don A. Cargill *(Pres. & Chief Exec. Officer)*
George Homanick *(V.P.-Mfg.)*
Mike Edwards *(Treas.)*
John C. Emery, Jr. *(Sec.)*
Fred R. Eldridge *(Mgr.-Pur.)*

Outside Service Firm(s):

Plante & Moran*(Auditors)*
Southfield, MI

N.B.D. Bank, N.A.*(Major Banking Relationship)*
611 Woodward Ave.
Detroit, MI 48226
Tel.: 313-225-1122
Fax: 313-225-3420

CARGILL INC.

15407 McGinty Rd. W.
Wayzata, MN 55391-2399
Mailing Address:
P.O. Box 9300
Minneapolis, MN 55440
Tel.: 612-475-7575
Fax: 612-475-6301
Year Founded: 1865
Sales Range: $1 Billion +
Emp.: 61,000
Processing, Marketing & Exporting of Grains; Vegetable Oils/Meals; Flour, Corn Milling; Corn Starches & Syrups; Nutrena Feeds; Hybrid Seed; Oil Based Chemicals; Bulk Commodities Including Salt, Molasses, Fertilizers; Bulk Transportation Service
S.I.C.: 0211; 0252; 1479; 2011; 2015; 2041; 2046; 2047; 2048; 2075; 2076; 2821; 2819; 2874; 3312; 3317; 4424; 4449; 5153; 2083; 5051; 5144; 5159; 5191; 6221; 6289; 6159; 6211; 5172; 6282
Whitney MacMillan *(Chm. Bd. & Chief Exec. Officer)*
William R. Pearce *(Vice Chm.)*
Heinz F. Hutter *(Pres. & Chief Oper. Officer)*
Robert L. Lumpkins *(V.P. & Chief Fin. Officer)*
James M. Wallace *(Mgr.-Corp. Communications)*
Daryl Wikstrom *(Mgr.-Pension Trust)*
Norm Erickson *(Supvr.-Mktg. Services)*

Divisions:

Cargill Financial Markets Div. **(1)**
P.O. Box 9300
Minneapolis, MN 55440
Tel.: 612-475-5286
Financial Services
S.I.C.: 6282
David W. Raisbeck *(Chief Oper. Officer)*

Cargill Flour Milling Div. **(1)**
P.O. Box 9300
Minneapolis, MN 55440
Tel.: 612-475-7575
Fax: 612-475-5062
Emp.: 1,000
Flour Milling; Food Processing; Grocery Product Manufacturing
S.I.C.: 2041
Larry DeWitt *(Pres.)*
Dan Dougherty *(V.P.-Sls.)*

Cargill Nutrena Feed **(1)**
P.O. Box 9300
Minneapolis, MN 55440
Tel.: 612-475-7413
Fax: 612-475-6391
Nutrena Livestock & Poultry Feeds, Nutrena Pet Food, Pro Energy Pet Food Brand
S.I.C.: 0213; 2048
Dave Larson *(Pres.)*
Lloyd Whiting *(Mktg. Mgr.)*
Norm Erickson *(Supvr.-Mktg. Services)*

Division:

Walnut Grove-Nutrena Feed Div., Cargill, Inc. **(2)**
Second & Linn Sts.
Atlantic, IA 50022
Tel.: 712-243-1030
Fax: 712-243-6360/3622
Approx.Sls.: $60,000,000
Emp.: 450
Fiscal Year-end: 5/31/91
Animal Feeds & Feed Supplements
S.I.C.: 2048
Andrew Loder *(Dir.-Opers.)*
Ray Underwood *(Dir.-Mktg. & Production)*
Roberta Beschorner *(Mgr.-Human Resources)*
Eileen Johnson *(Mgr.-Mktg. Services)*

Cargill Salt Division **(1)**
P.O. Box 9300,
Minneapolis, MN 55440
Tel.: 612-475-7575
Mineral Mining
S.I.C.: 1479
Tyrone Thayer *(Pres.)*
Bob North *(Dir.-Mktg.)*

Cargill Seed Div. **(1)**
P.O. Box 9300
Minneapolis, MN 55440
Tel.: 612-475-7575
Emp.: 500
Farm Seeds
S.I.C.: 5191; 0115
Bruce Priebe *(Pres.)*
Dick Johnson *(V.P.-Sls.)*

Emge Packing Co., Inc. **(1)**
Red Bank Rd.
Fort Branch, IN 47648
Tel.: 812-753-3214
Approx.Sls.: $185,000,000
Emp.: 650
Beef & Pork Packing
S.I.C.: 2011
Warren Mirtching *(Pres.)*

Excel Corp. **(1)**
151 N. Main
Wichita, KS 67202
Meat Products
S.I.C.: 2013; 2011
Bill Fielding *(Pres.)*
Dale Rodman *(Exec. V.P.)*

Subsidiaries:

Cargill Citro-America, Inc. **(1)**
P.O. Box 9300
Minneapolis, MN 55440
Tel.: 612-475-6456
Approx.Sls.: $200,000,000
Emp.: 35
Mfr. of Fresh Fruit Juices
S.I.C.: 2033
Douglas Linder *(Pres.)*
Richard L. Kellor *(V.P.)*

Cargill Fertilizer, Inc. **(1)**
8813 Highway 41 South
Riverview, FL 33569
Tel.: 813-677-9111
Approx.Sls.: $250,000,000
Emp.: 665
Fiscal Year-end: 5/31/91
Computer Systems/Hardware:
IBM System 38, Model 20
Mining and Mfr. of Agricultural Chemicals & Fertilizers
S.I.C.: 1475; 2874; 2873
Henk Mathot *(Pres. & Chief Exec. Officer)*
Jerry Hammond *(V.P., Treas. & Sec.)*
H. Gray Gordon *(V.P.-Personnel)*
Elsie Ritter *(Mgr.-Information Systems)*

Cargill Investor Services, Inc. **(1)**
141 W. Jackson Blvd., Ste. 1800
Chicago, IL 60604
Tel.: 312-435-8300
Approx.Sls.: $63,000,000
Emp.: 440
Commodity & Security Brokers; Security Dealers
S.I.C.: 6221; 6211
Hal T. Hansen *(Pres.)*

Cargill Marine & Terminal **(1)**
15407 McGinty Rd.
Wayzata, MN 55391
Tel.: 612-475-7575
Approx.Sls.: $80,000,000
Emp.: 480
Deep Sea Domestic Transportation of Freight; Transportation on Bays & Sounds of the Ocean; Marine Terminals; Stevedoring
S.I.C.: 4424; 4449; 4491
Allen A. Housh *(Pres.)*

Cargill Petroleum, Inc. **(1)**
295 Eastern Ave.
Chelsea, MA 02150
Tel.: 617-286-3400
Petroleum Brokers
S.I.C.: 5172
Yannick Lecamp *(Gen. Mgr.)*

Ladish Malting Co. **(1)**
P.O. Box 2044
Milwaukee, WI 53201
Tel.: 414-271-4763
Mfr. of Malt
S.I.C.: 2082
John H. Ladish *(Chm. Bd. & Chief Exec. Officer)*

North Star Steel Co. **(1)**
P.O. Box 9300, Dept. 51
Minneapolis, MN 55440
Tel.: 612-475-5471
Fax: 612-475-5474
Approx.Sls.: $750,000,000
Emp.: 3,400
Export
Blast Furnaces & Steel Mills; Fabricated Pipe & Fittings
S.I.C.: 3312; 5051
Robert A. Garvey *(Pres.)*
Harvey Anderson *(V.P.-Fin.)*
James Thompson *(V.P.-Mktg.)*

Subsidiaries:

North Star Steel Houston **(2)**
8603 Sheldon Rd.
Houston, TX 77049
Tel.: 713-456-9716
Emp.: 150
Oil Field Services
S.I.C.: 1389
Chuck Stanley *(Plant Mgr.)*

North Star Steel Kentucky, Inc. **(2)**
Old Coke Plant Rd.
Calvert City, KY 42029
Tel.: 502-395-3100
Approx.Sls.: $40,000,000
Emp.: 230
Mfr. of Steel Cold-Finished Bars & Bar Shapes
S.I.C.: 3312
Ron Phillips *(Plant Mgr.)*

North Star Steel Texas, Inc. **(2)**
Old Hwy. 90
Beaumont, TX 77704
Tel.: 409-768-1211
Approx.Sls.: $240,000,000
Emp.: 664
Mfr. of Rods, Iron & Steel Made In Steel Mills; Steel Nails; Wire
S.I.C.: 3312; 3315
Mike Coleman *(Gen. Mgr.)*

Wilbur Chocolate Co., Inc. **(1)**
48 No. Broad St.
Lititz, PA 17543
Tel.: 717-626-1131
Fax: 717-626-4227
Approx.Sls.: $100,000,000
Emp.: 350
Fiscal Year-end: 1/31/91
Chocolate Coatings to Candy Mfrs., Bulk Cocoas, Chocolate Chips & Drops, Ice Cream Mixes to Bakery & Ice Cream Industries, Candy Bars
S.I.C.: 2066; 2099
William J. Shaughnessy *(Pres. & Chief Exec. Officer)*
J.A. Maddox *(V.P.-Mktg. & Sls.)*
E.A. Maksel *(V.P. & Controller)*
J. Urbanski *(V.P.)*

Non-U.S. Holdings:

Cargill Agricola S.A. **(1)**
Rua Olavo Bilac 157 Sto. Amaro, 04671
P.O. Box 9333,
Sao Paulo, S.P. Brazil
Tel.: 11 545-0211
Telex: 11-56341 CARG BR
Fax: 11 246-4571
Mfr. of Soybeans, Frozen Concentrate Orange Juice, Cacau Beans
S.I.C.: 2075; 2037; 2095; 2066

Cargill International S.A. **(1)**
Geneva, Switzerland (100%)
N. Leonard Alderson *(Chm. Bd.)*

Cargill Ltd. **(1)**
The Cargill Bldg., 300-240 Graham Ave.
Box 5900,
Winnipeg, MB R3C 4C5, Canada
Tel.: 204-947-0141 (100%)
Telex: 07-57759 CARGILL WPG
Fax: 204-947-6220
Mfr. of Nutrena Feeds, Hybrid Seeds
S.I.C.: 0181; 2048; 5191
Kerry Hawkins *(Pres.)*

Plant:

Cargill Ltd. **(2)**
627 Plinquet
Saint Boniface, MB R2J 2W9, Canada
Tel.: 204-947-6100
Mfr. of Hybrid Seed & Nutrena Feeds Production
S.I.C.: 0181; 2048

Cargill NV **(1)**
Muisbroeklaan, Kaai 506 B-2030
Antwerp, Belgium
Tel.: 32 03 540 1811
Mfr. of Chemicals
S.I.C.: 2819

Cargill Trading Ltd. **(1)**
5th Fl., Hyundai Cheil Bldg., 80 Cheokseon-Dong, Chongro-Ku
Seoul, 110-052, Korea
Tel.: 82-02-733-0271
Telex: CARGILL K26704
Fax: 82-02-797-9605
Trading in Hybrid Seeds, Animal Feed
S.I.C.: 5191

Cargill UK Ltd. **(1)**
Fairmile Lane Knowle Hill Park, Cobham, Surrey KT11 2PD, United Kingdom
Tel.: 44-936-861000 (100%)
Trading in Hybrid Seed, Animal Feed
S.I.C.: 5191

CARGILL SALT
7200 Central Ave.
Newark, CA 94560-4206
Mailing Address:
P.O. Box 364
Newark, CA 94560
Tel.: 510-797-1820
Tel.: 800-321-1458
Telex: 910-381-6047
Fax: 510-790-8162
Approx.Sls.: $50,000,000
Emp.: 400
Export
Leslie Salt
S.I.C.: 2899
Ty Thayer *(Pres.)*
G.O. Rohlfson *(V.P. & Gen. Mgr.)*
Charlie Westmoreland *(V.P. & Opers. Mgr.)*
Maureen Dolan *(Sec. & Treas.)*
Bob North *(Exec. Mktg. Dir.)*
Roger Salmon *(Dir.-Sls.)*
Rod Christianson *(Mgr.-Mfg.)*
Lori Johnson *(Mgr.-Pub. Rels.)*
Bill Britt *(Government Affairs)*
Dave Rose *(Dir.-Pur.)*
Clem Teeters *(Mgr.-Consumer Products)*
Dave Rose *(Pur. Agent)*

Computer Systems/Hardware:
IBM

Division:

Dispensing Systems Div. **(1)**
2016 Clement Ave.
Alameda, CA 94501
Tel.: 510-523-6191
Fax: 510-523-7698
Export
Joe Esmond *(Mgr.)*

CARGOCAIRE ENGINEERING CORPORATION
79 Monroe St.
Amesbury, MA 01913
Mailing Address:
P.O. Box 640,
Amesbury, MA 01913-0640
Tel.: 508-388-0600
Tel.: 800-843-5360
Telex: 947476
Fax: 508-388-4556
Year Founded: 1939
Approx.Sls.: $22,653,000
Emp.: 160
Fiscal Year-end: 12/31/90
Manufactures Dehumidifiers & Heat Exchangers
S.I.C.: 3585
Sven Lundin *(Pres.)*
Robert P. Thompson *(V.P.-Fin.)*
Gail Cassin *(Controller)*
Doug Kosar *(Dir.-Mktg.)*
Dick Reiley *(Dir.-Sls.)*
Craig Fillmann *(Gen. Mgr.)*

CARHARTT, INC.
1 Parklane Blvd.
Dearborn, MI 48126
Mailing Address:
P.O. Box 600
Dearborn, MI 48121
Tel.: 313-271-8460
Tel.: 800-358-3825 **MI**
Fax: 313-271-3455
Year Founded: 1889
Approx.Sls.: $86,000,000
Emp.: 1,500
Fiscal Year-end: 9/30/91
Export
Manufacture Work Clothes, Outerwear & Hunting Clothes
S.I.C.: 2326; 2329; 2325
Robert C. Valade *(Pres. & Chief Exec. Officer)*
Gust Feles *(Exec. V.P. & Sec.)*
Verlon Prewitt *(V.P.-Mfg.)*
Peter Krause *(Treas.)*
Joe Berkowski *(Controller)*
Hugh Corteville *(Mgr.-Data Processing)*
Principal(s):
Robert C. Valade
Gust Feles

No. of Mfg. Plants/Facilities: 7

Computer Systems/Hardware:
IBM System AS400

Outside Service Firm(s):

Plante & Moran*(Auditors)*
Southfield, MI

Comerica Bank*(Major Banking Relationship)*
211 W. Fort St.
Detroit, MI 48226
Tel.: 313-222-3300

CARIBE EXPRESS
405 Hangar Ramey Base
Aguadilla, PR 00604
Mailing Address:
P.O. Box 460 Ramey,
Aguadilla, PR 00604
Tel.: 809-890-7000
Fax: 809-890-7004
Air Freight Service & Transportation
S.I.C.: 4522
Joseph R. Chatt *(Pres.)*
Oscar Allende *(V.P.)*
Nestor Gonzalez *(Gen. Mgr.)*
Joseph Cardona *(Dir.-Sls.)*
Bernardo Espinosa *(Mgr.-Admin.)*
Sylvia Medina *(Mgr.-Customer Service)*

Branches:

Caribe Express **(1)**
6901 L. Downwind Rd.
Greensboro, NC 27409
Tel.: 919-668-9370
Air Freight Customer Service
S.I.C.: 4522
John Ford *(Pres.)*

Caribe Express Latin American Div. **(1)**
6704 N.W. 82nd. Ave.
Miami, FL 33144
Tel.: 305-477-7757
Air Freight Service & Transportation
S.I.C.: 4522
Rachel Caribe *(Pres.)*

Caribe Express Pace Air Freight **(1)**
330 W. Wall Street Pike
Indianapolis, IN 46234
Tel.: 317-839-6515
Tel.: 800-752-1418
Air Freight Service & Transportation
S.I.C.: 4522
Robert Pfeffer *(Pres.)*

Caribe Freight **(1)**
Edificio Caribe Freight, Aeropuerto International de las Americas
Santo Domingo, PR
Tel.: 809-549-0161
Tel.: 809-549-0131
Air Freight Services
S.I.C.: 4522
Rafael Cuello *(Pres.)*

CARLES INC.
130 E. 59th St.
New York, NY 10022
Tel.: 212-755-9400
Year Founded: 1986
Approx.Billings: $10,000,000
Emp.: 12
Consumer Products, Direct Mktg.
John B. Carles *(Pres.)*

THE P.J. CARLIN CONSTRUCTION COMPANY
140 Huguenot St.
New Rochelle, NY 10801
Tel.: 914-632-7400
Fax: 914-632-9348
Year Founded: 1852
Approx.Sls.: $70,000,000
Emp.: 300
Fiscal Year-end: 3/31/92
General Building Construction & Development
S.I.C.: 1542; 1522
Edward E. Lustbader *(Chm. Bd., Pres., Chief Exec. Officer & Treas.)*
Brian G. Lustbader *(Exec. V.P., Gen. Counsel & Sec.)*
Jules Price *(V.P.-Pur.)*
Robert M. Slochover *(V.P.)*
Alan B. Stembridge *(V.P.-Admin. & Fin.)*
Jeffrey Schwartz *(Controller)*
Rose Ann Sperandio *(Dir.-Personnel)*
Principal(s):
Edward E. Lustbader
Brian G. Lustbader

Outside Service Firm(s):

J. H. Cohn & Co.*(Auditors)*
Newark, NJ

Empire Blue Cross & Blue Shield*(Group Insurer)*
New York, NY

Chemical Banking Corp.*(Major Banking Relationship)*
277 Park Ave.
New York, NY 10041
Tel.: 212-310-6407
Fax: 212-310-4526

Manhattan Life*(Pension Manager)*
New York, NY

CARLISLE EQUIPMENT COMPANY
840 Licking Pike
Wilder, KY 41076
Tel.: 606-441-7400
Fax: 606-441-7400, Ext. 280
Distribute Heavy Construction Equipment
S.I.C.: 5082
Wayne Carlisle *(Pres.)*
Gary Hoffman *(V.P.-Sls.)*
Gary Strassel *(Dir.-Admin.)*

Outside Service Firm(s):

Arthur Andersen & Co.*(Auditors)*
425 Walnut St.
Cincinnati, OH 45202
Tel.: 513-381-6900

Dinsmore & Shohl*(Legal Firm)*
2100 Fountain Square Plaza
Cincinnati, OH 45202-3172
Tel.: 513-977-8200

Provident National Bank*(Major Banking Relationship)*
4140 Hamilton Ave.
Cincinnati, OH
Tel.: 513-681-3900

Branch:

Carlisle Equipment Company **(1)**
3800 Crittenden Dr.
Louisville, KY 40217
Tel.: 502-361-7000
Emp.: 110
Distribute Heavy Construction Equipment
S.I.C.: 5082
Wayne Carlisle *(Pres.)*
J.H. Sorg *(V.P.-Fin.)*
Thomas F. McGuire *(V.P.-Sls.)*
W.T. Kitchen *(Gen Sls. Mgr.)*
Louise M. Davis *(Sec.)*
Tom Cook *(Dir.-Personnel)*
Jim Isaacs *(Mgr.-Data Processing)*

CARLISLE RETAILERS, INC.
4509 Main Ave.
Ashtabula, OH 44004
Tel.: 216-997-5111
Fax: 216-992-1375
Year Founded: 1860
Approx.Sls.: $46,000,000
Emp.: 750
Fiscal Year-end: 2/ 2/91
Dept. Store
S.I.C.: 5311
L. T. Carlisle III *(Chm., Pres. & Chief Exec. Officer)*
Raymond J. Miller *(Sr. V.P. Fin. & Chief Fin. Officer)*
Vincent L. Coneglio *(V.P.-Admin & Sec.)*
Susan Lagoni *(Controller)*
Debbi Bratt *(Dir.-Mngmt. Information Systems)*

JOHN CARLO INC.
21570 Hall Rd.
Mount Clemens, MI 48046
Mailing Address:
P.O. Box 8,
Mount Clemens, MI 48046
Tel.: 313-465-6232
Fax: 313-465-3932
Approx.Sls.: $51,000,000
Emp.: 443
Highway & Street Construction
S.I.C.: 1611
Carlo J. Catenacci *(Pres.)*
Joseph E. Catenacci *(V.P.)*
Jack Robson *(Treas.)*

Outside Service Firm(s):

Michigan National Bank*(Major Banking Relationship)*
Detroit, MI

CARLSBERG FINANCIAL CORP.
2800 28th St., Ste. 200
Santa Monica, CA 90405
Tel.: 310-450-9700 **DE**
Approx.Rev.: $33,921,000
Emp.: 627
Mfr. Prefab Bldgs; Mortgage Banking; Developers; Real Estate Brokers
S.I.C.: 1521; 2452; 6162; 6531; 8721
Richard P. Carlsberg *(Pres.)*
Ronald S. Tankersley *(Exec. V.P.)*

CARLSON COMPANIES, INC.
Carlson Parkway
Minneapolis, MN 55459
Mailing Address:
P.O. Box 59159
Minneapolis, MN 55459
Tel.: 612-540-5000 **MN**
Telex: 29 0996
Fax: 612-540-5832
Year Founded: 1938
Approx.Rev.: $9,300,000,000
Emp.: 90,000
Fiscal Year-end: 12/31/91
Import Export
Holding Company; Hotels; Inns; Resorts; Trading Stamps, Incentive & Premium Promotions; Restaurants; Real Estate; Financial; Design & Construction; Travel Agencies & Tour Companies
S.I.C.: 4724; 4725; 5812; 6719; 7011; 7389; 5023; 5021; 5141; 2499; 5099
Curtis L. Carlson *(Chm. Bd., Pres. & Chief Exec. Officer)*
Edwin C. Gage *(Vice Chm.)*
Marilynn C. Nelson *(Vice Chm.)*
Juergen Bartels *(Exec. V.P.)*
Charles W. Schmid *(Exec. V.P.)*
Lee Bearmon *(V.P., Sec. & Gen. Counsel)*
Joel E. Burke *(V.P.)*
Terry Butorac *(V.P.-Human Resources)*
John M. Diracles, Jr. *(V.P. & Treas.)*
James Goodlett *(V.P. & Chief Information Officer)*
D.M. Hamann *(V.P.-Tax)*
Thomas D. Jardine *(V.P.-Pub. Rels. & Pub. Affairs)*
D.H. Kemnitz *(V.P.-Employee Benefits)*
Mark Larson *(V.P.-Intl. Devel.)*
John R. Nagel *(V.P.-Investments)*
J.A. Norlander *(V.P.)*
Bruce Paulsen *(V.P. & Controller)*
Ann Richardson *(V.P.-Admin.)*
Kurt E. Retzler *(V.P.-Acquisitions Devel.)*

R.M. Wilson *(V.P.)*

No. of Mfg. Plants/Facilities: 945
No. of Foreign Offices: 678

Computer Systems/Hardware:
IBM

Outside Service Firm(s):

Arthur Andersen & Co.*(Auditors)*
45 S. 7th St.
Minneapolis, MN 55402

First Bank of Austin*(Major Banking Relationship)*
Austin, MN

First Bank Minneapolis*(Major Banking Relationship)*
Minneapolis, MN

Marquette Bank, N.A.*(Major Banking Relationship)*
Sixth & Marquette
Minneapolis, MN 55402
Tel.: 612-341-5651

Travelers Insurance Co.*(Group Insurer)*
1 Tower Square
Hartford, CT 06183-2492
Tel.: 203-277-4542
Fax: 203-277-5038

Groups:

Carlson Marketing Group, Inc. **(1)**
P.O. Box 59159, Carlson Parkway
Minneapolis, MN 55459
Tel.: 612-540-5288 (100%)
Approx.Sls.: $900,000,000
Motivational Training, Marketing & Incentive Travel Organization
S.I.C.: 7389
C.L. Carlson *(Chm.)*
Charles W. Schmid *(Pres.)*
Walter W. Erickson *(Exec. V.P.)*
Thomas N. Wilkolak *(Exec. V.P.)*
Mark Larson *(V.P.-Fin.)*

Divisions:

Carlson International Division **(2)**
P.O. Box 59159, Carlson Parkway
Minneapolis, MN 55459
Tel.: 612-540-5288
International Services
S.I.C.: 7389

E. F. MacDonald Motivation Div. **(2)**
P.O. Box 59159
Minneapolis, MN 55459
Tel.: 612-540-5000
Incentive & Motivation Firm
S.I.C.: 7389
Charles Schmid *(Pres.)*

Carlson Promotion Division **(2)**
P.O. Box 59159, Carlson Parkway
Minneapolis, MN 55459
Tel.: 612-540-5887
Creator of Logo Identified Specialty Advertising Products & Custom-Made Catalogs, Mail Order Sales & Fulfillment
S.I.C.: 7311
Walter W. Erickson *(Exec. V.P. & Gen. Mgr.)*

Carlson Retail Marketing **(2)**
Carlson Parkway
Minneapolis, MN 55459-8207
Tel.: 612-449-3704
Fax: 612-449-3752
Emp.: 650
Fiscal Year-end: 12/31/91
Trading Stamp Services
S.I.C.: 7389
Mike Simpson *(Pres.)*
Dick Shinofield *(V.P.-Legal)*
Pat Stoup *(V.P.-Human Rels.)*
Bob Crump *(Mktg. Dir.)*
Mal Anderson *(Sls. Dir.)*
James L. Doonan *(Natl. Sls. Mgr.)*

Subsidiaries:

K-Promotions, Inc. **(2)**
3825 W. Green Tree Rd.
Milwaukee, WI 53209
Tel.: 414-352-3450 (100%)
Mail Order
S.I.C.: 7389
Thomas V. Belle *(Exec. V.P.)*

Carlson Learning Company **(2)**
Carlson Parkway
Minneapolis, MN 55459
Tel.: 612-540-5100 (100%)
Offers Training Seminars & Learning Programs
S.I.C.: 8741
Thomas V. Belle *(Pres. & Chief Exec. Officer)*

Carlson Hospitality Group, Inc. **(1)**
P.O. Box 59159, Carlson Parkway
Minneapolis, MN 55459-8204
Tel.: 612-540-5526 (100%)
Approx.Sls.: $2,100,000,000
Hospitality Operations, Including Hotels, Resorts & Restaurants
S.I.C.: 7011; 5812
Juergen Bartels *(Pres. & Chief Oper. Officer)*

Divisions:

Radisson Hotels International Inc. **(2)**
P.O. Box 59159, Carlson Pkwy.
Minneapolis, MN 55459
Tel.: 612-540-5226
Hotels
S.I.C.: 7011
Juergen Bartels *(Pres.)*

Division:

Radisson Hotel Corporation **(3)**
Carlwon Pkwy.
Minneapolis, MN 55459-8204
Tel.: 612-540-5526
Tel.: 800-333-3333
Fax: 612-449-3400
Emp.: 350
Fiscal Year-end: 12/31/90
Management, Franchising, Ownership of Hotels, Inns & Resorts
S.I.C.: 7011
Curtis L. Carlson *(Chm. Bd.)*
John Norlander *(Pres.)*
Peter Blyth *(Exec. V.P.-Devel.)*
Tom Jardine *(V.P.-Pub. Rels.)*
Sue Gordon *(V.P.-Personnel)*
Geof Rochester *(V.P.-Mktg.)*
Alice Anderson *(Adv. Dir.)*

Subsidiary:

National Hotel Corp. **(4)**
P.O. Box 59159, Carlson Parkway
Minneapolis, MN 55459
Tel.: 612-540-5283 (100%)
Hotel Management
S.I.C.: 7011
John Norlander *(Pres.)*

Colony Hotels & Resorts, Inc. **(2)**
Carlson Parkway
Minneapolis, MN 55459
Tel.: 612-540-5000
Resort Management
S.I.C.: 7011
Joan A. Sills *(Pres.)*

TGI Friday's, Inc. **(2)**
14665 Midway Rd.
Addison, TX 75244
Tel.: 214-450-5400
Owns, Operates & Licenses Restaurant Chain
S.I.C.: 5812
Richard Rivera *(Pres. & Chief Exec. Officer)*
Nicholas Galanos *(Exec. V.P.-Opers.)*
Wallace Doolin *(Exec. V.P.-Franchise & Corp. Devel.)*
Stephen M. King *(V.P. & Chief Oper. Officer)*

Hospitality Procurement Division **(2)**
Carlson Pkwy, P.O. Box 59159,
Minneapolis, MN 55459-8202
Tel.: 612-540-5361 (100%)
Emp.: 20
Design/Construction Corporation Working Closely with Radisson Hotel Corp. on Interior Design/Construction
S.I.C.: 7389
Ann Richardson *(Pres.)*

Carlson Travel Group, Inc. **(1)**
P.O. Box 59159, Carlson Parkway
Minneapolis, MN 55459
Tel.: 612-540-5000 (100%)
Travel Agency
S.I.C.: 4724
Charles W. Schmid *(Pres. & Chief Oper. Officer)*

Divisions:

Carlson Travel Network-Commercial **(2)**
Carlson Parkway
Minneapolis, MN 55459
Tel.: 612-449-2280
Fax: 612-540-0259
Approx.Rev.: $6,100,000,000
376 Business Travel Agencies
S.I.C.: 4724
John Reiner *(Pres.-Carlson Travel Network-Cmml.)*
Charles W. Schmid *(Pres. & Chief Oper. Officer)*
Ron Letterman *(Pres.-Carlson Travel Network-Retail)*
Paul Vornle *(V.P. & Gen Mgr.-Carlson Travel Network-Intl.)*

Subsidiary:

Carlson Travel Network-Retail **(3)**
P.O. Box 59159, Carlson Parkway
Minneapolis, MN 55459
Tel.: 612-332-4323 (100%)
Emp.: 35
S.I.C.: 4724
Charles W. Schmid *(Pres.)*

Carlson Travel Network International **(2)**
P.O. Box 59159, Carlson Pkwy.
Minneapolis, MN 55459
Tel.: 612-540-5000
International Network Delivering Commerical & Leisure Travel Services to Clients in Western Europe & the Pacific Rim
S.I.C.: 4724

Carlson Travel Network Retail **(2)**
P.O. Box 59159, Carlson Pkwy.
Minneapolis, MN 55459
Tel.: 6013-540-5000
National Network Delivering a Consistently High Level of Leisure & Local Commercial Travel Services
S.I.C.: 4724

Subsidiaries:

Carlson Leasing, Inc. **(1)**
P.O Box 59159, Carlson Parkway
Minneapolis, MN 55459-8215
Tel.: 612-540-5840 (100%)
Equipment Leasing
S.I.C.: 7359
John R. Nagel *(Pres.)*

Subsidiary:

North American Financial Corp. **(2)**
Carlson Parkway
Minneapolis, MN 55459
Tel.: 612-540-5000 (100%)
Equipment Leasing
S.I.C.: 7359
John Nagel *(Pres. & Chief Exec. Officer)*

Carlson Real Estate Company **(1)**
45 S. 7th St., Ste. 2222
Minneapolis, MN 55402
Tel.: 612-333-9898 (100%)
Approx.Sls.: $40,000,000
Emp.: 40
Real Estate
S.I.C.: 6514
Dean A. Rieson *(Pres.)*
Mark Herreid *(V.P.-Fin.)*
Brad Lis *(Dir.-Investments)*

Non-U.S. Holdings:

Carlson Marketing Group Ltd. **(1)**
5353 Dundas Street West
Islington, ON Canada M9B 6J3
Tel.: 416-236-1991 (100%)
Telex: 06-969 550
Emp.: 131
Business Services
S.I.C.: 7389
Terry Rumsey *(Pres.)*

Carlson Marketing Group Japan Co. Ltd. **(1)**
Aoyama Bldg., Room 802
Tokyo, 107, Japan
Tel.: 03-3405-1911
Trading Stamp Services
S.I.C.: 7389
Peter Kenyon *(Pres.)*
J.C. Carlson *(V.P. & Chief Fin. Officer)*

Carlson Marketing Group (Aust.) Pty. Limited **(1)**
P.O. Box 474,
Edgecliff, N.S.W. 2027, Australia
Tel.: 61 2 327 8160 (100%)
Fax: 61 2 327 2748
Emp.: 3
Business Services
S.I.C.: 7389
Noel Rugg *(Mng. Dir.)*

P. Lawson Travel, Ltd. **(1)**
5353 Dundas St., W., Ste. 400
Islington, ON M9B 6J3, Canada
Tel.: 416-236-1921 (100%)
Travel Agency
S.I.C.: 4724
John Powell *(Pres. & Chief Oper. Officer)*

Carlson Marketing Group (U.K.) Limited **(1)**
Belgrave House, 1 Grey Friars, 7th Fl.
Northampton, NN 12LQ, United Kingdom
Tel.: 44 604 20035 (100%)
Telex: 312478 EFMNORG
Fax: 011-44-604-230219
Emp.: 100
Sales & Incentives
S.I.C.: 7389
Joe Thomas *(Mng. Dir.)*

Bernard Krief Motivation, S.A., Carlson Marketing Group **(1)**
115, rue du Bac
Paris, 75007, France
Emp.: 35
Sales Incentives
S.I.C.: 7389
Bernard Krief *(Pres.)*

The E. F. MacDonald Verkaufsforderung GmbH **(1)**
Vprgeborgstrasse 1 5000
Cologne, 1, Germany
Tel.: 49 221 380373 (100%)
Telex: 841-888 1180
Fax: 49-221-341-837
Emp.: 15
Sales & Incentives
S.I.C.: 7389
Gertjen Keg *(Dir.)*

Motivation S.P.A. **(1)**
Corso, Italia 17 20122
Milan, Italy
Tel.: 39 2 8891
Telex: 313147
Emp.: 85
Sales & Incentives
S.I.C.: 7389
Mario Grisorio *(Chm. Bd.)*

Premiums Intl. Ltd. **(1)**
Park & Charlotte St.
Port of Spain, Trinidad & Tobago
Tel.: 809-623-1209 (100%)
Sales & Incentives
S.I.C.: 7389

Saproma S.A. **(1)**
Avenue Edouard Lacomble 21 1040
Brussels, Belgium
Tel.: 32-2-736-8925
Telex: 846-25465
Emp.: 8
Business Services
S.I.C.: 7389
Rene Embrechts *(Mng. Dir.)*

Carlson Marketing Group Scandinavia Motivation Service AB **(1)**
Box 225, S-18252
Djursholm, Sweden
Tel.: 46-8-753-0195
Telex: 15287
Business Services
S.I.C.: 7389
Ulf Landgren *(Mng. Dir.)*

American Motivation (N.Z.) Ltd. **(1)**
5 Porters Ave. Eden Terrace,
Auckland, 1, New Zealand
Tel.: 64 9 396800
Fax: 64 9 392098
Emp.: 15
Business Services
S.I.C.: 7389
Noel Rugg *(V.P.)*

Carlson Companies, Inc.—(Continued)

Carlson Marketing Group Japan KK **(1)**
8F Helios Bldg., 5-1-3 Nishi-Gotanda
Shimayawa-ku,
Tokyo, 141, Japan
Tel.: 03-3491-4681
Fax: 81 3 491 6920
Emp.: 3
Business Services
S.I.C.: 7389
Peter Kenyon *(Gen. Mgr.)*

CDHM
CARLSON, DEL GALDO, HOAG, MATTHEI ADVERTISING INC.

CARLSON, DELGALDO, HOAG, MATTHEI ADVERTISING, INC.
One Main Place, 750 E. Main St.
Stamford, CT 06902
Tel.: 203-967-7200
Year Founded: 1988
Approx.Billings: $13,875,000
Emp.: 18
Consumer & Business-to-Business Adv.
Joseph A. DelGaldo *(Pres. & Chief Exec. Officer)*
William K. Hoag *(Exec. V.P. & Dir. Media & Mktg. Services)*
C. Chandler Pohl *(Sr. V.P.)*
Gary W. Sumple *(Dir.-Corp. Devel.& New Bus. Contact)*
Gerald E. Fox *(V.P.)*
Walter C. Smith *(Controller)*
Anthony Cassalia *(Mgr.-Studio)*
Diane Sweeney *(Mgr.-Office)*
Lola Hazzard *(Telecommunications)*

Computer Systems/Hardware:
IBM System 36

CARLSON & PARTNERS, INC.
950 Third Ave.
New York, NY 10022
Tel.: 212-754-6050
Year Founded: 1989
Approx.Billings: $40,000,000
Emp.: 27
Fashion & Fragrance Adv.
Sandra Carlson *(Pres. & Dir.-Creative)*
C. Scott Hawley *(Dir.-Pub. Rels.)*

CARLTON MANUFACTURING, INC.
317 W. Franklin St.
Elkhart, IN 46516
Tel.: 219-293-4507 **IN**
Fax: 219-293-3669
Year Founded: 1976
Approx.Sls.: $27,000,000
Emp.: 350
Mfr. of Upholstered On Wood Frames Couches, Sofas, Chairs & Rockers
S.I.C.: 2512
Ed Haradine *(Chm. Bd.)*
Douglas Mercier *(Pres.)*
Forest Hudspeth *(V.P.)*
Jean Rowe *(Controller)*

Outside Service Firm(s):

Crowe, Chizaek & Co.*(Auditors)*
Elkhart, IN

Warrick, Weaver, Boyn*(Legal Firm)*
Midwest Commerce Bldg., 121 W. Franklin St.
Elkhart, IN 46516

AmeriTrust National Bank*(Major Banking Relationship)*
Elkart, IN

CARLYLE & CO. JEWELERS
4615 Dundas Dr.
Greensboro, NC 27407
Mailing Address:
P.O. Box 21768,
Greensboro, NC 27420
Tel.: 919-294-2450
Fax: 919-294-2679
Year Founded: 1922
Approx.Sls.: $62,000,000
Emp.: 700
Fiscal Year-end: 3/31/91
Jewelry Retailer; 69 Stores in 11 States
S.I.C.: 5944
Lawrence M. Cohen *(Chm. Bd.)*
Russell Cohen *(Vice Chm. & Co-Chief Exec. Officer)*
John K. Cohen *(Pres. & Chief Exec. Officer)*
Richard I. Backer *(Exec. V.P.-Devel. & Asst. Sec.)*
Martin M. Bernstein *(Exec. V.P.-Real Estate)*
Ann I. Cranford *(V.P.-Store Opers.)*
Reuben E. Mercer *(V.P.-Credit & Sls.)*
Tom A. Heltsley *(Controller)*
Dru Michaels *(Mgr.-Adv.)*

CARLYLE HOLDING CORPORATION
1001 Pennsylvania Ave. N.W.
Washington, DC 20004
Tel.: 202-347-2626 **DE**
Sales Range: $80-99 Million
Venture Capital, Merchant Banking Holding Company, Real Estate
S.I.C.: 6799; 6099; 6719; 6531
Stephen L. Norris *(Chm. Bd.)*
William E. Conway Jr. *(Pres.)*

Subsidiary:

The Carlyle Group **(1)**
1001 Pennsylvania Ave. N.W.
Washington, DC 20004
Tel.: 202-347-2626 (100%)
Fax: 202-347-1818
Venture Capital Investors, Merchant Bankers, Real Estate
S.I.C.: 6799; 6099; 6531
Frederic Malek *(Sr. Advisor)*
Kevin Carney *(Comptroller)*

Subsidiaries:

CB Commercial Real Estate Group, Inc. **(2)**
533 Fremont Ave., Ste. 1000
Los Angeles, CA 90071
Tel.: 213-613-3241
Earnings: ($84,400,000)
Approx.Rev.: $339,500,000
Real Estate Brokers
S.I.C.: 6531
James J. Didion *(Co-Chm. Bd.)*
Frederic Malek *(Co-Chm. Bd.)*
Gary Beban *(Pres.)*
Stephen Tinsley *(Exec. V.P.)*
David A. Davidson *(Treas.)*

Divisions:

CB Commercial Real Estate Group Central Division **(3)**
2500 W. Loop S., Ste. 100
Houston, TX 77027
Tel.: 713-840-6500
Fax: 713-960-8583
Real Estate Brokers
S.I.C.: 6531
Kenneth Sandstad *(Exec. V.P. & Gen. Mgr.)*
Donna Ramsdell Kolius *(Sr. V.P.-Portfolio Services Div.)*

CB Commercial Real Estate Group Eastern Division **(3)**
1600 Summer St.
Stamford, CT 06905
Tel.: 203-329-7900
Fax: 203-348-4743
Real Estate Broker
S.I.C.: 6531
Boyd Van Ness *(Exec. V.P.-Eastern Div.)*

CB Commercial Real Estate Group, New York **(3)**
437 Madison Ave.
New York, NY 10022
Tel.: 212-223-7171
Real Estate Broker
S.I.C.: 6531

Claire Manufacturing Co. **(2)**
500 Vista Ave.
Addison, IL 60101
Tel.: 708-543-7800
Fax: 708-543-4310
Mfr. of Aerosols for Sanitary Supply
S.I.C.: 2842; 2879
Thomas Ehler *(Pres.)*

GDE Systems **(2)**
Approx.Sls.: $310,000,000
Emp.: 2,300
Mfr. of Space Electronics, Navigation Equip, Tactical Radios, Airborne & Surveillance Radar, Automatic Ground Support Equip.
S.I.C.: 3669; 3679

Reilly-Whiteman Inc. **(2)**
6801 Washington St.
Conshohocken, PA 19428
Tel.: 215-828-3800
Mfr. of Industrial Process Oils & Metal-Working Compounds, Basic Refiner of Fatty Oils
S.I.C.: 2842; 2869
Donald Segars *(Pres.)*

Sprayway, Inc. **(2)**
600 Vista Ave.
Addison, IL 60101
Tel.: 708-628-0998
Mfr. of Aerosol Bombs
S.I.C.: 2879
Maurice Aronson *(Pres.)*

Joint Venture:

Vought Aircraft Co. **(1)**
9314 W. Jefferson Blvd.
Dallas, TX 75211
Tel.: 214-266-2011
Fax: 214-266-1989
Aircraft Mfg; 51%-Owned by Carlyle Holding Corp. and 49% Owned by Northrop Corp.
S.I.C.: 3721

CARMICHAEL LYNCH, INC.
800 Hennepin Ave.
Minneapolis, MN 55403
Tel.: 612-334-6000
Fax: 612-334-6090
Year Founded: 1962
Approx.Billings: $110,000,000
Emp.: 168
Leland T. Lynch *(Chm. & Chief Exec. Officer)*
Louis Bacig *(Pres.)*
Charlie Anderson *(Chief Fin. Officer & Mng. Partner)*
Bob Genello *(Grp. Acct. Dir.)*
Doug Spong *(Dir.-Pub. Rels. & Mng. Partner)*
Janet Van Fossan *(Dir.-Human Resources & Sr. Partner)*
Principal(s):
Leland T. Lynch
Louis Bacig
Bob Genello

CARNEGIE ASSOCIATES, INC.
6545 Carnegie Ave.
Cleveland, OH 44103
Tel.: 216-881-3000
Year Founded: 1979
Approx.Billings: $14,000,000
Emp.: 72
Sweepstakes, Contests & Games, Training, Motivation, Inter-Active Systems & Marketing Tactics
Walter L. Schaffer *(Mng. Dir.)*
Jerry Franklin *(V.P.-Fin.)*
Bill Prytherch *(Dir.-Creative & Strategic Plng.)*
Donna Miller *(Mgr.-Human Resources)*

CARNEY/MOHLIN & COMPANY
7 Kimball Lane
Lynnfield, MA 01940
Tel.: 617-246-0782
Fax: 617-246-2406
Year Founded: 1985
Approx.Billings: $10,200,000
Emp.: 11
Advertising, Marketing & Corporate Design
C. Rick Mohlin *(Pres.)*
Renee Farrington *(Dir., Mktg. Services)*

Computer Systems/Hardware:
Apple

CARNIVAL CREATIONS
180 Madison Ave., Suite 901
New York, NY 10016
Tel.: 212-532-0810
Fax: 212-889-6675
Year Founded: 1947
Approx.Sls.: $15,000,000
Emp.: 500
Export
Mfr. Brassieres, Girdles & Panty Girdles
S.I.C.: 2342
Frank Klein *(Pres.)*
Murray Kelberman *(V.P.-Mktg.)*
Frank Solecitto *(Pur. Agent)*

CARNRICK LABS., INC.
65 Horsehill Rd.
Cedar Knolls, NJ 07927
Tel.: 201-267-2670
Fax: 201-267-2728
Year Founded: 1899
Approx.Sls.: $14,000,000
Emp.: 120
Fiscal Year-end: 12/31/91
Mfr. of Pharmaceuticals for Amenorrhea, Obesity, Pain, Headaches, Allergies, Colds, Muscaloskeletal Spasm, Arthritis & Diarrhea
S.I.C.: 2834
Edmond Bergeron *(Pres.)*
Fred Weinstein *(V.P.-Quality Control)*
Donna Vanden Bosch *(V.P. -Fin.)*
Robert G. Davis *(Dir.-Adv.)*
John Visconti *(Mgr.-Quality Control)*

Subsidiary:

Rystan Company, Inc. **(1)**
47 Center Ave.
Little Falls, NJ 07424-0214
Tel.: 201-256-3737
Emp.: 20
Fiscal Year-end: 12/31/91
Mfr. of Chloresium, Panafil, Prophyllin, Derifil
S.I.C.: 2834
Edmund Bergeron *(Pres.)*
Donald H. Leaman, Jr. *(Dir.-Mktg.)*
Robert G. Davis *(Adv. Dir.)*
Herb Wagner *(Plant Mgr.)*

CAROLINA BIOLOGICAL SUPPLY CO.
2700 York Rd.
Burlington, NC 27215
Tel.: 919-584-0381
Tel.: 800-334-5551 **NC**
Telex: 574-354
Fax: 919-584-3399
Year Founded: 1927
Sales Range: $40-59 Million
Emp.: 400
Fiscal Year-end: 5/31/92
Import Export
Mail Order Biological Supplies to Educational Institutions, Living & Preserved Animals & Plants, Visual Aids, Microscope Slides, Microscopes, Biological Models, Lab

Supplies & Chemicals, Books & Computer Programs, Physics & Earth Sciences Materials, Space Science Materials
S.I.C.: 2836; 3821
T.E. Powell III *(Pres.)*
Raymond O. Flagg *(V.P.)*
Daniel E. James *(V.P.)*
James B. MacDonald *(V.P.)*
A.E. Wolfe *(V.P.)*
Robert L. Saffelle, Jr. *(Treas.)*
Charles R. Cote *(Controller)*
Caroline E. Powell *(Sec.)*
Eddie Chrismon *(Dir.-Human Resources)*
Gregg Lee *(Dir.-Import & Pur.)*
Wesley Reynolds, Sr. *(Dir.-Data Processing)*
Harry Shoffner *(Dir.-Mktg. & Pub. Rels.)*
Charles Matthews *(Mgr.-Export)*

Computer Systems/Hardware:
IBM AS400

Outside Service Firm(s):

Wachovia Bank & Trust Co.*(Major Banking Relationship)*
Burlington, NC

Division:

Powell Laboratories **(1)**
P.O. Box 187
Gladstone, OR 97027
Tel.: 503-656-1641
Tel.: 800-547-1733
Fax: 503-656-4208
Sell Biological Materials To Educational Institutions
S.I.C.: 5961
James B. McDonald *(Gen. Mgr.)*

CAROLINA BUILDERS CORPORATION
3227 Wellington Ct.
Raleigh, NC 27615
Mailing Address:
P.O. Box 58515
Raleigh, NC 27658
Tel.: 919-850-8270 **NC**
Fax: 919-850-8280
Assets: $191,000,000
Liabilities: $80,000,000
Net Worth: $111,000,000
Approx.Sls.: $200,000,000
Emp.: 750
Fiscal Year-end: 7/31/91
Import
Manufacture & Distribute Wood Building Products
S.I.C.: 2431; 2439; 2452; 5031
David Dibben *(Chm. Bd.)*
Fenton N. Hord *(Pres. & Chief Exec. Officer)*
Gary Robinette *(Chief Fin. Officer & V.P.)*

Computer Systems/Hardware:
Data General

Outside Service Firm(s):

Price Waterhouse*(Auditors)*
1800 One Triad Plaza
Winston-Salem, NC 27101
Tel.: 919-725-0691
Fax: 919-725-5022

NationsBank Carolinas*(Major Banking Relationship)*
Raleigh, NC

CAROLINA GLOVE CO.
Drawer 820
Newton, NC 28658
Tel.: 704-464-1132
Fax: 704-464-1710
Approx.Sls.: $25,000,000
Emp.: 820
Manufacture Gloves
S.I.C.: 2381; 2259; 3151
Fred Abernethy *(V.P.-Mfg.)*
James S. Abernethy *(V.P.-Sls.)*
J.W. Abernethy III *(V.P.-Sls.)*
Robert C. Abernethy *(Sec.)*
Marshall Fisher *(Dir.-Mktg.)*

Outside Service Firm(s):

McGladrey & Pullen*(Auditors)*
Hickory, NC

Corne, Pitts, Corne & Grant*(Legal Firm)*
Newton, NC

Peoples Bank*(Major Banking Relationship)*
Newton, NC

CAROLINA MILLS, INC.
618 Carolina Ave.
Maiden, NC 28650
Mailing Address:
P. O. Box 157
Maiden, NC 28650
Tel.: 704-428-9911 **NC**
Fax: 704-428-2335
Assets: $108,549,107
Earnings: $7,555,101
Liabilities: $32,603,955
Net Worth: $75,945,152
Approx.Sls.: $178,782,000
Emp.: 2,450
Fiscal Year-end: 9/30/91
Export
Textiles
S.I.C.: 2211; 2231; 2281; 2299; 5021
E.P. Schrum *(Pres., Chief Exec. Officer & Treas.)*
J.G. Harbison *(V.P.-Admin. & Sec.)*
Clyde Hawn *(Pur. Dir.-Supplies)*
Ralph Kendrick *(Pur. Dir.-Fibres)*
Nancy Schrum *(Dir.-Human Resources)*
Mark Midgett *(Dir.-Data Processing)*

No. of Mfg. Plants/Facilities: 13
No. of U.S. Offices: 2

Computer Systems/Hardware:
IBM 4361

Subsidiaries:

Carolina Maiden Corp. **(1)**
Maiden, NC 28650
Tel.: 704-428-9911 (100%)
Emp.: 10
Yarn Sales
S.I.C.: 2284
George A. Moretz *(Pres.)*

CM Furniture, Inc. **(1)**
Hwy. 321 N.
Maiden, NC 28650
Tel.: 704-428-9978
Approx.Sls.: $8,000,000
Emp.: 365
Mfr. & Wholesale Exposed Wood & Fully Upholstered Family Room Furniture
S.I.C.: 2512; 5021
Edward P. Schrum *(Chm. Bd.)*
John Wells *(Pres.)*

CAROLINA MIRROR COMPANY
Hwy. 268 East
North Wilkesboro, NC 28659
Mailing Address:
P.O. Box 548
North Wilkesboro, NC 28659
Tel.: 919-838-2151
Tel.: 800-334-7245
Fax: 919-838-9734
Year Founded: 1936
Approx.Sls.: $37,000,000
Emp.: 550
Fiscal Year-end: 12/31/90
Mfg. Signet Mirrors
S.I.C.: 3231
Tommy Huskey *(Pres. & Chief Exec. Officer)*
Richard Holt *(Exec. V.P. & Gen. Mgr.-Decorative Prods.)*
Bill Anderson *(V.P.-Opers.)*
James Charles *(V.P.-Indus. Prod. Grp.)*
Howard James *(V.P.-Mfg. Prods.)*
W.R. McNeil *(V.P., Treas. & Sec.)*

Division:

Carolina Mirror-Houston **(1)**
17015 Park Row
Houston, TX 77084
Tel.: 800-231-5990
Fax: 713-492-8604
S.I.C.: 3231
Jim Sands *(Gen. Mgr.)*

CAROLINA STEEL CORPORATION
1451 S. Elm St.
Greensboro, NC 27406
Mailing Address:
P.O. Box 20888
Greensboro, NC 27420
Tel.: 919-275-9711 **NC**
Fax: 919-691-5801
Approx.Sls.: $220,000,000
Emp.: 1,250
Fiscal Year-end: 12/29/91
Import Export
Fabricators of Structural Steel, Prestressed Concrete Products; Steel Service Centers
S.I.C.: 3441; 5051; 3272
Hugh H. Williamson III *(Chm. Bd., Pres. & Chief Exec. Officer)*
William J. Bolton *(V.P.-Fin. & Sec.)*
Ronald H. Davis *(V.P.-Admin.)*
Michael DePopas *(Treas.)*
W.C. Summerlin *(Controller)*
Sadie Cox *(Mgr.-Personnel)*
Bob Steelman *(Mgr.-Pur.)*

No. of Mfg. Plants/Facilities: 20
No. of U.S. Offices: 20

Computer Systems/Hardware:
IBM 4341

Outside Service Firm(s):

NationsBank Carolinas*(Major Banking Relationship)*
P.O. Box 21848,
Greensboro, NC 27420

Pilot Life*(Group Insurer)*
Greensboro, NC

Adams, Kleemeier, Hagan, Hannah & Fauts*(Legal Firm)*
Greensboro, NC
Tel.: 919-373-1600

Wachovia Bank & Trust Co.*(Pension Manager)*
P.O. Box 21048,
Greensboro, NC 27402

Subsidiary:

CSC Erectors, Inc. **(1)**
Sandy Ridge Road
Greensboro, NC 27402
Tel.: 919-668-2742 (100%)
Emp.: 35
Structural Erector
S.I.C.: 1741

Manufacturing Plants:

Arnold Concrete Products-Greensboro **(1)**
P.O. Box 3346,
Greensboro, NC 27402
Tel.: 919-668-2742 (100%)
Mfr. of Pre Cast Concrete
S.I.C.: 3272
Ben Wiley *(Pres. - Concrete Prods.)*

Arnold Concrete Products-Raleigh Div. **(1)**
P.O. Box 1604,
Oxford, NC 27565
Tel.: 919-693-1200 (100%)
Mfr. Pre Cast Concrete Panels
S.I.C.: 3272
Ben Wiley *(Gen. Mgr.)*

Carolina Steel-Greenville Plant **(1)**
P.O. Box 128,
Greenville, SC 29602
Tel.: 803-244-3510 (100%)
Metal Service Centers & Offices
S.I.C.: 5051
Christopher Columbus *(Mgr.)*

Carolina Steel-Hickory Plant **(1)**
1115 3rd Ave. N.W.
Hickory, NC 28601
Tel.: 704-322-9420 (100%)
Fabricated Steel
S.I.C.: 3441
Steve Blakeley *(Plant Mgr.)*

Carolina Steel-Salem Plant **(1)**
1725 Vargrave St.
Winston-Salem, NC 27107
Tel.: 919-725-0521 (100%)
Fabricated Steel
S.I.C.: 3441
Mike Carcieri *(Plant Mgr.)*

Service Center Divisions:

Augusta Service Center **(1)**
911 Hayes Drive
Augusta, GA 30903
Tel.: 706-722-9631
Sales & Service
S.I.C.: 5051
Jay Kornegay *(Mgr.)*

Carolina Steel Service Center Plant **(1)**
360 Thompson Rd.
Lexington, KY 40510
Tel.: 606-253-2415
S.I.C.: 5051
Roger Shelton *(Mgr.)*

Carolina Steel Service Center Plant **(1)**
401 Driftwood St.
Nashville, TN 37210
Tel.: 615-254-1311
Alvin Ball *(Mgr.)*

Lynchburg Service Center **(1)**
Elon Industrial Park
Lynchburg, VA 24501
Tel.: 804-929-6801
Sales & Service
S.I.C.: 5051
Gary Mobley *(Mgr.)*

Richmond Service Center **(1)**
Seven Hills & Settlers Roads
Richmond, VA 23231
Tel.: 804-222-5146
Sales & Service
S.I.C.: 5051
Larry Ham *(Mgr.)*

Roinoke Service Center **(1)**
Botetourt Industrial Park, Industrial Park Drive
Hollins, VA 24033
Tel.: 703-992-5252
Sales & Service
S.I.C.: 5051
Gary Mobley *(Mgr.)*

Wilson Service Center **(1)**
2711 Commerce Rd.
Wilson, NC 27893
Tel.: 919-291-4111
Sales & Service
S.I.C.: 5051
Bruce Goodrich *(Mgr.)*

CAROLINA TRACTOR & EQUIPMENT CO.
9000 Stateville Rd.
Charlotte, NC 28213
Mailing Address:
P.O. Box 26665
Charlotte, NC 28221
Tel.: 704-596-6700
Fax: 704-596-1672
Year Founded: 1926
Sales Range: $100-499 Million
Emp.: 400
Fiscal Year-end: 12/31/89
Import Export
Distribution, Parts & Service of Heavy Construction & Industrial Equipment
S.I.C.: 5082; 5084
Ed Weisiger *(Chm. Bd.)*
Ed Weisiger, Jr. *(Pres.)*
John A. Hendrix *(Exec. V.P. & Gen. Mgr.)*
R.G. Harris *(V.P.-Lift Truck Div.)*
Alex Weaver *(V.P.-Parts Div.)*

Carolina Tractor & Equipment Co.—(Continued)

M.C. Fisher *(Controller)*
F. Griffin *(Dir.-Data Processing)*
Ben Putman *(Dir.-Pur.)*
D.P. Saunders *(Dir.-Personnel & Industrial Rels.)*
Ned Story *(Dir.-Construction & Equipment Sls.)*
William R. Padula *(Mgr.-Engine Div.)*
Doug Summers *(Mgr.-Mktg.)*
Principal(s):
Ed Weisiger, Jr.
William R. Padula

No. of U.S. Offices: 5

Computer Systems/Hardware:
IBM AS/400

Outside Service Firm(s):

Price Waterhouse*(Auditors)*
One NationsBank Plaza, Ste. 3200
Charlotte, NC 28280
Tel.: 704-372-9020

Wachovia Bank & Trust Co.*(Major Banking Relationship)*
Charlotte, NC

Marsh & McLennan*(Group Insurer)*
Charlotte, NC

Parker, Poe, Adams & Bernstein*(Legal Firm)*
2600 Charlotte Plaza
Charlotte, NC 28244
Tel.: 704-372-9000

DANIEL CARON LTD.
205 W. 39th St.
New York, NY 10018
Tel.: 212-719-3160 **NY**
Fax: 212-921-4273
Year Founded: 1979
Approx.Sls.: $220,000,000
Emp.: 140
Fiscal Year-end: 12/31/90
Import Export
Manufacturer & Wholesale Distributor of Women's & Children's Clothing
S.I.C.: 5137
Andrew Lee *(Chm. Bd., Pres. & Chief Oper. Officer)*
Dianna Lee *(Exec. V.P. & Sec.)*
Ronald Demichael *(V.P.-Fin.)*
Joseph O'Donnell *(Controller)*
Jamie Yu *(Mgr.-Mngmt. Info. Systems)*
Maurice Zeitouni *(Mgr.-Export/Import)*

No. of Mfg. Plants/Facilities: 3
No. of U.S. Offices: 2

Computer Systems/Hardware:
WANG

Outside Service Firm(s):

Mahoney Cohen & Co., P.C.*(Auditors)*
New York, NY

Fireman's Fund Insurance Co.*(Commercial Insurance Carrier)*
Parsippany, NJ

Chubb Life America*(Group Insurer)*
8 Sylvan Way
Parsippany, NJ

Chemical Banking Corp.*(Major Banking Relationship)*
277 Park Ave.
New York, NY 10041
Tel.: 212-310-6407
Fax: 212-310-4526

Subsidiary:

Faddaley Enterprises Inc. **(1)**
241 W. 37th St.
New York, NY 10018
Tel.: 212-827-0880
Emp.: 40
Mfr. of Women's & Children's Clothing & Accessories
S.I.C.: 2331
Albert Tang *(Pres.)*
Bruce Allen *(V.P.-Fin.)*

CAROUSEL SNACK BARS OF MINNESOTA
9549 Penn Ave., S.
Minneapolis, MN 55431
Tel.: 612-887-5399 **MN**
Fax: 612-881-8286
Year Founded: 1966
Assets: $17,700,000
Liabilities: $7,100,000
Net Worth: $10,600,000
Approx.Sls.: $54,900,000
Emp.: 2,500
Fiscal Year-end: 12/31/92
Restaurant
S.I.C.: 5812
Stephen Lieberman *(Pres., Chief Exec. & Chief Oper. Officer)*
Sanford J. Goldberg *(Sr. V.P.-Fin.)*
Anthony E. Dammicci *(V.P.-Real Estate)*
Harold Lieberman *(V.P. & Controller)*
David Lieberman *(Treas.)*
Harold Okinow *(Sec.)*
Terry Forsman *(Dir.-Personnel)*
Sue Vogt *(Dir.-Pur.)*

Principal(s):
Stephen Lieberman
David Lieberman

Outside Service Firm(s):

Lurie, Besikof, Lapidus & Co.*(Auditors)*
Minneapolis, MN

Phillips, Gross & Aaron*(Legal Firm)*
Minneapolis, MN

Norwest Bank Minnesota, N.A.*(Major Banking Relationship)*
Minneapolis, MN

Norwest Bank Minnesota, N.A.*(Pension Manager)*
6th St. & Marquette Av.
Minneapolis, MN 55479
Tel.: 612-667-1234

E. R. CARPENTER CO.
5016 Monument Ave.
Richmond, VA 23230
Mailing Address:
P.O. Box 27205
Richmond, VA 23261
Tel.: 804-359-0800
Fax: 804-257-5482
Approx.Sls.: $367,000,000
Emp.: 6,200
Manufacture Polyester Fiber Battings, Plastic Foams
S.I.C.: 2299; 3089
Stanley F. Pauley *(Chm. Bd. & Chief Exec. Officer)*
G. Loving *(V.P.-Sls.)*
A.F. Markey *(V.P. & Treas.)*
D. Friend *(Chief Engr.)*
B. Blackwell *(Dir.-Data Processing)*
Dave Harned *(Dir.-Personnel)*
Marti Proctor *(Mgr.-Employee Benefits)*

Computer Systems/Hardware:
IBM 3083

Outside Service Firm(s):

KPMG Peat Marwick*(Auditors)*
1021 E. Cary St., Ste. 1900
Richmond, VA 23219
Tel.: 804-649-9091

McGuire, Woods, Battle & Boothe*(Legal Firm)*
One James Ctr., 801 E. Main St.
Richmond, VA 23220
Tel.: 804-644-4131

Sovran Bank*(Major Banking Relationship)*
Sovran Center, 1111 E. Main St.
Richmond, VA 23219
Tel.: 804-788-2000

CARPENTER RIGGING
222 Napolean St.
San Francisco, CA 94124
Tel.: 415-285-1954
S.I.C.: 5085
Barnard Martin *(Pres.)*

Subsidiary:

Hood Industries Inc. **(1)**
2459 Fruitdale Ave., Unit 3
Bakersfield, CA 93313
Tel.: 805-833-0354

CARPETERIA, INC.
28159 Ave. Stanford
Valencia, CA 91355
Mailing Address:
P.O. Box 5902,
Santa Clarita, CA 91355
Tel.: 805-295-1000
Tel.: 800-FLOOR ME **CA**
Fax: 805-257-4958
Year Founded: 1960
Approx.Sls.: $90,000,000
Emp.: 300
Fiscal Year-end: 7/31/91
Retail Floor Covering Specialty Stores
S.I.C.: 5713
Corporate Giving Program: Local Community Support Programs Which are Education, or Youth/Children Oriented
Ted Haserjian *(Chm. Bd. & Sec.)*
Harold Haserjian *(Pres.)*
Bryan Haserjian *(Exec. V.P. & Treas.)*
Rockton Haserjian *(Exec. V.P.-Admin.)*
Ruth Dugan *(Exec. Admin. Assis.)*
Terry Mansky *(Grp. V.P.-Franchise)*
Brian Layfield *(V.P. & Chief Fin. Officer)*
Gary Liebman *(V.P.-Mktg.)*
Terry Mansky *(Gen. Counsel)*
Alek Poulatian *(Controller)*
George Holder *(Exec. Dir.-Company & Franchise Services)*
Steven Davidson *(Dir.-Products & Services)*
Stan Langer *(Dir.-Adv.)*
Sharon Hagen *(Mgr.-Personnel)*
Rocky Rogers *(Mgr.-Pur.)*
Natalie Wooldridge *(Mgr.-Pub. Rels.)*
Tracy Yu *(Mgr.-Mngmt. Information Systems)*

Computer Systems/Hardware:
NCR; Wyse

Outside Service Firm(s):

Philadelphia National Bank*(Major Banking Relationship)*
Philadelphia, PA

Carpro, Inc.
(See listing under Carpeteria, Inc.)

CARQUEST
715 Bypass North
Andalusia, AL 36420
Mailing Address:
P.O. Box 1488,
Andalusia, AL 36420
Tel.: 205-222-7501
Fax: 205-222-7925
Year Founded: 1968
Approx.Sls.: $52,000,000
Emp.: 415
Franchised Auto Parts Distributor
S.I.C.: 5531
Temple Sloan III *(Pres.)*
Dan Studstill *(V.P.)*
Alan Till *(Sec. & Treas.)*

Outside Service Firm(s):

Ernst & Young*(Auditors)*
Harbert Plaza, 1900 AmSouth
Birmingham, AL 35243

Albrith & Givhan*(Legal Firm)*
Birmingham, AL

Central Bank*(Major Banking Relationship)*
Birmingham, AL

Subsidiaries:

All Pro, Inc. **(1)**
208 E. 3 Notch St.
Andalusia, AL 36420
Tel.: 205-222-2414
Emp.: 50
Franchised Auto Parts Distr.
S.I.C.: 6794
Dan Studstill *(Pres.)*
Mark Wiggins *(V.P. & Gen. Mgr.)*
Clark Wilson *(Dir.-Adv.)*

Automotive Marketing Assoc. **(1)**
1645 Murfreefboro Rd., Ste. A
Nashville, TN 37217
Tel.: 615-361-7914
Distr. Lisenced Auto Parts
S.I.C.: 5531
Chuck Rider *(Chm., Pres. & Chief Exec. Officer)*

CARQUEST CORPORATION
580 White Plains Rd.
Tarrytown, NY 10591
Tel.: 914-332-1515
Year Founded: 1974
Automotive Supplies & Parts
S.I.C.: 5013; 5531
Neil Stockel *(Chm. Bd.)*
Daniel M. Bock *(Pres.)*
Tom Kirby *(V.P.)*
Peter Korrafel *(Sec. & Treas.)*
Tom Easton *(Dir.-Training)*
Len Hoppe *(Dir.-Adv.)*
Mike Leach *(Dir.-Mktg.)*
Jennifer Zezza *(Gen. Mgr.)*
Barbara Kuzemczak *(Asst. Mgr.-Adv.)*
Dave Loew *(Asst. Mgr.-Adv.)*

Distribution Centers:

ADI Warehouse Division, Carquest Corp. **(1)**
3155 Terrace St.
Kansas City, MO 64111
Tel.: 816-753-6660
Automotive Supplies & Parts
S.I.C.: 5013; 5531
Martin Brown *(Chm.)*
Dan Myers *(Pres.)*

Automotive Warehouse, Inc. **(1)**
2760 Waiwai Loop
Honolulu, HI 96819
Tel.: 808-836-0331
Automotive Supplies & Parts
S.I.C.: 5013; 5531
Kenneth Kaminaka *(Gen. Mgr.)*

BWP Distributors, Inc. **(1)**
1055 Bronx River Ave.
Bronx, NY 10472
Tel.: 718-991-9000
Automotive Supplies & Parts; Branches In Bristol, CT & Fairfield, NJ
S.I.C.: 5013; 5531
Neil Stockel *(Pres.)*

Cardis Corporation **(1)**
12950 E. Alondra Blvd.
Cerritos, CA 90701
Tel.: 310-926-4492
Automotive Supplies & Parts; Distribution Centers In Anaheim, Buena Park, Compton, Fresno, Hayward, Sacramento, San Diego & Ventura, CA
S.I.C.: 5013; 5531
Ken Cleveland *(Pres. & Chm. Bd.)*

Fremont Electric Company **(1)**
744 N. 34th St.
Seattle, WA 98103
Tel.: 206-633-2323
Automotive Supplies & Parts; Branches In Yakima, WA
S.I.C.: 5013; 5531
Moore McKinley, Jr. *(Pres.)*

General Parts, Inc. **(1)**
2635 Millbrook Rd.
Raleigh, NC 27604
Tel.: 919-876-9813

Automotive Supplies & Parts; Distribution Centers In Albany, GA, Lexington, KY; Bay City & Lansing, MI; Jackson, MS; Lakeville, MN; Billings, MT; Memphis & Nashville, TN; Asheville, Raleigh, NC, Indianapolis, IN; Montgomery & Andalusia, AL; Marshfield, WI; Portland, OR & Lemont, IL
S.I.C.: 5013; 5531
O. Temple Sloan, Jr. *(Chm. Bd.)*
Joseph Owen *(Pres.)*
C. Hamilton Sloan *(Exec. V.P.)*
Malcolm C. Graham *(Sec.)*
John Gardner *(Treas.)*

Hatch Grinding Company **(1)**
320 S. Lipan St.
Denver, CO 80223
Tel.: 303-744-7114
Automotive Supplies & Parts; Branch In Albuquerque, NM
S.I.C.: 5013; 5531
Peter Kornafel *(Pres.)*

A.E. Lottes Company **(1)**
800 N. 17th
St. Louis, MO 63106
Tel.: 314-436-4000
Automotive Supplies & Parts
S.I.C.: 5013; 5531
A.E. Lottes, III *(Pres.)*

Muffler Warehouse, Inc. **(1)**
1161 Wilson St.
Pocatello, ID 83201
Tel.: 208-237-6606
Automotive Supplies & Parts; Branches In Boise & Idaho Falls, ID
S.I.C.: 5013; 5531
John Albano *(Gen. Mgr.)*

PSC Distributing, Inc. **(1)**
702 N. 21st Ave.
Phoenix, AZ 85009
Tel.: 602-257-0605
Automotive Supplies & Parts; Branches In Mesa, Phoenix & Tuscon, AZ
S.I.C.: 5013; 5531
James Eaton *(Pres.)*

Parts Wholesalers, Inc. **(1)**
155 Perry Rd.
Bangor, ME 04401
Tel.: 207-941-1230
Automotive Supplies & Parts
S.I.C.: 5013; 5531
Earl Seymour *(Gen. Mgr.)*

Strafco **(1)**
1964 S. Alamo St.
San Antonio, TX 78204
Tel.: 210-226-0101
Automotive Supplies & Parts; Distribution Centers In Amarillo, Dallas, El Paso & Houston, TX
S.I.C.: 5013; 5531
David J. Straus *(Chm.)*

Sussen, Inc. **(1)**
600 Carnegie Ave.
Cleveland, OH 44103
Tel.: 216-361-1700
Automotive Supplies & Parts; Branches In Columbus & Youngstown, OH & Buffalo, NY
S.I.C.: 5013; 5531
Joseph J. Sussen *(Chm. Bd.)*
Daniel C. Sussen, Sr. *(Pres.)*
Bernard S. Lindway *(V.P.-Fin., Treas. & Sec.)*
William G. Fording *(V.P.-Mktg.)*
William Eickenberry *(V.P.-Pur.)*
Lynn Demeter *(V.P.-Personnel)*
Robert Broadman *(Mgr.-Sls.)*

CARR GOTTSTEIN FOODS
6411 A Street
Anchorage, AK 99518
Tel.: 907-561-1944
Fax: 907-564-2351
Sales Range: $10-19 Million
Grocery Stores
S.I.C.: 5499
Mark Williams *(Pres.)*

THE OLIVER CARR CO.
1700 Pennsylvania Ave. N.W., Ste. 900
Washington, DC 20006
Tel.: 202-624-1700
Fax: 202-737-0410
Fax: 202-737-2345
Year Founded: 1962
Approx.Sls.: $299,000,000
Emp.: 750
Real Estate Developer & Manager
S.I.C.: 6531; 6552
Oliver Carr *(Chm. Bd.)*
Robert O. Carr *(Pres.)*
Steven N. Bralower *(Sr. V.P.-Leasing)*
John J. Donovan, Jr. *(Sr. V.P.-Leasing)*
James S. Williams *(V.P.-Design & Construction)*

Principal(s):
Oliver Carr

Outside Service Firm(s):

Metropolitan Life Insurance Co.*(Group Insurer)*
Washington, DC

Stohlman Beuchert Egan & Smith*(Legal Firm)*
Washington, DC

Subsidiary:

Carpark **(1)**
1700 Pennsylvania Ave.
Washington, DC 20006
Tel.: 202-383-6250
Parking Management Company; Monthly & Daily Parking for Cars
S.I.C.: 7521
Phillip R. Carr *(Pres.)*

CARRAFIELLO, DIEHL & ASSOCIATES, INC.
90 N. Broadway
Irvington, NY 10533
Tel.: 914-591-9191
Fax: 914-591-9146
Fax: 914-591-4060
Year Founded: 1973
Approx.Billings: $68,500,000
Emp.: 90
Consumer & Medical Adv.
A. Louis Carrafiello *(Pres., Treas. & Chief Exec. Officer)*
Don J. Guarnieri *(Exec. V.P., Chief Fin. Officer)*
Robert M. Lynch *(Exec. V.P., Chief Oper. Officer)*
Robert C. Brandt *(Exec. V.P.)*
C. Patrick Mandarano *(Exec. V.P.)*
John F. Carlucci *(Sr. V.P.)*
Edward Cohen *(Sr. V.P.)*
John H. Kane *(Sr. V.P.)*
Marguerite E. Kennedy *(Sr. V.P., Media Dir.)*
Ruth L. McCarthy *(Sr. V.P.)*
Robert LaRocca *(Sr. V.P.)*
Robert Leung *(Sr. V.P.)*
Robert J. Morais *(Sr. V.P.)*
Steven Roth *(Sr. V.P.)*
Thomas G. Shea *(Sr. V.P.)*
Stanley M. Turk *(Sr. V.P.)*
Al Jacobsen *(V.P.)*
Robert J. Burriesci *(V.P.)*
Leonard F. Fiore *(V.P.)*
Tyler G. Kaus *(V.P.)*
Rudolph Kluck *(V.P.)*
Melinda Schmitz *(V.P.)*
Arthur Richenthal *(Gen. Counsel, Corp. Sec.)*
Ann Keely *(Mgr. Sec. Services)*

CARRIER VIBRATING EQUIPMENT, INC.
3400 Fern Valley Rd.
Louisville, KY 40213
Mailing Address:
P.O. Box 37070
Louisville, KY 40233
Tel.: 502-969-3171 **KY**
Fax: 502-969-3172
Approx.Sls.: $16,000,000
Emp.: 104
Fiscal Year-end: 10/31/90

Import Export
Manufactures Vibrating Conveyors, Feeders, Process Equipment, Bin & Pile Dischargers; Screw Feeders
S.I.C.: 3535
Ken N. Patel *(Pres. & Chief Exec. Officer)*
Brian M. Trudel *(Mgr.-Sls.)*
C.E. Heitmiller *(Mgr.-Engrng.)*
Ceil Platt *(Mgr.-Adv.)*

CARRIS REELS, INC.
Depot Lane
Rutland, VT 05701
Mailing Address:
P.O. Box 696
Rutland, VT 05702
Tel.: 802-773-9111 **VT**
Fax: 802-773-9112
Year Founded: 1980
Approx.Sls.: $44,000,000
Emp.: 400
Mfr. of Plywood Reels & Wood Spools
S.I.C.: 2499
William Carris *(Pres.)*
Marilynn Dalick *(Sec.)*

Outside Service Firm(s):

First Vermont Bank & Trust*(Major Banking Relationship)*
Rutland, VT

CARROLL'S FOODS, INC.
Hwy. 24 W.
Warsaw, NC 28398
Mailing Address:
P.O. Box 856
Warsaw, NC 28398
Tel.: 919-293-3434 **NC**
Fax: 919-293-7551
Year Founded: 1939
Approx.Sls.: $250,000,000
Emp.: 630
Fiscal Year-end: 12/31/91

Export
Producers of Hogs & Turkeys
S.I.C.: 0213; 0253
Joyce Carroll Matthews *(Chm. Bd., Sec. & Treas.)*
F.J. Faison, Jr. *(Pres.)*
Roger H. Kramer *(Chief Fin. Officer)*
Carroll Matthews Arthur *(V.P.)*
James Matthews *(V.P.)*
Jeffrey Matthews *(V.P.)*
Gregg Schmidt *(V.P.-Production)*
Billy Holt *(Pur. Agent)*
Barbara McLawhon *(Mgr.-Data Processing)*
Jay Thomas *(Mgr.-Human Resources)*
Don Butler *(Dir.-Real Estate)*
Dr. Shannon Jennings *(Poultry Veterinarian)*
Dr. Harry Snelson *(Swine Veterinarian)*
Lisa Blackburn *(Exec. Sec.)*

Principal(s):
Joyce Carroll Matthews
Carroll Matthews Arthur
James Matthews
Jeffrey Matthews

Computer Systems/Hardware:
IBM AS 400

Outside Service Firm(s):

Rabobank Neduland*(Auditors)*
New York, NY

Cape Fear Farm Credit*(Group Insurer)*
Clinton, NC

Ward & Smith*(Legal Firm)*
P.O. Box 867,
New Bern, NC 28560
Tel.: 919-633-1000

NationsBank Carolinas*(Major Banking Relationship)*
Kenansville, NC

CARROLS CORPORATION
968 James St.
Syracuse, NY 13203
Mailing Address:
P.O. Box 6969
Syracuse, NY 13217
Tel.: 315-424-0513 **DE**
Fax: 315-425-8874
Assets: $130,433,000
Earnings: ($2,774,000)
Liabilities: $132,998,000
Net Worth: $2,565,000
Approx.Rev.: $150,105,000
Emp.: 5,900
Fiscal Year-end: 12/31/90
Operates 164 Franchised Fast Food Restaurants Under the Burger King Trade Name in 9 States
S.I.C.: 5812; 5149
Alan Vituli *(Chm. Bd.)*
David J. Connor *(Pres. & Chief Exec. Officer)*
Daniel T. Accordino *(Exec. V.P.-Opers.)*
Richard V. Cross *(Exec. V.P.-Fin.)*
Paul P. Drotar *(V.P., Corp. Controller & Sec.)*
Richard W. Wessels *(V.P.-Information Systems)*
Michael A. Biviano *(V.P. & Reg. Mgr.)*
George Shore *(V.P. & Reg. Mgr.)*
David Smith *(V.P. & Reg. Mgr.)*
James Tunnessen *(V.P. & Reg. Mgr.)*
Marie Irwin *(Dir.-Mktg.)*

Outside Service Firm(s):

Coopers & Lybrand*(Auditors)*
One Lincoln Center
Syracuse, NY 13202
Tel.: 315-474-8541
Fax: 315-474-0259

Subsidiary:

Quanta Advertising Corporation **(1)**
968 James St.
Syracuse, NY 13203
Tel.: 315-424-7700 (100%)
Emp.: 14
Advertising Agency
S.I.C.: 7311

CARSE OIL CO. INC.
1700 S. Bumby Ave.
Orlando, FL 32806
Tel.: 407-898-9494 **FL**
Fax: 407-894-0755
Year Founded: 1972
Approx.Sls.: $50,000,000
Emp.: 250
Retail Gasoline & Groceries; Wholesale Petroleum Products
S.I.C.: 5541; 5411; 5172
Wayne L. Carse *(Pres.)*
Jimmie L. Carse *(Sec. & Treas.)*
Katherine Spivey *(Comptroller)*

Outside Service Firm(s):

Geller, Ragans, James, Oppenheimer & Creel*(Auditors)*
Orlando, FL

Barnett Banks Trust Company, N.A.*(Major Banking Relationship)*
Orlando, FL

CARSTENS HEALTH INDUSTRIES, INC.
7310 W. Wilson Ave.
Chicago, IL 60656
Tel.: 708-867-5550
Tel.: 800-782-1524
Fax: 708-867-0215
Approx.Sls.: $17,000,000
Emp.: 130
Fiscal Year-end: 12/31/90

Export
Mfr. Hospital & Long Term Care Patient Charting Systems; Customline & Design-A-Line Patient Chart Racks, Card-Indexers (Medix-Visitray); Pressure Sensitive Labels, Record Guard
S.I.C.: 3469; 2759; 3841
George P. Block *(Pres.)*
Barbara VanderKloot *(Exec. V.P.)*
Alan G. Kogerup *(Gen. Sls. Mgr.)*
Duane Conwell *(Controller)*
Nancy J. Pigoni *(Dir.-Adv.)*
Frank Raimondi *(Pur. Agent)*

CARSTENSEN FREIGHT LINE, INC.
(d/b/a Clinton Disposal Co.)
3008 Lincoln Way
Clinton, IA 52732
Tel.: 319-242-5110 **IA**
Fax: 319-242-5110, Ext. 113
Year Founded: 1920
Emp.: 100
Heavy Hauling; Garbage Collection & Transport, No Disposal
S.I.C.: 4213; 4212
David N. Carstensen *(Pres.)*
James A. Carstensen *(Treas.)*
Richard Carstensen *(Sec.)*

Outside Service Firm(s):

McGladrey & Pullen*(Auditors)*
Clinton, IA

CARTER
1275 Peachtree St. N.E., Suite 100
Atlanta, GA 30367-1801
Tel.: 404-888-3300
Fax: 404-888-3308
Sales Range: $100-499 Million
Emp.: 750
Real Estate Developer & Broker
S.I.C.: 6552; 6531
James B. Carson, Jr. *(Chm. & Chief Exec. Officer)*
Daniel B. Rather *(Vice Chm. & Sr. Mktg. Dir.)*
William A. Mitchell, Jr. *(Pres.)*
James Bealle *(Exec. V.P.)*

CARTER CHAMBERS SUPPLY, INC.
6819 S. Choctaw Dr.
Baton Rouge, LA 70806
Tel.: 504-926-2123 **LA**
Emp.: 76
Industrial Machinery & Equipment; Valves & Fittings; Valve Repair
S.I.C.: 5084; 5085; 7699
Brent Rhodes *(Pres. & Chief Exec. Officer)*
John Davis *(V.P.)*
Will Simoneaux *(Controller)*

Outside Service Firm(s):

Kean, Miller, Hawthorne, D'Armond, McCowan & Jarman*(Legal Firm)*
Baton Rouge, LA

Hibernia National Bank*(Major Banking Relationship)*
Baton Rouge, LA

CARTER COMPANIES
100 Northwest Pkwy.
Kansas City, MO 64068
Mailing Address:
P.O. Box 14216
Parkville, MO 64152
Tel.: 816-746-4700
Fax: 816-746-5544
Year Founded: 1962
Emp.: 100
Petroleum Transporters, Wholesalers & Retailers
S.I.C.: 5172; 5541
Sam Carter *(Chm. Bd. & Pres.)*
Bryan Beaber *(V.P.-Mktg.)*
Lonnie Buerge *(V.P.-Fin. Services)*
Melanie Carter *(V.P.-ASAP Div.)*
Fran Richman *(V.P.-Personnel)*

Computer Systems/Hardware:
IBM

Outside Service Firm(s):

Meyer & Hoffman & McCann*(Auditors)*
Kansas City, KS

Farmland Insurance*(Group Insurer)*
Des Moines, IA

THE WILLIAM CARTER COMPANY
112 W. 34th St.
New York, NY 10120
Tel.: 212-868-1600 **MA**
Fax: 203-925-0436
Year Founded: 1865
Approx.Sls.: $207,000,000
Emp.: 5,000
Fiscal Year-end: 12/31/90
Import Export
Mfr. of Childrens, Boys & Womens Underwear & Nightwear; Children's Outerwear
S.I.C.: 2341; 2253; 2322
Frederick J. Rowan II *(Pres. & Chief Exec. Officer)*
Dave Brown *(Chief Oper. Officer)*
Joe Pacifico *(Exec. V.P.-Mktg.)*
Charlie Whetzel *(Exec. V.P.-Mfg. & Opers.)*
Jay Berman *(Sr. V.P. & Chief Fin. Officer)*
John Deakins *(Sr. V.P.-Sls.)*
Jack MacEachern *(Sr. V.P.-Sls.)*
Lou Falanga *(V.P.-Fin.)*
Dave Tobin *(V.P. & Gen. Counsel)*
Suzanne B. Calkins *(V.P.-Mktg.)*
Bob Zitnay *(Controller)*
Paul Seal *(Dir.-Human Rels.)*
Ray Pelletier *(Dir.-Mngmt. Information Services)*

Outside Service Firm(s):

Price Waterhouse*(Auditors)*
One Financial Plaza
Hartford, CT 06103
Tel.: 203-240-2000

Metropolitan Life Insurance Co.*(Group Insurer)*
One Madison Ave.
New York, NY 10010-3690
Tel.: 215-578-9292

The Bank of New York*(Major Banking Relationship)*
One Wall Street
New York, NY 10286
Tel.: 212-635-6805
Fax: 212-635-3201

CARTER DAY INDUSTRIES, INC.
500 73rd Ave., N.E.
Minneapolis, MN 55432
Tel.: 612-571-1000 **NY**
Fax: 612-571-3012
Year Founded: 1959
Earnings: $142,000
Approx.Sls.: $16,965,000
Emp.: 140
Fiscal Year-end: 3/31/92
Import Export
Mfr. & Marketer of Equipment for Agricultural & General Industrial Applications
S.I.C.: 3523
Paul W. Ernst *(Pres. & Chief Exec. Officer)*
David A. Hauch *(V.P.-Engrng.)*
Jerry Slater *(V.P.-Mfg.)*
Wayne Wellan *(V.P.-Indus. Sls.)*
A.G. Laos *(V.P.-Bus. Devel.)*
Randy Herman *(V.P., Controller & Sec.)*
Myron Thiel *(Mgr.-Adv.)*

Subsidiary:

Hart-Carter Co. **(1)**
500 73rd Ave., N.E.
Minneapolis, MN 55432
Tel.: 612-571-1000 (100%)
Mfr. of Agricultural Equipment
S.I.C.: 3523
Paul W. Ernst *(Pres.)*
Bob Kilper *(Distr. Sls.)*
Harold Brown *(Dir.-Pur.)*
Stella M. Bauer *(Adv. & Promo.)*

Subsidiaries:

Carter Day Co. **(2)**
500 73rd Ave., N.E.
Minneapolis, MN 55432
Tel.: 612-571-1000 (100%)
Fax: 612-571-3012
Approx.Sls.: $10,234,000
Emp.: 100
Export
Computer Systems/Hardware:
IBM 36
Mfr. of Grain Cleaning & Sizing Equipment, Food Products Machinery; Wholesaler of Commercial & Industrial Machines & Equipment
S.I.C.: 3523; 3556; 3559; 5046; 5084
Paul W. Ernst *(Pres. & Chief Exec. Officer)*
A.G. Laos *(Dir.-Mktg. & Sls.)*
Myron Thiel *(Mgr.-Adv.)*

Carter Day International, Inc. **(2)**
500 73rd Ave., N.E.
Minneapolis, MN 55432
Tel.: 612-571-1000 (100%)
Approx.Sls.: $3,334,000
Emp.: 6
Sls. of Industrial Machinery & Equipment
S.I.C.: 5084
Paul W. Ernst *(Pres. & Chief Exec. Officer)*
A.G. Laos *(Dir.-Sls. & Mktg.)*
Myron Thiel *(Mgr.-Adv.)*

Non-U.S. Holding:

Carter Day Industries (Canada) Ltd. **(1)**
1425 Whyte Ave.
Winnipeg, MB R3E 1V7, Canada
Tel.: 204-786-5781
Emp.: 128
Designs; Mfrs. & Marketers; Implements Related to Harvesting & Dry Cereal Grain & Seeds
S.I.C.: 3523; 3564
Paul W. Ernst *(Pres.)*

J. C. CARTER COMPANY, INC.
671 W. 17th St.
Costa Mesa, CA 92627
Tel.: 714-548-3421
Fax: 714-752-2997
Year Founded: 1945
Approx.Sls.: $38,000,000
Emp.: 280
Fiscal Year-end: 9/30/88
Manufacture Aerospace Valves & Pumps, Cryogenic Pumps, Ground Fueling Equipment
S.I.C.: 3561; 3599; 3728
Robert Veloz *(Pres.)*
B. Baldauf *(V.P.-Fin.)*
Richard Graves *(V.P.-Mktg.-Aerospace & Comml. Fueling)*

Computer Systems/Hardware:
IBM PC's

Outside Service Firm(s):

Ernst & Young*(Auditors)*
515 S. Flower St.
Los Angeles, CA 90071
Tel.: 213-621-1666

Security Pacific National Bank*(Major Banking Relationship)*
333 So. Hope
Los Angeles, CA 90051

JERRY C. CARTER, INC.
1325 S. Bradford
Gainesville, GA 30503
Mailing Address:
P.O. Box 18,
Gainesville, GA 30503
Tel.: 706-534-5129
Year Founded: 1970
Approx.Sls.: $10,000,000
Fiscal Year-end: 6/30/91
Gas & Oil Product Distributors
S.I.C.: 5172
Jerry C. Carter *(Chm. Bd., Pres. & Chief Exec. Officer)*
Nelson Carter *(Treas. & Chief Fin. Officer)*

Outside Service Firm(s):

Alexander & Felton*(Auditors)*
Gainsville, GA

Robert Lawson*(Legal Firm)*
Gainsville, GA

Georgia First*(Major Banking Relationship)*
Gainsville, GA

CARTER-JONES LUMBER COMPANY
601 Tallmadge Rd.
Kent, OH 44240
Tel.: 216-673-6100
Fax: 216-678-6134
Year Founded: 1934
Approx.Sls.: $200,000,000
Emp.: 1,000
Fiscal Year-end: 12/31/91
Special Trade Contractors; Retail Building Materials & Garden Supplies
S.I.C.: 5031; 5211
Neil Sackett *(Pres.)*
Edith Beverly *(Controller)*
Jeff Seder *(Dir.-Data Processing)*

Computer Systems/Hardware:
IBM System 38

Outside Service Firm(s):

Ernst & Young*(Auditors)*
1300 Huntington Bldg.
Cleveland, OH 44115
Tel.: 216-861-5000
Fax: 303-291-6234

Blue Cross & Blue Shield in Eastern Ohio*(Group Insurer)*
Youngstown, OH

National City Bank*(Major Banking Relationship)*
P.O. Box 92301, Corp. Trust Dept.
Cleveland, OH 44101
Tel.: 216-575-2000

CARTON-CRAFT CORPORATION
115-121 Ash St.
Buffalo, NY 14204
Tel.: 716-852-7910
Fax: 716-856-7787
Sales Range: $10-19 Million
Emp.: 150
Mfr. of Folding Cartons & Novelties
S.I.C.: 2657
Timothy S. Ortolani *(Chm. Bd., Pres. & Chief Exec. Officer)*
Thecly L. Ortolani *(Sec. & Treas.)*
Kenneth E. Wagner *(Mgr.-Sls.)*
John S. Ortoloni *(Plant Mgr.)*

Outside Service Firm(s):

Price Waterhouse*(Auditors)*
3600 Marine Midland Center
Buffalo, NY 14203
Tel.: 716-856-4650

Connecticut National Bank*(Major Banking Relationship)*
777 Main St.
Hartford, CT 06115
Tel.: 203-728-2000

CARTWRIGHT COMMUNICATIONS CO.
7812 Red Sky Dr.
Cincinnati, OH 45249
Tel.: 513-489-1755 **OH**
Telex: 888663
Fax: 513-489-1449
Year Founded: 1968
Emp.: 33
Wholesale Distribution of Two-Way Radio Communications Equipment
S.I.C.: 5063
William Y. Cartwright *(Pres., Chief Exec., Chief Fin. Officer & Treas.)*
Ron Resch *(Mgr.-Opers.)*

Computer Systems/Hardware:
Sentinel

Outside Service Firm(s):

Mowery & Co.*(Auditors)*
Wilmington, OH

Aetna Life & Casualty*(Group Insurer)*
425 Fifth Ave.
New York, NY 10018
Tel.: 212-512-0777

Santen & Hughes*(Legal Firm)*
Cincinnati, OH

Star Bank*(Major Banking Relationship)*
425 Walnut Street
Cincinnati, OH 45202
Tel.: 513-632-4000

CARUS CORPORATION
315 Fifth St.
Peru, IL 61354-2857
Tel.: 815-223-1500
Tel.: (IL)-800-892-6831
Tel.: 800-435-6850 **DE**
Telex: 6731015
Fax: 815-223-4486
Year Founded: 1969
Assets: $37,581,947
Earnings: ($237,872)
Liabilities: $35,531,566
Net Worth: $2,050,381
Approx.Sls.: $59,100,000
Emp.: 388
Fiscal Year-end: 12/31/90
Import Export
Chemical Mfr., Potassium Permanganate; Rare Permanganates, Textbooks & General Books; Cricket: The Magazine for Children; Ladybug: The Magazine for Young Children
S.I.C.: 2819; 2731; 2721
M. Blouke Carus *(Chm. Bd., Pres., Chief Exec. & Chief Oper. Officer)*
Paul Carus *(Exec. V.P. & Treas.)*
Ivan H. Berke *(Sr. V.P.-Fin. & Admin.)*
J.C. Wilkes *(V.P.-Human Resources)*
Alan Aronson *(Legal Officer & Sec.)*
Chris A. Noll *(Controller, Asst. Sec. & Asst. Treas.)*
Dan Serafini *(Dir.-Organizational Devel. & Trng.)*
Ray Vitkus *(Dir.-Mngmt. Information Systems)*
Robert J. Willmot *(Dir.-Corp. Communications)*
Bobby Hemmerde *(Supvr.-Network/ Telecommunications)*
Mary Stachowicz *(Asst. Sec.)*

No. of Mfg. Plants/Facilities: 1
No. of U.S. Offices: 3

Computer Systems/Hardware:
Data Dec 4300, Dec 8530 & Dec Microvax II

Outside Service Firm(s):

Brook, Weiner, Scred, Kreger & Weinberg*(Auditors)*
225 N. Michigan Ave., Ste. 1830
Chicago, IL 60601

Willis Corroon Corp. of Illinois*(Commercial Insurance Carrier)*
135 S. La Salle St.
Chicago, IL 60603
Tel.: 312-621-4700

North American Life*(Group Insurer)*
Minneapolis, MN

UNUM Corporation*(Group Insurer)*
2211 Congress St.
Portland, ME 04122
Tel.: 207-770-2211
Fax: 207-770-4387

American National Bank & Trust Company of Chicago*(International Bank Affiliate)*
33 N. LaSalle St.
Chicago, IL 60602
Tel.: 312-661-5000
Fax: 312-661-6417

American National Bank & Trust Company of Chicago*(Investment Banker)*
33 N. LaSalle St.
Chicago, IL 60602
Tel.: 312-661-5000
Fax: 312-661-6417

Margolin & Aronson*(Legal Firm)*
Chicago, IL

Winston & Strawn*(Legal Firm)*
One 1st Natl. Plaza, No. 5000
Chicago, IL 60603
Tel.: 312-558-5600

American National Bank & Trust Company of Chicago*(Major Banking Relationship)*
33 N. LaSalle St.
Chicago, IL 60602
Tel.: 312-661-5000
Fax: 312-661-6417

The Principal Financial Group*(Pension Manager)*
711 High St.
Des Moines, IA 50309
Tel.: 515-247-4593
Tel.: 800-543-4015

Divisions:

Carus Chemical Company, Chemical Div. **(1)**
1001 Boyce Meml. Dr.
Ottawa, IL 61350
Tel.: 815-433-9070 (100%)
Fax: 815-433-9075
Approx.Sls.: $34,600,000
Emp.: 335
Mfr. of Industrial Chemicals
S.I.C.: 2819
Tyrone G. Goodart *(Pres. & Chief Exec. Officer)*
Howard M. Berthold *(V.P.-Sls.)*
Robert Willmot *(Dir.-Corp. Communications)*
K.J. Ficek *(Dir.-Drinking Water Treatment)*

Carus Publishing Company **(1)**
315 5th St.
Peru, IL 61354
Tel.: 815-223-1500
Approx.Sls.: $24,500,000
Andre W. Carus *(Pres. & Chief Oper. Officer)*
M. Blouke Carus *(Chief Exec. Officer)*

Divisions:

Open Court Publishing Company **(2)**
407 S. Dearborn, Ste. 1300
Chicago, IL 60605
Tel.: 312-939-1500
Tel.: 800-852-0790 (100%)
Fax: 312-939-8150
Emp.: 130
Fiscal Year-end: 12/31/92
Textbook Publishers
S.I.C.: 2731
M. Blouke Carus *(Chm. Bd. & Chief Exec. Officer)*
Andre W. Carus *(Pres.)*
Karen Hansill *(V.P.-Sls.-Eastern Div.)*
Gary Blauser *(V.P.-Sls.-Western Div.)*
RuthAnn Green *(V.P. & Gen. Mgr.)*
Alan A. Aronson *(Gen. Counsel)*
Dan Serafini *(Human Resources Coord.)*
Barbara Conteh *(V.P.-Publr.)*

Open Court Publishing Co.-General Books **(2)**
315 5th St.
Peru, IL 61354
Tel.: 815-223-2520
Tel.: 800-435-6850
Tel.: (IL)-800-892-6831
Fax: 815-223-1350
Emp.: 3
S.I.C.: 5192
M. Blouke Carus *(Chm. Bd. & Chief Exec. Officer)*
Andre W. Carus *(Pres.)*
David Ramsay Steele *(Editorial Dir. & Mgr.)*
Chris Vancalbergh *(Dir.-Production & Mfg.)*

Subsidiaries:

Cricket Magazine **(2)**
315 Fifth St.
Peru, IL 61354
Tel.: 815-223-2520
Tel.: 800-892-6831 IL
Tel.: 800-435-6850 (100%)
Telex: 798927
Fax: 815-223-4486
Emp.: 18
Childrens Magazine Publishers
S.I.C.: 2721
Marianne Carus *(Editor-in-Chief)*
Robert W. Harper *(V.P. & Publ.)*

Ladybug Magazine **(2)**
315 Fifth St.
Peru, IL 61354
Tel.: 815-223-2520
Telex: 789727
Fax: 815-223-4486
Childrens Magazine Publisher
S.I.C.: 2721
Robert Harper *(Gen. Mgr.)*
Marianne Carus *(V.P. & Editor-in-Chief)*

Carver Boat Corp.
(Acquired by Minstar, Inc.)

CARVER, INC.
P.O. Box 7849
Garden City, GA 31418
Mailing Address:
115 Coleman Blvd.
Savannah, GA 31408
Tel.: 912-748-5000 **TX**
Fax: 912-748-0500
Year Founded: 1842
Approx.Sls.: $10,000,000
Emp.: 80
Export
Mfr. of Oil Seed Processing Machinery
S.I.C.: 3559
John E. Lee *(Pres. & Chief Exec. Officer)*
Robert E. Lee *(V.P.-Fin.)*
Mike Mizer *(V.P.-Engrng.)*
Louis Gejoff *(Treas., Controller, Sec. & Chief Fin. Officer)*
Dave McKinley *(Mgr.-Mktg.)*
Kirk C. Wiggins *(Mgr.-Commercial)*
Louis Benoit *(Agt.- Purch.)*

No. of U.S. Offices: 3
No. of Foreign Offices: 1

Outside Service Firm(s):

Evans Porter Bryan*(Auditors)*
Atlanta, GA

Prudential Insurance Co. of America*(Group Insurer)*
751 Broad St.
Newark, NJ 07102-3777
Tel.: 201-802-6000

Baker & Botts*(Legal Firm)*
3000 One Shell Plaza
Houston, TX 77002
Tel.: 713-229-1789

The Principal Financial Group*(Pension Manager)*
711 High St.
Des Moines, IA 50309
Tel.: 515-247-4593
Tel.: 800-543-4015

CASANOVA PENDRILL PUBLICIDAD INC.
3333 Michelson Dr., Ste. 300
Irvine, CA 92715
Tel.: 714-474-5001
Year Founded: 1984
Approx.Billings: $40,000,000
Emp.: 60
Hispanic Adv.
Paul L. Casanova *(Pres., Sec. & New Bus. Contact)*
Barbara Casanova *(Treas.)*

CASCHEM INC.
40 Ave. A
Bayonne, NJ 07002
Tel.: 201-858-7900
Fax: 201-437-2728
Sales Range: $40-59 Million
Emp.: 220
Manufacture Specialty Chemicals Derived from Castor Oil & Urethanes
S.I.C.: 2076; 2822
Al Islander *(Pres.)*
Bruce Sielzkowski *(V.P.-Opers.)*
Laurence S. Slovin *(V.P.-Sls.)*

Computer Systems/Hardware:
Hewlett Packard

Outside Service Firm(s):

KPMG Peat Marwick*(Auditors)*
345 Park Ave.
New York, NY 10154
Tel.: 212-758-9700
Fax: 212-872-3308

Midlantic National Bank*(Major Banking Relationship)*
Metro Park, NJ

CASCINO PURCELL FREEBAIRN
East Tower, 3343 Peachtree Rd., Ste. 1220
Atlanta, GA 30326
Tel.: 404-237-9945
Fax: 404-231-2214
Year Founded: 1980
Approx.Billings: $11,000,000
Emp.: 18
Alfred M. Cascino *(Chm. Bd. & Chief Exec. Officer)*
John C. Freebairn *(Pres. & Chief Oper. Officer)*
Antoinette Cooper *(V.P. & Chief Fin. Officer)*
Emory M. Jones *(V.P.-Pub. Rels.)*

CASE FOLEY SACKETT, INC.
708 North 1st St., Ste. 110
Minneapolis, MN 55401
Tel.: 612-338-1841
Fax: 612-338-9824
Year Founded: 1986
Approx.Billings: $24,000,000
Emp.: 23
Financial Services, Healthcare, Retail
Ron Sackett *(Pres. & Dir. Creative Services)*
John Foley *(Chief Exec. Officer, Dir.-Client Services & New Bus. Contact)*
Kathlynn Kieselbach *(Dir.-Fin.)*

Computer Systems/Hardware:
Macintosh

CASE FOODS, INC.
1325 Mt. Herman Rd.
Salisbury, MD 21801
Tel.: 410-749-3202
Fax: 410-749-4919
Year Founded: 1987
Emp.: 1,050
Food Distribution & Processors
S.I.C.: 5144; 5149
Thomas R. Shelton *(Pres.)*
Mike Popowycz *(Dir.-Fin. & Plng.)*

No. of Mfg. Plants/Facilities: 4
No. of U.S. Offices: 1

Outside Service Firm(s):

Frost & Co.*(Auditors)*
Little Rock, AR

Calfee, Halter & Griswold*(Legal Firm)*
800 Superior Ave., Ste. 1800
Cleveland, OH 44115-2688
Tel.: 216-622-8200
Fax: 216-241-0816

The Bank of New York*(Major Banking Relationship)*
One Wall Street
New York, NY 10286
Tel.: 212-635-6805
Fax: 212-635-3201

Subsidiaries:

Case Farms, Inc. **(1)**
P.O. Box 308
Morganton, NC 28655
Tel.: 704-438-6900
Emp.: 400
Poultry Farm
S.I.C.: 0253; 0251
Leroy Cook *(Gen. Mgr.)*

Case Farms of Ohio **(1)**
P.O. Box 185
Winesbury, OH 44690
Tel.: 216-359-7141
Emp.: 400
Poultry Farm
S.I.C.: 0253; 0251
David Erens *(Gen. Mgr.)*

CASE-SWAYNE CO. INC.
1632 E. 4th St.
Santa Ana, CA 92702
Mailing Address:
P.O. Box 1678,
Santa Ana, CA 92702
Tel.: 714-558-8861
Fax: 714-558-7392
Year Founded: 1943
Approx.Sls.: $45,000,000
Emp.: 150
Fiscal Year-end: 3/31/91
Export
Mfr. Portion Packed, Sauces & Dry Specialty Food Products
S.I.C.: 2099; 2033
Amos Swayne *(Chm. Bd.)*
Keith Swayne *(Pres.)*
Joe McCarthy *(Chief Fin. Officer)*
Michael Wetterauer *(Sr. V.P.-Sls. & Mktg.)*
Alan Wright *(Sr. V.P.-Opers.)*
Yolanda Guibert *(V.P.-Human Resources)*
Kathy Ware *(V.P.-Quality Assurance)*
Jan Mendenhall *(Dir.-Research & Devel.)*
Dave Berner *(Mgr.-Pur./Inventory)*
Monica Guy *(Mgr.-Human Resources)*
Richard Hood *(Mgr.-Natl. Sls.)*
Patricia Tappan *(Mgr.-Personnel Training & Devel.)*

Computer Systems/Hardware:
Hewlett Packard

CASEY CO.
7845 Panama Lane
Bakersfield, CA 93307
Tel.: 805-845-0761
Fax: 805-845-0330
Petroleum Products Wholesaler
S.I.C.: 5172
Larry Delpit *(Pres.)*

Subsidiary:

Casey Co. **(1)**
180 E. Ocean Blvd., Ste. 910
Long Beach, CA 90802
Tel.: 310-590-8835
Fax: 213-432-4711
Approx.Sls.: $450,000,000
Emp.: 15
Wholesale Distributor of Petroleum Products
S.I.C.: 5172
Steve Christovich *(Dir.-Fin.)*

CASH & CARRY GROCER INC.
2844 W. Armitage Ave.
Chicago, IL 60647
Tel.: 312-486-5403 **IL**
Fax: 312-772-7410
Year Founded: 1981
Approx.Sls.: $18,000,000
Emp.: 11
Wholesale & Self Service Grocer
S.I.C.: 5411
Arnulfo Vargas *(Pres., Chief Exec. Officer & Investor Rels. Dir.)*
Alex Vargas *(V.P., Chief Oper. Officer & Pur. Dir.)*
Andres Vargas *(Dir.-Personnel)*
Ignacio Gonzales *(Gen. Counsel & Dir.-Data Processing)*
Principal(s):
Arnulfo Vargas

Outside Service Firm(s):

Bank of Puerto Rico*(Major Banking Relationship)*
Chicago, IL

CASH PLUS, INC.
222 S. Ninth St., Ste. 2200
Minneapolis, MN 55402
Tel.: 612-347-6900
Year Founded: 1976
Approx.Sls.: $120,000,000
Emp.: 31
Broadcast Buying & Syndication Services
Charles Percival *(Chm. Bd.)*
Dale M. Applequist *(Pres., Chief Exec. Officer & New Bus. Contact)*
Julie Golden *(V.P., Dir. Program Acquisitions)*
Maurice McKay *(Dir. Opers.)*
Shelley Plumb *(Program Distr.)*

Computer Systems/Hardware:
Donovan Data Systems

CASHCO, INC.
Hwy. 140 W.
Ellsworth, KS 67439
Mailing Address:
P.O. Box 6
Ellsworth, KS 67439
Tel.: 913-472-4461
Fax: 913-472-3539
Year Founded: 1915
Approx.Sls.: $11,000,000
Emp.: 130
Fiscal Year-end: 12/31/90
Cashco Regulators, Reducing & Relief Valves, Control Valves
S.I.C.: 3491; 3494
P.G. Rodgers *(Pres.)*
John C. Reid *(Mgr.-Tech. Services)*
Bruce Shiffer *(Mgr.-Prod.)*
R.L. Widdows *(Mgr.-Control Valve Production)*
Bridget Vanek *(Admin. Asst.)*
Scott Burns *(Pur. Agent)*

CASKET SHELLS, INC.
First St.
Eynon, PA 18403
Tel.: 717-876-2642
Fax: 717-876-5613
Approx.Sls.: $19,000,000
Emp.: 250
Manufacture Metal Caskets
S.I.C.: 3995
Joseph R. Semon *(Pres.)*
Elizabeth S. Bonczar *(V.P.-Fin.)*
Lawrence J. Bonczar *(V.P.-Engrng.)*
William Semon *(V.P.-Mfg.)*

Outside Service Firm(s):

Scrudata & Associates*(Auditors)*
Scranton, PA

Oliver, Price & Rhodes*(Legal Firm)*
Scranton, PA

First National Bank*(Major Banking Relationship)*
Scranton, PA

CASS-CLAY CREAMERY
1220 Main Ave.
Fargo, ND 58108
Mailing Address:
P.O. Box 2947
Fargo, ND 58108
Tel.: 701-232-1566
Fax: 701-232-9234
Year Founded: 1934
Approx.Sls.: $104,000,000
Emp.: 430
Fiscal Year-end: 12/31/90
Mfr. Dairy Products
S.I.C.: 2021; 2026
Robert Gee *(Chm. Bd.)*
Donald Ommodt *(Pres. & Chief Exec. Officer)*
Cliff Hagen *(V.P.-Sls.)*
Al Nielsen *(V.P.-Production)*
Mel Verbout *(V.P.-Milk Procurement)*
Marv Conant *(Chief Fin. Officer)*
Gene Johnston *(Sec.)*

Computer Systems/Hardware:
IBM

CASSANO'S INC.
1700 E. Stroop Rd.
Dayton, OH 45429
Tel.: 513-294-8400
Fax: 513-294-8107
Year Founded: 1953
Approx.Sls.: $20,600,000
Emp.: 775
Fiscal Year-end: 12/31/90
Fast Food Pizza Chain in OH
S.I.C.: 5812
Victor J. Cassano, Jr. *(Chm. Bd.)*
Randy Leasher *(Pres.)*
Richard O. Soehner *(Sr. V.P.)*
J. Lawson *(V.P.-Opers.)*
B.J. Middleton *(Controller)*

CASSENS TRANSPORT COMPANY
145 N. Kansas
Edwardsville, IL 62025
Mailing Address:
P.O. Box 468
Edwardsville, IL 62025
Tel.: 618-656-3006 **IL**
Fax: 618-692-7316
Year Founded: 1936
Approx.Sls.: $86,000,000
Emp.: 850
Specialized Trucking-Automobile Carrier; Automobile Dealership
S.I.C.: 4212; 4213; 5511
Albert Cassens *(Chm. Bd.)*
Allen Cassens *(Pres.)*
Richard Suhre *(Exec. V.P.)*
James E. Walker *(V.P.-Opers.)*
Kay Cassens *(Sec. & Treas.)*
Dwight Kay *(Dir.-Admin. Services)*
Robert Stevens *(Dir.-Mngmt. Information Systems)*

Computer Systems/Hardware:
IBM; Wang

Outside Service Firm(s):

Baird, Kurtz & Dobson*(Auditors)*
St. Louis, MO

Bank of Edwardsville*(Major Banking Relationship)*
Edwardsville, IL

CASTCRAFT INDUSTRIES, INC.
3649 W. Chase Ave.
Skokie, IL 60076
Tel.: 708-675-6530 **IL**
Fax: 708-675-6563
Year Founded: 1936
Emp.: 45
Import Export
Manufacture & Distribution of Graphic Arts Supplies
S.I.C.: 3861; 5199; 2791
Harry Kreiter *(Chm. Bd. & Pres.)*
Ned Kreiter *(Chief Oper. Officer, Treas. & Gen. Mgr.)*
Fredric J. Kreiter *(Chief Fin. Officer & Legal Counsel)*
Abe E. Kreiter *(Exec. V.P.)*
Sally M. Keene *(V.P.)*
Herbert M. Kreiter *(V.P.-Foreign Affairs)*

Outside Service Firm(s):

Continental Bank N. A.*(Major Banking Relationship)*
231 S. LaSalle St.
Chicago, IL 60697
Tel.: 312-828-2345
Tel.: 800-426-5754
Telex: 312-828-1783

Divisions:

Castcraft Software Optifont **(1)**
3649 W. Chase Ave.
Skokie, IL 60076
Tel.: 708-675-6530
Fax: 708-675-6563
Type Settings
S.I.C.: 2791
Abe E. Kreiter *(Chief Oper. Officer)*

Transfertech, Inc. **(1)**
3649 W. Chase Ave.
Skokie, IL 60076
Tel.: 708-675-6530
Fax: 708-675-6563
Herbert M. Kreiter *(V.P.)*

Type Films of Chicago Co. **(1)**
3649 W. Chase Ave.
Skokie, IL 60076
Tel.: 708-675-6563
Fax: 708-675-6563
Herbert M. Kreiter *(V.P.)*

Type Founders of Chicago **(1)**
3649 W. Chase Ave.
Skokie, IL 60076
Tel.: 708-675-6530
Fax: 708-675-6563
Abe E. Kreiter *(Chief Oper. Officer)*

CASTEX INDUSTRIES INC.
4240 Blue Star Hwy.
Holland, MI 49423
Tel.: 616-392-6966
Tel.: 800-283-7871 **MI**
Fax: 616-392-2886
Year Founded: 1972
Approx.Sls.: $20,000,000
Emp.: 125
Export
Manufacture Carpet Cleaning Equipment & Carpet Maintenance
S.I.C.: 3589; 7217
Harold Streur *(Chm. Bd.)*
Wayne A. Streur *(Pres.)*
Tom Vander Bie *(Exec. V.P.)*
Steve Lubbars *(V.P. & Treas.)*
Wayne Boeve *(V.P.-Mfg.)*

Barry Johnson *(V.P.-Exports)*
Laura Anthony *(Dir.-Mktg.)*
Bill Reddy *(Dir.-Pur.)*
Nancy Bulson *(Dir.-Human Resources)*

Principal(s):
Wayne A. Streur

No. of Mfg. Plants/Facilities: 1
No. of U.S. Offices: 1

Computer Systems/Hardware:
IBM

CASTING MATERIAL COMPANY
1610 Charter St.
Chattanooga, TN 37402
Tel.: 615-756-0011
Fax: 615-756-0114
Approx.Sls.: $10,000,000
Emp.: 20
Fiscal Year-end: 9/30/90
Foundry Products
S.I.C.: 2899; 5051
Mel Hartman *(Pres.)*
E. Antes *(Dir.-Adv. & Gen. Mgr.)*

CASTLE-HARLAN, INC.
150 E. 58th St.
New York, NY 10155
Tel.: 212-644-8600 **DE**
Fax: 212-207-8042
Year Founded: 1987
Earnings: $240,000,000
Approx.Assets: $1,700,000,000
Corporate Real Estate Office; Merchant Banking Firm
S.I.C.: 6531
John Castle *(Chm. Bd.)*
Leonard Harlan *(Pres.)*

Outside Service Firm(s):

KPMG Peat Marwick*(Auditors)*
444 S. Fifth St.
Louisville, KY 40202
Tel.: 502-587-0535
Fax: 502-587-1549

First Security National Bank & Trust Co.*(Major Banking Relationship)*
One First Security Plaza,
Lexington, KY 40507
Tel.: 606-231-1000

Subsidiary:

Jerrico, Inc. **(1)**
101 Jerrico Dr.
Lexington, KY 40509
Tel.: 606-263-6000
Fax: 606-263-6509
Emp.: 18,100
Restaurants & Wholesale Restaurant Supplies
S.I.C.: 5812; 5141; 6794
John K. Castle *(Chm. Bd.)*
Clinton A. Clark *(Pres. & Chief Exec. Officer)*
Anthony M. Lavely *(Exec. V.P.-Mktg.)*
William G. Mahony *(Exec. V.P.-Opers.)*
William E. Anderson II *(Sr. V.P., Sec. & Gen. Counsel)*
William P. Connery *(Sr. V.P.-Opers.)*
Bruce C. Cotton *(Sr. V.P.-Pub. Affairs)*
Gerald W. Deitchle *(Sr. V.P.-Fin. & Chief Fin. Officer)*
R. William Flock *(Sr. V.P.-Human Resources)*
Howard J. Singer *(Sr. V.P.-Devel.)*
Jack Zinga *(Sr. V.P.-Oper.)*
Larry D. Bowles *(V.P. & Treas.)*
Jeff Chasney *(V.P.-Mngmt. Information Systems)*
Brian C. Dixon *(V.P.-Mktg. Services)*
Franz X. Ecker *(V.P.-Food & Beverage)*
Eugene O. Getchell *(V.P.-Franchise)*
Doug Higdon *(V.P.-Personnel)*
Michael J. Kupstas *(V.P.-Field Mktg. & Promo.)*
David R. Smith *(Controller)*
Paul Bramel *(Dir.-Facilities, Maintenance & Telephones)*

Subsidiaries:

QSC, Inc. **(2)**
Foulkstone Plaza, 1105 N. Market St.
Wilmington, DE 19899
Tel.: 302-478-5015 (100%)
Fax: 302-478-5370
Investment Holding Company
S.I.C.: 6719

Subsidiary:

Long John Silver's, Inc. **(3)**
101 Jerrico Dr.
Lexington, KY 40509
Tel.: 606-263-6000 (100%)
Approx.Sls.: $720,000,000
Emp.: 18,000
Fiscal Year-end: 6/30/93
Import
Restaurant Operations & Franchisor Company
S.I.C.: 5812; 6794
Leonard Harlan *(Chm. Bd.)*
Clinton A. Clark *(Pres. & Chief Exec. Officer)*
William G. Mahony *(Exec. V.P.-Opers.)*
Anthony M. Lavely *(Exec. V.P.-Adv. & Mktg.)*
Gerald W. Deitchle *(Exec. V.P.-Fin. & Chief Fin. Officer)*
William E. Anderson II *(Sr. V.P., Sec. & Gen. Counsel)*
William Flock *(Sr. V.P.-Human Resources)*
Bruce C. Cotton *(Sr. V.P.-Pub. Affairs)*
Larry D. Bowles *(Sr. V.P.-Budgeting & Treasury Opers.)*
Jim Everett *(V.P.-Procurement)*
Brian Dixon *(V.P.-Mktg. Services)*
Donald Naught *(V.P.-Communications & Training)*
David Smith *(V.P.-Fin. & Acctg.)*
Bob Brutt *(V.P.-Franchising)*
George Souza *(V.P.-Sourcing)*
Jeff Chasney *(V.P.)*
Bonnie Mace *(Dir.-Quality Assurance)*
Patty Brophy *(Dir.-Conventions & Travel)*
Mary Roseman *(Dir.-Consumer Nutrition Information)*
Bruce Hinton *(Dir.-Communications)*
Paul Bramel *(Dir.-Facilities Maintenance)*
Carol Caskey *(Dir.-Employee Rels.)*

Lexington Equipment Co. **(2)**
101 Jerrico Dr.
Lexington, KY 40509
Tel.: 606-263-6000 (100%)
Fax: 606-263-6145
Approx.Sls.: $4,671,000
Emp.: 30
Equipment Sales to Company & Franchised Restaurants
S.I.C.: 5044
Ron W. Cegnar *(Chief Oper. Officer)*

CASTLEBERRY'S FOOD COMPANY
1621 15th Street
Augusta, GA 30901
Tel.: 706-733-7765
Fax: 706-733-5079
Year Founded: 1965
Approx.Sls.: $60,000,000
Emp.: 400
Mfr. Beef Stew & Canned Meats From Purchased Meat; Chili With & Without Meat
S.I.C.: 2013; 2032
Robert Kirby *(Pres.)*
Dave Carmany *(V.P.-Fin., Treas. & Controller)*
Beth Cleveland *(Sec.)*

CASTOR ADVERTISING CORP.
122 East 25th St.
New York, NY 10010
Tel.: 212-995-5900 **NY**
Fax: 212-995-5984
Year Founded: 1969
Sales Range: $40-59 Million
Emp.: 50
Spanish Language Advertising Agency
S.I.C.: 7311
Castor A. Fernandez *(Pres. & Chief Exec. Officer)*
Hector F. Elizalde *(Sr. Exec. V.P., Acct. Services & Chief Oper. Officer)*
David Halpern *(V.P., Chief Fin. Officer)*

Outside Service Firm(s):

David Gronsbell & Co.*(Auditors)*
New York, NY

Hanover Insurance Co.*(Commercial Insurance Carrier)*
Worcester, MA

Bank of New York*(Investment Banker)*
90 Washington St.
New York, NY 10015

Chemical Bank*(Investment Banker)*
450 West 33rd St.
New York, NY 10001
Tel.: 212-613-7197
Fax: 212-947-7628

Phillips, Nizer, Benjamin, Krim & Ballon*(Legal Firm)*
40 W. 57th St.
New York, NY 10019
Tel.: 212-977-9700

Subsidiary:

Castor Advertising Corp. **(1)**
11693 San Vicente Blvd., #266
Los Angeles, CA 90049
Tel.: 310-447-3690
Emp.: 2
Advertising Agency
S.I.C.: 7311
Hector Elizalde *(Sr. V.P.)*

CASTRO CONVERTIBLE CORPORATION
1990 Jericho Turnpike
New Hyde Park, NY 11040
Tel.: 516-488-3000
Fax: 516-488-3213
Year Founded: 1931
Approx.Sls.: $50,000,000
Emp.: 600
Fiscal Year-end: 6/30/91
Mfrs. & Retailers of Convertible Furniture
S.I.C.: 2515
Eugene Staudt *(Chm. Bd. & Chief Exec. Officer)*
Bernadette Castro Guida *(Pres.)*
Charles J. Harrington *(V.P.)*

Outside Service Firm(s):

European American Bank*(Major Banking Relationship)*
Mineola, NY

CASWELL/MASSEY CO. LTD.
121 Fieldcrest Ave.
Edison, NJ 08837
Tel.: 908-225-2181
Fax: 908-225-2385
Year Founded: 1752
Emp.: 180
Fiscal Year-end: 1/30/92
Import Export
Retail Fragrance Stores
S.I.C.: 5999
Edward Hung *(Pres.)*
Jacquelyn Hadley *(Chief Exec. Officer)*
Martin Latman *(Chief Fin. Officer)*

Outside Service Firm(s):

Chemical Banking Corp.*(Major Banking Relationship)*
277 Park Ave.
New York, NY 10041
Tel.: 212-310-6407
Fax: 212-310-4526

CATALINA YACHTS, INC.
21200 Victory Blvd.
Woodland Hills, CA 91367
Tel.: 818-884-7700 **CA**
Fax: 818-884-3810
Year Founded: 1968
Approx.Sls.: $25,000,000
Emp.: 650
Mfr. of Sailboats, Building & Repairing
S.I.C.: 3732
Frank W. Butler *(Pres.)*
Sharon Day *(Treas. & Sec.)*

CATERAIR HOLDINGS CORP.
7811 Montrose Rd.
Potomac, MD 20854
Tel.: 301-309-2800
Airline Passenger Catering
S.I.C.: 5812
Daniel Altobello *(Chm. Bd.)*
Angelo D. Bizarro *(Chief Fin. Officer)*

Subsidiary:

Caterair International **(1)**
7811 Montrose Rd.
Potomac, MD 20854
Tel.: 301-309-2800
Airline Passenger Catering
S.I.C.: 5812
Daniel Altobello *(Chm., Pres. & Chief Exec. Officer)*

CATHOLIC ORDER OF FORESTERS
P.O. Box 3012,
Naperville, IL 60566
Year Founded: 1883
Approx.Sls.: $175,000,000
Emp.: 100
Fiscal Year-end: 12/31/90
Fraternal Life Insurance Society
S.I.C.: 6311
John A. Gorski *(High Chief Ranger)*
John M. Spilar *(Vice High Chief Ranger)*
Bernard F. Milota *(High Sec. & Treas.)*
James Rial *(Admin. Dir.)*
Thomas Karleski *(Dir.-Sls. & Mktg.)*
Barbara Cunningham *(Editor-Catholic Forester Mag.)*

Computer Systems/Hardware:
IBM AS/400

JIM CAUSLEY PONTIAC GMC INC.
38111 Gratiot Ave.
Mt. Clemens, MI 48043
Tel.: 313-776-4455 **DE**
Fax: 313-463-9850
Year Founded: 1957
Assets: $7,900,000
Liabilities: $3,000,000
Net Worth: $4,900,000
Approx.Sls.: $79,900,000
Emp.: 117
Fiscal Year-end: 6/30/88
Automobile & Truck Dealerships
S.I.C.: 5511
James Causley, Sr. *(Pres.)*
Dan Weis *(Treas.)*

CAVALIER CORPORATION
1105 East 10th
Chattanooga, TN 37403
Tel.: 615-267-6671
Tel.: 800-251-6386
Fax: 615-267-5099
Year Founded: 1865
Emp.: 150

Export
Manufacture & Sale of Vending Machines
S.I.C.: 3581; 5046
Norman Sarkisian *(Chm. Bd.)*
Vernon D. Camp *(Pres.)*
Lawrence P. Hauser *(V.P.-Sls. & Mktg.)*
Brenda Camp *(Dir.-Pur.)*
Andrew Duffy *(Dir.-Fin.)*
James S. Floyd *(Dir.-Human Resources)*

Computer Systems/Hardware:
IBM PC

CAWSL CORPORATION
7 Wynnewood Rd.
Wynnewood, PA 19096
Mailing Address:
P.O. Box 280
Devault, PA 19432
Tel.: 215-649-3210
Fax: 215-649-5475
Year Founded: 1981
Sales Range: $60-79 Million
Manufacture Metal Tubing
S.I.C.: 3312; 3317; 3351
Paul E. Kelly, Sr. *(Chm. Bd., Chief Exec. & Fin. Officer)*
Paul E. Kelly, Jr. *(Pres.)*
Philip C. Howse *(V.P.)*
Joe Clock *(Treas.)*

Computer Systems/Hardware:
IBM System 41, IBM PC-XT

Outside Service Firm(s):

Coopers & Lybrand*(Auditors)*
2400 Eleven Penn Center
Philadelphia, PA 19103-2962
Tel.: 215-963-8000

Saul, Ewing, Remick & Saul*(Legal Firm)*
1500 Market St.
Philadelphia, PA 19102
Tel.: 215-972-7777

Philadelphia National Bank*(Major Banking Relationship)*
P.O. Box 13834, Broad & Chestnut Streets
Philadelphia, PA 19101-7618
Tel.: 215-973-8327

Aetna Life & Casualty*(Pension Manager)*
151 Farmington Avenue
Hartford, CT 06156
Tel.: 203-273-2128
Fax: 203-729-4295

Union National Bank*(Pension Manager)*
Pittsburgh, PA

Wood Asset Management*(Pension Manager)*
Philadelphia, PA

Subsidiaries:

Anchor Darling Industries Inc. **(1)**
919 Conestoga Rd., Ste. 305, Bldg. Two
Rosemont, PA 19010
Tel.: 215-527-9000 (100%)
Management Holding Company
S.I.C.: 6719
Andrew Bozzelli *(Pres.)*
Paul E. Kelly *(V.P.)*
P.C. Howse *(Treas.)*
Paul E. Kelly, Jr. *(Sec.)*

Subsidiaries:

Anchor Darling Valve Co. **(2)**
P.O. Box 3428, 701 First St.
Williamsport, PA 17701
Tel.: 717-327-4800
Telex: 759953
Fax: 717-327-4805
Custom Engineering Valves
S.I.C.: 3494

Pressure Products Industries **(2)**
900 Louis Dr.
Warminster, PA 18974
Tel.: 215-675-1600
General Industrial Machinery
S.I.C.: 3569

Williams & Company, Inc. **(1)**
901 Pennsylvania Ave.
Pittsburgh, PA 15233
Tel.: 412-237-2211
Emp.: 680
Ferrous & Non-Ferrous Metal & Industrial Service Centers; 11 Full Line Service Centers, 1 Processing Center & 9 Refrigeration Stores
S.I.C.: 5051; 5078
Roger R. Gaillard *(Pres., Chief Oper. & Chief Exec. Officer)*
Guy Dille *(V.P.-Fin. & Treas.)*
R.L. Finley *(V.P.-Sls.)*
Thomas H. Horsman *(V.P.-Pur. & Inventory Mngmt.)*
W.R. Miller *(V.P.-Opers.)*

Subsidiary:

Williams House of Metals, Inc. **(2)**
901 Pennsylvania Ave.
Pittsburgh, PA 15233
Tel.: 412-237-2211
Warehouse for Metals

THE CAXTON PRINTERS LTD.
312 Main St.
Caldwell, ID 83605
Tel.: 208-459-7421
Fax: 208-459-7450
Approx.Sls.: $14,000,000
Emp.: 50
Commercial Printers; Textbook Publishers; Distribution of School Supplies
S.I.C.: 2731; 2752; 5112
G. Gipson *(Pres.)*
D. Gipson *(V.P. & Pur. Dir.-Comml. Printing)*
Robert Tyson *(Pur. Dir.-School Supplies)*
Jim Stewart *(Pur. Dir.-Textbooks)*

Outside Service Firm(s):

Missouri, Bates & Gibbon*(Auditors)*
Caldwell, ID

Connolly & Smyser*(Legal Firm)*
Boise, ID

West One Bank*(Major Banking Relationship)*
Coldwell, ID

W.C. CAYE & COMPANY, INC.
787 Windsor St., S.W.
Atlanta, GA 30315
Mailing Address:
P.O. Box 4508
Atlanta, GA 30302
Tel.: 404-688-2177
Tel.: 800-282-6802 **GA**
Fax: 404-688-2189
Year Founded: 1946
Assets: $5,600,000
Liabilities: $1,700,000
Net Worth: $3,900,000
Approx.Sls.: $17,000,000
Emp.: 80
Fiscal Year-end: 12/31/91
Distributor For Commercial Building Supplies
S.I.C.: 5211; 5082; 3441
Charles G. Caye, Sr. *(Chm. Bd.)*
Charles G. Caye, Jr. *(Pres.)*
Andrew Avera *(V.P.)*
Morris G. Caye *(V.P.)*
W.L. Craddock, Jr. *(V.P.)*
Michael Johnson *(V.P.)*
Katherine M. Carr *(Controller)*

Computer Systems/Hardware:
IBM RS6000 Model 520H

Outside Service Firm(s):

Marshall Jones & Co.*(Auditors)*
Atlanta, GA

Blanchard & Calhoun*(Commercial Insurance Carrier)*
Augusta, GA

Blanchard & Calhoun*(Group Insurer)*
Augusta, GA

Smith, Gambrell & Russell*(Legal Firm)*
2400 First Atlanta Tower
Atlanta, GA 30383
Tel.: 404-656-1800
Fax: 404-264-2652

First Union National Bank*(Major Banking Relationship)*
Atlanta, GA

Massachusetts Mutual Life Insurance Co.*(Pension Manager)*
Atlanta, GA

Divisions:

W.C. Caye & Co. **(1)**
1468 Gordon Hwy.
Augusta, GA 30901
Tel.: 706-798-8744
Tel.: 800-842-0778
Fax: 706-798-8734
Kenny Avera *(Mgr.)*

W.C. Caye & Co. **(1)**
3761 Martinez Blvd.
Martinez, GA 30907
Tel.: 706-868-8683
Fax: 706-860-4379
Virginia Chambliss *(Mgr.)*

W.C. Caye & Co. **(1)**
1300 C E. President St.
Savannah, GA 31404
Tel.: 912-232-2833
Tel.: 800-673-6375
Ray Bryant *(Mgr.)*

W.C. Caye & Co. **(1)**
4560 Pionono Ave.
Macon, GA 31206
Tel.: 912-788-3008
Fax: 912-788-2967
Joey Stevens *(Mgr.)*

W.C. Caye & Co. **(1)**
1016 Virginia St.
Columbus, GA 31904
Tel.: 706-322-0573
Fax: 706-571-3225
Eric Bader *(Mgr.)*

Techsteel, Inc. **(1)**
2145 Plaster Bridge Rd.
Atlanta, GA 30324
Tel.: 404-873-1244
Fax: 404-876-6385
C. G. Caye *(Pres.)*

CE DE CANDY, INC.
1091 Lousons Rd.
Union, NJ 07083
Tel.: 908-964-0660
Tel.: 800-631-7968
Fax: 908-964-0911
Approx.Sls.: $20,000,000
Emp.: 125
Fiscal Year-end: 10/31/90
Import Export
Manufacturer of Candies
S.I.C.: 2064
Edward Dee *(Chm. Bd.)*
Jonathan Dee *(Pres.)*
Gordon Cameron *(V.P.-Mfg.)*
Eric Ostrow *(V.P.-Sls.)*
Marcia Weisman *(Mgr.-Sls.)*
Dorothy Wood *(Pur. Agent)*

Outside Service Firm(s):

Eisner & Tennenbaum*(Auditors)*
Woodbridge, NJ

Freundich & Reiser*(Legal Firm)*
Union, NJ

United Jersey Bank*(Major Banking Relationship)*
Clifton, NJ

CEBCOR (CONSOLIDATED EMPLOYMENT BENEFITS CORP.)
332 S. Michigan Ave., Ste. 850
Chicago, IL 60604
Tel.: 312-922-9798 **IL**
Fax: 312-922-1097
Year Founded: 1985
Approx.Billings: $51,000,000
Emp.: 49
Fiscal Year-end: 12/31/90
Payroll & Benefits Administration; Management Services & Risk Management Services
S.I.C.: 8741; 8742
Charles E. Stevenson, Jr. *(Chm., Pres. & Chief Exec. Officer)*
Walter Geyer *(V.P.-Plng. & Devel.)*
Wendy Hartmann *(V.P.-Admin.)*
Don Moore *(V.P. & Auditor)*
Anthony Proto *(V.P.-Mktg. & Sls.)*
Irwin Persin *(V.P.-Fin.)*
Milano Harden *(Mgr.-Adv. & Pub. Rels.)*

Outside Service Firm(s):

Coopers & Lybrand*(Auditors)*
203 N. LaSalle St.
Chicago, IL 60601
Tel.: 312-701-5500

Ray, Rizowy & Fleischer*(Legal Firm)*
Chicago, IL

LaSalle National Bank*(Major Banking Relationship)*
135 S. LaSalle St.
Chicago, IL 60603
Tel.: 312-443-2440
Fax: 312-443-2819

CEDAR FARMS COMPANY, INC.
2609 E. York St.
Philadelphia, PA 19125
Tel.: 215-739-7100
Tel.: 800-220-2217 **PA**
Fax: 215-739-6664
Year Founded: 1965
Assets: $5,000,000
Liabilities: $3,800,000
Net Worth: $1,200,000
Approx.Sls.: $38,000,000
Emp.: 80
Fiscal Year-end: 7/30/91
Wholesale Dairy Prods., Poultry, Frozen Foods, Meats & Meat Products
S.I.C.: 5143; 5144; 5142; 5147
Gus P. Pahidis *(Pres.)*
Peter Pahidis *(Exec. V.P. & Sec.)*
Mike Essaf *(Mgr.-Sls.)*

No. of Mfg. Plants/Facilities: 1
No. of U.S. Offices: 1

Computer Systems/Hardware:
IBM

Outside Service Firm(s):

Rudolph, Palitz & Co.*(Auditors)*
Philadelphia, PA

Continental Bank N. A.*(Major Banking Relationship)*
231 S. LaSalle St.
Chicago, IL 60697
Tel.: 312-828-2345
Tel.: 800-426-5754
Telex: 312-828-1783

THE CEDARWOOD COMPANIES
1765 Merriman Rd.
Akron, OH 44313
Tel.: 216-836-9971 **OH**
Fax: 216-864-8094
Year Founded: 1972
Approx.Sls.: $90,000,000
Emp.: 215
Fiscal Year-end: 12/31/88
Real Estate Development; General Contractor Commercial Buildings & Condominiums
S.I.C.: 1542; 1522; 6512; 6552
Anthony A. Petrarca *(Pres.)*
Lenora Petrarca *(Treas.)*
John S. Steinhauer *(Sec.)*

Outside Service Firm(s):

Coopers & Lybrand*(Auditors)*
P.O. Box 538, 800 Akron Centre Plaza
Akron, OH 44308

CEILING & PARTITIONS, INC.
8812 Spectrum Dr.
Landover, MD 20785
Tel.: 301-808-1400
Fax: 301-808-1405
Approx.Sls.: $10,000,000
Emp.: 160
Plastering, Drywall & Insulation
S.I.C.: 1742

John F. Hallam *(Pres. & Owner)*

Outside Service Firm(s):

Maryland National Bank*(Major Banking Relationship)*
10 Light St.
Baltimore, MD 21203
Tel.: 410-244-5000

CELENTANO BROTHERS
225 Bloomfield Ave.
Verona, NJ 07044
Tel.: 201-239-8444 **NJ**
Fax: 201-239-6351
Year Founded: 1947
Assets: $5,000,000
Liabilities: $2,000,000
Net Worth: $3,000,000
Approx.Sls.: $29,000,000
Emp.: 140
Fiscal Year-end: 6/30/90
Import
Italian Frozen Foods
S.I.C.: 2038
Domenick Celentano, Sr. *(Chm. Bd. & Pres.)*
Domenick A. Celentano, Jr. *(V.P.-Mktg.)*
Leslie Celentano *(Treas.)*
Doris Celentano *(Sec.)*

No. of Mfg. Plants/Facilities: 2
No. of U.S. Offices: 2

Computer Systems/Hardware:
IBM

Outside Service Firm(s):

T. Tibaldi*(Auditors)*
Cedar Grove, NJ

Blue Cross of New Jersey*(Group Insurer)*
Newark, NJ

Wolff, Sampson*(Legal Firm)*
5 Becker Farm Rd.
Roseland, NJ

CELESTIAL SEASONINGS
4600 Sleepytime Dr.
Boulder, CO 80301-3292
Tel.: 303-530-5300
Fax: 303-442-2177
Year Founded: 1970
Approx.Sls.: $50,000,000
Emp.: 220
Export
Herb Teas, Specialty Black Teas & Earth Wise Household Cleaning Products
S.I.C.: 2099
Corporate Giving Program: Colorado Organizations Only
Mo Siegel *(Chm. Bd. & Chief Exec. Officer)*
Barney Feinblum *(Vice Chm.)*
John Hale *(V.P.-Opers.)*
Felix Maez *(V.P.-Sls.)*
Mike Mondello *(V.P.-Mktg.)*
Steven I. McIntosh *(Gen. Counsel)*
Gary Stoker *(Controller)*
Steve Costello *(Mgr.-Mktg.)*
Randy Rush *(Mgr.-Sls. & Plng.)*
Mike Biery *(Dir.-Human Resources)*
Michael Chapman *(Quality Control)*
Blair Hansen *(Dir.-Pur.)*
Larry Bosch *(Export Sls. Mgr.)*
Lindsay Moore *(Dir.-Mktg. Services)*
Kathryn Besemer *(Dir.-Strategic Plng.)*
Mary Mulry *(Dir.-Res. & Devel.)*

No. of Mfg. Plants/Facilities: 1
No. of U.S. Offices: 1

Outside Service Firm(s):

Colorado National Bank*(Major Banking Relationship)*
17th & Champa
Denver, CO 80217

CELLO BAG COMPANY, INC.
P.O. Box 58810
Tukwila, WA 98138
Tel.: 206-251-8666
Fax: 206-251-8278
Approx.Sls.: $15,000,000
Emp.: 125
Flexible Packaging Materials, Polyethylene Film, Polyethylene Tubing
S.I.C.: 3081; 3084
James Ball *(Pres.)*
Charles Thomas *(Comptroller)*
Douglas Haughton *(Sec.)*
Kevin Mulvihill *(Dir.-Pur.)*

Outside Service Firm(s):

Otto Enger*(Auditors)*
Seattle, WA

Stafford, Frey, Cooper & Stewart*(Legal Firm)*
Seattle, WA

Seattle First National Bank*(Major Banking Relationship)*
701 Fifth Avenue
Seattle, WA 98104
Tel.: 206-358-3035

CELLULAR SERVICE, INC.
6100 San Fernando Rd.
Glendale, CA 91201
Tel.: 818-242-2567
Fax: 818-242-0802
Year Founded: 1984
Approx.Sls.: $30,800,000
Emp.: 55
Cellular Telephone Service
S.I.C.: 4812
Ray Ambraziunas *(Pres.)*
David Nelson *(Chief Exec. Officer)*

Outside Service Firm(s):

Sterling Bank*(Major Banking Relationship)*
Glendale, CA

CENEX (FARMERS UNION CENTRAL EXCHANGE, INC.)
5500 Cenex Dr.
Inver Grove Heights, MN 55075
Mailing Address:
P.O. Box 64089
St. Paul, MN 55164
Tel.: 612-451-5151
Tel.: 800-232-3039
Telex: 297-060
Year Founded: 1931
Assets: $734,034,000
Liabilities: $368,518,000
Net Worth: $365,516,000
Approx.Sls.: $1,685,905,000
Emp.: 2,500
Fiscal Year-end: 9/30/91
Import Export
Farm Supply Co-Operative; Petroleum Products; Fertilizer; Agriculture Chemicals; Tires; Batteries & Accessories; Agriculture Equipment; Farm Management Services
S.I.C.: 2911; 2992; 2999; 4226; 5013; 5072; 5083; 5172; 5191
Corporate Giving Program: Limited to Agriculture & Rural Development Programs
Elroy Webster *(Chm. Bd.)*
Noel Estenson *(Pres.)*
Duane Halverson *(Grp. V.P.-Members Services, Cenex/Land O'Lakes)*
David E. Johnson *(Grp. V.P.-Agronomy, Cenex/Land O'Lakes)*
Joel Koonce *(Grp. V.P.-Fin. & Chief Fin. Officer)*
Maurice Miller *(V.P.-Mktg. Communications)*
David Baker *(Corp. Counsel & Asst. Sec.)*
Richard Baldwin *(Dir.-Human Resources)*
Jennifer Mamer *(Dir.-Meetings Plng.)*
Frank Bezdicek *(Mgr.-Adv.)*
Mary Kaste *(Mgr.-Cenex Foundation)*
Roger Tschida *(Mgr.-Real Estate)*

No. of Mfg. Plants/Facilities: 16
No. of U.S. Offices: 2

Computer Systems/Hardware:
IBM: Hewlett Packard 2000

Outside Service Firm(s):

Coopers & Lybrand*(Auditors)*
1000 TCF Bldg.
Minneapolis, MN 55402
Tel.: 612-293-2929
Fax: 612-370-9395

Nationwide Insurance*(Group Insurer)*
One Nationwide Plaza
Columbus, OH 43216
Tel.: 614-249-6488

Dougherty, Rumble & Butler*(Legal Firm)*
St. Paul, MN

First Trust Company, Inc.*(Major Banking Relationship)*
First Trust Center, 180 E. Fifth St.
St. Paul, MN 55164

Saint Paul Bank for Cooperatives*(Major Banking Relationship)*
Saint Paul, MN

Subsidiaries:

CENEX AG Inc. **(1)**
200 W. Mercer
Seattle, WA 98119
Tel.: 206-282-2451
Don Haggarth *(Gen. Mgr.)*

CENEX Inc. **(1)**
P.O. Box 64089
Saint Paul, MN 55164
Tel.: 612-451-4930
Paul Rhein *(Gen. Mgr.)*

CENEX Ltd. **(1)**
P.O. Box 64089
Saint Paul, MN 55164
Tel.: 612-451-4930
Tom Erickson *(Gen. Mgr.)*

CENEX Petroleum Inc. **(1)**
P.O. Box 64089
Saint Paul, MN 55164
Tel.: 612-451-4930
Leon Westbrock *(Gen. Mgr.)*

CENEX Service Company **(1)**
P.O. Box 64089
Saint Paul, MN 55164
Tel.: 612-451-4930

Full Circle **(1)**
P.O. Box 64089
St. Paul, MN 55164
Tel.: 612-451-4930
Tom Erickson *(Gen. Mgr.)*

Pax Company **(1)**
580 W. 13th St., S.
Salt Lake City, UT 84115
Tel.: 801-973-2800
Robert Bess *(Gen. Mgr.)*

Joint Venture:

Cenex/Land O'Lakes, Inc. **(1)**
P.O. Box 64089
Saint Paul, MN 55164
Tel.: 612-451-5151 (50%)
Telex: 297-060
Fax: 612-451-5568
Assets: $606,016,000
Earnings: $12,060,000
Liabilities: $320,677,000
Net Worth: $285,339,000
Emp.: 700
Computer Systems/Hardware:
Hewlett Packard 922 & 955; IBM 3084QX
Plant Foods & Chemicals
S.I.C.: 2873; 2874
Noel Estenson *(Pres. & Chief Exec. Officer-Cenex Inc.)*
John Gherty *(Pres. & Chief Exec. Officer-Land O'Lakes Inc.)*
Al Giese *(V.P.-Agronomy & Food)*
Dave Johnson *(V.P. & Chief Oper. Officer)*
Joel Koonce *(V.P.-Fin. & Chief Fin. Officer)*
Paul Rhein *(V.P.-Agronomy Chemicals)*
Stan Marquart *(Dir.-Sls.)*
Frank Bezdizek *(Mgr.-Adv.)*
Annette Degnan *(Mgr.-Adv.)*

CENTERMARK PROPERTIES, INC.
(Formerly May Centers, Inc.)
611 Olive St.
Saint Louis, MO 63101
Tel.: 314-342-6200
Fax: 314-342-6100
Approx.Sls.: $68,000,000
Emp.: 800
Shopping Center, Property Operation Only
S.I.C.: 6512
William E. Grafstrom *(Chm. Bd.)*
Robert L. Ferguson *(Pres. & Chief Exec. Officer)*
Peter McMillan *(Chief Fin. Officer)*
Roger Burghdorf *(Sr. V.P.-Leasing)*
James Dausch *(Sr. V.P.-Devel.)*
Richard L. Taylor *(Sr. V.P., Center Mngmt.)*
Robert G. Vidal *(Sr. V.P.-Human Resources)*
James P. Whitcome *(Sr. V.P.-Capitol Improvements)*
Thomas E. Frost *(V.P. & Gen. Counsel)*

Outside Service Firm(s):

Arthur Andersen & Co.*(Auditors)*
1010 Market St.
St. Louis, MO 63101

CENTIMARK CORPORATION
3000 Industrial Blvd.
Bethel Park, PA 15102
Tel.: 412-833-4900 **PA**
Fax: 412-831-0149
Year Founded: 1968
Assets: $27,000,000
Liabilities: $12,000,000
Net Worth: $15,000,000
Sales Range: $60-79 Million
Emp.: 900
Fiscal Year-end: 4/30/92
Export
Contractors Engaged in the Installation of Flooring & Roofing
S.I.C.: 1752; 1761
Edward B. Dunlap *(Chm Bd., Pres., & Chief Exec. Officer)*
Daniel J. McVay *(Comptroller)*
John A. Rudzik *(Sr. V.P.-Fin., Chief Fin. Officer, & Treas.)*
John P. Liekar, Jr. *(Sr. V.P. & Sec.)*
Barry Budkey *(Sr. V.P.)*
Robert Fulton *(Sr. V.P.)*
Joseph Urbanic *(Sr. V.P.)*
Mildred Bradley *(Dir.-Mktg.)*
Stephen Hecht *(Dir.-Sls.)*
John P. Liekar Jr. *(Gen. Counsel & Sec.)*

No. of U.S. Offices: 42

Computer Systems/Hardware:
SEQUENT

Outside Service Firm(s):

Ernst & Young*(Auditors)*
2000 Pittsburgh Natl. Bldg.
Pittsburgh, PA 15222
Tel.: 412-644-7800
Fax: 412-644-7419

Pittsburgh National Bank*(Major Banking Relationship)*
5th Ave. & Wood St.
Pittsburgh, PA 15222
Tel.: 412-355-3000

CENTRAL ADVERTISING AGENCY

One Tandy Ctr., Ste. 300
Fort Worth, TX 76102
Tel.: 817-390-3554

Central Advertising Agency—(Continued)

Twx: 910-893-4053
Year Founded: 1963
Approx.Billings: $50,000,000
Emp.: 6

CENTRAL ALLIED ENTERPRISES
1243 Raff Rd., S.W.
Canton, OH 44710
Mailing Address:
P.O. Box 80449
Canton, OH 44708
Tel.: 216-477-6751 **OH**
Fax: 216-477-6751
Approx.Sls.: $45,000,000
Emp.: 250
Fiscal Year-end: 12/31/90
Asphalt & Asphatic Paving Mixtures; Bituminous Concrete; Ready-mixed Concrete; Highway & Street Construction; Sand & Gravel Construction
S.I.C.: 2951; 3273; 1611; 1442
J.A. Woodhall, Jr. *(Chm. Bd., Pres. & Chief Exec. Officer)*
Gerald Orn *(Exec. V.P. & Treas.)*
G.F. Braden *(Sr. V.P.)*
R.G. Johnson *(V.P.)*
Douglas A. Woodhall *(V.P.)*
Robert C. Woodhall *(V.P.)*

Outside Service Firm(s):

Bruner, Cox, Lotz, Syler & Graves*(Auditors)*
Canton, OH

Black, McCuskey, Souers & Arbaugh*(Legal Firm)*
1200 Harter Bank Bldg.
Canton, OH 44702
Tel.: 216-456-8341

Society National Bank*(Major Banking Relationship)*
Canton, OH

Divisions:

A-E Division **(1)**
1243 Raff Rd., S.W.
Canton, OH 44710
Tel.: 216-477-6751
Highway & Street Construction
S.I.C.: 1611
J.W. Woodhall, Jr. *(Chm. Bd., Pres. & Chief Fin. Officer)*

Canton Aggregate Division **(1)**
1243 Raff Rd., S.W.
Canton, OH 44710
Tel.: 216-477-6751
Ready-mixed Concrete
S.I.C.: 3273
J.A. Woodhall, Jr. *(Chm. Bd., Pres. & Chief Exec. Officer)*

Ohio Tar Asphalt **(1)**
1243 Raff Rd., S.W.
Canton, OH 44710
Tel.: 216-477-6751
Bituminous Road Materials
S.I.C.: 2951
J.A. Woodhall, Jr. *(Chm. Bd., Pres. & Chief Exec. Officer)*

CENTRAL COCA-COLA BOTTLING COMPANY, INC.
Corporate Headquarters, 1706 Roseneath Rd.
Richmond, VA 23230
Tel.: 804-359-3759
Tel.: 800-359-3759 **VA**
Fax: 804-358-5822
Year Founded: 1919
Approx.Sls.: $57,800,000
Emp.: 425
Fiscal Year-end: 12/31/91
Mfr. & Distribute Coca-Cola & Flavored Soft Drinks; Coca-Cola Classic & Allied Brands, A & W Root Beer & Creme Soda, Sunkist, Nestea, Yoo-Hoo & Minute Maid Juice-to-Go, Pocono Spring Water & Mistic Spring Water Juice
S.I.C.: 2086; 5962
Betty S. Christian *(Chm. Bd., Pres. & Chief Exec. Officer)*
L. T. Christian, IV *(Plan V.P.)*
Mark A. Christian *(Plan V.P. & Sec.)*
W. Lee Christian *(Plan V.P.)*
Norma J. Rist *(Plan V.P. & Gen. Mgr.)*
Colie Rowell *(Controller)*
Bradley A. Bachtell *(Dir.-Sls. & Opers.)*
Laurence M. Caramela *(Dir.-Sls. & Mktg., Bottle/Can)*
David D. Compton *(Dir.-Opers.)*
Principal(s):
Betty S. Christian

No. of Mfg. Plants/Facilities: 2
No. of U.S. Offices: 11

Computer Systems/Hardware:
IBM System 36

Outside Service Firm(s):

Deloitte & Touche*(Auditors)*
700 Bldg.,Suite 1800, 700 E. Main St.
Richmond, VA 23219-2619
Tel.: 804-697-1543
Fax: 804-697-1859

Aetna Life & Casualty*(Group Insurer)*
151 Farmington Avenue
Hartford, CT 06156
Tel.: 203-273-2128
Fax: 203-729-4295

Williams, Mullen, Christian & Dobbins*(Legal Firm)*
P.O. Box 1320, United Bank Bldg., 9th & Main
Richmond, VA 23210
Tel.: 804-643-1991

Crestar Bank*(Major Banking Relationship)*
P.O. Box 26665,
Richmond, VA 23261
Tel.: 804-782-5995

CENTRAL DATA CORPORATION
1602 Newton Dr.
Champaign, IL 61821
Tel.: 217-359-8010
Fax: 217-359-6904
Year Founded: 1975
Emp.: 42
Manufacture of SCSI Terminal Connectivity
S.I.C.: 3679
Jeffrey J. Roloff *(Chm. Bd. & Chief Exec. Officer)*
Earl D. Jacobsen *(Pres. & Chief Oper. Officer)*
Robert Koski *(V.P.-Mktg.)*
Terry Cornell *(Dir.-Pur.)*
Avon Morgan *(Dir.-Sls.)*

No. of Mfg. Plants/Facilities: 1
No. of U.S. Offices: 3

Computer Systems/Hardware:
Novelle LAN

Outside Service Firm(s):

McGladrey & Pullen*(Auditors)*
Champaign, IL

Erwin, Martinkus, Cole & Ansel*(Legal Firm)*
Champaign, IL

Harris Trust & Savings Bank*(Major Banking Relationship)*
111 W. Monroe St.
Chicago, IL 60690
Tel.: 312-461-2265
Tel.: 800-858-0840

Marine Bank*(Major Banking Relationship)*
Champaign, IL

CENTRAL DUPAGE HEALTH SYSTEM
(Formerly Healthcorp Affiliates)
1151 E. Warrenville Rd.
Naperville, IL 60563
Tel.: 708-505-8860
Emp.: 1,700
Hospital & Health Care Mgmnt. Srvcs.; Hospital & Specialty Outpatient Clinic Opers.
S.I.C.: 8742; 8062; 8093
James D. Anderson *(Pres. & Chief Exec. Officer)*
Paul Piro *(V.P.-Fin.)*
James Giger *(Controller)*

Subsidiaries:

Alcoholism Treatment Center **(1)**
27 W. 350 High Lake Rd.
Winfield, IL 60190
Tel.: 708-653-4000
Emp.: 60
Outpatient Alcohol Treatment Services
S.I.C.: 8093
David Fox *(Pres.)*

Central DuPage Hospital Association **(1)**
25 N. Winfield Rd.
Winfield, IL 60190
Tel.: 708-682-1600
Emp.: 1,500
General In-Patient Hospital Services
S.I.C.: 8062
George Holzhauer *(Pres. & Chief Exec. Officer)*

CENTRAL FEED MILLS, INC.
311 Maple St.
Snohomish, WA 98290
Mailing Address:
P.O. Box 237
Snohomish, WA 98290
Tel.: 206-568-2109 **WA**
Fax: 206-568-2834
Year Founded: 1950
Sales Range: $10-19 Million
Emp.: 50
Manufacturer of Feeds
S.I.C.: 2048
Mel Erickson, Sr. *(Pres., Sec. & Treas.)*
Mel E. Erickson, Jr. *(Exec. V.P. & Gen. Mgr.)*
Principal(s):
Mel Erickson, Sr.

No. of Mfg. Plants/Facilities: 1
No. of U.S. Offices: 1

Outside Service Firm(s):

KPMG Peat Marwick*(Auditors)*
3100 Two Union Square, 601 Union St., Ste. 3100
Seattle, WA 98101
Tel.: 206-292-1500

Frontier Bank*(Group Insurer)*
Everett, WA

Jewell & Thorpe*(Legal Firm)*
Seattle, WA

CENTRAL FREIGHT LINES INC.
5601 W. Waco Dr.
Waco, TX 76710
Mailing Address:
P.O. Box 2638
Waco, TX 76702
Tel.: 817-772-2120 **TX**
Fax: 817-772-4944
Year Founded: 1925
Approx.Sls.: $196,400,000
Emp.: 4,100
Common Motor Carrier
S.I.C.: 4213
C. Tom Clowe *(Pres. & Chief Exec. Officer)*
Joe Hall *(Chief Oper. Officer & Sr. V.P.-Opers.)*
Doyle Byrd *(Sr. V.P.-Human Resources & Devel.)*
Doug Quicksall *(V.P., Chief Fin. Officer & Treas.)*
Diana Callan Braswell *(Sec.)*
Principal(s):
Employee Owned

Outside Service Firm(s):

Sheehy, Lovelace & Mayfield*(Legal Firm)*
Waco, TX

NationsBank Texas*(Major Banking Relationship)*
P.O. Box 830345
Dallas, TX 75283-0345
Tel.: 214-508-1782

CENTRAL GROCERS CO-OP
3701 N. Centrella St.
Franklin Park, IL 60131
Tel.: 708-678-0660
Fax: 708-678-0859
Approx.Sls.: $386,000,000
Emp.: 225
Distributor to Independent Grocers
S.I.C.: 5141
John Logli *(Chm.)*
John Cortesi *(Pres.)*
Joe Caccamo *(Exec. V.P. & Gen. Mgr.)*
James Denges *(V.P.-Mktg. & Pur.)*
Tony Iori *(V.P.-Produce)*
Robert Wagner *(V.P. & Asst Gen. Mgr.)*
Tom Woodlock *(V.P.)*
Frank Vantil *(Treas.)*
Joseph Mazzuca *(Sec.)*

Computer Systems/Hardware:
Data General MV 20000

Outside Service Firm(s):

Affiliated Bank of Franklin Park*(Major Banking Relationship)*
Franklin Park, IL

CENTRAL ILLINOIS STEEL COMPANY
P.O. Box 78
Carlinville, IL 62626
Tel.: 217-854-3251
Fax: 217-854-3251, Ext. 333
Year Founded: 1967
Sales Range: $20-39 Million
Emp.: 100
Export
Steel Slitting, Shearing & Decoiling Steel Manufacture, Wire Roof Plates
S.I.C.: 3441; 3317; 3443
Dan Millard *(Chm. Bd., Pres., Chief Exec. & Chief Oper. Officer)*
Tim Millard *(V.P.)*
James Boland *(Dir.-Data Processing, Pension Admin., Controller & Sec.)*
Tom Drake *(Plant Mgr.)*

No. of Mfg. Plants/Facilities: 3
No. of U.S. Offices: 1

Outside Service Firm(s):

Carlinville National Bank*(Major Banking Relationship)*
Carlinville, IL

CENTRAL LIFE ASSURANCE CO.
611 5th Ave.
Des Moines, IA 50309
Mailing Address:
P.O. Box 1555
Des Moines, IA 50306
Tel.: 515-283-2371 **IA**
Fax: 515-242-4692
Year Founded: 1896
Assets: $2,238,376,339
Liabilities: $2,085,675,696
Net Worth: $152,700,643
Approx.Premiums: $403,048,265
Emp.: 300

Fiscal Year-end: 12/31/91
Life, Health & Annuity Insurance; Group & Individual
S.I.C.: 6311; 6321; 6324
D.T. Doan *(Pres.)*
Alfred Paynter Moore *(Pres.-Central Resource Grp.)*
Roger K. Brooks *(Chief Exec. Officer)*
Wayne Keith Gunzenhauser *(Exec. V.P.-Fin.)*
George Thomas Eldrige *(Sr. V.P.-Services)*
Franklin Leroy Lundquist *(V.P.-Individual Insurance)*
Lance Shaylor Nelson *(V.P.-Securities)*
Freddie Christensen O'Dell *(V.P.-Individual Admin.)*
Stephen Bennett Parrish *(V.P.-Mktg. Services)*
James Andrew Smallenberger *(V.P., Gen. Counsel & Sec.)*
George Joseph Syata *(V.P.-Mortgage Loan)*

Computer Systems/Hardware:
IBM

Outside Service Firm(s):

Coopers & Lybrand*(Auditors)*
Des Moines, IA

Norwest Bank Iowa N.A.*(Major Banking Relationship)*
666 Walnut
Des Moines, IA

CENTRAL LIVESTOCK ASSOCIATION, INC.
Exchange Bldg.
South St. Paul, MN 55075
Mailing Address:
P.O. Box 419
South St. Paul, MN 55075
Tel.: 612-451-1844
Fax: 612-451-1774
Year Founded: 1921
Assets: $10,418,821
Earnings: $360,000
Liabilities: $8,957,269
Net Worth: $1,461,552
Approx.Rev.: $4,216,525
Emp.: 80
Fiscal Year-end: 12/31/90
Livestock Selling Agency; Co-Op
S.I.C.: 7389; 5154
Quentin Heldberg *(Chm. Bd.)*
Lloyd Bauman *(1st Vice Chm.)*
William Eastgate *(2nd Vice Chm.)*
Donald G. Kampmeier *(Pres. & Gen. Mgr.)*
Doug Appleby *(V.P. & Asst. Gen. Mgr.)*
Curt Zimmerman *(V.P.-Mktg.)*
Carrol Boehnke *(Treas.)*
William Sarette *(Controller & Asst. Treas.)*
John M. Tiffany *(Sec.)*

Computer Systems/Hardware:
IBM

Outside Service Firm(s):

Cooperative Auditing Services*(Auditors)*
Minneapolis, MN

Paul Julian & Company*(Auditors)*
7301 Zane Ave., No.
Minneapolis, MN 55443
Tel.: 612-561-6867

Doherty, Rumble & Butler*(Legal Firm)*
2800 Minnesota World Trade Center
St. Paul, MN 55101-4999
Tel.: 612-291-9333

Drovers First American Bank of South St. Paul*(Major Banking Relationship)*
633 S. Concord St.
South St. Paul, MN
Tel.: 612-4516822

Northwestern National Bank of South St. Paul*(Major Banking Relationship)*
South St. Paul, MN

Subsidiary:

Central Livestock Order Buying Company **(1)**
Exchange Bldg.
South St. Paul, MN 55075
Tel.: 612-451-1844 (100%)
Purchasing & Mktg.
S.I.C.: 5154

CENTRAL MUTUAL INSURANCE CO.
800 S. Washington
Van Wert, OH 45891
Mailing Address:
P.O. Box 351,
Van Wert, OH 45891
Tel.: 419-238-1010
Year Founded: 1876
Approx.Sls.: $140,000,000
Emp.: 460
Fiscal Year-end: 12/31/91
Property & Casualty Insurance
S.I.C.: 6351; 6361
F.W. Purmort, Jr. *(Chm. Bd. & Pres.)*
Gerald D. Thatcher *(Sr. V.P., Chief Fin. Officer & Treas.)*
Roy Sauders Jr. *(Sr. V.P.)*
F.W. Purmort III *(V.P. & Sec.)*
Edward R. Buhl *(V.P.-Mktg.)*
Wayne N. Kilton *(V.P.-Personnel)*
Karl A. Waite *(V.P.-Fin.)*
James P. Cahoon *(Gen. Counsel)*

Computer Systems/Hardware:
IBM

Divisions:

Central Regional Office **(1)**
800 South Washington St
Van Wert, OH 45891
Tel.: 419-238-1010
F.W. Purmort III *(Res. V.P. & Sec.)*
Richard P. Bogart *(Asst. V.P.-Sls.)*

Northeastern Regional Office **(1)**
P.O. Box 9124, 404 Wyman Street
Waltham, MA 02254-9124
Tel.: 617-890-1752
Richard R. Bennett *(Mgr.-Sls.)*

Southeastern Regional Office **(1)**
5895 Windward Pkwy.
Alpharetta, GA 30201
Tel.: 404-740-8000
Roy P. Lein *(Resident V.P.)*
Warren C. Philipps *(Mgr.-Sls.)*

Southwestern Regional Office **(1)**
P.O. Box 152010, 1200 Walnut Hill Lane
Irving, TX 75015
Tel.: 214-550-1300
C.W. Wassberg *(Resident V.P.)*

Subsidiaries:

All America Insurance Company **(1)**
800 So. Washington
Van Wert, OH 45891
Tel.: 419-238-1010
Fax: 419-238-1010
F.W. Purmort, Jr. *(Pres.)*
Edward R. Buhl *(V.P.-Mktg.)*

Cafco **(1)**
800 So. Washington
Van Wert, OH 45891
Tel.: 419-238-1010
Fax: 419-238-1010
F.W. Purmort, Jr. *(Pres.)*
Gerald D. Thatcher *(Sr. V.P. & Treas.)*

Central-United Life Insurance Co. **(1)**
4301 Sergeant Rd.
Sioux City, IA 51102
Tel.: 712-276-8000
Jerry E. Wooldridge *(Pres.)*
Kenneth J. Dove *(V.P.-Agency)*
Robert J. Hartman *(V.P. & Treas.)*

CMI Lloyds **(1)**
1200 Walnut Hill Lane
Irving, TX 75062
Tel.: 214-550-1300
C.W. Wassberg *(Attorney-in-Fact)*
Jim Covey *(Dir.-Communications)*

CENTRAL NATIONAL-GOTTESMAN INC.
3 Manhattanville Rd.
Purchase, NY 10577-2110
Tel.: 914-696-9000
Fax: 914-696-1066
Year Founded: 1886
Sales Range: $1 Billion +
Emp.: 700
Import Export
Distribute Pulp, Paper, Lumber & Plywood
S.I.C.: 5031; 5113; 2671; 2672; 5111
Ira D. Wallach *(Chm. Bd.)*
James G. Wallach *(Pres. & Chief Exec. Officer)*
Leo Schenker *(Sr. Exec. V.P.)*
Joseph V. Flaherty *(Exec. V.P.)*
Lars E. Londen *(Exec. V.P.)*
Kenneth L. Wallach *(Sr. V.P.)*
Peter Siegfried *(V.P., Gen. Counsel & Sec.)*
Joshua J. Eisenstein *(Treas.)*

No. of U.S. Offices: 5
No. of Foreign Offices: 18

Computer Systems/Hardware:
IBM System 38

Divisions:

Lindenmeyr Central **(1)**
3 Manhattanville Rd.
Purchase, NY 10577-2100
Tel.: 212-696-9000

Lindenmeyr Munroe **(1)**
Corporate Headquarters, One Second St., Box 3637
Peabody, MA 01961-3637
Tel.: 617-595-4006
Tel.: 800-237-2737
Fax: 508-531-4478
Printing Papers
S.I.C.: 5111
Arthur Anderson *(Pres.)*
Joseph DuCharme *(V.P. & Gen. Mgr.)*
Judith A. Finlay *(Mgr.-Adv. & Mktg.)*

Branches:

Lindenmeyr Munroe **(2)**
240 Forbes Blvd.
Mansfield, MA 02048
Tel.: 508-339-6161
Tel.: 800-343-7782
Fax: 508-339-1996
David Manning *(Branch Mgr.)*

Lindenmeyr Munroe **(2)**
P.O. Box 3046, 249 Research Drive
Milford, CT 06460
Tel.: 203-878-9900
Tel.: 800-624-3281
Fax: 203-878-9686
Michael Foye *(Branch Mgr.)*

Lindenmeyr Munroe **(2)**
468 Pepsi Road
Manchester, NH 03103
Tel.: 603-627-1320
Tel.: 800-462-1911
Fax: 603-627-4816
Arthur J. Anderson *(Branch Mgr.)*

Lindenmeyr Munroe **(2)**
510 County Road
Westbrook, ME 04092
Tel.: 207-874-9000
Tel.: 800-442-1390
Fax: 207-874-0653
Mike Gibson *(Branch Mgr.)*

Lindenmeyr Munroe **(2)**
301 Veterans Blvd.
Rutherford, NJ 07070-2706
Tel.: 201-935-2900
Tel.: 800-631-0193
Fax: 201-935-5264
Printing Papers
S.I.C.: 5111
Stephen E. Oblet *(V.P. & Gen. Mgr.)*
L. R. Pasbach *(V.P.-Mktg.)*
William C. Meany *(Mgr.-Sls.)*

Lindenmeyr Munroe **(2)**
1845 New Highway
Farmingdale, NY 11735
Tel.: 516-293-0505
Kenneth Obletz *(V.P. & Gen. Mgr.)*

Lindenmeyr Munroe **(2)**
919 Wallace St.
Philadelphia, PA 19123
Tel.: 215-235-9000
Tel.: 800-342-2215
Fax: 215-236-1686
James W. Barrett *(Branch Mgr.)*

Lindenmeyr Munroe **(2)**
3041 Industry Drive
Lancaster, PA 17603-4025
Tel.: 717-393-2111
Tel.: 800-222-4908
Fax: 717-393-0948
Dale Rohrer *(Branch Mgr.)*

Lindenmeyr National **(1)**
919 Wallace St.
Philadelphia, PA 19123
Tel.: 215-235-3270
Fax: 215-763-6040

Lindenmeyr Paper **(1)**
100 Park Ave.
New York, NY 10017
Tel.: 212-532-7300

Branches:

Lindenmeyr Paper **(2)**
990 Washington Street
Boston, MA 02026

Lindenmeyr Paper **(2)**
2694 Bishop Drive
San Ramon, CA 94583

Lindenmeyr Paper **(2)**
541 North Fairbanks
Chicago, IL 60611
Tel.: 312-222-1890

Lindenmeyr Paper **(2)**
544 Fleetwood Court
Kingsport, TN 37662

Process Materials **(1)**
100 Park Avenue
New York, NY 10017

CENTRAL PAPER COMPANY
60 McClellan St.
Newark, NJ 07114
Tel.: 201-622-6377
Fax: 201-623-4323
Approx.Sls.: $140,000,000
Emp.: 100
Fine & Printing Papers, Copy Papers, Envelopes
S.I.C.: 5111; 5112
Robert H. Berkowitz *(Chm. Bd.)*
David H. Berkowitz *(Pres.)*
Donald A. Berkowitz *(Exec. V.P.-Sls. & Mktg.)*
Joseph Englander *(V.P.-Personnel & Pur.)*
K.H. Englander *(V.P.-Mktg.)*
Allen Levicky *(V.P.-Systems Analyst)*
Anne Sornstein *(V.P.-Admin. & Asst. Treas. & Sec.)*

No. of Mfg. Plants/Facilities: 4
No. of U.S. Offices: 4

Computer Systems/Hardware:
Quantel; IBM

Outside Service Firm(s):

Bederson & Company*(Auditors)*
West Orange, NJ

Central Paper Company—(Continued)

National Westminster Bank plc*(Major Banking Relationship)*
Astor Plaza, 1515 Broadway
New York, NY 10036

Division:

George W. Millar Co. (1)
161 6th Ave.
New York, NY 10013
Tel.: 212-645-7200
Paper Broker
S.I.C.: 5111

Affiliates:

Central Paper Co. (1)
1004 Wayhead Rd. Ext.
Trenton, NJ 08638
Tel.: 609-883-7500
Fine & Printing Paper, Envelopes & Copy Paper
S.I.C.: 5111; 5112
David Relles *(Div. Mgr.)*

First State Paper, Inc. (1)
P.O. Box 10007
Wilmington, DE 18950
Tel.: 302-656-6546
Fine & Printing Papers
S.I.C.: 5111
David Berkowitz *(Chief Oper. Officer)*

Marquardt & Co. (1)
161 6th Ave.
New York, NY 10013
Tel.: 212-645-7200
Paper Brokers
S.I.C.: 5111

Pick Quick Papers, Inc. (1)
60 McClellan St.
Newark, NJ 07114
Tel.: 201-622-6377
Wholesale Paper
S.I.C.: 5112
Donald Berkowitz *(Chief Oper. Officer)*

CENTRAL PARKING CORP.
2401 21st St., Ste. 300
Nashville, TN 37212
Tel.: 615-297-4255
Arrangement of Passenger Transportation
S.I.C.: 4729
James H. Bond *(Pres.)*
Robert Mitchell *(V.P.-Human Resources)*
Henry J. Abbott *(Sec.)*

Subsidiary:

Central Parking Corp. (1)
937 Church St.
Nashville, TN 37203
Tel.: 615-259-3898
Fax: 615-242-7801
Approx.Sls.: $225,000,000
Emp.: 1,800
Fiscal Year-end: 9/30/91
Computer Systems/Hardware:
MAI Basic 4
Parking Management; Transportation Services
S.I.C.: 7521; 4729
Monroe Carell, Jr. *(Chm. Bd. & Chief Exec. Officer)*
James H. Bond *(Pres.)*
Henry J. Abbott *(Sec.)*
Robert Mitchell *(V.P.-Human Resources)*
Randy Winton *(Corp. Controller)*

CENTRAL PHARMACEUTICALS, INC.
120 E. Third St.
Seymour, IN 47274
Mailing Address:
P.O. Box 328
Seymour, IN 47274
Tel.: 812-522-3915
Fax: 812-522-4963
Year Founded: 1904
Approx.Sls.: $15,000,000
Emp.: 150
Fiscal Year-end: 6/30/91
Export
Pharmaceuticals
S.I.C.: 2834
Joseph F. Connelly *(Chm. Bd.)*
H.A. Toulmin, Jr. *(Pres. & Treas.)*
Daniel J. Desmond *(Exec. V.P. & Chief Oper. Officer)*
Chand Jhaveri *(V.P.-Res. & Devel.)*
Jerry Wolfe *(V.P.-Sls.)*

Computer Systems/Hardware:
MAI/Basic Four

CENTRAL POINT SOFTWARE, INC.
15220 N.W. Greenbriar Pkwy., No. 200
Beaverton, OR 97006
Tel.: 503-690-8080
Tel.: 503-690-8090
Telex: 757710
Fax: 503-690-7133
Year Founded: 1981
Approx.Sls.: $17,800,000
Emp.: 130
Fiscal Year-end: 3/31/90
Produces Utility Programs for Computers
S.I.C.: 7372
Charles M. Boesenberg *(Pres. & Chief Oper. Officer)*
Corey Smith *(Chief Exec. Officer)*
David J. Roux *(Sr. V.P.-Mktg.)*
Phil Catterall *(V.P.-Sls.)*
Sal D'Auria *(V.P.-Installed Base)*
John Hotchman *(V.P.-Fin.)*
Thomas Darnell *(Dir.-Marcom)*
Ellen W. Pfeifer *(Mgr.-Marcom Communications)*

CENTRAL/SHIPPEE, INC.
46 Star Lake Rd.
Bloomingdale, NJ 07403
Mailing Address:
P.O. Box 135
Bloomingdale, NJ 07403
Tel.: 201-838-1100
Fax: 201-838-8273
Year Founded: 1926
Emp.: 50
Import Export
Felt Manufacturer
S.I.C.: 2231
Cornelius A. Hubner *(Chm. Bd.)*
Donald A. Hubner *(Pres.)*
C.E. Hubner, Jr. *(Exec. V.P.)*
James R. Nelson *(V.P.-Sls. & Adv.)*

Outside Service Firm(s):

John D. Carrico & Associates, CPA*(Auditors)*
Butler, NJ

Steel/Village Agency*(Commercial Insurance Carrier)*
Wayne, NJ

Johnson, Murphy, Hubner, McKeon & Wubbenhorst*(Legal Firm)*
51 Rte. 23 South
Riverdale, NJ 07457

Lakeland State Bank*(Major Banking Relationship)*
Lakeland, NJ

G. E. Hubner, Jr.*(Pension Manager)*
Bloomingdale, NJ

Group:

Allied Felt Group (1)
46 Star Lake Rd.
Bloomingdale, NJ 07403
Tel.: 201-838-1616
Fax: 201-838-8273
Emp.: 30
Felt for Crafts & Hobbies
S.I.C.: 5199
Cornelius A. Hubner *(Chm. Bd.)*
Donald A. Hubner *(Pres.)*
Jim Nelson *(V.P.-Sls.)*
Eric Hubner *(Treas.)*

CENTRAL STATES DIVERSIFIED, INC.
9322 Manchester Rd.
Saint Louis, MO 63119
Tel.: 314-961-4300
Fax: 314-961-1089
Year Founded: 1921
Assets: $18,000,000
Liabilities: $12,000,000
Net Worth: $6,000,000
Approx.Sls.: $56,000,000
Emp.: 500
Fiscal Year-end: 12/31/90
Manufacture Paper Bags; Polyethylene Show Bags; Consumer Products of Paper & Flexible Plastics; Disposable Paper Medical Products; POP Posters & Inflatables, Kites, Window Banners, Premiums
S.I.C.: 2674; 2676; 2679; 2656; 2759; 3089
J. Russell Flowers *(Chm. Bd.)*
R.S. Prince *(Pres. & Chief Oper. Officer)*
Charles Aebel *(Chief Fin. Officer)*
David L. Coe *(Exec. V.P.)*

No. of Mfg. Plants/Facilities: 4

Computer Systems/Hardware:
IBM System 38

Outside Service Firm(s):

Alexander & Alexander*(Auditors)*
St. Louis, MO

Thompson & Mitchell*(Legal Firm)*
One Mercantile Center
Saint Louis, MO 63101

Mark Twain St. Louis Bank*(Major Banking Relationship)*
1630 S. Lindbergh Blvd.
St. Louis, MO 63131

CENTRAL STATES ENTERPRISES, INC.
300 International Pkwy., Suite 150
Heathrow, FL 32746
Mailing Address:
P.O. Box 13339
Fort Wayne, IN 46868-3339
Tel.: 407-333-3503 **IN**
Fax: 407-333-2022
Year Founded: 1980
Assets: $33,300,000
Liabilities: $26,800,000
Net Worth: $6,500,000
Approx.Sls.: $116,000,000
Emp.: 65
Fiscal Year-end: 4/30/92
Export
Grain Elevators; Production & Feeding of Hogs
S.I.C.: 5153; 0213
Richard Shura *(Pres.)*
Robert Pegan *(Exec. V.P.)*
Kenneth Cupples *(V.P.-Sls.)*
Robert Godfrey *(Sec. & Treas.)*

Principal(s):
Richard Shura

Outside Service Firm(s):

Coopers & Lybrand*(Auditors)*
490 Lincoln Bank Tower
Fort Wayne, IN 46802
Tel.: 219-423-1531
Fax: 219-426-7870

Miller & Miller*(Legal Firm)*
New Haven, IN

Fort Wayne National Bank*(Major Banking Relationship)*
110 W. Berry St.
Fort Wayne, IN 46802
Tel.: 219-426-0555

CENTRAL SUPPLY CO., INC.
8900 E. 30th St.
Indianapolis, IN 46219
Mailing Address:
P.O.Box 1982,
Indianapolis, IN 46206
Tel.: 317-898-2411
Fax: 317-899-6421
Year Founded: 1976
Approx.Sls.: $54,600,000
Emp.: 159
Fiscal Year-end: 12/31/91
Wholesale Plumbing, Heating, Cooling, Electrical, Industrial & Mill Supplies
S.I.C.: 5074; 5063; 5075; 5085
John Carr, III *(Pres. & Chief Exec. Officer)*
David Hughes *(Treas.)*
Michael Bray *(Dir.-Data Processing)*

Principal(s):
Employee-Owned

Computer Systems/Hardware:
NCR 8555 Model 2

Outside Service Firm(s):

Roy J. Pile & Co.*(Auditors)*
Indianapolis, IN

Dutton & Overman*(Legal Firm)*
710 Century Building, 36 S. Pennsylvania St.
Indianapolis, IN 46204
Tel.: 317-633-4000

INB National Bank*(Major Banking Relationship)*
One Indiana Sq.
Indianapolis, IN 46266
Tel.: 317-266-6000

CENTRAL TRANSPORT INC.
Uwharrie Rd.
High Point, NC 27264
Mailing Address:
P.O. Box 7007,
High Point, NC 27264
Tel.: 919-431-9186 **NC**
Fax: 919-431-9186, Ext. 111
Approx.Sls.: $53,000,000
Emp.: 560
Fiscal Year-end: 12/31/89
Motor Freight Carrier of Bulk Commodities
S.I.C.: 4213
Archie L. Honbarrier *(Pres.)*
G. L. Honbarrier *(V.P.)*
Hezzie Hodges *(V.P.-Fin.)*
Don Webb *(V.P.-Sls. & Mktg.)*
Louise B. Honbarrier *(Sec. & Treas.)*
Len Fletcher *(Dir.-Opers.)*
Ben Keller, III *(Dir.-Data Processing)*

Outside Service Firm(s):

Dixon, Odom & Co.*(Auditors)*
Concord, NC

NationsBank Carolinas*(Major Banking Relationship)*
One NCNB Plaza T18-7
Charlotte, NC 28255

CENTURY AMERICA CORPORATION
875 No. Michigan Ave.
Chicago, IL 60611
Tel.: 312-266-1025
Fax: 312-266-7746
Approx.Sls.: $90,000,000
Emp.: 400
Fiscal Year-end: 12/31/91
Real Estate Investors; Steel Warehousing
S.I.C.: 5051; 6799
Myron Hokin *(Pres. & Chief Exec. Officer)*
Mark Gelfeld *(V.P. & Chief Fin. Officer)*
Jonathon Strauss *(Corp. Sec.)*
Debbie Cygan *(Dir.-Tax & Acct.)*

Computer Systems/Hardware:
Data General

Outside Service Firm(s):

Coopers & Lybrand*(Auditors)*
203 N. LaSalle St.
Chicago, IL 60601
Tel.: 312-701-5500

First National Bank of Chicago*(Major Banking Relationship)*
One First National Plaza
Chicago, IL 60670
Tel.: 312-732-9781
Tel.: 312-732-4050
Fax: 312-732-4840
Fax: 312-732-3055

CENTURY AUTOLINE
1700 S. Caton Ave.
Baltimore, MD 21227
Tel.: 410-368-5000
Tel.: 800-776-0368
Fax: 301-368-5019
Year Founded: 1832
Approx.Sls.: $10,000,000
Emp.: 60
Fiscal Year-end: 3/31/91
Lubricating Oils & Greases
S.I.C.: 2992
Edward J. Peres *(Pres.)*
Robert D. Scott *(V.P.)*

CENTURY BUSINESS CREDIT CORPORATION
119 W. 40th St.
New York, NY 10018
Tel.: 212-703-3500 **NY**
Sales Range: $500-999 Million
Emp.: 100
Factoring, Accounts Receivable Financing
S.I.C.: 6153
Stanley Tananbaum *(Chm. Bd. & Chief Exec. Officer)*
Andrew Tananbaum *(Pres. & Chief Fin. Officer)*
David Finkelstein *(Exec. V.P.)*
Howard Moore *(Sr. V.P.)*
Tom Pizzo *(Sr. V.P.-New Business Factoring)*
Anthony Sarcone *(Sr. V.P.)*
Robert Swanzey *(Sr. V.P.-Human Resources & Opers.)*
Allen Vogel *(Sr. V.P.-New Business Accounts Receivable Financing)*
Hugo Friedlaender *(V.P.)*
Alan Sasloff *(V.P.)*
Henry Gerstman *(Sec., Treas. & Controller)*

Outside Service Firm(s):

Ernst & Young*(Auditors)*
787 Seventh Ave.
New York, NY 10019
Tel.: 212-773-1243

Kronish, Lieb, Weiner & Hellman*(Legal Firm)*
1345 Ave. of the Americas
New York, NY 10105
Tel.: 212-841-6246

Chase Manhattan Bank, N.A.*(Major Banking Relationship)*
One Chase Manhattan Plaza
New York, NY 10081
Tel.: 212-552-2222
Tel.: 800-526-0801
Fax: 212-552-7175

Subsidiary:

Century Data Services, Inc. **(1)**
119 W. 40th St.
New York, NY 10018
Tel.: 212-703-3500 (79%)
Licensing of Computer Software Packages
S.I.C.: 6794
Andrew Tananbaum *(Pres.)*
Robert Swanzey *(Exec. V.P.)*
William Fish *(V.P.)*
Henry Gerstman *(Treas.)*

CENTURY COMPUTER MARKETING
4755 Alla Rd.
Marina Del Rey, CA 90292-6378
Tel.: 310-827-0999 **CA**
Fax: 310-578-2160
Year Founded: 1984
Approx.Sls.: $35,000,000
Emp.: 150
Export
Distributes Microcomputer Service Parts, Including Complete Systems, Peripherals, Enhancements and Data Communications Equipment. Refurbish Complete Systems & Parts.
S.I.C.: 5065; 7378
Dan Firestone *(Chief Exec. Officer)*
Mike Wolfe *(Pres.)*
Gary Owen *(Chief Fin. Officer)*
Dennis Cagan *(V.P.-Mktg. & Strategic Plng.)*

No. of U.S. Offices: 2
No. of Foreign Offices: 2

CENTURY DATA SYSTEMS
506 N. Harrington St.
Raleigh, NC 27603
Mailing Address:
P.O. Box 27884
Raleigh, NC 27611
Tel.: 919-821-5696
Fax: 919-821-2325
Year Founded: 1975
Approx.Sls.: $20,000,000
Emp.: 250
Fiscal Year-end: 6/30/90
Sell & Service Electronic Cash Registers & Computer Systems
S.I.C.: 5044; 5045
Clarence R. Wiggins *(Chm. Bd., Pres. & Chief Exec. Officer)*
Ken Wurtz *(Chief Fin. Officer & Controller)*
D. Wayne Williams *(Exec. V.P.)*
Bobby R. Young *(Exec. V.P.)*
R. T. Bailey *(Treas.)*
Kenneth Wertz *(Asst. Treas.)*
Fred Allen *(Dir.-Data Processing)*

Computer Systems/Hardware:
Texas Instruments A990

Outside Service Firm(s):

Smith, Allen, Hodge, Burn & Thomas*(Auditors)*
Raleigh, NC

Protective Life Insurance*(Group Insurer)*
Box 11407,
Birmingham, AL 35246

First Union National Bank*(Major Banking Relationship)*
Raleigh, NC

CENTURY FENCE COMPANY
N 11 West 24711 Silvernal Rd.
Pewaukee, WI 53072
Mailing Address:
P.O. Box 466,
Waukesha, WI 53187-0466
Tel.: 414-547-3331
Fax: 414-547-0669
Approx.Sls.: $10,000,000
Emp.: 110
Fiscal Year-end: 12/31/90
Chain Link Fence & Gates, Steel Beam Guard Rail, Athletic Back Stops & Tennis Courts, Interstate Hwy. Fencing & Signing, Traffic Pavement Markings
S.I.C.: 3315; 3312; 3949; 1629
A.W. Bryant *(Pres. & Treas.)*
W.O. Hoye *(Exec. V.P. & Sec.)*
Don Lucas *(V.P.-Sls.)*
Joseph Tenke *(V.P.-Construction)*
L. Fix *(Pur. Agent)*

Division:

Century Fence Co. **(1)**
P. O. Box 100
Forest Lake, MN 55025
Tel.: 612-464-7373
Fax: 612-464-7377
S.I.C.: 3315; 3312; 3949; 1629
D.D. Delage *(V.P. & Div. Mgr.)*

CENTURY FURNITURE INDUSTRIES
401 11th St., N.W.
Hickory, NC 28601
Mailing Address:
P.O. Box 608
Hickory, NC 28603
Tel.: 704-328-1851
Tel.: 800-852-5552 **NC**
Fax: 704-328-2176
Year Founded: 1948
Approx.Sls.: $120,000,000
Emp.: 1,600
Import Export
Mfr. of Case-Goods: Bedroom & Dining Room Furniture, Upholstered Chairs, Loveseats, Sofas, Dining Room & Occasional Chairs, Occasional Tables
S.I.C.: 2511; 2512
Harley F. Shuford, Sr. *(Chm. Bd.)*
Harley F. Shuford, Jr. *(Pres.)*
Charles B. Sutton *(Pres.-Sutton Div.)*
Nancy S. Dowdy *(Sr. V.P.-Adv. & Mktg.)*
David L. Leffler *(Sr. V.P.-Sls.)*
A. Alex Shuford *(Sr. V.P.-Upholstery Div.)*
Robert E. Bliss *(V.P.-Chair Div.)*
Larry MacBean *(V.P.-Intl.)*
Eric S. Schenk *(V.P.-Upholstery Opers.)*
George K. Snow, Jr. *(V.P.-Case-Good Opers.)*
Robert K. Johnson *(Treas.)*
David Whisant *(Dir.-Data Processing)*
Terry Guthrie *(Mgr.-Indus. Rels.)*

Outside Service Firm(s):

McGladrey & Pullen*(Auditors)*
Hickory, NC

Patrick, Harper & Dixon*(Legal Firm)*
Hickory, NC

First Union National Bank*(Major Banking Relationship)*
Hickory, NC

CENTURY PRODUCTS CO.
9600 Valley View Rd.
Macedonia, OH 44056-9989
Tel.: 216-468-2000
Fax: 216-650-2875
Year Founded: 1964
Emp.: 1,100
Import Export
Mfr. of Children's Products, Car Seats, Strollers, Infant Carriers; Nursery Furniture; Developmental Toys, Stuffed Animals
S.I.C.: 3944; 2511; 3942
Jim Callier *(Chm. Bd.)*
Frank E. Rumpeltin *(Pres.)*
Harold Krider *(V.P.-Fin.)*
Roger Faulb *(V.P.-New Mkt. Devel.)*
Patrick Osborne *(V.P.-Human Resources)*
Jim Geeslin *(V.P. Sls.)*
John Ragsdale *(Controller)*
Shelly DiMattio *(Mgr.-Adv.)*

Subsidiary:

Okla Homer Smith Furniture Co. **(1)**
P.O. Box 1148
Fort Smith, AR 72902
Tel.: 501-783-6191 (100%)
Mfr. of Nursery Furniture
S.I.C.: 2511
Okla Ben Smith *(Pres.)*
Charles Lensing *(V.P.-Fin.)*
Drew Warner *(Dir.-Sls.)*

CENTURY PUBLISHING COMPANY
990 Grove St.
Evanston, IL 60201
Tel.: 708-491-6440 **IL**
Fax: 708-491-0459
Year Founded: 1969
Approx.Sls.: $50,000,000
Emp.: 50
Fiscal Year-end: 5/31/92
Export
Publisher Sports, Travel, Movies & Video Magazines
S.I.C.: 2721
Norman Jacobs *(Chm. Bd. & Pres.)*
Jerry L. Croft *(Sr. V.P.)*
Victor Arnopolin *(V.P.)*
Judith Arnopolin *(Sec.)*

No. of U.S. Offices: 2

Computer Systems/Hardware:
Honeywell/Bull

Subsidiaries:

Inside Sports, Inc. **(1)**
990 Grove St.
Evanston, IL 60201
Tel.: 708-491-6440
Sports Magazine
S.I.C.: 2721
Norman Jacobs *(Pres.)*

World Publishing Company **(1)**
990 Grove St.
Evanston, IL 60201
Tel.: 708-491-6440
Fax: 708-491-0459
Travel, Video & Movie Magazines
S.I.C.: 2721
Norman Jacobs *(Pres.)*

CENTURY SEAFOOD INC.
3121-25 S. Lawrence St.
Philadelphia, PA 19148
Tel.: 215-336-9000 **PA**
Fax: 215-468-0881
Approx.Sls.: $80,000,000
Emp.: 150
Fiscal Year-end: 12/31/89
Wholesale Fish & Seafood
S.I.C.: 5146
Lawrence L. Soloff *(Pres. & Chief Exec. Officer)*
Don Haberle *(Controller)*

Outside Service Firm(s):

Simonson, Lipschutz & Fogel*(Auditors)*
Philadelphia, PA

CENTURY 21 AGMONT REAL ESTATE, INC.
3407 W. Lawrence Ave.
Chicago, IL 60625
Tel.: 312-463-3021 **IL**
Fax: 312-463-4901
Year Founded: 1983
Approx.Sls.: $21,000,000
Emp.: 15
Real Estate Sales
S.I.C.: 6531
Amalia Monteroso *(Pres.)*

Outside Service Firm(s):

G.P.S. Accounting Firm*(Auditors)*
Chicago, IL

Scott Berman*(Legal Firm)*
Chicago, IL

Albany Bank*(Major Banking Relationship)*
Chicago, IL

CENVILL DEVELOPMENT CORP.
(Filed Ch. 11 Bankruptcy, 8/92)
2601-21 S. Militar Trail
West Palm Beach, FL 33415
Tel.: 407-641-5900 **DE**
Assets: $282,945,000
Liabilities: $185,888,000
Net Worth: $97,057,000
Approx.Rev.: $202,837,000
Emp.: 670
Fiscal Year-end: 10/31/90
Construction, Development, Marketing & Operation of Condo Communities & Single-Family Homes
S.I.C.: 1521; 1542; 6411
Robert Seldomridge *(Pres.)*
Norma Tredwell *(V.P.-Fin.)*

Subsidiaries:

Bencart, Inc. **(1)**
North Haverhill Road
West Palm Beach, FL 33417
Tel.: 305-683-4767 (100%)
Approx.Sls.: $425,000
Emp.: 13
Insurance Broker
S.I.C.: 6411
Ronald Reshevsky *(Pres.)*

Boca Hamptons Management, Inc. **(1)**
North Haverhill Rd.
West Palm Beach, FL 33417
Tel.: 305-683-4767 (100%)
Single Family Home Developer; Inactive
S.I.C.: 1521
Mark Shevory *(Pres.)*

C. V. Investments, Inc. **(1)**
North Haverhill Rd.
West Palm Beach, FL 33417
Tel.: 305-683-4767 (100%)
Approx.Sls.: $48,000
Holding Company
S.I.C.: 6719
Craig Dougherty *(Pres.)*

C.V.W. Ltd. Partnership **(1)**
North Haverhill Road
West Palm Beach, FL 33409
Tel.: 305-683-4767 (100%)
Real Estate Developers
S.I.C.: 6552

Century Financial Services **(1)**
North Haverhill Road
West Palm Beach, FL 33417
Tel.: 305-683-4767 (100%)
Emp.: 4
Insurance
S.I.C.: 6411
Ronald Reshevsky *(Pres.)*

Century Golf Courses, Inc. **(1)**
North Haverhill Road
West Palm Beach, FL 33417
Tel.: 305-683-4767 (100%)
Golf Course
S.I.C.: 7992
Richard Siemens *(Pres.)*

Century Real Estate, Inc. **(1)**
North Haverhill Road
West Palm Beach, FL 33417
Tel.: 305-683-4767 (100%)
Approx.Sls.: $705,000
Emp.: 10
Real Estate Broker
S.I.C.: 6531
John DeLuca *(Pres.)*

Century Utilities, Inc. **(1)**
North Haverhill Road
West Palm Beach, FL 33417
Tel.: 305-683-4767 (100%)
Approx.Sls.: $1,000,000
Emp.: 14
Water & Sewage Treatment
S.I.C.: 4952
Richard Siemens *(Pres.)*

Cenvill Management, Inc. **(1)**
North Haverhill Road
West Palm Beach, FL 33417
Tel.: 305-683-4767 (100%)
General Contractor; Inactive
S.I.C.: 1541
Richard Siemens *(Pres.)*

Cenvill Recreation, Inc. **(1)**
North Haverhill Road
West Palm Beach, FL 33417
Tel.: 305-683-4767 (100%)
Approx.Sls.: $7,000,000
Emp.: 119
Recreation Administration
S.I.C.: 7032
Richard Siemens *(Pres.)*

Cenvill Services **(1)**
North Haverhill Road
West Palm Beach, FL 33417
Tel.: 305-683-4767 (100%)
Approx.Sls.: $261,000
Emp.: 41
Miscellaneous Corporate Services
S.I.C.: 8741
Richard Siemens *(Pres.)*

Subsidiaries:

Wynville Realty **(2)**
North Haverhill Road
W. Palm Beach, FL 33417
Tel.: 305-683-4767 (100%)
Approx.Sls.: $67,000
Emp.: 5
Real Estate
S.I.C.: 6552
James A. Paul *(Pres.)*

Comark, Inc. **(2)**
North Haverhill Road
West Palm Beach, FL 33417
Tel.: 305-683-4767 (100%)
Management & Marketing for Cable System
S.I.C.: 4813

F.W.D.C., Inc. **(1)**
North Haverhill Road
West Palm Beach, FL 33417
Tel.: 305-683-4767 (100%)
Real Estate Builder & Developer
S.I.C.: 1531; 6552
Richard Siemens *(Pres.)*

G.D.C. Business Systems, Inc. **(1)**
North Haverhill Road
West Palm Beach, FL 33417
Tel.: 305-683-4767 (100%)
Approx.Sls.: $1,000,000
Emp.: 18
Data Processing Center
S.I.C.: 7374
Thomas Johannes *(Pres.)*

Prestcon, Inc. **(1)**
North Haverhill Road
West Palm Beach, FL 33417
Tel.: 305-683-4767 (100%)
Approx.Sls.: $2,000,000
Emp.: 28
Precast Construction of Condominiums
S.I.C.: 1522
Richard Siemens *(Pres.)*

Wynmoor Homes, Inc. **(1)**
North Haverhill Road
West Palm Beach, FL 33417
Tel.: 305-683-4767 (100%)
Emp.: 1
Real Estate Development
S.I.C.: 6552
Mark Shevory *(Pres.)*

Wynmoor Ltd. Partnership **(1)**
North Haverhill Rd.
West Palm Beach, FL 33417
Tel.: 305-683-4767 (100%)
Approx.Sls.: $19,000,000
Emp.: 100
Condominium Community Developer
S.I.C.: 1531; 6552
Richard Siemens *(Chief Oper. Officer)*

Wynmoor Management & Co., Inc. **(1)**
North Haverhill Road
West Palm Beach, FL 33417
Tel.: 305-683-4767 (100%)
Approx.Sls.: $1,000,000
Management Services
S.I.C.: 8741
Richard Siemens *(Pres.)*

CERRITOS FORD, INC.
18900 Studebaker Rd.
Cerritos, CA 90701
Tel.: 310-865-5554 **CA**
Fax: 310-402-5759
Year Founded: 1981
Approx.Sls.: $67,000,000
Emp.: 165
Retail Sales of New & Used Automobiles
S.I.C.: 5511
Ronald Gregoire *(Pres.)*
David S. Smokler *(V.P.)*

CERTIFIED CORP.
170 Oak Hill Way
Brockton, MA 02401
Tel.: 508-584-8100
Fax: 508-584-8704
Approx.Sls.: $20,000,000
Emp.: 600
Fiscal Year-end: 12/31/90
Mfr. of Pharmaceuticals; Metal Mesh Gloves; Metal Mesh Handbags
S.I.C.: 3171; 5137; 5145
Maurice Liberman *(Pres.)*
Basil F. Perry *(V.P.-Fin.)*
Joseph Callaghan *(V.P.-Opers.)*

No. of Mfg. Plants/Facilities: 2
No. of U.S. Offices: 5

Computer Systems/Hardware:
MAI Basic 4

Outside Service Firm(s):

Arthur Andersen & Co.*(Auditors)*
One Intl. Place, 100 Oliver St.
Boston, MA 02110
Tel.: 617-330-4000
Fax: 617-439-9731

Zurich American Insurance Co.*(Commercial Insurance Carrier)*
New York, NY

State Mutual Life Assurance Co. of America*(Group Insurer)*
Boston, MA

Hale and Dorr*(Legal Firm)*
60 State St.
Boston, MA 02109-6098
Tel.: 617-526-6000

Bank of New England*(Major Banking Relationship)*
28 State Street
Boston, MA 02109
Tel.: 617-742-4000

William M. Mercer Incorporated*(Pension Manager)*
3700 Georgia Pacific Center
Atlanta, GA 30303
Tel.: 404-521-2200
Fax: 404-521-2200

Subsidiaries:

Powers Pharmaceutical **(1)**
170 Oak Hill Way
Brockton, MA 02401
Tel.: 508-584-8100
Fax: 508-584-8704
Approx.Sls.: $15,000,000
Emp.: 125
Fiscal Year-end: 12/31/90
Export
Mfr. of Over-the-Counter Pharmaceuticals
S.I.C.: 2834
Joseph Callaghan *(Pres.)*
Jack Bullock *(V.P.-Mktg. & Sls.)*
Paul Donavan *(Controller)*
Susan Medros *(Dir.-Pur.)*
Mike Barna *(Mgr.-Personnel)*

Whiting & Davis Company **(1)**
23 W. Bacon St.
Plainville, MA 02762
Tel.: 508-699-4411
Fax: 508-695-7606
Approx.Sls.: $16,000,000
Emp.: 500
Fiscal Year-end: 12/31/90
Mfrs. of Mesh Handbags & Accessories; Mesh Jewelry; Mesh Safety Equipment
S.I.C.: 3171; 3961; 3496
Curtis R. Smith *(Pres.)*
Ann Marie Lynch *(Pur. Agent)*

CERTIFIED GROCERS ADVERTISING CO.
(House Agency)
2601 S. Eastern Ave.
Los Angeles, CA 90040
Tel.: 213-726-2601
Assets: $277,659,000
Earnings: $1,532,000
Approx.Sls.: $1,797,602,000
Emp.: 2,775
Fiscal Year-end: 08/31/85
Food & Kindred Products.; Trucking & Warehousing; Wholesale Trade-Nondurable Goods; Insurance Carriers; Wholesale Food Distributor
S.I.C.: 5141; 5149; 5142; 5143; 5147; 5045
Donald W. Dill *(Sr. V.P.)*
Donald Grose *(V.P.-Human Resources)*
Jerry Lauer *(V.P.-Info. Services)*
Edward Collins *(Treas.)*
Jerry Lauer *(Dir.)*

CERTIFIED GROCERS MIDWEST, INC.
One Certified Dr.
Hodgkins, IL 60525-4894
Tel.: 708-579-2100
Fax: 708-579-9874
Year Founded: 1940
Assets: $125,000,000
Earnings: $16,000,000
Liabilities: $99,000,000
Net Worth: $26,000,000
Approx.Sls.: $650,000,000
Emp.: 720
Fiscal Year-end: 8/31/91
Food & Kindred Products; Wholesale Trade-Nondurable Goods
S.I.C.: 5141; 5149; 5142
Carl Zeman *(Chm. Bd.)*
Elwood Winn *(Pres. & Chief Exec. Officer)*
Steve D. Seder *(V.P. & Chief Exec. Officer)*
Edward Bradley *(V.P.-Opers.)*
John Abernathy *(V.P.-Mngmt. Info. Systems)*
Buzz Lindoo *(V.P.-Meat Opers.)*
Bill Schmidt *(V.P.-Produce Opers.)*
Chuck Chiodo *(V.P.-Bakery Opers.)*
Ted Clinnin *(V.P.-Human Resources)*
Jim Risley *(V.P.-Pur.)*
Elwood F. Winn *(Sec., Treas. & Chief Fin. Officer)*

No. of Mfg. Plants/Facilities: 4
No. of U.S. Offices: 1

Computer Systems/Hardware:
IBM 4110

Outside Service Firm(s):

Coopers & Lybrand*(Auditors)*
203 N. LaSalle St.
Chicago, IL 60601
Tel.: 312-701-5500

Jackson, Long & Associates, Inc.*(Commercial Insurance Carrier)*
Chicago, IL

John Hancock Mutual Life Insurance Co.*(Group Insurer)*
John Hancock Place, P.O. Box 111
Boston, MA 02117

Rudnick & Wolfe*(Legal Firm)*
203 N. LaSalle St.
Chicago, IL 60602
Tel.: 312-368-4000

American National Bank & Trust Company of Chicago*(Major Banking Relationship)*
33 N. LaSalle St.
Chicago, IL 60602
Tel.: 312-661-5000
Fax: 312-661-6417

Chicago Title & Trust Co.*(Pension Manager)*
111 W. Washington St.
Chicago, IL 60602
Tel.: 312-630-2000

Fax: 312-368-4736

CERTIFIED GROCERS OF CALIFORNIA
2601 S. Eastern Ave.
Los Angeles, CA 90040
Mailing Address:
Terminal Annex, P.O. Box 3396
Los Angeles, CA 90051
Tel.: 213-723-7476 **CA**
Fax: 213-726-2336
Year Founded: 1925
Assets: $495,000,000
Earnings: $2,332,000
Liabilities: $419,900,000
Net Worth: $75,100,000
Approx.Sls.: $2,742,000,000
Emp.: 2,700
Fiscal Year-end: 8/31/91

Import Export
Wholesale Groceries; Trucking & Warehousing; Insurance Carriers
S.I.C.: 5141; 5149; 5142; 5143; 5147; 5046; 2051; 5148; 6399
Lou Amen *(Chm. Bd.)*
Everett W. Dingwell *(Pres. & Chief Exec. Officer)*
Jerry Friedler *(Grp. Pres.-Services Companies)*
Rodney J. Love *(Grp. Pres.-Southern Calif)*
Chuck Pilliter *(Grp. Pres.-North CA)*
Donald W. Dill *(Sr. V.P. Admin.)*
Donald Grose *(Sr. V.P.-Human Resources)*
Herman Hensley *(Sr. V.P.-Distr.)*
Alfred Plamann *(Sr. V.P.-Fin. & Chief Fin. Officer)*
John Boukather *(Sr. V.P.-Retail)*
Jerry Lauer *(V.P.-Information Services)*
Paul Rohde *(V.P.-Human Resources)*
James Davidson *(Controller)*
David A. Woodward *(Sec. & Treas.)*
Bob De Paszthory *(Dir.-Export & Mktg. Plng.)*
Jim Rager *(Dir.-Real Estate)*
Bernie Vaaler *(Mgr.-Procurement)*

Computer Systems/Hardware:
IBM 3081

Outside Service Firm(s):

Coopers & Lybrand*(Auditors)*
350 S. Grand Ave.
Los Angeles, CA 90071
Tel.: 213-481-1000
Fax: 213-482-6440

Pacific Mutual*(Group Insurer)*
700 Newport Center Dr.
Newport Beach, CA 92660
Tel.: 714-640-3011
Fax: 714-759-3372

Algemene Bank Nederland*(International Bank Affiliate)*
Los Angeles, CA

Burke, Williams, Sorenson*(Legal Firm)*
Los Angeles, CA

National Australia Bank*(Major Banking Relationship)*
Los Angeles, CA

Security Pacific National Bank*(Major Banking Relationship)*
333 S. Beaudry Ave., 24th Fl.
Los Angeles, CA 90017
Tel.: 213-345-2829

Siebel Capital Management Co.*(Pension Manager)*
Larkspur, CA

Wells Fargo Bank*(Pension Manager)*
420 Montgomery St.
San Francisco, CA 94104

Subsidiaries:

Crown Grocers, Inc. **(1)**
2601 S. Eastern Ave.
Los Angeles, CA 90040
Tel.: 213-726-0939
Emp.: 20
Retail Grocery Store
Rodney Love *(Pres.)*

Grocers & Merchants Insurance Service **(1)**
874 S. Village Oak Dr.
Covina, CA 91724
Tel.: 818-915-1951
Fax: 818-332-2149
Emp.: 85
Bob Mason *(V.P.)*

Grocers Capital Co. **(1)**
2601 So. Eastern Ave.
Los Angeles, CA 90040
Tel.: 213-726-2601 (100%)
Fax: 213-721-0939
Emp.: 3
Financing Company
Everett W. Dingwell *(Pres.)*

Grocers Development Center **(1)**
2601 S. Eastern Ave.
Los Angeles, CA 90040
Tel.: 213-726-2601 (100%)
Fax: 213-721-0939
Temporary Help Service
S.I.C.: 7373
Donald Grose *(Pres.)*

Grocers Equipment Co. **(1)**
5577 Sheila St.
Los Angeles, CA 90040
Tel.: 213-728-3322
Fax: 213-722-4440
Emp.: 55
Import Export
Equipment Sales & Market Services
Rodney Love *(Pres.)*

Grocers General Merchandise Company **(1)**
2601 S. Eastern Ave.
Los Angeles, CA 90040
Tel.: 213-726-2601
General Merchandise Distributor
Jerry Friedler *(Pres.)*

Grocers Specialty Co. **(1)**
2601 S. Eastern Ave.
Los Angeles, CA 90040
Tel.: 213-726-2601
Wholesale Grocer
S.I.C.: 5141
Jerry Friedler *(Pres.)*

Pacific Economy Company **(1)**
2601 S. Eastern Ave.
Los Angeles, CA 90040
Tel.: 213-726-2601
General Merchandise Distributor
Everett W. Dingwell *(Pres.)*

CERTIFIED GROCERS OF FLORIDA, INC.
8305 SE 58th Ave.
Ocala, FL 32671
Tel.: 904-245-5151
Fax: 904-245-0459
Approx.Sls.: $395,000,000
Emp.: 870
Warehouse Groceries, Tobacco, Frozen Food, Dairy & Meat Products, Produce; Health & Beauty Aids; General Merchandise
S.I.C.: 4221; 4222; 4225
Lester Scaff *(Chm. Bd.)*
Chip Webb *(Vice Chm.)*
Tony DeMarco *(Pres.)*
Gene Morrison *(Treas.)*
Eric Jacobsen *(V.P.-Admin.)*
Paul Aaron *(Dir.-ISD)*

Outside Service Firm(s):

Deloitte & Touche*(Auditors)*
Jacksonville, FL

McKeeven & Pattilo*(Legal Firm)*
Ocala, FL

Barnett Banks Trust Company, N.A.*(Major Banking Relationship)*
Ocala, FL

CERTIFIED HOLDING CORP.
(Moving to New Address as of 1/1/93)
11410 Beverly Park Rd.
Everett, WA 98204
Tel.: 206-356-2626 **WA**
Holding Company; Custom Machinery; Aircraft Assemblies; Subassemblies & Parts
S.I.C.: 3728; 6719
R. Michael Briggs *(Pres. & Chief Exec. Officer)*
Brian P. Alleman *(V.P.-Fin.)*

Subsidiary:

ZMP, Inc. **(1)**
540 W. Chevy Chase Dr.
Glendale, CA 91204
Tel.: 818-241-5121
Fax: 800-500-7239
Sales Range: $20-39 Million
Aircraft Parts & Equipment
S.I.C.: 3728; 3599
T.D. Miller *(Chm. Bd.)*
R. Michael Briggs *(Chief Exec. Officer)*
Brian P. Alleman *(Sec. & Treas.)*

Subsidiary:

Adams Rite Products Inc. **(2)**
540 W. Chevy Chase Dr.
Glendale, CA 91204
Tel.: 818-241-5121
Fax: 818-500-7239
Approx.Sls.: $11,000,000
Emp.: 160
Fiscal Year-end: 6/30/90
Aircraft Controls & Locks
S.I.C.: 5088
Perry Cook *(Gen. Mgr.)*
Roger Snyder *(Dir.-Mktg.)*

CERWIN VEGA, INC.
555 E. Easy St.
Simi Valley, CA 93065
Tel.: 805-584-9332
Fax: 805-583-0865
Approx.Sls.: $21,000,000
Emp.: 250
Speaker Systems
S.I.C.: 3651
Eugene Czerwinski *(Pres.)*
Connie Czerwinski *(V.P., Sec. & Treas.)*
Ray Miranda *(Controller)*

Outside Service Firm(s):

Antous & Antous*(Auditors)*
Encino, CA

Antin, Stern, Litz & Grebow*(Legal Firm)*
Century City, CA

Security Pacific National Bank*(Major Banking Relationship)*
333 S. Beaudry Ave., 24th Fl.
Los Angeles, CA 90017
Tel.: 213-345-2829

CHADWICK-HELMUTH COMPANY, INC.
4601 N. Arden Dr.
El Monte, CA 91731
Tel.: 818-575-6161
Fax: 818-350-4236
Approx.Sls.: $10,000,000
Emp.: 95
Vibration Meters, Analyzers & Calibrators; Electric Lamps
S.I.C.: 3829; 3641
James R. Chadwick *(Pres.)*
William Chadwick *(V.P.)*
Jim Hart *(Dir.-Mktg.)*
John W. Beach, Jr. *(Mgr.-Sls.)*
Beth Hudson *(Mgr.-Contracts)*
Gary Taylor *(Mgr.-Opers.)*

Outside Service Firm(s):

Robert H. Peart*(Auditors)*
Los Angeles, CA

Hill, Betts & Nash*(Legal Firm)*
Los Angeles, CA

CHADWICK-MILLER INC.
10 Pequot Way
Canton, MA 02021
Mailing Address:
P.O. Box 9106,
Canton, MA 02021
Tel.: 617-828-8300 **MA**
Fax: 617-828-7840
Year Founded: 1948
Assets: $25,000,000
Liabilities: $19,500,000
Net Worth: $5,500,000
Approx.Sls.: $55,000,000
Emp.: 425
Fiscal Year-end: 3/31/91

Import Export
Import Distr. of Housewares, Notions, & Giftwares
S.I.C.: 5199; 5942
Thomas H. Lee *(Chm. Bd.)*
Gary Miller *(Pres. & Chief Exec. Officer)*
Steve Kuptsis *(V.P.-Admin. & Chief Fin. Officer)*
Richard LeBovidge *(V.P.-Quality Control)*
Robert Pugatch *(V.P.-Sls.)*
Bette Brophy *(Import Manager)*

No. of U.S. Offices: 1
No. of Foreign Offices: 2

Computer Systems/Hardware:
IBM System 36

Outside Service Firm(s):

Coopers & Lybrand*(Auditors)*
1 Post Office Square
Boston, MA 02110
Tel.: 617-574-5000
Fax: 617-345-0398

Ropes & Gray*(Legal Firm)*
One International Place
Boston, MA 02110
Tel.: 617-423-6100

Subsidiaries:

DeWolfe & Fiske Inc. **(1)**
P. O. Box 510, Pequot Industrial Pk
Canton, MA 02021
Tel.: 617-828-8300 (100%)
Book Wholesaler & Distributor
S.I.C.: 5199
Robert Leckinger *(Chief Exec. Officer)*
Danny Gurr *(Pres.)*

Lauriat Inc. **(1)**
Pequot Industrial Pk
Canton, MA 02021
Tel.: 617-828-8300 (100%)
Approx.Sls.: $32,000,000
Emp.: 200
Retail Book Stores, 20 Units
S.I.C.: 5942
Robert Leckinger *(Chief Exec. Officer)*
Danny Gurr *(Pres.)*

Non-U.S. Holdings:

Chadwick-Miller Intl. Ltd. **(1)**
Hang Seng Bank Bldg.
Hong Kong, Hong Kong
Tel.: 3-673149 (100%)
Import-Export of Housewares & Gifts
S.I.C.: 5199

Chadwick-Miller Inc. **(1)**
4th Fl., 36 Tah Hwei St.
Taipei, Taiwan (100%)
Import-Export
S.I.C.: 5199

CHAFFEE CASE & PARTNERS
196 Richmond St.
Providence, RI 02903
Tel.: 401-831-1430

Chaffee Case & Partners—(Continued)

Fax: 401-861-0680
Year Founded: 1982
Approx.Billings: $12,200,000
Emp.: 20
David S. Chaffee *(Pres.)*
Harry L. Case *(Exec. V.P.)*
Kathy P. McCabe *(Exec. V.P.)*
Edward Nowak *(Sr. V.P.)*
Mary C. Wyatt *(Sr. V.P., Pub. Rels.)*
Denis Deslauriers *(V.P., Finance)*
Peter Kelly *(V.P.)*

Computer Systems/Hardware:
IBM, Macintosh

CHAGNON LUMBER COMPANY, INC.
145 Temple St.
Nashua, NH 03060
Tel.: 603-883-7776 **NH**
Fax: 603-883-1959
Emp.: 40
Lumber & Other Building Materials; Trusses, Wooden Roof
S.I.C.: 5211; 2439
Emile A. Chagnon, Jr. *(Pres. & Treas.)*
Brit A. Chagnon *(V.P.)*

Outside Service Firm(s):

Prunier, Leonard & Bolton*(Legal Firm)*
Nashua, NH

Indian Head Bank*(Major Banking Relationship)*
Nashua, NH

CHALEK & CHALEK, INC.
380 Lexington Ave.
New York, NY 10017
Tel.: 212-972-3222
Fax: 212-557-7585
Year Founded: 1985
Approx.Billings: $14,500,000
Emp.: 21
Consumer Products & Services
Morton J. Chalek *(Chief Exec. Officer)*
Mitchel J. Chalek *(Pres.)*

CHALK & PARTNERS, LTD.
79 Fifth Ave.
New York, NY 10003
Tel.: 212-633-1200
Year Founded: 1986
Approx.Billings: $11,500,000
Emp.: 10
Howard W. Chalk *(Pres., New Bus. Contact & Creative Dir.)*

CHALLENGE GRAPHICS EQUIPMENT CO.
1810 E. Industrial Park Dr.
Grand Haven, MI 49417
Tel.: 616-842-8300
Fax: 616-842-6511
Mfr. of Printing, Folding, & Precision Products
S.I.C.: 3554; 3545; 5084
James C. Gould *(Chm. Bd.)*
William Smith *(Pres.)*

Subsidiary:

Challenge Technologies **(1)**
1433 Fulton St.
Grand Haven, MI 49417
Tel.: 616-847-6660
Fax: 616-847-6665
Approx.Sls.: $28,000,000
Emp.: 270
Export
Mfr. of Printing, Folding & Precision Products
S.I.C.: 3555; 3545
Larry J. Ritsema *(Pres.)*
James C. Gould *(Chief Exec. Officer)*
C. Edward Wiers *(Treas.)*
Sara Lee Rizzolo *(Sec.)*
Tom Crum *(Pur. Agent)*

Thomas L. Wood *(Natl. Sls. Mgr.)*

CHAMBERLAIN HEALTH & BEAUTY AIDS COMPANY
4000 N. W. 100th
Des Moines, IA 50322
Mailing Address:
P.O. Box 3570
Des Moines, IA 50322
Tel.: 515-276-1586
Year Founded: 1897
Emp.: 30
Health Care & Beauty Products
S.I.C.: 2844
A.D. Peters *(Pres.)*
Joseph M. Peters *(V.P. & Dir.-Mktg.)*
Sheryl Munyon *(Mgr.-Adv.)*

CHAMPAIGN LANDMARK
304 Bloomfield Ave.
Urbana, OH 43078
Tel.: 513-652-2135
Grains, Livestock Feed & Fertilizers
S.I.C.: 2048; 2875; 5153; 5191; 5172
Arthur Bullard *(Chm. Bd.)*
Arthur Gainer *(Treas. & Sec.)*
Harold Fourman *(Gen. Mgr.)*

Subsidiary:

Champaign Landmark **(1)**
140 S. Main St.
Mechanicsburg, OH 43044
Tel.: 513-834-2416
Fax: 513-834-2416, Ext. 252
Approx.Sls.: $49,000,000
Emp.: 75
Grains; Livestock Feeds; Fertilizers, Mixing Only
S.I.C.: 5153; 2048; 2875
Harold Fourman *(Gen. Mgr.)*

CHAMPION ALUMINUM CORPORATION
140 Eileen Way
Syosset, NY 11791
Tel.: 516-921-6200
Fax: 516-921-6370
Approx.Sls.: $20,000,000
Emp.: 140
Mfr. of Aluminum Replacement Windows
S.I.C.: 3442
Thomas Arcati *(Chm. Bd.)*
Fortunato Arcati *(Pres.)*
James Trupiano *(Controller)*
Vincent Parlato *(Dir.-Sls.)*

Outside Service Firm(s):

Siegel & Weill*(Auditors)*
New York, NY

European American Bank*(Major Banking Relationship)*
New York, NY

CHAMPION BOXED BEEF
5850 York St.
Denver, CO 80216
Mailing Address:
P.O. Box 16303,
Denver, CO 80216
Tel.: 303-288-0766
Fax: 303-287-7697
Year Founded: 1941
Assets: $15,600,000
Liabilities: $4,490,000
Net Worth: $11,110,000
Approx.Sls.: $225,000,000
Emp.: 250
Distributor of Beef, Fabricated Cuts
S.I.C.: 2011; 5147
Leonard Litvak *(Chm. Bd., Pres. & Chief Exec. Officer)*
Richard Sheldon *(Exec. V.P. & Dir.-Pur.)*
Jake Litvak *(V.P.)*
Sandra M. Solove *(Chief Fin. Officer & Controller)*
Joe Gangle *(Chief Engr.)*
Principal(s):
Leonard Litvak

No. of Mfg. Plants/Facilities: 1
No. of U.S. Offices: 1

Computer Systems/Hardware:
IBM

Outside Service Firm(s):

Deloitte & Touche*(Auditors)*
1560 Broadway, Ste. 1800
Denver, CO 80202-5626
Tel.: 303-837-3000
Fax: 303-825-0567

Aetna Life & Casualty*(Commercial Insurance Carrier)*
151 Farmington Avenue
Hartford, CT 06156
Tel.: 203-273-2128
Fax: 203-729-4295

First Interstate Bank*(International Bank Affiliate)*
Denver, CO
Tel.: 303-293-5456

Sherman & Howard*(Legal Firm)*
633 17th St.
Denver, CO 80202
Tel.: 303-297-2900

Colorado National Bank*(Major Banking Relationship)*
17th & Champa
Denver, CO 80217

CHAMPION BUSINESS FORMS
1966 Quincy
Glendale Heights, IL 60139
Mailing Address:
P.O. Box 5038
Glendale Heights, IL 60139
Tel.: 708-893-2940
Fax: 708-893-3077
Sales Range: $10-19 Million
Manufacture Business Forms
S.I.C.: 2752
Roger W. Swanson *(Pres.)*
Robert Donner *(V.P.)*

Outside Service Firm(s):

Seymour Greene & Associates*(Auditors)*
Chicago, IL

LaSalle National Bank*(Major Banking Relationship)*
120 S. LaSalle St.
Chicago, IL 60603
Tel.: 312-781-8000

CHAMPION, INC.
105 East A St.
Iron Mountain, MI 49801
Tel.: 906-779-2300
Fax: 906-779-2326
Approx.Sls.: $24,000,000
Emp.: 100
Electrical Supplies; Institutional Building Construction; Ready-Mixed Concrete; Mining Machinery & Equipment Except Petroleum; General Construction Machinery & Equipment
S.I.C.: 5063; 1542; 3273; 5082
Louis C. Verrette *(Chm. Bd. & Chief Exec. Officer)*
William C. Verrette *(Pres.)*
G.R. Benjamin *(Sr. V.P.)*
L.P. Bonicatto *(Sr. V.P.)*

Outside Service Firm(s):

Fleury, Singer & Co.*(Auditors)*
Iron Mountain, MI

Mouw & Celello, P.C.*(Legal Firm)*
Iron Mountain, MI

CHAMPION PNEUMATIC MACHINERY CO., INC.
1301 N. Euclid Ave.
Princeton, IL 61356
Tel.: 815-875-3321
Fax: 815-872-0421
Year Founded: 1919

Approx.Sls.: $28,000,000
Emp.: 180
Fiscal Year-end: 6/30/90
Import Export
Air Compressors
S.I.C.: 3563
Corporate Giving Program: United Way Bureau County
Gilbert Williamson *(Pres.)*
Leonard Krieger *(Sr. V.P.)*
H. Gene Klocke *(V.P.-Engrng.)*
H. Rhees *(V.P.-Mktg.)*
K. Nolden *(Mgr.-Mfg.)*
R.L. Hamrick *(Mgr.-Gen. Sls.)*
David Booth *(Service Mgr.)*

Computer Systems/Hardware:
IBM System 36

CHANCE INDUSTRIES, INC.
4219 Irving
Wichita, KS 67209
Mailing Address:
P.O. Box 12328,
Witchita, KS 67277-2328
Tel.: 316-942-7411 **KS**
Fax: 316-945-3498
Year Founded: 1985
Approx.Sls.: $35,000,000
Emp.: 379
Export
Mfr. of Carnival & Amusement Park Machines & Equipment; Assembly of All Types of Buses
S.I.C.: 3599; 3711
Richard G. Chance *(Pres.)*
Leon F. Metzinger *(V.P.-Fin. & Admin.)*
Robert Johnson *(Controller)*
Robert Buche *(Mgr.-Mngmt. Informations Systems)*
Steve Jacobson *(Mgr.-Human Resources)*

Outside Service Firm(s):

Peterson, Peterson & Goss*(Auditors)*
Wichita, KS

First National Bank*(Major Banking Relationship)*
Wichita, KS

Subsidiaries:

Chance Operations, Inc. **(1)**
4219 Irving
Wichita, KS 67209
Tel.: 316-942-7411
Mfr. of Amusement Park Equipment
S.I.C.: 3599; 3711
Richard G. Chance *(Pres.)*
Leon Metzinger *(Chief Fin. Officer)*
Jim Ramsey *(Dir.-Pur.)*

Chance Rides, Inc. **(1)**
4219 Irving
Wichita, KS 67209
Tel.: 316-942-7411
Tel.: 800-242-6231
Fax: 316-942-7416
Wholesale Distribution of Carnival & Amusement Park Equipment
S.I.C.: 5087
Richard G. Chance *(Pres.)*
Leon Metzinger *(Chief Fin. Officer)*
Ben Arnold *(V.P.-Sls. & Mktg.)*

CHANNEL HOME CENTERS INC.
945 Route 10
Whippany, NJ 07981
Tel.: 201-887-7000 **DE**
Fax: 201-887-4299
Year Founded: 1908
Approx.Sls.: $400,000,000
Emp.: 5,100
Fiscal Year-end: 7/31/91
Import
Home Improvement Centers
S.I.C.: 5211; 5251; 5231; 5261
Joseph Nusim *(Chm., Pres. & Chief Exec. Officer)*
Richard Kramer *(Acting Chief Fin. Officer)*
Paul Abate *(V.P.-Opers.)*

Thomas Ercolano *(V.P.-Real Estate)*
Robert Furlong *(V.P.-Store Activities)*
Marc Hettinger *(V.P.-Human Resources)*
Ron Niemiec *(V.P.-Adv.)*
Dan Sorell *(V.P.-Traffic & Distribution)*
Robert Anderson *(Asst. Treas.)*
Jill Miller *(Sec.)*
Lisa Kitzmiller *(Mgr.-Leasing)*

Computer Systems/Hardware:
IBM 3081

Outside Service Firm(s):

Deloitte & Touche*(Auditors)*
1 World Trade Center
New York, NY 10048
Tel.: 212-669-5000

Latham & Watkins*(Legal Firm)*
885 Third Ave.
New York, NY 10022
Tel.: 212-906-1200

Bankers Trust Co.*(Major Banking Relationship)*
130 Liberty St., 20th Fl.
New York, NY 10006
Tel.: 212-250-2737

Latham & Watkins*(Pension Manager)*
885 Third Ave.
New York, NY 10022
Tel.: 212-906-1200

Division:

Channel Home Centers, Central Region **(1)**
7909 Fredericksburg Rd., Ste. 134
San Antonio, TX 78229
Tel.: 210-696-7667
Emp.: 400
S.I.C.: 5211; 5231; 5251; 5261

CHANNEL TECHNOLOGIES, INC.
839 Ward Dr.
Santa Barbara, CA 93111
Tel.: 805-967-0171
Fax: 805-683-3420
Emp.: 90
Export
Holding Company
S.I.C.: 6719; 3679; 3812
Robert F. Carlson, Sr. *(Chm. Bd., Chief Exec. Officer & Treas.)*
Robert M. Callahan *(Pres.)*

No. of Mfg. Plants/Facilities: 1

Outside Service Firm(s):

Harris W. Seed*(Legal Firm)*
Santa Barbara, CA

Subsidiaries:

Channel Industries, Inc. **(1)**
839 Ward Dr.
Santa Barbara, CA 93111
Tel.: 805-967-0171
Telex: 658416
Fax: 805-683-3420
Emp.: 90
Piezoelectric Ceramic Materials
S.I.C.: 3679
Robert M. Callahan *(Pres.)*

Channel Products, Inc. **(1)**
7100-T Wilson Mills Rd.
Chesterland, OH 44026
Tel.: 216-423-0113
Telex: 980173
Fax: 216-423-1502
Emp.: 120
Controls, Filters & Tranducers
S.I.C.: 3679
Ken Pim *(V.P.)*

Electro Optical Ind. **(1)**
839 Ward Dr.
Santa Barbara, CA 93111
Tel.: 805-967-0171
Fax: 805-683-3420
Electronic Components
S.I.C.: 3679
Margret Cassen *(V.P.)*

International Transducer Corporation **(1)**
869 Ward Dr.
Santa Barbara, CA 93111
Tel.: 805-683-2575
Fax: 805-967-8199
Emp.: 70
Oceanographic Instruments, Underwater Sound Equipment
S.I.C.: 3812
William A. Bunker *(Pres.)*

Seabeam Ind., Inc. **(1)**
33 S.W. Industrial Park
Westwood, MA 02090
Tel.: 617-326-7815
Electronic Components
S.I.C.: 3679
Robert F. Carlson, Jr. *(Pres.)*

Sonatech, Inc. **(1)**
879 Ward Dr.
Santa Barbara, CA 93111
Tel.: 805-683-1431
Oceanographic Instruments
S.I.C.: 3812
Reginald J. Cyr *(Pres.)*

CHANNELLOCK, INC.
1306 S. Main St.
Meadville, PA 16335
Mailing Address:
P.O. Box 519
Meadville, PA 16335
Tel.: 814-724-8700
Telex: 550854
Fax: 800-962-2583
Year Founded: 1886
Approx.Sls.: $30,000,000
Emp.: 500
Fiscal Year-end: 7/31/91
Export
Manufacture of Hand Tools
S.I.C.: 3423
George S. DeArment *(Co-Chm. Bd.)*
William A. DeArment *(Co-Chm. Bd.)*
William S. DeArment *(Pres. & Gen. Mgr.)*
W.J. Walsh *(Chief Oper. Officer)*
Robert E. Cannon *(V.P.-Sls. & Mktg.)*
Donald A. Hornstein *(V.P.-Human Resources)*
William Leffingwell *(Chief Fin. Officer)*
James R. Stimpson *(Treas., Controller & Sec.)*
Kimberly Steider *(Data Processing Mgr.)*
Rita Schlosser *(Pur. Agent)*

No. of Mfg. Plants/Facilities: 2
No. of U.S. Offices: 1

Computer Systems/Hardware:
IBM AS/400

Outside Service Firm(s):

Pashke, Twargowski & Lee*(Auditors)*
Erie, PA

Mellon Bank, N.A.*(Major Banking Relationship)*
Four Station Sq., Third Fl.
Pittsburgh, PA 15219
Tel.: 412-326-8000

Subsidiary:

Hold-E-Zee, Ltd. **(1)**
99 Ling Road
Rochester, NY 14612
Tel.: 716-663-5373
Tel.: 800-622-5832
Emp.: 30
Import Export
Hold-E-Zee Screw Holding Screw Drivers & Nut Drivers, Upson 4 N 1 Screwdrivers, Standard Screw Drivers
S.I.C.: 3423
W.S. De Arment *(Chief Exec. Officer)*
Neil R. Oblom *(V.P.-Opers. & Chief Oper. Officer)*

CHAPMAN PRINTING COMPANY
2450 290 First Ave.
Huntington, WV 25703
Mailing Address:
P.O. Box 2968
Huntington, WV 25728
Tel.: 304-528-2791
Fax: 304-528-2746
Approx.Sls.: $18,000,000
Emp.: 257
Commercial Printing & Wholesale Office Supplies
S.I.C.: 5112
Marshall T. Reynolds *(Pres.)*
Tony K. Adkins *(Treas.)*
Jim Doyle *(Dir.-Personnel)*
Robert G. McKinney *(Mgr.-Sls.)*
Walter R. Sansom *(Pur. Agent)*

Outside Service Firm(s):

Coopers & Lybrand*(Auditors)*
100 E. Broad St.
Columbus, OH 43215

Huddleston, Bolen Batty, Porter & Copen*(Legal Firm)*
Huntington, WV

First Huntington National Bank*(Major Banking Relationship)*
Huntington, WV

CHARAN INDUSTRIES, INC.
370 Old Country Rd.
Garden City, NY 11530
Tel.: 516-747-6500 **NY**
Fax: 516-747-6554
Year Founded: 1937
Approx.Sls.: $60,000,000
Emp.: 900
Fiscal Year-end: 8/31/91
Commercial Real Estate & Bowling Operations
S.I.C.: 6512; 6552; 7933
Charles P. Ryan, Jr. *(Chm. Bd., Pres.)*
Robert J. McDermott *(V.P. & Chief Fin. Officer)*
John J. Ryan *(V.P. & Treas.)*
Kevin T. Ryan *(V.P. & Sec.)*
Thomas San Antonio *(Controller)*
Fred Kaplowitz *(Mgr.-Mktg.)*

Outside Service Firm(s):

A. Sheiffer & Co.*(Auditors)*
Westbury, NY

Subsidiaries:

Bowling Corp. of America **(1)**
370 Old Country Rd.
Garden City, NY 11530
Tel.: 516-747-6500 (100%)
Fax: 516-747-6551
Emp.: 800
Bowling, Bar, Restaurant, Pro Shops, Vending, Game Machines
S.I.C.: 7999; 7933; 5812
Kevin J. Ryan *(Pres. & Chief Oper. Officer)*

Charan Realty Group **(1)**
370 Old Country Rd.
Garden City, NY 11530
Tel.: 516-747-6500
REAL ESTATE
S.I.C.: 6531
John J. Ryan *(Pres. & Chief Oper. Officer)*

Seaway Shopping Centers, Inc. **(1)**
370 Old Country Rd.
Garden City, NY 11530
Tel.: 516-747-6500 (100%)
Emp.: 2
Owner, Operator 5 Shopping Centers
S.I.C.: 6512
John J. Ryan *(Chief Oper. Officer)*

THE CHARDON RUBBER CO.
373 Washington St.
Chardon, OH 44024
Tel.: 216-285-2161 **OH**
Fax: 216-286-8422
Year Founded: 1978
Approx.Sls.: $81,844,000
Emp.: 1,100
Fiscal Year-end: 12/31/90
Manufacture Mechanical Goods, Molded & Extruded Products
S.I.C.: 3089; 3069; 3061
J.W. Keener, Jr. *(Pres., Chief Exec. Officer & Treas.)*
John R. Cross *(V.P.-Sls. & Sec.)*
John R. Weber *(V.P.-Fin. & Chief Fin. Officer)*
John Noga *(Controller)*
P. Bongiovanni *(Gen. Mgr.)*
Rick Ford *(Dir.-Employee Benefits)*
D.W. Grepp *(Dir.-Mktg.)*
Patrick O'Neal *(Dir.-Human Resources & Personnel)*

Outside Service Firm(s):

Price Waterhouse*(Auditors)*
BP America Bldg., 200 Public Square, 27th Floor
Cleveland, OH 44114-2301
Tel.: 216-781-3700

Rosenfeld, Meyer & Susman*(Legal Firm)*
9601 Wilshire Blvd.
Beverly Hills, CA 90210
Tel.: 310-858-7700

Society National Bank*(Major Banking Relationship)*
900 Euclid Ave., P.O. Box 6477
Cleveland, OH 44101-6477
Tel.: 216-737-5000
Fax: 216-566-8947

Plants:

CEC Inc. **(1)**
P.O. Box 638,
Greeneville, TN 37744
Tel.: 615-638-1381
Manufacture Rubber Molding
S.I.C.: 3069; 3061
Jack Dawson *(Mgr.-Plant)*

Industrial Rubber Goods **(1)**
1776 Hilltop Rd.
Saint Joseph, MI 49085

RIM Development Center **(1)**
15825 Armour Rd.
Alliance, OH 44601

Subsidiary:

Beebe Rubber Company **(1)**
25 Marshall St.
Nashua, NH 03060
Tel.: 603-883-5577
Custom Molded Industrial & Automotive Parts, Rubber to Metal Bonding, Footwear Products
S.I.C.: 3061

CHARING CROSS GROUP
1330 S. Third St.
Louisville, KY 40208
Tel.: 502-635-7433
Approx.Sls.: $13,000,000
Emp.: 1,000
Contract Services Including Commercial Cleaning, Landscaping, Apartment Management & Physical Plant Maintenance; Owns & Manages Apartment Buildings
S.I.C.: 6513; 6552; 6531; 8741; 7349; 0781
Charles D. Scudder *(Chm. Bd. & Chief Exec. Officer)*
J.A. Barker *(Pres.)*
Principal(s):
Charles D. Scudder
D.L. Scudder

Outside Service Firm(s):

Charles W. Hebel, Jr.*(Legal Firm)*
Louisville, KY

CHARLES CURTAIN COMPANY, INC.
1352 Crampton St.
Dallas, TX 75207
Tel.: 214-630-7967 **TX**

Charles Curtain Company, Inc.—(Continued)

Fax: 214-630-7969
Year Founded: 1936
Emp.: 25
Export
Manufacture & Retail Drapes, Curtains & Bedspreads
S.I.C.: 2391; 2392; 5714; 5719
Robert I. Ross *(Chm. Bd.)*
Charles M. Ross *(Pres.)*
Jack M. Greenbert *(V.P.-Personnel)*

Outside Service Firm(s):

Philip Vogel & Co.*(Auditors)*
Dallas, TX

Alfred Sallenger*(Legal Firm)*
Dallas, TX

NationsBank Texas*(Major Banking Relationship)*
Dallas, TX

CHARLES MACHINE WORKS, INC.
1959 W. Fir Ave.
Perry, OK 73077
Tel.: 405-336-4402 **OK**
Fax: 405-336-3458
Year Founded: 1948
Approx.Sls.: $100,000,000
Emp.: 700
Export
Mfr. of Trenching Machinery
S.I.C.: 3531
Edwin Malzahn *(Chm. Bd. & Pres.)*
Mary Malzahn *(Vice Chm.)*
Dr. Donald Malzahn *(V.P.)*
Terry Wilcox *(Treas. & Sec.)*

Outside Service Firm(s):

First National Bank & Trust Co.*(Major Banking Relationship)*
Perry, OK

CHARLES RIVER DATA SYSTEMS, INC.
983 Concord St.
Framingham, MA 01701
Tel.: 508-626-1000
Tel.: 800-229-1900 **MA**
Fax: 508-626-1046
Year Founded: 1973
Sales Range: $20-39 Million
Fiscal Year-end: 6/30/92
Export
Development, Manufacture and Sale of Computer Systems
S.I.C.: 3575
Richard B. Shapiro *(Chm. Bd., Pres. & Chief Exec. Officer)*
John Owens *(Exec. V.P.)*
Joseph Disabato *(V.P.-Mfg.)*
Robert Sonnabend *(V.P.-Sls.)*
John O'Brien *(Chief Fin. Officer& Dir.-F & I)*
Susan E. Hadahan *(Controller)*
Robert Corbin *(Dir.-Human Resources)*
David Greer *(Dir.-Universe Sls. & Mktg.)*
John O'Brien *(Dir.-Human Resources)*
Kenneth Osowski *(Dir.-Systems Mktg.)*
Michael Bernardi *(Sr. Buyer)*

Computer Systems/Hardware:
Universe

Outside Service Firm(s):

Deloitte & Touche*(Auditors)*
125 Summer St.
Boston, MA 02110
Tel.: 617-261-8000
Fax: 617-261-8111

Chubb Group*(Commercial Insurance Carrier)*
Boston, MA

First National Bank of Boston*(Investment Banker)*
P.O. Box 644,
Boston, MA 02102-0644
Tel.: 617-575-2900
Fax: 617-575-2549

Goldstein & Manello*(Legal Firm)*
265 Franklin St.
Boston, MA 02110
Tel.: 617-329-3350

CHARLES RIVER FOODS, INC.
1 Widett Circle
Boston, MA 02118
Tel.: 617-269-4414
Fax: 617-269-4417
Year Founded: 1981
Approx.Sls.: $15,000,000
Emp.: 150
Fiscal Year-end: 12/31/90
Export
Processed Fresh Chicken
S.I.C.: 2015
Lester Stein *(Pres.)*
Stanley Weiss, Jr. *(Chief Exec. Officer & Treas.)*

No. of Mfg. Plants/Facilities: 2
No. of U.S. Offices: 1

CHARLES TOWN RACES, INC.
Flowing Springs Rd.
Charles Town, WV 25414
Mailing Address:
P.O. Box 551
Charles Town, WV 25414
Tel.: 304-725-2021 **WV**
Fax: 304-725-6979
Year Founded: 1983
Approx.Sls.: $36,000,000
Emp.: 400
Thoroughbred Horse Racing
S.I.C.: 7948
D. Keith Wagner *(Pres.)*
George Yeatras *(V.P.)*
Donald E. Hudson *(Gen. Mgr.)*
Ronald L. Evans *(Sec.)*
John Propst *(Treas.)*

CHARMGLOW INDUSTRIES, INC.
500 South Madison
DuQuoin, IL 62832
Tel.: 618-542-4468
Fax: 618-542-6138
Approx.Sls.: $60,000,000
Emp.: 400
Fiscal Year-end: 10/31/90
Manufacturer of Gas & Electric Grills
S.I.C.: 3589
Robert E. Feigenbaum *(Pres.)*
Larry L. Maxwell *(V.P.-Sls.)*

CHARRON, SCHWARTZ & PARTNERS, INC.
405 Lexington Ave., 63rd Fl.
New York, NY 10174
Tel.: 212-687--5555
Fax: 212-687--5591
Year Founded: 1989
Approx.Billings: $35,500,000
Emp.: 22
Norman S. Schwartz *(Chm. Bd. & Chief Oper. Officer)*
Theodore J. Charron *(Pres., Chief Exec. Officer & Creative Dir.)*
Ellen Taylor *(Chief Fin. Officer)*
Marjorie Charron *(Treas. & Gen. Mgr)*
Charles Napier Miller *(Dir. New Bus. Devel.)*

CHARTER HOUSE GROUP
535 Madison Ave., 28th Fl.
New York, NY 10022
Tel.: 212-421-3125
Motor Vehicle Parts & Accessories
S.I.C.: 3429
Jerome Katz *(Pres.)*
A.L. Fagan *(Exec. V.P.)*
P.R. Merrick *(Exec. V.P.)*

Outside Service Firm(s):

Coopers & Lybrand*(Auditors)*
1301 Avenue of The Americas
New York, NY 10019
Tel.: 212-536-2000

Subsidiary:

AP Parts Manufacturing Company **(1)**
One John Goerlich Square
Toledo, OH 43697-0965
Tel.: 419-259-3461
Fax: 419-259-3051
Approx.Sls.: $250,000,000
Emp.: 1,800
Fiscal Year-end: 12/31/90
Import Export
Computer Systems/Hardware:
Bull
Manufacturer of Automotive Exhaust Systems for Car Manufacturers & Replacement Markets; Supplier of Brakes, Shocks, Struts, Coil Springs, Steering & Suspension Parts to the Replacement Market
S.I.C.: 3714
Tom Thibert *(Pres.-Mktg.)*
J.R. Hall *(Pres.-Mfg.)*
James Clayton *(V.P.-Sls.)*
A.M. DelGozzo *(V.P.-Sls.)*
W.F. Newell *(V.P. & Controller)*
Bruno Rosa *(V.P.-Engrng. & Pur.)*
G.A. Worny *(V.P.-Mktg.)*
Jim Gerber *(Dir.-Prod. & Mktg. Devel.)*
J.V. Morsillo *(Dir.-Sls., West)*
F.L. Kohler *(Dir.-Distr. Opers.)*
B.J. Golatka *(Dir.-Customer Services & Admin.)*
Ken Vesey *(Gen. Sls. Mgr.-OEM)*
Sandra Tosha *(Dir.-Employee Rels.)*
Bonnie Schuff *(Dir.-Adv.)*
H.E. Deakin *(Mgr.-Pur.)*

CHARTWAY TECHNOLOGIES
20 W. Gude Dr.
Rockville, MD 20850
Tel.: 301-294-1000 **DE**
Fax: 301-294-1007
Year Founded: 1986
Assets: $12,793,256
Earnings: $1,737,031
Liabilities: $9,723,028
Net Worth: $3,070,228
Approx.Sls.: $27,804,801
Emp.: 200
Fiscal Year-end: 1/31/88
Manufacture, Sales & Service of Computer Software
S.I.C.: 7372
Larry G. Settle *(Chm. Bd.)*
Howard M. Arnold *(Pres. & Chief Exec. Officer)*
Thomas J. Rege *(Chief Fin. Officer, Sec., Treas. & Controller)*
Peter L. Garahan *(V.P.)*
Phil Kiviat *(V.P.)*
Barbara Duchez *(Dir.-Plng. & Devel.)*
Linda Sievering *(Mgr.-Office Services)*

No. of U.S. Offices: 4

Computer Systems/Hardware:
IBM

Outside Service Firm(s):

Arthur Andersen & Co.*(Auditors)*
1666 K Street, N.W.
Washington, DC 20006

State Mutual Life Assurance Co. of America*(Group Insurer)*
440 Lincoln St.
Worcester, MA 01605
Tel.: 508-852-1000

Schulman, Rodgers, Pordy, Gandel, Ecker*(Legal Firm)*
Silver Spring, MD

First American Bank of Virginia*(Major Banking Relationship)*
1970 Chain Bridge Rd.
McLean, VA 22102
Tel.: 703-821-7777
Fax: 703-760-6355

CHASE CHEVROLET CO.
Miner & Hunter
Stockton, CA 95201
Mailing Address:
P.O. Box 1969
Stockton, CA 95201
Tel.: 209-946-6600
Fax: 209-946-6625
Year Founded: 1944
Assets: $8,750,000
Liabilities: $6,820,000
Net Worth: $1,930,000
Approx.Sls.: $45,000,000
Emp.: 96
Fiscal Year-end: 12/31/89
Retail Car Dealership
S.I.C.: 5511
William K. Chase *(Chm. of Bd.)*
Cherly Arana *(Treas. & Sec.)*
John W. Chase *(Pres.)*
Charlotte Chase *(V.P.)*
Principal(s):
William K. Chase

Outside Service Firm(s):

Grant Thornton*(Auditors)*
Stockton, CA

Bank of America NT&SA*(Major Banking Relationship)*
Sacramento, CA

Subsidiary:

Chase Chrysler/Plymouth **(1)**
2979 Auto Center
Stockton, CA 95212
Tel.: 209-956-7600
Emp.: 26
Chrysler Plymouth Automobile Dealership
S.I.C.: 5511
Ken Watts *(Pres.)*

F. H. CHASE, INC.
69 Elm St.
Foxboro, MA 02035
Mailing Address:
P.O. Box 377
Foxboro, MA 02035
Tel.: 617-237-2000 **MA**
Fax: 508-543-5858
Year Founded: 1973
Assets: $3,909,940
Earnings: $80,000
Liabilities: $2,841,819
Net Worth: $1,068,121
Approx.Sls.: $11,000,000
Emp.: 100
Fiscal Year-end: 12/31/91
Sale & Installation of Interior Building Systems
S.I.C.: 1796; 1742
Francis H. Chase III *(Chm. Bd., Pres., Chief Exec., Chief Fin. Officer & Treas.)*
Eric L. Gray *(V.P.-Sls.)*
Michael V. Minutolo *(V.P.-Sls.)*
Domenic Russo *(V.P.-Opers.)*
Mary Brassard *(Corp. Sec. & Controller)*
Anne Burke *(Dir.-Pur.)*
Kathleen M. Howard *(Meetings Planner)*

No. of Mfg. Plants/Facilities: 3
No. of U.S. Offices: 3

Computer Systems/Hardware:
IBM

Outside Service Firm(s):

Loberfeld, Sherman*(Auditors)*
Newton, MA

Blue Cross & Blue Shield of Rhode Island*(Group Insurer)*
Providence, RI

Andover Bank*(Investment Banker)*
61 Main St.
Andover, MA 01810
Tel.: 508-475-6103
Fax: 508-475-6011

Cessari & McKenna*(Legal Firm)*
Boston, MA

Gaffin & Krattenmaker, PC*(Legal Firm)*
Boston, MA

Andover Bank*(Major Banking Relationship)*
61 Main St.
Andover, MA 01810
Tel.: 508-475-6103
Fax: 508-475-6011

ADQ, Inc.*(Pension Manager)*
Waltham, MA

CHATSWORTH DATA CORPORATION
20710 Lassen St.
Chatsworth, CA 91311
Tel.: 818-341-9200
Fax: 818-341-3002
Approx.Sls.: $15,000,000
Emp.: 120
Optical Scanning Devices, Test Equipment For Electronic & Electrical Circuits; Instruments for Measuring & Testing of Impacts; Impact Recording Equipment; Underground Cable Testing Equipment
S.I.C.: 3577
William H. Moothart *(Pres.)*
Carl G. Bohman *(V.P.)*
Frank J. Lefkowitz *(V.P.)*
Hannes G. Boehm *(Sec.)*

Outside Service Firm(s):

Bank of America NT&SA*(Major Banking Relationship)*
Chatsworth, CA

CHATTANOOGA CHOO-CHOO HOLIDAY INN
1400 Market St.
Chattanooga, TN 37402
Tel.: 615-266-5000
Tel.: 800-TRACK 29
Fax: 615-265-4635
Year Founded: 1972
Approx.Sls.: $15,000,000
Emp.: 400
30 Acre Vacation Complex Including Holiday Inn Hotel, Restaurants, Lounges, Gift Shops, Pools & Tennis; Railroad Museum with HO Gauge Model Railroad
S.I.C.: 5812; 7011; 5813
David Latture *(Gen. Mgr.)*
Chris Johnson *(Resident Mgr.)*
Russell Baker *(Controller)*
Lynne DeMatteo *(Sec.)*
Annie Still *(Dir.-Sls.)*
Vivian Cubb *(Dir.-Human Resources)*
Kelly Courter *(Dir.-Catering)*
Julie Dodson *(Corp. Sls. Mgr.)*
Joe Kilgore *(Mgr.-Mktg. & Pub. Rels.)*
Joy Nolan *(Mgr.-Convention Sls.)*
Karen Suttles *(Mgr.-Tour & Travel Sls.)*

Computer Systems/Hardware:
Holidex Reservations System

CHATTANOOGA GROUP
4717 Adams Rd.
Hixson, TN 37343
Tel.: 615-870-2281 **TN**
Fax: 615-875-5497
Physical Therapy & Exercise Equipment
S.I.C.: 3842; 3949
John H.P. Maley *(Pres. & Chief Exec. Officer)*
D.C. Linville *(Exec. V.P.-Mktg.)*
Claude McCormick *(Exec. V.P.-Opers.)*
Henry Kanies *(Sr. V.P.)*
Jack Kilgore *(V.P.-Fin.)*
Peggy Greever *(Sec.)*

Outside Service Firm(s):

Arthur Andersen & Co.*(Auditors)*
734 Market St.
Chattanooga, TN 37402
Tel.: 615-756-5000
Fax: 615-265-3869

American National Bank & Trust Co.*(Major Banking Relationship)*
Chattanooga, TN

CHEF ITALIA, INC.
2317 Vestal Pkwy., E.
Vestal, NY 13850
Tel.: 607-754-1070
Fax: 607-786-0233
Approx.Sls.: $21,000,000
Emp.: 100
Restaurant Chain; Manufacture Meatballs & Sausage
S.I.C.: 5812; 2013
Guido Iacovelli *(Chm. Bd. & Pres.)*
David Iacovelli *(Sec. & Treas.)*
Cameron T. Robert *(Consultant)*

Outside Service Firm(s):

Piaker & Lyons*(Auditors)*
Vestal, NY

Chernin & Gold*(Legal Firm)*
Vestal, NY

Chase Lincoln First Bank, N.A.*(Major Banking Relationship)*
Vestal, NY

CHELSEA MILLING CO.
201 North St.
Chelsea, MI 48118
Tel.: 313-475-1361
Approx.Sls.: $75,000,000
Emp.: 300
Manufacture Flour & Cake Mixes
S.I.C.: 2045
Howard S. Holmes *(Pres.)*
Dudley K. Holmes, Jr. *(V.P.)*
Howard S. Holmes, Jr. *(V.P.)*
Howdy Holmes *(V.P.)*
Mary B. Holmes *(Treas.)*

Outside Service Firm(s):

Chelsea State Bank*(Major Banking Relationship)*
Chelsea, MI

CHELSEA MOORE COMPANY
Fifth Third Center, Ste. 2200,
511 Walnut St.
Cincinnati, OH 45202-3118
Tel.: 513-621-1161
Tel.: 800-669-1161
Fax: 513-721-4611
Sales Range: $100-499 Million
Emp.: 85
Real Estate Brokerage, Leasing, Property Management, Financial Services, Tenant Representation
S.I.C.: 6512; 6513; 6531
Alfred A. Moore *(Chm. Bd.)*
William L. Whithouse, III *(Pres.)*
Scott N. Berlekamp *(Sr. V.P.-Commercial Mngmt. Services)*
N. Thomas Jochum *(Sr. V.P.-Residential Mngmt. Services)*
Michael H. Ward *(Sr. V.P.-Commercial Leasing Services)*
Judith T. Boschert *(Controller)*

Outside Service Firm(s):

Lincoln National Life Insurance Co.*(Group Insurer)*
PO Box 208, 1300 S. Clinton
Fort Wayne, IN 46801
Tel.: 219-455-2926
Fax: 219-455-7619

The Central Trust Company, N.A.*(Major Banking Relationship)*
201 E. Fifth
Cincinnati, OH 45202
Tel.: 513-651-8255

CHELSEA STATE BANK
305 S. Main St.
Chelsea, MI 48118
Tel.: 313-475-1355 **MI**
Fax: 313-475-7740
Year Founded: 1897
Emp.: 35
State Commercial Bank
S.I.C.: 6022
Paul G. Schaible, Jr. *(Chm. Bd., Pres. & Chief Exec. Officer)*
Scott Tanner *(V.P. & Cashier)*

CHEM-TAINER CORPORATION
361 Neptune Ave., N.
Brooklyn, NY 11704
Tel.: 516-661-8300 **NY**
Fax: 516-661-8923
Year Founded: 1958
Sales Range: $10-19 Million
Emp.: 225
Mfr. of Rotationally Molded Plastic Containers
S.I.C.: 3089
Stuart Pivar *(Chm. Bd.)*
James Glen *(Pres.)*
Anthony Lamb *(Exec. V.P.)*

Outside Service Firm(s):

Gregory Chios*(Auditors)*
Plainview, NY

Chemical Banking Corp.*(Major Banking Relationship)*
277 Park Ave.
New York, NY 10041
Tel.: 212-310-6407
Fax: 212-310-4526

CHEMCENTRAL CORPORATION
7050 W. 71st St.
Bedford Park, IL 60638
Mailing Address:
P.O. Box 730,
Bedford Park, IL 60499-0730
Tel.: 708-594-7000 **IL**
Fax: 708-594-7022
Fax: 708-594-6328
Year Founded: 1926
Approx.Sls.: $565,000,000
Emp.: 760
Import
Wholesale Solvents & Chemicals
S.I.C.: 5169
Richard T. Hough *(Chm. Bd.)*
H.D. Wenstrup *(Pres. & Chief Exec. Officer)*
D.W. Courtney *(V.P. & Dir.-Mktg.)*
A.L. Haines *(V.P., Treas., Controller & Chief Fin. Officer)*
W.D. Mulliken *(V.P., Sec. & Gen. Counsel)*
K.J. Krausz *(Treas.)*
Janette Linhart *(Mgr.-Mktg.)*
K.J. Dixon *(Plant Supvr.)*
Principal(s):
Richard T. Hough

No. of Mfg. Plants/Facilities: 43
No. of U.S. Offices: 35
No. of Foreign Offices: 1

Computer Systems/Hardware:
IBM AS 400

Outside Service Firm(s):

KPMG Peat Marwick*(Auditors)*
Peat Marwick Plaza, 303 E. Wacker Dr.
Chicago, IL 60601
Tel.: 312-938-1000

McDermott, Will & Emery*(Legal Firm)*
111 W. Monroe
Chicago, IL 60603
Tel.: 312-372-2000

Harris Trust & Savings Bank*(Major Banking Relationship)*
111 W. Monroe St.
Chicago, IL 60690
Tel.: 312-461-2265
Tel.: 800-858-0840

Subsidiaries:

CHEMCENTRAL/Atlanta **(1)**
1 Alchemy Pl.
Doraville, GA 30340
Tel.: 404-448-7123
Fax: 404-446-8922
Emp.: 27
S.I.C.: 5169
R.B. Reeves *(Gen. Mgr.)*
F.J. Buytendorp *(Reg. Mgr.)*

CHEMCENTRAL/Buffalo **(1)**
3709 River Rd.
Tonawanda, NY 14150
Tel.: 716-874-1600
Fax: 716-874-3607
Emp.: 22
S.I.C.: 5169
R.C. Wells *(Gen. Mgr.)*

CHEMCENTRAL/Chicago **(1)**
7050 W. 71st St.
Bedford Park, IL 60638
Tel.: 708-594-7000
Fax: 708-594-7022
Emp.: 61
W.R. Hough *(Gen. Mgr.)*
K.M. Jaggers *(Reg. Mgr.)*

CHEMCENTRAL/Cincinnati **(1)**
12 Standen Dr.
Hamilton, OH 45015
Tel.: 513-874-7766
Fax: 513-874-8173
Emp.: 40
S.I.C.: 5169
R.R. Wester *(Gen. Mgr.)*
T.E. Shumate *(Reg. Mgr.)*

CHEMCENTRAL/Cleveland **(1)**
21600 Drake Rd.
Strongsville, OH 44136
Tel.: 216-238-8550
Fax: 216-238-4690
Emp.: 31
S.I.C.: 5169
W.L. Zorn *(Gen. Mgr.)*

CHEMCENTRAL/Dallas **(1)**
2500 Vinson St.
Dallas, TX 75212
Tel.: 214-637-3450
Fax: 214-638-3818
Emp.: 28
S.I.C.: 5169
J.D. Sweatt *(Gen. Mgr.)*

CHEMCENTRAL/Detroit **(1)**
13395 Huron River Dr.
Romulus, MI 48174-0906
Tel.: 313-941-4800
Fax: 313-941-7140
Emp.: 61
S.I.C.: 5169
B.M. Machado *(Gen. Mgr.)*

CHEMCENTRAL/Fort Wayne **(1)**
7415 Nelson Rd. E.
Fort Wayne, IN 46803
Tel.: 219-749-5153
Fax: 219-749-8196
Emp.: 17
S.I.C.: 5169
M.W. Rost *(Gen. Mgr.)*

CHEMCENTRAL/Grand Rapids **(1)**
2940 Stafford Ave., S.W.
Wyoming, MI 49548
Tel.: 616-245-9111
Fax: 616-245-8669
Emp.: 25
S.I.C.: 5169
H.R. Edwards *(Gen. Mgr.)*

CHEMCENTRAL/Greensboro **(1)**
108 Oakdale Rd.
Jamestown, NC 27282-0100
Tel.: 919-454-1161
Fax: 919-887-0786
Emp.: 19
S.I.C.: 5169
J.J. McQuillan *(Gen. Mgr.)*

CHEMCENTRAL/Houston **(1)**
8425 Market St.
Houston, TX 77029-2419
Tel.: 713-675-5241
Fax: 713-675-3237
Emp.: 35
S.I.C.: 5169
C.B. Ruzicka *(Gen. Mgr.)*

CHEMCENTRAL Corporation—(Continued)

V.B. Hester *(Reg. Mgr.)*

CHEMCENTRAL/Indianapolis (1)
5850 W. 82nd St.
Indianapolis, IN 46278
Tel.: 317-876-0777
Fax: 317-872-7917
Emp.: 17
S.I.C.: 5169
G.W. Kreil *(Gen. Mgr.)*

CHEMCENTRAL/Kansas City (1)
910 No. Prospect Ave.
Kansas City, MO 64120-1685
Tel.: 816-241-3223
Fax: 816-241-6132
S.I.C.: 5169
J.M. Williams *(Gen. Mgr.)*

CHEMCENTRAL/Los Angeles (1)
13900 S. Carmenita Rd.
Santa Fe Springs, CA 90670-4997
Tel.: 213-773-3471
Fax: 213-921-8294
Emp.: 51
S.I.C.: 5169
D.M. Fogarty *(Gen. Mgr.)*
A.M. Schulten *(Reg. Mgr.)*

CHEMCENTRAL/Louisville (1)
1825 Appleton Ln.
Louisville, KY 40256
Tel.: 502-448-5111
Fax: 502-447-8639
Emp.: 18
S.I.C.: 5169
J.K. Van De Ryt *(Gen. Mgr.)*

CHEMCENTRAL/Milwaukee (1)
2400 S. 170th St.
New Berlin, WI 53151
Tel.: 414-784-2400
Fax: 414-784-4582
Emp.: 26
S.I.C.: 5169
J.R. Yanney *(Gen. Mgr.)*

CHEMCENTRAL/Minnesota (1)
21675 Hamburg Ave.
Lakeville, MN 55044
Tel.: 612-469-1500
Fax: 612-469-1585
Emp.: 14
S.I.C.: 5169
D.J. Frede *(Gen. Mgr.)*

CHEMCENTRAL/New Orleans (1)
333 River Rd.
Jefferson, LA 70121
Tel.: 504-837-8585
Fax: 504-837-8629
Emp.: 14
S.I.C.: 5169
R.J. Michalik *(Gen. Mgr.)*

CHEMCENTRAL/Odessa (1)
105 Pronto
Odessa, TX 79762
Tel.: 915-367-6087
Fax: 915-367-6195
Emp.: 10
S.I.C.: 5169
D.A. Daniels *(Branch Mgr.)*

CHEMCENTRAL/Oklahoma City (1)
7301 S.W. 29th
Oklahoma City, OK 73179
Tel.: 405-745-2341
Fax: 405-745-4730
Emp.: 14
S.I.C.: 5169
G.T. Ackerman *(Gen. Mgr.)*

CHEMCENTRAL/Orlando (1)
8120 S. Orange Ave.
Orlando, FL 32809
Tel.: 407-851-1101
Fax: 407-240-8724
Emp.: 20
S.I.C.: 5169
F.W. Cox *(Gen. Mgr.)*

CHEMCENTRAL/Pittsburgh (1)
Parkway West, Montour Run Exit
Coraopolis, PA 15108
Tel.: 412-923-2570
Fax: 412-787-5284
Emp.: 18
S.I.C.: 5169
J.W. Osegueda *(Gen. Mgr.)*

CHEMCENTRAL/Portland (1)
10821 N. Lombard St.
Portland, OR 97203
Tel.: 503-286-5821
Fax: 503-286-4580
Emp.: 12
S.I.C.: 5169
C.J. Colbert *(Gen. Mgr.)*

CHEMCENTRAL/St. Louis (1)
2646 Metro Blvd.
Maryland Heights, MO 63043
Tel.: 314-739-6600
Fax: 314-739-5249
Emp.: 27
S.I.C.: 5169
C.F. McCoy *(Gen. Mgr.)*

CHEMCENTRAL/Salt Lake City (1)
2465 S. 1100 W.
Woods Cross, UT 84087
Tel.: 801-292-0437
Fax: 801-298-7529
Emp.: 10
S.I.C.: 5169
W.F. Bellamy *(Gen. Mgr.)*

CHEMCENTRAL/San Antonio (1)
1107 E. Southcross Blvd.
San Antonio, TX 78214
Tel.: 210-533-0123
Fax: 210-533-3223
Emp.: 13
S.I.C.: 5169
P.A. Scafido *(Gen. Mgr.)*

CHEMCENTRAL/San Francisco (1)
31702 Hayman
Hayward, CA 94544
Tel.: 510-471-5420
Fax: 510-471-2983
Emp.: 23
S.I.C.: 5169
R.B. Dinneen *(Gen. Mgr.)*

CHEMCENTRAL/Seattle (1)
7601 So. 190th St.
Kent, WA 98032
Tel.: 206-251-8500
Fax: 206-251-6099
Emp.: 11
S.I.C.: 5169
E.D. Cleland *(Gen. Mgr.)*

CHEMCENTRAL/Spokane (1)
6308 E. Sharp
Spokane, WA 99212
Tel.: 509-535-0519
Fax: 509-535-9019
Emp.: 4
S.I.C.: 5169
J.D. Zinda *(Branch Mgr.)*

CHEMCENTRAL/Toledo (1)
4051 South Ave.
Toledo, OH 43615
Tel.: 419-536-3771
Fax: 419-531-8552
Emp.: 18
S.I.C.: 5169
D.O. Ziolkowski *(Gen. Mgr.)*

CHEMCENTRAL/Tulsa (1)
4500 N. Peoria Ave.
Tulsa, OK 74148
Tel.: 918-425-1306
Emp.: 13
S.I.C.: 5169
J.H. Lambert *(Gen. Mgr.)*

CHEMICAL EXCHANGE INDUSTRIES
3813 Buffalo Speedway
Houston, TX 77098
Mailing Address:
P.O. Box 812
Houston, TX 77001
Tel.: 713-526-8291
Fax: 713-522-9392
Mfr. Specialty Chemicals
S.I.C.: 2819; 2869
David M. Smith *(Pres. & Chief Exec. Officer)*
Peter R. Buenz *(Exec. V.P.-Opers.)*
Richard M. Wall *(Exec. V.P.-Mktg.)*
Mark W. Davis *(V.P.-Fin.)*
Leslie J. Jeko *(V.P.)*
Troy Gaddie *(Controller)*

Outside Service Firm(s):

Arthur Andersen & Co.*(Auditors)*
711 Louisiana, Ste. 1300
Houston, TX 77002-2323
Tel.: 713-237-2793

Cox & Smith*(Legal Firm)*
2000 NBC Bank Plaza, 112 E. Pecan St.
San Antonio, TX 78205
Tel.: 210-554-5500

Subsidiary:

Advanced Aromatics, Inc. (1)
5501 Baker Rd.
Baytown, TX 77520
Tel.: 713-526-8291
Fax: 713-522-9392
Approx.Sls.: $35,000,000
Emp.: 70
Manufacture Organic Chemicals
S.I.C.: 2869
Peter Buenz *(Pres.)*

CHEMOIL
750 Battery St., 6th Fl.
San Francisco, CA 94111
Tel.: 415-956-3834
Bunkering Petroleum to Barges
S.I.C.: 5172
Antonio Garcia *(Chm. Bd.)*
Robert Chandran *(Pres.)*

CHEMSTONE CORP.
P.O. Box 71
Strasburg, VA 22657
Tel.: 703-465-5161
Fax: 703-465-5150
Approx.Sls.: $10,000,000
Emp.: 139
Fluxstone Lime Mining
S.I.C.: 1411
Stillman A. Louis *(Pres.)*
Richard C. Culp *(V.P. & Gen. Mgr.)*
Robert O. Pecha *(V.P.-Sls. & Mktg.)*
William B. Reid *(V.P. & Controller)*

Computer Systems/Hardware:
IBM

CHEMTECH INDUSTRIES, INC.
1655 Des Peres Rd.
Saint Louis, MO 63131
Mailing Address:
P.O. Box 31000
St. Louis, MO 63131
Tel.: 314-966-9900
Tel.: 800-325-3332 **MO**
Twx: 910-997-0511
Fax: 314-966-2907
Year Founded: 1956
Assets: $38,638,606
Earnings: $1,389,467
Liabilities: $24,367,779
Net Worth: $14,270,827
Approx.Sls.: $120,000,000
Emp.: 300
Fiscal Year-end: 6/30/91
Import Export
Distr. Indus. Chemicals; Mfr. & Reseller of Specialty Chemicals
S.I.C.: 5169; 2899; 2819; 5171; 2843
William F. Schierholz *(Chm. Bd.)*
H.E. Griter *(Pres.-Dist. Div.)*
Mark E. Looney *(V.P. & Gen. Mgr.)*
Ronald L. Cox *(Controller)*
Yvonne Stewart *(Mgr.-Personnel)*
Tom Warren *(Mgr.-Data Processing)*

No. of Mfg. Plants/Facilities: 10

Computer Systems/Hardware:
Burroughs System A3

Outside Service Firm(s):

Arthur Andersen & Co.*(Auditors)*
1010 Market St.
St. Louis, MO 63101

Schoenbeck, Schoenbeck & Luther*(Legal Firm)*
St. Louis, MO

Mercantile Commerce Trust*(Major Banking Relationship)*
Saint Louis, MO

J. H. Ellwood & Associates*(Pension Manager)*
175 West Jackson Blvd., Ste. A-1827
Chicago, IL 60604
Tel.: 312-782-5432
Fax: 312-782-7494

CHEMUNG FORD, INC.
Rte. 14
Elmira, NY 14902
Tel.: 607-734-1681 **DE**
Fax: 607-737-0247
Year Founded: 1982
Approx.Sls.: $14,000,000
Emp.: 58
New & Used Automobiles & Pickups
S.I.C.: 5511
John Hartman *(Pres.)*
Pete Hartman *(Treas. & Sec.)*

Outside Service Firm(s):

Elmira Savings Bank*(Major Banking Relationship)*
Elmira, NY

CHENEY COMPANY
2445 S. Calhoun Rd.
New Berlin, WI 53151
Mailing Address:
P.O. Box 51188
New Berlin, WI 53151
Tel.: 414-782-1100
Tel.: 800-568-1222
Fax: 414-782-7442
Year Founded: 1935
Approx.Sls.: $18,000,000
Emp.: 125
Fiscal Year-end: 6/30/92
Export
Mfr. Stairway Elevators, Wheelchair Lifts
S.I.C.: 3534
Thomas Landgraf *(General Mgr.)*
Thomas Lieven *(Mgr.-Fin.)*
Jerry Voors *(Mgr.-Sls. & Mktg.)*
John Prendergast *(Mgr.-Res. & Devel.)*
Mark Soddors *(Mgr.-Mfg.. Sls.)*

CHERAW YARN MILLS, INC.
U.S. Hwy. 1
Cheraw, SC 29520
Mailing Address:
P.O. Box 807
Cheraw, SC 29520
Tel.: 803-537-7846 **SC**
Fax: 803-537-7665
Year Founded: 1917
Approx.Sls.: $45,000,000
Emp.: 300
Fiscal Year-end: 11/30/90
Import Export
Manufacture of Knitting Yarn; Cotton, Synthetic & Blends
S.I.C.: 2281
W. Manning Malloy *(Pres. & Treas.)*
H. Malloy Evans, Jr. *(V.P.)*
H. Malloy Evans, III *(V.P.)*
Edwin Malloy, Jr. *(Sec.)*
Bill Malloy *(Mgr.-Sls.)*
Fred Craft, Jr. *(Mgr.-Human Resources)*
Harold Hunter *(Dir.-Pur.)*
Luke Thurman *(Dir.-Data Processing)*

No. of U.S. Offices: 1

Outside Service Firm(s):

McGladrey & Pullen*(Auditors)*
Drawer G-2, 230 N. Elm St.
Greensboro, NC 27402
Tel.: 919-273-4461

Miller, Taylor, Johnson & Allison*(Legal Firm)*
Charlotte, SC

South Carolina National Bank*(Major Banking Relationship)*
Columbia, SC

THE CHERENSON GROUP
3 Regent St.
Livingston, NJ 07039
Tel.: 201-992-7800
Fax: 201-992-7250
Year Founded: 1961
Approx.Billings: $20,000,000
Emp.: 53
Advertising Agency
S.I.C.: 7311
Lee Cherenson *(Pres.)*
Ira Barcan *(Treas.)*
Connie Garb *(Dir.-Human Rels.)*
Peter Gavigan *(Dir.-Pub. Rels.)*
Valerie Rahn *(Dir.-Data Processing)*

Branch:

Success Advertising, Inc. **(1)**
3 Regent St.
Livingston, NJ 07039
Tel.: 201-535-9300
Tel.: 800-848-4323
Fax: 201-992-7250
Approx.Billings: $3,000,000
Emp.: 7
Corporate Recruitment Advertising
Kurt Schwartz *(Pres.)*

CHERNIN'S SHOES
1001 S. Clinton
Chicago, IL 60607
Tel.: 312-922-5900
Fax: 312-922-3673
Year Founded: 1907
Approx.Sls.: $80,000,000
Emp.: 500
Shoe Stores
S.I.C.: 5661
Harris Chernin *(Founder)*
Donald Lord *(Pres.)*
Keith Kohen *(V.P.-Retail Opers.)*
Steve Larrick *(V.P.)*
Gary Siegel *(V.P.-Pur.-Women's Shoes)*
Corey Simonson *(V.P.-Pur.-Mens' Shoes)*
Jim Lubinski *(Controller)*

Subsidiary:

Shoemart Express **(1)**
1001 S. Clinton
Chicago, IL 60607
Tel.: 312-922-5900
Self-Serve Shoe Store
S.I.C.: 5661
Don Lord *(Pres.)*

CHERNOFF/SILVER & ASSOCIATES
801 Gervais St.
Columbia, SC 29201
Tel.: 803-765-1323
Fax: 803-765-1485
Year Founded: 1974
Approx.Billings: $28,000,000
Emp.: 88
Business-to-Business, Healthcare, Travel & Tourism, Governmental Relations, Utilities & Services
Marvin Chernoff *(Chm.)*
A. Richard Silver *(Exec. V.P.)*
Rodney R. Hull *(Pres.)*
Timothy J. Koch *(Chief Fin. Officer)*
Taj Shiben *(Treas.)*
Doug Williams *(Sec.)*
Annette Budzak *(Mktg. & New Bus. Dir.)*
Erin MacLellan *(Pub. Rels. Dir.)*

CHEROKEE BRICK & TILE CO.
3250 Waterville Rd.
Macon, GA 31206
Mailing Address:
P.O. Box 4567,
Macon, GA 31213
Tel.: 912-781-6800
Fax: 912-781-6802
Approx.Sls.: $12,000,000
Emp.: 200
Mfr. Bricks
S.I.C.: 3291; 3259; 3297; 3255; 3271; 3299
Kenneth W. Dunwody, Jr. *(Chm. Bd.)*
Kenneth D. Sams *(Pres.)*
Jim Owens *(Gen. Mgr.-Opers.)*

Computer Systems/Hardware:
IBM System 36

Outside Service Firm(s):

McNair, McLemore, Middlebrooks*(Auditors)*
Macon, GA

Aetna Life & Casualty*(Group Insurer)*
Macon, GA

Jones, Cork & Miller*(Legal Firm)*
1st Natl. Bank Bldg.
Macon, GA 31208
Tel.: 912-745-2821

Citizens & Southern National Bank*(Major Banking Relationship)*
Macon, GA

THE CHEROKEE GROUP
9545 Wentworth St.
Sunland, CA 91040
Tel.: 818-951-1002 **CA**
Fax: 818-352-1851
Year Founded: 1972
Assets: $214,130,000
Earnings: $10,397,000
Liabilities: $198,861,000
Net Worth: $15,269,000
Approx.Sls.: $169,357,000
Emp.: 710
Fiscal Year-end: 5/27/91
Import Export
Designs, Manufactures & Markets Apparel for Men & Women, Women's Footwear; Licenses the Manufacturer of Compatible Cherokee & Code Bleu Brand Name Apparel, Shoes & Accessories; Operates & Franchises Specialty Retail Stores
S.I.C.: 2321; 2331; 3143; 3144; 2387; 2361; 3171; 3999; 2322; 2341; 5621; 6794; 3149
Robert Margolis *(Chm. & Chief Exec. Officer)*
Jay Kester *(Pres.)*
Mark Taxe *(Pres.-Shoe Div.)*
Cary D. Cooper *(Exec. V.P. & Chief Fin. Officer)*
Barry Lublin *(Chief Oper. Officer)*
Michael Seyhun *(Controller)*
John Dye *(Data Processing Mgr.)*

Computer Systems/Hardware:
HP 300 Model 960

Outside Service Firm(s):

Ernst & Young*(Auditors)*
515 S. Flower St.
Los Angeles, CA 90071
Tel.: 213-621-1666

Buchalter, Nemer, Fields & Younger*(Legal Firm)*
601 S. Figueroa St., Ste. 2500
Los Angeles, CA 90017-5704
Tel.: 213-891-0700

Subsidiaries:

Cherokee Apparel Corp. **(1)**
9545 Wentworth St.
Sunland, CA 91040
Tel.: 818-951-1002 (100%)
Approx.Sls.: $113,056,000
S.I.C.: 2321; 2331
Jay L. Kester *(Pres.)*

Cherokee Shoe Company, Inc. **(1)**
2985 E. Hillcrest Dr.
Westlake Village, CA 91362
Tel.: 805-496-1777
Approx.Sls.: $21,373,000
Mark Taxe *(Pres.)*

Pallmark International, Inc. **(1)**
2985 E. Hillcrest Dr.
Westlake Village, CA 91362
Tel.: 805-496-1777 (100%)
Import of Shoes
S.I.C.: 5139
Mark Taxe *(Pres.)*

Priority Finishing Corp. **(1)**
One Middle St.
Fall River, MA 02724
Tel.: 508-676-8235
Commissioned Dyer
S.I.C.: 2261; 2262
Thomas Melucci *(Pres.)*

CHERRY CENTRAL COOPERATIVE
1771 N. US 31 South
Traverse City, MI 49685
Mailing Address:
P.O. Box 988,
Traverse City, MI 49685-0988
Tel.: 616-946-1860
Fax: 616-941-4167
Year Founded: 1973
Approx.Sls.: $104,000,000
Emp.: 47
Fiscal Year-end: 4/30/91
Import Export
Processor of Fruits & Vegetables, Mktg. of Fresh Fruit & Vegetables
S.I.C.: 5148; 2033
John Minnema *(Pres. & Gen. Mgr.)*
Richard Bogard *(V.P.-Opers. & Fin.)*
James Giannestras *(V.P.-Mktg. & Sls.)*

Computer Systems/Hardware:
IBM

CHESAPEAKE FINANCIAL CORP.
6917 Collins Ave.
Miami Beach, FL 33141
Mailing Address:
P.O. Drawer K,
Miami Beach, FL 33141
Tel.: 305-866-7771 **DE**
Year Founded: 1903
Approx.Sls.: $250,000,000
Emp.: 4,800
Fiscal Year-end: 12/31/90
Manufacturer of Concentrates, Branded Soft Drinks; Franchises & Operates Fast Food Restaurants
S.I.C.: 2086; 2087; 5812; 2037; 3645; 2499; 2511
Victor Posner *(Chm. Bd., Pres. & Chief Exec. Officer)*
James W. Harralson *(Exec. V.P. & Chief Oper. Officer)*
Jack Coppersmith *(Sr. V.P. & Chief Fin. Officer)*
Renee Mottram-Doss *(Sr. V.P.-Admin.)*
Phillip A. Smalley, Jr. *(Sr. V.P.-Human Resources)*
Principal(s):
Victor Posner

Computer Systems/Hardware:
IBM System 36

Outside Service Firm(s):

Arthur Andersen & Co.*(Auditors)*
2100 One Biscayne Tower
Miami, FL 33131
Tel.: 305-374-3700

Subsidiaries:

Arby's, Inc. **(1)**
6917 Collins
Miami Beach, FL 33141
Tel.: 305-866-1904 (100%)
Fax: 305-866-7771
Approx.Rev.: $150,000,000
Emp.: 5,000
Fiscal Year-end: 12/31/90
Fast Food Restaurants
S.I.C.: 5812
Leonard Roberts *(Pres.)*
Kam Nassar *(Exec. V.P.-Fin., Admin. & Chief Fin. Officer)*
Larry Krueger *(Exec. V.P.-Mktg.)*
George Nadvit *(Exec. V.P.-Opers.)*
Barry Russo *(Sr. V.P.-Mktg.)*
Leo Johnson *(Sr. V.P.-Fin.)*
Joe Langteau *(Sr. V.P.-Opers.)*
Gaylon Smith *(Sr. V.P.-Franchising)*
Jack Wiles *(V.P.-Tech Services)*

Royal Crown Cola Co. **(1)**
6917 Collins Ave.
Miami Beach, FL 33141
Tel.: 305-866-3281 (100%)
Fax: 305-866-3281
Approx.Sls.: $100,000,000
Emp.: 230
Fiscal Year-end: 12/31/90
Soft Drinks
S.I.C.: 2086; 2087
Victor Posner *(Chm. Bd. & Pres.)*
Michael Coyne *(V.P.-Sls.)*
Cary Keane *(V.P.-Mktg.)*
Carter Stalvey *(Dir.-Adv.)*
Philip J. Mastrovito, Jr. *(Dir.-Mktg. Res.)*
Burt Zurdeeg *(Nehi Products Mgr.)*

THE CHESAPEAKE LIFE INSURANCE CO.
Gold's Galleria, 1033 O St., Ste. 5
Lincoln, NE 65808
Tel.: 402-479-8300
Year Founded: 1956
Assets: $55,088,031
Liabilities: $46,708,450
Net Worth: $8,379,581
Approx.Rev.: $10,008,368
Emp.: 15
Fiscal Year-end: 12/31/89
Life Insurance
S.I.C.: 6311
James M. Fail *(Chm. Bd. & Chief Exec. Officer)*
Charles D. Casper *(Pres. & Chief Oper. Officer)*
Denny L. Lett *(Sec.)*
Clifford G. Smith II *(Treas.)*
Theodore L. Kessner *(Legal Officer)*

Affiliates:

Farm & Home Life Insurance Co. **(1)**
300 W. Osborn Rd.
Phoenix, AZ 85013
Tel.: 602-264-9851
Life Insurance
S.I.C.: 6311

LSC-Marketing, Inc. **(1)**
300 W. Osborn Rd.
Phoenix, AZ 85013
Tel.: 602-264-9851
Insurance Marketing
S.I.C.: 6411

Life Insurance Co. of Arizona **(1)**
300 W. Osborn Rd.
Phoenix, AZ 85013
Tel.: 602-264-9851
S.I.C.: 6311

Lifeshares Group, Inc. **(1)**
300 W. Osborn Rd.
Phoenix, AZ 85013
Tel.: 602-264-9851
Holding Company
S.I.C.: 6719

Lifeshares Services Co. **(1)**
Gold's Galleria, 1033 "O" St., Ste. 5
Lincoln, NE 68508
Tel.: 402-479-8300
Tel.: 800-279-0269
Services Life Insurance Policies
S.I.C.: 6411

Underwriters National Assurance Co. **(1)**
300 W. Osborn Rd.
Phoenix, AZ 85013
Tel.: 620-264-9851
Life Insurance Company
S.I.C.: 6311

CHESSCO INDUSTRIES, INC.
1300 Post Rd. East
Westport, CT 06880
Tel.: 203-255-2804 **DE**
Year Founded: 1968
Approx.Sls.: $16,000,000
Emp.: 55
Fiscal Year-end: 12/31/90
Import Export
Manufacture Specialty Chemicals Used in the Medical, Auto & Electronic Industries
S.I.C.: 2899; 2819; 2891
Louis Radler *(Chm. Bd., Pres. & Chief Exec. Officer)*
Jeffrey Radler *(V.P.-Fin. & Chief Fin. Officer)*
Michael J. Daly *(Treas.)*
Albert J. Kleban *(Sec. & Gen. Counsel)*

No. of Mfg. Plants/Facilities: 2
No. of U.S. Offices: 4

Outside Service Firm(s):

Deloitte & Touche*(Auditors)*
1600 Summer St.
Stamford, CT 06905-5121
Tel.: 203-351-4600

Kleban & Samor*(Legal Firm)*
Southport, CT

State Street Bank & Trust Co.*(Major Banking Relationship)*
P.O. Box 366,
Boston, MA 02101
Tel.: 617-426-5523

Division:

Chessco Process Research Products Div. **(1)**
1013 Whitehead Rd. Ext.
Trenton, NJ 08638
Tel.: 609-882-0400
Emp.: 27
Produces Coolants & Finishing Compounds Used in the Manufacturing of Electronic Devices, Ball Bearings & Automotive Parts
S.I.C.: 2899
Anthony Broomer *(Pres.)*
John Santoro *(V.P.-Mktg.)*
Michael Kelly *(V.P.-Admin.)*

Subsidiaries:

Chemionics Corporation **(1)**
390 S. Munroe Falls Rd.
Tallmadge, OH 44278
Tel.: 216-733-8834 (100%)
Emp.: 40
Manufacture Latexes, Water-based Adhesives, Plastisols & Epoxy Polymer Systems; Suppliers of Quality Compounds, Coating & Adhesives
S.I.C.: 2891
Cyrus Blackfan *(Pres.)*

Chessco Capital Corp. **(1)**
1300 Post Rd. East
Westport, CT 06880
Tel.: 203-255-2804
Equipment Leasing
S.I.C.: 7359
Jeff Radler *(Pres.)*

A.W. CHESTERTON COMPANY
Middlesex Industrial Park, 225 Fallon Rd.
Stoneham, MA 02180
Tel.: 617-438-7000
Fax: 617-438-2930
Approx.Sls.: $32,000,000
Emp.: 600
Mechanical Packing Seals, Pumps & Special Technical Products
S.I.C.: 3053; 2842; 3561
James D. Chesterton *(Pres. & Chief Exec. Officer)*
Richard Hoyle *(Exec. V.P.)*
Doug Burke *(V.P.-Intl Sls.)*
Steve Chapman *(V.P.-Opers.)*
Peter Lowrey *(V.P.-Natl. Sls.)*
Joseph Marsico *(V.P.-Mfg.)*
Chester M. Howe *(Gen. Counsel)*

Outside Service Firm(s):

Deloitte & Touche*(Auditors)*
125 Summer St.
Boston, MA 02110
Tel.: 617-261-8000
Fax: 617-261-8111

First National Bank of Boston*(Major Banking Relationship)*
P.O. Box 644,
Boston, MA 02102-0644
Tel.: 617-575-2900
Fax: 617-575-2549

CHEVY CHASE CARS & GEO
7725 Wisconsin Ave.
Bethesda, MD 20814
Tel.: 301-657-4000
Fax: 301-907-8536
Year Founded: 1939
Approx.Sls.: $44,000,000
Emp.: 150
Retail New & Used Automobiles
S.I.C.: 5511
John Bowis *(Pres.)*
Frank Burroughs *(V.P.)*
D. Dabney *(Sec. & Treas.)*

Outside Service Firm(s):

Councilor, Buchanan & Mitchell*(Auditors)*
Washington, DC

Goldstein Blitz & Rosenberg*(Legal Firm)*
Bethesda, MD

Bank of Bethesda*(Major Banking Relationship)*
Bethesda, MD

CHEYENNE OUTFITTERS, INC.
P.O. Box 12013
Cheyenne, WY 82003
Tel.: 307-775-7500
Fax: 307-775-7569
Approx.Sls.: $11,000,000
Emp.: 100
Retail & Mail Order Western Fashion Apparel & Footware
S.I.C.: 5699; 5661; 5961
Frederick W. Wojcik *(Pres.)*
Jack Luedtke *(V.P. & G.M.)*
Cary Noteboom *(Dir.-Catalog)*

CHI SYSTEMS, INC.
(Formerly The Chi Group)
130 S. First St.
Ann Arbor, MI 48104
Tel.: 313-761-3912
Tel.: 800-521-7210 **MI**
Fax: 313-761-9366
Year Founded: 1969
Approx.Sls.: $10,000,000
Emp.: 60
Fiscal Year-end: 4/30/92
Export
Holding Company; Health Care Management & Consultants
S.I.C.: 6719
Karl G. Bartscht *(Chm. Bd. & Chief Exec. Officer)*
Steven P. Gray *(Pres.)*
Alan M. Zuckerman *(Exec. V.P.)*
Cynthia Hayward *(Sr. V.P.)*
H. Dominic Covvey *(V.P.)*
Evelyn S. Grindstaff *(V.P.)*
Joseph M. Spallina *(V.P.)*
James G. Lifton *(V.P.)*

No. of U.S. Offices: 3
No. of Foreign Offices: 2

Outside Service Firm(s):

C. H. Rubin & Co.*(Auditors)*
Ann Arbor, MI

Great Lakes Bancorp*(Major Banking Relationship)*
Ann Arbor, MI
Tel.: 313-769-8300

Chiat/Day/Mojo

CHIAT/DAY/MOJO INC. ADVERTISING
(Corporate Headquarters)
340 Hampton Dr.
Venice, CA 90291
Tel.: 310-314-5000 **DE**
Fax: 310-396-1273
Year Founded: 1968
Approx.Billings: $980,000,000
Emp.: 1,028
Advertising Agency
S.I.C.: 7311
Jay Chiat *(Chm. Bd., Chief Exec. Officer (Worldwide))*
Lee Clow *(Pres., Exec. Creative Dir.)*
Bob Wolf *(Chm. Bd., Chief Exec. Officer (North America))*
Simon Bax *(Exec. V.P., Chief Fin. Officer-Worldwide)*
Adelaide Horton *(Sr. V.P., Chief Opers. Officer)*
Jeff Blish *(Sr. V.P., Dir.-Plng.)*
Steve Alburty *(V.P., Dir. of Mngmt. Information Systems)*
Peter Rothenberg *(V.P., Gen. Counsel)*
Colette Chestnut *(V.P., Corp. Finance Dir.)*

No. of U.S. Offices: 3

Computer Systems/Hardware:
Wang

Outside Service Firm(s):

Coopers & Lybrand*(Auditors)*
350 S. Grand Ave.
Los Angeles, CA 90071
Tel.: 213-481-1000
Fax: 213-482-6440

First Business Bank*(Major Banking Relationship)*
Los Angeles, CA

Connecticut General Life Insurance Co.*(Group Insurer)*
P.O. Box 2975,
Hartford, CT 06104
Tel.: 203-726-6000

Maxicare*(Group Insurer)*
Los Angeles, CA

First Chicago Shareholder Services Trust Co.*(International Bank Affiliate)*
153 West 51st St.
New York, NY 10019
Tel.: 212-791-6422
Fax: 212-385-9798

Whitman & Ransom*(Legal Firm)*
200 Park Ave.
New York, NY 10166
Tel.: 212-351-3000

Branches:

Anderson & Lembke Inc. **(1)**
79 Fifth Ave., 7th Fl.
New York, NY 10003
Tel.: 212-886-2100
Fax: 212-989-2200
Steve Trygg *(Chm., Chief Creative Dir.)*
Larry McNaughton *(V.P., Gen. Mgr.)*
Don Hov *(Chief Fin. Officer, Fin. & Admin.)*

Anderson & Lembke, Inc. **(1)**
77 Maiden Lane
San Francisco, CA 94108
Tel.: 415-394-5990
Hans Ullmark *(Pres. & Chief Exec. Officer)*
Riley Warren *(Dir.-Fin./Admin.)*
Peter MacKey *(Gen. Mgr.)*

Chiat/Day/Mojo/New York **(1)**
79 5th Ave.
New York, NY 10003
Tel.: 212-807-4000
Fax: 212-675-5514
Jay Chiat *(Chm./Chief Exec. Officer-Worldwide)*
Doug Watson *(Pres./Chief Exec. Officer-New York)*
Jane Newman *(Vice Chm., Dir.-Strategic Plng.)*
Adelaide Horton *(Sr. V.P., Chief Opers. Officer-Worldwide)*
Stacey Lippman *(Sr. V.P., Corp. Media Dir.)*
Mary Morton *(Sr. V.P., Grp. Mngmt. Supvr.)*
Bob Zach *(Sr. V.P., Media Dir.)*
Steve Alburty *(V.P., Dir. M.I.S.-Worldwide)*
Colette Chestnut *(V.P., Corp. Fin. Dir.)*
Cheryl Gittelman *(V.P., Fin. Dir.)*
Steve Hancock *(Sr. V.P., Plng. Dir.)*
Dion Hughes *(V.P., Assoc. Creative Dir.)*
Gwen Lipsky *(V.P., Plng. Dir.)*
Eve Luppert *(V.P., Personnel Dir.)*
Peter Rothenberg *(V.P., Corp. Gen. Counsel)*

Chiat/Day/Mojo Inc. Advertising **(1)**
77 Maiden
San Francisco, CA 94108
Tel.: 415-445-3000
Fred Goldberg *(Pres. & Chief Exec. Officer-SF)*
Rosalinde Estes *(V.P., Mgr. Creative/ Admin.)*
Bob Marscovetra *(V.P., Dir. Finance)*
Catrina Wallace *(V.P., Dir. Acct. Planning)*

Jessica Dee Communications Public Relations **(1)**
733 Third Ave., 7th Floor
New York, NY 10017
Tel.: 212-476-4000
Emp.: 35
Patrice Tanaka *(V.P., Gen. Mgr., Creative Dir.)*
Michael Cassady *(Dir., Fin.)*

Perkins/Butler Direct Marketing **(1)**
79 Fifth Ave., 6th Fl.
New York, NY 10003
Tel.: 212-243-6868
Fax: 212-633-8010
Direct Marketing
Don Peppers *(Pres. & Chief Exec. Officer)*
Eva Luppert *(V.P., Personnel Mgr.)*
Kerry Ernst *(Fin. Mgr.)*

Bob Thomas & Associates, Inc. Public Relations **(1)**
340 Main St.
Venice, CA 90291
Tel.: 310-314-6696
Fax: 310-374-1020
Approx.Billings: $30,000,000
Emp.: 50
Consumer Prods., Automotive, Sport Mktg. & Consumer Electronics
Bob Thomas *(Chm.)*
Jerry Giaquinta *(Pres./Chief Exec. Officer)*
Jonathan Higgins *(Chief Opers. Officer)*

Bob Thomas & Associates **(1)**
77 Maiden Ln., 2nd Fl.
San Francisco, CA 94108
Tel.: 415-788-8944
Fax: 415-788-8910
Bob Thomas *(Chm.)*
Jerry Giaquinta *(Pres./Chief Exec. Officer)*
Jonathan Higgins *(Chief Opers. Officer)*

Bob Thomas Associates **(1)**
10 Lower Spadina Ave.
Toronto, ON M5V 2Z1, Canada
Tel.: 416-585-2266
Fax: 416-599-0004
Bob Thomas *(Chm.)*
Jerry Giaquinta *(Pres./Chief Exec Officer)*
Jonathan Higgins *(Chief Opers. Officer)*

Regional Offices:

Chiat/Day/Mojo/Atlanta **(1)**
200 Galleria Pkwy.
Atlanta, GA 30339
Tel.: 404-955-1880
Fax: 404-955-1880
John Upton *(V.P., Nissan Reg. Mktg. Acct. Dir.)*
Larry Saunders *(V.P., Field Acct. Dir.)*

Chiat/Day/Mojo/Chicago **(1)**
AT&T Plaza, 1111 West 22nd St.
Oak Brook, IL 60521
Tel.: 708-574-8030
Fax: 708-574-8085
John Upton *(V.P., Nissan Reg. Mktg. Acct. Dir.)*
Peter Renschler *(V.P. Field Acct. Dir.)*

Chiat/Day/Mojo/Dallas **(1)**
600 East Las Colinas Blvd.
Irving, TX 75039
Tel.: 214-556-0006
Fax: 214-556-0280

John Upton *(V.P., Nissan Reg. Mktg. Acct. Dir.)*
Peter Rentschler *(V.P., Field Acct. Dir.)*

Chiat/Day/Mojo/San Francisco **(1)**
77 Maiden Lane
San Francisco, CA 94108
Tel.: 415-445-3000
Fax: 415-433-6735
John Upton *(V.P., Nissan Reg. Mktg. Acct. Dir.)*

Non U.S. Holdings:

Chiat/Day/Mojo **(1)**
339 Military Rd.
Cremorne, N.S.W. 2090, Australia
Tel.: 61-2-908-6666
Telex: 73444
Fax: 61-2-953-5203
Ad Agency
S.I.C.: 7311
Graeme Wills *(Mng. Dir.)*
Ian Ballard *(Finance Dir.)*

Chiat/Day/Mojo **(1)**
55 Southbank Blvd.
South Melbourne, Victoria 3205, Australia
Tel.: 03 685-3444
Fax: 03-685-3434
Ad Agency
S.I.C.: 7311
Ric Otton *(Exec. Dir.)*
David Guthrie *(Finance Dir.)*

Chiat/Day/Mojo **(1)**
Berkshire House, 168-178 High Holborn
London, WC1V 7AA, United Kingdom
Tel.: 44-71-497-3575
Fax: 44-71-379-9844
Approx.Billings: $59,000,000
Emp.: 32
Full Service Advertising
M.T. Rainey *(Mng. Dir.)*
Julian Martin *(Sr. V.P., Acct. Dir.)*
Jerry Wales *(V.P., Finance Dir.)*

Chiat/Day/Mojo **(1)**
Kenwyn St./St. Georges Bay Rd. Parnell,
Auckland, New Zealand
Tel.: 64-9-393-859
Fax: 64-309-4173
Approx.Billings: $28,000,000
Emp.: 43
Full Service Agency
S.I.C.: 7311
Graeme Wills *(Chief Exec. Officer)*
Greg Eichmann *(Gen. Mgr.)*
Trish Scantlebury *(Finance Dir.)*

Chiat/Day/Mojo Inc. Advertising **(1)**
10 Lower Spadina
Toronto, ON M5V 2Z1, Canada
Tel.: 416-585-9992
Fax: 416-599-0004
Ad Agency
S.I.C.: 7311
Ira Matathia *(Pres., Chief Exec. Officer)*
Paul Rosenman *(V.P., Dir. Finance)*

Chiat/Day/Mojo Pty. Ltd. **(1)**
69 Shafston Ave.
Kangaroo Point, Queensland 4169, Australia
Tel.: 07-896-5666
Fax: 07-896-5614
Emp.: 42
Consumer Advertising
Austin Kelly *(Mng. Dir.)*
Bob Kilah *(Finance Dir.)*

Chiat/Day/Mojo Pty. Ltd. **(1)**
33 Broadway
Nedlands, W.A. 6009, Australia
Tel.: 61-9-386-8311
Fax: 61-9-386-6420
Ad Agency
S.I.C.: 7311
Simon Furzer *(Mng. Dir.)*

Chiat/Day/Mojo **(1)**
Level 2, Wool Store, 262-264 Thorndon
Quay P.O. Box 2118,
Wellington, New Zealand
Tel.: 64-4-499-4377
Fax: 64-4-499-4373
Greg Eichmann *(Gen. Mgr.)*
Trish Scantlebury *(Finance Mgr.)*

CHICAGO CONVENTION & TOURISM BUREAU
McCormick Place-on-the-Lake
Chicago, IL 60616
Tel.: 312-567-8500
Fax: 312-567-8533
Approx.Sls.: $285,541,533
Emp.: 50
Promotion of Conventions & Tourism for the City of Chicago
S.I.C.: 9611
Gregory Saunders *(Chm. Bd.)*
Gerald Roper *(Pres. & Chief Exec. Officer)*
Mel Patla *(V.P.-Mktg. & Sls.)*
Marilyn Miglin *(Treas.)*
Jack Jeffries *(Gen. Counsel)*
Susan M. Zdebski *(Controller)*
William T. Hogan *(Sec.)*
William C. Mitchell *(Fin. Exec.)*
Kate Haymaker *(Mgr.-Pub. Rels.)*
Donald J. DePorter *(Mgr.-Govt. Affairs)*
Patti Hooper-Evans *(Office Mgr./ Mngmt. Information Systems)*

CHICAGO EXTRUDED METALS CO.
1601 S. 54th Ave.
Cicero, IL 60650
Tel.: 708-656-7900
Fax: 708-780-3479
Approx.Sls.: $40,000,000
Emp.: 200
Copper Alloy Rod, Wire & Shapes
S.I.C.: 3351
Davis G. Anderson *(Pres.)*
Eugene A. Riccio *(V.P. & Gen. Mgr.)*
Kirk Cahill *(Controller)*

No. of Mfg. Plants/Facilities: 1

Computer Systems/Hardware:
IBM System 36

Outside Service Firm(s):

Sidley & Austin*(Legal Firm)*
One First National Plaza, 42nd Fl.
Chicago, IL 60603
Tel.: 312-853-7000
Fax: 312-853-7036

Lake Shore National Bank*(Major Banking Relationship)*
605 N. Michigan Ave.
Chicago, IL 60611
Tel.: 312-787-1900

THE CHICAGO FAUCET CO.
2100 S. Clearwater Dr.
Des Plaines, IL 60018-5999
Tel.: 708-803-5000
Fax: 708-298-3101
Year Founded: 1901
Emp.: 300
Fiscal Year-end: 9/30/90
Export
Mfr. Faucets & Brass Plumbing Fittings
S.I.C.: 3432
John S. Cook *(Chm. Bd.)*
Alan T. Lougee *(Pres.)*
Theodore K. Moore *(V.P.-Sls. & Mktg.)*
Richard H. Swiers *(V.P.-Opers.)*
Jim Carroll *(Treas., Chief Fin. Officer & Sec.)*
Bill Butchart *(Dir.-Data Proc.)*
Brian Downing *(Mgr.-Personnel)*
Michele Hudec *(Mgr.-Mktg.)*
Robert Swanson *(Pur. Agent)*

Computer Systems/Hardware:
IBM 38

Outside Service Firm(s):

Deloitte & Touche*(Auditors)*
Two Prudential Plaza, 180 N. Stetson
Chicago, IL 60601
Tel.: 312-946-2039

Katten, Muchin & Zavis*(Legal Firm)*
525 W. Monroe St., Ste. 1600
Chicago, IL 60661-3693
Tel.: 312-902-5200

First National Bank*(Major Banking Relationship)*
Des Plaines, IL

CHICAGO HEIGHTS STEEL
211 E. Main
Chicago Heights, IL 60411
Mailing Address:
P.O. Box 129,
Chicago Heights, IL 60411
Tel.: 708-756-5619
Tel.: 800-424-4487 **IL**
Year Founded: 1985
Approx.Sls.: $40,000,000
Emp.: 250
Fiscal Year-end: 4/30/92
Manufacturer Shapes, Bars & Posts for Fabricated Metal Products
S.I.C.: 3312
Frank Corral *(Pres.)*
Ron Owczarzak *(V.P.)*
Al DeBow *(Treas.)*

No. of Mfg. Plants/Facilities: 1
No. of U.S. Offices: 1

Computer Systems/Hardware:
Burroughs 900

Outside Service Firm(s):

Miller-Cooper & Co., Ltd.*(Auditors)*
Chicago, IL

Bell, Boyd & Lloyd*(Legal Firm)*
Three First National Plaza
Chicago, IL 60602
Tel.: 312-372-1121

LaSalle National Bank*(Major Banking Relationship)*
120 S. LaSalle St.
Chicago, IL 60603
Tel.: 312-781-8000

CHICAGO HOLDINGS, INC.
1000 RIDC Plaza
Pittsburgh, PA 15238
Tel.: 412-963-9870 **DE**
Fax: 412-963-9841
Year Founded: 1969
Sales Range: $60-79 Million
Emp.: 20
Holding Company; Equipment Rental & Leasing & Buying of Installment Contracts
S.I.C.: 6719; 7359; 6153
Burton W. Kanter *(Chm.)*
Richard J. Uhl *(Pres. & Chief Exec. Officer)*
Frank Jackson *(V.P. & Chief Acctg. Officer)*
Harold L. Lehman *(V.P. & Treas.)*
Thomas Galey *(Sec.)*
Pamela Diarla *(Gen. Counsel)*
Linda Johnson *(Dir.-Admin.)*
Robert Pickett *(Dir.-Contracts)*
Raymond Ritchie *(Dir.-Data Processing)*

Computer Systems/Hardware:
IBM System 34

Outside Service Firm(s):

Ernst & Young*(Auditors)*
2000 Pittsburgh Natl. Bldg.
Pittsburgh, PA 15222
Tel.: 412-644-7800
Fax: 412-644-7419

Pittsburgh National Bank*(Major Banking Relationship)*
Stock Transfer Dept., Fifth & Wood Streets
Pittsburgh, PA 15265

CHICAGO LOCK COMPANY
4311 W. Belmont Ave.
Chicago, IL 60641
Tel.: 312-282-7177
Fax: 312-282-8199
Year Founded: 1920
Emp.: 340
Export
Mfr. of Cam Locks, Switch Locks, High Security & Special Purpose Locks
S.I.C.: 3429
Lyle B. Shinn, Jr. *(Pres.)*
William R. Shinn *(Treas. & Sec.)*
Kenneth L. Blade *(Controller)*
Bill Gedwill *(Mgr.-Pur.)*
Dale Padjen *(Mgr.-Sls.)*
Jeff McVicker *(Chief Engr.)*
Bob Steinbach *(Design Engr.)*

Computer Systems/Hardware:
IBM System 36

Outside Service Firm(s):

Deloitte & Touche*(Auditors)*
Two Prudential Plaza, 180 N. Stetson
Chicago, IL 60601
Tel.: 312-946-2039

Traeger, Bolger & Traeger*(Legal Firm)*
Chicaog, IL

American National Bank & Trust Company of Chicago*(Major Banking Relationship)*
33 N. LaSalle St.
Chicago, IL 60602
Tel.: 312-661-5000
Fax: 312-661-6417

CHICAGO MECHANICAL, INC.
1400 E. 97th Pl.
Chicago, IL 60628
Tel.: 312-374-6700
Fax: 312-374-8801
Approx.Sls.: $50,000,000
Emp.: 100
Metal Contractor & Fabricator
S.I.C.: 3444; 1711
Lloyd Ulrich *(Pres. & Chief Exec. Officer)*
Nick Choksi *(V.P.)*

Computer Systems/Hardware:
IBM System 38

Outside Service Firm(s):

Doty, Jarrow & Co.*(Auditors)*
960 Industrial Dr.
Elmhurst, IL 60126
Tel.: 708-833-6500

The Principal Financial Group*(Group Insurer)*
Des Moines, IA

Cohon Raizes Regal*(Legal Firm)*
Chicago, IL

CHICAGO MERCANTILE EXCHANGE
30 So. Wacker Dr.
Chicago, IL 60606
Tel.: 312-930-1000
Fax: 312-930-8219
Year Founded: 1898
Approx.Sls.: $13,097,956
Emp.: 1,000
Fiscal Year-end: 12/31/90
Futures & Options Exchange for Cattle, Hogs, Pork Bellies, Lumber; Foreign Currencies, U. S. Treasury Bills 90-Day Certificates of Deposit, 90-Day Eurodollars; Stock Indexes & Stock Index Options; Also Options in Futures
S.I.C.: 6231
Jack Sandner *(Chm. Bd.)*
William J. Brodsky *(Pres.)*
Barbara Richards *(Sr. V.P.-Mktg.)*
Gail Osten *(V.P.-Adv. & Mktg. Services)*

CHICAGO READER, INC.
11 E. Illinois, 2nd Fl.
Chicago, IL 60611
Tel.: 312-828-0350
Fax: 312-828-0682
Year Founded: 1971
Approx.Rev.: $10,000,000
Emp.: 70
Fiscal Year-end: 12/31/91
Publisher of a Weekly Alternative Newspaper in Chicago
S.I.C.: 2711
Robert Roth *(Pres. & Publisher)*
Michael Lenehan *(Editor)*
Robert McCamant *(V.P.)*
Thomas Yoder *(Treas. & Adv. Dir.)*
Peter Bell *(Sec.)*

Computer Systems/Hardware:
Texas Instruments

Outside Service Firm(s):

Checkers, Simon & Rosner*(Auditors)*
Chicago, IL

Keck, Mahin, Cate & Koehler*(Legal Firm)*
8300 Sears Tower, 233 S. Wacker Dr.
Chicago, IL 60606
Tel.: 312-876-3400

Subsidiary:

Ruxton Group **(1)**
11 E. Illinois
Chicago, IL 60611
Tel.: 312-828-0564
Sells National Ads in Twelve Alternative Weekly Newspapers
S.I.C.: 7313
Susan Belair *(Sls. Mgr.)*

CHICAGO SHOW PRINTING CO.
8330 No. Austin Ave.
Morton Grove, IL 60053
Tel.: 708-470-5300 **IL**
Fax: 708-470-0318
Year Founded: 1902
Sales Range: $10-19 Million
Emp.: 90
Fiscal Year-end: 12/31/91
Import
Creative Designers & Producers of Point-of-Sale Advertising Displays & Mdsg. Programs
S.I.C.: 3993; 7319
R.R. Snediker *(Chm. Bd.)*
James M. Snediker *(Pres.)*
Gregg R. Pospisil *(V.P.-Fin.)*
M.B. Snediker *(Treas.)*
Kathryn Snediker *(Gen. Mgr.-Promos.)*
Principal(s):
R.R. Snediker

No. of Mfg. Plants/Facilities: 2
No. of U.S. Offices: 5

Computer Systems/Hardware:
DEC

Outside Service Firm(s):

Freidman, Eisenstein, Raemer & Schwartz*(Auditors)*
Chicago, IL

Harris Trust & Savings Bank*(Major Banking Relationship)*
111 W. Monroe St.
Chicago, IL 60690
Tel.: 312-461-2265
Tel.: 800-858-0840

Chapman & Cutler*(Legal Firm)*
111 W. Monroe
Chicago, IL 60603
Tel.: 312-845-3000

Plant:

Manufacturing Plant **(1)**
234 Lakewood Ave.
Waukegan, IL 60085
Tel.: 708-623-5200
Ken Dawson *(Mgr.)*

CHICAGO TUBE & IRON CO.
2531 W. 48th St.
Chicago, IL 60632
Tel.: 312-523-1441
Tel.: 800-972-0217 (IL)
Tel.: 800-621-8542 **IL**
Fax: 312-523-1375
Year Founded: 1914
Approx.Sls.: $140,000,000
Emp.: 340
Fiscal Year-end: 11/30/90
Export
Steel Service Center Warehouse
S.I.C.: 5051
Robert B. Haigh *(Chm., Chief Exec. Officer & Treas.)*
Donald R. McNeeley *(Pres. & Chief Oper. Officer)*
John F. McGlone *(V.P. & Chief Fin. Officer)*
James W. Ashley *(Sec.)*
Janet E. Gill *(Dir.-Exec. Services & Meetings Planner)*
Thomas M. Moran *(Dir.-Mngmt. Information Systems)*
Earl F. Pulte, Jr. *(Dir.-Sls. & Mktg.)*
Daniel L. Shoaf *(Dir.-Personnel)*

No. of U.S. Offices: 8

Computer Systems/Hardware:
Prime 9950

Outside Service Firm(s):

Liberty Mutual*(Group Insurer)*
Portland, ME

McDermott, Will & Emery*(Legal Firm)*
227 W. Monroe St.
Chicago, IL 60606-5096
Tel.: 312-372-2000

The Northern Trust Co.*(Major Banking Relationship)*
50 S. LaSalle St.
Chicago, IL 60675
Tel.: 312-630-6000
Fax: 312-630-6516

The Boston Company*(Pension Manager)*
260 Franklin St.
Boston, MA 02110
Tel.: 617-439-6619

Subsidiaries:

CT&I Corp. of Wisconsin **(1)**
6030 North 60th St.
Milwaukee, WI 53218
Tel.: 414-535-1331 (100%)
Fax: 414-535-1598
Steel Service Center Warehouse
S.I.C.: 5051

Chicago Tube & Iron Company of Minnesota **(1)**
2940 Eagandale Blvd.
Saint Paul, MN 55121
Tel.: 612-454-6800
Fax: 612-456-9547
Steel Service Center Warehouse
S.I.C.: 5051

Monticello Tank, Inc. **(1)**
806 N. First St.
Monticello, IN 47960
Tel.: 219-583-4311
Fax: 219-583-3011
S.I.C.: 3443

CHICAGO WEST PULLMAN CORPORATION
2300 Star Bank Center
Cincinnati, OH 45202
Tel.: 513-721-3900 **OH**
Fax: 513-721-6035
Year Founded: 1983
Emp.: 825
Fiscal Year-end: 6/30/90
Holding Company; Railroads & Steel
S.I.C.: 4011; 4013; 5051; 6719; 3499; 3743; 8741
John Weld Peck *(Chm. Bd.)*
Roger W. Ach, II *(Pres. & Chief Exec. Officer)*
Dennis N. Lindberg *(Exec. V.P. & Chief Oper. Officer)*
Jeffrey P. Noyce *(Exec. V.P. & Chief Fin. Officer)*
Andrea Scola *(V.P.-Admin. & Sec.)*

Outside Service Firm(s):

Arthur Andersen & Co.*(Auditors)*
425 Walnut St.
Cincinnati, OH 45202
Tel.: 513-381-6900

Thompson, Hine & Flory*(Legal Firm)*
1100 Natl. City Bank Bldg.
Cleveland, OH 44125
Tel.: 216-566-5500

The Central Trust Company, N.A.*(Major Banking Relationship)*
201 E. Fifth
Cincinnati, OH 45202
Tel.: 513-651-8255

Subsidiaries:

American Steel & Wire Corporation **(1)**
4300 E. 49th St.
Cuyahoga Heights, OH 44125
Tel.: 216-883-3800 (51%)
Fax: 216-883-4678
Earnings: ($1,440,000)
Approx.Sls.: $209,731,000
Emp.: 400
Fiscal Year-end: 6/30/92
Mfr. of Steel Rods & Wire
S.I.C.: 3312
Thomas Tyrrell *(Pres. & Chief Exec. Officer)*
Walter Robertson *(Exec. V.P. & Chief Oper. Officer)*
C.V. Meserole *(Exec. V.P. & Chief Fin. Officer)*
R.A. Dauk *(V.P.-Human Resources)*
Daniel Sholtis *(V.P.-Fin.)*

Chicago West Pullman Heavy Industries **(1)**
2300 Star Bank Center
Cincinnati, OH 45202
Tel.: 513-721-3900 (100%)
Fax: 513-721-6035
Heavy Industries
S.I.C.: 3531
Toby E. Croyle *(Pres.)*
Henry N. Parrish *(V.P. & Treas.)*
Dennis N. Lindberg *(Treas.)*

Subsidiaries:

Berwick Freight Car Co. **(2)**
Third & Oak Sts.
Berwick, PA 18603
Tel.: 717-752-1197
Fax: 717-752-2334
Manufacture of Freight Cars
S.I.C.: 3743
Walter S. Poque *(Pres.)*
Robert C. Ortner *(V.P. & Sec.)*
Henry N. Parrish *(V.P. & Treas.)*

Chicago West Pullman Financial Corporation **(2)**
2300 Star Bank Center
Cincinnati, OH 45202
Tel.: 513-721-3900 (100%)
Fax: 513-721-6035
Financial Services
S.I.C.: 6159
Jeffrey P. Noyce *(Pres.)*

Maxon Marine, Inc. **(2)**
South Boundary St.
Tell City, IN 47586
Tel.: 812-547-6451
Fax: 812-547-3045
Ship Building & Repairing
S.I.C.: 3731
Toby N. Croyle *(Pres.)*
Ralph W. Emerson *(V.P.)*
Henry N. Parrish *(V.P. & Treas.)*

Chicago West Pullman Transportation Corporation **(1)**
2728 E. 104th St.
Chicago, IL 60617-5766
Tel.: 312-374-4800 (100%)
Fax: 312-374-7713
Emp.: 50
Freight Cars, Steel, Billets, Grain, Wheat, Pulp & Board Products
S.I.C.: 0111; 0119; 2611; 2675; 3312; 3316
Roger W. Ach, II *(Chm. Bd.)*
Robert E. Smith *(Pres. & Chief Exec. Officer)*
Edwin E. Ellis *(Exec. V.P.)*
Robert C. Finley *(V.P.)*
Lawrence J. Looby *(V.P. & Sec.)*
Dennis N. Lindgerg *(Treas.)*

Subsidiaries:

Chicago Rail Link **(2)**
2728 E. 104th St.
Chicago, IL 60617-5766
Tel.: 312-721-4000
Fax: 312-374-7713
Railroad
S.I.C.: 4011
Robert E. Smith *(Pres.)*

Chicago West Pullman & Southern R.R. Co. **(2)**
2728 E. 104th St.
Chicago, IL 60617
Tel.: 312-374-4800 (100%)
Emp.: 5
Railroad Switching & Terminal Services
S.I.C.: 4013
R.E. Smith *(Pres.)*

Georgia Woodlands Railroad Co. **(2)**
P.O. Box 549, One Harris Rd.
Washington, GA 30673-0549
Tel.: 706-678-3000
Fax: 706-678-2341
Railroad
S.I.C.: 4011
Robert E. Smith *(Pres.)*

Manufacturers' Junction Railroad Company **(2)**
2335 S. Cicero Ave.
Cicero, IL 60650-2451
Tel.: 312-863-1717
Railroad
S.I.C.: 4011
Robert E. Smith *(Pres.)*

Newburgh & South Shore Railroad Company **(2)**
4200 E. 71st St.
Cleveland, OH 44105-5726
Tel.: 216-271-1183
Fax: 216-271-5304
Railroad
S.I.C.: 4011
Robert E. Smith *(Pres.)*

Wisconsin & Calumet Railroad Company **(2)**
203 S. Pearl St.
Janesville, WI 53545-4521
Tel.: 608-754-3630
Fax: 608-754-3651
Railroad
S.I.C.: 4011
Robert E. Smith *(Pres.)*

Main Line Management Services, Inc. **(1)**
Ste. 200, 533 Fellowship Rd.
Mount Laurel, NJ 08054
Tel.: 609-727-5000 (80%)
Fax: 609-727-0864
Management Services
S.I.C.: 8741
Carlton F. Wood *(Pres.)*
Douglas S. Golden *(V.P.)*
Robert J. Russell *(V.P. & Treas.)*
Martin Sigel *(V.P.)*

Vortec Corporation **(1)**
10125 Carver Rd.
Cincinnati, OH 45242
Tel.: 513-891-7474 (100%)
Fax: 513-891-4092
Approx.Sls.: $4,614,154
Fiscal Year-end: 12/31/90
Mfr. Compressed Air Handling & Air Conditioning Products
S.I.C.: 3585; 3499
Michael L. York *(Pres.)*
Michael T. Rawlings *(V.P.)*
Richard D. Rogers *(V.P.)*
Karen Brown *(Dir.-Mktg.)*

CHICAGO WHITE METAL CASTING, INC.
Rt. #83 & Fairway Dr.
Bensenville, IL 60106
Tel.: 708-595-4424
Fax: 708-595-4470
Approx.Sls.: $17,000,000
Emp.: 180

Zinc, Aluminum & Magnesium Die Castings
S.I.C.: 3363; 3364
Walter G. Treiber, Jr. *(Pres. & Chief Oper. Officer)*
Bill Baraglia *(V.P.-Mfg.)*
A.R. Cocco *(V.P.-Fin.)*
Peter M. Schelhas *(V.P.-Sls., Sec. & Treas.)*
Tom Mrock *(Mgr.-Pur.)*

Outside Service Firm(s):

John R. Waters & Co.*(Auditors)*
Chicago, IL

Harris Trust & Savings Bank*(Major Banking Relationship)*
111 W. Monroe St.
Chicago, IL 60690
Tel.: 312-461-2265
Tel.: 800-858-0840

CHICK-FIL-A, INC.
5200 Buffington Rd.
Atlanta, GA 30349
Tel.: 404-765-8000
Fax: 404-765-8140
Year Founded: 1967
Approx.Sls.: $325,000,000
Emp.: 160
Fiscal Year-end: 12/31/91
Fast Food Restaurant Chain
S.I.C.: 5812
S. Truett Cathy *(Founder)*
James L. S. Collins *(Pres.)*
James B. McCabe *(Chief Fin. Officer & V.P.-Fin.)*
Dan T. Cathy *(V.P.-Opers.)*
Bureon E. Ledbetter *(V.P. & Gen. Counsel)*
Perry A. Ragsdale *(V.P.-Design & Construction)*
Steven A. Robinson *(V.P.-Mktg.)*
David Salyers *(Dir.-Store Mktg.)*
Greg Ingram *(Mgr.-Natl. Adv.)*

Outside Service Firm(s):

KPMG Peat Marwick*(Auditors)*
277 Lakeshore Road East
Oakville, ON Canada
Tel.: 416-842-4722

Troutman, Sanders, Lockerman & Ashmore*(Legal Firm)*
600 Peachtree St., Ste. 5200
Atlanta, GA 30308-2216
Tel.: 404-885-3000

NationsBank*(Major Banking Relationship)*
35 Broad St.
Atlanta, GA 30303
Tel.: 404-581-2121
Tel.: 800-848-8198

CHICORP, INC.
208 S. La Salle St., Ste. 220
Chicago, IL 60604
Tel.: 312-855-7600 **DE**
Fax: 312-855-7642
Year Founded: 1965
Sales Range: $100-499 Million
Emp.: 725
Fiscal Year-end: 3/31/92
Holding Company; Dealer & Underwriters Security; Equipment & Vehicle Finance Leasing Company; Commodity Contracts Brokers & Dealers
S.I.C.: 6719; 6211; 6159; 6221
John A. Wing *(Chm. Bd. & Chief Exec. Officer)*
Robert R. Rudolph *(Vice Chm.)*
Wilbert Thiel *(Pres.)*
Paul Oliver *(Chief Fin. Officer)*

Outside Service Firm(s):

Ernst & Young*(Auditors)*
233 S. Wacker Dr.
Chicago, IL 60606
Tel.: 312-368-1800
Fax: 312-645-3095

Rollins Burdick Hunter*(Commercial Insurance Carrier)*
123 N. Wacker Dr.
Chicago, IL 60606
Tel.: 312-701-4000

Aetna Life & Casualty*(Group Insurer)*
151 Farmington Avenue
Hartford, CT 06156
Tel.: 203-273-2128
Fax: 203-729-4295

Continental Bank N. A.*(Major Banking Relationship)*
231 S. LaSalle St.
Chicago, IL 60697
Tel.: 312-828-2345
Tel.: 800-426-5754
Telex: 312-828-1783

Subsidiaries:

Chicago Corp. **(1)**
208 S. La Salle St., Ste. 220
Chicago, IL 66004
Tel.: 312-855-7600
Fax: 312-855-2864
Approx.Sls.: $76,000,000
Emp.: 694
Stock Brokers & Dealers; Investment Bankers
S.I.C.: 6211
John A. Wing *(Chm. Bd., Pres. & Chief Exec. Officer)*
Robert R. Rudolph *(Vice Chm.)*
Michael F. Brookins *(Vice Chm.)*
Thomas J. McCausland, Jr. *(Vice Chm.)*
Wilbert Thiel *(Exec. V.P. & Treas.)*
Robert T. Brehm *(Exec. V.P.)*
John C. Harris *(Exec. V.P.)*
Paul W. Oliver, Jr. *(Exec. V.P.)*
Jay K. Buck *(Sr. V.P.)*
Walter D. Fitzgerald *(Sr. V.P.)*
Kenneth H. McLellan, Jr. *(Sr. V.P.)*
Kenneth F. Puglisi *(Sr. V.P.-Bank Research)*
Perry Taylor *(Sr. V.P. & Corp. Counsel)*
W. Peter Williams *(Sr. V.P.)*

Chicorp Financial Services **(1)**
208 S. La Salle St., Ste. 220
Chicago, IL 60604
Tel.: 312-855-5880
Fax: 312-855-6001
Emp.: 20
Equipment & Vehicle Finance Leasing Companies
S.I.C.: 6159
Timothy O'Gorman *(Pres.)*

Chicorp Management Inc. **(1)**
208 S. LaSalle St., Ste. 1680
Chicago, IL 60604
Tel.: 312-855-6202
Fax: 312-855-8910
Charles Moore *(Pres.)*

CHIEF INDUSTRIES, INC.
3942 W. Old Hwy. 30
Grand Island, NE 68803
Mailing Address:
P.O. Box 2078,
Grand Island, NE 68802-2078
Tel.: 308-382-8820 **DE**
Fax: 308-381-8475
Year Founded: 1954
Approx.Sls.: $90,000,000
Emp.: 1,200
Fiscal Year-end: 6/30/91
Export
Grain Bins, Metal Building Systems; Factory Built Homes; Recreational Vehicles; Cabinets & Components; Electronic Display Systems; Wastewater Treatment Systems; Concrete Breaking Machines, Aeration Systems, Pole Buildings & Correctional Products; Ethanol Fuel
S.I.C.: 3444; 2451; 3589
Virgil Eihusen *(Chm. Bd. & Chief Exec. Officer)*
Robert Eihusen *(Pres.)*
Rollie Stroh *(Sr. V.P.-Adv.)*
Ron Johnson *(V.P.-Procurement)*
Linda Berney *(Controller)*
Dennis Jakob *(Dir.-Data Processing)*
Robert Summers *(Dir.-Human Resources)*
Barbara Saladen *(Asst. Sec.)*

No. of Mfg. Plants/Facilities: 9
No. of Foreign Offices: 1

Computer Systems/Hardware:
IBM; Vax

Outside Service Firm(s):

Deloitte & Touche*(Auditors)*
1040 NBC Center
Lincoln, NE 68508

Howard Tracy*(Legal Firm)*
Grand Island, NE

Boatmen's Trust Company*(Major Banking Relationship)*
100 North Broadway
St. Louis, MO 63102
Tel.: 314-466-2469

Divisions:

Caldwell Manufacturing **(1)**
P.O. Box 338
Kearney, NE 68847
Tel.: 308-237-3186
Fax: 308-237-2650
Export
Computer Systems/Hardware:
IBM; VAX
Grain Drying & Handling Equipment
S.I.C.: 3589
Ed Benson *(Gen. Sls. Mgr.)*

Chief Construction **(1)**
P.O. Box 2078,
Grand Island, NE 68802-2078
Tel.: 308-384-6600
Fax: 308-389-7393
Computer Systems/Hardware:
IBM; VAX
General Contractor
S.I.C.: 1542; 1522
Larry Williams *(Gen. Mgr.)*

Chief Financial Services **(1)**
1811 W. 2nd St., Ste. 425
Grand Island, NE 68803
Tel.: 308-381-8181
Fax: 308-381-8477
Financial Planning of RV & Housing Divisions
S.I.C.: 6282
Charles Gibson *(Gen. Mgr.)*

Chief Industries - Agri Products Div. **(1)**
P.O. Box 2078
Grand Island, NE 68802
Tel.: 308-382-8820
Fax: 308-381-8475
Export
Computer Systems/Hardware:
IBM; VAX
Grain Bins, Handling & Drying Equipment, Farm Buildings, Post Frame Buildings
S.I.C.: 3448; 3589
John Kerr *(Pres.)*

Chief Industries - Buildings Div. **(1)**
P.O. Box 2078
Grand Island, NE 68802
Tel.: 308-382-8820
Fax: 308-381-8475
Export
Computer Systems/Hardware:
IBM; VAX
Commercial Metal Building Systems & Components
S.I.C.: 3448
Don Anderson *(Pres.)*

Chief Industries - Housing Div. **(1)**
P.O. Box 127
Aurora, NE 68818
Tel.: 402-694-5250
Fax: 402-694-5873
Export
Computer Systems/Hardware:
IBM
Mobile Homes & Modular Homes
S.I.C.: 2451; 1521
Mel Auch *(Pres.)*

Chief E-Z Breaker, Inc. **(1)**
2809 E. Hwy. 30
Grand Island, NE 68801
Tel.: 308-381-7383
Fax: 308-381-7721
Export
Computer Systems/Hardware:
IBM
Concrete Breaking Machines
S.I.C.: 3589
Frank Vivian *(Mgr.-Sls.)*

Custom Product Div. **(1)**
P.O. Box 2078,
Grand Island, NE 68802
Tel.: 308-382-8820
Fax: 308-389-7484
Computer Systems/Hardware:
IBM; VAX
Hollow Metal & Furniture; Windows, Doors
S.I.C.: 3448
Dave Schocke *(Pres.)*

Custom Products Division **(1)**
P.O. Box 2078,
Grand Island, NE 68802-2078
Tel.: 308-382-8820
Fax: 308-382-3911
Mfr. Hollow Metal, Furniture, Windows, Doors & Other Items for Detention Facilities
S.I.C.: 3442; 2514; 2599
David Schocke *(V.P. & Gen. Mgr.)*

Ecology System Dept. **(1)**
P.O. Box 2078
Grand Island, NE 68802
Tel.: 308-382-8820
Fax: 308-389-7484
Export
Computer Systems/Hardware:
IBM
Sewage Treatment Systems for Sub-Divisions
S.I.C.: 3589
Bob Eversoll *(Mktg. Mgr.)*

Electronic Display Systems (Kallego) **(1)**
2813 E. Hwy. 30
Grand Island, NE 68801
Tel.: 308-384-6860
Fax: 308-381-7721
Export
Computer Systems/Hardware:
IBM
Electronic Signage
S.I.C.: 3589
John Price *(Gen. Mgr.)*

King of the Road Div. **(1)**
P.O. Box 553
Russell, KS 67665
Tel.: 913-483-2138
Fax: 913-483-4973
Export
Computer Systems/Hardware:
IBM
Mfg. of Recreational Vehicles
S.I.C.: 3792
Eugene Ewers *(Pres.)*

Subsidiaries:

Chief Ethanol Fuels, Inc. **(1)**
P.O. Box 488,
Hastings, NE 68902-0488
Tel.: 402-463-6885
Fax: 402-462-9931
Computer Systems/Hardware:
IBM
Mfr. Ethanol Fuel
S.I.C.: 2869
Roger Burken *(Gen. Mgr.)*

Grand Island Contract Carriers & Brokerage, Inc. **(1)**
P.O. Box 2078,
Grand Island, NE 68802-2078
Tel.: 308-382-4330
Fax: 308-389-7487
Computer Systems/Hardware:
IBM
Common & Contract Motor Carrier
S.I.C.: 6399
Bob Winter *(Gen. Mgr.)*

Indianhead Golf Club **(1)**
4100 Husker Hwy.
Grand Island, NE 68803
Tel.: 308-381-4653
Public 18 Hole Golf Course & Club House
S.I.C.: 7992; 5813
Randy Carlson *(Gen. Mgr.)*

Non-U.S. Holding:

Chief Industries UK Ltd. **(1)**
Bentall Industrial Estate
Malton, Essex CM9 7NW, United Kingdom
Tel.: 0621 859211 (100%)
Fax: 0621 850771
Mfrs. Grain Bins
S.I.C.: 3448
Charles Frost *(Mgr.)*

THE CHILDREN'S PLACE RETAIL STORES, INC.
25 Riverside Dr.
Pine Brook, NJ 07058
Tel.: 201-227-8900
Fax: 201-227-0321
Year Founded: 1969
Approx.Sls.: $120,000,000
Emp.: 1500
Fiscal Year-end: 1/31/91
Import
Retail Children's Clothing Stores
S.I.C.: 5641
Ezra Dabah *(Chm. Bd. & Chief Exec. Officer)*
Bill Lee *(Pres.)*
Stan Silver *(Chief Oper. Officer & Exec. V.P.)*
Charlie Naff *(Sr. V.P.-Opers.)*
Ed DeMartino *(V.P.-Data Processing)*
Seth Udasin *(Controller)*
Jack Esses *(Dir.-Pur.)*
Alan Odell *(Mgr.-Pur.)*
Mark Rose *(Mgr.-Imports)*
Carol Auten *(Corp. Travel Planner)*

Computer Systems/Hardware:
IBM

CHILEWICH PARTNERS
12 Water St.
White Plains, NY 10601
Tel.: 914-997-2000
Fax: 914-997-2122
Approx.Sls.: $1,000,000,000
Emp.: 850
Import Export
Commodity Trading, Cattle, Meatpacking
S.I.C.: 5159; 6799
Simon Chilewich *(Pres. & Chief Exec. Officer)*
Art Anker *(V.P.)*
Peter Billig *(V.P.)*
Bruce Bowers *(V.P.)*
Edward G. Newman *(V.P.)*
David Peters *(V.P.)*
Principal(s):
Simon Chilewich
Peter Billig
Bruce Bowers
Edward G. Newman

Outside Service Firm(s):

Warshaw, Burstein, Cohen, Schlesinger & Kuh*(Legal Firm)*
55 Fifth Ave.
New York, NY 10017

Chase Manhattan Bank, N.A.*(Major Banking Relationship)*
One Chase Manhattan Plaza
New York, NY 10081
Tel.: 212-552-2222
Tel.: 800-526-0801
Fax: 212-552-7175

CHIP SUPPLY INC.
7725 N. Orange Blossom Trail
Orlando, FL 32810
Tel.: 407-298-7100 **FL**
Fax: 407-290-0164
Year Founded: 1978
Approx.Sls.: $16,000,000
Emp.: 235
Processor & Packager of Semiconductor Dice
S.I.C.: 5065
Patrick Perrott *(Chm. Bd.)*
Edward J. Perott *(Pres.)*
Donald C. Harris *(Chief Exec. Officer)*
Dale R. Pullis *(V.P.-Fin.)*

Outside Service Firm(s):

Carlisle, Hand, Storer & McCall*(Auditors)*
Winter Park, FL

Dean, Mead, Egerton, Bloodworth*(Legal Firm)*
Orlando, FL

Florida Union National Bank*(Major Banking Relationship)*
Orlando, FL

CHIPMAN-UNION, INC.
500 Sibley Ave.
Union Point, GA 30669
Tel.: 706-486-2112 **GA**
Fax: 706-486-4963
Approx.Sls.: $47,000,000
Emp.: 600
Mfr. of Mens's, Boys' & Girls' Hosiery
S.I.C.: 2252
F. Sibley Bryan, Jr. *(Pres. & Chief Exec. Officer)*
A. Henry Reynolds *(V.P.-Admin.)*

Outside Service Firm(s):

Ernst & Young*(Auditors)*
1221 McKinney, Ste. 2400
Houston, TX 77010
Tel.: 713-750-1200

Hull, Towill, Norman & Barrett*(Legal Firm)*
P.O. Box 1564,
Augusta, GA 30913
Tel.: 706-722-4481

Trust Company Bank*(Major Banking Relationship)*
Trust Co. Tower
Atlanta, GA 30303
Tel.: 404-588-7963

Division:

Manufacturing Division **(1)**
500 Sibley Ave.
Union Point, GA 30669
Tel.: 706-486-2112
Mfr. of Men's, Boys' & Girls' Hosiery
S.I.C.: 2252
Carl E. Hagen *(Pres.)*

CHISWICK TRADING INC.
33 Union Ave.
Sudbury, MA 01776
Tel.: 508-443-9592
Fax: 508-443-8091
Year Founded: 1973
Assets: $4,300,000
Earnings: $400,000
Net Worth: $4,300,000
Approx.Sls.: $25,000,000
Emp.: 130
Fiscal Year-end: 12/31/90
Indus. Distributors, Flexible Pkgng.
S.I.C.: 5113
Theodore Pasquarello *(Pres. & Chief Exec. Officer)*
Barbara Scalzi *(Controller)*
Barbara Fallon *(Dir.-Personnel & Investor Rels.)*
Kenneth Murphy *(Dir.-Pur.)*
Joel Karsh *(Computer Info. Systems)*

Computer Systems/Hardware:
IBM System 38

Outside Service Firm(s):

Bernard F. Garrett C.P.A.*(Auditors)*
Needham, MA

First National Bank of Boston*(Major Banking Relationship)*
P.O. Box 644,
Boston, MA 02102-0644
Tel.: 617-575-2900
Fax: 617-575-2549

CHITTENDEN & EASTMAN CO.
401 S. Roosevelt
Burlington, IA 52601
Tel.: 319-753-2811
Fax: 319-752-1163
Approx.Sls.: $30,000,000
Emp.: 200
Import
Manufacturer of Mattresses; Distributor of Upholstered Furniture
S.I.C.: 5021; 2515
A.R. Weiler *(Chm. Bd. & Chief Exec. Officer)*
D.H. Robb *(Pres. & Chief Oper. Officer)*
Keith E. Bloomquist *(V.P.-Fin. & Admin.)*
N.L. Butler *(V.P.-Mfg.)*
R.H. Gainsforth *(V.P.-Sls.)*
R.A. Sarlo *(V.P.-Retail Stores)*

Computer Systems/Hardware:
HP 3000

Outside Service Firm(s):

Grant Thornton*(Auditors)*
700 One Prudential Plaza, 130 East Randolph St.
Chicago, IL 60601
Tel.: 312-856-0200
Fax: 312-565-4719

Farmers & Merchants Bank*(Major Banking Relationship)*
Burlington, IA

CHIVAS PRODUCTS LTD.
42555 Merrill Rd.
Sterling Heights, MI 48314-3266
Tel.: 313-254-3535 **MI**
Fax: 313-254-4910
Year Founded: 1974
Approx.Sls.: $30,000,000
Emp.: 310
Manufacture & Distribute Automotive Interior & Exterior Trim
S.I.C.: 3465; 5013
Ronald D. Moore *(Chm. Bd.)*
Frank N. Sheckell, Jr. *(Pres.)*
Edward G. Doyle *(V.P.)*
Charles H. Jehle *(V.P.-Fin.)*

Outside Service Firm(s):

Deloitte & Touche*(Auditors)*
200 Renaissance Center, 16th Fl.
Detroit, MI 48243
Tel.: 313-396-3000
Fax: 313-259-8087

National Bank of Detroit*(Major Banking Relationship)*
Warren, MI

CHOCTAW ELECTRIC CO-OP
Hwy. 93 N.
Hugo, OK 74743
Tel.: 405-326-6486
Fax: 405-326-2492
Approx.Sls.: $12,000,000
Emp.: 63
Electric Co-Operative
S.I.C.: 4911
Bill Easterwood *(Pres.)*
Joey Hairrell *(V.P.)*
Lela Campbell *(Treas. & Sec.)*
Mickie Braudrick *(Mgr.)*
Johnie Grimes *(Mgr.-Opers.)*
Sandra Pharis *(Mgr.-Admin. Services)*

Outside Service Firm(s):

Briscoe Robinson Company*(Auditors)*
Tulsa, OK

Security First National Bank*(Major Banking Relationship)*
Hugo, OK

George Walters*(Legal Firm)*
Broken Bow, OK

CHOCTAW, INC.
1184 Tupelo St.
Memphis, TN 38108
Tel.: 901-458-4481
Fax: 901-458-3444
Approx.Sls.: $37,000,000
Emp.: 275
Manufacture Concrete & Metal Drainage Pipe & Precast Bridges; Rental & Service Contruction Equipment & Supplies
S.I.C.: 3272; 3499; 5082
W.L. Quinlen, III *(Pres.)*
Troy Mashburn, Jr. *(Sec. & Treas.)*

Outside Service Firm(s):

Ernst & Young*(Auditors)*
1400 One Commerce Sq.
Memphis, TN 38103

First Tennessee Bank, N.A.*(Major Banking Relationship)*
Memphis, TN

LENA CHOW, INC.
627 Emerson St.
Palo Alto, CA 94301
Tel.: 415-324-3580
Fax: 415-324-4728
Year Founded: 1984
Approx.Billings: $10,000,000
Emp.: 15
Scientific & Medical Adv.
Lena Chow *(Pres. & New Bus. Contact)*
Robert M. Kuhar *(V.P., Gen. Mgr.)*
Christine Kelson *(Sec.)*

CHRISTENSON, BARCLAY & SHAW, INC.
9300 Metcalf, Ste. 900
Overland Park, KS 66212
Tel.: 913-341-0030
Tel.: 800-456-2678
Fax: 913-341-4922
Approx.Billings: $18,000,000
Yellow Pages
Jerry Christenson *(Pres.)*
Charles Schollenberger *(V.P., Pub. Rels.)*
Linda Meldrum *(Dir., Yellow Pages Div.)*
Sharon Rainwater *(Mgr., Yellow Pages Div.)*

CHRISTENSON ELECTRIC, INC.
111 S.W. Columbia, Ste. 480
Portland, OR 97201
Tel.: 503-241-4812
Fax: 503-241-0519
Approx.Sls.: $50,000,000
Emp.: 300
General Electrical Contractor
S.I.C.: 1731
Eric Christenson, Jr. *(Chm. Bd.)*
Brian Christopher *(Pres.)*
Vicky L. Bacon *(V.P.-Mktg. & Service Oper.)*
Larry Rominger *(V.P.-Construction)*
Peter Schwarzenberger *(V.P.-Fin.)*

Outside Service Firm(s):

Robert E. Hormel*(Auditors)*
Portland, OR

Miller, Nash, Wiener, Hager & Carlsen*(Legal Firm)*
900 S.W. Fifth Ave.
Portland, OR 97204
Tel.: 503-224-5858

United States National Bank of Oregon*(Major Banking Relationship)*
Portland, OR

CHRISTIAN CHILDREN'S FUND, INC.
2821 Emerywood Pkwy.
Richmond, VA 23261-6484
Mailing Address:
P.O. Box 26484,
Richmond, VA 23261-6484
Tel.: 804-756-2700
Tel.: 800-776-6767

Telex: 6844270 CCF UW
Fax: 804-756-2718
Year Founded: 1938
Approx.Sls.: $110,000,000
Emp.: 200
Fiscal Year-end: 6/30/91
Charitable Child Sponsorship Organization; Child Care & Community Development World-Wide
S.I.C.: 6732
Rev. Dr. R. Jackson Sadler *(Pres.)*
Dr. Paul F. McCleary *(Exec. Dir. & Chief Oper. Officer)*
James Brennan *(Comptroller)*
Lewis Booker *(Gen. Counsel)*
Jack Hinkle *(Acting Dir.-Fin.)*
W.R. Dixon *(Deputy Dir.-Devel.)*
Richard Wong *(Deputy Dir.-Plng. & Devel.)*
Ralph Black *(Dir.-Human Resources)*
William Gilbert *(Dir.-Information Services)*
Ellen Lambkin *(Dir.-Personnel Training & Devel.)*
Robert Gleason *(Mgr.-Admin. Services)*
Ann West *(Corp. Travel Planner)*
Miriam Ackley *(Librarian)*

Computer Systems/Hardware:
IBM Mainframe

Branch:

Los Angeles Regional Office **(1)**
9229 Sunset Blvd.
Los Angeles, CA 90069
Tel.: 310-550-6212
Fax: 310-550-5943

CHRISTIAN MEMORIAL CULTURAL CENTER
521 E. Hamlin Rd.
Rochester Hills, MI 48307
Tel.: 313-651-8192
Fax: 313-651-3169
Year Founded: 1961
Sales Range: $10-19 Million
Cemetery & Mausoleum
S.I.C.: 6553
Bernard LePage *(Pres.)*
Rebecca LePage *(V.P. & Mgr.-Sls.)*
Karl Schuster *(Gen. Counsel)*
Principal(s):
Bernard LePage

Outside Service Firm(s):

Karpus & Karpus*(Auditors)*
Madison Heights, MI

Continental Western Insurance*(Group Insurer)*
Rochester, MI

First of America Bank*(Major Banking Relationship)*
Rochester, MI

CHRISTIANITY TODAY, INC.
465 Gundersen Dr.
Carol Stream, IL 60188
Tel.: 708-260-6200 **IL**
Fax: 708-260-0114
Year Founded: 1955
Approx.Sls.: $15,000,000
Emp.: 100
Fiscal Year-end: 12/31/91
Publisher Christian Magazines
S.I.C.: 2721
Billy Graham *(Chm. Bd.)*
B. Clayton Bell, Sr. *(Exec. Chm.)*
Harold Myra *(Chief Exec. Officer)*
Paul Robbins *(Chief Oper. Officer)*
Roy Coffman *(Sr. V.P.)*
David O. Stewart *(Sr. V.P.)*
Keith Stonehocker *(Sr. V.P.)*
Nate Adams *(V.P.-Mktg.)*
Christopher Grant *(V.P.-Sls.)*
Walter Bottorff *(Controller)*
Jo Selander *(Dir.-Human Resources)*
Jonathan Thigpen *(Mgr.-Adv.)*

Computer Systems/Hardware:
Atex

Outside Service Firm(s):

Arthur Andersen & Co.*(Auditors)*
33 W. Monroe St.
Chicago, IL 60603-4067
Tel.: 312-580-0033
Fax: 312-507-6748

CHRISTIANSEN & FRITSCH, INC.
1008 Western Ave.
Seattle, WA 98104
Tel.: 206-223-6464
Year Founded: 1988
Approx.Billings: $25,000,000
Emp.: 35
Direct Response Advertising
Ron Christiansen *(Chm.)*
Bill Fritsch *(Pres.)*
Cynthia Grant *(Gen. Mgr.-Portland)*
David Giesdorf *(Gen. Mgr.-Seattle)*

Computer Systems/Hardware:
32 Macs Completely Networked. Desktop Publishing

CHRISTIE ELECTRIC CORPORATION
18120 S. Broadway
Gardena, CA 90248
Tel.: 310-715-1402
Fax: 310-618-8368
Approx.Sls.: $13,000,000
Emp.: 100
Mfr. of DC Power Supplies, Battery Chargers & Testers
S.I.C.: 3612; 3825; 3827
Tom E. Christie *(Chm. & Chief Exec. Officer)*
Raymond M. White *(Pres. & Chief Oper. Officer)*
Jack Kline *(V.P.-Mktg.)*
Merlyn Johnson *(Controller)*

CHRISTOPHER THOMAS ASSOCIATES INC.
1101 Stewart Ave.
Garden City, NY 11530
Tel.: 516-794-2400
Fax: 516-794-2551
Approx.Billings: $35,800,000
Emp.: 45
Christopher B. Santry *(Chm. & Chief Exec. Officer)*
Thomas M. Petrocine *(Pres. & Chief Oper. Officer)*
Russel R. Petrocine *(Sr. V.P., Gen. Mgr.)*
Gail Hoffman *(V.P., Controller)*
Donna Wick *(Office Mgr.)*

CHRISTY'S MARKETS, INC.
22 Christy's Drive
Brockton, MA 02401
Tel.: 508-586-0475
Fax: 508-588-4787
Emp.: 1,300
Wholesale Distribution of Perishables to Convenience Food Stores
S.I.C.: 5148
Christy Mihos *(Pres.)*
John McDonald *(Sr. V.P.)*
Enzo F. Rotatori *(V.P.-Mktg.)*
James Peter *(Treas.)*
William Reynolds *(Dir.-Human Resources)*

Outside Service Firm(s):

First National Bank of Boston*(Major Banking Relationship)*
P.O. Box 644,
Boston, MA 02102-0644
Tel.: 617-575-2900
Fax: 617-575-2549

CHROMA CORPORATION
3900 Dayton St.
McHenry, IL 60050
Tel.: 815-385-8100 **DE**
Fax: 815-385-1518
Emp.: 120
Plastic Color Pellets
S.I.C.: 2821
Robert D. Swain *(Chm. Bd.)*
Gary G. Bryan *(V.P.-Mfg.)*
Stewart D. Swain *(V.P.-Admin.)*

Outside Service Firm(s):

American National Bank*(Major Banking Relationship)*
33 North LaSalle St.
Chicago, IL 60690
Tel.: 312-661-6967

CHURCH & CHURCH INC.
(d/b/a Church's Lumber Yards)
7669 Auburn Rd.
Utica, MI 48317
Mailing Address:
P.O. Box 189-005
Utica, MI 48318
Tel.: 313-731-2050
Fax: 313-731-2579
Year Founded: 1890
Approx.Sls.: $76,000,000
Emp.: 550
Retail Lumber & Building Materials
S.I.C.: 5211
Roy B. Church *(Chm. Bd.)*
William R. Church *(Pres. & Chief Exec. Officer)*
Richard E. Wozniak *(Treas.)*

Outside Service Firm(s):

Ernst & Young*(Auditors)*
One Detroit Center, 500 Woodward, Ste. 1700
Detroit, MI 48243
Tel.: 313-259-9600

Chiro Herrinton Runstadler & Thomas*(Legal Firm)*
2833 Crooks Rd.
Troy, MI 40875

N.B.D. Bank, N.A.*(Major Banking Relationship)*
611 Woodward Ave.
Detroit, MI 48226
Tel.: 313-225-1122
Fax: 313-225-3420

CIMINELLI DEVELOPMENT COMPANY, INC.
350 Effjay Rd., Ste. 101
Williamsville, NY 142221
Tel.: 716-631-8000
Fax: 716-631-8034
Year Founded: 1961
Approx.Sls.: $38,000,000
Emp.: 200
Real Estate
S.I.C.: 6552
Frank L. Ciminelli *(Chief Exec. Officer)*

Outside Service Firm(s):

Trossman & Trossman*(Auditors)*
Buffalo, NY

Subsidiary:

Frank L. Ciminelli Construction Co. **(1)**
369 Franklin St.
Buffalo, NY 14202
Tel.: 716-855-1200
Fax: 716-835-2749
General Contractor
S.I.C.: 1522; 1542
Louis P. Ciminelli *(Pres.)*
Robert Mortellaro *(V.P.)*
Michael Schwimmer *(V.P.-Fin.)*

CIMLINC INC.
1222 Hamilton Parkway
Itasca, IL 60143
Tel.: 708-250-0090 **DE**
Fax: 708-250-8513
Approx.Sls.: $28,000,000
Emp.: 240
Computer-aided Design (CAD) Systems Support Service For Graphics Industry
S.I.C.: 5065; 5045; 8731; 7373
John A. West *(Pres.)*
David Auer *(V.P.)*
John Parson *(Dir.-Corp. Fin.)*

Outside Service Firm(s):

Kirkland & Ellis*(Legal Firm)*
200 E. Randolph Dr.
Chicago, IL 60601
Tel.: 312-861-2000
Fax: 312-861-2200

Harris Trust & Savings Bank*(Major Banking Relationship)*
111 W. Monroe St.
Chicago, IL 60690
Tel.: 312-461-2265
Tel.: 800-858-0840

CINAMERICA THEATRES, L.P.
9200 Sunset Blvd.
Los Angeles, CA 90069
Mailing Address:
P.O. Box 60909
Los Angeles, CA 90060
Tel.: 310-273-3336
Year Founded: 1973
Approx.Sls.: $196,000,000
Fiscal Year-end: 12/31/90
Theatre Exhibitors
S.I.C.: 7832
Kenneth Crowe *(Treas.)*

Computer Systems/Hardware:
IBM

THE CINCINNATI CORDAGE & PAPER COMPANY
800 E. Ross Ave.
Cincinnati, OH 45217
Mailing Address:
P.O. Box 17125
Cincinnati, OH 45217
Tel.: 513-242-3600 **OH**
Telex: 854 358 CORDAGE
Fax: 513-242-4307
Year Founded: 1892
Assets: $30,000,000
Liabilities: $15,000,000
Net Worth: $15,000,000
Approx.Sls.: $148,000,000
Emp.: 300
Fiscal Year-end: 12/31/90
Wholesale Paper Distributor
S.I.C.: 5111
John F. Church, Jr. *(Pres.)*
Paul J. Ruffing *(Chief Fin. Officer & V.P.)*
Richard G. Evans, Jr. *(Exec. V.P.)*
John A. McMinn *(Sr. V.P.-Admin.)*
David Pullman *(Dir.-Communications & Adv.)*
Anne Y. Hennen *(Mgr.-Human Resouces)*
Principal(s):
John F. Church, Jr.

No. of Mfg. Plants/Facilities: 11

Computer Systems/Hardware:
IBM 9221/120

Outside Service Firm(s):

Arthur Andersen & Co.*(Auditors)*
425 Walnut St.
Cincinnati, OH 45202
Tel.: 513-381-6900

Frost & Jacobs*(Legal Firm)*
2500 Central Trust Ctr.
Cincinnati, OH 45202
Tel.: 513-651-6800

Star Bank*(Major Banking Relationship)*
425 Walnut Street
Cincinnati, OH 45202
Tel.: 513-632-4000

James Investment*(Pension Manager)*
Alpha, OH

The Cincinnati Cordage & Paper Company—(Continued)

Ohio National Life*(Pension Manager)*
Cincinnati, OH

CINCINNATI GEAR COMPANY
5657 Wooster Pike
Cincinnati, OH 45227
Tel.: 513-271-7700
Fax: 513-271-6964
Emp.: 300
Mfr. of Gears & Marine Drives
S.I.C.: 3566
Walter L. Rye *(Chm. Bd.)*
Frank J. Posinski *(Pres. & Chief Oper. Officer)*
Charles W. Gay *(V.P.-Opers.)*
Octave Labath *(V.P.-Engrng.)*
David Bardill *(Mgr.-Mktg. & Adv.)*

Outside Service Firm(s):

Grant Thornton*(Auditors)*
1600 Atrium One
Cincinnati, OH 45202
Tel.: 513-762-5000

Fifth Third Bank*(Major Banking Relationship)*
Corporate Trust Services, 38 Fountain Square Plaza
Cincinnati, OH 45263

CINCINNATI INCORPORATED
7420 Kilby Rd.
Harrison, OH 45030
Mailing Address:
P.O. Box 11111,
Cincinnati, OH 45211
Tel.: 513-367-7100
Fax: 513-367-7552
Year Founded: 1898
Approx.Sls.: $50,000,000
Emp.: 650
Fiscal Year-end: 12/31/90
Mfrs. of Metal Working Equipment
S.I.C.: 3542; 3541; 3599
Perrin G. March III *(Chm. Bd. & Chief Exec. Officer)*
Charles R. Turner *(Pres.)*
Richard V. Pradetto *(Sr. V.P.-Mktg.)*
Dave Ertel *(V.P.-Opers.)*
Ed Silva *(V.P.-Fin. & Treas.)*
Marilyn Bourguein *(Dir.-Data Processing)*

Computer Systems/Hardware:
IBM 4341

Outside Service Firm(s):

Ernst & Young*(Auditors)*
1300 Chiquita Center, 250 E. Fifth St.
Cincinnati, OH 45202
Tel.: 513-621-6454

Prudential Insurance Co. of America*(Group Insurer)*
525 Vine St.
Cincinnati, OH 45202
Tel.: 513-784-7500

Dinsmore & Shohl*(Legal Firm)*
2100 Fountain Square Plaza
Cincinnati, OH 45202-3172
Tel.: 513-977-8200

The Central Trust Company, N.A.*(Major Banking Relationship)*
201 E. Fifth
Cincinnati, OH 45202
Tel.: 513-651-8255

CINCINNATI SUB-ZERO PRODUCTS, INC.
12011 Mosteller Rd.
Cincinnati, OH 45241-1528
Tel.: 513-772-8810
Fax: 513-772-9119
Approx.Sls.: $16,000,000
Emp.: 120
Fiscal Year-end: 9/ 1/90
Export
Mfr. Production Chilling Chambers; Environmental Test Equip.; Cryogenic Equip.; Hyper/Hypothermia Equip.
S.I.C.: 3841
Leonard Berke *(Pres.)*
Robert Schroeder *(V.P.-Production)*
Steve Berke *(V.P.)*
Russell Pennavaria *(Dir.-Mktg., Medical Div.)*

CINCINNATI UNITED CONTRACTORS
9501 Union Cemetery Rd.
Loveland, OH 45140
Tel.: 513-677-0060 **OH**
Fax: 513-677-1121
Year Founded: 1978
Approx.Sls.: $24,000,000
Emp.: 70
New Construction of Industrial & Commercial Buildings; Remodeling & Repairs of Industrial & Commercial Buildings; Structural Steel Erection; Self-propelled Aircraft
S.I.C.: 1541; 1542; 1791
Charles Kubicki *(Pres.)*
Dennis H. Eaton *(V.P.-Fin.)*

Outside Service Firm(s):

Rippie & Kingston*(Auditors)*
Cincinnati, OH

CINCOM SYSTEMS, INC.
2300 Montana Ave.
Cincinnati, OH 45211
Tel.: 513-662-2300 **OH**
Fax: 513-662-1086
Year Founded: 1968
Approx.Sls.: $158,011,000
Emp.: 1,400
Fiscal Year-end: 9/30/91
Import Export
Mfr. of Computer Software
S.I.C.: 7371; 7372
Thomas M. Nies *(Chm. Bd., Pres. & Chief Exec. Officer)*
Tom McLean *(V.P.-System Software Div.)*
Bill Dorece *(V.P.-Mfg. Solution Div.)*
Gerald Shawhan *(V.P.-Fin.)*
Barry Sargeant *(V.P.-Intl. Opres.)*
Ernest W. Tobler *(Treas.)*
Eric Lange *(Dir.-Mktg.)*
Ron Hank *(Dir.-Corp. Rels.)*

Outside Service Firm(s):

KPMG Peat Marwick*(Auditors)*
1600 Central Trust Ctr., 201 East Fifth St.
Cincinnati, OH 45202
Tel.: 513-421-6430

The Provident Bank*(Major Banking Relationship)*
One E. Fourth St.
Cincinnati, OH 45202
Tel.: 513-579-2000

CINE MAGNETICS, INC.
606 Halstead Ave.
Mamaroneck, NY 10543
Tel.: 914-698-3434 **NY**
Fax: 914-698-1847
Year Founded: 1972
Approx.Sls.: $38,000,000
Emp.: 250
Film Processing, Editing & Titling; Motion Picture Photographer, Still or Video; Photofinishing Laboratory; Laser Printing
S.I.C.: 7819; 7221; 3861; 7384; 2759
Helen Abbott *(Chm. Bd.)*
Joseph J. Barber, Jr. *(Pres.)*
Robert Pastore *(Exec. V.P.)*
Sidney Weisser *(Exec. V.P.)*
Michael J. Herschchuk *(Controller)*
Stephen J. Kushel *(Sec.)*

Outside Service Firm(s):

Konigberg, Wolf & Co.*(Auditors)*
New York, NY

Manufacturers Hanover Trust Co.*(Major Banking Relationship)*
P.O. Box 24935, Church St. Station
New York, NY 10249
Tel.: 212-613-7147

Division:

F.R. Chems Div. **(1)**
606 Halstead Ave.
Mamaroneck, NY 10543
Tel.: 914-698-3434
Photographic Processing Chemicals
S.I.C.: 3861
Joseph J. Barber, Jr. *(Pres.)*

CIOCIOLA & COMPANY ADVERTISING, INC.
475 Park Ave. South
New York, NY 10016
Tel.: 212-447-8400
Fax: 212-447-8400
Year Founded: 1983
Approx.Billings: $32,300,000
Emp.: 32
Mel Ciociola *(Chm. & Exec. Creative Dir.)*
Diane Ashley *(Pres.)*
Gwen Lato *(Sr. V.P., Fin.)*
Ernie Mannix *(Music Dir.)*

CIRCLE A.W. PRODUCTS, CO.
13885 S.W. 72nd Ave.
Portland, OR 97223
Mailing Address:
P.O. Box 23455
Portland, OR 97223
Tel.: 503-620-6635
Fax: 503-620-7751
Approx.Sls.: $20,000,000
Emp.: 210
Electric Metal Products, Wiring & Gutter Fittings, Transformer Cabinets, Cabinet Boxes, Meter & Breaker Assemblies, Screw Cover Boxes, Panel Boards, Switch Boards
S.I.C.: 3643; 3612; 3613; 3699
Arthur King *(Chief Exec. Officer)*
Thomas Ruddy *(Pres. & Gen. Mgr.)*
Mike Hollowell *(Chief Fin. Officer)*
Francis Marta *(V.P.-Engrng.)*
John Wilson *(Dir.-Acctng.)*
Doyle Lsngford *(Mgr.-Total Quality)*

Outside Service Firm(s):

Bronson, Bronson & McKinnon*(Legal Firm)*
555 California St.
San Francisco, CA 94104

Bank of America NT&SA*(Major Banking Relationship)*
Modesto, CA

CITATION COMPANIES, INC.

CITATION COMPANIES, INC.
175 Citation Ct.
Birmingham, AL 35209
Tel.: 205-942-6022
Fax: 205-942-1507
Year Founded: 1972
Approx.Billings: $15,000,000
Emp.: 30
Development of Consumer Loyalty Programs, Retail Continuity Promotions, Consumer Games, Contests, Sweepstakes & Special Events
Lance Britt *(Pres.)*
Dan Wallace *(Chief Exec. Officer)*
Steve Wright *(Exec. V.P.)*
John G. Harbuck *(V.P., Sls. & Mktg.)*

CITIZENS GAS & COKE UTILITY
2020 N. Meridian St.
Indianapolis, IN 46202
Tel.: 317-924-3341
Fax: 317-927-4395
Year Founded: 1935
Assets: $452,300,000
Earnings: ($3,600,000)
Liabilities: $268,000,000
Net Worth: $184,300,000
Approx.Sls.: $267,400,000
Emp.: 1,150
Fiscal Year-end: 9/30/91
Gas Distribution Company; Manufacture Foundry Coke & Blast Furnace Coke
S.I.C.: 4932; 4925
D.L. Lindemann *(Pres. & Chief Exec. Officer)*
James Chenoweth *(Chief Fin. Officer & V.P.-Fin.)*
William M. Ramey *(Sr. V.P.-Mktg.)*
G.F. Clancy *(V.P.-Information Services)*
Martin C. Dusel *(V.P.-Mfg.)*
Fredrick L. Leske *(V.P.-Gas Opers.)*
C.B. Lykins *(V.P.-Customer Service & Rates)*
M.J. Richcreek *(V.P.-Human Resources)*
S.F. Shay *(Controller-Mfg.)*
W.L. Zellers *(Controller-Gas Opers.)*
H.V. Huffman *(Assoc. Counsel)*
James D. Calhoun *(Exec. Dir.-Mktg.)*
D. A. Kaiser *(Dir.-Budget & Planning)*
Charles M. Lane *(Dir.-Treas. Srvcs.)*
Thomas Moorman *(Buyer)*

Computer Systems/Hardware:
Burroughs

Outside Service Firm(s):

Coopers & Lybrand*(Auditors)*
2900 One American Square, Box 82002
Indianapolis, IN 46282
Tel.: 317-639-4161

Aetna Life & Casualty*(Group Insurer)*
151 Farmington Avenue
Hartford, CT 06156
Tel.: 203-273-2128
Fax: 203-729-4295

Smith Morgan & Ryan*(Legal Firm)*
1900 Indiana Tower, One Indiana Sq.
Indianapolis, IN 46204
Tel.: 317-636-5401

Bank One, Indianapolis, N.A.*(Major Banking Relationship)*
111 Monument Circle, Ste. 1611
Indianapolis, IN 46204-1611
Tel.: 317-321-8110

INB National Bank*(Major Banking Relationship)*
One Indiana Sq.
Indianapolis, IN 46266
Tel.: 317-266-6000

CITIZENS NATIONAL BANCSHARES INC.
201 N.W. Railroad Ave.
Hammond, LA 70401
Mailing Address:
P.O. Box 2188,
Hammond, LA 70404
Tel.: 504-542-2265
Fax: 504-542-2350
Year Founded: 1983
Approx.Assets: $160,815,000
Fiscal Year-end: 12/31/90
Bank Holding Company
S.I.C.: 6712
Corporate Giving Program: Unitco Way
Hans Schneider *(Chm. Bd.)*
Phil K. Livingston *(Pres. & Chief Exec. Officer)*
Mayson H. Foster *(Sec. & Treas.)*

Computer Systems/Hardware:
IBM S/36

Subsidiary:

Citizens National Bank **(1)**
201 N.W. Railroad Ave.
Hammond, LA 70401
Tel.: 504-542-2265 (100%)
Fax: 504-542-2350
Approx.Assets: $182,980,000
Emp.: 101
Computer Systems/Hardware:
IBM S/36
Banking
S.I.C.: 6021
Mayson H. Foster *(Pres. & Chief Oper. Officer)*
David B. Daniel *(Controller)*
Jerry Correjoiles *(V.P.-Bus. Devel.)*
Christina Buchler *(V.P.-Mktg. & Human Resources)*
Sheila Tallia *(Pur. Agent)*

CITIZENS REALTY & INSURANCE INC.
111 S.E. 3rd St.
Evansville, IN 47708
Mailing Address:
P.O. Box 99
Evansville, IN 47701
Tel.: 812-428-2898 **IN**
Fax: 812-428-0990
Year Founded: 1937
Assets: $6,800,872
Liabilities: $4,905,469
Net Worth: $1,895,403
Approx.Sls.: $100,000,000
Emp.: 120
Fiscal Year-end: 12/31/91
Insurance & Real Estate Agents; Operates Apartment Buildings
S.I.C.: 6411; 6531; 6513
Stephan G. Miller *(Pres.)*
Allan R. Adams *(Pres.-Insurance Div.)*
Joe Wallace *(Exec. V.P.)*
Marian A. Thomas *(Sec.)*
Dennis Riffert *(Controller & Treas.)*

Outside Service Firm(s):

George S. Olive & Co.*(Auditors)*
201 N. Illinois St.
Indianapolis, IN 46204

Bowers, Harrison, Kent & Miller*(Legal Firm)*
Evansville, IN

Citizens National Bank*(Major Banking Relationship)*
20 NW Third St.
Evansville, IN 47739-0001
Tel.: 812-464-3400

CITRUS WORLD INC.
Hwy. 27 North
Lake Wales, FL 33853
Mailing Address:
P.O. Box 1111
Lake Wales, FL 33859
Tel.: 813-676-1411 **FL**
Year Founded: 1934
Assets: $160,000,000
Liabilities: $87,000,000
Net Worth: $73,000,000
Approx.Sls.: $330,000,000
Emp.: 950
Fiscal Year-end: 8/31/92
Export
Citrus Processors
S.I.C.: 2037; 0723
Frank M. Hunt *(Chm. Bd. & Pres.)*
Joseph D. Marshburn *(Chief Exec. Officer)*
Stephen M. Caruso *(Chief Oper. Officer)*
Walt Lincer *(V.P.-Sls. & Mktg.)*
William J. Hendry *(Treas.)*
David C. Latham *(Gen. Counsel)*
Dan McSpadden *(Mgr.-Mktg.)*
Principal(s):
Agricultural Cooperative

No. of Mfg. Plants/Facilities: 3
No. of U.S. Offices: 3

Computer Systems/Hardware:
Wang V5; Wang VS 100

Outside Service Firm(s):

KPMG Peat Marwick*(Auditors)*
650 Town Center Dr.
Costa Mesa, CA
Tel.: 714-850-4300

Heritage Consultants*(Group Insurer)*
Auburndale, FL

Foley & Lardner*(Legal Firm)*
Orlando, FL

First Union National Bank*(Major Banking Relationship)*
Lake Wales, FL

Subsidiary:

Wales Industries, Inc. **(1)**
Hwy. 27 No.
Lake Wales, FL 33853
Tel.: 813-676-7641 (100%)
Citrus Processor
S.I.C.: 0723; 2037
Don Sims *(Dir.)*

CITY BEVERAGE CO.
566 Wells St., S.W.
Atlanta, GA 30312
Tel.: 404-522-4200
Fax: 404-688-2148
Approx.Sls.: $12,000,000
Emp.: 81
Wine & Beer Distr.
S.I.C.: 5181; 5182
H. Jerome Russell *(Chm. Bd.)*
Jerome Russell *(Pres. & Gen. Mgr.)*
Areen Kao *(Controller)*
Brenda Robinson *(Dir.-Personnel & Admin. Mgr.)*

CITY MACHINE TOOL & DIE COMPANY
1302 E. Washington St.
Muncie, IN 47305
Tel.: 317-288-4431
Fax: 317-286-0217
Emp.: 155
Machine Tools, Metal Cutting, Dies & Die Holders For Metal Cutting, Forming, Die Casting
S.I.C.: 3541; 3544
John R. Wagner *(Pres.)*
James Allen Wagner *(Exec. V.P.)*
Michael R. Goodman *(V.P.-Fin. & Sec.)*
Bob Haack *(V.P.-Sls.)*

Outside Service Firm(s):

Whitinger & Company*(Auditors)*
Muncie, IN

Lincoln National Bank*(Major Banking Relationship)*
Fort Wayne, IN

CITY MEATS & PROVISIONS CO.
P.O. Box 27243,
Tucsan, AZ 85726
Year Founded: 1979
Assets: $10,860,000
Liabilities: $6,128,000
Net Worth: $4,732,000
Approx.Sls.: $55,000,000
Emp.: 170
Fiscal Year-end: 12/27/92
Export
Wholesaler Fresh Meats, Seafood & Poultry
S.I.C.: 5147; 5146; 5144
Employee Matching Gifts Program: 401K Plan
Robert B. McMahon *(Chm. Bd.,Chief Exec. Officer, Treas., & Sec.)*
Mike Brown *(Pres. & Exec. V.P.)*
LaDonna Ford *(Controller)*
John Scott Butler *(Gen. Mgr.)*

Computer Systems/Hardware:
MAI Basic Four

Outside Service Firm(s):

Coopers & Lybrand*(Auditors)*
Tucson, AZ

Royal Insurance Co.*(Commercial Insurance Carrier)*
Reno, NV

Great West Life Insurance*(Group Insurance Broker/Consult)*
Horsham, PA

Valley National Bank*(Major Banking Relationship)*
241 North Central Ave., 11th Floor
Phoenix, AZ 85001

Division:

Barone Sausage Company **(1)**
345 S. King Pkwy.
Tucson, AZ 85733
Tel.: 602-623-8571
Manufacture Meat Products
S.I.C.: 2013
Frank Sweeney *(Gen. Mgr.)*

CITY POSTAL, INC.
421 7th Ave.
New York, NY 10001
Tel.: 212-279-4300
Fax: 212-629-8998
Year Founded: 1977
Approx.Sls.: $12,500,000
Emp.: 350
Fiscal Year-end: 6/30/90
Time-Critical Air Courier & Freight; International Courier & International Remail
S.I.C.: 4513
Norman Broudski *(Pres. & Chief Exec. Officer)*
Albert Hernandez *(V.P.-Intl.)*
John Palmer *(Controller)*
Allen Gottlieb *(Mgr.-Sls.)*
Principal(s):
Norman Broudski

No. of U.S. Offices: 10

Computer Systems/Hardware:
IBM System 38-Model 40

Outside Service Firm(s):

Deloitte & Touche*(Auditors)*
1900 M St. N.W., 4th Fl.
Washington, DC 20036

Network Health Plan*(Group Insurer)*
Washington, DC

Silver, Friedman & Taff*(Legal Firm)*
1735 Eye St., N.W., 11th Fl.
Washington, DC 20006
Tel.: 202-429-6100
Fax: 202-833-3295

First American Bank, N.A.*(Major Banking Relationship)*
McLean, VA

Subsidiaries:

Aeromail, Inc. **(1)**
1851 Alexander Bell Dr.
Reston, VA 22091
Tel.: 703-620-5400
S.I.C.: 4513
Irving Rosenberg *(Chief Oper. Officer)*

Video Air Express **(1)**
1851 Alexander Bell Dr.
Reston, VA 22091
Tel.: 703-620-5400
S.I.C.: 4513
Gilbert Carpel *(Chief Oper. Officer)*

CIVES CORP.
411 Rouse Ln.
Roswell, GA 30076
Tel.: 404-993-4424 **DE**
Fax: 404-998-2361
Year Founded: 1952
Sales Range: $100-499 Million
Emp.: 1,000
Fiscal Year-end: 12/31/91
Howard Lechler *(Chm. Bd.)*
Ronald W. Shaw *(Pres. & Chief Exec. Officer)*
John S. Donovan *(Exec. V.P.-Fin., Admin. & Gen. Counsel)*
John M. Connor *(Controller)*

No. of Mfg. Plants/Facilities: 9
No. of U.S. Offices: 14
No. of Foreign Offices: 2

Computer Systems/Hardware:
MacIntosh

Outside Service Firm(s):

Wausau Insurance*(Group Insurer)*
New York, NY

First Atlanta Bank*(Major Banking Relationship)*
Atlanta, GA

CLAREMONT FLOCK CORPORATION
169 Main St.
Claremont, NH 03743
Tel.: 603-542-5151
Emp.: 25
Cotton, Rayon & Synthetic Flock For Compounding & Surface Coating Applications
S.I.C.: 2261; 2262
Burt McIntyre *(Pres.)*
Peter Hadley *(V.P.-Opers.)*
Carl F. Steinfield *(V.P.-Mktg.)*

Outside Service Firm(s):

Midlin, Clarino & Stevens*(Auditors)*
Rutland, VT

Shawmut Bank*(Major Banking Relationship)*
446 Main St.
Worcester, MA 01608
Tel.: 617-793-4000

Division:

Vertipile **(1)**
Scott Dr.
Leominster, MA 01453
Tel.: 508-534-6191
Fabrics
S.I.C.: 2261; 2262
Peter Hadley *(V.P.-Opers.)*

Clarity Coverdale Rueff

CLARITY COVERDALE RUEFF ADVERTISING
415 First Ave. N.
Minneapolis, MN 55401
Tel.: 612-339-3902
Fax: 612-339-7358
Year Founded: 1979
Approx.Billings: $32,000,000
Emp.: 25
Advertising Agency
S.I.C.: 7311
Corporate Giving Program: Cash Contributions to YMCA, United Way, Madd
Tim B. Clarity *(Pres.)*
Bob Rueff *(Chief Exec. Officer & Mktg. Dir.)*
Gary Hellmer *(V.P., Opers.)*
Karen E. Kaiser *(Mgr.-Mktg. Research.)*

TJ CLARK ADVERTISING/PR
99 Derby St.
Hingham, MA 02043
Tel.: 617-740-1155
Fax: 617-749-8662
Year Founded: 1986

TJ Clark Advertising/PR—(Continued)

Approx.Billings: $18,400,000
Emp.: 25
Hi-Tech, Consumer Products, Retail, Business-to-Business & Marketing Communications
Thomas J. Clark *(Pres.)*
Anthony Price *(V.P., Acct. Services & Controller)*
Michael J. Patton *(Dir., Pub. Rels.)*
Claire Pratt *(Pub. Rels. & Acct. Exec.)*

CLARK CONSTRUCTION GROUP
7500 Old Georgetown Rd.
Bethesda, MD 20814
Tel.: 301-657-7100
Fax: 301-657-7263
Year Founded: 1906
Approx.Sls.: $965,521,287
Emp.: 5,000
General Building Contractors; Heavy Construction
S.I.C.: 1541; 1542; 1623; 1629
Corporate Giving Program: Supports Education
Employee Matching Gifts Program: Dollar for Dollar Matches up to $3, 000; Post-Secondary Educational Institutions Only
A. James Clark *(Chm. Bd., Pres. & Chief Exec. Officer)*
Lawrence Nussdorf *(Exec. V.P.)*
Kathy Taub *(Gen. Counsel)*
Terry Clatzkin *(Controller)*
Andrea Danko-Koenig *(Dir.-Compensation & Benefits)*
Louise E. Pulizzi *(Dir.-Corp. Communications)*

Computer Systems/Hardware:
IBM System 38

Outside Service Firm(s):

Arthur Andersen & Co.*(Auditors)*
1666 K Street, N.W.
Washington, DC 20006

Hartford Life Insurance Co.*(Commercial Insurance Carrier)*
Hartford, CT 06104-2999

Metropolitan Life Insurance Co.*(Group Insurer)*
One Madison Ave.
New York, NY 10010-3690
Tel.: 215-578-9292

Arent, Fox, Kintner, Plotkin & Kahn*(Legal Firm)*
1815 H St. N.W.
Washington, DC 20006
Tel.: 202-857-6000

American Security Bank, N.A.*(Major Banking Relationship)*
1501 Pennsylvania Ave. N.W.
Washington, DC 20013
Tel.: 202-624-4000

Subsidiary:

Clark Enterprises, Inc. **(1)**
7500 Old Georgetown Rd.
Bethesda, MD 20814
Tel.: 301-657-7100
Fax: 301-657-7263
Emp.: 5,000
Industrial & Heavy Construction Contractor
S.I.C.: 1629; 6719; 1771
A. James Clark *(Chm. Bd. & Pres.)*
Lawrence C. Nussdorf *(Exec. V.P. & Treas.)*
Florence E. Allen *(Sec.)*

DAVID CLARK COMPANY, INC.
360 Franklin St.
Worcester, MA 01604
Tel.: 508-756-6216 **MA**
Fax: 508-753-5827
Approx.Sls.: $27,000,000
Emp.: 345
Radio Headphones; Electric Intercommunication Systems; Personal Safety Equipment; Fire Resistant & Protective Clothing
S.I.C.: 3679; 3669; 3842
Darald R. Libby *(Chm. Bd. & Chief Fin. Officer)*
Robert A. Vincent *(Pres.)*
John E. Flagg *(Treas.)*
Rosella T. Knipe *(Sec.)*

Outside Service Firm(s):

KPMG Peat Marwick*(Auditors)*
One Boston Place
Boston, MA 02108
Tel.: 617-723-7700

Bank of New England*(Major Banking Relationship)*
28 State Street
Boston, MA 02109
Tel.: 617-742-4000

CLARK DOOR CO., INC.
2564 Metro Blvd.
Maryland Heights, MO 63043
Tel.: 314-432-3112
Fax: 314-432-2296
Approx.Sls.: $10,000,000
Emp.: 125
Prest-O-Matic Automatic Doors, Shock Absorber, Fuse-O-Link, Durador, Fire Chief & Fire Man Fire Doors, Kayon Door Covering, Thermadoor Cold Storage & Fire Door Combination
S.I.C.: 3442; 3499
Rex Palmatier *(Pres.)*

Division:

Specialty Engineered Doors-Clark Door Co. **(1)**
2366 Center Line Industrial Dr.
Saint Louis, MO 63146
Tel.: 314-432-3112
S.I.C.: 3442; 3499

CLARK FOODSERVICE, INC.
950 Arthur Ave.
Elk Grove Village, IL 60007
Tel.: 708-956-1730 **IL**
Fax: 708-956-0199
Year Founded: 1912
Approx.Sls.: $312,000,000
Emp.: 1,100
Distributor of Paper, Plastic & Food Specialty Products to Restaurants, Hospitals & Hotels
S.I.C.: 5113; 5199
Don J. Hindman *(Chm. Bd. & Chief Exec. Officer)*
Tom DeAngelo *(Pres.)*
James A. Couch *(V.P.-Fin., Treas. & Chief Fin. Officer)*
Patrick Conoboy *(V.P.-Mngmt. Information Services)*
Thomas C. Deangelo *(V.P.-Opers.)*
Brian G. Fraser *(V.P.-Admin. & Gen. Counsel)*
Robert R. Sears *(Controller & Sec.)*
Principal(s):
Don J. Hindman

No. of Mfg. Plants/Facilities: 17
No. of U.S. Offices: 17

Computer Systems/Hardware:
Sequoia

Outside Service Firm(s):

Grant Thornton*(Auditors)*
700 One Prudential Plaza, 130 East Randolph St.
Chicago, IL 60601
Tel.: 312-856-0200
Fax: 312-565-4719

Continental Bank N. A.*(Major Banking Relationship)*
231 S. LaSalle St.
Chicago, IL 60697
Tel.: 312-828-2345
Tel.: 800-426-5754
Telex: 312-828-1783

Blue Cross & Blue Shield Association*(Group Insurer)*
233 N. Michigan Ave.
Chicago, IL 60601

Winston & Strawn*(Legal Firm)*
One 1st Natl. Plaza, No. 5000
Chicago, IL 60603
Tel.: 312-558-5600

Chicago Corporation*(Pension Manager)*
Chicago, IL

First National Bank of Chicago*(Pension Manager)*
One First National Plaza
Chicago, IL 60670
Tel.: 312-732-9781
Tel.: 312-732-4050
Fax: 312-732-4840
Fax: 312-732-3055

Divisions:

Chicago Division **(1)**
950 Arthur Ave.
Elk Grove Village, IL 60007
S.I.C.: 5113; 5199

Cincinnati Division **(1)**
2503 Commodity Cir.
Sharonville, OH 45241
S.I.C.: 5113; 5199

Cleveland Division **(1)**
5370 Naiman Pky.
Solon, OH 44139
S.I.C.: 5113; 5199

Columbus Division **(1)**
5310 Kreiger Ct.
Columbus, OH 43228
S.I.C.: 5113; 5199

Detroit Division **(1)**
6635 Sterling Dr. S.
Sterling Heights, MI 48077
S.I.C.: 5113; 5199

Indianapolis Division **(1)**
5525 W. Minnesota
Indianapolis, IN 46241
S.I.C.: 5113; 5199

Louisville Division **(1)**
4830 Jennings Lane
Louisville, KY 40218
S.I.C.: 5113; 5199

Riviera Beach Division **(1)**
1160 W. 13th St.
Riviera Beach, FL 33404
S.I.C.: 5113; 5199

Roseland Division **(1)**
2900 W. 127th St.
Blue Island, IL 60406
S.I.C.: 5113; 5199

Milwaukee Division **(1)**
17155 W. Glendale Dr.
New Berlin, WI 53151
S.I.C.: 5113; 5199

Orlando Division **(1)**
4060 Doctor Love Rd.
Orlando, FL 32810
S.I.C.: 5113; 5199

Ozark Division **(1)**
623-25 E. Tampa St.
Springfield, MO 65805
S.I.C.: 5113; 5199

Peoria Division **(1)**
1616-C W. Chanute Rd.
Peoria, IL 61615
S.I.C.: 5113; 5199

St. Louis Division **(1)**
8979 Seeger Industrial Dr.
Saint Louis, MO 63134
S.I.C.: 5113; 5199

Twin Cities Division **(1)**
432 Front Ave.
Saint Paul, MN 55117
S.I.C.: 5113; 5199

South Bend Division **(1)**
1901 Bendix Dr.
South Bend, IN 46628
S.I.C.: 5113; 5199

Mid-State Division **(1)**
8311 E. 34 Mile Rd, Box 359
Cadillac, MI 49601
S.I.C.: 5113; 5199

Clark-Simon, Inc. **(1)**
1901 Bendix Dr.
South Bend, IN 46628
Tel.: 219-234-5011
Emp.: 210
Distributor of Groceries, Frozen Foods, Fresh Produce, Paper & Sanitation Supplies
S.I.C.: 5113; 5141; 5142; 5149

CLARK GUM COMPANY
1300 S. Grove Ave.
Barrington, IL 60010
Tel.: 708-382-3502
Fax: 708-382-3509
Year Founded: 1912
Approx.Sls.: $10,000,000
Emp.: 7
Fiscal Year-end: 12/31/90
Gum Manufacturer
S.I.C.: 2067
Michael Maude *(Chm. Bd.)*
Earl Manhold III *(Pres.)*
John Abbs *(Controller)*
Nancy Tabb *(Credit Mgr.)*

Outside Service Firm(s):

Korman & Deutsch*(Auditors)*
Northbrook, IL

Parkway Bank*(Major Banking Relationship)*
Chicago, IL

A.D. CLARK, INC.
12901 W. Jefferson Blvd.
Los Angeles, CA 90066
Tel.: 310-306-4435 **CA**
Fax: 310-578-2385
Year Founded: 1959
Approx.Sls.: $115,000,000
Emp.: 1,200
Drug, Proprietary & Liquor Stores
S.I.C.: 5912; 5921
Richard Bromboch *(Co-Pres.)*
Ralph Wood *(Co-Pres.)*
James B. O'Shea *(Controller)*

Outside Service Firm(s):

Union Bank*(Major Banking Relationship)*
3810 Wilshire Blvd.
Los Angeles, CA 90010
Tel.: 213-480-6566

Keith Clark
(See listing under A.D. Clark, Inc.)

CLARK OIL & REFINING CORPORATION
8182 Maryland Ave.
Saint Louis, MO 63105
Tel.: 314-854-9696
Telex: 434509
Fax: 314-854-1580
Emp.: 5,500
Fiscal Year-end: 12/31/90
Refining, Marketing & Transportation of Petroleum Products
S.I.C.: 2911; 4925
Paul Melnuk *(Chm. Bd.)*
Paul D. Melnuk *(Pres. & Chief Oper. Officer)*
Richard P. Nelson *(V.P.-Refinery Opers.)*

M.R. Burmaster *(V.P.-Sec. & Head Legal Dept.)*
Thomas G. Henning *(V.P.-Retail Mktg.)*
Barry W. Frazier *(V.P.-Supply & Distr.)*
Donald H. Nonnenkamp *(Treas.)*
John Lindblad *(Controller)*
Peggy L. Danley *(Dir.-Personnel)*
James Jozwiakowski *(Dir.-Pur.)*
Scott Anderson *(Mgr.-Communications)*
Buddy L. Green *(Mgr.-Computer Services)*

Outside Service Firm(s):

Coopers & Lybrand*(Auditors)*
1200 West One Plaza
Boise, ID 83702
Tel.: 208-343-4301

Refineries:

Clark Oil & Refining Corporation--Blue Island Refinery **(1)**
131st & Kedzie Ave.
Blue Island, IL 60406
Tel.: 708-385-5000 (100%)
Refinery
S.I.C.: 2911

Clark Oil & Refining Corporation--Wood River Refinery **(1)**
P.O. Box 87,
Hartford, IL 62048
Tel.: 618-254-7301 (100%)
Refinery
S.I.C.: 2911

CLARK & POPE, INC.
41 East 42nd St.
New York, NY 10017
Tel.: 212-286-9339
Fax: 212-682-4748
Year Founded: 1982
Approx.Billings: $12,400,000
Emp.: 11
Marketing Communications
Herbert H. Clark *(Chm.)*
Wendell E. Pope *(Pres.)*
Lee W. Hill *(Mktg. Dir.)*
Eva-Susan Ruedel *(Admin.)*

CYRUS CLARK CO., INC.
267 Fifth Ave.
New York, NY 10016
Tel.: 212-684-5312
Fax: 212-481-3528
Year Founded: 1925
Approx.Sls.: $14,000,000
Emp.: 25
Fiscal Year-end: 12/31/91
Export
Printed Cotton, Chintz and Other Cottons: Think Chintz, Think Cyrus Clark, Converters of 100% Cotton Chintz, Decorative Printed Fabrics, Traditional & Contemporary Designs
S.I.C.: 2211
Cyrus Clark, Jr. *(Chm. Bd.)*
Cyrus Clark III *(Pres.)*
James V. Ponte *(Dir.-Mktg. & Adv.)*

Computer Systems/Hardware:
Wang

CLARKE GOWARD FITTS MATTESON, INC.
535 Boylston St.
Boston, MA 02116
Tel.: 617-536-7611
Fax: 617-536-4288
Year Founded: 1977
Approx.Billings: $21,200,000
Emp.: 25
Terence M. Clarke *(Chm.)*
William C. Matteson *(Pres. & Chief Exec. Officer)*
Michael Mroz *(V.P., Dir., CGFM Direct)*
Matthew Kelly *(V.P., Fin. & Admin.)*
Stephen Larkin *(Acct. Exec., New Bus. Devel.)*

CLARKLIFT OF MINNESOTA, INC.
501 W. 78th St.
Bloomington, MN 55420
Tel.: 612-887-5400
Fax: 612-881-3030
Year Founded: 1949
Approx.Sls.: $17,000,000
Emp.: 96
Forklift Truck Dealership; Service, Sale of Parts & Rental
S.I.C.: 3537; 7538; 7359
Clayton Schubert *(Pres.)*
Sid Lemcke *(Mgr.-Parts)*
Tom Roytek *(Mgr.-Sls.)*
Jeff Schubert *(Mgr.-Rental/Used Equip.)*
Tom Showalter *(Mgr.-Service)*

Outside Service Firm(s):

Booth Machowicz Hop & Co.*(Auditors)*
Minneapolis, MN

LeVander, Zotaley, Vander Linden & Rydland*(Legal Firm)*
Minneapolis, MN

American State Bank of Bloomington*(Major Banking Relationship)*
Bloomington, MN

CLARKSON CONSTRUCTION COMPANIES
4133 Gardner Ave.
Kansas City, MO 64120
Tel.: 816-483-8800
Fax: 816-241-6823
Year Founded: 1947
Approx.Sls.: $101,000,000
Emp.: 946
General Contractors Heavy Construction
S.I.C.: 1629
William E. Clarkson *(Pres.)*
D.J. Clarkson *(V.P.)*
Janice Clarkson *(Sec.)*
Robert B. Snapp, Jr. *(Asst. Sec. & Treas.)*

Outside Service Firm(s):

Baird, Kurtz & Dobson*(Auditors)*
Commerce Tower, 911 Main, Ste. 1900
Kansas City, MO
Tel.: 816-221-7544

Husch, Eppenberger, Donohue, Dobson & Cornfeld*(Legal Firm)*
Kansas City, MO

The Merchants Bank*(Major Banking Relationship)*
Kansas City, MO

CLASSIC MARKETS CORP.
6689-L Peachtree Industrial Blvd.
Norcross, GA 30092
Tel.: 404-447-9494
Fax: 404-242-0923
Year Founded: 1970
Approx.Sls.: $10,000,000
Emp.: 6
Fiscal Year-end: 12/31/92
Premium Sales Management: Houswares, Giftwares, Personal Care Prods, Incentive Travel, Promotional Television Representation
S.I.C.: 7389
Jay C. Standish *(Chm. Bd.)*
Carolyn S. Stiffler *(Pres. & Chief Exec. Officer)*
Richard Smith *(V.P.)*
Judith R. Standish *(Corp. Travel Planner)*

Computer Systems/Hardware:
IBM Compatable

CLAY-PARK LABS, INC.
Bathgate Industrial Park, 1700 Bathgate Ave.
Bronx, NY 10457
Tel.: 718-901-2800 **NY**
Fax: 718-294-8324
Assets: $22,900,000
Liabilities: $12,700,000
Net Worth: $10,200,000
Approx.Sls.: $42,000,000
Emp.: 450
Fiscal Year-end: 12/31/91
Import Export
Pharmaceuticals
S.I.C.: 2834
Bernard Ettinger *(Pres.)*
Morton Katz *(V.P. & Treas.)*
Steven Ettinger *(V.P.)*
Jack H. Vogel *(Chief Fin. Officer)*
Samuel Sirkin *(Sec.)*

Principal(s):
Bernard Ettinger
Morton Katz
Steven Ettinger
Jack H. Vogel
Samuel Sirkin

Outside Service Firm(s):

Eisner & Lubin*(Auditors)*
New York, NY

Banco Popular de Puerto Rico*(Major Banking Relationship)*
New York, NY

CLAYSON KNITTING CO. INC.
Hwy. 220 S.
Star, NC 27356
Mailing Address:
P.O. Box 39
Star, NC 27356
Tel.: 919-428-2171
Fax: 919-428-1133
Sales Range: $20-39 Million
Emp.: 765
Manufacture Men's & Children's Athletic Socks
S.I.C.: 2252
Joe E. Richardson *(Chief Exec. Officer)*
C. Vance Richardson *(Pres.)*
Jane Maxwell *(V.P.-Fin.)*
John M. Richardson *(V.P.)*

Outside Service Firm(s):

KPMG Peat Marwick*(Auditors)*
Two First Union Center
Charlotte, NC
Tel.: 704-335-5300

First Union National Bank*(Major Banking Relationship)*
CMG-5, Two First Union Center
Charlotte, NC 28288-1154
Tel.: 704-374-2698
Fax: 704-374-6987

A.T. CLAYTON & COMPANY, INC.
10 E. 40th St.
New York, NY 10016
Tel.: 212-689-1190
Fax: 212-213-9113
Approx.Sls.: $200,000,000
Emp.: 45
Paper Brokers; Printing & Writing
S.I.C.: 5111
W.F. Vallely, Jr. *(Chm. Bd.)*
Mark J. Vallely *(Pres.)*
Richard Crai *(Chief Fin. Officer)*
Scott Vallely *(Exec. V.P.)*

Outside Service Firm(s):

Chase Manhattan Bank, N.A.*(Major Banking Relationship)*
One Chase Manhattan Plaza
New York, NY 10081
Tel.: 212-552-2222
Tel.: 800-526-0801
Fax: 212-552-7175

CLAYTON CORPORATION
866 Horan Dr.
Fenton, MO 63026-2416
Tel.: 314-349-5333 **DE**
Fax: 314-349-5335
Assets: $8,000,000
Liabilities: $4,000,000
Net Worth: $4,000,000
Approx.Sls.: $18,000,000
Emp.: 110
Fiscal Year-end: 12/31/91
Import Export
Mfr. of Aerosol Valves, Accessories & Consumer Energy Saving Sealant Products Sold to Retail Trade
S.I.C.: 2891; 3089
Aaron S. Lapin *(Chm. Bd.)*
Byron R. Lapin *(Pres.)*
George E. McDowell *(V.P., Sec. & Treas.)*
Joseph C. Lott *(V.P.-Res. & Devel.)*
Dan L. Ranson *(V.P.-Mfg.)*
Gene Lapin *(Dir.-Pur.)*

No. of Mfg. Plants/Facilities: 1
No. of U.S. Offices: 1

Outside Service Firm(s):

Grant Thornton*(Auditors)*
53 State St.
Boston, MA 02109
Tel.: 617-723-7900

Mercantile Trust Co., N.A.*(Major Banking Relationship)*
One Mercantile Center, Mercantile Tower
St. Louis, MO 63101
Tel.: 314-425-2393

Subsidiaries:

Clayton Metals Corp. **(1)**
866 Horan Dr.
Fenton, MO 63026-2416
Tel.: 314-349-5333 (100%)
Fax: 314-349-5335
Mfr. of Metal Stampings
S.I.C.: 3469
Byron Lapin *(Pres.)*

Clayton Plastics Corp. **(1)**
866 Horan Dr.
Fenton, MO 63026-2416
Tel.: 314-349-5333 (100%)
Fax: 314-349-5335
Mfr. of Injection Molding
S.I.C.: 3089
Byron Lapin *(Pres.)*

Convenience Products, Inc. **(1)**
866 Horan Dr.
Fenton, MO 63026-2416
Tel.: 314-349-5333 (100%)
Fax: 314-349-5335
Mfr. of Consumer Energy Saving Sealant Products Sold To Retail Trade: Touch 'N Foam, Touch 'N Stick, Touch 'N Charge, Touch 'N Patch
Byron Lapin *(Pres.)*

CLAYTON-DAVIS & ASSOCIATES, INCORPORATED
8229 Maryland
Saint Louis, MO 63105
Tel.: 314-862-7800
Fax: 314-721-5171
Year Founded: 1953
Approx.Billings: $21,500,000
Emp.: 35
Advertising & Public Relations Agency
S.I.C.: 7311; 8743
Irvin Davis *(Chm. Bd. & Pres.)*
Faye Neves *(Chief Fin. Officer)*
Adrienne Davis *(Sec. & Treas.)*
Lee Gerstenhaber *(Controller, Mgr.-Office & Oper.,Telecommunications)*
Marge Futuran *(Dir.-Pub. Rels.)*
Walt Williams *(Dir.-Radio & T.V.)*
Lee Clark *(Mgr.-Publications)*
Steve Pezold *(Coord.-Direct Mail)*
Sharon Mooney *(Librarian)*

CLAYTON INDUSTRIES CO.
4213 N. Temple City Blvd.
El Monte, CA 91731
Mailing Address:
P.O. Box 5530
El Monte, CA 91734
Tel.: 818-443-9381 **CA**
Fax: 818-442-1701
Year Founded: 1935
Approx.Sls.: $24,000,000
Emp.: 300
Fiscal Year-end: 9/30/92
Export
Steamin' Demon, Clean-Master Steam Cleaners, HP-800 High Pressure Washer, Liquidemon Steam Cleaning Solvent, Kleen-Koil, Steam-Safe 20, Kermeed, Kerlite, Karbonoff, Kaystrip, Kerful, Wonderwash Compound, CSS/1200 & CD/410 Diagnostic Instrumentation Equipment
S.I.C.: 3635; 2842
William Clayton, Jr. *(Pres.)*
Allen Cluer *(Exec. V.P. & Gen. Mgr.)*
Boyd Calvin *(Chief Fin. Officer)*
Katie Gore *(Dir.-Pur.)*
Brooke W. Lammot *(Dir.-Dynamic Equip. Div.)*
George Licon *(Dir.-Personnel)*
Anthony J. Spicer *(Dir.-Sls.-Intl. Div.)*
Ruben Torres *(Dir.-Data Processing)*

Outside Service Firm(s):

KPMG Peat Marwick*(Auditors)*
725 S. Figueroa St.
Los Angeles, CA 90017
Tel.: 213-972-4000

Lillick McHose & Charles*(Legal Firm)*
707 Wilshire Blvd.
Los Angeles, CA 90017
Tel.: 213-620-9000

Bank of America NT&SA*(Major Banking Relationship)*
El Monte, CA

Divisions:

Clayton Manufacturing Div., Dynamic Equipment **(1)**
24750 Swanson Rd.
Southfield, MI 48034
Tel.: 313-354-2220
Service Steam Generators
S.I.C.: 7699
Brooke Lammot *(Dir.-Sls.)*

International Div. **(1)**
4213 N. Temple City Blvd.
El Monte, CA 91731
Tel.: 818-443-9381
Mfrs., Sls. & Service Steam Generators
S.I.C.: 3569; 7699
Anthony J. Spicer *(Dir.-Sls.)*

Non-U.S. Holding:

Maquiladora Clamaq S.A. de C.V. **(1)**
Calle 7 Sur No. 108, Ciudad Industrial
Tijuana, B.C. 22500, Mexico
Tel.: 23-41-41
Emp.: 60
Export
Mfrs. Industrial Boilers
S.I.C.: 3443

CLAYTON, WILLIAMS & SHERWOOD, INC.
800 Newport Center Dr., Ste. 400
Newport Beach, CA 92660
Tel.: 714-640-4200 **NV**
Fax: 714-640-4931
Year Founded: 1969
Assets: $500,000,000
Liabilities: $300,000,000
Net Worth: $200,000,000
Sales Range: $100-499 Million
Emp.: 400
Fiscal Year-end: 9/30/90
Real Estate Investments; Housing, Mobile Home Parks & Apartments
S.I.C.: 6798; 6515; 6513; 6514
Byron Williams *(Chm. Bd. & Sec.)*
Steven Sherwood *(Pres.)*
Ken Howell *(Chief Fin. Officer)*
Timothy T. Green *(Chief Oper. Officer)*
Dwight Frindt *(Sr. V.P.)*
Tom Kuk *(Treas.)*
Gary Walsh *(Controller)*
Jaci Whitmittmeyer *(Dir.-Investor Rels.)*
Principal(s):
Byron Williams
Steven Sherwood

No. of Mfg. Plants/Facilities: 65
No. of U.S. Offices: 4
No. of Foreign Offices: 1

Computer Systems/Hardware:
IBM

Outside Service Firm(s):

BDO Seidman*(Auditors)*
Tustin, CA

Riordan and McKinzie*(Legal Firm)*
523 W. 6th
Los Angeles, CA 90802
Tel.: 213-629-4824

Liberty National Bank & Trust Co.*(Major Banking Relationship)*
Huntington Beach, CA

Scudder, Stevens & Clark*(Pension Manager)*
333 S. Hope St., 37th Fl.
Los Angeles, CA 90071

CLEANERS HANGER CO.
3055 Reun Rd.
Palm Harbor, FL 34682
Mailing Address:
P.O. Box 9100
Palm Harbor, FL 34682
Tel.: 813-789-3000
Fax: 813-787-2317
Approx.Sls.: $50,000,000
Emp.: 500
Manufacture Wire Garment Hangers, Wire, Pulpboard Paper
S.I.C.: 3496; 2611; 3315
Richard W. Ruen, Sr. *(Chm. Bd.)*
Dennis A. Mele *(Pres.)*
John H. Ruen, Jr. *(V.P.)*
Richard W. Ruen, Jr. *(V.P.)*
Tony Palombo *(Treas.)*
Daniel P. Ruen *(Sec.)*

Outside Service Firm(s):

Arthur Andersen & Co.*(Auditors)*
Tampa, FL

Joseph, Wolf & Endean*(Legal Firm)*
Detroit, MI

N.B.D. Bank, N.A.*(Major Banking Relationship)*
611 Woodward Ave.
Detroit, MI 48226
Tel.: 313-225-1122
Fax: 313-225-3420

CLEAR SPRINGS FOODS, INC.
P.O. Box 712
Buhl, ID 83316
Tel.: 208-543-4316
Fax: 208-543-5608
Year Founded: 1966
Approx.Sls.: $25,000,000
Emp.: 380
Fiscal Year-end: 8/31/92
Import Export
Production of Rainbow Trout & Pacific Oysters
S.I.C.: 0273
Larry W. Cope *(Pres. & Chief Exec. Officer)*
Keith Quigley *(V.P. & Chief Fin. Officer)*
J. Robert Tullis *(Treas.)*
John C. Hepworth *(Sec.)*
Chris Howard *(Dir.-Mktg.)*
Stan Ayers *(Natl. Sls. Mgr.)*

CLEARING INTERNATIONAL, INC.
(Formerly Hitachi Zosen Clearing, Inc.)
6499 W. 65th St.
Chicago, IL 60638
Tel.: 312-767-8700
Fax: 708-458-9019
Year Founded: 1933
Approx.Sls.: $31,000,000
Emp.: 350
Fiscal Year-end: 3/31/91
Import
Mfr. of Metal Stamping Machines for the Automotive Industry
S.I.C.: 3542; 3599
John Comley *(Pres.)*
M.G. Kaldubowski *(V.P. & Controller)*

Outside Service Firm(s):

Price Waterhouse*(Auditors)*
200 E. Randolph
Chicago, IL 60601
Tel.: 312-565-1500

Continental Bank N. A.*(Major Banking Relationship)*
231 S. LaSalle St.
Chicago, IL 60697
Tel.: 312-828-2345
Tel.: 800-426-5754
Telex: 312-828-1783

CLEARPOINT RESEARCH CORPORATION
35 Parkwood Dr.
Hopkinton, MA 01748
Tel.: 508-435-2000
Fax: 508-435-7396
Approx.Sls.: $75,000,000
Emp.: 50
Manufacture Computer Memory Equipment
S.I.C.: 3674
Vincent Bono *(Pres.)*
Mary Savage *(Exec. V.P.)*
Robert Mulcahy *(Dir.-Mktg.)*

Outside Service Firm(s):

Price Waterhouse*(Auditors)*
160 Federal St.
Boston, MA 02110
Tel.: 617-439-3308
Fax: 617-439-3308

CLEMCO INDUSTRIES
One Cable Car Dr.
Washington, MO 63090
Tel.: 314-239-0300
Fax: 314-239-0788
Import Export
Manufacture Specialized Equipment
S.I.C.: 3589; 3599
Mark Cleary *(Pres.)*
Arnie Sallaberry *(V.P. & Gen. Mgr.)*
Scott Blackburn *(V.P.-Sls.)*
John Douglas *(Chief Fin. Officer)*

Subsidiaries:

Aerolyte Systems **(1)**
One Cable Car Dr.
Washington, MO 63090
Tel.: 314-239-0300
Tad Tassone *(Mgr.-Mktg.)*

Aerolyte Systems **(1)**
1657 Rollins Rd.
Burlingame, CA 94010
Tel.: 415-570-0217
Mfr. of Plastic Equip.
S.I.C.: 3559
Tad Tassone *(Mktg. Mgr.)*

Clemco Industries Corp. **(1)**
One Cable Car Dr.
Washington, MO 63090
Tel.: 314-239-0300
Telex: 184909
Fax: 314-239-0788
Approx.Sls.: $26,000,000
Emp.: 125
Import Export
Mfr. of a Full Range of Blast Machines & Specialized Equipment
S.I.C.: 3589; 3599
Mark Cleary *(Pres.)*
F. Scott Blackburn *(V.P.-Sls.)*
Patti Roman *(V.P.-Mktg.)*
Arnie Sallaberry *(V.P. & Gen. Mgr.)*
Peter Blackmur *(Mgr.-Export)*
Jed C. Heastrup *(Mgr.-Zero Product Sls.)*

CLEMENS MARKETS INC.
616 E. Main St.
Lansdale, PA 19446
Tel.: 215-855-9960 **PA**
Fax: 215-855-0237
Year Founded: 1939
Sales Range: $100-499 Million
Emp.: 1,700
Supermarkets
S.I.C.: 5411
Jack S. Clemens *(Pres. & Chief Exec. Officer)*
Alfred L. Krout *(V.P.-Human Resources)*
Thomas Roesener *(V.P.-Store Opers.)*
David Friesen *(Treas. & Asst. Sec.)*
Tom Hughes *(Dir.-Adv.)*
Ronald Hunsberger *(Dir.-Mktg.)*

No. of Mfg. Plants/Facilities: 10

Computer Systems/Hardware:
IBM 3600

Outside Service Firm(s):

Price Waterhouse*(Auditors)*
30 S. 17th St.
Philadelphia, PA 19103
Tel.: 215-665-9500

Pearlstine/Salkin, Associates*(Legal Firm)*
Lansdale, PA

Union National Bank*(Major Banking Relationship)*
10 W. Broad St.
Souderton, PA
Tel.: 215-721-2455

CLEMENTS FOODS CO.
6601 N. Harvey
Oklahoma City, OK 73116
Mailing Address:
P.O. Box 14538
Oklahoma City, OK 73113
Tel.: 405-842-3308
Tel.: 800-654-8355 **OK**
Fax: 405-843-6894
Assets: $12,600,000
Liabilities: $2,786,000
Net Worth: $9,814,000
Approx.Sls.: $40,000,000
Emp.: 125
Fiscal Year-end: 2/27/91
Import Export
Manufacture of Jellies, Preserves, Mayonnaise, Salad Dressing, Syrups, Mustard, Vinegar, Peanut Butter
S.I.C.: 2033; 2035; 2099
Richard H. Clements *(Chm. Bd., Pres. , & Chief Fin. Officer)*
Edward B. Clements *(V.P. & Chief Exec. Officer)*
Robert H. Clements *(V.P.)*
Gunner Anderson *(Controller & Asst. Sec.)*
Edward Clements *(Mgr.-Sls.)*
Principal(s):
Richard H. Clements
Edward B. Clements
Robert H. Clements
Mary L. Clements

No. of Mfg. Plants/Facilities: 2

Computer Systems/Hardware:
IBM

Outside Service Firm(s):

Cole-Reed*(Auditors)*
Oklahoma City, OK
Fax: 415-349-5207

Monnet, Hayes, Bullis, Thompson & Edwards*(Legal Firm)*
Oklahoma City, OK

Subsidiaries:

American Nut Co. **(1)**
Lewisville, TX
Tel.: 214-436-4596
Peanut Butter Manufacturer
S.I.C.: 2099
Edward B. Clements *(V.P.)*

Clements Nut Co. **(1)**
P.O. Box 247, 614 E. Main St.
Lewisville, TX 75067
Tel.: 214-436-4596
Export
Mfr. Peanut Butter
S.I.C.: 2099
Edward B. Clements *(V.P.)*

Clements Vinegar Company **(1)**
1734 N.W. 6th St.
Oklahoma City, OK 73106
Tel.: 405-232-7068 (100%)
Import Export
Mfr. Vinegar
S.I.C.: 2099
Wilson Mankins *(Mgr.)*

CLEVELAND BROTHERS EQUIPMENT CO.
5300 Paxton St.
Harrisburg, PA 17105
Mailing Address:
P.O. Box 2535,
Harrisburg, PA 17105
Tel.: 717-564-2121
Fax: 717-564-6931
Approx.Sls.: $45,000,000
Emp.: 200
Fiscal Year-end: 10/31/91
Caterpillar Tractor Dealer for Central Pennsylvania
S.I.C.: 5012; 5083
Jay W. Cleveland *(Pres. & Treas.)*
Michael A. Ryan *(Chief Fin. Officer & V.P.)*
William T. Kirchhoff *(Exec. V.P.)*
Gabe Plebani *(Controller)*

Computer Systems/Hardware:
Burroughs

Outside Service Firm(s):

KPMG Peat Marwick*(Auditors)*
P.O. Box 1190, 225 Market St., Ste. 300
Harrisburg, PA 17108-1190
Tel.: 717-238-7131

McNee's, Wallace, & Nurick*(Legal Firm)*
100 Pine St.
Harrisburg, PA 17108-1166

Dauphin Deposit Bank & Trust Co.*(Major Banking Relationship)*
213 Market St.
Harrisburg, PA 17101

Hamilton Bank*(Major Banking Relationship)*
Harrisburg, PA

CLEVELAND CHAIR COMPANY
370 Ninth St. S.E.
Cleveland, TN 37311
Mailing Address:
P.O. Box 159
Cleveland, TN 37311
Tel.: 615-476-8544
Fax: 615-476-8544, Ext. 241
Emp.: 450
Manufacture Catnapper Reclining Chairs
S.I.C.: 2511; 2514
W. Ronald Jackson *(Chm. Bd. & Pres.)*
Roger Jackson *(V.P.)*
Leo Matheny *(V.P.)*
Tony Bartolo *(Mgr.-Adv.)*

Computer Systems/Hardware:
IBM System 38

Outside Service Firm(s):

Union Trust*(Major Banking Relationship)*
Danbury, CT

CLEVELAND GROUP, INC.
2690 Cumberland Pkwy., Ste. 200
Atlanta, GA 30339
Tel.: 404-436-0879 **GA**
Fax: 404-434-4583
Year Founded: 1925
Assets: $39,206,902
Liabilities: $28,625,713
Net Worth: $10,581,189
Sales Range: $100-499 Million
Emp.: 1,450
Import Export
Electrical, Mechanical, Instrumentation Construction; Sales & Service; General Construction & Construction Management
S.I.C.: 1731; 1629; 1711; 5063; 7694; 8741
L. W. Cleveland, Sr. *(Chm. Emeritus)*
James R. Cleveland, Sr. *(Chm. Bd., Pres. & Chief Exec. Officer)*
Louie W. Cleveland, Jr. *(V.P.)*
James R. Cleveland, Jr. *(V.P.)*
Vann Cleveland *(Sec.)*
Fred A. Harkleroad *(Treas., Controller & Chief Fin. Officer)*
George Miller *(Data Processing Dir.)*
Principal(s):
L. W. Cleveland, Sr.
James R. Cleveland, Sr.
Louie W. Cleveland, Jr.
Vann Cleveland

No. of U.S. Offices: 7

Computer Systems/Hardware:
MAI Basic 4 Model 8030

Outside Service Firm(s):

Ross Lane & Company*(Auditors)*
Atlanta, GA

Robinson Humphrey Company, Inc.*(Investment Banker)*
3333 Peachtree Rd., N.E.
Atlanta, GA 30326
Tel.: 404-266-6000

Liberty Mutual*(Commercial Insurance Carrier)*
Atlanta, GA

Liberty Mutual*(Group Insurer)*
Atlanta, GA

Shapiro, Fussell & Genberg*(Legal Firm)*
Atlanta, GA

First Wachovia Bank & Trust Co.*(Major Banking Relationship)*
2 Peachtree St., NW
Atlanta, GA 30383
Tel.: 404-332-4000

Subsidiaries:

Aviation Constructors, Inc. **(1)**
2690 Cumberland Pkwy., Suite 200
Atlanta, GA 30339
Tel.: 404-434-0800
Emp.: 50
General Construction & Construction Management
S.I.C.: 1629
Fred A. Harkleroad *(Chief Exec. Officer)*
Terry A. Stratton *(Pres.)*

Cleveland Consolidated Inc. **(1)**
1281 Fulton Industrial Blvd. NW
Atlanta, GA 30336
Tel.: 404-696-4550
Plumbing, Heating & Air Conditioning Installation
S.I.C.: 1711; 1731
James R. Cleveland, Jr. *(Pres.)*

Cleveland Electric Co. **(1)**
3980 Martin Luther King Dr.
Atlanta, GA 30336
Tel.: 404-696-4550
Sales & Repair Electric Motors & Apparatus
S.I.C.: 7694; 5063
James R. Cleveland, Jr. *(Pres.)*

Cleveland Electric Company of Arkansas **(1)**
3401 West 65th St.
Little Rock, AR 72209
Tel.: 501-565-7561
Frank Johnson *(V.P.)*

CLEVELAND MACHINE CONTROLS
7550 Hub Pkwy.
Cleveland, OH 44125
Tel.: 216-524-8800
Approx.Sls.: $40,000,000
Emp.: 250
Mfr. of Controls for Adjustable Speed Drives & Web Tension Control Equipment; Numerical Controls; Measuring Tools & Machines
S.I.C.: 3625; 3545; 3566
William M. Jones *(Chm. Bd.)*
Michael E. Behary *(Pres.)*
Robert P. Bajko *(V.P.-Sls. & Mktg.)*
Robert G. Klimo *(V.P.-Engrng.)*
J.M. Lekan *(Comptroller)*
Donald R. Tomko *(Mgr.-Mktg.)*
Darla S. Wilk *(Mgr.-Pur.)*

CLEVELAND WRECKING COMPANY
2833 Leonia Blvd.
Los Angeles, CA 90058
Tel.: 213-269-0633
Fax: 213-581-3358
Year Founded: 1909
Approx.Sls.: $73,000,000
Emp.: 1,500
Demolition of Buildings & Other Structures
S.I.C.: 1795
Marvin H. Rose *(Chm. Bd.)*
W.M. Fenning *(Pres.)*
Harvey S. Stern *(Exec. V.P.)*
Al McHugh *(Gen. Mgr.)*
Gordon J. Webster *(Sec. & Treas.)*

Outside Service Firm(s):

BDO Seidman*(Auditors)*
1900 Avenue of the Stars, 11th Fl.
Los Angeles, CA 90067-6008
Tel.: 310-557-0300

Bank of America NT&SA*(Major Banking Relationship)*
555 So. Flower St., 5th Fl.
Los Angeles, CA 90071
Tel.: 213-228-3526
Fax: 213-228-4062

CLIGGOT PUBLISHING
55 Holly Hill Lane
Greenwich, CT 06830
Tel.: 203-661-0600
Fax: 203-661-8163
Year Founded: 1970
Approx.Sls.: $12,000,000
Emp.: 55
Medical Magazine Publishing
S.I.C.: 2721
Richard Cliggot *(Pres.)*
Ronald E. March *(Exec. V.P. & Chief Oper. Officer)*
Jonathan L. Bigelow *(V.P.)*
Judith S. Frisch *(V.P.)*
Kenneth A. Sylvia *(V.P.)*
Kenneth D. Watkins *(V.P.)*

THE CLIMATIC CORP.
2270 LeGrand Rd.
Columbia, SC 29223
Mailing Address:
P.O. Box 25189
Columbia, SC 29224
Tel.: 803-736-7770 **SC**
Fax: 803-736-7841
Year Founded: 1959
Approx.Sls.: $90,000,000
Emp.: 150
Wholesale Distributors of Microwave Ovens; Wholesale Televisions, Air Conditioners & Heaters
S.I.C.: 3631; 5064; 5075
John H. Bailey *(Chm. Bd., Pres., Chief Exec. & Chief Oper. Officer)*
Richard F. Smith *(Exec. V.P.)*
Cindee Bailey *(V.P.-Human Resources)*
John L. Bouknight *(V.P.-Assets)*
Bob Harden *(V.P. & Gen. Mgr.-S. Central Div.)*
Tom Huntington *(V.P.-Sls.)*
Billy Hagen *(Dir.-Data Processing & Software Sls.)*
Principal(s):
John H. Bailey

No. of Mfg. Plants/Facilities: 13
No. of U.S. Offices: 13

Computer Systems/Hardware:
IBM

Outside Service Firm(s):

Arthur Andersen & Co.*(Auditors)*
Columbia, SC

American States*(Commercial Insurance Carrier)*
Columbia, SC

American States Insurance Co.*(Commercial Insurance Carrier)*
500 N. Meridian St.
Indianapolis, IN 46204-1275
Tel.: 317-262-6262
Fax: 317-262-6290

General Administrators*(Group Insurer)*
Greenville, SC

SCN*(Investment Banker)*
Columbia, SC

Berry-Dunbar*(Legal Firm)*
Columbia, SC

South Carolina National Bank*(Major Banking Relationship)*
700 Main St.
Columbia, SC 29201

SCN*(Pension Manager)*
Columbia, SC

Subsidiary:

The Climatic Corporation **(1)**
3700 W. 65th St.
Little Rock, AR 72209
Tel.: 501-562-7600
Robert Harden *(V.P. & Gen. Mgr.)*

CLINE, DAVIS & MANN, INC.
450 Lexington Ave.
New York, NY 10022
Tel.: 212-907-4300
Year Founded: 1984
Approx.Billings: $93,880,000
Emp.: 76
Healthcare
Morgan E. Cline *(Chm. Bd. & Pres.)*
Fredric I. Mann *(Exec. V.P., Sec. & Creative Dir.)*
Clyde P. Davis *(Exec. V.P., Treas. & Creative Dir.)*
Carol Di Santo *(Sr. V.P., Dir. Proworx)*
Stacy Alabardo *(Network & Applications Mgr.)*
Anne Auld *(Chief Editor)*
Awilda Pinillos *(Sr. Project Dir.-Proworx Div.)*
Joe Magnemi *(Controller)*

THE CLINIPAD CORPORATION
66 High St.
Guilford, CT 06437
Mailing Address:
P.O. Box 387
Guilford, CT 06437
Tel.: 203-453-6543
Tel.: 800-243-6548 NY
Fax: 203-453-8347
Year Founded: 1970
Approx.Sls.: $30,000,000
Emp.: 400
Export
Packaging of Towelettes, Prep Pads, Swab Sticks & Antibiotics
S.I.C.: 2834; 2676; 3842; 3800
David A. Greenberg *(Pres.)*
Stephen N. Young *(Sr. V.P.)*
Principal(s):
David A. Greenberg

No. of Mfg. Plants/Facilities: 3

Outside Service Firm(s):

Deloitte & Touche*(Auditors)*
New Haven, CT

Connecticut National Bank*(Major Banking Relationship)*
New Haven, CT

Clinton Lumber Co.
(See Elk Supply Company Listing)

CLIPPER EXXPRESS CO.
15700 W. 103rd St.
Lemont, IL 60439
Tel.: 708-739-0700
Fax: 708-739-0097
Year Founded: 1938
Approx.Sls.: $46,500,000
Emp.: 213
Freight Forwarder
S.I.C.: 4731
Evelyn Chambers *(Chm. Bd.)*
Andy Sze *(Pres. & Chief Exec. Officer)*
Merle Chambers *(Chm. of the Exec. Committee)*
Gary Colbert *(V.P.-Sls.)*
Robert Wallace *(V.P.-Fin.)*
Vincent Battaglia *(Dir.-Data Processing)*
Principal(s):
Merle Chambers

No. of U.S. Offices: 31

Computer Systems/Hardware:
IBM System A 5400

Outside Service Firm(s):

KPMG Peat Marwick*(Auditors)*
Peat Marwick Plaza, 303 E. Wacker Dr.
Chicago, IL 60601
Tel.: 312-938-1000

Continental Bank N. A.*(Major Banking Relationship)*
231 S. LaSalle St.
Chicago, IL 60697
Tel.: 312-828-2345
Tel.: 800-426-5754
Telex: 312-828-1783

CLOUD CORPORATION
424 Howard Ave.
Des Plaines, IL 60018
Tel.: 708-390-9410 DE
Fax: 708-390-6170
Approx.Sls.: $16,000,000
Emp.: 180
Packaging & Labeling Services; Packaging Machinery
S.I.C.: 7389; 3565
Lyle Douglas Robison *(Pres.)*
Ted Husak *(V.P.-Sls.)*
Donn A. Hartman *(V.P.-Engrng.)*
Roy W. Wright *(Treas.)*
Robert W. Wright *(Sec.)*

Outside Service Firm(s):

Benjamin & Rees Ltd.*(Auditors)*
Chicago, IL

American National Bank*(Major Banking Relationship)*
33 North LaSalle St.
Chicago, IL 60690
Tel.: 312-661-6967

Plant:

Cloud Corporation **(1)**
7455 N. St. Louis Ave.
Skokie, IL 60076
Tel.: 708-679-4322
Charles E. Cloud *(Pres.)*

CLOVER FINANCIAL CORPORATION
23 W. Park Ave.
Merchantville, NJ 08109
Tel.: 609-662-1116
Fax: 609-662-6303
Sales Range: $20-39 Million
Emp.: 840
Fiscal Year-end: 11/30/88
Real Estate Investment Firm
S.I.C.: 6552; 6798
Donald Love *(Pres.)*
Robert L. Hogan *(V.P.)*
Steve Zalkind *(V.P.)*
Principal(s):
Donald Love
Robert L. Hogan
Steve Zalkind

Outside Service Firm(s):

Sherman, Silverstein, Kohl, Rose & Podolsky*(Legal Firm)*
Pennsauken, NJ

CLOVERDALE EQUIPMENT CO.
13133 Cloverdale
Oak Park, MI 48237
Tel.: 313-399-6600 MI
Fax: 313-399-7730
Year Founded: 1963
Assets: $13,276,000
Liabilities: $10,851,000
Net Worth: $2,425,000
Approx.Sls.: $13,500,000
Emp.: 70
Fiscal Year-end: 5/31/92
Sales & Rental of Construction & Industrial Equipment, Parts & Service
S.I.C.: 5082; 7359
Ben C. Maibach, Jr. *(Chm. Bd.)*
Thomas A. Moilanen *(Pres. & Chief Exec. Officer)*
John Buchan *(Exec. V.P.)*
Scott D. Packard *(Sec. & Treas.)*
Cynthia Gioia *(Telecommunications)*
Principal(s):
Thomas A. Moilanen
John Buchan

Computer Systems/Hardware:
Hewlett Packard

Outside Service Firm(s):

Doeren & Mayhew*(Auditors)*
Troy, MI

Blue Cross & Blue Shield of Michigan*(Group Insurer)*
Detroit, MI

Phoenix Mutual Life Insurance Co.*(Group Insurer)*
Hartford, CT

Michigan Mutual Insurance Co.*(Group Insurer)*
Detroit, MI

Stark, Reagan & Finnerty*(Legal Firm)*
Troy, MI
Tel.: 313-641-3955

Manufacturers National Bank N.A.*(Major Banking Relationship)*
38th Fl., 100 Renaissance Center
Detroit, MI 48243
Tel.: 313-222-4227

Subsidiary:

Hasper Equipment Co. **(1)**
3662 Airline Rd.
Muskegon, MI 49444
Tel.: 616-739-9525
Fax: 616-733-4601
S.I.C.: 5082; 7359
Mark Carr *(V.P. & Gen. Mgr.)*

CLOVERHILL BAKERY
2020 N. Parkside Ave.
Chicago, IL 60639
Tel.: 312-745-9800 IL
Fax: 312-745-1647
Year Founded: 1961
Approx.Sls.: $10,000,000
Emp.: 46
Mfr. of Frozen Bakery Products, Except Bread; Cakes, Pies & Pasteries
S.I.C.: 2053; 2051
William Gee, III *(Pres.)*
Robert Gee *(V.P.-Sls.)*
William A. Gee, IV *(V.P.-Plant Opers.)*
Edward Gee *(Treas. & Sec.)*

Outside Service Firm(s):

Frank L. Sassetti & Co.*(Auditors)*
Chicago, IL

CLUB CORPORATION INTERNATIONAL
3030 LBJ Freeway, Ste. 500
Dallas, TX 75234
Mailing Address:
P.O. Box 819012
Dallas, TX 75381
Tel.: 214-243-6191 NV
Fax: 214-888-7721
Year Founded: 1957
Assets: $2,289,305,000
Liabilities: $1,923,945,000
Net Worth: $365,360,000
Approx.Sls.: $700,311,000
Emp.: 16,000
Fiscal Year-end: 12/25/91
Owns & Operates Sports Clubs: Pinehurst Hotel & Country Club, Pinehurst, NC; Firestone Country Club, Akron, OH; Inverrary Country Club, Ft. Lauderdale, FL; Barton Creek Resort, Austin, TX
S.I.C.: 7997
Corporate Giving Program: United Way
Employee Matching Gifts Program: United Way
Robert H. Dedman, Sr. *(Chm. Bd. & Chief Exec. Officer)*
James E. Maser *(Vice Chm. Bd.)*
Robert H. Dedman, Jr. *(Pres. & Chief Oper. Officer)*
John H. Gray *(Exec. V.P. & Chief Admin. Officer)*
Terry Taylor *(Sr. V.P., Gen. Counsel & Sec.)*
Albert Chew *(Sr. V.P.-Human Resources)*
James P. McCoy, Jr. *(Chief Fin. Officer)*
Dan Barth *(Dir.-MIS)*
Jerry Dickenson *(Dir.-Quality Control)*
Principal(s):
Robert H. Dedman, Sr.
Robert H. Dedman, Jr.
Nancy M. Dedman
Patricia Dedman Dietz

No. of Mfg. Plants/Facilities: 230
No. of U.S. Offices: 5

Computer Systems/Hardware:
IBM 4341

Outside Service Firm(s):

KPMG Peat Marwick*(Auditors)*
1601 Elm St., Ste. 1600
Dallas, TX 75201
Tel.: 214-754-2000
Fax: 214-754-2297

Page & Addison*(Legal Firm)*
Dallas, TX

Subsidiaries:

Club Corporation Of America **(1)**
3030 LBJ Freeway, Ste. 500
Dallas, TX 75234
Tel.: 214-243-6191
Holding Company for Approximately 175 Private Clubs
S.I.C.: 6719
Robert Dedman, Jr. *(Chm. Bd.)*
Robert H. Johnson *(Chief Oper. Officer)*
Terry Taylor *(Gen. Counsel, Sec. & Dir.)*

Club Corp Realty **(1)**
3030 LBJ Freeway, Ste. 700
Dallas, TX 75234
Tel.: 214-243-6191
David L. Leinniger *(Chm. Bd. & Chief Exec. Officer)*

Club Resorts, Inc. **(1)**
3030 LBJ Freeway, Ste. 700
Dallas, TX 75234
Tel.: 214-243-6191
Operates Resorts
S.I.C.: 7011
Jerry W. Dickenson *(Chm. Bd. & Chief Exec. Officer)*
Mike Dempsey *(Chief Fin. Officer)*
Al Anderson *(Dir.)*

THE COAKLEY HEAGERTY COMPANIES, LTD.
1155 N. First St., Ste. 201
San Jose, CA 95112
Tel.: 408-275-9400
Fax: 408-995-0600
Year Founded: 1961
Approx.Billings: $11,900,254
Emp.: 17
Financial & Land Development
David A. Heagerty *(Chm. Bd. & Chief Exec. Officer)*
John D. Heagerty *(Pres.)*
Susann Rivera *(V.P.)*
Mark Klein *(Pub. Rels. News Dir.)*
Jan Silverstein *(Accounting)*
Terry Chamberlain *(Acct. Asst.)*

COAKLEY & WILLIAMS INC.
7500 Greenway Center Dr.
Greenbelt, MD 20770
Tel.: 301-345-9730
Fax: 301-982-4574
Year Founded: 1961
Assets: $30,000,000
Net Worth: $30,000,000
Approx.Sls.: $50,000,000
Emp.: 1,100
Fiscal Year-end: 12/31/91
General Contractor For Commercial Building; Real Estate Agents
S.I.C.: 1542; 6531
Corporate Giving Program: To the Columbia Lighthouse for the Blind, Approximately $20-30,000 per Year
Neil T. Coakley *(Chm. Bd., Sec. & Treas.)*
Fred G. Williams, Jr. *(Pres.)*
Terrance Coakley *(Exec. V.P.)*
Gary Williams *(Exec. V.P.)*
Brian Coakley *(V.P.)*

COAST GRAIN COMPANY, INC.
5355 E. Airport Dr.
Ontario, CA 91761
Tel.: 909-983-9766
Fax: 909-983-3822
Year Founded: 1938
Emp.: 232
Wholesale Feed & Grain
S.I.C.: 5153
Marsha Weinberg *(Chm. Bd.)*
Rhona Weinberg *(Pres.)*

Ray Moline *(Gen. Mgr.)*

Outside Service Firm(s):

Frazer & Torbet*(Auditors)*
City of Industry, CA

Demetriau Del Guercio & Lovejoy*(Legal Firm)*
Los Angeles, CA

Security Pacific National Bank*(Major Banking Relationship)*
Long Beach, CA

COAST MANUFACTURING COMPANY
200 Corporate Blvd.
Yonkers, NY 10701
Tel.: 914-376-1500
Fax: 914-376-0400
Approx.Sls.: $25,000,000
Emp.: 200
Mfr. of Photographic, Audio & Video Cases & Accessories
S.I.C.: 3161
Joseph Kappel *(Chm. Bd.)*
William E. Mooar *(Pres.)*
Richard Goldberg *(Exec. V.P.)*

Outside Service Firm(s):

Deloitte & Touche*(Auditors)*
50 Fountain Plaza
Buffalo, NY 14202
Tel.: 716-843-7200

Luppes, Kaminsky, Silverstein, Porter, Mathias & Wexler*(Legal Firm)*
Buffalo, NY

The Bank of New York*(Major Banking Relationship)*
One Wall Street
New York, NY 10286
Tel.: 212-635-6805
Fax: 212-635-3201

COAST PACKING COMPANY
3275 E. Vernon Ave.
Vernon, CA 90058
Tel.: 213-587-8141
Fax: 213-587-9199
Year Founded: 1922
Approx.Sls.: $23,000,000
Emp.: 62
Manufacture Vegetable Oils & Animal Fats, Baking & Frying Shortening Products
S.I.C.: 2076; 2077; 2079
Mel A. Gustafson *(Pres.)*
Ronald R. Gustafson *(Chief Oper. Officer)*
William F. Roth *(V.P.)*
Adele R. Gustafson *(Asst. Sec.)*

Outside Service Firm(s):

Nathan Fligsten & Company*(Auditors)*
Los Angeles, CA

Albert Dorn*(Legal Firm)*
Los Angeles, CA

Tokai Bank of California*(Major Banking Relationship)*
Los Angeles, CA

COAST TO COAST STORES, INC.
501 S. Cherry St.
Denver, CO 80222
Mailing Address:
P.O. Box 5820,
Denver, CO 80222
Tel.: 303-377-8400
Approx.Sls.: $354,361,000
Emp.: 950
Fiscal Year-end: 1/31/91
Holding Company
S.I.C.: 6719
Ken Hoffman *(Chief Exec. Officer)*
Ken Durrett *(Chief Fin. Officer)*
David Bowman *(V.P. & Gen. Counsel)*
Rollie Carlson *(V.P.-Mktg.)*
Charles Green *(V.P.-Data Processing)*

Computer Systems/Hardware:
IBM 4341

COASTAL DAIRY PRODUCTS, INC.
400 S. Douglas St.
Wilson, NC 27894
Tel.: 919-243-6161
Year Founded: 1945
Approx.Sls.: $11,000,000
Emp.: 125
Mfr. Ice Cream, Frozen Desserts & Dairy Products
S.I.C.: 2024
Richard J. Barnes *(Pres.)*
Thomas H. Barnes *(V.P.-Opers.)*
Thomas E. Beaman *(Controller)*
Bill Banker *(Product Mgr.)*
C.L. Boykin *(Personnel Mgr.)*
Edward Castle *(Sls. Mgr.)*
Richard A. McKellar *(Plant Mgr.)*

COASTAL LUMBER COMPANY
Green St. Extension
Weldon, NC 27890
Mailing Address:
P.O. Box 829
Weldon, NC 27890
Tel.: 919-536-4211
Tel.: 800-735-2727 **NC**
Fax: 919-536-3102
Year Founded: 1937
Approx.Sls.: $180,000,000
Emp.: 1,300
Fiscal Year-end: 10/ 3/90
Export
Hardwood Lumber, Pine Lumber & Plywood Treated Wood Products
S.I.C.: 2421; 2499
Paul B. Barringer, II *(Pres. & Chief Exec. Officer)*
S.H. Conger *(Exec. V.P.)*
Barry L. Cook *(V.P.-Opers.)*
Ronald F. Seay *(V.P. & Controller)*
L.C. Shipley *(V.P.-Mktg.)*

Outside Service Firm(s):

Davis & Company*(Auditors)*
Columbia, SC

United Virginia Bank*(Major Banking Relationship)*
Richmond, VA

Branch:

Coastal Lumber Company **(1)**
P.O. Box 237
Hazelton, WV 26535
Tel.: 304-379-7377
Manufacturer of Hardwood Dimension Products
S.I.C.: 2426
Greg Lottes *(Gen. Mgr.)*

Division:

Kemp Furniture Co. **(1)**
700 W. Elm St.
Goldsboro, NC 27530
Tel.: 919-580-0077
Furniture-Dimension Plant
S.I.C.: 5712
Sam Moss *(Gen. Mgr.)*

COASTAL WHOLESALE, INC.
500 E. Grainger
Kinston, NC 28503
Mailing Address:
P.O. Box 1375
Kinston, NC 28501
Tel.: 919-523-0101 **NC**
Fax: 919-523-7333
Assets: $8,134,445
Liabilities: $5,895,494
Net Worth: $2,238,951
Approx.Sls.: $130,000,000
Emp.: 150
Fiscal Year-end: 12/31/89
Wholesale Food Distributor; Manufacture Dairy Products
S.I.C.: 5141; 2026; 2022; 2024
Merle W. Edwards, Sr. *(Chm. Bd.)*
T.L. Edwards *(Chief Exec. Officer)*
Merle W. Edwards, Jr. *(Pres.)*
William R. Hawkins *(Controller)*
Debbie Chewning *(Dir.-Pur.)*
Rhonda S. Faulkner *(Dir.-Data Processing)*

COAT, APRON & LINEN SUPPLY
(Formerly A & P Apron & Linen Supply)
40 W. 170th St.
Bronx, NY 10452
Tel.: 718-681-2966 **NY**
Fax: 718-293-9622
Year Founded: 1966
Approx.Sls.: $18,000,000
Emp.: 325
Linen Supply
S.I.C.: 7213
Bernard Potack *(Chm. Bd.)*
Michael R. Potack *(Pres.)*
Martin P. Miner *(Sec.)*
Harvey Rosenberg *(Controller)*

THE COATES AGENCY
320 S.W. Oak, Ste. 300
Portland, OR 97204
Tel.: 503-241-1124
Year Founded: 1983
Approx.Billings: $10,000,000
Emp.: 17
Jean Pettijohn Coates *(Pres., Treas. & Creative Dir.)*
Michael R. Coates *(Exec. V.P., Sec. & Dir. Client Services)*
Susan Lucke *(Pub. Rels. Dir.)*

COBLE DAIRY PRODUCTS CO-OP
707 N. Main St.
Lexington, NC
Tel.: 704-249-9931 **NC**
Fax: 704-249-3116
Year Founded: 1955
Approx.Sls.: $80,000,000
Emp.: 680
Fluid Milk; Ice Cream & Frozen Deserts
S.I.C.: 2026; 2024
William V. Davis *(Pres.)*
Paul G. Parrish *(Chief Exec. Officer & Exec. V.P.)*
Jerry Smith *(Chief Fin. Officer & Controller)*
Roy D. Long *(V.P.)*
Kenneth A. Gray *(V.P.)*
Jimmie B. Sink *(Treas.)*
Charlotte Cook *(Sec.)*
Rusty Eaker *(Sec.)*
Ray Binkley *(Dir.-Mfg.)*
Jim Gandy *(Dir.-Sls.)*
Mikrel Sherman *(Dir.-Pur.)*

No. of U.S. Offices: 9

Outside Service Firm(s):

Todd, Coleman & Levangie*(Auditors)*
Winter Park, FL

Lexington State Bank*(Major Banking Relationship)*
Lexington, NC

COCA-COLA BOTTLING CO. OF CHICAGO
7400 N. Oak Park Ave.
Niles, IL 60714
Tel.: 708-647-0200
Fax: 708-647-7104
Approx.Sls.: $450,000,000
Emp.: 1,800
Soft Drinks
S.I.C.: 2086
Marvin J. Herb *(Chm. Bd. & Chief Exec. Officer)*
William F. O'Rourke *(Pres.)*
William A. Fullerton *(V.P. & Treas.)*
R. Palo *(V.P.-Personnel)*
Jerome Moza *(Controller)*

Computer Systems/Hardware:
IBM System 38

Outside Service Firm(s):

Ernst & Young*(Auditors)*
233 S. Wacker Dr.
Chicago, IL 60606
Tel.: 312-368-1800
Fax: 312-645-3095

First National Bank of Chicago*(Major Banking Relationship)*
One First National Plaza
Chicago, IL 60670
Tel.: 312-732-9781
Tel.: 312-732-4050
Fax: 312-732-4840
Fax: 312-732-3055

COCA-COLA BOTTLING CO. OF THE SOUTHWEST
#1 Coca Cola Place
San Antonio, TX 78219
Mailing Address:
P.O. Box 58
San Antonio, TX 78291
Tel.: 210-225-2601 **DE**
Fax: 210-229-0437
Year Founded: 1926
Approx.Sls.: $100,000,000
Emp.: 900
Soft Drink Bottler
S.I.C.: 2086
Edmund Hoffman *(Chm. Bd.)*
Toby Summers *(Pres. & Chief Oper. Officer)*
David Green *(Chief Fin. Officer & Dir.-Investor Rels.)*
Richard Smith *(Dir.-Personnel)*
Principal(s):
Texas Bottling Group

No. of Mfg. Plants/Facilities: 1
No. of U.S. Offices: 1

Computer Systems/Hardware:
Hewlett-Packard

Outside Service Firm(s):

Arthur Andersen & Co.*(Auditors)*
300 Convent St.
San Antonio, TX 78205
Tel.: 210-223-6511

Brock & Kelfer*(Legal Firm)*
San Antonio, TX

COCA COLA BOTTLING CO. UNITED, INC.
4600 East Lake Blvd.
Birmingham, AL 35217
Mailing Address:
P.O. Box 2006
Birmingham, AL 35201
Tel.: 205-841-2653 **AL**
Fax: 205-849-4679
Year Founded: 1902
Assets: $294,000,000
Liabilities: $229,000,000
Net Worth: $65,000,000
Approx.Sls.: $302,000,000
Emp.: 2,200
Fiscal Year-end: 12/31/91
Soft Drink Bottlers
S.I.C.: 3221; 5149
Crawford Johnson, III *(Chm. Bd.)*
Claude B. Nielsen *(Pres. & Chief Exec. Officer)*
Elbert N. Mullis, Jr. *(Exec. V.P. & Chief Admin. & Fin. Officer)*
Robert B. Lovell *(V.P.-Mktg. & Adv.)*
Fred E. Sims *(V.P.-Information Systems & Chief Info. Officer)*
Stevan D. Williams *(Treas. & Controller)*
Debra W. Myles *(Human Resources)*
Dixie A. Bauder *(Sec.)*

No. of Mfg. Plants/Facilities: 4
No. of U.S. Offices: 17

Coca Cola Bottling Co. United, Inc.—(Continued)

Computer Systems/Hardware:
IBM

Outside Service Firm(s):

KPMG Peat Marwick*(Auditors)*
1200 Financial Center
Birmingham, AL 35203
Tel.: 205-324-2495

Aetna Life & Casualty*(Group Insurer)*
Birmingham, AL

Bradley, Arant, Rose & White*(Legal Firm)*
1400 Park Place Tower
Birmingham, AL 35203
Tel.: 205-521-8000

American National Bank & Trust Company of Chattanooga*(Major Banking Relationship)*
736 Market St.
Chattanooga, TN 37402
Tel.: 615-757-3011

Subsidiary:

ABI Food Services, Inc. **(1)**
4600 East Lake Blvd.
Birmingham, AL 35217
Tel.: 205-841-2653
Emp.: 500
Food Service-Vending
S.I.C.: 5963
Frank A. Feist *(Pres.)*

COCA-COLA BOTTLING COMPANY OF ELIZABETHTOWN
1201 N. Dixie
Elizabethtown, KY 42701
Mailing Address:
P.O. Box 647
Elizabethtown, KY 42702-0647
Tel.: 502-737-4000 **KY**
Fax: 502-737-6665
Year Founded: 1920
Approx.Sls.: $25,000,000
Emp.: 155
Soft Drink Bottler
S.I.C.: 2086
William B. Schmidt *(Chm. Bd., Pres. & Treas.)*
Pam B. Just *(V.P. & Controller)*
Janet Schmidt *(V.P.)*
Larry Schmidt *(V.P.-Opers.)*

Outside Service Firm(s):

James A. Matthews & Co.*(Auditors)*
Memphis, TN

Citizens Fidelity Bank & Trust Co.*(Major Banking Relationship)*
500 W. Jefferson
Louisville, KY 40202
Tel.: 502-581-3389

GEORGE W. COCHRAN CO., INC.
2951 V St., N.E.
Washington, DC 20018
Tel.: 202-832-4700
Fax: 202-832-4908
Year Founded: 1847
Approx.Sls.: $74,000,000
Emp.: 69
Wholesale Distributor Of Tobacco, Confections & Convenience Store Items
S.I.C.: 5194
E.V. Young, Jr. *(Pres.)*
R.J. Young *(V.P.)*
W.E. Young *(Sec. & Treas.)*
Roy Kaufmann *(Gen. Counsel)*
Robert Essex *(Controller)*
Ray Worso *(Dir.-Pur.)*
John Joseph *(Mgr.-Admin.)*
Principal(s):
E.V. Young, Jr.
R.J. Young
W.E. Young

No. of U.S. Offices: 1

Computer Systems/Hardware:
Quantel System

Outside Service Firm(s):

Beers & Cutler*(Auditors)*
Washington, DC

Charter Corporation*(Commercial Insurance Carrier)*
Baltimore, MD

Kaufmann & Associates*(Legal Firm)*
Washington, DC

Sovran Bank*(Major Banking Relationship)*
Washington, DC

COCHRANE FURNITURE CO., INC.
Hwy. 321 N., Box 220
Lincolnton, NC 28092
Tel.: 704-732-1151
Year Founded: 1910
Approx.Sls.: $460,000,000
Emp.: 950
Mfr. of Wood Dining Room & Bedroom Furniture; Upholstery
S.I.C.: 2511; 2512
Jerry W. Cochrane *(Pres.)*
Bruce R. Cochrane *(Exec. V.P.-Mfg.)*
Neal H. Rhyne *(V.P.-Fin., Sec. & Treas.)*
Calvin J. Nantz *(Dir.-Pur.)*
Terri Cochrane *(Dir.-Galleries & Showrooms)*
Joel Cochrane *(Natl. Sls. Mgr.-Case Div.)*

Division:

Warrenton Division **(1)**
P.O. Box 539
Warrenton, NC 27589
Tel.: 919-257-2156
Wood Househole Furniture
S.I.C.: 2511
Robert Harold *(Gen. Mgr.)*

BARTLETT COCKE JR. CONSTRUCTION CO.
4359 Industrial Center
San Antonio, TX 78217
Tel.: 210-655-1031
Fax: 210-655-1327
Year Founded: 1959
Sales Range: $20-39 Million
Emp.: 75
General Contractor
S.I.C.: 1542; 1521
Bartlett Cocke, Jr. *(Chm. Bd. & Chief Exec. Officer)*
Duane C. Pozza *(Pres.)*
Nelson J. Jonas *(Sr. V.P.-Construction Opers.)*
Arlon W. Bruemmer *(V.P.-Pur.)*
Principal(s):
Bartlett Cocke, Jr.

No. of U.S. Offices: 1

Outside Service Firm(s):

Broadway National Bank*(Major Banking Relationship)*
San Antonio, TX

CODE-A-PHONE CORP.
16261 S.E. 130th Ave.
Clackamas, OR 97015
Mailing Address:
P.O. Box 5656
Portland, OR 97228
Tel.: 503-655-8940 **DE**
Fax: 503-655-0555
Year Founded: 1958
Approx.Sls.: $95,000,000
Emp.: 117
Fiscal Year-end: 12/31/91
Export
Sales & Marketing of Telephones, Answering Machines, Cordless Phones, Other Telephone Equipment
S.I.C.: 3661
Corporate Giving Program: Donations of CAP Products Only
Employee Matching Gifts Program: United Way
Loh Shiew Pin *(Chm. Bd.)*
Charles B. Huber *(Sr. V.P.)*
Jon Jurevic *(V.P.-Fin.)*
Karen Hilmoe *(V.P.-Intl. Sls. & Mktg.)*
Marty Mechanick *(V.P.-Sls.)*
Ruth J. Cummings *(Dir.-Human Resources)*
Jan Smith *(Dir.-Mktg.)*
Alma Allen *(Mgr.-Sls. Admin.)*
Lynn Brown *(Mgr.-Cost Acctg. & Mngmt. Information System)*
Carol Dewey *(Mgr.-Matl. Control)*
Tom LLona *(Mgr.-Intl. Sls. & Mktg.)*
Horst Raustein *(Mgr.-Quality Assurance)*
Elaine DiNucci *(Sls. Coordinator)*

No. of Mfg. Plants/Facilities: 4
No. of U.S. Offices: 7
No. of Foreign Offices: 1

Outside Service Firm(s):

Price Waterhouse*(Auditors)*
1221 S.W. Morrison, Suite 1800
Portland, OR 97204
Tel.: 503-224-9040

Rollins Burdick Hunter*(Commercial Insurance Carrier)*
1211 S.W. Fifth, Ste. 600
Portland, OR 97204-3799

Kaiser Permanente*(Group Insurer)*
Portland, OR

Stoel, Rives, Boley, Jones & Grey*(Legal Firm)*
900 S.W. Fifth Ave., Ste. 2300
Portland, OR 97204-1268
Tel.: 503-224-3380
Fax: 503-220-2480

First Interstate Bank*(Major Banking Relationship)*
P.O. Box 3131,
Portland, OR 97208
Tel.: 503-220-4855
Fax: 503-225-7153

CODE, HENNESSY & SIMMONS
10 S. Wacker, Ste. 3175
Chicago, IL 60606
Tel.: 312-876-1840
Fax: 312-876-3854
Investment Company
S.I.C.: 6211
Andrew W. Code *(Gen. Partner)*
Daniel J. Hennessy *(Gen. Partner)*
Brian P. Simmons *(Gen. Partner)*

Subsidiary:

Hirsh Company **(1)**
8051 Central Park Ave.
Skokie, IL 60076
Tel.: 708-673-6610
Tel.: 800-USA-EASY
Approx.Sls.: $55,000,000
Emp.: 200
Export
Computer Systems/Hardware:
IBM 38
Shelving for Home, Office & Factory; Hardware Prods.; Work Benches; Tool Accessories; Storage Prods.
S.I.C.: 2542; 2599; 3423; 3429; 3553
Dan Hennesy *(Chm. Bd.)*
Jack Larson *(Chief Fin. Officer)*
P. Barnett *(Exec. V.P.-Sls.)*
Ted Lucore *(Exec. V.P.-Opers.)*
Philip Barnett *(Exec. V.P.-Mtkg.)*
Nelson Head *(V.P.)*
Mike Zofkie *(Controller)*
Nelson Head *(Fin. Dir.)*
Richard Sylvan *(Dir.-Adv., Research & Devel.)*
GeryKwiatkowshi *(Dir.-Mfr. Services)*
Richard Sylvan *(Dir.-Adv.)*
Toni Gibson *(Dir.-Human Resources)*
Jack Frigo *(Plant Mgr.)*

CODISCO INC.
601 Codisco Way
Sanford, FL 32771
Tel.: 407-323-8500 **FL**
Fax: 407-323-0308
Year Founded: 1958
Assets: $35,808,000
Liabilities: $29,911,000
Net Worth: $5,897,000
Approx.Sls.: $78,900,000
Emp.: 500
Fiscal Year-end: 12/31/90
Export
Holding Co.; Mfr. & Wholesale Air Distribution Prods.
S.I.C.: 6719; 5075; 3444
Donald C. Bauerle, Sr. *(Chm. Bd.)*
James P. Walker *(Chief Fin. Officer)*
Donald C. Bauerle, Jr. *(Pres.)*
James W. Boykin *(Sr. V.P.)*
James Brown *(Dir.-Pur.)*
Vincent Caschetta *(Dir.-Data Processing)*
John Hamm *(Dir.-Sls. & Mktg.)*
Lynn Quigley *(Dir.-Personnel)*

No. of Mfg. Plants/Facilities: 1
No. of U.S. Offices: 30

Computer Systems/Hardware:
IBM

Outside Service Firm(s):

Deloitte & Touche*(Auditors)*
200 S. Orange Ave., Ste. 1800
Orlando, FL 32801
Tel.: 407-246-8200
Fax: 407-422-0936

J. Rolfe Davis*(Commercial Insurance Carrier)*
Orlando, FL

Mateer, Harbert & Bates, P.A.*(Legal Firm)*
Orlando, FL

Sun Bank, N.A.*(Major Banking Relationship)*
222 E. Robinson St., Ste. 350
Orlando, FL 32801

THE COE MFG. CO.
609 Bank St.
Painesville, OH 44077
Tel.: 216-352-9381
Fax: 216-352-1487
Approx.Sls.: $20,000,000
Emp.: 400
Drying Machines, Veneer & Plywood Machinery, Fibre & Gypsum Wallboard Machinery, Lumber Dry Kilns, OSB & Particleboard Machinery
S.I.C.: 3553; 2421; 2429; 3275
F.W. Fields *(Pres.)*
R.G. Gage *(V.P.)*
G.B. Milbourn *(V.P.-Sls.)*
Nathan R. Rutherford *(V.P.-Mktg.)*
Mike Coleman *(Controller)*
Walter Halyn *(Pur. Agent)*

Divisions:

United States Machinery **(1)**
P.O. Box 520
Painesville, OH 44077
Tel.: 216-352-9381
Fax: 215-352-1487
E.A. Bischoff *(Export Mgr.)*

United States Wallboard Machinery **(1)**
P.O. Box 520
Painesville, OH 44077
Tel.: 215-352-9381
Fax: 215-352-1487
N.C. Oehling *(V.P.)*

COGENTRIX INCORPORATED
9405 Arrowpoint Blvd.
Charlotte, NC 28273
Tel.: 704-525-3800 **NC**
Telex: 704-529-5313

Fax: 704-527-4413
Year Founded: 1983
Sales Range: $100-499 Million
Emp.: 380
Develop, Own & Operate Coal-Fired Energy & Steam Production Facilities
S.I.C.: 1221; 4961
George T. Lewis *(Chm. Bd. & Chief Exec. Officer)*
Bruce McMillan *(Chief Fin. Officer)*
Robert F. Weidaw *(Pres. & Chief Oper. Officer)*
Robert W. Anderson, Jr. *(Pres.-Development Co.)*
David J. Lewis *(Sr. V.P.-Environmental)*
James E. Lewis *(Sr. V.P.-Opers.)*
Thomas F. McCracken *(V.P.-Human Resources)*
William E. Clerke *(Dir.-Pur.)*
Thomas F. Schwartz *(Dir.-Acctg.)*

Principal(s):
George T. Lewis
Robert W. Anderson, Jr.
James E. Lewis
Donald A. Dowling

No. of Mfg. Plants/Facilities: 7
No. of U.S. Offices: 3

Computer Systems/Hardware:
H.P. Min.

Outside Service Firm(s):

Arthur Andersen & Co.*(Auditors)*
2300 Charlotte Plaza
Charlotte, NC 28244
Tel.: 704-332-0092

Johnson & Higgins*(Commercial Insurance Carrier)*
One First Union Center, Ste. 3900
Charlotte, NC 28202
Tel.: 704-374-1845
Fax: 704-374-1202

Salomon Brothers*(Investment Banker)*
7 World Trade Center
New York, NY 10048
Tel.: 212-783-7000

Moore & Van Allen*(Legal Firm)*
3000 NCNB Plaza
Charlotte, NC 28280
Tel.: 704-554-8510

NationsBank Carolinas*(Major Banking Relationship)*
One NCNB Plaza T18-7
Charlotte, NC 28255

The Principal Financial Group*(Pension Manager)*
711 High St.
Des Moines, IA 50309
Tel.: 515-247-4593
Tel.: 800-543-4015

COGGIN-O'STEEN INVESTMENT CORP.
7400 Bay Meadows Way
Jacksonville, FL 32256
Tel.: 904-730-2464
Fax: 904-730-2883
Approx.Sls.: $40,000,000
Automobile Dealerships
S.I.C.: 5511
Luther Coggin *(Pres. & Chief Exec. Officer)*
Harold S. O'Steen *(V.P. & Treas.)*
Howard K. O'Steen *(V.P.)*

Subsidiary:

Coggin Pontiac-GMC Inc. **(1)**
9201 Atlantic Blvd.
Jacksonville, FL 32211
Tel.: 904-724-2310
Fax: 904-721-6983
Approx.Sls.: $40,000,000
Emp.: 182
Automobile Dealerships
S.I.C.: 5511
Luther Coggin *(Pres. & Chief Exec. Officer)*
Howard K. O'Steen *(V.P.)*
Harold S. O'Steen *(V.P. & Treas.)*

LESTER COGGINS TRUCKING
Hwy. 33 S.
Okahumpka, FL 34762
Mailing Address:
P.O. Box 55
Okahumpka, FL 34762
Tel.: 904-326-8900 **FL**
Approx.Sls.: $20,500,000
Emp.: 325
Long-Distance Trucking
S.I.C.: 4213
Lester A. Coggins, Sr. *(Pres.)*
John Glover *(Exec. V.P.)*
Lester Coggins, Jr. *(Sec. & Treas.)*
G.E. Thompson *(Controller)*
Jack Glover *(Dir.-Mktg.)*
Fred Palmer *(Dir.-Maintenance)*
Richard Brock *(Mgr.-Opers.)*

Outside Service Firm(s):

Harmon Peaslee*(Auditors)*
Plant City, FL

Barnett Banks Trust Company, N.A.*(Major Banking Relationship)*
9000 Southside Blvd., P.O. Box 40200
Jacksonville, FL 32202-0200
Tel.: 904-464-2802

COGIFER INC.
5038 Beech St.
Cincinnati, OH 45212
Tel.: 513-631-3440
Fax: 513-366-4681
Approx.Sls.: $13,000,000
Emp.: 50
Import Export
Mfr. Railroad Track Components
S.I.C.: 3321; 3743; 3312
Clifford Turrell *(Pres., Chief Exec. Officer & Chief Fin. Officer)*
Jim Kindsvatter *(Chief Fin. Officer)*
Mike Klima *(Dir.-Sls.)*
Roger Stuart *(Chief Engr.)*

COGSDILL TOOL PRODUCTS, INC.
1001 Guion Dr.
Lugoff, SC 29078
Tel.: 803-438-4000
Fax: 803-438-5263
Sales Range: $10-19 Million
Emp.: 165
Fiscal Year-end: 12/31/91
Export
Metal Tools
S.I.C.: 3545; 3548
Margaret J. Walters *(Chm. Bd.)*
Kay Fife *(Vice Chm.)*
William Westerman *(Pres. & Chief Oper. Officer)*
Don Mitchell *(Exec. V.P.)*
Mike Burr *(V.P.-Engrng.)*
Warren B. Depperman *(V.P.-Res. & Devel.)*
Richard M. Quigley *(V.P.-Mfg.)*
Gordon Robinson *(V.P.-Sls.)*
John C. Schwab *(V.P.-Fin.)*
Gordon White *(V.P.-Sls.)*
Fred Ogburn *(Mgr.-Corp. Communications)*
Nathan Burr *(Pur. Agent)*

Principal(s):
Employee Owned

No. of Mfg. Plants/Facilities: 2
No. of U.S. Offices: 2
No. of Foreign Offices: 1

Computer Systems/Hardware:
IBM System 36

Outside Service Firm(s):

Citizens Southern National Bank*(Major Banking Relationship)*
Camden, SC

Non-U.S. Holding:

Cogsdill-Nuneaton, Ltd. **(1)**
Tenlons Road
Nuneaton, United Kingdom
Tel.: 203-383792
Telex: 311117
Fax: 203-344433
Emp.: 50
Mfr. Precision Metalworking Tools
S.I.C.: 3545
Keith Johnson *(Mng. Dir.)*

COHEN/JOHNSON, INC.
2029 Century Park E., Ste. 1300
Los Angeles, CA 90067
Tel.: 310-553-2300
Fax: 310-553-3626
Year Founded: 1985
Approx.Billings: $72,000,000
Emp.: 50
Howard Cohen *(Chm. Bd. & Exec. Creative Dir.)*
Mark Johnson *(Pres. & New Bus. Contact)*
Mara Friedman *(V.P., Dir. Research & Planning)*
Leslie Salowitz *(V.P., Admin.)*
Perry Freedman *(Acctg. Supvr.)*

Porteous Mitchel & Braun Company
(See listing under Cohen/Johnson, Inc.)

SIGMUND COHN CORP.
121 S. Columbus Ave.
Mount Vernon, NY 10553
Tel.: 914-664-5300
Fax: 914-664-5377
Approx.Sls.: $20,000,000
Emp.: 70
Fiscal Year-end: 8/31/92
Precision Manufacturing
S.I.C.: 3496; 3316
Richard Cohn *(Pres.)*
James Cohn *(Exec. V.P.)*
Thomas Cohn *(V.P. & Dir.-Personnel & Communications)*
Charles Boyet *(Controller & Treas.)*
Virigina Iozzo *(Dir.-Pur.)*
Frank Fitzpatrick *(Dir.-Res. & Devel.)*
Walter Rapp *(Dir.-Engrng.)*
Sharon Sheridan *(Dir.-Data Processing)*

COILCRAFT, INC.
1102 Silver Lake Rd.
Cary, IL 60013
Tel.: 708-639-2361
Fax: 708-639-1469
Year Founded: 1960
Approx.Sls.: $34,000,000
Emp.: 1,800
Export
Mfr. Radio & Intermediate Frequency Coils; Power Transformers; Industrial Coils; Transformers
S.I.C.: 3677; 3612
Charles Liebman *(Pres.)*
Raymond J. Roberts *(Treas.)*
William Desmond *(Dir.-Pur.)*
Paul Liebman *(Mgr.-Mktg.)*
L. Thompson *(Mgr.-Sls.)*

COKEN COMPANY, INC.
150 Colfax St.
Providence, RI 02905
Tel.: 401-785-9310
Fax: 401-467-6453
Approx.Sls.: $15,000,000
Emp.: 160
Electrical Work
S.I.C.: 1731
Gerald Russeth *(Pres. & Chief Exec. Officer)*
Elaine Barone *(V.P., Sec. & Treas.)*
Joseph Bellucci *(V.P.)*
David Evangelista *(V.P.)*
Ray Lambert *(V.P.)*

Outside Service Firm(s):

Ernst & Young*(Auditors)*
One Old Stone Square
Providence, RI 02903
Tel.: 401-331-7000

Pucci & Goldin*(Legal Firm)*
123 Dyer St.
Providence, RI 02909
Tel.: 401-861-7400

COLAD GROUP INC.
701 Seneca St.
Buffalo, NY 14210
Tel.: 716-849-1776
Tel.: 800-333-0189 **DE**
Fax: 716-849-1753
Year Founded: 1946
Approx.Sls.: $18,000,000
Emp.: 155
Fiscal Year-end: 12/31/91
Import
Mfr. Presentation Matls. & Product Information Packaging
S.I.C.: 2679; 2675; 2782
William P. Bresnahan *(Pres.)*
Mike Ferguson *(Exec. V.P.-Sls. & Mktg.)*
Robert Boychieder *(V.P.-Sls. & Alternative Channels)*
Mike Militello *(V.P. & Plant Mgr.)*
Kevin Erstice *(Controller)*
Tom James *(Plant Mgr.)*

COLD HEADING CO.
4600 Bellevue Ave.
Detroit, MI 48207
Tel.: 313-923-7800
Fax: 313-923-0812
Approx.Sls.: $54,000,000
Emp.: 200
Manufacture Screws, Nuts, Bolts, Rivets
S.I.C.: 3452
Paul Morath *(Chief Exec. Officer)*
Elizabeth Stevens *(Pres.)*
Bill Deason *(Chief Engineer)*

Outside Service Firm(s):

N.B.D. Bank, N.A.*(Major Banking Relationship)*
611 Woodward Ave.
Detroit, MI 48226
Tel.: 313-225-1122
Fax: 313-225-3420

COLD SPRING GRANITE COMPANY
601 Lakeshore Pkwy.
Minnetonka, MN 55305
Tel.: 612-449-4950
Telex: 753588
Fax: 612-449-5582
Year Founded: 1898
Approx.Sls.: $140,000,000
Emp.: 1,300
Fiscal Year-end: 12/31/90
Granite Quarry & Fabricating
S.I.C.: 1411; 5032
Patrick D. Alexander *(Pres. & Chief Exec. Officer)*
Steve Duncan *(V.P.-Sls. & Mktg.)*
Alfred Frasier *(V.P.-Opers.)*
Rosemary Alexander *(Sec.)*
Nick Khalil *(Controller)*
Dan Loraas *(Dir.-Mktg.)*
George Sehepf *(Dir.-Fin)*

No. of Mfg. Plants/Facilities: 4
No. of U.S. Offices: 3

Outside Service Firm(s):

KPMG Peat Marwick*(Auditors)*
4200 Norwest Center, 90 S. 7th St.
Minneapolis, MN 55402
Tel.: 612-341-2222

Cold Spring Granite Company—(Continued)

Marsh & McLennan*(Group Insurer)*
Minneapolis, MN

Norwest Bank Minnesota, N.A.*(International Bank Affiliate)*
Seventh & Marquette Ave.
Minneapolis, MN 55479
Tel.: 612-667-4296

Robins, Kaplan, Miller & Ciresi*(Legal Firm)*
1800 International Center, 900 Second Ave. So.
Minneapolis, MN 55402

Norwest Bank Minnesota, N.A.*(Major Banking Relationship)*
6th St. & Marquette Av.
Minneapolis, MN 55479
Tel.: 612-667-1234

Divisions:

Granit-Bronz, Inc. **(1)**
202 S. 3rd Ave.
Cold Spring, MN 56320
Tel.: 612-685-3621
Fax: 612-685-8490

Royal Melrose Granites **(1)**
202 S. 3rd Ave.
Cold Spring, MN 56320
Tel.: 612-685-3621
Fax: 612-685-8490

Subsidiaries:

Capital Marble & Granite Co. Inc. **(1)**
P.O. Box 1239,
Marble Falls, TX 78054
Tel.: 210-598-2593
Fax: 210-598-6589
S.I.C.: 1411; 5032

Lake Placid Granite Co. **(1)**
P.O. Box I
Au Sable Forks, NY 12912
Tel.: 518-645-8192
Fax: 518-647-8340

Raymond Granite Co. **(1)**
36772 Rd. 606
Raymond, CA 93653
Tel.: 209-689-3257
Fax: 209-689-3207

Texas Granite Corp. **(1)**
Hwy. 1431 West
Marble Falls, TX 78654
Tel.: 210-693-4316
Fax: 210-598-6589

COLDWATER SEAFOOD CORPORATION

133 Rowayton Ave.
Rowayton, CT 06853
Tel.: 203-852-1600
Fax: 203-866-4871
Approx.Sls.: $250,000,000
Emp.: 450
Fiscal Year-end: 12/31/90
Producer of Fresh/Frozen Seafood
S.I.C.: 2092
M. Gustafsson *(Pres.)*
G. Clarke *(Exec. V.P.)*
J.B. Jones *(V.P.-Sls. & Mktg.)*
L. Stange *(V.P.)*
Petur Masson *(Dir.-Mktg.)*
Pat Russo *(Asst. Mgr.-Adv.)*

Outside Service Firm(s):

Blue Cross & Blue Shield Association*(Group Insurer)*
Hartford, CT

Divisions:

Coldwater Seafood Corp. **(1)**
60 Commercial St.
Everett, MA 02149
Tel.: 617-387-2050

Coldwater Seafood Corp. **(1)**
Woods Rd.
Cambridge, MD 21613
Tel.: 410-228-7500
Jay Book *(Plant Mgr.)*
Pall Petursson *(Mgr.-Quality Assurance)*
Ronald Sasiela *(Dir.-Tech. Services)*

COLDWELL BANKERS/ SCHLOTT REALTORS

(Formerly Schlott Realtors)
1550 Rte. 23 North
Wayne, NJ 07470
Tel.: 201-633-5000
Year Founded: 1971
Sales Range: $100-499 Million
Emp.: 650
Real Estate Services
S.I.C.: 6531
Richard L. Schlott *(Pres.)*
Matt Broderick *(Sr. V.P.)*
Judith O'Brien *(V.P.-Admin.)*
Bruce Zipf *(Controller)*
Barbara Sullivan *(Mgr.-Employee Rels.)*

Computer Systems/Hardware:
Wang VS 100

Outside Service Firm(s):

Ernst & Young*(Auditors)*
433 Hackensack Ave.
Hackensack, NJ 07601
Tel.: 201-343-4095

Hogan & Palace*(Legal Firm)*
Hackensack, NJ

Citizens First National Bank*(Major Banking Relationship)*
Glen Rock, NJ

First Fidelity Bank, N.A.*(Major Banking Relationship)*
Totowa, NJ

COLE HENDERSON DRAKE, INC.

400 Colony Square, 1201 Peachtree St. NE, Ste. 500
Atlanta, GA 30361
Tel.: 404-892-4500
Fax: 404-892-4522
Approx.Billings: $24,000,000
Emp.: 48
Robert E. Cargill *(Chm.)*
Richard Henderson *(Chief Exec. Officer & Creative Dir.)*
John H. Drake *(Pres.)*
James P. Cole *(Exec. V.P.)*

COLE HERSEE COMPANY

20 Old Colony Ave.
Boston, MA 02127-2467
Tel.: 617-268-2100
Telex: 94-0901
Fax: 617-268-9490
Emp.: 475
Automotive Electrical Electronic Equipment: Switches, Connectors, Solenoids, Battery Isolators, Alarms, Indicator Lights, Plugs, Sockets, Temperature Sending Units, Terminal & Junction Blocks, Electrical Safety Devices
S.I.C.: 5531; 5015; 5013
Robert Mayer *(Pres.)*
Carl Price *(Gen. Sls. Mgr.)*
John R. West *(Sls. Mgr.-Aftermarket)*
J. Ranger *(Mgr.-Adv.)*
J.J. Santisi, Jr. *(Pur. Agent)*

COLE NATIONAL CORPORATION

(Formerly CNC Holding Corporation)
5915 Landerbrook Dr.
Cleveland, OH 44124
Tel.: 216-449-4100 **DE**
Year Founded: 1984
Assets: $225,754,000
Liabilities: $343,644,000
Net Worth: $117,890,000
Approx.Sls.: $426,453,000
Emp.: 7,800
Fiscal Year-end: 2/ 1/92
Import Export
Holding Company
S.I.C.: 6719; 5999; 7699; 5947
Jeffrey A. Cole *(Chm. Bd. & Chief Exec. Officer)*
Brian Smith *(Pres. & Chief Oper. Officer)*
John F. Downie *(Sr. V.P., Sec. & Gen. Counsel)*
Joseph Gagliotti *(V.P. & Treas.)*
Lisa Yager *(Mgr.-Fin.)*
Principal(s):
Jeffrey A. Cole

Computer Systems/Hardware:
IBM System 3083

Outside Service Firm(s):

Arthur Andersen & Co.*(Auditors)*
1717 E. 9th St.
Cleveland, OH 44114
Tel.: 216-781-2140
Fax: 216-781-3683

Prudential Insurance Co. of America*(Group Insurer)*
751 Broad St.
Newark, NJ 07102-3777
Tel.: 201-802-6000

Jones, Day, Reavis & Pogue*(Legal Firm)*
901 Lakeside Ave.
Cleveland, OH 44114
Tel.: 216-586-3939
Fax: 216-579-0212

Bankers Trust Co.*(Major Banking Relationship)*
Los Angeles, CA

National City Bank*(Major Banking Relationship)*
P.O. Box 92301, Corp. Trust Dept.
Cleveland, OH 44101
Tel.: 216-575-2000

Subsidiaries:

Cole Key Corporation **(1)**
5340 Avion Park Dr.
Cleveland, OH 44143
Tel.: 216-473-2000 (100%)
Approx.Sls.: $46,900,000
Emp.: 1,700
Import
Computer Systems/Hardware:
IBM
Leased Key Departments in Major Retail Stores
S.I.C.: 7699; 5947; 3479
Jeffrey A. Cole *(Chm. Bd.)*
Bryan Smith *(Pres.)*
Suzanne Sutter *(Sr. V.P.)*
Joseph Gagliotti *(V.P. & Treas.)*
John F. Downie *(Sec. & Gen. Counsel)*

Cole Vision Corporation **(1)**
18903 S. Miles
Cleveland, OH 44128
Tel.: 216-475-8925 (100%)
Approx.Sls.: $204,700,000
Emp.: 2,400
Retail Optical Dispensing, Leased Depts. in Dept. Stores
S.I.C.: 5999
Jeffrey A. Cole *(Chm. Bd.)*
Brian Smith *(Pres. & Chief Oper. Officer)*
John F. Downie *(Sec. & Gen. Counsel)*
Dennis Osgood *(Exec. V.P.)*
J. David Pierson *(Exec. V.P.)*
Mark Valentine *(Exec. V.P.)*
S. Drum *(V.P.-Mktg.)*
Joseph Gagliotti *(V.P. & Treas.)*

Things Remembered **(1)**
5340 Avion Park Dr.
Cleveland, OH 44143
Tel.: 216-473-2000 (100%)
Approx.Sls.: $174,800,000
Emp.: 2,900
Import
Computer Systems/Hardware:
IBM
Engraved Gifts, Stores, Personalizing
S.I.C.: 5947
Jeffrey A. Cole *(Chm. Bd.)*
Brian B. Smith *(Pres.)*
Jeffrey R. Doshan *(Exec. V.P.)*
Suzanne Sutter *(Exec. V.P.)*
Charles Kahn *(Exec. V.P.)*
John F. Downie *(Sr. V.P.)*
William Lahiff *(V.P. & Controller)*
Thomas C. Quayle *(V.P. & Gen. Mgr.)*
Leonard Barry *(V.P.-Stores)*
David Wicker *(V.P.-Mktg.)*
Suzanne Forsythe *(V.P.-Human Resources)*
Joseph Gagliotti *(Treas.)*

COLE PAPERS INC.

1300 38th St., N.
Fargo, ND 58108
Mailing Address:
P.O. Box 2967
Fargo, ND 58108
Tel.: 701-282-5311 **ND**
Fax: 701-282-5513
Year Founded: 1918
Approx.Sls.: $29,000,000
Emp.: 90
Industrial Papers, Printing Papers, Wholesale Floor & Counter Coverings
S.I.C.: 5023; 5111; 5113
Charles Perkins *(Pres.)*
Lloyd L. Anderson *(Chief Fin. Officer)*
Brad Carlson *(V.P.-Floor Covering Div.)*
Gregory Hanson *(V.P.-Mktg.)*
Kenneth Dahl *(Mgr.-Credit)*
Gerard Dompke *(Mgr.-Mktg., Printing Paper)*

Outside Service Firm(s):

Eide, Helmeke & Co.*(Auditors)*
Moorhead, MN

Conmy, Feste, Bossart, Hubbard & Corwin, Ltd.*(Legal Firm)*
Fargo, ND

Norwest Bank North Dakota, N.A.*(Major Banking Relationship)*
Fargo, ND

COLE TAYLOR FINANCIAL GROUP

350 E. Dundee Rd., Ste. 200
Wheeling, IL 60090
Tel.: 708-459-1111
Fax: 708-537-7627
Approx.Assets: $1,100,000,000
Emp.: 800
Bank Holding Co.; Two Community Banks Performing Commercial, Consumer Banking & Lease Financing Activities
S.I.C.: 6712; 6022; 6159
Sidney J. Taylor *(Chm. Bd. & Chief Exec. Officer)*
Irwin H. Cole *(Deputy Chm. Bd.)*
Joe Kristie *(V.P.-Corporate Mktg.)*

Banking Subsidiaries:

Cole Taylor Bank **(1)**
850 W. Jackson Blvd.
Chicago, IL 60607
Tel.: 312-738-2000
Full Service Bank; Other Locations: 47th & Ashland, 7601 So. Cicero Ave., 1965 N. Milwaukee Ave., all in Chgo., Il; Burbank, Il., Wheeling, Il., Skokie., Il.
S.I.C.: 6022
Jeffrey W. Taylor *(Chm. & Chief Exec. Officer)*
Bruce W. Taylor *(Pres. & Chief Oper. Officer)*
Mark T. Neil *(Grp. Exec. V.P.-Trust Services)*
Robert F. Corey *(Exec. V.P.-Govt. Rels.)*
Gerald A. Hawk *(Sr. V.P.)*
Edward H. Parsons *(Sr. V.P.)*
John J. Crotty *(Sr. V.P.-Correspondent Banking)*
William S. Race *(Chief Fin. Officer)*

Cole Taylor/Yorktown **(1)**
One Yorktown Center
Lombard, IL 60148
Tel.: 708-629-3800
Full Service Bank
S.I.C.: 6022
Sidney J. Taylor *(Chm. Bd. & Chief Exec. Officer)*
Irwin H. Cole *(Deputy Chm. Bd.)*
Bruce W. Taylor *(Pres. & Chief Exec. Officer)*
Jean M. Dierlam *(Gen. Mgr.)*

COLEMAN CABLE SYSTEMS, INC.
2500 Commonwealth Ave.
North Chicago, IL 60064
Tel.: 708-689-9090
Tel.: 800-323-9355 IL
Telex: 756634 COLEMAN CBL
Fax: 708-689-1192
Year Founded: 1971
Approx.Sls.: $110,300,000
Emp.: 300
Fiscal Year-end: 6/30/92
Import Export
Drawing & Insulating of Wire
S.I.C.: 3355; 3351; 3357
Allan Coleman *(Chm. Bd.)*
Jim Coleman *(Pres. & Chief Exec. Officer)*
William Vranek *(Chief Fin. Officer)*
Peter Leeb *(Exec. V.P. & Corp. Sec.)*
Mark Andrews *(Dir.-Data Processing)*
Catherine Roy *(Dir.-Pur.)*
Roger Davis *(Mgr.-Credit)*

No. of Mfg. Plants/Facilities: 3
No. of U.S. Offices: 3
No. of Foreign Offices: 1

Computer Systems/Hardware:
IBM System AS 400

Outside Service Firm(s):

Deloitte & Touche*(Auditors)*
Two Prudential Plaza, 180 N. Stetson
Chicago, IL 60601
Tel.: 312-946-2039

Gallagher-Bassett Services, Inc.*(Group Insurer)*
Arlington Heights, IL

Shefsky & Froehlich*(Legal Firm)*
Chicago, IL

First National Bank of Chicago*(Major Banking Relationship)*
One First National Plaza
Chicago, IL 60670
Tel.: 312-732-9781
Tel.: 312-732-4050
Fax: 312-732-4840
Fax: 312-732-3055

Chicago Title & Trust Co.*(Pension Manager)*
111 W. Washington St.
Chicago, IL 60602
Tel.: 312-630-2000
Fax: 312-368-4736

Subsidiaries:

Electrical Conductors, Inc. **(1)**
2500 Commonwealth Ave.
North Chicago, IL 60064
Tel.: 708-689-9090

Nehring Electrical Works Company **(1)**
813 E. Locust St.
De Kalb, IL 60115
Tel.: 815-756-2741
Fax: 815-756-7048
Emp.: 75
Draw, Insulates Copper & Aluminum Cable
S.I.C.: 3357
Ray Hott *(Pres.)*

COLEMAN CADILLAC INC.
(d/b/a Jim Coleman Cadillac)
10400A Auto Park Ave.
Bethesda, MD 20817
Tel.: 301-469-6600
Fax: 301-469-2113
Year Founded: 1954
Approx.Sls.: $37,000,000
Emp.: 150
New & Used Automobile Dealership
S.I.C.: 5511; 5531
William H. Coleman, Jr. *(Chm. Bd.)*
James R. Coleman *(Pres.)*
William H. Coleman, III *(V.P.)*
Gordon Price *(Controller, Treas. & Sec.)*
Sonny Durham *(Dir.-Fin.)*

Outside Service Firm(s):

Smithers & Southerly*(Auditors)*
Fairfax, VA

McNamee, Hosea & Jernigan*(Legal Firm)*
Greenbelt, MD

Maryland National Bank*(Major Banking Relationship)*
Baltimore, MD 21202

COLEMAN & CHRISTISON, INC.
506 Fort Rd.
Saint Paul, MN 55102
Tel.: 612-227-9391
Fax: 612-292-9452
Year Founded: 1966
Approx.Billings: $31,000,000
Emp.: 33
Richard J. Christison *(Pres.)*
Robert E. Goff *(Exec. V.P.)*
Kenneth D. Rowe *(Sr. V.P.)*
Roger Moe *(V.P.)*

Computer Systems/Hardware:
Macintosh/Data General

COLEMAN DAIRY INC.
5801 Asher Ave.
Little Rock, AR 72204
Tel.: 501-565-1551
Year Founded: 1862
Approx.Sls.: $44,200,000
Emp.: 300
Dairy Foods & Ice Cream
S.I.C.: 2024; 2022; 2026
Walter C. Coleman, Jr. *(Chm. Bd.)*
Walter C. Coleman III *(Pres.)*
Duane Osam *(V.P.-Production)*
Richard Beauford *(Controller)*
David Hall *(Dir.-Quality Control)*
Dodie Osam *(Dir.-Personnel)*
Bob Coleman *(Gen. Mgr.-Sls. & Sec.)*
Cherb Coleman *(Mgr.-Traffic & Distr.)*
Robert Hill *(Mgr.-Milk Production)*
Larry McBride *(Mgr.-Data Processing)*
Phil McBride *(Mgr.-Southern Div.)*
Ron Whaley *(Mgr.-Southern Div.)*

Principal(s):
Walter C. Coleman, Jr.
Walter C. Coleman III

Outside Service Firm(s):

L. Cotton Thomas, CPA's*(Auditors)*
Little Rock, AR

Wright, Lindsey, & Jennings*(Legal Firm)*
2200 Worthen Bank Bldg.
Little Rock, AR 72201
Tel.: 501-371-0808
Fax: 501-375-1617

NBD Business Finance, Inc.*(Major Banking Relationship)*
8001 Lincoln Ave.
Skokie, IL 60077

COLES EXPRESS
444 Perry Rd.
Bangor, ME 04401
Mailing Address:
P.O. Box 918
Bangor, ME 04401
Tel.: 207-942-7311
Fax: 207-942-7311 Ext. 268
Approx.Sls.: $18,000,000
Emp.: 250
Common Carrier
S.I.C.: 4212
Galen L. Cole *(Chm. Bd.)*
Garret Cole *(V.P.-Admin.)*
Len Cole *(Gen. Mgr.)*
Janet Cole *(Mgr.-Mktg.)*
Tom Weeks *(Mgr.-Human Resources & Safety)*

COLFAX ENVELOPE CORPORATION
951 Commerce Ct.
Buffalo Grove, IL 60089
Tel.: 708-215-1122 ILL
Fax: 708-215-1145
Year Founded: 1966
Approx.Sls.: $19,000,000
Emp.: 101
Import Export
Manufacturer of Lithographed Envelopes
S.I.C.: 2752
Charles R. Patten *(Chm. Bd. & Pres.)*
Fred Clanton *(V.P.-Opers.)*
Kathy Yudys *(V.P.-Customer Service)*
Jane Zimmet *(Dir.-Mktg.)*

Principal(s):
Charles R. Patten
Fred Clanton

No. of Mfg. Plants/Facilities: 1
No. of U.S. Offices: 1

Outside Service Firm(s):

Detterbeck & Associates*(Auditors)*
Chicago, IL

Blue Cross & Blue Shield Association*(Group Insurer)*
233 N. Michigan Ave.
Chicago, IL 60601

Meeker-Magner*(Commercial Insurance Carrier)*
Park Ridge, IL

Pope & John*(Legal Firm)*
Chicago, IL

Lakeshore National Bank*(Major Banking Relationship)*
Chicago, IL

COLFAX, INC.
38 Colfax St.
Pawtucket, RI 02860
Tel.: 401-724-3800
Fax: 401-724-4313
Approx.Sls.: $102,000,000
Emp.: 150
Vegetable Oil Mills; Vegetable Shortenings; Animal & Marine Fats & Oils
S.I.C.: 2076; 2079; 2077; 6512
Sidney Dressler *(Pres.)*
Abbott W. Dressler *(Exec. V.P. & Sec.)*
Michael B. Dressler *(Treas.)*

Outside Service Firm(s):

Goluses & Company*(Auditors)*
Pawtucket, RI

Fleet National Bank*(Major Banking Relationship)*
Corporate Trust Department, 125 Dupont Dr.
Providence, RI 02907
Tel.: 401-278-5400

COLIN SERVICE SYSTEMS, INC.
1 Brockway Place
White Plains, NY 10601
Tel.: 914-328-0800 NY
Fax: 914-328-7849
Approx.Sls.: $81,000,000
Emp.: 3,500
Building Maintenance, Except Repairs; Protective Guard Services
S.I.C.: 7349; 7381
George Colin *(Chm. Bd.)*
Jay B. Colin *(Vice Chm.)*
Lawrence Colin *(Pres. & Chief Exec. Officer)*
Bernard Blum *(Chief Fin. Officer)*
Robert Diamond *(V.P.)*

Outside Service Firm(s):

The Bank of New York*(Major Banking Relationship)*
One Wall Street
New York, NY 10286
Tel.: 212-635-6805
Fax: 212-635-3201

COLLE & McVOY, INC.
ADVERTISING / DIRECT MARKETING / PUBLIC RELATIONS / MARKET RESEARCH

COLLE & MCVOY, INC.
7900 International Dr.
Minneapolis, MN 55425
Tel.: 612-851-2500
Fax: 612-851-2583
Year Founded: 1935
Approx.Billings: $58,067,090
Emp.: 101
Advertising Agency
S.I.C.: 7311
Clarence Thompson *(Chm. Bd.)*
Allan Hietala *(Chief Exec. Officer)*
Jim Bergeson *(Pres.)*
James J. Heinz *(Exec. V.P., Consumer Div. Mgr.)*
Wayne Engelman *(Sr. V.P., Sec. & Treas.)*
Phil Johnson *(Sr. V.P., Agribusiness)*
Janet McGrath *(Grp. V.P., Pet Prods. Mgr.)*
Bob Hettlinger *(V.P., Human Resources)*
Steve Akerson *(Sr. V.P., Mktg. Research Dir.)*
Deborah Becker *(Sr. V.P., Pub. Rels. Dir.)*
Mary Ross *(V.P., Direct Mktg. Dir.)*
Steve Plagens *(V.P., Special Projects)*
Lucy Desteian *(Recording Sec.)*

Computer Systems/Hardware:
Mac Word Processing, Marketing Resources Plus, Market Manager, DEC MACII, MAC II Fax, Computer Graphics Integrator, Q&A

Outside Service Firm(s):

Larson, Allen, Weishair & Co.*(Auditors)*
Minneapolis, MN

Fredrikson & Byron, P.A.*(Legal Firm)*
1100 International Centre, 900 2nd Ave. S.
Minneapolis, MN 55402
Tel.: 612-347-7000

Norwest Bank Minnesota, N.A.*(Major Banking Relationship)*
Minneapolis, MN

Norwest Bank of Calhoun Isles*(Major Banking Relationship)*
Minneapolis, MN

Branch:

Colle & McVoy Public Relations **(1)**
7900 International Dr., Ste. 700
Minneapolis, MN 55425
Tel.: 612-851-2500
Fax: 612-851-2583
Approx.Billings: $8,210,000
Emp.: 11
Marketing Communications
S.I.C.: 8743
Clarence Thompson *(Chm. Bd.)*
James Trevis *(V.P., Agri-Business Pub. Rel. Mgr.)*
Bill Gnatzig *(V.P., Agricultural Pub. Rels.)*

COLLEGEVILLE FLAG MFG. COMPANY
4th Ave. & Walnut St.
Collegeville, PA 19426
Mailing Address:
P.O. Box 98,
Collegville, PA 19426
Tel.: 215-489-4131 PA

Collegeville Flag Mfg. Company—(Continued)

Fax: 215-489-4164
Year Founded: 1902
Assets: $10,000,000
Liabilities: $2,000,000
Net Worth: $8,000,000
Approx.Sls.: $23,000,000
Emp.: 275
Fiscal Year-end: 12/31/90
Manufacturer of Flags, Banners & Accessories
S.I.C.: 2399
David A. Cornish *(Pres. & Chief Exec. Officer)*
D. Samuel Cornish *(Pres.-Collgeville Imagingeering Div.)*
Richard Stanislaw *(Chief Fin. Officer)*
Douglas Cornish *(V.P.)*
Steven Cornish *(Mgr.-Sls.)*
Timothy Sanborn *(Mgr.-Opers.)*

Outside Service Firm(s):

Dreslin & Co.*(Auditors)*
Norristown, PA

Wisler, Pearlstine & Talone*(Legal Firm)*
Norristown, PA

Provident National Bank*(Major Banking Relationship)*
1000 Westlakes Dr.
Berwyn, PA 19312

COLLEGEVILLE/ IMAGINEERING L.P.
4th Ave. & Walnut Sts.
Collegeville, PA 19426
Mailing Address:
P.O. Box 808
Collegeville, PA 19426
Tel.: 215-489-4131
Fax: 215-489-4164
Year Founded: 1991
Mfr. of Halloween Costumes, Make-up & Accessories
S.I.C.: 2399
David A. Cornish *(Chm. Bd.)*
D. Samuel Cornish *(Pres.)*
Richard Stanislaw *(Chief Fin. Officer)*
Lawrence Liff *(Exec. V.P.)*
Gregg Lachenmayer *(V.P. & Sec.)*
Lucinda Smith *(Mgr.-Natl. Sls.)*

Outside Service Firm(s):

Dreslin & Co.*(Auditors)*
Norristown, PA

Wisler, Pearlstine & Talone*(Legal Firm)*
Norristown, PA

Provident National Bank*(Major Banking Relationship)*
1000 Westlakes Dr.
Berwyn, PA 19312

COLLEGIATE CONCEPTS INC.
1751 Montreal Circle
Tucker, GA 30084
Mailing Address:
P.O. Box 450388,
Atlanta, GA 30345
Tel.: 404-938-1700 **GA**
Fax: 404-491-6927
Year Founded: 1983
Approx.Sls.: $10,000,000
Emp.: 55
Fiscal Year-end: 1/ 1/91
Public Relations & Sales Representative For American Higher Education
S.I.C.: 8743
Russell G. Smith *(Chm. Bd. & Pres.)*
Eileen W. Smith *(Chief Oper. Officer)*
Walter E. Moore *(V.P. & Dir.-Sls.)*
Tracy Henson *(Mgr.-Acctg.)*
Patrick Stansbury *(Mgr.-Sls.)*
Christine Whiteside *(Office Mgr.)*

COLLIN STREET BAKERY
401 W. Seventh Ave.
Corsicana, TX 75110
Tel.: 903-872-8111 **TX**
Fax: 903-872-6879
Year Founded: 1896
Approx.Sls.: $25,000,000
Emp.: 72
Fiscal Year-end: 9/30/91
Export
Deluxe Fruit Cakes via Direct Mail
S.I.C.: 5961
L.W. McNutt, Jr. *(Pres.)*
Norman Shaw *(Exec. V.P.)*
Maurice Pollock *(V.P., Treas. & Controller)*
Robert McNutt *(V.P.-Opers.)*
John Crawford *(V.P.-Sls.)*

No. of Mfg. Plants/Facilities: 1
No. of U.S. Offices: 1
No. of Foreign Offices: 1

Computer Systems/Hardware:
IBM & Datapoint

Outside Service Firm(s):

Anderson & Associates, P.C.*(Auditors)*
Corsicana, TX

Ray Bailey Agency*(Commercial Insurance Carrier)*
Dallas, TX

NationsBank Texas*(Major Banking Relationship)*
Corsicana, TX

Wyatt Co.*(Pension Manager)*
2121 San Jacinto St., #2400
Dallas, TX
Tel.: 214-978-3400

COLLINS & AIKMAN GROUP INC.
3340 Ocean Park Blvd. Ste. 2000
Santa Monica, CA 90405
Mailing Address:
P.O. Box 4056,
Santa Monica, CA 90405
Tel.: 310-452-0161
Fax: 310-452-9509
Assets: $2,816,772,000
Earnings: ($233,858,000)
Liabilities: $1,083,581
Net Worth: $2,815,688,419
Approx.Sls.: $2,991,845,000
Emp.: 29,500
Fiscal Year-end: 1/30/92
Automotive & Industrial Products; Wallcoverings & Decorative Fabrics
S.I.C.: 2211; 2221; 2273; 2257; 2258; 2262; 2269; 2281; 2282; 2295; 2679; 3069; 3089; 3341; 3351; 3451; 3357; 3354; 3365
James R. Birle *(Co-Chm. & Co-Chief Exec. Officer)*
Bruce Wasserstein *(Co-Chm & Co-Chief Exec. Officer)*
Robert S. Fenton *(Exec. V.P. & Sec.)*
Michael A. Jamieson *(V.P. & Treas.)*
Elizabeth Philipp *(V.P. & Gen. Counsel)*

Operating Units:

Collins & Aikman Textile Group **(1)**
701 McCullough Dr.
Charlotte, NC 28262
Tel.: 704-547-8500
Fax: 704-548-2145
Approx.Sls.: $1,200,000,000
Emp.: 12,500
Fiscal Year-end: 1/31/91
Export
Computer Systems/Hardware:
IBM AS 400
Mfr. Textiles, Wallcoverings & Bath Fashions
S.I.C.: 2273; 2258; 2211; 2231; 2281; 2282; 2299; 2621; 2257
Corporate Giving Program: Matching Gifts to Colleges for Employees; Wickes Foundation Grants
Employee Matching Gift Program: Matching Gifts for Colleges & Universities (Academics Only)
James Birle *(Chm. Bd.)*
Thomas E. Hannah *(Pres. & Chief Exec. Officer)*
Andrew Major *(Pres.-Decorative Fabrics Grp.)*
Harold L. Sunday *(V.P.-Human Resources)*
Gary Hoskins *(V.P.-MIS)*
J.B. Cooper *(V.P.-Corp. Engrng.)*
Paul Weinle *(V.P.-Res. & Devel.)*
Anthony Hardwick *(Controller)*
Ronald Lindsay *(Chief Counsel)*
G. Clark Michael *(Dir.-Industrial Rels.)*
J.D.M. O'Hara *(Dir.-Corp. Communications)*
John Gunn *(Dir.-Corp. Pur.)*
Rogers Eads *(Dir.-Training & Devel.)*
David Perryman *(Mgr.-Telecommunications)*
Chip Moore *(Mgr.-Environmental Affairs)*

Operating Divisions:

Builders Emporium **(2)**
40 Parker
Irvine, CA 92718-1633
Tel.: 714-454-1090 (100%)
Fax: 714-454-6055
Approx.Sls.: $500,000,000
Emp.: 6,000
Fiscal Year-end: 1/31/91
Import
Retail Home Improvement Materials
S.I.C.: 5251
John Kearney *(Acting Pres.)*
Darrell Hevn *(V.P.-Mktg. & Store Plng.)*
Debra Scheibel *(Dir.-Adv.)*

C&A Automotive Group **(2)**
P.O. Box 580
Albemarle, NC 28001
Tel.: 704-983-5166
Mfr. of Automotive Textiles
S.I.C.: 2399
John Moose *(Pres.)*

Division:

Decorative Fabrics - Cavel **(3)**
1803 Main St.
Roxboro, NC 27573
Tel.: 919-599-1111
Plush or Velvet-Style Upholstery Fabric for Automotive Use Primarily
S.I.C.: 2273; 2231
John Moose *(Pres.)*

C&A Floor Coverings **(2)**
311 Smith Industrial Blvd.
Dalton, GA 30720
Tel.: 706-259-9711
Export
Computer Systems/Hardware:
AS 400
Commercial & Institutional Carpeting
S.I.C.: 2273
Charles Eitel *(Pres.)*

C&A Wallcoverings **(2)**
23645 Mercantile Rd.
Cleveland, OH 44122
Tel.: 216-464-3700
Approx.Sls.: $400,000,000
Emp.: 1,600
Residential & Commercial Wallcoverings
S.I.C.: 2621; 2679
William A. Foley *(Pres.)*
John A. Fitzgerald *(Exec. V.P.)*
David Lushin *(Gen. Mgr.-Mktg. Services)*

C&A Yarn Division **(2)**
Hwy. 52
Norwood, NC 28128
Tel.: 919-572-3615
Spun & Textured Yarns, Dyed Yarns & Sewing Threads
S.I.C.: 2282
John Montgomery *(V.P.-Mfg.)*

Decorative Fabrics - Mastercraft **(2)**
P.O. Box 125,
Spindale, NC 28160
Tel.: 704-286-4811
Telex: 704-287-8237
Fax: 704-287-8207
Flat Woven Jacquard & Dobby Upholstery Fabric
S.I.C.: 2221
Andrew Major *(Pres.)*
William Brucchieri *(Exec. V.P.)*
Harry Shoen *(Exec. V.P.)*
Thomas Byrnes *(V.P.-Mktg.)*
John Beason *(V.P.-Mktg.-Contract)*
Don Millwater *(Controller)*
Joe Coble *(Dir.-Pur.)*

Subsidiaries:

The Akro Corporation **(3)**
1212 7th St. S.W.
Canton, OH 44707
Tel.: 216-456-4543
Fax: 216-456-6760
Approx.Sls.: $100,000,000
Emp.: 1,250
Fiscal Year-end: 1/31/91
Export
Computer Systems/Hardware:
AS 400
Mfr. Carpet-to-Vinyl Mats & Matting; Carpet-to-Rubber Floor Tile; All Rubber Mats; Carpet-to-Rubber Automotive Floor Mats; Rubber Molded Parts
S.I.C.: 2273
Robert L. Narens *(Pres.)*
E. Buxbaum *(V.P.-Sls. & Mktg.)*
Dale Kaskey *(Controller)*
John Flasco *(Dir.-Pur.)*

Greeff Fabrics **(3)**
150 Midland Ave.
Port Chester, NY 10573
Tel.: 914-935-5700
Tel.: 800-223-0357
Telex: 12506
Fax: 914-935-5717
Approx.Sls.: $9,000,000
Emp.: 90
Fiscal Year-end: 1/25/91
Export
Fabrics & Wallcoverings
S.I.C.: 2231; 2679
Bill Foley *(Chief Exec. Officer)*
James Brucchieri *(Exec. V.P.)*
John Dull *(Gen. Mgr.)*
Marion Kaufman *(Dir.-Mktg.)*
Ray Dittmar *(Dir.-Sls.)*

Wickes Mfg. Co. **(3)**
P.O. Box 999
Southfield, MI 48037-0999
Tel.: 313-355-8000
Approx.Sls.: $1,000,000,000
Emp.: 13,000
Mfg. Screw, Nuts & Bolts
S.I.C.: 3452; 3465; 3569; 3714
Roney Klemens *(V.P.-Admin.)*

Divisions:

Dura Convertible Systems Div. **(4)**
1365 E. Beecher St.
Adrian, MI 49221
Tel.: 517-263-7864
Automotive Parts
S.I.C.: 3714
Reed White *(V.P. & Gen. Mgr.)*

H. Koch & Sons **(4)**
5410 E. La Palma Ave.
Anaheim, CA 92807
Tel.: 714-779-7000
Fax: 714-779-7141
Approx.Sls.: $6,000,000
Emp.: 55
S.I.C.: 3728
William Raftery *(Pres.)*
Charles Fiely *(Controller)*
Joe Martin *(Dir.-Engrng.)*
J. E. Masterson *(Dir.-Mktg.)*
H. Kowalski *(Pur. Agent)*

Wickes Bumper Division **(4)**
1860 Alpine N.W.
Grand Rapids, MI 49504
Tel.: 616-363-4847
Mfr. of Automotive Products
S.I.C.: 3714
David Rector *(Plant Mgr.)*

Kayser-Roth Hosiery, Inc. **(2)**
4905 Koger Blvd.
Greensboro, NC 27407
Tel.: 919-852-2030
Fax: 919-854-4352
Approx.Sls.: $500,000,000
Emp.: 6,000
Fiscal Year-end: 1/31/92
S.I.C.: 2389; 2251; 2252
Robert Seelert *(Pres. & Chief Exec. Officer)*
Gary N. Malloch *(Pres.-Sheer Hosiery Div.)*
David R. Preston *(Pres.-Sock Div.)*
Joseph A. Horne *(Pres.-Rolane Div.)*
Frank B. Stull *(Chief Fin. Officer)*
Jane Martin *(V.P.-Total Quality Mgmt.)*
Carol K. Burke *(V.P. & Gen. Mgr.-Consumer Direct)*
Tom Kuhn *(V.P.-Mktg., Sheer Hosiery)*
H.D. Kenan *(V.P.-Human Resources)*
J.A. Perlmutter *(V.P. & Gen. Counsel)*

Divisions:

Kayser-Roth Corporation **(3)**
210 Madison Ave.
New York, NY 10016
Tel.: 212-578-1282
Approx.Sls.: $1,000,000,000
Emp.: 12,400
Sales & Mktg. of Hosiery
S.I.C.: 5136; 5137; 2251; 2252; 2253

Rolane Corporation **(3)**
P.O. Box 5407,
Greensboro, NC 27403
Tel.: 919-299-8831
Fax: 919-852-8007
S.I.C.: 5136
Joseph A. Horne *(Pres.)*

Sheer Hosiery Div. **(3)**
4905 Koger Blvd.
Greensboro, NC 27407
Tel.: 919-852-2030
Women's Hosiery
S.I.C.: 2251
Gary N. Malloch *(Pres.)*
Tom Kuhn *(V.P.-Mktg.)*
Kevin Toomey *(V.P.-Sls.)*

Socks Division **(3)**
4905 Koger Blvd.
Greensboro, NC 27407
Tel.: 919-852-2030
Mfg.-Socks
S.I.C.: 2389
David Preston *(Pres.)*
Jack Watson *(V.P.-Mktg.)*
Dick Dally *(V.P.-Sls.)*

Wickes Engineering Group **(1)**
280 Adams St.
Manchester, CT 06040
Tel.: 203-643-2473
S.I.C.: 3599
George A. Longtin *(Pres.)*

Divisions:

Cepco **(2)**
280 Adams St.
Manchester, CT 06040
Tel.: 203-643-2473
Surface Finishing for Jet Engine Parts
S.I.C.: 3471
George A. Longtin *(Pres.)*

Klock Co. **(2)**
1366 Tolland Turnpike
Manchester, CT 06040
Tel.: 203-646-0700
S.I.C.: 3398
Gunnar Hicks *(Exec. V.P.)*

Mal Tool & Engineering Co. **(2)**
273 Adams St.
Manchester, CT 06040
Tel.: 203-643-2473
Produces Prototype & Production Parts for Jet Engines including Fan & Compressor Blades & Vanes, Turbine Blades & Discs, Seals & Shrouds, & Replacement Blades & Vanes for Stationary Gas & Steam Turbines
S.I.C.: 3599; 3728; 3564
George A. Longtin *(Pres.)*

Subsidiary:

Collins & Aikman Inc. **(1)**
The Centre at Purchase, Two Manhattanville Rd.
Purchase, NY 10577
Tel.: 516-997-9560
Holding Co.
S.I.C.: 6719
James R. Birle *(Chief Exec. Officer)*

COLLINS CHEVROLET, GEO
717 W. Broadway
Louisville, KY 40202
Tel.: 502-582-2531
Fax: 502-585-2528
Sales Range: $10-19 Million
Automobile Sales & Service
S.I.C.: 5511; 7538
Kevin Collins *(Pres.)*
Joe Scrogins, Jr. *(Gen. Mgr.)*
Principal(s):
Kevin Collins

COLLINS ELECTRIC COMPANY, INC.
53 Second Ave
Chicopee, MA 01020
Tel.: 413-592-9222 **MA**
Fax: 413-592-4157
Approx.Sls.: $11,000,000
Emp.: 150
General Electrical Contractor
S.I.C.: 1731
William A. Collins *(Pres.)*
Emil Krupke *(V.P.)*
Donald F. Collins *(Treas. & Sec.)*

Outside Service Firm(s):

BayBank Valley Trust Co.*(Major Banking Relationship)*
1500 Main St.
Springfield, MA 01101
Tel.: 413-781-7575

BILL COLLINS FORD INC.
3610 Bargetown Rd.
Louisville, KY 40218
Tel.: 502-459-9550 **DE**
Fax: 502-459-9550, Ext. 191
Year Founded: 1969
Sales Range: $80-99 Million
Emp.: 304
Auto & Yacht Sales & Leasing
S.I.C.: 5511; 5551
William Collins *(Pres. & Chief Exec. Officer)*
Kevin Collins *(Chief Oper. Officer & V.P.)*
Christine Collins *(V.P.)*
William K. Collins *(Treas.)*
John Maher *(Sec.)*

Outside Service Firm(s):

Citizens Fidelity Bank & Trust Co.*(Major Banking Relationship)*
P.O. Box 33000-Citizens Plaza
Louisville, KY 40232
Tel.: 502-581-3381

WARREN E. COLLINS, INC.
220 Wood Rd.
Braintree, MA 02184
Tel.: 617-843-0610
Fax: 617-843-4024
Sales Range: $10-19 Million
Emp.: 80
Mfr. of Pulmonary Function Testing Systems & Stress Testing Systems
S.I.C.: 3841; 3842; 3800
W. Collins III *(Chm. Bd. & Pres.)*
James McCollum *(Chief Oper. Officer)*
Cosimo Cariolo *(Dir.-Sls. & Mktg.)*

Outside Service Firm(s):

Sullivan & Worcester*(Legal Firm)*
One Post Office Square, 100 Federal St.
Boston, MA 02110
Tel.: 617-338-2800

South Shore Bank*(Major Banking Relationship)*
Quincy, MA

COLLINS OLDSMOBILE INC.
P.O. Box 24009, 4080 Lafayette Rd.
Indianapolis, IN 46254
Tel.: 317-293-5900 **IN**
Fax: 317-293-0937
Year Founded: 1961
Approx.Sls.: $76,000,000
Emp.: 165
Fiscal Year-end: 12/31/91
Retail Automotive Sales & Service
S.I.C.: 5511
Joseph E. Myers *(Chm. Bd. & Pres.)*
Mike Cook *(Sec. & Treas.)*
Jeff Drake *(Mgr.-Sls.)*
Jim Boyd *(Dir.-Pur.)*
Principal(s):
Joseph E. Myers

Computer Systems/Hardware:
Reynolds & Reynolds ERA

Outside Service Firm(s):

George S. Olive & Co.*(Auditors)*
201 N. Illinois St.
Indianapolis, IN 46204

Commercial Union Insurance*(Commercial Insurance Carrier)*
Indianapolis, IN

Key Benefit Administrators*(Group Insurer)*
Indianapolis, IN

Steers, Sullivan, McNamar & Rogers*(Legal Firm)*
Indianapolis, IN

Benefit Consultants*(Pension Manager)*
Indianapolis, IN

COLLMAN GRAPHICS, INC.
1820 Portal St.
Baltimore, MD 21224
Tel.: 410-633-4200
Fax: 410-633-1228
Approx.Premiums: $35,000,000
Emp.: 295
Commercial Printers
S.I.C.: 2752
Nicholas J. Collman *(Chm., Pres. & Chief Exec. Officer)*
Jerad Welsh *(Exec. V.P.)*
James M. Brown *(V.P.-Fin. & Admin.)*
Robert Fox *(V.P.-Pharmaceutical Sls.)*
Robert Janes *(V.P.-Sls.)*
Sidney Wicks *(V.P.-Sls. Publ.)*
Dale Terzigne *(Controller)*

Outside Service Firm(s):

First America Bank*(Major Banking Relationship)*
Baltimore, MD

Subsidiary:

John D. Lucas Printing Company **(1)**
1820 Portal St.
Baltimore, MD 21224
Tel.: 410-633-4200
Fax: 410-633-1228
Sales Range: $20-39 Million
Emp.: 295
Commercial Printers
S.I.C.: 2752
Nicholas Collman *(Chm., Pres. & Chief Exec. Officer)*
Jerad Welsh *(Exec. V.P.)*
James M. Browne *(V.P.-Fin. & Admin.)*
Bob Fox *(V.P.-Pharmaceutical Sls.)*
Sidney Wicks *(V.P.-Publ. Sls.)*
Robert Janes *(Controller)*
Robert E. Kirkner *(Dir.-Sls.)*

COLMAN TOYOTA
9292 Airline Hwy.
Baton Rouge, LA 70895
Tel.: 504-925-2525
Fax: 504-926-2045
Year Founded: 1985
Approx.Sls.: $21,000,000
Emp.: 70
Retail New & Used Automobiles
S.I.C.: 5511
Bob Colman *(Owner)*
Kenny Hamilton *(Gen. Mgr.-Sls.)*
Principal(s):
Bob Colman

COLONIAL BEEF CO.
3333 S. Third St.
Philadelphia, PA 19148
Tel.: 215-467-0900
Fax: 215-336-6025
Approx.Sls.: $60,000,000
Emp.: 200
Wholesale Meats, Specializing in Portion Control
S.I.C.: 5147
Mr. Katoh *(Pres.)*
Donald McKay *(Dir.-Sls. & Mktg.)*
Joseph Delfini *(Sec. & Treas.)*
Leo Gessford *(Chief Engineer)*
Simon Katz *(Mgr.-Intl. Sls.)*
Dick Soyel *(Mgr.-Natl. Sls.)*
Larry Vasquez *(Pur. Agent)*

Outside Service Firm(s):

Isdaner & Co.*(Auditors)*
Philadelphia, PA

Wolf, Block, Schorr & Solis-Cohen*(Legal Firm)*
Packard Bldg., 12th Fl., 15th & Chestnut Sts.
Philadelphia, PA 19102
Tel.: 215-569-4000

Philadelphia National Bank*(Major Banking Relationship)*
P.O. Box 13834, Broad & Chestnut Streets
Philadelphia, PA 19101-7618
Tel.: 215-973-8327

COLONIAL DODGE INC.
24200 Gratiot
East Detroit, MI 48021
Tel.: 313-778-1800
Fax: 313-778-1890
Approx.Sls.: $30,000,000
Emp.: 95
Retail Automobiles & Trucks
S.I.C.: 5511
Arthur J. Roshak *(Pres.)*
Darryl A. Pavlik *(V.P.)*
Pamela M. Bartling *(Office Mgr.)*

Outside Service Firm(s):

Comerica Bank*(Major Banking Relationship)*
211 W. Fort St.
Detroit, MI 48226
Tel.: 313-222-3300

COLONIAL METALS CO.
217 Linden St.
Columbia, PA 17512
Tel.: 717-684-2311 **PA**
Fax: 717-684-9555
Year Founded: 1979
Sales Range: $60-79 Million
Emp.: 150
Metal Smelters
S.I.C.: 3341; 5093
David Serls *(Pres.)*
Phillip Serls *(Exec. V.P.)*
Michael R. Mann *(V.P.-Pur.)*
Don McVay *(V.P.-Fin.)*
Don Saffer *(V.P.-Mktg.)*
James Rowe *(Dir.-MIS)*

Outside Service Firm(s):

York Bank & Trust Co.*(Major Banking Relationship)*
York, PA

COLONIAL OIL INDUSTRIES
N. Lathrop Ave.
Savannah, GA 31402
Mailing Address:
P.O. Box 576,
Savannah, GA 31402
Tel.: 912-236-1331 **GA**
Telex: 804729
Fax: 912-235-3881
Year Founded: 1921
Assets: $112,000,000
Net Worth: $112,000,000
Approx.Sls.: $287,000,000
Emp.: 200
Fiscal Year-end: 9/30/92
Import
Special Trade Contractors; Service Stations; Miscellaneous Retail Stores; Real Estate Developer; Wholesale & Retail Distributor of Petroleum & Petroleum Products
S.I.C.: 7549; 5983; 6552; 5172
Robert H. Demere *(Chm. Bd. & Chief Exec. Officer)*
Robert H. Demere, Jr. *(Pres. & Chief Oper. Officer)*
Francis A. Brown *(V.P.-Fin.)*

Colonial Oil Industries—(Continued)

William A. Baker *(V.P.-Opers.)*
John W. Getty *(V.P.-Admin.)*
James B. Mercer *(V.P.-Enmark Stations, Inc.)*
Schaffer B. Wimbish, Jr. *(V.P.-Sls.)*
Charles Hodges *(Treas. & Controller)*
John McElveen *(Gen. Counsel)*
E.M. Almeida, III *(Dir.-Personnel)*
Stan Lancaster *(Dir.-Pur.)*

Computer Systems/Hardware:
IBM 4331-2

Outside Service Firm(s):

Price Waterhouse*(Auditors)*
Savannah, GA

Adams, Gardner & Ellis*(Legal Firm)*
Savannah, GA

C & S National Bank*(Major Banking Relationship)*
Savannah, GA

Subsidiaries:

Chatham Towing Company, Inc. **(1)**
P.O. Box 576
Savannah, GA 31402
Tel.: 912-236-1331
Barge & Towing Services
S.I.C.: 4731

Colonial Drilling & Exploration Corporation **(1)**
P.O. Box 576
Savannah, GA 31402
Tel.: 912-236-1331
Land Investments
S.I.C.: 1381; 1382; 6531

Colonial Marine Industries, Inc. **(1)**
26 E. Byron St.
Savannah, GA 31401
Tel.: 912-233-7000
Ocean-Going Vessel Management, Agency & Chartering
S.I.C.: 4731
John DeMere *(Pres.)*

Enmark Stations, Inc. **(1)**
P.O. Box 576
Savannah, GA 31402
Tel.: 912-236-1331
Operators of Enmark Service Stations
S.I.C.: 5541
James B. Mercer *(V.P.)*

Colonial Terminals, Inc. **(1)**
P.O. Box 576
Savannah, GA 31402
Tel.: 912-236-1331
Bulk Liquid & Dry Products Terminalling(Clay & Kaolin)
S.I.C.: 5171; 1455

COLONIAL PETROLEUM CO.
P.O. Box 307,
Cliffside, NC 28024
Tel.: 704-453-7351
Approx.Sls.: $20,000,000
S.I.C.: 1389
Mike Frost *(Pres.)*
Hampton C. Hager *(Exec. V.P.)*

Subsidiary:

Petroleum World **(1)**
Hwy. 120
Cliffside, NC 28024
Tel.: 704-453-7351
Petroleum Jobber & Distribution
S.I.C.: 1389
Hampton C. Hager *(Exec. V.P.)*

COLONIAL PIPELINE COMPANY
945 E. Paces Ferry Rd., N.E.
Atlanta, GA 30326-0855
Mailing Address:
P.O. Box 18855,
Atlanta, GA 30326
Tel.: 404-261-1470
Tel.: 800-277-6457 **DE**
Telex: 361-116
Fax: 404-237-2315
Year Founded: 1962
Assets: $867,389,000
Earnings: $155,531,208
Liabilities: $818,185,000
Net Worth: $49,204,000
Approx.Sls.: $527,136,000
Emp.: 676
Fiscal Year-end: 12/31/90
Common Carrier Pipeline of Refined Petroleum Products
S.I.C.: 4613
Corporate Giving Program: United Way
Employee Matching Gifts Program: Educational Contributions by Employees & Spouses on a 2 to 1 Basis on First $1,000; On a 1 to 1 Basis up to $4,000
B. Walker *(Chm. Bd.)*
D.R. Brinkley *(Pres. & Chief Exec. Officer)*
C.W. Crider *(V.P.-Admin.)*
T.H. Norris *(V.P.-Opers.)*
K. Jones *(Corp. Sec.)*
P.A. Morrison *(Attorney)*
J.B. Nelson *(Treas.)*
E.H. Cooper *(Controller)*
R.E. Ahlfinger *(Dir.-Human Resources)*
V.A. Yarborough *(Dir.-Engrng.)*
R.F. Calupca *(Sr. Mgr.-Western Region)*
W.E. Copenhaver *(Sr. Mgr.-Opers. Control)*
H.R. Melendy *(Sr. Mgr.-Eastern Region)*
J.M. Blakely *(Mgr.-Scheduling, Shipper Rels.)*
N.J. Edmonds *(Mgr.-Opers. Plng. & Pipeline Control)*
G.L. French *(Mgr.-Plng. & Business Devel.)*
K.W. Lanman *(Mgr.-Pur.)*
O.L. Lowe *(Mgr.-Information Systems)*
R.B. Rondem *(Mgr.-Employee Rels.)*
Principal(s):
Amoco Pipeline Co.
Atlantic Richfield Co.
BP Oil Co.
Citgo Pipeline Investment Co.
Conoco Pipe Line Co.
Mobil Pipe Line Co.
Phillips Petroleum International Investment Co.
Texaco Trading & Transportation Inc.
Union Oil Co. of California

No. of Mfg. Plants/Facilities: 48
No. of U.S. Offices: 10

Computer Systems/Hardware:
STRATUS

Outside Service Firm(s):

Ernst & Young*(Auditors)*
600 Peachtree St. N.E.
Atlanta, GA 30308
Tel.: 404-874-8300

Northwestern National Life*(Group Insurer)*
20 Washington Ave. S.
Minneapolis, MN 55401

Shearson Lehman Hutton, Inc.*(Investment Banker)*
American Express Tower, World Financial Center
New York, NY 10285
Tel.: 212-298-2000

NationsBank*(Major Banking Relationship)*
35 Broad St.
Atlanta, GA 30303
Tel.: 404-581-2121
Tel.: 800-848-8198

First National Bank of Atlanta*(Major Banking Relationship)*
2 Peachtree Street N.W.
Atlanta, GA 30383

Equitable Capital*(Pension Manager)*
1221 Avenue of the Americas
New York, NY 10020
Tel.: 212-382-8099
Fax: 212-382-8089

INVESCO Capital Management*(Pension Manager)*
Ste. 300, 1315 Peachtree St., N.E.-Ste. 300
Atlanta, GA 30309
Tel.: 404-892-0896

COLONIAL SUPPLY CORPORATION
25 Union St.
Manchester, NH 03103
Tel.: 603-669-2334 **NH**
Fax: 603-669-0229
Year Founded: 1946
Approx.Sls.: $20,000,000
Emp.: 70
Wholesale Distribution of Plumbing & Hydronic Heating Supplies & Air Conditioning Equipment, Except Room Units
S.I.C.: 5074; 5075
Bernard Garrell *(Pres.)*
Peter Garrell *(V.P.)*
John Monson *(Sec.)*

Outside Service Firm(s):

First New Hampshire Bank*(Major Banking Relationship)*
Manchester, NH

COLONIAL WILLIAMSBURG FOUNDATION
Henry St. & Prince George St.
Williamsburg, VA 23187
Mailing Address:
P.O. Drawer 1776
Williamsburg, VA 23187
Tel.: 804-229-1000
Fax: 804-220-7685
Year Founded: 1926
Approx.Sls.: $100,000,000
Emp.: 4,000
Fiscal Year-end: 12/31/90
Adv. & Promo of the Restoration of Colonial Williamsburg & Visitor Services Including Williamsburg Inn, Williamsburg Lodge, The Motor House & Governors Inn
S.I.C.: 7311
Charles Longsworth *(Chm., Pres. & Chief Exec. Officer)*
J.C. Miles *(V.P.-Hotels & Restaurants)*
Randall J. Foskey *(Dir.-Mktg.)*

COLONNA BROS., INC.
4102 Bergen Tpke.
North Bergen, NJ 07047
Mailing Address:
P. O. Box 808
No. Bergen, NJ 07047
Tel.: 201-864-1115
Fax: 201-864-0144
Year Founded: 1918
Approx.Sls.: $10,000,000
Emp.: 39
Fiscal Year-end: 12/31/90
Import
Distributes Colonna Italian Kitchen Grated Cheese, Colonna Flavored Bread Crumbs, Plain Bread Crumbs, Private Label Packaging
S.I.C.: 5451
Leonard Colonna *(Chm. Bd.)*
Peter Colonna *(Pres., Chief Exec. Officer & Mng. Dir.)*
Mark Colonna *(Exec. V.P., Chief Oper. Officer-Mktg, Dir.Sls. Promo & Mgr.-Adv.)*
Diane Maniscalco *(Chief Fin. Officer-Admin./Opers.-Sec. & Treas.)*
Dennis Da Puzzo *(Dir.-Sls.)*

COLONY LIQUOR DISTRIBUTORS, INC.
132 Flatbush Ave.
Kingston, NY 12401
Tel.: 914-338-2740
Fax: 914-338-9385
Year Founded: 1935
Approx.Sls.: $45,000,000
Emp.: 150
Wholesale Distributor of Wines & Liquors
S.I.C.: 5182
Vincent J. Andretta *(Pres., Chief Exec. Officer & Treas.)*
Maureen Nerone *(V.P., Controller & Chief Fin. Officer)*

Computer Systems/Hardware:
Sperry IVAC System 80

Outside Service Firm(s):

Hiltzik Schneider Ehrlich & Co.*(Auditors)*
Great Neck, NY

Rogers & Wells*(Legal Firm)*
200 Park Ave.
New York, NY 10166
Tel.: 212-878-8000

Key Bank*(Major Banking Relationship)*
Kingston, NY

COLOR ARTS, INC.
1840 Oakdale Ave.
Racine, WI 53406
Tel.: 414-633-7751
Fax: 414-633-3008
Approx.Sls.: $12,000,000
Emp.: 175
Screen Printing
S.I.C.: 2759
William Nahikian *(Pres.)*
Daniel Mouw *(V.P.-Admin.)*
James Pekar *(V.P. & Controller)*
John Csepella *(Treas.)*
William F. Kolbe *(Sec.)*

Outside Service Firm(s):

DeMark, Kolbe & Brodek*(Legal Firm)*
Racine, WI

Marine Bank*(Major Banking Relationship)*
Racine, WI

COLOR CUSTOM, INC.
24060 Hoover Rd.
Warren, MI 48089
Tel.: 313-755-1010
Fax: 313-755-9808
Approx.Sls.: $34,000,000
Emp.: 100
Compounding & Extruding; Injection Molding
S.I.C.: 3089; 3087
Peter C. Schmitt *(Chm. Bd.)*
Paul Dettloff *(Pres.)*

Outside Service Firm(s):

Fletcher, Hugh Himmbispach*(Legal Firm)*
Detroit, MI

N.B.D. Bank, N.A.*(Major Banking Relationship)*
611 Woodward Ave.
Detroit, MI 48226
Tel.: 313-225-1122
Fax: 313-225-3420

COLOR GRAPHICS, INC.
4540 Frederick Dr., S.W.
Atlanta, GA 30336
Tel.: 404-696-1515
Fax: 404-691-8024
Emp.: 117
Commercial Lithographic Printing
S.I.C.: 2752
Maurice J. Towery *(Chm. Bd. & Chief Exec. Officer)*
John G. Glover *(Pres.)*
Odell Parson *(V.P.)*

Outside Service Firm(s):

Post & Associates*(Auditors)*
East Point, GA

COLORADO BOXED BEEF CO.
302 Progress Rd.
Auburndale, FL 33823
Mailing Address:
P.O. Box 899,
Winter Haven, FL 33882
Tel.: 813-967-0636
Fax: 813-965-2222
Year Founded: 1975
Assets: $22,851,615
Liabilities: $15,104,183
Net Worth: $7,747,432
Approx.Sls.: $231,558,154
Emp.: 205
Fiscal Year-end: 3/28/92
Import Export
Wholesale Meat Distributor
S.I.C.: 5147
John Roden *(Sr. V.P. & Gen. Mgr.)*
Bryan Saterbo *(Sr. V.P. & Treas.)*
Stephen Saterbo *(Sr. V.P.-Sls. & Mktg.)*
Jerry Heyman *(V.P.-Human Resources)*
Charles Chilton *(Gen. Counsel)*
Edith Saterbo *(Sec.)*
Sue Godfrey *(Dir.-Data Processing)*
Principal(s):
Bryan Saterbo
Stephen Saterbo

No. of Mfg. Plants/Facilities: 1
No. of U.S. Offices: 1

Computer Systems/Hardware:
IBM System AS-400

Outside Service Firm(s):

Beckert, Price & Rowse*(Auditors)*
Winter Haven, FL

Mutual of Omaha Insurance Company*(Group Insurer)*
Mutual of Omaha Plaza,
Omaha, NE 68175
Tel.: 800-228-7775

NationsBank*(Investment Banker)*
Winter Haven, FL

Sharit, Bunn, Chilton & Holden*(Legal Firm)*
Winter Haven, FL

NationsBank*(Major Banking Relationship)*
Winter Haven, FL

COLORADO LOTTERY
720 S. Colorado Blvd., Ste. 110
Denver, CO 80222
Tel.: 303-759-3552
Fax: 303-759-6847
Year Founded: 1983
Approx.Sls.: $185,000,000
Emp.: 111
Fiscal Year-end: 6/30/91
State Lottery
S.I.C.: 7999
George Turner *(Dir.)*
Bill Russell *(Deputy Dir.)*
Dan Noreen *(Dir.-Mktg. & Sls.)*
Mary Brown *(Assoc. Dir.-Mktg.)*
Alan Hoffman *(Mgr.-Mktg. & Promo.)*

COLORFORMS
133 Williams Dr.
Ramsey, NJ 07446
Tel.: 201-327-2600 **NJ**
Fax: 201-327-2506
Sales Range: $10-19 Million
Emp.: 300
Fiscal Year-end: 12/31/90
Pre-School Toys, Puzzles, Games & Activity Sets
S.I.C.: 3944
Harry Kislevitz *(Chm. Bd.)*
David Kislevitz *(Sr. V.P.)*
Joshua Kislevitz *(Mng. Dir.)*
Dennis J. Eckardt *(Controller)*
Margie Moss *(Dir.-Sls. Admin.)*

No. of Mfg. Plants/Facilities: 1
No. of U.S. Offices: 1
No. of Foreign Offices: 1

Computer Systems/Hardware:
MAI Basic 4

COLORTYME, INC.
P.O. Box 1781,
Athens, TX 75751
Tel.: 903-675-9291
Approx.Sls.: $100,000,000
Emp.: 45
Franchiser of Rent-to-Own Stores
S.I.C.: 6794
Willie Talley *(Chm. Bd., Pres. & Chief Exec. Officer)*
Jim Crysdale *(Chief Fin. Officer)*
Thom E. Webb *(V.P.-Adv. & Mktg.)*
Sandra Blackwell *(Dir.-Franchise Compliance)*

COLSKY MEDIA, INC.
2740 Van Ness Ave., Ste. 220
San Francisco, CA 94109
Tel.: 415-673-5400
Year Founded: 1973
Approx.Billings: $20,000,000
Emp.: 10
TV & Radio Media Planning & Buying
Richard A. Colsky *(Pres. & Chief Exec. Officer)*
Ho Chang Lam *(Controller)*
Stephen Trauner *(Dir.-Mktg.)*

Computer Systems/Hardware:
Marketing Resources Plus; IBM & Macintosh Capabilities

COLUMBIA CORPORATION
Kingsport Bldg., 215
Centerview Dr., Ste. 143
Brentwood, TN 37027
Tel.: 615-370-0180
Fax: 615-370-8736
Year Founded: 1984
Approx.Rev.: $60,000,000
Emp.: 355
Nursing Home Owner & Operator
S.I.C.: 8051
Patrick M. Dray *(Pres.)*
Ray Gann *(V.P.-Fin.)*

Computer Systems/Hardware:
IBM System 38 & 5381

Outside Service Firm(s):

Prudential Insurance Co. of America*(Group Insurer)*
Nashville, TN

First American Bank, N.A.*(Major Banking Relationship)*
Nashville, TN

COLUMBIA FALLS ALUMINUM COMPANY
2000 Aluminum Dr.
Columbia Falls, MT 59912
Mailing Address:
P.O. Box 10,
Columbia Falls, MT 59912
Tel.: 406-892-3261
Fax: 406-892-5317
Approx.Sls.: $200,000,000
Emp.: 750
Primary Aluminum, Primary Aluminum Ingots
S.I.C.: 3334
Brack Duker *(Chm. Bd.)*
Jerome T. Broussard *(Gen. Mgr.)*
Jerry Miller *(Fin. Coord.)*

Outside Service Firm(s):

Ernst & Young*(Auditors)*
50 S. Main, Ste. 1400
Salt Lake City, UT 84144
Tel.: 801-538-2500

Norwest of Kalispell*(Major Banking Relationship)*
Kalispell, MT

COLUMBIA FARMS INC.
Hwy. #23
Leesville, SC 29070
Tel.: 803-532-4488 **SC**
Fax: 803-532-0056
Sales Range: $40-59 Million
Emp.: 200
Poultry Dressing Plants
S.I.C.: 2015
Albin S. Johnson *(Chm. & Chief Exec. Officer)*
James G. Mabe *(Pres.)*
Donald K. Potter *(Treas.)*

Outside Service Firm(s):

Valley National Bank*(Major Banking Relationship)*
Leesville, SC

COLUMBIA LUMBER & MANUFACTURING CO.
P.O. Box 23289
Columbia, SC 29224
Tel.: 803-788-8950 **SC**
Fax: 803-736-6172
Year Founded: 1898
Sales Range: $20-39 Million
Emp.: 160
Wholesale & Retail Lumber & Building Materials; Manufacture Architectural Woodwork & Pressure-Treated Lumber
S.I.C.: 5031; 5211; 2452
William L. Otis, Jr. *(Chm. Bd. & Pres.)*

Outside Service Firm(s):

Ernst & Young*(Auditors)*
P.O. Box 627, 1611 Devonshire Dr.
Columbia, SC 20202
Tel.: 803-254-4700
Fax: 803-252-4090

Sinkler & Boyd*(Legal Firm)*
P.O. Box 1889,
Columbia, SC 29211

Citizens & Southern National Bank*(Major Banking Relationship)*
Columbia, SC

Subsidiary:

Colwood Co., Inc. **(1)**
P.O. Box 23289,
Columbia, SC 29224
Tel.: 803-788-5033
Emp.: 25
Pressure Treated Lumber
S.I.C.: 5211
James W. Bartz *(Pres.)*

THE COLUMBIA MFG. COMPANY, INC.
Cycle St.
Westfield, MA 01085
Mailing Address:
P.O. Box 1230
Westfield, MA 01086
Tel.: 413-562-3664
Approx.Sls.: $50,000,000
Emp.: 350
Fiscal Year-end: 12/31/90
Mfr. Bicycles & School Furniture
S.I.C.: 3751; 2531
Kenneth Howard *(Pres.)*
Bruce Turcotte *(Treas.)*

COLUMBIA NATIONAL GROUP, INC.
6600 Grant Ave.
Cleveland, OH 44105
Tel.: 216-883-4972 **OH**
Fax: 216-883-3483
Year Founded: 1984
Approx.Sls.: $200,000,000
Emp.: 250
Fiscal Year-end: 12/31/91
Holding Company for Steel Related Businesses; Scrap Steel Brokerage, Processing & Steel Service Centers
S.I.C.: 5093; 5051
David Miller *(Pres. & Chief Exec. Officer)*
Ronald Chawdowsky *(Chief Fin. Officer & V.P.-Fin.)*
Stephen Ruscher *(V.P., Treas. & Controller)*
Malvin Bank *(Sec.)*
Charles Hudson *(Dir.-Mngmt. Information Systems)*
Richard Vanco *(Mgr.-Pur.)*

Computer Systems/Hardware:
IBM System RS6000

Outside Service Firm(s):

Arthur Andersen & Co.*(Auditors)*
1717 E. 9th St.
Cleveland, OH 44114
Tel.: 216-781-2140
Fax: 216-781-3683

Thompson, Hine & Flory*(Legal Firm)*
1100 National City Bank Bldg.
Cleveland, OH 44114
Tel.: 216-566-5500

National City Bank*(Major Banking Relationship)*
P.O. Box 92301, Corp. Trust Dept.
Cleveland, OH 44101
Tel.: 216-575-2000

Subsidiaries:

Atlas Lederer Co. **(1)**
P.O. Box 20190
Cleveland, OH 44120
Tel.: 216-231-2430
David P. Miller *(Chm. Bd.)*
Ronald A. Bone *(Pres.)*
James D. Larr *(V.P.-Fin. & Treas.)*

Columbia Iron & Metal Co. **(1)**
6600 Grant Ave.
Cleveland, OH 44105
Tel.: 216-883-4972
S.I.C.: 5051; 5093
Ronald A. Bone *(Pres.)*
James D. Larr *(V.P.-Fin. & Treas.)*
Gerald Mink *(V.P.-Mktg.)*

Grant Steel Corp. **(1)**
3rd & Oliver
Pittsburgh, PA 15110
Tel.: 412-281-0300
S.I.C.: 5051
David P. Miller *(Chm. Bd.)*
Ronald A. Bone *(Pres.)*
James D. Larr *(V.P.-Fin. & Treas.)*

The Universal Steel Co. **(1)**
6600 Grant
Cleveland, OH 44105
Tel.: 216-883-4972
S.I.C.: 5051
David P. Miller *(Chm. Bd.)*
Lawrence Edleman *(Pres.)*
James D. Larr *(V.P.-Fin. & Treas.)*
David P. Massini *(V.P.-Mktg.)*
Michael Morgus *(V.P.-Admin.)*

COLUMBIA PAINT CO.
P.O. Box 4569
Spokane, WA 99202
Tel.: 509-535-9741
Fax: 509-535-3421
Year Founded: 1947
Approx.Sls.: $25,000,000
Emp.: 200
Fiscal Year-end: 10/31/92
Mfg., Distr. & Retailing Paint & Related Items
S.I.C.: 1721

Columbia Paint Co.—(Continued)

H.H. Larison *(Pres.)*
Thomas Wellborn *(Exec. V.P.)*
Jeff Bartsch *(V.P.-Sls.-Eastern Reg.)*
R. Guiles *(V.P.-Mfg., Res. & Devel.)*
E. Schindler *(V.P.-Fin.)*
Martin Wilson *(V.P.-Sls.-West. Reg.)*
Pamela Larison *(Mgr.-Mktg. & Personnel Devel.)*

COLUMBIA PIPE & SUPPLY COMPANY
1120 W. Pershing Rd.
Chicago, IL 60609
Tel.: 312-927-6600 **IL**
Fax: 312-927-8415
Approx.Sls.: $49,000,000
Emp.: 170
Plumbing & Hydronic Heating Supplies; Industrial Fittings
S.I.C.: 5074; 5085
Julius T. Arenberg *(Chm. Bd.)*
William D. Arenberg *(Pres. & Chief Exec. Officer)*
Daniel R. Arenberg *(Exec. V.P.)*
Tim P. Arenberg *(V.P.)*
Frank L. Bridgeford *(V.P.)*
Thomas Ryan *(V.P.)*
J. Steven Harrison *(Treas.)*
Norman E. Shoff *(Sec.)*

COLUMBIA SUSSEX CORPORATION
207 Grandview
Fort Mitchell, KY 41017
Tel.: 606-331-0091
Fax: 606-331-6383
Assets: $181,500,000
Liabilities: $153,000,000
Net Worth: $28,500,000
Approx.Sls.: $40,000,000
Emp.: 1,500
Owns & Operates Motels & Restaurants
S.I.C.: 7011; 5812
William J. Yung *(Pres. & Chief Exec. Officer)*
William Beegle *(Exec. V.P.)*
Stan Clayton *(V.P.)*
Joseph E. Marquet *(V.P.-Fin.)*
Ted Mitchell *(Treas. & Sec.)*
Tom Day *(Controller)*
Christopher Rhode *(Dir.-Personnel)*
Joe Rywe *(Pur. Agent)*

Outside Service Firm(s):

The Huntington National Bank *(Major Banking Relationship)*
Cincinnati, OH

COLUMBIAN ADVERTISING INC.

COLUMBIAN ADVERTISING INC.
201 E. Ohio St.
Chicago, IL 60611
Tel.: 312-943-7600 **DE**
Year Founded: 1960
Approx.Billings: $60,000,000
Emp.: 59
Fiscal Year-end: 12/13/91
Import
Merchandising, Sales Promotion & Direct Marketing
S.I.C.: 7311
Bernard J. Miller, Jr. *(Chm. Bd.)*
Bernard J. Miller III *(Pres.)*
Michael P. Slott *(Exec. V.P.)*
Ann McConville *(V.P.)*
Jeffrey B. Miller *(Treas.)*
Louis S. Geisman *(Comptroller)*

Computer Systems/Hardware:
IBM System 37 & PC, MAC

Outside Service Firm(s):

Klayman & Korman *(Auditors)*
Chicago, IL

Guardian Life Insurance Co. *(Group Insurer)*
Chicago, IL

Martin, Craig, Chester & Sonnenschein *(Legal Firm)*
Chicago, IL

LaSalle National Bank *(Major Banking Relationship)*
120 S. LaSalle St.
Chicago, IL 60603
Tel.: 312-781-8000

Division:

Columbian Direct Marketing **(1)**
201 East Ohio St.
Chicago, IL 60611
Tel.: 312-943-7600
Emp.: 28
Bernard J. Miller III *(Pres.)*

COLUMBIAN MUTUAL LIFE INSURANCE CO.
P.O. Box 1381,
Binghamton, NY 13902
Tel.: 607-724-2472 **NY**
Fax: 607-722-0328
Year Founded: 1882
Assets: $337,311,000
Liabilities: $313,594,000
Net Worth: $23,717,000
Sales Range: $1 Billion +
Emp.: 175
Life & Health Insurance
S.I.C.: 6311; 6321
John G. Shillestad *(Chm. Bd., Pres. & Chief Exec. Officer)*
Frank Crisafulli *(Exec. V.P.)*
Bart Bozzi, Jr. *(V.P.-Admin.)*
John J. Gately *(V.P. & Chief Actuary)*
Lillian M. Heilbron *(V.P.)*
Eric K. Rasanen *(V.P.)*
Tom Rattmann *(V.P.)*
Peter Young *(V.P.)*
Tanya Schmeller *(Sec.)*

Outside Service Firm(s):

KPMG Peat Marwick *(Auditors)*
345 Park Ave.
New York, NY 10154
Tel.: 212-758-9700
Fax: 212-872-3308

Marine Midland Bank *(Major Banking Relationship)*
Syracuse, NY

Subsidiaries:

Columbian Life Insurance Company **(1)**
P.O. Box 1381,
Binghamton, NY 13902
Tel.: 607-724-2472 (100%)
Life & Health Insurance
S.I.C.: 6311; 6321
John G. Shillestad *(Chm. Bd., Pres. & Chief Oper. Officer)*

Washington National Life Insurance Co. of New York **(1)**
120 W. 45th St.
New York, NY 10036
Tel.: 212-719-4300
Approx.Sls.: $48,000,000
Life Insurance & Annuities
S.I.C.: 6311
K.L. Carver *(Pres.)*

COLUMBIAN ROPE COMPANY
145 Towery St.
Guntown, MS 38849-0270
Mailing Address:
P.O. Box 270
Guntown, MS 38849-0270
Tel.: 601-348-2241 **DE**
Fax: 601-348-5749
Year Founded: 1903
Approx.Sls.: $20,000,000
Emp.: 250
Import Export
Manufacture & Distribute Rope, Twine & Industrial Fiber Products
S.I.C.: 2298; 2679; 3589
D.B. Chapman *(Chm. Bd)*
S.G. Ludt *(Pres., Chief Exec. Officer & Treas.)*
J.E. Richardson *(V.P.-Sls.)*
Charles Hankins *(Mgr.-Pur.)*
Jerry Lamontagne *(Mgr.-Tech Servs.)*
Joe Westmoreland *(Plant Mgr.)*
Chris Zuercher *(Mgr.-Sls.)*

No. of Mfg. Plants/Facilities: 3
No. of U.S. Offices: 4

Computer Systems/Hardware:
IBM

Outside Service Firm(s):

Nail, McKinney, Tate, Robinson *(Auditors)*
Tupelo, MS

Subsidiaries:

Monorail, Inc. **(1)**
23 N. Division St.
Auburn, NY 13021
Tel.: 315-253-3285 (100%)
Manufacture Car Wash Equipment
S.I.C.: 3589
B.S. Metcalf *(Gen. Mgr.)*
G. Servais *(Mgr.-Sales)*

Plymkraft Inc. **(1)**
P.O. Box 1577, Warwick Station
Newport News, VA 23601
Tel.: 804-595-0364 (100%)
Manufacture Twisted Paper Products
S.I.C.: 2679
N.W. Bergeron *(Exec. V.P. & Gen. Mgr.)*
G. Cabral *(Mgr.-Sls.)*

Non-U.S. Holdings:

Columbian Philippines Inc. **(1)**
P.O. Box 7501
Manila, Philippines
Tel.: 2-471421
Holding Co., Investments; Travel Agency
S.I.C.: 4724; 6719; 6211
Jose R. Mejia *(Chief Oper. Officer)*

TCG Fibers, Philippines **(1)**
Sasa,
Davao, 950L, Philippines
Tel.: 35-71979
Manufacture & Distribute Rope, Twine & Industrial Fiber Prods.
S.I.C.: 2298
J. Mejia *(Chief Oper. Officer)*

COLUMBINE SYSTEMS INC.
1707 Cole Blvd.
Golden, CO 80401-3296
Tel.: 303-237-4000
Fax: 303-237-0085
Year Founded: 1971
Assets: $4,000,000
Net Worth: $4,000,000
Approx.Sls.: $15,400,000
Emp.: 220
Fiscal Year-end: 3/31/91
Wholesale Computers, Peripheral Equipment & Computer Forms
S.I.C.: 5112
Wayne Ruting *(Chm. Bd.)*
Neil Hamilton *(Dir.-European Opers.)*
Wayne Ruting *(Pres. & Chief. Exec. Officer)*
Catherine P. Cole *(Chief Oper. Oficer & Sec.)*
David C. Hall *(Treas.)*
Dave Paulsen *(Controller & Dir.-Fin. & Treasury)*
Principal(s):
Wayne Ruting
Catherine P. Cole

No. of U.S. Offices: 2
No. of Foreign Offices: 1

Outside Service Firm(s):

Deloitte & Touche *(Auditors)*
1560 Broadway, Ste. 1800
Denver, CO 80202-5626
Tel.: 303-837-3000
Fax: 303-825-0567

Sherman & Howard *(Legal Firm)*
Denver, CO

Colorado National Bank *(Major Banking Relationship)*
17th & Champa
Denver, CO 80217

COLUMBUS MCKINNON CORP.
140 J.J. Audubon Pkwy.
Amherst, NY 14228-1197
Tel.: 716-689-5400 **NY**
Telex: 6854301
Fax: 716-689-5644
Year Founded: 1879
Approx.Sls.: $120,000,000
Emp.: 1,140
Fiscal Year-end: 3/31/92
Import Export
Manufacture Materials Handling Equipment, Hoists, Chains, Forgings, Trolleys and Volume Reduction Products, Tire-Shredders & Paper Shredders, Manipulators
S.I.C.: 3536; 3462
E.W. Duffy *(Chm. Bd.)*
H.P. Ladds, Jr. *(Pres. & Chief Exec. Officer)*
R.L. Montgomery *(Chief Fin. Officer, Exec. V.P. & Treas.)*
F.D. DeVilline *(V.P.-Sls. & Mktg.)*
P.A. Grant *(V.P.-Human Resources)*
K.G. McCreadie *(V.P. & Controller)*
T.T. Tevens *(V.P.-Info. Services)*
Lois Demler *(Sec.)*
William F. Ryan *(Asst. Treas.)*
Charles Astafan *(Mgr.-Shredder Sls.)*
W. Blizard *(Mgr.-Field Sls.-Hoist & Chain)*
Craig Johnston *(Mgr.-Intl.)*

No. of Mfg. Plants/Facilities: 7
No. of Foreign Offices: 4

Computer Systems/Hardware:
Honeywell DPS-6

Outside Service Firm(s):

Ernst & Young *(Auditors)*
1400 Key Tower - 50 Fountain Plaza
Buffalo, NY
Tel.: 716-843-5000
Fax: 716-847-6949

Fleet Bank *(International Bank Affiliate)*
Deer Park, NY 14202

Phillips, Lytle, Hitchcock, Blaine & Huber *(Legal Firm)*
3400 Marine Midland Center
Buffalo, NY 14203
Tel.: 716-847-8400

Fleet Bank *(Major Banking Relationship)*
Deer Park, NY 14202

Divisions:

CM Chain Division **(1)**
State Road 22A
Lexington, TN 38351
Tel.: 716-689-5400
Earl Loeswick *(Gen. Mgr.)*

CM Hoist Division **(1)**
Audubon & Sylvan Pkwys.
Amherst, NY 14228
Tel.: 716-689-5400

CM Mechanical Handling Systems **(1)**
140 J.J. Audubon Pkwy
Amherst, NY 14228-1187
Tel.: 716-689-5400

CM Shredder Div. **(1)**
140 J.J. Audubon Pkwy.
Amherst, NY 14228-1197
Tel.: 716-689-5400

Midland Forge Division **(1)**
101 S. Ave., S.W.
Cedar Rapids, IA 52406
Tel.: 319-362-1111
Gary Eckley *(Gen. Mgr.)*

Subsidiaries:

Dixie Industries, Inc. **(1)**
3510 N. Orchard Knob Ave.
Chattanooga, TN 37406
Tel.: 615-698-3323
Zane Goggin *(Pres.)*

Positech Corporation **(1)**
Rush Lake Rd.
Laurens, IA 50554
Tel.: 712-845-4548
Fax: 712-845-4765
Manufacture Manipulators & Hydraulic Cylinders
S.I.C.: 3593; 3536
Peter Hong *(Pres.)*

COLUMBUS MILLS, INC.
4600 River Rd.
Columbus, GA 31904
Mailing Address:
P.O. Box 1560,
Columbus, GA 31993
Tel.: 706-324-0111 **GA**
Fax: 706-322-4378
Year Founded: 1946
Approx.Sls.: $170,000,000
Emp.: 1,100
Fiscal Year-end: 7/31/90
Export
Manufacture Carpets & Rugs
S.I.C.: 2298
George P. Swift, Jr. *(Chm. Bd. & Chief Exec. Officer)*
John Dixon *(Pres. & Chief Oper. Officer)*
W. Howard Parham *(Exec. V.P.-Pur. & Mfg.)*
Larry Cooper *(V.P.-Sls.)*
James T. Tapscott *(Sec. & Treas.)*
Dave Bonaker *(Controller)*
Rodney Fuller *(Dir.-Human Resources)*
Stephen Howard *(Dir.-Mktg. Services)*
Nelson Hartman *(Dir.-Data Processing)*

Outside Service Firm(s):

Dougherty, McKinnon & Greenwald*(Auditors)*
Columbus, GA

Trust Company Bank*(Major Banking Relationship)*
P.O. Box 4655,
Atlanta, GA 30302

King & Spalding*(Legal Firm)*
Trust Co. Tower
Atlanta, GA 30303
Tel.: 404-572-4600

Division:

Lotus Carpet Division **(1)**
4500 River Rd.
Columbus, GA 31904
Tel.: 706-324-0111
Manufacture Carpets & Rugs
S.I.C.: 2298
Roy Hickman *(Pres.)*
William P. McGuigen *(V.P.-Prod. Plng. & Mfg.)*
H. David Murray *(V.P.-Sls.)*

Showroom:

Columbus Mills, Inc. **(1)**
Atlanta Merchandise Mart Space 309
Atlanta, GA 30303
Tel.: 404-577-4430
S.I.C.: 5023

COLUMBUS PIPE & EQUIPMENT COMPANY
773 E. Markison Ave.
Columbus, OH 43207
Tel.: 614-444-7871 **OH**
Fax: 614-444-0949
Emp.: 40
Steel Plumbing Fittings & Supplies
S.I.C.: 5051; 5074
Bruce Jay Silberstein *(Pres.)*
John Silberstein *(Asst. V.P.)*
Harry H. Brinkman *(Treas.)*
Dr. Jack Silberstein *(Sec.)*

Outside Service Firm(s):

Schwartz, Kelm, Warren & Rubenstein*(Legal Firm)*
250 E. Broad St.
Columbus, OH 43215
Tel.: 614-224-3168

COLUMBUS SHOW CASE COMPANY
850 W. 5th Ave.
Columbus, OH 43212
Tel.: 614-299-3161
Tel.: 800-848-3573
Fax: 614-297-0741
Year Founded: 1895
Approx.Sls.: $18,000,000
Emp.: 200-250
Fiscal Year-end: 2/28/92
Import Export
Manufacture Show Cases, Wall Systems, Custom Counters, Bakery Cases, Refrigerated Cases & Open Refrigerated Cases
S.I.C.: 2542; 2541
Carl J. Aschinger, Jr. *(Chm. Bd., Pres. & Chief Exec. Officer)*
George W. Anderson II *(Chief Fin. Officer)*
Paul Cianelli *(V.P.-Sls.)*
Michael Gray *(V.P.-Mfg. & Dir.-Columbus Opers.)*
Ken Jones *(V.P.-Pur. & Matls. Control)*
Frank Kates *(Controller)*
Chris Aschinger *(Dir.-Ashland Opers.)*
Bonnie Bates *(Mgr.-Human Resources)*
Carolyn Ferguson *(Mgr.-Natl. Mktg.)*

No. of Mfg. Plants/Facilities: 2
No. of U.S. Offices: 1

Computer Systems/Hardware:
IBM Systems 38

Outside Service Firm(s):

Deloitte & Touche*(Auditors)*
155 E. Broad St.
Columbus, OH 43215
Tel.: 614-221-1000
Fax: 614-229-4647

Thompson, Hine & Flory*(Legal Firm)*
100 E. Broad St., Ste. 1700
Columbus, OH 43215
Tel.: 614-228-1541

The Huntington National Bank*(Major Banking Relationship)*
41 S. High St.
Columbus, OH 43216

Division:

Columbus Showcase, Ashland Division **(1)**
P.O. Box 1387,
Ashland, KY 41105
Tel.: 606-324-5184
Manufacture Showcases, Wall Systems, Custom Counters, Bakery Cases, Refrigerated Cases, & Open Refrigerated Cases
S.I.C.: 2541; 2542

COLUMBUS STEEL DRUM COMPANY
1385 Blatt Blvd.
Blacklick, OH 43004
Tel.: 614-864-1900 **OH**
Fax: 614-860-0028
Approx.Sls.: $33,000,000
Emp.: 240
New & Reconditioned Drums
S.I.C.: 5085
S. Blatt *(Pres. & Treas.)*
Eliot Bank *(Exec. V.P.)*
William Neville *(V.P.)*
Robert Hinson *(Controller)*
Gary Weckerly *(Gen. Mgr.)*
Bill Blakeman *(Dir.-Engrng.)*
Selma K. Blatt *(Sec.)*

Outside Service Firm(s):

Banc One Columbus*(Major Banking Relationship)*
Columbus, OH

COLUSA ELEVATOR CO.
P.O. Box 26,
Colusa, IL 62329
Tel.: 217-755-4221
Fax: 217-755-4202
Year Founded: 1944
Approx.Sls.: $30,000,000
Emp.: 20
Grain Elevator; Drying & Storage
S.I.C.: 4221; 5153
Donald P. Griffiths, Sr. *(Pres. & Chief Exec. Officer)*
John B. Griffiths *(V.P.)*
Dale Griffiths *(Gen. Mgr.)*
Donald P. Griffiths, Jr. *(Gen. Mgr.)*
Phyllis J. Griffiths *(Treas.)*

Outside Service Firm(s):

McGladrey & Pullen*(Auditors)*
Burlington, IA

Apelmeier, Fisch, Power, Warner & Engberg*(Legal Firm)*
Nauvoo, IL

Farmers & Merchants Bank & Trust*(Major Banking Relationship)*
Nauvoo, IL

COLWELL INDUSTRIES, INC.
123 N. 3rd St.
Minneapolis, MN 55401
Tel.: 612-340-0365
Fax: 612-340-0231
Year Founded: 1951
Assets: $35,000,000
Earnings: $1,098,000
Net Worth: $35,000,000
Approx.Sls.: $42,000,000
Emp.: 600
Fiscal Year-end: 12/31/90
Manufacturer of Mdsg. Aids for All Industries Using Color; Medium Run Web Printer of Magazines.
S.I.C.: 2752; 2796; 2754; 2731; 3952
Corporate Giving Program: Contact Company for Information
Thomas G. Colwell *(Chm. Bd., Pres. & Chief Exec. Officer)*
Richard J. Schoen *(V.P.-Mngmt. Information Systems)*

COMARK
471 Brighton Dr.
Bloomingdale, IL 60108
Tel.: 708-351-9700 **IL**
Fax: 708-351-7204
Year Founded: 1977
Assets: $16,000,000
Liabilities: $12,500,000
Net Worth: $3,500,000
Approx.Sls.: $100,000,000
Emp.: 150
Fiscal Year-end: 12/31/91
Distribute Computer Media & Peripheral Equipment
S.I.C.: 5045
Philip Corcoran *(Chm., Chief Exec. & Chief Oper. Officer)*
Charles Wolande *(Pres. & Chief Fin. Officer)*
David W. Keilman *(Treas. & Controller)*

Computer Systems/Hardware:
IBM AS 400

Outside Service Firm(s):

Grant Thornton*(Auditors)*
700 One Prudential Plaza, 130 East Randolph St.
Chicago, IL 60601
Tel.: 312-856-0200
Fax: 312-565-4719

Schwartz & Freeman*(Legal Firm)*
Chicago, IL

Gary Wheaton Bank*(Major Banking Relationship)*
Wheaton, IL

COMBE INCORPORATED
1101 Westchester Ave.
White Plains, NY 10604
Tel.: 914-694-5454
Fax: 914-694-1585
Year Founded: 1949
Approx.Sls.: $100,000,000
Emp.: 200
Fiscal Year-end: 12/31/90
Manufacture Toiletries, Cosmetics, Pharmaceuticals
S.I.C.: 2834; 2844
Ivan D. Combe *(Chm. Bd.)*
Chapin Nolen *(Pres.)*
T.C. Infantino *(Exec. V.P.-Opers.)*
Douglas McGraime *(V.P. & Controller)*
Dominic P. DeMain *(V.P. & Grp. Mktg. Dir.)*
Clark R. Allen *(V.P. & Grp. Mktg. Dir.)*
Howard O. Colwell *(V.P.-Adv.)*
Ray H. Duane *(V.P.-Sls.)*
Christopher B. Combe *(V.P.-Mktg.)*
R.H. Kreissman *(V.P.-Fin. & Plng.)*
Herbert Lapidus *(V.P.-Res. & Devel.)*
Gail R. Perlow *(V.P.-Media)*
Anne York *(Dir.-Pub. Rels.)*

Computer Systems/Hardware:
IBM

Outside Service Firm(s):

Empire Blue Cross & Blue Shield*(Group Insurer)*
New York, NY

Travelers Insurance Co.*(Group Insurer)*
80 John St.
New York, NY 10038
Tel.: 212-574-2536
Fax: 212-574-2545

COMBS & HEATHCOTT
3426 Old Cantrell Rd.
Little Rock, AR 72202
Tel.: 501-664-3000
Fax: 501-664-4016
Year Founded: 1972
Approx.Billings: $15,000,000
Emp.: 26
Advertising, Direct Response Mktg. & Pub. Rels.
Bennett A. Combs *(Pres.)*
Gary Heathcott *(Exec. V.P.)*
J. Sam Smith *(Sr. V.P., Pub. Rels.)*
Jean Harvey *(Sec. & Treas.)*

COMBUSTION POWER COMPANY
(Sub. of National Power Co.)
1020 Marsh Rd.
Menlo Park, CA 94025
Tel.: 415-324-4744
Fax: 415-324-0788
Year Founded: 1967
Approx.Sls.: $30,000,000
Emp.: 60
Fiscal Year-end: 12/31/90
Mfr. of Fluidized Bed Boilers; Engineered Waste-to-Energy Systems; Fluidized Bed Systems; Research & Development
S.I.C.: 3433; 3443; 8711; 8731
Frank H. Walton *(Pres.)*
Mike O'Hagan *(Exec. V.P. & Chief Oper. Officer)*

Combustion Power Company—(Continued)

Gerhart Goldbach *(V.P.-Technology & Devel.)*
Joe O'Donnel *(V.P.-Engrng.)*
W.A. Romatowski *(V.P.-Fin. & Admin.)*
Norm Ziomek *(V.P.-Opers.)*

COMLINEAR CORPORATION
4800 Wheaton Dr.
Fort Collins, CO 80525
Tel.: 303-226-0500
Tel.: 800-776-0500
Fax: 303-226-0564
Year Founded: 1980
Approx.Sls.: $13,000,000
Emp.: 145
Fiscal Year-end: 9/30/91
Export
Mfr. of Hi-Speed Amplifiers, Signal Processing Components
S.I.C.: 3699
D. Nelson *(Chief Exec. Officer)*
Barry Rowen *(Chief Fin. Officer)*
David Ford *(V.P.-Mktg.)*
Bud McGuire *(Mgr.-Human Resources)*
K.J. Yurkewitz *(Public Rels. Coord.)*
Leslie Bledsoe *(Corp. Travel Planner)*

COMMAND PLASTIC CORPORATION
674 Carroll St.
Akron, OH 44304
Tel.: 216-434-3497 **OH**
Fax: 216-434-8316
Year Founded: 1971
Emp.: 95
Fiscal Year-end: 12/31/90
Manufacture Heat Sealed Vinyl Packaging for Banking, Music, Collectibles & Tool Pouch Industries
S.I.C.: 3089
Richard S. Ames *(Chm. & Chief Exec. Officer)*
Joe Samaco *(Pur. Agent)*

No. of Mfg. Plants/Facilities: 1
No. of U.S. Offices: 2

Computer Systems/Hardware:
IBM System 34

Outside Service Firm(s):

Hausser & Taylor*(Auditors)*
Cleveland, OH

Benesch, Friedlander, Coplan & Aronoff*(Legal Firm)*
1100 Citizens Bldg.
Cleveland, OH 44114
Tel.: 216-363-4500

Society National Bank*(Major Banking Relationship)*
800 Superior Ave.
Cleveland, OH 44114
Tel.: 216-689-5931
Fax: 216-689-3814

COMMANDER OIL CORPORATION
One Commander Sq.
Oyster Bay, NY 11771
Tel.: 516-922-9700 **NY**
Fax: 516-922-7256
Sales Range: $40-59 Million
Emp.: 50
Fiscal Year-end: 12/31/91
Mfr. & Distribute Fuel Oil
S.I.C.: 2911; 5172
Albert Shapiro *(Pres.)*
Harold D. Shapiro *(Exec. V.P.)*
Joseph G. Shapiro *(Exec. V.P.)*
Leonard H. Shapiro *(V.P.)*
Edgar J. Barnett, Jr. *(Asst. V.P.)*
Principal(s):
Albert Shapiro
Harold D. Shapiro
Joseph G. Shapiro

No. of Mfg. Plants/Facilities: 6

Computer Systems/Hardware:
IBM; ICC

Outside Service Firm(s):

United Amalgamated Local 355*(Group Insurer)*
New York, NY

Norstar Bank, N.A.*(Major Banking Relationship)*
Long Island, NY

COMMERCIAL & ARCHITECTURAL PRODUCTS INC.
(d/b/a Marlite)
202 Harger St.
Dover, OH 44622
Mailing Address:
P.O. Box 250
Dover, OH 44622
Tel.: 216-343-6621
Fax: 216-343-7296
Year Founded: 1989
Approx.Sls.: $42,000,000
Emp.: 225
Import Export
Marlite Brand Paneling, Toilet Partitions, Displawall, FRP Panels, Firetest II, Firetest Plank, Doors & Frames, Visual Mdsg. Prods., Custom Store Fixtures
S.I.C.: 2431; 2541; 3429
R.S. Campbell *(Pres. & Chief Exec. Officer)*
Tony De Crescenzo *(Chief Oper. Officer & Exec. V.P.)*
Don Froelich *(V.P.-Fin. & Admin.)*
David Johnson *(V.P.-Mfg.)*
L.D. Murphy *(V.P.-Mktg.)*
L. Graham *(Pur. Agent)*

No. of Mfg. Plants/Facilities: 2
No. of U.S. Offices: 5
No. of Foreign Offices: 1

Outside Service Firm(s):

Arthur Andersen & Co.*(Auditors)*
1717 E. 9th St.
Cleveland, OH 44114
Tel.: 216-781-2140
Fax: 216-781-3683

Divisions:

Midwest Operations **(1)**
P.O. Box 250
Dover, OH 44622
Tel.: 216-364-7561
S.I.C.: 2431
S. Taylor *(Opers. Mgr.)*

Northeast Operations **(1)**
80 Newfield Center
Edison, NJ 08837
Tel.: 908-225-1650
S.I.C.: 2431
Larry Soloway *(Opers. Mgr.)*

Southeast Operations **(1)**
1721 Marietta Blvd.
Atlanta, GA 30318
Tel.: 404-691-1234
S.I.C.: 2431
L.F. Kiefer *(Opers. Mgr.)*

Southwest Operations **(1)**
1184 113th St.
Grand Prairie, TX 75050
Tel.: 214-660-6443
S.I.C.: 2431
J.A. DeMichelle *(Opers. Mgr.)*

Western Operations **(1)**
16024 Phoebe Ave.
La Mirada, CA 90638
Tel.: 714-523-2500
S.I.C.: 2431
R. Baxter *(Opers. Mgr.)*

THE COMMERCIAL BANK
230 E. Second St.
Delphos, OH 45833
Mailing Address:
P.O. Box 429,
Delphos, OH 45833
Tel.: 419-695-1055 **OH**
Fax: 419-695-5749
Year Founded: 1877
Assets: $134,661,716
Earnings: $1,832,383
Liabilities: $121,372,370
Net Worth: $13,289,346
Approx.Sls.: $12,262,624
Emp.: 55
Fiscal Year-end: 12/31/91
Banking
S.I.C.: 6022
Elmer J. Helmkamp *(Chm. Bd.)*
Robert E. Nartker *(Vice Chm.)*
Paul G. Wreede *(Pres.)*
Ronald R. Elwer *(Exec. V.P. & Sec.)*
Thomas L. Grothouse *(V.P.-Personal Loans)*
Elizabeth J. McKowen *(V.P.-Human Resources)*
Rebecca L. Minnig *(V.P. & Cashier)*
Max E. Stover *(V.P.-Bus. Devel.)*
James W. Vincent *(V.P.-Commercial Loans)*
Neil S. Bair *(Asst. V.P. & Branch Mgr.)*
Kathleen A. Miller *(Controller)*
Rhonda L. Blockberger *(Loan Officer)*
Matthew F. Suever *(Loan Officer)*
Michael J. Swick *(Loan Officer)*
Mary Jo Duncan *(Acctg. Officer)*
M. Jann Bonifas *(Auditor)*
Nancy J. Fischer *(Asst. Cashier)*
Janis A. Owens *(Branch Mgr.)*
Ruth A. Eilerman *(Branch Mgr.)*

COMMERCIAL & INDUSTRIAL ADMINISTRATION CO. INC
1265 El Camino Real
Santa Clara, CA 95052
Mailing Address:
P.O. Box 26,
Santa Clara, CA 95052
Tel.: 408-984-7101 **CA**
Fax: 408-984-1563
Year Founded: 1977
Earnings: $185,000
Approx.Sls.: $25,000,000
Emp.: 80
Fiscal Year-end: 1/31/92
Third Party Administrators for Group Medical & Life Insurance Benefits
S.I.C.: 6411
Miles H. Barber *(Chm. Bd. & Chief Exec. Officer)*
Bernadine Printz *(Pres.)*
Gordon Likens *(Controller)*

No. of U.S. Offices: 1

Computer Systems/Hardware:
Prime

COMMERCIAL LIGHT COMPANY
245 Fence Lane
Hillside, IL 60162-6006
Mailing Address:
P.O. Box 6006
Hillside, IL 60162
Tel.: 708-449-6900 **IL**
Fax: 708-449-6942
Year Founded: 1915
Assets: $11,118,435
Liabilities: $8,524,867
Net Worth: $2,593,568
Approx.Sls.: $29,000,000
Emp.: 250
Fiscal Year-end: 3/31/92
General Electrical Contractor
S.I.C.: 1731
Thomas C. Halperin *(Chm Bd., Pres. & Chief Exec. Officer)*
Lawrence R. Dolan *(Exec. V.P. & Chief Oper. Officer)*
W.J. Bortman *(Sr. V.P.)*
S.J. Morris *(V.P.-Telecommunications)*
Stuart Edelstein *(Gen. Counsel)*
Michael R. Sorden *(Sec. & Treas.)*
D.R. Halperin *(Dir.-Media)*
P.J. Halperin *(Mgr.-Systems)*
Valery Ridgway *(Coord.-Data Processing)*
Donald Scaperdine *(Pur. Agent)*
S.F. Macioce *(Asst. Sec.)*
Principal(s):
Thomas C. Halperin
D.R. Halperin
P.J. Halperin

No. of Mfg. Plants/Facilities: 1
No. of U.S. Offices: 1

Computer Systems/Hardware:
Hewlett Packard; IBM P.C.'s

Outside Service Firm(s):

Arthur Andersen & Co.*(Auditors)*
Oakbrook Terrace, IL

CNA Insurance*(Commercial Insurance Carrier)*
CNA Plaza,
Chicago, IL 60685
Tel.: 312-822-5000

Prudential Insurance Co. of America*(Group Insurance Broker/ Consult)*
Minneapolis, MN

Marovitz & Edelstein*(Legal Firm)*
180 N. LaSalle St., St. 1601
Chicago, IL :60601-2697

Mid-City National Bank*(Major Banking Relationship)*
Chicago, IL

Retirement Programs Corp.*(Pension Manager)*
7630 S. County Line Rd.
Burr Ridge, IL 60521

Affiliate:

Advanced Technology Systems, Inc. **(1)**
7641 Currency Dr.
Orlando, FL 32819
Tel.: 407-856-8770
Fax: 407-856-1984
Emp.: 12
Communication/Computer Installation Company; Electrical Wiring Contractor
S.I.C.: 1731
William Gentry *(Gen. Mgr.)*

COMMERCIAL PLASTICS & SUPPLIES CORP.
98-31 Jamaica Ave.
Richmond Hill, NY 11418
Tel.: 718-441-1500
Fax: 718-847-6614
Year Founded: 1945
Approx.Sls.: $10,000,000
Rubber & Miscellaneous Plastic Products; Fabricated Metal Products; Wholesale Plastic Sheets, Rods & Tubes
S.I.C.: 3011; 3021; 3052; 3069; 3089
Morton R. French *(Chm. Bd., Pres., Chief Exec. & Chief Fin. Officer)*
Morton R. French, Jr. *(V.P. & Treas.)*
Norge Stratigos *(Asst. to the Pres.)*
Walter Taubert *(Dir.-Mngmt. Information Systems)*
Tim Ring *(Mgr.-Opers.)*

Computer Systems/Hardware:
IBM System 34

COMMERCIAL PRINTERS OF CONNECTICUT
3 Hilltop Rd.
Norwich, CT 06360
Tel.: 203-886-0541
Fax: 203-886-5805
Approx.Sls.: $12,000,000
Emp.: 120

Lithographic Commercial Printing
S.I.C.: 2752
Martin Lower *(Chm. Bd.)*
James Lower *(Pres.)*
Richard Gooding *(Exec. V.P.)*
James Peterson *(Sec.)*

Outside Service Firm(s):

Ernst & Young*(Auditors)*
Goodwyn Sq., 225 Asylum St.
Hartford, CT 06103
Tel.: 203-247-3100

State Street Bank & Trust Co.*(Major Banking Relationship)*
225 Franklin St.
Boston, MA 02101
Tel.: 617-654-3652

Ropes & Gray*(Legal Firm)*
One International Place
Boston, MA 02110
Tel.: 617-951-7000

Commercial Roof Decks
(See Beacon Sales Corporation Listing)

COMMERCIAL TRAVELERS MUTUAL INSURANCE COMPANY
70 Genesee
Utica, NY 13502
Tel.: 315-797-5200
Fax: 315-797-3198
Year Founded: 1883
Approx.Sls.: $10,000,000
Emp.: 100
Fiscal Year-end: 12/31/90
Accident & Health Insurance
S.I.C.: 6321
Herbert E. Trevvett *(Pres. & Chief Exec. Officer)*
Richard C. Nevins *(V.P.-Adv.)*
Vincent J. Keaveney *(Mktg. Mgr.)*

Monitor Life Insurance Company of New York **(1)**
70 Genesee St.
Utica, NY 13502
Tel.: 315-797-5200
Donald E. Joslin *(Pres. & Chief Exec. Officer)*

COMMODORE CRUISE LINE, LTD.
800 Douglas Rd.
Coral Gables, FL 33134
Tel.: 305-529-3000
Tel.: 800-237-5361
Telex: 441-7905
Fax: 305-567-9481
Year Founded: 1967
Approx.Sls.: $85,000,000
Emp.: 1125
Fiscal Year-end: 12/31/91
Cruise Ships; Caribe, Enchanted Isle, Enchanted Seas
S.I.C.: 4481
Ove Nordquist *(Pres. & Chief Exec. Officer)*
Patrick Doyle *(Exec V.P. & Chief Fin. Officer)*
Roy Fox *(Sr. V.P.-Hotel Services)*
David Christopher *(Sr. V.P.-Mktg. & Sls.)*
David Levene *(V.P.-Sls.)*
Lourdes Padilla *(Controller)*
Nancy Loewenherz *(Dir.-Pub. Rels.)*
Robert Garrity *(Mktg. Dir.)*
Deborah Booth *(Adv. Mgr.)*

Division:

Crown Cruise Line **(1)**
800 Douglas Rd., Ste. 700
Coral Gables, FL 33134
Tel.: 305-529-3000
Tel.: 800-822-5220
Telex: 441-7905
Fax: 305-567-9481
Cruise Line
S.I.C.: 4841
Ove Nordquist *(Pres. & Chief Exec. Officer)*

COMMONS BROS., INC.
55 Hunter Lane
Elmsford, NY 10523
Tel.: 914-347-5505
Tel.: 800-548-0016
Sales Range: $100-499 Million
Wholesale Distributor of Drugs
S.I.C.: 5122; 3993
Robert Castello *(Chm.)*
Jonathan Tendler *(Chief Exec. Officer)*

Subsidiary:

Commons Metro Inc. **(1)**
16 Rewe St.
Brooklyn, NY 11211
Tel.: 718-963-1606
Fax: 718-384-1195
Approx.Sls.: $111,000,000
Emp.: 110
Wholesale Distributor of Drugs, Drug Proprietaries & Sundries
S.I.C.: 5122
Robert Castello *(Chm. Bd.)*

COMMONWEALTH TOY & NOVELTY COMPANY
45 W. 25th St., 5th Fl.
New York, NY 10010
Tel.: 212-242-4070 **NY**
Fax: 212-645-4279
Year Founded: 1934
Approx.Sls.: $45,000,000
Emp.: 80
Mfr. & Wholesale Distribution of Stuffed Toys; Sales Promotion
S.I.C.: 5092; 3942; 8743
Harvey Greenfield *(Chm. Bd.)*
Steven Greenfield *(Pres.)*
Betty Greenfield *(V.P. & Sec.)*
Lee Schneider *(V.P.-Sls.)*
Stacy Baumer *(V.P.-Mktg.)*

No. of Mfg. Plants/Facilities: 2
No. of U.S. Offices: 5

Outside Service Firm(s):

Mahoney Cohen & Co., P.C.*(Auditors)*
New York, NY

European American Bank*(Major Banking Relationship)*
New York, NY

COMMTEK COMMUNICATIONS
8330 Boone Blvd., Ste. 600
Vienna, VA 22180
Tel.: 703-827-0511 **ID**
Fax: 703-356-6179
Year Founded: 1978
Assets: $13,000,000
Liabilities: $10,500,000
Net Worth: $2,500,000
Sales Range: $10-19 Million
Emp.: 40
Fiscal Year-end: 12/31/88
Publisher of Consumer & Trade Magazines, for Satellite Dish TV Business & Satellite TV Programming
S.I.C.: 2721
David G. Wolford *(Pres., Chief Exec. Officer & Publr.)*
Pamella D. Waite *(V.P. & Corp. Sec.)*
Michael A. Covington *(Controller)*
William Outlaw *(Dir.-Circulation)*
Principal(s):
David G. Wolford

No. of Mfg. Plants/Facilities: 1
No. of U.S. Offices: 2

Computer Systems/Hardware:
DEC VAX 785

Outside Service Firm(s):

Arthur Andersen & Co.*(Auditors)*
1666 K Street, N.W.
Washington, DC 20006

Union Mutual Life Insurance Co.*(Group Insurer)*
Portland, ME

Hogue, Speck, Anestad*(Legal Firm)*
Ketchum, ID

Sovran Bank*(Major Banking Relationship)*
Bethesda, MD

Employee Plan Assoc.*(Pension Manager)*
Vienna, VA

COMMUNICATION & DESIGN AGENCY INC.
4 Avis Dr.
Latham, NY 12110
Tel.: 518-783-0001
Fax: 518-783-6587
Year Founded: 1977
Approx.Billings: $19,000,000
Emp.: 35
Intergrated Marketing Communications
Francis J. Lipari *(Pres. & Chief Exec. Officer)*
Marshall S. Dickman *(Dir., Mktg. & Acct. Mngmt.)*
Joanne Beckmann *(Electronic Graphics Mgr.)*
Catherine Karamanus *(Asst. Production Mgr.)*
Carol L. Reiser *(Pub. Rels. Specialist)*

Computer Systems/Hardware:
IBM System 36, TSI, MM+, Financial, Media, Production, Traffic; Apple, MacIntosh IIci (Graphics Systems)

COMMUNICATION TRENDS, INC.
Bldg. 30, 3715 Northside Pkwy., Ste. 550
Atlanta, GA 30327
Tel.: 404-262-2900
Fax: 404-266-3645
Year Founded: 1974
Approx.Billings: $11,935,000
Emp.: 15
Direct Broadcast, Cable Television & Broadcast Syndication
Toni A. Dwyer *(Chm. & Pres.)*
Arthur A. Dwyer *(Exec. V.P.)*
Elizabeth Maury *(Controller)*
Beth Maury *(Mgr.-Bus.)*

COMMUNICATIONS CONCEPTS
3131 Executive Pkwy.
Toledo, OH 43606
Tel.: 419-531-5550
Fax: 419-531-5908
Year Founded: 1967
Approx.Billings: $23,000,000
Emp.: 24
Marketing Communications & Public Relations
James L. Appt *(Pres. Treas. & New Bus. Contact)*
Eric A. Lehman *(Exec. V.P.)*
Deatra Appt *(Gen. Mgr.)*

COMMUNICATIONS DIVERSIFIED
440 Park Ave., South
New York, NY 10016
Tel.: 212-213-3300
Fax: 212-213-2740
Year Founded: 1979
Approx.Billings: $51,500,000
Emp.: 40
Promotion, Direct Mktg. & Sport Mktg.
William H. Hennesberry *(Chm. Bd.)*
David H. Soskin *(Pres. & Chief Oper. Officer)*
Patrick J. Shannon *(Exec. V.P.)*
Steve Leicht *(Exec. V.P.)*
Stuart Fleischer *(Sr. V.P.)*

COMMUNICATIONS INTERNATIONAL
6020 Unity Dr., Ste. G
Norcross, GA 30071
Tel.: 404-447-1830 **GA**
Fax: 404-662-8133
Year Founded: 1979
Assets: $11,257,574
Liabilities: $10,471,783
Net Worth: $785,791
Approx.Sls.: $15,000,000
Emp.: 200
Fiscal Year-end: 9/30/89
Telecommunications Systems Integration
S.I.C.: 1731; 5999; 3661; 3663; 3812; 3829; 3699; 4812; 4822; 3669; 3679; 1623; 3571; 3572; 3575; 3577; 3578; 7379
Joe Profit *(Pres. & Chief Exec. Officer)*
Henry Myles *(V.P.-Human Resources)*
Casandra Harmon *(Dir.-Personnel)*
Principal(s):
Joe Profit
Spencer Jourdain

COMMUNICATIONS INTERNATIONAL
488 Madison Ave.
New York, NY 10022
Tel.: 212-826-9450
Fax: 212-826-9496
Approx.Sls.: $50,000,000
Emp.: 150
Publishing & Communications
S.I.C.: 2731; 2741
Arthur Hill Diedrick *(Chm. Bd., Pres. & Chief Exec. Officer)*
Christine Fontana *(Exec. V.P.)*
Seija Goldstein *(Chief Fin. Officer)*
Joseph Allen *(Controller)*
Peggy Shadwick *(Personnel Dir.)*

Outside Service Firm(s):

Arthur Andersen & Co.*(Auditors)*
Norcross, GA

Division:

Aetna Life & Casualty*(Commercial Insurance Carrier)*
151 Farmington Avenue
Hartford, CT 06156
Tel.: 203-273-2128
Fax: 203-729-4295

Rhode Island Monthly **(1)**
60 Branch Ave.
Providence, RI 02904
Tel.: 401-421-2552
Monthly Magazine
S.I.C.: 2741

Blue Cross & Blue Shield of Georgia, Inc.*(Group Insurer)*
Atlanta, GA

Jenner & Block*(Legal Firm)*
One IBM Plaza
Chicago, IL 60611
Tel.: 312-222-9350

Citizens Trust*(Major Banking Relationship)*
Atlanta, GA

Subsidiary:

International Microwave Corporation **(1)**
25 Van Zant St.
East Norwalk, CT 06855
Tel.: 203-857-4222
Telecommunications Systems Integrator
S.I.C.: 3661; 3674
Anthony Acri *(Pres.)*

Communications Plus, Inc.—(Continued)

COMMUNICATIONS PLUS, INC.
ADVERTISING · DIRECT MARKETING · SALES PROMOTION

COMMUNICATIONS PLUS, INC.
102 Madison Ave.
New York, NY 10016
Tel.: 212-686-9570
Fax: 212-686-9687
Year Founded: 1975
Approx.Billings: $19,000,000
Emp.: 50
Max Bodden *(Pres. & Chief Exec. Officer)*
Earl Bahler *(Exec. V.P., Mng. Dir.)*
Chris Bodden *(Sr. V.P.)*
Nora Reyes *(Sec./Treas.)*

COMMUNICO

COMMUNICO
(A member of The Jackson Group)
1101 Southeastern Ave.
Indianapolis, IN 46202
Tel.: 317-266-2777
Fax: 317-639-6809
Year Founded: 1990
Approx.Billings: $22,550,000
Emp.: 37
Advertising & Sales Promotion With Emphasis on Medical Marketing
Ron Jackson *(Chm. & Creative Dir.)*
Walt Bagot *(Vice Chm.)*
Brad Unroe *(Pres. & Chief Exec. Officer)*
Jim Adams *(V.P., Performance Programs)*
Kathy Jackson *(Chief Fin. Officer)*
Becky Massa *(Controller)*
Denise Trine *(Mgr., Personnel & Payroll)*

COMMUNITY CASH STORES
3001 No. Blackstock Rd.
Spartanburg, SC 29301
Mailing Address:
P.O. Box 5688
Spartanburg, SC 29304
Tel.: 803-576-0260
Fax: 803-574-1612
Year Founded: 1921
Approx.Sls.: $124,000,000
Emp.: 1,109
Fiscal Year-end: 12/31/91

Export
Food Stores
S.I.C.: 5411
B.R. Littlejohn, Jr. *(Chm. Bd.)*
B.R. Littlejohn III *(Pres. & Chief Exec. Officer)*
Albert M. Lord *(V.P.-Fin.)*
Anne L. Gowan *(Sec.)*
M. Glenn Walters *(Dir.-Opers.)*
Russell West *(Dir.-Personnel)*
Marty Yarborough *(Dir.-Mngmt. Information Systems)*
Beverly Aycoth *(Mgr.-Employee Benefits)*

Computer Systems/Hardware:
IBM

Outside Service Firm(s):

Holcombe, Bomar & Gunn*(Legal Firm)*
Spartanburg, SC

South Carolina National Bank*(Major Banking Relationship)*
P.O. Box 3128,
Spartanburg, SC 29304
Tel.: 803-596-4200

COMPEL
MARKETING INC.
A SALES PROMOTION AGENCY

COMPEL MARKETING, INC.
P.O. Box 35565,
Greensboro, NC 27425
Tel.: 919-886-4913
Fax: 919-886-4242
Year Founded: 1982
Approx.Billings: $13,000,000
Emp.: 20
Strategic Promotion Planning
Mark Herpel *(Pres.)*
Donald White *(Exec. V.P.)*
Joe Bucci *(V.P. & Gen. Mgr.)*

COMPENDIUM SYSTEMS
535 5th Ave.
New York, NY 10017
Tel.: 212-687-7344 **DE**
Telex: 212-557-5258
Fax: 212-682-7060
Year Founded: 1973
Assets: $14,600,000
Earnings: $2,400,000
Net Worth: $14,600,000
Sales Range: $40-59 Million
Emp.: 13
Magazine Publication Syndication
S.I.C.: 2721
John McAuliffe *(Chm. Bd. & Pres.)*
Blair Howell *(Chief Exec. Officer)*
Joan McAuliffe *(Chief Fin. Officer & Gen. Counsel)*
Kevin McGivney *(Sr. V.P. & Treas.)*
Bill Eastern *(V.P.)*
Hawley H. McAuliffe *(Controller)*
Hilton McAuliffe *(Trustee)*
Duncan Wagner *(Dir.-Computer Information System)*
Brenda Nichols *(Mgr.-Intl.)*

No. of Mfg. Plants/Facilities: 2

Computer Systems/Hardware:
DEC

Outside Service Firm(s):

Hayes & Co., C.P.A.*(Auditors)*
New York, NY

Chubb Group*(Commercial Insurance Carrier)*
P.O. Box 1615,
Warren, NJ 07061
Tel.: 201-580-2000

Chemical Bank*(International Bank Affiliate)*
450 West 33rd St.
New York, NY 10001
Tel.: 212-613-7197
Fax: 212-947-7628

Guardian Life Insurance Co.*(Group Insurer)*
New York, NY

Shearson Lehman Brothers, Inc.*(Investment Banker)*
World Financial Center
New York, NY 10285
Tel.: 212-298-2000

Gellis deMellinger*(Legal Firm)*
New York, NY

Chemical Bank*(Major Banking Relationship)*
450 West 33rd St.
New York, NY 10001
Tel.: 212-613-7197
Fax: 212-947-7628

E.F. Hutton*(Pension Manager)*
New York, NY

COMPLETE INTERIORS INC.
435 Douglas Ave.
Altamonte Springs, FL 32714
Tel.: 407-862-3203 **FL**
Year Founded: 1974
Assets: $70,000,000
Liabilities: $33,000,000
Net Worth: $37,000,000
Approx.Sls.: $52,000,000
Emp.: 140
Fiscal Year-end: 12/13/89
Real Estate Developer; General Contractor; Shopping Centers, Office Buildings, Single Family Homes
S.I.C.: 6552; 1542; 1521
Linda Carole Clark *(Pres.)*
Carole Warmington *(Sec. & Treas.)*
David Meadows *(Gen. Mgr.)*
Jessica Ery *(Dir.-Personnel)*
Principal(s):
Linda Carole Clark

Outside Service Firm(s):

Jung, Blosch & Scearce*(Auditors)*
Orlando, FL

American Pioneer Savings Bank*(Major Banking Relationship)*
Orlando, FL

COMPLEX INDUSTRY CORPORATION
37 W. 37th St.
New York, NY 10018
Tel.: 212-398-9450
Fax: 212-719-9697
Approx.Sls.: $21,000,000
Emp.: 110
Women's Sportswear
S.I.C.: 2339
Robert Kaplan *(Pres.)*
Rod Malijan *(Controller)*

Outside Service Firm(s):

BDO Seidman*(Auditors)*
1430 Broadway
New York, NY
Tel.: 212-765-7500

Proskauer, Rose, Goetz & Mendelsohn*(Legal Firm)*
New York, NY

Manufacturers Hanover Trust Co.*(Major Banking Relationship)*
4 New York Plaza
New York, NY 10015
Tel.: 212-623-3157

COMPONENT TECHNOLOGY CORP.
3409 W. 14th St.
Erie, PA 16505
Tel.: 814-838-1971 **DE**
Year Founded: 1982
Approx.Sls.: $22,000,000
Emp.: 275
Fiscal Year-end: 12/31/91
Mfr. Thermoplastic Injection Molding
S.I.C.: 3089
Tom Gaffney *(Chm. Bd.)*
Richard Brooks *(Pres.)*
Lance Erlick *(Chief Fin. Officer & Controller)*

Subsidiary:

R & R Plastics **(1)**
P.O. Box 177,
Swanton, OH 43558
Tel.: 419-825-2311 (100%)
Injection Molding of Thermoplastic Materials
S.I.C.: 3089
Tom Gaffney *(Chm. Bd.)*
Richard Brooks *(Pres.)*
Lance Erlick *(Chief Fin. Officer & Controller)*

COMPONENTS CORPORATION OF AMERICA
717 N. Harwood #2555
Dallas, TX 75201
Tel.: 214-969-0166 **NY**
Fax: 214-969-5905
Year Founded: 1916
Assets: $14,522,020
Liabilities: $5,944,822
Net Worth: $8,577,198
Approx.Sls.: $18,812,737
Emp.: 300
Fiscal Year-end: 12/31/90
Import Export
Manufacture Electronic Inductors & Electric Components
S.I.C.: 3612; 3677; 3643; 3679
Cary M. Maguire *(Chm. Bd.)*
Frank E. Castle *(Pres. & Chief Exec. Officer)*
William Powell *(V.P.-Fin. & Chief Fin. Officer)*
Walter L. Landergan, Jr. *(Sec. & Legal)*

No. of Mfg. Plants/Facilities: 3
No. of U.S. Offices: 4

Computer Systems/Hardware:
Prime Computers

Outside Service Firm(s):

KPMG Peat Marwick*(Auditors)*
1601 Elm St., Ste. 1600
Dallas, TX 75201
Tel.: 214-754-2000
Fax: 214-754-2297

Rich, May, Bilodeau & Flaherty P.C.*(Legal Firm)*
294 Washington St.
Boston, MA 02108
Tel.: 617-482-1360

Texas Commerce Bank*(Major Banking Relationship)*
2200 Ross Ave.
Dallas, TX 75266

Subsidiaries:

Para Systems Inc. **(1)**
1455 Le May Dr.
Carrollton, TX 75007
Tel.: 214-446-7363
Tel.: 800-238-7272
Mfr. Power Supply
S.I.C.: 3612
Steve Lam *(Pres.)*

StacoEnergy Products Co. **(1)**
301 Gaddis Blvd.,
Dayton, OH 45403
Tel.: 513-253-1191
Approx.Sls.: $8,260,000
Emp.: 100
Electronic & Electromechanical Manufacturer
S.I.C.: 3612; 3677
Fred Weigle *(Pres.)*
C.W. Parker *(Controller)*
R. Simpson *(V.P.-Mktg.)*
J. Redmyer *(V.P.-Engrng.)*
R. Hosler *(V.P.-Opers.)*

Stacoswitch, Inc. **(1)**
1139 Baker St.
Costa Mesa, CA 92626
Tel.: 714-549-3041
Approx.Sls.: $8,062,000
Emp.: 100
Manufacture Electronic & Electromechanical Switches
S.I.C.: 3643
James F. Gust *(Pres.)*
D. Dietz *(Treas.)*
D. Sugg *(V.P.-Sls.)*
T. Nichols *(V.P.-Engrng.)*
W. Swan *(V.P.-Opers.)*

Thordarson Meissner, Inc. **(1)**
628 Belmont St.
Mount Carmel, IL 62863
Tel.: 618-262-5121
Tel.: 800-851-3583 (100%)
Fax: 618-263-3150
Approx.Sls.: $2,500,000

Emp.: 65
Mfr. of Electronics Including Transformers For Indus., Military & Comml. Use
S.I.C.: 3677; 3612
F. Castle *(Pres.)*
R. Hogen *(Controller)*
Lori L. Jeffries *(Sls. Mgr.)*
Nancy Garrett *(Personnel Admin.)*

COMPUADD CORPORATION
12303 Technology Blvd.
Austin, TX 78727
Tel.: 512-250-1489 **TX**
Telex: 763543
Fax: 512-250-3528
Year Founded: 1982
Approx.Sls.: $400,100,000
Emp.: 1,000
Fiscal Year-end: 12/31/91
Import Export
Manufacture & Distribute Computer Hardware
S.I.C.: 5961; 7372
Bill Hayden *(Chm. Bd.)*
John Pope *(Dir.-Corp. Rels.)*

Outside Service Firm(s):

KPMG Peat Marwick*(Auditors)*
3000 Republic Bank Center
Houston, TX 77002
Tel.: 713-224-4262
Fax: 713-224-4566

Baker, Mills & Glast*(Legal Firm)*
Austin, TX

First Interstate Bank of Washington, N.A.*(Major Banking Relationship)*
P.O. Box 21927, 999 Third Ave.
Seattle, WA 98111
Tel.: 206-292-3522
Tel.: 800-522-6645

COMPUTER DYNAMICS, INC.
4452 Corporation Ln., Ste. 300
Virginia Beach, VA 23462
Tel.: 804-490-1234 **DE**
Fax: 804-490-8353
Year Founded: 1979
Assets: $10,200,000
Earnings: $600,000
Liabilities: $5,500,000
Net Worth: $4,700,000
Approx.Sls.: $32,000,000
Emp.: 558
Fiscal Year-end: 9/30/90
Computer Engineering Services
S.I.C.: 7372; 7379; 3571; 8711
Robert L. Starer *(Chief Exec. Officer)*
Kenneth Bowab *(Chief Fin. Officer)*
Joe Corcoran *(Exec. V.P.)*
Vickie Anderson *(Dir.-Human Resources)*
Richard Babb *(Dir.-Admin.)*
Percy Twine *(Dir.-Mngmt. Information Systems)*
Patti Hawkins *(Mgr.-Sls.)*
Nancy Barnard *(Coord.-Pub. Rels.)*
Linda Holland *(Corp. Travel Planner)*
Principal(s):

No. of Mfg. Plants/Facilities: 1
No. of U.S. Offices: 11
No. of Foreign Offices: 6

Computer Systems/Hardware:
Wang

Outside Service Firm(s):

Ernst & Young*(Auditors)*
Norfolk, VA

Liberty Mutual*(Commercial Insurance Carrier)*
Richmond, VA

Blue Cross & Blue Shield of Virginia*(Group Insurer)*
2015 Staples Mill Rd.
Richmond, VA 23230
Tel.: 804-359-7000
Fax: 804-354-7397

Crestar Bank*(Investment Banker)*
P.O. Box 2642,
Norfolk, VA 23514
Tel.: 804-624-5507
Fax: 804-624-5538

Saul, Ewing, Remick & Saul*(Legal Firm)*
Washington, DC

Crestar Bank*(Major Banking Relationship)*
P.O. Box 26665,
Richmond, VA 23261
Tel.: 804-782-5995

IDS Financial Services*(Pension Manager)*
Washington, DC

COMPUTER INSTRUMENTS CORPORATION
1000 Shames Dr.
Westbury, NY 11590
Tel.: 516-876-8400 **NY**
Fax: 516-876-9153
Year Founded: 1949
Assets: $12,186,000
Liabilities: $1,645,000
Net Worth: $10,541,000
Approx.Sls.: $10,850,000
Emp.: 57
Fiscal Year-end: 12/31/91
Import Export
Design, Manufacture & Sale Electronic Components & Instrumentation, Primarily of Pressure Transducers, Aircraft & Industrial Control Modules, Component Test Equipment
S.I.C.: 3825; 3812; 3829; 3823
Don Wilen *(Pres.)*
John Bang *(Controller)*

No. of Mfg. Plants/Facilities: 1
No. of U.S. Offices: 1

Outside Service Firm(s):

Ernst & Young*(Auditors)*
One Old Stone Square
Providence, RI 02903
Tel.: 401-331-7000

Johnson & Higgins*(Auditors)*
125 Broad St.
New York, NY 10004-2424
Tel.: 212-574-7000
Fax: 212-574-8988

Barclays Bank plc*(Major Banking Relationship)*
75 Wall St.
New York, NY 10265
Tel.: 212-412-4000

Citibank N.A.*(Major Banking Relationship)*
Corporate Trust Services, 399 Park Ave.
New York, NY 10043
Tel.: 212-559-1605

European American Bank*(Major Banking Relationship)*
New York, NY

COMPUTER METHODS CORPORATION
13740 Merriman St.
Livonia, MI 48150
Tel.: 313-522-5187 **MI**
Fax: 313-522-2705
Year Founded: 1977
Assets: $6,000,000
Liabilities: $4,500,000
Net Worth: $1,500,000
Approx.Sls.: $24,000,000
Emp.: 340
Fiscal Year-end: 6/30/92
Export
Computer Software Services; Systems Sales & Service
S.I.C.: 7372; 7379
Andrew K. Stewart *(Chm. Bd., Pres. & Chief Exec. Officer)*
Vahan Shahinian *(Pres.-Tech. Opers.)*
Charles Finney *(Chief Fin. Officer & Treas.)*
Cynthia Blake *(Controller)*
Charles Kovsky *(Gen. Counsel & Sec.)*
Ed Panyard *(Dir.-Telecommunication)*
Principal(s):
Andrew K. Stewart

No. of U.S. Offices: 8

Computer Systems/Hardware:
IBM; NCR

Outside Service Firm(s):

Follmer, Rudzewicz & Co.*(Auditors)*
Southfield, MI

Bituminous Casualty*(Commercial Insurance Carrier)*
Rock Island, IL

Blue Cross & Blue Shield of Michigan*(Group Insurer)*
Detroit, MI

Charles Kovsky*(Legal Firm)*
Detroit, MI

Manufacturers National Bank N.A.*(Major Banking Relationship)*
38th Fl., 100 Renaissance Center
Detroit, MI 48243
Tel.: 313-222-4227

CIGNA*(Pension Manager)*
Los Angeles, CA

COMPUTER SALES INTERNATIONAL INC.
10845 Olive St., 3rd Fl.
Saint Louis, MO 63141
Mailing Address:
P.O. Box 16264,
St. Louis, MO 63105
Tel.: 314-997-7010 **MO**
Fax: 314-997-7844
Year Founded: 1971
Approx.Sls.: $100,000,000
Emp.: 135
Computer Distributor & Leasing
S.I.C.: 5045; 7377
Kenneth Steinback *(Chm. Bd. & Chief Exec. Officer)*
Al Smith *(Pres.)*
E. William Gillula *(Chief Fin. Officer & Sr. V.P.)*
Larry Schinsky *(Sr. V.P.-Sls.)*
Lorraine Cherrick *(V.P. & Assoc. Gen. Counsel)*
Stephen G. Hamilton *(V.P. & Sec.)*
Loren Larsen *(V.P.-Opers)*
Sandra Workman *(Dir.-Personnel)*

Outside Service Firm(s):

Ernst & Young*(Auditors)*
701 Market St.
St. Louis, MO 63101
Tel.: 314-259-1000

Stolar Partnership*(Legal Firm)*
St. Louis, MO

Mark Twain St. Louis Bank*(Major Banking Relationship)*
1630 S. Lindbergh Blvd.
St. Louis, MO 63131

Subsidiary:

ReCon Services, Inc. **(1)**
6647 Romiss Ct.
Berkeley, MO 63134
Tel.: 314-521-0480
Emp.: 30
Computer Reconditioning, Refurbishing & Storage
S.I.C.: 7378
Frank Pike *(Pres.)*

Computerland
(See Bellwether Technology Corporation Listing)

COMPUTERLAND CORPORATION
5964 W. La Positas
Pleasanton, CA 94566-8575
Mailing Address:
P.O. Box 9012,
Pleasanton, CA 94566-9012
Tel.: 510-734-4000
Fax: 415-734-4802
Earnings: $5,000,000
Approx.Sls.: $1,700,000,000
Emp.: 650
Fiscal Year-end: 9/30/91
Franchisors of ComputerLand Stores
S.I.C.: 6794; 5734
William Y. Tauscher *(Pres. & Chief Exec. Officer)*
Ed Anderson *(Pres.-USA)*
Richard F. Vitkus *(Sr. V.P., Gen. Counsel & Dir.-Devel.)*
Marian Murphy *(Sr. V.P.-Mktg.)*
Barbara Belman *(Adv. Mgr.)*

Subsidiary:

Computerland **(1)**
621 Six Flags Dr.
Arlington, TX 76011
Tel.: 817-640-7274
Fax: 817-649-4430
Assets: $16,814,542
Earnings: $24,853
Liabilities: $8,189,987
Net Worth: $8,624,555
Approx.Rev.: $22,369,421
Emp.: 244
Fiscal Year-end: 12/31/90
PC Network Sales; Test Program Sets Which Consist of Detailed Performance & Diagnostic Test Programs Written in Computer Code
S.I.C.: 5045; 7371
Thomas M. Cracraft *(Pres. & Chief Exec. Officer)*

Non-U.S. Holding:

ComputerLand Canada Ltd. **(1)**
2000 Clark Blvd.
Brampton, ON L6T 4M7, Canada
Tel.: 416-793-9000 (100%)
Computer Store Franchisor
S.I.C.: 5734; 6794
Brian D. Childs *(Pres. & Chief Oper. Officer)*
Kauko Aronaho *(Sr. V.P. & Chief Fin. Officer)*
E. Victor Oliver *(Sr. V.P.)*

COMPUWARE CORPORATION
31440 Northwestern Hwy.
Farmington Hills, MI 48334-2564
Mailing Address:
P.O. Box 9080,
Farmington Hills, MI 48333-9080
Tel.: 313-737-7300
Tel.: 800-292-7432 **MI**
Telex: 235559
Fax: 313-737-7108
Year Founded: 1973
Approx.Sls.: $175,000,000
Emp.: 1,500
Fiscal Year-end: 3/31/92
Export
Data Processing Professional Services, & System Software Products
S.I.C.: 7374; 7372; 7379
Peter Karmanos, Jr. *(Chm. Bd. & Chief Exec. Officer)*
Thomas Thewes *(Vice Chm. & Exec. V.P.-Finance)*
Michael Lobsinger *(Exec. V.P.-Corp. Plng.)*
Ralph A. Caponigro *(Sr. V.P.-Fin. & Chief Fin. Officer)*
W. James Prowse *(Sr. V.P.-MIS, Human Resources & Recruiting)*
Joseph A. Nathan *(Sr. V.P. & Chief Oper. Officer-System Software Div.)*
Jack Shevillo *(Sr. V.P. & Chief Oper. Officer-Professional Service Div.)*
Dar Brown *(V.P.-Corp. Information Systems)*

Compuware Corporation—(Continued)

Karl Christen *(V.P.-Product Devel. & Support)*
Thomas Costello *(Gen. Counsel)*
Nick Trapani *(Controller)*
Ralph E. Mechler *(Dir.-Human Resources)*
Christopher M.F. Norris *(Dir.-Corp. Communications)*
Denise Knobblock *(Dir.-Facilities & Admin., & Corp. Admin.)*
D'Arcie Glaesmer *(Travel Coord.)*
Angela Sad *(Supvr.-Pur.)*

Principal(s):
Peter Karmanos, Jr.

No. of U.S. Offices: 5
No. of Foreign Offices: 6

Computer Systems/Hardware:
System Software Products

Outside Service Firm(s):

BDO Seidman*(Auditors)*
Detroit, MI

Aetna Life & Casualty*(Group Insurer)*
151 Farmington Avenue
Hartford, CT 06156
Tel.: 203-273-2128
Fax: 203-729-4295

Kemp, Klein, Humphrey, Edelman & Beer*(Legal Firm)*
Birmingham, MI

Comerica Bank*(Major Banking Relationship)*
Birmingham, MI

Comerica Bank*(Major Banking Relationship)*
211 W. Fort St.
Detroit, MI 48226
Tel.: 313-222-3300

Subsidiaries:

Power Base **(1)**
32100 Telegraph Rd.
Birmingham, MI 48010
Tel.: 313-540-0900
Data Processing Professional Services, & System Software Products
S.I.C.: 7374
Peter Karmanos, Jr. *(Chm. Bd.)*

XA Systems Corporation **(1)**
983 University Av.
Los Gatos, CA 95030
Tel.: 408-395-1800
Data Processing Professional Services, & System Software Products
S.I.C.: 7372; 7374; 7379
Peter Karmanos, Jr. *(Chm. Bd.)*

CONAIR CORPORATION
1 Cummings Point Rd.
Stamford, CT 06904
Tel.: 203-351-9000 **DE**
Fax: 203-964-8306
Approx.Sls.: $303,000,000
Emp.: 295
Distribute Personal Care Products; Telecommunications
S.I.C.: 3089; 3634; 2844
Leandro P. Rizzuto *(Chm. Bd. & Pres.)*
Maurice Lucas *(Exec. V.P.)*
Ronald T. Diamond *(Sr. V.P. & Gen. Mgr.-Consumer Appliances & Toiletries Div.)*
Barry Haber *(Sr. V.P. & Gen. Mgr.-Consumer Electronics Div.)*
John Mayorek *(Sr. V.P.)*
John Denis *(V.P.-Consumer Toiletries Sls.)*
Edward Doyle *(V.P.-Engnrg.)*
John Errett *(V.P.-Strategic Services)*
Harvey Frisch *(V.P. & Mgr.-Credit)*
Gerald Hogan *(V.P.-Consumer Appliance Sls.)*
Francis Lindsey *(V.P.-Consumer Appliance Mktg.)*
Eugene Morata *(V.P.-Professional Div. Mktg.)*
Jules Nachtigal *(V.P.-Res. & Devel.)*
Patrick P. Yanotta *(V.P.-Fin.)*
James A. Porcelli *(Controller)*
Sylvia Stropkai *(Dir.-Personnel)*
Joyce Varrone *(Dir.-Adv.)*

Outside Service Firm(s):

Deloitte & Touche*(Auditors)*
1 World Trade Center
New York, NY 10048
Tel.: 212-669-5000

Margulies & Margulies, P.C.*(Legal Firm)*
60 E. 42nd St.
New York, NY 10017
Tel.: 212-682-0334

Citibank N.A.*(Major Banking Relationship)*
Corporate Trust Services, 399 Park Ave.
New York, NY 10043
Tel.: 212-559-1605

Philadelphia National Bank*(Major Banking Relationship)*
5th & Market Sts.
Philadelphia, PA 19101
Tel.: 215-629-3100
Fax: 215-834-2069

Division:

Cuisinarts Inc. **(1)**
1 Cummings Point Rd.
Stamford, CT 06904
Tel.: 203-351-9000
Approx.Rev.: $50,000,000
Emp.: 18
Manufacture, Import & Wholesale Cooking Equipment; Cuisinart Food Processors & Cookware
S.I.C.: 5046; 3556
Barry Haber *(Gen. Mgr.)*
Paul Ackles *(V.P.-Mktg.)*
Patric Nugent *(Dir.-Adv.)*

Non-U.S. Holdings:

Conair Pacific Equipment Pte. Ltd. **(1)**
10 Jln. Kilang Timor #03-04
Singapore, Singapore
Tel.: 468 9955

Continental Conair, Ltd. **(1)**
Rm. 604, New World Centre 18-24 Salisbu,
Kowloon, Hong Kong (100%)
Wholesale Personal Care Products
S.I.C.: 5064; 5131

Continental Electric Industries, Ltd. **(1)**
16 Argyle St., Mongkok
Kowloon, Hong Kong (33.33%)
S.I.C.: 5064

Tatung/Conair Corporation **(1)**
22 Chungshan No. Rd.
Taipei, Taiwan (50%)
S.I.C.: 3634

THE CONAIR GROUP, INC.
20 Stanwix St., Ste. 620
Pittsburgh, PA 15222
Mailing Address:
P.O. Box 790,
Franklin, PA 16323
Tel.: 412-261-3488 **DE**
Fax: 412-261-3482
Assets: $65,000,000
Net Worth: $65,000,000
Approx.Sls.: $100,000,000
Emp.: 700
Manufactures Auxiliary Plastic Machinery & Equipment; Installs Systems to Handle Plastic Powder & Particles
S.I.C.: 3559
G. Watts Humphrey, Jr. *(Chm. Bd. & Chief Exec. Officer)*
E. Niles Kenyon *(Pres. & Chief Oper. Officer)*
Robert W. Riordan *(Sec.)*

No. of Mfg. Plants/Facilities: 6

Computer Systems/Hardware:
Honeywell DPS 7 & 675; Control Data Cyber 180

Outside Service Firm(s):

Arthur Andersen & Co.*(Auditors)*
Five Penn Center, Ste. 2600
Pittsburgh, PA 19103

Liberty Mutual*(Group Insurer)*
175 Berkeley St.
Boston, MA

Buchanan, Ingersoll p.c.*(Legal Firm)*
600 Grant St., 57th Flr.
Pittsburgh, PA 15219
Tel.: 412-562-8800

Fleet National Bank*(Major Banking Relationship)*
Corporate Trust Department, 125 Dupont Dr.
Providence, RI 02907
Tel.: 401-278-5400

CONBRACO INDUSTRIES INC.
701 Matthews-Mint Hill Rd.
Matthews, NC 28105
Mailing Address:
P.O. Box 247,
Matthews, NC 28106
Tel.: 704-847-9191
Fax: 704-841-6021
Year Founded: 1935
Sales Range: $60-79 Million
Emp.: 1,300
Fiscal Year-end: 12/31/91
Manufacture Valves & Cylinders
S.I.C.: 3494; 3443
Carl L. Mosack *(Pres.)*
Cal C. Mosack *(V.P.-Sls.)*
Glenn L. Mosack *(V.P.-Opers.)*
Everet Lowery *(Controller)*
Robert Fisher *(Pur. Mgr.)*
Carole Mosack-Lee *(Dir.-Adv. & Communications)*
Dan Davis *(Mgr.-Personnel)*
Marvin Barbour *(Data Processing Mgr.)*

Principal(s):
Carl L. Mosack
Everet Lowery

No. of Mfg. Plants/Facilities: 3

Computer Systems/Hardware:
IBM System 38

Outside Service Firm(s):

Dickson Odom & Co.*(Auditors)*
6525 Morrison Blvd. #516
Charlotte, NC 28211
Tel.: 704-364-5414

Weinstein & Sturges*(Legal Firm)*
1100 S. Tryon St.
Charlotte, NC 28203
Tel.: 704-372-4800

First Union National Bank*(Major Banking Relationship)*
CMG-5, Two First Union Center
Charlotte, NC 28288-1154
Tel.: 704-374-2698
Fax: 704-374-6987

Division:

RP & C **(1)**
701 Industrial Dr.
Monroe, NC
Tel.: 704-289-2821
S.I.C.: 3494; 3443

Concept Omega Corporation
(Name Changed to Thoroughbred Software International, Inc.)

CONCORD ASSETS GROUP, INC.
5200 Town Center Circle
Boca Raton, FL 33486
Tel.: 407-394-9260
Fax: 407-392-8311
Emp.: 100
Corporate Real Estate Investor & Broker/Dealer
S.I.C.: 6552; 6153
Leonard Mandor *(Chm. Bd. & Chief Exec. Officer)*
Robert Mandor *(Pres.)*
Harvey Shore *(Exec. V.P.)*
Joan Levine *(Sr. V.P.)*
Jo Otto *(Sr. V.P.)*

CONCORD LITHO CO., INC.
P.O. Box 464
Concord, NH 03301-0464
Tel.: 603-225-3328 **NH**
Fax: 603-225-6120
Year Founded: 1958
Approx.Sls.: $36,300,000
Emp.: 260
Fiscal Year-end: 12/31/91
Full Color Printing & Bronzing; Specialists in Greeting Cards, Direct Mail & Large Format Printing
S.I.C.: 2752; 2789
James D. Cook *(Chm. Bd. & Chief Exec. Officer)*
Michael D. Coughlin *(Pres.)*
James Brink *(Sec.)*
Rick Manburg *(Controller)*
William Nourse *(Dir.-Sls.)*
Phil Desiere *(Dir.-Mfg.)*
Richard King *(Dir.-Human Resources)*
Gene Bilodeau *(Dir.-Quality Control)*
Al Bodi *(Gen. Mgr.)*

Principal(s):
James D. Cook

No. of Mfg. Plants/Facilities: 1

Computer Systems/Hardware:
VAX III; CRC

Outside Service Firm(s):

Price Waterhouse*(Auditors)*
160 Federal St.
Boston, MA 02110
Tel.: 617-439-3308
Fax: 617-439-3308

Fleet National Bank*(Major Banking Relationship)*
Corporate Trust Dept., 125 Dupont Dr.
Providence, RI 02907
Tel.: 617-426-9555

CONCORDIA PUBLISHING HOUSE
3558 S. Jefferson
Saint Louis, MO 63118
Tel.: 314-268-1000
Tel.: 800-325-3040
Fax: 314-268-1FAX
Year Founded: 1869
Approx.Sls.: $32,000,000
Emp.: 349
Fiscal Year-end: 12/31/91
Import Export
Religious Publications, Periodicals & Merchandise
S.I.C.: 2741
Albert Moeller *(Chm. Bd.)*
Jack Gerber *(Pres. & Chief Exec. Officer)*
Steve Carter *(V.P.-Editorial)*
Herb Hinsch *(V.P.-Opers.)*
Alan Meyer *(V.P.-Fin.)*
George Oehlert *(V.P.-Sls.)*
John Schiller *(V.P.-Mktg.)*
Steve Schanot *(Controller)*
Gerry Puglisi *(Dir.-Mktg. Services)*
Jim Ruff *(Dir.-Human Resources)*
Larry Van de Riet *(Dir.-Fin.)*
Rich Talley *(Mgr.-Personnel)*
Dave Koch *(Dir.-Res. & Devel.)*

Computer Systems/Hardware:
DEC

CONCORP, INC.
P.O. Box 425
Nitro, WV 25143
Tel.: 304-755-8178
Fax: 304-755-3453
Approx.Sls.: $100,000,000
Emp.: 3,000

Holding Company; Mechanical Contractors; Steel Plate Fabrication
S.I.C.: 6719; 1711; 3443
T.J. McDavid *(Pres.)*
R.S. McDavid *(V.P.)*
Fred D. Young, Jr. *(Treas.)*
Gardner M. Stultz *(Sec.)*

Outside Service Firm(s):

Ernst & Young*(Auditors)*
Charleston, WV

Bowles, McDavid, Graff & Love*(Legal Firm)*
Charleston, WV

Subsidiary:

Union Boiler Co. **(1)**
P.O. Box 425
Nitro, WV 25143
Tel.: 304-755-8171
Approx.Sls.: $97,000,000
Emp.: 2,000
Mechanical & Electrical Construction; Steel Plate Fabrication
S.I.C.: 1711; 1731; 3443
Randall S. McDavid *(Chm. Bd. & Pres.)*
Roger W. Magaw *(Exec. V.P. & Treas.)*
Oney McDavid *(Exec. V.P.-Equip.)*
Arnold E. Burdette *(V.P.-Pur.)*
Robert L. Pennington *(V.P. & Controller)*
Randall S. McDavid *(Asst. to Pres.-Fin. & Sec.)*

CONCRETE CONSTRUCTION COMPANY
886 McKinley Ave.
Columbus, OH 43222
Tel.: 614-228-1029 **OH**
Fax: 614-228-7065
Year Founded: 1947
Approx.Sls.: $18,000,000
Emp.: 200
Heavy Highway, Residential & Pipeline Construction
S.I.C.: 1611; 1623; 1629; 6552
John Gallucci *(Chm. Bd., Pres. & Treas.)*
Alfred Gallucci *(Exec. V.P., Sec. & Personnel Dir.)*
James Braden *(V.P.-Sls. & Pur. & Chief Estimator)*
John Lusignolo *(V.P.-Construction)*
R. William Lauder *(Treas. & Controller)*
Robert Daley *(Mgr.-Maintenance)*
John Gallucci, III *(Mgr.-Data Processing)*

Outside Service Firm(s):

Pritchett, Dlusky & Saxe*(Auditors)*
Columbus, OH

OCA*(Group Insurer)*
Columbus, OH

BancOhio National Bank*(Major Banking Relationship)*
Columbus, OH

CONCRETE PIPE & PRODUCTS CO. INC.
P.O. Box 1223
Richmond, VA 23209
Tel.: 804-233-5471
Fax: 804-232-1213
Approx.Sls.: $35,000,000
Emp.: 900
Manufacture Concrete Pipe, Solite-Concrete Masonry Units, Pre-Cast Concrete Products
S.I.C.: 3272
Stanley R. Navas *(Pres.)*
Ronald L. Caricofe *(Treas.)*

Outside Service Firm(s):

Mitchell, Wiggins & Co.*(Auditors)*
Richmond, VA

Christian, Barton, Epps, Brent & Chappell*(Legal Firm)*
1200 Mutual Bldg.
Richmond, VA 23219
Tel.: 804-644-7851

Crestar Bank*(Major Banking Relationship)*
P.O. Box 26665,
Richmond, VA 23261
Tel.: 804-782-5995

Subsidiary:

Concrete Pipe & Products Co., Inc. of California **(1)**
P.O. Box 28758
Sacramento, CA 95828
Tel.: 916-381-3910
Mfr. of Concrete Pipe
S.I.C.: 3272
John LaGros *(V.P. & Gen. Mgr.)*

Plant:

Concrete Pipe & Products Co., Inc. of California **(2)**
P.O. Box 103
Lockeford, CA 95237
Tel.: 209-369-7487
Approx.Sls.: $10,000,000
Emp.: 155
Manufacture Concrete Pipe & Machinery
S.I.C.: 3272; 3599
Stanley R. Navas *(Pres. & Chief Exec. Officer)*

CONCRETE TECHNOLOGY CORP.
1123 Port of Tacoma Rd.
Tacoma, WA 98421
Mailing Address:
P.O. Box 2259,
Tacoma, WA 98401
Tel.: 206-383-3545
Fax: 206-572-9386
Approx.Sls.: $17,000,000
Emp.: 200
Manufacture Prestressed & Precast Concrete
S.I.C.: 3272
Charles Knight, Jr. *(Chm.Bd.)*
James R. Anderson *(Pres.)*
Lawrence M. Christiansen *(Controller)*
Dennis Merwood *(Dir.-Opers.)*
Larry P. Norton *(Dir.-Mktg.)*

Computer Systems/Hardware:
Hewlett Packard

Outside Service Firm(s):

Knight, Vale & Gregory*(Auditors)*
Tacoma, WA

Gordon, Thomas, Honeywell, Malanca, Peterson & Daheim*(Legal Firm)*
Tacoma, WA

First Interstate Bank*(Major Banking Relationship)*
Tacoma, WA

CONDERE CORPORATION
2750 Dixwell Ave.
Hamden, CT 06518
Tel.: 203-287-2200 **DE**
Fax: 203-287-2278
Year Founded: 1987
Approx.Sls.: $120,000,000
Emp.: 850
Retail Sales of Bus or Truck Tires; Pneumatic Automotive Tires; Automobile & Truck Retreading & Repair Shops; Automobile Road Service, Batteries
S.I.C.: 3011; 5531; 7534; 7549
Dennis Terwillger *(Chm. Bd. & Pres.)*
Wally Kirk *(Sr. V.P.)*
James Flynn *(V.P.-Personnel)*
Donald J. Paris *(V.P.-Fin. & Treas.)*

Outside Service Firm(s):

Ernst & Young*(Auditors)*
Goodwyn Sq., 225 Asylum St.
Hartford, CT 06103
Tel.: 203-247-3100

CONDON OIL COMPANY, INC.
126 E. Jackson St.
Ripon, WI 54971
Mailing Address:
P.O. Box 184,
Ripon, WI 54971
Tel.: 414-748-3186
Fax: 414-748-3201
Year Founded: 1939
Approx.Sls.: $50,282,000
Emp.: 35
Fiscal Year-end: 6/30/92
Oil Distr.
S.I.C.: 5171; 5172; 5541; 1711
B. Kent Bauman *(Pres. & Chief Fin. Officer)*
Lee F. Fenendael *(Treas.)*
LeRoy Kempf *(Controller & Sec.)*
Denise McCauley *(Dir.-Data Processing)*

Computer Systems/Hardware:
Datapoint

Outside Service Firm(s):

Marousek Inc.*(Auditors)*
Oshkosh, WI

Federated Mutual Insurance Co.*(Group Insurer)*
Owatonna, MN

Dempsey, Magnusen, Williamson & Lampe*(Legal Firm)*
One Pearl Ave.
Oshkosh, WI 54901
Tel.: 414-235-7300

First National Bank Ripon*(Major Banking Relationship)*
Ripon, WI

CONDOR D.C. POWER SUPPLIES INC.
(Formerly Condor Inc.)
2311 Statham Pkwy.
Oxnard, CA 93033
Tel.: 805-486-4565
Tel.: 800-235-5929 **CA**
Fax: 805-487-8911
Year Founded: 1979
Assets: $3,950,000
Earnings: $900,000
Liabilities: $1,120,000
Net Worth: $2,830,000
Approx.Sls.: $11,400,000
Emp.: 460
Fiscal Year-end: 12/31/91
Manufacture Electronic Subassemblies
S.I.C.: 3629; 3679
Len Wallace *(Chm. Bd.)*
Tom Ingman *(Pres. & Chief Oper. Officer)*
Suzanne Roedl *(Chief Fin. Officer)*
Mark Goldberg *(Dir.-Data Processing & Pur.)*

Principal(s):
Tom Ingman

No. of Mfg. Plants/Facilities: 2
No. of Foreign Offices: 1

Computer Systems/Hardware:
Alpha Micro AM 1042

Outside Service Firm(s):

Arthur Andersen & Co.*(Auditors)*
6320 Canoga Ave.
Woodland Hills, CA 91367

Subsidiary:

Electronica Condor De Mexico **(1)**
Costa Rica #14
Col. Cuauhemoc, Mexicali, BC Mexico
Tel.: 706-568-1640
Emp.: 250
Manufacturer of D.C. Power Supplies
S.I.C.: 3629

CONDOR PACIFIC INDUSTRIES, INC.
8053 Deering Ave.
Canoga Park, CA 91304
Tel.: 818-347-8331
Fax: 818-713-0162
Year Founded: 1963
Approx.Sls.: $15,000,000
Emp.: 125
Mfr. of Gyroscopes
S.I.C.: 3812
Sidney Meltzner *(Chief Fin. Officer)*
Charles Chuman *(Controller)*
Ed Shaw *(Dir.-Mktg.)*

Outside Service Firm(s):

Bank of America*(Major Banking Relationship)*
701 S. Western Ave.
Los Angeles, CA 91201

CONE-BLANCHARD MACHINE COMPANY
7 Everett Lane
Windsor, VT 05089
Mailing Address:
P.O. Box 27,
Windsor, VT 05089
Tel.: 802-674-2161
Fax: 802-674-2071
Sales Range: $10-19 Million
Emp.: 190
Manufacture Metal Working Equipment
S.I.C.: 5084
George T. Caccavaro *(Pres.)*
Elizabeth Ryan *(Dir.-Personnel)*
Kenneth Scully *(Dir.-Data Processing)*
Raymond G. Morse *(Mgr.-Customer Service)*

No. of Mfg. Plants/Facilities: 1
No. of U.S. Offices: 1

Outside Service Firm(s):

Howard Bank*(Major Banking Relationship)*
Burlington, VT

CONESTOGA HOLDINGS, INC.
72 Cummings Point Rd.
Stamford, CT 06902
Tel.: 203-977-1139 **NY**
Fax: 203-967-2886
Year Founded: 1983
Approx.Sls.: $106,000,000
Emp.: 350
Import Export
Holding Company; Industrial & Personal Service Paper; Janitorial Supplies; Plastics Materials
S.I.C.: 6719; 5113; 5087; 5162
J.H. Ogden, Jr. *(Chm. Bd. & Chief Exec. Officer)*

CONESTOGA WOOD SPECIALTIES, INC.
P.O. Box 158,
Earl, PA 17519
Tel.: 215-445-6701
Fax: 215-445-4433
Year Founded: 1964
Approx.Sls.: $60,000,000
Emp.: 600
Export
Mfr. of Raised Panel Doors, Drawer Fronts & Moldings, Millwork
S.I.C.: 2431
Norman Hahn *(Pres. & Chm. Bd.)*
Louis R. Green *(Chief Fin. Officer)*
Sam Hahn *(V.P.-New Products & Engnrg.)*
George Mabarak *(V.P.-Oper.)*
Roger Kloos *(Dir.-Sls. & Mktg.)*
Elizabeth Hahn *(Sec.)*

Conestoga Wood Specialties, Inc.—(Continued)

Outside Service Firm(s):

Blue Ball National Bank*(Major Banking Relationship)*
Blue Ball, PA

Conference Management Corporation
(Name Changed to Full Circle Media Corp.)

CONGAREE CONSTRUCTION CO., INC.
1634 Pineview Rd.
Columbia, SC 29209
Mailing Address:
P.O. Box 90446,
Columbia, SC 29290-1446
Tel.: 803-783-7812/7814/7815
Fax: 803-783-7816
Year Founded: 1964
Sales Range: $40-59 Million
Emp.: 100-300
General Contractor, Construction Management, Water & Sewer Treatment Plants
S.I.C.: 8711; 1542; 1622; 1623; 1629
John Curt Gwinn *(Chm. Bd.)*
John C. Gwinn, Jr. *(Pres.)*
Robert Layton Gwinn *(V.P.)*
Joyce M. Sawyer *(Sec.)*

Computer Systems/Hardware:
IBM

Outside Service Firm(s):

J. W. Hunt & Co.*(Auditors)*
Middleburg Office Park, 1607 St. Julian Place
Columbia, SC 29202
Tel.: 803-254-8196

Barnes, Alford, Stork & Johnson*(Legal Firm)*
Columbia, SC

South Carolina National Bank*(Major Banking Relationship)*
Columbia, SC

CONGOLEUM CORPORATION
3705 Quakerbridge Rd.
Mercerville, NJ 08619
Tel.: 609-584-3000
Year Founded: 1886
Emp.: 1,000
Export
Resilient Sheet Vinyl Flooring
S.I.C.: 3996
Corporate Giving Program: $25 to $1,000
William Canavan *(Chm. Bd.)*
Edwin Cowherd *(Pres.)*
Francis O'Neill *(Sr. V.P.-Sls. & Mktg.)*
Howard N. Feist *(V.P.-Fin.)*
S.A Giddings *(V.P.-Mfg.)*
George Tattersfield *(V.P.-Sls.)*
Mike Pomianoski *(V.P.-Mktg.)*
Doreen Trager *(Dir. of Communications)*
Elizabeth Charbonneau *(Dir.-Retail Mktg. & Sls. Promotion)*
James Snyder *(Dir.-Human Resources)*
Toby Majdan *(Adv. Service Mgr.)*

Conill Advertising, Inc.

CONILL ADVERTISING, INC.
100 Ave. of the Americas
New York, NY 10013
Tel.: 212-274-7500
Fax: 212-274-7550
Year Founded: 1968
Approx.Billings: $40,000,000
Emp.: 45
Hispanic Market
Carlos R. Rossi *(Chm. Bd. & Chief Exec. Officer)*
Michelle Aragon *(Vice Chm. & Chief Creative Officer)*
Paul Melter *(V.P., Fin. Controller)*
Libby Fine *(Bus. Mgr., Production)*

CONKLIN CO. INC.
551 Valley Park Dr.
Shakopee, MN 55379
Mailing Address:
P.O. Box 155
Shakopee, MN 55379
Tel.: 612-445-6010 **MN**
Fax: 612-496-4280
Year Founded: 1954
Approx.Sls.: $55,000,000
Emp.: 170
Manufacture Specialty Chemicals
S.I.C.: 2952; 2873; 2992; 2834; 2843; 2842
Charles Herbster *(Chm. Bd. & Pres.)*
Kent Bensen *(Chief Exec. Officer)*
Steve Korty *(V.P.-Opers.)*
Gordon Pryor *(Dir.-Res. & Devel.)*

No. of U.S. Offices: 2

Outside Service Firm(s):

KPMG Peat Marwick*(Auditors)*
1600 Meritor Tower, 444 Cedar St.
St. Paul, MN 55102

Best & Flanagan*(Legal Firm)*
3500 IDS Ctr.
Minneapolis, MN 55402
Tel.: 612-339-7121

National City Bank*(Major Banking Relationship)*
75 S. Fifth St.
Minneapolis, MN 55402

CONKLIN INSTRUMENT CORPORATION
West Road
Pleasant Valley, NY 12569
Mailing Address:
P.O. Box 650, West Rd.
Pleasant Valley, NY 12569
Tel.: 914-635-2136
Fax: 914-635-2510
Year Founded: 1957
Approx.Sls.: $10,000,000
Emp.: 100
Import Export
Mfr. of Telecommunications Equipment
S.I.C.: 3661; 3663
Charles E. Conklin *(Pres. & Chief Exec. Officer)*
Larry Bishop *(Sr. V.P.)*
David J. Conklin *(Exec. V.P.)*
D.J. Romeo *(V.P.-Sls.)*
Ida Mikula *(Controller)*
M.E. Conklin *(Corp. Sec.)*
M. Mikula *(Pur. Dir.)*

CONLEY FROG & SWITCH COMPANY
387 E. Bodley
Memphis, TN 38109
Mailing Address:
P.O. Box 9188,
Memphis, TN 38109
Tel.: 901-948-4593 **TN**
Fax: 901-948-4921
Year Founded: 1907
Sales Range: $20-39 Million
Emp.: 250
Export
Railroad Track Material & Commercial Forgings
S.I.C.: 3531
W.G. Crone *(Chm. Bd. & Chief Exec. Officer)*
E.M. Lyons *(Pres.)*
Darrell Dugan *(Chief Fin. Officer & Chief Info. Officer)*
R.L. Lyons *(V.P.-Pur.)*
P. Reilly *(V.P.-Mfg.)*
W.C. Reilly, III *(V.P.-Sls.)*
F.J. Hauser *(Sec. & Treas.)*
John Farris *(Gen. Counsel)*
D. Erb *(Mgr.-Human Resources)*
Greg Orman *(Mgr.-Quality Control)*

No. of Mfg. Plants/Facilities: 1
No. of U.S. Offices: 1

Computer Systems/Hardware:
IBM AS/400

Outside Service Firm(s):

Reynolds, Bone & Greisbeck*(Auditors)*
Memphis, TN

National Bank of Commerce*(Major Banking Relationship)*
Memphis, TN

Farris, Hancock, Gillman Branan & Hellen*(Legal Firm)*
Memphis, TN

CONNECTICUT CONTAINER CORPORATION
455 Sackett Point Rd.
North Haven, CT 06473
Tel.: 203-248-2161 **CT**
Fax: 203-248-0241
Year Founded: 1946
Approx.Sls.: $35,000,000
Emp.: 250
Fiscal Year-end: 12/31/91
Corrugated Shipping Containers
S.I.C.: 2653
Lawrence Perkins *(Chm. Bd., Pres. & Treas.)*
Harry Perkins *(Sr. V.P.)*
Louis L. Ceruzzi *(V.P.)*
Steven Egmont *(Dir.-Engrng.)*
Frank Damone *(Mgr.-Data Processing)*
John Sutliff *(Mgr.-Mfg.)*

No. of Mfg. Plants/Facilities: 4
No. of U.S. Offices: 4

Outside Service Firm(s):

Wald & Wald*(Auditors)*
New York, NY

Rubin & Rudman*(Legal Firm)*
Boston, MA

Union Trust*(Major Banking Relationship)*
New Haven, CT

Subsidiary:

Massachusetts Container Corporation **(1)**
300 Cedar Hill St.
Marlborough, MA 01752
Tel.: 508-481-1100
Corrugated Boxes
S.I.C.: 2653
Louis Ceruzzi *(V.P. & Sec.)*
Terry Moore *(Sls. Mgr.)*
Michael Feehly *(Prod. Mgr.)*

CONNECTICUT DRIVE SHAFT, INC.
470 Naugatuck Ave.
Milford, CT 06460
Mailing Address:
P.O. Box 2-188,
Milford, CT 06460
Tel.: 203-877-2716
Tel.: 800-243-2757 **CT**
Fax: 203-877-7486
Year Founded: 1971
Sales Range: $10-19 Million
Emp.: 100
Fiscal Year-end: 12/31/91
Export
Manufacture Auto & Truck Drive Shafts; Truck Parts
S.I.C.: 3714
Joseph A. Honek *(Chm. Bd.)*
J. Frank Honek *(Pres.)*
Andrew P. Honek *(V.P.)*
Anna B. Honek *(Sec.)*
Chris Derosa *(Mgr.-Opers.)*
Andrew D. Mirmina *(Mgr.-Sls.)*
Richard Dlugos *(Pur. Agent)*

Principal(s):
Joseph A. Honek
J. Frank Honek
Andrew P. Honek

No. of U.S. Offices: 5

Computer Systems/Hardware:
NCR 32/700 Mini-Computer 64 User

Outside Service Firm(s):

Levitsky & Berney*(Auditors)*
Woodbridge, CT

Stark & DeMatteo*(Legal Firm)*
Milford, CT

Bank of Boston*(Major Banking Relationship)*
Milford, CT

Division:

Newhouse Brake Division **(1)**
59 Kelso Ave.
West Springfield, MA 01089
Tel.: 413-736-7207
Tel.: 800-443-4013
Fax: 413-733-6713
Manufacturer of Auto Parts
S.I.C.: 3714
John F. Dolan *(Div. Mgr.)*

CONNECTICUT MUTUAL LIFE INSURANCE COMPANY
140 Garden St.
Hartford, CT 06154
Tel.: 203-987-6500 **CT**
Fax: 203-987-6532
Year Founded: 1846
Assets: $12,122,700,000
Earnings: $44,000,000
Liabilities: $11,484,500,000
Net Worth: $638,200,000
Approx.Income: $2,160,600,000
Emp.: 1,975
Fiscal Year-end: 12/31/91
Life Insurance, Disability Income Insurance, Group Pension Investments, Equity Products, Real Estate Investments
S.I.C.: 6311; 6371; 6798
Corporate Giving Program: Grants of $1,000,000 Per Year are Made to Non-Profit Organizations Which Focus on Education, Housing & Health Issues in the Hartford Area
Employee Matching Gifts Program: Employee Gifts up to $750 Per Year to a Credited Educational Institution are Matched
Myron P. Curzan *(Vice Chm.-Investment Policy & Sr. Exec. Consultant)*
Denis F. Mullane *(Pres. & Chief Exec. Officer)*
Robert K. Dickson *(Exec. V.P.-Fin. Services)*
Paul E. Petry *(Exec. V.P., Chief Fin. Officer & Treas.)*
Donald H. Pond *(Exec. V.P.-Individual Insurance)*
Walter Gorski *(Sr. V.P. & Gen. Counsel)*
Marnie W. Mueller *(Sr. V.P.-Corp. Resources)*
Rebeka J. Scalia *(V.P. & Controller)*
Robert R. Benton *(V.P.-Human Resources)*
Ann F. Lomeli *(Corp. Sec.)*
Lori Beauchemin *(Dir.-Meetings Planner)*

Computer Systems/Hardware:
IBM System 3081

Outside Service Firm(s):

Arthur Andersen & Co.*(Auditors)*
One Financial Plaza
Hartford, CT 06103
Tel.: 203-280-0649
Fax: 203-280-0898

CIGNA*(Group Insurer)*
Los Angeles, CA

Connecticut Bank & Trust*(Major Banking Relationship)*
One Constitution Plaza,
Hartford, CT 06115

Connecticut National Bank*(Major Banking Relationship)*
777 Main St.
Hartford, CT 06115
Tel.: 203-728-2000

Subsidiaries:

Bristol Recreation Systems, Inc. **(1)**
140 Garden St.
Hartford, CT 06154
Tel.: 203-727-6500 (100%)
Approx.Sls.: $767,537,000
Emp.: 2,200
Life Insurance
S.I.C.: 6311
Denis F. Mullane *(Chief Exec. Officer)*

CM Life Insurance Company **(1)**
140 Garden St.
Hartford, CT 06154
Tel.: 203-727-6500 (100%)
Fax: 203-727-6644
Approx.Sls.: $100,428,000
Life Insurance
S.I.C.: 6311
Donald H. Pond, Jr. *(Chief Oper. Officer)*

Connecticut Mutual Financial Services **(1)**
140 Garden St.
Hartford, CT 06154
Tel.: 203-727-6500 (100%)
Fax: 203-293-5236
Emp.: 60
Broker-Dealer & Investment Advisor
S.I.C.: 6211; 6282
Gerald J. Randall *(Chief Oper. Officer)*

Diversified Insurance Services of America **(1)**
140 Garden St.
Hartford, CT 06154
Tel.: 203-727-6500 (100%)
Fax: 203-727-6644
Emp.: 20
Procurement of Insurance Contracts from Various Insurance Companies
S.I.C.: 6411
Irving N. Stein *(Chief Oper. Officer)*

GroupAmerica Insurance Co. **(1)**
140 Garden St.
Hartford, CT 06105
Tel.: 203-727-6500 (100%)
Grp. Life & Disability Insurance
S.I.C.: 6311; 6321
Dennis Hardcastle *(Chief Oper. Officer)*

Urbco, Inc. **(1)**
140 Garden St.
Hartford, CT 06105
Tel.: 203-727-6500 (100%)
Fax: 203-293-5217
Real Estate Developer
S.I.C.: 6552
Robert N. Hunter *(Chief Oper. Officer)*

Non-U.S. Holding:

CM Transnational **(1)**
15 Blvd. Royal L-2449
Luxembourg, Luxembourg
Tel.: 352 4705 22 (100%)
Fax: 352 4705 14
Life Insurance
S.I.C.: 6311
Les Ennis *(Mng. Dir.)*

CONNECTICUT SPRING & STAMPING CORPORATION
5 Spring Lane
Farmington, CT 06032
Tel.: 203-677-1341
Fax: 203-677-7199
Sales Range: $20-39 Million
Emp.: 450
Precision Springs, Compression, Extension Torision, Wire Forms & Stampings; Power Press Stampings & Four Slide
S.I.C.: 3469; 3495; 3496
Peter Youmans *(Owner & Chief Exec. Officer)*
Julius Galin *(Pres.)*
Raymond Hunt *(Exec. V.P.)*
Ronald Bottino *(Gen. Mgr.)*
Gilman Cote *(Sec. & Treas.)*
Douglas Delfini *(Pur. Agent)*

Principal(s):
Peter Youmans

Outside Service Firm(s):

Blum, Shapiro & Co.*(Auditors)*
West Hartford, CT

CONNECTICUT STATE LOTTERY
Russell Rd.
Newington, CT 06111
Tel.: 203-566-2912
Fax: 203-665-1198
Approx.Sls.: $525,000,000
Emp.: 70
Fiscal Year-end: 12/31/90
State Lottery
S.I.C.: 7999
Susan H. White *(Lottery Unit Chief)*
Barbara Porto *(Mktg. Coord.)*

CONNELL LIMITED PARTNERSHIP
Fort Hill Square, One International Pl., #310
Boston, MA 02110-2635
Tel.: 617-737-2700 **DE**
Fax: 617-737-1617
Year Founded: 1987
Approx.Sls.: $1,000,000,000
Emp.: 3,200
Fiscal Year-end: 12/31/90
Export
Ferrous Scrap Brokerage & Processing; Aluminum Recycling; Secondary Aluminum Processing; Precision Metal Fabrication; Manufacture Machine Tools & Metalworking Tooling; Manufacture Heat Transfer Equipment
S.I.C.: 3443; 3544; 3341; 5093; 3542; 3484
William F. Connell *(Chm. Bd. & Chief Exec. Officer)*
Maurice R. Heller *(V.P.-Industrial Rels.)*
Edward J. Joyce *(V.P. & Gen. Counsel)*
Kathleen A. Murphy *(V.P. & Treas.)*
Arnold S. Ray *(V.P. & Controller)*

Principal(s):
William F. Connell

No. of Mfg. Plants/Facilities: 28
No. of U.S. Offices: 17
No. of Foreign Offices: 2

Computer Systems/Hardware:
IBM

Outside Service Firm(s):

Coopers & Lybrand*(Auditors)*
1 Post Office Square
Boston, MA 02110
Tel.: 617-574-5000
Fax: 617-345-0398

Blue Cross & Blue Shield of Illinois*(Group Insurer)*
100 Tower Drive
Burr Ridge, IL 60521
Tel.: 708-323-3666

Skadden, Arps, Slate, Meagher & Flom*(Legal Firm)*
913 Third Ave.
New York, NY 10022
Tel.: 212-371-6000

First National Bank of Boston*(Major Banking Relationship)*
P.O. Box 644,
Boston, MA 02102-0644
Tel.: 617-575-2900
Fax: 617-575-2549

Divisions:

Danly Die Set Division **(1)**
2115 S. 54th Ave.
Cicero, IL 60650
Tel.: 708-863-2800
S.I.C.: 3544
David Lowam *(Div. Pres.)*
Richard Barr *(V.P.-Mktg.)*
John Salamone *(V.P.- Oper.)*
David Samuelsen *(Dir.-Human Resources)*

Danly-Komatsu L.P. **(1)**
2115 S. 54th Ave.
Cicero, IL 60650
Tel.: 708-863-2800 (70%)
Fax: 708-780-1140
Approx.Sls.: $120,000,000
Emp.: 500
Fiscal Year-end: 12/31/90
Export
Mfr. of Presses; Press Automation Equipment; A Joint Venture; Danly 70% & Komatsu 30%
S.I.C.: 3542
Ronald Cantrell *(Pres.)*
Tasuo Suzuki *(Sr. V.P.-Engrng.)*
Bob Matsumoto *(V.P.-Sls., N. America)*
Michael J. Murphy *(V.P.-Mktg. & Sls.)*
N. Shibasaki *(V.P.-Quality Control)*
Mark Daniel *(Controller)*
D.J. Hawthorne *(Dir.-Sls. Admin.)*
G.A. Elliott *(Dir.-Employee Rels.)*
Ralph LaBrach *(Mgr.-Quality Control)*

Luria Bros. Division **(1)**
20521 Chagrin Blvd.
Cleveland, OH 44122
Tel.: 216-752-4000
S.I.C.: 5093
J. Robert Hahn *(Pres.)*
John Dilaqua *(V.P.-Fin.)*
Derek Harold *(V.P.-Mill Service)*
Ronald E. Messner *(V.P.-Human Resources)*

Mayville Metal Products Division **(1)**
First & Highland, P.O. Box 28
Mayville, WI 53050
Tel.: 414-387-3000
Emp.: 1,000
Contract Manufacturing; Office Machines, Dental Lab & Hospital Equipment, Electrical Control Cabinets & Switch Boxes, Fabricated Metal Components & Electro/ Mechanical Assemblies, Tubing Frames
S.I.C.: 3444; 3499
William A. Clapp *(Pres.)*
Russell Gessner *(V.P.-Mfg.)*
Larry Huser *(V.P.-Sls. & Mktg.)*
Chris Cummins *(Controller)*
Kenneth E. Oechsner *(Dir.-Human Resources)*

Wabash Alloys Division **(1)**
P.O. Box 466,
Wabash, IN 46992
Tel.: 219-563-7461
S.I.C.: 3341
Joseph Viland *(Pres.)*
Howard Sinclair *(V.P.-Fin.)*
Donald Pfanstiel *(V.P.-Sls.)*
William D. Chalfin *(V.P.-Human Resources)*

Yuba Heat Transfer Division **(1)**
2121 N. East Ave., P.O. Box 3158
Tulsa, OK 74116
Tel.: 918-234-6000
S.I.C.: 3443
Harold Lawrence *(Pres.)*
Brent Thompson *(V.P.-Sls.)*
Jack Meyer *(Controller)*
Phillip Kates *(Dir.-Human Resources)*

CONNELL RICE & SUGAR CO.
45 Cardinal Dr.
Westfield, NJ 07090
Tel.: 908-233-0700 **NJ**
Fax: 908-233-1070
Year Founded: 1926
Approx.Sls.: $1,200,000,000
Emp.: 150
Importer & Distributor of Food Products; Food Processing; Heavy Equipment Leasing
S.I.C.: 5141; 5142; 5146; 5147; 5153; 7359
Grover Connell *(Chm. Bd. & Pres.)*
George I. Alayeto *(Exec. V.P.)*
Ted Connell *(Exec. V.P.)*
R.C. Connolly *(Exec. V.P.)*
Terry Connell *(Sr. V.P. & Treas.)*
Richard F. Purcell *(Sr. V.P. & Sec.)*
Martin S. Simon *(Sr. V.P.)*
Robert Spalteholz *(V.P.-Real Estate Devel.)*

CONNELLY CONTAINERS, INC.
Righters Ferry Rd.
Bala-Cynwyd, PA 19004
Tel.: 215-839-6400 **PA**
Fax: 215-664-2926
Year Founded: 1989
Approx.Sls.: $62,067,000
Emp.: 475
Mfr. Corrugated Cartons, Fibreboard & Triple-Wall; Canned Food; Shipping Containers; Bulk Shippers
S.I.C.: 2621; 2035; 2032; 2653
Thomas S. Connelly *(Chm. Bd., Pres., Chief Exec. & Chief Oper. Officer)*
Charles J. LaGrossa *(Pres.-Paper Div.)*
Charles Boy *(V.P.-Opers.)*
Bernard Campbell *(V.P.-Sls.)*
Leon A. Wojnowski *(Sec., Treas. & Chief Fin. Officer)*
Morris Gerber *(Gen. Counsel)*
Mary Ann Albright *(Dir.-Personnel)*

Outside Service Firm(s):

Gerber & Gerber*(Legal Firm)*
One Montgomery Plaza, Ste.500
Norristown, PA 19401
Tel.: 215-279-6700

Philadelphia National Bank*(Major Banking Relationship)*
P.O. Box 13834, Broad & Chestnut Streets
Philadelphia, PA 19101-7618
Tel.: 215-973-8327

Subsidiaries:

Connelly Containers, Inc. of Philadelphia **(1)**
4368 Main St.
Philadelphia, PA 19127
Tel.: 215-839-6400 (100%)
Emp.: 60
Paper Mill
S.I.C.: 2621
Charles Lagrossa *(Pres.)*

Mrs. Schlorer's, Inc. **(1)**
270 N. Mill Rd.
Vineland, NJ 08360
Tel.: 609-921-2100 (100%)
Mayonnaise, Syrups; Condiments
S.I.C.: 2035
Dale Guhr *(Pres.)*

Venice Maid Co., Inc. **(1)**
270 N. Mill Rd.
Vineland, NJ 08360
Tel.: 609-691-2100 (100%)
Emp.: 150
Canning Food Products Under Private Label
S.I.C.: 2032

CONNORS BRUNSWICK, INC.
778 Main St.
South Portland, ME 04106
Mailing Address:
P.O. Box 540
Scarborough, ME 04070-0540
Tel.: 207-775-5777
Tel.: 800-334-3696
Fax: 207-775-6745
Approx.Sls.: $390,000,000
Emp.: 20
Fiscal Year-end: 12/31/91
Import Export
Canners of Sardines, Fish & Lobster
S.I.C.: 2091; 2092

Connors Brunswick, Inc.—(Continued)

Terry Alcorn *(V.P.-North American Sls.)*
Henry Johnson *(Controller)*
Sharon Dadiego *(Mktg. Admin.)*

Computer Systems/Hardware:
IBM Word Processor

Outside Service Firm(s):

Grant Thornton*(Auditors)*
53 State St.
Boston, MA 02109
Tel.: 617-723-7900

Shawmut Bank*(Major Banking Relationship)*
1 Federal St.
Boston, MA 02110
Tel.: 617-292-3715

Division:

Port Clyde Foods Co. **(1)**
778 Main St.
South Portland, ME 04106
Tel.: 207-775-5777
Tel.: 800-334-3696
Fax: 207-775-6745
Import Export
Computer Systems/Hardware:
IBM
Canners of Sardines, Fish Steaks & Kippered Snacks: Port Clyde, Booth, Holmes
S.I.C.: 2091; 2092
Terry Alcorn *(V.P.-N. American Sls.)*
Alan Carr *(V.P.-United States Sls.)*

CONQUEST CARPET MILLS
950 Riverbend Dr.
Dalton, GA 30720
Tel.: 706-226-8066
Fax: 706-226-8893
Approx.Sls.: $135,000,000
Emp.: 700
Manufacture Tufted Carpet
S.I.C.: 2273
Thomas Bouckaert *(Pres.)*
Norman Clapp *(Chief Fin. Officer)*
Terry Crump *(V.P.-Mktg.)*

Outside Service Firm(s):

First Union*(Major Banking Relationship)*
Dalton, GA

CONSO PRODUCTS COMPANY
P.O. Box 326
Union, SC 29379
Tel.: 803-427-9004
Fax: 803-427-0722
Sales Range: $20-39 Million
Emp.: 450
Export
Drapery & Upholstery Trimmings, Workroom Supplies, Notions; Decorative Trimmings Manufacturer
S.I.C.: 2396
Cary Findlay *(Chm. Bd. & Pres.)*
Gil Bartell *(V.P.-Fin.)*
Tony Esposito *(V.P.-Natl. Accts.)*
Konstance J.K. Findlay *(V.P.)*
William Stewart *(V.P.-Mfg.)*
Jo Davis *(Corp. Sec.)*
Butch Williams *(Dir.-Data Processing)*
Sherri Duncan *(Mgr.-Employee Benefits)*
Koni Findlay *(Mgr.-Export)*
Betsy O'Shields *(Mgr.-Mktg.)*
David Sears *(Mgr.-Sls.)*
Ken Easler *(Pur. Agent)*

No. of Mfg. Plants/Facilities: 2
No. of U.S. Offices: 2

Outside Service Firm(s):

Deloitte & Touche*(Auditors)*
1200 NCNB Plaza, 7 N. Laurens St.
Greenville, SC 29601
Tel.: 803-242-3640

CONSOLIDATED BEVERAGES, INC.
12 St. Mark St.
Auburn, MA 01501
Mailing Address:
P.O. Box 410
Auburn, MA 01501
Tel.: 508-832-5311
Fax: 508-832-9831
Approx.Sls.: $22,000,000
Emp.: 85
Wholesale Beer
S.I.C.: 5181
Ronald Field *(Pres.)*
John O'Shaughnessy *(Treas.)*
Page O'Berg *(Controller)*
John Kazlo *(Mgr.-Sls.)*

Principal(s):
Ronald Field
John O'Shaughnessy

Outside Service Firm(s):

Singer & Lusardi*(Auditors)*
Worcester, MA

Shawmut Bank*(Major Banking Relationship)*
Worcester, MA

CONSOLIDATED CIGAR CORPORATION
5900 N. Andrews Ave., Ste. 700
Fort Lauderdale, FL 33309
Tel.: 305-772-9000
Fax: 305-938-7811
Approx.Sls.: $120,000,000
Emp.: 3,000
Fiscal Year-end: 12/31/90
Import Export
Mfr. Cigars, Smoking Tobacco, Lighters
S.I.C.: 2121; 2131; 3999
Theodore W. Folz *(Pres. & Chief Exec. Officer)*
Richard DiMeola *(Exec. V.P. & Chief Oper. Officer)*
Gary Ellis *(Sr. V.P. & Chief Fin. Officer)*
James Colucci *(Sr. V.P. Sls. & Mktg.)*
George F. Gershel, Jr. *(Sr. V.P.-Tobacco)*
Denis McQuillen *(Sr. V.P. Mfg.)*
Eric Workman *(V.P.)*
David Goldfarb *(Dir.-Mktg.)*

Outside Service Firm(s):

Ernst & Young*(Auditors)*
787 Seventh Ave.
New York, NY 10019
Tel.: 212-773-1243

Citibank N.A.*(Major Banking Relationship)*
Corporate Trust Services, 399 Park Ave.
New York, NY 10043
Tel.: 212-559-1605

Divisions:

Allied Products **(1)**
5900 N. Andrews Ave., Ste. 700
Fort Lauderdale, FL 33309
Tel.: 305-772-9000
Fax: 305-938-7811
Approx.Sls.: $10,000,000
Emp.: 150
Fiscal Year-end: 12/31/90
Mixture 79 Regular & Cherry Pipe Tobacco, Dutch Masters Pipe Tobacco, China Black Pipe Tobacco, Rogers Tobacco Pouches, Complete Line of Smoking Accessories
S.I.C.: 5199; 3069; 3999; 3172; 2131
James Colucci *(Sr. V.P.-Sls. & Mktg.)*
Eric Workman *(V.P.-Natl. Accts.)*

Domestic Cigars **(1)**
5900 N. Andrews Ave., Ste. 700
Fort Lauderdale, FL 33309
Tel.: 305-772-9000

Premium Products Division **(1)**
5900 N. Andrews Ave., Ste. 700
Fort Lauderdale, FL 33309
Tel.: 305-772-9000
Import Export
Richard DiMeola *(Pres.)*

CONSOLIDATED COMPANIES INC. (CONCO)
3000 34th St.
Metairie, LA 70001
Mailing Address:
P.O. Box 6096,
Metairie, LA 70009
Tel.: 504-834-4082 **LA**
Fax: 504-834-2572
Approx.Sls.: $246,000,000
Emp.: 800
Import
Wholesale Groceries, Frozen Foods, Druggist Products & Sundries, Meats, Institutional Merchandise
S.I.C.: 5141; 5142; 5122; 5148; 5147
Victor J. Kurzweg III *(Chm. Bd. & Chief Exec. Officer)*
Winslow Chadwick, Jr. *(Pres. & Chief Fin. Officer)*
Hamilton J. Chauvin *(Exec. V.P.-Admin. & Sec.)*
George Beaver *(V.P.-Convenience Store Opers.)*
William E. Nelson *(V.P.-Procurement)*

Outside Service Firm(s):

Coopers & Lybrand*(Auditors)*
New Orleans, LA

First National Bank of Commerce*(Major Banking Relationship)*
New Orleans, LA

CONSOLIDATED CO-OP
R.F.D., P.O. Box 48
Gowrie, IA 50543
Tel.: 515-352-3851 **IA**
Fax: 515-352-3865
Year Founded: 1973
Assets: $7,808,862
Earnings: $262,256
Liabilities: $4,258,400
Net Worth: $3,550,462
Approx.Sls.: $28,500,000
Emp.: 65
Fiscal Year-end: 8/31/92
Farm Supply Co-operative: Petroleum Products, Grain
S.I.C.: 5153; 5172; 5191
James Stewart *(Chm. Bd. & Pres.)*
Alan Kohtz *(Chief Exec. Officer)*
Audra Cordle *(Chief Fin. Officer, Treas. & Controller)*
James Schleisman *(Dir.-Safety & Mgr.-Personnel)*
John Graney *(Mgr.-Data Processing)*

Outside Service Firm(s):

Gardiner & Co.*(Auditors)*
Des Moines, IA

Tri-State Insurance*(Commercial Insurance Carrier)*
Lawrence, MN

Mutual Service Life Insurance Co.*(Group Insurer)*
Arden Hills, MN

Johnson, Erb, Latham, Gibb*(Legal Firm)*
Ft. Dodge, IA

Omaha Bank for Co-ops*(Major Banking Relationship)*
Omaha, NE

Associated Benefits Corp.*(Pension Manager)*
2929 Westown Pkwy.
Des Moines, IA 50265

CONSOLIDATED INDUSTRIAL CORPORATION
430 N. Woodward Ave.
Birmingham, MI 48009
Tel.: 313-647-3337 **MI**
Emp.: 125
Rubber Ballons; Injection Molding Of Plastics
S.I.C.: 3069; 3089
Clark D. Matthews *(Pres.)*
John W. Burns *(Exec. V.P., Sec. & Treas.)*

Outside Service Firm(s):

MHB Company*(Auditors)*
Bloomfield Hills, MI

Comerica Bank*(Major Banking Relationship)*
Birmingham, MI

CONSOLIDATED INDUSTRIES, INC.
677 Mixville Rd.
Cheshire, CT 06410
Tel.: 203-272-5371
Fax: 203-272-5672
Approx.Premiums: $11,000,000
Emp.: 102
Ferrous & Non-ferrous Die Forgings
S.I.C.: 3365; 3462; 3463
Joseph P. Valentine *(Pres.)*
Ronald J. Clayton *(Exec. V.P.)*
Donald A. Luedke *(V.P.-Sls.)*
William T. Soltis *(Mgr.-Indus. Rels.)*

Outside Service Firm(s):

Arthur Andersen & Co.*(Auditors)*
One Financial Plaza
Hartford, CT 06103
Tel.: 203-280-0649
Fax: 203-280-0898

Connecticut National Bank*(Major Banking Relationship)*
Cheshire, CT

CONSOLIDATED LUMBER CO.
808 N. 4th St.
Stillwater, MN 55082
Mailing Address:
P.O. Box 288
Stillwater, MN 55082
Tel.: 612-439-3138
Fax: 612-439-9756
Approx.Sls.: $23,000,000
Emp.: 110
Wholesale & Retail Lumber & Building Materials; Architectural Services
S.I.C.: 5211; 5199; 8712
Dale H. Remus *(Pres.)*
David L. Majeski *(V.P.)*
John E. Stensvold *(V.P.)*
Jerome J. Oberembet *(Sec. & Treas.)*

Outside Service Firm(s):

McGladrey & Pullen*(Auditors)*
Stillwater, MN

Marquette Bank*(Major Banking Relationship)*
777 Marquette Ave.
Minneapolis, MN 55402
Tel.: 612-370-2182

Division:

Arrow Building Centers **(1)**
808 N. 4th St.
Stillwater, MN 55082
Tel.: 612-439-3138
Retail & Wholesale Lumber & Building Materials
S.I.C.: 5211; 5199; 8712
Dale H. Remus *(Pres.)*

CONSOLIDATED METAL PRODUCTS, INC.
1028 Depot St.
Cincinnati, OH 45204
Tel.: 513-251-2624

Fax: 513-251-2488
Approx.Sls.: $10,000,000
Emp.: 80
Import Export
Mfr. of Threaded Steel Bar Products
S.I.C.: 3316
Hugh Gallagher, Jr. *(Pres.)*
Robert L. Martz *(V.P.-Mktg.)*
Charles S. Schmidt *(V.P.-Fin.)*

CONSOLIDATED METCO, INC.
13940 N. Rivergate Blvd.
Portland, OR 97203
Mailing Address:
P.O. Box 83201
Portland, OR 97283-0201
Tel.: 503-286-5741
Tel.: 800-547-9473
Fax: 503-240-5443
Year Founded: 1964
Approx.Sls.: $75,000,000
Emp.: 500
Fiscal Year-end: 1/31/91
Export
Permanent Mold, Low Pressure & Die Castings Aluminum Foundry; Fuel/ Water Separators; Engineered Structural Foam, Heavy Duty Aluminum Truck/Trailer Hubs
S.I.C.: 3365; 3363; 3714
Ed J. Oeltjen *(Pres.)*
Michael J. Harman *(Exec. V.P.-Sls. & Mktg.)*
John Waters *(Controller)*
Mark Eaton *(Mgr.-Natl. Sls. & Mktg.)*

CONSOLIDATED MIDWEST, INC.
3600 Hwy. 157
La Crosse, WI 54603
Mailing Address:
P.O. Box 429
La Crosse, WI 54602
Tel.: 608-781-1010
Approx.Sls.: $25,000,000
Emp.: 194
Gases, Liquefied Petroleum, Butane Gas, Gasoline, Propane Gas, Natural Gas Distribution
S.I.C.: 5172; 5984
James A. Senty *(Chm. Bd. & Pres.)*
John L. Senty *(V.P. & Sec.)*
Richard A. Linton *(Controller & Asst. Treas.)*

Outside Service Firm(s):

Wipfli, Ullrich, Bertleson*(Auditors)*
Eau Claire, WI

Phillip & Sletteland*(Legal Firm)*
Milwaukee, WI

Marquette Bank, N.A.*(Major Banking Relationship)*
Sixth & Marquette
Minneapolis, MN 55402
Tel.: 612-341-5651

Subsidiary:

Midwest Bottle Gas Company **(1)**
3600 Hwy. 157
La Crosse, WI 54602
Tel.: 608-781-1010
Emp.: 192
Retail Liquefied Petroleum Gas & Appliances, Refined Gasoline & Fuel Oils
S.I.C.: 5984; 5722; 5983
James A. Senty *(Chm. Bd. & Pres.)*
John L. Senty *(V.P., Sec. & Treas.)*
Richard A. Linton *(Controller & Dir.-Personnel & Data Processing)*

CONSOLIDATED PIPE & SUPPLY COMPANY
1205 Hilltop Pkwy.
Birmingham, AL 35204
Mailing Address:
P.O. Box 2472,
Birmingham, AL 35201
Tel.: 205-323-7261
Fax: 205-323-7261 x291
Year Founded: 1964
Assets: $25,196,640
Earnings: $1,125,805
Net Worth: $25,196,640
Approx.Sls.: $90,000,000
Emp.: 250
Fiscal Year-end: 12/31/91
Wholesale & Retail Distributor of Steel Pipe, Valves & Fittings; Manufacture PVC Pipe, Coat & Wrap Pipe, Fusion Bond Coat Steel Pipe
S.I.C.: 5051; 5074; 5251; 3498; 3317; 3444
Howard J. Kerr *(Chm. Bd., Pres. & Chief Exec. Officer)*
C. A. Mock *(V.P., Sec. & Chief Fin. Officer)*
George Johnson *(Treas.)*
Ed Williamson *(Controller)*
David Faile *(Dir.-Mngmt. Info. Systems)*

Computer Systems/Hardware:
IBM System 38

Outside Service Firm(s):

Bradley, Arant, Rose & White*(Legal Firm)*
1400 Park Place Tower
Birmingham, AL 35203
Tel.: 205-521-8000

First Alabama Bank*(Major Banking Relationship)*
Birmingham, AL

Manufacturers Hanover Trust Co.*(Major Banking Relationship)*
270 Park Ave.
New York, NY 10017
Tel.: 212-286-3229

CONSOLIDATED PUBLISHING COMPANY
(d/b/a The Anniston Star)
216 W. 10th St.
Anniston, AL 36201
Mailing Address:
P.O. Box 189
Anniston, AL 36202
Tel.: 205-236-1551
Fax: 205-231-0027
Approx.Sls.: $10,000,000
Emp.: 185
Publisher of the Annison Star, A Daily Newspaper
S.I.C.: 2711
P.A. Sanguinetti *(Pres.)*
H.B. Ayers *(V.P.)*
E. Cody Hall *(Editor-in-Chief)*
A.J. Thornton *(Sec. & Treas.)*
Sam C. Ogle, Jr. *(Mgr.-Circulation)*
John C. Childs *(Bus. Mgr.)*

Outside Service Firm(s):

Camp & Associates*(Auditors)*
Talladega, AL

Merrill, Porch, Doster & Dillon*(Legal Firm)*
Anniston, AL

South Trust Bank of Calhoun County, N.A.*(Major Banking Relationship)*
Anniston, AL

CONSOLIDATED SYSTEMS, INC.
650 Rosewood Dr.
Columbia, SC 29201
Tel.: 803-771-7920 **SC**
Fax: 803-779-4649
Year Founded: 1968
Approx.Sls.: $147,000,000
Emp.: 275
Sheet Metalwork; Coating of Metals & Formed Products; Trucking Except Local
S.I.C.: 3443; 3479; 4213
G.W. Rogers *(Chm. Bd.)*
W.M. Trotter *(Pres. & Chief Exec. Officer)*
Edward M. Ringley *(Treas.)*

Outside Service Firm(s):

J.W. Hunt & Co.*(Auditors)*
Columbia, SC

South Carolina National Bank*(Major Banking Relationship)*
1426 Main St.
Columbia, SC 29226
Tel.: 803-765-3000
Fax: 803-765-4333

CONSTRUCTION COUNSELLORS, INC.
118 Mill Rd.
Park Ridge, NJ 07656
Tel.: 201-930-0300
Emp.: 50
General Contracting, Construction, Real Estate Development
S.I.C.: 1541; 1542; 6411; 6552
Robert Frankel *(Chief Exec. & Chief Fin. Officer)*

Subsidiaries:

Tennanah Lake Golf & Tennis Club, Inc. **(1)**
118 Mill Rd.
Park Ridge, NJ 07656
Tel.: 201-930-0300 (100%)
Golf Club
S.I.C.: 7997

Titan PRT **(1)**
118 Mill Rd.
Park Ridge, NJ 07656
Tel.: 201-930-0300 (100%)
Insurance
S.I.C.: 6411

CONSTRUCTION MACHINERY COMPANY
Glenwood & Vinton
Waterloo, IA 50704
Mailing Address:
P.O. Box 120
Waterloo, IA 50704
Tel.: 612-454-4300
Fax: 319-235-9998
Approx.Sls.: $10,000,000
Emp.: 80
Concrete Mixers, Hoists, Earth Drilling Equip. & Pipe Pushing Equip.
S.I.C.: 5082
Alex Stamatakis *(Chm. & Pres.)*
Carl M. Wright *(Sr. V.P.)*

CONSTRUCTION MANAGEMENT SERVICE
3600 Silverside Rd.
Wilmington, DE 19810
Mailing Address:
P.O. Box 7499
Wilmington, DE 19803
Tel.: 302-478-4200
Fax: 302-478-2750
Year Founded: 1984
Approx.Sls.: $45,000,000
Emp.: 400
Construction Management; General Electric Contractors
S.I.C.: 8741; 1731
John S. Adams *(Pres.)*
Scott W. Clark *(Sec. & Treas.)*

Outside Service Firm(s):

Horty & Horty*(Auditors)*
Welmington, DE

Chase Manhattan Bank, N.A.*(Major Banking Relationship)*
One Chase Manhattan Plaza
New York, NY 10081
Tel.: 212-552-2222
Tel.: 800-526-0801
Fax: 212-552-7175

CoreStates First Pennsylvania Bank, N.A.*(Major Banking Relationship)*
1500 Chestnut
Philadelphia, PA 19102

Subsidiary:

Hatzel & Buehler, Inc. **(1)**
3600 Silverside Rd.
Wilmington, DE 19810
Tel.: 302-478-4200
General Electrical Contractor
S.I.C.: 1731
William A. Goeller *(Pres. & Chief Exec. Officer)*
John S. Adams *(V.P. & Treas.)*
Michael C. Goeller *(Sec. & Gen. Counsel)*

CONSTRUCTION SPECIALTIES, INC.
55 Winans Ave.
Cranford, NJ 07016
Tel.: 908-272-5200 **NJ**
Telex: 138296
Approx.Sls.: $120,000,000
Emp.: 720
Fiscal Year-end: 4/30/92
Mfr. of Architectural Building Products in Aluminum
S.I.C.: 3442; 1799; 3585
Ellen H. Hakes *(Chm. Bd.)*
Robert H. Thomson *(Pres. & Chief Exec. Officer)*
Ronald F. Dadd *(Chief Oper. Officer)*
Frederick D. Smith *(Treas. & Chief Fin. Officer)*
Arthur C. Culbertson *(Sec. & Gen. Counsel)*
Roger C. Conrad *(Dir.-Personnel)*
Robert Olsen *(Chief Engineer)*
A.J. LaPoine *(Gen. Mgr.)*
Julian Sterns *(Adv. Mgr.)*

No. of Mfg. Plants/Facilities: 9
No. of U.S. Offices: 4
No. of Foreign Offices: 5

Computer Systems/Hardware:
Basic Four MAI System 740

Outside Service Firm(s):

KPMG Peat Marwick*(Auditors)*
150 John F. Kennedy Pkwy.
Short Hills, NJ 07078
Tel.: 201-467-9650

Toronto Dominion Bank*(Major Banking Relationship)*
42 Wall St.
New York, NY 10005-1924
Tel.: 212-820-2160

Subsidiaries:

Construction Specialties of California **(1)**
55 Winans Ave.
Cranford, NJ 07016
Tel.: 908-272-5200 (100%)
Approx.Sls.: $7,000,000
Emp.: 50
Mfr. of Building Products
S.I.C.: 3354
R.H. Thomson *(Pres.)*

Data Aire, Inc. **(1)**
7442 Orangewood
Garden Grove, CA 92675
Tel.: 714-891-3471 (100%)
Approx.Sls.: $5,000,000
Emp.: 40
Mfr. of Air Conditioners
S.I.C.: 3585
W. Hoover *(Pres.)*

Datasphere, Inc. **(1)**
49 Meeker Ave.
Cranford, NJ 07016
Tel.: 908-272-1810 (100%)
Approx.Sls.: $2,000,000
Emp.: 6
Computer Related Services
S.I.C.: 7379
R.F. Dadd *(Pres.)*

Special Erection Services, Inc. **(1)**
55 Winans Ave.
Cranford, NJ 07016
Tel.: 908-272-5200 (100%)
Approx.Sls.: $300,000
Emp.: 4
Installation of Aluminum Products
S.I.C.: 1799
Robert H. Thomson *(Pres.)*

CONSUMERS MARKETS INC.
639 W. Chestnut Expwy
Springfield, MO 65802
Tel.: 417-866-4305 **MO**
Year Founded: 1948
Sales Range: $100-499 Million
Emp.: 2,200
Grocery Stores
S.I.C.: 5411
Jesse Lewis *(Chm. Bd., Pres. & Chief Exec. Officer)*
Jerry Sutherland *(Sr. V.P., Treas. & Sec.)*

Computer Systems/Hardware:
IBM System 38

Outside Service Firm(s):

Baird, Kurtz & Dobson*(Auditors)*
Springfield, MO

CONTAINER PRODUCTS INC.
20245 W. 12 Mile Rd., Ste. 200
Southfield, MI 48076
Tel.: 313-827-7720 **MI**
Year Founded: 1984
Approx.Sls.: $85,000,000
Emp.: 500
Mfr. & Distributor of Steel Drums
S.I.C.: 3412
Irving A. Rubin *(Chm. Bd., Pres. & Chief Exec. Officer)*
Robert Bonczyk *(Exec. V.P.)*
Sally Leny *(V.P.-Mktg.)*

No. of Mfg. Plants/Facilities: 7

Computer Systems/Hardware:
Basic Four

Plants:

CP Illinois, Inc. **(1)**
P.O. Box 70, County Road
Jerseyville, IL 62052
Tel.: 618-498-6434
Mfr. of Industrial Packaging & Plastic Pails
S.I.C.: 3089
Donald Schaaf *(Plant Mgr.)*

CPI Plastics, Inc. **(1)**
P.O. Box 639, 434 Corinth Rd.
Newnan, GA 30264
Tel.: 706-253-7176
Mfr. of Industrial Packaging, Plastic Pails & Chicken Coops
S.I.C.: 3089
Harland J. Stone *(Plant Mgr.)*

Subsidiaries:

Container Products Inc. **(1)**
2391 Cassens Dr.
Fenton, MO 63026
Tel.: 314-343-7333
Mfr. of Metal Shipping Barrels, Drums & Kegs
S.I.C.: 3412
William Woodruff *(Gen. Mgr.)*

Container Products Inc. **(1)**
7838 Iron St.
Masury, OH 44438
Tel.: 800-321-2741
Mfr. of Metal Shipping Barrels, Drums & Kegs
S.I.C.: 3412
Thomas Seelig *(Gen. Mgr.)*

Container Products Inc. **(1)**
P.O. Box 23250, 6000 Jefferson Hwy.
New Orleans, LA 70123
Tel.: 504-733-6644
Mfr. of Metal Shipping Barrels, Drums & Kegs
S.I.C.: 3412
Doug Brooks *(Gen. Mgr.)*

Container Products Inc. **(1)**
P.O. Box 9556, 3717 W. 21st St.-Rte. 9
Tulsa, OK 74107
Tel.: 918-599-9010
Metal Shipping Barrels, Drums, Kegs, Pails
S.I.C.: 3412
Larry Patterson *(Plant Mgr.)*

CONTEC INTERNATIONAL
1023 State St.
Schenectady, NY 12307
Mailing Address:
P.O. Box 739
Schenectady, NY 12301
Tel.: 518-382-8000
Telex: 650 262 1964
Fax: 518-382-8452
Year Founded: 1977
Assets: $11,700,000
Earnings: $3,400,000
Liabilities: $8,400,000
Net Worth: $3,300,000
Approx.Sls.: $30,000,000
Emp.: 700
Fiscal Year-end: 9/30/88
Import
Manufacture, Sell & Service Cable TV Components, Primarily Converters
S.I.C.: 3575; 3621; 3663
Richard Monks *(Pres., Chief Exec. Officer & Chief Oper. Officer)*
Caroll Foreman *(V.P.-Opers.)*
Harold C. Petrie *(V.P.-Information Systems)*
Thomas Delaney *(Controller)*

No. of Mfg. Plants/Facilities: 5
No. of U.S. Offices: 5

Computer Systems/Hardware:
IBM AS/400

Outside Service Firm(s):

Coopers & Lybrand*(Auditors)*
80 State Street
Albany, NY 12207

Phoenix Mutual Life Insurance Co.*(Group Insurer)*
Hartford, CT

Arnold C. Peer*(Legal Firm)*
Schenectady, NY

Chemical Bank*(Major Banking Relationship)*
450 West 33rd St.
New York, NY 10001
Tel.: 212-613-7197
Fax: 212-947-7628

Key Bank*(Major Banking Relationship)*
Albany, NY

CONTICO INTERNATIONAL, INC.
1101 N. Warson
Saint Louis, MO 63132
Tel.: 314-997-5900
Fax: 314-997-1270
Year Founded: 1964
Approx.Sls.: $100,000,000
Emp.: 2,400
Fiscal Year-end: 5/31/91
Import Export
Manufacture & Distribute Plastic & Metal Janitorial Supplies, Automobile & Truck Accessories, Storage Containers
S.I.C.: 3089; 3469; 3714
Lester Miller *(Chm. Bd.)*
Larry M. Hill *(Vice Chm.-Admin.)*
Harlan Hoffman *(Vice Chm.-Opers.)*
Bill Miller *(Pres., Chief Exec. & Chief Oper. Officer)*
David C. Cooksey *(V.P., Chief Fin. Officer & Sec.)*
Sharon Ovey *(V.P.-Human Resources)*
Richard K. Meinkoth *(Treas. & Controller)*
Principal(s):
Lester Miller
Bill Miller

No. of Mfg. Plants/Facilities: 9
No. of Foreign Offices: 2

Computer Systems/Hardware:
IBM

Outside Service Firm(s):

Arthur Andersen & Co.*(Auditors)*
1010 Market St.
St. Louis, MO 63101

Popkin & Stern*(Legal Firm)*
St. Louis, MO

Bank of New England*(Major Banking Relationship)*
28 State Street
Boston, MA 02109
Tel.: 617-742-4000

CONTINENTAL AMERICAN CORP. D/B/A PIONEER BALLOON COMPANY
555 N. Woodlawn
Wichita, KS 67208
Tel.: 316-685-2266 **KS**
Fax: 316-685-2409
Year Founded: 1974
Import Export
Manufacturer & Printer of Latex & Metallic Balloons
S.I.C.: 3069
Ted A. Vlamis *(Pres.)*
Betty Vlamis *(Exec. V.P.)*
Joe Dillard *(Treas.)*

CONTINENTAL CABLEVISION
The Pilot House, Lewis Wharf
Boston, MA 02110
Tel.: 617-742-9500 **DE**
Fax: 617-742-0530
Year Founded: 1963
Assets: $2,082,182,000
Liabilities: $4,001,707,000
Net Worth: $1,919,525,000
Approx.Sls.: $1,039,163,000
Emp.: 7,000
Fiscal Year-end: 12/31/91
Operates Multiple Cable TV Systems
S.I.C.: 4841
Amos B. Hostetter, Jr. *(Chm. Bd. & Chief Exec. Officer)*
Timothy Neher *(Vice Chm.)*
Michael J. Ritter *(Pres. & Chief Oper. Officer)*
Andrew Dixon *(Sr. V.P. -Human Resources)*
Nancy Hawthorne *(Sr. V.P. & Treas.)*
Richard Hoffstein *(Sr. V.P. & Controller)*
Frederick C. Livingston *(Sr. V.P.-Mktg.)*
W. Lee H. Dunham *(Corp. Sec.)*
Linda Maslin *(Dir.-Adv. & Natl. Promo.)*
Steve Spinelli *(Dir.-Training)*
Peggy Wilcox *(Mgr.-Benefits)*
Edward J. Handlin *(Coord.-Data Processing)*

Computer Systems/Hardware:
Wang VS, PC's

Outside Service Firm(s):

Deloitte & Touche*(Auditors)*
125 Summer St.
Boston, MA 02110
Tel.: 617-261-8000
Fax: 617-261-8111

Sullivan & Worcester*(Legal Firm)*
One Post Office Square, 100 Federal St.
Boston, MA 02110
Tel.: 617-338-2800

CONTINENTAL CIRCUITS CORP.
3502 E. Roeser
Phoenix, AZ 85040
Tel.: 602-268-3461 **AZ**
Fax: 602-268-0208
Year Founded: 1971
Assets: $42,558,000
Liabilities: $26,384,000
Net Worth: $16,174,000
Approx.Sls.: $68,300,000
Emp.: 850
Fiscal Year-end: 7/31/92
Export
Manufacture Printed Circuit Boards
S.I.C.: 3679
Steven Fisher *(Chm. Bd., Pres. & Chief Exec. Officer)*
Thomas E. Linnen *(V.P.-Fin., Treas. & Sec.)*
John Maddux *(V.P.-Quality Assurance)*
William Moore *(V.P.-Opers.)*
Lee Small *(V.P.-Mktg.)*
Donald Schasane *(Dir.-Pur.)*
Principal(s):
Steven Fisher
Michael O. Flatt

No. of Mfg. Plants/Facilities: 4
No. of U.S. Offices: 4

Computer Systems/Hardware:
Qantel

Outside Service Firm(s):

Deloitte & Touche*(Auditors)*
2901 North Central Ave., Ste. 1200
Phoenix, AZ 85012
Tel.: 602-234-5100
Fax: 602-234-5186

St. Paul Insurance Companies*(Commercial Insurance Carrier)*
Phoenix, AZ

Blue Cross & Blue Shield of Arizona, Inc.*(Group Insurer)*
Phoenix, AZ

Gaston, Snow, Moya, Bailey, Bowers & Jones*(Legal Firm)*
Phoenix, AZ

Citibank N.A.*(Major Banking Relationship)*
Phoenix, AZ

CONTINENTAL COIN CORPORATION
5627 Sepulveda Blvd.
Van Nuys, CA 91411
Tel.: 818-781-4232 **CA**
Fax: 818-782-6779
Year Founded: 1971
Approx.Sls.: $100,000,000
Emp.: 30
Wholesale Distributor of Precious Metals, Coins, Jewelry & Precious Stones; Foreign Currency Exchange
S.I.C.: 5094; 5944; 6099
Gordon O'Rourke *(Pres.)*
Rod Schilling *(V.P.-Fin. & Sec.)*
Joe Buzanowski *(Dir.-Mktg.)*

Outside Service Firm(s):

Good, Gagerman & Berns*(Auditors)*
Los Angeles, CA

Bank of America NT&SA*(Major Banking Relationship)*
Van Nuys, CA

CONTINENTAL EAGLE CORPORATION
Gin Shop Hill Rd.
Prattville, AL 36067
Mailing Address:
P.O. Box 1000,
Prattville, AL 36067
Tel.: 205-365-8811 **DE**
Telex: 682 7211
Fax: 205-361-7627
Year Founded: 1832
Approx.Sls.: $30,000,000
Emp.: 550
Fiscal Year-end: 12/31/90
Manufacture Cotton Gins & Related Products
S.I.C.: 3523; 3559
Joseph C. Fermon *(Chm. Bd. & Chief Exec. Officer)*
R. Joseph Gray *(Pres.)*
Roger Fermon *(Exec. V.P.)*
Robert D. Doss *(V.P.-Fin. & Chief Fin. Officer)*
Paul Wilson *(V.P.-Sls.)*

Lothar Zell *(V.P.-Opers.)*
John Fiddler *(Dir.-Personnel)*
Jim Stanfield *(Dir.-Data Processing)*
Joe Thomas *(Dir.-Research & Devel.)*
Archie Taylor *(Mgr.-Export)*
Tommy Brown *(Adv. Coord.)*
Joe Dan Plunk *(Sls. Admin.)*
Rick, Rhodes *(Pur. Agent)*

Outside Service Firm(s):

Price Waterhouse*(Auditors)*
Birmingham, AL

Hill & Hill*(Legal Firm)*
Montgomery, AL

Bank of Boston*(Major Banking Relationship)*
Atlanta, GA

Branches:

Continental/Murray **(1)**
703 Slaton Hwy.
Lubbock, TX 79404
Tel.: 806-745-4501
Fax: 806-745-3744
Sales & Distribution
S.I.C.: 5084
Gary Weaver *(Branch Mgr.)*

Continental/Murray **(1)**
2011 W. Side Dr.
Augusta, GA 30907
Tel.: 706-868-8639
Sales Offices
S.I.C.: 5084
Bill Kelley *(Branch Mgr.)*

Continental/Murray **(1)**
3176 Trainquilty
Memphis, TN 38186
Tel.: 901-345-3300
Fax: 901-332-0723
Sales Offices
S.I.C.: 5084
George Barna *(Branch Mgr.)*

Continental/Murray **(1)**
3912 S. Front
Fresno, CA 93725
Tel.: 209-442-4570
Fax: 209-442-0670
Sales Offices
S.I.C.: 5084
Leland Stevens *(Branch Mgr.)*

Continental/Murray **(1)**
1805 E. Jefferson
Phoenix, AZ 85036
Tel.: 602-253-2496
Fax: 602-252-7115
Sales Offices
S.I.C.: 5084

Continental/Murray **(1)**
1305 E. Oklahoma
Harlingen, TX 78550
Tel.: 210-423-3964
Fax: 210-423-2853
Sales Offices
S.I.C.: 5084
Phil Watts *(Branch Mgr.)*

Continental/Murray **(1)**
Hwy. 80 E.
Rayville, LA 71269
Tel.: 318-728-4162
Sales Offices
S.I.C.: 5084

Continental/Murray **(1)**
215 S. Main
Altus, OK 73521
Tel.: 405-477-1825
Sales Offices
S.I.C.: 5084

CONTINENTAL FORGE COMPANY
512 E. Carlin St.
Compton, CA 90222
Mailing Address:
P.O. Box 4789
Compton, CA 90224-4789
Tel.: 213-774-3220
Fax: 310-631-7223
Approx.Sls.: $12,000,000
Emp.: 220
Import Export
Aluminum Forgings
S.I.C.: 3463
Charles Haueisen *(Pres.)*
Margaret A. Haueisen *(Treas.)*
Stan Curtis *(Asst. Sec. & Treas.)*
Earl F. Kelso *(Pur. Agent)*

Outside Service Firm(s):

Sansiveri, Ryan & Sullivan*(Auditors)*
Providence, RI

Bank of America NT&SA*(Major Banking Relationship)*
555 So. Flower St.
Los Angeles, CA 90071
Tel.: 213-683-3868

CONTINENTAL GRAIN COMPANY
277 Park Ave.
New York, NY 10172
Tel.: 212-207-5100
Telex: 12-5708
Fax: 212-207-5181
Year Founded: 1813
Approx.Sls.: $15,000,000,000
Emp.: 14,500
Fiscal Year-end: 3/30/92
Poultry Production & Processing; Manufacture & Preparation of Animal Food & Feeds, Whole Grains; Soybean Oil Mills; Beef Cattle Production; Countertrade; Commodity Merchandising
S.I.C.: 0212; 0251; 0119; 2048; 2075; 6221
Michel Fribourg *(Chm. Bd.)*
Donald L. Staheli *(Pres. & Chief Exec. Officer)*
James J. Bigham *(Exec. V.P. & Chief Fin. Officer)*
Paul J. Fribourg *(Exec. V.P. & Grp. Pres.-World Grain & Oilseeds)*
Sheldon L. Berens *(Sr. V.P. & Gen. Counsel)*
Thomas H. Dean *(Sr. V.P.-Corp. Devel.)*
Edmund P. Karam *(Sr. V.P. & Grp. Pres.-General Commodities)*
Dale F. Larson *(Sr. V.P. & Grp. Pres.-World Milling Industries)*
Bernard Steinweg *(Sr. V.P.-Govt. & Trade Policy)*
Dwight Coffin *(V.P.-Human Resources)*
Daryl C. Natz *(V.P.-Public Affairs)*
Daniel J. Willett *(V.P. & Treas.)*
William Cafarella *(Dir.-Employee Benefits)*
Jacqueline Levine *(Dir.-Treasury Opers.)*

No. of Mfg. Plants/Facilities: 200
No. of U.S. Offices: 24

Computer Systems/Hardware:
IBM 4381; IBM 3083

Outside Service Firm(s):

Arthur Andersen & Co.*(Auditors)*
1345 Ave. of the Americas
New York, NY 10105
Tel.: 212-708-4000

Non-U.S. Holding:

Finagrain, Cie Commerciale Agricole et Financiere S.A. **(1)**
P.O. Box 327, 16, Avenue Eugen-Pittard 1211
Geneva, 25, Switzerland
Tel.: 022/47 93 11
Telex: 422 375
Emp.: 125
Purchase and Sales of Grain, Feed, Seeds and Vegetable Oils
S.I.C.: 5153
Poul Schroeder *(Pres.)*
Rico Stroemer *(Gen. Mgr.)*

CONTINENTAL GRAPHICS HOLDINGS, INC.
4525 Wilshire Blvd., Suite 203
Los Angeles, CA 90010
Tel.: 213-930-2281
Fax: 213-930-0178
Year Founded: 1988
Holding Company
S.I.C.: 6719
Curtis F. Bourland *(Pres. & Chief Exec. Officer)*

Outside Service Firm(s):

Arthur Andersen & Co.*(Auditors)*
633 W. Fifth St.
Los Angeles, CA 90071
Tel.: 213-614-6500

Munger, Tolles & Olson*(Legal Firm)*
355 S. Grand
Los Angeles, CA 90071
Tel.: 213-683-9100

Security Pacific National Bank*(Major Banking Relationship)*
333 S. Beaudry Ave., 24th Fl.
Los Angeles, CA 90017
Tel.: 213-345-2829

Divisions:

Arts & Crafts Press **(1)**
3590 Kettner Blvd.
San Diego, CA 92101
Tel.: 619-297-0261
Printers
S.I.C.: 2752
Ray Ehlers *(Pres.)*

Continental Graphics Corporation **(1)**
4525 Wilshire Blvd., Suite 203
Los Angeles, CA 90010
Tel.: 213-930-2281
Approx.Sls.: $158,695,000
Emp.: 2,940
Printers
S.I.C.: 2752
Curtis F. Bourland *(Pres. & Chief Exec. Officer)*
Richard J. Agosinelli *(Sr. V.P. & Chief Fin. Officer)*

Subsidiaries:

Dauman Displays, Inc. **(1)**
1970 W. 139th
Gardena, CA 90247
Tel.: 213-321-2351
Point-of-Purchase Displays
S.I.C.: 3993
Sidney Dauman *(Pres.)*

Delmar Photographic and Printing Company **(1)**
9601 Monroe Rd.
Charlotte, NC 28212
Tel.: 704-847-9801
Advertising Specialty; Printing; General Commercial Printing; Yearbooks
S.I.C.: 2732
W. T. Smith, Jr. *(Pres.)*

Delmar Studios **(1)**
9555 Monroe Rd.
Charlotte, NC 28222
Tel.: 704-845-2002
Emp.: 273
School Pictures
S.I.C.: 7335
J.E. Peters *(Pres.)*

Franklin Press **(1)**
1001 S. Arrowhead Ave.
San Bernardino, CA 92412
Tel.: 714-889-9773
Printers
S.I.C.: 7335
A. Charles Super *(Pres.)*

Graphic Arts Center **(1)**
2000 N.W. Wilson St.
Portland, OR 97209
Tel.: 503-224-7777
Commercial Printers
S.I.C.: 2752
Kraig W. Kramers *(Pres.)*

Rush Press **(1)**
8835 Complex Dr.
San Diego, CA 92123
Tel.: 619-292-6906
Printers
S.I.C.: 2752
Ray W. Ehlers *(Chm.)*

CONTINENTAL MACHINES, INC.
5505 W. 123rd St.
Savage, MN 55378
Tel.: 612-890-3300 **MN**
Fax: 612-895-6450
Year Founded: 1927
Approx.Sls.: $35,000,000
Emp.: 380
Mfr. of Bond Saws, Surface Grinders, Gaging Equipment, Hydraulic Pumps & Valves & Power Units
S.I.C.: 3541; 3494; 3545; 3561; 3621
Charles T. Peterson *(Actng. Pres.)*
Gary A. Heist *(Chief Fin. Officer & Treas.)*
Leighton A. Wilkie *(Exec. V.P.)*
James W. Parkin *(Sr. V.P.-Mfg.)*
Mike Johnson *(V.P.-Sls.)*
Tim Konkler *(V.P.-Engrng.)*
A.J. Klaasen *(Sec.)*
Thomas L. Hunt *(Gen. Mgr.-Hydraulics)*

Outside Service Firm(s):

Ernst & Young*(Auditors)*
1400 Pillsbury Center
Minneapolis, MN 55402
Tel.: 612-343-1000

Norwest Bank Minnesota, N.A.*(Major Banking Relationship)*
P.O. Box 738, 161 N. Concord Exchange
South St. Paul, MN 55075-0738
Tel.: 800-468-9716

CONTINENTAL/MIDLAND, INC.
25000 S. Western Ave.
Park Forest, IL 60466
Tel.: 708-747-1200
Fax: 708-747-9373
Approx.Sls.: $30,000,000
Emp.: 269
Fiscal Year-end: 9/30/90
Export
Specialty Cold-Headed Fasteners & Power Actuated Tools
S.I.C.: 3452; 3546
R.S. Kaminski *(Chm. & Pres.)*
John Fuerst *(Chief Oper. Officer)*
Tom Hafner *(Chief Fin. Officer)*
Bill Erickson *(Pur. Agent)*

Computer Systems/Hardware:
BAMACS

CONTINENTAL MILLS, INC.
18125 Andover Pk. W.
Tukwila, WA 98188
Tel.: 206-872-8400
Fax: 206-872-7954
Year Founded: 1928
Approx.Sls.: $62,000,000
Emp.: 200
Manufacture Prepared Flour
S.I.C.: 2045
John M. Heily *(Chm. Bd., Pres. & Chief Exec. Officer)*
Ronald Wise *(Exec. V.P.-Sls. & Mktg.)*
James M. Hershberger *(V.P.-Fin.)*
Jon Gentry *(Dir.-Engrng.-Dry Mix Plant)*
Dave Sloan *(Dir.-Engrng.-Frozen Mix Plants)*

Outside Service Firm(s):

Moss Adams*(Auditors)*
1001 4th Ave., Ste. 2900
Seattle, WA 98154-1106
Tel.: 206-223-1820

Perkins Company*(Legal Firm)*
Seattle, WA

Continental Mills, Inc.—(Continued)

Security Pacific National Bank*(Major Banking Relationship)*
Bellevue, WA

CONTINENTAL NATIONAL AMERICAN REAL ESTATE INC.
830-5 Jury Ct.,
San Jose, CA 95112
Tel.: 408-998-5599 **NV**
Fax: 408-998-5598
Year Founded: 1977
Assets: $400,000,000
Liabilities: $43,000,000
Net Worth: $357,000,000
Sales Range: $100-499 Million
Emp.: 16
Fiscal Year-end: 12/31/90
Property Investment Firm
S.I.C.: 6531; 6719
J.J. Graham *(Chm.)*
John Parker *(Pres., Chief Exec. & Oper. Officer)*
John C. Rogers *(Chief Fin. Officer)*

Outside Service Firm(s):

Edward Padella*(Auditors)*
San Jose, CA

Home Savings*(Major Banking Relationship)*
San Jose, CA

CONTINENTAL OZARK, INC.
280 N. College, Ste. 500
Fayetteville, AR 72701
Mailing Address:
P.O. Box 1503
Fayetteville, AR 72702
Tel.: 501-521-5565 **AR**
Fax: 501-442-4650
Year Founded: 1977
Approx.Sls.: $314,000,000
Emp.: 70
Petroleum Bulk Stations
S.I.C.: 5171
E.G. Bradberry *(Pres.)*
Robert W. Bradberry *(Exec. V.P.)*

Outside Service Firm(s):

First National Bank*(Major Banking Relationship)*
Fayetteville, AR

CONTINENTAL PAPER & SUPPLY CO.
6400 E. Eight Mile Rd.
Detroit, MI 48234
Tel.: 313-892-7600 **MI**
Fax: 313-892-5510
Approx.Sls.: $21,900,000
Emp.: 84
Wholesale Industrial Paper Products, Packaging Materials & Janitorial Supplies; Warehousing & Delivery Services
S.I.C.: 5113; 5087; 4214
Michael A. Pisa, Sr. *(Chm. Bd. & Chief Exec. Officer)*
Michael A. Pisa, Jr. *(Pres.)*
Carlo Daniele *(V.P.)*
Veronica Pisa *(Sec.)*
David Marshall *(Controller)*

Outside Service Firm(s):

Frontiera & Pokart*(Auditors)*
Detroit, MI

Comerica Bank*(Major Banking Relationship)*
211 W. Fort St.
Detroit, MI 48226
Tel.: 313-222-3300

CONTINENTAL PLASTIC CARD CO.
3651 N.W. 120th Ave.
Coral Springs, FL 33065
Tel.: 305-753-0670
Tel.: 800-543-0670
Fax: 305-341-3479
Year Founded: 1974
Sales Range: $10-19 Million
Emp.: 118
Mfr. of Plastic Cards/Security ID
S.I.C.: 2671
Gordon M. Kramer *(Chm. Bd., Pres. & Chief Exec. Officer)*
Robert Thomson *(Controller)*
Paul Drozdowski *(Gen. Mgr.)*
Desso, Herara *(Dir.-Environmental & Natural Resources)*
Ivan Milo *(Dir.-Data Processing)*
Debbie Divinney *(Supvr.-Graphics)*
Jordan Manolakis *(Supvr.-Production)*
Amy Heimlich *(Mktg. Asst.)*
Sam Marks *(Mktg. Consultant)*
Principal(s):
Gordon M. Kramer

Outside Service Firm(s):

M.A. Cabrera & Co.*(Auditors)*
Ft. Lauderdale, FL

Shutts & Bowen*(Legal Firm)*
201 S. Biscayne Blvd., 1500 Miami Center
Miami, FL 33131

Citibank, N.A.*(Major Banking Relationship)*
Miami, FL

CONTINENTAL WATER COMPANY
535 N. New Ballas Rd.
Saint Louis, MO 63141
Tel.: 314-997-1662 **MO**
Fax: 314-997-2451
Year Founded: 1973
Approx.Sls.: $100,000,000
Emp.: 1,000
Holding Company; Water Utilities
S.I.C.: 6719; 4941
Robert A. Dolson *(Pres. & Chief Exec. Officer)*
C.A. Buescher *(Exec. V.P.)*
Phillip H. Peters *(Treas. & Comptroller)*
R.T. Ciottone *(Sec.)*

Outside Service Firm(s):

Coopers & Lybrand*(Auditors)*
One Metropolitan Square
St. Louis, MO 63102
Tel.: 314-436-3200

Bryan, Cave, McPheeters & McRoberts*(Legal Firm)*
One Metropolitan Sq.
St. Louis, MO 63102
Tel.: 314-259-2000

Boatmen's Trust Company*(Major Banking Relationship)*
100 North Broadway
St. Louis, MO 63102
Tel.: 314-466-2469

CONTINENTAL WEB PRESS, INC.
1430 Industrial Dr.
Itasca, IL 60143
Tel.: 708-773-1903 **IL**
Fax: 708-773-1909
Year Founded: 1973
Assets: $48,000,000
Liabilities: $36,000,000
Net Worth: $12,000,000
Approx.Sls.: $70,000,000
Emp.: 900
Fiscal Year-end: 12/31/90
Commercial Offset Printer
S.I.C.: 2752; 7331
Kenneth W. Field *(Pres. & Chief Exec. Officer)*
Diane Field *(V.P. & Treas.)*
John DeBerge *(Chief Fin. Officer)*
Dennis Allen *(Dir.-Sls.)*
Alan Bose *(Dir.-Data Processing)*
Michael Kraun *(Dir.-Human Resources)*
Donald Wiencek *(Dir.-Mfg. & Pur.)*
Pat LaPato *(Corp. Travel Planner)*

No. of Mfg. Plants/Facilities: 1
No. of U.S. Offices: 3

Computer Systems/Hardware:
Hewlet Packard

Outside Service Firm(s):

Deloitte & Touche*(Auditors)*
Two Prudential Plaza, 180 N. Stetson
Chicago, IL 60601
Tel.: 312-946-2039

Merrill Lynch*(Investment Banker)*
Hilton Head, SC

Rosenthal & Scanfield*(Legal Firm)*
Chicago, IL

LaSalle National Bank*(Major Banking Relationship)*
120 S. LaSalle St.
Chicago, IL 60603
Tel.: 312-781-8000

CONTRACT FREIGHTERS, INC.
2900 Davis Blvd.
Joplin, MO 64804
Tel.: 417-623-5229 **MO**
Fax: 417-623-8974
Approx.Sls.: $100,000,000
Emp.: 1,400
Trucking, Except Local
S.I.C.: 4212
Glenn Brown *(Pres.)*
Angelo Ianello *(V.P.-Fin. & Treas.)*

Outside Service Firm(s):

Mercantile Bank*(Major Banking Relationship)*
Joplin, MO

CONTRACT FURNISHINGS & SYSTEMS, LTD.
20 W. 22nd St.
New York, NY 10010-5804
Mailing Address:
P.O. Box 2049,
New York, NY 10010-5048
Tel.: 212-727-3800 **DE**
Fax: 212-727-1775
Year Founded: 1977
Assets: $9,600,000
Liabilities: $6,500,000
Net Worth: $3,100,000
Approx.Sls.: $30,000,000
Emp.: 85
Fiscal Year-end: 12/31/88
Office Furniture Dealership & Representation
S.I.C.: 5021
Charles L. Berman *(Exec. V.P.)*
William O'Reilly *(Controller)*
Peg Warren *(Dir.-Personnel)*
Daniel Weiner *(Dir.-Data Processing)*
Brian L. Carlo *(Dir.-Admin.)*

No. of U.S. Offices: 2

Computer Systems/Hardware:
DEC VAX 8250

Outside Service Firm(s):

Richard A. Bisner & Company*(Auditors)*
New York, NY

Aetna Life & Casualty*(Commercial Insurance Carrier)*
425 Fifth Ave.
New York, NY 10018
Tel.: 212-512-0777

United States Life Insurance Co.*(Group Insurer)*
New York, NY

Robinson, Brog & Leinwand*(Legal Firm)*
1345 Ave. of the Americas
New York, NY 10105
Tel.: 212-586-4050

National Westminster Bank plc*(Major Banking Relationship)*
Astor Plaza, 1515 Broadway
New York, NY 10036

Intac Actuarial Services, Inc.*(Pension Manager)*
Ramsey, NJ

CONTRACT INTERIORS INC.
10 Oak Hollow, Suite 200
Southfield, MI 48034
Tel.: 313-358-2000 **MI**
Fax: 313-358-4847
Year Founded: 1975
Assets: $11,809,582
Liabilities: $10,141,066
Net Worth: $1,668,516
Approx.Sls.: $58,200,000
Emp.: 200
Fiscal Year-end: 12/31/91
Wholesale Office Furniture; Interior Design Services
S.I.C.: 5021; 7389
Robert Spradlin *(Pres. & Chief Exec. Officer)*
Garland O. Snyder *(Sr. V.P.-Design/ Sls.)*
Tom Warniack *(Sr. V.P. & Chief Fin. Officer)*
Mary J. Jevahirian *(Controller)*
Barbara Frazier *(Mgr.-Whsle. Admin.)*
Joseph P. Lozowski *(Dir.-Bus. Devel.)*
Julie McKee *(Dir.-Employee Ben.)*
Donna Metzger *(Dir.-Mktg.)*
Pamela Smith *(Dir.-Major Accts.)*
Lorie Wyant *(Dir.- Training& Quality)*
Val Meinzinger *(Corp. Lib.)*
Karen Helber *(Exec. Asst.)*

Outside Service Firm(s):

Arthur Andersen & Co.*(Auditors)*
400 Renaissance Center
Detroit, MI 48243
Tel.: 313-259-8100

National Bank of Detroit*(Major Banking Relationship)*
611 Woodward Ave.
Detroit, MI 48226

CONTRACTORS STEEL COMPANY
36555 Amrhein Rd.
Livonia, MI 48150
Tel.: 313-464-4000 **MI**
Fax: 313-464-0098
Year Founded: 1960
Approx.Sls.: $60,000,000
Emp.: 165
Import
Steel Service Center
S.I.C.: 5051
Donald R. Simon *(Chm. Bd., Pres. & Treas.)*
Esther Simon *(Sec.)*
Eli E. Robinson *(Controller)*
Glen Dusek *(Dir.-Mktg. & Adv.)*
Robert Simon *(Dir.-Data Processing)*
Cynthia Wagner *(Dir.-Pur.)*
Marcus J. Bokas, Sr. *(Gen. Mgr.)*

No. of Mfg. Plants/Facilities: 3

Computer Systems/Hardware:
Digital

Outside Service Firm(s):

Katz, Victor & Yolles*(Legal Firm)*
Detroit, MI

First of America Bank*(Major Banking Relationship)*
Detroit, MI

CONTRACTORS SUPPLIES, INC.
303 Webber
Lufkin, TX 75901
Tel.: 409-634-3341 **TX**
Fax: 409-634-7869
Approx.Sls.: $12,000,000
Emp.: 125
Lufkin Redi-Mix Concrete; Concrete Or Cinder Blocks
S.I.C.: 3273; 3271
Thomas H. Moore *(Chm. Bd.)*
Henry Holubec *(Pres.)*
Sam Pirtie *(V.P.)*
Bert McKinney *(Sec. & Treas.)*

Outside Service Firm(s):

Axley & Rode*(Auditors)*
Lufkin, TX

First Bank, N.A.*(Major Banking Relationship)*
Lufkin, TX

John Sloan*(Legal Firm)*
Lufkin, TX

CONTRACTORS SUPPLY COMPANY, INC.
800 E. 18th St.
Kansas City, MO 64108
Tel.: 816-221-7788 **MO**
Fax: 816-221-0817
Approx.Sls.: $29,000,000
Emp.: 113
Wholesale Distributor of General Construction Machinery & Equipment
S.I.C.: 5082
Richard J. Knopke *(Pres.)*
Don P. Knopke *(V.P. & Sec.)*
David Knopke *(V.P.)*
Robert E. McGurn *(Treas.)*

Outside Service Firm(s):

Commerce Bank of Kansas City*(Major Banking Relationship)*
10th & Walnut
Kansas City, MO 64141
Tel.: 816-234-2000
Fax: 816-234-2548

CONTRAN CORPORATION
3 Lincoln Ctr., 5430 LBJ Freeway, Ste. 1700
Dallas, TX 75240
Tel.: 214-233-1700
Fax: 214-385-0586
Year Founded: 1968
Assets: $3,517,394,000
Earnings: $55,674,000
Liabilities: $3,240,711,000
Net Worth: $276,683,000
Approx.Sls.: $2,129,675,000
Emp.: 18,000
Fiscal Year-end: 12/31/90
Holding Company; Chemicals, Petroleum Services, Refined Sugar, Forest Products, Fast Foods, Titanium Metals, Hardware Products, Steel Rod, Wire & Wire Products
S.I.C.: 6719; 4731; 3312; 2911
Harold C. Simmons *(Chm. Bd., Pres. & Chief Exec. Officer)*
Michael A. Snetzer *(Pres.)*
William C. Timm *(Chief Fin. Officer & V.P.-Fin.)*
E.K. Anderson *(V.P.-Cash Mngmt.)*
J. Thomas-Montgomery *(V.P. & Controller)*
Steven L. Watson *(V.P. & Sec.)*
Mark Hollingsworth *(Gen. Counsel)*
Keith Johnson *(Mgr.-Employee Benefits)*
Jim Kruse *(Mgr.-Real Estate)*

Computer Systems/Hardware:
IBM PC

Outside Service Firm(s):

Deloitte & Touche*(Auditors)*
1400 Lincoln Plaza, LB-4
Dallas, TX 75201-3302
Tel.: 214-220-8000

American Heritage Life Insurance Co.*(Group Insurer)*
Jacksonville, FL

Kirkland & Ellis*(Legal Firm)*
200 E. Randolph Dr.
Chicago, IL 60601
Tel.: 312-861-2000
Fax: 312-861-2200

MBank Dallas*(Major Banking Relationship)*
1900 Pacific
Dallas, TX 75265

CONTROL SYSTEMS INC.
2675 Patton Rd.
Saint Paul, MN 55113
Mailing Address:
P.O. Box 64750
St. Paul, MN 55164
Tel.: 612-631-7800
Tel.: 800-627-8478 **MN**
Fax: 612-631-8424
Year Founded: 1976
Approx.Sls.: $21,000,000
Emp.: 100

Export
Mfr. Graphic Accellerator Boards & Semiconductors
S.I.C.: 3579
Robert B. Beale *(Pres.)*
Rebecca Beale *(V.P.)*
Robert Brandenburg *(Gen. Mgr.)*
Horace Beale *(V.P. & Sec.)*
Thomas Carretta *(Gen. Counsel)*
Jim Triggs *(Dir.-Mktg. & Mdse.)*
Greg Powell *(Dir.-Sls.)*
Brian Benda *(Dir.-Mfg.)*
Joan Brown *(Dir.-Human Resources & Employee Benefits)*
Peggy Noto *(Dir.-Pub. Rels.)*

Principal(s):
Robert B. Beale

No. of U.S. Offices: 1
No. of Foreign Offices: 5

Subsidiary:

Artist Graphics **(1)**
2675 Patton Rd.
Saint Paul, MN 55113
Tel.: 612-631-7800
Computer Technology
S.I.C.: 3579
Robert B. Beale *(Pres.)*

CONTROLLED SYSTEMS OF WISCONSIN, INC.
W32882 Watertown Plank Rd.
Nashotah, WI 53058
Mailing Address:
P.O. Box 240
Nashotah, WI 53058
Tel.: 414-367-4400
Fax: 414-367-4495
Year Founded: 1974
Emp.: 10
Heating, Air Conditioning & Ventilating Contractors
S.I.C.: 1711
Jeffrey E. Spence *(Chm. Bd., Pres., Controller & Chief Exec. & Fin. Officer)*
Ann Spence *(Treas.)*

Computer Systems/Hardware:
IBM

Outside Service Firm(s):

Donald Carlson*(Auditors)*
Nashotah, WI

Valley Bank*(Major Banking Relationship)*
Hartland, WI

CONVENIENT FOOD MART, INC.
929 N. Plum Grove Rd.
Schaumburg, IL 60173
Tel.: 708-995-1100
Year Founded: 1958
Approx.Sls.: $800,000,000
Emp.: 30
Fiscal Year-end: 12/31/90
Franchisor of Convenience Stores
S.I.C.: 5411
Richard Harper *(Pres.)*
Neil Wykes *(Chief Fin. Officer)*
Martin Venturini *(Sr. V.P.-Mktg.)*
John Manske *(V.P.-Corp. Devel.)*
Kathryn Friedman *(Gen. Counsel)*
David Stasiewicz *(Controller)*
Mike Kotel *(Opers.)*

CONVERSE PROFESSIONAL GROUP, INC.
3393 E. Foothill Blvd.
Pasadena, CA 91107
Tel.: 818-351-4741 **CA**
Year Founded: 1946
Approx.Sls.: $26,000,000
Emp.: 285
Engineering Services
S.I.C.: 8711
Al Liskys *(Chm. Bd.)*
Richard D. Gilbert *(Pres.)*
Joseph M. Desalvo *(V.P. & Asst. Sec.)*
Robert M. Pride *(V.P. & Treas.)*
Patricia M. Entrekin *(Mgr.-Personnel)*

Outside Service Firm(s):

McGladrey & Pullen*(Auditors)*
Pasadena, CA

CONWAY CORPORATION
1319 Prairie
Conway, AR 72032
Mailing Address:
P.O. Box 99
Conway, AR 72032
Tel.: 501-450-6000 **AR**
Year Founded: 1928
Assets: $116,138,236
Liabilities: $44,149,996
Net Worth: $71,988,240
Approx.Sls.: $27,066,262
Emp.: 109
Fiscal Year-end: 12/31/91
Electric Services; Water Supply; Cable & other Pay Television Services
S.I.C.: 4911; 4841
Frank Robins, III *(Chm. Bd.)*
William Hegeman *(Gen. Mgr.)*
Leo Crafton, III *(Sec.)*

Outside Service Firm(s):

Ernst & Young*(Auditors)*
Conway, AR

First National Bank Conway*(Major Banking Relationship)*
Conway, AR

Worthen National Bank & Trust, N.A.*(Major Banking Relationship)*
Conway, AR

CONWAY IMPORT CO. INC.
5 Warehouse Lane
Elmsford, NY 10523
Tel.: 914-592-1310 **NY**
Fax: 914-592-1104
Year Founded: 1910
Approx.Sls.: $15,000,000
Emp.: 12
Mfr. of Condiments; French Dressing, Mayonnaise, Processed Oil
S.I.C.: 2035
Nicholas A. Heineman *(Pres. & Chief Exec. Officer)*
Norman Domash *(Sr. V.P.)*
Gregg J. Heineman *(V.P.-Opers., Sec. & Treas.)*
Brett D. Heineman *(Sec. & Mgr.-East Reg. Sls.)*
Ethel Coletti *(Mgr.-Quality Control)*

Principal(s):
Nicholas A. Heineman
Norman Domash
Gregg J. Heineman
Brett D. Heineman
Scott Heineman
Theresa Heineman

No. of Mfg. Plants/Facilities: 1
No. of U.S. Offices: 3

Computer Systems/Hardware:
Burroughs

Outside Service Firm(s):

Paul J. Letwin*(Auditors)*
Buffalo Grove, IL
Tel.: 312-634-1776

Israeloff Trather & Co*(Auditors)*
New York, NY

Aetna Life & Casualty*(Group Insurer)*
620 Erie Blvd. W.
Syracuse, NY 13221
Tel.: 800-331-2595
Fax: 315-474-0781

Rosenman & Colin*(Legal Firm)*
575 Madison Ave.
New York, NY 10022
Tel.: 212-940-8800

Chemical Bank*(Major Banking Relationship)*
450 West 33rd St.
New York, NY 10001
Tel.: 212-613-7197
Fax: 212-947-7628

Divisions:

Conway Import Co. Inc. **(1)**
11051 W. Addison St.
Franklin Park, IL 60131
Tel.: 708-455-5600
Mfr. of Salad Dressings
S.I.C.: 2035
Scott Heinemann *(Pres.)*
Robert D. Burns *(V.P.-Sls. & Mktg.)*
Alvaro Romero *(V.P.-Mfg.)*

Conway Import Co. Inc. **(1)**
2242 Quimby Rd.
San Jose, CA 95122
Tel.: 408-238-1463
Distribution Center for Salad Dressings
S.I.C.: 5149
Bob Patrician *(Mgr.)*

CONWOOD COMPANY L.P.
813 Ridge Lake Blvd.
Memphis, TN 38120
Mailing Address:
P.O. Box 217
Memphis, TN 38101
Tel.: 901-761-2050 **DE**
Fax: 901-767-1302
Year Founded: 1985
Sales Range: $100-499 Million
Emp.: 1,014
Manufactures Chewing Tobacco & Snuff
S.I.C.: 2131
W.M. Rosson *(Chm. Bd.)*
J.S. Wilson, Jr. *(Pres. & Chief Exec. Officer)*
T.F. McCormack *(V.P.-Sls.)*
J.W. Cothren *(V.P.-Mktg.)*
D.L. Simpson III *(Sec. & Gen. Counsel)*
Don Odom *(Controller)*
J.G. Metz *(Dir.-Personnel)*
Ian Robinson *(Dir.-Pur.)*
W.A. Moore *(Mgr.-Data Processing)*
Anna Parker *(Mgr.-Cash)*
David Cash *(Mgr.-Export)*
T.H. Combs *(Prod. Mgr.-Tobacco Prods.)*
K.R. Schultz *(Prod. Mgr.-Tobacco Prods.)*

Computer Systems/Hardware:
IBM 4341

Conwood Company L.P.—(Continued)

Outside Service Firm(s):

KPMG Peat Marwick*(Auditors)*
Memphis, TN
Tel.: 901-725-3131

Equitable Real Estate Investment Managment Inc.*(Group Insurer)*
3414 Peachtree Rd. N.E.
Atlanta, GA 30326-1162

First Tennessee Bank, N.A.*(Major Banking Relationship)*
Memphis, TN

Wachovia Bank & Trust Co.*(Major Banking Relationship)*
P.O. Box 3001,
Winston-Salem, NC 27102
Tel.: 800-633-4236

Divisions:

Scott Tobacco **(1)**
939 Adams, P.O. Box 658
Bowling Green, KY 42101
Tel.: 502-842-5727
Emp.: 85
Manufacture & Process Twist Chewing Tobacco
S.I.C.: 2131
D.A. Howell *(Chief Oper. Officer)*

Taylor Bros. **(1)**
2415 Stratford Rd., S.W.
Winston-Salem, NC 27103-0597
Tel.: 919-768-4630
Manufacture & Process Loose-Leaf Chewing Tobacco
S.I.C.: 2131
M.A. Smith, Jr. *(Chief Oper. Officer)*

COOK HOLDING CORPORATION
P.O. Box 1597
Haines City, FL 33845
Tel.: 813-422-1121
Fax: 813-422-6907
Holding Company
S.I.C.: 6719; 0174; 0723; 0762; 6519
Bud Cook *(Chm. Bd. & Pres.)*

Outside Service Firm(s):

Annis, Mitchell, Cookey, Edwards & Roehn*(Legal Firm)*
Haines City, FL

NCNB National Bank*(Major Banking Relationship)*
Haines City, FL

Subsidiary:

B.C. Cook & Sons Enterprises, Inc. **(1)**
413 N. 12th St.
Haines City, FL 33844
Tel.: 813-422-1121
Fax: 813-422-6907
Approx.Sls.: $37,000,000
Emp.: 175
Citrus Marketing & Processing; Grove Leasing & Caretaking
S.I.C.: 0174; 0723; 0762; 6519
Burren Cook, Sr. *(Chm. Bd. & Pres.)*
Ron Haag, Jr. *(Exec. V.P.)*
R.H. Cook, Sr. *(Treas. & Sec.)*
Mary S. Williams *(Comptroller)*
Dewayne Cliett *(Mgr.-Sls.)*

COOK MANUFACTURING CORPORATION
3920 S. 13th St.
Duncan, OK 73533
Mailing Address:
P.O. Box 1737
Duncan, OK 73534
Tel.: 405-252-1699 **OK**
Fax: 405-252-2970
Year Founded: 1956
Sales Range: $10-19 Million
Emp.: 20
Fiscal Year-end: 12/31/90
Export
Computer System for Numerical Control Machines; Tape Twin Numerical Control Computer System for CNC Machines; CMC Powerlift Jackplates & Power Tilts for Outboard Motor Boats
S.I.C.: 3714; 3823; 3499
Greg Cook *(Pres. & Chief Oper. Officer)*
Rick Presley *(V.P.-Sls.)*
Debbie Cook *(Sec. & Treas.)*
Principal(s):
Greg Cook

No. of Mfg. Plants/Facilities: 1
No. of U.S. Offices: 1

Computer Systems/Hardware:
CMC Tape Twin System, CMC Jack Plates & Power Tilts for Outboard Motor Boats

Outside Service Firm(s):

Kornfeld & Franklin*(Auditors)*
Oklahoma City, OK

Liberty Mutual*(Commercial Insurance Carrier)*
Boston, MA

Equitable Plan Services*(Group Insurer)*
Oklahoma City, OK

North American Life*(Group Insurer)*
Minneapolis, MN

First Bank, N.A.*(Investment Banker)*
Duncan, OK

Liberty National Bank & Trust Co.*(Pension Manager)*
P.O. Box 25848,
Oklahoma City, OK 73125-0848
Tel.: 800-395-2662

COOK MOVING SYSTEMS, INC.
1845 Dale Rd.
Buffalo, NY 14225
Tel.: 716-897-0700 **NY**
Fax: 716-893-0500
Year Founded: 1912
Approx.Sls.: $15,000,000
Emp.: 200
Moving & Storage of Household Goods, Machine Electronics, Art & Special Products
S.I.C.: 4213; 4214
Joseph H. Conley, Jr. *(Pres. & Chief Exec. Officer)*
Gregory Fierle *(V.P.)*
Robert J. Glenn *(V.P.)*
Debra R. Fierle *(Sec.)*
William H. Launder *(Comptroller)*
Sid Binks *(Dir.-Adv.)*

No. of Mfg. Plants/Facilities: 6
No. of U.S. Offices: 6

Outside Service Firm(s):

Deloitte & Touche*(Auditors)*
50 Fountain Plaza
Buffalo, NY 14202
Tel.: 716-843-7200

Manufacturers & Traders Trust Company*(Major Banking Relationship)*
1 M & T Plaza
Buffalo, NY 14240
Tel.: 716-842-4200

Subsidiaries:

Sarasota Moving Systems Inc. **(1)**
4505 30th St., W.
Bradenton, FL 34207
Tel.: 813-755-2631

Tampa Bay Moving Systems Inc. **(1)**
5105 W. Clifton Ave
Tampa, FL 33634
Tel.: 813-885-6771

DAVID C. COOK PUBLISHING CO.
850 N. Grove Ave.
Elgin, IL 60120
Tel.: 708-741-2400
Tel.: 800-533-2201 **IL**
Fax: 708-741-2444
Year Founded: 1875
Approx.Sls.: $30,000,000
Emp.: 850
Fiscal Year-end: 5/31/90
Export
Publishers of Christian Educational Materials; Children's Books, Christian Inspirational Books, Videos & Films, Christian Greeting Cards
S.I.C.: 2731; 2771
David L. Mehlis *(Chm. Bd., Pres. & Chief Exec. Officer)*
David Hachtel *(V.P.-Fin.)*
Dick Robinson *(Dir.-Personnel)*
Therese Cox *(Asst. to Pres.)*

No. of Mfg. Plants/Facilities: 2
No. of U.S. Offices: 6
No. of Foreign Offices: 2

Computer Systems/Hardware:
IBM 4381

Outside Service Firm(s):

Randolph Shaw & Co.*(Auditors)*
Elgin, IL

Continental Bank N. A.*(Major Banking Relationship)*
231 S. LaSalle St.
Chicago, IL 60697
Tel.: 312-828-2345
Tel.: 800-426-5754
Telex: 312-828-1783

Subsidiary:

Outreach Publications **(1)**
P.O. Box 1010
Siloam Springs, AR 72761
Tel.: 501-524-9301
Emp.: 350
Greeting Cards
S.I.C.: 2771
Dean Kerns *(Pres. & Chief Exec. Officer)*

THE WILLIAM COOK AGENCY, INC.
225 Water St., Ste. 1600
Jacksonville, FL 32202
Tel.: 904-353-3911
Twx: 810-827-0575
Fax: 904-353-8165
Year Founded: 1965
Approx.Billings: $70,170,000
Emp.: 97
Advertising Agency
S.I.C.: 7311
Corporate Giving Program: Limited to Selected Local Charitable Organizations
Bernard C. Schramm, Jr. *(Chm. Bd.)*
J. Carson Eddings *(Pres. & Chief Exec. Officer)*
Lura Benton *(Sr. V.P.)*
David Curling *(Sr. V.P.)*
Brice McIntosh *(Sr. V.P., Dir. Mktg. Services)*
Michael Russell *(Sr. V.P.)*
Roger Schillig *(V.P.)*
Stephen D. Golden *(V.P., Controller)*
Glyn Denton *(V.P.)*
Marty Lynch *(V.P.)*
Dick Matthews *(V.P.)*
Patricia McCauley *(V.P.)*
Kate Ramono-Norton *(V.P.)*
Tony Testino *(Telecommunications)*

No. of U.S. Offices: 4

Outside Service Firm(s):

First Union National Bank*(Major Banking Relationship)*
Jacksonville, FL

Branches:

The William Cook Agency, Inc. **(1)**
1110 Brickell Ave., Ste. 430
Miami, FL 33131
Tel.: 305-379-8207

The William Cook Agency, Inc. **(1)**
Two First Union Center, 301 S. Tryon St., Ste. 310
Charlotte, NC 28202
Tel.: 704-377-7083
Ned Flemming *(Sr. V.P., Gen. Mgr.)*

William Cook Public Relations, Inc. **(1)**
225 Water St., Ste. 1600
Jacksonville, FL 32202
Tel.: 904-353-3911
Fax: 904-353-2847
J. Carson Eddings *(Pres., Chief Exec. Officer)*
Leo J. Bottary *(V.P.)*

JACK KENT COOKE, INC.
Kent Farms, P.O. Box 2110
Middleburg, VA 22117
Tel.: 703-687-4000
Fax: 703-687-5615
Emp.: 3,000
Commercial & Industrial Building Operations; Cable TV Services, Horse Farm, Newspapers, Publishing & Printing; Washington Redskins
S.I.C.: 2711; 0272; 1799; 7941
Jack Kent Cooke *(Pres.)*
John Kent Cooke *(V.P.)*
Wanda G. Wiser *(V.P.-Fin.)*

Outside Service Firm(s):

Middleburg National Bank*(Major Banking Relationship)*
Middleburg, VA

Subsidiary:

Cooke Media Group, Inc. **(1)**
P.O. Box 4200
Woodland Hills, CA 91365
Tel.: 818-713-3000
Fax: 818-713-3825
Approx.Sls.: $62,000,000
Emp.: 1,125
Newspaper Publishing: The Daily News
S.I.C.: 2711
Jack Kent Cooke *(Pres.)*
David Auger *(Publisher)*
Robert Berdick *(Editor)*

COOLEY, INC.
50 Esten Ave.
Pawtucket, RI 02862
Tel.: 401-724-9000
Fax: 401-726-8799
Emp.: 130
Coated Fabrics for Building Materials
S.I.C.: 2295; 2394
P. Robert Siener, Jr. *(Chm. Bd.)*
John P. Cunnigham *(Pres.)*
Peter H. Scott *(V.P.-Tech.)*
Chris Semonelli *(V.P.-Sls.)*

Outside Service Firm(s):

Sansiveri, Ryan & Sullivan*(Auditors)*
Providence, RI

Hinkley, Allen, Snyder & Comen*(Legal Firm)*
1500 Fleet Ctr.
Providence, RI 02903
Tel.: 401-274-2000

Fleet National Bank*(Major Banking Relationship)*
Corporate Trust Department, 125 Dupont Dr.
Providence, RI 02907
Tel.: 401-278-5400

THE COON-DE VISSER CO.
1500 N. Stephenson Hwy.
Royal Oak, MI 48068
Tel.: 313-399-6000
Approx.Sls.: $22,900,000
Emp.: 81

Distribute Industrial Pipes, Valves, Fittings, Air Compressors & Pumps
S.I.C.: 5084; 5085
Joseph S. Schiciano *(Pres.)*
R.J. Hall *(Exec. V.P.)*

Outside Service Firm(s):

Deloitte & Touche*(Auditors)*
200 Renaissance Center, 16th Fl.
Detroit, MI 48243
Tel.: 313-396-3000
Fax: 313-259-8087

N.B.D. Bank, N.A.*(Major Banking Relationship)*
611 Woodward Ave.
Detroit, MI 48226
Tel.: 313-225-1122
Fax: 313-225-3420

COOPER COMMUNITIES, INC.
1801 Forest Hills. Blvd.
Bella Vista, AR 72714
Tel.: 501-855-6151
Tel.: 800-648-6401 **DE**
Fax: 501-855-6256
Year Founded: 1954
Assets: $203,028,000
Liabilities: $76,622,000
Net Worth: $126,406,000
Approx.Sls.: $87,246,000
Emp.: 500
Fiscal Year-end: 12/31/91
Real Estate Developer; Residential Building Contractor; Construction Management; Engineering
S.I.C.: 6552; 1521; 8711; 8741; 6411
John A. Cooper, Jr. *(Chm. Bd.)*
Roger N. McMennamy *(Pres. & Chief Exec. Officer)*
Richard H. Smith *(Sr. V.P. & Gen. Counsel)*
Jay Neff Basore, Jr. *(Sr. V.P.-Human Resources)*
Barry W. Ellis *(Sr. V.P.-Devel.)*
Gary L. Newman *(Exec. V.P.)*
Jasper T. Neal *(V.P. & Treas.)*
Michael C. Dial *(Sr. V.P.-Fin.)*
Kevin T. McKiever *(V.P.-Mktg.)*
Larry B. Cooper *(Pres., Bella Vista Village)*
L. Randy Brucker *(Pres., Hot Springs Village)*
Daniel W. Cooper *(Pres., Tellico Village)*
Dewitt Smith *(Pres., Savannah Lakes)*

No. of U.S. Offices: 5

Outside Service Firm(s):

Coopers & Lybrand*(Auditors)*
1999 Bryan St., Ste. 3000
Dallas, TX 75201
Tel.: 214-754-5000

Subsidiaries:

Cooper Ventures, Inc. **(1)**
1801 Forest Hills Blvd.
Bella Vista, AR 72714 (75%)
Real Estate Leasing
S.I.C.: 6552
Roger N. McMennamy *(Chm. Bd., Pres. & Chief Exec. Officer)*

Ecco Services, Inc. **(1)**
1801 Forest Hills Blvd.
Bella Vista, AR 72714
Tel.: 501-855-6151 (75%)
Waste Treatment
S.I.C.: 1629
Roger N. McMennamy *(Chm. Bd.)*
Gary Carnahan *(Pres.)*

COOPER INSTRUMENT CORP.
Reeds Gap Rd.
Middlefield, CT 06455
Tel.: 203-349-3473
Tel.: 800-835-5011
Fax: 203-347-5135
Year Founded: 1885
Approx.Sls.: $10,000,000
Emp.: 80
Fiscal Year-end: 12/31/91
Import Export
Mfg. Household & Industrial Thermometers, Weather Instruments, Electronic Temperature Instruments
S.I.C.: 3829; 3823
Floyd Wallace *(Chief Exec. Officer)*
Dorothy Rusica *(Sec.)*
Wallace Perry *(Controller)*
Art Aloise *(Mgr.-Res. & Devel.)*
Paul Olore *(Mgr.-Mfg.)*
Gary Supeau *(Mgr.-Pur.)*
Carol DuPlessis *(Mgr.-Personnel)*
Frank Seaforth *(Mgr.-Data Processing)*
David Sebastianelli *(Mgr.-Natl. Sls.)*
Deborah Fitzgerald *(Mktg. & Sls. Specialist)*

COOPER LEDER MARCOMM
3000 Marcus Ave.
Lake Success, NY 11042
Tel.: 516-488-4800
Fax: 516-488-4828
Year Founded: 1971
Approx.Billings: $12,000,000
Emp.: 18
Indus., High-Tech, Business-to-Business, Healthcare, Real Estate, Travel & Resorts
Ronald E. Leder *(Principal)*
Marvin Lebowitz *(Principal)*
Bob Lipp *(Principal)*

Computer Systems/Hardware:
Adman/IBM, Apple Desktop

COOPERHEAT, INC.
1021 Centennial Ave.
Piscataway, NJ 08854
Tel.: 908-981-0800
Tel.: 800-526-4233
Fax: 908-981-0850
Year Founded: 1958
Sales Range: $40-59 Million
Emp.: 500
Metal Heat Treating; Heating Units & Devices; Fuel-fired Furnaces & Ovens
S.I.C.: 3398; 3567
Geoff Bond *(Pres. & Chief Oper. Officer)*
Emmett J. Lescroart *(Chief Exec. Officer)*
Nicholas Davy *(Chief Fin. Officer)*
Joseph S. Sink, Jr. *(Controller)*
Leah Tarlow *(Mgr.-Mktg.)*
Jim Obendorfer *(Pur. Agent)*

No. of U.S. Offices: 20
No. of Foreign Offices: 5

Outside Service Firm(s):

W.M. Ross & Company*(Commercial Insurance Carrier)*
42 Upper Montclair Plaza
Upper Montclair, NJ

Lum, Hoens, Abeles, Conant & Danzis*(Legal Firm)*
Newark, NJ

National Westminster Bank*(Major Banking Relationship)*
1125 Route 22 West
Bridgewater, NJ

Divisions:

Sandtex **(1)**
32980 Alvarado-Niles Rd., Ste. 820
Union City, CA 94587
Tel.: 800-962-1414

Thermojet **(1)**
125 Pillow St.
Butler, PA 16003
Tel.: 412-285-4706
Tel.: 800-253-1992

Thermojet **(1)**
1950 N. Griffith Blvd., Ste. A
Griffith, IN 46319
Tel.: 800-253-1993

COOPERS & LYBRAND
1301 Ave. of the Americas
New York, NY 10019
Tel.: 212-259-2431
Year Founded: 1898
Approx.Sls.: $5,000,000,000
Emp.: 67,000
Fiscal Year-end: 9/30/91
Certified Public Accountants & Consultants
S.I.C.: 8721
Employee Matching Gifts Program: The Coopers & Lybrand Foundation Matches Gifts of Individuals Associated With Coopers & Lybrand (United States), Whether or not Resident in the United States
Eugene M. Freedman *(Chm. Bd. & Chief Exec. Officer)*
Anthony J. Conti *(Vice Chm.-Human Resources)*
Harris J. Amhowitz *(Deputy Chm.)*
Steven W. McKessy *(Deputy Chm.)*
William K. O'Brien *(Deputy Chm.)*
Vincent M. O'Reilly *(Deputy Chm.)*
John J. Roberts *(Deputy Chm.)*
Frank Scalia *(Chief Fin. Officer)*
Philip Copans *(Natl. Controller)*
Hugo J. Bartell *(Dir.-Personnel Training & Devel.)*
Sal Luiso *(Dir.-Natl. Mktg.)*
David L. Nestor *(Dir.-Natl Pub. Rels.)*
Ronald H. Schirripa *(Dir.-Mngmt. Information System)*
Allen J. Weltmann *(Dir.-Govt. Affairs)*
James Lennon *(Corp. Travel Planner)*
K.E. Kennedy *(Dir.-Communications)*

Computer Systems/Hardware:
AT&T

Outside Service Firm(s):

Coopers & Lybrand*(Auditors)*
1301 Avenue of The Americas
New York, NY 10019
Tel.: 212-536-2000

Hughes, Hubbard & Reed*(Legal Firm)*
One Wall St.
New York, NY 10005
Tel.: 212-943-6500

Manufacturers Hanover Trust Co.*(Major Banking Relationship)*
270 Park Ave.
New York, NY 10017
Tel.: 212-286-3229

COORDINATED APPAREL, INC.
350 Fifth Ave., Room 1400
New York, NY 10118
Tel.: 212-613-9200
Fax: 212-613-9282
Emp.: 4,000
Administrative Services
S.I.C.: 8741
Frederick B. Dean *(Chm. Bd.)*
Richard T. Lewis *(Pres.)*
Ellen Constantinides *(Exec. V.P. & Treas.)*
C. Peter Cora *(V.P.)*
Dudley Van Vlack *(V.P. & Sec.)*
Fred C. Scribner *(Dir.)*

Outside Service Firm(s):

Townley & Updike*(Legal Firm)*
220 E. 42nd St.
New York, NY 10017
Tel.: 212-682-4567

Chemical Banking Corp.*(Major Banking Relationship)*
277 Park Ave.
New York, NY 10041
Tel.: 212-310-6407
Fax: 212-310-4526

Subsidiaries:

American Argo Corp. **(1)**
350 Fifth Ave.
New York, NY 10118
Tel.: 212-613-9200
Mfr. of Knit Sportswear
S.I.C.: 2253
Frederick Dean *(Pres.)*

Roydon Wear, Inc. **(1)**
350 Fifth Ave.
New York, NY 10118
Tel.: 212-268-1800
Mfr. of Boys' & Girls' Sportswear
S.I.C.: 2329; 2361
R.T. Lewis *(Pres.)*

Plant:

Roydon Wear, Inc. **(2)**
1409 E. Oak St.
McRae, GA 31055
Tel.: 912-868-6444
Mfr. of Boys' & Girls' Sportswear
S.I.C.: 2329; 2361
D.M. Billing *(V.P.-Prod. & Gen. Mgr.)*

AL COPELAND ENTERPRISES, INC.
1333 S. Clearview Pkwy.
Jefferson, LA 70121
Tel.: 504-733-4300 **LA**
Fax: 504-733-7551
Year Founded: 1972
Approx.Sls.: $1,000,000,000
Emp.: 15,000
Fiscal Year-end: 12/31/91
Export
Copeland Fast Food Restaurants Specializing in Fried Chicken; Franchise Service For Popeye's Famous Fried Chicken & Church's Fried Chicken
S.I.C.: 5812
Carl Hays *(Chief Oper. Officer)*
Jack Cook *(Sr. V.P.-Devel.)*
Chris Miller *(Sr. V.P. & Gen. Mgr. Popeyes)*
William Copeland *(Sr. Exec. V.P.-Franchising)*
Charles T. Coffman *(V.P.-Mktg.-Popeyes)*
Jim Husk *(V.P.-Pur.)*
Thomas P. Lally *(V.P.-Real Estate)*
Darrell Stutes *(V.P. & Gen. Counsel)*
Mary Ann Toliver-Ream *(V.P.-Mngmt. Information Systems)*
Larry Jackson *(Dir.-Telecommunications)*
Rody Scheib *(Dir.-Mktg.-Churches)*
Marjorie Cartwright *(Fin. Rels. Coord.)*

No. of Mfg. Plants/Facilities: 650
No. of U.S. Offices: 6

Computer Systems/Hardware:
IBM System 38

Outside Service Firm(s):

Whitney National Bank of New Orleans*(Major Banking Relationship)*
New Orleans, LA

Divisions:

Al Copeland Enterprises, Inc. **(1)**
Bldg. 700, 3980 DeKalb Technology Pkwy., Ste. 775
Atlanta, GA 30340
Tel.: 404-451-5411
Regional Opers. for Franchised & Company Owned Churches & Popeyes Fast Food Chicken Restaurants
S.I.C.: 5812
Rick Kilinski *(Dir.-Opers.-Churches)*
Jim Sanders *(Dir.-Opers.-Popeyes)*
Renee Cureton *(Mktg. Mgr.-Popeyes Fried Chicken)*

Popeye's Famous Fried Chicken **(1)**
2918 Dupree St.
Houston, TX 77054
Tel.: 713-666-8686
S.I.C.: 5812

Popeye's Famous Fried Chicken **(1)**
1405 Airline Hwy.
Metairie, LA 70001
Tel.: 504-834-3750
S.I.C.: 5812

Popeye's Famous Fried Chicken **(1)**
5510 Cherokee Ave., Ste. 230
Alexandria, VA 22312
Tel.: 703-354-0511

Al Copeland Enterprises, Inc.—(Continued)

Regional Opers. For Popeyes Fast Food Chicken Restaurants
S.I.C.: 5812
John Fajfar *(V.P.-Mktg.)*

Popeye's Famous Fried Chicken **(1)**
5864-66 Semoran Blvd., S.
Orlando, FL 32812
Tel.: 407-282-0415
S.I.C.: 5812

Popeye's Famous Fried Chicken **(1)**
10600 W. Higgins Rd., Ste. 512
Rosemont, IL 60018
Tel.: 708-699-9980
Regional Headquarters For Franchised & Company Owned Fast Food Chicken Restaurants: Churches Fried Chicken & Popeyes Famous Fried Chicken
S.I.C.: 5812
Sarah Bailey *(Mktg. Mgr.-Popeyes)*
Jeanne Debruler *(Mktg. Mgr.-Churches)*

Subsidiary:

Church's Fried Chicken, Inc. **(1)**
1333 S. Clearview Pkwy.
Jefferson, LA 70121
Tel.: 504-733-4300
Assets: $344,787,000
Earnings: $14,459,000
Liabilities: $86,346,000
Net Worth: $258,441,000
Approx.Rev.: $426,400,000
Emp.: 13,700
Fiscal Year-end: 12/25/91
Computer Systems/Hardware:
Norand
1,075 Takeout Stores Located in 25 States
S.I.C.: 5812
Alvin C. Copeland *(Chm. Bd.)*
Carl Hays *(Chief Oper. Officer)*
Ernest Renaud *(Acting Pres.)*
John F. Barteau *(Sr. V.P.-Devel. & Mfg.)*
Steve Clark *(Sr. V.P.-Church's)*
Chris Miller *(Sr. V.P.-Popeye's)*
Charles T. Coffman *(V.P.-Mktg.)*
Jim Husk *(V.P.-Pur.)*
Thomas P. Lally *(V.P.-Real Estate)*
Rody Scheib *(V.P.-Mktg.)*
Darrell Stutes *(V.P. & Gen. Counsel)*
Mary Ann Tolliver-Ream *(V.P.-Mngmt. Information Systems)*
Larry Jackson *(Dir.-Telecommunications)*
Marjorie Cartwright *(Fin. Rels. Coord.)*

Subsidiary:

Far West Products, Inc. **(2)**
P.O. Box 5369, 302 Spencer Lane
San Antonio, TX 78201
Tel.: 210-737-5758 (100%)
Emp.: 30
Mfr. Modular Buildings
S.I.C.: 2452
Joseph A. C. Cote *(Pres.)*

COPELAND LUMBER YARD, INC.
901 NE Glisan St.
Portland, OR 97232
Tel.: 503-232-7181
Approx.Sls.: $84,000,000
Emp.: 650
Retail Building Materials & Garden Supplies
S.I.C.: 5031; 5211; 5261
Helen J. Whitsell *(Chm. Bd., Chief Exec. Officer & Treas.)*
William A. Whitsell *(Pres.)*
M. D. Anderson *(Chief Fin. Officer)*

Outside Service Firm(s):

Arthur Andersen & Co.*(Auditors)*
111 S.W. Columbia, Ste. 1400
Portland, OR 97201
Tel.: 503-226-1331

First Interstate Bank*(Major Banking Relationship)*
P.O. Box 3131,
Portland, OR 97208
Tel.: 503-220-4855
Fax: 503-225-7153

JOHN COPES FOOD PRODUCTS, INC.
156 W. Harrisburg Ave.
Rheems, PA 17570
Mailing Address:
P.O. Box 419
Rheems, PA 17570
Tel.: 717-367-5142
Fax: 717-367-7317
Approx.Sls.: $10,000,000
Emp.: 80
Fiscal Year-end: 12/31/90
Dehydrated Sweet Corn & Sweet Corn Powder, John Cope's Frozen White & Yellow Corn, Popcorn, Frozen Corn-on-the-Cob, Frozen Peas, Flash Blanched Mushrooms
S.I.C.: 2034; 2037; 2099
Thomas L. Cope *(Pres.)*
Mike Schmid *(Dir.-Sls. & Mktg.)*
Jerry Keperling *(Oper. Mgr.)*
Dale Boyer *(Plant Supt.)*
Ruth Cope *(Sec. & Office Mgr.)*

COPLAND FABRICS, INC.
P.O. Box 1208
Burlington, NC 27216
Tel.: 919-226-0272 **NC**
Fax: 919-229-9551
Year Founded: 1941
Emp.: 700
Manufacture Broad Woven Synthetic Fabrics
S.I.C.: 2221
James R. Copland III *(Pres., Chief Exec. Officer & Treas.)*
Ronald G. Copland *(V.P. & Sec.)*
Melvin Butler *(Plant Mgr.)*

No. of Mfg. Plants/Facilities: 4

Computer Systems/Hardware:
IBM System 36

Outside Service Firm(s):

McGladrey & Pullen*(Auditors)*
Drawer G-2, 230 N. Elm St.
Greensboro, NC 27402
Tel.: 919-273-4461

Provident Life & Accident Insurance Co.*(Group Insurer)*
P.O. Box 12015
Chattanooga, TN 37401
Tel.: 615-755-7088

THE COPLEY PRESS, INC.
7776 Ivanhoe Ave.
La Jolla, CA 92037
Mailing Address:
P.O. Box 1530
La Jolla, CA 92038
Tel.: 619-454-0411 **IL**
Fax: 619-454-5014
Year Founded: 1905
Approx.Sls.: $408,000,000
Emp.: 3,700
Fiscal Year-end: 12/31/90
Newspaper Publishing
S.I.C.: 2711
Helen K. Copley *(Chm. Bd. & Chief Exec. Officer)*
Hubert L. Kaltenbach *(Vice Chm.)*
David C. Copley *(Pres.)*
Robert F. Crouch *(Sr. V.P.)*
Harold W. Fuson, Jr. *(V.P.-Legal Affairs)*
Carmi Hodge *(V.P.-Human Resources)*
Charles F. Patrick *(V.P.-Fin.)*
John P. Clarke *(V.P.)*
John W. Curley *(V.P.)*
George H. Fisk *(V.P.)*
Herbert G. Klein *(V.P.)*
Glenn W. Pfeil *(V.P.)*
Robert Propernick *(V.P.)*
David M. Stamps *(V.P.)*
Bertram E. Winrow *(V.P.)*
Dean P. Dwyer *(Treas.)*
Mary Lou Washatka *(Controller)*
Samuel G. Hunt, Jr. *(Mgr.-Info. Systems)*

Principal(s):
Helen K. Copley

No. of Mfg. Plants/Facilities: 8
No. of U.S. Offices: 11

Computer Systems/Hardware:
DEC

Outside Service Firm(s):

Ernst & Young*(Auditors)*
501 W. Broadway, Ste. 1200
San Diego, CA 92101

Aetna Life & Casualty*(Group Insurer)*
San Diego, CA

O'Melvney & Myers*(Legal Firm)*
Los Angeles, CA

Union Bank*(Major Banking Relationship)*
8155 Mercury Ct., P.O. Box 2529
San Diego, CA 92112

Divisions:

The Beacon-News **(1)**
101 S. River St.
Aurora, IL 60506
Tel.: 708-844-5844
Newspaper
S.I.C.: 2711
David M. Stamps *(Publr.)*

The Daily Breeze **(1)**
5215 Torrance Blvd.
Torrance, CA 90509
Tel.: 310-540-5511
Newspaper
S.I.C.: 2711
Bertram E. Winrow *(Publr.)*

Daily Courier-News **(1)**
300 Lake St.
Elgin, IL 60120
Tel.: 708-888-7800
Newspaper
S.I.C.: 2711
Robert C. Propernick *(Publr.)*

The Daily Journal (IL) **(1)**
362 Schmale Rd.
Wheaton, IL 60187
Tel.: 708-653-1100
Newspaper
S.I.C.: 2711
Robert C. Propernick *(Publr.)*

Union-Tribune Publishing Company **(1)**
350 Camino de la Reina
San Diego, CA 92108-4106
Tel.: 619-299-3131
Fax: 619-299-6822
Emp.: 1,700
Newspaper
S.I.C.: 2711
Helen K. Copley *(Publisher)*
Gene Bell *(Pres., Chief Exec. Officer)*
Blake Oversmith *(Controller)*
Gerry Wilson *(Dir.-Adv. Sls.)*
Dexter LaPierre *(Mgr.-Display Adv.)*
Mindy Rawers *(Mktg. Mgr.)*
Nancy Coleman *(Classified Adv. Mgr.)*
Diane Jordan *(Pur. Dir.)*
Greg Shaughnessy *(Major Accts., Adv.)*
Al Larranaga *(Reg. Sls. Mgr.)*
Pete Rice *(Natl. Sls. Mgr.)*

Herald-News **(1)**
300 Caterpillar Dr.
Joliet, IL 60436
Tel.: 815-729-6161
Newspaper
S.I.C.: 2711
George H. Fisk *(Publr.)*

The News-Pilot **(1)**
362 W. Seventh St.
San Pedro, CA 90731
Tel.: 310-832-0221
Newspaper
S.I.C.: 2711
Bertram E. Winrow *(Publr.)*

The State Journal-Register **(1)**
One Copley Plaza
Springfield, IL 62705
Tel.: 217-788-1300
Newspaper
S.I.C.: 2711
John P. Clarke *(Publr.)*

The Outlook **(1)**
1920 Colorado Ave.
Santa Monica, CA 90406
Tel.: 310-829-6811
Newspaper
S.I.C.: 2711
Bertram E. Winrow *(Publr.)*

The News-Sun **(1)**
100 W. Madison Ave.
Waukegan, IL 60085
Tel.: 708-336-7000
Newspaper
S.I.C.: 2711
Glenn W. Pfeil *(Publr.)*

Lincoln Courier **(1)**
601 Pulaski St.
Lincoln, IL 62656
Tel.: 217-732-2101
Newspaper
S.I.C.: 2711
John P. Clarke *(Publr.)*

COPPER & BRASS SALES, INC.
17401 Ten Mile Rd.
East Detroit, MI 48021
Tel.: 313-775-7710
Fax: 313-775-5078
Year Founded: 1931
Approx.Sls.: $222,000,000
Emp.: 978
Wholesale Non-Ferrous Metals; Manufacture Tubular Parts, Assemblies
S.I.C.: 5051
William K. Howenstein *(Chm. Bd. & Chief Exec. Officer)*
Michael J. Fitzsimons *(Pres. & Chief Oper. Officer)*
Wayne C. Wright *(Chief Fin. Officer, Treas. & Sec.)*
Kim Cleary *(Mgr.-Data Processing)*
Mary Ellen Goodrow *(Mgr.-Employee Rel.)*

Computer Systems/Hardware:
IBM

Outside Service Firm(s):

Arthur Andersen & Co.*(Auditors)*
400 Renaissance Center
Detroit, MI 48243
Tel.: 313-259-8100

Prudential Insurance Co. of America*(Group Insurer)*
751 Broad St.
Newark, NJ 07102-3777
Tel.: 201-802-6000

N.B.D. Bank, N.A.*(Major Banking Relationship)*
611 Woodward Ave.
Detroit, MI 48226
Tel.: 313-225-1122
Fax: 313-225-3420

Subsidiary:

Fitzsimons Manufacturing Co. **(1)**
3775 E. Outer Dr.
Detroit, MI 48234
Tel.: 313-891-4800

COPPERWELD STEEL COMPANY
(Sub. of CSC Industries, Inc.)
4000 Mahoning Ave.
Warren, OH 44482
Tel.: 216-841-6011
Fax: 216-841-7108
Year Founded: 1987
Approx.Sls.: $175,000,000
Emp.: 1,300
Export
Mfr. Steel Alloy Bars & Billetts
S.I.C.: 3312; 3316
D. Caiazza *(Pres. & Chief Exec. Officer)*
J. Duncan *(Controller)*
D. Kane *(V.P.-Opers.)*
R. Pastoreil *(V.P.-Quality Assurance)*

Art Lattanzi *(V.P.-Sls.)*
Joseph A. Hoffman *(Mgr.-Mktg. & Prod. Devel.)*
William Pounds *(Mgr.-Personnel)*

THE COPPS CORP.
2828 Wayne St.
Stevens Point, WI 54481
Tel.: 715-344-5900
Fax: 715-344-7378
Approx.Sls.: $170,000,000
Emp.: 2,500
Wholesale & Retail Groceries, Meat, Produce, Frozen Foods
S.I.C.: 5411; 5147
Michael W. Copps *(Chm. Bd. & Chief Exec. Officer)*
Timothy J. Copps *(Pres.)*
Frederick C. Copps *(Exec. V.P.-Wholesale)*
Donald C. Copps *(V.P.-Mdsg.)*
Thomas R. Copps *(V.P.-Pub. Rels.)*
Edwin S. Flatoff *(V.P.)*
Walter Geis *(V.P.-Human Devel. & Personnel Services)*
J. Keith Hyland *(V.P.)*
J. Thomas Sievwright *(V.P.-Fin.)*
Principal(s):
Michael W. Copps
Timothy J. Copps
Frederick C. Copps
Donald C. Copps
Thomas R. Copps

Computer Systems/Hardware:
IBM

Outside Service Firm(s):

Arthur Andersen & Co.*(Auditors)*
777 E. Wisconsin Ave., P.O. Box 1215
Milwaukee, WI 53202
Tel.: 414-271-5100
Fax: 414-283-3200

Michael, Best & Friedrich*(Legal Firm)*
100 East Wisconsin Avenue
Milwaukee, WI 53202
Tel.: 414-271-6560

Norwest Bank Minnesota, N.A.*(Major Banking Relationship)*
St. Paul, MN

COPPUS ENGINEERING CORP.
Millbury Industrial Park, Rte. 20
Millbury, MA 01527
Mailing Address:
Box #15003
Worcester, MA 01615-0003
Tel.: 508-756-8391
Telex: 200046
Fax: 508-798-3131
Year Founded: 1909
Assets: $38,900,000
Liabilities: $31,000,000
Net Worth: $7,900,000
Approx.Sls.: $59,400,000
Emp.: 540
Fiscal Year-end: 12/31/91
Export
Steam Turbines, Blowers & Exhausters, Fanmix Gas-Oil Burners, Marine Ventilators
S.I.C.: 3511; 3564
Donald E. Hare *(Pres. & Chief Exec. Officer)*
William F. Jones *(Exec V.P.)*
Robert C. Macomber *(V.P.-Fin.)*
Edwin W. Wyle *(Dir.-Human Resources)*
Chris Vaughn *(Mgr.-Portable Ventilator Mktg.)*
Jim Pitney *(Mgr.-Turbine Mktg.)*
Joseph Gaul *(Pur. Agent)*
Duane T. Sargisson *(Sec.)*

No. of Mfg. Plants/Facilities: 2
No. of U.S. Offices: 35
No. of Foreign Offices: 65

Computer Systems/Hardware:
IBM AS 400; IBM System 38

Outside Service Firm(s):

KPMG Peat Marwick*(Auditors)*
One Boston Place
Boston, MA 02108
Tel.: 617-723-7700

Fleet National Bank*(Major Banking Relationship)*
Corporate Trust Dept., 125 Dupont Dr.
Providence, RI 02907
Tel.: 617-426-9555

Murray Turbomachinery Corporation **(1)**
1106 Washington St.
Burlington, IA 52601
Tel.: 319-753-5431
Fax: 319-752-1616
Emp.: 170
Export
Computer Systems/Hardware:
IBM AS 400; IBM System 38
Mfr. of Steam Turbines
S.I.C.: 3511
John G. Popek *(Gen. Mgr.)*

CORA TEXAS MANUFACTURING CO.
Texas Rd.
White Castle, LA 70788
Mailing Address:
P.O. Box 280
White Castle, LA 70788
Tel.: 504-545-3679
Fax: 504-545-8360
Approx.Sls.: $22,000,000
Emp.: 80
Raw Sugar & Blackstrap Molasses
S.I.C.: 2061; 2062
Paul Kessler *(Chm. Bd.)*
Mel E. Schudmak *(Pres.)*
Claiborne Dugas *(V.P.)*
Walter Gilbert *(Treas.)*
Paul B. Kessler *(Sec.)*
John Engolio, Jr. *(Plant Mgr.)*
Jose Spinoso *(Mgr.-Prod.)*
Principal(s):
Mel E. Schudmak

Computer Systems/Hardware:
Wang

Outside Service Firm(s):

Postlethwaite & Netterville*(Auditors)*
Baton Rouge, LA

Bank of Commerce*(Major Banking Relationship)*
White Castle, LA

CORAL PETROLEUM CORPORATION
600 Travis, Ste. 6120
Houston, TX 77002
Tel.: 713-222-7109 **TX**
Fax: 713-984-2232
Year Founded: 1973
Approx.Sls.: $100,000,000
Fiscal Year-end: 8/31/91
Producers of Petroleum & Contractors in Shaft Drilling Industry
S.I.C.: 5172
David B. Chalmers *(Chm. Bd., Pres. & Chief Exec. Officer)*
William Spence *(Sr. V.P.)*
E. Ben Elledge *(Sr. V.P.)*
Mary Jenkins *(Sec. & Treas.)*

No. of Foreign Offices: 2

Computer Systems/Hardware:
Prime 750

Outside Service Firm(s):

Prudential Insurance Co. of America*(Group Insurer)*
751 Broad St.
Newark, NJ 07102-3777
Tel.: 201-802-6000

Chase Manhattan Bank, N.A.*(Major Banking Relationship)*
One Chase Manhattan Plaza
New York, NY 10081
Tel.: 212-552-2222
Tel.: 800-526-0801
Fax: 212-552-7175

Subsidiaries:

Coral Petroleum Development **(1)**
908 Town & Country Blvd.
Houston, TX 77024
Tel.: 713-467-2311 (100%)

Coral Petroleum International, Inc. **(1)**
908 Town & Country Blvd.
Houston, TX 77024
Tel.: 713-467-2311 (100%)

Non-U.S. Holdings:

Coral Energy Ltd. **(1)**
P.O. Box 1651
Hamilton, Bermuda
Tel.: 809-292-0225 (100%)
Emp.: 7
Mktg. Crude Oil & Petroleum Prods. Worldwide
S.I.C.: 5172

Coral International Ltd. **(1)**
Box 1651
Hamilton, Bermuda
Tel.: 809-292-0225 (100%)
Emp.: 7
Mktg. Crude Oil & Petroleum Prods. Worldwide
S.I.C.: 5172

Coral Petroleum Ltd. **(1)**
P.O. Box 500
Georgetown, Grand Cayman Cayman Islands (100%)
Mktg. Crude Oil & Petroleum Prods. Worldwide
S.I.C.: 5172
David B. Chalmers *(Chm. Bd.)*

CORBER CORPORATION
400 Newark Pompton Turnpike
Wayne, NJ 07470
Tel.: 201-696-8080
Sales Range: $100-499 Million
S.I.C.: 2512
Ronald Cordover *(Chm. Bd.)*

Subsidiary:

The Berkline Corporation **(1)**
One Berkline Dr.
Morristown, TN 37813
Tel.: 615-585-1500
Fax: 615-585-1760
Approx.Rev.: $114,000,000
Emp.: 2,200
Fiscal Year-end: 12/30/90
Manufacture Upholstered Furniture; Holding Company
S.I.C.: 2512; 6719
Ronald H. Cordover *(Chm. Bd.)*
Alan Cole *(Pres.)*
Tom Cunningham *(Sr. V.P.-Sls. & Mktg.)*
Terry Hunt *(Sr. V.P.-Opers.)*
Andrew J. Powell *(Sr. V.P.-Mfg. & Mfg. Services)*
Joel Stepakoff *(V.P.-Natl. Accts.)*
Donald A. Essenberg *(V.P.-Corp. Sls.)*
Larry Musick *(V.P.-Admin. & Human Resources)*
Marvin Yost *(V.P.-Sls.-West)*
Ryan Einhorn *(V.P.-Sls.-East)*
Robert Caplan *(V.P.-Gallery Program & Adv.)*
Bruce Jones *(Pur. Dir.)*
David Popkin *(Dir.-Sls Admin.)*

Subsidiaries:

Berkline Limited **(2)**
One Berkline Drive
Morristown, TN 37814
Tel.: 615-585-1500 (100%)
Approx.Sls.: $10,000,000
Emp.: 100
Manufacture Wood & Upholstered Household Furniture
S.I.C.: 2512

Dual Manufacturing & Engineering, Inc. **(2)**
80 Bigelow St.
Holyoke, MA 01040
Tel.: 413-536-4940 (100%)
Manufacture Metal Stampings
S.I.C.: 3469

Non-U.S. Holding:

Berkline, Inc. **(2)**
8491 Ernest Cormier
Ville d'Anjou, PQ H1J 1B5, Canada
Tel.: 514-352-8880 (100%)
Approx.Sls.: $8,500,000
Emp.: 190
Manufacture Upholstered Furniture
S.I.C.: 2512
Fred Purkey *(V.P.- Opers.)*

CORCORAN MFG. CO., INC.
1140 E. Howell St.
Anaheim, CA 92805
Mailing Address:
P.O. Box 4465
Anaheim, CA 92803
Tel.: 714-634-8854
Fax: 714-634-9066
Year Founded: 1952
Sales Range: $10-19 Million
Emp.: 35
Foam Paint Applicators, Brooms & Waxers
S.I.C.: 3991
Oliver Gardner *(Pres.)*
Gregory Isaac *(V.P.-Sls.)*

Outside Service Firm(s):

Lincoln National Life Insurance Co.*(Group Insurer)*
Fort Wayne, IN

National Bank of Southern California*(Major Banking Relationship)*
Santa Ana, CA

Subsidiary:

Belmont Plastics Co. **(1)**
1745 S. Haster St.
Anaheim, CA 92802
Tel.: 714-999-1012
Emp.: 15
Manufacture Bank Specialty Equipment
S.I.C.: 3089

CORCORAN TRUCKING COMPANY
221 Lomond Lane
Billings, MT 59101
Mailing Address:
P.O. Box 1472
Billings, MT 59103
Tel.: 406-245-6065 **MT**
Fax: 406-245-8598
Emp.: 40
Import Export
Long Distance Refrigeration Trucking & Hauling
S.I.C.: 4213
John E. Corcoran *(Pres.)*

Outside Service Firm(s):

Randall J. Kanuit*(Auditors)*
2108 Broadway, Upper Level
Billings, MT 59102
Tel.: 406-652-2161

Olsen, Christenson & Gannett*(Legal Firm)*
Billings, MT

First Interstate Bank*(Major Banking Relationship)*
Billings, MT

CORDOVA ENTERPRISE
P.O. Box 922079,
Sylmar, CA 91391-2079
Tel.: 818-361-7724
Holding Company
S.I.C.: 6719
Sam Cordova *(Chm. Bd.)*
Steve Cordova *(Chief Exec. Officer)*

Cordova Enterprise—(Continued)

Subsidiary:

Cordova Laboratories **(1)**
13177 Foothill Blvd.
San Fernando, CA 91342
Tel.: 818-361-7724
Sales Range: $20-39 Million
Emp.: 127
Mosquito Repellants; Sporting Equipment
S.I.C.: 4959; 5091
Sam Cordova *(Gen. Partner)*
Stephen Cordova *(Chief Exec. Officer)*

Division:

Cordova Laboratories-I.A.F. Div. **(2)**
13177 Foothill Blvd.
San Fernando, CA 91342
Tel.: 818-361-7724
Training School for Stock Brokers
S.I.C.: 6211

CORHAM, INC.
300 Central Ave.
White Plains, NY 10106
Tel.: 914-946-7373 **NY**
Fax: 914-946-7375
Year Founded: 1931
Approx.Sls.: $45,000,000
Emp.: 270
Import
Mail Order House For Flowers, Plants & Bulbs; Nurseries & Garden Centers; Artifical Flowers
S.I.C.: 5961; 5261; 5193
Ronald Corelli *(Pres.)*
John Corelli *(V.P.)*
Randall Corelli *(V.P.)*
Christopher Corelli *(Treas. & Sec.)*
Thomas Mignanelli *(Controller)*

Subsidiary:

Petals **(1)**
300 Central Ave.
White Plains, NY 10606
Tel.: 914-946-7373
Mail Order House
S.I.C.: 5961
Richard Corelli *(Pres.)*

Corinthian

CORINTHIAN MEDIA, INC.
845 Third Ave.
New York, NY 10022
Tel.: 212-371-5225 **DE**
Fax: 212-753-1379
Year Founded: 1976
Approx.Billings: $300,000,000
Emp.: 75
Fiscal Year-end: 12/31/91
Broadcast Media Buying Service
S.I.C.: 7319
Larry Miller *(Chm. Bd., Pres. & Chief Exec. Officer)*
Robert Ingram *(Exec. V.P.)*
Bob Klein *(V.P.)*
Joel Wolk *(V.P.- Dir. Plng.)*
Jon Zimmerman *(V.P.)*
Charles Greenman *(Gen. Counsel)*
Charlotte Pelcman *(Mgr.- Opers.)*
Clair Pride *(Mgr.-Billing)*
David Mozes *(Sls. Devel.)*

No. of Mfg. Plants/Facilities: 1
No. of U.S. Offices: 3

Computer Systems/Hardware:
DEC VAX; Honeywell

Outside Service Firm(s):

Block & Block*(Auditors)*
New York, NY

John Hancock Mutual Life Insurance Co.*(Group Insurer)*
John Hancock Place, P.O. Box 111
Boston, MA 02117

Prudential-Bache*(Investment Banker)*
9 West 57th St.
New York, NY 10019
Tel.: 212-415-5800
Fax: 212-415-5885

Parker, Chapin, Flattau & Klimpl*(Legal Firm)*
530 Fifth Ave.
New York, NY 10011
Tel.: 212-840-6200

Subsidiary:

Corinthian Direct **(1)**
845 Third Ave.
New York, NY 10022
Tel.: 212-371-5225
Emp.: 27
Direct Response Advertising
S.I.C.: 7331
Larry Schneiderman *(V.P.)*

CORMIER CHEVROLET COMPANY, INC.
2201 E. 223 St.
Long Beach, CA 90810
Tel.: 310-830-5100 **CA**
Fax: 310-830-1730
Year Founded: 1951
Approx.Sls.: $79,000,000
Emp.: 180
Retail Sales of New & Used Automobiles
S.I.C.: 5511
Leonard L. Cormier, III *(Pres.)*
Timothy Lewis *(V.P.-Fin.)*
John J. Peterson *(V.P.)*
J.C. Willis *(Treas. & Sec.)*

Outside Service Firm(s):

City National Bank*(Major Banking Relationship)*
22400 Hawthorne Blvd.
Torrance, CA 90505

CORMIER RICE MILLING COMPANY, INC.
501 W. 3rd Ave.
De Witt, AR 72042
Mailing Address:
P.O. BOx 152
De Witt, AR 72042
Tel.: 501-946-3561
Fax: 501-946-3029
Assets: $2,743,597
Liabilities: $346,091
Net Worth: $2,397,506
Sales Range: $10-19 Million
Emp.: 32
Fiscal Year-end: 7/31/91
Export
Head Rice, Brewers' Rice, Bran, Rice & Organic Brown Rice
S.I.C.: 2044
Harry W. Cormier, Jr. *(Pres.)*
J.T. Ferguson *(V.P.)*
Carol Cormier Ellis *(Sec. & Treas.)*
Principal(s):
Harry W. Cormier, Jr.
Carol Cormier Ellis

Outside Service Firm(s):

Priddy Crigger & Holifield*(Auditors)*
Little Rock, AR

Claude Jenkins*(Legal Firm)*
De Witt, AR

First National Bank*(Major Banking Relationship)*
De Witt, AR

CORN STATES HYBRID SERVICE, INCORPORATED
2505 McKinley Ave.
Des Moines, IA 50321
Tel.: 515-285-3091
Fax: 515-285-6802
Approx.Sls.: $25,000,000
Emp.: 32
Foundation Seed Stocks, Storage, Processing Equipment for Seed & Grain Companies, Seed Dryers, Seed Protectants, Seed Treatment Equipment, Automatic Baggers & Quality Control Automatic Samplers; Whizzer Bag Closer
S.I.C.: 3523
Dave Vandervelde *(Pres.)*
Tony Wolfe *(Exec. V.P.)*
Terry Parkinson *(Sec. & Treas.)*

CORNELL FORGE COMPANY
6666 W. 66th St.
Chicago, IL 60638
Tel.: 312-767-4242
Fax: 312-767-9443
Approx.Sls.: $15,000,000
Emp.: 200
Steel Drop & Press Forgings
S.I.C.: 3462
Alverin M. Cornell *(Chm. Bd. & Chief Exec. Officer)*
Sanderson Smith *(Pres.)*
Peter Stanley *(Treas.)*
Phil John *(Gen. Mgr.)*
Robert Vidas *(Mgr.-Matls.)*
Donald Wratney *(Chief Engr.)*

Outside Service Firm(s):

Harry F. Shea & Co.*(Auditors)*
Chicago, IL

LaSalle National Bank*(Major Banking Relationship)*
135 S. LaSalle St.
Chicago, IL 60603
Tel.: 312-443-2440
Fax: 312-443-2819

CORNELL IRON WORKS, INC.
Crestwood Industrial Park
Mountaintop, PA 18707
Tel.: 717-474-6773
Tel.: 800-233-8366 **NY**
Fax: 800-526-0841
Year Founded: 1828
Sales Range: $10-19 Million
Emp.: 130
Import Export
Manufacture Metal Doors, Grilles & Shutters
S.I.C.: 3442
M. Keen Cornell *(Pres. & Chief Exec. Officer)*
David Connell *(V.P.-Fin. Services)*
Richard Knupp *(V.P.-Mfg.)*
J. Walsh *(V.P.-Engrng.)*
Gary Tombasco *(Mgr.-Computer Services)*
Principal(s):
M. Keen Cornell

No. of Mfg. Plants/Facilities: 1
No. of U.S. Offices: 1

Computer Systems/Hardware:
IBM System 34

Outside Service Firm(s):

Hanover Bank*(Major Banking Relationship)*
Wilkes-Barre, PA

Subsidiary:

Cornell Storefront Systems, Inc. **(1)**
Crestwood Industrial Park
Mountaintop, PA 18707
Tel.: 800-882-6773
Closure Products & Service for Store Chains
S.I.C.: 3442
Christopher B. Slocum *(Pres.)*

CORNER POCKETS OF AMERICA
1445 Broadwater
Billings, MT 59102
Tel.: 406-248-8728
Fax: 406-248-8716
Year Founded: 1973
Emp.: 50
Billard & Pool Establishment & Drinking Place
S.I.C.: 5813
George Frank *(Pres.)*
Judy Frank *(Sec.)*

Outside Service Firm(s):

KPMG Peat Marwick*(Auditors)*
1000 1st. Interstate Center, 401 N. 31st. St.
Billings, MT 59103

Dixon & Dixon*(Legal Firm)*
Omaha, NE

First Citizens Bank & Trust Co.*(Major Banking Relationship)*
Billings, MT

Subsidiary:

CNJ Distributing **(1)**
1445 Broadwater
Billings, MT 59102
Tel.: 406-248-8728

CORNERSTONE
519 W. Pratt
Baltimore, MD 21201
Tel.: 410-727-2131
Fax: 410-783-0335
Year Founded: 1980
Approx.Billings: $18,600,000
Emp.: 17
Greg DesRoches *(Pres.)*

CORNNUTS INC.
1320 Harbor Bay Pkwy., Ste. 250
Alameda, CA 94501
Mailing Address:
P O. Box 6759
Oakland, CA 94603
Tel.: 510-523-3949
Tel.: 800-347-6428
Fax: 510-523-9094
Year Founded: 1936
Approx.Sls.: $45,000,000
Emp.: 250
Fiscal Year-end: 12/31/91
Export
Mfg. of Toasted Corn Food Snacks
S.I.C.: 2096
Corporate Giving Program:
Contributes To The United Way & The Environmental Federation
M.E. Holloway *(Chief Exec. Officer)*
Joe Heaney *(Pres. & Chief Oper. Officer)*
Richard Bell *(V.P.-Sls. & Mktg.)*
Robert Boesch *(V.P.-Opers.)*
R.K. Holloway *(V.P.)*
Jerry Smith *(V.P.-Agriculture)*
Joseph G. Bauer *(V.P.-Admin.)*
Joe Bauer *(V.P.-Admin.)*
Suzanne Gerber *(Sls. Mgr.)*
John Kauke *(Export Mgr.)*
Lori Melin *(Product Mgr.)*

No. of Mfg. Plants/Facilities: 3
No. of U.S. Offices: 1

Outside Service Firm(s):

Hood & Strong*(Auditors)*
Oakland, CA

Thelen, Marrin, Johnson & Bridges*(Legal Firm)*
Oakland, CA

Wells Fargo Bank*(Major Banking Relationship)*
Oakland, CA

CORNUCOPIA, INC.
(d/b/a Todds Enterprises)
1722 Kettering
Irvine, CA 92714
Tel.: 714-250-4080
Fax: 714-724-1338
Year Founded: 1942
Approx.Sls.: $12,000,000
Emp.: 127
Import Export
Manufacture Salad Dressings, Sauces & Soups for Restaurants
S.I.C.: 2032; 2035
Philip DeCarion *(Pres.)*
Al F. Mayo *(V.P.)*
Roger McFarland *(Treas.)*
Roy Oakley *(Sec.)*

Outside Service Firm(s):

Al Mayo and Company*(Auditors)*
Irvine, CA

Anderson & Anderson*(Group Insurer)*
Costa Mesa, CA

Beverly Hills Business Bank*(Major Banking Relationship)*
Laguna Niguel, CA

Subsidiary:

Central Commissary, Inc. **(1)**
610 S. 56th Ave.
Phoenix, AZ 85043
Tel.: 602-242-6344
Emp.: 35
Mfg. Soups & Salad Dressings
S.I.C.: 2032; 2035
Richard Burns *(Pres.)*
Jerry Law *(V.P.-Sls.)*

CORPORATE TRAVEL SERVICES
300 Lakeside Dr., Ste. 250
Oakland, CA 94612
Tel.: 510-832-3100 **CA**
Fax: 510-987-7930
Approx.Sls.: $100,000,000
Emp.: 190
Tourist Agency Arranging Transport, Lodging & Car Rental
S.I.C.: 4724
Harry Scott *(Pres. & Chief Exec. Oper.)*

Outside Service Firm(s):

Bank of America*(Major Banking Relationship)*
701 S. Western Ave.
Los Angeles, CA 91201

CORPOREX COMPANIES, INC.
50 E. River Center Blvd.
Covington, KY 41011
Tel.: 606-292-5500 **KY**
Fax: 606-292-5599
Year Founded: 1965
Assets: $305,000,000
Liabilities: $218,000,000
Net Worth: $87,000,000
Approx.Sls.: $57,000,000
Emp.: 135
Fiscal Year-end: 12/31/88
Commercial & Industrial Operative Builders & Developers
S.I.C.: 1541; 1542; 6512; 6552
Corporate Giving Program: United Way
William Butler *(Chm. Bd., Pres., Chief Exec. Officer & Treas.)*
J. William Blackham *(Exec. V.P.)*
Richard Krzyminski *(Sr. V.P.-Admin. & Controller)*
Fran Saele *(V.P.)*
Karen Myer *(Corp. Sec.)*

Computer Systems/Hardware:
IBM System 36

Outside Service Firm(s):

Deloitte & Touche*(Auditors)*
Chiquita Center, 250 E. 5th St., Ste. 1900
Cincinnati, OH 45202
Tel.: 513-784-7100

Katz, Teller, Brant & Hild*(Legal Firm)*
Cincinnati, OH

First National Bank of Louisville*(Major Banking Relationship)*
P.O. Box 36000,
Louisville, KY 40233

R.J. CORR NATURALS, INC.
14828 McKinley
Posen, IL 60469
Mailing Address:
P.O. Box 1240,
Gary, IN 46407
Tel.: 708-389-4200
Fax: 219-886-1416
Approx.Sls.: $10,000,000
Emp.: 8
Fiscal Year-end: 12/31/90
Mfr. & Distr. Soft Drinks
S.I.C.: 2086; 5149
Robert Corr *(Pres.)*
Laurie Peters *(Controller)*
Alex Coronado *(Dir.-New Prod. Devel. & Natl. Sls. Mgr.)*

CORRECT CRAFT, INC.
6100 So. Orange Ave.
Orlando, FL 32809
Tel.: 407-855-4141 **FL**
Fax: 407-851-7844
Year Founded: 1925
Approx.Sls.: $27,000,000
Emp.: 200
Export
Manufacture Boats
S.I.C.: 3732
Ralph C. Meloon, Sr. *(Chm. Bd.)*
Walter N. Meloon *(Pres. & Chief Exec. Officer)*
Mike Elrod *(V.P.-Prod.)*
Larry Meddock *(V.P.-Mktg.)*
Jeff Hadley *(Controller)*
Walter O. Meloon *(Treas.)*
Jim Welch *(Gen. Counsel)*
Terry Dunagin *(Mgr.-Adv.)*
Debbie Johnston *(Mgr.-Human Resources)*
Bill Snook *(Mgr.-Research & Devel.)*
Gary Meloon *(Pur. Agent)*
Angela Pilkington *(Office Admin.)*
Principal(s):
Ralph C. Meloon, Sr.
Walter O. Meloon

No. of Mfg. Plants/Facilities: 1
No. of U.S. Offices: 3

Outside Service Firm(s):

NationsBank Florida*(Major Banking Relationship)*
Orlando, FL

Divisions:

Mid-Atlantic Correct Craft, Inc. **(1)**
P.O. Box 403, Rt. 173
Bloomsbury, NJ 08804
Tel.: 908-479-6810
Fax: 908-479-6680
Boat Building
S.I.C.: 3732
Walter N. Meloon *(Pres.)*

Mid West Correct Craft, Inc. **(1)**
P.O. Box 216
Angola, IN 46703
Tel.: 219-833-2226
Fax: 219-833-2190
Boat Building
S.I.C.: 3732

New England Correct Craft, Inc. **(1)**
142 Flagg Rd.
Rochester, NH 03867
Tel.: 603-332-5739
Boat Building
S.I.C.: 3732
Bob Warner *(Pres.)*

Southeast Correct Craft, Inc. **(1)**
P.O. Box 13117
Orlando, FL 32859
Tel.: 407-851-1965
Fax: 407-240-0898
Boat Building
S.I.C.: 3732
Walter N. Meloon *(Pres.)*

West Coast Correct Craft, Inc. **(1)**
11371 Pyrites Way
Rancho Cordova, CA 95670
Tel.: 916-635-9110
Fax: 916-638-9822
Boat Building
S.I.C.: 3732
Walter N. Meloon *(Pres.)*

CORRIGAN BROS., INC.
3545 Gratiot
Saint Louis, MO 63103
Tel.: 314-771-6200
Fax: 314-771-8537
Approx.Sls.: $40,000,000
Emp.: 400
Warm Air Heating & Air Conditioning Contractor; Sheet Metal Work; Rental of Heavy Construction Equipment
S.I.C.: 1711; 1761
Dennis Corrigan *(Pres.)*

Outside Service Firm(s):

Anders, Minkler & Diehl*(Auditors)*
St. Louis, MO

Armstrong, Teasdale, Schlafly, Davis & Dicus*(Legal Firm)*
One Metropolitan Square
St. Louis, MO 63102
Tel.: 314-621-5065
Fax: 314-621-5065

Boatmen's National Bank of St. Louis*(Major Banking Relationship)*
One Boatmen's Plaza, 800 Market St.
St. Louis, MO 63101
Tel.: 314-466-6000

Division:

Corrigan Company Mechanical Contractors **(1)**
3545 Gratiot
St. Louis, MO 63103
Tel.: 314-771-6200
Approx.Sls.: $40,000,000
Emp.: 320
Thomas J. Corrigan, Jr. *(Pres.)*
James A. Corrigan, Jr. *(V.P.)*

CORRUGATED METALS, INC.
4800 S. Hoyne
Chicago, IL 60609
Tel.: 312-254-1611
Fax: 312-254-1106
Sales Range: $10-19 Million
Emp.: 100
Mfr. of Corrugated Roofing & Siding
S.I.C.: 3444
Edward Carlton, Jr. *(Pres. & Chief Exec. Officer)*
Thomas J. Carlton *(V.P.-Sls. & Mktg.)*
Thomas Schmitz *(V.P.-Midwest Opers.)*
Dorothy Carlton *(Sec. & Treas.)*

Outside Service Firm(s):

Gershon, Pierce & Co.*(Auditors)*
Morristown, NJ

Ron, Davison, Gern & Steiber*(Legal Firm)*
Morristown, NJ

First Fidelity Bank, N.A.*(Major Banking Relationship)*
Morristown, NJ

Corson Furniture Industries
(See Listing Under Norwalk Furniture Corporation; Name Changed To Hickory Hill Furniture Corporation)

CORTEC GROUP
200 Park Ave.
New York, NY 10166
Tel.: 212-370-5600
Fax: 212-682-4195
Year Founded: 1984
Mfr. Adhesives, Tapes & Glue
S.I.C.: 6719
Gerald Rosenberg *(Chm.)*
R. Scott Shafler *(Pres.)*
Stanley Barow *(Treas.)*

Subsidiary:

LePage's, Inc. **(1)**
120 Delta Drive
Pittsburgh, PA 15238
Tel.: 412-967-0250
Tel.: 800-628-5702 (100%)
Fax: 412-967-0255
Emp.: 300
Export
Adhesives; Tapes & Glue
S.I.C.: 2891; 2672
Jerry N. Graf *(Chm. Bd.)*
W. Les Baggett *(Pres. & Chief Exec. Officer)*
Gary Dean *(Chief Fin. Officer)*
Jack C. Jacobson *(Sr. V.P.-Sls.)*
Richard Ward *(V.P.-Sls.)*
James C. Kowieski *(V.P.-Commercial Div.)*
Ron Clark *(Data Processing Mgr.)*
Joe Orlando *(Quality Control)*

CORTLAND LINE CO., INC.
3736 Kellogg Rd.
Cortland, NY 13045
Mailing Address:
P.O. Box 5588,
Cortland, NY 13045
Tel.: 607-756-2851 **NY**
Fax: 607-753-8835
Year Founded: 1915
Assets: $3,910,000
Liabilities: $2,675,000
Net Worth: $1,235,000
Approx.Sls.: $8,000,000
Emp.: 90
Fiscal Year-end: 8/31/92
Import Export
Manufacture & Distribute Sport Fishing Lines
S.I.C.: 5091; 2298
Richard B. Sanders *(Chm. Bd.)*
S.M. Zattosky *(Pres., Chief Exec. Officer & Treas.)*
Brian P. Ward *(V.P.-Sls. & Mktg.)*
Genevieve Duca *(Dir.-Personnel)*
Emil Pollansky *(Dir.-Mfg. & Engrng.)*
Tom Kanalley *(Pur. Agent)*

Computer Systems/Hardware:
IBM/ALR

Outside Service Firm(s):

Ciaschi, Dieters-Hayen, Mickelson & Schaufler*(Auditors)*
Ithaca, NY

Fitzgerald, Taylor & Pomeroy*(Legal Firm)*
Cortland, NY

Key Bank*(Major Banking Relationship)*
Syracuse, NY

COSCO, INC.
2525 State St.
Columbus, IN 47201
Tel.: 812-372-0141
Fax: 812-372-0911
Year Founded: 1935
Approx.Sls.: $85,000,000
Emp.: 1,100
Manufacture Metal & Wooden Household Furniture, Metal & Plastic Juvenile Products
S.I.C.: 2514; 2515; 2599; 2511; 2519
Nick Costides *(Pres.)*
Scott Lancashire *(V.P.-Sls.)*
Jonathan P. Reynolds *(V.P., Gen. Counsel & Sec.)*
Roy Schwartzkopf *(V.P.-Mfg.)*

Cosco, Inc.—(Continued)

Bob Fierke *(Controller)*
Bud Burkett *(Mgr.-Adv.)*

Outside Service Firm(s):

George S. Olive & Co.*(Auditors)*
201 N. Illinois St.
Indianapolis, IN 46204

Society National Bank*(Major Banking Relationship)*
900 Euclid Ave., P.O. Box 6477
Cleveland, OH 44101-6477
Tel.: 216-737-5000
Fax: 216-566-8947

COSCO INDUSTRIES
56 Church St.
Spring Valley, NY 10977
Tel.: 914-356-4300
Fax: 914-356-6757
Year Founded: 1880
Assets: $25,500,000
Net Worth: $25,500,000
Approx.Sls.: $43,000,000
Emp.: 1,550
Mfr. Marking & Identification Products; Advertising Specialties; Printing Services; Metal Stampings
S.I.C.: 3953; 2752; 3469; 3993; 3999; 3089
Robert F. Schmidt *(Chm. Bd. & Chief Exec. Officer)*
David E. Tittle *(Chief Fin. Officer)*
Paul Becker *(V.P., Sec., Treas. & Gen. Counsel)*
Robert Saperstein *(Controller)*

No. of Mfg. Plants/Facilities: 10

Computer Systems/Hardware:
IBM System 36

Outside Service Firm(s):

Coopers & Lybrand*(Auditors)*
P.O. Box 10108, One Canterbury Green
Stamford, CT 06904-2108
Tel.: 203-326-8400
Fax: 203-323-0771

Connecticut General Life Insurance Co.*(Group Insurer)*
P.O. Box 2975,
Hartford, CT 06104
Tel.: 203-726-6000

Shea & Gould*(Legal Firm)*
1251 Ave. of the Americas
New York, NY 10020
Tel.: 212-827-3000

The Bank of New York*(Major Banking Relationship)*
One Wall Street
New York, NY 10286
Tel.: 212-635-6805
Fax: 212-635-3201

Subsidiary:

C&D/Hit Inc. **(1)**
7150 Bryan Dairy Rd.
Largo, FL 34647
Tel.: 813-541-5561

COSMETIQUE, INC.
200 Corporate Woods Pkwy.
Vernon Hills, IL 60061
Tel.: 708-913-9099 **IL**
Fax: 708-913-9496
Approx.Sls.: $25,000,000
Emp.: 200
Import Export
Mail Order Beauty Clubs
S.I.C.: 5961
June Giugni *(Pres.)*
Chuck Campbell *(Exec. V.P.)*
Ed Allen *(V.P.)*
August Keller *(Controller)*

Computer Systems/Hardware:
IBM

Outside Service Firm(s):

Benefit Trust & Life Insurance*(Group Insurer)*
P.O. Box 7915,
Lake Forest, IL

Harris Trust & Savings Bank*(Major Banking Relationship)*
111 W. Monroe St.
Chicago, IL 60690
Tel.: 312-461-2265
Tel.: 800-858-0840

COSMOPULOS CROWLEY DALY/CKG
250 Boylston St.
Boston, MA 02116
Tel.: 617-266-5500
Fax: 617-236-1177
Year Founded: 1982
Approx.Billings: $25,000,000
Emp.: 30
Advertising Agency
S.I.C.: 7311
Corporate Giving Program: United Way
Harold E. Daly, Jr. *(Mng. Partner)*
R. Barry Chalfin *(Mng. Partner)*
Peter Kostopoulos *(Mng. Partner)*
Thomas Clark *(Exec. V.P.)*
Mario Lucca *(V.P./Finance)*
Liz Pappas *(V.P./Opers.)*
Principal(s):
Harold E. Daly, Jr.

COSMOS COMMUNICATIONS, INC.
11-05 44th Dr.
Long Island City, NY 11101
Tel.: 718-482-1800
Fax: 718-482-1968
Sales Range: $10-19 Million
Emp.: 190
Commercial Printing, Prepress Services
S.I.C.: 2752; 2791
Arnold Weiss *(Pres.)*
Jerome Skapof *(V.P.-Mktg.)*
Michael Sommers *(Controller)*
Gerald Weiss *(Treas.)*

Outside Service Firm(s):

Grant Thornton*(Auditors)*
605 Third Ave.
New York, NY 10158
Tel.: 212-599-0100
Fax: 212-370-4520

Chase Manhattan Bank, N.A.*(Major Banking Relationship)*
One Chase Manhattan Plaza
New York, NY 10081
Tel.: 212-552-2222
Tel.: 800-526-0801
Fax: 212-552-7175

COSTA CRUISE LINES, N.V.
World Trade Center, 80 SW 8th St.
Miami, FL 33130-3097
Mailing Address:
P.O. Box 019614,
Miami, FL 33101-9865
Tel.: 305-358-7325
Tel.: 800-462-6782
Fax: 305-375-0676
Year Founded: 1990
Assets: $23,290,431
Liabilities: $22,475,031
Net Worth: $815,400
Approx.Sls.: $70,000,000
Emp.: 172
Fiscal Year-end: 7/31/92
International Cruise Lines
S.I.C.: 4481
Bruce Nierenberg *(Pres. & Chief Exec. Officer)*
Klaus Wombacher *(Exec. V.P.)*
Edward N. Levitan *(Sr. V.P.-Fin & Admin.)*
Mitchell Schlesinger *(Sr. V.P.-Mktg.)*
Jim Applebaum *(V.P.-Field Sales)*
Nina Cohen *(V.P.-Mktg. Services)*
Dennis Shine *(V.P.-Sls. Promotion)*
David Stafford *(V.P.-Intl. Sls.)*
Stephanie Hofmeister *(PR Coordinator)*
Gregor Blaise *(Controller)*
Sherry Karley *(Dir.-Employee Benefits)*
Claudia Guerrero *(Mgr.-Personnel)*
Jennifer Lawrence Schott *(Mgr.-Pub. Rels.)*

No. of U.S. Offices: 1

Computer Systems/Hardware:
IBM System AS400 Model 60, Model 35

H. COTLER COMPANY
10 W. 33rd St.
New York, NY 10001
Tel.: 212-971-6464
Fax: 212-239-1861
Emp.: 200
Men's & Young Men's Slacks, Jeans & Shirts
S.I.C.: 2325; 2321
Howard Cotler *(Chm. Bd.)*
Leslie B. Cotler *(Pres.)*
Alan Sussman *(Chief Oper. Officer)*
Gerald Sholtz *(Exec. V.P. & Chief Exec. Officer)*
Irv Beck *(Mgr.-Sls.)*

Outside Service Firm(s):

KPMG Peat Marwick*(Auditors)*
345 Park Ave.
New York, NY 10154
Tel.: 212-758-9700
Fax: 212-872-3308

Manufacturers Hanover Trust Co.*(Major Banking Relationship)*
4 New York Plaza
New York, NY 10015
Tel.: 212-623-3232

COTTER & COMPANY
2740 N. Clybourn Ave.
Chicago, IL 60614-1088
Tel.: 312-975-2700 **DE**
Fax: 312-975-1712
Year Founded: 1948
Approx.Rev.: $2,140,000,000
Emp.: 4,000
Fiscal Year-end: 12/28/91
Mfr. & Wholesale Distributor of Hardware, Farm & Garden Equipment for over 7,000 True Value Hardware & V&S Variety Stores Nationally
S.I.C.: 5083; 5023; 5072
William Claypool III *(Chm. Bd.)*
Daniel A. Cotter *(Pres. & Chief Exec. Officer & Dir.)*
Paul F. Fee *(Exec. V.P.)*
Daniel Burns *(V.P. & Gen. Counsel)*
Dan Burton *(V.P.-Member Services & Devel.)*
Kerry Kirby *(V.P. & Chief Fin. Officer)*
John Semkus *(V.P.-Distr.)*
Tom Filipski *(Controller)*
Frank Hashimoto *(Dir.-Cash Mngmt.)*
Bob Johnson *(Dir.-Information Services)*
Fred Lobo *(Dir.-Human Resources)*
Bill Messmer *(Dir.-Personnel Training & Devel.)*
Nancy Nasser *(Dir.-Employee Benefits)*
Jerry Thompson *(Dir.-Adv.)*
Gary Coppinger *(Mgr.-Adv.)*
Tom Sweenie *(Mgr.-Fin.)*

No. of Mfg. Plants/Facilities: 18
No. of U.S. Offices: 1

Computer Systems/Hardware:
IBM 3090

Outside Service Firm(s):

Ernst & Young*(Auditors)*
1100 Independence Center
Charlotte, NC 28246
Tel.: 704-372-6300

Harris Trust & Savings Bank*(Major Banking Relationship)*
111 W. Monroe St.
Chicago, IL 60690
Tel.: 312-461-2265
Tel.: 800-858-0840

Divisions:

General Power Equipment Co. **(1)**
201 E. Brink St.
Harvard, IL 60033
Tel.: 815-943-7411
Fax: 815-943-7888
Mfr. of Lawn Chief Lawn Mowers, Tillers & Riders; Snow Chief Snowblowers; Atlas Lawnmowers & Wheeler Lawnmowers
S.I.C.: 3524
Bob Simmons *(Gen. Mgr.)*
Ted Behle *(Sls. Mgr.-Lawn Chief & Snow Chief)*
Nevin I. Gage *(Sls. Mgr.-Atlas & Wheeler Div.)*

Tru-Test Mfg. Co. **(1)**
201 Jandus Rd.
Cary, IL 60013
Tel.: 708-639-5383
Fax: 708-639-2058
Mfr. of Tru-Test Paint
S.I.C.: 5198
Rick Hille *(Gen. Mgr.)*

Subsidiaries:

Cotter Acceptance Co., Inc. **(1)**
2740-52 N. Clybourn
Chicago, IL 60614
Tel.: 312-975-2890 (100%)
Financial Services
S.I.C.: 6159

Cotter Finance Co., Inc. **(1)**
2740-52 N. Clybourn Ave.
Chicago, IL 60614
Tel.: 312-975-2700 (100%)
Emp.: 1
Real Estate & Finance Services
S.I.C.: 6531; 7389

Wheeler Manufacturing Co. **(1)**
201 E. Brink
Harvard, IL 60033
Tel.: 815-943-7417 (100%)
Emp.: 5
Mfr. of Lawn Equipments
S.I.C.: 3524
Glenn Alexander *(Pres.)*

COTTMAN TRANSMISSION SYSTEMS, INC.
240 New York Dr.
Fort Washington, PA 19034
Tel.: 215-643-5885
Fax: 215-643-2519
Year Founded: 1962
Approx.Sls.: $45,000,000
Emp.: 60
Franchise Co. Serving Automotive Aftermarket
S.I.C.: 7537
Michael Ambrose *(Pres. & Gen. Mgr.)*
Edward W. Kelly, Jr. *(Exec. V.P. & Chief Fin. Officer)*
James Corkran *(Exec. V.P.)*
Todd Leff *(Gen. Counsel)*
Harry Kalish *(Adv. Dir.)*
Ellen Crawford *(Office Mgr.)*

Subsidiary:

A-1 Transmissions **(1)**
240 New York Dr.
Fort Washington, PA 19034
Tel.: 215-643-5885
Fax: 215-643-2519

COTTON ELECTRIC CO-OP
226 N. Broadway
Walters, OK 73572
Tel.: 405-875-3351 **OK**
Year Founded: 1938
Approx.Sls.: $27,000,000
Emp.: 114
Distribution of Electric Power
S.I.C.: 4911
Bruce Scott *(Pres.)*
Thomas Jones, Jr. *(V.P.)*

Clyde Johnson *(Gen. Mgr.)*

Outside Service Firm(s):

Briscoe Robinson Company*(Auditors)*
Tulsa, OK

Walters Bank & Trust Company*(Major Banking Relationship)*
Walters, OK

F.X. COUGHLIN CO.
27050 Wick Rd.
Taylor, MI 48180
Tel.: 313-946-9510
Telex: 4320046
Fax: 313-946-6945
Approx.Sls.: $75,000,000
Emp.: 260
Import Export
Freight Forwarder; Custom House Broker
S.I.C.: 3412
F.X. Coughlin *(Pres. & Treas.)*
Joseph Coughlin *(V.P. & Sec.)*
William B. Larkin *(V.P.)*

Outside Service Firm(s):

Pannell Kerr & Forster*(Auditors)*
Detroit, MI

COUGLE COMMISSION COMPANY, INC.
345 N. Aberdeen
Chicago, IL 60607
Tel.: 312-666-7861 **IL**
Fax: 312-666-6434
Approx.Sls.: $21,000,000
Emp.: 35
Fresh & Frozen Meat & Poultry
S.I.C.: 5144; 5147
Edgar Freidheim *(Chm. Bd.)*
Louis Friedheim *(Pres. & Chief Exec. Officer)*
John Freidheim *(V.P. & Sec.)*

Outside Service Firm(s):

Wolf & Co.*(Auditors)*
Chicago, IL

COULTER CORPORATION
601 Coulter Way
Hialeah, FL 33010
Mailing Address:
P.O. Box 2145, 601 West Coulter Way
Hialeah, FL 33012-0145
Tel.: 305-885-0131
Tel.: 800-327-6531
Fax: 305-883-6820
Year Founded: 1958
Emp.: 2,000
Fiscal Year-end: 3/31/89
Medical Equipment & Diagnostic Test Kit Manufacturer; Chemicals & Allied Products
S.I.C.: 3826
Wallace Coulter *(Chm. Bd. & Chief Exec. Officer)*
Joseph R. Coulter, Jr. *(Pres.)*
Udo Henseler *(Chief Fin. Officer)*
Sue Van *(Treas.)*
Luis Reyes *(Controller)*
Wayne Barlin *(Gen. Counsel)*
Laura Coulter-Jones *(Dir.-Project Planning)*
Albert Evans *(Dir.-Personnel)*
Anne-Lynne Keplar *(Dir.-Bus. Dev.)*
James Ring *(Dir.-Human Resources)*
Matt Smith *(Dir.-International)*
Bob Sheppard *(Dir.-Marketing Communication Exhibit)*
Ted Desibio *(Mgr.)*
Betsy Cole *(Mgr.-Training & Dev.)*
Dominick DiBiase *(Mgr.-Pur.)*
James Leeman *(Mgr.-Data Processing)*
Robert T. Godfrey *(Asst. Treas.)*

Computer Systems/Hardware:
IBM Systems 38 & 3083

Outside Service Firm(s):

Arthur Andersen & Co.*(Auditors)*
2100 One Biscayne Tower
Miami, FL 33131
Tel.: 305-374-3700

Silverman, Cass & Singer, Ltd.*(Legal Firm)*
Chicago, IL

Continental Bank N. A.*(Major Banking Relationship)*
231 S. LaSalle St.
Chicago, IL 60697
Tel.: 312-828-2345
Tel.: 800-426-5754
Telex: 312-828-1783

M.D. Sass Investors*(Pension Manager)*
New York, NY

COUNTRY CLASSIC DAIRIES, INC.
(d/b/a Darigold Farms)
P.O. Box 968
Bozeman, MT 59715
Tel.: 406-586-5426 **MT**
Fax: 406-586-5110
Year Founded: 1932
Approx.Sls.: $23,000,000
Emp.: 62
Co-op: Milk Processing; Ice Milk Packaged; Creamery Butter; Natural Cheese
S.I.C.: 2026; 2024; 2021; 2022
Keith Nye *(Gen. Mgr.)*

Outside Service Firm(s):

First Bank, N.A.*(Major Banking Relationship)*
Billings, MT

COUNTRY COMPANIES INSURANCE GROUP
1711 GE Rd.
Bloomington, IL 61704
Mailing Address:
P.O. Box 2000,
Bloomington, IL 61702-2000
Tel.: 309-557-2111 **IL**
Fax: 309-829-9430
Year Founded: 1929
Assets: $2,132,098,000
Earnings: $17,130,238
Liabilities: $1,770,654,000
Net Worth: $361,444,000
Approx.Sls.: $288,916,000
Emp.: 519
Fiscal Year-end: 12/31/90
Life Insurance
S.I.C.: 6311; 6321; 6331; 6726; 6719
John White, Jr. *(Pres.)*
Duane L. Miller *(Exec. V.P. & Chief Exec. Officer)*
Donald J. Engelkes *(V.P. & Gen. Mgr.)*
Robert W. Weldon *(V.P.-Fin. & Treas.)*
Barbara A. Baurer *(V.P.-Mngmt. Information Systems)*
Peter J. Borowski *(V.P.-Admin.)*
Deanna L. Frautschi *(V.P.-Communications & Human Resources)*
Michael J. Still *(V.P.-Agency)*
Enid Schlipf *(V.P.)*
Alan Dale *(V.P.)*
John Blackburn *(Reg. V.P.-Agency)*
Ted Giannoni *(Reg. V.P.-Agency)*
Donald J. Speichinger *(Reg. V.P.-Agency)*
Jerome Weiss *(Gen. Counsel)*
Linda Faull *(Sec.)*
Jeffrey Dillon *(Controller)*
Richard Gudeman *(Dir.-Actuary)*
Roger Rheeling *(Dir.-Grp. Health Insurance)*
Dennis Feicke *(Dir.-Human Resources)*
Tim Kelly *(Dir.-Life Insurance & Annuities)*
Mitchell Kosek *(Dir.-Corp. Support Services)*
Jean B. Lawyer *(Dir.-Corp. Communications)*
Bryce A. Sides *(Dir.-Adv. & Promo.)*
Paul Belyea *(Dir.-Underwriting)*
Jack Malehorn *(Dir.-Mktg. & Consumer Res.)*
James A. Bilyeu *(Medical Director)*

No. of Mfg. Plants/Facilities: 1
No. of U.S. Offices: 1

Computer Systems/Hardware:
IBM System 3090

Outside Service Firm(s):

Ernst & Young*(Auditors)*
233 S. Wacker Dr.
Chicago, IL 60606
Tel.: 312-368-1800
Fax: 312-645-3095

KPMG Peat Marwick*(Auditors)*
Peat Marwick Plaza, 303 E. Wacker Dr.
Chicago, IL 60601
Tel.: 312-938-1000

Member Companies:

Country Life Insurance Company **(1)**
1701 Towanda Ave.
Bloomington, IL 61702-2040
Tel.: 309-557-3000
Fax: 309-829-9430
Assets: $1,998,001,000
Liabilities: $1,644,825,000
Net Worth: $353,176,000
Approx.Premiums: $246,854,000
Emp.: 528
Fiscal Year-end: 12/31/90
Life Insurance Company
S.I.C.: 6311
John White, Jr. *(Pres.)*
Duane L. Miller *(Exec. V.P. & Chief Exec. Officer)*
Robert W. Weldon *(V.P.-Fin. & Treas.)*
Barbara A. Baurer *(V.P.-Mngmt. Information Systems)*
Peter J. Borowski *(V.P.-Admin.)*
Donald J. Engelkes *(V.P. & G.M.)*
Deanna L. Frautschi *(V.P.-Communications & Human Resources)*
Michael J. Still *(V.P.-Agency)*
Alan Dale *(V.P.)*
Enid Schlipf *(V.P.)*
Jerome Weiss *(Gen. Counsel)*
Norma Maney *(Sec.)*
Jeff Dillon *(Controller)*
Richard Gudeman *(Chief Actuary)*
Paul Belyea *(Dir.-Underwriting/Policy Issue)*
James A. Bilyeu *(Medical Dir.)*
Dennis Feicke *(Dir.-Human Resources)*
Tim Kelly *(Dir.-Life Insurance & Annuities)*
Mitchell Kosek *(Dir.-Support Services)*
Jerry G. Kownacki *(Dir.-Grp. & Health Insurance)*
Jean B. Lawyer *(Dir.-Corp. Rels.)*
Bryce A. Sides *(Dir.-Adv. & Sls. Promo.)*

Subsidiary:

Country Investors Life Assurance Company **(2)**
1701 Towanda Ave.
Bloomington, IL 61702-2040
Tel.: 309-829-3000 (100%)
Life & Health Insurance, Annuities
S.I.C.: 6311
John White, Jr. *(Pres.)*

CC Services **(2)**
1701 Towanda Ave.
Bloomington, IL 61702-2020
Tel.: 309-557-3000
Fax: 309-829-9430
Emp.: 1,141
Fiscal Year-end: 12/31/91
John White, Jr. *(Pres.)*
Duane L. Miller *(Exec. V.P. & Chief Exec. Officer)*
Barbara A. Baurer *(V.P.-Mngmt Information Systems)*
Peter J. Borowski *(V.P.-Admin.)*
Deanna L. Frautschi *(V.P.-Communications & Human Resources)*
Michael J. Still *(V.P.-Agency)*
Robert W. Weldon *(V.P.-Fin. & Treas.)*
Alan Dale *(V.P.)*
Enid Schlipf *(V.P.)*
Linda Faull *(Sec.)*
John Butler *(Controller)*
Jerome Weiss *(Gen. Counsel)*
Robert Bouck *(Dir.-Fleet & Leasing)*
Dennis Feicke *(Dir.-Corp. Human Resources)*
Jim Hanfland *(Dir.-Mngmt. Information Systems & Property/Casualty Agency System)*
Mike Howard *(Dir.-Agency Admin.)*
Robert Hunsacker *(Dir.-Mngmt. Information Systems & Data Processing)*
Mitchell Kosek *(Dir.-Corp. Support Services)*
Jean B. Lawyer *(Dir.-Corp. Communications)*
Steward Lyman *(Dir.-Insurance Brokerage Services)*
Paul Packard *(Dir.-Corp. Agency Training)*
Bryce A. Sides *(Dir.-Corp. Adv. & Sls. Promo.)*
Al Semmler *(Dir.-Fin. Services)*
Bob Turnbull *(Dir.-Mngmt. Information Systems-Life & Health Systems)*
Ken Wagner *(Dir.-Mngmt. Information Systems & Systems Support)*
Bill Wills *(Dir.-Corp. Agency Mngmt. Devel.)*

Country Mutual Insurance Company **(1)**
1700 Towanda Ave.
Bloomington, IL 61702-2100
Tel.: 309-557-3000
Fax: 309-829-9430
Assets: $980,095,000
Liabilities: $560,691,000
Net Worth: $419,404,000
Approx.Rev.: $498,153,000
Emp.: 1,263
Fiscal Year-end: 12/31/91
Property, Casualty & Liability Insurance, Specializing in Personal Lines
S.I.C.: 6331
John White, Jr. *(Pres.)*
Duane L. Miller *(Exec. V.P. & Chief Exec. Officer)*
Robert W. Weldon *(V.P.-Fin. & Treas.)*
Barbara A. Baurer *(V.P.-Mngmt. Information Systems)*
Peter J. Borowski *(V.P.-Admin.)*
Deanna L. Frautschi *(V.P.-Communications & Human Resources)*
Charles L. Jones *(V.P. & Gen. Mgr.)*
Michael J. Still *(V.P.-Agency)*
Alan Dale *(V.P.)*
Enid Schlipf *(V.P.)*
John Blackburn *(Reg. V.P.-Agency)*
Ted Giannoni *(Reg. V.P.-Agency)*
Donald J. Speichinger *(Reg. V.P.-Agency)*
Earl L. Mcintyre *(Reg. V.P.)*
James R. Wenckus *(Reg. V.P.)*
Jerome Weiss *(Gen. Counsel)*
Linda Faull *(Sec.)*
Matthew Kopff *(Controller)*
Bruce Lawson *(Reg. Controller)*
Richard Bill *(Dir.-Actuary)*
Duane Chisman *(Dir.-Claims)*
Dennis Feicke *(Dir.-Human Resources)*
Linda Hutchins *(Dir.-Opers.)*
Mitchell Kosek *(Dir.-Support Services)*
Jean B. Lawyer *(Dir.-Communications)*
Jack Malehorn *(Dir.-Mktg. & Consumer Res.)*
Bryce A. Sides *(Dir.-Adv. & Sls. Promo.)*
Jerome Tegenkamp *(Dir.-Underwriting)*
Edward M. Phelps *(Reg. Dir.-Opers.)*
Carter G. Thomas *(Reg. Dir.-Claims)*

Subsidiaries:

Country Casualty Insurance Company **(2)**
P.O. Box 2100, 1701 Towanda Ave.
Bloomington, IL 61702-2000
Tel.: 309-557-3000 (100%)
Casualty Insurance
S.I.C.: 6331
John White, Jr. *(Pres.)*

Country Preferred Insurance Company **(2)**
P.O. Box 2100, 1701 Towanda Ave.
Bloomington, IL 61702-2100
Tel.: 309-557-3000 (100%)
Insurance
S.I.C.: 6331
John White, Jr. *(Pres.)*

Northwest Farm Bureau Insurance Company **(2)**
P.O. Box 2100, 1701 Towanda Ave.
Bloomington, IL 61702-2100
Tel.: 309-557-3000 (100%)
Insurance
S.I.C.: 6331
John White, Jr. *(Pres.)*

Regional Office:

Country Mutual Northwest Regional Office **(1)**
2150 Country Dr. S.
Salem, OR 97302-2209
Tel.: 503-375-2710
Fax: 503-362-0325
Property, Casualty Insurance, Liability Insurance
S.I.C.: 6331

COUNTRY FRESH, INC.
2555 Buchanan Ave., S.W.
Grand Rapids, MI 49518
Tel.: 616-243-0173
Fax: 616-243-5926
Approx.Sls.: $135,000,000
Emp.: 290
Mfr. & Distributor of Milk, Ice Cream, Cottage Cheese & Yogurt
S.I.C.: 2026; 2024
Delton C. Parks *(Pres. & Gen. Mgr.)*
John Williams *(Controller)*

Outside Service Firm(s):

Deloitte & Touche*(Auditors)*
Grand Rapids, MI

Warner, Norcross & Judd*(Legal Firm)*
Grand Rapids, MI

Old Kent Bank*(Major Banking Relationship)*
Grand Rapids, MI

COUNTRY HOME BAKERY, INC.
1700-1722 Barnum Ave.
Bridgeport, CT 06610
Mailing Address:
P.O. Box 2327
Bridgeport, CT 06608
Tel.: 203-333-2151
Fax: 203-333-7728
Year Founded: 1959
Approx.Sls.: $150,000,000
Emp.: 1,500
Fiscal Year-end: 12/31/91
Mfr. of Frozen Bread & Other Bakery Products
S.I.C.: 2053
Chester E. Borck *(Chm. Bd.)*
Don K. Vance *(Pres.)*
Judith L. Borck *(Chief Exec. Officer)*
Steven F. Ambrose *(Exec. V.P.)*
Robert Beckerman *(V.P.-Mktg.)*
Charles R. Cullen *(V.P.-Fin.)*
George Green *(Dir.-Res. & Devel.)*
James W. Shaw *(Dir.-Corp. Mfg.)*
Richard L. Warren *(Dir.-Corp. Pur.)*
Linda Gentile *(Corp. Travel Coord. & Exec. Sec.)*

COUNTRYMARK COOPERATIVE, INC.
950 N. Meridian St., Ste. 0700
Indianapolis, IN 46204-3909
Tel.: 317-685-3000
Tel.: 800-562-2622
Year Founded: 1926
Assets: $190,000,000
Liabilities: $95,000,000
Net Worth: $95,000,000
Approx.Sls.: $2,000,000,000
Emp.: 1,800
Fiscal Year-end: 8/31/92
Export
Grain Storage & Marketing; Petroleum Refining & Sales; Farm Products Distribution
S.I.C.: 5153; 5159; 5031; 5191; 2873; 2999; 8611
Larry Curless *(Chm. Bd.)*
Philip French *(Pres. & Chief Exec. Officer)*
William Paddack *(Sr. V.P.)*
Norman Brandley *(V.P.-Human Resources)*
Paul Weinstein *(V.P.-Mktg. & Plng.)*
Robert Werner *(V.P.-Fin.)*
Robert Delambo *(Gen. Counsel)*
Ed Bryan *(Mgr.-Information Systems)*
Jeffrey Harper *(Mgr.-Mktg.)*
James Kapp *(Mktg. Communications Specialist)*
Principal(s):
Member-Owned

No. of U.S. Offices: 1

Computer Systems/Hardware:
IBM 4381

Outside Service Firm(s):

KPMG Peat Marwick*(Auditors)*
135 N. Pennsylvania St.
Indianapolis, IN 46204
Tel.: 317-636-5592
Fax: 317-635-3314

Farm Bureau Insurance*(Group Insurer)*
Indianapolis, IN

INB National Bank*(Major Banking Relationship)*
One Indiana Sq.
Indianapolis, IN 46266
Tel.: 317-266-6000

Merchants National Bank & Trust Company of Indianapolis*(Major Banking Relationship)*
One Merchants Plaza, Ste. 901E
Indianapolis, IN 46255
Tel.: 317-267-7109

Farm Bureau Insurance*(Pension Manager)*
Indianapolis, IN

Subsidiaries:

Countrymark Co-Op Inc. **(1)**
4565 Columbus Pike, Rte. 23 N.
Delaware, OH 43015
Tel.: 614-548-8200
Fax: 614-548-8422
Assets: $192,000,000
Earnings: $600,000
Liabilities: $126,000,000
Net Worth: $66,000,000
Approx.Sls.: $929,000,000
Emp.: 850
Fiscal Year-end: 8/31/90
Computer Systems/Hardware:
IBM 4341 P3
Agricultural Co-operative
S.I.C.: 5153; 5191; 2048; 2875; 5169; 5172
Philip French *(Pres.)*
Robert Werner *(V.P.-Fin.)*
Robert Wolf *(V.P.-Admin.)*
Jeffrey Price *(Treas.)*
Mark Stewart *(Legal Officer)*
Carmen Avogaro *(Dir.-Investor Rels. & Mgr.-Cash)*
Tom Scribner *(Dir.-Data Processing)*

Farbest Inc. **(1)**
950 N. Meridian
Indianapolis, IN 46204
Tel.: 317-685-3000
Tel.: 800-562-2622
Emp.: 3
Farm Products Distribution
S.I.C.: 5153; 5159
Philip French *(Pres.)*

COUNTY SEAT STORES, INC.
17950 Preston Rd.
Dallas, TX 75252
Tel.: 214-248-5100
Approx.Sls.: $250,000,000
Emp.: 5,400
Specialty Retailer of Apparel & Accessories
S.I.C.: 2389
Barry Parker *(Pres.)*
Louis Cabrera *(Sr. V.P.-Fin.)*
Linda Baker *(Dir.-Mktg. & Mdsg.)*
Michael Doarn *(Dir.-Pur.)*
Tom Grissom *(Dir.-Personnel)*

COURISTAN INC.
2 Executive Dr.
Fort Lee, NJ 07024
Tel.: 201-585-8500
Fax: 201-585-8552
Year Founded: 1926
Approx.Sls.: $50,000,000
Emp.: 100
Import & Manufacture Oriental Design Rugs, Oriental Rugs & Fine Broadloom
S.I.C.: 2273; 5023
George G. Couri *(Chm. Bd.)*
Walter West *(Pres.)*
Ronald J. Couri *(Treas.)*
Steven G. Couri *(Sec.)*
Saula Vetter *(Dir.-Adv.)*
Sid Spinner *(Mgr.-Credit)*

Divisions:

C&C Associates **(1)**
919 Third Ave.
New York, NY 10022
Tel.: 212-371-4200
S.I.C.: 5023; 2273

Couri Carpet Co. **(1)**
919 Third Ave.
New York, NY 10022
Tel.: 212-371-4200
S.I.C.: 5023; 2273

Couri-Murad & Co. **(1)**
919 Third Ave.
New York, NY 10022
Tel.: 212-371-4200
S.I.C.: 5023; 2273

U.S. Carpet Co. **(1)**
919 Third Ave.
New York, NY 10022
Tel.: 212-371-4200
S.I.C.: 5023; 2273

THE COURT COMPANY
5389 Estate Office Dr.
Memphis, TN 38119
Tel.: 901-682-2600
Fax: 901-682-2836
Emp.: 15
Builders of Racquetball Courts
S.I.C.: 1542
Randy Stafford *(Pres. & Chief Exec. Officer)*
Mike Mattingly *(Treas., Controller & Chief Fin. Officer)*

Outside Service Firm(s):

Crump Life & Health Distributors*(Auditors)*
5350 Poplar Ave., P.O. Box 171377
Memphis, TN 38187
Tel.: 901-761-1550

NBC Bank*(Major Banking Relationship)*
Memphis, TN

NBC Bank*(Pension Manager)*
Memphis, TN

COURTESY CHEVROLET & IMPORTS INC.
(Formerly Sim Fryson Chevrolet & Import Auto Plaza)
370 Elmira Rd.
Ithaca, NY 14850
Tel.: 607-272-7353 DE
Fax: 607-277-1940
Year Founded: 1969
Emp.: 110
Retail Automobile Dealerships
S.I.C.: 5511
John F. Wilson *(Pres.)*

No. of U.S. Offices: 2

Computer Systems/Hardware:
IBM System 36

COVALENT SYSTEMS CORPORATION
47436 Fremont Blvd.
Fremont, CA 94538-5026
Tel.: 510-683-3900 CA
Fax: 510-683-6779
Year Founded: 1982
Approx.Sls.: $20,000,000
Emp.: 140
Fiscal Year-end: 12/31/90
Business Management & Press Control Systems for the Graphic Arts Industry
S.I.C.: 7372
Dave Hannebrink *(Pres. & Chief Exec. Officer)*
Ron Burke *(Chief Fin. Officer)*
Greg Doudna *(V.P.-Customer Support)*
Paul Wyatt *(V.P.-Engrng.)*
Stephanie Palmer *(Mgr.-Mktg. Communications)*

Outside Service Firm(s):

Deloitte & Touche*(Auditors)*
60 S. Market St., Ste. 800
San Jose, CA 95113-2303
Tel.: 408-998-7111
Fax: 408-298-5782

Wilson, Sonsini, Goodrich & Rosati*(Legal Firm)*
Two Palo Alto Square
Palo Alto, CA 94304
Tel.: 415-493-9300

Silicon Valley Bank*(Major Banking Relationship)*
3000 Lakeside Dr.
Santa Clara, CA 95054

Coventry Financial, Inc.
(Name Changed to Del Webb's Coventry)

COVENTRY HOTELS ASSOCIATION
50 Kenney Pl.
Saddle Brook, NJ 07662
Tel.: 201-845-6200
Fax: 201-843-7172
Year Founded: 1912
Approx.Sls.: $30,000,000
Emp.: 2,300
Inns, Hotels, Resorts
S.I.C.: 7011
Gary Avigne *(Pres.)*
Gerald Katz *(Mgr.-Mktg.)*

COVINGTON FOODS, INC.
316 Second St.
Covington, IN 47932
Tel.: 317-793-2352 IN
Fax: 317-793-0209
Year Founded: 1959
Approx.Sls.: $38,000,000
Emp.: 335
Supermarkets
S.I.C.: 5411
Donald A. Clark *(Pres.)*
Jeff Clark *(V.P.)*
Margaret Clark *(Treas. & Sec.)*

Outside Service Firm(s):

Bank of Western Indiana*(Major Banking Relationship)*
Covington, IN

COVINGTON INDUSTRIES
2625 Cumberland Pkwy.
Atlanta, GA 30339
Tel.: 404-434-9210
Approx.Sls.: $20,000,000
Emp.: 7
Men's, Women's & Children Slacks, Jeans, Shirts & Jackets; Gelati
S.I.C.: 2325; 2369; 2253; 2361; 2321; 2329; 2339
Sidney Timbi *(Chief Exec. Officer)*
Robert Ingram *(V.P.-Sls.)*

Subsidiary:

Game Winner, Inc. **(1)**
2625 Cumberland Pkwy., No. 205
Atlanta, GA 30339
Tel.: 404-434-9210
Fax: 404-434-9215
Emp.: 700
Hunting & Shooting Clothing
S.I.C.: 2329
Sidney Timbi *(Pres.)*
Robert F. Ingram *(V.P.-Sls. & Mktg.)*

COWBOY OIL COMPANY
2700 S. 5th Ave.
Pocatello, ID 83204
Tel.: 208-232-7814 ID
Fax: 208-234-7245
Approx.Sls.: $28,000,000
Emp.: 120

Wholesale Distributor of Petroleum Products; Gasoline Stations
S.I.C.: 5172; 5541
Dick G. Geisler *(Pres.)*
Rita Geisler *(V.P.)*
Dale D. Hancock *(V.P. & Sec.)*
Mary Jean Hancock *(V.P.)*

Outside Service Firm(s):

Hansen, Barnett & Maxwell*(Auditors)*
Salt Lake City, UT

Idaho First National Bank*(Major Banking Relationship)*
Pocatello, ID

COWDEN METAL SPECIALTIES, INC.
4626 Eucalyptus Ave.
Chino, CA 91708
Mailing Address:
P.O. Box 336
Chino, CA 91708-0336
Tel.: 909-597-7861 **CA**
Fax: 909-597-2284
Year Founded: 1958
Approx.Sls.: $12,000,000
Emp.: 200
Export
Mfg. of Metal Stampings & Sheet Metal Fabricator
S.I.C.: 3469
Earl E. Payton *(Chm. Bd., Chief Exec. Officer & Sec.)*
Nancy L. Clark *(V.P.- Fin.)*
Peter Polston *(V.P.-Sls. & Mktg.)*
Jeffery J. Stump *(V.P.-Mfg.)*
Marvin Angel *(Dir.-Engrng.)*
Kerrie King *(Dir.-Pur.)*
Rizwan Khan *(Mgr.-Quality Control)*

Outside Service Firm(s):

Alan M. Rosen*(Auditors)*
Beverly Hills, CA

Union Bank*(Major Banking Relationship)*
City of Industry, CA

Branches:

Modern Wood Products, Inc. **(1)**
14211 Ramona Ave.
Chino, CA 91710
Tel.: 909-393-0885
Gary Smith *(Mgr.-Sls.)*
Steve Smith *(Dir.-Engrng.)*

Taylor's Hitek Product Finishing, Inc. **(1)**
14450 Yorba Ave.
Chino, CA 91710
Tel.: 909-597-4838
Paint & Silkscreen
S.I.C.: 7336
John Sandoual *(Gen. Mgr.)*

Taylor's Hitek Product Finishing, Inc. **(1)**
14165 Ramona Ave.
Chino, CA 91710
Tel.: 909-597-2178
Paint & Silkscreen
S.I.C.: 7336
John Sandoual *(Gen. Mgr.)*

Taylor's Hitek Product Finishing, Inc. **(1)**
P.O. BOx 336
Chino, CA 91708
Tel.: 909-597-2178
John Sandoual *(Gen. Mgr.)*

COWEN & COMPANY
Financial Square
New York, NY 10005-3597
Tel.: 212-495-6000
Tel.: 800-221-5616
Fax: 212-495-6020
Year Founded: 1918
Assets: $811,821,287
Liabilities: $720,319,664
Net Worth: $91,501,623
Approx.Sls.: $250,000,000
Emp.: 1,300
Fiscal Year-end: 3/31/91
Security Commission Brokers
S.I.C.: 6211
Joseph M. Cohen *(Chm.)*
Edward I. Herbst *(Chief Oper. Officer & Mng. Dir.)*
Creighton Peet *(Chief Admin. Officer & Mng. Dir.)*
Charles Peterson *(Chief Fin. Officer & Mng. Dir.)*
John L. Picard *(Dir.-Mktg.)*

No. of U.S. Offices: 13
No. of Foreign Offices: 5

Computer Systems/Hardware:
IBM; Tandem

Outside Service Firm(s):

Price Waterhouse*(Auditors)*
1251 Ave. of the Americas
New York, NY 10020
Tel.: 212-819-5000
Telex: 12-6798

Wilkie, Farr, & Gallagher*(Legal Firm)*
New York, NY

COWIN & COMPANY, INC.
301 Industrial Dr.
Birmingham, AL 35211
Mailing Address:
P.O. Box 19009
Birmingham, AL 35219
Tel.: 205-945-1300 **AL**
Fax: 205-945-1441
Year Founded: 1924
Approx.Sls.: $15,000,000
Emp.: 175
Fiscal Year-end: 12/31/90
Underground & Mine Construction
S.I.C.: 1629
John J. Cowin *(Chm. Bd., Pres. & Treas.)*
Peter G. Cowin *(V.P.)*
B. M. Roberts *(V.P.)*
Dan Searcy *(Sec.)*
Alwyn Protheroe *(Chief Engineer)*
Principal(s):
John J. Cowin
Peter G. Cowin

No. of U.S. Offices: 2

Outside Service Firm(s):

Hardman, Guess, Frost & Cummings*(Auditors)*
Birmingham, AL

COWLES MAGAZINES, INC.
P.O. Box 8200,
Harrisburg, PA 17105
Approx.Sls.: $38,600,000
Emp.: 105
Fiscal Year-end: 3/31/91
Publishers of Aviation Heritage, Great Battles, America's Civil War, Military History, Wild West, Vietnam, World War II, Vegetarian Times, II Mio Cavallo
S.I.C.: 2721
Employee Matching Gifts Program: Matching Gifts to Educational Institutions, Non-Profit Radio & T.V. Stations & Charities to which the Employee Personally Belongs
Christopher Little *(Pres.)*
Hal Oringer *(V.P.-Circulation & Mktg.)*
Phil Penny *(V.P.-Fin.)*
Steve Norton *(Gen. Mgr.-Life Style Grp.)*
Harry Myers *(Gen. Mgr.-Outdoor Skills Grp.)*
Nick Elsner *(V.P.-Production)*
Patricia Graybill *(Adv. Promo. Coord.)*

Subsidiaries:

Empire Press **(1)**
602 S. King St., Ste. 300
Leesburg, VA 22075
Tel.: 703-771-9400
S.I.C.: 2721

Vegetarian Times **(1)**
P.O. Box 570
Oak Park, IL 60303
Tel.: 708-848-8100
Fax: 708-848-8175
S.I.C.: 2721

COWLES MEDIA COMPANY
329 Portland Ave.
Minneapolis, MN 55415
Tel.: 612-673-7100 **DE**
Fax: 612-673-7020
Year Founded: 1935
Assets: $237,640,000
Earnings: $10,231,000
Liabilities: $256,700,072,000
Net Worth: $256,462,432,000
Approx.Sls.: $303,574,000
Emp.: 2,808
Fiscal Year-end: 3/28/92
Newspaper Publisher
S.I.C.: 2711
Corporate Giving Program: Contributes 5% Pretax Earnings; Emphasis on Contributions that Improve Life in Community, Literacy & Other Programs on Communication
David Kruidenier *(Chm. Bd.)*
David C. Cox *(Pres. & Chief Exec. Officer)*
Roger P. Parkinson *(Exec. V.P.)*
James A. Alcott *(V.P.-Admin.)*
John Grieman *(V.P.)*
Pamela Sveinson *(V.P.-Human Resources)*
James J. Viera *(V.P. & Chief Fin. Officer)*
Karen Larson *(Treas.)*
William R. Busch, Jr. *(Sec.)*

No. of U.S. Offices: 6

Computer Systems/Hardware:
IBM

Outside Service Firm(s):

KPMG Peat Marwick*(Auditors)*
4200 Norwest Center, 90 S. 7th St.
Minneapolis, MN 55402
Tel.: 612-341-2222

Faegre & Benson*(Legal Firm)*
2200 Norwest Ctr., 90 S. 7th St.
Minneapolis, MN 55402-3901
Tel.: 612-336-3000
Fax: 612-336-3026

First National Bank of Minneapolis*(Major Banking Relationship)*
Minneapolis, MN

Norwest Bank of Minneapolis N.A.*(Major Banking Relationship)*
P.O. Box 738, 161 N. Concord Exchange
So. St. Paul, MN 55075-0738
Tel.: 612-450-4064
Fax: 612-450-4078

Alliance Capital Management*(Pension Manager)*
1345 Avenue of the Americas
New York, NY 10017

Boatmen's Trust Company*(Pension Manager)*
100 North Broadway
St. Louis, MO 63102
Tel.: 314-466-2469

Garrison Koegh*(Pension Manager)*
New York, NY

Pacific Financial Research*(Pension Manager)*
9601 Wilshire Blvd., Ste. 828
Beverly Hills, CA 90210
Tel.: 213-278-4461
Fax: 213-278-4497

Division:

Star Tribune, Minneapolis-St. Paul **(1)**
425 Portland Ave.
Minneapolis, MN 55488
Tel.: 612-673-4000
Fax: 612-673-4359
Emp.: 2,500
Fiscal Year-end: 3/31/91
Computer Systems/Hardware:
IBM, Atex
Newspaper Publishing
S.I.C.: 2711
Corporate Giving Program: Company Will Contribute 5% of Pre-Tax Profits Annually Through Our Corporate Foundation & Cowles Media Foundation
Employee Matching Gift Program: Limited Program Focusing on Higher Education and United Way
Roger P. Parkinson *(Pres. & Publisher)*
Joel Kramer *(Exec. Editor)*
Jim Diaz *(V.P.-Adv.)*
Tom Mohr *(Classified Adv. Dir.)*
Bette Fenton *(Dir.-Pub. Rels. & Communications)*
Charles Hoag *(Dir.-Retail Adv.)*

Subsidiaries:

Cowles Magazines, Inc. **(1)**
6405 Flank Dr.
Harrisburg, PA 17105
Tel.: 717-657-9555 (100%)
Emp.: 152
Magazine Publisher
S.I.C.: 2721
Christopher M. Little *(Pres.)*

Scottsdale Publishing, Inc. **(1)**
7320 E. Earll Dr.
Scottsdale, AZ 85251
Tel.: 602-941-2300 (100%)
Emp.: 115
Newspaper Publishing
S.I.C.: 2711
Charles Pettit *(Pres. & Publisher)*

Cowles Business Media, Inc. **(1)**
6 River Bend
Stamford, CT 06907
Tel.: 203-358-9900 (100%)
Emp.: 161
Magazine Publisher
S.I.C.: 2721
Hershel B. Sarbin *(Pres. & Chief Exec. Officer)*

COWPER & SIEGFRIED
201 Ganson St.
Amherst, NY 14226
Mailing Address:
P.O. Box 1068,
Buffalo, NY 14240
Tel.: 716-675-1200 **NY**
Fax: 716-845-6895
Year Founded: 1915
Assets: $27,000,000
Liabilities: $20,000,000
Net Worth: $7,000,000
Approx.Sls.: $65,000,000
Emp.: 100
General Contractors, Construction Managers, Engineers
S.I.C.: 1522; 1541; 1542; 6512; 8711
Lewis E. Markle *(Pres. & Chief Oper. Officer)*
Richard B. Luczywek *(V.P.)*
Patricia Wallace *(Sec.)*
Jon Neenos *(Asst. Treas.)*

Computer Systems/Hardware:
Prime 750

Outside Service Firm(s):

Deloitte & Touche*(Auditors)*
50 Fountain Plaza
Buffalo, NY 14202
Tel.: 716-843-7200

Saperston & Day, P.C.*(Legal Firm)*
Buffalo, NY

Marine Midland Bank*(Major Banking Relationship)*
P.O. Box 803, 1 Marine Midland Center, 23rd Floor
Buffalo, NY 14203
Tel.: 716-841-2582

The Principal Financial Group*(Pension Manager)*
711 High St.
Des Moines, IA 50309
Tel.: 515-247-4593
Tel.: 800-543-4015

COWTOWN BOOT COMPANY
11401 Gateway W.
El Paso, TX 79936
Tel.: 915-593-2565
Approx.Sls.: $30,000,000
Emp.: 400
Wholesale, Retail & Manufacture Western Boots
S.I.C.: 3143; 5139; 5661
Paul Calcattera *(Pres.)*
Joe Calcattera *(V.P.)*
Ed Mounsey *(Comptroller)*

Outside Service Firm(s):

Diaz & Associates*(Auditors)*
El Paso, TX

Texas Commerce Bank*(Major Banking Relationship)*
P.O. Box 140
El Paso, TX 79980
Tel.: 602-253-9600

COX ADVERTISING
379 W. Broadway
New York, NY 10012
Tel.: 212-334-9141
Fax: 212-334-9179
Year Founded: 1986
Approx.Billings: $10,000,000
Emp.: 12
Consumer, Business-to-Business, Design, Direct Response & Sales Promotions
Michael Cox *(Chm. Bd. & Chief Exec. Officer)*
Jack Maged *(Pres. & Chief Oper. Officer)*
Jim Fairbrother *(Exec. V.P., Creative Dir.)*
Marc Rubin *(Sr. V.P., Assoc. Creative Dir.)*

Computer Systems/Hardware:
Macintosh

COX & COMPANY, INC.
200 Varick St., 4th Fl.
New York, NY 10014
Tel.: 212-366-0200 **NY**
Fax: 212-366-0222
Year Founded: 1944
Sales Range: $20-39 Million
Emp.: 260
Export
Mfr. of Aircraft Parts & Equipment
S.I.C.: 3728
H. George LeClerc *(Chm. Bd.)*
Warren Achenbaum *(Pres.)*
Milton M. Meinck *(V.P., Gen. Mgr. & Sec.)*
Dennis Phillips *(V.P.-Mktg.)*

Outside Service Firm(s):

Marine Midland Bank*(Major Banking Relationship)*
P.O. Box 803, 1 Marine Midland Center, 23rd Floor
Buffalo, NY 14203
Tel.: 716-841-2582

COX ENTERPRISES, INC.
1400 Lake Hearn Dr.
Atlanta, GA 30319
Mailing Address:
P.O. Box 105357,
Atlanta, GA 30348
Tel.: 404-843-5000 **GA**
Fax: 404-843-5142
Year Founded: 1968
Approx.Sls.: $2,300,000,000
Emp.: 30,000
Fiscal Year-end: 12/31/91
Broadcasting; Cable Television Systems; TV Sales Representative; Auto Auctions; Newspaper Publishing
S.I.C.: 4833; 4841; 4832; 2711; 2741; 5012
James C. Kennedy *(Chm. & Chief Exec. Officer)*
John R. Dillon *(Chief Fin. Officer & Sr. V.P.)*
Preston B. Barnett *(V.P. & Dir.-Taxation)*
John G. Boyette *(V.P. & Controller)*
Timothy W. Hughes *(V.P.-Human Resources)*
William L. Killen, Jr. *(V.P.-Plng. & Analysis)*
Alexander V. Netchvolodoff *(V.P.-Govt. Affairs)*
John C. Mellott *(Treas.)*
Richard J. Jacobson *(Asst. Treas.)*
Janet M. Lavine *(Asst. Treas. & Asst. Sec.)*
James A. Hatcher *(Sec. & Gen. Counsel)*
John H. Robinson *(Dir.-Corp. Information Systems)*
Lynda J. Stewart *(Dir.-Communications)*

Outside Service Firm(s):

Deloitte & Touche*(Auditors)*
100 Peachtree St., Ste. 1700
Atlanta, GA 30303-1943
Tel.: 404-220-1500
Fax: 404-220-1583

Aetna Life & Casualty*(Group Insurer)*
100 N. Riverside Plaza
Chicago, IL 60606

Dow, Lohnes & Albertson*(Legal Firm)*
1225 Connecticut Ave.
Washington, DC 20036
Tel.: 202-862-8000

First National Bank of Atlanta*(Major Banking Relationship)*
2 Peachtree Street N.W.
Atlanta, GA 30383

Texas Commerce Bank*(Major Banking Relationship)*
717 Travis St.
Houston, TX 77002
Tel.: 713-236-4636
Fax: 713-236-5476

Astrop Advisory Services*(Pension Manager)*
Atlanta, GA

Atlanta Capital Management*(Pension Manager)*
Atlanta, GA

Haven Capital Management*(Pension Manager)*
New York, NY
Tel.: 212-953-2327
Fax: 212-878-9044

Trust Company Bank*(Pension Manager)*
Stock Trans. Dept. P.O.B. 4625, Trust Company of Georgia Bldg.
Atlanta, GA 30302
Tel.: 404-588-7831

Division:

Cox Enterprises Newspaper Division **(1)**
1400 Lake Hearn Dr.
Atlanta, GA 30319
Tel.: 404-843-5000
Newspaper Operations
S.I.C.: 2711
David E. Easterly *(Pres.)*
Arnold Rosenfeld *(Sr. V.P.)*
Jay C. Campbell *(Grp. V.P.)*
David Scott *(V.P.)*
Caroline C. John *(V.P.-New Ventures)*
Cathey B. Coffey *(V.P.-Adv.)*
Brian G. Cooper *(V.P.-Fin. & Controller)*
James A. Cooper *(V.P.-Opers.)*
James T. McKnight *(V.P.-Telecommunications)*
James A. Hatcher *(Sec.)*

Subsidiaries:

Atlanta Newspapers **(2)**
72 Marietta St., N.W.
Atlanta, GA 30303
Tel.: 404-526-5151
Newspaper Publishing
S.I.C.: 2711
Jay R. Smith *(Publ.)*

Cox Arizona Publications, Inc. **(2)**
120 W. First Ave.
Mesa, AZ 85202
Tel.: 602-898-6500
Newspaper Publishing
S.I.C.: 2711
Miguel A. Laosa *(Publisher)*

Cox Texas Publications, Inc. **(2)**
1400 Lake Hearn Dr.
Atlanta, GA 30319
Tel.: 404-843-5000
Publishing
S.I.C.: 2711

Dayton Newspapers, Inc. **(2)**
Fourth & Ludlow Sts.
Dayton, OH 45402
Tel.: 513-225-2000
Newspaper Publishing
S.I.C.: 2711
J. Bradford Tillson *(Publisher)*

Grand Junction Newspapers, Inc. **(2)**
734 S. Seventh St.
Grand Junction, CO 81501
Tel.: 303-242-5050
Newspaper Publishing
S.I.C.: 2711
George Orbanek *(Publisher)*

Palm Beach Newspapers, Inc. **(2)**
2751 So. Dixie Hwy.
West Palm Beach, FL 33416
Tel.: 407-837-4100
Newspaper Publishing
S.I.C.: 2711
Tom A. Giuffrida *(Publisher)*

Springfield Newspapers, Inc. **(2)**
202 N. Limestone St.
Springfield, OH 45503
Tel.: 513-328-0300
Newspaper Publishing
S.I.C.: 2711
Charles R. Rinehart *(Publisher)*

Sun Printing Company **(2)**
2055 Arizona Ave.
Yuma, AZ 85364
Tel.: 602-783-3333
Printing Co.
S.I.C.: 2711
Samuel J. Pepper *(Publisher)*

Subsidiaries:

Bing Crosby Productions, Inc. **(1)**
610 South Ardmore Avenue
Los Angeles, CA 90005
Tel.: 213-487-7150
Sells Previously Produced Movies & TV Programs through Distributors & Syndicators
S.I.C.: 7822

Subsidiaries:

ASCO Music **(2)**
610 South Ardmore Avenue
Los Angeles, CA 90005
Tel.: 213-487-7150
Sells Previously Produced Movies & Television Programs through Distributors & Syndicators
S.I.C.: 7822

BeePee Music **(2)**
610 South Ardmore Avenue
Los Angeles, CA 90005
Tel.: 213-487-7150
S.I.C.: 7822

Cox Communications, Inc. **(1)**
1400 Lake Hearn Dr. N.E.
Atlanta, GA 30319
Tel.: 404-843-5000 (100%)
Holding Company for CEI's Broadcasting Division, Automobile Auction Division & Cable Division Subsidiaries
S.I.C.: 6719
John R. Dillon *(Pres.)*

Divisions:

Broadcast Division **(2)**
1400 Lake Hearn Dr. N.E.
Atlanta, GA 30319
Tel.: 404-843-5000
Radio & Television Broadcasting
S.I.C.: 4832; 4833
Nicholas D. Trigony *(Pres.)*
Kevin P. O'Brien *(Exec. V.P.-Independents)*
Michael J. Faherty *(Exec. V.P.-Radio)*
Andrew S. Fisher *(Exec. V.P.-Affiliates)*
Marc W. Morgan *(Reg. V.P.-West)*
Robert F. Neil *(Reg. V.P.-East)*
Patrick J. Gmiter *(V.P.-Mktg.)*
Thomas E. McClendon *(V.P. & Dir.-Res.)*
John J. Rouse, Jr. *(V.P. & Controller)*
John F. Swanson *(V.P.-Engrng.)*
James A. Hatcher *(Sec.)*

Subsidiaries:

KFI, Inc. **(3)**
610 S. Ardmore Ave.
Los Angeles, CA 90005
Tel.: 213-385-0101 (100%)
Radio Broadcasting
S.I.C.: 4832
Howard E. Neal *(V.P. & Gen. Mgr.)*

KTVU Inc. **(3)**
Two Jack London Sq.
Oakland, CA 94607
Tel.: 510-834-1212
Television Broadcasting
S.I.C.: 4833
Kevin P. O'Brien *(V.P. & Gen. Mgr.)*

WCKG, Inc. **(3)**
150 N. Michigan Ave., Ste. 1040
Chicago, IL 60601
Tel.: 312-781-7300
Radio Broadcasting
S.I.C.: 4832
Marc W. Morgan *(V.P. & Gen. Mgr.)*

WFTV, Inc. **(3)**
639 W. Central Blvd.
Orlando, FL 32801
Tel.: 407-841-9000
Television Broadcasting
S.I.C.: 4833
Merritt S. Rose, Jr. *(V.P. & Gen. Mgr.)*

WHIO, Inc. **(3)**
1414 Wilmington Ave.
Dayton, OH 45420
Tel.: 513-259-2111
Radio Broadcasting
S.I.C.: 4832
James R. Browning *(V.P. & Gen. Mgr.)*

Miami Valley Broadcasting Corporation, d/b/a WHIO-TV **(3)**
1414 Wilmington Ave.
Dayton, OH 45420
Tel.: 513-259-2111 (100%)
Television Broadcasting
S.I.C.: 4833
David B. Lippoff *(V.P. & Gen. Mgr.)*

WIOD, Inc. **(3)**
1401 N. Bay Causeway
Miami, FL 33141
Tel.: 305-759-4311
Radio Broadcasting
S.I.C.: 4832
Michael G. Disney *(V.P. & Gen. Mgr.)*

WKBD, Inc. **(3)**
26905 W. 11 Mile Rd.
Southfield, MI 48034
Tel.: 313-444-8500
Television Broadcasting
S.I.C.: 4833
Duane G. Kell *(V.P. & Gen. Mgr.)*

WPXI Inc., d/b/a WPXI-TV **(3)**
11 Television Hill
Pittsburgh, PA 15214
Tel.: 412-237-1100
Television Broadcasting
S.I.C.: 4833
John A. Howell, III *(V.P. & Gen. Mgr.)*

WSB, Inc. **(3)**
1601 W. Peachtree St., N.E.
Atlanta, GA 30309
Tel.: 404-897-7000 (100%)
Radio Broadcasting
S.I.C.: 4832
Robert F. Neil *(V.P. & Gen. Mgr.)*

Georgia Television Company **(3)**
1601 W. Peachtree St. N.E.
Atlanta, GA 30309
Tel.: 404-897-7000
Television Broadcasting
S.I.C.: 4833
Gregory J. Stone *(V.P. & Gen. Mgr.)*

WSB, Inc. d/b/a KLRX (FM) **(3)**
3625 N. Hall St.
Dallas, TX 75219
Tel.: 214-522-0979
Radio Broadcasting
S.I.C.: 4832
Gregg A. Lindahl *(V.P. & Gen. Mgr.)*

WSOC Radio, Inc. **(3)**
1901 N. Tryon St.
Charlotte, NC 28206
Tel.: 704-335-4700
S.I.C.: 4832
Todd P. Leiser *(V.P. & Gen. Mgr.)*

WSOC Television, Inc. **(3)**
1901 N. Tryon St.
Charlotte, NC 28206
Tel.: 704-335-4700
S.I.C.: 4833
Bruce R. Baker *(V.P. & Gen. Mgr.)*

WWRM, Inc. **(3)**
877 Executive Center Drive, W., Ste. 300
Saint Petersburg, FL 33702
Tel.: 813-576-1073
Radio Broadcasting
S.I.C.: 4832
Robert E. Huntley *(V.P. & Gen. Mgr.)*

TeleRep, Incorporated **(3)**
875 Third Ave.
New York, NY 10022
Tel.: 212-759-8787
Radio & Television Advertising Representative; Sells Time on TV Stations to National Advertisers Through Advertising Agencies
S.I.C.: 7313
Alfred M. Masini *(Pres.)*

Automobile Auction Division **(2)**
1400 Lake Hearn Drive, N.E.
Atlanta, GA 30319
Tel.: 404-843-5000 (80%)
Wholesale Automobile Auctions
S.I.C.: 5012
Warren V. Young *(Vice Chm.)*
Darryll M. Ceccoli *(Pres.)*
Robert E. Gartin *(V.P. & Chief Fin. Officer)*
Walter P. Bodine, Jr. *(V.P.-Admin.)*
Michael F. Moumousis *(V.P.-Mktg.)*
Richard E. Deckard *(V.P. & Chief Information Officer)*
David Harrison *(V.P.-Oper. West Reg.)*
John E. Stower *(V.P.-Oper. East Reg.)*
Louis A. Fazio *(V.P.-Factory/Fleet)*
Leon L. Lyon *(V.P.)*
Frank J. Mayer *(V.P.)*
Douglas E. Sifford *(V.P.)*
Donald R. Kolb *(V.P.)*
James A. Hatcher *(Sec.)*

Subsidiaries:

Arizona Auction Services, Inc., d/b/a Southwest Auto Auction **(3)**
400 No. Beck Ave.
Chandler, AZ 85226
Tel.: 602-894-2211
Wholesale Automobile Auctions
S.I.C.: 5012
Thomas A. Bishop *(Gen. Mgr.)*

Arizona Auction Services, Inc. d/b/a Arizona Auto Auction **(3)**
3420 S. 48th St.
Phoenix, AZ 85040
Tel.: 602-894-2400
Whlsle. Auto Auctions
S.I.C.: 5012
David M. Berkstresser *(Gen. Mgr.)*

Atlanta Auto Auction, Inc. **(3)**
4900 Buffington Rd.
Red Oak, GA 30272
Tel.: 404-762-9211
Wholesale Automobile Auction
S.I.C.: 5012
Charles N. Sanders *(Gen. Mgr.)*

Bay Cities Auto Auction **(3)**
29900 Auction Way
Hayward, CA 94544
Tel.: 510-786-4500
Fax: 510-786-2338
Wholesale Automobile Auctions
S.I.C.: 5012
Jack Green *(Gen. Mgr.)*

California Auto Dealers Exchange, Inc. **(3)**
1320 N. Tustin Ave.
Anaheim, CA 92817
Tel.: 714-996-2400
Wholesale Automobile Auction
S.I.C.: 5012
John Dorming *(Gen. Mgr.)*

California Auto Dealers Exchange, Inc. **(3)**
6446 Fremont Street
Riverside, CA 92504
Tel.: 914-689-6000
Wholesale Automobile Auction
S.I.C.: 5012
Robert Mowers *(Gen. Mgr.)*

Clanton's Auto Auction **(3)**
Highway 34 West
Darlington, SC 29532
Tel.: 803-393-2861
Fax: 803-395-1521
Wholesale Automobile Auctions
S.I.C.: 5012
Ray Clanton, Sr. *(Gen. Mgr.)*

Colorado Auction Services Corporation **(3)**
6955 E. 50th Ave.
Commerce City, CO 80022
Tel.: 303-287-8077
Wholesale Auto Auction
S.I.C.: 5012
Bradley Sturgeon *(Gen. Mgr.)*

Dealers Auto Auction of Dallas, Inc. **(3)**
2717 East Main
Grand Prairie, TX 75050
Tel.: 214-642-3900
Wholesale Auto Auction
S.I.C.: 5012
Anthony J. Giurato *(Gen. Mgr.)*

Denver Auto Auction **(3)**
17400 E. 31st Ave.
Aurora, CO 80011
Tel.: 303-343-3443
Fax: 303-343-6466
Wholesale Automobile Auctions
S.I.C.: 5012
Dave Caflik *(Gen. Mgr.)*

Florida Auction Services Corporation **(3)**
310 County Line Rd.
Lakeland, FL 33805
Tel.: 813-688-8458
Wholesale Auto Auction
S.I.C.: 5012
Nicholas R. Pund *(Gen. Mgr.)*

Florida Auto Auction of Orlando, Inc. **(3)**
600 West Hwy. 50
Ocoee, FL 32761
Tel.: 407-656-6200
Wholesale Auto Auction
S.I.C.: 5012
Joseph C. Greco *(Gen. Mgr.)*

Fort Worth Auto Auction **(3)**
2245 Jacksboro Hwy.
Fort Worth, TX 76114
Tel.: 817-626-5494
Fax: 817-624-2207
Wholesale Automobile Auctions
S.I.C.: 5012
Jim Scott *(Gen. Mgr.)*

Fredericksburg Auto Auction **(3)**
4907 Jefferson Davis Hwy.
Fredericksburg, VA 22401
Tel.: 703-898-4900
Wholesale Auto Auction
S.I.C.: 5012
James G. Grab *(Gen. Mgr.)*

Fresno Auto Dealers Auction **(3)**
278 North Marks
Fresno, CA 93706
Tel.: 209-268-8051
Wholesale Automobile Auctions
S.I.C.: 5012
Rodney J. Hacker *(Gen. Mgr.)*

Georgia Auction Services, Inc. **(3)**
2244 Stewart Avenue
Atlanta, GA 30315
Tel.: 404-766-5461
Wholesale Automobile Auction
S.I.C.: 5012
Gary M. Charlesworth *(Gen. Mgr.)*

Georgia Auction Services, Inc. d/b/a Community Aution Resale Services **(3)**
5900 Brook Hollow Parkway
Norcross, GA 30071
Tel.: 404-441-2277
Wholesale Auto Auction
S.I.C.: 5012
William R. Kuhn *(Gen. Mgr.)*

Georgia Dealers Auto Auction **(3)**
7205 Campbellton Rd.
Atlanta, GA 30331
Tel.: 404-349-5555
Fax: 404-349-9951
Wholesale Automobile Auctions
S.I.C.: 5012
Charles Sanders *(Gen. Mgr.)*

Greater Chicago Auto Auction **(3)**
12000 S. Cicero Ave.
Chicago, IL 60658
Tel.: 708-597-3600
Fax: 708-597-1692
Wholesale Automobile Auction
S.I.C.: 5012
Greg Kobel *(Gen. Mgr.)*

Greater Tampa Bay Auto Auction **(3)**
401 S. 50th St.
Tampa, FL 33619
Tel.: 813-247-1666
Fax: 813-247-1714
Wholesale Automobile Auctions
S.I.C.: 5012
Nick Pund *(Gen. Mgr.)*

Harrisonburg Auto Auction **(3)**
Exit 62 & Interstate 81, 3560 Early Rd.
Harrisonburg, VA 22801
Tel.: 703-434-5991
Fax: 703-434-6813
Wholesale Automobile Auction
S.I.C.: 5012
Jim Wheatley *(Gen. Mgr.)*

Kansas City Auto Auction **(3)**
3901 No. Great Midwest Dr.
Kansas City, MO 64161
Tel.: 816-452-4084
Wholesale Automobile Auctions
S.I.C.: 5012
James E. Orr *(Gen. Mgr.)*

Lakeland Auto Auction **(3)**
P.O. Box 90007, Interstate 4 & Hwy. 33
Lakeland, FL 33804
Tel.: 813-984-1551
Wholesale Automobile Auction
S.I.C.: 5012
Cliff Patterson *(Gen. Mgr.)*

Los Angeles Dealers Auto Auctions **(3)**
8001 Garvey Ave.
Rosemead, CA 92770-1053
Tel.: 818-573-8001
Fax: 818-307-0491
Wholesale Automobile Auctions
S.I.C.: 5012
John Duca *(Gen. Mgr.)*

Minneapolis Auto Auction **(3)**
8001 Jefferson Hwy.
Maple Grove, MN 55369
Tel.: 612-425-7653
Wholesale Automobile Auctions
S.I.C.: 5012
Chuck Eck *(Gen. Mgr.)*

Missouri Auction Services Corp. d/b/a 166 Auto Action **(3)**
2944 West Sunshine
Springfield, MO 65807
Tel.: 417-882-1666
Wholesale Automobile Auction
S.I.C.: 5012
Jamie D. Porter *(Gen. Mgr.)*

New England Auto Auction, Inc. **(3)**
123 Williams St.
North Dighton, MA 02764
Tel.: 508-823-6600
Wholesale Automobile Auctions
S.I.C.: 5012
John F. Sirianni *(Gen. Mgr.)*

National Auto Dealers Exchange **(3)**
P.O. Box 188, Route 206 S.
Bordentown, NJ 08505
Tel.: 609-298-3400
Wholesale Automobile Auctions
S.I.C.: 5012
Jack N. Leauber *(Gen. Mgr.)*

Newburgh Auto Auction **(3)**
Route 17K, P.O. Box 2426
Newburgh, NY 12550
Tel.: 914-562-0700
Fax: 914-562-0095
Wholesale Automobile Auctions
S.I.C.: 5012
Keith Williams *(Gen. Mgr.)*

Ohio Auto Auction **(3)**
3905 Jackson Pike
Columbus, OH 43123
Tel.: 614-871-2771
Fax: 614-871-6831
Wholesale Automobile Auctions
S.I.C.: 5012
David Munnikhuysen *(Gen. Mgr.)*

Pennsylvania Services Corporation **(3)**
Kramer Road
Gibsonia, PA 15044
Tel.: 412-443-7211
Wholesale Automobile Auctions
S.I.C.: 5012
Tom Davis *(Gen. Mgr.)*

Pennsylvania Services Corp. **(3)**
R.D. 1, Route 72
Manheim, PA 17545
Tel.: 717-665-3571 (100%)
Wholesale Automobile Auctions
S.I.C.: 5012
M. Gregory Gehman *(Gen. Mgr.)*

Portland Auto Auction **(3)**
3000 N. Hayden Island Dr.
Portland, OR 97217
Tel.: 503-286-3000
Fax: 503-283-3317
Fax: 503-286-3899
Wholesale Automobile Auction
S.I.C.: 5012
John Honegger *(Gen. Mgr.)*

St. Louis Auto Auction **(3)**
13813 St. Charles Rock Rd.
Bridgeton, MO 63045
Tel.: 314-739-1300
Fax: 314-739-1301
Wholesale Automobile Auctions
S.I.C.: 5012
Dutch Hauhe *(Gen. Mgr.)*

St. Pete Auto Auction **(3)**
14950 Roosevelt Blvd.
Clearwater, FL 34622
Tel.: 813-531-7717
Fax: 813-539-0912
Wholesale Automobile Auctions
S.I.C.: 5012
Joe Carollo *(Gen. Mgr.)*

San Antonio Auto Auction **(3)**
1500 Ackerman Rd.
San Antonio, TX 78219
Tel.: 210-661-4200
Wholesale Automobile Auctions
S.I.C.: 5012
Jeff Corigliano *(Gen. Mgr.)*

South Seattle Auto Auction **(3)**
19443 77th Ave. So.
Kent, WA 98064-5189
Tel.: 206-872-6800
Fax: 206-395-3342
Wholesale Automobile Auctions
S.I.C.: 5012
Greg Mahugh *(Gen. Mgr.)*

Southern California Auto Auction **(3)**
10700 Beech Ave.
Fontana, CA 92335
Tel.: 909-822-2261
Fax: 909-829-1370
Wholesale Automobile Auctions
S.I.C.: 5012
Rob Mowers *(Gen. Mgr.)*

Cox Enterprises, Inc.—(Continued)

Texas Auto Auction Services, Inc. d/b/a Big H Auto Auction **(3)**
14450 West Rd.
Houston, TX 77041
Tel.: 713-890-4300
Wholesale Automobile Auctions
S.I.C.: 5012
Thomas J. Nohstadt *(Gen. Mgr.)*

Texas Hobby Auto Auction **(3)**
800 Brisbane Rd.
Houston, TX 77061
Tel.: 713-649-8233
Fax: 713-640-8315
Wholesale Automobile Auctions
S.I.C.: 5012
Jim Smythe *(Gen. Mgr.)*

Utah Auto Auction **(3)**
1650 W. 500 S.
West Bountiful, UT 84087
Tel.: 801-298-7900
Fax: 801-298-9209
Wholesale Auto Auctions
S.I.C.: 5012
Dave McComb *(Gen. Mgr.)*

Wisconsin Services Corp. **(3)**
561 S. Highway 41
Caledonia, WI 53108
Tel.: 414-835-4436
Wholesale Automobile Auctions
S.I.C.: 5012
Dennis B. Worthy *(Gen. Mgr.)*

Cable Division **(2)**
1400 Lake Hearn Dr., N.E.
Atlanta, GA 30319
Tel.: 404-843-5000
Cable Television
S.I.C.: 4899
James O. Robbins *(Pres.)*
Jimmy W. Hayes *(Sr. V.P.-Fin. & Admin.)*
Barry R. Elson *(Sr. V.P.-Opers.)*
Robert C. O'Leary *(Sr. V.P.-Opers.)*
Ajit M. Dalvi *(Sr. V.P.-Mktg.)*
Alex B. Best *(Sr. V.P.-Engrng.)*
David C. Andersen *(V.P.-Public Affairs)*
L. Roy Prater *(V.P.-Mngmt. Information Systems)*
Patrick J. Esser *(V.P.-Adv. Sls.)*
Judy S. Henke *(V.P.-Human Resources)*
Robert N. Redella *(V.P.-Programing & Investments)*
Terri Thompsen *(V.P.-Mktg.)*
Richard A. Mueller *(V.P.-Engrng.)*
David M. Woodrow *(V.P.-Opers.)*
James A. Hatcher *(Sec.)*

Subsidiaries:

Cox Cable Bakersfield, Inc. **(3)**
820 22nd St.
Bakersfield, CA 93301
Tel.: 805-327-0821
Cable Television
S.I.C.: 4841
Peter Leveroni *(V.P. & Gen. Mgr.)*

Cox Cable Cedar Rapids, Inc. **(3)**
1939 Blairs Ferry Road, N.E.
Cedar Rapids, IA 52402
Tel.: 319-395-7960
Cable Television
S.I.C.: 4841
Charles V. DiToro *(V.P. & Gen. Mgr.)*

Cox Cable Cleveland Area, Inc. **(3)**
12221 Plaza Dr.
Parma, OH 44130
Tel.: 216-676-8300
Cable Television
S.I.C.: 4841
Ronald A. Hammaker *(V.P. & Gen. Mgr.)*

Cox Cable Rhode Island, Inc. **(3)**
111 Comstock Parkway
Cranston, RI 02920
Tel.: 401-943-7930
Cable Television
S.I.C.: 4841
Gary M. Perrelli *(V.P. & Gen. Mgr.)*

Cox Cable Greater Hartford, Inc. **(3)**
801 Parker Street
Manchester, CT 06040
Tel.: 203-646-6400
Cable Television
S.I.C.: 4841
Jayson R. Juraska *(V.P. & Gen. Mgr.)*

Cox Cable Hampton Roads, Inc. **(3)**
5200 Cleveland Street
Virginia Beach, VA 23462
Tel.: 804-497-1071
Cable Television
S.I.C.: 4841
Franklin R. Bowers *(V.P. & Gen. Mgr.)*

Cox Cable Humboldt, Inc. **(3)**
911 W. Wabash
Eureka, CA 95501
Tel.: 707-443-3127
Cable Television
S.I.C.: 4841
Dorothy A. Lovfald *(V.P. & Gen. Mgr.)*

Cox Cable Jefferson Parish, Inc. **(3)**
338 Edwards Ave.
Harahan, LA 70123
Tel.: 504-733-5680
Cable Television
S.I.C.: 4841
William K. Geppert *(Gen. Mgr.)*

Cox Cable Lubbock, Inc. **(3)**
6710 Hartford Avenue
Lubbock, TX 79413
Tel.: 806-793-7475
Cable Television
S.I.C.: 4841
Frank R. Wink *(V.P. & Gen. Mgr.)*

Cox Cable Middle Georgia, Inc. **(3)**
252 Holt Ave.
Macon, GA 31201
Tel.: 912-745-4145
Cable Television
S.I.C.: 4841
Claus F. Kroeger *(V.P. & Gen. Mgr.)*

Cox Cable New Orleans, Inc. **(3)**
2120 Canal Street
New Orleans, LA 70112
Tel.: 504-522-3838
Cable Television
S.I.C.: 4841
C. Ray Nagin *(V.P. & Gen. Mgr.)*

Cox Cable Greater Ocala, Inc. **(3)**
2410 S.W. 27th Street
Ocala, FL 32674
Tel.: 904-854-0055
Cable Television
S.I.C.: 4841
Gary E. Cassard *(V.P. & Gen. Mgr.)*

Cox Cable Oklahoma City, Inc. **(3)**
2312 N.W. 10th Street
Oklahoma City, OK 73107
Tel.: 405-525-2771
Cable Television
S.I.C.: 4841
J. Curt Hockemeier *(V.P. & Gen. Mgr.)*

Cox Cable Omaha, Inc. **(3)**
11505 W. Dodge Rd.
Omaha, NE 68154
Tel.: 402-330-2314
Cable Television
S.I.C.: 4841
Richard A. Hook *(V.P. & Gen. Mgr.)*

Cox Cable Pensacola, Inc. **(3)**
2205 LaVista Ave.
Pensacola, FL 32504
Tel.: 904-477-2695
Cable Television
S.I.C.: 4841
Larry F. Lewis *(V.P. & Gen. Mgr.)*

Cox Cable Quad Cities, Inc. **(3)**
3900 26th Ave.
Moline, IL 61265
Tel.: 309-797-2580
Cable Television
S.I.C.: 4841
Kay A. Galligan *(V.P. & Gen. Mgr.)*

Cox Cable Roanoke, Inc. **(3)**
1909 Salem Ave. S.W.
Roanoke, VA 24016
Tel.: 703-982-1110
Cable Television
S.I.C.: 4841
Bernard W. Langheim *(V.P. & Gen. Mgr.)*

Cox Cable Saginaw, Inc. **(3)**
720 North Bates St.
Saginaw, MI 48602
Tel.: 517-799-5080
Cable Television
S.I.C.: 4841
Darrell F. Wells *(V.P. & Gen. Mgr.)*

Cox Cable San Diego, Inc. **(3)**
5159 Federal Blvd.
San Diego, CA 92105
Tel.: 619-263-9251
Cable Television
S.I.C.: 4841
Robert G. McRann *(V.P. & Gen. Mgr.)*

Cox Cable Santa Barbara, Inc. **(3)**
22 S. Fairview
Goleta, CA 93117
Tel.: 805-683-7751
Cable Television
S.I.C.: 4841
Thomas H. Leone *(V.P. & Gen. Mgr.)*

Cox Cable South Carolina, Inc. **(3)**
1907 Oak Street
Myrtle Beach, SC 29577
Tel.: 803-448-7858
Cable Television
S.I.C.: 4841
Gretchen Shine *(V.P. & Gen. Mgr.)*

Cox Cable Spokane, Inc. **(3)**
1717 E. Buckeye
Spokane, WA 99207
Tel.: 509-484-4931
Cable Television
S.I.C.: 4841
Alan D. Collins *(V.P. & Gen. Mgr.)*

Cox Cable Staten Island (Partnership) **(3)**
100 Cable Way
Staten Island, NY 10303
Tel.: 718-447-7000
Cable Television
S.I.C.: 4899

Cox Cable University City, Inc. **(3)**
1115 N.W. 4th Street
Gainesville, FL 32601
Tel.: 904-377-2368
Cable Television
S.I.C.: 4841
Joseph F. Brewster *(V.P. & Gen. Mgr.)*

Video Service Company **(3)**
1400 Lake Hearn Dr. N.E.
Atlanta, GA 30319
Tel.: 404-843-5000
Cable Television
S.I.C.: 4841

CableRep, Inc. **(3)**
1400 Lake Hearn Drive, N.E.
Atlanta, GA 30319
Tel.: 404-843-5000
Cable Sales Representation Firm; Selling Advertising on Cox's Cable Television Systems
S.I.C.: 7313

Non-U.S. Holdings:

Manheim's Oshawa Dealers Exchange **(1)**
Hwy. 401 at Exit 425 Cortice Road,
Newcastle, ON Canada
Tel.: 416-428-6633
Tel.: 416-576-6633
Auto Auction
S.I.C.: 5012
Michael V. Kelly *(Auction Mgr.)*

Toronto Auto Auction **(1)**
8277 Lawson Road
Milton, ON Canada
Tel.: 416-275-3000
Auto Auction
S.I.C.: 5012
Ruth Hart-Stephens *(Gen. Mgr.)*

COX FURNITURE
Highway 74 W.
Maxton, NC 28364
Tel.: 919-844-3501
Fax: 919-844-3960
Mfr. Case Goods
S.I.C.: 2512
Charles Cox *(Pres. & Owner)*
Richard Cox *(V.P. & Sec.)*
Andy Bliggi *(Chief Fin. Officer)*

Outside Service Firm(s):

Dickson Odom & Co.*(Auditors)*
6525 Morrison Blvd. #516
Charlotte, NC 28211
Tel.: 704-364-5414

First Scotland Bank*(Major Banking Relationship)*
Laurinburg, NC

Subsidiary:

Selig Manufacturing Company **(1)**
Hwy. 421 N.
Siler City, NC 27344
Tel.: 919-742-4126
Fax: 919-742-2164
Assets: $4,000,000
Liabilities: $3,100,000
Net Worth: $900,000
Sales Range: $10-19 Million
Fiscal Year-end: 6/30/91
Manufacture Upholstered Furniture
S.I.C.: 2512
Andy Bliggi *(Chief Oper. Officer)*

COX HOBBIES, INC.
350 W. Rincon St.
Corona, CA 91720
Tel.: 909-278-1282
Fax: 909-278-2981
Approx.Sls.: $12,000,000
Emp.: 145
Import Export
Mfr. of Model Airplanes, Cars, Radio Systems, Engines & Accessories
S.I.C.: 3944
Doy B. Henley *(Chm. Bd.)*
William H. Selzer *(Pres. & Chief Exec. Officer)*
Ronald L. Koberg *(V.P. & Chief Oper. Officer)*
Chris Sousoures *(V.P.-Fin. & Controller)*
Patricia Moore *(Mgr.-Sls.)*
Dennis Riggs *(Mgr.-Mktg.)*

No. of Mfg. Plants/Facilities: 1
No. of U.S. Offices: 1

Computer Systems/Hardware:
IBM System 36

Outside Service Firm(s):

Union Bank*(Major Banking Relationship)*
Trust Dept., 8155 Mercury Ct.
San Diego, CA 92112
Tel.: 619-230-4487

COX LANDEY
AND PARTNERS, INC.

COX LANDEY AND PARTNERS, INC.
501 Madison Ave.
New York, NY 10022
Tel.: 212-838-5900
Fax: 212-486-7982
Approx.Billings: $35,000,000
Martin H. Landey *(Chm. & Chief Exec. Officer)*
Bob Cox *(Pres. & Creative Dir.)*
Terence Galvin *(V.P., Opers. & Production)*
Fran Bainbridge *(Comptroller)*

COX LUMBER CO.
3300 Fairfield Ave. S.
Saint Petersburg, FL 33712
Tel.: 813-327-4503
Fax: 813-327-5393
Approx.Sls.: $63,800,000
Emp.: 510
Retail Lumber & Other Building Materials
S.I.C.: 5211

Linton N. Tibbetts *(Chm. Bd. & Chief Exec. Officer)*
Robert Fehr *(Pres.)*
Russell P. Brandes *(Exec. V.P.-Fin.)*
Juan Quesada *(Exec. V.P.-Sls., Mktg. & Adv.)*
Daniel Tibbetts *(Exec. V.P.-Intl. Opers.)*
Arlen Tillis *(V.P.-Sls. & Mktg.)*

Outside Service Firm(s):

Grant Thornton*(Auditors)*
St. Petersburg, FL

Southeast Bank, N.A.*(Major Banking Relationship)*
Tampa, FL

COX WOOD PRESERVING CO.
Cannon Bridge Rd.
Orangeburg, SC 29116
Mailing Address:
P.O. Box 1124,
Orangeburg, SC 29116
Tel.: 803-534-7467 **SC**
Fax: 803-534-6328
Approx.Sls.: $34,000,000
Emp.: 180
Fiscal Year-end: 12/31/91
Manufacture & Wholesale Pressure-Treated Lumber & Related Wood Products
S.I.C.: 2491; 5031
William B. Cox *(Chm. Bd.)*
William B. Cox, Jr. *(Pres.)*
James D. Johnson *(V.P. & Treas.)*
H.E. Brickle *(Chief Credit Officer)*
Carl Mutch *(Chief Information Officer)*
Lovett Kitchens *(Sec.)*
Greg Campbell *(Dir.-Quality Control)*
Dixie Headden *(Dir.-Telecommunications)*
Cathy Johnson *(Dir.-Employee Benefits)*
Bruce Palmer *(Mgr.-Sls.)*

Outside Service Firm(s):

J. W. Hunt & Co.*(Auditors)*
Middleburg Office Park, 1607 St. Julian Place
Columbia, SC 29202
Tel.: 803-254-8196

Horger, Horger & Barnwell*(Legal Firm)*
Orangeburg, SC

First National Bank of Orangeburg*(Major Banking Relationship)*
Orangeburg, SC

J.B. COXWELL CONTRACT, INC.
6741 Lloyd Rd. W.
Jacksonville, FL 32254-1249
Tel.: 904-786-1120
Fax: 904-783-2970
Approx.Sls.: $15,000,000
Emp.: 130
Grading & Paving Contractor
S.I.C.: 1611
John B. Coxwell *(Pres.)*
Keith Corwin *(V.P.)*
Frances Coxwell *(Sec. & Treas.)*

Outside Service Firm(s):

William H. O'Byrne*(Auditors)*
Jacksonville, FL

CRADDOCK DEVELOPMENT CO., INC.
228 N. Cascade, Ste. 301
Colorado Springs, CO 80903
Mailing Address:
P.O. Box 2929
Colorado Springs, CO 80901
Tel.: 719-630-2233 **CO**
Fax: 719-630-2239
Year Founded: 1968
Assets: $67,695,982
Liabilities: $84,188,945
Net Worth: $16,492,963
Approx.Sls.: $51,000,000
Emp.: 400
Fiscal Year-end: 12/31/89
Subdivides & Develops Hotel, Commercial & Industrial Buildings, Marketing & Leasing
S.I.C.: 1541; 1542; 6512; 6531; 6552; 7011
James Berry Craddock *(Pres.)*
Ronald L. Walden *(Exec. V.P.)*
Marcia Roe-Wentworth *(Controller)*
Principal(s):
James Berry Craddock

Outside Service Firm(s):

Deloitte & Touche*(Auditors)*
Ste. 200, Two Windsor Dr., 7540 Windsor Dr.
Allentown, PA 18195
Tel.: 215-366-5100

Lawrence Hamil*(Legal Firm)*
Denver, CO

First Bank of Westland*(Major Banking Relationship)*
Denver, CO

Crafco, Inc.
(See listing under Craddock Development Co., Inc.)

CRAFTEX MILLS INC. OF PENNSYLVANIA
450 Sentry Parkway
Blue Bell, PA 19422-0795
Mailing Address:
P.O. Box 3017
Blue Bell, PA 19422-0795
Tel.: 215-941-1212 **PA**
Fax: 215-941-7171
Year Founded: 1903
Assets: $13,000,000
Liabilities: $8,500,000
Net Worth: $4,500,000
Approx.Sls.: $27,500,000
Emp.: 260
Fiscal Year-end: 12/31/90
Export
Manufacture Upholstery Materials & Fabrics
S.I.C.: 2211; 2221; 2231
Jeffrey A. Seder *(Chm. Bd.)*
Robert M. Blum *(Pres.)*
Jack Egar *(V.P.-Mktg.)*
Robert Proske *(V.P.-Fin.)*
Bruce Shawlis *(Dir.-Pur.)*

No. of Mfg. Plants/Facilities: 2
No. of U.S. Offices: 7

Outside Service Firm(s):

Coopers & Lybrand*(Auditors)*
2400 Eleven Penn Center
Philadelphia, PA 19103-2962
Tel.: 215-963-8000

Kleinbard, Bell & Brecker*(Legal Firm)*
30 S. 17th St.
Philadelphia, PA 19103
Tel.: 215-568-2000

CoreStates First Pennsylvania Bank, N.A.*(Major Banking Relationship)*
1500 Chestnut
Philadelphia, PA 19102

CRAFTY BEAVER HOME CENTER
4811 Oakton
Skokie, IL 60076
Tel.: 708-677-2106 **IL**
Fax: 708-677-2155
Approx.Sls.: $10,000,000
Emp.: 200
Retail Building & Related Products
S.I.C.: 5211
Donald R. Beres *(Chm. Bd.)*
Gary S. Beres *(Pres.)*
Richard R. Olswang *(V.P. & Treas.)*
Paul M. Puttrich *(V.P. & Pur. Agent)*
Ray Votzmeyer *(Adv. Mgr.)*

Outside Service Firm(s):

Glenn Ingram & Co.*(Auditors)*
Chicago, IL

Winston & Strawn*(Legal Firm)*
One 1st Natl. Plaza, No. 5000
Chicago, IL 60603
Tel.: 312-558-5600

North Shore National Bank*(Major Banking Relationship)*
Chicago, IL

CRAIN COMMUNICATIONS, INC.
1400 Woodbridge Ave.
Detroit, MI 48207
Tel.: 312-649-5200 **IL**
Fax: 312-280-3179
Year Founded: 1916
Approx.Sls.: $150,000,000
Emp.: 900
Fiscal Year-end: 2/31/91
Publishes Business, Trade & Consumer Periodicals
S.I.C.: 2711; 2721
Gertrude R. Crain *(Chm. Bd.)*
S.R. Bernstein *(Chm.-Exec. Committee)*
Keith E. Crain *(Vice Chm.)*
Rance E. Crain *(Pres.)*
William Morrow *(Exec. V.P.-Opers.)*
Joe Cappo *(Sr. V.P. & Grp. Publisher)*
Robert C. Adams *(V.P.-Production)*
William Strong *(V.P.-Circulation)*
Mary Kay Crain *(Treas.)*
Merrilee P. Crain *(Sec.)*
Frances Scott *(Dir.-Personnel)*
Penelope A. Geismar *(Mgr.-Corp. Communications)*

Computer Systems/Hardware:
IBM

Outside Service Firm(s):

Rollins Burdick Hunter*(Group Insurer)*
123 N. Wacker Dr.
Chicago, IL 60606
Tel.: 312-701-4000

Fiduciary Management, Inc.*(Pension Manager)*
Chicago, IL

Loomis, Sayles & Co., Inc.*(Pension Manager)*
3 First National Plaza, Suite 5450
Chicago, IL
Tel.: 312-346-9750

Renaissance Invest. Mgmt.*(Pension Manager)*
Cincinnati, OH

Publications:

Advertising Age **(1)**
740 N. Rush St.
Chicago, IL 60611
Tel.: 312-649-5200
Fax: 312-649-5331
Approx.Sls.: $35,000,000
Emp.: 100
Fiscal Year-end: 12/31/90
Advertising & Marketing Magazine
S.I.C.: 2721
Gertrude Crain *(Chm. Bd.)*
Keith Crain *(Vice Chm.)*
Rance Crain *(Pres. & Editor-in-Chief)*
Joe Cappo *(Sr. V.P.-Publishing Dir.)*
Edward R. Erhardt *(Publisher)*
Dennis Chase *(Exec. Editor)*
Fred Danzig *(Editor)*
Christina M. Frohock *(Dir.-Mktg. & Communications)*
Dave Kelley *(Circulation Mgr.)*

Automotive News **(1)**
1400 Woodbridge Ave.
Detroit, MI 48207
Tel.: 313-446-6000
Fax: 313-446-1680
Magazine Covering Current Events & Developments in the Automotive Trade
S.I.C.: 2721
Keith E. Crain *(Publisher)*

Business Insurance **(1)**
740 Rush St.
Chicago, IL 60611-2590
Tel.: 312-649-5275
Fax: 312-280-3174
Fax: 312-649-7799
Weekly Magazine Covering Risk Management, Insurance, Reinsurance
S.I.C.: 2721
Kathryn J. McIntyre *(Publisher)*

Business Marketing **(1)**
740 Rush St.
Chicago, IL 60611
Tel.: 312-649-5260
Fax: 312-649-5462
Monthly Magazine Covering Marketing, Sales & Advertising of Business-to-Business Products & Services
S.I.C.: 2721
J. Clifford Mulcahy *(Publisher)*

City & State **(1)**
740 Rush St.
Chicago, IL 60611
Tel.: 312-649-5220
Fax: 312-649-7799
Biweekly Business Newspaper for Government Managers
S.I.C.: 2711
Dan Miller *(Publisher)*

Crain's Chicago Business **(1)**
740 Rush St.
Chicago, IL 60611
Tel.: 312-649-5370
Fax: 312-649-5415
Chicago Metropolitan Area Business News & Information
S.I.C.: 2721
Gloria Scoby *(V.P. & Publisher)*

Crain's Cleveland Business **(1)**
700 West St. Clair
Cleveland, OH 44113
Tel.: 216-522-1383
Fax: 216-694-4264
Cleveland Metropolitan Area Business News & Information
S.I.C.: 2721
Brian Tucker *(Publisher/Editorial Dir.)*

Crain's Detroit Business **(1)**
1400 Woodbridge Ave.
Detroit, MI 48207-3187
Tel.: 313-446-6032
Fax: 313-446-1680
Detroit Metropolitan Business News & Information
S.I.C.: 2721
Keith E. Crain *(Publisher)*

Crain's New York Business **(1)**
220 E. 42nd St.
New York, NY 10017
Tel.: 212-210-0259
Fax: 212-210-0799
New York Local Business News & Information
S.I.C.: 2721
Alair Townsend *(Publisher)*

Electronic Media **(1)**
740 Rush St.
Chicago, IL 60611
Tel.: 312-649-5200
Weekly Magazine Concerning Management of Broadcast Media
S.I.C.: 2721
Ron Aldridge *(V.P. & Editor/Publisher)*

Modern Healthcare **(1)**
740 Rush St.
Chicago, IL 60611
Tel.: 312-649-5341
Fax: 312-280-3189
Monthly Magazine Covering the Business Aspects of Healthcare Management
S.I.C.: 2721
Charles S. Lauer *(Publisher)*

Pensions & Investments **(1)**
740 Rush St.
Chicago, IL 60611
Tel.: 312-649-5280
Magazine Published 27 Times Yearly Covering News for Credit, Capital & Investment Management
S.I.C.: 2721
William T. Bisson *(V.P. & Publisher)*

Crain Communications, Inc.—(Continued)

RCR Publications **(1)**
1728 Downing St.
Denver, CO 80218
Tel.: 303-832-6000
Publisher of RCR Radio Communications Report, a Newspaper for the Wireless Communication Industry
S.I.C.: 2721
John Sudmeier *(Publisher)*

Non-U.S. Holding:

Advertising Age International **(1)**
Cowcross Court 75-77 Cowcross St.,
London, EC1M 6BP, United Kingdom
Tel.: 071-608-2774 (100%)
Fax: 071-608-1173
International Advertising News Magazine
S.I.C.: 2731
Nancy Giges *(Intl. Editor)*
Julie Skur Hill *(Asst. Intl. Editor)*
Laurel Wentz *(European Editor)*
Ilse Cermak *(Intl. Copy Editor)*
Geoffrey Shives *(Design Dir.)*

CRAMER COMPANY
139 Mill Rock Rd. E.
Old Saybrook, CT 06475-1261
Tel.: 203-388-3574
Fax: 203-388-9831
Year Founded: 1936
Approx.Sls.: $15,000,000
Emp.: 130
Fiscal Year-end: 10/31/91
Import Export
Manufactures Reset, Interval, Cycle, Delay Timers & Elapsed Time Indicators, Subfractional Motors
S.I.C.: 3625
James W. Pogmore *(Pres.)*
Everett Latourette *(Reg. Sls. & Adv. Mgr.)*
Warren James *(Pur. Mgr.)*
Allan G. Larson *(Reg. Sls. Mgr.)*

CRAMER INC.
625 Adams St.
Kansas City, KS 66105
Tel.: 913-621-6700
Tel.: 800-366-6700
Fax: 913-621-1133
Year Founded: 1886
Approx.Sls.: $12,000,000
Emp.: 125
Fiscal Year-end: 12/31/90
Mfr. & Wholesale Distr. of Office & Factory Ergonomically Designed Chairs; Hospital, Hotel, Restaurant & Institutional Chairs; Office Desks & Tables; Ladders & Step Stools; Metal Files & Open Office Systems
S.I.C.: 2522; 2521; 2542; 2599
Charles Curtis *(Pres. & Chief Exec. Officer)*
Rick Mudge *(V.P.-Mktg. & Sls.)*
Ed Orr *(V.P.-Fin.)*
R. Wehner *(V.P.-Engrng.)*
Mark Rhoades *(Natl. Sls. Mgr.)*
Debra Wilmot *(Asst. Prod. Mgr.)*

CRAMER
C/K
KRASSELT

CRAMER-KRASSELT
733 N. Van Buren
Milwaukee, WI 53202
Tel.: 414-227-3500
Fax: 414-276-8710
Year Founded: 1898
Approx.Billings: $141,600,000
Emp.: 192
Advertising Agency
S.I.C.: 7311
Paul S. Counsell *(Chm. Bd. & Chief Exec. Officer)*
Peter G. Krivkovich *(Pres. & Chief Oper. Officer)*
William D. Faude *(Sr. V.P., Sec.)*
Robert J. Bradley *(V.P., Treas.)*

No. of U.S. Offices: 4

Computer Systems/Hardware:
IBM System 36

Outside Service Firm(s):

Arthur Andersen & Co.*(Auditors)*
777 E. Wisconsin Ave., P.O. Box 1215
Milwaukee, WI 53202
Tel.: 414-271-5100
Fax: 414-283-3200

First Bank Milwaukee*(Major Banking Relationship)*
201 W. Wisconsin Ave.
Milwaukee, WI 53259
Tel.: 414-278-6000

Branches:

Cramer-Krasselt **(1)**
733 N. Van Buren
Milwaukee, WI 53202
Tel.: 414-227-3500
Fax: 414-276-8710
S.I.C.: 7311
Paul S. Counsell *(Chm. Bd. & Chief Exec. Officer)*
Paul M. Bentley *(Sr. V.P., Dir. Client Services)*
Kenneth R. Lamm *(Sr. V.P.)*
Don Ingle *(V.P., Dir. Pub. Rels.)*
Norbert D. Berg *(V.P.)*
Susan Bishop *(V.P.)*
John Melamed *(V.P.)*

Cramer-Krasselt **(1)**
1420 E. Missouri Ave., Ste. 100
Phoenix, AZ 85014
Tel.: 602-277-0600
Fax: 602-234-1446
Advertising Agency
S.I.C.: 7311
Rolf G. Normann *(Exec. V.P., Gen. Mgr.)*
Berkley Cooke *(Sr. V.P.)*
Brian Landauer *(V.P.)*
Anne Johns *(Dir., Pub. Rels.)*
Tony Kingsbaker *(Asst. Dir., Pub. Rels.)*

Cramer-Krasselt **(1)**
225 N. Michigan Ave.
Chicago, IL 60601
Tel.: 312-616-9600
Fax: 312-938-3157
Advertising Agency
S.I.C.: 7311
Peter G. Krivkovich *(Pres.)*
Don Brashears *(Sr. V.P.)*
Bradley Tips *(Sr. V.P.)*
Susan Prather *(V.P., Dir. Pub. Rels.)*
Cathy Beres *(V.P.)*
Nick Bothfeld *(V.P.)*
Donna Noonan *(V.P.)*
Karen Seamen *(V.P.)*

Cramer-Krasselt **(1)**
225 E. Robinson St., Ste. 490
Orlando, FL 32802
Tel.: 407-236-8300
Fax: 407-425-6137
Advertising Agency
S.I.C.: 7311
Francesca Mathews *(Dir., Client Services)*

Cramer-Krasselt/Direct **(1)**
225 N. Michigan Ave.
Chicago, IL 60601
Tel.: 312-616-9600
Fax: 312-938-3157
Phil May *(Exec. V.P., Gen. Mgr.)*

CRANE CARRIER COMPANY
1925 N. Sheridan
Tulsa, OK 74151
Mailing Address:
P.O. Box 582891
Tulsa, OK 74158
Tel.: 918-836-1651
Fax: 918-832-7348
Approx.Sls.: $120,000,000
Emp.: 550
Heavy Duty On-Off Highway Carriers for Concrete Mixers, Refuse, Drilling Rigs; for Bulk Materials Handling, Century, Corsair, Centurion
S.I.C.: 3711; 3715
Ed Mascarin *(Pres.)*
Jerry Redwine *(V.P.-Pur.)*
Jim Wade *(V.P.-Sls. & Mktg.)*
Reg Wallace *(V.P.-Fin.)*

CRANE & CO., INC.
30 South St.
Dalton, MA 01226
Tel.: 413-684-2600
Fax: 413-684-0726
Year Founded: 1801
Approx.Rev.: $143,000,000
Emp.: 1,150
Fiscal Year-end: 12/31/90
Manufacture Papers; Stationery, Bond, Filtration, Tracing, Carbon
S.I.C.: 2621; 2761; 3955
Lansing E. Crane *(Chm. Bd.)*
Thomas A. White *(Pres. & Chief Exec. Officer)*
Stephen H. Wismer *(Exec. V.P. & Treas.)*
John Kittredge *(V.P.-Mfg.)*
J. Barrett McInerney *(V.P.-Mktg. & Sls.)*
J.D. Manning *(Dir.-Personnel)*
John R. Hansen *(Mgr.-Mktg.-Social Stationery)*
R.W. Kerans *(Mgr.-Commercial Paper Sls.)*
Paul C. LeBlanc *(Mgr.-New Prods. Sls.)*
D.H. Shiverick *(Pur. Agent)*

Computer Systems/Hardware:
IBM System 36

Outside Service Firm(s):

Grant Thornton*(Auditors)*
53 State St.
Boston, MA 02109
Tel.: 617-723-7900

First Agricultural Bank*(Major Banking Relationship)*
Pittsfield, MA

Subsidiaries:

Byron Weston Paper Co. **(1)**
30 South St.
Dalton, MA 01226
Tel.: 413-684-1234
Emp.: 305
Cotton Fiber, Bond, Ledger & Index, Super Sulphite, & Related Paper Specialties
S.I.C.: 2621; 2678
B.J. Sullivan *(Chm. & Chief Exec. Officer)*
T.H. White *(Pres. & Chief Oper. Officer)*

Excelsior Printing Co. **(1)**
60 Roberts Dr.
North Adams, MA 01247
Tel.: 413-663-3771

Excelsior Process & Engraving Co. **(1)**
Curan Hwy., Rte. 8
North Adams, MA 02147
Tel.: 413-664-4321

Standard Process & Engraving Co. **(1)**
2763 Teagarden St.
San Leandro, CA 94577
Tel.: 510-352-6900

CRANE CONSTRUCTION CO.
343 Wainwright Dr.
Northbrook, IL 60062
Tel.: 708-291-3400
Fax: 708-291-1691
Approx.Sls.: $95,000,000
Emp.: 225
General Contractor
S.I.C.: 1522; 1542
Jeffrey D. Crane *(Pres.)*
Ron Moser *(Chief Fin. Officer)*

Principal(s):
Jeffrey D. Crane

Computer Systems/Hardware:
Texas Instruments

Outside Service Firm(s):

Beatch, Rich & Nadler*(Auditors)*
Chicago, IL

LaSalle National Bank*(Major Banking Relationship)*
120 S. LaSalle St.
Chicago, IL 60603
Tel.: 312-781-8000

CRANE PLASTICS COMPANY
2141 Fairwood Ave.
Columbus, OH 43207
Mailing Address:
P.O. Box 1047
Columbus, OH 43216
Tel.: 614-443-4891 **DE**
Fax: 614-443-1436
Year Founded: 1947
Approx.Sls.: $120,000,000
Emp.: 650
Mfr. of Vinyl House Siding; Custom Extruded Thermoplastics
S.I.C.: 3089
Robert S. Crane, Jr. *(Chm. Bd.)*
Jameson Crane *(Pres.)*
Gary C. Fulmer *(Exec. V.P.)*
Arthur Korney *(V.P.-Research)*
Raymond J. Strutner *(V.P.-Mfg.)*
Philip Stobart *(V.P.-Prod. Devel.)*
John Wolff *(V.P.-Sls. & Mktg.)*

Outside Service Firm(s):

Deloitte & Touche*(Auditors)*
155 E. Broad St.
Columbus, OH 43215
Tel.: 614-221-1000
Fax: 614-229-4647

Bank One*(Major Banking Relationship)*
Columbus, OH

CRANFORD JOHNSON ROBINSON WOODS
303 W. Capitol Ave.
Little Rock, AR 72201
Tel.: 501-376-6251
Fax: 501-376-4241
Year Founded: 1961
Approx.Billings: $40,000,000
Emp.: 98
Advertising Agency
S.I.C.: 7311
Wayne Cranford *(Chm. & Chief Exec. Officer)*
Ron Robinson *(Pres. & Chief Oper. Officer)*
Shelby Woods *(Exec. V.P. & Chm.-Exec. Committee)*
Jim Johnson *(Sr. V.P.- Creative Services)*
Wayne Woods *(Sr. V.P.)*
Bob Anderson *(V.P. & Dir.-Opers.)*
Frank Cox *(V.P. & Dir.-Assoc.)*
Mike Dandurand *(V.P. & Dir.-Field Services)*
Bernie Jungkind *(V.P. & Dir.-Photography)*
Brenda Scisson *(V.P. & Dir.-Pub. Rels.)*
Dennis Schultz *(Controller & Mgr.-Acctg.)*
Ramon Greenwood *(Gen. Counsel)*
Greg Shira *(Mgr.-Print Production-Travel & Tourism Div.)*
Beverly Trimble *(Travel Planner)*

Computer Systems/Hardware:
Apple MacIntosh, PROSOFT-UNISYS, Microsoft Mail, Compuserve

Outside Service Firm(s):

Frost & Co.*(Auditors)*
Little Rock, AR

Arkansas Blue Cross & Blue Shield, Inc.*(Group Insurer)*
Little Rock, AR

First Commercial Bank*(Major Banking Relationship)*
P.O. Box 1331,
Little Rock, AR 72201

CRANSTON PRINT WORKS COMPANY
1381 Cranston St.
Cranston, RI 02920
Tel.: 401-943-4800 **RI**
Fax: 401-943-3971
Year Founded: 1824
Assets: $150,000,000
Earnings: $4,000,000
Liabilities: $111,000,000
Net Worth: $39,000,000
Approx.Sls.: $253,000,000
Emp.: 1,700
Fiscal Year-end: 6/30/89
Textile Printing & Converting
S.I.C.: 2261; 2262; 2869; 2899
Frederic L. Rockefeller *(Chm. Bd.)*
George Shuster *(Pres.)*
Robert Mandeville *(Chief Fin. Officer & Treas.)*
Pierre Conopack *(Dir.-Data Processing)*
Herbert Gray *(Dir.-Human Resources)*
Dennis Prior *(Dir.-Pur.)*

No. of Mfg. Plants/Facilities: 6
No. of U.S. Offices: 8

Computer Systems/Hardware:
Burroughs V530

Outside Service Firm(s):

Deloitte & Touche*(Auditors)*
125 Summer St.
Boston, MA 02110
Tel.: 617-261-8000
Fax: 617-261-8111

Corroon & Black*(Commercial Insurance Carrier)*
One Exeter Plaza
Boston, MA 02116
Tel.: 617-437-6900

Prudential Insurance Co. of America*(Group Insurer)*
751 Broad St.
Newark, NJ 07102-3777
Tel.: 201-802-6000

Travelers Insurance Co.*(Group Insurer)*
1 Tower Square
Hartford, CT 06183-2492
Tel.: 203-277-4542
Fax: 203-277-5038

Edwards & Angell*(Legal Firm)*
2700 Hospital Trust Twr.
Providence, RI 02903
Tel.: 401-274-9200

Chase Manhattan Bank, N.A.*(Major Banking Relationship)*
One Chase Manhattan Plaza
New York, NY 10081
Tel.: 212-552-2222
Tel.: 800-526-0801
Fax: 212-552-7175

Citibank N.A.*(Pension Manager)*
Corporate Trust Services, 399 Park Ave.
New York, NY 10043
Tel.: 212-559-1605

Travelers Insurance Co.*(Pension Manager)*
1 Tower Square
Hartford, CT 06183
Tel.: 203-222-7821
Fax: 203-222-7813

Subsidiary:

Bercen Inc. **(1)**
1381 Cranston St.
Cranston, RI 02920
Tel.: 401-943-7400
Emp.: 40
Chemicals
S.I.C.: 2899
John W. Wright *(Pres.)*

Crate & Barrel
(See Cranston Print Works Company)

CRAWFORD FITTINGS & CO.
29500 Solon Rd.
Solon, OH 44139
Tel.: 216-248-4600
Mfr. of Tube Fittings
S.I.C.: 3492
Joseph Callahan *(Pres.)*

THE CRAWFORD GROUP
26650 Lakeland Blvd.
Cleveland, OH 44132
Tel.: 216-261-7000
Holding Company
S.I.C.: 6719
Edward Crawford *(Chm. Bd.)*
Teri Arcaro *(Corp. Sec.)*

Outside Service Firm(s):

Society National Bank*(Major Banking Relationship)*
900 Euclid Ave., P.O. Box 6477
Cleveland, OH 44101-6477
Tel.: 216-737-5000
Fax: 216-566-8947

CRAY COMMUNICATIONS INC.
(Formerly Dowty Communications, Inc.)
9020 Junction Dr.
Annapolis Junction, MD 20701
Tel.: 301-317-7710
Fax: 301-317-7220
Year Founded: 1973
Approx.Sls.: $50,000,000
Emp.: 400
Fiscal Year-end: 3/31/91
Export
Data Communications Equip., High Speed Modems, Communications Processors, Network Mngmt. Systems
S.I.C.: 3577; 3669; 3679
Mike Lindsay *(Pres. & Chief Exec. Officer)*
P.G. Narayanan *(V.P.-Engrng. & Mktg.)*
Steve Feldstein *(V.P.-Sls. & Service)*
Mark Cummings *(V.P.-Mfg.)*
Gil Goldbeck *(Mgr.-Fin.)*
Leamar Capototh *(Mgr.-Sls. Promo.)*
Corrine Rawlins *(Mgr.-Personnel)*
Brian Gunn *(Mgr.-MIS)*
John Keating *(Mgr.-Personnel Training & Devel.)*
Bill Conroy *(Govt. Affairs)*

CREAM PRODUCTS CO., INC.
3 Westbrook Corp. Ctr.
Westchester, IL 60154
Tel.: 708-531-9779
Tel.: 800-535-5990
Fax: 708-531-1902
Year Founded: 1938
Approx.Sls.: $20,000,000
Emp.: 45
Fiscal Year-end: 12/31/90
Import Export
Manufacturer of Non-Dairy Products
S.I.C.: 5411
Jack Bluemke *(Chm. Bd.)*
John Bluemke, Jr. *(Pres.)*
David Bluemke *(Exec. V.P.)*
Don Bluemke *(V.P.-Opers.)*
Gerard Leganski *(V.P.-Fin.)*
James Vincent *(V.P.-Sls.)*
Thomas Hootman *(Mgr.-Adv.)*

CREATION WINDOWS OF INDIANA, INC.
53061 Ada Dr.
Elkhart, IN 46514
Mailing Address:
P.O. Box 1046
Elkhart, IN 46515
Tel.: 219-264-3131
Tel.: 800-862-3131
Fax: 219-264-9725
Year Founded: 1970
Approx.Sls.: $37,000,000
Emp.: 400
Fiscal Year-end: 12/31/91
Export
Mfr. of Windows & Doors for RV Indus.
S.I.C.: 3442
Robert Hotovy *(Chm. Bd.)*
Tim Nevelle *(Pres.)*
Martin J. Kuhar *(V.P., Sec. & Treas.)*
Joe Trippel *(V.P.-Fin.)*
Kenneth Koenig *(Controller)*
William Cowan *(Gen. Counsel)*
Donald Ravenscroft *(Dir.-Data Processing)*
Mary Lee Murray *(Mgr.-Personnel)*
Eric Wong *(Mgr.-Engrng.)*
Bob Weltz *(Mgr.-Quality Control)*

Computer Systems/Hardware:
IBM System 36

CREATIVE ALLIANCE, INC.
222 S. First St., Ste. 400
Louisville, KY 40202
Tel.: 502-584-8787
Fax: 502-589-9900
Year Founded: 1987
Approx.Billings: $45,415,772
Emp.: 56
Debbie Scoppechio *(Pres., New Bus. Contact & Mktg. Dir.)*
Wes Burgiss *(Exec. V.P., Sec.)*
Joe Adams *(Exec. V.P., Treas.)*
Mike Miller *(V.P., Devel.)*
Susan Kannapell *(V.P., Mktg.)*

CREATIVE DIRECT MARKETING GROUP, INC.
1815 West 213th St., Ste. 210
Torrance, CA 90501
Tel.: 310-212-5727
Year Founded: 1985
Approx.Billings: $12,206,000
Emp.: 18
Direct Response Adv.
Craig Huey *(Pres.)*

Computer Systems/Hardware:
Macintosh Network

CREATIVE HAIRDRESSERS
2815 Hartland Rd.
Falls Church, VA 22043
Tel.: 703-698-7090
Year Founded: 1974
Approx.Sls.: $92,000,000
Emp.: 4,500
Chain of Hair Salons
S.I.C.: 7231
Dennis Ratner *(Pres.)*
Warren Ratner *(V.P.)*
Barbara Salvucci *(Dir.-Adv.)*

Division:

The Hair Cuttery **(1)**
2815 Hartland Rd.
Falls Church, VA 22043
Tel.: 703-698-7090
Beauty Shops
S.I.C.: 7231
Dennis Ratner *(Pres.)*

CREATIVE MARKETING ALLIANCE INC.
34-c Washington Rd.
Princeton Junction, NJ 08550
Tel.: 609-799-4900
Fax: 609-799-7032
Year Founded: 1986
Approx.Billings: $11,000,000
Emp.: 20
Industrial, Commercial, Business-to-Business & Association Management
Jeffrey E. Barnhart *(Pres.)*
Russ B. Mykytyn *(Exec. V.P.)*
Burton W. Lambert *(Chief Fin. Officer & V.P., Opers.)*
Mary Kay Metcalf *(Mgr.-Communications & Bus.-to-Bus.)*
Craig DiLouie *(Mgr.-Communications, Indus. & Commercial)*

CREATIVE MARKETING INTERNATIONAL CORP.
31W001 North Ave.
West Chicago, IL 60185
Tel.: 708-293-9600
Fax: 708-293-6909
Year Founded: 1986
Approx.Billings: $55,000,000
Automotive, Ad Groups, Direct Marketing
Patrick J. O'Rahilly *(Pres.)*
Dick Ferguson *(Exec. V.P.)*
Michael Moody *(Exec. V.P.)*
Chuck Randazzo *(V.P., Automotive Div.)*
M. Bouzide *(V.P., Operations)*
Robert A. Gancarz *(Treas.)*
Chris Cantele *(Pub. Rels. Dir., New Bus. Contact)*
Robert L. Harris *(Mktg. Dir.)*

CREATIVE MARKETING RESOURCE, INC.
919 N. Michigan Ave., 1st Fl.
Chicago, IL 60611
Tel.: 312-943-6266
Fax: 312-787-8586
Year Founded: 1965
Approx.Billings: $21,000,000
Emp.: 14
Jacqueline Wagner *(Pres.)*
Larry Gillespie *(Controller)*
James Haddon *(Gen. Counsel & Sec.)*
Rochelle Cobar *(Travel Planner & Office Mgr.)*

Computer Systems/Hardware:
IBM, LAN

CREATIVE PLAYTHINGS LTD.
33 Loring Dr.
Framingham, MA 01701
Tel.: 508-620-0900
Fax: 508-872-3120
Approx.Sls.: $10,000,000
Emp.: 100
Manufacture & Retail Childrens Outdoor Playground Equipment
S.I.C.: 3949; 5941
Donald Hoffman *(Pres. & Treas.)*
Richard Kaplan *(V.P.)*
Robert E. Murphy *(V.P. & Chief Fin. Officer)*

Outside Service Firm(s):

James J. Sherry*(Auditors)*
Framingham, MA

First National Bank of Boston*(Major Banking Relationship)*
P.O. Box 644,
Boston, MA 02102-0644
Tel.: 617-575-2900
Fax: 617-575-2549

CREATIVE PRODUCTIONS
7500 Thomas Blvd.
Pittsburgh, PA 15208
Tel.: 412-731-8500
Approx.Sls.: $10,000,000
Emp.: 75
Designers and Builders of Exhibits and Dimensional Presentations
S.I.C.: 3999; 7389
Clifford Hellberg *(Chm. Bd., Pres., Chief Exec. Officer)*
C.E. Hellberg *(Chief Oper. Officer)*
C. Alan Cordial *(Exec. V.P.)*
S.W. Hellberg *(Sr. V.P.)*
Andrew Sovich *(Treas.)*
Marvin Aaron *(Pur. Agent)*

CREATIVE SALON FURNITURE INC.
(Formerly Tuscany Kolcraft Industries)
1768 E. 49th St.
Brooklyn, NY 11234
Tel.: 718-253-7373

Creative Salon Furniture Inc.—(Continued)

Fax: 718-258-9073
Sales Range: $10-19 Million
Emp.: 30
Manufacture Beauty Salon Furniture
S.I.C.: 2541; 2542; 2599; 3999
Emanuel Ferrigno *(Pres.)*
Salvador Chiesso *(V.P.-Mktg.)*
James Ravino *(Treas.)*

Outside Service Firm(s):

Empire Blue Cross & Blue Shield*(Group Insurer)*
New York, NY

Citibank N.A.*(Major Banking Relationship)*
Corporate Trust Services, 399 Park Ave.
New York, NY 10043
Tel.: 212-559-1605

CREDIT UNION NATIONAL ASSOCIATION
5710 Mineral Point Rd.
Madison, WI 53705
Mailing Address:
P.O. Box 431
Madison, WI 53701
Tel.: 608-231-4000
Year Founded: 1934
Approx.Sls.: $10,700,000
Emp.: 190
National Trade Association for Credit Unions
S.I.C.: 8611
Christie Eugene *(Chm. Bd.)*
Gary Janacek *(Vice Chm.)*
Ralph Swoboda *(Pres.)*
Durant Abernathy *(Sr. V.P. & Gen. Counsel)*
Chuck Zuver *(Sr. V.P. & Dir.-Govt. Affairs)*
Greg Moser *(Sr. V.P.-Admin. & Internal Audit)*
Lucy Harr *(V.P.-Communications)*
Dean Archer *(V.P.-Meetings & Special Events)*
Joellyn Quinn *(V.P.-Corp. Rels. & Asst. Sec.)*
Jerome Rather *(V.P.-Fin. & Controller)*
Rae Miles *(V.P.-New Product Devel.)*
Mark Condon *(Asst. V.P.-Communications)*
E.E. Levins *(Treas.)*
Matt Solomon *(Information Specialist)*
Peter DiSylvester *(Sec.)*
Lyle Baez *(Mgr.-Pur.)*
Diane Rahm *(Mgr.-Employment)*
Linda Vahldieck *(Mgr.-Training & Devel.)*
Anne Reynolds *(Mgr.-Information Resource Center)*
Caryn Ernst *(Coord.-Telephone Services)*
Karen Hoff *(Supvr.-Support Services)*

Computer Systems/Hardware:
IBM PC-based LAN Network

Affiliates:

Association of Credit Union League Executives **(1)**
P.O. Box 431
Madison, WI 53701-0431
Tel.: 608-231-4018
Tel.: 800-356-9655
An Association of Credit Union League Presidents from each State, & Associate Members Who are Also League Personnel
S.I.C.: 8611
Charles Sullivan *(Chm. Bd.)*
Pete Crear *(Exec. Dir.)*

CUNA Foundation **(1)**
805 15th N.W., Ste. 300
Washington, DC 20005
Tel.: 202-682-4200

CUNA Service Group, Inc. **(1)**
P.O. Box 431,
Madison, WI 53705
Tel.: 608-231-4000
Tel.: 800-356-9140
Provides Financial Products & Services for Credit Unions & Their Members Through Credit Union Leagues
S.I.C.: 8611
Ralph Swoboda *(Pres.)*
Jerome Rather *(V.P.-Fin. & Controller)*
Mark Condon *(V.P.-Publications/Mktg.)*
Darlene Brightbill *(Adv. Mgr.)*
Lyle Baez *(Pur. Mgr.)*

CUNA Mortgage Corporation **(1)**
8410 Greenbay Blvd.
Middleton, WI 53562
Tel.: 608-828-3000
S.I.C.: 8611
Brad Murphy *(Pres.)*

Credit Union Benefits Services, Inc. **(1)**
5710 Mineral Point Road
Madison, WI 53705
Tel.: 608-231-4101
S.I.C.: 8611
Lorence Wheeler *(Pres.)*

Defense Credit Union Council **(1)**
805 15th St. N.W.
Washington, DC 20005
Tel.: 202-628-5993
Serves the Needs of Credit Unions Having Primarily Military Fields of Membership & Represents Defense Credit Unions with the Department of Defense
S.I.C.: 8611
James W. Rowe *(Pres. & Chief Exec. Officer)*

Filene Research Institute **(1)**
5910 Mineral Point Rd.
Madison, WI 53705
Tel.: 608-231-8550
S.I.C.: 8611
Robert Hoel *(Exec. Dir.)*

National Federation of Community Development Credit Unions **(1)**
59 John St., 8th Fl.
New York, NY 10038
Tel.: 212-513-7191
S.I.C.: 8611
Cliff Rosenthal *(Exec. Dir.)*

United States Central Credit Union **(1)**
7300 College Boulevard,Ste.600
Overland Park, KS 66210
Tel.: 913-661-3800
Tel.: 800-255-0413
Financial Intermediary Between Corporates & Credit Unions & the Remainder of the Financial Community; Provides Liquidity, Credit & Settlement Services for Credit Unions
S.I.C.: 8611
James Bell *(Pres.)*

World Council of Credit Unions **(1)**
5810 Mineral Point Rd.
Madison, WI 53705
Tel.: 608-231-7130
S.I.C.: 8611
Al Charbonneau *(Chief Exec. Officer)*

CRENLO, INC.
1600 Fourth Ave., NW
Rochester, MN 55901
Tel.: 507-289-3371 **DE**
Fax: 507-287-3405
Year Founded: 1951
Approx.Sls.: $92,000,000
Emp.: 800
Fiscal Year-end: 8/ 2/92
Import
Manufactures Custom Metal Sheet Housing & Frames, Tractor Cabs & Related Sheet Metal Products, Electronic Modular Enclosures
S.I.C.: 3713; 3499; 3523; 3531; 3699
Charles A. Elliott *(Chm. Bd., Pres. & Chief Exec., Officer)*
Roger A. Carlson *(V.P.-Fin.)*
Gary P. Ellis *(V.P.-Sls. & Mktg.)*
Wayne De Bruin *(Dir.-Indus. Rels.)*
Gary J. Huck *(Dir.-Materials)*
Bradley D. O'Connell *(Dir.-Mfg.)*

No. of Mfg. Plants/Facilities: 2

Computer Systems/Hardware:
IBM System 4341

Outside Service Firm(s):

Arthur Andersen & Co.*(Auditors)*
45 S. 7th St.
Minneapolis, MN 55402

Faegre & Benson*(Legal Firm)*
2200 Norwest Ctr., 90 S. 7th St.
Minneapolis, MN 55402-3901
Tel.: 612-336-3000
Fax: 612-336-3026

Marquette Bank*(Major Banking Relationship)*
Rochester, MN

CRES-COR/CROWN-X
12711 Taft Ave.
Cleveland, OH 44108-1683
Tel.: 216-851-6800
Tel.: 800-321-7174
Telex: 703 049
Fax: 216-851-9734
Year Founded: 1936
Approx.Sls.: $20,000,000
Emp.: 200
Fiscal Year-end: 8/31/92
Export
Cres-Cor Mobile Aluminum Equip. & Infra-Red Food Warmers, Food Serving Warmers, Self Service Mobile Units, Food Service Equip., Crown-X Convection Oven, Roast-N-Hold Cooking Equipment
S.I.C.: 3499; 3589
George T. Baggott *(Chm. Bd.)*
George E. Baggott *(Pres.)*
Clifford D. Baggott *(Chief Opers. Officer)*
Tom Doorley *(Production Control Mgr.)*
James Miller *(Corp. Chef)*
Marlene Hanna *(Exhibits Coord.)*
Mary Schoeniger *(Pub. Rels. Coord.)*
Jerry Petac *(Pur. Dir.)*

CRESCENT ELECTRIC SUPPLY CO.
Dunleith Drive
East Dubuque, IL 61025
Mailing Address:
P.O. Box 500,
East Dubuque, IL 61025
Tel.: 815-747-3145
Fax: 815-747-7720
Year Founded: 1919
Emp.: 650
Fiscal Year-end: 12/31/90
Electrical Wholesaler
S.I.C.: 5063; 5064
James A. Schmid *(Pres. & Chief Exec. Officer)*
James Etheredge *(V.P.-Fin.)*
Wayne Alderson *(Treas.)*
Ronald Mahannah *(Mgr.-Traffic)*
Ken Snodgrass *(Mgr.-Data Processing)*

Computer Systems/Hardware:
Sperry Univac 1172

Outside Service Firm(s):

McGladrey & Pullen*(Auditors)*
Dubuque, IA

SISCO*(Group Insurer)*
East Dubuque, IL

O'Connor Thomas*(Legal Firm)*
Dubuque, IL

First National Bank of Chicago*(Major Banking Relationship)*
One First National Plaza
Chicago, IL 60670
Tel.: 312-732-9781
Tel.: 312-732-4050
Fax: 312-732-4840
Fax: 312-732-3055

The Principal Financial Group*(Pension Manager)*
711 High St.
Des Moines, IA 50309
Tel.: 515-247-4593
Tel.: 800-543-4015

CRESCIVE DIE & TOOL, INC.
905 Woodland Dr.
Saline, MI 48176
Tel.: 313-429-9451
Fax: 313-429-9047
Automotive Stampings, Die Sets for Metal Stamping Presses
S.I.C.: 3465; 3544
Joseph A. Butcko *(Chm. Bd.)*
Joseph D. Butcko *(Pres.)*
James M. Butcko *(V.P.)*
Mae Alice Butcko *(Sec. & Treas.)*

Outside Service Firm(s):

St. John Raham & Weidmayer*(Auditors)*
Ann Arbor, MI

Jackson, Lamb & Duerr*(Legal Firm)*
Ypsilanti, MI

Society Bank*(Major Banking Relationship)*
Ann Arbor, MI

Division:

Cresive Milan Division **(1)**
555 Platt
Milan, MI 48160
Tel.: 813-439-1546
Automotive Stampings
S.I.C.: 3465
Larry Paquin *(Plant Mgr.)*

CRESMER, WOODWARD, O'MARA & ORMSBEE
866 Third Ave.
New York, NY 10022
Tel.: 212-750-4040 **NY**
Fax: 212-935-9514
Year Founded: 1962
Approx.Sls.: $14,000,000
Emp.: 125
Newspaper Advertising Representative
S.I.C.: 7313
States D. Tompkins *(Pres. & Chief Exec. Officer)*
Robert T. Weber *(Exec. V.P.-Fin.)*
Thomas Clifford *(Exec. V.P.)*
Robert LaFontaine *(Exec. V.P.)*
Richard A. Mitchell *(Sr. V.P.)*
Marcia Jasuiklo *(Sec.)*

Outside Service Firm(s):

KPMG Peat Marwick*(Auditors)*
345 Park Ave.
New York, NY 10154
Tel.: 212-758-9700
Fax: 212-872-3308

CREST CADILLAC COMPANY
2121 Metro Center Blvd.
Nashville, TN 37228
Tel.: 615-242-4242
Fax: 615-242-2635
Year Founded: 1985
Approx.Sls.: $25,000,000
Emp.: 115
Retail New & Used Automobiles
S.I.C.: 5511
Mike Kitzmiller *(Pres.)*
Connie Carvin *(Chief Fin. Officer)*

Outside Service Firm(s):

George B. Jones & Co.*(Auditors)*
Memphis, TN

CREST DISTRIBUTING COMPANY, INC.
595 S. 200 E.
Provo, UT 84601
Tel.: 801-373-7970 **UT**
Fax: 801-373-7976
Approx.Sls.: $12,000,000
Emp.: 65
Petroleum Bulk Stations; Convenience Store Chain
S.I.C.: 5171; 5411
Todd Christensen *(Pres.)*

Outside Service Firm(s):

Central Bank*(Major Banking Relationship)*
Provo, UT

CRESTED BUTTE MOUNTAIN RESORT, INC.
500 Gothic Rd.
Mount Crested Butte, CO 81225
Mailing Address:
P.O. Box A
Mt. Crested Butte, CO 81225
Tel.: 303-349-2333
Tel.: 800-544-8448
Telex: 4953858
Fax: 303-349-2250
Year Founded: 1961
Approx.Sls.: $18,000,000
Emp.: 600
Skiing Resort Vacationing for Summer and Winter; Food and Beverage
S.I.C.: 7011
Corporate Giving Program: Inquire Via Letter; Committee of Two Determine Appropriateness.
R.O. Walton *(Chm. Bd.)*
Howard Bo Callaway *(Chief Exec. Officer)*
Edward C. Callaway *(Pres.)*
Debbie Fox *(V.P.-Sls.)*
Mike Busby *(Chief Fin. Officer, Treas. & Controller)*
Kim Gailey *(Dir.-Personnel)*
Mark Hartley *(Mgr.-Telecommunications)*
Gina Kroft *(Mgr.-Pub. Rels. & Special Events)*
Wanda Dimon *(Mgr.-Adv., Mktg. Promo. & Pub. Rels.)*

CRETE CARRIER CORP.
400 N.W. 56th
Lincoln, NE 68528
Mailing Address:
P.O. Box 81228
Lincoln, NE 68501
Tel.: 402-475-9521
Fax: 402-479-2074
Year Founded: 1966
Assets: $97,516,106
Liabilities: $18,144,244
Net Worth: $79,371,862
Approx.Sls.: $150,000,000
Emp.: 500
Fiscal Year-end: 9/30/90

Import Export
Transport of Dry & Temperature Controlled Products; Common & Contract Haulers; Truck Rental With Drivers; Commercial Building Leasing Operators
S.I.C.: 4213; 4212; 6512
Duane W. Acklie *(Chm.)*
Tonn Ostergard *(Pres. & Chief Exec. Officer)*
Karel Znamenacek *(Exec. V.P. & Treas.)*
Jack Peetz *(Exec. V.P.)*
Phyllis A. Acklie *(V.P. & Sec.)*
Ray Coulter *(V.P.)*
Raymond Dunn *(V.P.)*
Jon Huwe *(V.P.)*
James Krejci *(V.P.)*
Holly Ostergard *(V.P.)*

Outside Service Firm(s):

KPMG Peat Marwick*(Auditors)*
1600 FirsTier Bank Bldg., 13th & M Streets, Ste. 1600
Lincoln, NE 68508
Tel.: 402-476-1216

Union Bank & Trust Co.*(Major Banking Relationship)*
Lincoln, NE

Subsidiary:

Sunflower Carriers **(1)**
P.O. Box 9
York, NE 68467
Tel.: 402-363-7491
Emp.: 400
Refrigerated Transportation
S.I.C.: 4212; 4213
Roy Wallace *(Pres.)*
Dean Troester *(V.P.)*

THE CRETEX COMPANIES
311 Lowell Ave.
Elk River, MN 55330
Tel.: 612-441-2121
Fax: 612-441-3585
Year Founded: 1917
Concrete Products
S.I.C.: 3451; 3272
J.H. Bailey *(Chm. Bd. & Chief Exec. Officer)*
Charles A. Gallagher *(Pres.)*
D.A. Schumacher *(Chief Fin. Officer & Treas.)*
Dennis Wold *(Controller)*
Ron Ellingson *(Dir.-Data Processing)*

Computer Systems/Hardware:
IBM System 36

Outside Service Firm(s):

Ernst & Young*(Auditors)*
1400 Pillsbury Center
Minneapolis, MN 55402
Tel.: 612-343-1000

Dorsey & Whitney*(Legal Firm)*
2200 First Bank Place East
Minneapolis, MN 55402
Tel.: 612-340-2600
Fax: 612-340-2600

First Bank Minneapolis*(Major Banking Relationship)*
Minneapolis, MN

Norwest Bank Minnesota, N.A.*(Major Banking Relationship)*
6th St. & Marquette Av.
Minneapolis, MN 55479
Tel.: 612-667-1234

Subsidiary:

Juno Tool & Plastic Corporation **(1)**
1809 S. Plymouth Rd.
Minnetonka, MN 55343
Tel.: 612-593-1252
Custom Molded Injection & Compression Plastic Components
S.I.C.: 3089
Thomas C. Bender *(Pres.)*
Don Johnson *(Mgr.-Sls. & Mktg.)*

CRISA CORPORATION
(Sub. of Vitrocrisa Cristaleria, S.A., Monterrey, Mexico)
101 E. Park Blvd., Suite 805
Plano, TX 75074
Tel.: 214-881-9031
Fax: 214-422-5284
Year Founded: 1984
Approx.Sls.: $50,000,000
Emp.: 200
Fiscal Year-end: 12/31/91
Handblown Crystal, Glassware & Giftware
S.I.C.: 3229; 5023; 3231
Jorge Escamez *(Pres.)*
Rafael Melo *(Exec. V.P.)*
Mark Glazer *(V.P.-Sls. & Mktg.)*
Roberto M. Garcia *(Controller)*

THE CRISPIN COMPANY
2929 Allen Pkwy. Ste. 2222
Houston, TX 77019
Tel.: 713-224-8000 **TX**
Telex: 203353 CRISP UR
Fax: 713-224-1120
Year Founded: 1949
Approx.Sls.: $100,000,000
Emp.: 10
Fiscal Year-end: 8/31/89
Import Export
Wholesale Iron & Steel Products, International Trading-Marketing of Steel Products & Other Metals
S.I.C.: 5051
Robert Servais *(Chm. Bd.)*
Andre A. Crispin *(Pres. & Chief Exec. Officer)*
Jacques Bouchez *(V.P. & Chief Oper. Officer)*
B.R. Dickerson *(Gen. Counsel)*
Principal(s):
Robert Servais
Andre A. Crispin
Jacques Bouchez

Computer Systems/Hardware:
IBM PC

Outside Service Firm(s):

Aetna Life & Casualty*(Group Insurer)*
151 Farmington Avenue
Hartford, CT 06156
Tel.: 203-273-2128
Fax: 203-729-4295

Bracewell & Patterson*(Legal Firm)*
2900 South Tower, Pennzoil Place
Houston, TX 77002
Tel.: 713-223-2900

First City National Bank*(Major Banking Relationship)*
1301 Fannin St., Ste. 2215
Houston, TX 77002

CRISPIN & PORTER ADVERTISING INC.
2699 S. Bayshore Dr.
Miami, FL 33133
Tel.: 305-859-2070 **FL**
Fax: 305-854-3419
Year Founded: 1965
Approx.Billings: $30,000,000
Emp.: 38
Advertising Agency
S.I.C.: 7311
Charles Crispin *(Pres.)*
Charles Porter *(Chm. & Dir.-Creative)*
Margaret Megee *(V.P.- Travel & Tourism)*
John Stofka *(Controller)*

Computer Systems/Hardware:
Comprehensive Micro Network Invovling IBM PC's & MacIntosh Computers

Outside Service Firm(s):

Rachlin & Cohen*(Auditors)*
Miami, FL

THE CRITERION GROUP

THE CRITERION GROUP, INC.
12 Piedmont Center, Ste. 100
Atlanta, GA 30305
Tel.: 404-237-8618
Fax: 404-262-3299
Year Founded: 1982
Approx.Billings: $11,000,000
Emp.: 18
Hospitality, Travel & Entertainment
William J. McGregor *(Pres. & Creative Dir.)*
Sara Jones *(Controller & Chief Fin. Officer)*
Mark Goldman *(Sr. V.P., Mng. Dir.)*
Cheryl McGregor *(V.P., Opers.)*
Richard Shaw *(V.P. & Assoc. Creative Dir.)*
Kim Glover *(Pub. Rels. Dir.)*
David Hutchens *(Copywriter)*

Computer Systems/Hardware:
Adman, Macintosh

THE CROCKER-FELS COMPANY
1900 Stelton Rd.
Cincinnati, OH 45237
Tel.: 513-458-2342 **OH**
Fax: 513-458-2342
Year Founded: 1882
Approx.Sls.: $40,000,000
Emp.: 150
Import Export
Wholesaler of Medical & Surgical Supplies & Equipment
S.I.C.: 5047; 5122; 5100
John Armstrong *(Pres.)*
Robert D. Fighter *(V.P.-Sls. & Mktg.)*
Clyde Zizkuhr *(V.P.-Sls. & Mktg.)*
Principal(s):
John Armstrong

Outside Service Firm(s):

KPMG Peat Marwick*(Auditors)*
1600 Central Trust Ctr., 201 East Fifth St.
Cincinnati, OH 45202
Tel.: 513-421-6430

Star Bank*(Major Banking Relationship)*
425 Walnut Street
Cincinnati, OH 45202
Tel.: 513-632-4000

H. S. CROCKER CO., INC.
Valley Forge Square, 660 American Ave., Ste. 102
King of Prussia, PA 19406
Tel.: 215-768-7070 **CA**
Fax: 215-768-7082
Year Founded: 1856
Approx.Sls.: $20,000,000
Emp.: 125
Fiscal Year-end: 3/31/91
Printers of Pharmaceutical & Pressure Sensitive Labels, Folding Cartons & Portion Pack Lids
S.I.C.: 2759; 3086
Richard N. Kauffman *(Chm. Bd. & Chief Exec. Officer)*
Steven B. Campbell *(Pres. & Chief Fin. Officer)*
Albert M. Trice *(V.P.-Mktg.)*
Richard R. Sica *(Mgr.-Sls.)*
Thomas J. Sheehan *(Corp. Controller)*

No. of Mfg. Plants/Facilities: 3

Computer Systems/Hardware:
VAX VMS-Digital

Outside Service Firm(s):

Steinhart & Falconer*(Legal Firm)*
333 Market St.
San Francisco, CA 94105
Tel.: 415-777-3999

CoreStates Financial Corp.*(Major Banking Relationship)*
Philadelphia, PA

Divisions:

H.S. Crocker Co., Inc. **(1)**
12100 Smith Drive
Huntley, IL 60142
Tel.: 708-669-3600
Printers of Pharmaceutical & Pressure Sensitive Labels, Folding Cartons & Portion Pack Lids
S.I.C.: 2759; 3086
Ron Giordano *(V.P.)*

H.S. Crocker Co., Inc. **(1)**
Eagleview Corporate Center, 400 Eagleview Blvd.
Exton, PA 19341
Tel.: 215-458-7434
Export
Printers of Pharmaceutical & Pressure Sensitive Labels, Folding Cartons & Portion Pack Lids
S.I.C.: 2759; 3086
Tom Tyberg *(Plant Mgr.)*

H.S. Crocker Co., Inc. **(1)**
Valley Forge Corp. Ctr.
Norristown, PA 19403

H. S. Crocker Co., Inc.—(Continued)

Terry Jonardi *(Plant Mgr.)*

Lockwood Folding Box **(1)**
Valley Forge Corp. Ctr.
Norristown, PA 19403
Tel.: 215-666-6116
Printers of Pharmaceutical & Pressure Sensitive Labels, Folding Cartons & Portion Pack Lids
S.I.C.: 2759; 3086

CROFT METAL INC.
124 24th St.
McComb, MS 39648
Mailing Address:
P.O. Box 826,
McComb, MS 39648
Tel.: 601-684-6121
Fax: 601-684-5134
Emp.: 1,500
Fiscal Year-end: 12/31/91
Manufacture Metal Windows & Doors
S.I.C.: 3442; 3449; 3334; 3354; 3363; 2851
Joseph C. Bancroft *(Chm. Bd.)*
Gerald M. Abdalla *(Exec. V.P., Gen. Counsel & Sec.)*
Edwin Plemons *(Exec. V.P.-Sls.)*
Charles McGhee *(V.P. & Dir.-Mfg.)*
Gery Jones *(Dir.-Mngmt. Information Systems)*
Don Nixon *(Dir.-Customer Service)*

Computer Systems/Hardware:
IBM 4381

Outside Service Firm(s):

Coopers & Lybrand*(Auditors)*
1000 Morgan-Keegan Tower, 50 N. Front St.
Memphis, TN 38103
Tel.: 901-529-1100

CNA Insurance*(Group Insurer)*
CNA Plaza,
Chicago, IL 60685
Tel.: 312-822-5000

Subsidiary:

Croft Metals, Inc. of NC **(1)**
Hwy. 71
Lumber Bridge, NC 28357
Tel.: 919-843-3391

HEATHER CROLIE, INC.
(Formerly Michaels, Stern & Co.)
87 N. Clinton Ave.
Rochester, NY 14604
Tel.: 716-454-5265 **NY**
Year Founded: 1849
Sales Range: $10-19 Million
Emp.: 10
Fiscal Year-end: 12/31/91
Real Estate Operators
S.I.C.: 6512
Annabel E. Frankenstein *(Pres.)*
Arnold Taylor *(Treas. & Sec.)*

Outside Service Firm(s):

Ceibert, Murray & Sealfan*(Auditors)*
Rochester, NY

Woods, Oviatt, Gilman, Sturman & Clarke*(Legal Firm)*
44 Exchange St.
Rochester, NY 14614
Tel.: 716-454-5370

CROLL-REYNOLDS COMPANY
751 Central Ave.
Westfield, NJ 07090
Tel.: 908-232-4200
Fax: 908-232-2146
Year Founded: 1917
Approx.Sls.: $10,000,000
Emp.: 41
Export
Mfr. of Vacuum Pumps & Pollution Control Equipment
S.I.C.: 3561; 3563; 3564
Samuel W. Croll III *(Pres.)*
Louis O. Decker *(V.P. & Gen. Mgr.)*
Phillip Reynolds *(V.P.)*
James F. Reynolds *(Treas. & Dir.-Pur.)*
Karen Hahn *(Mgr.-Adv.)*
Helen Sorrentino *(Mgr.-Personnel)*
Russell Ojala *(Chief Engr.)*

CRONIN & COMPANY, INC.
50 Nye Rd.
Glastonbury, CT 06033
Tel.: 203-659-0514
Fax: 203-659-3455
Year Founded: 1948
Approx.Billings: $15,600,000
Emp.: 29
Consumer, Retail, Business-to-Business, Financial Services
William J. Cronin, Sr. *(Chm. Bd.)*
William J. Cronin, Jr. *(Pres.)*
John N. Riccio *(Principal)*
Michael G. Wheeler *(Principal)*
Elizabeth Vogt *(V.P., Dir. Strategic Plng.)*
Patti Stern *(Dir., Pub. Rels.)*

Computer Systems/Hardware:
Mac-Creative, IBM-Fiscal

CROOKS SUPERMARKET INC.
(d/b/a Steven's Supermarkets)
P.O. Box 50028,
Nashville, TN 37205-0028
Tel.: 615-352-2999
Fax: 615-356-3554
Year Founded: 1974
Approx.Sls.: $37,000,000
Emp.: 430
Grocery Stores
S.I.C.: 5411
Steven E. Crook *(Pres. & Chief Exec. Officer)*
C. Hackney *(Sr. V.P.)*
Gary Walker *(Comptroller)*

Computer Systems/Hardware:
Texas Instruments 372A

Outside Service Firm(s):

Marlin & Edmondson CPA'S*(Auditors)*
Nashville, TN

First American Bank, N.A.*(Major Banking Relationship)*
Nashville, TN

CROSBY & OVERTON, INC.
1610 W. 17th St.
Long Beach, CA 90813
Tel.: 310-432-5445
Tel.: 800-8CROSBY **CA**
Fax: 310-436-7540
Year Founded: 1950
Assets: $14,870,000
Liabilities: $6,913,000
Net Worth: $7,957,000
Approx.Sls.: $30,000,000
Emp.: 350
Fiscal Year-end: 8/31/92
Ship Cleaning; Local Petrolelum Haulage
S.I.C.: 4499; 4212; 8734; 8999
James R. Dent *(Chm. Bd & Pres.)*
Robert L. Dent *(Exec. V.P. & Treas.)*
John D. Saenz *(Exec. V.P.-Opers.)*
M.M. Dundee *(V.P. & Gen. Mgr.)*
Michael Shloub *(V.P.-Special Projects)*
Jack Tarrango *(V.P.-Opers.-CA)*
Paul R. Dent *(Sec.)*
Lelan Allen *(Controller)*
Larry Boyle *(Dir.-Environment/Natural Resources)*
Toni Carothers *(Dir.-Pur.)*
Herman Pinto *(Dir.-Personnel Training & Devel.)*
Milton Sanders *(Dir.-Tech./Engrng./Tech. Services)*

No. of U.S. Offices: 5

Computer Systems/Hardware:
Data General

Outside Service Firm(s):

Andersen, Lynn, Bezick & Wierks*(Auditors)*
Long Beach, CA

Sedgwick James*(Commercial Insurance Carrier)*
3435 Wilshire Blvd., 5th Fl.
Los Angeles, CA 90010
Tel.: 213-385-0545

Russell & Mirkovich*(Legal Firm)*
Long Beach, CA

Union Bank*(Major Banking Relationship)*
Long Beach, CA

Subsidiary:

Crosby & Overton Transportation Co. **(1)**
1610 W. 17th
Long Beach, CA 90813
Tel.: 310-432-5445
Approx.Sls.: $33,000,000
Emp.: 28
Local Trucking Without Storage
S.I.C.: 4212
J.R. Dent *(Pres.)*
Robert L. Dent *(Exec. V.P.)*
John Saenz *(V.P.)*
Paul Dent *(Treas. & Sec.)*

CROSCILL, INC.
261 Fifth Ave.
New York, NY 10016
Tel.: 212-689-7222 **NY**
Fax: 212-779-3580
Approx.Sls.: $90,000,000
Emp.: 1,000
Textile Home Furnishings; Window Treatments & Bed Coverings
S.I.C.: 2391; 2392
Myron Kahn *(Pres.)*
Anthony Cassella *(V.P.-Fin. & Controller)*
Ron Emery *(V.P.-Mfg.)*
Bill Hammon *(V.P.-Mktg.)*
David Kahn *(V.P.)*
Stanley Kahn *(V.P., Sec. & Treas.)*
Joe Osborne *(V.P.-Sls.)*
David Talbert *(V.P.)*

Outside Service Firm(s):

Yohalem, Gillman, Field & Agler*(Auditors)*
New York, NY

Marine Midland Bank*(Major Banking Relationship)*
250 Park Ave.
New York, NY 10017
Tel.: 212-503-6642

CROSS MOTORS CORP.
Watterson Expwy. at Newburg Rd.
Louisville, KY 40232
Tel.: 502-459-9900
Fax: 502-459-9900
Year Founded: 1934
Automobile Dealership Selling New Pontiac & Jeep/Eagle Cars & Jeeps
S.I.C.: 5511
Joe D. Cross, Sr. *(Chm.)*
Joe D. Cross, Jr. *(Pres.)*
James Tansellie *(Comptroller)*
David Moser *(Gen. Mgr.)*
Tom Jesukaitis *(Mgr.-Gen. Sls.)*

Computer Systems/Hardware:
BTI

THE CROSSET COMPANY INC.
205 Central Ave.
Cincinnati, OH 45202
Tel.: 513-421-5511 **OH**
Fax: 513-421-8773
Approx.Sls.: $86,000,000
Emp.: 300
Wholesale Distribute Fresh Fruits, Vegetables & Flowers
S.I.C.: 5148; 5193
Roger J. Schorr *(Pres. & Chief Exec. Officer)*
Brian R. Campbell *(V.P.-Fin. & Admin.)*
Elizabeth Garey *(Division Controller)*
Bruce Krahl *(Dir.-Opers.)*
Alice Schadler *(Mgr.-Human Resources)*
Neal Stout *(Mgr.-EDP)*
Don Webster *(Mgr.-Sls.)*
Howard Pippine *(Head Buyer)*

Outside Service Firm(s):

Arthur Andersen & Co.*(Auditors)*
425 Walnut St.
Cincinnati, OH 45202
Tel.: 513-381-6900

Klaine, Wiley, Hoffmann & Meurer*(Legal Firm)*
Cincinnati, OH

Society Bank*(Major Banking Relationship)*
Cincinnati, OH

Continental Associates*(Pension Manager)*
Cincinnati, OH

CROSSMAN CORP.
Routes 5 & 20
East Bloomfield, NY 14443
Tel.: 716-657-6161
Mfr. Toys & Games
S.I.C.: 3944
Ken Scheele *(Pres.)*
Tammy Boda *(Sec.)*

Subsidiaries:

Benjamin Sheridan Co. **(1)**
2600 Chicory Rd.
Racine, WI 53403
Tel.: 414-554-7900
Tel.: 800-837-4353
Fax: 414-554-8057
Emp.: 75
Export
Computer Systems/Hardware:
IBM System 3656
Air Rifles, Air Pistols, Slingshots, Paint Ball Guns
S.I.C.: 3944
Ray Katt *(Chm. Bd.)*
George Ribert *(Pres.)*
David Katt *(V.P.)*

Ranging **(1)**
Routes 5 & 20
East Bloomfield, NY 14443
Tel.: 716-657-6161
Fax: 716-657-5405
Approx.Sls.: $1,300,000
Emp.: 18
Fiscal Year-end: 12/31/90
Mfr. of Range Finders, Rangematic Optical Viewing & Measuring Devices, Optical Tapemeasure, Binoculars, Archery Access.
S.I.C.: 3861; 3827
Kenneth Scheele *(Pres.)*
Jim Jereckos *(Sr. V.P.-Opers.)*
Mitch Riccione *(Treas.)*
Thomas Campbell *(V.P.-Sls. & Mktg.)*
Lynn Searls *(V.P.-Human Resources)*
Pete Spencer *(Dir.-Mfg.)*
Tom Hughes *(Dir.-Engrng.)*
Barbara Schubert *(Dir.-Matls.)*
Ted Horrocks *(Mktg. Mgr.)*
Jim Callahan *(Mgr.-Data Processing)*
Terri Schinsing *(Mktg. Coord.)*

Division:

Fajen & Blair Division **(2)**
400 So. Walnut
Stover, MO 65078
Tel.: 314-377-2608

CROTON WATCH COMPANY
15 W. 37th St.
New York, NY 10018
Tel.: 800-443-7639
Sales Range: $10-19 Million
Emp.: 75
Croton Watches
S.I.C.: 3873

David Mermelstein *(Pres.)*

CROUCH SUPPLY COMPANY, INC.
902 S. Jennings Ave.
Fort Worth, TX 76104
Mailing Address:
P.O. Box 163829
Fort Worth, TX 76161-3829
Tel.: 817-332-2118 **TX**
Fax: 817-332-6511
Year Founded: 1944
Approx.Sls.: $10,000,000
Emp.: 45
Fiscal Year-end: 4/30/90
Distribute Food Product Machinery & Equipment; Chemicals
S.I.C.: 5169; 5046
Bradford Barnes *(Chm. Bd. & Chief Exec. Officer)*
Glen Woodson, II *(Pres. & Chief Oper. Officer)*
Michael Davis *(Chief Fin. Officer)*
David Pohlman *(Dir.-Pur.)*
Glen Rector *(Mgr.-Sls.)*
Paul Ingalls *(Project Engr.)*
Principal(s):
Barnes & Woodson, Inc.

No. of U.S. Offices: 6

Computer Systems/Hardware:
IBM

Outside Service Firm(s):

Rylander, Clay & Opitz*(Auditors)*
Fort Worth, TX

Kelly, Hart & Hallman*(Legal Firm)*
2500 First City Bank Tower
Ft. Worth, TX 76102
Tel.: 817-332-2500

Bank One*(Major Banking Relationship)*
Fort Worth, TX

Bank One*(Pension Manager)*
Fort Worth, TX

CROWDER CONSTRUCTION CO.
1123 E. 10th St.
Charlotte, NC 28230
Tel.: 704-372-3541 **NC**
Fax: 704-376-3573
Sales Range: $40-59 Million
Emp.: 500
Street & Site Development, Industrial, Bridge, Elevated Highway & Water & Sewer Plant Construction
S.I.C.: 1611; 1622; 1629
Otis A. Crowder *(Pres. & Chief Exec. Officer)*
Otis P. Crowder *(Sr. V.P.)*
W.T. Crowder *(Sr. V.P.)*
W.T. Crowder, Jr. *(V.P.-Equip. & Fixed Assets)*
Eugene P. Kiser *(V.P.-Fin.)*
F.L. Lancaster *(V.P.)*
C.E. Tucker *(V.P.-Opers.-Structural Div.)*
Bob Halton *(Dir.-Personnel & Safety)*

Outside Service Firm(s):

Deloitte & Touche*(Auditors)*
Lenoir, NC

NationsBank Carolinas*(Major Banking Relationship)*
One NCNB Plaza T18-7
Charlotte, NC 28255

CROWE ROPE COMPANY
P.O. Box 479
Warren, ME 04864
Tel.: 207-273-2426 **ME**
Fax: 207-273-2405
Year Founded: 1957
Approx.Sls.: $35,000,000
Emp.: 500
Export
Mfr. of Rope, Except Abestos & Wire; Twine
S.I.C.: 2298
Byron A. Crowe *(Pres.)*
Robert Ames *(V.P.-Engrng.)*
William McGonagle *(V.P.-Sls.)*
John Patterson *(Sec.)*

Outside Service Firm(s):

Connecticut National Bank*(Major Banking Relationship)*
777 Main St.
Hartford, CT 06115
Tel.: 203-728-2000

CROWELL, WEEDON & CO.
One Wilshire Boulevard
Los Angeles, CA 90017
Tel.: 213-244-9234
Fax: 213-620-1302
Year Founded: 1932
Emp.: 332
Personal Financial Planning; Municipal & Corporate Bonds; Municipal Bond Funds; Preferred & Common Stocks; Money Market Funds; Tax Sheltered Investments; Tax Deferred Annuities; Mutual Funds & Options; Underwritings & Private Placements; Mergers & Acquisitions; Corporate Evaluations; Institutional & Corporate Services; A Full-Service Brokerage & Investment Banking Firm
S.I.C.: 6211
Donald W. Crowell *(Mng. Partner)*
D.A. Bonet *(Partner & Mgr.-Opers.)*
Stephen S. Brixey, Jr. *(Partner/ Director-Retail Sls. Office Admin.)*
Walter T. Anderson *(Partner, Los Angeles)*
Radoslav A. Artukovic *(Partner, Los Angeles)*
Jacques Bellesiles *(Partner, Los Angeles)*
John J. Connelly *(Partner, Los Angeles)*
William Council *(Partner, Carlsbad)*
Charles O. Doud *(Partner, Los Angeles)*
Richard L. Goforth *(Partner, Los Angeles)*
Robert A. Gore *(Partner, Los Angeles)*
Lloyd Graham *(Partner, Pasadena)*
Alan S. Hackett *(Partner, Carlsbad)*
John M. Hales *(Partner, Newport Beach)*
Harold Harrington *(Partner, Los Angeles)*
Robert A. Hartley *(Partner, Los Angeles)*
John L. Herron *(Partner, Los Angeles)*
Robert M. Horn *(Partner, Newport Beach)*
Homer L. Hutchings *(Partner, Long Beach)*
Steven C. Jackson *(Partner, Los Angeles)*
Richard W. Jacobson *(Partner, Encino)*
Cameron L. Karg *(Partner, Newport Beach)*
Bryan A. Mascoe *(Partner, Los Angeles)*
Robert L. McManus *(Partner, Los Angeles)*
Alan F. McQueen *(Partner, Long Beach)*
Jerome E. Murphy, III *(Partner, Los Angeles)*
Theodore R. Paulson *(Partner, Newport Beach)*
Lynn P. Reitnouer *(Partner)*
Frank E. Ronald, Jr. *(Partner, Newport Beach)*
Murray H. Sandler *(Partner, Los Angeles)*
Norman R. Sarafian *(Partner, Pasadena)*
Robert Smith *(Partner, Los Angeles)*
Eugene H. Springborn *(Partner, Los Angeles)*
Allen N. Strand *(Partner, Los Angeles)*
Jim D. Waymire *(Partner)*
John A. Willett, Jr. *(Partner, Long Beach)*
David C. Williams *(Partner, Los Angeles)*
Otis H. Blasingham *(Limited Partner, Laguna Hills)*
Sara Wenkle *(Limited Partner, Long Beach)*

Outside Service Firm(s):

Deloitte & Touche*(Auditors)*
1000 Wilshire Blvd.
Los Angeles, CA 90017-2472
Tel.: 213-688-0800
Fax: 213-688-0100

Bank of America NT&SA*(Major Banking Relationship)*
555 So. Flower St.
Los Angeles, CA 90071
Tel.: 213-228-3868

CROWLEY MARITIME CORPORATION
155 Grand Ave.
Oakland, CA 94612
Tel.: 510-251-7500 **DE**
Fax: 510-251-7625
Year Founded: 1892
Approx.Sls.: $1,200,000,000
Emp.: 5,000
Fiscal Year-end: 12/31/90
Worldwide Marine Transportation
S.I.C.: 4492; 4491; 4226; 7699; 1629; 4213; 3731
Thomas B. Crowley *(Chm. Bd. & Chief Exec. Officer)*
James Rettig *(Pres.)*
Robert Andres *(Sr. V.P.-Admin.)*
Robert Hood *(Sr. V.P. & Chief Fin. Officer)*
William Pennella *(Sr. V.P.-Human Resources)*
William Verdon *(Sr. V.P. & Gen. Counsel)*
Dick Simpson *(V.P.-Mktg. & Pub. Rels.)*
Tana Shipman *(Sec.)*
Principal(s):
Thomas B. Crowley

Computer Systems/Hardware:
IBM 8100

Outside Service Firm(s):

Deloitte & Touche*(Auditors)*
50 Fremont St.
San Francisco, CA 94105-2230
Tel.: 415-393-4300
Fax: 415-227-0452

Derby, Cook, Quinby, Tweed*(Legal Firm)*
San Francisco, CA

Kominer & Fort*(Legal Firm)*
Washington, DC

The Bank of California, N.A.*(Major Banking Relationship)*
400 California
San Francisco, CA 94104
Tel.: 415-765-0400

Wells Fargo Bank*(Major Banking Relationship)*
420 Montgomery St.
San Francisco, CA 94104

CROWLEY WEBB & ASSOCIATES
268 Main St., Ste. 400
Buffalo, NY 14202
Tel.: 716-856-2932
Fax: 716-856-2940
Year Founded: 1986
Approx.Billings: $26,000,000
Emp.: 30
Consumer, Medical & Industrial Adv.
John R. Webb *(Chm.)*
Joseph J. Crowley *(Pres.)*
Ellen Ott *(V.P., Chief Fin. Officer)*

Computer Systems/Hardware:
Adman

CROWN AMERICAN CORPORATION
Pasquerilla Plaza
Johnstown, PA 15907
Mailing Address:
P.O. Box 879,
Johnstown, PA 15901
Tel.: 814-536-4441 **PA**
Fax: 814-535-9343
Year Founded: 1950
Assets: $1,265,240,000
Liabilities: $1,235,324,000
Net Worth: $29,916,000
Approx.Rev.: $791,412,000
Emp.: 12,000
Fiscal Year-end: 1/31/92
Import
Real Estate, 5 Office Buildings, 21 Hotels, 72 Department Stores, 33 Enclosed Shopping Malls, 9 Community Shopping Centers
S.I.C.: 6512; 5311; 7011; 6552
Frank J. Pasquerilla *(Chm. Bd. & Chief Exec. Officer)*
Mark E. Pasquerilla *(Pres.)*
Nicholas O. Antonazzo *(Exec. V.P.-Real Estate Devel.)*
Marlin R. Havener *(Exec. V.P.-Hotel Div.)*
Curtis C. Costlow *(Sr. V.P.-Property Management)*
Nicholas J. Pasquerilla *(Sr. V.P.-Facilities Plng. Dept.)*
Michael Ballow *(V.P.-Real Estate Leasing)*
James Bambrey *(V.P.-Hotel Opers.)*
Michael Chlebovec *(V.P.-Fin. Services)*
Patrick Galla *(V.P.-Human Resources)*
Robert J. Griffith *(V.P.-Real Estate Leasing)*
Christine Menna *(V.P.-Pub. Rels.)*
Thomas E. Myers *(V.P.-Real Estate Leasing)*
Michael E. Shutack *(V.P.-Mngmt. Information Systems)*
Timothy Trabold *(V.P.-Real Estate Leasing)*
Gary J. Thirkell *(V.P.-Hotel Opers.)*
John A. Washko *(V.P. & Controller)*
Patrick Miniutti *(Chief Fin. Officer)*
Donato Zucco, Ph.D *(Chief Admin. Officer)*
Ronald Rusinak *(Corp. Sec. & Gen. Counsel)*
Leah M. Pasquerilla *(Special Asst. to Chm.)*
Bill Riner *(Dir.-Pur.)*
Hope Slagel *(Mgr.-Employee Benefits)*
Leona Szala *(Mgr.-Travel)*
Melissa Updegraff *(Mgr.-Special Event)*
Principal(s):
Frank J. Pasquerilla

Computer Systems/Hardware:
IBM System 38

Outside Service Firm(s):

Barnes, Saly & Co.*(Auditors)*
Allentown, PA

Gleason Agency*(Commercial Insurance Carrier)*
Johnstown, PA

Gleason, DiFrancesco, Shade & Markovitz*(Legal Firm)*
Penn Traffic Building,
Johnstown, PA 15907
Tel.: 814-535-5561

U.S. National Bank*(Major Banking Relationship)*
Main & Franklin Sts.
Johnstown, PA
Tel.: 814-533-5300

Crown American Corporation—(Continued)

Divisions:

Crown American Facilities Planning Div. (1)
Pasquerilla Plaza
Johnstown, PA 15907
Tel.: 814-536-4441
Fax: 814-535-9305
Computer Systems/Hardware:
IBM/AS 400
Responsible for All Properties Under Construction
S.I.C.: 6552
Nicholas J. Pasquerilla *(Sr. V.P.)*

Crown American Hotel Division (1)
Pasquerilla Plaza
Johnstown, PA 15907
Tel.: 814-536-4441
Fax: 814-535-9499
Computer Systems/Hardware:
IBM System AS400
9 Holiday Inns; 2 Best Western; 2 Super 8 Motels; 7 Comfort Inns; 1 Courtyard by Marriott
S.I.C.: 6512
Marlin R. Havener *(Exec. V.P)*
Gary J. Thirkell *(V.P.-Opers. & Budget)*
Jim Bambrey *(V.P.-Full Service Opers.)*
Ron Hildebrand *(Dir.-Pur. Hotels)*

Crown American Real Estate Division (1)
Pasquerilla Plaza
Johnstown, PA 15907
Tel.: 814-536-4441
Fax: 814-535-9499
30 Enclosed Shopping Malls; 9 Community Centers
S.I.C.: 6512
Nicholas O. Antonazzo *(Exec. V.P.)*
Robert Griffith *(Sr. V.P.-Real Estate Leasing-Key Accts.)*
Michael Ballow *(V.P.-Real Estate Leasing)*
Thomas Myers *(V.P.-Leasing)*
Timothy Trahold *(V.P.-Leasing)*
Joy Miller *(Dir.-Retail Devel.)*
George Lulos *(Dir.-Land Devel.)*

Subsidiary:

Hess's Department Stores, Inc. (1)
Hamilton Mall at 9th
Allentown, PA 18101
Tel.: 215-821-4377 (99%)
Emp.: 15,000
Import
73 Retail Units
S.I.C.: 6512; 5311
Robert O'Connell *(Chm. Bd. & Chief Exec. Officer)*
Stephen J. Furst *(Pres. & Chief Oper. Officer)*
Fred Bentelspacher *(Sr. V.P.-Gen. Mdsg.)*
Kenneth A. Hinkle III *(Sr. V.P.-Fin. & Treas.)*
Susan Hartman *(V.P.-Sls.)*
William Jenkins *(V.P.-Data Processing)*
Bruce Kratz *(V.P.-Personnel)*
Adolf Klova *(V.P. & Adv. Dir.)*
Richard Kula *(V.P. & Dir.-Mngmt. Information Systems)*
James Quigley *(V.P. & Dir.-Distr.)*
James Miller *(V.P. & Dir.-Distr.)*
John Belliti *(V.P. & Reg. Dir.)*
Scott Ratarsky *(V.P. & Reg. Dir.)*
Carl Matichack *(V.P. & Reg. Dir.)*
Nicholas Baxevane *(V.P.-Men's Mdsg.)*
John Murphy *(V.P. & Dir.-Plng.)*

CROWN BUICK, INC.
2121 Clearview Pkwy.
Metairie, LA 70001
Tel.: 504-455-6666
Fax: 504-455-4757
Approx.Sls.: $26,000,000
Emp.: 77
Retail New & Used Automobiles
S.I.C.: 5511
Larry Oggs *(Pres.)*
Gerry Groetsch *(V.P.)*
Bud Weekley *(V.P.)*
Wallace Lancaster *(Sec. & Treas.)*

Outside Service Firm(s):

Jefferson Bankshares, Inc.*(Major Banking Relationship)*
Metairie, LA

CROWN COAL & COKE CO. INC.
200 Nine Parkway Center
Pittsburgh, PA 15220
Tel.: 412-921-1950 **PA**
Fax: 412-921-2938
Year Founded: 1920
Approx.Sls.: $99,000,000
Emp.: 22
Diversified Natural Resources & Energy Services
S.I.C.: 1221; 1222
Albert C. Muse *(Pres. & Chief Exec. Officer)*
Charles H. Muse, Jr. *(Treas. & Chief Fin. Officer)*
Principal(s):
Albert C. Muse
Charles H. Muse, Jr.

Outside Service Firm(s):

Coopers & Lybrand*(Auditors)*
600 Grant St., 35th Fl.
Pittsburgh, PA 15219
Tel.: 412-355-8000
Fax: 412-355-8089

Connecticut General Life Insurance Co.*(Group Insurer)*
P.O. Box 2975,
Hartford, CT 06104
Tel.: 203-726-6000

Pittsburgh National Bank*(Major Banking Relationship)*
Stock Transfer Dept., Fifth & Wood Streets
Pittsburgh, PA 15265

Connecticut Mutual*(Pension Manager)*
Hartford, CT

CROWN FENCE CO.
939 S. Fair Oaks Ave.
Pasadena, CA 91105
Mailing Address:
P.O. Box 50290
Pasadena, CA 91115
Tel.: 818-799-1172 **CA**
Fax: 818-799-1520
Year Founded: 1923
Approx.Sls.: $13,000,000
Emp.: 120
Fiscal Year-end: 12/31/90
Import
Steel Fencing Contractor
S.I.C.: 1799
Paula P. Fiedler *(Chm. Bd. & Sec.)*
Richard D. Fiedler *(Pres.)*
Eric W. Fiedler *(V.P.)*
Gwen Miller *(V.P.)*
Gordon Allen *(Treas. & Controller)*

No. of Mfg. Plants/Facilities: 2
No. of U.S. Offices: 2

Outside Service Firm(s):

Morgan, Lewis & Bockius*(Legal Firm)*
801 S. Grand Ave.
Los Angeles, CA 90017
Tel.: 213-612-5000

Sanwa Bank*(Major Banking Relationship)*
55 East 52nd St.
New York, NY 10055
Tel.: 212-339-6300
Fax: 212-754-1337

CROWN FOODS INC.
5243 Manchester
Saint Louis, MO 63110
Tel.: 314-645-5300 **MO**
Fax: 314-645-1671
Year Founded: 1975
Approx.Sls.: $55,000,000
Emp.: 210
Wholesale Fresh Meats, Poultry & Frozen Foods; Retail Meats & Produce
S.I.C.: 5147; 5144; 5142; 5421; 5431
Larry Stein *(Pres.)*
Don Kohl *(Controller)*

Outside Service Firm(s):

Rubin Brown Gornstein & Co.*(Auditors)*
230 S. Bemiston Ave.
St. Louis, MO 63105
Tel.: 314-727-8150

Boatmen's Trust Company*(Major Banking Relationship)*
100 North Broadway
St. Louis, MO 63102
Tel.: 314-466-2469

CROWN HOLDINGS, INC.
2500 W. County Rd. C
Roseville, MN 55113
Mailing Address:
P.O. Box 1364
Minneapolis, MN 55440
Tel.: 612-639-8900
Fax: 612-639-8051
Approx.Sls.: $24,000,000
Emp.: 60
Import Export
Holding Company; Manufacturer of Heavy Machinery, Metalworking Machinery & Special Industrial Machinery
S.I.C.: 3531; 3549; 3559; 6719
Clifford I. Anderson *(Chm. Bd. & Pres.)*
George E. Anderson *(V.P. & Sec.)*
Glenn D. Breuske *(V.P.-Mktg.)*
Bruce A. Wandrei *(Treas.)*
Sherry Stevenson *(Dir.-Personnel)*
Paul C. Ell *(Mgr.-Export)*
James W. Kenney *(Mgr.-Pur.)*
William L. Stevenson *(Mgr.-Res.)*

Outside Service Firm(s):

Boulay, Heutmaker, Zibell & Co.*(Auditors)*
Minneapolis, MN

Mackall, Crounse & Moore*(Legal Firm)*
1600 TCF Tower
Minneapolis, MN 55402
Tel.: 612-333-1341

Norwest Bank Minnesota, N.A.*(Major Banking Relationship)*
P.O. Box 738, 161 N. Concord Exchange
South St. Paul, MN 55075-0738
Tel.: 800-468-9716

Subsidiary:

Crown Iron Works Company (1)
2500 W. County Rd. C
Roseville, MN 55113
Tel.: 612-639-8900
Fax: 612-639-8051
Emp.: 76
Metal Processing Equipment
S.I.C.: 3559; 3531; 3549; 5084
Clifford I. Anderson *(Chm. Bd. & Pres.)*
George E. Anderson *(V.P. & Sec.)*
Bruce Wandrei *(Treas. & Controller)*
James W. Kenney, III *(Pur. Agent)*

CROWN INTERNATIONAL, INC.
P.O. Box 1000
Elkhart, IN 46514
Tel.: 219-294-8000
Fax: 219-294-8329
Approx.Sls.: $34,000,000
Emp.: 500
Fiscal Year-end: 12/31/90
Export
Mfr. Power Amplifiers; Pressure Zone Microphones & Hand-Held Microphones
S.I.C.: 3651
Ruby Moore Hunsberger *(Chm. Bd.)*
Clyde W. Moore *(Pres.)*
Edwin Moore *(Chief Exec. Officer)*
Dave Bowers *(Chief Fin. Officer)*
James S. Beattie *(Sls. Mgr.)*
Dave McLaughlin *(Forecasting Mgr.)*
Gerry Barclay *(Mgr.-Mktg. Srvcs.)*
Bill Gohen *(Export Mgr.)*
Gerald Stanley *(Res. & Devel.)*

CROWN PRINCE, INC. (CA)
17031 Green Dr.
City of Industry, CA 91745
Mailing Address:
Box 3568,
City of Industry, CA 91744
Tel.: 818-912-3700
Tel.: 800-447-2524
Telex: 69-8508
Fax: 818-913-6953
Emp.: 30
Import
Canned Sea Food Importer
S.I.C.: 5149
Robert Hoffman *(Pres.)*
Elvest Hawkins *(Controller)*
James Corbett *(Dir.-Sls. & Mktg.)*
Linda Guiney *(Mktg. Mgr.)*

Outside Service Firm(s):

First Interstate Bank*(Major Banking Relationship)*
City of Industry, CA

Division:

Crown Prince Divisional Office (1)
1675 Lakes Pkwy., Ste. 115
Lawrenceville, GA 30243

CROWN TEXTILE COMPANY
Three Valley Sq.
Blue Bell, PA 19422
Tel.: 215-641-9900
Fax: 215-641-9941
Year Founded: 1895
Approx.Sls.: $50,000,000
Emp.: 650
Fiscal Year-end: 7/31/92
Export
Specialty Textile Producer of Fusible & Sew-In Interfacings, Waistbandings, Cap Stiffeners, Interlinings, Underlinings in Wovens, Non-Wovens & Weft Insertion & Composites; Stylus Non-Woven, Armo-Wool, Armo Press, Acro & Fusible Acro, Fino II (P-1), P-26 Red Edge, SRF-Stretch Recovery Fusbile Armoflexxx, Fusible P-91, Armoite, So Sheer, Armo Fleece & Industrial Fabrics
S.I.C.: 2211; 2396
Richard C. Sheerr *(Chm. Bd., Pres & Chief Exec. Officer)*
Frank Engels *(Sr. V.P.-Mktg.)*
Anthony Hall *(V.P.-Mktg. & Sls.)*
Byron Hannon *(V.P.-Human Resources)*
Martin Lightman *(V.P.-Oper. Services)*
James Pope *(Controller)*
Joseph Sabatini *(Dir.-Mfg. Services)*
Carol Weber *(Dir.-Sls. & Mktg.)*

No. of Mfg. Plants/Facilities: 4

Outside Service Firm(s):

KPMG Peat Marwick*(Auditors)*
1600 Market St.
Philadelphia, PA 19103
Tel.: 215-299-3100

Wolf, Block, Schorr & Solis-Cohen*(Legal Firm)*
111 S. 15th
Philadelphia, PA 19102
Tel.: 215-569-4000

Provident National Bank*(Major Banking Relationship)*
Collegeville, PA

CRUCIBLE MATERIALS CORP.
State Fair Blvd.
Syracuse, NY 13209
Mailing Address:
P.O. Box 977
Syracuse, NY 13201
Tel.: 315-487-4111
Year Founded: 1983
Sales Range: $100-499 Million
Emp.: 2,500

CPM & Conventional Tool & High Speed Steels, Stainless, Die Steels, High Temperature Alloys, Stainless & Special Alloy Pipe & Tube, Alnico, Ferrite & Rare Earth Permanent Magnets, Superalloy & Titanium Powder
S.I.C.: 3312; 3339; 3499
John Vensel *(Chm. Bd., Pres. & Chief Exec. Officer)*
Gene Jaggers *(V.P.-Fin. & Treas.)*
James M. Stevenson *(V.P.-Admin.)*
Harvey O. Simmons III *(Gen. Counsel & Sec.)*
Y.O. Reich *(Mgr.-Adv.)*

No. of Mfg. Plants/Facilities: 7
No. of U.S. Offices: 7
No. of Foreign Offices: 1

Computer Systems/Hardware:
IBM System 36

Outside Service Firm(s):

KPMG Peat Marwick*(Auditors)*
345 Park Ave.
New York, NY 10154
Tel.: 212-758-9700
Fax: 212-872-3308

Mellon Bank*(Major Banking Relationship)*
New York, NY

Non-U.S. Holding:

Crusteel Ltd. **(1)**
Rutland Way
Sheffield, S3 8DG, United Kingdom
Tel.: 44-742-760651 (100%)
Distr. of Tool Steel, Stainless Steel Bars & Other Specialty Steel
S.I.C.: 5051
Max Brown *(Dir.)*

CRUM ELECTRIC SUPPLY CO., INC.
460 Circle Drive
Casper, WY 82601
Tel.: 307-266-1278
Fax: 307-235-2041
Year Founded: 1976
Assets: $3,883,813
Liabilities: $2,611,879
Net Worth: $1,271,934
Approx.Sls.: $12,758,509
Emp.: 55
Fiscal Year-end: 3/30/92
Supply Electrical Equipment & Parts to Electrical Contractors, Industrial Users, Utilities & Equipment Builders
S.I.C.: 5063
David H. Crum *(Pres., Chief Exec. & Chief Fin. Officer)*
Mary M. Crum *(Treas. & Sec.)*
Jim Roden *(Controller)*
Pat Eisenhauer *(V.P.-Sales & Mktg.)*
Steven Shepherd *(V.P. & Dir.-Inventory)*

Outside Service Firm(s):

Porter & Muirhead*(Auditors)*
Casper, WY

First Interstate Bank*(Major Banking Relationship)*
Casper, WY

Lincoln National Life Insurance Co.*(Group Insurer)*
Omaha, NE

CRUSTBUSTER, INC.
4 Dodge Rd.
Dodge City, KS 67801
Tel.: 316-227-7106
Fax: 316-385-2429
Approx.Sls.: $10,000,000
Emp.: 110
Manufacture Farm Tillage & Seeding Equipment
S.I.C.: 3524; 3523
Donald F. Hornung *(Pres. & Gen. Mgr.)*
Ronald Hornung *(V.P.)*
Nancy Hutton *(Sec., Treas. & Controller)*
Wayne Daubert *(Mgr.-Sls.)*

Outside Service Firm(s):

Grant Thornton*(Auditors)*
800 Fourth Financial Center
Wichita, KS 67202

First National Bank*(Major Banking Relationship)*
Spearville, KS

CRYSTAL CABINET WORKS, INC.
1100 Crystal Dr.
Princeton, MN 55371
Tel.: 612-389-4187 **MN**
Fax: 612-389-5749
Year Founded: 1965
Approx.Sls.: $45,000,000
Emp.: 610
Manufacture Wooden Kitchen Cabinets
S.I.C.: 2434
Jeffrey S. Haehn *(Pres.)*
Brad Lewis *(V.P.-Sls. & Mktg.)*
Robert Nardland *(Controller)*
Char Gatewood *(Dir.-Personnel)*

Outside Service Firm(s):

National City Bank*(Major Banking Relationship)*
75 S. Fifth St.
Minneapolis, MN 55402

CRYSTAL CLEAR INDUSTRIES COMPANY
2 Bergen Turnpike
Ridgefield Park, NJ 07660
Tel.: 201-440-4200
Fax: 201-440-1758
Sales Range: $40-59 Million
Emp.: 300
Import Export
Crystal Table & Floor Lamps
S.I.C.: 3229; 3645
Leopold Lefkowitz *(Pres.)*
Abraham Lefkowitz *(Chief Exec. Officer)*
Mike Gelb *(Sr. V.P.-Sls.)*
Bernard Camens *(Sr. V.P.-Sls-Lighting Div.)*
Dennis Sussman *(Sr. V.P.-Sls.-Lighting Div.)*
Zev Rosengarten *(V.P.-Pur.)*
Morton Roth *(V.P.-Fin.)*
Melissa Schwartz *(Dir.-Mktg.)*
Jeff Teller *(V.P.-Mktg.)*
Gregory J. Perrin *(Gen. Counsel)*

Outside Service Firm(s):

Saul Friedman Co.*(Auditors)*
Brooklyn, NY

First Fidelity Bank, N.A.*(Major Banking Relationship)*
Ridgefield Park, NJ

Greg Perrin*(Legal Firm)*
Ridgefield, NJ

CRYSTAL CREAM & BUTTER COMPANY
1013 D St.
Sacramento, CA 95814
Mailing Address:
P.O. Box 1313
Sacramento, CA 95806
Tel.: 916-444-7200
Fax: 916-448-0284
Approx.Sls.: $140,000,000
Emp.: 400
Manufacture Dairy Products
S.I.C.: 2026; 2021; 2024
K.W. Hansen *(Chm. Bd.)*
D.K. Hansen *(Pres.)*
C.R. Hills *(V.P.-Mktg.)*
D.W. Stimson *(Controller)*

Computer Systems/Hardware:
IBM System 38

Outside Service Firm(s):

Rossmann & Co.*(Auditors)*
Sacramento, CA

Foundation Health*(Group Insurer)*
Sacramento, CA

Bank of America NT&SA*(Investment Banker)*
Sacramento, CA

California Western Life*(Pension Manager)*
Sacramento, CA

Subsidiaries:

McColls Dairy **(1)**
2500 Angelo Ave.
Redding, CA 96001
Tel.: 916-241-4713
Manufacture Milk; Distribute Dairy Products
S.I.C.: 2026
Arnold Stein *(Pres.)*

Vitafreze Frozen Confections **(1)**
P.O. Box 1313
Sacramento, CA 95806
Tel.: 916-455-3030
S.I.C.: 2024

CRYSTAL FLASH PETROLEUM CORP.
5221 Ivy Tech Dr.
Indianapolis, IN 46268
Mailing Address:
P.O. Box 684
Indianapolis, IN 46206
Tel.: 317-879-2849 **IN**
Fax: 317-879-2855
Year Founded: 1930
Approx.Sls.: $50,000,000
Emp.: 225
Retail Gas & Convenience Stores
S.I.C.: 5541; 5411
Frank B. Fehsenfeld *(Chm. Bd.)*
Mac Fehsenfeld *(Pres. & Chief Exec. Officer)*
Greg Cobb *(V.P.-Opers.)*
Fred M. Fehsenfeld *(V.P. & Treas.)*
Lewis Davis *(Sec.)*
Principal(s):
Frank B. Fehsenfeld
Mac Fehsenfeld
Fred M. Fehsenfeld

Outside Service Firm(s):

R. J. Pile & Co.*(Auditors)*
Indianapolis, IN

Kunz & Kunz*(Legal Firm)*
Indianapolis, IN

INB National Bank*(Major Banking Relationship)*
One Indiana Sq.
Indianapolis, IN 46266
Tel.: 317-266-6000

CRYSTAL GEYSER
501 Washington
Calistoga, CA 94515
Mailing Address:
P.O. Box 304
Calistoga, CA 94515
Tel.: 707-942-0500 **CA**
Fax: 707-942-0647
Sales Range: $10-19 Million
Emp.: 50
Mfr. & Distributor of Sparkling Mineral Water, Natural Beverages & Vitamin Fortified Beverages
S.I.C.: 5149; 2086; 5499
Peter Gordon *(Chm. Bd.)*
Leo Soong *(Pres.)*
Kevin McClanahan *(V.P.-Mktg.)*
Connie Dempsey *(Dir.-Fin.)*
Principal(s):
Peter Gordon
Leo Soong

Computer Systems/Hardware:
Tatung Taxan Supercomputer

Outside Service Firm(s):

Grant Thornton*(Auditors)*
San Francisco, CA

Napa Valley Bank*(Major Banking Relationship)*
Calistoga, CA

THE CRYSTAL TISSUE CO.
3120 S. Verity Pkwy.
Middletown, OH 45042
Mailing Address:
P.O. Box 500
Middletown, OH 45042
Tel.: 513-423-0731 **DE**
Fax: 513-423-0516
Year Founded: 1894
Approx.Sls.: $45,000,000
Emp.: 325
Fiscal Year-end: 12/31/90
Import Export
Manufactures Commercial & Specialty Tissues, Gift Wraps, Tissue Folds
S.I.C.: 2678; 2621
William C. Akers *(Chm. Bd.)*
James F. Akers *(Pres. & Chief Exec. Officer)*
C. Robert Keener *(Exec. V.P. & Chief Oper. Officer)*
E. Randall Laubach *(V.P.-Fin., Chief Fin. Officer, Treas. & Admin.)*
S.W. Kelly *(Dir.-Sls. & Mktg.)*
Daniel Price *(Dir.-Purch.)*
R. Keith Singleton *(Mgr. -Indus. Relations)*

Outside Service Firm(s):

Deloitte & Touche*(Auditors)*
Chiquita Center, 250 E. 5th St., Ste. 1900
Cincinnati, OH 45202
Tel.: 513-784-7100

Smith & Schnacke*(Legal Firm)*
Cincinnati, OH

Bank One of Middletown*(Major Banking Relationship)*
Middletown, OH

Bank One*(Major Banking Relationship)*
100 E. Broad St.
Columbus, OH 43216
Tel.: 614-248-5995

CUBIX CORPORATION
2800 Lockheed Way
Carson City, NV 89706
Tel.: 702-883-7611 **DE**
Year Founded: 1975
Assets: $15,191,000
Earnings: $2,074,000
Liabilities: $2,835,000
Net Worth: $12,356,000
Approx.Sls.: $22,100,000
Emp.: 120
Fiscal Year-end: 11/30/88
Mfr. Microcomputers
S.I.C.: 3575
Don Lehr *(Chm. Bd. & Chief Exec. Officer)*
Al Fiegehen *(Pres.)*
Ron Law *(V.P., Treas. & Chief Fin. Officer)*
Robert Eichenberger *(Dir.-Opers.)*
Joanne Lanigir *(Dir.-Personnel)*
Richard Vogt *(Dir.-Fin.)*
Jim Zakzeski *(Dir.-Mktg.)*

No. of Mfg. Plants/Facilities: 1
No. of U.S. Offices: 3
No. of Foreign Offices: 1

Computer Systems/Hardware:
L.F. Technologies Model 1650; Cubix Unix System

Cubix Corporation—(Continued)

Outside Service Firm(s):

Price Waterhouse*(Auditors)*
660 Newport Center Dr., Ste. 600
Newport Beach, CA 92660
Tel.: 714-640-9200

Crowell, Susich, Owen & Tackes Ltd.*(Legal Firm)*
Carson City, NV

VINCE CULLERS ADVERTISING INC.
676 St. Clair, Ste. 2222
Chicago, IL 60611
Tel.: 312-649-7777 IL
Fax: 312-649-1957
Year Founded: 1956
Approx.Billings: $18,000,000
Emp.: 20
Fiscal Year-end: 3/31/91
Advertising for the Black Consumer Market
S.I.C.: 7311
Vincent T. Cullers *(Pres., Chief Exec. Officer & Treas.)*
Marian B. Cullers *(Exec. V.P. & Sec.)*
George Boykin *(Dir.-Mktg.)*
Carmelita R. Cullers *(Dir.-Pub. Rels. & Special Events Coord.)*

Computer Systems/Hardware:
Unisys 5000 C (Mini), Hewlett Packard PC, Macintosh PC

CULLMAN PRODUCTS CORPORATION
1909 Beach Ave. S.E.
Cullman, AL 35055
Mailing Address:
P.O. Box 489
Cullman, AL 35056
Tel.: 205-734-4921
Fax: 205-734-0380
Year Founded: 1959
Approx.Sls.: $75,000,000
Emp.: 500
Fiscal Year-end: 12/31/90
Mfr. of Mouldings
S.I.C.: 3469; 3442; 3471
Pete Sims *(Mgr.-Human Resources)*
John E. Leigeber *(Mgr.-Customer Service)*
John DiOrio *(Pur. Agent)*

CULLMAN VENTURES, INC.
767 Third Ave.
New York, NY 10017
Tel.: 212-751-6655
Fax: 212-888-7709
Approx.Sls.: $200,000,000
Emp.: 800
Holding Company: Calendars, Appointment Books & Catalogs; Co-op Advertising; Buying Group of Independent National Pharmacies
S.I.C.: 6719; 2678; 2759; 2761
Lewis B. Cullman *(Pres.)*
G. Thomas Hargrove *(Exec. V.P.)*
James O. Moore *(V.P.-Fin., Treas. & Asst. Sec.)*
Mildred F. Eisenmayer *(Sec. & Asst. Treas.)*

Outside Service Firm(s):

Ernst & Young*(Auditors)*
787 Seventh Ave.
New York, NY 10019
Tel.: 212-773-1243

Paul, Weiss, Rifkind, Wharton & Garrison*(Legal Firm)*
345 Park Ave.
New York, NY 10022
Tel.: 212-644-8000

National Westminster Bank plc*(Major Banking Relationship)*
175 Water St.
New York, NY 10038-4924
Tel.: 212-602-3364

Subsidiaries:

Associated Druggists **(1)**
3131 W. Pawnee
Wichita, KS 67213
Tel.: 316-943-2500
Approx.Sls.: $100,000,000
Emp.: 3,000
Voluntary Co-op Advertising & Buying Group of Independent Retail Pharmacies Participating in Program Sponsored by Member Wholesale Drug Companies
S.I.C.: 7319
Tom Turner *(Pres. & Chief Exec. Officer)*
Jerry Combs *(Sr. V.P. & Gen. Mgr.)*
Rene Koepsel *(Dir.-Adv.)*

Keith Clark **(1)**
101 O'Neil Rd.
Sidney, NY 13838
Tel.: 607-563-9411
Fax: 607-563-8811
Approx.Sls.: $100,000,000
Emp.: 950
Computer Systems/Hardware:
IBM System 38
Offset Printing; Calendars, Appointment Books & Other Desk Prods.
S.I.C.: 2782; 2752
G. Thomas Hargrove *(Chm. Bd.)*
Douglas Willies *(Pres.)*
Leonard Grecco *(V.P.-Fin.)*
Joseph P. Forgiano *(V.P.-Mfg.)*
David Williamson *(V.P.-Mktg. & Sls.-Office Prods. Div.)*
Clay Conover *(V.P.-Adv. Specialty)*
Donald Stone *(Mktg. Mgr.)*
Gary Schoonover *(Design Supvr.)*

Affiliate:

Pharmacists Public Relations Bureau **(1)**
1515 Broadway
New York, NY 10036
Tel.: 212-642-9590
S.I.C.: 7319
Tom Turner *(Pres.)*

Cullum Companies, Inc.
(Acquired by Randall's Food Markets, Inc., name changed to Tom Thumb Food & Drugs Inc.)

CULVER & ASSOCIATES, INC.
533 North 86th St.
Omaha, NE 68114
Tel.: 402-393-5435
Year Founded: 1983
Approx.Billings: $14,000,000
Emp.: 43
Advertising, Marketing, Market Research & Public Relations
Robert H. Culver *(Pres.)*
Mary N. Culver *(Corp. V.P.)*
John Lee *(V.P., Strategic Services)*
Craig Vance *(V.P., Controller)*
Nancy Etheredge *(Dir., Pub. Rels., A.P.R.)*
Robert H. Culver, Sr. *(Data Processing Mgr.)*
Carol Ladd-Wright *(Business Mgr.)*

CULVER TEXTILE CORPORATION
525 52nd St.
West New York, NJ 07093
Tel.: 201-866-6200
Fax: 201-865-0591
Sales Range: $10-19 Million
Emp.: 120
Manufacture Yarn
S.I.C.: 2282
Bruce Goldwyn *(Pres.)*
Sandra Goldwyn *(V.P. & Chief Exec. Officer)*

CUMBERLAND FARMS, INC.
777 Dedham St.
Canton, MA 02021
Mailing Address:
P.O. Box 58,
Canton, MA 02021
Tel.: 617-828-4900
Fax: 617-828-5246
Approx.Sls.: $1,900,000,000
Emp.: 10,000
Convenience Stores; Petroleum Distr.; Gasoline Service Stations
S.I.C.: 5399; 5172; 5541
Demetrios B. Haseotes *(Chm. Bd.)*
Harry Brenner *(Sr. V.P.-Sls.)*
Steven Haranga *(Dir.-Pur.)*
Alvin McKay *(Dir.-Mktg.)*

Computer Systems/Hardware:
IBM

Division:

Gulf Oil **(1)**
165 Flanders Road
Westborough, MA 01581
Tel.: 508-366-4445
Telex: 989349
Fax: 508-898-3230
Gasoline Service Stations
S.I.C.: 5541
J.C. Wansiewicz *(Pres.)*
J.G. Buckley *(V.P.-Wholesale Mktg.)*
G.J. Catenza *(V.P. & Controller)*
D.A. Oliver *(V.P.-Supply & Distr.)*
Robert M. Quinlan *(V.P.-Mktg.)*

CUMBERLAND PACKING CORP.
2 Cumberland St.
Brooklyn, NY 11205
Tel.: 718-858-4200
Fax: 718-260-9017
Approx.Sls.: $60,000,000
Emp.: 300
Mfr. Sugar & Salt Substitutes
S.I.C.: 2099
Benjamin Eisenstadt *(Chm. Bd.)*
Marvin Ernest Eisenstadt *(Pres.)*
Tony Buccola *(V.P.-Sls. & Mktg.)*
Ira A. Eisenstadt *(V.P.)*
Gil Mederos *(V.P.-Fin.)*
Michael Pedeond *(Mgr.-Adv.)*

Outside Service Firm(s):

Chemical Bank*(Major Banking Relationship)*
450 West 33rd St.
New York, NY 10001
Tel.: 212-613-7197
Fax: 212-947-7628

CUMBERLAND-SWAN, INC.
One Swan Drive
Smyrna, TN 37167
Mailing Address:
P.O. Box 129
Smyrna, TN 37167
Tel.: 615-459-8900 TN
Fax: 615-355-6728
Year Founded: 1898
Approx.Sls.: $70,000,000
Emp.: 750
Mfr. & Distr. of Health Care Products & Proprietary Drugs
S.I.C.: 2833; 2834; 5122; 5100
Lonnie L. Smith *(Pres. & Chief Exec. Officer)*
Randall M. Goldstein *(Exec. V.P.)*
Tony Schofield *(Sr. V.P.-Fin.)*
Michael R. Simon *(Sr. V.P.-Human Resources)*
Joe Mitchell *(V.P.-Tech. Affairs)*
Herbert R. Rich *(Gen. Counsel)*
Jesse Jackson *(Treas. & Controller)*
Linda Jones *(Sec. & Sr. Buyer)*
Bill Hale *(Mgr.-Plant)*
Gary Hodge *(Dir.-Data Processing)*
Richard L. Randolph *(Dir.-Pur.)*

No. of Mfg. Plants/Facilities: 2
No. of U.S. Offices: 2

Computer Systems/Hardware:
IBM AS/400

Outside Service Firm(s):

Kraft Bros., Esstman, Patton & Harrell*(Auditors)*
Nashville, TN

Third National Bank*(Major Banking Relationship)*
Nashville, TN

Subsidiary:

Cumberland Freight Line, Inc. **(1)**
13th Ave. & D St.
Smyrna, TN 37167
Tel.: 615-459-8900
Trucking Co.
S.I.C.: 4213
Tom Meyers *(Pres.)*

CUMMINGS INC.
200 12th Ave. S.
Nashville, TN 37203
Tel.: 615-244-5555
Fax: 615-255-6718
Year Founded: 1946
Sales Range: $40-59 Million
Emp.: 357
Fiscal Year-end: 12/31/90
Manufacture & Install Electrical Signs
S.I.C.: 3993; 1731
Thomas L. Cummings, Jr. *(Chm. Bd. & Chief Exec. Officer)*
George Roberts *(Vice Chm.)*
Thomas L. Cummings, III *(Pres. & Chief Oper. Officer)*
Jerry E. Morrison *(Sr. Exec. V.P.-Mktg.)*
W.T. Everett *(Exec. V.P.-Fin. & Admin.)*
Timothy J. Cummings *(V.P.-Engrng.)*
Ruth Binkley *(Controller)*
Richard Head *(Dir.-Pur.)*

No. of Mfg. Plants/Facilities: 4
No. of U.S. Offices: 8

Computer Systems/Hardware:
IBM PC; Unisys 5000-90

Outside Service Firm(s):

Deloitte & Touche*(Auditors)*
424 Church St., Ste. 2400
Nashville, TN 37219-2396

Third National Bank in Nashville*(Major Banking Relationship)*
Nashville, TN

CUMMINS-AMERICAN CORP.
891 Feehanville Dr.
Mount Prospect, IL 60056
Tel.: 708-299-9550 IN
Fax: 708-299-4939
Year Founded: 1956
Assets: $39,000,000
Earnings: $4,000,000
Liabilities: $11,000,000
Net Worth: $28,000,000
Approx.Sls.: $66,000,000
Emp.: 763
Fiscal Year-end: 10/31/91
Import Export
Holding Co.; Banks; Mfr. of Small Business Machines, Coin Counters & Wrappers; Coupon Books
S.I.C.: 6712; 2752; 3578; 3579; 6022
John E. Jones *(Chm. Bd.)*
Joseph Thomas *(Pres.)*
William H. Klotz *(Sr. V.P.)*
Leon R. Cheesbrough *(V.P.-Fin. & Acctg.)*
James L. Briggs *(V.P.)*
John C. Diedrich *(Chief Fin. Officer & Treas.)*

No. of Mfg. Plants/Facilities: 57
No. of U.S. Offices: 57

Computer Systems/Hardware:
IBM System 38

Outside Service Firm(s):

Ernst & Young*(Auditors)*
233 S. Wacker Dr.
Chicago, IL 60606
Tel.: 312-368-1800
Fax: 312-645-3095

McDermott, Will & Emery*(Legal Firm)*
227 W. Monroe St.
Chicago, IL 60606-5096
Tel.: 312-372-2000

Continental Bank N. A.*(Major Banking Relationship)*
231 S. LaSalle St.
Chicago, IL 60697
Tel.: 312-828-2345
Tel.: 800-426-5754
Telex: 312-828-1783

William M. Mercer Incorporated*(Pension Manager)*
Deerfield, IL

Subsidiaries:

Cummins-Allison Corp. **(1)**
891 Feehanville Dr.
Mount Prospect, IL 60056
Tel.: 708-299-9550 (100%)
Emp.: 500
Coin & Currency Handling & Packaging Equip.; Office Machines; Mortgage & Installment Loan Coupon Payment Systems; Paper Shredders, Perforators; Check Signers & Endorsers
S.I.C.: 3578; 3579
Joseph H. Thomas *(Pres. & Chief Oper. Officer)*
John Jones *(Chief Exec. Officer)*
W.H. Klotz *(Exec. V.P.-Intl. Sls.)*
Larry Lorenz *(V.P.-Mktg.)*
Joe Panarale *(V.P.-Employee Rels.)*
Sheldon Goldstein *(Pur. Agent)*

Division:

Allison Payment Systems Div. **(2)**
2200 Production Dr.
Indianapolis, IN 46241
Tel.: 317-244-2440
Joseph H. Thomas *(Chief Exec. Officer)*
Richard Lippitz *(V.P.-Sls.)*
John Mentzer *(V.P.-Admin.)*

Glenview State Bank **(1)**
800 Waukegan Rd.
Glenview, IL 60025
Tel.: 708-729-1900 (95%)
Emp.: 225
Computer Systems/Hardware:
IBM 4381/PC-Network
State Bank
S.I.C.: 6022
John E. Jones *(Chm. Bd. & Chief Exec. Officer)*
James S. Mentzer *(Vice Chm.)*
Paul A. Jones *(Pres.)*

CUMMINS CUMBERLAND INC.
9822 Bluegrass Pkwy.
Louisville, KY 40299
Tel.: 502-491-6060 **KY**
Fax: 502-499-2908
Approx.Sls.: $60,000,000
Emp.: 350
Wholesale Diesel Engines & Industrial Equipment; Franchised Distributor for the Cummins Engine Co.
S.I.C.: 5084; 7538
P. Jack Apple *(Pres.)*
Edward F. Surgeon *(V.P.-Opers.)*
Louis A. Willinger *(Treas.)*
Tim Wells *(Comptroller)*

Outside Service Firm(s):

Deloitte & Touche*(Auditors)*
510 W. Broadway
Louisville, KY 40202
Tel.: 502-562-2000

Robert Ackerson*(Legal Firm)*
Louisville, KY

Citizens Fidelity Bank & Trust Co.*(Major Banking Relationship)*
P.O. Box 33000-Citizens Plaza
Louisville, KY 40232
Tel.: 502-581-3381

CUMMINS INTERMOUNTAIN DIESEL
1030 Gale St.
Salt Lake City, UT 84101
Tel.: 801-355-6500 **UT**
Fax: 801-524-1351
Year Founded: 1953
Approx.Sls.: $61,000,000
Emp.: 370
Mfr. & Distributor of Diesel Engines & Parts; Gasoline Engines; Refrigeration Units; Motor Vehicles
S.I.C.: 5084; 3519; 5078
Loren Pugh *(Pres.)*
Bayne McMillan *(Exec. V.P.)*
Frank Stilper *(Chief Fin. Officer & Treas.)*

Outside Service Firm(s):

Zions First National Bank*(Major Banking Relationship)*
One South Main St.
Salt Lake City, UT 84111
Tel.: 801-582-4812

CUMMINS MID-SOUTH, INC.
666 Riverside Dr.
Memphis, TN 38103
Tel.: 901-577-0666 **TN**
Fax: 901-522-8758
Year Founded: 1972
Approx.Sls.: $57,000,000
Emp.: 255
Diesel Engines & Parts; Diesel Engine Repair; Automotive Generators, Electronic Parts & Equipment
S.I.C.: 5084; 7538; 5063; 5999
W.J. Hergenrader *(Chm. Bd.)*
Richard L. Penn *(Pres.)*
Sally Hergenrader *(Treas.)*
Barbara Penn *(Sec.)*

Outside Service Firm(s):

Deposit Guaranty National Bank*(Major Banking Relationship)*
One Deposit Guaranty Plaza,
Jackson, MS 39201

CUMMINS SOUTHWEST INC.
2239 N. Black Canyon Hwy.
Phoenix, AZ 85009
Mailing Address:
P.O. Box 6688,
Phoenix, AZ 85005
Tel.: 602-252-8021 **AZ**
Fax: 602-253-6725
Year Founded: 1968
Assets: $16,500,000
Liabilities: $15,900,000
Net Worth: $600,000
Sales Range: $40-59 Million
Emp.: 320
Wholesale & Service Cummins Diesel Engines & Generator Sets, Thermo King Refrigeration, Onan Generator Sets, Small Engines
S.I.C.: 5084; 7699; 7623
W. Patrick Snyder *(Pres.)*
Thomas R. Campbell *(Exec. V.P.-Fin.)*
Kurt Peterson *(Controller)*

No. of Mfg. Plants/Facilities: 5
No. of U.S. Offices: 5

Computer Systems/Hardware:
Concurrent

Outside Service Firm(s):

Arthur Andersen & Co.*(Auditors)*
33 W. Monroe St.
Chicago, IL 60603-4067
Tel.: 312-580-0033
Fax: 312-507-6748

The Atlantic Companies*(Commercial Insurance Carrier)*
New York, NY

Provident Mutual*(Group Insurer)*
Los Angeles, CA

Allen, Kimmerer & LaVelle*(Legal Firm)*
Phoenix, AZ

Citibank N.A.*(Major Banking Relationship)*
Phoenix, AZ

CUNNINGHAM-LIMP DEVELOPMENT CO.
5800 Crooks, Ste. 100
Troy, MI 48098
Tel.: 313-828-4000
Fax: 313-828-3312
Emp.: 50
Fiscal Year-end: 12/31/91
Holding Co.; Designers, Engineers & Builders
S.I.C.: 8711; 1522; 1541; 1542; 1629; 6719
J. Bennett Donaldson *(Pres., Chief Exec. Officer & Sec.)*
Don Kegley *(Chief Fin. Officer & Controller)*

Outside Service Firm(s):

Plante & Moran*(Auditors)*
Southfield, MI

Dahlberg, Mallender & Gawne*(Legal Firm)*
Detroit, MI

NBD Bank, N.A.*(Major Banking Relationship)*
Troy, MI

Subsidiary:

Cunningham Engineers, Inc. **(1)**
5800 Crooks Rd.
Troy, MI 48098
Tel.: 313-828-4000 (100%)
Engineering Co.; Architectural Design & Planning Service
S.I.C.: 8711; 8742
William H. Gillet *(Pres.)*

CUPLEX, INC.
1500 E. Hwy. 66
Garland, TX 75040
Tel.: 214-276-0333 **TX**
Fax: 214-276-3401
Approx.Sls.: $26,000,000
Emp.: 375
Printed Circuit Boards
S.I.C.: 3672
Ronald P. Ryno *(Chm. Bd. & Pres.)*
J. Jeff Ryno *(Exec. V.P. & Sec.)*
Robert D. Keeler *(V.P.-Fin. & Treas.)*

Outside Service Firm(s):

Ernst & Young*(Auditors)*
2121 San Jacinto, Ste. 500
Dallas, TX 75201
Tel.: 214-969-8000

CURRAN CONTRACTING CO.
7502 S. Main St.
Crystal Lake, IL 60014
Tel.: 815-455-5100 **IL**
Fax: 815-455-7894
Approx.Sls.: $65,000,000
Emp.: 300
Highway & Street Paving Contractor; Ceramic Wall & Floor Tile; Sod Farms; Grass Seed; Nursery Stock Seeds & Bulbs; Railroad Equipment & Supplies
S.I.C.: 1611; 3253; 0181; 5191; 5088
John H. Curran *(Chief Exec. Officer)*
William Curran *(Pres.)*
Michael Curran *(V.P.)*
Jack E. Krejca *(Treas.)*
Catherine Curran *(Sec.)*

Outside Service Firm(s):

Deloitte & Touche*(Auditors)*
Two Prudential Plaza, 180 N. Stetson
Chicago, IL 60601
Tel.: 312-946-2039

LaSalle National Bank*(Major Banking Relationship)*
135 S. La Salle St.
Chicago, IL 60690

THE CURRY CORPORATION
727 Central Ave.
Scarsdale, NY 10583
Tel.: 914-723-9200
Fax: 914-723-3469
Approx.Sls.: $454,000,000
Emp.: 600
Fleet & Individual Leasing & Sale of Automobiles, Trucks & Equipment
S.I.C.: 5511; 7359; 7513; 7515
Bernard F. Curry, Jr. *(Pres.)*
Gilbert L. Fitzpatrick *(Exec. V.P. & Sec.)*
Casper LaBarbera *(V.P.)*
Barbara A. Curry *(Treas.)*

Outside Service Firm(s):

Bennett Kielson Co.*(Auditors)*
New Rochelle, NY

CURTIS INSTRUMENTS, INC.
200 Kisco Ave.
Mount Kisco, NY 10549
Tel.: 914-666-2971 **NY**
Fax: 914-666-2188
Year Founded: 1960
Approx.Sls.: $25,000,000
Emp.: 325
Export
Mfr. of Instruments For Measuring Electrical Quantities; Test Equipment For Electronic & Electrical Circuits; Integrated Circuit Testers; Electrical Battery Testers; Speed Indicators & Recorders
S.I.C.: 3825; 3824
Edward M. Marwell *(Pres.)*
Eugene Finger *(V.P.-Engrng.)*
Erland Hagman *(V.P.-Sls.)*
Stuart E. Marwell *(V.P.-Fin.)*
Carol Niebler *(V.P.-Mfg.)*
Anne Papaelias *(V.P.-Human Resources)*
Stephen Post *(V.P.)*

Outside Service Firm(s):

Coopers & Lybrand*(Auditors)*
P.O. Box 10108, One Canterbury Green
Stamford, CT 06904-2108
Tel.: 203-326-8400
Fax: 203-323-0771

Barclays Bank plc*(Major Banking Relationship)*
75 Wall St.
New York, NY 10265
Tel.: 212-412-4000

CURTIS LUMBER COMPANY
885 Rte. 67
Ballston Spa, NY 12020
Tel.: 518-885-5311
Fax: 518-885-1126
Approx.Sls.: $57,000,000
Emp.: 270
Retail Lumber & Building Supplies; Lumber Manufacturing
S.I.C.: 2421; 5211
Jay Curtis *(Chm. Bd.)*
John Honhalligren *(V.P.)*
Joyce H. Curtis *(Sec.)*
Dave Boloski *(Gen. Mgr.)*

Outside Service Firm(s):

Deloitte & Touche*(Auditors)*
One Lincoln First Square
Rochester, NY 14604
Tel.: 716-232-1200

Ballston Spa National Bank*(Major Banking Relationship)*
Ballston Spa, NY

CURTIS MEDIA GROUP INC.
3012 Highwoods Blvd.
Raleigh, NC 27604
Tel.: 919-876-0674
Radio Broadcasting
S.I.C.: 4832
Donald Curtis *(Pres.)*
Joseph Bell *(Exec. V.P.)*

Divisions:

WBBB **(1)**
Box 1119, 1109 Tower Dr.
Burlington, NC 27216
Tel.: 919-584-0126
Tel.: 800-832-0101
Fax: 919-584-0126
News/Talk AM Radio Station
S.I.C.: 4832
Jack Weinlein *(Gen. Mgr.)*

WCPS **(1)**
Box 100, 3403 Main St.
Tarboro, NC 27886
Tel.: 919-823-2191
Southern Gospel Music Radio
S.I.C.: 4832
Tony Denton *(Gen. Mgr.)*

WEWO **(1)**
Box 529, Hwy. 74
Laurinburg, NC 28352
Tel.: 919-276-2965
Radio Broacasting
S.I.C.: 4832
Jack Inman *(Gen. Mgr.)*

WGBR **(1)**
914 W. Grantham St.
Goldsboro, NC 27530
Tel.: 919-736-1150
Fax: 919-736-3876
AM Radio Station, Adult Programming
S.I.C.: 4832
Walter Sturdivant *(Gen. Mgr.)*

WKTC **(1)**
914 W. Grantham St.
Goldsboro, NC 27530
Tel.: 919-736-1150
Fax: 919-736-3876
FM Radio Station Featuring Modern Country Music
S.I.C.: 4832
Walter Sturdivant *(Gen. Mgr.)*

WMXF AM/FM **(1)**
Box 529, Hwy. 74
Laurinburg, NC 28352
Tel.: 919-276-2965
Tel.: 800-235-9787
General Interest Radio
S.I.C.: 4832
Jack Inman *(Gen. Mgr.)*

WPCM **(1)**
Box 1119, 1109 Tower Dr.
Burlington, NC 27216
Tel.: 919-584-0126
Tel.: 800-832-0101
Fax: 919-584-0739
FM Radio Station Featuring Country Music
S.I.C.: 4832
Jack Weinlein *(Gen. Mgr.)*

WPTF **(1)**
3012 Highwoods Blvd.
Raleigh, NC 27604
Tel.: 919-876-0674
Adult General Interest Radio Programming
S.I.C.: 4832
Joseph Bell *(Exec. V.P. & Gen. Mgr.)*
Don Fowler *(Sales Mgr.)*

WQDR **(1)**
3012 Highwoods Blvd.
Raleigh, NC 27604
Tel.: 919-876-0674
Country Music Radio
S.I.C.: 4832
Donald Curtis *(Gen. Mgr.)*
Mack A. Moore *(Sales Mgr.)*
Barbara G. Price *(Natl. Sales Mgr.)*

WTAB **(1)**
Hwy. 701 Bypass & Avon St.
Tabor City, NC 28463
Tel.: 919-653-2131
Adult Interest AM Radio Station
S.I.C.: 4832
Chuck Lewis *(Gen. Mgr.)*

WYNA **(1)**
Hwy. 701 Bypass & Avon St.
Tabor City, NC 28463
Tel.: 919-653-2131
FM Radio Station, Country Music
S.I.C.: 4832
Chuck Lewis *(Gen. Mgr.)*

THE CURTIS PUBLISHING COMPANY
1000 Waterway Blvd.
Indianapolis, IN 46202
Tel.: 317-636-1000
Fax: 317-634-1791
Approx.Sls.: $30,000,000
Emp.: 250
Magazine Publisher
S.I.C.: 2741
Beurt SerVaas *(Chm. Bd. & Pres.)*
Paul SerVaas *(V.P.)*
Clarence Ormsby *(Sec. & Treas.)*

Subsidiaries:

Creative Marketing Group, Inc. **(1)**
1000 Waterway Blvd.
Indianapolis, IN 46202
Tel.: 317-633-2053

Curtis Intl. Ltd. **(1)**
1000 Waterway Blvd.
Indianapolis, IN 46202
Tel.: 317-633-2048

Curtis Management Group **(1)**
1000 Waterway Blvd.
Indianapolis, IN 46202
Tel.: 317-633-2050
Fax: 317-633-2047
Emp.: 25
Fiscal Year-end: 12/31/91
Manages Estates of Entertainers & Athletes for Licensing, Advertising & Promotional Purposes
S.I.C.: 8741
Mark Roesler *(Pres. & Chief Exec. Officer)*

U.S. Rubber Reclaiming, Inc. **(1)**
2000 Rubber Way Rd.
Vicksburg, MS 39182
Tel.: 601-636-7071
Fax: 601-638-0151
Approx.Sls.: $10,000,000
Emp.: 101
Fiscal Year-end: 7/31/92
Import Export
Recycled Rubber, Slabs and Reclaimed Rubber
S.I.C.: 3069
Bobby D. LaGrone *(Pres.)*
Arthur L. Hawkins *(V.P.-Sls.)*
Eugene D. Payne *(V.P.-Mfg.)*
Terry Guynes *(Mgr.-Quality Control)*

CURTIS SCREW CO., INC.
1130 Niagara St.
Buffalo, NY 14213
Tel.: 716-885-0110
Fax: 716-885-0561
Year Founded: 1905
Approx.Sls.: $15,200,000
Emp.: 138
Manufacture Precision Custom Components for Automobiles, Pumps, Quick Connects & Hand Tools
S.I.C.: 3451
John T. Hoskins *(Chm.)*
Robert C. Squier *(Pres.)*
Michael Taeger *(V.P.)*

L.N. CURTIS & SONS
1800 Peralta St.
Oakland, CA 94607
Tel.: 510-839-5111 **CA**
Fax: 510-839-5325
Approx.Sls.: $30,000,000
Emp.: 66
Municipal & Industrial Fire Protection & Safety Equipment
S.I.C.: 5087
Roger William Curtis *(Chm. Bd., Chief Exec. Officer & Sec.)*
Paul F. Curtis *(Pres., Chief Oper. Officer & Treas.)*
Steven L. Chandler *(Sr. V.P.)*
Tim D. Beth *(V.P.)*
Donald E. Miller *(V.P.)*
T.D. Beth *(Dir.-Pur.)*
William M. Curtis *(Dir.-Mktg.)*
Mark Dolim *(Dir.-Sls.)*

Outside Service Firm(s):

Leighton, Carter & Bonovich*(Auditors)*
San Rafael, CA

Bank of America NT&SA*(Major Banking Relationship)*
Oakland, CA

CURTIS-TOLEDO, INC.
1905 Kienlen Ave.
Saint Louis, MO 63133
Tel.: 314-383-1300
Fax: 314-381-1439
Approx.Sls.: $15,000,000
Emp.: 135
Fiscal Year-end: 12/31/91
Import
Mfr. Curtis Air Compressors; Clutch Discs; Toledo Pipe Threading Tools; Hose Cutting Machines
S.I.C.: 3563; 3541; 3291
K.M. Carpenter *(Pres.)*
Karen L. Carpenter *(Exec. V.P. & Sec.)*
D. Parsons *(V.P.-Fin.)*
Al Jerrigan *(V.P.-Sls.)*
Gary Lawson *(V.P.-Opers.)*

CURVCRAFT
600 Powell Ave.
Dunn, NC 28334
Mailing Address:
P.O. Box 946,
Dunn, NC 28334
Tel.: 919-892-4025
Tel.: 800-544-2612
Fax: 919-892-2494
Year Founded: 1967
Approx.Sls.: $10,000,000
Emp.: 120
Fiscal Year-end: 12/31/91
Import
Mfr. of Office Seating
S.I.C.: 2522; 2521
Henry Bandremer *(Pres.)*
Andrew Bandremer *(V.P.)*

Computer Systems/Hardware:
Zenix; WYSE

CUSTOM CONTROL SENSORS, INC.
21111 Plummer St.
Chatsworth, CA 91311
Mailing Address:
P.O. Box 2516
Chatsworth, CA 91313
Tel.: 818-341-4610
Approx.Sls.: $17,000,000
Emp.: 350
Pressure Flow & Temperature Switches
S.I.C.: 3822; 3625; 3823
Allen V.C. Davis *(Chm. Bd. & Pres.)*
Robert L. Powell *(Exec. V.P.)*
Philip Daley *(Chief Engr.)*

Outside Service Firm(s):

KPMG Peat Marwick*(Auditors)*
725 S. Figueroa St.
Los Angeles, CA 90017
Tel.: 213-972-4000

Walter, Finestone, Richter & Kane*(Legal Firm)*
Los Angeles, CA

First Interstate Bank of California, N.A.*(Major Banking Relationship)*
P.O. Box 3667,
Los Angeles, CA 90051
Tel.: 213-614-4000

CUSTOM DECOR, INC.
1196 South Little Creek Rd.
Dover, DE 19901
Mailing Address:
P.O. Box 538
Dover, DE 19903
Tel.: 302-734-9414 **DE**
Fax: 302-734-9419
Year Founded: 1974
Emp.: 12
Importer/Wholesaler of Giftware & Decorative Accessories
S.I.C.: 5199
William P. Scotton *(Pres.)*

No. of U.S. Offices: 1

Computer Systems/Hardware:
MAI Basic 4

Outside Service Firm(s):

Bill Witham*(Legal Firm)*
Dover, DE

CUSTOM PAK, INC.
P.O. Box 3083
Clinton, IA 52732
Tel.: 319-242-1801 **IA**
Year Founded: 1974
Approx.Sls.: $40,000,000
Emp.: 585
Mfr. of Blow Molded Finished Plastic Products
S.I.C.: 3089
Richard Olsen *(Pres.)*
Louise Laurent *(Treas. & Sec.)*
Paul Nugent *(V.P. & Gen. Mgr.)*
Jon Newsome *(Mgr.-Sls.)*

Outside Service Firm(s):

Clifton Gunderson*(Auditors)*
Clinton, IA

Clinton National Bank*(Major Banking Relationship)*
Clinton, IA

Subsidiary:

Midwest Poly **(1)**
PO Box 3023,
Clinton, IA 52732
Tel.: 319-243-4858
Bill Huginin *(Gen. Mgr.)*

CUSTOM SHOP SHIRTMAKERS INC.
18 E. 50th St., 10th fl.
New York, NY 10022
Tel.: 212-223-3600
Fax: 212-223-3608
Year Founded: 1937
Sales Range: $40-59 Million
Emp.: 650
Fiscal Year-end: 12/31/90
Custom Made Men's Shirts
S.I.C.: 2321; 5699
Mortimer Levitt *(Chm. Bd.)*
Tom Rinehart *(Pres.)*
Jules Seiden *(V.P.)*

Outside Service Firm(s):

Edward Isaacs & Co.*(Auditors)*
New York, NY

National Community Bank*(International Bank Affiliate)*
Jefferson, NJ

Malcolm Chaifetz*(Legal Firm)*
New York, NY

Subsidiary:

Morley Shirt Company **(1)**
Rte. 23
Franklin, NJ 07416
Tel.: 201-827-9135
Emp.: 750
Made-to Measure Men's Shirts
S.I.C.: 2321; 5611
Peter Kimmelman *(Pres.)*

H.H. CUTLER COMPANY
120 Ionia Ave., S. W.
Grand Rapids, MI 49501
Mailing Address:
P. O. Box 2488
Grand Rapids, MI 49501
Tel.: 616-459-9101
Approx.Sls.: $100,000,000
Emp.: 1,500
Infants & Children's Wearing Apparel
S.I.C.: 2369
William F. Cutler *(Co-Chm. Bd.)*
Richard F. Cutler *(Co-Chm. Bd.)*
Hal C. Smith *(Pres.)*
Terry Wagner *(V.P.-Mktg.)*
Greg Lamdert *(Sec. & Treas.)*

Subsidiaries:

Cutler Manufacturing Corp. **(1)**
2455 Oak Industrial Dr. N.E.
Grand Rapids, MI 49505
Tel.: 616-774-2258

Midwest Fashions, Inc. **(1)**
4550 Clyde Park S.W.
Grand Rapids, MI 49509

CUTLER MANUFACTURING CORPORATION
5204 U. S. Hwy. 98 South
Highland City, FL 33846
Mailing Address:
Drawer M
Eaton Park, FL 33840
Tel.: 813-644-3573
Fax: 813-646-4517
Approx.Sls.: $10,000,000
Emp.: 125
Fiscal Year-end: 12/31/90
Mfrs. of Pneumatic Tubes & Mail Boxes - U.S. Postal Service Approved; Gravity Flow Trash & Linen Chutes, Tenant Storage Lockers.
S.I.C.: 3579; 2531; 3089; 5087
James I. Botkin *(Pres.)*
L. Holder *(V.P.-Mfg.)*
D. Woodington *(V.P.-Fin.)*
Lori Ladoucer *(Mgr.-Sls.)*
Richard Shumite *(Mgr.-Mktg.)*

CUTTER FLYING SERVICE, INC.
2502 Clark Carr, Loop S.E.
Albuquerque, NM 87106
Mailing Address:
P.O. Box 274
Albuquerque, NM 87103
Tel.: 505-842-4169 **NM**
Fax: 505-842-4405
Year Founded: 1927
Approx.Sls.: $10,000,000
Emp.: 83
Self-propelled Aircraft, Flying Charter Service, Aircraft Radio Equipment & Repair; Janitorial Service
S.I.C.: 5599; 4581; 4522; 7622
W.R. Cutter *(Chm. Bd. & Pres.)*
Lowell Whitten *(Pres. & Gen. Mgr.)*
Charles Leonard *(V.P.-Opers.)*

Outside Service Firm(s):

Pannell Kerr & Foster*(Auditors)*
Albuquerque, NM

Sun West Bank of Albuquerque*(Major Banking Relationship)*
P.O. Box 25500
Albuquerque, NM 87125-0500
Tel.: 505-765-2698
Fax: 505-842-6661

Keleher & McLeod*(Legal Firm)*
P.O. Drawer AA
Albuquerque, NM 87103
Tel.: 505-842-6262

CYBER SYSTEMS, INC.
2570 E. Cerritos Ave.
Anaheim, CA 92806
Tel.: 714-634-2800 **CA**
Fax: 714-937-1955
Year Founded: 1977
Earnings: $180,914
Emp.: 30
Fiscal Year-end: 6/30/91
Export
Mfr. Computer-Based Data Acquisition & Load Control Systems & Instruments Primarily for Aerospace & Automotive Industry Applications
S.I.C.: 3825
Robert A. De Vito *(Chm. Bd., Pres., Chief Exec. & Chief Oper. Officer)*
Wanda L. Bowland *(Mgr.-Human Resources)*

No. of Mfg. Plants/Facilities: 1
No. of U.S. Offices: 1

Computer Systems/Hardware:
Digital Electronics PDP 11/73; Data General Desktop Generator

Outside Service Firm(s):

Talley & Company*(Auditors)*
Orange, CA

Travelers Insurance Co.*(Commercial Insurance Carrier)*
One Tower Square
Hartford, CT 06183-6130
Tel.: 203-277-4542
Fax: 203-277-5038

Humana Health Care Plan*(Group Insurer)*
St. Louis, MO

Obegi & Brewer*(Legal Firm)*
Newport Beach, CA

Union Bank*(Major Banking Relationship)*
Orange, CA

CYBEREX, INC.
7171 Industrial Park Blvd.
Mentor, OH 44060
Tel.: 216-946-1783
Tel.: 800-631-1236
Telex: 980644
Fax: 216-946-5963
Year Founded: 1969
Approx.Sls.: $10,000,000
Emp.: 120
Import Export
Manufactures Solid State Uninterruptible Power Supplies & Various Power Conditioning Products
S.I.C.: 3612; 3621; 3613; 3625
Edward J. Yohman *(Chm. Bd. & Chief Exec. Officer)*
Gus Stevens *(Pres. & Chief Oper. Officer)*
James E. Murray *(V.P.-Sls.)*
Edward Tornberg *(Sec.)*
Richard Christensen *(Dir.-Standard Prod. Sls.)*
Robert J. Resch *(Dir.-Res. & Devel.)*
Vincent Pona *(Treas.)*
Principal(s):
Edward J. Yohman

No. of Mfg. Plants/Facilities: 1
No. of U.S. Offices: 3

Computer Systems/Hardware:
VAX 4000

Outside Service Firm(s):

Deloitte & Touche*(Auditors)*
1717 East Ninth St.
Cleveland, OH 44114
Tel.: 216-589-1300

Chubb Group*(Commercial Insurance Carrier)*
P.O. Box 1615,
Warren, NJ 07061
Tel.: 201-580-2000

St. Paul Insurance Companies*(Group Insurer)*
St.Paul, MN

Travelers Insurance Co.*(Group Insurer)*
1 Tower Square
Hartford, CT 06183-2492
Tel.: 203-277-4542
Fax: 203-277-5038

Hahn, Loeser & Parks*(Legal Firm)*
Natl. City E. 6 Bldg.
Cleveland, OH 44114
Tel.: 216-621-0150

Scheinfeld, Makey & Kaye*(Major Banking Relationship)*
Houston, TX

The Principal Financial Group*(Pension Manager)*
711 High St.
Des Moines, IA 50309
Tel.: 515-247-4593
Tel.: 800-543-4015

CYBORG SYSTEMS, INC.
2 N. Riverside Plaza, 12th Fl.
Chicago, IL 60606
Tel.: 312-454-1865 **IL**
Fax: 312-930-1033
Year Founded: 1974
Assets: $12,800,000
Liabilities: $10,600,000
Net Worth: $2,200,000
Approx.Sls.: $20,300,000
Emp.: 150
Fiscal Year-end: 2/28/90
Computer Software
S.I.C.: 7372
Michael D. Blair *(Pres. & Chief Exec. Officer)*
James Pierce *(Exec. V.P.)*
Joseph Heery *(V.P. & Chief Fin. Officer)*
John Kluska *(V.P.-Products & Services)*
Alan Ross *(V.P.-New Business Devel.)*
Richard Skibski *(V.P.-Research & Devel.)*
Gary Tarr *(V.P.-Sls.)*
Mary Beth Riordan *(Controller)*
John Gorman *(Payroll Accountant)*
Dennis Johnson *(Mgr.-Quality Assurance & Installation)*
Cy Rappaport *(Mgr.-Human Resources)*
Principal(s):
Michael D. Blair
James Pierce

No. of U.S. Offices: 4
No. of Foreign Offices: 2

Computer Systems/Hardware:
IBM

Outside Service Firm(s):

Coopers & Lybrand*(Auditors)*
203 N. LaSalle St.
Chicago, IL 60601
Tel.: 312-701-5500

Arthur J. Gallagher & Co.*(Commercial Insurance Carrier)*
Chicago, IL

Travelers Insurance Co.*(Group Insurer)*
200 W. Madison St., Ste. 2100
Chicago, IL 60606
Tel.: 312-750-2800

Joel Greenburg Ltd.*(Legal Firm)*
221 N. Lasalle
Chicago, IL

Colonial Bank & Trust Co.*(Major Banking Relationship)*
Chicago, IL

Chicago Corporation*(Pension Manager)*
Chicago, IL

Non-U.S. Holdings:

Cyborg Systems of Canada **(1)**
1274 Pitt St.
Cornwall, Ontario K6J3T5, Canada
Tel.: 613-938-7431
Emp.: 10
Computer Software
S.I.C.: 7372
William Robinson *(Pres.)*

Cyborg Systems (UK) Ltd. **(1)**
Central Ct. Knoll Rise,
Orpington, Kent BR6 OJA, United Kingdom
Emp.: 40
Computer Software
S.I.C.: 7372
William Robinson *(Mng. Dir.)*

D&H DISTRIBUTING COMPANY
2525 N. 7th St.
Harrisburg, PA 17110
Tel.: 717-236-8001
Fax: 717-255-7838
Year Founded: 1918
Approx.Sls.: $100,000,000
Emp.: 250
Fiscal Year-end: 4/30/92
Export
Wholesale Distribution of Major Household Appliances & Related Parts; Kitchen Cabinets; Sound Systems; Closed Circuit & Other TV & Audio Products; Computer & Home Office Electronic Products
S.I.C.: 5064; 5045; 5078; 5099
S.E. Lavine *(Pres. & Chief Oper. Officer)*
Israel Schwab *(V.P.-Sls.)*
Morton Spector *(V.P. & Treas.)*
Morris Schwab *(Sec.)*

D & K OPTICAL, INC.
4415 Poplar Level Rd.
Louisville, KY 40213
Mailing Address:
P.O. Box 37410
Louisville, KY 40233
Tel.: 502-459-6722 **MN**
Fax: 502-458-5919
Year Founded: 1983
Assets: $9,000,000
Net Worth: $9,000,000
Approx.Sls.: $55,000,000
Emp.: 450
Fiscal Year-end: 12/31/90
Import Export
Optical Goods Stores; Optical Lenses of all Types Except Ophthalmic
S.I.C.: 3827; 5995
Employee Matching Gifts Program:
United Way
Larry Joel *(Chm. & Pres.)*
George Tokarczyk *(Sr. V.P.)*
George Brown *(V.P.-Admin.)*
James Kool *(V.P.)*
John Roos *(V.P.-Fin. & Treas.)*

Outside Service Firm(s):

Norwest Bank Minnesota, N.A.*(Major Banking Relationship)*
P.O. Box 738, 161 N. Concord Exchange
South St. Paul, MN 55075-0738
Tel.: 800-468-9716

D&L VENTURE CORP.
227 Main St.
New Britain, CT 06051
Tel.: 203-223-3655
Fax: 203-223-0750
Approx.Sls.: $87,000,000
Emp.: 1,200
Holding Company; Retail Clothing Stores Weathervane, D & L, J. Putnam
S.I.C.: 6719; 5621; 5611
Donald Davidson *(Co-Chm. Bd. & Chief Exec. Officer)*
Phillip T. Davidson *(Co-Chm. Bd.)*
Patrick Quay *(Exec. V.P. & Gen. Mgr.)*
Karl Kochman *(Sr. V.P. & Controller)*

D & R ADVERTISING
100 Jeffryn Blvd.
Deer Park, NY 11729
Tel.: 516-243-4700
Tel.: 800-800-9697
Year Founded: 1987
Approx.Billings: $10,000,000
Emp.: 27
Advertising - Trade, Consumer, Sales Promotion, Travel & Leisure
Walter J. Dygus *(Pres.)*
Anne Mendes *(V.P., Gen. Mgr.)*
Pat Passarellic *(Dir., Fin.)*
Jeffrey Landis *(Pres.-Travel & Leisure Div./Landis & Dygus)*

Computer Systems/Hardware:
Macintosh & IBM PC

D & W FOOD CENTERS, INC.
3001 Orchard Vista Dr., SE
Grand Rapids, MI 49546
Mailing Address:
P.O. Box 878
Grand Rapids, MI 49588-0878
Tel.: 616-940-3580 **MI**
Fax: 616-940-3159
Approx.Sls.: $158,000,000
Emp.: 3,500
Retail Grocery Stores
S.I.C.: 5411
Jeff Gietzen *(Pres.)*
Bob Woodrick *(Chief Exec. Officer)*
Rob Woodrick *(Exec. V.P.-Sls. & Mktg.)*
Doug Blease *(Sr. V.P.-Opers.)*
Jerry Matthews *(Sr. V.P.-Fin.)*
Robert Dykhouse *(V.P.-Store Devel.)*
Doug Scholma *(V.P.-Grocery Sls.)*
John Cromer *(Dir.-MIS)*
Michael Ross *(Dir.-Mktg.)*

Computer Systems/Hardware:
NCR

Outside Service Firm(s):

Deloitte & Touche*(Auditors)*
Grand Rapids, MI

Chary, Nantz, Wood & Hoffius*(Legal Firm)*
Grand Rapids, MI

Michigan National Bank*(Major Banking Relationship)*
77 Monroe Center
Grand Rapids, MI 49501
Tel.: 616-451-7600

DAQ ELECTRONICS INC.
252 Lackland Dr. East
Middlesex, NJ 08846
Tel.: 908-560-0050
Fax: 908-560-8885
Earnings: $150,000
Emp.: 70
Fiscal Year-end: 5/31/90
Develop & Manufacture Computers & Software for Remote Acquisition Control
S.I.C.: 3571; 7372
Stanley Green *(Pres., Chief Exec. & Chief Fin. Officer)*
Philip Epstein *(V.P.)*
Alan Rosenfeld *(V.P. & Sec.)*
Cliff Williams *(V.P.-Mktg. & Sls.)*
Gerald Bellina *(Treas.)*
Sue Kutner *(Mgr.-Fin.)*

Computer Systems/Hardware:
Burroughs B25

Outside Service Firm(s):

Howard Hirschhorn*(Auditors)*
Matawan, NJ

Podvey & Sachs*(Legal Firm)*
Newark, NJ

Central Jersey Bank*(Major Banking Relationship)*
Matawan, NJ

DBM HATCH, INC.
2304 Troy Ave.
El Monte, CA 91733
Tel.: 818-442-8522
Fax: 818-442-2256
Year Founded: 1967
Approx.Sls.: $10,000,000
Emp.: 120
Masonry Contractor
S.I.C.: 1741
C. Dewitt Brown *(Pres.)*
Jim Hensley *(V.P.)*
Danny Kinneson *(Sec. & Treas.)*

D.C. Lottery and Charitable Games Control Board

D.C. LOTTERY & CHARITABLE GAMES CONTROL BOARD
2101 Martin Luther King, Jr. Ave. S.E.
Washington, DC 20020
Tel.: 202-433-8000
Fax: 202-433-7987
Year Founded: 1982
Approx.Sls.: $149,182,000
Emp.: 126
Fiscal Year-end: 9/30/91
Lottery & Public Gaming
S.I.C.: 7999
Barbara Clark *(Chm. Bd.)*
Kenneth Brewer *(Vice Chm.)*
Anthony S. Cooper *(Exec. Dir.)*
Sylvia M. Kinard *(Deputy Exec. Dir.)*
Paul Kuntzler *(Treas.)*
Mona Blake *(Gen. Counsel)*
Dorothy L. Wade *(Chief-Lottery Opers. Div.)*
Arville Brock-Smith *(Chief-Div. Automated Information Services)*
James A. Thompson, Jr. *(Chief-Security & Audit Programs)*
Rosalind R. Inge *(Charitable Games Officer)*
Ivan Read *(Sls. Officer)*
Karen M. Rooths *(Procurement Officer)*
Andrea Murray *(Deputy Public Information Officer)*
Eugene Lyons *(Dir.-Mktg.)*
Robert N. Reid *(Mgr.-Fin. Program & Services)*
William Robinson *(Asst. Mgr.-Fin. Program & Services)*
Carlene Reid-Funn *(Mgr.-Human Resourse Devel.)*
Fran Harris-Stewart *(Public Affairs Specialist)*

Computer Systems/Hardware:
Wang, Honeywell

D.C.I., INC.
600 5th Ave., N.
Saint Cloud, MN 56301
Mailing Address:
P.O. Box 1227,
St. Cloud, MN 56302
Tel.: 612-252-8200 **MN**
Fax: 612-252-0866
Year Founded: 1955
Sales Range: $10-19 Million
Emp.: 230
Fiscal Year-end: 4/30/90
Manufacture Stainless Steel Vessels
S.I.C.: 3443; 3499
Corporate Giving Program: D.C.I. Donates to the Arts, Education & Organizations That Involve Our Employees
Gerald T. Howard *(Pres. & Chief Exec. Officer)*
Steve Stonestrom *(V.P.-Sls.)*
David Saucier *(V.P.-Engrng.)*
Wayne Brickman *(V.P.-Procurement & Human Resources)*
LeRoy L. Erickson *(Sec., Treas. & Chief Fin. Officer)*
Dennis McCarty *(Mgr.-Mfg.)*

No. of Mfg. Plants/Facilities: 1
No. of U.S. Offices: 1

Computer Systems/Hardware:
DEC

Outside Service Firm(s):

McMahon, Hartmann & Amundson*(Auditors)*
St. Cloud, MN

Hoolihan & Neils, P.A.*(Legal Firm)*
St. Cloud, MN

First American National Bank*(Major Banking Relationship)*
Saint Cloud, MN

Western National Bank*(Major Banking Relationship)*
St. Cloud, MN

DCI MARKETING
2727 W. Good Hope Rd.
Milwaukee, WI 53209
Tel.: 414-228-7000
Fax: 414-228-3421
Year Founded: 1944
Approx.Billings: $65,000,000
Emp.: 320
Sls. Promo., Merchandising, POP, Telemarketing & Direct Response
Ronald C. Chimenti *(Pres. & Chief Exec. Officer)*
Robert W. Kraft *(Exec. V.P., Chief Oper. Officer, POP Display & Mdsg. Systems Div.)*
Charles L. Knudtson *(Sr. V.P.-Mktg., New Bus. Devel.)*

DDC PERTEC
(Formerly Digital Development Corporation)
2705 E. Medina, Ste. 161
Tucson, AZ 85706
Tel.: 602-573-1113
Telex: 910-494-2093
Fax: 818-772-6609
Year Founded: 1959
Approx.Sls.: $50,000,000
Emp.: 450
Fiscal Year-end: 12/31/90
Export
Mfr. & Lessor Computer Products
S.I.C.: 3571; 3572; 3577; 7377
W.A. Lowrey *(Chm. Bd., Pres. & Chief Exec. Officer)*
John Lowrey *(Chief Fin. Officer)*
Leland Aids *(Gen. Counsel)*
William Jones *(Controller)*
Harry Lyons *(Dir.-Special Projects)*

Outside Service Firm(s):

Deloitte & Touche*(Auditors)*
21550 Oxnard St., Ste. 800
Woodland Hills, CA 91367-7100
Tel.: 818-593-4800
Fax: 818-347-4278

Security Pacific National Bank*(Major Banking Relationship)*
San Diego, CA

DDF&M
Dudreck DePaul Ficco & Morgan Inc.

DDF&M INC. DUDRECK DEPAUL FICCO & MORGAN INC.
200 First Ave.
Pittsburgh, PA 15222
Tel.: 412-261-2580 **PA**
Fax: 412-261-2682
Year Founded: 1961
Approx.Billings: $18,700,000
Emp.: 34
Fiscal Year-end: 12/31/90
Advertising Agency
S.I.C.: 7311
Albert W. Dudreck *(Chm. Bd. & Chief Exec. Officer)*
John DePaul *(Pres.)*
Gary Doughty *(Sr. V.P., Fin.)*
Mary Ann Miller *(Pub. Rels. Dir.)*
Principal(s):
Albert W. Dudreck
John DePaul

No. of Mfg. Plants/Facilities: 1
No. of U.S. Offices: 1

Computer Systems/Hardware:
IBM, ADMAN

Outside Service Firm(s):

Ernst & Young*(Auditors)*
2000 Pittsburgh Natl. Bldg.
Pittsburgh, PA 15222
Tel.: 412-644-7800
Fax: 412-644-7419

Houston Harbaugh*(Legal Firm)*
Pittsburgh, PA

Branch:

DDF&M Direct **(1)**
200 First Ave.
Pittsburgh, PA 15222
Tel.: 412-471-5400
Fax: 412-261-2682
Peter Waterkotte *(V.P., Gen. Mgr.)*

DEC INTERNATIONAL, INC.
1919 S. Stoughton Rd.
Madison, WI 53716
Mailing Address:
P.O. Box 8050,
Madison, WI 53708
Tel.: 608-222-3484 **WI**
Telex: 265489
Fax: 608-222-9314
Year Founded: 1939
Liabilities: $13,000,000
Net Worth: $13,000,000
Approx.Sls.: $70,000,000
Emp.: 625
Fiscal Year-end: 12/31/90
Holding Company; Manufactures Food Processing & Dairy Farming Equipment
S.I.C.: 6719; 3523; 3556
Randal A. Albrecht *(Chm. Bd.)*
Henrik Moe *(Pres., Chief Oper. & Exec. Officer)*
Robert W. Smith *(V.P. & Gen. Counsel)*
Donald R. Hildewig *(Dir.-Fin.)*
John Perez *(Mgr.-Sls.)*
Bob Reichert *(Mgr.-Adv.)*
John Drydyk *(Mgr.-Personnel)*
Principal(s):
Randal A. Albrecht

No. of Mfg. Plants/Facilities: 7
No. of U.S. Offices: 6
No. of Foreign Offices: 1

Computer Systems/Hardware:
IBM; Hewlett-Packard; Apple

Outside Service Firm(s):

Arthur Andersen & Co.*(Auditors)*
777 E. Wisconsin Ave., P.O. Box 1215
Milwaukee, WI 53202
Tel.: 414-271-5100
Fax: 414-283-3200

First Wisconsin National Bank*(Major Banking Relationship)*
Madison, WI

The Principal Financial Group*(Pension Manager)*
711 High St.
Des Moines, IA 50309
Tel.: 515-247-4593
Tel.: 800-543-4015

First Wisconsin National Bank*(Pension Manager)*
Madison, WI

Divisions:

DEC Alkar Div. **(1)**
105 Spring St.
Lodi, WI 53555
Tel.: 608-592-3211
Emp.: 130
Mfr. of Meat Processing Equipment
S.I.C.: 3565
P. Hinderaker *(Pres.)*

Berg Co. **(1)**
1911 S. Stoughton Rd.
Madison, WI 53716
Tel.: 608-221-4281
Emp.: 32
Mfr. of Liquor Dispensers
S.I.C.: 2541
Del Lins *(Pres.)*

DEC/Bou-Matic **(1)**
1919 S. Stoughton Rd.
Madison, WI 53716
Tel.: 608-222-3484
Fax: 608-222-9314
Emp.: 300
Fiscal Year-end: 12/31/90
Import Export
Mfr. of Milking Equipment; Farm Milk Coolers, Heat Recovery Systems & Heat Pump Water Heaters
S.I.C.: 3585; 3559; 3556; 3523; 3565
Paul Thompson *(Pres.)*
Robert Kmoch *(Controller)*
John Perez *(Dir.-Sls.)*
Terry Mullen *(Dir.-Engrng. & Mktg.)*
Joe Drydyk *(Dir.-Personnel)*
R.J. Reichert *(Mgr.-Mktg. Services)*
Joe Prazak *(Mgr.-Farm-Lines Mktg.)*
Ed Joseph *(Prod. Mgr.-Sanitation)*
John Brezezinski *(Prod. Mgr.-Dari-Kool)*
Don Murphy *(Pur. Mgr.)*

Sani-Matic Systems **(1)**
1915 S. Stoughton Rd.
Madison, WI 53708
Tel.: 608-222-2399
Emp.: 40
Mfr. of Sanitation Equipment
S.I.C.: 3565
R. Gerner *(Pres.)*

Stanley Drying Company **(1)**
P.O. Box 120,
Stanley, WI 54768
Tel.: 715-644-5827
Emp.: 18
Wholesale of Custom Drying
S.I.C.: 5131
D. Marquardt *(Gen. Mgr.)*

Non-U.S. Holdings:

DEC AG **(1)**
Poststrasse 14 CH-6300
Zug, Switzerland
Tel.: 042-217070
Mfr. of Food Processing & Dairy Farming Equipment
S.I.C.: 3523; 3556
Peter Hubler *(Chief Oper. Officer)*

Fabdec Ltd. **(1)**
Grange Road
Ellesmere Port, Salop SY12 9DG, United Kingdom
Tel.: 069171-2811
Mfr. of Farm Milk Coolers, Cellar Tanks, Electronic Liquor Dispensers
S.I.C.: 3565; 3523
Brian Colley *(Chief Oper. Officer)*

DFA Advertising, Inc.

D.F.A. ADVERTISING
161 W. 53rd St., Ste. 802
New York, NY 10019
Tel.: 212-247-0215
Year Founded: 1989
Approx.Billings: $11,650,000
Direct Marketing
Ed Forti *(Pres.)*
Pat Royall *(Sec.)*

DGWB, INC.
20 Executive Park, Ste. 200
Irvine, CA 92714
Tel.: 714-863-0404
Fax: 714-863-0933
Year Founded: 1988
Approx.Billings: $20,000,000
Emp.: 27
Daniel Ginsberg *(Pres.)*
James L. deYong *(Exec. V.P.)*
Cindy Melton *(Chief Fin. Officer)*
Michael Weisman *(V.P., Gen. Mgr.)*

DHL CORPORATION
333 Twin Dolphin Dr.
Redwood City, CA 94065
Tel.: 415-593-7474
Tel.: 800-CALL-DHL CA
Telex: 263014
Year Founded: 1969
Approx.Sls.: $600,000,000
Emp.: 7,500
Import Export
Holding Company; Worldwide Document, Small Package and Airfreight Delivery Service
S.I.C.: 6719; 4513; 4215
Patrick Foley *(Chm., Pres. & Chief Exec. Officer)*
Stephen L. Waller *(Sr. V.P.-Opers.)*
Lawrence Hughes *(Sr. V.P.-Airline & Hub Opers.)*
Garry Sellers *(Sr. V.P.-Personnel)*
Don Cullis *(V.P.-Sls.)*
Michael Lanier *(Chief Information Officer)*
Vic Guinasso *(Chief Oper. Officer)*
Ted Orme *(Gen. Counsel)*
Dean Christon *(Mgr.-Pub. Rels.)*
Rich Tuttle *(Mgr.-Adv. & Direct Response)*

Subsidiary:

DHL Airways, Inc. **(1)**
333 Twin Dolphin Dr.
Redwood City, CA 94065
Tel.: 415-593-7474
Tel.: 800-CALL-DHL (100%)
Telex: 263014
Fax: 415-593-1689
Approx.Sls.: $500,000,000
Emp.: 6,000
Fiscal Year-end: 12/31/90
Worldwide Delivery of Documents & Small Packages
S.I.C.: 4513
Patrick Foley *(Chm., Pres. & Chief Exec. Officer)*
Vic A. Guinasso *(Chief Oper. Officer)*
Stephen L. Waller *(Sr. V.P.-Opers.)*
Brian Billings *(Sr. V.P.-Mktg. & Plng.)*
Garry Sellers *(V.P.-Human Resources)*
Pam Rhodes *(Dir.-Mktg.)*
Dean Christon *(Mgr.-Mktg. Communications)*

Non-U.S. Holdings:

DHL Handling Mexicana, S.A. de C.V. **(1)**
Prol. Madero 255 Oriente Col. Lindavista, 67130
Guadalupe, N.L. Mexico
Tel.: 77-6191 (100%)
Courier Service
S.I.C.: 4513

DHL International AB **(1)**
Lastbilsv. 6
Sollentuna, Vaxel Sweden
Tel.: 35 94 40 (100%)
Telex: 15818 dhstop
Intl. Document & Small Package Courier Service
S.I.C.: 4513

DHL International BV **(1)**
Parnassusweg 203
Amsterdam, Netherlands
Tel.: 73 97 71 (100%)
Intl. Document & Small Package Courier Service
S.I.C.: 4513

DHL International Courier Service GmbH **(1)**
Karl Hammerschmidt 5
Munich, Germany
Tel.: 90 90 50 (100%)
Intl. Document & Small Package Courier Service
S.I.C.: 4513

DHL International Express Ltd. **(1)**
6390 Northwest Dr.
Toronto, ON L4V 1S1, Canada
Tel.: 416-677-3767 (100%)
Intl. Courier Services
S.I.C.: 4513
Cal Tobias *(Pres.)*

DHL International (Hong Kong) Ltd. **(1)**
13 Mok Cheong St. Tokwawan, Kowloon, Hong Kong
Tel.: 3-341431 (100%)
Telex: 45154 CHLHK
Fax: 123 4105
Intl. Document & Small Parcel Express Service
S.I.C.: 4513

DHL International N.V. **(1)**
Rue du Moyer 211 1040
Brussels, Belgium
Tel.: 32-2-735-7255 (100%)
International Document Courier Service
S.I.C.: 4513

DHL International S.A. **(1)**
Picassopl. 4 4002
Basel, Switzerland
Tel.: 22 61 77 (100%)
Intl. Document & Small Package Courier Service
S.I.C.: 4513

DHL International (U.K.) Ltd. **(1)**
Kings House, Great West Road
Brentford, United Kingdom
Tel.: 01-994-6433 (100%)
Document Courier Service
S.I.C.: 4513

D. M. MANAGEMENT COMPANY
25 Recreation Pk. Dr., Ste. 200
Hingham, MA 02043
Tel.: 617-740-2718
Fax: 617-749-8523
Year Founded: 1987
Approx.Sls.: $30,000,000
Emp.: 150
Fiscal Year-end: 6/30/91
Import
Specialty Mail Order Catalog Co.
S.I.C.: 5961
Sam Shanaman *(Chief Exec. Officer)*
George Burman *(Pres.)*
Kenneth Canaway *(V.P.-Opers., New Hampshire)*
Dave Walde *(Controller)*
Cindy de Grasse *(Mktg. Dir.)*
Leslie Charney *(Creative Dir.)*
Patricia Phelps *(Product Mgr.)*

DMI THE HEALTHCARE AGENCY
211 E. Ontario St.
Chicago, IL 60611
Tel.: 312-280-0700
Fax: 312-280-9506
Year Founded: 1972
Approx.Billings: $20,000,000
Emp.: 22
Marketing Loyalty Programs, Compliance, Training, Strategic Planning, Full Service Creative Ads, Healthcare, Video & CME
Dan Williams *(Pres. & Chief Exec. Officer)*
Paul Reynolds *(Admin.)*
Barbara Balasi *(Treas.)*
Peggy Sharp *(Librarian)*
Barb Williams *(Data Base Dir.)*

DMI, INC.
Rte. 150 E.
Goodfield, IL 61742
Tel.: 309-965-2233
Fax: 309-965-2520
Approx.Sls.: $25,000,000
Emp.: 295
Tractor Dual Wheels, Wagons, Plows & Fertilizer Application Equipment, Dump Truck Bodies, Truck Bumpers
S.I.C.: 3523; 3714
William H. Schmidtgall *(Pres.)*
Richard A. Brown *(V.P.-Mktg.)*
John R. Faklaris *(Treas.)*
Doris Blunier *(Sec.)*

Outside Service Firm(s):

Heinold-Banwart*(Auditors)*
East Peoria, IL

Sutkowski & Washkuhn*(Legal Firm)*
Jefferson Bank Bldg., Ste. 505, 123 S.W. Adams St.
Peoria, IL 61602
Tel.: 309-673-4500

Commercial National Bank*(Major Banking Relationship)*
Peoria, IL

DRK

DRK INC.
101 Summer St., Church Green
Boston, MA 02110
Tel.: 617-542-5848
Year Founded: 1979
Approx.Billings: $14,377,000
Emp.: 22
Clients Marketing Computer Products
David R. Kasabian *(Pres. & Creative Dir.)*
Annie Kasabian *(Exec. V.P., Gen. Mgr.)*
Steve Gray *(V.P., Dir. Mktg. Services)*
Bennette Hirsch *(V.P., Admin.)*
Victoria Litch *(Admin. Asst.)*

Computer Systems/Hardware:
IBM, Novell

D.S.U.-PETERBILT & GMC, INC.
4810 N. Basin Ave.
Portland, OR 97208
Tel.: 503-285-7771 OR
Fax: 503-286-4645
Year Founded: 1945
Assets: $18,300,000
Liabilities: $14,400,000
Net Worth: $3,900,000
Approx.Sls.: $50,300,000
Emp.: 208

D.S.U.-Peterbilt & GMC, Inc.—(Continued)

Fiscal Year-end: 9/30/90
Parts & Service for Trucks & Other Vehicles; New and Used Truck Sales
S.I.C.: 7538; 7539
Wallace H. Yost *(Chm. Bd. & Chief Exec. Officer)*
M.N. Plowman *(Pres.)*
Thomas R. Stassens *(V.P. & Service Mgr.)*
Jan Yost *(Treas. & Sec.)*
John W. Ryan *(Controller)*
Steve Morrison *(Parts Mgr.)*

No. of U.S. Offices: 2

Computer Systems/Hardware:
Microdata

Outside Service Firm(s):

Yergen & Meyer*(Auditors)*
Portland, OR

Safeco Insurance Co. of America*(Commercial Insurance Carrier)*
Seattle, WA

Blue Cross & Blue Shield of Oregon*(Group Insurer)*
Portland, OR

Gleason & Scarborough*(Legal Firm)*
Portland, OR

Seattle First National Bank*(Major Banking Relationship)*
Portland, OR

Russell Garvin*(Pension Manager)*
San Francisco, CA

Subsidiary:

DSU Leasing, Inc. **(1)**
4810 North Basin Ave.
Portland, OR 97217
Tel.: 503-285-7771
Fax: 503-286-4645
Emp.: 5
Leasing of Trucks & Trailers
S.I.C.: 7513
David Koon *(Lease & Rental Mgr.)*

DVC INDUSTRIES
1440 Fifth Ave.
Bay Shore, NY 11706
Tel.: 516-968-8500
Tel.: 800-865-8588
Fax: 516-968-8522
Year Founded: 1928
Approx.Sls.: $20,000,000
Emp.: 300
Fiscal Year-end: 8/31/90
Advertising Aids, Presentations, Sales Manuals & Loose Leaf Binders
S.I.C.: 2782; 2789
Employee Matching Gifts Program:
Employee Stock Ownership Plan
Henri L. Bertuch *(Pres.)*
Arthur P. Cappa *(V.P.-Sls.)*
Richard Jansen *(V.P.-Mktg.)*
Ron Simmons *(V.P.-Mfg.)*
Michael Bertuch *(V.P.-Mktg.)*
Raymond Schoeck *(Chief Fin. Officer)*
Dean Zimet *(Dir.-Pur.)*

Computer Systems/Hardware:
AS 400

DACOR CORPORATION
161 Northfield Rd.
Northfield, IL 60093
Tel.: 708-446-9555
Telex: 289499
Fax: 708-446-7547
Year Founded: 1954
Emp.: 125
Import Export
Mfr. of SCUBA & Skin Diving Equipment
S.I.C.: 3021; 3069; 3089; 3949
Joan Davison *(Chm. Bd.)*
A. Richard Michka *(Pres.)*
Joseph Perotti *(Controller)*
William Bowden *(Dir.-Matl. Mngmt.)*
Michael Martin *(Dir.-Sls.)*
Ron Pavelka *(Dir.-Mktg.)*
Robert Barr *(Mgr.-Pur.)*
Ray Fundora *(Mgr.-Export Sls.)*
John Sabala *(Mgr.-Mngmt. Information Systems)*
Vern Pedersen *(Master Service Technician)*

Outside Service Firm(s):

Coopers & Lybrand*(Auditors)*
203 N. LaSalle St.
Chicago, IL 60601
Tel.: 312-701-5500

Washington National Insurance*(Group Insurer)*
Evanston, IL

Pierce & Eslick, Ltd.*(Legal Firm)*
Chicago, IL

First National Bank of Chicago*(Major Banking Relationship)*
One First National Plaza
Chicago, IL 60670
Tel.: 312-732-9781
Tel.: 312-732-4050
Fax: 312-732-4840
Fax: 312-732-3055

DAD'S PRODUCTS CO., INC.
Mill St.
Meadville, PA 16335
Mailing Address:
P.O. Box 451-D
Meadville, PA 16335
Tel.: 814-724-7710
Fax: 814-337-2743
Approx.Sls.: $50,000,000
Emp.: 150
Manufacturers & Marketers of Dry & Canned Pet Foods; Dad's Meal, Chunx Dog & Cat Foods
S.I.C.: 2047; 2048
G. Thomas Lang *(Pres.)*
Richard A. Lang, Sr. *(Exec. V.P.)*
Richard A. Lang, Jr. *(V.P.-Adv., Sls. & Mktg.)*
Rick Moyer *(V.P.-Fin.)*

Outside Service Firm(s):

Marine Bank*(Major Banking Relationship)*
Erie, PA

D'AGOSTINO SUPERMARKETS INC.
1385 Boston Post Rd.
Larchmont, NY 10538
Tel.: 914-833-4000 **NY**
Fax: 914-576-2231
Approx.Sls.: $200,000,000
Emp.: 2,000
Supermarket Chain
S.I.C.: 5411
Nicholas D'Agostino, Jr. *(Chm. Bd.)*
Ronald Nevers *(Pres.)*
I. Steven D'Agostino *(V.P.-Sls. & Mdse.)*
Salvatore Garguilo *(V.P.)*
Peter Nero *(V.P.-Opers.)*
Roi R. Tucker *(V.P.-Human Resources)*
Fred Turrin *(V.P.-Fin.)*

Outside Service Firm(s):

Chemical Banking Corporation*(Major Banking Relationship)*
450 W. 33rd. St.
New York, NY 10001
Tel.: 212-613-7147

DAHLEM COMPANY, INC.
6200 Dutchman Lane
Louisville, KY 40205
Tel.: 502-452-1151
Fax: 501-452-0291
Approx.Sls.: $21,000,000
Emp.: 12
New Construction Of Commercial, Office & Industrial Buildings, Revovation & Repair; Commercial & Industrial Building Operations
S.I.C.: 1542; 1541; 6512
Bernard A. Dahlem *(Chm. Bd.)*
Floyd G. Hinton *(Pres.)*
Michael Connaughton *(Treas.)*
Karen Dahlem *(Sec.)*

Outside Service Firm(s):

Deloitte & Touche*(Auditors)*
510 W. Broadway
Louisville, KY 40202
Tel.: 502-562-2000

Brown, Todd & Heyburn*(Legal Firm)*
Citizens Plaza, 16th Fl.
Louisville, KY 40202
Tel.: 502-589-5400

First National Bank*(Major Banking Relationship)*
Louisville, KY

DahlinSmithWhite

DAHLIN SMITH WHITE, INC.
4 Triad Center, Ste. 400
Salt Lake City, UT 84180
Tel.: 801-364-0919
Fax: 801-536-7350
Year Founded: 1986
Approx.Billings: $60,000,000
Emp.: 90
Business-to-Business & High-Tech Adv.
John D. Dahlin *(Pres.)*
David C. Boede *(V.P., Grp. Acct. Supvr.)*
Alan K. Reigard *(V.P., Grp. Acct. Supvr.)*
Doug Folsom *(Dir., Fin.)*
Jennifer J. Johnson *(Dir., Indus. Rels.)*
Richard Schroader *(MIS Dir.)*
Sharon Larsen *(Office Mgr.)*

Computer Systems/Hardware:
Apple, Macintosh

DAHLSTEN TRUCK LINE, INC.
101 W. Edgar St.
Clay Center, NE 68933
Tel.: 402-762-3511 **NE**
Fax: 402-762-3812
Year Founded: 1979
Approx.Sls.: $11,000,000
Emp.: 170
Commercial & Contract Haulers; General Line of Groceries & Liquor
S.I.C.: 4213; 5182; 5141
Wanda Dahlsten *(Pres.)*
Vayle Hayes *(V.P. & Sec.)*
Donna Lukash *(Treas.)*

Outside Service Firm(s):

Commercial State Bank*(Major Banking Relationship)*
Clay Center, NE

DAHLSTROM MANUFACTURING COMPANY, INC.
443 Buffalo St.
Jamestown, NY 14702-0640
Mailing Address:
P.O. box 640,
Jamestown, NY 14702-0640
Tel.: 716-487-0111
Fax: 716-664-0890
Year Founded: 1904
Approx.Sls.: $27,000,000
Emp.: 425
Precision Fabricated Sheet Metal; Precision Roll Forming; Electro-Mechanical Assembly; Engineering Services
S.I.C.: 8711; 3469; 3449
Craig P. Colburn *(Pres.)*
Brian J. Sweeney *(Treas.)*
Rebecca Colburn *(Sec.)*
Carolyn French *(Dir.-Mktg.)*
W. Berg *(Dir.-Tech.)*
Mike Zorckler *(Mgr.-Specility Products Div.)*
Steve LaFuria *(MVC Division Mgr.)*
Hank Lachajczyk *(Mgr.-Finishing Div.)*
Pete Laughlin *(Mgr.-Rollforming Div.)*
L. McNallie *(Mgr.-Pur.)*
Mitch Klein *(Gen. Sls. Mgr.)*

Outside Service Firm(s):

Weinaug, Pensa, Buffamente & Co.*(Auditors)*
Jamestown, NY

Hiscock & Barclay*(Legal Firm)*
Buffalo, NY

Norstar Bank, N.A.*(Major Banking Relationship)*
Jamestown, NY

Division:

Dahlstrom Manufacturing Co., Inc.-Safeway Division **(1)**
110 S.W. 16th Ave.
Pompano Beach, FL 33069
Tel.: 305-972-1827
Fax: 305-977-2495
Manufacture Machine Parts & Assembly
S.I.C.: 3469
Mark White *(Gen. Mgr.)*

Subsidiary:

Dahlstrom Manufacturing B.V. **(1)**
Coolcock Industrial Estate Coolcock, Dublin, 17, Ireland
Tel.: 353 18 47 37 00
Fax: 353 18 47 35 85
Emp.: 70
Sheet Metal Fabrication Assembly
S.I.C.: 3469
Alan Mangan *(Gen. Mgr.)*

DAIDONE ELECTRICAL INC.
200 Raymond Blvd.
Newark, NJ 07105
Tel.: 201-690-5216 **NJ**
Fax: 201-344-3645
Electrical contractor.
S.I.C.: 1731
John Daidone *(Pres.)*

DAIGLE OIL CO.
44 Main St.
Fort Kent, ME 04743
Mailing Address:
P.O. Box 328
Fort Kent, ME 04743
Tel.: 207-834-5027
Fax: 207-834-5050
Emp.: 80
Wholesale & Retail Petroleum Products
S.I.C.: 5172; 5983; 5541
Richard Daigle *(Pres.)*
Leo Robichaud *(V.P.)*

No. of U.S. Offices: 3

Computer Systems/Hardware:
DEC

Outside Service Firm(s):

Chester Kearny Co.*(Auditors)*
Presque Isle, ME

Maine Oil Dealers Association Trust*(Group Insurer)*
Portland, ME

Salomon, Paige & Hunter*(Legal Firm)*
Caribou, ME

Maine National Bank*(Major Banking Relationship)*
Portland, ME

DAIRY FRESH CORP.
903 Tuscaloosa St.
Greensboro, AL 36744
Mailing Address:
P.O. Box 159
Greensboro, AL 36744
Tel.: 205-624-3041
Approx.Sls.: $65,000,000
Emp.: 650
Process & Distribute Milk & Ice Cream
S.I.C.: 2024; 2026; 5143
W. E. Burt *(Chm. Bd., Pres., & Chief Exec. Officer)*
W. L. York *(Chief Fin. Officer & Treas.)*

No. of Mfg. Plants/Facilities: 6

Computer Systems/Hardware:
IBM; Radio Shack

Outside Service Firm(s):

Robert E. Thompson*(Auditors)*
Tuscaloosa, AL

J.H. Seal, II*(Legal Firm)*
Tuscaloosa, AL

First National Bank of Mobile*(Major Banking Relationship)*
Mobile, AL

DAIRYGOLD INC.
635 Elliot Ave. W.
Seattle, WA 98119
Mailing Address:
P.O. Box 79007,
Seattle, WA 98119
Tel.: 206-284-7220
Fax: 206-281-3456
Emp.: 150
Mfr. of Dairy Products
S.I.C.: 2021; 2022; 2023; 5143; 5451
Wesley Eckert *(Pres.)*
Ronald Furrer *(Treas.)*
Douglas Marshall *(Corp. Counsel & Sec.)*
Oscar Ringness *(Dir.-Information Resources)*
Vesetn Yates *(Dir.-Human Resources)*
James Robson *(Gen. Mgr.-Sls. & Mktg.)*
John Usherwood *(Mgr.-Production)*

Outside Service Firm(s):

Deloitte & Touche*(Auditors)*
101 S. Capitol Blvd.
Boise, ID 83702
Tel.: 208-342-5361

Alexanderson, Davis, Rainey, Whitney & Kerrick*(Legal Firm)*
Boise, ID

West One Bank*(Major Banking Relationship)*
P.O. Box 7928
Boise, ID 83707
Tel.: 208-383-7098

Subsidiary:

Dairygold, Inc. **(1)**
Fifth & Albany
Caldwell, ID 83605
Tel.: 208-459-3687
Approx.Sls.: $141,000,000
Emp.: 105
Producers of Fluid Milk, Powdered Milk, Butter & Cheese
S.I.C.: 2021; 2022; 2023; 5143; 5451
Frank Krone *(Gen. Mgr.)*

DAIRYLAND POWER COOPERATIVE
3200 East Ave. S.
La Crosse, WI 54602-0817
Tel.: 608-788-4000
Fax: 608-787-1420
Approx.Sls.: $165,880,000
Emp.: 673
Electrical Energy
S.I.C.: 4911
Wayne L. Willink *(Pres.)*
Frank Bohte *(1st V.P.)*
Art Remer *(2nd V.P.)*
William Berg *(Gen. Mgr.)*
Leo Byrnes *(Treas.)*
Leo A. Wallace *(Sec.)*

Computer Systems/Hardware:
IBM

Outside Service Firm(s):

Arthur Andersen & Co.*(Auditors)*
45 S. 7th St.
Minneapolis, MN 55402

Wheeler, Van Sickle, Anderson, Norman & Harvey*(Legal Firm)*
La Crosse, WI

Norwest Bank Minnesota, N.A.*(Major Banking Relationship)*
La Crosse, WI

DAIRYLEA COOPERATIVE INC.
5001 Brittonfield Pkwy.
East Syracuse, NY 13057
Mailing Address:
P.O. Box 4844,
Syracuse, NY 13221-4844
Tel.: 315-433-0100 **NY**
Fax: 315-433-2345
Year Founded: 1919
Assets: $42,000,000
Earnings: $500,000,100,000
Liabilities: $33,800,000
Net Worth: $8,200,000
Approx.Sls.: $306,000,000
Emp.: 80
Fiscal Year-end: 3/31/92
Marketing of Bulk Raw Milk
Clyde E. Rutherford *(Chm. Bd. & Pres.)*
Richard P. Smith *(Exec. V.P. & Chief Exec. Officer)*
Edward Bangel *(V.P.-Fin.)*
Alex Baruch *(Controller)*
Ellen LaBerge *(Gen. Counsel)*
Mark Kenville *(Dir.-Member Relations & Communications)*
Deborah Canfield *(Mgr.-Information Systems)*

No. of U.S. Offices: 1

Computer Systems/Hardware:
Hewlett-Packard 6000, Series 68

Outside Service Firm(s):

Coopers & Lybrand*(Auditors)*
Buffalo, NY

Bond, Schoeneck & King*(Legal Firm)*
One Lincoln Center
Syracuse, NY 13202
Tel.: 315-422-0121

Subsidiary:

Agri-Service Agencies, Inc. **(1)**
P.O. Box 4910,
Syracuse, NY 13221
Tel.: 315-433-2332 (100%)
Emp.: 600
Insurance Services
S.I.C.: 6399
Edward Bangel *(Pres.)*

DAIRYMEN, INC.
10140 Linn Station Rd.
Louisville, KY 40223
Tel.: 502-426-6455
Fax: 502-423-6739
Year Founded: 1968
Assets: $227,479,000
Earnings: $3,452,000
Liabilities: $148,378,000
Net Worth: $79,101,000
Approx.Sls.: $984,687,000
Emp.: 3,500
Fiscal Year-end: 8/31/91
Marketing & Processing of Milk & Milk Products
S.I.C.: 5143; 2026; 5451; 2021; 2022; 2024
Bucky Jones *(Pres.)*
James W. McDowell *(Exec. V.P. & Chief Exec. Officer)*
James E. Mueller *(Sr. V.P. & Chief Fin. Officer)*
Tom Bean *(V.P.-Fin. Services)*
John W. Mays *(V.P.-Admin.)*
Jerome Roadcap *(V.P.-Human Resources)*
Dale Yost *(V.P. & Controller)*
Bill Arledge *(Dir.-Quality Control)*
Bill Boston *(Dir.-Real Estate)*
Jeff Durden *(Dir.-Mktg. & Sls.)*
David Lardner *(Dir.-Mngmt. Information Systems)*
Daniel G. Shaw *(Dir.-Corp. Communications)*
Peggy Arbuckle *(Corp. Travel Planner)*
Principal(s):
Bucky Jones
James W. McDowell

No. of Mfg. Plants/Facilities: 16

Computer Systems/Hardware:
IBM 3081 & 4341; Microvax II; IBM PC & XT; AT&T 6300 Plus

Outside Service Firm(s):

KPMG Peat Marwick*(Auditors)*
4905 Tildgman St.
Allentown, PA 18104
Tel.: 215-391-6380

Barnett & Alagia*(Legal Firm)*
Louisville, KY

Subsidiaries:

Flav-O-Rich, Inc. **(1)**
10140 Linn Station Rd.
Louisville, KY 40223
Tel.: 502-426-6455
Steven G. Conerly *(Chief Exec. Officer)*
Anthony Haynes *(V.P. & Controller)*
Robert Bell *(V.P.-Mktg.)*
Jeff Durden *(Dir.-Mktg. Services)*

Promotion Services, Inc. **(1)**
10140 Linn Station Rd.
Louisville, KY 40223
Tel.: 502-426-6455

DAKCO DISTRIBUTORS, INC.
101 E. Central
Minot, ND 58701
Mailing Address:
P.O. Box 5009,
Minot, ND 58702
Tel.: 701-857-1140 **ND**
Fax: 701-857-1161
Year Founded: 1973
Approx.Sls.: $50,000,000
Emp.: 66
Fiscal Year-end: 12/31/90
Import
Wholesaler of Drugs, Sundries, Store Fixtures, Sporting Goods, Electronic Computers & Computer Service
S.I.C.: 5122; 5045; 5091; 5113; 5145; 5194; 7372; 7374; 5100
R.F. Saunders *(Chm. Bd. & Chief Exec. Officer)*
Jerome Schmidt *(Pres.)*
Beulah Saunders *(Sec. & Treas.)*

Computer Systems/Hardware:
DEC VAX System

Outside Service Firm(s):

Brady, Martz & Associates*(Auditors)*
Minot, ND

Eaton, Van de Street & Ward*(Legal Firm)*
Minot, ND

Norwest Bank of North Dakota*(Major Banking Relationship)*
Minot, ND

Subsidiaries:

Dakota Drug, Inc. **(1)**
28 N. Main St.
Minot, ND 58701
Tel.: 701-852-2141
Fax: 701-857-1133
Assets: $12,498,901
Earnings: $603,523
Liabilities: $6,833,545
Net Worth: $5,665,356
Approx.Sls.: $38,000,000
Emp.: 41
Fiscal Year-end: 11/30/90
Import
Computer Systems/Hardware:
DEC VAX System
Wholesaler of Drugs & Drug Proprietaries
S.I.C.: 5122; 5100
Allen O. Svare *(Pres. & Gen. Mgr.)*
Richard F. Saunders *(Chief Exec. Officer)*
Orren Anderson *(V.P. & Mgr.-Sls.)*
Ted Scherr *(Sec. & Treas.)*

Midco Data Systems, Inc. **(1)**
101 E. Central
Minot, ND 58701
Tel.: 701-852-2141
Approx.Sls.: $600,000
Emp.: 9
Fiscal Year-end: 12/31/90
Computer Systems/Hardware:
DEC VAX System
Data Processing Srvcs.
S.I.C.: 7374
R.F. Saunders *(Chm. Bd.)*

Nodak Distributor **(1)**
18 2nd St. N.E.
Minot, ND 58701
Tel.: 701-857-1177
Approx.Sls.: $7,000,000
Emp.: 29
Computer Systems/Hardware:
DEC VAX System
Wholesale Distr. of Candy & Tobacco
S.I.C.: 5145; 5194
R.F. Saunders *(Chm. Bd.)*
Jim Aamodt *(Gen. Mgr.)*

Northland Sports Inc. **(1)**
P.O. Box 5009, 308 8th St. NE
Minot, ND 58701
Tel.: 701-852-2141
Approx.Sls.: $5,000,000
Emp.: 17
Fiscal Year-end: 12/31/90
Computer Systems/Hardware:
DEC VAX System
Wholesale Sporting Goods
S.I.C.: 5091
R.F. Saunders *(Chm. Bd.)*
Mark Slater *(Gen. Mgr.)*

DAKIN, INC.
Worldwide Headquarters, 1649 Adrian Rd.
Burlingame, CA 94010
Mailing Address:
P.O. Box 7746
San Francisco, CA 94120
Tel.: 415-692-1555
Telex: 278029
Fax: 415-259-2525
Year Founded: 1955
Approx.Sls.: $75,000,000

Dakin, Inc.—(Continued)

Emp.: 250
Fiscal Year-end: 12/31/91
Import
Gift Products; Stuffed Animals Toys, Dolls, Baby Products
S.I.C.: 3942; 5092; 3269; 5112; 2499
Robert Solomon *(Chm. Bd., Pres. & Chief Exec. Officer)*
Jack Morrow *(Exec. V.P.)*
Nannette Griswold *(Chief Fin. Officer)*
Stace Chapman *(Dir.-Mngmt. Information Systems)*
Pamela McSweeney *(Dir.-Mktg.-Executive Center, Woodland Hills, CA)*

DAKOTA ELECTRIC ASSOCIATION
4300 220th St. W.
Farmington, MN 55024
Tel.: 612-463-7134 **MN**
Fax: 612-463-6256
Year Founded: 1937
Assets: $116,085,448
Liabilities: $82,732,899
Net Worth: $33,352,549
Approx.Sls.: $71,737,466
Emp.: 192
Fiscal Year-end: 12/31/91
Electrical Co-Operative
S.I.C.: 4911
Corporate Giving Program: $500 per Agency without Board Authorization
Arthur Volkert *(Pres.)*
Ronald Swagger *(V.P.)*
Ray Nicolai *(Sec.)*
Carl Potter *(Treas.)*
Harold LeVander, Jr. *(Gen. Counsel)*
Wayne Briesacher *(Mgr.-Fin.)*
Malinda Mehrhoff *(Dir.-Human Resources)*
Eldon Johnson *(Gen. Mgr.)*
Robert Broderick *(Asst. Gen. Mgr.)*
Dale Detjen *(Mgr.-Member Services)*
Bill Trevis *(Mgr.-Data Processing)*
Alyn Angus *(Pur. Agent)*
LaDonna Riste *(Community Rels. Coord.)*
Ken LaBoone *(Communications Coord.)*
Principal(s):
Dakota Electric Association Members

No. of U.S. Offices: 1

Computer Systems/Hardware:
IBM

Outside Service Firm(s):

Olsen, Thielen & Co.*(Auditors)*
223 Little Canada Rd.
St. Paul, MN 55117

Reliance Insurance Co.*(Commercial Insurance Carrier)*
Philadelphia, PA

National Rural Electric Cooperative Association*(Group Insurer)*
Washington, DC

National Rural Utilities Cooperative Finance Corp.*(Investment Banker)*
2201 Cooperative Way
Herndon, VA

Maun & Simon*(Legal Firm)*
2300 World Trade Center, 30 E. 7th St.
St. Paul, MN 55101
Tel.: 612-229-2900

First National Bank-Farmington*(Major Banking Relationship)*
324 Oak St.
Farmington, MN

DAKOTAH, INC.
N. Park Lane
Webster, SD 57274
Mailing Address:
P.O. Box 120
Webster, SD 57274
Tel.: 605-345-4646 **SD**
Fax: 605-345-3300
Year Founded: 1971
Approx.Sls.: $15,000,000
Emp.: 300
Fiscal Year-end: 12/31/91
Export
Bedspreads & Bed Sets
S.I.C.: 2392
George C. Whyte, Jr. *(Chm. Bd., Pres. & Chief Exec. Officer)*
Terry Sampson *(Exec. V.P.)*
Georgie Olson *(Natl. Sls. Mgr.)*
Tim Knott *(Mfg. Mgr.)*

No. of Mfg. Plants/Facilities: 3
No. of U.S. Offices: 2

Outside Service Firm(s):

Grant Thorton*(Auditors)*
Sioux Falls, SD

Davenport, Evans, Hurwitz & Smith*(Legal Firm)*
Sioux Falls, SD

First Bank of South Dakota*(Major Banking Relationship)*
Sioux Falls, SD

DAKTRONICS, INC.
331 32nd Ave.
Brookings, SD 57006
Mailing Address:
P.O. Box 5128
Brookings, SD 57006
Tel.: 605-697-4000
Tel.: 800-843-5843 **SD**
Fax: 605-697-4700
Year Founded: 1968
Approx.Sls.: $25,000,000
Emp.: 440
Fiscal Year-end: 4/30/92
Export
Electric Scoreboards, Voting Machines; Printed Circuit Boards; Electric Timing Devices; Machine Shop Jobbing & Repair
S.I.C.: 3993; 3579; 3672
Dr. Aelred J. Kurtenbach *(Pres.)*
James Morgan *(V.P.)*
Dr. Charles Roberts *(V.P.)*
Dan Kondzjolka *(Controller)*
Dr. Duane E. Sander *(Sec.)*
Frank Kurtenbach *(Mgr.-Sls.)*
Jeff Robbins *(Mgr.-Pur.)*
Mike Charles *(Dir.-Mfg.)*
Carla Gatzke *(Dir.-Human Resources)*
Paul Weinand *(Dir.-Fin.)*
Mark Steinkamp *(Coord.-Pub. Rels & Adv.)*

Outside Service Firm(s):

McGladrey & Pullen*(Auditors)*
Sioux Falls, SD

LeWayne Erickson*(Legal Firm)*
Brookings, SD

First Bank of South Dakota*(Major Banking Relationship)*
Sioux Falls, SD

Subsidiary:

Star Circuits **(1)**
405 Railroad St.
Brookings, SD 57006
Tel.: 605-697-4650
Fax: 605-697-4666
Emp.: 20
Mfg. of Circuit Boards
S.I.C.: 3672
Carla Gatzke *(Pres.)*

DAL-TILE CORP.
7834 Hawn Freeway
Dallas, TX 75217
Tel.: 214-398-1411
Fax: 214-944-4390
Year Founded: 1947
Approx.Sls.: $100,000,000
Emp.: 1,800
Manufacturer & Distributor of Ceramic Tiles
S.I.C.: 3253; 5032
Bill Cox *(Chm. Bd. & Chief Exec. Officer)*
Charles Nies *(Chief Fin. Officer & Treas.)*
Larry Stringer *(Controller)*

Computer Systems/Hardware:
IBM 4331

Outside Service Firm(s):

Northwestern National Life*(Group Insurer)*
20 Washington Ave. S.
Minneapolis, MN 55401

Scoggins & Blanchard*(Legal Firm)*
Dallas, TX

NationsBank Texas*(Major Banking Relationship)*
901 Main St., 16th Fl.
Dallas, TX 75202
Tel.: 214-922-5000

Subsidiary:

Tileways Inc. **(1)**
7834 Hawn Freeway
Dallas, TX 75217
Tel.: 214-398-1411

DALE INDUSTRIES INC.
6455 Kingsley Ave.
Dearborn, MI 48126
Tel.: 313-846-9400 **MI**
Fax: 313-846-7128
Year Founded: 1951
Approx.Sls.: $35,000,000
Emp.: 100
Fiscal Year-end: 12/31/91
Import Export
Mfr. Steel & Aluminum Bldg. Components, Louvers, Roof Vents, Steel Studs, Gutters
S.I.C.: 3444
Albert Fruman *(Chm. Bd.)*
Jay Tate *(Pres.)*
Edward Kloop *(Dir.-Pur.)*

No. of Mfg. Plants/Facilities: 4

Computer Systems/Hardware:
Altos

Outside Service Firm(s):

Oppenheim, Appel, Dixon & Co.*(Auditors)*
New York, NY

Manufacturers National Bank*(Major Banking Relationship)*
23208 Van Dyke
Warren, MI 48089
Tel.: 313-759-1500

Subsidiary:

Incor, Inc. **(1)**
4601 N. Point Blvd.
Baltimore, MD 21219
Tel.: 410-477-4000
Emp.: 30
Manufacture of Steel & Aluminum Building Components
S.I.C.: 3444

DALFORT CORP.
7701 Lemmon Ave.
Dallas, TX 75209
Mailing Address:
P.O. Box 7556
Dallas, TX 75209
Tel.: 214-358-7415
Fax: 214-902-0938
Year Founded: 1928
Approx.Sls.: $284,000,000
Emp.: 1,400
Aircraft Maintenance Services & Ground Equipment Leasing
S.I.C.: 4581
Peter K. Chapman *(Pres. & Chief Exec. Officer)*
Sandra Holbrook *(Chief Fin. Officer)*
Joseph Gullion *(V.P.-Opers.)*
Harold S. Handelsman *(V.P., Sec. & Gen. Counsel)*
Dan Malin *(V.P.-Human Resources)*
A.S. Maurstad *(V.P.-Mktg.)*
Kenneth R. Posner *(V.P. & Treas.)*
Bobby Joe Rader *(Sr. Dir.-Quality Control)*
Ken Suarez *(Sr. Dir.-New Bus. Devel. & Program Mngmt.)*
Principal(s):
Pritzker Family

Outside Service Firm(s):

KPMG Peat Marwick*(Auditors)*
1601 Elm St., Ste. 1600
Dallas, TX 75201
Tel.: 214-754-2000
Fax: 214-754-2297

Neal, Gerber & Eisenburg*(Legal Firm)*
2 N. LaSalle St.
Chicago, IL 60605

DALLAS PETERBILT, INC.
515 N. Loop 12
Irving, TX 75061
Tel.: 214-445-7505 **TX**
Fax: 214-438-5196
Approx.Sls.: $75,000,000
Emp.: 125
Sales, Leasing & Service of New & Used Trucks, Tractors & Parts
S.I.C.: 5511; 7532
Jesse Kirk *(Chm. Bd. & Pres.)*
Frank Brown *(Gen. Counsel)*
Milo Kirk *(Sec.)*
Paul Rutledge *(Gen. Mgr.)*
Diane Neil *(Dir.-Personnel & Pur.)*

Computer Systems/Hardware:
IBM System 38

Outside Service Firm(s):

Coopers & Lybrand*(Auditors)*
1999 Bryan St., Ste. 3000
Dallas, TX 75201
Tel.: 214-754-5000

Mankoff, Hill, Held & Goldburg*(Legal Firm)*
Dallas, TX

American Bank*(Major Banking Relationship)*
Herst, TX

DALLY ADVERTISING, INC.
University Centre II, 1320 S. University Dr., Ste. 501
Fort Worth, TX 76107
Tel.: 817-332-5299
Fax: 817-870-1607
Year Founded: 1959
Approx.Billings: $20,000,000
Emp.: 34
Full Service
Scott Dally *(Pres. & Chief Exec. Officer)*
Pat McGeeny *(V.P., Acct. Planning)*
Janice Williams *(V.P., Pub. Rels.)*

Computer Systems/Hardware:
IBM, MacIntosh

WAYNE DALTON CORPORATION
4576 County Rd., 160
Mount Hope, OH 44660
Tel.: 216-674-7015
Fax: 216-674-1857
Approx.Sls.: $200,000,000
Emp.: 1,250
Import Export
Wood, Aluminum, Fiberglass & Steel Overhead Garage Doors
S.I.C.: 2431; 3442
Willis Mullet *(Chm. Bd. & Chief Exec. Officer)*
Thomas Bert Bennett *(Pres.)*
Joe Pedro *(Chief Fin. Officer)*
Geoff Forman *(V.P.-Sls.)*

George Keller *(V.P.-Opers.)*
Rick Kunko *(Controller)*

Outside Service Firm(s):

Arthur Andersen & Co.*(Auditors)*
1717 E. 9th St.
Cleveland, OH 44114
Tel.: 216-781-2140
Fax: 216-781-3683

The Central Trust Company, N.A.*(Major Banking Relationship)*
Cleveland, OH

Branch:

Kinnear Door **(1)**
P.O. Box 10823
Columbus, OH 43201
Tel.: 614-294-5508
Sls. & Mktg. Overhead Doors & Accessories
S.I.C.: 5211
Randy Kelly *(Gen. Mgr.)*

LEO A. DALY COMPANY
8600 Indian Hills Dr.
Omaha, NE 68114
Tel.: 402-391-8111 **NE**
Fax: 402-391-8564
Year Founded: 1915
Approx.Sls.: $55,000,000
Emp.: 709
Fiscal Year-end: 2/28/91
Export
Architecture, Engineering Planning & Interiors Professional Services
S.I.C.: 8711; 8712
Leo A. Daly *(Chm. Bd., Pres. & Treas.)*
Edward F. Cambridge *(Sr. V.P. & Chief Oper. Officer)*
Ronald Leiferman *(Sr. V.P. & Chief Fin. Officer)*
Charles Tvrdik *(V.P.-Personnel Training & Devel.)*
Robert Luhrs *(Controller)*
Jerry Norris *(Gen. Counsel)*
J.G. Daly *(Corp. Sec.)*

No. of U.S. Offices: 10
No. of Foreign Offices: 5

Computer Systems/Hardware:
DEC VAX 11/780

Outside Service Firm(s):

KPMG Peat Marwick*(Auditors)*
Two Central Park Plaza,
Omaha, NE 68102
Tel.: 402-348-1450

Aetna Life & Casualty*(Group Insurer)*
151 Farmington Avenue
Hartford, CT 06156
Tel.: 203-273-2128
Fax: 203-729-4295

Mathews & Cannon*(Legal Firm)*
Omaha, NE

Norwest Bank Minnesota, N.A.*(Major Banking Relationship)*
Omaha, NE

First Manhattan Capital Mgmt.*(Pension Manager)*
437 Madison Ave.
New York, NY 10022

M.J. DALY & SONS, INC.
P.O. Box 2797, 541 Bank St.
Waterbury, CT 06720
Tel.: 203-753-5131 **CT**
Fax: 203-597-0227
Year Founded: 1882
Approx.Sls.: $24,000,000
Emp.: 250
Fire Protection Power Piping, Heating, Ventilating, Plumbing, Sheet Metal Contractors, Air Conditioning & Sprinkler Pipe Fabrication
S.I.C.: 1711; 1761
Jan A. Dembinski *(Pres., Chief Exec. Officer & Treas.)*
Clifton C. Cotter *(Sr. V.P.)*
Janet Blumberg *(V.P.)*
Tom Dembinski *(V.P.)*
Joe Parton *(Controller)*
Michael J. Daly III *(Sec.)*

No. of Mfg. Plants/Facilities: 1
No. of U.S. Offices: 2

Outside Service Firm(s):

Deloitte & Touche*(Auditors)*
New Haven, CT

Atlantic Mutual Insurance*(Commercial Insurance Carrier)*
New York, NY

Bank of Boston*(Major Banking Relationship)*
81 W. Main St.
Waterbury, CT 06702
Tel.: 203-574-7000

DAN DEE PRETZEL & POTATO CHIP CO.
(Div. of Troyer Farms)
Route 97 South
Waterford, PA 16441
Mailing Address:
P.O. Box 676
Waterford, PA 16441
Tel.: 814-796-2611
Approx.Sls.: $12,000,000
Emp.: 60
Fiscal Year-end: 12/31/90
Potato Chips, Pretzels, Golden Wave Pretzel Sticks, Corn Snack Products
S.I.C.: 2052; 2096
Clifford Troyer *(Pres.)*
Daryl Troyer *(V.P.-Sls.)*

Subsidiary:

American Specialty Foods **(1)**
R.D. #1 Box 216B
Canonsburg, PA 15317
Tel.: 412-746-1161

DAN RIVER INC.
2291 Memorial Dr.
Danville, VA 24541
Mailing Address:
P. O. Box 6126
Greenville, SC 29606
Tel.: 804-799-7000 **VA**
Fax: 804-799-7276
Year Founded: 1882
Approx.Sls.: $292,000,000
Emp.: 5,105
Fiscal Year-end: 12/31/91
Textile Manufacturer
S.I.C.: 2211; 2221; 2273
J.L. Lanier, Jr. *(Chm. Bd. & Chief Exec. Officer)*
R.L. Williams *(Pres. & Chief Oper. Officer)*
B.F. Shea *(V.P.-Fin. & Chief Fin. Officer)*
E. Linwood Wright *(V.P.-Quality Service & Devel.)*
W.J. Mika *(V.P.-Indus. Rels.)*
H.L. Goodrich *(Sec. & Gen. Counsel)*
Larry W. Van de Visser *(Controller)*
C.S. Bolt, Jr. *(Treas.)*
W.E. Rodgers, Jr. *(Dir.-Pur.)*
S.D. Batson *(Dir.-Fin.)*

No. of Mfg. Plants/Facilities: 8
No. of U.S. Offices: 28

Outside Service Firm(s):

KPMG Peat Marwick*(Auditors)*
One Shelter Place, Box 10529
Greenville, SC 29603

Liberty Life Assurance Company*(Group Insurer)*
Greenville, SC

Life of Virginia*(Group Insurer)*
Richmond, VA

C&S Sovran Bank*(Pension Manager)*
P.O. Box 26904,
Richmond, VA 23261
Tel.: 804-344-1359

Equitable Life*(Pension Manager)*
1221 Ave. of the Americas
New York, NY 10022
Tel.: 212-382-8038
Fax: 212-382-8089

John Hancock Mutual Life Insurance Co.*(Pension Manager)*
John Hancock Place, P.O. Box 111
Boston, MA 02117

South Carolina National Bank*(Pension Manager)*
101 Greystone Blvd.
Columbia, SC 29226

Divisions:

Dan River Danville Mfg. Div. **(1)**
P.O. Box 261,
Danville, VA 24543
Tel.: 804-799-7000
Emp.: 6,969
Printed, Colored Yarn; Permanent Press Fabrics; Sheets & Pillowcases; Knit Velour
S.I.C.: 2281; 2299; 2211; 2221
Taylor M. Bruce *(V.P.-Mfg.)*

Dan River Apparel Fabrics Marketing Div. **(1)**
111 W. 40th St.
New York, NY 10018
Edward F. Delfoe, III *(V.P.-Mktg., Heavyweight Fabrics)*
C.E. Wyatt *(V.P. & Asst. to the Pres.)*
N.B. Woodworth *(V.P.-Mktg., Lightweight Fabrics)*

Dan River Inc.-Home Furnishings & Related Prods., Div. I **(1)**
P.O. Box 261,
Danville, VA 24543
Tel.: 804-799-7000
Textile Mfr.
S.I.C.: 2299
William Fine *(Pres.-Home Furnishings Mktg.)*
W.D. Price, Jr. *(Mgr.)*

Dan River Cotton Co., Inc. **(1)**
P.O. Box 1568, 2291 Memorial Dr.
Danville, IL 61834
Tel.: 804-799-7000 (100%)
Cotton buying, Classing, Warehousing
S.I.C.: 5159
G.W. Herron *(V.P.)*

Plants:

Dan River Inc.-Finishing Div. **(1)**
P.O. Box 261,
Danville, VA 24541
Tel.: 804-799-7000
S.I.C.: 2299
J.W. Ogle *(Mgr.-Apparel Finishing Div.)*

Dan River Inc.-Riverside Div. **(1)**
P.O. Box 261,
Danville, VA 24543
Tel.: 804-799-7000
Textile Mfr.
S.I.C.: 2257
Paul Mahaffey *(Div. Mgr.)*

Dan River Inc.-Wetumpka Plant **(1)**
1305 Parker
Wetumpka, AL 36092
Tel.: 205-567-8423
Yarn Mfr.
S.I.C.: 2281
R.D. Landers *(Plant Mgr.)*

Dan River Inc.-Yarn Dyed Apparel Fabrics, Div. II **(1)**
P.O. Box 261,
Danville, VA 24541
Tel.: 804-799-7000
Textile Mfr.
S.I.C.: 2299
Kenneth Massey *(Div. Mgr.)*

Subsidiary:

Danville Marketing **(1)**
111 W. 40th St.
New York, NY 10018
Tel.: 212-554-5555
S.I.C.: 5099
R.C. Crawford *(Chief Oper. Officer)*

DANA COMMUNICATIONS, INC.
2 E. Broad St.
Hopewell, NJ 08525
Tel.: 609-466-9187
Fax: 609-466-9608
Year Founded: 1979
Approx.Billings: $12,126,759
Emp.: 25
Hospitality, Office Products, Computers, Voice Processing
Michael D. Prewitt *(Chm.)*
Thomas H. Paine, Jr. *(Pres.)*
Robert F. Prewitt *(Exec. V.P.)*
Eugene Underwood *(Sr. V.P.)*
Kathy Walker *(Controller)*

Computer Systems/Hardware:
MacIntosh, IBM

DANA PERFUMES CORP.
(Sub. of Les Parfums de Dana, Inc.)
635 Madison Ave.
New York, NY 10022
Tel.: 212-751-3700
Fax: 212-371-7868
Year Founded: 1932
Manufactures Perfume, Cologne, Related Fragrance & Bath Products
S.I.C.: 2844
William Quinn *(Pres. & Chief Oper. Officer)*
Richard Scanlon *(V.P.-Sls.)*
Elizabeth Cohen *(Dir.-Mktg.)*
Eugene Morrissey *(Sec.)*
Madeleine Morrissey *(Dir.-Adv. & Pub. Rels.)*
Ruth Monstvilas *(Dir.-Pkgng. Devel.)*
Robert Boyd *(Pur. Agent)*

Computer Systems/Hardware:
NCR 8555

Outside Service Firm(s):

KPMG Peat Marwick*(Auditors)*
345 Park Ave.
New York, NY 10154
Tel.: 212-758-9700
Fax: 212-872-3308

Steckler, Gutman, Morrisey & Murray*(Legal Firm)*
New York, NY

Chemical Bank*(Major Banking Relationship)*
450 West 33rd St.
New York, NY 10001
Tel.: 212-613-7197
Fax: 212-947-7628

DANAFILMS, INC.
5 Otis St.
Westborough, MA 01581
Tel.: 508-366-8884
Fax: 508-898-0106
Approx.Sls.: $17,000,000
Emp.: 100
Manufacture Polyethylene Films & Plastic Display Clases
S.I.C.: 3089
Sherman V. Olson *(Pres. & Treas.)*
Walter Frick *(Controller)*
Robert P. Simoncini *(Mgr.-Sls.)*
Elaine L. Olson *(Clerk)*

Outside Service Firm(s):

Shawmut Bank*(Major Banking Relationship)*
446 Main St.
Worcester, MA 01608
Tel.: 617-793-4000

DANBURY PRINTING & LITHOGRAPH, INC.
One Prindle Lane
Danbury, CT 06811
Mailing Address:
P.O. Box 2479
Danbury, CT 06811
Tel.: 203-792-5500 CT
Fax: 203-744-5633
Year Founded: 1946
Offset Commercial Printig
S.I.C.: 2752
Melissa Previdi *(Pres. & Chief Exec. Officer)*
Bill Sherman *(V.P.-Sls. & Mktg.)*
Robert Mulrooney *(Controller)*
Jim O'Brien *(Mgr.-Personnel)*

DANCKER, SELLEW & DOUGLAS, INC.
53 Park Pl., Ste. 602
New York, NY 10007
Tel.: 212-619-7171 NY
Fax: 212-349-0695
Year Founded: 1949
Approx.Sls.: $57,000,000
Emp.: 170
Wholesale Distribution of Office Furniture
S.I.C.: 5021
Paul W. Dancker *(Chm. Bd.)*
J. Scott Douglas *(Pres.)*
Joan M. Dancker *(V.P.)*
Lawrence Katz *(V.P.)*
Gerard Kehoe *(V.P. & Treas.)*
James Davidson *(Sec.)*

Outside Service Firm(s):

Ernst & Young*(Auditors)*
787 Seventh Ave.
New York, NY 10019
Tel.: 212-773-1243

JOHN W. DANFORTH CO.
1940 Fillmore Ave.
Buffalo, NY 14214
Tel.: 716-832-1940
Fax: 716-832-2388
Year Founded: 1884
Approx.Sls.: $23,000,000
Emp.: 210
Mechanical Contractors; Industrial & Process Piping, Plumbing & Fire Protection Services
S.I.C.: 1711; 1799
Wayne R. Reilly *(Chm. Bd. & Chief Exec. Officer)*
Richard A. Grupka *(Sec. & Treas.)*

Outside Service Firm(s):

Gaines, Emhoff, Metzler & Co.*(Auditors)*
Buffalo, NY

Damon & Morey*(Legal Firm)*
1000 Cathedral Plaza
Buffalo, NY
Tel.: 716-856-5500
Fax: 716-856-5510

Key Bank*(Major Banking Relationship)*
Kingston, NY

DANFOSS DUKES FLUID POWER INC.
(Formerly Dukes Fluid Power Inc.)
950 State Ave.
Saint Charles, IL 60174
Tel.: 708-584-9544
Fax: 708-584-9128
Approx.Sls.: $10,000,000
Emp.: 80
Fiscal Year-end: 12/31/90
Hydraulic Directional Control Valves
S.I.C.: 3592
Fred Cregier *(Pres. & Chief Exec. Officer)*
Bob Paoli *(V.P.-Sls.)*
Robert Swanson *(V.P.-Fin., Sec., Treas. & Chief Fin. Officer)*

THE DANIEL CO. OF SPRINGFIELD
3725 W. Division
Springfield, MO 65803
Tel.: 417-869-7511 MO
Fax: 417-869-0240
Year Founded: 1973
Assets: $2,500,000
Liabilities: $260,000
Net Worth: $2,240,000
Sales Range: $10-19 Million
Emp.: 75
Fiscal Year-end: 12/31/89
Interstate Trucking
S.I.C.: 4213
Larry Daniel *(Pres. & Chief Exec. & Chief Fin. Officer)*
Ron Daniel *(V.P., Dir.-Personnel & Sec.)*
Todd Donaldson *(Controller)*

Principal(s):
Larry Daniel
Ron Daniel

No. of Mfg. Plants/Facilities: 1
No. of U.S. Offices: 1

Computer Systems/Hardware:
COMPAQ 386 LAN

Outside Service Firm(s):

Elliot, Robinson & Co.*(Auditors)*
Springfield, MO

Transport Insurance*(Commercial Insurance Carrier)*
Dallas, TX

Harold F. Glass & Assoc.*(Legal Firm)*
Springfield, MO

Commerce Bank*(Major Banking Relationship)*
Springfield, MO

Commerce Bank*(Pension Manager)*
Springfield, MO

C.R. DANIELS, INC.
3451 Ellicott Center Dr.
Ellicott City, MD 21043
Tel.: 301-461-2100 NY
Fax: 301-461-2987
Year Founded: 1918
Approx.Sls.: $20,000,000
Emp.: 450
Import Export
Mfr. Fabric Products; Materials Handling Containers; Plastic Tote Boxes & Systems; Conveyor & Elevator Belting, Aviation Products
S.I.C.: 2394; 2299; 2399; 3052; 3089; 3171
Harry F. Lee *(Chm. Bd.)*
Vernon T. Abel *(Vice Chm.)*
Gary V. Abel *(Pres.)*
John E. Frangos *(V.P.-Mfg. & Sec.)*
Harold M. Burgard *(V.P.-Pur.)*
Hugh A. Blaha *(V.P.-Export & Govt. Sls.)*
Grahame Poferl *(V.P.)*
M.J. Ahearn *(Controller)*
Peter Turner *(Mgr.-Sls.)*

Outside Service Firm(s):

J. H. Cohn & Co.*(Auditors)*
75 Eisenhower Pkwy.
Roseland, NJ 07068-1697
Tel.: 201-228-3500

Niles, Barton & Wilmer*(Legal Firm)*
Baltimore, MD

Signet Bank*(Major Banking Relationship)*
P.O. Box 1077, 7 St. Paul St.
Baltimore, MD 21203

DANIELS MANUFACTURING CORPORATION
526 Thorpe Rd.
Orlando, FL 32824
Tel.: 407-855-6161 FL
Fax: 407-855-6884
Year Founded: 1949
Approx.Sls.: $16,000,000
Emp.: 140
Export
Mfr. of Hand & Edge Tools; Power-Driven Handtools
S.I.C.: 3423; 3546
William A. Daniels *(Chm. Bd. & Pres.)*
James D. Vargo *(Sec. & Treas.)*

Outside Service Firm(s):

Sun Bank, N.A.*(Major Banking Relationship)*
200 S. Orange Ave., 8th Fl. SOAB
Orlando, FL
Tel.: 407-237-4141

DANIELS PRINTING COMPANY
40 Commercial St.
Everett, MA 02149
Tel.: 617-389-7900
Fax: 617-389-5520
Approx.Sls.: $37,000,000
Emp.: 280
Commercial & Financial Printing
S.I.C.: 2752
Lee S. Daniels *(Pres.)*
James E. Gately *(Treas.)*
William J. Merchant *(Mgr.-Fin.)*

Outside Service Firm(s):

Mintz, Levin, Cohn, Ferris, Glovsky & Popeo, P.C.*(Legal Firm)*
One Financial Center
Boston, MA 02111
Tel.: 617-542-2241

Brown Brothers, Harriman & Co.*(Major Banking Relationship)*
Boston, MA

DANIS INDUSTRIES CORPORATION
(Formerly Dayton Superior Corporation)
Mailing Address:
P.O. Box 725,
Dayton, OH 45401
Assets: $134,806,000
Earnings: $9,172,000
Liabilities: $101,978,000
Net Worth: $32,828,000
Approx.Sls.: $210,000,000
Emp.: 600
Fiscal Year-end: 12/31/91
Construction Company; Commercial Real Estate Developer
S.I.C.: 1541; 1629; 6512; 6552; 1611
Corporate Giving Program: The Danis Foundation Contributes to Charitable, Educational & Religious Causes.
Thomas J. Danis *(Chm. Bd.)*
Richard R. Danis *(Vice Chm.)*
Glenn P. Schimpf *(Pres. & Chief Exec. Officer)*
Richard C. Russell *(Sr. V.P., Chief Fin. Officer & Treas.)*
C. Ronald McSwiney *(Gen. Counsel & Sec.)*
Gregory McCann *(Corp. Counsel & Asst. Sec.)*
Scott Browning *(Dir.-Taxes)*
Michael N. Matzko *(Dir.-Human Resources)*

No. of U.S. Offices: 2

Computer Systems/Hardware:
Sperry System 1100

Outside Service Firm(s):

Ernst & Young*(Auditors)*
2300 Kettering Tower
Dayton, OH 45423
Tel.: 513-223-2000

Massachusetts Mutual Life Insurance Co.*(Group Insurer)*
1295 State St.
Springfield, MA 01111
Tel.: 413-788-8411
Fax: 413-730-6144

Bank One*(Investment Banker)*
Kettering Tower
Dayton, OH 45401
Tel.: 513-449-8600

Thompson, Hine & Flory*(Legal Firm)*
P.O. Box 8801, 2000 Courthouse Plaza N.E.
Dayton, OH 45401-8801
Tel.: 513-443-6500

Bank One*(Major Banking Relationship)*
Kettering Tower
Dayton, OH 45401
Tel.: 513-449-8600

Capital Guardian Trust*(Pension Manager)*
333 South Hope Street
Los Angeles, CA 90071
Tel.: 213-486-9334

Fidelity Management Trust*(Pension Manager)*
82 Devonshire St.
Boston, MA 02109
Tel.: 617-570-5627
Fax: 617-423-9014

Society National Bank*(Pension Manager)*
Dayton, OH

Groups:

Danis Building Construction Group **(1)**
2 River Place, Ste. 100
Dayton, OH 45405
Tel.: 513-228-1225
Building Construction
S.I.C.: 1541
Thomas P. Hammelrath *(Pres.)*

Danis Heavy Construction Group **(1)**
2 River Place, Ste. 200
Dayton, OH 45405
Tel.: 513-228-1225
Heavy Construction
S.I.C.: 1629
Herbert T. Schutte *(Pres.)*

Danis Highway Construction Group **(1)**
1518 E. First St.
Dayton, OH 45402
Tel.: 513-228-1225
Highway Construction
S.I.C.: 1611
James Ahern *(Pres.)*

DANN DEE DISPLAY FIXTURES
350 N. Orleans, Ste.1000
Chicago, IL 60654-1898
Tel.: 312-527-5820
Tel.: 800-888-8515
Fax: 312-527-9561
Year Founded: 1945
Approx.Sls.: $19,000,000
Emp.: 82
Fiscal Year-end: 6/30/92
Import
Store Displays, Fixturing & Racks
S.I.C.: 2541; 2542
Earl Dann *(Pres.)*
John Vacala *(Chief Oper. Officer)*
Linda Basgall *(Admin./Opers.)*
Dave King *(Controller)*
Elene Dann-Gobin *(Dir.-Mktg.)*
Larry Chronowski *(Dir.-Pur.)*
Beth Bauer *(Mgr.-Personnel)*
Mike McGee *(Mgr.-Data Processing)*

DAN'S SUPREME SUPER MARKETS INC.
474 Fulton Ave.
Hempstead, NY 11550
Tel.: 516-483-7046 NY

Fax: 516-483-1586
Sales Range: $100-499 Million
Emp.: 1,500
Grocery Stores
S.I.C.: 5411
Emerick Gross *(Pres. & Chief Exec. Officer)*
Richard Grobman *(V.P.)*
Donald Gross *(V.P., Treas. & Sec.)*
David Swissa *(Controller & Chief Fin. Officer)*

Computer Systems/Hardware:
IBM System 36

Outside Service Firm(s):

Yorkes, Ross & Co.*(Auditors)*
New York, NY

Liberty Mutual*(Group Insurer)*
175 Berkeley St.
Boston, MA

Arnold Tenney*(Legal Firm)*
New York, NY

Star Bank*(Major Banking Relationship)*
425 Walnut Street
Cincinnati, OH 45202
Tel.: 513-632-4000

National Bank of America*(Pension Manager)*
80 Pine St.
New York, NY 10005
Tel.: 212-623-4000

DANUSER MACHINE CO.
500 East Third
Fulton, MO 65251
Mailing Address:
P.O. Box 368
Fulton, MO 65251
Tel.: 314-642-2246 **MO**
Fax: 314-642-2240
Year Founded: 1910
Emp.: 60
Export
Mfr. Danuser Digger Tractor Attachments, Post Drivers, Earth Drills, Hydraulic Earth Scrapers & Specialized OEM Metal Components
S.I.C.: 3523; 3531; 3452
Jerry Danuser *(Pres.)*
Jack Thomas *(V.P. & Gen. Mgr.)*
Earl L. O'Rourke *(Gen. Mgr.-Sls.)*
Roland Bartley *(Mgr.-Sls. Promo.)*
Ron Dooley *(Pur. Agent)*

No. of Mfg. Plants/Facilities: 1
No. of U.S. Offices: 1

Outside Service Firm(s):

Baird, Kurtz & Dobson*(Auditors)*
St. Louis, MO

South Side National Bank*(Major Banking Relationship)*
3606 Gravois Av.
St. Louis, MO 63116
Tel.: 314-776-7000

DARDA INC. (USA)
(Div. of Life-Like Products)
1600 Union Ave.
Baltimore, MD 21211
Tel.: 410-889-1023
Fax: 410-889-0503
Approx.Sls.: $10,000,000
Emp.: 100
Import Export
Manufacturing & Wholesale Distributor of Toys & Games
S.I.C.: 3944; 5092
Jerry Kandel *(Pres.)*
Ed Weiss *(V.P.-Mktg.)*
Herbert Burk *(V.P.)*
Jay Kramer *(V.P.-Mktg. Services)*
Ed Byczynski *(V.P.-Plng. & Devel.)*
Chris Keller *(Controller & Treasurer)*
Butch Holt *(Dir.-Personnel)*
Bob Scheide *(Mgr.-Pur.)*
Bob Muskett *(Mgr.-Data Processing)*
Elfriede Neuhaus *(Mgr.-Export)*

Computer Systems/Hardware:
IBM System 38, PCs, Macintosh II

Outside Service Firm(s):

Equitable Bank, N.A.*(Major Banking Relationship)*
100 S. Charles St.
Baltimore, MD 21201
Tel.: 410-547-4000

Division:

Hinkle Easter Products **(1)**
1600 Union Ave.
Baltimore, MD 21211
Tel.: 410-889-1023
Mfr. Easter Egg Decorating Kits
S.I.C.: 2865
Jerry Kandel *(Pres.)*

DARIEN&KILBURG

DARIEN & KILBURG, INC.
2099 Gateway Pl.
San Jose, CA 95110
Tel.: 408-436-0900
Fax: 408-436-0959
Year Founded: 1982
Approx.Billings: $12,100,000
Emp.: 15
Consumer, Retail, Technology & Business-to-Business
Frank Darien *(Pres.)*
Frank Darien, Sr. *(Exec. V.P.)*
Paul Cohune *(Exec. V.P., New Bus. Contact)*
Ruth Branch *(Controller)*

Computer Systems/Hardware:
IBM, Macintosh

DARIGOLD, INC.
635 Elliott Ave., W.
Seattle, WA 98119
Mailing Address:
P.O. Box 79007,
Seattle, WA 98119
Tel.: 206-284-7220
Tel.: 800-333-MILK **WA**
Fax: 206-281-3456
Year Founded: 1918
Assets: $225,000,000
Liabilities: $127,000,000
Net Worth: $98,000,000
Approx.Sls.: $785,000,000
Emp.: 1,700
Fiscal Year-end: 3/31/92
Export
Wholesale Dairy Products
S.I.C.: 6531; 6719; 5812; 6512; 2026
Wesley Eckert *(Pres. & Chief Exec. Officer)*
Ron Furrer *(Treas. & Controller)*
Douglas Marshal *(Sec. & Gen. Counsel)*
Bob Lukaris *(Asst. to the Pres., Plng. & Devel.)*
Oscar Ringness *(Dir.-Mngmt. Information Systems)*
Veseth Yates *(Dir.-Human Resources)*
John Underwood *(Mgr.-Pur.)*
James Robson *(Gen. Mgr.-Sls. & Mktg.)*

Computer Systems/Hardware:
IBM 8100 & 3090-200

Outside Service Firm(s):

Deloitte & Touche*(Auditors)*
700 Fifth Ave., Suite 4500
Seattle, WA 98104-5044
Tel.: 206-292-1800

Alexander & Alexander*(Commercial Insurance Carrier)*
Seattle, WA

Bankers Life & Casualty*(Group Insurer)*
Chicago, IL

Blue Cross of Washington & Alaska*(Group Insurer)*
Seattle, WA

Graham & Dunn*(Legal Firm)*
1301 5th Ave., 34th Floor
Seattle, WA 98101
Tel.: 206-624-8300

Sea-First Bank*(Major Banking Relationship)*
Seattle, WA

Bankers Life & Casualty*(Pension Manager)*
Chicago, IL

Subsidiary:

Dairy Export Co., Inc. **(1)**
635 Elliott Ave.
Seattle, WA 98119
Tel.: 206-284-7220
Emp.: 60
Feed Mills & Farm Store
S.I.C.: 0723; 5451; 5399

DARLENE JEWELRY MANUFACTURING COMPANY
483 Main St.
Pawtucket, RI 02860
Tel.: 401-728-3300 **RI**
Fax: 401-722-4930
Sales Range: $10-19 Million
Emp.: 160
Fiscal Year-end: 12/31/90
Import Export
Costume Jewelry
S.I.C.: 3961
Bernard E. Baccari *(Pres.)*
John Baccari *(V.P.)*
Vincent Baccari *(V.P.)*
M.B. Colantino *(Sec.)*

Outside Service Firm(s):

Stephen Pascarella, Jr.*(Auditors)*
Providence, RI

Citizens Trust Company*(Major Banking Relationship)*
870 Westminster
Providence, RI 02903
Tel.: 401-456-7000

DARLING-DELAWARE CO., INC.
251 O'Connor Ridge Blvd., Ste. 300
Irving, TX 75038
Tel.: 214-717-0300 **DE**
Fax: 214-717-1588
Year Founded: 1882
Sales Range: $100-499 Million
Emp.: 55
Processing Animal By-Products
S.I.C.: 2077; 2048; 3111; 2841
Frank Miller *(Pres.)*
John Stine *(Controller)*
Ken Ghazey *(Exec. V.P. & Chief Fin. Officer)*
Christopher Roland *(Exec. V.P.-Mktg.)*
Alan Z. Sachter *(Exec. V.P.)*
Ron Cummings *(V.P.-Mngmt. Information Systems)*
Daryl Steinberg *(Corp. Counsel)*
Kevin Levy *(Asst. Sec.)*
Olivia Harndem *(Dir.-Cash Mngmt.)*
Jennifer Pateet *(Mgr.-Ins.)*
R. Sleeper *(Mgr.-Data Processing)*

No. of Mfg. Plants/Facilities: 40

Outside Service Firm(s):

KPMG Peat Marwick*(Auditors)*
1601 Elm St., Ste. 1600
Dallas, TX 75201
Tel.: 214-754-2000
Fax: 214-754-2297

Kelly, Hart & Hallman*(Legal Firm)*
2500 First City Bank Tower
Ft. Worth, TX 76102
Tel.: 817-332-2500

Harris Trust & Savings Bank*(Major Banking Relationship)*
111 W. Monroe St.
Chicago, IL 60690
Tel.: 312-461-2265
Tel.: 800-858-0840

First National Bank of Boston*(Major Banking Relationship)*
P.O. Box 644,
Boston, MA 02102-0644
Tel.: 617-575-2900
Fax: 617-575-2549

DARLING ENVELOPE CORPORATION
5400 Antioch Dr.
Shawnee Mission, KS 66202
Mailing Address:
P.O. Box 657
Shawnee Mission, KS 66201-0657
Tel.: 913-831-2525 **MO**
Fax: 913-831-2582
Year Founded: 1921
Emp.: 135
Mfr. of Envelopes
S.I.C.: 2677
Albert Darling *(Chm. Bd.)*
John P. Davis *(Vice. Chm.)*
Albert Darling, Jr. *(Pres.)*

Outside Service Firm(s):

United Missouri Bank*(Major Banking Relationship)*
P.O. Box 226
Kansas City, MO 64141
Tel.: 816-556-7000

DARLING'S
153 Perry Rd.
Bangor, ME 04401
Tel.: 207-941-1240 **ME**
Fax: 207-941-1206
Year Founded: 1976
Approx.Sls.: $32,000,000
Emp.: 169
Retail Sales of New & Used Automobiles & Motorcycles; Wholesale Distribution of Motor Vehicle Supplies & New Parts
S.I.C.: 5511; 5013
John B. Darling *(Pres.)*
Charles Rohn *(V.P.)*
Timothy Daugherty *(Treas.)*

Outside Service Firm(s):

Berry, Dunn & McNeill*(Auditors)*
Portland, ME

DARLINGTON VENEER COMPANY
225 4th St.
Darlington, SC 29532
Tel.: 803-393-3861
Fax: 803-393-8243
Emp.: 125
Hardwood & Plywood
S.I.C.: 2435
Jack Ramsey *(Pres.)*
Reginald H. Hubbard *(Gen. Mgr.)*
Jimmy Spears *(Sec.)*
Hugh M. Reynolds *(Mgr.-Sls.)*

Computer Systems/Hardware:
IBM System 36

Darlington Veneer Company—(Continued)

Outside Service Firm(s):

Coopers & Lybrand*(Auditors)*
1850 Charlotte Plaza
Charlotte, NC 28244
Tel.: 704-375-8414
Fax: 704-347-1601

Paulling & James*(Legal Firm)*
Darlington, SC

CNS Bank*(Major Banking Relationship)*
Darlington, SC

Subsidiary:

Diamond Hill Plywood Company **(1)**
600 E. Broad St.
Darlington, SC 29532
Tel.: 803-393-2803
Wholesale Plywood & Other Building Materials
S.I.C.: 5031; 5099
J.S. Ramsey, Jr. *(Chm. Bd.)*
John C. Ramsey *(Pres. & Gen. Mgr.)*
James H. Ramsey *(Exec. V.P.)*
Dave Hood *(V.P.-Sls.)*
William W. Abbott, Jr. *(V.P.-Data Processing)*
Dane Smyre *(Sec. & Treas.)*

DART CONTAINER CORP.
500 Hogsback Rd.
Mason, MI 48854
Tel.: 517-676-3800
Plastic Products; 13 Manufacturing Plants Throughout the U.S.
S.I.C.: 3089
William A. Dart *(Chm.)*
Robert C. Dart *(Pres.)*
William Myers *(Treas.)*

DART TRANSIT COMPANY, INC.
800 Lone Oak Rd.
Eagan, MN 55121
Mailing Address:
P.O. Box 64110
St. Paul, MN 55164
Tel.: 612-688-2000
Fax: 612-688-2015
Approx.Sls.: $97,000,000
Emp.: 155
Motor Carrier
S.I.C.: 4213
Donald G. Oren *(Pres.)*
Alan D. Swenson *(Exec. V.P.)*
Beverly J. Oren *(V.P.-Human Resources)*
Neil A. DuJardin *(Chief Oper. Officer)*
Darrell J. Egertson *(Chief Fin. Officer)*
David D. Oren *(Dir.-Information Systems)*

Outside Service Firm(s):

First Bank Minneapolis*(Major Banking Relationship)*
P.O. Box A700, 120 S. Sixth St.
Minneapolis, MN 55480
Tel.: 612-370-4141

THE DARTNELL CORPORATION
4660 N. Ravenswood Ave.
Chicago, IL 60640
Tel.: 312-561-4000
Tel.: 800-621-5463 **DE**
Fax: 312-561-3801
Year Founded: 1917
Emp.: 150
Fiscal Year-end: 12/31/91
Export
Publisher of Business Books; Newsletters, Training Films & Seminars
S.I.C.: 2731; 2741; 8748; 7812
Clark W. Fetridge *(Pres. & Chief Exec. Officer)*
Joseph Drago *(Chief Fin. Officer)*
George Economos *(Sr. V.P. & Dir.-Mktg.)*
Eugene Dombrowski *(V.P.-Intl.)*
Scott Pemberton *(V.P. & Editorial Dir.)*
Susan Keyes *(Controller)*
Bonnie Jean Fetridge *(Sec.)*
Thomas Johnson *(Dir.-Data Processing)*
Conrad Kamer *(Dir.-Human Resources)*
Chuck Pearl *(Dir.-Adv.)*
Ron Swenson *(Dir.-Pur.)*
Nancy Harbutte *(Mgr.-Telemarketing)*
Juanita Roberts *(Corp. Librarian)*

No. of Mfg. Plants/Facilities: 2
No. of U.S. Offices: 2
No. of Foreign Offices: 3

Outside Service Firm(s):

Ernst & Young*(Auditors)*
233 S. Wacker Dr.
Chicago, IL 60606
Tel.: 312-368-1800
Fax: 312-645-3095

William Blair & Co.*(Investment Banker)*
135 S. LaSalle St.
Chicago, IL 60603
Tel.: 312-236-1600

Bell, Boyd & Lloyd*(Legal Firm)*
Three First National Plaza
Chicago, IL 60602
Tel.: 312-372-1121

Bank of Ravenswood*(Major Banking Relationship)*
Chicago, IL

Division:

Cambridge Associates **(1)**
164 Canal St.
Boston, MA 02116
Tel.: 617-723-5969
Fax: 617-227-6982
Emp.: 10
Advertising Newsletters
S.I.C.: 2731
Herbert Motley *(Gen. Mgr.)*
Kent Krizik *(Mgr.-Sls.)*
Judy Wolfer *(Mgr.-Pur.)*

DATA DOCUMENTS HOLDINGS, INC.
4205 S. 96th St.
Omaha, NE 68127
Tel.: 402-339-0900
Fax: 402-339-0485
Holding Company
S.I.C.: 6719
Walter J. Kearns *(Chm. Bd. & Pres.)*

Outside Service Firm(s):

Deloitte & Touche*(Auditors)*
1000 Wilshire Blvd.
Los Angeles, CA 90017-2472
Tel.: 213-688-0800
Fax: 213-688-0100

Gibson, Dunn & Crutcher*(Legal Firm)*
333 S. Grand Ave.
Los Angeles, CA 90067
Tel.: 310-552-8500
Fax: 310-277-5827

Wells Fargo Bank*(Major Banking Relationship)*
333 S. Grand
Los Angeles, CA 90071
Tel.: 213-253-6836

Subsidiary:

Data Documents, Inc. **(1)**
4205 S. 96th St.
Omaha, NE 68127
Tel.: 402-339-0900
Approx.Sls.: $180,000,000
Emp.: 1,290
Manufacture Business Forms, Pressure Sensitive Labels, Variable Imaged Mailing Services, Tabulation Cards & Other Computer Supplies
S.I.C.: 2761
Walter J. Kearns *(Pres. & Chief Exec. Officer)*
Joseph C. Addison *(V.P.-Fin.)*
Morris W. Caudle *(V.P.-Sls.)*
Allyn D. Plejdrup *(V.P.-Data Label)*
William Rinehart *(V.P.-Mfg.)*
John S. Schulte *(V.P.)*

DATA INSTRUMENTS, INC.
100 Discovery Way
Acton, MA 01720
Tel.: 508-264-9550
Tel.: 800-333-DATA
Fax: 508-263-0630
Approx.Sls.: $23,000,000
Emp.: 230
Fiscal Year-end: 5/31/91
Export
Pressure Transducers, Linear Transducers, Load Cells & Instrumentation Transducer Products
S.I.C.: 3829; 3679
E.M. Colbert *(Chm. Bd.)*
Peter R. Russo *(Pres.)*
Mark Hatch *(V.P.-Mktg.)*
Daniel Weber *(V.P.-Engrng.)*
H. Erichson *(Chief Tech. Officer)*
Betty Berndt *(Adv. Mgr.)*
A. Bhide *(Mktg. Mgr.-Wintriss Products)*
P. Grad *(Intl. Sls. Mgr.)*
B. Hodges *(Mktg. Mgr.-Transducer Products)*
E.C. Lutfy *(Natl. Sls. Mgr.)*

Outside Service Firm(s):

Deloitte & Touche*(Auditors)*
125 Summer St.
Boston, MA 02110
Tel.: 617-261-8000
Fax: 617-261-8111

DATABASE AMERICA COMPANIES
100 Paragon Dr.
Montvale, NJ 07645-0419
Tel.: 201-476-2000
Fax: 201-476-2138
Data Processing
S.I.C.: 7374; 7379
Paul Goldner *(Pres.)*
Jeff Brenner *(Controller)*

Subsidiary:

Information Systems **(1)**
100 Paragon Dr.
Montvale, NJ 07645
Tel.: 201-476-2000
Fax: 914-592-3556
Assets: $7,167,123
Liabilities: $8,743,245
Net Worth: $1,576,122
Approx.Sls.: $9,170,952
Emp.: 87
Fiscal Year-end: 12/31/90
Application of Computer Technology to the Production of Products and Services including Direct Marketing, Manufacture of Business Slides and Commercial Application of Computer Graphics; Provide Direct Mktg. Data Processing Services to the Mktg. Industry
S.I.C.: 7379; 7374; 7336
Thomas Zukas *(Chief Exec. Officer)*
Michael Frost *(Pres. & Chief Oper. Officer)*
Bill McGlynn *(Mktg. Mgr.)*

DATABILITY, INC.
One Palmer Terrace
Carlstadt, NJ 07072
Tel.: 201-438-2400
Tel.: 800-456-7844 (Outside NJ)
Fax: 201-438-2688
Year Founded: 1977
Approx.Sls.: $25,000,000
Emp.: 100
Fiscal Year-end: 9/30/90
Export
Mfr. Software & Hardware
S.I.C.: 7371
Ron Howard *(Pres. & Chief Exec. Officer)*
Richard Rupp *(Exec. V.P.)*
James Gallagher *(V.P.-Sls.)*
Jerry Meyers *(V.P.)*
Frank Tolocka *(Chief Fin. Officer)*
Thomas DeQuincy Jefferson *(Dir.-Mktg.)*
Mario Saavides *(Dir.-Human Resources)*
Greg McAdoo *(Dir.-Res. & Devel.)*
Linda Ruvo/Everk *(Mgr.-Channel Mktg.)*
Terri Drexler *(Mgr.-Mktg. & Events)*

DATAMEDIA CORPORATION
20 Trafalgar Sq.
Nashua, NH 03063
Tel.: 603-886-1570 **DE**
Fax: 603-886-1782
Approx.Sls.: $65,000,000
Emp.: 100
Personal Computers & Software Security
S.I.C.: 3571
Roger Grower *(Pres.)*
Bernard J. Coker *(V.P.-Fin.)*

Outside Service Firm(s):

Arthur Andersen & Co.*(Auditors)*
One Intl. Place, 100 Oliver St.
Boston, MA 02110
Tel.: 617-330-4000
Fax: 617-439-9731

Midlantic National Bank*(Major Banking Relationship)*
6000 Midlantic Dr.
Mount Laurel, NJ 08054-6000
Tel.: 609-778-2675

Testa, Hurwitz & Thibeault*(Legal Firm)*
53 State St.
Boston, MA 02109
Tel.: 617-248-7000
Fax: 617-248-7100

DATRON INCORPORATED
2300 N. Barrington Rd., Ste. 600
Hoffman Estates, IL 60195
Tel.: 708-519-1100
Holding Company
S.I.C.: 6719
Henry Peppers *(Pres.)*

Subsidiaries:

All American Industries, Inc. **(1)**
P.O. Box 3010
Boca Raton, FL 33431
Tel.: 407-998-7777 (100%)
Emp.: 800
Aluminum Forgings, Aircraft Arresting Gear, Ordnance & Missile Motor Casings
S.I.C.: 3441; 3483; 3443
Arthur M. Goldberg *(Chm. Bd.)*
Jay H. Harris *(Pres. & Chief Oper. Officer)*

Subsidiaries:

All American Engineering Co. **(2)**
725 Dawson Dr.
Newark, DE 19711
Tel.: 302-453-8100 (100%)
Emp.: 129
Aircraft Arresting Gear & Catapults
S.I.C.: 3728
Edward J. Fahey *(Pres.)*

Anchor Metals, Inc. **(2)**
P.O. Box 157,
Hurst, TX 76053
Tel.: 817-268-1311 (100%)
Emp.: 363
Electrical Transmission Towers & Poles
S.I.C.: 3441
Wilburn Currence *(Pres.)*

Intercontinental Mfg. Co. **(2)**
P.O. Box 461148,
Garland, TX 75046
Tel.: 214-276-5131 (100%)
Emp.: 450
Ordnance & Missile Motor Casings, Aluminum & Magnesium Forgings
S.I.C.: 3769
Phillip B. Laquey *(Pres. & G.M.)*

Subsidiary:

Bergman Manufacturing **(3)**
1200 No. Glenbrook, P.O. Box 461148
Garland, TX 75040
Tel.: 214-276-5131

Forgings
S.I.C.: 3312
Howard Mihms *(V.P. & G.M.)*
Eugene L. Bausman *(V.P.)*

Datron Systems, Inc. **(1)**
P.O. Box 3010,
Boca Raton, FL 33431
Tel.: 407-997-7400 (100%)
Earnings: $3,456,000
Approx.Sls.: $73,101,000
Emp.: 1,000
Fiscal Year-end: 3/31/92
Electronics, Electro & Hydro Mechanical Assemblies
S.I.C.: 3679; 3694; 3494
Jay H. Harris *(Pres.)*

Division:

Eemco Div. **(2)**
4585 Electronics Place
Los Angeles, CA 90039
Tel.: 818-247-7060 (100%)
Emp.: 285
Electro & Hydro Mechanical Actuators
S.I.C.: 3674
William J. Forcey *(V.P. & G.M.)*

Subsidiary:

Tech Systems Corp. **(2)**
401 Watertown Rd.
Thomaston, CT 06787
Tel.: 203-283-5801 (100%)
Emp.: 400
Microwave Components, Electric Motors & Controls
S.I.C.: 3621
Stuart Litt *(Pres.)*

Non-U.S. Holding:

AAI International Ltd. **(1)**
Berkshire House, 3rd Flr., Queen St.
Maidenhead, Berkshire SL6 1NF, United Kingdom
Tel.: Maidenhead 32005 (100%)
Emp.: 16
Aircraft Arresting Systems Technical Liaison
S.I.C.: 3728

Non-U.S. Joint Ventures:

Befab-Safeland, Ltd. **(1)**
Bay 15, Industrial Estates
Shannon, County Clare Ireland
Tel.: Shannon 61844 (100%)
Emp.: 55
Aircraft Arresting Gear
S.I.C.: 3728

Elektro Metall Export Gmbh **(1)**
Manchingerstrasse 116
Ingolstadt, D-8070, Germany
Tel.: 0841/69017 (100%)
Emp.: 50
Electro Mechanical Assembly
S.I.C.: 3449

DAUBERT INDUSTRIES, INC.
One Westbrook Corp. Center, Ste. 1000
Westchester, IL 60154
Tel.: 708-409-5000
Fax: 708-409-5196
Year Founded: 1935
Approx.Sls.: $86,000,000
Emp.: 430
Fiscal Year-end: 12/31/91
Export
Holding Company for the Daubert Group; Nox-Rust Systems & Undercoatings; Daubond Adhesives; Easy Mask Masking Tape; VCI Volatile Corrosion Paper & Films; Silicone Coated Release Papers & Films, Cutting & Grinding Fluids & Auto Rust Proofing
S.I.C.: 6719; 2891; 2821; 3479; 2992
Harry A. Fischer, Jr. *(Chm. Bd.)*
M. Lawrence Garman *(Pres. & Chief Exec. Officer)*
S.A. Scott *(Sr. V.P.-Fin. & Admin.)*
J.R. Cosbey *(V.P., Sec. & Treas.)*
R.E. Blake *(V.P. & Controller)*
W.A. Gaeth *(V.P.-Human Resources)*
P.L. Nevell *(V.P.-Mngmt. Information Services)*

No. of Mfg. Plants/Facilities: 4

Computer Systems/Hardware:
IBM System 38

Outside Service Firm(s):

Arthur Andersen & Co.*(Auditors)*
33 W. Monroe St.
Chicago, IL 60603-4067
Tel.: 312-580-0033
Fax: 312-507-6748

American National Bank & Trust Company of Chicago*(Major Banking Relationship)*
33 N. LaSalle St.
Chicago, IL 60602
Tel.: 312-661-5000
Fax: 312-661-6417

Sonnenschein, Nath & Rosenthal*(Legal Firm)*
Sears Tower
Chicago, IL 60606
Tel.: 312-876-8000

Subsidiaries:

Daubert Chemical Company, Inc. **(1)**
4700 So. Central Ave.
Chicago, IL 60638
Tel.: 708-496-3750
Fax: 708-496-7367
Nox-Rust Rust Preventive Wax, Grease, Oil Coatings, Cutting Fluids, Mill, Stamping & Process Oils, Specialty Metalworking Compounds; Daubond, Laminating, Hot Melt, Structural Adhesives, Specialty Formulated Bonding Systems
S.I.C.: 2891; 3089; 3479; 2992
M.A. Dwyer *(Pres. & Chief Exec. Officer)*
P.T. Marek *(V.P.-Quality Assurance)*
Mark Pawelski *(Gen. Mgr.-Mfg.)*

Daubert Coated Products, Inc. **(1)**
One Westbrook Corp. Center, Suite 900
Westchester, IL 60154
Tel.: 708-409-5000
Tel.: 800-634-1303
Daubert Controlled Release Papers & Films, Nox-Rust Volatile Corrosion Inhibitor (VCI) Protective Packaging for Metal Surfaces; Easy-Mask Paint Masking & Protective Tapes, Coated & Laminated Products for the Health Care Industry
S.I.C.: 2891; 3089; 3479; 2992
M. Lawrence Garman *(Pres. & Chief Exec. Officer)*
J.L. Taylor *(V.P.-Mfg.)*
W.P. McBain *(V.P.-Sls. & Mktg.)*
S.L. Maher *(V.P.-Research & Devel.)*

ECP Incorporated **(1)**
One Westbrook Corp. Center, Suite 1000
Westchester, IL 60154
Tel.: 708-409-5000
Tel.: 800-323-3521
Fax: 708-409-5195
Auto Armor Rust Protection, Paint Protection, Interior Protection Packaged Systems for the Automobile Dealer; Specialty Chemical Private Label Manufacturing & Packaging; Management & Marketing Services
S.I.C.: 2992; 2671; 2819; 8742
M.L. Garman *(Chm. Bd.)*
Larry Bottendorf *(Pres. & Chief Exec. Officer)*
R.A. Remiasz *(Dir.-Tech. Services)*
M. Feely *(Natl. Sls. Mgr.)*
S.J. Haik *(Dir.-Corp. Devel & Admin.)*

DAV-EL SERVICES, INC.
North River, Pier 62
New York, NY 10011
Tel.: 212-645-9555 NY
Fax: 212-463-8620
Year Founded: 1966
Assets: $7,000,000
Liabilities: $6,000,000
Net Worth: $1,000,000
Approx.Sls.: $14,000,000
Fiscal Year-end: 12/31/90
Luxury Limousine Service
S.I.C.: 4119
Scott Solombrino *(Chm. Bd., Pres. & Chief Exec. Officer)*
Stephen M. Paluska *(Controller)*
Principal(s):
Scott Solombrino

No. of U.S. Offices: 350

Computer Systems/Hardware:
MAI Basic 4

Outside Service Firm(s):

KPMG Peat Marwick*(Auditors)*
345 Park Ave.
New York, NY 10154
Tel.: 212-758-9700
Fax: 212-872-3308

Rose & Snyder*(Auditors)*
Los Angeles, CA

Bank Leumi le-Israel B.M.*(Major Banking Relationship)*
New York, NY

Fireman's Fund Insurance Co.*(Commercial Insurance Carrier)*
New York, NY

Fireman's Fund Insurance Co.*(Group Insurer)*
New York, NY

Bankers Life & Casualty*(Group Insurer)*
Chicago, IL

Connecticut General Life Insurance Co.*(Group Insurer)*
P.O. Box 2975,
Hartford, CT 06104
Tel.: 203-726-6000

Morrison, Cohen & Singer*(Legal Firm)*
750 Lexington Ave.
New York, NY 10022
Tel.: 212-735-8600

Subsidiaries:

Dav-El Washington D.C., Inc. **(1)**
318 "I" Street, N.E.
Washington, DC 20002
Tel.: 202-543-2300
Emp.: 50
Limousine Service
S.I.C.: 4119
Jon Goldberg *(Chief Oper. Officer)*

Dav-El West **(1)**
9641 Sunset Blvd.
Beverly Hills, CA 90210
Tel.: 310-550-0070
Emp.: 150
Limousine Service
S.I.C.: 4119
Jerrie Heslov *(Chief Oper. Officer)*

J.T. DAVENPORT & SONS, INC.
Hwy. 42 East
Sanford, NC 27330
Tel.: 919-774-9444
Fax: 919-774-4282
Year Founded: 1917
Sales Range: $60-79 Million
Emp.: 110
Convenience Store Supplier
S.I.C.: 5411
J.T. Davenport, Jr. *(Pres. & Treas.)*
John Musselwhite *(Mgr.-Sls.)*
Graham Parker *(Mgr.-Mktg.)*
Jim Mize *(Dir.-Information Mngmt.)*
Sylvia Gordon *(Dir.-Personnel)*

Outside Service Firm(s):

Deloitte & Touche*(Auditors)*
Hickory, NC

Southern National Bank*(Major Banking Relationship)*
Sanford, NC

THE DAVEY TREE EXPERT COMPANY
1500 N. Mantua St.
Kent, OH 44240
Tel.: 216-673-9511 OH
Fax: 216-673-9843
Year Founded: 1880
Assets: $72,000,000
Liabilities: $36,000,000
Net Worth: $36,000,000
Approx.Sls.: $184,000,000
Emp.: 4,600
Fiscal Year-end: 12/31/90
General Tree & Lawn Care Service; Utility Line Maintenance; Interior Plant Care; Tree Nursery
S.I.C.: 0782; 0783
John W. Joy *(Chm. Bd.)*
R. Douglas Cowan *(Pres. & Chief Exec. Officer)*
David E. Adante *(V.P., Chief Fin. Officer & Sec.)*
Dr. Roger Funk *(V.P.-Human & Technical Resources)*
Gordon Ober *(V.P.-New Ventures)*
James J. Reed *(V.P. & Treas.)*
Bradley Comport *(Controller)*
Roger Beal *(Mgr.-Information Systems)*
Robert Browne *(Mgr.-Pur. & Properties)*
Ward Peterson *(Mgr.-Human Resources)*

Computer Systems/Hardware:
IBM

Outside Service Firm(s):

Deloitte & Touche*(Auditors)*
One Cascade Plaza, Ste. 1600
Akron, OH 44303-1187
Tel.: 216-253-2022

Johnson & Higgins*(Commercial Insurance Carrier)*
Akron, OH

Prudential Insurance Co. of America*(Group Insurer)*
751 Broad St.
Newark, NJ 07102-3777
Tel.: 201-802-6000

Thomson, Hine & Flory*(Legal Firm)*
Cleveland, OH

National City Bank*(Major Banking Relationship)*
P.O. Box 92301, Corp. Trust Dept.
Cleveland, OH 44101
Tel.: 216-575-2000

Society National Bank*(Major Banking Relationship)*
800 Superior Ave.
Cleveland, OH 44114
Tel.: 216-689-5931
Fax: 216-689-3814

Alliance Capital Management*(Pension Manager)*
1345 Avenue of the Americas
New York, NY 10017

Society National Bank*(Pension Manager)*
800 Superior Ave.
Cleveland, OH 44114
Tel.: 216-689-5931
Fax: 216-689-3814

Subsidiary:

Davey Tree Surgery Co. **(1)**
2617 S. Vasco Rd.
Livermore, CA 94550
Tel.: 510-443-1723
S.I.C.: 0783
Howard Bowles *(V.P. & Gen. Mgr.)*

Non-U.S. Holdings:

Vancouver Tree People **(1)**
2869 Norland Ave.
Burnaby, BC V5B 3A6, Canada
Tel.: 604-987-2084 (100%)
Tree Surgery
S.I.C.: 0783
Neil Wilson *(Gen. Mgr.)*

Canadian Shade Tree Service, Ltd. **(1)**
1540 Claire Crescent
Lachine, PQ H8S 4E6, Canada
Tel.: 514-634-7046 (100%)
Tree Surgery
S.I.C.: 0783

The Davey Tree Expert Company—(Continued)

High Tree Services Ltd. **(1)**
P.O. Box 186, Island Highway South
Nanaimo, BC V9R 5K9, Canada
Tel.: 604-245-7104
Tree Services
S.I.C.: 0783

D.A. DAVIDSON & CO.
Davidson Building
Great Falls, MT 59401
Mailing Address:
P.O. Box 5015
Great Falls, MT 59403
Tel.: 406-727-4200
Fax: 406-791-7315
Year Founded: 1935
Approx.Sls.: $23,000,000
Emp.: 237
Fiscal Year-end: 9/28/90
Investment Brokerage Service Firm
S.I.C.: 6211
Ian B. Davidson *(Chm. Bd. & Chief Exec. Officer)*
Vincent M. Purpura *(Pres. & Chief Oper. Officer)*
Eugene S. Hufford *(Sr. V.P.)*
Stuart C. Nicholson *(Sr. V.P.-Opers.)*
Gerald L. Meyer *(V.P.-Mktg. & Exec. Devel.)*
Charles C. Abernathy, Jr. *(V.P.-Sydnicate Dept.)*
James L. Bellessa, Jr. *(V.P.-Research)*
Darlene Miller *(Dir.-Public Rels.)*

No. of U.S. Offices: 14

Outside Service Firm(s):

Douglas Wilson & Co.*(Auditors)*
Great Falls, MT

Dorsey & Whitney*(Legal Firm)*
2200 First Bank Place East
Minneapolis, MN 55402

First Interstate Bank of Great Falls*(Major Banking Relationship)*
Great Falls, MI

Subsidiaries:

Financial Aims Corporation **(1)**
Davidson Building
Great Falls, MT 59401
Tel.: 406-727-6111
Investment Brokerage Service
S.I.C.: 6211
Eugene P. Lewis *(Pres.)*
Jack Davant *(V.P.)*

TrustCorp. **(1)**
Davidson Building
Great Falls, MT 59401
Tel.: 406-791-7320
Trust Company
S.I.C.: 6021
Robert Bragg *(Pres.)*

DAVIDSON MARKETING, INC.
54 W. Hubbard St.
Chicago, IL 60610
Tel.: 312-527-3900
Fax: 312-527-3327
Year Founded: 1979
Approx.Billings: $27,999,000
Emp.: 31
Developing Sls. Promo. Programs
Jay Farrell *(Pres. & New Bus. Contact)*

DAVIS ADVERTISING INC.
1700 Market St., Ste. 2626
Philadelphia, PA 19103
Tel.: 215-851-8600 **PA**
Fax: 215-851-0450
Year Founded: 1904
Approx.Billings: $15,000,000
Emp.: 40
Import Export
Agency Specializing in Recruitment Advertising
S.I.C.: 7311
George G. Griffin *(Chm. Bd., Pres. & Treas.)*
Christopher J. Taylor *(V.P.)*
Joseph Trzuskowski *(V.P.)*
Steven Mayer *(Sec.)*
Charles Lawson *(Acctg. Mgr.)*

DAVIS, BALL & COLOMBATTO ADVERTISING, INC.
865 S. Figueroa
Los Angeles, CA 90017
Tel.: 213-688-7000
Fax: 213-688-7288
Year Founded: 1958
Approx.Billings: $152,769,000
Emp.: 105
Consumer Retail Chains and Products, With an Emphasis on Broadcasting
Robert M. Davis *(Chm., Sec. & Treas.)*
Brad A. Ball *(Pres. (Odd Days), Exec. Creative Dir.)*
Mark D. Davis *(Pres. (Even Days))*
Robert J. Colombatto *(Dir.)*
Steve Orenstein *(Chief Fin. Officer)*
Paula Freeman *(Sr. V.P.)*
Jim McKenna *(Sr. V.P.)*
Roy Cowan *(Sr. V.P.)*
Lee Dick *(Sr. V.P.)*
George Milliken *(Sr. V.P.)*
John Turner *(Sr. V.P.)*
Tony Raymond *(Sr. V.P., Dir. Bus. Devel.)*
Bonnie Logan *(V.P., Dir. Human Resources)*
Sherry Rahbar *(V.P., Controller)*

BUD DAVIS CADILLAC, INC.
5433 Poplar Ave.
Memphis, TN 38119
Tel.: 901-761-1900 **TN**
Fax: 901-685-7431
Year Founded: 1974
Approx.Sls.: $40,000,000
Emp.: 150
Retail Sales of New & Used Automobiles
S.I.C.: 5511
Kindle Davis *(Pres.)*
David Ferraez *(V.P.)*
Gary K. Davis *(Treas. & Sec.)*

Outside Service Firm(s):

United American Bank*(Major Banking Relationship)*
Memphis, TN

DAVIS COMPANIES
2121 Ave. of the Stars, Ste. 2800
Los Angeles, CA 90067
Tel.: 310-551-1470
Fax: 310-556-3766
Holding Company
S.I.C.: 6719
Marvin Davis *(Pres.)*

Subsidiaries:

SPI Holdings **(1)**
1501 N. Plano Rd.
Richardson, TX 75061
Tel.: 214-234-2721
Fax: 214-669-1200
Holding Company
S.I.C.: 6719
James Boso *(Pres. & Chief Exec. Officer)*

Spectradyne Inc. **(1)**
1501 N. Plano Rd.
Richardson, TX 75061
Tel.: 214-669-1290
Emp.: 570
Provides Pay-Per-View & Satellite Delivered Programs Free To The Guest Lodging Industry
S.I.C.: 3663; 4833; 4841
James Boso *(Chief Exec. Officer)*
Sydney L. Bayer *(Pres.)*
John Aylsewarte *(V.P.-Fin.)*
David Tripp *(V.P. & Gen. Counsel)*
Nancy Deemer *(Controller)*

DAVIS ELECTRICAL CONSTRUCTORS, INC.
429 N. Main St.
Greenville, SC 29602
Mailing Address:
P.O. Box 1907
Greenville, SC 29602
Tel.: 803-250-2500
Tel.: 800-849-3284 **SC**
Fax: 803-233-3784
Approx.Sls.: $60,000,000
Emp.: 2,000
Import Export
Electrical & Instrumentation Contractor
S.I.C.: 1731
J.B. Stevens *(Chm. Bd.)*
J.M. Stephens *(Pres. & Chief Exec. Officer)*
J. C. Henderson *(V.P.-Construction)*
J. Lowell Hughes *(V.P. & Sec.)*
William M. Sumerel *(V.P.-Construction)*
Stan Turner *(Dir.-Mktg. & Adv.)*
Bill Dyar *(Dir.-Personnel)*
R. S. Passmore *(Dir.-Engrng.)*
Rob Robinson *(Dir.-Pur.)*
Bill Noel *(Dir.-Data Processing)*

Outside Service Firm(s):

Elliott, Davis & Co.*(Auditors)*
Greenville, SC

South Carolina National Bank*(Major Banking Relationship)*
7515 Northside Dr.
Greenville, SC
Tel.: 803-577-8280

JIMMY DAVIS ENTERPRISES, INC.
420 Lake Shore Dr.
Madison, FL 32340
Tel.: 904-973-2215 **FL**
Fax: 904-973-8386
Year Founded: 1965
Approx.Sls.: $22,000,000
Emp.: 165
Gasoline Service Stations; Eating Places; Gift Shops; Independent Grocery Stores
S.I.C.: 5541; 5812; 5947; 5411
James B. Davis, Jr. *(Pres.)*
James B. Davis, III *(V.P.)*
Hank Davis *(V.P.)*
Martha O. Davis *(Sec. & Treas.)*

Outside Service Firm(s):

Wesley Catledge & Company Associates*(Auditors)*
Madison, FL

Bank of Madison City*(Major Banking Relationship)*
Madison City, FL

JOSEPH DAVIS, INC.
120 W. Tupper St.
Buffalo, NY 14201
Tel.: 716-842-1500
Fax: 716-842-0124
Year Founded: 1948
Approx.Sls.: $47,000,000
Emp.: 275
General Mechanical Contractors
S.I.C.: 1711; 1623; 1731
Jeffrey J. Davis *(Pres.)*
Lawrence E. Davis *(V.P.)*
Donald A. DeMeo *(V.P. & Treas.)*
Edward Halady *(V.P.-Engrng.)*
Joseph Kuckowski *(V.P.-Estimating & Sec.)*
Peter Orendorf *(V.P.-Sls. & Adv.)*

Outside Service Firm(s):

Lucker, Kennedy & Felmeden*(Auditors)*
Buffalo, NY

Saperston & Day, P.C.*(Legal Firm)*
Buffalo, NY

Marine Midland Bank*(Major Banking Relationship)*
P.O. Box 803, 1 Marine Midland Center, 23rd Floor
Buffalo, NY 14203
Tel.: 716-841-2582

DAVIS INDUSTRIES INC.
19250 Plymouth Rd.
Detroit, MI 48228
Tel.: 313-835-6000
Fax: 313-837-7720
Year Founded: 1921
Approx.Sls.: $57,000,000
Emp.: 450
Fiscal Year-end: 9/27/92
Export
Manufacture Metal Stampings; Assemblies & Prototypes
S.I.C.: 3469; 3465
Richard Davis *(Chm. Bd. & Pres.-Davis Industries)*
Richard L. Davis, II *(Pres.)*
Kim E. Davis *(Pres.-DATEC Ind., Inc.)*
Merle Embry *(Pres.-Multi-Plex, Inc.)*
Lorne Greenwood *(Pres.-Davis Tool & Engineering Co.)*
Jeffery H. Davis *(V.P.)*
Conrad D. Chapman *(Sec.)*
Dale Martin *(Treas.)*
Scott Nelson *(Dir.-Sls.)*
Steve Nelson *(Dir.-Personnel)*

No. of Mfg. Plants/Facilities: 3

Computer Systems/Hardware:
AS400

Outside Service Firm(s):

Plante & Moran*(Auditors)*
Southfield, MI

Powers, Chapman, De Agostino*(Legal Firm)*
Troy, MI 48084

National Bank of Detroit*(Major Banking Relationship)*
611 Woodward Ave.
Detroit, MI 48226

Subsidiaries:

Davis Tool & Engineering Co. **(1)**
19250 Plymouth Rd.
Detroit, MI 48228
Tel.: 313-835-6000
Emp.: 350
Automotive Metal Stampings & Assemblies
S.I.C.: 3465
L. Greenwood *(Pres.)*
John Svendor *(V.P.)*
Michael Burns *(Controller)*

Multi-Plex, Inc. **(1)**
State Rd. 9 N.
Howe, IN 46746
Tel.: 219-562-2911
Emp.: 100
Merl Emery *(Pres.)*
Michael Cling *(Controller)*

DAVIS MECHANICAL CONTRACTORS, INC.
7640 Pelham Rd.
Greenville, SC 29615
Mailing Address:
P.O. Box 1847,
Greenville, SC 29602
Tel.: 803-288-7430 **SC**

Fax: 803-288-6115
Year Founded: 1965
Approx.Sls.: $62,000,000
Emp.: 1,100
Mechanical Contractors: Heating, Plumbing, Ventilating, Air Conditioning & Process Piping
S.I.C.: 1711
F. Harold Gillespie *(Chm. & Chief Exec. Officer)*
James F. Fero, Jr. *(Sr. V.P.)*
Tommy Park *(V.P.-Construction)*
Jim Trout *(Treas.)*

Outside Service Firm(s):

Ernst & Young*(Auditors)*
C & S Bank Tower, Two Shelter Centre, Ste. 800
Greenville, SC 29603

Wyche, Burgess, Freeman & Parham, P.A.*(Legal Firm)*
44 E. Camperdown Way
Greenville, SC 29602
Tel.: 803-242-3131

Citizens & Southern Trust Company, Inc*(Major Banking Relationship)*
Albany, GA

DAVIS MINING & MANUFACTURING

Miners Professional Bldg., Colburn, VA 24230
Tel.: 703-395-3354
Year Founded: 1985
Approx.Sls.: $242,000,000
Emp.: 1,600
Mfr. of Wood Turnings, Explosives, Mining Machinery & Equipment; Underground Mining; Wholesale Distributor of Construction & Mining Equipment
S.I.C.: 2892; 5082; 1222; 2426
William Jack Davis *(Chm. Bd. & Pres.)*
L. Jack Davis *(V.P.)*
Deborah Karen Davis *(Sec.)*
Joseph Funk *(Controller)*

Outside Service Firm(s):

Tri-City Bank & Trust Co.*(Major Banking Relationship)*
Blountville, TN

Division:

Allen-Rogers Co. **(1)**
P.O. Box 637,
Laconia, NH 03246
Tel.: 603-524-2060
Wood Products
S.I.C.: 2499; 2421
R.V. Guptill *(Pres. & Chief Oper. Officer)*

DAVIS-MOORE OLDSMOBILE, INC.

6215 E. Kellogg
Wichita, KS 67218
Tel.: 316-685-0211
Fax: 316-685-3011
Year Founded: 1956
Approx.Sls.: $73,000,000
Emp.: 175
Retail Automobiles, Recreational & Ulitity Trailers & General Automotive Repair
S.I.C.: 5511; 5561; 7538
T. Grant Davis, Jr. *(Pres.)*
Ted Davis, III *(Gen. Mgr.)*
Lois M. Smith *(Sec. & Treas.)*

Subsidiary:

Davis-Moore Recreational Vehicle Center **(1)**
6215 E. Kellogg
Wichita, KS 67218
Tel.: 316-685-0211
Recreational & Utility Trailers
S.I.C.: 5561
T. Grant Davis, Jr. *(Pres.)*

DAVIS-NEWMAN-PAYNE

4700 Coster Rd.
Knoxville, TN 37912
Mailing Address:
P.O. Box 12128,
Knoxville, TN 37912
Tel.: 615-688-3151
Fax: 615-687-4233
Year Founded: 1950
Approx.Billings: $19,000,000
Emp.: 30
Hal B. Atwater *(Chm. Bd.)*
Victor H. McLean *(Pres. & Chief Exec. Officer)*

DAVIS PAINT COMPANY

1311 Iron St.
Kansas City, MO 64116
Mailing Address:
P.O. Box 7589
Kansas City, MO 64116
Tel.: 816-471-4447
Tel.: 800-821-2029
Fax: 816-471-1460
Year Founded: 1921
Approx.Sls.: $12,000,000
Emp.: 130
Fiscal Year-end: 10/31/90
Paint Mfg.
S.I.C.: 2851; 5072
James L. Davis *(Chm. Bd. & Chief Exec. Officer)*
Kevin C. Ostby *(Pres.)*
Jeff Lee *(Exec. V.P.)*
Gladys Rains *(Chief Fin. Officer)*
Steve Bussjaeger *(V.P.-Tech.)*
Sandy Haskins *(V.P.-Industrial)*
Christine Wise *(Corp. Sec.)*
Karl Floth *(Sls. Mgr.)*
Bill Claibourn *(Mfg. Mgr.)*
Virginia Ellington *(Buyer)*

DAVIS & PHILLIPS, INC.

121 College Place
Norfolk, VA 23510
Mailing Address:
P.O. Box 3826,
Norfolk, VA 23514
Tel.: 804-627-7373
Fax: 804-627-4257
Year Founded: 1976
Approx.Billings: $20,775,000
Emp.: 37
Jerome R. Davis *(Pres.)*
Michael R. O'Neal *(Controller)*

DAVIS WIRE CORPORATION

5555 N. Irwindale
Irwindale, CA 91706
Tel.: 818-969-7651
Fax: 818-813-9985
Year Founded: 1927
Approx.Sls.: $100,000,000
Emp.: 1,000
Mr. of Wire & Wire Products
S.I.C.: 3496
E.A. Roskovensky *(Pres.)*
Steve Frediani *(V.P.-Mfg.)*

Outside Service Firm(s):

Arthur Andersen & Co.*(Auditors)*
33 W. Monroe St.
Chicago, IL 60603-4067
Tel.: 312-580-0033
Fax: 312-507-6748

McDermott, Will & Emery*(Legal Firm)*
227 W. Monroe St.
Chicago, IL 60606-5096
Tel.: 312-372-2000

Bank of America NT&SA*(Major Banking Relationship)*
555 So. Flower St.
Los Angeles, CA 90071
Tel.: 213-683-3868

DAVLIN PAINT COMPANY, INC.

P.O. Box 2308, 700 Alston Way
Berkeley, CA 94702
Tel.: 510-848-2863
Fax: 510-848-1464
Year Founded: 1968
Sales Range: $10-19 Million
Emp.: 26
Manufacture & Retail Paint
S.I.C.: 2851
David DeRuiter *(Pres.)*
Dennis Wilkens *(V.P.)*

Principal(s):
David DeRuiter
Dennis Wilkens

DAW TECHNOLOGIES, INC.

2700 South 900 West
Salt Lake City, UT 84119
Tel.: 801-977-3100 **UT**
Fax: 801-973-6640
Year Founded: 1974
Approx.Sls.: $28,000,000
Emp.: 170
Fiscal Year-end: 9/30/90

Export
Clean Room Design, Manufacture & Installation
S.I.C.: 1542; 7389
Ronald W. Daw *(Chm. Bd. & Chief Exec. Officer)*
Susan Mooney *(Pres. & Treas.)*
Kevan Blair *(Chief Fin. Officer)*
Kevin Blair *(Chief Info. Officer (MIS))*
Steve Burt *(Group V.P.-Asia/Pacific)*
Ryan S. Daw *(Group V.P.-Europe)*
Mike Wilkinson *(Gen. Counsel)*
Dallis Christensen *(Treas. & Chief Information Officer)*
F. Ray Hawkins *(Dir.-Human Resources)*
K. Barr Anderson *(Mgr.-Purch.)*
Pete Spransy *(Mgr. Res. & Devel.)*

No. of U.S. Offices: 1
No. of Foreign Offices: 1

Computer Systems/Hardware:
MIPS

Outside Service Firm(s):

Arthur Andersen & Co.*(Auditors)*
717 17th St., Ste. 1900
Denver, CO 80202
Tel.: 303-296-2121

Intermountain Health Care*(Group Insurance Broker/Consult)*
Salt Lake City, UT

DAWAHARES, INC.

1845 Alexandria Dr.
Lexington, KY 40504
Tel.: 606-278-0422
Fax: 606-277-5673
Approx.Sls.: $25,000,000
Emp.: 650
Retail Family Department Store
S.I.C.: 5651
Oscar D. Dawahare *(Acting Chm. Bd.)*
A.F. Dawahare *(Pres. & Dir.-Sls. & Mktg.)*
Harding E. Dawahare *(V.P. & Dir.-Pub. Rels.)*
Hoover Dawahare *(V.P.)*
S. Frank Dawahare, Jr. *(V.P.)*
Martin Dawahare *(Sec. & Treas.)*
Joe Dawahare *(Dir.-Govt. Affairs & Gen. Counsel)*
Michael Dawahare *(Dir.-Adv. & Media)*
Becky Marafet *(Dir.-Data Processing)*
Dee Shinnick *(Dir.-Human Resources, Personnel Training & Devel.)*
Norm Cron *(Controller)*
Kinch Query *(Corporate Travel Planner)*

Outside Service Firm(s):

Dulworth & Breeding*(Auditors)*
Lexington, KY

Bank of Whitesburg, Inc.*(Major Banking Relationship)*
Whitesburg, KY

DAWN FOOD PRODUCTS, INC.

2021 Micor Dr.
Jackson, MI 49203
Tel.: 517-789-4400 **MI**
Fax: 517-789-4465
Year Founded: 1955
Approx.Sls.: $190,000,000
Emp.: 800
Mfr. of Doughnut & Cake Mixes Prepared From Purchased Flour, Extracts Flavoring; Syrups; Colorings; Bakery Machinery; Condiments
S.I.C.: 2045; 2087; 3556; 5149
Ronald L. Jones *(Pres.)*
Steven M. Jones *(Exec. V.P.)*
Phillip W. Crow *(V.P.-Sls.)*
John R. Dixon *(V.P.)*
Miles E. Jones *(V.P.)*
Harry P. Wulff *(V.P.)*
Dale Curdin *(Gen. Mgr.)*
Marvel C. Jones *(Sec.)*
Peter Staelens *(Treas. & Asst. Sec.)*

Outside Service Firm(s):

Price Waterhouse*(Auditors)*
67 W. Michigan Mall
Battle Creek, MI 49017

Divisions:

Dawn/BESCO, Inc. **(1)**
2021 Micor Dr.
Jackson, MI 49302
Tel.: 517-789-4400
Mfr. of Extracts; Food Coloring; Food Preparations
S.I.C.: 2087; 2099

Dawn Food Products Frozen Div. **(1)**
2021 Micor Dr.
Jackson, MI 49203
Tel.: 517-789-4400
Mfr. of Croissants & Pastries, Except Frozen; Sweet Yeast Goods, Except Frozen
S.I.C.: 2051

Regency Creative Foods **(1)**
2021 Micor Dr.
Jackson, MI 49203
Tel.: 517-789-4400
Mfr. of Prepared Flour Mixes & Doughs
S.I.C.: 2045

DAWN JOY FASHIONS, INC.

501 7th Ave.
New York, NY 10018
Tel.: 212-354-9840
Fax: 212-944-7853
Approx.Sls.: $61,000,000
Emp.: 100
Women's, Juniors & Misses Dresses
S.I.C.: 2335
Martin Stein *(Pres. & Chief Exec. Officer)*
Richard Morabito *(V.P.-Controller)*

Outside Service Firm(s):

Chemical Banking Corp.*(Major Banking Relationship)*
277 Park Ave.
New York, NY 10041
Tel.: 212-310-6407
Fax: 212-310-4526

Subsidiary:

Sherri Martin **(1)**
501 7th Ave.
New York, NY 10018
Tel.: 212-354-9840
Women's, Juniors & Misses Dresses
S.I.C.: 2335
Martin Stein *(Pres.)*

DAXUS CORPORATION
One Oliver Plaza
Pittsburgh, PA 15222-2603
Tel.: 412-566-4900 **PA**
Fax: 412-566-3284
Year Founded: 1974
Sales Range: $10-19 Million
Emp.: 120
Designs & Installs Computer Integrated Industrial Automation Systems for Process & Discrete Parts Manufacturing Industries
S.I.C.: 7371; 7372; 7373; 7374; 7376; 7379
W. S. Brown IV *(Pres. & Chief Exec. Officer)*
Patricia M. Rogan *(Chief Fin. Officer)*
Daniel McDermott *(V.P.)*
Frank J. Guarnaccio *(Controller)*
Kerry P. Lamson *(Dir.-Mktg.)*
Thomas Kennedy *(Dir.-Engrng.)*
John D. Fader *(Natl. Sls. Mgr.)*

No. of Mfg. Plants/Facilities: 1
No. of U.S. Offices: 2

Computer Systems/Hardware:
IBM; DEC VAX; Apple

Outside Service Firm(s):

Alpern, Rosenthal & Company*(Auditors)*
Pittsburgh, PA

Equibank*(Major Banking Relationship)*
Two Oliver Plz.
Pittsburgh, PA 15222
Tel.: 412-288-5000

DAY & ZIMMERMANN, INC.
280 King of Prussia Rd.
Radnor, PA 19087
Tel.: 215-299-8000
Tel.: 800-523-0786 **MD**
Telex: 845192
Fax: 215-299-8030
Year Founded: 1901
Assets: $119,000,000
Liabilities: $62,500,000
Net Worth: $56,500,000
Approx.Sls.: $625,000,000
Emp.: 12,800
Fiscal Year-end: 12/31/91
Export
Diversified Professional Service Firm Providing Engineering Design, Architecture, Construction Management, Plant Operations, Naval Ship System Support, Mass Appraisal of Real Estate, Contract Technical Personnel & Nuclear Plant Security Services
S.I.C.: 8742; 8711; 8712; 7363; 6531
Employee Matching Gifts Program: Full Time, Regular Employees in the Delaware Valley Area may give up to Eight Hours of Pay to One of 20 Designated Institutions Through Payroll Deduction; This will be Matched, Dollar-For-Dollar, by Company Funds; Employee Contributions & Company Matching Funds Are Deducted Once Each Year, in the Fall, & Forwarded to Recipient..
Harold L. Yoh, Jr. *(Chm. Bd., Pres. & Chief Exec. Officer)*
Jack A. Apperson *(Pres.-Defense Systems Grp.)*
Benjamin J. Pellegrini *(Pres.-Mngmt. Services Grp.)*
Stephen Bushnell *(Chief Information Officer)*
John P. Follman *(Chief Fin. Officer & Sr. V.P.-Fin.)*
Barry L. Buechner *(Sr. V.P.-Bus. Plng. & Systems)*
Anthony Bosco *(V.P.-Bus. Analysis & Systems)*
F.A. Greenhalgh *(V.P. & Treas.)*
William R. Hamm *(V.P.-Admin.)*
Karen R. Lautzenheiser *(V.P.-Communications)*
Anthony G. Natale *(V.P.-Human Resources)*
Joseph Ritzel *(V.P. & Controller)*
James A. Goodman *(Gen. Counsel & Sec.)*
Dale Biegelman *(Asst. Treas.)*
Stephen P. Bushnell *(Dir.-Mngmt. Information Systems)*
Principal(s):
Harold L. Yoh, Jr.

No. of U.S. Offices: 60

Computer Systems/Hardware:
Hewlett-Packard 3000; Amdahl; IBM 536, 538, AS 400, 370, 4300, 3090; UNISYS

Outside Service Firm(s):

Deloitte & Touche*(Auditors)*
1700 Market St.
Philadelphia, PA 19103
Tel.: 215-246-2322
Fax: 215-569-2441

Marsh & McLennan*(Commercial Insurance Carrier)*
3 Parkway
Philadelphia, PA 19102
Tel.: 215-963-2800

Equitable Real Estate Investment Managment Inc.*(Group Insurer)*
3414 Peachtree Rd. N.E.
Atlanta, GA 30326-1162

Blank, Rome, Comisky & McCauley*(Legal Firm)*
Four Penn Center Plaza
Philadelphia, PA 19103
Tel.: 215-209-3700

Equitable Life*(Pension Manager)*
1221 Ave. of the Americas
New York, NY 10022
Tel.: 212-382-8038
Fax: 212-382-8089

New York Life*(Pension Manager)*
51 Madison Ave.
New York, NY 10010
Tel.: 212-576-6367
Fax: 212-576-6630

Divisions:

Aquidneck Data Company **(1)**
170 Enterprise Center
Middletown, RI 02840
Tel.: 401-847-7260
Provides Computer Software & Systems Engineering To Federal Government
S.I.C.: 7376; 7373
Kenneth A. Parker *(Pres.)*
Robert Fye *(V.P.)*
Patty Sweeney *(Treas.)*
John Park *(Controller)*
John Murray *(Dir.-Computer Information Systems)*
Robert Maddock *(Mgr.-Human Resources)*

Barry Services Company **(1)**
222 Continental Dr., Ste. 200
Newark, DE 19713
Tel.: 302-453-8000
Provides Recruiting & Placement Services for Clerical, Secretarial, Administrative, Graphic Communications & Light Industrial Personnel in Both Temporary & Permanent Positions
S.I.C.: 7363
Bonnie Wingate *(Exec. V.P.)*

Cole-Layer-Trumble Company (CLT) **(1)**
3199 Klepinger
Dayton, OH 45406
Tel.: 513-276-5261
Emp.: 500
Mass Appraisal of Real Estate; Data Systems for Public Administration
S.I.C.: 6531
Bruce Nagel *(Pres.)*

Day Data Systems **(1)**
280 King of Prussia Rd.
Radnor, PA 19087
Tel.: 215-975-6840
Recruiting & Placement Services for Data Processing & Data Communications Personnel in Temporary Positions
S.I.C.: 7363
Stephen J. Fierberg *(Pres.)*

Day & Zimmerman Kansas Division **(1)**
Hwy. 160 E.
Parsons, KS 67357-9106
Load, Assemble & Packaging of Conventional Ammunition Products for the Army; Also Provides Both Products & Manufacturing Services for Prime Weapon System Contractors & State Department-Approved Foreign Allies
S.I.C.: 3483
Joel Gregory *(Gen. Mgr.)*

Landisc Systems **(1)**
3199 Klepinger Rd.
Dayton, OH 45406
Tel.: 513-278-3800
Develops Applicaions for Laser Videodisc-Based Information Systems
S.I.C.: 7379

Lone Star Division **(1)**
Hwy. 82 W.
Texarkana, TX 75501-1800
Loading, Assembling & Packaging of Conventional Ammunition Products For The Army; Also Provides Both Products & Manufacturing Services For Prime Weapon System Contractors & State Department-Approved Foreign Allies
S.I.C.: 3483
Jerry Smith *(Gen. Mgr.)*

Munitions Technology Division **(1)**
4626 Summerhill Rd.
Texarkana, TX 75503
Engineering, Design, Procurement, Installation, Training & Start-Up Services for Equipment Used in Ammunition Production Lines
S.I.C.: 8711

H. L. Yoh Company **(1)**
280 King of Prussia Rd.
Radnor, PA 19087
Tel.: 215-975-6925 (100%)
Emp.: 2,500
Contract Technical Personnel
S.I.C.: 7363
Lawrence W. Suwak *(Pres.)*

Division:

Salem Technical Services **(2)**
1200 Jorie Blvd.
Oak Brook, IL 60521-9981
Tel.: 708-990-8800
Contract Engineering Services, Specialized Temporary Support & Personnel, Engineering, Design, Drafting & Technical
S.I.C.: 7363

Protection Technology **(1)**
280 King of Prussia Rd.
Radnor, PA 19087
Tel.: 215-341-3605 (100%)
Emp.: 3,100
Security Services for Nuclear Utilities, Industrial & Government Facilities
S.I.C.: 7382
Daniel J. Gallagher *(Pres.)*

Systems Engineering Associates Co. (SEACOR) **(1)**
200 East Park Dr.
Mount Laurel, NJ 08054
Tel.: 609-866-2400 (100%)
Emp.: 1,100
Naval Ship Systems Engineering, Training, Logistics Support & Modernization Program Management
S.I.C.: 8711; 8742
Jon Groff *(Chm. Bd. & Chief Exec. Officer)*

Subsidiaries:

D&Z, Inc. **(1)**
1818 Market St.
Philadelphia, PA 19103
Tel.: 215-299-8000
Professional Engineering, Architectural, Construction Management, Maintenance & Ancillary Service
S.I.C.: 8711; 8712; 8741
Floyd G. Walters *(Pres.)*

Divisions:

Day Engineering **(2)**
6302 Fairview Rd.
Charlotte, NC 28210
Tel.: 704-364-8431
Engineering Support Services for Modernization & Expansion Program for Du Pont Facilities
S.I.C.: 8711

Day Maintenance **(2)**
1818 Market St.
Philadelphia, PA 19103
Managed Plant Operations & Maintenance Support Services to Light & Heavy Industrial Plants in the Process Industries
S.I.C.: 8742

Day Products **(2)**
540 Pedricktown Rd.
Bridgeport, NJ 08014
Tel.: 609-467-5522
Recycle Plastic Products
S.I.C.: 3089
Terry Williams *(Pres.)*

Engineering & Construction Division **(2)**
1818 Market St.
Philadelphia, PA 19103
Tel.: 215-299-8000
Engineering, Design, Procurement & Construction Services to a Diverse Private & Government Client Base in the Specific Business Areas of Chemical, Oil, Food & Beverage, Industrial Manufacturing
S.I.C.: 8711
Lawrence W. Dooley *(Pres.)*

Life Sciences International **(2)**
1818 Market St.
Philadelphia, PA 19103
Tel.: 215-299-8506
Fax: 215-299-2273
Emp.: 230
Architectural & Engineering Services; Construction of Biotechnology & Pharmaceutical Facilities
S.I.C.: 8711
Robert J. Giorgio *(Pres.)*
John F. Gilmore *(Chief Exec. Office)*
Andrew D. Skibo *(Exec. V.P.-Sls. & Mktg.)*
V. Kumar Gupta *(V.P.-Pharmaceuticals)*
Michael M. Kaplan *(V.P.-Sls. & Mktg.)*
Frank J. Knoll *(V.P.-Opers.)*
James W. Hunt *(Dir.-Bus. Devel.)*
Susan M. Kearney *(Mgr.-Sls. & Mktg. Communications)*

Branch:

Life Sciences International-California **(3)**
7031 Koll Center Pkwy.; Ste. 300
Pleasanton, CA 94566
Tel.: 415-426-6500
Fax: 415-426-6555
Engrng. & Architectural Services; Construction of Pharmaceutical & Biotechnological Facilities
S.I.C.: 8711

MDC Systems **(2)**
280 King of Prussia Rd.
Radnor, PA 19087
Tel.: 215-975-6600 (100%)
Emp.: 100
Construction Management Services, Claims Analysis, Litigation Support
S.I.C.: 8711; 8742
John B. Stetson *(Pres.)*

Operating Plant Services **(2)**
1818 Market St.
Philadelphia, PA 19103
Maintenance & Plant Betterment, Design Engineering, Technical Support Personnel to Operating Industrial & Utility Clients
S.I.C.: 8742; 8711
Lawrence Newhart *(Pres.)*

Transportation & Distribution Associates **(2)**
280 King of Prussia Rd.
Radnor, PA 19087
Tel.: 215-975-6650 (100%)
Management, Operations & Maintenance Consulting to the Rail Transportation & Transit Industry
S.I.C.: 8744
John B. Stetson *(Pres.)*

Advanced DZign Systems **(2)**
201 Schuylkill Ave.
Reading, PA 19603
Tel.: 215-376-8451
Emp.: 100
Architects, Engineers-Micro Electronic Facilities
S.I.C.: 8711; 8712

David Watson *(Pres.)*

Subsidiaries:

NPS Energy Services, Inc. **(2)**
950 West Valley Rd., Ste. 2800
Wayne, PA 19087
Tel.: 215-341-3651
Provides General Maintenance & Overhaul for Large Industrial Facilities & Rotating Equipment
S.I.C.: 8742
Lawrence E. Newhart *(Acting Pres.)*

NPS, Inc. **(2)**
950 West Valley Rd., Ste. 2800
Wayne, PA 19087
Tel.: 215-341-3652
Engineering & Programmed Software Development to the Nuclear Power Industry & Close-in Photogrammetry Services
S.I.C.: 7371; 8711
Paul Greer *(Pres.)*

Day & Zimmermann, Inc. **(1)**
P.O. Box 15,
Hawthorne, NV 89415-0015
Tel.: 702-945-7658
Operates the Hawthorne Army Ammunition Plant Under Contract to the U.S. Army
S.I.C.: 8742

SEACOR Services, Inc. (SSI) **(1)**
200 East Park Drive, Suite 600
Mount Laurel, NJ 08054
Tel.: 609-866-2400
Water/Wastewater Operations & Base Operations Support Services
S.I.C.: 4953

Joint Venture:

Costain/Life Sciences International **(1)**
Costain House, Styal Rd.
Manchester, M22 5WN, United Kingdom
Tel.: 011-44-61-499-3030
Fax: 011-44-61-437-5829
Architectural & Engineering Services; Joint Venture of D&Z, Inc.
S.I.C.: 8711
Ian Thompson *(Grp. Mgr.)*

DAYCON PRODUCTS COMPANY, INC.
9001 E. Hampton Dr.
Capitol Heights, MD 20791
Tel.: 301-499-2600
Fax: 301-499-1659
Approx.Sls.: $12,000,000
Emp.: 80
Wholesale Janitorial Products
S.I.C.: 5087
Robert N. Cohen *(Pres.)*
Harry Feldman *(V.P.)*
John Poole *(Sec. & Treas.)*

Outside Service Firm(s):

Understein & Associates*(Auditors)*
Bethesda, MD

David M. Kanter*(Legal Firm)*
Washington, DC

Sovran Bank*(Major Banking Relationship)*
Bethesda, MD

DAYTON ROGERS MFG. CO.
2824 13th Ave., S.
Minneapolis, MN 55407
Tel.: 612-871-2471
Fax: 612-871-2646
Year Founded: 1929
Approx.Sls.: $30,000,000
Emp.: 500
Fiscal Year-end: 6/30/91
Export
Stampings (Small & Medium Lot); Die Cushions; Shell Trimmers; Layout Fluid
S.I.C.: 3469
John Seeger *(Chm. Bd.)*
John Seeger Jr. *(Pres.)*
Robert Gold *(V.P.-Engrng.)*
Steve Wennes *(V.P.-Opers.)*
James L. Hoopes *(V.P.-Sls. & Pub. Rels.)*
John O'Mally *(V.P.-Fin.)*
John Moylan *(V.P.-Human Resources)*
Tom Pilon *(Mgr.-Information Services)*
Steve Ekblad *(Mgr.-Quality Assurance)*
Philip Bryans *(Sls. Promo. Mgr.)*

Computer Systems/Hardware:
IBM 3600

Subsidiaries:

Dayton Rogers of Ohio **(1)**
2309 McGaw Rd. West
Columbus, OH 43207
Tel.: 614-491-1477
Stamping Metal for the Trade
S.I.C.: 3469

Dayton Rogers of Texas **(1)**
1107 Commercial Blvd. No.
Arlington, TX 76017
Tel.: 817-467-1261
Stamping Metal for the Trade
S.I.C.: 3469

Federal Stampings of California **(1)**
13630 Saticoy St.
Van Nuys, CA 91402
Tel.: 818-787-6670
Stamping Metal for the Trade
S.I.C.: 3469

Federal Stampings of Florida **(1)**
7205 30th Ave. No.
St. Petersburg, FL 33710
Tel.: 813-347-4137
Stamping Metal for the Trade
S.I.C.: 3469

Federal Stampings of New York **(1)**
1455 Emerson St.
Rochester, NY 14606
Tel.: 716-254-0220
Stamping Metal for the Trade
S.I.C.: 3469

Federal Stampings of Oregon **(1)**
4277 West 5th
Eugene, OR 97402
Tel.: 503-686-8530
Stamping Metal for the Trade
S.I.C.: 3469

Dayton Superior Corporation
(Name Changed to Danis Industries Corporation)

DAZEY CORPORATION
One Dazey Circle
Industrial Airport, KS 66031 **MO**
Tel.: 913-782-7500
Fax: 913-829-1485
Year Founded: 1899
Approx.Sls.: $60,000,000
Emp.: 350
Fiscal Year-end: 12/31/90
Import Export
Manufactures Electric Kitchen Appliances, Personal Care & Hydro-Therapy Products
S.I.C.: 3631; 3632; 3999
H. Stephen Talge *(Pres.)*
Lewis A. Mendelson *(Exec. V.P.-Mktg.)*
Foster L. Talge, Jr. *(Exec. V.P.-Engrng.)*
Jay Howard *(V.P.-Mfg.)*
Donald Drescher *(Sec. & Treas.)*
Joe Wempe *(Controller)*
Sam Dawdy *(Dir.-Personnel)*
Jerry Davis *(Dir.-Data Processing)*
Susan Gregory *(Mgr.-Adv.)*
Thomas Collins *(Pur. Agent)*
Principal(s):
H. Stephen Talge

No. of Mfg. Plants/Facilities: 1
No. of U.S. Offices: 3
No. of Foreign Offices: 1

Computer Systems/Hardware:
IBM System 38

Outside Service Firm(s):

KPMG Peat Marwick*(Auditors)*
1000 Walnut St.
Kansas City, MO 64106

Kuraner & Schwegler*(Legal Firm)*
Kansas City, MO

United Missouri Bank*(Major Banking Relationship)*
Tenth & Grand
Kansas City, MO 64106
Tel.: 816-556-7000

DE FRANCISCI MACHINE CORP.(DEMACO)
46-25 Metropolitan Ave.
Ridgewood, NY 11385
Tel.: 718-456-6600
Telex: 710-584-2449
Fax: 718-417-9264
Year Founded: 1911
Sales Range: $10-19 Million
Emp.: 100
Export
Manufacture Food Processing Equipment
S.I.C.: 3565
Ignatius DeFrancisci *(Chm. Bd.)*
Leonard DeFrancisci *(Pres. & Chief Exec. Officer)*
Jack Steinberg *(Controller)*
Joseph DeFrancisci, Jr. *(Sec.)*
Joseph DeFrancisci *(Dir.-Mktg.)*
Yvette Rodriguez *(Office Mgr.)*

Computer Systems/Hardware:
IBM System 34

Outside Service Firm(s):

Anchin, Block & Anchin*(Auditors)*
1375 Broadway
New York, NY 10018

Group Health Insurance (GHI)*(Group Insurer)*
New York, NY

Chemical Banking Corp.*(Major Banking Relationship)*
277 Park Ave.
New York, NY 10041
Tel.: 212-310-6407
Fax: 212-310-4526

PAUL A. DE JESSE, INC. ADVERTISING
Professional Plaza, Broad St.
Freehold, NJ 07728
Tel.: 908-780-6909
Year Founded: 1980
Approx.Billings: $19,000,000
Emp.: 25
Health Care Adv.
Paul A. De Jesse *(Pres.)*
Dr. Rudy Borgersen *(Medical Dir.)*
Allan Cohen, LLD *(Medical & Legal)*
Dr. William Cohen *(Assoc. Medical Dir.)*
Leila Coyle *(Controller)*
Ron Leavsley *(Dir., Mktg. & Strategic Plng.)*
June Sheehan *(Administrations Mgr.)*

DE NOVO CORPORATION
48380 Van Dyke
Utica, MI 48317
Mailing Address:
P.O. Box 180162,
Utica, MI 48318
Tel.: 313-739-5520 **MI**
Fax: 313-739-8351
Year Founded: 1950
Approx.Sls.: $125,000,000
Emp.: 10
Franchisors of Tastee Freez
S.I.C.: 5812
David Chapoton *(Chm. Bd.)*
James P. Brasier *(Pres.)*
Deanna Erickson *(Dir.-Mktg.)*
Richard Joy *(Dir.-Opers.)*
Principal(s):
David Chapoton

Computer Systems/Hardware:
IBM 50Z

Outside Service Firm(s):

Plante & Moran*(Auditors)*
Mt. Clemens, MI

Blue Cross & Blue Shield of Michigan*(Group Insurer)*
Detroit, MI

Michigan National Bank*(Major Banking Relationship)*
Dearborn, MI

Subsidiary:

Tastee Freez Intl. Inc. **(1)**
48380 Van Dyke
Utica, MI 48317
Tel.: 313-739-5520
Fax: 313-739-8351
Franchisors of Tastee Freez & Big T Family Restaurants
S.I.C.: 5812; 6794
David Chapoton *(Chm. Bd.)*
James Brasier *(Pres.)*
Deanna Erickson *(Dir.-Mktg.)*
Dick Joy *(Dir.-Opers.)*

DE VONS JEWELERS
1910 29th St.
Sacramento, CA 95816
Tel.: 916-451-6583
Fax: 916-456-2514
Approx.Sls.: $11,000,000
Emp.: 102
Retail Jewelers
S.I.C.: 5944
Gerald M. Merksamer *(Pres.)*
Jon R. Merksamer *(V.P. & Sec.)*
Steven A. Merksamer *(Asst. Sec.)*
Larry S. Miller *(Comptroller)*

Outside Service Firm(s):

Coopers & Lybrand*(Auditors)*
P.O. Box 538, 800 Akron Centre Plaza
Akron, OH 44308

Weintraub, Genshlea, Hardy, Erich & Brown*(Legal Firm)*
Sacramento, CA

Bank of America NT&SA*(Major Banking Relationship)*
Sacramento, CA

DEAD RIVER COMPANY
1 Dana St.
Portland, ME 04112
Mailing Address:
P.O. Box 7438 D.T.S.,
Portland, ME 04112
Tel.: 207-773-5841 **ME**
Telex: 350210
Fax: 207-773-1302
Year Founded: 1907
Sales Range: $100-499 Million
Emp.: 770
Fiscal Year-end: 12/28/90
Export
Forestry, Lumber & Wood Products; Wholesale Nondurable Goods; Service Stations; Miscellaneous Retail Stores; Real Estate Management
S.I.C.: 5172; 5983; 5984; 5541; 2499; 6531
P. Andrews Nixon *(Chm. Bd., Pres. & Chief Exec. Officer)*
Rollin F. Haynes *(V.P.-Real Estate)*
Walter L. Hunt *(V.P.-Human Resources & Sec.)*
F. Michael McClain *(V.P.-Petroleum Grp.)*
Richard M. Roderick *(V.P.-Fin.)*
Reginald B. Elwell *(Gen. Mgr.-Forest Prods. Grp.)*

No. of Mfg. Plants/Facilities: 1
No. of U.S. Offices: 40

Dead River Company—(Continued)

Computer Systems/Hardware:
Prime 750 & 2665

Outside Service Firm(s):

Ernst & Young*(Auditors)*
Portland, ME

Sedgwick James*(Commercial Insurance Carrier)*
Portland, ME

Pierce, Atwood, Scribner, Allen, Smith & Lancaster*(Legal Firm)*
Portland, ME

First National Bank of Boston*(Major Banking Relationship)*
P.O. Box 644,
Boston, MA 02102-0644
Tel.: 617-575-2900
Fax: 617-575-2549

Fleet National Bank*(Major Banking Relationship)*
Bangor, ME

State Street Bank & Trust Co.*(Major Banking Relationship)*
P.O. Box 366,
Boston, MA 02101
Tel.: 617-426-5523

State Street Bank & Trust Co.*(Pension Manager)*
225 Franklin St.
Boston, MA 02101
Tel.: 617-654-3652

Subsidiaries:

Dead River Forest Products **(1)**
55 Broadway
Bangor, ME 04401
Tel.: 207-947-8641 (100%)
Timberland Management
S.I.C.: 0811
Reginald B. Elwell *(Gen. Mgr.)*

Dead River Petroleum Co. **(1)**
55 Broadway
Bangor, ME 04401
Tel.: 207-947-8641 (100%)
Marketing of Petroleum Products; Gasoline, Fuel Oil & Propane
S.I.C.: 5172
F. Michael McClain *(V.P.)*

Dead River Properties **(1)**
13 Atlantic Place
South Portland, ME 04106
Tel.: 207-773-5868 (100%)
Management of Commercial Real Estate Properties
S.I.C.: 6512
Rollin F. Haynes *(V.P.)*

Scott Motor Transport **(1)**
55 Broadway
Bangor, ME 04401
Tel.: 207-947-8641 (100%)
Trucking
S.I.C.: 4213
Marvin F. Peters *(Gen. Mgr.)*

DEALERS ELECTRICAL SUPPLY CO.
2320 Columbus Ave.
Waco, TX 76703
Mailing Address:
P.O. Box 2676
Waco, TX 76703
Tel.: 817-756-7251
Fax: 817-756-0133
Year Founded: 1949
Approx.Sls.: $115,000,000
Emp.: 454
Fiscal Year-end: 4/30/90
Wholesale Electrical, Hardware & Construction Supplies
S.I.C.: 5063
Morris W. Bracey *(Chm. Bd., Pres., Chief Exec. & Chief Oper. Officer)*
Bob Stahl *(Exec. V.P.)*
Calvin Sanders *(Sr. V.P.)*
Richard Decker *(V.P.-Pur.)*
Anthony Newberg *(V.P.-Mktg. & Data Processing)*
Ernest A. West *(V.P.-Credit)*
David Bryant *(Controller)*
Carol Ann Jones *(Sec. & Treas.)*

Computer Systems/Hardware:
Burroughs B340

Outside Service Firm(s):

KPMG Peat Marwick*(Auditors)*
Waco, TX

T. D. Howe*(Commercial Insurance Carrier)*
15995 N. Barkers Landing
Houston, TX 77079
Tel.: 713-558-8585

Naman, Howell, Smith & Lee*(Legal Firm)*
Waco, TX

Republic Bank Waco*(Major Banking Relationship)*
Waco, TX

Aetna Life & Casualty*(Pension Manager)*
151 Farmington Avenue
Hartford, CT 06156
Tel.: 203-273-2128
Fax: 203-729-4295

DEALERS MANUFACTURING COMPANY
5130 Main St. N.E.
Minneapolis, MN 55421
Tel.: 612-572-1800
Fax: 612-572-0532
Approx.Sls.: $19,000,000
Emp.: 220
Remanufacture Automobiles & Truck Engines & Related Parts
S.I.C.: 3714
Employee Matching Gifts Program: United Way
D.W. Goodwin *(Pres.)*
John P. Mathiesen *(V.P.-Quality Control & Mfg.)*
Douglas Frank *(Chief Fin. Officer)*
Gene Olson *(Sls. & Mktg. Mgr.)*
Steve Schwartz *(Plant Mgr.)*
Ken Neubeck *(Mgr.-Matls.)*
Charles Giles *(Dir.-Data Processing)*

Outside Service Firm(s):

McGladrey & Pullen*(Auditors)*
Minneapolis, MN

Parsiner, Bowman & Levy*(Legal Firm)*
Minneapolis, MN

Norwest Bank of Minneapolis N.A.*(Major Banking Relationship)*
P.O. Box 738, 161 N. Concord Exchange
So. St. Paul, MN 55075-0738
Tel.: 612-450-4064
Fax: 612-450-4078

DEALERS TRANSPORT COMPANY, INC.
5405 Fox Plaza Dr., Ste. 107
Memphis, TN 38115
Tel.: 901-795-1199 **TN**
Fax: 901-795-1494
Year Founded: 1958
Retail Sales of New & Used Automobiles; Industrial Machinery & Equipment
S.I.C.: 5511; 5084
Harry Smith *(Chm. Bd.)*
Rex Jones *(Pres.)*

Outside Service Firm(s):

First Tennessee Bank, N.A.*(Major Banking Relationship)*
Memphis, TN

Subsidiaries:

Schilling Enterprises **(1)**
5405 Fox Plaza Dr., Ste. 107
Memphis, TN 38115
Tel.: 901-795-1199

Schilling Motors, Inc. **(1)**
963-87 Union Ave.
Memphis, TN 38104
Tel.: 901-525-1550
Retail Sales of New & Used Automobiles
S.I.C.: 5511
Rex Jones *(Pres.)*

DEAN OPERATIONS INC.
1201 W. 31st St.
Kansas City, MO 64108
Tel.: 816-753-5300 **MO**
Fax: 816-753-6005
Approx.Sls.: $57,000,000
Emp.: 240
Holding Company; Distribute Construction & Paving Equipment; Commercial Real Estate Subdividers & Developers
S.I.C.: 6719; 5082; 6552
Lester M. Dean, Sr. *(Chm. Bd. & Chief Exec. Officer)*
Curt Stokes *(Pres. & Chief Exec. Officer)*
Ted Roberts *(V.P.-Sls.)*
E. R. Sullivan *(V.P.-Mktg.)*
Robert Cohan *(Treas.)*
Leonard D. Moore *(Controller)*
Steve Butters *(Mgr.-Fin.)*
Barbara Jacobs *(Mgr.-Pur.)*
Jakcie Stokes *(Mgr.-Sls.)*

Outside Service Firm(s):

Coopers & Lybrand*(Auditors)*
Kansas City, MO

United Missouri Bank*(Major Banking Relationship)*
P.O. Box 226
Kansas City, MO 64141
Tel.: 816-556-7000

DEANS PHOTO SERVICE, INC.
4575 Mission George Pl.
San Diego, CA 92120
Tel.: 619-287-5811 **CA**
Fax: 619-287-2101
Year Founded: 1966
Approx.Sls.: $30,000,000
Emp.: 400
Film Processing & Finishing; Distribution of Photographic Cameras, Projectors, Equipment & Supplies
S.I.C.: 7384; 5043
David S. Price *(Chm. Bd.)*
Adele Hendricks *(Pres.)*
John Bond *(V.P.)*
Don L. Hedge *(V.P.-Opers.)*
John Jones *(V.P.-Tech. Services)*
Dale Powers *(V.P.-Mktg. & Sls.)*
David Erickson *(Treas.)*

Outside Service Firm(s):

Tenney, Wade & Seidinger*(Auditors)*
San Diego, CA

Union Bank*(Major Banking Relationship)*
La Mesa, CA

Subsidiaries:

Fuji TruColor Foto **(1)**
4686 Mission Gorge Pl.
San Diego, CA 92120
Tel.: 619-286-0500
Photofinishing Laboratory
S.I.C.: 7384
John A. Price *(Chief Fin. Officer)*

Presto Prints **(1)**
4575 Mission Gorge Pl.
San Diego, CA 92120
Tel.: 619-287-5811
Photofinishing Laboratories
S.I.C.: 7384

DEARBORN GAGE COMPANY
32330 Ford Rd.
Garden City, MI 48135
Tel.: 313-422-8300
Fax: 313-422-4445
Year Founded: 1936
Approx.Sls.: $13,000,000
Emp.: 95
Import
Mfr. Gages
S.I.C.: 3545
Elmer Ellstrom, Jr. *(Chm. Bd & Chief Exec. Officer)*
Olof W. Ellstrom, Jr. *(Pres.)*
Olof W. Ellstrom *(Exec. V.P.)*
Richard Ellstrom *(V.P.)*
Robert Sramek *(V.P.-Sls.)*
M. Sciberras *(Sec., Treas. & Comptroller)*
Russ Morgan *(Mgr.-Mfr.)*
Robert Bartelt *(Pur. Agent)*
Principal(s):
Elmer Ellstrom, Jr.
Olof W. Ellstrom, Jr.
Olof W. Ellstrom
Richard Ellstrom

Outside Service Firm(s):

Plante & Moran*(Auditors)*
Southfield, MI

Michigan National Bank*(Major Banking Relationship)*
Troy, MI

THE DEARBORN GROUP
33 N. Dearborn St., Ste. 1030
Chicago, IL 60602
Tel.: 312-726-9855
Fax: 312-726-1413
Year Founded: 1974
Sales Range: $40-59 Million
Emp.: 150
Real Estate Investment, Syndication, Development; Pension Fund Management
S.I.C.: 6722; 6798; 6799; 6371
Leonard M. Schiller *(Owner & Dir.-Acquisitions)*
Phil Schiller *(Owner)*
Tim Frazier *(Gen. Mgr.)*
Karyn Lev *(Controller)*
Principal(s):
Leonard M. Schiller
Phil Schiller

Computer Systems/Hardware:
MAI Basic Four

Outside Service Firm(s):

Wells & Co.*(Commercial Insurance Carrier)*
Indianapolis, IN

RMSCO Management*(Group Insurer)*
Chicago, IL

Katten, Muchin & Zavis*(Legal Firm)*
525 W. Monroe St., Ste. 1600
Chicago, IL 60661-3693
Tel.: 312-902-5200

American National Bank & Trust Company of Chicago*(Major Banking Relationship)*
33 N. LaSalle St.
Chicago, IL 60602
Tel.: 312-661-5000
Fax: 312-661-6417

The Northern Trust Co.*(Major Banking Relationship)*
50 S. LaSalle St.
Chicago, IL 60675

DEARDEN'S, INC.
700 S. Main St.
Los Angeles, CA 90014
Tel.: 213-362-9600 **CA**
Fax: 213-624-0775
Year Founded: 1910
Approx.Sls.: $20,000,000
Emp.: 160
Retailer Furniture, Appliances, TV & Audio Equipment, Fine Jewelry
S.I.C.: 5712; 5722; 5731; 5944
Douglas E. Dearden *(Chief Exec. Officer & Personnel Dir.)*
Rachel Bensimon *(Pres. & Chief Fin. Officer)*
William Opdike *(Sec.)*

Ron Bensimon *(Mgr.-Sls.)*
Principal(s):
Douglas E. Dearden

No. of Mfg. Plants/Facilities: 4

Computer Systems/Hardware:
Hewlett-Packard 3000

Outside Service Firm(s):

Ernst & Young*(Auditors)*
515 S. Flower St.
Los Angeles, CA 90071
Tel.: 213-621-1666

Sheppard, Mullin, Richter & Hampton*(Legal Firm)*
333 S. Hope Street, 48th Fl.
Los Angeles, CA 90071

Security Pacific Corporation*(Major Banking Relationship)*
Security Pacific Plaza
Los Angeles, CA 90071
Tel.: 213-345-6211
Fax: 213-625-0809

DEARDORFF-JACKSON COMPANY
P.O. Box 1188, 1120 Mountain View Ave.
Oxnard, CA 93032
Tel.: 805-487-7801
Fax: 805-483-1286
Year Founded: 1950
Approx.Sls.: $20,000,000
Emp.: 200
Grow, Pack & Ship Fresh Fruits & Vegetables
S.I.C.: 0161; 0171; 0723
T.D. Deardorff *(Chm. Bd. & Pres.)*
E.D. Williams *(V.P.-Field Opers.)*
Jim Boner *(Treas.)*
W.W. Deardorff, Jr. *(Mgr.-Sls. & Sec.)*

Outside Service Firm(s):

Dick Richards*(Legal Firm)*
Oxnard, CA

First Interstate Bank*(Major Banking Relationship)*
Oxnard, CA

DEARE MARKETING INC./ MATTHEW-LAWRENCE ADVERTISING & SALES PROMOTION INC.
322 8th Ave.
New York, NY 10001
Tel.: 212-929-1313
Fax: 212-929-1396
Fax: 212-929-1559
Year Founded: 1960
Approx.Billings: $36,685,000
Emp.: 22
Business-to-Business Sls. Promo. & Adv.; Direct Mail Packages, Tie-in Programs & Strategic Planning
Jennifer Deare *(Pres./DMI)*
Lawrence Danziger *(Pres./ML Div.)*
Denise Martinez *(Fin. Office Mgr.)*
Tracy Inserra *(Acct. Coord./Pub. Rels. Asst.)*
Bruce Schneider *(Computer Consultant)*
Dawn Ressy *(Admin. Asst.)*

DEB HOLDINGS, INC.
302 Waller St.
Saginaw, MI 48605
Tel.: 517-799-4941
Holding Company for Manufacturing Hand Cleaners
S.I.C.: 6719; 5122; 2841

Subsidiary:

SBS Products, Inc. **(1)**
302 Waller
Saginaw, MI 48602
Tel.: 517-799-4941
Tel.: 800-248-7190 (100%)
Fax: 800-367-7408
Approx.Sls.: $10,000,000
Emp.: 55
Fiscal Year-end: 12/31/92
Export
Mfr. of Industrial & Institutional Skin Care Products
S.I.C.: 2844; 2841
John Garrison *(Pres.)*
Robert L. Blasko *(Exec. V.P.)*
Mary Pierce *(Controller)*
Leslie Hersh *(Tech. Dir.)*
Dan Stacey *(Sls. Mgr.-Commercial Div.)*
Vera Vlassis *(Mgr.-Admin.)*
Peg Russell *(Pur. Agent)*

THE EDWARD J. DEBARTOLO CORPORATION
7620 Market St.
Youngstown, OH 44513-6085
Mailing Address:
P.O. Box 3287
Youngstown, OH 44513
Tel.: 216-758-7292
Fax: 216-758-3598
Year Founded: 1944
Approx.Rev.: $750,000,000
Emp.: 17,300
Develop, Own & Operate Retail Malls, Convenience & Theme Centers, Office Projects, Hotel Developments, Sports Enterprises & Sports/Entertainment Complexes
S.I.C.: 6512; 6552; 7941; 7948
Edward J. DeBartolo *(Chm. Bd. & Chief Exec. Officer)*
Edward J. DeBartolo, Jr. *(Pres. & Chief Admin. Officer)*
Marie Denise DeBartolo York *(Exec. V.P.-Corp. Mktg. & Communications)*
J. Paul Martha *(Exec. V.P. & Gen. Counsel-Civic Arena)*
Anthony W. Liberati *(Sr. V.P.-Corp. Plng. & Fin.)*
William D. Moses *(Sr. V.P.-Real Estate Leasing/Opers.)*
Richard S. Sokolov *(Sr. V.P.-Devel. & Gen. Counsel)*
Lynn E. Davenport *(V.P. & Treas.)*
Peter S. Frank *(V.P. & Controller)*
Dick A. Greco, Jr. *(V.P.-Devel. & Govt. Rels.)*
David H. Curl *(V.P.-Devel. Plng. & Mngmt.)*
John G. Mitchell *(V.P.-Leasing)*
Kim A. Rieck *(V.P. & Deputy Gen. Counsel)*
Jerry Scott *(V.P.-Mngmt. Services Div.)*
James Sebastian *(V.P.-Construction Services)*
Robert C. Stephenson *(V.P.-Office/ Industrial Properties)*
A. D. Wolfcale *(V.P., Deputy Gen. Counsel & Sec.)*
Louis A. Zarlenga *(V.P.-Engrng.)*
Floyd J. Zdrojkowski *(V.P.-Constuction & Engrng. Pur. Divs.)*
Jack Lambert *(V.P.)*
R. Lynn Squire *(V.P.)*
Marie Izzo Cartwright *(Asst. V.P.-Corp. Mktg. & Communications)*
Harry Connors *(Asst. V.P.-Devel.)*
Kenneth H. Lokiec *(Asst. V.P.-Shopping Ctr. Oper.)*
Mary B. Rutkoski *(Asst. V.P.-Shopping Ctr. Mktg.)*
James L. Donofrio *(Asst. V.P.-Leasing)*
Dean Kissos *(Asst. V.P. & Asst. Treas.)*
Irving Kravitz *(Asst. V.P.-Human Resources)*
Stanley S. Sams *(Asst. V.P.-Security)*
Paul E. Villani *(Asst. V.P.-Opers. & Facilities)*
Edward A. Ahlswede *(Dir.-Fin. Analysis)*
Steve E. Platz *(Dir.-Land Devel.)*
Michael D. Horvath *(Dir.-Corp. Insurance)*
Alan R. Huff *(Dir.-Flight Opers.)*
Ronald C. Jayne *(Dir.-Technical Services)*
Michael S. Kulyk *(Dir.-Taxes)*
Kenneth H. Lokiec *(Dir.-Shopping Center Opers.)*
Stephen E. Platz *(Dir.-Land Devel.)*
Thomas J. Poplar *(Dir.-Retail Services Div.)*
Richard L. Quasey *(Dir.-Pur.)*
Mary Rutkoski *(Dir.-Shopping Center Mktg.)*
Shirley A. Sikora *(Dir.-Compensation, Employee Benefits & Personnel)*
John E. Vavrus *(Dir.-Extra Income)*
Linda Pierce *(Sec.-Human Resources)*
Principal(s):
Edward J. DeBartolo
Edward J. DeBartolo, Jr.
Marie Denise DeBartolo York

Outside Service Firm(s):

Blue Cross & Blue Shield of Worthington*(Commercial Insurance Carrier)*
Worthington, OH

Subsidiary:

Louisiana Downs **(1)**
8000 E. Texas
Bossier City, LA 71111
Tel.: 318-742-5555
Approx.Sls.: $230,000,000
Emp.: 1,200
Thoroughbred Horse Racing
S.I.C.: 7948
E.J. DeBartolo *(Chm. Bd.)*
Thomas S. Sweeney *(Sr. V.P. & Gen. Mgr.)*
Paul Kuerzi *(Dir.-Opers.)*
Ray Tromba *(Dir.-Pub. Rels. & Mktg.)*
Rebecca Walker *(Dir.-Promo. & Mktg.)*

DEBRUCE GRAIN INC.
2702 Rockcreek Pkwy., Ste. 400
North Kansas City, MO 64117
Tel.: 816-421-8182 **MO**
Fax: 816-421-0962
Year Founded: 1978
Approx.Sls.: $670,000,000
Emp.: 165
Grain Merchandising; Wholesale Custom Cattle Feed
S.I.C.: 5153; 5191
Paul DeBruce *(Chm. Bd.)*
Larry Kittoe *(Pres.)*
Dale Feitz *(V.P.)*
Norman C. Guettermann *(V.P.)*
Gerald Byrnes *(Corp. Controller)*

Outside Service Firm(s):

John W. Meara & Co.*(Auditors)*
Kansas City, MO

DECAL ENTERPRISES, INC.
140 Franklin St.
New York, NY 10013
Tel.: 212-431-1700
Fax: 212-226-0694
Emp.: 282
Equipment & Supplier For Marine & Industrial Use
S.I.C.: 5084; 5085; 5088
John Calicchio *(Pres.)*
Lisa Calicchio *(V.P.)*
Steven Calicchio *(V.P.)*
Thomas Calicchio *(V.P.)*
John Santacroce *(V.P.-Fin.)*
Milton Rubin *(Sec.)*

Outside Service Firm(s):

Citibank N.A.*(Major Banking Relationship)*
Corporate Trust Services, 399 Park Ave.
New York, NY 10043
Tel.: 212-559-1605

Subsidiary:

Argo International **(1)**
140 Franklin St.
New York, NY 10013
Tel.: 212-431-1700
Emp.: 431
Distribution, Machinery & Electrical Components For Marine & Industrial Use
S.I.C.: 5084; 5063
John Calicchio *(Chm. Bd. & Chief Exec. Officer)*

DECATUR NEWS PUBLISHING COMPANY, INC.
739 Dekalb Industrial Way
Decatur, GA 30033
Tel.: 404-292-3536 **GA**
Year Founded: 1949
Approx.Sls.: $13,600,000
Emp.: 219
Fiscal Year-end: 12/31/91
Import
Suburban Weekly Newspaper Publishing; Commercial Web Printing
S.I.C.: 2711
Corporate Giving Program: Gives to the United Way
William C. Crane *(Chm. Bd.)*
Gerald Crane *(Pres.)*
R.S. Sauers *(Sr. V.P.-Mktg. & Sls.)*
Mary Louise Crane *(Treas. & Sec.)*
John Hewit *(Dir.-Adv.)*
Judy Thompson *(Mgr.-Data Processing)*

Outside Service Firm(s):

Haligan & Associates*(Auditors)*
Atlanta, GA

MacKay, Cordes, Daniel & King*(Legal Firm)*
Atlanta, GA

Bank South, N.A.*(Major Banking Relationship)*
P.O. Box 4387
Atlanta, GA 30302
Tel.: 404-529-4111

DECHERT PRICE & RHOADS
4000 Bell Atlantic Tower, 1717 Arch St.
Philadelphia, PA 19103-2793
Tel.: 215-994-4000
Fax: 215-994-2222
Year Founded: 1875
Approx.Billings: $100,000,000
Emp.: 940
Fiscal Year-end: 12/31/91
Law Firm
S.I.C.: 8111
Thomas B. Morris, Jr. *(Chm. Policy Committee, Mng. Ptnr. & Chief Exec. Officer))*
Marie Hoplamazian *(Admin. Dir.)*
Susan Alford *(Corp. Librarian)*

No. of U.S. Offices: 6
No. of Foreign Offices: 2

DECISION DATA INC.
One Progress Ave.
Horsham, PA 19044
Tel.: 215-956-6700
Tel.: 800-933-9897 **PA**
Fax: 215-443-0943
Year Founded: 1969
Sales Range: $100-499 Million
Emp.: 1,650
Fiscal Year-end: 6/30/91
Export
Mfr. & Sales of Computer Peripheral Equipment & Systems; System Leasing; Trade-Ins & Upgrades
S.I.C.: 3577; 7377; 7379
Don E. Ackerman *(Chm. Bd.)*
Ken Draeger *(Pres. & Chief Exec. Officer)*
Robert Rao *(Sr. V.P.-Sls.)*
Anthony P. Bamber *(V.P. & Chief Fin. Officer)*
Vincent M. Dadamo *(V.P. & Legal Counsel)*
E. Bock *(V.P.-Human Resources)*
Len Von Vital *(Controller)*
Brian Shemilt *(Dir.-Mktg. & Engrng.)*
E.W. Buckley *(Dir.-Corp. Services)*
J. Houdret *(Dir.-Communications)*
Mary Beth Ford *(Mgr.-Telecommunications)*
James K. Boyle *(Mgr.-Employee Compensation & Benefits)*
Cathy Ludlam *(Mgr.-Property Mngmt.)*
Tina R. DeLo *(Coord.-Mktg. Communications)*

Decision Data Inc.—(Continued)

Outside Service Firm(s):

Stradley, Ronon, Stevens & Young*(Legal Firm)*
2600 Commerce Sq.
Philadelphia, PA 19103
Tel.: 215-564-8000

Division:

Decision Data **(1)**
One Progress Ave.
Horsham, PA 19044
Tel.: 215-956-6700
Tel.: 800-933-9894
Fax: 215-443-0943
Computer Equipment Service
S.I.C.: 7379

Divisions:

Decision Data Direct **(2)**
One Progress Ave.
Horsham, PA 19044
Tel.: 215-443-0555
Computer Equipment Service
S.I.C.: 7379

Jones Business System **(2)**
6120 West by Northwest Blvd.
Houston, TX 77040
Tel.: 713-895-0600 (100%)
Services & Sells Texas Instrument Co. Equipment
S.I.C.: 7379
Bruce E. Slaven *(Gen. Mgr.)*

Non-U.S. Holdings:

Decision Data Computer Intl. S.A. **(1)**
18 Boulevard De Perolles P.O. Box 363, CH1701
Fribourg, Switzerland
Tel.: 0784-62421 (100%)
Emp.: 350
Sales & Services Computer Peripherals
S.I.C.: 5045
Guy Schaub *(V.P.-Intl.)*

Decision Data Computer (S.A.) **(1)**
9 Cour des Petits Ecuries 75010
Paris, France
Tel.: 31-1-246-7533 (100%)
Sales of Computers & Computer Pheripheral Equipment & Software
S.I.C.: 5045

Decision Data Computer GmbH **(1)**
Bergundestr. 51 400
Dusseldorf, 11, Germany
Tel.: 02 11-50-70-04 (100%)
Mfr. of Computer Peripheral Equipment
S.I.C.: 3577

Decision Data Computer (Belgium) S.A. **(1)**
Chausse de La Hulpe, 122 B1050
Brussels, Belgium
Tel.: 3-673-81-10 (100%)
Sales of Computers & Computer Peripheral Equipment & Software
S.I.C.: 5045; 7372

Decision Data Computer (GB) Ltd. **(1)**
Corrie House, 48-54 London Road
Staines, Middlesex TW18 4HQ, United Kingdom
Tel.: 932 7887 88
Sales of Computers & Computer Peripheral Equipment & Software
S.I.C.: 5045; 7372

DECK HOUSE INC.
930 Main St.
Acton, MA 01720
Tel.: 508-263-7000
Tel.: 800-727-3325
Fax: 508-263-4159
Year Founded: 1960
Approx.Sls.: $20,000,000
Emp.: 100
Fiscal Year-end: 9/30/91
Export
Manufacture Pre-Engineered Houses
S.I.C.: 2452
Michael S. Harris *(Pres. & Chief Exec. Officer)*
Donald Cameron *(V.P.-Design)*
Wayne Ferreira *(V.P.-Mfg.)*
Edward Tabor *(Treas.)*
D. Scott Adams *(Natl. Sls. Mgr.)*
Katherine Beach *(Mgr.-Mktg.)*
Steve Harlow *(Mgr.-Product Planning)*
Judith C. Berkes *(Program Mgr.-Exports)*

Principal(s):
Judith C. Berkes
William Morton, Jr.
Myrna Zaffina

No. of Mfg. Plants/Facilities: 2
No. of U.S. Offices: 9

Computer Systems/Hardware:
IBM 36 Mainframe; IBM PC

Outside Service Firm(s):

Tofias, Fleischman & Shapiro*(Auditors)*
Cambridge, MA

Fleet Bank*(Investment Banker)*
Boston, MA

Goodwin, Procter & Hoar*(Legal Firm)*
Exchange Place
Boston, MA 02109-2881
Tel.: 617-570-1000

DECKER RICKARD

99 Citizens Dr.
Glastonbury, CT 06033
Tel.: 203-659-1311
Fax: 203-659-3062
Year Founded: 1977
Approx.Billings: $13,000,000
Emp.: 24
James Decker *(Chm. & Dir. Creative Services)*
Craig Cheyne *(Pres. & Dir. Acct. Mngmt.)*
Albert D. Mason *(Chief Exec. Officer & New Bus. Contact)*
William Ludkiewicz *(V.P., Chief Fin. Officer)*
Ilaina Clement *(V.P., Pub. Rels.)*
Susan Wallace *(Pub. Rels. Acct. Mgr.)*

Computer Systems/Hardware:
NCR, MacIntosh

DECO PRODUCTS CO.
506 Sanford
Decorah, IA 52101
Tel.: 319-382-4264
Fax: 319-382-9845
Year Founded: 1960
Approx.Sls.: $18,000,000
Emp.: 300
Fiscal Year-end: 12/31/90
Export
Fast Lok, Hose Clamps; Aluma-Lok Hardware; Zinc Die Castings, Mechanical & Electrical Assemblies
S.I.C.: 3429; 5072; 3369; 3364
Thomas J. Henderson *(Chief Exec. Officer)*
Lew Storlie *(Gen. Mgr.)*
Richard Averill *(Natl. Sls. Mgr.)*
Larry Dwyer *(Asst. Mgr. & Pur. Mgr.)*

DECOR CORPORATION
1519 Alum Creek Dr.
Columbus, OH 43209
Tel.: 614-258-2871
Fax: 614-251-1005
Year Founded: 1981
Approx.Sls.: $14,700,000
Emp.: 700
Retail Art Stores
S.I.C.: 5999
Jeffrey Gilbert *(Pres.)*
Ed Redensek *(Asst. V.P.-Adv.)*

DECORATIVE CRAFTS, INC.
50 Chestnut St.
Greenwich, CT 06830
Tel.: 203-531-1500
Tel.: 800-431-4455 **NY**
Fax: 203-531-1590
Year Founded: 1928
Approx.Sls.: $14,000,000
Emp.: 50
Import
Wholesale Distribution of Funriture & Accesssories
S.I.C.: 5021
Richard Cohn *(Pres.)*
Jeffrey Cohn *(V.P.)*
Carol Cohn *(Treas. & Sec.)*

Outside Service Firm(s):

Fleet National Bank*(Major Banking Relationship)*
Hartford, CT

DEDERT CORPORATION
20000 Governors Dr.
Olympia Fields, IL 60461
Tel.: 708-747-7000
Fax: 708-755-8815
Year Founded: 1970
Approx.Sls.: $26,000,000
Emp.: 35
Provides Engineering Services; Mfr. of Dehydrating Equipment; Evaporation & Solvent Recovery Systems
S.I.C.: 8711; 3556; 3443
William G. Dedert *(Pres.)*
Thomas W. Dedert *(V.P.-Opers.)*
Jack Brown *(Treas.)*
Kay Burghard *(Dir.-Mktg.)*

DEE PAPER COMPANY
Front & Broomall
Chester, PA 19016-0320
Mailing Address:
P.O. Box 320
Chester, PA 19016
Tel.: 215-876-9285
Tel.: 800-359-0041
Fax: 215-876-7040
Year Founded: 1921
Approx.Sls.: $14,000,000
Emp.: 130
Fiscal Year-end: 12/31/90
Mfr. of Folding Paper Boxes
S.I.C.: 2657
Robert Dee *(Pres.)*
William Allaire *(V.P.)*
Jay Dee *(Treas. & Sec.)*
David Culley *(Controller)*
Joel Kramer *(Dir.-Sls.)*

No. of Mfg. Plants/Facilities: 1
No. of U.S. Offices: 1

Outside Service Firm(s):

Glickman Berkovitz Levinson Weiner*(Auditors)*
Fort Washington, PA

Schnader, Harrison, Segal & Lewis*(Legal Firm)*
Philadelphia, PA

Philadelphia National Bank*(Major Banking Relationship)*
5th & Market Sts.
Philadelphia, PA 19101
Tel.: 215-629-3100
Fax: 215-834-2069

Division:

Diamond Paper Box Co. **(1)**
1330-40 Unity St.
Philadelphia, PA 19124
Tel.: 215-831-8300
Mfr. of Folding Cartons
S.I.C.: 2657

DEEN WHOLESALE MEAT COMPANY, INC.
813 E. Northside Dr.
Fort Worth, TX 76102
Tel.: 817-335-2257 **TX**
Fax: 817-870-9107
Approx.Sls.: $13,000,000
Emp.: 50
Fresh Meats
S.I.C.: 5147
George C. Deen *(Pres.)*
Craig Deen *(V.P.)*
Danny Deen *(V.P.)*
Debbie Deen *(V.P.)*
Nancy Deen *(Sec. & Treas.)*

Outside Service Firm(s):

Charles E. Roach*(Auditors)*
Fort Worth, TX

DEERFIELD MANUFACTURING CO., INC.
408 Fourth Ave.
Mason, OH 45040
Tel.: 513-398-2010
Fax: 513-398-2014
Approx.Sls.: $45,000,000
Emp.: 400
Mfr. Metal Stampings
S.I.C.: 3469
Michael H. Norris *(Pres.)*
James L. Uehlein *(V.P.)*
Rose Ruffner *(Mgr.-Personnel)*
Richard Smith *(Opers. Mgr.)*
Charles Harrah *(Pur. Agent)*

DEERSKIN TRADING POST, INC.
(Div. of Initio, Inc.)
725 Dell Rd.
Carlstadt, NJ 07072
Tel.: 201-935-2450
Fax: 201-935-2092
Year Founded: 1944
Approx.Sls.: $16,000,000
Emp.: 120
Fiscal Year-end: 4/30/92
Import
Catalog Sales of Leather, Suede & Fur Products Including Garments For Men, Women & Children, Gloves, Coats ,Shoes, Boots, Wallets, Pocketbooks & Accessories; Direct Mail
S.I.C.: 5961; 5632; 5661; 5948
Martin Fox *(Chm. Bd.)*
Daniel A. DeStefano *(Pres.)*
Vic Vicich *(V.P.-Opers.)*
Debra Solan *(V.P.-Pur.)*
Audrey Remes *(Treas. & Chief Fin. Officer)*
Michael DeVarti *(Mgr.-MIS)*

Computer Systems/Hardware:
Data General

DEFENDER SERVICES, INC.
9031 Garners Ferry Rd.
Columbia, SC 29209
Mailing Address:
P.O. Box 1775,
Columbia, SC 29202
Tel.: 803-776-4220 **SC**
Fax: 803-783-2311
Fax: 803-776-1580
Year Founded: 1958
Assets: $12,670,000
Liabilities: $10,950,000
Net Worth: $1,720,000
Approx.Sls.: $64,000,000
Emp.: 6,100
Fiscal Year-end: 9/30/92
Industrial Maintenance Services; General Contractors Industrial Buildings & Warehouses; Wholesale Service Establishment Equipment & Supplies; Security Services
S.I.C.: 7381; 7349; 5087
G. Hollis Cone *(Chm. Bd., Pres. & Chief Exec. Officer)*

Roy D. Shiver *(Exec. V.P.-Opers.)*
John N. McCarter, Jr. *(Sr. V.P.)*
Robert G. Meyers *(Sr. V.P.)*
Billy E. Mitchum *(Sec. & Treas.)*
Principal(s):
G. Hollis Cone
Roy D. Shiver
John N. McCarter, Jr.
Robert G. Meyers
Billy E. Mitchum

No. of Mfg. Plants/Facilities: 400
No. of U.S. Offices: 3

Computer Systems/Hardware:
IBM AS400

Outside Service Firm(s):

Arthur Andersen & Co.*(Auditors)*
Columbia, SC

Aetna Life & Casualty*(Group Insurer)*
151 Farmington Avenue
Hartford, CT 06156
Tel.: 203-273-2128
Fax: 203-729-4295

Nelson, Mullins, Riley & Scarborough*(Legal Firm)*
Keenan Bldg., 1330 Lady St., 3rd Floor
Columbia, SC 29201
Tel.: 803-799-2000
Fax: 803-256-7500

First Union National Bank*(Major Banking Relationship)*
Two First Union Center
Charlotte, NC 28288-1154
Tel.: 704-374-2698

DEITSCH PLASTICS COMPANY
14 Farwell St.
West Haven, CT 06516
Tel.: 203-934-6601 CT
Fax: 203-933-4763
Assets: $15,000,000
Liabilities: $7,000,000
Net Worth: $8,000,000
Sales Range: $20-39 Million
Emp.: 100
Fiscal Year-end: 8/31/90
Export
Flocked Fabrics
S.I.C.: 3083; 2261
David Deitsch *(Pres.)*
Jacob Pinson *(V.P.)*
Joseph Deitsch *(V.P.)*
Sara Deitsch *(Sec.)*
Charles Terrill *(Controller)*
Marvin Kornfeld *(Mgr.-Sls.)*

No. of Mfg. Plants/Facilities: 2
No. of U.S. Offices: 2

Computer Systems/Hardware:
WYSE/IBM

Outside Service Firm(s):

Weinstein & Anastasio*(Auditors)*
Woodbridge, CT

Tick & Co.*(Commercial Insurance Carrier)*
Lake Success, NY

Susman, Duffy & Segaloff*(Legal Firm)*
West Haven, CT

Fleet National Bank*(Major Banking Relationship)*
555 Long Wharf Dr.
New Haven, CT 06511

Fleet Norstar Employee Benefits Service*(Pension Manager)*
Albany, NY

Subsidiary:

Deitsch Plastic Export Co. **(1)**
535 Broadway
New York, NY 10012
Tel.: 212-925-7070
Emp.: 7
Sale & Exportation of Flocked Fabrics
S.I.C.: 5199
Mordecai Deitch *(Pres.)*

MARCEL DEKKER, INC.
270 Madison Ave.
New York, NY 10016
Tel.: 212-696-9000 NY
Fax: 212-685-4540
Year Founded: 1963
Approx.Sls.: $30,000,000
Emp.: 165
Fiscal Year-end: 12/31/91
Export
Scientific Book & Journal Publishing
S.I.C.: 2731; 2721
Marcel Dekker *(Chm. Bd. & Pres.)*
Graham Garratt *(Exec. V.P. & Publr.)*
Wallace Kluberdanz *(Sr. V.P.-Fin.)*
Eridania Perez *(V.P.)*
Sandra Beberman *(Asst. V.P.)*
Henry Secor *(Asst. V.P.- Sls.)*
Edward Pelisson *(Controllor)*
Michelle Molloy *(Mgr.-Personnel)*
Bruno Baumgartner *(Mgr.- Intl. Div.)*
Eileen Nebhut *(Coord.-Bilk Sls.)*

No. of U.S. Offices: 2
No. of Foreign Offices: 2

Outside Service Firm(s):

Delmastro & Greeley*(Auditors)*
New York, NY

Cummings & Lockwood*(Legal Firm)*
P.O. Box 120, Ten Stamford Forum
Stamford, CT 06904
Tel.: 203-327-1700

DEKTAS & EGER, INC.
30 W. Third St.
Cincinnati, OH 45202
Tel.: 513-621-7070
Fax: 513-621-7271
Year Founded: 1978
Approx.Billings: $12,660,000
Emp.: 15
Michael C. Dektas *(Pres.)*
Donald L. Eger, Jr. *(Exec. V. P.)*
Lee Siegmund *(New. Bus. Devel.)*
Martin Pressman *(Controller)*

DEL AMERICAN PROPERTIES, INC.
1101 N. Lake Destiny Dr., Ste. 400
Maitland, FL 32751
Tel.: 407-660-8666 FL
Fax: 407-875-0219
Year Founded: 1982
Approx.Sls.: $30,000,000
Emp.: 40
Real Estate Development, General Contractor & Property Management
S.I.C.: 6552; 6531
Christopher Del Guidice *(Chm. Bd. & Pres.)*
Fred Del Guidice *(Vice Chm.)*
Donald L. Kafka *(Exec. V.P.)*
P.M. Lombardo *(Sr. V.P.)*
John Terrell *(Controller)*

DEL MAR AVIONICS
1601 Alton Ave.
Irvine, CA 92714
Tel.: 714-250-3200
Fax: 714-261-0529
Year Founded: 1952
Approx.Sls.: $25,000,000
Emp.: 500
Biomedical Instrumentation Systems, Holter Ambulatory ECG, Exerstress Testing Systems; Firetrac Laser Disc Mastering Systems; Hydra-Set Load Positioners
S.I.C.: 3841; 3699; 3829; 3845
Bruce Del Mar *(Pres. & Treas.)*
R. Cherry *(Sr. V.P.-Engrng.)*
Robert Costanza *(V.P.-Opers.)*
Dave Johnson *(V.P.-Sls. & Mktg.)*
John Christian *(V.P.-Customer Service & Engineering)*
John Zemar *(V.P.-Mfg.)*
John Gibbs *(V.P.-Fin.)*
Lois Machida *(Sec.)*

Frank Gunning *(Pur. Agent)*

Outside Service Firm(s):

First Interstate Bank*(Major Banking Relationship)*
Irvine, CA

DEL MONTE FOODS
One Market Plaza
San Francisco, CA 94105
Mailing Address:
P.O. Box 193575,
San Francisco, CA 94119-3575
Tel.: 415-442-5034 NY
Fax: 415-442-5024
Approx.Sls.: $1,400,000,000
Emp.: 20,000
Fiscal Year-end: 6/30/91

Import Export
Canned Fruits & Vegetable Products
S.I.C.: 2033; 2032; 2034; 2035; 2099; 5149; 4213; 3411
Employee Matching Gifts Program: Contributions to Non-Profit Matched $1 to $1. Includes Annual Maximum And Per Gift Minimum
Dr. Robert J. Carbonell *(Chm. Bd.)*
A. Ewan Macdonald *(Pres. & Chief Exec. Officer)*
Norman Mackenzie *(Exec. V.P.-Worldwide Opers.)*
Robert W. D'Ornellas *(Sr. V.P.-Mktg.)*
Kay Dryden *(Sr. V.P., Sec. & Legal Counsel)*
David M. Little *(Sr. V.P.-Admin.)*
David L. Meyers *(Sr. V.P. & Chief Fin. Officer)*
Michael J. Stieger *(Sr. V.P-Sls.)*
DeeAnn Campbell *(V.P.-Communications)*
Jeffry Helfer *(V.P.-Bus. Devel.)*
Irvin R. Holmes, Jr. *(V.P.-Mktg., Fruits)*
Tom Gibbons *(Treas.)*
Laura Munro *(Dir.-Mktg., Beverages)*
JoAnn Sheehy *(Dir.-Mktg., Tomatoes & Vegetables)*
David Karasch *(Dir.-Mktg., Tomatoes)*
Mark Buxton *(Dir.-Personnel)*
JoAnn Sheehy *(Dir.-Mktg., Vegetables)*

Plant:

Del Monte Corp. **(1)**
2009 Maplewood Ave., P.O. Box 747
De Kalb, IL 60115
Tel.: 815-758-3431
Canned Vegetables
S.I.C.: 2033
Gary Brown *(Plant Mgr.)*

DEL TACO, INC.
345 Baker St.
Costa Mesa, CA 92626
Tel.: 714-540-8914
Year Founded: 1965
Approx.Sls.: $200,000,000
Emp.: 8,000
Fiscal Year-end: 12/31/90
Holding Co.: Del Taco Restaurants
S.I.C.: 6719
Kevin Moriarty *(Pres. & Chief Exec. Officer)*
Harold Fox *(Exec. V.P. & Chief Fin. Officer)*
Paul Hitzelberger *(Exec. V.P.-Mktg. & Sec.)*
Donald Stoops *(Exec. V.P.-Opers.)*
Janet Simmons *(V.P.-Pur.)*
Peter Solomon *(Controller)*
James Farley *(Dir.-Real Estate & Franchise Opers.)*
Holly Kruger *(Dir.-Mktg.)*
Linda Oliver *(Dir.-Research & Devel.)*
Ed Rabella *(Dir.-Human Resources)*

Computer Systems/Hardware:
IBM

Division:

Del Taco/Naugles **(1)**
345 Baker St.
Costa Mesa, CA 92626
Tel.: 714-540-8914
Fax: 714-641-3612
Emp.: 11,180
Fiscal Year-end: 12/31/90
Mexican/American Fast Food Restaurant Chain
S.I.C.: 5812
Kevin K. Moriarty *(Pres. & Chief Exec. Officer)*
Harold Fox *(Exec. V.P.-Fin. & Treas.)*
Paul Hitzelberger *(Exec. V.P.-Mktg. & Sec.)*
Don Stoops *(V.P.-Opers.)*

DEL-VAL MANUFACTURING COMPANY
200 Park Ave.
Warminster, PA 18974
Tel.: 215-674-4700
Fax: 215-957-0544
Sales Range: $10-19 Million
Emp.: 25

Import
Mfr. of Residential Electrical Lighting Fixtures
S.I.C.: 3645
Kenneth H. Spear *(Chm. Bd., Pres. & Chief Exec. Officer)*
Christopher J. Heise *(V.P.-Fin. & Admin.)*
Carol Spear *(Sec.)*
Anthony Scarcelli *(Mgr.-Opers.)*
Katherine Peppiatt *(Personnel Administrator)*

No. of Mfg. Plants/Facilities: 1

Outside Service Firm(s):

Arthur Andersen & Co.*(Auditors)*
1601 Market St.
Philadelphia, PA 19103
Tel.: 215-241-7300

Wolf, Block, Schorr & Solis-Cohen*(Legal Firm)*
Packard Bldg.
Philadelphia, PA 19102
Tel.: 215-977-2000

Meridian Bank*(Major Banking Relationship)*
One Meridian Plaza, 36th Fl.
Philadelphia, PA
Tel.: 215-854-3900

DELAGRA CORPORATION
P.O. Box 126
Bridgeville, DE 19933
Tel.: 302-337-8206 DE
Fax: 302-337-3387
Year Founded: 1975
Approx.Sls.: $10,000,000
Emp.: 117
Process Quick, Frozen & Cold Pack Vegetables
S.I.C.: 2037
Charles West *(Pres.)*
Sandra Webb *(Treas. & Sec.)*

DELAWARE ELECTRIC CO-OP
Rte. 13
Greenwood, DE 19950
Mailing Address:
P.O. Box 600
Greenwood, DE 19950
Tel.: 302-349-4571 DE
Fax: 302-349-5891
Year Founded: 1936
Approx.Sls.: $36,000,000
Emp.: 119
Distribution of Electric Power
S.I.C.: 4911
William Wells *(Pres.)*
Albert Lank *(V.P.)*
E. Paul Bienvenue *(Gen. Mgr.)*
Betty Benson *(Treas. & Sec.)*

Delaware Electric Co-Op—(Continued)

Outside Service Firm(s):

Wilmington Trust Co.*(Major Banking Relationship)*
Rodney Square North
Wilmington, DE 19890
Tel.: 302-651-1000

DELAWARE LOTTERY
Bluehen Mall, Ste. 202
Dover, DE 19901
Tel.: 302-739-5291
Fax: 302-739-6706
Approx.Sls.: $67,200,000
Emp.: 22
Fiscal Year-end: 6/30/91
State lottery
S.I.C.: 7999
Wayne Lemmons *(Dir.)*
Ted Manno *(Sls. & Mktg. Admin.)*
Frank Brown *(Deputy Dir.)*

DELAWARE NORTH COMPANIES, INC.
438 Main St.
Buffalo, NY 14202
Tel.: 716-858-5000 **DE**
Fax: 716-858-5266
Year Founded: 1915
Approx.Sls.: $1,200,000,000
Emp.: 40,000
Fiscal Year-end: 12/31/91
Holding Co.; Airport Food Service, Metals; Printing; Sports Concessions; Owner of Boston Garden Arena
S.I.C.: 6719; 3341; 3356; 5812; 7948
Corporate Giving Program:
Contributions on Individual Basis, Administered by V.P. Public Affairs
Jeremy M. Jacobs *(Chm. & Chief Exec. Officer)*
Stanley F. Phillips *(Vice Chm.)*
Richard T. Stephens *(Pres. & Chief Oper. Officer)*
Clifford R. Kaeser *(Sr. Exec. V.P.)*
Stanley R. Mills *(V.P., Gen. Counsel & Sec.)*
G. Gail Edwards *(V.P.-Finance & Treas.)*
Gary Fraker *(V.P.-Pur. & Food Service)*
Marlene J. Galla *(V.P.-Human Resources)*
Samuel L. Gifford II *(V.P.-Pub. Affairs & Adv.)*
Andrew Nicol *(V.P.-Real Estate)*
Bruce Carlson *(Corp. Controller)*
Peter Palumbo *(Dir.-Mngmt. Information Systems)*
Susan Scott *(Dir.-Employee Benefits)*
Robert Matson *(Mgr.-Telecommunications)*
Diane Kanicki *(Corp. Travel Planner)*

Principal(s):
Jeremy M. Jacobs

No. of U.S. Offices: 2

Computer Systems/Hardware:
Burroughs B6810

Outside Service Firm(s):

Price Waterhouse*(Auditors)*
3600 Marine Midland Center
Buffalo, NY 14203
Tel.: 716-856-4650

Johnson & Higgins*(Commercial Insurance Carrier)*
New York, NY

Blue Cross & Blue Shield of Indiana*(Group Insurer)*
P.O. Box 7700,
Indianapolis, IN 46277-3772

Independent Health Association*(Group Insurer)*
777 International Dr.
Buffalo, NY
Tel.: 716-631-5392

Dean Witter Reynolds*(Investment Banker)*
Two World Trade Ctr.
New York, NY 10048

Goldman, Sachs & Co.*(Investment Banker)*
85 Broad St.
New York, NY 10004
Tel.: 212-902-1000
Fax: 212-902-4451

Merrill Lynch*(Investment Banker)*
North Tower, 28th Fl., 4 World Financial Center
New York, NY 10281-1200
Tel.: 212-449-1000

Marine Midland Bank*(Major Banking Relationship)*
P.O. Box 803, 1 Marine Midland Center, 23rd Floor
Buffalo, NY 14203
Tel.: 716-841-2582

Marine Midland Bank*(Pension Manager)*
P.O. Box 803, 1 Marine Midland Center, 23rd Floor
Buffalo, NY 14203
Tel.: 716-841-2582

Subsidiaries:

Concession Air Corporation **(1)**
One Delaware North Place, 438 Main St.
Buffalo, NY 14202
Tel.: 716-858-5000 (100%)
Approx.Sls.: $26,000,000
Emp.: 3,080
Airport & In-Flight Food & Beverage Services, Retail Mdsg. & Parking Services
S.I.C.: 5812; 7521; 5947
Jon Luther *(Pres.)*
John Fernbach *(V.P.-Fin.)*
Gary Fraker *(V.P.-Pur.)*
Thomas Keon *(Dir.-Mktg.)*

Arrow Typographers, Inc. **(1)**
2-14 Liberty St.
Newark, NJ 07102
Tel.: 201-622-0111 (100%)
Approx.Sls.: $4,700,000
Emp.: 80
Specialty Typesetting Services
S.I.C.: 2791
Reuben Friedman *(Pres. & Chief Exec. Officer)*

Sportsystems Corporation **(1)**
One Delaware North Place, 438 Main St.
Buffalo, NY 14202
Tel.: 716-858-5000
Approx.Sls.: $30,000,000
Management of Racing Facilities
S.I.C.: 7948
William J. Bissett *(Pres.)*
Randa Kahn *(V.P.-Mktg.)*
Thomas Murrer *(Chief Fin. Officer)*

Sportservice Corporation **(1)**
One Delaware North Place, 438 Main St.
Buffalo, NY 14202
Tel.: 716-858-5000 (100%)
Approx.Sls.: $150,000,000
Emp.: 10,000
Concessionaire
S.I.C.: 5812
Michael F. Thompson *(Pres.-Sportservice)*
John Fernbach *(V.P.-Fin.)*
Gary Fraker *(V.P.-Pur.)*
Thomas Keon *(Dir.-Mktg.)*

DELAWARE RIBBON MANUFACTURERS, INC.
2531 Trenton Ave.
Philadelphia, PA 19125
Tel.: 215-425-8060 **PA**
Fax: 215-425-4710
Year Founded: 1940
Emp.: 85
Mfr. Ribbon
S.I.C.: 2241
Thomas R. Lodge *(Pres.)*
Thomas R. Lodge, Jr. *(V.P.)*
Susan M. Lodge *(Sec.)*

Outside Service Firm(s):

Continental Bank N. A.*(Major Banking Relationship)*
231 S. LaSalle St.
Chicago, IL 60697
Tel.: 312-828-2345
Tel.: 800-426-5754
Telex: 312-828-1783

DELLA CONSTRUCTION CO. INC.
1 Depot Hill Rd.
Enfield, CT 06082
Mailing Address:
P.O. Box 1290
Enfield, CT 06082
Tel.: 203-627-5141 **CT**
Fax: 203-627-0522
Year Founded: 1967
Assets: $16,201,943
Liabilities: $12,186,841
Net Worth: $4,015,102
Approx.Sls.: $26,000,000
Emp.: 350
Fiscal Year-end: 6/30/90
General Contractors Highway & Streets, Excavation, Foundation Work, Water Mains, Sewers & Pipelines
S.I.C.: 1611; 1741; 1623; 1794
Stephen J. Dellaquila *(Pres. & Treas.)*
Thomas F. Lepore *(Exec. V.P.)*
Robert McDiarmid *(Sr. V.P.)*
Christopher Toomey *(Sr. V.P.-Equip.)*
Jeffrey D. Schwarz *(V.P. & Chief Fin. Officer)*
John Standial *(V.P.-Acctg.)*
Dennis Keiser *(V.P.-Hwy. & Site Div.)*
Regina Dugan *(Mgr.-Personnel)*
James Pace *(Mgr.-Data Processing)*

Outside Service Firm(s):

Arthur Andersen & Co.*(Auditors)*
One Financial Plaza
Hartford, CT 06103
Tel.: 203-280-0649
Fax: 203-280-0898

Reide & Riege*(Legal Firm)*
Hartford, CT

Bank of New England*(Major Banking Relationship)*
Springfield, MA

DELOITTE & TOUCHE
(Member of Deloitte Touche Tohmatsu International)
Ten Westport Rd.
Wilton, CT 06897-0820
Mailing Address:
P.O. Box 820,
Wilton, CT 06897-0820
Tel.: 203-761-3000
Fax: 203-834-2200
Year Founded: 1895
Approx.Rev.: $2,000,000,000
Emp.: 15,300
Fiscal Year-end: 5/31/92
Accounting, Auditing, Tax & Management Consulting Services
S.I.C.: 8721
Corporate Giving Program:
Educational Institutions
Employee Matching Gifts Program:
Educational Institutions
J. Michael Cook *(Chm. Bd. & Chief Exec. Officer)*
Edward A. Kangas *(Mng. Partner)*
Howard J. Krongard *(Gen. Counsel)*
Robert W. Pivik *(Chief Fin. Officer)*
Carl Burton *(Dir.-Adv.)*
Mary F. Smith *(Dir. Mktg./ Communications)*

No. of U.S. Offices: 200

Outside Service Firm(s):

Blue Cross & Blue Shield of Connecticut, Inc.*(Group Insurer)*
North Haven, CT

Prudential Insurance Co. of America*(Group Insurer)*
Box 9300, 1 Campus Dr.
Parsippany, NJ 07054

THE DELPHI GLASS CORP.
DELPHI STAINED GLASS CENTERS
2116 E. Michigan Ave.
Lansing, MI 48912
Tel.: 517-482-2617
Fax: 517-482-4028
Year Founded: 1973
Assets: $1,133,441
Earnings: $607,467
Liabilities: $525,974
Net Worth: $607,467
Approx.Sls.: $10,000,000
Emp.: 21
Fiscal Year-end: 5/31/88
Stained Glass Wholesalers & Retailers; Franchisor of Delphi Stained Glass Centers for Stained Glass Hobbyists; International Mail Order Catalogs
S.I.C.: 5961; 5999; 5099; 6794
Daniel L. Fattaleh *(Chm. Bd., Pres., Chief Exec. Officer & Treas.)*
Alice C. Fattaleh *(Controller)*
Tom Donaldson *(Gen. Mgr.)*

Computer Systems/Hardware:
Hewlett-Packard 250

Outside Service Firm(s):

Danielson, Schultz, & Co.*(Auditors)*
Lansing, MI

Plante & Moran*(Auditors)*
Lansing, MI

Foster, Swift, Collins & Smith*(Legal Firm)*
Lansing, MI

First American Bank, N.A.*(Major Banking Relationship)*
Lansing, MI

DELTA EDUCATION, INC.
5 Hudson Park Dr.
Hudson, NH 03051
Mailing Address:
P.O. Box 915,
Hudson, NH 03051
Tel.: 603-889-8899
Fax: 603-880-6520
Year Founded: 1973
Approx.Sls.: $17,000,000
Emp.: 130
Fiscal Year-end: 12/31/91
Import Export
Publisher & Manufacturer of Elementary School Science & Math Materials
S.I.C.: 2731
Thomas Richardson *(Chm. Bd., Pres. & Chief Exec. Officer)*
Ken Lunoi *(Chief Oper. Officer & Exec. V.P.)*
Alexandria Hayes *(V.P.-Mktg.)*
Bill McGinnis *(V.P.-Sls.)*
Mike Mizara *(V.P.-Fin.)*
Harvey Richardson *(V.P.-Admin.)*
June Conant *(Dir.-Personnel)*
Grant Gardner *(Dir.-Pur.)*

No. of Mfg. Plants/Facilities: 1
No. of U.S. Offices: 2

Computer Systems/Hardware:
MicroVax II

Outside Service Firm(s):

Coopers & Lybrand*(Auditors)*
Manchester, NH

Commercial Union Insurance Co.*(Commercial Insurance Carrier)*
Boston, MA

Phoenix Mutual Life Insurance Co.*(Group Insurer)*
Hartford, CT

The Bigelow Company*(Investment Banker)*
Boston, MA

Devine, Millimet & Branch*(Legal Firm)*
Manchester, NH

First New Hampshire Bank*(Major Banking Relationship)*
Manchester, NH

Roberts Planning Group*(Pension Manager)*
Manchester, NH

Delta Ford Truck Sales, Inc.
(Name Changed To Mid-South Ford Truck Sales, Inc.)

DELTA FOREMOST CHEMICAL CORP.
3915 Air Park St.
Memphis, TN 38118
Mailing Address:
P.O. Box 30310,
Memphis, TN 38130-0310
Tel.: 901-363-4340
Tel.: 800-238-5150
Fax: 901-375-3600
Year Founded: 1947
Approx.Sls.: $15,000,000
Emp.: 200
Mfr. of Industrial Cleaning Chemicals
S.I.C.: 2819
H. Cooper *(Pres.)*
L. Schneider *(Dir.-Mktg.)*

Computer Systems/Hardware:
IBM 38

DELTA INDUSTRIES
Bradley Park Rd.
East Granby, CT 06026
Tel.: 203-653-5041
Fax: 203-653-5792
Sales Range: $20-39 Million
Emp.: 107
Machine Shop, Jet Engine Components
S.I.C.: 3443; 3444; 3724
Richard Jaquith *(Pres.)*
William Evans *(V.P.)*
John Garrott *(Mgr.-Sls.)*
Bob Kincaid *(Mgr.-Personnel)*

Outside Service Firm(s):

Hinden, Sievers & Company*(Auditors)*
New York, NY

Connecticut National Bank*(Major Banking Relationship)*
East Grandby, CT

DELTA LIFE CORPORATION
530 Oak Court, Ste. 200
Memphis, TN 38117
Tel.: 901-683-1222 **DE**
Year Founded: 1979
Emp.: 75
All Lines of Insurance; Personal Financial Services; Title Insurance; Bond & Mortgage Companies
S.I.C.: 7299; 6311; 6162
Robert Wallace *(Pres.)*
Marilyn D. Johnson *(V.P.)*
Louanne Martin *(Exec. Sec.)*
Betty Adams *(Sec.)*

Outside Service Firm(s):

Coopers & Lybrand*(Auditors)*
1000 Morgan-Keegan Tower, 50 N. Front St.
Memphis, TN 38103
Tel.: 901-529-1100

Union Planters National Bank*(Major Banking Relationship)*
P.O. Box 387,
Memphis, TN 38147
Tel.: 901-523-6865
Fax: 901-523-6490

Subsidiary:

Delta Life & Annuity Co. **(1)**
530 Oak Court, Ste. 200
Memphis, TN 38117
Tel.: 901-683-1222
Personal Financial Services; Life Insurance
S.I.C.: 6311
Marilyn D. Johnson *(V.P.)*

DELTA PRIDE CATFISH, INC.
Industrial Park
Indianola, MS 38751
Mailing Address:
P.O. Box 850
Indianola, MS 38751
Tel.: 601-887-5401
Tel.: 800-421-1045 **MS**
Fax: 601-887-5950
Year Founded: 1981
Assets: $59,802,000
Liabilities: $19,665,000
Net Worth: $40,137,000
Approx.Sls.: $150,000,000
Emp.: 1,800
Fiscal Year-end: 6/28/92
Export
Processing & Marketing of Fresh & Frozen Farm-Raised Catfish
S.I.C.: 0273; 2092; 5146
Robert R. White, Jr. *(Chm. Bd.)*
Harrell Potter *(Vice Chm.)*
Larry W. Joiner *(Pres.)*
Paul A. McIntyre *(V.P.-Opers.)*
Sissy Sullivan *(V.P.-Sls.-Western Zone)*
Jimmie Blount *(Sec., Treas. & Controller)*
Richard Noble *(Gen. Counsel)*
Burton Ely *(Asst. Controller)*
Billy Boswell *(Dir.-Data Processing)*
Charles Langley *(Dir.-Quality Assurance)*
Larry Steed *(Dir.-Pur.)*
Walter Harrison *(Mgr.-Pub. Rels.)*
Gerry Holaday *(Mgr.-Export)*

No. of Mfg. Plants/Facilities: 3
No. of U.S. Offices: 1

Computer Systems/Hardware:
NCR 9300

Outside Service Firm(s):

Baird & Stallings, P.A.*(Auditors)*
Indianola, MS

Todd-Davis-Chandler*(Commercial Insurance Carrier)*
Jackson, MS

Blue Cross & Blue Shield Association*(Group Insurer)*
Greenville, MS

Townsend, McWilliams & Holladay*(Legal Firm)*
Indianola, MS

Citizen's Bank*(Major Banking Relationship)*
Belzoni, MS

Peoples Bank*(Major Banking Relationship)*
Indianola, MS

DELTA RESINS & REFRACTORIES, INC.
6263 N. Teutonia Ave.
Milwaukee, WI 53209
Tel.: 414-462-1200
Year Founded: 1935
Approx.Sls.: $25,000,000
Emp.: 78
Export
Mfr. of Specialty Resins & Foundry Additives; Core & Mold Coatings, Partings, Adhesives; Industrial Oils & Tool Mfg.
S.I.C.: 2821; 2891; 2899; 2952; 2992; 2999; 3599; 5162; 5169
Donald W. Hansen *(Chm. Bd. & Pres.)*
Daniel Yrigoyan *(Sr. V.P.-Sls. & Mktg.)*
Thomas Mooneyham *(V.P.-Technology)*
Roy O'Doherty *(V.P.-Mfg.)*

DELTA RUBBER COMPANY
Rte. 12
Danielson, CT 06239
Mailing Address:
P.O. Box 300
Danielson, CT 06239
Tel.: 203-779-0300
Fax: 203-774-0402
Approx.Sls.: $10,000,000
Emp.: 200
Molded Rubber Goods, Compression, Transfer, Injecting Molding; Rubber To Metal Bonding; Precision Rubber Seals; Compounding To Specifications; Design Service; Mold Design
S.I.C.: 3061; 3053; 3069
David A. Harrington *(Pres.)*
Christopher Andrews *(V.P.-Engrng.)*
Milton Oliveira *(V.P.-Opers.)*
Frederick Duda *(Controller)*

Outside Service Firm(s):

Sansiveri, Ryan & Sullivan*(Auditors)*
Providence, RI

Worcester County Institution for Savings*(Major Banking Relationship)*
Worcester, MA

DELTA SUGAR CORPORATION
35265 Willow Ave., P.O. Box 58
Clarksburg, CA 95612
Tel.: 916-665-1840
Fax: 916-744-1516
Approx.Sls.: $23,000,000
Emp.: 75
Granulated Sugar From Sugar Beets
S.I.C.: 2063
Joseph Borges *(Chm. Bd.)*
A.L. Sandberg *(Pres. & Chief Exec. Officer)*
Gonzalo J. Gomez *(V.P.-Fin.)*
Walter R. Higgins *(V.P.-Mktg. & Sls.)*
David Voit *(V.P.-Opers.)*

Outside Service Firm(s):

First Interstate Bank*(Major Banking Relationship)*
Whittier, CA

DELTA SURPRENANT WIRE & CABLE, INC.
172 Sterling St.
Clinton, MA 01510
Tel.: 508-365-6331
Fax: 508-365-4054
Year Founded: 1941
Approx.Sls.: $50,000,000
Emp.: 400
Import Export
Low Voltage Power Control Instrument Cable & Wire for Use in Indus., Military & Comml. Electronic Application
S.I.C.: 3496
Garo Artinian *(Pres.)*
Brian Lesperance *(V.P.-Finance & Admin.)*
Steve Harney *(Mgr.-Opers.)*
Nancy Sarafian *(Mgr.-Sls. & Mktg.)*

Computer Systems/Hardware:
Digital

DELUXE HOMES OF PENNSYLVANIA, INC.
499 W. Third St.
Berwick, PA 18603
Mailing Address:
P.O. Box 323
Berwick, PA 18603
Tel.: 717-752-5914
Fax: 717-752-6904
Year Founded: 1965
Sales Range: $40-59 Million
Emp.: 400
Export
Modular Housing; Wood & Steel Fabrication
S.I.C.: 2452; 3448
Donald E. Meske *(Pres.)*
Rick Guyer *(V.P. & Gen. Mgr.)*
Dan Meske *(V.P.-Pur.)*
Donald Shiner *(V.P.)*
William Duffy *(Controller)*

No. of Mfg. Plants/Facilities: 2

Outside Service Firm(s):

Parente, Randolph, Orlando, Carey & Associates*(Auditors)*
46 Public Square
Wilkes-Barre, PA 18701-2681
Tel.: 717-820-0100
Fax: 717-824-9865

Hourigan, Kluger, Spohrer, Quinn & Myers*(Legal Firm)*
Wilkes-Barre, PA

First Eastern Bank N.A.*(Major Banking Relationship)*
11 West Market St.
Wilkes-Barre, PA 18768
Tel.: 717-826-4603

DEMARIA BUILDING CO. INC.
45500 Grand River Ave.
Novi, MI 48376
Mailing Address:
P.O. Box 8018,
Novi, MI 48376
Tel.: 313-348-8710 **MI**
Fax: 313-348-6251
Year Founded: 1969
Approx.Sls.: $55,200,000
Emp.: 150
Fiscal Year-end: 12/31/90
General Contractor; Construction Managers
S.I.C.: 1542; 1541
Joseph A. DeMaria, Sr. *(Chm. Bd. & Chief Exec. Officer)*
Richard J. DeMaria *(Pres.)*
Joseph A. DeMaria, Jr. *(Exec. V.P.)*
Steven G. Sovinsky *(Controller)*
Joe Dilorio *(Dir.-Client Devel.)*

Computer Systems/Hardware:
NCR Tower 32-600

Outside Service Firm(s):

Swad & Company*(Auditors)*
Livonia, MI

Liberty Mutual*(Commercial Insurance Carrier)*
Novi, MI

Manufacturers National Bank N.A.*(Major Banking Relationship)*
38th Fl., 100 Renaissance Center
Detroit, MI 48243
Tel.: 313-222-4227

THE DEMARS CORP.
1919 N. Meridian St.
Indianapolis, IN 46202
Mailing Address:
P.O. Box 887
Indianapolis, IN 46206
Tel.: 317-924-9192 **IN**
Fax: 317-925-7415
Year Founded: 1927
Approx.Sls.: $220,000,000
Emp.: 200

The DeMars Corp.—(Continued)

Construction Management, General Contracting, Real Estate Development
S.I.C.: 1542; 1541; 8741; 6552
Richard B. DeMars *(Chm. Bd.)*
Dan R. DeMars *(Pres.)*
Charles E. Kendall *(Exec. V.P.-Mktg. & Admin.)*
Michael A. Peterson *(Exec. V.P.-Fin. & Legal)*
Gilbert P. Hammond, Jr. *(V.P.-Human Resources)*
Robert M. Olberding *(V.P.-Mgr. of Information & Support Services)*
Principal(s):
DeMars Family

Outside Service Firm(s):

Ernst & Young*(Auditors)*
One Indiana Square, Ste. 3400
Indianapolis, IN 46204
Tel.: 317-236-1100

Ice, Miller, Donadio & Ryan*(Legal Firm)*
One American Square, Box 82001
Indianapolis, IN 46282
Tel.: 317-236-2219

INB National Bank*(Major Banking Relationship)*
One Indiana Sq.
Indianapolis, IN 46266
Tel.: 317-266-6000

Subsidiaries:

Challenger Construction, Inc. **(1)**
2021 N. Meridan St.
Indianapolis, IN 46202
Tel.: 317-923-9450
Fax: 317-923-5733
Emp.: 19
C.L. Flaugher *(Pres.)*

DeMars Haka Development, Inc. **(1)**
1919 N. Meridan St.
Indianapolis, IN 46202
Tel.: 317-924-9192
Emp.: 7
Commercial Development
S.I.C.: 6552
David E. Carley *(Pres.)*

DeMars Program Management, Inc. **(1)**
1919 N. Meridan St.
Indianapolis, IN 46202
Tel.: 317-924-9192

Geupel DeMars, Inc. **(1)**
1919 N. Meridan St.
Indianapolis, IN 46202
Tel.: 317-924-9192
Dan R. DeMars *(Pres.)*

DEMCO INC.
4810 Forest Run Rd.
Madison, WI 53704
Mailing Address:
P.O. Box 7488
Madison, WI 53707
Tel.: 608-241-1201
Approx.Sls.: $30,000,000
Emp.: 260
Fiscal Year-end: 12/31/90
Business Educational & Library Supplies
S.I.C.: 3271; 3272; 5211
Greg Larson *(Pres.)*
John E. Wall *(Chief Exec. Officer)*
Larry Sobyak *(V.P., Treas. & Personnel Mgr.)*
Patrick Wall *(V.P.-Mktg.)*
Bill Erickson *(V.P.-Opers. & Production Mgr.)*
Colleen Goltz *(Coord.-Mktg.)*

DEMERT & DOUGHERTY, INC.
Five Westbrook Corp. Center, Ste. 900
Westchester, IL 60154
Tel.: 708-409-9000 **IL**
Fax: 708-409-9006
Year Founded: 1919
Assets: $20,700,000
Liabilities: $5,600,000
Net Worth: $15,100,000
Approx.Sls.: $52,000,000
Emp.: 210
Fiscal Year-end: 3/22/92
Export
Chemicals & Allied Products; Wholesale Trade-NonDurable Goods; Personal Care Products; Automotive Additive Products; Contract Packaging
S.I.C.: 2844; 2899; 2992; 7389
Leonard B. Drell *(Chm. Bd., Pres., Chief Exec. & Chief Oper. Officer)*
Steven Drell *(Exec. V.P. & Sec.)*
Peter C. Miehl *(V.P.-Fin. & Treas.)*
Gerald Sullivan *(Controller)*
N. Kubina *(Dir.-Human Resources)*
Jane Parker *(Dir.-Pur.)*
J. Young *(Dir.-Opers.)*
Charles Scott *(Dir.-Govt. Affairs)*
William Weker *(Dir.-Res. & Devel.)*
Karen Mansfield *(Travel Coord.)*
William Coburn *(Gen. Mgr.-Beauty)*
Liza Kristy *(Mgr.-Data Processing)*
Howard Cain *(Adv. Consultant)*
Principal(s):
Leonard B. Drell

No. of Mfg. Plants/Facilities: 2
No. of U.S. Offices: 1

Computer Systems/Hardware:
IBM AS 400

Outside Service Firm(s):

Coopers & Lybrand*(Auditors)*
203 N. LaSalle St.
Chicago, IL 60601
Tel.: 312-701-5500

Marsh & McLennan*(Commercial Insurance Carrier)*
222 S. Riverside Plaza
Chicago, IL 60606
Tel.: 312-648-6652

Jackson, Long & Associates, Inc.*(Group Insurer)*
19900 Governers Dr.
Olympia Fields, IL

Kidder, Peabody & Co.*(Investment Banker)*
125 South Wacker
Chicago, IL

Shefsky & Froehlich*(Legal Firm)*
Chicago, IL

First National Bank of Chicago*(Major Banking Relationship)*
One First National Plaza
Chicago, IL 60670
Tel.: 312-732-9781
Tel.: 312-732-4050
Fax: 312-732-4840
Fax: 312-732-3055

Pittsburgh National Bank*(Major Banking Relationship)*
500 W. Madison St., Ste. 3140
Chicago, IL 60606
Tel.: 312-906-3400
Fax: 312-906-3420

Divisions:

Aeropak **(1)**
5 Westbrook Corp. Center Suite 900
Westchester, IL 60154
Tel.: 708-409-9000
Fax: 708-409-9006
Export
Contract Packaging
James Gleichman *(Sls. Mgr.)*

Beauty-Professional **(1)**
5 West Brook Corp. Center
Westchester, IL 60159
Tel.: 708-409-9000
All Set, AVEC, Aerolak, Bland, Directress, Perceptions, The Look. Honey Almond Shampoo, Golden Wehatgerm Shampoo, Essential Collection
S.I.C.: 2844
David Doyle *(Sls. Mgr.)*

Beauty Retail Products **(1)**
5 Westbrook Corp. Center,Ste. 900
Westchester, IL 60154
Tel.: 708-409-9000
Import
All Set, Aerolak, Bland Hair Spray, Honey Almond Shampoo, Permessentials, Professional One
William Coburn *(Natl. Sls. Mgr.)*

Heet Automotive **(1)**
5 Westbrook Corp. Ctr., Suite 900
Westchester, IL 60154
Tel.: 708-409-9000
Tel.: 800-532-5111
Fax: 708-409-9006
Approx.Sls.: $15,000,000
Emp.: 60
Fiscal Year-end: 3/31/91
Export
Heet Fuel System Dryer & Anti Freeze, Clindo Cleaner, Satin Glo Polish
S.I.C.: 2899
Leonard Drell *(Chm. Bd.)*
Steven Drell *(Chief Oper. Officer)*
Peter Miehl *(Chief Fin. Officer)*
Ken Sedin *(Natl. Sls. Mgr.)*
Bill Weber *(Res. & Devel.)*

DEMETER, INC.
98 South & East, Ste. A
Fowler, IN 47944
Mailing Address:
P.O. Box 465
Fowler, IN 47944
Tel.: 317-884-0600 **IN**
Fax: 317-884-0933
Year Founded: 1964
Approx.Sls.: $104,000,000
Emp.: 150
Grain Drying, Merchandising & Storage
S.I.C.: 5153
Donald G. Brouillette *(Pres. & Chief Exec. Officer)*
Marilyn S. Brouillette *(Exec. V.P.)*
Phillis M. Henady *(Treas.)*
Kenneth E. Klemme *(Sec.)*
Principal(s):
Donald G. Brouillette

Outside Service Firm(s):

Joseph F. Glotzbach*(Auditors)*
Hammond, IN

Fowler State Bank*(Major Banking Relationship)*
Fowler, IN

JACK DEMMER FORD, INC.
37300 Michigan Ave.
Wayne, MI 48184
Tel.: 313-721-2600 **MI**
Fax: 313-721-0616
Year Founded: 1957
Approx.Sls.: $35,000,000
Emp.: 110
Retail Automobiles
S.I.C.: 5511; 5521; 7538
John E. Demmer *(Chief Exec. Officer)*
William J. Demmer *(Pres.)*
James Demmer *(V.P.)*

Outside Service Firm(s):

First of America Bank*(Major Banking Relationship)*
Wayne, MI

DEMOCRAT PRINTING & LITHOGRAPH COMPANY
114-22 E. 2nd St.
Little Rock, AR 72201
Mailing Address:
P.O. Box 191
Little Rock, AR 72203
Tel.: 501-374-0271
Fax: 501-374-1610
Approx.Sls.: $19,000,000
Emp.: 200
Commercial Printing Publications & Catalogs
S.I.C.: 2752
F.H. Parke, Jr. *(Chm.)*
Haynes Whitney Jr. *(Pres.)*
Larry Brown *(V.P.)*
R.E. Hill *(Sec. & Treas.)*

Outside Service Firm(s):

Frost & Co.*(Auditors)*
Little Rock, AR

Worthen National Bank of Arkansas*(Major Banking Relationship)*
P.O. Box 1681, 200 W. Capitol
Little Rock, AR 72201
Tel.: 501-378-1209
Fax: 501-378-1062

DEMOULAS SUPER MARKETS
875 East St.
Tewksbury, MA 01876
Tel.: 508-851-8000
Fax: 508-851-3942
Approx.Sls.: $940,000,000
Emp.: 2,400
Fiscal Year-end: 3/31/92
Retail Grocery Chain
S.I.C.: 5411
Telemachus A. DeMoulas *(Pres. & Chief Exec. Officer)*
Julian Lacourse *(Exec. V.P.)*
James D. Miamis *(Exec. V.P.)*
D. Harold Sullivan *(V.P., Treas. & Chief Fin. Officer)*
Donald Mulligan *(V.P. & Controller)*

Computer Systems/Hardware:
Honeywell DPS; Level 7; Digital 1144 & 1173

Outside Service Firm(s):

Sullivan & Bille*(Auditors)*
Boston, MA

Goldman & Curtis*(Legal Firm)*
Lowell, MA

Bank of New England North*(Major Banking Relationship)*
Lowell, MA

Shawmut Arlington Bank*(Major Banking Relationship)*
Lawrence, MA

DEMPSTER, INC.
P.O. Box 1338
Toccoa, GA 30577
Tel.: 706-886-2327
Fax: 706-886-4318
Approx.Sls.: $40,000,000
Emp.: 150
Fiscal Year-end: 3/31/91
Export
Manufacturer of Dempster Dumpmaster Front Loader Truck Mounted Compaction Body; Dempster Dumpster Hoist Unit; Dempster Dinosaur Hydraulic Tilting Frame; Route-King Refuse Collection Truck And Recycle Bodies
S.I.C.: 3489
Charles W. Walton *(Pres. & Chief Exec. Officer)*
B. Whitescarver *(Exec. V.P. & Chief Oper. Officer)*
John Thomas *(V.P.-Sls.)*
Forrest Hayes *(Chief Fin. Officer)*
Thomas Martin *(Controller)*

DEN-MAT CORPORATION
2727 Skyway Dr.
Santa Maria, CA 93455
Mailing Address:
P.O. Box 1729,
Santa Maria, CA 93456
Tel.: 805-922-8491 **DE**
Fax: 805-922-6933
Year Founded: 1974
Sales Range: $10-19 Million
Emp.: 400
Fiscal Year-end: 8/31/90

Development & Sales of Dental Products
S.I.C.: 3841
Dr. Robert Ibsen *(Chm. Bd., Pres., Chief Exec. Officer & Treas.)*
Noreen Freitas *(Exec. V.P.)*
Sandy Savinsky *(Controller)*

No. of Mfg. Plants/Facilities: 1
No. of U.S. Offices: 7
No. of Foreign Offices: 2

Computer Systems/Hardware:
AS 400

Outside Service Firm(s):

Ernst & Young*(Auditors)*
515 S. Flower St.
Los Angeles, CA 90071
Tel.: 213-621-1666

Richard Weldon*(Legal Firm)*
Santa Monica, CA

Bank of Santa Maria*(Major Banking Relationship)*
Santa Maria, CA

DENA CORPORATION
850 Nicholas Blvd.
Elk Grove Village, IL 60007
Tel.: 708-593-3041 IL
Year Founded: 1968
Approx.Sls.: $10,000,000
Emp.: 70
Fiscal Year-end: 12/31/91
Export
Manufacturer of Hair Care Products
S.I.C.: 2844
Hasan M. Elkhatib *(Pres.)*
Nelson Hanna *(Asst. to Pres.)*
Louis Berton *(Controller)*
Principal(s):
Hasan M. Elkhatib

Outside Service Firm(s):

Deloitte & Touche*(Auditors)*
Two Prudential Plaza, 180 N. Stetson
Chicago, IL 60601
Tel.: 312-946-2039

CNA Insurance*(Commercial Insurance Carrier)*
CNA Plaza,
Chicago, IL 60685
Tel.: 312-822-5000

Winston & Strawn*(Legal Firm)*
1 First National Plza.
Chicago, IL 60603
Tel.: 312-786-5600

Harris Trust & Savings Bank*(Major Banking Relationship)*
111 W. Monroe St.
Chicago, IL 60690
Tel.: 312-461-2265
Tel.: 800-858-0840

Subsidiary:

Meta International, Inc. **(1)**
850 Nicholas Blvd.
Elk Grove Village, IL 60007
Tel.: 708-593-3044
Approx.Sls.: $7,000,000
Emp.: 40
Manufacture & Distributor Of Hair Care Products
S.I.C.: 2844
Hasan M. Elkhatib *(Pres. & Chief Exec. Officer)*

DENLINGER, INC.
3246 Lincoln Hwy. E
Paradise, PA 17562
Mailing Address:
P.O. Box 369
Paradise, PA 17562
Tel.: 717-768-8244
Fax: 717-768-3460
Emp.: 220
Retail Lumber, Millwork, Roofing, Roof & Floor Trusses, Pre-Fabricated Wall Sections
S.I.C.: 5211
John M. Denlinger *(Pres. & Gen. Mgr.)*
Stephanie R. Carbaugh *(V.P.)*
Robert Hamor *(Treas.)*
Vera M. Denlinger *(Exec. Sec.)*

Outside Service Firm(s):

Sager, Swisher & Company*(Auditors)*
Lancaster, PA

Barley, Snyder, Cooper & Barber*(Legal Firm)*
Lancaster, PA

Farmers First Bank*(Major Banking Relationship)*
Intercourse, PA

DENNIS CHEMICAL COMPANY, INC.
2700 Papin St.
Saint Louis, MO 63103
Tel.: 314-771-1800 MO
Fax: 314-771-8399
Year Founded: 1936
Approx.Sls.: $25,000,000
Emp.: 75
Export
Manufacture Polymeric Compounds, Lacquers Allied Products, Adhesives & Sealants
S.I.C.: 2821; 2851; 2891
Aaron S. Dennis *(Pres. & Treas.)*
Robert Cunningham *(V.P.-Sec.)*
Kevin McCullough *(V.P.-Mfg.)*
Charles F. Seger, III *(V.P.-Sls. & Mktg.)*
Dolores Lada *(Comptroller)*
Carl Berry *(Mgr.-Data Processing)*
Robert Glaub *(Pur. Agent)*

No. of Mfg. Plants/Facilities: 2

Computer Systems/Hardware:
IBM AS 400 Model 20

Outside Service Firm(s):

Flom & Lopapata*(Auditors)*
St. Louis, MO
Tel.: 314-241-8881

Husch, Eppenberger, Donohue, Elson & Cornfield*(Legal Firm)*
100 N. Broadway
St. Louis, MO 63102
Tel.: 314-421-4800

United Missouri Bank*(Major Banking Relationship)*
Saint Louis, MO

Subsidiary:

Diversified Compounders **(1)**
5701 E. Union Pacific Blvd.
Los Angeles, CA 90022
Tel.: 213-728-3000
Manufacture of Plastic Compounds
S.I.C.: 2821
Yousof Nathie *(Plant Mgr.)*

W.J. DENNIS CO.
1111 Davis Rd.
Elgin, IL 60123-1388
Tel.: 708-697-4800 DE
Fax: 708-697-4821
Year Founded: 1900
Approx.Sls.: $12,000,000
Emp.: 60
Fiscal Year-end: 12/31/90
Import
Ideal Window & Floor Squeegees, Draft Seal, Vinyl King, Silver King Weatherstripping, Vinyl Wall Base
S.I.C.: 3429
H.C. Dennis *(Pres.)*
T.I. Anderson *(V.P. & Sec.)*

Outside Service Firm(s):

Hart Davis & Co., Ltd.*(Auditors)*
Chicago, IL

Keck, Mahin, Cate & Koehler*(Legal Firm)*
8300 Sears Tower, 233 S. Wacker Dr.
Chicago, IL 60606
Tel.: 312-876-3400

First Chicago Bank*(Major Banking Relationship)*
Oak Park, IL

DE NOOYER CHEVROLET INC.
127 Wolf Rd.
Albany, NY 12205
Tel.: 518-458-7700
Fax: 518-458-8263, Ext. 215
Approx.Sls.: $45,000,000
Emp.: 118
Retail Automobiles
S.I.C.: 5511
James S. De Nooyer *(Pres.)*
William J. Cass *(V.P.)*
Doreen Vogt *(Sec. & Treas.)*

Outside Service Firm(s):

Bryan Leyden*(Auditors)*
Albany, NY

DENTEC CORPORATION
1181 S. Rogers Circle, Unit 14
Boca Raton, FL 33487
Mailing Address:
P.O. Box 810573
Boca Raton, FL 33481-0573
Tel.: 407-241-5966 DE
Fax: 407-241-0323
Year Founded: 1985
Import Export
Mfr. Tooth Brush Sanitizer
S.I.C.: 2842
A. Wayne Lackey *(Chm. Bd. & Pres.)*
Sharon H. Woodruff *(Office Mgr., Asst. Sec. & Treas.)*

No. of U.S. Offices: 1

Outside Service Firm(s):

Grant Thornton*(Auditors)*
500 E. Broward Blvd.
Fort Lauderdale, FL 33994-3095
Tel.: 305-358-0077

American National Bank*(Major Banking Relationship)*
Ft. Lauderdale, FL

DENTON ENTERPRISES INC.
20415 Mack Ave.
Grosse Pointe, MI 48236
Tel.: 313-884-5530 MI
Fax: 313-884-5132
Approx.Sls.: $30,000,000
Emp.: 100-500
Highway & Street Construction
S.I.C.: 1611
Leet E. Denton *(Pres.)*
Barry J. Adams *(V.P.)*
Samuel L. Carman *(V.P.)*
Donald W. Riddell, III *(V.P.-Data Processing)*
Leatha Denton *(Asst. Sec.)*

Outside Service Firm(s):

Plante & Moran*(Auditors)*
Southfield, MI

Butzel Long*(Legal Firm)*
Madden Bldg., 150 W. Jefferson, Ste. 900
Detroit, MI 48226-4430
Tel.: 313-225-7000
Fax: 313-225-7080

Manufacturers National Bank N.A.*(Major Banking Relationship)*
38th Fl., 100 Renaissance Center
Detroit, MI 48243
Tel.: 313-222-4227

DENTSPLY INTERNATIONAL INC.
570 W. College Ave.
York, PA 17405
Mailing Address:
P.O. Box 872
York, PA 17405
Tel.: 717-845-7511 DE
Fax: 717-854-2343
Year Founded: 1899
Sales Range: $100-499 Million
Emp.: 3,500
Fiscal Year-end: 12/31/91
Import Export
Holding Company for the Manufacturer & Wholesaler of Dental Equipment, Dental Supplies & Medical Supplies
S.I.C.: 5047; 3843; 5049; 6719
Burton C. Borgelt *(Chm. & Chief Exec. Officer)*
John C. Miles *(Pres. & Chief Oper. Officer)*
Michael R. Crane *(Sr. V.P.-Intl. Opers.)*
John H. Weiland *(Sr. V.P.-N. American Opers.)*
Edward D. Yates *(Sr. V.P.-Fin.)*
Robert D. Brennan *(V.P. & Gen. Mgr.-York Div.)*
Emery Dougherty *(V.P.-Res. & Devel.)*
J. Patrick Clark *(Gen. Counsel)*
Timothy S. Warady *(Controller)*
Marcus Dixon *(Treas.)*
Michael D. Hanson *(V.P.-Corp. Plng.)*
George R. Rhodes *(V.P.-Corp. Communications & Professional Rels.)*
J. Robert Wingert *(Dir.-Corp. Human Resources)*
Lawrence C. Kimble *(Asst. Treas.)*

No. of Mfg. Plants/Facilities: 27
No. of U.S. Offices: 10
No. of Foreign Offices: 17

Computer Systems/Hardware:
IBM

Outside Service Firm(s):

Price Waterhouse*(Auditors)*
30 S. 17th St.
Philadelphia, PA 19103
Tel.: 215-665-9500

Travelers Insurance Co.*(Group Insurer)*
1 Tower Square
Hartford, CT 06183-2492
Tel.: 203-277-4542
Fax: 203-277-5038

Schnader, Harrison, Segal & Lewis*(Legal Firm)*
1600 Market Street
Philadelphia, PA 19103
Tel.: 215-751-2000

Chemical Banking Corp.*(Major Banking Relationship)*
277 Park Ave.
New York, NY 10041
Tel.: 212-310-6407
Fax: 212-310-4526

Commonwealth National Bank*(Major Banking Relationship)*
Philadelphia, PA

First National Bank of Minneapolis*(Major Banking Relationship)*
Minneapolis, MN

CoreStates First Pennsylvania Bank, N.A.*(Major Banking Relationship)*
Center Sq. West Tower, 15th & Market Streets
Philadelphia, PA 19101

National Westminster Bank plc*(Major Banking Relationship)*
Astor Plaza, 1515 Broadway
New York, NY 10036

Dentsply International Inc.—(Continued)

Wilmington Trust Co.*(Major Banking Relationship)*
Rodney Square North
Wilmington, DE 19890
Tel.: 302-651-1000

Divisions:

L. D. Caulk Div. (1)
Lakeview & Clarke Ave.
Milford, DE 19963
Tel.: 302-422-4511
Mfr. & Wholesale Distr. of Dental Supplies
S.I.C.: 3843; 5047
Thomas L. Whiting *(V.P. & Gen. Mgr.)*
William Broomfield *(Adv. Mgr.)*

Ceramco (1)
6 Terri Lane
Burlington, NJ 08016
Tel.: 609-386-8900
Mfr. of Dental Porcelains
S.I.C.: 3843
James M. Mandell *(V.P. & Gen. Mgr.)*

Dentsply/Implant Division (1)
15821 Ventura Blvd.
Encino, CA 91436
Tel.: 818-783-1517
Mfr. of Dental Implant Instruments
S.I.C.: 3843
Kelly F. Sheehan *(Gen. Mgr.)*

Ransom & Randolph Div. (1)
120 W. Wayne St.
Maumee, OH 43537
Tel.: 419-893-9497
Mfr. & Wholesale Distr. of Dental Supplies
S.I.C.: 3843; 5047
Dr. Karl E. Hoekstra *(V.P. & Gen. Mgr.)*

Subsidiary:

Ash, U.S.A. (1)
570 W. College Ave.
York, PA 17405
Tel.: 717-845-7511 (100%)
Mktg. of Dental Instruments
S.I.C.: 5049
F. Al King *(Gen. Mgr.)*

Non-U.S. Holdings:

AD Plastics Ltd. (1)
Clifton Rd. Marton,
Blackpool, FY 4QF, United Kingdom
Mfr. of Dental Plastics
S.I.C.: 3843
K. Dronsfield *(Chief Oper. Officer)*

Ash Instruments Division, Dentsply Ltd. (1)
Penny Cross Close Beacon Park,
Plymouth, PL2 3NY, United Kingdom
Mfr. of Dental Instruments
S.I.C.: 3843
Ben Hamlin *(Dir.-Opers.)*

C.M.W. Laboratories Dentsply, Ltd. (1)
Cornford Rd.,
Blackpool, Lancashire FY4 4QQ, United Kingdom
Tel.: 0253-65167
Telex: 677412 ADIVPL G
Fax: 0253-697431
Mfr. & Wholesale Distr. of Bone Cement
S.I.C.: 5047; 3843
John Paxman *(Chief Oper. Officer)*

L. D. Caulk Co. of Canada Div. (1)
1100 Lodestar Rd., Unit 8
Downsview, ON M3J 2Z4, Canada
Tel.: 416-635-7662
Wholesale Distr. of Dental Supplies & Equipment
S.I.C.: 5047
S. Cannon *(Chief Oper. Officer)*

De Art S.R.L. (1)
Via Rimini 22 20142
Milan, Italy
Mfr. & Wholesale Distr. of Dental Supplies & Equipment
S.I.C.: 5047; 3843
M. Lago *(Chief Oper. Officer)*

Detrey Dentsply AG (1)
Nordstrasee 89 CH-8037
Zurich, Switzerland
Wholesale Distr. of Dental Supplies & Equipment
S.I.C.: 5047
W.W. Weston *(Chief Oper. Officer)*

Detrey Dentsply S.A. (1)
72, rue du General LeClex 92270
Bois-Colombes, France
Wholesale Distr. of Dental Supplies & Equipment
S.I.C.: 5047
T. Baccuche *(Chief Oper. Officer)*

Dentsply Argentina S.A.C.I. (1)
3933/35 Zabala
Buenos Aires, Argentina
Wholesale Distr. of Dental Equipment & Supplies
S.I.C.: 5047
N. Alvarez *(Chief Oper. Officer)*

Dentsply (Australia) Pty. Ltd. (1)
58 Rupert Col.
Collingwood, Victoria 3066, Australia
Tel.: 3 417 1666
Wholesale Distr. of Dental Supplies & Equipment
S.I.C.: 5047
R. Chancellor *(Chief Oper. Officer)*

Dentsply Canada Ltd. (1)
1100 Lodestar Ave, Unit 8
Toronto, ON M3J 2V4, Canada
Tel.: 416-635-7070
Wholesale Distr. of Dental Supplies & Equipment
S.I.C.: 5047
G. Osterbauer *(Chief Oper. Officer)*

Dentsply Caulk de Mexico, S.A. de C.V. (1)
Calz. Vallejo 846, Col. Industrial Vallejo Del. Azcapotzalco, 02300
Mexico, D.F. Mexico
Tel.: 5 567 9989
Mfr. of Dental Supplies & Equipment
S.I.C.: 3843
Dr. Luis Quinoz *(Gen. Dir.)*
Raul Gonzalez *(Mgr.-Fin.)*
Francisco Carranza *(Mgr.-District)*

Dentsply GmbH (1)
Eisenbahnstrasse 180 Postfach 101074, D-6072
Dreieich, Germany
Tel.: 06103 6 07 0
Telex: 413 870 TREY D
Fax: 06103 60 73 33
Mfr. & Wholesale Distr. of Dental Supplies & Equipment
S.I.C.: 5047; 3843
G. Schmidt *(Chief Oper. Officer)*

Detrey Dentsply (1)
De-Trey-Strasse 1 Postfach 5346, D-7750
Constance, 12, Germany
Tel.: 07531 5 83-0
Telex: 7 33 313 dent d
Fax: 07531 583 104
Mfr. & Wholesale Distr. of Dental Supplies & Equipment
S.I.C.: 3843; 5047
W.W. Weston *(Chief Oper. Officer)*

Dentsply Industria e Comercio Ltda. (1)
R Alice Herve 86-Bigen
Petropolis, 25600, Brazil
Tel.: 55-242-42-1262
Telex: 2131569DSPY
Mfr. & Wholesale Distr. of Dental Supplies & Equipment
S.I.C.: 5047; 3843
R. Figueinas *(Chief Oper. Officer)*

Dentsply Ltd. (1)
Ham Moor Lane, Addlestone
Weybridge, Surrey KT15 2SE, United Kingdom
Tel.: 0932-853422
Telex: 893012 DETREY G
Fax: 0932 840168
Mfr. & Wholesale Distr. of Dental Supplies & Equipment
S.I.C.: 3843; 5047
S. Lozenby *(Plant Mgr.)*

Dentsu,Young & Rubicam Partnerships

DENTSU, YOUNG & RUBICAM PARTNERSHIPS
810 Seventh Ave.
New York, NY 10019
Tel.: 212-408-2100
Fax: 212-957-9512/408-2292
Approx.Billings: $884,000,000
Emp.: 2,138
Advertising
S.I.C.: 7311
Shinzo Ueno (Tokyo) *(Chm.)*
Gary Burandt (NY) *(Pres. & Chief Exec. Officer)*
Naoki Kobuse (Tokyo) *(Sr. Exec. V.P., Dir. WW Mktg.)*
Alain Rousset (Hong Kong) *(Sr. Exec. V.P., Chief Fin. Officer)*
Lori Kafafian *(V.P., Dir.-Human Resources)*
Ada Tse *(Supvr.-Intl. Coordination)*

Non-U.S. Holdings:

Dentsu, Sudler & Hennessey (1)
Tsukiji MK Bldg., 2-11-26, Tsukiji Chuo-ku, Tokyo, 104, Japan
Tel.: 81-3-3546-0451
Telex: 781-22596
Fax: 3-35460455
Approx.Sls.: $27,000,000
Emp.: 28
Advertising
S.I.C.: 7311
Akira Tanaka *(Pres.)*
Takayoshi Akimoto *(Exec. V.P.)*

Dentsu, Young & Rubicam, Alcantara/Manila (1)
704 Vito Cruz P.O. Box 2251,
Manila, 2801, Philippines
Tel.: 632-257-4681/4689
Telex: 742-27770
Fax: 632-521-8129
Approx.Billings: $11,000,000
Emp.: 132
Full Service Advertising
S.I.C.: 7311
Severo Alcantara *(Chm.)*
Antero B. Javier *(Pres.)*

Dentsu, Young & Rubicam/Bangkok (1)
Maneeya Centre, 8th Fl., 518/5 Ploenchit Rd.
Bangkok, 10330, Thailand
Tel.: 662-254-8267/75
Telex: 788 20713
Fax: 662-254-8276
Fax: 662-254-8156 (Reg. Off.)
Approx.Billings: $25,000,000
Emp.: 125
Full Service Advertising
S.I.C.: 7311
David Sia *(Exec. V.P. & Reg. Dir.-South & East Asia)*
Teddy Spha Palasthira *(Chm.)*

Dentsu, Young & Rubicam/Beijing (1)
10th Fl., Asia-Pacific Bldg., No. 8, Ya Bao Lu, Chaoyang District
Beijing, 100020, People's Republic of China
Tel.: 1-5125559
Telex: 716-211209
Fax: 1-5125988
Approx.Billings: $3,000,000
Emp.: 31
Advertising
S.I.C.: 7311
Xiong Yao Hua *(Chm.)*
Wang Xin *(Dep. Gen. Mgr.)*
Melvin Song *(Dep. Gen. Mgr.)*

Dentsu, Young & Rubicam/Shanghai (1)
Rm. 1206, Shanghai International Trade Centre 2200 Yan An Rd. West,
Shanghai, 200335, People's Republic of China
Tel.: 21-2752949
Telex: 716-30029
Fax: 21-2754202
Approx.Billings: $3,000,000
Emp.: 30
Advertising
S.I.C.: 7311
Gregg Loveall *(Chief Rep.)*

Dentsu, Young & Rubicam/Hong Kong (1)
418 Mount Parker House, 1111 King's Rd.
Hong Kong, Hong Kong
Tel.: 852-884-6668
Telex: 86012 HDMHK HX
Fax: 852-885-3208/886-0989
Approx.Billings: $61,000,000
Emp.: 149
Full Service Advertising
S.I.C.: 7311
Horst Beck *(Reg. Mgr.)*
James Ng *(Mng. Dir.)*
Yukio Nakano *(Deputy Reg. Dir.-E. Asia & Deputy Mng. Dir.-DY&R Hong Kong)*

Dentsu, Young & Rubicam/Kuala Lumpur (1)
6th Fl., Wisma MBSB, 48 Jalan Dungun
Damansara Heights, 50490
Kuala Lumpur, Malaysia
Tel.: 60-3-255-2600
Telex: 784-31096
Fax: 60-3-255-1289
Approx.Billings: $25,000,000
Emp.: 87
Full Service Advertising
S.I.C.: 7311
Rishya Joseph *(Mng. Dir., V.P. & Reg. Mgr.)*
Eddy Chin *(Dir.-Mktg.)*

Dentsu, Young & Rubicam/Seoul (1)
5/6 Fl., Woomi Bldg., 98-6, Nonhyun-dong, Kangnam-ku
Seoul, Korea
Tel.: 82-2-548-7150
Fax: 82-2-548-8639
Approx.Billings: $10,000,000
Emp.: 30
Advertising
S.I.C.: 7311
Bon Hyung Woo *(Pres.)*
Jim Foley *(Exec. V.P.)*
Semin Kim *(Exec. Dir.)*

Dentsu, Young & Rubicam/Singapore (1)
6th Fl., 20 Kallang Ave.
Singapore, 1233, Singapore
Tel.: 65-2950025
Telex: 786-35001
Fax: 65-2962016
Approx.Billings: $28,000,000
Emp.: 85
Full Service Advertising
S.I.C.: 7311
Yoichi Kawashima *(Deputy Reg. Dir.-So. Asia)*

Dentsu, Young & Rubicam/Taipei (1)
6th Fl., 146 Sung Chiang Rd.
Taipei, Taiwan R.O.C.
Tel.: 886-2-521-9322
Telex: 785-13457
Fax: 886-2-521-9249
Approx.Billings: $11,000,000
Emp.: 56
Full Service Advertising
S.I.C.: 7311
James Herendeen *(Deputy Mng. Dir.)*
Richard Hsiung *(Mng. Dir. & Creative Dir.)*

Dentsu, Young & Rubicam/Tokyo (1)
Kyobashi K-1 Bldg., 2-7-12 Yaesu, Chuo-ku
Tokyo, 104, Japan
Tel.: 81-3-3278-4811
Telex: 781-2738
Fax: 81-3-3278-4809
Approx.Billings: $300,000,000
Emp.: 262
Advertising
S.I.C.: 7311
Kakuichi Murakami *(Pres. & Reg. Dir.)*
Derek Hall *(Exec. V.P.)*
Koh Okada *(Sr. Mng. Dir.)*
Kazuhiko Moriya *(Sr. Mng. Dir.)*
Makoto Yamazaki *(Sr. Mng. Dir.)*
Christian Worth *(Dir. of Intl. Bus. Devel.)*

Marketforce Advertising Philippines Inc. (1)
S-341 3rd Fl., Secretariat Bldg., PICC, CCP Complex Roxas Blvd.,
Manila, Philippines
Tel.: 632-832-0309 (x 7627)
Telex: 742-27770
Fax: 632-521-8129
Advertising
S.I.C.: 7311
Severo Alcantara *(Pres.)*
Antero B. Javier *(Mng. Dir.)*

Mattingly & Partners Group Pty Ltd. (1)
21-31 Goodwood St.
Richmond, Victoria 3121, Australia
Tel.: 61-3-426-1111
Fax: 61-3-426-1188
Advertising
S.I.C.: 7311
David Mattingly *(Grp. Chm.)*

Mattingly & Partners/Melbourne (1)
21-31 Goodwood St.
Richmond, Victoria 3121, Australia
Tel.: 61-3-426-1111
Fax: 61-3-426-1188
Approx.Billings: $191,000,000
Emp.: 110
Full Service Advertising
S.I.C.: 7311
David Mattingly *(Chm.)*
Geoff Ingall *(Mng. Dir.)*

Mattingly & Partners/Auckland (1)
4th Fl., Cnr. Augustus Terrace & Parnell Rise Parnell,
Auckland, New Zealand
Tel.: 64-9-309-2840
Fax: 64-9-309-6357
Approx.Billings: $33,000,000
Emp.: 50
Full Service Advertising
S.I.C.: 7311
Ross Jackson *(Mng. Dir.)*

Mattingly & Partners/Sydney (1)
83 Alexander St.
Crows Nest, N.S.W. 2065, Australia
Tel.: 61-2-906-3708
Fax: 61-2-906-2450
Approx.Billings: $20,000,000
Emp.: 30
Full Service Advertising
S.I.C.: 7311
Barry Anderson *(Mng. Dir.)*
Tim Edwards *(Gen. Mgr.)*

Metro (1)
Samudera Indonesia Bldg., 5th Fl., Jl. Jend. S. Parman Kav. 35 Slipi,
Jakarta, 11480, Indonesia
Tel.: 62-21-59-3277
Fax: 62-21-548-0870
Approx.Billings: $4,000,000
Emp.: 25
Full Service Advertising
Hendra Soesanto *(Chm. & Fin. Dir.)*
Henry Saputra *(Mng. & Creative Dir.)*

Oriental Source (1)
2nd Fl., Mount Parker House, 1111 King's Rd.
Hong Kong, Hong Kong
Tel.: 2-886-5184
Fax: 2-886-5468
Premiums
S.I.C.: 7311
Rodney Tam *(Reg. Dir. & Gen. Mgr.)*

Rediffusion (1)
Readymoney Terrace, 1st Fl., 167 Dr. Annie Besant Rd. Worli,
Bombay, 400 018, India
Tel.: 91-22-493-5945/1566/6800
Telex: 953-1175537
Fax: 91-22-493-6557
Approx.Billings: $19,000,000
Emp.: 180
Full Service Advertising
S.I.C.: 7311
Arun Nanda *(Chm. & Mng. Dir.)*
Ashoke Bjapurkar *(Sr. Gen. Mgr.)*
Conrad Saldanha *(Gen. Mgr.-Opers. & Bus. Devel.)*
V. Shantakumar *(Gen. Mgr. (Creative))*
H.V. Subramaniam *(Gen. Mgr. (Bombay))*

Triangle Pacific (1)
2nd Fl., Mount Parker House, 1111 King's Rd.
Hong Kong, Hong Kong
Tel.: 2-886-5128
Fax: 2-886-5470
Approx.Billings: $5,000,000
Emp.: 20
Sales Promotion
S.I.C.: 7311
Rodney Tam *(Reg. Dir. & Gen. Mgr.)*

Wunderman (1)
4th Fl., Mount Parker House, 1111 King's Rd.
Hong Kong, Hong Kong
Tel.: 2-884-6668
Telex: 780-86012
Fax: 2-567-5701
Approx.Billings: $3,000,000
Emp.: 8
Direct Marketing
S.I.C.: 7311
Tracy Richardson *(V.P., Mng. Dir.)*

DENVER EQUIPMENT COMPANY
621 S. Sierra Madre
Colorado Springs, CO 80903
Mailing Address:
P.O. Box 340,
Colorado Springs, CO 80901
Tel.: 719-471-3443
Telex: 168169
Fax: 719-471-4469
Year Founded: 1927
Approx.Sls.: $70,000,000
Emp.: 235
Fiscal Year-end: 2/26/93
Export
Mineral Recovery & Chemical Processing Equipment
S.I.C.: 3532; 3561; 3565; 3554; 3569
Ronald Robinson *(Chm. Bd. & Chief Exec. Officer)*
Jack Lundberg *(Pres.)*
A.G. Cipoletti *(Chief Fin. Officer)*
W.E. Troyer *(V.P.-Opers.)*
Frederick R. Coumbe *(Controller)*
M.P. O'Dell *(Sec.)*
Thomas Conrad *(Dir.-Pur.)*
Keith Johnson *(Dir.-Human Resources)*
Thomas Smith *(Dir.-Mngmt. Information Systems)*
Frank Marconi *(Mgr.-Adv.)*
John Novoselac *(Mgr.-Mktg. & Sls.)*

No. of Mfg. Plants/Facilities: 5
No. of U.S. Offices: 5
No. of Foreign Offices: 4

Computer Systems/Hardware:
IBM 9370

Outside Service Firm(s):

Grant Thornton*(Auditors)*
Colorado Springs, CO

United Bank*(Major Banking Relationship)*
Colorado Springs, CO

Subsidiaries:

Denver Autometrics (1)
6235 Lookout Rd.
Boulder, CO 80301
Tel.: 303-530-1600
Fax: 303-530-5210
Emp.: 35
Mineral Recovery & Processing Control Equipment
S.I.C.: 3532; 3443; 3569
Jim Shotton *(Pres.)*

Denver Thomas, Inc. (1)
P.O. Box 96
Birmingham, AL 35201
Tel.: 205-599-6600
Fax: 205-599-6610
Emp.: 250
Mineral Recovery & Chemical Processing Equipment
S.I.C.: 3561; 3321; 3322; 3325
George Sheehy *(Pres.)*

Non-U.S. Holdings:

Denver Equipment Pty., Ltd. (1)
1st. Fl., 40 Dickson Ave. P.O. Box 365,
Artarmon, N.S.W. Australia
Tel.: 02 439 6699
Emp.: 10
Mineral Recovery & Chemical Processing Equip.
S.I.C.: 3532; 3561
Allan Nuttall *(Mng. Dir.)*

Denver Process Equipment, Ltd. (1)
Stocks House, 9 No. St.
Leatherhead, Surrey KT22 7AX, United Kingdom
Tel.: 0372-379-313
Emp.: 90
Mineral Recovery, Chemical Processing & Environmental System Equipment
S.I.C.: 3532
Allan Manning *(Mng. Dir.)*

DENVER WHOLESALE FLORISTS COMPANY
4800 Dahlia St.
Denver, CO 80216
Mailing Address:
P.O. Box 173354
Denver, CO 80217-3354
Tel.: 303-399-0970
Tel.: 800-776-2055
Telex: 45-0075
Fax: 303-322-7307
Year Founded: 1909
Approx.Sls.: $38,000,000
Emp.: 275
Fiscal Year-end: 7/31/92
Import
Colorado Carnations, Roses, Cut Flowers & Florist Supplies
S.I.C.: 5193; 5992
Marion Elliot *(Pres.)*
John Shelton *(Gen. Mgr. & Sec.)*
Larry Hagen *(Controller)*
Joy Harrison *(Mgr.-Data Processing)*
David Gaul *(Mgr.-Sls. & Adv.)*

Computer Systems/Hardware:
IBM

Subsidiaries:

DWF of Cincinnati, Inc. (1)
1220 Findley St.
Cincinnati, OH 45214
Tel.: 513-621-2217
Fax: 513-621-2699
Kathy Beasley *(Gen. Mgr.)*

DWF of Flint, Inc. (1)
5100 Exchange Dr.
Flint, MI 48507
Tel.: 313-733-5100
Fax: 313-733-8530
David Oatley *(Mgr.)*

DWF of Milwaukee, Inc. (1)
425 W. Walnut
Milwaukee, WI 53212
Tel.: 414-263-8400
Fax: 414-263-8407

DWF of Norfolk (1)
5315 Henneman Dr.
Norfolk, VA 23513
Tel.: 804-857-4007
Fax: 804-857-9720
Shirley Stowe *(Mgr.)*

DWF of North Kansas City (1)
21 W. 13th Ave.
North Kansas City, MO 64116
Tel.: 816-474-9705
Fax: 816-842-7342
Import
Rick Harper *(Mgr.)*

DWF of Omaha (1)
9312 G Street
Omaha, NE 68127
Tel.: 402-339-5080
Fax: 402-339-9557
John Adams *(Mgr.)*

DWF of Saint Louis, Inc. (1)
2715 LaSalle St.
Saint Louis, MO 63104
Tel.: 314-772-0254
Fax: 314-772-0254
Ron Gainey *(Gen. Mgr.)*

DWF of Salt Lake, Inc. (1)
1765 S. 300 W.
Salt Lake City, UT 84115
Tel.: 801-487-6221
Fax: 801-467-4991
Phillip James *(Mgr.)*

DWF of Seattle (1)
330 Terry Ave. No.
Seattle, WA 98109
Tel.: 206-624-6545
Fax: 206-622-4136
Patrick Layhon *(Mgr.)*

DWF of Tacoma (1)
5211 S. Washington
Tacoma, WA 98406
Tel.: 206-473-4343
Fax: 206-473-5510

Dallas Flower Market, Inc. (1)
2636 Farrington St.
Dallas, TX 75207
Tel.: 214-631-3280
Fax: 214-634-1593
Pete Anderson *(Mgr.)*

DEPEW DEVELOPMENT INC.
4429 Walden Ave.
Lancaster, NY 14086
Tel.: 716-685-1610 **NY**
Fax: 716-685-1616
Year Founded: 1971
Approx.Sls.: $11,500,000
Emp.: 100
Highway, Bridge & Sewer Line Contractor
S.I.C.: 1611; 1622; 1623
John Arcadi *(Pres.)*
Vincent Arcadi *(Sec. & Treas.)*

Outside Service Firm(s):

Edward Jarosz*(Auditors)*
Buffalo, NY

A.N. DERINGER, INC.
64-66 N. Main St.
Saint Albans, VT 05478
Tel.: 802-524-5975
Fax: 802-524-5975
Emp.: 400
Custom House Brokerage; Insurance Agents
S.I.C.: 4731; 6411
Kenneth J. Holzcheiter *(Pres. & Gen. Mgr.)*
Robert L. Bronson *(V.P.)*
Carl W. Klaszky *(Sec. & Treas.)*

Outside Service Firm(s):

KPMG Peat Marwick*(Auditors)*
St. Albans, VT

Franklin Lamoille Bank*(Major Banking Relationship)*
St. Albans, VT

DERST BAKING COMPANY, INC.
1311 W. 52nd St. Extn.
Savannah, GA 31405
Tel.: 912-233-2235 **GA**
Fax: 912-234-3611
Year Founded: 1946
Approx.Sls.: $33,000,000
Emp.: 474
Mfr. & Wholesale Distribution of Bread, Cake & Other Related Products
S.I.C.: 2051; 5461
Edward J. Derst, Jr. *(Chm. Bd.)*
Edward J. Derst, III *(Pres. & Chief Exec. Officer)*
Marvin K. Boggs *(V.P.-Sls.)*
Heather Burton *(V.P.-Fin.)*
Catherine D. Miller *(Treas.)*

Outside Service Firm(s):

NationsBank*(Major Banking Relationship)*
Savannah, GA

DESA INTERNATIONAL, INC.
2701 Industrial Dr.
Bowling Green, KY 42101
Tel.: 502-781-9600

Desa International, Inc.—(Continued)

Fax: 502-781-9669
Year Founded: 1985
Approx.Sls.: $51,000,000
Emp.: 500
Mfr. of Heating Equipment, Except Electric; Portable Chain Saws
S.I.C.: 3433; 3546
Robert H. Elman *(Chm. Bd. & Chief Exec. Officer)*
Damon S. Vitale *(Pres. & Chief Oper. Officer)*
Donald W. Denton *(V.P.-Engrng.)*
John M. Kelly *(V.P.-Mktg. & Sls.)*
Dirk D. Miller *(V.P.-Mfg. Services)*
Richard Miller *(V.P.-Human Resources)*
William A. Parsons, Jr. *(V.P.-Intl.)*
Jim Phillip *(V.P.-Mfg. & Opers.)*
Ralph Pratt *(V.P.-Tech. Services & Quality Control)*
Douglas D. Rohrtree *(V.P.-Engrng., Specialty Products)*
Terry G. Scariot, Sr. *(V.P.-Fin. & Sec.)*

Outside Service Firm(s):

The Citizens National Bank*(Major Banking Relationship)*
Bowling Green, KY

DESCO CORPORATION
150 E. Campus View Blvd., Suite 250
Columbus, OH 43235
Tel.: 614-888-8855
Fax: 614-888-3779
Year Founded: 1974
Approx.Sls.: $150,000,000
Emp.: 2,500
Export
Mfr. of Motor Vehicle Parts & Accessories; Measuring Controlling & Counting Devices; Timers; Fabricated Metal Products; Nonresidential Building Operators; Oil & Natural Gas Producers
S.I.C.: 3499; 3714; 3823; 3824; 6512
Arnold B. Siemer *(Chm. Bd. & Pres.)*
Denny Burns *(Grp. V.P.-Process)*
Gary Fought *(Grp. V.P.-Construction)*
Clyde R. Fobes *(V.P. & Treas.)*
James Zins *(Controller)*
Russell M. Gertmenian *(Sec.)*
Diane Kana *(Dir.-Human Resources)*
Anna Greashaber *(Mgr.-Mktg.)*
Barbara J. Siemer *(Intl. Mktg. Coord.)*
Principal(s):
Arnold B. Siemer

No. of Mfg. Plants/Facilities: 12
No. of U.S. Offices: 1
No. of Foreign Offices: 3

Outside Service Firm(s):

Ernst & Young*(Auditors)*
One Columbus, 10 W. Broad St.
Columbus, OH 43215
Tel.: 614-224-5678

Alexander & Alexander*(Commercial Insurance Carrier)*
1328 Dublin Road
Columbus, OH 43216
Tel.: 614-486-9571
Fax: 614-488-2394

Vorys, Sater, Seymour & Pease*(Legal Firm)*
P.O. Box 1008, 52 E. Gay St.
Columbus, OH 43216
Tel.: 614-464-6258

Society National Bank*(Major Banking Relationship)*
900 Euclid Ave., P.O. Box 6477
Cleveland, OH 44101-6477
Tel.: 216-737-5000
Fax: 216-566-8947

Division:

Desco Advertising & Marketing **(1)**
959 Cheney Ave.
Marion, OH 43302
Tel.: 614-382-6001
Advertising & Marketing Services; Administrative Services for Automatic Timing & Controls
S.I.C.: 7311; 8741
Anna Greashaber *(Mgr.-Mktg.)*
Douglas Wearn *(Chief Oper. Officer-Administrative Services)*

Plant:

Automatic Timing & Controls, Inc. **(1)**
201 S. Gulph Rd.
King of Prussia, PA 19406
Tel.: 215-992-9800 (100%)
Mfr. of Timers & Counters
S.I.C.: 3625; 3824
Douglas Wearn *(Gen. Mgr.)*

DESERET MANAGEMENT CORPORATION
36 S. State St., Ste. 1825
Salt Lake City, UT 84111
Tel.: 801-538-0651
Fax: 801-538-0655
Emp.: 9
Holding Co.
S.I.C.: 6719
Gordon B. Hinckley *(Chm. Bd.)*
Robert Hales *(Pres.)*
Floyd Moon *(Treas. & Asst. Sec.)*

Computer Systems/Hardware:
Televideo 950

Outside Service Firm(s):

Deloitte & Touche*(Auditors)*
50 S. Main St., Ste. 1800
Salt Lake City, UT 84144
Tel.: 801-328-4706

Deseret Mutual Benefit Association*(Group Insurer)*
Salt Lake City, UT

Kirton, McConkie & Poelman*(Legal Firm)*
Salt Lake City, UT

Subsidiaries:

Beneficial Life Insurance **(1)**
36 S. State St.,Ste. 1310
Salt Lake City, UT 84111
Tel.: 801-538-0651
S.I.C.: 6311
Gordon B. Hinckley *(Chm.)*

Bonneville International Corp. **(1)**
Broadcast House, No. 5 Triad Center
Salt Lake City, UT 84180
Tel.: 801-575-7500
Broadcasting
S.I.C.: 4832; 4833
Gordon B. Hinckley *(Chm.)*
Robert A. Johnson *(V.P.-Sec. & Gen. Counsel)*

Divisions:

KSL Radio **(2)**
Broadcast House
Salt Lake City, UT 84110-1160
Tel.: 801-575-7230
Adult Programming-Radio
S.I.C.: 4832
F. Russell Wood *(Gen. Mgr.)*
Darryl Steele *(Natl. Sls. Mgr.)*
Larry Anderson *(Gen. Sls. Mgr.)*
Maggie St. Claire *(Dir.-Mktg. & Community Affairs)*

KSL-TV **(2)**
Broadcast House
Salt Lake City, UT 84180-1160
Tel.: 801-575-5555
Twx: 910-925-5822
Fax: 801-575-5830
Television Station
S.I.C.: 4833

Deseret Book Co. **(1)**
P.O. Box 30178, 40 E. Temple South
Salt Lake City, UT 84130
Tel.: 801-534-1515
Publication of General Trade Hardcovers & Paperbacks, Juveniles, Bibles, Cookbooks, Religion, General Nonfiction
S.I.C.: 2731
Ronald A. Millet *(Gen. Mgr.)*

Deseret News **(1)**
157 Regent St.
Salt Lake City, UT 84111
Tel.: 801-237-2721
Fax: 801-237-2775
Publishes Morning & Sunday Tribune, Evening & Saturday Deseret News
S.I.C.: 2711
Dominic Welch *(Pres.)*

Zion's Securities Corp. **(1)**
102 E.S. Social Hall Ave.
Salt Lake City, UT 84111
Tel.: 801-321-8700
Rental Property
S.I.C.: 6531

DESIGN 1 INTERIORS
2049 Century Park E., Ste. 3000
Los Angeles, CA 90067
Tel.: 310-553-5032 **CA**
Fax: 310-785-0445
Year Founded: 1976
Sales Range: $10-19 Million
Emp.: 60
Fiscal Year-end: 10/31/91
Export
Commercial Interior Design
S.I.C.: 7389
Sue Firestone *(Pres. & Chief Exec. Officer)*
Gary Owen *(Chief Fin. Officer & Controller)*
Jeanne James *(Sr. V.P.)*
Sandy Tubis *(Sr. V.P.)*
Teresa Chester *(V.P.)*
Steve Firestone *(V.P.)*
Ron Zamir *(V.P. & Gen. Mgr.)*
Principal(s):
Sue Firestone
Jeanne James
Sandy Tubis
Teresa Chester
Steve Firestone

No. of Mfg. Plants/Facilities: 2
No. of U.S. Offices: 1
No. of Foreign Offices: 1

Computer Systems/Hardware:
Altos & IBM

Outside Service Firm(s):

Ernst & Young*(Auditors)*
1999 Avenue of the Stars
Century City, CA 90067
Tel.: 310-553-2800
Fax: 310-556-8309

Emmett & Chandler*(Commercial Insurance Carrier)*
Los Angeles, CA

Security Pacific Corporation*(Major Banking Relationship)*
Security Pacific Plaza
Los Angeles, CA 90071
Tel.: 213-345-6211
Fax: 213-625-0809

Despatch

DESPATCH INDUSTRIES
63 St. Anthony Pkwy.
Minneapolis, MN 55418
Mailing Address:
P.O Box 1320,
Minneapolis, MN 55440
Tel.: 612-781-5363
Tel.: 800-328-5476
Fax: 612-781-5353
Year Founded: 1902
Assets: $25,000,000
Liabilities: $18,000,000
Net Worth: $7,000,000
Approx.Sls.: $40,000,000
Emp.: 342
Fiscal Year-end: 12/31/90
Import Export
Designers & Manufacturers of Heat Processing & Environmental Testing Equipment & Systems
S.I.C.: 3567; 3821; 3569; 3829; 3823
Warren G. Christianson *(Chm. Bd.)*
Sid D. Johnston *(Pres. & Chief Exec. Officer)*
John Allyn *(V.P.-Opers.)*
Hans L. Melgaard *(V.P.-Technology)*
Jeff Ogden *(V.P.-Admin. & Chief Fin. Officer)*
Barbara Barnes *(Mgr.-Materials)*
Gail Hanson *(Mgr.-Personnel)*
Patricia Jensen *(Dir.-Mngmt. Information Systems)*
Steve Jones *(Div. Mgr.-Applied Prods.)*
Corey Minnich *(Div. Mgr.-Engrng. Systems)*
Kent Phillips *(Div. Mgr.-Service Prods.)*
Principal(s):
Warren G. Christianson
Sid D. Johnston

No. of Mfg. Plants/Facilities: 2
No. of U.S. Offices: 2

Computer Systems/Hardware:
IBM System 38

Outside Service Firm(s):

Deloitte & Touche*(Auditors)*
900 Pillsbury Ctr.
Minneapolis, MN 55402
Tel.: 612-332-2301
Fax: 612-375-5418

Fredrikson & Byron, P.A.*(Legal Firm)*
1100 International Centre, 900 2nd Ave. S.
Minneapolis, MN 55402
Tel.: 612-347-7000

Norwest Bank Minnesota, N.A.*(Major Banking Relationship)*
6th St. & Marquette Av.
Minneapolis, MN 55479
Tel.: 612-667-1234

Affiliate:

Ransco Industries, Inc. **(1)**
1400 E. Statham Pkwy.
Oxnard, CA 93033
Tel.: 805-487-7777
Fax: 805-486-7024
Emp.: 101
James A. Wasson *(Pres.)*

DESTINY INDUSTRY INC.
Industrial Park
Moultrie, GA 31768
Mailing Address:
P.O. Box 1766,
Moultrie, GA 31776
Tel.: 912-985-6100
Fax: 912-985-5346
Approx.Sls.: $56,000,000
Emp.: 710
Fiscal Year-end: 9/30/90
Manufacturer of Mobile Homes
S.I.C.: 2451
William G. Edwards *(Pres.)*
John Benny Alderman *(V.P.-Fin.)*
Donny E. Edwards *(V.P.-Sls.)*

Outside Service Firm(s):

William O. Pifer*(Auditors)*
Moultrie, GA

Moultrie National Bank*(Major Banking Relationship)*
Moultrie, GA

DETECTO SCALE COMPANY
(Div. of Cardinal Scale Mfg. Co.)
203 E. Daugherty
Webb City, MO 64870
Mailing Address:
P.O. Box 151,
Webb City, MO 64870
Tel.: 417-673-4631
Tel.: 800-641-2008
Fax: 417-673-5001
Year Founded: 1953
Approx.Sls.: $14,000,000
Emp.: 400
Fiscal Year-end: 6/31/90
Export
Mfr. Detecto Beam Clinical Scales, Detecto Digital Clinical Scales, Detecto Industrial Dial & Beam Scales, Detecto Industrial Digital Scales, Detecto Commercial Scales; Detecto Food Scales; Detecto Consumer Scales, Detecto Postal Scales, Detecto Sporting Goods Scales
S.I.C.: 3596; 3821
William H. Perry *(Chief Exec. Officer)*
David H. Perry *(Pres.)*
Herbert A. Harwood *(Exec. V.P.)*
H. Schoener *(V.P.)*
Marion E. Perry *(Sec. & Treas.)*

DETEX CORPORATION
302 Detex Dr.
New Braunfels, TX 78130
Tel.: 210-629-2900
Tel.: 800-729-3839
Telex: 261701
Fax: 210-620-6711
Year Founded: 1923
Approx.Sls.: $11,500,000
Emp.: 120
Fiscal Year-end: 12/31/90
Import Export
Watchman's Clocks & Exit Control Locks & Alarms; Entry Control (DENTCO) Systems, Remote Indicating Panels (Annunciators)
S.I.C.: 3873; 3469; 3699; 3825
Corporate Giving Program: United Way
Philip H. Haselton *(Chm. Bd.)*
Philip N. Haselton *(Pres.)*
Anthony L. Mudford *(V.P. & Gen. Mgr.)*
John H. Blodgett *(Treas.)*
R.R. MacDonald *(Dir.-Sls.)*
P. deBergeois *(Dir.-Mktg.)*
E. Boratko *(Dir.-Mfg.)*
Virginia E. Tamweber *(Mgr.-Data Processing)*
J.F. Fornadel *(Mgr.-Engrng.)*

DETROIT CITY DAIRY, INC.
15004 Third Ave.
Highland Park, MI 48203
Tel.: 313-868-5511
Fax: 313-868-0134
Year Founded: 1938
Assets: $9,300,000
Liabilities: $3,975,000
Net Worth: $5,325,000
Approx.Sls.: $83,000,000
Emp.: 240
Wholesale Dairy Products
S.I.C.: 5143
Meyer Must *(Chm. Bd.)*
Alan Must *(Pres.)*
Joel Must *(Pres.-Warehouse)*
James A. Mrowka *(Controller)*
Mary Must *(Treas.)*
Principal(s):
Meyer Must
Alan Must
Joel Must

No. of Mfg. Plants/Facilities: 1
No. of U.S. Offices: 1

Computer Systems/Hardware:
IBM System 36

Outside Service Firm(s):

Kleiman, Carney & Greenbaum*(Auditors)*
Farmington Hills, MI

General Underwriters*(Group Insurer)*
Southfield, MI

Comerica Bank*(Investment Banker)*
211 W. Fort St.
Detroit, MI 48226
Tel.: 313-222-3300

Merrill Lynch*(Investment Banker)*
Detroit, MI

Barris, Sott, Denn, Dricker*(Legal Firm)*
Detroit, MI

Comerica Bank*(Major Banking Relationship)*
211 W. Fort St.
Detroit, MI 48226
Tel.: 313-222-3300

Merrill Lynch*(Pension Manager)*
Detroit, MI

DETROIT COIL COMPANY
2435 Hilton Rd.
Ferndale, MI 48220
Tel.: 313-398-5600
Fax: 313-398-0481
Approx.Sls.: $10,000,000
Emp.: 100
Industrial Solenoids, Electro Magnetic Coils
S.I.C.: 3679; 3677
A.C. Jenckes *(Pres.)*
David C. Jencks *(V.P. & Gen. Mgr.)*
Hollis W. Jencks, III *(V.P.-Engrng.)*
John E. Sloan *(Controller)*
Larry Williamson *(Chief Engnr.)*
Charles Swords *(Pur. Agent)*
Tom Dougherty *(Mgr.-Sls.)*
Robert Dugan *(Plant Mgr.)*

Outside Service Firm(s):

NBD Bank, N.A.*(Major Banking Relationship)*
611 Woodward Ave.
Detroit, MI 48226
Tel.: 313-225-1122

DETTRA FLAG COMPANY
120 Montgomery Ave.
Oaks, PA 19456
Mailing Address:
P.O. Box 408,
Oaks, PA 19456-0408
Tel.: 215-666-5050 **PA**
Fax: 215-666-1466
Year Founded: 1901
Approx.Sls.: $15,000,000
Emp.: 180
Export
Mfr. of Flags, Banners, Cloth Decorations & Flag Accessories
S.I.C.: 2399
William C. Spangler *(Pres.)*
Joseph E. McIntyre *(V.P.-Sls.)*
Joseph Price *(V.P.-Mfg. & Sec.)*
Malcolm Campbell *(V.P.)*
Francis P. Loeber *(V.P.)*
Elmer Bauer *(Treas.)*
John Thomas *(Dir.-Pur.)*
Donald Batzel *(Mgr.-Facilities)*
Frank Hicks *(Mgr.-Sls.)*
Kathleen Kehan *(Mgr.-Human Resources)*
William Paterson *(Indus. Engr.)*

Outside Service Firm(s):

Deloitte & Touche*(Auditors)*
1700 Market St.
Philadelphia, PA 19103
Tel.: 215-246-2322
Fax: 215-569-2441

Stradley, Ronon, Stevens & Young*(Legal Firm)*
2600 Commerce Sq.
Philadelphia, PA 19103
Tel.: 215-564-8000

Fidelity Bank*(Major Banking Relationship)*
Broad & Walnut St.
Philadelphia, PA 19109

Subsidiary:

Sirtex Printing Company **(1)**
East Main St.
Old Mystic, CT 06372
Tel.: 203-536-8320
Textile Printing on Flags
S.I.C.: 2399
Harold Burns *(Gen. Mgr.)*

Deutsch

DEUTSCH/DWORIN, INC.
(Formerly Deutsch, Inc.)
215 Park Ave. South
New York, NY 10003
Tel.: 212-995-7500
Fax: 212-353-9659
Year Founded: 1969
Approx.Billings: $135,000,000
Emp.: 120
Advertising Agency
S.I.C.: 7311
David Deutsch *(Chm. Bd.)*
Steve Dworin *(Pres.)*
Cheryl Greene *(Sr. V.P., Dir. Acct. Planning)*
Brian Martin *(Sr. V.P., Dir.-New Bus.)*
Paul Lubarsky *(V.P., Controller)*

Computer Systems/Hardware:
IBM PC

Outside Service Firm(s):

Weisbarth, Altman & Miller*(Auditors)*
New York, NY

Nixon, Hargrave, Devans & Doyle*(Legal Firm)*
30 Rockefeller
New York, NY
Tel.: 212-586-4100

Republic National Bank*(Major Banking Relationship)*
355 Lexington Ave.
New York, NY 10017
Tel.: 212-573-5514

Branch:

Deutsch Direct **(1)**
215 Park Ave. South
New York, NY 10003
Tel.: 212-995-7500
Fax: 212-254-2253
Steve Dworin *(Pres.)*

DEUTSCH, SHEA & EVANS, INC.
601 Gateway Blvd., Ste. 950
South San Francisco, CA 94080
Tel.: 415-244-4800
Fax: 415-244-4807
Year Founded: 1939
Approx.Billings: $40,500,000
Charles L. Gould *(Chm. & Chief Exec. Officer)*
Joel R. Spiegel *(Pres.)*
Carmen Monte *(V.P., Fin. & Admin.)*
Paul R. Tully *(V.P., New Bus. Devel.)*

THE DEUTSCH COMPANY
2444 Wilshire Blvd., Rm. 600
Santa Monica, CA 90403
Tel.: 310-453-0055
Fax: 310-453-6467
Emp.: 4,000
Mfr. of Aerospace Parts-Primarily Fasteners & Connectors
S.I.C.: 3452; 3769; 3728
Alex Deutsch *(Chm. Bd. & Chief Exec. Officer)*
Carl Deutsch *(Pres.)*
Lester Deutsch *(Exec. V.P.)*
W. E. Haller *(V.P.-Fin., Chief Fin. Officer & Treas.)*

Outside Service Firm(s):

First Interstate Bank of California, N.A.*(Major Banking Relationship)*
P.O. Box 3667,
Los Angeles, CA 90051
Tel.: 213-614-4000

DEVAULT FOODS
Devault Lane
Devault, PA 19432
Tel.: 215-644-2536
Tel.: 800-HAMBURG
Fax: 215-644-2631
Sales Range: $80-99 Million
Emp.: 145
Fiscal Year-end: 9/30/91
Import
Meat Processing
S.I.C.: 2011
Thomas A. DiFillippo *(Chm. Bd. & Pres.)*
Lucy R. DiFillippo *(Exec. V.P.)*
Henry Jankowski *(V.P.-Opers.)*
Carl L. Sorzano *(Treas.)*
Pauli Rubino *(Gen. Counsel)*
Holly Brown *(Dir.-Sls.)*
Sue Ramberg *(Dir.-Personnel)*

No. of Mfg. Plants/Facilities: 1

Computer Systems/Hardware:
IBM 36

Outside Service Firm(s):

T. Nanni*(Auditors)*
Chester, PA

Meridian Bank*(Major Banking Relationship)*
Reading, PA

DEVELOPERS DIVERSIFIED
34555 Chagrin Blvd.
Moreland Hills, OH 44022
Tel.: 216-247-4700
Fax: 216-247-1118
Emp.: 50
Real Estate Developers & Brokers
S.I.C.: 6552; 6513
Bert L. Wolstein *(Chief Exec. Officer)*
John R. McGill *(Pres.)*
Loren F. Henry *(Pres.-Mngmt.)*
Joan Allgood *(Gen. Counsel)*
David E. Frantz *(Dir.-Mktg. & Pub. Rels.)*
Stuart R. Holmquist *(Dir.-Mall Opers.)*

DEVINE & PEARSON, INC.
Crown Colony Office Park, 300 Congress St.
Quincy, MA 02169
Tel.: 617-472-2700
Fax: 617-472-8880
Year Founded: 1965
Approx.Billings: $22,000,000
Emp.: 31
Hugh T. Devine *(Pres. & New Bus. Contact)*
Matthew Devine *(Sr. V.P.)*
Thomas Devine *(Sr. V.P.)*
Philip Mathews *(V.P.)*
Charlotte Delaney *(V.P., Fin.)*

DEVLIEG BULLARD SERVICES GROUP
(Formerly DeVlieg Inc.)
10100 Forest Hills Rd.
Rockford, IL 61115
Tel.: 815-547-5321
Approx.Sls.: $54,000,000
Emp.: 275
Boring & Milling Machines, Machine Tools, Cutting Tools
S.I.C.: 3541

DeVlieg Bullard Services Group—(Continued)

Ron Cantrell *(Pres.)*
Lawrence Holmes *(V.P.-Fin.)*

Outside Service Firm(s):

Deloitte & Touche*(Auditors)*
200 Renaissance Center, 16th Fl.
Detroit, MI 48243
Tel.: 313-396-3000
Fax: 313-259-8087

Kerr, Russell & Weber*(Legal Firm)*
Detroit, MI

DEVLIN LUMBER & SUPPLY CORP.
1540 Rockville Pike
Rockville, MD 20852
Mailing Address:
P.O. Box 1306
Rockville, MD 20849-1306
Tel.: 301-881-1000
Fax: 301-468-0628
Year Founded: 1949
Approx.Sls.: $30,000,000
Emp.: 130
Fiscal Year-end: 3/31/90
Export
Retail Lumber, Millwork, Building Materials
S.I.C.: 5211; 5251
Jonathan S. England *(Chm. Bd.)*
James L. Quinn *(Pres.)*
Joseph R. Hallett *(V.P.)*
Donald Miller *(V.P.)*

No. of Mfg. Plants/Facilities: 3

Outside Service Firm(s):

Matthews, Carter & Boyce*(Auditors)*
McLean, VA

E. Austin Carlin*(Legal Firm)*
Bethesda, MD

Sovran Bank*(Major Banking Relationship)*
Rockville, MD

Subsidiaries:

Maryland Wood Preserving Corp. **(1)**
1540 Rockville Pike
Rockville, MD 20852
Tel.: 410-881-1000

Taylor Lumber & Supply Corp. **(1)**
1540 Rockville Pike
Rockville, MD 20852
Tel.: 410-881-1000

DEVOE PAINT CORPORATION
2179 South 300 West, #1
Salt Lake City, UT 84115
Tel.: 801-486-2211
Fax: 801-486-2286
Approx.Sls.: $15,000,000
Emp.: 24
Fiscal Year-end: 12/31/90
Distr. of Ameritone & Devoe Paint Prods.
S.I.C.: 2851
S. Lynn Bullock *(Mgr.-Reg.)*
Bruce Moore *(Mgr.-Stores)*
Linda Hardman *(Mgr.-Reg. Admin.)*

DEVON DIRECT MARKETING & ADVERTISING, INC.
200 Berwyn Park
Berwyn, PA 19312
Tel.: 215-644-0333
Year Founded: 1983
Approx.Billings: $99,100,000
Emp.: 98
Consumer Direct Mktg. & Adv.
Ronald D. Greene *(Mng. Dir.)*
Anne Jadick *(Chief Fin. Officer)*
Ronald Goldstein *(V.P., New Acct. Devel.)*
Robert DeCurtis *(Dir. Human Resources)*
Linda Bessette *(Fulfillment Services Dir.)*
Victoria Hills *(Mktg. Services Dir.)*

DEWBERRY & DAVIS
8401 Arlington Blvd.
Fairfax, VA 22031
Tel.: 703-849-0100
Fax: 703-849-0118
Sales Range: $80-99 Million
Emp.: 1,000
Engineers, Architects & Surveyors
S.I.C.: 8711; 8712; 8713
Sidney O. Dewberry *(Mng. Partner)*
Barry K. Dewberry *(Gen. Partner)*
Allen C. Skiles *(Pres.-Tolk, Inc.)*
Glen R. Harrah *(Chief Fin. Officer)*
Carl Keisler *(Controller)*
Mark F. Davis *(Gen. Counsel)*
William H. Edwards *(Mng. Principal-Southern Branches)*
Douglas R. Fahl *(Mng. Principal-Land Design & Survey Div.)*
John P. Fowler, II *(Mng. Principal-Transportation/Structures)*
William G. Fru *(Mng. Principal-Mngmt. Engrng. & Tech. Services)*
Albert C. Gray, Ph.D *(Mng. Principal-Water Resources & Municipal Engrng.)*
David P. Habib *(Mng. Principal-Architecture)*
Robert T. Skunda *(Mng. Principal-Mktg.)*
Dan M. Pleasant *(Principal Branch Mgr.-Danville Office)*
Thomas L. Wiley *(Principal)*
Jefferson L. DeHoff *(Dir.-Mktg.)*
Alan L. Dodd *(Dir.-Human Resources)*
Troy Mitchell *(Dir.-Pur.)*
Blair Ashworth-McSpadden *(Corporate Travel & Meetings Planner)*
Cindy Taylor-Willis *(Assoc. Mgr.-Public Rels.)*
Richard Penner *(Admin.-Employee Benefits)*
Principal(s):
Thomas L. Wiley

No. of U.S. Offices: 17

Outside Service Firm(s):

First Virginia Bank*(Major Banking Relationship)*
Arlington, VA

Subsidiaries:

Goodkind & O'Dea, Inc. **(1)**
60 Feronia Way
Rutherford, NJ 07070
Tel.: 201-438-6166
Fax: 201-438-9168
Approx.Sls.: $12,000,000
Emp.: 170
Design & Inspection of Bridges, Roads, Transportation Facilities, Urban Infrastructures, Water Resources, Drainage & Flood Control; Architecture, Interior Design, Building Engineering, Land design Landscape Architecture, Surveying, Mapping, Program Management
S.I.C.: 4785; 8711; 7389; 0781; 8713; 4941; 1629
John P. Fowler, II *(Pres.)*
Glen Harrah *(Treas.)*
James Boyd *(Sec.)*

The Office of Lee Kendrick **(1)**
8401 Arlington Blvd.
Fairfax, VA 22031
Tel.: 703-849-0100
Mechanical & Electrical Engineering
S.I.C.: 8711
Allan Skiles *(Pres.)*
Bert Hobbs *(Pres.)*

DEWEESE INC.
1825 S. Hill St.
Los Angeles, CA 90015
Tel.: 213-746-0990
Fax: 213-748-4919
Approx.Sls.: $15,000,000
Emp.: 300
Fiscal Year-end: 7/31/90
Import Export
DeWeese Women's Swimwear & Beachwear
S.I.C.: 2339
John Weingarten *(Pres.)*
Mary Ann DeWeese *(Chief Exec. Officer)*
James Weingarten *(V.P.-Opers.)*
Bette Merrillees *(Controller)*
Lynn Ferris *(Dir-Adv.)*

Computer Systems/Hardware:
Hewlett Packard

DEWEY CORPORATION
5500 U.S. Hwy. 80 W.
Jackson, MS 39209
Tel.: 601-922-8331 **MS**
Fax: 601-922-9058
Year Founded: 1986
Approx.Sls.: $74,000,000
Emp.: 1,100
Common & Contract Carrier
S.I.C.: 4213
James A. Miller *(Pres.)*

Outside Service Firm(s):

Deloitte & Touche*(Auditors)*
Jackson, MS

Deposit Guaranty National Bank*(Major Banking Relationship)*
One Deposit Guaranty Plaza,
Jackson, MS 39201

Subsidiary:

Miller Transporters, Inc. **(1)**
5500 U.S. Hwy. 80 W.
Jackson, MS 39209
Tel.: 601-922-8331
Common & Contract Carrier
S.I.C.: 4213; 4231
Scott F. Miller *(Pres.)*
Richard L. Miller *(Exec. V.P., Treas. & Sec.)*
Dennis M. Miller *(V.P.)*
Harold D. Miller, Jr. *(V.P.)*

DEWITT MEDIA, INC.
460 Park Ave. South
New York, NY 10016
Tel.: 212-545-0120
Fax: 212-545-0138
Year Founded: 1984
Approx.Billings: $147,000,000
Emp.: 37
Media Consulting & Management
Gene DeWitt *(Pres.)*
Merlie Elizes *(Comptroller)*

DEXOL INDUSTRIES, INC.
1450 W. 228th
Torrance, CA 90501
Tel.: 310-326-8373
Fax: 310-325-0120
Year Founded: 1911
Approx.Sls.: $15,000,000
Emp.: 50
Mfr. of Insecticides, Fungicides, Weed Killers & Garden Tools
S.I.C.: 2879; 3423
Jane Donalson *(Pres.)*
Tom Batdorff *(V.P.-Sls.)*
John Prues *(Dir.-Mktg.)*
Bill Eastwood *(Plant Mgr.)*

DEXTER CHEMICAL CORP.
845 Edgewater Rd.
Bronx, NY 10474
Tel.: 718-542-7700 **NY**
Fax: 718-991-7684
Year Founded: 1945
Sales Range: $10-19 Million
Emp.: 75
Fiscal Year-end: 12/31/91
Export
Textile, Paper, Cosmetic & Industrial Chemicals
S.I.C.: 2816; 2819; 2865
Dr. Sidney M. Edelstein *(Chm. Bd.)*
Leo Goldberg *(Pres.)*
Leonard A. Sitver *(Exec. V.P.)*
Mark L. Goldstein *(Treas. & Sec.)*
Principal(s):
Dr. Sidney M. Edelstein

Computer Systems/Hardware:
Burroughs

Outside Service Firm(s):

Connecticut General Life Insurance Co.*(Group Insurer)*
P.O. Box 2975,
Hartford, CT 06104
Tel.: 203-726-6000

Manufacturers Hanover Trust Co.*(Major Banking Relationship)*
270 Park Ave.
New York, NY 10017
Tel.: 212-286-3229

DEXTER COMPANY
501 N. 8th St.
Fairfield, IA 52556
Tel.: 515-472-5131
Fax: 515-472-6336
Year Founded: 1912
Approx.Sls.: $30,000,000
Emp.: 365
Export
Commercial Laundry Machinery & Equipment
S.I.C.: 3582; 3321
R.J. Crockett *(Pres. & Chief Exec. Officer)*
Ray W. Hackney *(V.P.-Foundry Opers.)*
A.D. Ehret *(V.P., Sec. & Treas.)*
D.R. Fenton *(Dir.-Engrng.)*
Gary Morris *(Dir.-Data Processing)*
Tom Kunkle *(Mgr.-Indus. Rels.)*
D.L. Swan *(Pur. Agent)*

Computer Systems/Hardware:
IBM System 36 Model 5360

Outside Service Firm(s):

KPMG Peat Marwick*(Auditors)*
2500 Ruan Center
Des Moines, IA 50309
Tel.: 515-288-7465

Austin & Gaudineer*(Legal Firm)*
Des Moines, IA

Norwest Bank Minnesota, N.A.*(Major Banking Relationship)*
Des Moines, IA

DEXTER SHOE COMPANY
Railroad Ave.
Dexter, ME 04930
Tel.: 207-924-7341
Fax: 207-924-5802
Approx.Sls.: $150,000,000
Emp.: 2,500
Mfr. Dexter Shoes
S.I.C.: 3143; 3144; 3149; 3142
Harold Alfond *(Chm. Bd.)*
Keith Burden *(Chief Fin. Officer)*
Peter Lunder *(Pres., Chief Oper. Officer & Sec.)*
Gerald Hyde *(Pres.-Athletic Div.)*
Daniel Miller *(Pres.-Mktg.)*
Theodore Alfond *(Exec. V.P.)*
Susan Regan *(V.P.-Adv.)*
Richard Rubin *(V.P.-Mktg.)*

Outside Service Firm(s):

Ernest M. Shapiro & Co.*(Auditors)*
Lewiston, ME

Merrill Bank*(Major Banking Relationship)*
Bangor, ME

DI GIORGIO CORPORATION
2 Executive Dr., Ste. 400
Somerset, NJ 08873
Tel.: 908-469-4444 **DE**

Fax: 908-469-9151
Year Founded: 1920
Approx.Sls.: $1,000,000,000
Emp.: 2,900
Fiscal Year-end: 12/31/90
Food Processing & Distribution; Building Materials
S.I.C.: 2013; 2431; 3442; 5031; 5141
Arthur Goldberg *(Chm. Bd., Pres. & Chief Exec. Officer)*
Richard Neff *(Chief Fin. Officer)*
Susan Dullabh *(Cash Mgr.)*
Carrie Garitano *(Mgr.)*

Outside Service Firm(s):

Price Waterhouse*(Auditors)*
555 California
San Francisco, CA 94104
Tel.: 415-393-8500

Divisions:

Las Plumas Lumber North Division **(1)**
1245 Oro Dam Blvd.
Oroville, CA 95965
Tel.: 916-533-5313
Fax: 916-534-3815
Precut Houseframes
S.I.C.: 2452
Richard Neff *(Pres.)*

Las Plumas Lumber South Division **(1)**
6464 33rd St.
Riverside, CA 92509
Tel.: 909-681-2211
Precut Houseframes
S.I.C.: 2452
Roger T. Manwell *(Pres.)*

Subsidiary:

White Rose Corporation **(1)**
2 Frozen Food Plaza
Secaucus, NJ 07096
Tel.: 201-864-8880
Distributes Frozen Foods
S.I.C.: 5142; 5143
Jay Zdatny *(Mgr.)*

Divisions:

White Rose Dairy **(2)**
1200 Harrison
Kearny, NJ 07032
Tel.: 201-955-2100
Distributes Dairy Products
S.I.C.: 5143
Joseph Fantozzi *(V.P. & Gen. Mgr.)*

White Rose Food **(2)**
150 Price Pkwy.
Long Island City, NY 11735
Tel.: 516-293-9600
Fax: 516-293-9610
Emp.: 750
Wholesale Food Distribution: Canned & Frozen Goods, Candy, Baby Foods, Dairy & Meats
Arthur M. Goldberg *(Chm. Bd.)*
Stephen R. Bokser *(Pres. & Chief Oper. Officer)*
John Giglia *(Sr. V.P. & Treas.)*
Selma Silverman *(V.P. & Sec.)*
Lester Ratzken *(Adv. Mgr.)*

DIADORA AMERICA, INC.
21527 88th Place S.
Kent, WA 98031
Tel.: 206-395-4644
Tel.: 800-423-9958
Fax: 206-395-4931
Year Founded: 1985
Approx.Sls.: $25,000,000
Emp.: 15
Fiscal Year-end: 12/31/90
Wholesale & Import Athletic Shoes
S.I.C.: 5139
Galliano Mondin *(Chief Exec. Officer)*
Jay Piccola *(V.P.-Sls. & Mktg.)*
Anne McIntosh *(Mgr.-Adv. & Mdsg.)*

DIAGRAPH CORPORATION
3401 Rider Trail S.
Earth City, MO 63045-1110
Tel.: 314-739-1221
Tel.: 800-722-1125
Fax: 314-770-5700
Year Founded: 1893
Approx.Sls.: $50,000,000
Emp.: 440
Fiscal Year-end: 5/31/92

Export
Mfr. of Bar Coding Systems for Industry & Retail Including Electronic Label Printing Systems & Ink Jet Coding Systems. Plus a Complete Line of Marking, Coding & Shipping Room Supplies
S.I.C.: 3953
James R. Brigham, Sr. *(Chm. Bd.)*
James R. Brigham, Jr. *(Pres.)*
Daniel E. Finke *(Group V.P.-Coding & Mktg. Systems)*
Steve Mitchell *(Group V.P.-Labeling Systems)*
Sarah Brigham *(V.P.-Human Resources & Intl.)*
Dan Finke *(V.P.-Coding & Marking System)*
Ken Gardner *(V.P.-Sls.)*
Roger Hopkins *(V.P.-Engrng.)*
Christopher Kline *(V.P.-Corp. Devel.)*
Steve Mitchell *(V.P.-Labeling Systems)*
Roger Patterson *(V.P.-Fin.)*
Gene Turner *(V.P.-Mfg.)*
Barbie Brigham *(Sec.)*
John Slattery *(Controller)*
Victoria A. Holmes *(Dir.-Coding Systems)*
Susan Itter *(Dir.-Mngmt. Information Systems)*
Glenda W. O'Neill *(Dir.-Mktg.)*
Diane Commens *(Mgr.-Human Resources)*
Kevin Gold *(Mgr.-Professional Devel.)*
Tracy Evans *(Mgr.-Mktg. Services)*
Quentin Griesenauer *(Mgr.-Mktg. Communications)*
Kathy Halstead *(Mgr.-Customer Service)*
Victoria Holmes *(Mgr.-Intl. Sls.)*
Roger Harrison *(Pur. Agent)*

No. of Mfg. Plants/Facilities: 3
No. of U.S. Offices: 11
No. of Foreign Offices: 3

Computer Systems/Hardware:
IBM AS/400

Outside Service Firm(s):

Arthur Andersen & Co.*(Auditors)*
1010 Market St.
St. Louis, MO 63101

Commerce Bank of St. Louis*(Major Banking Relationship)*
Saint Louis, MO

Plant:

Diagraph Corp. **(1)**
P.O. Box 520
Herrin, IL 62949
Tel.: 618-997-3321
Mfr. of Rubber & Metal Marking Devices
S.I.C.: 3953

DIAMOND BRANDS, INC.
1800 Cloquet Ave.
Cloquet, MN 55720
Tel.: 218-879-6700
Tel.: 800-777-7942
Fax: 218-879-6700
Year Founded: 1986
Approx.Assets: $15,000,000
Emp.: 400
Fiscal Year-end: 12/31/90
Import Export
Mfr. of Matches & Bar-B-Que Starter, Tooth Picks, Ice Cream Sticks, & Corn Dog Sticks
S.I.C.: 3999; 2499; 2899
Edward A. Michael *(Pres. & Chief Exec. Officer)*
John Young *(V.P.-Sls. & Mktg.)*
Phillip J. LeBrasseur *(Controller)*

Subsidiary:

Universal Match Corp. **(1)**
3740 Florida Ave., Ste. 1
Kenner, LA 70065
Tel.: 218-878-0200
Sales & Marketing
S.I.C.: 5199
Charles Gudger *(V.P.-Sls. & Mktg.)*

DIAMOND CHEMICAL CO., INC.
Page & Schulyer
Lyndhurst, NJ 07071
Tel.: 201-935-4300
Fax: 201-935-6997
Sales Range: $10-19 Million
Emp.: 57
Dry Cleaning, Laundry & Dish Washing Soaps & Detergents
S.I.C.: 2841; 2842
Abraham L. Diamond *(Pres. & Chief Exec. Officer)*
Frederic Diamond *(Exec. V.P., Sec. & Treas.)*
Harold Diamond *(Dir.-Mktg.)*

Outside Service Firm(s):

Anthony Gagliardi*(Auditors)*
New Brunswick, NJ

National Community Bank*(Major Banking Relationship)*
Lyndhurst, NJ

T.L. DIAMOND COMPANY
30 Rockefeller Plaza
New York, NY 10112
Tel.: 212-582-0420
Fax: 212-582-3412
Approx.Sls.: $15,000,000
Emp.: 175
Export
Primary Smelting & Refining Of Nonferrous Metals
S.I.C.: 3339
Theodore L. Diamond *(Pres.)*
Allen S. Perl *(V.P.)*
Clare W. Diamond *(Sec. & Treas.)*

Subsidiaries:

Eagle Zinc Co. **(1)**
P.O. Box 340, Rural Rte. 1
Hillsboro, IL 62049
Tel.: 217-532-3971
Sharon Becker *(Pur. Agent)*

Meadowbrook Co. **(1)**
P.O. Box 184, Main St.
Spelter, WV 26438
Tel.: 304-623-2916
Fay Palmer *(Office Mgr.)*

DIAMOND CRYSTAL SPECIALTY FOODS, INC.
10 Burlington Ave.
Wilmington, MA 01887
Tel.: 508-658-3131
Fax: 508-657-7944
Approx.Sls.: $26,000,000
Emp.: 312
Fiscal Year-end: 3/31/91
Individually Packaged Condiments & Food Service Kits
S.I.C.: 2099
Ronald J. Kunkel *(Pres.)*
Ronald M. Tarantino *(V.P.-Sls.)*
Jim Ellis *(Natl. Sls. Mgr.)*
M.Y. LaBarre *(Grp. Mktg. Mgr.)*
Don Hargesheimer *(Natl. Acct. Mgr.)*
Ed Martin *(Pur. Agent)*

DIAMOND ELECTRONICS, INC.
P.O. Box 200,
Lancaster, OH 43130
Tel.: 614-756-9222
Fax: 614-756-4237
Year Founded: 1946
Approx.Sls.: $15,000,000
Emp.: 140
Fiscal Year-end: 12/31/90
Manufacturer of TV Cameras, Electronic Security, Access Control Systems, Data Acquisition and Process Monitoring Systems
S.I.C.: 3663
John Biddinger *(Chm. Bd.)*
Richard Tompkins *(Pres.)*
Richard L. Grover *(V.P.-Mktg.)*

DIAMOND MOTORS INC.
12422 Florida Blvd.
Baton Rouge, LA 70815
Tel.: 504-272-9330
Fax: 505-272-5484
Year Founded: 1965
Approx.Sls.: $18,511,890
Emp.: 62
Retail New & Used Automobiles
S.I.C.: 5511
Benny Andre *(Pres.)*
Barry Andre *(V.P.)*
Gillis Leger *(Gen. Mgr.)*
Principal(s):
Benny Andre

Outside Service Firm(s):

Guaranty Bank*(Major Banking Relationship)*
Zachary, LA

DICK CORPORATION
900 Rte. 51
Large, PA 15025
Mailing Address:
P.O. Box 10896
Pittsburgh, PA 15236
Tel.: 412-384-1000 **PA**
Fax: 412-384-1150
Approx.Sls.: $550,000,000
Emp.: 2,500
General Contractors for Construction of Industrial & Other Nonresidential Buildings
S.I.C.: 1541; 1542
Dorsey W. Dick *(Chm. Bd.)*
A.T. McLaughlin, Jr. *(Pres.)*
Douglas P. Dick *(Sr. V.P.-Sls. & Mktg.)*
David E. Dick *(Sr. V.P.)*
Stephen K. Peary *(Chief Fin. Officer)*
Roger J. Peters *(Gen. Counsel)*
Lon Susack *(Treas.)*
Leroy Trimbath *(Controller)*
G.W. Lotz *(Dir.-Bus. Devel.)*
Principal(s):
Dorsey W. Dick
Douglas P. Dick
David E. Dick

No. of Mfg. Plants/Facilities: 1
No. of U.S. Offices: 1

Computer Systems/Hardware:
IBM System 38

Outside Service Firm(s):

S. R. Snodgrass & Co.*(Auditors)*
Beaver Falls, PA

CNA Insurance*(Group Insurer)*
CNA Plaza,
Chicago, IL 60685
Tel.: 312-822-5000

Pittsburgh National Bank*(Major Banking Relationship)*
5th Ave. & Wood St.
Pittsburgh, PA 15222
Tel.: 412-355-3000

THE DICKERSON GROUP, INC.
1501 Charlotte Ave.
Monroe, NC 28111
Mailing Address:
P.O. Box 5011
Monroe, NC 28111
Tel.: 704-289-3111 **NC**
Fax: 704-282-0650
Assets: $29,800,000
Earnings: $12,000,000
Liabilities: $9,800,000
Net Worth: $20,000,000

The Dickerson Group, Inc.—(Continued)

Approx.Sls.: $75,000,000
Emp.: 600
Highway Construction & Real Estate Management, Development & Sales
S.I.C.: 1611; 6531
N.K. Dickerson III *(Chm. Bd.)*
Kenton R. Gebert *(Pres., Chief Exec. & Chief Oper. Officer)*
Ted H. Tyson *(Exec. V.P.)*
John F. Joyner *(V.P.-Fin.)*
R. Nickles *(Treas. & Sec.)*

Computer Systems/Hardware:
IBM System 36

Subsidiaries:

CTB, Inc. **(1)**
P.O. Box 5011
Monroe, NC 28111
Tel.: 704-289-3111 (100%)
Mngmt. & Rental of Real Estate & Mining Properties
S.I.C.: 6531

Dickerson Carolina, Inc. **(1)**
P.O. Box 400,
Monroe, NC 28110
Tel.: 704-289-3111 (100%)
Approx.Sls.: $22,000,000
Emp.: 75
Highway & Street Construction; Bridges & Utilities
S.I.C.: 1611
K. R. Gebert *(Pres. & Chief Oper. Officer)*

Dickerson, Inc. **(1)**
P.O. Box 400,
Monroe, NC 28110
Tel.: 704-289-3111 (100%)
Approx.Sls.: $25,000,000
Emp.: 417
S.I.C.: 1611; 1622
Ken Gebert *(Pres.)*

Dickerson Realty Corp. **(1)**
P.O. Box 400,
Monroe, NC 28110
Tel.: 704-289-3111 (100%)
Approx.Sls.: $1,200,000
Real Estate Mngmt., Devel. & Sls.
S.I.C.: 6531
K. R. Gebert *(Pres.)*

Dickerson Realty Florida, Inc. **(1)**
P.O. Box 719,
Stuart, FL 33494
Tel.: 305-287-6820 (96%)
Approx.Sls.: $360,000
S.I.C.: 6531
K. R. Gebert *(Pres.)*

South Atlantic Equipment, Inc. **(1)**
P.O. Box 5011
Monroe, NC 28111
Tel.: 704-289-3111 (100%)
Equipment Rental & Repair
S.I.C.: 7359

Affiliate:

Commercial Products, Inc. **(1)**
P.O. Box 400,
Monroe, NC 28110
Tel.: 704-289-3111
Approx.Sls.: $3,700,000
Ready-Mixed Concrete
S.I.C.: 3273
Ken Gebert *(Pres.)*

DICKINSON PRESS, INC.
5100 33rd St. S.E.
Grand Rapids, MI 49512
Tel.: 616-957-5100 MI
Fax: 616-957-1261
Year Founded: 1963
Approx.Sls.: $17,000,000
Emp.: 130
Fiscal Year-end: 12/31/91
Lithographic Offset Printing
S.I.C.: 2752
LaVerne DeWeerd *(Pres.)*
Norman DeWeerd *(V.P.-Personnel & Opers.)*
William Krombeen *(V.P.)*
Bob Worcester *(Mgr.-Sls.)*
Everett Kwizema *(Pur. Agent)*
Theodore Markus *(Asst. Treas.)*
No. of Mfg. Plants/Facilities: 1

Outside Service Firm(s):

Deloitte & Touche*(Auditors)*
Grand Rapids, MI

Varnum, Riddering, Schmidt & Howlett*(Legal Firm)*
666 Old Kent Bldg.
Grand Rapids, MI 49502
Tel.: 616-459-4186

Michigan National Bank*(Major Banking Relationship)*
77 Monroe Center
Grand Rapids, MI 49501
Tel.: 616-451-7600

DICKTEN & MASCH MANUFACTURING CO.
N44 W. 3341 Watertown Plank Rd.
Nashotah, WI 53058
Tel.: 414-367-5200 WI
Fax: 414-367-5630
Year Founded: 1941
Approx.Sls.: $24,000,000
Emp.: 260
Custom Molded Plastic Products
S.I.C.: 3089
Erich Dickten *(Chm. Bd.)*
John Owzik *(Pres.)*
Thomas P. Guenther *(Exec. V.P. & Treas.)*
A. William Asmuth, Jr. *(Sec.)*
Principal(s):
Erich Dickten

No. of Mfg. Plants/Facilities: 2
No. of U.S. Offices: 2

Computer Systems/Hardware:
IBM AS/400

Outside Service Firm(s):

Arthur Andersen & Co.*(Auditors)*
777 E. Wisconsin Ave., P.O. Box 1215
Milwaukee, WI 53202
Tel.: 414-271-5100
Fax: 414-283-3200

Bank One Milwaukee, N.A.*(Major Banking Relationship)*
111 E. Wisconsin Ave.
Milwaukee, WI
Tel.: 414-765-3000

DIDDE WEB PRESS
1200 Graphic Arts Rd.
Emporia, KS 66801
Tel.: 316-342-4740
Fax: 316-342-7383
Year Founded: 1954
Approx.Sls.: $60,000,000
Emp.: 400
Printing Equipment
S.I.C.: 3555
Carl Didde *(Chm. Bd.)*
David D. Didde *(Pres. & Chief Exec. Officer)*
William D. Vancelette *(Chief Oper. Officer & Exec. V.P.)*
Les Hassell *(Sr. V.P.)*
Keith Durall *(Sec.)*
Cecil Bollinger *(Mgr.-Mngmt. Information Systems)*
Cathy Pierson *(Mgr.-Mktg.)*
Principal(s):
Carl Didde
David D. Didde

Outside Service Firm(s):

Deloitte & Touche*(Auditors)*
1010 Grand Ave.
Kansas City, MO 64106-2232
Tel.: 816-474-6180

DIE CAST PRODUCTS, INC.
621 W. Rosecrans Ave.
Gardena, CA 90248
Tel.: 213-321-1561 CA
Fax: 213-327-6345
Year Founded: 1988
Approx.Sls.: $14,000,000
Emp.: 140
Zinc & Zinc-Base Alloy Die-Castings; Aluminum Die-Castings
S.I.C.: 3364; 3363
Gerald Plantz *(Pres.)*
Lewis McGinnis *(Chief Fin. Officer)*

Outside Service Firm(s):

Marine Midland Bank*(Major Banking Relationship)*
Long Beach, CA

DIEBEL MANUFACTURING CO.
6505 Oakton St.
Morton Grove, IL 60053
Mailing Address:
P.O. Box 549
Morton Grove, IL 60053
Tel.: 708-967-5678 DE
Fax: 708-967-0655
Year Founded: 1937
Approx.Sls.: $17,000,000
Emp.: 98
Metal Stampings, Parts Machining, Assembly-Mechanical, Tools & Dies & Contract Manufacturing
S.I.C.: 3469; 3544; 3429
Robert Diebel *(Pres.)*
Werner Gruse *(V.P.-Tooling)*
H. Harris *(V.P. & Gen. Mgr.)*
Steven B. Sandstrom *(V.P.-Fin. & Admin.)*
Eugene Bielski *(Pur. Agent)*
Bob Bates *(Mgr.-Mfg.)*
Janice Hoye *(Mgr.-Human Resources)*
Judy Seppanen *(Mgr.-Matls.)*
Principal(s):
Robert Diebel

No. of Mfg. Plants/Facilities: 1
No. of U.S. Offices: 1

Computer Systems/Hardware:
Unisys/Jobtrack

Outside Service Firm(s):

Kelly, Olson, Rogan & Siepker*(Legal Firm)*
Chicago, IL

American National Bank & Trust Company of Chicago*(Major Banking Relationship)*
33 N. LaSalle St.
Chicago, IL 60602
Tel.: 312-661-5000
Fax: 312-661-6417

DIEHL SPECIALTIES INTL.
24 N. Clinton St.
Defiance, OH 43512
Tel.: 419-782-5010
Fax: 419-784-5924
Year Founded: 1982
Approx.Sls.: $4,700,000
Emp.: 110
Fiscal Year-end: 12/31/90
Export
Mfr. of Evaporated Milk, & Coffee Creamer
S.I.C.: 2023; 2026
William A. Diehl *(Chm. Bd.)*
John P. Speiser *(Pres.)*
Peter Diehl *(V.P. & Sec.)*
Thomas Diehl *(V.P.)*
Craig M. Cox *(Treas.)*
Robert Hulbert *(Controller)*
Thomas Mekus *(Dir.-Sls. & Mktg.)*
Richard Bream *(Dir.-Quality Control)*
Joe Huff *(International Sls. Mgr.)*
Robert Switzer *(Pur. Agent)*

Outside Service Firm(s):

Nachtrab, Cousino & O'Neil*(Auditors)*
Toledo, OH

Weaner, Zimmerman, Bacon & Yoder*(Legal Firm)*
Defiance, OH

Society Bank*(Major Banking Relationship)*
Toledo, OH

Subsidiary:

Diehl, Inc. **(1)**
24 N. Clinton St.
Defiance, OH 43512
Tel.: 419-782-5010
Fax: 419-784-5924
Emp.: 115
Export
Mfr. of Wilson's Evaporated Milk; Wilson's Non-Dairy Coffee Creamer
S.I.C.: 2023
John P. Speiser *(Pres.)*
John Diehl *(V.P.)*
Thomas A. Mekus *(Mgr.-Sls. & Mktg.)*

DIELINE CORPORATION
3755 36th St. S.E.
Kentwood, MI 49512
Tel.: 616-956-0081
Fax: 616-956-0999
Year Founded: 1982
Approx.Sls.: $12,000,000
Emp.: 115
Designs & Mfrs. Chassis & Body Stamping Dies for Car Manufacturers
S.I.C.: 3465
Roger Schiefler *(Chm. & Chief Oper. Officer)*
Jay Groendyke *(Pres. & Chief Exec. Officer)*
Dennis Doyle *(V.P.-Mfg.)*
Owen Weldy *(V.P.-Sls.)*

DIEMAKERS, INC.
801 Secont St.
Monroe City, MO 63456
Mailing Address:
P.O. Box 278
Monroe City, MO 63456
Tel.: 314-735-4577 MO
Fax: 314-735-2978
Approx.Sls.: $50,000,000
Emp.: 700
Zinc, Magnesium And Aluminum Die Castings
S.I.C.: 3364; 3363; 3544
Albert E. Davis *(Pres.)*
Don L. Hays *(Chief Fin. Officer & Treas.)*
Dean W. Akerson *(V.P.-Mktg.)*
Herman Hirner *(V.P. & Magnesium Plant Mgr.)*
Howard Truesdell *(V.P. & Zinc Plant Mgr.)*
Barbara K. Broughton *(Sec.)*

Outside Service Firm(s):

Coopers & Lybrand*(Auditors)*
One Metropolitan Square
St. Louis, MO 63102
Tel.: 314-436-3200

Richard K. Jeydel*(Legal Firm)*
New York, NY

Boatmen's National Bank of St. Louis*(Major Banking Relationship)*
One Boatmen's Plaza, 800 Market St.
St. Louis, MO 63101
Tel.: 314-466-6000

DIEMOLDING CORP.
125 Rasbach St.
Canastota, NY 13032
Tel.: 315-697-2221
Fax: 315-697-8083
Year Founded: 1920
Approx.Sls.: $30,000,000
Emp.: 375
Custom Molding of Plastics & Proprietary Products for Medical & Automotive Industries
S.I.C.: 3089
Donald F. Dew *(Chm. Bd., Pres. & Chief Exec. Officer)*
B. Jarvis Dew *(Vice Chm.)*
Bruce J. Dew *(Sec.)*
Edward McManus *(Chief Fin. Officer)*
Principal(s):

Donald F. Dew
B. Jarvis Dew
Bruce J. Dew
Donald H. Dew

Computer Systems/Hardware:
Unisys A-3

Outside Service Firm(s):

Price Waterhouse*(Auditors)*
One Mony Plaza
Syracuse, NY 13202

Bond, Schoeneck & King*(Legal Firm)*
One Lincoln Center
Syracuse, NY 13202
Tel.: 315-422-0121

Norstar Bank, N.A.*(Major Banking Relationship)*
Syracuse, NY

DIERBERGS MARKETS INC.
1422 Elbridge Payne Rd.
Chesterfield, MO 63006
Mailing Address:
P.O. Box 1070
Chesterfield, MO 63006
Tel.: 314-532-8884 **MO**
Fax: 314-532-8759
Year Founded: 1854
Approx.Sls.: $300,000,000
Emp.: 3,000
Supermarkets
S.I.C.: 5411
Robert J. Dierberg *(Pres., Chief Exec. Officer & Treas.)*
F. Roger Dierberg *(V.P. & Sec.)*
Fred Martels *(Dir.-Personnel)*
John Muckerman *(Dir.-Mktg. & Adv.)*
Bob Francis *(Mgr.-Store Devel.)*

Outside Service Firm(s):

Baird, Kurtz & Dobson*(Auditors)*
St. Louis, MO

First Missouri Bank & Trust Co.*(Major Banking Relationship)*
St. Louis, MO

DIETRICH'S MILK PRODUCTS, INC.
100 McKinley Ave.
Reading, PA 19605-2117
Tel.: 215-929-5736
Fax: 215-921-5695
Approx.Sls.: $115,000,000
Emp.: 150
Fiscal Year-end: 12/31/92
Manufacturer of Industrial Food Ingredients
S.I.C.: 2021; 2022; 2023
Thomas W. Dietrich *(Pres. & Chief Exec. Officer)*
Jeffery A. Nilsson *(V.P.-Opers.)*
Kerry Dietrich *(Chief Fin. Officer & Treas.)*
Michael Barr *(Controller)*
Patricia Miller *(Dir.-Human Resources)*
Richard J. Nikola *(Dir.-Sls.)*

DIETZGEN CORPORATION
250 Wille Rd.
Des Plaines, IL 60018
Tel.: 708-635-5200
Tel.: 800-473-1270 **DE**
Fax: 708-635-5210
Year Founded: 1885
Emp.: 300
Mfr. & Sale of Drafting & Reprographic Equipment & Related Supplies
S.I.C.: 2679; 3861; 3829; 5049
W.J. Driscoll *(Chm. Bd.)*
L. Kujovich *(Pres. & Chief Exec. Officer)*
A. Gutierrez *(V.P.-Fin. & Treas.)*
T. LaQuintano *(V.P.-Sls. & Mktg.)*
R. Smith *(V.P.-Opers.)*
J.S. Micallef *(Sec.)*
C. Conlin *(Dir.-Data Processing)*
J. Curtin *(Dir.-Pur.)*
Horst Hunt *(Dir.-Research & Devel.)*
William Sullivan *(Dir.-Personnel)*
David West *(Mgr.-International)*

No. of Mfg. Plants/Facilities: 9
No. of U.S. Offices: 14

Computer Systems/Hardware:
IBM 4381

Outside Service Firm(s):

KPMG Peat Marwick*(Auditors)*
Peat Marwick Plaza, 303 E. Wacker Dr.
Chicago, IL 60601
Tel.: 312-938-1000

Marsh & McLennan*(Group Insurer)*
222 S. Riverside Plaza
Chicago, IL 60606
Tel.: 312-648-6652

First Bank of St. Paul*(Major Banking Relationship)*
St. Paul, MN

Non-U.S. Holding:

Dietzgen de Mexico S.A. de C.V. **(1)**
Belisario Dominquez No. 151-A Colonia Coyoacan,
Mexico, D.F. 04100, Mexico
Tel.: 554-6820
Sl. & Distr. of Drafting Equip.
S.I.C.: 5049

DIFCO, INC.
1501 N. Main St.
Findlay, OH 45840
Mailing Address:
P.O. Box 238
Findlay, OH 45840
Tel.: 419-422-0525
Fax: 419-422-1275
Approx.Sls.: $10,000,000
Emp.: 100
Air Dump & Mine Cars; Rotary Car Dumpers
S.I.C.: 3532
D.F. Flowers *(Chm. Bd.)*
Wayne S. Westlake *(Pres.)*
John Murray *(V.P.-Engrng.)*
R.J. Ward *(V.P. & Sls. Mgr.)*
Tom Baker *(Dir.-Mfg.)*

Computer Systems/Hardware:
IBM

DIFEO AUTOMOTIVE NETWORK
947 Communipaw Ave.
Jersey City, NJ 07304
Tel.: 201-451-3111
Fax: 201-451-4885
Approx.Sls.: $448,000,000
Emp.: 950
Retail New & Used Automobiles
S.I.C.: 5511
Samuel X. DiFeo *(Pres.)*
Joseph C. DiFeo *(Sec.)*
Joseph J. Mitolo *(Comptroller)*

Outside Service Firm(s):

Joseph J. Mitolo*(Auditors)*
Jersey City, NJ

Trust Company Bank*(Major Banking Relationship)*
201 Newark Ave.
Jersey City, NJ 07302

J.D. DIFFENBAUGH, INC.
2375 Chicago Ave.
Riverside, CA 92507
Tel.: 909-684-2820
Fax: 909-684-3604
Approx.Sls.: $20,000,000
Emp.: 100
Commercial Construction Contractors
S.I.C.: 1542
Marvin J. Hawkins, Sr. *(Chm. Bd. & Pres.)*
D. Flanigan *(Exec. V.P. & Treas.)*
Vernon R. Orr *(V.P., Sec. & Controller)*
Principal(s):
Marvin J. Hawkins, Sr.

Outside Service Firm(s):

BR Sharp*(Auditors)*
Riverside, CA

Reid & Hellyer*(Legal Firm)*
Riverside, CA

Security Pacific National Bank*(Major Banking Relationship)*
Riverside, CA

DIGITAL ELECTRONIC AUTOMATION
37000 Plymouth Rd.
Livonia, MI 48150
Tel.: 313-591-3800
Fax: 313-591-3850
Approx.Sls.: $30,000,000
Emp.: 100
Import Export
Manufactures CMMS
S.I.C.: 3823
Keith Mills *(Pres.)*
Maurizo Parigi *(V.P.)*
Terrance K. Jolly *(Sec.)*
Otto Geiserman *(Dir.-Mktg. & Mgr.-Reg. Sls.)*
William Sumerton *(Dir.-Fin.)*

DIGITAL PATHWAYS INC.
201 Ravendale Drive
Mountain View, CA 94043
Tel.: 415-964-0707
Fax: 415-961-7487
Year Founded: 1970
Approx.Sls.: $10,000,000
Emp.: 80
Fiscal Year-end: 4/30/92
Export
Communication Security Products
S.I.C.: 3669
Mel Schwartz *(Chm. Bd.)*
Chuck Erickson *(Pres. & Chief Exec. Officer)*
Ainslie Mayberry *(Chief Fin. Officer)*
Len Birkwood *(Exec. V.P.)*
Dan Samuels *(V.P.-Chief Scientist)*
Bruce Johnson *(Dir.-Sls., Western Region)*
Dan Permenter *(Dir.-Sls., Eastern Region)*
David Rodgers *(Mgr.-Mktg.)*

DIGITRON TOOL CO., INC.
8641 Washington Church Rd.
Miamisburg, OH 45342
Tel.: 513-435-5710 **OH**
Fax: 513-435-3464
Year Founded: 1971
Approx.Sls.: $39,000,000
Emp.: 550
Motor Vehicle Parts & Accessories; Aircraft Parts & Equipment; Special Dies & Tools; Jig & Fixtures
S.I.C.: 3714; 3728; 3544
Nestor Fernandez *(Pres. & Chief Exec. Officer)*
Bob Folkerth *(Chief Fin. Officer)*
Nancy Fernandez *(Treas.)*
Anita Adams *(Dir.-Human Resources)*
Ray Wolfe *(Mgr.-Mktg.)*

Outside Service Firm(s):

Ernst & Young*(Auditors)*
2300 Kettering Tower
Dayton, OH 45423
Tel.: 513-223-2000

Bank One*(Major Banking Relationship)*
Kettering Tower
Dayton, OH 45401
Tel.: 513-449-8600

DILLINGHAM CONSTRUCTION CORPORATION
5960 Inglewood Dr.
Pleasanton, CA 94588-8535
Mailing Address:
P.O. Box 1089,
Pleasanton, CA 94566
Tel.: 510-463-3300 **NV**
Telex: 6771209 DHMC UW
Fax: 510-463-1571
Year Founded: 1902
Assets: $213,900,000
Liabilities: $173,700,000
Net Worth: $40,200,000
Approx.Rev.: $770,000,000
Emp.: 1,050
Fiscal Year-end: 10/31/91
General Contractors Active In Commercial, Industrial, Heavy And Maritime Construction Disciplines With Design-Build And Construction Management Capabilities
S.I.C.: 1771; 1522; 1541; 1542; 1611; 1622; 1623; 1629
Donald K. Stager *(Chm. Bd., Pres. & Chief Exec. Officer)*
Larry L. Magelitz *(V.P.-Fin.)*
Dennis P. Haist *(V.P., Gen. Counsel & Sec.)*
Julien R. Hansen *(V.P.-Human Resources)*
Peter C. Freeman *(Treas.)*
Paul Y. Nakama *(Controller)*
Lenore J. Thielen *(Mgr.-Mktg. & Pub. Rels.)*
James L. Todt *(Mgr.-Mngmt. Info. Services)*
Bonnie Husted *(Meetings Planner)*
Lois Guinlivan *(Dir.-Pension Admin.)*

No. of Mfg. Plants/Facilities: 36
No. of U.S. Offices: 5
No. of Foreign Offices: 6

Computer Systems/Hardware:
DEC VAX; IBM PC; Wang-OIS; Apple Macintosh Plus

Outside Service Firm(s):

Arthur Andersen & Co.*(Auditors)*
Spear Street Tower, One Market Plaza, Ste. 3500
San Francisco, CA 94105
Tel.: 415-546-8200

Fireman's Fund Insurance Co.*(Commercial Insurance Carrier)*
Novato, CA

Metropolitan Life Insurance Co.*(Group Insurer)*
One Madison Ave.
New York, NY 10010-3690
Tel.: 215-578-9292

Thelen, Marrin, Johnson & Bridges*(Legal Firm)*
Two Embarcadero Center
San Francisco, CA 94111
Tel.: 415-392-6320

Thelen, Marrin, Johnson & Bridges*(Legal Firm)*
Oakland, CA

Thelen, Marrin, Johnson & Bridges*(Legal Firm)*
333 S. Grand Ave., 34th Fl.
Los Angeles, CA 90071
Tel.: 213-621-9800
Fax: 213-623-4742

Delaware Investment Advisors*(Pension Manager)*
One Commerce Square
Philadelphia, PA 19103

Lehman Capital Management*(Pension Manager)*
55 Water St., 34th Fl.
New York, NY 10041
Tel.: 212-668-5447

Dillingham Construction Corporation—(Continued)

Subsidiaries:

Dillingham Construction N.A., Inc. **(1)**
P.O. Box 1089, 5960 Inglewood Dr.
Pleasanton, CA 94588
Tel.: 510-463-3300 (100%)
Fax: 510-463-1571
Emp.: 227
Commercial, Industrial, Heavy & Maritime Construction Srvcs.
S.I.C.: 1741; 1522; 1541; 1542; 1611; 1622; 1623; 1629; 3272; 3498; 3499; 1742; 1793; 1796; 1799; 3271; 3273; 3299; 3494; 1442
John M. Jacobs *(Pres. & Chief Exec. Officer)*

Divisions:

Basalt Precast Division **(2)**
2301 Napa Vallejo Hwy., P.O. Box 2490
Napa, CA 94558
Tel.: 707-257-7111 (100%)
Emp.: 23
Precast Concrete Products
S.I.C.: 3272
Walter J. Sweetman *(Pres.)*

Dillingham Construction N.A., Inc. **(2)**
135 West Victoria St.
Long Beach, CA 90805
Tel.: 310-603-9633 (100%)
Emp.: 30
Commercial Construction
S.I.C.: 1522; 1542
R.L. Johnson *(V.P.)*

Dillingham Construction International, Inc. **(1)**
5960 Inglewood Dr.
Pleasanton, CA 94588-8535
Tel.: 510-463-3300 (100%)
Fax: 510-463-0559
Emp.: 40
General Contractors Active in Commercial, Industrial, Heavy & Maritime Contstruction with Design-Build & Construction Mngmt. Capabilities
S.I.C.: 1622; 1541; 1542; 1611; 1623; 1629; 1741; 1522
Michael MacGregor *(Pres.)*

Dillingham Construction Pacific, Ltd. **(1)**
614 Kapahulu Ave.
Honolulu, HI 96812
Tel.: 808-735-3211 (100%)
Fax: 808-735-7416
Emp.: 405
General Contractors Active in Commercial, Industrial, Heavy and Maritime Construction Disciplines with Design/Build and Construction Managmeent Capabilities
S.I.C.: 1442; 1521; 1522; 1541; 1542; 1611; 1622; 1623; 1629; 8711
James R. Perry *(Pres. & Chief Exec. Officer)*

Subsidiaries:

Hawaiian Bitumuls & Paving Company **(2)**
P.O. Box 2240, 110 Puuhole St.
Honolulu, HI 96804
Tel.: 808-845-3391
Emp.: 37
Paving, Concrete & Rock Products Contractor
S.I.C.: 1442; 1611; 1771; 1799; 3271; 3273
William J. Wilson *(Pres.)*

Hawaiian Dredging & Construction Company **(2)**
614 Kapahulu Ave.
Honolulu, HI 96812
Tel.: 808-735-3211
Emp.: 361
General Contractors Active in Commercial, Industrial, Heavy and Maritime Construction Disciplines with Design/Build and Construction Management Capabilities
S.I.C.: 1521; 1522; 1541; 1542; 1611; 1622; 1623; 1629; 1442; 1796; 8711
James R. Perry *(Pres. & Chief Exec. Officer)*

Unconsolidated Holding:

Watkins Engineers & Constructors, Inc. **(1)**
P.O. Box 2194, 1238 Airport Ave.
Tallahassee, FL 32316
Tel.: 904-576-7181
Emp.: 65
Comml. & Industrial Construction
S.I.C.: 1521; 1522; 1541; 1542; 8711
Donald E. Sundgren *(Pres.)*

Non-U.S. Holding:

Dillingham Construction (H.K.) Limited **(1)**
Easey Commercial Bldg., Room 1803-1805
253-261 Hennessy Rd.,
Wanchai, Hong Kong
Tel.: 832-5816
Fax: 834-3521
Commercial , Industrial & Heavy Construction
S.I.C.: 1522; 1541; 1542; 1611; 1622; 1623; 1629
M.T. Slayton *(Mng. Dir.)*

DIMAC CORPORATION
One Corporate Woods Dr.
Bridgeton, MO 63044-3838
Tel.: 314-344-8000
Fax: 314-344-8099
Approx.Sls.: $139,000,000
Emp.: 600
Fiscal Year-end: 12/31/91
Holding Company For Direct Marketing Agencies
S.I.C.: 6719; 7311
Carl Thoma *(Chm. Bd.)*
Michael T. McSweene *(Pres. & Chief Exec. Officer)*
T.G. Beffa *(V.P. & Chief Fin. Officer)*
Wm. K. Myers *(V.P.-Mktg.)*
F.G. Kerr *(V.P.-Opers.)*
M.Z. Sincoff *(V.P.-Human Resources)*

Outside Service Firm(s):

Ernst & Young*(Auditors)*
701 Market St.
St. Louis, MO 63101
Tel.: 314-259-1000

Bryan, Cave, McPheeters & McRoberts*(Legal Firm)*
One Metropolitan Sq.
St. Louis, MO 63102
Tel.: 314-259-2000

Boatmen's Bank of St. Louis*(Major Banking Relationship)*
1 Boatmen's Plaza
St. Louis, MO

Subsidiaries:

DIMAC DIRECT **(1)**
One Corporate Woods Dr.
Bridgeton, MO 63044-3838
Tel.: 314-344-8000
Fax: 314-344-8099
Approx.Billings: $139,000,000
Emp.: 600
Fiscal Year-end: 12/31/88
Computer Systems/Hardware:
IBM
Direct Mail Advertising
S.I.C.: 7331
Michael T. McSweeney *(Pres. & Chief Exec. Officer)*
William K. Myers *(Sr. V.P., Mktg.)*
Timothy G. Beffa *(Sr. V.P., Fin., Chief Fin. Officer)*
F. Gene Kerr *(Sr. V.P., Opers.)*
Michael Z. Sincoff *(Sr. V.P., Human Resources)*
Gary Vest *(V.P., Tech. Services)*
Alex Crohn *(V.P., Bus. Devel.)*
Betty Sphar *(V.P., Research, Media & Database Plng.)*
Earl Malin *(Dir., Total Quality Mngmt.)*

Dimac Direct **(1)**
1400 Evans Ave.
San Francisco, CA 94124-0527
Tel.: 415-550-3301
Fax: 415-550-3391
Emp.: 125
Paul Sekins *(Gen Mgr., Opers.)*
Dick Silviera *(Dir., Comml. Sls.)*
Diane Broch *(Dir., Retail Sls.)*

Branch:

Dimac Direct **(2)**
690 Canton St.
Westwood, MA 02090-2322
Tel.: 617-329-8100
Fax: 617-329-3326
Emp.: 15
Francis Cesare *(V.P., Gen. Mgr.)*

DIMAC DIRECT **(1)**
1236 Wellesley Ave. #4
Los Angeles, CA 90025
Tel.: 310-207-0792
Fax: 310-820-9400
Marshall Richman *(Reg. Acct. Mgr.)*

DIMAC DIRECT **(1)**
2632 East Ave, Q-14
Palmdale, CA 93550
Tel.: 805-273-4991
Fax: 805-273-4804
Tammy Crownover *(Acct. Supervisor)*

DIMCO-GRAY COMPANY
8200 S. Suburban Rd.
Dayton, OH 45458
Tel.: 513-433-7600
Fax: 513-433-0520
Year Founded: 1944
Approx.Sls.: $10,000,000
Emp.: 150
Fiscal Year-end: 10/31/90
Export
Electric Timing Devices, Molded Plastic Knobs & Handles, Snap Slide Fasteners
S.I.C.: 3625; 3089; 3429
Norm Brennan *(Chm. Bd.)*
N. Brennan *(Chief Exec. Officer)*
Norman Brennan *(Pres.)*
T. Horton *(Gen. Counsel)*
V. Fushimi *(Sec.)*
A. Raybon *(Personnel Dir.)*
H. McCarty *(Dir.-Data Processing)*
H. Helgeson *(Dir.-Quality Control)*
Vincent Ferraro *(Pur. Dir.)*
James L. Harl *(Sls. & Mktg. Mgr.)*

Computer Systems/Hardware:
IBM 400

DIMEO CONSTRUCTION COMPANY
75 Chapman St.
Providence, RI 02905
Tel.: 401-781-9800
Fax: 401-461-4586
Year Founded: 1931
Sales Range: $100-499 Million
Emp.: 175
General Contractor & Construction Manager
S.I.C.: 1542; 1711
Thomas P. Dimeo *(Chm. Bd.)*
Harry C. Van Matre *(Pres.)*
John A. Coxall *(V.P.-Pur.)*
Stephen F. Rutledge *(V.P.-Opers.)*
Linda S. Stubbs *(V.P.-Admin. & Human Resources)*
John V. Gibbons, III *(Controller)*
Principal(s):
Thomas P. Dimeo

No. of U.S. Offices: 3

Outside Service Firm(s):

Ernst & Young*(Auditors)*
One Old Stone Square
Providence, RI 02903
Tel.: 401-331-7000

Hinkley, Allen, Snyder & Comen*(Legal Firm)*
1500 Fleet Ctr.
Providence, RI 02903
Tel.: 401-274-2000

Fleet National Bank*(Major Banking Relationship)*
125 Dupont Dr.
Providence, RI 02907-3178
Tel.: 401-278-5335

DINAIRE CORP.
145 Gruner Rd.
Buffalo, NY 14227
Tel.: 716-894-1201 **NY**
Year Founded: 1946
Approx.Sls.: $20,000,000
Emp.: 300
Export
Manufacture Solid Oak & Hardwood Chairs, Dinettes & Junior Dining Room Furniture
S.I.C.: 2511
Carmelo Gugino, Jr. *(Pres. & Treas.)*
Elizabeth W. Gugino *(V.P.)*
John S. Waliszewski *(V.P.-Fin.)*
Donald J. Holzman *(Sec. & Gen. Counsel)*
Principal(s):
Carmelo Gugino, Jr.

No. of Mfg. Plants/Facilities: 2
No. of U.S. Offices: 1

Computer Systems/Hardware:
Rexxon

Outside Service Firm(s):

Schunk & Wilson*(Auditors)*
Buffalo, NY

Duke, Holzman, Yaeger & Radlin*(Legal Firm)*
Buffalo, NY

Fleet Bank*(Major Banking Relationship)*
Deer Park, NY 14202

DINE OUT ADVERTISING CORP.
(House Agency)
2000 Las Vegas Blvd. South
Las Vegas, NV 89104
Tel.: 702-382-2000
Fax: 702-383-0664
Year Founded: 1977
Approx.Billings: $21,134,000
Emp.: 15
Direct Response
Bob Stupak *(Pres. & New Bus. Contact)*
Jerry Mansel *(Fin. Mgr.)*

DINWIDDIE CONSTRUCTION CO.
275 Battery St. #300
San Francisco, CA 94111
Tel.: 415-986-2718
Approx.Sls.: $275,000,000
Emp.: 150
Fiscal Year-end: 6/30/90
General Building Contractors
S.I.C.: 1542
Don Dreusike *(Pres. & Chief Exec. Officer)*
David Lee *(V.P., Treas., Sec. & Controller)*
Mark Liew *(Dir.-Mngmt. Information Systems)*

Computer Systems/Hardware:
IBM System 36

Outside Service Firm(s):

KPMG Peat Marwick*(Auditors)*
3 Embarcadero Center
San Francisco, CA 94111
Tel.: 415-951-0100
Fax: 415-397-1129

Equitable Life*(Group Insurer)*
1221 Ave. of the Americas
New York, NY 10022
Tel.: 212-382-8038
Fax: 212-382-8089

Morrison & Foerster*(Legal Firm)*
345 California St.
San Francisco, CA 94104
Tel.: 415-677-7000

Bank of America, N.T. & S.A.*(Major Banking Relationship)*
P.O. Box 37002,
San Francisco, CA 94137

Wells Fargo Bank*(Major Banking Relationship)*
420 Montgomery St.
San Francisco, CA 94104

Wells Fargo Bank*(Pension Manager)*
420 Montgomery St.
San Francisco, CA 94104

DIRECT COMMUNICATIONS CORPORATION
45 Kraft Ave.
Bronxville, NY 10708
Tel.: 914-237-7931
Fax: 914-237-7618
Year Founded: 1987
Approx.Billings: $44,610,000
Emp.: 33
Toys, Dolls, Games, Sporting Goods & Electronics
Richard Blank *(Chm. Bd. & Pres.)*
Pamela Daniels *(Sec. & Production Dir.)*
Roslyn Shaw *(Treas.)*

THE DIRECT MARKETING GROUP INC.
757 Third Ave., Third Fl.
New York, NY 10017
Tel.: 212-355-2530 **NY**
Fax: 212-355-5022
Year Founded: 1970
Approx.Billings: $150,000,000
Emp.: 450
Direct Mail & Direct Response Advertising
S.I.C.: 7311
John A. De Pasquale *(Chm. Bd.)*
Dennis Veccia *(Sr. V.P., Fin.)*
William Forlenza *(Sr. V.P., Bus. Devel.)*
Burton Rubin *(Gen. Counsel)*
William Marano *(Pres.-Computer & Lettershop Divs.)*
Ellen Sanger *(Pres.-Telemarketing Div.)*
Robert Lubcker *(Gen. Mgr.-Fulfillment Div.)*
Aileen Neill *(Gen. Mgr.-List Div.)*
Charles Lindberg *(Dir.-Personnel)*

No. of Mfg. Plants/Facilities: 1
No. of U.S. Offices: 3
No. of Foreign Offices: 5

Computer Systems/Hardware:
IBM 4341 Group II Equivalent

Outside Service Firm(s):

Leslie Sufrin*(Auditors)*
New York, NY

Utica Mutual Insurance*(Commercial Insurance Carrier)*
Utica, NY

Prudential Insurance Co. of America*(Group Insurer)*
751 Broad St.
Newark, NJ 07102-3777
Tel.: 201-802-6000

Morgan Guaranty Trust Company of New York*(Investment Banker)*
23 Wall St.
New York, NY 10015
Tel.: 212-483-2323

Citibank N.A.*(Major Banking Relationship)*
Corporate Trust Services, 399 Park Ave.
New York, NY 10043
Tel.: 212-559-1605

Leslie Sufrin*(Pension Manager)*
New York, NY

Subsidiaries:

Creative Technical Services **(1)**
40 Daniel St.
Farmingdale, NY 11735
Tel.: 516-752-9500
Emp.: 350
Direct Mail Production Services
S.I.C.: 7331
William Marano *(Chief Oper. Officer)*

Response Communications, Inc. **(1)**
933 Western Dr.
Indianapolis, IN 46241
Tel.: 317-244-7600
Emp.: 400
Telemarketing
S.I.C.: 7389
George Bradbury *(Chief Exec. Officer)*

DIRECT PRESS MODERN LITHO CORPORATION
386 Oakwood Rd.
Huntington Station, NY 11746
Tel.: 516-271-7000
Fax: 516-271-7008
Year Founded: 1917
Approx.Sls.: $28,000,000
Emp.: 320
Commercial Lithographers
S.I.C.: 2752
Pierre Humbert *(Pres.)*
Jose Humbert *(Sec. & Treas.)*

Outside Service Firm(s):

Chase Manhattan Bank, N.A.*(Major Banking Relationship)*
One Chase Manhattan Plaza
New York, NY 10081
Tel.: 212-552-2222
Tel.: 800-526-0801
Fax: 212-552-7175

Meyer, Suozzi, English & Klein*(Legal Firm)*
Long Island, NY

DIRECT RESPONSE BROADCASTING NETWORK

DIRECT RESPONSE BROADCASTING NETWORK, INC.
1101 Market St., Ste. 1300
Philadelphia, PA 19107
Tel.: 215-925-8585
Fax: 215-925-8562
Year Founded: 1972
Approx.Billings: $25,000,000
Emp.: 25
Direct Response Broadcasting
Larry Magill *(Pres.)*
Brad R. Magill *(Exec. V.P. & Chief Oper. Officer)*
Michael Spena *(Opers. Mgr.)*
Frank Corso *(Controller)*
Kimberly Cusick *(Office Mgr.)*

DIRECTORY DISTRIBUTING ASSOCIATES, INC.
4363 Woodson Rd.
Saint Louis, MO 63134
Mailing Address:
P.O. Box 10066
St. Louis, MO 63145
Tel.: 314-427-2800 **MO**
Fax: 314-427-2044
Year Founded: 1947
Approx.Sls.: $49,000,000
Emp.: 2,500
Fiscal Year-end: 6/30/92
Export
Distributor of Telephone Directories & Catalogs
S.I.C.: 7389
John W. Runk *(Chm. Bd. & Pres.)*
Gary Grimes *(V.P.-Opers., Southwestern Bell)*
Michael Shelton *(V.P. & Treas.)*
Stan Snori *(V.P.-Opers., Bell South Region)*
Judith Runk *(Sec.)*
John Richardson *(Dir.-Personnel)*
Robert Fischer *(Mgr.-Data Processing)*

Principal(s):
John W. Runk

No. of U.S. Offices: 35
No. of Foreign Offices: 1

Computer Systems/Hardware:
Unisys A6NS

Outside Service Firm(s):

Grace & Co.*(Auditors)*
St. Louis, MO

Concannon/Mitchell Corp.*(Commercial Insurance Carrier)*
St. Louis, MO

DBL Benefits*(Group Insurer)*
St. Louis, MO

Barry & Bresnahan*(Legal Firm)*
St. Louis, MO

United Missouri Bank*(Major Banking Relationship)*
Ferguson, MO

United Missouri Bank*(Major Banking Relationship)*
Saint Louis, MO

Subsidiary:

Directory Distributing Associates, Inc. **(1)**
1800 Ellesmere Ave.
Scarborough, ON M1H 2V5, Canada
Tel.: 419-438-6333 (100%)
Directory Distribution
S.I.C.: 7389

DISCOUNT DRUG MART INC.
211 Commerce Dr.
Medina, OH 44256
Tel.: 216-725-2340 **OH**
Fax: 216-722-2990
Year Founded: 1969
Approx.Sls.: $87,000,000
Emp.: 2,000
Retail Drugstore Chain
S.I.C.: 5912
Parviz Boodjeh *(Pres. & Chief Exec. Officer)*
David Boodjeh *(V.P.-Mktg.)*
Tom McConnell *(V.P.-Fin.)*
John Wright *(V.P. & Opers. Mgr.)*

Outside Service Firm(s):

Arthur Andersen & Co.*(Auditors)*
1717 E. 9th St.
Cleveland, OH 44114
Tel.: 216-781-2140
Fax: 216-781-3683

Society National Bank*(Major Banking Relationship)*
900 Euclid Ave., P.O. Box 6477
Cleveland, OH 44101-6477
Tel.: 216-737-5000
Fax: 216-566-8947

Discount Tire Co.
(See Reinalt-Thomas Corp. Listing)

THE DISPATCH PRINTING COMPANY
34 S. Third St.
Columbus, OH 43216-1289
Tel.: 614-461-5211
Telecopier: 614-461-5210
Year Founded: 1871
Emp.: 1,300
Fiscal Year-end: 12/31/90
Import
Publishers of The Columbus Dispatch
S.I.C.: 2711
John W. Wolfe *(Chm. Bd.)*
John F. Wolfe *(Pres., Chief Exec. Officer & Publisher)*
Richard M. Franks *(Exec. V.P. & Gen. Mgr.)*
A. Kenneth Pierce, Jr. *(V.P. & Chief Fin. Officer)*
Thomas B. Sherrill *(V.P.-Mktg.)*
John A. Witzel *(Controller)*
Floyd V. Jones *(Dir.-Employee & Labor Rels.)*
Robert L. Tucker *(Dir.-Production)*
Ronald J. Trubisky *(Dir.-Indus.& Plng.)*
Gary D. Merrell *(Dir.-Adv.)*
Richard M. Franks *(Exec. V.P. & Gen. Mgr.)*
Mark Barebo *(Mgr.-Retail Adv.)*
Bill Goddard *(Mgr.-Classified Adv.)*
Gary Scott *(Mgr.-Pur.)*
Leonard A. Zane *(Mgr.-Natl. Adv.)*
Robert B. Smith *(Editor)*

No. of Mfg. Plants/Facilities: 2

Computer Systems/Hardware:
IBM XT; Digital

Outside Service Firm(s):

KPMG Peat Marwick*(Auditors)*
Two Nationwide Plaza
Columbus, OH 43215
Tel.: 614-249-2300

Insurance Ohio*(Commercial Insurance Carrier)*
Columbus, OH

Insurance Ohio*(Group Insurer)*
Columbus, OH

Jones, Day, Reavis & Pogue*(Legal Firm)*
901 Lakeside Ave.
Cleveland, OH 44114
Tel.: 216-586-3939
Fax: 216-579-0212

Seyfarth, Shaw, Fairweather & Geraldson*(Legal Firm)*
520 Madison Ave.
New York, NY 10022
Tel.: 212-715-9000

BancOhio National Bank*(Major Banking Relationship)*
Columbus, OH

BancOhio National Bank*(Pension Manager)*
Columbus, OH

Subsidiary:

Dispatch Consumer Services **(1)**
7801 N. Central, P.O. Box 206
Westerville, OH 43081
Tel.: 614-548-5555
Emp.: 70
Comml. Printing
S.I.C.: 2741
Richard M. Franks *(Chm. Bd. & Pres.)*

DISPLAY TECHNOLOGIES, INC.
1355 Holmes Rd.
Elgin, IL 60123
Tel.: 708-931-2100
Tel.: 800-544-8823
Fax: 708-931-2120
Approx.Sls.: $54,000,000
Emp.: 250
Manufacture, Repair & Maintain CRT Equipment
S.I.C.: 3577; 7378
Thomas Corcoran *(Chm. Bd.)*
John D. Watson *(Pres. & Chief Exec. Officer)*
Bonnie Penera *(Exec. Sec.)*
Daniel Czuba *(Sec.)*

THE DISSTON CO.
7345 G. West Friendly Ave.
Greensboro, NC 27410
Tel.: 919-852-9220

The Disston Co.—(Continued)

Fax: 919-299-0616
Year Founded: 1840
Approx.Sls.: $50,000,000
Emp.: 300
Import Export
Power Tool Accessories; Lawn & Garden Products; Hand Cutting Tools; Chain Saw Accessories; Tool Boxes
S.I.C.: 3546; 3469; 3524; 3425; 3423
Henry G. Libby *(Chm. Bd. & Pres.)*
Mike Field *(V.P.-Sls.)*
Rebecca J. Smith *(V.P.-Mktg.)*
Pam Hundley *(Controller)*
Terry Haraway *(Dir.-Human Resources)*

Outside Service Firm(s):

Arthur Andersen & Co.*(Auditors)*
One Southern Life Center
Greensboro, NC 27401
Fax: 919-378-1445

Meade, Tate & Daniel*(Legal Firm)*
Danville, VA

Smith, Helms, Mullis & Moore*(Legal Firm)*
227 North Tryon St.
Charlotte, NC 28231

NationsBank Carolinas*(Major Banking Relationship)*
Greensboro, NC

DISTRIBUTION AMERICA
2700 River Rd.
Des Plaines, IL 60018
Tel.: 708-699-2323
Fax: 708-699-7098
Approx.Sls.: $650,000,000
Emp.: 3,200
Hardware Merchandising Group; Sentry, Minuteman, Val-U-Line Hardware & Houseware Items; 38 Distributors
S.I.C.: 5251
John Mize *(Chm. Bd.)*
Ronald A. Pink *(Pres.)*
Ronald L. Draghi *(Chief Fin. Officer & V.P.-Fin. & MIS)*
Curtis Burdick *(V.P.-Sls. & Sls. Promo)*
Rob Liebgott *(V.P.-Mdse., Adv. & Lumber Bldg. Matls.)*
Robert E. Guido *(Dir.-Natl. Acct. Sls.)*
Gregory J. Hauche *(Dir.-Retail Service)*
Greg Thomas *(Dir.-Mktg.)*
Paul Michalowski *(Dir.-Mdse. & Mktg.)*
Wayne Wiggleton *(Dir.-Lumber Bldg. Matls.)*
Carol Jones *(Dir.-Adv.)*
Ruth N. McDermott *(Mgr.-Personnel & Communications)*
Tom Fromelt *(Program Mgr.-Trustworthy Stores)*

Affiliates:

Baker-Hamilton **(1)**
721 Eubanks Dr.
Vacaville, CA 95688
Tel.: 707-447-3812

Blish-Mize Co. **(1)**
223 So. 5th St.
Atchison, KS 66002
Tel.: 913-367-1250
John Mize, Jr. *(Pres. & Chief Exec. Officer)*

California Hardware Co. **(1)**
13085 East Temple
City of Industry, CA 91746
Tel.: 818-369-9411
T.L. Smith *(Pres.)*

General Hardware Co.-Div. Hdqtrs. **(1)**
217 Luckie St.
Atlanta, GA 30301
Tel.: 404-521-2010
Jerry Barton *(Pres.)*

General Hardware Co.-Atlanta **(1)**
217 Luckie St.
Atlanta, GA 30301
Tel.: 404-521-2010
Gary Mattson *(Pres.)*

General Hardware Co.-Greensboro **(1)**
1010 Scott Ave.
Greensboro, NC 27403
Tel.: 919-299-9121
M.D. Stout, III *(Pres.)*

General Hardware Co.-Jacksonville **(1)**
3031 Westside Blvd.
Jacksonville, FL 32209
Tel.: 904-768-3421
Richard Paige *(Pres.)*

General Hardware Co.-St. Petersburg **(1)**
4650 Ulmerton Rd.
Clearwater, FL 34622
Tel.: 813-577-2345
William E. Siviter *(Pres.)*

Hall & Knight Hardware Co. **(1)**
20 Chapel St.
Lewiston, ME 04240
Tel.: 207-784-5721
Fred Hall *(V.P.)*

Henderson & Baird Hardware Co., Inc. **(1)**
1100 Sycamore St
Greenwood, MS 38930
Tel.: 601-453-3221
Harry Carter *(Pres.)*

Masback Hardware Co. **(1)**
2400 83rd St.
North Bergen, NJ 07047
Tel.: 201-861-2900
E.R. Masback, Jr. *(Pres.)*

S & T Wholesale Hardware, Inc. **(1)**
3230 Industrial Pkwy.
Jeffersonville, IN 47130
Tel.: 812-283-6661
Charles Redmon *(Pres.)*

South States Inc. **(1)**
P.O. Box 3945, Woolworth Rd.
Shreveport, LA 71133
Tel.: 318-686-8527
Approx.Sls.: $23,000,000
Emp.: 115
Distributor of Hardware, Electrial, Plumbing Fittings & Industrial Supplies
S.I.C.: 5072; 5063; 5074; 5085
Louie R. Davis *(Chm. Bd.)*
Keeney Beauvis *(V.P.)*
Bill Burgin *(V.P.-Opers.)*
Edna R. Davis *(Sec. & Treas.)*

West Texas Wholesale Supply Co. **(1)**
4th & Plum
Abilene, TX 79604
Tel.: 915-677-2851
Marshal M. Kellar *(Pres.)*

Witte Hardware Corp. **(1)**
4600 Goodfellow
Saint Louis, MO 63120
Tel.: 314-381-1900
Neil Margolis *(Pres.)*

Wright & Wilhelmy Co. **(1)**
10th & Jackson St.
Omaha, NE 68102
Tel.: 402-341-1362
Warren R. Daasch *(Pres.)*

DISTRIBUTORS OIL COMPANY, INC.
4085 Florida Blvd.
Baton Rouge, LA 70806
Tel.: 504-344-3314
Fax: 504-338-9714
Year Founded: 1959
Approx.Sls.: $32,000,000
Emp.: 24
Wholesale Distribution of Gasoline, Lubricating Oils & Greases
S.I.C.: 5172
Winslow J. Chadwick *(Chm. Bd.)*
Bobby A. Lax *(Pres. & Gen. Mgr.)*
Hamilton J. Chauvin *(Sec.)*
Eugene Sanchez *(Treas.)*

Outside Service Firm(s):

Whitney National Bank of New Orleans*(Major Banking Relationship)*
P.O. Box 61260
New Orleans, LA 70161
Tel.: 504-586-7422

DISTRICT PETROLEUM PRODUCTS, INC.
1832 Milan Rd.
Sandusky, OH 44870
Tel.: 419-625-8373
Fax: 419-625-8907
Year Founded: 1950
Approx.Sls.: $40,000,000
Emp.: 250
Wholesale & Retail Petroleum Products
S.I.C.: 5983; 5172
John S. Stipp *(Chm. Bd. & Chief Exec. Officer)*
Scott L. Stipp *(Pres.)*
Timothy J. Donnelly *(V.P.-Fin.)*
Principal(s):
John S. Stipp

Outside Service Firm(s):

Ernst & Young*(Auditors)*
1300 Huntington Bldg.
Cleveland, OH 44115
Tel.: 216-861-5000

Buckingham, Holzapfel, Zeiher, Waldock & Schell*(Legal Firm)*
Sandusky, OH

BancOhio National Bank*(Major Banking Relationship)*
Sandusky, OH

DIVANE BROS. ELECTRIC CO.
2424 N. 25th Ave.
Franklin Park, IL 60131
Tel.: 708-455-7143
Fax: 708-455-7899
Year Founded: 1922
Approx.Sls.: $14,000,000
Emp.: 125
Electrical Contractors & Engineers
S.I.C.: 1731; 8711
William T. Divane Jr. *(Pres. & Treas.)*
Charles J. Sugrue *(Exec. V.P.)*
John T. Raiche *(Sec. & Controller)*
Principal(s):
William T. Divane Jr.

Outside Service Firm(s):

Harry F. Shea & Co.*(Auditors)*
Chicago, IL

Daley & George*(Legal Firm)*
Chicago, IL

Continental Bank N. A.*(Major Banking Relationship)*
231 S. LaSalle St.
Chicago, IL 60697
Tel.: 312-828-2345
Tel.: 800-426-5754
Telex: 312-828-1783

DIVERSIFIED COMMUNICATIONS
5 Milk St.
Portland, ME 04101
Mailing Address:
P.O. Box 7437,
Portland, ME 04112 **ME**
Tel.: 207-774-5981
Fax: 207-761-7915
Year Founded: 1970
Assets: $91,500,000
Liabilities: $70,600,000
Net Worth: $20,900,000
Sales Range: $40-59 Million
Emp.: 507
Communications; Broadcasting, Publishing, Cable Television, Expositions, Newsletters
S.I.C.: 4833; 2741; 7999; 4841
Josephine H. Detmer *(Chm. Bd.)*
Horace A. Hildreth, Jr. *(Pres. & Sec.)*
Garry H. Ritchie *(Pres.-Broadcasting Div.)*
David Lowell *(Exec. V.P.-Opers.)*
Paul G. Clancy *(Treas.)*
Principal(s):
Horace A. Hildreth, Jr.

Computer Systems/Hardware:
Wang

Outside Service Firm(s):

KPMG Peat Marwick*(Auditors)*
100 Middle St. Plaza
Portland, ME

Continental Insurance*(Group Insurer)*
Portland, ME

Richardson & Troubh*(Legal Firm)*
Portland, ME

First National Bank of Boston*(Major Banking Relationship)*
P.O. Box 644,
Boston, MA 02102-0644
Tel.: 617-575-2900
Fax: 617-575-2549

DIVERSIFIED DYNAMICS INC.
1681 94th Lane N.E.
Minneapolis, MN 55434
Tel.: 612-788-6318
Telex: 29-0276
Fax: 612-780-2958
Holding Company, Pumps
S.I.C.: 6719; 3561
W.L. Bruggeman *(Chm. & Chief Exec. Officer)*
Steven Bruggeman *(Pres.)*

Non-U.S. Holdings:

Cat Pumps AG **(1)**
Loretohohe 5 CH-6300
Zug, Switzerland
Tel.: 042 21 31 40 (100%)
Fax: 042 21 81 33
Mktg. & Distr. of Pumps
S.I.C.: 5084

Cat Pumps Corporation **(1)**
1681 94th Lane N.E.
Minneapolis, MN 55434
Tel.: 612-780-5440 (100%)
Fax: 612-780-2958
Mfr. of High Pressure Industrial Piston & Ceramic Plunger Pumps
S.I.C.: 3561
W.L. Bruggeman *(Chm. Bd. & Chief Exec. Officer)*
Steven Bruggeman *(Pres.)*
K. Shultis *(Mgr.-Tech. Services)*
D.J. Thompson *(Mgr.-Mktg. Services)*

Cat Pumps Deutschland GmbH **(1)**
Rostockerstr. 9 D-6200
Wiesbaden-Bierstadt, Germany
Tel.: 0611 50 10 44-45 (100%)
Fax: 0611 50 10 46
Mfr. of Pumps
S.I.C.: 3561

Cat Pumps International N.V. **(1)**
Harmoniestr. 29 B-2018
Antwerp, Belgium
Tel.: 03-237-7225 (100%)
Mktg. & Sale of Pumps
S.I.C.: 5084

Cat Pumps (UK) Ltd. **(1)**
27 Station Industrial Estate
Fleet, Hampshire GU13 8QY, United Kingdom
Tel.: 0252 622031 (100%)
Telex: 858898 CATPUK G
Fax: 0252 626655
Mfr. of Pumps
S.I.C.: 3561

DIVERSIFIED GROUP, INC.
5801 Citrus Blvd.
Harahan, LA 70123
Tel.: 504-733-2800
Fax: 504-733-2884
Approx.Sls.: $40,000,000
Emp.: 15
Holding Company; Power Line Construction & Maritime Repairs
S.I.C.: 1623; 1629; 6719
H.D. Hughes *(Chm. Bd., Pres., Chief Exec. Officer & Sls. Dir.)*
Thomas P. Buddie *(V.P.)*
Vicki Kihnemann *(Mgr.-Office)*

Outside Service Firm(s):

Price Waterhouse*(Auditors)*
601 Poydras, Ste. 2000
New Orleans, LA 70130
Tel.: 504-529-2000

Hibernia National Bank*(Major Banking Relationship)*
New Orleans, LA

DIX & EATON INCORPORATED
1010 Euclid Ave.
Cleveland, OH 44115
Tel.: 216-241-0405
Fax: 216-241-0832
Year Founded: 1952
Approx.Billings: $34,000,000
Emp.: 60
Public Relations, Investor Relations & Marketing Communications
Henry F. Eaton *(Chm. & Chief Exec. Officer)*
Edward M. Stevens *(Group Pres.)*
Scott Chaikin *(Grp. Pres.)*
Hugh J. Brown *(Exec. V.P.)*
Elizabeth L. Sislak *(V.P., Chief Fin. Officer)*
Patricia L. Cochrum *(V.P., Asst. to Chm.)*

DIXIE BREWING CO., INC.
2537 Tulane Ave.
New Orleans, LA 70119
Tel.: 504-822-8711
Fax: 504-827-0410
Year Founded: 1907
Approx.Sls.: $11,000,000
Emp.: 85
Export
Dixie Beer, Dixie Amber Light, New Orleans Best, New Orleans Best Light, Dixie Blackened Voodoo Lager
S.I.C.: 2082
Kendra Elliott Bruno *(Pres.)*
Joseph Bruno *(Exec. V.P.)*
J. Michael Bruno *(Natl. Sls. Mgr.)*

DIXIE DAIRY COMPANY
1200 W. 15th Ave.
Gary, IN 46407
Tel.: 219-885-6101 **IL**
Fax: 219-882-7533
Year Founded: 1899
Approx.Sls.: $20,000,000
Emp.: 75
Milk & Dairy Products
S.I.C.: 5143; 5451
Thomas T. Eskilson *(Pres.)*
Arnold J. Eskilson *(Sec. & Treas.)*
Jack Fowler *(Comptroller)*
Edward Stark *(Mgr.-Sls.)*

No. of Mfg. Plants/Facilities: 1
No. of U.S. Offices: 1

Outside Service Firm(s):

Raymond S. Blunt & Co.*(Auditors)*
Chicago, IL

Gainer Bank*(Major Banking Relationship)*
Gary, IN

DIXIE ELECTRIC COOPERATIVE
402 E. Blackman St.
Union Springs, AL 36089
Tel.: 205-738-2500
Fax: 205-738-2527
Sales Range: $10-19 Million
Emp.: 56
Electric Utility
S.I.C.: 4911
R.E. Adams *(Pres.)*
C.S. Paul *(V.P.)*
Jerry Twigs *(Gen. Mgr.)*
B.B. Spratling, Jr. *(Sec. & Treas.)*
John T. Hall *(Controller)*
Gary Harrison *(Mgr.-Engrng. Oper.)*
David E. Watson *(Pur. Agent)*
Bobbie Pike *(Supvr.-Data Processing)*

Outside Service Firm(s):

Jackson Thornton*(Auditors)*
Montgomery, AL

Rushton, Stakely, Johnston & Garrett*(Legal Firm)*
P.O. Box 270
Montgomery, AL 36195
Tel.: 205-834-8480

American National Bank*(Major Banking Relationship)*
Union Springs, AL

DIXIE OIL COMPANY
U.S. Hwy. 82 E.
Tifton, GA 31793-1007
Mailing Address:
P.O. Box 1007,
Tifton, GA 31743
Tel.: 912-382-2700
Approx.Sls.: $23,000,000
Emp.: 55
Wholesale Bulk Petroleum & Petroleum Products; Retail Gasoline
S.I.C.: 5171; 5541
W. Fred Lindsey *(Chm. Bd.)*
Bobby Lindsey *(Pres.)*
W.A. McCall *(Sec., Treas., Controller & Data Processing Mgr.)*

Outside Service Firm(s):

Watson & Purvis*(Auditors)*
Tifton, GA

Seymour Owens*(Legal Firm)*
Tifton, GA

Citizens Bank*(Major Banking Relationship)*
Tifton, GA

Dixie Reel Co.
(See Lone Star Corrugated Container Corporation Listing)

DIXON VALVE & COUPLING COMPANY
800 High St.
Chestertown, MD 21620
Tel.: 410-778-2000
Fax: 410-778-9655
Approx.Sls.: $30,000,000
Emp.: 400
Valves, Hydraulic, Aircraft, Hose & Tube Fittings & Assemblies, Founderies; Ductile Iron Castings, Brass & Bronze Die-castings, Aluminum & Aluminum-Based Alloy Castings
S.I.C.: 3492; 3429; 3322; 3321; 3364; 3365
Richard B. Goodall *(Chm. Bd. & Chief Exec. Officer)*
Richard L. Goodall *(Pres.)*
Douglas K. Goodall *(Exec. V.P.)*
James F. Canalchio *(V.P. & Treas.)*
Louis F. Farina *(V.P.)*
Richard F. Flaherty *(V.P.-Sls.)*
Paramjit Singh *(V.P.-Engrng.)*
John E. Myers *(Sec.)*
Richard Gentry *(Dir.-Adv.)*
Lucien Jacquet *(Dir.-Data Processing)*

Outside Service Firm(s):

Chestertown Bank of Maryland*(Major Banking Relationship)*
Chestertown, MD

Subsidiaries:

Predco, Inc. **(1)**
P.O. Box 520
Pennsauken, NJ 08110
Tel.: 609-665-2644
Fax: 609-663-2732
Approx.Sls.: $30,000,000
Emp.: 200
Fiscal Year-end: 12/31/90
Manufacture Metal Fabrication, Marine Equipment & Bulk Material Handling Systems
S.I.C.: 3499
Richard B. Goodall *(Chm. Bd.)*
Anthony J. Frascella *(Pres.)*
Glenn L. Brown *(V.P.-Adv.)*
Richard Tew *(V.P. & Treas.)*
Robert Hayes *(V.P.)*
Joseph R. Ford *(V.P.)*

Yardley Products Corporation **(1)**
10 W. College Ave.
Yardley, PA 19068
Tel.: 215-493-2723
Fax: 215-493-6796
Approx.Sls.: $2,000,000
Emp.: 15
Fiscal Year-end: 12/31/90
Manufacture Metal Fasteners Intro-Sert, Speed-Pin, Tri-Sert, Fiber-Sert, Zap-Sert, Sharp-Sert
S.I.C.: 3429; 3452
J. DeHaven *(Pres.)*
Tim Bailey *(V.P.-Sls.)*

DIXSON, INC.
287 27 Rd.
Grand Junction, CO 81503
Tel.: 303-244-1241 **CO**
Fax: 303-245-6267
Year Founded: 1958
Assets: $7,062,048
Liabilities: $1,437,300
Net Worth: $5,624,748
Approx.Sls.: $17,000,000
Emp.: 250
Fiscal Year-end: 9/30/90
Mfr. of Auto Aftermarket, Test & Tune Equipment, Electric Panel Meters; Heavy Duty Tachometers & Speedometers; Automotive Instruments, Cultured Quartz, Dixco, Thermo Dynamics
S.I.C.: 3824; 3714; 3825
Knute S. Knudson *(Pres. & Chief Oper. Officer)*
C. Huston *(V.P.-Mktg. & Sls.)*
Dennis Coleman *(V.P.-Engrng.)*
Sara Hunt *(Dir.-Personnel)*
Nannette Pond *(Mgr.-Automotive Prods.)*
Pam Stephens *(Mktg. Coord.)*

Outside Service Firm(s):

Dalby, Wendland & Co.*(Auditors)*
Grand Junction, CO

W. E. Foster*(Legal Firm)*
Grand Junction, CO 81501

Central Bank of Denver*(Major Banking Relationship)*
P.O. Box 315, Peck Slip Station
New York, NY 10038

First Interstate Bank*(Major Banking Relationship)*
Denver, CO
Tel.: 303-293-5456

Divisions:

Electronic Instruments **(1)**
287 - 27 Rd.
Grand Junction, CO 81501
Tel.: 303-242-8863
Approx.Sls.: $5,900,000
Heavy Duty Tachometers & Speedometers; Electrical Panel Meters; Bar Graphs
S.I.C.: 3694; 3825
Charles Husten *(Mgr.-Mktg.)*
Dennis Coleman *(Mgr.-Engnrg.)*
Al Hale *(Quality Control Mgr.)*

Products Division **(1)**
287 - 27 Rd.
Grand Junction, CO 81501
Tel.: 303-242-8863
Approx.Sls.: $2,000,000
Manufacture Auto After Market, Test & Tune Equipment
S.I.C.: 3694
Dan Kopsell *(Mgr.-Div.)*

Subsidiary:

Thermo Dynamics, Inc. **(1)**
Fox Ridge Dr.
Shawnee Mission, KS 66202
Tel.: 913-384-3100 (100%)
Approx.Sls.: $2,600,000
Emp.: 50
Cultured Quartz
S.I.C.: 3679
Knute Knudson *(Pres.)*
Richard Monley *(Gen. Mgr.)*

DOALL COMPANY
254 N. Laurel
Des Plaines, IL 60016
Tel.: 708-824-1122
Tel.: 800-75DOALL
Fax: 708-699-7524
Year Founded: 1940
Approx.Sls.: $120,000,000
Emp.: 125
Fiscal Year-end: 5/31/91
Import Export
Machine Tools, Cutting Tools, Industrial Supplies, Precision Gages, Measuring Equipment & Cutting Fluids
S.I.C.: 3825; 3545
Michael L. Wilkie *(Chm. Bd., Pres., Chief Exec. & Chief Oper. Officer)*
L.A. Wilkie *(Chm.-Exec. Committee)*
John Klaasen *(Chief Fin. Officer, V.P.-Fin. & Treas.)*
C.T. Peterson *(Sr. V.P.)*
R.A. Bedell *(V.P.-Intl. Sls.)*
David Crawford *(V.P.-Sls.)*
Jon Henricks *(V.P.-Corp. Affairs)*
Herbert Kemp *(V.P.-Data Processing)*
Theodore Timm *(Sec. & Gen. Counsel)*
Daniel M. McGivern *(Dir.-Mktg.)*
David Rollins *(Dir.-Logistics)*
Al Bielsky *(Gen. Mgr.)*
Dick Lowe *(Mgr.-Employee Benefits)*

Computer Systems/Hardware:
Sequoia

Outside Service Firm(s):

Ernst & Young*(Auditors)*
233 S. Wacker Dr.
Chicago, IL 60606
Tel.: 312-368-1800
Fax: 312-645-3095

Jenner & Block*(Legal Firm)*
One IBM Plaza
Chicago, IL 60611
Tel.: 312-222-9350

Continental Bank N. A.*(Major Banking Relationship)*
231 S. LaSalle St.
Chicago, IL 60697
Tel.: 312-828-2345
Tel.: 800-426-5754
Telex: 312-828-1783

Branch:

Sacramento Industrial Supply **(1)**
330 Commerce Circle
Sacramento, CA 95815
Tel.: 916-929-6795
Industrial Supplies
S.I.C.: 5085

Division:

Mac's Machinery & Supply **(1)**
7755 Mossy Cup
Boise, ID 83709-2846
Tel.: 208-362-6209
Industrial Equipment & Supplies Distributor
Mac McKnight *(Pres.)*

DoAll Company—(Continued)

Subsidiary:

Southwest Doall Industrial Supply (1)
514 Riverdale Dr.
Glendale, CA 91204
Tel.: 818-243-3153
Fax: 818-240-3569
Approx.Sls.: $30,000,000
Emp.: 145
Industrial Supplies& Tools
S.I.C.: 5085
David Crawford *(Pres.)*

DOANE PRODUCTS CO.
W. 20th & State Line Rd.
Joplin, MO 64802
Mailing Address:
P.O. Box 879
Joplin, MO 64802
Tel.: 417-624-6166
Fax: 417-624-1666
Year Founded: 1956
Approx.Sls.: $100,000,000
Emp.: 600
Export
Private Label Pet Food
S.I.C.: 2047
Herbert L. Tessereau *(Vice Chm. & Chief Exec. Officer)*
Bob Robinson *(Pres.)*
Dick H. Weber *(V.P.-Mktg.)*
Paul Peterson *(V.P.-Procurement)*
R. Gene Hess *(V.P. & Controller)*
Steve Wawrzyniak *(V.P.-Tech. Services)*

Division:

Doane Products Co., Branded Sales Div. (1)
W. 20th & State Line
Joplin, MO 64804
Tel.: 417-624-6166
Tel.: 800-641-4718
Fax: 417-624-1666
Approx.Sls.: $28,000,000
Emp.: 88
Fiscal Year-end: 12/31/90
Export
Pet Foods, Field & Show Pet Foods, Winner Pet Food,
S.I.C.: 2047
Bob Robinson *(Pres. & Chief Exec. Officer)*
Dick H. Weber *(V.P.-Sls. & Mktg.)*
R. Gene Hess *(Chief Fin. Officer)*
Robert L. Junk *(Mgr.-Sls./Private Label)*
Lorn E. McLeod *(Mgr.-Sls./Grocery Div.)*

DOBBS BROTHERS MANAGEMENT
5170 Sanderlin Ave.
Memphis, TN 38117
Mailing Address:
P.O. Box 241750
Memphis, TN 38124-1750
Tel.: 901-685-8881
Fax: 901-685-9053
Management Company
S.I.C.: 8742
James K. Dobbs, III *(Partner)*
John C. Dobbs *(Partner)*
John Shanks *(Chief Exec. Officer)*

Outside Service Firm(s):

Boatmen's Bank of Tennessee*(Major Banking Relationship)*
200 Madison
Memphis, TN
Tel.: 901-529-5900

DOBLES CHEVROLET, INC.
1250 S. Willow St.
Manchester, NH 03103
Tel.: 603-669-2450
Fax: 603-622-2413
Year Founded: 1955
Approx.Sls.: $39,000,000
Emp.: 135
Retail Sales & Service Of New Automobiles
S.I.C.: 5511
Arthur J. Dobles *(Chm. Bd.)*
Gerald Montembeault *(Pres.)*
Edward Zimmerman *(Sec., Treas. & Personnel Mgr.)*
David Turner *(Dir.-Sls. & Mktg.)*

Outside Service Firm(s):

Gerald Dupont Accounting Firm*(Auditors)*
Manchester, NH

Devine, Millimet & Branch*(Legal Firm)*
Manchester, NH

DOBSON & JOHNSON, INC.
4522 Harding Rd.
Nashville, TN 37205
Mailing Address:
P.O. Box 50889,
Nashville, TN 37205
Tel.: 615-386-9400
Fax: 615-269-3755
Year Founded: 1955
Approx.Sls.: $267,000,000
Emp.: 203
Real Estate, Mortgage Financing
S.I.C.: 6531
Al Johnson *(Chm. Bd.)*
Al Johnson II *(Pres.)*
Judith Brock *(V.P.)*

Computer Systems/Hardware:
IBM PC-XT

Outside Service Firm(s):

Price Waterhouse*(Auditors)*
4400 Harding Rd.
Nashville, TN 37205
Tel.: 615-292-5000

Commerce Union*(Major Banking Relationship)*
Nashville, TN

Third National Bank in Nashville*(Major Banking Relationship)*
Nashville, TN

DOCK FOUNDRY COMPANY
428 Fourth St.
Three Rivers, MI 49093
Tel.: 616-278-1765
Fax: 616-279-5820
Sales Range: $10-19 Million
Emp.: 92
Gray Iron Castings
S.I.C.: 3321
Fitzmaurice Coghlin *(Chm. Bd.)*
John F. Coghlin *(Pres.)*
Robert Grimm *(Chief Fin. Officer)*

Outside Service Firm(s):

Ernst & Young*(Auditors)*
1100 Old Kent Bank Bldg.
Kalamazoo, MI 49007
Tel.: 616-349-6671

First American Bank, N.A.*(Major Banking Relationship)*
Three Rivers, MI

DR PEPPER/SEVEN-UP COMPANIES, INC.
8144 Walnut Hill Lane
Dallas, TX 75231
Mailing Address:
P.O. Box 655086,
Dallas, TX 75265
Tel.: 214-360-7000 **DE**
Fax: 214-360-7980
Year Founded: 1988
Approx.Sls.: $600,000,000
Emp.: 915
Fiscal Year-end: 12/31/91
Export
Beverage Holding Company
S.I.C.: 6719
John R. Albers *(Chm. Bd., Pres. & Chief Exec. Officer)*
True H. Knowles *(Chief Oper. Officer)*
Ira M. Rosenstein *(Exec. V.P. & Chief Fin. Officer)*
Charles P. Grier *(Sr. V.P.-Opers.)*
Jim Ball *(V.P.-Communications)*
Daniel O'Neill *(V.P.-Intl.)*
John L. Quigley, Jr. *(V.P.-Admin.)*
Randy Slaughter *(V.P.-Franchise)*
Nelson A. Bangs *(V.P., Gen Counsel & Sec.)*
Michael R. Buiter *(V.P. & Treas.)*
Myron Semrad *(Controller)*
Roger Pickett *(Dir.-Training)*
John Stevenson *(Dir.-Data Processing)*
Mike Beaird *(Dir.-Pur.)*

No. of Mfg. Plants/Facilities: 1

Computer Systems/Hardware:
IBM 4381

Outside Service Firm(s):

KPMG Peat Marwick*(Auditors)*
1601 Elm St., Ste. 1600
Dallas, TX 75201
Tel.: 214-754-2000
Fax: 214-754-2297

Metropolitan Life Insurance Co.*(Group Insurer)*
Tampa, FL

Subsidiaries:

Dr Pepper Company (1)
8144 Walnut Hill Lane
Dallas, TX 75231
Tel.: 214-360-7000
Fax: 214-360-7980
Sales Range: $100-499 Million
Fiscal Year-end: 12/31/90
Soft Drinks; Dr Pepper, Seven-Up, Diet Seven-Up, Cherry Seven-Up, Welch's Carbonated Soft Drinks & I.B.C. Root Beer & Creme Soda
S.I.C.: 2086; 2087
John R. Albers *(Chm. & Chief Exec. Officer)*
True H. Knowles *(Pres. & Chief Oper. Officer)*
John M. Kilduff *(Sr. V.P.-Sls.)*
John Clarke *(Sr. V.P.-Mktg.)*
Bill Tolany *(V.P.-Mktg. Services)*

Subsidiary:

Premier Beverages (2)
8144 Walnut Hill Ln.
Dallas, TX 75231
Tel.: 214-360-7000
Fax: 214-360-7980
Bottler of Soft Drinks
S.I.C.: 2086; 2087
Michael S. McGrath *(V.P. & Gen. Mgr.)*
Jim Tebillcack *(V.P.-Mktg.)*

Subsidiaries:

I.B.C. Root Beer Company (3)
8144 Walnut Hill Lane
Dallas, TX 75231
Tel.: 214-360-7000
Fax: 214-360-7980
Emp.: 200
Soft Drink Bottling Co.
S.I.C.: 2086
Michael S. McGrath *(V.P. & Gen. Mgr.)*
Harry V. Ingram III *(Dir.-Mktg.)*
Pam Jones *(Mgr.-Mktg. Systems)*

Welch's Carbonated Beverages (3)
8144 Walnut Hill Lane
Dallas, TX 75231
Tel.: 214-360-7000
S.I.C.: 2086
Edward Orick *(V.P.-Sls.)*

The Seven-Up Company (1)
8144 Walnut Hill Lane
Dallas, TX 75231
Tel.: 214-360-7000
Fax: 214-360-7980
Sales Range: $100-499 Million
Emp.: 400
Computer Systems/Hardware:
IBM
Soft Drinks
S.I.C.: 2086
Francis I. Mullin *(Pres. & Chief Oper. Officer)*
Russell Klein *(Sr. V.P.-Mktg.)*
Bob Quirk *(Sr. V.P.-Sls.)*
Jim Watkins *(V.P.-Mktg. Services)*

Non-U.S. Holding:

Dr Pepper Japan Co. (1)
Hibiva Bldg., 1-1-1 Shinbashi Minato-ku, Tokyo, 105 Japan
Tel.: 0303591-7361
Soft Drink Franchise Co.
S.I.C.: 2086
True H. Knowles *(Chief Oper. Officer)*

DODSON GROUP
9201 State Line Rd.
Kansas City, MO 64114
Tel.: 816-361-3400
Tel.: 800-825-5535 **MO**
Year Founded: 1900
Assets: $207,000,000
Liabilities: $174,000,000
Net Worth: $33,000,000
Approx.Sls.: $110,300,000
Emp.: 315
Fiscal Year-end: 12/31/90
Fire, Marine, Casualty & Worker's Compensation Insurance
S.I.C.: 6331
Cathleen Dodson *(Chm. Bd. & Chief Exec. Officer)*
Donald E. McCandless *(Vice Chm.)*
James R. Jones *(Pres. & Chief Oper. Officer)*
Glen E. Williams, Jr. *(Exec. V.P. & Chief Fin. Officer)*
James C. Cook *(V.P.-Research & Devel.)*
Kenneth J. Holferty *(V.P.-Client Services)*
Linda J. Miller *(V.P.-Human Resources)*
J. Larry Odom *(V.P.-Claims)*
John M. Stubbs *(V.P.-Mktg.)*
Clyde J. Rayburn *(Gen. Counsel)*
Jack E. Casper *(Dir.-Actuarial Services)*
James A. Hitchcock *(Dir.-Internal Audit)*
Virginia Johnson *(Dir.-Admin. Services)*
Timothy J. Morehead *(Dir.-Underwriting)*
Gary D. Kohlstaedt *(Mgr.-Personal Lines)*

Computer Systems/Hardware:
IBM

Outside Service Firm(s):

Cuneo, Lawson, Shay, Staley*(Auditors)*
Kansas City, MO

Shook, Hardy & Bacon*(Legal Firm)*
One Kansas City Place
Kansas City, MO 64105
Tel.: 816-474-6550

United Missouri Bank*(Major Banking Relationship)*
P.O. Box 226
Kansas City, MO 64141
Tel.: 816-556-7000

DOE-ANDERSON ADVERTISING AGENCY, INC.
223 E. Broadway
Louisville, KY 40202
Tel.: 502-589-1700 **KY**
Fax: 502-587-8349
Year Founded: 1915
Approx.Billings: $34,288,000
Emp.: 68
Fiscal Year-end: 12/31/91
Advertising Agency
S.I.C.: 7311
Robert S. Allison *(Chm. & Chief Exec. Officer)*
David G. Wilkins *(Pres. & Chief Oper. Officer)*
James S. Lindsey *(Exec. V.P.)*
Philip D. Payne *(Exec. V.P.)*
Kenneth R. Hoskins *(V.P., Mng. Dir.-Pub. Rels.)*
Bruce J. Skinner *(V.P., Dir.-Brdcst. Services)*
Steven H. Aronson *(V.P.)*
Bobbi F. Davis *(V.P.)*

Douglas C. Gabbert *(V.P.)*
Thomas A. Mudd *(Sec. & Treas.)*

No. of Mfg. Plants/Facilities: 1
No. of U.S. Offices: 1

Outside Service Firm(s):

Coopers & Lybrand*(Auditors)*
Louisville, KY 46201

Blue Cross & Blue Shield of Kentucky*(Group Insurer)*
9901 Linn Station Rd.
Louisville, KY 40223
Tel.: 502-426-3700

First National Bank of Louisville*(Major Banking Relationship)*
P.O. Box 36000,
Louisville, KY 40233

DOE SPUN, INC.
100 W. 33rd St.
New York, NY 10001
Tel.: 212-736-1945 **DE**
Fax: 212-279-6916
Assets: $18,000,000
Liabilities: $7,885,000
Net Worth: $10,115,000
Approx.Sls.: $43,000,000
Emp.: 450
Fiscal Year-end: 4/30/91
Import
Mfr. of Children's Knit & Woven Outerwear & Sportswear
S.I.C.: 2253; 2369
Barry Schwartz *(Chm. Bd. & Chief Exec. Officer)*
Daniel Schwartz *(Pres.)*
Steven Schwartz *(Chief Oper. Officer)*
Stanley Oremland *(Chief Fin. Officer)*
Bob Zelen *(Sr. V.P.-Sls.)*
Kenneth Miller *(Controller)*
Eugene Feldman *(Sec. & Legal Officer)*

No. of Mfg. Plants/Facilities: 5
No. of U.S. Offices: 7
No. of Foreign Offices: 1

Computer Systems/Hardware:
IBM System 400

Outside Service Firm(s):

BDO Seidman*(Auditors)*
1430 Broadway
New York, NY
Tel.: 212-765-7500

Goldstick, Weinberger, Feldman, Alperstein & Taishoff*(Legal Firm)*
551 Fifth Ave.
New York, NY 10017
Tel.: 212-682-0700

Chemical Banking Corporation*(Major Banking Relationship)*
450 W. 33rd. St.
New York, NY 10001
Tel.: 212-613-7147

Subsidiaries:

Bambinaggine **(1)**
100 W. 33rd St.
New York, NY 10001
Tel.: 21-279-6916
Mfr. of Children Clothing
S.I.C.: 5641
Barry Schwartz *(Chm. Bd. & Chief Exec. Officer)*

Calabash Ltd. **(1)**
100 West 33rd St.
New York, NY 10001
Tel.: 212-736-1945 (100%)
Approx.Sls.: $8,000,000
Emp.: 40
Mfr. of Jeans, Sportswear, Shirts, Knit Tops, Sweaters
S.I.C.: 2253
Steven Schwartz *(Chief Oper. Officer)*

Mia Bambini **(1)**
100 W. 33rd St.
New York, NY 10001
Tel.: 212-736-1945
Mfr. of Children Clothing
S.I.C.: 5641
Barry Schwartz *(Chm. Bd. & Chief Exec. Officer)*

THE F. DOHMEN COMPANY
P.O. Box 9, W 194 N 11381 McCormick Dr.
Germantown, WI 53022
Tel.: 414-255-0022
Fax: 414-255-0041
Year Founded: 1858
Emp.: 175
Pharmacy Wholesaler
S.I.C.: 5122
Erwin Dohmen *(Chm. Bd.)*
Robert Wendland *(Pres.)*
John Dohmen *(Exec. V.P.)*
Robert Dohmen *(Sec.)*
Barbara Ziller *(Treas.)*

Outside Service Firm(s):

Arthur Andersen & Co.*(Auditors)*
777 E. Wisconsin Ave., P.O. Box 1215
Milwaukee, WI 53202
Tel.: 414-271-5100
Fax: 414-283-3200

Churchill, Duback & Smith*(Legal Firm)*
Milwaukee, WI

Marshall & Ilsley Trust Company*(Major Banking Relationship)*
770 N. Water St.
Milwaukee, WI

Subsidiary:

Northwestern Drug Company **(1)**
2001 N.E. Kennedy
Minneapolis, MN 55413
Tel.: 612-331-6550
Fax: 612-378-1549
Assets: $17,500,000
Liabilities: $12,079,000
Net Worth: $5,421,000
Approx.Sls.: $100,000,000
Emp.: 102
Fiscal Year-end: 12/31/90
Computer Systems/Hardware:
NCR
Wholesaler of Drugs & Supplies
S.I.C.: 5122; 5100
Russell Bodgren *(Chm. Bd.)*
Kent F. Olson *(Pres. & Chief Exec. Officer)*
Allan Lueck *(Chief Fin. Officer)*
Robert H. Brix *(Treas.)*
James M. Schneider *(Sec.)*
Marvin Jesinoski *(Mgr.-Sls.)*
Harold Hedger *(Dir.-Mngmt. Information Systems)*

DOMBROWSKI & HOLMES, INC.
5051 S. Western Blvd.
Chicago, IL 60609
Tel.: 312-889-1882
Year Founded: 1970
Emp.: 45
Underground Sanitation & Waste Hauling
S.I.C.: 4953
George B. Holmes *(Pres., Chief Exec. & Chief Fin. Officer)*
Vic Churna *(Gen. Counsel)*

Outside Service Firm(s):

Greenman & Assocs.*(Auditors)*
Chicago, IL

American Crown Life Insurance Co.*(Group Insurer)*
New York, NY

Victor Churma*(Legal Firm)*
Chicago, IL

Republic National Bank*(Major Banking Relationship)*
Chicago, IL

Subsidiary:

D & H Piping **(1)**
5051 S. Western Blvd.
Chicago, IL 60609
Tel.: 312-889-1882

DOMECQ IMPORTERS INC.
143 Sound Beach Ave.
Old Greenwich, CT 06870
Tel.: 203-637-6500
Tel.: 800-366-8721
Fax: 203-637-6599
Year Founded: 1981
Approx.Sls.: $70,000,000
Emp.: 60
Fiscal Year-end: 12/31/92
Import
Distr. of Wine & Spirits
S.I.C.: 5182
J. Joaquin Ysasi Ysasmandi *(Chm. Bd.)*
Michael Domecq *(Pres. & Chief Exec. Officer)*
Alfredo Valdes *(V.P.-Fin., Opers., Corp. Sec. & Treas.)*
Gabriel Sagaz *(V.P.-Mktg. & Natl. Accts.)*
Thomas Kaminsky *(V.P. & Natl. Sls. Mgr.)*
Richard Kapp *(Controller)*
Robert Cooke *(Dir. Information Systems)*
Ronald Ossip *(Dir.-Mktg.)*
Hersey Eqquiqfm *(Dir.-Mktg.)*
Audry Settember *(Mgr.-Human Resources & Office Services)*

Computer Systems/Hardware:
LAN With Client Saver Technology

DOMESTIC LINEN SUPPLY & LAUNDRY CO.
3800 18th St.
Detroit, MI 48208
Tel.: 313-831-6700
Fax: 313-831-2617
Approx.Sls.: $40,000,000
Emp.: 1,000
Linen Supply; Garment Rental
S.I.C.: 7213; 7211; 7299; 7218
Sol Colton *(Chm. Bd.)*
Bruce L. Colton *(Pres. & Chief Exec. Officer)*
Maynard Kalef *(V.P.-Fin.)*
Patrick Tienanelli *(V.P.-Mktg.)*
Michael DeFortuna *(V.P.-Admin.)*
Diane Colton *(V.P.)*
David J. Colton *(V.P.)*
Leonard H. Colton *(Treas.)*

Outside Service Firm(s):

Gross, Bornstein, Grey & Co.*(Auditors)*
Southfield, MI

Levin, Levin, Garvett & Dill*(Legal Firm)*
3000 Tower Ctr., Ste. 1800
Southfield, MI 48075
Tel.: 313-352-8200

Manufacturers National Bank N.A.*(Major Banking Relationship)*
38th Fl., 100 Renaissance Center
Detroit, MI 48243
Tel.: 313-222-4227

Plant:

Domestic Linen Supply Co. **(1)**
1321 No. 17th St.
Richmond, VA 23219
Tel.: 804-643-6731
Industrial Laundry
S.I.C.: 7218
Bernadette Corrigan *(Gen. Mgr.)*

DOMINICK & DOMINICK, INCORPORATED
90 Broad St.
New York, NY 10004
Tel.: 212-558-8800
Fax: 212-797-5268
Year Founded: 1870
Emp.: 500
Security & Commodity Brokers & Services
S.I.C.: 6211; 6221
Peter M. Kennedy, III *(Pres.)*
Paul L. Kennedy *(Exec. V.P.)*
Paul Morgante *(Exec. V.P. & Chief Fin. Officer)*
Frederick P. Shields *(Sr. V.P.-Opers. & Admin.)*
Robert Harrison *(V.P. & Gen. Counsel)*
Arthur LeClair *(V.P.-Mngmt. Information Systems)*
Jenny Roman *(Mgr.-Personnel)*

Outside Service Firm(s):

Aetna Life & Casualty*(Group Insurer)*
151 Farmington Avenue
Hartford, CT 06156
Tel.: 203-273-2128
Fax: 203-729-4295

White & Case*(Legal Firm)*
1155 Avenue of The Americas
New York, NY 10036

Bankers Trust Co.*(Major Banking Relationship)*
P.O. Box 318, Church St. Station
New York, NY 10008
Tel.: 212-454-2212
Fax: 212-454-2783

Chemical Banking Corp.*(Major Banking Relationship)*
277 Park Ave.
New York, NY 10041
Tel.: 212-310-6407
Fax: 212-310-4526

Chemical Bank*(Major Banking Relationship)*
450 West 33rd St.
New York, NY 10001
Tel.: 212-613-7197
Fax: 212-947-7628

Subsidiary:

Dominick Futures Corporation **(1)**
90 Broad St.
New York, NY 10004
Tel.: 212-558-8800
Securities Brokerage
S.I.C.: 6211

DOMINICK'S FINER FOODS
505 Railroad Ave.
Northlake, IL 60164
Tel.: 708-562-1000 **DE**
Fax: 708-409-6021
Year Founded: 1925
Approx.Sls.: $2,000,000,000
Emp.: 18,000
Fiscal Year-end: 10/31/91
Owns & Operates 99 Grocery Stores
S.I.C.: 5411
Corporate Giving Program: United Way & Crusade of Mercy
Dominick DiMatteo *(Chm. Bd.)*
James DiMatteo *(Vice Chm. & Chief Exec. Officer)*
Daniel Josephs *(Pres. & Chief Oper. Officer)*
Charles Brazik *(Sr. V.P.-Human Resources)*
Bob McCoy *(Sr. V.P.-Opers.)*
Rick Weber *(Sr. V.P. & Chief Fin. Officer)*
Herb Young *(Sr. V.P.-Mktg.)*
Hal Raiman *(V.P.-Real Estate)*
Thomas Roti *(V.P. & Gen. Counsel)*
Lori Marin *(Controller)*
Bill Berryman *(Mgr.-Mngmt. Information Systems)*
Principal(s):
Dominick DiMatteo
James DiMatteo

No. of Mfg. Plants/Facilities: 95
No. of U.S. Offices: 1

Computer Systems/Hardware:
IBM

Outside Service Firm(s):

Ernst & Young*(Auditors)*
233 S. Wacker Dr.
Chicago, IL 60606
Tel.: 312-368-1800
Fax: 312-645-3095

Dominick's Finer Foods—(Continued)

Chemical Banking Corp.*(Investment Banker)*
277 Park Ave.
New York, NY 10041
Tel.: 212-310-6407
Fax: 212-310-4526

Harris Trust & Savings Bank*(Major Banking Relationship)*
111 W. Monroe St.
Chicago, IL 60690
Tel.: 312-461-2265
Tel.: 800-858-0840

Subsidiary:

OMNI Superstores **(1)**
505 Railroad Ave.
Northlake, IL 60164
Tel.: 708-562-1000
Retail Grocery Business
S.I.C.: 5411
Nina Walchirk *(Controller)*

DOMINO'S PIZZA INC.
30 Frank Lloyd Wright Dr.
Ann Arbor, MI 48106
Mailing Address:
P.O. Box 997,
Ann Arbor, MI 48106
Tel.: 313-930-3030 **MI**
Fax: 313-668-1946
Year Founded: 1960
Earnings: $5,400,000
Approx.Rev.: $2,500,000,000
Emp.: 145,000
Fiscal Year-end: 12/31/91
Chain of 5,450 Delivery Pizza Restaurants
S.I.C.: 5812
Thomas S. Monaghan *(Chm. Bd., Pres. & Chief Exec. Officer)*
Don Vlcek *(Pres.-Distr.)*
Tim Carr *(V.P. & Treas.)*
Stuart Mathis *(V.P.-Franchise Opers.)*
John McDevitt *(V.P.-Fin. & Admin.)*
Nickep Romyananda *(V.P.-Corp. Opers.)*
James Stitley *(V.P.-Consumer/Product Research)*
Joe Davis *(Corp. Grant Contact)*
Harry Silverman *(Controller)*
Ken Herr *(Dir.-Data Processing)*
Walter Power *(Dir.-Training)*
Mitch Srail *(Dir.-Human Services)*
Robert Totte *(Dir.-Taxes)*

Principal(s):
Thomas S. Monaghan

No. of U.S. Offices: 9
No. of Foreign Offices: 6

Computer Systems/Hardware:
IBM System 36 & 4341; NCR

Outside Service Firm(s):

Arthur Andersen & Co.*(Auditors)*
400 Renaissance Center
Detroit, MI 48243
Tel.: 313-259-8100

Great-West Life Assurance Co.*(Group Insurer)*
8505 East Orchard Rd.
Englewood, CO 8011
Tel.: 800-537-2033

National Bank of Detroit*(Major Banking Relationship)*
611 Woodward
Detroit, MI 48226
Tel.: 313-225-1000

Subsidiaries:

Domino's Pizza Distribution Corp. **(1)**
P.O. Box 990
Ann Arbor, MI 48106
Tel.: 313-663-6300 (100%)
Distributor of Food, Equipment & Supplies
S.I.C.: 5141
Don Vlcek *(Pres.)*

Domino's Pizza International, Inc. **(1)**
P.O. Box 997
Ann Arbor, MI 48106
Tel.: 313-665-5500
Emp.: 6,450
International Franchising
S.I.C.: 6794
Gary McCausland *(V.P.)*

EDWARD DON & COMPANY OF ILLINOIS
2500 S. Harlem Ave.
North Riverside, IL 60546
Tel.: 708-442-9400 **IL**
Fax: 708-442-0491
Year Founded: 1921
Approx.Sls.: $230,000,000
Emp.: 1,100
Fiscal Year-end: 12/31/90

Import Export
Distribute Food Service Equipment, Furnishings & Supplies
S.I.C.: 5021; 5046; 5087
Robert E. Don *(Chm. Bd. & Chief Exec. Officer)*
Robert S. Vor Broker *(Pres.)*
Paul F. Burgoyne *(V.P.-Mktg.)*
Jim Cornelius *(V.P.-Sls.)*
Ken Cotuno *(V.P.-Natl. Accounts & Specialty Sls.)*
Leon Ellin *(V.P.-Fin.)*
Edward Fromkin *(V.P.-Information Systems)*
Jim Walsh *(V.P.-Human Resources)*
Paul Burgoyne *(Mgr.-Mdsg. & Adv.)*

Computer Systems/Hardware:
IBM

Outside Service Firm(s):

Altschuler, Melvoin & Glasser*(Auditors)*
30 S. Wecker Dr.
Chicago, IL 60606
Tel.: 312-207-2800

Aetna Life & Casualty*(Group Insurer)*
100 N. Riverside Plaza
Chicago, IL 60606

Katten, Muchin & Zavis*(Legal Firm)*
525 W. Monroe St., Ste. 1600
Chicago, IL 60661-3693
Tel.: 312-902-5200

Continental Bank N. A.*(Major Banking Relationship)*
231 S. LaSalle St.
Chicago, IL 60697
Tel.: 312-828-2345
Tel.: 800-426-5754
Telex: 312-828-1783

Branches:

Edward Don & Company of Florida-Fort Lauderdale Branch **(1)**
2200 S.W. 45th St.
Fort Lauderdale, FL 33312
Tel.: 305-983-3000
Richard Piontkowski *(V.P. & Gen. Mgr.)*

Edward Don & Company of Georgia-Clarkston Branch **(1)**
696 Park N. Blvd.
Clarkston, GA 30021
Tel.: 404-297-7000
Mike Cunningham *(Gen. Mgr.)*

Edward Don & Company of New Jersey-Mt. Laurel Branch **(1)**
820 Eastgate Dr.
Mount Laurel, NJ 08054
Tel.: 609-234-8700
Mark Miller *(Gen Mgr.)*

Edward Don & Company of Texas-Dallas Branch **(1)**
2005 McDaniel
Carrollton, TX 75006
Tel.: 214-484-2300
Jerry Ridenour *(Pres.)*

Subsidiary:

Montgomery-Green Co. **(1)**
1200 New Hope Rd. Ext.
Raleigh, NC 27620
Tel.: 919-250-9311
Approx.Sls.: $16,000,000
Distributor of Commercial Ranges & Other Heavy Kitchen Equipment
S.I.C.: 5046; 5087
Mike Fasig *(V.P. & Gen. Mgr.)*

DONAHOE & PUROHIT, INC.
One O'Hare Centre, Ste. 5060,
6250 N. River Rd.
Rosemont, IL 60018
Tel.: 708-825-8010
Fax: 708-825-8019
Year Founded: 1985
Approx.Billings: $12,000,000
Emp.: 11
Healthcare/Medical Adv.
Edward J. Donahoe *(Chm. Bd., Pres. & Acct. Supvr.)*
Scott Kale, M.D. *(Medical Dir.)*

DONAHUE, INC., ADVERTISING
227 Lawrence St.
Hartford, CT 06106
Tel.: 203-728-0000
Fax: 203-247-9247
Year Founded: 1978
Approx.Billings: $12,000,000
Emp.: 18
Automotive, High-Tech., Financial & Business-to-Business Adv.
James C. Donahue *(Pres. & Chief Exec. Officer)*
Blaine G. Murphy *(Exec. V.P.)*
Duoglas P. Shea *(Treas.)*

Computer Systems/Hardware:
IBM, Macintosh, Wang

DONALDSON GROUP
27 Maiden Lane, 7th Floor
San Francisco, CA 94108
Tel.: 415-989-2400
Fax: 415-989-0500
Year Founded: 1988
Approx.Billings: $32,000,000
Emp.: 24
Bruce Donaldson *(Pres.)*
Ira Zuckerman *(Dir., Bus. Devel.)*
Keith Louie *(Controller)*

W.B. DONER

W.B. DONER & COMPANY
(Co-Headquarters)
25900 Northwestern Hwy.
Southfield, MI 48075
Tel.: 313-354-9700
Fax: 313-827-8448
Year Founded: 1937
Approx.Billings: $425,000,000
Emp.: 540
Advertising Agency
S.I.C.: 7311
Herbert D. Fried *(Chm. of Exec. Committee)*
John Decerchio *(Vice Chm. & Exec. Creative Dir.)*
Alan Kalter *(Pres. & Chief Oper. Officer)*
John DeCerchio *(Vice Chm. & Exec. Creative Dir.)*
John Considine *(Exec. V.P. & Dir.-Strategic Planning)*
Dean Friedman *(Sr. V.P. & Grp. Mgmt. Supvr.)*
H. Barry Levine *(Sr. V.P. & Chief Fin. Officer)*
Fred Toettcher *(Sr. V.P. & Dir.-Mktg.)*
Michael Kneffel *(V.P. & Assoc Dir.-Mktg.)*
Andrew McMechin *(V.P. & Dir.-Media Plng.)*
Patricia Simpson *(Dir.-Pub. Rels.)*

Outside Service Firm(s):

Arthur Andersen & Co.*(Auditors)*
400 Renaissance Center
Detroit, MI 48243
Tel.: 313-259-8100

Manufacturers National Bank N.A.*(Major Banking Relationship)*
38th Fl., 100 Renaissance Center
Detroit, MI 48243
Tel.: 313-222-4227

Non-U.S. Holdings:

Doner & Company Limited **(1)**
Oriel Bldg., 10-13 Margaret St.
London, W1N 7LF, United Kingdom
Tel.: 071-436-7195
Advertising
S.I.C.: 7311
Don Riesett *(Pres.)*
David Foxon *(V.P. & Gen. Mgr.)*

Doner Schur Peppler **(1)**
90 Eglinton Ave. W.
Toronto, ON M4R 1K8, Canada
Tel.: 416-485-9901
Telex: 485-4357
Emp.: 54
Advertising
S.I.C.: 7311
Dan Peppler *(Chm., Natl. Creative Dir., Chief Exec. Officer)*
Tony Scala *(Sr. V.P., Retail Grp. Head)*
Adrian Branch *(Sr. V.P., Dir. Client Services)*

Doner Schur Peppler **(1)**
2020 University Ave.
Montreal, PQ H3A 2A5, Canada
Tel.: 514-842-3757
Emp.: 20
Advertising
S.I.C.: 7311
Marie Gordon *(Sr. V.P., Media Dir.)*
Brandy Cote *(V.P., Assoc. Media Dir.)*

Affiliate:

Luscombe and Partners Pty. Ltd. **(1)**
60 Stokes St. P.O. Box 69,
Port Melbourne, Victoria 3207, Australia
Tel.: 03-645-2255
Telex: 151868
Fax: 03-646-5305
Approx.Billings: $30,000,000
Emp.: 50
Kevin Luscombe *(Chm. Bd. & Mng. Dir.)*
David Brocklehurst *(Fin. Dir. & Sec.)*

Donino&Partners, inc.

DONINO & PARTNERS, INC.
3350 Cumberland Circle, Ste. 1950
Atlanta, GA 30339
Tel.: 404-618-5000
Fax: 404-618-5007
Year Founded: 1986
Approx.Billings: $15,500,000
Emp.: 22
Technology, Sports Marketing, Cable & Entertainment
Frank Donino *(Pres. & Chief Exec. Officer)*
Eldridge W. White *(Exec. V.P. & Partner)*
Donna Rice *(V.P., Fin.)*
S. Cronin *(Sec.)*

DONLEE TECHNOLOGIES INC.
693 N. Hills Rd.
York, PA 17402
Tel.: 717-755-1081 **DE**
Fax: 717-755-0020
Year Founded: 1986
Approx.Assets: $20,000,000
Emp.: 175
Import Export
Manufactures Heating & Cooling Equipment & Pressure Tanks
S.I.C.: 3443; 3433; 3567; 3585; 3479
David C. Alcorn *(Chm. Bd. & Chief Exec. Officer)*
Donald K. Eyster *(Vice Chm. & Chief Fin. Officer)*
Charles S. Alcorn *(Pres. & Chief Oper. Officer)*
Jane Smith *(Chief Information Officer (MIS))*
Jonathan Shipper *(Controller)*
Lynn Haunrick *(Mgr.-Promo.)*
Mary Wagner *(Mgr.-Indus. Rels.)*
Jerry Zoldos *(Mgr.-Pur.)*

No. of Mfg. Plants/Facilities: 1
No. of U.S. Offices: 135
No. of Foreign Offices: 3

Computer Systems/Hardware:
IBM AS-400; Data-3 System

Outside Service Firm(s):

Arthur Andersen & Co.*(Auditors)*
Lancaster, PA

Continental Insurance*(Commercial Insurance Carrier)*
180 Maiden Lane
New York, NY

Pennsylvania Blue Shield*(Group Insurance Broker/Consult)*
Philadelphia, PA

Meridian Bank*(Investment Banker)*
York, PA

Smith, Anderson, Baker, Long & Rausch*(Legal Firm)*
124 E. Market St.
York, PA 17401
Tel.: 717-845-9641

Meridian Bank*(Major Banking Relationship)*
York, PA

DONLEN CORP.
500 Lake Cook Rd.
Deerfield, IL 60015
Tel.: 708-831-0400 **IL**
Fax: 708-831-0483
Year Founded: 1965
Approx.Sls.: $66,000,000
Emp.: 75
Fiscal Year-end: 8/31/87
Fleet Leasing & Management
S.I.C.: 7513
Don Rappeport *(Chm. Bd. & Chief Exec. Officer)*
G. Rappeport *(Pres.)*
Zeno Wisniewski *(V.P. & Claims Rels.)*
William C. Bush *(V.P.-Sls., Western Region)*
Gerald Witt *(V.P.-Sls., Central Region)*
Steve Sammis *(V.P.-Sls., Eastern Region)*
Paul B. Hieder *(V.P.-Maintenance Mngmt.)*
B. Birndorf *(Gen. Counsel)*
Principal(s):
Don Rappeport

No. of U.S. Offices: 6

Computer Systems/Hardware:
IBM System 38

Outside Service Firm(s):

BDO Seidman*(Auditors)*
111 E. Wacker Dr.
Chicago, IL 60601

Beryl A. Birndorf*(Legal Firm)*
Chicago, IL

Harris Trust & Savings Bank*(Major Banking Relationship)*
111 W. Monroe St.
Chicago, IL 60690
Tel.: 312-461-2265
Tel.: 800-858-0840

Harris Trust & Savings Bank*(Pension Manager)*
111 W. Monroe St.
Chicago, IL 60690
Tel.: 312-461-2265
Tel.: 800-858-0840

DONLEY'S, INC.
5430 Warner Rd.
Cleveland, OH 44125
Tel.: 216-524-6800 **OH**
Fax: 216-642-3216
Year Founded: 1941
Approx.Sls.: $12,000,000
Emp.: 225
Fiscal Year-end: 11/30/90
General Commercial & Industrial Contracting, Concrete Contracting
S.I.C.: 1541; 1542; 1771; 3272
Terrance K. Donley *(Pres. & Treas.)*
Patrick Powers *(Chief Fin. Officer)*
Mac Donley *(Exec. V.P.)*
Charles E. Zumpkehr *(Sec.)*

Computer Systems/Hardware:
IBM System 36

Outside Service Firm(s):

Arthur Andersen & Co.*(Auditors)*
1717 E. 9th St.
Cleveland, OH 44114
Tel.: 216-781-2140
Fax: 216-781-3683

Calfee, Halter & Griswold*(Legal Firm)*
800 Superior Ave., Ste. 1800
Cleveland, OH 44115-2688
Tel.: 216-622-8200
Fax: 216-241-0816

Society National Bank*(Major Banking Relationship)*
900 Euclid Ave., P.O. Box 6477
Cleveland, OH 44101-6477
Tel.: 216-737-5000
Fax: 216-566-8947

DONNKENNY, INC.
1411 Broadway
New York, NY 10018
Tel.: 212-730-7770 **NY**
Fax: 212-398-1787
Year Founded: 1931
Assets: $69,662,237
Liabilities: $63,295,155
Net Worth: $6,367,082
Approx.Sls.: $100,000,000
Emp.: 2,000
Fiscal Year-end: 12/ 1/90
Import Export
Mfr. of Women's Clothing
S.I.C.: 2331; 2341; 2335
Richard Rubin *(Chm., Pres., Chief Exec. & Chief Oper. Officer)*
Edward Creevy *(Chief Fin. Officer)*
Ronald Hollandsworth *(Controller)*
Diane Gubotosi *(Dir.-Pur.)*
Michael Holliday *(Dir.-Data Processing)*
Eileen Pack *(Dir.-Personnel)*

No. of Mfg. Plants/Facilities: 8
No. of U.S. Offices: 6

Computer Systems/Hardware:
IBM

Outside Service Firm(s):

KPMG Peat Marwick*(Auditors)*
345 Park Ave.
New York, NY 10154
Tel.: 212-758-9700
Fax: 212-872-3308

Hartford Life Insurance Co.*(Commercial Insurance Carrier)*
Hartford, CT 06104-2999

Squadron, Ellenoff, Plesent & Lehrer*(Legal Firm)*
551 Fifth Ave.
New York, NY 10017
Tel.: 212-661-6500

Division:

Mickey & Company **(1)**
1411 Broadway
New York, NY 10018
Tel.: 212-730-7770
Mfr. Apparel
S.I.C.: 2331
Michael O'Malley *(Pres.)*

Subsidiary:

Christiansburg Garment Co. Inc. **(1)**
1411 Broadway
New York, NY 10018
Tel.: 212-730-7770
Ladies' Sportswear
S.I.C.: 2339
Richard Rubin *(Pres.)*

THE DONOHOE COMPANIES, INC.
2101 Wisconsin Ave. N.W.
Washington, DC 20007
Tel.: 202-333-0880 **DE**
Fax: 202-333-5394
Year Founded: 1884
Approx.Sls.: $113,000,000
Emp.: 550
Building Developer & Contractor
S.I.C.: 1531; 1542; 6552
Richard J. Donohoe *(Chm. Exec. Committee)*
James A. Donohoe, III *(Pres. & Chief Exec. Officer)*
W. Michael Gorsage *(Pres.-Donohoe Real Estate Services)*
Robert C. Herr *(Pres.-Construction Co.)*
Robert A. Plitt *(Sr. V.P.)*
William M. Weistling, Sr. *(Sr. V.P.)*
John H. Clagett *(V.P.-Construction)*
Gerard Goeke *(V.P.-Information Services & Controller)*
Keith P. MacKinnon *(V.P.-Construction)*
William J. Walsh, III *(V.P. & Pres.-Property Mngmt. & Leasing)*
Joseph E. Widmayer *(V.P. & Pres.-Complete Bldg. Services)*
John E. Stinchfield *(Sec. & Gen. Counsel)*

Outside Service Firm(s):

Thomas Havey & Co.*(Auditors)*
Washington, DC

Melrod, Redman, Gartland*(Legal Firm)*
1801 K St., N.W., Ste. 1100
Washington, DC 20006
Tel.: 202-822-5300

American Security Bank, N.A.*(Major Banking Relationship)*
1501 Pennsylvania Ave. N.W.
Washington, DC 20013
Tel.: 202-624-4000

DONREY MEDIA GROUP
3600 Wheeler Ave.
Fort Smith, AR 72901
Mailing Address:
P.O. Box 17017
Fort Smith, AR 72917-7017
Tel.: 501-785-7810 **NV**
Fax: 501-785-9430
Year Founded: 1940
Assets: $330,000,000
Earnings: $25,000,000
Net Worth: $330,000,000
Approx.Sls.: $302,000,000
Emp.: 4,160
Fiscal Year-end: 6/30/89
Newspaper Publishing, Outdoor Advertising, Cable Television & Television Broadcasting
S.I.C.: 7312; 4832; 4833; 2711
Donald W. Reynolds *(Chm. Bd.)*
Fred W. Smith *(Pres. & Chief Exec. Officer)*
E.H. Patterson *(Exec. V.P. & Chief Fin. Officer)*
Ross Pendergrast *(Exec. V.P. & Chief Oper. Officer)*
Don R. Burns *(Sr. V.P.-Outdoor T.V. & Cable)*
Don R. Burris *(V.P.)*
Emmett Jones *(V.P.-Eastern Newspaper Group)*
Darrell W. Lofton *(V.P., Treas. & Controller)*
David A. Osborn *(V.P.-Western Newspaper Group)*
Gary Peterson *(Dir.-Mngmt. Information Systems)*
Principal(s):
Donald W. Reynolds

Computer Systems/Hardware:
IBM 4361

Outside Service Firm(s):

Deloitte & Touche*(Auditors)*
One Williams Center, Ste. 2400
Tulsa, OK
Tel.: 918-586-8800

Continental Bank N. A.*(Major Banking Relationship)*
231 S. LaSalle St.
Chicago, IL 60697
Tel.: 312-828-2345
Tel.: 800-426-5754
Telex: 312-828-1783

First Interstate Bank*(Major Banking Relationship)*
P.O. Box 98511,
Las Vegas, NV 89193-8511

NationsBank Carolinas*(Major Banking Relationship)*
One NCNB Plaza T18-7
Charlotte, NC 28255

Subsidiary:

Donrey Inc. TX **(1)**
306 E. California
Gainesville, TX 76240
Tel.: 817-665-5511
Newspaper Publishing
S.I.C.: 2711
Jerry Prickett *(Mng. Editor)*

DONTECH
(A Partnership Between Ameritech Publishing & Donnelley Directory)
205 N. Michigan Ave.
Chicago, IL 60601
Tel.: 312-861-3500
Fax: 312-856-8678
Year Founded: 1990
Approx.Sls.: $500,000,000
Emp.: 750
Fiscal Year-end: 12/31/90
Publishers of Ameritech PagesPlus, White & Yellow Page Directories in Illinois & Northwest Indiana; Moneysavers Coupons; Tel-Key & Street Address Directories
S.I.C.: 2741
Corporate Giving Program: Focus on Literary & Environmental Issues
Employee Matching Gifts Program: Matches Employee Contributions to Qualified Educational Institutions
Roger T. Hughes *(Pres. & Chief Exec. Officer)*
Carol Calzaretta *(V.P.-Human Resources)*
William Cooke *(V.P.-Strategic Plng. & Mktg.)*
Richard Cussigh *(V.P. & Chief Fin. Officer)*
Charles Sieber *(V.P.-Sls.)*
Edward Riehl *(V.P.-Law)*
Richard Boulton *(Dir.-Communications)*

DonTech—(Continued)

Peter Szalkowski *(Dir.-Mktg.)*
Sue Vittorio *(Sls. Promo. Mgr.)*
Kate Cleary *(Public Rels. Mgr.)*
Julie Hubbard *(Personnel Mgr.)*

Donut Equipment & Supply Co.
(See Yum Yum Donut Shop, Inc. Listing)

DOONAN & SONS, INC.
Jct. Hwy. 56 & 156
Great Bend, KS 67530
Mailing Address:
P.O. Box 1286
Great Bend, KS 67530
Tel.: 316-792-2494 **KS**
Fax: 316-792-2494, Ext. 122
Year Founded: 1978
Approx.Sls.: $48,000,000
Emp.: 120
Wholesale Distribution of New & Used Commercial Trucks & Trailers For Trucks
S.I.C.: 5012
Wendell M. Doonan *(Pres.)*
Kenneth C. Doonan *(V.P.)*
Jack Bunn *(Mgr.-Personnel)*

Outside Service Firm(s):

First National Bank & Trust Co.*(Major Banking Relationship)*
Great Bend, KS

Subsidiary:

Doonan Truck & Equipment, Inc. **(1)**
Jct. Hwy. 56 & 156
Great Bend, KS 67530
Tel.: 316-792-2494
Approx.Sls.: $46,000,000
Wholesael Distribution of New & Used Commercail Trucks & Trailer For Trucks
S.I.C.: 5012
Wendell M. Doonan *(Pres.)*

DOOR STORE, INC.
3140 M St. N.W.
Washington, DC 20007
Tel.: 202-333-8170 **DC**
Fax: 202-337-8647
Year Founded: 1957
Assets: $3,879,687
Liabilities: $2,005,375
Net Worth: $1,874,312
Approx.Sls.: $15,000,000
Emp.: 90
Fiscal Year-end: 12/31/91
Retail Contemporary Furniture
S.I.C.: 5712
Norman N. Tolkan *(Chm. Bd. & Pres.)*
Victor K. Tolkan *(Sec. & Treas.)*
Jaro Pacachek *(Dir.-Adv.)*
Ed Mendoza *(Supvr.-Payroll)*

Outside Service Firm(s):

Garner, Bloom & Klein*(Auditors)*
Chevy Chase, MD

First National Bank of Maryland*(Major Banking Relationship)*
25 S. Charles St.
Baltimore, MD 21201
Tel.: 410-244-4025

ACE DORAN HAULING & RIGGING COMPANY
1601 Blue Rock St.
Cincinnati, OH 45223
Tel.: 513-681-7900
Tel.: 800-829-0929 **OH**
Fax: 513-681-7900, Ext. 214
Year Founded: 1911
Assets: $11,199,000
Earnings: $11,199,000
Liabilities: $4,759,000
Net Worth: $6,440,000
Approx.Sls.: $30,000,000
Emp.: 120
Fiscal Year-end: 12/31/90
Transportation of General Commodities
S.I.C.: 4213
Robert J. Doran *(Pres. & Treas.)*
John R. Doran *(Exec. V.P.-Opers.)*
Patrick J. Doran *(V.P.)*
John Herbert *(Gen. Counsel & Sec.)*
Terry Sexton *(Comptroller)*
George W. Brown *(Mgr.-Data Processing)*
Cork Doran *(Mgr.-Adv.)*
Pat Cummings *(Dir.-Safety)*
Principal(s):
Robert J. Doran

Computer Systems/Hardware:
IBM System 38

Outside Service Firm(s):

Walter P. Plattenburg & Assoc.*(Auditors)*
8230 Montgomery Rd., Ste. 100
Cincinnati, OH
Tel.: 513-891-2722

Provident National Bank*(Major Banking Relationship)*
4140 Hamilton Ave.
Cincinnati, OH
Tel.: 513-681-3900

Lindhorst & Dreidame*(Legal Firm)*
1700 Central Trust, 201 E. Fifth St.
Cincinnati, OH 45202
Tel.: 513-421-6630

DORAN TEXTILES INC.
Hwy. 226
Shelby, NC 28151
Mailing Address:
P.O. Box 9000,
Shelby, NC 28151
Tel.: 704-487-2000 **NC**
Fax: 704-487-2218
Approx.Sls.: $230,000,000
Emp.: 2,500
Mfr. Drapery & Apparel Fabrics, Yarns & Home-Furnishing Fabrics
S.I.C.: 2211; 2221
John Fox, Jr. *(Chm.)*
David Roberts *(Pres. & Chief Oper. Officer)*
Chris Wallace *(Controller)*
Dean Garver *(Dir.-Human Resources)*

Outside Service Firm(s):

Coopers & Lybrand*(Auditors)*
1850 Charlotte Plaza
Charlotte, NC 28244
Tel.: 704-375-8414
Fax: 704-347-1601

First National Bank of Shelby*(Major Banking Relationship)*
Shelby, NC

Subsidiary:

Doran Mill Co. **(1)**
Drawer A
Shelby, NC 28151
Tel.: 704-487-2000
Broad Woven Fabric Mill
S.I.C.: 2211
John Fox, Jr. *(Chm. Bd.)*
David Roberts *(Pres. & Chief Oper. Officer)*
Chris Wallace *(Controller)*
Dean Garver *(Dir.-Human Resources)*

DORLAND SWEENEY JONES
701 Market St., Ste. 2000
Philadelphia, PA 19106
Tel.: 215-625-0111
Fax: 215-625-9037
Year Founded: 1883
Approx.Billings: $40,100,000
Emp.: 67
Healthcare Marketing
Harry A. Sweeney, Jr. *(Pres.)*
Dick Jones *(Exec. V.P. & Design Dir.)*
Robert Morrison *(Exec. V.P. & Creative Dir.)*
Charles J. Santangelo *(Exec. V.P., Fin. & Opers.)*
Barbara Zehender *(Exec. V.P., Grp. Dir.)*
Mike Hill *(Exec. V.P., Mktg.)*
Nancy B. Long *(Acct. Supvr.-Pub. Rels.)*

DORMAN-ROTH FOODS, INC.
14 Empire Blvd.
Moonachie, NJ 07074
Tel.: 201-440-3600
Approx.Sls.: $250,000,000
Emp.: 500
Endeco, LoChol Cheeses, Joan of Arc
S.I.C.: 2022
Richard Dietterich *(Pres.)*
William Urich *(V.P.-Fin.)*
Ned Dorman *(V.P.-Food Service-Mktg. & Sls.)*
Steve Bullard *(V.P.-Retail Mktg.)*
Mark Ruchheim *(V.P.-Opers.)*
Steve Flintosh *(Controller)*
Gary Graf *(Dir.-Procurement)*
Steve Vanacore *(Dir.-Mngmt. Information Systems)*

Division:

Dorman-Roth Foods Div., Inc. **(1)**
105 Third St.
Monroe, WI 53566
Tel.: 608-325-2187
Fax: 608-325-2177

DORMEYER INDUSTRIES
3418 N. Milwaukee Ave.
Chicago, IL 60641
Tel.: 312-775-3600
Fax: 312-283-4927
Year Founded: 1950
Approx.Sls.: $11,000,000
Emp.: 250
Fiscal Year-end: 7/31/90
Mfr. Solenoids, Transformers, Coils, Converter/Chargers
S.I.C.: 3625; 3677; 3629
John Armour *(Pres.)*
Larry Harney *(Exec. V.P.)*
Bonnie Merry *(Treas.)*
Bob Steinberg *(Dir.-Sls.)*
Bill Gerhard *(Mgr.-Natl. Sls.)*
Ed Weber *(Pur. Agent)*

EDWARD G. DORN & ASSOCIATES, INC.
1801-H S. Hicks Rd.
Rolling Meadows, IL 60008
Tel.: 708-991-1270
Fax: 708-991-1519
Year Founded: 1971
Approx.Billings: $15,280,000
Emp.: 20
Industrial, Hi-Tech, Automotive & Consumer
Edward G. Dorn *(Chm. Bd. & Pres.)*
John Andersen *(Exec. V.P.)*
Bob Skolnick *(V.P., Dir. Sls. & New Bus. Contact)*
Cecilia A. Dorn *(Sec. & Treas.)*
Linda Dorn *(Pub. Rels. Dir.)*
Elayne Sivertsen *(Desk Top Publr.)*
Kathleen Williams *(Mktg. Dir.)*

ERNST W. DORN CO., INC.
15905 S. Broadway
Gardena, CA 90248
Tel.: 310-770-8080 **CA**
Approx.Sls.: $24,000,000
Emp.: 94
Fiscal Year-end: 12/31/91
Import Export
Supplies & Equipment for Screen Printing
S.I.C.: 5084; 5198
Ernst W. Dorn, II *(Pres.)*
James C. Walker *(Exec. V.P.)*
Thomas E. MacDonald *(Chief Fin. Officer)*
Harry K. Padveen *(Treas.)*
Vera Benson *(Sec. & Controller)*
Principal(s):
Ernst W. Dorn, II

Computer Systems/Hardware:
IBM 3600

Outside Service Firm(s):

Latham & Watkins*(Legal Firm)*
633 West Fifth St.
Los Angeles, CA 90071
Tel.: 213-485-1234
Fax: 213-643-9086

Community Bank*(Major Banking Relationship)*
Pasadena, CA

DORON PRECISION SYSTEMS, INC.
174 Court St.
Binghamton, NY 13902
Mailing Address:
Box 400
Binghamton, NY 13902
Tel.: 607-772-1610 **DE**
Fax: 607-772-6760
Year Founded: 1973
Assets: $6,780,000
Liabilities: $3,543,000
Net Worth: $3,237,000
Sales Range: $10-19 Million
Emp.: 102
Fiscal Year-end: 9/30/91
Export
Simulation Systems for Auto, Truck, Bus; Multi-Media/Student Response Systems; Simulated Amusement Rides
S.I.C.: 3663; 7373; 7372
Employee Matching Gifts Program: Matches Twenty Percent of Employee's First Five Percent
Carl J. Wenzinger, Jr. *(Chm. Bd.)*
Karl J. Hirshman *(Pres.)*
W. Ralph Price *(Exec. V.P.)*
Ken Kittinger *(V.P.)*
Robert J. Nole *(Treas. & Mgr.-Mngmt. Information Systems)*
W.K. Adams *(Mgr.-Curriculum)*
David Lindsey *(Mgr.-Mktg.)*
O.W. Murray *(Mgr.-Intl. Sls.)*
James Paff *(Mgr.-Customer Service)*
Margurite Rush *(Mgr.-Pur.)*
Robert C. Pettit *(Chief Engr.)*

Computer Systems/Hardware:
IBM System 36

Outside Service Firm(s):

Bonadio, Insero & Co.*(Auditors)*
Rochester, NY 11604

Kemper Insurance*(Commercial Insurance Carrier)*
Johnson City, NY

Binghamton Savings Bank*(Investment Banker)*
Binghamton, NY 13902

Sherburne, Powers & Needham*(Legal Firm)*
Boston, MA

Chase Lincoln First Bank, N.A.*(Major Banking Relationship)*
P.O. Box 1250,
Rochester, NY 14603
Tel.: 716-232-5000

Subsidiary:

Foron International Sales Corp. **(1)**
P.O. Box 400,
Binghamton, NY 13902
Tel.: 607-772-1610
Emp.: 90
K.J. Hirshman *(Pres.)*
O.W. Murray *(V.P.)*
R.J. Nole *(Treas.)*

DORR-OLIVER INCORPORATED
612 Wheeler's Farms Rd.
Milford, CT 06460
Mailing Address:
P.O. Box 3819
Milford, CT 06460
Tel.: 203-876-5400
Telex: 965912
Fax: 203-876-5432
Approx.Sls.: $150,000,000
Emp.: 700
Fiscal Year-end: 3/31/91
Export
Processing Equipment & Systems; Food Processing Machinery, General & Specialized Industrial Machinery; Separators for Gas, Air, Steam & Vapor; Chemical Engineering
S.I.C.: 3532; 3554; 3561; 3559; 3567; 3569
E.J. Finn *(Chm. Bd.)*
C.J. Barton *(Pres.)*
M.S. Madigan *(Sr. V.P.-Fin.)*
L. Bonnyay *(V.P.-Europe)*
C.J. Patten *(V.P. & Gen. Counsel)*
R.E. Coomes *(V.P. & Controller)*
J.J. Murphy *(U.S. Mktg. Mgr.)*

THE DORRIS LUMBER & MOULDING CO.
2601 Redding Ave.
Sacramento, CA 95820
Tel.: 916-452-7531
Fax: 916-452-0377
Year Founded: 1924
Approx.Sls.: $34,000,000
Emp.: 170
Import Export
Millwork, Mouldings
S.I.C.: 2431
Chase Israelson *(Pres.)*
Bob Pascuzzi *(Chief Fin. Officer & Sec.)*
Erik Israelson *(V.P.)*
Dan Mathes *(V.P.)*
Robert J. Reynolds *(V.P.)*
Joshua Tyler *(V.P.)*

Outside Service Firm(s):

Ross, McDonald & Bonetti*(Auditors)*
Sacramento, CA

Diepenbrock, Wulff, Plant & Hannegan*(Legal Firm)*
Sacramento, CA

Wells Fargo Bank*(Major Banking Relationship)*
420 Montgomery St.
San Francisco, CA 94104

DORRITIE LYONS & NICKEL, INC.
655 Third Ave.
New York, NY 10017
Tel.: 212-687-9394
Fax: 212-983-6946
Year Founded: 1979
Approx.Billings: $60,505,500
Emp.: 69
Health Care Adv.
Michael J. Lyons *(Chm. & Chief Exec. & Creative Officer)*
Albert G. Nickel *(Pres. & Chief Oper. Officer)*
Thomas J. Velardi *(Exec. V.P., Assoc. Creative Dir.-Art)*
Marilyn Hertzberg *(V.P., Fin. & Office Services)*

DORSEY TRAILERS, INC.
One Paces W. #1700, 2727 Paces Ferry Rd.
Atlanta, GA 30339
Tel.: 404-438-9595 **GA**
Fax: 404-438-8190
Year Founded: 1911
Approx.Sls.: $100,000,000
Emp.: 1,000
Fiscal Year-end: 12/31/91
Mfr. of Truck Trailers, Container Chassis, Dump Trailers, Refrigerated Trailers, Platform Trailers, Refuse Trailers
S.I.C.: 3715
Marilyn Marks *(Pres. & Chief Exec. Officer)*
T. Charles Chitwood *(Chief Fin. Officer)*
Nick Culich *(V.P. & Gen. Mgr.)*
Charles W. Mudd *(V.P.-Sls. & Mktg.)*
Paul Morrow *(V.P.-Admin.)*
Kenny Sawyer *(Dir.-Human Resources)*
Barbara Owen *(Dir.-Admin. Services)*
Principal(s):
Marilyn Marks

No. of Mfg. Plants/Facilities: 2
No. of U.S. Offices: 3

Computer Systems/Hardware:
IBM System 38

Outside Service Firm(s):

Price Waterhouse*(Auditors)*
100 Cumberland Circle, Ste. 1400
Atlanta, GA 30339

Blue Cross & Blue Shield of Alabama*(Group Insurer)*
450 Riverchase Pkwy. East
Birmingham, AL 35298
Tel.: 205-988-2245

The Robinson-Humphrey Company, Inc.*(Investment Banker)*
3333 Peachtree Road
Atlanta, GA 30326
Tel.: 404-266-6000

Alston & Bird*(Legal Firm)*
One Atlantic Center, 1201 West Peachtree St.
Atlanta, GA 30309-3424
Tel.: 404-881-7000

Congress Financial Corp.*(Major Banking Relationship)*
Atlanta, GA

Plant:

Dorsey Trailers, Inc. **(1)**
1409 Hickman St.
Elba, AL 36323
Tel.: 205-897-5711
Fax: 205-897-5345
Mfr. of Truck Trailers, Container Chassis, Dump Trailers, Refrigerated Trailers, Platform Trailers, Refuse Trailers
S.I.C.: 3715
Marilyn R. Marks *(Pres.)*

DOT PRINTER, INC.
2424 McGaw Ave.
Irvine, CA 92714
Tel.: 714-474-1100
Fax: 714-474-1263
Approx.Sls.: $25,000,000
Emp.: 145
Lithographic Printing
S.I.C.: 2752
Charles L. Massingil *(Chm. Bd.)*
Bruce M. Carson *(Pres.)*
Eric C. Pepys *(Sec. & Treas.)*
Cindy Brown *(Payroll Admin.)*

Dothan Mfg. Co.
(See Listing Under Host Apparel, Inc.; Name Changed To Dothan Apparel, Inc.)

DOUBLE AA BUILDERS, LTD.
7319 N. 16th St., Ste. 200
Phoenix, AZ 85020
Tel.: 602-944-0544 **AZ**
Fax: 602-944-0610
Year Founded: 1989
Assets: $1,359,486
Liabilities: $1,240,569
Net Worth: $118,917
Sales Range: $10-19 Million
Emp.: 10
Fiscal Year-end: 6/31/90
Export
General Contractor of Commercial Buildings
S.I.C.: 1542
Geoffrey E. Schwan *(Pres.)*
Robert J. Rohn *(V.P.-Field Opers. Mgr.)*
Edward O. Burke *(Gen. Counsel)*

Principal(s):
Geoffrey E. Schwan
Robert J. Rohn

No. of Mfg. Plants/Facilities: 1
No. of U.S. Offices: 1

Computer Systems/Hardware:
CDCI; IPM PC-AT

Outside Service Firm(s):

David R. Nicholas*(Auditors)*
Phoenix, AZ

Aetna Life & Casualty*(Commercial Insurance Carrier)*
151 Farmington Avenue
Hartford, CT 06156
Tel.: 203-273-2128
Fax: 203-729-4295

Safeco Insurance Co. of America*(Group Insurer)*
Phoenix, AZ

First Interstate Bank*(Major Banking Relationship)*
P.O. Box 53441,
Phoenix, AZ 85072-3441
Tel.: 602-229-4049

THE DOUBLE-COLA COMPANY
3350 Broad St.
Chattanooga, TN 37408
Tel.: 615-267-5691
Telex: 558-436 DBL COLA CTA
Fax: 615-267-0793
Year Founded: 1927
Approx.Sls.: $19,000,000
Emp.: 24
Fiscal Year-end: 12/31/90
Import Export
Flavor Mfr., Double Cola, Ski, Jumbo, Diet Double Cola, Chaser
S.I.C.: 2086; 2087
Noorally K. J. Dhanani *(Chm. Bd.)*
Alnoor K.J. Dhanani *(Vice Chm.)*
L.E. Shanks *(Pres.)*
John H. Kirby *(V.P.-Sls.)*
Karl Sooder *(V.P.-Mktg.)*
M. H. Sanborn, Jr. *(V.P. & Dir.-Intl. Sls.)*
Leland Myers *(Controller)*

Computer Systems/Hardware:
IBM; Apple

JON DOUGLAS COMPANY
427 N. Camden Dr.
Beverly Hills, CA 90210
Tel.: 310-859-7007 **CA**
Fax: 310-859-7481
Year Founded: 1971
Approx.Sls.: $100,000,000
Emp.: 2000
Full Service Residential Real Estate Brokerage & Development Company
S.I.C.: 6552
Jon A. Douglas *(Pres. & Chief Exec. Officer)*
Lou Piatt *(Exec. V.P. & Chief Oper. Officer)*
John Mortenson *(Sr. V.P.-Opers.)*
Barbara Orr *(V.P. & Chief Fin. Officer)*

No. of U.S. Offices: 32

Outside Service Firm(s):

Kenneth Leventhal & Co.*(Auditors)*
Los Angeles, CA

DOUGLAS ELLIMAN-GIBBONS & IVES, INC.
575 Madison Ave.
New York, NY 10022
Tel.: 212-832-4100
Fax: 212-891-7239
Approx.Sls.: $12,000,000
Emp.: 250
Real Estate Management & Brokerage
S.I.C.: 6531
Howard P. Milstein *(Chm. & Chief Exec. Officer)*
John P. Clancy *(Sr. V.P. & Controller)*
Nicholas Dana *(Sr. V.P.)*
Frank W. Doelger *(Sr. V.P.)*
Jeffery Urstadt *(Sr. V.P.)*

Divisions:

Douglas Elliman-Gibbons & Ives, Inc. **(1)**
30 Morristown Rd.
Bernardsville, NJ 07924
Tel.: 908-221-1244

Douglas Elliman-Haldenstein **(1)**
2112 Broadway
New York, NY 10023
Tel.: 212-362-9600

Douglas Elliman, Inc. **(1)**
41 Meeting House Lane
Southampton, NY 11968
Tel.: 516-283-0303
Cynthia Gay *(Sr. V.P.)*
Gordon Hamersley *(Sr. V.P.)*

Douglas Elliman-Jane Hayes, Inc. **(1)**
71 Forest Ave.
Locust Valley, NY 11560
Tel.: 516-759-0400
Louise O'Rourke *(V.P.)*

Douglas Elliman Knight Frank Inc. **(1)**
10 Rooney Circle
West Orange, NJ 07052
Tel.: 201-864-9400
Thomas Glerum *(Exec. V.P.)*

Douglas Elliman Pickering Assoc., Inc. **(1)**
30 Milbank Ave.
Greenwich, CT 06830
Tel.: 203-869-7800
Rosamond Pickering Shannon *(Pres.)*

DOUGLAS STEEL FABRICATING CORPORATION
1312 S. Waverly Rd.
Lansing, MI 48917
Mailing Address:
P.O. Box 27277
Lansing, MI 48909
Tel.: 517-322-2050
Fax: 517-322-0050
Approx.Sls.: $17,000,000
Emp.: 100
Import Export
Steel Fabricator
S.I.C.: 3441
Ronald Beckwith *(Pres.)*
John M. Rogers *(Exec. V.P.)*
Lee Tucker *(Controller)*
Michael J. Szostak *(Dir.-Mktg. & Sls.)*
Ruth Essenberg *(Sec.)*

Outside Service Firm(s):

Dickinson Wright Moon VanDusen & Freeman*(Legal Firm)*
Lansing, MI

Manufacturers Bank*(Major Banking Relationship)*
Lansing, MI

DOUGLAS STEPHEN PLASTICS, INC.
22-36 Green St.
Paterson, NJ 07501
Mailing Address:
P.O. Box 2775,
Paterson, NJ 07501
Tel.: 201-523-3030 NJ
Fax: 201-523-0643
Year Founded: 1959
Sales Range: $10-19 Million
Emp.: 140
Plastic Food Containers, Cutlery Catering Trays, Kits
S.I.C.: 3089; 3085
Stewart Graff *(Pres.)*
Douglas Graff *(V.P.)*
M. Graff *(Treas. & Sec.)*
Brian McCullough *(Mgr.-Sls.)*

Outside Service Firm(s):

Shulman & Solomon, pc*(Auditors)*
Hasbrouck Heights, NJ

Badd, Larner, Gross & Picillo*(Legal Firm)*
Short Hills, NJ

Hudson United Bank North*(Major Banking Relationship)*
Paterson, NJ

DOWNEY DESIGNS INTERNATIONAL, INC.
2265 Executive Dr.
Indianapolis, IN 46241
Tel.: 317-248-9888
Fax: 317-244-6823
Approx.Sls.: $49,000,000
Emp.: 210
Jewelry, Precious & Semi-precious Stones & Metals
S.I.C.: 3911; 5094
David G. Downey *(Chm. Bd. & Chief Exec. Officer)*
Robert B. Sloan *(Pres., Chief Oper. Officer & Treas.)*
Nancy M. Mills *(Chief Fin. Officer & V.P.)*
Michael A. Hasten *(Exec. V.P.)*
David Henry *(V.P.)*
Cynthia Smith *(Coord.-Human Resources)*

Outside Service Firm(s):

Gottlieb & Schwartz*(Legal Firm)*
69 Washington
Chicago, IL 60602
Tel.: 312-726-2122

Bank One, Indianapolis, N.A.*(Major Banking Relationship)*
111 Monument Circle, Ste. 1611
Indianapolis, IN 46204-1611
Tel.: 317-321-8110

DOWNEY PRINTING
400 Deming Ave.
Waukee, IA 50263
Mailing Address:
P.O. Box 489
Waukee, IA 50263
Tel.: 515-987-5100
Fax: 515-987-5155
Assets: $3,850,000
Earnings: $300,000
Net Worth: $3,850,000
Sales Range: $10-19 Million
Emp.: 114
Commercial & Telephone Directory Printing; Commercial Catalogs
S.I.C.: 2759
John M. Downey *(Chm. Bd.)*
J. Michael Downey *(Pres.)*
Cynthia S. Craigmile *(Chief Fin. Officer & V.P.)*
Kim Roach *(Mgr.-Acctg.)*

Computer Systems/Hardware:
IBM 5211; McDonald Douglas 6000

Outside Service Firm(s):

McGladrey & Pullen*(Auditors)*
Des Moines, IA

Blue Cross of Iowa*(Group Insurer)*
Des Moines, IA

TONY DOWNS FOODS COMPANY
400 Armstrong Blvd. N.
Saint James, MN 56081
Tel.: 507-375-3111 MN
Fax: 507-375-3048
Year Founded: 1947
Approx.Sls.: $40,000,000
Emp.: 550
Processes, Freezes & Cans Chickens; Manufacturer of Frozen Entrees
S.I.C.: 2038; 2013
Richard Downs *(Chm. Bd. & Chief Exec. Officer)*
David Sawyer *(Pres.)*
Dale Grothe *(Dir.-Human Resources)*
Patricia M. Johnson *(Dir.-Fin., Treas. & Sec.)*

Outside Service Firm(s):

Ernst & Young*(Auditors)*
111 E. Kilbourn Ave., Ste. 900
Milwaukee, WI 53202
Tel.: 414-273-5900

M & I Marshall & Ilsley Bank*(Major Banking Relationship)*
770 N. Water St.
Milwaukee, WI 53202
Tel.: 414-765-8700

THE DOWNS GROUP, INC.
120 Greenwich Rd.
Charlotte, NC 28211
Tel.: 704-364-4133
Fax: 704-365-3184
Year Founded: 1975
Approx.Billings: $11,000,000
Emp.: 15
Business-to-Business & High Technology
William F. Downs *(Chm. Bd.)*
Beverly B. Downs *(Vice Chm., Chief Exec. Officer & Treas.)*
Tyler E. Glenn, Jr. *(Pres. & Chief Oper. Officer)*

DOYLE MCKENNA BAYER BROWN
1175 Harvard Way
Reno, NV 89502
Tel.: 702-323-2181
Fax: 702-329-5899
Year Founded: 1955
Approx.Billings: $15,000,000
Emp.: 32
Eugene M. McKenna *(Pres.)*
Mark Bayer *(Exec. V.P.)*
Ray Brown *(Exec. V.P.)*
Lynnae Hornbarger *(V.P., Admin., Media Services Dir.)*

DRACKETT & LAVIDGE, INC.
6263 N. Scottsdale Rd., Ste. 190
Scottsdale, AZ 85250
Tel.: 602-998-2600
Fax: 602-998-5525
Year Founded: 1982
Approx.Billings: $15,000,000
Emp.: 29
William R. Lavidge *(Pres.)*
Mark Hiegel *(Gen. Mgr.)*
Susan Smith *(Fin. Mgr.)*
Helen Prorock *(Receptionist)*

Computer Systems/Hardware:
MacIntosh; IBM-Adman (Accounting)

DRAFTING GRAPHICS, INC.
1250 Pratt Blvd.
Elk Grove Village, IL 60007
Tel.: 708-593-0500
Fax: 708-593-1164
Emp.: 35
Printers for Engineering & Drafting Companies
S.I.C.: 2759
Grant S. Antink *(Pres. & Chief Exec. Officer)*
Mary Hartman *(Dir.-Mktg.)*

Computer Systems/Hardware:
IBM

Outside Service Firm(s):

Lakeside Bank*(Investment Banker)*
Chicago, IL

Daniel Marsch*(Legal Firm)*
Chicago, IL

Lakeside Bank*(Major Banking Relationship)*
Chicago, IL

DRAPER CORPORATION
5644 Hornaday Rd.
Greensboro, NC 27409
Mailing Address:
P.O. Box 18100,
Greensboro, NC 27419-8100
Tel.: 919-852-4200 GA
Fax: 919-855-1122
Approx.Sls.: $40,000,000
Emp.: 375
Fiscal Year-end: 3/31/91
Import Export
Mfr. Textile Looms & Parts
S.I.C.: 3552
Edward J. Bauman *(Chm. Bd.)*
William O. Cordes *(Pres. & Chief Exec. Officer)*
James F. Arpe *(Chief Fin. Officer)*
C. Denny Walker *(Sec. & Dir.-Personnel)*
Keith Garber *(Dir.-Materials & Info. Systems)*
Harry Gainey *(Dir.-Mktg. Communications)*

No. of Mfg. Plants/Facilities: 5
No. of U.S. Offices: 3
No. of Foreign Offices: 2

Computer Systems/Hardware:
IBM 4341

Outside Service Firm(s):

Arthur Andersen & Co.*(Auditors)*
One Southern Life Center
Greensboro, NC 27401
Fax: 919-378-1445

Smith, Melns, McMullis & Moore*(Legal Firm)*
Greensboro, NC

First Union National Bank*(Pension Manager)*
Two First Union Center CMG-5-1154
Charlotte, NC 28288-1154
Tel.: 704-374-6250

Division:

Seabrook Inc. **(1)**
410 Shockley Rd.
Anderson, SC 29622
Tel.: 803-224-5671
Mfr. of Replacement Parts for Textile Mills
S.I.C.: 3552
W.O. Cordes *(Pres.)*

Non-U.S. Holdings:

Draper de Mexico S.A. de C.V. **(1)**
Norte 75, 2591 Colonia Xochimanca
Mexico, D.F. 16, Mexico
Tel.: 905-399-5499 (100%)
Loom Parts Mfr.
S.I.C.: 3552
W.O. Cordes *(Pres.)*

Draper Erin Ltd. **(1)**
Dock Rd., Corcanree Industrial Estate
Limerick, Ireland
Tel.: 353-61-28555 (100%)
Loom Parts Mfr.
S.I.C.: 3552
W.O. Cordes *(Pres.)*

DRAPER DANIELS MEDIA SERVICES, INC.
2525 Armitage Ave.
Melrose Park, IL 60160
Tel.: 708-450-3000
Year Founded: 1980
Approx.Billings: $43,500,000
Emp.: 7
Advertising Agency Specializing in Media Plng. & Buying
S.I.C.: 7311; 7319
Marilyn Lunenfeld *(V.P.)*
Michelle Dirks *(Network Opers. Supvr.)*

Dravo Automation Sciences, Inc.
(Name Changed To Daxus Corporation)

DREISBACH & SONS CADILLAC COMPANY
24600 Grand River Ave.
Detroit, MI 48219
Tel.: 313-531-2600 MI
Fax: 313-531-0196
Year Founded: 1965
Approx.Sls.: $32,000,000
Emp.: 105
Retail Sales & Service of New & Used Automobiles
S.I.C.: 5511; 7538
Thomas S. Dreisbach *(Chm. Bd. & Chief Oper. Officer)*
Mark L. Dreisbach *(Pres.)*
John F. Noonan *(Sec.)*
David Porter *(Treas.)*
Bill Rocker *(Dir.-Sls.)*

Outside Service Firm(s):

Paul V. Engstrom & Co.*(Auditors)*
Southfield, MI

Troy Noonan*(Legal Firm)*
Detroit, MI

NBD Bank, N.A.*(Major Banking Relationship)*
P.O. Box 222,
Detroit, MI 48232
Tel.: 313-225-4414
Fax: 313-225-3420

LOUIS DREYFUS CORPORATION
10 Westport Rd.
Wilton, CT 06897
Tel.: 203-761-9700
Fax: 203-761-2375
Year Founded: 1941
Emp.: 240
Agricultural Services; Trucking & Warehousing; Commodity Exporters
S.I.C.: 4214; 4221; 5153; 5144; 5147
John Finlayson *(Chm. Bd.)*
Jerome Dubrowski *(V.P., Treas. & Chief Fin. Officer)*
Peter Griffin *(Controller)*
Leon Nackenson *(Sec.)*
Thomas Scheuer *(Legal Counsel & Asst. Sec.)*

Computer Systems/Hardware:
IBM System 36

Outside Service Firm(s):

Ernst & Young*(Auditors)*
Six Landmark Square
Stamford, CT 06901
Tel.: 203-348-3700

Dewey Ballantine*(Legal Firm)*
1301 Avenue of Americas
New York, NY 10019-6092
Tel.: 212-820-1100

Subsidiary:

Louis Dreyfus Natural Gas **(1)**
14000 Quail Springs Pkwy., Ste. 600
Oklahoma City, OK 73134
Tel.: 405-749-1300
Fax: 405-848-1197
Assets: $43,499,000
Earnings: ($657,000)
Liabilities: $23,118,000
Net Worth: $20,381,000
Approx.Rev.: $16,811,000
Emp.: 175
Fiscal Year-end: 9/30/90
Oil & Gas Exploration
S.I.C.: 1311
John Finlayson *(Chm. Bd.)*

DRI MARK PRODUCTS, INC.
15 Harbor Park Dr.
Port Washington, NY 11050
Tel.: 516-484-6200 **NY**
Fax: 516-484-6279
Year Founded: 1960
Sales Range: $10-19 Million
Emp.: 100
Fiscal Year-end: 10/31/91
Import Export
Markers & Office Supplies
S.I.C.: 3951
Charles Reichmann *(Chief Exec. Officer)*
Louis Reichmann *(Pres.)*
Ellen Samra *(V.P.-Sls. & Mktg.)*
Cathy Williams *(Controller)*
Joan Stern *(Mgr.-Pur.)*

No. of Mfg. Plants/Facilities: 1
No. of U.S. Offices: 1

Computer Systems/Hardware:
IBM PC

DRI-PRINT FOILS
329 New Brunswick Ave.
Rahway, NJ 07065
Tel.: 908-382-6800
Fax: 908-382-8760
Approx.Sls.: $20,000,000
Emp.: 200
Mfr. of Hot Stamping Foils & Application Machinery; Dri-Cal
S.I.C.: 3497
George Shouldis *(V.P.-Opers. & Fin.)*
John Porto *(V.P.-Sls. & Mktg.)*

DRIBECK IMPORTERS, INC.
57 Old Post Road No. 2
Greenwich, CT 06830
Mailing Address:
P. O. Box 4000
Greenwich, CT 06836
Tel.: 203-622-1124
Fax: 203-622-0533
Year Founded: 1964
Approx.Sls.: $120,000,000
Emp.: 57
Import
Importers of Beck's Beer, Dribeck Light Beer & Haake-Beck Non-Alcoholic Beer
S.I.C.: 5181
John J. Kucich *(Pres. & Chief Exec. Officer)*
Thomas H. Schwalm *(Exec. V.P.-Sls. & Mktg.)*
Thomas Angelo *(Exec. V.P.-Fin.)*
Virgil Abbatiello *(V.P.-Sls.)*

L.F. DRISCOLL CO.
P.O. Box 468, 9 Presidential Blvd.
Bala-Cynwyd, PA 19004
Tel.: 215-668-0950 **PA**
Fax: 215-668-9425
Year Founded: 1929
Approx.Sls.: $126,000,000
Emp.: 250
General Contractor; Industrial & Nonresidential Building, Warehouse Construction
S.I.C.: 1541; 1542
Edward C. Driscoll *(Chm. Bd., Chief Exec. Officer & Treas.)*
Thomas J. Tobin, Jr. *(Pres.)*
John J. Donnelly *(Exec. V.P.-Construction)*
Mary Leach Colen *(Sr. V.P.-Mktg.)*
Joe Saggisi *(Chief Fin. Officer)*

Outside Service Firm(s):

Coopers & Lybrand*(Auditors)*
2400 Eleven Penn Center
Philadelphia, PA 19103-2962
Tel.: 215-963-8000

Wolf, Block, Schorr & Solis-Cohen*(Legal Firm)*
Packard Bldg., 12th Fl., 15th & Chestnut Sts.
Philadelphia, PA 19102
Tel.: 215-569-4000

Provident National Bank*(Major Banking Relationship)*
1000 Westlakes Dr.
Berwyn, PA 19312

DRIVE TRAIN INDUSTRIES
3301 Brighton Blvd.
Denver, CO 80217
Mailing Address:
P.O. Box 5845,
Denver, CO 80217
Tel.: 303-292-1100 **CO**
Fax: 303-297-0473
Approx.Sls.: $19,000,000
Emp.: 154
Wholesale Heavy Duty Truck Parts; General Automotive Repair
S.I.C.: 5013; 7538
R. James Burke *(Pres.)*
Paul T. Burke *(V.P.-Opers.)*
Richard J. Switzer *(Sec. & Treas.)*

Outside Service Firm(s):

Grant Thornton*(Auditors)*
Denver, CO

Wade, Ash, Word, Hill & Guthery*(Legal Firm)*
Denver, CO

First Interstate Bank*(Major Banking Relationship)*
Denver, CO
Tel.: 303-293-5456

ROBERT F. DRIVER CO., INC.
1620 Fifth Ave.
San Diego, CA 92101-2703
Mailing Address:
P.O. Box 670,
San Diego, CA 92112-4121
Tel.: 619-238-1828 **CA**
Fax: 619-699-1323
Year Founded: 1925
Assets: $23,474,000
Earnings: $215,000
Liabilities: $21,526,000
Net Worth: $1,948,000
Approx.Sls.: $209,900,000
Emp.: 221
Fiscal Year-end: 7/31/91
Insurance Brokers & Service
S.I.C.: 6411; 6311; 6321
Robert F. Driver *(Chm. Bd. Emeritus)*
Irwin B. Sklar *(Chm. Bd.)*
George F. Driver *(Pres. & Chief Oper. Officer)*
Richard B. Gulley *(Chief Exec. Officer)*
John Freeman *(Chief Fin. Officer, V.P., Treas. & Sec.)*
Roger G. Combe *(Exec. V.P.)*
Thomas W. Corbett *(Exec. V.P. & Dir.-Newport Beach Office)*
Martin Heflin *(V.P. & Dir.-Marine Div.)*
Robert L. Mikels *(V.P. & Dir.-Information Services)*
Robert D'Angelo *(V.P. & Mgr.-Employee Benefits)*
Thomas P. Brady *(V.P. & Mgr.-Escond Office)*
Barbara A. Clady *(V.P. & Mgr.-Mktg.)*
Donetta Francis *(V.P. & Controller)*
Thomas W. Buschmann *(Asst. V.P. & Dir.-Admin.)*
Deborah Knutson *(Asst. V.P. & Dir-Human Resources)*
Didi Standard *(Asst. Controller)*
Tom Buschmann *(Dir.-Admin. & Telecommunications & Corp. Video Systems)*
Alpha Johnson *(Dir.-Personnel Training)*
Mark Winter *(Dir.-Pur.)*
Principal(s):
Robert F. Driver
Irwin B. Sklar

No. of U.S. Offices: 3

Computer Systems/Hardware:
DELPHI; IBM RS6000

Outside Service Firm(s):

West, Johnston, Turnquist & Schmitt*(Auditors)*
2550 Fifth Ave.
San Diego, CA 92103
Tel.: 619-234-6775

Aetna Life & Casualty*(Group Insurer)*
San Diego, CA

Sullivan, Cummins, Wartz, McDade & Wallace*(Legal Firm)*
945 4th Ave.
San Diego, CA 92101
Tel.: 619-233-1888

Security Pacific National Bank*(Major Banking Relationship)*
San Diego, CA

Lawrence S. Branton*(Pension Manager)*
San Diego, CA

Branches:

Robert F. Driver & Co., Inc. **(1)**
3636 Birch St., Ste. 230
Newport Beach, CA 92660-2619
Tel.: 714-756-0271
Fax: 714-756-2713
Insurance Broker & Service
S.I.C.: 6411

Robert F. Driver & Co., Inc. **(1)**
613 W. Valley Pkwy., Ste. 220
Escondido, CA 92025-2550
Tel.: 619-578-3341
Fax: 619-745-5815
Insurance Broker & Service
S.I.C.: 6411

Subsidiary:

Premium Advance Company **(1)**
1620 5th Ave., P.O. Box 670
San Diego, CA 92101
Tel.: 619-238-1828 (100%)
Fax: 619-699-1323
Emp.: 184
Premium Financing
S.I.C.: 6289

DRUG EMPORIUM OF ARIZONA, INC.
13402 N. Scottsdale Rd., Ste. B160
Scottsdale, AZ 85254
Tel.: 602-948-2266 **AZ**
Fax: 602-951-9145
Year Founded: 1979
Assets: $14,400,000
Earnings: $1,620,000
Liabilities: $12,700,000
Net Worth: $1,700,000
Approx.Sls.: $79,100,000
Emp.: 425
Fiscal Year-end: 8/31/91
Retail Drug Store Franchise
S.I.C.: 5912
Richard L. Henderson *(Pres.)*
Gregg C. Roberson *(Sr. V.P. & Chief Oper. Officer)*
Malvern D. Crowley *(V.P.-Fin. & Treas.)*
Barbara Henderson *(V.P. & Sec.)*
Principal(s):
Richard L. Henderson
Gregg C. Roberson
Malvern D. Crowley

Outside Service Firm(s):

Deloitte & Touche*(Auditors)*
2901 North Central Ave., Ste. 1200
Phoenix, AZ 85012
Tel.: 602-234-5100
Fax: 602-234-5186

Polese, Hiner & Nolan*(Legal Firm)*
Phoenix, AZ

Valley National Bank*(Major Banking Relationship)*
241 N. Central Ave.
Phoenix, AZ 85073
Tel.: 602-261-2900

DRUG GUILD DISTRIBUTORS, INC.
350 Meadowland Pkwy.
Secaucus, NJ 07094
Tel.: 201-348-3700
Fax: 212-608-3893
Approx.Sls.: $145,000,000
Emp.: 300
Wholesaler of Drugs
S.I.C.: 5122; 5100
Al Hertel *(Chm. Bd.)*
Roman Englander *(Pres.)*
Alan Glenn *(Sr. V.P.)*
Gary Merten *(V.P.)*
Harold Miller *(V.P.)*
Jay Reba *(Controller)*

Outside Service Firm(s):

Anchin, Block & Anchin*(Auditors)*
1375 Broadway
New York, NY 10018

Scheichet & Davis*(Legal Firm)*
New York, NY

DRUMM & ASSOCIATES, INC.
110 Veterans Blvd., Ste. 350
Metairie, LA 70005
Tel.: 504-837-9244
Fax: 504-835-5924
Emp.: 75
Real Estate Investment & Syndication Firm
S.I.C.: 6722; 6726
Streuby L. Drumm, Jr. *(Pres.)*

Computer Systems/Hardware:
IBM System 36

Outside Service Firm(s):

Hibernia National Bank*(Major Banking Relationship)*
New Orleans, LA

DRUMMOND COMPANY, INC.
3000 Hwy. 78 East
Jasper, AL 35501
Mailing Address:
P.O. Box 1549,
Jasper, AL 35501
Tel.: 205-387-0501 **AL**
Fax: 205-384-2456
Year Founded: 1935
Approx.Sls.: $734,000,000
Emp.: 2,800
Fiscal Year-end: 12/31/90
Coal Mining
S.I.C.: 1221; 1222; 3312
Garry N. Drummond *(Chief Exec. Officer)*
E.A. Drummond *(Vice Chm.)*
H.D. Dahl *(Pres. & Chief Oper. Officer)*
Walter Johnsey *(Exec. V.P.-Admin., Chief Fin. Officer & Treas.)*

Drummond Company, Inc.—(Continued)

Donald Baxter *(Exec. V.P.-Coal Opers.)*
John M. Pearson *(Sr. V.P.-ABC Coke)*
William B. Long *(V.P. & Gen. Counsel)*
Thomas M. Walters *(V.P. & Controller)*
Joseph T. Bilich *(V.P.-Human Resources)*
James H. Strickland *(Dir.-Pub. Rels.)*
Principal(s):
Garry N. Drummond
E.A. Drummond

No. of Mfg. Plants/Facilities: 10
No. of U.S. Offices: 3
No. of Foreign Offices: 5

Computer Systems/Hardware:
Amdahl 470V8

Outside Service Firm(s):

Kaye, Scholer, Fierman, Hays & Handler*(Legal Firm)*
New York, NY

Citibank N.A.*(Major Banking Relationship)*
Corporate Trust Services, 399 Park Ave.
New York, NY 10043
Tel.: 212-559-1605

DRUTHER'S INTERNATIONAL, INC.
1 Oxmoor Pl.
Louisville, KY 40222
Mailing Address:
101 Bullet Lane, Ste. 475
Louisville, KY 40222
Tel.: 502-426-0110
Fax: 502-429-6009
Year Founded: 1963
Approx.Sls.: $95,000,000
Emp.: 4,500
Fiscal Year-end: 10/29/90
Franchisers of Dairy Queen; Dairy Queen Braziers Restaurants
S.I.C.: 5812; 6794
Thomas L. Hensley *(Pres. & Chief Exec. Officer)*
Robert Gatewood *(Sr. Exec. V.P.-Legal Affairs & Sec.)*
Michael J. Kull *(Sr. Exec. V.P.-Mktg.)*
Dave Newman *(V.P.-Pur.)*
Don E. Saylor *(V.P.-Franchise Devel. & Real Estate)*
Scott J. Carpenter *(Controller)*
Jerome C. Blair *(Dir.-Mngmt. Information Systems)*
Bill Bond *(Dir.-Training)*
Sandy Hensley *(Dir.-Office Admin.)*
Roy Price *(Dir.-Cash Mngmt.)*
Don Saylor *(Dir.-Real Estate)*
Mike Super *(Dir.-Human Resources)*

Outside Service Firm(s):

KPMG Peat Marwick*(Auditors)*
444 S. Fifth St.
Louisville, KY 40202
Tel.: 502-587-0535
Fax: 502-587-1549

DRY STORAGE CORPORATION
1750 So. Wolf Rd.
Des Plaines, IL 60018
Tel.: 708-390-6800 **IL**
Fax: 708-390-7276
Year Founded: 1960
Sales Range: $100-499 Million
Emp.: 1,500
Distribution Services
S.I.C.: 4225
James A. McIlrath *(Pres.)*
Ann M. Drake *(Chief Exec. Officer)*
Seshan Rammohan *(Chief Fin. Officer)*
Robert M. Waller *(Chief Oper. Officer)*
Thomas Smith *(V.P., Treas. & Gen. Counsel)*
Edward Odmark *(V.P. & Controller)*
Frank Merrick *(V.P.-Human Resources)*
Carl Rhyan *(V.P.-Customer Rels.)*
Marilee Tatalias *(V.P.-Real Estate)*
Dennis Waliczek *(V.P.-Information Services)*
Principal(s):
James A. McIlrath
Ann M. Drake

No. of Mfg. Plants/Facilities: 22
No. of U.S. Offices: 22

Computer Systems/Hardware:
IBM AS 400

Outside Service Firm(s):

Ernst & Young*(Auditors)*
233 S. Wacker Dr.
Chicago, IL 60606
Tel.: 312-368-1800
Fax: 312-645-3095

Jacobson, Brandvik & Anderson*(Legal Firm)*
Chicago, IL

Continental Bank N. A.*(Major Banking Relationship)*
231 S. LaSalle St.
Chicago, IL 60697
Tel.: 312-828-2345
Tel.: 800-426-5754
Telex: 312-828-1783

LaSalle National Bank*(Major Banking Relationship)*
135 S. LaSalle St., Rm.260
Chicago, IL 60603

DUALITE INC.
One Dualite Lane
Williamsburg, OH 45176
Tel.: 513-724-7100
Fax: 513-724-9029
Year Founded: 1947
Approx.Sls.: $28,000,000
Emp.: 285
Fiscal Year-end: 6/30/91
Import Export
Illuminated Indoor & Outdoor Signs, Clocks, Neon & Menu Signs, Illuminated Awnings
S.I.C.: 3993; 7312
Frank W. Schube *(Pres. & Chief Exec. Officer)*
Kenneth W. Buns *(Exec. V.P.)*
Kenneth E. Syberg *(V.P.-Mktg.)*
Dennis Emery *(V.P.-Sls.)*
Greg Schube *(V.P.-Sls.)*
Marvin Jett *(V.P. & Treas.)*
Ralph Laxton *(V.P. & Sec.)*
E. Lynn Webb *(V.P.-Admin.)*
Robert Ferguson *(Mgr.-Adv. & Sls. Promo.)*
Bill Schroer *(Pur. Agent)*

Subsidiary:

Dualite Sales & Service, Inc. **(1)**
One Dualite Ln.
Williamsburg, OH 45176
Tel.: 513-724-7100
Import Export
Mfr. of Indoor & Outdoor Signs, Clocks, Neon Signs, Menu Signs, Illuminated Awnings
S.I.C.: 3993; 7312
Greg Schube *(Chief Exec. Officer)*
Kenneth W. Buns *(Pres.)*
E. Lynn Webb *(V.P.-Treas.)*
Kenneth E. Syberg *(V.P.-Mktg.)*
Kevin M. Syberg *(V.P.-Sls.)*
Dennis Emery *(V.P.-Sls.)*
Paula Mueller *(Sec.)*
Patrick J. Seggerson *(Dir.-Design & Res.& Devel.)*
J. Robert Ferguson *(Mgr.-Adv. & Sls. Promo.)*

DUANE READE
49-29 30th Place
Long Island City, NY 11101
Tel.: 718-784-8503 **NY**
Fax: 718-361-1784
Approx.Sls.: $200,000,000
Emp.: 1,100
Retail Drug Chain; 37 Stores; Prescription Service, Cosmetics, Tobacco, Photographic Supplies, Candy, Food & Housewares
S.I.C.: 5912; 5441; 5719; 5949; 5993; 5999
Abraham D. Cohen *(Chm. Bd.)*
Eli D. Cohen *(Pres., Chief Oper. Officer & Treas.)*
Hyman Needleman *(Chief Fin. Officer)*
Leon E. Cohen *(Exec. Sr. V.P.)*
Joseph Cohen *(Sr. V.P.-Real Estate)*
Ronald E. Cohen *(Sr. V.P.)*
Mery Altman *(Controller)*
Marvin Sklamberg *(Gen. Counsel)*
Jack Cohen *(Sec.)*
Joseph Dweck *(Dir.-Data Processing)*

Outside Service Firm(s):

Richard Eisner*(Auditors)*
New York, NY

Fried, Frank, Harris, Shriver & Jacobson*(Legal Firm)*
1 New York Plaza
New York, NY 10004
Tel.: 212-820-8000

Chemical Banking Corp.*(Major Banking Relationship)*
277 Park Ave.
New York, NY 10041
Tel.: 212-310-6407
Fax: 212-310-4526

DUARY/J.F. DUNCAN INDUSTRIES, INC.
9301 Steward & Gray Rds.
Downey, CA 90241
Tel.: 310-862-4269 **CA**
Fax: 310-869-1850
Year Founded: 1988
Approx.Sls.: $20,000,000
Emp.: 82
Mfr. of Commercial Cooking Equipment; Food Products Machinery
S.I.C.: 3589; 3556
John C. Durward *(Chm. Bd.)*
John E. Wong *(Pres.)*
Donald L. Durward *(V.P.)*

Outside Service Firm(s):

First Interstate Bank*(Major Banking Relationship)*
P.O.Box 54168, Terminal Annex
Los Angeles, CA 90054-0168
Tel.: 800-522-6645

DUBIN-CLARK & COMPANY
289 Greenwich Ave.
Greenwich, CT 06830
Tel.: 203-629-2030
Fax: 203-629-2235
Holding Company
S.I.C.: 6719; 3317; 2891; 3423; 3312; 5051
Ronald N. Dubin *(Chm. Bd.)*
J. Thomas Clark *(Pres.)*
Jean Pierre Dammann *(Chief Fin. Officer)*
Peter Howard *(Partner)*
Christy Sadler *(Partner)*

Subsidiaries:

Precision Specialty Metals, Inc. **(1)**
3301 Medford St.
Los Angeles, CA 90063
Tel.: 213-267-3200
Fax: 213-267-3252
Manufacturer & Wholesaler of Stainless Steel Sheet Strips & Coils
S.I.C.: 3312; 5051
C. Edwin Brady *(Pres.)*

Rath Manufacturing **(1)**
2505 Foster Ave.
Janesville, WI 53545
Tel.: 608-754-2222
Fax: 608-754-0889
Emp.: 110
Mfr. Stainless Steel Tubing
S.I.C.: 3317
Frank Fenton *(Pres.)*

Roberts Consolidated Industries **(1)**
600 N. Baldwin Park Blvd.
City of Industry, CA 91749
Tel.: 818-369-7311
Fax: 818-369-7311
Emp.: 200
Floor Coverings & Accessories
S.I.C.: 2891; 3423
Carl Watson *(Pres.)*

DUCHOSSOIS INDUSTRIES, INC.
845 Larch Ave.
Elmhurst, IL 60126
Tel.: 708-279-3600 **DE**
Fax: 708-530-6091
Year Founded: 1983
Approx.Rev.: $1,000,000,000
Emp.: 6,000
Manufacture & Leasing of Railroad Cars, Garage Door Openers & Electronic Products; Research & Development; Communications; Manufacture Waxers & Polishers; Storm Doors
S.I.C.: 3743; 4741; 3639; 3489; 8731; 3442; 3669; 3699
Richard L. Duchossois *(Chm. Bd. & Chief Exec. Officer)*
Craig J. Duchossois *(Pres.)*
Gerald F. Lahey *(Exec. V.P.)*
R.H. Irving *(V.P. & Gen. Counsel)*
Joseph H. Michalcewicz *(V.P.-Human Resources)*
L.S. Minkel *(V.P.-Fin.)*
Sally Anderson *(Mgr.-Adv. & Sls. Promo.)*

No. of Mfg. Plants/Facilities: 22
No. of U.S. Offices: 22

Computer Systems/Hardware:
IBM System 4341

Outside Service Firm(s):

Arthur Andersen & Co.*(Auditors)*
33 W. Monroe St.
Chicago, IL 60603-4067
Tel.: 312-580-0033
Fax: 312-507-6748

Bank of America, N.T. & S.A.*(Major Banking Relationship)*
P.O. Box 37002,
San Francisco, CA 94137

Harris Trust & Savings Bank*(Major Banking Relationship)*
111 W. Monroe St.
Chicago, IL 60690
Tel.: 312-461-2265
Tel.: 800-858-0840

David J. Greene & Co.*(Pension Manager)*
30 Wall St.
New York, NY
Tel.: 212-344-5180

Subsidiaries:

The Chamberlain Group, Inc. **(1)**
845 Larch Ave.
Elmhurst, IL 60126
Tel.: 708-279-3600 (100%)
Emp.: 2,000
Mfr. Garage Door Openers, Electronic Prods., Premium Storm Doors
S.I.C.: 3442; 3679; 3699
Robert Baker *(Pres.)*
D. Rolls *(V.P.-Mktg.)*
Robert Markwart *(Dir.-Mktg.)*
Charlie Franke *(Mgr.-Natl. Sls.)*
Sally Anderson *(Mgr.-Adv. & Sls. Promo.)*

Chamberlain Manufacturing Corp. **(1)**
845 Larch Ave.
Elmhurst, IL 60126
Tel.: 708-279-3600
Emp.: 2,000
Ordnance Products, Research & Development
S.I.C.: 3489
Merton L. Townsend *(Pres.)*

Thrall Car Mfg. Co. **(1)**
2541 State St.
Chicago Heights, IL 60411-0218
Tel.: 708-757-5900 (100%)
Fax: 708-757-4112
Approx.Sls.: $250,000,000
Emp.: 1,400
Computer Systems/Hardware:
AS400
S.I.C.: 3743
C.J. Duchossois *(Chm. Bd.)*
J.E. Carrol *(Pres.)*
H.P. Hahn *(Exec. V.P.)*
Martin Graham *(Sr. V.P.-Northern Opers.)*
Lee K. Johnson *(Sr. V.P.-Engrng., Mktg. & Sls.)*
M.B. Leeser *(Sr. V.P.-Sls. & Mktg.)*
Jack Lynch *(V.P.-Sls.-General Freight Car Prods.)*
P.G. Ledebuhr *(Controller)*
P.L. Sereta *(Treas.)*
E.E. Engle *(Dir.-Mktg.)*
J.S. Kink *(Mgr.-Mfg.)*
C.P. Dowden *(Mgr.-Personnel)*
K.W. Strawbridge *(Mgr.-Mkt. Research)*
M.A. McDonald *(Mgr.-Telecommunications)*
H.C. Schmalbruch *(Mgr.-Quality Control)*
J.T. Sabatino *(Mgr.-Pur.)*
R.C. Amstein *(Mgr.-Data Processing)*

DUCKWALL-ALCO STORES, INC.
401 Cottage St.
Abilene, KS 67410
Tel.: 913-263-3350 **KS**
Fax: 913-263-7531
Year Founded: 1901
Sales Range: $100-499 Million
Emp.: 3,500
Fiscal Year-end: 1/31/92
Import
Chain of Discount Stores
S.I.C.: 5311; 5331
Glen L. Shank *(Pres., Chief Exec. & Oper. Officer)*
Dennis Alesio *(V.P.-Personnel)*
Charles E. Bogan *(V.P. & Gen. Counsel)*
Bryan DeCordova *(V.P. & Chief Fin. Officer)*
Gary W. Lowry *(V.P. & Controller)*
James Schoenbeck *(V.P.-Opers.)*
Charles L. Verble *(V.P.-Real Estate)*
Dan Curoe *(Dir.-Training)*
Dorothy Haslouer *(Dir.-Adv.)*
John E. Hedeen *(Dir.-Real Estate)*
Jack McCart *(Dir.-Mngmt. Information Systems)*
Steven Marsh *(Dir.-Planning & Analysis)*

Computer Systems/Hardware:
IBM 4361

Outside Service Firm(s):

KPMG Peat Marwick*(Auditors)*
Wichita, KS

Blue Cross & Blue Shield of Kansas*(Group Insurer)*
1133 S.W. Topeka
Topeka, KS 66612

Fourth National Bank Wichita*(Major Banking Relationship)*
Wichita, KS

Reimer & Koger Assocs.*(Pension Manager)*
Mission, KS

A. DUDA & SONS INC.
1975 W. State Rd. 426
Oviedo, FL 32765
Mailing Address:
P.O. Box 257,
Oviedo, FL 32765
Tel.: 407-365-2111 **FL**
Fax: 407-365-2148
Year Founded: 1926
Approx.Sls.: $282,000,000
Emp.: 1,500
Fiscal Year-end: 8/21/92
Agribusiness & Real Estate; Vegetable & Citrus Growers, Cattle, Crop Preparation, Wholesale Farm Equipment & Fresh Fruits & Vegetables
S.I.C.: 0161; 0174; 0212; 0723; 5083; 5148
Edward D. Duda *(Chm. Bd.)*
Ferdinand S. Duda *(Pres.)*
Andrew L. Duda *(Exec. V.P.)*
Joseph A. Duda *(Exec. V.P.-Real Estate & Pres.-Viera Co.)*
Charles L. Ashley *(V.P. & Treas.)*
Luther Duda *(V.P. & Sec.)*
Hugh English *(V.P.-Citrus Div.)*
Francis J. McCarthy *(V.P.-Mktg. & Sls.)*
Bruce Paschal *(V.P.-Sls.)*
Calvin J. Livingston *(Gen. Counsel)*

Outside Service Firm(s):

Price Waterhouse*(Auditors)*
Orlando, FL

Dean, Mead, Egerton, Bloodworth*(Legal Firm)*
Orlando, FL

Sun Bank, N.A.*(Major Banking Relationship)*
200 S. Orange Ave., 8th Fl. SOAB
Orlando, FL
Tel.: 407-237-4141

Subsidiaries:

Gene Jackson Farms **(1)**
P.O. Box 5147
Oxnard, CA 93031
Tel.: 805-984-7494
Gene Jackson *(Pres.)*

Valley Onions **(1)**
P.O. Box 2345
McAllen, TX 78502
Tel.: 210-631-3311
Mike Kirby *(Pres.)*

The Viera Company **(1)**
7380 Murrell Rd., Ste. 201
Melbourne, FL 32900
Tel.: 407-242-1200
Real Estate Company
S.I.C.: 6531
Joseph A. Duda *(Pres.)*

DUDEK & BOCK SPRING MANUFACTURING COMPANY
5100 W. Roosevelt Rd.
Chicago, IL 60650
Tel.: 312-379-4100 **IL**
Fax: 312-379-4108
Year Founded: 1946
Approx.Sls.: $24,000,000
Emp.: 385
Export
Mfr. of Steel Springs, Except Wire; Miscellaneous Fabricated Wire Products
S.I.C.: 3493; 3496; 3469
Thersea Dudek Schneider *(Chm. Bd.)*
Walter Dudek *(Pres.)*
John Dudek *(Chief Oper. Officer)*
Richard Sandlow *(Chief Fin. Officer)*
Robert Pacana *(Sr. V.P.)*
John E. Schneider *(V.P.-Sls. & Mktg.)*
William Mauk *(V.P.-Opers.)*
Nicholas Kuhn *(V.P.-Scheduling)*
Patricia Mauk *(Treas. & Sec.)*
Bob Kula *(Mgr.-Engrng.)*
Carole Jacklin *(Dir.-Human Resources)*

Outside Service Firm(s):

Rattner, Sandlow & Associates*(Auditors)*
Chicago, IL

DUDNYK ADVERTISING
Commonwealth Corp. Center,
100 Tournament Dr.
Horsham, PA 19044
Tel.: 215-443-9406
Fax: 215-675-3952
Year Founded: 1981
Approx.Billings: $29,200,000
Emp.: 54
Advertising, Marketing Communications, Sales Promotion, Direct Mail and Public Relations Planning & Implementation for Clients in Agri-Business, Business-to-Business, Healthcare and Consumer Sectors
Edward K. Dudnyk *(Pres.)*
Edward J. Shields *(Exec. V.P.)*
Scott D. Tattar *(V.P., Dir. Pub. Rels.)*
Richard Sutliff *(Chief Fin. Officer)*
Jennifer Cole *(Mgr., Opers. & Admin., Corp. Travel Planner)*
Marilyn Cummins *(Dir. Mktg. Services, New Bus. Contact)*

Computer Systems/Hardware:
Noell Network (PC Based)

DUFFY & SHANLEY, INC.
The Penthouse, 222 Richmond St.
Providence, RI 02903
Tel.: 401-274-0001
Fax: 401-278-4491
Year Founded: 1973
Approx.Billings: $25,300,000
Emp.: 38
Full Service Advertising, Public Relations & Direct Marketing Agency
David A. Duffy *(Pres.)*
Robert L. Newbert *(Exec. V.P., Adv.)*
Paul Fleming *(Sr. V.P., Mktg. Services)*
Steven Maurano *(V.P., Pub. Rels.)*
Robert Hart *(V.P., Fin.)*
Patricia Campellone *(V.P.)*
Rose M. Giusti *(Dir., Admin. Services)*
David Sarlitto *(Mgr.-Duffy & Shanley Direct)*

DUGAN & MEYERS INTERESTS, INC.
11110 Kenwood Rd.
Cincinnati, OH 45242
Tel.: 513-891-4300 **OH**
Fax: 513-891-0704
Year Founded: 1935
Assets: $50,939,942
Liabilities: $37,447,452
Net Worth: $13,492,490
Sales Range: $100-499 Million
Emp.: 55
Fiscal Year-end: 12/31/90
Holding Company; Building Construction
S.I.C.: 6719
Francis R. Dugan *(Chm. & Chief Exec. Officer)*
Jerome E. Meyers, Jr. *(V.P.-Mktg. & Bus. Devel.)*

Principal(s):
Francis R. Dugan

No. of U.S. Offices: 3

Computer Systems/Hardware:
Honeywell; IBM PC

Outside Service Firm(s):

Storch, White & Forrester*(Auditors)*
Milford, OH

Liberty Mutual*(Commercial Insurance Carrier)*
175 Berkeley St.
Boston, MA

Porter, Wright, Morris & Arthur*(Legal Firm)*
41 S. High St.
Columbus, OH 43215
Tel.: 614-227-2000
Fax: 614-227-2100

Gradison & Co.*(Pension Manager)*
Cincinnati, OH

Subsidiaries:

Dugan & Meyers Construction Co. **(1)**
11110 Kenwood Rd.
Cincinnati, OH 45242
Tel.: 513-891-4300 (100%)
Fax: 513-891-0704
General Contractor-Commercial
S.I.C.: 1531; 1541; 1542; 6719
Francis Dugan *(Pres.)*

Monitor Construction Co. **(1)**
P.O. Box 42337,
Cincinnati, OH 45242
Tel.: 513-791-0301 (100%)
General Contractor-Commercial
S.I.C.: 1531; 1541; 1542
Jerome Myers *(Pres.)*

Riverside Development Corp. **(1)**
11110 Kenwood Rd.
Cincinnati, OH 45242
Tel.: 513-891-0704 (100%)
Real Estate Holdings; Investments
S.I.C.: 6799
Francis Dugan *(Pres.)*

DUGAN, VALVA ASSOCIATES
10 Park Ave.
Morristown, NJ 07960
Tel.: 201-539-8880
Tel.: 800-526-8712
Fax: 201-984-2320
Year Founded: 1985
Approx.Billings: $20,000,000
Emp.: 31
Providing Strategic Marketing & Sales Promotion Programs that Always Reinforce Brand Image, are Class-of Trade Specific, & are Executed with an Extraordinarily High Level of Precision
Peter Dugan *(Chm.)*
George Valva *(Pres.)*
Gene Foley *(Controller)*

Computer Systems/Hardware:
Macintosh, IBM

DUGGAN INDUSTRIES, INC.
3901 S. Lamar St.
Dallas, TX 75215
Tel.: 214-428-8336 **TX**
Fax: 214-428-1929
Year Founded: 1946
Approx.Sls.: $21,000,000
Emp.: 45
Ferrous Metal Scrap & Waste; Steel Pipe & Tubing
S.I.C.: 5093; 5051
Joel E. Duggan *(Pres.)*
Edwin L. Duggan, Sr. *(Exec. V.P.)*
Joe D. Duggan *(V.P. & Treas.)*
Ruby Duggan *(V.P. & Sec.)*
Edwin L. Duggan, Jr. *(V.P.)*

Outside Service Firm(s):

KPMG Peat Marwick*(Auditors)*
1601 Elm St., Ste. 1600
Dallas, TX 75201
Tel.: 214-754-2000
Fax: 214-754-2297

Division:

Ace Iron & Metal Div. **(1)**
4603 Irving Blvd.
Dallas, TX 75215
Tel.: 214-428-8336
Ferrous Metal Scrap & Waste
S.I.C.: 5093; 5051
Joel E. Duggan *(Pres.)*

DUKANE CORPORATION
2900 Dukane Dr.
Saint Charles, IL 60174
Tel.: 708-584-2300 **DE**
Telex: 72-0426
Fax: 708-584-2370
Year Founded: 1922
Approx.Sls.: $69,000,000
Emp.: 750
Export

Dukane Corporation—(Continued)

Mfr. of Telephone & Communications Equipment, Industrial Controls, Audio-Visual Equipment, Ultrasonic Plastics Assembly Equipment, Underwater Locator Beacons & Alignment Equipment for Opto-Electronic Device Assembly
S.I.C.: 3661; 3669; 3577; 3861; 3699; 3823; 3812
John McWilliams Stone, Jr. *(Chm. Bd. & Chief Exec. Officer)*
Charles Clark *(Pres. & Chief Oper. Officer)*
L.E. Harris *(V.P. & Treas.)*
B.M. Johnston *(V.P.-Human Resources)*
J. Nechay *(V.P.-Mfg.)*
C.E. Zolper *(Controller)*
John Koziol *(Data Processing Dir.)*
Ed Sitar *(Intl. Procurement Dir.)*
Don Beck *(Librarian)*
Elizabeth M. Fiden *(Mktg. Communications Mgr.)*
J. Savanyu *(Dir.-Total Quality Mgmnt.)*
M.M. Ozgowicz *(Matls. Mgr.)*
B. Koehling *(Plant Mgr.)*
Susan M. Mizanin *(Mktg. Communications Specialist)*

No. of Mfg. Plants/Facilities: 2
No. of U.S. Offices: 2

Computer Systems/Hardware:
Honeywell 6000

Outside Service Firm(s):

Coopers & Lybrand*(Auditors)*
203 N. LaSalle St.
Chicago, IL 60601
Tel.: 312-701-5500

R. H. Wine & Co.*(Group Insurer)*
Elmhurst, IL

Sidley & Austin*(Legal Firm)*
One First National Plaza, 42nd Fl.
Chicago, IL 60603
Tel.: 312-853-7000
Fax: 312-853-7036

Divisions:

Dukane Audio Visual Div. **(1)**
2900 Dukane Dr.
Saint Charles, IL 60174
Tel.: 708-584-2300
Fax: 708-584-5156
Audio Visual Equip. for Schools & Business
S.I.C.: 3577; 3861
Peter A. Fredriksen *(Div. Pres.)*
Glen Schrader *(Dir.-Sls. & Mktg.)*

Dukane Communications Systems Div. **(1)**
2900 Dukane Dr.
Saint Charles, IL 60174
Tel.: 708-584-2300
Fax: 708-584-2792
Mfr. of Communications Equipment for Industrial & Commercial Markets
S.I.C.: 3661; 3669
Steven L. Deppe *(Pres.)*
Warren Anderson *(Ntl. Sls. Mgr.)*

Dukane Microrobotics Division **(1)**
2900 Dukane Dr.
Saint Charles, IL 60174
Tel.: 708-584-2300
Fax: 708-584-2370
Mfr. of Robot Systems for Assembly of Opto-Electronic Devices
S.I.C.: 3699
Keith Watkins *(Pres.)*
Charles Petus *(Mktg. Mgr.)*

Dukane SeaCom Division **(1)**
2900 Dukane Dr.
Saint Charles, IL 60174
Tel.: 708-584-2300
Fax: 708-584-5154
Mfr. of Underwater Locator Beacons for Aircraft & Offshore Drilling
S.I.C.: 3812
Joseph H. Lyon *(Pres.)*
Tom Greenacre *(V.P.)*

Dukane Ultrasonics Div. **(1)**
2900 Dukane Dr.
Saint Charles, IL 60174
Tel.: 708-584-2300
Fax: 708-584-5154
Mfr. of Ultrasonic Welding Equipment for Plastics Industry
S.I.C.: 3699; 3669; 3823
Franklin R. Link *(Pres.)*
Bill Lynch *(V.P.-Sls. & Mktg.)*
Doug Robertson *(Ntl. Sls. Mgr.)*
Jeff Sherry *(Intl. Sls. Mgr.)*
Fred McGowen *(Intl. Sls. Mgr.)*

Subsidiaries:

Alessi Incorporated **(1)**
35 Parker
Irvine, CA 92718
Tel.: 714-830-0660 (100%)
Fax: 714-863-9461
Approx.Sls.: $5,000,000
Emp.: 30
Mfr. of Electronic Test Equipment
S.I.C.: 3825
Alan J. Spriet *(Pres.)*
Don Miller *(Sls. Mgr.)*

Trilan Systems Corporation **(1)**
2900 Dukane Dr.
Saint Charles, IL 60174
Tel.: 708-584-2300
Fax: 708-584-3162
Transmission of Voice, Data & Video Over a Single Cable Equipment
S.I.C.: 3661; 3669
Robert Sexton *(Pres.)*
Ron Lewen *(Dir.-Engrng.)*
Ronald Lewen *(Dir.-Engrng.)*

Non-U.S. Holdings:

Dukane Canada Ltd. **(1)**
461 Manitou Dr.
Kitchener, ON N2C 1L5, Canada
Tel.: 519-748-5352
Fax: 519-748-9221
Mfr. of Communications Equipment
S.I.C.: 3661
Bernard Poetker *(Pres.)*
Douglas Hainsworth *(Controller)*

AB Sonic International Aps **(1)**
Gerdasgade13-15 2500
Valby, Denmark
Mfr. of Ultrasonic Welding Equipment for Plastics Industry
S.I.C.: 3699
Poul L. Soerensen *(Pres.)*

DUKE MANUFACTURING CO., INC.
2305 No. Broadway
Saint Louis, MO 63102
Mailing Address:
P.O. Box 5426
St. Louis, MO 63147
Tel.: 314-231-1130
Fax: 314-231-5074
Year Founded: 1923
Approx.Sls.: $25,000,000
Emp.: 250
Fiscal Year-end: 12/31/90
Thurmaduke, Aerohot & Duke Food Warmers, Cafeteria Counters & Other Food Service Equip.
S.I.C.: 3589
J.D. Johnson *(Pres.)*
J.J. Hake *(Chief Fin. Officer)*
M.R. Andrus *(Natl. Sls. Mgr.)*

DULING OPTICAL CORPORATION
4415 Poplar Level Rd.
Louisville, KY 40213
Tel.: 502-459-6722
Fax: 502-458-5919
Sales Range: $40-59 Million
Emp.: 450
165 Retail Optical Stores
S.I.C.: 3229; 3851
Larry Joel *(Chm. Bd.)*
George Pokarczyk *(Pres. & Chief Oper. Officer)*
John Roos *(Chief Fin. Officer)*
Mike Yager *(Dir.-Mktg.)*
Alice Harris *(Office Mgr.)*

Principal(s):
Larry Joel

No. of U.S. Offices: 163

Computer Systems/Hardware:
M.A.I.

Subsidiaries:

Kindy Optical **(1)**
4415 Poplar Level Rd.
Louisville, KY 40233
Tel.: 502-458-5919
Retail Optical Stores
S.I.C.: 5995

Monfried Optical **(1)**
4415 Poplar Level Rd.
Louisville, KY 40233
Tel.: 502-459-5919
Retail Optical Stores
S.I.C.: 5995

DUMORE CORPORATION
1030 Veteran St.
Mauston, WI 53948
Tel.: 608-847-6420
Fax: 1-800-338-6673
Year Founded: 1914
Approx.Sls.: $12,000,000
Emp.: 150
Export
Industrial Power Equip. Including Automatic Drill Units, Portable Machining Units, Hand & Flexible Shaft Grinders, Tool Post Grinders; FHP Motors & Gear Motors Including Permanent Magnet, Shunt-Type & Series Universal Type
S.I.C.: 3545; 3546
Employee Matching Gifts Program: Corporation Participates in a 401K Plan
R.L. Harrington *(Chm. Bd.)*
Lawrence F. Piet *(Pres.)*
Allen D. Boyle *(Exec. V.P.)*
Gale Poquette *(Dir.-Pur.)*
Thomas Evans *(Mgr.-Sls. & Mktg.-Indus. Div.)*

Computer Systems/Hardware:
IBM System 400

Outside Service Firm(s):

Wipfli, Ullrich, Bertelson*(Auditors)*
Green Bay, WI

Foley & Lardner*(Legal Firm)*
777 E. Wisconsin Ave.
Milwaukee, WI 53202
Tel.: 414-271-2400

M & I Marshall & Ilsley Bank*(Major Banking Relationship)*
770 N. Water St.
Milwaukee, WI 53202
Tel.: 414-765-8700

DUNAVANT ENTERPRISES, INC.
3797 New Getwell Rd.
Memphis, TN 38118
Tel.: 901-369-1500
Fax: 901-369-1608
Year Founded: 1990
Approx.Sls.: $300,000,000
Emp.: 600
Cotton Merchandising
S.I.C.: 5159
W.B. Dunavant, Jr. *(Chm. Bd.)*
Samuel T. Reeves *(Pres.)*
Louis Baioni *(Exec. V.P. & Treas.)*
Robert J. Hussey *(Exec. V.P.)*
William B. Dunavant, III *(V.P.)*
H.J. Weathersby *(V.P.)*
William Stubblefield *(Sec.)*

Outside Service Firm(s):

Valley National Bank*(Major Banking Relationship)*
141 N. Central Ave.
Phoenix, AZ 85001
Tel.: 602-261-2614

Subsidiary:

Dunavant Enterprises **(1)**
1410 F St.
Fresno, CA 93771
Tel.: 209-485-1800
Fax: 209-485-7364
Domestic & International Cotton Trading
S.I.C.: 5159
Samuel T. Reeves *(Pres.)*
Allen Knepper *(Dir.-Data Processing)*

Subsidiary:

Dunavant Commodity Corp. **(2)**
114 Liberty St.
New York, NY 10006
Tel.: 212-775-1596
Commodity Brokerage
S.I.C.: 6221
Louis Canario *(V.P.)*

DUNCAN EQUIPMENT COMPANY
1005 S. Second
Duncan, OK 73533
Mailing Address:
P.O. Box 40
Duncan, OK 73533
Tel.: 405-255-1216 **OK**
Fax: 405-255-0409
Year Founded: 1948
Approx.Sls.: $21,000,000
Emp.: 93
Wholesale Distribution of Pumps & Pumping Equipment & Industrial Supplies
S.I.C.: 5084; 5085
David Ragland *(Chm. Bd.)*
John O. Moore *(Pres. & Chief Exec. Officer)*
Judy Ragland *(V.P. & Sec.)*
John B. Smith *(Treas.)*

Outside Service Firm(s):

Security National Bank*(Major Banking Relationship)*
Duncan, OK

DUNDEE MILLS, INC.
Railroad Ave.
Griffin, GA 30224
Mailing Address:
P.O. Drawer E,
Griffin, GA 30224
Tel.: 706-227-5581
Fax: 706-227-5581
Year Founded: 1888
Earnings: $240,000,000
Approx.Sls.: $200,000,000
Emp.: 4,000
Fiscal Year-end: 8/30/91
Export
Mfr. Bathroom Towels, Baby Products, Healthcare Products
S.I.C.: 2211
John T. Newton *(Chm. Bd.)*
J. Henry Walker *(Pres.)*
R. Wayne Boyd *(Pres.-Sls.)*
David D. Blalock, Jr. *(Exec. V.P.-Sls.)*
John C. Bray *(Exec. V.P.-Sls.)*
Clarence J. McMerty *(Exec. V.P.-Mktg.-Baby Prods.)*
David J. Taylor *(Exec. V.P.-Mktg.)*
J. Gilliam Cheatham *(V.P.-Sls.)*
Howard B. Gossett *(V.P.-Fin. & Credit Mgr.)*
Douglas R. Tingle *(Sec.)*
Wayne H. Brown *(Dir.-Personnel)*

Outside Service Firm(s):

Ernst & Young*(Auditors)*
600 Peachtree St. N.E.
Atlanta, GA 30308
Tel.: 404-874-8300

Cumming, Cumming & Esary*(Legal Firm)*
Griffin, GA

First National Bank of Griffin*(Major Banking Relationship)*
Griffin, GA

DUNES HOTELS AND CASINOS INC.
3650 Las Vegas Blvd., S.
Las Vegas, NV 89109
Tel.: 702-737-4110
Fax: 702-737-4893
Earnings: $2,626,000
Approx.Sls.: $109,998,600
Emp.: 1,300
Holding Co.; Amusement & Recreation Services; Coin Operated Amusement Devices; Hotel Casinos; Eating Establishments
S.I.C.: 7999; 7993; 7011; 5812; 6719
Donald Hinkle *(Chm.-Exec. Committee)*
Fred Houghland *(Dir.-Personnel)*

Outside Service Firm(s):

McGladrey & Pullen*(Auditors)*
300 S. Fourth St., Ste. 900
Las Vegas, NV 89101
Tel.: 702-386-5800

Valley Bank of Nevada*(Major Banking Relationship)*
300 S. Fourth St.
Las Vegas, NV 89101

S. P. DUNHAM & CO.
Rte. 1, Texas Ave.
Lawrenceville, NJ 08648
Tel.: 609-989-7777
Fax: 609-883-7213
Approx.Sls.: $10,000,000
Emp.: 300
Department Store
S.I.C.: 5311
Allan R. Plapinger *(Chm. Bd.)*
Mervyn J. Platt *(Vice Chm. & Sec.)*
Harold Koslow *(Pres.)*

No. of Mfg. Plants/Facilities: 3

Outside Service Firm(s):

Louis H. Linowitz & Co.*(Auditors)*
Trenton, NJ

Central Jersey Bank & Trust*(Major Banking Relationship)*
Freehold, NJ

DUNHAM'S ATHLEISURE CORPORATION
5000 Dixie Hwy.
Waterford, MI 48329
Tel.: 313-674-4991 **DE**
Fax: 313-674-4980
Year Founded: 1937
Sales Range: $100-499 Million
Emp.: 1,400
Fiscal Year-end: 1/31/91
Import
64 Discount Sporting Goods & Athletic Apparel Stores
S.I.C.: 5699; 5941
Jeffrey G. Lynn *(Chm. Bd., Pres. & Chief Exec. Officer)*
Marshall A. Sosne *(Chief Fin. Officer & V.P.)*
James A. Nelson *(V.P.-Distribution)*
Steven J. Sander *(V.P.-Store Opers.)*
John Palmer *(Sec. & Gen. Counsel)*
Joan M. Long *(Controller)*
Daniel Cieslak *(Mng. Dir-Human Resources)*
Michael F. Taylor *(Mng. Dir.-Mngmt. Information Systems)*

Outside Service Firm(s):

Coopers & Lybrand*(Auditors)*
400 Renaissance Center
Detroit, MI 48243
Tel.: 313-446-7100
Fax: 313-446-7117

National Bank of Detroit*(Major Banking Relationship)*
611 Woodward Ave.
Detroit, MI 48226

DUNKIRK ICE CREAM CO., INC.
One Ice Cream Dr., Rte. 60 N.
Dunkirk, NY 14048
Tel.: 716-366-5400
Fax: 716-366-5400, Ext. 222
Year Founded: 1914
Sales Range: $60-79 Million
Emp.: 350
Fiscal Year-end: 11/30/91
Mfr. Ice Cream
S.I.C.: 2024
William M. Wells *(Chm. Bd.)*
Richard D. Coulcher *(V.P.)*
James DePerno *(V.P.)*
John Dyckes *(Controller)*
Carla Seiler *(Mktg. Coord.)*

DUNLAP & CO. INC.
P.O. Box 328
Columbus, IN 47202
Tel.: 812-376-3021 **IN**
Fax: 812-372-7876
Year Founded: 1873
Approx.Sls.: $20,000,000
Emp.: 200
Mechanical & General Industrial & Non-Residential Buildings Contractor
S.I.C.: 1542; 1711
Dennis E. King *(Pres.)*
Laura Stanton *(V.P., Sec. & Treas.)*
Principal(s):
Dennis E. King
Laura Stanton

No. of Mfg. Plants/Facilities: 1
No. of U.S. Offices: 1

Computer Systems/Hardware:
IBM PC/AT

Outside Service Firm(s):

George S. Olive & Co.*(Auditors)*
201 N. Illinois St.
Indianapolis, IN 46204

Beck & Harrison*(Legal Firm)*
231 Washington St.
Columbus, IN 47201
Tel.: 812-372-8858

Irwin Bank & Trust*(Major Banking Relationship)*
Irwin, PA

THE DUNLAP COMPANIES
200 Greenleaf
Fort Worth, TX 76107
Tel.: 817-336-4985
Fax: 817-877-1302
Year Founded: 1947
Sales Range: $100-499 Million
Emp.: 2,500
Department Stores
S.I.C.: 5311
Ret Martin *(Chm. Bd. & Chief Exec. Officer)*
Edward Martin *(Pres.)*
Tom Hoskins *(Exec. V.P.)*
Don Bullock *(Sr. V.P.)*
Ira G. Dunlap *(Sr. V.P.)*
R. Neil Ellis *(V.P. & Gen. Mgr.)*
Craig P. Peterson *(V.P. & Controller)*
Gerald L. Stallard *(V.P.-Fin.)*

Outside Service Firm(s):

Arthur Andersen & Co.*(Auditors)*
Fort Worth, TX

United States National Bank*(Major Banking Relationship)*
2201 Market St., P.O. Box 179
Galveston, TX 77553
Tel.: 713-763-1151

Subsidiaries:

M. M. Cohn Co., Inc. **(1)**
300 S. University Ave.
Little Rock, AR 72201
Tel.: 501-664-5501
Department Stores
S.I.C.: 5311
John Land *(Chm. Bd.)*

Porteous **(1)**
500 Main Mall
South Portland, ME 04106-3293
Tel.: 207-775-6066
Fax: 207-775-1009
Emp.: 600
Department Stores
S.I.C.: 5311
L. Robert Porteous, Jr. *(Chm. Bd., Sec. & Treas.)*
Joseph Hofkin *(Pres.)*
Joseph Garneau *(V.P.-Stores)*
Paul Chamberlain *(V.P.-Personnel)*

Steketee Paul & Sons Company, Inc. **(1)**
86 Monroe Center
Grand Rapids, MI 49503-3215
Tel.: 616-456-6588
Department Stores
S.I.C.: 5311
Keith Lang *(Chm. Bd.)*

DUNMORE CORPORATION
207 Penns Trail
Newtown, PA 18940
Mailing Address:
P.O. Box 1067,
Newtown, PA 18940
Tel.: 215-968-0442
Tel.: 800-444-0242 **PA**
Telex: 831848
Fax: 215-968-7471
Year Founded: 1970
Approx.Sls.: $25,000,000
Emp.: 180
Fiscal Year-end: 3/31/91
Import Export
Metallizing, Coatings, Laminating, Printing Of Plastics Films, Papers & Fabrics
S.I.C.: 3479; 3083; 3089
Michael L. Sullivan *(Pres.)*
Robert E. Dalton *(Exec. V.P. & Chief Oper Officer)*
Barry N. Skolnick *(V.P.-Res. & Devel.)*
Michael T. Sullivan *(V.P.-Mfg.)*
Michael Zelno *(Controller)*
William H. Piercy *(Sec. & Treas.)*
Massino Petrei *(Chief Engr.)*
Stephen A. Clow *(Dir.-Quality Assurance)*
Joseph P. Duke *(Mgr.-Pur.)*
Laura Fiscus *(Mgr.-Human Relations)*
Mark Gold *(Mgr.-Data Processing)*
Daniel J. Sullivan *(Mgr.-Customer Service)*

Computer Systems/Hardware:
IBM System 36, Microvax II Model Q4

Outside Service Firm(s):

KPMG Peat Marwick*(Auditors)*
1600 Market St.
Philadelphia, PA 19103
Tel.: 215-299-3100

Diamond, Polsky & Bauer*(Legal Firm)*
Philadelphia, PA

Fidelity Bank*(Major Banking Relationship)*
Broad & Walnut St.
Philadelphia, PA 19109

Division:

Dunmore Corporation/Brewster **(1)**
Rte. 6
Brewster, NY 10509
Tel.: 914-279-5061
Tel.: 800-422-6822
Fax: 914-279-5231
Import Export
Computer Systems/Hardware:
Micro Vax II Model Q4
Metallizing, Coatings, Laminating, Printing of Plastics Films, Papers & Fabrics
S.I.C.: 3479; 3083; 2671
Michael L. Sullivan *(Pres.)*

CHARLES DUNN COMPANY-REALTORS
1200 Wilshire Blvd.
Los Angeles, CA 90017
Tel.: 213-481-1800
Fax: 213-481-0758
Emp.: 200
Real Estate Investor & Syndicator; Insurance; Property Management
S.I.C.: 6531; 6552; 6331
Joseph C. Dunn *(Mng. Partner)*
Richard C. Dunn *(Mng. Partner)*
Michael Faxworthy *(Partner)*
Melanie Clarke *(Office Mgr.)*
William P. Harrison *(Mgr.-Sls.)*
Pamela Mosher *(Mgr.-Pub. Rels.)*

Computer Systems/Hardware:
IBM PC; Texas Instruments

Outside Service Firm(s):

PruCare of California*(Group Insurer)*
Los Angeles, CA

First Interstate Bank of California, N.A.*(Major Banking Relationship)*
P.O. Box 3667,
Los Angeles, CA 90051
Tel.: 213-614-4000

DUNN-EDWARDS CORPORATION
4885 East 52nd Place
Los Angeles, CA 90040
Tel.: 213-771-3330 **CA**
Year Founded: 1925
Assets: $85,000,000
Liabilities: $21,000,000
Net Worth: $64,000,000
Sales Range: $100-499 Million
Emp.: 1,200
Fiscal Year-end: 12/31/90
Import Export
Manufactures Paint & Distributes Wallcoverings
S.I.C.: 2851; 5198
Robert E. Mitchell *(Chm. Bd.)*
John B. Teets *(Pres. & Chief Exec. Officer)*
Dennis R. Kromer *(Chief Fin. Officer, Treas. & Controller)*
James R. Edwards *(V.P.)*
Lynn P. McGinnis *(V.P.)*
Kenneth N. Edwards *(Sec.)*
Gary Jones *(Dir.-Human Resources)*
George Mathew *(Dir.-Opers.)*
Gil Mislang *(Dir.-Res. & Devel.)*
Bob Pacelli *(Dir.-Mktg.)*
Ralph Peyton *(Dir.-Mngmt. Information Systems)*
Paul Sarto *(Gen. Sls. Mgr.)*

No. of Mfg. Plants/Facilities: 3

Outside Service Firm(s):

Winds & McClaughy*(Auditors)*
Long Beach, CA

Bolton Co.*(Commercial Insurance Carrier)*
Los Angeles, CA

Sanwa Bank*(Major Banking Relationship)*
601 S. Figueroa St.
Los Angeles, CA 90017
Tel.: 213-896-7817
Fax: 213-489-1977

Security Pacific National Bank*(Major Banking Relationship)*
Long Beach, CA

Churchill Management*(Pension Manager)*
Los Angeles, CA

NWQ Investment Management*(Pension Manager)*
655 S. Hope St.
Los Angeles, CA
Tel.: 213-624-6700
Fax: 213-689-4757

Dunn-Edwards Corporation—(Continued)

Subsidiary:

Wellborn - DE Corp. (1)
215 Rossmoor Rd., S.W.
Albuquerque, NM 87125
Tel.: 505-877-5050
Emp.: 125
Paint Mfr. & Retail Store Chain
S.I.C.: 2816; 2851; 5231
Bob Cummins *(Pres.)*
Randy Fuller *(Controller)*

DUNN INDUSTRIES INC.
929 Holmes
Kansas City, MO 64106
Tel.: 816-474-8600 **MO**
Fax: 816-391-2510
Year Founded: 1924
Approx.Sls.: $252,000,000
Emp.: 7
Holding Company
S.I.C.: 6719
William H. Dunn *(Chm. Bd.)*
Barrett Brady *(Pres. & Chief Exec. Officer)*
Stephen D. Dunn *(V.P.)*
Terrance P. Dunn *(V.P.)*
William H. Dunn, Jr. *(V.P.)*
Dale E. Shikles *(V.P.)*
Ardyth L. Wendte *(Sec.)*

Computer Systems/Hardware:
Qantel System 64 Minicomputers

Outside Service Firm(s):

Grant Thornton*(Auditors)*
1101 Walnut, Ste. 1600
Kansas City, MO 64106

Seigfreid, Bingham, Levy, Selze & Gee*(Legal Firm)*
Kansas City, MO

Commerce Bank of Kansas City*(Major Banking Relationship)*
10th & Walnut
Kansas City, MO 64141
Tel.: 816-234-2000
Fax: 816-234-2548

Subsidiary:

J.E. Dunn Construction Co. (1)
929 Holmes
Kansas City, MO 64106
Tel.: 816-474-8600
Emp.: 400
Gen. Contractor Nonresidential Bldgs.; Construction Mngmt. & Consulting
S.I.C.: 1542
William H. Dunn *(Chm. Bd.)*
Terrence P. Dunn *(Pres. & Chief Exec. Officer)*
Barrett Brady *(Exec. V.P.-Admin. & Treas.)*
Frederick Shipman III *(Exec. V.P.-Construction Opers.)*
Bernard Jacquinot *(Exec. V.P.-Field Oper.)*
C.J. Cianciaruso *(Sr. V.P.-Mktg.-Special Projects)*
Louis M. Hilker *(Sr. V.P.-Coord. Scheduling)*
Dale Shikles *(Sr. V.P. & Controller)*
Ardyth L. Wendte *(Sr. V.P. & Sec.)*

DUNN REBER GLENN MARZ
50 Washington St.
Reno, NV 89503
Tel.: 702-786-4900
Fax: 702-786-9327
Year Founded: 1969
Approx.Billings: $31,000,000
Emp.: 62
John J. Glenn *(Chm. Bd., Chief Exec. Officer)*
Rick Atchison *(Exec. V.P.)*
Kenneth K. Kenevan *(V.P., Chief Fin. Officer)*
Scott Voeller *(V.P., Dir. Res. & Strategic Plng.)*

DUO-FAST

DUO-FAST CORPORATION
3702 River Rd.
Franklin Park, IL 60131
Tel.: 708-678-0100
Tel.: 800-752-5207 **IL**
Telex: 62053554
Fax: 708-678-6824
Year Founded: 1937
Nailers, Staplers, Tackers, Nails, Staples, Self-Feeding Electric Screw Drivers
S.I.C.: 3423; 3399; 3315
Robert H. Torstenson *(Chm. Bd. & Pres.)*
Steve Wilson *(V.P.-Engrng.)*
Dave Kalous *(V.P.-Mktg.)*
Pat Fitzgibbon *(V.P.-Mfg.)*
Art Morissette *(Controller)*
Robert Grimley *(Sec. & Treas.)*
Holly Roberts *(Dir.-Human Resources)*
Charles Harper *(Dir.-Matl. Procurement)*
Roy Kibbe *(Mgr.-Gen. Sls.)*
Antonio Nieves *(Mgr.-Export Sls.)*
Alan Moon *(Mgr.-Intl. Sls.)*
Robert Saunders *(Mgr.-Mnmgt. Information Systems)*
Paul Johnson *(Mgr.-Mktg.)*
Mary Beth Smith *(Asst. Mgr.-Mktg. Communications)*

Computer Systems/Hardware:
IBM 4381

Division:

Duo-Fast Corporation (1)
800 N. Pearman
Cleveland, MS 38732
Tel.: 601-843-0100
S.I.C.: 3423
Dick Vrastiak *(Gen. Mgr.)*

DUPEY MANAGEMENT CORP.
9015 Sterling St.
Irving, TX 75063
Tel.: 214-929-8595
Fax: 214-929-8283
Year Founded: 1977
Sales Range: $60-79 Million
Emp.: 1,900
Retail & Wholesale Art Supplies
S.I.C.: 5199; 5999
Michael Dupey *(Chm. Bd. & Chief Exec. Officer)*
Patricia Dupey *(Pres.)*
Andy Jones *(Chief Fin. Officer)*
Belinda Neal *(Mgr.-Personnel)*
Principal(s):
Michael Dupey
Patricia Dupey

No. of Mfg. Plants/Facilities: 1
No. of U.S. Offices: 27

Computer Systems/Hardware:
IBM PC-XT; Wang PC

Outside Service Firm(s):

Grant Thornton*(Auditors)*
1445 Ross Ave.
Dallas, TX 75202
Tel.: 214-855-7300

Allied Bank*(Major Banking Relationship)*
Dallas, TX

G.B. DUPONT CO., INC.
500 W. Long Lake Rd.
Troy, MI 48098
Tel.: 313-879-0200
Fax: 313-879-1001
Year Founded: 1939
Approx.Sls.: $36,000,000
Emp.: 280
Mfr. Bolts, Nuts & Screws
S.I.C.: 3452
Kent G. DuPont *(Pres.)*
Richard D. Reynolds *(Exec. V.P.)*
Walter A. Marks *(V.P.-Sls.)*
Richard A. Robertson *(Treas.)*
Lorraine K. Marks *(Sec.)*

Outside Service Firm(s):

Deloitte & Touche*(Auditors)*
200 Renaissance Center, 16th Fl.
Detroit, MI 48243
Tel.: 313-396-3000
Fax: 313-259-8087

Levin, Levin, Garvett & Dill*(Legal Firm)*
3000 Tower Ctr., Ste. 1800
Southfield, MI 48075
Tel.: 313-352-8200

Michigan National Bank*(Major Banking Relationship)*
Detroit, MI

DUPPS COMPANY
548 N. Cherry St.
Germantown, OH 45327
Tel.: 513-855-6555
Fax: 513-855-6554
Approx.Sls.: $32,000,000
Emp.: 180
Export
Rendering & Meat Packing, House Machines & Meat Processing Equipment
S.I.C.: 3556; 3559
John A. Dupps, Jr. *(Pres.)*
Frank N. Dupps *(Exec. V.P.)*
R.H. Graman *(V.P.-Fin.)*
W.F. Schottelkotte *(V.P.-Engrng.)*
David M. Dupps *(Treas. & Sec.)*
V.L. Campbell *(Mgr.-Matls.)*

Outside Service Firm(s):

Coopers & Lybrand*(Auditors)*
Dayton, OH

Coolidge, Wall, Womsley & Lombard*(Legal Firm)*
33 W. First St., Ste. 600
Dayton, OH 45402
Tel.: 513-223-8177
Fax: 513-223-6705

Fifth Third Bank*(Major Banking Relationship)*
Dayton, OH
Tel.: 513-461-9990

DURACO PRODUCTS, INC.
1109 E. Lake St.
Streamwood, IL 60107
Tel.: 708-837-6615
Tel.: 800-888-7687 **DE**
Telex: 206-055
Fax: 708-837-7136
Year Founded: 1966
Approx.Sls.: $50,000,000
Emp.: 225
Fiscal Year-end: 12/31/91
Export
Plastic Horticulture Ware; Garden Planterware & Horticultural Accessories
S.I.C.: 3089
J.M. Licht *(Pres. & Chief Exec. Officer)*
L.C. Frank *(V.P.-Fin. & Chief Fin. Officer)*
R.E. Husby *(V.P.-Mktg.)*
C.J. Piec *(V.P.-Mfg.)*
K.L. Sanderson *(V.P.-Plng. & Devel.)*
D.G. Grimaldi *(Dir.-Human Resources)*
M.J. Vasquez *(Mgr.-Pur.)*

No. of Mfg. Plants/Facilities: 4

Computer Systems/Hardware:
IBM System 38, AS400

Outside Service Firm(s):

KPMG Peat Marwick*(Auditors)*
Schaumburg, IL

Prudential Insurance Co. of America*(Group Insurer)*
Chicago, IL

First National Bank of Boston*(Major Banking Relationship)*
P.O. Box 644,
Boston, MA 02102-0644
Tel.: 617-575-2900
Fax: 617-575-2549

Division:

Duraco Products Inc. of South Carolina (1)
P.O. Box 867, Hwy. 9 Adamsburg
Union, SC 29379
Tel.: 803-427-6202
Export
Computer Systems/Hardware:
IBM System 38
Mfg. Textile, Handmade Products
S.I.C.: 3089
Carl Patrick *(Plant Mgr.)*

DUREX INDUSTRIES INC.
(Formerly William Recht Company, Inc.)
1183 W. Side Ave.
Jersey City, NJ 07306
Tel.: 201-792-6350
Fax: 201-792-5599
Emp.: 250
Manufacture Printing Ink, Paints & Allied Products; Lead Pencils & Art Goods; Printing Trades Machinery
S.I.C.: 2851; 2893; 3555; 3952
William Recht, Jr. *(Pres.)*
Mike Raio *(V.P.)*

Outside Service Firm(s):

Kelly, Lee & Company*(Auditors)*
Jersey City, NJ

Midwest Bank*(Major Banking Relationship)*
Jersey City, NJ

DURHAM TRANSPORTATION, INC.
Travis Bldg, Ste. 200, 9171 Capital of Texas Highway N.
Austin, TX 78759-7252
Tel.: 512-343-6292
Fax: 512-343-6596
Year Founded: 1917
Approx.Sls.: $67,000,000
School Bus & Local Bus Charter Service
S.I.C.: 4151; 4141
Larry K. Durham *(Pres.)*
John Edney *(Sr. V.P.)*
Edwin P. LeCroy, Jr. *(Sr. V.P.)*
David Delamatte *(V.P.)*
J.B. Durham *(V.P.)*
Winston Mitchell *(Treas.)*

Outside Service Firm(s):

Central Reserve Life Insurance Co.*(Legal Firm)*
Durham, NC

Community Bank*(Major Banking Relationship)*
Pasadena, CA

Union Bank*(Major Banking Relationship)*
3810 Wilshire Blvd.
Los Angeles, CA 90010
Tel.: 213-480-6566

DURLACHER & CO., INC.
47-11 Van Dam St.
Long Island City, NY 11101
Tel.: 718-706-1700 **NY**
Fax: 718-729-4749
Year Founded: 1908
Approx.Sls.: $20,000,000

Emp.: 150
Mfr. of Women's & Childrens Accessories
S.I.C.: 2339; 2353
Jules C. Ventura *(Pres.)*
Arnold Sabin *(V.P.)*
Arthur Shuldiner *(Treas.)*
Donald Levenson *(Sec.)*

Outside Service Firm(s):

Patrusky, Mintz & Semel*(Auditors)*
22 Cortlandt St.
New York, NY 10007
Tel.: 212-732-2600
Fax: 212-374-1967

Wachtell, Lipton, Rosen & Katz*(Legal Firm)*
299 Park Ave.
New York, NY 10171

Chemical Banking Corp.*(Major Banking Relationship)*
277 Park Ave.
New York, NY 10041
Tel.: 212-310-6407
Fax: 212-310-4526

Division:

Accessory Institute Div. **(1)**
411 Fifth Ave.
New York, NY 10016
Tel.: 212-684-7117
Jules C. Ventura *(Pres.)*

A. K. DURNIN CHRYSLER PLYMOUTH, INC.
6815 Florida Blvd.
Baton Rouge, LA 70806
Mailing Address:
P.O. Box 64848
Baton Rouge, LA 70896
Tel.: 504-927-3900 **LA**
Fax: 504-927-3907
Year Founded: 1971
Assets: $6,039,218
Earnings: $150,000,000
Liabilities: $4,833,478
Net Worth: $1,205,740
Approx.Sls.: $23,000,000
Emp.: 60
Fiscal Year-end: 7/31/92
Retail New & Used Automobiles
S.I.C.: 5511
Douglas K. Durnin *(Pres.)*
Terry J. Durnin *(V.P.)*
Jerry L. Durnin *(Sec. & Treas.)*

Outside Service Firm(s):

Jules Prokop*(Auditors)*
Hammond, LA

Glusman, Moore & Wilkinson*(Legal Firm)*
Baton Rouge, LA

National Bank of Commerce*(Major Banking Relationship)*
Baton Rouge, LA

DURO DYNE CORPORATION
P.O. Box 117
Farmingdale, NY 11735
Tel.: 516-249-9000
Tel.: 800-899-3876
Fax: 516-249-8346
Year Founded: 1952
Approx.Sls.: $25,000,000
Emp.: 165
Import Export
Mfr. of Sheet Metal & Accessories For the HVAC Industry; Flexible Duct Connectors & Insulation Fastening Machinery
S.I.C.: 3444; 3564; 3569
Milton Hinden *(Pres.)*
Carole D'Agosta *(V.P.-Opers.)*
Randy Hinden *(V.P.)*
John Lyons *(V.P.-Res. & Devel.)*
Paul Thompson *(V.P.-Sls.)*
Principal(s):
Milton Hinden

No. of Mfg. Plants/Facilities: 3
No. of U.S. Offices: 3
No. of Foreign Offices: 3

Outside Service Firm(s):

The Bank of New York*(Major Banking Relationship)*
One Wall Street
New York, NY 10286
Tel.: 212-635-6805
Fax: 212-635-3201

DURO-LAST ROOFING, INC.
525 Morley Dr.
Saginaw, MI 48601
Tel.: 517-753-6486
Tel.: 800-248-0280 **MI**
Fax: 517-753-4472
Year Founded: 1981
Approx.Sls.: $30,000,000
Emp.: 150
Fiscal Year-end: 12/31/89
Custom Fabricated Single-Ply Roofing Systems
S.I.C.: 2295
John R. Burt *(Chm. Bd. & Pres.)*
Kathy L. Allen *(V.P.)*
Thomas J. Lawler *(V.P. & Gen. Counsel)*
Sharon Sny *(Chief Fin. Officer & Treas.)*
Mitch Fournier *(Controller)*
Steve Hetzman *(Dir.-Pur.)*
Principal(s):
John R. Burt

No. of Mfg. Plants/Facilities: 2

Computer Systems/Hardware:
IBM

Outside Service Firm(s):

Yeo & Yeo, CPA*(Auditors)*
Saginaw, MI

DURO PAPER BAG MANUFACTURING CO.
Davies & Oak Sts.
Ludlow, KY 41016
Tel.: 606-581-8200
Fax: 606-581-1829
Approx.Sls.: $200,000,000
Emp.: 1,000
Fiscal Year-end: 2/29/91
Mfr. of Paper & Plastic Grocery Bags & Sacks, Merchandise Bags & Shopping Bags; Carrier Boxes
S.I.C.: 3089
Charles Shor *(Pres.)*
Chick Glabman *(Pres.-Specialty Prod. Sls.)*
Ivan Hughes *(Sr. V.P.-Mfg.)*
John Baumann *(V.P.-Fin.)*
David Davis *(V.P.-Mktg. & Transportation)*
Paul Feldman *(V.P.-Sls.)*
Walt Kramer *(V.P. & Pur.-Paper)*

Outside Service Firm(s):

Arthur Andersen & Co.*(Auditors)*
425 Walnut St.
Cincinnati, OH 45202
Tel.: 513-381-6900

Taft, Stettinius & Hollister*(Legal Firm)*
First Natl. Bank Center
Cincinnati, OH 45202
Tel.: 513-381-2838

Star Bank*(Major Banking Relationship)*
425 Walnut Street
Cincinnati, OH 45202
Tel.: 513-632-4000

Divisions:

Duro Paper Bag Mfg. Co. **(1)**
P.O. Box 4380
Brownsville, TX 78523
Tel.: 210-831-4207
Mfr. of Plastic & Paper Bags
S.I.C.: 3089
Carlos Billarreal *(Gen. Mgr.)*

Duro Paper Bag Mfg. Co. **(1)**
1301 Madison Ave.
Covington, KY 41011
Tel.: 606-431-5011
Mfr. of Plastic & Paper Bags
S.I.C.: 3089

Duro Paper Bag Mfg. Co. **(1)**
P.O. Box 247
Hudson, WI 54016
Tel.: 715-386-9386
Mfr. of Plastic & Paper Bags
S.I.C.: 3089
Paul Frye *(Gen. Mgr.)*

Duro Paper Bag Mfg. Co. **(1)**
P.O. Box 5004
Tampa, FL 33675
Tel.: 813-247-4737
Mfr. of Plastic & Paper Bags
S.I.C.: 3089
Arvel Bailey *(Gen. Mgr.)*

Duro Paper Bag Mfg. Co. **(1)**
Richwood Industrial Pk., Shoreland Dr.
Walton, KY 41094
Tel.: 606-485-6188
Mfr. of Plastic & Paper Bags
S.I.C.: 3089
Jim Wilson *(Mgr.-Plant)*

DURO-TEST CORPORATION
9 Law Dr.
Fairfield, NJ 07004
Tel.: 201-808-1800
Tel.: 800-289-3876 **NY**
Telex: 139287
Fax: 201-808-6622
Year Founded: 1929
Approx.Sls.: $75,000,000
Emp.: 1,700
Fiscal Year-end: 7/31/91
Export
Manufacture Light Bulbs; Manufacture & Marketing of Incandescent, Fluorescent & High-Intensity-Discharge Type Lights for Commercial & Industrial Use
S.I.C.: 3641
Dan E. Picini *(Chm. Bd., Pres. & Chief Oper. Officer)*
Bernard J. Conboy *(V.P.-Admin.)*
Anthony Cavalieri *(Chief Fin. Officer)*
John Andreacci *(Controller)*
David Goldman *(Legal Officer & Sec.)*
James Stoddard *(Dir.-Mktg.)*
James Arricale *(Dir.-Mngmt Information Systems)*
Valerie Hunter *(Mgr.-Benefits & Compensation)*
Vincent Giambalvo *(Mgr.-Personnel Training & Devel.)*
Shirley Benson *(Personnel Mgr.)*
Joe Johnson *(Export Mgr.)*
Miguel Diaz *(Gen. Mgr.)*

Outside Service Firm(s):

Arthur Andersen & Co.*(Auditors)*
P.O. Box 221, 101 Eisenhower Pkwy.
Roseland, NJ 07068
Tel.: 201-403-6100
Fax: 201-403-0579

Brenner, Saltzman, Wallman & Goldman*(Legal Firm)*
271 Whitney Ave.
New Haven, CT 06511
Tel.: 203-772-2600
Fax: 203-562-2098

Chemical Banking Corp.*(Major Banking Relationship)*
277 Park Ave.
New York, NY 10041
Tel.: 212-310-6407
Fax: 212-310-4526

Subsidiaries:

Duro Lite Lamps, Inc. **(1)**
9 Law Dr.
Fairfield, NJ 07004
Tel.: 201-808-0902
Tel.: 800-526-7193 (100%)
Fax: 201-808-6622
Markets Light Sources For Residential Use
S.I.C.: 5063
Jim Stoddard *(Mktg. Dir.)*

Duro-Test Intl. Corp. **(1)**
9 Law Dr.
Fairfield, NJ 07004
Tel.: 201-808-1800 (100%)
Telex: 139287
Fax: 201-808-6622
Export
Sales Co. For Lighting Products
S.I.C.: 5063
Mike Diaz *(Dir.-Intl. Opers.)*

Non-U.S. Holdings:

Duro-Test Canada **(1)**
419 Attwell Dr.
Rexdale, ON M9W 5W5, Canada
Tel.: 416-675-1623 (100%)
Emp.: 110
Sales Co. for Lighting Products
S.I.C.: 5063
Tony Mastrovito *(Gen. Mgr.)*

Duro-Test de Mexico, S.A. **(1)**
Paseo de la Reforma 195-10O Piso 5
Mexico, D.F. Mexico
Tel.: 5-5921477 (100%)
Emp.: 150
Sales Co. for Lighting Products
S.I.C.: 5063
Jorge Wilson *(Gen. Mgr.)*

DURON, INC.
10406 Tucker St.
Beltsville, MD 20705
Tel.: 301-937-4600 **MD**
Fax: 301-937-6708
Year Founded: 1949
Approx.Sls.: $160,000,000
Emp.: 1,200
Fiscal Year-end: 12/31/91
Export
Paint, Wallcoverings; Sundries
S.I.C.: 2851; 5231
Harry Feinberg *(Chm. Bd.)*
Robert Feinberg *(Pres.)*
George W. Aman *(Exec. V.P.-Data Processing)*
Peter Pittroff *(Sr. V.P.-Sls.)*
Doug Veum *(Sr. V.P.-Mfg.)*
Robert Clark *(V.P.-Fin.)*
Tom Schwartzbeck *(V.P.-Sls. & Mktg.)*
Michael Hanlon *(Controller)*
Paul Harab *(Controller & Sec.)*
James Felsecker *(Asst. Sec.)*
Albert R. Munita *(Asst. Sec.)*
Tom Brice *(Dir.-Envir. & Natl. Resources)*
David Ellwood *(Dir.-Pur.)*
William Horan *(Dir.-Telecommunications)*
Walter Masal *(Dir.-Data Processing)*
Andrea Steele *(Dir.-Personnel)*
Rick Vain *(Dir.-Mktg.)*
Ron Wells *(Dir.-Taxes)*
Scott Wilson *(Dir.-Real Estate)*
Gloria Brown *(Employee Benefits Admin.)*

No. of Mfg. Plants/Facilities: 2
No. of U.S. Offices: 1

Outside Service Firm(s):

Harab, Kamerow & Associates*(Auditors)*
Washington, DC

Kemper Financial Services*(Commercial Insurance Carrier)*
Baltimore, MD

Paley, Rothman, Goldstein, Rosenberg & Cooper*(Legal Firm)*
Bethesda, MD

Maryland National Bank*(Major Banking Relationship)*
Baltimore, MD 21202

NationsBank Carolinas*(Pension Manager)*
One NCNB Plaza,
Charlotte, NC 28255
Tel.: 704-374-5000

JOHN DUSENBERY CO., INC.
220 Franklin Rd.
Randolph, NJ 07869
Tel.: 201-366-7500
Fax: 201-366-7453
Approx.Sls.: $30,000,000
Emp.: 134
Fiscal Year-end: 12/31/91
Import Export
Mfr. & Design Paper Film & Foil Converting Machinery, Slitting Accessories & Parts; Auto Tensioneer, Dusinkoter
S.I.C.: 3599
John Wilkes *(Pres.)*
Jim Olwell *(Sr. V.P.-Fin.)*
Joseph Benyo *(V.P.-Sls.)*
John F. Dusenbery *(Chief Exec. Officer)*
A.M. Guber *(Controller)*
Principal(s):
John F. Dusenbery

Outside Service Firm(s):

Kelley Drye & Warren*(Legal Firm)*
350 Park Ave.
New York, NY 10022
Tel.: 212-752-5800
Fax: 212-808-7800

Chemical Bank*(Major Banking Relationship)*
Newark, NJ

DUTTON-LAINSON CO.
451 W. 2nd
Hastings, NE 68902
Mailing Address:
P.O. Box 729
Hastings, NE 68902
Tel.: 402-462-4141 **NE**
Fax: 402-462-2971
Year Founded: 1886
Approx.Sls.: $25,000,000
Emp.: 400
Fiscal Year-end: 9/30/90
Import Export
Hand Winches, Electric Winches, Brake Winches, Tongue Jacks, Couplers, Wheel Bearing Protectors, Trailer Accessories, Fuel Filters, Grease Guns, Pump Oil Cans, Oil Funnels & Lube Spouts, Tire Pumps, Fence Stretcher/Splicer, Spare Tire Carrier
S.I.C.: 3531; 5084
Hal Lainson *(Chm. Bd.)*
Charles Hermes *(Pres.)*
Jeremy Daniels *(V.P.)*
Ron Michalek *(V.P.)*
G.E. McClure *(V.P.)*
Dale Gray *(V.P. & Treas.)*
Jorn Olsen *(V.P. & Controller)*
J.J. Lainson *(Sec.)*
Clark Hansel *(Dir.-Pur.)*
Dean Poppe *(Mgr.-Personnel)*

Outside Service Firm(s):

Deloitte & Touche*(Auditors)*
1040 NBC Center
Lincoln, NE 68508

KPMG Peat Marwick*(Auditors)*
1600 FirsTier Bank Bldg., 13th & M Streets, Ste. 1600
Lincoln, NE 68508
Tel.: 402-476-1216

Brown & Brown*(Legal Firm)*
Lincoln, NE

City National Bank*(Major Banking Relationship)*
Lincoln, NE

Division:

Sanitas Healthcare Div. **(1)**
451 W. 2nd
Hastings, NE 68904
Tel.: 402-462-4141
Whirlpool Healthcare Tubs
S.I.C.: 3842
Jim Vander Heiden *(Dir.-Sls. & Mktg.)*

DUVAL & PARTNERS
585 Commercial St.
Boston, MA 02109
Tel.: 617-248-1881
Fax: 617-248-1874
Year Founded: 1961
Approx.Billings: $19,000,000
Emp.: 31
Marketing Evolutionary Products & Services
Betsyann Duval *(Pres.)*
Dorothy Woglom *(Exec. V.P., Acct. Principal)*
David Domeshek *(V.P., Pub. Rels.)*
Diana Pohly *(V.P., Bus. Devel.)*
Mara Levy *(Opers./Human Resources Dir.)*

Computer Systems/Hardware:
MacIntosh

DWECK & CAMPBELL, INC.
536 Broadway
New York, NY 10012
Tel.: 212-219-0600
Year Founded: 1991
Approx.Billings: $14,000,000
Emp.: 7
Michael Dweck *(Pres. & New Bus. Contact)*

DWYER INSTRUMENTS INC.
102 Highway 212
Michigan City, IN 46360
Mailing Address:
P.O. Box 373,
Michigan City, IN 46360
Tel.: 219-879-8000 **IN**
Cable: 25916
Fax: 219-872-9057
Year Founded: 1931
Approx.Sls.: $55,700,000
Emp.: 850
Fiscal Year-end: 12/31/91
Export
Mfr. Industrial Instruments & Controls
S.I.C.: 3823; 3812; 3829; 3822; 3824
James G. Dwyer *(Chm. Bd.)*
Edwin J. Clark *(Pres. & Chief Exec. Officer)*
Stephen S. Clark *(Chief Oper. Officer & Exec. V.P.)*
T.M. D'Haeze *(V.P.-Fin. & Acctg., Treas. & Sec.)*
Gregg P. Miller *(V.P.-Indus. Rels.)*
J. Barry *(Dir.-Sls.)*
Donald E. Dewitt *(Dir.-Engrng.)*
Al Richardson *(Dir.-Mfg.)*
Dave Decker *(Mktg. Coord.)*
Principal(s):
Edwin J. Clark

No. of Mfg. Plants/Facilities: 10
No. of U.S. Offices: 5
No. of Foreign Offices: 2

Computer Systems/Hardware:
Compaq 386; IBM System 34, 36 & AS 400

Outside Service Firm(s):

Price Waterhouse*(Auditors)*
202 S. Michigan
South Bend, IN 46624

Society Bank*(Major Banking Relationship)*
South Bend, IN

Divisions:

W.E. Anderson Div. **(1)**
P.O. Box 358,
Michigan City, IN 46360
Tel.: 219-879-8000
Fax: 219-872-9057
Export
S.I.C.: 3822; 3823

Mercoid Div. **(1)**
P.O. Box 258
Michigan City, IN 46360
Tel.: 219-879-8000
Fax: 219-872-9057
Export
Mfr. Mercoid Pressure, Temperature & Level Controls
S.I.C.: 3822; 3823

Value Assemblers & Manufacturers, Inc. **(1)**
Kansas City, MO
Tel.: 213-773-1272

Affiliates:

Love Controls Corporation **(1)**
1475 S. Wheeling Rd.
Wheeling, IL 60090
Tel.: 708-541-3232
Telex: 297115 LOVE UR
Fax: 708-541-7366
Manufacture of Temperature Sensors & Controls
S.I.C.: 3822; 3823
Stephen S. Clark *(Pres. & Chief Oper. Officer)*

Proximity Controls Corp. **(1)**
P.O. Box 386, Route 6
Fergus Falls, MN 56537
Tel.: 218-739-3364
Tel.: 800-642-4755 (MN)
Tel.: 800-346-9819
Fax: 218-739-2734
Manufacture of Liquid & Dry Bulk Level Controls & Valve Position Indicating Switches & Transmitters
S.I.C.: 3822; 3823

DYATRON/BONDO CORPORATION
3700 Atlanta Industrial Pkwy. N.W.
Atlanta, GA 30331
Tel.: 404-696-2730
Fax: 404-699-0073
Emp.: 193
Manufacture & Wholesale Autobody Repair Products
S.I.C.: 3714; 5013
J.Q. Machamer *(Chm. Bd. & Chief Exec. Officer)*
Lamont Machamer *(V.P.-Sls. & Mktg.)*
Abdul Razzak *(V.P.-Tech. Services)*

Outside Service Firm(s):

Smith & Radigan*(Auditors)*
Atlanta, GA

First National Bank of Atlanta*(Major Banking Relationship)*
2 Peachtree Street N.W.
Atlanta, GA 30383

Subsidiary:

Fibertec Inc. **(1)**
35 Scotland St.
Bridgewater, MA 02324
Tel.: 508-697-5100
Manufacturer of Laminex; Polyester Compound used in FRP Fabrication
Joseph Aten *(Pres.)*

DYKE INDUSTRY, INC.
309 Center St.
Little Rock, AR 72201
Tel.: 501-376-2921
Fax: 501-374-4922
Year Founded: 1965
Approx.Sls.: $92,000,000
Emp.: 500
Wholesale Distributor of Rough, Dressed & Finished Lumber, Plywood & Millwork
S.I.C.: 5031
James T. Dyke *(Chm. Bd.)*
Fred W. Edick *(Pres.)*
Carl D. McVay *(V.P.-Opers.)*
Wendy Buste *(Treas.)*
Wayne Syler *(Regional Mgr.)*

Outside Service Firm(s):

Ernst & Young*(Auditors)*
425 W. Capitol, Ste. 3600
Little Rock, AR 72201
Tel.: 501-372-5443
Fax: 501-372-6288

Union National Bank*(Major Banking Relationship)*
P.O. Box 1541
Little Rock, AR 72203
Tel.: 501-378-4213

DYNAMIC CONTROLS CORP.
8 Nutmeg Rd. S.
South Windsor, CT 06074
Mailing Address:
P.O. Box 73
South Windsor, CT 06074
Tel.: 203-528-9971 **CT**
Fax: 203-289-6163
Approx.Sls.: $31,000,000
Emp.: 350
Manufacture Aircraft Equipment
S.I.C.: 3728
Thomas P. Farkas *(Pres.)*
R. Matiasek *(V.P.-Mfg.)*
T. A. Phillips *(V.P.-Engrng.)*
C. A. DeAndrea *(Mgr.-Personnel)*
R. J. Kowalski *(Mgr.-Mktg.)*
R. K. Sceery *(Mgr.-Admin.)*

Outside Service Firm(s):

Greenberg, Rosenblatt, Kull & Bitsoli*(Auditors)*
306 Main St.
Worcester, MA 01608
Tel.: 508-791-0901

Reide & Riege*(Legal Firm)*
Hartford, CT

BayBank Valley Trust Co.*(Major Banking Relationship)*
1500 Main St.
Springfield, MA 01101
Tel.: 413-781-7575

DYNAMIC METAL PRODUCTS COMPANY
967 Parker St.
Manchester, CT 06040
Tel.: 203-646-4048 **CT**
Fax: 203-647-7175
Year Founded: 1963
Approx.Sls.: $18,000,000
Emp.: 145
Export
Precision Sheet Metal Work, Dies, Tools, Die Sets, Jigs & Fixtures
S.I.C.: 3444; 3544
James Melo *(Chm. Bd. & Treas.)*
Howard Miller *(Vice Chm. & Sec.)*
Joseph Kuronya *(Pres.)*
James Downey, Jr. *(Chief Fin. Officer)*
Mario Facchini *(Exec. V.P.)*
Alan Kick *(V.P.-Sls. & Mktg.)*
Norman Letendre *(V.P.-Engrng.)*
Stephen Olander *(Controller)*
Thomas Decker *(Dir.-Pur.)*
Mary DelGaudio *(Dir.-Human Resources & Employee Benefits)*
L. Donald Isabelle *(Dir.-Quality Control)*
N. Letendre *(Dir.-Res. & Devel.)*
Ralph Rawson *(Dir.-Engrng. & Tech. Services)*

No. of Mfg. Plants/Facilities: 1
No. of U.S. Offices: 1
No. of Foreign Offices: 1

Outside Service Firm(s):

Bardaglio, Hart & Schuman*(Auditors)*
Windsor Locks, CT

Coopers & Lybrand*(Auditors)*
280 Trumbull St.
Hartford, CT 06103

Reide & Riege*(Legal Firm)*
Hartford, CT

Rogin, Nassau, Caplan, Lassamn & Hirtle*(Legal Firm)*
Hartford, CT

Fleet National Bank*(Major Banking Relationship)*
Vernon, CT

THE DYSON-KISSNER-MORAN CORPORATION
230 Park Ave., Ste. 659
New York, NY 10169
Tel.: 212-661-4600 **DE**
Fax: 212-986-8016
Year Founded: 1954
Sales Range: $1 Billion +
Import Export
Private Investment Company
S.I.C.: 6159
Ernest H. Lorch *(Chm. Bd. & Chief Exec. Officer)*
Robert R. Dyson *(Pres. & Chief Oper. Officer)*
C. Richard Owens *(Sr. V.P. & Chief Fin. Officer)*
Paul Rossetti *(Sr. V.P.-Devel.)*
Joseph L. Aurichio *(Sr. V.P.-Opers.)*
John S. Wehrle *(V.P.-Fin. Plng.)*
Goran G. Diedrichs *(V.P.-European Opers.)*
John Carleton *(V.P.)*
Robert D. Farley *(V.P.)*
John H. Fitzsimons *(Sec. & Gen. Counsel)*
Edmund G. McElroy, Jr. *(Treas.)*
Harry Ploaskier *(Controller)*

No. of U.S. Offices: 1

Computer Systems/Hardware:
IBM PC

Outside Service Firm(s):

Arthur Andersen & Co.*(Auditors)*
1345 Ave. of the Americas
New York, NY 10105
Tel.: 212-708-4000

Division:

J. A. Sexauer **(1)**
531 Central Park Ave.
Scarsdale, NY 10583
Tel.: 914-472-7500
Fax: 914-472-3774
Emp.: 300
Import Export
Computer Systems/Hardware:
IBM System 38
Wholesalers of Plumbing, Electrical & Heating Supplies
S.I.C.: 5074
Gil Silva *(Pres.)*
Carmen Sbezzi *(V.P.-Sls. & Mktg.)*
Vin Pescosolido *(V.P.-Fin.)*
Anthony Shiavo *(V.P.-Pur.)*
Rick Coalter *(Dir.-Mktg. Communications)*
Raymond Carioscia *(Personnel Dir.)*

Subsidiaries:

Arrow Group Industries, Inc. **(1)**
P.O. Box 928,
Wayne, NJ 07474-0928
Approx.Sls.: $60,000,000
Emp.: 300
Fiscal Year-end: 1/31/91
Export
Manufacture Steel, Aluminum & Wood Outdoor Storage Buildings
S.I.C.: 3448
Ernest M. Simon *(Chm. & Chief Exec. Officer)*
George J. Smith *(Pres. & Chief Oper. Officer)*
Paul A. Mees *(V.P.-Fin.)*
John Franklin *(V.P.-Des. & Engrng.)*
Luke Hosenitz *(Controller)*
Jerry Saul *(Adv. & Sls. Promo. Mgr.)*
Barbara Capo *(Mgr.-Natl. Accts. & Foreign Sls.)*

Burner Systems International, Inc. **(1)**
700 East 10th St.
Chattanooga, TN 37402
Tel.: 800-251-6318
Mfr. of Gas Burners and Manifolds for Use in Furnaces, Water Heaters and Commercial Cooking Appliances
S.I.C.: 3433; 3498
Robert R. Dyson *(Chm. & Chief Exec. Officer)*
Michael Frost *(Pres.)*

CCC Conveyors, Inc. **(1)**
P.O. Box 59448, 2466 Glenda Lane
Dallas, TX 75229-4511
Tel.: 214-620-7090
Fax: 214-620-7239
Manufacture Conveyor Systems For Airport Baggage Handling Systems & Post Offices
Robert R. Dyson *(Chm. Bd.)*
Dan Quinn *(Pres.)*
Marc F. Harris *(V.P. & Treas.)*
John H. FitzSimons *(V.P. & Sec.)*

Centre Foundry & Machine Co. **(1)**
74 Warnwood Ave.
Wheeling, WV 26003
Tel.: 304-277-3600
Mfr. of Specialty Gray Iron
S.I.C.: 3321
Hans A. Schmidt *(Pres.)*
Ernest M. Simon *(V.P.)*
John H. FitzSimons *(Sec.)*
Edmund G. McElroy, Jr. *(Treas.)*
William O'Mudge *(V.P.)*

M.S. Chambers & Son, Inc. **(1)**
132 W. Main St.
Baltic, CT 06330
Tel.: 203-822-8213
Commercial Printers; Rotogravure, Embossing & Flexographic Roller Engraving
S.I.C.: 2754; 2759
Martin C. Shapiro *(Pres.)*

Cissell Manufacturing Company **(1)**
831 First St.
Louisville, KY 40203
Tel.: 502-581-1292
Emp.: 450
Mfr. of Commercial Dry Cleaning Equipment & Clothes Dryers
S.I.C.: 3582; 3589
Milton E. Milam *(Pres.)*
R. Kevin Hobbs *(V.P.-Fin.)*
Tony Polliam *(V.P.-Engrng.)*
Roberto Rubini *(V.P.-Mktg.)*

Consolidated Group, Inc. **(1)**
P.O. Box 33669,
Charlotte, NC 28233
Tel.: 800-483-4536
Supplies Anilox, Rotogravure and Flexographic Rolls, Textile Screens to the Printing Industry
S.I.C.: 2754; 2759
James H. Dickson *(Pres.)*
Jerry Glenn *(V.P.-Fin. & Treas.)*
Ernest M. Simon *(V.P.)*
John H. FitzSimons *(Sec.)*

Consolidated Screen-Makers, Inc. **(1)**
P.O. Box 28233,
Charlotte, NC 28233
Tel.: 800-438-4536
Supplies Textile Screens
S.I.C.: 3953
James H. Dickson *(Pres.)*
Jerry Glenn *(V.P.-Fin. & Treas.)*
Ernest M. Simon *(V.P.)*

Consolidated Engravers-East, Inc. **(1)**
P.O. Box 28233,
Charlotte, NC 28233
Tel.: 800-438-4536
Supplies Anilox and Rotogravure and Flexographic Rolls, Textile Screens to the Printing Industry
S.I.C.: 2754; 2759; 2796
James H. Dickson *(Pres.)*
Jerry Glenn *(V.P.-Fin. & Treas.)*
Ernest M. Simon *(V.P.)*
John H. FitzSimons *(Sec.)*

DKM Building Enterprises, L.P. **(1)**
Princeton Pike Park Corp. Ctr., 1009 Lenox Dr.
Lawrenceville, NJ 08648-2316
Tel.: 609-895-1433
Fax: 609-895-1540
Manufactures & Markets Primarily Residential Modular Houses
Ronald Berman *(Chm. Bd.)*
Paul Rossetti *(Pres.)*
Robert J. Baker *(Sr. V.P. & Chief Oper. Officer)*
George Manukas *(Sr. V.P. & Chief Fin. Officer)*

DKM, Ltd. **(1)**
230 Park Ave.
New York, NY 10169
Ernest H. Lorch *(Chm. & Chief Exec. Officer)*
Robert R. Dyson *(Pres. & Chief Oper. Officer)*
C. Richard Owens *(Sr. V.P. & Chief Fin. Officer)*

DKM Properties Corporation **(1)**
1009 Lenox Dr.
Lawrenceville, NJ 08648
Tel.: 609-896-2160
Real Estate Investment, Development & Construction
S.I.C.: 6552
Robert S. Powell, Jr. *(Pres.)*
George Manukas *(V.P., Treas. & Asst. Sec.)*

DKM Resources, Inc. **(1)**
Interfirst Plaza, 1100 Louisiana St.,Ste.4550
Houston, TX 77002
Tel.: 713-739-0312
Acquires Oil & Gas Production Facilities & Reserves
S.I.C.: 6799
Sidney F. Jones *(Pres. & Chief Exec. Officer)*
Susan E. Wellborn *(V.P., Chief Fin. Officer, Controller, & Asst. Sec.)*

Kearney-National, Inc. **(1)**
5 Corporate Park Dr.,Ste.114
White Plains, NY 10604-3805
Tel.: 914-694-6700 (100%)
Fax: 914-694-6513
Approx.Sls.: $180,775,000
Emp.: 1,800
Fiscal Year-end: 12/31/90
Mfr. of Electrical & Electronic Components, Electrical Power Distribution Equip. & Computer Memory Products
S.I.C.: 3629
Robert R. Dyson *(Chm. Bd.)*
Joseph L. Aurichio *(Pres. & Chief Exec. Officer)*
James F. Zyboyovsky *(Sr. V.P.)*
Matthew J. Zilinskas *(Controller)*

Divisions:

Coto Wabash **(2)**
55 Dupont Dr.
Providence, RI 02907
Tel.: 401-943-2686
Fax: 401-942-0920

Hapco/American Div. **(2)**
Hillman Hwy.
Abingdon, VA 24210
Tel.: 703-628-7171 (100%)
Aluminum Lighting & Traffic Signal Support Structures
S.I.C.: 3446
David L. O'Brien *(Pres. & G.M.)*
J.F. Zboyovsky *(Grp. V.P.)*
William B. Corcoran *(Controller)*
Milton C. Webber *(Gen. Sls. Mgr.)*

Kearney **(2)**
1928 Montreal Rd.
Tucker, GA 30084
Tel.: 404-939-6011 (100%)
Fax: 404-938-5790
Approx.Sls.: $55,000,000
Emp.: 400
Electric Equipment for Transmission & Distribution Systems
S.I.C.: 3613; 3643
Richard Prusiewicz *(Pres.)*
Tom Boyd *(Exec. V.P.)*
Richard Brogan *(V.P.-Human Resources)*
Robert A. Duncan *(V.P.-Mktg.)*
Greg Rufus *(V.P.-Fin.)*
Jack L. Williamson *(V.P.-Sls.)*
Alan Myers *(Controller)*
Donna Perrone *(Mgr.-Adv. & Communications)*
Sam Guza *(Adv. Coord.)*

Manufacturing Facility:

Kearney Div. **(3)**
3660 So. School St.
Fayetteville, AR 72701
Tel.: 501-521-3700 (100%)
Fax: 501-521-0816
Approx.Sls.: $33,000,000
Emp.: 190
Mfr. of Electrical Components
S.I.C.: 3613; 3643
Eldon Henninger *(Mgr.-Mfg.)*

Kearney-Western Power Products, Inc. **(2)**
900 Portway Ave.
Hood River, OR 97031
Tel.: 503-386-4581 (100%)
Approx.Sls.: $5,900,000
Emp.: 50
Manufacture of Fiberglass Enclosures to House Electrical Equipment & Other Equipment
S.I.C.: 2221
Richard Prosiewicz *(Pres.)*
Jim D. Coon *(V.P. & Plant Mgr.)*
Lynn Beier *(Plant Mgr.)*

Spectrol Electronics Corp. **(2)**
40-51 Grey Stone Dr.
Ontario, CA 01761
Tel.: 909-923-3313
Fax: 909-923-3503

Wabash Magnetics **(2)**
First & Webster St.
Wabash, IN 46992
Tel.: 219-563-2191 (100%)
Approx.Sls.: $9,600,000
Mfr. of Automotive Sensors
S.I.C.: 3679; 3829
Mike Buis *(Pres.)*
Dave Ogram *(V.P.-Fin.)*
Lawrence R. Denbo *(Chief Fin. Officer)*

Wabash Magnetics **(2)**
810 N. Cass St.
Wabash, IN 46992
Tel.: 219-563-3111 (100%)
Approx.Sls.: $7,400,000
Mfr. of Automotive Sensors
S.I.C.: 3679; 3829

Manufacturing Facility:

Wabash Magnetics **(3)**
1222 Seymour Dr.
South Boston, VA 24592
Tel.: 804-575-7911 (100%)
Approx.Sls.: $9,000,000
Mfr. of Automotive Sensors
S.I.C.: 3679; 3829

Leader National Corporation **(1)**
4807 Rockside Rd.
Independence, OH 44131
Tel.: 216-447-1660
Casualty Insurer Specializing in Non-Standard Automotive Coverage
S.I.C.: 6331
Donald C. Kintzing *(Pres. & Chief Exec. Officer)*
Gerald F. Burke *(Sr. V.P.-Fin.)*

Pentek Corporation **(1)**
8502 Brookville Rd.
Indianapolis, IN 46239-9427
Tel.: 317-359-3858
Manufacture Custom Material Handling Equipment-Belt-Powered Roller Conveyors, Pushers, Transfer Cars, Turntables & Other Unit-Load Equipment Primarily for the Shipping Container Industry
S.I.C.: 3535
Dan Quinn *(Pres.)*
Mark F. Farris *(V.P.-Fin.)*

Plaid Enterprises Inc. **(1)**
P.O. Box 7600, 1649 International Blvd.
Norcross, GA 30091
Tel.: 404-923-8200
Designs, Manufactures and Sells a Broad Line of Craft Products
S.I.C.: 3944; 5945
Ernest M. Simon *(Pres., Chief Exec. & Oper. Officer)*
John S. Michalek *(V.P.-Fin. & Chief Fin. Officer)*
John F. McDonald *(V.P.-Mktg.)*

The RAL Corporation **(1)**
P.O. Box 1405, 131 Rte. 46 West
Fairfield, NJ 07006
Tel.: 201-227-9100
Wholesale Distribution of Plumbing, Heating & Air Conditioning Equipment in New York & New Jersey
S.I.C.: 5074
David E. Berman *(Pres.)*
Murray J. Zucker *(V.P., Chief Fin. Officer & Treas.)*

Thetford Corporation **(1)**
7101 Jackson Rd.
Ann Arbor, MI 48103
Tel.: 313-769-6000
Telex: 810-223-6010
Fax: 313-769-2023
Assets: $35,700,948
Liabilities: $14,747,067
Net Worth: $20,953,881
Approx.Sls.: $70,000,000
Emp.: 340

Fiscal Year-end: 12/31/90
Export
Manufacture & Sales of Sanitation Products & Systems
S.I.C.: 2842; 3088; 3589; 3089
Charles L. Sargent *(Chm. Bd. & Chief Exec. Officer)*
John R. Arlen *(Pres.)*
John M. Antos *(V.P.-Engrng.)*
Michael W. Larime *(V.P.-Sls. & Mktg.)*
Victor Silles *(Chief Fin. Officer & Treas.)*
Frederick A. Tomczyk *(Mgr.-Mktg. Services)*
Armin L. Luzi *(Mgr.-Mktg.)*
James F. Janowski *(Mgr.-Natl. Sls.)*
Jerry Wireman *(Mgr.-Mfg.)*
Brian Hall *(Mgr.-Pur.)*
Jack Quigley *(Dir.-Personnel)*
John Goedert *(Mgr.-Information Systems)*

Divisions:

Thetford Corp. Mfg. Facility **(2)**
800 Baker Rd.
Dexter, MI 48130
Tel.: 313-769-6000
Manufacture Plastic Plumbing Fixtures
S.I.C.: 3088

Thetford Corp., Warehouse Div. **(2)**
2700-B Saturn
Brea, CA 92621
Tel.: 714-993-7500
Fax: 714-993-3861
Import & Export of Sanitation Products
S.I.C.: 4225
Ken West *(Reg. Sls. Mgr.)*

Thetford Corp., Warehouse Div. **(2)**
55712-B County Rd. 15
Elkhart, IN 46514
Tel.: 219-274-6491
Emp.: 2
S.I.C.: 4225
Robert Watts *(Reg. Sls. Mgr.)*

Subsidiary:

Thetford Systems, Inc. **(2)**
7101 Jackson Road
Ann Arbor, MI 48106
Tel.: 313-769-6000
Approx.Sls.: $834,000
Emp.: 13
Service Industry Machines
S.I.C.: 3589
Edward Jordan *(Pres.)*

Trayco of S.C., Inc. **(1)**
1307 National Cemetary Rd.
Florence, SC 29502
Tel.: 803-669-5462
James Hulsman *(Pres.)*
Gil V. Silva *(V.P.)*
Ernest M. Simon *(V.P.)*
Erich Grotti *(Treas.)*

Affiliate:

Varlen Corp. **(1)**
305 East Shuman Blvd.
Naperville, IL 60566
Tel.: 708-420-0400 (31.8%)
Approx.Sls.: $169,869,000
Fiscal Year-end: 1/31/88
(See Separate Listing)
Richard L. Wellek *(Pres. & Chief Exec. Officer)*

Non-U.S. Holdings:

Campa Products B.V. **(1)**
29 Nijverheidsweg PO Box 169, 4870-AD
Etten-Leur, Netherlands
Tel.: 01608-15944
S.I.C.: 2842; 3088

Camptel International SPA **(1)**
Sede amm. e. stabil.:, Via G. Di Vittorio, 358 20099
Milan, Italy
Tel.: 02-240-5251
Fax: 02-240-5686
Mfg. of Commercial Laundry Dry Cleaning & Pressing Machines
G. Nalin *(Gen. Mgr.)*

Furigas NV **(1)**
J.C. van Markenstraat 19 9403 AC
Assen, Netherlands
Tel.: 59 20 45 145
Mfr. of Gas Burners for use in Furnaces
S.I.C.: 3443

Kearney-National Canada Ltd. **(1)**
280 Speedvale Ave. W.
Guelph, ON N1H 1C4, Canada
Tel.: 519-822-3670 (100%)
Holding Company
S.I.C.: 6719; 3612
John Richardson *(Pres.)*

Subsidiary:

Les Appareillager Electriques Kearney-National **(2)**
9240 Langelier Blvd.
Saint Leonard, PQ H1P 2E1, Canada
Tel.: 514-323-1274
Mfrs. Electric Power Equipment
S.I.C.: 3612
Michel St-Onge *(Mgr.)*

MultiServ International Ltd. **(1)**
Piccadilly House, 33 Regent St.
London, SW1Y 4NB, United Kingdom
Tel.: 44-71-439-6661

Pantex Cissell **(1)**
9672 AP Winschoten 27
Industrieweg, Netherlands
Tel.: 05970-12300
Fax: 05970-12723
Mfg. of Commercial Laundry Dry Cleaning & Pressing Machines

Spectrol Electronics **(1)**
Drakes Way Swindon
Wiltshire, SNE 3HY, United Kingdom
Tel.: 011-44-79-353-5211
Fax: 011-44-79-353-9255

Thetford (Aqua) Products, Ltd. **(1)**
Centrovell Indus. Estate, Caldwell Rd.
Nuneaton, Warwickshire United Kingdom
Tel.: 0203-341941
Plastic Products
S.I.C.: 2842; 3088

Thetford GmbH **(1)**
Schallburch 14 5657
Haan, 1, Germany
Tel.: 0202/39-30-57
Plastic Products, Enameled Iron & Metal Sanitary Ware
S.I.C.: 2842; 3088

Thetford Producten B.V. **(1)**
29 Nijverheidsweg P.O. Box 169, 4870-AD
Etten-Leur, Netherlands
Tel.: 01608-15944
Distribution of Sanitary Ware
S.I.C.: 5074

Thetford Sanitation Ltd. **(1)**
2299 Drew Rd.
Mississauga, ON L5S 1A1, Canada
Tel.: 416-671-0255
Mfrs. Plastic & Plumbing Fixtures & Supplies
S.I.C.: 2842; 3088
Graham Chignal *(Mgr.)*

E & A INDUSTRIES, INC.
101 W. Ohio, Ste. 1840
Indianapolis, IN 46204
Tel.: 317-684-3150 **IN**
Fax: 317-684-3164
Year Founded: 1977
Assets: $11,000,000
Liabilities: $5,000,000
Net Worth: $6,000,000
Approx.Sls.: $21,000,000
Emp.: 100
Fiscal Year-end: 12/31/90
Export
Mfr. Chemicals, Auto Reconditioning Products; Real Estate
S.I.C.: 2842; 6531
Edwin H. Klink *(Chm. Bd. & Pres.)*
John M. Campbell *(Chief Oper. Officer)*
Ronald L. Wise *(Treas. & Sec.)*
Robert Hunt *(Controller)*
Mike Kelsch *(Dir.-Import)*
Patti Kottkamp *(Dir.-Human Resources)*
Scott Neese *(Dir.-Research & Devel.)*
Sean O'Farrell *(Dir.-Mngmt. Information Systems)*
John Ranshaw *(Dir.-Export & Intl. Mgr.)*
Principal(s):
Edwin H. Klink

No. of Mfg. Plants/Facilities: 2
No. of U.S. Offices: 1
No. of Foreign Offices: 1

Computer Systems/Hardware:
IBM System 36

Outside Service Firm(s):

Ernst & Young*(Auditors)*
One Indiana Square, Ste. 3400
Indianapolis, IN 46204
Tel.: 317-236-1100

Wells & Co.*(Commercial Insurance Carrier)*
Indianapolis, IN

Bank of Nova Scotia*(International Bank Affiliate)*
44 King St. West
Toronto, ON MH5 1E2, Canada

Bank of Nova Scotia*(International Bank Affiliate)*
P.O. Box 70,
Halifax, NS D3J 2MI, Canada
Tel.: 902-420-4901

McDonald & Co.*(Investment Banker)*
2100 Society Bldg.
Cleveland, OH 44114

Ice, Miller, Donadio & Ryan*(Legal Firm)*
One American Square, Box 82001
Indianapolis, IN 46282
Tel.: 317-236-2219

INB National Bank*(Major Banking Relationship)*
One Indiana Sq.
Indianapolis, IN 46266
Tel.: 317-266-6000

INB National Bank*(Pension Manager)*
Indianapolis, IN

Subsidiaries:

Car Brite Distributing, Inc. **(1)**
1855 S. Draper St.
Indianapolis, IN 46203
Tel.: 317-781-2768
Fax: 317-781-3292
Distribution of Automotive Reconditioning Chemicals & Supplies
S.I.C.: 5169

Car Brite, Inc. **(1)**
1910 S. State St.
Indianapolis, IN 46203
Tel.: 317-788-9925 (100%)
Fax: 317-788-9930
Approx.Sls.: $12,000,000
Emp.: 70
Mfr. Auto Reconditioning Products
S.I.C.: 2842
Edwin H. Klink *(Chm. Bd.)*
John Campbell *(Pres.)*
Michael D. Wasson *(V.P.)*
Robert E. Fuller *(V.P.)*
Ronald L. Wise *(Sec. & Treas.)*

H & K Realty Co. Inc. **(1)**
101 West Ohio, Ste. 1840
Indianapolis, IN 46204
Tel.: 317-684-3150 (100%)
Fax: 317-684-3164
Approx.Sls.: $1,000,000
Emp.: 7
Rental of Real Estate
S.I.C.: 6531
Edwin H. Klink *(Chm. Bd. & Pres.)*
Ronald L. Wise *(Sec. & Treas.)*

E-B ADVERTISING DISPLAY INC.
2037 Wales Rd., N.E.
Massillon, OH 44646
Tel.: 216-833-4101
Tel.: 800-321-9869
Fax: 216-833-9844
Year Founded: 1952
Approx.Billings: $12,000,000
Emp.: 140
W.E. Baucom *(Chm.)*
Betty Denaro-Baucom *(Pres.)*
Archer Wright *(Sr. V.P., Sls.)*
Dick Loxley *(Sr. V.P., Sls.)*
Bruce Moore *(V.P., Sls.)*
Dee Tremba *(V.P., Sls.)*
Bob Russell *(V.P., Gen. Mgr.)*
Theresa Moore *(V.P. Admin.)*
Janet Baylor *(Sls. Service Mgr.)*

E & G FOODS
7007 N.W. 37th Ave.
Miami, FL 33147
Tel.: 305-691-3535 **FL**
Fax: 305-691-2015
Approx.Sls.: $146,000,000
Emp.: 180
Wholesale Meat & Seafood
S.I.C.: 5146; 5147
Guillermo Quirch, Sr. *(Pres.)*
Guillermo Quirch, Jr. *(V.P.)*
Eduardo Quirch *(Treas.)*
Teresita Del Calvo *(Controller & Dir.-Data Processing)*

Outside Service Firm(s):

Berges, Guardado & San Miguel*(Auditors)*
Miami, FL

Republic National Bank*(Major Banking Relationship)*
Miami, FL

E-II HOLDINGS, INC.
(Entered Ch. 11 bankruptcy protection 7-92)
600 Madison Ave.
New York, NY 10022
Tel.: 212-307-8100 **DE**
Holding Company, Consumer Products
S.I.C.: 6719; 3589; 3161; 2047; 2048
Stephen J. Green *(Chm. Bd.)*

Subsidiaries:

Culligan International Company **(1)**
One Culligan Pkwy.
Northbrook, IL 60062
Tel.: 708-205-6000
Approx.Sls.: $290,000,000
Emp.: 1,500
Fiscal Year-end: 1/31/90
Water Conditioning Products & Services
S.I.C.: 3589
I. Donald Rosuck *(Pres.)*
Harold Stafford *(Pres.-North America)*
Lee Strain *(V.P.-Mfg.)*
Larry Holzman *(Adv. & Mktg. Dir.)*
Dave Horslev *(Dir.-Human Resources)*

Subsidiary:

Everpure Inc. **(2)**
660 N. Blackhawk Dr.
Westmont, IL 60559
Tel.: 708-654-4000
Water Conditioning & Filtration Products
S.I.C.: 3589
Jim Vosseller *(Pres.)*
James V. Bove, Jr. *(Mktg. Mgr.-Consumer Prods.)*
Richard N. Verson *(Mgr.-Mktg. Communications)*

Pet Specialties, Inc. **(1)**
109 Park Dr., Ste. 360
Brentwood, TN 37027
Tel.: 615-377-3790
Mfr. of Pet Foods
S.I.C.: 2047; 2048

Samsonite Corporation **(1)**
11200 E. 45th Ave.
Denver, CO 80239
Tel.: 303-373-2000
Fax: 303-373-6300
Emp.: 4,500
Import Export
Mfr. of Samsonite Luggage & Business Cases
S.I.C.: 3161
Thomas Leonard *(Pres.-USA)*
Nick Noell *(Pres.-Intl. & Chief Fin. Officer)*
Roger Keehn *(V.P.-Human Resources)*
Frank Steed *(V.P.-Sls. & Mktg.)*
Jim Ray *(V.P.-Opers.)*
D. Michael Clayton *(Gen. Counsel)*
Paige Miller *(Dir.-Mktg. Services)*

Subsidiary:

Lark Luggage Company, Inc. **(2)**
11200 E. 45th Ave.
Denver, CO 80239-0094
Tel.: 303-373-6200
Tel.: 800-421-LARK
Fax: 303-373-6300
Approx.Sls.: $10,000,000
Emp.: 20
Fiscal Year-end: 2/28/91
Manufacture Luggage
S.I.C.: 3161
Tom Leonard *(Pres.)*
Stephen Green *(Chief Exec. Officer)*
Roger Coe *(V.P. & Gen. Mgr.)*

EAC CORPORATION
(d/b/a/ EckAdams)
347 N. Lindbergh Blvd.
Saint Louis, MO 63141
Tel.: 314-993-8100 **DE**
Fax: 314-993-1260
Year Founded: 1977
Approx.Sls.: $24,000,000
Emp.: 250
Mfr. Metal & Wood Office & Institutional Furniture
S.I.C.: 2521; 2522; 2531
M. Weldon Rogers III *(Chm. Bd., Pres. & Chief Exec. Officer)*
Joseph M. Mooney *(Sr. V.P.-Opers.)*
Norman F. Clements *(V.P., Sec. & Treas.)*

No. of U.S. Offices: 3

Outside Service Firm(s):

KPMG Peat Marwick*(Auditors)*
1010 Market St.
Saint Louis, MO 63101
Tel.: 314-444-1400

Bryan, Cave, McPheeters & McRoberts*(Legal Firm)*
One Metropolitan Sq.
St. Louis, MO 63102
Tel.: 314-259-2000

Southwest Bank*(Major Banking Relationship)*
St. Louis, MO

Divisions:

Flewelling Div. **(1)**
12411 Industrial Ave., Box 2247
South Gate, CA 90280
Tel.: 213-636-9874
Fax: 213-531-1859
Emp.: 85
Mfr. of Office Seating
S.I.C.: 2521; 2522

Osceola Div. **(1)**
Hwy. 61 South
Osceola, AR 72370
Tel.: 501-563-2900
Fax: 501-563-2939
Emp.: 120
Mfr. of Office Seating
S.I.C.: 2521; 2522

E B 5 CORPORATION
111 S.W. 5th Ave., Suite 2650
Portland, OR 97204
Tel.: 503-222-0061
Fax: 503-659-7352
Approx.Sls.: $17,000,000
Emp.: 10
Fiscal Year-end: 12/31/90
Cosmetic Company Specializing in Creams & Lotions
S.I.C.: 5999
Robert C. Heldfond *(Pres.)*
Richard Morrell *(Exec. V.P.)*
Robert D. Heldfond *(V.P.-Mktg.)*
Dan Wendell *(V.P.-Adv.)*

EBM SYSTEMS, INC.
7701 Greenbelt Rd.
Greenbelt, MD 20770
Tel.: 301-441-8200 **MD**
Fax: 301-220-5482
Year Founded: 1954
Emp.: 200
Third-Party Maintenance of Minicomputers, PCs, Peripherals, Typewriters & Computer Networks Plus Sls. of Typing Systems & Equipment Supplies
S.I.C.: 5045; 7629
Joseph McDermott, Jr. *(Pres. & Chief Exec. Officer)*
Kirk D. Brown *(Chief Fin. Officer & Exec. V.P.-Systems)*
Frank Shartle *(Sr. V.P.)*

No. of U.S. Offices: 1

Computer Systems/Hardware:
IBM System 36; DEC PDP 1134

Outside Service Firm(s):

Hyatt & Rhoads*(Legal Firm)*
Washington, DC

EBSC CORPORATION
5045 Broadway
Gary, IN 46409
Tel.: 219-769-1363 **IN**
Fax: 219-887-0210
Year Founded: 1917
Assets: $5,000,000
Net Worth: $5,000,000
Emp.: 500
Fiscal Year-end: 12/31/91
Building Maintenance Services
S.I.C.: 7349
Michael Saks *(Pres.)*
Allan Saks *(Gen. Mgr.)*

Computer Systems/Hardware:
IBM Clones

Division:

Technicare Cleaning Systems Inc. **(1)**
2720 N. College
Indianapolis, IN 46204
Tel.: 317-926-1221
Janitorial & Auto Reconditioning Services
S.I.C.: 2842
Edwin H. Klink *(Chm. & Pres.)*
Gary Kramer *(V.P. & Gen. Mgr.)*
Allan B. Hubbard *(Treas.)*
Ronald L. Wise *(Sec.)*

E.C.D., INC.
Bldg. 798, 171 Central Ave.
Hillside, NJ 07205
Tel.: 201-926-4242 **DE**
Fax: 201-926-1632
Approx.Sls.: $27,000,000
Emp.: 82
Import
Cold Drawn Carbon, Stainless & Alloy Wire
S.I.C.: 3315
Anthony J. Russo *(Chm. Bd. & Pres.)*
Lou Arcuri *(Exec. V.P.-Sls.)*
William J. Hughes *(V.P.-Admin. & Fin.)*
Richard A. Rafanello *(Treas. & Sec.)*
Cheryl Coelho *(Mgr.-Matls.)*

No. of Mfg. Plants/Facilities: 2

Outside Service Firm(s):

United Jersey Bank/Central N.A.*(Major Banking Relationship)*
Somerset, NJ

Wiss & Company*(Auditors)*
354 Eisenhower Pkwy.
Livingston, NJ 07039
Tel.: 201-994-9400

Shain, Schaffer & Rafanello*(Legal Firm)*
Parsippany, NJ

Subsidiary:

E.C.D. Inc. **(1)**
1201 Jersey Ave.
North Brunswick, NJ 08902
Tel.: 908-247-3131
Emp.: 20
Cold Drawn Carbon, Stainless & Alloy Wire
S.I.C.: 3315
Nick Russo *(Gen. Mgr.)*

ECRM
554 Clark Rd.
Tewksbury, MA 01876
Tel.: 508-851-0207
Fax: 508-851-7016
Emp.: 250
Manufacture of Laser Scanning Equipment, Graphic Digitizers, Laser Image Recorders, Laser Graphic Systems
S.I.C.: 3829
William Givens *(Pres.)*
Paul Markham *(V.P.-Sls.)*

EDI INTERNATIONAL, INC.
525 Carr St.
Cincinnati, OH 45203
Mailing Address:
P.O. Box 958,
Cincinnati, OH 45201-0958
Tel.: 513-621-0662
Tel.: 800-733-0663 **IN**
Telex: 21-4500 EARLYDAN CIN
Fax: 513-621-4248
Year Founded: 1821
Assets: $33,000,000
Liabilities: $30,000,000
Net Worth: $3,000,000
Approx.Sls.: $100,000,000
Emp.: 195
Fiscal Year-end: 12/31/90
Import Export
Holding Company/Grain Merchant
S.I.C.: 2041
Samuel M. Harrell *(Chm. Bd., Pres. & Chief Exec. Officer)*

Outside Service Firm(s):

Ernst & Young*(Auditors)*
One Indiana Square, Ste. 3400
Indianapolis, IN 46204
Tel.: 317-236-1100

Baker & Daniels*(Legal Firm)*
810 Fletcher Bldg., 108 N. Pennsylvania
Indianapolis, IN 46204
Tel.: 317-237-4535

The Central Trust Company, N.A.*(Major Banking Relationship)*
Columbus, OH

Subsidiaries:

E & D Grain Marketing Co **(1)**
525 Carr St.
Cincinnati, OH 45203
Tel.: 513-621-0662
Fax: 513-621-4248
Grain Merchant
S.I.C.: 2041
Tom Couch *(Pres.)*
Samual D. Harrell *(Dir.-Mktg.)*
James Messer *(Dir.-Sls.)*

The Early & Daniel Company, Inc. **(1)**
525 Carr St.
Cincinnati, OH 45203
Tel.: 513-621-0662 (100%)
Approx.Sls.: $69,000,000
Emp.: 85
Export
Merchandise & Storage of Grain
S.I.C.: 5153
Tom D. Couch *(Pres.)*

Tidewater Grain Co. **(1)**
525 Carr St.
Cincinnati, OH 45203
Tel.: 513-621-0662 (100%)
Sales Range: $100-499 Million
Emp.: 3
Grain Export
S.I.C.: 5153
Robert C. Hall *(Pres.)*

EFCO CORPORATION
County Rd. & Bridle Ln.
Monett, MO 65708
Mailing Address:
P.O. Box 609
Monett, MO 65708
Tel.: 417-235-3193
Tel.: 800-221-4169 **MO**
Fax: 417-235-7313
Year Founded: 1953
Approx.Sls.: $70,000,000
Emp.: 900
Fiscal Year-end: 9/30/90
Export
Manufacturer of Aluminum Windows & Custom Curtainwall, Store Front & Entry Doors
S.I.C.: 3442
William Terry Fuldner *(Chm. Bd. & Chief Exec. Officer)*
Christopher T. Fuldner *(Pres.)*
Jack Appel *(V.P.-Engrng.)*
Scott Beckwith *(V.P.-Mfg.)*
Bret Baker *(Chief Fin. Officer)*
Don Kellhofer *(Sec. & Treas.)*
John Beckwith *(Mgr.-Data Processing)*
Mark Cox *(Mgr.-Eastern Sls.)*
John E. Fuldner *(Mgr.-Mktg. & Adv.)*
Bart Kay *(Mgr.-Western Sls.)*
Randy Mackey *(Mgr.-Pur.)*
Mona Workes *(Mgr.-Personnel)*
Principal(s):
Christopher T. Fuldner

No. of Mfg. Plants/Facilities: 1
No. of U.S. Offices: 3

Computer Systems/Hardware:
IBM AS 400

Outside Service Firm(s):

Germanese & Sitton*(Auditors)*
St. Louis, MO

United Missouri Bank*(Major Banking Relationship)*
Tenth & Grand
Kansas City, MO 64106
Tel.: 816-556-7000

E F INDUSTRIES
16434 Ishida Ave.
Carson, CA 90248
Tel.: 310-754-2295
Fax: 213-754-2295
Approx.Sls.: $10,000,000
Emp.: 119
Computer Repair & Maintenance
S.I.C.: 7379
Edward Farris *(Pres.)*
Mark Farris *(V.P.-Mktg. & Sls.)*

Outside Service Firm(s):

Bernstein & Fox Accounting*(Auditors)*
Los Angeles, CA

Fine, Persik & Freidman*(Legal Firm)*
Los Angeles, CA

Union Bank*(Major Banking Relationship)*
445 S. Figueroa St.
Los Angeles, CA 90071
Tel.: 213-236-5076

EGC MEDIA GROUP, INC.
15 Bay Ave.
Hicksville, NY 11801
Tel.: 516-935-4944
Fax: 516-935-7030
Year Founded: 1985
Approx.Billings: $10,300,000
Emp.: 12
Business-to-Business, Corp. Identity, Video Production, Consumer Package, Design, In-Store Merchandising, Franchises, Retail Chains & Automotive
Ernest G. Canadeo *(Chm. Bd. & Pres.)*
Cynthia Smith *(Mgr., Pub. Rels.)*

Computer Systems/Hardware:
MacIntosh

ELE INTERNATIONAL, INC.
(Formerly Soiltest Inc.)
86 Albrecht Dr.
Lake Bluff, IL 60044
Mailing Address:
P.O. Box 8004
Lake Bluff, IL 60044
Tel.: 708-295-9400
Tel.: 800-323-1242
Fax: 708-295-9414
Approx.Sls.: $14,000,000
Emp.: 100
Export
Mfr. Engineering Test Equip. for Construction Materials, Including Soils, Rock, Concrete & Asphalt; Mfr. Agricultural Test Equip.Memory-Scout, Porta Probe, Strata-Scout, Versa-Tester, Volumeasure, Stratameter. A Soiltest Products Division.
S.I.C.: 3825
Michael Head *(Pres.)*
Richard Brusko *(V.P.-Opers.)*
Terry Flanagan *(V.P.-Sls.)*
Ken Kober *(V.P.-Fin.)*
Jeff Weaver *(Dir.-Mktg.)*

ENI
100 Highpower Rd.
Rochester, NY 14623
Tel.: 716-427-8300
Year Founded: 1968
Approx.Sls.: $30,000,000
Emp.: 400
Fiscal Year-end: 12/31/90
Mfr. RF Amplifiers & RF Plasma Generators
S.I.C.: 3663
John Stratakos *(Pres.)*
Ed Maier *(V.P.-Sls.)*
Jonathan Gorbold *(V.P.-Engrng. & Mktg.)*

E.P. GRAPHICS, INC.
(Formerly Economy Printing Concern, Inc.)
169 S. Jefferson
Berne, IN 46711
Tel.: 219-589-2145 **IN**
Fax: 219-589-2810
Approx.Sls.: $22,000,000
Emp.: 240
Prints & Binds Magazines & Books
S.I.C.: 2721; 2731; 2789
Carl H. Muselman *(Chm. Bd.)*
Arthur K. Muselman *(Pres.)*
Thomas Muselman *(V.P.-Mfg.)*
Roger Muselman *(V.P.-Sls.)*

Outside Service Firm(s):

Ernst & Young*(Auditors)*
2300 Fort Wayne Natl. Bank Bldg.
Fort Wayne, IN 46802

First Bank, N.A.*(Major Banking Relationship)*
Berne, IN

ERA REAL ESTATE
(Electronic Realty Associates, Inc., L.P.)
4900 College Blvd.
Overland Park, KS 66211
Mailing Address:
P. O. Box 2974
Shawnee Mission, KS 66201
Tel.: 913-491-1000
Fax: 913-451-6476
Year Founded: 1971
Approx.Sls.: $20,000,000,000
Emp.: 360
International Real Estate Franchise Assoc.; Home Warranties; Referral & Relocations Services; Sellers Security Plan; Buyers Protection Plan
S.I.C.: 6531
Victor Goulet *(Pres. & Chief Exec. Officer)*
Robert Purcell *(Chief Oper. Officer & Chief Fin. Officer)*
Mac Heavener *(Pres.-Servicenter Div.)*
Tom Schmitt *(Pres.-Network Div.)*
Tony DiBenedetto *(V.P.-Legal Counsel)*
Ken Channell *(V.P.-Mktg.)*
Terri F. Mueller *(Dir.-Corp. Communications)*

Subsidiary:

ERA General Agency Corp. **(1)**
P.O. Box 2983
Shawnee Mission, KS 66201
Tel.: 913-631-1545
Real Estate
S.I.C.: 6531

ERB LUMBER COMPANY
375 S. Eton Rd.
Birmingham, MI 48009
Mailing Address:
P.O. Box 3013,
Birmingham, MI 48012
Tel.: 313-644-5300 **MI**
Year Founded: 1913
Assets: $139,000,000
Liabilities: $102,000,000
Net Worth: $37,000,000
Approx.Sls.: $325,000,000
Emp.: 1,800
Fiscal Year-end: 12/31/90
Manufacture & Distribute Lumber & Building Materials; Real Estate Operations
S.I.C.: 2431; 5031; 5211; 6513
Fred A. Erb *(Chm., Pres. & Chief Exec. Officer)*
Noel Goulston *(Exec. V.P. & Chief Oper. Officer)*
Bob Hall *(V.P.-Builder Sls.)*
Carl Craft *(V.P. & Chief Fin. Officer)*
Daniel DiBardino *(V.P.-Loss Prevention)*
John M. Erb *(V.P.-Opers.)*
Richard A. Kramer *(V.P.-Personnel)*
George L. Erb *(Treas. & Sec.)*

No. of Mfg. Plants/Facilities: 50

Outside Service Firm(s):

Coopers & Lybrand*(Auditors)*
400 Renaissance Center
Detroit, MI 48243
Tel.: 313-446-7100
Fax: 313-446-7117

Jaffe, Snider, Raitt & Heuer*(Legal Firm)*
1800 First Natl. Bldg.
Detroit, MI 48226
Tel.: 313-761-8380

Comerica Bank*(Major Banking Relationship)*
211 W. Fort St.
Detroit, MI 48226
Tel.: 313-222-3300

Divisions:

Lumber & Building Materials Div. **(1)**
375 S. Eton Rd.
Birmingham, MI 48009
Tel.: 313-644-5300
Emp.: 700
Lumber/Building Materials
S.I.C.: 5031; 5211
J.M. Erb *(Operations)*
H. Bock *(Builder)*
Phil Pescarino *(Retail-Dir.)*

McClelland & Duff, Inc. **(1)**
375 S. Eton Rd.
Birmingham, MI 48009
Tel.: 313-644-5300
Emp.: 25
Lumber
S.I.C.: 2431
Fred A. Erb *(Pres.)*

Real Estate Div. **(1)**
375 S. Eton Rd.
Birmingham, MI 48012
Tel.: 313-644-5300
Emp.: 10
Buildings (Operation of)
S.I.C.: 6159; 6512; 6513; 6552
Fred A. Erb *(Pres.)*

Subsidiaries:

Erb Lumber Co. of Indiana **(1)**
910 State Hwy. 212
Michigan City, IN 46360
Tel.: 219-872-8663 (60%)
Emp.: 20
Distribute Lumber
S.I.C.: 5211
Rob McFarland *(Chief Oper. Officer)*

Peter Kuntz Company **(1)**
Hulman Bldg., 120 W. Second, 10th Fl.
Dayton, OH 45402
Tel.: 512-461-3870
Operates Lumber Outlets
S.I.C.: 2431; 5211

THE ERM GROUP
855 Springdale Dr.
Exton, PA 19341
Tel.: 215-524-3500
Tel.: 800-544-3117 **PA**
Fax: 215-524-7335
Year Founded: 1977
Approx.Sls.: $270,209,000
Emp.: 2,100
Fiscal Year-end: 3/31/92
Environmental Engineering & Consulting
S.I.C.: 8711
Corporate Giving Program: United Way.
Paul H. Woodruff *(Chm. Bd., Pres. & Chief Exec. Officer)*
Kent E. Patterson *(Chief Oper. Officer)*
Daniel M. Sevick *(Chief Fin. Officer & Treas.)*
Leonard Brown *(Controller)*
Arnon E. Garonzik *(Gen. Counsel & Sec.)*
Bradley Bernosky *(Dir.-Mngmt. Information Systems)*
Dorothy Buffington *(Dir.-Communications)*
Jack Newell *(Dir.-Mktg., Communications & Adv.)*
Susan Lee *(Mgr.-Human Resources)*
Linda Perry *(Mgr.-Employee Benefits)*

No. of U.S. Offices: 43
No. of Foreign Offices: 10

Computer Systems/Hardware:
IBM; Macintosh; DEC

Outside Service Firm(s):

Arthur Andersen & Co.*(Auditors)*
1601 Market St.
Philadelphia, PA 19103
Tel.: 215-241-7300

AIG (American International Group)*(Commercial Insurance Carrier)*
Philadelphia, PA

Lloyds Bank plc*(Commercial Insurance Carrier)*
71 Lombard St.
London, EC3 EBS, United Kingdom
Tel.: 071-626 1500
Telex: 888301

Johnson & Higgins*(Group Insurer)*
Two Logan Square
Philadelphia, PA
Tel.: 215-246-1058

MacElree, Harvey, Gallagher & Featherman*(Legal Firm)*
West Chester, PA

Morgan, Lewis & Bockius*(Legal Firm)*
2000 One Logan Square
Philadelphia, PA 19103
Tel.: 215-963-5000

Philadelphia National Bank*(Major Banking Relationship)*
P.O. Box 734, 50 W. Market St.
West Chester, PA 19381-0734
Tel.: 215-692-1526

Johnson Companies*(Pension Manager)*
One Summit Square, Rt. 413 & Double Woods Road
Newtown, PA 18940
Tel.: 215-860-3742

Vanguard Group*(Pension Manager)*
Vanguard Financial Center
Valley Forge, PA 19482
Tel.: 215-648-6000
Fax: 215-648-6114

Affiliates:

ERM-Computer Services, Inc. **(1)**
865 Springdale Dr.
Exton, PA 19341
Tel.: 215-524-3600
Emp.: 35
Computer & Engineering Services
S.I.C.: 7379; 7372
Brian Gurnham *(Pres.)*

ERM-EnviroClean **(1)**
855 Springdale Dr.
Exton, PA 19341
Tel.: 215-524-3550
Emp.: 30
Construction Management
S.I.C.: 8742; 8741
Stanley Porfido *(Pres.)*

ERM-Midwest, Inc. **(1)**
450 W. Wilson Bridge Rd.
Columbus, OH 43085
Tel.: 614-433-7900
Engineering Services
S.I.C.: 8711
Neil L. Drobny *(Pres.)*

ERM-New England, Inc. **(1)**
205 Portland St.
Boston, MA 02114
Tel.: 617-742-8228
Engineering Services
S.I.C.: 8711
John A.S. McGlennon *(Pres.)*

ERM-North Central, Inc. **(1)**
102 Wilmot Rd., Ste. 300
Deerfield, IL 60015
Tel.: 708-940-7200
Engineering Services
S.I.C.: 8711
James W. Polich *(Pres.)*

ERM-Northeast, Inc. **(1)**
175 Froehlich Farm Blvd.
Woodbury, NY 11797
Tel.: 516-921-4300
Engineering Services
S.I.C.: 8711
John A. DeFillippi *(Pres.)*

ERM-Northwest, Inc. **(1)**
2821 Northrup Way
Bellevue, WA 98004
Tel.: 206-827-9440
Engineering Services
S.I.C.: 8711
Michael Bacon *(Pres.)*

ERM-Rocky Mountain, Inc. **(1)**
5950 South Willow Dr., Ste. 310
Englewood, CO 80111
Tel.: 303-741-5050
Engineering Services
S.I.C.: 8711
Robert A. Arnott *(Pres.)*

ERM-South, Inc. **(1)**
9501 Princess Palm Ave., Ste. 100
Tampa, FL 33619
Tel.: 813-622-8727
Engineering Services
S.I.C.: 8711
Paul Gruber *(Pres.)*

ERM-Southeast, Inc. **(1)**
215 Centerview Dr., Ste. 110
Brentwood, TN 37024
Tel.: 615-373-3350
Engrng. Services
S.I.C.: 8711
Fred Ziegler *(Pres.)*

ERM-Southwest, Inc. **(1)**
16000 Memorial Dr., Ste. 200
Houston, TX 77079
Tel.: 713-496-9600

Engineering Services
S.I.C.: 8711
Douglas S. Diehl *(Pres.)*

ERM-West, Inc. **(1)**
1777 Botelho Dr., Ste. 260
Walnut Creek, CA 94596
Tel.: 510-946-0455
Engineering Services
S.I.C.: 8711
Richard W. Stone *(Pres.)*

ERS ADVERTISING, INC.

P.O. Box 4500, 500 College Rd., E.
Princeton, NJ 08543
Tel.: 609-243-6346
Fax: 609-243-6971
Year Founded: 1971
Approx.Billings: $14,000,000
Emp.: 32
Health Care Adv.

ESSTAR INCORPORATED
(Merger of Amstar Corporation & Essex Industries)
555 Long Wharf Dr.
New Haven, CT 06511
Mailing Address:
P.O. Box 9804,
New Haven, CT 06536-0804
Tel.: 203-777-2274 DE
Fax: 203-785-8851
Year Founded: 1989
Approx.Sls.: $450,000,000
Emp.: 3,400
Fiscal Year-end: 12/31/91
Import Export
Manufactures & Distributes Industrial & Technical Products
S.I.C.: 3423; 3429
Howard B. Wentz *(Chm. Bd.)*
Robert A. Haversat *(Pres. & Chief Exec. Officer)*
Roger D. Chesley *(V.P. & Gen. Counsel)*
Jeffrey A. Mereschuk *(V.P. & Chief Fin. Officer)*
Richard L. Hoffmann *(V.P.-Corp. Plng. & Taxes)*
Kenneth J. Jones *(Sec.)*
David C. Figurelli *(Treas.)*
John D. Speridakos *(Controller)*

Outside Service Firm(s):

Arthur Andersen & Co.*(Auditors)*
One Financial Plaza
Hartford, CT 06103
Tel.: 203-280-0649
Fax: 203-280-0898

The Bank of New York*(Major Banking Relationship)*
One Wall Street
New York, NY 10286
Tel.: 212-635-6805
Fax: 212-635-3201

Subsidiaries:

Amstar Corporation **(1)**
555 Long Wharf Dr.
New Haven, CT 06511
Tel.: 203-777-2274 (100%)
Robert A. Haversat *(Pres.)*

Subsidiaries:

Amstar Technical Products Co., Inc. **(2)**
555 Long Wharf Dr.
New Haven, CT 06511
Tel.: 203-777-2274 (100%)
Technical Prod.
Howard B. Wentz, Jr. *(Chm. & Pres.)*

Division:

Graham Mfg. Co. **(3)**
1920 E. 26th St.
Marshfield, WI 54449
Tel.: 715-387-2581
Fax: 715-387-0739
Manufactures Wooden Flush Doors
S.I.C.: 2431

Patrick Moran *(Gen. Mgr.)*

Milwaukee Electric Tool Corp. **(2)**
13135 W. Lisbon Rd.
Brookfield, WI 53005
Tel.: 414-781-3600
Telex: 910-262-3043
Fax: 414-781-3611
Emp.: 2,150
Import Export
Computer Systems/Hardware:
IBM
Mfr. Portable Electric Power Tools: Sawzalls, Hole-Shooters, Vac-U-Rig, Dymorig Drills, Hole Hawg, Screw-Schooter
S.I.C.: 3546
Richard C. Grove *(Pres.)*
J.W. Ames *(V.P.-Fin., Treas. & Sec.)*
Mike Schmidt *(V.P.-Mktg.)*
Vic Delisle *(V.P.-Mfg.)*
Dan Perry *(V.P.-Sls.)*
Dennis Schmidt *(Controller)*
D.J. Reed *(Personnel Dir.)*
Dick Wilhelm *(Gen. Sls. Mgr.-West)*
Tom Kennedy *(Gen. Sls. Mgr.-East)*
Debra Sajkowski *(Adv. Mgr.)*

Essex Industries **(1)**
Long Wharf Maritime Center, 555 Long Wharf Dr.
New Haven, CT 06511
Tel.: 203-777-2274 (100%)
Fax: 203-785-8851
Approx.Sls.: $234,000,000
Emp.: 1,800
Fiscal Year-end: 12/31/90
Import Export
Computer Systems/Hardware:
IBM
Mfr. of Architectural Hardware; Wood & Metal Doors, Locks & Hinges for Commercial & Non-Residential Markets
S.I.C.: 3429
Robert A. Haversat *(Chm. Bd., Pres. & Chief Exec. Officer)*
Jeffrey A. Mereschuk *(V.P. & Chief Fin. Officer)*
Roger D. Chesley *(V.P. & Gen. Counsel)*
Jerry N. Currie *(Grp. V.P.)*
David C. Figurelli *(Treas.)*
John D. Speridakos *(Controller)*

Subsidiaries:

Curries Company **(2)**
525 9th St. S.E.
Mason City, IA 50401
Tel.: 515-423-1334
Emp.: 500
Mfr. of Steel Doors & Frames
S.I.C.: 3442
Robert A. Hubbard *(Gen. Mgr.)*
Richard C. Amick *(V.P.-Mktg.)*
Kenneth L. Krahn *(V.P.-Indus. Rels.)*
David W. Underwood *(Treas.)*
Jeff Mereschuk *(Sec.)*
Dick Ebeling *(Adv. Mgr.)*

Sargent Manufacturing Company **(2)**
100 Sargent Dr.
New Haven, CT 06511
Tel.: 203-562-2151
Fax: 203-776-5992
Approx.Sls.: $50,000,000
Emp.: 900
Import Export
High Quality Architectural Hardware, Locks, Door Closers, Exit Devices
S.I.C.: 3429
J.A. Figurelli *(Pres.)*
Mary K. O'Meara *(Dir.-Adv.)*
S. Davi *(Pur. Agent)*

Non-U.S. Holding:

Milwaukee Electric Tool (Canada) Ltd. **(1)**
755 Progress Ave.
Scarborough, ON M1H 2W7, Canada
Tel.: 416-439-4181 (100%)
Approx.Sls.: $10,000,000
Emp.: 100
Sls. & Services Heavy-Duty Electric Tools
S.I.C.: 7629; 7359

ETL TESTING LABORATORIES, INC
Rt. 11 Industrial Park
Cortland, NY 13045
Mailing Address:
P.O. Box 2040,
Cortland, NY 13045
Tel.: 607-753-6711
Year Founded: 1896
Approx.Sls.: $10,000,000
Emp.: 175
Independent Testing Lab.
S.I.C.: 8734
Pedro Guzman *(Pres.)*
James R. Williams *(V.P.)*
Kenneth Ash *(Mgr.-Mktg.)*

Divisions:

Georgia Div. **(1)**
5855-P Oakbrook Pky.
Norcross, GA 30093
Tel.: 404-446-7294
S.I.C.: 8734
Peter Balint *(V.P.)*

West Coast Div. **(1)**
660 Forbes Blvd.
South San Francisco, CA 94080
Tel.: 415-871-1414
S.I.C.: 8734

EWI, INC.
100 S. Broadway Ave.
Salem, OH 44460
Tel.: 216-337-1113
Fax: 216-337-1119
Assets: $10,000,000
Liabilities: $9,000,000
Net Worth: $1,000,000
Approx.Sls.: $35,000,000
Emp.: 400
Metal Stampings
George S. Hofmeister *(Chm. Bd. & Pres.)*
Joseph Dominijanni *(Treas. & V.P.-Finance)*
James E. Phillips *(Corp. Sec.)*
John Nolan *(Mgr.-Sls.)*
Dennis Peterson *(Mgr.-Mfg.)*
Robert Shurkey *(Dir.-Engineering)*
Dee Dee Baker *(Dir.-Human Resources)*

No. of Mfg. Plants/Facilities: 1
No. of U.S. Offices: 2

Computer Systems/Hardware:
Altos

Subsidiary:

EWI, Inc.-Stamping & Die Div. **(1)**
500 Stephenson Hwy., Ste. 203
Troy, MI 48084
Tel.: 313-588-0044
Emp.: 3
Sales of Stamping & Die
S.I.C.: 5084

Plant:

South Bend Stamping Div. **(2)**
601 W. Broadway
South Bend, IN 46624
Tel.: 219-282-8200
Emp.: 419
Metal Stamping
S.I.C.: 3465
Dennis J. Peterson *(Gen. Mgr.)*

E Z LOADER BOAT TRAILERS, INC.
N. 717 Hamilton
Spokane, WA 99202
Mailing Address:
P.O. Box 3263
Spokane, WA 99202
Tel.: 509-489-0181
Fax: 509-489-5729
Assets: $15,000,000
Liabilities: $6,000,000
Net Worth: $9,000,000
Sales Range: $40-59 Million
Emp.: 40
Export
Boat Trailers
S.I.C.: 3792
Randy D. Johnson *(Pres.)*
David Thielman *(Chief Exec. Officer)*
Ralph Carlsberg *(Chief Fin. Officer)*
Marc D. Johnson *(Treas.)*
Ken Vorhees *(Controller)*
Jim Dillon *(Gen. Mgr.)*
Daryl Hammers *(Gen. Mgr.)*
William D. Baker *(Dir.-Human Resources)*
Principal(s):
Randy D. Johnson
David Thielman

Outside Service Firm(s):

LeMasters & Daniels*(Auditors)*
Spokane, WA

Lukins & Annis*(Legal Firm)*
Spokane, WA

United States Bank*(Major Banking Relationship)*
Spokane, WA

Washington Trust Bank*(Major Banking Relationship)*
Spokane, WA

E-Z MART STORES, INC.
602 W. Falvey
Texarkana, TX 75501
Mailing Address:
P.O. Box 1426
Texarkana, TX 75501
Tel.: 903-838-0558
Fax: 903-832-7903
Approx.Sls.: $146,000,000
Emp.: 2,500
Convenience Stores; Wholesale Gasoline & Service Station Equipment
S.I.C.: 5441; 5087; 5172
Jim Yates *(Chm. Bd.)*
Tom Coleman *(Pres.)*
Eric Bishop *(Gen. Counsel)*
Sonja Hubbard *(Controller, Treas & Sec.)*
Stacy Floyd *(Asst. Controller)*

Outside Service Firm(s):

Grier, Reeves & Lawley*(Auditors)*
Texarkana, TX

Hubbard, Patton, Peek, Haltom & Roberts*(Legal Firm)*
Texarkana, TX

First State Bank*(Major Banking Relationship)*
500 Chestnut St.
Abilene, TX 79602

E-Z SERVE CORP.
10700 North I45, Ste. 500
Houston, TX 77037
Mailing Address:
P.O. Box 3579,
Abilene, TX 79602
Tel.: 713-591-1111
Fax: 713-847-4739
Approx.Sls.: $896,000,000
Emp.: 550
Petroleum Refining; Gen. Mdse. Stores; Automotive Dealer & Service Stations
S.I.C.: 2911; 5541
R. McGlothlin, Jr. *(Chm. Bd. & Chief Exec. Officer)*
G. R. Nicholson *(Pres.)*
Roland C. Orr *(Sr. V.P.)*
J. Denson *(Controller)*
John Hemthill *(Sec.)*
Weldon Martin *(Treas.)*
Robert Muzaka *(Dir.-Real Estate)*
Tom Sorrells *(Data Processing Dir.)*

Computer Systems/Hardware:
Hewlett-Packard 3000

Outside Service Firm(s):

KPMG Peat Marwick*(Auditors)*
1601 Elm St., Ste. 1600
Dallas, TX 75201
Tel.: 214-754-2000
Fax: 214-754-2297

Aetna Life & Casualty*(Group Insurer)*
151 Farmington Avenue
Hartford, CT 06156
Tel.: 203-273-2128
Fax: 203-729-4295

E-Z Serve Corp.—(Continued)

Jack C. Currey*(Legal Firm)*
Abilene, TX

First National Bank of Abilene*(Major Banking Relationship)*
400 Pine St., P.O. Box 701
Abilene, TX 79604
Tel.: 915-675-7000

First National Bank of Abilene*(Pension Manager)*
400 Pine St., P.O. Box 701
Abilene, TX 79604
Tel.: 915-675-7000

Subsidiary:

TOC Retail, Inc. **(1)**
10700 North I-45, Ste. 500
Houston, TX 77037
Tel.: 713-591-1111
Fax: 713-847-4739
Emp.: 6,000
930 Convenience Food Stores; 207 Company-Owned/Operated & Franchised World Bazaar Imported Home Accessories Stores
S.I.C.: 5411; 5719
Neil H. McLaurin *(Pres.)*

Division:

Magic Market Convenience Stores **(2)**
10700 North I45, Ste. 500
Houston, TX 77037
Tel.: 713-591-1111
Convenience Stores
S.I.C.: 5411

EAGER BEAVER
4425 Hwy 27 S.
Lake Wales, FL 33853
Tel.: 813-638-1421
Tel.: 800-257-8163
Telex: 510-686-8977
Fax: 813-638-2028
Year Founded: 1950
Approx.Sls.: $20,000,000
Emp.: 120
Export
Road Rollers, Pavers, Eager Beaver Trailers, Recycling Trucks & Trailers
S.I.C.: 3715; 3531
F.W. Flowers, Jr. *(Pres.)*
George MacConnell *(Gen. Mgr.)*
Tom Tompkins *(Sls. Mgr.)*
Carol Flowers *(Adv. & Mktg. Mgr.)*

Division:

General Engines Co., Inc. **(1)**
4425 Hwy. 27 South
Lake Wales, FL 33853
Tel.: 813-638-1421
Trailers, Rollers & Recyclers
S.I.C.: 3715

Affiliate:

Electric Mobility Co. **(1)**
591 Mantua Blvd.
Sewell, NJ 08080
Tel.: 800-662-5489
Export
3-Wheel Electric Carts for Disabled
S.I.C.: 3842

EAGLE BUTTON CO., INC.
415 Fourteenth St.
Carlstadt, NJ 07072
Tel.: 201-935-3990
Approx.Sls.: $10,000,000
Emp.: 55
Export
Buttons, Buckles, Tabs, Hangers, Toggles, Elbow Paches, Draw Cords & Braid
S.I.C.: 3965; 2241; 3496
Arthur Simon *(Chm. Bd. & Treas.)*
Edward Simon *(Pres.)*
Kevin Casey *(V.P.)*
Bob Colby *(V.P.)*
Paul Martin *(V.P.)*
Robert Clark *(Sec.)*
Herbert Gitin *(Comptroller)*
Mitch State *(Mgr.-Sls.)*
Al Rokowski *(Chief Engr.)*

Outside Service Firm(s):

Arthur Andersen & Co.*(Auditors)*
1345 Ave. of the Americas
New York, NY 10105
Tel.: 212-708-4000

Fox, Colby, Smith & Greene*(Legal Firm)*
New York, NY

National Community Bank*(Major Banking Relationship)*
Carlstadt, NJ

EAGLE

EAGLE ELECTRIC MFG. CO., INC.
45-31 Court Square
Long Island City, NY 11101
Tel.: 718-937-8000
Fax: 718-482-0160
Year Founded: 1920
Approx.Sls.: $100,000,000
Emp.: 2,000
Import Export
Switches, Receptacles, Wallplates & Weatherproof Devices, Range, Dryer, Power Devices, & Power Cord Sets, Wire Connectors, Ceiling Receptacles, Two Pole, Two Wire Straight Blade Caps Connectors, Two Pole, Three Wire Straight Blade Caps Connectors, Kwiklok Nylon Caps Connectors, Egalok Locking Devices, Transformers, Bells, Buzzers, Chimes, Wire Starters, Push Buttons, Household Devices, Fuses-Plugs & C
S.I.C.: 3643; 3082; 3613; 3644
Melvin Ludwig *(Chm. Bd. & Pres.)*
N. Kluger *(Exec. V.P.)*
S. Fradkin *(Sr. V.P.)*
Warren Cohen *(V.P.-Sls. & Mktg.)*
C. Eisner *(V.P.-Pur.)*
Joseph Elmaleh *(V.P.-Intl. Mktg. & Sls.)*
A. Gish *(V.P.-Consumer Sls.)*
M. Schneider *(V.P.-Fin.)*
James F. Cook *(Dir.-Mktg.)*
R. Lofgren *(Dir.-Sls./Electrical Distr.)*
J. Mannarino *(Mgr.-O.E.M. Sls.)*
T. Maynard *(Mgr.-Mktg.)*
Seth W. Rose *(Mgr.-Adv.)*
M. Carlin *(Pur. Agent)*

Computer Systems/Hardware:
IBM

Outside Service Firm(s):

BDO Seidman*(Auditors)*
1430 Broadway
New York, NY
Tel.: 212-765-7500

Manufacturers Hanover Trust Co.*(Major Banking Relationship)*
P.O. Box 24935, Church St. Station
New York, NY 10249
Tel.: 212-613-7147

EAGLE LINCOLN MERCURY INC.
6116 Lemmon Ave.
Dallas, TX 75209
Tel.: 214-357-0461 **KS**
Fax: 214-353-3528
Year Founded: 1959
Approx.Sls.: $50,000,000
Emp.: 350
Fiscal Year-end: 6/30/91
Retail New & Used Automobiles; Automobile Rental, Leasing & Repair; Paint Shop
S.I.C.: 5511; 7514; 7515; 7532; 7538
Robert M. Eagle *(Chm. Bd. & Chief Exec. Officer)*
John R. Eagle *(Pres. & Chief Oper. Officer)*
Phyllis Carnes *(Exec. V.P., Comptroller, Legal Officer & Dir.-Investor Rels.)*
James Darren Eagle *(V.P.)*
Judy Strickland *(Dir.-Personnel, Data Processing & Telecommunications)*
Gary Wilson *(Mgr.-Gen. Sls.)*
Principal(s):
Robert M. Eagle
John R. Eagle

Computer Systems/Hardware:
Reynolds & Reynolds

Outside Service Firm(s):

George B. Jones & Co.*(Auditors)*
Memphis, TN

Travelers Insurance Co.*(Group Insurer)*
Dallas, TX

Melton, Melton & Whaley*(Legal Firm)*
Dallas, TX

Bank One Texas*(Major Banking Relationship)*
1717 Main St.
Dallas, TX 75201
Tel.: 214-290-2367

R.W. EAKEN, INC.
P.O. Box 171
Leesport, PA 19533
Tel.: 215-926-2136 **PA**
Fax: 215-926-2864
Year Founded: 1932
Approx.Sls.: $17,000,000
Emp.: 34
Fiscal Year-end: 4/30/92
Wholesale Distributor of Solvents & Chemicals
S.I.C.: 5169
R. William Eaken *(Chm. Bd.)*
William G. Mills *(Pres.)*
John P. Schreffler *(V.P.)*
Barbara J. Eaken *(Sec., Treas. & Comptroller)*

Outside Service Firm(s):

Beard & Company*(Auditors)*
Reading, PA

Stevens & Lee*(Legal Firm)*
607 Washington St.
Reading, PA 19603
Tel.: 215-376-9781

First National Bank*(Major Banking Relationship)*
Leesport, PA

EARLE INDUSTRIES, INC.
Hwy. 64 E.
Earle, AR 72331
Mailing Address:
P.O. Box 28
Earle, AR 72331
Tel.: 501-792-8694 **AR**
Fax: 501-792-7100
Year Founded: 1962
Approx.Sls.: $17,000,000
Emp.: 280
Closet Items & Accessories: Mfr. of Bags, Garment Storage; Shoe Bags; Plastic Blanket Bags
S.I.C.: 2392
Donald Felsenthal *(Pres.)*
Jim Felsenthal *(V.P.)*
Peter Felsenthal *(V.P.)*
Roland Harrison *(Controller)*

Outside Service Firm(s):

First Southern Bank*(Major Banking Relationship)*
Earle, AR

EARNHARDT'S AUTO CENTER
7777 E. Baseline
Tempe, AZ 85283
Mailing Address:
P.O. Box 26878
Tempe, AZ 85285
Tel.: 602-838-6000 **AZ**
Fax: 602-831-5379
Approx.Sls.: $98,000,000
Emp.: 500
New & Used Automobiles, Vans & Pickups; New & Used Automotive Parts; General Automotive Repair Shops; Motor Homes
S.I.C.: 5511; 5531; 7538; 5561
Hal J. Earnhardt, Jr. *(Chm. Bd.)*
Hal J. Earnhardt, III *(Pres.)*
Robbyn McDowell *(Chief Fin. Officer)*
Jim Babe Earnhardt *(Sec. & Treas.)*

Outside Service Firm(s):

First Interstate Bank*(Major Banking Relationship)*
P.O. Box 53441,
Phoenix, AZ 85072-3441
Tel.: 602-229-4049

EARP MEAT COMPANY
6550 Kansas Ave.
Kansas City, KS 66111
Tel.: 913-287-3311 **KS**
Fax: 913-287-3297
Year Founded: 1962
Approx.Sls.: $106,525,000
Emp.: 125
Distribute Food, Beverages & Operating Supplies to McDonald's Restaurants
S.I.C.: 5142; 5143; 5147; 5149; 5113; 5199
Donald C. Earp *(Pres.)*
James J. Earp *(V.P.)*
Marie Earp *(Sec. & Treas.)*
Willard Small *(Mgr.-Opers.)*

Outside Service Firm(s):

Security National Bank*(Major Banking Relationship)*
Kansas City, KS

EAST JORDAN IRON WORKS
301 Spring St.
East Jordan, MI 49727
Tel.: 616-536-2261
Fax: 616-536-7058
Gray & Ductile Iron Castings, Brake Drums, Fire Hydrants, Street Castings, Gate Valves, Industrial Castings
S.I.C.: 3321
F.F. Malpass *(Pres.)*
W.J. Hauck *(V.P.-Mfg.)*
W.J. Lorne *(Sec.)*

Outside Service Firm(s):

BDO Seidman*(Auditors)*
99 Monroe Ave. NW, Ste. 800
Grand Rapids, MI 49503
Tel.: 616-774-7000
Fax: 616-451-2096

Northwestern State Bank*(Major Banking Relationship)*
East Jordan, MI

EAST KENTUCKY POWER CO-OP
4758 Lexington Rd.
Winchester, KY 40392
Mailing Address:
P.O. Box 707
Winchester, KY 40392
Tel.: 606-744-4812 **KY**
Fax: 606-744-6008
Year Founded: 1941
Assets: $940,867,000
Liabilities: $884,499,000
Net Worth: $56,368,000
Approx.Sls.: $253,019,000
Emp.: 633

Fiscal Year-end: 12/31/91
Electrical Power Generation & Transmission
S.I.C.: 4911
E.A. Gilbert *(Chm. Bd.)*
J.L. Burton *(Vice Chm.)*
Donald R. Norris *(Pres. & Gen. Mgr.)*
Foster J. Collis *(Gen. Counsel)*
Richard E. Crutcher *(Treas. & Sec.)*
Paul Atchison *(Dir.-Electric Opers. Div.)*
Ron Brown *(Dir.-Plng. & Engrng. Div.)*
David Eames *(Dir.-Fin. Div.)*
Bob Miller *(Dir.-Mktg. & Communications Div.)*
Robert Sherman *(Dir.-Pur.)*
Hubert Smith *(Dir.-Power Prod. Div.)*
Bill Starcher *(Dir.-Admin. Div.)*
George Carruba *(Mgr.-Systems Planning)*
Dave Drake *(Mgr.-Mktg.)*
Harry Enoch *(Mgr.-Res. & Devel.)*
Ray Gillespie *(Mgr.-Information Systems)*
Robert Hughes *(Mgr.-Environmental Affairs)*
Margaret Jeffiers *(Mgr.-Training & Admin. Services)*
Barry Mayfield *(Mgr.-Public Affairs)*
Michael McCarthy *(Mgr.-Personnel Services)*
Don Miller *(Mgr.-Acctg.)*
Frank Oliva *(Mgr.-Fin.)*
Brenda Eames *(Supvr.-Transportation & Meetings)*
Robert Sherman *(Supvr.-Pur.)*
Joe Smothers *(Supvr.-Benefits)*

No. of Mfg. Plants/Facilities: 3
No. of U.S. Offices: 1

Computer Systems/Hardware:
IBM System 4381

Outside Service Firm(s):

Coopers & Lybrand*(Auditors)*
Louisville, KY 46201

AEGIS*(Commercial Insurance Carrier)*
Harborside Financial Center, 700 Plaza Two
Jersey City, NJ 07311
Tel.: 201-915-7200
Fax: 201-451-3472

Liehman Brothers*(Investment Banker)*
American Express Tower, World Financial Center
New York, NY 10285

Brown, Todd & Heyburn*(Legal Firm)*
Citizens Plaza, 16th Fl.
Louisville, KY 40202
Tel.: 502-589-5400

Bank One, Clark County*(Major Banking Relationship)*
Winchester, KY

NRECA*(Pension Manager)*
1800 Massachusetts Ave., N.W.
Washington, DC 20036

EAST MOLINE METAL PRODUCTS COMPANY
1201 7th St.
East Moline, IL 61244
Tel.: 309-752-1350 **IL**
Fax: 309-752-1380
Year Founded: 1946
Approx.Sls.: $15,000,000
Emp.: 150
Export
Manufacture Metal Stampings; Fabricated Structural Metal Welding; Hydraulic Hammers & Hoists; Industrial Cranes; Cement Finishing Equipment; Personnel Lifts
S.I.C.: 3469; 3441; 3536
William J. Dowsett *(Chm. Bd.)*
Patrick W. Dowsett *(Pres.)*
Connie Dowsett *(Chief Fin. Officer & Treas.)*
Milt Chaney *(Mgr.-Opers.)*
Alan Griffin *(Mgr.-Quality Control)*
Tim Johnson *(Mgr.-Mfg.)*
Art Roady *(Mgr.-Pur.)*
Nancy Tragarz *(Mgr.-Personnel)*

Computer Systems/Hardware:
IBM PC

Outside Service Firm(s):

McGladrey & Pullen*(Auditors)*
Moline, IL

First National Bank of East Moline*(Major Banking Relationship)*
East Moline, IL

EAST RIVER ELECTRICAL POWER CO.
121 S.E. First St.
Madison, SD 57042
Tel.: 605-256-4536 **SD**
Fax: 605-256-3980
Year Founded: 1949
Approx.Sls.: $59,000,000
Emp.: 100
Distribution of Electric Energy
S.I.C.: 4911
Jeffrey L. Nelson *(Gen. Mgr.)*

Outside Service Firm(s):

Norwest Bank Minnesota, N.A.*(Major Banking Relationship)*
Madison, SD

EASTERN AIR DEVICES, INC.
One Progress Dr.
Dover, NH 03820
Tel.: 603-742-3330
Fax: 603-742-9080
Year Founded: 1942
Sales Range: $10-19 Million
Emp.: 150
Export
Precision Motors, Rotating Components, Blowers & Fans
S.I.C.: 3621
Logan Delany *(Chm. Bd.)*
Lee Perlman *(Pres.)*
Daryle Cooper *(V.P.-Mktg. & Sls.)*
Dominick D. More *(Chief Fin. Officer)*
Karen L. Russo *(Adv. Mgr.)*
A. Paquette *(Pur. Agent)*

Computer Systems/Hardware:
DEC VAX

Outside Service Firm(s):

Purdy, Bornstein Associates*(Auditors)*
Portsmouth, NH

Donahue, McCaffrey, Sisemoore & Tucker*(Legal Firm)*
Dover, NH

Security Pacific National Bank*(Major Banking Relationship)*
Dover, NH

EASTERN AMERICAN ENERGY CORPORATION
501 E. 56th St.
Charleston, WV 25304-2393
Tel.: 304-925-6100 **WV**
Fax: 304-925-3285
Year Founded: 1972
Assets: $135,000,000
Liabilities: $116,000,000
Net Worth: $19,000,000
Approx.Sls.: $30,000,000
Emp.: 220
Fiscal Year-end: 6/30/89
Oil & Gas Production & Exploration
S.I.C.: 1311
John Mork *(Pres.)*
Joseph E. Casabona *(Exec. V.P.)*
Donald Supcoe *(V.P.-Admin.)*
Cheryl Bowman *(Admin. Asst.)*

Outside Service Firm(s):

Arthur Andersen & Co.*(Auditors)*
Five Penn Center, Ste. 2600
Pittsburgh, PA 19103

McDonough Caperton Insurance Group*(Commercial Insurance Carrier)*
Charleston, WV

Goodwin & Goodwin*(Legal Firm)*
Charleston, WV

Chase Manhattan Bank, N.A.*(Major Banking Relationship)*
One Chase Manhattan Plaza
New York, NY 10081
Tel.: 212-552-2222
Tel.: 800-526-0801
Fax: 212-552-7175

Subsidiary:

Eastern American Energy Corp. **(1)**
2281 Airport Prof. Bldg.
Indiana, PA 15701
Tel.: 412-463-8400
Ali Rdissi *(Mgr.)*

EASTERN CANVAS PRODUCTS, INC.
50 Rogers Rd.
Ward Hill, MA 01830
Tel.: 508-373-1581 **MA**
Fax: 508-374-0967
Year Founded: 1972
Approx.Sls.: $30,000,000
Emp.: 80
Mfr. of Canvas, Webbing, Synthetic Fabric Products, Daypacks, Backpacks, Travel Bags & Carry Alls
S.I.C.: 2211; 2241; 2391; 3161
Monte Goldman *(Pres.)*
Robert Frank *(Gen. Mgr. & Chief Engr.)*
Norman Jacobs *(Mgr.-Natl. Sls.)*
Jeanette Cormier *(Office Mgr.)*

Outside Service Firm(s):

Levine, Zidman & Ditch*(Auditors)*
Boston, MA

State Street Bank & Trust Co.*(Major Banking Relationship)*
225 Franklin St.
Boston, MA 02101
Tel.: 617-328-5000

EASTERN COLOR PRINTING COMPANY
60 Security Dr.
Avon, CT 06001
Mailing Address:
P.O. Box 646
Avon, CT 06001
Tel.: 203-673-0461 **CT**
Fax: 203-675-9309
Year Founded: 1926
Approx.Sls.: $23,000,000
Emp.: 100
Fiscal Year-end: 12/31/92
Import
Printing Newspaper Supplements, Advertising Circulars & Pamphlets
S.I.C.: 2759; 2752
A. Robert Palmer *(Pres. & Chief Exec. Officer)*
William A. Manthey *(V.P.-Fin.)*
Scott Campbell *(Dir.-Pur.)*
Ronald E. Goen *(Dir.-Engrng.)*
Anthony Melillo *(Mgr.-Customer Service)*
Raymond Mead *(Supvr.-Pressroom)*
William Streich *(Supvr.-Prep. Dept.)*
Thomas Teasdale *(Sec.)*

No. of Mfg. Plants/Facilities: 1
No. of U.S. Offices: 1

Outside Service Firm(s):

Arthur Andersen & Co.*(Auditors)*
One Financial Plaza
Hartford, CT 06103
Tel.: 203-280-0649
Fax: 203-280-0898

Reid & Riege*(Legal Firm)*
Hartford, CT

Connecticut National Bank*(Major Banking Relationship)*
777 Main St.
Hartford, CT 06615

EASTERN FINE PAPER, INCORPORATED
517 S. Main St.
Brewer, ME 04412
Mailing Address:
P.O. Box 129,
Brewer, ME 04412
Tel.: 207-989-7070
Tel.: 800-341-1750 **ME**
Fax: 207-989-2149
Year Founded: 1888
Approx.Sls.: $100,000,000
Emp.: 465
Export
Paper Products, Minimum 50% Recycled: Certificate 25% Bond (50), Atlantic Bond & Offset (55/10), Premium Bristol Card Stock (50), Schooner Text & Cover (50), Eastern Opaque (55/10)--Coated Products: Silicone Release Coated, Dry Gum
S.I.C.: 2621; 2672; 2674
Joseph H. Torras *(Chm. Bd. & Pres.)*
John H. Harker *(Exec. V.P.)*
Jackson A. Libby *(Exec. V.P.-Mktg.)*
Robert W. Sullivan *(Exec. V.P.)*
Page Best *(V.P.-Sls.)*
N.C. Collins *(V.P.-Fin.)*
Donna M. Holland *(Mgr.-Personnel)*

No. of Mfg. Plants/Facilities: 2

Computer Systems/Hardware:
IBM

EASTERN FLAT BED SYSTEMS
1928 Wilson Rd.
Newberry, SC 29108
Tel.: 803-276-2031 **SC**
Fax: 803-276-9327
Approx.Sls.: $21,200,000
Emp.: 350
Common Carrier Trucking
S.I.C.: 4213
John Miller *(Pres.)*

No. of U.S. Offices: 4

Outside Service Firm(s):

Frederick Crawford*(Legal Firm)*
Newberry, SC

NationsBank South Carolina*(Major Banking Relationship)*
Columbia, SC

EASTERN MILK PRODUCERS COOPERATIVE ASSN., INC.
2401 Burnet Ave.
Syracuse, NY 13206
Mailing Address:
P.O. Box 601
Syracuse, NY 13214
Tel.: 315-463-0781
Fax: 315-437-1225
Year Founded: 1923
Approx.Sls.: $250,200,000
Emp.: 200
Fiscal Year-end: 3/31/91
Milk & Milk Products Association
S.I.C.: 5963; 2026
Lewis Gardner *(Pres.)*
Michael Donovan *(Gen. Mgr.)*
Robert Stronach *(Mgr.-Communications)*
Paula Agor *(Personnel Mgr.)*

EASTERN SMELTING & REFINING CORPORATION
37-39 Bubier St.
Lynn, MA 01901
Tel.: 617-599-9000
Fax: 617-598-4880
Approx.Sls.: $30,000,000
Emp.: 70
Precious Metals
S.I.C.: 1099
John R. Friberg *(Pres., Chief Exec. Officer & Sec.)*

Eastern Smelting & Refining Corporation—(Continued)

Kenneth B. Rosenberg *(Exec. V.P.-Fin. & Treas.)*
Stuart A. Alperin *(V.P.-Sls.)*

Outside Service Firm(s):

KPMG Peat Marwick*(Auditors)*
One Boston Place
Boston, MA 02108
Tel.: 617-723-7700

Bank of Boston*(Major Banking Relationship)*
Lynn, MA

EASTERN TECHNOLOGIES LTD
10 Industrial Way
Amesbury, MA 01913
Tel.: 508-388-5662 **MA**
Fax: 508-388-0845
Year Founded: 1982
Approx.Sls.: $70,000,000
Emp.: 500
Fiscal Year-end: 6/30/91
Export
Mfr. of Tankers, Fuel Oil Trucks, Firetrucks, Buses, Containment Shelters, Trailers & Low Level Defense Equipment
S.I.C.: 3443; 3711; 3715; 3728
Harley Waite, Jr. *(Chm. Bd., Pres. & Chief Exec. Officer)*
R. Vorias *(Pres.-Craig Systems)*
L. Kurpis *(Chief Fin. Officer)*
Robert Sanders *(Exec. V.P.)*
G. Nevison *(Sr. V.P.-Mktg. & Sls.)*
P. Patuto *(Sr. V.P.-Fin.)*
T. Vorias *(V.P.-Admin.)*
Karen Waite *(Mgr.-Pub. Rels.)*

No. of Mfg. Plants/Facilities: 4
No. of U.S. Offices: 3
No. of Foreign Offices: 6

Outside Service Firm(s):

Feeley & Driscoll*(Auditors)*
Boston, MA

Peabody & Brown*(Legal Firm)*
101 Federal St.
Boston, MA 02110-1832

Bank IV*(Major Banking Relationship)*
Boston, MA

Subsidiaries:

AES **(1)**
10 Industrial Way
Amesbury, MA 01913
Tel.: 508-388-5662

Craig Systems **(1)**
10 Industrial Way
Amesbury, MA 01913
Tel.: 508-388-0845
R. Vorias *(Pres.)*

RES-Q-TECH Inc. **(1)**
10 Industrial Way
Amesbury, MA 01913
Tel.: 508-388-5662

Techweld Ltd. **(1)**
10 Industrial Way
Amesbury, MA 01913
Tel.: 508-388-5662

Transit Systems Inc. **(1)**
10 Industrial Way
Amesbury, MA 01913
Tel.: 508-388-5662

EASTLAND SHOE MANUFACTURING CORPORATION
5 Park St.
Freeport, ME 04032
Tel.: 207-865-6314
Fax: 207-865-6791
Approx.Sls.: $40,000,000
Emp.: 400
Machine Sewn Women's Loafers
S.I.C.: 3144
Jonas B. Klein *(Pres. & Treas.)*
James B. Klein *(V.P.-Sls.)*
H. Vance Smith *(V.P.-Fin.)*
Russ Moors *(Pur. Agent-Findings)*

Outside Service Firm(s):

Albin, Randall & Bennett*(Auditors)*
Portland, ME

Bernstein, Shur, Sawyer & Nelson*(Legal Firm)*
1 Monument Sq.
Portland, ME 04111
Tel.: 207-774-6291

Sterling National Bank*(Major Banking Relationship)*
540 Madison Ave.
New York, NY 10022
Tel.: 212-826-2271

EASTMAN MACHINE CO.
779 Washington St.
Buffalo, NY 14203
Tel.: 716-856-2200
Fax: 716-856-1140
Year Founded: 1889
Approx.Sls.: $18,000,000
Emp.: 265
Manufacture Industrial Cloth Cutting & Spreading Equipment
S.I.C.: 3552
Charles P. Stevenson *(Chm. Bd. Emeritus)*
Robert L. Stevenson *(Pres. & Treas.)*
Roy Stevenson *(V.P.)*
Wade Stevenson *(V.P.)*
Diane C. Vandermeer *(Controller)*

Outside Service Firm(s):

Lucker, Kennedy & Felmeden*(Auditors)*
Buffalo, NY

Fleet Bank*(Major Banking Relationship)*
Deer Park, NY 14202

EASTWAY DELIVERY SERVICE OF HOUSTON, INC.
8211 Laporte Frwy.
Houston, TX 77012
Mailing Address:
P.O. Box 15290
Houston, TX 77002
Tel.: 713-967-7000
Tel.: 800-364-5623 **TX**
Fax: 713-967-7055
Year Founded: 1977
Assets: $2,580,000
Liabilities: $1,450,000
Net Worth: $1,130,000
Approx.Sls.: $12,000,000
Emp.: 70
Fiscal Year-end: 12/31/91
Delivery Service within the Houston Commercial Zone
S.I.C.: 4212
John R. Oren *(Chm. Bd. & Chief Exec. Officer)*
Rick M. McCormick *(Pres. & Chief Oper. Officer)*
Daniel Massalone *(V.P.-Sls.)*
Karen Oren *(Sec.)*
Marlise C. Skinner *(Controller)*
Donna Brown *(Dir.-Personnel)*
Richard Young *(Dir.-Data Processing)*
Principal(s):
John R. Oren
Rick M. McCormick

No. of U.S. Offices: 1

Computer Systems/Hardware:
IBM RS 6000

Outside Service Firm(s):

White Petrov McHone*(Auditors)*
Houston, TX

Fizer, Beck, Webster & Bentley*(Legal Firm)*
Houston, TX

Post Oak Bank*(Major Banking Relationship)*
2200 Post Oak Blvd.
Houston, TX 77056
Tel.: 713-966-2200

Subsidiaries:

Eastway Air Cartage, Inc. **(1)**
757 Kenrick
Houston, TX 77060
Tel.: 713-847-4000
Emp.: 12
Delivery Service of Airfrieght within the Houston Commercial Zone
S.I.C.: 4212
John R. Oren *(Chm. Bd. & Chief Exec. Officer)*
Rick McCormick *(Pres. & Chief Oper. Officer)*
Dennis Stalcup *(V.P.)*

Eastway Delivery Service of Austin, Inc. **(1)**
1300 Smith Rd., Ste. 102
Austin, TX 78762
Tel.: 512-389-2292
Fax: 512-476-0711
Emp.: 15
Delivery Service within the Austin Comml. Zone
S.I.C.: 4212
John R. Oren *(Chm. Bd. & Chief Exec. Officer)*
Rick McCormick *(Pres. & Chief Oper. Officer)*
Charles Davenport *(V.P.)*

Eastway Delivery Service of Dallas, Inc. **(1)**
1200 E. Northwest Hwy., Ste. 300
Grapevine, TX 76051
Tel.: 817-329-0046
Fax: 817-488-5587
Emp.: 22
Delivery Service Within The Dallas/Ft. Worth Commercial Zone
S.I.C.: 4212
John R. Oren *(Chm. Bd. & Chief Exec. Officer)*
Rick McCormick *(Pres. & Chief Oper. Officer)*
Paul Skinner *(V.P.)*

Eastway Transportation Services, Inc. **(1)**
5821 Kelley St.
Houston, TX 77026
Tel.: 713-967-7070
Tel.: 800-725-3874
Fax: 713-967-7055
Emp.: 25
Intrastate Hauling of Oilfield Equipment & Miscellaneous Goods
S.I.C.: 4212
John R. Oren *(Chm. Bd. & Pres.)*
Rick McCormick *(V.P. & Chief Oper. Officer)*
Tim Lerchbacker *(V.P.)*

EASY DAY MANUFACTURING COMPANY, INC.
P.O. Box 8000
Holliston, MA 01746
Tel.: 508-429-8100
Fax: 508-429-1289
Emp.: 60
Mops, Brooms, Brushes, Sponges, Ironing Board Cover Sets, Dust Pans
S.I.C.: 2392; 2674; 3069; 3991
Harold Footer *(Chm. Bd. & Chief Exec. Officer)*
Alan P. Michelson *(Pres.)*
John W. Cooke *(V.P.-Sls.)*
Harris Footer *(V.P.-Pur.)*
Jeri Weinstein *(Comptroller)*

EAT N PARK RESTAURANTS
100 Park Manor Dr.
Pittsburgh, PA 15205
Tel.: 412-923-1000
Fax: 412-787-1771
Year Founded: 1949
Approx.Sls.: $100,000,000
Emp.: 5,000
Family Restaurants in Western PA, OH & WV
S.I.C.: 5812
James Broadhurst *(Chm., Pres. & Chief Exec. Officer)*
D. Wohleber *(Exec. V.P.-Fin.)*
Basil Cox *(Exec. V.P.-Mktg.)*
David Shaw *(V.P.-Design & Construction)*
Ronald Champe *(V.P.-Pur.)*

EATEL CORPORATION
913 S. Burnside Ave.
Gonzales, LA 70737
Tel.: 504-621-4200
Fax: 504-647-5252
Approx.Sls.: $13,500,000
Emp.: 88
Holding Company; Telephone Communications
S.I.C.: 4812; 6719
Charles King *(Pres.)*
Mike Czerwinski *(Exec. V.P.)*
Arthur G. Scanlan III *(V.P., Sec. & Treas.)*
Clarence J. Porta, Jr. *(Dir.-Comptroller & Data Processing)*

Outside Service Firm(s):

Hawthorn, Waymouth & Carroll*(Auditors)*
Baton Rouge, LA
Tel.: 504-923-3000

Pescy, Holdridge & Willis*(Legal Firm)*
Baton Rouge, LA

First National Bank*(Major Banking Relationship)*
Gonzales, LA

Subsidiary:

East Ascension Telephone Company **(1)**
913 S. Burnside Ave.
Gonzales, LA 70737
Tel.: 504-621-4200
Albert J. Banker *(Pres.)*
Charles M. King, Jr. *(Exec. V.P.)*
Arthur G. Scanlan *(V.P. Sec. & Treas.)*

EATON EQUIPMENT CORP.
250 Lake Ave.
Blasdell, NY 14219
Mailing Address:
P.O. Box 250,
Blasdell, NY 14219
Tel.: 716-822-2020 **NY**
Year Founded: 1935
Approx.Sls.: $23,800,000
Emp.: 70
Wholesale Distributor of Outdoor Power Equipment, Golf Course Equipment & Supplies
S.I.C.: 5083; 5091; 5084
Wyndham Eaton *(Pres. & Chief Exec. Officer)*
W. Thompson Eaton *(Exec. V.P.-Sls.)*
John Bailie *(Treas.)*

Outside Service Firm(s):

Morgan & Beyer C.P.A.*(Auditors)*
Buffalo, NY

Williams, Stevens, McCarvle, Frizl*(Legal Firm)*
Buffalo, NY

Fleet Bank*(Major Banking Relationship)*
Deer Park, NY 14202

EATON OFFICE SUPPLY CO., INC.
180 John Glenn Dr.
Amherst, NY 14226-9500
Tel.: 716-691-6100 **NY**
Fax: 716-691-0074
Year Founded: 1915
Approx.Sls.: $25,000,000
Emp.: 49

Commercial Office Supply Dealer
S.I.C.: 5112; 5021
Bruce C. Eaton *(Pres.)*
Shirley Learman *(Office Mgr.)*

Principal(s):
Bruce C. Eaton

Computer Systems/Hardware:
Hewlett Packard

EBCO MFG. COMPANY
265 N. Hamilton Rd.
Columbus, OH 43213
Tel.: 614-861-1350
Fax: 614-861-1357
Sales Range: $60-79 Million
Emp.: 425
Fiscal Year-end: 1/31/91

Export
Electric Water Coolers & Dehumidifiers
S.I.C.: 3585; 3634
T.R. Benua, Jr. *(Pres. & Treas.)*
P.L. Benua *(Exec. V.P. & Sec.)*
George P. Buena *(V.P.)*
M.J. Blackstone *(Dir.-Mktg.)*
F.T. Jones *(Dir.-Pur.)*
C.R. Harmon *(Gen. Sls. Mgr.)*
Michael C. Pastor *(Chief Fin. Mgr.)*
A. Abolins *(Adv. Mgr.)*
Jeanne Clegg *(Personnel Mgr.)*
C.L. Parker *(Mgr.-Computer Services)*

Computer Systems/Hardware:
IBM AS/400

Outside Service Firm(s):

John Hancock Mutual Life Insurance Co.*(Group Insurer)*
One Financial Center, 44th Floor
Boston, MA 02111
Tel.: 617-348-3707
Fax: 617-350-0305

BancOhio National Bank*(Major Banking Relationship)*
Columbus, OH

EBELING & REUSS COMPANY
333 Court
Allentown, PA 18105
Mailing Address:
P.O. Box 1289,
Allentown, PA 18105-1289
Tel.: 215-776-7100
Fax: 215-776-7102
Year Founded: 1886
Approx.Sls.: $20,000,000
Emp.: 46
Fiscal Year-end: 12/31/90
Importers of Fine Giftware, Dinnerware & Stemware
S.I.C.: 5023
Ronald D. Rapelje *(Pres. & Chief Exec. Officer)*
Sam Ghazaleh *(Treas.)*

EBERLE DIRECT MARKETING GROUP, INC.
Ste. 700, 8245 Boone Blvd.
Vienna, VA 22182
Tel.: 703-893-1095 **VA**
Fax: 703-821-0920
Year Founded: 1974
Assets: $5,000,000
Liabilities: $3,400,000
Net Worth: $1,600,000
Fiscal Year-end: 6/30/90
Holding Co.
S.I.C.: 6719
Bruce Eberle *(Chm. Bd. & Chief Exec. Officer)*
M. Declan Bransfield, III *(Pres.)*
Ted Kocur *(Chief Fin. Officer)*
Kimberly Bellissimo *(Dir.-Pur.)*

No. of U.S. Offices: 2

Computer Systems/Hardware:
IBM

Outside Service Firm(s):

Thompson, Greenspon & Co.*(Auditors)*
Fairfax, VA

Main Street Investments*(Investment Banker)*
Falls Church, VA

Guardian Life Insurance Co.*(Group Insurer)*
New York, NY

Continental Insurance*(Commercial Insurance Carrier)*
180 Maiden Lane
New York, NY

Fred Codding*(Legal Firm)*
Fairfax, VA

Subsidiaries:

Bruce W. Eberle & Associates **(1)**
Ste. 700, 8245 Boone Blvd.
Vienna, VA 22182
Tel.: 703-821-1550 (100%)
Approx.Sls.: $1,200,000
Emp.: 8
Computer Systems/Hardware:
1 IBM System
Direct Marketing Agency, Creative Agency & Fundraising
S.I.C.: 7311; 7331; 7389
M. Declan Bransfield III *(Pres.)*
Ted A. Kocur *(V.P.)*
Katherine M. Eberle *(Treas.)*

Omega List Company **(1)**
8245 Boone Blvd.
Vienna, VA 22182
Tel.: 703-821-1890 (100%)
Approx.Sls.: $2,000,000
Emp.: 6
List Brokerage & List Mangement For Business Services
S.I.C.: 7331; 7389

EBSCO INDUSTRIES, INC.
P.O. Box 1943
Birmingham, AL 35201
Tel.: 205-991-6600
Telex: 78-2661
Fax: 205-991-1479
Year Founded: 1944
Sales Range: $100-499 Million
Emp.: 3,000
Fiscal Year-end: 6/30/91

Import Export
Furniture & Fixtures; Printing & Publishing; Leather & Leather Products; Fabricated Metal Products; Miscellaneous Manufacturing Industries
S.I.C.: 5199; 2542; 5021; 5091; 7389; 2782; 7375
Elton B. Stephens *(Chm. Bd.)*
J.T. Stephens *(Pres., Chief Exec. Officer & Chief Oper. Officer)*
Virgil Wells *(Treas.)*
Jack H. Breard *(Dir.-Mktg.)*
P.R. Sisbarro *(Dir.-Personnel)*
Joe K. Weed *(Dir.-Adv.)*
John Fitts *(Gen. Mgr.-Data Processing)*

Principal(s):
Elton B. Stephens
J.T. Stephens

No. of Mfg. Plants/Facilities: 8
No. of U.S. Offices: 60
No. of Foreign Offices: 5

Outside Service Firm(s):

Bradley, Arant, Rose & White*(Legal Firm)*
1400 Park Place Tower
Birmingham, AL 35203
Tel.: 205-521-8000

Chase Manhattan Bank, N.A.*(Major Banking Relationship)*
One Chase Manhattan Plaza
New York, NY 10081
Tel.: 212-552-2222
Tel.: 800-526-0801
Fax: 212-552-7175

Citibank N.A.*(Major Banking Relationship)*
Corporate Trust Services, 399 Park Ave.
New York, NY 10043
Tel.: 212-559-1605

SouthTrust Bank*(Major Banking Relationship)*
Birmingham, AL
Tel.: 205-254-5068

Subsidiaries:

Ebsco Graphics **(1)**
1223 Linwood
Oklahoma City, OK 73106
Tel.: 405-235-3344
J.T. Stephens *(Chief Oper. Officer)*

Ebsco Investment Services, Inc. **(1)**
P.O. Box 1943
Birmingham, AL 35201
Tel.: 205-991-6600
J.T. Stephens *(Chief Oper. Officer)*

Luxor Corporation **(1)**
2245 Delany Rd.
Waukegan, IL 60087
Tel.: 708-244-1800
Emp.: 60
Manufacturer of Audio Visual Material Storage Cabinets, Microfiche Filing Systems, Video Consoles & Office Furniture Equipment, AV Equipment Stands & Computer Stands
S.I.C.: 2522; 2542
Donald Nichoalds *(Pres.)*
Robert Raw *(Gen. Mgr.)*
George Swallow *(Controller)*
Jane Yarnall *(Natl. Sls. Dir.)*
Heidi Fredricksen *(Mgr.-Mktg.)*
Jerry Sabal *(Mgr.-Pur.)*

Plastics Research & Development Co. **(1)**
3601 Jenny Land
Fort Smith, AR 72914
Tel.: 501-782-8971

EBY BROWN CO.
1001 Sullivan Rd.
Aurora, IL 60506
Tel.: 708-897-8792
Fax: 708-897-9220
Approx.Sls.: $950,000,000
Emp.: 830
Distributor Of Candy, Food, Tobacco & Merchandise
S.I.C.: 5149
Richard Wake *(Co-Pres.)*
Tom Wake *(Co-Pres.)*
Chris Timmons *(Branch Mgr.)*

Principal(s):
Richard Wake
Tom Wake

Outside Service Firm(s):

The Merchants National Bank of Aurora*(Major Banking Relationship)*
Aurora, IL

Subsidiary:

Eby Brown Co. **(1)**
5820 Fortune Circle
Indianapolis, IN 46251
Tel.: 317-248-6930
Wholesale Distributor Of Candy, Tobacco, Automotive Parts & Groceries
S.I.C.: 5013; 5141; 5145; 5194
Pat Reynolds *(Gen. Mgr.)*

EBY CORPORATION
610 N. Main St.
Wichita, KS 67201
Tel.: 316-268-3500
Fax: 316-268-3649
Year Founded: 1937
Approx.Sls.: $240,000,000
Holding Company
S.I.C.: 6719
Martin K. Eby *(Chm. Bd. & Pres.)*

Outside Service Firm(s):

Grant Thornton*(Auditors)*
800 Fourth Financial Center
Wichita, KS 67202

Subsidiary:

Martin K. Eby Construction Company, Inc. **(1)**
610 Main St.
Wichita, KS 67201
Tel.: 316-268-3500
Approx.Sls.: $200,000,000
Emp.: 1,300
Heavy Construction General Contractors Nonresidential & Industrial Buildings & Warehouses, Bridge Tunnel, Elevated Highway, Water Sewer Pipe Line Communication & Power Plant Construction
S.I.C.: 1541; 1542; 1622; 1623; 1629
Martin K. Eby, Jr. *(Chm. Bd. & Chief Exec. Officer)*
James R. Grier III *(Pres.)*
C. Ed Coon *(Exec. V.P.)*
Charles K. Eby *(Exec. V.P.)*
Jess Myers *(V.P. & Gen. Counsel)*
Ralph N. Townsend *(V.P.-Personnel)*
Roberta D. Nielsen *(Sec.)*

ECHEVARRIA ANGEL CO., INC.
(d/b/a Somma Mattress)
3760 Union Pacific Ave.
Los Angeles, CA 90023
Mailing Address:
P.O. Box 23399,
Los Angeles, CA 90023
Tel.: 213-260-7951
Tel.: 800-22-SOMMA **CA**
Fax: 213-266-3082
Year Founded: 1966
Assets: $7,789,000
Liabilities: $5,402,000
Net Worth: $2,387,000
Approx.Sls.: $20,096,000
Emp.: 110
Fiscal Year-end: 10/31/91

Export
Mfr. of Mattresses & Waterbed Flotation
S.I.C.: 2515
Angel Echevarria *(Pres. & Chief Exec. Officer)*
Michael Echevarria *(Chief Oper. Officer & Exec. V.P.)*
Michael D. Joyce *(Chief Fin. Officer)*
David Tenura *(Dir.-Sls. & Mktg.)*

Principal(s):
Angel Echevarria
Michael Echevarria
Robert Echevarria
Angel L. Perez Echevarria

No. of Mfg. Plants/Facilities: 1
No. of U.S. Offices: 1

Computer Systems/Hardware:
Quantel 64

Outside Service Firm(s):

Arthur Andersen & Co.*(Auditors)*
6320 Canoga Ave.
Woodland Hills, CA 91367

Kindel & Anderson*(Legal Firm)*
555 S. Flower, Ste. 2600
Los Angeles, CA 90071
Tel.: 213-680-2222

Sanwa Bank*(Major Banking Relationship)*
601 S. Figueroa St.
Los Angeles, CA 90017
Tel.: 213-896-7817
Fax: 213-489-1977

ECHO DESIGN GROUP, INC.
10 E. 40th St.
New York, NY 10016
Tel.: 212-686-8771
Fax: 212-686-5017
Sales Range: $20-39 Million
Emp.: 10
Design & Manufacture Ladies Outerwear, Mufflers, Ties & Belts
S.I.C.: 2339; 2253; 2387

Echo Design Group, Inc.—(Continued)

Dorothy H. Roberts *(Chief Exec. Officer)*
Charles T. Williams *(Pres.)*
Katherine Adler *(V.P.-Mktg.)*
Jennifer Mead *(V.P.-Sls.)*
Lynn T. Roberts *(V.P.-Adv.)*

Outside Service Firm(s):

Spicer & Oppenheim *(Auditors)*
7 World Trade Center,
New York, NY 10048
Tel.: 212-422-1000

Webster & Sheffield *(Legal Firm)*
One Rockefeller Plaza
New York, NY 10004-2594
Tel.: 212-957-9800

The Bank of New York *(Major Banking Relationship)*
One Wall Street
New York, NY 10286
Tel.: 212-635-6805
Fax: 212-635-3201

PAUL ECKE RANCH, INC.
441 Saxony Rd.
Encinitas, CA 92024
Tel.: 619-753-1134 **CA**
Year Founded: 1930
Approx.Sls.: $10,000,000
Emp.: 300
Poinsettias Grown In Field Nurseries
S.I.C.: 0181
Paul Ecke, Jr. *(Chm. Bd.)*
Paul Ecke, III *(Pres.)*
David Garcia *(Dir.-Personnel)*

Outside Service Firm(s):

First Interstate Bank *(Major Banking Relationship)*
P.O. Box 53441,
Phoenix, AZ 85072-3441
Tel.: 602-229-4049

JACK ECKERD CORPORATION
8333 Bryan Dairy Rd.
Largo, FL 34647
Mailing Address:
P.O. Box 4689,
Clearwater, FL 34618
Tel.: 813-397-7461 **FL**
Fax: 813-398-8369
Year Founded: 1952
Assets: $1,362,499,000
Earnings: ($759,000)
Liabilities: $1,625,855,000
Net Worth: $263,356,000
Approx.Sls.: $3,562,197,000
Emp.: 39,800
Fiscal Year-end: 2/ 1/92

Import
Retail Drug Stores
S.I.C.: 5912
Employee Matching Gifts Program: $50 Minimum/$1,000 Maximum Per Calendar Year
Stewart Turley *(Chm. Bd., Pres. & Chief Exec. Officer)*
Harry Lambert *(Pres.-Eckerd Drug Co.)*
John W. Boyle *(Sr. V.P.-Fin. & Admin.)*
Ronald Peterson *(Sr. V.P.-Mktg.)*
Richard Roberson *(Sr. V.P.-Eckerd Vision Grp.)*
Ken Banks *(V.P.-Adv.)*
Robert D. Boos *(V.P.)*
James M. Santo *(V.P.-Legal Affairs & Sec.)*
Wayne A. Saunders *(V.P.-Human Resources)*
Thomas E. Whiddon *(V.P. & Treas.)*
Samuel G. Wright *(V.P. & Controller)*
Michael Zagorac *(V.P.-Pub. Affairs)*
David Durfee *(Dir.-Treas. Services)*
Leonard F. Barker *(Mgr.-Fin. Reporting)*

Outside Service Firm(s):

KPMG Peat Marwick *(Auditors)*
201 N. Franklin St., Ste. 3000
Tampa, FL 33602
Tel.: 813-223-1466
Fax: 813-229-3976

Travelers Insurance Co. *(Group Insurer)*
One Tower Square
Hartford, CT 06183-6130
Tel.: 203-277-4542
Fax: 203-277-5038

Shackleford, Farrior, Stallings & Evans, P.A. *(Legal Firm)*
501 E. Kennedy Blvd., Ste. 1400
Tampa, FL 33602
Tel.: 813-273-5000

Divisions:

Eckerd Drug Co. **(1)**
2100 Directors Row
Orlando, FL 32809
Tel.: 305-851-4120
Retail Drug Stores
S.I.C.: 5912
Jerry Stettner *(V.P.)*

Eckerd Drug Co. **(1)**
8333 Bryan Dairy Rd.
Largo, FL 34647
Tel.: 813-397-7461
Retail Drug Stores
S.I.C.: 5912
Les Reagin *(Sr. V.P.)*

Eckerd Drug Co. **(1)**
824 S. Military Trail
Deerfield Beach, FL 33442
Tel.: 305-428-2830
Retail Drug Stores
S.I.C.: 5912
Thomas Kaplan *(V.P.)*

Eckerd Drug Co. **(1)**
825 Pride Blvd.
Hammond, LA 70401
Tel.: 504-542-9400
Retail Drug Stores
S.I.C.: 5912
Larry Tucker *(V.P.)*

Eckerd Drug Co. **(1)**
1776 Statesville Ave.
Charlotte, NC 28231
Tel.: 704-371-8000
Retail Drug Stores
S.I.C.: 5912
David Hensley *(V.P.)*

Eckerd Drug Co. **(1)**
4409 Action St.
Garland, TX 75042
Tel.: 214-272-0411
Retail Drug Stores
S.I.C.: 5912
Oren Peacock *(Sr. V.P.)*

Eckerd Drug Co. **(1)**
2061 Interstate 45 S.
Conroe, TX 77302
Tel.: 713-273-1141
Retail Drug Stores
S.I.C.: 5912
Ernie Zost *(V.P.)*

Eckerd Drug Co. **(1)**
36 Herring Rd.
Newnan, GA 30265
Tel.: 706-253-9620
Retail Drug Stores
S.I.C.: 5912
Dick Sullivan *(V.P.)*

ECKMAN CONSTRUCTION COMPANY
84 Palomino Lane
Bedford, NH 03110
Tel.: 603-623-1713 **NH**
Fax: 603-623-1713
Year Founded: 1974
Approx.Sls.: $30,000,000
Emp.: 50
Fiscal Year-end: 12/31/91
All Forms of General Construction & Construction Management, including Commercial & Industrial Buildings
S.I.C.: 1542
Harold R. Eckman *(Pres.)*
Amy Eckman *(V.P. & Gen. Counsel)*

Principal(s):
Harold R. Eckman
Amy Eckman

Outside Service Firm(s):

Leone, Bigalo & McDonald *(Auditors)*
Wolfeboro, NH

First New Hampshire Bank *(Major Banking Relationship)*
Manchester, NH

ECLIPSE, INC.
1665 Elmwood Rd.
Rockford, IL 61103
Tel.: 815-877-3031 **IL**
Telex: 257438
Fax: 815-877-2656
Year Founded: 1908
Approx.Sls.: $75,000,000
Emp.: 650
Fiscal Year-end: 3/31/91

Export
Mfr. of Industrial Heating, Brass Foundry, Gas Meter Connectors, Valves, Brass Plumbing Products, Exchangers, Recuperators & Controls, Burners, Blowers
S.I.C.: 3567; 3433; 3494; 3364; 3491
A. Campbell Perks *(Chm. Bd. & Chief Exec. Officer)*
Douglas Perks *(Pres. & Chief Oper. Officer)*
Gerry Sibley *(Exec. V.P.)*
Lachlen Perks *(V.P.-Mktg.)*
Richard Russell *(V.P.-Combustion U.S.A.)*
Harry F. Steltmann *(V.P., Chief Fin. Officer, Treas & Sec.)*
Greg Bubp *(Controller)*
Jan Downey *(Admin. Asst.)*
Paul Carpenter *(Dir.-Fin.)*
Jack O'Brien *(Dir.-Adv.)*
James Volkening *(Dir.-Pur.)*
Ray Meyers *(Dir.-Mngmt. Information Systems)*

No. of Mfg. Plants/Facilities: 13
No. of U.S. Offices: 42
No. of Foreign Offices: 75

Computer Systems/Hardware:
IBM System 4381

Outside Service Firm(s):

Coopers & Lybrand *(Auditors)*
6000 E. State St.
Rockford, IL 61108
Tel.: 815-394-0300

M & I Marshall & Ilsley Bank *(Major Banking Relationship)*
770 N. Water St.
Milwaukee, WI 53202
Tel.: 414-765-8700

Division:

Eclipse Thermal Systems **(1)**
6117 No. Elston Ave.
Chicago, IL 60646
Tel.: 312-775-4800 (100%)
Approx.Sls.: $2,500,000
Emp.: 8
Wholesale of Industrial Heating Equipment
S.I.C.: 5084
Al Benz *(Gen. Mgr.)*

Subsidiaries:

Eclipse-Combustion **(1)**
1665 Elmwood Rd
Rockford, IL 61103 (100%)
Approx.Sls.: $22,000,000
Emp.: 210
Mfr. & Wholesale of Burners, Blowers & Valves
S.I.C.: 3564; 5084
Richard Russell *(Gen. Mgr.)*

Eclipse-Controls **(1)**
1665 Elmwood Rd.
Rockford, IL 61103 (100%)
Approx.Sls.: $3,500,000
Emp.: 6
Mfr. of Heat Process Controls
S.I.C.: 3585
James White *(Gen. Mgr.)*

Exothermics-Eclipse, Inc. **(1)**
5040 Enterprise Blvd.
Toledo, OH 43612
Tel.: 419-729-9726 (100%)
Fax: 419-729-9705
Approx.Sls.: $5,000,000
Emp.: 25
Wholesale of Heat Exchangers
S.I.C.: 5084
Bruce McKenna *(Gen. Mgr.)*

Rockford-Eclipse **(1)**
1665 Elmwood Rd.
Rockford, IL 61103
Tel.: 815-877-3031 (100%)
Approx.Sls.: $20,000,000
Emp.: 140
Mfr. of Gas Meter Connectors, Valves & Brass Plumbing Products
S.I.C.: 3491; 3494
Gene Wheeler *(Gen. Mgr.)*

Sall-Eclipse **(1)**
2320 Kishwaukee St.
Rockford, IL 61108
Tel.: 815-877-3031 (100%)
Approx.Sls.: $6,000,000
Emp.: 60
Brass Foundry
S.I.C.: 3364
Chuck Cushing *(Gen. Mgr.)*

Southern Combustion & Controls, Inc. **(1)**
401 N. Market St.
Chattanooga, TN 37405
Tel.: 615-266-4831 (100%)
Approx.Sls.: $1,800,000
Emp.: 15
Sales Office for Industrial Heating Equipment
S.I.C.: 5084
Bill Bulger *(Gen. Mgr.)*

Non-U.S. Holdings:

Eclipse Combustion & Industrial Equipment Pty. **(1)**
Glen Waverley, Australia (50%)
Mfr. of Combustion Control Instruments & Industrial Equipment
S.I.C.: 3823

Eclipse Thermal Systems **(1)**
1145 Westport Crescent
Mississauga, ON L5T 1E8, Canada
Tel.: 416-670-1222 (100%)
Telex: 06-963507
Emp.: 23
Mfr. of Gas & Oil Burners, Gas & Air Valves, Air/Gas Mixers, Blowers, Control Panels for Process Heating Applications
S.I.C.: 3433; 3491
Bill Butler *(V.P. & Gen. Mgr.)*

Eclipse Thermal Systems **(1)**
2095 Madison
Montreal, PQ H43 2T2, Canada
Tel.: 514-482-9770 (100%)
Brass Foundry
S.I.C.: 3364
Harry Sutton *(Gen. Mgr.)*

Eclipse Thermal Systems, Ltd. **(1)**
Wassage Way, Hampton Lovett Indus. Estate Kidderminster Road,
Droitwich, Worcestershire WR9 0NX, United Kingdom
Tel.: 44-90-577-3661 (100%)
Fax: 334177
Emp.: 25
Mfr. of Industrial Heating
S.I.C.: 3433
John Darby *(Chief Oper. Officer)*
David Powell *(Gen. Mgr.)*

Enterprise S.A. de C.V. **(1)**
Rodriguez Saro 424 Col. Del Valle, Del. B. Juarez,
Mexico, D.F. Mexico
Tel.: 905-534-6020 (23%)
Emp.: 200

Mfr. of Industrial Controls, Automation & Combustion Systems
S.I.C.: 3625
Jorge Alvarez *(Gen. Mgr.)*

Flameco-Eclipse B.V. **(1)**
Zwolleweg 5 2803 PS
Gouda, Netherlands
Tel.: 311820-15988 (100%)
Fax: 311820-33269
Emp.: 105
Mfr. of Industrial Heating Equipment
S.I.C.: 3433
Cor Havelaar *(Chief Oper. Officer)*

Vulcan - Eclipse **(1)**
Mahalaymi Chambers, Bhulabhai Desai Rd.
Bombay, 26, India (39%)
Mfr. of Industrial Heating Equipment
S.I.C.: 3433

ECLIPSE MANUFACTURING COMPANY
1828 Oakland Ave.
Sheboygan, WI 53082-0788
Tel.: 414-457-2311 **WI**
Fax: 414-457-4935
Approx.Sls.: $17,000,000
Emp.: 140
Stamping Metal For The Trade
S.I.C.: 3469
Richard F. Leicht *(Chm. Bd.)*
Richard F. Leicht, Jr. *(Pres.)*
Jeffrey Leicht *(V.P.-Mfg.)*
Robert C. Senkbell *(V.P.-Mktg.)*

No. of Mfg. Plants/Facilities: 2

Computer Systems/Hardware:
IBM

Outside Service Firm(s):

Rohde, Neuses & Dales*(Legal Firm)*
Sheboygan, WI

First Wisconsin National Bank*(Major Banking Relationship)*
Sheboygan, WI

ECO WATER SYSTEMS
P.O. Box 64420
Saint Paul, MN 55125
Tel.: 612-739-5330
Tel.: 800-86 WATER
Fax: 612-739-4547
Year Founded: 1945
Approx.Sls.: $60,000,000
Emp.: 500
Fiscal Year-end: 12/31/90
Import Export
Mfr. Water Softeners, Water Filtration Equipment, Purifiers & Pumps
S.I.C.: 3589; 7389; 7629
Edward J. Fierko *(Pres.)*
Mike Reid *(Controller)*
Kent Hemminger *(Dir.-Fin. Services)*
Charles Anderson *(Dir.-Mfg.)*
John M. Scott *(Dir.-Mktg.)*
Donald D. Johnson *(Mgr.-Natl. Sls.)*
Floyd Smith *(Mgr.-Adv.)*
David Kell *(Mgr.-Personnel)*
Anne Gedelman *(Mgr.-Sls. Promo.)*
Mike Kopacz *(Mgr.-Intl. Mktg.)*
Jerry Johnson *(Mgr.-Mktg. Services)*
Peggy Leutele *(Mgr.-Telemarketing)*
Tim O'Malley *(Mgr.-Quality Control)*
Mike Schlitt *(Mgr.-Pur.)*

Computer Systems/Hardware:
IBM

ECONOCOM-USA INC.
4400 S. Mendehall, Ste. 8
Memphis, TN 38141
Tel.: 901-367-1105 **TN**
Fax: 901-367-2176
Year Founded: 1985
Approx.Sls.: $120,000,000
Emp.: 175
Computer Hardware Rental or Leasing, Except Finance Leasing; Data Processing Consultant; Computer & Data Processing Equipment Repair/Maintenance; Equipment Rental & Leasing; Telephone Equipment
S.I.C.: 7377; 5045; 7379; 7378; 7359; 5065
Pierre J. Verbeke *(Pres.)*
J.D. Bartow *(V.P. & Controller)*
Mitchell Lansky *(V.P. & Gen. Counsel)*
Kevin Thomas *(Controller)*

Outside Service Firm(s):

Meritor Financial*(Major Banking Relationship)*
Philadelphia, PA

ECONOLITE CONTROL PRODUCTS, INC.
3360 E. La Palma Ave.
Anaheim, CA 92806
Tel.: 714-630-3700 **CA**
Fax: 714-630-6349
Year Founded: 1933
Approx.Sls.: $26,000,000
Emp.: 150
Fiscal Year-end: 12/ 1/91
Export
Traffic Control Systems
S.I.C.: 3669
M.C. Doyle *(Chm. Bd.)*
S.R. Onderdonk *(Pres. & Chief Exec. Officer)*
F. Klaben *(Sr. V.P. & Gen. Mgr.)*
D. Adams *(V.P.-Opers.)*
G. Duncan *(V.P.-Engrng.)*
W. Russell *(V.P.-Mktg.)*
J. Spinazzi *(V.P.-Mktg.)*
D. Palmer *(Controller)*
T. Smith *(Dir.-Pur.)*
J. Scalise *(Mgr.-Human Resources)*

No. of U.S. Offices: 8
No. of Foreign Offices: 2

Outside Service Firm(s):

Arthur Andersen & Co.*(Auditors)*
Costa Mesa, CA

Stone & Doyle*(Legal Firm)*
Anaheim, CA

Community Bank*(Major Banking Relationship)*
Burbank, CA

Subsidiary:

Econolite Canada, Inc. **(1)**
1650 Midland Ave. M1P 3C2
Scarborough, Ontario Canada
Tel.: 416-752-4252
Fax: 416-752-6357
Emp.: 20
Traffic Control Systems
S.I.C.: 3669
P. Keen *(Gen. Mgr.)*

THE ECONOMICS PRESS, INC.
12 Daniel Rd.
Fairfield, NJ 07004
Tel.: 201-227-1224
Fax: 201-227-9742
Year Founded: 1959
Approx.Sls.: $15,000,000
Emp.: 180
Publisher of Training Materials for Industry & Schools
S.I.C.: 2741
John L. Beckley *(Chm. Bd.)*
Michael LoRusso *(Pres.)*
Robert Kleinmanns *(V.P., Sec. & Treas.)*
Alan Yohalem *(V.P. & Controller)*

Computer Systems/Hardware:
Hewlett-Packard

Outside Service Firm(s):

KPMG Peat Marwick*(Auditors)*
Newark, NJ

Orbe, Nugent & Collins*(Legal Firm)*
Fairfield, NJ

New Jersey Bank*(Major Banking Relationship)*
Newark, NJ

ECONOMY FOLDING BOX CORP.
LaSalle & 26th Sts.
Chicago, IL 60616
Tel.: 312-225-2000 **IL**
Fax: 312-225-3082
Year Founded: 1954
Assets: $9,919,000
Liabilities: $2,970,000
Net Worth: $6,949,000
Approx.Sls.: $15,460,000
Emp.: 140
Fiscal Year-end: 12/31/91
Folding Boxes
S.I.C.: 2657
J. Clifford Moos *(Chm., Pres. & Chief Exec. Officer)*
Michael M. Mitchel *(V.P.)*
Richard Bartle *(Controller)*
Edward Fellin *(Treas.)*
Ray Horkman *(Mgr.-Sls.)*
Shirley Levin *(Mgr.-Adv.)*
P. Bose *(Pur. Agent)*
Principal(s):
J. Clifford Moos
Michael M. Mitchel
Edward Fellin
Emily A. Moos
Jane K. Moos
Joseph D. Moos
Carol Mitchel

No. of Mfg. Plants/Facilities: 1
No. of U.S. Offices: 1

Outside Service Firm(s):

Grant Thornton*(Auditors)*
700 One Prudential Plaza, 130 East Randolph St.
Chicago, IL 60601
Tel.: 312-856-0200
Fax: 312-565-4719

Continental Bank N. A.*(Major Banking Relationship)*
231 S. LaSalle St.
Chicago, IL 60697
Tel.: 312-828-2345
Tel.: 800-426-5754
Telex: 312-828-1783

ECUATORIANA AIRLINES
7270 N.W. 12th St., Ste. 400
Miami, FL 33126
Tel.: 305-593-9955
Fax: 305-593-7986
Approx.Sls.: $48,000,000
Emp.: 130
Fiscal Year-end: 12/31/90
Intl. Scheduled Air Lines; Empresa Ecuatoriana De Aviacion
S.I.C.: 4729
Hernan Moscoro *(Reg. Mgr.)*

EDDINS-WALCHER COMPANY
P.O. Box 1920, 2506 West Wall Ave.
Midland, TX 79702
Tel.: 915-684-4423
Fax: 915-684-4030
Year Founded: 1937
Approx.Sls.: $50,000,000
Emp.: 178
Fiscal Year-end: 12/31/88
Markets Refined Petroleum Products
S.I.C.: 5172
Jack Walcher *(Chm., Pres. & Chief Exec. Officer)*
Ralph Arrell *(Exec. V.P.)*
Glen Cavitt *(Exec. V.P.)*
Dan T. Moody *(Exec. V.P.)*
Gary Willis *(V.P.-Fin., Chief Fin. Officer & Treas.)*
Principal(s):
Jack Walcher

No. of U.S. Offices: 18

Computer Systems/Hardware:
IBM System 34

Outside Service Firm(s):

Philadelphia Life Insurance Co.*(Group Insurer)*
Houston, TX

Lynch, Chappell, Allday & Alsup*(Legal Firm)*
1600 1st Natl. Bank Bldg.
Midland, TX 79701
Tel.: 915-683-3351

Travelers Insurance Co.*(Pension Manager)*
1 Tower Square
Hartford, CT 06183
Tel.: 203-222-7821
Fax: 203-222-7813

EDELBROCK CORP.
2700 California St.
Torrance, CA 90503
Tel.: 310-781-2222
Fax: 310-230-1187
Year Founded: 1938
Assets: $45,000,000
Liabilities: $28,000,000
Net Worth: $17,000,000
Sales Range: $40-59 Million
Emp.: 176
Fiscal Year-end: 6/30/90
Import Export
Mfr. Performance Automotive Equipment
S.I.C.: 3694; 3559
Victor Edelbrock *(Chm. Bd., Pres. & Chief Exec. Officer)*
Jeffrey L. Thompson *(Exec. V.P.)*
Tony Hollis *(V.P.-Fin.)*
Wayne Murray *(V.P.-Mfg.)*
Jack Ring *(V.P.-Corp. Devel.)*
John Towle *(V.P.-Sls.)*
Nancy Edelbrock *(Sec.)*
Katherine Higgins *(Treas.)*
Jody Scott *(Controller)*
Camee Edelbrock-Isom *(Dir.-Adv.)*
Marvin Griffin *(Dir.-Data Processing)*
Jackie Langlais *(Dir.-Personnel)*
Nancy Smith *(Dir.-Pur.)*
Principal(s):
Victor Edelbrock

No. of Mfg. Plants/Facilities: 1
No. of U.S. Offices: 1

Computer Systems/Hardware:
Hewlett-Packard

Outside Service Firm(s):

Ernst & Young*(Auditors)*
21300 Victory Blvd., Ste. 1000
Woodland Hills, CA 91367
Tel.: 818-703-4700

Dodge, Warren & Peters*(Commercial Insurance Carrier)*
Torrance, CA

Blue Cross of California*(Group Insurer)*
2101 Western St.
Oakland, CA 94659
Tel.: 800-645-3000

Bank of America NT&SA*(International Bank Affiliate)*
555 So. Flower St., 5th Fl.
Los Angeles, CA 90071
Tel.: 213-228-3526
Fax: 213-228-4062

City National Bank*(International Bank Affiliate)*
120 S. Spalding Dr.
Beverly Hills, CA 90213
Tel.: 310-550-5821

Arant, Kleinberg & Lerner*(Legal Firm)*
Los Angeles, CA

Edelbrock Corp.—(Continued)

Bateman, Eichler, Hill, Richards*(Pension Manager)*
Los Angeles, CA

Divisions:

Edelbrock Corp. **(1)**
2700 California St.
Torrance, CA 90503
Tel.: 310-781-2222

Edelbrock Development **(1)**
2700 California St.
Torrance, CA 90503
Tel.: 310-781-2222

EDELMANN DIV. OF STANT, INC.
111 Deer Lake Rd., Ste. 110
Deerfield, IL 60015
Tel.: 708-405-9400
Approx.Sls.: $20,000,000
Emp.: 600
Mfr. of Edelmann Fuel Lines; Automotive Parts; Anti-Freeze, Battery & Cooling System Testers; Locking Gas Caps, Gasoline Tank Caps; Radiator & Oil Caps; Thermostats; Brass Fittings; Steel Brake Lines; Power Steering Products; Fuses; Hydraulics
S.I.C.: 3714
David Paridy *(Pres.)*
Donald Edelmann *(Grp. V.P.)*
Paul Lederer *(V.P.)*
Eric S. Arroyo *(Gen. Mgr.)*
Ralph Magden *(Dir.-Pur.)*
Brian Markus *(Mgr.-Mktg.)*
Leslie Tokay *(Export Mgr.)*

EDELMANN SCOTT, INC.
629 E. Main St.
Richmond, VA 23219
Tel.: 804-643-1931
Fax: 804-643-1934
Year Founded: 1979
Approx.Billings: $10,500,000
Emp.: 16
Edgar S. Edelmann *(Pres. & Mktg. Dir.)*
Richard J. Scott *(Chief Exec. Officer & Creative Dir.)*
Terry Fink *(Sr. V.P., Media Dir.)*
Patricia Martino-Alspaugh *(Office Mgr.)*

EDELSON & SONS CORPORATION
44 E. 32nd St.
New York, NY 10016
Tel.: 212-685-2752
Fax: 212-685-5702
Approx.Sls.: $14,000,000
Emp.: 400
Womens & Childrens Underwear; Robes & Dressings Gowns; Womens & Children Clothing
S.I.C.: 2341; 2384; 5137
Norman Edelson *(Pres.)*

Outside Service Firm(s):

Weinick, Sanders & Co.*(Auditors)*
New York, NY

Chase Manhattan Bank, N.A.*(Major Banking Relationship)*
One Chase Manhattan Plaza
New York, NY 10081
Tel.: 212-552-2222
Tel.: 800-526-0801
Fax: 212-552-7175

EDELSTEIN ASSOCIATES ADVERTISING INC.
2030 First Ave., 3rd Fl.
Seattle, WA 98121
Tel.: 206-448-4888
Fax: 206-448-8513
Year Founded: 1977
Approx.Billings: $10,000,000
Emp.: 45
David Edelstein *(Chm. Bd. & Pres.)*
Gregg Blodgett *(V.P., Fin.)*
Nancy Edelstein *(Sec.)*

EDERER INC.
2925 First Ave., S.
Seattle, WA 98134
Mailing Address:
P.O. Box 24708
Seattle, WA 98124
Tel.: 206-622-4421 **WA**
Fax: 206-623-8583
Year Founded: 1901
Approx.Sls.: $18,000,000
Emp.: 130
Fiscal Year-end: 9/30/92
Import Export
Overhead, Gantry, Revolver and Container Cranes; Motor Speed Controls, Cableways, Concrete Cars Trolleys, Crane Uprating, Crane Refurbishment, Hoist Safety Systems
S.I.C.: 3536
Don Miller *(Pres. & Chief Exec. Officer)*
Joe Busch *(V.P.-Oper.)*
Jim Nelson *(Dir.-Sls. & Mktg.)*
Jerry Bement *(Pur. Agent)*
Principal(s):
Don Miller

No. of U.S. Offices: 2

Computer Systems/Hardware:
Northgate

Outside Service Firm(s):

Coopers & Lybrand*(Auditors)*
1800 First Interstate Center, 999 Third Ave.
Seattle, WA 98104-4098
Tel.: 206-622-8700

McDonald Insurance*(Commercial Insurance Carrier)*
Seattle, WA

Raleigh, Schwarz & Powell*(Commercial Insurance Carrier)*
1119 Pacific Ave.
Seattle, WA 98402
Tel.: 206-624-4860

Stoel, Rives, Boley, Jones & Grey*(Legal Firm)*
3600 One Union Sq., 600 University
Seattle, WA 98101
Tel.: 206-624-0900
Fax: 206-386-7500

Seafirst Bank*(Major Banking Relationship)*
Columbia-SeaFirst Center, 701 5th Ave., 11th Flr.
Seattle, WA 98124
Tel.: 206-358-3039
Fax: 206-358-3113

Divisions:

Ederer Cranes **(1)**
2925 First Ave. So.
Seattle, WA 98134
Tel.: 206-622-4421
Fax: 206-623-8583
Emp.: 130
Import Export
Overhead Cranes
S.I.C.: 3536
Jim Nelson *(Dir.-Sls. & Mktg.)*

Meta Services Inc. **(1)**
2925 First Ave., So.
Seattle, WA 98134
Tel.: 206-622-4421
Fax: 206-623-8583
Export
Dam Construction Equipment & Consulting
S.I.C.: 3536
P.L. Longthorpe *(Project Mgr.)*

Star Cranes **(1)**
2925 First Ave. So.
Seattle, WA 98134
Tel.: 206-622-4421
Fax: 206-623-8583
Export
Overhead Cranes
S.I.C.: 3536
Jim Nelson *(Dir.-Sls. & Mktg.)*

Washington Cranes **(1)**
2925 First Ave. So.
Seattle, WA 98134
Tel.: 206-622-4421
Fax: 206-623-8583
Export
Overhead Cranes
S.I.C.: 3536
Jim Nelson *(Dir.-Sls. & Mktg.)*

EDGAR B. FURNITURE CO.
P.O. Box 849
Clemmons, NC 27012
Tel.: 919-766-7321
Fax: 919-766-8308
Year Founded: 1979
Approx.Sls.: $18,000,000
Emp.: 80
Direct Marketing of Household Furniture Through Catalogs
S.I.C.: 5961
J. Edgar Broyhill II *(Pres.)*
Phred Huber *(V.P.-Sls.)*
Carl D. Sawyer *(V.P.-Opers.)*
T. Paul Hendrick *(Legal Officer)*
Principal(s):
J. Edgar Broyhill II

No. of U.S. Offices: 2

Computer Systems/Hardware:
IBM System 36

Outside Service Firm(s):

Root, Sawyer, Wilkerson & Woods*(Auditors)*
Winston-Salem, NC

NationsBank Carolinas*(International Bank Affiliate)*
Winston-Salem, NC

Hendrick, Zotian & Cocklereece*(Legal Firm)*
Winston-Salem, NC

EDGEWATER CORPORATION
300 College Ave.
Oakmont, PA 15139-2199
Tel.: 412-826-7200
Tel.: 800-245-6202 **PA**
Fax: 412-826-7210
Year Founded: 1916
Assets: $19,728,000
Earnings: $362,000
Liabilities: $19,252,000
Net Worth: $476,000
Approx.Sls.: $45,000,000
Emp.: 500
Fiscal Year-end: 12/31/90
Export
Mfr. of Circular Metal Products: Rail Road Wheels, Jet Engine Rings, Bearing Races & Metal Rings
S.I.C.: 3312; 3462
J.H. Kirkwood *(Chm., Pres. & Chief Exec. Officer)*
G.F. Kutzmark *(Exec. V.P. & Chief Oper. Officer)*
W.K. Squires *(V.P.-Mktg.)*
Joseph R. Rosati *(V.P.-Indus. Rels.)*
R.L. Ross *(Sec., Treas. & Controller)*
J.E. Jablonowksi *(Mgr.-Plant)*
H.T. Bryer *(Mgr.-Data Processing)*
M.L. Shoenberger *(Mgr.-Quality & Prod. Devel.)*
T.H. Frazer *(Asst. Treas.)*

No. of Mfg. Plants/Facilities: 1
No. of U.S. Offices: 6

Computer Systems/Hardware:
IBM AS-400

Outside Service Firm(s):

Alpern, Rosenthal & Company*(Auditors)*
Pittsburgh, PA

Houston Harbaugh*(Legal Firm)*
Pittsburgh, PA

Fidelcor Business Credit Corp.*(Major Banking Relationship)*
810 7th Ave.
New York, NY 10019
Tel.: 212-333-7445

Fidelity Bank*(Major Banking Relationship)*
Broad & Walnut St.
Philadelphia, PA 19109

Equitable Real Estate Investment Managment Inc.*(Pension Manager)*
3414 Peachtree Rd. N.E.
Atlanta, GA 30326-1162

Mid Atlantic Capital Corporation*(Pension Manager)*
912 Fifth Ave.
Pittsburgh, PA 15219
Tel.: 412-391-7077

Division:

Edgewater Steel Co. **(1)**
300 College Ave.
Oakmont, PA 15139
Tel.: 412-826-7200
Tel.: 800-245-6202
Export
Iron & Steel Forgings
S.I.C.: 3312; 3462

EDGEWOOD TOOL & MANUFACTURING COMPANY
8900 Inkster Rd.
Romulus, MI 48174
Tel.: 313-946-1300 **MI**
Fax: 313-946-1339
Year Founded: 1936
Assets: $14,677,000
Liabilities: $11,323,000
Net Worth: $3,354,000
Approx.Sls.: $32,500,000
Emp.: 130
Fiscal Year-end: 7/31/91
Import Export
Mfr. Automotive Metal Stampings, Tools & Dies
S.I.C.: 3714; 3465; 3545
James R. Lozelle *(Pres. & Chief Exec. Officer)*
James McClain *(V.P. & Gen. Mgr.)*
William D. Belisle *(V.P.-Engrng.)*
John L. Daly *(V.P.-Fin.)*
David J. Wacnik *(Controller)*
Fred V. Feiler *(Dir.-Pur.)*
Brian Fiebernitz *(Dir.-Personnel Training & Devel.)*
Richard Jones *(Dir.-Sls.)*
Terrence Vessey *(Dir.-Quality)*
Joe Knapp *(Mgr.-Data Processing)*
Principal(s):
James R. Lozelle

No. of Mfg. Plants/Facilities: 3
No. of U.S. Offices: 2
No. of Foreign Offices: 1

Outside Service Firm(s):

Coopers & Lybrand*(Auditors)*
400 Renaissance Center
Detroit, MI 48243
Tel.: 313-446-7100
Fax: 313-446-7117

Hooper, Hathaway, Price & Beuche*(Legal Firm)*
Ann Arbor, MI

Comerica Bank*(Major Banking Relationship)*
211 W. Fort St.
Detroit, MI 48226
Tel.: 313-222-3300

Affiliate:

Ann Arbor Assembly Corporation **(1)**
251 Airport Industrial Dr.
Ypsilanti, MI 48198
Tel.: 313-484-0380
Emp.: 90
Assembly
S.I.C.: 3714
Larry Byrne *(Pres.)*
Bryan Cody *(V.P.)*

EDLUND COMPANY, INC.
159 Industrial Pkwy.
Burlington, VT 05401
Mailing Address:
P.O. Box 929,
Burlington, VT 05402
Tel.: 802-862-9661
Fax: 802-862-4822
Year Founded: 1926
Approx.Sls.: $10,000,000
Emp.: 100
Import Export
Mfr. of Can Openers & Can Opening Systems; Scales; Sliders; Commercial & Industrial Food Service Equipment
S.I.C.: 3423; 3596
Willett S. Foster IV *(Pres. & Chief Exec. Officer)*
James B. Foster *(V.P.-Real Estate)*
Stephen P. Foster *(V.P. & Treas.)*
Peter Nordell *(Dir.-Mktg. & Sls.)*
Cathy Mitchelities *(Pur. Agent)*
Peter Doremus *(Sec.)*

Outside Service Firm(s):

KPMG Peat Marwick*(Auditors)*
Burlington Business Ctr. II, 77 S. Bedford St.
Burlington, MA 01803

Doremus Associates*(Legal Firm)*
Burlington, VT

Howard Bank*(Major Banking Relationship)*
Burlington, VT

EDMONSON WHEAT GROWERS, INC.
Hwy. 194
Edmonson, TX 79032
Mailing Address:
P.O. Box 32
Edmonson, TX 79032
Tel.: 806-864-3327
Fax: 806-864-3325
Year Founded: 1934
Assets: $6,399,102
Earnings: $595,000
Liabilities: $2,349,256
Net Worth: $4,049,846
Approx.Sls.: $20,000,000
Emp.: 25
Fiscal Year-end: 7/31/90
Agriculture Production-Crops; Agriculture Services; Membership Organization
S.I.C.: 5153; 5191; 4221; 5261; 8611
Delbert Howell *(Pres.)*
Steve Lee *(V.P.)*
Guy Snelling *(Sec. & Treas.)*
Don Ketchum *(Gen. Mgr.)*
Royce Duckett *(Asst. Mgr.)*

Computer Systems/Hardware:
Point Four

Outside Service Firm(s):

Ridley, Baker & Co.*(Auditors)*
Lubbock, TX

Farmland Insurance*(Commercial Insurance Carrier)*
Des Moines, IA

Malcom Tisedale*(Legal Firm)*
Plainview, TX

Hale County State Bank*(Major Banking Relationship)*
Plainview, TX

Texas Bank for Co-operatives*(Major Banking Relationship)*
Austin, TX

EDMUND SCIENTIFIC COMPANY
101 E. Gloucester Pike
Barrington, NJ 08007-1380
Tel.: 609-573-6250
Fax: 609-573-6295
Year Founded: 1942
Sales Range: $10-19 Million
Emp.: 150
Import Export
Distribute Astronomical, Optical & Scientific Items; Manufacture Optical Products
S.I.C.: 3827; 5049; 5961
Norman W. Edmund *(Chm. Bd.)*
Robert M. Edmund *(Pres. & Chief Exec. Officer)*
Frank S. DiMinno, Jr. *(V.P.-Indus. Opers.)*
Gwynne Edmund *(V.P.-Mktg.)*
Dave McGonigle *(V.P.-Opers.)*
Joan Costa *(Dir.-Opers.)*
Virginia Lamelas *(Mgr.-Personnel)*
Judy Thomas *(Controller)*

No. of U.S. Offices: 1
No. of Foreign Offices: 2

Computer Systems/Hardware:
Hewlett-Packard 3000

Outside Service Firm(s):

W. H. Webster & Co.*(Auditors)*
Philadelphia, PA

Lowell S. Thomas, Jr.*(Legal Firm)*
Philadelphia, PA

Saul, Ewing, Remick & Saul*(Legal Firm)*
Philadelphia, PA

Continental Bank N. A.*(Major Banking Relationship)*
231 S. LaSalle St.
Chicago, IL 60697
Tel.: 312-828-2345
Tel.: 800-426-5754
Telex: 312-828-1783

Subsidiary:

Anchor Optical Co., Inc. **(1)**
97 E. Gloucester Pike
Barrington, NJ 08007
Tel.: 609-573-6231

EDUCATIONAL INSIGHTS, INC.
19560 Rancho Way
Dominguez Hills, CA 90220
Tel.: 213-979-1955
Tel.: 800-933-3277 **CA**
Fax: 310-605-5048
Year Founded: 1962
Approx.Sls.: $10,000,000
Emp.: 175
Import Export
Design, Manufacture & Distribute Educational Toys, Games & Teaching Aides
S.I.C.: 3999
Burton Cutler *(Chm. Bd.)*
Jay Cutler *(Pres.)*
Diana Cutler *(V.P. & Sec.)*
Dennis Graham *(V.P.-Bus. Devel.)*
Jim Whitney *(V.P.-Sls. & Mktg.)*
Candace Dominguez *(Controller)*
Virginia Bowling *(Mgr.-Personnel)*
Sue Brown *(Mgr.-Adv.)*
Principal(s):
Burton Cutler
Jay Cutler
Carol Cutler-Csapo
Corey Cutler
Karen Cutler

No. of Mfg. Plants/Facilities: 2
No. of U.S. Offices: 1
No. of Foreign Offices: 1

Outside Service Firm(s):

Simon, Steemke & Co.*(Auditors)*
Los Angeles, CA

Union Bank*(Major Banking Relationship)*
Torrance, CA

EDUCATIONAL PUBLISHING CORPORATION
11000 S. Lavergne Ave.
Oak Lawn, IL 60453
Tel.: 708-425-0800 **DE**
Fax: 708-425-7916
Year Founded: 1898
Assets: $72,000,000
Liabilities: $67,000,000
Net Worth: $5,000,000
Approx.Sls.: $55,000,000
Emp.: 225
Fiscal Year-end: 12/31/90
Holding Company; Markets & Creates Educational Materials
S.I.C.: 6719; 2741; 3421
William M. Barnum *(Chm. Bd. & Chief Exec. Officer)*
Guy W. Fiske *(Vice Chm.)*
John T. Kersic *(Publisher & Pres.-Educational Publ. Grp.)*
Joseph Vecchiolla *(Exec. V.P., Chief Fin. Officer & Sec.)*
Brian Watts *(V.P. & Controller)*
James Murphy *(Dir.-Human Resources)*
Rita O'Toole *(Dir.-Pur.)*
Craig Adkins *(Acctg. Mgr.)*

No. of Mfg. Plants/Facilities: 4
No. of U.S. Offices: 5

Computer Systems/Hardware:
IBM

Outside Service Firm(s):

Ernst & Young*(Auditors)*
Portland, ME

CNA Insurance*(Commercial Insurance Carrier)*
CNA Plaza,
Chicago, IL 60685
Tel.: 312-822-5000

New England Mutual Life Insurance Co.*(Group Insurer)*
Chicago, IL

Shearson Lehman Brothers, Inc.*(International Bank Affiliate)*
Tower C, World Financial Center
New York, NY 10285
Tel.: 212-298-2000

Paul, Hastings, Janofsky & Walker*(Legal Firm)*
Santa Monica, CA

American National Bank & Trust Company of Chicago*(Major Banking Relationship)*
33 N. LaSalle St.
Chicago, IL 60602
Tel.: 312-661-5000
Fax: 312-661-6417

Kemper Insurance*(Pension Manager)*
500 W. Madison St., Ste. 1100
Chicago, IL

Subsidiaries:

Creative Publications **(1)**
11000 S. LaVergne Ave.
Oak Lawn, IL 60453
Tel.: 708-425-0800
John T. Kersic *(Chief Oper. Officer)*
Jack Dorris *(Dir.-Pur.)*

Ideal School Supply Company **(1)**
11000 S. LaVergne Ave.
Oak Lawn, IL 60453
Tel.: 708-425-0800
Jeff Abraham *(Dir.-Data Processing)*
Rita O'Toole *(Dir.-Pur.)*

Ideal School Supply Corporation **(1)**
11000 S. Lavergne Ave.
Oak Lawn, IL 60453
Tel.: 708-425-0800

Instructional Fair, Inc. **(1)**
2400 Turner Ave.
Grand Rapids, MI 49501
Tel.: 616-363-1290
Jerry Pelak *(Controller & Mgr.-Opers.)*

Priss Prints, Inc. **(1)**
3960 Broadway, Ste. 105
Garland, TX 75043
Tel.: 214-278-5600
Toni Fisher Moratt *(Chief Oper. Officer)*

Whitehall Educational Toys **(1)**
11000 S. Lavergne Ave.
Oak Lawn, IL 60453
Tel.: 708-425-0800

EDUSERV
(Formerly Hemar Group)
85 E. 7th Pl., Ste. 400
Saint Paul, MN 55101
Tel.: 612-227-6735 **MN**
Year Founded: 1982
Approx.Sls.: $35,000,000
Emp.: 800
Student Loan Servicing
S.I.C.: 7374; 6351
Mark Nonnelly *(Chm. Bd.)*
C.R. Michell *(Vice Chm. Bd. & Treas.)*
Carl Keil *(Pres.)*

Outside Service Firm(s):

Coopers & Lybrand*(Auditors)*
1000 TCF Bldg.
Minneapolis, MN 55402
Tel.: 612-293-2929
Fax: 612-370-9395

Norwest Bank Minnesota, N.A.*(Major Banking Relationship)*
P.O. Box 738, 161 N. Concord Exchange
South St. Paul, MN 55075-0738
Tel.: 800-468-9716

EDWARDS BAKING CO.
1 Lemon Lane N.E.
Atlanta, GA 30307
Tel.: 404-377-0511
Fax: 404-377-0788
Approx.Sls.: $40,000,000
Emp.: 220
Fiscal Year-end: 12/31/90
Mfr. of Frozen Dessert Concepts & Portion Control Desserts; Distr. to Retail & Food Service Industry
S.I.C.: 2051; 2053; 5142
Joel Edwards *(Chm. Bd. & Chief Exec. Officer)*
Donald S. Patterson *(Sr. V.P.)*
Sam Tidwell *(Sr. V.P.)*
Bobby W. Payne *(V.P.)*
Jim Miller *(V.P.)*
Dale Caldwell *(V.P.-Mktg.)*

EDWARDS BROTHERS, INC.
2500 S. State St.
Ann Arbor, MI 48106
Mailing Address:
P.O. Box 1007
Ann Arbor, MI 48106
Tel.: 313-769-1000
Year Founded: 1893
Approx.Sls.: $54,000,000
Emp.: 650
Fiscal Year-end: 9/30/91
Export
Manufacture of Books & Journals
S.I.C.: 2731; 2721
Corporate Giving Program: Largely local area colleges, hospitals, and charities.
Martin H. Edwards *(Pres.)*
Douglas Weber *(Treas.)*
William Kasdorf *(V.P.-Electronic Publishing)*
John W. Pugsley *(V.P.-Mktg. & Sls.)*
Martin B. Stadtmiller *(V.P.-Mfg.)*
Joan Schneider *(Dir.-Personnel)*

No. of Mfg. Plants/Facilities: 3
No. of U.S. Offices: 7

Outside Service Firm(s):

Deloitte & Touche*(Auditors)*
101 N. Main Street
Ann Arbor, MI 48104-1411
Tel.: 313-769-6200

Edwards Brothers, Inc.—(Continued)

Great Lakes Bancorp*(Major Banking Relationship)*
Ann Arbor, MI
Tel.: 313-769-8300

Plant:

Impressions Inc. **(1)**
2016 Winnebago St.
Madison, WI 53704
Tel.: 608-244-6218
Books & Journals
S.I.C.: 2731; 2721

Subsidiary:

Edwards Brothers - Carolina **(1)**
800 Edwards Dr.
Lillington, NC 27546
Tel.: 919-893-2717
Emp.: 150
Books & Journals
S.I.C.: 2721; 2731

EDWARDS ENGINEERING CORPORATION

101 Alexander
Pompton Plains, NJ 07444
Tel.: 201-835-2800
Tel.: 800-526-5201
Telex: 130-131
Fax: 201-835-3222
Year Founded: 1947
Approx.Sls.: $20,000,000
Emp.: 145
Fiscal Year-end: 12/31/91
Import Export
Zone-A-Matic Zone Control Heating, Box-Fin & Quiet/Slide Valance Units & Baseboard Radiation; Water Chillers, Vapor Recovery Units, Coaxial Heat Transfer Units
S.I.C.: 3585; 3433
R.C. Edwards *(Chm. Bd. & Pres.)*
C.W. Dittig *(V.P.-Mfg.)*
D.S. Edwards *(V.P.-Prod. Engrng.)*
R. Rendall Banks *(V.P.-Fin.)*
R.E. Waldrop *(V.P.-Sls.)*
T.J. Pierson *(Dir.-Mktg.)*
E.A. Bogucz *(Mgr.-Adv.)*
R. Lewin *(Mgr.-Personnel)*
E. Bigliamo *(Pur. Agent)*

Computer Systems/Hardware:
NCR

J.D. EDWARDS & COMPANY

8055 E. Tufts Ave., Ste. 1331
Denver, CO 80237
Tel.: 303-488-4000 **CO**
Fax: 303-488-4675
Year Founded: 1977
Assets: $45,100,000
Liabilities: $30,000,000
Net Worth: $15,100,000
Approx.Rev.: $79,900,000
Emp.: 1,100
Fiscal Year-end: 12/31/91
Export
Computer Software For IBM Midrange Systems
S.I.C.: 7372
C. Edward McVaney *(Chm. Bd., Pres. & Chief Exec. Officer)*
Ron Harris *(Exec. V.P.-Client Services)*
Lawrence A. Mueller *(Exec. V.P.-Worldwide Sls. & Mktg.)*
Rick Allen *(V.P.- Fin., Admin. & Chief Fin. Officer)*
Buffy Collison *(V.P.-Software Devel.)*
Mike Iiams *(V.P.-Mktg.)*
Rod McDonald *(V.P. & Dir. European Sls.)*
Robert C. Newman *(V.P.-Complementary Prods.)*
Richard G. Snow, Jr. *(V.P.- Gen. Counsel & Sec.)*
Jack L. Thompson *(V.P.-Heavy Tech.)*
Steve Attaway *(Dir.-Pur.)*
John Cannington *(Dir.-Worldwide Opers.& Mgr.-Large Accts.)*
Fred Wahlstrom *(Dir.-Corp. Communications)*
Greg Dixon *(Mgr.-Human Resources)*
Helen Tueffel *(Mgr.-Sls. Promo. & Adv.)*
Fred Wahlstrom *(Pub. Rels. Specialist)*
Judy Albright *(Supvr.-Travel)*

Principal(s):
C. Edward McVaney
Jack L. Thompson

No. of U.S. Offices: 34
No. of Foreign Offices: 10

Computer Systems/Hardware:
IBM

Outside Service Firm(s):

Arthur Andersen & Co.*(Auditors)*
717 17th St., Ste. 1900
Denver, CO 80202
Tel.: 303-296-2121

EDWARDSTONE & COMPANY, INC.

(Formerly Edwardstone Partners)
600 Madison Ave., 26th Fl.
New York, NY 10022
Tel.: 212-832-2700 **DE**
Holding Company
S.I.C.: 6719
Nick Toms *(Pres.)*

Divisions:

Manhattan Electric Cable Corporation **(1)**
Station Plaza
Rye, NY 10580
Tel.: 914-967-8000
Tel.: 800-228-6322
Approx.Sls.: $50,000,000
Emp.: 135
Wholesale Electric Cable & Wire
S.I.C.: 5063; 5065
Scott Cannold *(Pres.)*
George C. Graeber *(Chief Oper. Officer)*
Stanley R. Small *(V.P. & Controller)*
Donald W. Bowley *(Chief Fin. Officer)*
Sarah Sheehan *(Mgr.-Sls. Opers.)*
Allan P. Marconi *(Dir.-Mktg.)*
Robert W. Goodwins *(Dir.-Pur.)*

Seacoast Electric Company **(1)**
Station Plaza
Rye, NY 10580
Tel.: 914-967-8000
Distribute Wire & Cable For U.S. Navy
S.I.C.: 5063
George C. Graeber *(Chief Oper. Officer)*
Donald W. Rowley *(Chief Fin. Officer)*
Sarah Sheehan *(Mgr.-Sls. Opers.)*
Allan P. Marconi *(Dir.-Mktg.)*
Robert Goodwins *(Dir.-Pur.)*

Edwin Bird Wilson, Inc.
(Name Changed To Adler Boschetto Peebles & Partners, Inc.)

EFFECTIVE MANAGEMENT SYSTEMS

12000 W. Park Place
Milwaukee, WI 53224-3026
Tel.: 414-359-9800
Tel.: 800-962-1279 **WI**
Fax: 414-359-9011
Year Founded: 1978
Approx.Sls.: $29,000,000
Emp.: 499
Fiscal Year-end: 11/30/90
Provides Business Computers, Software (Customer Serv./ Distributors, Control, Manufacturing Systems, Finance & Accounting, Marketing & Sales, Engineering, Office Automation, Data Processing) & Services (Project Mnagement, Telephone Support, Training Software, Customization & Technical Consultants) to Manufacturers, Vending, Food Service, Office Coffee Service, & Music & Games Operations
S.I.C.: 7372; 7379; 5962; 5963
Michael D. Dunham *(Pres.)*
Thomas G. Allen *(V.P.-Sls. & Mktg.)*
Thomas M. Dykstra *(V.P. & Treas.)*
Jeffrey J. Fossum *(V.P. & Chief Fin. Officer)*
Donald W. Vahlsing *(V.P. & Sec.)*
Gary Kohls *(Dir.-Research)*
Robert Johnson *(Gen. Mgr.-Vending)*
Robert Weisenberg *(Gen. Mgr.)*
Carol Dolge *(Mgr.-Acctg.)*
Jane Karrels *(Mgr.-Meetings Planning)*
Ellen P. Kohls *(Mgr.-Mktg.)*
Gail Peters *(Mgr.-Sales Services)*
Dawn Ray *(Mgr.-Personnel Training & Devel.)*
Nancy Theis *(Mgr.-Quality Control)*
Bonnie R. Jaskie *(Corp. Librarian)*
Jeanne Batchelor *(Benefits Admin.)*

Principal(s):
Michael D. Dunham
Thomas G. Allen
Thomas M. Dykstra
Donald W. Vahlsing
Gary Kohls
Robert Weisenberg
Wayne T. Wedell
Roger K. Miller

No. of Mfg. Plants/Facilities: 17
No. of U.S. Offices: 17
No. of Foreign Offices: 4

Computer Systems/Hardware:
Digital; Compaq; Printronix

Outside Service Firm(s):

Ernst & Young*(Auditors)*
111 E. Kilbourn Ave., Ste. 900
Milwaukee, WI 53202
Tel.: 414-273-5900

CNA Insurance*(Commercial Insurance Carrier)*
Milwaukee, WI

Robertson-Ryan*(Commercial Insurance Carrier)*
Milwaukee, WI
Tel.: 414-277-5591

Aetna Life & Casualty*(Group Insurer)*
151 Farmington Avenue
Hartford, CT 06156
Tel.: 203-273-2128
Fax: 203-729-4295

First Bank Brown Deer*(Investment Banker)*
Milwaukee, WI

Rich Koenigs*(Legal Firm)*
Milwaukee, WI

First Bank Brown Deer*(Major Banking Relationship)*
Milwaukee, WI

Branches:

EMS Central Regional Office (Corporate) **(1)**
12000 W. Park Pl.
Milwaukee, WI 53224
Tel.: 414-359-9800
Fax: 414-359-9012

EMS Eastern Regional Office **(1)**
100 Foxboro Blvd.
Foxboro, MA 02035
Tel.: 508-698-0800
Fax: 508-698-0116
Paul Lavallee *(Pres.)*

EMS Southwest Region Office **(1)**
433 E. LAS Calinas Blvd., Suite 940
Irving, TX 75039-5611
Tel.: 214-869-1719

Affiliates:

Automation Resources **(1)**
One Urban Center, 4830 W. Kennedy Blvd., Suite 665
Tampa, FL 33609
Tel.: 813-287-2747

Broadway & Seymour **(1)**
128 S. Tryon St.
Charlotte, NC 28202
Tel.: 704-372-4281
Fax: 704-343-9608

Built Environment Services **(1)**
660 Linton Blvd., Suite 205B
Delray Beach, FL 33444
Tel.: 407-272-7710
Fax: 407-278-4830

Computer Systems of Long Island **(1)**
Atrium Executive Center, 80 Orville Dr.
Bohemia, NY 11716
Tel.: 516-563-7258
Fax: 516-563-4208

Computer Technologies, Inc. **(1)**
317 Ridgecrest Dr.
Lexington, NC 27292
Tel.: 919-547-1407
Fax: 919-632-8924

Darwin Data Systems **(1)**
1380 Energy Lane, Suite 202
Saint Paul, MN 55108
Tel.: 612-647-9946
Fax: 612-647-1621

EMS-Illinois **(1)**
600 N. Commons Dr.
Aurora, IL 60504
Tel.: 708-820-0060
Emp.: 36
Daniel E. Long *(Pres.)*

EMS-Michigan **(1)**
37610 Hillstech Dr.
Farmington Hills, MI 48018
Tel.: 313-553-4555
Emp.: 9
Provides Business Computers, Software & Services
S.I.C.: 7372; 7379
Cary Tripp *(Chief Oper. Officer)*

EMS-Ohio **(1)**
147 Bell St.
Cleveland, OH
Tel.: 216-247-2779
Emp.: 7
Joseph Schlanser *(Chief Oper. Officer)*

EMS-West **(1)**
22 Executive Park
Irvine, CA 92714
Tel.: 714-263-1000
Fax: 714-261-4013
Michelle Monnin *(Chief Oper. Officer)*

Integrated Business Systems **(1)**
3001 McInley Ave.
Des Moines, IA 50321
Tel.: 515-285-5582
Fax: 515-287-6800

MFG Systems **(1)**
Gamma Building, 4068 Mount Royal Blvd.
Allison Park, PA 15101
Tel.: 412-487-3410
Fax: 412-486-4190

Total Management Systems **(1)**
147 Bell St.
Chagrin Falls, OH 44022
Tel.: 216-247-2779
Fax: 216-247-4840

Wipfli, Ullrich, Bertelson **(1)**
119 Scott Street
Wausau, WI 54402
Tel.: 214-869-1719
Fax: 214-869-3749

Word-Tech Business Systems **(1)**
5625 Foxridge Dr.
Mission, KS 66202
Tel.: 913-722-3334
Fax: 913-722-3491

Non-U.S. Holdings:

Hitachi Zosen Systems, Inc **(1)**
Minato-Ku, 1-4-10, Takanawa,
Tokyo, 108, Japan
Tel.: 011-81-3-3473-7603
Fax: 011-81-6-448-6135

Jitachi Zosen Systems, Inc. **(1)**
Nishi-Ku, 1-22-17, Edobri,
Osaka, 550, Japan
Tel.: 011-81-6-448-5081
Fax: 011-81-6-448-6135

Open Systems Consulting **(1)**
#516 Teheran Officetel, Kangnam-Ku, 707-38 Yeoksam-Dong,
Seoul, Korea
Tel.: 011-82-2-568-8017

Open Systems Consulting **(1)**
79-6 Susung-3GA Susung-Gu,
Daegu, Korea
Tel.: 011-82-53-761-9071
Fax: 011-82-53-761-9073

EFFICIENT ENGINEERING CO.
130 Town Center Dr.
Troy, MI 48084
Tel.: 313-528-2888
Fax: 313-689-2117
Year Founded: 1939
Approx.Sls.: $14,000,000
Emp.: 300
Engineering, Drafting & Design of Tools, Dies, Special Machines, Welding Equipment & Computer Graphics
S.I.C.: 8711; 3541; 3542; 3544; 3549; 3559
Robert E. Baer *(Pres.)*
Sylvia Baer *(V.P.)*
Russ Imus *(V.P.-Sls.)*
Carol Camimer *(Treas.)*
Herb Brown *(Mgr.-Personnel)*
Principal(s):
Robert E. Baer

Computer Systems/Hardware:
NCR/IBM

Outside Service Firm(s):

Mellen, Seal & Pivoz*(Auditors)*
Birmingham, MI

Liberty Bank & Trust*(Major Banking Relationship)*
Troy, MI

EFFINGHAM-CLAY SERVICE CO.
410 S. Willow
Effingham, IL 62401
Tel.: 217-342-9231
Assets: $10,059,000
Earnings: $360,000
Net Worth: $10,059,000
Approx.Sls.: $36,000,000
Emp.: 100
Farmer-Owned; Sales Of Grain, Agricultural Supplies, Petroleum, Feed & Seed, Fertilizer, Chemicals, Livestock & Farm Equipment
S.I.C.: 5191; 5083; 5153; 5154; 5172
Phillip Hartke *(Pres.)*
Bill Kitley *(V.P.)*
Michael Buzzard *(Sec.)*
Stephen Wissink *(Controller)*
Robert Faulkner *(Gen. Mgr.)*
Robert Hoffman *(Mgr.-Opers.)*
Principal(s):
Phillip Hartke
Gerald Quade

Computer Systems/Hardware:
Honeywell

Outside Service Firm(s):

Illinois Auditors Association*(Auditors)*
Chicago, IL

Schneiderjon, Weber, Harvey & Stephens*(Legal Firm)*
Effingham, IL

First National Bank of Effingham*(Major Banking Relationship)*
Effingham, IL

EGAN COS.
7100 Medicine Lake Rd.
Minneapolis, MN 55427
Tel.: 612-544-4131 **MN**
Fax: 612-591-5560
Emp.: 350
Warm Air Heating & Air Conditioning Contractor
S.I.C.: 1711; 4911; 3086
Gerald L. Egan *(Pres. & Chief Exec. Officer)*
Edward J. Kocourek *(V.P., Sec. & Treas.)*

Outside Service Firm(s):

KPMG Peat Marwick*(Auditors)*
4200 Norwest Center, 90 S. 7th St.
Minneapolis, MN 55402
Tel.: 612-341-2222

O'Connor & Hannan*(Legal Firm)*
3800 IDS Tower, 80 S. 8th St.
Minneapolis, MN 55402
Tel.: 612-343-1124

First Bank Minneapolis*(Major Banking Relationship)*
P.O. Box A700, 120 S. Sixth St.
Minneapolis, MN 55480
Tel.: 612-370-4141

Subsidiaries:

Egan McKay Electrical Contractors **(1)**
7100 Medicine Lake Rd.
Minneapolis, MN 55427
Tel.: 612-544-4131
Fax: 612-591-5560
Electric Company
S.I.C.: 4911
Gerald L. Egan *(Pres.)*

Egan & Sons Co. **(1)**
7100 Medicine Lake Rd.
Minneapolis, MN 55427
Tel.: 612-544-4131
Approx.Sls.: $26,000,000
Warm Air Heating & Air Conditioning Contractor
S.I.C.: 1711
Ken Schultz *(Pres.)*
David Egan *(V.P.)*
Joe Egan *(V.P.)*
Edward J. Kocourek *(V.P., Sec. & Treas.)*
Richard L. Lebrun *(V.P.-Service Dept.)*

Egan & Sons Air Conditioning Co. **(1)**
7100 Medicine Lake Rd.
Minneapolis, MN 55427
Tel.: 612-544-4131
Fax: 612-591-5560
Approx.Sls.: $9,000,000
Warm Air Heating & Air Conditioning Contractor
S.I.C.: 1711
John A. Fischer *(Pres.)*
Edward J. Kocourek *(V.P.)*
Gerald L. Egan *(Sec. & Treas.)*

Egan & Sons Insulation **(1)**
7100 Medicine Lake Rd.
Minneapolis, MN 55427
Tel.: 612-544-4131
Fax: 612-591-5560
Insulation Company
S.I.C.: 3086
Gerald L. Egan *(Pres.)*

EGG HARBOR YACHT CO., INC.
801 Philadelphia Ave.
Egg Harbor City, NJ 08215
Tel.: 609-965-2300
Fax: 609-965-2870
Approx.Sls.: $31,100,000
Emp.: 225
Fiscal Year-end: 10/31/90
Fiberglass Pleasure Boats
S.I.C.: 3732
Charlie Underwood *(Pres.)*
Donald C. Leek *(V.P.)*
Rudy Lehnert *(V.P.)*

Outside Service Firm(s):

Zelnich & Associates*(Auditors)*
Philadelphia, PA

Pluese & Libotz*(Legal Firm)*
Cherry Hill, NJ

Midlantic National Bank/South*(Major Banking Relationship)*
Egg Harbor City, NJ

EGGLAND'S BEST, INC.
(Formerly C. R. Eggs, Inc.)
842 First Ave.
King of Prussia, PA 19406
Tel.: 215-265-6500
Fax: 215-265-8380
Year Founded: 1988
Emp.: 10
Fiscal Year-end: 12/31/90
Export
Marketing Services for Egglands Best Eggs
S.I.C.: 5144; 8742
Lucas J. Leone *(Chm. Bd.)*
Robert J. Fuhrman *(Pres.)*
Charles T. Lanktree *(Exec. V.P.)*
Kurt Misialek *(V.P.)*
Jeffrey L. Garwin, M.D., Ph.D. *(V.P.-Medical & Quality Assurance)*

Computer Systems/Hardware:
PC LAN

Outside Service Firm(s):

Arthur Andersen & Co.*(Auditors)*
1601 Market St.
Philadelphia, PA 19103
Tel.: 215-241-7300

Janney, Montgomery, Scott*(Investment Banker)*
16th & Market Sts.
Philadelphia, PA

Morgan, Lewis & Bockius*(Legal Firm)*
123 So. Broad St.
Philadelphia, PA 19109
Tel.: 215-875-2500

Meridian Bank*(Major Banking Relationship)*
One Meridian Plaza, 36th Fl.
Philadelphia, PA
Tel.: 215-854-3900

EGIZII ELECTRIC, INC.
700 N. MacArthur Blvd.
Springfield, IL 62702
Tel.: 217-528-4001 **IL**
Fax: 217-528-1677
Year Founded: 1959
Approx.Sls.: $14,000,000
Emp.: 205
Electrical Work; Commercial & Office Building New Construction; Warm Air Heating & Air Conditioning Contractor; Ventilation & Duct Work Contractor; Plumbing Contractors
S.I.C.: 1731; 1542; 1711
Robert Egizii *(Pres. & Chief Exec. Officerf)*
Danyal Mutman *(V.P. & Chief Fin. Officer)*
Howard Heppler *(V.P.)*
Dorse Taylor *(V.P.)*
Mervin Thompson *(V.P.)*

Outside Service Firm(s):

Pehlman & Dold*(Auditors)*
Springfield, IL

First National Bank*(Major Banking Relationship)*
Springfield, IL

EGYPTIAN LACQUER MANUFACTURING COMPANY, INC.
555 Sagamore Pkwy., S.
Lafayette, IN 47905
Mailing Address:
P.O. Box 4449,
Lafayette, IN 47903
Tel.: 317-447-2136 **IN**
Fax: 317-447-0249
Year Founded: 1876
Approx.Sls.: $14,000,000
Emp.: 110
Mfr. of Enamels, Lacquer, Bases, Dopes, Thinner; Chemical Coatings
S.I.C.: 2851
George H. DeVault *(Pres.)*
Robert A. Richardson *(V.P. & Gen. Mgr.)*
Principal(s):
Louis A. Ruckgaber, Jr.

Outside Service Firm(s):

Lafayette National Bank*(Major Banking Relationship)*
Lafayette, IN

Subsidiary:

Egyptian Lacquer Mfg. Co. **(1)**
4 Fort Granger Dr.
Franklin, TN 37064
Tel.: 615-798-3881
Mfr. of Chemical Coatings
S.I.C.: 2851
George Bruner *(V.P. & Gen. Mgr.)*

800-FLOWERS
1600 Stewart Ave.
Westbury, NY 11590
Tel.: 516-237-6000
Fax: 516-237-6060
Approx.Sls.: $50,000,000
Emp.: 350
Flower & Gift Giving Services, Direct Marketing
S.I.C.: 5992
James McCann *(Pres.)*
Chris McCann *(V.P.-Opers.)*
Susan Ashbridge *(V.P.-Prod. Devel.)*
Glenn Reed *(Chief Fin. Officer)*
Susan Lesica *(Dir.-Adv.)*
Tracey Gittere *(Dir.-Communications)*
Alyson Graci *(Mgr.-Mngmt. Information Systems)*
Beverly Thurber *(Mgr.-Mngmt. Information Systems)*

84 LUMBER CO.
St. Rte. #519
Eighty Four, PA 15384
Tel.: 412-228-8820
Fax: 412-225-2530
Approx.Sls.: $800,000,000
Emp.: 3,800
Retail Lumber & Home Building Supplies
S.I.C.: 5211
Joseph A. Hardy, Sr. *(Chm., Pres. & Chief Exec. Officer)*
Jerry Smith *(Exec. V.P.)*
Denny Brua *(V.P.-Pur.)*
Kurt Stump *(V.P.-Fin.)*
Jeanen Tomshay *(V.P.-Mktg.)*
Sid McCallister *(Dir.-Mngmt. Information Service)*

Outside Service Firm(s):

Deloitte & Touche*(Auditors)*
2400 One PPG Place
Pittsburgh, PA 15222
Tel.: 412-281-2232

EINSTEIN MOOMJY INC.
20 Hook Mountain Rd.
Pine Brook, NJ 07058
Mailing Address:
P.O. Box 673,
Pine Brook, NJ 07058
Tel.: 201-575-0895

Einstein Moomjy Inc.—(Continued)

Fax: 201-575-4306
Year Founded: 1953
Approx.Sls.: $15,600,000
Emp.: 150
Retail Floor Covering; Einstein Moomjy, The Carpet Department Store
S.I.C.: 5713
Walter Moomjy *(Chm. Bd.)*
Ted Einstein *(Pres.)*
Albert Moomjy *(V.P.)*
Ernst Einstein *(Sec. & Treas.)*
Vincent M. Dailey, Sr. *(Comptroller)*

eire PARTNERS INC.

EIRE PARTNERS, INC.
230 W. Superior St., Ste. 600
Chicago, IL 60610
Tel.: 312-335-4330
Fax: 312-335-8339
Year Founded: 1987
Approx.Billings: $35,000,000
Emp.: 40
Advertising, Sales Promo. & Direct Mktg.
Corporate Giving Program: Charity SIDS Foundation
David F. Sheehan *(Mng. Partner & Chief Exec. Officer)*
Anne H. Cox *(Mng. Partner & Chief Fin. Officer)*
E. James Kearney *(Mng. Partner & Chief Oper. Officer)*
Jarrett M. Nathan *(Mng. Partner & Creative Dir.)*
Ellissa Polston *(V.P., Mngmt. Supvr.)*
Janet Kelly *(V.P., Media Dir.)*
Marcia Rubino *(Controller)*
Anne Brennan *(Accounting Clerk)*

Computer Systems/Hardware:
IBM, MacIntosh

EJL
EISAMAN, JOHNS & LAWS ADVERTISING, INC.

EISAMAN, JOHNS & LAWS ADVERTISING, INC.
5700 Wilshire Blvd.
Los Angeles, CA 90036
Tel.: 213-932-1234
Fax: 213-965-6134
Year Founded: 1959
Approx.Billings: $165,000,000
Emp.: 210
Dennis R. Coe *(Pres.)*
Dean R. Laws *(Pres.)*
Michele (Mike) de Maio *(Pres., Central Div., Chicago)*
Richard J. Westman *(Pres., Southwest Div., Houston)*
Adrienne Hall *(Vice Chm.)*
Jack J. Leener *(Exec. V.P.)*
Anna Laws *(Sec. & Controller)*
Joe R. Eisaman *(Chm. Emeritus)*

LEO EISENBERG & CO., INC.
1101 Walnut, Ste. 800
Kansas City, MO 64106
Tel.: 816-221-8000
Fax: 816-346-6355
Emp.: 200
Real Estate Developers & Brokers
S.I.C.: 6552; 6531
Irv Maizlish *(Chm. Bd.)*
Bob Johnson *(Pres.)*
Ron Bennett *(Exec. V.P.)*
Bill Knoth *(Exec. V.P.)*
Richard Baier *(Sr. V.P.)*
John Rubinstein *(Sr. V.P.)*
Cindi Dodson *(Dir.-Pub. Rels.)*

No. of U.S. Offices: 9

Outside Service Firm(s):

Mercantile Bank of Missouri*(Major Banking Relationship)*
Kansas City, MO

EISNER & ASSOCIATES, INC.
ADVERTISING•PUBLIC RELATIONS

EISNER & ASSOCIATES, INC.
12 W. Madison St.
Baltimore, MD 21201
Tel.: 410-685-3390
Fax: 410-685-0387
Year Founded: 1939
Approx.Billings: $65,000,000
Emp.: 65
Advertising, Public Relations, Graphic Design, Sales Promotion, Direct Marketing & Commercial Production
Henry W. Eisner *(Chm. Emeritus)*
Steven C. Eisner *(Pres. & Chief Exec. Officer)*
Sharyn Williamson *(Exec. V.P., Strategic Plng.)*
John Ciotti *(Exec. V.P., Chief Fin. Officer)*
Joseph Bruce *(Sr. V.P., Strategic Plng.)*
Julie Mercer *(Sr. V.P., Corp. Devel.)*
Linda Stanley *(Dir., Office Services)*

WILLIAM EISNER & ASSOCIATES INC.
P.O. Box 28800
Milwaukee, WI 53220
Tel.: 414-425-8800
Fax: 414-425-0021
Year Founded: 1959
Approx.Billings: $27,400,000
Emp.: 48
Strategic Planning, In-House Broadcast Facilities, Spot Market Media Negotiation, Data Base Research, Broadcast Retail Services
Corporate Giving Program: Greater Milwaukee Initiative, Charitable contributions equivalent to 2% or more of average domestic pre-tax earnings in a year.
Employee Matching Gifts Program: 401 (k) Plan.
Elaine B. Eisner *(Chm. Bd.)*
Bill Eisner, Jr. *(Pres., Chief Exec. Officer & Creative Dir.)*
Craig L. Gruenberg *(Exec. V.P., Chief Oper. Officer)*
Barb Olson *(Admin. & Opers.)*
Jon P. Glass *(Controller)*

EL CAMINO RESOURCES, LTD.
8550 Balboa Blvd., Ste. 140
Northridge, CA 91325
Tel.: 818-895-6600 **CA**
Fax: 818-894-3589
Year Founded: 1979
Assets: $186,282,314
Liabilities: $168,280,709
Net Worth: $18,001,605
Approx.Sls.: $255,000,000
Emp.: 175
Fiscal Year-end: 4/30/88
Import Export
Retail & Lease Computers
S.I.C.: 5734; 7377
David E. Harmon *(Chm. Bd., Pres., Chief Exec. & Chief Oper. Officer)*
Mel Kleinman *(V.P.-Sls.)*
Brian O'Fria *(V.P.-Fin.)*
David Wolfs *(V.P.-Mktg.)*
Mike Lockwood *(Gen. Counsel)*
Principal(s):
David E. Harmon
Mel Kleinman
David Wolfs

No. of U.S. Offices: 10

Computer Systems/Hardware:
Point Four

Outside Service Firm(s):

Mutual of New York*(Group Insurer)*
New York, NY

Continental Bank N. A.*(Major Banking Relationship)*
231 S. LaSalle St.
Chicago, IL 60697
Tel.: 312-828-2345
Tel.: 800-426-5754
Telex: 312-828-1783

EL DORADO TIRE CO.
1120 E. Long Lake Rd.
Troy, MI 48098
Tel.: 313-528-3020 **MI**
Fax: 313-528-8132
Year Founded: 1966
Approx.Sls.: $48,000,000
Emp.: 10
Tire & Inner Tube Sls.
S.I.C.: 5014
Herman R. Calamari *(Chm. Bd.)*
James Tyler *(Pres.)*
Thomas O. Murphy *(V.P.-Fin.)*
Marvin Fox *(Treas.)*

EL TORITO RESTAURANTS, INC.
2450 White Rd.
Irvine, CA 92417
Tel.: 714-863-6400
Fax: 714-863-8617
Year Founded: 1954
Approx.Sls.: $318,000,000
Emp.: 9,612
Mexican Restaurant Chain
S.I.C.: 5812
Norm Haberman *(Chm. Bd.)*
Martin M. Casey *(Pres. & Chief Exec. Officer)*
James W. Stryker *(Chief Fin. Officer)*
Russ Bendel *(Exec. V.P.-Opers.)*
Richard Butler *(Exec. V.P.-Mktg.)*
Mark Carneal *(V.P.-Human Resources)*
Marc Faircloth *(V.P.-Facilities)*
Ed Bartholemy *(V.P.-Fin.)*

ELAN FOODS
28 Church Street, Ste. 206
Buffalo, NY 14202
Tel.: 716-854-2444
Fax: 716-854-5235
Sales Range: $10-19 Million
Emp.: 8
Fiscal Year-end: 3/31/91
Export
Markets Elan Premium Frozen Yogurt
S.I.C.: 5143
James Biltekoff *(Pres.)*
Joanne Biltekoff *(V.P.)*
Bruce Johnson *(Controller)*

ELASTIC MATERIALS, INC.
200 Wellar Dr.
Smithville, OH 44677
Mailing Address:
P.O. Box 257,
Smithville, OH 44677
Tel.: 216-669-3441
Fax: 216-669-2291
Approx.Sls.: $10,000,000
Emp.: 12
Manufacture Thermoplastic Tar Emulsion & Pavement Sealer, Primarily for Construction Industry
S.I.C.: 2951; 1791
Robert D. Harris *(Pres. & Chief Oper. Officer)*
Jeffrey Blank *(Sec. & Dir.-Mktg.)*
Principal(s):
Robert D. Harris
Jeffrey Blank

Outside Service Firm(s):

Wayne County National Bank*(Major Banking Relationship)*
Wooster, OH

ELASTOMERIC TECHNOLOGIES, INC.
2940 Turnpike Dr.
Hatboro, PA 19040
Tel.: 215-672-0787 **PA**
Telex: 387236
Fax: 215-672-4633
Emp.: 50
Fiscal Year-end: 3/31/91
Project Engineering & Management
S.I.C.: 3678; 8711
Robin Weber *(Chm. Bd. & Pres.)*
Andrew Strange *(V.P.-Engrng.)*
David J. Zecchin *(V.P.-Fin.)*
Jane K. Kunihiro *(Dir.-Mfg.)*
Thomas G. Campbell *(Mgr.-Reg. Sls.)*
George Glatts, III *(Mgr.-Eastern Reg. Sls. Engrng.)*
Naomi McAuliff *(Mgr.-Quality Assurance)*
Richard Rosenberger *(Mgr.-Matls.)*
John Seibert *(Mgr.-Western Reg. Sls. Engrng.)*

No. of Mfg. Plants/Facilities: 1
No. of U.S. Offices: 1

Outside Service Firm(s):

Kreischer, Miller & Company*(Auditors)*
Horsham, PA

Wolf, Block, Schorr & Solis-Cohen*(Legal Firm)*
Packard Bldg.,
Philadelphia, PA 19102

Meridian Bank*(Major Banking Relationship)*
Malvern, PA

ELBECO INCORPORATED
4207 Pottsville Pike
Reading, PA 19603
Mailing Address:
P.O. Box 13099
Reading, PA 19612
Tel.: 215-921-0651
Fax: 215-921-8651
Emp.: 600
Mfr. of Elbeco Men's Shirts & Trousers
S.I.C.: 2321; 2325
Lee H. Lurio *(Pres. & Treas.)*
John J. Campbell *(Sr. V.P.)*
David Lurio *(V.P.-Mktg.)*
Mary Seiders *(V.P.-Sls.)*

ELBERTA CRATE & BOX COMPANY
P.O. Box 795, 606 Dorthan Hwy.
Bainbridge, GA 31717
Tel.: 912-246-2266 **GA**
Fax: 912-246-0387
Year Founded: 1928
Approx.Sls.: $25,000,000
Emp.: 400
Import Export
Mfr. of Wood Fruit Crates; Wirebound; Boxes; Pallets
S.I.C.: 2449; 2448
John M. Simmons *(Chm. Bd.)*
D. Ramsay Simmons, Jr. *(Pres.)*
D. Ramsay Simmons, III *(V.P., Sec. & Treas.)*

Outside Service Firm(s):

Redford A. Cherry*(Auditors)*
Tallahasee, FL

Bainbridge National Bank*(Major Banking Relationship)*
Bainbridge, GA

Kirbo & Bridges*(Legal Firm)*
Bainbridge, GA

THE ELDER-BEERMAN STORES CORP.
3155 El-Bee Rd.
Dayton, OH 45439
Mailing Address:
P.O. Box 1448,
Dayton, OH 45401-1448
Tel.: 513-296-2700 **OH**
Fax: 513-296-2915 (Buyers)
Fax: 513-296-4625 (Exec.)
Fax: 513-296-4597 (Mlrm.)
Year Founded: 1883
Sales Range: $100-499 Million
Emp.: 8,500
Import
Retail Department & Furniture Stores
S.I.C.: 5712; 5311; 5661
Herbert O. Glaser *(Chm. Bd. & Chief Oper. Officer)*
Barbara B. Weprin *(Vice Chm.)*
Milton E. Hartley *(Pres. & Chief Exec. Officer)*
Bruce A. Macke *(Chief Fin. Officer & Exec. V.P.)*
Donald L. DeGraeve *(Exec. V.P.-Mdsg.)*
Kenneth R. Epstein *(Exec. V.P.-Stores)*
Leonard B. Peal *(Exec. V.P.-Cost & Leased Depts.)*
Raymond Blanton *(Sr. V.P.)*
Rafael Furst *(Sr. V.P. & Treas.)*
Patricia L. Gifford *(Sr. V.P.-Human Resources)*
James A. Lance *(Sr. V.P.)*
David W. Lovejoy *(Sr. V.P. & Controller)*
James A. Lance *(Sr. V.P.-Mngmt. Info. Systems)*
Jack Mullen *(Sr. V.P.-Adv. & Sls. Promo.)*
Jeff Brown *(V.P.-Store Planning)*
Guenter C. Kass *(V.P.-Pur.)*
David H. McDonald *(V.P.-Real Estate)*
David E. Matson *(V.P. & Corp. Dir.-Asset Protection)*
Raymond Clayman *(Gen. Counsel)*
Harry Jensen *(Sec.)*
Marilyn Molnar *(Dir.-Personnel Training & Devel.)*
Larry Washing *(Dir.-Employee Benefits)*
Max Gutmann *(Merger & Acquisition Mgr.)*
Evelyn L. Collier *(Exec. Sec.)*

Computer Systems/Hardware:
Tandem, NCR

Outside Service Firm(s):

Deloitte & Touche*(Auditors)*
1700 Courthouse Plaza NE
Dayton, OH 45401
Tel.: 513-223-8821

Factory Mutual*(Commercial Insurance Carrier)*
Cleveland, OH

Clayman & Williamson*(Legal Firm)*
11 W. Monument Bldg., Ste. 402
Dayton, OH 45402
Tel.: 513-224-1461

Bank One*(Major Banking Relationship)*
Kettering Tower
Dayton, OH 45401
Tel.: 513-449-8600

Divisions:

Bee-Gee Shoe Div. **(1)**
153 E. Helena St.
Dayton, OH 45404
Tel.: 513-223-4241 (100%)
Fax: 513-223-4435
Emp.: 7,000
Import
Computer Systems/Hardware:
Tandem, NCR
108 El-Bee Shoe Outlet Stores
S.I.C.: 5661
Raymond L. Blanton *(Pres. & Chief Exec. Officer)*
Jay D. Gutmann *(Exec. V.P.)*
Robert D. Wolf *(Sr. V.P.)*
Alan R. Berman *(V.P. & Controller)*
Troy E. Hayward *(V.P.-Human Resources)*
Michael C. Kruthaupt *(V.P. & Dir.-Stores, Outlet Div.)*

Elder-Beerman Stores Div. **(1)**
3155 El-Bee Road
Dayton, OH 45439
Tel.: 513-296-2700
Fax: 513-296-2915
Import
Computer Systems/Hardware:
Tandem, NCR
Operator of 47 Total Dept. Stores
S.I.C.: 5311
Herbert O. Glaser *(Chm. Bd. & Chief Oper. Officer)*
Bruce A. Macke *(Exec. V.P. & Chief Fin. Officer)*
Donald L. DeGraeve *(Exec. V.P.-Mdsg.)*
Charles P. Shaffer *(Sr. V.P. & Gen. Mgr.-Soft Home, Hard Lines & Cosmetics Divisions)*
John H. Snyder *(Sr. V.P. & Dir. -Stores)*
Thomas K. Kingery *(Sr. V.P. & Dir.-Stores)*
Carol L. Bernstein *(V.P. & Group Dir. of Stores, Northern Div.)*
James A. Lance *(Sr. V.P.-Information Systems)*
James A. Hopp *(Sr. V.P. & Gen. Mdsg. Mgr.-Women's Apparel)*
Jack Mullen *(V.P.-Adv.)*
Guenter C. Kass *(V.P.-Pur.)*
Patricia L. Gifford *(V.P. & Dir.-Human Resources)*
Jeff Brown *(V.P.-Store Plng.)*
Anthony A. Singleton *(V.P.-Data Processing)*

Subsidiaries:

The El-Bee Chargit Corp. **(1)**
3155 Elbee Road
Dayton, OH 45439
Tel.: 513-296-2700 (100%)
Fax: 513-296-4674
Computer Systems/Hardware:
Tandem, NCR
Credit Financing Sub.
S.I.C.: 6153
Herbert O. Glaser *(Chm. Bd.)*
Rafael Furst *(Pres. & Treas.)*
Timothy W. Broderick *(V.P.)*
David W. Lovejoy *(V.P.)*
Deanna R. Leadingham *(V.P.)*
Harry A. Jensen *(Sec.)*

Margo's La Mode, Inc. **(1)**
3909 Live Oak Dr.
Dallas, TX 75204
Tel.: 214-824-7080 (100%)
Fax: 214-823-6757
Approx.Sls.: $44,000,000
Emp.: 680
Fiscal Year-end: 12/31/90
Import
Operator of 102 Specialty Stores for Misses
S.I.C.: 5632
Tom Unrine *(Pres. & Chief Oper. Officer)*
Mary M. Stafford *(V.P.-Human Resources)*
Michael W. Webb *(V.P., Controller & Asst. Treas.)*
Shirley Holly *(Sec.)*

Affiliate:

All World Travel Service, Inc. **(1)**
111 West First St.
Dayton, OH 45402
Tel.: 513-222-1220 (50%)
Travel Bureau
S.I.C.: 4724
Wes S. Hamden *(Pres.)*
Rafael Furst *(V.P.)*
Bruce A. Macke *(V.P.)*
David W. Lovejoy *(V.P. & Treas.)*
Douglas DeRose *(Controller)*
Harry A. Jensen *(Sec.)*

ELDER MANUFACTURING COMPANY
12747 Olive St.
Creve Coeur, MO 63166
Mailing Address:
P.O. Box 273
St. Louis, MO 63166
Tel.: 314-469-1120
Approx.Sls.: $20,000,000
Emp.: 1,000
Fiscal Year-end: 12/31/90
Tom Sawyer & Elderado Apparel for Boys & Young Men, Men's Shirts
S.I.C.: 2321; 2311; 2322; 2325; 2326; 2329; 2331; 2335; 2337; 2339
Ronald Cher *(Pres.)*
Joe Mercurio *(V.P.)*

ELDORADO CHEMICAL COMPANY
14350 Lookout Rd.
San Antonio, TX 78233
Mailing Address:
P.O. Box 34837,
San Antonio, TX 78265-4837
Tel.: 210-653-9323
Fax: 210-653-0825
Approx.Sls.: $11,000,000
Emp.: 50
Manufacture Speciality Cleaning Products
S.I.C.: 2842
Joseph Fredrickson *(Pres.)*
Pat Smith *(V.P.)*
Kandee Jo Walker *(Sec. & Treas.)*

Outside Service Firm(s):

Crawford, Lawlor, Iverson & Company*(Auditors)*
San Antonio, TX

ELECTRIC FURNACE CO.
435 W. Wilson St.
Salem, OH 44460-0150
Tel.: 216-332-4661 **OH**
Telex: 98-2459
Fax: 216-332-1853
Year Founded: 1923
Approx.Sls.: $40,000,000
Emp.: 197
Fiscal Year-end: 9/30/90
Export
Custom Design, Mfr. & Installation of Industrial Heat Processing Equipment; Commercial Heat Treating; Machine Fabricators
S.I.C.: 3567
Corporate Giving Program: United Way
Jacob O. Kamm *(Chm. Bd., Pres. & Chief Exec. Officer)*
R.E. Coe *(Vice Chm.)*
J.O. Kamm *(Chief Fin. Officer)*
D. Hessler *(Sec. & Gen. Counsel)*
William Ferguson *(Dir.-Pur.)*
J.O. Kamm, II *(Dir.-Pur.)*
C.P. Kamm *(Mgr.-Pension Admin. & Risk Mngmt.)*
G.J. Greenisen *(Mgr.-Sls.)*
J.M. Magyaros *(Mgr.-Intl. Sls.)*
P.A. Simonsic *(Mgr.-Pension Admin. & Risk Mngmt.)*
James Barclay *(Mgr.-Chief Chemist)*
Bruce Hoyt *(Quality Control)*

No. of Mfg. Plants/Facilities: 3
No. of U.S. Offices: 2
No. of Foreign Offices: 4

Computer Systems/Hardware:
UNISYS 1860

Outside Service Firm(s):

Ernst & Young*(Auditors)*
1300 Huntington Bldg.
Cleveland, OH 44115
Tel.: 216-861-5000

Aetna Life & Casualty*(Group Insurer)*
151 Farmington Avenue
Hartford, CT 06156
Tel.: 203-273-2128
Fax: 203-729-4295

Hornblower & Weeks*(Investment Banker)*
New York, NY

Squire, Sanders & Dempsey*(Legal Firm)*
41 S. High Street
Columbus, OH 43215

Midwest Bank & Trust Co.*(Major Banking Relationship)*
Cleveland, OH

Division:

Industrial Products Division **(1)**
435 W. Wilson St.
Salem, OH 44460
Tel.: 216-332-4661 (100%)
Fax: 216-332-1853
Approx.Sls.: $1,000,000
Machine Fabricators
S.I.C.: 3599
B. Rhodes *(Mgr.-Oper.)*
J.O. Kamm *(Chief Fin. Officer)*

Subsidiaries:

Turner Machine Company **(1)**
435 W. Wilson St.
Salem, OH 44460
Tel.: 216-332-4661 (100%)
Fax: 216-332-1853
Emp.: 17
Export
Machine Fabrication
S.I.C.: 3599
Barry Rhodes *(Chief Oper. Officer)*
Phil Greenisen *(Mktg.)*
S. Mix *(Purchasing)*

Wilkinson Company, Inc. **(1)**
1530 Commerce Dr.
Stow, OH 44224
Tel.: 216-686-9922 (100%)
Fax: 216-686-9412
Approx.Sls.: $4,000,000
Emp.: 70
Export
Design, Mfr. & Installation of Chutes for the Construction Industry
S.I.C.: 3443
J.O. Kamm *(Chm. & Chief Exec. Officer)*
T.J. Hoover *(V.P.-Sls.)*
T.J. Hoover *(V.P.-Sls.)*
W. Ferguson *(Dir.-Pur.)*
G. Greenisen *(Dir.-Mktg.)*
C.P. Kamm *(Treas.)*

Non-U.S. Holdings:

Canefco Limited **(1)**
50 Milne Ave.
Scarborough, ON M1L 1K3, Canada
Tel.: 416-691-2117 (100%)
Approx.Sls.: $12,000,000
Emp.: 17
Custom Design, Mfr. & Installation of Industrial Heat Processing Equipment, Specializing in the Aluminum Industry
S.I.C.: 3433
J.O. Kamm *(Chm.)*
Robert F. Carmichael *(Pres.)*
M. Dick *(Sales)*

Electric Furnace France S.A.R.L. **(1)**
32, Place St. Geoges 75009
Paris, France
Tel.: 33-01-8789247 (95%)
Emp.: 3
Industrial Heat Processing Equipment
S.I.C.: 5074
Franis Simoni *(Chief Oper. Officer)*
A.G. Cornet *(Mgr.)*

Electric Furnace Germany, GmbH **(1)**
Ringstrasse 54, Postfach 306 416
Kleve, Germany (100%)
Industrial Heat Processing Equipment
S.I.C.: 3567
A. G. Cornet *(Mng. Dir.)*

ELECTRIC POWER EQUIPMENT CO.
60 E. Spring St.
Columbus, OH 43215
Tel.: 614-224-5215 **OH**
Fax: 614-461-9098
Year Founded: 1920
Assets: $4,745,800
Liabilities: $558,000

Electric Power Equipment Co.—(Continued)

Net Worth: $4,187,800
Sales Range: $10-19 Million
Emp.: 70
Fiscal Year-end: 1/31/92
Electrical Construction & Maintenance
S.I.C.: 1731
James C. McAtee *(Pres.)*
Robert E. Lash *(V.P. & Data Processing Dir.)*
W.B. Langley *(Treas.)*
James B. Feibel *(Sec. & Gen. Counsel)*
J.K. Jansen *(Pur. Dir.)*

Principal(s):
James C. McAtee

No. of Mfg. Plants/Facilities: 1
No. of U.S. Offices: 1

Computer Systems/Hardware:
DEC 1180

Outside Service Firm(s):

Ickert & Mahoney*(Auditors)*
Columbus, OH

Benesch, Friedlander, Coplan & Aronoff*(Legal Firm)*
Columbus, OH

Fifth Third Bank*(Major Banking Relationship)*
Columbus, OH

The Huntington National Bank*(Major Banking Relationship)*
41 S. High St.
Columbus, OH 43216

ELECTRIC SPECIALTY & SUPPLY CORP.
817 Albany St.
Boston, MA 02119
Tel.: 617-442-6400 **MA**
Fax: 617-442-9155
Year Founded: 1948
Approx.Sls.: $38,000,000
Emp.: 120
Fiscal Year-end: 12/31/90
Wholesale of Electric Supplies Including Wire & Cable
S.I.C.: 5063
Douglas A. Hoffman *(Pres.)*
Simon Feuz *(Chief Fin. Officer)*
Richard DeMarco *(V.P.-Sls.)*
David Ogilvy *(Controller)*
Jay Skarbinski *(Pur. Agent)*

No. of U.S. Offices: 7

Computer Systems/Hardware:
Basic 4

Outside Service Firm(s):

Baril & Smith*(Auditors)*
Wakefield, MA

Guardian Life Insurance Co.*(Group Insurer)*
New York, NY

Medical Claims Service*(Group Insurer)*
Quincy, MA

Sullivan & Worcester*(Legal Firm)*
One Post Office Square, 100 Federal St.
Boston, MA 02110
Tel.: 617-338-2800

Bank of New England*(Major Banking Relationship)*
28 State Street
Boston, MA 02109
Tel.: 617-742-4000

First National Bank of Boston*(Major Banking Relationship)*
Mail Stop 44-02-09, P.O. Box 644
Boston, MA 02102-0644
Tel.: 617-575-2555

Subsidiaries:

Electric Specialty & Supply **(1)**
71 Lowell Rd.
Salem, NH 03079
Tel.: 603-893-3004
Emp.: 7
Electrical Wholesale Supplies
S.I.C.: 5063
Don Babin *(Branch Mgr.)*

Electric Specialty & Supply **(1)**
20 Sturtevant St.
Somerville, MA 02143
Tel.: 617-625-6400
Emp.: 28
Electrical Wholesale Supplies
S.I.C.: 5063
Howard Garber *(Branch Mgr.)*

Electric Specialty & Supply **(1)**
389 N. Frontage Rd., I 95
New London, CT 06320
Tel.: 203-443-7191
Emp.: 11
Electrical Wholesale Supplies
S.I.C.: 5063

Electric Specialty & Supply **(1)**
2100 Thomaston Ave.
Waterbury, CT 06704
Tel.: 203-754-0433
Emp.: 10
Electrical Wholesale Supplies
S.I.C.: 5063
Tom Riffle *(Branch Mgr.)*

ELECTRICAL EQUIPMENT COMPANY
1440 Diggs Dr.
Raleigh, NC 27603-2755
Tel.: 919-828-5411
Fax: 919-832-6306
Approx.Sls.: $30,000,000
Emp.: 65
Distributor & Service Electrical Motors & Equipment
S.I.C.: 5063; 7629; 7694
T.J. Walker *(Gen. Mgr. & Sec.)*

Outside Service Firm(s):

McGladrey & Pullen*(Auditors)*
Raleigh, NC

Wolff & Martin*(Legal Firm)*
Raleigh, NC

Wachovia Bank of North Carolina, N.A.*(Major Banking Relationship)*
P.O. Box 27886, 227 Fayetteville St.
Raleigh, NC 27611
Tel.: 919-755-7730

Branch:

Electrical Equipment Company **(1)**
1807 Blvd. W.
Richmond, VA 23230
Tel.: 804-353-7841
Emp.: 225
Distributes & Services Electrical Motors & Equipment
S.I.C.: 5063; 7629; 7694
Richard L. Hedgepath *(Pres. & Gen. Mgr.)*
J. Allen Warren *(V.P.)*

ELECTRICAL INSULATION SUPPLIERS
300 N. Mannheim Rd.
Hillside, IL 60162
Tel.: 708-547-5400
Fax: 708-547-7538
Approx.Sls.: $65,000,000
Emp.: 35
Fiscal Year-end: 10/31/91
Distr. of Industrial & Electrical Equip.; 3M Tape, GE Parts & Brushes & Electronic Materials for Manufacturing & Assembly
S.I.C.: 5063
Steve Kendall *(Chief Exec. Officer)*
Charles Schoen *(Pres.)*
Dwane Thomas *(V.P.-Opers.)*
Bill Knight *(V.P.-Opers.)*
Robert Watts *(Chief Fin. Officer)*
Mark Brayman *(Controller)*
Bob Gannon *(Gen. Mgr.-Central Div.)*
Dave Bradfield *(Gen. Mgr.-Eastern Div.)*
Joe Rodgers *(Gen. Mgr.-Pacific Div.)*
Robert Smith *(Mgr.-Data Processing)*
Ed Partyka *(Mgr.-Mktg.)*
Bob McCarley *(Mgr.-Mktg.)*
John Howell *(Mgr. Pur.)*
Lou Ann Melton *(Mgr.-Payroll & Benefits)*
Risa Fischer *(Asst. Corp. Admin.)*
Pauline Bailey *(Adv. Coord.)*
Howard Hintermister *(Mgr.-Export Sls.)*

Computer Systems/Hardware:
IBM AS/400

Divisions:

Conductors Unlimited **(1)**
4934 Distribution Dr.
Tampa, FL 33605
Tel.: 813-248-1620
Distr. of Industrial & Electrical Equipment
S.I.C.: 5063
Ron Novak *(Branch Mgr.)*

Missile Supply Co. **(1)**
1347 S. 300 West
Salt Lake City, UT 84115
Tel.: 801-483-1226
Distr. of Industrial & Electrical Equipment
S.I.C.: 5063
Gary Johnson *(Business Mgr.)*

ELECTRICAL WHOLESALE SUPPLY COMPANY, INC.
P.O. Box 1835, 1990 Rollandet Ave.
Idaho Falls, ID 83403
Tel.: 208-523-2800 **ID**
Fax: 208-522-0212
Year Founded: 1962
Approx.Sls.: $17,000,000
Emp.: 49
Import Export
Wholesale Distribution of Electrical Construction Materials
S.I.C.: 5063
Corporate Giving Program: United Way, Local Charities & Colleges; All Set by the Board of Directors
Harold Davis *(Chm.)*
Reeve Norman *(Vice-Chm., Pres. & Chief Exec. Officer)*
John M. Sharp *(Sec.)*
Richard Webster *(Pur. Agent)*

Principal(s):
Harold Davis
Reeve Norman
Gary Gardner

Outside Service Firm(s):

Burnett, Humphreys & Mason*(Auditors)*
Idaho Falls, ID

West One Bancorp*(Major Banking Relationship)*
Idaho Falls, ID

ELECTRO AD AGENCY, INC.

10950 Washington Blvd.
Culver City, CA 90230
Tel.: 310-558-2645
Fax: 310-558-2494
Year Founded: 1957
Approx.Billings: $10,600,000
Emp.: 20
Electronic Components & Computer Products
Tom Thorson *(V.P., Dir. Adv.)*
Pat Green *(Office Mgr.)*

ELECTRO BRAND, INC.
5410 W. Roosevelt Rd.
Chicago, IL 60650
Tel.: 312-261-5000 **IL**
Fax: 312-261-5091
Year Founded: 1961
Emp.: 20
Import Export
Wholesale Distributor of Television Sets, Radios, High Fidelity Equipment, Tape Players & Recorders
S.I.C.: 5064
Richard Ettelson *(Chm. Bd. & Pres.)*
Stephen Ettelson *(V.P. & Sec.)*

Outside Service Firm(s):

LaSalle National Bank*(Major Banking Relationship)*
135 S. LaSalle St.
Chicago, IL 60603
Tel.: 312-443-2440
Fax: 312-443-2819

ELECTRO-COATINGS, INC.
(Sub. of EC Industries, Inc.)
1401 Park Ave.
Emeryville, CA 94608
Tel.: 510-653-5303
Fax: 510-428-1551
Year Founded: 1947
Approx.Sls.: $12,000,000
Emp.: 100
Industrial Metal Coatings & Finishes
S.I.C.: 2899
Kent Garvens *(Pres.)*
Kathy Poling *(Sec.)*

ELECTRO DYNAMICS CRYSTAL CORPORATION
9075 Cody
Overland Park, KS 66214
Tel.: 913-888-1750
Fax: 913-888-1260
Emp.: 100
Quartz Crystals
S.I.C.: 3679
John Hardesty *(Pres.)*
Tim Abbott *(V.P.-Sls. & Gen. Mgr.)*
Karen Hadley *(Mgr.-Sls.)*
Janice Smeall *(Mgr.-Mktg.)*
Jennine Stump *(Dir.-Mfg.)*

ELECTRO FIBEROPTICS CORPORATION
56 Hudson St.
Northborough, MA 01532
Tel.: 508-393-3753
Tel.: 800-445-7016 **MA**
Fax: 508-393-7360
Year Founded: 1991
Emp.: 45
Fiscal Year-end: 12/31/91
Import Export
Designs, Manufactures & Sells Fiberoptic Components & Illumination Systems For Microscopy, Traffic Signs & Pedestrian Signals
S.I.C.: 3669; 3829
Konrad Lisi *(Pres.)*
Bradley Goodrich *(V.P.-Fin. & Treas.)*
Elizabeth Cusanello *(Dir.-Sls. Admin.)*
Timothy Hales *(Mgr.-Opers.)*
Henry Kroll *(Mgr.-Engrng.)*
Roy Lesage *(Mgr.-Pur.)*
Raymond Rossatti *(Mgr.-Quality Control)*
William Corson Wyman *(Mgr.-Personnel)*

No. of Mfg. Plants/Facilities: 1
No. of U.S. Offices: 1

Computer Systems/Hardware:
IBM

Outside Service Firm(s):

O'Connor, Maloney & Co.*(Auditors)*
Worcester, MA

Safety Fund National Bank*(Major Banking Relationship)*
Northborough, MA

ELECTRO-MATIC PRODUCTS INC.
23409 Industrial Park Ct.
Farmington Hills, MI 48335
Tel.: 313-478-1182 **MI**

Fax: 313-478-1472
Approx.Sls.: $32,000,000
Emp.: 65
Manufacture & Wholesaler Of Industrial Apparatus
S.I.C.: 3612; 3625; 3548; 3678; 5063
Raymond J. Persia *(Pres.)*
Robert Waldie *(V.P.)*
Tom Moore *(Sec.)*

Outside Service Firm(s):

National Bank of Detroit*(Major Banking Relationship)*
Plymouth, MI

ELECTRO MECHANICAL DESIGN SERVICES, INC.
16618 Oakmont Ave.
Gaithersburg, MD 20877
Tel.: 301-840-5710
Fax: 301-840-8589
Year Founded: 1975
Emp.: 60
Fiscal Year-end: 12/31/89
Mfr. Printed Circuit Boards; Provides CAD Design Services & Precision Reprographics
S.I.C.: 3679
Patrick E. Roney *(Chm. Bd., Pres. & Chief Exec. Officer)*
Davis L. Hooper *(Comptroller)*
Shirley Settle *(Mgr.-Personnel)*
Michelle Demoss *(Dir.-Mngmt. Information Systems)*

Computer Systems/Hardware:
IBM System 36

Outside Service Firm(s):

Franzoni & Assocs.*(Auditors)*
Gaithersburg, MD

Donahue & McDonald*(Legal Firm)*
Rockville, MD

Maryland National Bank*(Major Banking Relationship)*
2 N. Charles St.
Baltimore, MD 21201

ELECTRO METHODS INC.
330 Governors Hwy.
South Windsor, CT 06074
Mailing Address:
P.O. Box 54
South Windsor, CT 06074
Tel.: 203-289-8661 **CT**
Fax: 203-289-1868
Approx.Sls.: $32,000,000
Emp.: 190
Mfr. Jet Engine Parts
S.I.C.: 3724
Donald Judson *(Pres.)*
Paul Keller *(Dir.-Fin.)*
John Wolanski *(Dir.-Data Processing)*
Maurice Avery *(Mgr.-Quality Control)*
Peter Burhans *(Mgr.-Mfg.)*
Joyce O'Donnell *(Mgr.-Pur.)*
Louis Tavano *(Mgr.-Tech. Services)*

Principal(s):
Al Stangier

No. of Mfg. Plants/Facilities: 3
No. of U.S. Offices: 2

Computer Systems/Hardware:
DEC, PDP & VAX

Outside Service Firm(s):

Arthur Andersen & Co.*(Auditors)*
One Financial Plaza
Hartford, CT 06103
Tel.: 203-280-0649
Fax: 203-280-0898

Byrne, Slater, Sandler, Shulman & Rouse*(Legal Firm)*
Hartford, CT

ELECTRO-SCIENCE LABORATORIES, INC.
416 E. Church Rd.
King of Prussia, PA 19406-1533
Mailing Address:
P.O. Box 1533,
King of Prussia, PA 19406
Tel.: 215-272-8000 **PA**
Fax: 215-272-6759
Year Founded: 1962
Emp.: 85
Import Export
Electronic Materials, Laser systems
S.I.C.: 8731; 3825; 3676
Dr. Sidney J. Stein *(Chm. Bd., Chief Exec. Officer)*
Michael Alan Stein *(Pres. & Chief Oper. Officer)*
Cornelius Y.D. Huang *(V.P.-Research)*
Edwin J. Kohl *(Dir.-Fin.)*
Gerald Lorenz *(Dir.-Sales & Mktg.)*
Loretta Spadafora *(Dir.-Mfg.)*
Dr. Richard L. Wahlers *(Mgr.-Res. & Devel.)*

Computer Systems/Hardware:
IBM Display Writer

Outside Service Firm(s):

Deloitte & Touche*(Auditors)*
1 World Trade Center
New York, NY 10048
Tel.: 212-669-5000

Non-U.S. Holdings:

ESL S.N.C. **(1)**
7 rue de l'Avenir 92360
Meudon-la-Foret, France
Tel.: 6318945 (95%)
Sls., Distr. & Warehousing, Technical Service Laboratory
S.I.C.: 8731
Michael Alan Stein *(Pres.)*

Electro-Science Deutschland **(1)**
5, Stock, Sendlinger-Tor-Platz 8 8000
Munich, 2, Germany (100%)
Sls., Warehousing, Importation, Technical Services
S.I.C.: 8731
Michael Stein *(Pres.)*

ESL-Nippon Co. Ltd. **(1)**
Sukegawa Bldg., 1-3-4 Yanagi Bashi Taito-ku,
Tokyo, 111, Japan
Tel.: 03-3864-8521
Fax: 03-3864-9240
H. Wada *(Mng. Dir.)*

Non-U.S. Affiliate:

Agmet Ltd. **(1)**
38 Bennet Road
Reading, Berkshire 01144, United Kingdom
Tel.: 734-873-139
Research & Development
S.I.C.: 8731
Richard D. Tate *(Mng. Dir.)*

ELECTRO-WIRE PRODUCTS, INC.
17000 Executive Plaza Dr.
Dearborn, MI 48126
Tel.: 313-336-9393
Mfr. of Wiring Harnesses
S.I.C.: 3315
Thomas Wheeler *(Pres.)*

Subsidiary:

Electro-Wire Products, Inc. **(1)**
1900 S. Livernois
Rochester Hills, MI 48309
Tel.: 313-656-2800
Mfr. of Electrical Wire & Cable Products for the Automotive Industry
S.I.C.: 3357; 3714
J. Ronald Bishop *(Pres.)*
John J. Murray *(V.P.-Fin., Sec. & Treas.)*

Plants:

Electro-Wire, Inc. **(2)**
200 N. Industrial Pk. Rd.
Excelsior Springs, MO 64024
Tel.: 816-637-3193
Mfr. of Industrial Battery Cables & Ground Straps
S.I.C.: 3357; 3643
Linda Chrane *(Plant Mgr.)*

Electro-Wire, Inc. **(2)**
421 Haven Hill Rd.
Shelbyville, KY 40065
Tel.: 502-633-5440
Mfr. of Electrical Wiring Harnesses
S.I.C.: 3357; 3643
Frank Wilkerson *(Plant Mgr.)*

ELECTROCATALYTIC, INC.
2 Milltown Ct.
Union, NJ 07083
Tel.: 908-851-2277
Fax: 908-851-6906
Approx.Sls.: $19,000,000
Emp.: 110
Design & Produce Electro Mechanical Equipment
S.I.C.: 3822
John M. Scansaroli *(Pres.)*
Walter L. Scruggs *(Chief Fin. Officer)*
Dr. David B. Blum *(V.P.-Engrng.)*
Paul B. Byrne *(V.P.)*
Emil J. Litwin *(V.P.)*

Outside Service Firm(s):

Chemical Banking Corp.*(Major Banking Relationship)*
277 Park Ave.
New York, NY 10041
Tel.: 212-310-6407
Fax: 212-310-4526

THE ELECTRON CORP.
5101 S. Rio Grande St.
Littleton, CO 80120
Tel.: 303-794-4392
Fax: 303-798-6619
Approx.Sls.: $34,000,000
Emp.: 350
Fiscal Year-end: 10/31/90
Gray Ductile Iron Castings, V-Belt Pulleys
S.I.C.: 3321
Pierce Marshall *(Chm. Bd.)*
James Cartwright *(Pres.)*
Larry Z. Harvey *(V.P.-Sls. & Mktg.)*
Kevin Hocum *(Chief Fin. Officer)*
Robert Coutts *(Mgr.-Mfg.)*
Hal Davenport *(Pur. Agent)*

Computer Systems/Hardware:
Qantel

Division:

Electron Corp. **(1)**
Blackwell, OK 74631
Tel.: 918-363-3115
Import Export
Heavy Construction Facility
S.I.C.: 3321
Larry Z. Harvey *(V.P.-Sls. & Mktg.)*
Richard Hicks *(Plant Mgr.)*

ELECTRONIC DATA MAGNETICS, INC.
210 Old Thomasville Rd.
High Point, NC 27264
Tel.: 919-882-8115 **NC**
Fax: 919-882-0106
Emp.: 190
Mfr. of Computer Tab Cards
S.I.C.: 2675
Richard Hallman *(Pres.)*
James C. Hall *(Sr. V.P.-Mktg.)*
William H. Jones *(Sr. V.P.-Mfg.)*
Sid Childress *(V.P.-Engrng.)*
Elmer George *(V.P.-Sls.)*
Charles L. Weisner *(V.P.-Fin. & Sec.)*

Outside Service Firm(s):

Dixon, Odom & Co.*(Auditors)*
Greensboro, NC

NationsBank Carolinas*(Major Banking Relationship)*
One NCNB Plaza,
Charlotte, NC 28255
Tel.: 704-374-5000

Division:

Farm & Ticket Tag Div. **(1)**
210 Old Thomasville Rd.
High Point, NC 27264
Tel.: 919-882-8115
Mfr. of Computer Tab Cards
S.I.C.: 2675
Vern Cuerden *(V.P.)*

ELECTRONIC DRIVES AND CONTROLS
17 Eastmans Rd.
Parsippany, NJ 07054
Tel.: 201-428-0500
Fax: 201-428-0135
Year Founded: 1968
Sales Range: $10-19 Million
Emp.: 30
Mfg., Service &Supply Parts for Industrial Adjustable Speed Drives
S.I.C.: 3625; 7694; 5065
Henry Dillard, III *(Pres.)*

Computer Systems/Hardware:
IBM-PC Compatible LAN-MAS 90

Outside Service Firm(s):

The Mutual Group*(Group Insurer)*
Milwaukee, WI

United Jersey Bank, N.W.*(Major Banking Relationship)*
Randolph, NJ

ELECTRONICS STAMPING CORP.
19920 S. Alameda St.
Rancho Dominguez, CA 90220
Tel.: 310-639-2120 **DE**
Fax: 310-639-2479
Emp.: 50
Bussing Systems
S.I.C.: 3679
Hangup Moon *(Pres.)*
Royal Colquhoun *(V.P.-Electronic Stamping Corp.)*
Bob McCartney *(Controller)*
Shirley Berry *(Dir.-Human Resources)*

No. of U.S. Offices: 20

Computer Systems/Hardware:
IBM System 36

Outside Service Firm(s):

Sanwa Bank*(Major Banking Relationship)*
Long Beach, CA

ELEK-TEK, INC.
7350 N. Linder Ave.
Skokie, IL 60077
Tel.: 708-677-7660
Tel.: 800-395-1000 **IL**
Fax: 708-677-7168
Approx.Sls.: $148,000,000
Emp.: 600
Computer & Software Stores; Personal & Home Entertainment Computers & Accessories; Computer & Peripheral Equipment; Mail Order Computer Software
S.I.C.: 5734; 5045; 5961
Mort Goldman *(Chm. Bd.)*
Hal Goldman *(Pres.)*
Cameron Estes *(V.P. & Gen. Mgr.)*

Outside Service Firm(s):

Coopers & Lybrand*(Auditors)*
203 N. LaSalle St.
Chicago, IL 60601
Tel.: 312-701-5500

Melvin L. Goodman*(Auditors)*
Chicago, IL

Elek-Tek, Inc.—(Continued)

Eisenman, Allsopp & Strack*(Major Banking Relationship)*
100 Crossways Park West
Woodbury, NY 11797
Tel.: 516-364-3190

ROBERT ELEN & ASSOCIATES
6430 Sunset Blvd., Ste. 1000
Los Angeles, CA 90028
Tel.: 213-464-3536
Fax: 213-464-8927
Year Founded: 1976
Approx.Billings: $19,000,000
Emp.: 25
Robert W. Elen *(Pres. & Creative Dir.)*
O.B. Benskin *(Sr. V.P.)*
Joe Greenberg *(V.P., Media/Mktg.)*

ELGIN-HONEY HILL CORPORATION
3707 W. Harrison St.
Chicago, IL 60624
Tel.: 312-722-7100
Fax: 312-722-3230
Assets: $8,901,000
Liabilities: $5,542,000
Net Worth: $3,359,000
Approx.Sls.: $32,000,000
Emp.: 65
Fiscal Year-end: 1/31/90
Import
Ice Cream & Ice Milk Mixes, Cream, Milk & Whipped Cream Topping, Non Dairy Creamer & Whip Topping
S.I.C.: 2024; 2026
Kenneth Gignac *(Chm. Bd. & Pres.)*
Stanley Lehman *(V.P.-Opers.)*
Leland D. Roberts *(Sec. & Dir.-Pur.)*
Edward Gignac *(Controller & Dir.-Data Processing)*
Cheryl Pieper *(Mgr.-Quality Control)*

No. of Mfg. Plants/Facilities: 1
No. of U.S. Offices: 1

Outside Service Firm(s):

Arthur Andersen & Co.*(Auditors)*
33 W. Monroe St.
Chicago, IL 60603-4067
Tel.: 312-580-0033
Fax: 312-507-6748

Harris Trust & Savings Bank*(Investment Banker)*
111 W. Monroe St.
Chicago, IL 60690
Tel.: 312-461-2265
Tel.: 800-858-0840

Levin & Ginsburg, Ltd.*(Legal Firm)*
Chicago, IL

Harris Trust & Savings Bank*(Major Banking Relationship)*
111 W. Monroe St.
Chicago, IL 60690
Tel.: 312-461-2265
Tel.: 800-858-0840

ELGIN WATCH INTERNATIONAL, INC.
33-00 Northern Blvd.
Long Island City, NY 11101
Tel.: 718-361-7720
Fax: 718-367-1705
Approx.Sls.: $45,000,000
Emp.: 120
Fiscal Year-end: 12/31/90
Mfr. Elgin, Waltham & Nelsonic Watches
S.I.C.: 3873
Joseph Mermelstein *(Chm. Bd.)*
Bernard Mermelstein *(Pres. & Chief Exec. Officer)*
Adam Dabin *(V.P.-Sls.)*
Robert Grossinger *(V.P.-Mfg.)*
Karen Weiss *(Adv. Mgr.)*

ELIAS BROTHERS RESTAURANTS, INC.
4199 Marcy Rd.
Warren, MI 48091
Tel.: 313-759-6000
Fax: 313-757-4737
Year Founded: 1938
Approx.Sls.: $470,000,000
Emp.: 17,000
Restaurants & Food Manufacturing
S.I.C.: 5812
Fred Elias *(Chm. Bd.)*
Louis Elias *(Pres.)*
William H. Morgan *(Exec. V.P. & Dir.-Communications)*
Richard Hamlyn *(Legal Officer)*
Charles Anders *(Dir.-Training)*
Chris Hines *(Dir.-Personnel)*
Joe Michaels *(Dir.-Pur.)*
Tony Michaels *(Dir.-Mktg.)*
Principal(s):
Fred Elias
Louis Elias

Computer Systems/Hardware:
IBM System 38

Outside Service Firm(s):

Deloitte & Touche*(Auditors)*
2 Ruan Center
Des Moines, IA 50309
Tel.: 515-288-1200

Michigan National Bank*(Major Banking Relationship)*
Detroit, MI

Division:

Big Boy Restaurant System (1)
Marriott Dr.
Washington, DC 20058
Tel.: 301-897-9000
Approx.Sls.: $150,000,000
Emp.: 7,000
Fiscal Year-end: 12/31/90
Restaurants
S.I.C.: 5812
Daniel Bloodwell *(V.P.-Opers.)*
Jon Jameson *(V.P.-Mktg. & Adv.)*
Steve Sunkhouser *(V.P.-Opers.)*

ELI'S CHICAGO'S FINEST, INC.
6510 W. Dakin Ave.
Chicago, IL 60634
Tel.: 312-736-3417
Tel.: 800-999-8300
Fax: 314-736-1169
Approx.Sls.: $15,000,000
Emp.: 100
Manufacturer & Distributor of Cheese Cakes & Muffins
S.I.C.: 2051; 2053; 5142
Marc S. Schulman *(Pres.)*
Walter Babian *(Sr. V.P.)*
Peter Filippelli *(V.P.-Mktg. & Sls.)*
Jolene Worthington *(V.P.-Opers.)*
Patti Carroll *(Reg. V.P.)*
Esther Schulman *(Treas.)*
Maureen Schulman *(Dir.-Pub. Rels.)*
Charlene Meir *(Mgr.-Customer Service)*
Brian Smith *(Plant Mgr.)*

ELITE LAMP, INC.
P.O. Box 591
West Memphis, AR 72301
Tel.: 501-735-1826 **AR**
Fax: 501-735-7643
Year Founded: 1963
Approx.Sls.: $12,000,000
Emp.: 225
Mfr. of Table & Floor Lamps
S.I.C.: 3645
Matthew Lee Pike, III *(Pres.)*
Roma I. Pike *(V.P.)*
Martha Pike Rhodes *(V.P.)*
Mary Anne Pike *(Treas. & Sec.)*

Outside Service Firm(s):

Citizens Bank*(Major Banking Relationship)*
Marion, AR

ELIXIR INDUSTRIES
17925 S. Broadway
Gardena, CA 90248
Mailing Address:
P.O. Box 470,
Gardena, CA 90247
Tel.: 213-321-1191 **CA**
Fax: 213-323-1467
Year Founded: 1949
Approx.Sls.: $122,000,000
Emp.: 1050
Fiscal Year-end: 12/31/91
Import Export
Manufacture & Distribute Component Parts for Mobile Homes & Recreational Vehicles, Aluminum Siding, Doors, Roofs, Windows, Paint

S.I.C.: 3442; 2851; 3444; 2891; 3341; 3353; 3714; 5013
Roland R. Sahm *(Chm. Bd. & Chief Exec. Officer)*
David Whitt *(Pres. & Chief Oper. Officer)*
Hoss Rassouli *(V.P.-Pur.)*
Steven L. Solomon *(V.P. Fin., Chief Fin. Officer & Treas.)*
Robert Pollack *(Controller)*
Steve McBride *(Chief Info. Officer & Dir.-MIS)*
Leslie Moreau *(Dir.-Human Res.)*
Julie Cameron *(Mgr.-Intl. Sls.)*
Lea Gerber *(Mgr.-Risk)*
Principal(s):
Roland R. Sahm

No. of Mfg. Plants/Facilities: 25
No. of U.S. Offices: 25

Computer Systems/Hardware:
IBM 4341

Outside Service Firm(s):

Coopers & Lybrand*(Auditors)*
350 S. Grand Ave.
Los Angeles, CA 90071
Tel.: 213-481-1000
Fax: 213-482-6440

Fulbright & Jaworski*(Legal Firm)*
700 Flower St.
Los Angeles, CA 90017

The Bank of New York*(Major Banking Relationship)*
One Wall Street
New York, NY 10286
Tel.: 212-635-6805
Fax: 212-635-3201

Divisions:

Elixir Industries (1)
17770 E. Rowland
City of Industry, CA 91748
Tel.: 213-965-4958
Custom Vacuum Forming
S.I.C.: 3443
Mario Guzman *(Gen. Mgr.)*

Elixir Industries (1)
2040 Industrial Parkway
Elkhart, IN 46516
Tel.: 219-294-5685
Manufacturer of Mobile Homes Siding, Aluminum Parts
S.I.C.: 3442
Roger Roderictz *(Gen. Mgr.)*

Elixir Industries (1)
3443 Airport Rd.
Sacramento, CA 95834
Tel.: 916-929-9262
Manufacturer of Mobile Home Parts
S.I.C.: 3442
Tom Murray *(Gen. Mgr.)*

Elixir Industries (1)
Hwy. 20, Alt. 72 East
Tuscumbia, AL 35674
Tel.: 205-381-5932
Manufacturer of Metal Siding & Roofing for Mobile Homes
S.I.C.: 3442
Jerry Anglin *(Gen. Mgr.)*

Elixir Industries (1)
219 S. Mulberry
Mesa, AZ 85202
Tel.: 602-834-1484
Manufacturer of Fabricated Aluminum & Galvanized Materials
S.I.C.: 3443
Fred Desi *(Gen. Mgr.)*

Elixir Industries (1)
Southside Industrial Park
Douglas, GA 31533
Tel.: 912-384-2078
Manufacturer of Metal Siding, Mobile Home Doors & Aluminum Extrusions
S.I.C.: 3442
Archie Brown *(Gen. Mgr.)*

Elixir Industries (1)
Fitzgerald, GA 31750
Tel.: 912-423-4024
Manufacturer of Aluminum Parts for Mobile Homes
S.I.C.: 3442
Willie Hester *(Gen. Mgr.)*

Elixir Industries (1)
501 N. Eagle Rd.
Boise, ID 83707
Tel.: 208-888-1511
Manufacturer of Mobile Home Skirting, Metal Fabrication, Roofs for Mobile Homes
S.I.C.: 3442
Ed Dormeyer *(Gen. Mgr.)*

Elixir Industries (1)
640 Collins Rd.
Elkhart, IN 46516
Tel.: 219-862-4911
Extrude Aluminum Products
S.I.C.: 3341
Doug Wyrt *(Gen. Mgr.)*

Elixir Industries (1)
19527 Grim Rd.
Aurora, OR 97002
Tel.: 503-981-0181
Manufacturer of Mobile Home & RV Supplies, Doors, Aluminum Siding
S.I.C.: 3442
Wally Hucker *(Gen. Mgr.)*

Elixir Industries (1)
304 East Main, P.O. Box 312
Leola, PA 17540
Tel.: 717-656-2831
Manufacturer of Siding for Mobile Homes
S.I.C.: 3442
Ron Rose *(Gen. Mgr.)*

Elixir Industries (1)
Bldg. #3, 2000 East Columbia Way
Vancouver, WA 98661
Tel.: 206-693-1471
Manufacturer of Travel Trailer Awnings & Vacuum Forms
S.I.C.: 3442
Keith Lords *(Gen. Mgr.)*

Elixir Industries (1)
1203 Freeway Dr.
Reidsville, NC 27320
Tel.: 919-342-2353
Manufacturer of Mobile Home Products
S.I.C.: 3442
Tim Suttles *(Gen. Mgr)*

Elixir Industries/Alum-A-Form Div. (1)
17905 S. Broadway
Gardena, CA 90248
Tel.: 213-321-1191
Aluminum Fabrication
S.I.C.: 3365
Tom Murray *(Gen. Mgr.)*

ELK SUPPLY COMPANY
(d/b/a Clinton Lumber Co.)
103 Choctaw Ave.
Clinton, OK 73601
Tel.: 405-323-1250 **OK**
Fax: 405-323-1639
Year Founded: 1976
Approx.Sls.: $18,000,000
Emp.: 105
Retail Sales of Lumber & Other Building Materials Primarily To Construction Contractors
S.I.C.: 5211
Calvin D. Browning *(Pres.)*

Susan Browning *(V.P.)*
Deanne Johnson *(Treas. & Sec.)*

Outside Service Firm(s):

Bank of the West*(Major Banking Relationship)*
Clinton, OK

ELKAY MANUFACTURING COMPANY
2222 Camden Ct.
Oak Brook, IL 60521
Tel.: 708-574-8484
Fax: 708-574-5012
Year Founded: 1920
Approx.Sls.: $150,000,000
Emp.: 1,400
Export
Stainless Steel Kitchen & Cabinet Sinks; Comml. Water Coolers & Faucets
S.I.C.: 3431; 3585
Ronald C. Katz *(Chm. Bd. & Chief Exec. Officer)*
David F. Craigmile *(Pres.)*
Clark Carpenter *(V.P. & Treas.)*
Thomas M. Kodosky *(Controller)*
John E. Graves *(Sec.)*
Richard Steckel *(Dir.-Employee Rels.)*
Richard J. Hartmann *(Mgr.-Mktg. Communications)*

Computer Systems/Hardware:
IBM PC

Outside Service Firm(s):

Ernst & Young*(Auditors)*
233 S. Wacker Dr.
Chicago, IL 60606
Tel.: 312-368-1800
Fax: 312-645-3095

Jenner & Block*(Legal Firm)*
One IBM Plaza
Chicago, IL 60611
Tel.: 312-222-9350

First National Bank of Chicago*(Major Banking Relationship)*
One First National Plaza
Chicago, IL 60670
Tel.: 312-732-9781
Tel.: 312-732-4050
Fax: 312-732-4840
Fax: 312-732-3055

Division:

Cordley Temprite **(1)**
2222 Camden St.
Oak Brook, IL 60521
Tel.: 708-573-8840
Mfr. Water Coolers
S.I.C.: 3585
Dennis Scully *(Pres.)*

Factory:

Elkay Manufacturing **(1)**
2700 S. 17th Ave.
Broadview, IL 60153
Tel.: 708-681-1880
Stan Bandur *(Plant Mgr.)*

Subsidiary:

Halsey Taylor **(1)**
2222 Camden Ct.
Oak Brook, IL 60521
Tel.: 708-574-3500
Fax: 708-574-3503
Emp.: 884
Fiscal Year-end: 12/31/90
Export
Mfr. of Drinking Fountains & Electric Water Coolers
S.I.C.: 3585
Richard Gatehouse *(Pres.)*
Al Huneycutt *(Dir.-Mktg.)*

ELKAY PLASTICS COMPANY, INC.
4380 Ayers Ave.
Los Angeles, CA 90023
Mailing Address:
P.O. Box 23008
Los Angeles, CA 90023
Tel.: 213-263-7073
Tel.: 800-421-7002 **CA**
Fax: 213-263-0059
Year Founded: 1966
Assets: $4,527,305
Liabilities: $1,357,803
Net Worth: $3,169,502
Approx.Sls.: $20,000,000
Emp.: 81
Fiscal Year-end: 12/31/89
Import
Nondurable Goods; Manufacture Miscellaneous Plastic Products
S.I.C.: 3089; 5199
Louis Kestenbaum *(Chm.)*
Louis Chertkow *(Chief Exec. Officer)*

No. of Mfg. Plants/Facilities: 1

Computer Systems/Hardware:
Ultimate

Outside Service Firm(s):

Arthur Andersen & Co.*(Auditors)*
633 W. Fifth St.
Los Angeles, CA 90071
Tel.: 213-614-6500

Quinlan Insurance*(Commercial Insurance Carrier)*
Newport Beach, CA

Metplans*(Group Insurer)*
Orange, CA

Riordan and McKinzie*(Legal Firm)*
523 W. 6th
Los Angeles, CA 90802
Tel.: 213-629-4824

First Business Bank*(Major Banking Relationship)*
Los Angeles, CA

Transamerica Insurance Co.*(Pension Manager)*
1150 S. Olive St.
Los Angeles, CA 90015
Tel.: 213-742-4249

Branches:

Elkay Plastics Co., Inc., Stock Service Center **(1)**
500 S. Brandon
Seattle, WA 98108
Tel.: 206-763-3230
Tel.: 800-333-5529
Fax: 206-767-0710
Distribution & Service
S.I.C.: 5162
Don Giarde *(Gen. Mgr.)*

Elkay Plastics Co., Inc., Stock Service Center **(1)**
1580 North I-35
Carrollton, TX 75006
Tel.: 214-242-1466
Tel.: 800-521-0919
Fax: 214-466-1416
Distribution & Service
S.I.C.: 5162
Patrick Nuccio *(Gen. Mgr.)*

Elkay Plastics Co., Inc., Stock Service Center **(1)**
14600 E. 35th Pl., Unit H
Aurora, CO 80011
Tel.: 303-375-0174
Tel.: 800-634-8921
Fax: 303-375-0174
Distribution & Service
S.I.C.: 5162
Dave Bates *(Gen. Mgr.)*

ELKAY PRODUCTS, INC.
(Sub. of Labsystems, OY, Helsinki, Finland)
800 Boston Turnpike
Shrewsbury, MA 01545
Mailing Address:
P.O. Box 5247
Shrewsbury, MA 01545
Tel.: 508-845-2116
Tel.: 800-522-7763 **MA**
Fax: 508-842-1338
Year Founded: 1964
Sales Range: $10-19 Million
Emp.: 260
Fiscal Year-end: 12/31/90
Import Export
Mfr. of Plastic Laboratory Products
S.I.C.: 3821; 3089
Leo V. Heikkinen *(Pres.)*
Larry Amato *(Chief Fin. Officer, Treas. & Sec.)*
Richard Fask *(V.P.-Mfg.)*
Edward Jaye *(V.P.-Mktg. & Sls.)*
Sol Saltiel *(V.P.-Mngmt. Information Systems)*
Sandra Wiggins *(V.P.-Quality Control)*
Jan T. Mathieu *(Controller)*
Stacey Almelba *(Dir.-Employee Benefits)*
Peter Costas *(Dir.-Prod. Devel. & Mktg.)*
Steve Foley *(Dir.-Data Processing)*
Steven Grinley *(Dir.-Direct Mktg.)*
Charles Kozuck *(Dir.-Mfg.)*
Frank Quinn *(Dir.-Human Resources & Personnel Training & Devel.)*
Gail Wairstrom *(Dir.-Export)*
Paula Caouette *(Mgr.-Pur.)*
Kevin Kelliher *(Natl. Sls. Mgr.)*
Sue Breen *(Admin. Asst.)*

No. of Mfg. Plants/Facilities: 4
No. of U.S. Offices: 3
No. of Foreign Offices: 2

Computer Systems/Hardware:
Digital VAX 8300

Outside Service Firm(s):

KPMG Peat Marwick*(Auditors)*
One Boston Place
Boston, MA 02108
Tel.: 617-723-7700

Cuddy, Lynch, Manzi & Bixby*(Legal Firm)*
Boston, MA

Mechanics Bank*(Major Banking Relationship)*
Worcester, MA

ELKINGTON REALTY & DEVELOPMENT
168 Beal St.
Memphis, TN 38103
Tel.: 901-526-0110 **TN**
Fax: 901-763-4290
Year Founded: 1976
Sales Range: $20-39 Million
Emp.: 15
Real Estate Development & Construction
S.I.C.: 6552; 1522; 1541
John Elkington *(Pres.)*
Principal(s):
John Elkington

Computer Systems/Hardware:
IBM PC 50-150

Outside Service Firm(s):

Pannell, Kerr & Forster*(Auditors)*
Memphis, TN

James & Co.*(Commercial Insurance Carrier)*
Memphis, TN

Blue Cross & Blue Shield of Memphis*(Group Insurer)*
85 N. Danny Thomas Blvd.
Memphis, TN 38103

Hank Shelton*(Legal Firm)*
Memphis, TN

First Tennessee Bank, N.A.*(Major Banking Relationship)*
Memphis, TN

ELKINS CONSTRUCTORS, INC.
4501 Beverly Ave.
Jacksonville, FL 32210
Mailing Address:
P.O. BOX 2396
Jacksonville, FL 32203
Tel.: 904-384-6455 **FL**
Fax: 904-387-1303
Year Founded: 1984
Assets: $6,279,196
Liabilities: $4,432,446
Net Worth: $1,846,750
Approx.Sls.: $42,000,000
Emp.: 115
Fiscal Year-end: 12/31/90
Industrial, Commercial Buildings, Medical Facilities & Water Treatment & Waste Treatment Plant Construction
S.I.C.: 1541; 1542
C.F. Lieske *(Chm. Bd.)*
Barry L. Allred *(Pres., Chief Oper. Officer & Treas.)*
J.L. Gajewski *(V.P. & Sec.)*
S.B. Sgroi *(Controller)*
T.G. Butler *(Dir.-Commercial Div.)*
M.J. Coan *(Dir.-Bus. Devel.)*
M.D. Welch *(Dir.-Utility Div.)*
C.P. Woodman *(Dir.-Sarasota Medical Div.)*

No. of U.S. Offices: 2

Outside Service Firm(s):

Gunn, Patterson, Spaulding & Bohn*(Auditors)*
Jacksonville, FL

Herke Insurance Center, Inc.*(Commercial Insurance Carrier)*
Indianapolis, IN

Ulmer, Murchison, Ashby & Taylor*(Legal Firm)*
P. O. Box 479
Jacksonville, FL 32201
Tel.: 904-354-5652

Barnett Banks Trust Company, N.A.*(Major Banking Relationship)*
9000 Southside Blvd., P.O. Box 40200
Jacksonville, FL 32202-0200
Tel.: 904-464-2802

Merchants National Bank & Trust Company of Indianapolis*(Major Banking Relationship)*
One Merchants Plaza, Ste. 901E
Indianapolis, IN 46255
Tel.: 317-267-7109

Division:

Elkins Constructors **(1)**
747 N. Washington Blvd.
Sarasota, FL 34236
Tel.: 813-365-0757
Emp.: 15
Peter Woodman *(Mgr.-Branch)*

ELKMAN ADVERTISING & PUBLIC RELATIONS
150 Monument Rd.
Bala-Cynwyd, PA 19004
Tel.: 215-668-1100
Fax: 215-668-2586
Fax: 215-668-2064
Year Founded: 1954
Approx.Billings: $47,400,000
Emp.: 73
Advertising Agency
S.I.C.: 7311
Stanley Elkman *(Chm. Bd.)*
Donald M. Tuckerman *(Pres. & Chief Exec. Officer)*
Donald Rosenblit *(Sr. Exec. V.P., Dir. Acct. Services)*

Elkman Advertising & Public Relations—(Continued)

Bernadette Alexander *(Exec. V.P., Res. Dir.)*
Sam Rogers *(Exec. V.P., Pub. Rels. Dir.)*
Edwin M. Wilder *(V.P.)*

Computer Systems/Hardware:
NBI

Branches:

Elkman Advertising, Public Relations Div. **(1)**
150 Monument Rd.
Bala-Cynwyd, PA 19004
Tel.: 215-668-1100
Fax: 215-668-2586
Fax: 215-668-2064
Emp.: 11
Media & Community Relations, Special Events, Product Introductions, Re-Staging & Special Communications Programs
Stanley Elkman *(Chm.)*
Donald M. Tuckerman *(Pres. & Chief Exec. Officer)*
Sam Rogers *(Exec. V.P., Pub. Rels. Dir.)*

ELLERBE BECKET, INC.
800 LaSalle Av.
Minneapolis, MN 55402
Tel.: 612-376-2000
Fax: 612-376-2271
Year Founded: 1909
Approx.Sls.: $93,573,323
Emp.: 996
Fiscal Year-end: 12/31/91
Architecture; Health Care, Educational, Corporate, Hospitality, Governmental; Devel.; Engrng. Services; Sports, World Trade Centers & Construction Services
S.I.C.: 8712
John C. Gaunt *(Pres. & Chief Exec. Officer)*
Robert Degenhardt *(Exec. V.P. & Chief Oper. Officer)*
Richard Broeker *(Sr. V.P. & Chief Development Officer)*
Darrell I. Sykes *(Sr. V.P. & Chief Fin. Officer)*
Doug Green *(Sr. V.P. & Gen. Counsel)*
Julienne D. Sprint *(Sr. V.P. & Dir.-Human Resources)*
Jack L. Hunter *(Dir.-Minneapolis-CCI)*
Jim Jenkins *(Dir.-Minneapolis-Medical)*
Ron Turner *(Dir.-Kansas City)*
Mike Hallmark *(Dir.-Los Angeles)*
Rick Lincicome *(Dir.-Washington, D.C./New York)*
Gerald Simons *(Dir.-Tokyo)*
John J. Kulas *(Dir.-Information Systems)*
David Fey *(Dir.-Pub. Rels.)*
Jeanne Aamodt *(Dir.-Pub. Rels.)*

No. of U.S. Offices: 7
No. of Foreign Offices: 1

Computer Systems/Hardware:
IBM

Branches:

Ellerbe Becket-Kansas City **(1)**
605 West 47th
Kansas City, MO 64112
Tel.: 816-561-4443
Fax: 816-561-2863

Ellerbe Becket-New York **(1)**
200 Madison Ave.
New York, NY 10016
Tel.: 212-685-9191
Fax: 212-685-9214

Ellerbe Becket-Minneapolis **(1)**
800 LaSalle Ave.
Minneapolis, MN 55425
Tel.: 612-376-2000
Fax: 612-376-2271

Ellerbe Becket-Los Angeles **(1)**
Colorado Place, 2501 Colorado Ave.
Santa Monica, CA 90404-3585
Tel.: 310-829-4000
Fax: 310-828-7215

Ellerbe Becket-Washington **(1)**
1875 Connecticut Ave. N.W., Ste. 600
Washington, DC 20009
Tel.: 202-986-2000
Fax: 202-986-9130

Subsidiary:

Ellerbe Becket Construction Services **(1)**
800 LaSalle Ave.
Minneapolis, MN 55425
Tel.: 612-853-2000
Fax: 612-376-2271
Construction Services; Design/Build
S.I.C.: 8741
Brad Hornburg *(Pres.)*
Darrell Sykes *(Treas.)*
David Whitehouse *(Sr. V.P. & Sec.)*
Gregg Judge *(Sr. V.P.)*
Lauson Kostka *(Sr. V.P.)*

ELLICOTT MACHINE CORP.
1611 Bush St.
Baltimore, MD 21230
Tel.: 410-837-7900 **MD**
Fax: 410-752-3294
Year Founded: 1885
Approx.Sls.: $60,000,000
Emp.: 550
Export
Railroad Car Parts, Dredges & Dredging Machinery; Contract Machining, Fabrication & Assembly Services
S.I.C.: 3743
Richard E. Bowe *(Chm. Bd. & Pres.)*
Charles R. Kreter *(Chief Fin. Officer)*
T.K. Galvin, Jr. *(Exec. V.P.)*
Peter A. Bowe *(V.P. & Pres.-Dredge Div. & Ellicott Engrng., Inc.)*
Steve Glagola *(V.P.-Personnel)*
D.J. Piper *(V.P.)*
Martin E. Barnes *(Dir.-Major Projects)*

No. of Mfg. Plants/Facilities: 4

Computer Systems/Hardware:
Honeywell

Outside Service Firm(s):

Ernst & Young*(Auditors)*
1 N. Charles St.
Baltimore, MD 21201
Tel.: 410-539-7940
Fax: 410-783-3832

ELLIOTT COMPANY
N. Fourth St.
Jeannette, PA 15644
Tel.: 412-527-2811 **DE**
Fax: 412-527-8442
Approx.Sls.: $226,000,000
Emp.: 1,860
Fiscal Year-end: 5/31/92
Import Export
Manufacture Equipment for the Power & Process Industry; Plant Air Compressors, Air & Gas Compressors, Steam Turbines, Tube Maintenance Tools, Turbine Generators, Power Recovery Turbines
S.I.C.: 3563; 3511
Paul R. Smiy *(Chm. Bd. & Chief Exec. Officer)*
Ronald D.V. Turner *(Pres. & Chief Oper. Officer)*
John J. Lapina *(Chief Fin. Officer & V.P.-Fin.)*
Samuel R. Ferari *(V.P.-Engrng. Prods.)*
Klaus P. Fischer *(V.P., Gen. Counsel & Sec.)*
Janice O. Garlock *(V.P.-Human Resources)*
Adrian G.P. Jansen *(V.P.-Europe, Mideast & Africa)*
Donal P. Maloney *(V.P.-ESS Sls. & Mktg.)*
Frank N. Rossmann *(V.P.-Tech.)*
Gary R. Vaughn *(V.P.-Engrng. & Indus. Prods.)*
Richard Sowerby *(Controller)*
John Brenzia *(Treas.)*
David J. Jefferiss *(Dir.-Indus. Prods/ Service Parts)*
Frank Rassmann *(Dir.-Engineering)*

Outside Service Firm(s):

KPMG Peat Marwick*(Auditors)*
1 Mellon Bank Ctr.
Pittsburgh, PA 15219
Tel.: 412-391-9710

Non-U.S. Holdings:

Elliott Turbomachinery S.A. **(1)**
Zucherstrasse 4 8842
Altendorf, Switzerland
Tel.: 556-12100 (100%)
Telex: 817 275
Telecopier: 556-36212
Emp.: 19
Sales & Service of Elliot Products
S.I.C.: 5084
Adrian G.P. Jansen *(V.P.-Foreign Opers.)*

Elliott Turbomachinery Ltd. **(1)**
120 Thornycroft Indus. Estate, Worting Rd.
Basingstoke, Hampshire RG21 1SD, United Kingdom
Tel.: 256-54334
Telex: 739717 ELLIOT G
Fax: 256-22464
Compressor & Turbine Services
S.I.C.: 7699

Elliott Turbomachinery Canada, Inc. **(1)**
955 Maple
Burlington, ON L7S 1W6, Canada
Tel.: 416-333-4101
S.I.C.: 5084

MICHAEL R. ELLISON INC.
4455 E. Camelback, Ste. C-240
Phoenix, AZ 85060
Tel.: 602-952-1400
Twx: 910-950-1170
Fax: 602-952-9423
Year Founded: 1972
Approx.Billings: $10,000,000
Emp.: 15
Ministry Development & Religious Adv.
Michael R. Ellison *(Pres.)*
Don Kurtenbach *(Chief Fin. Officer)*
Doug Preudhomme *(V.P., Opers.)*
Susan Ellison *(Sec. & Treas.)*

Ray Ellison Industries
(Name Changed to Ray Co., Inc.)

ELLWOOD CITY FORGE
Commercial Ave.
Ellwood City, PA 16117
Tel.: 412-752-0055
Tel.: 800-843-0166
Fax: 412-752-3449
Year Founded: 1910
Approx.Sls.: $60,000,000
Emp.: 310
Fiscal Year-end: 12/31/90
Export
Mfr. of Steel Forgings & Open Die
S.I.C.: 3462
Robert Barensfeld *(Chm. Bd.)*
Kevin J. Handerhan *(Pres.)*
Larry L. Symons *(V.P. & Chief Fin. Officer)*
Michael A. Kamnikar *(V.P.-Mktg.)*
David E Barensfeld *(Chief Exec. Officer)*
Dolores M. Dean *(Controller)*
Sunil Ahuja *(Dir.-Mngmt. Information Services)*
Wayne L. Simon *(Dir.-Human Resources)*
Steve Peck *(Dir.-Plng. & Analysis)*
Glenn Fegely *(Dir.-Intl. Sls.)*
Michael Addessi *(Dir.-Pur.)*
Joanna Ashburn *(Admin. Asst.)*
Jorn Jensen *(Mgr.-Engrng.)*
Kim Senchak *(Mgr.-Quality Control)*

e&a
elser & aucone, inc.

ELSER & AUCONE, INC.
420 Lexington Ave.
New York, NY 10170
Tel.: 212-867-3300
Fax: 212-867-3761
Year Founded: 1985
Approx.Billings: $15,650,000
Emp.: 20
Arnold J. Elser *(Pres., Dir. Creative Services)*
Stephen A. Elser *(Sr. V.P., Mktg. & Bus. Devel.)*
Maria DiChiara *(V.P., Opers. Dir.)*
Robert J. Bauhofer *(V.P., Mktg. Res.)*
Joseph Cantwell *(V.P., Plng. & Devel.)*

Computer Systems/Hardware:
Apple Macintosh

THE ELWELL-PARKER ELECTRIC CO.
4205 St. Clair Ave.
Cleveland, OH 44103
Tel.: 216-881-6200
Telex: 980-207
Fax: 216-391-7708
Year Founded: 1893
Approx.Sls.: $16,000,000
Emp.: 200
Fiscal Year-end: 12/31/90
Export
Power Industrial, Electric & I. C. Trucks, Tractors, Cranes & Sideloaders
S.I.C.: 3537
S.K. Towson, Jr. *(Pres.)*
L.J. Wareham *(V.P.-Fin.)*
Andrew H. Minda *(Dir.-Personnel)*
Robert S. Vale *(Mgr.-Mfg.)*
R.J. Marshik *(Mgr.-Mktg.)*
D.J. Stankiewicz *(Mgr.-Intl. Sls.)*
Norma Zumbach *(Dir.-Pur.)*
D.J. STankiewicz *(Mgr.-Int'l. Sls.)*

ELYRIA FOUNDRY COMPANY
120 Filbert St.
Elyria, OH 44036
Tel.: 216-322-4657
Approx.Sls.: $25,000,000
Emp.: 260
Mfr. of Gray & Ductile Iron Castings
S.I.C.: 3321
Robert L. Gollmar *(Chm. Bd.)*
Gregg L. Foster *(Pres.)*
David J. Knapp *(Exec. V.P.-Opers.)*
Floyd Baum *(V.P.)*
Beverly Houts *(Controller)*
Kim Bevington *(Mgr.-Sls.)*

Emb-Tex Corp.
(See Elyria Foundry Company)

EMERALD CORPORATION
1775 E. 45th St.
Cleveland, OH 44103
Tel.: 216-431-8070 **OH**
Fax: 216-431-6924
Year Founded: 1917
Approx.Sls.: $48,000,000
Emp.: 250
Warm Air Heating & Air Conditioning Contractor; Plumbing Contractors; Ventilation & Duct Work Contractor; Water, Sewer & Utility Lines
S.I.C.: 1711; 1623

David K. Nachman *(Pres. & Chief Exec. Officer)*
George W. Spahn *(V.P.)*
Dennis A. Spahn *(Sec.)*
David T. Spahn *(Treas. & Asst.Sec.)*

Outside Service Firm(s):

Ciulla Stephens & Company*(Auditors)*
Cleveland, OH

AmeriTrust Company, N.A.*(Major Banking Relationship)*
P.O. Box 5937, 900 Euclid Ave.
Cleveland, OH 44101-0937

EMERY WATERHOUSE COMPANY
Rand Road
Portland, ME 04104
Tel.: 207-775-2371
Fax: 207-775-5206
Year Founded: 1842
Approx.Sls.: $100,000,000
Emp.: 275
Wholesale & Retail Hardware, Paints, Building Materials, Major Appliances, Housewares & Supplies
S.I.C.: 3999; 5039; 5072; 5085; 5198
Charles L. Hildreth, Jr. *(Chm. Bd.)*
Stuart Welch *(Pres.)*
Bob Morrill *(V.P.-Oper.)*
Kirby Kramer *(V.P.-Fin.)*
Bill Brown *(V.P.-Sls.)*
Ernie Lebel *(V.P.-Human Resources)*
Peter Plowman *(Dir.-Pur.)*

Outside Service Firm(s):

Coopers & Lybrand*(Auditors)*
P.O. Box 538, 800 Akron Centre Plaza
Akron, OH 44308

Richardson & Troubh*(Legal Firm)*
Portland, ME

EMIGRANT SAVINGS BANK
5 E. 42nd St.
New York, NY 10017
Tel.: 212-883-5800
Fax: 212-957-9090
Approx.Sls.: $3,200,000,000
Emp.: 800
Savings Banking, Real Estate Mortgage & Personal Loans
S.I.C.: 6036
Raymond V. O'Brien, Jr. *(Chm. Bd.)*
Franklin R. Saul *(Pres.)*
James C. Woolsey *(Exec. V.P. & Comptroller)*
Francis A. Balzarini *(Sr. V.P. & Mortgage Officer)*
Eileen Trawinski *(V.P.-Mktg.)*

EMKAY, INC.
805 W. Thorndale
Itasca, IL 60143
Tel.: 708-250-7400
Year Founded: 1946
Approx.Sls.: $50,000,000
Emp.: 105
Fiscal Year-end: 2/28/91
Daily Rental, Long Term Fleet Leasing & Vehicle Management
S.I.C.: 7515; 4119
Samuel A. Rea *(Chm. Bd.)*
Gary L. Tepas *(Pres. & Chief Exec. Officer)*
Robert J. Kaiser *(Sr. V.P.- Sls.)*
Steven J. Derus *(V.P.-Admin.)*
Gary L. Ellison *(V.P.-Fin.)*
Jack Reynolds *(V.P.-Client Services)*

JOHN EMMERLING INC.
135 East 55th St.
New York, NY 10022
Tel.: 212-751-7460
Fax: 212-371-6365
Year Founded: 1976
Approx.Billings: $21,000,000
Emp.: 17
John A. Emmerling *(Chm. Bd., Pres. & Chief Exec. Officer)*
Russell G. Finley *(Sr. V.P., Mktg./Media)*
Ann Levin *(Controller)*
Russell S. Berman *(Sec.)*

Computer Systems/Hardware:
IBM RS 6000/Macintosh

EMPIRE AIRLINES
11101 Airport Dr.
Hayden Lake, ID 83835
Tel.: 208-772-4048 **ID**
Fax: 208-772-7892
Year Founded: 1977
Assets: $5,594,282
Liabilities: $4,093,745
Net Worth: $1,500,537
Sales Range: $10-19 Million
Emp.: 150
Fiscal Year-end: 12/31/91
Import Export
Aviation Services; Large Aircraft Contracting & Commuter Airlines
S.I.C.: 4512
M.E. Spelde *(Chm. Bd., Pres. & Chief Exec. Officer)*
William Thois *(Chief Fin. Officer, Treas., Sec. & Dir.-Admin. & Opers.)*
Nick Chenoweth *(V.P. & Gen. Counsel)*
Victor Walters *(V.P. & Dir.-Flight)*
Ann Farrar *(Controller)*
Michael Cyper *(Dir.-Data Processing)*
Judy Spelde *(Dir.-Human Resources)*
Mel Spelde *(Dir.-Govt. Affairs)*
Tim Swanson *(Dir.-Personnel Training & Devel.)*
Larry Tucker *(Dur.-Pur.)*
Kim Upshaw *(Dir.-Mktg., Sls., Adv. & Pub. Rels.)*
Kathy Califand *(Corp. Travel Planner)*
Principal(s):
M.E. Spelde
Nick Chenoweth
Victor Walters

No. of U.S. Offices: 6

Computer Systems/Hardware:
Novell/Platinum

Outside Service Firm(s):

Arthur Andersen & Co.*(Auditors)*
999 Main St.
Boise, ID 83702

Johnson & Higgins*(Commercial Insurance Carrier)*
877 Main St., Ste. 707
Boise, ID 83702
Tel.: 208-338-1006
Telex: 208-338-1015

West One Bank*(Major Banking Relationship)*
Cour d'Alene, ID

West One Bank*(Pension Manager)*
101 S. Capitol Blvd.
Boise, ID 83701
Tel.: 208-383-7947
Fax: 208-383-3870

EMPIRE BLUE CROSS & BLUE SHIELD
622 Third Ave.
New York, NY 10017
Tel.: 212-476-1000
Year Founded: 1935
Approx.Sls.: $3,100,000,000
Emp.: 10,000
Fiscal Year-end: 12/31/90
Health Care Insurance & Travel Protection Insurance
S.I.C.: 6321
Albert A. Cardone *(Chm. & Chief Exec. Officer)*
Donald L. Morchower *(Exec. V.P. & Chief Oper. Officer)*
Bernard Schoen *(V.P.-Sls.)*
Eric S. Schlesinger *(Chief Mktg. Officer)*
Thomas F. Salvia *(Adv. Mgr.)*

EMPIRE BRUSHES, INC.
U. S. Hwy. 13 North
Greenville, NC 27835
Mailing Address:
P.O. Box 1606
Greenville, NC 27835
Tel.: 919-758-4111
Fax: 919-758-4302
Year Founded: 1909
Approx.Sls.: $60,000,000
Emp.: 600
Fiscal Year-end: 12/31/90
Import Export
Mfr. Household, Maintenance & Personal Brushes, Sponge Mops, Dust Mops, Wet Mops, Auto Brushes, Paint Sundry Brushes, Upright Brooms, Push Brooms
S.I.C.: 3991
Joseph Gantz *(Pres.)*
Fred Strom *(Exec. V.P.)*
Jim Sloan *(Sr. V.P.-Corp. Devel.)*
Jim Lewis *(V.P.-Field Sls. West)*
Cary Eubank *(V.P.-Field Sls. East)*
Fred S. Nover *(V.P.-Sls., Mktg. & Distr.)*
Charles Price *(Comptroller)*
Walter Horne *(Dir.-Sls. Admin.)*
Paul Ricciarelli *(Dir.-Mktg.)*
Stan Zicherman *(Pur. Mgr.)*

Computer Systems/Hardware:
IBM AS 400

EMPIRE DIAMOND CORPORATION
350 Fifth Ave.
New York, NY 10001
Tel.: 212-564-4777
Fax: 212-564-4960
Year Founded: 1931
Approx.Sls.: $16,000,000
Emp.: 17
Fiscal Year-end: 9/30/90
Import Export
Diamonds & Jewelry
S.I.C.: 5094
Irven J. Brod *(Pres.)*
Gregory Herdemian *(Chief Oper. Officer)*
Spencer Brod *(Sec. & Treas.)*
David Cohen *(Treas.)*
Jack Brod *(Adv. Dir.)*

EMPIRE ELECTRIC ASSOCIATION
Drawer K
Cortez, CO 81321
Tel.: 303-565-8534 **CO**
Fax: 303-565-8534, Ext. 4444
Year Founded: 1939
Approx.Sls.: $18,000,000
Emp.: 62
Co-operative; Distrubtion of Electric Power
S.I.C.: 4911
Floyd Ray *(Pres.)*
Jack N. Young *(V.P.)*
Dorthy M. Kruse *(Sec.)*
Neal Stevens *(Gen. Mgr.)*

Outside Service Firm(s):

Citizens State Bank*(Major Banking Relationship)*
Cortez, CO

EMPIRE KOSHER POULTRY, INC.
River Road
Mifflintown, PA 17059
Mailing Address:
P.O. Box 165,
Mifflintown, PA 17059
Tel.: 717-436-5921
Tel.: 800-233-7177
Fax: 717-436-9269
Year Founded: 1938
Emp.: 1,100
Fiscal Year-end: 5/31/91
Export
Processors & Packers of Kosher Poultry & Foods
S.I.C.: 0251; 2015; 2099
Murray L. Katz *(Pres.)*
Ronald Swanger *(Exec. V.P.)*
Alan Katz *(V.P.-Mktg. & Sls.)*
Steven Katz *(V.P.-Opers.)*
Matthew Soccio *(Controller)*
Birgitta Wade *(Dir.-Adv.)*
Harry Geedey *(Mgr.-Sls.)*

Outside Service Firm(s):

Haas & Co.*(Auditors)*
Philadelphia, PA

Subsidiaries:

K & L Feeds **(1)**
R.D. 1
Selinsgrove, PA 17870
Tel.: 717-374-0501
S.I.C.: 0251
Greg Gillespie *(V.P.)*

Mattern Hatchery **(1)**
Route 1, Box 240
Beaver Springs, PA 17812
Tel.: 717-658-8211
S.I.C.: 0251
Mickey Baugher *(Gen. Mgr.)*

EMPIRE NATIONAL BANK
1227 E. Front St.
Traverse City, MI 49684
Mailing Address:
P.O. Box 1220,
Traverse City, MI 49685-1220
Tel.: 616-922-2111
Approx.Rev.: $19,090,000
Regional Bank
S.I.C.: 6021
James E. Dutmers, Jr. *(Chm. Bd.)*
Robert L. Israel *(Pres.)*

EMPIRE PETROLEUM, INC.
2959 Nebraska Ave.
Toledo, OH 43607
Mailing Address:
P.O. Box 4036
Toledo, OH 43609
Tel.: 419-534-6025
Tel.: 800-837-6025 **OH**
Fax: 419-534-6032
Year Founded: 1972
Sales Range: $20-39 Million
Emp.: 25
Export
Petroleum Bulk Stations; Gasoline Stations
S.I.C.: 5171; 5541
Robert J. Mallendick *(Pres. & Treas.)*
Carol Mallendick *(V.P. & Sec.)*

Outside Service Firm(s):

TrustCorp Bank*(Major Banking Relationship)*
Three Seagate
Toledo, OH 43604
Tel.: 419-244-8000

EMPIRE SOUTHWEST CO.
1725 S. Country Club Rd.
Mesa, AZ 85210
Mailing Address:
P.O. Box 2985,
Phoenix, AZ 85062
Tel.: 602-898-4400 **AZ**
Telex: 165-207
Fax: 602-898-4489
Year Founded: 1959
Assets: $120,000,000
Liabilities: $85,000,000
Net Worth: $35,000,000
Approx.Sls.: $200,000,000
Emp.: 715
Fiscal Year-end: 10/31/89
Caterpillar & John Deere Farm Equipment Dealer
S.I.C.: 5082; 5083; 7359; 3531

Empire Southwest Co.—(Continued)

Jack W. Whiteman *(Chm. Bd. & Chief Exec. Officer)*
John O. Whiteman *(Pres.-Empire Machinery)*
John R. Slentz *(V.P. & Gen. Mgr.-M.C.T. Prop. & Empire Transport)*
Mary Kay Lorona *(Corp. Counsel)*
Rich Mente *(V.P.-Fin. & Controller)*
Dee Robb *(Dir.-Personnel)*
Marti Soza *(Office Pur.-Buyer)*
Principal(s):
John O. Whiteman

No. of U.S. Offices: 14

Computer Systems/Hardware:
NCR

Outside Service Firm(s):

Deloitte & Touche*(Auditors)*
2901 North Central Ave., Ste. 1200
Phoenix, AZ 85012
Tel.: 602-234-5100
Fax: 602-234-5186

Ryley, Carlock & Applewhite*(Legal Firm)*
Phoenix, AZ

Security Pacific Bank Arizona*(Major Banking Relationship)*
Phoenix, AZ

Smoot Knoche & Co.*(Pension Manager)*
Salt Lake City, UT

Strong/Corneliuson Capital Management Inc.*(Pension Manager)*
Milwaukee, WI

EMPIRE STEEL TRADING COMPANY
80 Wall St.
New York, NY 10005
Tel.: 212-344-9700 **NY**
Fax: 212-344-9715
Year Founded: 1940
Sales Range: $20-39 Million
Emp.: 35
Export
Steel Traders
S.I.C.: 5051
Walter Kahn *(Pres.)*
Simon Kahn *(Sec.)*

EMPIRE WEST COMPANIES, INC.
6700 N. Oracle, Ste. 100
Tucson, AZ 85704
Tel.: 602-297-9000 **CA**
Fax: 602-297-9134
Emp.: 250
Real Estate Management & Developers
S.I.C.: 6531
Cary Marmis *(Chm. Bd. & Pres.)*
Michael Bartz *(Sr. V.P. & Gen. Counsel)*
Ronald Priestley *(Sr. V.P.-Fin.)*

No. of U.S. Offices: 1

Outside Service Firm(s):

Ernst & Young*(Auditors)*
1100 CitiBank Tower, One S. Church Ave.
Tucson, AZ 85701
Tel.: 602-622-5801

Travelers Insurance Co.*(Commercial Insurance Carrier)*
1 Tower Square
Hartford, CT 06183-2492
Tel.: 203-277-4542
Fax: 203-277-5038

ALTA Health Strategies*(Group Insurer)*
Phoenix, AZ

Citibank N.A.*(Major Banking Relationship)*
Phoenix, AZ

Western Savings & Loan*(Major Banking Relationship)*
Tucson, AZ

EMPLOYERS INSURANCE OF WAUSAU A MUTUAL CO.
(Affiliate of Nationwide Mutual Insurance Co., Columbus, OH)
2000 Westwood Dr.
Wausau, WI 54401
Mailing Address:
P.O. Box 8017
Wausau, WI 54402-8017
Tel.: 715-845-5211 **WI**
Fax: 715-842-6947
Year Founded: 1911
Assets: $2,915,585,000
Liabilities: $2,486,785,000
Net Worth: $428,800,000
Sales Range: $1 Billion +
Emp.: 5,600
Property & Casualty Insurance
S.I.C.: 6331
John E. Fisher *(Gen. Chm.)*
Arden Shisler *(Chm. Bd.)*
Leon J. Weinberger *(Pres. & Chief Exec. Officer)*
Thomas E. Kryshak *(Exec. V.P.-Fin.)*
Gordon E. McCutchan *(Exec. V.P. & Gen. Counsel)*
Carl J. Santillo *(Exec. V.P.-Opers.)*
Bill D. Wymore *(Exec. V.P.-Admin. Services)*
Dwight Davis *(Sr. V.P.-Western Division)*
Scott Isaacson *(Sr. V.P.-Mktg.)*
David R. Jahn *(Sr. V.P.-South Central Division)*
J.M. Magalska *(Sr. V.P., Grp. & Retire Oper.)*
Richard J. Byron *(V.P., Assoc. Gen. Counsel & Sec.)*
Warren L. Fabel *(V.P.-Personnel)*
Mark E. Fiebrink *(V.P. & Actuary)*
W.H. Gustavson *(V.P. & Dir.-Med.)*
Floyd R. Luettgens *(V.P.-Audit)*
Virden H. Morrison *(V.P.-Office Services)*
Willard C. Sanford *(V.P. & Treas.)*
Bruce Thornton *(V.P. & Controller)*
Phil Wirtanen *(V.P. & Dir.-Sls.)*
Vicki Amundson *(Asst. Treas.)*
Brad Zweck *(Mgr.-Pub. Rels.)*

Computer Systems/Hardware:
IBM 3090, 200 & 3081

Outside Service Firm(s):

KPMG Peat Marwick*(Auditors)*
Peat Marwick Plaza, 303 E. Wacker Dr.
Chicago, IL 60601
Tel.: 312-938-1000

Subsidiaries:

Wausau Life Insurance Company **(1)**
2000 Westwood Dr.
Wausau, WI 54401
Tel.: 715-845-5211
Life Insurance Services
S.I.C.: 6311
James M. Magalska *(Exec. V.P.)*

Wausau Underwriters Life Insurance Company **(1)**
2400 Westwood Dr.
Wausau, WI 54401
Tel.: 715-845-5211
Life Insurance Services
S.I.C.: 6311
James M. Magalska *(Exec. V.P.)*

Non-U.S. Holding:

Wausau Insurance Company (U.K.), Ltd. **(1)**
85 Greenchurch St.
London, EC3 V0HA, United Kingdom
Tel.: 071-488-8111 (100%)
Emp.: 5,600
Property & Casualty Insurance Services
S.I.C.: 6331

EMRICK CHEVROLET SALES CORPORATION
1801-11 Chamberlayne Ave.
Richmond, VA 23222
Tel.: 804-321-5000 **VA**
Fax: 804-229-2017
Approx.Sls.: $24,000,000
Emp.: 60
New & Used Automobiles, Trucks, Tractors & Trailers
S.I.C.: 5511
Charles W. Appich, Jr. *(Pres.)*
Donald L. Appich *(V.P. & Treas.)*
A. Melton Williams *(V.P. & Sec.)*
Ron Marker *(Controller)*

Outside Service Firm(s):

KPMG Peat Marwick*(Auditors)*
1021 E. Cary St., Ste. 1900
Richmond, VA 23219
Tel.: 804-649-9091

Parker, Pollard & Brown*(Legal Firm)*
Richmond, VA

EMSON RESEARCH, INC.
1100 Boston Ave.
Bridgeport, CT 06610
Tel.: 203-366-4501
Fax: 203-332-1803
Approx.Sls.: $20,000,000
Emp.: 350
Mfr. of Aerosol Valves & Pump Sprayers
S.I.C.: 3499
Emil Meshberg *(Chief Exec. Officer)*
John Clark *(V.P.-Mfg.)*
Brian Connelly *(V.P.-Sls. & Mktg.)*
Greg Stillwagon *(Controller)*
John Farrell *(Mgr.-Personnel)*
James Tamborra *(Dir.-Engrg.)*

Outside Service Firm(s):

Deloitte & Touche*(Auditors)*
1633 Broadway
New York, NY 10019
Tel.: 212-489-1600

Goldman, Rosen & Willinger*(Legal Firm)*
177 State St.
Bridgeport, CT 06604
Tel.: 203-366-4726

Connecticut Bank & Trust*(Major Banking Relationship)*
Bridgeport, CT

ENABLING TECHNOLOGIES COMPANY
3102 S.E. Jay St.
Stuart, FL 34997
Tel.: 407-283-4817 **FL**
Fax: 407-220-2920
Year Founded: 1973
Approx.Sls.: $10,000,000
Emp.: 29
Design, Manufacture, Market & Service Computer Aids For The Blind & Visually Handicapped; Custom Programming & Software Development For Business Systems
S.I.C.: 8742; 7382
Tony Schenk *(Chm. Bd., Pres. & Chief Exec. Officer)*

No. of Mfg. Plants/Facilities: 1
No. of U.S. Offices: 6

Computer Systems/Hardware:
IBM

Outside Service Firm(s):

John Alden Life Insurance Co.*(Group Insurer)*
Miami, FL

Sun Bank, N.A.*(Major Banking Relationship)*
Stuart, FL

ENCO MATERIALS, INC.
211-214 Boscobel St.
Nashville, TN 37213
Tel.: 615-256-3192 **TN**
Fax: 615-259-3589
Approx.Sls.: $29,000,000
Emp.: 190
Mfr. & Marketing of Concrete Reinforcing Bars; Fabricated Steel; Iron or Steel Structural Shapes
S.I.C.: 3449; 5051
Wilbur Sensing, Jr. *(Chm. Bd.)*
C.E. Thames *(Pres.)*
Billy Potter *(V.P.)*
Philip Hood *(Controller)*
Homer Lane *(Pur. Agent)*
Ronald Campbell *(Sec.)*

Outside Service Firm(s):

Alfred T. Adams, Jr.*(Legal Firm)*
Nashville, TN

First American National Bank*(Major Banking Relationship)*
First American Center
Nashville, TN 37237
Tel.: 615-748-2000

Division:

Enco-Johnson City Division **(1)**
2704 S. Roan St.
Johnson City, TN 37601
Tel.: 615-928-3176
Mfr. of Concrete Reinforcing Bars & Fabricated Steel Iron or Steel Structural Shapes
S.I.C.: 3449
Jerry McKinney *(Gen. Mgr.)*

ENCORE MARKETING INTERNATIONAL
4501 Forbes Blvd.
Lanham, MD 20706
Tel.: 301-459-8020
Fax: 301-731-0525
Year Founded: 1978
Approx.Sls.: $37,000,000
Emp.: 900
Discount Travel Services
S.I.C.: 4724
Patrick J. Gorman *(Co-Pres. & Chief Exec. Officer)*
Martin D. Gorman *(Co-Pres. & Chief Oper. Officer)*
Gale Lanier *(V.P.-Client Services & Sec.)*
Albert F. Baumann *(Treas.)*

ENCORE SHOE CORPORATION
51 Wakefield St.
Rochester, NH 03867
Mailing Address:
P.O. Box 1920,
Rochester, NH 03867
Tel.: 603-332-8000
Fax: 603-332-8027
Approx.Sls.: $59,000,000
Emp.: 250
Fiscal Year-end: 12/31/90
Mfr. Men's & Women's Shoes & Boots
S.I.C.: 3143; 3144
Earl L. Katz *(Chm. Bd. & Chief Exec. Officer)*
James M. Katz *(Pres.)*
Ronald A. Katz *(Exec. V.P.)*
Dennis Corliss *(Controller)*

Computer Systems/Hardware:
Wang

Outside Service Firm(s):

Brown, Rudnick, Freed & Gesmer*(Legal Firm)*
One Financial Center
Boston, MA 02111
Tel.: 617-330-9000

Capitol Bank & Trust*(Major Banking Relationship)*
Rochester, NH

ENCYCLOPAEDIA BRITANNICA EDUCATIONAL CORPORATION
310 S. Michigan Ave.
Chicago, IL 60604
Tel.: 312-347-7900
Fax: 312-347-7903
Year Founded: 1929
Approx.Sls.: $25,000,000
Emp.: 120
Fiscal Year-end: 9/30/90
Audiovisual Educational Materials
S.I.C.: 7812
Joseph E. Elliott *(Pres.)*
Jim Decker-Ward *(Exec. V.P.-Mktg.)*
Robert Whitworth *(Exec. V.P.)*
Harry Joy *(Mgr.-Legal)*

ENCYCLOPAEDIA BRITANNICA, INC.
310 S. Michigan Ave.
Chicago, IL 60604
Tel.: 312-347-7000 NY
Telex: 190203 EBINCUT
Year Founded: 1768
Assets: $598,000,000
Liabilities: $423,000,000
Net Worth: $175,000,000
Approx.Sls.: $627,000,000
Emp.: 2,300
Fiscal Year-end: 9/30/91
Publishing
S.I.C.: 2731; 2741
Robert P. Gwinn *(Chm. Bd. & Chief Exec. Officer)*
Peter B. Norton *(Pres. & Chief Oper. Officer)*
Fred H. Figge, Jr. *(Exec. V.P. & Chief Fin. Officer)*
Stanley D. Frank *(Exec. V.P. & Pres.-Compton's Multimedia Publ. Grp.)*
David Van Tosh *(Exec. V.P.-North American Adv. & Mktg.)*
Patricia A. Wier *(Exec. V.P. & Pres.-EBNA)*
Karen M. Barch *(V.P.-Editorial Devel.)*
William J. Bowe *(V.P., Sec. & Gen. Counsel)*
Norman Braun *(V.P.-Pub. Affairs)*
Raymond Majesty *(V.P.-Mfg.)*
Robert McHenry *(V.P. & Gen. Editor)*
Karl Steinberg *(V.P.-Human Resources)*
Woodrow A. Sutton *(Treas.)*
Randall Johnson *(Controller)*
Lisa McLaughlin *(Dir.-Corp. Communications)*

Principal(s):
William Benton Foundation

No. of U.S. Offices: 100
No. of Foreign Offices: 50

Computer Systems/Hardware:
IBM 3090 - Model 180

Outside Service Firm(s):

Price Waterhouse*(Auditors)*
200 E. Randolph
Chicago, IL 60601
Tel.: 312-565-1500

Marsh & McLennan*(Commercial Insurance Carrier)*
1166 Avenue of the Americas
New York, NY 10036
Tel.: 212-345-6000
Fax: 212-345-3285

Equitable Real Estate Investment Managment Inc.*(Group Insurer)*
3414 Peachtree Rd. N.E.
Atlanta, GA 30326-1162

Mayer, Brown & Platt*(Legal Firm)*
190 S. LaSalle St., Ste. 3900
Chicago, IL 60603
Tel.: 312-782-0600

First National Bank of Boston*(Major Banking Relationship)*
P.O. Box 644,
Boston, MA 02102-0644
Tel.: 617-575-2900
Fax: 617-575-2549

Frank Russell Company*(Pension Manager)*
909 A St.
Tacoma, WA 98402

Divisions:

Britannica Home Library Services **(1)**
310 S. Michigan Ave.
Chicago, IL 60604
Tel.: 312-347-7000
Publishing
S.I.C.: 2731

Great Books of the Western World **(1)**
310 S. Michigan Ave.
Chicago, IL 60604
Tel.: 312-347-7000
Book Publisher
S.I.C.: 2731

EB (NA) **(1)**
310 S. Michigan Ave.
Chicago, IL 60604
Tel.: 312-347-7000 (100%)
Publishing
S.I.C.: 2731
Patricia A. Wier *(Pres.)*
Robert L. Baseman *(Exec. V.P.-Sls.)*
James D. Battin *(Exec. V.P.-Adv. & Mktg.)*
Frank E. Holmes *(Exec. V.P. & Reg. Mgr.)*
Normand T. LaJoie *(Exec. V.P.-Admin.)*
David J. Van Tosh *(Exec. V.P.-Sls.)*
Nathan Taylor *(V.P.)*
Michael Bearden *(V.P. & Reg. Mgr.)*
Edward J. Gagliardi *(V.P. & Reg. Mgr.)*
Howard N. Scaife *(V.P.-Sls. Support)*
Anthony J. Migas *(V.P.-Information Services)*
Harold J. Silver *(V.P.-Third Party Mktg.)*
Gregory J. Parker *(V.P.-Fin. Services)*
Nick Ventresca *(V.P. & Reg. Mgr.)*
Robert Schmieder *(V.P. & Reg. Mgr.)*
John V. Henrici *(V.P. & Reg. Mgr.)*
Alan M. Komensky *(Gen. Counsel)*

Division:

Britcom Telemarketing Division **(2)**
2200 S. Main
Lombard, IL 60148
Tel.: 708-932-7300
Telemarketing Services
S.I.C.: 7389
Nathan Taylor *(V.P. & Gen. Mgr.)*

Subsidiaries:

American Learning Corp. **(1)**
310 S. Michigan Ave.
Chicago, IL 60604
Tel.: 312-939-0303 (83%)
Fax: 312-939-1680
Approx.Rev.: $16,200,000
Emp.: 1,200
Learning Centers
S.I.C.: 8299
Peter B. Norton *(Chm. Bd. & Chief Exec. Officer)*
Douglas Paul *(Pres. & Chief Oper. Officer)*
Paula Singer *(V.P.)*
Nancy L. Behrendt *(Mgr.-Personnel)*
Brian K. Larson *(Mgr.-Pur.)*
Cindy Nunez *(Adv. Coordinator)*

Compton's New Media Inc. **(1)**
310 S. Michigan Ave.
Chicago, IL 60604
Tel.: 312-347-7000 (100%)
Text Search & Retrieval Software
S.I.C.: 7372; 7375
Norman Bastin *(Sr. V.P. & Gen. Mgr.)*

Encyclopaedia Britannica Educational Corporation **(1)**
310 S. Michigan
Chicago, IL 60604
Tel.: 312-347-7000
S.I.C.: 2731
Joseph Elliott *(Pres.)*
James Decker-Ward *(Exec. V.P.-Mktg.)*

Merriam-Webster, Inc. **(1)**
47 Federal St.
Springfield, MA 01102
Tel.: 413-734-3134
Tel.: 800-828-1880
Fax: 413-731-5979
Emp.: 100
Fiscal Year-end: 9/31/90
Computer Systems/Hardware:
Hewlett-Packard
Publishing of Reference Books
S.I.C.: 2731
Joseph Esposito *(Pres.)*
Donald F. Miller *(V.P.-Sls.)*
James Withgott *(V.P.-Admin.)*
Tom Coopee *(Treas.)*
Susan Leslie *(Dir.-Mktg.)*
Leslie Manganaro *(Asst. Dir.-Mktg.)*
John Hughes *(Mgr.-Mfg.)*
Dolores Goncalves *(Pur. Agent)*

Enercon Data Corp.
(Name Changed To Integrated Energy Controls Corp.)

ENERFAB INC.
4955 Spring Grove Ave.
Cincinnati, OH 45232
Tel.: 513-641-0500
Fax: 513-242-6833
Approx.Sls.: $30,000,000
Emp.: 250
Fiscal Year-end: 9/31/90
Export
Stainless Steel & Steel Lined Food & Beverage Process Vessels; Storage Tanks & Pressure Vessels
S.I.C.: 3443; 3589
John Davies *(Chm. Bd.)*
David F. Herche *(Chief Exec. Officer)*
Terry W. Pfister *(V.P.-Fin., Chief Fin. Officer, Sec. & Treas.)*
Jeff Raasch *(V.P.-Sls.)*
Terrence J. Byrnes *(Dir.-Mktg.)*

ENERGY BROKERS GUILD
(Div. of Transworld Indus.)
2961 W. Glenlord Rd.
Stevensville, MI 49127
Tel.: 616-429-8706
Year Founded: 1948
Approx.Sls.: $81,000,000
Emp.: 34
Fiscal Year-end: 9/ 1/90
Kitchen & Bathroom Cabinets & Energy Savings Products for the House & Industry Including Waterquest KDF Water Filtration Products for Residential, Domestic & Foreign Markets
S.I.C.: 2514
S. Casavant *(Partner)*
G.P. Busca *(Sr. V.P.-Sls. & Mktg. & Chief Oper. Officer)*
Robert Saxon *(Dir.-Mktg.)*
B. Price *(Dir.-New Products)*

ENERGY & ENVIRONMENTAL RESEARCH CORP.
18 Mason Rd.
Irvine, CA 92718
Tel.: 714-859-8851
Fax: 714-859-3194
Emp.: 180
Fiscal Year-end: 1/31/92
Consulting Firm Doing Research on Fuel Combustion
S.I.C.: 8711
Dr. Thomas J. Tyson *(Chm. Bd., Pres. & Chief Exec. Officer)*
Kay Grenda *(Dir.-Personnel)*
Evan Gruber *(Dir.-Fin.)*
Wayne Plizga *(Controller)*

No. of U.S. Offices: 4

Computer Systems/Hardware:
IBM PC; XEROX PC; PDP 11

Outside Service Firm(s):

Ernst & Young*(Auditors)*
18400 Von Karman
Irvine, CA 92715
Tel.: 714-863-3010

Aetna Life & Casualty*(Group Insurer)*
Irvine, CA

Sheppard, Mullin, Richter & Hampton*(Legal Firm)*
Newport Beach, CA

Bank of America NT&SA*(Major Banking Relationship)*
Anaheim, CA

ENERGY FUELS DEVELOPMENT CORPORATION
(d/b/a Enviro Fuels)
320 S. Boston, Ste. 1501
Tulsa, OK 74103
Tel.: 918-592-0300
Fax: 918-492-0355
Approx.Sls.: $10,000,000
Emp.: 3
Manufacture Ethanol For Motor Fuel Additive
S.I.C.: 2869
Ben G. Henneke, Jr. *(Pres.)*
Charles Henneke Jr. *(V.P.)*

Outside Service Firm(s):

KPMG Peat Marwick*(Auditors)*
Topeka, KS

Doerner, Stuart, Saunders, Daniel & Anderson*(Legal Firm)*
1000 Atlas Life Bldg., 415 S. Boston
Tulsa, OK 74103
Tel.: 918-582-1211

Bank of New England*(Major Banking Relationship)*
28 State Street
Boston, MA 02109
Tel.: 617-742-4000

ENERGY MINERALS CORPORATION
999 Eighteenth St., Ste. 3100
Denver, CO 80202
Tel.: 303-571-1010 CO
Fax: 303-571-1030
Year Founded: 1969
Sales Range: $10-19 Million
Emp.: 19
Fiscal Year-end: 6/30/90
Oil & Gas Exploration
S.I.C.: 1382
E.E. Runyan *(Chm. Bd.)*
Robert L. Marolda *(Pres.)*
Donald M. Johnson *(V.P.-Opers. & Chief Oper. Officer)*
Steven R. Matre *(V.P.-Fin., Chief Fin. Officer & Sec.)*
John A. McKnight *(V.P.-Land)*
James R. Gooding *(Admin. Mgr.)*

Computer Systems/Hardware:
Hewlett-Packard 260

Outside Service Firm(s):

Deloitte & Touche*(Auditors)*
1560 Broadway, Ste. 1800
Denver, CO 80202-5626
Tel.: 303-837-3000
Fax: 303-825-0567

Insurance Management Assoc.*(Commercial Insurance Carrier)*
Denver, CO

Principal Mutual Life Insurance Co.*(Group Insurer)*
711 High St.
Des Moines, IA 50309

Shaw, Spangler & Roth*(Legal Firm)*
1700 Broadway
Denver, CO 80202
Tel.: 303-861-2223

United Bank of Denver*(Major Banking Relationship)*
P.O. Box 5247
Denver, CO 80217
Tel.: 303-861-8811

United Asset Management Services*(Pension Manager)*
Denver, CO

Subsidiary:

BMR Corporation **(1)**
999 Eighteenth St., #3100
Denver, CO 80202
Tel.: 303-296-4900
Crude Petroleum & Natural Gas
S.I.C.: 1311
R.L. Marolda *(Chief Exec. Officer)*

ENGER-KRESS COMPANY
151 Wisconsin St.
West Bend, WI 53095
Tel.: 414-334-3456
Tel.: 800-367-7547
Fax: 414-334-6185
Year Founded: 1885
Approx.Sls.: $10,000,000
Emp.: 200
Fiscal Year-end: 3/31/92
Export
Leather Goods; Heritage, Jake Johnson
S.I.C.: 3172
W.A. Bauman *(Pres. & Treas.)*
Wm. M. Hemmings *(V.P.-Sls. & Mktg. & Corp. Sec.)*

ENGINEERED PRODUCTS, INC.
1844 Ardmore Blvd.
Pittsburgh, PA 15221
Tel.: 412-242-6900
Fax: 412-242-5205
Approx.Sls.: $25,000,000
Emp.: 150
Wholesale Construction Materials; Manufacture Sheet Metal; Bridge Repair
S.I.C.: 1622; 3444; 5039
Otto W. Abraham *(Chm. Bd. & Pres.)*
Joseph Stein *(V.P.-Opers.)*
C.J. Trakofler *(V.P.-Fin & Dir.-Data Processing)*
Martin B. Colnes *(Sec. & Treas.)*

Outside Service Firm(s):

Deloitte & Touche*(Auditors)*
2400 One PPG Place
Pittsburgh, PA 15222
Tel.: 412-281-2232

Warman & Crone*(Legal Firm)*
Pittsburg, PA

Union National Bank*(Major Banking Relationship)*
Pittsburgh, PA

ENGINEERING SERVICE, INC.
21556 Telegraph Rd.
Southfield, MI 48034
Mailing Address:
P.O. Box 7
Southfield, MI 48037
Tel.: 313-357-3800
Fax: 313-350-1949
Year Founded: 1941
Sales Range: $10-19 Million
Emp.: 150
Engineering Services; Computer Graphics, Robotics, Tool Path Generation
S.I.C.: 8711; 3569
James Karchon *(Pres.)*
Howard D. Star *(Chief Oper. Officer)*

Outside Service Firm(s):

Price Waterhouse*(Auditors)*
200 Renaissance Center, Ste. 3900
Detroit, MI 48243

National Bank of Detroit*(Major Banking Relationship)*
611 Woodward Ave.
Detroit, MI 48226

ENGINEERING TECHNOLOGY LTD. (E.T.)
777 Chicago Rd.
Troy, MI 48083
Tel.: 313-588-4280 **MI**
Fax: 313-588-8252
Year Founded: 1973
Approx.Sls.: $31,000,000
Emp.: 350
Product Design, Engineering & Styling
S.I.C.: 8711
George Milidrag *(Chm. Bd.)*
James Kidd *(Pres.)*
John Bamibery *(Chief Fin. Officer)*

ENGLEFIELD, INC.
(Formerly Englefield Oil Co.)
447 James Parkway
Newark, OH 43055
Tel.: 614-928-8215 **OH**
Fax: 614-928-3844
Year Founded: 1961
Assets: $19,500,000
Liabilities: $14,500,000
Net Worth: $5,000,000
Approx.Sls.: $200,000,000
Emp.: 1,021
Fiscal Year-end: 6/30/92
Automotive Dealer; Service Stations; Convenience Stores
S.I.C.: 5541; 5172; 5171; 5411
F.W. Englefield, III *(Chm. Bd.)*
F.W. Englefield, IV *(Co-Pres., Chief Exec. & Chief Fin. Officer)*
Benjamin B. Englefield *(Co-Pres.)*
Frank McManus *(V.P.)*
Ed Stephens *(V.P.-Opers.)*
Fred Kaseman *(Controller)*

Computer Systems/Hardware:
Burroughs

Outside Service Firm(s):

Blackman Kallick Bartelstein*(Auditors)*
300 Riverside Plaza
Chicago, IL 60606
Tel.: 312-207-1040

J. Robert Beam*(Legal Firm)*
Zanesville, OH

BancOhio National Bank*(Major Banking Relationship)*
Columbus, OH

ENIDINE INCORPORATED
Seven Centre Dr.
Orchard Park, NY 14127
Tel.: 716-662-1900
Fax: 716-662-1909
Approx.Sls.: $10,000,000
Emp.: 150
Industrial & Aerospace Shock Absorbers
S.I.C.: 3399
Patrick P. Lee *(Chm. Bd. & Pres.)*
Malcolm Gibbins *(V.P.-Intl. Opers.)*
Benjamin T. Houghton *(V.P.-Engrng.)*
Richard Ryan *(V.P.-Fin.)*
Barry Mann *(Dir.-Sls. & Mktg.)*
Dick Delislee *(Mgr.-Opers.)*

Outside Service Firm(s):

Ernst & Young*(Auditors)*
1400 Key Tower - 50 Fountain Plaza
Buffalo, NY
Tel.: 716-843-5000
Fax: 716-847-6949

Fleet Bank*(Major Banking Relationship)*
Deer Park, NY 14202

The Enro Shirt Company, Inc.
(See listing under Enidine Incorporated)

ENSONIQ CORPORATION
155 Great Valley Pkwy.
Malvern, PA 19355
Tel.: 215-647-3930
Fax: 215-647-8908
Approx.Sls.: $23,000,000
Emp.: 180
Electronic Keyboards, Pianos & Organs; Hearing Aids
S.I.C.: 3931
Bruce Crockett *(Pres.)*
Al Charpentier *(V.P.)*
Daniel Garrett *(V.P.-Sls.)*
David Meehan *(V.P.-Sound Selector)*
Bob Parke *(V.P.-Mktg.)*
Malcolm Walter *(Chief Fin. Officer)*
Bob Yannes *(Treas.)*

Outside Service Firm(s):

Arthur Andersen & Co.*(Auditors)*
Hackensack, NJ

Continental Bank, N.A.*(Major Banking Relationship)*
Norristown, PA

THE ENSTAR GROUP, INC.
172 Commerce St., 3rd Fl.
Montgomery, AL 36104
Tel.: 205-834-5483 **DE**
Fax: 205-834-2530
Year Founded: 1969
Emp.: 7
Import Export
Holding Co.
S.I.C.: 6035
Nimrod T. Frazer *(Chm. & Pres.)*
Cheryl D. Davis *(Chief Fin. Officer, V.P.-Taxes & Sec.)*
Amy M. Dunaway *(Treas. & Controller)*

Subsidiaries:

American Savings of Florida, ESB **(1)**
17801 N.W. 2nd Ave.
Miami, FL 33169
Tel.: 305-770-2400 (50%)
Assets: $4,660,920,000
Liabilities: $4,322,585,000
Net Worth: $338,335,000
Approx.Income: $266,190,000
Emp.: 1,016
Federally Insured Thrift Institution
S.I.C.: 6035
Charles Kimbrel *(Chm. Bd.)*
Stephen D. Taylor *(Pres. & Chief Exec. Officer)*
Alan B. Goldstein *(Exec. V.P., Sec. & Gen. Counsel)*
Barbara E. Mahoney *(Exec. V.P.-Retail Banking)*
Robert Radler *(Sr. V.P.-Mktg.)*
Elise Boston *(Adv. Mgr.)*

Bargain Town U.S.A., Inc. **(1)**
One Retail Dr.
Montgomery, AL 36110
Tel.: 205-270-5700 (100%)
Fax: 205-263-7812
Earnings: $3,102,000
Approx.Sls.: $57,079,000
Emp.: 1,120
Fiscal Year-end: 12/31/90
Fashion Retailing at Discount Prices
S.I.C.: 5651
Jim Scarborough *(Pres.)*
Judy Bonzo *(Dir.-Adv.)*

Shoe City Corporation **(1)**
One Retail Dr.
Montgomery, AL 36110
Tel.: 205-270-6300
Fax: 205-270-5705
Earnings: $1,455,000
Approx.Rev.: $51,125,000
Emp.: 1,445
Family Shoe Stores
S.I.C.: 5661
Morris Capp *(Pres.)*
George Bixler *(V.P.-Opers.)*
Mike Dobbs *(V.P.-Warehousing)*
Wade Gafford *(Comptroller)*
Judy Bonzo *(Adv. Dir.)*

ENTERPRISE PRESS, INC.
627-631 Greenwich St.
New York, NY 10014
Tel.: 212-741-2111 **NY**
Fax: 212-627-7937
Year Founded: 1915
Approx.Sls.: $18,000,000
Emp.: 180
Offset Printing
S.I.C.: 2752
Robert Hort *(Chm. Bd. & Sec.)*
Michael Hort *(Pres.)*
Irene Szeglin *(Controller)*

Outside Service Firm(s):

Chemical Banking Corp.*(Major Banking Relationship)*
277 Park Ave.
New York, NY 10041
Tel.: 212-310-6407
Fax: 212-310-4526

ENTERPRISE PRODUCTS COMPANY
2727 N. Loop W., Ste. 700
Houston, TX 77008
Tel.: 713-880-6500
Fax: 713-880-6573
Approx.Sls.: $110,000,000
Emp.: 925
Wholesale Petroleum, Bulk Station & Terminal
S.I.C.: 1321; 4922
Dan L. Duncan *(Chm. Bd. & Chief Exec. Officer)*
O.S. Andras *(Pres.)*
Gary L. Miller *(Chief Fin. Officer)*
John Tomerlin *(V.P.-Human Resources)*
Mike Knesek *(Controller)*

Outside Service Firm(s):

Deloitte & Touche*(Auditors)*
333 Clay St., Ste. 2300
Houston, TX 77002
Tel.: 713-756-2000

ENTERPRISE RENT-A-CAR COMPANY
8850 Ladue Rd.
Saint Louis, MO 63124
Tel.: 314-863-7000 **MO**
Fax: 314-863-7000
Year Founded: 1957
Approx.Rev.: $889,000,000
Emp.: 7,000
Automobile Leasing & Rental
S.I.C.: 7515; 7514
Jack C. Taylor *(Chm. Bd.)*
Andrew C. Taylor *(Pres. & Treas.)*
Douglas S. Brown *(Exec. V.P.)*
Warren Knaup *(Sr. V.P. & Sec.)*
Donald L. Ross *(Sr. V.P.)*
Steve Smith *(Adv. & Mktg. Dir.)*

Outside Service Firm(s):

Commerce Bank of Kansas City*(Major Banking Relationship)*
10th & Walnut
Kansas City, MO 64141
Tel.: 816-234-2000
Fax: 816-234-2548

ENTERPRISES INTERNATIONAL INC.
Blaine & Firman
Hoquiam, WA 98550
Mailing Address:
P.O. Box 293
Hoquiam, WA 98550
Tel.: 206-533-6222 **WA**
Fax: 206-532-2792
Approx.Sls.: $70,000,000
Emp.: 3
Fiscal Year-end: 12/31/90
Export
Holding Company; Paper Pulp for Printing Industry
S.I.C.: 3554; 6719
Isabelle S. Lamb *(Chm. Bd., Pres. & Treas.)*
Larry B. Lock *(Controller & Sec.)*

No. of Mfg. Plants/Facilities: 11
No. of U.S. Offices: 3
No. of Foreign Offices: 8

Outside Service Firm(s):

Moss Adams*(Auditors)*
1001 4th Ave., Ste. 2900
Seattle, WA 98154-1106
Tel.: 206-223-1820

Marsh & McLennan*(Commercial Insurance Carrier)*
720 Olive Way
Seattle, WA 98101
Tel.: 206-223-1240
Fax: 206-224-0637

William M. Mercer Incorporated*(Group Insurance Broker/Consult)*
One Union Square, Ste. 3200
Seattle, WA 98101-3137

Tel.: 206-292-7000
Fax: 206-382-0627

U.S. Bank of Washington*(Investment Banker)*
1414 Fourth Ave.
Seattle, WA 98101
Tel.: 206-344-2300

Gordon, Thomas, Honeywell, Malanca, Peterson & Daheim*(Legal Firm)*
Tacoma, WA

U.S. Bank Of Washington*(Major Banking Relationship)*
Seattle, WA

Gardner, Preston & Moss, Inc.*(Pension Manager)*
Boston, MA

Subsidiary:

Ovalstrapping Inc. **(1)**
710-8th St.
Hoquiam, WA 98550
Tel.: 206-532-9101
Fax: 206-532-1792
Emp.: 110
Export
Paper Pulp for Printing Industry
S.I.C.: 3554
Isabelle S. Lamb *(Pres.)*
Jim Pasic *(Gen. Mgr.)*

Non-U.S. Holding:

Lamb AG **(1)**
Landstrasse 15 CH-5430
Wettingen, Switzerland
Tel.: 056 26 55 44
Telex: 826306
Fax: 056 26 55 95
Distr. of Paper Machinery
S.I.C.: 5084
Hans Kaiser *(Mng. Dir.)*

ENTRON INDUSTRIES LIMITED PARTNERSHIP
(Formerly Entron, Inc.)
70-31 84th St.
Glendale, NY 11385
Tel.: 718-894-8100 DE
Fax: 718-326-9405
Year Founded: 1964
Emp.: 150
Mfg. Electronics
S.I.C.: 3674; 3679
Joseph Ross *(Pres. & Chief Exec. Officer)*
Doris Beal *(V.P.-Mfg.)*
A. Allan Riech *(V.P.-Contracts)*
Raymond H. Gaughran *(Treas.)*
Kay Sears *(Chief Engineer)*

No. of Mfg. Plants/Facilities: 1
No. of U.S. Offices: 1

Computer Systems/Hardware:
IBM PC

Outside Service Firm(s):

Coopers & Lybrand*(Auditors)*
1301 Avenue of The Americas
New York, NY 10019
Tel.: 212-536-2000

Olwine, Connelly, Chase, O'Donnell & Weyher*(Legal Firm)*
750 7th Ave.
New York, NY 10019
Tel.: 212-326-3500
Fax: 212-308-2041

Central Jersey Bank*(Major Banking Relationship)*
Matawan, NJ

THE ENTWISTLE COMPANY
Bigelow St.
Hudson, MA 01749
Tel.: 508-481-4000 RI
Fax: 508-562-4808
Year Founded: 1914
Assets: $32,755,000
Liabilities: $11,297,000
Net Worth: $21,458,000
Approx.Sls.: $46,371,000
Emp.: 380
Fiscal Year-end: 9/30/91
Machinery for Insulated Wire & Cable; Electro-Mechanical Equipment For The Government
S.I.C.: 3549
Herbert I. Corkin *(Chm. Bd., Pres., Chief Exec. & Chief Oper. Officer)*
Thomas E. Robinson *(Sr. V.P. & Sec.)*
Dale F. Eck *(V.P. & Treas.)*
Steven Wentzell *(Dir.-Rur.)*

Outside Service Firm(s):

Grant Thornton*(Auditors)*
53 State St.
Boston, MA 02109
Tel.: 617-723-7900

Edwards & Angell*(Legal Firm)*
2700 Hospital Trust Twr.
Providence, RI 02903
Tel.: 401-274-9200

Divisions:

Entwistle Defense Technology Div. **(1)**
3909 Hulen
Fort Worth, TX 76107
Tel.: 817-738-3535
Mfr. of Defense Technology
S.I.C.: 3549
Larry Hove *(Pres.)*

Lockley Manufacturing Division **(1)**
310 Grove St.
New Castle, PA 16103
Tel.: 412-658-1551 (100%)
Mfr. of Defense Technology
S.I.C.: 3812
Norman Smilek *(Pres.)*
George Frederick *(V.P.)*

Divisions:

Snark Boats Div. **(2)**
P.O. Box 2360, Industrial St.
New Castle, PA 16102
Tel.: 412-658-6555
Mfr. of Small Sail Boats
S.I.C.: 3732
Robin Holder *(Dir.-Mktg.)*

Triangle Parachute **(2)**
1335 Durham Rd.
Roxboro, NC 27573
Tel.: 919-597-2225
Mfr. of Parachutes
S.I.C.: 3569
N. Wilkersonerson *(Plant Mgr.)*

Subsidiary:

The Entwistle Export Co., Inc. **(1)**
Bigelow St.
Hudson, MA 01749
Tel.: 508-481-4000 (100%)
Mfr. of Metalworking Machinery
S.I.C.: 3549

ENVIRODYNE INDUSTRIES, INC.
701 Harger Rd., Ste. 121
Oak Brook, IL 60521
Tel.: 708-571-8800 DE
Fax: 708-571-0959
Year Founded: 1970
Assets: $1,086,457,000
Earnings: ($31,755,000)
Liabilities: $1,126,760,000
Net Worth: $40,303,000
Approx.Sls.: $543,969,000
Emp.: 4,600
Fiscal Year-end: 12/26/91
Mfr. Cellulosic Casings; Shrinkable Plastic Bags; Plastic Flatware; Drinking Straws; Plastic Packaging Films; Thermoformed Plastic Containers
S.I.C.: 3089
Donald P. Kelly *(Chm. Bd., Pres. & Chief Exec. Officer)*
John S. Corcoran *(Exec. V.P. & Chief Fin. Officer)*
F. Edward Gustafson *(Exec. V.P. & Chief Oper. Officer)*
Stephen M. Schuster *(V.P., Sec. & Gen. Counsel)*
Gordon S. Donovan *(Treas.)*
Sandra L. Musachia *(Controller)*

Outside Service Firm(s):

Coopers & Lybrand*(Auditors)*
203 N. LaSalle St.
Chicago, IL 60601
Tel.: 312-701-5500

Continental Bank N. A.*(Major Banking Relationship)*
231 S. LaSalle St.
Chicago, IL 60697
Tel.: 312-828-2345
Tel.: 800-426-5754
Telex: 312-828-1783

Subsidiaries:

Clear Shield National, Inc. **(1)**
1175 Wheeling Rd.
Wheeling, IL 60090
Tel.: 708-541-2900 (100%)
Approx.Sls.: $66,000,000
Emp.: 500
Mfrs. Disposable Plastic Flatware, Drinking Straws, Custom Disposable Dining Kits & Related Prods. for the Institutional Mkt. & Retail Consumer Market
S.I.C.: 3089
Denis Davison *(Pres.)*
Luther Haskins *(V.P.-Fin.)*
Jim Couris *(V.P.-Mfg.)*
Keith A. Johnson *(Mgr.-Natl. Sls.)*

Sandusky Plastics, Inc. **(1)**
400 Broadway
Sandusky, OH 44870
Tel.: 419-626-8980
Mfg. Thermoformed Plastic Containers
S.I.C.: 3089
Thomas J. Aylward *(Pres.)*

Viskase Corporation **(1)**
6855 W. 65th St.
Bedford Park, IL 60638
Tel.: 708-496-4200
Emp.: 1500
Mfr. of Cellulosic Casings, Shrinkable Plastic Bags & Plastic Films
S.I.C.: 3089
F. Edward Gustafson *(Pres.)*
J.E. King *(Dir.-Sls.)*
W. K. Goerich *(Dir.-Mktg.)*

Division:

Filmco Industries, Inc. **(2)**
1450 S. Chillicothe Rd.
Aurora, OH 44202
Tel.: 216-562-6111 (100%)
Manfacture Plastic Packaging Film
S.I.C.: 3089
John Onesta *(Gen. Mgr.)*

Non-U.S. Holdings:

Envirodyne Limited **(1)**
Salters Lane Sedgefield, Stockton-on-Tees, Cleveland United Kingdom
Tel.: 44-0740 20751
Telex: 58460 FILMCO G
Fax: 44-0740 21358
Mfr. of Plasticized Polyvinyl Chloride Films
S.I.C.: 2821

Viskase **(1)**
Kingsway Fforestfach, Swansea, United Kingdom
Tel.: 44-0792 582585
Telex: 48237 VISKAS G
Fax: 44-0792 582574
Mfr. of Cellulosic Casings for Sausages, Hams & Other Foods
S.I.C.: 3089

Viskase Canada Inc. **(1)**
150 Colborne St. E.
Lindsay, ON K9V 5P6, Canada
Tel.: 705-324-2101
Tel.: 800-461-0330
Fax: 705-324-4377
Cellulose Food Casings, Food Packaging Equipment
S.I.C.: 3089
N. Hamilton *(Plant Mgr.)*

ENVIRONETICS
(Formerly Access Medical Systems)
21 Business Park Dr.
Branford, CT 06405
Tel.: 203-481-3073 DE
Year Founded: 1983
Approx.Sls.: $10,000,000
Emp.: 26
Fiscal Year-end: 9/30/92
Mfr. & Wholesale Distr. of Diagnostic Products
S.I.C.: 2835; 5047
J.L. Cohoon *(Chm. Bd.)*
Mark Kaufman *(Chief Exec. Officer)*
Richard L. Musser *(V.P.-Fin. & Opers.)*
Dean T. Layton *(V.P.)*

ENVIRONMENTAL INDUSTRIES, INC.
24121 Ventura Blvd.
Calabasas, CA 91302
Tel.: 818-223-8500 CA
Fax: 818-223-8142
Year Founded: 1949
Approx.Sls.: $221,000,000
Emp.: 3,500
Fiscal Year-end: 4/30/92
Landscape Construction & Maintenance, Tree Growing
S.I.C.: 0781; 0782; 0783
Burton S. Sperber *(Chm. Bd., Pres. , & Chief Exec. Officer)*
David Rose *(Exec. V.P. & Chief Fin. Officer)*
William N. Cohen *(V.P., Gen. Counsel, & Sec.)*
Stanley A. Colton *(V.P.)*
Michael L. Dingman *(V.P.)*
S. Gene Giannulli *(V.P.)*
Andres A. Martinez *(V.P. & Controller)*
Richard Sperber *(V.P.)*
Stuart J. Sperber *(V.P.-Tree Div.)*
Bruce K. Wilson *(V.P.-Maintenance Div.)*
Barbara Royce Extract *(Dir.-Corp. & Public Rels.)*

Outside Service Firm(s):

Security Pacific National Bank*(Major Banking Relationship)*
333 S. Hope St.
Los Angeles, CA 90017
Tel.: 213-613-6211

Division:

Environmental Landscape Products **(1)**
2209 E. Orangewood Ave.
Anaheim, CA 92806
Tel.: 714-978-6200
Fax: 714-978-0188
Landscaping Supplies
S.I.C.: 0781
Roger Laguna *(Gen. Mgr.)*

EON LABS, INC.
207 Westminister
Lake Forest, IL 60045
Tel.: 708-615-1966
Emp.: 600
Fiscal Year-end: 12/31/91
Mfg. & Distribute Generic Pharmaceutical
S.I.C.: 2834
Gary Nei *(Pres. & Chief Exec. Officer)*
James Kenton *(Chief Fin. Officer)*

No. of U.S. Offices: 6

Subsidiary:

Vitarine Pharmaceuticals, Inc. **(1)**
227-15 N. Conduit Ave.
Springfield Gardens, NY 11413
Tel.: 718-276-8600
Sales Range: $100-499 Million
Fiscal Year-end: 9/30/91
Manufacture Pharmaceuticals
S.I.C.: 2834

Eon Labs, Inc.—(Continued)

Roger Jordon *(Pres.)*
Dr. Seymour Hyden *(Exec. V.P.)*
Gail Prince *(V.P.-Regulatory Affairs)*
Michael Raya *(V.P.-Quality Control)*
William Eversgerd *(V.P.-Material Mngmt.)*
David H. Gransec *(Sec.)*

Subsidiaries:

Crown Drug **(2)**
1640 W. Fulton St.
Chicago, IL 60612
Tel.: 312-666-0981
Mfr. of Pharmaceuticals
S.I.C.: 2834
Fred Bondy *(Gen. Mgr.)*

Ellis Pharmaceuticals **(2)**
355 Tomoka Ave.
Ormond Beach, FL 32174
Tel.: 904-672-0611
Mfr. of Pharmaceuticals
S.I.C.: 2834

Major Pharmaceuticals Corp. **(2)**
3720 Lapeer Rd.
Auburn Hills, MI 48326
Tel.: 313-370-0680
Mfr. of Pharmaceuticals
S.I.C.: 2834
Bill Farber *(Chief Exec. Officer)*

Michigan Pharmacal **(2)**
3720 Lapeer Rd.
Auburn Hills, MI 48326
Tel.: 313-370-0680
Mfr. of Pharmaceuticals
S.I.C.: 2834
Bill Farber *(Chief Exec. Officer)*

Murray Drug **(2)**
415 S. Fourth St.
Murray, KY 42071
Tel.: 502-753-6654
Mfr. of Pharmaceuticals
S.I.C.: 2834
Steve Dublin *(Chief Oper. Officer)*

Texas Drug Reps **(2)**
11722 Warfield
San Antonio, TX 78216
Tel.: 210-349-2695
Mfr. of Pharmaceuticals
S.I.C.: 2834

Ultra Drug **(2)**
8330 Arjons Dr.
San Diego, CA 92126
Tel.: 619-693-6080
Mfr. of Pharmaceuticals
S.I.C.: 2834
Steve Strand *(Chief Oper. Officer)*

Vitarine Pharmaceuticals of the Virgin Islands Inc. **(2)**
P.O. Box 3016
Kingshill, VI 00824

EPEC, INC.
New Bedford Industrial Park
New Bedford, MA 02747
Tel.: 508-995-5171 **MA**
Fax: 508-995-3691
Year Founded: 1981
Approx.Sls.: $10,000,000
Emp.: 170
Mfr. of Printed Circuit Boards
S.I.C.: 3672
Ralph Calico *(Pres.)*
Michael Navoy *(Treas.)*
Anthony Perritano *(Controller)*
Russ Girard *(Mgr.-Quality Control)*
Kristin Hannigan *(Mgr.-Pur.)*

Outside Service Firm(s):

Bank of New England*(Major Banking Relationship)*
New Bedford, MA

EPIC HEALTHCARE GROUP
3333 Lee Parkway
Dallas, TX 75265-0398
Mailing Address:
PO Box 650398,
Dallas, TX 75219
Tel.: 214-443-3333
Own & Manage Hospitals
S.I.C.: 8069
Ken George *(Chief Exec. Officer)*

No. of U.S. Offices: 39

EPOXYLITE CORPORATION
9400 Toledo Way
Irvine, CA 92718
Mailing Address:
P.O. Box 19671,
Irvine, CA 92713
Tel.: 714-951-3231
Fax: 714-472-0980
Emp.: 100
Epoxy & Polyurethane Formulation, Adhesives, Coatings
S.I.C.: 2821; 2891; 3561
P.A. Timmins *(Chm. Bd.)*
Peter A. Dorsa *(Pres.)*
Ron Grant *(V.P.)*
Dennis Shephard *(V.P.)*

Outside Service Firm(s):

Sweek, Connolly & Torre*(Auditors)*
Santa Ana, CA

Irsfeld, Irsfeld & Younger*(Legal Firm)*
Glendale, CA

First Business Bank*(Major Banking Relationship)*
Los Angeles, CA

A. EPSTEIN AND SONS, INTL., INC.
600 W. Fulton St.
Chicago, IL 60661-1199
Tel.: 312-454-9100
Telex: 254314
Fax: 312-559-1217
Year Founded: 1921
Assets: $11,500,000
Earnings: $62,100,000
Liabilities: $5,300,000
Net Worth: $6,200,000
Approx.Rev.: $55,000,000
Emp.: 600
Fiscal Year-end: 12/31/90
Designs & Manages Construction of Buildings & Building Systems
S.I.C.: 1541; 8711; 8742; 8712
Sidney Epstein *(Chm. Bd.)*
Melvin Kupperman *(Pres. & Chief Exec. Officer)*
Gerald E. Tomaszewski *(V.P. & Chief Fin. Officer)*

No. of U.S. Offices: 3
No. of Foreign Offices: 4

Computer Systems/Hardware:
IBM PC; Apollo

Outside Service Firm(s):

Grant Thornton*(Auditors)*
700 One Prudential Plaza, 130 East Randolph St.
Chicago, IL 60601
Tel.: 312-856-0200
Fax: 312-565-4719

Altheimer & Gray*(Legal Firm)*
10 S. Wacker Dr.
Chicago, IL 60606
Tel.: 312-715-4000

Harris Trust & Savings Bank*(Major Banking Relationship)*
111 W. Monroe St.
Chicago, IL 60690
Tel.: 312-461-2265
Tel.: 800-858-0840

Subsidiaries:

Architectural Interiors, Inc. **(1)**
600 W. Fulton
Chicago, IL 60606
Tel.: 312-454-9100 (100%)
Fax: 312-559-1217
Approx.Sls.: $2,000,000
Emp.: 33
Space Planning; Interior Design
S.I.C.: 8742; 8712; 8744
Jean Bellas *(Pres.)*

Computer Technology Management Inc. **(1)**
600 West Fulton St.
Chicago, IL 60606
Tel.: 312-454-9100
Fax: 312-559-1217
Emp.: 12
Computer Support & Consultancy Services
S.I.C.: 7371; 7372; 7373; 7374; 7379; 8742
Kristine Fallon *(Pres.)*

Epstein Civil Engineering, Inc. **(1)**
600 W. Fulton
Chicago, IL 60606
Tel.: 312-454-9100 (100%)
Fax: 312-559-1217
Approx.Sls.: $5,000,000
Emp.: 30
Municipal Engineering; Highway & Bridge Construction; Pollution Control, Land Development; Sitework for Buildings
S.I.C.: 8711; 8713
William Rynearson *(Pres.)*

Epstein Construction Inc. **(1)**
600 W. Fulton
Chicago, IL 60606
Tel.: 312-454-9100 (100%)
Fax: 312-559-1217
Approx.Sls.: $100,000,000
Emp.: 44
Construction; Construction Management
S.I.C.: 1522; 1542; 1629; 8742; 1541
Richard O. Lober *(Pres.)*

Epstein Engineering, Inc. **(1)**
600 W. Fulton St.
Chicago, IL 60606-1199
Tel.: 312-454-9100
Fax: 312-559-1217
Emp.: 110
Structural, Mechanical & Electrical Engineering Services
S.I.C.: 8711
Maurice Spang *(Pres.)*

Epstein Engineering Export, Ltd. **(1)**
600 W. Fulton
Chicago, IL 60606
Tel.: 312-454-9100 (100%)
Fax: 312-559-1217
Approx.Sls.: $10,000,000
Emp.: 7
Engineering; Industrial & Commercial Construction
S.I.C.: 1541; 1542; 8711; 8712; 8742; 1629
Maciej Raczkiewicz *(Pres.)*
Thomas J. Einbecker *(V.P.)*

Epstein Material Handling Engineering, Inc. **(1)**
600 W. Fulton
Chicago, IL 60606
Tel.: 312-454-9100 (100%)
Fax: 312-559-1217
Approx.Sls.: $15,000,000
Emp.: 28
Analysis of Warehousing & Distribution Problems; Material Handling Systems Design; Crane Engineering Design Services
S.I.C.: 8711; 8742
Wayne Schild *(Pres.)*

Epstein Process Engineering, Inc. **(1)**
600 W. Fulton
Chicago, IL 60661-1199
Tel.: 312-454-9100 (100%)
Fax: 312-559-1217
Emp.: 39
Food, Pharmaceutical & Industrial Process Design Services
S.I.C.: 8711; 8742
Mickey Kupperman *(Pres.)*
Toni Nessi *(V.P.-Mktg.)*

A. Epstein & Sons (California) Inc. **(1)**
1440 South Sepulveda Blvd.
Los Angeles, CA 90025
Tel.: 310-473-5358 (100%)
Fax: 310-473-4908
Approx.Sls.: $5,000,000
Emp.: 15
General Architectural and Engineering Services
S.I.C.: 8712; 8711
Jerrold Penrose *(Pres.)*

A. Epstein & Sons, Inc. **(1)**
600 W. Fulton
Chicago, IL 60606
Tel.: 312-454-9100 (100%)
Fax: 312-599-1217
Approx.Sls.: $60,000,000
Emp.: 79
Architects
S.I.C.: 8712
Mike Damore *(V.P. & Dir. of Architecture)*

Interior Design Inc. **(1)**
1440 South Sepulveda Blvd.
Los Angeles, CA 90025
Tel.: 310-473-5358 (100%)
Fax: 310-473-4908
Approx.Sls.: $4,000,000
Emp.: 19
Space Planning; Interior Design
S.I.C.: 8742; 8744
Marjorie Platzker *(Pres.)*

Interior Space Design Inc., (ISD) **(1)**
600 W. Fulton St.
Chicago, IL 60606
Tel.: 312-454-9100
Space Planning, Interior Design
S.I.C.: 8742; 8744
Jean Bellas *(Exec. V.P.)*

Non-U.S. Holdings:

Epstein Engineering Export (Warsaw), Ltd. **(1)**
Biuro Nadzora w Warszawie, Al 1 Armii Wojska Polskiego, 16 M 3
Warsaw, 00-582, Poland
Tel.: 28 84 33
Tel.: 29 13 88
Fax: 28 84 33
Emp.: 36
Engineering; Industrial & Commercial Construction
S.I.C.: 1541; 1542; 8711; 8712; 8742; 1629
Maciej A. Raczkiewicz *(Pres. & Chief Oper. Officer)*

A. Epstein & Sons (France) Inc. **(1)**
Tour Pariferic 93306
Aubervilliers, Cedex France
Tel.: 1-48-39-86-18
Fax: 1-48-39-29-87
Approx.Sls.: $10,000,000
Emp.: 11
Architecture; Engineering; General Contracting
S.I.C.: 8711; 8712
Boyana Zec *(Pres.)*

A. Epstein & Sons (Israel) Ltd. **(1)**
P.O. Box 50003, The Industry House, 29 Hamered St.
Tel Aviv, 68125, Israel
Tel.: 3-664-511
Tel.: 3-662-905
Fax: 3-510-3689
Approx.Sls.: $30,000,000
Emp.: 50
Architecture; Engineering; General Contracting
S.I.C.: 8711; 8712; 1541
Yoav Sarne *(Pres.)*

A. Epstein & Sons (U.K.) Ltd. **(1)**
Vincent House Vincent Square,
London, SW1P 2NB, United Kingdom
Tel.: 071-834-5062
Fax: 011-44-1-630-5956
Approx.Sls.: $30,000,000
Emp.: 7
Architecture; Engineering; General Contracting
S.I.C.: 8711; 8712
Marty Buchalski *(Pres.)*

EQUINOX ADVERTISING, INC.
980 N. Michigan Ave., Ste. 1180
Chicago, IL 60611
Tel.: 312-951-5366
Year Founded: 1986
Approx.Billings: $20,000,000
Emp.: 20
Commercial Adv.
William Daniel *(Sec. & Dir.-Art)*
Stuart Rankin *(Treas. & New Bus. Contact)*
William Izzo *(Dir.-Production)*

Bernard Washington *(Dir.-Creative)*

THE EQUION CORPORATION
555 Long Wharf Dr., 12th Fl.
New Haven, CT 06511
Tel.: 203-777-7367 **DE**
Fax: 203-787-5707
Approx.Sls.: $75,000,000
Emp.: 600
Fiscal Year-end: 7/31/90
Automotive, Truck & Off-Highway Air Conditioning & Heating Units
S.I.C.: 3714; 3585
Sam Reisman *(Chm. Bd.)*
Barry Banducci *(Pres. & Chief Exec. Officer)*
Richard E. Gregerson *(V.P.-Fin.)*
Charles E. Johnson *(V.P.)*
Mark D. Williams *(Dir.-Plng & Mktg. Devel.)*

Outside Service Firm(s):

Ernst & Young*(Auditors)*
1000 Brown & Williamson Tower
Louisville, KY 40202
Tel.: 502-585-1400

Kramer, Levin, Nessen, Kamin & Frankel*(Legal Firm)*
919 Third Ave.
New York, NY 10022
Tel.: 212-688-1100

Manufacturers Hanover Trust Co.*(Major Banking Relationship)*
40 Wall St.
New York, NY 10005
Tel.: 212-623-4444

Subsidiaries:

Hayden, Inc. **(1)**
P.O. Box 848, 1531 Pomona Rd.
Corona, CA 91720
Tel.: 909-736-2665
Mfrs. Oil-to-Air Transfer Devices for Vehicular & Stationary Devices
S.I.C.: 3585; 3714
Paul T. Loomis *(Pres.)*
Eugene Boyer *(Exec. V.P.-Opers.)*
James Wright *(V.P.-Fin.)*
Donald Cox *(V.P.-Mfg.)*
Stephen Price *(V.P.-Engrng.)*

Signet Systems, Inc. **(1)**
Tapp Road
Harrodsburg, KY 40330
Tel.: 606-734-7711
Automotive, Truck & Off-Highway Air Conditioning & Heating Units
S.I.C.: 3585; 3714
Charles E. Johnson *(Pres. & Chief Exec. Officer)*
Thomas Campbell *(Exec. V.P.-Opers.)*
Robert Hange *(V.P.-Sls. & Mktg.)*
Lawrence Mentzer *(V.P.-Engrng.)*
William C. Pellisero *(V.P.-Fin. & Admin.)*

EQUIPMENT MANUFACTURING, INC.
21550 Hoover Rd.
Warren, MI 48089
Mailing Address:
P.O. Box 748,
Warren, MI 48090
Tel.: 313-755-6600
Fax: 313-755-0255
Approx.Sls.: $15,000,000
Emp.: 200
Racks for Material Handling & Storage
S.I.C.: 3441; 3531
Dave Foran *(Pres.)*
Gary Burgess *(V.P., Treas. & Pur. Agent)*
Lowell G. Steffens *(V.P.-Sls. & Adv.)*

EQUITABLE BAG COMPANY
37-11 35th Ave.
Long Island City, NY 11101
Tel.: 718-786-0620 **NY**
Fax: 718-361-1815
Year Founded: 1919
Approx.Sls.: $140,000,000
Emp.: 1,200
Fiscal Year-end: 12/31/90
Export
Manufacture Paper Bags
S.I.C.: 2673; 2674
Robert A. Krissel *(Pres. & Chief Oper. Officer)*
Jonathon S. Canno *(Exec. V.P.)*
Harvey J. Burstein *(V.P.-Opers.)*
William Maher *(V.P.-Sls. Admin.)*
Harold Mills *(V.P. & Gen. Mgr.-Southern Division)*
C. Charles Pearl *(V.P.-Tech. Oper.)*
Lawrence Pinchuck *(V.P.-Sls.)*
Paul Shackford *(V.P.-Fin. & Admin.)*
James Stepp *(V.P. & Gen. Mgr.-Midwest Division)*
Michael A. Doris *(Controller)*
Jeffrey R. Greene *(Dir.-Human Resources)*
Ralph Solimano *(Dir.-Mngmt. Information Service)*
Thomas Zink *(Dir.-Pur.)*

No. of Mfg. Plants/Facilities: 3
No. of U.S. Offices: 3

Computer Systems/Hardware:
AS 400

Outside Service Firm(s):

Ernst & Young*(Auditors)*
787 Seventh Ave.
New York, NY 10019
Tel.: 212-773-1243

Citibank N.A.*(Major Banking Relationship)*
Corporate Trust Services, 399 Park Ave.
New York, NY 10043
Tel.: 212-559-1605

EQUITABLE BANKSHARES OF COLORADO, INC.
P.O. Box 8779,
Denver, CO 80201
Tel.: 303-534-2265 **CO**
Fax: 303-293-0700
Year Founded: 1980
Assets: $96,809,000
Earnings: $754,000
Liabilities: $88,665,000
Net Worth: $8,144,000
Approx.Income: $9,172,000
Emp.: 67
Fiscal Year-end: 6/30/92
Banking; Financial Holding Co.
S.I.C.: 6021; 6712
Judith B. Wagner *(Chm.)*
Joy S. Burns *(Vice Chm.)*
B. La Rae Orullian *(Pres. & Chief Exec. Officer)*
Thora A. Aarvig *(Sec.)*

Computer Systems/Hardware:
HP-3000

Subsidiaries:

Equitable Bank of Littleton, N.A. **(1)**
101 W. Mineral Ave.
Littleton, CO 80120
Tel.: 303-797-2265 (100%)
Fax: 303-730-8430
Approx.Assets: $6,418,000
Banking
S.I.C.: 6021
Darrell J. Schulte *(Pres. & Chief Exec. Officer)*
James D. Campbell *(Cashier & Asst. V.P.)*

The Women's Bank, N.A. **(1)**
821 17th St.
Denver, CO 80202
Tel.: 303-293-2265 (99%)
Approx.Assets: $57,264,000
Emp.: 36
Banking
S.I.C.: 6021
B. La Rae Orullian *(Chm. & Chief Exec. Officer)*
Jean H. Peden *(Pres.)*
Benjamin P. Garneau *(Sr. V.P.-Compliance)*
Nancy P. Gruber *(V.P.)*
Jean K. Matsuda *(Auditor)*

EQUITY FUND ADVISORS INC.
Ste. 500, 550 Post Oak Blvd.
Houston, TX 77027
Tel.: 713-960-0250 **TX**
Fax: 713-960-1205
Sales Range: $100-499 Million
Emp.: 30
Real Estate Developers & Brokers
S.I.C.: 6552; 6153
Dennis R. Ranzau *(Pres.)*
Marty Hogan *(V.P.-Fin.)*
Micky D. Altman *(Sec.)*
William L. Paulk *(Dir.-Design & Construction)*

EQUITY GROUP INVESTMENTS
2 N. Riverside Plaza, Ste. 600
Chicago, IL 60606
Tel.: 312-454-0100
Holding Company
S.I.C.: 6719
Samuel Zell *(Chm. Bd. & Pres.)*
Arthur A. Greenburg *(Sr. V.P & Chief Fin. Officer)*

Outside Service Firm(s):

Eisenstein, Raemer & Schwartz*(Auditors)*
Chicago, IL

First National Bank of Commerce*(Major Banking Relationship)*
210 Baronne St.
New Orleans, LA 70112
Tel.: 504-561-1371

Subsidiary:

Delta Queen Steamboat Company **(1)**
Robin St. Wharf
New Orleans, LA 70130-1890
Tel.: 504-586-0631
Tel.: 800-543-1949
Telex: 5101007509
Fax: 504-585-0630
Approx.Sls.: $61,000,000
Emp.: 448
Fiscal Year-end: 3/31/92
Steamboat Cruises; Delta Queen, Mississippi Queen
S.I.C.: 4489
Cody Engle *(Chm. Bd.)*
Patrick Fahey *(Pres. & Chief Exec. Officer)*
Jeffrey Krida *(Exec. V.P. & Chief Oper. Officer)*
Scott Young *(Exec. V.P.)*
Russell E. Varvel *(Sr. V.P.-Sls.)*
James German *(V.P.-Mktg.)*
Richard Kerr *(V.P.-Finance)*
David Kish *(V.P.-Admin. & Gen. Counsel)*
Len Morissette *(V.P.-Hotel Oper.)*
Wes Payne *(V.P.-Entertainment & Cruise Programs)*
Patricia Young *(V.P.-Pub. Rels.)*
Steve Isaacson *(Chief Fin. Officer)*
Minette Bruce *(Controller)*
Alva Head *(Exec. Asst.)*
William Beal *(Dir.-Reservations)*
Homer Ellis *(Dir.-Pur.)*
Connie Fox *(Dir.-Corp. Affairs)*
David Snow *(Dir.-Mktg.)*
Barbara Ewell *(Mgr.-Human Resources)*
Terry Westerfield *(Mgr.-Pub. Rels.)*
Lauren Pettingill *(Mgr.-Retail)*

EQUITY SUPPLY COMPANY
P.O. Box 579
Kalispell, MT 59901
Tel.: 406-755-7400 **MT**
Fax: 406-257-3542
Year Founded: 1917
Approx.Sls.: $11,000,000
Emp.: 54
Cream; Aerated Grain Elevators; Fertilizer & Fertilizer Materials; Gasoline Stations; Builders Hardware
S.I.C.: 2026; 5153; 5159; 5541
Nathan L. Byrd *(Gen. Mgr.)*
Rose Ann Stafford *(Sec. & Treas.)*
Ron Hartsock *(Chief Engr.)*

Outside Service Firm(s):

Hamilton Misfeldt & Co.*(Auditors)*
Great Falls, MT

Norwest Bank Kalispell, N.A.*(Major Banking Relationship)*
P.O. Box 88,
Kalispell, MT 59901
Tel.: 406-756-4000

ERDLE PERFORATING CO.
100 Pixley Indus. Pkwy.
Rochester, NY 14624
Tel.: 716-247-4700 **NY**
Fax: 716-247-4716
Year Founded: 1870
Approx.Sls.: $15,000,000
Emp.: 100
Manufacture Perforated Metals
S.I.C.: 3469
William J. Erdle, III *(Chm. Bd. & Pres.)*
C. Roy Cooke *(V.P.-Opers.)*
Ronald L. Dewey *(Dir.-Fin. & Sec.)*
Karen Thomas *(Dir.-Pur.)*

Principal(s):
William J. Erdle, III

Outside Service Firm(s):

Cortland L. Brovitz & Co.*(Auditors)*
Rochester, NY

Harter, Secrest & Emery*(Legal Firm)*
700 Midtown Tower
Rochester, NY 14604
Tel.: 716-232-6500

Marine Midland Bank*(Major Banking Relationship)*
One Marine Midland Plaza
Rochester, NY

Subsidiaries:

Erdle Perforating of Carolina **(1)**
10721 John Price Rd.
Charlotte, NC 28217
Tel.: 704-588-4380 (100%)
Manufacture Perforated Metals
S.I.C.: 3469
George Erdle *(Pres.)*

Erdle Perforating Co. Ltd. **(1)**
22 Bowden St.
Fort Erie, ON Canada L2A 5M9
Tel.: 416-871-8481 (100%)
Manufacture Perforated Metals
S.I.C.: 3469
John Gibson *(Chief Oper. Office)*

MARSHALL ERDMAN AND ASSOCIATES, INC.
5117 University Ave.
Madison, WI 53705
Mailing Address:
P.O. Box 5249,
Madison, WI 53705
Tel.: 608-238-0211
Fax: 608-238-5604
Year Founded: 1951
Approx.Sls.: $150,000,000
Emp.: 800
Fiscal Year-end: 12/31/90
Import
Design, Engineering, Prefabrication, & Construction of Medical Buildings, Techline Furniture & Cabinetry
S.I.C.: 1629
Corporate Giving Program: United Way
Marshall Erdman *(Chm. Bd.)*
Roger Hauck *(Pres.)*
Bill Madden *(Controller)*
Alice D'Alessio *(Dir.-Communications)*
Jim Curtis *(Dir.-Pur.)*

Divisions:

Marshall Erdman & Assoc., Inc. **(1)**
3097 Presidential Dr.
Atlanta, GA 30340
Tel.: 404-451-2752
S.I.C.: 1629
Bill Wakefield *(V.P. & Gen. Mgr.)*

Marshall Erdman and Associates, Inc.—(Continued)

Marshall Erdman & Assoc., Inc. (1)
891 Interlocken Pkwy.
Broomfield, CO 80020
Tel.: 303-466-5111
S.I.C.: 1629

Marshall Erdman & Assoc., Inc. (1)
880 Dorothy Dr., Ste. 800
Richardson, TX 75081
Tel.: 214-231-5321
S.I.C.: 1629
Dan Figert *(V.P. & Gen. Mgr.)*

Marshall Erdman & Assoc., Inc. (1)
7 Thompson Rd.
East Windsor, CT 06088
Tel.: 203-623-9487
S.I.C.: 1629
Marv Wiehe *(Gen. Mgr.)*

Marshall Erdman & Assoc., Inc. (1)
8550 Cinder Bed Rd., #1300
Newington, VA 22122
Tel.: 703-370-9047
S.I.C.: 1629
Don Kayon *(Gen. Mgr.)*

ERGON, INC.
202 E. Pearl Rd.
Jackson, MS 39201
Mailing Address:
P.O. Drawer 1639
Jackson, MS 39215
Tel.: 601-948-3472
Fax: 601-948-3472, Ext. 333
Approx.Sls.: $100,000,000
Emp.: 1,000
Gasoline; Greases; Lubricating; Asphalt Or Asphaltic Materials Made In Refineries; Liquid Petroleum Transport; Crude Petroleum Pipeline
S.I.C.: 2911; 4213; 4449; 5171; 5984
Leslie B. Lampton, Sr. *(Chm. Bd. & Pres.)*
George Ishee *(Sr. V.P.)*
James Jones *(Sr. V.P.)*
Leslie B. Lampton, III *(V.P.)*
Lee C. Lampton *(V.P.)*
Martin Howard *(V.P. & Controller)*
Kathy Stone *(V.P., Treas. & Sec.)*

Outside Service Firm(s):

First National Bank of Commerce*(Major Banking Relationship)*
New Orleans, LA

Subsidiary:

Crafco, Inc. (1)
6975 W. Crafco Way
Chandler, AZ 85226
Tel.: 602-276-0476
Fax: 602-961-0513
Approx.Sls.: $13,000,000
Emp.: 125
Manufacture Road Repair Machines; Asphalt Based Sealant Products
S.I.C.: 2951; 3531
Donald M. Brooks *(V.P. & Gen. Mgr.)*

ERICKSON DIVERSIFIED CORP.
509 1/2 Second St.
Hudson, WI 54016
Tel.: 715-386-9315 **WI**
Fax: 715-386-9315, Ext. 32
Year Founded: 1928
Sales Range: $100-499 Million
Emp.: 1,500
Fiscal Year-end: 12/31/91
Chain of 16 Combination Food & Drug Stores
S.I.C.: 5411; 5912
Dean Erickson *(Pres.)*
Thomas Williamson *(V.P. & Controller)*
Doug Driscoll *(V.P.)*
Steve Erickson *(V.P.)*
David Hacker *(V.P. & Dir.-Human Resources)*
Greg Erickson *(Sec. & Gen. Counsel)*
Tom Boron *(Dir.-Data Processing)*
Terry Giebel *(Asst. Controller)*

Principal(s):
Dean Erickson

No. of Mfg. Plants/Facilities: 22
No. of U.S. Offices: 1

Computer Systems/Hardware:
IBM

Outside Service Firm(s):

Bartz, Postl & Associates*(Auditors)*
Milwaukee, WI

American Family Insurance Group*(Commercial Insurance Carrier)*
Madison, WI

Liberty Mutual*(Commercial Insurance Carrier)*
Madison, WI

Northwestern National Life*(Group Insurer)*
St. Paul, MN

Wausau Insurance*(Group Insurer)*
2000 Westwood Dr.
Wausau, WI 54401-7881
Tel.: 715-842-6902
Fax: 715-847-8534

Norwest Bank Minnesota, N.A.*(Major Banking Relationship)*
Norwest, MN

ERICKSON OIL PRODUCTS, INC.
1231 Industrial St.
Hudson, WI 54016
Tel.: 715-386-8241 **WI**
Fax: 715-386-2022
Year Founded: 1950
Approx.Sls.: $65,000,000
Emp.: 500
Retail Gasoline Service Station & Convenience Store
S.I.C.: 5411; 5541
Claire L. Erickson *(Pres.)*
David B. Erickson *(Exec. V.P.)*
Gary D. VanderVorst *(V.P. Fin. & Treas.)*

Outside Service Firm(s):

McGladrey & Pullen*(Auditors)*
1800 Town Square, 445 Minnesota St.
St. Paul, MN 55101

Winthrop & Weinstine*(Legal Firm)*
444 Cedar Street
St. Paul, MN 55101

Norwest Bank Minnesota, N.A.*(Major Banking Relationship)*
6th St. & Marquette Ave.
Minneapolis, MN 55479-0065
Tel.: 612-667-8101

ERICKSON TRANSPORT CORPORATION
2255 N. Packer Rd.
Springfield, MO 65803
Tel.: 417-862-6741 **WI**
Fax: 417-862-4992
Year Founded: 1940
Approx.Sls.: $12,000,000
Emp.: 105
Contract Haulers
S.I.C.: 4213
John H. Erickson *(Pres.)*
Alf L. Erickson *(V.P.)*
Howard J. Erickson *(V.P.)*
Leif V. Erickson *(Treas. & Sec.)*

Outside Service Firm(s):

Commerce Bank*(Major Banking Relationship)*
Springfield, MO

ERICO INTERNATIONAL
30000 Aurora Rd. #102
Cleveland, OH 44139
Tel.: 216-349-2630 **OH**
Fax: 216-349-2996
Year Founded: 1903
Approx.Sls.: $90,000,000
Emp.: 1,200
Electrical Connectors & Welding Equipment, Rail Bonds, Industrial Fasteners, Reinforcing Bar Connections
S.I.C.: 3548; 3429; 3643
A.M. Kies *(Pres. & Chief Exec. Officer)*
R.D. Church *(Sec. & Treas.)*
S. Buncher *(Controller)*

No. of Mfg. Plants/Facilities: 1
No. of U.S. Offices: 1

Computer Systems/Hardware:
IBM Compatibles

Outside Service Firm(s):

Ernst & Young*(Auditors)*
1300 Huntington Bldg.
Cleveland, OH 44115
Tel.: 216-861-5000

Jones, Day, Reavis & Pogue*(Legal Firm)*
901 Lakeside Ave.
Cleveland, OH 44114
Tel.: 216-586-3939
Fax: 216-579-0212

ERICSON MARKETING COMMUNICATIONS
1130 Eighth Ave. South
Nashville, TN 37203
Tel.: 615-242-1050
Year Founded: 1969
Approx.Billings: $44,348,552
Emp.: 103
Janice Wendell *(Chm.)*
Gary Haynes *(Pres., Chief Exec. Officer)*
Phil Martin *(Pres., Ericson Pub. Rels.)*
Walt Baker *(Sr. V.P., Dir. Client Services)*
Mark Wright *(Sr. V.P., Mktg. Services)*
Ralph Langreck *(V.P., Gen. Mgr., Ericson Small Bus.)*
Connie Carter *(V.P.,Res. Services, Production Coord.)*
Tommy Pugh *(V.P., Res. Services, Production Coord.)*
Margie Whitmore *(Mgr., Corp. Sec.)*
Susan Henderson *(Promo. Dir.)*

ERIE FAMILY LIFE INSURANCE COMPANY
100 Erie Insurance Place
Erie, PA 16530
Tel.: 814-870-2000 **PA**
Year Founded: 1967
Assets: $226,082,111
Earnings: $5,865,994
Liabilities: $173,041,084
Net Worth: $53,041,027
Approx.Rev.: $31,216,284
Emp.: 60
Fiscal Year-end: 12/31/90
Underwriting & Selling Non-Participating Individual, Group & Universal Life Insurance Policies; Individual & Group Annuities
S.I.C.: 6311
Thomas B. Hagen *(Chm. Bd. & Chief Exec. Officer)*
John M. Petersen *(Pres., Chief Fin. Officer & Treas.)*
Jan R. Van Gorder *(Exec. V.P., Sec. & Gen. Counsel)*
John J. Brinling, Jr. *(Exec. V.P.)*
Robert H. Dreyer *(Sr. V.P. & Chief Actuary)*
Philip A. Garcia *(V.P.)*
Bruno Pisano *(V.P.)*

Outside Service Firm(s):

KPMG Peat Marwick*(Auditors)*
1500 National City Center
Cleveland, OH 44114
Tel.: 216-696-9100

Subsidiaries:

Erie Indemnity Company (1)
100 Erie Insurance Place
Erie, PA 16530
Tel.: 814-870-2000
Insurance Adjusters
S.I.C.: 6411
Thomas B. Hagen *(Chm. Bd. & Chief Exec. Officer)*
John M. Petersen *(Pres., Chief Fin. Officer & Treas.)*
Jan R. Van Gorder *(Exec. V.P., Sec. & Gen. Counsel)*

Erie Insurance Exchange (1)
100 Erie Insurance Place
Erie, PA 16530
Tel.: 814-870-2000
Reciprocal Insurance Exchange
S.I.C.: 6411
Thomas B. Hagen *(Chm. Bd. & Chief Exec. Officer)*
John M. Petersen *(Pres., Chief Fin. Officer & Treas.)*
Jan R. Van Gorder *(Exec. V.P., Sec. & Gen. Counsel)*

Erie Insurance Group (1)
100 Erie Insurance Place
Erie, PA 16530
Tel.: 814-870-2000
Life Insurance
S.I.C.: 6311
Thomas B. Hagen *(Chm. Bd. & Chief Exec. Officer)*
John M. Petersen *(Pres., Chief Fin. Officer & Treas.)*
Jan R. Van Gorder *(Exec. V.P., Sec. & Gen. Counsel)*

Flagship City Insurance Company (1)
100 Erie Insurance Place
Erie, PA 16530
Tel.: 814-870-2000
Assigned Risk Insurance
S.I.C.: 6411
Thomas B. Hagen *(Chm. Bd. & Chief Exec. Officer)*

ERIE PRESS SYSTEMS
1253 W. 12th
Erie, PA 16512
Tel.: 814-871-1600
Tel.: 800-222-3608
Fax: 814-871-1608
Year Founded: 1895
Approx.Sls.: $15,000,000
Emp.: 211
Fiscal Year-end: 6/30/92
Export
Forging Equip., Hydraulic Presses, Mechanical Presses & Molding
S.I.C.: 3542
Gary Lunger *(Pres.)*
William R. Carpenter *(Mktg. Mgr.)*
Carl Bodendorfer *(Mfg. Mgr.)*

Computer Systems/Hardware:
WANG

Subsidiary:

Van Air Systems, Inc. (1)
350 Mechanic St.
Lake City, PA 16423

ERIEZ MAGNETICS
Asbury Road at Airport
Erie, PA 16506
Mailing Address:
P.O. Box 10608
Erie, PA 16514-0608
Tel.: 814-833-9881
Tel.: 800-345-4946
Telex: 17-0922
Fax: 814-838-4960
Year Founded: 1942
Approx.Sls.: $50,000,000
Emp.: 250
Fiscal Year-end: 12/31/90

Export
Magnetic, Vibratory Equip. and Metal Detection For Industry
S.I.C.: 3569; 3559; 3823; 3825; 8731; 8734
R.A. Merwin *(Chm. Bd.)*
C.F. Giermak *(Pres.)*
R.F. Merwin *(Chm.-Exec. Committee)*
B.M. Merwin *(Sec.)*
Keith W. Jones *(Mgr.-Mktg. Communications)*
E.S. Twichell *(Sls. Mgr.)*
D.L. Ross *(Pur. Agent)*
J.E. Lutton *(Mgr.-Mfg.)*
R.A. Cook *(Mgr.-Personnel)*
D.L. Salsbury *(Controller)*

Computer Systems/Hardware:
IBM System 38

THE ERIN COMPANY
500 Main St.
Bangor, ME 04401
Tel.: 207-947-8651
Fax: 207-945-6575
Year Founded: 1969
Sales Range: $20-39 Million
Emp.: 600
Real Estate Developer; Owns & Operates Holiday Inns
S.I.C.: 6552
Peter H. Daigle *(Pres.)*

No. of U.S. Offices: 7

Computer Systems/Hardware:
IBM

Outside Service Firm(s):

Barry, Dunn, McNeil, Parker*(Auditors)*
Bangor, ME

Blue Cross & Blue Shield of Connecticut, Inc.*(Group Insurer)*
North Haven, CT

Rudman & Winchell*(Legal Firm)*
84 Harlow St.
Bangor, ME 04401
Tel.: 207-947-4501

ERIN GROUP ADMINISTRATORS, INC.
2260 Erin Ct.
Lancaster, PA 17604
Mailing Address:
P.O. Box 7777
Lancaster, PA 17604
Tel.: 717-299-1201
Tel.: 800-433-3746 **PA**
Fax: 717-392-4779
Year Founded: 1977
Assets: $1,056,255
Liabilities: $835,894
Net Worth: $220,361
Sales Range: $10-19 Million
Emp.: 68
TPA Admin. Employee Benefit Plans
S.I.C.: 6311; 6321; 6324
Lucille Werts *(Pres.)*
Sara A. Dadds *(Sec.)*
Mary Caci *(Dir.-Pur. & Personnel)*
Donald Cromer *(Mktg. Rep.)*

Outside Service Firm(s):

Insurance Company of North America*(Commercial Insurance Carrier)*
One Logan Square
Philadelphia, PA 19103
Tel.: 215-241-4000

Appel, Yost & Sorrentino*(Legal Firm)*
Lancaster, PA

Fulton Bank*(Major Banking Relationship)*
110 Penn Sq.
Lancaster, PA 17602
Tel.: 717-291-2411

Subsidiaries:

American Sentinel Insurance Company **(1)**
P.O. Box 1651,
Harrisburg, PA 17105
Tel.: 717-238-4559
Insurance
S.I.C.: 6321
Dorothy Cole *(Mgr.-Office)*

Sentinel Management Services, Inc. **(1)**
2250 Erin Ct.
Lancaster, PA 17604
Tel.: 717-291-1760
Tel.: 800-432-8877
Insurance
S.I.C.: 6321
Amy Krow *(Mgr.-Office)*

N. ERLANGER, BLUMGART & COMPANY, INC.
1450 Broadway
New York, NY 10018
Tel.: 212-221-7100
Approx.Sls.: $70,000,000
Emp.: 110
Earl-Glo Fabrics; Erlanger Fashion Fabrics, Linings, Shirtings, & Home Furnishings
S.I.C.: 2211; 2392
Girard Iason *(Chm.)*
John Iason *(Pres.)*
Bruce Freeman *(V.P.)*
Mike Manis *(Sls. Mgr.)*
Tony Diresta *(Controller & Treas.)*
Toni Shore *(Publicity Dir.)*

Division:

Pearloom Fabrics **(1)**
261 5th Ave.
New York, NY 10016
Tel.: 212-221-7100

ERMCO, INC.
151 S. East St.
Indianapolis, IN 46202
Tel.: 317-634-2923 **IN**
Fax: 317-634-2853
Emp.: 250
General Electrical Contractor
S.I.C.: 1731
Edward M. Gossett *(Chm. Bd.)*
James A. Maddox *(Pres.)*
Darrell Gossett *(Exec. V.P., Sec. & Treas.)*
Rox F. Bumpas *(V.P.)*
Ronald J. Goad *(V.P.)*
W. Thomas Woods *(V.P.-Engrng.)*

Outside Service Firm(s):

Bagley, Hoage & Harrison*(Auditors)*
Indianapolis, IN

Cottrell, Itenbach & Helbert*(Legal Firm)*
Indianapolis, IN

Banc One Indiana*(Major Banking Relationship)*
Indianapolis, IN

ERNEST PAPER PRODUCTS, INC.
2424 E. 26th St.
Los Angeles, CA 90058
Tel.: 213-583-6561 **CA**
Fax: 213-588-1049
Year Founded: 1946
Approx.Sls.: $28,000,000
Emp.: 85
Wholesale Distributor of Industrial & Personal Service Paper
S.I.C.: 5113
A.C. Wilson *(Chm. Bd. & Chief Exec. Officer)*
Tim Wilson *(Pres.)*
Ben Alhadeff *(V.P.-Fin.)*

Outside Service Firm(s):

Mitsui Manufacturers Bank*(Major Banking Relationship)*
Los Angeles, CA

ERNST HOME CENTER, INC.
1511 6th Ave.
Seattle, WA 98101
Tel.: 206-621-6700
Approx.Sls.: $253,000,000
Emp.: 3,000
Retail Home Improvement Products
S.I.C.: 5211; 5311; 5251
Hal Smith *(Pres.)*
Monty Reese *(Sr. V.P.-Mktg.)*
Michael Baumann *(Chief Fin. Officer)*
Thomas Stanton *(Dir.-Opers.)*

ERNST & YOUNG
277 Park Ave.
New York, NY 10172
Tel.: 212-773-3000
Telex: 177704 Ans bk YOUNGUT
Fax: 212-773-1996
Year Founded: 1894
Approx.Sls.: $2,200,000,000
Emp.: 20,000
Fiscal Year-end: 9/30/91
Professional Services Firm Providing Accounting, Auditing, Entrepreneurial, Management Consulting, Tax Services, & Business Advisory Services
S.I.C.: 8721; 7389; 8742
Ray J. Groves *(Chm. Bd.)*
Robert J. Kelly *(Co-Chm.-Opers.)*
William A. Grant, Jr. *(Co-Chm.-Opers.)*
Jesse M. Miles *(Co-Chm.-Intl. Fin.)*
Robert D. Neary *(Co-Chm.-Professional Services)*
Michael Grobstein *(Vice Chm.-Plng., Mktg. & Industry Services)*
Robert K. Herdman *(Vice Chm.-Acctg. Services)*
Michael Henning *(Vice Chm.-Tax Services)*
Charles J. Reynolds *(Vice Chm.-Auditing Services)*
Robert G. Streit *(Vice Chm.-Fin. & Admin.)*
Roger R. Nelson *(Vice Chm.-Mngmt. Consulting Services)*
James C. Boland *(Vice Chm. & Mng. Partner-N. Central Reg.)*
H. Ray Eanes *(Vice Chm. & Mng. Partner-SE Reg.)*
William L. Kimsey *(Vice Chm. & Mng. Partner-West Reg.)*
Philip A. Laskawy *(Vice Chm. & Mng. Partner-NY Metro Reg.)*
Robert Center *(Vice Chm. & Mng. Partner-MW Reg.)*
Richard A. Young *(Vice Chm. & Mng. Partner-East Reg.)*
David Reed *(Vice Chm. & Deputy Mng. Partner-SW Reg.)*
Paul Ostling *(Vice Chm.-Human Resources)*
Carl D. Liggio *(Gen. Counsel)*
Herbert J. Lerner *(Natl. Dir.-Tax Services)*
Mort Meyerson *(Natl. Dir.-Pub. Communications)*

No. of U.S. Offices: 100
No. of Foreign Offices: 480

Computer Systems/Hardware:
UNISYS 1100/92

Non-U.S. Holdings:

ATAG Allgemeine Treuhand AG **(1)**
Bandenerstrasse 47 P.O. Box 5272, CH-8022
Zurich, Switzerland
Tel.: 202-54-50
Telex: 815515 ANSBK ATAG CH
Telecopier: 242-54-22
Emp.: 25
Public Accountants
S.I.C.: 8721
Heinrich Gehring *(Partner & Chief Exec. Officer)*
Karl Meile *(Vice Chm.)*

ATAG Fiduciaire Generale SA **(1)**
6, rue d'Italie P.O. Box 326, CH-1211
Geneva, 3, Switzerland
Tel.: 021-35-27
Telex: 428260 And bk FGSA CH
Fax: 021-95-38
Emp.: 25
Public Accountants
S.I.C.: 8721
Jean Kettiger *(Partner)*

Ernst & Young **(1)**
Becket House, 1 Lambeth Palace Rd.
London, SE1 7EU, United Kingdom
Tel.: 071-928-2000
Telex: 885234
Fax: 071-928-1345
S.I.C.: 8721
Elwyn O.M. Eilledge *(Mng. Dir.)*
Harold Cottam *(Mng. Dir.)*

ERSHIGS, INC.
742 Marine Dr.
Bellingham, WA 98225
Tel.: 206-733-2620
Fax: 206-733-2628
Approx.Sls.: $19,000,000
Emp.: 150
Plastic Pipe, Fiberglass Tanks & Ducting
S.I.C.: 3084; 3089
A. Herbert Ershig *(Chm. Bd.)*
Richard Sumner *(Pres.)*
Robert Becker *(Sec. & Treas.)*

Outside Service Firm(s):

Moss Adams*(Auditors)*
Bellingham, WA

U. S. Bank*(Major Banking Relationship)*
Seattle, WA

ERVIN INDUSTRIES, INC.
3893 Research Park Dr.
Ann Arbor, MI 48108
Mailing Address:
P.O. Box 1168
Ann Arbor, MI 48106
Tel.: 313-769-4600
Fax: 313-663-0136
Year Founded: 1920
Approx.Sls.: $75,000,000
Emp.: 230
Mfr. of Metal Abrasives
S.I.C.: 3291; 5085
John Pearson *(Pres.)*
Kenneth Prior *(V.P.-Mfg.)*
W.R. Rhodaberger *(V.P.-Sales)*
Lynn H. Rogers *(V.P. & Gen. Mgr.-Georg Fischer Amasteel S.A.)*
Vince P. Sardone *(V.P.-Fin. & Chief Fin. Officer)*
Kathryn Welch *(Treas.)*
Richard Conn *(Controller)*

No. of Mfg. Plants/Facilities: 3

Outside Service Firm(s):

Deloitte & Touche*(Auditors)*
101 N. Main Street
Ann Arbor, MI 48104-1411
Tel.: 313-769-6200

Hooper, Hathaway, Price & Beuche*(Legal Firm)*
Ann Arbor, MI

Comerica Bank*(Major Banking Relationship)*
211 W. Fort St.
Detroit, MI 48226
Tel.: 313-222-3300

Divisions:

Ervin Amasteel Div. **(1)**
915 Tabor
Adrian, MI 49221
Tel.: 517-265-6118
Mfr. of Abrasives
S.I.C.: 3291
Jim Lemon *(Plant Mgr.)*

Ervin Industries, Inc.—(Continued)

Ervin Amasteel Div. **(1)**
681 E. Butler Rd.
Butler, PA 16001
Tel.: 412-282-1060
Mfr. of Abrasives
S.I.C.: 3291
Don Gerhart *(Plant Mgr.)*

Non-U.S. Joint Venture:

Georg Fischer Amasteel S.A. **(1)**
Muhlenstrasse 105 Postfach, CH-8201
Schaffhausen, Switzerland
Tel.: 053-81 11 11 (50%)
Mktg. of Abrasives; Joint Venture of Ervin Industries Inc. and Georg Fischer AG
S.I.C.: 5085
Lynn R. Rogers *(V.P. & Gen. Mgr.)*

ERVING PAPER MILLS
Arch St.
Erving, MA 01344
Mailing Address:
P.O. Box 38, Arch St.
Erving, MA 01344-0038
Tel.: 508-544-2711 **MA**
Fax: 508-544-7506
Year Founded: 1905
Sales Range: $60-79 Million
Emp.: 475
Import Export
Manufacture Jumbo Rolls Tissue, Market Pulp, Napkins, Consumer, Food Service & Healthcare Products
S.I.C.: 2621; 2671; 2676
Employee Matching Gifts Program: Gifts of $25 or More, to Eligible Educational Institutions (Non-Profit, Accredited, Graduate or Professional Schools, Colleges and Post-Secondary Technical Institutions), Matched up to a Maximum of $200 per Employee or Director per Calendar Year
Charles B. Housen *(Chm. Bd., Pres. & Chief Exec. Officer)*
Ronald Marsh *(Dir.-Mngmt. Information Systems)*
Dawn M. Williams *(Dir.-Admin. & Sec.)*
Lawrence A. Zanga *(Dir.-Pur.)*
Denis L. Emmett *(Treasurer)*
Paul R. Dise *(Controller)*
Laurence S. Dunning *(Grp. Dir.-Healthcare Div.)*
David G. Oxley *(Grp. Dir.-Food Service Div.)*
Robert L. Howes *(Grp. Dir.-Packaged Prods. Div.)*
Raymond F.J. Smith *(Grp. Dir.-Paper Mill Div.)*
Lydia J. Bailey *(Mgr.-Personnel)*
Paul W. Sullivan *(Engr.)*
Sandra L. Misiun *(Art Dir.)*
Principal(s):
Charles B. Housen
Anna Housen

No. of Mfg. Plants/Facilities: 6
No. of U.S. Offices: 2

Computer Systems/Hardware:
IBM 4341

Outside Service Firm(s):

Coles & Bodoin*(Auditors)*
Boston, MA

Bingham, Dana & Gould*(Legal Firm)*
150 Federal St.
Boston, MA 02110
Tel.: 617-951-8000
Fax: 617-951-8736

Bank of New England*(Major Banking Relationship)*
28 State Street
Boston, MA 02109
Tel.: 617-742-4000

Bay Bank Harvard Trust Company*(Pension Manager)*
Boston, MA

Affiliate:

Flamingo Products **(1)**
3095 E. 11th Ave.
Hialeah, FL 33013
Tel.: 305-691-4641

ESCO CORPORATION
2141 NW 25th Ave.
Portland, OR 97210
Mailing Address:
P.O. Box 10123,
Portland, OR 97210
Tel.: 503-228-2141 **OR**
Fax: 503-778-6330
Year Founded: 1913
Emp.: 3,000
Import Export
High Alloy Castings; Earth Moving & Forest Products; Stainless Steel & Aluminum Rolling Mill Products, Aerospace Investments Castings
S.I.C.: 3316; 3531; 3355
Henry T. Swigert *(Chm. Bd.)*
Nicholas P. Collins *(Pres. & Chief Exec. Officer)*
Steven D. Pratt *(Pres.-Propriety Prods. Grp.)*
Bill Weber *(Pres.-ISC Grp.)*
Colin Hill *(Sr. V.P.-Casting Grp.)*
Gene K. Huey *(V.P.-Fin.)*
Ken McCaw, Jr. *(V.P. & Gen. Counsel)*
Joe Smith *(Dir.-Human Resources)*
Ken Horung *(Mgr.-Adv.)*
Dale MacHaffie *(Mgr.-Real Estate)*
Jim Songer *(Mgr.-Intl. Fin.)*
Mary Egan *(Legal Admin.)*
Mike Jubinville *(Pur. Agent)*

No. of Mfg. Plants/Facilities: 4
No. of U.S. Offices: 3
No. of Foreign Offices: 4

Computer Systems/Hardware:
Burroughs Systems A-10 & A-15

Outside Service Firm(s):

Grant Thornton*(Auditors)*
Portland, OR

Black, Helterline, Beck & Rappleyea*(Legal Firm)*
Bank of California Tower
Portland, OR 97205
Tel.: 503-224-5560

The Bank of California, N.A.*(Major Banking Relationship)*
Portland, OR

Columbia Mngmt. Co.*(Pension Manager)*
1300 S.W. Sixth Ave.
Portland, OR 97207
Tel.: 503-222-3600

FJW Financial Management*(Pension Manager)*
Portland, OR

Divisions:

Custom Casting **(1)**
2141 N.W. 25th Ave.
Portland, OR 97210
Tel.: 503-228-2141
Mfr. of High Alloy Castings
S.I.C.: 3365; 3369
Robert Davis *(V.P.)*

Earthmoving Equipment Div. **(1)**
2141 N.W. 25th Ave.
Portland, OR 97210
Tel.: 503-228-2141
Mfr. of Earthmoving Equipment
S.I.C.: 3531
Colin Hill *(V.P.)*

Esco Industrial Service Center **(1)**
2141 N.W. 25th Ave.
Portland, OR 97210
Tel.: 503-228-2141
Fax: 503-778-6330
Industrial Service Center
S.I.C.: 5051
William Weber *(Gen. Mgr.)*

Esco International **(1)**
2141 N.W. 25th Ave.
Portland, OR 97210
Tel.: 503-228-2141
Wholesale of Metals
S.I.C.: 5051
James Songer *(V.P.)*

Proprietory Products Group **(1)**
2141 N.W. 25th Avenue
Portland, OR 97210
Tel.: 503-228-2141
Fax: 503-778-6330
Forestry Services
S.I.C.: 0851
Steve Pratt *(Pres.)*

Subsidiaries:

Bucyrus Blades Inc. **(1)**
260 E. Beal Ave.
Bucyrus, OH 44820
Tel.: 419-562-6015
Tel.: 800-532-5233 (100%)
Fax: 419-562-8360
Approx.Sls.: $23,000,000
Emp.: 190
Cutting Edges & Related Wearing Parts For Dozers, Scrapers, Front-End Loaders, Graders & Snow Plows; Snow Plow Shoes, Nose Pieces & Wear Plates; Fasteners
S.I.C.: 3581
Larry Huget *(Pres.)*
John Spiegel *(Sec. & Treas.)*
Joseph J. Diederich *(V.P.-Sls.)*

Division:

Bucyrus Blades of Georgia **(2)**
7134 Hwy. 54
Morrow, GA 30260
Tel.: 404-968-4636
Mfr. of Cutting Edges
S.I.C.: 3531
Larry Huget *(Pres.)*

PTI Technologies **(1)**
2323 Teller Rd.
Newbury Park, CA 91320
Tel.: 805-499-2661
Fax: 805-375-2258
Advanced Technology Filters & Filter Systems for Military & Commercial Aerospace Markets
S.I.C.: 3599
Jan O. Johnson *(Pres.)*

Non-U.S. Holdings:

Bucyrus Blades of Canada Ltd. **(1)**
199 St. David St.
Lindsay, ON K9V 5K7, Canada
Tel.: 705-328-3222 (100%)
Fax: 705-328-2857
Mfr. of Blades
S.I.C.: 3531

Bucyrus Blades de Mexico **(1)**
Apartado Postal No. 32659,
Mexico, D.F. 1, Mexico (100%)
Mfr. of Blades
S.I.C.: 3531

Esco, Europe S.A. **(1)**
Rue des Frous-Chaux 7230
Frameries, Belgium
Mfr. of Construction Machinery
S.I.C.: 3531

Esco Ltd. **(1)**
1855 Kingsway
Port Coquitlam, BC Canada B3C 1C1
Tel.: 604-942-7261
Mfr. of Steel Castings
S.I.C.: 3325
Robert Bowyer *(Mgr.)*

Esco, S.A. **(1)**
Boite Postal 229 69803
Saint-Priest, France
Mfr. of Construction Equipment
S.I.C.: 3531

ESCO ELEVATORS, INC.
4720 Esco Dr.
Fort Worth, TX 76140
Mailing Address:
P.O. Box 445
Fort Worth, TX 76101
Tel.: 817-478-4251
Fax: 817-478-4421
Approx.Sls.: $25,000,000
Emp.: 200
Import Export
Manufactures & Installs Freight, Passenger & Residence Elevators
S.I.C.: 3534
Jim Swanson *(Chief Exec. Officer)*
Dick Davis *(Pres. & Chief Exec. Officer)*
J.H. McMillan *(Sr. V.P.-Construction)*
Jim R. Jeoffroy *(V.P.-Sls.)*
Sam Merserve *(V.P.)*
George Ring *(V.P.-Field Opers.)*
Wm. Thomas Coon *(Controller)*
Phillip Basford *(Dir.-Research & Devel.)*
Roger Bowyer *(Dir.-Quality Control)*
Johnny Roberts *(Dir.-Engrng.)*
Roger Westerfield *(Dir.-Pur.)*

Computer Systems/Hardware:
IBM System 36

Outside Service Firm(s):

Barg & Associates*(Auditors)*
Fort Worth, TX

Cantey & Hanger*(Legal Firm)*
2100 1st Republic Bank Tower, 801 Cherry St.
Ft. Worth, TX 76102
Tel.: 817-877-2800

North Ft. Worth Bank*(Major Banking Relationship)*
Fort Worth, TX

ESPRIT DE CORP.
900 Minnesota St.
San Francisco, CA 94107
Tel.: 415-648-6900
Fax: 415-641-5964
Sales Range: $500-999 Million
Emp.: 3,700
Manufacture & Wholesaler of Women's & Children's Clothing. Retailer
S.I.C.: 2331; 2335; 5137
Isaac Stein *(Chm. Bd.)*
Fritz Ammann *(Pres. & Chief Exec. Officer)*
Lisa Engler *(Pres.-Retail)*
Phil Lighty *(V.P.-Sourcing)*
Sue Thomas *(V.P.-Human Resources)*
Peter Buckley *(Dir.-Intl.)*
Neil Kraft *(Dir.-Image)*

Computer Systems/Hardware:
IBM 3081

Outside Service Firm(s):

Moss Adams*(Auditors)*
San Francisco, CA

Wells Fargo Bank*(Major Banking Relationship)*
420 Montgomery St.
San Francisco, CA 94104

Divisions:

Esprit Accessories **(1)**
900 Minnesota St.
San Francisco, CA 94107
Tel.: 415-648-6900
Lynn Miller *(Pres.)*

Esprit Department **(1)**
900 Minnesota St.
San Francisco, CA 94107
Tel.: 415-648-6900
Ed Jones *(Pres.)*

Esprit Kids **(1)**
900 Minnesota St.
San Francisco, CA 94107
Tel.: 415-648-6900
Dan Danford *(Pres.)*

Esprit Sport **(1)**
900 Minnesota St.
San Francisco, CA 94107
Tel.: 415-648-6900
Dick Baker *(Pres.)*

ESROCK ADVERTISING
14550 South 94th Ave.
Orland Park, IL 60462
Tel.: 708-349-8400
Fax: 708-349-8471
Year Founded: 1978
Approx.Billings: $18,000,000
Emp.: 28
Business-to-Business Adv.
Jack Coughlin *(Pres. & Exec. Creative Dir.)*
Ron Brennan *(Group V.P., Gen Mgr.)*
Ciela Quitsch *(Group V.P., Adv./Mktg.)*
Larry Ryan *(V.P., Mktg. & Media)*

ESSEX GRAIN PRODUCTS, INC.
9 Lee Blvd.
Frazer, PA 19355
Tel.: 215-647-3800
Fax: 215-647-4990
Year Founded: 1972
Approx.Sls.: $20,000,000
Emp.: 30
Warehousing & Wholesale Food Ingredients Distributor
S.I.C.: 4221; 5153; 5149
William Bierer *(Chm. Bd. & Chief Exec. Officer)*
Alice Bierer *(Pres. & Chief Fin. Officer)*
Roy Day *(Exec. V.P.)*
Luke Palante *(V.P.-Sls. & Mktg.)*

No. of Mfg. Plants/Facilities: 2

Computer Systems/Hardware:
MAI Basic Four

Outside Service Firm(s):

Philadelphia National Bank*(Major Banking Relationship)*
West Chester, PA

ESSEX GROUP, INC.
1601 Wall St.
Fort Wayne, IN 46802
Mailing Address:
P.O. Box 1601,
Ft. Wayne, IN 46801
Tel.: 219-461-4000
Year Founded: 1930
Approx.Sls.: $992,000,000
Emp.: 3,700
Fiscal Year-end: 12/31/90

Export
Mfr. Electrical, Electronic & Communications Wires & Cables for Appliance, Automotive, Construction, Telephone & Electrical Equip. Mfrs.; Magnet Wires for Electric Motors, Electrical Insulating Materials
S.I.C.: 3357; 3351; 3355; 3356
Stanley Craft *(Chm., Pres. & Chief Exec. Officer)*
David Menzie *(Chief Fin. Officer & V.P.-Fin.)*
Gunther Guckel *(Chief Information Officer)*
Mark Beck *(V.P.-Metals)*
Thomas E. Castaldi *(V.P.-Communications)*
Anthony Criso *(V.P., Legal Counsel & Sec.)*
John Suddarth *(V.P.-Human Resources)*
David Owen *(Treas.)*
James Rice *(Controller)*
Dominic Lucenta *(Dir.-Human Resources)*
Curt Norton *(Dir.-Pur.)*
Frederick Zinser *(Intl. Business Contact)*

Computer Systems/Hardware:
IBM 3084

Divisions:

Industrial Products Div. **(1)**
1601 Wall St.
Fort Wayne, IN 46802
Tel.: 219-461-4000
Mfr. Electrical, Electronic & Communications Wires & Cables for Appliance, Automotive, Construction, Telephone & Electrical Equip. Mfrs.; Magnet Wires for Electric Motors, Electrical Insulating Materials
S.I.C.: 3355; 3356; 3357; 3351
Steven R. Abbott *(Pres.)*

Telecommunication Products Div. **(1)**
800 E. Garfield
Decatur, IL 62521
Tel.: 217-429-2531
Mfr. of Telephone Cables
S.I.C.: 3661
Frederick Zinser *(Pres.)*

Wire & Cable Div. **(1)**
1601 Wall St.
Fort Wayne, IN 46802
Tel.: 219-461-4000
Mfr. of Wire and Cable
S.I.C.: 5063; 4822; 2298; 4813
Thomas Twehues *(Pres.)*

ESSKAY MANUFACTURING CO.
122 Stribling St.
San Antonio, TX 78204
Mailing Address:
P.O. Box 830648
San Antonio, TX 78283-0648
Tel.: 210-222-9585
Fax: 210-222-1326
Approx.Sls.: $22,000,000
Emp.: 250
Import
Boy's Wear-Suits, Sport Coats, Slacks, Dress Shirts & Sweaters
S.I.C.: 2311
Ray Patterson *(Chief Exec. Officer)*
Edward May *(V.P.-Opers.)*
Bruce Bennett *(V.P.-Personnel)*
Hugh Patterson *(V.P.-Production)*
Glen Kuhns *(Controller)*

Computer Systems/Hardware:
IBM

THE ESTEE CORPORATION
169 Lackawanna Ave.
Parsippany, NJ 07054
Tel.: 201-335-1000
Fax: 201-335-0899
Year Founded: 1946
Approx.Sls.: $50,000,000
Emp.: 300
Fiscal Year-end: 12/31/90
Preserves; Jellies; Low Calorie Foods, Confections & Gelatin Desserts; Estee Diet Control Prods.; Louis Sherry Sugarless Confections; China Bowl Oriental Condiments
S.I.C.: 2033
Steven Silk *(Chief Exec. Officer)*
Marie DuBois *(Chief Information Officer)*
Tom Ruggerio *(Chief Fin. Officer)*
James Donegan *(V.P.-Sls.)*
Annette Hartmann *(V.P.-Mfg.)*
Darlene Allen *(Dir.-Health Care Mktg.)*
Josephine Hawthorne *(Dir.-Mktg.)*
Dorothy Radlicz *(Mktg. Dir.-Estee)*

ESTEE LAUDER, INC.
767 Fifth Ave.
New York, NY 10153
Tel.: 212-572-4200 **DE**
Fax: 212-572-3941
Approx.Sls.: $1,350,000,000
Emp.: 10,000
Fiscal Year-end: 12/31/90
Cosmetics & Fragrances
S.I.C.: 2844
Estee Lauder *(Chm. Bd.)*
Leonard Lauder *(Pres. & Chief Exec. Officer)*
Robin Burns *(Pres.-Estee Lauder USA)*
Fred Langhammer *(Exec. V.P. & Chief Oper. Officer)*
Evelyn Lauder *(Exec. V.P.)*
Robert Aquilina *(Sr. V.P. & Chief Fin. Officer)*
Ed Callahan *(Sr. V.P.-Human Resources-Worldwide)*
Muriel Gonzalez *(Sr. V.P.-Mktg.)*
June Leaman *(Sr. V.P.-Creative Mktg.)*
Sharon LeVan *(Sr. V.P.-Creative Mktg. Devel.)*
Saul Magram *(Sr. V.P. & Gen. Counsel)*
Rebecca C. McGreevy *(Sr. V.P.-Pub. Rels.)*
Daria Myers *(V.P.-Mktg.)*
Dominique Szabo *(V.P.-Makeup Mktg.)*
Edward Silverman *(Treas.)*
Carolyn Preiss *(Dir.-Compensation & Benefits)*
Michael Naylor *(Controller)*
John Howard *(Dir.-Mngmt. Information Systems)*

Computer Systems/Hardware:
IBM

Outside Service Firm(s):

Price Waterhouse*(Auditors)*
153 E. 53rd St., 44th Fl.
New York, NY 10022
Tel.: 212-371-2000

Travelers Insurance Co.*(Group Insurer)*
1 Tower Square
Hartford, CT 06183-2492
Tel.: 203-277-4542
Fax: 203-277-5038

Krieger & Tick*(Legal Firm)*
New York, NY

Chemical Bank*(Major Banking Relationship)*
450 West 33rd St.
New York, NY 10001
Tel.: 212-613-7197
Fax: 212-947-7628

Chemical Banking Corp.*(Pension Manager)*
277 Park Ave.
New York, NY 10041
Tel.: 212-310-6407
Fax: 212-310-4526

Division:

Len Ron Mfg. Co. Inc. **(1)**
350 S. Service Rd.
Melville, NY 11747-3233
Tel.: 516-454-7000
Mfr. of Cosmetics
S.I.C.: 2844
John Sheldon *(Corp. Mfg.)*

Subsidiaries:

Estee Lauder, Intl. **(1)**
767 Fifth Ave.
New York, NY 10153
Tel.: 212-572-4600 (100%)
Distr. of Products
S.I.C.: 5122
Jeanette S. Wagner *(Pres.)*
Robert J. Aquilina *(Exec. V.P.)*
Raymond Bermay *(Sr. V.P.)*
Peter Pflugk *(Sr. V.P.)*

Origins Natural Resources Inc. **(1)**
767 Fifth Ave.
New York, NY 10153
Tel.: 212-572-4200
Skin Care, Body Products, Aromatherapy & Makeup
S.I.C.: 2844
William Lauder *(Pres. & Gen. Mgr.)*

Affiliates:

Aramis, Inc. **(1)**
767 Fifth Ave.
New York, NY 10153
Tel.: 212-572-3700
Fragrances & Products for Men
S.I.C.: 2844
Robert Nielsen *(Pres.)*
Sharon Le Van *(Sr. V.P.-Mktg. & Creative Services)*

Clinique Laboratories, Inc. **(1)**
767 Fifth Ave.
New York, NY 10153
Tel.: 212-572-3800
Cosmetics Aromatics Elixir Fragrance; Treatment Program for Face & Body
S.I.C.: 2844
Carol Phillips *(Chm. Bd.)*
Daneil J. Brestle *(Pres.)*
Eunice Valdiva *(Exec. V.P.-Mktg. & Fin.)*

Prescriptives, Inc. **(1)**
767 Fifth Ave.
New York, NY 10022
Tel.: 212-572-4400
Fax: 212-572-6645
Cosmetics & Treatment Program for Skin
S.I.C.: 2844
Daniel J. Brestle *(Pres.)*
James Bunn *(V.P. & Gen. Mgr.)*

Non-U.S. Holdings:

Estee Lauder K.K. **(1)**
Shin Aoyama Bldg., Nishi-kan 1-1, Minami Aoyama 1-chome
Tokyo, Japan
Tel.: 03-3405-6211
Cosmetics
S.I.C.: 2844

Estee Lauder N.V. **(1)**
15, Nijverheidsstraat 2431
Oevel-Westerlo, Netherlands
Tel.: 014 21.67.20 (100%)
Cosmetics & Fragrances
S.I.C.: 2844

ESTES EXPRESS LINES, INC.
1100 Commerce Rd.
Richmond, VA 23224
Tel.: 804-232-6793 **VA**
Fax: 804-233-1436
Year Founded: 1936
Approx.Sls.: $112,000,000
Emp.: 2,200
Less-Than-Truckload Transport
S.I.C.: 4213
Robey W. Estes, Sr. *(Chm. Bd. & Chief Exec. Officer)*
Robey W. Estes, Jr. *(Pres. & Treas.)*
Michael T. Chapura *(V.P.-Claims)*
John T. Johnson *(V.P.-Opers.)*
William T. Hupp *(V.P.-Sls.)*
Leo L. Lively *(V.P.-Natl. Accts.)*
Ray G. Williams *(V.P.-Maint.)*
Kenneth W. Witt *(V.P.-Safety)*
Paul J. Dugent *(Dir.-Pricing)*
Trafton T. Hardison *(Asst. V.P.-Sls.)*
Gary D. Oakes *(Corp. Sec.)*
Andrew L. Rice *(Asst. Treas.)*

Outside Service Firm(s):

NationsBank*(Major Banking Relationship)*
4th Fl. Pavillon, 1111 E. Main St.
Richmond, VA
Tel.: 804-788-2551

ESTHER WILLIAMS SWIMMING POOL CO.
8600 River Rd.
Delair, NJ 08110
Tel.: 609-663-2900
Fax: 609-663-1297
Approx.Sls.: $20,000,000
Emp.: 175
Fiscal Year-end: 12/31/90
Mfr. of Above Ground & In Ground Swimming Pools
S.I.C.: 3949; 2452
Frank Kessler *(Chm. Bd.)*
Michael R. Bettar *(Pres.)*
Donald Levy *(V.P.-Sls.)*

ALEX J. ETKIN, INC.
31440 Northwestern Hwy., Ste. 150
Farmington Hills, MI 48334-2533
Mailing Address:
P.O. Box 9061
Farmington Hills, MI 48333-9061
Tel.: 313-737-5800 **MI**
Fax: 313-737-5801
Year Founded: 1939
Approx.Sls.: $131,000,000
Emp.: 100
Fiscal Year-end: 1/31/92
General Contractors, Construction Management
S.I.C.: 1542; 8741
Alex J. Etkin *(Chm. Bd.)*
Thomas H. Landry *(Pres.)*
James J. Cole, Jr. *(Exec. V.P.)*
Andrea Atherton *(V.P.-Pre-Construction Services)*
Richard Brennan *(V.P.-Project Admin.)*
George J. Fadool *(V.P.-Construction)*
Donald N. Sielaff *(V.P.-Estimating)*
Karen Kelly *(Mktg.)*
Michael J. Doubles *(Controller)*
Toby Etkin *(Sec.)*

No. of U.S. Offices: 2

Computer Systems/Hardware:
IBM-Personal Computers

Outside Service Firm(s):

Bodman, Longley & Dahling*(Legal Firm)*
100 Renaissance Center
Detroit, MI 48243
Tel.: 313-259-7777

Michigan National Bank*(Major Banking Relationship)*
Detroit, MI

Subsidiary:

A.J. Etkin Construction Co. **(1)**
P.O. Box 9061, 31440 Northwestern Hwy., Ste. 150
Farmington Hills, MI 48018
Tel.: 313-737-5800
Fax: 313-737-5801
Emp.: 100
Gen. Contractors, Construction Mngmt., Interiors
S.I.C.: 1542; 1541; 8741
Thomas H. Landry *(Pres.)*

EUROMARKET DESIGNS, INC.
(Crate & Barrel Stores)
725 Landwehr Rd.
Northbrook, IL 60062
Tel.: 708-272-2888 **IL**
Fax: 708-272-5276
Year Founded: 1962
Assets: $54,386,000
Liabilities: $22,121,000
Net Worth: $32,265,000
Approx.Sls.: $150,000,000
Emp.: 1,800
Fiscal Year-end: 2/ 3/91
Import
Operation of 36 Crate & Barrel Specialty Houseware Stores Nationwide Carrying Housewares, Culinary Items, Dinnerware & Glassware, Home Furnishings, Accessories & Gifts; Operation of 5 Crate & Barrel Furniture Stores; Catalog Sales
S.I.C.: 5712; 5719; 5311
Gordon I. Segal *(Pres. & Chief Exec. Officer)*
Barbara Turf *(Exec. V.P.)*
Bruce W. Schneidewind *(Chief Fin. Officer)*
Adrienne Litwin *(Media Coord.)*
Bette Kahn *(Mgr.-Pub. Rels. & Community Affairs)*

Outside Service Firm(s):

Kupferberg, Goldberg & Neimark*(Auditors)*
Chicago, IL

Much, Shelist, Freed, Denenberg, Ament & Eiger*(Legal Firm)*
Chicago, IL

Harris Trust & Savings Bank*(Major Banking Relationship)*
111 W. Monroe St.
Chicago, IL 60690
Tel.: 312-461-2265
Tel.: 800-858-0840

EVA-TONE INC.
4801 Ulmerton Rd.
Clearwater, FL 34622
Mailing Address:
P.O. Box 7020
Clearwater, FL 34618
Tel.: 813-572-7000
Tel.: 800-382-8663
Fax: 813-572-6214
Approx.Sls.: $15,000,000
Emp.: 250
Mfr. Eva-Tone Thin Flexible Vinyl Phonograph Records, High Speed, High Quality Audio Cassette Duplication, Commercial Printing, Direct Mail Services, Videocassette Duplication, CD Replication
S.I.C.: 3651; 5099; 7331
R. Evan Evans *(Pres.)*
Norman H. Welch, Jr. *(Exec. V.P.-Audio Sls.)*
Mark Evans *(Dir.-Human Resources)*
Patrick Augustine *(Mgr.-Natl. Mktg.)*
Joseph DeMasso *(Mgr.-Natl. Sls.)*
Lawrence S. Johnson *(Mgr.-Adv.)*

EVANA AUTOMATION
5825 Old Boonville Hwy.
Evansville, IN 47715
Tel.: 812-479-8246
Fax: 812-474-3138
Approx.Sls.: $12,000,000
Emp.: 75
Import Export
Robotic Conveyors
S.I.C.: 3535
Charles M. Walker *(Chm. Bd.)*
Gerald Niehaus *(Pres. & Chief Exec. Officer)*
Delores Brothers *(Sec., Treas. & Chief Fin. Officer)*
Greg Claspell *(Dir.-Mktg.)*
Randy Wire *(Dir.-Admin. & Opers.)*

Outside Service Firm(s):

Bamberger, Foreman, Oswald & Hahn*(Legal Firm)*
708 Hulman Bldg.
Evansville, IN 47708
Tel.: 812-425-1591

Citizens National Bank*(Major Banking Relationship)*
20 NW Third St.
Evansville, IN
Tel.: 812-464-3400

EVANGELINE MEDICAL & X-RAY DISTRIBUTORS
6781 Cezanne Ave.
Baton Rouge, LA 70806
Mailing Address:
P.O. Box 64851
Baton Rouge, LA 70896
Tel.: 504-927-3522 **LA**
Fax: 504-926-9371
Year Founded: 1972
Assets: $3,503,936
Liabilities: $1,452,581
Net Worth: $2,051,355
Approx.Sls.: $15,000,000
Emp.: 52
Fiscal Year-end: 12/31/91
Retailer of X-Ray Film Chemicals & Equipment
S.I.C.: 5047

E.J. Cop *(Chm. Bd.)*
Mike Pritchett *(Pres. & Chief Exec. Officer)*
Larry Chauvin *(V.P.-Fin. & Opers.)*
Robert Escher *(Mgr.-Opers.)*

Outside Service Firm(s):

Morton, Plaisance, White & Company*(Auditors)*
Baton Rouge, LA

Hartford Life Insurance Co.*(Commercial Insurance Carrier)*
Hartford, CT 06104-2999

Premier Bank*(Major Banking Relationship)*
P.O. Box 1511
Baton Rouge, LA 70821

EVANS ADHESIVE CORP.
925 W. Henderson Rd.
Columbus, OH 43220
Tel.: 614-451-2665
Tel.: 800-888-0925
Fax: 614-451-1373
Year Founded: 1900
Approx.Sls.: $11,500,000
Emp.: 76
Mfr. of Industrial & Commercial Adhesives & Related Products
S.I.C.: 2891
Arthur E. Loos *(Chm. Bd.)*
R.S. Kowaluk *(Pres.)*
Peggy Rinehart *(V.P.)*
T.M. Schueler *(Asst. Treas.)*
Jack Ford *(Natl. Sls. Mgr.)*
Susan Burbacher *(Asst. Sls. Mgr.)*

EVANS BROTHERS COMPANY, INC.
W. 229 N. 1492 Westwood Dr.
Waukesha, WI 53187
Tel.: 414-549-6200
Approx.Sls.: $90,000,000
Emp.: 180
Wholesale Industrial & Personal Service Paper; Commercial Machines & Equipment; Frozen Foods; Confectionery
S.I.C.: 5113; 5142; 5145
Raymond Marshall *(Pres.)*
John R. Evans *(Chief Exec. Officer)*
William M. Evans *(V.P.-Sls., Adv. & Mktg.)*

Outside Service Firm(s):

Vrakas Blum*(Auditors)*
Brookfield, WI

Smith & O'Neill*(Legal Firm)*
Milwaukee, WI

M & I Northern Bank*(Major Banking Relationship)*
Brookfield, WI

EVANS FABRICATION, INC.
1255 Peters Rd.
Harvey, LA 70058
Tel.: 504-368-6000
Fabrication & Construction
S.I.C.: 1799; 3499
Gary Hamilton *(Pres.)*

EVANS, HARDY & YOUNG, INC.
829 De la Vina St.
Santa Barbara, CA 93101
Tel.: 805-963-5841
Fax: 805-564-4279
Year Founded: 1986
Approx.Billings: $25,000,000
Emp.: 21
Jim Evans *(Pres. & Chief Exec. Officer)*
John Hickman *(Sr. V.P., St Louis Office)*
David Gordon *(V.P., Los Angeles Office)*
Sue Andrews *(V.P., Chief Fin. Officer)*

Computer Systems/Hardware:
Gable Systems, MM-Plus

EVANS INDUSTRIES, INC.
200 Renaissance Center
Detroit, MI 48243
Tel.: 313-259-2266
Fax: 313-259-4687
Approx.Sls.: $70,000,000
Emp.: 800
Mfr. Plastic Molded Parts, Inboard Gas, Process Equip.-Feed Mills & Diesel Engines, Engine Generator Sets, Aluminum & Brass Castings, Automotive after Market Appearance Kits, Concrete Blocks, Silica Sand/ Indus. Sand, Rubber Molded Parts, Adhesives, Urethane Chemicals & Casters
S.I.C.: 3089; 3363; 3364; 3511; 3519; 3531; 3087; 3271; 3429; 3061; 3714
Robert B. Evans, Sr. *(Chm. Bd. & Chief Exec. Officer)*
Barry Woodrow *(Pres.)*
Patricia Varcalli *(Controller)*

Outside Service Firm(s):

Ernst & Young*(Auditors)*
One Detroit Center, 500 Woodward, Ste. 1700
Detroit, MI 48243
Tel.: 313-259-9600

Reynolds, Beeby & Magnuson*(Legal Firm)*
Detroit, MI

Manufacturers National Bank N.A.*(Major Banking Relationship)*
38th Fl., 100 Renaissance Center
Detroit, MI 48243
Tel.: 313-222-4227

STU EVANS LINCOLN-MERCURY INC.
16800 Fort St.
Southgate, MI 48195
Tel.: 313-285-8800
Fax: 313-285-4570
Approx.Sls.: $115,800,000
Emp.: 211
Retail New & Used Motor Vehicles
S.I.C.: 5511
Stewart E. Evans *(Chm. Bd.)*
John Evans *(Pres. & Gen. Mgr.)*
Ann Fitzgerald *(Controller)*

EvansGroup

EVANSGROUP
110 Social Hall Ave.
Salt Lake City, UT 84111
Tel.: 801-364-7000
Fax: 801-364-0431
Year Founded: 1943
Approx.Billings: $200,000,000
Emp.: 368
Fiscal Year-end: 12/31/91
Advertising Agencies, Public Relations & Publicity
S.I.C.: 7311; 8743
Jon L. Johnson *(Pres., Chief Exec. Officer & Dir.)*
Donald B. Kraft *(Chm. & Dir.)*
L. Glen Snarr *(Chm., Exec. Comm. & Dir.)*
Charles R. Bartholomew *(Chief Exec. Officer (Los Angeles) & Dir.)*
Bernard J. Cummins *(Pres. & Chief Exec. Officer (San Francisco) & Dir.)*
Kelli McDonald Kurz *(Pres. & Chief Oper. Officer (Denver) & Dir.)*
Lon LaFlamme *(Pres. & Chief Exec. Officer (Seattle) & Dir.)*

Craig McKenzie *(Pres. & Chief Exec. Officer (Phoenix) & Dir.)*
Philip A. Motta *(Chief Exec. Officer (Dallas) & Dir.)*
Harry Roberts *(Pres. & Chief Exec. Officer (Portland) & Dir.)*
David G. Thomas *(Chief Exec. Officer (Salt Lake City) & Dir.)*
George L. Arnold *(Pres. & Chief Oper. Officer (Dallas) & Dir.)*
John Eastham *(Exec. V.P. (Seattle) & Dir.)*
Wayne C. Evans *(Sr. V.P. (Salt Lake City) & Dir.)*
Thomas A. Weinberg *(Pres. & Chief Oper. Officer (Los Angeles) & Dir.)*
James L. Winters *(Exec. V.P., Exec. Creative Dir. (Dallas) & Dir.)*
Bradley J. Nordgren *(Sr. V.P. & Chief Fin. Officer)*
Dennis R. Whicker *(Sr. V.P., Fin. Services)*
Marion Woodfield *(Sr. V.P., Acctg. Services)*

Principal(s):
100% of Stock Owned By 70 Employees

No. of U.S. Offices: 10

Outside Service Firm(s):

Terry, Price & Wunderli*(Auditors)*
Salt Lake, UT

Van Cott, Bagley, Cornwall & McCarthy*(Legal Firm)*
50 S. Main St., Ste. 1600
Salt Lake City, UT 84144
Tel.: 801-532-3333

Zions First National Bank*(Major Banking Relationship)*
One S. Main St.
Salt Lake City, UT 84111
Tel.: 801-524-4808

Branches:

Ellis & Ross Advertising & Design **(1)**
Museum Square Penthouse #1, 5757 Wilshire Blvd.
Los Angeles, CA 90036
Tel.: 213-938-2230
John Ellis *(Pres.)*

Evans Food Group **(1)**
Evans/Kraft Bldg., 190 Queen Anne North
Seattle, WA 98109-4924
Tel.: 206-285-5522
Dee Munson *(Pres.)*
Linda Hrdlicka *(V.P., Dir. Food Service)*
Donna Roberts *(V.P., Dir. Consumer)*
Jane Morimoto *(Dir. Test Kitchens)*

Evans/Public Relations **(1)**
Evans/Kraft Bldg., 190 Queen Anne Ave., North
Seattle, WA 98109-4924
Tel.: 206-285-5522
John Eastham *(Chm.)*
Arline Andre *(Pres., Home Product & Pub. Rels.)*
Dee Munson *(Pres., Food Group)*

EvansGroup **(1)**
4131 N. Central Expwy., Ste. 510
Dallas, TX 75204
Tel.: 214-521-6400
Philip A. Motta *(Chief Exec. Officer)*
George L. Arnold *(Pres. & Chief Oper. Officer)*
Jim Winters *(Exec. V.P., Exec. Creative Dir.)*
Steve Dodd *(Sr. V.P., Acct. Supvr.)*
Dave Winslow *(Exec. V.P., Dir. Acct. Services)*
Sherry Revord *(V.P., Creative Dir.)*

EvansGroup **(1)**
Prudential Plaza, 1050 17th St., Ste. 700
Denver, CO 80202
Tel.: 303-534-2343
Charles R. Bartholomew *(Chief Exec. Officer)*
Larry Norman *(Exec. V.P. & Creative Dir.)*
Kelli McDonald *(Pres., Chief Oper. Officer)*
Kathleen K. Brock *(Exec. V.P.)*
Lew Cady *(V.P., Creative)*
Mike Lane *(V.P., Acct. Supvr.)*
Jay G. Marks *(V.P., Acct. Supvr.)*
James P. House *(Pub. Rels. Dir.)*

EvansGroup **(1)**
Evans/Kraft Bldg., 190 Queen Anne Ave. North
Seattle, WA 98109-4924
Tel.: 206-285-2222
Fax: 206-286-8388
Donald B. Kraft *(Chm. Bd.)*
Lon LaFlamme *(Pres. & Chief Oper. Officer)*
Michael Mogelgaard *(Co-Chm. & Creative Dir.)*
Jack Ehrig *(Vice Chm.)*
Andy Keehn *(Sr. V.P., Dir. Planning)*
Dennis Gregg *(Sr. V.P., Chief Fin. Officer)*
James Clarke *(Sr. V.P.)*
Leah Hall *(V.P., Opers.)*
Brian Bradley *(V.P.)*
Sean Clark *(V.P.)*
Nancy Eastham *(V.P.)*
Dick Ehrig *(V.P.)*
Mike Ready *(V.P.)*
Dale Simpson *(V.P.)*
David Owens *(V.P.)*
Ronald Hughes *(Pres., Rep Force)*
Arline Andre *(Pres., Home Products Group)*
Dee Munson *(Pres., Evans Food Group)*

EvansGroup **(1)**
308 S.W. First Ave., Ste. 200
Portland, OR 97204
Tel.: 503-227-3921
Fax: 503-228-0006
Harry Roberts *(Pres.)*

EvansGroup **(1)**
Museum Square Penthouse #1, 5757 Wilshire Blvd.
Los Angeles, CA 90036
Tel.: 213-954-3000
Charles R. Bartholomew *(Chief Exec. Officer)*
Tom Weinberg *(Pres., Chief Oper. Officer)*
Ronnie Greenfield *(Sr. V.P., Acct. Service)*
Karen Whaley *(Office Mgr.)*

EvansGroup **(1)**
Biltmore Financial Center, 2390 E. Camelback, Ste. 325
Phoenix, AZ 85016
Tel.: 602-957-6636
Craig McKenzie *(Pres. & Chief Exec. Officer)*
David Gilbertson *(V.P., Pub. Rels.)*

EvansGroup **(1)**
690 Fifth St.
San Francisco, CA 94107
Tel.: 415-957-0300
Mick Cummins *(Pres. & Chief Exec. Officer)*

EvansGroup **(1)**
110 Social Hall Ave.
Salt Lake City, UT 84111
Tel.: 801-364-7000
David G. Thomas *(Chief Exec. Officer)*
Ronald A. Stone *(Pres. & Chief Creative Officer)*
Mike Korologos *(Exec. V.P., Dir. Pub. Rels.)*
Mike Rodriguez *(Exec. V.P., Dir. Acct. Services)*
Wayne C. Evans *(V.P. & Sec.)*
Daniel R. Huch *(V.P.)*
Lex L. Larsen *(V.P.)*
Dennis M. Newbold *(V.P.)*

Rep Force **(1)**
Evans/Kraft Bldg., 190 Queen Anne Ave. North
Seattle, WA 98109-4924
Tel.: 206-285-2222
Ron Hughes *(Pres.)*

Division:

Winslow Taylor Public Relations **(1)**
4131 N. Central Expwy., Ste. 510
Dallas, TX 75204
Tel.: 214-528-6863
Karen Taylor *(V.P., Gen. Mgr. & Acct. Supvr.)*

EVANSVILLE BREWING COMPANY
1301 W. Pennsylvania Ave.
Evansville, IN 47710
Mailing Address:
1301 W. Lloyd Expwy.
Evansville, IN 47710
Tel.: 812-425-7101
Fax: 812-425-7150
Year Founded: 1988
Approx.Sls.: $27,000,000
Emp.: 100
Export
Mfr. of Beer
S.I.C.: 2082
Mark S. Mattingly *(Chm. Bd. & Chief Exec. Officer)*
John Hellweg *(Pres.)*
Tom Bryant *(V.P.-Sls.)*
John Stone *(V.P.-Fin. & Admin.)*
Clarence Powell *(V.P.-Opers.)*
Mark S. Mattingly *(V.P.)*
Terry Southerland *(Dir.-Mktg.)*

Computer Systems/Hardware:
IBM-Compatible

EVCON HOLDINGS
3110 N. Mead
Wichita, KS 67219
Tel.: 316-832-6300
Approx.Sls.: $120,000,000
Fiscal Year-end: 12/31/91
Robert Hoffman *(Pres.)*
Ronald Buss *(V.P.-Fin.)*

Subsidiary:

Home Heating & Air Conditioning **(1)**
250 N. St. Francis Ave.
Wichita, KS 67202
Tel.: 316-261-3211
Approx.Sls.: $106,000,000
Emp.: 696
Mfg. & Sls. of Heat Pumps, Electric & Gas Furnaces & Air Conditioning for Residential, Mobile Home; Air Conditioning & Furnaces for RV
S.I.C.: 3585; 3699
Donald V. Berchtold *(Exec. V.P. & G.M.)*
Robert Hoffman *(Mgr. Res.)*
Joe Nold *(Mgr. Mfg. Housing)*
Melvin L. Adams *(Mgr., R.V. Products Div.)*

Subsidiary:

Red T. Products **(2)**
5004 South St.
Nacogdoches, TX 75961
Tel.: 409-560-3553
Refrigerant Coils & Air Handlers
S.I.C.: 3585
Howard Wilson *(Opers. Mgr.)*

EVENING POST PUBLISHING CO.
134 Columbus St.
Charleston, SC 29403-4800
Tel.: 803-577-7111
Fax: 803-577-7111, Ext. 483
Approx.Sls.: $11,000,000
Emp.: 700
Publishing of Daily Newspapers
S.I.C.: 2711
Peter Manigault *(Chm. Bd.)*
Ivan V. Anderson, Jr. *(Pres.)*
Joseph F. Smoak *(V.P., Gen. Mgr. & Treas.)*
James W. Martin *(Controller)*
Arthur M. Wilcox *(Sec.)*
Ernest R. Adams *(Dir.-Sls. & Mktg.)*
J. Douglas Donehue *(Dir.-Corp. Communications)*
James T. Eddins *(Dir.-Circulation)*
Paul Sharry *(Mgr.-Personnel)*
Pam W. Gill *(Pur. Agent)*

Outside Service Firm(s):

Price Waterhouse*(Auditors)*
Columbia, SC

Metropolitan Life Insurance Co.*(Group Insurer)*
One Madison Ave.
New York, NY 10010-3690
Tel.: 215-578-9292

EVERBRITE, INC.
4949 S. 110th St.
Greenfield, WI 53228
Mailing Address:
P.O. Box 20020
Greenfield, WI 53220
Tel.: 414-529-3500
Tel.: 800-558-3888 **WI**
Fax: 414-529-7191
Year Founded: 1928
Approx.Sls.: $95,000,000
Emp.: 1,300
Export
Outdoor & Indoor Point-of-Purchase Signs
S.I.C.: 3993
Carl H. Wamser *(Chm. Bd.)*
Charles E. Trame *(Vice Chm.)*
William J. Fritz *(Pres.)*
Perry Ankerson *(Pres.-Point of Pur. Div.)*
Robert Harruff *(Pres.-Identity System Div.)*
Tom Donnelly *(V.P.-Human Resources)*
Barbara Laughter *(Dir.-Mktg.)*

Outside Service Firm(s):

Arthur Andersen & Co.*(Auditors)*
777 E. Wisconsin Ave., P.O. Box 1215
Milwaukee, WI 53202
Tel.: 414-271-5100
Fax: 414-283-3200

Chernov, Croen & Stern*(Legal Firm)*
Milwaukee, WI

M & I Marshall & Ilsley Bank*(Major Banking Relationship)*
770 N. Water St.
Milwaukee, WI 53202
Tel.: 414-765-8700

Division:

Everbrite LaCrosse **(1)**
3145 Airport Rd.
La Crosse, WI 54601
Tel.: 608-781-8700
Mfr. Custom-Made Signs
S.I.C.: 3993
David Heuss *(Gen. Mgr.)*

Subsidiaries:

GHN **(1)**
24000 S. Vermont Rd.
Harbor City, CA 90710
Tel.: 310-530-7363
Mfr. of Neon Signs
S.I.C.: 3993

Mount Vernon Neon **(1)**
#1 Neon Dr.
Mount Vernon, IL 62864
Tel.: 618-242-0645
Mfr. of Neon Signs
S.I.C.: 3993
Mike Mateer *(Pres.)*

EVERFRESH BEVERAGES INC.
3333 N. Mt. Prospect Rd.
Franklin Park, IL 60131
Tel.: 708-833-8440
Fax: 708-833-8450
Approx.Sls.: $60,000,000
Emp.: 160
Mfr. of Fruit Juices & Other Beverages
S.I.C.: 2033; 2037
Mike Conde *(Pres. & Chief Exec. Officer)*
Andrew J. Brennan *(V.P.-Sls. & Mktg.)*
Patrick Crowley *(V.P.-Fin. Information Services)*
James Pratt *(V.P.-Opers.)*
Cheryl Yanello *(V.P.-Human Resources)*
Bruce Hesbon *(Pur. Agent)*

EVERGREEN HEALTHCARE LTD.
11350 North Meridian, Ste. 200
Carmel, IN 46032
Tel.: 317-580-8585
Management for Nursing Homes
S.I.C.: 8052; 8051
William Petty *(Pres.)*
Donald Finney *(Chief Oper. Officer)*

Evergreen Healthcare Ltd.—(Continued)

Subsidiary:

National Heritage, Inc. **(1)**
15770 N. Dallas Pkwy., 5th Fl.
Dallas, TX 75248
Tel.: 214-233-3900
Tel.: 800-677-6440
Fax: 214-490-6053
Assets: $33,134,000
Earnings: ($7,248,000)
Liabilities: $18,991,000
Net Worth: $14,143,000
Approx.Rev.: $51,396,000
Emp.: 2,358
Fiscal Year-end: 6/30/91
Computer Systems/Hardware:
IBM 4381 P-13 Mainframe Processor
Manages & Operates Intermediate & Skilled Long-Term Care Centers
S.I.C.: 8051; 8052

EVERGREEN INTERNATIONAL AVIATION, INC.
3850 Three Mile Lane
McMinnville, OR 97128-9496
Tel.: 503-472-9361
Fax: 503-472-1048
Approx.Sls.: $350,000,000
Emp.: 2,500
Import Export
Aviation Services
S.I.C.: 4512; 4522; 4581
Delford M. Smith *(Chm. Bd.)*
Joe Sharp *(Pres.)*
Robert I. Cantrell *(Sr. V.P.-Fin.)*
Donna G. Nelson *(V.P.-Admin.)*

Computer Systems/Hardware:
Hewlett-Packard 3000 System 70

Outside Service Firm(s):

Deloitte & Touche*(Auditors)*
3900 U.S. Bancorp Tower
Portland, OR 97204
Tel.: 503-222-1341
Fax: 503-224-2172

Miller, Nash, Wiener, Hager & Carlsen*(Legal Firm)*
900 S.W. Fifth Ave.
Portland, OR 97204
Tel.: 503-224-5858

United States National Bank of Oregon*(Major Banking Relationship)*
Portland, OR

L. G. EVERIST INC.
313 S. Phillips Ave.
Sioux Falls, SD 57102
Mailing Address:
P.O. Box 829
Sioux Falls, SD 57117
Tel.: 605-334-5000
Fax: 605-334-3656
Year Founded: 1914
Approx.Sls.: $20,000,000
Emp.: 200
Mining; Marine Construction
S.I.C.: 1411; 1499; 1629
C. Schulte *(Chm. Bd.)*
Thomas Everist *(Pres.)*
H.J. Schmidt *(Sec. & Treas.)*
George Spencer *(Chief Engr.)*

Computer Systems/Hardware:
IBM System 34

Outside Service Firm(s):

KPMG Peat Marwick*(Auditors)*
4200 Norwest Center, 90 S. 7th St.
Minneapolis, MN 55402
Tel.: 612-341-2222

Woods, Fuller, Schultz*(Legal Firm)*
Sioux Falls, SD

First National Bank of Minneapolis*(Major Banking Relationship)*
Minneapolis, MN

EVERLAST SPORTS MANUFACTURING CORP.
750 E. 132nd St.
Bronx, NY 10454
Tel.: 718-993-0100
Tel.: 800-221-8777
Telex: 287019 EVRSP
Fax: 718-665-4116
Approx.Sls.: $20,000,000
Emp.: 300
Mfr. of Sporting Goods & Gymnasium Equipment
S.I.C.: 3949
Ben J. Nadorf *(Pres. & Treas.)*
D.I. Golomb *(Exec. V.P. & Sec.)*
J.L. Toms *(V.P.-Admin. & Mktg.)*
Toni Prisciandaro *(Asst. V.P.)*
J.S. Begue *(Comptroller)*
Frank Lekram *(Dir.-Pur.)*

Outside Service Firm(s):

Traub & Lesser*(Legal Firm)*
Bronx, NY

Manufacturers Hanover Trust Co.*(Major Banking Relationship)*
350 Park Ave.
New York, NY 10022

EVY OF CALIFORNIA, INC.
10755 Venice Blvd.
Los Angeles, CA 90034
Tel.: 310-559-3000 **CA**
Fax: 310-837-2529
Year Founded: 1986
Approx.Sls.: $30,000,000
Emp.: 650
Mfr. of Girls' Dresses & Sportwear
S.I.C.: 2369; 2361
Kurt Krieser *(Pres.)*
Henry Cowen *(V.P.)*
Don Feldman *(V.P.-Sls.)*

Outside Service Firm(s):

Lasker, Kim & Co.*(Auditors)*
Beverly Hills, CA

Kindel & Anderson*(Legal Firm)*
555 S. Flower, Ste. 2600
Los Angeles, CA 90071
Tel.: 213-680-2222

Wells Fargo Bank*(Major Banking Relationship)*
333 S. Grand
Los Angeles, CA 90071
Tel.: 213-253-6836

EXACT EQUIPMENT CORPORATION
850 Town Center Dr.
Langhorne, PA 19047
Mailing Address:
P.O. Box 666,
Levittown, PA 19058
Tel.: 215-750-9090 **DE**
Fax: 215-741-1619
Year Founded: 1986
Sales Range: $10-19 Million
Emp.: 90
Import Export
Mfrs. & Mkts. Packaging Machinery & Weighing Equip.
S.I.C.: 3565; 3596
Robert C. Enichen *(Pres.)*
Stan Smith *(V.P.-Opers. & Pur. Dir.)*
J. Kirk *(Sec. & Treas.)*
F. Basil *(Dir.-Mktg.)*
F. Schwendeman *(Dir.-Data Processing)*
Principal(s):
Robert C. Enichen
Stan Smith

No. of Mfg. Plants/Facilities: 2
No. of U.S. Offices: 8

Computer Systems/Hardware:
IBM System 36

Outside Service Firm(s):

Meridian Bank*(Major Banking Relationship)*
Philadelphia, PA

Branch:

Exact Equipment Corporation **(1)**
1507 W. Elizabeth
Linden, NJ 07036
Tel.: 201-862-5311
Harry Haley *(Mgr.)*

EXCEL INDUSTRIES, INC.
200 S. Ridge Rd.
Hesston, KS 67062
Tel.: 316-327-4911
Fax: 316-327-2117
Year Founded: 1960
Approx.Sls.: $35,000,000
Emp.: 250
Fiscal Year-end: 10/30/92
Import Export
Mfr. Commercial Turf & Grounds Equipment
S.I.C.: 3524
Roy Mullet *(Chm. Bd.)*
Paul Mullet *(Pres.)*
Byron K. Henson *(Exec. V.P.)*
Vernon Nikkel *(V.P.-Personnel)*
Don Cuthbertson *(Dir.-Mfg.)*
Dave Welfelt *(Dir.-Sls. & Mktg.)*
Ken Raney *(Mgr.-Adv.)*

No. of Mfg. Plants/Facilities: 1
No. of U.S. Offices: 1

Computer Systems/Hardware:
IBM AS/400

Outside Service Firm(s):

Peterson & Peterson*(Auditors)*
Wichita, KS

First National Bank of Wichita*(Major Banking Relationship)*
Box One
Wichita, KS 67201
Tel.: 316-268-1201

EXCELL MANUFACTURING COMPANY
200 Chestnut St.
Providence, RI 02903
Tel.: 401-421-5957
Fax: 401-421-8387
Approx.Sls.: $10,000,000
Emp.: 65
Manufacture Jewelry Chains, Precious Metals
S.I.C.: 3911
Howard K. Kilguss *(Chm. Bd., Pres. & Treas.)*
Lawrence DeMichele *(V.P.)*

Outside Service Firm(s):

Ernst & Young*(Auditors)*
One Old Stone Square
Providence, RI 02903
Tel.: 401-331-7000

Connors & Kliquss*(Legal Firm)*
Providence, RI

Citizens Savings Bank*(Major Banking Relationship)*
Providence, RI

EXCELLED SHEEPSKIN & LEATHER COAT CORPORATION
350 5th Ave.
New York, NY 10018
Tel.: 212-594-5843
Fax: 212-967-5695
Year Founded: 1927
Assets: $25,000,000
Liabilities: $15,000,000
Net Worth: $10,000,000
Approx.Sls.: $40,000,000
Emp.: 250
Fiscal Year-end: 12/31/91
Import Export
Men's Outerwear, Leather, Suedes & Sheepskin
S.I.C.: 2386
Myron Goldman *(Pres.)*
Michael Holzberg *(V.P.)*
Dave Karreau *(V.P. & Gen. Mgr.)*
Principal(s):
Myron Goldman

No. of Mfg. Plants/Facilities: 2
No. of U.S. Offices: 6

Outside Service Firm(s):

Freedman, Alpren & Green*(Auditors)*
New York, NY

Kantor, Davidoff, Wolfe, Rabbino & Kass, P.C.*(Legal Firm)*
New York, NY

National Westminster Bank plc*(Major Banking Relationship)*
Astor Plaza, 1515 Broadway
New York, NY 10036

Subsidiary:

Empire Clothing **(1)**
1700 Burlington
Kewanee, IL 61443
Tel.: 309-852-3341
Emp.: 150
Mfg. Leather Coats
S.I.C.: 2386
Phil Dubow *(Pres.)*

EXCELSIOR MANUFACTURING & SUPPLY CORP.
1465 E. Industrial Dr.
Itasca, IL 60143
Tel.: 708-773-5500 **IL**
Fax: 708-773-1612
Year Founded: 1886
Assets: $10,984,290
Liabilities: $4,918,108
Net Worth: $6,066,182
Approx.Sls.: $24,000,000
Emp.: 170
Fiscal Year-end: 12/31/91
Import
Manufacture Metal Products; Distributor Heating & Cooling Equipment
S.I.C.: 3431; 3433; 5072; 5074; 5075
John Brady *(Pres. & Chief Oper. Officer)*
Gene Baker *(Chief Oper. Officer)*
Robert Clement *(Chief Fin. Officer & Sec.)*
Curtis R. Mangrum *(V.P.-Sls.)*
Tom Woessner *(V.P.-Mktg. & sls.)*
James H. Mangrum *(V.P.)*
Vicki M. Vetali *(Treas. & Controller)*
Dennis Juda *(Sec.)*

No. of Mfg. Plants/Facilities: 2
No. of U.S. Offices: 7

Computer Systems/Hardware:
Prime

Outside Service Firm(s):

Deloitte & Touche*(Auditors)*
Two Prudential Plaza, 180 N. Stetson
Chicago, IL 60601
Tel.: 312-946-2039

Hanover Insurance Co.*(Commercial Insurance Carrier)*
Itasca, IL

Gary Wheaton Bank*(Investment Banker)*
Wheaton, IL

Drendel, Schanlaber, Horwitz & Tatnall*(Legal Firm)*
Aurora, IL

LaSalle National Bank*(Major Banking Relationship)*
135 S. LaSalle St., Rm.260
Chicago, IL 60603

EXECUTIVE CAPITAL CORP.
Rte. 30
Big Rock, IL 60511
Tel.: 708-556-3731
Fax: 708-556-3017
Year Founded: 1968
Sales Range: $100-499 Million
Emp.: 150
Real Estate Investment Firm
S.I.C.: 6798
William R. Stahlke *(Pres.)*
Evon Rayman *(V.P.)*
Steve Schomer *(V.P.)*

Computer Systems/Hardware:
IBM; Toshiba; Compaq

EXECUTIVE CAR LEASING, INC.
7800 Santa Monica Blvd.
Los Angeles, CA 90046
Tel.: 213-654-5000 **NJ**
Fax: 213-654-1208
Year Founded: 1955
Emp.: 150
Passenger Car Leasing; Truck Leasing Without Drivers
S.I.C.: 7515; 7513
Samuel Goldman *(Pres.)*

Subsidiary:

Executive Car Leasing Company **(1)**
7807 Santa Monica Blvd.
Los Angeles, CA 90046
Tel.: 213-654-5000
Approx.Sls.: $28,000,000
Emp.: 190
Passenger Car Leasing; Truck Leasing Without Driver
S.I.C.: 7515; 7513
Samuel Goldman *(Pres.)*
Cyril Yedor *(Exec. V.P.)*
Nancy Kelley *(V.P.-Fin.)*
David Clark *(V.P.)*
Joe Shehab *(V.P.)*
Richard Schrieklin *(Controller)*
Fran Rycewicz *(Mgr.-Data Processing)*
Roslyn Boulianne *(Mgr.-Pur.)*

EXECUTIVE ENTERPRISES, INC.
22 W. 21st St.
New York, NY 10010
Tel.: 212-645-7880
Fax: 212-675-4883
Year Founded: 1971
Approx.Sls.: $19,900,000
Emp.: 85
Fiscal Year-end: 12/31/91
Export
Executive Seminars, Periodicals & Book Publishing
S.I.C.: 2731; 2721; 8299
J. Brian McGrath *(Chm. Bd.)*
James F. Slabe *(Pres. & Chief Oper. Officer)*
Principal(s):
J. Brian McGrath
James F. Slabe

No. of Mfg. Plants/Facilities: 1

Computer Systems/Hardware:
NIXDORF & Apple Mcintosh

Outside Service Firm(s):

Paul Czarnowski & Associates*(Auditors)*
New York, NY

Weil, Gotshal & Manges*(Legal Firm)*
767 5th Ave.
New York, NY 10153
Tel.: 212-310-8000

Marine Midland Bank*(Major Banking Relationship)*
250 Park Ave.
New York, NY 10017
Tel.: 212-503-6642

J. & W. Seligman*(Pension Manager)*
One Bankers Trust Plaza
New York, NY 10006
Tel.: 212-488-0200
Fax: 212-488-0876

Division:

Executive Enterprises Publications Co., Inc. **(1)**
22 W. 21st St.
New York, NY 10010
Tel.: 212-645-7880
Seminars, Periodicals & Book Publishing
S.I.C.: 2721; 2731; 8299
James F. Slabe *(Pres.)*

EXECUTIVE JET AVIATION, INC.
(Div. of RTS Capital Services, Inc.)
625 N. Hamilton Rd.
Columbus, OH 43219
Mailing Address:
P.O. Box 369099,
Columbus, OH 43239-9099
Tel.: 614-239-5500
Fax: 614-239-5589
Year Founded: 1966
Approx.Sls.: $30,000,000
Emp.: 140
Fiscal Year-end: 4/30/92
Business Jet Charter; Maintenance; Pilot Training; Avionics Service & Installation; Aircraft Brokerage, Sales, Leasing; Helicopter Leasing; Consultation, Engine Leasing; Helicopter Maintenance
S.I.C.: 4522
Richard T. Santulli *(Pres. & Chief Exec. Officer)*
Steve Speaks *(Dir.-Avionics)*
Richard G. Smith III *(Dir.-Opers.)*

Computer Systems/Hardware:
IBM system 36; Network PC Systems

EXIDE CORPORATION
P.O. Box 14205, 635 Penn St.
Reading, PA 19612
Tel.: 215-378-0500 **DE**
Fax: 215-378-0315
Year Founded: 1888
Assets: $478,000,000
Liabilities: $398,700,000
Net Worth: $79,300,000
Approx.Sls.: $570,000,000
Emp.: 4,600
Fiscal Year-end: 3/31/91
Import Export
Mfr. of Automotive Batteries
S.I.C.: 3691; 3692
Arthur M. Hawkins *(Pres. & Chief Exec. Officer)*
Richard L. Touve *(Chief Fin. Officer)*
Douglas N. Pearson *(Exec. V.P.)*
William Rankin *(Exec. V.P.-Engrng.)*
Joseph Calio *(V.P.-Sls. & Mktg.)*
Alan E. Gautnier *(V.P.-Fin. & Asst. Sec.)*
Jack J. Sosiak *(V.P.-Human Resources)*
Michael McCool *(Controller)*
Richard T. Kimball *(Dir.-Personnel)*
Principal(s):
Arthur M. Hawkins

No. of Mfg. Plants/Facilities: 24
No. of U.S. Offices: 2

Computer Systems/Hardware:
IBM

Outside Service Firm(s):

Arthur Andersen & Co.*(Auditors)*
Reading, PA

Wausau Insurance*(Commercial Insurance Carrier)*
Philadelphia, PA

Connecticut General Life Insurance Company*(Group Insurer)*
New York, NY
Tel.: 212-5754600

Kirkland & Ellis*(Legal Firm)*
200 E. Randolph Dr.
Chicago, IL 60601
Tel.: 312-861-2000
Fax: 312-861-2200

Chemical Bank*(Major Banking Relationship)*
70 W. Madison St.
Chicago, IL 60602

NBD Bank, N.A.*(Pension Manager)*
P.O. Box 222,
Detroit, MI 48232
Tel.: 313-225-4414
Fax: 313-225-3420

Division:

ESB Puerto Rico Corp. **(1)**
Industrial Park, 889 Julio N. Matos
Carolina, PR 00628
Emp.: 39
Mfr. of Automotive Batteries
S.I.C.: 3692
Al Mashado *(Chief Oper. Officer)*

EXPERIENCE IN SOFTWARE, INC.
2000 Hearst Ave. Ste 202
Berkeley, CA 94709
Tel.: 510-644-0694
Tel.: 800-678-7008 **CA**
Fax: 510-644-3823
Year Founded: 1983
Emp.: 3
Export
Manufacture Computer Software
S.I.C.: 7372
Roy A. Nierenberg *(Pres.)*
Carolyn Burd *(Mktg. Mgr.)*
Craig Settles *(Mgr.-Public Rels.)*

No. of U.S. Offices: 1

Computer Systems/Hardware:
IBM PC & Compatibles

Outside Service Firm(s):

Nationwide Insurance*(Group Insurer)*
Concord, CA

Wells Fargo Bank*(Major Banking Relationship)*
420 Montgomery St.
San Francisco, CA 94104

EXPO INDUSTRIES, INC.
7465 Carroll Rd.
San Diego, CA 92121
Tel.: 619-566-4343 **CA**
Fax: 619-566-0350
Year Founded: 1982
Approx.Sls.: $32,000,000
Emp.: 125
Exterior & Interior Building Materials; Stucco
S.I.C.: 5031; 3299
Robert P. Papera *(Pres.)*
David G. Crabtree *(V.P.)*
W. Dean Allen *(Chief Fin. Officer & Treas.)*
Chuck Opperman *(Sec.)*

Outside Service Firm(s):

Deloitte & Touche*(Auditors)*
701 "B" St., Ste. 1900
San Diego, CA 92101-8198

Wells Fargo Bank*(Major Banking Relationship)*
San Diego, CA

Express Services, Inc.
(See Gray-Pro, Inc. Listing)

EZON PRODUCTS, INC.
1900 Exeter Rd.
Germantown, TN 38138
Tel.: 901-755-5555 **TN**
Fax: 901-757-2728
Year Founded: 1952
Approx.Premiums: $200,000,000
Emp.: 375
Wholesale Distribution of Automotive Supplies & Parts; Garage Service Equipment; Chemical Preparations; Real Estate Managers
S.I.C.: 5013; 2899; 6531
Oscar J. Gomez, Jr. *(Chm. Bd.)*
Barry Gomez *(Pres.)*
Jack Packett *(V.P.)*

Outside Service Firm(s):

National Bank of Commerce*(Major Banking Relationship)*
Memphis, TN

F & B MANUFACTURING CO.
5480 N. Northwest Hwy.
Chicago, IL 60630
Tel.: 312-774-6300
Fax: 312-774-1373
Year Founded: 1922
Assets: $31,000,000
Liabilities: $16,000,000
Net Worth: $15,000,000
Approx.Sls.: $60,000,000
Emp.: 540
Fiscal Year-end: 6/30/92
Import Export
Manufacture Auto Replacement Parts
S.I.C.: 3694
Milada F. Anderson *(Pres.)*
Fred H. Vansice *(Exec. V.P.)*
Jim Grubb *(Chief Info. Officer)*
Daniel T. Powell *(Chief Fin. Officer)*
Ward Nieds *(Controller)*
Ted Thacker *(Gen. Mgr.)*
Gary Kroll *(Dir.-Purch.)*

Computer Systems/Hardware:
AS/400

Outside Service Firm(s):

Friedman, Eisenstein, Raemer & Schwartz*(Auditors)*
Chicago, IL

Hill, Van Santen, Steadman & Simpson*(Legal Firm)*
Chicago, IL

American National Bank*(Major Banking Relationship)*
33 North LaSalle St.
Chicago, IL 60690
Tel.: 312-661-6967

Subsidiary:

Filko/Cobra, Inc. **(1)**
5480 N. Northwest Hwy.
Chicago, IL 60630
Tel.: 312-774-1373
Emp.: 110
Mfr. Auto Parts
S.I.C.: 3694
Fred H. Vansice *(Pres.)*
Daniel T. Powell *(Chief Fin. Officer)*
Les Green *(V.P.-Sls.)*
Gary Kroll *(V.P.-Pur.)*
Ted Thacker *(Gen. Mgr.)*

F & M DISTRIBUTORS INC.
25800 Sherwood
Warren, MI 48091
Tel.: 313-758-1400
Fax: 313-758-3787
Year Founded: 1955
Approx.Sls.: $600,000,000
Emp.: 1,200
Retail Health & Beauty Aids; Household Supplies
S.I.C.: 5311; 5912; 5399
Randolph J. Agley *(Chm. Bd.)*
Frank A. Newman *(Pres. & Chief Exec. Officer)*
D. Zani *(V.P.-Human Resources)*
Patty Klein *(V.P.-Mktg.)*
Wayne Inman *(V.P.)*
Michael T. Timmis *(V.P.)*
Laura Kendall *(Chief Fin. Officer)*
Frank Jerneycic *(Sec. & Treas.)*

F & M Distributors Inc.—(Continued)

Outside Service Firm(s):

Arthur Andersen & Co.*(Auditors)*
400 Renaissance Center
Detroit, MI 48243
Tel.: 313-259-8100

Marco, Inman & Timmis*(Legal Firm)*
20180 Mack Ave.
Grosse Pointe Woods, MI 48236
Tel.: 313-885-8100

Manufacturers National Bank N.A.*(Major Banking Relationship)*
38th Fl., 100 Renaissance Center
Detroit, MI 48243
Tel.: 313-222-4227

F & W PUBLICATIONS, INC.
1507 Dana Ave.
Cincinnati, OH 45207
Tel.: 513-531-2222 **OH**
Fax: 513-531-4744
Fax: 513-531-1843
Year Founded: 1911
Approx.Sls.: $43,000,000
Emp.: 225
Fiscal Year-end: 12/31/91
Import Export
Magazine Publishing
S.I.C.: 2721
Corporate Giving Program: Fine Arts Fund; United Appeal
Richard H. Rosenthal *(Pres.)*
David R. Luppert *(Sr. V.P.-Fin. & Admin.)*
W. Budge Wallis *(Sr. V.P. & Gen. Mgr.-Book Div.)*
Jeff Lapin *(V.P. & Gen. Mgr.-Magazine & Educational Services Div.)*
Hugh Gildea *(Controller)*
Michael Hoover *(Dir.-Mfg.)*
Mert Ransdell *(Dir.-Book Club)*
Kathy Schneider *(Dir.-Personnel)*
Principal(s):
Richard H. Rosenthal

No. of U.S. Offices: 1

Outside Service Firm(s):

KPMG Peat Marwick*(Auditors)*
1600 Central Trust Ctr., 201 East Fifth St.
Cincinnati, OH 45202
Tel.: 513-421-6430

Blue Cross & Blue Shield Association*(Group Insurer)*
Cincinnati, OH

The Central Trust Company, N.A.*(Investment Banker)*
201 E. Fifth
Cincinnati, OH 45202
Tel.: 513-651-8255

Strauss & Troy*(Legal Firm)*
Cincinnati, OH

The Central Trust Company, N.A.*(Major Banking Relationship)*
201 E. Fifth
Cincinnati, OH 45202
Tel.: 513-651-8255

Star Bank*(Major Banking Relationship)*
425 Walnut Street
Cincinnati, OH 45202
Tel.: 513-632-4000

Divisions:

Betterway Publications Inc. **(1)**
P.O. Box 219,
Crozet, VA 22932
Tel.: 804-823-5661
Fax: 804-823-2047
Bob Hostage *(Pres.)*

Book Division **(1)**
1507 Dana Ave.
Cincinnati, OH 45207
Tel.: 513-531-2222
Fax: 513-531-4744
William Wallis *(V.P. & Gen. Mgr.)*

Education Division **(1)**
1507 Dana Ave.
Cincinnati, OH 45207
Tel.: 513-531-2222
Jeff Lapin *(V.P. & Gen. Mgr.)*

Magazine & Educational Services Division **(1)**
1507 Dana Ave.
Cincinnati, OH 45207
Tel.: 513-531-2222
Jeffry Lapin *(V.P. & Gen. Mgr.)*

F C L GRAPHICS
4600 N. Olcott
Harwood Heights, IL 60656
Tel.: 708-867-5500
Fax: 708-867-7768
Approx.Sls.: $18,000,000
Emp.: 148
Offset Printing
S.I.C.: 2752
Frank Calabrese *(Pres.)*
Phil Bauman *(V.P.)*

Outside Service Firm(s):

E.E. Warner & Co.*(Auditors)*
Des Plaines, IL

FCN ADVERTISING
10850 W. Park Place, Ste. 1200
Milwaukee, WI 53224
Tel.: 414-577-2000
Year Founded: 1939
Approx.Billings: $27,000,000
Emp.: 20
Business-to-Business, Marketing, Public Relations & Consulting
Andrew A. Vallozzi *(Pres. & Treas.)*
Rich Brayer *(V.P.)*
Ronald Caffrey *(V.P.)*
Phil Eckel *(V.P.-Production)*
Tom Hamilton *(V.P.)*
Janet Vallozzi *(V.P.)*

Computer Systems/Hardware:
Macintosh

FDL FOODS, INC.
701 E. 16th St.
Dubuque, IA 52001
Tel.: 319-588-5400
Fax: 319-588-5317
Year Founded: 1982
Approx.Sls.: $750,000,000
Emp.: 2,800
Fiscal Year-end: 10/30/90
Export
Wholesale & Retail Pork Products
S.I.C.: 5147
Robert H. Wahlert *(Chm. Bd., Pres. & Chief Exec. Officer)*
Mike McCoy *(V.P., Treas. & Chief Fin. Officer)*
Chuck Naylor *(V.P. & Gen. Counsel)*
Howard McLean *(V.P.-Opers.)*
Bob Urell *(V.P.-Engrng.)*
Neil Keith *(Dir.-Pur.)*
Diane Thoma *(Dir.-Personnel)*
Principal(s):
Robert H. Wahlert

No. of Mfg. Plants/Facilities: 2

Computer Systems/Hardware:
AS 400

Outside Service Firm(s):

McGladrey & Pullen*(Auditors)*
Chicago, IL

Cottingham & Butler*(Group Insurer)*
Dubuque, IA

FEL CORPORATION
Route 547 & Central Ave.
Farmingdale, NJ 07727
Tel.: 908-938-9000
Fax: 908-919-2482
Year Founded: 1976
Approx.Sls.: $36,000,000
Emp.: 450
Mfr. of Electrical Coils & Transformers
S.I.C.: 3677
William D. Hurley *(Chm. Bd.)*
Foster Hirsch *(Pres.)*
Benjamin Amato *(V.P.-Opers.)*
Joseph Gagliardi *(V.P.-Fin.)*

FGI
700 Eastowne Dr.
Chapel Hill, NC 27514
Tel.: 919-493-1670
Fax: 919-490-8829
Year Founded: 1982
Approx.Billings: $30,000,000
Emp.: 90
Adv.
Carl W. Nordgren *(Chief Exec. Officer)*
Jim Protzman *(Chm. Bd.)*

F J M CORPORATION
2150 Touhy Ave.
Elk Grove Village, IL 60007
Tel.: 708-364-4700 **IL**
Fax: 708-364-0852
Year Founded: 1945
Approx.Sls.: $11,000,000
Emp.: 21
Wholesale Distributor of Metalworking Machinery; Machine Tools & Accessories
S.I.C.: 5084
Francis J. Myers, Jr. *(Pres.)*
John Myers *(V.P.)*

Principal(s):
Francis J. Myers, Jr.
John Myers

Outside Service Firm(s):

American National Bank & Trust Company of Chicago*(Major Banking Relationship)*
33 N. LaSalle St.
Chicago, IL 60602
Tel.: 312-661-5000
Fax: 312-661-6417

FKQ ADVERTISING INC.
15351 Roosevelt Blvd.
Clearwater, FL 34620
Tel.: 813-539-8800
Fax: 813-530-5696
Year Founded: 1982
Approx.Billings: $24,000,000
Emp.: 31
Robert O. Faller *(Chm. Bd., Pres.)*
Lisa M. Faller *(Exec. V.P., Sec. & Client Services)*
Lou Carbone *(V.P., Mktg. & Strategic Plng.)*
Karen L. Gorenflo *(Fin. Mgr. & Treasurer)*
Kelly Besch *(Acctg.)*
Gillian Hegner *(Admin. Asst.)*
Tracy Davies *(Asst. Office Mgr.)*

Computer Systems/Hardware:
Macintosh

FM INDUSTRIES, INC.
8600 Will Rogers Blvd.
Fort Worth, TX 76140
Mailing Address:
P.O. Box 40555
Ft. Worth, TX 76140
Tel.: 817-293-4220
Fax: 817-551-5801
Year Founded: 1989
Assets: $10,750,000
Net Worth: $10,750,000
Sales Range: $10-19 Million
Emp.: 130
Fiscal Year-end: 12/31/89
Hydraulic Railcar Cushioning Devices, Hydraulic Demolition Hammers, Compactors, Booms and Pedestals and Railroad Locomotive Simulators
S.I.C.: 3743; 3533; 3561; 3563; 3531; 3532; 3699
Allan J. Kvasnicka *(Chm. Bd.)*
O. Elwyn Seay *(Pres. & Chief Exec. Officer)*
William R. Frazier *(Chief Fin. Officer & V.P.-Fin.)*
Maurice Dew *(V.P.-Mfg.)*
Richard Hodges *(V.P.-Engrng.)*
Tommy Howe *(V.P.-Sls.)*
Leo Kane *(V.P.-Contruction Equip.)*

Outside Service Firm(s):

Arthur Andersen & Co.*(Auditors)*
777 East Campbell Rd., Ste. 777
Richardson, TX 75081

Baker, Mills & Glast*(Legal Firm)*
500 Trammel Crow Center, Ste. 2001
Dallas, TX 75201-2916
Tel.: 214-220-8200

Everman Bank*(Major Banking Relationship)*
Ft. Worth, TX

FMS MANAGEMENT SYSTEMS, INC.
2655 N.E. 189th St.
North Miami Beach, FL 33180
Tel.: 305-931-5454 **MD**
Fax: 305-931-5454
Approx.Rev.: $50,000,000
Emp.: 1,500
Operates & Franchises 87 IHOP Restaurants Throughout FL
S.I.C.: 5812
Leslie Freedman *(Pres. & Chief Fin. Officer)*
Robert Leonard *(Chief Oper. Officer)*
Nathan Finkel *(V.P. & Sec.)*
Martin B. Freedman *(V.P. & Treas.)*
James E. Brown, Jr. *(V.P.-Finance)*
Principal(s):
Leslie Freedman
Nathan Finkel
Martin B. Freedman

Computer Systems/Hardware:
AT&T 4410, 3B-2400; Atlas 2086

Outside Service Firm(s):

KPMG Peat Marwick*(Auditors)*
One Independent Dr.
Jacksonville, FL 32201

Liberty Mutual*(Commercial Insurance Carrier)*
Boston, MA

FRABT*(Group Insurer)*
Maitland, FL

NationsBank Florida*(Major Banking Relationship)*
51 W. Forsyth St.
Jacksonville, FL 32202

F.P.A., INC.

(d/b/a Frank Parra Chevrolet)
1000 E. Airport Fwy.
Irving, TX 75062
Tel.: 214-721-4300 **TX**
Fax: 214-721-4463
Approx.Sls.: $130,000,000
Emp.: 275
Automobile Dealership
S.I.C.: 5511
Tim Parra *(Pres.)*
Mike Parra *(V.P.)*
Paul Morgan *(Treas. & Sec.)*
Principal(s):
Tim Parra

Computer Systems/Hardware:
ADP

Outside Service Firm(s):

Ernst & Young*(Auditors)*
2121 San Jacinto, Ste. 500
Dallas, TX 75201
Tel.: 214-969-8000

Texas Commerce Bank*(Major Banking Relationship)*
2200 Ross Ave.
Dallas, TX 75266

F. R. MANUFACTURING CORPORATION
(a/k/a/ Fran Rica)
2807 South Hwy. 99
Stockton, CA 95205
Mailing Address:
P.O. Box 30127
Stockton, CA 95213
Tel.: 209-948-2811
Fax: 209-948-5198
Year Founded: 1968
Approx.Sls.: $16,000,000
Emp.: 90
Fiscal Year-end: 12/31/90
Mfr. of Food Processing & Packaging Equip.
S.I.C.: 3411; 3089
J.M. Hougland *(Pres. & Chief Oper. Officer)*
Lloyd Hay *(Exec. V.P.)*
John Miller *(V.P. & Controller)*

FTD/FLORISTS' TRANSWORLD DELIVERY ASSOCIATION
29200 Northwestern Hwy.
Southfield, MI 48034
Mailing Address:
P.O. Box 2227,
Southfield, MI 48037
Tel.: 313-355-9300
Fax: 313-355-6350
Year Founded: 1910
Approx.Sls.: $700,000,000
Emp.: 379
Flowers-by-Wire
S.I.C.: 7389
John Borden *(Exec. V.P.)*
Jim Jordan *(Sr. Grp. Dir.-Membership Services)*
Doug Hagemann *(Grp. Dir.-Fin.)*
Roger Gullickson *(Grp. Dir.-Mktg.)*
Rick Sharpe *(Dir.-Consumer Mktg.)*
Richard Williams *(Mgr.-Consumer Communications)*

FWD CORPORATION
105 E. 12th St.
Clintonville, WI 54929
Tel.: 715-823-2141 **WI**
Fax: 715-823-5768
Year Founded: 1909
Approx.Sls.: $38,000,000
Emp.: 400
Fiscal Year-end: 9/30/91
Heavy Duty Specialized On-Off Highway Trucks, Crane Carriers, Utility Vehicles, Highway Maintenance Vehicles, Ready-Mix Chassis, Fire Apparatus
S.I.C.: 3711; 3531; 3537; 3799; 3569
Randolph W. Lenz *(Chm. Bd.)*
James M. Green *(Pres. & Chief Exec. Officer)*
Stephen Smith *(V.P.-Engrng.)*
Joseph L. Kaufmann *(Chief Fin. Officer & Treas.)*
John Roesnheim *(Controller)*
Wanda Tellock *(Sec.)*
Robert Hoffman *(Mgr.-Pur.)*
Ben Hoppe *(Mgr.-Sls.)*
Bill McGehee *(Mgr.-Mfg.)*

Principal(s):
Randolph W. Lenz

Computer Systems/Hardware:
IBM System 38

Outside Service Firm(s):

Deloitte & Touche*(Auditors)*
250 E. Wisconsin Ave.
Milwaukee, WI 53202-4283
Tel.: 414-271-3000

Foley & Lardner*(Legal Firm)*
777 E. Wisconsin Ave.
Milwaukee, WI 53202
Tel.: 414-271-2400

First Wisconsin Financial Services*(Major Banking Relationship)*
Milwaukee, WI
Tel.: 608-868-6000

Subsidiary:

Seagrave Fire Apparatus, Inc. **(1)**
105 E. 12th St.
Clintonville, WI 54929
Tel.: 715-823-3194
Approx.Sls.: $35,000,000
Emp.: 400
Fiscal Year-end: 9/30/91
Computer Systems/Hardware:
IBM
Manufactures Fire Apparatus
S.I.C.: 3669
James M. Green *(Pres. & Chief Exec. Officer)*
Joseph L. Kaufmann *(Treas. & Chief Fin. Officer)*
Steven Smith *(V.P.-Engrng.)*
Wanda D. Tellock *(Corp. Sec.)*
Ben Hoppe *(Mgr.-Sls.)*
William McGehee *(Mgr.-Mfg.)*
R.J. Hoffman *(Mgr.-Pur.)*
Roland Myers *(Mgr.-Product Support)*

FABER/CASTELL CORPORATION
4 Century Dr.
Parsippany, NJ 07054
Tel.: 201-539-4111 **NJ**
Fax: 201-537-4537
Year Founded: 1919
Approx.Sls.: $200,000,000
Emp.: 1,350
Fiscal Year-end: 12/31/90
Import Export
Manufacture & Import Writing Instruments
S.I.C.: 3951; 3161; 2893; 3952
Christopher M. Wiedenmayer *(Chm. Bd. & Chief Exec. Officer)*
Erik Jorgensen *(Pres. & Chief Oper. Officer)*
William B. Adams *(V.P.-Quality Systems)*
R. Asher *(V.P.-Sls.)*
Walter Charwath *(V.P. & Treas.)*
William G. Cook *(V.P.-Mktg.)*
Joseph T. LaPaglia *(V.P.-Fin. & Chief Fin. Officer)*
Mark Morris *(V.P.-Newark, NJ Location)*
Edmund Roberts *(V.P.-Mfg.)*
Michael Stanga *(V.P.-Retail Sls.)*
Edward J. Toner *(Sec. & Legal Officer)*
Robert R. Baker *(Controller)*
Kenneth A. Debrowski *(Asst. Treas.)*
Andrew Torok *(Dir.-Research & Devel.)*
Mac Bowden *(Mgr.-Communications)*
Diane Cimo *(Mgr.-Export)*
J. Gordon *(Mgr.-Matls.)*
John Lambert *(Mgr.-Human Resources)*

Principal(s):
Christopher M. Wiedenmayer
Erik Jorgensen

No. of Mfg. Plants/Facilities: 4
No. of U.S. Offices: 3
No. of Foreign Offices: 1

Computer Systems/Hardware:
IBM System AS 400

Outside Service Firm(s):

Price Waterhouse*(Auditors)*
4 Headquarters Plaza North, 9th Fl.
Morristown, NJ 07962
Tel.: 201-540-8980

Collins, Toner & Rusen*(Legal Firm)*
123 Columbia Turnpike
Florham Park, NJ 07932
Tel.: 201-377-0313

Midlantic National Bank*(Major Banking Relationship)*
Metro Park Plaza, P. O. Box 600
Edison, NJ 08818
Tel.: 908-321-8359

Non-U.S. Holding:

Faber/Castell Canada Ltd. **(1)**
1325 The Queensway
Toronto, ON M8Z 1S9, Canada
Tel.: 416-259-5051 (100%)
Emp.: 200
Mfr. of Pencils & Other Writing Instruments
S.I.C.: 3952
A. Victor Steele *(Pres.)*

FABER, COE & GREGG, INC.
10 Enterprise Av. N.
Secaucus, NJ 07094
Tel.: 201-330-1515 **NY**
Year Founded: 1848
Approx.Sls.: $54,270,933
Emp.: 600
Fiscal Year-end: 12/31/91
Retail Gift Shops & Newstands
S.I.C.: 5947; 5994
Edward Gropper *(Chm. Bd. & Pres.)*
Henry M. Hafer *(Exec. V.P.)*
Stanley Jersky *(Treas.)*
Charles D. Finkelstein *(Sec.)*

Subsidiaries:

Faber, Coe & Gregg of Chicago, Inc. **(1)**
449 E. Illinois
Chicago, IL 60611
Tel.: 312-670-2285
S.I.C.: 5194

Faber, Coe & Gregg of Pennsylvania, Inc. **(1)**
2627 Penn Ave
Pittsburgh, PA 15201
Tel.: 412-281-6700
S.I.C.: 5194

Moss & Lowenhaupt Cigar Co. **(1)**
723 Olive St.
Saint Louis, MO 63101
Tel.: 314-621-3770
Retail
S.I.C.: 5993
Martin P. Pearl *(Chief Opr. Officer)*

FABER ENTERPRISES, INC.
6606 Variel Ave.
Canoga Park, CA 91303
Tel.: 818-999-1300
Fax: 818-712-0512
Emp.: 134
Hydraulic Fittings
S.I.C.: 3728
Esther Faber *(Chm. Bd.)*
Ronald E. Spencer *(Pres.)*
Marilyn Spencer *(Sec. & Treas.)*
Mark Scatoloni *(Mgr.-Engrng.)*
Bob Ruble *(Pur. Agent)*

Outside Service Firm(s):

Goldfarb, Sturman, Muerback & Sturman*(Legal Firm)*
Encino, CA

neil faber media inc.

NEIL FABER MEDIA INC.
157 West 57th St.
New York, NY 10019
Tel.: 212-957-7660 **NY**
Fax: 212-265-3426
Year Founded: 1979
Approx.Billings: $67,300,000
Emp.: 27
Marketing & Media Consulting for all Media, Planning, Problem Solving, Buying & Analysis
S.I.C.: 7311
N. Faber *(Pres.)*
S. Somer *(Treas.)*

Computer Systems/Hardware:
Digital, Epson

Outside Service Firm(s):

Robert Braunschweig*(Auditors)*
New York, NY

Pryor, Cashmen Sherman & Flynn*(Legal Firm)*
410 Park Ave.
New York, NY 10022

Chemical Banking Corp.*(Major Banking Relationship)*
277 Park Ave.
New York, NY 10041
Tel.: 212-310-6407
Fax: 212-310-4526

FABEX INC.
42400 Grand River, Ste. 201
Novi, MI 48375
Tel.: 313-347-1041 **DE**
Twx: 810-242-8811
Fax: 313-347-3003
Approx.Sls.: $30,000,000
Emp.: 350
Manufacture Automotive Hoses & Tubes, Pipe & Pipe Fittings
S.I.C.: 3052; 3599; 3498
Thomas J. Manning, Sr. *(Chief Exec. Officer)*
Joseph Blouin *(Pres.)*
Michael Biber *(Treas.)*
Josephine Mowinski *(Sec.)*

Outside Service Firm(s):

Deloitte & Touche*(Auditors)*
200 Renaissance Center, 16th Fl.
Detroit, MI 48243
Tel.: 313-396-3000
Fax: 313-259-8087

Michigan National Bank*(Major Banking Relationship)*
P.O. Box 9065,
Farmington Hills, MI 48333-9065
Tel.: 313-473-3000

FSA
Fabianac, Stropes & Armstrong

FABIANAC, STROPES & ARMSTRONG, INC.
120 Broadway
San Francisco, CA 94111
Tel.: 415-421-8111 **CA**
Fax: 415-421-1594
Year Founded: 1986
Approx.Billings: $18,000,000
Emp.: 12
Fiscal Year-end: 7/31/90
Advertising Agency
S.I.C.: 7311
Ronald Armstrong *(Chm. Bd. & Creative Dir.)*
Larry Stropes *(Pres., Chief Exec. Officer & New Bus. Contact)*
Tony Biacci *(Chief Fin. Officer)*
Eneida Bolanos *(Office Admin.)*

Principal(s):
Ronald Armstrong
Larry Stropes

No. of U.S. Offices: 1

Fabianac, Stropes & Armstrong, Inc.—(Continued)

Computer Systems/Hardware:
Apple, MacIntosh

JOHN FABICK TRACTOR COMPANY
1 Fabick Dr.
Fenton, MO 63026
Tel.: 314-343-5900
Fax: 314-343-4910
Year Founded: 1917
Approx.Sls.: $100,000,000
Emp.: 400
Fiscal Year-end: 12/31/92
Sales & Service of Heavy Construction Machinery
S.I.C.: 5082; 7699
John Fabick *(Chm. Bd.)*
Harry Fabick *(Pres. & Chief Oper. Officer)*
Thomas A. Dinkins, III *(Exec. V.P.)*
John Fabick, IV *(V.P.-Pipeline Sls.)*
James Jansen *(V.P. & Treas.)*
Tom Victor *(V.P.-Domestic Sls.)*
Scott Borlinghaus *(Sec. & Controller)*
Ron Hult *(Mgr.-Mktg.)*
Principal(s):
John Fabick
Harry Fabick

Computer Systems/Hardware:
Honeywell

Outside Service Firm(s):

Deloitte & Touche*(Auditors)*
One City Centre
St. Louis, MO 63101
Tel.: 314-342-4900
Fax: 314-342-1100

Alexander & Alexander*(Commercial Insurance Carrier)*
St. Louis, MO

Bryan, Cave, McPheeters & McRoberts*(Legal Firm)*
One Metropolitan Sq.
St. Louis, MO 63102
Tel.: 314-259-2000

Boatmen's Trust Company*(Major Banking Relationship)*
100 North Broadway
St. Louis, MO 63102
Tel.: 314-466-2469

Subsidiaries:

Fabick & Company **(1)**
1 Fabick Dr.
Fenton, MO 63026
Tel.: 314-343-5900 (100%)
Fax: 314-343-4910
S.I.C.: 5082

Fabick Brothers Equipment **(1)**
1 Fabick Dr.
Fenton, MO 63026
Tel.: 314-343-5900 (100%)
Fax: 314-343-4910
S.I.C.: 5082

Fabick Machinery **(1)**
1 Fabick Dr.
Fenton, MO 63026
Tel.: 314-343-5900 (100%)
Fax: 314-343-4910
S.I.C.: 5082

Fabick Tractor **(1)**
1 Fabick Dr.
Fenton, MO 63026
Tel.: 314-343-5900 (100%)
Fax: 314-343-4910

FABREEKA INTERNATIONAL, INC.
1023 Turnpike St.
Stoughton, MA 02072
Mailing Address:
P.O. Box 210
Stoughton, MA 02072
Tel.: 617-341-3655
Twx: 94 0362
Fax: 617-341-3983
Year Founded: 1918
Approx.Sls.: $10,000,000
Emp.: 137
Import Export
Mfr. & Wholesale Anti-Shock & Vibration Pads; Rubber Composition Belting & Engineered Vibration Isolation Systems
S.I.C.: 3069; 5085
J. Patrick Norton *(Chm. Bd., Pres. & Chief Exec. Officer)*
Daniel R. Rork *(V.P. & Chief Oper. Officer)*
Charles E. Bradly *(Treas. & Controller)*
Agnes A. McGuire *(Sec.)*
Robert F. Delnegro *(Dir.-Engrng.)*
Gerald Hegarty *(Mgr.-Mktg.)*
William B. Sechler *(Mgr.-Sls.)*

Outside Service Firm(s):

Coopers & Lybrand*(Auditors)*
1 Post Office Square
Boston, MA 02110
Tel.: 617-574-5000
Fax: 617-345-0398

Palmer & Dodge*(Legal Firm)*
One Beacon St.
Boston, MA 02108

First National Bank*(Major Banking Relationship)*
Boston, MA

FABRIC WHOLESALERS, INC.
2035 N.E. 181st Ave.
Portland, OR 97230
Tel.: 503-666-4511
Approx.Sls.: $55,000,000
Fiscal Year-end: 6/30/90
Wholesale of Fabrics
S.I.C.: 5131
Tony J. Bosboom *(Pres. & Chief Exec. Officer)*
Judith A. Bennett *(V.P.-Mktg. & Pub. Rels.)*
Doug Caudell *(V.P.-Fin.)*
Myron Parry *(V.P.-Property Mngmt. & Real Estate)*
Ronald E. Westcott *(V.P.-Pur.)*
Jacques B. Nichols *(Treas. & Sec.)*

M. FABRIKANT & SONS, INC.
600 5th Ave.
New York, NY 10020
Tel.: 212-757-0790 **NY**
Fax: 212-262-9757
Approx.Sls.: $250,000,000
Emp.: 225
Wholesale Distributor of Diamonds & Jewelry
S.I.C.: 5094
Charles Fortgang *(Co.-Chm. Bd.)*
Philip J. Hahn *(Co.-Chm. Bd.)*
Mathew Fortgang *(Pres.)*
Michael Shaffet *(Treas.)*

Outside Service Firm(s):

Manufacturers Hanover Trust Co.*(Major Banking Relationship)*
4 New York Plaza
New York, NY 10015
Tel.: 212-633-7938

FABWEL INC.
1838 Middlebury St.
Elkhart, IN 46516
Tel.: 219-522-8473 **IN**
Fax: 219-522-5451
Year Founded: 1972
Assets: $56,000,000
Liabilities: $45,000,000
Net Worth: $11,000,000
Approx.Sls.: $110,000,000
Emp.: 305
Fiscal Year-end: 12/31/91
Import Export
Mfr. Metal & Aluminum Sheet Metal
S.I.C.: 3444; 3363
Edward P. Welter *(Pres. & Chief Oper. Officer)*
John W. Gardner *(V.P. & Chief Fin. Officer)*
Lew Rawels *(V.P.-Speciality Prods.)*
Raymond Stout *(V.P.-Metals Group)*
Principal(s):
Edward P. Welter

No. of Mfg. Plants/Facilities: 9
No. of U.S. Offices: 10

Computer Systems/Hardware:
IBM

Outside Service Firm(s):

Warrick, Weaver, Boyn*(Legal Firm)*
Midwest Commerce Bldg., 121 W. Franklin St.
Elkhart, IN 46516

Midwest Commerce Banking Co.*(Major Banking Relationship)*
Elkhart, IN

FACEMATE CORPORATION
5 W. Main St.
Chicopee, MA 01020
Tel.: 413-594-6661 **MA**
Twx: 955460
Fax: 413-594-8328
Year Founded: 1975
Approx.Sls.: $42,000,000
Emp.: 350
Fiscal Year-end: 12/31/91
Import Export
Mfr. & Retail Apparel Interlinings & Textile Finisher; Shirt & Apparel Interlinings, Industrial Linings, Home Furnishing Linings; Paint Strainers, Automotive Headliners; Lemon Wraps, Polishing Cloth; Military Bandages & Slings
S.I.C.: 2396; 2261; 2262; 2299
Walter F. Mrozinski *(Chm. Bd.)*
Michael Kohler *(Pres.)*
Robert C. McAdam *(Sr. V.P.-Mktg. & Sls.)*
William E. Tierney, Jr. *(Controller)*
Kathleen M. Soucy *(Dir.-Personnel)*
Rory Miller *(Pur. Agent)*
JoAnn Mrozinski *(Pur. Agent)*

No. of Mfg. Plants/Facilities: 5
No. of U.S. Offices: 8

Computer Systems/Hardware:
IBM A/S 400

Outside Service Firm(s):

Coopers & Lybrand*(Auditors)*
2300 Bay Bank Tower, 1500 Main St.
Springfield, MA 01101
Tel.: 413-781-7200

Bacon, Wilson, Ratner, Cohen, Salvage, Fialky & Fitzgerald, P.C.*(Legal Firm)*
Springfield, MA

Bay Bank Middlesex*(Major Banking Relationship)*
Burlington, MA

Subsidiary:

FaceMate Pond Lilt Great Falls **(1)**
200 Main St.
Somersworth, NH 03878
Tel.: 603-692-3622
Tel.: 800-258-7102
Emp.: 100
Textile Finishing, Napping, Dyeing, Bleaching
S.I.C.: 2261; 2262
Lomise Coffin *(Dir.-Sls.)*
Darlene Garmeau *(Dir.-Pur.)*

FADAL ENGINEERING COMPANY, INC.
7260 Atoll Ave.
North Hollywood, CA 91605
Tel.: 818-765-9838
Fax: 818-765-3054
Year Founded: 1951
Approx.Sls.: $75,000,000
Emp.: 200
Machine Tools, Numerical Controls
S.I.C.: 3541
Adrian X. de Caussin *(Pres.)*
David E. de Caussin *(V.P.)*
Larry F. de Caussin *(Treas.)*

Outside Service Firm(s):

William A. Knoppow*(Auditors)*
Sherman Oaks, CA

Buchalter, Nemer, Fields & Younger*(Legal Firm)*
601 S. Figueroa St., Ste. 2500
Los Angeles, CA 90017-5704
Tel.: 213-891-0700

Security Pacific National Bank*(Major Banking Relationship)*
Woodland Hills, CA

Fahlgren Martin

FAHLGREN MARTIN, INC.
Corporate Office:
Rosemar Rd. & Seminary Dr.
Parkersburg, WV 26102
Mailing Address:
P.O. Box 1628
Parkersburg, WV 26102
Tel.: 304-424-3591
Fax: 304-424-3515
Approx.Billings: $175,000,000
Emp.: 350
H. Smoot Fahlgren *(Chief Exec. Officer)*
David N. Martin *(Chm.)*
Ralph L. Thompson *(Pres. & Chief Oper. Officer)*
Steve Drongowski *(Sr. Exec. Partner)*
James R. Fankhauser *(Sr. Fin. Partner, Sec. & Treas.)*

FAIR LANES INC.
10944 Beaver Dam Rd.
Hunt Valley, MD 21030-2252
Tel.: 410-771-3800
Tel.: 800-338-2695 **MD**
Fax: 410-785-1227
Year Founded: 1923
Approx.Sls.: $110,000,000
Emp.: 4,700
Fiscal Year-end: 6/30/90
Operates Bowling Centers & Restaurants
S.I.C.: 5812; 7933
E.M. Clayton III *(Chm. Bd.)*
S.E. Carley *(Pres. & Chief Exec. Officer)*
Roy J. Schumacher *(Chief Fin. Officer, V.P.-Fin., Treas.)*
Thomas Carlucci *(V.P.-Pur. & Maintenance)*
David Gagnon *(V.P.-Opers.)*
J.N. Gruber *(V.P.-Human Resources)*
William Quigley *(V.P.-Mktg.)*
Wayne Strausburg *(V.P.-Real Estate & Devel.)*
John J. Gabinet *(Controller)*
Susan Nocitra *(Dir.-Mktg.)*
Clay Wildey *(Dir.-Manpower & Devel.)*
Bill Brennan *(Mgr.-Pur. & Maintenance)*
Dean Davidson *(Mgr.-Fin. Services)*
Stacy Karten *(Mgr.-Bowler Communications & Devel.)*
Jerry Reynolds *(Mgr.-Data Processing)*
Michelle Rokos *(Coord.-Mktg.)*

Computer Systems/Hardware:
NCR

Division:

Fair Lane Bowling Div. **(1)**
1112 N. Rolling Rd.
Baltimore, MD 21228
Tel.: 410-788-6300

Chain of Bowling Centers
S.I.C.: 7933
S.E. Carley *(Pres.)*
Thomas R. Carlucci *(V.P.-Pur. & Maintenance)*

FAIRBANKS MORSE PUMP CORPORATON
P.O. Box 999, 3601 Fairbanks Ave.
Kansas City, KS 66106-0999
Tel.: 913-371-5000 **KS**
Fax: 913-371-2272
Approx.Sls.: $60,000,000
Emp.: 350
Export
Mfr. Turbine & Centrifugal Pumps
S.I.C.: 3561
W. Jackson Letts *(Chm. Bd. & Pres.)*
Donald A. Robinson *(Exec. V.P.)*
Christopher B. Steinhoff *(Exec. V.P.)*
Virgil Beaty *(V.P.-Engrng.)*
Barry M. Krengel *(V.P.-Fin. & Treas.)*
Wayne O. Miller *(V.P.-Personnel)*
Daniel P. Weary *(Sec.)*
William G. Fivecoat *(Controller)*
Jim Hodes *(Mgr.-Pur.)*
Lee R. Rennison *(Dir.-Data Processing)*

Outside Service Firm(s):

Arthur Andersen & Co.*(Auditors)*
1500 Commerce Tower, 911 Main St.
Kansas City, MO 64105
Tel.: 816-221-4200
Fax: 816-221-7693

Blackwell, Sanders, Matheny, Weary & Lombardi*(Legal Firm)*
2300 Main Street
Kansas City, MO 64108
Tel.: 816-474-5700

FAIRFAX LUMBER & MILLWORK COMPANY INC.
7622 Backlick Rd.
Springfield, VA 22150
Mailing Address:
P.O. Box 5500,
Springfield, VA 22150
Tel.: 703-644-4045 **VA**
Fax: 703-644-4203
Year Founded: 1947
Assets: $7,100,000
Liabilities: $3,100,000
Net Worth: $4,000,000
Approx.Sls.: $15,000,000
Emp.: 70
Fiscal Year-end: 1/31/92
Lumber & Millwork
S.I.C.: 5211
John F. Dolan *(Chm. Bd. & Pres.)*
J.L. Peters, Jr. *(Vice Chm. & Treas.)*
David Doss *(Chief Oper. Officer)*
Timothy P. Tobin *(Exec. V.P.)*
Samuel N. Moore *(Sec.)*
John O'Donnol *(Dir.-Human Resources)*
Michael Fife *(Mgr.-Sls.)*
Principal(s):
John F. Dolan
J.L. Peters, Jr.
L. Hardbower

No. of Mfg. Plants/Facilities: 2
No. of U.S. Offices: 2

Computer Systems/Hardware:
IBM 36

Outside Service Firm(s):

Campbell, Veltrie & Clark*(Auditors)*
Vienna, VA

Sovran Bank*(Major Banking Relationship)*
Tysons Corner, VA

Subsidiary:

Fairfield Building Systems **(1)**
651 Maddox Dr.
Culpeper, VA 22701

FAIRFIELD ELECTRIC CO-OP
Highway 321 N.
Winnsboro, SC 29180
Mailing Address:
P.O. Box 150
Winnsboro, SC 29180
Tel.: 803-635-4621 **SC**
Fax: 803-635-9614
Year Founded: 1939
Approx.Sls.: $16,000,000
Emp.: 55
Distribution Of Electric Power
S.I.C.: 4911
Joe Sharp *(Pres.)*
James F. Wilkes *(V.P.)*
W.C. Good *(Treas.)*
Peggy B. Jeffcoat *(Sec.)*

Outside Service Firm(s):

Bank of Ridgeway*(Major Banking Relationship)*
Winnsboro, SC

THE FAIRFIELD LUMBER & SUPPLY COMPANY
185 Thorpe St.
Fairfield, CT 06430
Tel.: 203-259-1631
Fax: 203-254-8235
Sales Range: $20-39 Million
Emp.: 120
Cases, Boxes; Wholesale & Retail Building Materials, Pre-Fab Houses
S.I.C.: 3272; 2452; 5031; 5211
B. William Plotkin *(Pres. & Sec.)*
J.G. Reilly *(Exec. V.P. & Treas.)*
Joseph Butkus *(Chief Engr.)*
Diane Leahy *(Mgr.-Admin.)*
Gordon Ricker *(Mgr.-Sls.)*

Outside Service Firm(s):

Edward Isaacs & Co.*(Auditors)*
Stamford, CT

Merchants Bank & Trust Company*(Major Banking Relationship)*
Stamford, CT

FAIRFIELD MAXWELL LTD.
277 Park Ave.
New York, NY 10172
Tel.: 212-421-2850 **NY**
Fax: 212-355-1845
Year Founded: 1957
Approx.Sls.: $175,000,000
Emp.: 200
Management Services; Shipping Agents; Fuel Oil; Deep Sea Foreign Transportation of Freight
S.I.C.: 8741; 4731; 5172; 4412
Frank M. Kuwahara *(Chm. Bd.)*
Kaytaro G. Sugahara *(Pres.)*
Vincent Yax *(Sr. V.P. & Treas.)*
Robert Davis *(Controller)*
Constantine P. Roalli *(Gen. Counsel)*

Subsidiary:

Fairfield International Corporation **(1)**
277 Park Ave.
New York, NY 10172
Tel.: 212-421-2850
Fax: 212-355-1845
Approx.Sls.: $75,000,000
Emp.: 200
Financial Management For Business
S.I.C.: 8741
Kaytaro G. Sugahara *(Pres.)*
Vincent Yax *(V.P., Controller & Treas.)*
Brian Sugahara *(V.P.)*
Peter Siviglia *(Sec.)*

Subsidiary:

Fairfield Industries, Inc. **(2)**
10627 Kinghurst
Houston, TX 77099
Tel.: 713-981-8181
Approx.Sls.: $25,000,000
Emp.: 250
Geophysical Exploration
S.I.C.: 1382

Richard C. Anderson *(Pres. & Chief Exec. Officer)*

FAIRMONT HOMES, INC.
502 S. Oakland
Nappanee, IN 46550
Tel.: 219-773-7941
Fax: 219-773-3030
Year Founded: 1971
Approx.Sls.: $160,000,000
Emp.: 1,375
Manufacture Mobile Homes
S.I.C.: 2451
James F. Shea *(Chm. Bd.)*
Edward Ludwick *(Pres.)*
Kenneth W. Brink *(V.P.-Fin.)*
Jack Racolta *(V.P.-Opers.)*
Kenneth C. Brinkler *(Sec.)*
James F. Shea, Jr. *(Treas.)*

Outside Service Firm(s):

AmeriTrust National Bank*(Major Banking Relationship)*
Elkart, IN

THE FAIRMONT HOTELS
Atop Nob Hill
San Francisco, CA 94108
Tel.: 415-772-5000
Tel.: 800-527-4727 **CA**
Telex: 910-372-6002
Fax: 415-772-5086
Year Founded: 1906
Approx.Sls.: $10,000,000
Emp.: 5,000
Fiscal Year-end: 12/31/91
Hotel Ownership & Management
S.I.C.: 7011
Richard L. Swig *(Vice Chm.)*
Melvin Swig *(Vice Chm.)*
Robert Small *(Pres. & Chief Exec. Officer)*
Stan Boyd *(V.P.-Sls. & Mktg.)*
RoJean De Chantal *(V.P.-Human Resources)*
Liz Erikson *(V.P.-Convention Sls.)*
Larry Garfinkel *(V.P.-Devel.)*
John Ott *(V.P. & Chief Fin. Officer)*
Gordon Seaman *(V.P.-Opers.)*
Henry Bose *(Natl. Dir.-Adv. & Mktg. Programs)*
Susan Jacobs *(Natl. Dir.-Travel Industry Sls.)*
Patricia Winkler *(Mgr.-Mktg. Communications)*

Outside Service Firm(s):

Sedgwick James*(Group Insurer)*
600 Montgomery St., 7th Floor
San Francisco, CA 94111
Tel.: 415-983-5600

Titchell, Maltzman, Mark, Bass, Ohleyer & Mishel*(Legal Firm)*
650 California St.
San Francisco, CA 94137

First Interstate Bank*(Major Banking Relationship)*
345 California St., 8th Flr.
San Francisco, CA 94104
Tel.: 415-773-7801

FAIRVIEW CONSTRUCTION, INC
1100 N. Opdyke Rd.
Auburn Hills, MI 48326
Mailing Address:
1100 N. Opdyke Rd.
Auburn Hills, MI 48326
Tel.: 313-377-2600 **MI**
Fax: 313-377-2539
Year Founded: 1978
Assets: $3,033,933
Liabilities: $1,458,821
Net Worth: $1,575,112
Emp.: 12
Fiscal Year-end: 12/31/91
Commercial Buildings General Contractor
S.I.C.: 1542
Beverly Furnari *(Pres.)*
Michael Furnari *(V.P.)*
Michael Vavrek *(Controller)*
Johnathan Hilts *(Legal Counsel)*

Outside Service Firm(s):

Doeren & Mayhew*(Auditors)*
Troy, MI

Zervos Agency, Inc.*(Commercial Insurance Carrier)*
Southfield, MI

Construction Association of Michigan (CAM)*(Group Insurer)*
Detroit, MI

Manufacturers National Bank*(Major Banking Relationship)*
Sterling Heights, MI

FAIRWAY FORD, INC.
2323 Laurens Rd.
Greenville, SC 29607
Tel.: 803-242-5060 **SC**
Fax: 803-233-1301
Year Founded: 1966
Assets: $11,503,181
Liabilities: $8,542,895
Net Worth: $2,960,286
Approx.Sls.: $44,987,479
Emp.: 136
Fiscal Year-end: 8/31/92
Ford & Isuzu Cars & Trucks Dealership
S.I.C.: 5511
A. Foster McKissick, III *(Pres.)*
Ervin Williamson *(V.P.)*
Julius Boyd *(Sec. & Treas.)*
Jim Burns *(Mgr.-Used Car Sls.)*
Mike Cantrell *(Mgr.-F & I Sls.)*
Mack Charpia *(Mgr.-Vehicle Sls.)*
Tony Franklin *(Mgr.-Used Truck Sls.)*
Steve Jellen *(Mgr.-Service)*
Gary McAlister *(Mgr.-New Ford Sls.)*
Rion McKissick *(Mgr.-Quality Control)*
Rick Ramos *(Mgr.-F & I Sls.)*
Douglas Sanders *(Mgr.-Parts)*
Jim Wilbur *(Mgr.-F & I Sls.)*
Bill Ross *(Asst. Mgr.-New Ford Sls.)*
Principal(s):
A. Foster McKissick, III

No. of U.S. Offices: 1

Computer Systems/Hardware:
Texas Instrument-Winchester

Outside Service Firm(s):

Elliott, Davis & Co.*(Auditors)*
Greenville, SC

Corroon & Black*(Commercial Insurance Carrier)*
P.O. Box 2007, 111 Williams St.
Greenville, SC 29602

Blue Cross & Blue Shield of South Carolina*(Group Insurer)*
1517 Laurel St.
Columbia, SC 29201

J. C. Bradford & Co.*(Investment Banker)*
Pawleys Island, SC

Leatherwood, Walker, Todd & Mann*(Legal Firm)*
P.O. Box 2248
Greenville, SC 29602
Tel.: 803-242-6440

Carolina First Bank*(Major Banking Relationship)*
P.O. Box 1029, 102 Main St.
Greenville, SC 29602

NationsBank Carolinas*(Major Banking Relationship)*
One NCNB Plaza T18-7
Charlotte, NC 28255

Fairway Ford, Inc.—(Continued)

Divisions:

Blue Ridge Finance Co., Inc. (1)
P.O. Box 17974, Station B, 355 Woodruff Rd.
Greenville, SC 29606
Tel.: 803-458-7134
Financial Institution; Car Financing & Second Mortgages
S.I.C.: 6153; 6162
Julius Boyd *(Pres.)*
C. Tommy McIntyre *(Branch Mgr.)*
Shannan Campbell *(Asst. Branch Mgr.)*

Heritage Lincoln-Mercury (1)
2424 Laurens Rd.
Greenville, SC 29607
A. Foster McKissick *(Pres.)*
Ervin Williamson *(V.P.)*
Julius Boyd *(Sec. & Treas.)*

FALCON CANDY COMPANY
2300 Carpenter St.
Philadelphia, PA 19146
Tel.: 215-985-0774 **PA**
Fax: 215-985-0123
Approx.Sls.: $12,000,000
Emp.: 200
Export
Mfr. Candy & Candy Specialties
S.I.C.: 2064
Dominick Branca *(Pres.)*
Vincent Mitchell *(Exec. V.P.-Sls. & Mktg.)*
Mathias Schummer *(Sr. V.P.-Fin.)*
Pasquale Branca *(V.P.-Sls.)*
Carmela Branca *(Treas.)*
William Mercer *(Dir.-Engrng.)*
Peter Woodruff *(Dir.-Pur.)*

Outside Service Firm(s):

Haas & Co.*(Auditors)*
Philadelphia, PA

Weston C. Overholt, Jr.*(Legal Firm)*
Philadelphia, PA

Philadelphia National Bank*(Major Banking Relationship)*
P.O. Box 13834, Broad & Chestnut Streets
Philadelphia, PA 19101-7618
Tel.: 215-973-8327

FALCON SAFETY PRODUCTS INC.
25 Chubb Way
Branchburg, NJ 08876-1299
Mailing Address:
P.O. Box 1299,
Somerville, NJ 08876-1299
Tel.: 908-707-4900
Telex: 833542
Fax: 908-707-8855
Approx.Sls.: $11,000,000
Emp.: 50
Export
Mfr. of Safety Access., Photographic Chemistry, Photographic Accessories, Marine Accessories, Computer Cleaning Prods
S.I.C.: 3829; 3669
Phil Lapin *(Pres.)*
David Lieberman *(Chief Fin. Officer)*
Andrew Steinman *(Dir.-Mktg. & Sls.)*
Pat Vail *(Mgr.-Mktg.)*
Edward Nodelman *(Asst. Mgr.-Mktg.)*

Divisions:

William B. Bliss Div. (1)
25 Chubb Way
Somerville, NJ 08876-1299
Tel.: 908-707-4900
Export
Safety Division

Edwal Scientific Products Div. (1)
25 Chubb Way
Somerville, NJ 08876-1299
Tel.: 908-707-4900
Export
Photography Division

PETE FALL FORD INC.
2525 By Pass Rd.
Elkhart, IN 46514
Tel.: 219-294-1563 **IN**
Fax: 219-295-0169
Year Founded: 1961
Approx.Sls.: $26,000,000
Emp.: 75
Fiscal Year-end: 12/31/91
Automobile Dealership
S.I.C.: 5511
Gary Mc Afee *(Pres.)*
George Reichandter *(Gen. Mgr.)*
Lloyd Borkhoder *(Sec. & Controller)*

Computer Systems/Hardware:
Reynolds & Reynolds

Outside Service Firm(s):

First National Bank of Elkhart*(Major Banking Relationship)*
Elkhart, IN

FALLON COMMUNITY HEALTH PLAN
100 Hartwell St.
West Boylston, MA 01583
Tel.: 508-835-2550
Assets: $59,385,376
Earnings: $2,967,686
Liabilities: $37,894,939
Net Worth: $21,490,437
Approx.Rev.: $180,884,285
Fiscal Year-end: 12/31/90
Health Maintenance Organization
S.I.C.: 6324
John A. Duggan, M.D. *(Pres.)*
Christy W. Bell *(Exec. Dir.)*
Joel M. Kaufman, M.D. *(Medical Dir.)*
Charles S. Mills, M.D. *(Asst. Medical Dir.)*
Gary J. Zelch *(Assoc. Exec. Dir. & Dir.-Fin.)*
Denis J. FitzGerald, M.D. *(Treas.)*
Stuart H. Bentkover, M.D. *(Asst. Treas.)*
Alan M. Stoll *(Clerk)*
James J. Egan III *(Assoc. Dir.-Mktg.)*
Carolyn Hussey, R.N. *(Assoc. Dir.-Health Mngmt. Services)*
Harry Dodyk *(Dir.-Opers.)*
Ellen Sachs Leicher *(Dir.-Plng. & Devel.)*
Gary W. Thomas *(Dir.-Mktg. & Community Rels.)*

FAMILY INNS OF AMERICA, INC.
509 Tammy King Rd.
Pigeon Forge, TN 37863-0010
Mailing Address:
P.O. Box 10,
Pigeon Forge, TN 37868
Tel.: 615-453-4988 **TN**
Fax: 615-453-2120
Year Founded: 1972
Approx.Sls.: $24,000,000
Emp.: 500
Motels, Restaurants & Lounges
S.I.C.: 7011; 5812
Kenneth M. Seaton *(Chm. Bd., Pres. & Chief Exec. Officer)*
Beera Chopra *(V.P.-Opers. & Treas.)*
Randy Brooks *(Legal Dept. Admin.)*
Harold Foshie *(Comptroller)*
Dee Lundy *(Dir.-Sls. & Mktg.)*
Principal(s):
Kenneth M. Seaton

Computer Systems/Hardware:
IBM System 54

Outside Service Firm(s):

Blue Cross & Blue Shield of Tennessee*(Group Insurer)*
Chattanooga, TN

First American National Bank*(Major Banking Relationship)*
Knoxville, TN

Subsidiaries:

Airport '82 Associates Ltd. (1)
P.O. Box 10,
Pigeon Forge, TN 37863
Tel.: 615-453-1240 (100%)
Approx.Sls.: $700,000
Emp.: 15
David Hackett *(Chief Exec. Officer)*

Dixie Royal Homes, Inc. (1)
Cookeville, TN 38501
Tel.: 615-528-1589 (75%)
Manufactured Housing
S.I.C.: 2452
Kris Bellah *(Chief Oper. Officer)*

Family Inns of New Orleans, Inc. (1)
6303 Chef Menteur
New Orleans, LA 70126
Tel.: 504-246-2400 (100%)
Motel
S.I.C.: 7011
Kenneth M. Seaton *(Pres.)*

Growth Management Corp. (1)
4300 Rutledge Pike
Knoxville, TN 37914
Tel.: 615-546-3910 (51%)
Approx.Sls.: $1,500,000
Emp.: 24
Restaurant, Motel & Lounge
S.I.C.: 7011; 5812
Kenneth M. Seaton *(Chief Oper. Officer)*

Innco Management Corp. (1)
8167 Kingston Pike
Knoxville, TN 37919
Tel.: 615-693-1811 (33.33%)
Emp.: 74
Motel, Restaurant & Lounge
S.I.C.: 7011; 5812
Charles Frost *(Chief Oper. Officer)*

Lucky Inns of America, Inc. (1)
P.O. Box 10,
Pigeon Forge, TN 37863
Tel.: 614-453-1240 (100%)
Emp.: 69
Motel, Restaurant & Lounge
S.I.C.: 7011; 5812
Kenneth M. Seaton *(Chief Oper. Officer)*

Profit Management Corp. (1)
I-40 at Gallaher Rd.
Kingston, TN 37763
Tel.: 615-376-5573 (51%)
Emp.: 70
Motel, Restaurant & Lounge
S.I.C.: 7011; 5812
David Hackett *(Chief Oper. Officer)*

Regional Development Corp. (1)
P.O. Box 10,
Pigeon Forge, TN 37863
Tel.: 615-453-1240 (100%)
Emp.: 16
Real Estate Devel.
S.I.C.: 6552
Kenneth M. Seaton *(Chief Oper. Officer)*

Kenneth M. Seaton Enterprises (1)
P.O. Box 10,
Pigeon Forge, TN 37863
Tel.: 615-453-1240 (100%)
Emp.: 124
Motel & Real Estate Devel.
S.I.C.: 1522; 6552
Kenneth M. Seaton *(Chief Oper. Officer)*

Tri-Management Corp. (1)
P.O. Box 10,
Pigeon Forge, TN 37863
Tel.: 615-453-1240 (100%)
Approx.Sls.: $750,000
Emp.: 24
David Hackett *(Chief Exec. Officer)*

FAMTEC INTERNATIONAL, INC.
509 N. Third Ave.
Des Plaines, IL 60016
Tel.: 708-803-3200 **IL**
Telex: 726416
Fax: 708-803-9875
Year Founded: 1959
Approx.Sls.: $45,000,000
Emp.: 4
Fiscal Year-end: 5/31/91
Import Export
Holding Company; Mfr. of Machine Tools
S.I.C.: 3541; 3545; 6719
James N. Farley *(Pres. & Chief Exec. Officer)*
Makoto Kouzuma *(V.P. & Chief Oper. Officer)*
Roger Marach *(Chief Fin. Officer & Treas.)*
Charles A. Kelley *(Sec.)*

No. of Mfg. Plants/Facilities: 6
No. of U.S. Offices: 3
No. of Foreign Offices: 7

Outside Service Firm(s):

KPMG Peat Marwick*(Auditors)*
Peat Marwick Plaza, 303 E. Wacker Dr.
Chicago, IL 60601
Tel.: 312-938-1000

Chapman & Cutler*(Legal Firm)*
111 W. Monroe
Chicago, IL 60603
Tel.: 312-845-3000

First Wisconsin National Bank*(Major Banking Relationship)*
777 E. Wisconsin Ave.
Milwaukee, WI 53202
Tel.: 414-765-4321
Fax: 414-355-6903

Subsidiary:

SpeedFam Corporation (1)
509 N. 3rd Ave.
Des Plaines, IL 60016
Tel.: 708-803-3200 (100%)
Fax: 708-803-9875
Approx.Sls.: $30,000,000
Emp.: 75
Mfr. of Machine Tools, Abrasives & Coolants Instruments
S.I.C.: 3541
James N. Farley *(Chm. Bd.)*
Makoto Kouzuma *(Pres.)*
Christopher Augur *(V.P. & Gen. Mgr.)*
Richard Shocker *(V.P.-Mfg.)*

Non-U.S. Holdings:

FamTec AG (1)
Manchinenbau CH-3292
Busswil, Switzerland
Tel.: 32 8441 55 (100%)
Fax: 32 84 55 73
Emp.: 20
Mfr. of Machine Tools
S.I.C.: 3541

SpeedFam Machines Co. Ltd. (1)
Brindley Rd. Dodwells Bridge Indus. Estate, Hinckley, Leicestershire LE10 3B4, United Kingdom
Tel.: 455 631 707 (100%)
Fax: 455-611360
Emp.: 25
Mfr. of Machine Tools
S.I.C.: 3541

SpeedFam GmbH (1)
Borsteler Chaussee 287 D-2000
Hamburg, 61, Germany
Tel.: 841-212-072 (100%)
Fax: 553 7,2 00
Emp.: 5
Mfr. of Machine Tools
S.I.C.: 3541

Joint Venture:

SpeedFam Co Ltd. (1)
No. 2647 Haykawa
Ayase City, Kanagawa-Pref. Japan
Tel.: 0467 76 3131 (50%)
Fax: 0467-77-7159
Mfr. of Metalworking Machines; Joint Venture of FamTec International, Inc. & Obara Corporation
S.I.C.: 3541; 3542

Ardell Industries Inc.
(Acquired by Jordan Company)

FANTASTIC SAM'S INTERNATIONAL, INC.
3180 Old Getwell Rd.
Memphis, TN 38118
Mailing Address:
P.O. Box 18845
Memphis, TN 38181-0845
Tel.: 901-363-8624
Tel.: 800-844-7267 **TN**
Fax: 901-363-8946
Year Founded: 1974
Approx.Sls.: $12,000,000
Emp.: 50
Fiscal Year-end: 7/31/92
Franchisor of Hair Salons
S.I.C.: 7241; 7231
Curtis G. McCoy *(Chm. Bd. & Pres.)*
Mike Kemp *(Chief Fin. Officer & Controller)*
Alan Webb *(Pres.-Intl. Division)*
Lorraine Cauble *(Sr. V.P.-Regional Opers.)*
Amelia Blanton *(Gen. Counsel)*
Wilgus Wade Hogg *(Dir.-Mktg.)*
Kate Yarbro *(Mgr.-Office)*

Outside Service Firm(s):

Ernst & Young*(Auditors)*
1400 One Commerce Sq.
Memphis, TN 38103

Sovran Bank*(Major Banking Relationship)*
Memphis, TN

FARADAY, INC.
805 S. Maumee
Tecumseh, MI 49286
Tel.: 517-423-2111
Fax: 517-423-2320
Approx.Sls.: $12,000,000
Emp.: 245
Export
Fire Alarm Systems, Annunciator Systems, Signals, Farady Fire Alarm Systems & Signals; Faramod Fire Alarm Devices; FOS Signaling Devices, Clock Programming Systems, Standard Electric Time
S.I.C.: 3663; 3669
Robert Bell *(Pres.)*
R. Miller *(V.P.)*
David L. Hall *(Mktg. Mgr.)*

FARAGO ADVERTISING
101 Fifth Ave.
New York, NY 10003
Tel.: 212-243-0864
Year Founded: 1988
Approx.Billings: $25,068,000
Emp.: 22
Peter Farago *(Pres. & Creative Dir.)*
Elizabeth Gray *(Exec. V.P., Dir. Client Services, New Bus. Contact)*
Ralph Westerhoff *(Sr. V.P., Direct Mktg.)*
Pat Sergott *(Sr. V.P., Pub. Rels.)*
Julie Burton *(V.P., Research Dir.)*
Alex Stefanishin *(Studio Mgr.)*
Nancy Todd *(Controller)*
Rachel Olderman *(Office Mgr.)*

FARALLON COMPUTING, INC.
2000 Powell St., Ste. 600
Emeryville, CA 94608
Tel.: 510-596-9100
Fax: 510-596-9020
Year Founded: 1986
Approx.Sls.: $40,000,000
Emp.: 250
Export
Mfr. of Computer Peripheral Equipment; Prepackaged Software
S.I.C.: 3577; 7372
Reese Jones *(Pres.)*
Robert Herrington *(V.P.-Mfg.)*
Alan Ausing *(Chief Fin. Officer)*

FAREWAY STORES, INC.
2600 E. Eighth St.
Boone, IA 50036
Tel.: 515-432-2623
Year Founded: 1938
Assets: $57,275,239
Liabilities: $13,817,514
Net Worth: $43,457,725
Approx.Sls.: $325,000,000
Emp.: 2,500
Fiscal Year-end: 3/31/91
Retail Supermarkets
S.I.C.: 5411; 5421
F. W. Beckwith *(Chm. Bd., Pres. & Chief Exec. Officer)*
Robert Cramer *(Exec. V.P.)*
Robert G. Carper *(V.P.-Wholesale Pur.)*
Mike Campbell *(Controller & Sec.)*
John Wassenaar *(Treas.)*

Computer Systems/Hardware:
IBM System 36

Outside Service Firm(s):

Deloitte & Touche*(Auditors)*
2 Ruan Center
Des Moines, IA 50309
Tel.: 515-288-1200

Travelers Insurance Co.*(Group Insurer)*
1 Tower Square
Hartford, CT 06183-2492
Tel.: 203-277-4542
Fax: 203-277-5038

Courter, Doran & Quinn*(Legal Firm)*
Bonne, IA

Citizens National Bank*(Major Banking Relationship)*
Boone, IA

FARGO CLINIC LTD.
737 Broadway
Fargo, ND 58123
Tel.: 701-237-2000
Fax: 701-234-2316
Year Founded: 1919
Approx.Sls.: $30,000,000
Emp.: 500
Medical Services; Group Medical Practice
S.I.C.: 8011
Wallace Radtke *(Pres.)*
Roger Gilbertson *(V.P.)*
Thomas Ahlin *(Sec. & Treas.)*
Bruce Haga *(Chief Fin. Officer)*
Gary Gelder *(Data Processing Coord.)*

Computer Systems/Hardware:
Honeywell

Outside Service Firm(s):

Eide, Helmeke & Co.*(Auditors)*
Fargo, ND

Vogel, Brantner, Kelly, Knutson, Weir & Bye, Ltd.*(Legal Firm)*
Fargo, ND

First Bank of North Dakota*(Major Banking Relationship)*
Fargo, ND

FARGO GLASS & PAINT COMPANY
1801 7th Ave. N.
Fargo, ND 58102
Tel.: 701-235-4441
Fax: 701-235-3435
Approx.Sls.: $20,000,000
Emp.: 150
Fiscal Year-end: 12/31/91
Wholesale Glass Products, Paints, Varnishes, Floor Coverings
S.I.C.: 5023; 5039; 5064; 5198
Gerald Lovell *(Pres.)*
Gerald Hendricks *(V.P.-Sls.)*
Pete Pianka *(Dept. Mgr.)*
Mike MacDonald *(Dept. Mgr.)*
Ron Albrecht *(Dept. Mgr.)*
Dennis Dunlop *(Dept. Mgr.)*

Computer Systems/Hardware:
IBM System 36

Outside Service Firm(s):

Eide, Helmeke & Co.*(Auditors)*
Fargo, ND

Vogel, Brantner, Kelly, Knutson, Weir & Bye, Ltd.*(Legal Firm)*
Fargo, ND

FARIBAULT FOODS INC.
1050 Baker Bldg., 706 2nd Ave. S.
Minneapolis, MN 55402
Tel.: 612-333-6461
Fax: 612-342-2908
Year Founded: 1896
Approx.Sls.: $50,000,000
Emp.: 150
Fiscal Year-end: 3/31/91
Export
Canned Fruits & Vegetables, Tomato Products, Condiments
S.I.C.: 2033; 2035
E.B. MacDonald *(Chm. Bd.)*
Reid V. MacDonald *(Pres. & Chief Exec. Officer)*
Gary A. Kindseth *(Exec. V.P.)*
Michael S. Peroutka *(V.P.-Sls. & Mktg.)*
Darrell Charboneau *(Chief Fin. Officer)*
Principal(s):
Reid V. MacDonald
Gary A. Kindseth

No. of Mfg. Plants/Facilities: 6

Computer Systems/Hardware:
MAI Basic 4

Outside Service Firm(s):

Hutton, Nelson & McDonald*(Auditors)*
Chicago, IL

Divisions:

Butter Kernel Products **(1)**
706 2nd Ave., So.
Minneapolis, MN 55402
Tel.: 612-333-6461
Approx.Sls.: $6,000,000
Emp.: 10
Export
Canned Vegetables
S.I.C.: 2033
R.V. MacDonald *(Pres.)*
Michael S. Peroutka *(V.P.)*

Durand Canning Co. **(1)**
P.O. Box 188
Durand, WI 54736
Tel.: 715-672-8971
Canned Vegetables
R.V. MacDonald *(Pres.)*

Kuner-Empson Company **(1)**
221 No. Kuner Rd.
Brighton, CO 80601
Tel.: 303-659-1710
Fax: 303-659-7681
Approx.Sls.: $12,000,000
Emp.: 80
Canned Vegetables, Tomato Products & Condiments
S.I.C.: 2033
R.V. MacDonald *(Pres.)*
Mike Peroutka *(V.P.-Sls.)*
Robert Seifert *(Gen. Mgr.)*

Mrs. Grimes Foods **(1)**
512 N. Main St.
Grimes, IA 55435
Tel.: 612-333-6461

FARIBAULT WOOLEN MILL CO.
1500 Second Ave., N. W.
Faribault, MN 55021
Mailing Address:
P. O. Box 369
Faribault, MN 55021
Tel.: 507-334-6444
Fax: 507-332-2936
Year Founded: 1865
Approx.Sls.: $18,000,000
Emp.: 175
Export
Faribo Pak-a-Robes, Wool Blankets, Cotton Blankets, Acrylic Blankets, Afghan Throws
S.I.C.: 2231
Richard J. Klemer *(Chm. Bd.)*
Peter Johnson *(Pres.)*
Charles Champlin *(Sr. V.P.-Special Mkts.)*
Alan Woodside *(V.P.-Retail Sls.)*
Jeffrey Larsen *(Chief Fin. Officer)*
Richard Shaw *(Plant Mgr.)*

Computer Systems/Hardware:
IBM AS400

FARLEY CANDY COMPANY
2945 W. 31st St.
Chicago, IL 60623
Mailing Address:
P.O. Box 25,
Skokie, IL 60077
Tel.: 312-254-0900
Tel.: 800-225-7321 **DE**
Year Founded: 1891
Approx.Sls.: $200,000,000
Emp.: 1,400
Fiscal Year-end: 12/31/91
Import Export
Manufacture Candy, Chocolates, Fruit Snacks, Lozenges & Trail Mixes
S.I.C.: 2034; 2064; 2066
William H. Ellis *(Chm. Bd., Pres. & Chief Oper. Officer)*
E. George LeBreux *(Exec. V.P.)*
Ronald Cappadocia *(Sr. V.P.-Mktg. & Sls.)*
John Dobrozsi *(Sr. V.P.-Res. & Engrng.)*
Michael S. Gotkin *(Sr. V.P. & Gen. Counsel)*
Gary Ricco *(Sr. V.P.-Fin.)*
George Antoniadis *(V.P.-Grocery Sls.)*
David Barnett *(V.P.-Mktg.)*
Donald Laughlin *(V.P.-Intl.)*
Richard J. Parizek *(V.P.-National Accts.)*
Ronald Kowieski *(Dir.-Pur.)*
Bernice Panocha *(Dir.-Human Resources)*
Principal(s):
William H. Ellis

No. of Mfg. Plants/Facilities: 6
No. of U.S. Offices: 9

Computer Systems/Hardware:
IBM System 38

Outside Service Firm(s):

Ernst & Young*(Auditors)*
233 S. Wacker Dr.
Chicago, IL 60606
Tel.: 312-368-1800
Fax: 312-645-3095

Arthur J. Gallagher & Co.*(Commercial Insurance Carrier)*
Chicago, IL

Sidley & Austin*(Legal Firm)*
One First National Plaza, 42nd Fl.
Chicago, IL 60603
Tel.: 312-853-7000
Fax: 312-853-7036

Continental Bank, N.A.*(Major Banking Relationship)*
30 N. LaSalle St.
Chicago, IL 60693

FARLEY INDUSTRIES
233 S. Wacker Dr., Ste. 5000
Chicago, IL 60606
Tel.: 312-876-1724 **DE**
Fax: 312-993-1749
Year Founded: 1976
Approx.Rev.: $3,515,000,000
Emp.: 49,900
Fiscal Year-end: 12/31/90
Import Export
Mfr. of Men's, Women's & Children's Underwear, Screen Print Shirts, Fleecewear, Family Hosiery, Sheets, Towels, Footwear, Fleecewear, Sheets & Towels; Railroad Parts, Automotive Body Assemblies
S.I.C.: 2211; 2221; 3143; 3144; 2252; 2322; 2331; 2339; 2341; 2241; 2297; 2392
William F. Farley *(Chm. Bd. & Chief Exec. Officer)*
Richard C. Lappin *(Pres. & Chief Oper. Officer)*
Paul M. O'Hara *(Exec. V.P. & Chief Fin. Officer)*
Richard M. Cron *(Sr. V.P.-Devel.)*
Kenneth Greenbaum *(V.P. & Gen. Counsel)*
Earl C. Shanks *(V.P. & Dir.-Taxes)*
Michael F. Bogacki *(V.P. & Controller)*
Burgess D. Ridge *(V.P.-Admin.)*
Brian Hanigan *(Treas.)*
David Palmer *(Dir.)*

No. of Mfg. Plants/Facilities: 41

Computer Systems/Hardware:
IBM; DEC

Outside Service Firm(s):

Ernst & Young*(Auditors)*
233 S. Wacker Dr.
Chicago, IL 60606
Tel.: 312-368-1800
Fax: 312-645-3095

Travelers Insurance Co.*(Commercial Insurance Carrier)*
1 Tower Square
Hartford, CT 06183-2492
Tel.: 203-277-4542
Fax: 203-277-5038

Provident Life & Accident Insurance Co.*(Group Insurer)*
P.O. Box 12015
Chattanooga, TN 37401
Tel.: 615-755-7088

Katten, Muchin & Zavis*(Legal Firm)*
525 W. Monroe St., Ste. 1600
Chicago, IL 60661-3693
Tel.: 312-902-5200

Bankers Trust Co.*(Major Banking Relationship)*
P.O. Box 318, Church St. Station
New York, NY 10008
Tel.: 212-454-2212
Fax: 212-454-2783

Chemical Bank*(Major Banking Relationship)*
450 West 33rd St.
New York, NY 10001
Tel.: 212-613-7197
Fax: 212-947-7628

Advisory Research, Inc.*(Pension Manager)*
New York, NY

Divisions:

Farley, Inc. **(1)**
233 S. Wacker Dr., Ste. 5000
Chicago, IL 60606
Tel.: 312-876-7000
Holding Co.
S.I.C.: 6719

Divisions:

Magnus Metals **(2)**
S. Bell & Viaduct
Fremont, NE 68025
Tel.: 402-721-9540 (100%)
Mfr. Railroad Parts
S.I.C.: 3568
Steven S. Coleman *(Pres.)*
Richard Dischler *(Controller)*
John Macklin *(Plant Mgr.)*

Tool & Engineering Co. **(2)**
900 W. 18th St.
Chicago, IL 60608
Tel.: 312-876-1724 (100%)
Emp.: 280
Design & Mfr. Sheet Metal Prototype Parts, Sub-Assemblies & Body Assemblies for the Auto Industry
S.I.C.: 3711
Donald E. Williams *(Pres.)*
Alexander Zunich *(V.P.)*
Craig Williams *(Sls. Mgr.)*
Thomas Woods *(Controller)*

Subsidiary:

Acme Boot Co., Inc. **(2)**
1002 Stafford St.
Clarksville, TN 37040
Tel.: 615-552-2000 (100%)
Fax: 615-647-3566
Emp.: 1,600
Mfr. Leather Boots
S.I.C.: 3143
Michael Vogel *(Pres. & Chief Oper. Officer)*
Sam McConner *(Sr. V.P.-Sls.)*
Calvin McKay *(Sr. V.P. & Treas.)*
Andy Thompson *(Dir. Adv.-Acme Dan Post)*
Sheri Herndon *(Dir.-Adv.-Dingo)*

Fruit of the Loom **(1)**
#1 Fruit of the Loom Drive
Bowling Green, KY 42102
Tel.: 502-781-6400 (100%)
Fax: 502-781-6588
Earnings: $31,700,000
Approx.Sls.: $1,628,000
Emp.: 30,000
Fiscal Year-end: 12/31/92
Export
Mfr. Men's & Women's Underwear, Activewear & Socks
S.I.C.: 2322; 2341
Joe Medalie *(Vice Chm.)*
Jack Moore *(Pres.)*
John Holland *(Chief Exec. Officer)*
David Drescher *(Exec. V.P.-Mktg.)*
Hollis Hinton *(Exec. V.P.-Sls.)*
Richard Landau *(Exec. V.P.-Sls.)*
Leon Tonelson *(Exec. V.P.-Sls.)*
Ralph Wakeland *(Exec. V.P.-Fin.)*
L.B. McKeithen *(V.P.-Mktg. Services)*
Michael Sherlock *(V.P.-Mktg.-Underwear & Hosiery)*
John Wigodsky *(V.P.-Mktg.-Activewear)*
Janet Rosati *(Dir.-Consumer Relations)*
Michael Bonadio *(Dir.-Sls. Promo.)*

Union Underwear Co., Inc. **(1)**
1 Fruit of the Loom Dr.
Bowling Green, KY 42103
Tel.: 502-781-6400 (100%)
Fax: 502-781-6400
Earnings: $77,100,000
Approx.Sls.: $1,426,800,000
Emp.: 27,700
Fiscal Year-end: 12/31/90
Manufacturer of Underwear, Activewear, Family Hosiery, Fleecewear & Screen Print T-Shirts
S.I.C.: 2322; 2252; 2341; 2339; 2251
John B. Holland *(Chm. Bd. & Chief Exec. Officer)*
Joseph Medalie *(Vice Chm.)*
Jack Moore *(Pres.)*
Ralph Huschle *(Pres.-F.O.L. Intl. Div.)*
David R. Drescher *(Exec. V.P.-Mktg.)*
Hollis Hinton *(Exec. V.P.-Sls.)*
Richard Landau *(Exec. V.P.-Hosiery Sls.)*
Leon Tonelson *(Exec. V.P.-Sls.)*
Stan Vinson *(Exec. V.P.-Mfg.)*
Ralph Wakeland *(Exec. V.P.-Fin. & Treas.)*
Hugo Becker *(V.P.-Personnel)*
Gene Faller *(V.P.-Pur.)*
Lester Schwartz *(V.P.-Adv. & Sls. Promo. Mgr.)*

West Point-Pepperell, Inc. **(1)**
400 West 10th St.
West Point, GA 31833
Tel.: 706-645-4000
Assets: $2,935,276,000
Earnings: ($47,831,000)
Liabilities: $1,707,377,000
Net Worth: $1,227,899,000
Approx.Sls.: $1,213,616,000
Emp.: 19,900
Fiscal Year-end: 12/31/90
Mfr. of Linens & Towels Marketed Under Design Names Such as: Martex, Lady Pepperell, Utica, Tastemaker, Ralph Lauren & Vellux
S.I.C.: 2211; 2221; 2241; 2297; 2391
William Farley *(Chm. Bd. & Chief Exec. Officer)*
Edgar E. Davis *(Pres. & Chief Oper. Officer)*
Stan Kees *(Chief. Fin. Officer)*
Toni M. Cauble *(Dir.-Corp. Communications)*
William Lane *(Pur. Agent)*

Divisions:

Apparel Fabrics Div. **(2)**
1221 Ave. of the Americas
New York, NY 10020
Tel.: 212-382-5000
Cotton & Synthetic Apparel Fabrics & Finishing
S.I.C.: 2211; 2261
Warren Levitt *(Sr. V.P.-Sls.)*
W. Tony Freeman *(V.P.-Mfg. Knits & Specialties)*
Pamela Goehring *(Dir.-Mktg. Services)*

Plant:

Mission Valley Mills, Inc. **(3)**
P.O. Box 141,
New Braunfels, TX 78130
Tel.: 210-625-3411
Broadcloths, Denims, Body Goods, Ginghams, Chambrays, etc.
S.I.C.: 2211; 2221
Guadalupe Castaneda *(Plant Mgr.)*

Home Fashions Div. **(2)**
1185 Ave. of the Americas
New York, NY 10036
Tel.: 212-382-5000
Towels & Toweling, Bathroom Ensembles, Cotton & Synthetic Sheetings, Sheets & Pillow Cases, Blankets
S.I.C.: 2392
Robert A. Woithe *(Pres.)*
J. L. Grant *(V.P.-Sheet Mfg.)*
L. L. Bledsoe *(V.P.-Towel Mfg.)*
F. D. Gray *(V.P.-Admin. & Controller)*
C. S. Cilley *(V.P.-Sls.)*
William A. Lane *(Gen. Pur. Agent)*

Custom Fabrics Div. **(2)**
400 west 10th St.
West Point, GA 31833
Tel.: 706-645-4000
Woven Cotton & Synthetic Fabrics
S.I.C.: 2211; 2241
Allen Hinkle *(Pres.)*
Trey Hodges *(V.P.-Mfg.)*
Ralph Allen *(V.P.-Sls.)*
A. Ray Jones *(Controller)*
William A. Lane *(Gen. Pur. Agent)*

Subsidiaries:

Chattahoochee Valley Railway Company **(2)**
400 W. 10th St.
West Point, GA 31833
Tel.: 706-645-4000 (100%)
Kathleen Shaddix *(V.P. & G.M.)*

Stevens Home Fashions **(2)**
1185 Ave. of the Americas
New York, NY 10036
Tel.: 212-930-2000 (100%)
Fax: 212-930-2079
Assets: $1,200,338,000
Earnings: $1,865,547,000
Liabilities: $698,531,000
Net Worth: $501,807,000
Approx.Sls.: $1,698,284,000
Emp.: 23,000
Fiscal Year-end: 11/ 3/90
Mfr. Cotton & Synthetic Fabrics, Carpets, Sheets, Towels, Bath Rugs & Yarn
S.I.C.: 2211; 2273; 2221; 2281; 2262; 3069
Robert Woithe *(Pres.)*
Bryan Dixon *(Dir.-Adv.)*

Divisions:

Stevens Carpet Div. **(3)**
1185 Ave. of the Americas
New York, NY 10036
Tel.: 212-930-2000
Carpets & Rugs
S.I.C.: 2273
John Riley *(Div. Pres.)*
Brian Daniels *(Exec. V.P.-Mfg.)*

International Div. **(3)**
1185 Ave. of the Americas
New York, NY 10036
Tel.: 212-930-2000
Export of Bed Linens & Towels
S.I.C.: 5023
Donald P. Shaffer *(V.P. Intl. Sls. & Mktg.)*

Sheet & Bedroom Accessories Div. **(3)**
1185 Ave. of the Americas
New York, NY 10036
Tel.: 212-930-2000
S.I.C.: 2392
Richard Roman *(Pres.)*

Converter & Industrial Fabrics Div. **(3)**
1185 Ave. of the Americas
New York, NY 10036
Tel.: 212-930-2000
S.I.C.: 2299
William Donovan *(Pres.)*

Terry, Bath & Kitchen Products Div. **(3)**
1185 Ave. of the Americas
New York, NY 10036
Tel.: 212-930-2000
S.I.C.: 2392
R. A. Grissinger *(Pres.)*

Stevens Auto Products **(3)**
1185 Ave. of the Americas
New York, NY 10036
Tel.: 212-930-2000
S.I.C.: 2284
Robert B. Sparks *(Pres.)*

Subsidiaries:

Stevens Aviation, Inc. **(3)**
Greer, SC 29651
Tel.: 803-879-6000 (100%)
Aircraft Sales & Service
S.I.C.: 4581
Samuel S. Baker *(Pres.)*

Camp Hosiery **(3)**
350 Fifth Ave.
New York, NY 10118
Tel.: 212-760-8899 (100%)
Fax: 212-629-8676
Emp.: 35
Women's & Men's Hosiery
S.I.C.: 2252
Richard Landau *(Exec. V.P.)*
Victor Ricci *(V.P.-Mdsg. & Mktg.)*

Plants:

Camp Hosiery **(4)**
1801 No. 12th St.
Reading, PA 19604
Tel.: 215-921-0611
Men's Hosiery
S.I.C.: 2252
David Forester *(Plant Mgr.)*

Camp Hosiery **(4)**
P.O. Box 370, 213 Grand St.
Lenoir City, TN 37771
Tel.: 615-986-3531
Women's Hosiery
S.I.C.: 2251
Harry Pease *(Plant Mgr.)*

BVD Licensing Corporation **(3)**
P.O. Box 780,
Bowling Green, KY 42101
Tel.: 502-781-6400 (100%)
S.I.C.: 2322; 2341
David Drescher *(Exec. V.P.)*

Non-U.S. Holdings:

Fabrica de Valvulas **(1)**
Calle 5 No. 1906
Guadalajara, Jalisco 1-646, Mexico
Mfr. Petroleum Coal Prods.
S.I.C.: 2999

Codi International B.V. **(1)**
Verlaat 22
Veenendaal, U3900 AA, Netherlands (30%)
S.I.C.: 2321; 2325

Daisy de Venezuela C.A. **(1)**
Apdo 6601,
Caracas, Venezuela
Tel.: 49-20-53
Regional Offices
S.I.C.: 5136; 5137

Firet, B.V. **(1)**
Verlaat 22 U3900 AA
Veenendaal, Netherlands (50%)

Nonwovens
S.I.C.: 2297

Firet, G.m.b.H. **(1)**
Haibach, Germany (50%)
Nonwoven Fabrics
S.I.C.: 2297

S.A. Firet, N.V. **(1)**
Dandermondesti 51 1040
Brussels, Belgium
Tel.: 735-11-82 (50%)
Nonwoven Fabrics
S.I.C.: 2297

Van Raalte de Venezuela C.A. **(1)**
Apdo. 6601,
Caracas, 1010, Venezuela
Tel.: 443-1511
Mfr. Women's Lingerie, Swimwear, Blouses & Dresses
S.I.C.: 2331; 2335; 2339; 2341

Wool Filters Intl. **(1)**
Sydney, Australia (18.75%)
S.I.C.: 0214; 2231

West Point-Pepperel (U.K.) Ltd. **(1)**
6 Cavendish Square
London, W1, United Kingdom (100%)
Bed & Bath Furnishings
S.I.C.: 2392

FARM FAMILY MUTUAL INSURANCE CO.
Rte. 9 West
Glenmont, NY 12077
Mailing Address:
P.O. Box 656,
Albany, NY 12201
Tel.: 518-436-9751 **NY**
Fax: 518-436-5471
Year Founded: 1955
Assets: $140,245,000
Liabilities: $113,363,000
Net Worth: $26,882,000
Approx.Sls.: $75,000,000
Emp.: 200
Fiscal Year-end: 12/31/89
Property & Casualty Insurance
S.I.C.: 6331
William M. Stamp, Jr. *(Pres.)*
Philip P. Weber *(Exec. V.P. & Chief Exec. Officer)*
James Bettini *(Sr. V.P.-Opers.)*
William T. Conine *(Sr. V.P.-Information Services)*
Gerald L. McGregor *(Sr. V.P.-Claims)*
Raymond Osterhoust *(Sr. V.P.-Investments)*
Charles E. Simon *(Sr. V.P. & Chief Fin. Officer)*
Dell Wyman *(Sr. V.P.-Mktg.)*
Don R. Benton *(Treas.)*
Victoria Stanfor *(Gen. Counsel)*
Mary M. Schmitt *(Sec.)*

Outside Service Firm(s):

KPMG Peat Marwick*(Auditors)*
74 N. Pearl St.
Albany, NY 12207
Tel.: 518-455-8809

Key Bank*(Major Banking Relationship)*
Albany, NY

FARM FRESH, INC.
7530 Tidewater Drive
Norfolk, VA 23505
Mailing Address:
P.O. Box 1289
Norfolk, VA 23501
Tel.: 804-480-6700 **VA**
Fax: 804-480-6399
Year Founded: 1948
Assets: $269,887,182
Earnings: ($19,368,489)
Liabilities: $242,187,366
Net Worth: $27,699,816
Approx.Sls.: $763,000,000
Emp.: 4,200
Fiscal Year-end: 12/30/90
Retail Grocery, General Merchandise Stores
S.I.C.: 5411
Michael Julian *(Chm. Bd., Pres. & Chief Exec. Officer)*
Doug Voris *(Exec. V.P.-Store Opers.)*
Ron Johnson *(Sr. V.P.-Richmond Div.)*
Timothy E. Kullman *(Chief Fin. Officer)*
Susan T. Mayo *(V.P.-Pub. Rels. & Consumer Affairs)*
Al Wanzelak *(V.P.-Human Resources)*
Orville Crook *(Controller)*
Bob Beck *(Dir.-Mdsg. & Mktg.)*
Jim Jansen *(Dir.-Adv.)*
Glenn Sharpe *(Dir.-Mngmt.)*
Frankie Fells, Sr. *(Mgr.-Personnel Training & Devel.)*
Cheryle McHenry *(Mgr.-Compensation & Benefits)*

Computer Systems/Hardware:
IBM - Software International

Outside Service Firm(s):

Freedman, Levy, Kroll & Simonds*(Legal Firm)*
1050 Connecticut Ave.
Washington, DC 20036

Crestar Bank*(Major Banking Relationship)*
P.O. Box 26665,
Richmond, VA 23261
Tel.: 804-782-5995

FARM & HOME OIL COMPANY
420 State Rd.
Telford, PA 18969
Tel.: 215-257-0131 **PA**
Fax: 215-257-2088
Approx.Sls.: $70,000,000
Emp.: 125
Full Service Distributor & Retailer of Petroleum Products
S.I.C.: 5541; 5983; 5172
Kenneth A. Longacre *(Chief Exec. Officer)*
Daryl Hackman *(Pres.)*
Rod Durstein *(V.P.)*
Bryan Cassel *(Chief Fin. Officer)*

Outside Service Firm(s):

KPMG Peat Marwick*(Auditors)*
1600 Market St.
Philadelphia, PA 19103
Tel.: 215-299-3100

Butera, Hess, Beausang & Moyer*(Legal Firm)*
700 Valley Forge Plaza
King of Prussia, PA 19406
Tel.: 215-265-0800

Union National Bank*(Major Banking Relationship)*
10 W. Broad St.
Souderton, PA
Tel.: 215-721-2455

FARM JOURNAL, INC.
230 W. Washington Sq.
Philadelphia, PA 19106
Tel.: 215-829-4700
Fax: 215-829-4803
Year Founded: 1877
Approx.Sls.: $32,000,000
Emp.: 360
Magazine Publishing, Farm Journal
S.I.C.: 2721
Dale E. Smith *(Chm. Bd. & Pres.)*
Larry Campbell *(Exec. V.P., Sec. & Treas.)*
Earl Ainsworth *(Sr. V.P.-Editorial)*
Roger D. Randall *(Sr. V.P. & Publr.)*
Kenneth Venuti *(Controller)*

Outside Service Firm(s):

Deloitte & Touche*(Auditors)*
1700 Market St.
Philadelphia, PA 19103
Tel.: 215-246-2322
Fax: 215-569-2441

White & Williams*(Legal Firm)*
Philadelphia, PA

Meridian Bank*(Major Banking Relationship)*
One Meridian Plaza, 36th Fl.
Philadelphia, PA
Tel.: 215-854-3900

Subsidiary:

Rockwood Research **(1)**
1751 West County Rd. B
Saint Paul, MN 55113
Tel.: 612-631-1977
Market Research
S.I.C.: 8732
Dale Longfellow *(Exec. V.P.)*

FARM STORES, INC.
5800 N.W. 74th Ave.
Miami, FL 33166
Tel.: 305-592-3100
Fax: 305-591-4243
Approx.Sls.: $250,000,000
Emp.: 1,400
Convenience Food Stores; Gasoline Stations
S.I.C.: 5411; 5541
A.S. Fogg *(Chief Exec. Officer)*
A.S. Fogg, Jr. *(Pres. & Chief Oper. Officer)*
S.M. Fogg *(Exec. V.P.)*
J.L. LaFrankie *(V.P.-Mktg.)*
Richard D. Rentz *(V.P. & Gen. Counsel)*
N.W. Rasmussen *(V.P.-Mfg.)*

Outside Service Firm(s):

Greenberg, Traurig, Hoffman, Lipoff, Rosen & Quentel, P.A.*(Legal Firm)*
1221 Brickell Ave.
Miami, FL 33131
Tel.: 305-579-0500

Southeast Bank, N.A.*(Major Banking Relationship)*
One Southeast Financial Center
Miami, FL 33131

FARMERS AND TRADERS LIFE INSURANCE CO.
960 James St.
Syracuse, NY 13201
Mailing Address:
P.O. Box 1056,
Syracuse, NY 13201
Tel.: 315-471-5656
Tel.: 800-347-0960
Fax: 315-475-6612
Year Founded: 1912
Approx.Sls.: $230,000,000
Emp.: 90
Life Insurance & Annuities
S.I.C.: 6311
John J. Whittle *(Chm. Bd., Pres. & Chief Exec. Officer)*
William Hess *(Sr. V.P.-Mktg. & Sls.)*
Kenneth C. Sharkey *(V.P. & Treas.)*
John Luchsinger *(Sec.)*
Lynn A. Faulkner *(Dir.-Communications)*

FARMERS CO-OP MARKET INC.
Bowden & Co-op Road
Frisco City, AL 36445
Mailing Address:
P.O. Box 187
Frisco City, AL 36445
Tel.: 205-267-3175
Year Founded: 1949
Approx.Sls.: $10,278,000
Emp.: 45
Fiscal Year-end: 00/00/86
Cooperative for Farm Supplies
S.I.C.: 5191; 5999
Paul Watson *(Chm., Pres. & Chief Exec. Officer)*
Sam R. Carter *(Chief Fin. Officer & Treas.)*
Phyllis York *(Office Mgr.)*

FARMERS MARINE COPPER WORKS
1908 Strand Ave. B
Galveston, TX 77550
Mailing Address:
P.O. Box 748,
Galveston, TX 77553
Tel.: 409-765-6361 **TX**
Fax: 409-765-8513
Year Founded: 1920
Sales Range: $10-19 Million
Emp.: 110
Fiscal Year-end: 12/31/89
Manufacture Pipe; Machine Shop
S.I.C.: 3356; 3599
Bruce J. Farmer *(Pres. & Chief Exec. Officer)*
Thos E. Farmer *(V.P.)*
Donald Farmer *(V.P.)*
Sidney C. Farmer III *(V.P.)*
Carroll E. Effstrom *(Sec. & Treas.)*
Elizabeth Nerren *(Pur. Agent)*

Outside Service Firm(s):

Head, Maxwell & McKena*(Auditors)*
Galveston, TX

United States National Bank*(Major Banking Relationship)*
2200 Market
Galveston, TX 77550
Tel.: 713-763-1151

Subsidiary:

Farmer's Copper & Industrial Supply **(1)**
202 37th St.
Galveston, TX 77550
Tel.: 409-765-9003
Tel.: 800-231-9450
Emp.: 50
Sell Pipe Fittings & Sheet Metal
S.I.C.: 3356
Bruce J. Farmer *(Pres.)*

FARMERS MUTUAL HAIL INSURANCE CO.
2323 Grand Ave.
Des Moines, IA 50312
Tel.: 515-282-9104
Fax: 515-282-6303
Fax: 515-282-1220
Year Founded: 1893
Approx.Sls.: $78,000,000
Emp.: 125
Fiscal Year-end: 12/31/92
Insurance On Growing Crops; Poultry, Reinsurance
S.I.C.: 6411
Perry Rutledge *(Pres.)*
Albert B. Carter *(Sr. V.P. & Treas.)*
William A. Rutledge *(Sr. V.P. & Sec.)*
Donald R. Duwelius *(Sr. V.P.)*
Louis G. Bobinet *(V.P. & Personnel Mgr.)*
Myron Kumler *(V.P.-Sls.)*
Mark M. Mulvihill *(Asst. V.P.-Agency Services)*

Computer Systems/Hardware:
Unisys

FARMER'S PRIDE, INC.
West Main St.
Fredericksburg, PA 17026
Tel.: 717-865-6626
Fax: 717-865-7046
Year Founded: 1942
Approx.Sls.: $20,000,000
Emp.: 331
Poultry Dressing & Packing
S.I.C.: 2015
Scott I. Sechler *(Chm. Bd. & Pres.)*
Paul Swope, Jr. *(V.P. & Gen. Mgr.)*
Robert L. Walborn *(V.P.-Sls.)*
Bruno Schmalhoser *(Chief Fin. Officer)*

FARMERS RICE COOPERATIVE
2525 Natomas Park Dr.
Sacramento, CA 95833
Mailing Address:
P.O. Box 15223,
Sacramento, CA 95851
Tel.: 916-923-5100
Fax: 916-920-4295
Year Founded: 1944
Approx.Sls.: $150,000,000
Emp.: 275
Fiscal Year-end: 8/31/90
Export
Rice Milling & Marketing
S.I.C.: 2044; 5499
Alfred Montna *(Chm. Bd.)*
Ralph S. Newman, Jr. *(Pres. & Chief Exec. Officer)*
Paul C. Crutchfield *(Sr. V.P.-Oper.)*
James E. Dodson *(V.P.-Fin. & Admin.)*
William V. Huffman *(V.P.-Communications)*
Robert M. Sandrock *(V.P.-Field Services)*

Outside Service Firm(s):

Deloitte & Touche*(Auditors)*
50 Fremont St.
San Francisco, CA 94105-2230
Tel.: 415-393-4300
Fax: 415-227-0452

McCutchen, Doyle, Brown & Enerson*(Legal Firm)*
3 Embarcadero Center
San Francisco, CA 94111
Tel.: 415-393-2000

Bank of America NT&SA*(Major Banking Relationship)*
Sacramento, CA

FARMERS TELEPHONE CO-OP
1101 E. Main St.
Kingstree, SC 29556
Tel.: 803-382-2333 **SC**
Fax: 803-382-3909
Year Founded: 1952
Approx.Sls.: $28,000,000
Emp.: 223
Telephone Communication, Except Radio
S.I.C.: 4813
Aubrey E. Judy *(Chief Oper. Officer)*

Outside Service Firm(s):

Chemical Bank*(Major Banking Relationship)*
Garden City, NY

FARMERS UNION MARKETING & PROCESSING ASSOCIATION
Box 319
Redwood Falls, MN 56283
Tel.: 507-637-2938 **MN**
Fax: 507-637-5409
Year Founded: 1929
Approx.Sls.: $48,000,000
Emp.: 231
Inedible Grease & Tallow, Meat Scrapes & Tankage, Feather Meal, Hides, Services-Livestock Commission Sales, Insurance, Pet Food Ingredients
S.I.C.: 2077; 0291; 2011; 2048; 2076; 6399
Gordon K. Scherbing *(Pres. & Chief Exec. Officer)*

Outside Service Firm(s):

Deloitte & Touche*(Auditors)*
900 Pillsbury Ctr.
Minneapolis, MN 55402
Tel.: 612-332-2301
Fax: 612-375-5418

Gislason, Dosland, Hunter & Malecki*(Legal Firm)*
Minneapolis, MN

Minnesota Valley Bank*(Major Banking Relationship)*
Minneapolis, MN

FARMHAND, INC.
23610 Highway 7
Excelsior, MN 55331
Mailing Address:
P.O. Box 1500,
Excelsior, MN 55331
Tel.: 612-474-1941
Fax: 612-474-9247
Approx.Sls.: $30,000,000
Emp.: 200
Export
Farm Machinery
S.I.C.: 3523
Joe Lund *(Pres.)*
Tom Schaefer *(V.P.-Mktg.)*
J.D. Hardy *(V.P.-Fin.)*
Darlene Birkeland *(Mgr.-Adv.)*
Jerry Schler *(Mgr.-Sls.)*

FARMINGTON HILLS HOLDING COMPANY
35300 Grand River
Farmington, MI 48335
Tel.: 313-478-0500
Fax: 313-478-1925
Approx.Sls.: $40,000,000
Emp.: 170
Automotive Dealership
S.I.C.: 5511
Robert Mechigian, Sr. *(Pres.)*
Harley Adler *(V.P.)*
Keith Thornton *(Sec. & Treas.)*

Subsidiaries:

Bob Saks Jeep-Eagle **(1)**
35200 Grand River
Farmington, MI 48335
Tel.: 313-478-0500
Frank Lopez *(V.P. & Gen. Mgr.)*

Bob Saks Oldsmobile Inc. **(1)**
35200 Grand River
Farmington, MI 48335
Tel.: 313-478-0500
Robert Mechigian *(Pres.)*

Bob Saks Toyota **(1)**
35200 Grand River
Farmington, MI 48335
Tel.: 313-478-0500
Robert Mechigian *(Pres.)*

FARMLAND INDUSTRIES, INC.
3315 N. Oak Trafficway
Kansas City, MO 64116
Mailing Address:
P.O. Box 7305,
Kansas City, MO 64116
Tel.: 816-459-6000 **KS**
Fax: 816-459-6979
Year Founded: 1929
Assets: $1,369,231,000
Earnings: $42,693,000
Liabilities: $871,867,000
Net Worth: $497,364,000
Approx.Sls.: $3,600,000,000
Emp.: 7,400
Fiscal Year-end: 8/31/91
Manufacture & Distribute Animal Feed, Petroleum Products, Fertilizer, Chemicals & Technical Service
S.I.C.: 5172; 2992; 2048; 2873; 2819; 2851; 4221
Otis Molz *(Chm. Bd.)*
Harry C. Cleberg *(Pres. & Chief Exec. Officer)*
Wayne Rice *(Pres.-Farmland Foods, Inc.)*
Gary Evans *(Exec. V.P.)*
Robert E. Johanson *(Exec. V.P.-Membership & Communications)*
Robert Honse *(Exec. V.P.-Agriculture Opers.)*
John F. Berardi *(V.P.-Fin. & Treas.)*
Lewis Linville *(V.P., Controller & Asst. Treas.)*
George Richter *(V.P.-Mngmt. & Fin. Services)*
Steve Dees *(V.P.-Admin.)*
Harold Carter *(V.P.-Business Devel.)*
Tim Daugherty *(V.P.-Mngmt. Information Services)*
Bill Matteson *(V.P.-Pub. Affairs)*
Bernard Sanders *(V.P.-Plng.)*
Gary Morrison *(V.P.-Petroleum Opers.)*
F.E. Schrodt *(V.P.-Transportation & Logistics)*
Larry S. Jenkins *(Exec. Dir. Fin. & Lease)*
Jack Warren *(Exec. Dir.-Employee Trust)*
Roger Uher *(Dir.-Pur.)*
Holly Zermmerman *(Gen. Mgr.-Human Resources)*
Douglas A. Young Jr. *(Mgr.-Corp. Real Estate)*
Principal(s):
Otis Molz

Computer Systems/Hardware:
IBM Systems 37 & 38

Outside Service Firm(s):

KPMG Peat Marwick*(Auditors)*
1000 Walnut St.
Kansas City, MO 64106

Commerce Bank*(Major Banking Relationship)*
Springfield, MO

Subsidiaries:

The Cooperative Finance Assn., Inc. **(1)**
P.O. Box 7305, 3315 N. Oak Traffic Way
Kansas City, MO 64116
Tel.: 816-459-6000 (100%)
Commodity, Operating, Facility Loans for Local Coops.
S.I.C.: 6159

Cooperative Service Co. **(1)**
Culvert St.
Lincoln, NE 68506
Tel.: 402-423-2516
Auditing Insurance, Management Service for Local Coops.
S.I.C.: 8721

Farmers Chemical Co. **(1)**
P.O. Box 225
Joplin, MO 64802
Tel.: 417-624-5225 (100%)
Mfr. of Ammonium Phosphate Fertilizer Products
S.I.C.: 2874

Farmland Industries, Inc. **(1)**
Kansas City, MO

Farmland Industries, Intl., Inc. **(1)**
3315 N. Oak Trafficway
Kansas City, MO 64116
Tel.: 816-459-6000
Crude Oil Procurement
S.I.C.: 1311

Farmland Industries U.K. Ltd. **(1)**
3315 N. Oak Trafficway
Kansas City, MO 64116
Tel.: 816-459-6000
Crude Oil Services
S.I.C.: 1311

Farmland Insurance Agency, Inc. **(1)**
P.O. Box 7305, 3315 N. Oak Traffic Way
Kansas City, MO 64116
Tel.: 816-459-6000 (100%)
Insurance Agency
S.I.C.: 6311

Farmland Foods, Inc. **(1)**
10015 N. Executive Hills Blvd.
Kansas City, MO 64153
Tel.: 816-891-1200
Fax: 816-891-1258
Approx.Sls.: $711,500,000
Emp.: 2,426
Fiscal Year-end: 8/31/90
Pork Processing, Food Marketing; Hams, Bacon, Smoked & Fresh Sausage, Hot Dogs, Luncheon Meats, Dry Sausage, Fresh Pork
S.I.C.: 2011; 2013
Wayne Rice *(Pres.)*
Jerry L. Schwab *(Sec.)*
Sherm Robbs *(Mgr.-Mktg.)*

Farmland Securities Co. **(1)**
P.O. Box 7305, 3315 N. Oak Traffic Way
Kansas City, MO 64116
Tel.: 816-459-6000
Broker-Dealer for Farmland Securities
S.I.C.: 6211

Union Equity **(1)**
2300 N. 10th
Enid, OK 73702
Tel.: 405-233-5100
Telex: 227169
Fax: 405-233-9802
Export
Computer Systems/Hardware:
Sperry 1172
Agricultural Services; Marketing & Storage of Grain
S.I.C.: 5153; 4221; 0111; 0119
H.D. Cleybergn *(Pres.)*
Edwin Wallace *(Dir.-Fin. & Admin.)*
Bernard C. Sanders *(Corp. Sec.)*

Subsidiaries:

Equity Country Inc. **(2)**
P.O. Box 266
Darrouzett, TX
Tel.: 806-624-2311

Equity Export, Oil & Gas, Inc. **(2)**
2300 N. 10th
Enid, OK 73702
Tel.: 405-233-5100

Marine Terminal Shipping Co. **(2)**
2300 N. 10th
Enid, OK 73702
Tel.: 405-233-5100

Uneco Investor Services Inc. **(2)**
4800 Main St.
Kansas City, MO 64112
Tel.: 816-931-2661

Joint Venture:

Harvest Equity Inc. **(1)**
4535 Normal Blvd., Ste. 222
Lincoln, NE 68506
Tel.: 402-489-8105
50% Owned By Harvest States

FARMSTEAD FOODS, INC.
E. Main St., Box 1059
Albert Lea, MN 56007
Tel.: 507-377-4200
Fax: 507-477-4171
Year Founded: 1990
Approx.Sls.: $300,000,000
Emp.: 725
Meat Packing Plant
S.I.C.: 2011
Keith Barnes *(Pres.)*
Mark Campbell *(V.P. & Chief Fin. Officer)*

FARMWAY CO-OP INC.
204 East Court Street
Beloit, KS 67420
Mailing Address:
P.O. Box 568,
Beloit, KS 67420
Tel.: 913-738-2241
Year Founded: 1911
Assets: $18,020,150
Earnings: $1,356,476
Liabilities: $1,472,609
Net Worth: $16,547,541
Approx.Sls.: $37,000,408
Emp.: 110
Fiscal Year-end: 4/30/90
Grain Storage & Handling; Feed Manufacturing; Crop Production; Petroleum Sales & Service; Grain & Farm Supply; Cooperative Membership Organizations
S.I.C.: 4221; 5153; 5159; 5191; 5261; 5541
Robert Kirgis *(Chm. Bd. & Pres.)*
Byron Ulery *(Chief Exec. Officer & Gen. Mgr.)*

Phillip Kirchoff *(Chief Fin. Officer & Controller)*
Billie Albert *(Treas. & Sec.)*

FARNAM COMPANIES, INC.
301 W. Osborn Rd.
Phoenix, AZ 85013
Mailing Address:
P.O. Box 34820
Phoenix, AZ 85067-4820
Tel.: 602-285-1660 **AZ**
Fax: 602-285-1803
Year Founded: 1946
Approx.Sls.: $71,000,000
Emp.: 200
Fiscal Year-end: 12/31/91
Import Export
Mfr. & Distributor of Animal Health Care Products for Horses & Pets, Lawn & Garden Products & Livestock Products
S.I.C.: 2834; 2879; 3523; 3999; 2819
Charles Duff *(Chm. Bd. & Chief Exec. Officer)*
Tony Hyland *(Pres.)*
Ed Gower *(Chief Information Officer)*
Joseph C. Motola *(Chief Fin. Officer, V.P.-Fin. & Sec.)*
Bill Johnson *(Exec. V.P.)*
Stephen Davis *(Controller)*
Leslie Burger *(Dir.-Pur.)*
Andy Deer *(Dir.-Mktg.)*
Frank Siciliano *(Dir.-Intl. Sls. & Mktg.)*
Trish Spencer *(Dir.-Creative Services)*
Susan Stark *(Dir.-Personnel)*
Duke Hrabe *(Natl. Sls. Mgr.-H/P Div.)*
Edwin Gower *(Mgr.-Data Processing)*
Lee Veith, DVM *(Mgr.-Regulatory Affairs)*

Computer Systems/Hardware:
IBM AS/400

Outside Service Firm(s):

Eide Helmeke & Co.*(Auditors)*
Phoenix, AZ

Delta Dental of Arizona*(Group Insurer)*
Phoenix, AZ

Lincoln National Life Insurance Co.*(Group Insurer)*
Phoenix, AZ

Barry Becker*(Legal Firm)*
Phoenix, AZ

Thunderbird Bank*(Major Banking Relationship)*
Phoenix, AZ

Security Pacific National Bank*(Pension Manager)*
Phoenix, AZ

Division:

Sudbury Consumer Products Company **(1)**
301 W. Osborn
Phoenix, AZ 85013
Tel.: 602-285-1660
Fax: 602-285-1803
Approx.Sls.: $3,000,000
Emp.: 35
Fiscal Year-end: 11/30/91
Sudbury Soil Test Kits, Garden & Plant Meters, Tailor-Made Fertilizer, Sea Power Liquefied Seaweed, Seagreen Compost Maker, Chaperone Animal Repellents, Herbicide Applicators, Pressure Sprayers, Rodenticides, Insect Traps
S.I.C.: 2873; 2874; 2879
Charles B. Duff *(Chief Exec. Officer)*
Michael Kennedy *(Div. Mgr.)*
David Roatch *(Natl. Sls. Mgr.)*
Sheri Van Wormer *(Sls. Admin.)*
Wendy Marshall *(Mktg. Admin.)*

FARNSWORTH COMPANIES
460 S. Greenfield Rd.
Mesa, AZ 85206
Tel.: 602-832-6200 **AZ**
Sales Range: $40-59 Million
Holding Company; Subs. Involved in Construction, Real Estate
S.I.C.: 6719
Ross N. Farnsworth *(Pres.)*
David Palmer *(Treas. & Sec.)*
Principal(s):
Ross N. Farnsworth

Computer Systems/Hardware:
IBM

Outside Service Firm(s):

Pannell, Kerr, Forster*(Auditors)*
Phoenix, AZ

James Benefits*(Commercial Insurance Carrier)*
Mesa, AZ

James Benefits*(Group Insurer)*
Mesa, AZ

Valley National Bank*(Investment Banker)*
3636 N. Central Av.
Phoenix, AZ 85038
Tel.: 602-261-1313

E. Gene Wade Ltd.*(Legal Firm)*
Phoenix, AZ

Valley National Bank*(Major Banking Relationship)*
Shawano, WI

Subsidiaries:

Farnsworth Construction **(1)**
460 S. Greenfield Rd.
Mesa, AZ 85206
Tel.: 602-832-6200
Emp.: 200
Single & Multiple Residential Buildings, Commercial Buildings; Painting Contracting
S.I.C.: 1521; 1522; 1542; 1731
Ross N. Farnsworth *(Pres.)*
Tim R. Nielsen *(V.P.-Opers. & Engrng.)*
Craig Ahlstrom *(Mktg. Dir.)*
Pat Reilly *(Data Processing Dir.)*

Farnsworth Development Co. **(1)**
6065 E. University Dr.
Mesa, AZ 85205
Tel.: 602-832-6200
Real Estate Managers, Agents & Developers
S.I.C.: 6531; 6552
Ross N. Farnsworth *(Pres.)*
Craig Ahlstrom *(Dir.-Adv., Mktg., Opers. & Sls.)*
David Palmer *(Dir.-Fin. Opers.)*
Pat Reilly *(Dir.-Data Processing & Pur.)*

MEL FARR FORD, INC.
24750 Greenfield Rd.
Oak Park, MI 48237
Tel.: 313-967-3700
Fax: 313-967-3714
Year Founded: 1972
Approx.Sls.: $28,000,000
Emp.: 87
Automobile Sales & Service
S.I.C.: 7532
Mel Farr *(Pres.)*
Randall A. Secord *(V.P.)*
Principal(s):
Mel Farr

Outside Service Firm(s):

Follmer, Rudzewicz & Co.*(Auditors)*
Southfield, MI

First Independence National Bank*(Major Banking Relationship)*
Detroit, MI

FARRAR, STRAUS & GIROUX, INC.
19 Union Sq. W.
New York, NY 10003
Tel.: 212-741-6900 **NY**
Fax: 212-633-9385
Year Founded: 1946
Approx.Sls.: $25,000,000
Emp.: 120
Fiscal Year-end: 6/30/90
Book Publishers
S.I.C.: 2731
Roger W. Straus, Jr. *(Pres. & Chief Exec. Officer)*
Roger W. Straus, III *(Exec. V.P.)*
Samuel Kam *(V.P. & Treas.)*
Michael di Capua *(V.P. & Editor)*
Arthur Wang *(V.P.)*
Bridget Marmion *(V.P. & Dir.-Mktg. & Sls.)*
Dorris Janowitz *(V.P. & Production Mgr.)*
Margaret Miller *(Sec.)*

Outside Service Firm(s):

Grant Thornton*(Auditors)*
605 Third Ave.
New York, NY 10158
Tel.: 212-599-0100
Fax: 212-370-4520

Divisions:

Hill & Wang **(1)**
19 Union Sq. W.
New York, NY 10003
Tel.: 212-741-6900

Sunburst **(1)**
19 Union Sq. W.
New York, NY 10003
Tel.: 212-741-6900

FARRELL CMA
420 Lexington Ave., Ste. 1656
New York, NY 10170
Tel.: 212-983-7060
Fax: 212-983-6076
Year Founded: 1987
Approx.Billings: $25,000,000
Emp.: 5
Political Adv.
Catherine Farrell *(Pres.)*
Lorraine Di Sapio *(V.P.)*

Computer Systems/Hardware:
AS 400

FARRELL LINES INCORPORATED
1 Whitehall
New York, NY 10004
Tel.: 212-440-4200
Fax: 212-440-4645
Year Founded: 1925
Approx.Sls.: $126,800,000
Emp.: 222
Steamship Service
S.I.C.: 4731; 4412; 4491
George F. Lowman *(Chm. Bd.)*
Richard V. Parks *(Vice Chm.)*
Richard Gronda *(Pres.)*
James E. Bambrick *(Exec. V.P.)*
Nicholas F. Kondas *(V.P.-Plng., Systems & Profit Improvement)*
James G. Norton *(V.P. & Treas.)*
H. Underweiner *(V.P.-Mktg. & Sls.)*
C. Boyle *(Gen. Sls. Mgr.)*

Computer Systems/Hardware:
IBM 4341

Outside Service Firm(s):

KPMG Peat Marwick*(Auditors)*
345 Park Ave.
New York, NY 10154
Tel.: 212-758-9700
Fax: 212-872-3308

Willis Corroon*(Commercial Insurance Carrier)*
7 Hanover Square
New York, NY
Tel.: 212-837-0823
Fax: 212-344-8290

Travelers Insurance Co.*(Group Insurer)*
1 Tower Square
Hartford, CT 06183-2492
Tel.: 203-277-4542
Fax: 203-277-5038

Winthrop, Stimson, Putnam & Roberts*(Legal Firm)*
Financial Centre, 695 East Main St.
Stamford, CT 06904-6760
Tel.: 203-348-2300

Chemical Bank*(Major Banking Relationship)*
One Battery Park Plaza, 24 Whitehall St.
New York, NY 10004

Metropolitan Life Insurance Co.*(Pension Manager)*
One Madison Ave.
New York, NY 10010-3690
Tel.: 215-578-9292

FASHION SHOP OF KENTUCKY INC.
11008 Decimal Dr.
Louisville, KY 40299
Tel.: 502-267-5415
Fax: 502-267-0480
Approx.Sls.: $27,000,000
Emp.: 200
Women's Apparel Chain
S.I.C.: 5621
David Levine *(Pres.)*
Ann Zimmerman *(Chief Exec. Officer)*
Benjamin Levine *(V.P.)*
Lawrence Levine *(V.P.)*
Victoria Goldenberg *(Sec. & Treas.)*

No. of Mfg. Plants/Facilities: 7

FASTEC INDUSTRIAL
23348 County Rd. 6
Elkhart, IN 46515
Mailing Address:
P.O. Box 1048
Elkhart, IN 46514
Tel.: 219-262-2505
Fax: 219-262-8634
Approx.Sls.: $16,000,000
Emp.: 90
Fiscal Year-end: 12/31/91
Wholesale Distribution of Hardware & Related Products
S.I.C.: 5075; 5078
James L. Braddock *(Chm. Bd., Pres. & Treas.)*
Charles R. White *(Exec. V.P. & Chief Exec. Officer)*
Teresa Burns *(Mgr.-Data Processing)*

Outside Service Firm(s):

John F. Burnham & Assoc.*(Auditors)*
Elkhardt, IN

Benefit Trust & Life*(Group Insurer)*
South Bend, IN

Bernard Katz*(Legal Firm)*
Elkhardt, IN

Midwest Commerce Banking Co.*(Major Banking Relationship)*
Elkhart, IN

Subsidiaries:

Fastec SW Corporation **(1)**
23348 County Rd. 6, P.O. Box 1048
Elkhart, IN 46515
Tel.: 219-262-2505 (100%)

Fie Trading Corporation **(1)**
23348 County Rd. 6, P.O. Box 1048
Elkhart, IN 46515
Tel.: 219-262-2505 (100%)

FAUBER CONSTRUCTION COMPANY, INC.
2200 N. 9th St.
Lafayette, IN 47902
Tel.: 317-742-1081 **IN**
Fax: 317-423-1099
Year Founded: 1955
Approx.Sls.: $19,000,000
Emp.: 125
Highway & Street Paving Contractor
S.I.C.: 1611
Jerome J. McTague *(Chm. Bd.)*

Fauber Construction Company, Inc.—(Continued)

Michael McTague *(Pres. & Chief Exec. Officer)*

Outside Service Firm(s):

Ernst & Young*(Auditors)*
Lafayette, IN

Bank One Lafayette, N.A.*(Major Banking Relationship)*
Lafayette, IN

FAWN INDUSTRIES, INC.
311 Intl. Circle, Ste. 140
Hunt Valley, MD 21030
Tel.: 301-584-1300 **MD**
Fax: 301-584-1327
Year Founded: 1953
Approx.Sls.: $40,000,000
Emp.: 500
Manufacture Plastic Products; Electronic Assembly
S.I.C.: 3089; 3679
John B. Franzone *(Pres. & Chief Exec. Officer)*
Raymond Fioravante *(Controller)*
Bob Strange *(Dir.-Pur.)*

No. of Mfg. Plants/Facilities: 3
No. of U.S. Offices: 2

Computer Systems/Hardware:
IBM

Outside Service Firm(s):

KPMG Peat Marwick*(Auditors)*
111 S. Calvert St.
Baltimore, MD 21202
Tel.: 410-783-8300

Gordon, Feinblatt, Rothman, Hoffberger & Hollander*(Legal Firm)*
Redwood & South Sts.
Baltimore, MD 21202
Tel.: 410-752-4567

Maryland National Bank*(Major Banking Relationship)*
Baltimore, MD 21202

THE FAXON COMPANY, INC.
15 Southwest Park
Westwood, MA 02090
Tel.: 617-329-3350 **MA**
Fax: 617-329-9875
Assets: $49,203,409
Liabilities: $36,171,445
Net Worth: $13,031,964
Approx.Sls.: $380,000,000
Emp.: 650
Fiscal Year-end: 3/31/91
Library Magazine Subscription Agency
S.I.C.: 7389; 7375
Richard R. Rowe *(Chm. Bd., Pres. & Chief Exec. Officer)*
Allan Exon *(V.P.-Fin.)*
Joel H. Baron *(V.P.-Publr. Services)*
Marcella Nelson *(V.P.-Human Resources)*
Peter Pyclik *(V.P.-Info. Systems)*
Mark Zuroff *(Deputy Dir.-Fin.)*
John Woodland *(Dir.-Telecommunications)*

Outside Service Firm(s):

Deloitte & Touche*(Auditors)*
125 Summer St.
Boston, MA 02110
Tel.: 617-261-8000
Fax: 617-261-8111

State Street Bank & Trust Co.*(Major Banking Relationship)*
225 Franklin St.
Boston, MA 02110
Tel.: 617-985-8179
Fax: 617-985-9722

Subsidiary:

Turner Subscription Agency **(1)**
116 E. 16th St.
New York, NY 10003
Tel.: 212-254-4454
Library Subscription Service
S.I.C.: 7389

Non-U.S. Holdings:

Faxon Canada **(1)**
Ten Rutledge St.
Hyde Park, ON N0M 1Z0, Canada
Tel.: 416-287-6124 (100%)
Emp.: 25
Magazine Subscription Services
S.I.C.: 7389
Graham Yates *(Chief Oper. Officer)*

Faxon Europe **(1)**
Hogehilweg 10 1101 CC
Amsterdam, 20, Netherlands
Tel.: 31-20-910591 (100%)
Telex: 84414651
Emp.: 65
Library Subscription Services
S.I.C.: 7389

Nihon Faxon **(1)**
4th Fl., Kurihara Bldg. 7-8-13 Nishi Shinjuku-ku,
Tokyo, 160, Japan
Tel.: 03-3367-3081 (100%)
Telex: 232-5149
Emp.: 5
Library Subscription Service
S.I.C.: 7389
Minoru Taguchi *(Chief Oper. Officer)*

FAY, SPOFFORD & THORNDIKE, INC.
191 Spring St.
Lexington, MA 02173
Mailing Address:
P.O. Box 9117,
Lexington, MA 02173
Tel.: 617-863-8300 **MA**
Fax: 617-861-6915
Year Founded: 1914
Approx.Sls.: $16,000,000
Emp.: 200
Fiscal Year-end: 12/31/92
Consulting Engineers
S.I.C.: 8711
Robert T. Loney *(Pres.)*
Robert J. Caton *(Sr. V.P. & Treas.)*
William J. Glover, Jr. *(Sr. V.P. & Clerk)*
Emile J. Hamwey *(Sr. V.P. & Asst. Treas.)*
Edward A. Welch *(Sr. V.P.)*
Nicholas J. Pappas *(Sr. V.P.)*
James G. Rourke *(Sr. V.P. & Temp. Clerk)*
Max D. Sorota *(Consultant)*

Outside Service Firm(s):

Deloitte & Touche*(Auditors)*
125 Summer St.
Boston, MA 02110
Tel.: 617-261-8000
Fax: 617-261-8111

FEDCO, INC.
9300 Santa Fe Springs Rd.
Santa Fe Springs, CA 90670
Tel.: 310-946-2511
Fax: 310-903-3259
Year Founded: 1949
Approx.Sls.: $750,000,000
Emp.: 5,000
Department Stores
S.I.C.: 5311
Edward L. Butterworth *(Pres. & Chief Exec. Officer)*
Dennis Honaker *(V.P.)*
Roy L. Olofson *(Treas.)*

No. of Mfg. Plants/Facilities: 9

Computer Systems/Hardware:
IBM

Outside Service Firm(s):

KPMG Peat Marwick*(Auditors)*
725 S. Figueroa St.
Los Angeles, CA 90017
Tel.: 213-972-4000

Security Pacific Corporation*(Major Banking Relationship)*
Security Pacific Plaza
Los Angeles, CA 90071
Tel.: 213-345-6211
Fax: 213-625-0809

FEDERAL BUSINESS PRODUCTS, INC.
95 Main Ave.
Clifton, NJ 07014
Tel.: 201-667-9800
Fax: 201-667-7756
Approx.Sls.: $27,000,000
Emp.: 250
Printing Of Continuous, Snapout & Other Business Forms
S.I.C.: 2761
James J. Trainor *(Pres.)*
Lawrence A. Merse *(V.P.-Fin. & Sec.)*
Robert Wolff *(V.P. & Comptroller)*

Outside Service Firm(s):

Ernst & Young*(Auditors)*
Lyndhurst, NJ

FEDERAL CHICAGO CORPORATION
925 22nd St.
North Chicago, IL 60064
Tel.: 708-473-5077 **DE**
Fax: 708-689-1620
Year Founded: 1928
Approx.Sls.: $12,000,000
Emp.: 300
Export
Aluminum Die-castings; Zinc & Zinc-based Alloy Die-castings; Magnesium & Magnesium Base Alloy Die-castings;
S.I.C.: 3363; 3364
Raymond Cross, Sr. *(Chm. Bd.)*
Margaret M. Cross *(Vice Chm.)*
Charles F. Kerbs, Jr. *(Pres.)*
Malachy J. Cross *(V.P.)*
Mary Lenore Cross *(V.P. & Controller)*
Raymond Cross *(V.P. & Sec.)*
Raymond E. Cross, III *(V.P.)*
Al Ferriera *(V.P.)*
William Kleifgen *(V.P.)*
Anastasia Cross *(Pur. Agent)*

No. of Mfg. Plants/Facilities: 2
No. of U.S. Offices: 1

Outside Service Firm(s):

McMahan & Company*(Auditors)*
Lake Forest, IL

M.J. Caughlan & Associates*(Legal Firm)*
Chicago, IL

Lakeside Bank*(Major Banking Relationship)*
Chicago, IL

FEDERAL COMPRESS & WAREHOUSE COMPANY, INC.
165 Madison Ave., Suite 1400
Memphis, TN 38103
Tel.: 901-524-4000
Fax: 901-524-4050
Year Founded: 1977
Emp.: 500
Cotton Warehousing & Services
S.I.C.: 4226
Samuel B. Hollis *(Pres.)*
Robert B. Cohen *(V.P. & Treas.)*
Vicky L. Cortise *(V.P.-Personnel & Risk Mngmt.)*
W.J. Haneghan *(V.P.)*
Larry G. Lively *(V.P.-Mktg.)*
Charles S. Walker *(V.P.-Fin.)*

Outside Service Firm(s):

Arthur Andersen & Co.*(Auditors)*
165 Madison Ave., Ste. 165
Memphis, TN 38103
Tel.: 901-525-4451

Rickey & Bourland*(Legal Firm)*
Memphis, TN

First Tennessee Bank, N.A.*(Major Banking Relationship)*
Memphis, TN

FEDERAL DATA CORPORATION
4800 Hampton Lane
Bethesda, MD 20814
Tel.: 301-986-0800
Fax: 301-961-3892
Year Founded: 1970
Approx.Sls.: $112,000,000
Emp.: 230
Data Services; Government Contractor
S.I.C.: 7374
Robert Hanley *(Chm. Bd.)*
Daniel Young *(Pres.)*
Marvin Haber *(V.P. & Legal Counsel)*
Larry Smith *(V.P.)*
Paul Taltavull *(V.P.)*
John Wayne *(V.P.)*
Jim Dean *(Chief Fin. Officer)*
Harry Marren *(Pres. FDS Inc.)*

Outside Service Firm(s):

Price Waterhouse*(Auditors)*
1801 K. Street, N.W.
Washington, DC 20006
Tel.: 202-296-0800

FEDERAL DISTRIBUTING CORPORATION
57-01 49th St.
Maspeth, NY 11378
Tel.: 718-497-0100
Fax: 718-497-2062
Year Founded: 1921
Assets: $3,000,000
Liabilities: $1,500,000
Net Worth: $1,500,000
Approx.Billings: $10,000,000
Emp.: 70
Fiscal Year-end: 12/31/90
Sales Promotion Agency
S.I.C.: 7311
Bernard Greenfield *(Pres.)*
Kenneth Greenfield *(Exec. V.P.)*
Ronald Einziger *(V.P.-Direct Mail Sls.)*
Michael Weiss *(V.P.-Fin. & Admin.)*

FEDERAL FARM CREDIT BANKS FUNDING CORPORATION
10 Exchange Place
Jersey City, NJ 07302
Tel.: 201-200-8000 **NJ**
Fax: 201-200-8109
Year Founded: 1916
Assets: $7,492,088
Liabilities: $5,558,838
Net Worth: $1,933,250
Sales Range: $100-499 Million
Emp.: 53
Fiscal Year-end: 12/31/90
Agricultural Financial Services Institution
S.I.C.: 6061
David M. Muller *(Chm. Bd.)*
James A. Brickley *(Pres. & Chief Exec. Officer)*
Lee J. Nash *(Exec. V.P.-Fin. & ALM)*
Robert G. Williams *(Exec. V.P.-Fin. Mngmt.)*
Jane Hamburger *(Sr. V.P., Sec. & Dir.-Personnel)*
Alicia Blain *(V.P.-Information Systems)*
Maria E. Zielinski *(Controller)*
Laura A. Czysz *(Office Mgr.)*
Dolores Gill *(Admin. Asst.)*
Karen Wynne *(Coordinator-Admin.)*

Computer Systems/Hardware:
Sun Server

Outside Service Firm(s):

Price Waterhouse*(Auditors)*
7 St. Paul St.
Baltimore, MD 21202

Price Waterhouse*(Auditors)*
One Boatmen's Plaza
St. Louis, MO 63101
Tel.: 314-425-0500

Price Waterhouse*(Auditors)*
153 E. 53rd St., 44th Fl.
New York, NY 10022
Tel.: 212-371-2000

Sutherland, Asbill & Brennan*(Legal Firm)*
1275 Pennsylvania Ave., N.W.
Washington, DC 20004-2404
Tel.: 202-383-0100

Member Banking Affiliates:

CoBank **(1)**
5500 S. Quebec St.
Englewood, CO 80111
Tel.: 303-740-4000 (29.8%)
Fax: 303-740-4002
Emp.: 447
Agricultural Lending Institution
S.I.C.: 6159
W.M. Harding *(Pres.)*

Farm Credit Bank of Baltimore **(1)**
Farm Credit Bank Bldg., 14114 York Rd.
Sparks, MD 21152
Tel.: 410-329-5500 (5.4%)
Fax: 410-329-5705
Emp.: 803
Agricultural Lending Institution
S.I.C.: 6159
Gene L. Swackhamer *(Pres.)*

Farm Credit Bank of Columbia **(1)**
Farm Credit Bank Bldg., 1401 Hampton St.
Columbia, SC 29201
Tel.: 803-799-5000 (5.4%)
Fax: 803-254-1776
Emp.: 1,447
Agricultural Lending Institution
S.I.C.: 6159
Maxey D. Love, Jr. *(Pres.)*

Farm Credit Bank of Louisville **(1)**
Farm Credit Bank Bldg., 201 W. Main St.
Louisville, KY 40202
Tel.: 502-566-7000 (5.4%)
Fax: 502-566-7052
Emp.: 1,293
Agricultural Lending Institution
S.I.C.: 6159
Barney O. Barnett *(Pres.)*

Farm Credit Bank of Omaha **(1)**
Farm Credit Bank Bldg., 206 S. 19th St.
Omaha, NE 68102
Tel.: 402-348-3333 (5.4%)
Fax: 402-348-3699
Emp.: 913
Agricultural Lending Institution
S.I.C.: 6159
James D. Kirk *(Pres.)*

Farm Credit Bank of St. Louis **(1)**
1415 Olive St.
Saint Louis, MO 63103
Tel.: 314-342-3200 (5.4%)
Fax: 314-342-4592
Emp.: 1,151
Agricultural Lending Institution
S.I.C.: 6159
C.T. Fredrickson *(Pres.)*

Farm Credit Bank of St. Paul **(1)**
375 Jackson St.
Saint Paul, MN 55101
Tel.: 612-282-8800 (5.4%)
Fax: 612-282-8666
Emp.: 1,826
Agricultural Lending Institution
S.I.C.: 6159
Larry D. Bueglar *(Pres.)*

Farm Credit Bank of Spokane **(1)**
W. 601 First Ave.
Spokane, WA 99204
Tel.: 509-838-9300 (5.4%)
Fax: 509-838-9223
Emp.: 770
Agricultural Lending Institution
S.I.C.: 6159
Doyle Cook *(Pres.)*

Farm Credit Bank of Springfield **(1)**
Farm Credit Bank Bldg., 67 Hunt St.
Agawam, MA 01001
Tel.: 413-786-7600 (5.4%)
Fax: 413-789-0140
Emp.: 607
Agricultural Lending Institution
S.I.C.: 6159
James A. Pierson *(Chief Exec. Officer)*

Farm Credit Bank of Texas **(1)**
La Costa Office Park, 6210 Highway 290 East
Austin, TX 78723
Tel.: 512-465-0400 (5.4%)
Fax: 512-465-0675
Emp.: 816
Agricultural Lending Institution
S.I.C.: 6159
Arnold R. Henson *(Pres.)*

Farm Credit Bank of Wichita **(1)**
Farm Credit Bank Bldg., 245 No. Waco
Wichita, KS 67202
Tel.: 316-266-5100 (5.4%)
Fax: 316-266-5121
Emp.: 990
Agricultural Lending Institution
S.I.C.: 6159
Jerold L. Harris *(Pres.)*

Federal Intermediate Credit Bank of Jackson **(1)**
713 S. Pear Orchard Rd.
Ridgeland, MS 39157
Tel.: 601-977-8400 (2.7%)
Fax: 601-977-8383
Emp.: 296
Agricultural Lending Institution
S.I.C.: 6159
Don W. Oates *(Pres.)*

Saint Paul Bank for Cooperatives **(1)**
375 Jackson St.
Saint Paul, MN 55101
Tel.: 612-282-8200 (2.7%)
Fax: 612-282-8201
Emp.: 77
Agricultural Lending Institution
S.I.C.: 6159
Dennis Johnson *(Pres.)*

Springfield Bank for Cooperatives **(1)**
67 Hunt St.
Agawam, MA 01001
Tel.: 413-786-7600 (2.7%)
Fax: 413-789-0140
Emp.: 10
Agricultural Lending Institution
S.I.C.: 6159
James A. Pierson *(Pres.)*

Western Farm Credit Bank **(1)**
3636 American River Dr.
Sacramento, CA 95864
Tel.: 916-485-6000
Emp.: 400
Bank: Short, Intermediate & Long Term Agricultural Loans
S.I.C.: 6159
George D. Beitzel *(Pres.)*

FEDERATED MUTUAL INSURANCE COMPANY
121 E. Park Square
Owatonna, MN 55060
Tel.: 507-455-5200
Fax: 507-455-5199
Year Founded: 1904
Assets: $1,893,000,000
Liabilities: $1,490,000,000
Net Worth: $403,000,000
Approx.Sls.: $725,000,000
Emp.: 2,650
Fiscal Year-end: 12/31/91
Fire, Casualty, Accident & Health Insurance
S.I.C.: 6331; 6321
C.I. Buxton II *(Chm. Bd. & Chief Exec. Officer)*
Kirk N. Nelson *(Pres. & Chief Oper. Officer)*
A.T. Annexstad *(Sr. V.P.-Sls.)*
Donald R. Huff *(Sr. V.P.-Underwriting & Asst. Sec.)*
J.E. Meilahn *(Sr. V.P. & Chief Fin. Officer & Treas.)*
Lloyd Nelson *(Sr. V.P., Dir.-Admin. & Asst. Sec.)*
James L. Sheard *(Sr. V.P.-Human Resources)*
Jon Berglund *(1st V.P. & Dir.-Claims)*
F.H. Heiseke *(Sec.)*
Lois Ciffra *(Dir.-Telecommunications)*
Dean Fretheim *(Dir.-Corp. Travel Plnr. & Leasing)*
Howard Heckes *(Dir.-Personnel Training & Devel.)*
Dan Lewis *(Dir.-Meetings Plng.)*
Debra B. ReMine *(Dir.-Legal Counsel)*
Gary Tobiason *(Dir.-Data Processing)*
Brian Brose *(Mgr.-Personnel)*
Sherm Fjalstad *(Mgr.-Communications & Indus. Rels.)*
Tim Rice *(Mgr.-Adv. & Mdsg.)*
Steve Erdman *(Pur. Agent)*

Computer Systems/Hardware:
IBM

Outside Service Firm(s):

KPMG Peat Marwick*(Auditors)*
4200 Norwest Center, 90 S. 7th St.
Minneapolis, MN 55402
Tel.: 612-341-2222

Norwest Bank Minnesota, N.A.*(Major Banking Relationship)*
6th St. & Marquette Av.
Minneapolis, MN 55479
Tel.: 612-667-1234

FEED SERVICE CORP.
R.R. 1 Box 244A
Crete, NE 68333
Mailing Address:
P.O. Box 348,
Crete, NE 68333
Tel.: 402-826-2171 **NE**
Fax: 402-826-4646
Year Founded: 1951
Emp.: 35
Mfr. Feed & Nutrients
S.I.C.: 2048
Sam J. Brown *(Pres.)*
Edwin C. Brown *(Exec. V.P.)*
Larry Stallard *(Exec. V.P.)*

No. of Mfg. Plants/Facilities: 3

Outside Service Firm(s):

Fry, White & Guszak*(Auditors)*
Lincoln, NE

Alexander & Alexander*(Commercial Insurance Carrier)*
P.O. Box 82515
Lincoln, NE 68501-2515

Woods & Aitken*(Legal Firm)*
1500 American Charter Ctr., 206 S. 13th St.
Lincoln, NE 68508
Tel.: 402-474-0321

FEL-PRO INCORPORATED
7450 N. McCormick Blvd.
Skokie, IL 60076
Tel.: 708-674-7700
Telex: 4330056
Fax: 708-674-7700
Year Founded: 1918
Approx.Sls.: $275,000,000
Emp.: 2,000
Fiscal Year-end: 12/31/90
Import Export
Mfr. of Gaskets & Other Sealing Devices for the Internal Combustion Engine
S.I.C.: 3053; 3069; 3714; 5013; 5085
Ken Lehman *(Co-Chm. Bd.)*
David Weinberg *(Co-Chm.)*
Dennis Kessler *(Pres.)*
Guy Gunzberg *(V.P.-Data Processing)*
Paul Lehman *(V.P.)*
Robert O'Keefe *(V.P.-Indus. Rels.)*
Harold Rosen *(Controller)*
Richard Morris *(Mgr.-Mktg. Services)*

Computer Systems/Hardware:
IBM 4381

Outside Service Firm(s):

Altschuler, Melvoin & Glasser*(Auditors)*
30 S. Wecker Dr.
Chicago, IL 60606
Tel.: 312-207-2800

Washington National Insurance*(Group Insurer)*
Evanston, IL

First National Bank of Chicago*(Major Banking Relationship)*
One First National Plaza
Chicago, IL 60670
Tel.: 312-732-9781
Tel.: 312-732-4050
Fax: 312-732-4840
Fax: 312-732-3055

FELLERS & COMPANY
5918 W. Courtyard Dr., 5th Fl.
Austin, TX 78730
Tel.: 512-338-4500
Fax: 512-338-4510
Year Founded: 1969
Approx.Billings: $25,000,000
Emp.: 53
Recruitment, Healthcare, Oil Related Indus., Science & Technology, Telecommunications
Doyle Fellers *(Pres.)*
John Rasco *(Sr. V.P.)*
Angie Roberts *(Exec. Sec.)*

Computer Systems/Hardware:
DG, IBM, MacIntosh

FELLOWES MANUFACTURING CO.
1789 Norwood Ave.
Itasca, IL 60143-1095
Tel.: 708-893-1600 **IL**
Fax: 708-893-1648
Year Founded: 1917
Approx.Sls.: $150,000,000
Emp.: 1,000
Fiscal Year-end: 3/31/91
Mfr. Record Storage & Office Organization Products
S.I.C.: 2652; 3579; 3496; 3471
John Fellowes *(Chm. & Chief Exec. Officer)*
James E. Fellowes *(Pres. & Chief Oper. Officer)*
Clint Bull *(Exec. V.P.)*
Peter Fellowes *(Exec. V.P. & Sec.)*
Douglas P. Elder *(Sr. V.P. & Chief Fin. Officer)*
Robert L. Compagno *(V.P.-Sls.)*

Fellowes Manufacturing Co.—(Continued)

Arlis A. McLean *(V.P.-Human Resources)*
John Smith *(V.P.-Mfg. Devel.)*
Park Owens *(Dir.-Mktg.)*

Outside Service Firm(s):

KPMG Peat Marwick*(Auditors)*
Peat Marwick Plaza, 303 E. Wacker Dr.
Chicago, IL 60601
Tel.: 312-938-1000

Rooks, Pitts & Poust*(Legal Firm)*
55 W. Monroe St.
Chicago, IL 60603

Continental Bank N. A.*(Major Banking Relationship)*
231 S. LaSalle St.
Chicago, IL 60697
Tel.: 312-828-2345
Tel.: 800-426-5754
Telex: 312-828-1783

Divisions:

Bankers Box/Records Storage Systems **(1)**
1789 Norwood Ave.
Itasca, IL 60143
Tel.: 708-893-1600
Fax: 708-893-1648
S.I.C.: 2652

Copyholder Division **(1)**
1789 Norwood Ave.
Itasca, IL 60143
Tel.: 708-893-1600
Fax: 708-893-1648
S.I.C.: 2652

Information Processing Products **(1)**
1789 Norwood Ave.
Itasca, IL 60143
Tel.: 708-893-1600
Fax: 708-893-1648
S.I.C.: 3579

Power Shred Division **(1)**
1789 Norwood Ave.
Itasca, IL 60143
Tel.: 708-893-1600
Fax: 708-893-1648
S.I.C.: 3579

THE FELTERS COMPANY
22 West St.
Millbury, MA 01527
Tel.: 508-865-4401
Fax: 508-865-1367
Approx.Sls.: $16,000,000
Emp.: 500
Wool & Synthetic Felts & Felt Prods.
S.I.C.: 2231
Henry Ramella *(Pres.)*
Robert B. Coleman *(V.P.-Opers.)*
T.D. Knepper *(Dir.-Res. & Devel.)*

FELTON BRUSH INC.
315 Wilson St.
Manchester, NH 03103
Tel.: 603-669-1970
Tel.: 800-258-9702 **NH**
Fax: 603-669-0756
Year Founded: 1847
Sales Range: $10-19 Million
Emp.: 150
Import Export
Brushes
S.I.C.: 3991
Corporate Giving Program: Local Charities and Organizations Only
Richard H. Godfrey *(Chm. Bd.)*
Alan B. Jenkins *(Pres.)*
Alan Reischi *(Corp. Sec.)*
Mark Godfrey *(Mgr.-Opers.)*
D. Johnson *(Mgr.-Mktg.)*
Stephan Stone *(Mgr.-Data Processing)*
Sandra Boucher *(Dir.-Personnel)*
Stuart Rockwell *(Pur. Agent)*
Principal(s):
Richard H. Godfrey
Alan B. Jenkins
Mark Godfrey
D. Johnson
Stuart Rockwell

No. of Mfg. Plants/Facilities: 1

Computer Systems/Hardware:
IBM System 36

Outside Service Firm(s):

Coopers & Lybrand*(Auditors)*
Manchester, NH

Kendall Insurance Co.*(Commercial Insurance Carrier)*
P.O. Box 1840, 90 South Main Street
Rochester, NH 03867
Tel.: 603-332-5800
Telex: 94-4406

Sheehan, Phinney, Bass & Green*(Legal Firm)*
Manchester, NH

Bank East*(Major Banking Relationship)*
Manchester, NH

FENDER MUSICAL INSTRUMENTS
7975 N. Hayden Rd.
Scottsdale, AZ 85258
Tel.: 602-596-9690
Fax: 602-596-9690
Year Founded: 1985
Approx.Sls.: $25,000,000
Emp.: 450
Mfr. of Musical Instruments
S.I.C.: 3931
William Schultz *(Pres. & Chief Exec. Officer)*
Kurt J. Hemrich *(Exec V.P.-Opers. & Admin.)*
William L. Mendello *(Exec. V.P., Sec. & Treas.)*
Jim Cruickshank *(V.P.-Communications)*
Ed Rizzuto *(V.P.-Mktg., Acoustic Div.)*
Dan Smith *(V.P.-Mktg., Electric Guitars)*
Bill Hughes *(Dir.-Prod. Res. & Devel.)*

Outside Service Firm(s):

BankAmerica Corp.*(Major Banking Relationship)*
Anaheim, CA

FENNER MANHEIM
311 W. Stiegel St.
Manheim, PA 17545-1010
Tel.: 717-665-2421
Tel.: 800-243-3374
Fax: 717-665-2649
Year Founded: 1911
Approx.Sls.: $10,000,000
Emp.: 150
Fiscal Year-end: 8/31/92
Export
Shaft Mounts & Bushings: Shaft Mount, Keyless, Veelos Adjustable V-Belting, Transmission & Conveyor Belting, Manheim Variable Speed Belt
S.I.C.: 2141; 3714
Julian V. Bigden *(Pres.)*
John Mullineaux *(V.P.-Fin. & Gen. Mgr.)*
Ian L. Smith *(V.P.-Sls.)*

Computer Systems/Hardware:
IBM

H.G. FENTON MATERIAL COMPANY
7220 Trade St., Ste. 300
San Diego, CA 92121
Tel.: 619-566-2000 **CA**
Fax: 619-549-3589
Year Founded: 1951
Approx.Sls.: $63,000,000
Emp.: 520
Sand Construction; Gravel; Stone, Crushed or Broken; Cement; Calcareous Fufa, Crushed & Broken; Top Soil
S.I.C.: 5032; 1422; 5261
Henry F. Hunte *(Chm. Bd. & Chief Exec. Officer)*
David Vickers *(Pres. & Chief Oper. Officer)*
James Ruland *(Treas. & Sec.)*

Outside Service Firm(s):

Levitz, Zacks & Cicerie*(Auditors)*
San Diego, CA

San Diego Trust & Savings*(Major Banking Relationship)*
San Diego, CA

Subsidiary:

Pre-Mix Concrete Co. **(1)**
7220 Trade St., Ste.300
San Diego, CA 92121
Tel.: 619-586-2000
Ready-Mexed Concrete
S.I.C.: 3273
David Vickers *(Pres. & Chief Oper. Officer)*

FENTON PRESS, INC.
1544 Wrightwood
Addison, IL 60101
Tel.: 708-543-8114 **IL**
Fax: 708-543-8232
Year Founded: 1965
Assets: $8,174,000
Liabilities: $4,123,539
Net Worth: $4,050,461
Approx.Sls.: $16,000,000
Emp.: 116
Sheetfed & Lithographic Commercial Printing
S.I.C.: 2752
Ralph Tobiason *(Pres.)*
Alvin Blagaich *(V.P.-Sls. & Mktg.)*
Victor Franz *(V.P. & Sec.)*
Joseph Spokas *(V.P.-Fin.)*
Principal(s):
Ralph Tobiason
Alvin Blagaich
Victor Franz

Outside Service Firm(s):

Bauer, Morgan & VanLiere*(Auditors)*
Bloomingdale, IL

Harris Trust & Savings Bank*(Major Banking Relationship)*
111 W. Monroe St.
Chicago, IL 60690
Tel.: 312-461-2265
Tel.: 800-858-0840

FERGUSON ELECTRIC CONSTRUCTION CO., INC.
333 Ellicott St.
Buffalo, NY 14203
Tel.: 716-852-2010 **NY**
Fax: 716-852-2010
Year Founded: 1935
Approx.Sls.: $23,400,000
Emp.: 200
Electrical Contractor & Wholesale Electrical Equipment
S.I.C.: 1731; 5063
Whitworth Ferguson, Jr. *(Pres.)*
Robert A. Fredericks *(V.P.-Engrng.)*
Dean A. Little *(V.P.)*
Thomas K. Sonricker *(Controller)*
Jim Wachtel *(Dir.-Pur.)*

Outside Service Firm(s):

Lumsden McCormick & Co.*(Legal Firm)*
Buffalo, NY

FERGUSON INDUSTRIES
1900 W. Northwest Hwy.
Dallas, TX 75220
Tel.: 214-556-0010
Telex: 73-0915
Fax: 214-556-9149
Year Founded: 1953
Approx.Sls.: $15,000,000
Emp.: 20
Fiscal Year-end: 9/30/92
Export
Flex Poise Scales, Hopper Scales, Weigh Tanks, Liquid Mixers, Liquid Feed Blenders, Storage Systems, LP Gas Standby Systems, Gas Separators, Chemical Process Reactors, Chemical Process Systems, Oil Skimmers, Pollution Control Equipment
S.I.C.: 3596
Sam Ferguson *(Pres., Chief Exec. & Chief Oper. Officer)*
Sam Ferguson, Jr. *(Exec. V.P. & Dir.-Sls. & Mktg.)*
Harold E. Clark *(Mgr.-Adv. & Sls. Promo.)*
Jack Robertson *(Mgr.-Res. & Devel.)*

Computer Systems/Hardware:
Compaq-Network

Subsidiary:

Ferguson Industries International **(1)**
1900 W. Northwest Hwy.
Dallas, TX 75220
Tel.: 214-556-0010
Fax: 214-556-9149
Export
Mfr. of Weighing & Force-Measuring Machines & Devices
S.I.C.: 3596

FERGUSON MANUFACTURING & EQUIPMENT COMPANY
4900 Harry Hines Blvd.
Dallas, TX 75235
Tel.: 214-631-3000
Fax: 214-637-1530
Approx.Sls.: $17,000,000
Emp.: 70
Compaction Equipment Consisting Of Towed & Self-propelled Steel Wheel, Tamping, Pneumatic
S.I.C.: 3531
Dan Sheedan *(Pres.)*
Don Zimmermann *(V.P.-Opers.)*
Faye Zimmerman *(Coord.-Sls. & Mktg.)*

Outside Service Firm(s):

M Bank*(Major Banking Relationship)*
Dallas, TX

FERMAN OLDSMOBILE
1307 W. Kennedy Blvd.
Tampa, FL 33606
Mailing Address:
P.O. Box 1321
Tampa, FL 33601
Tel.: 813-253-0681 **FL**
Fax: 813-254-6430
Approx.Sls.: $100,000,000
Emp.: 550
New & Used Automobiles & Pickups
S.I.C.: 5511
James L. Ferman, Sr. *(Chm. Bd.)*
James L. Ferman, Jr. *(Pres.)*
Martha S. Ferman *(Sec. & Treas.)*

Outside Service Firm(s):

Ryals, Brimmer & Burek*(Auditors)*
Tampa, FL

Hill, Ward & Henderson*(Legal Firm)*
Tampa, FL

First Florida Bank*(Major Banking Relationship)*
P.O. Box 31265,
Tampa, FL 33631-3265
Tel.: 813-224-1475

Subsidiary:

Ferman Motor Car Co., Inc. **(1)**
1307 W. Kennedy Blvd.
Tampa, FL 33606
Tel.: 813-623-2411

New & Used Automobiles & Pickups
S.I.C.: 5511
James L. Ferman, Sr. *(Pres.)*

Fern/HanawayInc

FERN/HANAWAY, INC.
ADVERTISING/PUBLIC RELATIONS
Airport Professional Park,
2374 Post Rd.
Warwick, RI 02886
Tel.: 401-732-6610
Fax: 401-738-5027
Year Founded: 1952
Approx.Billings: $16,345,547
Emp.: 38
Full Service
Sanford M. Fern *(Pres.)*
James F. Hanaway, Jr. *(Exec. V.P., Treas.)*
Harold Tregar *(V.P.)*
Beverly A. Fern *(V.P., Fin.)*
Pasquale Sclama, Jr. *(V.P., Opers., Telecommunications)*
Diane DiLeo *(V.P.)*
David Hughes *(Dir., Pub. Rels.)*

Computer Systems/Hardware:
Desk Top, Publishing, Macs

FERRARA FOODS & CONFECTIONS, INC.
195 Grand St.
New York, NY 10013
Tel.: 212-226-6150
Telex: WVI 620070
Telex: RCA 232943
Fax: 212-226-0667
Year Founded: 1892
Approx.Sls.: $30,000,000
Emp.: 200
Fiscal Year-end: 6/30/90
Import Export
Torrone Ferrara Nougat Candy, Baba Au Rhum, Syrups For The Home & Commercial Use, Breadsticks From Italy, Motia Chocolate from Italy, Espresso Coffee & All Purpose Grind Coffee, Cannoli Shells, Almond Cookies, Pannettone Coffee Cake, Easter Candy, Clam Sauces, Mona Lisa Pasta From Italy
S.I.C.: 5145; 5141
Alfred Lepore *(Pres.)*
Eugene Marfuggi *(Exec. V.P.-Natl. Sls., Mktg. & Adv.)*
Ryan Bustros *(Chief Information Officer)*

JAMES FERRERA & SONS, INC.
135 Will Dr.
Canton, MA 02021
Tel.: 617-828-6150 **MA**
Fax: 617-821-2682
Year Founded: 1946
Assets: $18,000,000
Liabilities: $6,500,000
Net Worth: $11,500,000
Approx.Sls.: $280,000,000
Emp.: 950
Fiscal Year-end: 7/31/90
Wholesale Grocer
S.I.C.: 5141
Harold Ferrera *(Chief Exec. Officer)*
Kenneth G. Ferrera *(Pres.)*
James J. Ferrera *(Controller & Treas.)*
Michael Pessia *(Gen. Counsel)*
Diane Ferrera *(Dir.-Personnel)*
Alfred Ferrera *(Asst. Treas.)*
George Pereira *(Mgr.-Data Processing)*
Sandy Stewart *(Mgr.-Sls.)*
Principal(s):
Harold Ferrera

No. of U.S. Offices: 1

Computer Systems/Hardware:
IBM System 38

Outside Service Firm(s):

Bartz, Postl & Associates*(Auditors)*
Milwaukee, WI

Arkwright Mutual Insurance*(Commercial Insurance Carrier)*
225 Wyman St.
Waltham, MA 02254-9198
Tel.: 617-890-9300
Fax: 617-890-0075

Multibank*(International Bank Affiliate)*
Quincy, MA

Blue Cross of Massachusetts, Inc.*(Group Insurer)*
Boston, MA

Theise & Rosenthal*(Legal Firm)*
Boston, MA

South Shore Bank*(Major Banking Relationship)*
Quincy, MA

Subsidiaries:

First United Small Business Investment Co. **(1)**
135 Will Dr.
Canton, MA 02021
Tel.: 617-821-6150 (100%)
Fax: 617-821-2682
Small Business Investment
S.I.C.: 6159
Alfred Ferrera *(Chief Oper. Officer)*

Great Scott Food Markets, Inc. **(1)**
135 Will Dr.
Canton, MA 02021
Tel.: 617-821-6150
Fax: 617-821-2682
Emp.: 800
Retail Grocery Stores
S.I.C.: 5411
Paul Morley *(Chief Oper. Officer)*

Value King, Inc. **(1)**
135 Will Dr.
Canton, MA 02021
Tel.: 617-821-6150
Fax: 617-821-2682
Emp.: 120
Retail Grocery Stores
S.I.C.: 5411
Paul Morley *(Chief Oper. Officer)*

FERRELL COMPANIES INC./ FERRELLGAS
One Liberty Plaza
Liberty, MO 64068
Tel.: 816-792-1600 **MO**
Fax: 816-792-7985
Year Founded: 1939
Approx.Sls.: $500,000,000
Emp.: 3,000
Fiscal Year-end: 7/31/92
Import
Markets Propane, Natural Gas Liquids, Olefins, Butane & Other Natural Gas Liquid Products
S.I.C.: 5984
James E. Ferrell *(Chm. Bd., Pres. & Chief Exec. Officer)*
Geoffrey Ramsden *(Chief Fin. Officer)*
Bradley Cochennet *(V.P.)*
Stephen Mills *(Controller)*
Danley K. Sheldon *(Treas.)*
David Weinmeister *(Dir.-Information Systems)*
Rhonda Smiley *(Managing Dir.-Legal Affairs)*
Brian M. Smith *(Managing Dir.-Mktg. & Communications)*
Michelle Warner *(Managing Dir.-Employee Services)*
Noni Korst *(Mgr.-Pur.)*
Principal(s):
James E. Ferrell

No. of Mfg. Plants/Facilities: 525
No. of U.S. Offices: 525

Computer Systems/Hardware:
Data General DEC 6520, DEC 6410, DEC 3600, NCR 9400 (2 units)

Outside Service Firm(s):

Deloitte & Touche*(Auditors)*
1010 Grand Ave.
Kansas City, MO 64106-2232
Tel.: 816-474-6180

Reliance Insurance Co.*(Commercial Insurance Carrier)*
New York, NY

Aetna Life & Casualty*(Group Insurer)*
Philadelphia, PA

Smith, Gill, Fisher & Butts*(Legal Firm)*
One Kansas City Place, 35th Fl, 1200 Main St.
Kansas City, MO 64105
Tel.: 816-474-7400

Wells Fargo Bank*(Major Banking Relationship)*
New York, NY

Subsidiaries:

Ferrell North America **(1)**
16800 Greenspoint Park Dr.
Houston, TX 77060
Tel.: 713-874-9494
Fax: 713-872-7218
Emp.: 40
Import
S.I.C.: 5172
James Ferrell *(Chm.)*

Ferrellgas, Inc. **(1)**
One Liberty Plaza
Liberty, MO 64068
Tel.: 816-792-1600
Emp.: 3,002
S.I.C.: 5172; 5984
James Ferrell *(Pres.)*

FERRO UNION, INC.
1000 W. Francisco St.
Torrance, CA 90502
Tel.: 310-538-9900 **DE**
Fax: 310-768-0082
Year Founded: 1965
Approx.Sls.: $175,000,000
Emp.: 425
Mfr. of Steel; Aluminum Bars, Rods, Ingots, Sheets, Pipes & Plates; Seamless Steel Tubes
S.I.C.: 3317
Albert Perrish *(Chm. Bd.)*
Thomas W. Riodan *(Pres. & Chief Exec. Officer)*
William G. Bollman *(Exec. V.P.)*
Steven W. Scheinkman *(V.P.-Fin.)*
Thomas L. Thomas *(Treas.)*

Outside Service Firm(s):

Ernst & Young*(Auditors)*
Torrance, CA

Subsidiary:

Samsteel, Inc. **(1)**
1000 W. Francisco St.
Torrance, CA 90502
Tel.: 310-538-9900
Emp.: 425
Mfr. & Marketing of Steel; Seamless Steel Tubes
S.I.C.: 5051; 3317
Albert Perrish *(Chm. Bd.)*
Thomas W. Riodan *(Pres.)*
William G. Bollman *(Exec. V.P.)*
Steven W. Scheinkman *(V.P.-Fin.)*
Thomas L. Thomas *(Treas.)*

FERROUS PROCESSING & TRADING CO.
9100 John Kronk Ave.
Detroit, MI 48210
Tel.: 313-582-2910
Fax: 313-582-1949
Approx.Sls.: $50,000,000
Emp.: 125
Metal Scrap Processing
S.I.C.: 3312; 3313; 3469
Jeffrey N. Cole *(Chm.)*
John Morrissey *(Exec. V.P. & Chief Fin. Officer)*
Mark Sheffer *(V.P.)*
Ralph Tomlinson, Jr. *(V.P.)*
Gary W. Schier *(Treas.)*

Outside Service Firm(s):

N.B.D. Bank, N.A.*(Major Banking Relationship)*
611 Woodward Ave.
Detroit, MI 48226
Tel.: 313-225-1122
Fax: 313-225-3420

FERRY-MORSE SEED COMPANY
(Wholly-Owned Sub. of Limagrain S.A.)
555 Codoni St.
Modesto, CA 95354
Mailing Address:
P.O. Box 4938
Modesto, CA 95352-4938
Tel.: 209-579-7333
Approx.Sls.: $30,000,000
Emp.: 350
Fiscal Year-end: 6/30/90
Vegetable Seed, Flower Seed, Grass Seed
S.I.C.: 0181
Richard Parvel *(V.P.-Domestic Div.)*
R.P. Baermann *(V.P.-Plng.)*
Phil Robnett *(V.P.-Mktg. & Prod. Devel.)*
G.R. Allbritten *(Chief Oper. Officer)*

Divisions:

Advance Seed Co. **(1)**
600 Stephen Beale Dr.
Fulton, KY 42041
Tel.: 502-472-3400
Fax: 502-472-3402
Emp.: 135
Fiscal Year-end: 6/30/90
Import Export
Computer Systems/Hardware:
IBM 400
Packaged Vegetable, Flower & Lawn Seeds
S.I.C.: 0181
Jack Simpson *(Chief Exec. Officer)*
Chuck Atkins *(V.P.-Intl. Sls.)*
Francois Nicolas *(V.P.-Mktg.)*
Mike Tate *(Ntl. Sls. Mgr.)*
Michael Daniel *(Mktg. Mgr.)*
B. Miller *(Pur. Agent)*

International Div. **(1)**
P.O. Box 4938
Modesto, CA 95352
Tel.: 209-579-7333

Vegetable & Flower Div. **(1)**
P.O. Box 4938
Modesto, CA 95352
Tel.: 209-579-7333

FESSEL, SIEGFRIEDT & MOELLER, INC.
981 S. Third St.
Louisville, KY 40203
Mailing Address:
P.O. Box 1031,
Louisville, KY 40201
Tel.: 502-585-5154
Year Founded: 1955
Approx.Billings: $14,000,000
Emp.: 30
Rudy F. Moeller, Sr. *(Pres.)*
Rudy D. Moeller, Jr. *(Exec. V.P.)*
John W. Ellis *(V.P.)*
C. Daniel Hartlage *(V.P., Pub. Rels.)*
Timothy W. Wolf *(Sec., Treas.)*
Stephanie S. Coburn *(Office Mgr.)*
Andrea M. Cummings *(Dir., Mktg. Services)*
Donald R. Doninger *(Sr. Mktg. Consultant)*

Computer Systems/Hardware:
NCR-Tower 32/600

FEUER LEATHER CORPORATION
8 Skyline Dr.
Hawthorne, NY 10352
Tel.: 914-592-0073 **NY**
Fax: 914-592-0075
Year Founded: 1954
Approx.Sls.: $150,000,000
Emp.: 1,700
Import Export
Wholesale Distribution & Marketing of Leather & Cut Stock Hides
S.I.C.: 5159; 5199
Irwin Feuer *(Pres. & Chief Exec. Officer)*
Robert Watson *(Exec. V.P.)*
Myron Feuer *(Sec.)*

Outside Service Firm(s):

Irving Trust Co.*(Major Banking Relationship)*
One Wall St.
New York, NY 10015

FIBER MATERIALS, INC.
Biddeford Industrial Park, 5 Morin St.
Biddeford, ME 04005
Tel.: 207-282-5911
Twx: 944480
Fax: 207-282-7529
Year Founded: 1969
Approx.Sls.: $25,000,000
Emp.: 750
Develop & Manufacture High Temperature & Composite Materials
S.I.C.: 3999
Maurice H. Subilia *(Pres.)*
Dave Loper *(Mgr.-Opers.)*
David Hanrahan *(Pur. Agent)*

Outside Service Firm(s):

Coopers & Lybrand*(Auditors)*
Portland, ME

Foley, Hoag & Eliot*(Legal Firm)*
One Post Office Square
Boston, MA 02210
Tel.: 617-482-1390

First National Bank*(Major Banking Relationship)*
Boston, MA

FIBERESIN INDUSTRIES INC.
P.O. Box 88, 37031 E. Wisconsin Ave.
Oconomowoc, WI 53066
Tel.: 414-567-4427
Fax: 414-567-4814
Year Founded: 1946
Approx.Sls.: $27,000,000
Emp.: 210
Fiscal Year-end: 12/31/91
Export
Mfr. Decorative Laminated Particle Board
S.I.C.: 3089
Harland W. Huston *(Chm. & Pres.)*
William K. Keck *(V.P.)*
Wayne F. Schefelker *(Sec. & Treas.)*
Carlton Gieseke *(Mgr.-Sls. Promo)*
Ken Johnson *(Mgr.-Mfg.)*

Computer Systems/Hardware:
IBM

Subsidiary:

Rodman Industries **(1)**
2601 Cleveland
Marinette, WI 54143
Tel.: 715-735-9541
Fax: 715-735-6148
Approx.Sls.: $12,000,000
Emp.: 50
Fiscal Year-end: 12/31/90
Export
Resincore, Custom Particle Boards, Medium & High Densities, Urea Boards, Phenolic Urea-Formaldehyde Free Boards, HPL Cold-Pressing Service
S.I.C.: 2493
H.M. Huston *(Pres.)*
Tony Hopp *(Plant Mgr.)*
T.A. Klasell *(Sls. Mgr.)*
Sharon A. Brigham *(Asst. Sls. Mgr.)*

FIBRE GLASS-EVERCOAT COMPANY INC.
6600 Cornell Rd.
Cincinnati, OH 45242
Tel.: 513-489-7600
Telex: 214-645
Fax: 513-489-9229
Year Founded: 1953
Approx.Sls.: $27,000,000
Emp.: 170
Marine & Automotive Repair Products
S.I.C.: 3731; 3429; 3714; 3949
Larry Kaucheck *(Pres.)*
Ron Stibich *(Sr. V.P.-Mktg. & Sls.)*
Daman Infalvi *(V.P.-Fin. & Chief Fin. Officer)*
Gary Frederick *(Asst. Controller)*
Ron Dreyer *(Dir.-Opers.)*
Ron Smith *(Mgr.-Data Processing)*

No. of Mfg. Plants/Facilities: 5
No. of U.S. Offices: 4
No. of Foreign Offices: 1

Outside Service Firm(s):

Price Waterhouse*(Auditors)*
2200 Chemed Center, 255 E. 5th St.
Cincinnati, OH 45202-4798
Tel.: 513-621-1900

Milgrim Thomajan Jacobs & Lee, P.C.*(Legal Firm)*
53 Wall St.
New York, NY 10005-2815
Tel.: 212-858-5300

THE FIBRE-METAL PRODUCTS COMPANY
Baltimore Pike & S. Brenton Lake Rd.
Concordville, PA 19331
Mailing Address:
P.O. Box 248,
Concordville, PA 19331
Tel.: 215-459-5300
Fax: 215-358-9138
Approx.Sls.: $14,000,000
Emp.: 185
Industrial Safety & Welding Safety Equip.; Superlectric, Superglas, Superflex, Superlite, Scalpcap, Monarch, Eyeline, Tigerhood, Sologoggle, Noisegard, Slide-lok, Action-Specs
S.I.C.: 3842; 3548
Charles E. Bowers, Jr. *(Pres.)*
Deborah A. Schoultz *(Treas.)*
James Foster *(Pur. Dir.)*
Robert J. Ennamorato *(Mktg. Mgr.)*

FIBREBOND CORPORATION
1300 Davenport
Minden, LA 71055
Tel.: 318-377-1030 **LA**
Fax: 318-377-5756
Approx.Sls.: $14,000,000
Emp.: 177
Mfr. of Concrete Products & Suppressant Systems
S.I.C.: 3272; 1711
Claud B. Walker *(Chm. Bd.)*
Steven L. Schoonover *(Pres. & Chief Exec. Officer)*

Outside Service Firm(s):

James & James*(Auditors)*
Shreveport, LA

Peoples Bank & Trust*(Major Banking Relationship)*
Minden, LA

FICKS REED COMPANY
4900 Charlemar Dr.
Cincinnati, OH 45227
Tel.: 513-561-2100 **OH**
Fax: 513-561-1135
Year Founded: 1885
Sales Range: $10-19 Million
Emp.: 150
Fiscal Year-end: 12/31/91
Import of Rattan Furniture; Design & Production Of Upholstry
S.I.C.: 2519; 2512; 5021
Lee B. Ficks *(Pres., Chief Exec. Officer, & Treas.)*
Thomas D. Aders *(V.P.-Sls.)*
Roy Tate *(Chief Fin. Officer)*
Joy S. Ficks *(Sec.)*
Michael Hirschfeld *(Gen. Counsel & Asst. Sec.)*
Gerry S. Hinig *(Dir.-Fashion & Coord.-Design)*
Arthur A. Hensler *(Mgr.-Quality Control)*
Michael Marshall *(Mgr.-Engrng. & Sourcing)*
Donald Polochak *(Mgr.-Engrng.)*
Thomas Reenan *(Mgr.-Mfg.)*
Babu M. Thomas *(Mgr.-Data Processing)*
Chris Yaeger *(Mgr.-Pur. & Traffic)*
Principal(s):
Lee B. Ficks

No. of Mfg. Plants/Facilities: 2
No. of U.S. Offices: 3
No. of Foreign Offices: 1

Computer Systems/Hardware:
IBM System 36

Outside Service Firm(s):

Ernst & Young*(Auditors)*
1300 Chiquita Center, 250 E. Fifth St.
Cincinnati, OH 45202
Tel.: 513-621-6454

Paul V. Gosiger*(Commercial Insurance Carrier)*
602 Main Street
Cincinnati, OH

Walter P. Dolle*(Group Insurance Broker/Consult)*
49 E. 4th St., Ste. 600
Cincinnati, OH
Tel.: 513-421-6515

Graydon, Head & Ritchey*(Legal Firm)*
1900 Fifth Third Center
Cincinnati, OH 45202
Tel.: 513-621-6464

Star Bank*(Major Banking Relationship)*
425 Walnut Street
Cincinnati, OH 45202
Tel.: 513-632-4000

FIDELITY INVESTMENTS (FMR CORP.)
82 Devonshire St.
Boston, MA 02109
Tel.: 617-570-7000
Fax: 617-728-7258
Year Founded: 1946
Approx.Rev.: $1,473,700,000
Emp.: 7,700
Fiscal Year-end: 12/31/91
Fund Management
S.I.C.: 6722
Edward C. Johnson III *(Chm. & Chief Exec. Officer)*
Denis McCarthy *(Sr. V.P. & Chief Fin. Officer)*
Robert C. Pozen *(Sr. V.P. & Gen. Counsel)*
Dennis Driscoll *(Sr. V.P.-Adv.)*

Computer Systems/Hardware:
IBM

Outside Service Firm(s):

Coopers & Lybrand*(Auditors)*
1 Post Office Square
Boston, MA 02110
Tel.: 617-574-5000
Fax: 617-345-0398

Brown Brothers, Harriman & Co.*(Major Banking Relationship)*
Boston, MA

Brown Brothers, Harriman & Co.*(Major Banking Relationship)*
59 Wall St.
New York, NY 10005-2818
Tel.: 212-493-8029

Subsidiary:

FMR Corp. **(1)**
82 Devonshire St.
Boston, MA 02109
Tel.: 617-570-7000
Emp.: 100
Holding Co. & Mutual Funds
S.I.C.: 6719; 6722
Edward C. Johnson *(Chief Exec. Officer)*

FIDUCIARY TRUST CO. INTERNATIONAL
Two World Trade Center
New York, NY 10048-0772
Tel.: 212-466-4100
Year Founded: 1931
Approx.Sls.: $74,736,000
Emp.: 601
Fiscal Year-end: 12/31/91
Managers of Investments, Trustee & Executor
Lawrence S. Huntington *(Chm. Bd.)*
Jeremy H. Biggs *(Vice Chm.)*
Michael O. Magdol *(Vice Chm.-Chief Fin. Officer)*
Landon Thomas *(Vice Chm.)*
L. F. Boker Doyle *(Pres.)*
Anne M. Tatlock *(Exec. V.P.-Investment)*
James R. Deane *(Exec. V.P., Gen. Counsel & Sec.)*
Richard H. Turrell *(Sr. V.P.-Investment)*
Yvette C. Bockstein *(Sr. V.P.-Investment)*
Eleanor Schmidt *(Sr. V.P.-Investment)*
Donald L. Keene *(Sr. V.P.-Investment)*
Jeanne Y. Russell *(Sr. V.P.-Investment)*
Charles W. Beck, Jr. *(Sr. V.P.-Investment)*
Peter V. Haight *(Sr. V.P.-Investment)*
Christopher J. Elkus *(Sr. V.P.-Investment)*
Julia W. Linsley *(Sr. V.P.-Investment)*
William L. Strong *(Sr. V.P.-Investment)*
George J. Mullen *(Sr. V.P.-Mktg.)*
James E. Klein *(Sr. V.P.-Human Resources)*
David K. Stone *(Exec. V.P. & Dir.-Opers.)*
Richard J. Potter *(Sr. V.P.-Investment)*
Dino J. Veronese *(Sr. V.P.-Investment)*
Pascal F. Wirz *(Sr. V.P.-Investment)*
Edmond L. Murphy *(Sr. V.P.-Investment)*
Barry J. McKeon *(Sr. V.P. & Comptroller)*
Stuart C. Hochberger *(Sr. V.P.-Investment)*
Francis B. Shephard *(V.P.-Investment)*
Douglas Caverly *(V.P.-Investment)*
Sheila H. Coco *(Sr. V.P.-Investment)*
Donald F. Stubbs *(V.P. & Trust Counsel)*
Oscar G. Montes *(V.P. & Trust Officer)*
Robert D. Mattson *(V.P. & Trust Officer)*
Fredrick Yorke III *(V.P. & Treas.)*
Carlo J. Oliva *(Opers. Officer-Pur. Dir.)*
Eileen McEntegart *(Bus. Devel. Asst.)*

FIDUCIARY TRUST COMPANY INTERNATIONAL
Two World Trade Center
New York, NY 10048
Tel.: 212-466-4100
Investment Management, Trust Services
S.I.C.: 6022; 6733; 6282

Lawrence S. Huntington *(Chm. Bd. & Chief Exec. Officer)*
Jeremy Biggs *(Vice Chm.)*
Landon Thomas *(Vice Chm.)*
L. F. Boker Doyle *(Pres.)*
Michael O. Magdol *(Exec. V.P. & Chief Fin. Officer)*
James R. Deane *(Exec. V.P., Sec. & Gen. Counsel)*
Anne M. Tatlock *(Exec. V.P.)*
Barry J. McKeon *(Sr. V.P. & Comptroller)*
David K. Stone *(Sr. V.P. & Dir.-Opers.)*
James E. Klein *(Sr. V.P.-Human Resources)*
George J. Mullen, Jr. *(Sr. V.P.)*
J. Alan Steinkamp *(Sr. V.P.-Real Estate)*
Frederick Yorke, III *(V.P. & Treas.)*
Mary A. Mullen *(V.P. & Asst. Counsel)*

Non-U.S. Holdings:

Fiduciary Trust Company of New York Ltd. **(1)**
30 Old Burlington St.
London, W1, United Kingdom
Tel.: 071-734-2648 (100%)
Investments
S.I.C.: 6282
John A. Hockin *(Sr. V.P.)*

Fiduciary Trust (International) S.A. **(1)**
67, rue de Saint-Jean, P.O. Box 227 CH-1211
Geneva, 11, Switzerland
Tel.: 022 32 10 00 (100%)
Telex: 422 224
Fax: 022 31 43 91
Adamir Piaget *(V.P. & Controller)*

FIELD CONTAINER COMPANY, L.P.
(Formerly Field Container Corporation)
1500 Nicholas Blvd.
Elk Grove Village, IL 60007
Tel.: 708-437-1700 **DE**
Fax: 708-956-3249
Year Founded: 1942
Approx.Sls.: $350,000,000
Emp.: 2,000
Fiscal Year-end: 4/30/92
Manufacture of Folding Paper Cartons & Ink
S.I.C.: 2657; 2893
Eli Field *(Chm. Bd.)*
Lawrence Field *(Pres. & Chief Exec. Officer)*
James Eckstein *(Pres.-Elk Grove/Westfield)*
Michael Nussbaum *(Pres.-Acquisitions)*
Richard Sachse *(Chief Oper. Officer)*
Vincent J. Hotton *(V.P.-Fin.-Elk Grove/Westfield)*
Jay Nevins *(V.P.-Fin.)*
Kimberly Brown *(Sec.)*
Jeff Arnesen *(Corp. Controller)*
Dwight Lucia *(Dir.-Pur.)*
John Ozimek *(Mgr.-Data Processing)*
Principal(s):
Eli Field
Lawrence Field
Kimberly Brown
Barbara Field

Computer Systems/Hardware:
IBM System 36

Outside Service Firm(s):

BDO Seidman*(Auditors)*
111 E. Wacker Dr.
Chicago, IL 60601

Katten, Muchin & Zavis*(Legal Firm)*
525 W. Monroe St., Ste. 1600
Chicago, IL 60661-3693
Tel.: 312-902-5200

American National Bank & Trust Company of Chicago*(Major Banking Relationship)*
33 N. LaSalle St.
Chicago, IL 60602
Tel.: 312-661-5000
Fax: 312-661-6417

Subsidiary:

Handschy Industries **(1)**
120 25th St.
Bellwood, IL 60104
Tel.: 708-547-7500
Manufacture of Ink
S.I.C.: 2893
Jim Shaw *(Chief Oper. Officer)*

FIELD PACKING COMPANY
P.O. Box 766
Owensboro, KY 42302
Tel.: 502-926-2324
Fax: 502-926-5077
Year Founded: 1915
Approx.Sls.: $70,000,000
Emp.: 480
Import Export
Processor of Meat, Sausage & Smoked Meat Products
S.I.C.: 2011; 2013
Sam Wyse *(Pres.)*
Keith Luedke *(V.P.-Sls.)*
Michael Daniel *(Sec., Treas. & Controller)*
Ron Neal *(Dir.-Personnel)*
Joseph Roberts *(Dir.-Pur.)*
Kevin Dykman *(Dir.-Data Processing)*
Richard Barsky *(Dir.-Mktg. & Adv.)*

FIELDALE CORPORATION
P.O. Box 558
Baldwin, GA 30511-0558
Tel.: 706-778-5100
Fax: 706-778-3767
Year Founded: 1972
Approx.Sls.: $300,000,000
Emp.: 3,500
Fiscal Year-end: 9/30/92
Export
Poultry Processing
S.I.C.: 2015
Joe Hatfield *(Chm. Bd. & Chief Exec. Officer)*
Thomas A. Arrendale, Jr. *(Pres.)*
Tom Hensley *(V.P. & Chief Fin. Officer)*
Glenn Ingram *(Treas.)*
James Swain *(Dir.-Data Processing)*
Michael Riddell *(Mgr.-Data Processing)*

Computer Systems/Hardware:
IBM Systems 36 & 38

Outside Service Firm(s):

Price Waterhouse*(Auditors)*
100 Cumberland Circle, Ste. 1400
Atlanta, GA 30339

Alexander & Alexander*(Commercial Insurance Carrier)*
Two Piedmont Center, 3565 Piedmont Rd. N.E.
Atlanta, GA 30363

Alston & Bird*(Legal Firm)*
One Atlantic Center, 1201 West Peachtree St.
Atlanta, GA 30309-3424
Tel.: 404-881-7000

NationsBank*(Major Banking Relationship)*
35 Broad St.
Atlanta, GA 30303
Tel.: 404-581-2121
Tel.: 800-848-8198

NationsBank*(Pension Manager)*
35 Broad St.
Atlanta, GA 30303
Tel.: 404-581-2121
Tel.: 800-848-8198

FIESTA MART INC.
5235 Katy Fwy.
Houston, TX 77007
Mailing Address:
P.O. Box 7481
Houston, TX 77248-7481
Tel.: 713-869-5060 **TX**
Fax: 713-869-6197
Year Founded: 1972
Assets: $183,000,000
Liabilities: $97,000,000
Net Worth: $86,000,000
Approx.Sls.: $555,000,000
Emp.: 5,000
Fiscal Year-end: 5/31/92
Import Export
Retail Supermarkets
S.I.C.: 5411
Donald L. Bonham *(Chm. Bd. & Chief Exec. Officer)*
O.C. Mendenhall *(Vice Chm.)*
Louis Katopodis *(Pres. & Chief Oper. Officer)*
Bob Walker *(Exec. V.P. & Chief Fin. Officer)*
Liz Marshall *(Controller)*
Ray Rodriguez *(Treas.)*
Joe Jurica *(Gen. Mgr.)*
Allen Gray *(Mktg. Dir.)*
Gil Russell *(Data Processing Dir.)*
David Kayle *(Real Estate Dir.)*
Juanita Elizondo *(Human Resources Dir.)*
Keith Jacobsen *(Adv. Dir.)*
Joe Coronado *(Personnel Training & Devel.)*
Bernie Murphy *(Govt. Affairs)*
Brenda Gerland *(Corp. Grants Contact)*
Principal(s):
Donald L. Bonham
O.C. Mendenhall

Outside Service Firm(s):

Coopers & Lybrand*(Auditors)*
1100 Louisiana, Ste. 4100
Houston, TX 77002
Tel.: 713-757-5200
Fax: 713-757-5249

Willis Corroon*(Commercial Insurance Carrier)*
1225 N. Loop West, #700
Houston, TX 77008

MONY Capital Markets*(Investment Banker)*
Rockville, MD

Dickerson, Carmouche & Jones*(Legal Firm)*
Houston, TX

First City National Bank*(Major Banking Relationship)*
Houston, TX

THE FIGARO COMPANY, INC.
3601 Executive Blvd.
Mesquite, TX 75149
Mailing Address:
P.O. Box 850117
Mesquite, TX 75185-0117
Tel.: 214-288-3587
Fax: 214-288-1887
Year Founded: 1904
Emp.: 6
Fiscal Year-end: 12/31/90
Export
Hickory Liquid Barbecue Smoke, Artificial Liquid Sweetener, Fabuloso Fajitas Marinade, Figaro Mesquite Smoke Marinade
S.I.C.: 2033
J.S. McKenney *(Pres.)*
J.K. McKenney *(V.P.)*
M.P. McKenney *(Sec. & Treas.)*

FIKE CORPORATION
704 S. 10th St.
Blue Springs, MO 64015
Tel.: 816-229-3405
Fax: 816-228-9277
Year Founded: 1945
Approx.Sls.: $20,000,000
Emp.: 202
Export
Mfr. of Rupture Discs, Flanges, Pressure Relief Devices, Explosive Vents, Fire Extinguishing Systems & Components & Metal Fabrication Explosion Suppression Systems
S.I.C.: 3491; 3492; 3494; 3569
Lester L. Fike, Jr. *(Chm. Bd. & Chief Exec. Officer)*
Gary C. Batz *(Pres.)*
William A. Eckholm *(Grp. V.P.)*
Heikki Gronlund *(V.P.-Intl. Opers.)*
Maxwell Jewel *(V.P.-Fin.)*
Logan J. Wilson *(V.P.-Legal Affairs & Sec.)*
Bill Storck *(Controller)*
Charles Laitner *(Dir.-Engrng.)*
William Copelin *(Mgr.-Adv.)*
Hal Cross *(Mgr.-Data Processing)*
Jeannie Foster *(Mgr.-Customer Service-Rupture Discs)*
Marvin Griffey *(Mgr.-Quality Assurance)*
Edith Smith *(Mgr.-Personnel)*
Emmett Stewart *(Mgr.-Pur.)*

Outside Service Firm(s):

Ernst & Young*(Auditors)*
One Kansas City Place, 1200 Main St.
Kansas City, MO 64105

The Merchants Bank*(Major Banking Relationship)*
Kansas City, MO

FILCO, INC.
1433 Fulton Ave., Suite D
Sacramento, CA 95825
Tel.: 916-483-4526
Fax: 916-978-3455
Year Founded: 1972
Approx.Sls.: $30,000,000
Emp.: 80
Retail Televisions, Stereo Equipment, Cameras, Photographic Equipment, Major Household Appliances & Microwaves
S.I.C.: 5722; 5736; 5946
Tony Saca *(Pres.)*
Gabriel Batarseh *(Sec. & Treas.)*

Outside Service Firm(s):

Jim Rice & Associates*(Auditors)*
Sacramento, CA

Sanwa Bank*(Major Banking Relationship)*
Sacramento, CA

Filko Automotive Products
(See F & B Manufacturing Co. Listing)

FIMBEL DOOR CORPORATION
Coddington Rd.
Whitehouse, NJ 08888
Mailing Address:
P.O. Box 96
Whitehouse, NJ 08888
Tel.: 908-534-4151 **NJ**
Fax: 201-534-5682
Year Founded: 1924
Approx.Sls.: $16,000,000
Emp.: 225
Mfr. of Overhead Type Wood, Steel, Aluminum & Fiberglass Garage Doors, Electric Operators & Controls & Complete Repair Parts
S.I.C.: 2431; 3231; 3442; 3625
Edward Fimbel, Jr. *(Chm. Bd. & Pres.)*
Paul Fimbel *(V.P.)*
Edward Fimbel, III *(Sec.)*
Chandler Knight *(Mgr.-Sls.)*
James Wood *(Pur. Agent)*
Byron D. Ehlers, Jr. *(Chief Engr.)*

Fimbel Door Corporation—(Continued)

Outside Service Firm(s):

Dennis G. Barker*(Auditors)*
Hawthorne, NJ

Porzio, Bromberg & Newman, P.C.*(Legal Firm)*
Morristown, NJ

Midlantic National Bank*(Major Banking Relationship)*
Metro Park Plaza,
Edison, NJ 08818
Tel.: 908-321-8000

FINANCIAL ASSOCIATES
10977 Granada Lane
Overland Park, KS 66211
Mailing Address:
P.O. Box 7730
Overland Park, KS 66207
Tel.: 913-491-5200
Fax: 913-491-5204
Year Founded: 1976
Approx.Sls.: $15,500,000
Emp.: 21
Fiscal Year-end: 12/31/90
Health Insurance Brokerage
S.I.C.: 6411
Charles T. Stumpf *(Chm. Bd., Pres., Chief Exec. Officer & Treas.)*
Kimberly Beach *(V.P.-Admin.)*

Principal(s):
Charles T. Stumpf

No. of Mfg. Plants/Facilities: 1
No. of U.S. Offices: 1

Computer Systems/Hardware:
Cado; Epson

Outside Service Firm(s):

National Travelers Life*(Group Insurer)*
820 Keo Way
Des Moines, IA 50309-1527

FINANCIAL NETWORK INVESTMENT
2780 Skypark Dr.
Torrance, CA 90505
Tel.: 310-326-3100 CA
Fax: 213-316-0133
Year Founded: 1983
Approx.Sls.: $24,000,000
Emp.: 50
Security Brokers
S.I.C.: 6211
Miles Gordon *(Pres.)*
John Simmers *(Exec. V.P.)*

Outside Service Firm(s):

MetroBank*(Major Banking Relationship)*
Torrance, CA

FINANCIAL PROTECTION SERVICES INC.
6860 Commercial Dr.
Springfield, VA 22151-4208
Tel.: 703-941-3232
Fax: 703-256-4832
Holding Company
S.I.C.: 6719
David Phillips *(Chm. Bd. & Chief Exec. Officer)*

Outside Service Firm(s):

Price Waterhouse*(Auditors)*
Bethesda, MD

Subsidiaries:

CCC Information Services (1)
640 N. LaSalle
Chicago, IL 60610
Tel.: 312-787-2640
Fax: 312-944-2795
Vehicle Evaluations Due To Loss Or Damage
Howard A. Tullman *(Chm. Bd.)*
Dave Phillips *(Pres. & Chief Exec. Officer)*
David B. Mullen *(Chief Fin. Officer)*
Dan Dicaro *(Controller)*
Joe Fisher *(Legal Officer)*

Credit Card Service Corporation (1)
6860 Commercial Dr.
Springfield, VA 22150
Tel.: 703-941-3232
Fax: 703-256-4754
David Phillips *(Chm. Bd. & Chief Exec. Officer)*
Richard Flaherty *(Pres. & Chief Oper. Officer)*

FINANCIAL WORLD PARTNERS
1328 Broadway
New York, NY 10001
Tel.: 212-594-5030
Fax: 212-629-0021
Year Founded: 1902
Approx.Sls.: $20,000,000
Emp.: 100
Fiscal Year-end: 12/31/91
Export
Publishers
S.I.C.: 2741
M. Meagher *(Chm. Bd.)*
Douglas A. McIntyre *(Pres. & Chief Exec. Officer)*
James Schiavone *(Chief Fin. Officer & Exec. V.P.)*
John R. Campbell *(Sr. V.P. & Publisher)*
Lawrence Hedblom *(Sr. V.P.)*
Alan Schafer *(V.P.-Mfg. & Distr.)*
Ken Margiotta *(Controller)*
Debbie Kaplan *(Dir.-Mktg.)*
Tom Gibson *(Mgr.-Pub. Rels.)*
Alan Schafer *(Mgr.-Mfg.)*
Geoffrey Smith *(Editor)*

Computer Systems/Hardware:
IBM, Appel, Compugraphics

Outside Service Firm(s):

Horowitz & Ullman*(Auditors)*
New York, NY

Manufacturers Hanover Trust Co.*(Major Banking Relationship)*
4 New York Plaza
New York, NY 10015
Tel.: 212-623-3232

Division:

Corporate Finance Magazine (1)
1328 Broadway
New York, NY 10001
Tel.: 212-594-5030
S.I.C.: 2721
Margaret Elliott *(Editor)*

FINCH, PRUYN & CO., INC.
1 Glen St.
Glens Falls, NY 12801
Tel.: 518-793-2541
Fax: 518-793-7364
Year Founded: 1904
Approx.Sls.: $200,000,000
Emp.: 1,017
Fiscal Year-end: 12/29/92
Export
Printing, Publishing & Converting Papers
S.I.C.: 2621
Richard J. Carota *(Chm., Pres. & Chief Exec. Officer)*
Homer L. Feerer *(V.P.-Sls. & Mktg.)*
Daniel J. Gleason *(V.P.-Mfg.)*
David P. Manny *(V.P. & Sec.)*
John A. Shaffer *(V.P. & Chief Fin. Officer)*
John A. Sheldon *(V.P.-Pur.)*
Laurier J. Lavigne *(Treas.)*
Edward M. Palmer *(Dir.-Customer Service)*

No. of Mfg. Plants/Facilities: 1

Computer Systems/Hardware:
IBM System 400

Outside Service Firm(s):

Coopers & Lybrand*(Auditors)*
1301 Avenue of The Americas
New York, NY 10019
Tel.: 212-536-2000

Chemical Bank*(Major Banking Relationship)*
450 West 33rd St.
New York, NY 10001
Tel.: 212-613-7197
Fax: 212-947-7628

FINDLAY INDUSTRIES, INC.
4000 Fostoria Rd.
Findlay, OH 45840
Tel.: 419-422-1302
Fax: 419-422-0385
Approx.Sls.: $40,000,000
Emp.: 800
Sound & Heat Barriers Including Dash, Cowl, Wheelwell Insulators Package Trays, Molded Urethane Foam Seat Cushions & Backs, Interior Door Trim Panels, Interior Seat Covers
S.I.C.: 3714; 2299; 2295; 2396; 2821; 2822; 2824; 3086; 3089
Philip D. Gardner *(Pres. & Chief Exec. Officer)*
Philip J. Gardner *(Exec. V.P.)*
Michael Gardner *(V.P.-Opers.)*
Martin Terry *(V.P.-Human Resources)*

Outside Service Firm(s):

Ernst & Young*(Auditors)*
1100 Independence Center
Charlotte, NC 28246
Tel.: 704-372-6300

National Bank of Detroit*(Major Banking Relationship)*
P.O. Box 222,
Detroit, MI 48232
Tel.: 313-225-3423
Fax: 313-225-3420

WALLY FINDLAY GALLERIES INTERNATIONAL
814 N. Michigan Ave.
Chicago, IL 60611
Tel.: 312-649-1500
Fax: 312-943-9519
Year Founded: 1870
Approx.Sls.: $10,000,000
Emp.: 50
Fiscal Year-end: 9/30/92
Retail Original Oil Paintings
S.I.C.: 5999
Walstein C. Findlay, Jr. *(Pres.)*
Simone Karoff *(V.P.)*
Robert W. Ryan *(Treas.)*
Principal(s):
Walstein C. Findlay, Jr.

Computer Systems/Hardware:
Epson, Compac

Outside Service Firm(s):

Deloitte & Touche*(Auditors)*
Two Prudential Plaza, 180 N. Stetson
Chicago, IL 60601
Tel.: 312-946-2039

Burke, Wilson & McIlvaine*(Legal Firm)*
Chicago, IL
Tel.: 312-715-5000

Harris Trust & Savings Bank*(Major Banking Relationship)*
111 W. Monroe St.
Chicago, IL 60690
Tel.: 312-461-2265
Tel.: 800-858-0840

Subsidiaries:

Wally Findlay Galleries, Inc. (1)
165 Worth Ave.
Palm Beach, FL 33480
Tel.: 305-655-2090
Retail Original Oil Paintings
S.I.C.: 5999
Walstein C. Findlay Jr. *(Pres.)*

Wally Findlay Galleries, Inc. (1)
17 E. 57th St.
New York, NY 10022
Tel.: 212-421-5390
Retail Orginal Oil Painting
S.I.C.: 5999
Walstein C. Findlay Jr. *(Pres.)*

FINDLEY ADHESIVES, INC.
11320 Watertown Plank Rd.
Wauwatosa, WI 53226-3413
Tel.: 414-774-2250 DE
Fax: 414-774-8075
Year Founded: 1911
Approx.Sls.: $130,000,000
Emp.: 460
Fiscal Year-end: 12/31/92
Import Export
Manufacture Industrial Adhesives
S.I.C.: 2891
John Findley *(Pres.)*
Gary Delzell *(V.P.-Mfg.)*
David Jackson *(V.P.)*
Michael Klonne *(V.P.-Mktg. & Sls.)*
Kenneth Rader *(V.P.-Fin.)*
Andrea Sanders *(V.P.-Res. & Devel.)*
Robert Kruis *(Controller)*
James Schroeder *(Dir.-Regulatory Affairs)*
John Wagner *(Mgr.-Data Processing)*
Richard Bergmann *(Mgr.-Distr. & Customer Service)*
Richard Karrow *(Mgr.-Quality Assurance)*
Thomas Parry *(Mgr.-Res. & Devel., Gen. Pkgng.)*
Paul Schmitz *(Mgr.-Personnel)*
Gary Wilkes *(Mgr.-Pur.)*

No. of Mfg. Plants/Facilities: 12
No. of U.S. Offices: 10
No. of Foreign Offices: 2

Computer Systems/Hardware:
IBM System AS400

Outside Service Firm(s):

Deloitte & Touche*(Auditors)*
250 E. Wisconsin Ave.
Milwaukee, WI 53202-4283
Tel.: 414-271-3000

Kemper Insurance*(Commercial Insurance Carrier)*
Minneapolis, MN

Bank One Milwaukee, N.A.*(Investment Banker)*
111 E. Wisconsin Ave.
Milwaukee, WI
Tel.: 414-765-3000

Godfrey & Kahn*(Legal Firm)*
780 N. Water St.
Milwaukee, WI 53202
Tel.: 414-273-3500
Fax: 414-273-5198

Marshall & Ilsley Trust Company*(Pension Manager)*
770 N. Water St.
Milwaukee, WI

Subsidiary:

Automotive Chemical Corporation (1)
38855 Hills Tech Dr.
Flemington Hills, MI 48212-1199
Tel.: 313-553-7483
Manufacturer of Adhesives & Sealants
S.I.C.: 2891
Mary Lou Bagley *(Pres.)*
Andy Lacis *(Gen. Mgr.)*

Non-U.S. Holdings:

Findley Euro BV (1)
Zeggeveld #10 4705
Roosendaal, Netherlands

Manufacturer of Adhesives
S.I.C.: 2891
C. Van Osta *(Pres.)*

Findley France SA (1)
8, rue Denis Papian Zone Industrielle,
68000 Nord,
Colmar, France
Manufacturer of Ashesives
S.I.C.: 2891
Jean-Jacques Zingler *(Plant Mgr.)*

J.H. FINDORFF & SON, INC.
601 W. Wilson St.
Madison, WI 53703
Tel.: 608-257-5321
Fax: 608-257-5306
Year Founded: 1890
Approx.Sls.: $103,000,000
Emp.: 200
New Construction of Industrial, Commercial & Office Buildings; Institutional Building Construction; Waste Water & Sewage Treatment Plant Construction & Construction Managers
S.I.C.: 1542; 1541; 1629
Gerhard H. Zoller *(Chm. Bd.)*
Kenneth J. Krusha *(Pres. & Chief Exec. Officer)*
Daniel L. Petersen *(Chief Fin. Officer & Corp. Sec.)*
F. Curtis Hastings *(V.P. & Treas.)*
Chistopher J. Smocke *(V.P.)*
Tim Staplemin *(Controller)*
Robert Dunn *(Dir.-Mktg.)*

Outside Service Firm(s):

McGladrey & Pullen*(Auditors)*
Madison, WI

Stroud, Stroud, Willink, Thompson & Howard*(Legal Firm)*
Madison, WI

First Bank, N.A.*(Major Banking Relationship)*
201 W. Wisconsin Ave.
Milwaukee, WI 53203
Tel.: 414-278-6071

FINE ORGANICS CORP.
205 Main St.
Lodi, NJ 07644
Tel.: 201-472-6800
Tel.: 800-526-7480 DE
Fax: 201-472-6810
Year Founded: 1940
Approx.Sls.: $10,000,000
Emp.: 49
Fiscal Year-end: 9/30/91
Export
Mfr. Solvents & Maintenance Cleaners
S.I.C.: 2869; 2842
William J. Reidy *(Chm. & Chief Exec. Officer)*
Gary F. Straub *(Pres. & Chief Oper. Officer)*
Joseph J. Howanitz *(V.P. & Tech. Dir.)*
Cary S. Rosloff *(Controller)*
James R. Higdon *(Dir.-Opers. & Sec.)*
Lewis Goldberg *(Sls. Mgr.)*
Tim Damato *(Mgr.-Adv.)*
Samuel J. Damato *(Mgr.-Pur.)*
Dennis Esposito *(Mgr.-Customer Service)*
Charles J. Gentile *(Mgr.-Data Processing)*
Barbara L. Haas *(Personnel Admin.)*

No. of Mfg. Plants/Facilities: 2
No. of U.S. Offices: 2

Computer Systems/Hardware:
IBM

M. FINE & SONS MANUFACTURING CO., INC.
350 Fifth Ave.
New York, NY 10118
Tel.: 212-239-1111 NY
Fax: 212-714-9475
Year Founded: 1890
Sales Range: $40-59 Million
Emp.: 800
Fiscal Year-end: 12/31/89
Export
Manufacture & Distribute Men's & Boys' Flannel Shirts, Jeans & Casual Wear
S.I.C.: 2321; 2325; 2326
Leo Fine *(Chm. Bd.)*
Allan H. Fine *(Co-Pres.)*
Martin L. Fine *(Co-Pres.)*
Stephen L. Fine *(Co-Pres.)*
David Fine *(V.P.)*
Principal(s):
Leo Fine
Allan H. Fine
Martin L. Fine
Stephen L. Fine

No. of Mfg. Plants/Facilities: 4
No. of U.S. Offices: 2

Computer Systems/Hardware:
IBM S/38

Outside Service Firm(s):

S. P. Cooper & Co.*(Auditors)*
New York, NY

First Union Corp.*(Major Banking Relationship)*
First Union Plaza
Charlotte, NC 28288
Tel.: 704-374-6738

FINESILVER MANUFACTURING COMPANY
816 Cameron St.
San Antonio, TX 78296
Tel.: 210-227-5316
Year Founded: 1897
Emp.: 1,900
Manufacture Men's Work Clothes, Jeans & Shirts
S.I.C.: 5136; 2326
Lynn Finesilver *(Pres. & Chief Exec. Officer)*
Lynn Crystal *(Treas.)*
Sid Ozer *(Mgr.-Sls.)*

FINGER FURNITURE COMPANY, INC.
4001 Gulf Fwy.
Houston, TX 77003
Tel.: 713-221-4441
Fax: 713-227-0406
Approx.Sls.: $62,000,000
Emp.: 1,100
Retail Household & Office Furniture
S.I.C.: 5712; 5719
Robert Finger *(Pres.)*
Joe Kost *(Exec. V.P.)*
David W. Barg *(Treas.)*
Principal(s):
Robert Finger

Computer Systems/Hardware:
IBM

Outside Service Firm(s):

BDO Seidman*(Auditors)*
Houston, TX

Butler & Binion*(Legal Firm)*
1600 First Interstate Bank Plaza
Houston, TX 77002
Tel.: 713-237-3111

FINGERLE LUMBER CO.
617 S. Fifth Ave.
Ann Arbor, MI 48106
Mailing Address:
P.O. Box 1167
Ann Arbor, MI 48106
Tel.: 313-663-0581 MI
Fax: 313-663-2515
Year Founded: 1931
Approx.Sls.: $32,043,000
Emp.: 150
Fiscal Year-end: 12/31/90
Import Export
Lumber, Building Supplies, Hardware & Paint
S.I.C.: 5031; 2851; 3429; 5039; 5072; 5198; 5211; 5231; 5251
John B. Fingerle *(Pres.)*
Mark M. Fingerle *(V.P. & Dir.-Pur.)*
John H. Roose *(V.P.)*
Robert L. Shroup *(V.P.)*
Larry Fingerle *(Sec. & Treas.)*
Principal(s):
John B. Fingerle
Mark M. Fingerle
Larry Fingerle

Outside Service Firm(s):

Deloitte & Touche*(Auditors)*
101 N. Main Street
Ann Arbor, MI 48104-1411
Tel.: 313-769-6200

NBD Bank, N.A.-Ann Arbor*(Commercial Insurance Carrier)*
P.O. Box 8601, 125 S. Main St.
Ann Arbor, MI 48107
Tel.: 313-995-8111

A. FINKL & SONS CO.
2011 N. Southport Ave.
Chicago, IL 60614
Tel.: 312-975-2510 DE
Fax: 312-348-5347
Year Founded: 1879
Approx.Sls.: $60,000,000
Emp.: 445
Fiscal Year-end: 1/31/92
Export
Steel Manufacturer: Ingots, Forgings, Die Blocks & Hot Works, Forged Rolls, Open Die Forgings
S.I.C.: 3312
Charles W. Finkl *(Chm. Bd.)*
B.C. Liimatainen *(Pres.)*
C.P. Laurenson *(Sr. V.P.-Sls.)*
S.A. Witek *(V.P.-Sls.)*
Steve A. Witek *(V.P.-Mktg.)*
Joseph E. Curci *(Chief Fin. Officer)*
Otto E. Moll *(Controller)*
Richard J. Burgess *(Dir.-Indus. Rels.)*
S. Gebbia *(Plant Mgr.)*
C. Gelber *(Dir.-Pur.)*
Principal(s):
Charles W. Finkl

No. of U.S. Offices: 2

Computer Systems/Hardware:
Hewlett-Packard

Outside Service Firm(s):

Arthur Andersen & Co.*(Auditors)*
33 W. Monroe St.
Chicago, IL 60603-4067
Tel.: 312-580-0033
Fax: 312-507-6748

Ross & Hardies*(Legal Firm)*
1 IBM Plaza
Chicago, IL 60611
Tel.: 312-467-9300

The Northern Trust Co.*(Major Banking Relationship)*
50 S. LaSalle St.
Chicago, IL 60675
Tel.: 312-630-6000
Fax: 312-630-6516

FINLAY ENTERPRISES, INC.
521 5th Ave.
New York, NY 10175
Tel.: 212-382-7400
Fax: 212-557-3848
Holding Company; Fine Jewelry; Jewelry & Watch Repair; Cosmetics
S.I.C.: 6719; 7631; 2844
Harold Geneen *(Chm. Bd.)*
David Cornstein *(Pres. & Chief Exec. Officer)*
James Love *(V.P.-Data Processing)*
Bonnie Davis *(Gen. Counsel & Sec.)*

Computer Systems/Hardware:
IBM 3090

Subsidiary:

Finlay Fine Jewelry (1)
521 5th Ave.
New York, NY 10175
Tel.: 212-382-7400
Ronald Grudberg *(Chm. Bd.)*
Robert Lowenstein *(Vice Chm. Bd.)*

FINLEY FARMERS GRAIN ELEVATOR COMPANY
Burlington Northern Right-of-Way
Finley, ND 58230
Mailing Address:
P.O. Box 477
Finley, ND 58230
Tel.: 701-524-1500 ND
Fax: 701-524-2200
Year Founded: 1911
Approx.Sls.: $22,000,000
Emp.: 20
Fiscal Year-end: 2/31/91
Grain Elevators, Petroleum Products; Fertilizer & Fertilizer Materials
S.I.C.: 5153; 5172; 5191
Elton O. Lovro *(Gen. Mgr.)*

Outside Service Firm(s):

Arthur H. Wilson, Jr.*(Auditors)*
Finley, ND

Citizens State Bank*(Major Banking Relationship)*
Finley, ND

FINNAREN & HALEY, INC.
901 Washington St.
Conshohocken, PA 19428
Tel.: 215-825-1900
Fax: 215-825-1184
Approx.Sls.: $20,000,000
Emp.: 200
Mfr. & Retailer of Paint & Allied Products
S.I.C.: 5231
Daniel J. Haley, Jr. *(Chm. Bd.)*
Robert A. Haley *(Vice Chm.)*
Bernard J. Burke *(Pres.)*
Robert A. Haley, Jr. *(Exec. V.P.)*
Francis X. Connell *(Controller)*

Outside Service Firm(s):

Philadelphia National Bank*(Major Banking Relationship)*
5th & Market Sts.
Philadelphia, PA 19101
Tel.: 215-629-3100
Fax: 215-834-2069

FIRE CONTROL INSTRUMENTS, INC.
269 Grove St.
Newton, MA 02166
Tel.: 617-965-2010
Fax: 617-965-0659
Manufacture Fire Alarm Control Systems
S.I.C.: 3823
Frank Carideo *(Pres.)*
Arthur S. Appel *(Exec. V.P.)*
Hans Viezens *(Chief Fin. Officer)*

FIRST ABILENE BANKSHARES, INC.
400 Pine St.
Abilene, TX 79601
Mailing Address:
P.O. Box 701
Abilene, TX 79604
Tel.: 915-675-7155
Fax: 915-675-7342
Assets: $834,499,854
Earnings: $8,645,037
Liabilities: $760,972,441

First Abilene Bankshares, Inc.—(Continued)

Net Worth: $73,527,413
Approx.Income: $70,193,432
Emp.: 445
Fiscal Year-end: 12/31/91
Bank Holding Co.
S.I.C.: 6712
Kenneth T. Murphy *(Chm. Bd., Pres. & Chief Exec. Officer)*
Curtis R. Harvey *(Exec. V.P. & Chief Fin. Officer)*
Harold C. Quinton *(Sr. V.P. & Auditor)*
E.K. Hufstedler, III *(V.P.)*
Gary S. Gragg *(V.P.)*
Sandy Lester *(Sec.-Treas.)*
Sandi Hugg *(Asst. Auditor)*
Michael Kinard *(Asst. Sec.-Treas.)*

Banking Subsidiaries:

Eastland National Bank **(1)**
201 East Main St.
Eastland, TX 76448
Tel.: 817-629-8551 (100%)
Approx.Assets: $48,940,083
Fiscal Year-end: 12/31/91
Commercial Bank
S.I.C.: 6021
Grover Hallmark *(Pres.)*
Clint S. Ferguson *(Exec. V.P.)*
Joe W. Taylor *(Sr. V.P.)*
Jim Davidson *(V.P. & Cashier)*
Marcia Hale *(V.P.)*

First National Bank of Abilene **(1)**
400 Pine St.
Abilene, TX 79604
Tel.: 915-675-7000
Approx.Assets: $528,353,731
Fiscal Year-end: 12/31/91
Commercial Bank
S.I.C.: 6021
Kenneth T. Murphy *(Chm. Bd. & Chief Exec. Officer)*
F. Scott Dueser *(Pres.)*

First National Bank in Cleburne **(1)**
403 N. Main
Cleburne, TX 76031
Tel.: 817-641-6631 (100%)
Approx.Assets: $81,318,035
Fiscal Year-end: 12/31/91
Eddie Saylors *(Chm. Bd. & Chief Exec. Officer)*
William B. Wilson *(Pres.)*
Craig Beskow *(Sr. V.P. & Cashier)*
Ed Fitzhugh *(Sr. V.P.)*
Deloris Wolfe *(Sr. V.P.)*

First National Bank of Sweetwater **(1)**
201 Elm Street
Sweetwater, TX 79556
Tel.: 915-235-8631 (100%)
Approx.Assets: $101,623,300
Fiscal Year-end: 12/31/91
Commercial Bank
S.I.C.: 6021
Patrick N. Gerald *(Chm. Bd. & Pres.)*
Morris E. Hinshaw *(Exec. V.P.)*
Don Allen *(Sr. V.P. & Trust Officer)*
Lloyd F. Harris *(Sr. V.P.)*
Gary Conway *(V.P. & Controller)*
Fermin Garza *(V.P.)*
Bernie Hawley *(V.P.)*

Hereford State Bank **(1)**
212 East 3rd St.
Hereford, TX 79045
Tel.: 806-364-3456 (100%)
Approx.Assets: $77,740,520
Fiscal Year-end: 12/31/91
Commercial Bank
S.I.C.: 6022
Craig Smith *(Chm. Bd. & Pres.)*
Terry Bromlow *(Exec. V.P.)*
Waldo Baxter *(Sr. V.P.)*
Steve Gilbert *(V.P. & Cashier)*
Larry Alley *(V.P.)*
Jeff Brown *(V.P.)*
Mark Nicklaus *(V.P.)*

FIRST AMERICAN BANKSHARES, INC.
15th & H Sts. N.W.
Washington, DC 20005
Tel.: 202-383-1400 **VA**
Fax: 202-383-1444
Year Founded: 1925
Approx.Assets: $8,000,000,000
Emp.: 4,900
Fiscal Year-end: 12/31/91
Bank Holding Co.
S.I.C.: 6712; 6022
Employee Matching Gifts Program: Matches Dollar for Dollar with a Minimum of $25 & a Maximum of $500 per Year
Nicholas deB. Katzenbach *(Chm. Bd.)*
George L. Davis *(Pres. & Chief Exec. Officer)*
Paul G. Adams III *(Exec. V.P. & Chief Oper. Officer)*
John T. Davis *(Exec. V.P.)*
Michael M. Howard *(Sr. V.P.-Corp. Devel.)*
John F. Pipia *(Sr. V.P.-Credit Policy)*
David L. Pitelka *(Sr. V.P. & Controller)*
Janet Schmidt *(Sr. V.P.-Human Resources)*
Iris B. Wordsworth *(Sr. V.P. & Dir.-Corp. Rels.)*
Michael B. Johnson *(Sr. V.P.)*
James E. Lewis *(Sr. V.P.)*
Leonard B. Blank *(V.P.-Asset/Liability)*
Edward C. Cousins *(V.P.-Compensation & Benefits)*
John C. Henry *(V.P.-Gen. Counsel & Sec.)*

No. of U.S. Offices: 286

Computer Systems/Hardware:
DEC VAX 8530

Outside Service Firm(s):

Arthur Andersen & Co.*(Auditors)*
1666 K Street, N.W.
Washington, DC 20006

Cooke & Bieler, Inc.*(Investment Banker)*
1700 Market St., Ste. 3222
Philadelphia, PA 19103
Tel.: 215-567-1101

Clifford & Warnke*(Legal Firm)*
815 Connecticut Ave. N.W.
Washington, DC 20006
Tel.: 202-828-4200

First American Bank of Washington*(Major Banking Relationship)*
740 Fifteenth St., N.W.
Washington, DC 20005
Tel.: 202-637-4644

Chase Manhattan Bank, N.A.*(Pension Manager)*
One Chase Manhattan Plaza
New York, NY 10081
Tel.: 212-552-2222
Tel.: 800-526-0801
Fax: 212-552-7175

Subsidiaries:

First Advantage Mortgage Corporation **(1)**
8910 Rte. 108
Columbia, MD 21045
Tel.: 410-964-4800 (100%)
Fax: 410-964-4839
Emp.: 161
Mortgage Banking
S.I.C.: 6162
Albert C. Kocourek *(Pres. & Chief Exec. Officer)*
James W. Raker *(Sr. V.P. & Chief Fin. Officer)*

First American Bank of Georgia, N.A. **(1)**
34 Peachtree St., N.W.
Atlanta, GA 30303
Tel.: 404-951-4000 (100%)
Fax: 404-951-4599
Approx.Sls.: $154,602,000
Emp.: 967
National Commercial Banking
S.I.C.: 6021
Guy W. Freeman *(Chm. Bd. & Chief Exec. Officer)*
William R. Spradling *(Exec. V.P. & Chief Fin. Officer)*
Arthur P. Baxter *(Sr. V.P.-Mktg.)*

First American Metro Corp. **(1)**
1751 Pinnacle Dr.
McLean, VA 22102
Tel.: 703-821-7777
National Commercial Banking
S.I.C.: 6021
Fred L. Bollerer *(Chm. Bd. & Chief Exec. Officer)*
Bruce Genther *(Mgr.-Adv.)*
Joe Kwiatek *(Dir.-Pur.)*
Russ McNish *(Personnel Mgr.)*

Banking Subsidiary:

First American International Bank **(2)**
Brickell Bay Tower, 28th Fl., 1001 S. Bayshore Dr.
Miami, FL 33131
Tel.: 305-536-3950 (100%)
Fax: 305-579-9721
Approx.Sls.: $15,530,000
Emp.: 45
International Banking
S.I.C.: 6081
Vincent D. Cater *(Pres. & Chief Exec. Officer)*

First American Bank of Maryland **(1)**
8401 Colesville Rd.
Silver Spring, MD 20910
Tel.: 301-565-7000 (100%)
Fax: 301-565-7164
Approx.Rev.: $157,545,000
Emp.: 465
Banking
S.I.C.: 6022
Marlin K. Husted *(Pres. & Chief Exec. Officer)*

First American Bank of New York **(1)**
350 Park Ave.
New York, NY 10022
Tel.: 212-759-9898 (100%)
Fax: 212-418-5407
Approx.Rev.: $156,577,000
Emp.: 824
Banking
S.I.C.: 6022
William M. Duncan *(Chm. Bd., Pres. & Chief Exec. Officer)*
Thomas G. Jones *(Grp. V.P. & Mgr.)*
Raffaela Palmiere *(Assoc. V.P.)*

First American Bank, N.A., Washington, D.C. **(1)**
740 15th St. N.W.
Washington, DC 20005
Tel.: 202-637-6100 (100%)
Fax: 202-637-7729
Approx.Rev.: $181,276,000
Emp.: 546
Banking
S.I.C.: 6021
Joseph E. Foss *(Chm. Bd. & Chief Exec Officer)*
Larry Glasscock *(Pres. & Chief Oper. Officer)*

First American Bank of Virginia **(1)**
1970 Chain Bridge Rd.
McLean, VA 22102
Tel.: 703-821-7777 (100%)
Fax: 703-760-6355
Approx.Rev.: $369,598,000
Emp.: 1,420
Banking
S.I.C.: 6022
Fred L. Bollerer *(Chm. Bd. & Chief Exec. Officer)*
Richard L. Ripley *(Pres. & Chief Oper. Officer)*

FIRST COMPUTER CORPORATION
1740 Westwood Blvd.
Los Angeles, CA 90024
Tel.: 310-470-2501 **CA**
Fax: 310-470-3090
Year Founded: 1983
Approx.Sls.: $14,000,000
Emp.: 35
Fiscal Year-end: 12/31/91
Mfr. of Personal Computers
S.I.C.: 5734
Harry Cohen *(Pres.)*
Morris Cohen *(V.P.)*
Isaac Cohen *(Treas. & Sec.)*
Gail Eddy *(Dir.-Admin.)*

Outside Service Firm(s):

Mercantile National Bank*(Major Banking Relationship)*
Los Angeles, CA 90067

FIRST CONNECTICUT SBIC
(Filed Chapter 11 Bankruptcy)
(Plan of Reorganization Approved January 9, 1992)
1000 Lafayette Blvd.
Bridgeport, CT 06604
Tel.: 203-366-4726 **CT**
Year Founded: 1960
Industrial Loan Company (Non-Deposit Banking);
S.I.C.: 6159
James M. Breiner *(Chm. Bd. & Treas.)*
David Engelson *(Pres. & Chief Fin. Officer)*
Steven A. Breiner *(V.P.)*
Bruce Jacobson *(V.P.)*
Lawrence R. Yurdin *(V.P.)*
Jerome Goldman *(Sec.)*
Louis I. Cohen *(Asst. Treas. & Sec.)*

FIRST DISTRICT ASSOCIATION
216 W. Commercial St.
Litchfield, MN 55355
Tel.: 612-693-3236
Fax: 612-693-6708
Year Founded: 1921
Approx.Sls.: $140,000,000
Emp.: 160
Export
Cheese & Whey Products Cooperative
S.I.C.: 2022
Ron Leaf *(Pres.)*
Charles Hallberg *(Treas.)*
Ray Nelson *(Comptroller)*
Doug Loch *(Mgr.-Sls.)*
Les Young *(Pur. Agent)*

Outside Service Firm(s):

Paul Julian & Company*(Auditors)*
7301 Zane Ave., No.
Minneapolis, MN 55443
Tel.: 612-561-6867

Doherty, Rumble & Butler*(Legal Firm)*
2800 Minnesota World Trade Center
St. Paul, MN 55101-4999
Tel.: 612-291-9333

Center National Bank*(Major Banking Relationship)*
Litchfield, MN

FIRST ELECTRIC COOPERATIVE
901 N. First St.
Jacksonville, AR 72076
Tel.: 501-982-4545 **AR**
Fax: 501-982-8450
Year Founded: 1937
Approx.Sls.: $61,453,000
Emp.: 150
Fiscal Year-end: 12/31/91
Electrical Power Distribution
S.I.C.: 4911
Alton Higginbotham *(Chief Exec. Officer & Gen. Mgr.)*
Billy J. Swaffar *(Pres.)*
Finis R. Long *(V.P.)*
Robert M. Hill *(Sec. & Treas.)*
Joyce Howell *(Controller)*
Wayne Belinge *(Dir.-Pur.)*
James Carson *(Dir.-Engrng.)*
Brad Ford *(Asst. Mgr.)*

Outside Service Firm(s):

Baird, Kurtz & Dobson*(Auditors)*
Little Rock, AR

First Jacksonville Bank*(Major Banking Relationship)*
Jacksonville, AR

1ST FAMILY TRAVELERS HAWAII
2155 Kalakaua Ave., Ste. 716
Honolulu, HI 96815
Tel.: 808-971-7300
Tel.: 800-662-2329

Fax: 808-971-7337
Approx.Sls.: $40,000,000
Emp.: 100
Tour Operator (Wholesale)
S.I.C.: 4725
Semin Vilani *(Pres.)*

Divisions:

Trade Wind Tours **(1)**
1100 31st St.
Downers Grove, IL 60515
Tel.: 708-645-2000
Fax: 708-960-9258
S.I.C.: 4725
Bill Jones *(V.P.-Opers.)*

Trade Wind Tours **(1)**
150 Kaiulani Ave.
Honolulu, HI 96805
Tel.: 808-531-3788
S.I.C.: 4725
Glenn Tamaku *(V.P.-Fin.)*

FIRST FEDERAL SAVINGS AND LOAN ASSN. OF ROCHESTER
1 First Federal Plaza
Rochester, NY 14614
Tel.: 716-238-2100
Tel.: 800-462-4656
Year Founded: 1896
Approx.Rev.: $17,800,000
Emp.: 1,400
Fiscal Year-end: 12/31/90
Savings And Loan; Mortgage Loans
S.I.C.: 6035
Thomas N. Borshoff *(Pres. & Chief Exec. Officer)*
Thomas J. Mullin *(Sr. Exec. V.P.)*
Peter W. Sear *(Exec. V.P.)*
Kenneth D. Bell *(Sr. V.P.-Retail Banking Div.)*
Nicholas P. Comardello *(Sr. V.P.-Residential Mortgage Lending Div.)*
Mark H. Chaplin *(Sr. V.P.-Fin. Div. & Chief Fin. Officer)*
Theodore P. Katsampes *(Sr. V.P.-Plng. Div., Gen. Counsel & Sec.)*
George H. Murray, Jr. *(Sr. V.P.-Mktg. & Personnel Devel.)*
Edward C. Schultz *(Sr. V.P.-Real Estate Services Div.)*
Linda L. Williams *(Sr. V.P.-Opers. Div.)*
Mark A. Browning *(V.P.-Lending Admin.)*
John M. Corrigan *(V.P.-Retail Banking Div.)*
Terry A. Darveaux *(V.P.-Mktg. Services)*
Lynn C. Davison *(V.P.-Mktg. Resources)*
Jeffrey A. Denler *(V.P.-Real Estate Mngmt.)*
David C. Epke *(V.P.-Information Services)*
Dana C. Gavenda *(V.P.-Upstate Reg., Retail Banking Div.)*
Richard Hewitt *(V.P.-Fin. Analysis)*
James B. Howard *(V.P.-Human Resources)*
Richard A. Hurlbut *(V.P.-Document Processing)*
Fredrik J. Lindenhovius *(V.P.-Fin. Services & Cons. Lending)*
Robert Nolan *(V.P.-Pub. Rels.)*
Russell G. Rankin *(V.P.-Central Reg., Retail Banking Div.)*
David M. Sadowsky *(V.P.-Residential Mortgage Lending)*
James Stokes *(V.P.-Debt Admin.)*
Barbara J. Schrot *(V.P.-Compensation & Benefits)*
Clarence G. Simmons III *(V.P. & Treas.)*
Richard L. Steere *(V.P. & Chief Appraiser)*
Frank C. Szabo *(V.P. & Controller)*
Roger A. Youngs *(V.P.-Central Opers.)*
Ira M. Yourman *(V.P.-Mortgage Loan Opers.)*
Gary P. Zimmerman *(V.P.-Internal Audit)*
Jack Keck *(Dir.-Pur.)*
Debra Alley *(Mgr.-Adv. & Promo.)*

Computer Systems/Hardware:
IBM

FIRST FINANCIAL GROUP, INC.
(d/b/a American Beauty Homes)
16830 Ventura Blvd., Ste. 600
Encino, CA 91436
Tel.: 818-981-4900
Fax: 818-981-4821
Year Founded: 1972
Approx.Sls.: $50,000,000
Emp.: 80
New Construction of Single-Family Houses; Subdividers & Developers
S.I.C.: 1521; 6552
Jack Shine *(Chm. Bd.)*
Joel Shine *(Pres.)*
David Bock *(V.P.)*
Loretta Shine *(Treas. & Sec.)*

Outside Service Firm(s):

City National Bank*(Major Banking Relationship)*
8525 W. Pico Blvd.
Los Angeles, CA 90035
Tel.: 310-550-5690

FIRST FLORIDA EQUITIES, LTD.
7740 5 W. 104th St., Ste. 200
Miami, FL 33156
Tel.: 305-666-5588
Telex: 2798213
Fax: 305-666-5586
Sales Range: $40-59 Million
Emp.: 300
Real Estate Investment Firm; Syndicator; Commercial Real Estate Broker; Property Manager
S.I.C.: 6531; 6552
Claude Dorsy *(Pres.)*
Lincoln J. Herzeca *(V.P.-Acquisitions)*
Carol F. Keys *(Gen. Counsel)*

Principal(s):
Claude Dorsy
Tom Huston, Jr.
James R. Mitchell

Computer Systems/Hardware:
IBM System 38

Outside Service Firm(s):

Sun Bank, N.A.*(Major Banking Relationship)*
Miami, FL 33131

1ST FRANKLIN CORPORATION
213 E. Tugalo St.
Toccoa, GA 30577
Mailing Address:
P.O. Box 880,
Toccoa, GA 30577
Tel.: 706-886-7571 **GA**
Fax: 706-886-7639
Assets: $88,823,190
Earnings: $3,748,188
Liabilities: $64,416,931
Net Worth: $24,406,259
Approx.Rev.: $30,730,459
Emp.: 346
Fiscal Year-end: 12/31/91
Holding Company
S.I.C.: 6712
Ben F. Cheek III *(Chm. Bd. & Pres.)*
T. Bruce Childs *(V.P.-Opers.)*
Phoebe Martin *(V.P.-Mktg.)*
Linda S. Sessa *(Treas.)*
Lynn E. Cox *(Sec.)*
A. Roger Guimond *(Chief Fin. Officer)*
Phoebe Martin *(Dir.-Adv.)*
Herb Masten *(Dir.-Pur.)*

Subsidiaries:

First Franklin Financial Corp. **(1)**
213 E. Tugalo St.
Toccoa, GA 30577
Tel.: 706-886-7571 (100%)
Fax: 706-886-7369
Emp.: 343
Consumer Finance Company which Acquires & Services Direct Cash Loans, Real Estate Loans & Sales Financial Contracts
S.I.C.: 6159
Ben F. Cheek III *(Chm. Bd.)*
T. Bruce Childs *(Pres.)*
A. Roger Guimond *(Chief Fin. Officer)*
Linda S. Sessa *(Treas.)*
Lynn E. Cox *(Sec.)*
A. Roger Guimond *(Controller)*

Subsidiaries:

Frandisco Life Insurance Co. **(2)**
213 E. Tugalo St.
Toccoa, GA 30577
Tel.: 706-886-7571 (100%)
Fax: 706-886-7369
Emp.: 343
Credit Life/Accident & Health Insurance
S.I.C.: 6311; 6321
Ben Cheek III *(Pres.)*
A. Roger Guimond *(Chief Fin. Officer)*

Frandisco Property & Casualty Insurance **(2)**
213 E. Tugalo St.
Toccoa, GA 30577
Tel.: 706-886-7571 (100%)
Emp.: 343
Property & Casualty Insurance
S.I.C.: 6331
Ben Cheek III *(Pres.)*
A. Roger Guimond *(Chief Fin. Officer)*

Franklin Securities, Inc. **(2)**
213 E. Tugalo St.
Toccoa, GA 30577
Tel.: 706-886-7571 (100%)
Emp.: 5
Securities Dealer
S.I.C.: 6211
Ben Cheek III *(Pres.)*
A. Roger Guimond *(Chief Fin. Officer)*

FIRST GRAY LINE CORPORATION
335 N. Maple, Ste. 273
Beverly Hills, CA 90210
Tel.: 310-247-4800
Year Founded: 1969
Approx.Sls.: $102,000,000
Emp.: 1,100
Local Rent-a-Car Service
S.I.C.: 7514; 4142
Henry F. Burroughs, Jr. *(Chm. Bd.)*
James R. Burroughs *(Pres. & Chief Oper. Officer)*
Donald R. McCammack *(Exec. V.P.)*
Mary Anne Doms *(V.P. & Sec.)*
Harry E. Lewis *(V.P. & Sec.)*

FIRST MOUNT JOY CORPORATION
P.O. Box 308,
Mount Joy, PA 17552
Tel.: 717-653-1411 **DE**
Fax: 717-653-2302
Year Founded: 1988
Approx.Sls.: $49,000,000
Emp.: 370
Fiscal Year-end: 5/31/92
Gasoline Filling Stations; Petroleum Bulk Stations; Fuel Oil Dealers
S.I.C.: 5541; 5171; 5983
Franklin R. Eichler *(Pres.)*
Charles W. Ricedorf *(V.P.)*
Harrison L. Diehl *(Treas.)*
Darlene F. Halterman *(Sec. & Asst. Treas.)*

Outside Service Firm(s):

CoreStates Bank, N.A.*(Major Banking Relationship)*
Broad & Chestnut Sts.
Philadelphia, PA 19101
Tel.: 215-973-3100

Subsidiary:

Sisco Company **(1)**
P.O. Box 302
Mount Joy, PA 17552
Tel.: 717-653-1411
Approx.Sls.: $122,000,000
Emp.: 370
Gasoline Filling Stations; Petroleum Bulk Stations; Fuel Oil Dealers; Oil Burners; Air Conditioning Room Units, Self-contained; Oil Burner Repair Service
S.I.C.: 5541; 5171; 5983; 5074; 5722
Franklin R. Eichler *(Pres.)*
Charles W. Ricedorf *(V.P.-Opers.)*
Michael T. Reese *(V.P.-Mktg.)*
Harrison L. Diehl *(Treas.)*
Robert K. Shank *(Sec. & Asst. Treas.)*

FIRST NATIONAL BANK OF LOUISVILLE
(Sub. of First Kentucky National Corp.)
101 S. Fifth St.
Louisville, KY 40202
Tel.: 502-581-4200
Year Founded: 1863
Approx.Assets: $5,000,000,000
Emp.: 2,200
Fiscal Year-end: 12/31/90
Financial Services
S.I.C.: 6022
Morton Boyd, Jr. *(Pres. & Chief Exec. Officer)*

Affiliate:

First Kentucky Trust Company **(1)**
101 S. Fifth St.
Louisville, KY 40202
Tel.: 502-581-4200
S.I.C.: 6022

FIRST SOUTHWEST COMPANY
1700 Pacific Ave., Ste. 500
Dallas, TX 75201
Tel.: 214-953-4000 **TX**
Fax: 214-954-4339
Year Founded: 1946
Approx.Sls.: $20,000,000
Emp.: 140
Fiscal Year-end: 12/31/92
Investment Bankers
S.I.C.: 6211
Robert K. Utley III *(Chm. Exec. Committee & Co-Chief Exec. Officer))*
Hill Feinberg *(Vice Chm. & Co-Chief Exec. Officer)*
Richard Litton *(Mng. Dir.)*
Daniel P. Son *(Dir.)*

Outside Service Firm(s):

KPMG Peat Marwick*(Auditors)*
1601 Elm St., Ste. 1600
Dallas, TX 75201
Tel.: 214-754-2000
Fax: 214-754-2297

FIRST STATE FEDERAL SAVINGS & LOAN
201 Main St., S.
Hutchinson, MN 55350-2573
Tel.: 612-587-2000 **MN**
Fax: 612-587-2072
Year Founded: 1933
Assets: $144,278,000
Liabilities: $130,561,000
Net Worth: $13,717,000
Emp.: 72
Fiscal Year-end: 9/30/91
Savings & Loan Association
S.I.C.: 6035
Audrey C. Cox *(Chm. Bd.)*
Donald A. Glas *(Pres. & Chief Exec. Officer)*
Larry Romo *(Sr. V.P. & Dir. of Lending)*
Richard H. Burgart *(Chief Fin. Officer)*
Arliss Haag *(Sec.)*
Dale O. Ortloff *(Controller)*
Carol Haukos *(Dir.-Mktg. & Human Resources)*

First State Federal Savings & Loan—(Continued)

Outside Service Firm(s):

Bertram Cooper & Co.*(Auditors)*
Waseca, MN

Federal Home Loan Bank*(Major Banking Relationship)*
Des Moines, IA

Subsidiary:

Firstate Services, Inc. **(1)**
201 Main St., S.
Hutchinson, MN 55350-2573
Tel.: 612-587-8132
Emp.: 2
Insurance, Investments & Financial Planning
S.I.C.: 6282; 6211; 6411
David Wetterling *(Service Corp. Mgr.)*

FIRST WORTHING
8144 Walnut Hill Lane, Ste. 550
Dallas, TX 75231
Tel.: 214-739-8141 **TX**
Fax: 214-369-4130
Emp.: 450
Fiscal Year-end: 12/31/88
Real Estate Investment, Development
S.I.C.: 6552
Robert K. Utley, III *(Chm. Bd.)*
Mark R. Wagner *(Pres.)*
Fred Albrecht *(Exec. V.P.-Fin.)*

No. of U.S. Offices: 2

Computer Systems/Hardware:
Prime; Jonas & Erickson

Outside Service Firm(s):

Arthur Andersen & Co.*(Auditors)*
Austin, TX

Royal Insurance*(Group Insurer)*
9300 Arrowpoint Blvd.
Charlotte, NC 28217
Tel.: 704-522-2000
Fax: 704-522-3200

Liddell, Sapp, Zivley, Hill & LaBoon, L.L.P.*(Legal Firm)*
3400 Texas Commerce Tower
Houston, TX 77002
Tel.: 713-223-4151

NationsBank Texas*(Major Banking Relationship)*
901 Main St., 16th Fl.
Dallas, TX 75202
Tel.: 214-922-5000

FIRSTFED MICHIGAN CORPORATION
1001 Woodward Ave.
Detroit, MI 48226-1904
Tel.: 313-965-1400 **MI**
Year Founded: 1988
Assets: $9,415,180,000
Earnings: $34,040,000
Liabilities: $8,942,342,000
Net Worth: $472,838,000
Approx.Income: $901,315,000
Fiscal Year-end: 12/31/91
Holding Company for First Federal of Michigan Banks
S.I.C.: 6712; 6035
C. Gene Harling *(Chm. Bd., Pres. & Chief Exec. Officer)*
Richard W. Neu *(Treas.)*
Michael T. Welsh *(Sec.)*

Outside Service Firm(s):

KPMG Peat Marwick*(Auditors)*
Suite 1200, 150 W. Jefferson
Detroit, MI 48226

Subsidiary:

First Federal of Michigan **(1)**
1001 Woodward Ave.
Detroit, MI 48226-1904
Tel.: 313-965-1400
Federal Savings & Loan Institution; 82 Branch Offices In 3 States
S.I.C.: 6035

C. Gene Harling *(Chm. Bd., Pres. & Chief Exec. Officer)*
Richard W. Neu *(Exec. V.P. & Chief Fin. Officer)*
Richard Platt *(Exec. V.P.-Mktg. Div.)*
George M. Bourgon, Jr. *(Sr. V.P. & Dir.-Personnel)*
Allan D. Breyer *(Sr. V.P. & Mgr.-Mngmt. Information Systems)*
James Chomakos *(Sr. V.P. & Mgr.-Mktg. Admin.)*
Donald G. Franck *(Sr. V.P. & Mgr.-Commercial Real Estate Loans)*
Joyce K. Hancock *(Sr. V.P. & Controller)*
William A. Hoffhines *(Sr. V.P. & Mgr. Grand Rapids Div.)*
Albert R. King *(Sr. V.P. & Mgr.-Mortgage Opers.)*
F. William Manion *(Sr. V.P. & Mgr.-Branch Opers.)*
Malcolm R. Milne *(Sr. V.P. & Treas.)*
Donald W. Ruff *(Sr. V.P. & Mgr.-Corp. Opers & Auditing)*
Bruce E. Ruffin *(Sr. V.P. & Community Investment Officer)*
Michael T. Welsh *(Sr. V.P. & Sec.)*

Subsidiaries:

Bay Savings Bank, FSB **(2)**
2712 Washington Ave.
Newport News, VA 23607-3920
Tel.: 804-247-5275
Federal Savings Bank
S.I.C.: 6035

County Mortgage Corporation **(2)**
180 Oakland Ave.
Birmingham, MI 48009-3475
Tel.: 313-646-2810
Mortgage Loan Company
S.I.C.: 6035

Omni Savings Bank, FSB **(2)**
1940 Blossom St.
Columbia, SC 29205-2296
Tel.: 803-771-8919
Federal Savings Bank
S.I.C.: 6035

FISCA OIL CO., INC.
4830 Rainbow Blvd.
Westwood, KS 66205
Mailing Address:
P.O. Box 3363
Kansas City, KS 66103
Tel.: 913-236-7000
Fax: 913-236-7128
Approx.Sls.: $75,000,000
Emp.: 200
Fiscal Year-end: 9/30/89
Gasoline Service Stations
S.I.C.: 5541
M. R. Hudson *(Chm. Bd. & Pres.)*
Robert Crews *(V.P.)*
Arnold Alan *(Controller)*
George Burton *(Mgr.-Data Processing)*

Computer Systems/Hardware:
Univac

Outside Service Firm(s):

Ernst & Young*(Auditors)*
Topeka, KS

State Mutual Life Assurance Co. of America*(Group Insurer)*
440 Lincoln St.
Worcester, MA 01605
Tel.: 508-852-1000

Commercial National Bank*(Investment Banker)*
Topeka, KS

Weeks, Thomas & Lysaught*(Legal Firm)*
Kansas City, KS

Commercial National Bank*(Major Banking Relationship)*
Topeka, KS

Commercial National Bank*(Pension Manager)*
Topeka, KS

Subsidiary:

Meta Plant Food **(1)**
4830 Rainbow Blvd.
Westwood, KS 66205
Tel.: 913-236-7000
S.I.C.: 5541

FISCHBACH & DOUGHERTY, INC.
6065 Barfield Rd., Ste. 210
Atlanta, GA 30328
Tel.: 404-250-1300 **GA**
Fax: 404-250-4389
Year Founded: 1978
Sales Range: $10-19 Million
Emp.: 100
Real Estate Investment Firm
S.I.C.: 6531
R.L. Dougherty *(Pres.)*
Robert A. Fischbach *(V.P.)*

Computer Systems/Hardware:
IBM PC

Outside Service Firm(s):

Hishon Ranney*(Legal Firm)*
Atlanta, GA

NationsBank*(Major Banking Relationship)*
35 Broad St.
Atlanta, GA 30303
Tel.: 404-581-2121
Tel.: 800-848-8198

Subsidiary:

Metro Atlanta Properties **(1)**
6065 Barfield Rd., Ste. 210
Atlanta, GA 30328
Tel.: 404-250-1400
S.I.C.: 6531

FISCHER LIME & CEMENT COMPANY
3347 Pearson Road
Memphis, TN 38118
Tel.: 901-363-4986
Fax: 901-794-3569
Year Founded: 1972
Approx.Sls.: $50,000,000
Emp.: 350
Wholesale & Manufacture Concrete Blocks & Bricks; General Building Materials
S.I.C.: 3271; 5039
Tom Sheppard *(Pres.)*
Ed Kennedy *(V.P.)*
Dayton Phillips *(Sec. & Treas.)*

Outside Service Firm(s):

National Bank of Commerce*(Major Banking Relationship)*
Memphis, TN

L. FISH CORPORATION
4242 W. 42nd Pl.
Chicago, IL 60632
Tel.: 312-523-7700
Fax: 312-523-3533
Approx.Sls.: $35,000,000
Emp.: 285
Retail Furniture, Carpets, Rugs, Household Appliances
S.I.C.: 5713; 5712
Stephen M. Ehrlichman *(Pres.)*
Milton Fish, Jr. *(V.P. & Sec.)*
Robert J. Klosak *(V.P.-Data Processing & Personnel)*
Principal(s):
Milton Fish, Jr.

Computer Systems/Hardware:
IBM System 36

Outside Service Firm(s):

Altschuler, Melvoin & Glasser*(Auditors)*
30 S. Wecker Dr.
Chicago, IL 60606
Tel.: 312-207-2800

Jenner & Block*(Legal Firm)*
One IBM Plaza
Chicago, IL 60611
Tel.: 312-222-9350

American National Bank & Trust Company of Chicago*(Major Banking Relationship)*
33 N. LaSalle St.
Chicago, IL 60602
Tel.: 312-661-5000
Fax: 312-661-6417

Subsidiary:

Midwest Equipment Co. **(1)**
4242 W. 42nd Pl.
Chicago, IL 60632
Tel.: 312-523-7700
Stephen M. Ehrlichman *(Pres.)*

FISH ENGINEERING & CONSTRUCTION, INC.
1990 S. Post Oak Rd., Suite 200
Houston, TX 77056
Tel.: 713-621-8300 **TX**
Fax: 713-850-7682
Year Founded: 1962
Assets: $12,000,000
Earnings: $1,000,000
Net Worth: $12,000,000
Approx.Sls.: $60,000,000
Emp.: 1,500
Fiscal Year-end: 12/31/88
Engineering & Construction for Oil, Gas & Petrochemical Industry
S.I.C.: 1629; 8711
J.A. Boyd *(Chm. Bd., Pres. & Chief Exec. Officer)*
G.L. Turner *(Sr. V.P.)*
G.W. Alves *(Sr. V.P.)*
D.E. Lockwood *(Sr. V.P.)*
J.E. Dill *(V.P.)*
J. Napoli *(V.P.)*
E.M. Basco *(Treas.)*
Cooper Ford *(Dir.-Personnel)*
Steve Brunner *(Dir.-Data Processing)*
R.J. Schmidt *(Pur. Agent)*

No. of U.S. Offices: 1

Computer Systems/Hardware:
Novell

Outside Service Firm(s):

Grant Thornton*(Auditors)*
Houston, TX

Andrews & Kurth*(Legal Firm)*
4200 Texas Commerce Tower
Houston, TX 77002
Tel.: 713-220-4200

Bank One*(Major Banking Relationship)*
Houston, TX

Subsidiaries:

Fish International Co. **(1)**
1990 S. Post Oak Rd., Suite 200
Houston, TX 77056-3846
Tel.: 713-621-8300 (100%)
Engineering
S.I.C.: 8711; 1629

Fish International Engineers **(1)**
1990 S. Post Oak Rd., Suite 200
Houston, TX 77056-3846
Tel.: 713-621-8300 (100%)
S.I.C.: 1629; 8711

Fish Service Corporation **(1)**
1990 S. Post Oak Rd., Suite 200
Houston, TX 77056-3846
Tel.: 713-621-8300 (100%)
S.I.C.: 8711; 1629

FISHER COMPANIES, INC.
1525 One Union Sq.
Seattle, WA 98101-3211
Tel.: 206-624-2752
Fax: 206-682-7733
Year Founded: 1911

Holding Company; Flour Milling, Grain Processing Equipment, Broadcasting & Commercial Real Estate
S.I.C.: 6719; 2041; 4833; 6531
Donald G. Graham, Jr. *(Chm. Bd. & Chief Exec. Officer)*
William W. Krippaehne, Jr. *(Pres.)*
G.O. Fisher *(V.P. & Treas.)*
E.A. Gowey *(Sec.)*

Outside Service Firm(s):

Price Waterhouse*(Auditors)*
1001 Fourth Ave. Plaza
Seattle, WA 98154
Tel.: 206-622-1505

Graham & Dunn*(Legal Firm)*
1301 5th Ave., 34th Floor
Seattle, WA 98101
Tel.: 206-624-8300

Seattle First National Bank*(Major Banking Relationship)*
701 Fifth Avenue
Seattle, WA 98104
Tel.: 206-358-3035

Subsidiaries:

Fisher Broadcasting, Inc. **(1)**
100 Fourth Ave.N.
Seattle, WA 98109
Tel.: 206-443-4000
Fax: 206-443-8272
Emp.: 479
Radio & Television Broadcasting
S.I.C.: 4832; 4833
John F. Behnke *(Chm. Bd.)*
Patrick Scott *(Pres. & Chief Exec. Officer)*
Jay Giesa *(Exec. V.P.-Admin. & Sec.)*
James L. Boyer *(V.P. & Gen. Mgr.-KATU)*
Phelps K. Fisher *(V.P.-Mktg.)*
Robert D. Kalstad *(V.P.-Admin.)*
Richard Warsinske *(V.P. & Gen. Mgr.-KOMO TV)*
Howard W. Wilkinson *(V.P., Chief Exec. Officer, & Treas.)*
John Ulman *(Controller)*

Fisher Mills, Inc. **(1)**
3235 16th Ave., S.W.
Seattle, WA 98134
Tel.: 206-622-4430
Fax: 206-682-3676
Sales Range: $40-59 Million
Emp.: 175
Flour
S.I.C.: 2041
Terry Barrans *(Pres. & Chief Exec. Officer)*
C.E. Bowden *(V.P.-Grain/Traffic, Sec., & Treas.)*
Ronald H. Osborne *(V.P.-Logistics)*
Dale Pierce *(V.P.-Sls.)*

Fisher Properties Inc. **(1)**
1525 One Union Sq.
Seattle, WA 98101
Tel.: 206-682-7733
Fax: 206-682-7733
Real Estate
S.I.C.: 6531
William Krippaehne, Jr. *(Chm. Bd.)*
Mark A. Weed *(Pres. & Chief Exec. Officer)*

FISHER GRAPHIC INDUSTRIES
1137 Graphics Dr.
Modesto, CA 95351
Tel.: 209-577-0181
Fax: 209-577-0871
Year Founded: 1979
Emp.: 70
Fiscal Year-end: 6/30/91
Manufactures & Markets Flexographic Printing Plates
S.I.C.: 3555; 7311
Mike Fisher, Sr. *(Chm. Bd.)*
Mike Fisher, Jr. *(Pres. & Chief Exec. Officer)*
Scott Fisher *(V.P.)*
Norma Joe Fisher *(Treas., Controller & Chief Fin. Officer)*

Computer Systems/Hardware:
IBM AT

FISHER PEN COMPANY
9240 W. Belmont
Franklin Park, IL 60131
Tel.: 708-366-5030 **IL**
Fax: 708-366-5044
Year Founded: 1948
Approx.Sls.: $10,000,000
Emp.: 100
Export
Office, School & Gift Ball Point Pens; Ink Refills
S.I.C.: 3951; 2899
Paul C. Fisher *(Chm. Bd.)*
Bruce J. Brizzolara *(Pres. & Chief Exec. Officer)*
David Fall *(V.P.-Sls.)*
Principal(s):
Paul C. Fisher

No. of Mfg. Plants/Facilities: 2
No. of U.S. Offices: 2

Outside Service Firm(s):

Michael A. Lavelle*(Legal Firm)*
Chicago, IL

Subsidiary:

Fisher Pen Co. of Nevada **(1)**
711 Yucca St.
Boulder City, NV 89005
Tel.: 702-293-3011
Manufacture Ballpoint Pens
S.I.C.: 3951
Paul C. Fisher *(Pres.)*

FISHER SKYLIGHTS, INC.
50 Snake Hill Rd.
West Nyack, NY 10994
Tel.: 914-358-9000 **NY**
Fax: 914-358-9060
Year Founded: 1922
Approx.Sls.: $10,000,000
Emp.: 65
Fiscal Year-end: 12/31/90
Import Export
Mfr. of Custom Metal Framed Skylights, Stage Ventilators, Smoke, Fire & Explosion Vents
S.I.C.: 3444
Robert J. Fisher *(Pres.)*
Thomas J. Fisher *(Exec. V.P.)*
Joseph N. Fisher *(V.P.)*
Carol Parrish *(Sec.)*
Michael Fisher *(Pur. Agent & Expediter)*
Ronald Bodmer *(Plant Mgr.)*
Principal(s):
Robert J. Fisher
Thomas J. Fisher
Joseph N. Fisher

No. of Mfg. Plants/Facilities: 2
No. of U.S. Offices: 1
No. of Foreign Offices: 1

Computer Systems/Hardware:
Digital & Auto-Cad

Outside Service Firm(s):

Bernstein & Bernstein*(Auditors)*
New York, NY

Eifert, French & Ketchum Insurance*(Commercial Insurance Carrier)*
Pelham, NY 10803

David W. Bernstein, P.C.*(Legal Firm)*
New York, NY

Chemical Bank*(Major Banking Relationship)*
White Plains, NY

Shore & Reich*(Pension Manager)*
575 Lexington Ave.
New York, NY 10022
Tel.: 212-758-3330
Fax: 212-752-8304

FISHERIES SUPPLY COMPANY
1900 N. Northlake Way #10
Seattle, WA 98103
Tel.: 206-632-4462
Tel.: 800-426-6930 **WA**
Fax: 206-634-4600
Year Founded: 1928
Approx.Sls.: $16,000,000
Emp.: 60
Marine Supplies; Automotive Supplies & Parts
S.I.C.: 5088; 5551; 5013
C. Fain Sutter, Sr. *(Chm. Bd.)*
Carl F. Sutter, Jr. *(Pres.)*
Victoria Schneider *(V.P.)*
Ruth A. Sutter *(Treas.)*

Outside Service Firm(s):

Seafirst Bank*(Major Banking Relationship)*
Columbia-SeaFirst Center, 701 5th Ave., 11th Flr.
Seattle, WA 98124
Tel.: 206-358-3039
Fax: 206-358-3113

FISHERS BIG WHEEL INC.
102 Nesbitt Rd.
New Castle, PA 16105
Mailing Address:
P.O. Box 5189,
New Castle, PA 16105
Tel.: 412-658-3781 **PA**
Fax: 412-658-1134
Year Founded: 1935
Sales Range: $100-499 Million
Emp.: 4,500
Import
Discount Department Store
S.I.C.: 5311
Marshall Hess *(Chm. Bd.)*
Barry Gold *(Vice Chm. & Chief Admin. Officer)*
Robert Floum *(Pres. & Chief Exec. Officer)*
Albert A. Agostinelli *(Chief Fin. Officer & Exec. V.P.)*
Robert W. Lytle *(Exec. V.P.-Store Opers.)*
Rick Abraham *(Sr. V.P.-Strategic Plng. & New Bus. Devel.)*
Andy Hess *(Sr. V.P.-Corp. Apparel Mdse.)*
Carl Schwartz *(Sr. V.P.-Gen. Msde. Mgr., Hardlines)*
Regis Carozza *(V.P.-Human Resources)*
A. Cunningham *(V.P. & Treas.)*
Andy Danus *(V.P.-Mngmt. Information Systems)*
Rick Noca *(Dir.-Real Estate)*
Gabriella Budai *(Mgr.-Human Resources)*
Scott Campbell *(Mgr.-Procurement)*
Wayne Garrett *(Mgr.-Opers.)*
Terry Gillespie *(Mgr.-Training & Devel.)*

Principal(s):
Marshall Hess
Gail Wolpin
Ruth Ann Mendel
Marianne Hess

No. of U.S. Offices: 1

Outside Service Firm(s):

Coopers & Lybrand*(Auditors)*
600 Grant St., 35th Fl.
Pittsburgh, PA 15219
Tel.: 412-355-8000
Fax: 412-355-8089

Tucker Arensberg, P.C.*(Auditors)*
Pittsburgh, PA

Nadler, Nadler & Burdman*(Legal Firm)*
20 Federal Plaza West
Youngstown, OH 44503

Mellon Bank, N.A.*(Major Banking Relationship)*
P.O. Box 444,
Pittsburgh, PA 15230
Tel.: 412-236-8000
Tel.: 1-800-451-7392
Fax: 412-236-8157

FISHKING PROCESSORS, INC.
1320 Newton St.
Los Angeles, CA 90021
Mailing Address:
P.O. Box 21385, Market Station
Los Angeles, CA 90021
Tel.: 213-746-1307 **CA**
Twx: 674561
Fax: 213-746-4008
Year Founded: 1955
Approx.Sls.: $98,000,000
Emp.: 800
Fiscal Year-end: 3/31/89
Process Seafood, Breaded Shrimp & Specialty Items
S.I.C.: 2092
Tamotsu Furukawa *(Pres.)*
Norman Furukawa *(Co-Vice Chm.)*
Kiyoshi Kawaguchi *(Co-Vice Chm.)*
Gary Kawaguchi *(V.P.-Prod. & Sec.)*
Kenneth K. Kawaguchi *(V.P.-Mktg.)*
Albert Nigorizawa *(V.P.-Sls.)*

Outside Service Firm(s):

Deloitte & Touche*(Auditors)*
1000 Wilshire Blvd.
Los Angeles, CA 90017-2472
Tel.: 213-688-0800
Fax: 213-688-0100

Union Bank*(Major Banking Relationship)*
445 S. Figueroa St.
Los Angeles, CA 90071
Tel.: 213-236-5076

Subsidiary:

QF, Inc. **(1)**
Shell Belt Rd.
Bayou La Batre, AL 36509
Tel.: 205-824-4173
Emp.: 150
Processor of Fresh Shrimp & Breaded Shrimp Products
S.I.C.: 2092
George House *(Chief Oper. Officer)*

FISHMAN & TOBIN, INC.
176 W. Louden St.
Philadelphia, PA 19120
Tel.: 215-457-7300
Tel.: 800-367-2772 **PA**
Fax: 215-457-1726
Year Founded: 1913
Sales Range: $40-59 Million
Emp.: 1,400
Import
Mfr. Boys' & Men's Trousers & Clothing
S.I.C.: 2325; 2326; 2329
Sylvan M. Tobin *(Chm. Bd.)*
Bernard Fishman *(Chm.-Exec. Committee)*
Mark Fishman *(Pres.)*
Daniel Goldstein *(Dir.-Data Processing)*
Ed Kochman *(Dir.-Admin.)*
Nicholas Vetere *(Controller)*
Ed Riesenberg *(Mgr.-Prod.)*

Outside Service Firm(s):

Simonson, Lipschutz & Fogel*(Auditors)*
Philadelphia, PA

Horvitz, Fisher, Miller & Sedlack*(Legal Firm)*
Philadelphia, PA

Meridian Bank*(Major Banking Relationship)*
Philadelphia, PA

FISKE BROTHERS REFINING COMPANY
129 Lockwood St.
Newark, NJ 07105
Tel.: 201-589-9150

Fiske Brothers Refining Company—(Continued)

Mfr. of Cutting Oils & Compounds, Drawing Compounds & Other Metal Working Lubricants
S.I.C.: 2992
Fred J. Snyder, Jr. *(Pres. & Chief Exec. Officer)*
R.T. McCluskey *(V.P. & Treas.)*

Divisions:

Fiske Brothers Refining, Toledo Div. **(1)**
1500 Oakdale
Toledo, OH 43605
Tel.: 419-691-2491
Lubricating Oils
S.I.C.: 2992
Arthur Kontak *(V.P. & Gen. Mgr.)*

Lubriplate Div. of Fiske Bros. Refining Co. **(1)**
129 Lockwood St.
Newark, NJ 07105
Tel.: 201-589-9150
Fax: 201-489-4432
Emp.: 190
Lubriplate Lubricants
S.I.C.: 2992
Fred J. Snyder, Jr. *(Pres.)*
R.T. McCluskey *(V.P. & Treas.)*
T.A. Liddy III *(Pur. Agent)*
Lynn I. Lindsay *(Export Mgr.)*

FITZGERALD ADVERTISING INC.
1055 St. Charles Ave.
New Orleans, LA 70130
Tel.: 504-529-3161
Fax: 504-592-8223
Year Founded: 1926
Approx.Billings: $12,700,000
Emp.: 21
Donald C. Smith *(Chm. Bd.)*
Ronald J. Thompson *(Pres.)*
Laura Lee Killeen *(Exec. V.P., Copy Dir.)*
Sally O. Donlon *(V.P.)*
Randolph L. Seeling *(Treas.)*
Linda Vangilder *(Mktg. & Admin. Asst.)*
Jean Williams *(Asst. Controller)*

FITZGERALD & CO.
One Buckhead Plaza, 3060
Peachtree Rd. N.W., Ste. 500
Atlanta, GA 30305
Tel.: 404-262-8900
Fax: 404-239-0548
Year Founded: 1983
Approx.Billings: $42,000,000
Emp.: 62
David P. Fitzgerald *(Pres.)*
Greg Cahill *(Sr. V.P., Chief Fin. Officer)*
Rhonda Ratliff *(Systems Admin.)*

Computer Systems/Hardware:
MacIntosh, Wang, IBM

FITZGERALD & COMPANY, INC.
105 Sockanossett Cross Rd.
Cranston, RI 02920
Tel.: 401-275-5700
Fax: 401-275-5721
Year Founded: 1943
Approx.Billings: $16,000,000
Emp.: 33
Banking, Environmental, Business-to-Business & Retail
Saul Alden Fern *(Chm. Bd. & Chief Exec. Officer)*
William E. Smith *(Pres., Chief Oper. Officer & Sec.)*
Charles E. Petit *(Exec. V.P., Chief Fin. Officer & Treas.)*
Martha Parker *(Sr. V.P., Pub. Rels.)*
Yvette L. Ullom *(V.P., Fin., Human Resources & Pur.)*

FITZPATRICK & WELLER, INC.
12 Mill St.
Ellicottville, NY 14731
Mailing Address:
P.O. Box 490
Ellicottville, NY 14731
Tel.: 716-699-2393 **NY**
Fax: 716-699-2893
Year Founded: 1895
Approx.Sls.: $18,000,000
Emp.: 210
Fiscal Year-end: 9/30/91
Export
Manufacture of Lumber & Wood Products
S.I.C.: 2426
Gerard J. Fitzpatrick *(Pres.)*
Gregory J. Fitzpatrick *(V.P. & Treas.)*
Michael Fitzpatrick *(V.P. & Sec.)*
Ronald Mercer *(V.P.)*
Cheryl A. Schmidt *(Controller)*
Dana G. Fitzpatrick *(Mgr.-Intl.)*

Principal(s):
Gerard J. Fitzpatrick
Dana G. Fitzpatrick

No. of Mfg. Plants/Facilities: 1
No. of U.S. Offices: 1

Outside Service Firm(s):

Ernst & Young*(Auditors)*
1400 Key Tower - 50 Fountain Plaza
Buffalo, NY
Tel.: 716-843-5000
Fax: 716-847-6949

Shane & Franz*(Legal Firm)*
Olean, NY

Fleet Bank of New York, N.A.*(Major Banking Relationship)*
10 Fountain Plaza
Buffalo, NY 14202

FIVE DOLLAR CLOTHING STORES
2320 E. 49th St.
Los Angeles, CA 90058
Tel.: 213-587-5555
Tel.: 800-275-2744
Fax: 213-587-7324
Year Founded: 1981
Approx.Sls.: $45,000,000
Emp.: 700
Fiscal Year-end: 6/30/91
Retail Women's Wear
S.I.C.: 5621; 5632; 5137
Morrie Dym *(Pres. & Chief Exec. Officer)*
Larry Smith *(V.P. & Sec.)*
Miriam Knutson *(V.P.-Opers.)*
Virginia Solomon *(V.P.-Fin. & Info. Systems)*
Neal Marks *(Dir.-Pur.)*
Mario Acevedo *(Dir.-Distr. Center)*
Debbie Rosenberg *(Dir.-Personnel Training & Devel.)*
Bernie Labowitz *(Dir.-Leasing)*
Charles Rodriguez *(Dir.-Construction & Store Design)*
Nancy Carter *(Mgr.-Personnel)*

Computer Systems/Hardware:
IBM System 36, POS-NCR 2122

FLAIR COMMUNICATIONS AGENCY, INC.
Flair House, 214 W. Erie St.
Chicago, IL 60610
Tel.: 312-943-5959
Tel.: 800-621-8317
Fax: 312-943-0881
Year Founded: 1964
Approx.Billings: $37,000,000
Emp.: 120
Annual Planning/Execution, Trade Channel-Specific, Account-Specific, Point-of-Sale, Direct Response/ Database/Micro Marketing Events/ Special Markets
S.I.C.: 7311
Lee F. Flaherty *(Chm Bd. & Chief Exec. Officer)*
Allyn M. Miller *(Pres.)*
Al Fritsch *(Chief Oper. Officer & V.P.)*
August V. Comella *(Exec. V.P., Gen. Mgr.)*
Al Fritsch *(Dir.-Mktg.)*
Thomas Lynch *(Mgr.-Mktg. Plng.)*

Computer Systems/Hardware:
Four Phase

Outside Service Firm(s):

Friedman, Goldberg & Mintz*(Auditors)*
Chicago, IL

Sidley & Austin*(Legal Firm)*
One First National Plaza, 42nd Fl.
Chicago, IL 60603
Tel.: 312-853-7000
Fax: 312-853-7036

American National Bank & Trust Company of Chicago*(Major Banking Relationship)*
33 N. LaSalle St.
Chicago, IL 60602
Tel.: 312-661-5000
Fax: 312-661-6417

Branches:

Flair Communications Agency, Inc. **(1)**
246 East 62nd St.
New York, NY 10021
Tel.: 212-758-4487
Lee Flaherty *(Chm. & Chief Exec. Officer)*

Flair Communications Agency, Inc. **(1)**
4929 Wilshire Blvd., Ste. 650
Los Angeles, CA 90010
Tel.: 213-937-1511
David Flaherty *(V.P.-West Coast Opers.)*

Flair Communications Agency, Inc. **(1)**
150 Stratford Bldg., Ste. 280
Winston-Salem, NC 20174
Tel.: 919-722-1200

FLAKT INC., BAHNSON DIV.
3901 West Point Blvd.
Winston-Salem, NC 27103
Mailing Address:
P.O. Box 10458
Winston-Salem, NC 27108
Tel.: 919-760-3111
Fax: 919-760-1548
Approx.Sls.: $40,000,000
Emp.: 600
Fiscal Year-end: 12/31/90
Mfrs. Indus. Air Conditioning, Humidifying & Cleaning Equip. Contractors, Engineers & Contractors, Filtration
S.I.C.: 3585
F.L. Mangum *(Pres. & V.P.-Contracting Bus. Unit)*
Michael Heilig *(Dir.-Sls. & Mktg.)*
R.D. Flowers *(Mgr.-Pur.)*

FLANAGAN BROTHERS
400 Clark St.
Bear Creek, WI 54922
Mailing Address:
P.O. Box 217
Bear Creek, WI 54922
Tel.: 715-752-4105
Fax: 715-752-3432
Year Founded: 1924
Sales Range: $10-19 Million
Emp.: 100
Fiscal Year-end: 12/31/90
Import Export
Mfr. Sauerkraut in Cans, Polybags & Glass Jars
S.I.C.: 2035
David J. Flanagan, Jr. *(Pres.)*
Ryan A. Downs *(V.P.-Sls. & Mktg.)*
David D. Flanagan *(V.P.-Production)*
Debbie Wege *(Sec.)*
Marie F. Downs *(Treas.)*
Jill Johnson *(Controller)*
Ali Norder *(Asst. Mgr.-Sls.)*
Principal(s):
David J. Flanagan, Jr.
Ryan A. Downs
David D. Flanagan

Outside Service Firm(s):

Schenck & Associates*(Auditors)*
Appleton, WI

Foley & Lardner*(Legal Firm)*
Clintonville, WI

First State Bank*(Major Banking Relationship)*
Clintonville, WI

Subsidiary:

Flanagan Bros. Trucking Co. **(1)**
400 Clark St.
Bear Creek, WI 54922
Tel.: 715-752-4105
Emp.: 15
Transportation
S.I.C.: 4212
Deb Jarries *(Sec.)*

FLANDERS INDUSTRIES, INC.
1901 Wheeler Ave.
Fort Smith, AR 72901
Tel.: 501-785-2351 **AR**
Fax: 501-783-2694
Year Founded: 1970
Approx.Sls.: $39,000,000
Emp.: 460
Export
Mfr. of Metal Lawn & Garden Furniture; Fireplace Equipment, Andirons, Grates, Screens
S.I.C.: 2514; 3429
Don H. Flanders *(Chm. Bd.)*
Dudley K. Flanders *(Pres. & Chief Exec. Officer)*

Outside Service Firm(s):

Norris Taylor & Co.*(Auditors)*
Fort Smith, AR

First National Bank*(Major Banking Relationship)*
Fort Smith, AR

THE FLATLEY COMPANY
50 Braintree Hill Office Park
Braintree, MA 02184
Tel.: 617-848-2000
Fax: 617-849-5199
Approx.Sls.: $300,000,000
Emp.: 5,320
Cooperative Apartment Developers; Industrial Buildings, New Construction, Commercial & Office Buildings, New Construction; Commercial & Office Buildings,

Renovation & Repair; Shopping Center Construction; Auditorium Hall Operation; Apartment Hotel Operation; Franchised Hotel
S.I.C.: 1531; 1541; 1542; 6512; 6513; 7011

FLAVOR HOUSE PRODUCTS, INC.
2700 Horace Shepherd Dr.
Dothan, AL 36303
Mailing Address:
P.O. Box 8084,
Dothan, AL 36304
Tel.: 205-983-5643
Fax: 205-983-4796
Approx.Sls.: $35,000,000
Emp.: 125
Fiscal Year-end: 12/31/90
Dry Roasted & Oil Roasted Peanuts, Snack Nuts & Canister Snacks
S.I.C.: 2068
H.P. Byrd *(Chief Exec. Officer)*
Robert Fitzgerald *(Pres.)*
P.J. Simkus *(V.P.-Fin.)*
W.T. Chappelear, Jr. *(V.P.-Mktg.)*
David Kerper *(Dir.-Pur.)*

THE FLECTO CO., INC.
1000 45th St.
Oakland, CA 94608
Tel.: 510-655-2470
Tel.: 800-635-3286
Fax: 510-652-0969
Year Founded: 1934
Sales Range: $20-39 Million
Emp.: 100
Fiscal Year-end: 12/31/90
Wood & Metal Finishes; Special Coatings
S.I.C.: 2821; 2822; 2851
John E. Vetterli *(Pres.)*
Michael J. McCoy *(Chief Fin. Officer & V.P.)*
Richard Swanson *(V.P.-Opers. & Gen. Mgr.)*
Michael O. Vetterli *(V.P.-Mktg.)*
Wayne Schultz *(Dir.-Customer Service)*
Steve Boike *(Buyer)*

Computer Systems/Hardware:
Hewlett Packard System 3000

Outside Service Firm(s):

Deloitte & Touche*(Auditors)*
50 Fremont St.
San Francisco, CA 94105-2230
Tel.: 415-393-4300
Fax: 415-227-0452

Foley, McIntosh & Foley*(Legal Firm)*
Oakland, CA

C.B. FLEET COMPANY, INCORPORATED
4615 Murray Pl.
Lynchburg, VA 24506
Mailing Address:
P.O. Box 11349,
Lynchburg, VA 24506
Tel.: 804-528-4000 **VA**
Telex: 710 871 1501
Fax: 804-847-4219
Year Founded: 1869
Emp.: 300
Mfr. of Health & Beauty Aid Products
S.I.C.: 2834; 2844
William R. Chambers *(Chm. Bd. & Chief Exec. Officer)*
Brian Duffy *(Pres. & Chief Oper. Officer)*
George M. Hricz *(V.P.-Opers.)*
Lynn Farrar *(V.P.-Pur.)*
Jerry Johnson *(Dir.-Pur.)*
Wayne C. Johnson *(Dir.-Personnel)*
Frances Lee *(Dir.-Quality Assurnace)*
Robert A. Lemon *(Dir.-Fin.)*
James O'Reagan *(Dir.-Opers.)*
Judy Ryon *(Dir.-Sls. & Mktg.)*
Lisa Saunders *(Dir.-Distr.)*
Galen Collins *(Mgr.-Res. & Devel.)*
Charles R. Hudson *(Mgr.-Mngmt. Information Systems)*
Ezra Jenkins *(Mgr.-Employee Rels.)*
Robert W. Stevens *(Mgr.-Natl. Sls.)*

No. of Mfg. Plants/Facilities: 1
No. of U.S. Offices: 1

Computer Systems/Hardware:
IBM S38 AS400

Outside Service Firm(s):

Ernst & Young*(Auditors)*
One James Center, 901 E. Cary St.,Ste. 1000
Richmond, VA 23219
Tel.: 804-780-0010

Edmunds & Williams*(Legal Firm)*
Lynchburg, VA

Crestar Bank*(Major Banking Relationship)*
Lynchburg, VA

Non-U.S. Holdings:

E.C. DeWitt & Company (Aust.) Pty. Ltd. **(1)**
25 Macbeth St.
Braeside, Victoria 3195, Australia
Tel.: 03-580 2755
Fax: 03-580 2899
Emp.: 3
Import Export
Computer Systems/Hardware:
Total Peripherals 386-33 1922 MH2, 81 MBHD, EPSON LQ 1070
Mktg. & Sales of Chemicals & Over-the-Counter Pharmaceutical Products
S.I.C.: 5169; 5122; 5100
Denis Dikschei *(Mng. Dir.)*

E.C. DeWitt & Company Limited **(1)**
62-64 East Barnet Road
New Barnet, EN4 8RQ, United Kingdom
Tel.: 081-441-9310 (100%)
Mfr. of Pharmaceuticals, Toothpaste
S.I.C.: 2834; 2844
John James *(Mng. Dir.)*

DeWitt International (Singapore) Pte. Ltd. **(1)**
62 Tannery Lane
Singapore, 1334, Singapore
Tel.: 747 1172 (100%)
Fax: 745 4482
Sales & Marketing of DeWitt's Pills, Clinomint Smokers Toothpaste
S.I.C.: 5122
Tay Pan Ling *(Mng. Dir.)*

FLEET ENGINEERS, INC.
1800 E. Keating
Muskegon, MI 49442
Tel.: 616-777-2537
Fax: 616-777-5500
Sales Range: $10-19 Million
Emp.: 112
Fiscal Year-end: 12/31/90
Import Export
Motor Vehicle Parts & Accessories
S.I.C.: 3714
Louis E. Eklund, Jr. *(Chm. & Treas.)*
Wesley Eklund *(Pres.)*
Donald Jones *(Controller)*
Robert Eklund *(Gen. Counsel)*
Ann Eklund *(Sec.)*
M. Dewitt *(Dir.-Personnel)*
Jeff Beach *(Mgr.-Engrng.)*
Jerry Miller *(Mgr.-Mktg.)*

Outside Service Firm(s):

BDO Seidman*(Auditors)*
801 W. Norton
Muskegon, MI 49441
Tel.: 616-739-9441

CNA Insurance*(Commercial Insurance Carrier)*
Muskegon, MI

Parmenter, O'Toole, et al*(Legal Firm)*
Muskegon, MI

Comerica Bank*(Major Banking Relationship)*
Muskegon, MI

Subsidiary:

Lee Industries **(1)**
1800 E. Keating Ave.
Muskegon, MI 49442
Tel.: 616-777-2540
Emp.: 34
Assembly, Packaging, Painting & Finishing
S.I.C.: 3714
Wesley Eklund *(Pres.)*

FLEETWOOD ALUMINUM PRODUCTS
2485 Railroad St.
Corona, CA 91720
Tel.: 909-279-1070
Fax: 909-279-8068
Approx.Sls.: $10,000,000
Emp.: 95
Fiscal Year-end: 12/31/91
Aluminum Doors, Sash & Trim
S.I.C.: 3442
V. Glenn McCoy *(Pres.)*
Gerald Perryman *(V.P.)*
Janice McCoy *(Sec. & Treas.)*

THE FLEETWOOD COMPANY
1500 Brook Dr.
Downers Grove, IL 60515
Tel.: 708-495-9300
Year Founded: 1935
Approx.Sls.: $10,000,000
Emp.: 60
Export
Nil-O-Nal, Fayd Skin Cream, Wate-On Emulsions & Tablets, Cornmaster, Marlene's Hair Waving Shampoo, Rinsa-Rama, Super Wate On Tablets & Emulsion & Powder Packs, Tintz Creme Color Shampoo, Terri Cover Cream & Liquid, Floress Oil Wave Protein Shampoo, Spring Again Tropical Skin Moisturizer & Cleanser, Nailette Nail Toughener, Wate-Off Tablets, Tropical Skin Moisturizer & Cleanser
S.I.C.: 2844
Nelson McMahon, Jr. *(Pres.)*
D. R. Kloss *(Exec. V.P.-Sls.)*

Computer Systems/Hardware:
AT&T

FLEETWOOD SYSTEMS, INC.
621 E. Plainfield Rd.
Countryside, IL 60525
Tel.: 708-482-9696
Fax: 708-482-9776
Approx.Sls.: $30,000,000
Emp.: 300
Mfr. of Material Handling Equipment
S.I.C.: 3535; 3565
Wallace W. Mojden *(Chm. Bd.)*
Andrew E. Mojden *(Pres.)*
Edward Paben *(V.P.-Sls.)*
Lawrence S. Carlson *(Sec. & Treas.)*

FLEISCHLI OIL COMPANY, INC.
2234 W. Lincoln Way
Cheyenne, WY 82001
Mailing Address:
P.O. Box 487,
Cheyenne, WY 82003
Tel.: 307-634-4466 **WY**
Fax: 307-778-8036
Year Founded: 1955
Approx.Sls.: $60,000,000
Emp.: 71
Fiscal Year-end: 8/31/91
Petroleum Products
S.I.C.: 5172
Gus Fleischli *(Chm. Bd.)*
Gerald Loghry *(Pres.)*
Robert K. Jensen *(V.P.)*
W. Alan Hughes *(Treas. & Sec.)*

Outside Service Firm(s):

McGladrey & Pullen*(Auditors)*
320 W. 25th
Cheyenne, WY
Tel.: 307-634-2151

Dray, Madison & Thomson, P.C.*(Legal Firm)*
Cheyenne, WY

Norwest Bank*(Major Banking Relationship)*
Cheyenne, WY

FLEISHMAN HILLARD INC.
200 N. Broadway Ave.
Saint Louis, MO 63102
Tel.: 314-982-1700
Twx: 910-861-1198
Fax: 314-231-2313
Year Founded: 1946
Approx.Billings: $52,228,000
Emp.: 525
John D. Graham *(Chm. & Chief Exec. Officer)*
Royce L. Rollins *(Exec. V.P. & Chief Fin. Officer)*
Dan Huffer *(Exec. V.P. & Chief Oper. Officer)*
Alan W. Akerson *(Exec. V.P.)*
Joseph T. Finnigan *(Exec. V.P.)*
Linda S. Mills *(Exec. V.P.)*
James L. Morice *(Exec. V.P.)*
Paul J. Siemer *(Exec. V.P.)*

FLEMING PACKAGING CORP.
1028 S.W. Adams St.
Peoria, IL 61602
Tel.: 309-676-2121
Fax: 309-676-6138
Year Founded: 1934
Approx.Sls.: $100,000,000
Emp.: 900
Offset, Gravure, Flexo, Letterpress Printing: Commercial, Labels, Stamps; Direct Mail Advertising Services
S.I.C.: 2759; 2752; 7331
William J. Mannlein *(Pres. & Chief Exec. Officer)*
Wm. M. Fulton *(Pres.)*
Allyn G. Schmid *(Sr. V.P. & Treas.)*
Gerald T. Wombacher *(Sr. V.P.-Sls.)*
John F. Ryan *(V.P. & Sec.)*

Subsidiaries:

Budde & Westermann **(1)**
P.O. Box 177
Montclair, NJ 07042
Tel.: 201-744-5363
Jules Dahlman *(Gen. Mgr.)*

Fleming-Potter Co. **(1)**
1028 S.W. Adams St.
Peoria, IL 61602
Tel.: 309-676-2121
Bill Fulton *(Pres.)*

Fleming-Potter Fast Printing **(1)**
1114 S.W. Jefferson St.
Peoria, IL 61602
Tel.: 309-673-8183
Phil Haste *(Gen. Mgr.)*

Fleming-Potter Webkote **(1)**
1016 S.W. Adams
Peoria, IL 61602
Tel.: 309-676-2121
Greg Black *(Gen. Mgr.)*

fp CameoColor, Inc. **(1)**
700 Pinecrest Dr.
East Peoria, IL 61611
Tel.: 309-698-1600
John Watts *(Gen. Mgr.)*

fp Label, Inc. **(1)**
601 Airpark Rd.
Napa, CA 94558-6272
Tel.: 707-258-3900
Bob Pyburn *(Gen. Mgr.)*

fp Packaging, Inc. **(1)**
385 Oyster Point Blvd. Unit #3
South San Francisco, CA 94080
Tel.: 415-742-5400
Greg Fulford *(Gen. Mgr.)*

Fleming Packaging Corp.—(Continued)

fp Portocork, Inc. (1)
601 Airpark Rd.
Napa, CA 94558-6272
Tel.: 707-258-3930
James Herwatt *(Gen. Mgr.)*

Spiralkote (1)
1200 Central Florida Pkwy.
Orlando, FL 32837
Tel.: 407-859-7780
Bob Poppen *(Gen. Mgr.)*

J. H. FLETCHER & CO.
402 High St.
Huntington, WV 25702
Mailing Address:
P.O. Box 2187,
Huntington, WV 25722
Tel.: 304-525-7811 **DE**
Fax: 304-525-3770
Year Founded: 1937
Approx.Sls.: $30,000,000
Emp.: 150
Fiscal Year-end: 12/31/90
Export
Manufacture Underground Mine Equipment
S.I.C.: 3532
Corporate Giving Program: Based on a Percentage of Pretax Profit, Requests Must be Received in writing by December 1st
Employee Matching Gifts Program: Match Up to $200 per Employee for Gifts to Accredited Institutions of Higher Learning
James H. Fletcher *(Chm. & Chief Exec. Officer)*
Raymond F. Parks *(Pres. & Chief Oper. Officer)*
Philip E. Cline *(Sr. V.P. & Chief Fin. Officer)*
Jack W. Nistendirk *(Controller)*
Douglas R. Hardman *(Chief Engr.)*
William S. McIntyre *(Chief Design Engr.)*
David Cooper *(Dir.-Personnel)*
Charles C. Brown *(Mgr.-Mfg.)*
Billy D. Goad, Sr. *(Mgr.-Service)*
Steven Shirley *(Mgr.-Mtls..)*
Robert Stach *(Mgr.-Sls.)*
C. Maxwell Cassidy *(Pur. Agent)*

No. of Mfg. Plants/Facilities: 2
No. of U.S. Offices: 1

Computer Systems/Hardware:
IBM System AS 400

Outside Service Firm(s):

Taylor & Co.*(Auditors)*
Huntington, WV

Jenkins, Fenstermaker, Krieger, Kays & Farrell*(Legal Firm)*
Huntington, WV

First Huntington National Bank*(Major Banking Relationship)*
Huntington, WV

FLETCHER ENTERPRISES
2601 N. 32nd Ave.
Phoenix, AZ 85009
Tel.: 602-269-1351 **AZ**
Fax: 602-484-9279
Sales Range: $40-59 Million
Emp.: 250
Real Estate
S.I.C.: 6531
Robert Fletcher *(Pres.)*

Computer Systems/Hardware:
IBM System 38

Outside Service Firm(s):

CNA Insurance*(Commercial Insurance Carrier)*
CNA Plaza,
Chicago, IL 60685
Tel.: 312-822-5000

CNA Insurance*(Group Insurer)*
CNA Plaza,
Chicago, IL 60685
Tel.: 312-822-5000

First Interstate Bank*(Major Banking Relationship)*
P.O. Box 53441,
Phoenix, AZ 85072-3441
Tel.: 602-229-4049

Subsidiary:

Fletcher Cobre Tire Co. Inc. (1)
2601 N. 32nd Ave.
Phoenix, AZ 85009
Tel.: 602-269-1351
Retail Tires & Automotive Repair
S.I.C.: 5531; 7538
Gerald W. Fletcher *(Pres.)*

FHW
FletcherHuntWirthAssociatesInc

FLETCHER HUNT WIRTH ASSOCIATES, INC.
2405 Grand, Ste. 400
Kansas City, MO 64108
Tel.: 816-471-1880
Tel.: 800-659-6603
Year Founded: 1987
Approx.Billings: $14,200,000
Emp.: 27
Andy Fletcher *(Pres. & Chief Exec. Officer)*
Jon Cassat *(V.P.)*
Jeff Wirth *(V.P.)*
Wendy Fletcher *(V.P., Mktg. Services)*
Kathy Falcone *(V.P., Pub. Rels.)*
Bill Pajnic *(Controller)*

Computer Systems/Hardware:
Macintosh

FLEX-O-GLASS, INC.
1100 N. Cicero Ave.
Chicago, IL 60651
Tel.: 312-261-5200
Fax: 312-261-5422
Year Founded: 1924
Emp.: 250
Manufacture Plastic Film & Plastic Products
S.I.C.: 3089
Harold Warp *(Chm. Bd.)*
Harold G. Warp *(Pres.)*
Ellis Bogenholm *(Sec.)*
William Clarey *(Controller)*
Ross Fosbender *(Mgr.-Adv.)*
Jeff Whittington *(Mgr.-Sls.)*

Outside Service Firm(s):

Ernst & Young*(Auditors)*
233 S. Wacker Dr.
Chicago, IL 60606
Tel.: 312-368-1800
Fax: 312-645-3095

Pioneer Bank & Trust Co.*(Major Banking Relationship)*
Chicago, IL

Divisions:

Flex-O-Film Plastic Div. (1)
1100 N. Cicero Ave.
Chicago, IL 60651
Tel.: 312-379-7878

Warp Brothers (1)
4647 W. Augusta Blvd.
Chicago, IL 60651
Tel.: 312-261-5200
Fax: 312-261-5204
Approx.Sls.: $20,000,000
Emp.: 200
Export

Computer Systems/Hardware:
IBM System 36
Plastic Window Materials, Plastic Film & Sheeting, Other Plastic Prods.
S.I.C.: 3081
Harold G. Warp *(Pres.)*
Ross Fosbender *(Adv. Mgr.)*

FLEXEL, INC.
115 Perimeter Center Pl., Ste. 1100
Atlanta, GA 30346
Tel.: 404-393-0696 **GA**
Fax: 404-393-2174
Year Founded: 1985
Approx.Sls.: $150,000,000
Emp.: 1,000
Fiscal Year-end: 11/30/92
Import Export
Manufacture & Sale of Flexible Packaging Materials
S.I.C.: 3089
Corporate Giving Program: Donations *to Customer Functions & Trade* Functions
W. Lindsey Walters *(Chm. Bd. & Pres.)*
Calvin O. Walters *(Vice Chm.)*
Marty Benton *(V.P.-Human Resources)*
Tom McClimen *(V.P.-Mfg.)*
Robert Smelas *(V.P.-Fin.)*
Anthony Vaudo *(V.P.-Opers.)*
J.B. Brooks *(Sec. & Treas.)*
Harold Cannon *(Mgr.-Leasing)*
Scott Ellis *(Mgr.-Import)*
Max Hartman *(Pur. Agent)*
Debra Bottega *(Mktg. Coord.)*
Ann Riggs *(Benefits Admin.)*

No. of Mfg. Plants/Facilities: 4
No. of U.S. Offices: 3

Computer Systems/Hardware:
IBM System 38, 4300

Subsidiary:

Robert Williams (1)
115 Perimeter Center Pl., Suite 1100
Atlanta, GA 30346
Tel.: 404-392-9237
Emp.: 65
Flexible Pack Films; Slitter Distributor
S.I.C.: 3081
Dick Ploeger *(Pres.)*

FLEXFAB, INC.
1843 Gun Lake Rd.
Hastings, MI 49058
Tel.: 616-945-2433
Fax: 616-945-3442
Year Founded: 1961
Approx.Sls.: $32,000,000
Emp.: 300
Fiscal Year-end: 9/30/91
Export
Mfr. of Flexible Non-Metallic Hose & Ducting
S.I.C.: 3052; 3069
Willard G. Pierce *(Chm. Bd.)*
D.A. DeCamp *(Pres. & Chief Exec. Officer)*
J.R. Toburen *(V.P. & Sec.)*
Gerald Dyer *(V.P. & Gen. Mgr.)*
Hugh Boyce *(Dir.-Sls. & Mktg.)*
Principal(s):
Willard G. Pierce
D.A. DeCamp

Computer Systems/Hardware:
HP Network/Baan

Outside Service Firm(s):

Ernst & Young*(Auditors)*
171 Monroe Ave. NW
Grand Rapids, MI 49503
Tel.: 616-774-0710
Fax: 616-774-0190

Johnson & Higgins*(Commercial Insurance Carrier)*
Hastings, MI

Varnum, Riddering, Schmidt & Howlett*(Legal Firm)*
800 Prime Bank Bldg., Pearle & Monroe, NW
Grand Rapids, MI 49503
Tel.: 616-459-4186

American National Bank & Trust Co. of Michigan*(Major Banking Relationship)*
Grand Rapids, MI

Subsidiaries:

Associated Industrial Rubber (1)
5 Lemnah Dr.
St. Albans, VT 05478
Tel.: 802-527-0108
Emp.: 50
Mfr. Rubber Products
S.I.C.: 3052

Federal Hose Manufacturing Corp. (1)
25 Florence Ave.
Painesville, OH 44077
Tel.: 216-352-8927
Emp.: 48
Mfr. Rubber Products
S.I.C.: 3052

Pro Line (1)
1675 Gun Lake Rd.
Hastings, MI 49058
Tel.: 616-948-8026
Emp.: 50
Mfr. of Archery Equipment
S.I.C.: 3949

FLEXIBLE PRODUCTS COMPANY
1007 Industrial Park Dr.
Marietta, GA 30061
Mailing Address:
P.O. Box 3190,
Marietta, GA 30061
Tel.: 404-428-2684
Telex: 804670
Fax: 404-428-9431
Year Founded: 1951
Assets: $36,256,000
Earnings: $946,000
Liabilities: $26,858,000
Net Worth: $9,398,000
Approx.Sls.: $83,804,000
Emp.: 380
Fiscal Year-end: 5/31/92
Import Export
Mfr. of Urethane Foam Systems, Urethane Coatings & Vinyl Plastisol Inks
S.I.C.: 2821; 3086; 3087; 2899
J. Peter Henson *(Chm. Bd. & Chief Exec. Officer)*
B.J. Wolfson *(Pres. & Chief Oper. Officer)*
W.R. York *(Controller)*
T.R. Casey *(V.P.-Human Resources & Employee Benefits)*
D.J. Cruickshank *(V.P. & Chief Fin. Officer)*
R.L. Kells *(V.P.-Pur.)*
B.N. Dutenhoffer *(Dir.-Mngmt. Information Services)*
Principal(s):
Employee-Owned

No. of Mfg. Plants/Facilities: 3
No. of U.S. Offices: 3
No. of Foreign Offices: 2

Computer Systems/Hardware:
MICRO

Outside Service Firm(s):

Price Waterhouse*(Auditors)*
100 Cumberland Circle, Ste. 1400
Atlanta, GA 30339

Johnson & Higgins*(Commercial Insurance Carrier)*
25 Park Place, N.E.
Atlanta, GA 30303
Tel.: 404-658-9877

Johnson & Higgins*(Group Insurer)*
25 Park Place, N.E.
Atlanta, GA 30303
Tel.: 404-658-9877

Robinson Humphrey Company, Inc.*(Investment Banker)*
3333 Peachtree Rd., N.E.
Atlanta, GA 30326
Tel.: 404-266-6000

Alston & Bird*(Legal Firm)*
One Atlantic Center, 1201 West Peachtree St.
Atlanta, GA 30309-3424
Tel.: 404-881-7000

Subsidiary:

Insta-Foam Products, Inc. **(1)**
1500 Cedarwood Dr.
Joliet, IL 60435
Tel.: 815-741-6800 (100%)
Fax: 815-741-6822
Emp.: 135
Mfr. Urethane Foam Systems
S.I.C.: 2822
Joe Hall *(V.P. & Chief Oper. Officer)*

Non-U.S. Subsidiaries:

Euroflex Screen Print Supplies Ltd. **(1)**
P.O. Box 300,
Dartford, Kent DA1 1PQ, United Kingdom
Tel.: 44-3-227-7778 (100%)
Fax: 44-3-228-8370

Polyurethane International Division **(1)**
Excelsiorlaan 40 1930,
Zavemtem, Belgium
Tel.: 32-2-725-7879
Fax: 32-2-725-7887

Screen Products Australian Pty Ltd **(1)**
77 Parkhurst Dr. 3180
Knoxfield, Victoria Australia
Tel.: 03-887-1522 (80%)
Fax: 03-887-1711

FLEXONICS INC.
300 E. Devon Ave.
Bartlett, IL 60103
Tel.: 708-837-1811
Fax: 708-213-3052
Year Founded: 1902
Approx.Sls.: $35,000,000
Emp.: 350
Fiscal Year-end: 2/28/91
Export
Flexible Metal Hose, Expansion Joints, Compensators, Flexible Ducting & Connectors
S.I.C.: 3599; 3444
S.J. Perkins *(Pres.)*
W.J. Gonia *(V.P.-Sls. & Mktg.)*
W. Kowal *(Chief Fin. Officer)*

FLINN & DREFFEIN ENGINEERING CO.
3520 Commercial Ave.
Northbrook, IL 60062
Tel.: 708-272-6370
Fax: 708-272-6450
Approx.Sls.: $10,000,000
Emp.: 40
Export
Designer & Builder of Industrial Furnaces & Process Controls Systems
S.I.C.: 3567; 3823
R.A. Kelly *(Chm. Bd.)*
J.K. Balaz *(Pres. & Chief Exec. Officer)*
Robert A. Andreas *(V.P.-Sls.)*

FLINT INK CORP.
25111 Glendale Ave.
Detroit, MI 48239
Tel.: 313-538-6800 **MI**
Fax: 313-538-0730
Year Founded: 1920
Approx.Sls.: $415,000,000
Emp.: 2,650
Fiscal Year-end: 12/31/87
Chemicals & Allied Products; Petroluem Refining; Insurance Carriers
S.I.C.: 2816; 2865; 2911; 6399
Robert H. Flint *(Chm. Bd. & Chief Exec. Officer)*
H. Howard Flint, II *(Pres. & Chief Oper. Officer)*
Thomas W. Clarke *(V.P.-Fin. & Treas.)*
Henry J. Rosinski *(Controller)*
Richard Laber *(Dir.-Pur.)*
Michael S. Cain *(Mgr.-Mngmt. Information Systems)*
John H. Denler, Jr. *(Mgr.-Cash & Benefits)*

No. of Mfg. Plants/Facilities: 40

Computer Systems/Hardware:
IBM Systems 315D & 4361

Outside Service Firm(s):

Deloitte & Touche*(Auditors)*
200 Renaissance Center, 16th Fl.
Detroit, MI 48243
Tel.: 313-396-3000
Fax: 313-259-8087

Dykema, Gossett*(Legal Firm)*
400 Renaissance Ctr., 35th Fl.
Detroit, MI 48243
Tel.: 313-568-6800

Barnett Banks Trust Company, N.A.*(Major Banking Relationship)*
Miami, FL

Michigan National Bank*(Major Banking Relationship)*
Detroit, MI

Equitable Life*(Pension Manager)*
1221 Ave. of the Americas
New York, NY 10022
Tel.: 212-382-8038
Fax: 212-382-8089

Michigan National Investors*(Pension Manager)*
Detroit, MI

FLINT MANUFACTURING CO.
3084 E. Hemphill Rd.
Burton, MI 48529
Tel.: 313-742-8033
Fax: 313-742-5379
Approx.Sls.: $10,000,000
Emp.: 60
Fiscal Year-end: 12/31/91
Magic Heat, Heat Circulators, Fireplace Heaters
S.I.C.: 3567
James Lantz *(Pres.)*
Bruce Howard *(Exec. V.P.)*
Theodore Bunker *(Controller)*

Outside Service Firm(s):

Ernst & Young*(Auditors)*
101 N. Washington Ave.
Saginaw, MI 48607

Michigan National Bank*(Major Banking Relationship)*
Flint, MI

FLINT RIVER MILLS
1100 Dothan Rd.
Bainbridge, GA 31717
Mailing Address:
P.O. Box 278
Bainbridge, GA 31717
Tel.: 912-246-2232 **FL**
Fax: 912-246-2607
Year Founded: 1947
Approx.Sls.: $24,000,000
Emp.: 125
Mfr. of Poultry & Livestock Feeds
S.I.C.: 2048
A.L. Poitevint *(Chm. Bd. & Pres.)*
Fred Collins *(V.P. & Sec.)*
Hoke S. Grant *(V.P.)*
Henry Metcalf *(V.P.)*
Charles Drane Smith *(Treas.)*

Outside Service Firm(s):

James D. Holley & Co.*(Auditors)*
Tallahassee, FL

Lambert, Floyd & Conger*(Legal Firm)*
Bainbridge, GA

First Port City Bank*(Major Banking Relationship)*
Bainbridge, GA

Plant:

Flint River Mills **(1)**
1006 Dothan Rd.
Bainbridge, GA 31717
Tel.: 912-246-2232

FLO-PAC CORPORATION
700 N. Washington Ave., Ste. 400
Minneapolis, MN 55401
Tel.: 612-332-6240
Fax: 612-344-1663
Year Founded: 1913
Approx.Sls.: $20,000,000
Emp.: 225
Fiscal Year-end: 12/31/90
Flo-Pac Industrial & Domestic Brushes, Brooms
S.I.C.: 3991
Jeffrey A. Bowen *(Pres.)*
Leroy J. Schwartz *(V.P.-Adv.)*
Raymond R. Olson *(Treas.)*

Outside Service Firm(s):

Grant Thornton*(Auditors)*
500 Pillsbury Center
Minneapolis, MN 55402-1459

Faegre & Benson*(Legal Firm)*
2200 Norwest Ctr., 90 S. 7th St.
Minneapolis, MN 55402-3901
Tel.: 612-336-3000
Fax: 612-336-3026

Norwest Bank Minnesota, N.A.*(Major Banking Relationship)*
6th St. & Marquette Ave.
Minneapolis, MN 55479-0065
Tel.: 612-667-8101

Divisions:

Flour City Brush Co. **(1)**
918 N. 3rd St.
Minneapolis, MN 55401
Tel.: 612-332-8641
S.I.C.: 3991

Pacific Coast Brush Co. **(1)**
11690 Pacific Ave.
Fontana, CA 92335
Tel.: 909-681-3747
S.I.C.: 3991

South Eastern Brush Co. **(1)**
1120 Oakleigh Dr.
East Point, GA 30344
Tel.: 404-762-0131
S.I.C.: 3991

FLOATHE JOHNSON ASSOCIATES, INC.
550 Kirkland Way, Ste. 200
Kirkland, WA 98033
Tel.: 206-822-8400
Tel.: 800-356-2843
Fax: 206-822-0879
Year Founded: 1982
Approx.Billings: $35,000,000
Emp.: 76
Advertising & Public Relations & "TechnoBranding" (Process for Building Brands for High Technology Products & Companies)
Maury Floathe *(Chm. Bd. & Pres.)*
Greg Johnson *(Exec. V.P., Gen. Mgr., Branch Operations)*
Charles R. Pettis, III *(Sr. V.P. Mktg. & Business Development)*
Katherine James-Schuitemaker *(Sr. V.P., Gen. Mgr., Kirkland)*
Jim Rose *(V.P., Opers.)*
Joe LePla *(Gen. Mgr., Pub. Rels.)*
Ann Demitruk *(Grp. Mgr.)*
Suzette Cavanaugh *(Dir., Res. & Plng.)*

FLODSTROM CONSTRUCTION CO.
(Company is Voluntarily Inactive)
707 Lake Cook Rd.
Deerfield, IL 60015
Tel.: 708-498-0300 **IL**
Fax: 708-498-9981
Approx.Sls.: $11,000,000
Emp.: 25
New Construction Of Commercial, Office & Industrial Buildings
S.I.C.: 1542; 1541
Sven G. Flodstrom *(Chm. Bd.)*
Len Flodstrom *(Pres.)*
Majken Flodstrom *(Sec. & Treas.)*

Outside Service Firm(s):

DiMonte & Lizak*(Legal Firm)*
Chicago, IL

LaSalle Bank Northbrook*(Major Banking Relationship)*
Northbrook, IL

FLOJET CORPORATION
12 Morgan St.
Irvine, CA 92718
Tel.: 714-859-4945
Fax: 714-859-1153
Year Founded: 1975
Approx.Sls.: $25,000,000
Emp.: 250
Export
Manufacture Pumps and Pumping Equipment
S.I.C.: 3561
Ben R. Du *(Pres.)*
Ernest Burnett *(V.P.)*
Carmela Du *(Treas.)*
Michael Patrick *(Dir.-Pur.)*
Butch Valenzuela *(Mgr.-Data Processing)*

Outside Service Firm(s):

White Nelson*(Auditors)*
Anaheim, CA

Gary B. Ross*(Legal Firm)*
Anaheim, CA

Security Pacific National Bank*(Major Banking Relationship)*
333 S. Hope
Los Angeles, CA 90071
Tel.: 213-345-6211

THE FLOOD COMPANY
1212 Barlow Rd.
Hudson, OH 44236
Mailing Address:
P.O. Box 399
Hudson, OH 44236
Tel.: 216-650-4070
Tel.: 800-321-3444 **OH**
Fax: 216-650-1453
Year Founded: 1841
Sales Range: $20-39 Million
Emp.: 90
Fiscal Year-end: 12/31/91
Export
Mfr. of Paint Additives, Wood Preservatives & Waterproofing Products
S.I.C.: 2851
Earl F. Flood *(Chm. Bd.)*
Peter E. Flood *(Pres. & Chief Exec. Officer)*
Gordon C. Anthony *(Exec. V.P. & Treas.)*
Cecil Given *(V.P.-Sls.)*
Peter B. Statham *(V.P.-Mktg.)*
Karen J. Harris *(Corp. Sec.)*
James R. Vollan *(Controller & Chief Admin. Officer)*
David J. Harris *(Dir.-Pur.)*

The Flood Company—(Continued)

Lou Ann Lambert *(Dir.-Human Resources)*
Robert A. Siladie *(Dir.-Environment/ Natural Rsrcs.)*
Patricia Wagle *(Dir.-Res. & Devel.)*
Ann Mars *(Mgr.-Sls. & Mktg.)*
George Washington *(Mgr.-Adv.)*

Principal(s):
Earl F. Flood
Peter E. Flood

No. of Mfg. Plants/Facilities: 2
No. of U.S. Offices: 3

Computer Systems/Hardware:
IBM AS/400

Outside Service Firm(s):

Swearingen & Swearingen*(Auditors)*
Cleveland, OH

Schneider, Smeltz, Ranney & LaFond*(Legal Firm)*
Cleveland, OH

Society National Bank*(Major Banking Relationship)*
Cleveland, OH

Society National Bank*(Pension Manager)*
Cleveland, OH

FLORAL GLASS & MIRROR, INC.
895 Motor Parkway
Hauppauge, NY 11788
Tel.: 516-234-2200 **NY**
Fax: 516-234-8866
Year Founded: 1951
Approx.Sls.: $13,000,000
Emp.: 100
Mfr. of Glass Products & Mirrors, Tempered & Insulating Glass
S.I.C.: 3231; 3211
Charles Kaplanek, Sr. *(Chm. Bd.)*
Charles Kaplanek, Jr. *(Pres.)*
Paul D. Bieber *(Exec. V.P.)*
Stan Lane *(Chief Fin. Officer)*
Rosemary Kaplanek *(Sec. & Treas.)*

Outside Service Firm(s):

Holtz, Rubenstein & Co.*(Auditors)*
445 Broad Hollow Rd.
Melville, NY 11747-3696

Marine Midland Bank*(Major Banking Relationship)*
Hauppauge, NY

FLORASYNTH INC.
410 E. 62nd St.
New York, NY 10021
Mailing Address:
P.O. Box 190, FDR Station
New York, NY 10150
Tel.: 212-371-7700
Fax: 212-752-4012
Assets: $97,000,000
Liabilities: $45,000,000
Net Worth: $52,000,000
Sales Range: $100-499 Million
Emp.: 1,000
Fiscal Year-end: 12/31/91
Mfr. of Flavor & Fragrance Compounds; Essential Oils; Aromatic Chemicals
S.I.C.: 2844; 2087; 2899
Jack N. Friedman *(Chm. Bd., Pres. & Chief Exec. Officer)*
Enrique Vindel Martinez *(Pres.-Intl. Div.)*
Richard J. Coleman *(Exec. V.P.)*
Michael F. Mann *(Exec. V.P. & Chief Fin. Officer)*
Kenneth L. Rugg *(V.P.-Fragrance Div.)*
Jamie Stecher *(Gen. Counsel)*

Outside Service Firm(s):

David Berdon & Co.*(Auditors)*
415 Madison Ave.
New York, NY 10017
Tel.: 212-832-0400

Chemical Bank*(Major Banking Relationship)*
270 Park Ave.
New York, NY 10017
Tel.: 212-286-6000

Divisions:

Florasynth Inc. **(1)**
300 North St.
Teterboro, NJ 07608
Tel.: 201-288-5066

Florasynth Inc. **(1)**
3720 Touhy Ave.
Skokie, IL 60076
Tel.: 708-973-4640

Lautier S.A. **(1)**
410 E. 62nd St.
New York, NY 10021
Tel.: 212-371-7700

Non-U.S. Holdings:

Compania General de Esencias Grupo Florasynth S.A. **(1)**
Poligono Industrial Congost, Ave. San Julian 154 08400 Grupo C Nave 4, Barcelona, Spain
Tel.: 3-846 3086
Telex: 97166 ESEN E
Fax: 3-846 3568
Sales Office
S.I.C.: 5122; 2844
Juan Ciuro *(Mgr.)*

Florasynth Australasia Pty. Ltd. **(1)**
Unit 6, 181-187 Taren Point Rd.
Taren Point, NSW 2229, Australia
Tel.: 2-526-1644
Telex: 790-176470 FLORAA AA
Fax: 2-526-1477
Sales Office
S.I.C.: 2087; 2844
Barrie Dean *(Mng. Dir.)*

Florasynth Canada, Inc. **(1)**
5800 Andover Ave.
Mount Royal, PQ H4T 1H4, Canada
Tel.: 514-341-3785
Telex: 058-24554
Fax: 514-341-6525
Mfr. & Sales of Fragrance & Flavor
S.I.C.: 2087; 2844; 2899; 5149
Ralph Arsenault *(Pres.)*

Florasynth (Far East) Pte. Ltd. **(1)**
1304 World Trade Centre
Causeway Bay, Hong Kong
Tel.: 2-763682
Telex: 780-80432 FLOR HX
Fax: 890-7565
Mktg. & Distr. of Flavorings & Fragrance Compounds
S.I.C.: 2087; 2844; 2899; 5122; 5149
Gary Churchwell *(Mng. Dir.)*

Florasyntesis Fragrancias y Aromas Ltda. **(1)**
Calle 39 Bis B No. 80-82,
Bogota, Colombia
Tel.: 1-269-4608
Telex: 396-42410
Fax: 1-269-2779
Manufacture & Sales of Flavors & Fragrances
S.I.C.: 2087; 2899; 5149
Carlos Quintana *(Mng. Dir.)*

Florasynth Fragancias y Aromas Ltda. **(1)**
Rua Frei Fabiano N. 36 CEP 20780,
Engenho Novo,
Rio de Janeiro, Brazil
Tel.: 21-261 6107
Telex: 391-2130885 LAUT BR
Fax: 21-261 3177
Flavor & Fragrance Manufacturing & Sales
S.I.C.: 2087; 2844

Florasyntesis Fragrancias y Aromas Ltda.-Factory **(1)**
Mauel Larrea 1000
Quito, Ecuador
Tel.: 2-547 767
Telex: 393-2198 ALESCA ED
Fax: 2-564 912
Mfr. of Fragrances & Flavors
S.I.C.: 2087; 2844; 2899
Oswaldo Alvarez *(Mng. Dir.)*

Florasynth GMBH **(1)**
Mittelstr. 52-54 5000
Cologne, 1, Germany
Tel.: 221-235433
Telex: 841-8881675
Fax: 221-325436
Fragrance & Flavor Sales
S.I.C.: 5122; 2087; 2844
Gerd Sprendiano *(Pres.)*

Florasynth-Lautier K.K. **(1)**
Kanda Shibasaki Bldg., No. 16-7, 1-Chome Higashi Kanda Chiyoda-Ku,
Tokyo, 101, Japan
Tel.: 03-3865-3822
Telex: 781-25973 LAUTIER J
Fax: 3-865 3855
Mfr. & Sales of Fragrances & Flavors
S.I.C.: 2087; 2844; 2899; 5122
Kenjiro Niino *(Mng. Dir.)*

Florasynth S.A. de C.V. **(1)**
Apartado Postal 158,
Cuautitlan, Mexico CP 54800, Mexico
Tel.: 5-872 6998
Telex: 383-171345 FLORME
Fax: 5-872 4444
Mfr. & Sales of Frangrances & Flavors
S.I.C.: 2087; 2844; 2899; 5122
Joaquin Lanz *(Gen. Mgr.)*

Florasynth Limited **(1)**
Wentworth House, 2/4 High St.
Chalfont St. Peter, Buckinghamshire SL9 9QA, United Kingdom
Tel.: 0753-890 505
Telex: 851-846036
Fax: 0753-890 370
Emp.: 12
Fiscal Year-end: 12/31/90
Import
Sales of Fragrance & Flavor Compounds
S.I.C.: 5122; 5149
Derek Thipthorpe *(Mng. Dir.)*

I.C.S.A.-Florasynth **(1)**
Via F. LLI. Roselli, 5 20090
Premenugo di Settala, Milano Italy
Tel.: 2-95770212
Tel.: 95770044
Telex: 35768 ICSAF I
Fax: 2-957-7026
Mfr. Flavors
S.I.C.: 2087
Roberto Rosellini *(Gen. Mgr.)*

Lautier Florasynth S.A. **(1)**
4, Ave. Alphonse Morel 06332
Grasse, Cedex France
Tel.: 93-70 11 51
Telex: 842-970273 Lautier Gras
Fax: 93-78 80 28
Mfr. & Sales of Fragrance & Flavors
S.I.C.: 2087; 2844; 2899; 5122
Claude Benazeraf *(Gen. Mgr.)*
Nancy Jullien *(Co-Ordinator for U.S.)*

FLORENCE CORPORATION
1647 E. Jericho Turnpike
Huntington, NY 11743
Tel.: 516-499-6200
Fax: 516-499-0228
Year Founded: 1946
Approx.Sls.: $28,500,000
Emp.: 156
Wholesale Wood Framed Windows & Doors; Roofing & Siding Materials & Manufacture Metal Doors & Metal Framed Windows
S.I.C.: 5031; 5039; 3442
E. Richard Droesch *(Pres.)*
Greg Barnych *(V.P.)*
John Bieselin *(V.P.)*
Bob Buttermelch *(Controller)*

Outside Service Firm(s):

Albrecht, Viggiano Zuceck & Company*(Auditors)*
Farmingdale, NY

National Westminster Bank Plc*(Major Banking Relationship)*
Dix Hills, NY

FLORI CORP.
(d/b/a Turf Irrigation & Water Works Supply)
3622 S. 30th St.
Phoenix, AZ 85040
Tel.: 602-268-8781 **AZ**
Fax: 602-268-8973
Year Founded: 1965
Sales Range: $10-19 Million
Emp.: 48
Fiscal Year-end: 12/31/90
Distribute Water Works Supplies
S.I.C.: 5084
Robert D. Flori *(Chm. Bd. & Treas.)*
John R. Flori *(Pres. & Chief. Exec. Officer)*
James D. Flori *(V.P. & Sec.)*
Linda Williams *(V.P.)*
Kris Boyer *(Dir.-Pur.)*

Principal(s):
Robert D. Flori
Anita H. Flori

No. of Mfg. Plants/Facilities: 3
No. of U.S. Offices: 1

Computer Systems/Hardware:
Unisys

Outside Service Firm(s):

R. Steven Rhue & Co.*(Auditors)*
Phoenix, AZ

Orth-LaPrade Insurance*(Commercial Insurance Carrier)*
4722 N. 24th St., Ste. 172
Phoenix, AZ 85016-4838
Tel.: 602-957-2604
Fax: 602-957-2132

Orth-LaPrade Insurance*(Group Insurer)*
4722 N. 24th St., Ste. 172
Phoenix, AZ 85016-4838
Tel.: 602-957-2604
Fax: 602-957-2132

Plattner, Schneidman & Schneider*(Legal Firm)*
Phoenix, AZ

Valley National Bank*(Major Banking Relationship)*
3636 N. Central Av.
Phoenix, AZ 85038
Tel.: 602-261-1313

FLORIDA CRUSHED STONE COMPANY
1616 S. 14th St.
Leesburg, FL 34748
Mailing Address:
P.O. Box 490300,
Leesburg, FL 34749
Tel.: 904-787-0608
Fax: 904-728-5001
Approx.Sls.: $66,000,000
Emp.: 800
Crushed Limestone; Wholesale Sand, Cement & Lime
S.I.C.: 1422; 5032
F. Browne Gregg *(Chm. Bd. & Chief Exec. Officer)*
Carl Lunderstadt *(Pres. & Chief Oper. Officer)*
J.E. Allsopp, Jr. *(V.P.-Sls.)*
Joseph J. Piermatteo *(V.P.)*
Randy Simpson *(Chief Fin. Officer & V.P.)*
W. Reid Darnell *(Sec. & Treas.)*

Outside Service Firm(s):

Price Waterhouse*(Auditors)*
Orlando, FL

Holland & Knight*(Legal Firm)*
Lakeland, FL

THE FLORIDA LOTTERY
250 Marriott Dr.
Tallahassee, FL 32399-4000
Tel.: 904-487-7777
Fax: 904-487-4541
Year Founded: 1988
Approx.Sls.: $2,200,000,000
Emp.: 735
Fiscal Year-end: 6/31/91
State Lottery
S.I.C.: 7999
Dr. Marcia Mann *(Sec.)*
Sandy Koon *(Asst. Sec.)*
George Haynie *(Deputy Sec. Fin. & Admin.)*
David Colombo *(Deputy Sec.-Opers.)*
Kenneth Hart *(Gen. Counsel)*
Bernard Edwards *(Deputy Sec. & Mktg.)*
Bob Kowalczyk *(Dir.-Adv.)*
Carlos Ribero *(Dir.-Sls.)*
Ed George *(Dir.-Communications)*
Bill Hunter *(Dir.-IRM)*
Nancy Hawkin *(Mgr.-Special Events)*
Robert Gallo *(Mgr.-Adv.)*
Tom Napier *(Mgr.-Pur.)*
Bill Salokar *(Mgr.-Res.)*
David Weiss *(Legislative Liaison)*
Pat Koop *(Adv. Assoc.)*

FLORIG EQUIPMENT COMPANY, INC.
906 Ridge Pike
Conshohocken, PA 19428
Tel.: 215-825-0900
Fax: 215-825-0909
Year Founded: 1934
Sales Range: $10-19 Million
Emp.: 150
Fiscal Year-end: 12/31/91
Manufacture & Wholesale Truck & Trailer Equipment & Machinery
S.I.C.: 3713; 3715; 3599; 5013
Edward Florig *(Pres. & Treas.)*
Patrick McFeeley *(V.P. & Sec.)*
John Woodman *(V.P.-Mktg. & Sls.)*
Martin Blumenthal *(Mgr.-Sls.)*
James Maloney *(Mgr.-Data Processing)*
Edward Ocelus *(Pur. Agent)*

Outside Service Firm(s):

Jungers, O'Connell & Bacheier*(Auditors)*
Philadelphia, PA

Smith, Aker, Grossman & Norristown*(Legal Firm)*
Philadelphia, PA

Provident National Bank*(Major Banking Relationship)*
1000 Westlakes Dr.
Berwyn, PA 19312

THE FLORISTS ASSN. OF GREATER CLEVELAND, INC.
1070 Hanna Bldg.
Cleveland, OH 44115-2001
Tel.: 216-523-1341
Year Founded: 1930
Approx.Sls.: $15,000,000
Emp.: 275
Fiscal Year-end: 9/30/90
Import
Assn. of Retailers, Wholesalers, Growers
S.I.C.: 8611
Sharon Aitken *(Pres.)*
Harold Hansen *(V.P.)*
R.P. Richards *(Treas.)*
Harry Gard Shaffer, Jr. *(Exec. Sec.)*

FLORISTS' MUTUAL INSURANCE CO.
500 St. Louis St.
Edwardsville, IL 62025
Tel.: 618-656-4240
Fax: 618-656-7581
Year Founded: 1887
Approx.Premiums: $60,000,000
Emp.: 200
Direct Writing Full Line Insurance Company Serving Exclusively the Horticultural Industry
S.I.C.: 6311; 6321
Stephen B. Otte *(Pres. & Chief Exec. Officer)*
Kurt H. Seelbach *(Sr. V.P. & Treas.)*
Kenneth J. Von Forell, Jr. *(Sr. V.P.)*
Robert E. McClellan, Jr. *(Sr. V.P.)*
Jim V. Fosters *(V.P.-Mktg.)*
Carolee S. Kleffman *(Sec.)*

Computer Systems/Hardware:
DEC VAX

FLOWERS OF HAWAII
2304 Huntington Drive
San Marino, CA 91108
Tel.: 818-799-1234 CA
Fax: 818-286-5100
Year Founded: 1946
Emp.: 15
Export
Direct Mail of Vanda Orchids, Leis, Tropical Flowers, Arrangements, Lapel Vials, & Potted Orchid Plants
John Wm. Devereux, Jr. *(Pres.)*

Division:

Mauna Loa Orchids, Ltd. **(1)**
P.O. Box 4007
Hilo, HI 96720
Tel.: 808-959-5858
Tel.: 800-356-7244
Fax: 808-959-2121
Hawaiian Exotic Flowers
S.I.C.: 0181
Sonoko Tokusato *(Gen. Mgr.)*

Subsidiary:

Mauna Loa Orchids, Ltd., D/B/A Hawaiian Exotic Flowers **(1)**
P.O. Box 4007,
Hilo, HI 96722
Tel.: 808-959-5858
Tel.: 800-356-7244
Fax: 808-959-2121
Growers, Packagers & Shippers of Vanda Orchids, Leis, Hawaiian Tropicals, Orchid Plants, Lapel Vials & Potted Orchid Plants
S.I.C.: 0181

THE FLEXIBLE CORP.
970 Pittsburgh Dr.
Delaware, OH 43015
Tel.: 614-369-7671
Fax: 614-362-2600
Approx.Sls.: $196,000,000
Emp.: 1,200
Heavy Duty Transit Buses, After Market Bus Parts, Advanced Bus Remanufacturing, Comml. Chassis
S.I.C.: 3711; 3713; 3714
Cruse W. Moss *(Chm. Bd.)*
Mark J. Obert *(Vice Chm.)*
Edward N. Kravitz *(Pres. & Chief Oper. Officer)*
Eric Dardinger *(V.P.-Fin.)*
G. Robert Richards *(V.P. & Gen. Counsel)*
Warren Marsh *(Acting V.P.-Opers.)*
Robert Packham *(V.P.-Parts & Chassis Opers.)*
Jack Thompson *(Dir.-Indus. Rels.)*

FLYING FOOD FARE, INC.
5945 S. Keating Ave.
Chicago, IL 60629
Tel.: 312-581-3900 IL
Fax: 312-581-0014
Year Founded: 1983
Approx.Sls.: $10,000,000
Emp.: 290
Contract Food Services; Frozen Dinners
S.I.C.: 5142
Sue Ling Gin *(Chm. Bd. & Sec.)*

Outside Service Firm(s):

First Chicago Bank*(Major Banking Relationship)*
One First National Plaza
Chicago, IL 60670

FLYING J. INC.
50 W. 990 S.
Brigham City, UT 84302
Mailing Address:
P.O. Box 678,
Brigham City, UT 84302
Tel.: 801-734-6400
Tel.: 800-734-6400 UT
Fax: 801-734-6556
Year Founded: 1968
Approx.Sls.: $600,000,000
Emp.: 4,000
Mfr. Integrated Petroleum
S.I.C.: 1311; 5172; 5541
O. Jay Call *(Chm. Bd.)*
J. Phillip Adams *(Pres.)*
R. E. Germer *(Sr. V.P.)*
Ronald Parker *(V.P.)*
Barre G. Burgon *(V.P., Sec. & Corp. Counsel)*
R.W. Anderson *(Chief Fin. Officer)*
Robert Langford *(Personnel Dir.)*
Scott Vincent *(Dir.-Mktg. & Adv.)*
Gerald McCammon *(Dir.-Data Processing)*
Craig Toone *(Pur. Dir.)*

Computer Systems/Hardware:
IBM 4361

Outside Service Firm(s):

KPMG Peat Marwick*(Auditors)*
60 E. South Temple, Ste. 900
Salt Lake City, UT 84111
Tel.: 801-328-3000
Fax: 801-237-1552

Watkins & Faber*(Legal Firm)*
Salt Lake City, UT

First Security Bank of Utah*(Major Banking Relationship)*
Salt Lake City, UT

FLYNN/SABATINO
9049 Springboro Pike
Miamisburg, OH 45342
Tel.: 513-859-0599
Fax: 513-859-4081
Year Founded: 1938
Approx.Billings: $23,000,000
Emp.: 32
Gregory K. Sabatino *(Chm. Bd.)*
Terrance L. Flynn *(Pres. & Brdcst. Production)*
Garry L. Day *(Exec. V.P.)*
D. Ron Bott *(Sr. V.P., Acct. Service)*
William L. Coy *(V.P., Opers.)*
Sandra L. Clark *(V.P.)*
John Sillaman *(Asst. V.P., Acct Service)*

Computer Systems/Hardware:
Adds, NCR, IBM

FOGARTY & KLEIN/WINIUS BRANDON
7155 Old Katy Rd., Ste. 100
Houston, TX 77024
Tel.: 713-862-5100 TX
Fax: 713-869-6560
Year Founded: 1980
Approx.Billings: $87,388,550
Emp.: 86
Fiscal Year-end: 12/31/89
Advertising Agency
S.I.C.: 7311
William H. Fogarty *(Pres.)*
Scott Alyward *(Sr. V.P., Grp. Supvr.)*
Bill Penczak *(Sr. V.P., Grp. Supvr.)*
Roger Beckstead *(V.P., Chief Fin. Officer)*
Brad Fitch *(V.P., Grp. Supvr.)*
Susan Morrow *(V.P., Grp. Supvr.)*
Kim Paisley *(V.P., Grp. Supvr.)*
Bill Dunne *(Grp. Supvr.)*
Principal(s):
William H. Fogarty
Art Casper
Richard E. Klein

No. of U.S. Offices: 2

Outside Service Firm(s):

Fulbright & Jaworski*(Legal Firm)*
1301 McKinney St.
Houston, TX 77010
Tel.: 713-651-5151

First Interstate Bank*(Major Banking Relationship)*
First Interstate Plaza
Houston, TX 77210
Tel.: 713-224-6611

Subsidiaries:

Fogarty & Klein Public Relations **(1)**
7155 Old Katy Rd., Ste. 200
Houston, TX 77024
Tel.: 713-867-3200
Fax: 713-869-6566
Emp.: 8
Public Relations
S.I.C.: 8743
Alex Kopatic *(V.P., Gen. Mgr.)*
Roger Beckstead *(Chief Fin. Officer)*

Fogarty & Klein Sales Promotion, Inc. **(1)**
3303 Louisiana
Houston, TX 77006
Tel.: 713-862-5100
Fax: 713-869-6560
Sls. Promo. & Direct Response
S.I.C.: 7319; 7331

Fogarty & Klein Yellow Pages, Inc. **(1)**
1204 Lakeway Dr., #3
Austin, TX 78734
Tel.: 512-261-6816
Fax: 512-261-4624
Emp.: 7
Yellow Pages, Directory Advertising
S.I.C.: 7311
Cissy Arnold *(V.P., Gen. Mgr.)*
Roger Beckstead *(Chief Fin. Officer)*

FOJTASEK COMPANIES, INC.
2100 Union Bower Rd.
Irving, TX 75061-6957
Mailing Address:
P.O. Box 226957
Dallas, TX 75222
Tel.: 214-445-0040 TX
Fax: 214-554-6751
Approx.Sls.: $102,000,000
Emp.: 700
Fiscal Year-end: 6/30/90
Import
Manufacture Doors & Windows
S.I.C.: 2431
Joe Fojtasek *(Pres.)*
Richard Fojtasek *(V.P.)*
Louis W. Simi, Jr. *(V.P. & Gen. Mgr.)*
Shirley Crutcher *(Treas. & Sec.)*

Computer Systems/Hardware:
MAI Basic 48020

Outside Service Firm(s):

Davis & Clark*(Auditors)*
Dallas, TX

Texas Commerce Bank*(Major Banking Relationship)*
2200 Ross Ave.
Dallas, TX 75266

FOLAND'S JEWELRY BROKERS
4100 E. 14 Mile
Warren, MI 48092
Tel.: 313-264-0110
Fax: 313-246-0350
Approx.Sls.: $10,000,000
Emp.: 350
Retail Sales Of Jewelry, Appliances, Giftware, Domestics & Cameras
S.I.C.: 5944; 5946; 5947
A. Jerome Kroot *(Chm. Bd.)*

Outside Service Firm(s):

Plante & Moran*(Auditors)*
Livonia, MI

National Bank of Detroit*(Major Banking Relationship)*
Livonia, MI

FOLEY-BELSAW COMPANY
3300 E. Fifth St.
Minneapolis, MN 55418
Tel.: 612-789-8831 **MN**
Fax: 612-789-3185
Year Founded: 1926
Approx.Sls.: $56,000,000
Emp.: 150
Fiscal Year-end: 8/31/92
Import Export
Mfr. Saw Sharpening & Tool Maintenance Equip.; Correspondence Courses in Small Engine Repair, Locksmithing & Upholstery
S.I.C.: 3291; 3425; 8249
Walter M. Ringer, Jr. *(Chm. Bd. & Chief Exec. Officer)*
Walter M. Ringer III *(Co-Vice Chm.)*
John M. Ringer *(Co-Vice Chm.)*
Richard J. Hentges *(Pres. & Chief Oper. Officer)*
Gerald Mrnak *(V.P. & Controller)*

No. of Mfg. Plants/Facilities: 5
No. of U.S. Offices: 3

Computer Systems/Hardware:
IBM

Outside Service Firm(s):

KPMG Peat Marwick*(Auditors)*
4200 Norwest Center, 90 S. 7th St.
Minneapolis, MN 55402
Tel.: 612-341-2222

First Bank Systems*(Major Banking Relationship)*
120 So. Sixth St.
Minneapolis, MN 55402

Subsidiaries:

Foley Martens Company **(1)**
3300 E. Fifth St.
Minneapolis, MN 55418
Tel.: 612-789-8831
Emp.: 120
Mfg. of Wooden Products Including Cutting Boards, Tables & Lawn Furniture
S.I.C.: 2511
Thomas Renard *(Pres.)*

Foley-PLP Company **(1)**
1920 Lyell Ave.
Rochester, NY 14604
Tel.: 716-647-1538
Fax: 716-458-0800
Emp.: 120
Mfr. of Blades & Metal Forgings, Tractors, Lawn & Garden Equipment
S.I.C.: 3462
Walter M. Ringer, Jr. *(Chm. Bd.)*
John M. Ringer *(Pres.)*
John M. Comer *(Exec. V.P. & Gen. Mgr.)*
Norman D. Butler *(V.P.-Sls. & Mktg., Service Parts Div.)*
Scott T. Jonap *(V.P.-Sls. & Mktg., Consumer Prods. Div.)*
George O. Mosier *(V.P.-Sls. & Mktg., Intl. Div.)*
Richard J. Hentges *(Treas.)*
Gerald D. Mrnak *(Controller)*
Walter M. Ringer, III *(Sec.)*
David B. DeVos *(Dir.-Opers.)*
Ted Strohmeyer *(Mgr.-Pur.)*

STEVE FOLEY CADILLAC
100 Skokie Blvd.
Northbrook, IL 60062
Tel.: 708-564-4090 **DE**
Fax: 708-564-5787
Assets: $15,180,000
Liabilities: $10,900,800
Net Worth: $4,279,200
Approx.Sls.: $45,000,000
Emp.: 115
Fiscal Year-end: 12/31/91
New & Used Automobiles; Rent-a-car Service
S.I.C.: 5511; 7514
Stephen X. Foley *(Pres.)*
Mercedes Foley *(Vice Chm. & Sec.)*
Stephen X. Foley, Jr. *(Chief Oper. Officer)*
John F. Sheils *(Treas.)*

Outside Service Firm(s):

NBD Bank, N.A.*(Major Banking Relationship)*
Security Transfer Services, P.O. Box 330751
Detroit, MI 48232

FOLEY HOLDING COMPANY, INC.
1550 S. West St.
Wichita, KS 67213
Tel.: 316-943-4211 **KS**
Year Founded: 1987
Approx.Sls.: $34,000,000
Emp.: 210
Fiscal Year-end: 12/31/91
Wholesale Distribution of Construction & Mining Machinery; Industrial Machinery & Equipment; Heavy Construction Equipment Rental; Nonresidential Building Operators
S.I.C.: 5082; 5084; 7353; 6512
Paul J. Foley *(Chm. Bd.)*
Paul Foley, Jr. *(Pres.)*

Outside Service Firm(s):

First National Bank*(Major Banking Relationship)*
Wichita, KS

Subsidiary:

Foley Tractor Company, Inc. **(1)**
1550 S. West St.
Wichita, KS 67213
Tel.: 316-943-4211
Wholesale Distribution of General Construction Machinery & Equipment; Industrial Machinery & Equipment
S.I.C.: 5082; 5084
Paul J. Foley *(Chm. Bd.)*
Paul J. Foley, Jr. *(Pres.)*

FOLGER ADAM COMPANY
16300 W. 103rd St.
Lemont, IL 60439
Tel.: 708-739-3900
Fax: 708-739-6138
Security Alarm Systems
S.I.C.: 7382
Edgar B. Jewett, III *(Pres.)*

Outside Service Firm(s):

Ernst & Young*(Auditors)*
233 S. Wacker Dr.
Chicago, IL 60606
Tel.: 312-368-1800
Fax: 312-645-3095

Continental Bank, N.A.*(Major Banking Relationship)*
30 N. LaSalle St.
Chicago, IL 60693

Subsidiary:

Stewart Decatur Security Systems, Inc. **(1)**
P.O. Box 18700
Erlanger, KY 41018
Tel.: 606-371-6000
Installation of Security Systems
S.I.C.: 7382

FOLGER NOLAN FLEMING DOUGLAS
725 15th St., N.W.
Washington, DC 20005
Tel.: 202-783-5252 **DE**
Fax: 202-347-5474
Year Founded: 1889
Assets: $18,690,896
Liabilities: $5,273,471
Net Worth: $13,417,425
Emp.: 69
Fiscal Year-end: 3/31/92
Security Brokers; Investment Advisory Service
S.I.C.: 6211; 6282
Lee M. Folger *(Chm. Bd.)*
Robert W. Fleming *(Pres.)*
W. Leslie Douglas *(Sr. V.P.)*
Robert B. Leahy *(Sr. V.P.)*
John Rodler *(Sr. V.P.)*
John M. Glassic *(V.P. & Cashier)*
Richmond J. Cooper *(V.P.)*

Outside Service Firm(s):

Covington & Burling*(Legal Firm)*
120 Pennsylvania Ave. N.W.
Washington, DC 20044
Tel.: 202-662-6000
Fax: 202-662-6291

The Riggs National Bank*(Major Banking Relationship)*
1503 Pennsylvania Ave. N.W.
Washington, DC 20013
Tel.: 202-624-2000

FOLLETT CORPORATION
1000 W. Washington Blvd.
Chicago, IL 60607
Tel.: 312-666-4300 **IL**
Fax: 312-666-9213
Year Founded: 1957
Assets: $100,000,000
Net Worth: $100,000,000
Approx.Sls.: $400,000,000
Emp.: 4,000
Fiscal Year-end: 3/31/91
Contract Management of Bookstores; Wholesale Distributor of Textbooks, Library Books, Paper Products & School Supplies; Publishing of Computer Software
S.I.C.: 5199; 5942
Robert J. Follett *(Chm. Bd.)*
Paul R. Litzsinger *(Pres. & Chief Exec. Officer)*
R. Waichler *(V.P. & Dir.-Opers.)*
Kenneth J. Hull *(Chief Fin. Officer)*
LaVerne Hosek *(Gen. Counsel & Sec.)*

No. of Mfg. Plants/Facilities: 375
No. of U.S. Offices: 5

Computer Systems/Hardware:
IBM System 4831

Outside Service Firm(s):

Arthur Andersen & Co.*(Auditors)*
33 W. Monroe St.
Chicago, IL 60603-4067
Tel.: 312-580-0033
Fax: 312-507-6748

Kidder, Peabody & Co.*(Investment Banker)*
125 South Wacker
Chicago, IL

Seyfarth, Shaw, Fairweather & Geraldson*(Legal Firm)*
55 E. Monroe
Chicago, IL 60606
Tel.: 312-346-8000

Continental Bank N. A.*(Major Banking Relationship)*
231 S. LaSalle St.
Chicago, IL 60697
Tel.: 312-828-2345
Tel.: 800-426-5754
Telex: 312-828-1783

Divisions:

Follett College Resources **(1)**
1000 W. Washington Blvd.
Chicago, IL 60607
Tel.: 312-666-4300
Wholesale of Used College Texts to College Bookstores & Electronic Products & Services for Higher Education Purposes
S.I.C.: 5199; 5065
R.M. Traut *(Pres.)*

Follett Library Book Co. **(1)**
4506 Northwest Hwy.
Crystal Lake, IL 60014
Tel.: 815-455-1100
Wholesaler of Children's Books & Audio-Visual Materials
S.I.C.: 5199
C.R. Follett *(Pres.)*

Follett Software Company **(1)**
809 N. Front St.
McHenry, IL 60050-5589
Tel.: 815-455-1101
Sale of Software to Schools & Libraries
S.I.C.: 5045
C.R. Follett, Jr. *(Pres.)*

Wilcox & Follett Co. **(1)**
1000 W. Washington Blvd.
Chicago, IL 60607
Tel.: 312-666-5856
Wholesaler New, Rebound & Used Textbooks for Grades 1-12
S.I.C.: 5199
K.A. Follett *(Pres.)*

Subsidiaries:

Follett College Stores Corp. **(1)**
400 W. Grand
Elmhurst, IL 60126
Tel.: 708-279-2330 (100%)
Contract Management of College Bookstores
S.I.C.: 8741; 5942
L.D. Padgett *(Pres.)*

Subsidiary:

Brennan College Service, Inc. **(2)**
45 Island Pine Rd.
Springfield, MA 01118
Tel.: 413-737-0222
Management of College Bookstores
S.I.C.: 8741; 5942
Thomas Courtney *(Controller)*

Follett Service Corporation **(1)**
1000 W. Washington Blvd.
Chicago, IL 60607
Tel.: 312-666-4300 (100%)
Sale of Computers & Software for College Bookstores
S.I.C.: 5045
R.M. Traut *(Pres.)*

FOLMAR & ASSOCIATES
3472 Springhill Ave.
Mobile, AL 36608
Mailing Address:
P.O. Box 16765,
Mobile, AL 36616
Tel.: 205-343-3777
Fax: 205-343-1887
Real Estate Developer
S.I.C.: 6552
William Cooper *(Dir.-Property Mngmt.)*
Curt Wilson *(Dir.-Mktg.)*

No. of U.S. Offices: 2

FONES & MANN INC.
152 Madison Ave., 20th Fl.
New York, NY 10016
Tel.: 212-689-9870
Fax: 212-689-4004
Year Founded: 1974
Approx.Billings: $15,000,000
Emp.: 28
Maynard Fones *(Pres.)*
Terry Wright *(V.P., Sec. & Treas.)*
F.A. Wright *(Fin. Admin.)*
Mary Ellen Vogler *(Office Mgr.)*

Food Fair Supermarkets
(See Pacific Hawaiian Ltd. Listing)

FOOD & GAS, INC.
(Formerly The Russell Corporation)
4151 Memorial Dr., Ste. 206C
Decatur, GA 30032
Tel.: 404-294-6555 GA
Fax: 404-294-0041
Sales Range: $100-499 Million
Emp.: 92
Wholesale Distributor Petroleum Fuel
S.I.C.: 5541; 5169
Nancy H. Russell *(Pres.)*
Russ Clegg *(Chief Fin. Officer)*
Barron Jeff Russell *(Treas. & Sec.)*

Computer Systems/Hardware:
IBM-3637

Outside Service Firm(s):

Fidelity National Bank*(Major Banking Relationship)*
Decatur, GA

THE FOOD GROUP
292 Madison Ave., 7th Fl.
New York, NY 10017
Tel.: 212-725-5766
Fax: 212-686-2901
Year Founded: 1969
Approx.Billings: $30,500,000
Emp.: 45
Foodservice Adv.
Donald Axleroad *(Pres.)*
Richard Vetter *(V.P., Media Svcs./ Pub. Rels.)*
Genevieve Murphy *(Treas.)*
Leon Meizlik *(Controller)*
Melinda Pace *(Pub. Rels. Mgr.)*

Computer Systems/Hardware:
Computer Associates Software

FOOD SERVICES OF AMERICA
4025 Dell Ridge Way, S.W., Ste. 400
Seattle, WA 98106
Mailing Address:
P.O. Box 84628
Seattle, WA 98124-5928
Tel.: 206-933-5000 DE
Year Founded: 1986
Assets: $141,239,614
Liabilities: $87,353,727
Net Worth: $53,885,887
Approx.Sls.: $845,000,000
Emp.: 2,100
Fiscal Year-end: 12/31/90
Wholesale Fruits, Produce, Groceries & Frozen Foods; Trucking; Distributor of Paper Products
S.I.C.: 5148; 5411; 4213; 5142; 5141
Thomas J. Stewart *(Chm. Bd.)*
Dick Weis *(Pres. & Chief Exec. Officer)*
Paul J. Junker *(Chief Oper. Officer)*
Dennis Specht *(Chief Fin. Officer)*
John Michalak *(Sr. V.P.-Mktg. & New Bus. Devel.)*
Richard Duchaine *(V.P.-Mnmgt. Information Systems)*
Bill Floten *(V.P.-Opers.)*
Ernie Snyder *(V.P.-Fin. & Admin.)*
Rodger Toomey *(V.P.-Mdsg. & Pur.)*
Stan Sievsind *(Dir.-Adv.)*
Paula Weir *(Dir.-Employee Benefits)*

Outside Service Firm(s):

Security Pacific National Bank*(Major Banking Relationship)*
Security Pacific Tower, T21-7,
Seattle, WA 98124
Tel.: 206-621-5920

Subsidiaries:

AmeriFresh **(1)**
2715 E. Marginal Way S.
Seattle, WA 98134
Tel.: 206-767-3605
Also Located in CA, FL, OR, TX, AZ, CO, ID & WA
S.I.C.: 5148

Northwest Service, Inc. **(1)**
6737 Corson Ave. S.
Seattle, WA 98108
Tel.: 206-767-3605
Trucking Operation
S.I.C.: 7513

FOOTE & DAVIES INC.
3101 McCall Dr.
Atlanta, GA 30340
Mailing Address:
P.O. Box 4800,
Atlanta, GA 30362
Tel.: 404-451-4511 GA
Fax: 404-455-1012
Year Founded: 1887
Sales Range: $100-499 Million
Emp.: 1,450
Fiscal Year-end: 10/31/92
Commercial Printing
S.I.C.: 2752; 4214
Larry Burnette *(Pres.)*
Robert Lindsay *(V.P.-Data Processing)*
Bob Schick *(V.P.-Sls.)*
Robert Smith *(V.P.-Matls.)*
Bruce Thompson *(Gen. Counsel)*
Leslie Policky *(Dir.-Production Control)*
Edward L. Fay *(Mgr.-Credit Collections)*

No. of Mfg. Plants/Facilities: 2

Computer Systems/Hardware:
IBM 4381 & System 38

Outside Service Firm(s):

Kilpatrick & Cody*(Legal Firm)*
3100 Equitable Bldg., 100 Peachtree St. N.W.
Atlanta, GA 30343
Tel.: 404-572-6500

Bank South, N.A.*(Major Banking Relationship)*
P.O. Box 4387
Atlanta, GA 30302
Tel.: 404-529-4111

FORBES, INC.
60 Fifth Ave.
New York, NY 10011
Tel.: 212-620-2200
Telex: RCA 235948
Year Founded: 1917
Approx.Sls.: $150,000,000
Emp.: 450
Export
Forbes Magazine Publishing; Real Estate Investment
S.I.C.: 2721; 6798
Christopher C. Forbes *(Vice Chm.)*
Malcolm S. Forbes, Jr. *(Pres., Chief Exec. & Editor-in-Chief)*
Leonard H. Yablon *(Exec. V.P. & Chief Fin. Officer)*
Scott R. Yablon *(V.P.-Admin.)*
Joel B. Redler *(V.P. & Treas.)*
Stephen G. Nicoll *(V.P.-Adv. & Promo.)*
John M. Thornton *(V.P.-Consumer Mktg.)*
Caspar W. Weinberger *(Publisher)*
Jeffrey Cunningham *(Assoc. Publisher)*
James W. Michaels *(Editor)*
Lawrence Minard *(Mng. Editor)*
William Donald Garson *(Dir.-Corp. Communications)*
William J. Flatley *(Dir.-Adv.)*
Bruce H. Rogers *(Dir.-Mkt. Devel.)*
Joseph J. De Marte *(Dir.-Data Processing)*
George Clissold *(Mgr.-Consumer Adv.)*
Principal(s):
Malcolm S. Forbes, Jr.

No. of U.S. Offices: 11
No. of Foreign Offices: 6

Computer Systems/Hardware:
IBM Mainframe & PC

Outside Service Firm(s):

Ernst & Young*(Auditors)*
787 Seventh Ave.
New York, NY 10019
Tel.: 212-773-1243

Connecticut General Life Insurance Co.*(Group Insurer)*
P.O. Box 2975,
Hartford, CT 06104
Tel.: 203-726-6000

Chemical Banking Corp.*(Investment Banker)*
277 Park Ave.
New York, NY 10041
Tel.: 212-310-6407
Fax: 212-310-4526

Chemical Bank*(Major Banking Relationship)*
450 West 33rd St.
New York, NY 10001
Tel.: 212-613-7197
Fax: 212-947-7628

Chemical Banking Corp.*(Major Banking Relationship)*
277 Park Ave.
New York, NY 10041
Tel.: 212-310-6407
Fax: 212-310-4526

Chemical Banking Corp.*(Pension Manager)*
277 Park Ave.
New York, NY 10041
Tel.: 212-310-6407
Fax: 212-310-4526

Division:

Forbes Magazine Division **(1)**
60 Fifth Ave.
New York, NY 10011
Tel.: 212-620-2200
Magazine Publishing
S.I.C.: 2721
Caspar W. Weinberger *(Publisher)*
Jeffrey M. Cunningham *(Assoc. Publisher)*
James W. Michaels *(Editor)*
Lawrence Minard *(Mng. Editor)*

Subsidiary:

Sangre de Cristos Ranches Inc. **(1)**
60 Fifth Ave.
New York, NY 10011
Tel.: 212-620-2200
Leonard H. Yablon *(Pres.)*

FORD DEVELOPMENT CORPORATION
11148 Woodward Lane
Cincinnati, OH 45241
Tel.: 513-772-1521
Tel.: 800-643-8162 OH
Fax: 513-772-1556
Year Founded: 1971
Approx.Sls.: $19,000,000
Emp.: 120
Import Export
Excavation Work, Commercial & Industrial Concrete Work
S.I.C.: 1794; 1771; 1542
Robert J. Henderson, Sr. *(Chm. Bd., Pres. & Chief Exec. Officer)*
Robert F. Henderson *(V.P.)*
Barbara McDonald *(Chief Fin. Officer)*

Outside Service Firm(s):

Central Trust Bank*(Major Banking Relationship)*
201 E. Fifth St.
Cincinnati, OH 45202

FORD METER BOX COMPANY
775 Manchester Ave.
Wabash, IN 46992-0443
Mailing Address:
P.O. Box 443
Wabash, IN 46992-0443
Tel.: 219-563-3171
Tel.: 219-563-8441
Fax: 219-563-0167
Approx.Sls.: $60,000,000
Emp.: 600
Export
Mfr. Water Meter Setting & Testing Equipment, Valves & Fittings for Water Utility Industry
S.I.C.: 3494; 3823; 3829
John L. Ford, Jr. *(Chm. Bd.)*
Henry A. Leander *(Pres.)*
Terry Agness *(Exec. V.P.-Mfg.)*
Wayne Rennaker *(Sr. V.P.)*
Carl Doran *(Sr. V.P.-Export)*
Albro D. Daniel *(Sr. V.P.-Sls.)*
Thomas Hodson *(V.P.)*
William E. Kimmons *(V.P.)*
David Kunkel *(V.P.)*
Richard Prickett *(V.P.)*
Richard Swart *(V.P.)*
Ray Gillespie *(Sec. & Treas.)*
Charles Chapman *(Mgr.-Adv.)*
Robert Heath *(Pur. Agent)*

Computer Systems/Hardware:
Data General

FORD PRODUCTS CORPORATION
Ford Products Rd.
Valley Cottage, NY 10989
Mailing Address:
P.O. Box A,
Valley Cottage, NY 10989
Tel.: 914-358-8282
Fax: 914-358-8717
Approx.Sls.: $21,000,000
Emp.: 250
Fiscal Year-end: 12/31/90
Mfr. Oil, Solar & Electrical Water Heaters; Oil & Gas Burners & Warm Air Furnaces
S.I.C.: 3433; 3585; 3639
Charles L. Green *(Chm., Pres. & Chief Exec. Officer)*
George C. Farelli *(Chief Engineer)*
Michael Kaufmann *(Dir.-Sls. & Mktg.)*

FORD STEEL CO., INC.
2475 Rock Island Blvd.
Maryland Heights, MO 63043
Tel.: 314-567-4680 MO
Fax: 314-567-5762
Approx.Sls.: $11,000,000
Emp.: 35
Export
Marketing of Iron or Steel Semifinished Products; Metal Bars & Plates & Rough Castings
S.I.C.: 5051
James Curtis Ford *(Chm. Bd.)*
John S. Ford, Jr. *(Pres.)*
Anthony Morrison *(V.P.-Intl. Sls.)*

Outside Service Firm(s):

Price Waterhouse*(Auditors)*
One Boatmen's Plaza
St. Louis, MO 63101
Tel.: 314-425-0500

Centerre Bancorp*(Major Banking Relationship)*
St. Louis, MO

FORECAST MORTGAGE CORPORATION
10670 Civic Center Dr.
Rancho Cucamonga, CA 91730
Tel.: 909-987-7788 CA
Fax: 909-980-7305
Year Founded: 1971
Assets: $100,000,000
Liabilities: $50,000,000

Forecast Mortgage Corporation—(Continued)

Net Worth: $50,000,000
Approx.Sls.: $143,000,000
Emp.: 170
Fiscal Year-end: 10/31/90
Real Estate Investment & Development
S.I.C.: 6552; 6799
James Previti *(Chm. Bd, Pres. & Chief Exec. Officer)*
Jim Rankin *(Chief Oper. Officer)*
Linda Wallace *(Chief Fin. Officer & Treas.)*
Bruce Strickland *(Sr. V.P.-Land Acquisitions)*
Joe Carmen *(V.P.)*
Mibs Matthews *(Corp. Counsel)*
William Kasavan *(Chief Fin. Analyst)*

No. of U.S. Offices: 2

Outside Service Firm(s):

Kenneth Leventhal Co.*(Legal Firm)*
San Diego, CA

Sanwa Bank*(Major Banking Relationship)*
San Diego, CA

FOREIGN CANDY CO., INC.
451 Black Forest Rd.
Huff, IA 51239
Tel.: 712-439-1496 **IA**
Fax: 712-439-1434
Year Founded: 1978
Approx.Sls.: $11,000,000
Emp.: 45
Wholesale Distribution of Candy
S.I.C.: 5145
Peter W. DeYager *(Pres.)*
Betty J. DeYager *(Sec.)*

Outside Service Firm(s):

Cain Ellsworth & Co.*(Auditors)*
Sioux City, IA

Security National Bank*(Major Banking Relationship)*
Sioux City, IA

FORESTRY SUPPLIERS, INC.
205 W. Rankin St.
Jackson, MS 39201
Mailing Address:
P.O. Box 8397
Jackson, MS 39284
Tel.: 601-354-3565 **MS**
Year Founded: 1949
Approx.Sls.: $10,000,000
Emp.: 60
Fiscal Year-end: 12/31/92
Export
Wholesale Distributor of Surveyors' Instruments; Forestry Equipment & Environmental Supplies
S.I.C.: 5999; 5049; 5082
John R. Gwaltney *(Chm. Bd., Pres. & Chief Exec. Officer)*
Robert B. Middleton *(Exec. V.P. & Treas.)*
Ray N. Hansen *(V.P.-Mktg.)*
Jerry D. Pelly *(V.P.-Sls. , Customer Service & Sec.)*

Outside Service Firm(s):

Jeff Huff*(Auditors)*
Jackson, MS

Deposit Guaranty National Bank*(Major Banking Relationship)*
One Deposit Guaranty Plaza,
Jackson, MS 39201

FOREVER LIVING PRODUCTS
1200 S. Priest Rd.
Tempe, AZ 85281
Mailing Address:
P.O. Box 29041
Phoenix, AZ 85038
Tel.: 602-968-3999
Telex: 9109500150
Year Founded: 1978
Approx.Sls.: $264,000,000
Emp.: 500
Fiscal Year-end: 12/31/90
Direct Sales Diet & Nutritional Products
S.I.C.: 5141; 5122
Rex Maughan *(Chm. Bd., Pres. & Chief Exec. Officer)*
Tom Mace *(Exec. V.P.)*
Glen Banks *(Sr. V.P. & Treas.)*
Navaz Ghaswala *(V.P.-Admin.)*
Harold Greene *(V.P.-Sls.)*
Bill Lewis *(V.P.-Sls.)*
R. Jay Lloyd *(Legal Counsel)*

Principal(s):
Rex Maughan

No. of Mfg. Plants/Facilities: 2
No. of U.S. Offices: 12
No. of Foreign Offices: 7

Computer Systems/Hardware:
IBM System 3800

Outside Service Firm(s):

Schulman Klock*(Auditors)*
Phoenix, AZ

Cash, Sullivan & Cross*(Group Insurer)*
Phoenix, AZ

Lloyd, Joyce & Poole*(Legal Firm)*
Boise, ID

Streich Lang*(Legal Firm)*
2100 1st Interstate Bank Plaza, 100 W. Washington
Phoenix, AZ 85003
Tel.: 602-229-5538

First Interstate Bank*(Major Banking Relationship)*
P.O. Box 53441,
Phoenix, AZ 85072-3441
Tel.: 602-229-4049

Subsidiary:

Deco Container **(1)**
9600 Dilworth
Dallas, TX 75243
Tel.: 214-343-5700
Don Calhoun *(Exec. V.P.)*

FORMAC CORPORATION
4701 Humboldt Ave. N.
Minneapolis, MN 55430
Tel.: 612-521-5151
Fax: 612-521-2249
Approx.Sls.: $15,000,000
Emp.: 100
Machine Job Shop
S.I.C.: 3599
Dennis Strong *(Pres.)*
Robert F. Gustafson *(Chief Exec. Officer)*
Jennifer Asplund *(Dir.-Personnel)*
David C. Lemberg *(Mgr.-Pur.)*

Outside Service Firm(s):

Norwest Bank Minnesota, N.A.*(Major Banking Relationship)*
8th & Marquette
Minneapolis, MN 55479
Tel.: 612-372-8123

FORMAN BROTHERS, INC.
4235 Sheriff Rd., N.E.
Washington, DC 20019
Tel.: 202-388-8400 **DE**
Fax: 202-396-0810
Year Founded: 1946
Approx.Sls.: $53,000,000
Emp.: 160
Wholesale Distribution of Liquor; Wine
S.I.C.: 5182
Barry Forman *(Chm. Bd.)*
Hal Munter *(Pres.)*

Outside Service Firm(s):

First National Bank of Maryland*(Major Banking Relationship)*
Washington, DC

FORMATION, INC.
121 Whittendale Dr.
Moorestown, NJ 08057
Tel.: 609-234-5020
Fax: 609-234-8543
Approx.Sls.: $41,000,000
Emp.: 203
Fiscal Year-end: 7/31/92
Design & Manufacture Computer Peripheral Hardware
S.I.C.: 3571
A.D. Beard *(Chm. Bd. & Pres.)*
B.I. Kessler *(Exec. V.P. & Sec.)*
T.M. Valentine *(V.P.-Fin. & Treas.)*
R. Liberatore *(V.P.-Corp. Sls. & Mktg.)*
K.R. Dando *(V.P.-Networking Systems)*
S.L. Muir *(V.P.-Mfg.)*
J. Pierce *(V.P-Quality Assurance)*
C. Johnson *(Dir.-Human Resources)*

Outside Service Firm(s):

Arthur Young & Co.*(Auditors)*
Philadelphia, PA

Moss, Powers & Kugler*(Legal Firm)*
Philadelphia, PA

United Jersey Bank*(Major Banking Relationship)*
Philadelphia, PA

FORMS & SUPPLY, INC.
1733 University Commercial Place
Charlotte, NC 28213
Tel.: 704-598-8971
Fax: 704-596-6098
Year Founded: 1962
Approx.Sls.: $25,000,000
Emp.: 160
Fiscal Year-end: 5/31/92
Office Supplies
S.I.C.: 5112
Jimmy D. Godwin *(Pres.)*
Baron Culbertson *(V.P.)*
Ray Harrelson *(V.P.)*
Diane Godwin *(Mgr.-Personnel)*

Outside Service Firm(s):

Buford Griffin*(Auditors)*
Charlotte, NC

NationsBank Carolinas*(Major Banking Relationship)*
One NCNB Plaza,
Charlotte, NC 28255
Tel.: 704-374-5000

FORMU-3 INTERNATIONAL, INC.
4790 Douglas Circle N.W.
Canton, OH 44718
Tel.: 216-499-3334
Tel.: 800-525-6315
Fax: 216-499-8231
Year Founded: 1982
Approx.Sls.: $20,000,000
Emp.: 180
Fiscal Year-end: 12/31/89
Weight Reduction System
S.I.C.: 7299
Jeffrey Stone *(Pres.)*
Walter Poston *(V.P.-Franchise Devel.)*
Michelle Smith *(V.P.)*
Gary Tersingi *(V.P.-Admin.)*
Peter Ciofani *(Chief Fin. Officer)*
Robert Newbold *(Gen. Counsel)*
Kevin Gross *(Dir.-Pur.)*
Tom Scovell *(Dir.-Data Processing)*
Jody Tortora *(Dir.-Franchise Leads/ Telemktg.)*
Chris Thomas *(Dir.-Training)*
Marge Frease *(Gen. Acctg. Supv.)*
Christa Tersigni *(Coord.-Devel. & Special Projects)*

Outside Service Firm(s):

Black, McCuskey, Souers & Arbaugh*(Legal Firm)*
1200 Harter Bank Bldg.
Canton, OH 44702
Tel.: 216-456-8341

Society National Bank*(Major Banking Relationship)*
Canton, OH

HANK FORSSBERG, INC.
Two University Plaza, Ste. 208
Hackensack, NJ 07601
Tel.: 201-488-4800
Year Founded: 1969
Approx.Billings: $12,000,000
Emp.: 14
Upscale Products & Services
Henrik J. Forssberg *(Pres., Chief Exec. Officer & Creative Dir.)*
Nancy Talarico *(V.P., Chief Oper. Officer & Creative Dir.)*
Eileen Walton *(Opers. Mgr.)*

FORSTMANN & COMPANY, INC.
1185 Avenue of the Americas
New York, NY 10128
Tel.: 212-642-6900
Tel.: 800-233-2544 **GA**
Fax: 212-642-6870
Emp.: 2,700
Export
Global Textile Resource for Fashion Apparel Fabrics, Interior Textiles & Specialty Markets
S.I.C.: 2231
Christopher L. Schaller *(Chm., Pres. & Chief Exec. Officer)*
Fred D. Matheson *(Exec. V.P.-Mfg.)*
Richard Pactor *(Exec. V.P.-Prod. Devel. & Styling)*
William B. Towne *(Exec. V.P. & Chief Fin. Officer)*
Peter M. Roaman *(Exec. V.P.-Mktg.)*
Rod Peckham *(V.P. & Treas.)*
Brian Moorstein *(V.P.-Women's Wear)*
James Wallis *(V.P.-Men's Wear)*
Robert C. Christian *(V.P.-Human Resources)*
George J. Moran, Jr. *(V.P.-Coating & Specialty Fabrics)*
James Robinson *(V.P.-Opers.)*
Miles Glidden *(V.P.-Interior Textiles)*
Roy Edwards *(V.P.)*
John Doukas *(Dir.-Intl. Sales)*
Betsy Garder *(Mgr.-Mktg. Services)*

Outside Service Firm(s):

Powell, Goldstein, Frazer & Murphy*(Legal Firm)*
191 Peachtree St. NE, 16th Fl.
Atlanta, GA 30303
Tel.: 404-572-6700
Fax: 404-572-5958

Sales and Marketing Office:

Forstmann & Company, Inc. **(1)**
1185 Ave. of the Americas
New York, NY 10036
Tel.: 212-642-6900

Division:

Woolen Division **(1)**
P.O. Box 1049,
Dublin, GA 31040
Tel.: 912-275-5400
S.I.C.: 2231
J. Marshall McDuffie *(Gen. Mgr.)*

FORSTMANN LITTLE & CO.
767 Fifth Ave., 44th Fl.
New York, NY 10153
Tel.: 212-355-5656
Fax: 212-759-9059
Leveraged Buyout Investment & Mngmt. Firm
S.I.C.: 6719
Theodore J. Forstmann *(Partner)*

Nicholas C. Forstmann *(Partner)*
William Brian Little *(Partner)*

Companies:

Thomas & Betts Holdings, Inc. **(1)**
1555 Lynnfield Rd., Ste. 250
Memphis, TN 38119
Tel.: 901-682-7766
Telex: 980214
Assets: $691,685,000
Earnings: $456,749,000
Liabilities: $433,941,000
Net Worth: $257,744,000
Approx.Sls.: $714,586,000
Emp.: 3,300
Fiscal Year-end: 12/30/90
Computer Systems/Hardware:
IBM
Diversified Manfacture of Aerospace, Electrical & Electronic Products
S.I.C.: 3679; 3644; 3728
Clyde R. Moore *(Pres. & Chief Oper. Officer)*
William Turner *(Chief Exec. Officer)*
Van Kent *(V.P.-Human Resources)*
John R. Janulis *(Chief Fin. Officer)*
Donald R. Thau *(Treas.)*
Theodore W. Vogtman *(Controller)*
Louis D. Mattielli *(Sec.)*

General Instrument Corporation **(1)**
767 Fifth Ave.
New York, NY 10153
Tel.: 212-207-6200
(See Separate Listing)
Donald H. Rumsfeld *(Chm. & Chief Exec. Officer)*
George E. Safiol *(Pres. & Chief Exec. Officer)*
Christopher F. Sutphin *(Sr. V.P.)*
Thomas C. DeFazio *(V.P.-Fin. & Chief Fin. Officer)*
Mathew D. Miller *(V.P.-Technology)*
Lemuel A. Tarshis *(V.P.-Technology)*
Steven A. Davidson *(V.P.-Personnel & Organization)*
Richard Friedland *(V.P. & Controller)*
Roger L. Heffernan *(V.P.-Mfg.)*
Edward R. Kearney *(V.P.-Investor Rels. & Communications)*

Lear Siegler Diversified Holdings Corp. **(1)**
220 S. Orange Ave.
Livingston, NJ 07039
Tel.: 201-535-9522
Fax: 201-535-9837
Assets: $1,490,317,000
Earnings: $55,510,000
Liabilities: $848,118,000
Net Worth: $642,199,000
Approx.Sls.: $600,000,000
Emp.: 5,000
Computer Systems/Hardware:
IBM PC XT
Holding Company
S.I.C.: 6719
William J. Turner *(Chm. Bd., Pres. & Chief Exec. Officer)*
Henry S. Lager *(V.P.-Human Resources)*
Jim Mattews *(V.P. & Gen. Counsel)*

Lear Siegler Diversified Holdings Corp. **(1)**
220 S. Orange Ave.
Livingston, NJ 07039
Tel.: 201-535-9522
Fax: 201-535-9837
Assets: $1,490,317,000
Earnings: $55,510,000
Liabilities: $848,118,000
Net Worth: $642,199,000
Approx.Sls.: $600,000,000
Emp.: 5,000
Computer Systems/Hardware:
IBM PC XT
Holding Company
S.I.C.: 3715; 2531; 8711
William Turner *(Chm. Bd., Pres., Chief Exec. & Chief Oper. Officer)*
Henry S. Lager *(Sr. V.P.-Human Resources)*
Ronald B. Kalich *(Grp. V.P.)*
D. Craig Bowman *(V.P. & Assoc. Gen. Counsel)*

FORSYTHE MARCELLI JOHNSON ADVERTISING, INC.
610 Newport Center Dr.
Newport Beach, CA 92660
Tel.: 714-759-9500
Fax: 714-759-1265
Year Founded: 1980
Approx.Billings: $33,000,000
Emp.: 40
Business-to-Business & Healthcare Adv.
James Forsythe *(Pres.)*
Jeff Turcotte *(Exec. V.P.)*
Pat Schultheis *(V.P.-Controller)*
John Voigt *(V.P.-Mktg.)*

FORT DEARBORN LITHOGRAPH COMPANY
6035 Gross Point Rd.
Niles, IL 60714
Tel.: 312-774-4321
Fax: 312-774-1091
Lithographic Labels, General Printing
S.I.C.: 2752
Thomas W. Adler *(Pres.)*
Richard J. Adler *(V.P.-Sls. & Sec.)*

Outside Service Firm(s):

Francis Kuhn & Associates*(Auditors)*
Chicago, IL

Morton & Herman*(Legal Firm)*
Ft. Worth, TX

Team Bank*(Major Banking Relationship)*
500 Throckmorton
Fort Worth, TX 76102
Tel.: 817-884-4000

Division:

Ft. Dearborn Lithograph Graphic Arts Division **(1)**
P.O. Box 1293
Fort Worth, TX 76101
Tel.: 817-335-4677
Fax: 817-332-8068
Approx.Sls.: $16,000,000
Emp.: 99
Lithographic Labels, General Printing
S.I.C.: 2752
R. Bruce Besten *(Pres.)*
Gilbert Geesa *(V.P.-Sls.)*
Pauline Palmer *(Controller)*
Dick Macy *(Dir.-Mfg.)*

FORT HOWARD CORPORATION
1919 S. Broadway
Green Bay, WI 54307
Mailing Address:
P.O. Box 19130
Green Bay, WI 54307-9130
Tel.: 414-435-8821 **DE**
Fax: 414-435-3703
Year Founded: 1919
Approx.Sls.: $1,138,210,000
Emp.: 6,000
Fiscal Year-end: 12/31/91
Export
Mfr. & Distr. of Paper Related Products; Facial & Bathroom Tissues, Towels, Napkins & Wipers
S.I.C.: 2621; 2679; 2676; 2297
Donald H. DeMeuse *(Chm. Bd. & Chief Exec. Officer)*
Michael T. Riordan *(Pres. & Chief Oper. Officer)*
Kathleen J. Hempel *(Sr. Exec. V.P. & Chief Fin. Officer)*
Andrew W. Donnelly *(Exec. V.P.)*
John F. Rowley *(Exec. V.P.)*
Jeffrey P. Eves *(V.P.-Pub. Affairs)*
Leon Freischmidt *(V.P.)*
George F. Hartmann, Jr. *(V.P.)*
James W. Nellen II *(V.P., Gen. Counsel & Sec.)*
Daniel Platkowski *(V.P.)*
Timothy G. Reilly *(V.P.)*
Donald J. Schneider *(V.P.)*
R. Michael Lempke *(Treas.)*
Charles L. Szews *(Controller)*
David A. Stevens *(Asst. V.P.)*
Brian Baillie *(Dir.-Adv. & Sls. Promo.)*

Outside Service Firm(s):

Arthur Andersen & Co.*(Auditors)*
777 E. Wisconsin Ave., P.O. Box 1215
Milwaukee, WI 53202
Tel.: 414-271-5100
Fax: 414-283-3200

Morgan Stanley & Co.*(Pension Manager)*
1251 Avenue of the Americas
New York, NY 10020
Tel.: 212-703-8447
Fax: 212-703-6476

Subsidiary:

Fort Sterling Ltd. **(1)**
Mansell Way, Horwich
Bolton, BL6 6JL, United Kingdom
Tel.: 0204-68611
Telex: 63323 FORTS G
Fax: 0204-68302
Paper Converters & Manufacturers
S.I.C.: 3554

Subsidiary:

Stuart Edgar Ltd. **(2)**
South Lancashire Industrial Estate Lockett Rd., Bryn,
Wigan, Lancashire WN4 8DE, United Kingdom
Tel.: 44.942/719 600
Telex: 677404 sedgar g
Fax: 44.942/719 620
Mfr. of Tissue
S.I.C.: 2621

Tissue Facilities:

Fort Howard Paper Corporation **(1)**
5600 E. Chandler
Muskogee, OK 74402
Tel.: 918-683-7671 (100%)
Papermaking & Converting Facility
S.I.C.: 2621; 2679; 2676; 2297
Karl Meyers *(Gen. Mgr.)*

Fort Howard Paper Corporation **(1)**
Rte. 1 Baker Hill Rd.
Rincon, GA 31326
Tel.: 912-826-5216
Papermaking Facilities
S.I.C.: 2297; 2621; 2679; 2676
Carson Chapman *(Gen. Mgr.)*

FORT PITT ACQUISITIONS COMPANY, INC.
400 Chess St.
Coraopolis, PA 15108
Tel.: 412-269-2950
Sales & Marketing of Framesi/ Roffler, USA Hair Care Products
S.I.C.: 2844; 5087
Dennis Katowczik *(Pres.)*
Charles Hall *(Exec. V.P.)*
Bob Scott *(V.P.-Opers.)*
Robert Scott *(V.P.-Mktg.)*
Tom Andriz *(Controller)*

FORT WORTH LUMBER COMPANY
9101 South Freeway
Fort Worth, TX 76140
Tel.: 817-293-5211 **TX**
Fax: 817-293-3487
Emp.: 48
Rough, Dressed & Finished Lumber
S.I.C.: 5031
Earle N. Parker *(Chm. Bd.)*
Robert E. Fiesler *(Pres.)*
Lowell Bodifor *(Sec. & Treas.)*

Outside Service Firm(s):

Randy S. Meigs*(Legal Firm)*
Ft. Worth, TX

NationsBank Texas*(Major Banking Relationship)*
Ft. Worth, TX

FORTIFIBER CORPORATION
4489 Bandini Blvd.
Los Angeles, CA 90023
Tel.: 213-268-6783 **CA**
Fax: 213-264-8247
Approx.Sls.: $25,000,000
Emp.: 300
Fiscal Year-end: 12/31/91
Mfr. of Building Paper, Waterproof & Reinforced Wrapping Paper, Chemically Coated & Treated Industrial Paper, Plastic Film Sheeting & Bags, Extrusion Coated Paper & Foil
S.I.C.: 2679; 2671; 2672; 2673
G. Stuart Yount *(Chm. Bd., Chief Exec. & Chief Fin. Officer)*
Robert Thoms *(Pres. & Chief Oper. Officer)*
Carl Thoms *(Exec. V.P.)*
Walter Wey *(Controller)*

Outside Service Firm(s):

Edward White & Co.*(Auditors)*
Los Angeles, CA

Iverson, Yoakum, Papiano, & Hatch*(Legal Firm)*
Los Angeles, CA

Bank of America NT&SA*(Major Banking Relationship)*
555 So. Flower St., 5th Fl.
Los Angeles, CA 90071
Tel.: 213-228-3526
Fax: 213-228-4062

FORTUNE FASHION
(Formerly Harry Rosenblatt & Sons, Inc.)
1248 S. Flower St.
Los Angeles, CA 90015
Tel.: 213-746-3746
Fax: 213-748-3863
Emp.: 200
Distributor & Wholesaler of Unisex Activewear
S.I.C.: 5137
Fred Kayne *(Chief Exec. Officer)*

Outside Service Firm(s):

Good, Gagerman & Berns*(Auditors)*
Los Angeles, CA

Wells Fargo Bank*(Major Banking Relationship)*
333 S. Grand
Los Angeles, CA 90071
Tel.: 213-253-6836

FORTUNOFF
1300 Old Country Rd.
Westbury, NY 11590
Tel.: 516-832-9000
Fax: 516-832-9361
Approx.Sls.: $148,000,000
Emp.: 1,200
Retail Jewelry, China, Crystal, Furniture & Silverware
S.I.C.: 5944; 5719
Alan Fortunoff *(Pres.)*
Norman Goldberg *(Exec. V.P. & Chief Oper. Officer)*
Leonard Tabs *(Sr. V.P.-Fin.)*
Barbara Kaplan *(V.P.-Adv.)*
Helene Fortunoff *(Sec. & Treas.)*

Outside Service Firm(s):

Ernst & Young*(Auditors)*
395 N. Suce Road
Melville, NY 11747

Liebman & Schrier*(Legal Firm)*
New York, NY

National Westminster Bank Plc*(Major Banking Relationship)*
Carle Place, NY

THE FORUM CORPORATION
One Exchange Place
Boston, MA 02109
Tel.: 617-523-7300 **DE**
Fax: 617-723-5806
Year Founded: 1971
Assets: $13,562,000
Liabilities: $8,646,000
Net Worth: $4,916,000
Approx.Sls.: $41,000,000
Emp.: 300
Fiscal Year-end: 5/31/92

The Forum Corporation—(Continued)

International Training & Consulting Firm
S.I.C.: 8742
John W. Humphrey *(Chm. Bd.)*
Richard C. Whiteley *(Vice Chm.)*
John J. Bray *(Chm.-Forum Europe Ltd.)*
Thomas Keiser *(Pres.-Forum North America)*
Jane Carroll *(Chief Exec. Officer-Forum Europe & Forum Asia)*
David Blount *(Chief Fin. Officer)*
Diane Hessan *(Exec. V.P.-Corp.)*
Robert P. Boehm *(V.P.-Fin. & Opers., SAS)*
Elizabeth Sunelay *(V.P.-Mktg.)*
Melinda Gaeson *(Mgr.-Comml. Project)*
Susan Newhard *(Mgr.-Corp. Mktg.)*
Principal(s):
John W. Humphrey
John J. Bray

No. of U.S. Offices: 8
No. of Foreign Offices: 1

Computer Systems/Hardware:
IBM System 38

Outside Service Firm(s):

Deloitte & Touche*(Auditors)*
125 Summer St.
Boston, MA 02110
Tel.: 617-261-8000
Fax: 617-261-8111

Hartford Life Insurance Co.*(Commercial Insurance Carrier)*
Hartford, CT 06104-2999

Group Administration Services*(Group Insurer)*
Baltimore, MD

Ricklefs & Uehlein*(Legal Firm)*
Boston, MA

State Street Bank & Trust Co.*(Major Banking Relationship)*
P.O. Box 5003
Boston, MA 02107
Tel.: 617-786-6316

American Fiduciary Corp.*(Pension Manager)*
Newton, MA

Non-U.S. Holdings:

Forum Learning Systems of Canada, Ltd. **(1)**
10 Bay St., #1512
Toronto, BC M5J 2R8, Canada
Tel.: 416-360-8941
Sales & Mngmt. Training & Consulting
S.I.C.: 8742
Michael J. Pickering *(Sr. V.P.)*

FCS Forum s.s.r.o. **(1)**
Na Porici 12 115 30
Prague, 1, Czechoslovakia
Tel.: 2-287-2022
S.I.C.: 8742
Erika Maguire-Vyhnalek *(Gen. Mgr.)*

Forum Asia Pacific **(1)**
18th Fl., EIE Tower, Bond Center, 89 Queensway
Central, Hong Kong
Tel.: 2848-9260
S.I.C.: 8742
Galina V. Jeffrey *(Mng. Dir.-Asia)*

Forum Europe Ltd. **(1)**
Orion House, 5 Upper St. Martin's Lane
London, WC2H 9EA, United Kingdom
Tel.: 71-497-5555
S.I.C.: 8742
Jane Carroll *(Cheif Exec. Officer-Forum Europe)*

Affiliates:

EuroForm S.r.l. **(1)**
Via Montebello 30 20121
Milan, Italy
Tel.: 2-655-2880
S.I.C.: 8742
Maurizio Besozzi *(Mng. Dir.)*

Kasanen Training/BTC Forum **(1)**
Heikkilantie 6, PL 100 00211
Helsinki, Finland
Tel.: 0-682-1733
S.I.C.: 8742
Kari Kasanen *(Mng. Dir.)*

Training Dynamics **(1)**
275 Alfred St., 1st. Fl.
North Sydney, 2060, Australia
Tel.: 2-955-6361
S.I.C.: 8742
Stephen Solomons *(Mng. Dir.)*

Forum Compania deEntrenamiento **(1)**
Gerencial C.A., Av. Universidad, Esq.
Monroy Edif. Centro Parque Carabobo,
Piso, Ofc. 301,
Caracas, 1011, Venezuela
Tel.: 2-507-9547
S.I.C.: 8742
Alberto B'aez Duarte *(Mng. Dir.)*
Eulalia Vila *(Dir.)*

FORUM PUBLISHING COMPANY
P.O. Box 2020
Fargo, ND 58102
Tel.: 701-235-7311 **ND**
Fax: 701-241-5487
Year Founded: 1917
Approx.Sls.: $50,000,000
Emp.: 750
Newspaper Publishing; Television & Radio Broadcasting Stations; Commercial Printing
S.I.C.: 2711; 4833; 4832; 2752
William C. Marcil *(Pres. & Publr.)*
Lloyd Case *(V.P.)*
Charles Bolnet *(V.P.)*

Outside Service Firm(s):

Norwest Bank Fargo, N.A.*(Major Banking Relationship)*
Fargo, ND

FOSS MANUFACTURING COMPANY INCORPORATED
380 Lafayette Rd.
Hampton, NH 03842
Mailing Address:
P.O. Box 5000,
Hampton, NH 03842-5000
Tel.: 603-929-2111
Fax: 603-929-0061
Year Founded: 1954
Approx.Sls.: $60,000,000
Emp.: 500
Engineered Non-woven Textiles
S.I.C.: 2297
Stephen W. Foss *(Pres.)*
Bruce James *(Exec. V.P.)*
David Rowell *(V.P.-Opers.)*
Kevin Sexton *(V.P.-Fin.)*
Jean Foss *(Treas.)*

Outside Service Firm(s):

First National Bank of Boston*(Major Banking Relationship)*
P.O. Box 644,
Boston, MA 02102-0644
Tel.: 617-575-2900
Fax: 617-575-2549

FOSTER & GALLAGHER INC.
6523 N. Galena Rd.
Peoria, IL 61632
Tel.: 309-693-8600 **IL**
Fax: 309-691-2632
Sales Range: $100-499 Million
Emp.: 1,400
Retail Catalog Sales; Nursery Stock; Magazine Subscriptions; Children's Toys & Crafts; Specialty Foods
S.I.C.: 5961; 5261
Employee Matching Gifts Program:
Foster & Gallagher Foundation
Matches Employee Gifts ($10-$500) to Peoria, IL Tri-County Area Not-for-Profit Organizations
Thomas Foster *(Chm. Bd. & Chief Exec. Officer)*
Melvyn Regal *(Vice Chm.)*
A. Robert Pellegrino *(Pres.)*
Walter Deehring *(Exec. V.P.)*
Jerry Rathmann *(Sr. V.P.)*
Fred Stuber *(Sr. V.P.-Fin.)*
Bruce Wright *(Sr. V.P.-Adv.)*
James L. Burke *(V.P.-Opers.)*
James Daken *(V.P.-Resource Devel.)*
William Gehring *(V.P.-Mngmt. Information Systems)*
Principal(s):
Thomas Foster
Melvyn Regal

Computer Systems/Hardware:
IBM System 4381

Outside Service Firm(s):

Price Waterhouse*(Auditors)*
Peoria, IL

Commercial Bank of Peoria*(Major Banking Relationship)*
Peoria, IL

Divisions:

Brecks **(1)**
6523 N. Galena Rd.
Peoria, IL 61632
Tel.: 309-691-4610
Retail Catalog Nurseries
S.I.C.: 5261; 5961

David Kay, Inc. **(1)**
4509 Taylor Ln.
Cleveland, OH 44128
Tel.: 216-464-5125
Garden Gift Catalog Co.
S.I.C.: 5961
David Kay *(Pres.)*

Magazine Market Place, Inc. **(1)**
6523 N. Galena Rd.
Peoria, IL 61632
Tel.: 309-691-4610
Magazine Direct Mktg. Srvc.
S.I.C.: 5961

Spring Hill Nurseries Co. **(1)**
Elm St.
Tipp City, OH 45371
Tel.: 513-667-2491
Emp.: 200
Retail & Catalog Nursery Stock Sls.
S.I.C.: 5261; 5961
James H. Kyle *(V.P. & G.M.)*
Doreen Neff *(Office Mgr.)*

Limited Partnership:

Mauna Loa Macadamia Nut Co. **(1)**
827 Fort St.
Honolulu, HI 96813
Tel.: 808-544-6112
(See Separate Listing)

Subsidiaries:

HearthSong, Inc. **(1)**
400 Morris St.
Sebastopol, CA 95473
Tel.: 707-829-0900
Mail-Order Company For Toys
S.I.C.: 5961

The Popcorn Factory **(1)**
13970 W. Laurel Dr.
Lake Forest, IL 60045
Tel.: 708-362-0028
Fax: 708-362-7033
Emp.: 70
Fiscal Year-end: 9/30/90
Mfr. Large Gift Canisters of Popcorn
S.I.C.: 2096
Phyllis Cretors *(Pres.)*
Nancy Hensel *(V.P.-Mktg. & Mdsg.)*
Ann Bromley *(Mgr.-Mdse.)*
Karen Fornell *(Mgr.-Catalog)*
Karen Shutty *(Mgr.-Mktg.)*

FOSTER MEDICAL SUPPLY, INC.
275 Wyman St.
Waltham, MA 02154
Tel.: 617-890-4848 **DE**
Fax: 617-890-8446
Year Founded: 1987
Approx.Sls.: $150,000,000
Emp.: 500
Distribute Medical Apparatus & Supplies to Doctors, Clinics, Nursing Homes & Hospitals
S.I.C.: 5047
Robert L. Cohen *(Chm. Bd.)*
Robert W. Macleod *(Chief Fin. Officer)*
John Breen *(Treas.)*
Gordon Dalrymple *(Dir.-Mngmt. Information Systems)*

No. of U.S. Offices: 17

Outside Service Firm(s):

Bank of New England*(Major Banking Relationship)*
28 State Street
Boston, MA 02109
Tel.: 617-742-4000

FOSTER-MILLER, INC.
350 2nd Ave.
Waltham, MA 02154
Tel.: 617-890-3200 **MA**
Fax: 617-890-3489
Year Founded: 1956
Approx.Sls.: $33,000,000
Emp.: 273
Fiscal Year-end: 7/31/91
Production Machinery, Polymer Processing Technology, Remote Control Devices, Technology Development & Implementation, Design & Systems Integration
S.I.C.: 3559; 3822; 7373; 5162
E.L. Foster *(Chm. Bd.)*
C. Kojabashian *(Pres.)*
A.A. Aponick *(V.P.)*
James Bright *(V.P.)*
E.J. Goldman *(V.P.)*
A.R. Guzdar *(V.P.)*
E.H. Nahikian *(V.P.)*
R.R. Olander *(V.P.)*
W.A. Ribich *(V.P.)*

Outside Service Firm(s):

Kaitz, Levine & Ilacqua*(Auditors)*
Boston, MA

Bay Bank Harvard Trust Company*(Major Banking Relationship)*
Cambridge, MA

FOSTER PONTIAC, INC.
3636 S. 27th St.
Milwaukee, WI 53221
Tel.: 414-282-5000
Fax: 414-282-5855
Approx.Sls.: $36,000,000
Emp.: 67
Fiscal Year-end: 12/31/91
Retail Automobiles
S.I.C.: 5511
John Foster *(Pres.)*
Betty Foster *(V.P.)*
James Foster *(Treas.)*

Outside Service Firm(s):

Bank One Milwaukee, N.A.*(Major Banking Relationship)*
111 E. Wisconsin Ave.
Milwaukee, WI
Tel.: 414-765-3000

FOSTER REFRIGERATOR CORPORATION
Mill & No. Second
Hudson, NY 12534
Tel.: 518-828-3311
Fax: 518-828-3115
Year Founded: 1946
Approx.Sls.: $10,000,000
Emp.: 50
Fiscal Year-end: 12/31/90
Export

Comml. Refrigerators & Freezers, Pre-fabricated Walk-Ins Infrared & Convection Ovens, Lab. Refrigerators & Freezers, Bakery & Marine Refrigerators & Freezers
S.I.C.: 3585; 3589
Lawrence H. Foster *(Pres.)*
Jim Dillon *(V.P.-Sls. & Mktg.)*
Bob Delaney *(Personnel Admin.)*
R. Walsh *(Pur. Agent)*

FOSTORIA INDUSTRIES, INC.
1200 N. Main St.
Fostoria, OH 44830
Mailing Address:
P.O. Box E,
Fostoria, OH 44830-0986
Tel.: 419-435-9201 TN
Fax: 419-435-0842
Year Founded: 1917
Assets: $6,500,000
Liabilities: $1,300,000
Net Worth: $5,200,000
Approx.Sls.: $16,800,000
Emp.: 160
Fiscal Year-end: 9/30/91
Export
Industrial Lighting; Industrial Ovens; Industrial, Commercial & Residential Heating
S.I.C.: 3567; 3585; 3646
R.E. Henry, Sr. *(Chm. Bd.)*
E.N. Schalk *(Pres. & Chief Exec. Officer)*
Larry E. Dunlap *(V.P. & Gen. Prods. Div. Mgr.)*
W.M. Poma *(V.P. & Special Prods. Div. Mgr.)*
D.J. Bouillon *(Treas. & Chief Fin. Officer)*
Steve Fruth *(Dir.-Mktg.)*
T.L. Putnam *(Dir. Data Processing)*
Karl Williamson *(Dir.-Personnel)*
W.P. Eibner *(Mgr.-Process Heat Div.)*
G. Kimmel *(Mgr.-Adv. & Sls. Promo.-Process Heat)*
R.V. Klueter *(Mgr.-Adv.)*
J.B. Wetherill *(Pur. Agent)*

No. of Mfg. Plants/Facilities: 2
No. of U.S. Offices: 1

Computer Systems/Hardware:
IBM System 36

Outside Service Firm(s):

Price Waterhouse*(Auditors)*
One Seagate, Ste. 1800
Toledo, OH 43604
Tel.: 419-247-1800

Provident Life & Accident Insurance Co.*(Group Insurer)*
Knoxville, TN

FOTHERINGHAM & ASSOCIATES
215 S. State St., Ste. 300
Salt Lake City, UT 84111-2319
Tel.: 801-521-2903
Fax: 801-359-2420
Year Founded: 1971
Approx.Billings: $15,000,000
Emp.: 30
Robert S. Fotheringham *(Chm.)*
Bruce H. Jensen *(Pres.)*
Tony Thompson *(Controller)*
Hal Christensen *(Mktg. & Client Services Dir.)*
Tim Brown *(Pub. Rels. Dir.)*

FOTOUHI ALONSO INC. ADVERTISING & MARKETING
1901 Ave. of the Stars, Ste. 950
Los Angeles, CA 90067
Tel.: 310-553-8271
Fax: 213-553-0514
Year Founded: 1976
Approx.Billings: $19,870,000
Emp.: 18
Farida Fotouhi *(Pres.)*

FOULDS INC.
520 E. Church St.
Libertyville, IL 60048
Tel.: 708-362-3062
Fax: 708-362-6658
Year Founded: 1885
Approx.Sls.: $16,000,000
Emp.: 100
Fiscal Year-end: 12/31/90
Export
Mfr. of Spaghetti, Macaroni, Noodles; Kaboodles Egg Noodles, No Yolks Egg Noodle Substitute, No Yolks Egg Noodle Dumplings, Wacky Mac & Cheese Dinners
S.I.C.: 2098
Robert B. Strom *(Pres.)*
Joseph A. Bradley *(V.P.)*
Lowell Wilkins *(Controller)*
Jim Bauspies *(Plant Mgr.)*
Sharon Gilb *(Mgr.-Qual. Control)*
Gary Henke *(Natl. Sls. Mgr.)*
Principal(s):
Robert B. Strom
Joseph A. Bradley

Outside Service Firm(s):

Ernst & Young*(Auditors)*
233 S. Wacker Dr.
Chicago, IL 60606
Tel.: 312-368-1800
Fax: 312-645-3095

Chapman & Cutler*(Legal Firm)*
111 W. Monroe
Chicago, IL 60603
Tel.: 312-845-3000

American National Bank*(Major Banking Relationship)*
Chicago, IL

4C FOODS CORPORATION
580 Fountain Ave.
Brooklyn, NY 11208
Tel.: 718-272-4242
Fax: 718-272-2899
Year Founded: 1939
Approx.Sls.: $45,000,000
Emp.: 120
Fiscal Year-end: 12/31/90
Mfr. & Distribute Food Products
S.I.C.: 2034; 2045; 5141
John Celauro *(Pres.)*
Dan Swartz *(V.P.-Private Label Packing)*
Tony Landolfi *(Dir.-Mktg. & Mgr.-Natl. Sls.)*
Ronald Long *(Dir.-Personnel)*
Joseph Saratella *(Pur. Agent-Supplies)*

No. of Mfg. Plants/Facilities: 1
No. of U.S. Offices: 1

Computer Systems/Hardware:
Sperry Univac

Outside Service Firm(s):

Wiss & Company*(Auditors)*
Livingston, NJ

Principal Mutual Life Insurance Co.*(Group Insurer)*
711 High St.
Des Moines, IA 50309

European American Bank*(Major Banking Relationship)*
New York, NY

4DAY TIRE STORES
(Sub. of Lansdale Carr, Inc.)
17662 Armstrong Ave.
Irvine, CA 17662
Tel.: 714-250-9244
Fax: 714-261-5473
Approx.Sls.: $130,000,000
Emp.: 500
Fiscal Year-end: 4/30/92
54 Retail Tire Stores
S.I.C.: 5531
Donald Carr *(Pres.)*

Floyd Ewton *(Chief Fin. Officer)*
Peter Lewis *(Adv. Mgr.)*

FOUR SEASONS SOLAR PRODUCTS CORP.
5005 Veterans Memorial Hwy.
Holbrook, NY 11741
Tel.: 516-563-4000 NY
Fax: 516-563-4010
Year Founded: 1975
Approx.Sls.: $50,000,000
Emp.: 250
Mfr. & Distribute Solar Greenhouses & Solarium/Atrium Structures
S.I.C.: 3448
Chris Esposito *(Pres.)*
Joseph Esposito *(Exec. V.P.)*
Tony Russo *(V.P.-Franchise Sls.)*
Principal(s):
Chris Esposito
Joseph Esposito

No. of Mfg. Plants/Facilities: 2
No. of U.S. Offices: 5
No. of Foreign Offices: 2

Outside Service Firm(s):

Deloitte & Touche*(Auditors)*
Newark, NJ

Delson & Gordon*(Legal Firm)*
230 Park Ave.
New York, NY 10017
Tel.: 212-686-8030

Chemical Bank*(Major Banking Relationship)*
450 West 33rd St.
New York, NY 10001
Tel.: 212-613-7197
Fax: 212-947-7628

FRED V. FOWLER COMPANY, INC.
66 Rowe St.
Newton, MA 02166
Tel.: 617-332-7004 MA
Fax: 617-332-4137
Year Founded: 1946
Approx.Sls.: $20,000,000
Emp.: 53
Fiscal Year-end: 7/31/90
Import Export
Wholesaler & Distributor Of Mechanical & Electronic Precision Measuring Tools For the Metal Working Industry
S.I.C.: 5084; 5065; 5085
Corporate Giving Program: United Fund
Frederick V. Fowler, Jr. *(Chm. Bd., Pres. & Chief Exec. Officer)*
Uldis Uzolins *(Chief Fin. Officer & V.P.)*
Marshall Rakusin *(Sr. V.P.-Sls.)*
Charles Parrott *(Sec.)*
Monticello Abrahms *(Dir.-Quality Control)*
Jan Delaney *(Dir.-Import)*
Fred V. Fowler, III *(Dir.-Research & Devel.)*
Carol Kaufman *(Dir.-Adv.)*
Principal(s):
Frederick V. Fowler, Jr.
Uldis Uzolins

No. of U.S. Offices: 3

Outside Service Firm(s):

Peck Associates*(Auditors)*
Wellesley Hills, MA

Tucker Anthony Inc.*(Commercial Insurance Carrier)*
1 Beacon St.
Boston, MA 02108
Tel.: 617-725-2000
Fax: 617-725-2280

Sun Life*(Group Insurer)*
Boston, MA

Nutter, McClennen & Fish*(Legal Firm)*
One International Place
Boston, MA 02210-2699
Tel.: 617-439-2000

Shawmut Bank*(Major Banking Relationship)*
Newton, MA

Affiliate:

Fowler Tools of Canada **(1)**
24 E. McIntyre Pl.,
Kitchener, Ontario N2R 1G9, Canada
Tel.: 519-895-0970
Emp.: 4
Wholesale & Distribution of Measuring Tools in Canada
S.I.C.: 5084
Harry Scanlan *(Pres.)*
Janette Scanlan *(Chief Fin. Officer & Dir.-Pur.)*

FOWNES BROTHERS & CO., INC.
411 5th Ave.
New York, NY 10016
Tel.: 212-683-0150
Fax: 212-683-2832
Year Founded: 1921
Approx.Sls.: $35,000,000
Emp.: 250
Import Export
Mfr. of Fabric Dress & Work Gloves
S.I.C.: 2381
Thomas Gluckman *(Pres.)*
Arnold Jaffe *(V.P.)*
Helmut Dosch *(V.P.)*
Howard Chaiet *(Controller)*
Gladyee Gluckman *(Sec.)*
Lee Diack *(Dir.-Mktg.)*

C.B. FOX COMPANY
220 Camp St.
New Orleans, LA 70130
Tel.: 504-588-9211 DE
Fax: 504-588-9214
Approx.Sls.: $14,000,000
Emp.: 6
Export
Exporter of Corn, Wheat & Soybeans
S.I.C.: 5153
Richard B. Fox *(Pres.)*
David J. Conroy *(Sec.)*
Joel M. Pratt *(Comptroller)*

Outside Service Firm(s):

Bourgeois, Bennett & Thokey*(Auditors)*
New Orleans, LA

First National Bank of Commerce*(Major Banking Relationship)*
210 Baronne St.
New Orleans, LA 70112
Tel.: 504-561-1371

FOX-KNAPP INC.
(Div. of David Peyser Sport)
362 Fifth Ave., Ste. 601
New York, NY 10010
Tel.: 212-564-2486
Fax: 212-629-6714
Approx.Sls.: $10,000,000
Emp.: 650
Import Export
Mens, Ladies & Boys Sports Outerwear
S.I.C.: 2321; 2329; 2253
Elliott Singer *(Pres.)*
Arthur Pennick *(Dir.-Mktg.)*
Ydalia Diaz *(Mgr.-Adv.)*

FOX VALLEY CORPORATION
600 S. Vulcan St.
Appleton, WI 54915
Mailing Address:
P.O. Box 727
Appleton, WI 54912
Tel.: 414-739-8982 DE

Fox Valley Corporation—(Continued)

Fax: 414-733-2975
Approx.Sls.: $200,000,000
Emp.: 1,600
Fiscal Year-end: 3/31/92
Export
Mfr. of Gift Wrap, Ribbons, Bows & Fine Writing Papers; Holding Company
S.I.C.: 2671; 2678; 2679; 6719
Robert C. Buchanan *(Pres. & Chief Exec. Officer)*
Robert L. Esten *(V.P.)*
Richard W. Gygi *(V.P.)*
Lyle H. Richter *(V.P., Treas. & Sec.)*

Outside Service Firm(s):

Arthur Andersen & Co.*(Auditors)*
777 E. Wisconsin Ave., P.O. Box 1215
Milwaukee, WI 53202
Tel.: 414-271-5100
Fax: 414-283-3200

Subsidiaries:

CPS Corporation **(1)**
1715 Columbia Hwy.
Franklin, TN 37065
Tel.: 615-794-8000
Fax: 615-791-5131
Approx.Sls.: $100,000,000
Emp.: 780
Mfg. of Gift Wrap, Ribbons & Bows
S.I.C.: 2671; 2679
Richard W. Gygi *(Pres.)*
Philip Pageau *(V.P. & Controller)*
Nick Jordan *(V.P.-Sls.)*
Morris Patterson *(V.P.-Opers.)*
William Neal *(V.P.-Fund Raising)*
Marc English *(V.P.-Mktg.)*
Margaret Napier *(V.P.-Human Resources)*
Doug Carlson *(V.P.-Custom)*

Fox River Paper Company **(1)**
200 E. Washington St., Ste. 300
Appleton, WI 54913
Tel.: 414-733-7341
Tel.: 800-558-8327
Fax: 414-733-2975
Approx.Sls.: $100,000,000
Emp.: 700
Export
Mfr. of Stationery & Specialized Papers
S.I.C.: 2621
Robert L. Esten *(Pres.)*
D.J. Lang *(V.P.-Sls.)*
Jim Jacobson *(V.P.-Opers.)*
Oakie L. Sallee *(V.P.-Natl. Accts.)*
Charles Whitaker *(V.P.-Admin.)*
Lynn M. Yelton *(V.P.-Mktg.)*
D.L. Peotter *(Treas.)*

Divisions:

Howard Paper **(2)**
504 W. Church St.
Urbana, OH 43078
Tel.: 513-653-7151
Tel.: 800-543-5010
Fax: 513-653-7422
Approx.Sls.: $79,000,000
Emp.: 354
Fiscal Year-end: 3/31/92
Export
Computer Systems/Hardware:
IBM System 34
Fine Paper & Allied Products
S.I.C.: 2621
Tom Danz *(V.P.-Resident Mgr.)*
Ted Erickson *(Dir.-Engrng. & Maintenance)*
Robert Craine *(Mgr.-Data Processing)*
Donald Sprague *(Mgr.-Technical)*
Donald Baker *(Superintendent-Paper Mill)*
Stephen Phillip *(Sr. Process Engr.)*

Subsidiary:

Howard Paper Mills **(3)**
504 W. Church St.
Urbana, OH 43078
Tel.: 513-653-7151
Fine Paper & Allied Products
S.I.C.: 2621
Robert C. Buchanan *(Pres. & Chief Exec. Officer)*

Rising Paper Company **(2)**
295 Park St.
Housatonic, MA 01236
Tel.: 413-274-3345
Fax: 413-274-6684
Sales Range: $20-39 Million
Emp.: 160
Fiscal Year-end: 3/30/92
Export
Mfr. of Fine Writing, Business, Technical & Art Paper; Matboard
S.I.C.: 2621; 2631
Robert Buchanan *(Chm. Bd.)*
Robert Esten *(Pres.-Fox River Paper Co.)*
Kenneth Krukonis *(Tech. Dir.)*
John Coutu *(V.P. & Resident Mgr.)*
Robert Montana *(Mgr.-Admin.)*

FOXWORTH-GALBRAITH LUMBER CO.
17111 Waterview Parkway
Dallas, TX 75252
Mailing Address:
P.O. Box 799002
Dallas, TX 75379-9002
Tel.: 214-437-6100 **TX**
Fax: 214-437-4236
Year Founded: 1902
Approx.Sls.: $150,000,000
Emp.: 1,500
Wholesale & Retail Lumber & Building Materials
S.I.C.: 5031; 5039; 5211
J.C. Galbraith, Jr. *(Chm. Bd.)*
Walter L. Foxworth *(Pres.)*
Jack Foxworth *(V.P.)*
H. S. Galbraith *(V.P.)*
J. C. Galbraith, III *(V.P.-Sls. & Adv.)*
Billy White *(Treas.)*

Outside Service Firm(s):

H. V. Robertson & Co.*(Auditors)*
Amarillo, TX

Texas Commerce Bank*(Major Banking Relationship)*
2200 Ross Ave.
Dallas, TX 75266

Subsidiary:

Arizona Sash & Door Co. **(1)**
850 W. Lincoln St.
Phoenix, AZ 85002
Tel.: 602-253-3151
Millwork; Wooden Doors & Door Sashes; Rough, Dressed & Finished Lumber; Builders' Hardware
S.I.C.: 2431; 5031; 5072
Kenneth A. Mann *(Gen. Mgr.)*

FRAENKEL COMPANY
10600 S. Choctaw Dr.
Baton Rouge, LA 70815
Mailing Address:
P.O. Box 15385,
Baton Rouge, LA 70895
Tel.: 504-275-8111
Fax: 504-272-7319
Year Founded: 1959
Approx.Sls.: $35,000,000
Emp.: 285
Import Export
Wholesale Furniture; Manufacturer Of Mattresses, Bedsprings & Upholstered Furniture
S.I.C.: 2515; 5021; 2512
Albert Fraenkel *(Chm. Bd.)*
Harvey Hoffman *(Pres.)*
Bruce Minkoff *(Exec. V.P.)*
Mike Hirschman *(V.P.)*
Susan Pourciau *(Treas.)*
Eleanor Fraenkel *(Sec.)*

Outside Service Firm(s):

Postlethwaite & Netterville*(Auditors)*
Baton Rouge, LA

Watson Blanche Wilson & Posner*(Legal Firm)*
Baton Rouge, LA

Sun Burst*(Major Banking Relationship)*
Baton Rouge, LA

Subsidiaries:

Fraenkel Company **(1)**
8300 Industrial Dr.
Olive Branch, MS 38654
Tel.: 601-895-3800

FRAGRANCE RESOURCES, INC.
275 Clark St.
Keyport, NJ 07735
Tel.: 908-264-6767
Fax: 908-264-2933
Approx.Sls.: $20,000,000
Emp.: 58
Fiscal Year-end: 11/30/91
Manufacture Oils & Essential Oils
S.I.C.: 2899
Richard Carraher *(Chief Exec. Officer)*
Steve Coffey *(Pres.-Fragrances)*
Frank Mara *(V.P.-Opers.)*
Richard Timmes *(V.P.-Fin.)*

Outside Service Firm(s):

Kipnis & Karchmer*(Auditors)*
386 Park Ave. S.
New York, NY 10016
Tel.: 212-447-5588

ANDY FRAIN SERVICES, INC.
310 W. Chicago Ave.
Chicago, IL 60610
Tel.: 312-266-6900 **DE**
Fax: 312-266-8641
Year Founded: 1924
Sales Range: $20-39 Million
Emp.: 6,500
Fiscal Year-end: 6/30/91
Usher & Guard Services
S.I.C.: 7363; 7381
Stephen A. Cohen *(Chm. Bd. & Pres.)*
David Clayton *(Exec. V.P.)*
Christian Montgomery *(Exec. V.P.-Mktg.)*
Principal(s):
Stephen A. Cohen
David Clayton
Christian Montgomery
John Pressman

Subsidiary:

Andy Frain Aviation Services, Inc. **(1)**
310 W. Chicago Ave.
Chicago, IL 60610
Tel.: 312-266-6900
Airport Screening & Special Services
S.I.C.: 8744
Stephen A. Cohen *(Pres.)*

J. H. FRANCE REFRACTORIES CO.
1944 France Rd.
Snow Shoe, PA 16874
Tel.: 814-387-6811
Fax: 814-387-6209
Approx.Sls.: $17,000,000
Emp.: 175
Firebrick, Castables, Mortar, Plastic Fire Brick, Special Products
S.I.C.: 3255
William A. France, Jr. *(Pres.)*
D.W. Bates *(V.P. & Treas.)*
Larry Markol *(Comptroller & Sec.)*
N.C. Wiggin *(Mgr.-Mktg. Services)*
Scott Klinger *(Pur. Agent)*

Divisions:

Greenpoint Division **(1)**
25-39 Borden Ave.
Long Island City, NY 11101
Tel.: 718-729-8950
Emil Pilosi *(Gen. Mgr.)*

Van Brunt Division **(1)**
4041 Ridge Ave.
Philadelphia, PA 19129
Tel.: 215-848-7575
John Dunn *(Gen. Mgr.)*

FRANCHISE ENTERPRISES INC.
1313 Hardees Blvd.
Rocky Mount, NC 27804
Tel.: 919-977-0950 **NC**
Fax: 919-972-7702
Year Founded: 1961
Sales Range: $80-99 Million
Emp.: 3,300
Franchisee of Fast-Food Restaurants
S.I.C.: 5812
Albert H. Schnitzlein *(Pres. & Chief Exec. Officer)*
Fredrick Forsythe *(Exec. V.P.-Fin.)*
G. Randy Robinson *(Sr. V.P.-Sls.)*
Fred M. Tharrington *(Sr. V.P.-Devel.)*
Richard P. Wilson *(Sr. V.P.-Human Resources)*
Carolyn H. Burgess *(V.P.-Fin.)*
Ray Matthews *(V.P.)*
Principal(s):
Citicorp Capital Investors, Ltd.

Outside Service Firm(s):

Arthur Andersen & Co.*(Auditors)*
Raleigh, NC

Centura Bank*(Major Banking Relationship)*
Rocky Mount, NC

FRANCHISE FINANCE CORP. OF AMERICA
17207 N. Perimeter Dr.
Scottsdale, AZ 85255
Tel.: 602-585-4500
Year Founded: 1980
Approx.Rev.: $116,000,000
Emp.: 65
Fiscal Year-end: 12/31/91
Investment Mngmt.; Operates 1,200 Properties in 45 States
S.I.C.: 7389
Paul Bagley *(Chm. Bd.)*
Morton H. Fleischer *(Pres., Chief Exec. Officer & Treas.)*
Vivian L. Anderson *(Sr. V.P. & Sec.)*

FRANK CONSOLIDATED ENTERPRISES INC.
(d/b/a Wheels, Inc.)
666 Garland Place
Des Plaines, IL 60016
Tel.: 708-699-7000
Fax: 708-699-6494
Year Founded: 1939
Approx.Sls.: $1,345,000,000
Emp.: 1,826
Fleet Management & Leasing of Automobiles & Trucks; Corp. Travel Services
S.I.C.: 5511; 4724; 7513; 7514
Elaine S. Frank *(Chm. Bd.)*
James S. Frank *(Pres.)*
Ford G. Pearson *(Exec. V.P.)*
Theodore D. Less *(Sr. V.P.)*
Michael Christian *(V.P.-Midwest Sls.)*
Peter Egan *(V.P.-Eastern Sls.)*
Dennis LaLiberty *(V.P.-Mktg.)*
Principal(s):
James S. Frank

Computer Systems/Hardware:
IBM

Outside Service Firm(s):

Continental Bank N. A.*(Major Banking Relationship)*
231 S. LaSalle St.
Chicago, IL 60697
Tel.: 312-828-2345
Tel.: 800-426-5754
Telex: 312-828-1783

Subsidiary:

IVI Travel **(1)**
400 Skokie Blvd.
Northbrook, IL 60062-2887
Tel.: 708-480-8400 (100%)
Approx.Rev.: $240,000,000
Emp.: 475
Corporate Travel Management
S.I.C.: 4724
Walter G. Freedman *(Pres.)*
Lee Turner *(Exec. V.P. & Chief Fin. Officer)*
Louis Fischer *(Sr. V.P.-Sls.)*
Steve Weiner *(V.P.-Mktg.)*

FRANK INDUSTRIES, INC.
3950 Burnsline Rd.
Brown City, MI 48416
Tel.: 313-346-2771
Fax: 313-346-3553
Year Founded: 1967
Approx.Sls.: $12,000,000
Emp.: 100
Fiscal Year-end: 12/31/90
Mfr. of Xplorer Motor Homes, Cargo Vans & Commercial Vehicles
S.I.C.: 3792
Ronald R. Frank *(Chm. Bd. & Chief Exec. Officer)*
Gerrie E. Frank *(Pres. & Gen. Mgr.)*
Dave Weinsz *(Sls. Dir.)*
Joe Tyson *(Adv. Mgr.)*
Ray Burgess *(Pur. Dir.)*

Division:

Xplorer Motor Home Div. **(1)**
3950 Burnsline Rd.
Brown City, MI 48416
Tel.: 313-346-2771
Fax: 313-346-3553
Mfr. of Xplorer Motor Homes, Cargo Vans & Commercial Vehicles
S.I.C.: 3792

WALLY FRANK, LTD.
63-25 69th St.
Middle Village, NY 11379
Tel.: 212-326-2233
Fax: 718-326-0453
Year Founded: 1933
Approx.Sls.: $10,000,000
Emp.: 75
Fiscal Year-end: 8/31/90

Import
Wally Frank Pipes, Tobaccos & Cigars
S.I.C.: 2121; 2131; 3999
Larry Weinfeld *(Pres.)*
Stephan Frank *(V.P.)*
Wally Frank *(Treas.)*

S. M. FRANK & CO., INC.
P.O. Box 789,
Peekskill, NY 10566
Mailing Address:
P.O. Box 789
Peekskill, NY 10566
Year Founded: 1924
Emp.: 15

Import Export
Import & Mfg. Smokers Pipes & Smoking Articles
S.I.C.: 2131
W.F. Fuerbach, Jr. *(Chm. Bd., Pres. & Treas.)*
D.S. Fuerbach *(Sec.)*

Computer Systems/Hardware:
IBM PC AT

Outside Service Firm(s):

Walter Reinman*(Auditors)*
Goshen, NY

Blue Shield of Northeastern New York, Inc.*(Group Insurer)*
Albany, NY

Connecticut General Life Insurance Co.*(Group Insurer)*
P.O. Box 2975,
Hartford, CT 06104
Tel.: 203-726-6000

Peekskill Bank*(Major Banking Relationship)*
Peekskill, NY

Division:

Kaywoodie **(1)**
1000 N. Division St.
Peekskill, NY 10566
Tel.: 914-739-3100

Medico, Inc. **(1)**
1000 N. Division St.
Peekskill, NY 10566
Tel.: 914-739-3100

Yello-Bole **(1)**
1000 N. Division St.
Peekskill, NY 10566
Tel.: 914-739-3100

FRANKEL & COMPANY
111 E. Wacker Dr.
Chicago, IL 60601
Tel.: 312-938-1900
Year Founded: 1962
Approx.Billings: $160,000,000
Emp.: 270
Creative & Sales Promotion
Bernard Frankel *(Chm. & Chief Exec. Officer)*
Jim Mack *(Pres.)*
David Tridle *(Pres.-Frankel Service Grp.)*
Mike McCann *(Sr. V.P., Dir. Opers.)*
Joe Skarbek *(V.P., Plng. & Admin.)*
Muriel Glick *(V.P., Dir. Pub. Rels.)*
Mark Steinsdoerfer *(Dir., Systems & Analysis)*
George Soukup *(Controller)*
Chris Shoemaker *(Personnel Mgr.)*

Computer Systems/Hardware:
NCR-Tower-32850

FRANKENBERRY, LAUGHLIN & CONSTABLE, INC.
207 E. Michigan St.
Milwaukee, WI 53202
Tel.: 414-272-2400
Fax: 414-272-3056
Year Founded: 1976
Approx.Billings: $68,400,000
Emp.: 100
Steven L. Laughlin *(Partner & Creative Dir.)*
John Constable *(Partner & Exec. Art Dir.)*
Lawrence Freschl *(Exec. V.P., Opers.)*
Julie Tarney *(Sr. V.P., Pub. Rels.)*

Computer Systems/Hardware:
Wang VS

FRANKFURT GIPS BALKIND, ADVERTISING
(An Affil. of Frankfurt Gips Balkind Communications)
244 East 58th St.
New York, NY 10022
Tel.: 212-421-5888
Fax: 212-759-9284
Year Founded: 1991
Approx.Billings: $61,000,000
Emp.: 58
Steve Frankfurt *(Chm.)*
Aubrey Balkind *(Chief Exec. Officer)*
Lori Moskowitz *(Sr. V.P. & Dir., Acct. Services)*

Computer Systems/Hardware:
Apple MacIntosh

FRANKLIN BAKING CO., INC.
500 W. Grantham St.
Goldsboro, NC 27530
Mailing Address:
P.O. Drawer 228
Goldsboro, NC 27533
Tel.: 919-735-0344 **NC**
Fax: 919-735-6629
Year Founded: 1945
Approx.Sls.: $49,000,000
Emp.: 625
Baking & Distribution of Bread, Rolls & Other Bakery Products
S.I.C.: 2051
E. Thomas Franklin *(Chm., Pres. & Treas.)*
E. Thomas Franklin, Jr. *(Exec. V.P.)*
Jeffrey B. Franklin *(Sr. V.P.)*
Mozelle B. Franklin *(V.P.)*
Timothy K. Franklin *(V.P.)*
S.M. Franklin *(V.P.)*
Richard E. Askins *(Controller)*
J.D. Hood *(Dir.-Mfg.)*
William P. Pearman *(Dir.-Pur.)*
J.E. Smith *(Dir.-Personnel)*
Carl Wadsworth *(Dir.-Sls.)*
Tom Smith *(Chief Engineer)*
Harold McRoberts *(Mgr.-Product)*

No. of Mfg. Plants/Facilities: 4
No. of U.S. Offices: 1

Computer Systems/Hardware:
PC Network & IBM

Outside Service Firm(s):

KPMG Peat Marwick*(Auditors)*
3100 Smoketree Court
Raleigh, NC 27629
Tel.: 919-872-3600
Fax: 919-790-9731

M & M Company*(Commercial Insurance Carrier)*
Raleigh, NC

Chubb Group*(Group Insurer)*
Goldsboro, NC

M & M Company*(Group Insurer)*
Raleigh, NC

PMA*(Group Insurer)*
Goldsboro, NC

Dees, Smith, Powell, Jarrett, Dees & Jones*(Legal Firm)*
Raleigh, NC

Branch Banking & Trust Co.*(Major Banking Relationship)*
Raleigh, NC

FRANKLIN FEDERAL SAVINGS ASSOCIATION
One Franklin Plaza
Ottawa, KS 66067
Tel.: 913-894-9704 **KS**
Fax: 913-242-6023
Year Founded: 1889
Approx.Income: $100,000,000
Emp.: 375
Savings and Loan Association
S.I.C.: 6036
John A. Scowcroft *(Vice Chm.)*
Frank Mercandte *(Pres. & Chief Exec. Officer)*
Nancy L. Spovale *(Sr. V.P.-Opers.)*

FRANKLIN SPORTS INDUSTRIES
17 Campanelli Pkwy.
Stoughton, MA 02072
Tel.: 617-344-1111
Fax: 617-344-3220
Approx.Sls.: $65,000,000
Emp.: 175
Mfr. of Athletic & Sporting Goods
S.I.C.: 3949
Irving H. Franklin *(Chm. Bd. & Treas.)*
Larry Franklin *(Pres.)*
Richard Firenze *(V.P.-Sls.)*
George Small *(V.P. & Controller)*
Kurt Gluck *(Dir.-Pur.)*
John J. Cassidy *(Mgr.-Personnel)*

FRANKLIN STEEL COMPANY
600 Atlantic Ave.
Franklin, PA 16323
Mailing Address:
P.O. Box 671
Franklin, PA 16323
Tel.: 814-437-3726
Year Founded: 1901
Approx.Sls.: $40,000,000
Emp.: 385

Export
Mfr. of Concrete Reinforcing Bars; Merchant Bars & Shapes; Farm Fence Posts; Highway Sign Posts
S.I.C.: 3449; 3429
John F. O'Toole *(Pres.)*
B.W. Nerlich *(Exec. V.P.)*
W.G. Miller *(V.P.)*
M. Murphy *(V.P. & Chief Fin. Officer)*
W.P. Rhodes *(Pur. Agent)*
T.A. Spence *(Personnel Mgr.)*
Jim Young *(Sls. Mgr.)*

FRANKS SUPPLY COMPANY, INC.
3311 Stanford, N.E.
Albuquerque, NM 87107
Tel.: 505-884-0000 **NM**
Fax: 505-884-1787
Emp.: 55
Fiscal Year-end: 6/30/92
General Construction Machinery & Equipment; Equipment Rental & Leasing
S.I.C.: 5082; 7359
Dan Deaver *(Pres. & Chief Exec. Officer)*
Melissa Deaver *(V.P.)*
Harvey Copass *(Controller)*
Richard Crifasi *(Gen. Mgr.)*
Rick Lamb *(Mgr.-Sls.)*

Outside Service Firm(s):

Clifford Gunderson*(Auditors)*
Albuquerque, NM

Sun West Bank of Albuquerque*(Major Banking Relationship)*
P.O. Box 25500
Albuquerque, NM 87125-0500
Tel.: 505-765-2698
Fax: 505-842-6661

FRANTZ MANUFACTURING CO.
301 W. 3rd St.
Sterling, IL 61081
Tel.: 815-625-0163 **DE**
Fax: 815-626-0747
Sales Range: $40-59 Million
Emp.: 500

Export
Mfr. Overhead Garage Doors, Hardware, Conveyor Wheels & Bearings, Barn Tracks & Hangers
S.I.C.: 3442; 3399; 3429; 3568; 3562; 2431
H.B. Musgrove *(Chm. Bd., Pres. & Chief Exec. Officer)*
M. Anderson *(V.P.-Mktg.)*
E.L. Froeliger *(Sec., Treas. & Chief Fin. Officer)*
J.E. Ewald *(Dir.-Data Processing)*
L.L. Forristall *(Dir.-Personnel)*
O.D. Null *(Dir.-Pur.)*
A.P. Snelling *(Dir.-Oper., Sterling Door Div.)*
Jerry Knox *(Mgr.-Adv.)*
W.H. Stotzer *(Mgr.-Sls.)*

Outside Service Firm(s):

Arthur Andersen & Co.*(Auditors)*
33 W. Monroe St.
Chicago, IL 60603-4067
Tel.: 312-580-0033
Fax: 312-507-6748

Allendale Mutual Insurance Co.*(Commercial Insurance Carrier)*
1301 Atwood Ave.
Johnston, RI 02919
Tel.: 401-275-3000

Frantz Manufacturing Co.—(Continued)

Western Employers Insurance*(Commercial Insurance Carrier)*
Santa Ana, CA

Liberty Mutual*(Commercial Insurance Carrier)*
175 Berkeley St.
Boston, MA

Prudential Insurance Co. of America*(Group Insurer)*
Prudential Tower Suite 450, 800 Boylston St.
Boston, MA 02119

Boodell, Sears, Sugrue, Giambalvo & Crowley*(Legal Firm)*
69 W. Washington
Chicago, IL 60602

Bell, Boyd & Lloyd*(Legal Firm)*
Three First National Plaza
Chicago, IL 60602
Tel.: 312-372-1121

First National Bank of Sterling*(Major Banking Relationship)*
Sterling, IL

First Wisconsin Financial Services*(Major Banking Relationship)*
Milwaukee, WI
Tel.: 608-868-6000

Divisions:

Frantz Bearing Div. **(1)**
3201 W. LeFevre Rd.
Sterling, IL 61081
Tel.: 815-625-7063
Fax: 815-626-0747
Emp.: 100
Wheels & Bearings
S.I.C.: 3562; 2431
Larry L. Spaulding *(V.P.-Anti-Friction Group)*

Frantz Western Div. **(1)**
Roseburg, OR 97470
Tel.: 503-679-3111
Mfr. Doors
S.I.C.: 3442
E.E. Ufkin *(Gen. Mgr.)*
J.R. McCormick *(V.P.-Millwork Group)*

Sterling Steel Ball Div. **(1)**
3201 W. LeFevre Rd.
Sterling, IL 61081
Tel.: 815-625-2750
Fax: 815-626-0747
Emp.: 100
Mfg. Steel Balls
S.I.C.: 3562
Larry L. Spaulding *(Gen. Mgr.)*

Subsidiary:

Frantz Export Corp. **(1)**
301 W. 3rd St.
Sterling, IL 61081
Tel.: 815-625-0163
Hardware, Doors, Bearings & Balls
S.I.C.: 5072; 5085; 1751

FRASER PAPER, LTD.
9 W. Broad St.
Stamford, CT 06904
Mailing Address:
P.O. Box 10055
Stamford, CT 06904
Tel.: 203-359-2544
Approx.Sls.: $375,000,000
Emp.: 3,900
Export
Fine Paper Grades (Rolls)-Groundwood Publication Grades (Rolls)
S.I.C.: 2621
Niall O'Briain *(Pres.)*
A. Michael Moloney *(Sr. V.P.-Sls.)*
A.K. Bidwell *(Dir-Sls. Admin. & Adv. Mgr.)*

FRAZIER-WILLIAMS CHEVROLET GEO
1099 Lila Ave.
Milford, OH 45150
Tel.: 513-831-5555
Fax: 513-831-0836
Year Founded: 1958
Sales Range: $20-39 Million
Emp.: 25
Retail New & Used Automobiles; Car Rental & Leasing
S.I.C.: 5511; 7514; 7515
Robert Marlowe *(Pres.)*
Gary L. Grever *(V.P.)*
Jerry Quinlan *(V.P.)*
Tony Giordullo *(Sec. & Treas.)*

Outside Service Firm(s):

Bank One*(Major Banking Relationship)*
Cincinnati, OH

Fifth Third Bank*(Major Banking Relationship)*
Corporate Trust Services, 38 Fountain Square Plaza
Cincinnati, OH 45263

FREDERIC PRINTING COMPANY
14701 E. 38th Ave.
Aurora, CO 80011
Tel.: 303-371-7990 **CO**
Year Founded: 1878
Assets: $6,622,000
Liabilities: $2,607,000
Net Worth: $4,015,000
Sales Range: $10-19 Million
Emp.: 120
Import Export
Commercial Sheetfed Offset Printing; Literature Distribution Mailing
S.I.C.: 2752
Rand Frederic *(Pres. & Chief Exec. Officer)*
Barbara Benham *(Controller)*
Jon Smick *(Plant Mgr.)*
Bill Edmunds *(Fulfillment Mgr.)*
Principal(s):
Rand Frederic

No. of Mfg. Plants/Facilities: 1
No. of U.S. Offices: 2

Computer Systems/Hardware:
MAI Basic Four System 3000

Outside Service Firm(s):

Colorado National Bank*(Major Banking Relationship)*
17th & Champa
Denver, CO 80217

Arthur J. Gallagher & Co.*(Commercial Insurance Carrier)*
P.O. Box 24809,
Denver, CO 80224
Tel.: 303-773-9999

Blue Cross & Blue Shield Association*(Group Insurer)*
Denver, CO

Elrod, Katz, Preeo & Look*(Legal Firm)*
Denver, CO

Subsidiary:

Frederic Printing **(1)**
4500 S. Lakeshore Dr., Ste. #320
Tempe, AZ 85282
Tel.: 602-437-4544 (100%)
Emp.: 1
Literature Distribtuion Fulfillment Mailing
S.I.C.: 2752

FREDERICK TRADING COMPANY
7901 Trading Lane
Frederick, MD 21701
Mailing Address:
P.O. Box 400
Frederick, MD 21701
Tel.: 301-662-2161
Fax: 301-662-7243
Approx.Sls.: $65,000,000
Emp.: 390
Wholesale Hardware, Builders Hardware, Plumbing & Heating Supplies, Housewares, Paints, Electrical, Automotive & Farm Supplies
S.I.C.: 5072; 5013; 5015; 5039; 5063; 5065; 5074; 5075; 5191; 5198
Raymond L. Thomas *(Pres.)*
Richard C. Molesworth *(Exec. V.P.)*
Dennis M. Michael *(V.P.-Sls.)*
Nicolas Felsh *(V.P. & Treas.)*
Gary E. Duckworth *(Sec.)*
Henry E. Ponton *(Sls. Mgr.-Plumbing & Heating)*
Ben Lettie *(Sls. Mgr.-Mass Mdse. & Hardware)*
Lawrence Snyder *(Sls. Mgr.-Paint)*
Al Williams *(Sls. Mgr.-Promo.)*
Aubrey Hite *(Mgr.-Mktg.)*
Dana Rosendall *(Mgr.-Warehouse)*
David Hardy *(Asst. Mgr.-Sls.)*

Outside Service Firm(s):

McLean, Koehler, Sparks & Hammond*(Auditors)*
Baltimore, MD

Fredericktown Bank & Trust Co.*(Major Banking Relationship)*
Frederick, MD

FREDRICKSON MOTOR EXPRESS CORP.
3400 N. Graham St.
Charlotte, NC 28206
Mailing Address:
P.O. Box 5369
Charlotte, NC 28225
Tel.: 704-376-2471
Tel.: 800-426-9190 **NC**
Fax: 704-343-0435
Year Founded: 1919
Sales Range: $40-59 Million
Emp.: 1,094
Fiscal Year-end: 12/31/91
Regional Motor Freight Carrier of General Commodities
S.I.C.: 4212; 4213
John W. Fredrickson *(Pres.)*
Larry W. Hartsell *(Sr. V.P.)*
Chad Beatty *(V.P.-Oper.)*
John Luckadoo *(V.P.-Natl. Accts. & Traffic)*
Edward F. Wall *(V.P.-Sls.)*
Sidney L. Warren *(Treas.)*
Leslie F. Beatty *(Corp. Sec.)*
John Barrett *(Dir.-Maintenance)*
Patricia Dwiggins *(Dir.-Safety)*
Richard Henderson *(Dir.-Traffic)*
John Van Hoy *(Dir.-Data Processing)*

No. of Mfg. Plants/Facilities: 22

Computer Systems/Hardware:
UNISYS 2200

Outside Service Firm(s):

Cherry, Bekaert & Holland*(Auditors)*
Charlotte, NC

Weinstein & Sturges*(Legal Firm)*
1100 S. Tryon St.
Charlotte, NC 28203
Tel.: 704-372-4800

Rock Hill National Bank*(Major Banking Relationship)*
Fort Mill, SC

FREED & ASSOCIATES
3600 Clipper Mill Rd.
Baltimore, MD 21211
Tel.: 410-243-1421
Tel.: 800-366-1421
Fax: 410-235-2108
Year Founded: 1986
Approx.Billings: $10,700,000
Emp.: 18
Retail, New Products & Service Introductions, Collateral Production & Corporate Identity
Gloria Freed *(Pres.)*
David Rogers *(New Bus. Devel.)*

Computer Systems/Hardware:
MacIntosh-Aldus Page Maker, Adobe Illustrator, IBM Word Perfect, Lotus, Alpha Four, ADMAN, Quatro Pro

FREEDLAND INDUSTRIES CORPORATION
4200 Miller Rd.
Dearborn, MI 48126
Tel.: 313-584-3033
Fax: 313-584-7195
Emp.: 150
Automotive Stampings; Cold Finishing Of Steel Shapes
S.I.C.: 3465; 3316
Richard Freedland *(Pres.)*
Bruce Rosenthal *(Exec. V.P.)*
Benjamin Freedland *(V.P.)*
Ruth Freedland *(Treas.)*
Sukumar Joshipura *(Controller)*

Outside Service Firm(s):

Hertzberg & Noveck*(Legal Firm)*
Birmingham, MI

Comerica Bank*(Major Banking Relationship)*
211 W. Fort St.
Detroit, MI 48226
Tel.: 313-222-3300

FREEDMAN, GIBSON & WHITE INC.
814 Plum St.
Cincinnati, OH 45202
Tel.: 513-241-3900
Fax: 513-241-2220
Year Founded: 1959
Approx.Billings: $15,600,000
Emp.: 30
Leigh B. Miller *(Pres. & Chief Exec. Officer)*
Lauralee Sawyer *(Pub. Rels. Dir.)*
Marilyn Clements *(Controller)*

S. FREEDMAN & SONS, INC.
3322 Pennsy Dr.
Landover, MD 20785
Tel.: 301-322-5000 **MD**
Fax: 301-772-7563
Approx.Sls.: $43,000,000
Emp.: 150
Industrial & Personal Service Paper; Office Forms & Supplies; Janitors Supplies
S.I.C.: 5113; 5943; 5087
Mark Freedman *(Pres.)*
Barry Perlis *(Exec. V.P.)*
Robert Varnon *(V.P.)*
Louis Sacks *(Treas. & Sec.)*

Outside Service Firm(s):

Buchanan & Co.*(Auditors)*
Washington, DC

The Riggs National Bank*(Major Banking Relationship)*
1503 Pennsylvania Ave. N.W.
Washington, DC 20013
Tel.: 202-624-2000

FREEDOM FORGE CORPORATION
500 N. Walnut St.
Burnham, PA 17009
Tel.: 717-248-4911
Approx.Sls.: $165,000,000
Emp.: 1,600
A Holding Company
S.I.C.: 6719; 3724; 3541; 3728; 3592; 3312
Herbert C. Graves *(Pres.)*
James A. Spendiff *(Chief Fin. Officer & V.P.)*
David D. Barland *(Exec. V.P.)*
Jon C. Zimmerman *(V.P.-Engrd. Prods. Grp.)*

Outside Service Firm(s):

First Chicago Trust Co. of New York*(Major Banking Relationship)*
One First Natl. Plaza, Ste. 123
Chicago, IL 60670
Tel.: 312-407-4660

Divisions:

American Welding & Manufacturing Co. **(1)**
Dietz Rd.
Warren, OH 44483
Tel.: 216-393-2531
Approx.Sls.: $80,000,000
Emp.: 470
Mfg. of Rings, Flash Welded and Seamless
S.I.C.: 3724; 3423
D.G. Cook *(V.P. & Gen. Mgr.)*
Paul E. Emmerling *(V.P.-Sls. & Mktg.)*
C. Wheeler *(Asst. Treas., Asst. Sec. & Controller)*
Gary Coupland *(Dir.-Engrng.)*
D. Bevilagua *(Mgr.-Human Resources)*
D.A. Bonar *(Mgr.-Quality Control)*
H. Huffman *(Mgr.-Matls.)*
R.L. McCord *(Mgr.-Sls.)*
R.E. Nelson *(Pur. Agent)*
R.A. Humphries *(Buyer-Raw Matls.)*

Gentz Industries Inc. **(1)**
23600 Schoenherr
Warren, MI 48090
Tel.: 313-772-2500
Mfr. of Aircraft Engines & Parts
S.I.C.: 3724
Ed Kruske *(Pres.)*

Johnson Technology **(1)**
2034 Latimer Dr.
Muskegon, MI 49442
Tel.: 616-777-2685
Precision Machining, Laser Radial Grinding for the Aerospace Industry
S.I.C.: 3541; 3728
Ron Frederick *(Pres.)*

Standard Steel **(1)**
500 N. Walnut St.
Burnham, PA 17009
Tel.: 717-248-4911
Mfr. of Forgings, Steel & Iron; Ingots, Steel; Blooms, Steel; Axles, Rolled or Forged
S.I.C.: 3312
Herbert Graves *(Pres. & Chef Exec. Officer)*

FREEDOM NEWSPAPERS INC.
17666 Fitch
Irvine, CA 92714
Mailing Address:
P.O. Box 19549
Irvine, CA 92713
Tel.: 714-553-9292
Fax: 714-474-7675
Year Founded: 1927
Approx.Sls.: $375,000,000
Newspaper Publishing; Broadcasting
S.I.C.: 2711; 4832; 4833
James N. Rosse *(Pres.)*
David Kuykendall *(V.P. & Chief Fin. Officer)*
Penelope Troup *(V.P.-Risk Mngmt.)*
Richard K. Walker *(V.P.-Admin.)*

Computer Systems/Hardware:
IBM System 36

Outside Service Firm(s):

ALTA Health Strategies*(Group Insurer)*
Phoenix, AZ

Latham & Watkins*(Legal Firm)*
650 Town Center Dr., 20th Fl.
Costa Mesa, CA 92626-1918
Tel.: 714-540-1235

Bank of America, N.T. & S.A.*(Major Banking Relationship)*
P.O. Box 37002,
San Francisco, CA 94137

Division:

The Orange County Register **(1)**
625 N. Grand Ave.
Santa Ana, CA 92701
Tel.: 714-835-1234
Fax: 714-543-3904
Emp.: 2,600
Fiscal Year-end: 12/31/92
Daily Newspaper
S.I.C.: 2711
R. David Threshie, Jr. *(Publisher)*
Howard Grothe *(V.P.-Adv.)*
John Schueler *(V.P.-Circulation)*
Chris Anderson *(Editor)*
Richard Wallace *(Gen. Mgr.)*
Michael Weaver *(Comptroller)*
Rick Avery *(Dir.-Classified Adv.)*
Howard Griffin *(Dir.-Adv.)*
Ronna Kelly *(Dir.-Community Rels.)*
Jim Roe *(Dir.-Information Services)*
Larry Burkhart *(Mgr.-Retail Adv.)*
Mark Stange *(Mgr.-Classified Adv.)*

CARL M. FREEMAN ASSOCIATES, INC.
11325 Seven Locks Rd.
Potomac, MD 20854
Tel.: 301-983-0400 **MD**
Fax: 301-983-9289
Year Founded: 1958
Assets: $69,000,000
Earnings: $3,700,000
Liabilities: $44,000,000
Net Worth: $25,000,000
Approx.Sls.: $14,580,000
Emp.: 100
Fiscal Year-end: 12/31/91
Real Estate Development
S.I.C.: 6552
Carl M. Freeman *(Chm. Bd. & Chief Exec. Officer)*
Joshua M. Freeman *(Pres. & Chief Oper. Officer)*
Michael F. Lynn *(Exec. V.P.)*
William O. Eitze *(V.P.-Fin., Chief Fin. Officer, Controller & Treas.)*

Computer Systems/Hardware:
IBM PS2 & Prime

FREEMAN BLANSHEI PARTNERS
1714 Stockton St., 4th Fl.
San Francisco, CA 94133
Tel.: 415-434-2761
Fax: 415-434-1765
Year Founded: 1980
Approx.Billings: $10,000,000
Emp.: 7
Consumer & Packaged Goods Adv., New Products Consultation
Gary Freeman *(Pres.)*
Patricia Freeman *(Treas.)*
Lance Blanshei *(Gen. Mgr.)*
Lori Kleinen *(Mgr.-Admin.)*

FREEMAN COSMETIC CORP.
10474 Santa Monica Blvd., Ste. 300
Los Angeles, CA 90025
Mailing Address:
P.O. Box 4074
Beverly Hills, CA 90213
Tel.: 310-470-6840
Fax: 310-474-7149
Emp.: 90
Fiscal Year-end: 12/31/90
Export
Mfr. Of Hair & Skin Care Products
S.I.C.: 2844
Larry J. Freeman *(Pres. & Chief Exec. Officer)*
Patricia Limon *(Chief Fin. Officer)*
Gene Bartlett *(Sr. V.P.-Sls.)*
Chris Knerr *(V.P.-Mktg.)*
Mark S. Freeman *(Sec. & Dir.-Intl. Sls. & Mktg.)*
Adriene Cole *(Sr. Dir.-Mktg.)*
Jill Freeman *(Dir.-Mktg.)*
Nina Lenart *(Dir.-Pub. Rels.)*

FREEMAN DECORATING CO.
8801 Ambassador Row
Dallas, TX 75247-4622
Tel.: 214-638-6450 **IA**
Fax: 214-638-0905
Year Founded: 1927
Assets: $81,380,127
Liabilities: $30,417,502
Net Worth: $50,962,625
Approx.Sls.: $225,000,000
Emp.: 1,450
Fiscal Year-end: 4/30/91
Trade Show & Convention Service Contractor
S.I.C.: 7389
D.S. Freeman, Jr. *(Chm. Bd. & Chief Exec. Officer)*
Dale Van Ort *(Pres. & Chief Oper. Officer)*
Robert D. Lozier *(Exec. V.P.)*
James Howe *(Sr. V.P.)*
John O'Connell, Jr. *(Sr. V.P.)*
Larry Arnaudet *(V.P.-Sls.)*
John A. Boyd *(V.P.)*
Richard G. Huber *(V.P. & Controller)*
Donald D. Baughman *(V.P.)*
Barry G. Rappaport *(V.P.)*
George H. Reinschmidt *(V.P. & Treas.)*
Jack L. Scott *(V.P.-Data Mngmt. Services)*
Sandra L. Dowie *(Sec.)*
Ellen Bechert *(Dir.-Corp. Devel.)*
Jackie Bridges *(Dir.-Pur.)*
Richard O. Camp *(Dir.-Human Resources)*
Principal(s):
D.S. Freeman, Jr.
Sandra L. Dowie
The Freeman Decorating Co., ESOP

No. of Mfg. Plants/Facilities: 15
No. of U.S. Offices: 2

Outside Service Firm(s):

Ernst & Young*(Auditors)*
2121 San Jacinto, Ste. 500
Dallas, TX 75201
Tel.: 214-969-8000

Holmes, Murphy & Associates of Texas, Inc.*(Commercial Insurance Carrier)*
Dallas, TX

Passman, Jones, Andrews, Holly*(Legal Firm)*
Dallas, TX

NationsBank Texas*(Major Banking Relationship)*
P.O. Box 831000
Dallas, TX 75283-1000
Tel.: 214-508-0972

Subsidiary:

AVW Audiovisual, Inc. **(1)**
2241 Irving Blvd.
Dallas, TX 75207
Tel.: 214-634-9060
Fax: 214-905-9912
Rental & Sale of Audio-Visual Equipment;Production of Multimedia Presentations
S.I.C.: 7389
Marty Greenberg *(Pres.)*
Joe Dickinson *(V.P. & Controller)*

FREEMAN MANUFACTURING & SUPPLY COMPANY
1246 W. 70th St.
Cleveland, OH 44102
Tel.: 216-961-4200 **OH**
Fax: 216-961-9233
Year Founded: 1956
Approx.Sls.: $20,000,000
Emp.: 90
Export
Wholesale Distribution of Industrial Supplies; Polishing Preparations & Related Products; Industrial Machinery & Equipment
S.I.C.: 5085; 2842; 5084
Gerald W. Rusk *(Chm. Bd.)*
Lou Turco *(Pres.)*
Byron Krantz *(Sec.)*

FREEMAN SHOES COMPANY
1 Freeman Lane
Beloit, WI 53511
Tel.: 608-364-1200 **DE**
Fax: 608-364-1408
Year Founded: 1987
Assets: $24,000,000
Liabilities: $21,000,000
Net Worth: $3,000,000
Approx.Sls.: $43,000,000
Emp.: 450
Fiscal Year-end: 2/ 2/91
Import Export
Manufacture Men's Shoes
S.I.C.: 3143
Prasad Reddy *(Chm. Bd., Pres. & Chief Exec. Officer)*
Paul Haakenson *(V.P. & Chief Fin. Officer)*
Dan McGinley *(V.P.-Opers.)*
Chuck Reityell *(V.P.-Sls.)*
Carmen Harstad *(Dir.-Personnel)*

No. of Mfg. Plants/Facilities: 1
No. of U.S. Offices: 1
No. of Foreign Offices: 1

Computer Systems/Hardware:
IBM 38 Model 700

Outside Service Firm(s):

Ernst & Young*(Auditors)*
111 E. Kilbourn Ave., Ste. 900
Milwaukee, WI 53202
Tel.: 414-273-5900

Rollins Burdick Hunter*(Commercial Insurance Carrier)*
Milwaukee, WI

Rollins Burdick Hunter*(Investment Banker)*
Milwaukee, WI

M & I Marshall & Ilsley Bank*(Major Banking Relationship)*
Beloit, WI

H. FREEMAN & SON, INC.
3601 Island Rd.
Philadelphia, PA 19153
Mailing Address:
P.O. Box 16961
Philadelphia, PA 19142
Tel.: 215-365-7705
Year Founded: 1885
Approx.Sls.: $17,000,000
Emp.: 400
Mfr. Men's Tailored Clothing
S.I.C.: 2325
Benjamin H. Freeman II *(Pres.)*
Peter Marziano *(Sr. V.P.)*
Mayur Shah *(Treas.)*
Stanley Mastalski *(Mgr.-Customer Service)*

FREESON ADVERTISING AGENCY
(House Agency)
5980 Miami Lakes Dr.
Miami Lakes, FL 33014
Tel.: 305-362-2611
Year Founded: 1968
Approx.Sls.: $13,636,000
Personal Care Appliance Market
Belvin Friedson *(Chm. Bd.)*
David Friedson *(Pres. & Chief Exec. Officer)*
Barbara Friedson *(Exec. V.P.)*
Richard Bruno *(Corp. V.P., Mktg.)*
Burton A. Honig *(Chief Fin. Officer)*
Jerald I. Rosen *(Sec.)*
Mary Cwikla *(Mktg. Services Mgr.)*

FREEWAY CORPORATION
9301 Allen Dr.
Cleveland, OH 44125
Tel.: 216-524-9700
Fax: 216-524-7396
Year Founded: 1944
Approx.Sls.: $25,000,000
Emp.: 240
Fiscal Year-end: 12/31/91
Export
Metal Washers, Small Stampings & Unground Ball Bearing Assemblies
S.I.C.: 3452; 3469; 3562
Walter Sutowski *(Chm. Bd. & Chief Exec. Officer)*
Jerry Grams *(Pres. & Chief Oper. Officer)*
Pat Mowchan *(V.P.-Sls.)*
Gus Rinella *(Dir.-Pur.)*
Leo Mastalski *(V.P.-Mfg.)*

Computer Systems/Hardware:
DEC

Divisions:

Freeway Roanoke **(1)**
1401 Coulter Dr., N.W.
Roanoke, VA 24012
Tel.: 703-362-3006
Fax: 703-362-9022
Computer Systems/Hardware:
DEC
S.I.C.: 3452
Richard Ioffreda *(Gen. Mgr.)*

Freeway Rockford **(1)**
4701 Boeing Dr.
Rockford, IL 61109
Tel.: 815-397-6425
Fax: 815-397-8562
S.I.C.: 3452
Jack Sommers *(Gen. Mgr.)*

Subsidiaries:

Triangle Machine Product Co. **(1)**
6055 Hillcrest Dr.
Valley View, OH 44125
Tel.: 216-524-5872
Fax: 216-524-1052
S.I.C.: 3451
Lou Cado *(Gen. Mgr.)*

FREHNER CONSTRUCTION COMPANY, INC.
124 W. Brooks
North Las Vegas, NV 89030
Tel.: 702-649-6250 **NV**
Fax: 702-649-1167
Approx.Sls.: $48,000,000
Emp.: 100
General Contractors; Highway & Street Construction & Paving
S.I.C.: 1611
Garth E. Frehner *(Pres.)*
Don Grock *(V.P.)*
Robert C. Whitney *(Sec. & Treas.)*

Outside Service Firm(s):

McGladrey & Pullen*(Auditors)*
300 S. Fourth St., Ste. 900
Las Vegas, NV 89101
Tel.: 702-386-5800

Mike Leavitt*(Legal Firm)*
Las Vegas, NV

Valley Bank of Nevada*(Major Banking Relationship)*
300 S. Fourth St.
Las Vegas, NV 89101

THE FREMONT CO.
802 North Front
Fremont, OH 43420
Mailing Address:
P.O. Box 845,
Fremont, OH 43420
Tel.: 419-334-8995
Fax: 419-334-8120
Approx.Sls.: $31,000,000
Emp.: 200
Fiscal Year-end: 12/31/90
Frank's Quality Canned Foods: Kraut, Kraut Juice, Sweet Sour Red Cabbage, Dry Pack Beans, Tomatoes & Catsup
S.I.C.: 2033
Richard Smith *(Pres.)*
Frank Zigray *(Sec. & Treas.)*

Subsidiaries:

Fremont Canning Co. **(1)**
P. O. Box 27
Milford, IL 60953
Tel.: 815-889-4115

Fremont Co. **(1)**
P.O. Box 532
Bluffton, IN 46714
Tel.: 219-824-1422

Fremont Co. **(1)**
P. O. Box 242
Rockford, OH 45882
Tel.: 419-363-2924

FREMONT FOREST PRODUCTS
7200 Greenleaf Ave., Suite 310
Whittier, CA 90602
Tel.: 310-945-2911 **CA**
Fax: 310-696-8574
Year Founded: 1958
Approx.Sls.: $89,000,000
Emp.: 46
Wholesale Distribution of Rough, Dressed & Finished Lumber
S.I.C.: 5031
Peter V. Speek *(Pres. & Treas.)*
Blaine Smith *(V.P.)*
James R. Salo *(Controller)*
Edward Miller *(Sec.)*

Outside Service Firm(s):

Fedak & Zahn*(Auditors)*
Whittier, CA

First Interstate Bank*(Major Banking Relationship)*
Whittier, CA

I. H. FRENCH & CO. INC.
505 E. University
Champaign, IL 61820
Tel.: 217-351-1750 **DE**
Year Founded: 1895
Approx.Sls.: $225,000,000
Emp.: 7
Export
Own & Manage Apartments; Commodity Investment & Merchandising
S.I.C.: 6513; 6799
Eugene B. Tomlin *(Pres. & Chief Exec. Officer)*
Brant R. Moore *(Chief Fin. Officer, Treas. & Sec.)*
Principal(s):
Eugene B. Tomlin

No. of U.S. Offices: 2

Outside Service Firm(s):

Clifton Gunderson*(Auditors)*
Champaign, IL

Prudential Insurance Co. of America*(Group Insurer)*
751 Broad St.
Newark, NJ 07102-3777
Tel.: 201-802-6000

American National Bank*(Major Banking Relationship)*
Champaign, IL

American United Life*(Pension Manager)*
One American Square
Indianapolis, IN 46204
Tel.: 317-263-1877

Frenchy's Creole Fried Chicken, Inc.
(See A. Grace Development)

JIM FRESARD PONTIAC BUICK, INC.
400 N. Main St.
Royal Oak, MI 48067
Tel.: 313-547-6100
Fax: 313-547-2491
Year Founded: 1973
Approx.Sls.: $65,000,000
Emp.: 90
Fiscal Year-end: 12/31/91
Retail New & Used Automobiles
S.I.C.: 5511
F. James Fresard *(Pres.)*
Douglas J. Fresard *(V.P.)*
Judith Fresard *(V.P.)*
Cindy Gallagher *(Sec. & Treas.)*

FRESH MARK, INC.
1888 Southway S.E.
Massillon, OH 44646
Mailing Address:
P.O. Box 571,
Massillon, OH 44648
Tel.: 216-832-7491
Tel.: 800-860-6779 **OH**
Fax: 216-833-1329
Sales Range: $100-499 Million
Emp.: 1,500
Full Line Meat Packers
S.I.C.: 2011
Neil Genshaft *(Chm. Bd. & Chief Exec. Officer)*
Harry Valentino *(Pres. & Chief Oper. Officer)*
Vicky Kendrick *(Sec.. V.P.)*

No. of Mfg. Plants/Facilities: 4

Computer Systems/Hardware:
Honeywell

Outside Service Firm(s):

Ernst & Young*(Auditors)*
1300 Huntington Bldg.
Cleveland, OH 44115
Tel.: 216-861-5000
Fax: 303-291-6234

Krugliak, Wilkins, Griffith, Dougherty*(Legal Firm)*
Canton, OH

Central National Bank*(Major Banking Relationship)*
Cleveland, OH

The Central Trust Company, N.A.*(Major Banking Relationship)*
Canton, OH

Fifth Third Bank*(Major Banking Relationship)*
Corporate Trust Services, 38 Fountain Square Plaza
Cincinnati, OH 45263

The Central Trust Company, N.A.*(Pension Manager)*
Canton, OH

Fifth Third Bank*(Pension Manager)*
Corporate Trust Services, 38 Fountain Square Plaza
Cincinnati, OH 45263

Metropolitan Life Insurance Co.*(Pension Manager)*
One Madison Ave.
New York, NY 10010-3690
Tel.: 215-578-9292

Subsidiaries:

Leann, Inc. **(1)**
Southway S.E.
Massillon, OH 44646
Tel.: 216-832-7491

Sugardale Foods Inc. **(1)**
1600 Harmont Ave., N.E.
Canton, OH 44705
Tel.: 216-455-5253
Harry Valentino *(Chief Oper. Officer)*

Superior's Brand Meats **(1)**
1888 Southway, S.E.
Massillon, OH 44646
Tel.: 216-832-7491
Meat Prods.
S.I.C.: 2013
Harry Valentino *(Chief Oper. Officer)*

FREUDENBERG-NOK (MI)
47690 E. Anchor Ct.
Plymouth, MI 48170
Tel.: 313-451-0020
Fax: 313-451-0125
Year Founded: 1989
Approx.Sls.: $360,000,000
Emp.: 4,000
Fiscal Year-end: 12/31/90
Mfg. Oil Seals & Custom Molded Rubber Parts
S.I.C.: 3053
Joseph C. Day *(Chief Exec. Officer)*
Ed Barry *(Sr. V.P.-Sls.)*
Phil Storm *(Sr. V.P.-After Market Div.)*
Tom Takeda *(Sr. V.P.-Seals Div.)*
Syd Madeley *(Sr. V.P. & Gen. Mgr.-Vibration Control Div.)*
William Tobin *(V.P.-Corp. Devel. & Admin.)*
Bob Hangi *(V.P. & Gen. Mgr.-Plastic Products Div.)*
Ken Anderson *(Chief Fin. Officer)*
Joel Darcy *(Chief Info. Officer)*
Dan Klaiber *(Dir.-Personnel)*
Sharon Wenzl *(Mgr.-Adv. & Sls. Promo.)*

Divisions:

Automotive Aftermarket Division **(1)**
11617 State Rte. 13
Milan, OH 44846
Transmission Repair Kits, Power Stearing, CV Kits, Brake Kits, Replacement Heavy Duty Oil Bath Seals & Fluid Power Sealing Systems
S.I.C.: 7537

Plastic Products Division **(1)**
Grenier Industrial Park
Manchester, NH 03103
Reinforced Gaskets for Automotive Applications, Polyurethane Hydraulic Seals, Microcellular Urethane Jounce Jumpers, Composite Products, Lost Core Molded Intake Manifolds, Solid Injection Polyurethane Products, Microcelluar Foam Products, Suspension Parts for Automotive Applications, Piston, Speedometer Sleeves for Transmissions, Fuel Bodies, Spacers for Gaskets & Waterpumps
S.I.C.: 3053; 3592; 3561
Richard Hidy *(V.P.)*

Plastic Products Division **(1)**
100 W. Country Rd., P.O. Box 4452
Scottsburg, IN 47170-0452
Reinforced Gaskets for Automotive Applications; Polyurethane Hydraulic Seals; Microcellular Urethane Jounce Bumpers; Composite Products; Lost Core Molded Intake Manifolds; Solid Injection Polyurethane Products; Microcellular Foam

Products; Suspension Parts for Automotive Application; Pistons; Speedometer Sleeves for Transmissions; Fuel Bodies; Spacers for Gaskets & Waterpumps
S.I.C.: 3053; 3592; 3561
Leroy Whitcher *(Plant Mgr.)*

Rubber Products Division **(1)**
P.O. Box 38, State Rd. 44 W.
Shelbyville, IN 46176-0038
Rocker Cover, Electrical Sealing & Extrusion Gaskets; Electrical Connectors; Brake Parts
S.I.C.: 3053; 3678; 3714

Rubber Products Division **(1)**
P.O. Box 245, U.S. 52 W.
Morristown, IN 46161-0245
Rocker Cover, Electrical Sealing & Extrusion Gaskets; Electrical Connectors; Brake Parts
S.I.C.: 3053; 3678; 3714

Rubber Products Division **(1)**
P.O. Box 4452, Country Rd. 100 W.
Scottsburg, IN 47170-0452
Rocker Cover, Electrical Sealing & Extrusion Gaskets; Electrical Connectors; Brake Parts
S.I.C.: 3053; 3678; 3714

Seals Division **(1)**
Ragged Mountain Hwy., P.O. Box B
Bristol, NH 03222-0501
Tel.: 603-968-7876
Appliance Face, Radial Shaft, Engine Valve Stem, Strut, Oil & Water Pump Seals
S.I.C.: 3053

Seals Division **(1)**
P.O. Box 1879
Cleveland, GA 30528
Tel.: 603-286-8986
Appliance Face, Radial Shaft, Engine Valve Stem, Strut, Oil & Water Pump Seals
S.I.C.: 3053

Seals Division **(1)**
1618 Lukken Industrial Dr. W.
La Grange, GA 30240
Appliance Face, Radial Shaft, Engine Valve, Strut, Oil & Water Pump Seals
S.I.C.: 3053

Tool Shop **(1)**
P.O. Box 756, Main St.
Ashland, NH 03217

Vibration Control Division **(1)**
1497 Gerber St.
Ligonien, IN 46767
Drive Line Dampers, Half Shaft Dampers, Hydraulic Engine Mounts, Water Pump Dampers & Torsional Vibration Dampers
S.I.C.: 3829

Woodland Molded Plastics **(1)**
3110 SA. Twenty-Sixth Ave.
Broadview, IL 60153-4575
Reinforced Gaskets for Automotive Applications; Polyurethane Hydraulic Seals; Microcellar Urethane Jounce Bumpers; Composite Products; Lost Core Molded Intake Manifolds; Solid Injection Polyurethane Products; Microcellar Foam Products; Suspension Parts for Automotive Applications; Pistons; Speedometer Sleeves for Transmissions; Fuel Bodies; Spacers for Gaskets & Waterpumps
S.I.C.: 3053; 3592; 3561
Ty Huffman *(Plant Mgr.)*

Non-U.S. Division:

Rubber Products Division **(1)**
65 Spruce St. Box 100,
Tillsonburg, ON N4G 4H3, Canada
Rocker Cover, Electrical Sealing & Extrusion Gaskets; Electrical Connectors; Brake Parts
S.I.C.: 3053; 3678; 3714

JOHN S. FREY ENTERPRISES
1900 E. 64th St.
Los Angeles, CA 90001
Tel.: 213-583-4061 **CA**
Fax: 213-583-5571
Year Founded: 1950
Assets: $49,863,914
Liabilities: $14,144,746
Net Worth: $35,719,168
Approx.Sls.: $75,300,000
Emp.: 600
Fiscal Year-end: 3/31/92
Import Export
Fabrication & Erection of Steel Buildings; Canopies, Walk-In & Overhead Doors; School Lockers
S.I.C.: 3442
John S. Frey *(Chm. Bd. & Pres.)*
Robert E. Hansen *(V.P. & Dir.-Engrng.)*
Barbara A. Cruncleton *(Treas., Sec. & Dir.)*
Karl A. Schmidt *(Gen. Counsel)*
Geraldine R. Frey *(Dir.-Pub. Rels.)*
John Frey, Jr. *(Dir.)*

No. of Mfg. Plants/Facilities: 6
No. of U.S. Offices: 6

Computer Systems/Hardware:
AT&T Keymark Programs

Outside Service Firm(s):

Levine, Cooper, Spiegel & Co.*(Auditors)*
Los Angeles, CA

Pillsbury, Madison & Sutro*(Legal Firm)*
Los Angeles, CA

Bank of America NT&SA*(Major Banking Relationship)*
555 So. Flower St., 5th Fl.
Los Angeles, CA 90071
Tel.: 213-228-3526
Fax: 213-228-4062

Subsidiaries:

Finishline Industries Inc. of Arizona **(1)**
2308 S. 11th Ave.
Phoenix, AZ 85997
Tel.: 602-254-6144
Fax: 602-254-2231
Emp.: 8
Mfg. School Lockers & Misc. Sheet Metal Items
S.I.C.: 3442
Tillman Turley *(Gen. Mgr.)*

Finishline Industries Inc. of Georgia **(1)**
1275 S. Main St.
Conyers, GA 30207
Tel.: 404-483-7293
Fax: 404-483-3961
Emp.: 75
Mfg. Overhead & Walk-In Doors
S.I.C.: 3442
Marshall Granade *(Gen. Mgr.)*
Lois Brewer *(Pur. Mgr.)*

Madison, Inc. **(1)**
8500 New Sapulpa Rd.
Tulsa, OK 74131
Tel.: 918-224-6990
Fax: 918-224-7835
Emp.: 125
Fab/Erect Steel Bldgs., Canopies & Doors
S.I.C.: 3442
Bill Poole *(Gen. Mgr.)*
John Fitzwilson *(Sls. Mgr.)*
Steve Adams *(Mktg. Mgr.)*
Danny Kirk *(Pur. Mgr.)*

Madison Industries **(1)**
1900 E. 64th St.
Los Angeles, CA 90001
Tel.: 213-583-4061
Fax: 213-582-1015
Emp.: 130
Fab/Erect Steel Bldgs., Canopies & Doors
S.I.C.: 3442
John Frey *(Gen. Mgr.)*
Dan Ensman *(Sls. Mgr.)*
Tom Sentell *(Mktg. Mgr.)*
Crystal Thomas *(Pur. Mgr.)*

Madison Industries Inc. of Arizona **(1)**
2100 S. 11th Ave.
Phoenix, AZ 85007
Tel.: 602-252-3083
Fax: 602-254-7234
Emp.: 110
Fab/Erect Steel Bldgs., Canopies & Doors
S.I.C.: 3442
John Sentell *(Gen. Mgr.)*
Mike Sentell *(Mgr.-Sls.)*
Sam Long *(Mgr.-Pur.)*

Madison Industries Inc. of Georgia **(1)**
1035 S. Access Rd., S.W.
Conyers, GA 30207
Tel.: 404-483-4401
Fax: 404-785-6622
Emp.: 225
Fab/Erect Steel Bldgs., Canopies & Doors
S.I.C.: 3442
Mike Davis *(Gen. Mgr.)*
Chris Brown *(Sls. Mgr.)*
Joe Van Dover *(Mktg. Mgr.)*
Gene Whitley *(Pur. Mgr.)*

FRICKS & ASSOCIATES/ ADVERTISING INC.
Bldg. 500, 1100 Abernathy Rd. N.E., Ste. 1725
Atlanta, GA 30328
Tel.: 404-396-6206
Fax: 404-396-0207
Year Founded: 1987
Approx.Billings: $13,200,000
Emp.: 15
John Fricks *(Pres.)*

FRIEDMAN
BENJAMIN
ADVERTISING

FRIEDMAN BENJAMIN INC. ADV.
22 W. 23rd St.
New York, NY 10010
Tel.: 212-633-2600
Fax: 212-633-6011
Year Founded: 1985
Approx.Billings: $15,000,000
Emp.: 12
New Product Launches & Repositioning Using Media
Elizabeth A. Mason *(Pres.)*
Stephen Z. Friedman *(Chief Exec. Officer)*

Computer Systems/Hardware:
Macintosh

FRIEDMAN, EISENSTEIN, RAEMER & SCHWARTZ
401 N. Michigan Ave., Ste. 2600
Chicago, IL 60611
Tel.: 312-644-6000
Telex: 263111 SERV UR
Fax: 312-644-4423
Year Founded: 1972
Sales Range: $20-39 Million
Emp.: 240
Certified Public Accountants; Business & Personal Consultants
S.I.C.: 8721; 8748
Irwin Friedman *(Chm. Bd.)*
Irwin Steinberg *(Mng. Partner)*
Kevin Simpson *(Controller)*
Rick Jakubas *(Dir.-Mngmt. Information Systems)*
Anne McNicholl *(Dir.-Admin. Services)*
Lori Pedelty *(Dir.-Quality Devel.)*
Richard Wilkes *(Dir.-Opers.)*

No. of U.S. Offices: 2

Computer Systems/Hardware:
Hewlett Packard 3000; Compaq Microcomputer

Division:

Practice Development Institute **(1)**
401 N. Michigan Ave., #2600
Chicago, IL 60601
Tel.: 312-644-6000
Marketing Consultants
S.I.C.: 8742
Allan D. Koltin *(Pres.)*

FRIENDLY CHEVROLET CO. INC.
5601 Lemmon Ave.
Dallas, TX 75209
Mailing Address:
P.O. Box 7066,
Dallas, TX 75209
Tel.: 214-526-8811 **TX**
Year Founded: 1957
Assets: $58,116,000
Net Worth: $58,116,000
Approx.Sls.: $258,000,000
Emp.: 241
Retail New & Used Automobiles & Trucks; Commercial Building Operations; Automobile Supplies & Repair
S.I.C.: 5511; 7538; 6512; 5531
Roy A. Eddins *(Chm. Bd.)*
Mark A. Eddins *(Pres. & Chief Exec. Officer)*
Mitchell Vuckovich *(Chief Fin. Officer)*

Outside Service Firm(s):

KPMG Peat Marwick*(Auditors)*
1601 Elm St., Ste. 1600
Dallas, TX 75201
Tel.: 214-754-2000
Fax: 214-754-2297

SANUS*(Group Insurer)*
Dallas, TX

North Park National Bank*(Major Banking Relationship)*
Dallas, TX

FRIENDLY HOLIDAYS INC.
1983 Marcus Ave.
Lake Success, NY 11042
Tel.: 516-358-1320
Approx.Sls.: $30,000,000
Emp.: 75
Fiscal Year-end: 12/31/90
Travel (Tour Operator)
S.I.C.: 4724
Dorothy Mazzotta *(Pres.)*
Carlos Ibarguen *(V.P.)*
Patricia Stango *(Gen. Mgr.)*

FRIERSON MEE & HERMAN
215 Park Ave. South
New York, NY 10003
Tel.: 212-353-3500
Fax: 212-353-3694
Year Founded: 1978
Approx.Billings: $16,000,000
Emp.: 16
Financial Services, Publishing, Toys, Retail & Telecommunications

Computer Systems/Hardware:
Macintosh, Linotronic

FRIGID FOOD PRODUCTS, INC.
1599 E. Warren Ave.
Detroit, MI 48207
Tel.: 313-831-7900
Emp.: 152
Mfr. Frozen Foods, Fruits, Fruit Juices & Purees; Canned Fruits
S.I.C.: 2037
Jeffrey R. Roth *(Chief Fin. Officer)*
Karen Saint Jon *(Mgr.-Sls.)*

Outside Service Firm(s):

N.B.D. Bank, N.A.*(Major Banking Relationship)*
611 Woodward Ave.
Detroit, MI 48226
Tel.: 313-225-1122
Fax: 313-225-3420

BOB FRINK CHEVROLET G.E.O. MANAGEMENT
(Formerly Bob Frink Management)
4811 Madison Ave.
Sacramento, CA 95841
Mailing Address:
P.O. Box 41469,
Sacramento, CA 95841
Tel.: 916-331-6777
Fax: 916-332-9719
Approx.Sls.: $310,000,000
Emp.: 730
Owns & Operates Automobile Dealerships
S.I.C.: 5511
John McMichael *(Pres.)*

Principal(s):
John McMichael

Outside Service Firm(s):

Bank of America NT&SA*(Major Banking Relationship)*
Sacramento, CA

FRIONA INDUSTRIES, L.P.
900 Amarillo Bank Bldg., 410 S. Taylor St., Ste. 900
Amarillo, TX 79101
Mailing Address:
P.O. Box 15568,
Amarillo, TX 79105-5568
Tel.: 806-374-1811 **TX**
Fax: 806-374-1324
Year Founded: 1972
Approx.Sls.: $200,000,000
Emp.: 300
Commercial Cattle Feed; Marketing Animal Health Supplies; Grain; Cattle Feedlots
S.I.C.: 0211; 4221; 5191; 5153
James Herring *(Pres. & Chief Exec. Officer)*
Dal C. Reid *(V.P. & Chief Fin. Officer)*
Jim Small *(Treas.)*
Sam Curtsinger *(Mgr.-Data Processing)*

Computer Systems/Hardware:
Hewlett-Packard Series 58

Outside Service Firm(s):

KPMG Peat Marwick*(Auditors)*
600 First National Pl. II
Amarillo, TX 79101
Tel.: 806-373-6661

Insurance Management Assoc.*(Commercial Insurance Carrier)*
Wichita, KS

Provident Life & Accident Insurance Co.*(Group Insurer)*
Houston, TX

Hughes & Luce*(Legal Firm)*
Bank One Center, 1717 Main St.
Dallas, TX 75202
Tel.: 214-651-0477

Friona State Bank*(Major Banking Relationship)*
Friona, TX

Divisions:

Friona Feed Yard Div. **(1)**
P.O. Box 369,
Friona, TX 79035
Tel.: 806-265-3574
S.I.C.: 0211
David George *(Mgr.)*

Hi-Pro Animal Health Div. **(1)**
P.O. Box 519
Friona, TX 79035
Tel.: 806-247-2791
Mktg. of Animal Feed
S.I.C.: 5191
William Stovel *(Mgr.)*

Hi-Pro Feed Div. **(1)**
P.O. Box 519
Friona, TX 79035
Tel.: 806-247-2791
Mktg. of Animal Feed
S.I.C.: 5191
Jack Hamil *(Mgr.)*

Randall County Feed Yard **(1)**
Rte. 4, Box 99
Amarillo, TX 79119
Tel.: 806-499-3701
Kevin Thompson *(Gen. Mgr.)*

Spring Lake Feed Yard **(1)**
P.O. Box 718,
Earth, TX 78031
Tel.: 806-965-2163
Harold Greenhouse *(Gen. Mgr.)*

Swisher Country Cattle Co. **(1)**
P.O. Box 129,
Tulia, TX 79088
Tel.: 806-627-4231
Feed Yard
S.I.C.: 0211
John Bliss *(Gen. Mgr.)*

Subsidiary:

Friona Agriculture Credit Corp. **(1)**
P.O. Box 15568
Amarillo, TX 79105
Tel.: 806-374-1811 (100%)
S.I.C.: 6159
James Herring *(Actg. Pres.)*

FRITZ CHEMICAL COMPANY
500 Sam Houston Rd.
Mesquite, TX 75149
Mailing Address:
P.O. Drawer 17040
Dallas, TX 75217
Tel.: 214-285-5471
Tel.: 800-955-1323 **TX**
Fax: 214-270-0179
Year Founded: 1956
Assets: $17,023,142
Liabilities: $11,466,368
Net Worth: $5,556,774
Approx.Sls.: $51,297,000
Emp.: 280
Fiscal Year-end: 12/31/90
Import Export
Mfr. Industrial Inorganic Materials; Terrazzo Floor Tile, Concrete Admixtures, Oilfield Additives, Aquaculture Products, Pet Products; Wholesale Nondurable Goods
S.I.C.: 2819; 3272; 5051
Corporate Giving Program: Employee *Profit Sharing Plan*
C. Frederick Weisend *(Chm. Bd., Pres. & Chief Exec. Officer)*
Randy R. Klemmer *(Exec. V.P.-Opers. & Sls.)*
Garland A. Davis *(Sr. V.P.)*
Jack Edwards *(V.P.-Quality Control, Research & Devel.)*
Anita Walker *(Treas.& Sec.)*
Bud Kuykendal *(Chief Engineer)*
Kathryn Trull *(Dir.-Personnel)*
Bob Williams *(Dir.-Safety)*
Gabriel Ojeda *(Gen. Mgr.)*
Cecil Campbell *(Mgr.-Natl. Sls.)*
Charles E.E. Lowe *(Mgr.-Distr.)*
Judy Mulheirn *(Mgr.-Creative Services)*
Monica Robinson *(Mgr.-Employee Benefits)*
Jack Westerman *(Mgr.-Data Processing)*
Li-Hsiang Yu *(Mgr.-Far East. Opers.)*
Norman Haas *(Buyer)*
Kerry Weisend *(Intl. Buyer)*
Benita McCann *(Librarian)*

Principal(s):
C. Frederick Weisend

No. of Mfg. Plants/Facilities: 4
No. of U.S. Offices: 9
No. of Foreign Offices: 1

Computer Systems/Hardware:
IBM System 38, AS/400

Outside Service Firm(s):

Arthur Andersen & Co.*(Auditors)*
901 Main St., Ste. 5600
Dallas, TX 75202
Tel.: 214-741-8300

Alexander & Alexander*(Commercial Insurance Carrier)*
4099 McEwen, Ste. 700
Dallas, TX 75244
Tel.: 817-448-0700

Travelers Insurance Co.*(Group Insurer)*
Dallas, TX

Texas Commerce Bank*(Investment Banker)*
2200 Ross Ave.
Dallas, TX 75266

Johnson & Gibbs, P.C.*(Legal Firm)*
100 Founders Square, 900 Jackson St.
Dallas, TX 75202-4499
Tel.: 214-977-9000

Texas Commerce Bank*(Major Banking Relationship)*
2200 Ross Ave.
Dallas, TX 75266

Texas Commerce Bank*(Pension Manager)*
2200 Ross Ave.
Dallas, TX 75266

FRITZ CO. INC.
1912 Hastings Ave.
Newport, MN 55055
Tel.: 612-459-9751 **MN**
Fax: 612-459-7381
Approx.Sls.: $75,000,000
Emp.: 130
Fiscal Year-end: 12/31/91
Wholesale Confectionery & Tobacco Products
S.I.C.: 5145; 5194
James P. Fritz *(Chm. Bd., Pres. & Chief Exec. Officer)*
Chris Johnson *(Sec. & Treas.)*

Outside Service Firm(s):

Lethert, Skwira, Schultz & Co.*(Auditors)*
St. Paul, MN

Signal Hills State Bank*(Major Banking Relationship)*
West St. Paul, MN

FRITZ COMPANIES, INC.
706 Mission St.
San Francisco, CA 94103
Tel.: 415-904-8200
Fax: 415-904-8661
Year Founded: 1933
Emp.: 1,800
Customhouse Brokers
S.I.C.: 4731
Lynn C. Fritz *(Chm. Bd., Pres. & Chief Exec. Officer)*
Ron Marcillac *(Exec. Dir.)*
Dennis Pelino *(Exec. Dir.)*
Jed Williams *(Dir.-Mngmt. Information Systems)*

Outside Service Firm(s):

Security Pacific National Bank*(Major Banking Relationship)*
50 California, 13th Fl.
San Francisco, CA 94111

PHILIP FRITZE & SONS, INC.
10 School St.
Whippany, NJ 07981
Tel.: 201-887-0685
Fax: 201-887-6019
Sales Range: $20-39 Million
Emp.: 170
Fiscal Year-end: 9/30/92
Mfr. of Heating & Air Conditioning Equipment
S.I.C.: 3585
William Fritze *(Pres.)*
Kenneth Fritze *(V.P. & Sec.)*
Susan Fritze *(Mgr.-Office)*

Outside Service Firm(s):

Ferro, Berdon & Co.*(Auditors)*
New York, NY

Midlantic National Bank*(Major Banking Relationship)*
Metro Park Plaza,
Edison, NJ 08818
Tel.: 908-321-8000

FROG SWITCH & MANUFACTURING COMPANY
600 East High St.
Carlisle, PA 17013
Mailing Address:
P.O. Box 70,
Carlisle, PA 17013
Tel.: 717-243-2454 **PA**
Fax: 717-243-1385
Sales Range: $20-39 Million
Emp.: 260
Fiscal Year-end: 12/31/91
Indian Brand Manganese Steel Castings For Jaw & Gyratory Crushers, Hammer Mills & Impactors; High Chrome Iron Castings & For Ball & Rod Mills, Pulvomatic Impact Crusher
S.I.C.: 3312; 3325; 3462; 3531
Robert Lee Jacobs *(Chm. Bd.)*
Robert J. Sleeman *(Pres.)*
John Tasker *(V.P.-Mktg. & Sls.)*
Jerome E. Zary *(V.P., Sec., Chief Fin. Officer & Treas.)*

Outside Service Firm(s):

Boyer & Ritter*(Auditors)*
Carlisle, PA

Commonwealth National Bank*(Major Banking Relationship)*
Carlisle, PA

Frontier Enterprises
(See Hasslocher Enterprises, Inc. Listing)

FRONTIER FOUNDRIES, INC.
221 Perry St.
Titusville, PA 16354-0627
Tel.: 814-827-2244
Fax: 716-282-2377
Approx.Sls.: $15,000,000
Emp.: 160
Non-Ferrous & Aluminum Alloy Castings & CNC Machining
S.I.C.: 3365
William E. Gephardt, Jr. *(Pres. & Chief Exec. Officer)*
Timothy M. Booth *(V.P.-Sls.)*

Divisions:

Frontier Foundries, Inc. **(1)**
221 S. Perry St.
Titusville, PA 16354
Tel.: 814-827-1800
Aluminum Permanent Mold & Shell Precision Castings
S.I.C.: 3365
Cam Austin *(V.P.-Admin.)*

Supreme Machine Div. **(1)**
101-5 Industrial Pkwy.
Gardenville, NY 10923
Tel.: 716-668-5200
S.I.C.: 3365
Roger Metz *(V.P. & Gen. Mgr.)*

FRONTIER LUMBER COMPANY, INC.
1941 Elmwood Ave.
Buffalo, NY 14207
Tel.: 716-873-8500

Fax: 716-873-8509
Year Founded: 1940
Approx.Sls.: $10,000,000
Emp.: 75
Production & Retail Sale of Lumber; Architectural Millwork; Lumber Treatment
S.I.C.: 2491; 5031
Edward J. McDermid, Sr. *(Pres.)*
Edward G. Hoffman *(V.P.)*
Daniel V. Brennan *(Sec. & Controller)*
Edward J. McDermid, Jr. *(Treas.)*

Outside Service Firm(s):

Schunk & Wilson*(Auditors)*
Buffalo, NY

Watson, McGarvey, Bennett, Colligan & Johnson*(Legal Firm)*
Buffalo, NY

Key Bank*(Major Banking Relationship)*
Buffalo, NY

Subsidiary:

Wood Treaters of Buffalo Co., Inc. **(1)**
100 Botsford Place
Buffalo, NY 14216
Tel.: 716-874-6181
S.I.C.: 5031

FROST COMPANY
224 Andover St.
Andover, MA 01810
Mailing Address:
P.O. Box 608
Woburn, MA 01801
Tel.: 508-470-3772
Fax: 508-474-0451
Approx.Sls.: $15,000,000
Emp.: 38
Distributor Snapper Lawn Mowers & Riding Mowers, Giant Vac Vacuums & Leaf Blowers
S.I.C.: 5083
Stephen B. Frost *(Pres.)*
Thomas C. Frost *(V.P.-Mktg.)*
Robert Keon *(Oper. Mgr.)*

FROST INC.
2020 Bristol NW
Grand Rapids, MI 49504
Tel.: 616-453-7781 **MI**
Fax: 616-453-2161
Year Founded: 1913
Sales Range: $10-19 Million
Emp.: 120
Mfr. of Overhead Conveyor Components
S.I.C.: 3535
Chad Frost *(Pres.)*
Fred Sytsma *(Exec. V.P.-OEM Sls.)*
Terry McGovern *(Gen. Mgr.)*

Principal(s):
Chad Frost
Fred Sytsma

No. of Mfg. Plants/Facilities: 1

Computer Systems/Hardware:
IBM System 36

Outside Service Firm(s):

Crowe, Chizek & Co.*(Auditors)*
Grand Rapids, MI

Manufacturers National Bank N.A.*(Major Banking Relationship)*
38th Fl., 100 Renaissance Center
Detroit, MI 48243
Tel.: 313-222-4227

FRU-CON CONSTRUCTION CORPORATION
15933 Clayton Rd.
Ballwin, MO 63011
Mailing Address:
P.O. Box 100
Ballwin, MO 63022-0100
Tel.: 314-391-6700
Tel.: 800-937-8266 **DE**
Telex: 193168
Fax: 314-391-4513
Year Founded: 1872
Approx.Sls.: $587,000,000
Emp.: 2,450
Fiscal Year-end: 12/31/91

Export
Engineering & Architectural Consultants; Building Contractors; Heavy Construction Contractors
S.I.C.: 6719; 8711; 1542; 1622; 1623; 1629; 1541; 8712
Corporate Giving Program: Fru-Con Supports Two Programs: Scholarship Programs to both the University of Missouri in St. Louis and Purdue University. The Second Program is Financial Consideration to Organizations that Submit a Written Request to the Trustees of the Fru-Con Foundation. The Foundation Restricts Financial Consideration to Not-For-Profit Activities
Herbert Bodner *(Pres. & Chief Exec. Officer)*
Juerger Kaiser *(Exec. V.P. & Chief Fin. Officer)*
Stephen L. Drawe *(Exec. V.P.)*
Bruce A. Frost *(Sr. V.P.-Indus.)*
Juergen Kochannek *(Sr. V.P. & Treas.)*
Leonard R. Ruzicka *(Sr. V.P., Sec. & Gen. Counsel)*
Arnie Zehner *(Sr. V.P.-Energy)*
William S. Brooks *(V.P.-Process)*
James Coleman, Jr. *(V.P.-Human Resources)*
Bradley Lambert *(V.P.-Energy)*
Martin W. Schaper *(V.P. & Controller)*
F.A. Tucker *(V.P.-Bus. Devel.)*
Klaus Wegmann *(V.P.-Estimating)*
Granville White *(V.P.-Intl.)*
Thomas J. Franz *(Dir.-Pur.)*
Danae A. Goldsmith *(Dir.-Corp. Communications)*
Barton E. Jones *(Dir.-Data Processing)*

No. of U.S. Offices: 24

Computer Systems/Hardware:
Prime 9955-750

Outside Service Firm(s):

Coopers & Lybrand*(Auditors)*
One Metropolitan Square
St. Louis, MO 63102
Tel.: 314-436-3200

CIGNA Life Insurance Co.*(Group Insurer)*
St. Louis, MO

Wickwire, Gavin & Gibbs*(Legal Firm)*
8100 Boone Blvd., 6th & 7th Flrs.
Vienna, VA 22182-2642

Bank of America NT&SA*(Major Banking Relationship)*
One Allen Center, Ste. 3100
Houston, TX 77002
Tel.: 713-651-4872
Fax: 713-651-4841

Subsidiary:

Fru-Con Engineering Inc. **(1)**
15933 Clayton Rd.
Ballwin, MO 63011
Tel.: 314-391-6700
Fax: 314-391-4513
Emp.: 200
Engineering & Architectural Services
S.I.C.: 8712
Daniel M. Amsden *(Pres.)*

FRY/HAMMOND/BARR INCORPORATED
600 E. Washington St.
Orlando, FL 32801
Tel.: 407-849-0100
Fax: 407-849-0817
Year Founded: 1962
Approx.Billings: $25,000,000
Emp.: 28
Advertising Agency
S.I.C.: 7311
Charles F. Fry *(Pres.)*
Mary Alice Kolesar *(V.P. & Controller)*

Computer Systems/Hardware:
Data General

Outside Service Firm(s):

Sun Bank, N.A.*(Major Banking Relationship)*
Miami, FL 33131

THE FRYE COMPANY
1 Elm Sq.
Andover, MA 01810
Tel.: 508-475-7488
Tel.: 800-826-3793
Approx.Sls.: $10,000,000
Emp.: 250
Fiscal Year-end: 9/30/90
Mfr. Shoes & Boots
S.I.C.: 3149
Stanley Kravetz *(Pres.)*
Carl Derrick *(Dir.-Adv.)*

FUEL SOUTH, INC.
P.O. Box 572
Hazlehurst, GA 31539
Tel.: 912-375-5596
Fax: 912-375-2703
Year Founded: 1943
Sales Range: $80-99 Million
Emp.: 38
Fiscal Year-end: 12/31/92
Petroleum & Petroleum Products; Convenience Food Stores
S.I.C.: 5172; 5399
J.C. Jones III. *(Chm. Bd.)*
Jimmy Walker *(Pres.)*
Phil Wysong *(V.P. & Treas.)*
Jerry Wood *(Gen. Mgr.)*
Joanne McNeal *(Office Mgr.)*

No. of Mfg. Plants/Facilities: 1
No. of U.S. Offices: 1

Computer Systems/Hardware:
IBM System A/S 400

Outside Service Firm(s):

Grant Thornton*(Auditors)*
Atlanta, GA

Nationwide Insurance*(Commercial Insurance Carrier)*
Atlanta, GA

Barnes & Barnes*(Commercial Insurance Carrier)*
Macon, GA

Jones & Solomon*(Legal Firm)*
Alma, GA

Bank South, N.A.*(Major Banking Relationship)*
P.O. Box 4387
Atlanta, GA 30302
Tel.: 404-529-4111

FUGAZY INTERNATIONAL CORPORATION
555 Madison Ave., 12 Fl.
New York, NY 10022
Tel.: 212-838-7577
Fax: 212-752-9781
Approx.Sls.: $250,000,000
Emp.: 400
Fiscal Year-end: 12/31/90
Total Transportation Co. Travel Agencies, Including Franchises, Limousines, Buses & Rental Cars, Helicopter Charter
S.I.C.: 4724
William D. Fugazy *(Chm. Bd.)*
Roy D. Fugazy *(Pres. & Chief Exec. Officer)*
Joan Henderson *(V.P.)*

Divisions:

Fugazy Limousines **(1)**
2220 E. 40 st.
New York, NY 10022
Tel.: 612-689-0100
Roy D. Fugazy *(Chief Exec. Officer)*

Fugazy Travel **(1)**
555 Madison Ave., 12th Fl.
New York, NY 10022
Tel.: 212-838-7577
S.I.C.: 4724
Roy D. Fugazy *(Chief Exec. Officer)*

FUGRO-MCCLELLAND, INC.
6100 Hillcroft
Houston, TX 77081
Mailing Address:
P.O. Box 740010
Houston, TX 77274
Tel.: 713-772-3700
Telex: 762447
Fax: 713-778-5518
Year Founded: 1946
Approx.Sls.: $33,000,000
Emp.: 615
Geotechnical Engineering, Waste Management, Marine Geosciences, Environmental Services, Construction Services
S.I.C.: 8711; 1382; 1629; 4499; 4953
William J. Emrich *(Pres.)*
Harry M. Fong *(Treas.)*
Sundra Fontenot *(Sec.)*
G.J. Kramer *(Dir.)*

No. of U.S. Offices: 10
No. of Foreign Offices: 12

Outside Service Firm(s):

Ernst & Young*(Auditors)*
1 Houston Ctr., 1200 McKinney
Houston, TX 77002
Tel.: 713-750-1500

Sewell & Riggs*(Legal Firm)*
800 Capital Bank Plaza
Houston, TX 77002
Tel.: 713-652-8700

First City National Bank*(Major Banking Relationship)*
Houston, TX

Subsidiaries:

Fugro-McClelland **(1)**
98 Jalan SS 15/4 Subang Jaya, 47500
Petaling Jaya, Selangor Malaysia
Tel.: 734-3341
Tel.: 733-1820
Telex: 36120 PCTRAD MA

Fugro-McClelland Hong Kong, Ltd. **(1)**
11-F Park Commercial Centre, 2-12 Shelter St.
Coswaybay, Hong Kong

Fugro-McClelland, Ltd. **(1)**
McClelland House, Chantry Place off Headstone Lane
Harrow, Middlesex HA3 6NY, United Kingdom
Tel.: 01 421-2411
Telex: 925759

Fugro-McClelland, Ltd. **(1)**
510 Thomson Rd. #14-01 SLF Complex, Singapore, 1129, Singapore
Tel.: 337-9071
Telex: 21068 SOILMAC RS
Fax: 337-2849

Fugro-McClelland, Inc.—(Continued)

Fugro-McClelland Middle East **(1)**
1509 Dubai International Trade Center P.O. Box 9264,
Dubai, United Arab Emirates
Tel.: 375976
Telex: 45752 MIL EM

Fugro-McClelland, Ltd. **(1)**
18 Frogmore Rd. Hemel Hempstead, Herts HP3 9RT, United Kingdom
Tel.: 01 421-2411
Telex: 925759

Jacques/McClelland Geosciences, Inc. **(1)**
3 Spectacle Lake Dr.
Dartmouth, NS B3H 2Rl, Canada
Tel.: 902-468-8750
Telex: 01921745

McClelland Consultants Midwest, Inc. **(1)**
1601 Dielman Rd.
Saint Louis, MO 63141
Tel.: 314-993-1463

McClelland-Suhaimi, Ltd. **(1)**
P.O. Box 2165,
Dammam, 31451, Saudi Arabia
Tel.: 857-7491
Telex: 801477

N.B.K. Geosciences, Ltd. **(1)**
P.O. Box 318
Doha, Qatar
Tel.: 328211
Tel.: 417388

Newfoundland Geosciences, Ltd. **(1)**
607 Torbay Road P.O. Box 9370, Station B, Saint John's, NF A1A 2Y3, Canada
Tel.: 709 576-1428
Telex: 016-4148

FULL CIRCLE MEDIA CORP.
200 Connecticut Ave.
Norwalk, CT 06856-4990
Tel.: 203-852-0500
Fax: 203-838-3710
Year Founded: 1976
Approx.Rev.: $25,000,000
Emp.: 110
Fiscal Year-end: 9/30/92
Trade Shows & Trade Publications
S.I.C.: 7389
David Cheifetz *(Chm. Bd.)*
Richard Guerrein *(Co.-Chief Exec. Officer)*
Paul Mackler *(Co.-Chief Exec. Officer)*
Larry Henry *(Pres.)*
Nicholas Curci *(Chief Fin. Officer)*
Karin Ragonesi *(Dir.-Human Resources)*

No. of U.S. Offices: 4

Computer Systems/Hardware:
IBM AS/400

Outside Service Firm(s):

Nishball, Srebrick*(Auditors)*
Bridgeport, CT

Prudential Insurance Co. of America*(Group Insurer)*
Norwalk, CT

Flemming, Zulack & Williamson*(Legal Firm)*
New York, NY

Connecticut National Bank*(Major Banking Relationship)*
Westport, CT

Divisions:

Full Circle Communications **(1)**
23410 Civic Center Way, Ste. E 10
Malibu, CA 90265
Tel.: 213-456-2283
Bill Slapin *(Publr.)*

Viscom Enterprises **(1)**
656 E. Swedesford Rd., Ste. 218
Wayne, PA 19087
Tel.: 215-964-8801
Rich Guerrein *(Publr.)*

FULL SERVICE BEVERAGE COMPANY
2901 S. Kansas
Wichita, KS 67216
Tel.: 316-529-3777 **KS**
Fax: 316-529-1544
Year Founded: 1948
Sales Range: $40-59 Million
Emp.: 300
Fiscal Year-end: 9/30/90
Import Export
Soft Drink Company
S.I.C.: 2086
John L.D. Frazier *(Chm. Bd. & Chief Exec. Officer)*
Robert Westerfield *(Pres.)*
Kent Wilson *(V.P.-Fin. & Chief Fin. Officer)*
Patricia Pew *(Sec.)*

No. of Mfg. Plants/Facilities: 2
No. of U.S. Offices: 9

Computer Systems/Hardware:
DigaTex

Outside Service Firm(s):

KPMG Peat Marwick*(Auditors)*
Wichita, KS

Foulston & Siefkin*(Legal Firm)*
700 Fourth Financial Center
Wichita, KS 67202
Tel.: 316-267-6371

Bank IV*(Major Banking Relationship)*
P.O. Box 1122,
Wichita, KS 67201
Tel.: 316-261-4304

Division:

Full Service Beverage Company of Colorado **(1)**
2840 S. Zuni
Englewood, CO 80110
Tel.: 303-761-7777
Mfr. of Soft Drinks
S.I.C.: 2086

THE FULLER BRUSH COMPANY
Westport Addition, P.O. Box 729
Great Bend, KS 67530
Tel.: 316-792-1711 **KS**
Fax: 316-792-1906
Year Founded: 1906
Approx.Sls.: $50,000,000
Emp.: 480
Mfr. of Brushes & Cleaning Products for Home & Commercial Use
S.I.C.: 2842; 2899; 3991
H. Lee Turner *(Chm. Bd.)*
James Giesler *(Chief Oper. & Chief Fin. Officer)*
Elizabeth Turner *(Treas.)*
Gerald Nehra *(V.P.-Legal)*
Cindy Latham *(Dir.-Mktg.)*

Division:

The Fuller Brush Company **(1)**
3065 Center Green Dr.
Denver, CO 80301
Tel.: 303-440-9448
Fax: 316-792-1906
Approx.Sls.: $50,000,000
Emp.: 480
Marketing of Brushes & Cleaning Products for Home & Commercial Use
S.I.C.: 5963; 5961

GEORGE A. FULLER COMPANY
919 Third Ave.
New York, NY 10022
Tel.: 212-355-2700 **MD**
Fax: 212-752-8488
Year Founded: 1882
Assets: $19,000,000
Liabilities: $2,000,000
Net Worth: $17,000,000
Approx.Sls.: $400,000,000
Emp.: 400
Fiscal Year-end: 12/31/89
Construction, General Contracting & Construction Management Worldwide
S.I.C.: 1542; 1522; 1629; 8742
Wilfred G. Mango, Jr. *(Pres. & Chief Exec. Officer)*
Robert A. Musco *(Exec. V.P.-Opers.)*
Joseph A. Neeley *(Sr. V.P.-Mechanical Elec. Service)*
Francis P. Donelan *(V.P., Sec. & Gen. Counsel)*
Maurice Leonardi *(V.P.-Fin. & Admin.)*
Richard Schneider *(V.P.-Estimating)*
Lynda Hetterman *(Sr. Deputy Dir.-Oper.)*
Principal(s):
Wilfred G. Mango, Jr.
Francis P. Donelan
Thomas M. Haythe
Dimitri D. Papdopoulos

Computer Systems/Hardware:
Data General Eclipse MV/4000

Outside Service Firm(s):

Arthur Andersen & Co.*(Auditors)*
1345 Ave. of the Americas
New York, NY 10105
Tel.: 212-708-4000

FULLERTON METALS CO.
3000 Shermer Rd.
Northbrook, IL 60065-3002
Tel.: 708-291-2400 **IL**
Fax: 708-291-2475
Year Founded: 1943
Approx.Sls.: $95,000,000
Emp.: 150
Fiscal Year-end: 12/31/92
Primary Metal Industries; Fabricated Metal Prods.; Wholesale Trade-durable Goods
S.I.C.: 5051
Kenneth J. Riskind *(Pres. & Chief Exec. Officer)*
Joseph L. Marzullo *(Sr. V.P.-Fin.)*
William P. Eftax *(Controller)*
John Fugazy *(Dir.-Data Processing)*
Joseph Grano *(Gen. Mgr.)*

Computer Systems/Hardware:
Data General MV 18000

Outside Service Firm(s):

Ernst & Young*(Auditors)*
233 S. Wacker Dr.
Chicago, IL 60606
Tel.: 312-368-1800
Fax: 312-645-3095

D'Ancona & Pflaum*(Legal Firm)*
30 No. LaSalle St.
Chicago, IL 60602
Tel.: 312-580-2000

FURMAN FOODS, INC.
R.R. 2
Northumberland, PA 17857-0502
Tel.: 717-473-3516
Fax: 717-473-7367
Year Founded: 1921
Approx.Sls.: $45,000,000
Emp.: 250
Fiscal Year-end: 3/31/92
Import Export
Canned Vegetables
S.I.C.: 2033
David N. Geise *(Pres.)*
James F. Kohl *(Exec. V.P.)*
Paul S. Dubendorf *(V.P.-Fin.)*
Joel R. Furman *(V.P.-Sls. & Mktg.)*
William W. Furman, Jr. *(Treas. & Data Processing Mgr.)*
Franklin G. Furman *(Sec.)*
Kermit K. Kohl *(Dir.-Personnel)*
Marvin Klaassen *(Pur. Agent)*
Dave Betts *(Mgr.-Retail Sls.)*

Outside Service Firm(s):

KPMG Peat Marwick*(Auditors)*
P.O. Box 1190, 225 Market St., Ste. 300
Harrisburg, PA 17108-1190
Tel.: 717-238-7131

Carpenter, Diehl & Kivko*(Legal Firm)*
Sunbury, PA

Provident National Bank*(Major Banking Relationship)*
P.O. Box 7648
Philadelphia, PA 19101
Tel.: 215-585-5000

FURMAN LUMBER COMPANY
32 Manning Rd.
Billerica, MA 01821
Mailing Address:
P.O. Box 130,
Nutting Lake, MA 01865
Tel.: 508-670-3800
Tel.: 800-843-9663
Fax: 508-670-3999
Year Founded: 1956
Approx.Sls.: $300,000,000
Emp.: 287
Fiscal Year-end: 2/28/91
Lumber Company
S.I.C.: 5211
John R. Furman *(Chm. Bd.)*
Barry L. Kronick *(Pres. & Chief Exec. Officer)*
George Gray *(Chief Fin. Officer)*
Walter Cole *(Dir.-Data Processing & Telecommunications)*
Bill Perry *(Dir.-Personnel)*
Michael Scolavino *(Dir.-Pur. & Sls.)*
Richard Viola *(Dir.-Mktg.)*
Laura Schulze *(Mgr.-Adv. & Pub. Rels.)*

No. of U.S. Offices: 13

Computer Systems/Hardware:
IBM System 38

Outside Service Firm(s):

Arthur Andersen & Co.*(Auditors)*
901 Main St., Ste. 5600
Dallas, TX 75202
Tel.: 214-741-8300

Marsh & McLennan*(Commercial Insurance Carrier)*
1300 San Jacinto Tower, 2121 San Jacinto St.
Dallas, TX 75201-6789
Tel.: 214-979-9900

John Bromberg & Leeds*(Legal Firm)*
Dallas, TX

NationsBank Texas*(Major Banking Relationship)*
901 Main St., 16th Fl.
Dallas, TX 75202
Tel.: 214-922-5000

Subsidiary:

Slaughter Bros., Inc. **(1)**
11050 Plano Rd.
Dallas, TX 75238
Tel.: 214-341-9000 (100%)
Fax: 214-341-5320
Approx.Sls.: $60,000,000
Emp.: 160
Wholesale Distribution of Wood Products
S.I.C.: 5031
Timothy Thompson *(Pres.)*
R. Kephart *(V.P.-Treas. & Sec.)*
George Steele *(V.P.)*
Jack D. Mathews *(Data Processing Dir.)*

Divisions:

Furman Wholesale Lumber Div. **(2)**
1800 D Montreal Cir.
Atlanta, GA 30084
Tel.: 404-934-6800 (100%)
Approx.Sls.: $8,400,000
Emp.: 16
Wholesale Distributor of Lumber
S.I.C.: 5031
Dek Spaulding *(Mgr.)*

Furman Wholesale Lumber Div. (2)
4341 Old Lamar
Memphis, TN 38118
Tel.: 901-365-6500 (100%)
Approx.Sls.: $6,500,000
Emp.: 14
Wholesale Distributor of Lumber
S.I.C.: 5031
Earl Stephens *(Mgr.)*

Furman Wholesale Lumber Div. (2)
11050 Plano Rd.
Dallas, TX 75238
Tel.: 214-341-9000 (100%)
Approx.Sls.: $21,100,000
Emp.: 22
Wholesale Distributor of Lumber
S.I.C.: 5031
Darrel Bishop *(Mgr.)*

Furman Wholesale Lumber Div. (2)
2021 S. Division St.
Orlando, FL 32805
Tel.: 305-843-1340 (100%)
Approx.Sls.: $6,300,000
Emp.: 15
Wholesale Distributor of Lumber
S.I.C.: 5031
Charles Irvine *(Opr. Mgr.)*

Furman Wholesale Lumber Div. (2)
8446 Vidor
San Antonio, TX 78217
Tel.: 210-349-5381 (100%)
Approx.Sls.: $6,800,000
Emp.: 16
Wholesale Distributor of Lumber
S.I.C.: 5031
George Steele *(Mgr.)*
John Robinson *(Asst. Mgr.)*

Furman Wholesale Lumber Div. (2)
13246 Murphy Rd.
Stafford, TX 77477
Tel.: 713-499-5575 (100%)
Approx.Sls.: $10,700,000
Emp.: 20
Wholesale Distributor of Lumber
S.I.C.: 5031
George Steele *(Mgr.)*

FURMAN, ROTH ADV.
801 Second Ave.
New York, NY 10017
Tel.: 212-687-2300
Fax: 212-687-0858
Approx.Billings: $10,200,000
Emp.: 21
Retail, Food, Package Goods, Recruitment & Radio Advertising
Nat Roth *(Chm. & Chief Fin. Officer)*
Ernie Roth *(Pres. & New Bus. Contact)*
Estelle Krasna *(Sr. V.P., Controller, Corp. Sec.)*
Sally Mutafopulos *(Gen. Mgr.)*

FURNAS ELECTRIC COMPANY
1000 McKee St.
Batavia, IL 60510
Tel.: 708-879-6000 **DE**
Fax: 708-879-0867
Year Founded: 1932
Assets: $54,000,000
Liabilities: $12,000,000
Net Worth: $42,000,000
Approx.Sls.: $114,000,000
Emp.: 1,500
Fiscal Year-end: 12/31/91
Export
Controls for Electric Motors, Heating & Lighting Loads, Pilot Controls & Relays
S.I.C.: 3625
R.W. Hansen *(Chm. Bd., Pres. & Chief Exec. Officer)*
G.R. Nary *(Vice Chm.)*
Dennis Walstad *(Sr. V.P. & Chief Oper. Officer)*
T.J. McGavin *(Exec. V.P., Mktg. & Sls.)*
P.P. Welch *(V.P.-Sls.)*
R.C. Trumpy *(V.P.-Mfg.)*
T.F. Caughlin *(V.P.-Industrial Rels.)*
W.G. Lynch *(V.P.-Fin.)*
H. Nicholas Funk *(Controller)*
J.G. Hansen *(Sec.)*
P. Margitan *(Data Processing Dir.)*
G. Sampson *(Pur. Dir.)*
Jay Stoy *(Dir.-Adv. & Communications)*

Principal(s):
R.W. Hansen
J.G. Hansen
C.L. Hansen

No. of Mfg. Plants/Facilities: 3
No. of U.S. Offices: 67
No. of Foreign Offices: 1

Computer Systems/Hardware:
NAS 6620

Outside Service Firm(s):

Coopers & Lybrand*(Auditors)*
Aurora, IL

Harris Trust & Savings Bank*(International Bank Affiliate)*
111 W. Monroe St.
Chicago, IL 60690
Tel.: 312-461-2265
Tel.: 800-858-0840

Drendel, Schanlaber, Horwitz, Tatnall & McCracken*(Legal Firm)*
Chicago, IL

Harris Trust & Savings Bank*(Major Banking Relationship)*
111 W. Monroe St.
Chicago, IL 60690
Tel.: 312-461-2265
Tel.: 800-858-0840

Duff & Phelps*(Pension Manager)*
Chicago, IL

Subsidiaries:

Climco Coils Co. (1)
400 Oakwood
Morrison, IL 61270
Tel.: 815-772-2107
S.I.C.: 3625

Nordic Controls Co. (1)
155 N. Van Nortwick
Batavia, IL 60510
Tel.: 708-879-7500
S.I.C.: 3625

FURNITURE CONSULTANTS
11 W. 19th St.
New York, NY 10011
Tel.: 212-229-4500
Fax: 212-807-0036
Year Founded: 1978
Approx.Sls.: $66,000,000
Emp.: 150
Fiscal Year-end: 2/28/90
Contract Furniture Dealer
S.I.C.: 5021
John Varacchi *(Pres.)*
Richard Bascetta *(V.P.-Sls.)*
David Itkin *(V.P.-Mktg.)*
Herbert Krauss *(V.P.-Admin.)*
Lawrence Itkin *(Treas.)*
Howard Drucker *(Controller)*
Mike Mullman *(Gen. Counsel)*
Kate Eible *(Mgr.-Sls. Admin. & Personnel)*

No. of Mfg. Plants/Facilities: 1

Computer Systems/Hardware:
DEC VAX 750

Outside Service Firm(s):

Joseph Herbert & Co.*(Auditors)*
330 Seventh Ave.
New York, NY 10001

Allstate Insurance*(Group Insurer)*
Northbrook, IL

Schoenwald, Schafzin & Mullman*(Legal Firm)*
New York, NY

FURNIVAL/STATE MACHINERY CO.
(Formerly Seacorp National, Inc.)
1857 William Penn Way
Lancaster, PA 17601
Mailing Address:
P.O. Box 12399
Lancaster, PA 17605
Tel.: 717-397-7551
Fax: 717-397-6562
Approx.Sls.: $72,000,000
Emp.: 250
Mfr. General Construction Machinery & Equipment
S.I.C.: 5082; 7359; 5084
Robert G. Thomson *(Chief Exec. Officer)*
Dennis E. Levering *(Pres.)*
Jan Bailey *(Dir.-Communications)*

FURR'S SUPERMARKETS
1730 Montano Rd. NW
Albuquerque, NM 87184
Tel.: 505-344-6525
Grocery Store Chains
S.I.C.: 5411
Stuart Rosenthal *(Pres. & Chief Oper. Officer)*
Jan Friederich *(Chief Exec. Officer)*

THE FUSCO CORPORATION
555 Long Wharf Dr.
New Haven, CT 06511
Tel.: 203-777-7451
Fax: 203-782-0725
Year Founded: 1924
Approx.Sls.: $148,000,000
Emp.: 350
Fiscal Year-end: 3/31/91
Building Construction
S.I.C.: 1542; 1541; 6552
Edmund J. Fusco, Sr. *(Pres.)*
John Scaramozza *(V.P.-Opers.)*
Gerald Shearer *(V.P.-Engrng.)*
Lynn R. Fusco *(V.P.-Mktg.)*
Ronald Olson *(Comptroller)*
Paul F. Morris *(Treas.)*

Outside Service Firm(s):

Bailey, Moore, Glazer, Schaefer & Proto*(Auditors)*
10 Lunar Dr.
Woodbridge, CT

Pepe & Hazzard*(Legal Firm)*
Hartford, CT

Connecticut National Bank*(Major Banking Relationship)*
777 Main St.
Hartford, CT 06615

LOU FUSZ AUTOMOTIVE NETWORK
925 N. Lindbergh
Saint Louis, MO 63141
Tel.: 314-994-1500 **MO**
Fax: 314-993-4096
Year Founded: 1954
Approx.Sls.: $115,000,000
Emp.: 200
Holding Company: Automobile Dealership
S.I.C.: 6719; 5511
Louis Fusz *(Chm. Bd.)*
Louis Fusz, Jr. *(Pres.)*
Martha Fusz *(Treas.)*
Peter Ramey *(Chief Fin. Officer)*

No. of Mfg. Plants/Facilities: 5

Outside Service Firm(s):

Martin & Associates*(Auditors)*
St. Louis, MO

Boatmen's Trust Company*(Major Banking Relationship)*
100 North Broadway
St. Louis, MO 63102
Tel.: 314-466-2469

Subsidiary:

Lou Fusz Motor Company (1)
925 N. Lindbergh
Saint Louis, MO 63141
Tel.: 314-994-1500
Automobile Dealership
S.I.C.: 5511
Lou Fusz Jr. *(Pres.)*

FUTTER LUMBER CORPORATION
100 Merrick Rd.
Rockville Centre, NY 11570
Mailing Address:
P.O. Box 347,
Rockville Center, NY 11570
Tel.: 516-764-4445
Fax: 516-536-9503
Year Founded: 1944
Approx.Sls.: $78,000,000
Emp.: 20
Fiscal Year-end: 12/31/91
Import
Wholesale Lumber
S.I.C.: 5031
Bernard Futter *(Pres. & Chief Exec. Officer)*
Francine Scrivani *(Exec. V.P.)*
Kenneth Futter *(Sec. & Treas.)*
Ken Henderson *(Controller)*

No. of U.S. Offices: 1

Computer Systems/Hardware:
IBM System 400

Outside Service Firm(s):

Hiltzik Schneider Ehrlich & Co.*(Auditors)*
Great Neck, NY

Fried, Frank, Harris, Shriver & Jacobson*(Legal Firm)*
1 New York Plaza
New York, NY 10004
Tel.: 212-820-8000

Irving Trust Co.*(Major Banking Relationship)*
One Wall St.
New York, NY 10015

Bank of New York*(Major Banking Relationship)*
90 Washington St.
New York, NY 10015

FUTURE FOAM, INC.
25 Main Place, Ste. 500
Council Bluffs, IA 51503
Tel.: 712-323-9122 **NE**
Fax: 712-323-0158
Approx.Sls.: $66,000,000
Emp.: 400
Fiscal Year-end: 12/31/91
Plastic Foam Products; Insulation & Cushioning Material; Foamed Plastic; Ice Chests Or Portable Coolers
S.I.C.: 3086
Charles Schneider *(Chm. Bd.)*
William Grassman *(Pres.)*

Outside Service Firm(s):

Grant Thornton*(Auditors)*
Omaha, NE

R. David Garber*(Legal Firm)*
Omaha, NE

First National Bank of Omaha*(Major Banking Relationship)*
One First National Center
Omaha, NE 68102

FUTURE FORD/HUGO INC.
650 Auto Mall Dr.
Roseville, CA 95661
Tel.: 916-786-3673
Fax: 916-969-6493
Year Founded: 1981
Emp.: 92

Future Ford/Hugo Inc.—(Continued)

Retail Automobiles
S.I.C.: 5511
G. Steve Pleau *(Pres.)*
John Moisan *(V.P.)*
Gene Pleau *(Sec. & Treas.)*
Bob Crowe *(Mgr.-Sls.-New Car)*
Rocky Kness *(Mgr.-Sls.-Used Car)*

Outside Service Firm(s):

Winetrub Sundberg & Martinelli*(Auditors)*
Emeryville, CA

Bank of America NT&SA*(Major Banking Relationship)*
Roseville, CA

FUTURES PERSONNEL SERVICES
Maryland Exec. Park, Oxford Bldg., 8600 LaSalle Rd.
Baltimore, MD 21286
Tel.: 410-321-1984
Year Founded: 1976
Sales Range: $10-19 Million
Emp.: 15
Exec. Recruitment & Placement Service
S.I.C.: 7361
Daniel A. Otakie *(Chm., Pres., Chief Exec. Officer & Treas.)*
Principal(s):
Daniel A. Otakie

No. of U.S. Offices: 2

Outside Service Firm(s):

Wolpoff & Company*(Auditors)*
Baltimore, MD

Thompson & Jones*(Commercial Insurance Carrier)*
Baltimore, MD

Allen, Thiebolt & Alexander*(Legal Firm)*
Baltimore, MD

Equitable Bank, N.A.*(Major Banking Relationship)*
100 S. Charles St.
Baltimore, MD 21201
Tel.: 410-547-4000

Maryland National Bank*(Major Banking Relationship)*
10 Light St.
Baltimore, MD 21203
Tel.: 410-244-5000

FYRNETICS, INC.
1055 Stevenson Ct. Ste. 102W
Roselle, IL 60172
Tel.: 708-893-4592
Fax: 708-893-9967
Approx.Sls.: $25,000,000
Emp.: 17
Mfr. Smoke Alarms
S.I.C.: 3669
Thomas Russo *(Pres.)*
J. Sha *(Sec. & Treas.)*
Carl Pikus *(Dir.-Sls.)*

G & A COMMUNICATIONS
1401 Dove St., 5th Fl.
Newport Beach, CA 92660
Tel.: 714-476-1009
Year Founded: 1973
Approx.Billings: $15,000,000
Emp.: 20
High-Tech & Business-to-Business
Frank Galusha *(Pres.)*
Dan Krongaard *(Exec. V.P., Grp. Supvr.)*
Geri Schanz *(V.P., Dir. Pub. Rels.)*

G & L PRODUCTS, INC.
16900 W. Victor Rd.
New Berlin, WI 53151
Tel.: 414-784-7970
Fax: 414-784-7675
Fiscal Year-end: 12/31/92
Mfr. of Articulating Ladders
S.I.C.: 3499
Dave Lambert *(Chm. Bd.)*
Dave Lambert Jr. *(V.P.)*

Subsidiary:

G & L Products **(1)**
1200 Fisher Rd.
Charles City, IA 50616
Tel.: 515-228-3414
Fax: 515-228-3438
Emp.: 50
Computer Systems/Hardware:
IBM System 34
Manufacturer of Sprayers, Hi-Pressure Washers, Bin Floor Air Frames/Ladders
S.I.C.: 3629
Dave Lambert Sr. *(Pres.)*
W. Grunwald *(V.P.)*

G & W ELECTRIC CO.
3500 W. 127th St.
Blue Island, IL 60406
Tel.: 708-388-5010
Fax: 708-388-0755
Approx.Sls.: $20,000,000
Emp.: 270
High Voltage Electrical Equipment
S.I.C.: 3699
J.D. Mueller *(Chm. Bd.)*
James Acree *(Pres.)*
John H. Mueller *(V.P.-Opers.)*
L. Arends *(Mgr.-Mktg. Services)*

GAF CORPORATION
1361 Alps Rd.
Wayne, NJ 07470
Tel.: 201-628-4000 **DE**
Telex: 130374 GAF WANE
Fax: 201-628-4114
Year Founded: 1965
Assets: $1,865,722,000
Earnings: $210,383,000
Liabilities: $1,706,624,000
Net Worth: $159,098,000
Approx.Sls.: $925,614,000
Emp.: 4,075
Fiscal Year-end: 12/31/91
Import Export
Chemicals; Building Materials
S.I.C.: 2869; 2952; 3069; 4832; 3229; 5169; 3295; 3399; 5039; 2842
Samuel J. Heyman *(Chm. Bd. & Chief Exec. Officer)*
Thomas C. Bohrer *(Exec. V.P.-Chemicals)*
Carl R. Eckardt *(Exec. V.P.-Bus. Devel.)*
John M. Sergey *(Exec. V.P.-Bldg. Matls.)*
Stephen A. Block *(Sr. V.P. & Gen. Counsel)*
James J. Strupp *(Sr. V.P.-Human Resources)*
Jonathan H. Stern *(V.P. & Controller)*
Ron DeBiasse *(V.P.-Pur. & Real Estate)*
Bernard T. Schumacher *(V.P.-Mngmt. Information Systems)*
Robert H. Steinfeld *(V.P.-Taxation)*
John Tancredi *(V.P.-Res. & Devel.)*
Mark A. Presto *(Treas.)*
Eleanor Carlson *(Mgr.-Shareholder Rels. & Asst. Sec.)*
Arthur Clark *(Mgr.-Cash Mngmt.)*
Linda Marion *(Mgr.-Travel)*
William Roberts *(Asst. Controller)*

Outside Service Firm(s):

Arthur Andersen & Co.*(Auditors)*
P.O. Box 221, 101 Eisenhower Pkwy.
Roseland, NJ 07068
Tel.: 201-403-6100
Fax: 201-403-0579

Willis Corroon*(Commercial Insurance Carrier)*
7 Hanover Square
New York, NY
Tel.: 212-837-0823
Fax: 212-344-8290

Kramer, Levin, Nessen, Kamin & Frankel*(Legal Firm)*
919 Third Ave.
New York, NY 10022
Tel.: 212-688-1100

Chase Manhattan Bank, N.A.*(Major Banking Relationship)*
One Chase Manhattan Plaza
New York, NY 10081
Tel.: 212-552-2222
Tel.: 800-526-0801
Fax: 212-552-7175

Westwood Management*(Pension Manager)*
885 Third Ave.
New York, NY 10022-4802
Tel.: 212-688-2323

Subsidiaries:

GAF Broadcasting Co., Inc. **(1)**
1180 Ave. of the Americas
New York, NY 10036
Tel.: 212-730-9628 (100%)
Approx.Sls.: $5,800,000
Emp.: 35
Radio Broadcasting Company
S.I.C.: 4832
Samuel J. Heyman *(Pres.)*
Matthew Field *(V.P. & Gen. Mgr.)*
Jonathan H. Stern *(V.P. & Controller)*
Stephen A. Block *(V.P. & Sec.)*

GAF Building Materials Corporation **(1)**
1361 Alps Rd.
Wayne, NJ 07470
Tel.: 201-628-3000 (100%)
Approx.Sls.: $424,800,000
Emp.: 1,774
Mfr. of Building Products
S.I.C.: 2952; 3229; 5039
Samuel J. Heyman *(Chm. Bd.)*
James T. Sherwin *(Vice Chm.)*
John M. Sergey *(Pres.)*
Russell E. Kennedy *(V.P.-Sls. & Mktg.)*
Donald LaPalme *(V.P.-Mfg.)*
Leonard Goodman *(V.P.-Fin.)*
Robert Hodgson *(V.P.-Human Resources)*

GAF Export Corp. **(1)**
1361 Alps Rd.
Wayne, NJ 07470
Tel.: 201-628-3000 (100%)
Mktg. of Chemicals
S.I.C.: 5169
Carl R. Eckardt *(Pres.)*
Jonathan H. Stern *(V.P. & Treas.)*
Stephen A. Block *(Sec.)*

GAF International Corp. **(1)**
1361 Alps Road
Wayne, NJ 07470
Tel.: 201-628-3000
Inactive
Carl R. Eckardt *(Pres.)*
Jonathan H. Stern *(Treas.)*
Stephen A. Block *(Sec.)*

International Specialty Products, Inc. **(1)**
818 Washington St.
Wilmington, DE 19801
Tel.: 302-429-8554 (100%)
Assets: $1,074,724,000
Liabilities: $590,352,000
Net Worth: $484,372,000
Approx.Sls.: $525,786,000
Mfr. of Chemicals
S.I.C.: 2869; 3295; 3399
Samuel J. Heyman *(Chm. Bd.)*
Thomas C. Bohrer *(Pres.)*
Alan Z. Senter *(Exec. V.P.)*
David I. Burton *(Sr. V.P.-Specialty Derivitive Chemicals)*
Richard F. Bauman *(V.P.-Mktg. & Sls. Acetylenes)*
Arthur Dresner *(V.P.-Advanced Matls.)*
Abraham Lindenauer *(V.P.-Matls. Mngmt.)*
Richard B. Olsen *(V.P.-Fin.)*
James P. Rogers *(V.P. & Treas.)*
Raymond W. Smith *(V.P.-Intl.)*
James J. Strupp *(V.P.-Human Resources)*

Non-U.S. Holdings:

GAF (Australasia) Pty. Ltd. **(1)**
Beaconsfield P.O. Box 110,
Alexandria, Sydney 2015, Australia
Tel.: 61-2-6931433
Mktg. of Chemicals
S.I.C.: 5169

GAF (Belgium) N.V. **(1)**
Hoogkamerstraat 42
Sint-Niklaas, B-2700, Belgium
Tel.: 010-32 (3) 7766955
Mfr. & Mktg. of Chemicals & Building Materials
S.I.C.: 5169; 2819

GAF (Canada) Inc. **(1)**
1075 The Queensway East
Mississauga, ON L4Y 4C1, Canada
Tel.: 416-277-0381
Mfr. & Mktg. of Chemicals
S.I.C.: 5169; 2819

GAF Corp. de Mexico S.A. de C.V. **(1)**
Calle de Lopez No. 15
Mexico, D.F. 1, Mexico
Tel.: 525-905-747039
Mfr. & Mktg. of Chemicals
S.I.C.: 2819; 5169

GAF (Danmark) A/S **(1)**
Frederlksdalsvej 141
Virum, DK 2830, Denmark
Tel.: 010-45 (2) 552800
Mfr. & Mktg. of Chemicals
S.I.C.: 2819; 5169

GAF (Deutschland) GmbH **(1)**
Rudolf-Diesel-Strasse 25 Postfach 1380, 5020
Frechen, Germany
Tel.: 022341051
Mktg. of Chemicals
S.I.C.: 5169

GAF do Brasil Industria e Commercio, Ltda. **(1)**
Rua Major Sertorio 212-2 01222
Sao Paulo, Brazil
Tel.: 55-11-2591422
Mktg. of Chemicals
S.I.C.: 5169

GAF (France) S.A. **(1)**
Z.A.C. Paris-Nord 2 B.P. 50007, 95945
Roissy Charles de Gaulle, France
Tel.: 010-33-(1) 48632700
Mktg. of Chemicals
S.I.C.: 5169

GAF (Great Britain) Co. Ltd. **(1)**
Rythe House, 2 Littleworth Rd.
Esher, Surrey KT10 9PD, United Kingdom
Tel.: 44-61-998-1122
Mfr. & Mktg. of Chemicals
S.I.C.: 2819; 5169

GAF Huls Chemie GmbH **(1)**
Postfach 1320 D-4370
Marl, Recklinghausen Germany
Tel.: 49 (2365) 492984
Mfr. of Chemicals
S.I.C.: 2819

GAF Insurance Ltd. **(1)**
Victoria Hall, P.O. Box HM 1826
Hamilton, HMHX, Bermuda
Tel.: 809-292-4402
Insurance
S.I.C.: 6311

GAF (Italia) S.P.I. **(1)**
Via Lampedusa, 13 20141
Milan, Italy
Tel.: 010-39-2-8466741
Mktg. of Chemicals
S.I.C.: 5169

GAF (Japan) Ltd. **(1)**
Kogen Bldg. 67 No. 17-2 Shinbashi 6-chome, Minato-Ku,
Tokyo, 105, Japan
Tel.: 03-3434-7566
Mktg. of Chemicals
S.I.C.: 5169

GAF (Nederland) N.V. **(1)**
Olivier van Noortstraat 7 Postbus 4005,
Schiedam, NL-3102 GA, Netherlands
Tel.: 010-31-10-705044
Mfr. & Mktg. of Chemicals
S.I.C.: 2819; 5169

GAF (New Zealand) Pty., Ltd. **(1)**
2 Monmouth St. P.O. Box 78073,
Grey Lynn, Auckland New Zealand
Tel.: 64-(9)-761271
Mfr. & Mktg. of Chemicals
S.I.C.: 2819; 5169

GAF Norden AB **(1)**
Box 824 S-121
Johanneshov, 08, Sweden
Tel.: 46-8-188830
Mktg. of Chemicals
S.I.C.: 5169

GAF (Osterreich) GmbH **(1)**
Lutzowgasse 12-14 Postfach 119, A-1130
Vienna, Austria
Tel.: 010-43-222-947614
Mktg. of Chemicals
S.I.C.: 5169

GAF (Singapore) Pte. Ltd. **(1)**
8 N03-17 Chia Ping Rd. Jurong Industrial,
Singapore, 2261, Singapore
Tel.: 65-2612355
Mktg. of Chemicals
S.I.C.: 5169

GAF South Africa (Pty.), Ltd. **(1)**
P.O. Box 78838
Sandton, 2146, South Africa
Tel.: 27-11-7837465
Mktg. of Chemicals
S.I.C.: 5169

GAF Sucursal en Espana **(1)**
Loreto, 42 Entlo
Barcelona, 080 29, Spain
Tel.: 1-34-3 239-9185
Mktg. of Chemicals
S.I.C.: 5169

GAF (Switzerland) AG **(1)**
Gubelstrasse II 6300
Zug, Switzerland
Tel.: 41-42-217133
Mktg. of Chemicals
S.I.C.: 5169

GAI CONSULTANTS, INC.
570 Beatty Rd.
Monroeville, PA 15146
Tel.: 412-856-6400 **PA**
Fax: 412-856-4970
Year Founded: 1958
Approx.Sls.: $13,000,000
Emp.: 257
Consulting Services In All Areas of Civil, Environmental & Geotechnical Engineering Including Hydrology, Hydraulics, Solid & Hazardous Waste Management, Coastal & Land Use Planning, Site Development, Urban Engineering, Archaeology & Cultural Resources
S.I.C.: 8711; 8731
Anthony M. DiGioia, Jr. *(Pres.)*
Richard E. Gray *(Sr. V.P.)*
Thomas D. Donovan *(V.P.)*
John A. Hribar *(V.P.)*
Henry A. Salver *(V.P.-Corp. Devel.)*
Alfred C. Olson, Jr. *(Controller)*
Arlene G. Irwin *(Exec. Sec.)*
Raymond J. Giarrusso *(Sec. & Treas.)*
Mary Beth Pepper *(Dir.-Corp. Communication)*
R. Steven Atkins *(Mgr.-Computer Services)*
Charles R. Rogers *(Mgr.-Admin. Services)*
Barbara E. Reid *(Librarian)*
Principal(s):
Anthony M. DiGioia, Jr.
Lawrence R. Dodds
Thomas D. Donovan
Raymond J. Giarrusso
Richard E. Gray
John A. Hribar
Herbert M. Mandel
James E. Niece
Henry A. Salver
John W. Spires

No. of U.S. Offices: 5

Computer Systems/Hardware:
DEC VAX 11/730; CADD Systems; PC ATclass Micor-computers; Apple MacIntosch

Outside Service Firm(s):

R.S. Markovitz & Co., P.C.*(Auditors)*
Pittsburgh, PA

Liberty Insurance Co.*(Commercial Insurance Carrier)*
Mt. Lebanon, PA

Blue Cross of Western Pennsylvania*(Group Insurer)*
One Smithfield St.
Pittsburgh, PA 15222
Tel.: 1-800-242-6425

Rothman & Gordon*(Legal Firm)*
Pittsburgh, PA

Mellon Bank, N.A.*(Major Banking Relationship)*
Monroeville, PA

Griffith & Bennett*(Pension Manager)*
Pittsburgh, PA

Branches:

GAI Consultants, Inc. **(1)**
117 Airports N. Office Park
Fort Wayne, IN 46825
Tel.: 219-489-2900
Dr. James M. King *(Pres.)*

GAI Consultants, Inc. **(1)**
4715-C MacCorkle Ave., S.E.
Charleston, WV 25304
Tel.: 304-925-7730
Fax: 304-925-7776
Emp.: 15
Highway & Bridge Construction Projects
S.I.C.: 1622
Dana L. Burns *(Mgr.)*

GAI Consultants, Inc. **(1)**
300 Birchfield Dr., Ste. 301
Mount Laurel, NJ 08054
Tel.: 609-273-6585
Fax: 609-273-0050
Highway & Bridge Construction
S.I.C.: 1622
Raymond H. Aub *(Mgr.-Eastern Reg.)*

Subsidiaries:

GAI Construction Monitoring Services, Inc. **(1)**
570 Beatty Rd.
Monroeville, PA 15146
Tel.: 414-856-6400
Fax: 412-856-6400
Emp.: 20
Construction Monitoring Expertise In Highway & Bridge Construction Projects
S.I.C.: 1622
Lawrence R. Dodds *(Mgr.)*

GAI Construction Services, Inc. **(1)**
300 Birchfield Dr., Ste. 301
Mount Laurel, NJ 08054
Tel.: 609-273-6585
Fax: 609-273-0050
Emp.: 30
Construction Monitoring Expertise In Highway & Bridge Construction Projects
S.I.C.: 1622
Raymond H. Aub *(Dir.-Eastern Reg.)*

GAI Consultants-NC, Inc. **(1)**
401 Glenwood Ave.
Raleigh, NC 27603
Tel.: 919-828-0801
Fax: 919-833-2784
Emp.: 25
Consulting Services In Geotechnical & Civil-Structural Engineering With Emphasis On Highway & Bridge Design
S.I.C.: 1622
John W. Spires, Jr. *(Pres.)*

GAI Consultants-Southeast, Inc. **(1)**
1833 Edgewater Dr.
Orlando, FL 32804
Tel.: 407-423-8398
Fax: 407-843-1070
Emp.: 40
Consulting Services In Civil, Traffic & Structural Engineering & Construction Monitoring
S.I.C.: 8711
Gary M. DeJidas *(Pres.)*

GES INC.
Hwy. One Lee Shopping Center
Marianna, AR 72360
Mailing Address:
P.O. Box 649
Marianna, AR 72360
Tel.: 501-295-2484 **AR**
Fax: 501-295-3551
Year Founded: 1962
Approx.Sls.: $35,000,000
Emp.: 300
Fiscal Year-end: 12/31/91
Retail Grocery Stores: Food Giant
S.I.C.: 5411
Oral W. Edwards *(Chm. Bd. & Pres.)*
Steve Edwards *(Chief Oper. Officer & V.P.)*
W. Frank Morledge *(Gen. Counsel)*
Debbie Edwards *(Dir.-Personnel & Corp. Video Systems)*
Danny Donaldson *(Supvr.-Mngmt.)*
Principal(s):
Oral W. Edwards
Steve Edwards

No. of Mfg. Plants/Facilities: 7

Computer Systems/Hardware:
IBM PC

Outside Service Firm(s):

Jack R. Gentry, CPA*(Auditors)*
Marianna, AR

Planters Bank & Trust*(Major Banking Relationship)*
Forrest City, AR

GF INDUSTRIES, INC.
930 98th Ave.
Oakland, CA 94603
Tel.: 510-568-0711
Holding Co.
S.I.C.: 6719; 6512; 2052
Wilfred Uytengsu *(Pres.)*
Michael Roche *(Chief Fin. Officer)*
Marvin Bennett *(Controller)*
Linda Kilgore *(Admin. Asst.)*

Outside Service Firm(s):

Deloitte & Touche*(Auditors)*
50 Fremont St.
San Francisco, CA 94105-2230
Tel.: 415-393-4300
Fax: 415-227-0452

Wells Fargo Bank*(Major Banking Relationship)*
420 Montgomery St.
San Francisco, CA 94104

Subsidiaries:

GF Properties, Inc. **(1)**
930 98th Ave.
Oakland, CA 94603
Tel.: 510-568-0713
Real Estate
S.I.C.: 6512

Sunshine Biscuits, Inc. **(1)**
100 Woodbridge Center Dr.
Woodbridge, NJ 07095-1196
Tel.: 908-855-4000
Tel.: 800-242-7449 (100%)
Fax: 908-855-2944
Approx.Sls.: $750,000,000
Emp.: 3,998
Fiscal Year-end: 3/31/92
Export
Computer Systems/Hardware:
Unisys A 16
Cookies & Crackers
S.I.C.: 2052
Wilfred Uytengsu *(Chm. & Chief Exec. Officer)*
Arthur G. Murray *(Pres. & Chief Oper. Officer)*
Bernard Zitomer *(V.P.-Pur.)*
John M. Mayhew *(V.P.-Sls.)*
Gerald P. Jantzi *(V.P.-Mktg.)*
Alan R. Bird *(V.P.-Engrng.)*
Clement A. Calabrese *(V.P.-Retail Sls.)*
Robert J. Matson *(V.P.-Information Systems)*
Joseph V. Somers *(V.P.-Technical Services)*
Joseph Taranto *(V.P.-Foodservice & Ingredient Prods. Div.)*
Stephen R. Barbieri *(Sec. & Legal Counsel)*
Alexander Nichols *(Dir.-Adv. & Mktg. Services)*
James D. Ferber *(Dir.-Human Resources)*
Joseph M. Talmage *(Controller)*

Subsidiaries:

Blue Bell Potato Chip Co. **(2)**
100 N.E. Farragut St.
Portland, OR 97211
Tel.: 503-289-8851
Mfr. & Mktg. Potato Chips
S.I.C.: 2096

Sunshine/Salerno (IL) **(2)**
7777 N. Caldwell Ave.
Niles, IL 60648
Tel.: 708-967-6200
Fax: 708-967-1411
Approx.Sls.: $60,000,000
Emp.: 450
Fiscal Year-end: 3/31/91
Import
Computer Systems/Hardware:
Unisys; IBM; AS400
Cookie Products
S.I.C.: 2052
Wilfred Uytengsu *(Chm. & Chief Exec. Officer)*

Sunshine/Salerno, Inc. (NJ) **(2)**
P.O. Box 7
Sayreville, NJ 08872
Tel.: 908-254-2000
Emp.: 1,310
Manufacturer & Distributor of Cookies & Crackers
S.I.C.: 5141; 2052
Raymond Baxter *(Pres.)*
Tom J. Bartus *(V.P.-Opers.)*
Vickie Lamb *(Mgr.-Product)*

GF OFFICE FURNITURE LTD.
525 Steam Plant Rd.
Gallatin, TN 37066
Mailing Address:
P.O. Box 1918,
Gallatin, TN 37066
Tel.: 615-452-9120
Tel.: 800-624-9751 **OH**
Telex: 982474
Fax: 615-451-0820
Year Founded: 1902
Assets: $38,000,000
Liabilities: $33,000,000
Net Worth: $5,000,000
Approx.Sls.: $100,000,000
Emp.: 850
Fiscal Year-end: 12/31/90
Export
Mfr. of Metal & Wood Office Furniture & Systems
S.I.C.: 2522; 2521
Carl Zemenick *(Pres. & Chief Exec. & Chief Oper. Officer)*
Ronald W. Myers *(V.P.-Fin. & Admin. & Chief Fin. Officer)*
James Hildebrand *(V.P.-Sls. & Mktg.)*
James Barrows *(Dir.-Mktg.)*
Brian Good *(Dir.-Mfg.)*
Mike Griffin *(Dir.-Matls. & Human Resources)*
Van Walkenberg *(Dir.-Mngmt. Information Systems)*
Ed Zeock *(Dir.-Acctg.)*

Computer Systems/Hardware:
NEC/IBM

Subsidiary:

GF Office Furniture **(1)**
4944 Belmont Ave.
Youngstown, OH 44501
Tel.: 216-759-8888 (100%)
Approx.Sls.: $160,000,000
Emp.: 2,500
S.I.C.: 2522
Carl Zemenick *(Pres.)*
Ronald Myers *(V.P.-Fin. & Admin.)*
James Hildebrand *(V.P.-Sls. & Mktg.)*

GF Office Furniture Ltd.—(Continued)

Mike Griffin *(Dir.-Matls. & Human Resources)*

GFA BRANDS, INC.
211 Knickerbocker Rd.
Cresskill, NJ 07626
Mailing Address:
P.O. Box 397,
Cresskill, NJ 07626-0512
Tel.: 201-568-9300 **OH**
Fax: 201-568-6374
Year Founded: 1973
Approx.Sls.: $27,000,000
Emp.: 14
Fiscal Year-end: 12/31/91
Export
Sales & Marketing of Heart Beat Spread, Cheese, Salad Dressings & Mayonnaise, H-O Cereals, Mrs. Fanning's Pickles, Nucoa Margarine, Spin Blend Dressing & Smart Beat Foods
S.I.C.: 5149
Robert M. Harris *(Chm. Bd. & Chief Exec. Officer)*
James Harris *(Pres. & Chief Operating Officer)*
Cecily Harris *(Sec. & Treas.)*
W. Keane *(Controller)*
Howard Seiferas *(Dir.-Admin./Opers.)*
Peter Dray *(Mgr.-Mfg.)*

Outside Service Firm(s):

R. D. Hunter*(Auditors)*
Paramus, NJ

Schottenstein, Zox & Dunn*(Legal Firm)*
41 S. High St.
Columbus, OH 43215
Tel.: 614-221-3211

Midlantic National Bank*(Major Banking Relationship)*
Cresskill, NJ

G.I. JOE'S INC.
9805 Boeckman Rd.
Wilsonville, OR 97070
Tel.: 503-682-2242
Fax: 503-682-7200
Year Founded: 1982
Approx.Sls.: $133,000,000
Emp.: 900
Chain of Sporting Goods Stores
S.I.C.: 5311
David Orkney *(Pres.)*
Norman Daniels *(V.P.)*
Duane Mellen *(V.P.)*
Wayne Jackson *(Treas. & Sec.)*

G.L. ADVERTISING
25 Aladin Ave.
Dumont, NJ 07628
Tel.: 201-387-0360
Year Founded: 1987
Approx.Billings: $300,000,000
Emp.: 4
Health Care/Beauty Products
Dan Palmon *(Chm. Bd.)*
Reuven Gershoni *(Pres.)*
Sue Burickson *(Exec. V.P.)*
Sara McPherson *(Corp. Sec.)*

GNWC WIRE, CABLE & NETWORK PRODUCERS
1401 Brook Drive
Downers Grove, IL 60515
Tel.: 708-627-1777
Fax: 708-932-4342
Year Founded: 1983
Approx.Sls.: $50,000,000
Emp.: 200
Fiscal Year-end: 12/31/90
Distr. of Wire & Cable Prods.
S.I.C.: 3496
Jim Dellaripa *(Pres.)*
Tom Katsoulis *(Chief Exec. Officer)*
David Bemoras *(V.P.)*
Dianna Soust *(V.P. & Controller)*
Robert Bessler Jr. *(Dir.-Opers.)*
Mark Winkel *(Dir.-Pur.)*

GPD LIMITED
6753 Jones Mill Ct.
Norcross, GA 30092
Tel.: 404-840-7272
Fax: 404-840-7211
Wholesale Distributor of Compressor & Refrigeration Equipment
S.I.C.: 5084
John Dickerson *(Pres.)*
John Lange *(Sls. Mgr.-Whlse.)*

Outside Service Firm(s):

Ernst & Young*(Auditors)*
Calumet City, IL

Beverly Bank*(Major Banking Relationship)*
Calumet City, IL

GS&B
ADVERTISING

GS&B-LINTAS ADVERTISING
4104 Aurora St.
Coral Gables, FL 33146
Tel.: 305-444-4221 **FL**
Fax: 305-444-6327
Year Founded: 1982
Approx.Billings: $36,800,000
Emp.: 58
Retail & Hispanic Advertising Agency
S.I.C.: 7311
Al Garcia-Serra *(Chm. & Chief Exec. Officer)*
Jose Luis Castro *(Exec. V.P. & New Business Contact)*
Eduardo del Rivero *(Exec. V.P.-Acct. Services)*
Dennis Dunkelberger *(V.P. & Dir.-Caribbean)*
Olga Palma-Fernandez *(V.P.- Fin.)*
Luis G. Figueras *(V.P.- Consumer Promos./Pub. Rels.)*
K. Dickson *(Dir.- Human Resources)*
O. Chinea *(Admin. Asst.)*

Computer Systems/Hardware:
AS 400

GSC ENTERPRISES, INC.
130 Hillcrest Dr.
Sulphur Springs, TX 75482
Mailing Address:
P.O. Box 638
Sulphur Springs, TX 75482
Tel.: 903-885-7621
Tel.: 800-231-1938 **TX**
Fax: 903-885-6928
Year Founded: 1947
Assets: $95,668,279
Liabilities: $66,383,459
Net Worth: $29,284,820
Approx.Sls.: $623,109,597
Emp.: 1,500
Fiscal Year-end: 12/31/89
Export
Wholesale Food Products
S.I.C.: 5141; 5191
Kenneth McKenzie *(Chm. Bd.)*
Michael K. McKenzie *(Pres. & Chief Exec. Officer)*
Mike Mize *(V.P.-Corp. Plng. & Devel., Chief Fin. Officer, Sec. & Treas.)*
Travis Owens *(V.P.-Opers.)*

Computer Systems/Hardware:
IBM

Outside Service Firm(s):

Thomas & Thomas*(Auditors)*
Texarkana, AR

W.T. Allison, II*(Legal Firm)*
Dallas, TX

NationsBank Texas*(Major Banking Relationship)*
901 Main St., 16th Fl.
Dallas, TX 75202
Tel.: 214-922-5000

Branches:

GSC Distributing of Abilene **(1)**
841 Oak St.
Abilene, TX 79602
Tel.: 915-672-5694
Distribution Location for Food Products
S.I.C.: 5141
Glenn Carter *(Mgr.)*

GSC Distributing of Austin **(1)**
2832 M.L.K. Dr.
Austin, TX 78702
Tel.: 512-478-2548
Distribution Location for Food Products
S.I.C.: 5141
Tracy Stevens *(Mgr.)*

GSC Distributing of Corpus Christi **(1)**
711 Oak Park Ave.
Corpus Christi, TX 78408
Tel.: 512-887-9588
Distribution Location for Food Products
S.I.C.: 5141
Phillip Dromgoole *(Mgr.)*

GSC Distributing of Dallas **(1)**
1135 So. Lamar St.
Dallas, TX 75215
Tel.: 214-426-1755
Distribution Location for Food Products
S.I.C.: 5141
Kent Bolding *(Mgr.)*

GSC Distribution of Houston **(1)**
801 Service St.
Houston, TX 77009
Tel.: 713-864-4285
Wholesale Food Club
S.I.C.: 5411
Ray Janz *(Mgr.)*

GSC Distributing of Ft. Worth **(1)**
500 E. Rosedale
Fort Worth, TX 76104
Tel.: 817-429-0007
Distribution Location for Food Products
S.I.C.: 5141
Reg Arnold *(Mgr.)*

GSC Distributing of Houston **(1)**
801 Service Rd.
Houston, TX 70009
Tel.: 713-864-4285
Distribution Location for Food Products
S.I.C.: 5141
Ray Janz *(Mgr.)*

GSC Distributing of San Angelo **(1)**
1515 N. Chadbourne
San Angelo, TX 76903
Tel.: 915-655-6348
Distribution Location for Food Products
S.I.C.: 5141
Curtis Day *(Mgr.)*

GSC Distributing of Tyler **(1)**
2400 E. Gentry Pkwy.
Tyler, TX 75710
Tel.: 903-592-4215
Distribution Location for Food Products
S.I.C.: 5141
Billy Key *(Mgr.)*

GSC Distributing of Waco **(1)**
1809 Summer Ave.
Waco, TX 76708
Tel.: 817-756-5321
Distribution Location for Food Products
S.I.C.: 5141

GSC Distributing of Wichita Falls **(1)**
600 Ohio St.
Wichita Falls, TX 76301
Tel.: 817-723-6617
Distribution Location for Food Products
S.I.C.: 5141
G.B. Ritchie *(Mgr.)*

Joykist/GSC Distributing **(1)**
719 S. Santa Rosa
San Antonio, TX 78204
Tel.: 210-225-2663
Candy Distributors
S.I.C.: 5441
Ronnie Mitchell *(Mgr.)*

Divisions:

Consolidated Wholesale Company Division **(1)**
1740 W. Main St.
Oklahoma City, OK 73126
Tel.: 405-232-5593
Wholesale Food Products
S.I.C.: 5141
Jules J. Lehman *(Pres.)*
Elmer E. Wolf *(V.P.)*
William H. Wolf *(Mgr.-Sls.)*
Kenneth R. Cochran *(Mgr.-Warehouse)*
Robert D. Timmons *(Computer Analyst)*
H. Randall Shafer *(Buyer)*

Fidelity Express Money Order Company Division **(1)**
130 Hillcrest Dr.
Sulphur Springs, TX 75482
Tel.: 903-885-1283
Money Order Company
S.I.C.: 6099
Kerry Law *(Gen. Mgr.)*
Pat Odom *(Office Mgr.)*
Robert Gage *(Dir.-Sls.)*

GSC Distributing Companies Division **(1)**
942 Main St.
Sulphur Springs, TX 75482
Tel.: 800-231-1938
Distributors of Groceries, Tobacco & Candy
S.I.C.: 5141
Steve Shing *(Pres.)*
Ron Fergurson *(Controller)*
Mike Bain *(V.P.-Opers.)*
Mike Nottingham *(Mgr.-Sls.)*
Chad Bolton *(Mgr.-Data Processing)*

Grocery Supply Company Division **(1)**
130 Hillcrest Dr.
Sulphur Springs, TX 75482
Tel.: 903-885-7621
Wholesale Grocery Distributor
S.I.C.: 5141
Malcolm Kirkland *(Pres.)*
Jerry Gillem *(V.P.-Fin.)*
Dick Walker *(V.P.-Opers.)*
Paul Tipping *(V.P.-Pur.)*
John McCrary *(V.P.-Sls.)*
Theresa Collins *(Mgr.-Personnel)*
Jim Goggans *(Mgr.-Data Processing)*

Sweeney & Company Division **(1)**
2330 Roosevelt
San Antonio, TX 78210
Tel.: 210-533-1281
Grocery Warehouse
S.I.C.: 5141
Jim Davis *(Pres.)*
Gary Gresham *(V.P.-Fin.)*
Larry Morris *(V.P.-Opers.)*
Dan Biela *(Mgr.-Pur.)*
Henry Graeber *(Mgr.-Personnel)*
Jerry Donahoe *(Mgr.-Data Processing)*

GSC ENTERPRISES, INC.
737 N. Michigan Ave., Ste. 1200
Chicago, IL 60611
Tel.: 312-751-2990 **DE**
Fax: 312-751-2990, Ext. 247
Approx.Sls.: $480,000,000
Emp.: 1,100
Bank Holding Company
S.I.C.: 6712
Clyde W. Engle *(Chm. Bd., Pres. & Treas.)*
Amy Miller *(Chief Oper. Officer)*
W.N. Weaver, Jr. *(Sec.)*

Outside Service Firm(s):

Coronet Insurance Company*(Group Insurer)*
Chicago, IL

Subsidiaries:

Bank of Lincolnwood **(1)**
4433 W. Touhy Ave.
Lincolnwood, IL 60646
Tel.: 708-675-2800
Emp.: 125
Banking
S.I.C.: 6022
James L. Hamilton *(Pres.)*

Toulin Inc. **(1)**
625 N. Michigan
Chicago, IL 60611
Tel.: 312-751-2990
Roger Weston *(Pres.)*

GSD&M

GSD&M
(Gurasich, Spence, Darilek & McClure)
1250 Capital of Texas Hwy., Ste. 400
Austin, TX 78746
Tel.: 512-327-8810
Fax: 512-327-1775
Year Founded: 1971
Approx.Billings: $210,000,000
Emp.: 226
Steve Gurasich *(Chm.)*
Roy Spence *(Pres.)*
Bonnie Hunter *(Sr. V.P., Admin.)*
Marty Urbanovsky *(Sr. V.P., Fin.)*
Raoul Rodriguez *(Sr. V.P., Dir.-Hispanic Services)*
Joy Matheny *(Telecommunications)*

GSP MARKETING SERVICES, INC.
320 W. Ohio
Chicago, IL 60606
Tel.: 312-944-3000
Fax: 312-944-8587
Year Founded: 1978
Approx.Billings: $42,000,000
Emp.: 53
Direct Mktg.
Richard Grunsten *(Pres.)*
Michael Zarembra *(Exec. V.P.)*
Jim Clark *(V.P.)*

GWP, INC.
9080 Santa Monica Blvd.
Los Angeles, CA 90069
Tel.: 310-278-4900
Fax: 310-858-6842
Year Founded: 1963
Approx.Sls.: $62,000,000
Emp.: 58
Fiscal Year-end: 12/31/90
Operator & Owner of Real Estate, GWP, Inc., Tri-Palm Estates; Group 3 Design
S.I.C.: 6531
Andrew E. Stevens *(Chm. Bd., Pres., Mktg. & Pub. Rel. Dir.)*
Steve Kipnis *(V.P.-Adv. & Sls. Dir.)*
Glenn Stevens *(V.P.)*
Al Chicketti *(Gen. Mgr. & Mktg. Mgr.)*
Evelyn Bondoc *(Controller/Computer Operations)*
Kathy Walton *(Personnel Dir. & Admin. Office Mgr.)*

Subsidiaries:

Group 3 Design **(1)**
9080 Santa Monica Blvd.
Los Angeles, CA 90069
Tel.: 310-278-4900
Kathy Walton *(Admin.)*

Tri-Palm Estate **(1)**
32700 Desert Moon Dr.
Thousand Palms, CA 92276
Tel.: 619-343-3497
Fax: 619-343-2951
Mobile Home Community
S.I.C.: 6531
Barbara Schott *(Dir. of Admin.)*

GABBERT'S, INC.
3501 Galleria
Minneapolis, MN 55435
Tel.: 612-927-1500
Tel.: 612-828-8500
Fax: 612-828-8503
Fax: 612-927-1555
Year Founded: 1947
Approx.Sls.: $65,000,000
Emp.: 650
Retail Home Furnishings
S.I.C.: 5712
James D. Gabbert *(Chm. Bd., Pres. & Chief Exec. Officer)*
Gary Pedersen *(Chief Fin. Officer)*
Lois Turem *(Sec.)*

Outside Service Firm(s):

KPMG Peat Marwick*(Auditors)*
4200 Norwest Center, 90 S. 7th St.
Minneapolis, MN 55402
Tel.: 612-341-2222

First Bank Minneapolis*(Major Banking Relationship)*
Minneapolis, MN

THE GAGE COMPANY
3000 Liberty Ave.
Pittsburgh, PA 15201
Tel.: 412-471-6600
Fax: 412-255-6953
Year Founded: 1892
Approx.Sls.: $150,000,000
Emp.: 520
Fiscal Year-end: 12/31/90
Wholesaler of Pipes, Valves, Fittings, Abrasives, Fasteners, Power Transmission Products, Tools, Pumps, Compressors & Machinery , Plumbing & Heating Supplies
S.I.C.: 5085
Robert A. Chute *(Chm. Bd., & Chief Exec. Officer)*
G.A. Van Luven *(Vice Chm., Chief Fin. Officer, Treas. & Controller)*
Lloyd H. Morgan *(Pres. & Chief Oper. Officer)*
Principal(s):
G.A. Van Luven

Computer Systems/Hardware:
IBM AS 400

Outside Service Firm(s):

KPMG Peat Marwick*(Auditors)*
1 Mellon Bank Ctr.
Pittsburgh, PA 15219
Tel.: 412-391-9710

Branch:

Westco Industrial **(1)**
160 Target Circle
Bangor, ME 04401
Tel.: 207-945-0231
Distribute Industrial Supplies
S.I.C.: 5074; 5085
Walt Pieschke *(Gen. Mgr.)*

Subsidiary:

Westco Industrial Corporation **(1)**
145 Presumpscott
Portland, ME 04013
Tel.: 207-774-5812
Distribute Industrial Supplies
S.I.C.: 5074; 5085
Dan Buckley *(Gen. Mgr.)*

GAGE MARKETING GROUP
10000 Highway 55
Minneapolis, MN 55441-6365
Tel.: 612-595-3800
Fax: 612-831-8241
Approx.Billings: $120,000,000
Emp.: 1500
Edwin C. Gage *(Chm. & Chief Exec. Officer)*
Kenneth Gudorf *(Vice Chm.)*
Chris Boyle *(Pres., Adistra Corp.)*
James K. Pfleider *(Pres., Event Mktg. & Travel)*
Joseph R. Thomas *(Pres., Promo. Mngmt. Co.)*
G.A. Corky Hall *(Exec. V.P., Mktg. Communications)*
John C. Kalenberg *(Exec. V.P., Mktg. Services)*
Roberta Dircks *(V.P., Controller)*
Robert H. Sondag *(V.P., Fin. & Admin.)*
Joseph Potocki *(Sr. Exec.)*

GAGGENAU USA CORPORATION
425 University Ave.
Norwood, MA 02062
Tel.: 617-255-1766
Fax: 617-769-2212
Year Founded: 1980
Approx.Sls.: $17,000,000
Emp.: 15
Import
Mfr. of Built-In Ovens & Electrical Appliances; Plumbing Fittings & Supplies
S.I.C.: 5064; 5074
R.H. Rhinerson *(Pres.)*
Thomas Cutler *(V.P.)*
Peter Tarr *(Sec.)*

GAI'S SEATTLE FRENCH BAKING CO., INC.
2006 Weller St.
Seattle, WA 98144
Mailing Address:
P.O. Box 24327
Seattle, WA 98124
Tel.: 206-322-0931
Fax: 206-726-7555
Year Founded: 1930
Emp.: 575
Bread, Buns, Sweet Goods & Donuts
S.I.C.: 2051; 2052
Phillip H. Gai *(Chm. Bd.)*
Lawrence McDonald *(Pres. & Chief Exec. Officer)*
Donald P. Gai *(V.P. & Sec.)*

Outside Service Firm(s):

Sanborn & Associates, Inc.*(Auditors)*
Seattle, WA

Karr Tuttle & Koch*(Legal Firm)*
Seattle, WA

Seattle First National Bank*(Major Banking Relationship)*
701 Fifth Avenue
Seattle, WA 98104
Tel.: 206-358-3035

Subsidiary:

Langendorf Baking Company Of Seattle, Inc. **(1)**
2901 6th Ave., S.
Seattle, WA 98134
Tel.: 206-682-2244
Wholesale Bakery
S.I.C.: 2051; 2052
Phillip Gai *(Chm. Bd.)*
Tom Dagg *(V.P. & G.M.)*

GALARDI GROUP, INC.
4440 Von Karman
Newport Beach, CA 92660
Tel.: 714-752-5800
Fax: 714-851-2618
Year Founded: 1960
Approx.Sls.: $122,000,000
Emp.: 100
Fiscal Fast-end: 12/31/92
Retail Fast Food
S.I.C.: 5812
John N. Galardi *(Chm. Bd.)*
D. Tase *(Pres.-Wienerschnitzel Div. & Orig. Hamburger Stand)*
Alan B. Fuller *(Treas.)*
Tom Amberger *(Dir.-Mktg.)*

Computer Systems/Hardware:
IBM 400

R. J. GALLAGHER CO.
P.O. Box 20710
Houston, TX 77225
Tel.: 713-748-4501
Telex: 794377
Fax: 713-478-4510
Assets: $15,000,000
Earnings: $40,000,000
Net Worth: $15,000,000
Approx.Sls.: $650,000,000
Emp.: 175
Fiscal Year-end: 11/30/91
Wholesale Stainless Steel Metal Goods; Distribute Pipe, Tubing, Fittings, Valves & Flanges
S.I.C.: 5051; 5085; 5072
Robert J. Gallagher, Jr. *(Pres.)*
Michael Boyle *(Exec. V.P.)*
Don Callegari *(V.P.-Fin. & Acting Treas.)*
Ken Parks *(Mgr.-Pur.)*

Outside Service Firm(s):

Riquelny & Clesi*(Auditors)*
Houston, TX

Aetna Life & Casualty*(Commercial Insurance Carrier)*
151 Farmington Avenue
Hartford, CT 06156
Tel.: 203-273-2128
Fax: 203-729-4295

Lincoln National Life Insurance Co.*(Group Insurer)*
PO Box 208, 1300 S. Clinton
Fort Wayne, IN 46801
Tel.: 219-455-2926
Fax: 219-455-7619

Hoover, Bax & Shearer*(Legal Firm)*
Houston, TX

Texas Commerce Bank*(Major Banking Relationship)*
600 Travis Street, Suite 1150
Houston, TX 77002
Tel.: 713-236-4865

GALLAGHER-KAISER CORP.
13710 Mt. Elliot
Detroit, MI 48212
Tel.: 313-368-3100
Fax: 313-368-3109
Approx.Sls.: $105,000,000
Emp.: 125
Designs, Manfactures & Installs Paint Finishing Systems & Equipment, Ventilation Systems, Dust Collection Equipment, Acoustical Panel Systems
S.I.C.: 3564; 3567; 3296
Joseph P. Kaiser, Jr. *(Chm.)*
R. S. Kaiser *(Pres.)*
Jim McClean *(Mgr.-Engrng.)*

Outside Service Firm(s):

Plante & Moran*(Auditors)*
Southfield, MI

Stark, Reagan & Finnerty*(Legal Firm)*
Troy, MI
Tel.: 313-641-3955

Manufacturers National Bank N.A.*(Major Banking Relationship)*
38th Fl., 100 Renaissance Center
Detroit, MI 48243
Tel.: 313-222-4227

E & J GALLO WINERY
600 Yosemite Blvd.
Modesto, CA 95354
Mailing Address:
P.O. Box 1130
Modesto, CA 95353
Tel.: 209-579-3111
Fax: 209-579-3192
Year Founded: 1933
Approx.Sls.: $1,000,000,000
Emp.: 3,000
Export

E & J Gallo Winery—(Continued)

Production & Distribution of Wine & Wine Products
S.I.C.: 5182; 0172; 2084
Ernest Gallo *(Chm. Bd.)*
Julio Gallo *(Pres.)*
Robin W. Gould *(Chief Fin. Officer)*
A. P. Fenderson *(Exec. V.P.-Mktg.)*
Jack Dickman *(V.P. & Asst. Treas.)*
Gary Ippolito *(V.P.-Natl. Sls.)*
Sue McClelland *(V.P.-Media)*
Louis Friedman *(Treas.)*
Principal(s):
Ernest Gallo
Julio Gallo

Computer Systems/Hardware:
IBM System 36

Outside Service Firm(s):

Travelers Insurance Co.*(Pension Manager)*
1 Tower Square
Hartford, CT 06183
Tel.: 203-222-7821
Fax: 203-222-7813

Division:

Bartles & Jaymes **(1)**
600 Yosemite Blvd.
Modesto, CA 95354
Tel.: 209-579-3111
Telex: 209-579-6647
Fax: 209-579-4467
Export
Mfr. Wine Coolers
S.I.C.: 2084
Ernest Gallo *(Chm. Bd.)*
Julio Gallo *(Pres.)*
Sue McClelland *(V.P.-Media)*
Dan Solomon *(Communications Dir.)*

Affiliate:

Carlo Rossi Vineyards **(1)**
P.O. Box 1130
Modesto, CA 95353
Tel.: 209-579-3161
Emp.: 45
Winery
S.I.C.: 2084
Carlo Rossi *(Pres. & Gen. Mgr.)*
A.P. Fenderson *(Exec. V.P.-Mktg.)*

GAME TIME, INC.
150 Gametime Dr.
Fort Payne, AL 35967
Mailing Address:
P.O. Box 121
Fort Payne, AL 35967
Tel.: 205-845-5610 **AL**
Fax: 205-845-2649
Year Founded: 1929
Approx.Sls.: $30,000,000
Emp.: 300
Import Export
Mfr. Playground & Recreation Equipmemt;Wood Buildings, Shelters, Site Furnishings
S.I.C.: 2531; 3449; 3949; 2452
Ross D. Siragusa, Jr. *(Pres.)*
John R. Siragusa *(Exec. V.P. & Sec.)*
S. Scott Grupp *(V.P.)*
Richard D. Siragusa *(V.P.)*
Rick Kuhn *(Controller)*
Jim Collins *(Dir.-Personnel)*
Tom Mollet *(Dir.-Mktg.)*
Lance Benzing *(Mgr.-Pur.)*
Howell Helton *(Mgr.-Information Services)*
Mike McWilliams *(Mgr.-Quality Control)*
Bobby Starling *(Mgr.-Plant)*
L.J. Tschetter *(Mgr.-Exports)*
Glenda McDow *(Mktg. Coord.)*

Outside Service Firm(s):

Altschuler, Melvoin & Glasser*(Auditors)*
30 S. Wecker Dr.
Chicago, IL 60606
Tel.: 312-207-2800

Ross & Hardies*(Legal Firm)*
1 IBM Plaza
Chicago, IL 60611
Tel.: 312-467-9300

LaSalle National Bank*(Major Banking Relationship)*
135 S. LaSalle St., Rm.260
Chicago, IL 60603

GAMMA ONE, INC.
12 Corporate Dr.
North Haven, CT 06473
Tel.: 203-234-0440
Fax: 203-234-2015
Year Founded: 1980
Sales Range: $10-19 Million
Emp.: 140
Offset Color Separations
S.I.C.: 2796
David Pfeifer *(Pres.)*
Bryon J. Ramseyer *(Exec. V.P.)*
Kieran J. Doherty *(V.P.)*
Veronica Buczynski *(Controller)*

Outside Service Firm(s):

Levitsky & Berney*(Auditors)*
Woodbridge, CT

Sachs, Berman, Rashba & Shure*(Legal Firm)*
New Haven, CT

Union Trust*(Major Banking Relationship)*
New Haven, CT

GANAHL LUMBER COMPANY
1220 E. Ball Rd.
Anaheim, CA 92805-5993
Tel.: 714-772-5444
Fax: 714-772-0639
Approx.Sls.: $41,000,000
Emp.: 350
Wholesale & Retail Lumber, Building Materials & Hardware; Manufacture Millwork
S.I.C.: 2431; 5031; 5039; 5211
Peter Ganahl *(Pres.)*
Jim Taft *(Gen. Mgr.)*
John Ganahl *(Controller)*
Principal(s):
Peter Ganahl

Outside Service Firm(s):

McGladrey & Pullen*(Auditors)*
222 S. Harbor Blvd. #800
Anaheim, CA 92815

Bank of America NT&SA*(Major Banking Relationship)*
Anaheim, CA

GANNETT FLEMING AFFILIATES, INC.
P.O. Box 67100,
Harrisburg, PA 17106-7100
Tel.: 717-763-7211 **DE**
Fax: 717-763-8150
Year Founded: 1915
Approx.Sls.: $60,000,000
Emp.: 1,100
Fiscal Year-end: 12/31/88
Engineering Service In The Following Areas: Site Development, Building Rehabilitation, Highways & Traffic Structures, Mass Transit, Railroads, Valuation & Public Utility Rate Studies, Water Source & Treatment, Water Transmission & Pumping, Dams, Flood Protection, Environmental Quality Management, Wastewater & Treatment & Collection, Solid Waste & Hazardous Waste
S.I.C.: 8711
Maurice A. Wadsworth *(Chm. & Pres.)*
Walter K. Morris *(Sr. V.P.-Water Resources & Asst. Sec.)*
Harold T. Waddington *(Sr. V.P.-Valuation, Rates & Sec.)*
John E. Waters *(Sr. V.P.-Environment)*
Robert J. Dietz *(V.P.)*
Ronald J. Drnevich *(V.P.-Transportation)*
Lynn E. Knepp *(Controller)*
Walter P. Buehler *(Dir.-Personnel)*

No. of U.S. Offices: 24
No. of Foreign Offices: 2

Outside Service Firm(s):

Stambaugh, Dorgan & Co.*(Auditors)*
York, PA

Citibank N.A.*(International Bank Affiliate)*
Corporate Trust Services, 399 Park Ave.
New York, NY 10043
Tel.: 212-559-1605

Rhoads & Sinon*(Legal Firm)*
Harrisburg, PA

Wilmington Trust Co.*(Major Banking Relationship)*
Rodney Square North
Wilmington, DE 19890
Tel.: 302-651-1000

GUY GANNETT PUBLISHING COMPANY
1 City Center
Portland, ME 04101
Mailing Address:
P.O. Box 15277
Portland, ME 04101
Tel.: 207-780-9050 **ME**
Fax: 207-780-9355
Year Founded: 1921
Approx.Sls.: $140,000,000
Emp.: 1,700
Newspaper Publishing
S.I.C.: 2711
Jean Gannet Hawley *(Chm. Bd. & Publr.)*
Madeleine Corson *(Vice Chm.)*
James B. Shaffer *(Pres. & Chief Exec. Officer)*
James E. Baker *(V.P.-Fin. & Treas.)*
Jane Begert *(V.P.-Human Rels.)*
Michael Bock *(V.P.-Television)*
Gene Reardon *(Controller)*
Nancy L. Agler *(Corp. Sec.)*
Deborah Mahoney *(Corp. Benefits Mgr.)*
Margaret Flynn *(Communications Coordinator)*

Outside Service Firm(s):

Coopers & Lybrand*(Auditors)*
Portland, ME

Preti, Flaherty & Beliveau*(Legal Firm)*
Portland, ME

Subsidiaries:

Central Maine Morning Newspapers **(1)**
274 Western Ave.
Augusta, ME 04330

Minnesota Sun Publications **(1)**
7831 East Bush Lake Rd.
Bloomington, MN 55435

Portland Newspapers **(1)**
390 Congress St.
Portland, ME 04104

Shakopee Valley Printing Co. **(1)**
5101 Valley Industrial Blvd. South
Shakopee, MN 55379

KGAN-TV **(1)**
600-602 Old Marion Rd., N.E.
Cedar Rapids, IA 52406

WGGB-TV **(1)**
1300 Liberty St.
Springfield, MA 01102-0040

WGME-TV **(1)**
1335 Washington Ave.
Portland, ME 04104

WJCS-TV **(1)**
2680 East Cook St.
Springfield, IL 62703

GANNETT TRANSIT
666 Third Ave.
New York, NY 10017
Tel.: 212-867-4700
Fax: 212-297-6472
Approx.Sls.: $47,000,000
Emp.: 150
Fiscal Year-end: 12/31/90
Transit Advertising Car Cards, Posters, Special Displays, Bus Shelter Displays
S.I.C.: 7389
Marvin Schwartz *(Chm. Bd. & Chief Exec. Officer)*
Rick Domashco *(Pres.)*
Marc Valenti *(Sr. V.P. & Sls. Mgr.)*
Kenneth Kochan *(V.P.-Fin.)*
Andy Weitzer *(Dir.-Mktg.)*

Divisions:

Gannett Transit **(1)**
444 N. Michigan Ave.
Chicago, IL 60611
Tel.: 312-527-0550
James McGann *(V.P.)*

Gannett Transit **(1)**
1029 Sibley Tower Bldg.
Rochester, NY 14604
Tel.: 716-454-1399
Ed Saresky *(Gen. Mgr.)*

Gannett Transit **(1)**
88 Custer
Detroit, MI 48202
Tel.: 313-872-6030
Rocco Iacobellis *(Gen. Mgr.)*

Gannett Transit **(1)**
RJ Casey Industrial Park, Columbus & Preble Aves.
Pittsburgh, PA 15233
Tel.: 412-322-5050
Dave Lomburger *(Gen. Mgr.)*

Gannett Transit **(1)**
750 Third Ave.
New York, NY 10017
Tel.: 212-867-4700
Steve Feinberg *(V.P. & Gen. Mgr.)*

Gannett Transit **(1)**
1731 Workman St.
Los Angeles, CA 90031
Tel.: 310-846-9333
Doreen Roberts *(V.P. & Gen. Mgr.)*

GANS INK & SUPPLY COMPANY, INC.
1441 Boyd St.
Los Angeles, CA 90033
Tel.: 213-264-2200
Fax: 213-264-2916
Year Founded: 1950
Approx.Sls.: $17,000,000
Emp.: 160
Mfr. of Printing Inks
S.I.C.: 2893
Robert J. Gans *(Chm. Bd. & Pres.)*
Jeff Koppelman *(V.P.)*
Chuck Eugenio *(Controller)*

Outside Service Firm(s):

Arnold L. Lipkin*(Auditors)*
Los Angeles, CA

Bank of America*(Major Banking Relationship)*
701 S. Western Ave.
Los Angeles, CA 91201

THE GARBER COMPANY
600 Union St.
Ashland, OH 44805
Tel.: 419-289-2666
Fax: 419-281-5415
Year Founded: 1879

Approx.Sls.: $50,000,000
Emp.: 450
Export
Offset Printing on Folding Cartons, Promotional Contract Packaging
S.I.C.: 2752
Dean Bartosic *(Vice Chm.)*
John McMillen *(Pres.)*
Phil Falter *(V.P.-Fin.)*
Donald Foster *(V.P.-Mktg.)*
Robert Schoenfeld *(V.P.)*
M. Brekas *(Dir.-Engrng.)*
Laura Gustin *(Dir.-Pur.)*
Barry McGrath *(Mgr.-Mktg.)*

Computer Systems/Hardware:
IBM

GARBER, GOODMAN ADVERTISING, INC.
4500 Biscayne Blvd.
Miami, FL 33137
Tel.: 305-573-5177
Fax: 305-576-9059
Year Founded: 1963
Approx.Billings: $20,000,000
Emp.: 16
Real Estate, Travel, Resort, Financial & Manufacturing
Robert Goodman *(Pres.)*
Diane Goodman *(V.P.-Fin.)*
Maria A. Rodriguez *(Controller)*

GARDEN WAY, INC.
102nd St. & 9th Ave.
Troy, NY 12180
Tel.: 518-235-6010
Fax: 518-235-7544
Sales Range: $100-499 Million
Emp.: 1,400
Shredders, Rototillers, Mowers, Riding Mowers, Garden Tractors, Lawn Tractors, Snowthrowers, Lawn & Garden Products
S.I.C.: 3523; 3524
Jairo A. Estrada *(Chm. Bd. & Chief Exec. Officer)*
Nathaniel C. Stoddard *(Pres. & Chief Oper. Officer)*
Donald J. Wanst *(Sr. V.P.-Admin.)*
Michael Powers *(Chief Fin. Officer)*
Thomas Maher *(Treas.)*
Lucia Miller *(Sec.)*

Outside Service Firm(s):

KPMG Peat Marwick*(Auditors)*
74 N. Pearl St.
Albany, NY 12207
Tel.: 518-455-8809

Herzog, Engstrom, Burke, Koplovitz & Cavalier, P.C.*(Legal Firm)*
11 N. Pearl St.
Albany, NY 12210
Tel.: 518-465-7581

GARDINER METAL COMPANY
4820 S. Campbell Ave.
Chicago, IL 60632
Tel.: 312-847-0100
Tel.: 800-621-0870 **IL**
Fax: 312-847-2314
Year Founded: 1898
Approx.Sls.: $18,000,000
Emp.: 85
Fiscal Year-end: 6/30/92
Export
White Metal Alloys Solder, Babbitt, Cored Wire Solder, Came Lead, Fluxes, Preforms, Solder Paste, Flux Paste, Tin & Lead Atimony
S.I.C.: 3356
Scott Gardiner *(Chm. Bd., Pres., Chief Exec. & Chief Oper. Officer)*
Kenneth Hilger *(Treas. & Chief Fin. Officer)*
Karen G. Peiss *(Exec. V.P.)*
Linda G. Hicks *(Sec.)*
Thomas Wegner *(Plant Mgr.)*
Lois Meadows *(Dir.-Human Resources)*
Julie Bradbury *(Dir.-Res. & Devel.)*
Maxine Seef *(Exec. Sec.)*

Principal(s):
Scott Gardiner
Linda G. Hicks
Karen G. Peiss

No. of Mfg. Plants/Facilities: 3
No. of U.S. Offices: 3

Outside Service Firm(s):

Clifton Gunderson*(Auditors)*
Oak Brook, IL

Sentry Insurance*(Commercial Insurance Carrier)*
1800 N. Point Dr.
Stevens Point, WI 54481

Employee Benefit Plan*(Group Insurer)*
Des Plaines, IL

Peterson Ross*(Legal Firm)*
200 E. Randolph Dr.
Chicago, IL

Harris Trust & Savings Bank*(Major Banking Relationship)*
111 W. Monroe St.
Chicago, IL 60690
Tel.: 312-461-2265
Tel.: 800-858-0840

Divisions:

Gardiner Solder Company **(1)**
4820 S. Campbell Ave.
Chicago, IL 60632
Tel.: 312-847-0100
Fax: 312-847-2314
Emp.: 50
S.I.C.: 2899; 3356
Bob Nesnidal *(Natl. Accts. Mgr.)*

Johnson Manufacturing Co. **(1)**
114 Lost Grove Rd.
Princeton, IA 52768
Tel.: 319-289-5123
Fax: 319-289-3825
Emp.: 25
Manufacture Flux & Solder
S.I.C.: 2899; 3356
Alan Gickler *(V.P. & Gen. Mgr.)*
Larry LePrevost *(Natl. Sls. Mgr.)*

Techform Laboratories **(1)**
2021 N. Glassell
Orange, CA 92665
Tel.: 714-921-9054
Fax: 714-921-2119
Emp.: 10
Chemicals for the Electronics Industry
S.I.C.: 2819
Gary De Mello *(V.P. & Gen. Mgr.)*

GARDNER COMMUNICATIONS, INC.
77 Geary St., Ste. 500
San Francisco, CA 94108
Tel.: 415-434-2191
Fax: 415-434-8254
Year Founded: 1977
Approx.Billings: $20,000,000
Robert K. Gardner *(Pres. & Exec. Creative Dir.)*
Karen L. Young *(V.P., Gen. Mgr.)*
Gayle S. Geary *(V.P., Dir. Mktg. Services)*

GARDNER PUBLICATIONS, INC.
6600 Clough Pike
Cincinnati, OH 45244
Tel.: 513-231-8020
Fax: 513-231-2818
Sales Range: $10-19 Million
Emp.: 107
Publish Trade Journals & Books
S.I.C.: 2721; 2731
George Hay *(Chm. Bd.)*
Richard G. Kline *(Pres.)*
Jo Ann C. Dooley *(V.P., Sec. & Treas.)*
Donald E. Kline *(V.P.)*
Margaret Kline *(V.P.)*
Steven R. Kline *(V.P.)*

Outside Service Firm(s):

The Central Trust Company, N.A.*(Major Banking Relationship)*
201 E. Fifth
Cincinnati, OH 45202
Tel.: 513-651-8255

GARELICK FARMS, INC.
1199 W. Central St.
Franklin, MA 02038
Tel.: 508-528-9000
Fax: 508-520-3922
Approx.Sls.: $160,000,000
Emp.: 650
Milk, Dairy Prouducts, Plastic Containers
S.I.C.: 2026; 3089; 5143
Peter M. Bernon *(Chm. Bd. & Chief Exec. Officer)*
Alan J. Bernon *(Pres.)*
Stephen B. Lincoln, Jr. *(V.P.-Sls.)*

Outside Service Firm(s):

Coopers & Lybrand*(Auditors)*
1 Post Office Square
Boston, MA 02110
Tel.: 617-574-5000
Fax: 617-345-0398

Licht & Semonoff*(Legal Firm)*
Providence, RI

Shawmut Bank*(Major Banking Relationship)*
446 Main St.
Worcester, MA 01608
Tel.: 617-793-4000

GARNEY HOLDING COMPANY, INC.
1331 N.W. Vivion Rd.
Kansas City, MO 64118-4554
Tel.: 816-741-4600 **MO**
Fax: 816-741-4894
Year Founded: 1961
Approx.Sls.: $44,000,000
Emp.: 250
Water Main & Sewer Line Construction; New Construction of Office Buildings; Subdividers & Developers; Beef Cattle Feedlots
S.I.C.: 1623; 1542; 6552; 0211
Charles A. Garney *(Chm. Bd.)*
James I. Dorman, Jr. *(Pres.)*
Montie Tripp *(Exec. V.P.)*
John Dillingham *(Sr. V.P.-Sls. & Mktg.)*
J.W. Youngblood *(Sr. V.P.-Opers.)*
Thomas J. Dahl *(V.P.-Fin.)*
George Gunter *(V.P.)*
Steve McCandless *(V.P.)*
Steve Swatek *(V.P.)*
Tom Keitel *(Controller)*

Outside Service Firm(s):

Grant Thornton*(Auditors)*
Kansas City, MO

United Missouri Bank*(Major Banking Relationship)*
Kansas City, MO

Subsidiary:

Garney Companies, Inc. **(1)**
1331 N.W. Vivion Rd.
Kansas City, KS 64118-4554
Tel.: 816-741-4600

GARRISON-LONTINE ADVERTISING
1444 Wazee
Denver, CO 80202
Tel.: 303-571-5404
Year Founded: 1988
Approx.Billings: $21,200,000
Emp.: 26
Consumer Products & Foodservice Adv.
T. Paul Garrison *(Chm., Chief Exec. Officer)*
Rodney N. Lontine *(Vice Chm.)*
Roger Ruark *(Pres., Chief Fin. Officer)*
Brooks Augustine *(Partner, Promo. Services)*
Pat Murphy *(V.P.)*
David Baggs *(Office Mgr.)*

Computer Systems/Hardware:
Apple, MacIntosh

GARSITE/TSR, INC.
539 So. 10th
Kansas City, KS 66105
Tel.: 913-342-5600
Fax: 913-342-0638
Mfr. of Aircraft Refuelers
S.I.C.: 3728
Phillip Hodes *(Pres.)*
Melvyn Paul *(Treas.)*
Sally Lewis *(Sec.)*

Subsidiary:

Garsite/TSR, Inc. **(1)**
172 E. Industry Court
Deer Park, NY 11729
Tel.: 516-667-1010 (100%)
Mfr. of Aviation Ground Support Systems
S.I.C.: 3443; 3713; 3715; 3824
William Hodes *(Pres.)*

GARTNER GROUP, INC.
56 Top Gallant Rd.
Stamford, CT 06902
Mailing Address:
P.O. Box 10212
Stamford, CT 06904-2212
Tel.: 203-964-0096
Telex: 643 528
Fax: 203-324-7901
Year Founded: 1979
Approx.Sls.: $84,000,000
Emp.: 460
Fiscal Year-end: 9/30/90
Information Services for High-tech Industry
S.I.C.: 8999
Corporate Giving Program:
Corporation Supports and Participates in The United Way of Stamford.
Gideon I. Gartner *(Chm. Bd.)*
Manuel Fernandez *(Pres. & Chief Exec. Officer)*
Craig Symons *(Sr. V.P. & Chief Info. Officer)*
Grigsby C. Markham *(Chief Fin. Officer)*
Michael Kolesar *(Treas.)*
Tom Barry *(Dir.-Acctg.)*
Nancy Luzak *(Dir.-Admin. Services)*
Patricia Verbitsky *(Dir.-Employee Benefits)*

GARVEY ELEVATORS INC.
P.O. Box 1948
Hutchinson, KS 67504
Tel.: 316-662-5411
Assets: $25,966,000
Earnings: $1,100,000
Liabilities: $12,790,000
Net Worth: $13,176,000
Approx.Sls.: $85,000,000
Emp.: 125
Fiscal Year-end: 3/31/91
Agriculture Services; Trucking & Warehousing
S.I.C.: 5153; 4221
James S. Garvey *(Chm. Bd.)*
D. Mike Landers *(Pres.)*
Harold Deandoff *(Chief Operating Officer)*
R.W. Vogt *(Treas. & Chief Fin. Officer)*

Computer Systems/Hardware:
IBM Systems 36

GARVEY INDUSTRIES, INC.
301 N. Main, Ste. 860
Wichita, KS 67202
Tel.: 316-291-8390

Garvey Industries, Inc.—(Continued)

Fax: 316-291-8354
Year Founded: 1972
Crude Petroleum & Natural Gas Production & Wholesale Grain, Furnished Taxicab Service, Mortgage Bankers & Loan Correspondents, Subdividers & Developers & Operates Apartment Buildings
S.I.C.: 1311; 4121; 5153; 6162; 6513; 6552
Willard W. Garvey *(Chm. Bd., Pres. & Chief Exec. Officer)*
James H. Childers *(Exec. V.P.)*
Jean K. Garvey *(V.P. & Sec.)*

Outside Service Firm(s):

Grant Thornton*(Auditors)*
800 Fourth Financial Center
Wichita, KS 67202

Learned & Jordan*(Legal Firm)*
Wichita, KS

Bank IV*(Major Banking Relationship)*
P.O. Box 1122,
Wichita, KS 67201
Tel.: 316-261-4304

Harris Trust & Savings Bank*(Major Banking Relationship)*
111 W. Monroe St.
Chicago, IL 60690
Tel.: 312-461-2265
Tel.: 800-858-0840

Subsidiaries:

Builders Development Inc. **(1)**
301 N. Main, Ste. 800
Wichita, KS 67202
Tel.: 316-291-8300
Real Estate Developers, Operative Builders & Apartment
S.I.C.: 1531; 6513; 6552
Alexander Dean *(Pres.)*
James Childers *(V.P.)*
Bradley Smisor *(Sec. & Treas.)*

Builders Inc. **(1)**
301 N. Main, Ste. 800
Wichita, KS 67202
Tel.: 316-291-8300
Apartment & Nonresidential Bldg. Operator & Subdivider & Developer
S.I.C.: 6512; 6513; 6552
Willard W. Garvey *(Pres.)*
Alexander L. Dean *(Exec. V.P.)*
Harvey Childers *(V.P.)*
Bradley K. Smisor *(Sec.)*

Garvey Grain **(1)**
5255 S. Hoover
Wichita, KS 67202
Tel.: 316-522-4871
Dave Ensles *(Pres.)*

Garvey International, Inc. **(1)**
One Foxfield Sq.
St. Charles, IL 60174
Tel.: 708-377-9966
Wholesale Grain Merchandising, Processing & Storage
S.I.C.: 4221; 5153
Bob M. White *(Pres.)*
Bill Arnold *(V.P., Sls. & Intl. Mktg.)*
R. E. Dilger *(V.P., Admin.)*
Lita K. Jimenez *(V.P. & Treas.)*

Petroleum, Inc. **(1)**
301 N. Main, Ste. 860
Wichita, KS 67202
Tel.: 316-291-8390
Emp.: 70
Oil Company
S.I.C.: 1311
Willard W. Garvey *(Chm. Bd. & Chief Exec. Officer)*
James Williams *(Pres.)*
Robert C. Heaton *(Mgr.-Mktg.)*
Ben Whiteside *(Dir.-Data Processing)*

GARVIN FIRE PROTECTION SYSTEMS
501 W. Southern
Orange, CA 92665
Tel.: 714-974-8770 **AZ**
Fax: 714-974-3451
Year Founded: 1974
Approx.Sls.: $20,000,000
Emp.: 180
Fiscal Year-end: 2/28/90
Sprinkler System Installation Contractor
S.I.C.: 1711
John O'Connell *(Pres. & Chief Exec. Officer)*
Richard Farmer *(Exec. V.P. & Chief Fin. Officer)*
Terry Flynn *(V.P.)*
Gail Garvin *(Sec.)*

Principal(s):
Carroll Garvin

Outside Service Firm(s):

Price Waterhouse*(Auditors)*
660 Newport Center Dr., Ste. 600
Newport Beach, CA 92660
Tel.: 714-640-9200

Case, Schroeder, Knowlson, Mobley & Burnett*(Legal Firm)*
Irvine, CA

THE GARY GROUP
9046 Lindblade St.
Culver City, CA 90232
Tel.: 310-842-8400
Fax: 310-842-7114
Year Founded: 1976
Approx.Billings: $15,000,000
Emp.: 12
Entertainment
Richard M. Gary *(Pres. & New Bus. Contact)*
Elsa H. Gary *(Exec. V.P., Sec., Acct. Supvr. & Media Dir.)*

THE GARY-WILLIAMS COMPANY
370 17th St., Ste. 5300
Denver, CO 80202
Tel.: 303-628-3800
Fax: 303-628-0801
Sales Range: $500-999 Million
Emp.: 225
Oil & Gas Exploration, Extraction & Refining; Wholesale Petroleum Products
S.I.C.: 1311; 2911; 5172
Samuel Gary *(Chm. Bd.)*
Ronald Williams *(Pres. & Chief Exec. Officer)*
David Younggren *(Sr. V.P.)*
Sally Allen *(V.P.-Admin. & Governmental Affairs)*
James Greene *(Gen. Counsel)*

Computer Systems/Hardware:
IBM System 38

Outside Service Firm(s):

Arthur Andersen & Co.*(Auditors)*
717 17th St., Ste. 1900
Denver, CO 80202
Tel.: 303-296-2121

Mutual Administrators*(Group Insurer)*
Reno, NV

NationsBank*(Major Banking Relationship)*
Dallas, TX

Subsidiaries:

Bloomfield Refining Co. **(1)**
370 17th St., Ste. 5300
Denver, CO 80202
Tel.: 303-628-3800
S.I.C.: 1311

Gary-Williams Energy Corporation **(1)**
370 17th St., Ste. 5300
Denver, CO 80202
Tel.: 303-628-3800
S.I.C.: 1311
Samuel Gary *(Chm. Bd.)*
Ronald Williams *(Pres. & Chief Exec. Officer)*
A. Joe Warr *(Sr. V.P.)*
David Younggren *(Sr. V.P.)*
Sally Allen *(V.P.-Admin. & Governmental Affairs)*
Thomas Bruskotter *(V.P.-Supply, Distribution & Mktg.)*
James Greene *(Gen. Counsel)*

Western Slope Refining Co. **(1)**
370 17th. St., Ste. 5300
Denver, CO 80202
Tel.: 303-628-3800
S.I.C.: 1311

GAS EQUIPMENT COMPANY, INC.
11616 Harry Hines
Dallas, TX 75229
Mailing Address:
P.O. Box 29242
Dallas, TX 75229
Tel.: 214-241-2333 **TX**
Fax: 214-620-1403
Year Founded: 1937
Emp.: 560

Import Export
Manufacture Measuring & Controlling Devices; Investment Castings & Wholesale Industrial Machinery & Equipment
S.I.C.: 3322; 3369; 3829; 5084
Jack W. LaDue *(Pres. & Treas.)*
H.G. Ross *(Exec. V.P.)*
C.K. LaDue *(V.P.)*
M.J. LaDue, III *(V.P. & Sec.)*
Tom Simmons *(V.P.)*
Ron Horton *(Controller)*

No. of Mfg. Plants/Facilities: 6
No. of U.S. Offices: 6

Computer Systems/Hardware:
IBM AS/400

Outside Service Firm(s):

Hall & Hall*(Auditors)*
Dallas, TX

Bank One Texas*(Major Banking Relationship)*
1717 Main St.
Dallas, TX 75201
Tel.: 214-290-2367

Subsidiary:

Rochester Gauges Inc. Of Texas **(1)**
11616 Harry Hines Blvd.
Dallas, TX 75229
Tel.: 214-241-2161
Twx: 730913
Emp.: 300
Manufacture Electrical & Liquid Level Gauges; Industrial Thermometers
S.I.C.: 3829
Jack W. LaDue *(Pres. & Treas.)*
H.G. Ross *(Exec. V.P.)*
Al Wells *(Gen. Mgr.)*
Bud Barendsen *(Mgr.-Natl. Sls.)*
Jack R. LaDue *(Sec.)*
Harley Brisendine *(Pur. Agent)*
Ron Horton *(Controller)*
Sam Sims *(Mgr.-Personnel)*
Dave White *(Dir.-M.I.S.)*

GAS-FIRED PRODUCTS, INC.
305 Doggett St.
Charlotte, NC 28203
Mailing Address:
P.O. Box 36485
Charlotte, NC 28236
Tel.: 704-372-3485
Fax: 704-332-5843
Year Founded: 1949
Approx.Sls.: $10,000,000
Emp.: 50
Fiscal Year-end: 9/30/91

Import Export
Bulktobac & Gastobac Tobacco Curing System; Space-Ray, Gas-Fired Infra-Red Heating System; Sunstar Gas Room Heaters; Seahorse Outdoor Gas Water Heaters
S.I.C.: 3567
F.L. Horne *(Pres.)*
F.L. Horne, Jr. *(V.P. & Gen. Mgr.)*

Non-U.S. Holding:

Gas-Fired Products (U.K.) Ltd. **(1)**
4-6 Chapel Lane Claydon,
Ipswich, IP6 0JL, United Kingdom
Tel.: 0473 830 551 (100%)
Fax: 0473 832 055
Import Export
Mfr. of Heating Apparatus
S.I.C.: 3433
Brian Kitchener *(Mng. Dir.)*

GAST MFG. CORP.
2300 M-139
Benton Harbor, MI 49022
Mailing Address:
P. O. Box 97
Benton Harbor, MI 49023-0097
Tel.: 616-926-6171
Fax: 616-927-0808
Year Founded: 1920
Approx.Sls.: $40,000,000
Emp.: 700
Fiscal Year-end: 1/ 1/91

Export
Air Pumps & Pnuematic Motors
S.I.C.: 3724
Warren E. Gast *(Pres. & Gen. Mgr.)*
Les Peterson *(Dir.-Sls.)*
Roger Csepregi *(Mgr.-Mktg. Services)*
Allan Fisher *(Mgr.-Pur.)*
K.C. Gast *(Mgr.-Mktg. Devel.)*
Nancy Hendrix *(Mktg. Services Coord.)*

GASTON COUNTY DYEING MACHINE CO.
200 S. Main St.
Stanley, NC 28164
Mailing Address:
P.O. Box 308
Stanley, NC 28164
Tel.: 704-822-5000
Fax: 704-827-0476
Year Founded: 1921
Sales Range: $60-79 Million
Emp.: 550
Fiscal Year-end: 9/30/90

Export
Manufacture Textile Wet-Processing Machinery & Controls
S.I.C.: 3552; 3443; 3559; 3823
H. Max Craig, Jr. *(Pres.)*
Gordon Hacker *(Exec. V.P. & Gen. Mgr.)*
Chris W. Aurich *(Sr. V.P.-Res. & Devel.)*
Archie P. McKinnis *(Sr. V.P.-Fin. & Admin.)*
Ray Cooper *(V.P.-Sls.)*
Max N. Walker *(Treas. & Sec.)*
T.J. Hiley *(Dir.-Intl. Mktg.)*
William Query *(Dir.-Opers.)*
Glenda Bumgarner *(Mgr.-Pur.)*
Sally Davis *(Mgr.-Adv.)*

No. of Mfg. Plants/Facilities: 3
No. of U.S. Offices: 2

Outside Service Firm(s):

Arthur Andersen & Co.*(Auditors)*
2300 Charlotte Plaza
Charlotte, NC 28244
Tel.: 704-332-0092

First Citizens Bank & Trust Co.*(Major Banking Relationship)*
Charlotte, NC

Division:

Gaston County Carpet Div. **(1)**
P.O. Box 5409,
Fort Oglethorpe, GA 30742
Tel.: 706-866-6914
Emp.: 50
Carpet Manufacturing Machinery
S.I.C.: 3552; 3559
Delton Mullins *(Gen. Mgr.)*

GATE CITY BEVERAGE DISTRIBUTORS
2505 Steele St.
San Bernardino, CA 92408
Tel.: 909-799-1600 CA
Fax: 909-799-1615
Year Founded: 1941
Approx.Sls.: $50,000,000
Emp.: 180
Wholesale Distribution of Beer & Other Fermented Malt Liquors, Soft Drinks & Mineral or Spring Water Bottling
S.I.C.: 5181; 5149
Morton Aronoff *(Chm. Bd.)*
Leona Aronoff *(Chief Exec. Officer)*
Jack Aronoff *(Pres.)*
Barry Aronoff *(V.P.)*
David W. Dempsey *(Controller)*

Outside Service Firm(s):

Wells Fargo Bank*(Major Banking Relationship)*
San Bernadino, CA

GATE PETROLEUM COMPANY
9540 San Jose Blvd.
Jacksonville, FL 32257
Tel.: 904-737-7220
Fax: 904-448-3000
Year Founded: 1960
Approx.Sls.: $250,000,000
Emp.: 2,000
Service Station, Wholesale & Retail Fuel, Oil & Automotive Parts; Manufacture Asphalt Felts & Coating; Land Development & Sales
S.I.C.: 2952; 5013; 5172; 5541; 5983
Herbert H. Peyton *(Chm. Bd. & Pres.)*
Donald R. Davis *(V.P.-Corp. Rels.)*
Wayne M. Levitt *(V.P.-Mktg.)*
Jack C. Lueders, Jr. *(V.P.-Admin.)*
Joseph C. Luke *(V.P.-Construction Materials)*
Thomas W. Rhodes *(V.P.)*
P. Jeremy Smith, Jr. *(V.P.-Fin.)*
Louis M. Zemanek *(Sec. & Treas.)*

Outside Service Firm(s):

Smoak, Davis & Nixon*(Auditors)*
Jacksonville, FL

Rogers, Towers, Bailey, Jones, Gay*(Legal Firm)*
Jacksonville, FL

First Union National Bank*(Major Banking Relationship)*
Jacksonville, FL

THE GATES CORPORATION
900 S. Broadway
Denver, CO 80209
Mailing Address:
P.O. Box 5887
Denver, CO 80217-5887
Tel.: 303-744-1911 DE
Telex: 6837035
Fax: 303-744-4000
Year Founded: 1911
Approx.Sls.: $1,344,000,000
Emp.: 17,000
Fiscal Year-end: 12/31/91
Import Export
Holding Company; Manufacturer of Rubber Belts & Hoses for Automobiles & Industrial Drive Systems, Batteries, Formed-Fiber Plastics Products; Land Development; Power Drive Products (Tensioners, Pulleys, Power Drive Systems For Vehicles)
S.I.C.: 3061; 3069; 3692; 3714; 3052; 6531; 6719
Employee Matching Gifts Program: Higher Education Institutions Attended by Employees Only
Charles C. Gates *(Chm. Bd. & Chief Exec. Officer)*
Donald E. Miller *(Pres. & Chief Oper. Officer)*
Thomas Gibson *(Exec. V.P., Chief Fin. Officer, Sec. & Gen. Counsel)*
Robert L. Stamp *(V.P.-Fin., Treas. & Controller)*
Lewis P. Keim *(V.P.-Pub. Rels.)*
Jay T. Schmelter *(Dir.-Benefits)*

No. of Mfg. Plants/Facilities: 47
No. of U.S. Offices: 10
No. of Foreign Offices: 8

Computer Systems/Hardware:
IBM 3081

Outside Service Firm(s):

Ernst & Young*(Auditors)*
4300 Republic Plaza
Denver, CO 80202
Tel.: 303-628-4406

Aetna Life & Casualty*(Group Insurer)*
151 Farmington Avenue
Hartford, CT 06156
Tel.: 203-273-2128
Fax: 203-729-4295

Prudential Insurance Co. of America*(Group Insurer)*
751 Broad St.
Newark, NJ 07102-3777
Tel.: 201-802-6000

Bankers Trust Co.*(Major Banking Relationship)*
P.O. Box 318, Church St. Station
New York, NY 10008
Tel.: 212-454-2212
Fax: 212-454-2783

United Bank of Denver*(Major Banking Relationship)*
Denver, CO

Aetna Life & Casualty*(Pension Manager)*
151 Farmington Avenue
Hartford, CT 06156
Tel.: 203-273-2128
Fax: 203-729-4295

Bankers Trust Co.*(Pension Manager)*
One Bankers Trust Plaza
New York, NY 10006
Tel.: 212-250-6902

Chemical Bank*(Pension Manager)*
450 West 33rd St.
New York, NY 10001
Tel.: 212-613-7197
Fax: 212-947-7628

Thorndike, Doran, Paine & Lewis*(Pension Manager)*
Boston, MA

Wall, Patterson, McGrew & Hamilton*(Pension Manager)*
Atlanta, GA

Wentworth, Hauser & Violich*(Pension Manager)*
333 Sacramento St.
San Francisco, CA 94111
Tel.: 415-981-6911

Subsidiaries:

A Bar A Ranch **(1)**
900 S. Broadway
Denver, CO 80209
Tel.: 303-744-1911 (100%)
Emp.: 25
Cattle Ranch
S.I.C.: 0212
R.L. Stamp *(V.P.)*

Gates Energy Products, Inc. **(1)**
Hwy. 441 No.
Alachua, FL 32615
Tel.: 904-462-3911
Fax: 904-462-4726
Approx.Sls.: $200,000,000
Emp.: 3,000
Fiscal Year-end: 12/31/90
Export
Mfr. Rechargeable Batteries
S.I.C.: 3691
Kim Edwards *(Pres.)*
Ron Hammel *(V.P.)*
Bill Perusek *(V.P.)*
Steve Sanborn *(V.P.)*
Larry Stone *(Controller)*
Carol J. Ebert *(Dir.-Mktg. Communications & Pub. Rels.)*
Timothy L. Hill *(Dir.-Consumer Mktg. & Sls.)*
Shawn Griffin *(Natl. Sls. Mgr.)*

Gates Formed-Fibre Products **(1)**
P.O. Box 1300
Auburn, ME 04210-9156
Tel.: 207-784-1118 (100%)
Fax: 207-784-1123
Approx.Sls.: $30,000,000
Emp.: 300
Mfr. Molded Structures for Automotive & Aircraft Applications
S.I.C.: 3089
David M. MacMahon *(Pres.)*

Gates Land Co. **(1)**
202 E. Cheyenne Mountain Blvd., Ste. I
Colorado Springs, CO 80906
Tel.: 719-576-8500 (100%)
Emp.: 3
Land Development
S.I.C.: 6552
David K. Sunderland *(Pres.)*

Gates Power Drive Products, Inc. **(1)**
1133 W. Long Lake Rd., Ste. 201
Bloomfield Hills, MI 48013
Tel.: 313-540-4500 (100%)
Fax: 313-540-4885
Emp.: 155
Mfr. of Spun Steel Pulleys, Tensioners
S.I.C.: 3714
Robert D. Emrick *(Pres.)*

The Gates Rubber Company **(1)**
900 S. Broadway
Denver, CO 80209
Tel.: 303-744-1911
Approx.Sls.: $1,300,000,000
Emp.: 13,000
Fiscal Year-end: 12/31/90
Mfr. of Automotive Engine Belts & Hose; Industrial Drive Belts, Hose, Hydraulic Products & Molded Rubber Products
S.I.C.: 3061; 3069
Charles C. Gates *(Chm. Bd. & Chief Exec. Officer)*
Donald E. Miller *(Pres. & Chief Oper. Officer)*
L.G. Estenfelder *(Pres.-Intl. Div.)*
T.J. Gibson *(Exec. V.P. & Chief Fin. Officer)*
A.L. Stecklein *(Sr. V.P.-European Opers.)*
John M. Riess *(Grp. V.P.-U.S. Opers.)*
D.R. Ahlman *(V.P.-Admin.)*
W.J. Dotson *(V.P.-Auto Aftermarket Hardware Sls.)*
J.D. Hoesel *(V.P.-Acctg.)*
P.D. McFadden *(V.P.-Adv. Tech. & Engrng.)*
Donald Allendorf *(Dir.-Mktg. Communications & Res.)*
Robert Stedman *(Mgr.-Automotive Adv.)*
Larry Hennesy *(Mgr.-Indus. Adv.)*
David Wheeler *(Mgr.-Private Brand Adv.)*

Non-U.S. Holdings:

Gates do Brasil Ind. e Com. Ltda. **(1)**
Rua Cesario Alvim 602/634 03054,
Sao Paulo, S.P. Brazil
Tel.: 291-8822
Telex: 1121240
Fax: 55-11-933158
Mfr. of Belting
S.I.C.: 3052
Michael Shanklin *(Pres.)*

Gates Canada Inc. **(1)**
300 Henry St.
Brantford, ON N3T 5W1, Canada
Tel.: 519-759-4141
Fax: 519-759-4567
Mfr. of Automotive Hose & Belts, Industrial Belts & Hoses
S.I.C.: 3052
Tony Roberts *(Pres.)*
Bruce Hodgson *(V.P.)*
Thomas Malone *(V.P.-Fin.)*
Peter Tekker *(V.P.-Mfg.)*
Roman Wempe *(V.P.-Industrial Mfg.)*
Robert Scherer *(Dir.-Pur.)*

Gates Europe N.V. **(1)**
Dr. Carlierlaan 30 B-9440
Erembodegem, Belgium
Tel.: 053-762-711
Telex: 846-12322
Fax: 53-773-486
Emp.: 650
Mfr. of Belting & Hose
S.I.C.: 3052
L.G. Estenfelder *(Pres.)*

Gates Hydraulics Ltd. **(1)**
Station Road St. Neots,
Huntingdon, Cambs. PE19 1QF, United Kingdom
Tel.: 44 0480 75333
Mfr. of Hydraulic Hose & Coupling
S.I.C.: 3052; 3429
John Gardiner *(Mng. Dir.)*

The Gates Rubber Company **(1)**
Eisenbahnweg 50 Postfach 1428, D-5100,
Aachen, 1, Germany
Tel.: 241-5108-200
Fax: 24-5108-249
S.I.C.: 3052

The Gates Rubber Company Limited **(1)**
NCR House, 5th Floor, 2, Roseburn Gardens
Edinburgh, EH12 5NJ, United Kingdom
Tel.: 31-337-4007
Telex: 851-727576
Fax: 31-337-4042
Mfr. of Rubber
S.I.C.: 3052
Brian Corless *(Opers. Dir.)*

The Gates Rubber Company Ltd. **(1)**
Edinburgh Rd., Heathhall
Dumfries, DE1 1QA, United Kingdom
Tel.: 0387-53111
Telex: 778785 GATES G
Fax: 0387-68937
Emp.: 900
Fiscal Year-end: 12/31/88
Mfr., Sale & Distr. of Power Transmission Belts, Plastics, Waterproof Footwear, Carpet Underlay
S.I.C.: 3021; 3069; 3052
Brian Corless *(Mng. Dir.)*

Gates Rubber de Mexico **(1)**
Cerrada de Galeana No. 5 Fracc. Industrial La Loma, 54060
Tlalnepantla, Mexico
Tel.: 905-361-1313
Fax: 905-361-1813
Mfr. of Rubber
S.I.C.: 3052
Carlos Machorro *(Pres.)*

Gates Vulca Automotive Products Division **(1)**
Avenida de la Riera, 3-5 Apartado de Correos 7,
Barcelona, Spain
Tel.: 3473-3050
Fax: 3473-4021
Mfr. of Rubber Products for the Automotive Industry
S.I.C.: 3052
Antonio German *(V.P.)*

GATEWAY APPAREL, INC.
8500 Valcour
Saint Louis, MO 63123
Mailing Address:
P.O. Box 6990,
St. Louis, MO 63123
Tel.: 314-638-1500 MO
Fax: 314-631-6020
Year Founded: 1971
Assets: $66,732,000
Liabilities: $21,637,000
Net Worth: $45,095,000
Approx.Sls.: $200,000,000
Emp.: 4,500
Fiscal Year-end: 1/26/91
Women's Retail Specialty Stores; Fashionation; Show Off; Tempo; The Right Price; Fashion Gal; Something Special
S.I.C.: 5632; 5699
Carl Simons *(Pres.)*

Gateway Apparel, Inc.—(Continued)

Warren A. Davis *(Exec. V.P. & Chief Fin. Officer)*
Ronald Meyer *(Exec. V.P.-Opers.)*
Raymond C. Plas *(Exec. V.P.-Mktg. & Mdsg.)*
Bennett Lerner *(V.P.-Personnel)*
Fred Buckhold *(Dir.-Mngmt. Information)*

Principal(s):
Carl Simons
Warren A. Davis
Ronald Meyer
Raymond C. Plas

No. of U.S. Offices: 150

Computer Systems/Hardware:
IBM 4361

Outside Service Firm(s):

KPMG Peat Marwick*(Auditors)*
1010 Market St.
Saint Louis, MO 63101
Tel.: 314-444-1400

Husch, Eppenberger, Donohue, Elson & Cornfield*(Legal Firm)*
100 N. Broadway
St. Louis, MO 63102
Tel.: 314-421-4800

Boatmen's National Bank*(Major Banking Relationship)*
800 Market St.
St. Louis, MO 63166
Tel.: 314-554-6000

GATEWAY PRESS, INC.
4500 Robards Lane
Louisville, KY 40218
Tel.: 502-454-0431
Fax: 502-459-7930
Year Founded: 1950
Approx.Sls.: $35,000,000
Emp.: 286
Fiscal Year-end: 6/30/92
Commercial Lithography
S.I.C.: 2752
Christopher W. Georgehead, II *(Pres. & Chief Exec. Officer)*
Robert N. Burrice *(Exec. V.P. & Chief Oper. Officer)*
Joe Ackermann *(Sr. V.P.-Sls.)*
William S. Keeling *(Sr. V.P.-Production)*
Larry Siers *(V.P.)*
Dennis Brown *(Dir.-Res. Maintenance & Acquisitions)*
Phil H. Hinds *(Dir.-Personnel)*

Outside Service Firm(s):

Christen, Brown & Rufer*(Auditors)*
Louisville, KY

Ruck, Roseberry, Wilson & Cooper*(Legal Firm)*
Louisville, KY

Citizens Fidelity Bank & Trust Co.*(Major Banking Relationship)*
P.O. Box 33000-Citizens Plaza
Louisville, KY 40232
Tel.: 502-581-3381

GATEWAY 2000
610 Gateway Dr., N.
Sioux City, SD 57049
Tel.: 605-232-2000
Fax: 605-232-2023
Year Founded: 1985
Assets: $76,000,000
Liabilities: $34,100,000
Net Worth: $41,900,000
Sales Range: $60-79 Million
Emp.: 1,100
Fiscal Year-end: 12/31/90
Import Export
Computer & Software Stores; Computers, Peripherals & Software
S.I.C.: 5734; 5045
Ted Waitt *(Pres.)*
Richard Snyder *(Exec. V.P. & Sec.)*

GATOR FREIGHTWAYS, INC.
2483 St. Rt. 3 W.
Wilmington, OH 45177
Tel.: 513-382-1494
Tel.: 800-828-3209 **FL**
Year Founded: 1968
Assets: $14,766,718
Earnings: $525,000
Liabilities: $9,538,793
Net Worth: $5,227,925
Approx.Sls.: $20,290,057
Emp.: 473
Fiscal Year-end: 6/30/91
General Commodities Freight Carriers
S.I.C.: 4731
Ralph L. Roberts *(Chm. Bd. & Pres.)*
Tom Roberts *(Chief Oper. Officer)*
Lee R. Johnson *(Chief Fin. Officer)*
Bob Mullins *(V.P.-Sls.)*
Mike Murray *(V.P. & Gen. Counsel)*
Ronald Carey *(Corp. Sec.)*
Thomas E. Cavellier *(Controller)*
Roby Roberts *(Dir.-Cash Mngmt.)*
Patricia M. Spade *(Dir.-Data Processing)*

Principal(s):
Ralph L. Roberts

No. of U.S. Offices: 8

Computer Systems/Hardware:
MAI Basic Four

Outside Service Firm(s):

Mellott & Mellott*(Auditors)*
Suite 1217 Fourth & Race Tower
Cincinnati, OH 45202
Tel.: 513-241-2940

American Agency*(Group Insurer)*
P.O. Box 21997
Columbus, OH 43221
Tel.: 614-442-1400
Fax: 614-442-1419

Barnett Bank*(Major Banking Relationship)*
Orlando, FL

GATOR INDUSTRIES INC.
1000 S.E. 8th St.
Hialeah, FL 33010
Tel.: 305-888-5000 **FL**
Fax: 305-885-3869
Approx.Sls.: $60,000,000
Emp.: 970
Fiscal Year-end: 12/31/91
Import Export
Shoe Manufacture & Exporting; Custom Compounding Plastics & Rubber
S.I.C.: 2821; 2822; 3021; 5139
Guillermo Miranda, Jr. *(Chm. Bd. & Chief Exec. Officer & Pres.)*
Jose J. Miranda *(Chief Oper. Officer & Exec. V.P.)*
V. Mendoza *(Chief Fin. Officer & Chief Info. Officer & Treas. & Dir.-Data Pr)*
Mario Napolez *(Controllor)*
Rolando A. Perez *(V.P.-Plastics Div.)*
Luis Valeiras *(V.P.-Sls. , Mktg. & Adv., Dir.- Corp.Travel)*
A. Falcon *(Dir.-Purch.)*
C. Romero *(Dir. Human Res. & Pers. Training)*
G. Ruiz *(Dir. Mfr.)*

Outside Service Firm(s):

Carlos Arazoza & Co.*(Auditors)*
Coral Gables, FL

FRED P. GATTAS COMPANY, INC.
5000 Summer Ave.
Memphis, TN 38122
Tel.: 901-767-2930 **TN**
Fax: 901-682-6153
Year Founded: 1945
Approx.Sls.: $32,000,000
Emp.: 350
Catalog Showrooms; General Merchandise
S.I.C.: 5399
Fred P. Gattas, Jr. *(Pres.)*
James Wood Gattas *(Exec. V.P.)*
George Gattas *(V.P.)*
Tommy Gattas *(V.P.)*
Andrew D. Gattas *(Treas. & Sec.)*

Outside Service Firm(s):

First Tennessee Bank, N.A.*(Major Banking Relationship)*
P.O. Box 84
Memphis, TN 38101-0034
Tel.: 901-523-4541

GAY JOHNSON'S INC.
1154 N. 4th St.
Grand Junction, CO 81501
Mailing Address:
P.O. Box 1829
Grand Junction, CO 81502
Tel.: 303-245-7992 **CO**
Fax: 303-242-5663
Year Founded: 1941
Assets: $5,447,932
Liabilities: $1,758,092
Net Worth: $3,689,840
Approx.Sls.: $16,000,000
Emp.: 125
Fiscal Year-end: 2/28/90
Retail & Wholesale Fuel; New & Recap Tires; Property Lease & Rental; Restaurants & Convenience Stores
S.I.C.: 5812; 3011; 5172; 5531; 5983; 5984; 6519; 6531
Berton Johnson *(Pres.)*
Dee A. Brinegar *(Chief Fin. Officer)*
Gaynell Lenderman *(Sec.)*

Principal(s):
Berton Johnson
Gaynell Lenderman

Computer Systems/Hardware:
IBM

Outside Service Firm(s):

Miller, Thompson & Hocking, CPA's*(Auditors)*
Grand Junction, CO

Younge & Hockensmith*(Legal Firm)*
Grand Junction, CO

First Colorado Bank & Trust*(Major Banking Relationship)*
Denver, CO

Grand Valley National Bank*(Major Banking Relationship)*
Grand Junction, CO

GAYLORD ENTERTAINMENT CO.
2802 Opryland Dr.
Nashville, TN 37214
Tel.: 615-871-6776
Assets: $904,928
Liabilities: $878,620
Net Worth: $26,308
Approx.Rev.: $600,927
Emp.: 4,700
Fiscal Year-end: 12/31/91
Import Export
Operation of Entertainment, Cable Networks, Broadcasting & Cable Television Systems; Parent Company of the Grand Ole Opry, Opryland Park, Opryland Hotel, The Nashville Network, Country Music Television; WSM-AM/FM Radio in Nashville & WKY Radio in P Oklahoma City
S.I.C.: 4833; 4841; 7929; 7011
Edward G. Gaylord *(Chm. Bd.)*
Earl W. Wendell *(Pres. & Chief Exec. Officer)*
Terry E. London *(V.P. & Chief Fin. Officer)*
Michael Dimond *(V.P.-Mktg.)*
Edward H. Ellis *(Treas.)*
Francis M. Wentworth, Jr. *(Sec.)*

Subsidiary:

Oklahoma Publishing Company **(1)**
9000 N. Broadway
Oklahoma City, OK 73114
Tel.: 405-475-3311
Fax: 405-475-3128
Approx.Sls.: $800,000,000
Emp.: 10,000
Fiscal Year-end: 12/31/90
Computer Systems/Hardware:
IBM 4341
Newspaper Publishing & Broadcasting
S.I.C.: 2711; 4832; 4833
Edward L. Gaylord *(Pres. & Publisher)*
Thelma F. Gaylord *(V.P.)*
Edmund O. Martin *(V.P. & Gen. Mgr.)*
Glenn M. Stinchcomb *(V.P. & Treas.)*
Edith Gaylord Harper *(Sec.)*
Dick Dugan *(Dir.-Mktg. Services)*
John Harrington *(Dir.-Personnel)*
David Thompson *(Dir.-Adv.)*
Janet Tucker *(Mgr.-Pur.)*

Division:

The Daily & Sunday Oklahoman **(2)**
9000 N. Broadway
Oklahoma City, OK 73114
Tel.: 405-475-3311
Fax: 405-475-3128
Emp.: 1,000
Fiscal Year-end: 12/31/91
Newspaper Publishers
S.I.C.: 2711
Edward L. Gaylord *(Pres. & Publisher)*
Edmund O. Martin *(V.P.)*
Thelma Gaylord *(V.P.)*
G.M. Stinchcomb *(V.P. & Treas.)*
E.K. Gaylord, II *(V.P. & Asst. Sec.)*
Edith Gaylord Harper *(Sec.)*
David L. Thompson *(Adv. Dir.)*
Clydette Womack *(Mktg. Mgr.)*

Subsidiary:

Gaylord Broadcasting Co. **(2)**
10111 N. Central Expwy.
Dallas, TX 75231
Tel.: 214-363-8722 (100%)
Approx.Sls.: $300,000,000
Emp.: 8,000
S.I.C.: 4832; 4833
Edward L. Gaylord *(Chm. Bd. & Chief Exec. Officer)*
James R. Terrell *(Pres. & Chief Oper. Officer-TV Stations)*
Michael C. Schuch *(V.P. & Mgr.-WVTV)*
Kevin Hale *(V.P. & Mgr.-KSTW)*
Ed Trimble *(V.P. & Mgr.-KTVT)*
Steve Mauldin *(V.P. & Mgr.-KHTV)*
Jim Fisher *(Station Mgr.-WKY)*
G.M. Stinchcomb *(Treas.)*
Edith Gaylord Harper *(Sec.)*

Subsidiaries:

Cencom Cable Television **(3)**
2215 Mission Rd.
Alhambra, CA 91802
Tel.: 818-300-8228
Cable TV
S.I.C.: 4841
Craig Watson *(Pres.)*

Opryland USA, Inc. **(3)**
2804 Opryland Dr.
Nashville, TN 37214
Tel.: 615-889-6611
Emp.: 6,000
Entertainment & Hospitality Service
S.I.C.: 7922
Edward L. Gaylord *(Chm. Bd.)*
E.W. Wendell *(Pres.)*

GAYLORD PRINTING, INC.
15555 Woodrow Wilson
Detroit, MI 48238
Tel.: 313-883-7800
Tel.: 800-486-7746
Fax: 313-883-2917
Year Founded: 1938
Sales Range: $20-39 Million
Emp.: 180
Lithographing & Commercial Printing
S.I.C.: 2752
Charles F. Drebes *(Pres. & Chief Exec. Officer)*
Gary J. Abraham *(V.P.-Fin. & Gen. Counsel)*
William Chambo *(V.P.-Admin.)*
David L. Duncan *(V.P.-Sls.)*
John Dennison *(Controller)*
John S. Abbott *(Sec.)*

Craig Stevens *(Gen. Mgr.)*

No. of Mfg. Plants/Facilities: 2
No. of U.S. Offices: 2

Outside Service Firm(s):

Collins, Buri & McConkey*(Auditors)*
Birmingham, MI

Comerica Bank*(Major Banking Relationship)*
211 W. Fort St.
Detroit, MI 48226
Tel.: 313-222-3300

Divisions:

Gaylord Central Printing & Publishing Div. **(1)**
129 N. Grand Traverse
Flint, MI 48503
Tel.: 313-238-5900
Offset Commercial Printing
S.I.C.: 2752
Noreen Crosley *(Gen. Mgr.)*

Gaylord Lithograph Div.-Detroit **(1)**
1555 Woodrow Wilson
Detroit, MI 49238
Tel.: 313-883-7800
Markets Major Retail Chains In-Store Signing
S.I.C.: 2752
Charles F. Drebes *(Pres.)*

GAYMAR INDUSTRIES, INC.
10 Centre Drive
Orchard Park, NY 14127
Tel.: 716-662-2551
Tel.: 800-828-7341
Fax: 716-662-6120
Year Founded: 1956
Approx.Sls.: $41,000,000
Emp.: 200
Export
Manufacture Medical Equipment
S.I.C.: 3841
John K. Whitney *(Chm.)*
John K. Whitney, Jr. *(Exec. V.P.)*
Ray Blush *(V.P.-Human Resources)*
Frank J. Kopfer *(V.P.-Fin. & Chief Fin. Officer)*
Douglas R. Rash *(V.P.-Mktg.)*
William Cordes *(Controller)*
Jere Culp *(Dir.-Opers.)*
Thomas Wojcik *(Dir.-Info. Services)*
Samuel Baker *(Mgr.-Intl.)*
James Gotro *(Pur. Agent)*
Principal(s):
John K. Whitney

No. of Mfg. Plants/Facilities: 1
No. of U.S. Offices: 1

Outside Service Firm(s):

KPMG Peat Marwick*(Auditors)*
700 Empire Tower
Buffalo, NY 14202-3786
Tel.: 716-854-1830
Fax: 716-856-8063

Fleet Bank*(Major Banking Relationship)*
Deer Park, NY 14202

Subsidiaries:

Clinicare Systems, Inc. **(1)**
10 Center Dr.
Orchard Park, NY 14127
Tel.: 716-662-2551
Tel.: 800-825-7341
Fax: 716-662-0730
Emp.: 80
Medical Equipment Rental Services
S.I.C.: 7352
Doug Rash *(V.P. & Gen. Mgr.)*
Lonny L. Wolgemuth *(Mktg. Mgr.)*

Retec USA, Inc. **(1)**
10 Centre Dr.
Orchard Park, NY 14127
Tel.: 716-662-2551
Tel.: 800-877-3832
Emp.: 15
Mfr. of Wheelchairs
S.I.C.: 3842
John Whitney, Jr. *(V.P. & Gen. Mgr.)*

GAZETTE COMPANY, INC.
500 Third Ave., S.E.
Cedar Rapids, IA 52401
Tel.: 319-398-8211 **IA**
Fax: 319-398-8395
Year Founded: 1957
Approx.Sls.: $35,000,000
Emp.: 600
Publishing & Printing of Newspapers; Television Broadcasting Stations
S.I.C.: 2711; 4833
Joseph Hladky, Jr. *(Chm. Bd.)*
Joe Hladky *(Pres. & Publr.)*
Ken Slaughter *(V.P. & Treas.)*
Elizabeth T. Barry *(Sec.)*

Outside Service Firm(s):

Firstar Bank Cedar Rapids, N.A.*(Major Banking Relationship)*
222 Second Ave. S.E.
Cedar Rapids, IA 52406
Tel.: 319-398-4224

Gearon Hoffman Conlon &Nye

GEARON HOFFMAN CONLON & NYE ADVERTISING, INC.
1051 Franklin Ave.
Garden City, NY 11530
Tel.: 212-688-2400
Fax: 516-746-3889
Year Founded: 1982
Approx.Billings: $20,850,000
Emp.: 34
Robert Conlon *(Chm. & Co-Creative Dir.)*
Dan Gearon *(Vice Chm. & Chief Exec. Officer)*
Paul Nye *(Vice Chm. & Co-Creative Dir.)*
Russell Brown *(V.P., Gen. Mgr.)*
Amanda Davidson *(Office Mgr.)*

Computer Systems/Hardware:
IBM; Macintosh

GEBO DISTRIBUTING CO., INC.
P.O. Box 850
Plainview, TX 79072
Tel.: 806-293-4212
Approx.Sls.: $18,000,000
Emp.: 126
Retail Farm & Home Supplies; Clothing; Automotive Supplies Including Tires & Batteries
S.I.C.: 5719; 5261; 5531; 5651
Brenton T. Gebo *(Pres.)*
L. Evelyn Gebo *(V.P., Sec. & Treas.)*
Don Jones *(Chief Fin. Officer)*
Dick Crigger *(Dir.-Pur.)*

GEER, DUBOIS INC.
114 Fifth Ave.
New York, NY 10011
Tel.: 212-741-1900
Year Founded: 1947
Approx.Billings: $76,000,000
Emp.: 75
Rodney Underwood *(Chm. & Creative Dir.)*
Steve Bowen *(Pres., Chief Exec. Officer)*
Martyn Straw *(Exec. V.P., Dir. Strategic Services)*
Celine Hubler *(V.P., Dir. Agency Opers.)*
Harry Janavey *(V.P., Chief Fin. Officer)*

GEIGER BROTHERS
Mt. Hope Ave.
Lewiston, ME 04240
Tel.: 207-783-2001
Fax: 207-783-6418
Year Founded: 1878
Approx.Sls.: $58,000,000
Emp.: 400
Fiscal Year-end: 1/31/92
Print, Bookbinding, Leather Products, Calendars, Diaries, Year Books, Almanacs & Specialities for Advertising
S.I.C.: 2759; 2782; 2789; 3199; 3993
Raymond A. Geiger *(Chm. Bd.)*
Eugene G. Geiger *(Pres. & Treas.)*
Robert A. Shimko *(Exec. V.P.)*
David L. Cutter *(V.P.-Mngmt. Information Systems)*
Kenneth C. Geiger *(V.P. & Mgr.-Materials)*
Peter E. Geiger *(V.P.-Mktg. & Sls.)*
Ronald G. Giard *(V.P.-Mfg.)*
Peter D. Letourneau *(V.P.-Sls. Service)*
Ronald B. Reynolds *(V.P.-Admin. Service)*

Outside Service Firm(s):

Berry, Dunn & McNeill*(Auditors)*
Portland, ME

Skelton, Taintor & Abbott*(Legal Firm)*
95 Maine St.
Auburn, ME 04210
Tel.: 207-784-3200

Fleet National Bank*(Major Banking Relationship)*
Lewiston, ME

STEPHEN L. GELLER INC.
800 Second Ave.
New York, NY 10017
Tel.: 212-986-6642
Fax: 212-949-9392
Year Founded: 1973
Approx.Billings: $20,000,000
Emp.: 26
Direct Response Print Advertising
Sue Geller *(Chm. Bd. & New Bus. Contact)*
Stephen Geller *(Pres.)*
Marianna Morello *(Exec. V.P.)*
John Romano *(V.P., Sec. & Adv. Mgr.)*
Mary Ann Shraky *(V.P., Barter)*
Robert Ronzo *(Treas.)*
Che Roehner *(Dir.-Sls.)*

GEM-DANDY, INC.
P.O. Box 657
Madison, NC 27025
Tel.: 919-548-9624
Tel.: 800-334-5101
Year Founded: 1922
Approx.Sls.: $11,000,000
Emp.: 233
Import Export
Suspenders, Belts, Neckties, Ladies Panties & Lingerie
S.I.C.: 2389
Rahn Boyer *(Pres. & Chief Exec. Officer)*
Ray Kees *(Chief Fin. Officer, Corp. Sec. & Tres.)*
George R. Penn *(V.P.-Sls. & Mktg.)*
Don Wilson *(V.P.-Mfg. Mgr.)*
Ralph McDevit *(Dir.-Data Processing)*
Don Powers *(Dir.-Engr. & Quality Control)*
Dixie Martin *(Mgr.-Personnel)*
Pat Purdue *(Pur. Agent)*

Computer Systems/Hardware:
Wang

GEM, INCORPORATED
1 Gem Blvd.
Byhalia, MS 38611
Tel.: 601-838-2121
Fax: 601-838-4075
Approx.Sls.: $14,000,000
Emp.: 175
Fiscal Year-end: 10/31/91
Gem Dust Mops, Sponge Mops, Ironing Table Covers, Pads & Cover Sets, Laundry Access.; Cotton Maid Spray Starch; Lad Syrup, Olde Farm Syrup & Household Chemicals
S.I.C.: 2392; 2099; 2499; 2842
C. Sullivan *(Pres.)*
M. Grant *(V.P.-Mfg.)*

GEM INDUSTRIES FINANCE CORPORATION
Highway 123 N.
Toccoa, GA 30577
Mailing Address:
P.O. Box 400
Tocoa, GA 30577
Tel.: 706-886-8431
Fax: 706-886-5119
Year Founded: 1911
Assets: $16,160,889
Liabilities: $4,034,152
Net Worth: $12,126,737
Approx.Sls.: $20,000,000
Emp.: 380
Fiscal Year-end: 12/31/90
Import
Holding Company
S.I.C.: 6719
M.F. Rolla *(Pres. & Chief Oper. Officer)*
Edward E. Berriman *(Exec. V.P. & Gen. Supt.)*
Jerome De Franco *(V.P.-Nursing Home Furniture Div.)*
George Diamond *(V.P.-Contract Div.)*

No. of Mfg. Plants/Facilities: 5
No. of U.S. Offices: 1

Computer Systems/Hardware:
ALTO 500

Subsidiary:

Gem Industries, Inc. **(1)**
525 Parker St.
Gardner, MA 01440
Tel.: 508-632-6800 (100%)
Fax: 508-632-7439
Assets: $16,500,000
Liabilities: $5,695,400
Net Worth: $10,804,600
Approx.Sls.: $23,000,000
Emp.: 390
Fiscal Year-end: 12/31/90
Computer Systems/Hardware:
Altos 500
Mfr. of Metal & Wood Furniture & Hardware
S.I.C.: 2514; 5712; 3449
M.F. Rolla *(Pres. & Chief Oper. Officer)*
Edward E. Berriman *(Exec. V.P. & Gen. Supt.)*
Jerome De Franco *(V.P.-Nursing Home Furniture Div.)*
George Diamond *(V.P.-Contract Div.)*

Subsidiaries:

Benson Corp. **(2)**
512 N. Mill St.
Weyauwega, WI 54983
Tel.: 414-867-2143 (100%)
Approx.Sls.: $5,000,000
Emp.: 45
Mfr. of Metal Furniture & Hardware
S.I.C.: 2514; 3469
James Fredericks *(Chief Oper. Officer)*

Gem Southeast, Inc. **(2)**
Hwy. 123 N.
Toccoa, GA 30577
Tel.: 706-886-8431 (100%)
Approx.Sls.: $8,000,000
Emp.: 60
Mfr. of Work Aids, Metal Furniture, Hardware & Nursing Home Beds
S.I.C.: 2514; 3469; 2599; 2500
Mark Schindler *(Chief Oper. Officer)*

Mohawk Furniture, Inc. **(2)**
Five Mill St.
Broadalbin, NY 12025
Tel.: 518-883-3424 (100%)
Fax: 518-583-3424
Approx.Sls.: $4,000,000
Emp.: 90

Gem Industries Finance Corporation—(Continued)

Mfr. of Domestic Furniture & Dormitory Case Goods
S.I.C.: 2514; 2599; 5712
D.F. Peters *(Chief Oper. Officer)*

GEM TOP MFG., INC.
8811 S.E. Herbert Ct.
Clackamas, OR 97015
Tel.: 503-659-3733
Fax: 503-654-9101
Approx.Sls.: $20,000,000
Emp.: 222
Fiscal Year-end: 9/30/91
Export
Caps For Mounting On Trucks; Recreational Vehicle Parts & Accessories
S.I.C.: 3792; 5531
Judy Fuglestad *(Pres.)*
Henry O. Geisler *(Chief Exec. Officer)*
Gale Kingsbury *(Exec. V.P.-Opers.)*
Robert Forseth *(Dir.-Mfg.)*
Dan Willis *(Dir.-Engrng.)*
Steve Krezo *(Natl. Sls. Mgr.)*
Dwight Griffith *(Pur. Agent)*

Outside Service Firm(s):

Van Beek & Co.*(Auditors)*
Portland, OR

Key Bank*(Major Banking Relationship)*
1211 S.W. Fifth Ave., Suite 300
Portland, OR 97205
Tel.: 503-790-7500

Division:

Gem Top East Inc **(1)**
1124 Haley Rd.
Murfreesboro, TN 37130
Tel.: 615-890-0770
Gary Moss *(Gen. Mgr.)*

GEMINI ALUMINUM CORPORATION
3255 Pomona Blvd.
Pomona, CA 91768
Tel.: 909-595-7403
Fax: 909-594-7962
Sales Range: $40-59 Million
Emp.: 100
Aluminum Extrusions
S.I.C.: 3354
Allan J. Hardy *(Pres.)*
Frank Hogan *(V.P.)*
Lani Hardy *(Dir.-Admin.)*

GEMINI CONSULTING
25 Airport Road
Morristown, NJ 07960
Tel.: 201-285-9000
Fax: 201-285-9020
Year Founded: 1954
Approx.Sls.: $265,000,000
Emp.: 900
Fiscal Year-end: 12/31/91
Management Consulting Services
S.I.C.: 8742
David Teiger *(Chm. Bd.)*
Daniel J. Valentino *(Mng. Dir.-North America)*
James N. Kelly *(Mng. Dir.-Europe & Asia)*
Nicholas Zaccaria *(Treas.)*

Subsidiary:

ParcPlace Systems **(1)**
1550 Plymouth St.
Mountain View, CA 94043
Tel.: 415-691-6700
Mgmnt. Consulting Services
S.I.C.: 8742

Non-U.S. Subsidiaries:

Gemini Consulting-London **(1)**
11-14 Grafton St.
London, W1X 3LA, United Kingdom
Tel.: 71-4995-4006
Fax: 71-629-6128
Management Consulting Services
S.I.C.: 8742

M A C Group (Japan), Inc. **(1)**
JS Ichigaya Bldg., 4th Fl., 5 Goban-cho, Chiyoda-ku
Tokyo, 102, Japan
Tel.: 813-3265-8285
Fax: 813-3265-8540
Management Consulting Service
S.I.C.: 8742
James C. Abeggien *(Pres.)*
John Rolander *(Sr. V.P.)*

GENDERM CORPORATION
600 Knightsbridge Pkwy.
Lincolnshire, IL 60069
Tel.: 708-634-7373
Tel.: 800-325-7246 **DE**
Fax: 708-634-2008
Year Founded: 1983
Assets: $11,000,000
Earnings: $770,000
Liabilities: $8,000,000
Net Worth: $3,000,000
Approx.Sls.: $20,000,000
Emp.: 100
Fiscal Year-end: 12/31/91
Export
Mfr. of Pharmaceuticals
S.I.C.: 2834; 5122; 5100
Dr. Joel Bernstein *(Chm. Bd. & Chief Exec. Officer)*
Frank Pollard *(Pres. & Chief Oper. Officer)*
Edward J. O'Connell *(Chief Fin. Officer)*
Frank Brisben *(Exec. V.P.-Sls.)*
Norman Smagley *(Treas., Sec. & Risk Mngmt.)*
Ronald Russell *(Controller)*
Jessie Coe *(Dir.-Data Processing)*
Gary Knappenberger *(Dir.-Quality Control)*
Jean Rumsfield *(Dir.-Mktg.)*
Peggy Stefanski *(Dir.-Human Resources)*
Dennis West *(Dir.-Res. & Devel.)*

Computer Systems/Hardware:
Novell Network PC's

Subsidiary:

GalenPharma, Inc. **(1)**
600 Knightsbridge
Lincolnshire, IL 60069
Tel.: 708-634-7373
Tel.: 800-325-PAIN
Fax: 708-634-2008
Approx.Sls.: $3,000,000
Emp.: 6
Pharmaceutical Company
S.I.C.: 2834; 5122; 5100
Joel E. Bernstein *(Chm. Bd.)*
Frank Pollard *(Pres.)*

GENERAL AEROSPACE MATERIALS CORPORATION
95 E. Bathpage Rd.
Plainview, NY 11803
Tel.: 516-694-5700
Fax: 516-694-5718
Sales Range: $20-39 Million
Emp.: 150
Aluminum, Stainless Steel, Titanium & Special Metals
S.I.C.: 5051
Lester Kerner *(Pres.)*
George Elkins *(Exec. V.P.)*
Robert Price *(V.P.)*
Joseph Gemmo *(Chief Fin. Officer)*
Bertram Wagner *(Treas.)*

Outside Service Firm(s):

Ernst & Young*(Auditors)*
395 N. Suce Road
Melville, NY 11747

Moses & Singer*(Legal Firm)*
1271 Ave. of the Americas
New York, NY 10020
Tel.: 212-246-3700

NatWest Bank U.S.A.*(Major Banking Relationship)*
New York, NY

GENERAL ALUM & CHEMICAL
1145 Corporate Dr.
Holland, OH 43528
Mailing Address:
P.O. Box 819
Holland, OH 43528
Tel.: 419-865-8000
Tel.: 800-537-7561 **IN**
Fax: 419-865-6413
Year Founded: 1978
Approx.Sls.: $11,500,000
Emp.: 40
Chemical Producer of Aluminum Sulfate
S.I.C.: 2819
James Poure *(Chm. Bd., Pres. & Chief Exec. Officer)*
Timothy Poure *(Exec. V.P.)*
Barbara S. Haase *(V.P.-Admin. Services & Sec.)*
John Kevern *(V.P.-Fin. & Chief Fin. Officer)*
Frank Oddou *(V.P.)*
Denise D. Crouch *(Admin. Asst.)*

No. of Mfg. Plants/Facilities: 3
No. of U.S. Offices: 1

Computer Systems/Hardware:
IBM

Outside Service Firm(s):

Ernst & Young*(Auditors)*
One Sea Gate
Toledo, OH 43604
Tel.: 419-244-8000

Savage, Jordan, Giha & Ballard*(Legal Firm)*
Toledo, OH

Mid American National Bank*(Major Banking Relationship)*
800 Madison Ave.
Toledo, OH 43624
Tel.: 419-255-7434

GENERAL AMERICAN LIFE INSURANCE CO.
700 Market St.
St. Louis, MO 63101
Mailing Address:
P.O. Box 396,
St. Louis, MO 63166
Tel.: 314-231-1700 **MO**
Fax: 314-444-0486
Assets: $6,052,440,603
Earnings: $31,059,284
Liabilities: $5,820,131,641
Net Worth: $232,308,962
Approx.Sls.: $1,907,254,248
Emp.: 2,800
Fiscal Year-end: 12/31/91
Life & Health Insurance
S.I.C.: 6311; 6321
Corporate Giving Program: Majority of Available Funds Go To Health Care & Medical Research Causes.
H. Edwin Trusheim *(Chm. Bd.)*
Richard A. Liddy *(Pres. & Chief Exec. Officer)*
Michael Hogan *(Exec. Grp. V.P.-Life & Health)*
Leonard M. Rubenstein *(Exec. V.P. & Treas.)*
Phillip A. Schorr *(Exec. V.P.-Individual)*
Robert J. Banstetter *(V.P., Gen. Counsel & Sec.)*
John W. Barber *(V.P. & Controller)*
E. Tom Hughes *(V.P. & Actuary-Grp.)*
Michael P. Ingrassia *(V.P.-Grp. Opers.)*
George T. Lacy *(V.P.-Grp. Field Sls.)*
Larry Larance *(V.P.-Pub. Rels. & Human Resources)*
Robert C. Orton *(V.P.-Agency)*
Rowland R. Ricketts *(V.P.-Individual N.B. Claims)*
E. Christopher Simonds *(V.P.-Information Systems)*
Donald L. Smith *(V.P.-Mortgage Loan & Real Estate)*
Deborah Walters *(Second V.P.-Pension Admin.)*
Ruth A. Bradfield *(Dir.-Benefits Admin.)*
Mary Lou Lemley *(Dir.-Real Estate)*
Nancy McBride *(Dir.-Meetings Plng.)*
Orville Moore *(Dir.-Telecommunications)*
Jim Monahan *(Mgr.-Adv.)*
Kathy Spaeth *(Mgr.-Cash Mngmt.)*
John Vogel *(Pur. Agent)*

Computer Systems/Hardware:
Amdahl

Outside Service Firm(s):

KPMG Peat Marwick*(Auditors)*
1010 Market St.
Saint Louis, MO 63101
Tel.: 314-444-1400

General American Life Insurance Co.*(Group Insurer)*
700 Market
Saint Louis, MO 63101
Tel.: 314-525-5458
Fax: 314-525-3677

Subsidiaries:

Consultec, Inc. **(1)**
6065 Roswell Rd., N.E.
Atlanta, GA 30328
Tel.: 404-594-7799 (100%)
Insurance Consultants
S.I.C.: 6411
Gray Arnold *(Pres.)*

Genelco, Inc. **(1)**
1600 S. Brentwood., Ste. 500
Saint Louis, MO 63144
Tel.: 314-962-2040 (100%)
Insurance Consultants
S.I.C.: 6411
David Johnson *(Pres.)*

Paragon Life Insurance Co. **(1)**
7701 Forsyth
Clayton, MO 63105
Tel.: 314-862-2211 (100%)
Life & Health Insurance
S.I.C.: 6311
Carl H. Anderson *(Chief Oper. Officer)*

GENERAL AUTOMATION, INC.
3300 W. Oakton
Skokie, IL 60076
Tel.: 708-676-4004
Fax: 708-676-2213
Emp.: 100
Screw Machine Products
S.I.C.: 3451
Max J. Starr *(Pres.)*
Robert Chleboun *(Mgr.-Engrng.)*

Outside Service Firm(s):

Schwartz & Freeman*(Legal Firm)*
401 N. Michigan Ave., Suite 3400
Chicago, IL 60611
Tel.: 312-222-0800

American National Corporation*(Major Banking Relationship)*
Chicago, IL

GENERAL AUTOMOTIVE CORPORATION
2015 Washtenaw
Ann Arbor, MI 48104
Tel.: 313-994-8000 **DE**
Fax: 313-662-3600
Year Founded: 1979
Approx.Sls.: $310,000,000
Emp.: 1,600
Holding Company; Automotive Accessories; Buses
S.I.C.: 6719; 3711; 3714
Cruse W. Moss *(Chm. Bd. & Chief Exec. Officer)*
Mark J. Obert *(Pres.)*
G. Robert Richards *(Exec. V.P.-Fin. & Admin.)*
Principal(s):
Cruse W. Moss

No. of Mfg. Plants/Facilities: 7

No. of U.S. Offices: 7
No. of Foreign Offices: 1

Computer Systems/Hardware:
IBM

Outside Service Firm(s):

Ernst & Young*(Auditors)*
One Detroit Center, 500 Woodward, Ste. 1700
Detroit, MI 48243
Tel.: 313-259-9600

Seyfarth, Shaw, Fairweather & Geraldson*(Legal Firm)*
520 Madison Ave.
New York, NY 10022
Tel.: 212-715-9000

Massachusetts Mutual Life Insurance Co.*(Pension Manager)*
1295 State Street
Springfield, MA 01111
Tel.: 413-788-8411

Subsidiaries:

Flexible Corp. **(1)**
970 Pittsburgh Dr.
Delaware, OH 43015
Tel.: 614-362-2600 (100%)
Emp.: 1,100
Transit Bus Manufacturer
S.I.C.: 3711
Edward N. Kravitz *(Pres. & Chief Oper Officer)*

GENERAL AUTOMOTIVE SPECIALTY CO., INC.
Rtes. 1 & 130
North Brunswick, NJ 08902
Mailing Address:
P.O. Box 3042
North Brunswick, NJ 08902
Tel.: 908-545-7000
Fax: 908-545-7201
Sales Range: $40-59 Million
Emp.: 1,000
Mfr. of Electrical Switches, Trailer Connectors, Pigtails, Sockets & Locks
S.I.C.: 3678; 3613; 3679
Ronald B. Hermann *(Chm. & Pres.)*
Stanley Godt *(V.P.-Fin.)*
Jesse Hermann *(V.P.-Sls. & Mktg.)*
Mark Levine *(V.P.-Engrng.)*

Outside Service Firm(s):

Cole, Schotz, Bernstein, Meisel & Forman*(Legal Firm)*
New Rochelle, NJ

General Binding Corporation
(See listing under General Automotive Specialty Co., Inc.)

GENERAL BUSINESS SERVICES, INC.
7134 Columbia Gateway Dr.
Columbia, MD 21046
Tel.: 410-290-1040
Tel.: 800-638-7940
Fax: 410-290-1233
Approx.Sls.: $13,000,000
Emp.: 250
Fiscal Year-end: 3/31/91
Small Business Counseling Franchise
S.I.C.: 8742; 8748
Robert Pirtle *(Chm. & Pres.)*
Peter H. Johnson *(Exec. V.P.)*
Edward Arrington *(V.P.-Mktg.)*
Janet McGlynn *(V.P.-Training)*
Lois Giles *(Insurance Mgr.)*

GENERAL COMPUTER CORP. INC.
2045 Midway Dr.
Twinsburg, OH 44087
Tel.: 216-425-3241 **OH**
Fax: 216-425-3249
Year Founded: 1970
Assets: $10,685,935
Earnings: $706,143
Liabilities: $5,387,608
Net Worth: $5,298,327
Approx.Rev.: $13,238,074
Fiscal Year-end: 5/31/92
Computer Programming & Software Services, Data Processing Services
S.I.C.: 7371; 7372; 7374
Sidney Dworkin *(Chm. Bd.)*
Joseph E. Adams *(Vice Chm.)*
R.R. Pilarczyk *(Pres., Chief Exec. Officer & Treas.)*
Kenneth McClain *(Exec. V.P.-Mktg.)*
Thomas Stanek *(Exec. V.P.-Opers.)*
Robert M. Phillips *(Sr. V.P.-Services)*
David R. Stitt *(Sr. V.P.-Fin. & Admin.)*
James J. Mindala *(V.P.-Sls.)*

Subsidiary:

Mavis Industries, Inc. **(1)**
2976 Alhambra Dr.
Cameron Park, CA 95682
Tel.: 916-677-1234 (100%)
Provides Computer Systems & Services to Pharmacies
S.I.C.: 7371; 7372; 7374

GENERAL DRUG CO.
200 N. Fairfield Ave.
Chicago, IL 60612
Tel.: 312-826-4242 **IL**
Fax: 312-826-6231
Approx.Sls.: $23,000,000
Emp.: 43
Fiscal Year-end: 4/30/91
Wholesaler of Drugs
S.I.C.: 5122; 5100
Seymour Stoller *(Pres.)*
Sidney Gimbel *(Sec.)*

Outside Service Firm(s):

Richard Mann*(Auditors)*
Waukegan, IL

Holleb & Coff, Ltd.*(Legal Firm)*
55 E. Monroe, Suite 4100
Chicago, IL 60603
Tel.: 312-807-4600

LaSalle National Bank*(Major Banking Relationship)*
120 S. LaSalle St.
Chicago, IL 60603
Tel.: 312-781-8000

GENERAL ELECTRIC MASTER RETIREMENT TRUST
3003 Summer St.
Stamford, CT 06905
Tel.: 203-357-4100 **CT**
Fax: 203-326-4250
Year Founded: 1940
Approx.Sls.: $13,100,000,000
Emp.: 105
Investments & Trusts Management
S.I.C.: 6733
Dale F. Frey *(Chm. Bd. & Pres.)*
Arthur G. Bahr *(Trustee)*
Michael J. Cosgrove *(Trustee)*
Allan M. Lewis *(Trustee)*
John H. Myers *(Trustee)*
Eugene Bolton *(Trustee)*
John Reissberg *(Trustee)*

GENERAL GROWTH COMPANIES, INC.
215 Keo
Des Moines, IA 50309
Tel.: 515-281-9100 **MA**
Fax: 515-283-0635
Year Founded: 1964
Approx.Sls.: $110,000,000
Approx.Assets:$55,000,000
Emp.: 2,600
Fiscal Year-end: 12/31/91
Real Estate Development & Management
S.I.C.: 6552; 6531
Martin Bucksbaum *(Chm. Bd. & Chief Exec. & Info. Officer)*
Matthew Bucksbaum *(Pres., Treas. & Sec.)*
John Bucksbaum *(Exec. V.P.)*
Stanley Richards *(Exec. V.P. & Gen. Counsel)*
John Walker *(V.P.)*

No. of U.S. Offices: 3

Outside Service Firm(s):

Coopers & Lybrand*(Auditors)*
Des Moines, IA

Goldman, Sachs & Co.*(Investment Banker)*
85 Broad St.
New York, NY 10004
Tel.: 212-902-1000
Fax: 212-902-4451

CIGNA*(Group Insurance Broker/ Consult)*
Hartford, CT
Tel.: 203-726-6000

Wachtell, Lipton, Rosen & Katz*(Legal Firm)*
299 Park Ave.
New York, NY 10171

Citibank N.A.*(Major Banking Relationship)*
Corporate Trust Services, 399 Park Ave.
New York, NY 10043
Tel.: 212-559-1605

First Bank of St. Paul*(Major Banking Relationship)*
St. Paul, MN

Wells Fargo Bank*(Major Banking Relationship)*
420 Montgomery St.
San Francisco, CA 94104

Subsidiaries:

General Growth Center Companies, Inc. **(1)**
400 South Hwy. 169, Ste. 800
Minneapolis, MN 55426
Tel.: 612-525-1200 (100%)
Fax: 612-525-2192
Emp.: 1,650
Shopping Center Management
S.I.C.: 6512; 8741

General Growth of California, Inc. **(1)**
15821 Ventura Blvd., Ste. 525
Encino, CA 91436
Tel.: 818-907-3400 (100%)
Fax: 818-907-8841
Emp.: 40
Real Estate Development
S.I.C.: 6552

GENERAL HOMES CORPORATION
(Filed Chapter 11 Bankruptcy, January 10, 1991)
7322 Southwest Freeway
Houston, TX 77074
Tel.: 713-270-4177 **TX**
Year Founded: 1973
Assets: $339,490,000
Earnings: ($155,026,000)
Liabilities: $448,001,000
Net Worth: $108,511,000
Approx.Rev.: $258,460,000
Emp.: 988
Fiscal Year-end: 9/30/89
Volume Production & Sale of Moderately Priced Single-Family Homes & the Development of Related Subdivisions
S.I.C.: 1521
William A. LeSage *(Chm. Bd & Chief Exec. Officer)*
James C. Alexander *(V.P., Sec. & Treas.)*
Sidney H. Evans *(V.P. & Controller)*
Dennis Garrett *(V.P.)*
Jon W. Morris *(V.P.)*

Outside Service Firm(s):

Arthur Andersen & Co.*(Auditors)*
711 Louisiana, Ste. 1300
Houston, TX 77002-2323
Tel.: 713-237-2793

Baker & Botts*(Legal Firm)*
3000 One Shell Plaza
Houston, TX 77002
Tel.: 713-229-1789

Subsidiary:

FGMC, Inc. **(1)**
7322 Southwest Freeway
Houston, TX 77074
Tel.: 713-270-4177 (100%)
Mortgage Bankers
S.I.C.: 6162
James W. Olafson *(Pres.)*

GENERAL LATEX & CHEMICAL CORPORATION
675 Massachusetts Ave.
Cambridge, MA 02139
Tel.: 617-576-8000
Fax: 617-876-1010
Year Founded: 1927
Approx.Sls.: $120,000,000
Emp.: 300
Natural & Synthetic Latex & Resin Compounds, Urethane Foam Compounds
S.I.C.: 5162; 5169; 2822
Robert W. MacPherson *(Chm. Bd. & Chief Exec. Officer)*
William H. Jefferson *(Pres.)*
Jack E. Hobbs *(V.P.)*
Dean L. McGinis *(V.P.)*
James F. Twohig *(Pur. Agent)*

Outside Service Firm(s):

KPMG Peat Marwick*(Auditors)*
One Boston Place
Boston, MA 02108
Tel.: 617-723-7700

Shawmut Bank*(Major Banking Relationship)*
1 Federal St.
Boston, MA 02110
Tel.: 617-292-3715

Divisions:

General Latex & Chemical Corp (N.C.) **(1)**
P.O. Box 5487
Charlotte, NC 28225
Tel.: 704-376-3582
Fax: 704-342-1704
J.E. Hobbs *(V.P. & Gen. Mgr.)*

General Latex & Chemical Corp (Ohio) **(1)**
P.O. Box 498
Ashland, OH 44805
Tel.: 419-289-2727
Fax: 419-289-0779
Mfr. of Urethane Foam & Latex
S.I.C.: 2822
Sheldon Hopkins *(V.P. & Gen. Mgr.)*

General Latex & Chemical Corporation (Georgia) **(1)**
P.O. Box 709
Dalton, GA 30720
Tel.: 706-278-3622
Fax: 706-278-5462
Mfr. of Urethane & Latex Compounds
S.I.C.: 2822
J.E. Hobbs *(V.P. & Gen. Mgr.)*

General Latex & Chemical Corporation **(1)**
P.O. Box 748
Cucamonga, CA 91729
Tel.: 909-987-6261
Fax: 909-987-5504
Mfr. of Urethane & Latex Compounds
S.I.C.: 2822
Dean McGinnis *(Gen. Mgr.)*

General Latex & Chemical Corporation **(1)**
67 High St.
North Billerica, MA 01862
Tel.: 508-663-3485
Fax: 508-663-3488
John W. Blomstrom *(Gen. Mgr.)*

GENERAL MARINE INDUSTRIES, INC.
6725 Bay Line Dr.
Panama City, FL 32404
Mailing Address:
P.O. Box 15488,
Panama City, FL 32406
Tel.: 904-769-0311
Fax: 904-769-0731
Boat Building & Repair
S.I.C.: 3732
Terry Rutherford *(Pres.)*
Steve Johnson *(V.P.-Opers.)*
Mike Robinson *(V.P.-Sls. & Mktg.)*

Outside Service Firm(s):

Harold Harper*(Auditors)*
Tiftin, GA

Subsidiaries:

Century Boats By General Marine Industries **(1)**
6725 Bay Line Dr.
Panama City, FL 32404
Tel.: 904-769-0311
Fax: 904-769-0731
Approx.Sls.: $40,000,000
Emp.: 300
Export
Mfr. Fiberglass Pleasure Boats
S.I.C.: 3732
Richard Hostetter *(Chm. Bd.)*
Bill Whitfield *(Pres.)*
Rick Futrell *(Exec. V.P.-Sls.)*
Steve Johnson *(Exec. V.P.-Opers.)*
David P. Adam *(Chief Fin. Officer)*
Angie Hill *(Dir.-Human Resources)*
David Nix *(Dir.-Pur.)*
Virginia Holmes *(Sec.)*

GMI, Inc.-Glasstream **(1)**
6725 Bay Line Dr.
Panama City, FL 32404
Tel.: 904-769-0311
Fax: 904-769-0731
Approx.Sls.: $55,000,000
Emp.: 1,200
Export
Manufacture Fiberglass Boats
S.I.C.: 3732
William Whitfield *(Chm. Bd. & Pres.)*
Steve Johnson *(Exec. V.P.-Opers.)*
Rick Futrell *(V.P.-Sls.)*
Dave Adam *(Chief Fin. Officer)*
Diana Holmes *(Dir.-Mktg.)*
Hank Bennett *(Dir.-Tech. Engrng.)*
Glen Mattox *(Dir.-Natural Resources)*
Angie Hill *(Dir.-Personnel)*
Mike Serian *(Dir.-Data Processing)*
David Nix *(Pur. Dir.)*
Robert Fisher *(Mgr.-Matls.)*

GENERAL MEDIA PUBLISHING GROUP
1965 Broadway
New York, NY 10023
Tel.: 212-496-6100
Fax: 212-580-3693
Year Founded: 1965
Approx.Sls.: $185,000,000
Emp.: 438
Fiscal Year-end: 12/31/90
Publisher of Penthouse, The Girls of Penthouse, Penthouse Letters, Omni, Longevity, Compute, Four Wheeler, Open Wheel, Stock Car Racing Magazine, Superstock & Drag Illustrated, Variations, Forum, Special Magazines & Books, Foreign Editions
S.I.C.: 2721; 2731; 2741
Corporate Giving Program: City-Meals-On-Wheels, United Cerebral Palsy, Police Athletic League, Syracuse Cancer Research Institute, AMFAR
Employee Matching Gifts Program: Match City-Meals-On-Wheels & Others on a Case by Case Basis
Bob Guccione *(Chm. Bd., Chief Exec. Officer & Publr.)*
Kathy Keeton *(Pres. & Chief Oper. Officer)*
William Marlieb *(Pres.-Mktg. Div.)*
Jeri Winston *(Sr. V.P.-Admin.)*
Pat Gavin *(V.P.-Fin. & Chief Fin. Officer)*
Nancy Kestenbaum *(V.P. & Dir.-Group Adv. Sales)*
Anthony Guccione *(Sec. & Treas.)*
Larry Sutter *(Legal Officer)*
Avorey Arnold *(Dir.-Adv.)*
Dane Hall *(Dir.-Pub. Rels.)*
Bob Rattner *(Dir.-Res.)*
Robyn Wisneski *(Dir.-Personnel)*
Principal(s):
Kathy Keeton

Computer Systems/Hardware:
IBM PC & Apple

Outside Service Firm(s):

Grant Thornton*(Auditors)*
605 Third Ave.
New York, NY 10158
Tel.: 212-599-0100
Fax: 212-370-4520

Travelers Insurance Co.*(Group Insurer)*
1 Tower Square
Hartford, CT 06183-2492
Tel.: 203-277-4542
Fax: 203-277-5038

Divisions:

Omni Publications International Ltd. **(1)**
1965 Broadway
New York, NY 10023
Tel.: 212-496-6100
Emp.: 350
Magazine Publishing
S.I.C.: 2721
Bob Guccione *(Chm., Editor & Publisher)*
Kathy Keeton Guccione *(Pres.)*
Frank DeVino *(Sr. V.P. & Graphics Dir.)*
John Evans *(Sr. V.P. & Production Dir.)*
Linda Newman *(V.P. & Assoc. Publisher)*
Anthony J. Guccione *(Sec. & Treas.)*
Dane Hall *(Dir.-Pub. Rels.)*

Saturday Review Magazine **(1)**
1965 Broadway
New York, NY 10023
Tel.: 212-496-6100
Approx.Sls.: $3,530,000
Emp.: 18
S.I.C.: 2721
Bob Guccione *(Publr.)*

GENERAL MEDIA SERVICES, INC.
23 Meeker Rd.
Westport, CT 06880
Tel.: 203-222-0244
Fax: 203-227-0126
Year Founded: 1986
Approx.Billings: $10,800,000
Emp.: 8
Media Strategy, Planning, Buying
Richard Atkins *(Pres.)*
Susanne Atkins *(Exec. V.P.)*

GENERAL METALCRAFT, INC.
Mckee Rd.
Dover, DE 19903
Mailing Address:
P.O. Box 557,
Dover, DE 19903
Tel.: 302-678-3454
Fax: 302-678-0312
Approx.Sls.: $30,000,000
Emp.: 350
Fiscal Year-end: 6/30/92
Export
Manufacture Metal Office Furniture
S.I.C.: 2522
Edmond Spiegelman *(Pres. & Dir.-Mktg.)*
R. Burr *(V.P.-Sls.)*
M. Amsterdam *(Sec. & Treas.)*
C. Spiegelman *(Mgr.-Plant)*

Computer Systems/Hardware:
IBM

Outside Service Firm(s):

Kopple & Gottlieb*(Auditors)*
Philadelphia, PA

Kleinbard, Bell & Brecker*(Legal Firm)*
30 S. 17th St.
Philadelphia, PA 19103
Tel.: 215-568-2000

GENERAL SAFETY CORPORATION
23001 Industrial Dr. W.
Saint Clair Shores, MI 48080
Tel.: 313-777-6530
Fax: 313-772-8819
Approx.Sls.: $75,000,000
Emp.: 880
Mfr. Automobile Seat Belts & Hardware
S.I.C.: 2399; 3429
Alfred J. Fisher, Jr. *(Chm. Bd.)*
Alfred J. Fisher III *(Pres.)*
John Brownell *(V.P.)*
Michael R. Fisher *(V.P.)*
Richard Retman *(Treas.)*
Vince Mayer *(Dir.-Mfg.)*
Robert Mudloff *(Dir.-Pur.)*

Outside Service Firm(s):

Plante & Moran*(Auditors)*
Southfield, MI

Honigman, Miller, Schwartz & Cohn*(Legal Firm)*
2290 First National Bldg.
Detroit, MI 48226
Tel.: 313-256-7800

N.B.D. Bank, N.A.*(Major Banking Relationship)*
611 Woodward Ave.
Detroit, MI 48226
Tel.: 313-225-1122
Fax: 313-225-3420

General Science Corporation
(Acquired by Science Applications International Corporation)

GENERAL SERVICES CORPORATION
2922 Hathaway Rd.
Richmond, VA 23225
Tel.: 804-320-7101
Fax: 804-323-1747
Sales Range: $20-39 Million
Emp.: 350
Real Estate Investment; Apartment Owner & Manager
S.I.C.: 6513; 6531
Jonathan S. Perel *(Pres.)*
John Hunt *(V.P.-Apt. Property Mngmt.)*
Marianne Phillips *(V.P.)*
Winfrey Brooks *(Treas.)*
Principal(s):
Jonathan S. Perel

Computer Systems/Hardware:
IBM System 38

Outside Service Firm(s):

Blue Cross & Blue Shield of Virginia*(Group Insurer)*
2015 Staples Mill Rd.
Richmond, VA 23230
Tel.: 804-359-7000
Fax: 804-354-7397

Marks Stokes & Harrison*(Legal Firm)*
Hopewell, VA

Central Fidelity Bank*(Major Banking Relationship)*
Richmond, VA

GENERAL SHIP CORPORATION
300 Northern Ave.
Boston, MA 02210
Tel.: 617-261-4200 **MA**
Fax: 617-330-5399
Year Founded: 1932
Sales Range: $20-39 Million
Emp.: 250
Export
Shipbuilding & Ship Repairing, Machine & Job Shop Work, Heavy Metal Fabrication In Aluminium & Steel
S.I.C.: 3731; 3354; 3499; 3599
James Harvie *(Chm. Bd., Pres. & Chief Exec. Officer)*
Keith A. Brown *(Exec. V.P. & Treas.)*
Stephen G. Clark *(V.P.-Admin.)*
Richard H. Owen *(V.P.-Opers.)*
Michael McKinnon *(Controller)*
Thomas G. Gentile *(Mgr.-Pur.)*

No. of Mfg. Plants/Facilities: 2

Outside Service Firm(s):

Arthur Andersen & Co.*(Auditors)*
One Intl. Place, 100 Oliver St.
Boston, MA 02110
Tel.: 617-330-4000
Fax: 617-439-9731

Choate, Hall & Stewart*(Legal Firm)*
Exchange Place, 53 State St.
Boston, MA 02109
Tel.: 617-227-5020

U.S. Trust Co.*(Major Banking Relationship)*
40 Court St.
Boston, MA 02108
Tel.: 617-726-7371
Fax: 617-726-7380

GENERAL SPORTCRAFT COMPANY LTD.
140 Woodbine St.
Bergenfield, NJ 07621
Tel.: 201-384-4242
Fax: 201-387-8128
Year Founded: 1926
Approx.Sls.: $30,000,000
Emp.: 125
Fiscal Year-end: 12/31/90
Import Export
Mfr. & Distributor of Sports Equipment, Darts, Badminton, Table Tennis & Backyard Games
S.I.C.: 3949; 3944
Sophie Holdstein *(Chm. Bd.)*
Kenneth J. Edelson *(Pres. & Chief Exec. Officer)*
Michael J. Nally *(Exec. V.P. & Chief Oper. Officer)*
Michael A. Sloane *(V.P.-Sls.)*
Charles Sasjack, Jr. *(Chief Fin. Officer)*
Jill Edelson *(Sec.)*
Lawrence J. Gazlay *(Dir.-Mktg.)*
James O'Keeffe *(Dir.-Sls.)*
Maria Jen *(Mgr.-Data Processing)*
Michael A. Sloane *(Mgr.-Export & Intl. Bus. Cont.)*
Robert Weisinger *(Mgr.-Personnel)*

Computer Systems/Hardware:
IBM

GENERAL SPRING, INC.
(Formerly General Spring & Wire Company, Inc.)
P.O. Box 176
Hartsville, TN 37074-0176
Tel.: 615-374-9500
Fax: 615-374-9540
Assets: $8,000,000
Liabilities: $6,000,000
Net Worth: $2,000,000
Sales Range: $10-19 Million
Emp.: 82
Fiscal Year-end: 5/31/90
Mfr. Mechanical Wire Springs
S.I.C.: 3495
Ed Lang *(Pres.)*

No. of Mfg. Plants/Facilities: 1

Computer Systems/Hardware:
Novell

Outside Service Firm(s):

Collinsworth & Bright*(Auditors)*
Lebanon, TN

CNA Insurance*(Commercial Insurance Carrier)*
CNA Plaza,
Chicago, IL 60685
Tel.: 312-822-5000

Blue Cross & Blue Shield of Tennessee*(Group Insurer)*
Chattanooga, TN

Nutter, McClennen & Fish*(Legal Firm)*
600 Atlantic Ave.
Boston, MA 02210
Tel.: 617-973-9700

Worcester County Institution for Savings*(Major Banking Relationship)*
Worcester, MA

GENERAL TEXTILES
1690 Brandywine
Chula Vista, CA 91911
Tel.: 619-421-5777
Approx.Sls.: $36,000,000
Emp.: 570
Retail Family Clothing & Shoes
S.I.C.: 5651; 5661
Michael Weisberge *(Pres.)*
Andrew Rosenberg *(Dir.-Adv.)*

GENERAL TIME CORP.
520 Guthridge Ct.
Norcross, GA 30092
Mailing Address:
P.O. Box 4125,
Norcross, GA 30091-4125
Tel.: 404-447-5300 **DE**
Telex: 261314
Fax: 404-242-4009
Sales Range: $60-79 Million
Emp.: 900
Fiscal Year-end: 2/28/91
Import Export
Manufacture Clocks, Time & Precision Instruments
S.I.C.: 3873
Frederick M. Pistilli *(Chm. & Chief Exec. Officer)*
David A. Casselman *(V.P.-Fin., Controller, Sec. & Treas.)*
Bob L. Krecl *(V.P.-Mktg. & Sls.)*
Don Ragogna *(V.P.-Mfg.)*

No. of Mfg. Plants/Facilities: 1

Divisions:

Seth Thomas **(1)**
520 Guthridge Ct.
Norcross, GA 30092
Tel.: 404-447-0737
Telex: 261314
Clocks & Nautical Instruments
S.I.C.: 3873
Frederick M. Pistilli *(Chm. & Chief Exec. Officer)*
Dorothy Cox *(Mktg. Communications Coord.)*

Westclox **(1)**
520 Gutheridge Ct.
Norcross, GA 30092
Tel.: 404-447-5300
Telex: 261314
Fax: 404-242-4009
Emp.: 100
Westclox Spring Wound Clocks, Electric Clocks, Quartz Clocks, Wall Clocks & Solid State Alarm Clocks
S.I.C.: 3873
Frederick M. Pistilli *(Pres.)*
David Casselman *(Controller)*
Dorothy Cox *(Mktg. Communications Coord.)*
Robert Krecl *(Dir.-Mktg.)*

GENERAL TOOLS MFG.
80 White St.
New York, NY 10013
Tel.: 212-431-6100
Fax: 212-431-6499
Year Founded: 1922
Approx.Sls.: $15,000,000
Emp.: 50
Import Export
Mfr. of Hand & Precision Tools, Measuring Devices, Magnets, Magnetic Tools
S.I.C.: 3423; 3545; 3823
Gerald Weinstein *(Chm. Bd.)*
Peter Charnley *(Pres.)*
Leonard Hirsch *(V.P.-Fin. & Chief Fin. Officer)*
Tom McGannon *(V.P.-Mktg.)*
Martin Weinstein *(V.P.)*
Frank Taormina *(Mgr.-Adv.)*

Computer Systems/Hardware:
Basic Four

GENERAL WELDING SUPPLY CORPORATION
400 Shames Dr.
Westbury, NY 11590
Tel.: 516-334-8834 **NY**
Fax: 516-334-6943
Year Founded: 1962
Sales Range: $10-19 Million
Emp.: 35
Distribute Welding Products
S.I.C.: 5084
James P. Ruddy *(Pres.)*
Joanna Ruddy *(Sec.)*
Peter Dalal *(Controller)*

Outside Service Firm(s):

Black & Brownstein*(Legal Firm)*
Long Island, NY

Chemical Bank*(Major Banking Relationship)*
Long Island City, NY

GENERAL WHOLESALE COMPANY, INC.
1271 A Tacoma Dr.
Atlanta, GA 30318
Tel.: 404-352-1041 **GA**
Fax: 404-351-2502
Year Founded: 1982
Approx.Sls.: $75,000,000
Emp.: 200
Wholesale Distribution of Liquor, Wine, Beer & Other Fermented Malt Liquors
S.I.C.: 5182; 5181
Jane H. Young *(Chm. Bd.)*
William D. Young, Sr. *(Pres. & Chief Exec. Officer)*
E. Howard Young *(V.P.)*
William D. Young, Jr. *(V.P. & Sec.)*

GENERATION METALS CORP.
300 Oser Ave.
Hauppauge, NY 11788
Tel.: 516-273-0073
Fax: 516-434-1115
Approx.Sls.: $12,000,000
Emp.: 40
Fiscal Year-end: 10/31/91
Metals & Aerospace Parts Distributor
S.I.C.: 5088
Marvin Rubman *(Exec. V.P. & Adv. Dir.)*
Bernard Kole *(Exec. V.P.)*
Joseph Coonan *(Export Mgr.)*

GENERRA SPORTSWEAR COMPANY, INC.
18200 Segale Parkdrive B
Tukwila, WA 98188
Tel.: 206-728-6888 **WA**
Fax: 206-394-6208
Year Founded: 1980
Approx.Sls.: $160,000,000
Emp.: 550
Mfr. & Market Women's, Men's & Children's Sportswear Apparel
S.I.C.: 2329; 2339; 5137
Steven M. Miska *(Chm. Bd. & Chief Exec. Officer)*
Daniel F. Prentice *(Pres. & Chief Oper. Officer)*
Dwight D. Boyd *(Exec. V.P.-Opers.)*
Russell Riggins *(Exec. V.P.-Fin. & Legal Counsel)*
Helen M. Hull *(V.P.-Fin.)*
Paul Chan *(Sec. & Treas.)*

Principal(s):
Steven M. Miska
Daniel F. Prentice
Charles C.K. Yeung

No. of U.S. Offices: 1

Outside Service Firm(s):

KPMG Peat Marwick*(Auditors)*
3100 Two Union Square, 601 Union St., Ste. 3100
Seattle, WA 98101
Tel.: 206-292-1500

Security Pacific National Bank Washington*(Major Banking Relationship)*
Seattle, WA

Subsidiary:

Generra Sportswear (Hong Kong) Ltd. **(1)**
97 How Ming St. Kwun Tong, Kowloon, Hong Kong
Piece Goods Acquisition & Order Placement
S.I.C.: 2269
Kenny Won *(Pres.)*

GENESEE METAL STAMPINGS, INC.
975 John St.
West Henrietta, NY 14586
Tel.: 716-328-3351
Sales Range: $10-19 Million
Emp.: 35
Metal Stampings
S.I.C.: 3469
Gerard Caschette *(Pres. & Treas.)*
Dale Mallaber *(V.P.)*
Richard Whistler *(Mgr.-Sls.)*

Computer Systems/Hardware:
MAI Basic Four

Outside Service Firm(s):

Mengel, Metzer Barr & Co.*(Auditors)*
Rochester, NY

Woods, Oviatt, Gilman, Sturman & Clarke*(Legal Firm)*
44 Exchange St.
Rochester, NY 14614
Tel.: 716-454-5370

Marine Midland Bank*(Major Banking Relationship)*
One Marine Midland Plaza
Rochester, NY

GENEVA CORPORATION
300 N. Greene St.
Greensboro, NC 27401
Mailing Address:
P.O. Box 21962,
Greensboro, NC 27420
Tel.: 919-275-9936 **NC**
Fax: 919-274-4984
Approx.Sls.: $160,000,000
Emp.: 750
Export
Wholesale & Distribution of Cedar Products
S.I.C.: 5031; 5021
F. James Becher, Jr. *(Chm. Bd. & Pres.)*
William J. Armfield, IV *(V.P.)*
Thomas E. Grant *(V.P.-Human Resources)*
H. Michael Weaver *(V.P.)*
Russell R. Myers *(Controller)*

Outside Service Firm(s):

North Carolina National Bank*(Major Banking Relationship)*
Charlotte, NC 28255
Tel.: 704-374-5735

GENEVAR ENTERPRISES
1120-B Elkton Dr.
Colorado Springs, CO 80907
Tel.: 719-593-1015
Telex: 450827 SP
Fax: 719-590-7466
Holding Company
S.I.C.: 6719; 3577
Gene Rider *(Pres.)*
Lowell Bell *(V.P.-Opers.)*
Renee Anzuini *(Controller)*

Outside Service Firm(s):

Deloitte & Touche*(Auditors)*
P.O. Box 938,
Colorado Springs, CO 80901
Tel.: 719-636-5126

Sherman & Howard*(Legal Firm)*
633 17th St.
Denver, CO 80202
Tel.: 303-297-2900

First American Bank, N.A.*(Major Banking Relationship)*
Colorado Springs, CO

Subsidiary:

Brown Disc Products Company **(1)**
1120-B Elkton Dr.
Colorado Springs, CO 80907
Tel.: 719-593-1015 (100%)
Telex: 450827 SP
Mfr. of Flexible Diskettes
S.I.C.: 3577
Gene Rider *(Pres.)*
Harry McCreery *(V.P.-Fin.)*
Lowell Bell *(V.P.-Opers.)*

GENEVE CORPORATION
96 Cummings Point Rd.
Stamford, CT 06902
Tel.: 203-358-8000 **DE**
Year Founded: 1986
Approx.Sls.: $349,000,000
Emp.: 2,000
Financial Mail Orders & Metal Fabrication
S.I.C.: 6411; 5961; 2821
Edward Netter *(Chm. Bd. & Pres.)*
Steven B. Lapin *(Exec. V.P. Opers & Asst. Sec.)*
Ronald G. Strackbein *(Exec. V.P.)*
John Flack *(Sr. V.P.)*
Robert T. Keiser *(Sr. V.P.)*
Frederick G. Meyer *(Controller)*

Outside Service Firm(s):

Putnam Trust of Greenwich*(Major Banking Relationship)*
Greenwich, CT

Subsidiaries:

First International Reinsurance Company **(1)**
485 Madison Ave.
New York, NY 10022
Insurance
S.I.C.: 6411

Geneve Capital Group Inc. **(1)**
485 Madison Ave.
New York, NY 10022
Tel.: 212-355-4141
Insurance
S.I.C.: 6399

Independence Holding Company **(1)**
96 Cummings Point Rd.
Stamford, CT 06902
Tel.: 203-358-8000
Approx.Rev.: $53,057,000
Emp.: 360
Fiscal Year-end: 12/31/90
Life Insurance; Investment Management
S.I.C.: 6719; 6211
Edward Netter *(Chm. Bd. & Chief Exec. Officer)*
Steven B. Lapin *(Exec. V.P. Opers. & Asst. Sec.)*

Geneve Corporation—(Continued)

Madison National Life Insurance Co., Inc. **(1)**
6120 University Ave.
Middleton, WI 53562
Tel.: 608-238-2691 (100%)
Life Insurance
S.I.C.: 6311
Stephen McCormick *(Pres.)*

Nasco **(1)**
901 Janesville Ave.
Fort Atkinson, WI 53538
Tel.: 414-563-2446
Emp.: 400
Mail Order Catalog
S.I.C.: 5961
W. Phil Niemeger *(Exec. V.P. & Chief Exec. Officer)*
Phillip W. Niemeyer *(V.P.)*
Cynthia Ludeman *(Dir.-Personnel)*
Kent R. Parks *(Dir.-Adv.)*
Mike Wagner *(Dir.-Data Processing)*
Gordon Marquart *(Mgr.-Export)*
Curt Loeffler *(Pur. Agent)*

Southern Life and Health Insurance Company **(1)**
2101 Highland Ave.
Birmingham, AL 35205
Tel.: 205-933-1160
Insurance
S.I.C.: 6311; 6331
Jimmy E. Phillips *(Pres.)*
Hubert Stiles *(Sr. V.P.)*

Standard Security Life Insurance Company of New York **(1)**
485 Madison Ave.
New York, NY 10022
Tel.: 212-355-4141
Emp.: 48
Fiscal Year-end: 12/31/90
Insurance
S.I.C.: 6311
Morrison Rein *(Pres. & Chief Exec. Officer)*
Alex Giordano *(Sr. V.P.-Sls.)*

THE GENIE COMPANY
22790 Lakepark Blvd.
Alliance, OH 44601
Tel.: 216-821-5360 **OH**
Fax: 216-821-4702
Emp.: 600
Export
Mfr. of Residential Garage Door Opener System, Gate Openers, Wet/Dry Shop Vacuums and Garage Trash Compactors
S.I.C.: 3589; 3699; 3639
John T. Gray *(Pres. & Chief Exec. Officer)*
Jerry Haley *(V.P.-Opers.)*
Bennett Rubin *(V. P.-Mktg. & Sls.)*
Thomas Zilliox *(V.P.-Fin. & Admin.)*
John Mullen *(Dir.-Quality & Engrng.)*

Division:

The Genie Company **(1)**
2850 Gilchrist Rd.
Akron, OH 44305
Tel.: 216-798-6200
Fax: 216-798-6208
Mktg. of Garage Door Openers, Antenna Rotators, Trash Compactors
S.I.C.: 5065
Bennett Rubin *(V.P.-Mktg. & Sls.)*
Roger Robb *(V.P.-Sls., Professional Prods.)*
Jim Yezbak *(V.P.-Sls., Consumer Prods.)*
Keith Glover *(V.P.-Blue Max Div.)*
Randy Nelson *(Mgr.-Intl. Mktg.)*
Sharon Dack *(Mgr.-Adv.)*

GENIE MANUFACTURING CORP.
999 Rush-Henrietta, Townline Rd.
Rush, NY 14543
Mailing Address:
P.O. Box 299,
West Henrietta, NY 14586
Tel.: 716-359-4100 **NY**
Fax: 716-359-2627
Year Founded: 1973
Emp.: 50
Import Export
Manufacture Original Equipment Filters
S.I.C.: 3564
Sheldon Gleason *(Chm. Bd., Pres., Chief Exec. & Chief Fin. Officer & Controller)*
Jean Gleason *(V.P. & Treas.)*

No. of Mfg. Plants/Facilities: 5

Computer Systems/Hardware:
IBM 5160

Outside Service Firm(s):

Bonido, Insero & Co.*(Auditors)*
Rochester, NY

Chamberlain, D'Amanda, Oppenheimer & Greensfield*(Legal Firm)*
1600 Crossroads Office Bldg.,
Rochester, NY 14614
Tel.: 716-232-3730

Norstar Bank, N.A.*(Major Banking Relationship)*
Rochester, NY

Genova Hartwick Juliano

GENOVA HARTWICK JULIANO, INC.
15 Valley Dr.
Greenwich, CT 06831
Tel.: 203-629-8081
Fax: 203-531-4964
Year Founded: 1990
Approx.Billings: $22,500,000
Emp.: 16
Joseph Genova *(Chm. & Chief Exec. Officer)*
Sharon Hartwick *(Co-Chm.)*
Philip Juliano *(Pres.)*

GENOVA PRODUCTS, INC.
7034 E. Court St.
Davison, MI 48423
Mailing Address:
P.O. Box 309,
Davison, MI 48423
Tel.: 313-744-4500
Tel.: 800-521-7488 **MI**
Fax: 313-744-3130
Year Founded: 1962
Approx.Sls.: $70,000,000
Emp.: 65
Fiscal Year-end: 12/31/90
Export
Manufacture Plumbing Pipe & Fittings & Related Products
S.I.C.: 3432; 3088; 3084; 3089; 2891
Robert M. Williams *(Chm., Chief Exec. Officer & Treas.)*
Dwight P. Van Steenkiste *(Pres.)*
Jill L. Williams *(Sec.)*
Don Dinkgrave *(Dir.-Fin.)*
Bob Hunt *(Dir.-Mfg.)*
Jeanette Kellogg *(Dir.-Sls. & Mktg.)*
Jim Morrow *(Dir.-Engrng.)*
Dave Paige *(Dir.-Opers.)*
Theresa Bandkau *(Mgr.-Mktg.)*
Barry Brang *(Mgr.-Personnel)*
Lori Williams-Kirby *(Mgr.-Adv.)*
Wayne Gillmer *(Buyer)*

Computer Systems/Hardware:
IBM AS400

Outside Service Firm(s):

Arthur Andersen & Co.*(Auditors)*
400 Renaissance Center
Detroit, MI 48243
Tel.: 313-259-8100

Smith & Harris*(Legal Firm)*
Flint, MI

N.B.D. Bank, N.A.*(Major Banking Relationship)*
611 Woodward Ave.
Detroit, MI 48226
Tel.: 313-225-1122
Fax: 313-225-3420

Subsidiaries:

Genova-Indiana, Inc. **(1)**
9501 Airport Dr.
Fort Wayne, IN 46809
Tel.: 219-478-1639 (100%)
Mfr. Plumbing Pipe & Fittings & Warehousing
S.I.C.: 3088

Genova-Minnesota, Inc. **(1)**
500 N.W. 12th St.
Faribault, MN 55021
Tel.: 507-332-7421 (100%)
Mfr. of Plumbing Pipe & Fittings & Related Prods.
S.I.C.: 3088

Genova-Pennsylvania, Inc. **(1)**
PO Box 369, Forest Rd.
Hazleton, PA 18201
Tel.: 717-459-1436 (100%)
Mfr. of Plumbing Pipe & Fittings & Related Prods.
S.I.C.: 3088

Wiltic Chemical Manufacturing **(1)**
422 Rising St.
Davison, MI 48423
Tel.: 313-653-1890 (100%)
Mfg. of Solvents, Adhesives & Cleaners
S.I.C.: 2891

GENTEX OPTICS, INC.
324 Main St.
Simpson, PA 18407
Mailing Address:
P.O. Box 336
Carbondale, PA 18407
Tel.: 717-282-8600
Fax: 717-282-8555
Approx.Sls.: $20,000,000
Emp.: 300
Fiscal Year-end: 12/31/90
Mfr. Optical Products, Safety Lenses, Welding Filter Plates, Polycarbonate RX Lenses
S.I.C.: 3851
L. Peter Frieder, Jr. *(Pres.)*
R. Nahmias *(V.P.-Sls.)*
D. O'Hara *(V.P.-Opers.)*
H. Acker *(Chief Fin. Officer)*
J. McNamara *(Mgr.-Mktg.)*

GENUARDI SUPER MARKETS INC.
805 E. Germantown Pike
Norristown, PA 19401
Tel.: 215-277-6000 **PA**
Fax: 215-277-7783
Approx.Sls.: $230,000,000
Emp.: 1,800
Supermarkets; Wholesale Groceries
S.I.C.: 5141; 5142; 5411; 5147
Charles A. Genuardi *(Pres. & Chief Exec. Officer)*
Dominic Genuardi *(Treas.)*
Joseph Genuardi, Jr. *(Sec.)*
Jim Genuardi, Jr. *(Recording Sec.)*

GEO-CENTERS, INC.
7 Wells Ave.
Newton Center, MA 02159
Tel.: 617-964-7070
Fax: 617-527-7592
Approx.Sls.: $30,000,000
Emp.: 470
Fiscal Year-end: 12/31/90
High-Tech Research & Development
S.I.C.: 8742; 8731
Dr. Edward P. Marram *(Chm. Bd., Pres., Chief Exec. Officer & Treas.)*
Bruce G. Hain *(Chief Fin. Officer & V.P.)*
Brian K. Lavery *(Controller)*
James Kimball *(Dir.-Human Resources)*
Thomas DiGiuseppe *(Mgr.-Boston Opers.)*
Maridee Kirwin *(Mgr.-Govt. Procurement)*
Mark J. Levine *(Mgr.-Bus. Devel.)*
Stefanie Fish *(Librarian)*

Computer Systems/Hardware:
Micro-VAX 2; Compaq; Novell Network

Outside Service Firm(s):

Daniel Peck Assocs.*(Auditors)*
Wellesley, MA

Travelers Insurance Co.*(Commercial Insurance Carrier)*
One Tower Square
Hartford, CT 06183-6130
Tel.: 203-277-4542
Fax: 203-277-5038

Tanner Capital*(Investment Banker)*
Boston, MA

Fleet National Bank*(Major Banking Relationship)*
Corporate Trust Dept., 125 Dupont Dr.
Providence, RI 02907
Tel.: 617-426-9555

GMG

GEOGRAPHIC MARKETING GROUP (GMG)
The Curtis Center, Independence Square West
Philadelphia, PA 19105
Mailing Address:
P.O. Box 868,
Philadelphia, PA 19106
Tel.: 215-440-7800
Fax: 215-440-7813
Year Founded: 1983
Approx.Billings: $30,000,000
Emp.: 30
Advertising Agency
S.I.C.: 7311
Arthur G. Broll, Jr. *(Chm. Bd., Chief Fin. Officer & Treas.)*
Mel R. Korn *(Pres. & Chief Exec. Officer)*
Margaret P. Dembowczyk *(Exec. V.P., Chief Oper. Officer)*
Francie Truran *(Asst. Treas.)*

No. of U.S. Offices: 2

Computer Systems/Hardware:
IBM, Apple

Outside Service Firm(s):

Fidelity Bank*(Major Banking Relationship)*
Broad & Walnut St.
Philadelphia, PA 19109

Branch:

Geographic Marketing Group (GMG) **(1)**
301 Rte. 17 North, Ste. 204
Rutherford, NJ 07070
Tel.: 201-438-9200
S.I.C.: 7311

GEORGE LITHOGRAPH
650 Second St.
San Francisco, CA 94107
Tel.: 415-397-2400 **CA**
Fax: 415-267-4626
Year Founded: 1932
Sales Range: $20-39 Million
Emp.: 275
Lithographic Printers
S.I.C.: 2752; 2791

J. Curtiss Taylor *(Pres.)*
Mary Bull *(Chief Information Officer)*
Christopher Latchford *(Controller)*
Hartly Fleischmann *(Sec.)*
Richard Andreotti *(V.P.-Mfg.)*
Mark Lindsay *(V.P.-Sls. & Mktg.)*
Peter Tielborg *(Dir.-Human Resources)*
Kathy Fleming *(Mgr.-Admin.)*
James Mekis *(Mgr.-Technical Devel.)*

Principal(s):
J. Curtiss Taylor

No. of Mfg. Plants/Facilities: 2
No. of U.S. Offices: 1

Outside Service Firm(s):

Kimball, McKenna & Von Kaschnitz*(Auditors)*
Alameda, CA

Fleischmann & Fleischmann*(Legal Firm)*
650 California St., Ste. 2550
San Francisco, CA 94108-2606
Tel.: 415-981-0140

Sanwa Bank*(Major Banking Relationship)*
Oakland, CA

GEORGE TRANSFER, INC.
I-83 at Rte. 439
Parkton, MD 21120
Mailing Address:
P.O. Box 500
Parkton, MD 21120
Tel.: 410-329-4000
Fax: 410-329-6744
Approx.Sls.: $40,000,000
Emp.: 100
Motor Carrier
S.I.C.: 4213
T. Bayard Williams, Jr. *(Chm. Bd.)*
Edward A. Gallagher, IV *(Pres.)*
William J. Gallagher *(V.P.-Sls.)*
Michael Kelley *(V.P.)*
Merlin G. Tucker *(V.P.)*
Jerome H. Dolle *(Treas.)*
Robert W. Conner *(Mgr.-Safety)*
John Nickol *(Mgr.-Opers.)*
Terry Vaught *(Mgr.-Data Processing)*
Norma J. Lingenfelter *(Supvr.-Personnel)*

Outside Service Firm(s):

KPMG Peat Marwick*(Auditors)*
111 S. Calvert St.
Baltimore, MD 21202
Tel.: 410-783-8300

Lalos & Keegan*(Legal Firm)*
Washington, DC

Maryland National Bank*(Major Banking Relationship)*
Baltimore, MD 21202

GEORGETOWN INDUSTRIES, INC.
1901 Roxborough Rd., Suite 200
Charlotte, NC 28211
Tel.: 704-366-6901 **DE**
Fax: 704-365-4340
Year Founded: 1983
Approx.Sls.: $700,000,000
Emp.: 4,000
Fiscal Year-end: 12/31/90
Mfr. Wire, Wire Rod, Bars, Billets; Wholesaler & Retailer Bldg. Matls.; Retailer Specialty Home Furnishings & Wire Products
S.I.C.: 3312; 3315; 3496; 5031; 5032; 5211; 5719
Roger R. Regelbrugge *(Pres. & Chief Exec. Officer)*
Dennis F. Flint *(Exec. V.P.)*
Gerald L. Anderson *(V.P.-Fin. & Treas.)*
D.O. Shelley *(Controller)*

Outside Service Firm(s):

Arthur Andersen & Co.*(Auditors)*
2300 Charlotte Plaza
Charlotte, NC 28244
Tel.: 704-332-0092

Parker, Poe, Adams & Bernstein*(Legal Firm)*
Charlotte, NC

NationsBank Carolinas*(Major Banking Relationship)*
One NCNB Plaza
Charlotte, NC 28255

Subsidiaries:

Waccamaw Corporation **(1)**
3200 Pottery Dr.
Myrtle Beach, SC 29577
Tel.: 803-236-4606
Fax: 803-236-3666
Sales Range: $100-499 Million
Emp.: 2,275
Retail Home Furnishings & Gifts; Pottery; Waccamaw Pottery Stores
S.I.C.: 5719; 5947
John Cote *(Pres.)*
Andy Owczarek *(Sr. V.P.-Opers.)*

Western Lumber Company, Inc. **(1)**
2745 Tidelands
National City, CA 92050
Tel.: 619-474-3341
Wholesale & Retail Lumber & Building Materials
S.I.C.: 5031; 5211
Mike McMahan *(Exec. V.P. & Gen. Mgr.)*

GEORGIA CROWN DISTRIBUTING
7 Crown Circle
Columbus, GA 31907
Mailing Address:
PO Box 7908,
Columbus, GA 31908
Tel.: 706-568-4580
S.I.C.: 5182; 5181
Donald Leebern, Jr. *(Pres.)*
Ken Slay *(Exec. V.P.)*

GEORGIA DUCK & CORDAGE MILLS
21 Laredo Dr.
Scottdale, GA 30079
Tel.: 404-294-5172
Fax: 404-296-5165
Sales Range: $40-59 Million
Emp.: 400
Export
Conveyor Belting, Rubber & PVC Industrial Textiles
S.I.C.: 2821; 3535
Ray Willoch *(Pres.)*
Milton C. Scott *(Sec., Treas. & Exec. Office Mgr.)*
Ron Phillips *(Comptroller)*

Outside Service Firm(s):

Bruce A. Landers*(Auditors)*
Atlanta, GA

Bank South*(Major Banking Relationship)*
Scottdale, GA

GEORGIA IRON WORKS CO.
5000 Wrightsboro Rd.
Grovetown, GA 30813
Tel.: 706-863-1011
Fax: 706-860-5897
Approx.Sls.: $37,000,000
Emp.: 365
Mfr. of Solids Handling Pumps, Pump Parts
S.I.C.: 3561; 3321
Thomas W. Hagler, Jr. *(Chm. & Chief Exec. Officer)*
John W. Lee *(Pres. & Chief Oper. Officer)*
Graeme R. Addie *(V.P.-Engrng.)*
Lawrence R. Berry *(V.P.-Sls. & Engrng.)*
Jeffrey Jenkins *(V.P.-Mfg.)*
Horst Uzpurvis *(V.P.-Mktg.)*
Albert Wallace *(V.P. & Controller)*
Billie S. Hagler *(Treas.)*
Alice H. Lee *(Sec.)*
Leonard T. Martin *(Dir.-Pur.)*
James W. Herron *(Mgr.-Customer Service)*
Larry Lynn *(Mgr.-Data Processing)*

THE GEORGIA MARBLE COMPANY
1201 Roberts Blvd.
Kennesaw, GA 30144
Tel.: 404-421-6500
Fax: 404-421-6507
Year Founded: 1987
Approx.Sls.: $86,500,000
Emp.: 1,100
Fiscal Year-end: 12/31/91
Stone For Building Facades & Interiors, Memorial Monuments; Crushed & Ground Calcium Carbonate Products
S.I.C.: 1411; 1422
A.L. Gay, Jr. *(Pres.)*
E.G. Hartleb *(Chief Fin. Officer & V.P.)*
B.R. Addison *(V.P.-Consumer Prods.)*
J.W. Cline *(V.P.-Indus. Prods.)*
Ray Barker *(Dir.-Personnel)*

Outside Service Firm(s):

Ernst & Young*(Auditors)*
600 Peachtree St. N.E.
Atlanta, GA 30308
Tel.: 404-874-8300

Jones, Day, Reavis & Pogue*(Legal Firm)*
First Atlanta Tower,
Atlanta, GA 30303
Tel.: 404-521-3939

First National Bank of Atlanta*(Major Banking Relationship)*
P.O. 4148
Atlanta, GA 30302
Tel.: 404-588-5000

GEORGIAN PRESS, INC.
175 Varick St.
New York, NY 10014
Tel.: 212-924-4820
Fax: 212-627-9639
Approx.Sls.: $32,000,000
Emp.: 100
Holding Co.; Real Estate Investments
S.I.C.: 6719; 6798
Jessie J. Lehman *(Chm. Bd. & Sec.)*
Jonathan E. Lehman *(Pres. & Treas.)*

Outside Service Firm(s):

BDO Seidman*(Auditors)*
1430 Broadway
New York, NY
Tel.: 212-765-7500

National Westminster Bank plc*(Major Banking Relationship)*
Astor Plaza, 1515 Broadway
New York, NY 10036

GEORGIE BOY MANUFACTURING, INC.
69950 M 62
Edwardsburg, MI 49112
Tel.: 616-663-3415
Tel.: 800-521-8733 **MI**
Fax: 616-663-2065
Year Founded: 1967
Approx.Sls.: $75,000,000
Emp.: 500
Mfr. Motor Homes
S.I.C.: 3792
Daniel George *(Chm. Bd.)*
Virl Thompson *(Pres.)*
Art Colvin *(V.P.-Pur. Dir.)*
Fred Emmert *(V.P.-Sls. & Mktg.)*
Dick Yost *(V.P.-Customer Service)*
Gerald Jankowski *(Controller)*

No. of Mfg. Plants/Facilities: 1
No. of U.S. Offices: 1

Computer Systems/Hardware:
IBM; ADP

Outside Service Firm(s):

McGladrey & Pullen*(Auditors)*
Elkhart, IN

AmeriTrust National Bank*(Major Banking Relationship)*
Elkart, IN

GERBER ADVERTISING
209 S.W. Oak St.
Portland, OR 97204
Tel.: 503-221-0100 **OR**
Fax: 503-228-5315/7471
Year Founded: 1910
Assets: $3,102,549
Liabilities: $2,500,265
Net Worth: $602,284
Approx.Billings: $26,200,000
Emp.: 60
Advertising Agency
S.I.C.: 7311
Tom M. Hougan *(Chm.)*
Philip L. Stevens *(Pres. & Chief Exec. Officer)*
Sally Auguston *(Sr. V.P., Acct. Services Dir.)*
Don Dickinson *(Sr. V.P.)*
Elaine Miller *(Sr. V.P., Media & Support)*
Nanci Dickinson *(V.P., Controller)*
Olga Spencer *(Dir.-Pub. Rels.)*

No. of U.S. Offices: 1

Computer Systems/Hardware:
Data General; IBM PC, Macintosh, BCS, MM Plus

Outside Service Firm(s):

McDonald, Jacobs & Biskar*(Auditors)*
Portland, OR

Stoll & Stoll*(Legal Firm)*
Portland, OR

Key Bank*(Major Banking Relationship)*
1211 S.W. Fifth Ave., Suite 300
Portland, OR 97205
Tel.: 503-790-7500

Stonewall Pension Service*(Pension Manager)*
Portland, OR

Subsidiary:

Nu-Safe Reporting **(1)**
209 S.W. Oak
Portland, OR 92704
Tel.: 503-221-0100
Fax: 503-228-5315
Emp.: 2
Advertising Operations
S.I.C.: 7311
Philip L. Stevens *(Chief Oper. Officer)*

J. GERBER & CO. INC.
855 Ave. of Americas
New York, NY 10001
Tel.: 212-613-1100 **NY**
Fax: 212-613-1168
Year Founded: 1937
Assets: $60,000,000
Earnings: $800,000
Liabilities: $48,000,000
Net Worth: $12,000,000
Approx.Sls.: $200,000,000
Emp.: 115
Fiscal Year-end: 9/30/90
Import Export
Import & Export Steel, Metal & Agricultural Products
S.I.C.: 5051; 5013; 5078; 5191
G. Clain *(Pres., Chief Exec. & Chief Oper. Officer)*
R. Hartoch *(Exec. V.P.)*
P. Kemeny *(V.P.)*
Alan Mandell *(Controller)*
W. Rybnick *(Sec.)*
Aaron Gilman *(Dir.-Data Processing)*

J. Gerber & Co. Inc.—(Continued)

Barbara Rubenberg *(Mgr.-Employee Benefits)*

Computer Systems/Hardware:
Datapoint

Outside Service Firm(s):

Price Waterhouse*(Auditors)*
153 E. 53rd St., 44th Fl.
New York, NY 10022
Tel.: 212-371-2000

Phoenix Mutual Life Insurance Co.*(Group Insurer)*
Hartford, CT

Graubard, Moskowitz, McGoldrick, Dannett & Horowitz*(Legal Firm)*
345 Park Ave.
New York, NY 10022
Tel.: 212-593-3000

The Bank of New York*(Major Banking Relationship)*
One Wall Street
New York, NY 10286
Tel.: 212-635-6805
Fax: 212-635-3201

Irving Trust Co.*(Major Banking Relationship)*
New York, NY

Mellon Bank*(Major Banking Relationship)*
New York, NY

Standard Chartered Bank*(Major Banking Relationship)*
New York, NY

Segal Association*(Pension Manager)*
New York, NY

Subsidiary:

Gerber Agri-Export Inc. **(1)**
855 Ave. of Americas
New York, NY 10001
Tel.: 212-613-1100
S.I.C.: 5191

GERBER PLUMBING FIXTURES CORPORATION
4656 W. Touhy Ave.
Chicago, IL 60646
Tel.: 708-675-6570
Tel.: 800-5-GERBER **IL**
Fax: 708-675-5192 (IL)
Year Founded: 1932
Approx.Sls.: $85,000,000
Emp.: 850
Fiscal Year-end: 11/30/90
Export
Mfr. Vitreous China Fixtures, Brass Plumbing Fittings, Chrome & Decorated Faucets & Fittings
S.I.C.: 3261; 3432
Harriet G. Lewis *(Chm. Bd.)*
Alan G. Lewis *(Chief Exec. Officer)*
Jack Hanlon *(Pres. & Chief Oper. Officer)*
Robert C. Luker *(V.P. & Chief Fin. Officer)*
Ila J. Lewis *(Treas.)*
Jon Deiter *(Controller)*
Daryl Gerber *(Sec.)*
Douglas Elias *(Mgr.-Data Processing)*

No. of Mfg. Plants/Facilities: 4

Computer Systems/Hardware:
Unisys

Outside Service Firm(s):

Arthur Andersen & Co.*(Auditors)*
33 W. Monroe St.
Chicago, IL 60603-4067
Tel.: 312-580-0033
Fax: 312-507-6748

Metropolitan Life Insurance Co.*(Group Insurer)*
One Madison Ave.
New York, NY 10010-3690
Tel.: 215-578-9292

Harris Trust & Savings Bank*(Investment Banker)*
111 W. Monroe St.
Chicago, IL 60690
Tel.: 312-461-2265
Tel.: 800-858-0840

Shefsky & Froehlich*(Legal Firm)*
Chicago, IL

Harris Trust & Savings Bank*(Major Banking Relationship)*
111 W. Monroe St.
Chicago, IL 60690
Tel.: 312-461-2265
Tel.: 800-858-0840

Harris Trust & Savings Bank*(Pension Manager)*
111 W. Monroe St.
Chicago, IL 60690
Tel.: 312-461-2265
Tel.: 800-858-0840

Stein, Roe & Farnham*(Pension Manager)*
One S. Wacker Dr.
Chicago, IL 60606
Tel.: 312-368-7700

Subsidiaries:

AAA Plumbing Pottery Corp. **(1)**
4656 W. Touhy Ave.
Chicago, IL 60646
Tel.: 708-675-6570 (100%)
S.I.C.: 3261

Globe Valve Corporation **(1)**
4656 W. Touhy Ave.
Chicago, IL 60646
Tel.: 708-675-6570 (100%)
S.I.C.: 3432
James McNeany *(Chief Oper. Officer)*

Woodbridge Sanitary Pottery Corp. **(1)**
4656 W. Touhy Ave.
Chicago, IL 60646
Tel.: 708-675-6570 (100%)
S.I.C.: 3261

GERBIG, SNELL/WEISHEIMER & ASSOC., INC.
8000 Ravine's Edge Ct.
Worthington, OH 43085
Tel.: 614-848-4848
Fax: 614-848-3477 (Admin.)
Fax: 614-848-3777 (Creative)
Year Founded: 1977
Approx.Billings: $27,000,000
Emp.: 37
Healthcare Marketing
Robert L. Gerbig *(Pres. & Chief Exec. Officer)*
Christopher J. Snell *(Exec. V.P.)*
Richard A. Weisheimer *(Exec. V.P.)*
Mary Beth Schaper *(V.P., Bus. Devel.)*
Ann Dulin *(Treas.)*
Alice Wintersteller *(Telecommunications)*

GERLAND CORP.
2541 Gessner Dr.
Houston, TX 77080
Tel.: 713-462-9030 **TX**
Fax: 713-462-5726
Approx.Sls.: $167,000,000
Emp.: 1,300
Grocery Stores
S.I.C.: 5411
J.W. Morris *(Pres. & Chief Exec. Officer)*
Joseph P. Gerland *(Exec. V.P. & Sec.)*
Kevin Doris *(V.P.-Opers.)*
Rick Noeth *(V.P.-Bakery & Produce Opers.)*
Jeff Reeder *(V.P. & Treas.)*
Wayne Swift *(V.P.-Meat Opers.)*

Outside Service Firm(s):

Coopers & Lybrand*(Auditors)*
1100 Louisiana, Ste. 4100
Houston, TX 77002
Tel.: 713-757-5200
Fax: 713-757-5249

Crady & Jewett*(Legal Firm)*
Houston, TX

NationsBank Texas*(Major Banking Relationship)*
700 Louisiana
Houston, TX 77002
Tel.: 713-247-800

GERRARD AND COMPANY
400 E. Touhy Ave.
Des Plaines, IL 60018-2684
Tel.: 708-299-8000 **IL**
Twx: 910-233-2398
Fax: 708-803-5250
Year Founded: 1935
Approx.Sls.: $116,000,000
Emp.: 300
Fiscal Year-end: 3/31/91
Import Export
Mfr. Steel & Plastic Strapping, Strapping Seals, Strapping Tools, Automatic Strapping Machines, Wire Ties, Strip Steel
S.I.C.: 3089; 3423; 3315; 3496; 3499; 3316; 3993; 3535
Anthony Tako *(Chm. Bd. & Pres.)*
E. Michael Gerhardstein *(Exec. V.P.)*
Peter Rocush *(Sec. & Treas.)*
John Schramm *(Chief Engr.)*
Tom Driscoll *(Mgr.-Mktg.)*
James L. Heveran *(Mgr.-Pur.)*
Michael Molek *(Mgr.-Inventory Control)*

Computer Systems/Hardware:
IBM

Outside Service Firm(s):

Grant Thornton*(Auditors)*
700 One Prudential Plaza, 130 East Randolph St.
Chicago, IL 60601
Tel.: 312-856-0200
Fax: 312-565-4719

Rieck & Crotty*(Legal Firm)*
55 W. Monroe St.
Chicago, IL 60603

Continental Bank N. A.*(Major Banking Relationship)*
231 S. LaSalle St.
Chicago, IL 60697
Tel.: 312-828-2345
Tel.: 800-426-5754
Telex: 312-828-1783

GERRITY CO., INC.
90 Oak St.
Newton, MA 02164
Mailing Address:
P.O. Box 9111
Newton, MA 02164
Tel.: 617-244-1400
Tel.: 800-877-9663 **DE**
Fax: 617-244-0633
Year Founded: 1886
Assets: $62,000,000
Liabilities: $40,000,000
Net Worth: $22,000,000
Approx.Sls.: $197,000,000
Emp.: 692
Fiscal Year-end: 11/30/91
Import
Wholesale Lumber Traders & Retail Lumber Sls.
S.I.C.: 5031; 2439; 2499; 2431; 5211
J. Frank Gerrity II *(Chm. Bd. & Treas.)*
James F. Gerrity III *(Pres. & Chief Exec. Officer)*
Vincent J. Micale *(Sr. V.P. & Chief Oper. Officer)*
Albert Sabbag *(Chief Fin. Officer)*
L.B. Harding *(Chief Info. Officer)*
G.S. Fuller *(V.P.)*
R. Wall *(V.P.)*
Peter J. Young *(Gen. Counsel)*
Joseph Joyce *(Controller)*
T. O'Malley *(Dir.-Adv.)*
Peter Wilde *(Dir.-Mktg.)*
Jack Parquette *(Mgr.-Sls.)*
Principal(s):
J. Frank Gerrity II
James F. Gerrity III

No. of Mfg. Plants/Facilities: 19
No. of U.S. Offices: 19

Computer Systems/Hardware:
Sperry-Univac

Outside Service Firm(s):

Deloitte & Touche*(Auditors)*
125 Summer St.
Boston, MA 02110
Tel.: 617-261-8000
Fax: 617-261-8111

Alliance Insurance*(Commercial Insurance Carrier)*
Boston, MA

Lumbermans Underwriting*(Commercial Insurance Carrier)*
Boca Raton, FL

Rackman, Sawyer, Brewster*(Legal Firm)*
Boston, MA

Brown Brothers, Harriman & Co.*(Major Banking Relationship)*
Boston, MA

Brown Brothers, Harriman & Co.*(Major Banking Relationship)*
59 Wall St.
New York, NY 10005-2818
Tel.: 212-493-8029

Shawmut Bank*(Major Banking Relationship)*
1 Federal St.
Boston, MA 02110
Tel.: 617-292-3715

Bank of New England*(Pension Manager)*
One Washington Mall
Boston, MA 02108
Tel.: 617-742-4000

Subsidiaries:

Gerrity Lumber Co. **(1)**
Railroad Ave., Box 669
Meredith, NH 03253
Tel.: 603-279-7911
S.I.C.: 2421

Mt. Waldo Operations **(1)**
90 Oak St., Box 9111
Newton Upper Falls, MA 02164
Tel.: 617-244-1400
Real Estate
S.I.C.: 6552

GERSON & GERSON, INC.
462 7th Ave.
New York, NY 10018
Tel.: 212-279-1130 **NY**
Fax: 212-643-9130
Year Founded: 1933
Approx.Sls.: $20,000,000
Emp.: 50
Mfr. of Infants' & Children's Dresses
S.I.C.: 2361
Max Gerson *(Chm. Bd.)*
Matthew Gerson *(Pres.)*
Miriam Dubner *(Sec. & Treas.)*

Outside Service Firm(s):

Weiner & Co.*(Auditors)*
New York, NY

Marine Midland Bank*(Major Banking Relationship)*
140 Broadway
New York, NY 10015
Tel.: 212-658-1620

THE GERSTENSLAGER COMPANY
1425 E. Bowman
Wooster, OH 44691
Mailing Address:
P.O. Box 390
Wooster, OH 44691
Tel.: 216-262-2015
Telex: 216-262-4009
Fax: 216-262-3610
Approx.Sls.: $50,000,000
Emp.: 550
Mfr. Automotive Stampings & Weldments; Cathodic Electro-Coat Primer
S.I.C.: 3469; 3443; 3465
J.D. Wisner *(Chm. & Chief Exec. Officer)*
T.L. Iceman *(Pres.)*
K.L. Vagnini *(V.P., Sec. & Treas.)*
P. Hawkins *(Controller)*
R.H. Zeigler *(Dir.-Sls.)*
C. Edwards *(Dir.-Pur.)*
Steve Giauque *(Mgr.-Mfg.)*

Computer Systems/Hardware:
MAI Basic Four

Outside Service Firm(s):

Meaden & Moore*(Auditors)*
525 Metro Place North
Dublin, OH 43017
Tel.: 614-766-6991

Vorys, Sater, Seymour & Pease*(Legal Firm)*
52 E. Gay St.
Columbus, OH 43215
Tel.: 614-464-6400

BancOhio National Bank*(Major Banking Relationship)*
Columbus, OH

Division:

Stamping Division **(1)**
1425 E. Bowman, P.O. Box 390
Wooster, OH 44691
Tel.: 216-262-2015
Metal Stampings
S.I.C.: 3469
T.L. Iceman *(Pres.)*
K.L. Vagnini *(V.P.)*

Subsidiary:

Superior Die Tool And Machine Company **(1)**
2301 Fairwood Ave.
Columbus, OH 43207
Tel.: 614-444-2181
Fax: 614-444-8712
Richard Holstein *(V.P. & Gen. Mgr.)*

GESSNER INDUSTRIES
384 Faggart Ave.
Concord, NC 28025
Tel.: 704-782-3100 **NC**
Year Founded: 1964
Sales Range: $10-19 Million
Emp.: 89
Fiscal Year-end: 3/31/92
Manufacture Textile Machinery
S.I.C.: 3552; 5084
David Gessner *(Pres. & Treas.)*
Laura Gilleland *(Chief Fin. Officer & Controller)*

Computer Systems/Hardware:
Data General

GETMAN CORPORATION
6998 34th Ave.
Bangor, MI 49013
Mailing Address:
P.O. Box 70
Bangor, MI 49013
Tel.: 616-427-5611
Fax: 616-427-8781
Approx.Sls.: $12,000,000
Emp.: 90
Diesel Powered Trucks For Underground Mining
S.I.C.: 3532; 3531
D.S. Getman *(Chm. Bd. & Pres.)*
James F. Walker *(V.P.-Mfg.)*
Ruby Hebeeb *(Dir.-Fin.)*

Outside Service Firm(s):

Crowe, Chizek & Co.*(Auditors)*
South Bend, IN

Varnum, Ridderig, Schmidt & Howlett*(Legal Firm)*
Kalamazoo, MI

First America Bank*(Major Banking Relationship)*
Kalamazoo, MI

GEYER-MCALLISTER PUBLICATIONS, INC.
51 Madison Ave.
New York, NY 10010
Tel.: 212-689-4411
Fax: 212-683-7929
Approx.Sls.: $12,000,000
Emp.: 60
Trade & Business Publications; Shipping Digest, Gifts And Decorative Accessories, Playthings, The Gift And Decorative Accessory Buyers Directory, Playthings Directory Issue
S.I.C.: 2721; 2741
Donald McAllister, Jr. *(Chm. Bd.)*
Richard A. Duffy *(Pres.)*
Donald McAllister *(Chm.-Exec. Committee)*
Douglas P. Caffrone *(Exec. V.P.)*
Robert Chiara *(Sr. V.P.)*
Phyllis Sweed *(Sr. V.P.)*

GHAFARI ASSOCIATES, INC.
17101 Michigan Ave.
Dearborn, MI 48128
Tel.: 313-421-3900
Telex: 509741 GAI UD
Year Founded: 1982
Assets: $3,600,000
Liabilities: $2,400,000
Net Worth: $1,200,000
Sales Range: $10-19 Million
Emp.: 200
Export
Architectural, Engineering, CAD & Computer Services
S.I.C.: 8711; 8712; 7373
Yousif B. Ghafari *(Pres. & Chief Exec. & Chief Oper. Officer)*
Kouhaila G. Hammer *(Sr. V.P.-Fin. & Admin.)*
Laura Wilbanks *(Controller)*
Mara Kalnins-Ghafari *(Gen. Counsel)*
Mark Biokass *(Dir.-Mngmt. Info. Systems)*
Richard W. Butwin *(Dir.-Indianapolis Opers.)*
Richard Jablonski *(Dir.-Mktg.)*
Sandy Sinclair *(Dir.-Mktg.)*
Robert J. Faust *(Mgr.-Detroit Opers., GIS/AM/FM Div.)*
Lisa Jordan *(Mgr.-Bus. Devel.)*
Karen McNamara *(Mgr.-Bus. Devel.)*
Mary K. Mosey *(Mgr.-Bus. Devel.)*
Principal(s):
Yousif B. Ghafari

No. of U.S. Offices: 5

Computer Systems/Hardware:
DEC VAX 780 & 250

Outside Service Firm(s):

Arthur Andersen & Co.*(Auditors)*
400 Renaissance Center
Detroit, MI 48243
Tel.: 313-259-8100

Korotkin, Schlesinger & Associates*(Commercial Insurance Carrier)*
26877 Northwestern Hwy.
Southfield, MI
Tel.: 313-352-5140

Blue Cross & Blue Shield of Michigan*(Group Insurer)*
Detroit, MI

Hardy, Lewis, Pollard & Page*(Legal Firm)*
Birmingham, MI

Michigan National Bank*(Major Banking Relationship)*
P.O. Box 9065,
Farmington Hills, MI 48333-9065
Tel.: 313-473-3000

Manufacturers National Bank N.A.*(Pension Manager)*
38th Fl., 100 Renaissance Center
Detroit, MI 48243
Tel.: 313-222-4227

Divisions:

Ghafari Associates, Inc. **(1)**
6330 E. 75th St., Ste. 118
Indianapolis, IN 46250
Tel.: 317-845-9666
Emp.: 40
Architectural, Engineering, CAD, Intergraph, Interpro 2020 & Computer Services
S.I.C.: 7373; 8711; 8712
R. Butwin *(Gen. Mgr.)*

Ghafari Associates, Inc. **(1)**
41150 Technology Pky. Dr., Ste. 106
Sterling Heights, MI 48314
Tel.: 313-739-4300
Architectural, Engineering, CAD & Computer Services
S.I.C.: 7373; 8711; 8712
Bob Burgess *(Chief Oper. Officer)*

MacKenzie, Kuth & Klein Div. **(1)**
209 Avon St.
Flint, MI 48503
Tel.: 313-235-4681
Architectural, Engineering, CAD, Intergraph, Interpro 2020 & Computer Services
S.I.C.: 7373; 8711; 8712
Tom Brockway *(Gen. Mgr.)*

Eberle M. Smith Associates, Inc. **(1)**
14147 Farmington Rd.
Livonia, MI 48154
Tel.: 313-421-3900
Architectural Engineering, CAD, Intergraph, Interpro 2020 & Computer Services
S.I.C.: 7373; 8711; 8712
Harold Birden *(Pres.)*

Benjamin Woodhouse & Guenther **(1)**
14147 Farmington Rd.
Livonia, MI 48154
Tel.: 313-421-3900
Architectural, Engineering, CAD, Intergraph, Interpro 2020 & Computer Services
S.I.C.: 7373; 8711; 8712
Arthur R. Livermore *(Gen. Mgr.)*

GHENT MANUFACTURING, INC.
South Street at Cherry
Lebanon, OH 45036
Mailing Address:
P.O. Box 410,
Lebanon, OH 45036
Tel.: 513-932-3445
Fax: 513-932-9252
Year Founded: 1977
Approx.Sls.: $15,000,000
Emp.: 190
Fiscal Year-end: 12/31/90
Import Export
Mfr. Visual Communication Aids
S.I.C.: 3999
George Leasure *(Pres., Chief Exec. & Chief Fin. Officer & Treas.)*
Jean M. Behymer *(Controller)*
Julia McIntosh *(Pur. Agent)*

No. of Mfg. Plants/Facilities: 5
No. of U.S. Offices: 3

Computer Systems/Hardware:
MAI Basic 4

Outside Service Firm(s):

William Bachman*(Auditors)*
Lebanon, OH

Marsh & McLennan*(Commercial Insurance Carrier)*
1400 Central Trust Center
Cincinnati, OH 45202-4191
Tel.: 513-721-5557

The Central Trust Company, N.A.*(Investment Banker)*
201 E. Fifth
Cincinnati, OH 45202
Tel.: 513-651-8255

Graydon, Head & Ritchey*(Legal Firm)*
1900 Fifth Third Center
Cincinnati, OH 45202
Tel.: 513-621-6464

The Central Trust Company, N.A.*(Major Banking Relationship)*
201 E. Fifth
Cincinnati, OH 45202
Tel.: 513-651-8255

Star Bank*(Pension Manager)*
425 Walnut Street
Cincinnati, OH 45202
Tel.: 513-632-4000

Division:

Waddell Div. of Ghent Mfg. Co. **(1)**
512 S. Washington St.
Greenfield, OH 45123
Tel.: 513-981-7724
Approx.Sls.: $3,000,000
Emp.: 24
Manufacturer of Show Cases
S.I.C.: 2542; 2541
George Leasure *(Pres.)*
Eldon Fender *(Gen. Mgr.)*

G&M Gianettino & Meredith Advertising

GIANETTINO & MEREDITH ADVERTISING
788 Morris Turnpike
Short Hills, NJ 07078
Tel.: 201-376-2100
Fax: 201-376-3492
Year Founded: 1977
Approx.Billings: $83,500,000
Emp.: 70
Ronald J. Gianettino *(Chm. Bd. & Chief Exec. Officer)*
George Meredith *(Pres. & Creative Dir.)*
Norma J. Friend *(Exec. V.P., Chief Oper. Officer)*
Karen McAuvic *(Exec. V.P., Retail Div.)*
Dr. Dorothy Philips *(Exec. V.P., Health Care Div.)*
Tom Kuhn *(V.P., Automotive Div.)*
Francin M. Lytle *(V.P. & Dir., Mktg)*
Susan B. Rahausen *(V.P., Chief Fin. Officer)*

Computer Systems/Hardware:
MacIntosh

GIANT EAGLE, INC.
101 Kappa Dr.
Pittsburgh, PA 15238
Tel.: 412-963-6200
Fax: 412-963-7266
Approx.Sls.: $259,000,000
Emp.: 5,000
Wholesale Grocery Products
S.I.C.: 5411
Irwin Porter *(Chm. Bd.)*
Ray Burgo *(Pres.)*
David Shapira *(Chief Exec. Officer)*
Richard H. Nimtz *(Sr. V.P.)*
Sam Amoedo *(V.P. & Gen. Mgr.)*
Ray Huber *(V.P.-Personnel & Labor Rels.)*
Bob Irby *(V.P.-Mngmt. Information Systems)*
Lisa Kranz *(V.P.-Mktg.)*
Mark Minnaugh *(V.P.-Fin. & Accounting)*

Giant Eagle, Inc.—(Continued)

Computer Systems/Hardware:
Sperry 1100

Outside Service Firm(s):

Coopers & Lybrand*(Auditors)*
600 Grant St., 35th Fl.
Pittsburgh, PA 15219
Tel.: 412-355-8000
Fax: 412-355-8089

Connecticut General Life Insurance Co.*(Group Insurer)*
P.O. Box 2975,
Hartford, CT 06104
Tel.: 203-726-6000

Marcus & Shapira*(Legal Firm)*
One Oxford Centre
Pittsburgh, PA 15219
Tel.: 412-471-3490

Union National Bank*(Major Banking Relationship)*
Pittsburgh, PA

Union National Bank*(Pension Manager)*
Pittsburgh, PA

Subsidiaries:

FlexRx **(1)**
1810 Lincoln Hwy.
North Versailles, PA 15137
Tel.: 412-829-3200
Emp.: 200
Mail Service Prescriptions for Health Care Packages
S.I.C.: 5961
Ray Burgo *(Pres.)*
Linda Schuetz *(Dir.-Sls.)*
Jay Flanick *(Mgr.-Opers.)*

Giant Eagle Market Co. **(1)**
101 Kappa Dr.
Pittsburgh, PA 15238
Tel.: 412-963-6200
Approx.Sls.: $1,450,000,000
Emp.: 12,000
David Shapria *(Pres. & Treas.)*

Tamarkin Co., Inc. **(1)**
101 Kappa Dr.
Pittsburgh, PA 15238
Tel.: 412-963-6200
David Shapiro *(Pres. & Treas.)*

GIANT MARKETS INC.
501 So. Washington Ave.
Scranton, PA 18505
Mailing Address:
P.O. Box 2014,
Scranton, PA 18505
Tel.: 717-343-2401 **PA**
Fax: 717-961-8861
Year Founded: 1932
Assets: $8,000,000
Liabilities: $5,000,000
Net Worth: $3,000,000
Sales Range: $40-59 Million
Emp.: 385
Fiscal Year-end: 12/31/89
Retail Supermarket Chain of 6 Stores
S.I.C.: 5411
Joseph Hodin *(Chm., Pres. & Chief Exec. Officer)*
William Hodin *(V.P.)*
Erma Baracaia *(Corp. Sec.)*
Rita Bubernak *(Dir.-Personnel Training & Devel.)*
Ronald Wolff *(Dir.-Plng. & Devel.)*
Jane Foy *(Mgr.-Data Processing)*
Elizabeth Kaminskas *(Asst. Mgr.-Employee Benefits)*
Nancy Marchuck *(Asst. Mgr.-Employee Benefits)*
Principal(s):
Joseph Hodin
William Hodin

No. of Mfg. Plants/Facilities: 6
No. of U.S. Offices: 1

Computer Systems/Hardware:
IBM

Outside Service Firm(s):

Robert T. Kelly & Co.*(Auditors)*
Scranton, PA

Zurich American Insurance Co.*(Commercial Insurance Carrier)*
Schaumberg, IL

Blue Cross of Northeastern Pennsylvania*(Group Insurer)*
Wilkes-Barre, PA

Wormuth & Mey*(Legal Firm)*
Scranton, PA

Third National Bank*(Major Banking Relationship)*
Scranton, PA

Massachusetts Mutual Life Insurance Co.*(Pension Manager)*
1295 State Street
Springfield, MA 01111
Tel.: 413-788-8411

THE GIARDINI/RUSSELL GROUP
100 Galen St.
Watertown, MA 02172
Tel.: 617-926-5030
Fax: 617-926-9701
Year Founded: 1966
Approx.Billings: $20,000,000
Emp.: 25
High Tech, Medical Products, Business-to-Business & Consumer
Richard Warren *(Chm. & Chief Exec. Officer)*
Bob Russell *(Vice Chm.)*
Richard Haigis *(Pres.)*
Richard Lindner *(Chief Fin. Officer)*
Laurel McKenzie *(Controller)*

Computer Systems/Hardware:
IBM System 36

ROBERT GIBB & SONS, INC.
205 40th St. S.W.
Fargo, ND 58103
Mailing Address:
P.O. Box 10188
Fargo, ND 58106
Tel.: 701-282-5900 **ND**
Fax: 701-281-0819
Approx.Sls.: $14,000,000
Emp.: 100
Fiscal Year-end: 2/28/92
Plumbing Contractors; Heating & Air Conditioning Contractors; Fire Sprinkler System Installation; Sewer Line Construction; Water Main Construction
S.I.C.: 1711; 1623
Robert Gibb, Sr. *(Chm. Bd.)*
Robert Gibb, Jr. *(Pres.)*
Gregory Gibb *(V.P.)*
James Gibb *(V.P.)*
Steven Gibb *(V.P.)*
Bradley Gibb *(Sec. & Treas.)*

Outside Service Firm(s):

Nilles, Hansen & Davies Ltd.*(Legal Firm)*
1800 Radison Tower, 201 North 5th St.,
P.O. Box 2626
Fargo, ND 58102
Tel.: 701-237-5544

Norwest Bank Fargo, N.A.*(Major Banking Relationship)*
Fargo, ND

GIBBS WIRE & STEEL COMPANY, INC.
Metals Dr.
Southington, CT 06489
Tel.: 203-621-0121 **CT**
Telex: 710-473-3731
Fax: 203-628-7780
Year Founded: 1956
Assets: $19,709,465
Liabilities: $4,061,037
Net Worth: $15,648,428
Approx.Sls.: $50,000,000
Emp.: 130
Fiscal Year-end: 8/31/90
Metal Distr. & Processing
S.I.C.: 5051
Charles F. Gibbs *(Chm.)*
Charles W. Gibbs *(Pres.)*
John W. Cleaver *(V.P. & Sls. Mgr.)*
Robert Iorio *(V.P.-Pur.)*
Robert B. Johnson *(V.P. & Adv. Dir.)*
Thomas Molnar *(V.P.-Mktg.)*
William J. Torres *(V.P., Sec., Treas., Legal Officer & Telecommunications Dir.)*
Doris Ravasio *(Controller)*
Jeffry Reilly *(Mgr.-Corp. Pur.)*
Principal(s):
Charles F. Gibbs
Charles W. Gibbs

No. of Mfg. Plants/Facilities: 6
No. of U.S. Offices: 6

Computer Systems/Hardware:
IBM System 36

Outside Service Firm(s):

Dudzik & Beauchemin*(Auditors)*
Southington, CT

Chubb Group*(Group Insurer)*
Boston, MA

Mutual Benefit Life Insurance*(Group Insurer)*
520 Broad St.
Newark, NJ 07102-3184
Tel.: 201-481-8000

Elliott, Forgione, Stanek & Izzo*(Legal Firm)*
Southington, CT

Connecticut Bank & Trust*(Major Banking Relationship)*
One Constitution Plaza,
Hartford, CT 06115

Non-U.S. Holding:

Gibbs Wire & Steel Company of Canada Ltd. **(1)**
120 Walker Dr.
Brampton, ON L6T 4G9, Canada
Tel.: 416-791-6811 (100%)
Metal Distr. & Processing
S.I.C.: 5051
Charles W. Gibbs *(Pres.)*

GIBRALTAR

GIBRALTAR STEEL CORP.
635 S. Park Ave.
Buffalo, NY 14240
Tel.: 716-856-6500 **NY**
Fax: 716-856-0084
Year Founded: 1972
Assets: $65,000,000
Liabilities: $25,000,000
Net Worth: $40,000,000
Approx.Sls.: $154,000,000
Emp.: 600
Import Export
Processor High-Tech Cold Rolled Strip Steel; Mfr. Steel Strapping; Steel Service Center
S.I.C.: 3316; 3499; 5051
Brian J. Lipke *(Pres. & Chief Exec. Officer)*
Neil E. Lipke *(Exec. V.P.)*
Walter T. Erazmus *(V.P.-Fin.)*
John E. Flint *(V.P.-Acctg.)*
Richard M. O'Brien *(Sec. & Treas.)*
Charles Davitt *(Dir.-Personnel)*
Curtis Lipke *(Dir.-Strapping Opers.)*
Joseph A. Rosenecker *(Dir.-Cold Rolled Strip Opers.)*
Carl P. Spezio *(Dir.-Metals Processing Opers.)*
Principal(s):
Brian J. Lipke
Neil E. Lipke

No. of Mfg. Plants/Facilities: 6
No. of U.S. Offices: 6

Computer Systems/Hardware:
IBM

Outside Service Firm(s):

Price Waterhouse*(Auditors)*
3600 Marine Midland Center
Buffalo, NY 14203
Tel.: 716-856-4650

Albrecht, Maguire, Heffern & Gregg*(Legal Firm)*
Buffalo, NY

Chase Lincoln First Bank, N.A.*(Major Banking Relationship)*
295 Main St.
Buffalo, NY 14203
Tel.: 716-849-8531

THE GIBSON GROUP INC.
2727 Madison Road, Ste. 201
Cincinnati, OH 45209
Mailing Address:
P.O. Box 8028,
Cincinnati, OH 45208
Tel.: 513-871-9966 **OH**
Fax: 513-871-2380
Year Founded: 1981
Assets: $10,000,000
Liabilities: $9,000,000
Net Worth: $1,000,000
Sales Range: $40-59 Million
Emp.: 9
Wholesale Paper & Paper Products
S.I.C.: 5111; 5113
J.G. Donohoo *(Chm. Bd. & Pres.)*
Richard G. Donohoo *(V.P. & Sec.)*
William G. Donohoo *(V.P. & Treas.)*
Principal(s):
J.G. Donohoo

No. of U.S. Offices: 1

Computer Systems/Hardware:
IBM PC-AT

Outside Service Firm(s):

Ernst & Young*(Auditors)*
1300 Chiquita Center, 250 E. Fifth St.
Cincinnati, OH 45202
Tel.: 513-621-6454

Thompson, Hine & Flory*(Legal Firm)*
P.O. Box 8801, 2000 Courthouse Plaza N.E.
Dayton, OH 45401-8801
Tel.: 513-443-6500

First American National Bank*(Major Banking Relationship)*
First American Ctr.
Nashville, TN 37238
Tel.: 615-748-2441

GIBSON GUITAR CORPORATION, INC.
641 Massman Dr.
Nashville, TN 37210
Mailing Address:
P.O. Box 100087
Nashville, TN 37210
Tel.: 615-871-4500
Tel.: 800-4-GIBSON
Fax: 615-889-3216
Year Founded: 1894
Approx.Sls.: $25,000,000
Emp.: 600
Mfr. & Marketing of Musical Instruments: Gibson, Epiphone, Pearl Drums, Steinberger, Ramirez Classical, Gibson Strings & Accessories, Oberheim, Gibson Labs
S.I.C.: 3931
Henry E. Juszkiewicz *(Chm. Bd. & Chief Exec. Officer)*
David H. Berryman *(Pres.)*
Larry Bolland *(V.P.-Sls.)*

Paul Jernigan *(Dir.-Adv. & Public Rels.)*

Outside Service Firm(s):

Grant Thornton*(Auditors)*
Oaklahoma, OK

Farris, Warfield & Kanaday*(Legal Firm)*
Third Natl. Financial Ctr., 424 Church St., Ste. 1900
Nashville, TN 37219
Tel.: 615-244-5200
Fax: 615-726-3185

Barclays Bank plc*(Major Banking Relationship)*
Charlotte, NC

Division:

Pearl Drum Center **(1)**
408 Harding Indus. Dr.
Nashville, TN 37211
Tel.: 615-833-4477

THE GIBSON-HOMANS COMPANY
1755 Enterprise Pkwy.
Twinsburg, OH 44087
Tel.: 216-425-3255 **OH**
Fax: 216-425-2546
Year Founded: 1913
Approx.Sls.: $55,000,000
Fiscal Year-end: 12/31/91
Paint Specialties, Roof Coatings, Sealants, Caulks, Wood Preservers, Tile Adhesives
S.I.C.: 2952; 2891; 2951
Gary Golenberg *(Pres. & Chief Exec. Officer)*
Harry Novak *(Sr. V.P.-Fin. & Admin.)*
Pat Grieshammer *(V.P.-Mktg.)*
Mark Pfaff *(Dir.-Pur.)*
Camille DeRose *(Dir.-Adv.)*

Outside Service Firm(s):

Ernst & Young*(Auditors)*
1300 Huntington Bldg.
Cleveland, OH 44115
Tel.: 216-861-5000

Thompson, Hine & Flory*(Legal Firm)*
1100 National City Bank Bldg.
Cleveland, OH 44114
Tel.: 216-566-5500

National City Bank*(Major Banking Relationship)*
P.O. Box 92301, Corp. Trust Dept.
Cleveland, OH 44101
Tel.: 216-575-2000

Plant:

Gibson-Homans Baltimore Plant **(1)**
1101 Hanzlik Ave.
Baltimore, MD 21237
Tel.: 410-391-4500
Adhesives
S.I.C.: 2891

Divisions:

Gibson-Homans California Div. **(1)**
301 C-9th St.
Modesto, CA 95351

Gibson-Homans California Div. **(1)**
2457 E. 30th St.
Vernon, CA 90058
Tel.: 213-589-5317
Asphalt Mastics & Coatings
S.I.C.: 2952; 2891; 2851
Frank Nicholson *(Div. Mgr.)*

Gibson-Homans Conyers Div. **(1)**
1721 Old Covington Hwy.
Conyers, GA 30208
Tel.: 404-483-7272
S.I.C.: 2891

Ginson-Homans Iowa Div. **(1)**
1623 E. Euclid Ave.
Des Moines, IA 50316
Tel.: 515-262-9394
Asphalt Mastics & Coatings
S.I.C.: 2952; 2891; 2851

Alwyn J. Morgan *(Div. Mgr.)*

Gibson-Homans Texas Div. **(1)**
2800 N. Old 75 Hwy.
Ennis, TX 75119
Tel.: 214-875-8666
Asphalt Mastics & Coatings
S.I.C.: 2952; 2891; 2851
Wendell A. Bryant *(Div. Mgr.)*

Non-U.S. Holdings:

Gibson-Homans of Canada Ltd. **(1)**
2540 Rena Rd.
Mississauga, ON Canada L4T 3C9
Tel.: 416-677-5522 (100%)
Mfr. Roof Coatings, Adhesives, Sealants, Wood Preservers, Driveway Repair Products
S.I.C.: 2891; 2952
H. Frances *(Gen. Mgr.)*

Gibson-Homans of Canada Ltd. **(1)**
101 De LaBarre
Boucherville, PQ Canada J4B 2X6
Tel.: 514-655-9000 (100%)

GIBSON WINE COMPANY
9750 Kent St.
Elk Grove, CA 95624-0726
Mailing Address:
P.O. Box 726,
Elk Grove, CA 95759-0726
Tel.: 916-685-9594
Tel.: 800-748-6711
Fax: 916-685-1448
Year Founded: 1939
Approx.Sls.: $10,000,000
Emp.: 55
Fiscal Year-end: 6/30/91
Export
Table Wines, Vermouths, Dessert Wines, Fruit & Berry Wines; Hard Cider; Cooking Wines, Sparkling Wines, Varietals & Mid-Varietals
S.I.C.: 2084
William Boos *(Pres.)*
Rich Edwards *(V.P. & G.M.)*
Jerry Legge *(Sls. Mgr.)*
Lynda Cook *(Export Sls. Mgr.)*

Computer Systems/Hardware:
AS400

GIFFELS ASSOCIATES, INC.
25200 Telegraph Rd.
Southfield, MI 48034-2599
Mailing Address:
P.O. Box 5025
Southfield, MI 48086-5025
Tel.: 313-355-4600 **MI**
Fax: 313-948-6100
Year Founded: 1925
Assets: $17,137,000
Liabilities: $10,700,000
Net Worth: $6,437,000
Approx.Sls.: $44,510,000
Emp.: 503
Fiscal Year-end: 12/31/91
Architect & Engineering Services
S.I.C.: 8711; 8712
Daniel J. Bohn, Jr. *(Chm. Bd.)*
Richard A. Bither *(Pres.)*
Ralph W. Gudmundsen *(Sr. V.P. & Controller)*
David P. Bourgeois *(Sr. V.P.-Mktg.)*
Harutun Vaporciyan *(Grp. V.P. & Treas.)*
Richard Bland *(Dir.-Computer Services)*
R. Bruce *(Dir.-Pur. & Gen. Services)*
J. Collins *(Dir.-Human Resources)*
Deborah A. Ferris *(Dir.-Pub. Rels.)*
Helen Kott *(Corp. Librarian)*

No. of U.S. Offices: 2

Computer Systems/Hardware:
Intergraph Systems VAX 11/785, 11/780 & CADD Workstations; Hewlett-Packard System 3000

Outside Service Firm(s):

Plante & Moran*(Auditors)*
Southfield, MI

Centennial Insurance Co.*(Commercial Insurance Carrier)*
45 Wall St.
New York, NY 10005
Tel.: 212-943-1800

Prudential Insurance Co. of America*(Commercial Insurance Carrier)*
Minneapolis, MN

Lexington Insurance Co.*(Commercial Insurance Carrier)*
Boston, MA

UNUM Corporation*(Group Insurer)*
2211 Congress St.
Portland, ME 04122
Tel.: 207-770-2211
Fax: 207-770-4387

Manufacturers National Bank N.A.*(Investment Banker)*
38th Fl., 100 Renaissance Center
Detroit, MI 48243
Tel.: 313-222-4227

Allan D. Behrendt*(Legal Firm)*
W. Bloomfield, MI

Manufacturers National Bank N.A.*(Major Banking Relationship)*
38th Fl., 100 Renaissance Center
Detroit, MI 48243
Tel.: 313-222-4227

Subsidiary:

Giffels Hoyem Basso, Inc. **(1)**
3150 Livernois, Ste. 300
Troy, MI 48083
Tel.: 313-680-0680 (100%)
Fax: 313-680-1919
Approx.Sls.: $6,126,000
Emp.: 89
Architect & Engineering Services
S.I.C.: 8711; 8712
Daniel J. Bohn, Jr. *(Chm. Bd.)*
Paul Stachowiak *(Pres.)*
Harry Diamond *(Dir.-Mktg.)*

GIGANTE VAZ & PARTNERS
ADVERTISING, INC.

GIGANTE VAZ & PARTNERS ADVERTISING, INC.
169 Johnson Rd.
Parsippany, NJ 07054
Tel.: 201-644-2777
Fax: 201-644-4919
Year Founded: 1988
Approx.Billings: $22,000,000
Emp.: 15
Broadcast & Print Advertising, including OOH
Paul Gigante *(Pres. & Creative Dir.)*
Madeline Vaz *(Exec. V.P., Dir. Acct. Mngmt.)*

GILBANE BUILDING COMPANY
7 Jackson Walkway
Providence, RI 02940
Tel.: 401-456-5800 **RI**
Fax: 401-456-5936
Year Founded: 1873
Assets: $200,304,737
Net Worth: $200,304,737
Approx.Sls.: $1,250,000,000
Emp.: 900
Fiscal Year-end: 12/31/91
Construction Managers; General Contractors For Industry, Institutional & Commercial Facilities
S.I.C.: 1541; 1542
William J. Gilbane *(Chm. Bd.)*
Paul J. Choquette, Jr. *(Pres.)*
Joseph M. Donato *(Chief Fin. Officer)*
Albert Jaggears *(Chief Oper. Officer)*
Thomas F. Gilbane, Jr. *(Exec. V.P.)*
Norman E. Roy *(Sr. V.P.-Fin. & Treas.)*
David F. Chapman *(V.P. & Reg. Mgr.-Southwest)*
John W. DiNicola *(V.P. & Gen. Counsel)*
Dan M. Kelly *(V.P.-Human Resources)*
Ramon Lopez *(V.P.-Technical Services)*
Robert A. Manocchia *(V.P. & Reg. Bus. Devel. Mgr.-New England)*
John J. McCoy *(V.P.-Construction Opers.-New England)*
Walter McKelrey *(V.P. & Reg. Mgr.-Northeast)*
Stephen J. Muldoon *(V.P. & Chief Oper. Officer-Northeast)*
Alfred K. Potter II *(V.P.-Mktg.)*
Jean A. Gilbane *(Asst. Treas)*
Robert V. Gilbane *(Sec.)*

Principal(s):
William J. Gilbane
Thomas F. Gilbane, Jr.
David F. Chapman
Jean A. Gilbane
Robert V. Gilbane

Computer Systems/Hardware:
IBM System AS400

Outside Service Firm(s):

Arthur Andersen & Co.*(Auditors)*
One Intl. Place, 100 Oliver St.
Boston, MA 02110
Tel.: 617-330-4000
Fax: 617-439-9731

Aetna Life & Casualty*(Group Insurer)*
151 Farmington Avenue
Hartford, CT 06156
Tel.: 203-273-2128
Fax: 203-729-4295

John Hancock Mutual Life Insurance Co.*(Group Insurer)*
John Hancock Place, P.O. Box 111
Boston, MA 02117

Fleet National Bank*(Major Banking Relationship)*
125 Dupont Dr.
Providence, RI 02907-3178
Tel.: 401-278-5335

Rhode Island Hospital Trust National Bank*(Major Banking Relationship)*
Providence, RI

Subsidiaries:

B.T. Equipment Co., Inc. **(1)**
P.O. Box 17071, 115 Lydia Ann Rd.
Smithfield, RI 02917
Tel.: 401-456-5850
Sales & Rentals Of Heavy Equipments
S.I.C.: 5082

Gilbane Properties, Inc. **(1)**
7 Jackson Walkway
Providence, RI 02940
Tel.: 401-456-5800
Realestate Developer
S.I.C.: 6531

GILBERT & BENNETT
North Main St.
Georgetown, CT 06829
Mailing Address:
P.O. Box 385
Georgetown, CT 06829
Tel.: 203-544-8323
Fax: 203-544-8096
Year Founded: 1818
Approx.Sls.: $50,000,000
Emp.: 608
Fiscal Year-end: 9/30/90

Gilbert & Bennett—(Continued)

Wire Cloth, Netting, Hardware Wire Cloth, Perma Gard Welded Wire Fabric, Welded Fence, Flower Border, Fence Posts, Welded Mesh, Folding Fence, Mink Gard Welded Mesh
S.I.C.: 3496
Paul Gossling *(Chief Exec. Officer)*
Tom Rodel *(Exec. V.P.-Sls.)*
John Zimmerman *(V.P.-Fin.)*
Iris F. Kugel *(Adv. Mgr.)*

Divisions:

Gilbert & Bennett **(1)**
P.O. Box 56
Blue Island, IL 60406
Tel.: 708-233-0100

Gilbert & Bennett **(1)**
P.O. Box 1205
Toccoa, GA 30577
Tel.: 706-886-1447

Gilbert & Bennett **(1)**
P.O. Box 158
Dunbar, WV 25064
Tel.: 304-768-1268

Gilbert & Bennett **(1)**
P.O. Box 310
Scotland Neck, NC 27874
Tel.: 919-826-4151

Gilbert & Bennett **(1)**
P.O. Box 38
Carney, MI 49812
Tel.: 906-639-2132

N. G. GILBERT CORPORATION
700 S. Council St.
Muncie, IN 47305
Mailing Address:
P.O. Box 1032
Muncie, IN 47308
Tel.: 317-284-4461
Fax: 317-288-2125
Year Founded: 1939
Approx.Sls.: $60,000,000
Emp.: 1,000
Electric Utility Contracting
S.I.C.: 1731; 1623
Jan G. Gilbert *(Chm. Bd.)*
Robert L. Bowen *(Vice Chm.)*
John Price *(Pres.)*
Dan J. Hinds *(V.P. & Chief Fin. Officer)*
Karen E. Beard *(Sec. & Treas.)*

Outside Service Firm(s):

Arthur Andersen & Co.*(Auditors)*
111 Monument Circle, Ste. 4300
Indianapolis, IN 46204-5143
Tel.: 317-634-3210
Fax: 317-632-3973

Beasley, Gilkison, Retherford, Buckles & Clark*(Legal Firm)*
110 E. Charles St.
Muncie, IN 47305

Star Bank*(Major Banking Relationship)*
Indianapolis, IN

GILBERT MFG. CORP.
P.O. Box 165, Route 26
Locke Mills, ME 04255
Tel.: 207-875-2301 **ME**
Fax: 207-875-2303
Year Founded: 1985
Sales Range: $10-19 Million
Emp.: 100
Fiscal Year-end: 6/30/90
Export
Mfr. Wood Turnings, Cutlery Handles, Scraper Handles & Small Flatware Items
S.I.C.: 2499
Duane L. Gilbert *(Pres. & Owner)*
Robert Betz *(Mgr.-Plant)*
Harry Swan *(Mgr.-Pur.)*
Carol Whitman *(Mgr.-Office)*
Lillian Brooks *(Quality Control Inspector)*
Judith M. Foster *(Corp. Customer Liaison)*

Principal(s):
Duane L. Gilbert

No. of Mfg. Plants/Facilities: 1
No. of U.S. Offices: 1

Computer Systems/Hardware:
Burroughs

Outside Service Firm(s):

Sayer & Golden*(Legal Firm)*
Lisbon, MN

U.S. Trust Co.*(Major Banking Relationship)*
30 Court St.
Boston, MA 02108

GILBERT/ROBINSON, INC.
47th & Main
Kansas City, MO 64112
Tel.: 816-756-2200
Fax: 816-561-2842
Approx.Sls.: $300,000,000
Emp.: 14,000
Fiscal Year-end: 12/31/90
Family Type Restaurants; Houlihan's Old Place, Bristol Bar & Grill, Seaport Cafe & Bar, Lily's/Cricket's, Fred P. Ott's, Buena Vista, Plaza III, Lucille's Country Dinner House, Charley's Place Restaurants, Darryl's, Hogates, Ribsters, Phineas & Carnegies
S.I.C.: 5812; 5813
Frederick R. Hipp *(Pres.-Casual Restaurants Div.)*
Mary Bonono *(Dir.-Mktg. & Adv.)*

GW&J
GILBERT WHITNEY & JOHNS

GILBERT, WHITNEY & JOHNS, INC.
Jefferson Plaza, 110 S. Jefferson Rd.
Whippany, NJ 07981
Tel.: 201-386-1776
Fax: 201-386-0589
Year Founded: 1969
Approx.Billings: $41,500,000
Emp.: 55
Consumer Adv., Business-to-Business Adv. & Pub. Rels.
John Daltner *(Chm.)*
John P. Leonardi *(Pres.)*
James V. Polizzi *(Sr. V.P., Dir. Adv. Services)*
Richard Small *(Sr. V.P., Grp. Pub. Rels. Dir.)*
Michael Bratnick *(V.P., Acct. Supvr., Pub. Rels.)*
Robert Pantaliano *(V.P., Controller)*
Terrence J. Pranses *(V.P., Dir. Mktg. Devel.)*

Computer Systems/Hardware:
PC Network; Hewlett Packard-HP3000; DataTrack

GILES & RANSOME, INC.
2975 Galloway Rd.
Bensalem, PA 19020
Tel.: 215-639-4300 **PA**
Fax: 215-245-2831
Year Founded: 1916
Approx.Sls.: $175,000,000
Emp.: 425
Distributor Construction Equipment, Tractors, Industrial Trucks, Marine & Diesel Engines, Asphalt & Concrete Paving Equipment, Material Handling Equipment, Franchise Caterpillar Dealer
S.I.C.: 5082; 5083; 5084; 6794
Ernest L. Ransome, III *(Chm. Bd.)*
Percy A. Ransome, III *(Vice Chm.)*
Wayne L. Bromley, Jr. *(Pres.)*
Dennis R. Runyen *(V.P.-Fin.)*
James M. Vito *(V.P.-Sls.)*
Carl Wanjek *(Controller)*
John Colasurdo *(Dir.-Pur.)*
Dale Hulse *(Mgr.-Data Processing)*
Donald Sprague *(Legal Officer)*
Principal(s):
Ernest L. Ransome, III
Percy A. Ransome, III
Wayne L. Bromley, Jr.

No. of Mfg. Plants/Facilities: 12

Outside Service Firm(s):

Coopers & Lybrand*(Auditors)*
2400 Eleven Penn Center
Philadelphia, PA 19103-2962
Tel.: 215-963-8000

Dechert, Price & Rhoads*(Legal Firm)*
4000 Bell Atlantic Tower, 1717 Arch St.
Philadelphia, PA 19103
Tel.: 215-994-4000
Tel.: 2000

Philadelphia National Bank*(Major Banking Relationship)*
P.O. Box 13834, Broad & Chestnut Streets
Philadelphia, PA 19101-7618
Tel.: 215-973-8327

M.C. GILL CORPORATION
4056 Easy St.
El Monte, CA 91731
Tel.: 818-443-4022
Fax: 818-350-5880
Year Founded: 1945
Approx.Sls.: $25,000,000
Emp.: 200
Fiscal Year-end: 12/31/92
Import Export
Specialty Laminators Of Flat & Contoured Fiberglass Cloth, Reinforced Plastics & Sandwich Panels & Composites
S.I.C.: 2821; 3083; 3728; 3089
Merwyn C. Gill *(Chm. Bd.)*
Stephen E. Gill *(Pres. & Chief Exec. Officer)*
Phillip C. Gill *(V.P.-Mktg.)*
Howard C. Alphson *(Sec. & Gen. Counsel)*
Larry Russell *(Dir.-O.E.M. Sls.)*
Paul W. DeGood *(Mgr.-Mktg. Services)*
Dan Guerrero *(Mgr.-Human Resources)*
Dean Lundberg *(Mgr.-Quality Control)*
Larry Tomlinson *(Mgr.-Matls.)*
Bruce Stanford *(Chief Engr.)*
Principal(s):
Merwyn C. Gill
Stephen E. Gill
Phillip C. Gill

No. of Mfg. Plants/Facilities: 2
No. of U.S. Offices: 1

Outside Service Firm(s):

Lee, Sperling & Hisahume*(Auditors)*
Los Angeles, CA

Howard Alphson*(Legal Firm)*
Santa Monica, CA

Bank of America NT&SA*(Major Banking Relationship)*
El Monte, CA

Subsidiary:

Royal Plastic **(1)**
P.O. Box 380,
Minden, NE 68959
Tel.: 308-832-2760
Fax: 308-832-2214
Emp.: 25
Advanced Composites Contoured Parts
S.I.C.: 3089
Stephen Gill *(Pres.)*

THE GILLESPIE ORGANIZATION, INC.
International Corporate Center, P.O. Box 3333
Princeton, NJ 08543
Tel.: 609-799-6000
Fax: 609-799-6752
Year Founded: 1973
Approx.Billings: $89,000,000
Emp.: 95
Consumer, Business-to-Business, Direct Response
S.I.C.: 7311
Richard J. Gillespie *(Pres.)*
Suzanne Brown *(V.P., Fin.)*
Elizabeth Blazer *(V.P., Human Resources)*
Principal(s):
Richard J. Gillespie

Computer Systems/Hardware:
IBM

Subsidiaries:

Gillespie Advertising, Inc. **(1)**
International Corporate Center, P.O. Box 3333
Princeton, NJ 08543
Tel.: 609-799-6000
Fax: 609-799-6752
Approx.Billings:
Joseph Barone *(Pres.)*
Ray Hirschman *(Exec. V.P., Exec. Creative Dir.)*
Mike McCartan *(Exec. V.P., Gen. Mgr.)*
Bob Musial *(V.P., Dir.-Acct. Mngmt.)*
Marci Samat *(V.P., Mgmt. Supervisor)*
Mike McCartan *(V.P.)*
Daryl Delaney *(V.P.)*

Gillespie Public Relations, Inc. **(1)**
P.O. Box 3333,
Princeton, NJ 08543
Tel.: 609-799-4949
Fax: 609-799-6395
Approx.Billings: $500,000
Emp.: 7
Corporate Public Relations, Crisis Planning/ Management, Issues Management/Public Affairs, Publicity
Lou Grossman *(Pres.)*

Magazine Marketing, Inc. **(1)**
191 Clarksville Rd.
Lawrenceville, NJ 08648
Tel.: 609-452-1633
Fax: 609-520-1663
Jack Kent *(Pres.)*
Scott MacAdam *(V.P.)*

GILLETT HOLDINGS, INC.
555 17th St., Ste. 3300
Denver, CO 80202
Tel.: 303-292-0045 **DE**
Fax: 303-292-9603
Year Founded: 1977
Approx.Sls.: $800,000,000
Emp.: 4,000
Broadcasting, Beef Packing, Recreation & Real Estate
S.I.C.: 6719; 4833; 6531; 2011; 2013
George N. Gillett, Jr. *(Chm. Bd.)*
Larry Haugen *(V.P.)*
David Ramon *(V.P. & Chief Fin. Officer)*
Dave Dunham *(Controller)*
James G. Gorman *(Emp. Ben. Mgr.)*

Outside Service Firm(s):

Ernst & Young*(Auditors)*
4300 Republic Plaza
Denver, CO 80202
Tel.: 303-628-4406

Winston & Strawn*(Legal Firm)*
One 1st Natl. Plaza, No. 5000
Chicago, IL 60603
Tel.: 312-558-5600

First National Bank of Chicago*(Major Banking Relationship)*
One First National Plaza
Chicago, IL 60670

Tel.: 312-732-9781
Tel.: 312-732-4050
Fax: 312-732-4840
Fax: 312-732-3055

Subsidiaries:

GCC, Inc. **(1)**
555 17th Street, Suite 3300
Denver, CO 80202
Tel.: 303-292-0045 (100%)
Holding Co.
S.I.C.: 6719

GNG-1, Inc. **(1)**
555 17th St., Ste. 3300
Denver, CO 80202
Tel.: 303-292-0045 (100%)
Holding Co.
S.I.C.: 6719

GNG-3, Inc. **(1)**
555 17th St.
Denver, CO 80202
Tel.: 303-292-0045 (100%)
Holding Co.
S.I.C.: 6719

Gillett Broadcasting, Inc. **(1)**
555 17th St., Ste. 3300
Denver, CO 80202
Tel.: 303-292-0045 (100%)
Holding Co.(Inactive)
S.I.C.: 6719

Gillett Broadcasting of Maryland, Inc. WMAR-TV **(1)**
6400 York Rd.
Baltimore, MD 21212
Tel.: 410-377-2222 (100%)
S.I.C.: 4833
Arnold J. Kleiner *(Pres. & Gen. Mgr.)*

Gillett Broadcasting of Tennessee, Inc. **(1)**
555 17th St., Ste. 3300
Denver, CO 80202
Tel.: 303-292-0045 (100%)
Holding Company (Inactive)
S.I.C.: 6719

Gillett Corporation **(1)**
555 17th St., Ste. 3300
Denver, CO 80202
Tel.: 303-292-0045 (100%)
Holding Co.
S.I.C.: 6719

Gillett-GP Corporation **(1)**
555 17th St., Ste. 3300
Denver, CO 80202
Tel.: 303-292-0045 (100%)
Holding Co.
S.I.C.: 6719

Gillett Group, Inc. **(1)**
555 17th St., Ste. 3300
Denver, CO 80202
Tel.: 303-292-0045 (100%)
Holding Co.
S.I.C.: 6719

Gillett Group Management, Inc. **(1)**
555 17th St., Ste. 3300
Denver, CO 80202
Tel.: 303-292-0045 (100%)
Emp.: 20
Management Company for Gillett Holdings, Inc.
S.I.C.: 6719

Gillett Productions, Inc. **(1)**
555 17th St., Ste. 3300
Denver, CO 80202
Tel.: 303-292-0045 (100%)
Holding Co.
S.I.C.: 6719

KSBW, Inc. **(1)**
238 John St.
Salinas, CA 93901
Tel.: 408-758-8888 (100%)
Television Broadcasting
S.I.C.: 4833

KSBY, Inc. **(1)**
467 Hill St.
San Luis Obispo, CA 93401
Tel.: 805-541-6666 (100%)
Television Broadcasting
S.I.C.: 4833

Packerland Packing Co. **(1)**
2580 University Ave., P.O. Box 1184
Green Bay, WI 54302
Tel.: 414-468-4000 (100%)
Emp.: 1,100
Beef Packing & Processing
S.I.C.: 2011; 2013
David F. Backer *(Chief Oper. Officer)*

Vail Associates, Inc. **(1)**
P.O. Box 7
Vail, CO 81658
Tel.: 303-949-5750 (100%)
Emp.: 500
Ski Resorts
S.I.C.: 7011
George Gillett, Jr. *(Chm. Bd.)*

WLUC, Inc. **(1)**
555 17th Street, Suite 3300
Denver, CO 80202
Tel.: 303-292-0045 (100%)
S.I.C.: 4833
Guy Spitsberg *(Gen. Mgr.)*

Winnebago Color Press, Inc. **(1)**
555 17th Street
Denver, CO 80202
Tel.: 303-292-0045 (100%)
Emp.: 58
Holding Company (Inactive)
S.I.C.: 6719

GILLIS ADVERTISING & PUBLIC RELATIONS
3620 8th Ave. South
Birmingham, AL 35222
Tel.: 205-326-0200 **AL**
Fax: 205-326-8519
Year Founded: 1973
Assets: $4,745,449
Liabilities: $3,226,666
Net Worth: $1,518,783
Approx.Billings: $30,000,000
Emp.: 51
Advertising Agency
S.I.C.: 7311
Wayne H. Gillis *(Chm. Bd. & Pres.)*
Donald D. Dunham *(Exec. V.P., Acct. Service)*
Elizabeth M. Smith *(Exec. V.P., Media Dir.)*
Gail Wood *(Dir.-Fin.)*
Craig Woodward *(Dir.-Pub. Rels.)*
Principal(s):
Wayne H. Gillis

No. of U.S. Offices: 1

Computer Systems/Hardware:
IBM

Outside Service Firm(s):

Hawley, Beck & Company, P.C.*(Auditors)*
Birmingham, AL

Blue Cross & Blue Shield of Alabama*(Group Insurer)*
450 Riverchase Pkwy. East
Birmingham, AL 35298
Tel.: 205-988-2245

Nationwide Insurance*(Commercial Insurance Carrier)*
One Nationwide Plaza
Columbus, OH 43216
Tel.: 614-249-6488

Pritchard, McCall, Jones*(Legal Firm)*
Birmingham, AL

First Alabama Bank*(Major Banking Relationship)*
Birmingham, AL

A.A.A.A.*(Pension Manager)*
New York, NY

Branch:

Gillis Public Relations, Inc. **(1)**
3620 8th Ave. South
Birmingham, AL 35222
Tel.: 205-326-0200
Fax: 205-326-8519
Craig Woodward *(Pres.)*

GILLOGLY CHEVROLET INC.
1777 Union Rd.
West Seneca, NY 14224
Tel.: 716-674-5000 **NY**
Fax: 716-674-8802
Year Founded: 1948
Assets: $7,844,927
Liabilities: $5,544,975
Net Worth: $2,299,952
Approx.Sls.: $28,000,000
Emp.: 85
Fiscal Year-end: 12/31/89
Automobiles & Trucks Sales & Leasing
S.I.C.: 5511; 7515
Fred D. Gillogly *(Pres. & Treas.)*
Terry B. Gillogly *(V.P.)*
Roseanne L. Gillogly *(Sec.)*
Pete Kramer *(Mgr.-Sls.)*

Outside Service Firm(s):

Komlyn & Co.*(Auditors)*
Pittsburgh, PA

Watson, McGarvey, Bennett, Colligan & Johnson*(Legal Firm)*
Buffalo, NY

MNT Bank*(Major Banking Relationship)*
Buffalo, NY

MARTY GILMAN, INC.
30 Gilman Rd.
Gilman, CT 06336
Tel.: 203-889-7334
Tel.: 800-243-0398 **CT**
Fax: 203-823-1859
Year Founded: 1929
Sales Range: $10-19 Million
Emp.: 55
Mfr. Football Practice Equipment, Wrestling Equipment, Exercise Mats, Canvas Products, Marine Products, Stadium Cushions, Punching Bags, Karate & Judo Equipment
S.I.C.: 3949; 2394; 3089; 3429
Shirley J. Gilman *(Pres. & Treas.)*
Neil Gilman *(V.P. & Sec.)*
Richard Weis *(Gen. Mgr.)*
Geoffrey Gilman *(Mgr.-Sls.)*
Principal(s):
Shirley J. Gilman
Neil Gilman

Computer Systems/Hardware:
IBM

Outside Service Firm(s):

Bailey, Moore, Glazer, Schaefer & Proto*(Auditors)*
10 Lunar Dr.
Woodbridge, CT

Aetna Life & Casualty*(Commercial Insurance Carrier)*
151 Farmington Avenue
Hartford, CT 06156
Tel.: 203-273-2128
Fax: 203-729-4295

Aetna Life & Casualty*(Group Insurer)*
151 Farmington Avenue
Hartford, CT 06156
Tel.: 203-273-2128
Fax: 203-729-4295

Kirkpatrick & Lockhart*(Legal Firm)*
Boston, MA 02110

Bank of Boston*(Major Banking Relationship)*
100 Pearl St.
Hartford, CT 06103

GILMAN PAPER CO.
1000 Osborne St.
Saint Marys, GA 31558
Mailing Address:
P.O. Box 878,
St. Marys, GA 31558
Tel.: 912-882-4241
Tel.: 800-624-9657
Fax: 912-882-3591
Approx.Sls.: $440,000,000
Emp.: 2,500
Fiscal Year-end: 12/31/90
Export
Paper & Allied Products
S.I.C.: 2679
Corporate Giving Program: Match dollar for dollar up to $2,500
Howard Gilman *(Chm. Bd. & Chief Exec. Officer)*
William H. Davis *(Pres. & Chief Oper. Officer)*
John Faiella *(Treas.)*
Bernard Bergreen *(Gen. Counsel)*
Michael Pallen *(Controller)*
Allen Harrelson *(Dir.-Pur.)*
John Love *(Dir.-Personnel)*
Frank Ross *(Dir.-Data Processing)*
Principal(s):
Howard Gilman

No. of Mfg. Plants/Facilities: 2
No. of U.S. Offices: 1

Computer Systems/Hardware:
Honeywell

Outside Service Firm(s):

Grant Thornton*(Auditors)*
605 Third Ave.
New York, NY 10158
Tel.: 212-599-0100
Fax: 212-370-4520

Royal Insurance Co.*(Commercial Insurance Carrier)*
Charlotte, NC

Provident Life & Accident Insurance Co.*(Group Insurer)*
P.O. Box 12015
Chattanooga, TN 37401
Tel.: 615-755-7088

Bernard Bergreen*(Legal Firm)*
New York, NY

First Chicago Shareholder Services Trust Co.*(Major Banking Relationship)*
153 West 51st St.
New York, NY 10019
Tel.: 212-791-6422
Fax: 212-385-9798

First Chicago Shareholder Services Trust Co.*(Pension Manager)*
153 West 51st St.
New York, NY 10019
Tel.: 212-791-6422
Fax: 212-385-9798

Subsidiary:

Saint Marys Railroad Co. **(1)**
110 Osborne St., P.O. Box 520
Saint Marys, GA 31558
Tel.: 912-882-4301
Emp.: 28
Connecting Line Rail Service for Parent Co.
S.I.C.: 4731
Charles Chapman *(Pres.)*

GILMORE BROS., INC.
143 S. Kalamazoo Mall
Kalamazoo, MI 49007
Tel.: 616-345-3541
Fax: 616-345-0212
Year Founded: 1881
Approx.Sls.: $14,000,000
Emp.: 300
Department Store
S.I.C.: 5311
Martha Parfet *(Chm. Bd.)*
Jeffrey Hoffman *(Pres.)*
Timothy C. Watkins *(V.P. & Controller)*
Ray T. Parfet, Jr. *(Sec. & Treas.)*
Jim Hartill *(Dir.-Personnel)*
Barbara Frazier *(Mgr.-Adv.)*

Outside Service Firm(s):

Ernst & Young*(Auditors)*
1100 Old Kent Bank Bldg.
Kalamazoo, MI 49007
Tel.: 616-349-6671

Gilmore Bros., Inc.—(Continued)

Deming, Hughey, Lewis, Keiser, Allen & Chapman*(Legal Firm)*
Kalamazoo, MI

Old Kent Bank*(Major Banking Relationship)*
Kalamazoo, MI

GILMORE ENVELOPE CORP.
4540 Worth St.
Los Angeles, CA 90063
Tel.: 213-268-3401 **CA**
Fax: 213-264-2029
Year Founded: 1937
Approx.Sls.: $45,000,000
Emp.: 450
Mfr. Envelopes
S.I.C.: 2677
Howard N. Gilmore, Jr. *(Pres. & Chief Exec. Officer)*
George Duplisea *(V.P. & Gen. Mgr., Northern Div.)*
Dan Paracchini *(V.P. & Gen. Mgr., Southern Div.)*
Kathleen Gilmore *(Dir.-Mktg.)*
Principal(s):
Howard N. Gilmore, Jr.

No. of Mfg. Plants/Facilities: 2
No. of U.S. Offices: 8

Outside Service Firm(s):

Wells Fargo Bank*(Major Banking Relationship)*
333 S. Grand
Los Angeles, CA 90071
Tel.: 213-253-6836

GILPATRICK CONSTRUCTION COMPANY
714 W. Monroe
Riverton, WY 82501
Tel.: 307-856-2229 **WY**
Fax: 307-856-7165
Year Founded: 1943
Approx.Sls.: $10,000,000
Emp.: 25
General Contractors for Highway Construction; Wholesale Distribution of Sand & Gravel
S.I.C.: 1611; 5032
Rick Gilpatrick *(Pres.)*
Ronald Currier *(Sec. & Treas.)*

Outside Service Firm(s):

First Interstate Bank*(Major Banking Relationship)*
Riverton, WY

GILSTER MARY LEE CORP.
1037 State St.
Chester, IL 62233
Mailing Address:
P.O. Box 227
Chester, IL 62233
Tel.: 618-826-2361 **IL**
Fax: 618-826-2973
Approx.Sls.: $300,000,000
Emp.: 1,200
Export
Private Label & Contract Manufacturer Cake Mixes, Dry Drink Mixes, Dry Cereals, Macaroni, Potato Products, Popcorn
S.I.C.: 2045; 2098
Donald E. Welge *(Pres. & Gen. Mgr.)*
Michael W. Welge *(Exec. V.P., Sec., Treas. & Comptroller)*
Delbert Dethrow *(V.P. & Truck Mgr.)*
Sheldon Gitelman *(V.P.-Sls.)*
David Yu *(V.P. & Tech. Dir.)*
Ron Tretter *(Asst. V.P.-Engrng.)*
Rob Welge *(Dir.-Personnel)*

Outside Service Firm(s):

Kerbereck & Brareckel*(Auditors)*
Chester, IL

Buena Vista National Bank of Chester*(Major Banking Relationship)*
Chester, IL

Divisions:

Duff Mix Div. **(1)**
P.O. Box 227
Chester, IL 62233
Tel.: 618-826-2361
S.I.C.: 2045

Gilster Mary Lee Corp. **(1)**
305 E. Washington
Momence, IL 60954
Tel.: 815-472-6456
Mfr. Chocolate Drinks & Powder
S.I.C.: 2066
Gary Schultz *(Plant Supvr.)*

Party Pac Div. **(1)**
P.O. Box 227,
Chester, IL 62233
Tel.: 618-826-2361
S.I.C.: 2045

Py-O-My Div. **(1)**
P.O. Box 227
Chester, IL 62233
Tel.: 618-826-2361
S.I.C.: 2045; 2066

GILVIN-TERRILL INC.
P.O. Box 9027
Amarillo, TX 79105
Tel.: 806-374-0932
Fax: 806-944-5271
Approx.Sls.: $17,500,000
Emp.: 190
Heavy Highway Construction; Aggregate & Hot Mix Production
S.I.C.: 1611; 1622; 1629
Leon P. Gilvin *(Chm. Bd.)*
F. C. Chow *(Pres.)*
Shirley A. Vernon *(Sec. & Treas.)*

Outside Service Firm(s):

Gibson, Ochsner & Adkins*(Legal Firm)*
Amarillo, TX

First National Bank of Amarillo*(Major Banking Relationship)*
Amarillo, TX

GINGISS INTERNATIONAL
180 N. LaSalle St., Ste. 1111
Chicago, IL 60601
Tel.: 312-236-2333
Fax: 312-580-7170
Year Founded: 1985
Approx.Sls.: $60,000,000
Emp.: 175
Fiscal Year-end: 12/31/91
Franchise Development; Men's Formal Wear Stores, Rental & Sales
S.I.C.: 7299; 5611
Michael J. Corrao *(Chm. Bd., Pres. & Chief Exec. Officer)*
Richard Vanderwal *(Chief Fin. Officer & V.P.-Fin.)*
Anthony J. Grimaldi *(V.P.-Real Estate)*
John Heiser *(V.P.-Franchise Devel.)*
Roman Pisockyj *(V.P.)*
Richard E. Ovradnik *(V.P.)*
Timothy Smodilla *(V.P.-Franchise Opers.)*
Carol A. Oldberg *(Dir.-Communications)*

Outside Service Firm(s):

Grant Thornton*(Auditors)*
700 One Prudential Plaza, 130 East Randolph St.
Chicago, IL 60601
Tel.: 312-856-0200
Fax: 312-565-4719

American National Bank & Trust Company of Chicago*(Major Banking Relationship)*
33 N. LaSalle St.
Chicago, IL 60602
Tel.: 312-661-5000
Fax: 312-661-6417

GINSBERG'S INSTITUTIONAL FOODS, INC.
P.O. Box 17, Rte. 66
Hudson, NY 12534
Tel.: 518-828-4004 **NY**
Fax: 518-828-2630
Year Founded: 1909
Approx.Sls.: $26,000,000
Emp.: 90
Fiscal Year-end: 9/30/91
Distribute Institutional Food Supplies Under The NIFDA Label
S.I.C.: 5141
Morton A. Ginsberg *(Chm. Bd.)*
David M. Ginsberg *(Pres.)*
Ira M. Ginsberg *(V.P. & Sec.)*
David W. Hart *(Controller)*
Suzanne Kozel *(Dir.-Mktg.)*
Bill Merceirs *(Dir.-Admin. & Opers.)*
Robert Quenneville *(Dir.-Sls.)*
Robert J. Van Pelt *(Dir.-Pur.)*
Principal(s):
Morton A. Ginsberg
David M. Ginsberg
Ira M. Ginsberg

Computer Systems/Hardware:
DEC PDP 11/73, DEC VAK 80

Outside Service Firm(s):

Morton J. Glickman & Co.*(Auditors)*
Hudson, NY

Chemical Bank*(Major Banking Relationship)*
Albany, NY

Rapport, Meyers, Griffen & Whitbeck*(Legal Firm)*
Hudson, NY

GIRGENTI, HUGHES, BUTLER & MCDOWELL
100 6th Ave., 8th Fl.
New York, NY 10013-1687
Tel.: 212-966-0077
Fax: 212-966-7755
Year Founded: 1986
Approx.Billings: $40,000,000
Emp.: 40
Health Care Adv.
Steve Girgenti *(Pres. & New Bus. Contact)*
Bill Butler *(Exec. V.P.)*
Dennis Lantier *(V.P., Acct. Supvr.)*
George Lefeber *(V.P., Finance)*
Bob Ranieri *(V.P., Assoc. Creative Dir.)*

GISH, SHERWOOD & FRIENDS, INC.
460 Tenth Circle No.
Nashville, TN 37203
Tel.: 615-255-5600
Fax: 615-255-5655
Year Founded: 1978
Approx.Billings: $15,000,000
Emp.: 30
Dale L. Gish *(Chm. Bd. & Pres.)*
Karen Edwards *(V.P., Opers.)*
Laurel Conley *(V.P., Fin. Services)*
Marsha Wade *(Co-Op Service Dir.)*

GITANO GROUP INC.
1411 Broadway
New York, NY 10018
Tel.: 212-819-0707
Fax: 212-730-0319
Year Founded: 1971
Earnings: ($62,473,000)
Approx.Sls.: $780,444,000
Emp.: 4,000
Fiscal Year-end: 12/31/91
Women's, Men's & Children's Casual Clothing
S.I.C.: 5137; 5136
Morris Dabah *(Chm. Bd.)*
Peter C. Kells *(Vice Chm., Chief Fin. & Chief Oper. Officer)*
Haim Dabah *(Pres. & Chief Exec. Officer)*
Stanley Greenstein *(Exec. V.P.)*
Gustave Birnberg *(Sr. V.P.)*
Phillip Brader *(V.P. & Dir.-Global Sourcing)*
Pam Breeman *(V.P.-Adv.)*
David Keery *(Sr. Fin. Officer)*
Steven M. Gerber *(Gen. Counsel & Sec.)*
John Amodeo *(Adv. Mgr.)*
Ken Petti *(Pub. Rels. Mgr.)*
Ira Kolko *(Personnel Mgr.)*
Sam Nusenbaum *(Import Mgr.)*
Norman Berger *(Data Processing Mgr.)*

Divisions:

Gitano Boy's & Men's Division **(1)**
20 W. 33rd St.
New York, NY 10001
Tel.: 212-564-6100
Boy's & Men's Clothing
S.I.C.: 5136
Eli Harari *(Chief Oper. Officer)*

Gitano Girl's Division **(1)**
112 W. 34th Street
New York, NY 10120
Tel.: 212-563-5360
Girl's Clothing
S.I.C.: 5137
Ezra Dabah *(Chief Oper. Officer)*

Gloria Vanderbilt Division **(1)**
1411 Broadway
New York, NY 10018
Tel.: 212-819-0707
Women's Apparel
S.I.C.: 5137
Jack Gross *(Pres.)*

Non-U.S. Holdings:

Jamtex Ltd. **(1)**
51-52 Caracas Ave. Kingston Export Free Zone,
Kingston, 15, Jamaica (100%)
Mfr. of Jeans
S.I.C.: 2325

Noel of Jamaica Ltd. **(1)**
J.K.D.C. Complex 76 Market Gravity Dr.,
Kingston, 15, Jamaica (100%)
Mfr. Jeans
S.I.C.: 2325

GIUMARRA VINEYARDS
P.O. Bin 1969,
Bakersfield, CA 93303
Year Founded: 1974
Approx.Sls.: $17,000,000
Emp.: 150
Export
Winery; Giumarra Vineyards, Breckenridge Cellars & Grape King Grape Juice
S.I.C.: 2084
Sal Giumarra *(Pres.)*
John Giumarra, Jr. *(V.P.)*
William Butler *(Chief Fin. Officer)*
John A. Culver *(Dir.-Sls. & Mktg. & Adv. Mgr.)*
Jim Lawrence *(Winery Mgr.)*

GLAMORISE FOUNDATIONS, INC.
135 Madison Ave.
New York, NY 10016
Tel.: 212-684-5025
Fax: 212-689-7793
Year Founded: 1921
Emp.: 200
Export
Mfr. Bras & Girdles
S.I.C.: 2342
Richard Rosner *(Pres.)*
Morton Levine *(Exec. V.P.-Fin.)*
Bernard Pundyk *(Exec. V.P.)*

Gerold Kirschner *(Sr. V.P.)*
Donald Mullings *(V.P.)*
Jon R. Pundyk *(Dir.-Mktg.)*
Martin Gresack *(Mgr.-Sls.)*

Computer Systems/Hardware:
IBM System 34

GLASTEEL INDUSTRIAL LAMINATES
(Div. Alpha Corp.)
1727 Buena Vista
Duarte, CA 91010
Tel.: 818-444-4965
Tel.: 800-537-1306
Approx.Sls.: $19,000,000
Emp.: 60
Fiscal Year-end: 10/31/90
Mfr. Electrical Grade Laminates & Circuit Boards
S.I.C.: 3672
Dave Barrell *(Mgr.-Sls. & Mktg.)*

Division:

Glasteel Tennessee, Inc. **(1)**
P.O. Box 521
Collierville, TN 38017
Tel.: 901-853-2010
Architectural Work
Walt Ochinski *(Mgr.)*

GLAZERS WHOLESALE DRUG CO. INC.
14860 Landmark Blvd.
Dallas, TX 75240
Tel.: 214-702-0900
Fax: 214-702-8508
Emp.: 900
Liquor, Wine & Beer Wholesale Distributors
S.I.C.: 5181; 5182
Robert S. Glazer *(Chm. Bd., Pres. & Chief Exec. Officer)*
Cary Rossel *(V.P., Chief Fin. Officer & Admin.)*
Pat O'Shea *(V.P.-Pur.)*

Computer Systems/Hardware:
IBM System 36

Outside Service Firm(s):

Weiner, Wilheim & Dennis*(Auditors)*
Dallas, TX

Aetna Life & Casualty*(Group Insurer)*
151 Farmington Avenue
Hartford, CT 06156
Tel.: 203-273-2128
Fax: 203-729-4295

Tobolowsky Prager & Schlinger*(Legal Firm)*
Dallas, TX

MBank Dallas*(Major Banking Relationship)*
1900 Pacific
Dallas, TX 75265

MBank Dallas*(Pension Manager)*
1900 Pacific
Dallas, TX 75265

GLEN ELLEN WINERY
1883 London Ranch Rd.
Glen Ellen, CA 95442
Tel.: 707-935-3000
Fax: 707-935-4049
Year Founded: 1855
Approx.Sls.: $23,000,000
Emp.: 30
Fiscal Year-end: 12/31/90
California Winery Producing Premium Varietal Wines Under 4 Labels Including Glen Ellen, Benzinger, M.G. Vallejo & The Imagery Series, an Ultra Premium Limited Production Wine
S.I.C.: 2084; 5182
Michael Benziger *(Mng. Gen. Partner)*
Bruce Rector *(Mng. Gen. Partner & Winemaker)*
Rusty Eddy *(Dir.-Pub. Rels.)*
Tim Wallace *(Dir.-Mktg.)*

GLEN OAKS INDUSTRIES, INC.
16 E. 34th St.,20th Fl.
New York, NY 10016
Tel.: 212-679-9020
Fax: 212-779-0238
Approx.Sls.: $65,000,000
Emp.: 1,000
Men's Dress Slacks
S.I.C.: 2325
Milton Askinas *(Pres.)*
Stanley Bloomberg *(Exec. V.P. & Sec.)*
Joe Trapina *(Mktg. Dir.)*

Outside Service Firm(s):

Brecker, Schor & Company*(Auditors)*
New York, NY

Moser & Henkin*(Legal Firm)*
New York, NY

Bankers Trust Co.*(Major Banking Relationship)*
280 Park Ave.
New York, NY 10017
Tel.: 212-454-2647

GLEN RAVEN MILLS, INC.
(Executive Offices)
1831 N. Park Ave.
Glen Raven, NC 27217
Tel.: 919-227-6211 nc
Telex: 910-333-6959
Fax: 919-226-8133
Year Founded: 1880
Emp.: 2,500
Textile Mill Prods.
S.I.C.: 2251; 2281; 2262; 2269; 3552; 2221; 2211
Edmund R. Gant *(Chm. Bd. & Sec.)*
Roger Gant, Jr. *(Chm.-Exec. Committee)*
Allen E. Gant, Jr. *(Pres. & Asst. Treas.)*
G. Russell Gantt *(V.P., Treas. & Asst. Sec.)*
W.S. Chandler, Jr. *(V.P.-Devel.)*
Bruce Buchanan *(V.P. & Gen. Mgr.-Consumer Prods. Div.)*
Charles C. Grady *(V.P. & Gen. Mgr.-Glenspun Div.)*
Donald I. Burhoe *(V.P. & Gen. Mgr.-Filament Fabrics Div.)*
Charles McKeller *(V.P.-Mfg. Services)*
T. Scott Gillam *(V.P.)*
W. Richard Feroe *(Mgr.-Norlina Div. & Glen Touch Div.)*
S. Dan Sibley *(Mgr.-Finishing Div.)*
Monti Allison *(Mgr.-Pur.)*

No. of Mfg. Plants/Facilities: 10

Computer Systems/Hardware:
IBM 4300

Outside Service Firm(s):

McGladrey & Pullen*(Auditors)*
Drawer G-2, 230 N. Elm St.
Greensboro, NC 27402
Tel.: 919-273-4461

Wachovia Bank & Trust Co.*(Major Banking Relationship)*
P.O. Box 3001,
Winston-Salem, NC 27102
Tel.: 800-633-4236

Vernon, Vernon, Wooten, Brown, Andrews, & Garrett, P.A.*(Legal Firm)*

Divisions:

Glen Raven Marketing Corp. **(1)**
1350 Broadway
New York, NY 10018
Tel.: 212-629-9255
Fax: 212-629-9310
Provides Marketing and Sales Services for The Glenspun and Consumer Products Divisions
S.I.C.: 8742
Larry Yow *(V.P.-Mktg.-Glenspun Div.)*

Glen Raven Marketing Corporation **(1)**
1350 Broadway
New York, NY 10018
Tel.: 212-629-9255
Fax: 212-629-9310
Marketing & Sales Service for Glenspun & Consumer Products Division
Larry Yow *(V.P.-Mktg.-Glenspun Div.)*
Ken Brunini *(V.P. & Reg. Sls. Mgr.-Consumer Prods. Div.)*

Glen Raven Marketing Corporation **(1)**
One Blue Hill Plaza, 4th Fl.
Pearl River, NY 10965
Tel.: 914-735-0110
Fax: 914-735-0193
Marketing & Sales for the Filament Fabrics Division
Jack Derasmo *(V.P.-Mktg. & Sls. Mgr.)*

Glen Raven Mills, Inc.-Park Ave. Finishing Division **(1)**
PO Box 4268, 1821 North Park Ave.
Glen Raven, NC 27215
Tel.: 919-227-6211
Fax: 919-227-5650
Commision Dyer and Finisher Specializing in Knitted, Woven and Nonwoven Fabrics
S.I.C.: 2231
S. Dan Silbey *(Pres. & Gen. Mgr.)*

Glen Raven Mills, Inc.-Glenspun Division **(1)**
142 Raven Rd.
Glen Raven, NC 27217-1100
Tel.: 919-227-6211
Fax: 919-228-0530
Producer of Natural,Packaged Dyed, ProducerDyed and SolutionDyed Yarns-Both Ring and Open-End-for Knitted and Woven Apparel, Home Furnishings and Industrial End Uses
S.I.C.: 2231
Charles C. Grady *(V.P. & Gen. Mgr.)*

Plants:

Glen Raven Mills, Inc.-Kinston Plant **(2)**
P.O. Box 3485, 800 Manning St.
Kinston, NC 28502-3485
Tel.: 919-527-9036
Fax: 919-527-2226
Part of the Glenspun Division; Utilizes Both Ring and Open-End Spinning Technology to Produce Natural, Producer-Dyed and Solution Dyed Acrylic Yarns
S.I.C.: 2281

Glen Raven Mills, Inc.-Ultraspun Plant **(2)**
232 Glen Raven Rd.
Glen Raven, NC 27217-1100
Tel.: 919-227-6211
Fax: 919-570-2626
Part of the Glenspun Division; Produces World-Class Open-End Acrylic Yarn
S.I.C.: 2281

Glen Raven Mills, Inc.-Custom Fabrics Division **(1)**
.831 North Park Ave
Glen Raven, NC 27217-1100
Tel.: 919-227-6211
Fax: 399-229-409
Mfr. SUNBRELLA (R) Awning, Marine, Furniture and Indurtrial Fabrics
S.I.C.: 2394; 2399
David A. Edgerton *(V.P. & Gen. Mgr.)*

Plants:

Glen Raven Mills, Inc.-Custom Fabrics Division-Equinox Plant **(2)**
200 Jackson St.
Anderson, SC 29621
Tel.: 803-224-1671
Fax: 803-225-1273
Mfr. (spinning and weaving) Site for The Custom Fabrics Division
S.I.C.: 2231; 2211

Glen Raven Mills, Inc.-Custom Fabrics Division-Equinox Finishing Plant **(2)**
107 Service Rd.
Anderson, NC 29621
Tel.: 803-224-1671
Fax: 803-225-2948
Finishes Fabrics Produced by the Custom Fabrics Division
S.I.C.: 2231

Glen Raven Mills, Inc.-Textured Yarn Group-Norlina Division **(1)**
1831 North Park Ave.
Glen Raven, NC 27217-1100
Tel.: 919-227-6211
Fax: 919-226-8454
Texturizes Fine Denier Nylon for the Women's Hosiery Market
S.I.C.: 2251
W. Richard Feroe *(Pres.)*

Plant:

Glen Raven Mills, Inc.-Norlina Plant **(2)**
P.O. Box 518, Highway U.S. 1 South
Norlina, NC 27563
Tel.: 919-456-4141
Cable: 919-456-3959
Mfr. Textured Nylon Ladies Hosiery
S.I.C.: 2251

Glen Raven Mills, Inc.-Textured Yarn Group-Glen Touch Division **(1)**
1831 North Park Ave.
Glen Raven, NC 27217-1100
Tel.: 919-227-6211
Fax: 919-226-8454
Air Jet Textures Nylon, Polyester and Other Synthetic Filament Yarns; Designed for Use in Active Outerwear, Home Furnishings and Industrial Applications
S.I.C.: 2281
W. Richard Feroe *(Gen. Mgr.)*

Plant:

Glen Raven Mills, Inc.-Glen Touch Plant **(2)**
P.O. Box 278, 3726 Altamahaw-Union Ridge Rd.
Altamahaw, NC 27202
Tel.: 919-227-6211
Fax: 919-222-8165
Mfr. Variety of Synthetic Filament Yarns in a Broad Range of Deniers
S.I.C.: 2281

Glen Raven Mills, Inc.-Filament Fabrics Division **(1)**
Drawer 100, Highway 19 East
Burnsville, NC 28714
Tel.: 704-682-9710
Fax: 704-682-9710
Produces Filament Febrics Woven for Outerwear, Sport & Leisure Gear, Luggage, Interlinings, Pocketing, Upholstery, Flags & Industrial Uses
S.I.C.: 2211; 2221
Donald I. Burhoe *(V.P. & Gen. Mgr.)*

Glen Raven Mills Marketing Corp. **(1)**
4th Floor, One Blue Hill Plaza
Pearl River, NY 10965
Tel.: 914-735-0110
Fax: 914-735-0193
Marketing & Sales Functions for the Filament Fabrics Division
S.I.C.: 8742
Jack Derasmo *(V.P. Mktg. & Sls. Mgr.)*

Glen Raven Mills, Inc. **(1)**
1821 North Park Ave., P.O. Box 4268
Glen Raven, NC 27217
Tel.: 919-227-6211
Fax: 919-227-5650
Commission Dyer, Finisher Specializing in Knitted, Woven, & Nonwoven Fabrics
S. Dan Sibley *(Pres. & Gen. Mgr.)*

Glen Raven Mills, Inc.-Consumer Products Division **(1)**
3730 Altamahaw-Union Ridge Rd., P.O. Box 8
Altamahaw, NC 27202
Tel.: 919-227-6211
Fax: 919-570-3010
Markets Ladies Hosiery
Bruce Buchanan *(V.P. & Gen. Mgr.)*

Glen Raven Mills, Inc.-Consumer Products Division **(1)**
P.O. Box 8, 3730 Altamahaw-Union Ridge Rd.
Altamahaw, NC 27202
Tel.: 919-227-6211
Fax: 919-570-3010

Glen Raven Mills, Inc.—(Continued)

Markets Ladies Hosiey -Primarily for Customers' House Labels; Product Line Includes:Pantyhose, Knee Highs, Control Top Hosiery & Exercise Tights for Women
S.I.C.: 2251
Bruce Buchanan *(V.P. & Gen. Mgr.)*

Glen Raven Mills, Inc.-Custom Fabrics Div. **(1)**
1831 North Park Ave.
Glen Raven, NC 27217-1100
Tel.: 919-227-6211
Fax: 919-229-4039
Mfr. of Awning, Marine, Furniture & Industrial Fabrics
David A. Edgerton *(V.P. & Gen. Mgr.)*

Glen Raven Mills, Inc.-Glenspun Div. **(1)**
142 Glen Raven Rd.
Glen Raven, NC 27217-1100
Tel.: 919-227-6211
Fax: 919-228-0530
Natural Package Dyed, Producer Dyed, & Solution Acrylic Yarns, Both Ring & Open End, for Knitted & Woven Apparel, Home Furnishings & Industrial End Uses
Charles C. Grady *(V.P. & Gen. Mgr.)*

Glen Raven Mills, Inc.-Kingston Plant **(1)**
800 Manning St., P.O. Box 3485
Kingston, NC 28502-3485
Tel.: 919-527-9036
Fax: 919-527-2226
Natural, Producer Dyed & solution Dyed Acrylic Yarns

Glen Raven Mills, Inc.-Custom Fabrics Div., Equinox Plant **(1)**
200 Jackson St.
Anderson, SC 29621
Tel.: 803-224-1671
Fax: 803-225-1273
Mfg. for Custom Fabrics Div.

Glen Raven Mills, Inc.-Custom Fabrics Div., Equinox Finishing Plant **(1)**
107 Service Rd.
Anderson, SC 29621
Tel.: 803-224-1671
Fax: 803-225-2948

Glen Raven Mills, Inc.-Filament Fabrics Div. **(1)**
Hwy. 19 E., Drawer 100
Burnsville, NC 28714
Tel.: 704-682-2142
Fax: 704-682-9710
Filament Fabrics
Donald I. Burhoe *(V.P. & Gen. Mgr.)*
T. Scott Gillam Jr. *(V.P. & Mfg. Mgr.)*

Glen Raven Mills, Inc.-Glen Touch Plant **(1)**
3726 Altamahaw-Union Ridge Rd., P.O. Box 278
Altamahaw, NC 27202
Tel.: 919-227-6211
Fax: 919-222-8165
Mfr. of Synthetic Filament Yarn

Glen Raven Mills, Inc.-Norlina Plant **(1)**
Hwy. U.S. 1 S., P.O. Box 518
Norlina, SC 27563
Tel.: 919-456-4141
Fax: 919-456-3959
Mfr. of Textured Nylon

Glen Raven Mills, Inc.-Textured Mills Group, Glen Touch Div. **(1)**
1831 North Park Ave.
Glen Raven, NC 27217-1100
Tel.: 919-227-6211
Fax: 919-226-8454
Air Jets Nylon, Plyester & Other Synthetic Filament Yarns
W. Richard Feroe *(Gen. Mgr.)*

Glen Raven Mills, Inc.-Textured Yarn Group, Norlina Div. **(1)**
1831 North Park Ave.
Glen Raven, NC 27217-1100
Tel.: 919-227-6211
Fax: 919-226-8454
Texturizes Fine Denier Nylon for the Women's Hosiery Market
W. Richard Feroe *(Pres.-Norlina Mills)*

Glen Raven Mills, Inc.-Transportation Div. **(1)**
(Hwy. 87 North at Ossipee), 1831 Nroth Park Ave.
Glen Raven, NC 27217-1100
Tel.: 919-227-6211
Fax: 919-584-7216
Services Glen Raven Customers
Jimmy H. Coble *(Dir. of Transportation)*

Glen Raven Mills, Inc.-Transportation Division **(1)**
(Highway 87 N. at Ossipee), 1831 North Park Ave.
Glen Raven, NC 27217-1100
Tel.: 919-227-6211
Fax: 919-584-7216
Services Glen Raven Customers; Fleet Primarily Covers the Eastern Seaboard
Jimmy H. Coble *(Dir. - Trans.)*

Glen Raven Mills, Inc.-Ultraspun Plant **(1)**
232 Glen Raven Rd.
Glen Raven, NC 27217-1100
Tel.: 919-227-6211
Fax: 919-570-2626
Open End Acrylic Yarns

GLENAYRE TURNKEY TECHNOLOGIES, INC.
One Cornell Pkwy.
Springfield, NJ 07081
Tel.: 908-906-0600
Fax: 201-467-2387
Approx.Sls.: $10,000,000
Emp.: 100
Mfr. of Radio Paging & Intercom Systems
S.I.C.: 3663; 3669
John Badrick *(Pres.)*

GLENCRAFT LINGERIE, INC.
38 E. 32nd St.
New York, NY 10016
Tel.: 212-689-5990 **NY**
Fax: 212-545-0235
Year Founded: 1961
Approx.Sls.: $11,000,000
Emp.: 50
Mfr. of Women's, Misses', Children's & Infants Underware
S.I.C.: 2341
Irving Jacobson *(Pres.)*
Evelyn Jacobson *(V.P.)*
Harvey Jacobson *(Sec. & Treas.)*

Outside Service Firm(s):

Albert J. Hasson & Co.*(Auditors)*
New York, NY

Chase Manhattan Bank, N.A.*(Major Banking Relationship)*
One Chase Manhattan Plaza
New York, NY 10081
Tel.: 212-552-2222
Tel.: 800-526-0801
Fax: 212-552-7175

THE GLENNON COMPANIES
One City Centre
Saint Louis, MO 63101
Tel.: 314-436-5455
Year Founded: 1964
Approx.Billings: $28,752,000
Emp.: 65
Glennon D. Jamboretz *(Chm. Bd., Pres. & Chief Exec. Officer)*
Larry D. Mickey *(Pres.-The Lawrence Co.)*
Patrick Forrestal *(Pres.-The Patrick Co.)*
Debbie Carosella *(Exec. V.P., Gen. Mgr.-Adv.)*
Dennis Wilhelmi *(Sr. V.P., Chief Fin. Officer)*
Bruce M. Hagen *(V.P., Dir. Bus Devel.)*

GLENOIT MILLS, INC.
Hwy. 33 West
Tarboro, NC 27886
Mailing Address:
P.O. Box 1157
Tarboro, NC 27886
Tel.: 919-823-2124
Fax: 919-823-7181
Approx.Sls.: $58,000,000
Emp.: 450
Fiscal Year-end: 12/31/91
Export
Glenoit Deep-Pile Fabrics for Men's, Women's, Children's Outerwear; Homefurnishings, Rugs & Industrail Uses
S.I.C.: 2299; 2257; 2231; 2211; 2297; 2241
Thomas O'Gorman *(Pres.)*
Fred Keshner *(Sr. V.P.)*
John Wolf *(V.P.)*
Thomas L. Harrell *(V.P. & Treas.)*

Computer Systems/Hardware:
IBM AS 400

GLENROY CONSTRUCTION CO. INC.
450 S. Ritter Ave.
Indianapolis, IN 46219
Mailing Address:
P.O. Box 19383
Indianapolis, IN 46219
Tel.: 317-359-9501 **IN**
Fax: 317-352-7115
Year Founded: 1945
Approx.Sls.: $30,000,000
Emp.: 200
General Contractors; Construction Management
S.I.C.: 1541; 1542; 8741
Jesse N. Jones, III *(Pres. & Chief Exec. Officer)*
William E. Blevins *(V.P.)*
K.E. Jones *(V.P.)*
M.E. Meador *(Treas.)*

Outside Service Firm(s):

Katz, Sapper & Miller*(Auditors)*
Indianapolis, IN

Hughes & Hughes*(Legal Firm)*
Indianapolis, IN

INB National Bank*(Major Banking Relationship)*
One Indiana Sq.
Indianapolis, IN 46266
Tel.: 317-266-6000

GLENSHAW GLASS CO. INC.
William Flinn Hwy. 1101
Glenshaw, PA 15116
Tel.: 412-486-9100 **PA**
Year Founded: 1895
Assets: $24,500,000
Liabilities: $12,800,000
Net Worth: $11,700,000
Approx.Sls.: $49,000,000
Emp.: 475
Fiscal Year-end: 9/30/88
Mfr. Flint, Amber & Emerald Green Glass Containers
S.I.C.: 3221
John Ghaznavi *(Chm. Bd.)*
David T. Gutowski *(Treas.)*
Jeff Beattie *(Dir.-Data Processing)*
James Tolbert *(Dir.)*
Gerard T. Tremel *(Mgr.-Acctg.)*

No. of Mfg. Plants/Facilities: 1
No. of U.S. Offices: 1

Computer Systems/Hardware:
Sperry-Univac 9030

Outside Service Firm(s):

Love Scherle & Bauer*(Auditors)*
Pittsburgh, PA

Benefit Trust & Life*(Group Insurer)*
South Bend, IN

Reed, Smith, Shaw & McClay*(Legal Firm)*
Mellon Square, P.O. Box 2009
Pittsburgh, PA 15230
Tel.: 412-288-3131
Fax: 412-288-3063

Westinghouse Credit Corporation*(Major Banking Relationship)*
Pittsburgh, PA

GENE B. GLICK COMPANY, INC.
8330 Woodfield Crossing Blvd., Ste. 200
Indianapolis, IN 46240
Mailing Address:
P.O. Box 40177
Indianapolis, IN 46240
Tel.: 317-469-0400
Fax: 317-469-8142
Sales Range: $10-19 Million
Emp.: 546
Land Developer
S.I.C.: 6552
Eugene B. Glick *(Pres.)*
John Cottrell *(Chief Fin. Officer)*
Stephen L. Valinet *(Dir.-Res.)*
Michael D. White *(Dir.-Human Resources)*
John Despot *(Mgr.-Data Processing)*

Computer Systems/Hardware:
IBM PC XT

Outside Service Firm(s):

Ernst & Young*(Auditors)*
One Indiana Square, Ste. 3400
Indianapolis, IN 46204
Tel.: 317-236-1100

INB National Bank*(Major Banking Relationship)*
One Indiana Sq.
Indianapolis, IN 46266
Tel.: 317-266-6000

GLICO HARMONY FOODS CORPORATION
719 Swift St.
Santa Cruz, CA 95060
Mailing Address:
P.O. Box 1191
Santa Cruz, CA 95061
Tel.: 408-457-3200
Fax: 408-457-3230
Year Founded: 1990
Approx.Sls.: $25,000,000
Emp.: 500
Mfr. Quality Snacks, Confectionary Products
S.I.C.: 2099; 2064; 5149; 5145
Corporate Giving Program: Cases Are Reviewed On An Individual Basis
Yasuaki Honda *(Vice Chm. & Exec. V.P.)*
Stephen Kennedy *(Chief Fin. Officer & V.P.)*
Dan Haut *(V.P. & Chief Resource Officer)*
Eiichi Takano *(V.P. & Sec.)*
Edward Jacobs *(Treas. & Dir.-Fin. Services)*
William R. Dawson *(Gen. Counsel)*
Donna Ferris *(Dir.-Human Resources)*
Eric Mitchell *(Dir.-Mngmt. Information Systems)*
Dee Schabot *(Dir.-Employee Benefits)*

No. of Mfg. Plants/Facilities: 1
No. of U.S. Offices: 1

Computer Systems/Hardware:
H.P.

Outside Service Firm(s):

KPMG Peat Marwick*(Auditors)*
50 W. San Fernando
San Jose, CA 95113-2413
Tel.: 408-279-2000

Fireman's Fund Insurance Co.*(Commercial Insurance Carrier)*
San Francisco, CA

Aetna Life & Casualty*(Group Insurer)*
151 Farmington Avenue
Hartford, CT 06156
Tel.: 203-273-2128
Fax: 203-729-4295

Bancroft, Avery, McAlister*(Legal Firm)*
San Francisco, CA

First Interstate Bank*(Major Banking Relationship)*
San Jose, CA

Mutual of New York*(Pension Manager)*
New York, NY

GLINES & RHODES, INC.
189 East St.
Attleboro, MA 02703
Mailing Address:
P.O. Box 2285,
Attleboro, MA 02703
Tel.: 508-226-2000
Fax: 508-226-7136
Year Founded: 1915
Sales Range: $40-59 Million
Emp.: 35
Refining of Precious Metals
S.I.C.: 3341
Raymond E. Crowell *(Chm. Bd. & Pres.)*
Ralph Crowell *(Exec. V.P. & Treas.)*
William Atwell *(V.P.-Mfg.)*
Richard Lunn *(V.P.-Fin.)*
Michael Powers *(V.P.-Sls.)*
Willard G. McGraw *(Sec.)*

Outside Service Firm(s):

Cotta, Swenson & Oliveria*(Auditors)*
Attleboro, MA

Warner & Stackpole*(Legal Firm)*
75 State St.
Boston, MA 02109
Tel.: 617-227-7042

Rhode Island Hospital Trust National Bank*(Major Banking Relationship)*
Hospital Trust Tower
Providence, RI

GLOBAL MARKETING RESOURCES
551 Fifth Ave.
New York, NY 10176
Tel.: 212-297-0000
Fax: 212-297-0073
Year Founded: 1991
Approx.Billings: $29,000,000
Emp.: 26
Thomas J. Tanski *(Pres. & Chief Exec. Officer)*
Sharon Gerson *(Exec. V.P., Chief Oper. Officer)*
Paul L. Zeno *(Sr. V.P., Mktg. & Sls.)*
Tony Morgis *(V.P., Sls.)*
Mike Suscavage *(V.P., Sls.)*

GLOBAL PETROLEUM CORP.
800 South St.
Waltham, MA 02154
Tel.: 617-894-8800
Fax: 617-893-7642
Assets: $125,000,000
Net Worth: $125,000,000
Approx.Sls.: $1,243,000,000
Emp.: 250
Fiscal Year-end: 6/30/87
Retail Commercial & Industrial Fuels; Wholesale Distr. of Fuels through Subsidiary
S.I.C.: 5172; 5983
Alfred A. Slifka *(Pres. & Chief Exec. Officer)*
Richard Slifka *(Chief Fin. Officer & Treas.)*
Christopher Gorgone *(Controller)*

Outside Service Firm(s):

Ernst & Young*(Auditors)*
200 Clarendon St., 46th Fl.
Boston, MA 02116
Tel.: 617-266-2000

Guardian Life Insurance Co.*(Group Insurer)*
New York, NY

Sumner Fox*(Legal Firm)*
Boston, MA

First National Bank of Boston*(Major Banking Relationship)*
P.O. Box 644,
Boston, MA 02102-0644
Tel.: 617-575-2900
Fax: 617-575-2549

Welsh, Ives & Kotler*(Pension Manager)*
Boston, MA

GLOBAL STEEL PRODUCTS CORPORATION
95 Marcus Blvd.
Deer Park, NY 11729
Tel.: 516-586-3330
Fax: 516-586-3455
Approx.Sls.: $20,000,000
Emp.: 250
Mfr. of Toilet Partitions, Dressing Booths, Shower Stalls & Accessory Items
S.I.C.: 3431; 2542
M.F. Rolla *(Chm. Bd.)*
R. Strack *(Pres.)*
T. Cohen *(V.P.-Mfg.)*
L. Dibella *(V.P.-Admin.)*
R. St. Nicholas *(V.P.-Sls.)*

GLOBAL TURNKEY SYSTEMS INC.
Four North St.
Waldwick, NJ 07463
Tel.: 201-445-5050
Tel.: 800-524-2132 **DE**
Fax: 201-445-1648
Year Founded: 1985
Assets: $2,800,000
Liabilities: $2,000,000
Net Worth: $800,000
Sales Range: $10-19 Million
Emp.: 100
Fiscal Year-end: 12/31/91
Distributor of Turnkey Mini/Micro Computer Systems
S.I.C.: 3571
William J. Devers, Jr. *(Chm. Bd.)*
Robert E. Farina *(Pres.& Chief Exec. Officer)*
Michael Urban *(V.P.-Field Service & Mfg.)*
Michael Winer *(V.P. & Controller)*
Paul G. Lagano *(V.P.-Sls. & Mktg.)*

No. of Mfg. Plants/Facilities: 2
No. of U.S. Offices: 2

Computer Systems/Hardware:
IBM RS/6000 & Others

Outside Service Firm(s):

Rotenberg & Meril*(Auditors)*
Hackensack, NJ

Hopkins & Sutter*(Legal Firm)*
Three First Natl. Plaza
Chicago, IL 60602
Tel.: 312-558-6600

Chubb Group*(Commercial Insurance Carrier)*
New York, NY

Lincoln National Life Insurance Co.*(Group Insurer)*
Chicago, IL

Lake Shore National Bank*(Major Banking Relationship)*
605 N. Michigan Ave.
Chicago, IL 60611
Tel.: 312-787-1900

Division:

OMNI Industry **(1)**
1801 Broadway, Ste. 1700
Denver, CO 80202
Tel.: 303-293-2666
Fax: 303-293-8340
Computer Systems/Hardware:
IBM AS/400 & DEC VAX
Mfr. Software for Publishing Industry
S.I.C.: 7371
Lee Pierce *(Div. V.P.-Sls.)*
Gail Noyes *(Div. V.P.-Mktg.)*

GLOBE-AMERADA GLASS COMPANY
2001 Greenleaf Ave.
Elk Grove Village, IL 60007
Tel.: 708-364-2900
Tel.: 800-323-8776 **IL**
Telex: 280398
Fax: 708-364-2909
Year Founded: 1919
Assets: $11,593,000
Liabilities: $4,633,000
Net Worth: $6,960,000
Approx.Sls.: $30,000,000
Emp.: 300
Fiscal Year-end: 2/28/91
Import Export
Architectural & Security Glass Products; Automotive Replacement Glass & Installation
S.I.C.: 3211; 3231; 5013; 7539
Mildred Kellman *(Chm. Bd. & Pres.)*
Cheri Kellman *(V.P.-Architectural Div.)*
John Kellman *(V.P.-Retail Div.)*
Michael Kellman *(V.P.-Natl. Auto Glass Replacement Program)*
Robert Kellman *(V.P.-Auto Glass)*
Marvin Weitzenfeld *(Sec.)*
Rosann Holbrook *(Mgr.-Adv.)*
Charles Chewning *(Mgr.-Data Processing)*
Tammy Fleming *(Dir.-Pur.)*

No. of Mfg. Plants/Facilities: 1
No. of U.S. Offices: 26

Computer Systems/Hardware:
IBM System 36

Outside Service Firm(s):

Blackman Kallick Bartelstein*(Auditors)*
300 Riverside Plaza
Chicago, IL 60606
Tel.: 312-207-1040

Daley & George*(Legal Firm)*
Chicago, IL

LaSalle National Bank*(Major Banking Relationship)*
135 S. La Salle St.
Chicago, IL 60690

Subsidiary:

Assurance Glass Co. of Alabama **(1)**
Selfield Industrial Park
Selma, AL 36701
Tel.: 205-875-1900
Tel.: 800-633-2513
Emp.: 90
Mfr. Architectural & Security Glass and Glass-Clad Polycarbonate Prods.
S.I.C.: 3231
Cheri Kellman *(V.P.)*

GLOBE BUSINESS FURNITURE, INC.
90 Volunteer Dr.
Hendersonville, TN 37075
Tel.: 615-822-4968
Fax: 615-824-9755
Year Founded: 1897
Approx.Sls.: $100,000,000
Emp.: 900
Fiscal Year-end: 12/31/91
Import Export
Mfr. Wood & Metal Office Seating & Partitions
S.I.C.: 2521; 2522; 2541; 2542
Hanley Sayers *(Chm. Bd.)*
John W. Park *(Pres.)*
Daryl Anne Park *(Sr. V.P.-Mktg. & Sls.)*
James F. Mills, Jr. *(V.P.-Human Resources & Quality Control)*
Frank Patterson *(V.P.-Mfg.)*
Ken Wilmore *(V.P.-Sourcing & Acquisitions)*
John Speas *(Corp. Controller)*
Dennis Arnold *(Dir.-Nat'l. Acct. Sls.)*
Maurice Driver *(Dir.-Catalog Sls.)*
Danny Skeen *(Dir.-Sls.)*
Bill Wong *(Dir.-Mktg.)*
Principal(s):
John W. Park

No. of Mfg. Plants/Facilities: 6
No. of U.S. Offices: 2

Outside Service Firm(s):

Deloitte & Touche*(Auditors)*
424 Church St., Ste. 2400
Nashville, TN 37219-2396

Gullett, Sanford & Robinson*(Legal Firm)*
Nashville, TN

NationsBank*(Major Banking Relationship)*
35 Broad St.
Atlanta, GA 30303
Tel.: 404-581-2121
Tel.: 800-848-8198

Division:

Chairworld, Inc. **(1)**
2638 Yates Ave.
City of Commerce, CA 90040
Tel.: 213-728-3633
Fax: 213-888-0937
Import
Computer Systems/Hardware:
Wang VS
S.I.C.: 2522
John W. Park *(Pres.)*

GLOBE GLASS & MIRROR CO.
2 N. LaSalle, Ste. 2500
Chicago, IL 60602-3876
Tel.: 312-578-7200 **IL**
Fax: 312-278-2571
Year Founded: 1930
Assets: $33,000,000
Liabilities: $20,000,000
Net Worth: $13,000,000
Approx.Sls.: $102,000,000
Emp.: 1,000
Fiscal Year-end: 12/31/91
Repair & Replace Auto Glass Commercial & Residential Glazing
S.I.C.: 7536; 1793
Joseph Kellman *(Chm., Pres. & Chief Exec. Officer)*
Jack Kellman *(Exec. V.P.-Mktg. & Sls.)*
Robert Kubiak *(V.P.-Fin., Chief Fin. Officer & Sec.)*
Gladys Lazar *(V.P., Asst. to The Pres. & Asst. Sec.)*
Frank Nimesheim *(V.P.-Human Resources)*
Charlie Rogers *(V.P.-Customer Rels.)*
Jim Schmelzer *(V.P.-Materials & Specialty Products)*
Mark Sklenar *(V.P.-Info. Tech.)*
Scott Pettit *(Treas. & Asst. Sec.)*
Michael Podjasek *(Controller)*
Principal(s):
Joseph Kellman

No. of U.S. Offices: 100

Computer Systems/Hardware:
IBM 9121

Outside Service Firm(s):

KPMG Peat Marwick*(Auditors)*
Peat Marwick Plaza, 303 E. Wacker Dr.
Chicago, IL 60601
Tel.: 312-938-1000

Fireman's Fund Insurance Co.*(Commercial Insurance Carrier)*
Brea, CA

Globe Glass & Mirror Co.—(Continued)

LaSalle National Bank*(Major Banking Relationship)*
135 S. LaSalle St.
Chicago, IL 60603
Tel.: 312-443-2440
Fax: 312-443-2819

Subsidiaries:

CarComp Services, Inc. (1)
2 N. LaSalle St., Ste 2500
Chicago, IL 60602-3876
Tel.: 312-278-6900
Emp.: 40
Auto Glass Repair & Replacement
S.I.C.: 7536; 1793
Eddie Cheskis *(Chief Oper. Officer)*

USA-GLAS, Inc. (1)
1880 W. Fullerton Ave.
Chicago, IL 60614
Tel.: 312-278-6900
Emp.: 260
Automotive Glass Replacement & Repair
S.I.C.: 7536; 1793
Perry Ludy *(Chief Oper. Officer)*

U.S. Auto Glass Centers, Inc. (1)
2 N. LaSalle St., Ste. 2500
Chicago, IL 60602-3876
Tel.: 312-278-6900
Emp.: 730
Automotive Glass Service
S.I.C.: 7536; 1793
Richard Bergman *(Chief Oper. Officer)*

GLOBE INDUSTRIES, INC.
2638 E. 126th St.
Chicago, IL 60632
Tel.: 312-646-1300 **DE**
Fax: 312-646-7765
Year Founded: 1934
Approx.Sls.: $175,000,000
Emp.: 1500
Fiscal Year-end: 12/31/91
Mfr. of Automotive & Commercial Sound Control Materials
S.I.C.: 3714
Kingdon Gould, Jr. *(Chm. Bd.)*
Robert A. Christopher *(Pres. & Chief Exec. Officer)*
Donald E. Benson *(Exec. V.P. & Chief Fin. Officer)*
Gerald Barefoot *(V.P.-Sls.)*
Robert Gatti *(V.P.-Mfg.)*
Joseph Labak *(V.P. & Controller)*
Matthew Ostroski *(V.P.-Pur.)*
Frederick J. Zolla *(V.P. & Treas.)*
Anil Bhojawani *(Dir.-Mngmnt. Information Services)*
John Bidese *(Dir.-Human Resources)*
Hameed Kahn *(Dir.-Research & Devel.)*
Matthew Smith *(Dir.-Mktg.)*

Subsidiary:

Mastico Industries, Ltd. (1)
P.O. Box 400, 730 Goshen Rd.,
Tillsonburg, ON N4G 4H8, Canada
Tel.: 519-842-6411 (100%)
Mfr. of Automotive Soundproofing
S.I.C.: 3714
Jake Koke *(Gen. Mgr.)*

GLOBE INTERNATIONAL INC.
1400 Clinton St.
Buffalo, NY 14206
Mailing Address:
P.O. Box 1062
Buffalo, NY 14240
Tel.: 716-824-8484
Fax: 716-827-0375
Year Founded: 1916
Approx.Sls.: $20,706,000
Emp.: 200
Import Export
Manufacture & Wholesale Industrial Solid Woven Synthetic & Rubber Belting
S.I.C.: 2241; 3052; 3069; 5085
Harry M. Cardillo *(Pres.)*
Mark E. Hoffman *(Chief Fin. Officer)*
D.J. Beecher *(V.P.-Sls.)*
T.M. Hansen *(V.P.-Admin.)*
F.S. Zabron *(V.P.-Engrng.)*
John Brown *(Mgr.-Personnel)*

Computer Systems/Hardware:
Data General

Outside Service Firm(s):

Fleet Bank*(Major Banking Relationship)*
Deer Park, NY 14202

GLOBE MORTGAGE COMPANY
Two University Plaza
Hackensack, NJ 07602
Mailing Address:
P.O. Box 246,
Hackensack, NJ 07602
Tel.: 201-489-6120 **NJ**
Fax: 201-489-8165
Year Founded: 1957
Assets: $87,921,616
Liabilities: $71,664,419
Net Worth: $16,257,197
Sales Range: $500-999 Million
Emp.: 214
Fiscal Year-end: 6/30/92
Mortage Banking & Related Services
S.I.C.: 6162
Murray L. Beer *(Chm. Bd., Pres. & Chief Exec. Officer)*
Leonard J. Bendzin *(Exec. V.P. & Chief Oper. Officer)*
John G. Caruso *(Exec. V.P., Loan Admin. & Sec.)*
James A. Richmond *(Exec. V.P.-Mortgate Loans)*
Angelo Prieto *(Sr. V.P.-Fin. & Treas.)*

Principal(s):
Murray L. Beer
Leonard J. Bendzin
John G. Caruso
James A. Richmond
Brett M. Davis

No. of U.S. Offices: 8

Computer Systems/Hardware:
IBM

Outside Service Firm(s):

Deloitte & Touche*(Auditors)*
Newark, NJ

The Logberg Companies*(Commercial Insurance Carrier)*
Teaneck, NJ

Sills Cummis Zuckerman Radin Tischman Epstein & Gross*(Legal Firm)*
33 Washington St.
Newark, NJ 07102
Tel.: 201-643-3232

Bankers Trust Co.*(Major Banking Relationship)*
P.O. Box 318, Church St. Station
New York, NY 10008
Tel.: 212-454-2212
Fax: 212-454-2783

Chemical Banking Corp.*(Major Banking Relationship)*
277 Park Ave.
New York, NY 10041
Tel.: 212-310-6407
Fax: 212-310-4526

Midlantic National Bank*(Major Banking Relationship)*
Hackensack, NJ

National Community Bank*(Major Banking Relationship)*
Hackensack, NJ

National Westminster Bank plc*(Major Banking Relationship)*
175 Water St.
New York, NY 10038-4924
Tel.: 212-602-3364

Divisions:

Financial Resources Group (1)
Two University Plaza
Hackensack, NJ 07602
Tel.: 201-489-6120
Holding Company
S.I.C.: 6719
Murray L. Beer *(Chm. Bd., Pres. & Chief Exec. Officer)*

Global Financial Services, Inc. (1)
Two University Plaza
Hackensack, NJ 07602
Tel.: 201-489-6120
Tel.: 800-654-5623
Fax: 201-489-8165
Emp.: 214
Holding Company
S.I.C.: 6719
Murray L. Beer *(Chm. Bd., Pres. & Chief Exec. Officer)*

GLOBUS-GATEWAY/COSMOS TOURAMA
95-25 Queens Blvd.
Rego Park, NY 11374
Tel.: 718-268-1700
Tel.: 800-228-0211
Fax: 800-289-4646
Approx.Sls.: $10,000,000
Emp.: 110
Tours to U.S.A., Hawaii & Alaska, Mexico, Britain, Australia, New Zealand, Canada, Europe, the Orient & China, South Pacific
S.I.C.: 4725
John A. Martinen *(Pres.)*
Charles Maxwell *(Dir.-Mktg.)*
Bonnie Fragman *(Mktg. Coord.)*

GLORIA JEAN'S COFFEE BEAN CORP.
1001 Asbury
Buffalo Grove, IL 60089
Tel.: 708-808-0580 **IL**
Fax: 708-808-0593
Year Founded: 1976
Approx.Sls.: $50,000,000
Emp.: 50
Import Export
Franchise Chain For Retail Gourmet Coffee
S.I.C.: 6794; 5499
Gloria Jean Kvetko *(Owner)*
Edward C. Kvetko *(Pres.)*
Guy Wood *(Exec. V.P.)*
Stephen Cleary *(Corp. Counsel)*
Jim Dore *(Controller)*
Roger Badesch *(Dir.-Adv. & Pub. Rels.)*
Tom Jaworski *(Dir.-Leasing)*

Principal(s):
Gloria Jean Kvetko
Guy Wood

GODDESS BRA COMPANY
156 Porter St.
East Boston, MA 02128
Tel.: 617-569-3000 **MA**
Fax: 617-569-1120
Year Founded: 1945
Sales Range: $10-19 Million
Emp.: 270
Fiscal Year-end: 12/31/91
Import Export
Mfr. Goddess, Revelation Bras
S.I.C.: 2342
David H. Wilson *(Pres.)*
William Jacobson *(V.P.)*
Arnold B. Wilson *(V.P.)*
Arnold E. Jacobson *(Treas. & Dir.-Data Processing)*
Morris Lezar *(Mgr.-Office)*

Principal(s):
David H. Wilson
William Jacobson
Arnold B. Wilson
Arnold E. Jacobson

Outside Service Firm(s):

Kellem, Goodman & Cohen*(Auditors)*
Newton, MA

Bank of New England*(Major Banking Relationship)*
28 State Street
Boston, MA 02109
Tel.: 617-742-4000

GODFATHER'S PIZZA, INC.
9140 W. Dodge Rd.
Omaha, NE 68114
Tel.: 402-391-1452
Fax: 402-392-2357
Year Founded: 1973
Sales Range: $100-499 Million
Emp.: 4,000
Fiscal Year-end: 5/28/91
Pizza Restaurants
S.I.C.: 5812
Herman Cain *(Pres. & Chief Exec. Officer)*
Ronald B. Gartlan *(Exec. V.P. & Chief Oper. Officer)*
Gary Batenhorst *(V.P. & Gen. Counsel)*
William C. Methven *(V.P.-Opers.)*
Spencer Wiggins *(V.P.-Human Resources)*
Steve Frisbie *(Dir.-Mdse. & Pub. Rels.)*

Subsidiary:

Big Cheese Pizza Corporation (1)
1130 Haskell
Wichita, KS 67213
Tel.: 316-263-5577
Emp.: 350
Fiscal Year-end: 1/ 3/90
Chain of 58 Company-Owned & Franchised Pizza Restaurants
S.I.C.: 5812
James Stevens *(Pres. & Chief Exec. Officer)*
Thomas J. Ryan *(Exec. V.P.)*
Vernon Schroeder *(Treas. & Sec.)*

GODFREY ADVERTISING
2890 Hempland Rd.
Lancaster, PA 17601
Tel.: 717-393-3831
Fax: 717-393-1403
Year Founded: 1947
Approx.Billings: $22,000,000
Emp.: 40
Export
Business-to-Business, Industrial, Integrated Marketing Communications Programs & Services
Dennis F. Cox *(Pres.)*
C. David Kramer *(Sr. V.P.)*
Robert E. Vail *(Sr. V.P.)*
Russ Green *(V.P., Bus. Devel.)*
Charles Manners *(V.P.)*
Ken Jones *(V.P.)*
John Vastyan *(Dir., Pub. Rels.)*
Scott Kriner *(Dir., Photography)*

Computer Systems/Hardware:
Macintosh Design/Production; IBM/ Compatible Office/Copywriting

GODWIN ADVERTISING AGENCY, INC.
One Jackson Place, 188 E. Capitol, Ste. 800
Jackson, MS 39201
Mailing Address:
P.O. Box 531,
Jackson, MS 39205
Tel.: 601-354-5711
Year Founded: 1937
Approx.Billings: $20,000,000
Emp.: 48
George W. Godwin, Jr. *(Chm. & Chief Exec. Officer)*
Danny Mitchell *(Pres. & Chief Oper. Officer)*
Frank N. Arender *(Exec. V.P.)*
Philip Shirley *(Sr. V.P., Pub. Rels.)*
Lance Hopkins *(V.P., Mktg.)*
Steve Sewell *(V.P., Pub. Rels.)*

GOEBEL ART, INC.
3401 Coon Rapids Blvd.
Coon Rapids, MN 55433 **MN**
Tel.: 612-427-1120
Fax: 612-427-9373
Year Founded: 1954
Approx.Sls.: $32,000,000
Emp.: 77
Fiscal Year-end: 12/31/89
Retail New Automobiles
S.I.C.: 5511
Arthur F. Goebel *(Pres. & Treas.)*
Margaret E. Goebel *(Sec.)*
Tom Kulick *(Mgr.-Sls.)*
Donald Servin *(Gen. Mgr.)*

Principal(s):
Arthur F. Goebel
Margaret E. Goebel

No. of Mfg. Plants/Facilities: 1

Outside Service Firm(s):

First National Bank*(Major Banking Relationship)*
P.O. Box 1599
Midland, TX 79701
Tel.: 915-685-2000

GOHMANN ASPHALT & CONSTRUCTION INC.
1630 Broadway
Clarksville, IN 47129
Mailing Address:
P.O. Box 2428
Clarksville, IN 47131
Tel.: 812-282-1349 **IN**
Fax: 812-288-2168
Year Founded: 1959
Approx.Sls.: $50,000,000
Emp.: 453
Fiscal Year-end: 3/31/90
Highway Construction; Manufacturer Asphaltic Materials; Trucking; Quarrying
S.I.C.: 1611; 1629; 2951
J. Michael Gohmann *(Pres. & Chief Exec. Officer)*
Annette G. Dezelan *(V.P.)*
John R. Gohmann *(V.P., Chief Oper. Officer, Sec. & Dir.-Pur.)*
Richard L. Cripe *(Treas.)*
Raymond J. Brown *(Asst. Controller)*
Sandra Crutchfield *(Mgr.-Data Processing)*
David F. Hardin *(Chief Engr.)*

Principal(s):
J. Michael Gohmann
Annette G. Dezelan
John R. Gohmann

No. of Mfg. Plants/Facilities: 7
No. of U.S. Offices: 8

Computer Systems/Hardware:
Basic IV

Outside Service Firm(s):

Ernst & Young*(Auditors)*
1000 Brown & Williamson Tower
Louisville, KY 40202
Tel.: 502-585-1400

William T. Smith Co.*(Group Insurer)*
Louisville, KY

Citizens Fidelity Bank & Trust of Indiana*(Investment Banker)*
New Albany, IN
Tel.: 812-945-2265

Fifer, Lanum & Blau*(Legal Firm)*
Jeffersonville, IN 47130

Stites & Harbison*(Legal Firm)*
600 West Main St.
Louisville, KY 40202
Tel.: 502-587-3400

Citizens Fidelity Bank & Trust of Indiana*(Major Banking Relationship)*
New Albany, IN
Tel.: 812-945-2265

Subsidiaries:

Gohmann Asphalt & Construction of KY., Inc. **(1)**
P.O. Box 19257, 2001 Outer Loop
Louisville, KY 40219
Tel.: 502-969-1082 (100%)
Emp.: 6
Asphalt Mfg.
S.I.C.: 2951
Richard L. Cripe *(Treas. & Controller)*

Gohmann Asphalt & Construction of Texas, Inc. **(1)**
3609 Pinehurst Ct.
Plano, TX 75075
Tel.: 214-377-3801 (100%)
Fax: 214-248-0422
Emp.: 18
Asphalt Mfg.
S.I.C.: 2951
Charles Bauder *(V.P.)*

Mariana Corporation **(1)**
P.O. Box 2602
Clarksville, IN 47131
Tel.: 812-284-1515 (100%)
Emp.: 17
Aggregate Transportation
S.I.C.: 4789; 5032
Arthur S. Rose, II *(V.P.)*

Riverton Truckers, Inc. **(1)**
P.O. Box 2602
Clarksville, IN 47131
Tel.: 812-284-1515 (100%)
Emp.: 58
Aggregate Transportation
S.I.C.: 5032; 4789
Arthur S. Rose, II *(V.P.)*

Sellersburg Stone Company, Inc. **(1)**
P.O. Box D, 1019 Utica St.
Sellersburg, IN 47172
Tel.: 812-246-3383 (100%)
Emp.: 28
Stone Mfg.
S.I.C.: 3281
Kenneth Rush *(Gen. Mgr.)*

GOLD COAST ADVERTISING
3625 N.W. 82nd Ave., Ste. 404
Miami, FL 33166
Tel.: 305-592-1192 (Dade)
Tel.: 305-522-3338 (Broward)
Fax: 305-477-9551
Year Founded: 1982
Approx.Billings: $22,000,000
Emp.: 17
Retail, Consumer Products, Financial, Business-to-Business, Travel & Real Estate Advertising
Robert E. Utsman *(Chm., Sec. & Mktg. Dir.)*
Stuart R. Dornfield *(Pres., Creative, Radio, TV Production & New Bus. Contact)*
Robert Bidney *(Gen. Mgr.)*

GOLD KIST, INC.
244 Perimeter Center Pkwy., N.E.
Atlanta, GA 30346
Mailing Address:
P.O. Box 2210,
Atlanta, GA 30301
Tel.: 404-393-5000 **GA**
Fax: 404-393-5548
Year Founded: 1936
Assets: $671,756,000
Earnings: $32,933,000
Liabilities: $374,816,000
Net Worth: $296,940,000
Approx.Rev.: $1,290,000,000
Emp.: 9,000
Fiscal Year-end: 6/30/91
Export
Agribusiness Cooperative
S.I.C.: 2048; 2875; 2015; 5191
W.P. Smith *(Chm. Bd.)*
Harold Chitwood *(Chief Exec. Officer)*
Gaylord O. Coan *(Pres.)*
Kenneth N. Whitmire *(Grp. V.P.)*
Peter Gibbons *(V.P. & Chief Fin. Officer)*
Paul G. Brower *(V.P.-Communications)*
William A. Epperson *(V.P.-Human Resources)*
Jack K. Hogan *(V.P.-Admin.)*
Jack L. Lawing *(V.P.-Law & Sec.)*
John McLaughlin *(V.P.-Feed & Animal Health)*
Allen Merritt *(V.P.-Fertilizer & Chemicals)*
Lester F. Schinake *(V.P.-Retail Opers.)*
Jerry Stewart *(V.P.-Mktg. & Poultry Grp.)*
Stephen O. West *(Treas.)*
Walter F. Pohl, Jr. *(Controller)*
Roy Finley *(Dir.-Pur.)*
Glenn H. Glover *(Dir.-Plng.)*
Ken Walker *(Dir.-Real Estate)*

Computer Systems/Hardware:
IBM Systems 43,41 & 400

Groups:

Agri-Commodities Group **(1)**
244 Perimeter Center Pkwy. N.E.
Atlanta, GA 30346
Tel.: 404-393-5000
Peanuts, Grain, Soymeal & Soy Oil, Peanut Oil, Farm Mngmt.
S.I.C.: 0119; 0762

Agri-Commodities & Services Group **(1)**
244 Perimeter Center Pkwy. N.E.
Atlanta, GA 30346
Tel.: 404-393-5000
Chemicals & Farm Supplies, Including Agricommodities
S.I.C.: 2873; 2874; 2875; 5191
Allen Merritt *(V.P.)*

Poultry Group **(1)**
244 Perimeter Center Pkwy. N.E.
Atlanta, GA 30346
Tel.: 404-393-5000
Farm Coop.-Broilers, Eggs & Hogs
S.I.C.: 0252; 0213; 2011; 2015
Harold O. Chitwood *(Exec. V.P.)*

Subsidiaries:

Agvestments, Inc. **(1)**
244 Perimeter Center Pkwy. N.E.
Atlanta, GA 30346
Tel.: 404-393-5000

AgraTrade Financing, Inc. **(1)**
244 Perimeter Center Pkwy.
Atlanta, GA 30346
Tel.: 404-393-5000
Agricultural Loan Company
S.I.C.: 6159

Agri International, Inc. **(1)**
244 Perimeter Center Pkwy.
Atlanta, GA 30346
Tel.: 404-393-5000

Subsidiaries:

Agra Tech Seeds, Inc. **(2)**
244 Perimeter Center Pkwy. N.E.
Atlanta, GA 30346
Tel.: 404-393-5000

Golden Poultry Co., Inc. **(2)**
244 Perimeter Center Pkwy. N.E.
Atlanta, GA 30346
Tel.: 404-393-5000 (85%)
Earnings: ($3,295,000)
Approx.Sls.: $338,886,000
Fiscal Year-end: 6/27/92

Luker Engineering & Fabrication Group **(2)**
244 Perimeter Center Pkwy. N.E.
Atlanta, GA 30346
Tel.: 404-393-5000

Joint Venture:

Golden Peanut Company **(1)**
244 Perimeter Center Pkwy. N.E.
Atlanta, GA 30346
Tel.: 404-393-5000
Joint Venture of Gold Kist, Inc. (41%) & Archer Daniel Midland Co. (59%)

GOLD MEDAL PRODUCTS CO.
2001 Dalton Ave.
Cincinnati, OH 45214
Tel.: 513-381-1313
Tel.: 800-543-0862
Year Founded: 1931
Approx.Sls.: $30,000,000
Emp.: 250

Export
Concession, Snack Bar Turn Key Installations. Sno-Kone, Polar Pete Slush, Whiz Bang, Pop-A-Lot (Popcorn, Cotton Candy, Baked Hot Dog & Donut Machines), Coin Soap Detergent Vending Machines, Dogeroo Hot Dog Machine; Gay 90's Whiz-Bang Nostalgic Popcorn Machine; Econo-Pop Economy Priced Popcorn Machine, Italian Ice, Elephant Ears & Circus Waffle Machine, Cornado Hi-Volume Commercial Poppers
S.I.C.: 3581
J.C. Evans *(Chm. Bd.)*
Dan Kroeger *(Pres.)*
E.W. Tschan *(V.P.-Mfg.)*
Roger Frazier *(Dir.-Intl. Sls.)*
Mary Helen House *(Dir.-Mktg., Adv., Art, Audio/Visual & Communication Services)*
Dave Evans *(Pur. Agent)*

MORTON GOLDBERG ASSOCIATES, INC.
350 Park Ave.
New York, NY 10022
Tel.: 212-752-3552
Fax: 212-371-1910
Year Founded: 1983
Approx.Billings: $10,200,000
Emp.: 18
Sales Promotion/Marketing Consultants
Morton Goldberg *(Pres. & Treas.)*
Steven Shapiro *(Exec. V.P., Gen. Mgr.)*
Randy Sacks *(Controller & Sec.)*

Goldberg Fossa Seid
ADVERTISING, INC

GOLDBERG FOSSA SEID ADVERTISING, INC.
156 Fifth Ave.
New York, NY 10010
Tel.: 212-727-7400
Fax: 212-727-7899
Year Founded: 1988
Approx.Billings: $17,500,000
Emp.: 20
Ira Goldberg *(Partner & Dir. Acct. Services)*
Ernest Fossa *(Partner & Dir. Media Services)*
Steven Seid *(Partner & Dir. Opers.)*
Jill Post *(Controller)*

GOLDBERG MARCHESANO KOHLMAN INC.
1700 Wisconsin Ave. N.W.
Washington, DC 20007
Tel.: 202-337-0700
Fax: 202-298-3400
Year Founded: 1970
Approx.Billings: $26,700,000
Emp.: 45
Norman Goldberg *(Chm.)*
Carole Marchesano *(Pres.)*
Kris Kohlman *(Exec. V.P.)*
Sandra Socrates *(V.P., Opers.)*

GOLDBERG MOSER O'NEILL
77 Maiden Lane
San Francisco, CA 94108
Tel.: 415-677-1800
Year Founded: 1990
Approx.Billings: $100,000,000
Emp.: 90
Fred Goldberg *(Pres. & Chief Exec. Officer)*
Mike Massaro *(Exec. V.P., Chief Oper. Officer)*
Dennis O'Rourke *(Sr. V.P. & Chief Fin. Officer)*
Patrick Sherwood *(Sr. V.P., Dir. Bus. Devel.)*
Rosalinde Estes *(V.P., Dir. Admin.)*
Susan Satmary *(Dir., Pub. Rels.)*

Computer Systems/Hardware:
Dell; Hewlett Packard 3000; MacIntosh & Radius

GOLDBERGER DOLL MFG. COMPANY, INC.
538 Johnson Ave.
Brooklyn, NY 11237
Tel.: 718-366-5800 **NY**
Fax: 718-417-5587
Year Founded: 1916
Approx.Sls.: $20,000,000
Emp.: 400
Mfr. Goldberger, Softina Dolls
S.I.C.: 3942; 3944
Eugene Goldberger *(Pres.)*
Lawrence Doppelt *(Exec. V.P.)*
Seymour Goldberger *(Treas. & Adv. Dir.)*
Mel Rosenblum *(Mktg. Dir.)*
Principal(s):
Eugene Goldberger

Computer Systems/Hardware:
Qantel

Outside Service Firm(s):

Cohen, Friedman, Dorman, Spector & Co.*(Auditors)*
Union, NJ

Chase Manhattan Bank, N.A.*(Major Banking Relationship)*
One Chase Manhattan Plaza
New York, NY 10081
Tel.: 212-552-2222
Tel.: 800-526-0801
Fax: 212-552-7175

GOLDEN CORRAL CORPORATION
5151 Glenwood Ave.
Raleigh, NC 27612
Mailing Address:
P.O. Box 29502,
Raleigh, NC 27626
Tel.: 919-781-9310
Fax: 919-881-4485
Approx.Sls.: $400,000,000
Emp.: 16,000
Family Steakhouse Restaurant Chain
S.I.C.: 5812
James H. Maynard *(Chm. Bd.)*
Theodore M. Fowler, Jr. *(Pres. & Chief Exec. Officer)*
C. Lamar Bell *(V.P.-Fin.)*
Gordon L. Paulsen *(V.P.-Opers.)*
Alfred R. Seeley *(V.P.)*
John McCormick *(Sec.)*
Stephen Fortlouis *(Dir.-Adv. & Promo.)*

Outside Service Firm(s):

KPMG Peat Marwick*(Auditors)*
3100 Smoketree Court
Raleigh, NC 27629
Tel.: 919-872-3600
Fax: 919-790-9731

Shaw, Pittman, Potts & Trowbridge*(Legal Firm)*
2300 N St. N.W.
Washington, DC 20037
Tel.: 202-663-8000

Branch Banking & Trust Co.*(Major Banking Relationship)*
Raleigh, NC

Subsidiary:

SS Restaurant Corporation **(1)**
5151 Glenwood Ave.
Raleigh, NC 27612
Tel.: 919-781-9310
Fax: 919-881-4485
Fiscal Year-end: 12/31/90
Family Type Restaurants & Franchises
S.I.C.: 5812; 6794
Richard A. Urquahrt III *(Pres. & Treas.)*
Harold E. Piper *(V.P. & Asst. Sec.)*
Gene T. Aman *(V.P.)*
John M. McCormick *(Sec.)*

GOLDEN EAGLE DISTRIBUTORS, INC.
705 E. Ajo Way
Tucson, AZ 85713
Tel.: 602-884-5999 **AZ**
Fax: 602-884-1804
Sales Range: $60-79 Million
Emp.: 230
Wholesale Distributor Anheuser-Busch Products Inc.
S.I.C.: 5181
W.M. Clements *(Chm. Bd., Pres. & Chief Exec. Officer)*
Jim Grimes *(Exec. V.P.)*
Dale E. Nunn *(V.P.-Corp. Mktg.)*
E.A. Lefferts *(Chief Fin. Officer)*

Computer Systems/Hardware:
Digital Micro-Vax

Outside Service Firm(s):

KPMG Peat Marwick*(Auditors)*
Tucson, AZ

Flutes, Sakrison, Even, Grant & Pelander*(Legal Firm)*
Tucson, AZ

Valley National Bank*(Major Banking Relationship)*
241 North Central Ave., 11th Floor
Phoenix, AZ 85001

Branches:

Golden Eagle Distributors, Inc. **(1)**
100 N. Jefferson
Casa Grande, AZ 85222
Tel.: 602-836-2221
Beer Distributor
S.I.C.: 5181

Golden Eagle Distributor, Inc. **(1)**
P.O. Box 697
Buckeye, AZ 85326
Tel.: 602-386-6312
Beer Distributor
S.I.C.: 5181

Golden Eagle Distributors, Inc. **(1)**
550 S. Broad St.
Globe, AZ 85501
Tel.: 602-425-4831
Beer Distributor
S.I.C.: 5181

Golden Eagle Sales, Inc. **(1)**
U.S. Hwy. 66 W.
Holbrook, AZ 86025
Tel.: 602-524-3961
Beer Distributors
S.I.C.: 5181

Golden Eagle Sales, Inc. **(1)**
1850 E. Butler
Flagstaff, AZ 86002
Tel.: 602-779-3634
Beer Distributor
S.I.C.: 5181

GOLDEN GATE UNIVERSITY
536 Mission St.
San Francisco, CA 94105
Tel.: 415-442-7000
Fax: 415-495-2671
Year Founded: 1901
Approx.Sls.: $34,000,000
Emp.: 300
Fiscal Year-end: 6/30/90
University Education
S.I.C.: 8221
David M. Gregory *(Chm. Bd.)*
Otto Butz *(Pres. & Chief Exec. Officer)*
Susan Barney *(V.P.-Admin.)*
Anthony D. Branch *(V.P.-Academic)*
Richard Mazyrack *(V.P.-Fin.)*
Donald M. Chaffee *(Dean-Undergraduate)*
Harry L. Knight *(Dean-Academic Admin.)*
Tony Pagano *(Dean-Law)*
Patricia Fitzgerald *(Dir.-Personnel)*
Ken Kovacs *(Dir.-Pub. Rels. & Adv.)*

Computer Systems/Hardware:
Hewlett Packard

GOLDEN GEM GROWERS INC.
39017 Golden Gem Dr.
Umatilla, FL 32784
Mailing Address:
P.O. Drawer 9,
Umatilla, FL 32784
Tel.: 904-669-2101 **FL**
Fax: 904-669-1241
Year Founded: 1951
Assets: $58,443,140
Earnings: ($2,337,709)
Liabilities: $42,846,196
Net Worth: $15,596,944
Approx.Sls.: $120,864,349
Emp.: 727
Fiscal Year-end: 8/31/92
Agricultural Cooperative; Harvesting, Packing & Marketing Fresh Citrus Fruit; Processing & Marketing Frozen Concentrates, Citrus Feed & Oils; Grove Caretaking Services to Growers
S.I.C.: 0722; 0723; 0762; 2037; 2048; 5142; 5148
John F. Nelson *(Chm. Bd.)*
J. F. Nelson, Jr. *(Pres.)*
G. Martin Stephens *(Sr. V.P.)*
Thomas L. Burkett *(V.P. & Treas.)*
Brannan T. Collins *(V.P. & Dir.-Harvesting Opers.)*
Philip D. Conant *(V.P. & Sec.)*
J. Robert Crawford *(V.P. & Dir.-Concentrate Opers.)*
John M. Kennedy *(V.P.-Grove Care)*
John W. Prevatt *(V.P.-Sls. & Mktg.)*
John H. Schrieffer *(V.P.)*
Gary L. Brundage *(Dir.-Pur.)*
Ellen Justice *(Dir.-Employee Benefits)*
Dudley Zeller *(Dir.-Personnel & Risk Mngmt.)*

Outside Service Firm(s):

KPMG Peat Marwick*(Auditors)*
P.O. Box 3031, 111 N. Orange Ave., Suite 1600
Orlando, FL 32802
Tel.: 407-423-3426

Arkwright Mutual Insurance*(Commercial Insurance Carrier)*
2 Galleria Tower, 13455 Nole Rd., Suite 1900
Boston, MA 75240
Tel.: 214-233-1094
Fax: 214-333-0324

Travelers Insurance Co.*(Group Insurer)*
1 Tower Square
Hartford, CT 06183-2492
Tel.: 203-277-4542
Fax: 203-277-5038

C & S National Bank*(Major Banking Relationship)*
Atlanta, GA
Tel.: 404-392-2984

Columbia Bank for Cooperatives*(Major Banking Relationship)*
Columbia, SC

GOLDEN STATE FOODS CORP.
234 E. Colorado Blvd., 8th Flr.
Pasadena, CA 91101
Tel.: 714-252-2000 **DE**
Fax: 714-584-1803
Year Founded: 1965
Approx.Sls.: $900,000,000
Emp.: 1,700
Food Processing & Distributor for McDonald's
S.I.C.: 5141
James E. Williams *(Pres. & Chief Exec. Officer)*
Gene L. Olson *(V.P.-Fin. & Sec.)*
Walt Kersten *(Treas.)*
Thomas Throm *(Controller)*
Ron Childers *(Mgr.-Personnel)*
Richard Moretti *(Dir.-Data Processing)*

Computer Systems/Hardware:
IBM 4381

Outside Service Firm(s):

Arthur Andersen & Co.*(Auditors)*
633 W. Fifth St.
Los Angeles, CA 90071
Tel.: 213-614-6500

Aetna Life & Casualty*(Group Insurer)*
151 Farmington Avenue
Hartford, CT 06156
Tel.: 203-273-2128
Fax: 203-729-4295

O'Melveny & Myers*(Legal Firm)*
400 S. Hope St.
Los Angeles, CA 90071
Tel.: 213-669-6000

Bank of America NT&SA*(Major Banking Relationship)*
555 So. Flower St., 5th Fl.
Los Angeles, CA 90071
Tel.: 213-228-3526
Fax: 213-228-4062

Bank of America NT&SA*(Pension Manager)*
555 So. Flower St., 5th Fl.
Los Angeles, CA 90071
Tel.: 213-228-3526
Fax: 213-228-4062

Divisions:

Golden State Foods Corp.-City of Industry Div. **(1)**
640 Sixth Ave.
City of Industry, CA 91749
Tel.: 213-686-0347
Approx.Sls.: $189,379,000
Emp.: 476
Meat & Dairy Products Processing; Manufacturer of Syrups & Condiments & Distributor
S.I.C.: 5147
Robert M. McMaster *(Sr. V.P.)*

Golden State Foods Corp.-Georgia Div. **(1)**
P.O. Box 578,
Conyers, GA 30207
Tel.: 404-483-0711
Approx.Sls.: $76,702,000
Emp.: 282
Meat Processing; Syrups; Baking Goods
S.I.C.: 5147; 2038; 2051
Dwayne Salter *(Gen. Mgr.)*

Golden State Foods Corp.-Hawaii Div. **(1)**
94-069 Leonui St.
Waipahu, HI 96797
Tel.: 808-671-4017
Approx.Sls.: $22,399,000
Emp.: 31
Distribution Center
S.I.C.: 5141
Peter Avignone *(V.P.)*

Golden State Foods Corp.-North Carolina Div. **(1)**
P.O. Box 21366,
Greensboro, NC 27420
Tel.: 919-668-0011
Approx.Sls.: $134,423,000
Emp.: 232
Mfr. Bakery Products & Distribution Center
S.I.C.: 5461

John Tart *(Gen. Mgr.)*

Golden State Foods Corp.-Northwest Div. **(1)**
1409 Puyallup
Sumner, WA 98390
Tel.: 206-581-4460
Approx.Sls.: $58,267,000
Emp.: 80
Distribution Center
S.I.C.: 5141
Jim Karkosky *(Gen. Mgr.)*

Golden State Foods Corp.-Phoenix Div. **(1)**
5516 W. Buchanan St.
Phoenix, AZ 85043
Tel.: 602-258-4700
Approx.Sls.: $49,051,000
Emp.: 67
Distribution Center
S.I.C.: 5141
Al Schutza *(Gen. Mgr.)*

Golden State Foods Corp.-Rochester Div. **(1)**
41 Scutti Park Blvd.
Rochester, NY 14623
Tel.: 716-334-2400
Approx.Sls.: $48,951,000
Emp.: 58
Distribution Center
S.I.C.: 5141
Joe DePrimi *(Gen. Mgr.)*

GOLDEN STATE MUTUAL LIFE INSURANCE COMPANY
1999 W. Adams
Los Angeles, CA 90018
Mailing Address:
P.O. Box 2332
Los Angeles, CA 90051
Tel.: 213-731-1131
Tel.: 800-225-5476 **CA**
Fax: 213-733-0320
Year Founded: 1925
Assets: $105,643,181
Liabilities: $96,538,657
Net Worth: $9,104,524
Approx.Sls.: $35,895,136
Emp.: 335
Fiscal Year-end: 12/31/91
Life & Health Insurance
S.I.C.: 6311; 6321
Corporate Giving Program:
Community Organizations
Employee Matching Gifts Program:
Contributions to Known Charitable Organizations; Will Match Up to $300.00
Ivan J. Houston *(Chm. Bd.)*
Larkin Teasley *(Pres. & Chief Exec. Officer)*
Verdun J. Arnaud *(Sr. V.P. & Actuary)*
George E. Hill *(Sr. V.P.)*
Elroy Bond *(V.P. & Dir.-Data Processing)*
Charles L. James *(V.P. & Agency Dir.)*
Kenneth L. Watts *(V.P.-Real Estate Lending & Dir.-Admin. Services)*
Norman A. Houston *(Treas.)*
Sharon A. Smith *(Controller)*
Marvin Brown *(Dir.-Network Devel.)*
Gloria A. McDowell *(Dir.-Human Resources & Sec.)*
Harold Toliver *(Dir.-Mktg. & Public Rels.)*
Michael S. Webb *(Dir.-Training)*
Isaac Snowden *(Assoc. Dir.-Data Processing)*
Stella Owens-Murrell *(Gen. Counsel)*

No. of U.S. Offices: 18

Computer Systems/Hardware:
IBM 4381

Outside Service Firm(s):

Ernst & Young*(Auditors)*
515 S. Flower St.
Los Angeles, CA 90071
Tel.: 213-621-1666

Bank of America NT&SA*(Major Banking Relationship)*
555 So. Flower St., 5th Fl.
Los Angeles, CA 90071
Tel.: 213-228-3526
Fax: 213-228-4062

GOLDEN SUN FEEDS, INC.
Hwy. 4 South
Estherville, IA 51334-0517
Tel.: 712-362-3551
Fax: 712-362-3953
Year Founded: 1925
Approx.Sls.: $95,000,000
Emp.: 285
Fiscal Year-end: 6/30/91
Mfr. & Distributor Livestock & Poultry Feeds; Golden Sun Feeds
S.I.C.: 2048
H. C. Hauber *(Pres. & Chief Exec. Officer)*
Stan K. Thomsen *(Sr. V.P.-Admin. & Sec.)*
John Ball *(V.P. & Chief Fin. Officer)*
Maurice Show *(V.P. & Opers. Officer)*
Layne Anderson *(V.P. & Dir.-Research & Nutrition)*
Dick Potratz *(V.P. & Gen. Sls. Mgr.)*
Bruce Scott *(V.P.-Pur.)*
Jack L. Lloyd *(Dir.-Adv. & Mdsg.)*

Divisions:

Golden Sun Feeds, Inc. **(1)**
Danville, IL 61832
Tel.: 217-442-0290
S.I.C.: 2048
Orlynn Harms *(Mgr.-Plant & Sls.)*

Golden Sun Feeds, Inc. **(1)**
Grinnell, IA 50112
Tel.: 515-236-6565
S.I.C.: 2048
Ken Mergen *(Mgr.-Plant & Sls.)*

Golden Sun Feeds, Inc. **(1)**
Sioux Falls, SD 50112
Tel.: 605-336-0787
S.I.C.: 2048
Jerry Venjohn *(Mgr.-Plant & Sls.)*

Golden Sun Feeds, Inc. **(1)**
Estherville, IA 51344
S.I.C.: 2048
Robert Gee *(Mgr.-Plant & Sls.)*

Golden Sun Feeds, Inc. **(1)**
Maquoketa, IA 50260
Tel.: 319-652-4949
S.I.C.: 2048
Jack Tichy *(Mgr.-Plant & Sls.)*

Golden Sun Feeds, Inc. **(1)**
Fremont, NE 68025
Tel.: 402-721-4010
S.I.C.: 2048
Jerry Venjohn *(Mgr.-Plant & Sls.)*

GOLDEN WEST BROADCASTERS
5858 Sunset Blvd.
Los Angeles, CA 90028
Mailing Address:
P.O. Box 710,
Los Angeles, CA 90078
Tel.: 213-460-5672
Fax: 213-460-6621
Year Founded: 1952
Approx.Rev.: $40,000,000
Emp.: 126
Fiscal Year-end: 12/31/90
Own & Operate Radio Stations & Sports Team
S.I.C.: 4832; 7941
Gene Autry *(Chm. Bd., Pres. & Chief Exec. Officer)*
Jacqueline Autry *(Exec. V.P., Treas. & Chief Fin. Officer)*
Bill Ward *(Exec. V.P. & Gen. Mgr.)*
Bob Sponseller *(V.P. & Controller)*
Richard M. Brown, Esq. *(Gen. Counsel)*
Sue Hinshe *(Gen. Sls. Mgr.)*
Jim Patryla *(Dir.-Human Resources)*
Joanne Redmond *(Personnel Admin.)*

Computer Systems/Hardware:
IBM-PC

Outside Service Firm(s):

Arthur Andersen & Co.*(Auditors)*
633 W. Fifth St.
Los Angeles, CA 90071
Tel.: 213-614-6500

Sedgwick James*(Commercial Insurance Carrier)*
3435 Wilshire Blvd., 5th Fl.
Los Angeles, CA 90010
Tel.: 213-385-0545

Continental Insurance*(Group Insurer)*
180 Maiden Lane
New York, NY

Jeffer, Mangels, Butler & Marmaro*(Legal Firm)*
Los Angeles, CA

Security Pacific Corporation*(Major Banking Relationship)*
Security Pacific Plaza
Los Angeles, CA 90071
Tel.: 213-345-6211
Fax: 213-625-0809

Security Pacific Invest. Mgmt.*(Pension Manager)*
Los Angeles, CA

Subsidiary:

California Angels Baseball Club **(1)**
State College Blvd.
Anaheim, CA 92805
Tel.: 714-937-6700
Emp.: 200
Broadcasting; Baseball Club
S.I.C.: 7941; 4832
Jim Wilson *(V.P.-Fin.)*

GOLDEN WEST HOMES
1308 E. Wakeham Ave.
Santa Ana, CA 92705
Tel.: 714-835-4200 **CA**
Fax: 714-835-6232
Year Founded: 1965
Approx.Sls.: $74,000,000
Emp.: 625
Fiscal Year-end: 12/28/91
Mfr. of Mobile Home
S.I.C.: 2451; 2499
Harry Karsten, Jr. *(Chm. Bd. & Pres.)*
Robert J. Henry *(Sr. V.P.)*
Frank D. Jacobs *(V.P. & Chief Fin. Officer)*
Greg Avants *(Mgr.-Information Services & Telecommunications)*
Principal(s):
Harry Karsten, Jr.

No. of Mfg. Plants/Facilities: 4
No. of U.S. Offices: 5

Computer Systems/Hardware:
IBM System 38

Outside Service Firm(s):

Arthur Andersen & Co.*(Auditors)*
18500 Von Karman Ave. #1100
Irvine, CA
Tel.: 714-757-3100

Wells Fargo Bank*(Major Banking Relationship)*
420 Montgomery St.
San Francisco, CA 94104

Tausch Insurance Brokers*(Commercial Insurance Carrier)*
Santa Ana, CA

Prudential Insurance Co. of America*(Group Insurer)*
Prudential Tower Suite 450, 800 Boylston St.
Boston, MA 02119

Shaffer & Gold*(Legal Firm)*
Los Angeles, CA

Divisions:

Golden West Homes, Albany Div. **(1)**
2445 Pacific Blvd. S.
Albany, OR 97321
Tel.: 503-926-8631
Emp.: 125
Mfr. of Mobile Homes
S.I.C.: 2451
Bruce Stoyer *(Gen. Mgr.)*

Golden West Homes Perris Div. **(1)**
3100 N. Perris Blvd.
Perris, CA 92557
Tel.: 909-657-1611
Emp.: 250
Mfr. of Mobile Homes
S.I.C.: 2451
Clay Latimer *(Gen. Mgr.)*

Golden West Homes, Sacramento Div. **(1)**
9998 Old Placerville Rd.
Sacramento, CA 95827
Tel.: 916-363-2681
Emp.: 130
Mfr. of Mobile Homes
S.I.C.: 2451
Andy Karsten *(Gen. Mgr.)*

Goldfarb & COMPANY
ADVERTISING

GOLDFARB & COMPANY ADVERTISING
26250 Northwestern Hwy.
Southfield, MI 48076
Tel.: 313-350-8200
Fax: 313-350-8213
Year Founded: 1968
Approx.Billings: $24,525,000
Emp.: 35
Natl. Retail, Consumer Prods. & Co-op
Robert Goldfarb *(Pres.)*
Mark Dutil *(Sr. V.P. & Dir.-Creative)*
Marvin Hirsch *(Sr. V.P.)*
Morris Johnson *(Sr. V.P. & Exec. Dir.-Art)*
Chuck Rossi *(Sr. V.P.)*
Jacki Smoke *(Sr. V.P. & Mgr.-Opers.)*
Roy Youngmark *(Sr. V.P. & Dir.-Creative)*
Tom Bennett *(Dir.-Mktg. Devel.)*
Eileen Thomas *(Mgr.-Acctg.)*

THE GOLDHIRSH GROUP INC.
38 Commercial Warf
Boston, MA 02110
Year Founded: 1979
Approx.Sls.: $54,000,000
Emp.: 150
Fiscal Year-end: 12/31/90
Magazine Publisher; Goldhirsh Group
S.I.C.: 2721
Bernard A. Goldhirsh *(Chm. Bd.)*
Jay MacDonald *(Publisher)*
Howard Kaplan *(Dir.-Mktg. & Asst. Publisher)*
Sharon McKee *(Dir.-Sls. Devel.)*
Kristin Norrgard *(Dir.-Adv. & Assoc. Publisher)*
Anne Goldstein *(Dir.-Res.)*
Deborah Schalm *(Mgr.-Sls. Devel.)*
Nancy Kriskey *(Mktg. Asst.)*

S. I. GOLDMAN CO.
799 Bennett Dr.
Longwood, FL 32750
Mailing Address:
P.O. Box 526100,
Longwood, FL 32752-6100
Tel.: 407-830-5000 **FL**
Fax: 407-830-4969
Year Founded: 1959
Approx.Sls.: $25,200,000
Emp.: 190

S. I. Goldman Co.—(Continued)

Mechanical Contractor Plumbing, Heating & Air Conditioning; Fire Sprinklers
S.I.C.: 1711
Siegmund I. Goldman *(Chm. Bd. & Pres.)*
Marilyn S. Goldman *(Exec. V.P., Sec. & Treas.)*
Ronald Burkett *(V.P.-Opers.)*
Alan W. Mooney *(Controller)*
Ken Matthews *(Mgr.-Mktg.)*

Outside Service Firm(s):

Geller, Ragans, James, Oppenheimer & Creel *(Auditors)*
Orlando, FL

Mateer, Harbert & Bates, P.A. *(Legal Firm)*
Orlando, FL

Barnett Bank *(Major Banking Relationship)*
Orlando, FL

Subsidiary:

Southeast Fire Sprinkler Company (1)
799 Bennett Dr.
Longwood, FL 32750
Tel.: 305-331-7464
Emp.: 70
Fire Sprinkler Contractor
S.I.C.: 1711
S. I. Goldman *(Pres.)*
Ron Burkett *(V.P.-Opers.)*

GOLDMAN FINANCIAL GROUP
1 Post Office Sq. #41
Boston, MA 02109-2103
Tel.: 617-338-1200
Fax: 617-338-6444
Year Founded: 1982
Approx.Sls.: $325,000,000
Emp.: 2,000
Merger, Acquisition & Reorganization Research; Management Consulting Services; Blast Furnaces & Steel Mill; Chemical Preparations
S.I.C.: 8732; 8742; 3312; 2899
David Goldman *(Pres. & Treas.)*
Karen Chiampa *(Controller)*
Donald Paulson *(Sec.)*

Outside Service Firm(s):

Arthur Andersen & Co. *(Auditors)*
One Intl. Place, 100 Oliver St.
Boston, MA 02110
Tel.: 617-330-4000
Fax: 617-439-9731

Brown, Rudnick, Freed & Gesmer *(Legal Firm)*
One Financial Center
Boston, MA 02111
Tel.: 617-330-9000

Subsidiaries:

Broderick Company, Inc. (1)
Muncie, IN
High Quality Carbon & Alloy Steel Forgings
S.I.C.: 3325

Bryant Grinder Corp. (1)
257 Clinton St.
Springfield, VT 05156
Tel.: 802-885-5161 (100%)
Telex: 94-3427
Fax: 802-885-9444
Approx.Sls.: $29,000,000
Emp.: 350
Fiscal Year-end: 6/30/91
Import Export
Internal Grinders, External Form Grinders, Center Hole Grinders, External Centerless Grinders, Spindles & Spindle Systems
S.I.C.: 3541
R.E. Crossman *(Pres. & Gen. Mgr.)*
D.A. Shuffleburg *(Adv. Mgr.)*
R. Massucco *(Personnel Mgr.)*
D. Johnson *(Pur. Mgr.)*

The Hall Chemical Company (1)
Wickliffe, OH
Bulk Chemicals
S.I.C.: 5169

Hill-Loma, Inc. (1)
Gorham, ME
Metal Punching, Shearing, Grinding, Continuous and Semi-continuous Casting Equipment
S.I.C.: 7389; 3325

The Impex Group Limited (1)
Boston, MA
Foreign Trading Company
S.I.C.: 4226

J & L Metrology Company, Inc. (1)
Springfield, VT
Optical Comparators
S.I.C.: 3827

Jones & Lamson Waterbury Farrel Corp. (1)
181 W. Johnson Ave.
Cheshire, CT 06410
Tel.: 203-272-3271
Fax: 203-271-1322
Emp.: 1,940
Machine Tools
S.I.C.: 3542; 3541
David Goldman *(Owner)*
William Mayer *(Chief Exec. Officer)*
Ed Tenney *(Mgr.-Opers.)*
J.C. Cavanaugh *(Pur. Agent)*

Vermont USA Machine Tool Group (1)
Precision Dr.
North Springfield, VT 05150
Tel.: 802-886-8333
Mfr. of Gear Cutting & Finishing Machines; Optical Comparators
S.I.C.: 3541; 3827
Richard Crossman *(Pres.)*

Subsidiary:

Fellows Corporation (2)
Precision Dr.
North Springfield, VT 05150
Tel.: 802-886-8333
Mfr. of Gear Cutting & Finishing Machines; Optical Comparators
S.I.C.: 3541; 3827

GOLDMAN, SACHS & CO.
85 Broad St.
New York, NY 10004
Tel.: 212-902-1000
Telex: ITT421344 GOLSAX
Year Founded: 1869
Assets: $60,365,000,000
Liabilities: $57,888,000,000
Net Worth: $2,477,000,000
Approx.Rev.: $4,200,000,000
Emp.: 6,600
Fiscal Year-end: 11/30/90
Full-service International Investment Banking And Brokerage Firm
S.I.C.: 6211; 6221
John L. Weinberg *(Sr. Chm.)*
Robert E. Rubin *(Co-Chm. & Sr. Partner)*
Stephen Friedman *(Co-Chm. & Sr. Partner)*
Gordon McMahon *(Partner)*
Ann Gorski *(V.P.-Corp. Communications)*

No. of U.S. Offices: 11
No. of Foreign Offices: 6

Outside Service Firm(s):

Coopers & Lybrand *(Auditors)*
1301 Avenue of The Americas
New York, NY 10019
Tel.: 212-536-2000

Empire Blue Cross & Blue Shield *(Group Insurer)*
New York, NY

Sullivan & Cromwell *(Legal Firm)*
125 Broad St.
New York, NY 10004
Tel.: 212-558-4000

Subsidiaries:

Goldman Sachs (1)
85 Broad St.
New York, NY 10004
Tel.: 212-902-1000
Tel.: 800-323-5678
Fax: 212-902-3925
Emp.: 286
Commodities
S.I.C.: 6221
Mark Winkelman *(Partner)*
Ann Gorski *(V.P.-Corp. Communications)*

Goldman Sachs Money Markets Inc. (1)
85 Broad St.
New York, NY 10004
Tel.: 212-902-1000
Fax: 212-344-4010
Commercial Paper Dealer
S.I.C.: 6153

Non-U.S. Holdings:

J. Aron & Company (U.K.), Limited (1)
5 Old Bailey
London, EC4M 7AH, United Kingdom
Tel.: 071-248-6464
Fax: 071-489-2316
Commodity Dealers
S.I.C.: 6221

J. Aron & Company (U.K.), Limited (1)
8-10 New Fetter Lane
London, EC4A 1DB, United Kingdom
Tel.: 071-248-6464
Fax: 071-489-5067 (Coffee)

Goldman Sachs (Asia) Limited (1)
Edinburgh Tower, The Landmark, 35th Flr.
15 Queen's Rd. Central,
Hong Kong, Hong Kong
Tel.: 852-5-255078
Fax: 852-5-8681435
Investment Banking
S.I.C.: 6211; 6221

Goldman Sachs (Australia) Limited (1)
Grosvenor Place, 225 George St.
Sydney, N.S.W. 2000, Australia
Tel.: 02-251-6166
Fax: 61-2-251-6160

Goldman Sachs Canada (1)
150 King St., West, Suite 1201
Toronto, ON M5H 1J9, Canada
Tel.: 416-343-8900
Fax: 416-593-8506

Goldman Sachs Equity Securities (U.K.) Limited (1)
5 Old Bailey
London, EC4M 7AH, United Kingdom
Tel.: 071-248-6464
Fax: 071-489-2633

Goldman Sachs Finanz AG (1)
Talstrasse 82 8001
Zurich, Switzerland
Tel.: 1-211-8759
Fax: 41-1-211-6972
Investment Company
S.I.C.: 6211

Goldman Sachs Futures Limited (1)
5 Old Bailey
London, EC4M 7AH, United Kingdom
Tel.: 071-248-6464
Fax: 071-489-2607

Goldman Sachs Government Securities (U.K.) Limited (1)
5 Old Bailey
London, EC4M 7AH, United Kingdom
Tel.: 071-248-6464
Fax: 071-489-2873

Goldman Sachs International Limited (1)
5 Old Bailey
London, EC4M 7AH, United Kingdom
Tel.: 071-248-6464
Fax: 071-489-2911
Broker, Dealer Outside the U.S.
S.I.C.: 6211
Jeffrey Weingarten *(Mng. Dir.)*

Goldman Sachs International Limited et Cie. (1)
8, rue Halevy, 2nd Fl. 75009
Paris, France
Tel.: 01-42-66-94-71

Goldman Sachs International Finance Limited (1)
5 Old Bailey
London, EC4M 7AH, United Kingdom
Tel.: 071-248-6464
Fax: 071-489-2236

Goldman Sachs (Japan) Corp. (1)
ARK Mori Bldg., 10th Fl., 12-32, Akasaka 1-chome Minato-ku,
Tokyo, 107, Japan
Tel.: 03-3589-7000
Fax: 81-3-587-9260
Investment Banking
S.I.C.: 6211; 6221

Goldman Sachs Limited (1)
5 Old Bailey
London, EC4M 7AH, United Kingdom
Tel.: 071-248-6464
Fax: 071-489-5723

GOLDMARK INDUSTRIES, LTD.
437 Madison Ave.
New York, NY 10022
Tel.: 212-759-9080 **DE**
Fax: 212-759-0299
Year Founded: 1986
Sales Range: $10-19 Million
Fiscal Year-end: 1/31/91
Holding Company for Publishing Businesses
S.I.C.: 6719
Jeffrey M. Gold *(Chm. Bd. & Chief Exec. Officer)*
Lloyd Singer *(Vice Chm.)*
Walter J. Bembenista *(Sr. V.P. & Chief Fin. Officer)*
Lenore Gold *(Dir.-Personnel)*

No. of U.S. Offices: 2

Outside Service Firm(s):

Harris Trust Company of New York *(Major Banking Relationship)*
77 Water St.
New York, NY 10005
Tel.: 212-701-7600

The Bank of New York *(Major Banking Relationship)*
One Wall Street
New York, NY 10286
Tel.: 212-635-6805
Fax: 212-635-3201

Subsidiaries:

Art Publishing Co. (1)
437 Madison Ave.
New York, NY 10022
Tel.: 212-759-9080
Fax: 212-759-0299
Publishing Company
S.I.C.: 2731

Goldmark Industries (1)
437 Madison Ave.
New York, NY 10022
Tel.: 212-759-9080
Fax: 212-759-0299
Operating & Holding Company for Print Businesses
S.I.C.: 2741
Jeffrey M. Gold *(Chm. Bd., Pres. & Chief Exec. Officer)*
Lloyd W. Singer *(Vice Chm.)*

Scafa Tornabene (1)
100 Snakehill Rd.
West Nyack, NY 10994
Tel.: 914-358-7600
Emp.: 30
Art Publishing
S.I.C.: 2741
Arthur T. Castillo *(Chm. Bd. & Chier Exec. Officer)*

Affiliate:

Goldmark Partners **(1)**
437 Madison Ave.
New York, NY 10022
Tel.: 212-759-9080
Investment Banking
S.I.C.: 6211
Jeffrey M. Gold *(Chm. Bd. & Chief Exec. Officer)*
Walter J. Bembenista *(Mng. Dir.)*

GOLDSMITH | JEFFREY

GOLDSMITH/JEFFREY, INC.
31 West 21st St.
New York, NY 10010
Tel.: 212-691-4361
Year Founded: 1987
Approx.Billings: $35,000,000
Emp.: 30
Gary Goldsmith *(Chm. Bd., Sec. & Creative Dir.)*
Bob Jeffrey *(Pres., Treas. & New Bus. Contact)*
Stan Fessler *(Chief Fin. Officer)*
Jill Thurber *(Office Mgr.)*

GOLDSMITHS, INC.
151 N. Main St.
Wichita, KS 67202
Tel.: 316-263-0131 **KS**
Fax: 316-262-0691
Year Founded: 1960
Approx.Sls.: $28,000,000
Emp.: 110
Wholesale Distribution & Retail Sales of Office Furniture
S.I.C.: 5021; 5712
Maryon G. Arst *(Chm. Bd.)*
Mike Arst *(Pres.)*
Rodger M. Arst *(Chief Exec. Officer)*
James G. Hull *(V.P.)*
Patricia L. Arst *(Sec.)*
Max R. Sutton *(Treas.)*

Outside Service Firm(s):

First National Bank*(Major Banking Relationship)*
Wichita, KS

JOEL GOLDSTEIN MARKETING COMMUNICATIONS
2701 Ocean Park Blvd., Ste. 201
Santa Monica, CA 90405
Tel.: 310-450-2329
Fax: 310-450-7082
Year Founded: 1974
Approx.Billings: $14,000,000
Emp.: 18
Joel G. Goldstein *(Pres.)*
Kim Kusler *(Controller)*
Jennifer Lewis *(Pub. Rels.)*

GOLF HOSTS, INC.
36750 U.S. Hwy. 19 N.
Palm Harbor, FL 34684
Mailing Address:
P.O. Box 1088,
Tarpon Springs, FL 34688
Tel.: 813-942-2000 **FL**
Fax: 813-942-5579
Assets: $53,000,000
Liabilities: $41,000,000
Net Worth: $12,000,000
Approx.Sls.: $56,000,000
Emp.: 1,400
Fiscal Year-end: 12/31/91
Import Export
Resorts & Hotels; Real Estate Development
S.I.C.: 6513; 7011
Stanley Wadsworth *(Chm. Bd., Pres. & Chief Exec. Officer)*
C. James McCormick *(Vice Chm.)*
Richard S. Ferreira *(Exec. V.P. & Chief Fin. Officer)*
Richard L. Akin *(V.P. & Treas.)*
Lewis Hill, III *(Sec.)*

Outside Service Firm(s):

Arthur Andersen & Co.*(Auditors)*
Tampa, FL

Foley & Lardner*(Legal Firm)*
Tampa, FL

Barnett Bank of Pinellas County, N.A.*(Major Banking Relationship)*
1901 Central Ave.
Saint Petersburg, FL 33733
Tel.: 813-535-0711

Subsidiary:

Golf Host Resorts, Inc. **(1)**
P.O. Box 1088
Tarpon Springs, FL 34688
Tel.: 813-942-2000
Fax: 813-942-5579
Emp.: 1400
Resort Hotels, Condominiun Units; Operates Golf Club & Resort With Conference Facilities, Eating & Drinking Places
S.I.C.: 7011; 5812; 5813; 7997
Stanley D. Wadsworth *(Chm. Bd., Pres. & Chief Exec. Officer)*
C. James McCormick *(Vice Chm.)*
Richard S. Ferreira *(Exec. V.P. & Chief Fin. Officer)*
Richard L. Akin *(V.P. & Treas.)*
Lewis Hill, III *(Sec.)*

Divisions:

Innisbrook Division **(2)**
P.O. Drawer 1088
Tarpon Springs, FL 34688
Tel.: 813-942-2000
Emp.: 1100
Resort Hotels, Condominium Units, Operates Golf Club & Resorts With Conference Facilities, Eating & Drinking Places
S.I.C.: 5812; 5813; 7011; 7997
Richard Ferreria *(General Manager)*

Tamarron Division **(2)**
P.O. Box 3131
Dorango, CO 81302
Tel.: 303-259-2000
Resort Hotels, Condominium Units, Operates Golf Club & Resort With Conference Facilities, Eating & Drinking Places
S.I.C.: 5812; 5813; 7011; 7997
William Sageser *(Gen. Mgr.)*

LEON SHAFFER GOLNICK ADVERTISING, INC.
(Div. of the Golnick Company)
2817 E. Oakland Park Blvd.
Fort Lauderdale, FL 33306
Tel.: 305-563-5000
Tel.: 800-327-8320
Fax: 305-563-5000 ext. 388
Year Founded: 1946
Approx.Billings: $200,000,000
Emp.: 58
Syndication Adv. for Banks, Savings & Loan, Credit Unions, Auto Dealers & Hospitals
Leon S. Golnick *(Chm. Bd.)*
Marshall Golnick *(Exec. V.P.)*
Greg Golnick *(Sr. V.P.)*
Roger Maston *(Dir.-Client Rels.)*
George Harris *(Office Mgr.)*
Glen Anderson *(Sr. Studio)*
Steve Levine *(Dir., Computer Dept.)*

GOLODETZ CORPORATION
666 Fifth Ave.
New York, NY 10103
Tel.: 212-581-2400 **DE**
Fax: 212-307-1002
Year Founded: 1916
Approx.Sls.: $1,000,000,000
Emp.: 1,200
Fiscal Year-end: 6/30/89
Import Export
Steel Trading, Coal Export, Industrial Investments, Financial Services, Leasing, Agriculture, Real Estate Development, Liquid Storage Terminal
S.I.C.: 6159; 6282; 6552; 6799
Michele Golodetz *(Chm. Bd.)*
Gavin Parfit *(Pres.)*
Gavin J. Parfit *(Chief Fin. Officer)*
Sharon Roth *(V.P.-Fin.)*
David Ginzberg *(Treas.)*
Principal(s):
Michele Golodetz
Isaac Suder
Oscar Golodetz

No. of Mfg. Plants/Facilities: 10
No. of U.S. Offices: 12
No. of Foreign Offices: 9

Computer Systems/Hardware:
IBM

Outside Service Firm(s):

KPMG Peat Marwick*(Auditors)*
345 Park Ave.
New York, NY 10154
Tel.: 212-758-9700
Fax: 212-872-3308

Bankers Trust Co.*(Investment Banker)*
P.O. Box 318, Church St. Station
New York, NY 10008
Tel.: 212-454-2212
Fax: 212-454-2783

Morgan Stanley & Co.*(Investment Banker)*
1251 Avenue of the Americas
New York, NY 10020
Tel.: 212-703-8447
Fax: 212-703-6476

Roe & Kramer*(Legal Firm)*
New York, NY

Subsidiaries:

M. Golodetz Export Corp. **(1)**
666 Fifth Ave.
New York, NY 10103
Tel.: 212-581-2400
S.I.C.: 5149

Vector Realty Corp. **(1)**
666 Fifth Ave.
New York, NY 10103
Tel.: 212-581-2400
Real Estate Developer
S.I.C.: 6552

GOLUB & CO.
625 N. Michigan Ave. Ste.2000
Chicago, IL 60611
Tel.: 312-440-8800
Fax: 312-440-0809
Emp.: 40
Real Estate Investor, Developer, Broker
S.I.C.: 6531; 6552
Eugene Golub *(Chm. Bd. & Pres.)*
Christopher Milam *(Sr. V.P.)*
Michael H. Newman *(Sr. V.P.)*
Douglas E. Harness *(V.P.-Asset Mngmt.)*
Terry Sullivan *(Controller)*

Computer Systems/Hardware:
IBM System 36

Outside Service Firm(s):

Ernst & Young*(Auditors)*
233 S. Wacker Dr.
Chicago, IL 60606
Tel.: 312-368-1800
Fax: 312-645-3095

Greenburger Krause & Jacobs*(Legal Firm)*
Chicago, IL

American National Bank & Trust Company of Chicago*(Major Banking Relationship)*
33 N. LaSalle St.
Chicago, IL 60602
Tel.: 312-661-5000
Fax: 312-661-6417

GOLUB CORPORATION
501 Duanesburg Rd.
Schenectady, NY 12306
Mailing Address:
P.O. Box 1074,
Schenectady, NY 12301
Tel.: 518-355-5000 **NY**
Fax: 518-355-0843
Year Founded: 1932
Approx.Sls.: $1,066,000,000
Emp.: 11,000
Fiscal Year-end: 4/28/91
Retail Grocery Chain
S.I.C.: 5411
Lewis Golub *(Chm. Bd. & Chief Exec. Officer)*
Neil M. Golub *(Pres. & Chief Oper. Officer)*
Fred Bacheldor *(Sr. V.P.-Retail Opers.)*
Frank Lennon *(Sr. V.P.-Admin.)*
John Endres *(V.P. & Controller)*
Henry Gervais *(V.P.-Distr. Center)*
William Kenneally *(V.P., Sec. & Gen. Counsel)*
Lawrence G. Olsen *(V.P., Treas. & Chief Fin. Officer)*
Ronald Schleich *(V.P.-Real Estate)*
Curt Hopkins *(Dir.-Personnel)*
Frank Lorch *(Dir.-Non-Resale Pur.)*
Tom Nowak *(Dir.-Mngmt. Information Systems)*
Jennifer Kenneally *(Asst. Treas. & Mgr.-Treas. Services)*

Computer Systems/Hardware:
IBM 4381

Outside Service Firm(s):

Coopers & Lybrand*(Auditors)*
80 State Street
Albany, NY 12207

Empire Blue Cross & Blue Shield*(Group Insurer)*
New York, NY

Subsidiary:

Price Chopper **(1)**
501 Duanesburg Rd.
Schenectady, NY 12306
Tel.: 518-355-5000 (100%)
Fax: 518-355-0843
Approx.Sls.: $1,066,000,000
Emp.: 11,000
77 Supermarkets Located in NY, Western MA, VT & PA
S.I.C.: 5411
Lewis Golub *(Chm. Bd. & Chief Exec. Officer)*
Neil Golub *(Pres. & Chief Oper. Officer)*
Frank Lennon *(Sr. V.P.-Admin.)*
Lawrence G. Olsen *(V.P.-Fin., Treas. & Chief Fin. Officer)*
David Henry *(V.P.-Adv.)*

GOMAR MANUFACTURING CO., INC.
1501 W. Blancke St.
Linden, NJ 07036
Tel.: 908-862-0820
Fax: 908-862-6851
Approx.Sls.: $25,000,000
Emp.: 90
Mfr. of Metallized, Coated & Laminated Films & Sheetings
S.I.C.: 3081; 3497
P.J. Marks *(Pres.)*
Louis Friedman *(V.P.)*

GONNELLA BAKING CO.
2002-14 W. Erie St.
Chicago, IL 60612
Tel.: 312-733-2020
Fax: 312-733-7056
Year Founded: 1886
Approx.Sls.: $35,000,000
Emp.: 400
Fiscal Year-end: 12/31/90
Import Export

Gonnella Baking Co.—(Continued)

Bakers of French Bread & Rolls
S.I.C.: 2051
Louis L. Marcucci *(Chm. Bd. & Pres.)*
Robert Gonnella *(Chief Exec. Officer & Sec.)*
George Marcucci *(Chief Fin. Officer & Treas.)*
Roy Marcucci *(V.P.)*

No. of Mfg. Plants/Facilities: 4

Outside Service Firm(s):

Deloitte & Touche*(Auditors)*
Two Prudential Plaza, 180 N. Stetson
Chicago, IL 60601
Tel.: 312-946-2039

Meeker-Magner Company*(Group Insurer)*
Des Plaines, IL

Subsidiaries:

Gonnella Frozen Products **(1)**
1117 E. Wiley Rd.
Schaumburg, IL 60195
Tel.: 708-884-8829
Ken Gonnella *(Chief Fin. Officer)*
Ronald Lucchesi *(Chief Oper. Officer)*

Torino Baking Co. **(1)**
318 E. Kensington Ave.
Chicago, IL 60628
Tel.: 312-785-0751
Louis Gonnella *(V.P. & Chief Oper. Officer)*

GOOD COMPANIES
118 E. 223rd St.
Carson, CA 90745
Tel.: 213-775-8541 **CA**
Fax: 213-835-6039
Year Founded: 1956
Approx.Sls.: $40,000,000
Emp.: 600
Import Export
Wood Occasional Furniture, Tables & Bookcases
S.I.C.: 2511
David Finegood *(Pres.)*
Daniel Finegood *(First V.P.)*
Frank Garcia *(V.P.-Mktg.)*
Ronald Pinto *(V.P.-Fin.)*
Freddi Sue Finegood *(Sec.)*
J. Kaplan *(Dir.-Pur. & Traffic)*
Principal(s):
David Finegood
Daniel Finegood
Frank Garcia
Freddi Sue Finegood

No. of Mfg. Plants/Facilities: 1
No. of U.S. Offices: 1
No. of Foreign Offices: 1

Computer Systems/Hardware:
MIA BASIC FOUR

Outside Service Firm(s):

Breslow, Loeb & Associates*(Auditors)*
Los Angeles, CA

First Business Bank*(Major Banking Relationship)*
Los Angeles, CA

Non-U.S. Holding:

Muebles Fino Bueno **(1)**
Tiajuana, Mexico
Emp.: 500
Mfg.
Tom Pliner *(Gen. Mgr.)*

SHELDON GOOD & CO., INC.
333 W. Wacker Dr., Ste. 450
Chicago, IL 60606
Tel.: 312-346-1500 **DE**
Fax: 312-346-1233
Year Founded: 1965
Approx.Sls.: $430,000,000
Emp.: 500
Fiscal Year-end: 10/31/92
Commercial & Industrial Real Estate Marketing; Mortgage Financing; Real Estate Auctions; Consulting
S.I.C.: 6531; 7389; 6162
Sheldon F. Good *(Chm. & Chief Exec. Officer)*
Steven L. Good *(Pres.)*
Michael Whiteman *(Exec. V.P.)*
Gordon Greene *(Sr. V.P.)*
Michael Klimek *(Dir.-Fin.)*

No. of U.S. Offices: 11

Computer Systems/Hardware:
IBM

Outside Service Firm(s):

Altschuler, Melvoin & Glasser*(Auditors)*
30 S. Wecker Dr.
Chicago, IL 60606
Tel.: 312-207-2800

LaSalle National Bank*(Major Banking Relationship)*
120 S. LaSalle St.
Chicago, IL 60603
Tel.: 312-781-8000

Subsidiaries:

Real Estate Auctions, Inc. **(1)**
333 W. Wacker Dr., Ste. 450
Chicago, IL 60606
Tel.: 312-630-0915

Sheldon Good & Co. of California **(1)**
840 Newport Center Dr., Suite 110
Newport Beach, CA 92660
Tel.: 714-720-8022
Real Estate Marketing
S.I.C.: 6531

Sheldon Good & Company of Colorado, Inc. **(1)**
4600 S. Ulster St., Suite 700
Denver, CO 80737
Tel.: 303-740-6665

Sheldon Good & Company of Florida **(1)**
1300 S.E. 17th St., Suite 216
Fort Lauderdale, FL 33316
Tel.: 305-771-5544

Non-U.S. Holding:

Sheldon Good & Co. of Canada **(1)**
100 1 Evergreen Pl.,
Winnipeg, Manitoba R3L0E9, Canada
Tel.: 800-361-6027
Real Estate Marketing
S.I.C.: 6531

GOOD STUFF FOOD COMPANY, INC.
1771 W. Blake Ave.
Los Angeles, CA 90031
Tel.: 213-913-7200 **CA**
Fax: 213-913-7236
Year Founded: 1984
Approx.Sls.: $50,000,000
Emp.: 1,500
Mfr. of Bread, Cake & Related Products
S.I.C.: 2051
Weston L. Johnson *(Chm. Bd. & Pres.)*
Al Gates *(V.P.-Fin.)*
Stella Johnson *(Sec.)*

Outside Service Firm(s):

First Interstate Bank*(Major Banking Relationship)*
P.O.Box 54168, Terminal Annex
Los Angeles, CA 90054-0168
Tel.: 800-522-6645

W. B. GOODE COMPANY, INC.
3280 Formex Rd.
Richmond, VA 23224
Mailing Address:
P.O. Box 24159,
Richmond, VA 23224
Tel.: 804-231-0669 **VA**
Fax: 804-230-3934
Year Founded: 1937
Sales Range: $20-39 Million
Emp.: 220
Full Service Contractor to the Petroleum Marketing Industry
S.I.C.: 1799; 5013; 7699; 3448; 3441
Roy V. Sutton *(Pres. & Chief Exec. Officer)*
Thomas G. Theisen *(V.P.-Fin. & Chief Fin. Officer)*
Lee Bates *(V.P.)*
Wayne Hill *(V.P.)*
William Kinnan *(V.P.)*
Scott Johnston *(Controller)*
Jay Biggers *(Mgr.-Gen. Sls.)*
Principal(s):
Roy V. Sutton

No. of U.S. Offices: 5

Outside Service Firm(s):

KPMG Peat Marwick*(Auditors)*
1021 E. Cary St., Ste. 1900
Richmond, VA 23219
Tel.: 804-649-9091

Kaufman & Canoles*(Legal Firm)*
One Commercial Place
Norfolk, VA 23510

Crestar Bank*(Major Banking Relationship)*
P.O. Box 26665,
Richmond, VA 23261
Tel.: 804-782-5995

Branches:

W. B. Goode Company, Inc. **(1)**
1640 DeBaun Ave., P.O. Box 1294
Chesapeake, VA 23320
Tel.: 804-547-7191
Fax: 804-436-4908
Complete Sls., Installation & Service for all Manufacturers Represented; In-Shop, Field Installation & Subcontractor Services; Tank Testing; Card System & Bank Debit System Specialists; Fleet, Fuel Depots & Liquid Handling; 24-Hour, 7-Day Emergency Service Repair; Underground Storage Tank Installation, Repair, Testing & Removal
S.I.C.: 5084; 5082; 5013; 7699
Tommy Salamon *(Branch Mgr.)*
Joe Wrightson *(Service Mgr.)*

W. B. Goode Company, Inc. **(1)**
2800 Cofer Road, P.O. Box 14259
Richmond, VA 23224
Tel.: 804-233-6987
Fax: 804-230-0871
Complete Sales, Installation & Service for all Manufacturers Represented
S.I.C.: 5084; 5082; 5013; 7699
David Owen *(Branch Mgr.)*
Henry Young *(Construction Mgr.)*
Billy Williams *(Service & Electrical Mgr.)*

W. B. Goode Company, Inc. **(1)**
622 Mohawk Avenue, N.E., P.O. Box 13826
Roanoke, VA 24037
Tel.: 703-982-0124
Fax: 703-343-5918
Complete Sales, Installation & Service for All Manufacturers Represented
S.I.C.: 5084; 5082; 5013; 7699
Jerry Dobbins *(Branch Mgr.)*
Terry Kidman *(Service Mgr.)*

Subsidiaries:

Formex, Inc. - Permanent Steel Forms **(1)**
P.O. Box 24129, 2800 Cofer Rd.
Richmond, VA 23224
Tel.: 804-231-1988 (100%)
Fax: 804-232-6114
Curbing, Island Forms, Light & Sign Pole Bases in Steel, Stainless or Galvanized, Non-Hwy. Type Guard Rails, Dispenser Boxes, Dogbones Islands & Heavy U Shaped Pipe Guards
S.I.C.: 3448; 3312; 3441
Joe Fleming *(Pres.)*
Roger Atkins *(V.P.-Mfg.)*
Al Oliver *(Customer Rels.)*
Elenor Redford *(Customer Rels.)*

Magnum Building Systems **(1)**
1000 Jefferson Davis Hwy., P.O. Box 24159
Richmond, VA 23224
Tel.: 804-232-3000 (100%)
Fax: 804-230-3934
Emp.: 10
Pre-Engineered & Custom Mfr. of Canopies for Pump Islands, Service Stations, Convenience Stores & Store Front Fascia; Installation Available in Northeastern & Southeastern U.S.A.
S.I.C.: 3448
Andy Koval *(Mgr.-Opers.)*

Stone & Hoover Contracting, Inc. **(1)**
8433 Backlick Rd., Ste. 201
Lorton, VA 22079
Tel.: 703-550-7070 (100%)
Fax: 703-339-3723
Sls., Service & Installation of Petroleum Equip. inc. Customer Designed Dispensing Systems for Comml & Indust. Applications
S.I.C.: 8711; 1799; 1542
Dave Mederer *(Gen. Mgr.)*
Julius George *(Mgr.-Construction)*
Jonathan Wells *(Mgr.-Sls.)*

Affiliate:

GES Environmental, Inc. **(1)**
8040 Kimway Drive
Richmond, VA 23228
Tel.: 804-264-7095
Environmental Consulting & Contracting
Gene Watson *(V.P.)*

GOODHEART-WILLCOX CO., INC.
123 W. Taft Drive
South Holland, IL 60473
Tel.: 708-333-7200
Tel.: 800-323-0440
Fax: 708-333-9130
Year Founded: 1921
Approx.Rev.: $11,700,000
Emp.: 50
Fiscal Year-end: 4/30/92
Publisher of Mechanical, Technical & Home Economics Books
S.I.C.: 2731
George Fischer *(Chm. Bd.)*
John Flanagan *(Pres.)*
Dick Snyder *(V.P.-Sls.)*
Donald A. Massucci *(V.P.-Admin.)*
Kathleen McMillan *(Adv. Dir.)*

GOODMAN EQUIPMENT CORP.
5430 W. 70th Pl.
Bedford Park, IL 60638
Tel.: 708-496-1188 **DE**
Fax: 708-496-3939
Year Founded: 1971
Approx.Sls.: $18,000,000
Emp.: 85
Import Export
Mfr. Underground Mining & Tunneling Machinery, Material Handling Equipment, Plastics Blow Molding Machinery; Sale of Renewal Parts on Listed Equipment in Addition to Injection Molding Equipment (NATCO)
S.I.C.: 3559; 3532; 3531; 5084; 5082
Calvin A. Campbell, Jr. *(Chm. Bd., Pres. & Chief Exec. Officer)*
Thomas J. Schneider *(Exec. V.P.)*
Francis A. Horvath *(Pres.-Goodman Mfg. Co. of Canada, Ltd.)*
Donald L. Roach *(V.P.-Improved Parts & Service Div. & Data Processing Dir.)*
Samuel B. Fortenbaugh, III *(Gen. Counsel)*
Catherine A. Madden *(Controller)*
Valentine Gencius *(Dir.-Pur.)*
Paul Ernst *(Mgr.-Personnel)*
Silvio M. Martino *(Mgr.-Production)*

No. of Mfg. Plants/Facilities: 4
No. of U.S. Offices: 1

Computer Systems/Hardware:
Hewlett-Packard Model 922RX

Outside Service Firm(s):

Gimbel, Abrams & Singer Ltd.*(Auditors)*
Chicago, IL

Johnson & Higgins*(Commercial Insurance Carrier)*
New York, NY

The Northern Trust Co.*(International Bank Affiliate)*
50 S. LaSalle St.
Chicago, IL 60675
Tel.: 312-630-6000
Fax: 312-630-6516

Johnson & Higgins*(Group Insurer)*
New York, NY

Morgan, Lewis & Bockius*(Legal Firm)*
2000 One Logan Square
Philadelphia, PA 19103-6993
Tel.: 215-963-5000
Fax: 215-963-5299

The Northern Trust Co.*(Major Banking Relationship)*
50 S. LaSalle St.
Chicago, IL 60675
Tel.: 312-630-6000
Fax: 312-630-6516

William Blair & Co.*(Pension Manager)*
135 S. LaSalle St.
Chicago, IL 60603
Tel.: 312-236-1600

Subsidiary:

Improved Blow Molding Equipment Company, Inc. **(1)**
11 Sagamore Park Dr.
Hudson, NH 03051
Tel.: 603-889-8900
Plastics Blow Molding Equipment/Service
S.I.C.: 3089
Ronald R. Beaulieu *(Pres.)*
R. Dale Pleasant *(V.P.)*

GOODMANS, INC.
1400 E. Indian School Rd.
Phoenix, AZ 85014
Mailing Address:
P.O. Box 13289
Phoenix, AZ 85002
Tel.: 602-263-1110 **AZ**
Fax: 602-263-0624
Year Founded: 1953
Sales Range: $20-39 Million
Emp.: 230
Wholesale & Leasing Office Furniture
S.I.C.: 5021; 7359
Murray Goodman *(Pres. & Treas.)*
Bob Wood *(Chief Fin. Officer)*
Dorothy Goodman *(Sec.)*

Computer Systems/Hardware:
Prime

Outside Service Firm(s):

Valley National Bank*(Major Banking Relationship)*
241 North Central Ave., 11th Floor
Phoenix, AZ 85001

GOODPASTURE, INC.
214 S. 6th St.
Brownfield, TX 79316
Mailing Address:
P.O. Box 912
Brownfield, TX 79316
Tel.: 806-637-2541
Fax: 806-637-2541
Assets: $31,000,000
Net Worth: $31,000,000
Approx.Sls.: $31,000,000
Emp.: 150
Fertilizer; Grain Storage & Merchandising; Value Added Dealer for AT&T & IBM
S.I.C.: 5153; 4221; 2874
Molly Goodpasture *(Chm. Bd.)*
Ken Muldrow *(Pres. & Chief Exec. Officer)*
Tom Middleton *(Exec. V.P.)*
Sam Chaffin *(V.P.-Fin.)*
Donnie Wade *(Controller, Treas. & Sec.)*

Computer Systems/Hardware:
IBM Systems 36 & 4300

Outside Service Firm(s):

KPMG Peat Marwick*(Auditors)*
1000 Two First City Center, 550 W. Texas St.
Midland, TX 79701
Tel.: 915-682-3791

Aetna Life & Casualty*(Group Insurer)*
151 Farmington Avenue
Hartford, CT 06156
Tel.: 203-273-2128
Fax: 203-729-4295

Brownfield State Bank*(Investment Banker)*
Brownfield, TX

Thompson & Knight*(Legal Firm)*
3300 First City Center
Dallas, TX 75201
Tel.: 214-969-1700

Bank of America NT&SA*(Major Banking Relationship)*
One Allen Center, Ste. 3100
Houston, TX 77002
Tel.: 713-651-4872
Fax: 713-651-4841

Brownfield State Bank*(Major Banking Relationship)*
Brownfield, TX

Texas Commerce Bank*(Major Banking Relationship)*
Lubbock, TX

GOODRUM LEONARD & ASSOCIATES, INC.
4301 Hillsboro Rd.
Nashville, TN 37215
Tel.: 615-292-4431
Fax: 615-292-5059
Year Founded: 1971
Approx.Billings: $12,500,000
Emp.: 18
Harold Goodrum *(Chm. & Chief Exec. Officer)*
Miller Leonard *(Pres. & Creative Dir.)*
Bruce Hunt *(Exec. V.P.)*
Lucy Gibson *(Controller)*

GOODWAY TOOL CORPORATION
420 West Ave.
Stamford, CT 06902
Tel.: 203-359-4708
Tel.: 800-333-7467
Year Founded: 1966
Approx.Sls.: $10,000,000
Emp.: 44
Export
Mfr. High Pressure Hoses for Vacuums
S.I.C.: 3052; 3625
P.K. Reichborn *(Pres. & Treas.)*
Donald A. Bull *(Exec. V.P. & Sec.)*
Arvid K. Grimsley *(V.P.)*
Carole Jaehn *(Treas.)*

Computer Systems/Hardware:
Unisys

GOODWILL INDUSTRIES OF AMERICA, INC.
9200 Wisconsin Ave.
Bethesda, MD 20814
Tel.: 301-530-6500 **MD**
Fax: 301-530-1516
Year Founded: 1902
Assets: $4,641,865
Liabilities: $402,865
Net Worth: $4,239,000
Approx.Rev.: $664,000,000
Emp.: 65
Fiscal Year-end: 12/31/90
Nonprofit Provider of Vocational Rehabilitation & Employment Services for People With Disabilities And Others
S.I.C.: 8742; 7361
David M. Cooney *(Chm. Bd.)*
J. Michael Stephens *(Controller, Div. Dir.-Admin. Services & Personnel Dir.)*
Jean Robinson *(Gen. Counsel)*
David W. Barringer *(Dir.-Communications)*
Cecil E. McFarland *(Dir.-Membership Services Div.)*
Stephen L. Snyderman *(Dir.-Mngmt. Information Systems)*

No. of Mfg. Plants/Facilities: 200
No. of U.S. Offices: 179
No. of Foreign Offices: 44

Computer Systems/Hardware:
IBM 4331; IBM PC

Outside Service Firm(s):

KPMG Peat Marwick*(Auditors)*
2001 M St., N.W.
Washington, DC 20036
Tel.: 202-467-3800

Corporate Insurance Management*(Commercial Insurance Carrier)*
Alexandria, VA

Provident Life & Accident Insurance Co.*(Group Insurer)*
P.O. Box 12015
Chattanooga, TN 37401
Tel.: 615-755-7088

Maryland National Bank*(Major Banking Relationship)*
Washington, DC

Sovran Bank*(Major Banking Relationship)*
Virginia Beach, VA

Connecticut General*(Pension Manager)*
Seattle, WA

Mutual of New York*(Pension Manager)*
New York, NY

WILLIAM H. GOODWIN TRUST
1 James Ctr.
Richmond, VA 23219
Tel.: 804-643-4200
Approx.Sls.: $29,000,000
Bowling Alleys
S.I.C.: 3731; 7377
Juanita Gordon *(Controller)*
Norwood H. Davis, Jr. *(Trustee)*
L.F. Loree III *(Trustee)*

Subsidiaries:

AMF Bowling Centers Inc. **(1)**
7275 Glen Forest Dr.
Richmond, VA 23226-3755
Tel.: 804-282-6800
145 Bowling Centers Throughout the U.S.
S.I.C.: 7933
Beverly W. Armstrong *(Pres.)*

Subsidiaries:

AMF Azalea Bowl **(2)**
1741 Dumbarton Rd.
Richmond, VA 23227-3323
Tel.: 804-266-7405
AMF Bowling Centers
S.I.C.: 7933

AMF Lang's Bowlarama Inc. **(2)**
225 Niantic Ave.
Cranston, RI 02907-3121
Tel.: 401-944-0500
S.I.C.: 7933

AMF Bowling Centers Inc. **(1)**
4555 E. Red Bridge Rd.
Kansas City, MO 64131
Tel.: 816-941-2929
Bowling Alleys
S.I.C.: 7933
Bob Ludwig *(Mgr.)*

GOOLSBY FOODS, INC.
2219 Laurel Dr.
Columbus, GA 31907
Tel.: 706-563-4357
Fax: 706-569-9805
Approx.Sls.: $49,000,000
Emp.: 700
Goolsby Foods; Retail Groceries
S.I.C.: 5411
Robert Goolsby *(Chm. Bd. & Pres.)*
Bill Duffie *(Controller)*
Sharon Goolsby *(Asst. Sec.)*

Outside Service Firm(s):

Robinson, Grimes & Company*(Auditors)*
Columbus, GA

Thompson, Redmond & Nickols*(Legal Firm)*
Columbus, GA

Columbus Bank & Trust Company*(Major Banking Relationship)*
Trust Dept., P.O. Box 120
Columbus, GA 31902
Tel.: 706-649-2311

GORDON BROTHERS
40 Broad St.
Boston, MA 02109
Tel.: 617-426-3233
Fax: 617-422-6288
Year Founded: 1903
Assets: $9,287,000
Liabilities: $4,064,000
Net Worth: $5,223,000
Sales Range: $40-59 Million
Emp.: 14
Fiscal Year-end: 12/31/91
Jewelers
S.I.C.: 5944
Philip Gordon *(Chm. Bd.)*
Robert Sager *(Pres.)*
Michael Frieze *(Chief Exec. Officer)*

No. of U.S. Offices: 1

Outside Service Firm(s):

Coopers & Lybrand*(Auditors)*
1 Post Office Square
Boston, MA 02110
Tel.: 617-574-5000
Fax: 617-345-0398

Hinkley, Allen, Snyder & Comen*(Legal Firm)*
Providence, RI

Bank of Boston*(Major Banking Relationship)*
100 Federal St.
Boston, MA 02110
Tel.: 617-434-4322

Subsidiary:

Gordon Brothers Corporation **(1)**
40 Broad St.
Boston, MA 02109
Tel.: 617-426-3233
Emp.: 85
Jewelry
S.I.C.: 5944
Michael Frieze *(Pres. & Chief Exec. Officer)*
Alan Wong *(Chief Fin. Officer)*
Herman Snyder *(Sec.)*

GORDON & FERGUSON OF DELAWARE, INC.
2915 Niagara Lane
Plymouth, MN 55447
Mailing Address:
P.O. Box 47510
Minneapolis, MN 55447
Tel.: 612-559-8300
Telex: 29-1141
Fax: 612-559-2871
Year Founded: 1871
Emp.: 300

Gordon & Ferguson of Delaware, Inc.—(Continued)
Mfr. & Distributor of Men's & Boys' Outerwear, Leather Garments & Sportswear
S.I.C.: 2311; 2329; 5136
Ian Schaffer *(Pres.)*
Kristi L. Duffy *(Controller)*
D. Peterson *(Mgr.-Natl. Sls.)*

Outside Service Firm(s):

Divine, Scherzer & Brody*(Auditors)*
St. Paul, MN

GORDON FOOD SERVICE INC.
P.O. Box 1787, 333 50th St.
Grand Rapids, MI 49501
Tel.: 616-530-7000
Fax: 616-530-7165
Year Founded: 1900
Approx.Sls.: $365,000,000
Emp.: 950
Wholesale Food Distributor
S.I.C.: 5149; 5142; 5143; 5147; 5113; 5148
Paul B. Gordon *(Chm. Bd. & Chief Exec. Officer)*
Dan Gordon *(Pres.)*
John M. Gordon *(Chief Fin. Officer, Treas., Sec.)*
Paul Carpentier *(Controller)*
Jack Schultz *(Dir.-Benefits)*
Dave Vickery *(Dir.-Human Resources)*
Michael Clark *(Mgr.-Mngmt. Information Systems)*

Computer Systems/Hardware:
Burroughs 812

Outside Service Firm(s):

Deloitte & Touche*(Auditors)*
Grand Rapids, MI

Old Kent Bank & Trust Co.*(Major Banking Relationship)*
One Vandenberg Center
Grand Rapids, MI 49503
Tel.: 616-774-5000

KENNETH GORDON NEW ORLEANS, LTD.
1209 Distributors Row
New Orleans, LA 70123
Tel.: 504-734-1433 **LA**
Fax: 504-733-1625
Approx.Sls.: $26,000,000
Emp.: 300
Import Export
Manufacture Garments For Specialty Stores
S.I.C.: 2337; 5137
Kenneth Gordon *(Pres.)*
Harvey Herstein *(Sr. V.P. & Treas.)*
Marc Miller *(Sr. V.P. & Plant Mgr.)*
Betty Lachman *(V.P.-Office Admin. & Computer Opers.)*
Steven Lavin *(V.P.-Mktg.)*
J.B. Kiefer *(Gen. Counsel)*

Outside Service Firm(s):

Bain, Freibaum & Company*(Auditors)*
New Orleans, LA

Whitney National Bank of New Orleans*(Major Banking Relationship)*
P.O. Box 61260
New Orleans, LA 70161
Tel.: 504-586-7422

GORDON SIGN COMPANY
2930 W. 9th Ave.
Denver, CO 80204
Tel.: 303-629-6121
Fax: 303-629-1024
Year Founded: 1905
Approx.Sls.: $10,000,000
Emp.: 130
Electric Signs
S.I.C.: 3993
Jim Skagen *(Pres.)*
Curt Mateer *(Pur. Agent)*
William Brown *(Dir.-Fin.)*
Harry Grass *(Dir.-Sls. & Mktg.)*
Wayne Page *(Dir.-Opers.)*

Outside Service Firm(s):

Deloitte & Touche*(Auditors)*
Topeka, KS

United Bank of Denver*(Major Banking Relationship)*
Denver, CO

Subsidiary:

CBS Signs, Inc. **(1)**
1805 Pacific Ave.
Cheyenne, WY 82007
Tel.: 307-637-7446
Bill Brown *(Gen. Mgr.)*

GORDON & SMITH, INC.
7081 Consolidated Way
San Diego, CA 92121
Tel.: 619-549-2690
Fax: 619-549-3804
Approx.Sls.: $16,000,000
Emp.: 85
Mfr. Mens Sportswear & Surfboards; Wholesale & Retail Sporting Goods
S.I.C.: 2329; 3949; 5941
Laurence Gordon *(Pres. & Chief Exec. Officer)*
Gayle Gordon *(V.P.)*
Karen Woods *(Chief Fin. Officer, Dir.-MIS, & Mgr.-Opers.)*

Outside Service Firm(s):

Stonefield & Josephson*(Auditors)*
San Diego, CA

First National Bank of San Diego*(Major Banking Relationship)*
San Diego, CA

GORDY'S, INC.
1131 Oxford St.
Worthington, MN 56187
Tel.: 507-376-3197 **MN**
Fax: 507-376-9612
Year Founded: 1963
Sales Range: $80-99 Million
Emp.: 500
Retail Groceries
S.I.C.: 5411
Gordon B. Anderson *(Chm. Bd. & Pres.)*
Thomas G. Anderson *(Chief Oper. Officer, Chief Fin. Officer & V.P.)*
Bruce S. Anderson *(V.P.)*
Greg Pearson *(Gen. Mgr.)*
Principal(s):
Gordon B. Anderson
Thomas G. Anderson
Bruce S. Anderson

Outside Service Firm(s):

Turbes, Drealan, Haas & Co.*(Auditors)*
Worthington, MN

Hedeen & Hughes*(Legal Firm)*
Worthington, MN

Norwest Bank Worthington, N.A.*(Major Banking Relationship)*
Worthington, MN

W. L. GORE & ASSOCIATES, INC.
555 Paper Mill Rd.
Newark, DE 19714
Mailing Address:
P.O. Box 9329
Newark, DE 19714
Tel.: 302-738-4880
Fax: 302-738-7710
Year Founded: 1958
Approx.Sls.: $400,000,000
Emp.: 4,500
Manufacture Artificial Arteries & Prostheses; Special Wiring & Cable For Computers In Space; Waterproof Breathable Membranes
S.I.C.: 3357; 3552; 3841; 3679
Robert W. Gore *(Pres. & Chief Exec. Officer)*
Shanti Mehta *(Chief Fin. Officer)*
Dr. Genevieve W. Gore *(Treas. & Sec.)*

Computer Systems/Hardware:
IBM

Outside Service Firm(s):

Gunnip & Co.*(Auditors)*
Wilmington, DE

Blue Shield of New Jersey*(Group Insurer)*
Newark, NJ

Bank of Delaware*(Major Banking Relationship)*
Wilmington, DE

CHESTER GORE COMPANY INC.
780 Third Ave.
New York, NY 10017
Tel.: 212-754-9111
Fax: 212-759-7864
Year Founded: 1955
Approx.Billings: $15,000,000
Emp.: 18
Adv. Agency
S.I.C.: 7311
Chester Gore *(Pres. & Creative Dir.)*
Gerie Gore *(V.P., Admin.)*
Jerry Bindell *(Comptroller)*
Georgette Lordi *(Pub. Rels.)*
Principal(s):
Chester Gore
Gerie Gore

GORE GRAPHICS, INC.
340 N. Madison Ave.
Los Angeles, CA 90004
Tel.: 213-668-2111
Fax: 215-663-4052
Approx.Sls.: $23,000,000
Emp.: 215
Commercial Printing, Lithographic
S.I.C.: 2752; 2759
Jeffrey R. Gore *(Pres.)*
Roger Allen, Jr. *(Exec. V.P. & Sec.)*
Walter Schulte *(V.P.-Fin.)*
Roy Turman *(V.P.-Opers.)*

Outside Service Firm(s):

Arthur Andersen & Co.*(Auditors)*
633 W. Fifth St.
Los Angeles, CA 90071
Tel.: 213-614-6500

Imperial Bank*(Major Banking Relationship)*
Inglewood, CA

GOSHEN RUBBER CO., INC.
1525 S. 10th St.
Goshen, IN 46526
Mailing Address:
P.O. Box 517,
Goshen, IN 46526-0517
Tel.: 219-533-1111
Fax: 219-533-5332
Year Founded: 1916
Approx.Sls.: $68,000,000
Emp.: 700
Mfr. of Custom Molded & Automatic Machine-Cut Industrial & Mechanical Rubber Products
S.I.C.: 3069
Arthur McElwee *(Chm. Bd. & Pres.)*
Carroll D. Hobson *(Sr. V.P.-Mfg. & Engrng.)*
Robert S. Alexander *(V.P.-Fin.)*
J. Barnhill *(V.P.-Mfg.)*
John Gilleece *(V.P.-Sls.)*
Edward S. Johnson *(V.P.-Goshen Rubber of Canada, Ltd.)*
LaMar D. Malone *(V.P.-Product Devel.)*
Richard D. Robbins *(V.P.-Matls.)*
Principal(s):
Arthur McElwee

Computer Systems/Hardware:
Wang

Subsidiaries:

GNC Corp **(1)**
2600 Wilco Blvd.
Wilson, NC 27893
Tel.: 919-237-6171
Mfr. Rubber Seals & Gaskets
S.I.C.: 3053
Ken Krodel *(Plant Mgr.)*

GRN Corp. **(1)**
1000 12th Street
Gothenburg, NE 69138
Tel.: 308-537-3693
Mfr. O-Rings & Gaskets
S.I.C.: 3053
Larry Kauffman *(Plant Mgr.)*

GSH Corp. **(1)**
310 Kinggold Blvd.
Snow Hill, NC 28580
Tel.: 919-747-5947
Mfr. Rubber O-Rings & Gaskets
S.I.C.: 3053
Douglas Van Loue *(Plant Mgr.)*

Non-U.S. Holding:

Goshen Rubber of Canada Ltd. **(1)**
100 Stafford Drive
Brampton, ON L6W 1L4, Canada
Tel.: 416-457-5843
Mfr. Gaskets
S.I.C.: 3053
Ranjit Garcha *(Plant Mgr.)*

GOSIGER INC.
108 McDonough St.
Dayton, OH 45402
Tel.: 513-228-5174
Fax: 513-228-5189
Approx.Sls.: $50,000,000
Emp.: 80
Distribute Machine Tools & Machinery
S.I.C.: 5084
Jane Gosiger Haley *(Pres.)*
Jerry Gecowets *(Exec. V.P.)*
Ira H. Stanley *(V.P.-Fin. & Treas.)*
Hugh Wall, III *(Gen. Counsel)*

No. of U.S. Offices: 4

Outside Service Firm(s):

Crowe, Chizek & Co.*(Auditors)*
Dayton, OH

Coolidge, Wall, Womsley & Lombard*(Legal Firm)*
33 W. First St., Ste. 600
Dayton, OH 45402
Tel.: 513-223-8177
Fax: 513-223-6705

GOSNELL BUILDERS
2728 N. 24th St.
Phoenix, AZ 85008
Tel.: 602-956-4300 **AZ**
Fax: 602-954-0597
Year Founded: 1973
Sales Range: $100-499 Million
Emp.: 4,000
General Contractor Single Family Homes, Nonresidential & Industrial Buildings; Hotel & Warehouse Operators; Subdivider & Developer
S.I.C.: 1542; 1521; 1531; 6512; 7011; 6552
Corporate Giving Program: Make-A-Wish, March of Dimes, Fiesta Bowl
Robert A. Gosnell *(Chief Exec. Officer)*
Rick Kafka *(Pres. & Dir.-Mktg.)*
Brian Richards *(Pres.-Residential)*
Daniel F. Kelly *(Chief Fin. Officer)*
Lee Plozaj *(Exec V.P.-Construction)*
Stuart C. Berres *(V.P.-Constr. Opers.)*

Craig W. Bisch *(V.P.-Arch.)*
Patrick Donnelly *(V.P.-Engrng.)*
John O. Theobald *(Gen. Counsel)*
Principal(s):
Robert A. Gosnell

No. of U.S. Offices: 6
No. of Foreign Offices: 1

Outside Service Firm(s):

Toback & Company*(Auditors)*
Phoenix, AZ

Lewis & Roca*(Legal Firm)*
Phoenix, AZ

Valley National Bank*(Major Banking Relationship)*
241 North Central Ave., 11th Floor
Phoenix, AZ 85001

Subsidiary:

Point Builders **(1)**
3130 Bonita Rd.
San Diego, CA
Tel.: 619-691-1800

GOUCHENOUR ADV., INC.
(Formerly Gouchenour & Associates, Inc.)
455 South Orange Ave., 6th Fl.
Orlando, FL 32801-3356
Tel.: 407-841-8585
Fax: 407-425-5297
Year Founded: 1988
Approx.Billings: $12,500,000
Emp.: 21
Fiscal Year-end: 12/31/90
Advertising Agency: Marketing Research
S.I.C.: 7311; 8732
C. Lee Gouchenour *(Chm. & Chief Exec. Officer)*
Don Ratliff *(Pres. & Chief Oper. Officer)*
Tom Brinkmoeller *(V.P.- Pub. Rels.)*
Charles Fout *(V.P.- Fin. & Human Resources)*
Bernie Urban *(Mgr.-Computer Graphics)*
Melissa Ludwig *(Sec.)*

Computer Systems/Hardware:
IBM, MacIntosh, Olivetti, Data General

Outside Service Firm(s):

Forness, Graham & Cottrill*(Auditors)*
Orlando, FL

Hartford Life Insurance Co.*(Commercial Insurance Carrier)*
Hartford, CT 06104-2999

Aetna Life & Casualty*(Group Insurer)*
151 Farmington Avenue
Hartford, CT 06156
Tel.: 203-273-2128
Fax: 203-729-4295

Subin, Shams, Rosenbluth & Moran*(Legal Firm)*
Orlando, FL

Sun Bank, N.A.*(Major Banking Relationship)*
200 S. Orange Ave., 8th Fl. SOAB
Orlando, FL
Tel.: 407-237-4141

GOUGLER INDUSTRIES, INC.
705 Lake St.
Kent, OH 44240
Tel.: 216-673-5821 **OH**
Telex: 986403
Fax: 216-673-5824
Year Founded: 1924
Approx.Sls.: $25,000,000
Emp.: 275
Import Export
Mfr. & Assembler of Steel Molds for the Plastic Industry
S.I.C.: 3599; 3544; 3542; 3559; 3321

Corporate Giving Program: United Way
Hank Saito *(Pres.)*
Richard W. Hugill *(V.P.-Mfg.)*
L.D. Wittensoldner *(Controller)*

Principal(s):
Richard W. Hugill
Nicholas J. Mendiola

No. of Mfg. Plants/Facilities: 2

Computer Systems/Hardware:
UNISYS

Outside Service Firm(s):

Deloitte & Touche*(Auditors)*
One Cascade Plaza, Ste. 1600
Akron, OH 44303-1187
Tel.: 216-253-2022

Prudential Insurance Co. of America*(Commercial Insurance Carrier)*
751 Broad St.
Newark, NJ 07102-3777
Tel.: 201-802-6000

American Health Care Management*(Group Insurer)*
Canton, OH

Blue Cross & Blue Shield of Northern Ohio*(Group Insurer)*
2060 E. 9th St.
Cleveland, OH 44115
Tel.: 216-687-7000

Brouse & McDowell*(Legal Firm)*
500 First National Tower
Akron, OH 4308
Tel.: 216-535-5711

Society National Bank*(Major Banking Relationship)*
900 Euclid Ave., P.O. Box 6477
Cleveland, OH 44101-6477
Tel.: 216-737-5000
Fax: 216-566-8947

First National Bank of Ohio*(Pension Manager)*
Akron, OH

GOULD INVESTORS, L.P.
60 Cutter Mill Rd.
Great Neck, NY 11021
Tel.: 516-466-3100 **MA**
Fax: 516-466-3132
Assets: $141,031,417
Earnings: ($3,910,694)
Liabilities: $154,627,332
Net Worth: $13,595,915
Approx.Rev.: $33,777,709
Emp.: 25
Fiscal Year-end: 9/30/91
Real Estate, Mortgage Investments
S.I.C.: 6211
Fredric H. Gould *(Exec. Officer)*
Marshall Rose *(Exec. Officer)*
Robert Huhem *(V.P.-Sales)*
Karen Dunleavy *(Treas.)*
Simeon Brinberg *(Gen. Counsel)*

Managing General Partner:

Georgetown Partners, Inc. **(1)**
60 Cutter Mill Rd.
Great Neck, NY 11021
Tel.: 516-466-3100
Real Estate, Mortgage Investments
S.I.C.: 6211
Marshall Rose *(Chm. Bd.)*
Fredric Gould *(Pres.)*
Stuart S. Gould *(Chm. Exec. Committee)*
Nathan Kupin *(Vice Chm.)*
David Kalish *(Chief Fin. Officer)*
Simeon Brinberg *(Sr. V.P. & Sec.)*
Israel Rosenzweig *(Sr. V.P.)*
Matthew J. Gould *(Sr. V.P.)*
Myron Ginsburg *(V.P.)*
Seth Kobay *(V.P.-Opers. & Controller)*
Herbert Mendelson *(V.P. & Asst. Sec.)*
Daniel Lembo *(V.P.)*
Karen Dunleavy *(Treas.)*

GOULD PACKAGING, INC.
P.O. Box 61506,
Vancouver, WA 98666
Mailing Address:
Lock Box 14622
St. Louis, MO 63178
Tel.: 206-693-6757
Fax: 314-583-8187
Year Founded: 1923
Approx.Sls.: $11,000,000
Emp.: 80
Import Export
Package & Convert Friction, Rubber, Plastic, Painting & Masking Tape; Freezer & Strapping Tape; Weatherstripping; Sandpaper Products; Creative Tapes; Pretty-Up Bath Appliques; Stationery Tapes
S.I.C.: 3069; 2672; 3842; 2295; 3291; 3089
Steven Gould *(Pres.)*

Computer Systems/Hardware:
IBM 36

Subsidiary:

Gould Packaging, Inc. **(1)**
800 N. Oak St.
Union, MO 63084
Tel.: 314-583-4500
Tel.: 800-325-3556
Fax: 314-583-8187
Emp.: 80
Mfg. Paper & Plastic Products
S.I.C.: 2672; 3069; 3089
Steven Gould *(Pres.)*

GOULD PAPER CORPORATION
315 Park Ave. S.
New York, NY 10010
Tel.: 212-505-1000
Fax: 212-505-7599
Approx.Sls.: $300,000,000
Emp.: 130
Printing Papers, Paper Board
S.I.C.: 2621; 2631
Harry E. Gould, Jr. *(Chm. Bd. & Pres.)*
Robert I. Anderson *(Exec. V.P.-Sls.)*
D.J. Lala *(Exec. V.P.)*
Fred Balluff *(Sr. V.P.-Sls.)*
Cliff Chaplin *(Sr. V.P.-Sls.)*
Al Goldfarb *(Sr. V.P.-Sls.)*
Marion Hindenburg *(Sr. V.P.-Sls.)*
Rick Irwin *(Sr. V.P. Sls. & Gen. Mgr. Publication Papers Div.)*
Dan Jackino *(Sr. V.P.-Sls.)*
Richard Miner *(Sr. V.P.-Sls.)*
Gary Zipper *(Sr. V.P.-Sls.)*
Lowell Ash *(V.P.-Sls.)*
Joseph Bergman *(V.P. & Controller)*
Jerry Blumstein *(V.P. & Asst. Sls. Mgr.)*
Robert Colucco *(V.P.-Sls.)*
Morton Eisenberg *(V.P.-Sls.)*
Ted Marks *(V.P.-Sls.)*
Jules Meisel *(V.P.-Sls.)*
Carl Meisel *(V.P.-Opers.)*
Stephen Meyer *(V.P. & Asst. Sls.Mgr.)*
Jerry Mutchnick *(V.P.-Sls.)*
Joseph O'Neill *(V.P.-Sls.)*
William Paley *(V.P.-Sls.)*
John Petrucelli *(V.P.-Sls.)*
Philip Salzman *(V.P.-Sls.)*

Outside Service Firm(s):

BDO Seidman*(Auditors)*
1430 Broadway
New York, NY
Tel.: 212-765-7500

Gaston & Snow*(Legal Firm)*
New York, NY

Paul, Weiss, Rifkind, Wharton & Garrison*(Legal Firm)*
345 Park Ave.
New York, NY 10022
Tel.: 212-644-8000

Chemical Banking Corp.*(Major Banking Relationship)*
277 Park Ave.
New York, NY 10041
Tel.: 212-310-6407
Fax: 212-310-4526

Divisions:

Gould Paper Corporation **(1)**
532 Page St.
Stoughton, MA 02072
Tel.: 617-341-2141
Sales & Marketing Office
S.I.C.: 5111
Gerald M. Chisholm *(Sr. V.P. & Gen. Mgr.)*
William G. Monahan *(V.P.-Sls.)*

Gould Paper Corporation **(1)**
3003 Carlisle Ave.
Dallas, TX 75204
Tel.: 214-871-9501
Sales & Marketing Office
S.I.C.: 5111
Bill Crisler *(Sr. V.P. & Gen. Mgr.)*

Subsidiary:

Fibreweb International, Ltd. **(1)**
22 1/2 Lowndes Ave.
Norwalk, CT 06854
Tel.: 203-866-6290
Paper & Fiber Brokers
S.I.C.: 5113
C. William Anderson *(Chief Oper. Officer)*

STEPHEN GOULD PAPER CO., INC.
35 S. Jefferson Rd.
Whippany, NJ 07981
Tel.: 201-428-1500
Fax: 201-428-1610
Year Founded: 1939
Approx.Sls.: $92,000,000
Emp.: 300
Fiscal Year-end: 12/31/90
Packaging Consultant Firm; Manufacture, Marketing, Distributor, Design & Engineering of Packaging
S.I.C.: 2653; 3089; 2448
Michael Golden *(Pres.)*
David Golden *(Chief Fin. Officer, Treas. & Sec.)*
Dale Golden *(Exec. V.P.)*
John Golden *(Exec. V.P.)*
Peter Van Slyke *(Exec. V.P.)*
J. Gilbert Brown *(Controller)*
Gloria Sowizral *(Dir.-Pur.)*
Deborah J. Habbart *(Corp. Asst.)*
Principal(s):
Michael Golden
Dale Golden
John Golden
Peter Van Slyke

No. of U.S. Offices: 26

Computer Systems/Hardware:
Burroughs B-900

Outside Service Firm(s):

Lupo & Lazar*(Auditors)*
90 Woodbridge Center Dr.
Woodbridge, NJ 07095

United States Life Insurance Co.*(Group Insurer)*
New York, NY

Pitney, Hardin, Kipp & Szuch*(Legal Firm)*
163 Madison Ave.
Morristown, NJ 07960
Tel.: 201-267-3333

National Community Bank*(Major Banking Relationship)*
Maywood, NJ

Subsidiaries:

Gould Central Florida **(1)**
825 Sunshine Ln.
Altamonte Springs, FL 32701
Tel.: 407-788-0007
Fax: 407-774-0986
Sales & Marketing Office
S.I.C.: 5111

Stephen Gould Paper Co., Inc.—(Continued)

Gary White *(Mgr.)*

Gould Southern (1)
1826 A. Doan Way
Norcross, GA 30093
Tel.: 404-921-1111
Sales & Marketing Office
S.I.C.: 5111
Robert Sherman *(Mgr.)*

Stephen Gould Corporation (Plainview, NY) (1)
151 Fairchild Ave.
Plainview, NY 11803
Tel.: 516-576-0800
Sales & Marketing Office
S.I.C.: 5111
Lou Fusaro *(Mgr.)*

Stephen Gould Corporation (Rochester, NY) (1)
1200-C Scottsville Rd.
Rochester, NY 14624
Tel.: 716-328-2990
Sales & Marketing Office
S.I.C.: 5111
David Orange *(Mgr.)*

Stephen Gould IN (1)
P.O. Box 44, Rte. 7, Aztec & Bell Rds.
Warsaw, IN 46580
Tel.: 219-269-6755
Sales & Marketing Office
S.I.C.: 5111
William Barden *(Mgr.)*

Stephen Gould MD (1)
9480 Deereco Rd.
Lutherville, MD 21093
Tel.: 410-561-3100
Sales & Marketing Office
S.I.C.: 5111
Steve Carlin *(Mgr.)*

Stephen Gould MI (1)
37678 Enterprise Ct.
Farmington Hills, MI 48331
Tel.: 313-489-4040
Sales & Marketing Office
S.I.C.: 5111
David Schalte *(Mgr.)*

Stephen Gould/Midhudson (1)
1123 Rte. 52
Fishkill, NY 12524
Tel.: 914-896-7800
Sales & Marketing Office
S.I.C.: 5111
Rick Beckerman *(Mgr.)*

Stephen Gould Midwest (1)
1302 Clarkson/Clayton Center
Ellisville, MO 63011
Tel.: 314-394-2150
Sales & Marketing Office
S.I.C.: 5111
David Baldock *(Mgr.)*

Stephen Gould of Arizona, Inc. (1)
4041 S. McClintock
Tempe, AZ 85382
Tel.: 602-820-5000
Sales & Marketing Office
S.I.C.: 5111

Stephen Gould of California (1)
4633 Old Ironsides Dr.
Santa Clara, CA 95050
Tel.: 408-980-0770
Fax: 408-980-0903
Sales & Marketing Office
S.I.C.: 5111
Robert DeStefano *(Mgr.)*

Stephen Gould of California-North Bay (1)
1001 Marina Village Pkwy., 4th Fl.
Alameda, CA 94501
Tel.: 415-522-3200
Sales & Marketing Office
S.I.C.: 5111
Don Wallunas *(Mgr.)*

Stephen Gould of Carolina, Inc. (1)
9741-D Southern Pine Blvd.
Charlotte, NC 28210
Tel.: 704-522-0225
Sales & Marketing Office
S.I.C.: 5111
Chris Garvey *(Mgr.)*

Stephen Gould of Carolina, Inc. (1)
2500 Gateway Centre Blvd.
Morrisville, NC 27560
Tel.: 919-481-3700
Fax: 919-467-1367
Sales & Marketing Office
S.I.C.: 5111
Ed O'Brien *(Mgr.)*

Stephen Gould of Colorado, Inc. (1)
Unit 3, 4860 Ironton St.
Denver, CO 80239
Tel.: 303-373-1924
Sales & Marketing Office
S.I.C.: 5111

Stephen Gould of Connecticut Corp. (1)
291 Lambert Rd.
Orange, CT 06477
Tel.: 203-795-9753
Sales & Marketing Office
S.I.C.: 5111
William Meyers *(Mgr.)*

Stephen Gould of Florida, Inc. (1)
5723 Benjamin Center Dr.
Tampa, FL 33613
Tel.: 813-886-8460
Sales & Marketing Office
S.I.C.: 5111
Tom Titus *(Mgr.)*

Stephen Gould of Florida, Inc. (1)
652 S.W. 12th Ave.
Deerfield Beach, FL 33442
Tel.: 305-426-8800
Sales & Marketing Office
S.I.C.: 5111
Frank Taverrite *(Mgr.)*

Stephen Gould of Illinois, Inc. (1)
1051 Perimeter Dr.
Schawnburg, IL 60173-5055
Tel.: 708-834-8585
Sales & Marketing Office
S.I.C.: 5111
Willard Nye *(Mgr.)*

Stephen Gould of Indiana, Inc. (1)
8604 Allisonville Rd., Ste. 101
Indianapolis, IN 46250
Tel.: 317-577-5180
Sales & Marketing Office
S.I.C.: 5111

Stephen Gould of New England, Inc. (1)
30 Commerce Way
Tewksbury, MA 01876
Tel.: 508-581-2500
Sales & Marketing Office
S.I.C.: 5111
Jim Vitas *(Mgr.)*

Stephen Gould of Ohio, Inc. (1)
10227 Alliance Rd.
Cincinnati, OH 45242
Tel.: 513-793-1010
Sales & Marketing Office
S.I.C.: 5111
Harvey Cohen *(Mgr.)*

Stephen Gould of Pennsylvania Corp. (1)
6 Eves Dr.
Marlton, NJ 08053
Tel.: 609-985-8888
Sales & Marketing Office
S.I.C.: 5111
Stan Schneider *(Mgr.)*

Stephen Gould of Puerto Rico, Inc. (1)
884 Ashford Ave.
Condado, PR 00907
Tel.: 809-725-6385
Sales & Marketing Office
S.I.C.: 5111
David Wolff *(Mgr.)*

Stephen Gould of Tennessee (1)
Southern Station Bldg., 306 W. Depot Ave., Ste. 104
Knoxville, TN 34917
Tel.: 615-637-2020
Sales & Marketing Office
S.I.C.: 5111
Todd Fisher *(Mgr.)*

Stephen Gould of Texas, Inc. (1)
15820 Midway Rd.
Dallas, TX 75244
Tel.: 214-490-1373
Sales & Marketing Office
S.I.C.: 5111
Todd Harmon *(Mgr.)*

Stephen Gould OH (1)
4350 Emery Industrial Pkwy.
Cleveland, OH 44128
Tel.: 216-292-3500
Sales & Marketing Office
S.I.C.: 5111
Alan Malkin *(Mgr.)*

Stephen Gould Paper Co., Inc. (1)
35 S. Jefferson Rd.
Whippany, NY 07981
Tel.: 201-428-1500
Sales & Marketing Office
S.I.C.: 5111
Barry Osias *(Mgr.)*

GOYA FOODS, INC.
100 Seaview Dr.
Secaucus, NJ 07096
Tel.: 201-348-4900
Fax: 201-348-6609
Approx.Sls.: $330,000,000
Emp.: 600
Import
Wholesale Food Distributor & Manufacturing Companies in Puerto Rico, Spain, Santo Domingo & The Dominican Republic
S.I.C.: 5141; 5149
Joseph Unanue *(Pres.)*
Conrad O. Colon *(V.P.-Mktg.)*
Aldo Cunningham *(V.P.-Sls.)*
Carlos Ortiz *(Gen. Counsel)*
Joseph Perez *(Dir.-Pur.)*
Ralph Toro *(Dir.-Pub. Rels.)*
Gilberto Otero *(Mgr.-Personnel)*

Computer Systems/Hardware:
IBM

Outside Service Firm(s):

Polakoff & Leen*(Auditors)*
New York, NY

Allstate Insurance*(Group Insurer)*
Northbrook, IL

Altschuler, Melvoin & Glasser*(Group Insurer)*
30 S. Wecker Dr.
Chicago, IL 60606
Tel.: 312-207-2800

Chemical Bank*(Investment Banker)*
450 West 33rd St.
New York, NY 10001
Tel.: 212-613-7197
Fax: 212-947-7628

Skadden, Arps, Slate, Meagher & Flom*(Legal Firm)*
919 3rd Ave.
New York, NY 10022
Tel.: 212-371-6000
Fax: 212-735-2000

Chemical Bank*(Major Banking Relationship)*
450 West 33rd St.
New York, NY 10001
Tel.: 212-613-7197
Fax: 212-947-7628

Phoenix Mutual Life Insurance Co.*(Pension Manager)*
Hartford, CT

Subsidiaries:

Bison Canning Co., Inc. (1)
South Main St.
Angola, NY 14006
Tel.: 716-549-0076
Fax: 716-549-1506
Approx.Sls.: $15,000,000
Emp.: 150
Canned Foods, Dried Beans, Sloppy Joe Mix, Tomato Sauce, Corned Beef & Chicken
S.I.C.: 2032
Franklin J. Drago *(Pres.)*
Robert J. Drago *(V.P.)*
James B. Seeley *(Sec.)*
Greg F. Drago *(Mgr.-Sls.)*

Goya Foods of Florida (1)
1900 N.W. 92nd Ave.
Miami, FL 33172
Tel.: 305-592-3150
Canned Foods, Sausages & Meats
S.I.C.: 2032

A. GRACE DEVELOPMENT
(d/b/a Frenchy's Creole Fried Chicken, Inc.)
PO Box 670303,
Houston, TX 77267-0303
Tel.: 713-449-8681
Fax: 713-449-5935
Year Founded: 1967
Approx.Sls.: $10,000,000
Emp.: 300
Fast Food Restaurants
S.I.C.: 5812
Darryl King *(Pres.)*

No. of Mfg. Plants/Facilities: 16

Computer Systems/Hardware:
Burroughs System B-80

Outside Service Firm(s):

Ernst & Young*(Auditors)*
1 Houston Ctr., 1200 McKinney
Houston, TX 77002
Tel.: 713-750-1500

W. M. GRACE DEVELOPMENT
7575 N. 16th St., Ste. 1
Phoenix, AZ 85020
Tel.: 602-956-8254 **MO**
Fax: 602-943-3548
Assets: $200,000
Liabilities: $75,000
Net Worth: $125,000
Sales Range: $40-59 Million
Emp.: 25
Fiscal Year-end: 8/31/92
Real Estate Developer
S.I.C.: 6552
W.M. Grace *(Chm. Bd. & Pres.)*
Jim Stamatis *(Sr. V.P.)*
Howard T. Grace *(V.P. & Dir.-Leasing)*
Steve Mason *(V.P.-Fin.)*
Roy Collum *(Dir. Personnel)*
Ron Crouch *(Dir.-Design & Construction)*

No. of U.S. Offices: 2

Computer Systems/Hardware:
Texas Instruments #700

Outside Service Firm(s):

Aetna Life & Casualty*(Group Insurer)*
Phoenix, AZ

Gammage & Burnham*(Legal Firm)*
Phoenix, AZ

Security Pacific National Bank*(Major Banking Relationship)*
Phoenix, AZ

GRACE & ROTHSCHILD
114 Fifth Ave.
New York, NY 10011
Tel.: 212-366-1600
Fax: 212-989-0681
Year Founded: 1986
Approx.Billings: $55,000,000
Emp.: 55
Roy Grace *(Chm. Bd.)*
Diane Rothschild *(Pres.)*
Gordon C. Sleeper III *(Exec. V.P.)*

GRAF BERTEL
292 Madison Ave.
New York, NY 10017
Tel.: 212-679-7733
Fax: 212-689-5570
Year Founded: 1989

Approx.Billings: $20,000,000
Emp.: 12
Bertel Schmitt *(Chm. Bd. & Creative Dir.)*
Hubert Graf *(Chief Exec. Officer, Creative Dir. & New Bus. Contact)*

JOHN H. GRAHAM & CO., INC.
617 Oradell Ave.
Oradell, NJ 07649
Mailing Address:
P.O. Box 739
Oradell, NJ 07649
Tel.: 201-261-8100
Tel.: 800-800-7566
Fax: 201-261-3109
Year Founded: 1870
Emp.: 40
Fiscal Year-end: 12/31/91

Import Export
King Cotton Cordage
S.I.C.: 2281
George Graham *(Chm. Bd.)*
Robert Kramer *(Pres. & Treas.)*
Burke Carter *(V.P. & Gen. Mgr.)*
Peter Goldsmith *(V.P.-Import & Sec.)*
Emmanuel Barrientos *(Controller)*
Dale Kramer *(Mgr.-Sls.)*

No. of U.S. Offices: 1

Outside Service Firm(s):

Walker, Minkis & Gordon*(Auditors)*
North Brunswick, NJ

United Jersey Bank*(Major Banking Relationship)*
Oradell, NJ

GRAHAM GROUP, INC.
910 Grand Ave.
Des Moines, IA 50309
Tel.: 515-244-0387
Fax: 515-244-6815
Sales Range: $10-19 Million
Emp.: 50
Fiscal Year-end: 12/31/91
Real Estate Development Company
S.I.C.: 6552
George Milligan *(Pres.)*
Richard Hein *(V.P.)*
Jess Murillo *(V.P., Treas., Controller & Chief Fin. Officer)*
Charles Taylor *(Sec.)*

Computer Systems/Hardware:
IBM System 34 & 36

Outside Service Firm(s):

Denman & Co.*(Auditors)*
Des Moines, IA

HMO Iowa*(Group Insurer)*
Des Moines, IA

Bankers Trust Co.*(Major Banking Relationship)*
Des Moines, IA

First Interstate Bank*(Major Banking Relationship)*
Milwaukee, WI

Subsidiary:

MacMillan Oil Co., Inc. **(1)**
P.O. Box 4968
Des Moines, IA 50306
Tel.: 515-283-0631
Emp.: 65
Computer Systems/Hardware:
IBM System 34 & 36
Wholesale & Retail Sellers Of Petroleum Prods.
S.I.C.: 5172; 5983
John Graham *(Chm. Bd.)*
Jeff Murillo *(V.P., Treas., Controller & Chief Fin. Officer)*
John McGarvey *(Sec.)*

GRAHAM MAGNETICS, INC.
4001 Airport Frwy., Ste. 400
Bedford, TX 76021
Tel.: 817-868-5000
Tel.: 800-433-7632
Fax: 817-354-9145
Year Founded: 1964
Approx.Sls.: $80,000,000
Emp.: 400
Fiscal Year-end: 12/31/92

Export
Mfr. & Marketer of Data Storage Media Products & Equipment
S.I.C.: 3695; 3577; 5045
Scott D. Whittenburg *(Pres. & Chief Exec. Officer)*
John C. Belsly *(Exec. V.P.-Fin. & Chief Fin. Officer)*
Michael B. Bryan *(V.P.-Sls. & Mktg.)*
Whittington P. Vara *(Dir.-Mktg.)*

GRAHAM PAINT AND VARNISH COMPANY
4800 S. Richmond Ave.
Chicago, IL 60632
Tel.: 312-376-7676
Approx.Sls.: $10,000,000
Emp.: 70
Mfg. Graham & Hooker Paint
S.I.C.: 2851
Ray J. Shilvock *(Chm. Bd.)*
Frank Lilien *(Pres.)*
James Nass *(Mgr.-Sls.)*

GRAMEX CORPORATION
11966 St. Charles Rock Rd.
Bridgeton, MO 63044
Tel.: 314-739-8300
Fax: 314-291-7720
Year Founded: 1958
Approx.Sls.: $80,000,000
Emp.: 900
Retail Discount Chain, Sporting Goods, Micro Computer Sales & Service
S.I.C.: 5734; 5941
Jack Holley *(Chm. Bd.)*
Tom Holley *(Pres.)*
Fred Rudolph *(Exec. V.P. & Chief Fin. Officer)*

Outside Service Firm(s):

KPMG Peat Marwick*(Auditors)*
1010 Market St.
Saint Louis, MO 63101
Tel.: 314-444-1400

First Missouri Bank & Trust Co.*(Major Banking Relationship)*
St. Louis, MO

THE GRANADA GROUP
11000 Richmond
Houston, TX 77042
Tel.: 713-877-7000 **TX**
Fax: 713-783-2130
Approx.Sls.: $1,190,000,000
Emp.: 2,100
Beef Cattle Feedlots, Meat Processing & Distributor, Commodity Brokers & Dealers
S.I.C.: 0212; 0211; 0751; 6221
David G. Eller *(Pres. & Chief Exec. Officer)*
Thomas L. Easley *(Chief Fin. Officer & V.P.)*
James M. Eller, Jr. *(V.P.)*
Clarence Pett *(V.P.-Tax & Audit)*

Outside Service Firm(s):

Deloitte & Touche*(Auditors)*
333 Clay St., Ste. 2300
Houston, TX 77002
Tel.: 713-756-2000

Kech, Mahin & Cate*(Legal Firm)*
Houston, TX

NationsBank Texas*(Major Banking Relationship)*
Corporate Trust Department, 700 Louisiana St.
Houston, TX 77002
Tel.: 713-247-6000

Divisions:

Granada Financial Services **(1)**
11000 Richmond
Houston, TX 77042
Tel.: 713-783-1310
Bob Wilkens *(Pres.)*

Granada Management Division **(1)**
11000 Richmond
Houston, TX 77042
Tel.: 713-783-1310
Douglas L. McKinna *(Pres.)*

GRAND BANKS YACHTS, LTD.
(Sub. of American Marine Pte. Ltd., Singapore)
563 Steamboat Rd.
Greenwich, CT 06830
Tel.: 203-869-9274 **CT**
Fax: 203-869-1808
Year Founded: 1976
Assets: $13,130,000
Liabilities: $7,800,000
Net Worth: $5,330,000
Approx.Sls.: $38,300,000
Emp.: 680
Fiscal Year-end: 3/31/90
Mfr. Motor Yachts
S.I.C.: 3731
Robert Livingston *(Chm., Pres. & Chief Exec. Officer)*
Richard C. Loh *(V.P.)*
Robert L. Phillips *(Mktg. Mgr.-West Coast)*

No. of Mfg. Plants/Facilities: 1
No. of U.S. Offices: 2
No. of Foreign Offices: 1

Computer Systems/Hardware:
IBM 36

Outside Service Firm(s):

KPMG Peat Marwick*(Auditors)*
Stamford Square, 3001 Summer St.
Stamford, CT 06905
Tel.: 203-356-9800

Providence Insurance*(Group Insurer)*
Chattanooga, TN

Wardley Ltd.*(Investment Banker)*
Singapore, Singapore

GRAND PRAIRIE CO-OP, INC.
1 S. Calhoun
Tolono, IL 61880
Tel.: 217-485-5143 **IL**
Fax: 217-485-5143
Year Founded: 1981
Assets: $14,075,367
Earnings: $517,741
Liabilities: $8,572,185
Net Worth: $5,503,182
Approx.Sls.: $54,371,106
Emp.: 53
Fiscal Year-end: 6/30/90
Agricultural Production & Services
S.I.C.: 5153; 5191
Ronald Starwalt *(Pres.)*
Richard Wilken *(V.P.)*
Reid Anderson *(Treas.)*
Jim Deters *(Controller)*
Chris Wise *(Sec.)*
Roger Miller *(Dir.-Opers.)*
Dennis Montavon *(Gen. Mgr.)*

Computer Systems/Hardware:
IBM System 38

Outside Service Firm(s):

Illinois Agricultural Auditing*(Auditors)*
Bloomington, IL

Farmland Insurance*(Commercial Insurance Carrier)*
1963 Bell Ave.
Des Moines, IA 50315

Lawrence Eaton*(Legal Firm)*
Newton, IL

Co-Bank St. Louis Region*(Major Banking Relationship)*
1415 Olive St.
St. Louis, MO 63166

Branches:

Grand Prarie Co-op, Inc. **(1)**
Box 330, Fulls Siding, R.R. 1
Saint Joseph, IL 61873
Tel.: 217-469-7600
Agricultural Products & Services
S.I.C.: 5153; 5191
Thomas E. Billman *(Mgr.)*

Grand Prairie Co-op, Inc. **(1)**
108 N. Main St.
Saint Joseph, IL 61873
Agricultural Products & Services
S.I.C.: 5153; 5191
Thomas E. Billman *(Mgr.)*

Grand Prairie Co-op, Inc. **(1)**
Sloan Station, R.R. 1
Ivesdale, IL 61851
Tel.: 217-564-2274
Agriculatural Products & Services
S.I.C.: 5153; 5191
Craig Bush *(Mgr.)*

Grand Prairie Co-op, Inc. **(1)**
N. Harrison St.
Philo, IL 61864
Tel.: 217-684-2424
Agriculatural Products & Services
S.I.C.: 5153; 5191
Tom Sinder *(Mgr.)*

Grand Prairie Co-op, Inc. **(1)**
Deers, R.R. 3
Urbana, IL 61801
Agricultural Products & Services
S.I.C.: 5153; 5191
Tom Sinder *(Mgr.)*

Grand Prairie Co-op, Inc. **(1)**
Block, R.R. 1
Sidney, IL 61877
Agricultural Products & Services
S.I.C.: 5153; 5191
Tom Sinder *(Mgr.)*

Grand Prairie Co-op, Inc. **(1)**
Apex, R.R. 1
Tolono, IL 61880
Tel.: 217-485-6000
Tel.: 800-328-4724
Agricultural Products & Services
S.I.C.: 5153; 5191
Roger Miller *(Mgr.)*

Grand Prairie Co-op, Inc. **(1)**
P.O. Box 68,
Savoy, IL 61874
Tel.: 217-359-5500
Agricultural Products & Services
S.I.C.: 5153; 5191
Raphael Billman *(Mgr.)*

GRAND UNION HOLDINGS CORPORATION
(Formerly GND Holdings Corporation)
26 Meadow Road
Riverside, CT 06878
Tel.: 203-637-0511 **DE**
Year Founded: 1989
Assets: $1,512,100,000
Earnings: ($65,100,000)
Net Worth: $1,512,100,000
Approx.Sls.: $2,968,500,000
Emp.: 19,000
Fiscal Year-end: 3/28/92
Supermarkets
S.I.C.: 5411
Gary D. Hirsch *(Chm., Pres., Dir., & Treas.)*

Grand Union Holdings Corporation—(Continued)

Subsidiary:

Grand Union Capital Corporation **(1)**
26 Meadow Rd.
Riverside, CT

Subsidiary:

The Grand Union Company **(2)**
201 Willowbrook Blvd.
Wayne, NJ 07470
Tel.: 201-890-6000
Fax: 201-890-6671
Assets: $713,204,000
Liabilities: $438,212,000
Net Worth: $274,992,000
Approx.Sls.: $3,000,000,000
Emp.: 19000
Fiscal Year-end: 3/28/92
Retail Supermarket Chain; 311 Stores on the East Coast
S.I.C.: 5411
Gary D. Hirsch *(Chm. Bd.)*
Joseph J. McCaig *(Pres. & Chief Exec. Officer)*
William A. Louttit *(Exec. V.P. & Chief Oper. Officer)*
Charles J. Barrett *(Sr. V.P.-Personnel)*
R. Terence Galvin *(Sr. V.P. & Chief Fin. Officer)*
Robert J. Saba *(Sr. V.P.-No. Region)*
Darrell W. Stine *(Sr. V.P.-NY Region)*
Raymond Ayers *(V.P.-Real Estate)*
Kenneth Baum *(V.P. & Controller)*
L. Andrew De Paolis *(V.P.-Adv. & Sls. Promo.)*
Robert P. Ferla *(V.P.-Exec. Devel. & Training)*
James R. Holt *(V.P.-Southern Region)*
William E. Kinslow *(V.P. -Mngmt. Information Systems)*
Frank Nicastro *(V.P. & Treas.)*
Albert Rossi *(V.P.-Facilities Mngmt.)*
Donald C. Vaillancourt *(V.P.-Communications)*
G. Vuolo *(V.P.-Labor Rels.)*
Albert J. Meyer *(Gen. Counsel)*

THE GRANDOE CORPORATION

70-82 Bleecker St.
Gloversville, NY 12078
Mailing Address:
P.O. Box 713
Gloversville, NY 12078
Tel.: 518-725-8641 **NY**
Fax: 518-725-9088
Year Founded: 1919
Emp.: 2,000

Import Export
Men's & Ladies' Dress, Ski Golf & Hunting Gloves; Knit Headwear; Scarfs
S.I.C.: 2253; 2381; 3949
Richard J. Zuckerwar *(Chm. Bd. & Pres.)*
Eric D. Friedman *(V.P. & Sec.)*
Thomas Poliseno *(V.P.-Sls.)*
Paul G. Glotzbecker *(Chief Fin. Officer)*
Jane Zuckerwar *(Treas.)*

No. of Mfg. Plants/Facilities: 3
No. of U.S. Offices: 6
No. of Foreign Offices: 3

Computer Systems/Hardware:
Data General

Outside Service Firm(s):

Ekstein, Lutz, Cichy & Zeronda*(Auditors)*
Gloversville, NY

Key Bank*(Major Banking Relationship)*
Albany, NY

GRANDPA BRANDS COMPANY

317 E. 8th St.
Cincinnati, OH 45202
Tel.: 513-241-1677 **OH**
Fax: 513-241-1676
Year Founded: 1936
Sales Range: $10-19 Million
Emp.: 25

Export
Mfr. of Soaps, Novelties, Dental Aids & Antacid Tablets, Ear Wax Drops, Incense & Silver Plate-it
S.I.C.: 2841; 2834; 2899; 3999; 2844
Benjamin L. Pritz *(Chm. Bd., Pres. & Chief Exec. Officer)*
Phillip Steiner *(Sec.)*
Robert Steiner *(Treas.)*
Donna VonHandof *(Dir.-Customer Service)*
Claire Scudder *(Mgr.-Office)*

Principal(s):
Benjamin L. Pritz
Robert Steiner

Outside Service Firm(s):

Hukill, Hazlett & Harrington*(Group Insurer)*
Cincinnati, OH

The Central Trust Company, N.A.*(Major Banking Relationship)*
Cincinnati, OH
Tel.: 513-651-8896

Divisions:

C.S. Dent & Co. **(1)**
317 E. 8th St.
Cincinnati, OH 45202
Tel.: 513-241-1677
Fax: 513-241-1676
Export
Mfr. of Over-the-Counter Remedies; Incense & Silver-Plating Compounds
S.I.C.: 2834; 2899; 2844; 2841; 2842
Benjamin L. Pritz *(Pres.)*
Donna VonHandorf *(Sec. to the Pres.)*

Grandpa Soap Co. **(1)**
317 E. 8th St.
Cincinnati, OH 45202
Tel.: 513-241-1677
Mfr. of Grandpa's Wonder Pine Tar Soap
S.I.C.: 2841

A. J. Lehman Co. **(1)**
317 E. 8th St.
Cincinnati, OH 45202
Tel.: 513-241-1676
Fax: 513-241-1676
Emp.: 25
Fiscal Year-end: 12/31/89
Extracts & Flavors; Inactive
S.I.C.: 2082; 2086; 2087
Benjamin L. Pritz *(Pres.)*
Phillip Steiner *(Sec.)*
Donna VanNandorf *(Customer Service)*

Par Beverage Co. **(1)**
317 E. 8th St.
Cincinnati, OH 45202
Tel.: 513-241-1677
Mfr. of Novelties
S.I.C.: 5199
Benjamin Pritz *(Pres.)*
Robert L. Steiner *(Treas.)*
Philip Steiner *(Sec.)*

GRANDVILLE PRINTING COMPANY

P.O. Box 247,
Grandville, MI 49468
Year Founded: 1956
Approx.Sls.: $20,000,000
Emp.: 200
Advertising Inserts, Newspapers, Commercial Printing
S.I.C.: 2752
Jeffrey C. Brewer *(Chm. Bd.)*
Patrick Brewer *(Pres.)*
Todd Polavin *(Dir.-Fin.)*

Outside Service Firm(s):

Byker, Van Popering & Berysma*(Auditors)*
Grand Rapids, MI

Warner,Norcross & Judd*(Legal Firm)*
Grand Rapids, MI

Grand Valley National Bank*(Major Banking Relationship)*
Grand Rapids, MI

GRANDY'S, INC.

997 Grandy's Lane
Lewisville, TX 75067
Tel.: 214-317-8000
Fax: 214-317-8134
Fax: 214-317-5631
Year Founded: 1973
Approx.Sls.: $200,000,000
Emp.: 4,200
Fast Food Restaurant Chain
S.I.C.: 5812
Ralph Roberts *(Pres.)*
Robert Speck *(Chief Oper. Officer)*
Grant Miller *(V.P.-Franchising)*
Mary Palumbo *(V.P.-Mktg.)*
Juanita Dostal *(Pur. Dir.)*
Bob McGregor *(Dir.-Human Resources)*

Computer Systems/Hardware:
DEC PDP 11

GRANGER CONSTRUCTION CO.

(Formerly Granger Associates, Inc.)
6267 Aurelius Rd.
Lansing, MI 48909
Mailing Address:
P.O. Box 22187,
Lansing, MI 48909
Tel.: 517-393-1670
Fax: 517-393-1382
Year Founded: 1960
Approx.Sls.: $97,000,000
Fiscal Year-end: 11/30/91
General Construction; Refuse Handling; General Excavating; Solid Waste Disposal
S.I.C.: 1542; 4953
Alton L. Granger *(Chm. & Chief Exec. Officer)*
Gary Granger *(Pres.)*
Dennis Anderson *(V.P.)*
Ray Easton *(V.P., Controller)*
Glenn Granger *(V.P.)*
Jerry Granger *(V.P.)*
Gerry Massa *(V.P.-Estimating)*
David Rockey *(Dir.-Mngmt. Information Systems)*

Principal(s):
Alton L. Granger
Glenn Granger
Jerry Granger

Computer Systems/Hardware:
IBM System 36

Outside Service Firm(s):

Layton & Richardson*(Auditors)*
Lansing, MI

Michigan Mutual Insurance Co.*(Group Insurer)*
Lansing, MI

First of America Bank*(Investment Banker)*
Lansing, MI

First of America Bank*(Major Banking Relationship)*
Lansing, MI

First of America Bank*(Pension Manager)*
Lansing, MI

Division:

Functions **(1)**
6267 Aurelius Rd.
Lansing, MI 48909
Tel.: 517-393-1670
Fax: 517-393-1382
S.I.C.: 1542; 4953
Larry W. Moore *(Administrator)*

GRANITE STATE MANUFACTURING CO.

(An Allard Industries Company)
124 Joliette St.
Manchester, NH 03105
Tel.: 603-668-1900
Fax: 603-668-1906
Year Founded: 1938
Approx.Sls.: $20,000,000
Emp.: 100
Fiscal Year-end: 6/30/93

Export
Mfr. Antenna & Radar Systems, Industrial Transmissions, Specialty Machine Equip.
S.I.C.: 3559; 3663; 3812
Gerald R. Allard *(Chm. Bd.)*
Ronald A. Allard *(Pres.)*
Charles L. Ferguson *(Sr. V.P.)*
Robert Martin *(V.P.-New Bus. Devel.)*
Michael Allard *(V.P.-Opers.)*
Maurice E. Allard *(Treas. & Controller)*
Dennis Ringland *(Dir.-Sls. & Mktg.)*
Carlo Carluccio *(Div. Mgr.)*
Gary Pinard *(Mgr.-Pur.)*

Subsidiary:

Snow-Nabstedt Power Transmissions **(1)**
111 Joliette St.
Manchester, NH 03102
Tel.: 603-668-1900
Fax: 603-668-1906
Emp.: 100
Export
Industrial Transmissions
S.I.C.: 3599; 3568
R. Allard *(Pres.)*
C. Carluccio *(Div. Mgr.)*

GRANITE STATE PACKING CO.

(d/b/a Jac Pac Food)
163 Hancock St.
Manchester, NH 03101
Mailing Address:
P.O. Box 5220,
Manchester, NH 03108
Tel.: 603-669-3300 **NH**
Fax: 603-669-9886
Year Founded: 1929
Approx.Sls.: $90,000,000
Emp.: 350

Import Export
Mfr. of Frozen Meats From Purchased Meat
S.I.C.: 2011
Corporate Giving Program: 2nd Harvest
Irwin Muskat *(Chm. Bd., Pres. & Chief Exec. Officer)*
Charles Hungler *(Chief Fin. Officer)*
Theodore Krentzel *(Exec. V.P.)*
Darryl Armstrong *(V.P.-Sls.)*
Roger Sheely *(V.P.-Res. & Devel.)*
William S. Green *(Sec.)*
Richard A. Morse *(Gen. Counsel)*
Darryl Armstrong *(Dir.-Sls.& Mktg.)*
Mac Baker *(Dir.-Pur.)*
Ed McDougall *(Dir.-Human Resources)*

Outside Service Firm(s):

Tules, Miller & Co.*(Auditors)*
Boston, MA

Sheehan, Phinney, Bass & Green*(Legal Firm)*
Manchester, NH

Fleet National Bank*(Major Banking Relationship)*
Manchester, NH

GRANITEVILLE CO.
Marshall St.
Graniteville, SC 29829
Mailing Address:
P.O. Box 128,
Graniteville, SC 29829
Tel.: 803-663-7231 SC
Fax: 803-663-7316
Assets: $162,966,114
Liabilities: $75,831,173
Net Worth: $87,134,941
Approx.Sls.: $400,000,000
Emp.: 4,000
Mfr. & Finisher of Textiles
S.I.C.: 2211
Victor Posner *(Chm. Bd. & Chief Exec. Officer)*
Steven Posner *(Vice Chm.)*
Harold D. Kingsmore *(Pres. & Chief Oper. Officer)*
John L. Barnes, Jr. *(Exec. V.P.)*
William E. Johnson *(V.P.-Admin.)*
Ira E. Coward *(Chief Engineer)*
Frank Harling *(Personnel Dir.)*
Ron Knight *(Dir.-Mngmt. Information Systems)*
Principal(s):
Victor Posner
Steven Posner

No. of Mfg. Plants/Facilities: 4

Computer Systems/Hardware:
Burroughs; Wang

Outside Service Firm(s):

Arthur Andersen & Co.*(Auditors)*
Columbia, SC

National Union Fire Ins. Co. of Pittsburgh, Pa.*(Commercial Insurance Carrier)*
70 Pine St.
New York, NY 10270
Tel.: 212-770-7000

Divisions:

Gregg Div. **(1)**
Main St.
Graniteville, SC 29829
Tel.: 803-663-7231
Dyeing & Finishing Cotton & Polyester Yarns
S.I.C.: 2269
Craig M. Burgess *(Plant Mgr.)*

Hickman Div. **(1)**
Main St.
Graniteville, SC 29829
Tel.: 803-663-7231
S.I.C.: 2211
John Overstreet *(Plant Mgr.)*

Sibley Div. **(1)**
Goodrich St.
Augusta, GA 30904
Tel.: 706-724-8211
S.I.C.: 2211
Leighton C. Melendon, Jr. *(Plant Mgr.)*

Sutherland Div. **(1)**
Cottage St.
Augusta, GA 30901
Tel.: 706-722-8020
S.I.C.: 2211
Edgar S. Bell *(Plant Mgr.)*

Swint Div. **(1)**
Main St.
Graniteville, SC 29829
Tel.: 803-663-7231
S.I.C.: 2211
D. T. Atkinson *(Plant Mgr.)*

Townsend Div. **(1)**
Main St.
Graniteville, SC 29829
Tel.: 803-663-7231
S.I.C.: 2211
William R. Alexander *(Supt.)*

Warren Div. **(1)**
Marshall St.
Graniteville, SC 29829
Tel.: 803-663-7231

Woodhead Div. **(1)**
Main St.
Graniteville, SC 29829
Tel.: 803-663-7731
S.I.C.: 2211
Harry S. Witt *(Plant Mgr.)*

Subsidiary;

C. H. Patrick & Co., Inc. **(1)**
P.O. Box 2526,
Greenville, SC 29602
Tel.: 803-244-4831 (100%)
Emp.: 42
Chemicals
S.I.C.: 2819
John K. Boykin *(Pres.)*

GRANT/JACOBY, INC.

GRANT/JACOBY, INC.
737 N. Michigan Ave.
Chicago, IL 60611
Tel.: 312-664-2055
Fax: 312-664-3596
Year Founded: 1938
Approx.Billings: $65,845,000
Emp.: 100
Bruce I. Carlson *(Chm. & Chief Exec. Officer)*
R. Milton Lynnes *(Pres. & Chief Oper. Officer)*
Robert W. Lavender *(Sr. V.P., Opers.)*
Pam Prosch *(Sr. V.P., Dir. Strategic Devel.)*
Timothy J. Grob *(V.P., Chief Fin. & Admin. Officer)*
Marty Kierzek *(V.P., Controller)*
Tom Langner *(Dir.-Creative & Sls. Promo.)*
Debbie Leider *(Dir.-Pub. Rels.)*
Jim Head *(Sr. V.P., Co-Dir.)*
Peggy Nordeen *(Sr. V.P.)*

GRANT-LYDICK BEVERAGE CO.
(d/b/a Big Red Bottling Co. of San Antonio)
4518 Old Sequin Rd.
San Antonio, TX 78220
Mailing Address:
P.O. Box 200243
San Antonio, TX 78220
Tel.: 210-661-4271
Approx.Sls.: $25,000,000
Emp.: 185
Soft Drink Bottler
S.I.C.: 2086
H.L. Grant *(Chm. Bd.)*
J. Lee Lydick *(Pres.)*
Emery J. Bodnar *(Exec. V.P.)*
Kevin G. Donnellan *(V.P.-Mfg. Opers.)*
Cecil Sorsby *(V.P.-Sls.)*
Michael Grant *(Sec. & Treas.)*
Margaret L. Jones *(Controller)*

Divisions:

Big Red RC & 7-Up of LaGrange, TX **(1)**
189 S. Brown
La Grange, TX 78945
Tel.: 409-968-3451
S.I.C.: 2086

7UP/RC of Austin **(1)**
3411 Hidalgo St.
Austin, TX 78702
Tel.: 512038504477
S.I.C.: 2086

7UP of Corpus Christi **(1)**
3127 Cabaniss Pkwy.
Corpus Christi, TX 78415
Tel.: 512-851-9977
S.I.C.: 2086

7UP/RC of Harlingen **(1)**
915 Ed Carey Dr.
Harlingen, TX 78550
Tel.: 210-423-2705
S.I.C.: 2086

7Up of Victoria **(1)**
3704 Billy Dr.
Victoria, TX 77901
Tel.: 512-575-1721
S.I.C.: 2086

Grant
Marketing Communications Inc.

GRANT MARKETING COMMUNICATIONS INC.
2001 Joshua Rd.
Lafayette Hill, PA 19444
Tel.: 215-834-0550
Fax: 215-834-0524
Year Founded: 1976
Approx.Billings: $12,550,000
Emp.: 25
Advertising Agency
S.I.C.: 7311
Howard C. Grant *(Chm. & Pres.)*
John Seddon Wilson, III *(Sr. V.P.-Mktg. & Media Plng.)*
Ernst McKenna *(V.P. & Dir.-Grant Design)*
Ruth von Kummer *(V.P. & Dir.-Grant Direct)*
Shirley Grant *(Sec. & Treas.)*
Barbara Aumann Moss *(Dir.- Pub. Rels.)*

Subsidiaries:

Grant Design **(1)**
2001 Joshua Rd.
Lafayette Hill, PA 19444
Tel.: 215-834-0550
Ernst McKenna *(Dir.)*

Grant Promotion **(1)**
2001 Joshua Rd.
Lafayette Hill, PA 19444
Tel.: 215-834-0550
John Seddon Wilson, III *(Dir.)*

Grant Public Relations **(1)**
2001 Joshua Rd.
Lafayette Hill, PA 19444
Tel.: 215-834-0550
Public Relations
S.I.C.: 8743
Barbara Aumann Moss *(Dir.)*

GRANT THORNTON
Prudential Plaza, Ste. 800
Chicago, IL 60601
Tel.: 312-856-0001
Fax: 312-861-1340
Year Founded: 1924
Approx.Sls.: $215,000,000
Emp.: 2,500
Fiscal Year-end: 7/31/92
Import Export
Accounting, Auditing, Tax & Management Consulting Services
S.I.C.: 8721
Employee Matching Gifts Program: To Qualified Colleges & Universities
Robert E. Nason *(Exec. Partner)*
David H. Abramson *(Area Mng. Partner)*
John C. Burke *(Area Mng. Partner)*
Domenick J. Esposito *(Area Mng. Partner)*
Richard S. Delaney *(Area Mng. Partner)*
Burt Fischer *(Area Mng. Partner)*
James P. Hayden *(Area Mng. Partner)*
Edward J. Vonderbrink *(Area Mng. Partner)*
Robert A. Kleckner *(Mng. Dir. & Intl. Dir.)*
Patrick D. Zorsch *(Natl. Dir.-Mngmt. Consultant)*
Howard Groveman *(Natl. Dir.-Acct. & Audit)*
John M. Latta *(Natl. Dir.-Tax Practice)*
Daniel C. Shogren *(Natl. Dir.-Human Resources)*
Theodore J. Thompson *(Natl. Dir.-Fin. & Admin.)*

No. of U.S. Offices: 44
No. of Foreign Offices: 250

Computer Systems/Hardware:
IBM 9375

Outside Service Firm(s):

Metropolitan Life Insurance Co.*(Group Insurer)*
One Madison Ave.
New York, NY 10010-3690
Tel.: 215-578-9292

GRANTHAM COMPANY
2685 Hansrob Rd.
Orlando, FL 32804
Tel.: 407-299-6446 FL
Fax: 407-295-7104
Approx.Sls.: $53,000,000
Emp.: 110
Wholesale Beer, Wine & Liquor
S.I.C.: 5181; 5182
H. Varley Grantham *(Pres.)*
Linda Grantham *(Treas.)*

Outside Service Firm(s):

Forness, Graham & Cottrill*(Auditors)*
Orlando, FL

GRANTREE CORPORATION
9775 S.W. Gemini Dr.
Beaverton, OR 97005
Mailing Address:
P.O. Box 3210,
Portland, OR 97208
Tel.: 503-644-5500 OR
Fax: 503-520-0539
Year Founded: 1919
Assets: $15,875,000
Liabilities: $12,467,000
Net Worth: $3,408,000
Approx.Rev.: $40,000,000
Emp.: 460
Fiscal Year-end: 4/ 1/92
Import Export
Furniture Rental Services for Home & Office; Sale of Used Furniture
S.I.C.: 7359; 5712; 5932
Corporate Giving Program: United Appeal Only
Ralph Van Horne *(Chm. Bd.)*
Jerry L. Kilb *(Pres. & Chief Oper. Officer)*
Russell B. Jones *(Sr. V.P.-Fin., Treas., Chief Fin. Officer & Sec.)*
G. Drew Blevins *(V.P.-Adv. & Mktg.)*
Lee Dambis *(V.P.-Real Estate)*
Elizabeth Ettling *(Controller)*
Rick Hartman *(Dir.-Mngmt. Information Systems)*

Computer Systems/Hardware:
IBM/Hewlett-Packard

Outside Service Firm(s):

KPMG Peat Marwick*(Auditors)*
1211 S.W. Fifth Ave.
Portland, OR 97204

Miller, Nash, Wiener, Hager & Carlsen*(Legal Firm)*
Portland, OR

GranTree Corporation—(Continued)

First Interstate Bank*(Major Banking Relationship)*
P.O. Box 3131,
Portland, OR 97208
Tel.: 503-220-4855
Fax: 503-225-7153

Subsidiary:

Multiform Enterprises, Inc. **(1)**
2701 N.W. Vaughn, Ste. 890
Portland, OR 97201
Tel.: 503-223-1161 (100%)
Furniture Rental & Sls.
S.I.C.: 7359

GRAPHIC CENTER, INC.
26 Tobey Rd.
Bloomfield, CT 06002
Tel.: 203-522-2233 **CT**
Fax: 203-243-5002
Approx.Sls.: $12,000,000
Emp.: 155
Book & Commercial Printing, Typesetting
S.I.C.: 2732; 2752; 2791
Guy Hains *(Pres.)*
James Martocchie *(Sr. V.P.)*
Donald L. Cagenello *(Sec. & Treas.)*

Outside Service Firm(s):

Lenkowski, Lonergan & Company*(Auditors)*
Waterbury, CT

Silverstein & Osach*(Legal Firm)*
New Haven, CT

Connecticut Bank & Trust*(Major Banking Relationship)*
One Constitution Plaza,
Hartford, CT 06115

GRAPHIC CONTROLS, CORP.
(Formerly Graphic Controls, Inc.)
189 Van Rensselaer
Buffalo, NY 14210
Mailing Address:
P.O. Box 1271
Buffalo, NY 14240-1271
Tel.: 716-853-7500
Tel.: 800-669-1535
Telex: 200902 GRAP UR
Fax: 716-849-6404
Assets: $91,283,000
Liabilities: $106,404,000
Net Worth: $15,121,000
Approx.Sls.: $177,043,000
Emp.: 1,574
Fiscal Year-end: 12/31/91
Import Export
Mfr. of Chart & Graph Paper, Marking Devices; EKG & EEG Disposable Electrodes, Conductivity Gels, Pen Plotter Supplies & Facsimile Papers
S.I.C.: 3953; 2759; 2782; 3800
Corporate Giving Program: Approximately $100,000/Year
Employee Matching Gifts Program: 1 For 1 Match Up to $1,000/Employee Maximum
Donald P. Quinlan *(Chm. Bd., Pres. & Chief Exec. Officer)*
William C. Gates *(Chief Fin. Officer, V.P. & Treas.)*
Duane B. Hopper *(Exec. V.P.)*
Larry R. Drake *(V.P.-Human Resources & Information Services)*
Robert A. Evans *(V.P.)*
Anders E. Mailow *(V.P.-Intl. Opers. & New Devel.)*
Dennis Szywala *(Controller)*
Patricia Baubonis *(Sec. & Mgr.-Legal Services)*
Ron Liss *(Dir.-Data Processing)*
Felix Brown *(Mgr.-Res. & Devel.)*
Ron Fleissner *(Mgr.-Corp. Acctg.)*
May C. Randazzo *(Mgr.-Pub. Affairs/ Communication)*
Jannie Redmon *(Mgr.-Human Resources & Training & Devel.)*
E.M. Roth *(Mgr.-Sls.)*
Raul Saona *(Mgr.-Intl. Sls. & Mktg.)*
E. Sulick *(Gen. Sls. Mgr.-Medical)*
Jeff Westcott *(Mgr.-Telecommunications)*

No. of Mfg. Plants/Facilities: 10
No. of U.S. Offices: 10
No. of Foreign Offices: 7

Computer Systems/Hardware:
IBM 9000

Outside Service Firm(s):

Ernst & Young*(Auditors)*
1400 Key Tower - 50 Fountain Plaza
Buffalo, NY
Tel.: 716-843-5000
Fax: 716-847-6949

Alexander & Alexander*(Commercial Insurance Carrier)*
One Constitution Plaza
New York, NY 10036
Tel.: 617-241-9800

Atlantic Mutual Insurance*(Commercial Insurance Carrier)*
New York, NY

Johnson & Higgins*(Commercial Insurance Carrier)*
125 Broad St.
New York, NY 10004-2424
Tel.: 212-574-7000
Fax: 212-574-8988

Marsh & McLennan*(Commercial Insurance Carrier)*
10 Lafayette Sq.
Buffalo, NY
Tel.: 716-854-7290
Fax: 716-854-7120

Protection Mutual*(Commercial Insurance Carrier)*
Boston, MA

Damon & Morey*(Legal Firm)*
1000 Cathedral Plaza
Buffalo, NY
Tel.: 716-856-5500
Fax: 716-856-5510

Fleet Bank*(Major Banking Relationship)*
Deer Park, NY 14202

M & T Bank*(Major Banking Relationship)*
One M & T Plaza
Buffalo, NY
Tel.: 716-842-5073

Marine Midland Bank*(Major Banking Relationship)*
P.O. Box 803, 1 Marine Midland Center, 23rd Floor
Buffalo, NY 14203
Tel.: 716-841-2582

Templeton Investment Counsel*(Pension Manager)*
New York, NY

Divisions:

Graphic Controls Industrial Products Div. **(1)**
P.O. Box 1271
Buffalo, NY 14240
Tel.: 716-853-7500

Graphic Controls Medical Products Div. **(1)**
P.O. Box 1271
Buffalo, NY 14240
Tel.: 716-853-7500

Subsidiary:

Graphic Controls Corporation **(1)**
189 Van Rensselaer
Buffalo, NY 14210
Tel.: 716-853-7500
Tel.: 800-669-4428
Fax: 716-849-6404
Assets: $138,759,000
Earnings: $2,218,000
Liabilities: $128,465,000
Net Worth: $10,294,000
Approx.Sls.: $161,589,000
Emp.: 1,588
Fiscal Year-end: 12/31/90
Computer Systems/Hardware:
IBM 3081-6
Mfr. of Charts, Markers, Coated Papers, Disposable Medical Products, Recording Charts, Coated Products, EKG & EEG Disposable Electrodes, ECG Paper, Conductivity Gels, Lab Forms, Marking Systems, Pen Plotter Supplies & Facsimile Papers
S.I.C.: 3953; 2671; 3842; 3800
Donald P. Quinlan *(Chm. Bd., Pres., Chief Exec. & Chief Oper. Officer)*
Larry R. Drake *(V.P.-Human Resources & Information Services)*
Robert A. Evans *(V.P. & Gen. Mgr.-Information Prods.)*
William C. Gates *(V.P., Treas. & Chief Fin. Officer)*
Anders E. Mailow *(V.P.-New Devel.)*
Patricia Baubonis *(Sec.)*
Ron Liss *(Dir.-Data Processing)*
E. Sulick *(Gen. Sls. Mgr.-Medical)*
Felix Brown *(Mgr.-Res. & Devel.)*
Ron Fleissner *(Mgr.-Corp. Acctg.)*
May C. Randazzo *(Mgr.-Pub. Affairs & Communication)*
Jannie Redmon *(Mgr.-Personnel Training & Devel.)*
E.M. Roth *(Mgr.-Sls.-Information Prods.)*
Raul Saona *(Mgr.-Intl. Sls. & Mktg.)*
Jeff Westcott *(Mgr.-Telecommunications)*

GRAPHIC PRODUCTIONS COMPANY
5600 N.W. 32nd Ave.
Miami, FL 33142
Tel.: 305-635-8655
Tel.: 800-634-1304 **FL**
Fax: 305-638-4833
Approx.Sls.: $24,000,000
Emp.: 170
Commercial Printers
S.I.C.: 2752; 2759
Noel Hernandez *(Chm. Bd., Pres. & Chief Fin. Officer)*
George B. San Meguel *(V.P. & Comptroller)*
Thelma Rodriguez *(Grp. V.P. & Sec.)*
Georgette Franco *(Dir.-Human Resources)*
Fred Haas *(Gen. Mgr.)*

Outside Service Firm(s):

Andres J. Triaky, Jr.*(Auditors)*
Coral Gables, FL

Bank of Coral Gables*(Major Banking Relationship)*
Coral Gables, FL

GRAPHISPHERE HOLDING COMPANY
2170 So. Mannheim Rd.
Des Plaines, IL 60018
Tel.: 708-635-8000
Tel.: 800-552-0840
Fax: 708-635-0691
Approx.Sls.: $115,000,000
Emp.: 700
Holding Company for Printing Companies
S.I.C.: 6719; 2759; 2789
Gary Ingersoll *(Pres.)*
Elizabeth Kepuraitis *(Chief Fin. Officer)*
Mark Just *(V.P.-Sls.)*

No. of Mfg. Plants/Facilities: 3

Outside Service Firm(s):

Lakeshore National Bank*(Major Banking Relationship)*
Chicago, IL

Freeborn & Peters*(Legal Firm)*
11 S. LaSalle St.
Chicago, IL 60603
Tel.: 312-750-9500

Subsidiaries:

Bradley Printing Company **(1)**
2170 S. Mannheim Rd.
Des Plaines, IL 60018
Tel.: 708-635-8000
Tel.: 800-552-0840 (100%)
Fax: 708-635-5064
Approx.Sls.: $90,000,000
Emp.: 575
Fiscal Year-end: 12/31/91
Computer Systems/Hardware:
Data General
Off-Set Printers with Bindery Facilities
S.I.C.: 2759; 2789
Gary R. Ingersoll *(Pres. & Chief Exec. Officer)*
Elizabeth Kepuraitis *(Chief Fin. Officer & V.P.)*
Lawrence E. Just *(Asst. Sec. & Gen. Counsel)*
Mark Just *(V.P.-Sls.)*
Karl Saionz *(V.P.-Finishing)*
Charles Chalifoux *(V.P.-Mfg.)*
Robert Czerniak *(V.P.-Press Opers.)*
Michelle Coughlin *(Dir.-Pur.)*
Eric Schulz *(Dir.-Data Processing)*
Patricia De Marco *(Dir.-Personnel)*
Douglas M. Black *(Controller)*

Midwest Litho Arts **(1)**
125 E. Oakton
Des Plaines, IL 60018
Tel.: 708-296-2000 (100%)
Emp.: 120
Printing Company
S.I.C.: 2752
Larry Babka *(Pres.)*
Larry Menconi *(V.P.-Sls.)*
David Cimo *(Controller)*

Paper Express **(1)**
1605 Winthrop Ave.
Des Plaines, IL 60018
Tel.: 708-297-9950 (100%)
Printing And Wrighting Paper
S.I.C.: 5111

EARL G. GRAVES, LTD.
130 Fifth Ave.
New York, NY 10011
Tel.: 212-242-8000 **NY**
Fax: 212-886-9615
Approx.Sls.: $17,500,000
Emp.: 64
Communications
S.I.C.: 2721
Earl G. Graves *(Chm. Bd., Pres. & Chief Exec. Officer)*
Luther M. Ragin, Jr. *(Chief Fin. Officer)*
Earl G. Graves, Jr. *(Sr. V.P.-Sls. & Mktg.)*
Barbara Graves *(Gen. Mgr.)*
Principal(s):
Earl G. Graves

No. of U.S. Offices: 2

Outside Service Firm(s):

Mitchell Titus & Co.*(Auditors)*
New York, NY

Cowan, Liebowitz & Latman*(Legal Firm)*
New York, NY

Chase Manhattan Bank, N.A.*(Major Banking Relationship)*
One Chase Manhattan Plaza
New York, NY 10081
Tel.: 212-552-2222
Tel.: 800-526-0801
Fax: 212-552-7175

Subsidiary:

Earl G. Graves Publishing Co., Inc. **(1)**
130 Fifth Ave.
New York, NY 10011
Tel.: 212-242-8000 (100%)
Fax: 212-886-9615
Publishing Company
S.I.C.: 2721

GRAVYMASTER INC.
16 Business Park Dr.
Branford, CT 06405
Tel.: 203-481-2276
Fax: 203-488-8085
Year Founded: 1935
Emp.: 35
Export
Seasonings & Browning Sauce; Rock Candy Products
S.I.C.: 2099; 2033; 2064
John M. Mills *(Chm. Bd.)*
Stephen Besse *(Pres.)*

Richard M. Accola *(V.P.-Sls. & Mktg.)*

Computer Systems/Hardware:
Qantel

Division:

Dryden & Palmer Company **(1)**
16 Business Park Dr.
Branford, CT 06405
Tel.: 203-481-2276
Stephen A. Besse *(Pres. & Chief Oper. Officer)*
Richard M. Accola *(V.P.-Sls. & Mktg.)*

GRAY BAUMGARTEN LAYPORT, INC.
2275 Swallow Hill Rd
Pittsburgh, PA 15220
Tel.: 412-279-3732
Fax: 412-279-7870
Year Founded: 1977
Approx.Billings: $12,000,000
Emp.: 20
Full Service Advertising & Public Relations, With Extensive Experience in Health Care Advertising & Public Relations
Mark H. Gray *(Pres.)*
Ronald J. Baumgarten *(V.P., Opers.)*
Carol Gray *(Dir. Pub. Rels.)*
Sean Smith *(Acct. Mgr., Pub. Rels.)*
Anna Parisi *(Acctg.)*

Computer Systems/Hardware:
MacIntosh

JAMES N. GRAY CONSTRUCTION CO., INC.
250 W. Main St., Ste. 2500
Lexington, KY 40507-1760
Tel.: 606-281-5000 **KY**
Fax: 606-252-5300
Year Founded: 1960
Assets: $25,362,234
Liabilities: $16,049,158
Net Worth: $9,313,076
Sales Range: $100-499 Million
Emp.: 350
Fiscal Year-end: 3/31/91
Design, Engineering, Construction-Primarily for Industrial Manufacturing Plants
S.I.C.: 8711; 1541
Lois Howard Gray *(Chm. Bd.)*
C.C. Howard Gray *(Pres. & Chief Exec. Officer)*
James P. Gray, II *(Chief Oper. Officer)*
Franklin N. Gray *(Exec. V.P.)*
Danny B. Parrish *(V.P.-Fin., Asst. Sec. & Asst. Treas.)*
Alan L. Fowler *(V.P.-Mktg.)*
Kevin B. Burford *(Dir.-Personnel)*
Principal(s):
Lois Howard Gray
C.C. Howard Gray
James P. Gray, II
Franklin N. Gray

No. of U.S. Offices: 4
No. of Foreign Offices: 1

Computer Systems/Hardware:
IBM AS400

Outside Service Firm(s):

Ernst & Young*(Auditors)*
Lexington, KY

CNA Insurance*(Commercial Insurance Carrier)*
Indianapolis, IN

Blue Cross & Blue Shield of Kentucky*(Group Insurer)*
9901 Linn Station Rd.
Louisville, KY 40223
Tel.: 502-426-3700

Garmon & Goodman*(Legal Firm)*
Glasgow, KY

Liberty National Bank & Trust Co.*(Major Banking Relationship)*
416 W. Jefferson St.
Louisville, KY 40202
Tel.: 502-566-2000

Shearson Lehman Brothers, Inc.*(Pension Manager)*
Louisville, KY

GRAY KIRK/VANSANT ADVERTISING, INC.
The World Trade Center
Baltimore, MD 21202
Tel.: 410-539-5400
Fax: 410-234-2441
Year Founded: 1912
Approx.Billings: $75,000,000
Emp.: 75
Kenneth E. Mayhorne *(Chm.)*
Roger L. Gray *(Pres. & Chief Exec. Officer)*
Graham V. Kirk *(Sr. Exec. V.P., Chief Oper. Officer)*
Margot A. Amelia *(Sr. V.P., Acct. Admin.)*
Carolyn Bodie *(V.P., Pub. Rels.)*
Barbara Wells *(V.P., Controller)*

GRAY PRINTING CO.
401 E. North St.
Fostoria, OH 44830
Mailing Address:
P.O. Box 840
Fostoria, OH 44830
Tel.: 419-435-6638 **OH**
Fax: 419-435-9410
Year Founded: 1888
Sales Range: $10-19 Million
Emp.: 155
Commercial & Publication Printing
S.I.C.: 2731; 2759
Thomas M. Gray *(Chm. Bd.)*
Robert A. Gray *(Pres. & Chief Exec. Officer)*
Scott A. Gray *(V.P.-Sls. & Mktg.)*
Floyd J. Lawless *(Controller)*
Lisa Fisher *(Sec.)*
Robert Etzinger *(Dir.-Pur.)*
Maxine Mazza *(Dir.-Human Resources)*
Principal(s):
Thomas M. Gray
Robert A. Gray

Outside Service Firm(s):

Ernst & Young*(Auditors)*
One Sea Gate
Toledo, OH 43604
Tel.: 419-244-8000

Marshall & Melhorn*(Legal Firm)*
Toledo, OH

Fifth Third Bank*(Major Banking Relationship)*
Corporate Trust Services, 38 Fountain Square Plaza
Cincinnati, OH 45263

GRAY-PRO, INC.
(d/b/a Express Services, Inc.)
2741 Mapleton
Boulder, CO 80304
Mailing Address:
P.O. Box 7250
Boulder, CO 80306
Tel.: 303-443-1700 **CO**
Fax: 303-443-1939
Year Founded: 1973
Assets: $1,296,824
Liabilities: $2,072
Net Worth: $1,294,752
Approx.Sls.: $10,000,000
Emp.: 36
Fiscal Year-end: 12/31/91
Temporary Help Services
S.I.C.: 7361; 7363
James R. Gray *(Pres.)*
Miles Hamm *(V.P. & Gen. Mgr.)*
Carol G. Gray *(V.P.)*
Dorothy Van Treeck *(Sec. & Dir.-Data Processing)*
Jeffrey Gazaway *(Branch Mgr.)*
Marty Quigley *(Branch Mgr.)*
Jim Finnegan *(Admin. Asst.)*

No. of U.S. Offices: 4

Computer Systems/Hardware:
IBM System 36

Outside Service Firm(s):

William H. Bickell*(Auditors)*
Boulder, CO

Beeson Taggart & Assoc.*(Commercial Insurance Carrier)*
Boulder, CO

United Bank of Colorado*(Major Banking Relationship)*
Boulder, CO

JACK GRAY TRANSPORT, INC.
4600 E. 15th Ave.
Gary, IN 46403
Tel.: 219-938-7020 **IN**
Fax: 219-938-7020, Ext. 284
Approx.Sls.: $70,000,000
Emp.: 250
Fiscal Year-end: 12/31/91
Long Distance Trucking; Dry Bulk Commodities
S.I.C.: 4213
John S. Gray, Sr. *(Chm. Bd. & Pres.)*
Gary I. Goldberg *(Exec. V.P.)*
Duane O'Donnell *(Sr. V.P.)*
Carmen Mormino *(V.P.)*
Edwin L. Wesner *(V.P.-Fin.)*
Diane R. Jones *(Sec. & Dir.-Admin. Services)*
Barbara Milligan *(Controller)*

Outside Service Firm(s):

Ernst & Young*(Auditors)*
233 S. Wacker Dr.
Chicago, IL 60606
Tel.: 312-368-1800
Fax: 312-645-3095

Russell Millbrath & Associates*(Legal Firm)*
Winamac, IN

Mellon Bank N.A.*(Major Banking Relationship)*
1 Mellon Center
Pittsburgh, PA 15258

Division:

Lake & River Transfer Div. **(1)**
4600 E. 15th Ave.
Gary, IN 46403
Tel.: 219-938-7020
Heavy Hauling
S.I.C.: 4212
John S. Gray, Sr. *(Pres.)*

GRAYBAR ELECTRIC COMPANY, INC.
34 N. Meramec Ave.
Clayton, MO 63105
Mailing Address:
P.O. Box 7231
St. Louis, MO 63177
Tel.: 314-727-3900 **NY**
Fax: 314-727-0788
Year Founded: 1869
Approx.Sls.: $1,900,000,000
Emp.: 4,800
Fiscal Year-end: 12/31/91
Export
Trucking & Warehousing; Retail Stores; Electrical Wholesale Distributor
S.I.C.: 5063
E.A. McGrath *(Pres.)*
John R. Seaton *(V.P. & Comptroller)*
Aubrey A. Thompson *(V.P.-Mktg. & Sls.)*
G.S. Tulloch *(V.P., Sec. & Gen. Counsel)*
J.F. VanPelt *(V.P.-Human Resources)*
J.W. Wolf *(V.P. & Treas.)*
Roy J. McRee *(Dir.-Mngmt. Information Systems)*
Don Folkemer *(Natl. Mgr.-Adv. & Sls. Promo.)*
R.E. Lentes *(Mgr.-Empl. Ben.)*

No. of U.S. Offices: 200
No. of Foreign Offices: 5

Computer Systems/Hardware:
Honeywell

Outside Service Firm(s):

Towers, Perrin, Forster & Crosby*(Auditors)*
101 South Hanley
St. Louis, MO 63105
Tel.: 314-854-4900
Fax: 314-854-4953

Breed, Abbott & Morgan*(Legal Firm)*
Citicorp Center, 153 E. 53rd St.
New York, NY 10002
Tel.: 212-888-0800

Boatmen's Trust Company*(Major Banking Relationship)*
100 North Broadway
St. Louis, MO 63102
Tel.: 314-466-2469

Chase Manhattan Bank, N.A.*(Major Banking Relationship)*
One Chase Manhattan Plaza
New York, NY 10081
Tel.: 212-552-2222
Tel.: 800-526-0801
Fax: 212-552-7175

Chemical Bank*(Major Banking Relationship)*
450 West 33rd St.
New York, NY 10001
Tel.: 212-613-7197
Fax: 212-947-7628

Irving Trust Co.*(Major Banking Relationship)*
New York, NY

Mercantile Bank*(Major Banking Relationship)*
Saint Louis, MO

Equitable Real Estate Investment Managment Inc.*(Pension Manager)*
3414 Peachtree Rd. N.E.
Atlanta, GA 30326-1162

John Hancock Mutual Life Insurance Co.*(Pension Manager)*
John Hancock Place, P.O. Box 111
Boston, MA 02117

Subsidiary:

Graybar International, Inc. **(1)**
34 N. Meramec Ave.
Clayton, MO 63103
Tel.: 314-727-3900
Wholesale Electrical & Telecommunications Distribution
S.I.C.: 5063

GRAYCOR, INC.
One Graycor Dr.
Homewood, IL 60430
Tel.: 708-206-0500 **IL**
Fax: 312-221-7119
Year Founded: 1921
Approx.Sls.: $150,000,000
Emp.: 1,000
Fiscal Year-end: 9/30/91
Holding Company: General Contractor
S.I.C.: 6719; 1541; 1542; 1795; 1629
Melvin Gray *(Chm. & Chief Exec. Officer)*

Graycor, Inc.—(Continued)

R.E. Rolwing *(Pres.)*
Michael O. Mizanin *(V.P.-Fin.)*
Brian Redington *(V.P.-Mktg.)*
Principal(s):
Melvin Gray

Outside Service Firm(s):

Altschuler, Melvoin & Glasser*(Auditors)*
30 S. Wecker Dr.
Chicago, IL 60606
Tel.: 312-207-2800

Artex Insurance Agency, Inc.*(Commercial Insurance Carrier)*
12222 Merit Drive, Suite 1660
Dallas, TX 75251

Principal Mutual Life Insurance Co.*(Group Insurer)*
Rolling Meadows, IL

Altheimer & Gray*(Legal Firm)*
10 S. Wacker Dr.
Chicago, IL 60606
Tel.: 312-715-4000

American National Bank & Trust Company of Chicago*(Major Banking Relationship)*
33 N. LaSalle St.
Chicago, IL 60602
Tel.: 312-661-5000
Fax: 312-661-6417

Harris Associates, L.P.*(Pension Manager)*
Two North LaSalle St.
Chicago, IL 60606-3790
Tel.: 312-621-0600

Subsidiaries:

Chicago Blasting Company **(1)**
12233 Ave. O
Chicago, IL 60633
Tel.: 312-933-1100
Dynamiting
S.I.C.: 1795
J.D. Martin *(V.P.)*

The Edward Gray Corp. **(1)**
1 Graycor Dr.
Homewood, IL 60430
Tel.: 708-206-0500
Fax: 312-221-7119
Emp.: 900
General Building Contractors; Heavy Construction; Machinery Installations; Precision Blasting; Steel & Aluminum Mill Services
S.I.C.: 1541; 1542; 1629; 1795
Melvin Gray *(Chm. Bd. & Chief Exec. Officer)*
Robert Rolwing *(Pres.)*

Gray International **(1)**
1 Graycor Dr.
Homewood, IL 60430
Tel.: 708-206-0500
General Contractors
S.I.C.: 1541; 1542
Don Kaye *(V.P.)*

Inland Construction Company **(1)**
1 Graycor Dr.
Homewood, IL 60430
Tel.: 708-206-0500
General Contractor
S.I.C.: 1542
Melvin Gray *(Chm. Bd. & Chief Exec. Officer)*
Robert Rolwing *(Pres.)*

GRAYLINE HOUSEWARES
(Div. of C. R. L. Corp.)
1616 Berkley St.
Elgin, IL 60123
Tel.: 708-695-3900
Tel.: 800-222-7388
Fax: 708-695-4817
Approx.Sls.: $10,000,000
Emp.: 100
Fiscal Year-end: 6/30/91
Export
Mfr. Housewares
S.I.C.: 3496
Fred K. Rosen *(Pres.)*

Joe Petz *(Controller)*
Tony Martinello *(Dir.-Mktg.)*
Arlene Grzesiak *(Mgr.-Natl. Sls.)*

GRAYMILLS CORP.
3705 N. Lincoln Ave.
Chicago, IL 60613
Tel.: 312-477-4100
Fax: 312-477-8673
Year Founded: 1939
Approx.Sls.: $15,000,000
Emp.: 120
Import Export
Manufacture Pumping Units, Parts-Cleaning Systems & Control Systems for Printing & Machine Tool Industry
S.I.C.: 3492
Gerald N. Shields *(Chm. Bd., Pres. & Chief Exec. Officer)*
Linda L. Shields *(V.P.-Communications)*
Vincent Aquilino *(Sec.)*
R. Lichtenberger *(Mgr.-Intl. Sls.)*
Terri Katner *(Dir.-Personnel)*
John Bauer *(Dir.-Pur.)*
Principal(s):
Gerald N. Shields
Vincent Aquilino

No. of Mfg. Plants/Facilities: 1
No. of U.S. Offices: 1

Computer Systems/Hardware:
Honeywell; Ultimate

Outside Service Firm(s):

Deloitte & Touche*(Auditors)*
Chattanooga, TN

Chapman & Cutler*(Legal Firm)*
111 W. Monroe
Chicago, IL 60603
Tel.: 312-845-3000

NBD Skokie*(Major Banking Relationship)*
Skokie, IL

GREAT AMERICAN INDUSTRIES, INC.
300 Plaza Dr.
Vestal, NY 13850-3646
Tel.: 607-729-9331 **DE**
Fax: 607-797-7103
Approx.Sls.: $250,000,000
Emp.: 3,343
Fiscal Year-end: 12/31/90
Mfr. of Rubber Products, Diving Suits, Retail Scuba Diving & Underwater Equipment, Foam Products, Electro Mechanical Devices
S.I.C.: 3069; 3679; 3674; 3824
Burton I. Koffman *(Chm. Bd. & Pres.)*
Milton Koffman *(Exec. V.P., Sec. & Treas.)*
Richard E. Koffman *(Sr. V.P.)*
Leo P. Serowik *(V.P. & Controller)*

Outside Service Firm(s):

BDO Seidman*(Auditors)*
1430 Broadway
New York, NY
Tel.: 212-765-7500

Beveridge and Diamond, P.C.*(Legal Firm)*
1333 New Hampshire Ave. N.W.
Washington, DC 20036
Tel.: 202-828-0200

Subsidiaries:

Paeco Industries, Inc. **(1)**
One Executive Way
Toms River, NJ 08753
Tel.: 908-341-4444 (100%)
Bldg. Prods.
Milton Koffman *(Pres.)*

Subsidiary:

Allied Steel Products **(2)**
3201 N.W. 167th St.
Miami, FL 33169
Tel.: 305-624-3333 (100%)
Mfr. Steel Doors
S.I.C.: 3442

Parkway Fabricators, Inc. **(1)**
241 Raritan St.
South Amboy, NJ 08879
Tel.: 908-721-5300
Tel.: 800-472-7592 (100%)
Fax: 908-721-4016
Approx.Sls.: $7,000,000
Emp.: 100
Import Export
Production of Rubber Goods including Diving Suits; Mfr. of Regulators
S.I.C.: 3069; 3021; 3089; 3949
Frank N. Sanger *(Pres.)*
Richard F. Lafferty *(Exec. V.P.)*
Robert J. Reilly *(Chief Fin. Officer)*

Rubatex Corporation **(1)**
906 Adams St.
Bedford, VA 24523
Tel.: 703-586-2611 (100%)
Emp.: 850
Production of Rubber Goods
S.I.C.: 3069
R.L. Adams *(Pres. & Chief Exec. Officer)*
Larry Brookshier *(V.P.-Mktg.)*
Jackson Overstreet *(V.P.-Mfg.)*
J.T. Evans *(Treas.)*
C.R. Toms *(Sec. & Personnel Dir.)*
J.L. Coleman *(Gen. Sls. Mgr.)*
V.J. Lisa *(Pur. Dir.)*

Subsidiary:

Groendyk Mfg. Co., Inc. **(2)**
278 Main St.
Buchanan, VA 24066
Tel.: 703-254-1010 (100%)
Fax: 703-254-2400
Approx.Sls.: $10,000,000
Emp.: 105
Fiscal Year-end: 12/31/90
Export
Production of Rubber Goods
S.I.C.: 3069
R.L. Adams *(Pres.)*
M. Tsoleas *(Fin. Exec.)*
J. Evans *(Controller)*
H.J. McMillan *(Gen. & Sls. Mgr.)*
V. Seay *(Dir.-Personnel)*
H. Hairston *(Mgr.-Res. & Devel.)*
R. Lipes *(Mgr.-Pur.)*
J.W. McCabe *(Mgr.-Quality Control)*
B. Zimmerman *(Mgr.-Export)*

Tech-Aerofoam Products, Inc. **(1)**
3551 N.W. 116th St.
Miami, FL 33167
Tel.: 305-685-5995 (100%)
Emp.: 280
Mfg., Whlsle. & Mktg. of Flexible Foam Prods.
S.I.C.: 5039; 3086
David Melin *(Chief Oper. Officer)*

Warren Refrigerator Company, Inc. **(1)**
5110 Glenmont
Houston, TX 77081
Tel.: 713-666-2939 (100%)
Commercial Refrigerators
S.I.C.: 3585
John Canon *(Pres.)*

THE GREAT ATLANTIC COMPANIES
2 Eaton St., Ste. 1100
Hampton, VA 23669
Tel.: 804-722-5211 **VA**
Fax: 804-728-9683
Year Founded: 1963
Sales Range: $80-99 Million
Emp.: 700
Fiscal Year-end: 12/31/90
Real Estate Investment, Development & Management; Construction, Hotels
S.I.C.: 6531; 6552; 6798; 1531; 7389; 7011
Edwin Joseph *(Chm. Bd. & Pres.)*
Kenneth L. Allen *(Pres.-Homebuilding Div.)*
Bob G. Barnes *(V.P.-Hospitality)*
Richard Swift *(Chief Oper. Officer)*
Thomas G. Keefe *(Chief Fin. Officer)*
James R. Joseph *(Exec. V.P.)*
Principal(s):
Edwin Joseph

No. of Mfg. Plants/Facilities: 100
No. of U.S. Offices: 7

Computer Systems/Hardware:
IBM System 36

Outside Service Firm(s):

Rauch, Witt & Co.*(Auditors)*
Newport News, VA

Nationwide Insurance*(Commercial Insurance Carrier)*
Lynchburg, VA

Blue Cross & Blue Shield of Virginia*(Group Insurer)*
2015 Staples Mill Rd.
Richmond, VA 23230
Tel.: 804-359-7000
Fax: 804-354-7397

Crestar Bank*(Investment Banker)*
Bank-Newport News, V

Jones, Blechman, Woltz & Kelly*(Legal Firm)*
Newport News, VA

Crestar Bank*(Major Banking Relationship)*
P.O. Box 26665,
Richmond, VA 23261
Tel.: 804-782-5995

Massachusetts Mutual Life Insurance Co.*(Pension Manager)*
1295 State St.
Springfield, MA 01111
Tel.: 413-788-8411
Fax: 413-730-6144

Subsidiaries:

Atlantic Homes Corp. **(1)**
2 Eaton St., Ste. 1100
Hampton, VA 23669
Tel.: 804-722-5211
General Contractor
S.I.C.: 1521; 1531
Kenneth Allen *(Pres.)*

Great Atlantic Hospitality Co. Inc. **(1)**
2 Eaton St., Ste. 1100
Hampton, VA 23669
Tel.: 804-722-5211
Emp.: 135
Residential Property Sales; Hotels
S.I.C.: 6531; 7011
Bob G. Barnes *(V.P.)*

Great Atlantic Management Co. Inc. **(1)**
2 Eaton St., Ste. 1100
Hampton, VA 23669
Tel.: 804-722-5211
Commercial & Residential Property Management, Asset Management
S.I.C.: 6531
James Joseph *(V.P.)*

THE GREAT FRAME UP SYSTEMS, INC.
9335 Belmont Ave.
Franklin Park, IL 60131
Tel.: 708-671-2530
Approx.Sls.: $23,000,000
Emp.: 35
Fiscal Year-end: 4/30/91
Franchisor of Do-It-Yourself and Custom Picture Framing Stores; The Great Frame Up
S.I.C.: 7699
David Klitzky *(Pres.)*
Sheryl Solomon *(Dir.-Adv.)*

GREAT LAKES BANCORP
401 East Liberty St.
Ann Arbor, MI 48107
Tel.: 313-769-8300
Year Founded: 1890
Assets: $2,887,032,000
Earnings: ($564,000)
Liabilities: $2,737,740,000
Net Worth: $149,292,000
Approx.Income: $296,925,000
Fiscal Year-end: 12/31/91
S.I.C.: 6035
Roy E. Weber *(Chm. Bd.)*
Robert J. Delonis *(Pres. & Chief Exec. Officer)*

John G. Holbrock *(Pres.-Dollar Federal Savings)*
Lloyd E. Fairbanks *(Reg. Pres.-Northeast Michigan)*
Robert H. Porter *(Reg. Pres.-Central Michigan)*
Samuel B. Van Boven *(Reg. Pres.-West Michigan)*
Julie A. Gerschick *(Sr. V.P.-Control & Compliance)*
Joanne Hilgeneck *(Sr. V.P.-Human Resources)*
Alex F. Kato *(Sr. V.P.-Corp. Lending)*
Hans W. Maier *(Sr. V.P.-Opers.)*
Dennis E. Pearsall *(Sr. V.P.-Retail Banking)*
Kaye Ross *(Sr. V.P.-Quality Mngmt.)*
Thomas R. Bower *(First V.P.-Retail Loan Admin.)*
Kenneth E. Haist *(First V.P.-Income Property Lending)*
Douglas O. Hanton *(First V.P.-Corp. Services)*
Charles L. Henry, Jr. *(First V.P.-Mktg.)*
Alvin P. Lipnick *(First V.P.-Legal Services)*
Mark C. Ouimet *(First V.P.-Retail Banking Offices, SE Michigan Region)*
Alfred J.Paul *(First V.P.-Retail Loan Servicing)*
Peter W. Price *(First V.P.-Information Systems)*
Glen J. Ohl *(Treas. & Chief Fin. Officer)*
Bruce A. Hubbard *(Corp. Sec.)*
D. Kathryn Thompson *(Controller)*

THE GREAT LAKES CHEESE CO.
9988 Kinsman Rd.
Newbury, OH 44065
Mailing Address:
P.O. Box 335
Newbury, OH 44065
Tel.: 216-564-7181 **OH**
Fax: 216-564-7653
Year Founded: 1958
Approx.Sls.: $240,000,000
Emp.: 420
Fiscal Year-end: 12/29/90

Import
Manufacturing, Packaging & Distribution of Cheese
S.I.C.: 5143; 2022
Hans Epprecht *(Pres. & Chief Exec. Officer)*
John W. Epprecht *(V.P., Sec. & Treas.)*
William H. Andrews *(Dir.-Sls.)*
Michael Cefarati *(Dir.-Pur.)*
S. Heidi Eller *(Dir.-Mktg.)*
Russ Mollins *(Dir.-Fin.)*
Michael Smith *(Dir.-Data Processing)*
Beth Wendell *(Dir.-Personnel)*

No. of Mfg. Plants/Facilities: 3
No. of U.S. Offices: 6

Computer Systems/Hardware:
IBM

Outside Service Firm(s):

Deloitte & Touche*(Auditors)*
1717 East Ninth St.
Cleveland, OH 44114
Tel.: 216-589-1300

Hahn, Loeser & Parks*(Legal Firm)*
Natl. City E. 6 Bldg.
Cleveland, OH 44114
Tel.: 216-621-0150

National City Bank*(Major Banking Relationship)*
P.O. Box 92301,
Cleveland, OH 44101-0900
Tel.: 216-575-2529
Tel.: 800-622-6757
Fax: 216-575-9396

Subsidiaries:

Great Lakes Cheese Of New York, Inc. **(1)**
23 Phelps Rd.
Adams, NY 13605
Tel.: 315-232-4511
Emp.: 65
Manufacturer Of Cheddar Cheese & Dried Whey
S.I.C.: 2022
Max Badertscher *(Gen. Mgr.)*

Great Lakes Of Wisconsin **(1)**
801 South St.
Plymouth, WI 53073
Tel.: 414-893-1121
Emp.: 100
Assembler & Packager Of Natural Cheese
S.I.C.: 2022
Richard Metzler *(Gen. Mgr.)*

GREAT LAKES CONSTRUCTION CO.
6600 Schaaf Rd.
Cleveland, OH 44131
Tel.: 216-524-2970
Fax: 216-642-8693
Year Founded: 1948
Approx.Sls.: $50,000,000
Emp.: 500
Heavy & Highway Construction Contractors
S.I.C.: 1611
Bruce C. Gilbert *(Pres., Chief Exec. Officer & Treas.)*
Joseph W. Allen *(V.P.-Contract Mngmt.)*
Milton Kaplan *(V.P.-Engrng.)*
William J. Leonard *(V.P.-Fin.)*
Vincent A. Strazzo *(V.P.-Opers.)*
Andrew T. Ungar *(V.P.-Mktg.)*

Computer Systems/Hardware:
IBM

Outside Service Firm(s):

Arthur Andersen & Co.*(Auditors)*
1717 E. 9th St.
Cleveland, OH 44114
Tel.: 216-781-2140
Fax: 216-781-3683

Thompson, Hine & Flory*(Legal Firm)*
1100 National City Bank Bldg.
Cleveland, OH 44114
Tel.: 216-566-5500

Society National Bank*(Major Banking Relationship)*
900 Euclid Ave., P.O. Box 6477
Cleveland, OH 44101-6477
Tel.: 216-737-5000
Fax: 216-566-8947

Society National Bank*(Major Banking Relationship)*
Cleveland, OH

GREAT LAKES DREDGE & DOCK
2122 York Rd.
Oak Brook, IL 60521
Tel.: 708-574-3000
Tel.: 800-323-7100 **DE**
Telex: 25-4441
Fax: 708-574-2980
Year Founded: 1890
Approx.Rev.: $200,000,000
Emp.: 500
Fiscal Year-end: 12/31/91
Heavy Marine Construction, Primarily Dredging
S.I.C.: 1629
Witt Barlow *(Chm., Pres. & Chief Exec. Officer)*
D.B. Mackie *(Sr. V.P., Gen. Counsel & Sec.)*
Richard M. Lowry *(Sr. V.P. & Chief Engr.)*
Bruce J. Biemeck *(V.P. & Chief Fin. Officer)*
Deborah Wensel *(Controller)*
Sol Collura *(Dir.-Data Processing)*
R. Kilander *(Dir.-Pur.)*
Richard Adams *(Mgr.-Mktg. & Pub. Rels.)*

GREAT LAKES FINANCIAL RESOURCES, INC.
18600 S. Dixie Hwy.
Homewood, IL 60430
Tel.: 708-799-2805 **DE**
Fax: 708-799-3392
Year Founded: 1981
Assets: $408,851,000
Earnings: $3,036,000
Liabilities: $375,215,000
Net Worth: $33,636,000
Approx.Rev.: $39,020,000
Emp.: 11
Fiscal Year-end: 12/31/90
Multi-Bank Holding Company
S.I.C.: 6712; 6022
Corporate Giving Program: Donations *Made By Individual Banks To Entities* Active In Their Respective Trade Areas
Robert E. Field *(Chm. Bd.)*
Vincent C. Yager *(Pres. & Chief Exec. Officer)*
Thomas S. Agler *(V.P. & Chief Fin. Officer)*
Ronald L. Peacher *(V.P.-Review Services)*
James L. Calvert *(Asst. V.P. & Investment Officer)*
Susan M. Zibell *(Asst. V.P. & Dir. Personnel)*
Cynthia K. Zweigoron *(Asst. V.P.-Pur. & Acctg. Officer)*
Gail Byrnes *(Dir.-Human Resources)*
Mary Ann Diment *(Auditor)*
Margaret N. Jackson *(Auditor)*
Fred W. Mansfield *(Sec. & Treas.)*

No. of U.S. Offices: 4

Outside Service Firm(s):

Crowe, Chizek & Co.*(Auditors)*
P.O. Box 3687,
Oak Brook, IL 60822
Tel.: 708-954-7408
Fax: 708-799-1299

Freeman, Scanlon & Keefe*(Auditors)*
Chicago, IL

William Blair & Co.*(Investment Banker)*
135 S. LaSalle St.
Chicago, IL 60603
Tel.: 312-236-1600

Seyfarth, Shaw, Fairweather & Geraldson*(Legal Firm)*
55 East Monroe, 42nd Fl.
Chicago, IL 60603
Tel.: 312-346-8000

American National Bank*(Major Banking Relationship)*
33 North LaSalle St.
Chicago, IL 60690
Tel.: 312-661-6967

Subsidiaries:

Bank of Homewood **(1)**
2034 Ridge Rd.
Homewood, IL 60430
Tel.: 708-798-6060 (100%)
Fax: 708-798-3566
Emp.: 62
S.I.C.: 6022
Robert E. Field *(Chm. Bd.)*
William W. Addy *(Pres. & Chief Exec. Officer)*
Ronald T. Shropshire *(Exec. V.P. & Chief Credit Officer)*

Community Bank of Homewood-Flossmoor **(1)**
18600 Dixie Hwy.
Homewood, IL 60430
Tel.: 708-799-2800 (100%)
Fax: 312-799-1299
Emp.: 32
Commercial Bank
S.I.C.: 6022
Robert E. Field *(Chm. Bd.)*
William W. Addy *(Pres.)*
Robert W. Slowinski *(V.P. & Chief Credit Officer)*
Patricia A. Brackman *(V.P. & Compliance Officer)*
Jean van Brussel *(Asst. V.P.)*
Julie L. Maggio *(Asst. Trust Officer)*
Gayle A. Liskunas *(Cashier)*

First National Bank of Blue Island **(1)**
13057 S. Western Ave.
Blue Island, IL 60406
Tel.: 708-385-2200 (100%)
Fax: 708-385-5287
Emp.: 118
Commercial Bank
S.I.C.: 6021
Robert E. Field *(Chm. Bd.)*
Thomas L. Dockweiler *(Chm.-Exec. Committee & Chief Exec. Officer)*
Fred W. Mansfield *(Pres. & Chief Oper. Officer)*
James J. Jurik *(Sr. V.P. & Chief Credit Officer)*
Richard T. Hardy, Jr. *(V.P.-Mortgage Lending)*
William H. Thomson *(V.P. & Trust Officer)*
Sarah J. Wahlberg *(Sr. V.P.)*

GREAT LAKES LITHOGRAPH CO.
4005 Clark Ave.
Cleveland, OH 44109-1186
Tel.: 216-651-1500
Tel.: 800-765-4846 **OH**
Fax: 216-651-8311
Year Founded: 1931
Approx.Sls.: $14,000,000
Emp.: 105
Fiscal Year-end: 12/31/90
Commercial Lithographic Printing
S.I.C.: 2752
George E. Schultz *(Chm. Bd.)*
James R. Schultz *(Pres. & Chief Exec. Officer)*
Robert J. Schultz *(Chief Fin. Officer, Treas. & Sec.)*
William A. Meyer *(Sr. V.P.)*
J.A. Chinnici, Jr. *(V.P.-Sls.)*
Michael L. Nakonek *(V.P.-Opers.)*
Kostika Radivaj *(V.P.-Mfg.)*
Anthony Sanson *(V.P.-Fin.)*
Thomas A. Schultz *(V.P.-Mktg.)*
Michael Bangs *(Dir.-Pur.)*
Cindy Just *(Dir.-Mktg.)*
Terry McMilliam *(Mgr.-Sls. Devel.)*

No. of Mfg. Plants/Facilities: 1
No. of U.S. Offices: 3

Outside Service Firm(s):

Ernst & Young*(Auditors)*
1300 Huntington Bldg.
Cleveland, OH 44115
Tel.: 216-861-5000

Calfee, Halter & Griswold*(Legal Firm)*
800 Superior Ave., Ste. 1800
Cleveland, OH 44115-2688
Tel.: 216-622-8200
Fax: 216-241-0816

Society National Bank*(Major Banking Relationship)*
800 Superior Ave.
Cleveland, OH 44114
Tel.: 216-689-5931
Fax: 216-689-3814

Subsidiary:

PREPLINK **(1)**
25125 Detroit Rd.
Westlake, OH 44145
Tel.: 216-892-5575
Emp.: 6
Desktop Service Bureau; Imaging Service
S.I.C.: 2796
James Schultz *(Chief Oper. Officer)*
Dean Hanisko *(Dir.-Mktg.)*

GREAT LAKES RECREATION CO.
28900 Schoolcraft Rd.
Livonia, MI 48150
Tel.: 313-425-4870 **MI**
Emp.: 300
BowlingCenters
S.I.C.: 7933
Barbara Wachstein *(Pres. & Chief Exec. Officer)*
Kenneth Kubit *(V.P. & Controller)*

Great Lakes Recreation Co.—(Continued)

Subsidiaries:

Bowlerama Lanes, Inc. **(1)**
21630 W. Seven Mile Rd.
Detroit, MI 48225
Tel.: 313-737-9590
Bowling Center
S.I.C.: 7933

Cloverlanes, Inc. **(1)**
28900 Schoolcraft
Livonia, MI 48150
Tel.: 313-427-6410
Bowling Center
S.I.C.: 7933

Fairlanes Bowl, Inc. **(1)**
29600 Stephenson Hwy.
Madison Heights, MI 48071
Tel.: 313-548-9333
Bowling Center
S.I.C.: 7933

Great Lakes Bowling Centre, Inc. **(1)**
6366 Woodward Ave.
Detroit, MI 48202
Tel.: 313-875-6369
Bowling Center
S.I.C.: 7933

Ypsi-Arbor Lanes **(1)**
2985 Washtenaw
Ypsilanti, MI 48197
Tel.: 313-434-1110
Bowling Centers
S.I.C.: 7933

GREAT LAKES SPORTSWEAR MANUFACTURING INDUSTRIES
11371 E. State Fair
Detroit, MI 48234
Tel.: 313-372-4500
Fax: 313-372-5070
Men's & Boys' Sport Jackets
S.I.C.: 2329
Dynn Nick *(Pres. & Chief Exec. Officer)*

Outside Service Firm(s):

Albert Prest*(Legal Firm)*
Harper Woods, MI

Manufacturers National Bank N.A.*(Major Banking Relationship)*
38th Fl., 100 Renaissance Center
Detroit, MI 48243
Tel.: 313-222-4227

GREAT LAKES TECHNOLOGIES CORP.
300 S. Kalamazoo Mall, Ste. 210
Kalamazoo, MI 49007
Tel.: 616-385-2200 **MI**
Fax: 616-385-4684
Year Founded: 1977
Sales Range: $10-19 Million
Emp.: 20
Microfilms, Comfilms, Surveillance Films; Processing Labs
S.I.C.: 7384
Robin L. Marshall *(Pres. & Chief Exec. Officer)*
William Marvin *(V.P.)*
Chris Abruzzo *(Mgr.-Sls.)*
Rene Weber *(Mgr.-Data Processing)*

No. of Mfg. Plants/Facilities: 3
No. of U.S. Offices: 6
No. of Foreign Offices: 1

Computer Systems/Hardware:
NCR

Outside Service Firm(s):

First of America Bank*(Investment Banker)*
Kalamazoo, MI

First of America Bank*(Major Banking Relationship)*
Kalamazoo, MI

GREAT LAKES TERMINAL & TRANSPORT CORP.
1750 N. Kingsbury St.
Chicago, IL 60614
Tel.: 312-664-3500 **IL**
Year Founded: 1940
Approx.Sls.: $100,000,000
Emp.: 208
Fiscal Year-end: 11/30/90
Wholesale Derivatives, Fiberglass
S.I.C.: 5169
Louis H.T. Dehmlow *(Chm. Bd. & Chief Exec. Officer)*
Steven L. Dehmlow *(Pres. & Chief Oper. Officer)*
William F. Dvorak *(Treas.)*
James F. Pepelnjak *(Sec. & Dir.-Human Resources)*
Raymond Mochinski *(Dir.-Data Processing)*
David Forner *(Dir.-Personnel Devel.)*

Computer Systems/Hardware:
Sperry Univac OS/3

Outside Service Firm(s):

Arthur Andersen & Co.*(Auditors)*
33 W. Monroe St.
Chicago, IL 60603-4067
Tel.: 312-580-0033
Fax: 312-507-6748

CIGNA*(Group Insurer)*
Los Angeles, CA

Sidley & Austin*(Legal Firm)*
One First National Plaza, 42nd Fl.
Chicago, IL 60603
Tel.: 312-853-7000
Fax: 312-853-7036

The Northern Trust Co.*(Major Banking Relationship)*
30 S. LaSalle St.
Chicago, IL 60675
Tel.: 312-630-6000

CIGNA*(Pension Manager)*
Los Angeles, CA

Subsidiaries:

Alpha Resin Supply **(1)**
1750 N. Kingsbury St.
Chicago, IL 60614
Tel.: 312-664-3500
Distr. of Resins
S.I.C.: 5162; 3087
Louis H.T. Dehmlow *(Chm. Bd.)*

Argo Terminal Co. **(1)**
8800 W. 71st St.
Bedford Park, IL 60638
Tel.: 708-735-0586 (100%)
Emp.: 16
Terminal Management
S.I.C.: 4231
Nick Tepavich *(Gen. Mgr.)*

Great Lakes Terminal & Transport of Pennsylvania **(1)**
P.O. Box 281,
Industry, PA 15052
Tel.: 412-643-9450 (100%)
Emp.: 7
Terminal Management
S.I.C.: 4231
Thomas Gimbus *(Plant Mgr.)*

GREAT NECK SAW MANUFACTURERS, INC.
165 E. Second St.
Mineola, NY 11501
Tel.: 516-746-5352 **NY**
Fax: 516-746-5358
Year Founded: 1940
Approx.Sls.: $57,000,000
Emp.: 700
Mfr. of Hand Tools
S.I.C.: 3425
Richard Jacoff *(Chm. Bd.)*
Sydney Jacoff *(Pres.)*
Daniel Jacoff *(V.P.-Engrng.)*
Salem Jacoff *(V.P. & Sec.)*
Jay Fallstich *(Pur. Agent)*
Charles Harold *(Plant Mgr.)*

Outside Service Firm(s):

BDO Seidman*(Auditors)*
1430 Broadway
New York, NY
Tel.: 212-765-7500

Berlack, Israels & Lieberman*(Legal Firm)*
120 West 45th St.
New York, NY 10036
Tel.: 212-704-0100
Fax: 212-704-0196

National Westminster Bank plc*(Major Banking Relationship)*
175 Water St.
New York, NY 10038-4924
Tel.: 212-602-3364

GREAT PLAINS MANUFACTURING, INC.
Second & Center
Assaria, KS 67416
Mailing Address:
P.O. Box 218
Assaria, KS 67416
Tel.: 913-667-4755
Tel.: 800-255-0132
Fax: 913-667-2055
Year Founded: 1976
Approx.Sls.: $55,000,000
Emp.: 750
Fiscal Year-end: 12/31/90
Grain Drills, Hitches & Other Agricultural Implements
S.I.C.: 3523
Roy Applequist *(Pres.)*
Gary Lee *(V.P.-Fin.)*
Eric Lund *(V.P.-Mktg.)*
Eric Johnson *(V.P.-Engrng.)*
Linda League *(Adv. Coordinator)*
Jim Welch *(Pur. Agent)*

GREAT SALT LAKE MINERALS & CHEMICALS CORP.
P.O. Box 1190
Ogden, UT 84402
Tel.: 801-731-3100 **DE**
Fax: 801-731-4481
Year Founded: 1967
Assets: $47,800,000
Liabilities: $32,700,000
Net Worth: $15,100,000
Approx.Sls.: $54,700,000
Emp.: 279
Fiscal Year-end: 3/31/91
Export
Producer Of Sulfate Of Potash, Common Salt, Magnesium Chloride & Sodium Sulfate
S.I.C.: 2819
Richard J. Donahue *(Chm. Bd.)*
Peter Behrens *(Vice Chm.)*
William S. Holt *(Pres.)*
Grant H. Braun *(Sr. V.P.-Mktg.)*
Max J. Reynolds *(V.P.-Opers.)*
Kenneth L. Warnick *(V.P.-Admin., Sec. & Treas.)*
Sheldon K. Barfuss *(Controller)*
Clint Owen *(Dir.-Data Processing)*
Dan Richardson *(Dir.-Corp. Plng.)*
Bruce Wood *(Dir.-Human Resources)*
Principal(s):
Richard J. Donahue
Peter Behrens
William S. Holt

No. of Mfg. Plants/Facilities: 1
No. of U.S. Offices: 1

Computer Systems/Hardware:
Prime

Outside Service Firm(s):

Coopers & Lybrand*(Auditors)*
1700 Benneficial Life Tower
Salt Lake City, UT 84111
Tel.: 801-531-9666

Kimball, Parr, Crockett & Waddoups*(Legal Firm)*
Salt Lake City, UT

First Security Bank of Utah*(Major Banking Relationship)*
79 S. Main
Salt Lake City, UT 84111
Tel.: 801-350-5289

Subsidiary:

GSL Solar Consultants & Advisors, Inc. **(1)**
P.O. Box 1190
Ogden, UT 84401
Tel.: 801-731-3100
Management Services
S.I.C.: 8741
Peter Behrens *(Chief Oper. Officer)*

GREAT SCOTT ADVERTISING CO. INC.
1185 Ave. of the Americas
New York, NY 10036
Tel.: 212-921-2050
Fax: 212-921-2392/3
Year Founded: 1971
Approx.Billings: $51,000,000
Emp.: 72
Entertainment, Travel & Leisure, Consumer Products, Real Estate & Education
Lorraine Borden *(Chm. Bd., Chief Exec. Officer, Chief Fin. Officer, Pres.)*
Sherri Callan *(Exec. V.P., Dir.-West Coast Div.)*
Eunice Bellucci *(Exec. V.P.-Arts & Entertainment Div.)*
Scott Mauro *(Sr. V.P.-Arts & Entertainment Div.)*
Beverly Severino *(Sec. & Treas.)*
Fred Golden *(Exec. Dir.-Theatre Div.)*
Dale Marsilio *(Dir.-Personnel)*
Michael Whamond *(Dir.-Admin. West Coast Div.)*
Linde Liu *(Computer Graphics Supvr.)*

GREATBANC, INC.
105 East Galena Blvd.
Aurora, IL 60505
Tel.: 708-844-6110 **DE**
Fax: 708-844-6115
Assets: $321,601,000
Earnings: $3,940,000
Liabilities: $299,262,000
Net Worth: $22,339,000
Approx.Income: $28,455,000
Emp.: 232
Fiscal Year-end: 12/31/91
Bank Holding Company
S.I.C.: 6712
Roger L. Weston *(Chm. Bd., Pres. & Chief Exec. Officer)*
John A. Sheldon *(Vice Chm.)*
Steven R. Madlinger *(V.P., Chief Fin. Officer & Treas.)*
John P. Culhane *(V.P.-Corp. Funds & Mgr.-Investment)*
David R. Corydon *(V.P.)*
Michael Welgat *(V.P.-Fin. Services)*
Charles H. Perlman *(Sec.)*
Marian J. DePew *(Asst. Sec.)*
Michael Rouner *(Controller)*

Outside Service Firm(s):

Ernst & Young*(Auditors)*
150 S. Wacker Dr.
Chicago, IL 60606
Tel.: 312-368-1800

Subsidiaries:

Aurora National Bank **(1)**
2 So. Broadway
Aurora, IL 60505
Tel.: 708-844-7000
Banking
S.I.C.: 6021
Susan Horwitz *(Pres. & Chief Exec. Officer)*

Evanston Bank **(1)**
603 Main St.
Evanston, IL 60202
Tel.: 708-869-4500
Banking
S.I.C.: 6021
R. Dean Long *(Pres.)*

First National Bank in Chicago Heights **(1)**
100 First National Plaza
Chicago Heights, IL 60411
Tel.: 708-754-3100
Banking
S.I.C.: 6021

GREATER CONSTRUCTION CORP.
1105 Kensington Park Dr.
Altamonte Springs, FL 32714
Tel.: 407-869-0300 **FL**
Fax: 407-862-0057
Year Founded: 1965
Approx.Sls.: $33,000,000
Emp.: 40
Operative Residential Contractors
S.I.C.: 1531
Robert A. Mandell *(Pres.)*
Lester Mandell *(Chief Exec. Officer)*
Yim Bible *(V.P.)*
Simon Snyder *(V.P.)*
Steven Zimmerman *(V.P.)*
George Billings *(Treas.)*
Lester Zimmerman *(Sec.)*

Outside Service Firm(s):

Ernst & Young*(Auditors)*
390 N. Orange Ave., Ste. 1700
Orlando, FL 32801
Tel.: 407-872-6600

Lowndes, Drosdick, Doster, Kantor & Reed*(Legal Firm)*
Orlando, FL

First Union National Bank*(Major Banking Relationship)*
Orlando, FL

GREATER NEW YORK BOX CO.
149 Entin Rd.
Clifton, NJ 07014
Tel.: 201-472-3600
Fax: 201-472-5801
Year Founded: 1904
Approx.Sls.: $17,000,000
Emp.: 150
Mfr. of Corrugated Shipping Containers, Display Packaging; Linerboard Specialty Products, File Boxes, Pallets; Tote Boxes
S.I.C.: 2653; 2657
Irving Edelman *(Chm. Bd.)*
Leo Edelman *(Pres.)*
Jules Edelman *(Exec. V.P.)*
Allan Edelman *(V.P. & Controller)*
Mitchell Edelman *(Treas.)*

Outside Service Firm(s):

National Westminster Bank plc*(Major Banking Relationship)*
2 Montgomery St.
Jersey City, NJ 07302
Tel.: 201-547-7000

GREATER NEW YORK MUTUAL INSURANCE COMPANY
215 Lexington Ave.
New York, NY 10016
Tel.: 212-683-9700
Fax: 212-685-0826
Year Founded: 1917
Approx.Sls.: $125,000,000
Emp.: 350
Commercial Property & Casualty Insurance
S.I.C.: 6331
Alexander E. Rosenthal *(Chm. Bd.)*
Warren Heck *(Pres.)*
Lawrence C. Davis *(Sr. V.P.-Mktg.)*

GREATER ORLANDO AUTO AUCTION
9800 Bachman Rd.
Orlando, FL 32824
Tel.: 407 438 1000 **FL**
Fax: 407-850-2613
Assets: $5,200,000
Liabilities: $3,000,000
Net Worth: $2,200,000
Approx.Sls.: $40,000,000
Emp.: 122
Fiscal Year-end: 10/31/90
Wholesale Used Cars
S.I.C.: 5012
Denny Hecker *(Pres.)*
Allan Siskind *(Dir.-Mktg.)*

Principal(s):
Denny Hecker

No. of U.S. Offices: 2

Computer Systems/Hardware:
Novell

Outside Service Firm(s):

Blue Cross & Blue Shield Association*(Group Insurer)*
Orlando, FL

Mahaby, Baber & Leash*(Legal Firm)*
Orlando, FL

Southeast Bank, N.A.*(Major Banking Relationship)*
Orlando, FL

GREDE FOUNDRIES, INC.
9898 W. Bluemound Rd.
Milwaukee, WI 53226
Mailing Address:
P.O. Box 26499
Milwaukee, WI 53226
Tel.: 414-257-3600 **WI**
Fax: 414-257-4102
Year Founded: 1920
Assets: $125,000,000
Liabilities: $60,000,000
Net Worth: $65,000,000
Approx.Sls.: $225,000,000
Emp.: 2,700
Fiscal Year-end: 11/ 2/90
Export
Gray & Ductile Iron Foundry
S.I.C.: 3321; 3325
Burleigh E. Jacobs *(Chm. Bd.)*
Bruce E. Jacobs *(Pres.)*
R.J. Burns *(V.P., Sec. & Chief Fin. Officer)*
W. Stewart Davis Jr. *(V.P.-Human Resources)*
Jack F. Steele *(V.P.-Sls. & Mktg.)*
Walter S. Davis *(Gen. Counsel)*
G.E. Ertel *(Controller)*
Larry L. Duesing *(Dir.-Mngmt. Information Systems)*
Frank Haas *(Dir.-Pur.)*

Principal(s):
Burleigh E. Jacobs
Bruce E. Jacobs

No. of Mfg. Plants/Facilities: 10

Computer Systems/Hardware:
IBM

Outside Service Firm(s):

Arthur Andersen & Co.*(Auditors)*
777 E. Wisconsin Ave., P.O. Box 1215
Milwaukee, WI 53202
Tel.: 414-271-5100
Fax: 414-283-3200

First Wisconsin National Bank*(Major Banking Relationship)*
777 E. Wisconsin Ave.
Milwaukee, WI 53202
Tel.: 414-765-4321
Fax: 414-355-6903

M & I Marshall & Ilsley Bank*(Major Banking Relationship)*
770 N. Water St.
Milwaukee, WI 53202
Tel.: 414-765-8700

M & I Marshall & Ilsley Bank*(Pension Manager)*
770 N. Water St.
Milwaukee, WI 53202
Tel.: 414-765-8700

Subsidiaries:

Grede New Castle, Inc **(1)**
9898 W. Bluemound Rd
Milwaukee, WI 53226
Tel.: 414-257-3600
B.E. Jacobs *(Pres.)*
Bruce Jacobs *(V.P.)*

Grede Permcast, Inc. **(1)**
9898 W. Bluemound Rd.
Milwaukee, WI 53226
Tel.: 414-257-3600
B.E. Jacobs *(Pres.)*
Bruce Jacobs *(V.P.)*

Grede Transport, Inc. **(1)**
9898 W. Bluemound Rd.
Milwaukee, WI 53226
Tel.: 414-257-3600
B.E. Jacobs *(Pres.)*
Bruce Jacobs *(V.P.)*

Grede Vassar, Inc. **(1)**
9898 W. Bluemound Rd.
Milwaukee, WI 53226
Tel.: 414-257-3600
B.E. Jacobs *(Pres.)*
Bruce Jacobs *(V.P.)*

Roberts Foundry Co., Inc. **(1)**
9898 W. Bluemound Rd.
Milwaukee, WI 53226
Tel.: 414-257-3600
H. H. Robinson *(Chief Oper. Officer)*
B.E. Jacobs *(Pres.)*
Bruce Jacobs *(V.P.)*

GREECO BROTHERS, INC.
50 Island St.
Lawrence, MA 01840
Tel.: 508-686-3833
Fax: 508-686-9802
Approx.Sls.: $40,000,000
Emp.: 800
Southwick Clothes for Men
S.I.C.: 2321; 2325; 2326; 2329
Richard Greeco *(Pres.)*
Martin Danzig *(V.P.-Sls.)*
Anthony Satienza *(V.P.-Opers.)*
Kristin Hotchkins *(Adv. Mgr.)*

GREELEY GAS CO.
1301 Pennsylvania St., Ste. 800
Denver, CO 80203
Tel.: 303-861-8080 **CO**
Fax: 303-861-8080, Ext. 54
Approx.Sls.: $65,000,000
Emp.: 310
Natural Gas Distribution
S.I.C.: 4924
Lee E. Schlessman *(Chm. Bd. & Pres.)*
Richard Remley *(Sr. V.P.)*
David W. Adams *(V.P.)*
R.J. Durkin *(V.P.)*
Jerrel E. Green *(V.P.)*
David L. Meyer *(V.P. & Treas.)*
D. Allen Spaur *(V.P.)*
Donald P. Burman *(Controller)*
Susan Duncan *(Sec.)*

Outside Service Firm(s):

Ernst & Young*(Auditors)*
4300 Republic Plaza
Denver, CO 80202
Tel.: 303-628-4406

Kelly, Stansfield & O'Donnell*(Legal Firm)*
550 - 15th St.
Denver, CO 80202
Tel.: 303-571-7511

Central Bank*(Major Banking Relationship)*
Denver, CO

Division:

Greeley Gas Cane Division **(1)**
703 N. Main St.
Eureka, KS 67045
Tel.: 316-583-6341
Gas Production & Distribution
S.I.C.: 4924
Lee E. Schlessman *(Chm. Bd. & Pres.)*
Fred Stuber *(Gen. Mgr.)*

GREEN BAY PACKAGING INC.
1700 N. Webster Ave.
Green Bay, WI 54302
Mailing Address:
P.O. Box 19017
Green Bay, WI 54307
Tel.: 414-433-5311 **WI**
Year Founded: 1933
Approx.Sls.: $250,000,000
Emp.: 2,400
Manufacture Corrugated Boxes
S.I.C.: 2631; 2653; 2657
George F. Kress *(Chm. Bd.)*
James F. Kress *(Pres. & Chief Exec. Officer)*
Leo N. Crowley *(Exec. V.P.-Plng. & Admin.)*
Roger P. Hoffman *(Chief Oper. Officer)*
Fred J. Wakeman *(Chief Fin. Officer)*
John D. L. Droege *(V.P.-Indus. Rels.)*
R. James Smits *(Treas.)*
Walter J. Dauska *(Controller)*
John B. Dauska *(Dir.-Personnel)*

No. of Mfg. Plants/Facilities: 20
No. of U.S. Offices: 27

Computer Systems/Hardware:
IBM

Outside Service Firm(s):

Deloitte & Touche*(Auditors)*
250 E. Wisconsin Ave.
Milwaukee, WI 53202-4283
Tel.: 414-271-3000

Aetna Life & Casualty*(Group Insurer)*
151 Farmington Avenue
Hartford, CT 06156
Tel.: 203-273-2128
Fax: 203-729-4295

Gibbs, Roper, Loots & Williams*(Legal Firm)*
735 Water St.
Milwaukee, WI 53202
Tel.: 414-273-7010

M & I Marshall & Ilsley Bank*(Major Banking Relationship)*
770 N. Water St.
Milwaukee, WI 53202
Tel.: 414-765-8700

David J. Greene & Co.*(Pension Manager)*
30 Wall St.
New York, NY
Tel.: 212-344-5180

M & I Investment Management Corp.*(Pension Manager)*
Milwaukee, WI

GREEN BUS LINES, INC.
16525 147th Ave.
Jamaica, NY 11434
Tel.: 718-995-4700 **NY**
Fax: 718-995-4712
Year Founded: 1988
Approx.Sls.: $40,000,000
Emp.: 530
Bus Line Operations
S.I.C.: 4111

Green Bus Lines, Inc.—(Continued)

Burton Cooper *(Pres.)*
Martin Gottlieb *(V.P.)*
Jerome Cooper *(Sec.)*

Outside Service Firm(s):

Allen Warner & Co.*(Auditors)*
New York, NY

Chase Manhattan Bank, N.A.*(Major Banking Relationship)*
One Chase Manhattan Plaza
New York, NY 10081
Tel.: 212-552-2222
Tel.: 800-526-0801
Fax: 212-552-7175

THOMAS L. GREEN & CO., INC.
202 N. Miley Ave.
Indianapolis, IN 46222
Tel.: 317-263-6935
Telex: 27 2160 GREENCO IND
Fax: 317-263-6930
Year Founded: 1893
Approx.Sls.: $10,000,000
Emp.: 80
Fiscal Year-end: 12/31/91
Export
Mfr. Bakery Machinery; Greenco
S.I.C.: 3556
Mrs. Howard Caldwell *(Chm. Bd.)*
Thomas R. Lugar *(Pres.)*
Randy Wagoner *(V.P.-Admin.)*
Todd Lugar *(Sec. & Treas.)*

B. GREEN & CO.
3601 Washington Blvd.
Baltimore, MD 21227
Tel.: 301-247-8300
Tel.: 800-456-4733 **MD**
Fax: 301-247-2839
Year Founded: 1915
Assets: $650,000,000
Net Worth: $650,000,000
Approx.Sls.: $570,000,000
Emp.: 1,200
Fiscal Year-end: 6/30/90
Export
Food Distributor & Grocery Stores
S.I.C.: 5141
Judge Meyer Cardin *(Chm. Bd.)*
Bernard Green *(Pres.)*
Jesse Swartz *(Chief Fin. Officer)*
Benjamin L. Green *(Exec. V.P.)*
Charles Green *(V.P.)*
Benjamin L. Sigman *(V.P. & Sec.)*
John Urbain *(V.P. & Chief Information Officer)*
Judy Dyckman *(Controller)*
Leon Brafman *(Dir.-Mdsg. & Adv.)*
Howard Dunn *(Dir.-Pur.)*
Howard Everson *(Dir.-Warehousing)*
Vince Farace *(Dir.-Sls. & Mktg.)*
Win Grymes *(Dir.-Data Processing)*
Debi Marsh *(Dir.-Pur.)*
Bill Pollack *(Dir.-Quality Assurance)*
Jan Squitieri *(Dir.-Human Resources)*
George Whelan *(Dir.-Maintenance)*
Neil Yeakle *(Dir.-Pur.)*
Martin Brill *(Mgr.-Export)*
Bob Monsheimer *(Mgr.-Leasing)*
Carol Pullen *(Mgr.-Employee Benefits)*
Joni Abrams *(Admin. Asst.)*
Principal(s):
Judge Meyer Cardin
Bernard Green
Benjamin L. Green
Charles Green
Benjamin L. Sigman
Benjamin Cardin
Howard Cardin
Bernice Sigman

Computer Systems/Hardware:
IBM 4381

Outside Service Firm(s):

Arthur Andersen & Co.*(Auditors)*
120 E. Baltimore St.
Baltimore, MD 21202
Tel.: 301-727-5800

Marsh & McLennan*(Commercial Insurance Carrier)*
Baltimore, MD

Alta Administrators*(Group Insurer)*
Pittsburgh, PA

Venable, Baetjer & Howard*(Legal Firm)*
1800 Mercantile Bank Bldg., 2 Hopkins Plaza
Baltimore, MD 21201
Tel.: 410-244-7400

Maryland National Bank*(Major Banking Relationship)*
Baltimore, MD 21202

Subsidiary:

Monroe Foods/Dessert Masters **(1)**
6855 Rappahannock Dr.
Jessup, MD 20785
Tel.: 410-799-1134 (100%)
Emp.: 40
Meat & Ice Cream Distributor
S.I.C.: 5147; 5143

GREEN CONSTRUCTION OF INDIANA, INC.
Hwy. #41 N.
Oaktown, IN 47561
Mailing Address:
P.O. Box 150
Oaktown, IN 47561
Tel.: 812 886 4141 **IN**
Fax: 812 745 2315
Year Founded: 1939
Assets: $57,500,000
Liabilities: $32,700,000
Net Worth: $24,800,000
Approx.Sls.: $62,800,000
Emp.: 1,500
Fiscal Year-end: 12/31/89
Bituminous Coal Mining; Motor Hotels; Radio Stations
S.I.C.: 1221; 7011; 4832
Robert D. Green *(Pres. & Chief Exec. Officer)*
Thomas E. Green *(V.P.)*
Curtis V. Kimmell *(V.P.)*
Richard Fox *(Sec.)*
Tom Clary *(Treas.)*

No. of Mfg. Plants/Facilities: 4
No. of U.S. Offices: 5

Computer Systems/Hardware:
IBM

Outside Service Firm(s):

Sackrider & Co.*(Auditors)*
Terre Haute, IN

Kimmell, Funk & Cummings*(Legal Firm)*
Vincennes, IN

Bank One, Indianapolis, N.A.*(Major Banking Relationship)*
111 Monument Circle, Ste. 1611
Indianapolis, IN 46204-1611
Tel.: 317-321-8110

DANIEL GREEN CO.
1 Main St.
Dolgeville, NY 13329
Tel.: 315-429-3131
Fax: 315-429-8424
Year Founded: 1882
Approx.Sls.: $25,000,000
Emp.: 700
Mfr. of Comfy Felt, Leather and Fabric Slippers, Casual Footwear
S.I.C.: 3142; 3149
William E. Homrighaus *(Chm.)*
Warren J. Reardon, III *(Pres.)*
W. Lee Bynon *(V.P.-Sls.)*
Janet Cool *(Treas.)*
W. Lee Bynon *(Mgr.-Natl. Sls.)*

Outside Service Firm(s):

Deloitte & Touche*(Auditors)*
One Lincoln First Square
Rochester, NY 14604
Tel.: 716-232-1200

Sullivan & Worcester*(Legal Firm)*
One Post Office Square, 100 Federal St.
Boston, MA 02110
Tel.: 617-338-2800

Norstar Bank, N.A.*(Major Banking Relationship)*
Utica, NY

GREEN HOLDINGS, INC.
8055 E. Tufts Ave., Ste. 700
Denver, CO 80237-2898
Tel.: 303-850-7676
Tel.: 800-421-6972 **IA**
Fax: 303-779-5380
Year Founded: 1983
Assets: $103,200,000
Liabilities: $90,800,000
Net Worth: $12,400,000
Approx.Sls.: $162,300,000
Emp.: 1,000
Fiscal Year-end: 12/31/91
Export
Holding Company; Heavy Civil & Highway Construction, Mining, Construction Management & Engineering Services
S.I.C.: 6719; 1629; 1611; 1623; 1622; 8711; 8741
W.M. King *(Chm. Bd.)*
J. David McClung *(Pres. & Chief Exec. Officer)*
W.G. Scott *(Pres.-Green Mining)*
P.J. Moore *(Sr. V.P., Chief Oper. Officer, Chief Fin. Officer, Sec. & Treas.)*
D.D. Murray *(Treas. & Asst. Sec.)*
D.R. Martin *(Gen. Counsel)*
M.R. Schipper *(Asst. Sec. & Controller)*

Computer Systems/Hardware:
IBM AS/400

Outside Service Firm(s):

Coopers & Lybrand*(Auditors)*
370 17th St., Ste. 3300
Denver, CO 80202
Tel.: 303-573-2800

CIGNA*(Group Insurer)*
SW Regional Claim Office, Community Natl. Bank Bldg. 600 Taylor St
Sherman, TX 75090
Tel.: 918-664-1344
Fax: 918-663-6250

Barokas & Martin*(Legal Firm)*
1422 Bellevue Ave.
Seattle, WA 98122
Tel.: 206-621-1871

Continental Bank N. A.*(Major Banking Relationship)*
231 S. LaSalle St.
Chicago, IL 60697
Tel.: 312-828-2345
Tel.: 800-426-5754
Telex: 312-828-1783

Subsidiaries:

C.C. Conley & Sons, Inc. **(1)**
8055 E. Tufts Ave., Ste. 700
Denver, CO 80237
Tel.: 303-850-7676 (100%)
Fax: 303-779-5380
Coal Mining
S.I.C.: 1221; 1222
D.L. Finger *(Pres.)*
P.J. Moore *(Sr. V.P., Treas. & Sec.)*

Green International-Guyana, Inc. **(1)**
8055 E. Tufts Ave., Ste. 700
Denver, CO 80237
Tel.: 303-850-7676 (100%)
Fax: 303-779-5380
Metal Mining
W.G. Scott *(Pres.)*
P.J. Moore *(Sr. V.P., Sec. & Treas.)*

Green International, Inc. **(1)**
8055 E. Tufts Ave., Ste. 700
Denver, CO 80237
Tel.: 303-779-5360
Fax: 303-779-5380
Emp.: 200
Heavy, Civil, Highway, Industrial & Building Construction & Mining
S.I.C.: 1611; 1622; 1623; 1629
J. David McClung *(Pres. & Chief Oper. Officer)*
P.J. Moore *(Sr. V.P., Chief Fin. Officer, Sec. & Treas.)*
D.L. Finger *(Sr. V.P.)*
W.G. Scott *(Sr. V.P.)*
W.J. Roberts *(V.P.)*
R.K. Skerik *(V.P.)*
G.L. Wilson *(V.P.)*
J.M. Ebisa *(Asst. Sec.)*
D.L. Langerman *(Asst. Sec.)*
D.D. Murray *(Asst. Sec.)*
M.R. Schipper *(Asst. Sec.)*
R.P. Strouse *(Dir.-Bus. Devel.)*

Green Mining, Inc. **(1)**
8055 E. Tufts Ave., Ste. 700
Denver, CO 80237-2898
Tel.: 303-779-5360
Fax: 303-779-5380
Emp.: 60
Contract Mining; Coal, Gold, Bauxite, etc.; Heavy Construction; Metal Mining
S.I.C.: 1629; 1099; 1041
W.G. Scott *(Pres.)*
P.J. Moore *(Sr. V.P., Sec. & Treas.)*
M.R. Schipper *(V.P. & Asst. Sec.)*
W.G. McPherson *(V.P.)*
G.L. Wilson *(V.P.)*

Northland Alaska, Inc. **(1)**
125 W. 5th Ave.
Anchorage, AK 99501
Tel.: 907-279-5456
Fax: 907-258-7984
S.I.C.: 1623; 1629
W.G. Jenkins *(Pres.)*
P.J. Moore *(Sr. V.P.)*

JOHN E. GREEN CO.
220 Victor Ave.
Highland Park, MI 48203
Tel.: 313-868-2400 **MI**
Fax: 313-868-0011
Year Founded: 1909
Approx.Sls.: $45,000,000
Emp.: 250
Mechanical & Fire Protection Contractor
S.I.C.: 1711; 1799
Peter J. Green *(Pres.)*
Michael Brunett *(V.P.)*
Ray Brunett *(V.P.)*
Rex Millsap *(V.P.)*
John R. Green *(Sec. & Treas.)*

Outside Service Firm(s):

Plante & Moran*(Auditors)*
Southfield, MI

Morris Rowland*(Legal Firm)*
Troy, MI

N.B.D. Bank, N.A.*(Major Banking Relationship)*
611 Woodward Ave.
Detroit, MI 48226
Tel.: 313-225-1122
Fax: 313-225-3420

GREEN LEAF VENTURES, INC.
6610 Convoy Ct.
San Diego, CA 92111
Mailing Address:
P.O. Box 121513
San Diego, CA 92112
Tel.: 619-576-3800 **CO**
Fax: 619-278-4140
Year Founded: 1967
Sales Range: $100-499 Million
Emp.: 4,000
Fiscal Year-end: 10/31/90
Owns & Operates Restaurant Groups: J. Ross Browne's Whaling Stations, J. Ross Brown-Dry Dock, The Dock, Monterey Whaling Co., The Boat House, Rusty Pelican, Rusty Duck, Carlos Murphy's
S.I.C.: 5812
Gordon H. Miles *(Chm. Bd.)*
Scott Barnett *(Pres.-Seafood Div.)*
William Lewis *(Pres.-Casual Dining Div.)*
Daniel Bylund *(Chief Fin. Officer)*
Robert Radke *(V.P.-Real Estate)*

Nancy Huth *(Controller)*
Mary Laloggia *(Mktg. Admin. Asst.)*

Outside Service Firm(s):

Coopers & Lybrand*(Auditors)*
402 W. Broadway, Ste. 400
San Diego, CA 92109
Tel.: 619-232-8000

ALTA Health Strategies*(Group Insurer)*
Phoenix, AZ

Continental Bank N. A.*(Major Banking Relationship)*
231 S. LaSalle St.
Chicago, IL 60697
Tel.: 312-828-2345
Tel.: 800-426-5754
Telex: 312-828-1783

GREEN MOUNTAIN HOLDING CORPORATION
Ethan Allen Drive
Danbury, CT 06811
Tel.: 203-743-8000
Fax: 203-743-8298
Approx.Sls.: $320,000,000
Emp.: 5,700
Fiscal Year-end: 6/30/90
Holding Company, Fine Furniture
S.I.C.: 6719; 2511; 2512
M. Farooq Kathwari *(Chm., Pres. & Chief Exec. Officer)*

Subsidiary:

Ethan Allen, Inc. **(1)**
Ethan Allen Dr.
Danbury, CT 06811
Tel.: 203-743-8000
Fax: 203-743-8298
Approx.Sls.: $1,000,000,000
Emp.: 5,200
Furniture
S.I.C.: 2511; 2512
M. Farooq Kathwari *(Chm., Pres. & Chief Exec. Officer)*
Edward P. Schade *(V.P. & Chief Fin. Officer)*
Sharon A. Blonkoff *(Corp. Counsel)*
Lenora Kirkley *(Dir.-Adv.)*
Charles Farfaglia *(Dir.-Personnel)*

LEONARD GREEN & PARTNERS
333 S. Grand Ave., Suite 5400
Los Angeles, CA 90071
Tel.: 213-625-0005
Investment Banking Firm
S.I.C.: 6211
Leonard Green *(Partner)*

Subsidiary:

Thrifty Corporation **(1)**
3424 Wilshire Blvd.
Los Angeles, CA

GREEN SPOT PACKAGING INC.
100 S. Cambridge
Claremont, CA 91711-4842
Mailing Address:
P.O. Box 2001,
Claremont, CA 91711-9001
Tel.: 909-625-8771
Fax: 909-621-4634
Year Founded: 1981
Approx.Sls.: $11,000,000
Emp.: 100
Fiscal Year-end: 9/31/91
Import Export
Aseptic Packager of Fruit Flavored Soft Drinks, 100 % Fruit Juicers; Concentrate Packers; Water
S.I.C.: 2086
C. C. Cheung *(Chm. Bd. & Pres.)*
Roger Nordin *(Pres.)*
Stephen Leung *(Chief Fin. Officer)*
Wiley Jones *(Exec. V.P.)*
Samuel F. Marino *(Exec. V.P.)*
Don Koury *(Controller)*
Stephen Reed *(Sec.)*

JACK GREENBERG INC.
1717 N. Delaware Ave.
Philadelphia, PA 19125
Tel.: 215-426-7200
Tel.: 800-441-9449 **PA**
Fax: 215-426-8530
Year Founded: 1943
Approx.Sls.: $106,000,000
Emp.: 70
Fiscal Year-end: 6/26/92
Import
Imports & Distributes Cheese, Canned & Frozen Meat
S.I.C.: 5142; 5143
Emanuel Greenberg *(Pres.)*
Fred Greenberg *(Exec. V.P., Sec. & Sls. Mgr.)*
Steve Cohn *(Controller)*

Computer Systems/Hardware:
NCR

Outside Service Firm(s):

Grant Thornton*(Auditors)*
2000 Market St.
Philadelphia, PA 19101

Pennsylvania Blue Shield*(Group Insurer)*
Philadelphia, PA

Philadelphia National Bank*(Major Banking Relationship)*
Philadelphia, PA

Affiliate:

Valhalla Trading Co. **(1)**
1717 N. Delaware Rd.
Philadelphia, PA 19125
Tel.: 215-426-8607
Valhalla Danish Hams & Pork Prods., Cheeses, Danish Cookies & Corned Beef
S.I.C.: 5142; 5143

M. H. GREENEBAUM, INC.
7 Century Dr.
Parsippany, NJ 07054
Mailing Address:
P.O. Box 6192
Parsippany, NJ 07054
Tel.: 201-538-9200
Fax: 201-538-3599
Year Founded: 1894
Approx.Sls.: $24,000,000
Emp.: 7
Fiscal Year-end: 6/30/92
Import
Danish Crown Canned Hams, Austrian Alps Cheese, Queen Kristina Hams (Taiwan), Zagreb Hams (Yugoslavia), Green Tree Hams (Holland)
S.I.C.: 5143; 2013
Linda Jensen *(V.P.-Sls.)*
Edward McCormick *(V.P.-Fin.)*

GREENGAGE ASSOCIATES, INC.
Graybar Bldg., 420 Lexington Ave., Ste. 1830
New York, NY 10170
Tel.: 212-867-7300
Fax: 212-867-0162
Year Founded: 1974
Approx.Billings: $16,000,000
Emp.: 15
Travel & Tourism, Hotels, Re-Insurance
Richard Gaetano Ferrelli *(Pres. & Acct. Services)*
Judith Cremin *(Pub. Rels.)*
Carroll Dorrell *(Controller)*

GREENHORNE & O'MARA, INC.
9001 Edmonston Rd.
Greenbelt, MD 20770
Tel.: 301-982-2800 **MD**
Fax: 301-220-2483
Year Founded: 1950
Assets: $29,197,000
Liabilities: $15,388,000
Net Worth: $13,809,000
Approx.Sls.: $67,000,000
Emp.: 740
Fiscal Year-end: 10/31/91
Engineers, Architects, Planners Scientists, Surveyors and Photogrammetrists
S.I.C.: 8712; 8713
A. James O'Mara *(Chm. Bd. & Chief Exec. Officer)*
William A. Caruthers *(Pres.)*
Robert P. Schocke *(Chief Fin. Officer, Treas., Controller & Sec.)*
Thomas Chicca *(V.P.-Eastern Region)*
Lawrence Courtney *(V.P.-Southeast Region)*
Yoram Gordon *(V.P.-Environmental Div.)*
Lowell Jackson *(V.P.-Transportation Div.)*
Maureen Kirker *(V.P.-Human Resources)*
Alan Lockman *(V.P.-Architecture)*
Brandon Smith *(V.P.-Southwest Region)*
Oyton Terteniz *(V.P.-Mid Atlantic Region)*
Bruce Yoder *(V.P.-Plng. Div.)*
Robert Field *(Gen. Counsel)*
Richard Garber *(Dir.-Quality Control)*
Joseph Michard *(Dir.-Pur.)*
Principal(s):
A. James O'Mara
William A. Caruthers
Thomas Chicca
Lawrence Courtney
Oyton Terteniz
Bruce Yoder
Brandon Smith
Yoram Gordon

No. of U.S. Offices: 18

Computer Systems/Hardware:
Data General

Outside Service Firm(s):

Ernst & Young*(Auditors)*
1225 Connecticut Ave., NW
Washington, DC 20036

B & B*(Commercial Insurance Carrier)*
Rockville, MD

NCAS*(Group Insurer)*
Fairfax, VA

Fossett & Brugger*(Legal Firm)*
Seabrook, MD

Citizens Bank*(Major Banking Relationship)*
Laurel, MD

GREENSTONE ROBERTS
ADVERTISING

GREENSTONE ROBERTS ADVERTISING
1 Huntington Quadrangle
Melville, NY 11747
Tel.: 516-249-2121
Fax: 516-249-6877
Year Founded: 1972
Approx.Billings: $85,000,000
Emp.: 135
Advertising Agency
S.I.C.: 7311
Ronald Greenstone *(Chm. & Chief Exec. Officer)*
Gary Roberts *(Pres., Chief Oper. Officer)*
Lamberto Cruz *(Sr. V.P., Chief Fin. Officer)*
Denise Anderson *(V.P.)*
Deborah C. Abramowicz *(V.P.)*
Principal(s):
Ronald Greenstone

GREENSTRIPE MEDIA, INC.
1300 Quail St., Ste. 209
Newport Beach, CA 92660
Tel.: 714-752-9277
Fax: 714-752-2964
Year Founded: 1977
Approx.Billings: $17,800,000
Emp.: 7
Broadcast Planning & Placement, Syndication & Political Campaigns
Joe Winkelmann *(Chm. Bd., Pres. & Chief Exec. Officer)*
Tony De Dios *(Gen. Mgr.)*

GREENWAY CO-OP SERVICE
3520 Third Ave., N.E.
Rochester, MN 55903
Mailing Address:
P.O. Box 6878
Rochester, MN 55903
Tel.: 507-289-4086
Fax: 507-289-7653
Year Founded: 1930
Approx.Sls.: $18,000,000
Emp.: 60
Wholesale & Retail Gas & Oil; Manufacture Fertilizer; Retail Farm Supplies
S.I.C.: 2875; 5172; 5191; 5541
Richard Brennan *(Chm. Bd.)*
Wayne Searles *(Vice Chm.)*
Dan Wodrich *(Controller & Chief Exec. Officer)*
John King *(Sec. & Treas.)*

Outside Service Firm(s):

Coopers & Lybrand*(Auditors)*
411 East Wisconsin Bldg.
Milwaukee, WI 53202

Dunlop, Keith & Collin*(Legal Firm)*
Minneapolis, MN

Norwest Bank Minnesota, N.A.*(Major Banking Relationship)*
Rochester, MN

GREENWICH AIR SERVICES
Miami Intl. Airport, Bldg. 2146
Miami, FL 33122
Mailing Address:
P.O. Box 522187
Miami, FL 33152
Tel.: 305-871-5300
Approx.Sls.: $100,000,000
Emp.: 800
Aviation Maintenance Base
S.I.C.: 4581
Eugene P. Conese, Sr. *(Chm. Bd.)*
Eugene P. Conese, Jr. *(Pres. & Chief Exec. Officer)*
Odney Johnson *(Exec. V.P.-Opers.)*
Albert Millberg *(Exec. V.P.-Fin.)*

GREENWOOD MILLS, INC.
104 Maxwell Ave.
Greenwood, SC 29646
Tel.: 803-229-2571
Fax: 803-941-4060
Approx.Sls.: $500,000,000
Emp.: 7,800
Mfr. Fabrics for Men's, Women's & Children's Apparel, Uniforms & Home Furnishings
S.I.C.: 2211; 2221; 2231
J.C. Se[illegible], Jr. *(Chm. & Chief Exec. Officer)*
W.M. Self *(Pres. & Chief Oper. Officer)*
Ted Colcolough *(Exec. V.P.-Mfg.)*
John W. Davis *(Exec. V.P.-Non-Textile Opers.)*
Paul Welder *(Exec. V.P.-Fin.)*
Dale Boyd *(V.P.-Greige Mfg.)*
Wayne Justesen *(V.P., Sec. & Gen. Counsel)*
J.A. Pate *(V.P.-Electronic Data Processing Services)*
Frank Robertson *(V.P.-Engrng.)*

Greenwood Mills, Inc.—(Continued)

Jimmy Thompson *(V.P.-Greige Mfg.)*
E.S. Pettit *(Asst. Treas.)*
C.F. Garren *(Dir.-Deferred Ben.)*
Billy Whaly *(Dir.-Mktg.)*

Computer Systems/Hardware:
IBM 3083

Outside Service Firm(s):

Elliott, Davis & Co.*(Auditors)*
Greenwood, SC

Aetna Life & Casualty*(Group Insurer)*
100 N. Riverside Plaza
Chicago, IL 60606

Provident Life & Accident Insurance Co.*(Group Insurer)*
P.O. Box 12015
Chattanooga, TN 37401
Tel.: 615-755-7088

Ivins, Phillips & Barker*(Legal Firm)*
Washington, DC

Chemical Banking Corp.*(Major Banking Relationship)*
277 Park Ave.
New York, NY 10041
Tel.: 212-310-6407
Fax: 212-310-4526

Chemical Bank*(Major Banking Relationship)*
450 West 33rd St.
New York, NY 10001
Tel.: 212-613-7197
Fax: 212-947-7628

Subsidiaries:

Environmental Resorts Inc. **(1)**
Greenwood Bldg.
Greenwood, SC 29646
Tel.: 803-227-2121

Greenwood Cotton Co. **(1)**
Greenwood Bldg.
Greenwood, SC 29646
Tel.: 803-227-2121

Greenwood Development Co. **(1)**
Greenwood Bldg.
Greenwood, SC 29646
Tel.: 803-227-2121

Greenwood Mills, Inc. **(1)**
111 W. 40th St.
New York, NY 10018
Tel.: 212-398-9200
Emp.: 180
Sales & Marketing
S.I.C.: 2211; 5137; 5136
Eugene Bekaert *(V.P. & Dir.-Creative Services)*
Robert E. Kaplan *(V.P.-Opers. & Mktg. Services)*
Kitty Cox *(Dir.-Mktg. Communications)*

Greenwood Warehouse Co. **(1)**
Greenwood Bldg.
Greenwood, SC 29646
Tel.: 803-227-2121

GREENWOOD PACKING PLANT
Packer St.
Greenwood, SC 29648
Mailing Address:
Box 188
Greenwood, SC 29648
Tel.: 803-229-5611
Approx.Sls.: $150,000,000
Emp.: 520
Pork & Beef Meat Packer
S.I.C.: 2011
P. H. Barnette *(Chm. Bd.)*
W. A. Barnette, Jr. *(Pres.)*
Bill Wilkerson *(Treas., Controller & Sec.)*
C. J. Brabham, Jr. *(Asst. V.P.-Employee Rel.)*

Outside Service Firm(s):

Elliott, Davis & Co.*(Auditors)*
Greenville, SC

Provident Life & Accident Insurance Co.*(Group Insurer)*
Hartford, CT

South Carolina National Bank*(Major Banking Relationship)*
Greenwood, SC

NationsBank Carolinas*(Pension Manager)*
Spartanburg, SC

AUTRY GREER & SONS, INC.
2850 W. Main St.
Prichard, AL 36612
Tel.: 205-457-8655 **DE**
Fax: 205-457-8655, Ext. 198
Year Founded: 1916
Approx.Sls.: $70,000,000
Emp.: 725
Grocery Store Chain; General Line of Groceries
S.I.C.: 5411; 5141
J. Barton Greer, Jr. *(Chm. Bd.)*
Jack V. Greer, Sr. *(Pres.)*
O.M. Ottis, III *(Chief Fin. Officer)*
Jack Greer *(V.P. & Treas.)*
Robert A. Greer *(V.P. & Sec.)*

Outside Service Firm(s):

S. Felton Mitchell, Jr.*(Auditors)*
Mobile, AL

GREER STEEL CO.
624 Blvd.
Dover, OH 44622
Mailing Address:
P.O. Box 280,
Dover, OH 44622
Tel.: 216-343-8811
Fax: 216-343-1700
Year Founded: 1917
Sales Range: $40-59 Million
Emp.: 250
Fiscal Year-end: 12/31/91
Mfr. of Cold Rolled Strip Steel & Flat Wire
S.I.C.: 3316
Robert M. Withew *(Pres.)*
Paul H. Eagle *(Exec. V.P.)*
G. David Peters *(V.P.-Sls.)*
R.L. Powell *(V.P.-Opers.)*
Lee Hartline *(Treas. & Controller)*

No. of Mfg. Plants/Facilities: 2

Computer Systems/Hardware:
Hewlett Packard 9000

Outside Service Firm(s):

Ernst & Young*(Auditors)*
One Cascade Plaza
Akron, OH 44308

Chubb Group*(Commercial Insurance Carrier)*
P.O. Box 1615,
Warren, NJ 07061
Tel.: 201-580-2000

Black, McCuskey, Souers & Arbaugh*(Legal Firm)*
1200 Harter Bank Bldg.
Canton, OH 44702
Tel.: 216-456-8341

The Huntington National Bank*(Major Banking Relationship)*
Dover, OH

The Huntington National Bank*(Pension Manager)*
41 S. High St.
Columbus, OH 43216

GREGG APPLIANCES INC.
(d/b/a H.H. Gregg)
4151 E. 96th St.
Indianapolis, IN 46240
Tel.: 317-848-8710 **IN**
Fax: 317-848-8723
Year Founded: 1955
Approx.Sls.: $99,000,000
Emp.: 400
Retail Radio & Television, Major Appliances
S.I.C.: 5731; 5722
William G. Throgmartin *(Chief Exec. Officer)*
Jerry Throgmartin *(Pres.)*
Ken Beckley *(Exec. V.P.)*
Mike Stout *(Dir.-Sls.)*
Principal(s):
William G. Throgmartin

Outside Service Firm(s):

Ernst & Young*(Auditors)*
One Indiana Square, Ste. 3400
Indianapolis, IN 46204
Tel.: 317-236-1100

Merchants National Bank & Trust Company of Indianapolis*(Major Banking Relationship)*
One Merchants Plaza, Ste. 901E
Indianapolis, IN 46255
Tel.: 317-267-7109

GREGG INDUSTRIES, INC.
10460 Hickson St.
El Monte, CA 91734
Tel.: 818-575-7664
Fax: 818-401-0971
Year Founded: 1940
Approx.Sls.: $17,000,000
Emp.: 218
Manufacture Iron Castings
S.I.C.: 3321
Charles R. Gregg *(Chm. Bd.)*
Robert C. Gregg *(Pres.)*
Tom Hough *(Chief Fin. Officer)*
Chris Gregg *(V.P.)*
James Addis *(Mgr.-Sls.)*
Maria Kauffman *(Mgr.-Data Processing)*

Outside Service Firm(s):

McGladrey & Pullen*(Auditors)*
Pasadena, CA

Security Pacific National Bank*(Major Banking Relationship)*
El Monte, CA

GREGORY AFFILIATES, INC.
4800 S.W. Griffith Dr., Ste. 300
Beaverton, OR 97005
Tel.: 503-526-5600
Fax: 503-644-8428
Approx.Sls.: $72,000,000
Emp.: 475
Holding Company; Manufacture Lumber, Plywood & Veneer; Wholesale Forest Products
S.I.C.: 6719; 2421; 2435; 2411; 5031
William H. Gregory *(Chm. Bd. & Pres.)*
Marie Gregory *(V.P.)*
Noelle Statter *(Sec.)*
Lyle Adams *(Treas.)*

Outside Service Firm(s):

Price Waterhouse*(Auditors)*
1221 S.W. Morrison, Suite 1800
Portland, OR 97204
Tel.: 503-224-9040

U.S. National Bank*(Major Banking Relationship)*
309 S.W. Sixth Ave.
Portland, OR 97208
Tel.: 503-275-4942

GREGORY & CLYBURNE, INC.
45 Church St.
Stamford, CT 06906
Tel.: 203-327-6333
Fax: 203-353-8180
Year Founded: 1973
Approx.Billings: $12,000,000
Emp.: 18
Corporate Image Advertising
James R. Gregory *(Pres.)*
Tom Zara *(Exec. V.P.)*
Evelyn Clyburne *(Sec. & Treas.)*
Ann M. Gantz *(Controller)*
Jay Moody *(Dir.-Pub. Rels.)*

GRESS FOODS INC.
950 Industrial Blvd.
Gainesville, GA 30501
Tel.: 706-536-8818
Fax: 706-531-1487
Approx.Sls.: $71,000,000
Emp.: 900
Poultry Processor & Hatcheries
S.I.C.: 0254; 2015
Ronald D. Gress *(Pres.)*
Lee E. Ellenburg *(V.P.-Fin.)*
Peter Gress *(V.P.-Intl. Sls.)*
Diane Austin *(Dir.-Personnel)*
Bill Fissasloo *(Dir.-Pur., Sec. & Treas.)*

Outside Service Firm(s):

Wayne I. Bowen*(Auditors)*
Atlanta, GA

Whelchel Dunlap & Gignilliat*(Legal Firm)*
Atlanta, GA

First National Bank of Atlanta*(Major Banking Relationship)*
2 Peachtree Street N.W.
Atlanta, GA 30383

GREY EAGLE DISTRIBUTORS INC.
2340 Millpark Dr.
Maryland Heights, MO 63043
Tel.: 314-429-9100 **MO**
Fax: 314-429-9137
Year Founded: 1963
Approx.Sls.: $62,000,000
Emp.: 150
Beer Distributor
S.I.C.: 5181
Jerry Clinton *(Chm. Bd. & Pres.)*
Jeff Clinton *(V.P. & Gen. Mgr.)*
Steve Nolan *(Sec.)*
Steve Jones *(Mgr.-Mktg.)*
Buz Schoo *(Mgr.-Sls.)*

Outside Service Firm(s):

KPMG Peat Marwick*(Auditors)*
1010 Market St.
Saint Louis, MO 63101
Tel.: 314-444-1400

Commerce Bank of Kansas City*(Major Banking Relationship)*
10th & Walnut
Kansas City, MO 64141
Tel.: 816-234-2000
Fax: 816-234-2548

THE GRIEVE CORPORATION
500 Hart Rd.
Round Lake, IL 60073
Tel.: 708-546-8225 **IL**
Fax: 708-546-9210
Year Founded: 1949
Approx.Sls.: $10,000,000
Emp.: 150
Fiscal Year-end: 12/31/91
Export
Industrial Ovens & Furnaces
S.I.C.: 3567
G.P. Grieve *(Chm. Bd.)*
P.J. Calabrese *(Pres.)*
D.V. Grieve *(V.P.-Engrng.)*
H.W. Grieve *(Sec.)*
F.P. Calabrese *(Mgr.-Sls.)*
Principal(s):
G.P. Grieve
P.J. Calabrese

Outside Service Firm(s):

Defrees & Fiske*(Legal Firm)*
Chicago, IL

Manufacturers National Bank N.A.*(Major Banking Relationship)*
38th Fl., 100 Renaissance Center
Detroit, MI 48243
Tel.: 313-222-4227

GRIFFIN BACAL INC.
130 Fifth Ave.
New York, NY 10011
Tel.: 212-337-6300
Year Founded: 1978
Approx.Billings: $195,300,000
Emp.: 183
Kids & Families, Leisure & Lifestyle Marketing, Consumer Electronics, Sports/Sporting Goods, Packaged Goods, Business to Business, New Product Development & Licensing
Tom Griffin *(Co-Chm. & Chief Exec. Officer)*
Joe Bacal *(Co-Chm. & Dir. Creative Services)*
Paul Kurnit *(Pres. & Chief Oper. Officer)*
Myer Berlow *(Exec. V.P., Dir. of Bus. Devel.)*
Lenny Leokum *(Exec. V.P., Creative Dir.)*
Art Heller *(Exec. V.P., Dir. Media Services)*
Loretta Volpe *(Exec. V.P., Dir. Media/ Mktg. Services)*
Bill Beihl *(Sr. V.P., Chief Fin. Officer)*
Arnie Berger *(Sr. V.P., Grp. Dir.)*
David Biebelberg *(Sr. V.P., Grp. Dir.)*
Ned Clausen *(Sr. V.P., Grp. Dir.)*
Richard Conti *(Sr. V.P., Grp. Dir.)*
J. Edmund Keating *(Sr. V.P., Grp. Dir.)*
Bob Horne *(Sr. V.P., Grp. Dir.)*
Bob Kantor *(Sr. V.P., Grp. Dir.)*
Jeff Marks *(Sr. V.P., Grp. Dir.)*
Lisa Kaye *(V.P., Dir. Local TV)*
Sharyn Esposito *(V.P., Bus. Affairs)*
Janice Figueroa *(V.P., Strategic Plng.)*

GRIFFIN CORPORATION
P.O. Box 1847
Valdosta, GA 31603
Tel.: 912-242-8635
Fax: 912-244-5813
Year Founded: 1935
Sales Range: $80-99 Million
Emp.: 200
Fiscal Year-end: 9/30/90
Import Export
Production of Agriculture Chemicals
S.I.C.: 2879; 5191; 5169
Allen W. Mathis, Jr. *(Chm. Bd.)*
Michael R. Schimmenti *(Pres. & Chief Oper. Officer)*
Rutledge A. Griffin, Jr. *(Chief Exec. Officer)*
Ed Gaw *(Chief Fin. Officer, Treas. & Sec.)*
Theresa Lamie *(Dir.-Personnel)*
David Mims *(Mgr.-Mngmt. Information Systems)*

Principal(s):
Rutledge A. Griffin, Jr.

No. of Mfg. Plants/Facilities: 3
No. of U.S. Offices: 3
No. of Foreign Offices: 1

Computer Systems/Hardware:
IBM AS/400

Outside Service Firm(s):

Price Waterhouse*(Auditors)*
Savannah, GA

Alexander & Alexander*(Commercial Insurance Carrier)*
Two Piedmont Center, 3565 Piedmont Rd. N.E.
Atlanta, GA 30363

Tillman, McTier, Coleman, Talley & Newborn*(Legal Firm)*
Valdosta, GA

Citizens & Southern Trust Company, Inc.*(Major Banking Relationship)*
Valdosta, GA

Subsidiaries:

Griffin Ag Products Inc. **(1)**
P.O. Box 1847
Valdosta, GA 31603
Tel.: 912-242-8635

Griffin International **(1)**
P.O. Box 1848
Valdosta, GA 31603
Tel.: 912-242-8635

Griffin Mining Co. **(1)**
P.O. Box 1848
Valdosta, GA 31603
Tel.: 912-242-8635

Kocide Chemical Co. **(1)**
P.O. Box 1847
Valdosta, GA 31603
Tel.: 912-242-8635

GRIFFIN ENVELOPE, INC.
4301 E. Marginal Way S.
Seattle, WA 98134
Mailing Address:
P.O. Box 24267
Seattle, WA 98124
Tel.: 206-682-4400
Fax: 206-682-2170
Year Founded: 1912
Sales Range: $10-19 Million
Emp.: 80
Manufacturer Of Envelopes
S.I.C.: 2677
Donald Watson *(Pres.)*
Joe Ritchie *(V.P.-Sls.)*
Grant Woodfield *(Controller)*

GRIFFIN HOMES, INC.
24005 Ventura Blvd.
Calabasas, CA 91302
Tel.: 818-591-2500 **CA**
Fax: 818-591-0087
Year Founded: 1960
Approx.Sls.: $230,000,000
Emp.: 225
Speculative Builders of Single-Family Houses
S.I.C.: 1531
Paul E. Griffin *(Chm. Bd.)*
Bruce Freeman *(Pres.)*
Gloria Griffin *(Sr. V.P.)*

Outside Service Firm(s):

Pollick & Andreasen*(Auditors)*
Los Angeles, CA

BankAmerica Corp.*(Major Banking Relationship)*
Anaheim, CA

GRIFFIN INDUSTRIES, INC.
4221 Alexandria Pike
Cold Spring, KY 41076
Tel.: 606-781-2010 **KY**
Fax: 606-572-2575
Year Founded: 1943
Approx.Sls.: $108,000,000
Emp.: 850
Inedible Grease & Tallow Rendering
S.I.C.: 2077
John L. Griffin, Sr. *(Chm. Bd.)*
Dennis B. Griffin *(Pres. & Chief Exec. Officer)*
John M. Griffin *(Exec. V.P.)*
Robert A. Griffin *(V.P.)*

Divisions:

Atlanta Processing Co. Div. **(1)**
4413 Tanner Church Rd.
Ellenwood, GA 30049
Tel.: 404-363-1320
R. Barron *(Gen. Mgr.)*

Tampa Soap Div. **(1)**
10001 Orient Rd.
Tampa, FL 33619
Tel.: 813-626-1135
John Hardy *(Gen. Mgr.)*

GRIFFIN MANUFACTURING CO.
111 S. Cherokee
Muskogee, OK 74403
Mailing Address:
P.O. Box 1928,
Muskogee, OK 74402
Tel.: 918-687-6311
Fax: 918-687-3579
Year Founded: 1908
Approx.Sls.: $13,000,000
Emp.: 80
Fiscal Year-end: 6/30/91
Import
Griffin's Waffle Syrup, Coconut & Canned Foods, Preserves, Jellies, Salad Dressing, Mustards & Spices
S.I.C.: 2035; 2062
Martha Griffin *(Chm. Bd.)*
John W. Griffin *(Pres.)*
Bill Kennedy *(Chief Exec. Officer)*
Randy Webb *(Chief Fin. Officer)*
Mike Miller *(Dir.-Mktg.)*

Computer Systems/Hardware:
IBM System 34

GRIFFITH LABORATORIES WORLDWIDE, INC.
1 Griffith Center
Alsip, IL 60658
Tel.: 708-371-0900 **IL**
Telex: 190-143
Fax: 708-597-3294
Year Founded: 1919
Approx.Sls.: $338,000,000
Emp.: 2,500
Fiscal Year-end: 9/30/91
Mfr. Food Ingredients; Sterilization Services
S.I.C.: 2099
Dean L. Griffith *(Chm. Bd.)*
Hedric E. Rhodes *(Pres. & Chief Exec. Officer)*
B. Robert Kill *(Sr. V.P.-Intl. Accts.)*
Ralph A. Sair, Ph.D. *(Sr. V.P.-Worldwide Technical & Mktg.)*
Joseph R. Maslick *(Sr. V.P., Chief Fin. Officer & Sec.)*
William C. Frost *(V.P.-Fin. Services)*
James H. McClain *(V.P.-Human Resources)*
James S. Legg *(Gen. Counsel & Asst. Sec.)*
Brian J. Tuttle *(Treas.)*
Drew M. Bandusky *(Intl. Controller)*
Hugh Martin *(Dir.-Plng. & Devel.)*

Outside Service Firm(s):

KPMG Peat Marwick*(Auditors)*
Peat Marwick Plaza, 303 E. Wacker Dr.
Chicago, IL 60601
Tel.: 312-938-1000

Peers & Co.*(Investment Banker)*
Chicago, IL

Bell, Boyd & Lloyd*(Legal Firm)*
Three First National Plaza
Chicago, IL 60602
Tel.: 312-372-1121

Continental Bank N. A.*(Major Banking Relationship)*
231 S. LaSalle St.
Chicago, IL 60697
Tel.: 312-828-2345
Tel.: 800-426-5754
Telex: 312-828-1783

Northern Capital Management, Inc.*(Pension Manager)*
6510 Grand Teton Plaza, Suite 412
Madison, WI
Tel.: 608-829-2990

Subsidiaries:

Custom Food Products Inc. **(1)**
730 N. Albany
Chicago, IL 60612
Tel.: 312-722-7500
Mfr. of Private-Label Soup Bases, Gravies & Sauces for the Food Service Industry
S.I.C.: 2099
Martin Overton *(Chief Oper. Officer)*

Griffith Micro Science International Inc. **(1)**
200 S. Frontage Rd., Ste. 120
Burr Ridge, IL 60521
Tel.: 708-654-5150
Fax: 708-654-5181
Contract Gas Sterilization Service
S.I.C.: 8734
William Dow *(Pres.)*
Richard L. Rediehs *(Dir.-Fin.)*

Non-U.S. Holdings:

Griffith Colombia S.A. **(1)**
P.O. Box AA 8589 Carrera 51-A, No. 10-Sur-81,
Medellin, Colombia
Tel.: 4-285-3911
Fax: 4-285-0193
Mfr. of Food Ingredients
S.I.C.: 2099
Juan Carlos Eisen *(Pres.-Latin American Grp.)*

Griffith Laboratories (H.K.) Ltd. **(1)**
8th Flr., Unit A-B, Supreme Industrial Bldg.
15 Shan Mei St., Fo-Tan,
Shatin, N.T. Hong Kong
Tel.: 604-5008
Telex: 36819 GRIF HX
Fax: 694-9149
Mfr. of Food Ingredients
S.I.C.: 2099
Henry Szeto *(Chief Oper. Officer)*

Griffith Laboratories Iberia S.A. **(1)**
Apartado de Correos 78 E-43800
Valls, Tarragona Spain
Tel.: 77-602200
Telex: 56776 GRIL E
Mfr. of Food Ingredients
S.I.C.: 2099

Griffith Laboratories Ireland Limited **(1)**
Pineview Industrial Estate, Firhouse Road
Dublin, 16, Ireland
Tel.: 1-936-000
Telex: 93555
Fax: 1-936-151
Mfr. of Food Ingredients
S.I.C.: 2099

Griffith Laboratories Italia S.r.l. **(1)**
Via Cassia 640 00189
Rome, Italy
Tel.: 6-3666809
Telex: 621451
Fax: 6-3665377
Mfr. of Food Ingredients
S.I.C.: 2099
Maurizio Panzetti *(Chief Oper. Officer)*

Griffith Laboratories, K.K. **(1)**
NSS Building, 13-31, Kohnan 2-Chome
Minato-Ku,
Tokyo, 108, Japan
Tel.: 03-3450-1231
Telex: J34898 GLJTKO
Fax: 3-3450-2608
Mfr. of Food Ingredients
S.I.C.: 2099
Dr. Junzo Tokunaga *(Chief Oper. Officer)*

Griffith Laboratories Limited **(1)**
P.O. Box 22-434, 11-13 Bell Ave. Otahuhu,
Auckland, 6, New Zealand
Tel.: 9-592-059
Fax: 9-595-795
Mfr. of Food Ingredients
S.I.C.: 2099
Phil Taylor *(Chief Oper. Officer)*

Griffith Laboratories Limited **(1)**
482 Mu 19 Soi Pookmitr Rod Rang Kao Rd., Samrong Tai,
Samutprakan, 10130, Thailand
Tel.: 2 384 0036
Telex: 20538 GRIFLAB/TH
Fax: 2-384-0817
Mfr. of Food Ingredients
S.I.C.: 2099
Akom Palanuwech *(Chief Oper. Officer)*

The Griffith Laboratories, Ltd. **(1)**
Cannington, ON L0E 1E0, Canada
Tel.: 705-432-2682
Mfr. of Food Ingredients
S.I.C.: 2099

Griffith Laboratories Worldwide, Inc.—(Continued)

Griffith Laboratories Limited **(1)**
Cotes Park Estate
Somercotes, Derbyshire DE5 4NN, United Kingdom
Tel.: 773-832171
Telex: 37456 GRILAB G
Fax: 773-835-294
Mfr. of Food Ingredients
S.I.C.: 2099
James Nicholson *(Chief Oper. Officer)*

The Griffith Laboratories Ltd. **(1)**
757 Pharmacy Ave.
Scarborough, ON M1L 3J8, Canada
Tel.: 416-288-3050
Telex: 06 96 3562 GRIFLAB TOR
Fax: 416-288-3481
Mfrs. Food Preparations, Rice Milling & Food Prods. Machinery
S.I.C.: 2099; 2044; 3565
Alan Hawley *(Pres. & Chief Exec. Officer)*

Griffith Laboratories (Phils.) Inc. **(1)**
Building No. 2, Honeydew Rd. FT Complex, Tagig,
Manila, Philippines
Tel.: 2-816-28-91
Telex: 26433 GRIFLAB PH
Fax: 2-815-1788
Mfr. of Food Ingredients
S.I.C.: 2099
Joselito L. Lacson *(Chief Oper. Officer)*

Griffith Laboratories Pte. Ltd. **(1)**
1, Defu Lane 10, #03-567 Defu Industrial Park
Singapore, 1953, Singapore
Tel.: 286-9482
Fax: 382-2640
Mfr. of Food Ingredients
S.I.C.: 2099
Albert Tee *(Area Mgr.)*

Griffith Laboratories Pty., Ltd. **(1)**
23 Britton St.
Smithfield, N.S.W. 2164, Australia
Tel.: 2 604 1400 (100%)
Telex: AA 22430 GRIFLAB (Sydney)
Fax: 02-725-1360
Mfr. of Food Chemicals
S.I.C.: 2099

Griffith Laboratories Pty., Ltd. **(1)**
1 Griffith St.
Scoresby, Victoria 3179, Australia
Tel.: 3-763-5300
Telex: AA 32358 GRIFLAB
Fax: 3 763 4887
Mfr. of Food Ingredients
S.I.C.: 2099
Graham Robertson *(Chief Oper. Officer)*

N.V. Griffith Laboratories S.A. **(1)**
Toekomstlaan, Wolfstee Industriepark B-2200
Herentals, Belgium
Tel.: 14 21 50 00
Telex: 33791 griflab b
Fax: 14 22 00 53
Mfrs. Food Ingredients; Commercial Testing Laboratory
S.I.C.: 2099; 8734
Marc van Moerbeke *(Chief Oper. Officer)*

Griffith Panama S.A. **(1)**
via Argentina, Balmoral Building, 10th Flr., Apt. 10A P.O. Box 1391-9A,
Panama, Panama
Tel.: 507-63-7078
Telex: 3467 GRIFSA PG
Fax: 507-64-7370
Mfr. of Food Ingredients
S.I.C.: 2099
Ricardo A. Cavazos *(Chief Oper. Officer)*

Laboratorios Griffith de Centro America S.A. **(1)**
Apd. 7-2820 (1000),
San Jose, Costa Rica
Tel.: 39-01-36
Telex: 7510 LABGRIF
Fax: 39-19-42
Mfr. of Food Ingredients
S.I.C.: 2099
Juan Carlos Eisen *(Chief Oper. Officer)*

Laboratories Griffith de Mexico, S.A. de C.V. **(1)**
Apartado Postal 1832
Monterrey, N.L. Mexico
Tel.: 83-36-28-28
Telex: 0382-753 GRIFME
Fax: 838-80425
Mfr. of Food Ingredients
S.I.C.: 2099
Alvaro Palma *(Chief Oper. Officer)*
Raul de Jesus Sanchez *(Chief Fin. Officer)*

JACK GRIGGS INC.
1149 S. Kaweah
Exeter, CA 93221
Tel.: 209-592-3154 **CA**
Fax: 209-592-3583
Sales Range: $10-19 Million
Emp.: 33
Exxon Petroleum Jobbers; Propane or LPG Jobbers
S.I.C.: 7389; 5171
David Griggs *(Pres., Chief Exec. & Chief Fin. Officer & Treas.)*
Forest Griggs, III *(V.P.)*
Forest Griggs, Jr. *(Sec.)*
Principal(s):
David Griggs
Forest Griggs, III
Forest Griggs, Jr.

Computer Systems/Hardware:
NCR

Outside Service Firm(s):

J. Paul Kirth*(Auditors)*
Lindsey, CA

American Crown Life Insurance Co.*(Group Insurer)*
New York, NY

GRIMMER REALTY CO. INC.
2000 SouthBridge Pkwy., Ste. 100
Birmingham, AL 35209
Tel.: 205-879-2376 **AL**
Fax: 205-879-2410
Year Founded: 1962
Sales Range: $20-39 Million
Emp.: 6
Commercial Real Estate Developer & Broker
S.I.C.: 6552; 6153
James B. Grimmer *(Chm. Bd.)*
Park Grimmer *(Pres.)*
Susan L. Grimmer *(V.P. & Treas.)*
Rose J. Grimmer *(Sec.)*

No. of U.S. Offices: 1

GRINDMASTER CORPORATION
1733 Research Dr.
Louisville, KY 40299
Mailing Address:
P.O. Box 35020,
Louisville, KY 40232
Tel.: 502-499-0770
Tel.: 800-695-4500 **DE**
Fax: 502-499-0245
Year Founded: 1933
Sales Range: $10-19 Million
Emp.: 95
Fiscal Year-end: 12/31/91
Import Export
Manufacture Of Commercial Coffee & Peanut Grinders, Coffee Brewers & Beverage Dispensing Equipment
S.I.C.: 3556
Thomas C. McDonald *(Chm. Bd.)*
Karl D. Kuiper *(Pres.)*
Doug Dyke *(V.P.-Opers.)*
Larry Johnson *(V.P.-Sls.)*
Carl Smith *(V.P.-Fin.)*
Doug Nance *(Dir.-Sls.)*
Brian Newman *(Dir.-Research & Devel.)*
Karen Adams *(Mgr.-Plant & Pur.)*
Jim Cox *(Mfr. Engr.)*
Debbie Forns *(Office Mgr.)*
Ruth Keddem *(Pur. Mgr.-Canton)*
Steve Kirshaer *(Mgr.-Mngmt. Information Systems)*
Lisa Lancaster *(Mgr.-Mktg.)*
Principal(s):
Thomas C. McDonald
Karl D. Kuiper

No. of Mfg. Plants/Facilities: 2
No. of U.S. Offices: 2

Computer Systems/Hardware:
Hewlett Packard

Outside Service Firm(s):

Arthur Andersen & Co.*(Auditors)*
2300 Meidinger Tower
Louisville, KY 40202
Tel.: 502-589-4160

Alexander & Alexander*(Commercial Insurance Carrier)*
220 W. Main St., Ste. 1800
Louisville, KY 40202-1395
Tel.: 502-561-1500
Fax: 502-561-1535

Brown, Todd & Heyburn*(Legal Firm)*
Citizens Plaza, 16th Fl.
Louisville, KY 40202
Tel.: 502-589-5400

First National Bank of Louisville*(Major Banking Relationship)*
Louisville, KY

GRISANTI, INC.
9300 Shelbyville Rd., Ste. 1006
Louisville, KY 40222
Tel.: 502-429-0341
Approx.Sls.: $42,750,000
Emp.: 2,985
Chain of Italian Restaurants
S.I.C.: 5812
Michael J. Grisanti *(Pres. & Chief Exec. Officer)*
Patrick J. McGafferty *(Sec., Treas. & Chief Fin. Officer)*
John Greenuk *(Mgr.-Mktg.)*

GRISWOLD INDUSTRIES, INC.
1701 Placentia Ave.
Costa Mesa, CA 92627
Tel.: 714-548-2201 **CA**
Fax: 714-548-5441
Year Founded: 1970
Approx.Sls.: $25,000,000
Emp.: 450
Control Valves; Fluid Power; Hydraulic & Pneumatic; Sprinkler Systems
S.I.C.: 3492; 3494
Norbert M. Warkocki *(Chief Exec. Officer)*
Donald G. Griswold *(Pres.)*
Enn Rehaste *(Controller)*
Harold W. Ensign *(Dir.-Engrng.)*
Steve Merchant *(Dir.-Pur.)*

Outside Service Firm(s):

First Interstate Bank*(Major Banking Relationship)*
P.O. Box 53441,
Phoenix, AZ 85072-3441
Tel.: 602-229-4049

Divisions:

Cla-Val Div. **(1)**
P.O. Box 1325
Newport Beach, CA 92659
Tel.: 714-548-2201
Approx.Sls.: $25,000,000
Emp.: 450
Automatic Regulating Valves
S.I.C.: 3492
Donald G. Griswold *(Chm. Bd.)*
Enn Rehaste *(Controller)*
Geraldine Beegan *(Sec.)*

Soundcast Company **(1)**
1701 Placentia Ave.
Costa Mesa, CA 92627
Tel.: 714-548-2201
Castings, Except Die; Copper & Copper-base Alloy
S.I.C.: 3492; 3494
Donald G. Griswold *(Pres.)*

GRIZZARD ADVERTISING, INC.
1144 Mailing Ave., SE
Atlanta, GA 30315
Mailing Address:
P.O. Box 1563,
Atlanta, GA 30301
Tel.: 404-622-1501
Tel.: 800-241-9351
Fax: 404-627-7582
Year Founded: 1919
Approx.Billings: $23,490,000
Emp.: 125
Direct Mail Adv. & Direct Mail Fund Raising
Claude H. Grizzard, Sr. *(Chm. Bd.)*
Claude T. Grizzard, Jr. *(Vice Chm.)*
Roger Hackman *(Vice Chm.)*
Glenn W. Summerlin *(Pres.)*
Michael D. Dzvonik *(Exec. V.P.)*
Debbi B. Layfield *(Sr. V.P.)*
Ted W. Grigg *(V.P.)*
H. Gary Halperin *(V.P.)*
James P. Leak *(V.P.)*
James R. Todd *(V.P.)*
William C. Anderson *(V.P.)*
Clyde A. Tallent *(Dir., Pur.)*
Sylvia D. Estes *(Dir., Human Resources)*
Jody Adkison *(Data Entry Supvr.)*
Judy Howard *(Asst. Controller)*
Melissa Delk *(Human Resources Asst.)*

GROCERS BAKING CO.
210 28th St. S.E.
Grand Rapids, MI 49508
Tel.: 616-245-9127 **MI**
Fax: 616-245-2368
Year Founded: 1934
Approx.Sls.: $55,000,000
Emp.: 600
Cooperative; Wholesale Bread, Rolls, Sweet Rolls, Cakes, Doughnuts & Pies
S.I.C.: 5149
Walter Goff *(Chm. Bd.)*
Rod Folkert *(Pres. & Chief Exec. Officer)*
Keith Bazaire *(Treas.)*
Ray Van Haecke *(Dir.-Data Processing)*

No. of Mfg. Plants/Facilities: 1
No. of U.S. Offices: 12

Computer Systems/Hardware:
IBM System 36

Outside Service Firm(s):

Deloitte & Touche*(Auditors)*
Grand Rapids, MI

Comerica Bank International*(Major Banking Relationship)*
Grand Rapids, MI

Comerica Bank*(Major Banking Relationship)*
211 W. Fort St.
Detroit, MI 48226
Tel.: 313-222-3300

Subsidiary:

April Hill, Inc. **(1)**
190 28th St., SE
Grand Rapids, MI 49508
Tel.: 616-245-0595
Emp.: 75
Produces Frozen Bakery Foods
S.I.C.: 2051; 2053
Elmer Blatz *(Pres. & Chief Exec. Officer)*

GROCERS SUPPLY CO. INC.
3131 E. Holcombe Blvd.
Houston, TX 77021
Mailing Address:
P.O. Box 14200
Houston, TX 77221
Tel.: 713-747-5000
Fax: 713-749-9368
Year Founded: 1923

Approx.Sls.: $1,000,000,000
Emp.: 1,200
Independent Wholesale Food Distributor
S.I.C.: 5141; 5122; 5145; 5072
Milton Levit *(Pres.)*
Max Levit *(V.P.)*
Robert Ozmun *(Chief Fin. Officer & Controller)*
Gerald Levit *(Sec. & Treas.)*
Melvin Emmons *(Gen. Counsel)*
Clarence Chadwick *(Dir.-Human Rels.)*
James Nelson *(Mgr.-Credit)*
Robert Lowrey *(Acct. Mgr.)*
John Patrick *(Mgr.-Data Processing)*
Jack Todd *(Mgr.-Fin.)*

Outside Service Firm(s):

Arthur Andersen & Co.*(Auditors)*
711 Louisiana, Ste. 1300
Houston, TX 77002-2323
Tel.: 713-237-2793

Life Insurance Co. of the Southwest*(Group Insurer)*
Dallas, TX

Hirsch & Westheimer*(Legal Firm)*
Houston, TX

First City National Bank*(Major Banking Relationship)*
Houston, TX

Texas Commerce Bank*(Pension Manager)*
717 Travis St.
Houston, TX 77002
Tel.: 713-236-4636
Fax: 713-236-5476

Subsidiaries:

Grocers Supply Institution **(1)**
3131 E. Holcombe Blvd.
Houston, TX 77021
Tel.: 713-747-5000

Grocers Supply International **(1)**
411 Brisbane
Houston, TX 77061
Tel.: 713-641-9792

Grocers Supply Small Business **(1)**
3131 E. Holcombe Blvd.
Houston, TX 77021
Tel.: 713-747-5000

Masterbilt Fixtures, Inc. **(1)**
3131 E. Holcombe Blvd.
Houston, TX 77021
Tel.: 713-747-5000

GROENDYKE TRANSPORTS, INC.
2510 Rock Island Blvd.
Enid, OK 73701
Tel.: 405-234-4663 **OK**
Fax: 405-234-1216
Approx.Sls.: $76,000,000
Emp.: 1,000
Trucking Except Local
S.I.C.: 4213
John Groendyke *(Chm. Bd.)*
Max E. Barton *(Pres. & Chief Exec. Officer)*

Outside Service Firm(s):

Baird, Kurtz & Dobson*(Auditors)*
Enid, OK

Central National Bank*(Major Banking Relationship)*
Enid, OK

GROESBECK LUMBER & SUPPLY, INC.
23155 Groesbeck Hwy.
Warren, MI 48089
Tel.: 313-776-5410
Fax: 313-776-1540
Approx.Sls.: $15,000,000
Emp.: 30
Millwork & Lumber
S.I.C.: 5211
Robert D. Matuja *(Pres.)*
Dennis Matuja *(V.P.)*

Outside Service Firm(s):

Burnstein, Norris & Brown*(Auditors)*
Southfield, MI

Bailey & Tull*(Legal Firm)*
Utica, MI

Manufacturers National Bank N.A.*(Major Banking Relationship)*
38th Fl., 100 Renaissance Center
Detroit, MI 48243
Tel.: 313-222-4227

GROMER SUPER MARKETS, INC.
585 N. McLean Blvd.
Elgin, IL 60123
Tel.: 708-742-4460
Fax: 708-742-6310
Approx.Sls.: $20,000,000
Emp.: 175
Retail Super Markets
S.I.C.: 5411
Richard H. Gromer *(Pres. & Chief Exec. Officer)*
Bernice E. Gromer *(V.P. & Sec.)*
John Landeck *(Controller)*

Outside Service Firm(s):

Elgin State Bank*(Major Banking Relationship)*
Elgin, IL

JOHN GROSS & CO.
1521 Edgewood St.
Baltimore, MD 21227
Tel.: 410-646-1445
Approx.Sls.: $10,000,000
Emp.: 29
Fiscal Year-end: 12/31/90
Scotch Whisky: Black Bull, Drumochter, Excalibur, Glen Coull, Highland Park, McColl's, Regis Royal & Tomatin
S.I.C.: 2085
John J. Gross *(Partner)*
Milton M. Gross *(Partner)*
C. Lucas *(Office Mgr.)*
E. Wallens *(Sec.)*

GROSSENBURG IMPLEMENTS, INCORPORATED
P.O. Box 311
Winner, SD 57580-0311
Tel.: 605-842-2040
Fax: 605-842-3485
Approx.Sls.: $12,000,000
Emp.: 54
Wholesale & Retail Stores, Farm Machinery, Tires, Appliances
S.I.C.: 5014; 5064; 5083; 5699; 5722
Gene C. Grossenburg *(Pres.)*
Barry Grossenburg *(Exec. V.P.)*
Norman Nielson *(Treas.)*
Blanche Grossenburg *(Sec.)*
Rodney Grossenburg *(Mgr.-Sls.)*
Ray Hannedt *(Mgr.-Adv.)*

Outside Service Firm(s):

Kim Dean*(Auditors)*
Winner, SD

Day & Grossenburg*(Legal Firm)*
Winner, SD

First Fidelity Bank, N.A.*(Major Banking Relationship)*
Winner, SD

GROSSMAN IRON & STEEL COMPANY
5 N. Market
St. Louis, MO 63102
Tel.: 314-231-9423 **MO**
Fax: 314-231-6983
Wholesale Distribution of Nonferrous Scrap Metals; Ferrous Metal Scrap & Waste
S.I.C.: 5093
Sidney Grossman *(Chm. Bd.)*
David Grossman *(Pres.)*
John Lorinc *(V.P., Sec. & Treas.)*

Outside Service Firm(s):

Husch, Eppenberger, Donohue, Elson & Cornfield*(Legal Firm)*
100 N. Broadway
St. Louis, MO 63102
Tel.: 314-421-4800

Cass Bank*(Major Banking Relationship)*
St. Louis, MO

M. GROSSMAN SON, INC.
245 4th St.
Passaic, NJ 07055
Tel.: 201-779-4651
Fax: 201-473-9663
Year Founded: 1933
Approx.Sls.: $10,000,000
Emp.: 232
Manufacture Ladies Millinery
S.I.C.: 2353
Max Grossman *(Pres.)*
Bernard Grossman *(V.P.-Sls., Mktg. & Fin.)*
Elliott Taradash *(V.P.-Production, Sec. & Treas.)*
Carol Scidillo *(Pur. Agent)*

Outside Service Firm(s):

Sax, Macy, Fromm & Company*(Auditors)*
Clifton, NJ

Michael Sternick*(Legal Firm)*
Paterson, NJ

THE JOHN C. GROUB COMPANY INC.
900 A Ave. E., Freeman Field
Seymour, IN 47274
Tel.: 812-522-1374
Fax: 812-522-1374
Year Founded: 1863
Approx.Sls.: $121,000,000
Emp.: 650
Grocery Stores
S.I.C.: 5411
Don M. Bollinger *(Chm. Bd. & Chief Exec. Officer)*
James T. McCoy *(Pres. & Chief Oper. Officer)*
Ron Meyer *(Chief Fin. Officer)*
Tom Bollinger *(Mgr.-Sls. & Treas.)*
Mary Emily *(Sec.)*

Outside Service Firm(s):

R. J. Pile & Co.*(Auditors)*
Indianapolis, IN

Jackson County Bank*(Major Banking Relationship)*
Seymour, IN

GROUP DEKKO INTERNATIONAL INC.
Hwy. 6 & County Rd. 400 E.
Kendallville, IN 46755
Mailing Address:
P.O. Box 2000
Kendalville, IN 46755
Tel.: 219-347-0700 **IN**
Telex: 232416
Fax: 219-347-0700 EXT. 7363
Year Founded: 1953
Approx.Sls.: $110,000,000
Emp.: 800
Export
Manufacture of Electric Current-Carrying Wiring Devices
S.I.C.: 3643
Chester E. Dekko *(Chm. Bd., Pres. & Chief Exec. Officer)*
Robert Shuherk *(V.P.-Admin.)*
Lynn E. Slone *(V.P.-Acctg. & Taxation)*
M. Jo Dull *(Grp. Controller)*
Joe Marsh *(Dir.-Pur.)*
Nancy Moore *(Mgr.-Personnel)*
Joan Shepherd *(Mgr.-Information Services)*
George Wappes *(Mgr.-Training)*

Principal(s):
Chester E. Dekko

Outside Service Firm(s):

Coopers & Lybrand*(Auditors)*
490 Lincoln Bank Tower
Fort Wayne, IN 46802
Tel.: 219-423-1531
Fax: 219-426-7870

Barrett & McNagny*(Legal Firm)*
Lincoln Bank Tower, 3rd Fl.
Ft. Wayne, IN 46802
Tel.: 219-423-9551

Fort Wayne National Bank*(Major Banking Relationship)*
110 W. Berry St.
Fort Wayne, IN 46802
Tel.: 219-426-0555

Divisions:

Albion Wire, Inc. **(1)**
State Rd. 8 E
Albion, IN 46701
Tel.: 219-636-2107
Emp.: 124
Mfr. of Copper Wire
S.I.C.: 3351
Mark Lundquist *(Mgr.-Plant)*
Todd Eagan *(Mgr.-Sls.)*

Dekko Wire Div., Kendallville **(1)**
811 Commerce Dr.
Kendallville, IN 46755
Tel.: 219-347-5365
Mff. of Copper Wire
S.I.C.: 3351
Brian Stolte *(Gen. Mgr.)*
Todd Eagan *(Mgr.-Sls.)*

Indiana Insulated Wire **(1)**
State Rd 3, RR 700 S.
South Milford, IN 46786
Tel.: 219-351-2155
Mfr. Insulated Wire & Cable
S.I.C.: 3357
Dan Burtnette *(Gen. Mgr.)*

Affiliates:

Auto Jectors, Inc. **(1)**
1563 E. State Rd. 8
Albion, IN 46701
Tel.: 219-636-2133
Emp.: 48
Mfr. of Plastic Molding Machines
S.I.C.: 3559
Bill Carteaux *(Gen. Mgr.)*

Flex-Ohm, Inc. **(1)**
9455 W. Gilbert Lake Rd.
Cromwell, IN 46732
Tel.: 219-856-4884
Emp.: 75
Wire Drawing (Resistance Wire)
S.I.C.: 3357
Wayne Luckenbill *(V.P.)*

Heat Tech, Inc. **(1)**
100 Industrial Park East
Afton, IA 50830
Tel.: 515-347-5257
Emp.: 170
Mfr. of Heating Units, Resistor Units, Epoxy Sealers, Electric Current Carrying Devices
S.I.C.: 3634; 3643; 2891; 3625
Lyle Persels *(V.P.)*
Cory Coleman *(Gen. Mgr.)*

Heaters Engineering, Inc. **(1)**
Rte. 1 Backwater Rd,. Box 337
North Webster, IN 46555
Tel.: 219-834-2818
Mfr. of Heating Units, Epoxy Sealers & Resistor Units
S.I.C.: 3634; 3643; 2891; 3625
Jeff Thornburgh *(V.P.)*
Lee Haddock *(Mgr.-Pur.)*

Group Dekko International Inc.—(Continued)

Hoosier Wire, Inc. **(1)**
Progress Dr.
Avilla, IN 46710
Tel.: 219-897-2885
Emp.: 135
Mfr. & Distributor of Insulated Wire & Cable
S.I.C.: 3357
Robert Kozlowski *(Pres.)*

Iowa Assemblies, Inc. **(1)**
Hwy. 34 W.
Osceola, IA 50213
Tel.: 515-342-6559
Emp.: 380
Mfr. of Wiring Harnesses
S.I.C.: 3643
Lyle Persels *(Pres.)*
Lane Eddy *(Dir.-Sls.)*
Bev Carson *(Controller)*

Lyall Assemblies, Inc. **(1)**
St Rd. 9 & Cr 400 S.
Albion, IN 46701
Tel.: 219-636-2551
Emp.: 300
Mfr. of Electrical Wiring Assembly
S.I.C.: 3679
Chester Dekko *(Chm. Bd.)*

PVC Compounders **(1)**
6928 N - 400 E
Kendallville, IN 46755
Tel.: 219-347-4055
Emp.: 20
Mfr. of Polyvinyl Chloride Compounds
S.I.C.: 2821
Thomas J. Feichter *(V.P.)*
Brenda Sower-Koza *(Dir.-Sls.)*
Mark Shire *(Gen. Mgr.)*

Pent Assemblies, Inc. **(1)**
US 6 & Cr 400 E
Kendallville, IN 46755
Tel.: 219-347-5828
Emp.: 150
Mfr. of Wiring Harnesses & Wiring Devices
S.I.C.: 3679; 3643
John Gres *(Pres.)*
Steve Hankins *(V.P.)*
Diane Gerencer *(Controller)*

Pent Plastics, Inc. **(1)**
303 E. 4th St.
Avilla, IN 46710
Tel.: 219-897-3775
Mfr. of Molded Plastic Products
S.I.C.: 3089
Chester Dekko *(Pres.)*
Rick Nowels *(V.P.)*

Pent Products, Inc. **(1)**
US 6 & Cr 400 E
Kendallville, IN 46755
Tel.: 219-347-5828
Emp.: 160
Mfr. of Wiring Devices & Wiring Harnesses
S.I.C.: 3679; 3643
John Gres *(Pres.)*
Randy Sutton, Jr. *(V.P.)*

Reclaimers, Inc. **(1)**
6928 N - 400 E
Kendallville, IN 46755
Tel.: 219-347-5610
Emp.: 38
Copper Refining
S.I.C.: 3341; 5093
Thomas J. Feichter *(V.P.)*
Robert Van Vleet *(Gen. Mgr.)*

Silicones, Inc. **(1)**
US 6 & Cr 400 E
Kendallville, IN 46755
Tel.: 219-347-5793
Emp.: 37
Mfr. of Silicone, Insulated Wire
S.I.C.: 3357
Chester Dekko *(Pres.)*
Wayne Malcom *(Gen. Mgr.)*

Wire Tech, Inc. **(1)**
Progress Way
Avilla, IN 46710
Tel.: 219-897-3125
Emp.: 28
Wholesales Wire & Cable & Manufacturer of Wire & Cable
S.I.C.: 5051; 3315
Chester Dekko *(Pres.)*
Randy Wilson *(Group Mgr.)*

GROUP INSURANCE INC.
10932 Cloverland Ave.
Baton Rouge, LA 70809
Tel.: 504-293-1770 **LA**
Fax: 504-295-1996
Year Founded: 1972
Approx.Sls.: $25,000,000
Emp.: 22
Fiscal Year-end: 12/31/91
Medical Insurance Brokerage; Accident & Health
S.I.C.: 6321
Dan Jumonville *(Chm. Bd. & Pres.)*
Carla Jumonville *(Sec.)*
Carol Anglin *(Dir.-Pur.)*

Principal(s):
Dan Jumonville

No. of U.S. Offices: 4

Computer Systems/Hardware:
Tandy

Outside Service Firm(s):

Dyer & Vicknair*(Auditors)*
Baton Rouge, LA

Home Life Insurance Co.*(Group Insurer)*
Piscataway, NJ

Keisel Roy Aaron & Zwick*(Legal Firm)*
Baton Rouge, LA

Hancock Bank*(Major Banking Relationship)*
Baton Rouge, LA

Subsidiary:

Group Insurance of Colorado **(1)**
9101 E. Kenyon Ave., Ste. 3200
Denver, CO 80237
Tel.: 303-770-2501 (100%)
Medical Insurance Brokerage
S.I.C.: 6321; 6324
Mike Nelson *(Pres.)*

GROUP TWO ADVERTISING, INC.
2002 Ludlow St.
Philadelphia, PA 19103
Tel.: 215-561-2200
Fax: 215-561-2842
Year Founded: 1970
Approx.Billings: $18,150,000
Emp.: 17
Richard Elkman *(Pres. & Chief Exec. Officer)*
Jay Goldberg *(V.P.)*
Madalyn Corsey *(Asst. to Pres.)*
Dorothy Montgomery *(Comptroller)*

GROVE VALVE & REGULATOR COMPANY
6529 Hollis
Oakland, CA 94608
Tel.: 510-655-7700
Fax: 510-420-2150
Approx.Sls.: $50,000,000
Emp.: 165
Air Dome & Flexible Tube Regulators, Ball, Gate Valves
S.I.C.: 3491
John Tescher *(Pres.)*
Ken Banks *(V.P.-Fin., Sec. & Treas.)*
Jack Grimes *(V.P. & Plant Mgr.)*
Gary D. Bowman *(Mkt. Plng. Mgr.-Regulators)*
Jack Coulter *(Mgr.-Engrng.)*
Dick Golomb *(Gen. Sls. Mgr.)*
Steve Knutson *(Mgr.-Human Resources)*

S. J. GROVES & SONS COMPANY
10000 Hwy. 55 West
Minneapolis, MN 55441
Mailing Address:
P.O. Box 1267
Minneapolis, MN 55440
Tel.: 612-546-6943
Fax: 612-541-8147
Year Founded: 1905
Approx.Sls.: $262,000,000
Emp.: 500
Fiscal Year-end: 12/31/89
Heavy Construction Contractors
S.I.C.: 1611; 1622; 1629; 1623
Franklin N. Groves *(Chm. Bd. & Chief Exec. Officer)*
Roger J. Ludlam *(Pres. & Chief Oper. Officer)*
Paul Seppala *(Chief Fin. Officer)*
Sandra Martell *(Corp. Sec. & Gen. Counsel)*
R. C. Lunden *(Mgr.-Data Processing)*

Computer Systems/Hardware:
IBM 4341

Outside Service Firm(s):

KPMG Peat Marwick*(Auditors)*
4200 Norwest Center, 90 S. 7th St.
Minneapolis, MN 55402
Tel.: 612-341-2222

Mutual Benefit Life Insurance*(Group Insurer)*
Hartford, CT

First National Bank of Chicago*(Major Banking Relationship)*
One First National Plaza
Chicago, IL 60670
Tel.: 312-732-9781
Tel.: 312-732-4050
Fax: 312-732-4840
Fax: 312-732-3055

Norwest Bank Minnesota, N.A.*(Major Banking Relationship)*
6th St. & Marquette Av.
Minneapolis, MN 55479
Tel.: 612-667-1234

First National Bank of Minneapolis*(Major Banking Relationship)*
Minneapolis, MN

Metropolitan Life Insurance Co.*(Pension Manager)*
One Madison Ave.
New York, NY 10010-3690
Tel.: 215-578-9292

Piper, Jaffray & Hopwood, Inc.*(Pension Manager)*
Minneapolis, MN

GROWMARK, INC.
1701 Towanda Ave.
Bloomington, IL 61702
Mailing Address:
P.O. Box 2500
Bloomington, IL 61702-2500
Tel.: 309-557-6000 **DE**
Year Founded: 1927
Assets: $387,699,431
Liabilities: $166,420,915
Net Worth: $221,278,516
Approx.Sls.: $754,083,000
Emp.: 1,000
Fiscal Year-end: 8/31/92
Livestock & Poultry Feeds, Chemical Fertilizers, Petroleum, Seed Products, Livestock & Poultry Products; Grain Marketing
S.I.C.: 2048; 2874; 2911; 5153; 5191
O. Glenn Webb *(Chm. Bd. & Pres.)*
Douglas N. Scheider *(Vice Chm.)*
Daryle L. Stonier *(Vice Chm.)*
Norman T. Jones *(Chief Exec. Officer)*
Marvin Weisert *(Sr. V.P.-Member Services)*
Stephen R. Carr *(V.P. & Corp. Counsel)*
William Davisson *(V.P.-Fin.)*
John McClenathan *(V.P.-Grain Opers.)*
Vern McGinnis *(V.P.-Corp. Services)*
Stanley Nielsen *(V.P.-Distr.)*
William Erlenbush *(Controller)*
Thomas A. Seidel *(Sec.)*
Jeffrey M. Solberg *(Treas.)*
Stan Johnson *(Dir.-Mktg. Devel.)*
Steve Hammerschmidt *(Dir.-Adv.)*
Carter Priess *(Dir.-Data Processing)*
Dave Striegel *(Dir.-Mktg. Services)*
Donald Wilkey *(Dir.-Pur.)*
Don Donsbach *(Mgr.-Employment & Placement)*

Outside Service Firm(s):

Ernst & Young*(Auditors)*
233 S. Wacker Dr.
Chicago, IL 60606
Tel.: 312-368-1800
Fax: 312-645-3095

Anderson, Harmon & Quick*(Legal Firm)*
Bloomington, IL

GRYBAUSKAS & PARTNERS
24 East 21st St.
New York, NY 10010
Tel.: 212-979-0280
Fax: 212-979-0288
Year Founded: 1988
Approx.Billings: $16,750,000
Emp.: 20
Roland Grybauskas *(Pres. & Creative Dir.)*
Joseph G. Beatrice *(Exec. V.P., Mktg. Dir.)*
Lyn McDermott *(Dir., Finance & Admin.)*

GUARANTEE ELECTRICAL COMPANY
3405 Bent Ave.
Saint Louis, MO 63116
Tel.: 314-772-5400 **MO**
Fax: 314-772-9261
Year Founded: 1902
Approx.Sls.: $60,000,000
Emp.: 600
Industrial & Commercial Electrical Contractors
S.I.C.: 1731; 3613
Charles W. Oertli *(Chm. Bd.)*
Fred J. Oertli *(Chm. Exec. Committee)*
Fred G. Oertli, Jr. *(Pres.)*
J.J. Farina *(Pres.-Guarantee Indus. Systems of MO)*
Rick Ledbetter *(Exec. V.P.-Opers.)*
Roger S. Oertli *(Exec. V.P.-Construction Div.)*
Jerry Gassel *(V.P.-Sls.)*
G.E. Kirk *(V.P.-Estimating)*
David D. Metcalfe *(V.P.-Mktg.)*
Greg Diekemper *(Treas.)*

Principal(s):
Charles W. Oertli
Fred J. Oertli
Fred G. Oertli, Jr.
Richard Oertli
Thelma C. Oertli
Robert Oertli

Outside Service Firm(s):

Armstrong, Teasdale, Schlafly, Davis & Dicus*(Legal Firm)*
One Metropolitan Square
St. Louis, MO 63102
Tel.: 314-621-5065
Fax: 314-621-5065

Boatmen's National Bank of St. Louis*(Major Banking Relationship)*
One Boatmen's Plaza, 800 Market St.
St. Louis, MO 63101
Tel.: 314-466-6000

Subsidiaries:

Gismo Inc. **(1)**
3445 Bent Ave.
St. Louis, MO 63116
Tel.: 314-772-5440
Tel.: 800-325-9524
Emp.: 150
Mfr. 18-Wheeler Trailers
S.I.C.: 3715
Mark Morris *(Pres. & Chief Exec. Officer)*

Guarantee Interiors **(1)**
3415 Bent Ave.
Saint Louis, MO 63116
Tel.: 314-772-5400
Tel.: 800-325-9524
Emp.: 90
Commercial Interior Installation of Acoustical Ceilings, Drywall Partitions & Flooring
S.I.C.: 1742; 1752
Bob Farrell *(V.P.)*

GUARANTEE MUTUAL LIFE CO.
8801 Indian Hills Dr.
Omaha, NE 68114
Tel.: 402-390-7300 **NE**
Fax: 402-390-7577
Year Founded: 1901
Assets: $686,668,233
Earnings: $3,181,859
Liabilities: $624,903,518
Net Worth: $61,764,715
Approx.Premiums: $153,283,246
Emp.: 300
Fiscal Year-end: 12/31/90
Life & Health Insurance, Annuities
S.I.C.: 6311; 6321
Robert D. Bates *(Chm. Bd., Pres. & Chief Exec. Officer)*
R.L. Comeau *(Exec. V.P.-Grp. Div.)*
D.L. Bomberger *(Sr. V.P. & Treas.)*
T.L. Gilbert *(Sr. V.P.-Individual Div.)*
Richard A. Spellman *(Sr. V.P., Gen. Counsel & Sec.)*
M.C. Biggerstaff *(V.P.-Mortgage Loans)*
J.L. Broady *(V.P.-Information Systems)*
J.E. Burch *(V.P. & Controller)*
P.D. Ochsner *(V.P.-Plng. & Strategic Devel.)*
G.H. Rittenhouse *(V.P.-Grp. Mktg.)*
S.L. Ryan *(V.P.-Human Resources & Admin.)*
P.L. Shipley *(V.P. & Assoc. Gen. Counsel)*
J.V. Swallow *(V.P.-Agency)*
Michael P. Feimer *(Dir.-Res. & Devel.)*
M.C. McCaleb *(Dir.-Sls. Promo. & Adv.)*
Mark Peters *(Dir.-Meeting Planner)*

No. of U.S. Offices: 1

Computer Systems/Hardware:
IBM

Outside Service Firm(s):

Deloitte & Touche*(Auditors)*
2000 First National Center
Omaha, NE 68102
Tel.: 402-346-7788

Norwest Bank Minnesota, N.A.*(Major Banking Relationship)*
Omaha, NE

Subsidiary:

Guarantee American Life Company **(1)**
8801 Indian Hills Dr.
Omaha, NE 68114
Tel.: 402-390-7300
Non-Active Life Insurance
S.I.C.: 6311
E. A. Conley *(Chief Oper. Officer)*

GUARANTEE TITLE CO., INC.
4445 Lake Forest Dr., Suite 400
Cincinnati, OH 45242
Tel.: 513-563-8810
Holding Co.
S.I.C.: 6712

Subsidiary:

Charter Oak Financial Corporation **(1)**
4445 Lake Forest Dr.
Cincinnati, OH 45242
Tel.: 513-563-3300
Fax: 513-563-3372
Emp.: 232
Holding Company
S.I.C.: 6712
Leo H. Wiest *(Exec. V.P.)*
William J. Dries *(Sr. V.P. & Chief Fin. Officer)*
Gregory W. Meyers *(Sr. V.P.-Retail Banking)*
Ron L. Sebastian *(Sr. V.P.-Mortgage Banking)*

Subsidiaries:

Charter Oak Federal Savings Bank **(2)**
4411 Lake Forest Dr.
Cincinnati, OH 45242
Tel.: 513-563-5050
Savings Bank
S.I.C.: 6035

First Trust Savings Bank **(2)**
10601-36 San Jose Blvd.
Jacksonville, FL 32257
Tel.: 904-262-5555
Savings Bank
S.I.C.: 6035
James Follan *(Pres.)*

Heritage Service Corporation **(2)**
65 E. Kemper Rd.
Cincinnati, OH 45246
Tel.: 513-671-6812
Tax Exempt Investments
S.I.C.: 6035

GUARANTEED PRODUCTS, INC.
355 N. Vineland Ave.
City of Industry, CA 91746
Tel.: 818-968-5573 **CA**
Fax: 818-333-8562
Year Founded: 1988
Approx.Sls.: $45,000,000
Emp.: 350
Mfr. of Aluminum Extrusions & Frames
S.I.C.: 3355
Dick Russell *(Pres. & Chief Exec. Officer)*
John Coller *(V.P.-Engrng.)*
Stuart Reeves *(Controller)*
Ron Tuck *(Mgr.-Extrusions)*

GUARANTY CORPORATION
929 Government St.
Baton Rouge, LA 70802
Mailing Address:
P.O. Box 2231
Baton Rouge, LA 70821
Tel.: 504-383-0355
Fax: 504-343-0047
Year Founded: 1926
Assets: $162,868,000
Liabilities: $148,732,000
Net Worth: $14,136,000
Approx.Sls.: $17,425,000
Emp.: 90
Fiscal Year-end: 12/31/91
Life Insurance; Mortgage Banking: Broadcasting
S.I.C.: 4832; 6162; 6311
Corporate Giving Program: The United Way
G. A. Foster, Jr. *(Pres.)*
Thomas H. Clark *(Exec. V.P.)*
Randy W. Kendrick *(V.P.-Fin.)*
A. B. Rogers, Jr. *(Treas.)*
Janet Baldwin *(Sec.)*

Outside Service Firm(s):

Postlethwaite & Netterville*(Auditors)*
Baton Rouge, LA

Schanerville & Baringer*(Legal Firm)*
Baton Rouge, LA

Baton Rouge Bank & Trust Company*(Major Banking Relationship)*
Baton Rouge, LA

GUARD PUBLISHING COMPANY
975 High St.
Eugene, OR 97401
Mailing Address:
P.O. Box 10188
Eugene, OR 97440
Tel.: 503-485-1234 **OR**
Fax: 503-683-7622
Year Founded: 1961
Approx.Sls.: $19,000,000
Emp.: 340
Newspaper Publishing & Printing; Offset Commercial Printing
S.I.C.: 2711; 2752
Edwin M. Baker *(Chm. Bd.)*
Alton F. Baker, III *(Editor & Publisher)*
R. Fletcher Little *(V.P.)*
Ann Baker Mack *(Treas.)*
Bridget Baker *(Sec.)*
Cynthia Waldon *(Mgr.-Human Resources)*

Outside Service Firm(s):

First Interstate Bank*(Major Banking Relationship)*
Eugene, OR

GUARDIAN ALARM CO.
20800 Southfield Rd.
Southfield, MI 48075
Tel.: 313-423-1000 **MI**
Fax: 313-423-3009
Year Founded: 1930
Approx.Sls.: $50,000,000
Emp.: 2,000
Burglar Alarm Monitoring & Maintenance, Guards & Armored Trucks
S.I.C.: 7382; 7381
Milton Pierce *(Chm. Bd.)*
Charles May *(Pres.)*
Douglas Pierce *(V.P. & Chief Exec. Officer)*
Laurie Mickiewicz *(Controller)*
Richard Pierce *(Sec.)*
Paul Parr *(Gen. Mgr.)*
Gisela Foreman *(Dir.-Human Resources)*
Harry Haden *(Dir.-Mngmt. Information Systems)*

Outside Service Firm(s):

Follmer, Rudzewicz & Co.*(Auditors)*
Southfield, MI

N.B.D. Bank, N.A.*(Major Banking Relationship)*
611 Woodward Ave.
Detroit, MI 48226
Tel.: 313-225-1122
Fax: 313-225-3420

Division:

Det. Division of National Guardian & Beechwood Security of Cleveland **(1)**
Cleveland, OH

GUARDIAN INDUSTRIES CORP.
43043 W. Nine Mile Rd.
Northville, MI 48167
Tel.: 313-347-0100 **DE**
Fax: 313-349-5995
Assets: $518,182,000
Earnings: $223,788,000
Net Worth: $518,182,000
Approx.Sls.: $760,900,000
Emp.: 5,854
Mfr. of Insulation Materials; Flat Glass; Photo Development
S.I.C.: 3211; 3231; 7384
William Davidson *(Chm., Pres., Chief Exec. & Chief Oper. Officer)*
Jeffrey A. Knight *(V.P.-Fin.)*
Wallace L. Rueckel *(Treas.)*
Robert H. Gorlin *(Gen. Counsel)*
Alan L. Schlang *(Sec.)*
Kenneth Battjes *(Dir.-Personnel)*
Karl Straky *(Mgr.-Comml. & Architectural Glass)*

Outside Service Firm(s):

Coopers & Lybrand*(Auditors)*
400 Renaissance Center
Detroit, MI 48243
Tel.: 313-446-7100
Fax: 313-446-7117

Butzel Long*(Legal Firm)*
Madden Bldg., 150 W. Jefferson, Ste. 900
Detroit, MI 48226-4430
Tel.: 313-225-7000
Fax: 313-225-7080

Michigan National Bank*(Major Banking Relationship)*
Detroit, MI

Branches:

Glass Distribution **(1)**
1220 Menlo Dr. N.W.
Atlanta, GA 30318
Tel.: 404-351-2620 (100%)
Emp.: 9
Glass Distribution
S.I.C.: 5039
William Davidson *(Pres.)*

Glass Distribution **(1)**
367 Dorchester
South Boston, MA 02127
Tel.: 617-268-1020 (100%)
Emp.: 11
Glass Distribution
S.I.C.: 5039

Glass Distribution **(1)**
802 E. 140th St.
Bronx, NY 10454
Tel.: 718-585-1222 (100%)
Emp.: 14
S.I.C.: 3211

Glass Distribution **(1)**
1761 Olive St. N.E.
Capitol Heights, MD 20743
Tel.: 410-772-1100 (100%)
Emp.: 7
S.I.C.: 5039

Glass Distribution **(1)**
16401 Center Ave.
Harvey, IL 60426
Tel.: 708-596-0500 (100%)
Emp.: 9
Glass Distribution
S.I.C.: 5039
William Davidson *(Pres.)*

Glass Distribution **(1)**
4522 Indianola
Columbus, OH 43214
Tel.: 614-262-8241 (100%)
Emp.: 6
Glass Distribution
S.I.C.: 5039
William Davidson *(Pres.)*

Glass Distribution **(1)**
8408 Chancellor Row
Dallas, TX 75247
Tel.: 214-631-0060 (100%)
Emp.: 9
S.I.C.: 3211

Glass Distribution **(1)**
24150 Haggerty Rd.
Farmington Hills, MI 48018
Tel.: 313-471-0180 (100%)
Emp.: 7
S.I.C.: 5039
Shande Thorton *(Gen. Mgr.)*

Glass Distribution **(1)**
722 E. Zimmerly
Wichita, KS 67211
Tel.: 316-262-2488 (100%)

Guardian Industries Corp.—(Continued)

Emp.: 9
S.I.C.: 3211

Glass Distribution **(1)**
681 S. Clarence
Los Angeles, CA 90023
Tel.: 213-264-0161 (100%)
Emp.: 9
S.I.C.: 5039

Glass Distribution **(1)**
2952 N.W. Yeon
Portland, OR 97210
Tel.: 503-224-9545 (100%)
Emp.: 8
S.I.C.: 5039

Plants:

Glass Plant **(1)**
11535 E. Mountainvew
Kingsburg, CA 93631
Tel.: 209-896-6400
Emp.: 225
S.I.C.: 3211

Glass Plant **(1)**
14600 Romine Rd.
Carleton, MI 48117
Tel.: 313-962-2252 (100%)
Emp.: 649
S.I.C.: 3211
Ron Smith *(Plant Mgr.)*

Glass Plant **(1)**
3060 S.W. 2nd Ave.
Fort Lauderdale, FL 33315
Tel.: 305-525-3481 (100%)
Emp.: 75
Glass Distribution
S.I.C.: 5039
Richard Harss *(Gen. Mgr.)*

Glass Plant **(1)**
Cudworth Rd.
Webster, MA 01570
Tel.: 617-943-6600 (100%)
Emp.: 149
Architectural Facility
S.I.C.: 3211

Glass Plant **(1)**
3801 S. Hwy. 287
Corsicana, TX 75110
Tel.: 903-872-4871
Emp.: 272
Manufacture of Glass
S.I.C.: 3211
Walter Palmer, Jr. *(Plant Mgr.)*

Glass Plant **(1)**
R.R. 5 & S.R. 67
Upper Sandusky, OH 43351
Tel.: 419-294-4921 (100%)
Emp.: 436
Fabrication Facility
S.I.C.: 3211

Glass Plant **(1)**
1456 S. Manhattan Ave.
Fullerton, CA 92631
Tel.: 714-991-4431
Emp.: 27
Architectural Facility
S.I.C.: 3211

Glass Plant **(1)**
1901 Raymer Ave.
Fullerton, CA 92633
Tel.: 714-525-3528
Emp.: 73
Flat Glass
S.I.C.: 3211
Thomas Wunderoych *(Plant Mgr.)*

Glass Plant **(1)**
24145 W. Moline Martin Rd.
Millbury, OH 43447
Tel.: 419-855-7706
Emp.: 30
Glass Tempering & Shipping
S.I.C.: 3211; 5039
Jack Albano *(Plant Mgr.)*

Glass Plant **(1)**
1412 S. First St.
Rogers, AR 72756
Tel.: 501-636-0888
Emp.: 143
Architectural Facility
S.I.C.: 3211
Barrell Perez *(Plant Mgr.)*
John Fordman *(Gen. Mgr.)*

Guardian Glass Inc. **(1)**
P.O. Box 507,
West Elizabeth, PA 15088
Tel.: 412-384-3400 (55%)
Emp.: 227
Flat Glass
S.I.C.: 3211
Gary Cochran *(Plant Mgr.)*

Photo Plant **(1)**
43045 W. Nine Mile Rd.
Northville, MI 48167
Tel.: 313-349-6700 (100%)
Emp.: 286
Photo Devel.
S.I.C.: 7384
Don Steinbach *(Gen. Mgr.)*

Photo Plant **(1)**
16400 Lathrop Ave.
Harvey, IL 60426
Tel.: 708-596-4500 (100%)
Emp.: 189
Photo Devel.
S.I.C.: 7384
Ron Schopp *(Gen. Mgr.)*

Photo Plant **(1)**
3811 Ferguson Rd.
Fort Wayne, IN 46801
Tel.: 219-747-3102 (100%)
Emp.: 151
Photo Devel.
S.I.C.: 7384
Ernest Poise *(Gen. Mgr.)*

Photo Plant **(1)**
425 Live Oak St.
San Antonio, TX 78293
Tel.: 210-227-5025 (100%)
Emp.: 72
Photo Devel.
S.I.C.: 7384

Photo Plant **(1)**
L.B.I. No. 2, Race St.
Allentown, PA 18103
Tel.: 215-266-9431 (100%)
Emp.: 370
Photo Devel.
S.I.C.: 7384

Photo Plant **(1)**
10 Technology Dr.
Auburn, MA 01501
Tel.: 508-832-5741 (100%)
Emp.: 59
Photo Devel.
S.I.C.: 7384

Photo Plant **(1)**
9108 Bond
Overland Park, KS 66214
Tel.: 913-492-3515 (100%)
Emp.: 42
Photo Devel.
S.I.C.: 7384

Photo Plant **(1)**
1415 S. Monroe St.
Mason City, IA 50401
Tel.: 515-423-7412 (100%)
Emp.: 49
Photo Devel.
S.I.C.: 7384

Photo Plant **(1)**
P.O. Box 340, Grace City Rd.
Slippery Rock, PA 16057
Tel.: 412-794-4845
Emp.: 138
S.I.C.: 7384
Steve Vetuik *(Gen. Mgr.)*

Photo Plant **(1)**
2715 S.E. Raymond
Portland, OR 97202
Tel.: 503-234-0244
Emp.: 79
S.I.C.: 7384

Units:

Consulting Services, Inc. **(1)**
43043 W. 9 Mile Rd.
Northville, MI 48167
Tel.: 313-349-6700 (100%)
Emp.: 36
Data Processing
S.I.C.: 8741

Continental Mortgage Investors **(1)**
111 Devonshire St.
Boston, MA 02109
Tel.: 617-482-6201 (40%)
Emp.: 12
Real Estate Investment

Engineering Services **(1)**
43043 W. Nine Mile Rd.
Northville, MI 48167
Tel.: 313-349-6700
Emp.: 36
S.I.C.: 8711

Michigan Retail **(1)**
24150 Haggerty Rd.
Farmington Hills, MI 48018
Tel.: 313-471-0180 (100%)
Emp.: 36
S.I.C.: 3211

Ohio Retail **(1)**
830 E. 222nd St.
Euclid, OH 44123
Tel.: 216-731-7000 (100%)
Emp.: 34
S.I.C.: 3211

Photo Central Office **(1)**
43043 W. Nine Mile Rd.
Northville, MI 48167
Tel.: 313-349-6700
Emp.: 36
S.I.C.: 7384

West Virginia Retail **(1)**
1513 Seventh St.
Parkersburg, WV 26101
Tel.: 304-485-8591 (100%)
Emp.: 25
S.I.C.: 3211

Subsidiaries:

Cue Industries, Inc. **(1)**
3135 Highway M
Antonia, MO 63012
Tel.: 314-942-2253
Emp.: 650
Holding Co.; Importer and Mfr. of Women's Handbags; Mfr. Misc. Plastic Prods.
S.I.C.: 3089; 6719; 3171

Falconer Glass Industries, Inc. **(1)**
500 S. Work St.
Falconer, NY 14733
Tel.: 716-665-6422
Fax: 800-444-5278
Approx.Sls.: $60,000,000
Emp.: 800
Manufacture Mirrors, Tempered Flat Glass, Fabricator & Jobber Of Flat Glass, Glazing Contractor & Automobile Glass Installer, Laminated & Insulated Glass
S.I.C.: 3231; 1793; 3211; 5039; 5231
R.E. Turner, Sr. *(Chief Exec. Officer)*
Richard E. Turner, Jr. *(Pres.)*
Richard D. Thorpe *(V.P.-Opers.)*
Rick Hill *(Controller)*
Dennis J. Crandall *(Dir.-Human Resources)*

G.I.C. Financial Services Corporation **(1)**
9701 Higgins Rd.
Rosemont, IL 60018
Tel.: 708-823-6976
Emp.: 7
Leasing Subsidiary

Guardian Industries Corp. **(1)**
1000 E. North St.
Albion, MI 49224
Tel.: 517-629-9464 (100%)
Emp.: 177
Insulation Plant
S.I.C.: 3231

Guardian Transportation Corp. **(1)**
P.O. Box 162, Moline Martin Rd.
Millbury, OH 43447-0162
Tel.: 419-855-7707
Emp.: 39
Intercoastal Transportation
S.I.C.: 4424

Windsor Plastics, Inc. **(1)**
601 No. Congress Ave.
Evansville, IN 47715
Tel.: 812-477-6151 (100%)
Injection Moulding Manufacturing; Plastic Products
S.I.C.: 3089
Mary Henson *(Pres. & Gen. Mgr.)*

THE GUARDIAN LIFE INSURANCE COMPANY OF AMERICA

201 Park Ave. S.
New York, NY 10003
Tel.: 212-598-8000 **NY**
Fax: 212-533-5156
Assets: $4,168,496,831
Liabilities: $3,797,647,106
Net Worth: $370,849,725
Approx.Rev.: $2,000,000,000
Emp.: 2,400
Fiscal Year-end: 12/31/90
Insurance, Annuities
S.I.C.: 6321; 6311; 6036
Arthur V. Ferrara *(Pres. & Chief Exec. Officer)*
Peter Hutchings *(Exec. V.P. & Chief Fin. Officer)*
Joseph D. Sargent *(Exec. V.P.-Life Insurance)*
Edward K. Kane *(Sr. V.P. & Gen. Counsel)*
Douglas Kramer *(Sr. V.P.-Admin.)*
John J. Pallotta, Jr. *(Sr. V.P.-Grp. Insurance)*
John M. Smith *(Sr. V.P.-Equity Prods.)*
Thomas G. Kabele *(V.P. & Corp. Actuary)*
Frederick V. Kluth *(V.P.-Pensions)*
Frank Sorrentino *(V.P.-Health Insurance)*
Thomas Baker *(V.P.-Data Processing)*
Herbert N. Grolnick *(Sec.)*
Joseph Budani *(Pur. Agent)*

Computer Systems/Hardware:
IBM 3081 & 3083

Outside Service Firm(s):

Ernst & Young*(Auditors)*
787 Seventh Ave.
New York, NY 10019
Tel.: 212-773-1243

Chemical Banking Corp.*(Major Banking Relationship)*
277 Park Ave.
New York, NY 10041
Tel.: 212-310-6407
Fax: 212-310-4526

Subsidiaries:

Guardian Asset Management Corp. (GAMCORP) **(1)**
201 Park Ave. S.
New York, NY 10003
Tel.: 212-598-8000 (100%)
Large-Fund & Institutional Management
S.I.C.: 6726

The Guardian Insurance & Annuity Co. (GIAC) **(1)**
201 Park Ave., S.
New York, NY 10003
Tel.: 212-598-8000 (100%)
Stock Life Insurance & Equity Products
S.I.C.: 6311
John C. Angle *(Chm. Bd. & Chief Exec. Officer)*

Guardian Investor Services Corp. **(1)**
201 Park Ave. S.
New York, NY 10003
Tel.: 212-598-8000 (100%)
Broker-Dealer
S.I.C.: 6211
John M. Smith *(Pres.)*

Non-U.S. Subsidiary:

Guardian Baillie Gifford, Ltd. **(1)**
1 Rutland Ct.
Edinburgh, EH3 8EY United Kingdom
Insurance, Annuities
S.I.C.: 6311

GUARDSMARK, INC.
22 S. Second St.
Memphis, TN 38103
Mailing Address:
P.O. Box 45
Memphis, TN 38101
Tel.: 901-522-6000
Tel.: 800-238-5878 DE
Telex: 53-3230
Fax: 901-522-6013
Year Founded: 1963
Approx.Sls.: $100,000,000
Emp.: 8,000
Fiscal Year-end: 6/30/90
Uniformed Security Officer Services; Undercover Investigations; Technical Services
S.I.C.: 7382; 7381; 8748
Ira A. Lipman *(Chm. & Pres.)*
Mark Lipman *(Sr. Vice Chm.)*
W.B. Mallory III *(Vice Chm., Sec. & Gen. Counsel)*
Patricia D. Rogoski *(Sr. V.P., Treas. & Chief Fin. Officer)*
John F. Clark, Jr. *(Sr. V.P.)*
Peter R. Greenfield *(Sr. V.P.)*
Howard B. Spector *(Sr. V.P.)*
Ira E. Waldrup *(Sr. V.P.)*
James F. Antonelli *(V.P.)*
Charles E. Chumley *(V.P.)*
Steve Coulson, Jr. *(V.P.)*
Bernard A. Doyle *(V.P.)*
Jefferson D. Harris *(V.P.)*
O. Nathaniel Hilburn, Jr. *(V.P.)*
Robert T. Jensen *(V.P.)*
Kevin W. Kern *(V.P.)*
Alice Knowles *(V.P.)*
O. Franklin Lowie *(V.P.)*
Benjamin C. Oberholtzer *(V.P.)*
Robert W. Overman *(V.P.)*
Sandra E. Peiser *(V.P.)*
Terrence M. Randell *(V.P.)*
Michael J. Rice *(V.P.)*
Bruce A. Scherer *(V.P.)*
Neil L. Solomon *(V.P.)*
George F. Sullivan *(V.P.)*
Ernest L. Whitlow *(V.P.)*
Ashley G. Williams *(V.P.)*

No. of U.S. Offices: 86

Computer Systems/Hardware:
IBM System 36, IBM PC-XT & AT

Outside Service Firm(s):

Coopers & Lybrand*(Auditors)*
1000 Morgan-Keegan Tower, 50 N. Front St.
Memphis, TN 38103
Tel.: 901-529-1100

Rogovin, Huge & Schiller*(Legal Firm)*
Washington, DC

Morgan Guaranty Trust Company of New York*(Major Banking Relationship)*
23 Wall St.
New York, NY 10015
Tel.: 212-483-2323

Division:

Mark Lipman Div. **(1)**
22 S. Second St.
Memphis, TN 38103
Tel.: 901-522-7800
Fax: 901-522-7858
Detective Agency
S.I.C.: 7381
Mark Lipman *(Sr. Vice Chm.)*
John F. Clark *(Sr. V.P.)*
Benjamin C. Oberholtzer *(V.P.)*
Alice M. Knowles *(V.P.)*

Subsidiary:

Peoplemark, Inc. **(1)**
22 S. Second St.
Memphis, TN 38103
Tel.: 901-522-6000 (100%)
Fax: 901-522-6013
Emp.: 500
Temporary Help Service
S.I.C.: 7363
Ira A. Lipman *(Chm. Bd.)*
Patricia D. Rogoski *(Sr. V.P.)*
Robert W. Overman *(V.P.)*
Terri A. Duff *(V.P.)*
W.B. Mallory, III *(Sec.)*

GUESS ?, INC.
1444 S. Alameda
Los Angeles, CA 90021
Tel.: 213-765-3100 CA
Fax: 213-233-1889
Approx.Sls.: $80,000,000
Emp.: 750
Mfr. of Men's, Women's, & Children's Clothing
S.I.C.: 2339; 2329; 5611; 5621
George Marciano *(Chief Exec. Officer)*
Maurice Marciano *(Pres.)*
Armond Marciano *(Exec. V.P.)*

Outside Service Firm(s):

Bank of America*(Major Banking Relationship)*
701 S. Western Ave.
Los Angeles, CA 91201

Division:

Eyewear Division **(1)**
123 E. 35th St.
Los Angeles, CA 90011
Tel.: 213-235-3090
Mfr. of Eyeglasses
S.I.C.: 3851
Maurice Marciano *(Pres.)*

GUEST QUARTERS SUITE HOTELS
30 Rowes Wharf
Boston, MA 02110
Tel.: 617-330-1440
Tel.: 800-424-7900
Fax: 617-737-8752
Year Founded: 1972
Approx.Sls.: $120,000,000
Emp.: 2,500
Fiscal Year-end: 12/31/90
All-Suite Hotel Chain
S.I.C.: 7011
Richard M. Kelleher *(Pres.)*
William Perocci *(Chief Fin. Officer)*
Ronald Callentine *(Exec. V.P.)*
Bob Bitner *(Sr. V.P.-Sls.)*
Jim Flynn *(Sr. V.P.-Opers.)*
Jeff McIntyre *(Sr. V.P.-Opers.)*
Steve Pletcher *(Sr. V.P.-Technical Services)*
Mark van Hartesvelt *(Sr. V.P.-Sls. & Mktg.)*
Harvey Cannova *(V.P.-Reservations)*
John Weaver *(V.P.-Human Resources)*
Bob Provost *(Controller)*
Suzanne Erickson *(Exec. Sec.)*
Sheila Schofield *(Dir.-Communications)*
Brook Ethridge *(Mgr.-Adv.)*

GUEST SERVICES, INC.
3055 Prosperity Ave.
Fairfax, VA 22031
Tel.: 703-849-9300
Fax: 703-641-4690
Year Founded: 1917
Approx.Sls.: $100,000,000
Emp.: 3,500
Operates Lodging, Retail Food Service, Restaurants & Recreation Facilities
S.I.C.: 5812; 7011; 7999
Milton V. Peterson *(Chm. Bd.)*
S. J. DiMeglio *(Pres.)*
Logan Dowler *(V.P.)*
Gerard Gabrys *(V.P.-Fin. & Treas.)*
Sondra Gillice *(V.P.-Sls.)*
John Romer *(Comptroller)*
A. Carraway *(Gen. Counsel)*
J. Hughes *(Dir.-Pur.)*
M.J. Selario *(Dir.-Data Processing)*
Barbara Freeman *(Sec.)*

Outside Service Firm(s):

Arthur Andersen & Co.*(Auditors)*
1666 K Street, N.W.
Washington, DC 20006

First American of Virginia*(Major Banking Relationship)*
Alexandria, VA

GUIDEPOSTS ASSOCIATES, INC.
39 Seminary Hill Rd.
Carmel, NY 10512
Tel.: 914-225-3681 NY
Fax: 914-228-2056
Year Founded: 1944
Assets: $64,000,000
Liabilities: $40,000,000
Net Worth: $24,000,000
Approx.Sls.: $68,000,000
Emp.: 380
Fiscal Year-end: 6/30/91
Publishing Only of Periodials, Magazines & Books, Not Printed on Site
S.I.C.: 2721; 2731
Ruth Stafford Peale *(Chm.)*
John Temple *(Pres. & Chief Exec. Officer)*
Carl Piraneo *(Controller)*
Gerard Dickler *(Sec.)*
Vincent Daley *(Dir.-Fin.)*
John Downing *(Dir.-Mktg.)*
Richard Dulton *(Dir.-Mfg.)*
Joe Kelly *(Dir.-Human Resources)*
Paula Bernett *(Mgr.-Pub. Rels.)*
Norman Vincent Peale *(Publr.)*
Fulton Oursler, Jr. *(Editor)*

No. of U.S. Offices: 2

Outside Service Firm(s):

Sperduto, Spector & Co.*(Auditors)*
New York, NY

Hall, Dickler, Lawler, Kent & Friedman*(Legal Firm)*
460 Park Ave.
New York, NY 10017
Tel.: 212-838-4600

Bank of New York*(Major Banking Relationship)*
Brewster, NY

GUILFORD TRANSPORTATION INDUSTRIES INC.
7 Executive Park Dr.
Merrimack, NH 03054
Tel.: 603-429-1685 DE
Fax: 603 429 1755
Approx.Sls.: $275,000,000
Emp.: 2,250
Holding Company; New England Freight Rail Carries
S.I.C.: 4011; 6719
Timothy Mellon *(Chm. Bd. & Chief Exec. Officer)*
David Fink *(Pres.)*

Outside Service Firm(s):

Bank of Boston*(Major Banking Relationship)*
Guilford, CT

GULF COAST LEAD COMPANY, INC.
1901 N. 66th St.
Tampa, FL 33619
Tel.: 813-626-0303 FL
Fax: 813-662-8388
Year Founded: 1953
Approx.Sls.: $14,000,000
Emp.: 95
Lead Smelting & Refining, Secondary; Apartment Hotel Operation
S.I.C.: 3341; 6513
Willis M. Kitchen *(Pres.)*
Solomon Walker *(Treas.)*
Stephen Oster *(Sec.)*

Outside Service Firm(s):

First Florida Bank*(Major Banking Relationship)*
P.O. Box 31265,
Tampa, FL 33631-3265
Tel.: 813-224-1475

GULF DISTRIBUTION INC.
5959 N.W. 37th Ave.
Miami, FL 33142
Tel.: 305-634-6800
Fax: 305-635-0699
Approx.Sls.: $125,000,000
Emp.: 220
Fiscal Year-end: 6/30/92
Wholesaler of Pharmaceuticals & Toiletries
S.I.C.: 5122; 5100
Marvin I. Goldman *(Chm. Bd.)*
Howard Goldman *(Pres.)*
Robert Gasthalter *(V.P. & Treas.)*
Carol Goldman *(Sec.)*
Arnold Simon *(Dir.-Pub. Rels.)*

Outside Service Firm(s):

BDO Seidman*(Auditors)*
Miami, FL

Southeast Bank, N.A.*(Major Banking Relationship)*
One Southeast Financial Center
Miami, FL 33131

GULF EXPLORATION
1700 West Loop South
Houston, TX 77069
Tel.: 713-440-4007
Fax: 713-440-4008
Year Founded: 1984
Approx.Sls.: $12,000,000
Emp.: 5
Oil & Gas Exploration Services
S.I.C.: 1382
Robert R. Hillery *(Pres.)*
Wayne Aquinaldo *(Chief Fin. Officer)*

GULF LUMBER COMPANY, INC.
1850 Conception St.
Mobile, AL 36610
Tel.: 205-457-6872 DE
Fax: 205-452-7110
Year Founded: 1972
Approx.Sls.: $27,000,000
Emp.: 205
Rough, Sawed or Planed Lumber
S.I.C.: 2421
Fred T. Stimpson *(Pres. & Chief Exec. Officer)*
Robert M. Shackleford *(Exec. V.P.)*
William Sandy Stimpson *(Exec. V.P.)*
Gordon S. Stimpson *(Treas. & Sec.)*

Outside Service Firm(s):

Smith, Dukes & Buckalew*(Auditors)*
Mobile, AL

GULF STATES ASPHALT COMPANY, INC.
300 Christy Place
South Houston, TX 77587
Mailing Address:
P.O. Box 508
South Houston, TX 77587
Tel.: 713-941-4410
Tel.: 800-662-0987 TX
Fax: 713-947-4906
Year Founded: 1947
Approx.Sls.: $30,000,000
Emp.: 160
Fiscal Year-end: 2/28/92
Export
Manufacture Paving & Roofing Mixtures, Asphalt & Petroleum Products, Paints, Varnishes, Lacqueres & Enamels; Coatings, Adhesives, Waterproofing Mastics
S.I.C.: 2851; 2899; 2951; 2952; 2999

Gulf States Asphalt Company, Inc.—(Continued)

Reba H. Bramble *(Chm. Bd. & Chief Exec. Officer)*
Luis X. Pena *(Pres., Chief Exec. Officer & Chief Fin. Officer)*
Tim J. Callahan *(Exec. V.P.)*
Jayne G. Hawkins *(Dir.-Mktg. & Export)*
Tom Arlt *(Dir.-Pur.)*
Jerome Pye *(Dir.-Laboratory)*

No. of Mfg. Plants/Facilities: 2
No. of U.S. Offices: 2

Computer Systems/Hardware:
Novell Network

Outside Service Firm(s):

NationsBank Texas*(Major Banking Relationship)*
1100 Louisiana, 20th Fl.
Houston, TX 77002

Subsidiary:

Gulf Seal Specialties, Inc. **(1)**
P.O. BOx 508
South Houston, TX 77587
Tel.: 713-941-4410
Fax: 713-947-4906
Mfr. Sealant Tapes & Seam Sealers
S.I.C.: 2891
Mark Platz *(Sls. Mgr.)*

GULF STATES MANUFACTURERS, INC.
Airport Rd.
Starkville, MS 39759
Mailing Address:
P.O. Box 1128,
Starkville, MS 39759
Tel.: 601-323-8021
Fax: 601-324-2984
Approx.Sls.: $30,000,000
Emp.: 325
Fiscal Year-end: 12/31/92
Export
Pre-Engineered Steel Buildings
S.I.C.: 3448
W.L. Jones *(Pres.)*
Fred A. Jones *(V.P.)*
Clayton H. Richardson, Jr. *(Sec., Treas. & Gen. Mgr.)*
Thomas Southerland *(Mgr.-Mktg.)*
Tom Zeppelin *(Mgr.-Personnel)*

GULF STATES PAPER CORPORATION
1400 River Rd., N.E.
Tuscaloosa, AL 35404
Tel.: 205-553-6200 **DE**
Fax: 205-553-6095
Year Founded: 1884
Approx.Sls.: $200,000,000
Emp.: 2,000
Export
Mfr. of Paperboard Folding Cartons & Other Paper Prods.
S.I.C.: 2631; 2421; 2657; 2679
Jack Warner *(Chm. Bd. & Chief Exec. Officer)*
Jon Warner *(Pres. & Chief Oper. Officer)*
J J. O'Brien *(Sr. V.P. & Chief Fin. Officer)*
Charles Allison *(V.P., Sec. & Gen. Counsel)*
Jon Anderson *(V.P. & Treas.)*
Donald L. Stein *(V.P. & Controller)*
J. F. Vengrouskie, Jr. *(V.P.-Personnel)*
Dan Meissner *(Dir.-Corp. Communications)*
Mary Chism *(Pension Admin.)*

Computer Systems/Hardware:
IBM System 4361

Outside Service Firm(s):

Price Waterhouse*(Auditors)*
Birmingham, AL

Blue Cross & Blue Shield of Alabama*(Group Insurer)*
450 Riverchase Pkwy. East
Birmingham, AL 35298
Tel.: 205-988-2245

King & Spalding*(Legal Firm)*
Trust Co. Tower
Atlanta, GA 30303
Tel.: 404-572-4600

Chemical Bank*(Major Banking Relationship)*
450 West 33rd St.
New York, NY 10001
Tel.: 212-613-7197
Fax: 212-947-7628

First National Bank of Chicago*(Major Banking Relationship)*
One First National Plaza
Chicago, IL 60670
Tel.: 312-732-9781
Tel.: 312-732-4050
Fax: 312-732-4840
Fax: 312-732-3055

InterFirst Bank Dallas*(Major Banking Relationship)*
Dallas, TX

Wachovia Bank & Trust Co.*(Major Banking Relationship)*
P.O. Box 3001,
Winston-Salem, NC 27102
Tel.: 800-633-4236

First Union National Bank*(Pension Manager)*
Two First Union Center
Charlotte, NC 28288-1154
Tel.: 704-374-2698

Mitchell Hutchins Asset Management Inc.*(Pension Manager)*
1285 Avenue of the Americas
New York, NY 10019
Tel.: 212-713-1865

United Capital Management*(Pension Manager)*
One United Bank Center, 1700 Lincoln St., Ste. 3301
Denver, CO 80274-0077
Tel.: 303-831-9474

Subsidiary:

Westervelt Land Co. **(1)**
1400 River Rd.
Tuscaloosa, AL 35404
Tel.: 205-553-6200

GULF STATES TOYOTA
7701 Wilshire Pl.
Houston, TX 77040
Mailing Address:
P.O. Box 40306
Houston, TX 77240
Tel.: 713-744-3300
Fax: 713-744-3332
Approx.Sls.: $1,000,000,000
Emp.: 750
Distributor & Retailer Toyota Automobiles & Trucks
S.I.C.: 5012; 5511
Jerry H. Pyle *(Pres.)*
Don Bishop *(Grp. V.P.-Sls. & Mktg.)*
Chip Mason *(V.P.-Fin. & Chief Fin. Officer)*
Chuck Delacroix *(V.P.-Mktg.)*
Julie Distelrath *(Sec.)*
J.B. O'Hara *(Dir.-Admin.)*

Computer Systems/Hardware:
IBM System 39

GULFSTREAM HOLDINGS CORPORATION
500 Gulfstream Rd.
Savannah, GA 31402
Mailing Address:
P.O. Box 2206,
Savanah, GA 31402
Tel.: 912-964-3000 **DE**
Telex: 54-6470
Fax: 912-964-3775
Year Founded: 1990
Approx.Sls.: $1,000,000,000
Emp.: 4,600
Fiscal Year-end: 12/31/90
Import Export
Mfr. of Aircraft; Holding Company
S.I.C.: 3721; 3724; 3728
Allen E. Paulson *(Chm. Bd.)*
William C. Lowe *(Pres., Chief Exec. & Chief Oper. Officer)*

Divisions:

Gulfstream Aerospace Corp. **(1)**
1000 Wilson Blvd., Ste. 2701
Arlington, VA 22209
Tel.: 703-276-9500
Fax: 703-276-9504
Government & Military Relations Department
Douglas Wood *(V.P.-Govt. Sls.)*
Helen Newman *(V.P.-Govt. Rels.)*

Gulfstream Aerospace Corp. **(1)**
4150 Donald Douglas Dr.
Long Beach, CA 90808
Tel.: 310-420-1818
Fax: 310-420-4696
Jet Sales Office
S.I.C.: 5088

Gulfstream Aerospace Corp. **(1)**
Northeast Farmington Ave.
Farmington, CT 06032
Tel.: 203-677-7666
Jet Sales Office
S.I.C.: 5088

Gulfstream Aerospace Corp. **(1)**
3663 N. Belt E., Ste. 400
Houston, TX 77032
Tel.: 713-987-7300
Jet Sales Office
S.I.C.: 5088

Gulfstream Aerospace Corp. **(1)**
7200 Corporate Center Dr., Ste. 314
Miami, FL 33126
Tel.: 305-593-0500
Jet Sales Office
S.I.C.: 5088

Gulfstream Aerospace Technologies Corp. **(1)**
Box 22500, Wiley Post Airport
Oklahoma City, OK 73123
Tel.: 405-789-5000
Telex: 74-7193
Approx.Sls.: $30,000,000
Emp.: 605
Subcontracting of Aerospace Equipment for Industry & Governments
Robert Buckley *(Pres.)*

Gulfstream Marketing Midwest Region **(1)**
2001 Spring Rd.
Oak Brook, IL 60521
Tel.: 708-571-6606
Sales Office
S.I.C.: 5088

GUMP'S, INC.
250 Post St.
San Francisco, CA 94108
Tel.: 415-982-1616
Fax: 415-984-9390
Year Founded: 1861
Emp.: 300
Import
Specialty Gift Store
S.I.C.: 5947
Joseph Pickard *(Vice Chm. & V.P.-Mail Order)*
Dave Wiezel *(Chief Fin. Officer)*
Charles Dishman *(Exec. V.P.)*
Dottie Adams *(Exec. Dir.-Mail Order)*
Shelton Ellis *(Exec. Dir.-Stores)*
Michelene Adams *(Dir.-Gallery)*
Nina Beutel *(Dir.-Mktg.)*
Barbara Musante *(Dir.-MIS)*
Colleen Dillon *(Admin. Asst./Adv.)*

Subsidiary:

Gumps **(1)**
2800 Olympic Blvd., Ste. 203
Santa Monica, CA 90404
Tel.: 310-449-7747
S.I.C.: 5947

GUNDER & ASSOCIATES, INC.
270 Bradenton Ave.
Dublin, OH 43017
Tel.: 614-761-9600
Fax: 614-761-9666
Year Founded: 1972
Approx.Billings: $23,300,000
Emp.: 34
Consumer Advertising
Stephen Gunder *(Chm. Bd. & Pres.)*
Scott Lenz *(Exec. V.P.)*
Barbara Byrum *(Sr. V.P., Opers., Sec. & Treas.)*
Joseph Cattaneo *(Sr. V.P., Pub. Rels.)*
Alice Walters *(V.P., Dir. Pub. Rels.)*
Jim Beier *(Dir., Promo., Special Events, Meeting Plng.)*

CURTIS C. GUNN, INC.
7744 Broadway, Ste. 100
San Antonio, TX 78209
Tel.: 210-824-3208
Fax: 210-829-8226
Approx.Sls.: $160,000,000
Emp.: 550
Automobile Dealerships; Nonresidential Building Operator
S.I.C.: 5511; 6512
Curtis C. Gunn, Sr. *(Sr. Chm. Bd.)*
Curtis C. Gunn, Jr. *(Chm. Bd.)*
Robert Bomer *(Pres.)*

Outside Service Firm(s):

Mendelson & Mata*(Legal Firm)*
San Antonio, TX

NationsBank Texas*(Major Banking Relationship)*
San Antonio, TX

GUNNEBO FASTENING CORP.
180 S. Hartman St.
York, PA 17403
Mailing Address:
P.O. Box 1589
York, PA 17405
Tel.: 717-846-2200
Tel.: 800-336-1640
Fax: 717-852-0809
Approx.Sls.: $15,000,000
Emp.: 130
Fiscal Year-end: 12/31/90
Import Export
Mfr. Anchoring Devices & Allied Products
S.I.C.: 3462
David Jones *(Pres. & Chief Oper. Officer)*
Don Hogentogler *(Exec. V.P./Chief Exec. Officer)*
Bert Mayer *(Admin./Oper.)*
John Williams *(Controller)*
Ian Jones *(Dir.-Mktg.)*

Computer Systems/Hardware:
IBM

VINOD GUPTA COMPANY, INC.
5707 South 86th Circle
Omaha, NE 68127
Tel.: 402-331-7169
Fax: 402-331-1505
Year Founded: 1973
Approx.Billings: $31,000,000
Emp.: 102
Vin Gupta *(Pres.)*
Jack Betts *(Sr. V.P.)*
Glenn Prettymon *(V.P.)*

GURLEY MOTOR COMPANY
701 W. Coal Ave.
Gallup, NM 87301
Tel.: 505-722-6621
Fax: 505-722-3105
Year Founded: 1939
Approx.Sls.: $23,000,000
Emp.: 120
Retail Sales of New & Used Automobiles
S.I.C.: 5511
C.E. Gurley *(Chm. Bd.)*
Patrick J. Gurley *(Pres.)*
John Pena *(V.P. & Treas.)*
Mary Kimura *(Sec.)*

Outside Service Firm(s):

Sun West Bank*(Major Banking Relationship)*
Gallup, NM

GURNEY INDUSTRIES INC.
619 E. Price Ave.
Gastonia, NC 28054
Mailing Address:
P.O. Box 519,
Gastonia, NC 28053-0519
Tel.: 704-865-3441
Fax: 704-865-2061
Year Founded: 1965
Assets: $5,391,000
Earnings: $1,270,000
Net Worth: $5,391,000
Approx.Sls.: $18,000,000
Emp.: 250
Fiscal Year-end: 6/30/90
Mfr. of Knitted Products; Apparel & T-Shirts; Outside Finishing & Dyeing
S.I.C.: 2257; 2253
Robert J. Gurney, Jr. *(Chm. Bd., Pres. & Chief Exec. Officer)*
James Crosby *(V.P.-Mfg.)*
Cornelia Austin *(Sec.)*
Peter Lazare *(Dir.-Mktg.)*
John Roney *(Dir.-Personnel)*
Ramesh Bhalerao *(Asst. to Pres.)*

No. of Mfg. Plants/Facilities: 3
No. of U.S. Offices: 3

Outside Service Firm(s):

Cherry, Bekaert & Holland*(Auditors)*
Charlotte, NC

Thompson Insurance*(Commercial Insurance Carrier)*
Montgomery, AL

General Administrators*(Group Insurer)*
Charlotte, NC

Cannon & Blair*(Legal Firm)*
Charlotte, NC

Bank of Prattville*(Major Banking Relationship)*
Prattville, AL

Branch Banking & Trust Co.*(Major Banking Relationship)*
Gastonia, NC

GUSSO MANUFACTURING, INC.
5112 Second Ave.
Brooklyn, NY 11232
Tel.: 718-492-7900 **NY**
Fax: 718-492-0886
Year Founded: 1918
Approx.Sls.: $16,000,000
Emp.: 250
Mfr. of Index Cards, Indexes, File Folders & Transfer Files
S.I.C.: 2675
Joel Kremsdorf *(Pres.)*
Alan Snider *(V.P.-Sls. & Mktg.)*
Robert R. Sharp *(V.P. & Chief Fin. Officer)*
Wendy Kremsdorf *(Treas.)*
Arlene Kremsdorf *(Sec.)*
Samuel Meltzer *(Dir.-Pur.)*
David J. Weger *(Dir.-Sls.)*
Seymour Baum *(Mgr.-Plant)*
Diane A. Crosby *(Mgr.-Adv.)*

Outside Service Firm(s):

Miller Ellin & Co.*(Auditors)*
New York, NY

Warshaw, Burstein, Cohen, Schlesinger & Kuh*(Legal Firm)*
55 Fifth Ave.
New York, NY 10017

Manufacturers Hanover Trust Co.*(Major Banking Relationship)*
P.O. Box 24935, Church St. Sta.
New York, NY 10249
Tel.: 212-613-7191

THE GUTHRIE GROUP
477 Congress St.
Portland, ME 04101-3406
Tel.: 207-874-8000
Fax: 207-874-9826
Year Founded: 1989
Approx.Billings: $10,000,000
Emp.: 10
Francis J. Guthrie *(Pres.)*
Carol R. Potts *(Controller)*

THE GUTTMAN GROUP
200 Speers Rd.
Belle Vernon, PA 15012
Tel.: 412-483-3533
Fax: 412-483-5226
Sales Range: $100-499 Million
Emp.: 210
Marketing & Distribution of Petroleum Products; Gasoline, Diesel, Motor Oil, Greases & Home Heating; Towing
S.I.C.: 5172; 4492
Alan R. Guttman *(Pres. & Treas.)*
James Guttman *(Pres.-Mon River Towing, Inc.)*
Maury S. Guttman *(Exec. V.P.)*
Richard M. Guttman *(V.P.)*
Ivan I. Melnick *(V.P.-Fin.)*
Fred Perino *(V.P.-Liquid Div.)*
Donald F. Smith *(V.P.-Sls.)*
Dolores A. Harper *(Sec.)*
Daniel Matta *(Comptroller)*

Outside Service Firm(s):

Epstein, Tabor & Schorr*(Auditors)*
Pittsburgh, PA

Buchanan, Ingersoll p.c.*(Legal Firm)*
600 Grant St., 57th Flr.
Pittsburgh, PA 15219
Tel.: 412-562-8800

Union National Bank*(Major Banking Relationship)*
Pittsburgh, PA

H & D STEEL SERVICE, INC.
9960 York-Alpha Dr.
North Royalton, OH 44133
Tel.: 216-237-3390
Fax: 216-237-4540
Year Founded: 1973
Approx.Sls.: $30,000,000
Emp.: 36
Steel Service Center
S.I.C.: 5051
Raymond G. Schreiber *(Pres.)*
Philip Le Marquand *(Gen. Mgr.)*
Matt Smith *(Treas.)*
Barb Lorenz *(Sec.)*

No. of Mfg. Plants/Facilities: 1
No. of U.S. Offices: 1

Computer Systems/Hardware:
Data General

Outside Service Firm(s):

Hausser & Taylor*(Auditors)*
Cleveland, OH

Weston, Hurd, Fallon, Paisley & Howley*(Legal Firm)*
Cleveland, OH

The Huntington National Bank*(Major Banking Relationship)*
Strongsville, OH

H. GROUP HOLDING INC.
200W. Madison St., 39th fl.
Chicago, IL 60606
Tel.: 312-750-1234
Hotel Holding Company
S.I.C.: 6519
Jay Pritzker *(Chm. Bd. & Chief Exec. Officer)*
A.N. Pritzker *(Vice Chm.)*

Subsidiaries:

Hyatt Corporation **(1)**
200 W. Madison
Chicago, IL 60606
Tel.: 312-750-1234
Fax: 312-750-1417
Sales Range: $500-999 Million
Emp.: 40,000
Fiscal Year-end: 12/31/90
Computer Systems/Hardware:
IBM 4341
Holding Company; Hotels
S.I.C.: 7011; 6531; 6719
Jay A. Pritzker *(Chm. Bd.)*
Thomas J. Pritzker *(Pres.)*
Harold Handelsman *(Sr. V.P., Sec. & Gen. Counsel)*
Kenneth Posner *(Sr. V.P.-Fin.)*
Mark Pollock *(Dir.-Natl. Adv. & Promo.)*

Division:

Northridge Industries, Inc. **(2)**
202 E. Fremont St.
Las Vegas, NV 89101
Tel.: 702-385-4011
Approx.Sls.: $1,853,998
Emp.: 54
Developers & Operators of Hyatt Lodges
S.I.C.: 6531
Jeanne Hood *(Pres.)*
Jewell M. Bidelman *(V.P.-Treas.)*
H. Handelsman *(Sec.)*

Subsidiaries:

Classic Residence by Hyatt **(2)**
200 W. Madison
Chicago, IL 60606
Tel.: 312-750-1234
Senior Housing Industry
S.I.C.: 6513
Penny Pritzker *(Pres.)*

Hyatt Hotels Corporation **(2)**
200 W. Madison St.
Chicago, IL 60606
Tel.: 312-750-1234 (100%)
Fax: 312-750-8579
Approx.Sls.: $2,300,000,000
Emp.: 50,000
Hotels
S.I.C.: 7011
Darryl Hartley-Leonard *(Pres.)*
Albert J. Kelly *(Exec. V.P.)*
Ed Rabin *(Exec. V.P.)*
Marc Yanofsky *(Sr. V.P.-Mktg.)*
John Biggs *(Sr. V.P.-Fin. Admin.)*
Peter Connely *(Sr. V.P. & Gen. Counsel)*
Jim Evans *(Sr. V.P.-Sls.)*
Karine Armstrong *(V.P.-Mktg., Resorts)*
Karen Rugen *(V.P.-Pub. Rels.)*
David Marks *(Mgr.-Natl. Adv.)*
Jim Jones *(Dir.-Sls. Devel.)*
Barbara Strauss-Locke *(Dir.-Adv. & Promo.)*
Marvin Pollack *(Dir.-Adv.)*
Nan Krump-Moss *(Dir.-Mkt. Devel.)*
Brian Cassidy *(Dir.-Incentive Mkt. Sls.)*
Susie Gawriluk *(Dir.-Travel Industry Sls.)*
Brian Gamache *(Dir.-Resort Div. Sls. & Mktg.)*
Scott Walker *(Dir.-Western Div. Sls. & Mktg.)*
Fred Shea *(Dir.-Midwest Div. Sls. & Mktg.)*
Gary Sain *(Dir.-Natl. Accounts)*

Hyatt International Corporation **(2)**
200 W. Madison
Chicago, IL 60606
Tel.: 312-750-1234
Tel.: 800-233-1234
Approx.Sls.: $801,000,000
Emp.: 26,000
Management Company for Hyatt Hotels in Foreign Countries
S.I.C.: 8742
Bernd Chorengel *(Pres.)*
John Wallis *(V.P.-Sls. & Mktg.)*
Wendy Strachan *(V.P.-Human Resources)*
David Kan *(V.P.-Tech. Services)*
Len Stoga *(V.P.-Fin.)*
Michael Evanoff *(V.P.-Devel. & Gen. Counsel)*
Cristina Tabora *(Dir.-Mktg. Communications)*
Kristin Sandberg *(Mgr.-Pub. Rels.)*
Lisa Zimmer *(Mgr.-Mktg.)*

Affiliate:

Hyatt Air, Inc. **(2)**
200 W. Madison
Chicago, IL 60606
Tel.: 312-750-1234
Air Transportation
S.I.C.: 4512

H & H DISTRIBUTING COMPANY, INC.
304 S. Vine
West Union, IA 52175
Mailing Address:
P.O. Box 494
West Union, IA 52175
Tel.: 319-422-3846 **IA**
Fax: 319-422-3296
Year Founded: 1946
Approx.Sls.: $24,000,000
Emp.: 76
Fiscal Year-end: 6/30/91
General Line Of Groceries, Fresh Fruits, Vegetables; Candy; Tobacco; Restaurant Equipment & Supplies
S.I.C.: 5141; 5145; 5194; 5046
Donald E. Hansen *(Chm. Bd.)*
Sandra Baldwin *(Pres. & Treas.)*
Mike Baldwin *(Chief Oper. Officer)*
Ruth Hansen *(Exec. V.P. & Sec.)*
Carl Huber *(Chief Info. Officer)*
Principal(s):
Donald E. Hansen
Sandra Baldwin

Outside Service Firm(s):

O'Connor & Thomas*(Legal Firm)*
200 Cycare Plaza
Dubuque, IA 52001
Tel.: 319-557-8400

First National Bank*(Major Banking Relationship)*
Union, IA

H & H TUBE & MANUFACTURING CO.
108 Garfield St.
Vanderbilt, MI 49795
Mailing Address:
P.O. Box 455,
Vanderbilt, MI 49795
Tel.: 517-983-2800 **MI**
Fax: 517-983-2501
Year Founded: 1930
Approx.Sls.: $25,000,000
Emp.: 200
Fiscal Year-end: 6/30/92
Import Export
Copper Rolling & Drawing
S.I.C.: 3351; 3498
Larry B. Higgins *(Chm. Bd., Pres. & Chief Exec. Officer)*
Richard P. Watson *(Exec. V.P. & Chief Oper. Officer)*
Ronald V. DeBona *(Sec.)*
James Jury *(Controller)*
Hugh O. Thompson *(Mgr.-Sls.)*
Cynthia J. Hurst *(Dir.-Human Resources)*
Ronald C. Drake *(Pur. Agent)*

No. of Mfg. Plants/Facilities: 2

Outside Service Firm(s):

Gavigan, Burkhart, Freeman, Inc.*(Auditors)*
Gaylord, MI 49735

DeBona, Siebert & Lang*(Legal Firm)*
Livonia, MI

Manufacturers National Bank N.A.*(Major Banking Relationship)*
38th Fl., 100 Renaissance Center
Detroit, MI 48243
Tel.: 313-222-4227

HBE CORPORATION
11330 Olive St.
Saint Louis, MO 63141
Mailing Address:
P.O. Box 27339
St. Louis, MO 63141
Tel.: 314-567-9000 **DE**
Fax: 314-567-7731
Year Founded: 1959
Sales Range: $100-499 Million
Emp.: 3,500
Design & Build Hospitals, Banks, Medical Office Buildings, Retirement Communities; Hotel Ownership & Operation
S.I.C.: 1542; 7011; 6512; 7996
Fred S. Kummer *(Chm., Pres., Chief Exec. Officer, Treas. & Founder)*
Ronald J. Unterreiner *(V.P.-Fin. & Chief Fin. Officer)*
Robert Koester *(Gen. Counsel)*
Lynn Gibbs *(Dir.-Data Processing)*

Computer Systems/Hardware:
IBM System 38

Outside Service Firm(s):

Price Waterhouse*(Auditors)*
One Boatmen's Plaza
St. Louis, MO 63101
Tel.: 314-425-0500

Pension Associates*(Group Insurer)*
St. Louis, MO

Rollins Burdick Hunter*(Commercial Insurance Carrier)*
500 Washington Ave., Suite 1100
St. Louis, MO 63101
Tel.: 314-241-8013
Fax: 314-241-3248

Corroon & Black*(Commercial Insurance Carrier)*
St. Louis, MO

Peper, Martin, Jensen, Maichel & Hetlage*(Legal Firm)*
720 Olive St.
St. Louis, MO 63101
Tel.: 314-421-3850

Mercantile Bank*(Major Banking Relationship)*
Saint Louis, MO

Divisions:

Adam's Mark Hotels **(1)**
11330 Olive St. Rd.
Saint Louis, MO 63141
Tel.: 314-567-9000
Fax: 314-567-7675
Design/Build, Owner & Operator of Hotels
Fred Kummer *(Pres.)*

HBE Adam's Rib **(1)**
11330 Olive St. Rd.
Saint Louis, MO 63141
Tel.: 314-567-9000
Fax: 314-567-7731
Developers of International Year-Round Resort in Eagle, CO
Fred Kummer *(Pres.)*

HBE Bank Facilities **(1)**
11330 Olive St. Rd.
Saint Louis, MO 63141
Tel.: 314-567-9000
Design/Build Firm for Financial Institutions
Robert Keyes *(Exec. V.P.)*

HBE Medical Buildings **(1)**
11330 Olive St. Rd.
Saint Louis, MO 63141
Tel.: 314-567-9000
Fax: 314-567-7731
Design/Build Firm for Medical Office Buildings
Daniel W. Figert *(V.P.)*

HBE Retirement Communities **(1)**
11330 Olive St. Rd.
St. Louis, MO 63141
Tel.: 314-567-9000
Fax: 314-567-7731
Design/Build Firm & Developers of Retirement Villages
Fred Kummer *(Pres.)*

Hospital Building & Equipment Co. **(1)**
11330 Olive St. Rd.
Saint Louis, MO 63141
Tel.: 314-567-9000
Fax: 314-567-7731
Design/Build Firm for Health Care
Fred Kummer *(Pres.)*
Tom Spalding *(V.P.-Sls. & Mktg.)*

HCB CONTRACTORS
1401 Elm St., 46th Fl.
Dallas, TX 75202
Tel.: 214-747-8541
Fax: 214-748-5063
Year Founded: 1946
Approx.Sls.: $648,000,000
Emp.: 250
Fiscal Year-end: 12/31/90
General Building Contractors
S.I.C.: 6289; 1541; 1542; 6531; 6153; 1629
Henry C. Beck, Jr. *(Chm. Bd.)*
Lawrence A. Wilson *(Pres. & Chief Exec. Officer)*
Henry C. Beck III *(Chief Oper. Officer)*
Jerry D. Cooper *(V.P.-Human Resources)*
James F. Russell *(V.P.-Fin., Chief Fin. Officer & Sec.)*
Jerry W. Boggess *(Treas.)*

Computer Systems/Hardware:
IBM 4341

Outside Service Firm(s):

Coopers & Lybrand*(Auditors)*
1999 Bryan St., Ste. 3000
Dallas, TX 75201
Tel.: 214-754-5000

Locke, Purnell, Rain, Harrell*(Legal Firm)*
1415 S. Vernon St.
Dallas, TX 75224
Tel.: 214-943-7521

NationsBank Texas*(Major Banking Relationship)*
P.O. Box 2964,
Dallas, TX 75221

M Securities Corporation*(Pension Manager)*
Dallas, TX

HCC INDUSTRIES
4232 TempleCity Blvd.
Rosemead, CA 91770
Mailing Address:
P.O. Box 739,
Rosemead, CA 91770
Tel.: 818-443-8933
Fax: 818-575-2437
Year Founded: 1945
Assets: $27,000,000
Earnings: $1,000,000
Liabilities: $25,000,000
Net Worth: $2,000,000
Approx.Sls.: $30,000,000
Emp.: 450
Fiscal Year-end: 3/28/92
Import
Mfr. of Hermetic Seals & Power-Conversion Components
S.I.C.: 3679; 3678; 5084
Andrew Goldfarb *(Pres. & Chief Exec. Officer)*
Anthony F. Serge *(Chief Fin. Officer)*
Christopher H. Bateman *(V.P. & Sec.)*

Subsidiaries:

Glasseal Products, Inc. **(1)**
P.O. Box 978, 485 Oberlin
Lakewood, NJ 08701
Tel.: 908-370-9100 (100%)
Fax: 908-370-7107
Mfr. of Hermetic Sub-Miniature Rectangular Connectors
S.I.C.: 3678

Subsidiary:

Sealtron, Inc. **(2)**
9705 Redding Rd.
Cincinnati, OH 45215
Tel.: 513-733-8400 (100%)

Hermetic Seal Corp. **(1)**
4232 Temple City Blvd.
Rosemead, CA 91770
Tel.: 818-443-8931 (100%)

Division:

Hermetite Corp. **(2)**
485 Oberlin
Lakewood, NJ 08701
Tel.: 908-364-6868 (100%)

HLC INDUSTRIES
38880 Grand River
Farmington Hills, MI 48335
Tel.: 313-477-9600 **MI**
Fax: 313-477-3210
Approx.Sls.: $12,000,000
Emp.: 160
Hose & Tube Fittings & Assemblies, Hydraulic/pneumatic
S.I.C.: 3492
Paul Sowers *(Gen. Mgr.)*
David F. Boyle *(Treas.)*
John F. Burns *(Sec.)*
Pam Nichols *(Pur. Agent)*
Principal(s):
William Morrow
James Darling

Outside Service Firm(s):

John Burns*(Legal Firm)*
Detroit, MI

Manufacturers National Bank N.A.*(Major Banking Relationship)*
38th Fl., 100 Renaissance Center
Detroit, MI 48243
Tel.: 313-222-4227

HDS SERVICES
(Formerly Trettco, Inc.)
33469 W. 14 Mile Rd.
Farmington Hills, MI 48331
Tel.: 313-661-9000 **MI**
Fax: 313-661-8383
Year Founded: 1965
Approx.Sls.: $93,000,000
Emp.: 429
Fiscal Year-end: 12/31/91
Food Service Management Company for Hospitals, Long Term Care Facilities, Retirement Communities, Country Clubs, Yacht Clubs & Office Buildings
S.I.C.: 5812
William W. Triplett *(Chm. Bd. & Chief Exec. Officer)*
John H. King *(Pres. & Chief Oper. Officer)*
Jerry L. Fournier *(V.P.)*
Robert A. Wills *(V.P.-Opers.)*
Raymond F. Zall *(V.P.-Mktg.)*
George A. Cousins *(Treas.)*
Henry M. Campbell *(Gen. Counsel)*
Donna Belsky *(Dir.-Data Processing)*
Alvis Wilson *(Dir.-Pur.)*

No. of Mfg. Plants/Facilities: 121
No. of U.S. Offices: 5

Computer Systems/Hardware:
IBM AS 400; IBM Pc's

Outside Service Firm(s):

Ernst & Young*(Auditors)*
One Detroit Center, 500 Woodward, Ste. 1700
Detroit, MI 48243
Tel.: 313-259-9600

Alexander & Alexander*(Commercial Insurance Carrier)*
700 Fisher Bldg.
Detroit, MI 48202-3053
Tel.: 313-872-3300
Fax: 313-876-8953

Monaghan, Laprete & McDonald*(Legal Firm)*
Birmingham, MI

Comerica Bank*(Major Banking Relationship)*
211 W. Fort St.
Detroit, MI 48226
Tel.: 313-222-3300

H & H ADVERTISING
2620 Tillar Ave.
Fort Worth, TX 76107
Tel.: 817-332-4102 **TX**
Fax: 817-870-0334
Year Founded: 1957
Earnings: $150,000
Emp.: 35
Fiscal Year-end: 3/31/90
Advertising, Specializing in Door-to-Door Delivery of Circulars & Samples; Direct Mail; Printing
S.I.C.: 7319; 2752; 2754
Harold E. Hammond *(Pres. & Chief Exec. Officer)*
Michael Hammond *(V.P.,Treas., & Sec.)*

Computer Systems/Hardware:
IBM PC XT; Amstrad PC; Epsom Printer; Epsom 286

Outside Service Firm(s):

Brookshire & Assocs.*(Auditors)*
Ft. Worth, TX

Bernard Whitney*(Legal Firm)*
Ft. Worth, TX
Tel.: 817-332-4879

NationsBank Texas*(Major Banking Relationship)*
Ft. Worth, TX

Team Bank*(Major Banking Relationship)*
P.O. Box 2604,
Fort Worth, TX 76113
Tel.: 817-884-4614

Subsidiaries:

Direct Delivery Sevice **(1)**
2620 Tillar Ave.
Fort Worth, TX 76107
Tel.: 817-332-4102

H & H Printing **(1)**
2620 Tillar Ave.
Fort Worth, TX 76107
Tel.: 817-332-4102

Southwest Sample & Marketing **(1)**
2620 Tillar Ave.
Fort Worth, TX 76107
Tel.: 817-332-4102

HLB COMMUNICATIONS, INC.
875 N. Michigan Ave., Ste. 1330
Chicago, IL 60611
Tel.: 312-649-0371
Fax: 312-649-1119
Year Founded: 1978
Sales Range: $10-19 Million
Emp.: 17
Public Relations
S.I.C.: 8743
Harvey Haddon *(Chm. Bd.)*
Kathy Baughman *(Pres.)*
Kevin Lynch *(Exec. V.P.)*
Larry Gillespie *(Controller & Treas.)*
Principal(s):
Kathy Baughman
Kevin Lynch

No. of U.S. Offices: 1

Computer Systems/Hardware:
Prime

Outside Service Firm(s):

Ernst & Young*(Auditors)*
233 S. Wacker Dr.
Chicago, IL 60606
Tel.: 312-368-1800
Fax: 312-645-3095

Metropolitan Life Insurance Co.*(Group Insurer)*
Chicago, IL

James T. Haddon & Assoc.*(Legal Firm)*
Chicago, IL

HMC Corporation
(See HLB Communications, Inc.)

H M K ENTERPRISES, INC.
800 South St.
Waltham, MA 02154
Tel.: 617-891-6660
Fax: 617-891-9712
Year Founded: 1981
Approx.Sls.: $400,000,000
Emp.: 675
Mfr. of Steel Bar Products & Office Furniture Distribution
S.I.C.: 3639; 3585; 3743
Steven E. Karol *(Pres. & Chief Exec. Officer)*
Dale Okonow *(Chief Fin. Officer & Sr. V.P.)*
William J. Fitzgerald *(V.P. & Treas.)*

Outside Service Firm(s):

KPMG Peat Marwick*(Auditors)*
One Boston Place
Boston, MA 02108
Tel.: 617-723-7700

Mintz, Levin, Cohn, Ferris, Glovsky & Popeo, P.C.*(Legal Firm)*
One Financial Center
Boston, MA 02111
Tel.: 617-542-2241

Subsidiary:

H M K Industries Of Oklahoma **(1)**
800 South St.
Waltham, MA 02154
Tel.: 617-891-6660
Mfr. of Bars & Bar Shapes, Iron & Steel Fence Posts
S.I.C.: 3312
Robert W. Ackerman *(Pres. & Chief Exec. Officer)*

HMK ADVERTISING, INC.
210 Boylston St.
Chestnut Hill, MA 02167
Tel.: 617-969-7777
Fax: 617-969-1762
Year Founded: 1976
Approx.Billings: $14,000,000
Emp.: 20
Leisure Industries
Harvey M. Karp *(Pres.)*
Holly Patmore *(Sr. V.P.)*
Shelley Derby *(V.P., Acct. Services)*

THE HOH ORGANIZATIONS
180 N. Wabash Ave.
Chicago, IL 60601
Tel.: 312-346-8131
Telex: 703506
Fax: 312-782-4024
Year Founded: 1959
Sales Range: $10-19 Million
Emp.: 200
Holding Co.; Consulting Engineering & Architectural Services
S.I.C.: 6719; 8711; 8712
Harry O. Hefter *(Chm. Bd. & Pres.)*
Melvin E. Blank *(V.P.-Admin.)*
R. N. Mora *(Sec. & Gen. Counsel)*

Outside Service Firm(s):

Kupferberg, Goldberg & Neimark*(Auditors)*
Chicago, IL

Mora & Netzky*(Legal Firm)*
225 W. Washington St.
Chicago, IL

Boulevard Bank*(Major Banking Relationship)*
410 N. Michigan Ave.
Chicago, IL 60611
Tel.: 312-836-6500

Subsidiaries:

HOH Architects, Inc. **(1)**
180 N. Wabash Ave.
Chicago, IL 60601
Tel.: 312-346-8131
Architectural Design of Plants, Office Bldgs., Warehouses, Educational, Health & Computer Facilities
S.I.C.: 8712
Donald R. Michaelis *(V.P.)*

HOH Engineers, Inc. **(1)**
180 N. Wabash Ave.
Chicago, IL 60601
Tel.: 312-346-8131
Engineering Services for the Metals, Manufacturing, Food, Chemical and Pharmaceutical Industries, and for Environmental and Hazardous Wastes.
S.I.C.: 8711
Harry O. Hefter *(Chm. Bd. & Pres.)*

HOH International, Inc. **(1)**
Karaiskaki 10
Melissa, Attikis Greece 15127
Tel.: 30-1 724-5541
Telex: 218344 IBS GR
Zachery Fotinopolous *(Dir.-Intl. Opers.)*

HOH-Ohio **(1)**
130 Dewalt N.W.
Canton, OH 44702
Tel.: 216-456-1700
Ralph D. Wilson *(V.P.)*

Harry O. Hefter-Associates, Inc. **(1)**
180 N. Wabash Ave.
Chicago, IL 60601
Tel.: 312-346-8131
Engineering Services for Government Specializing in Transportation, Municipal Structures & Waterworks
S.I.C.: 8711
Don L. Ortinau *(V.P.)*

Milltech-HOH, Inc. **(1)**
4711 No. Brady St.
Davenport, IA 52806
Tel.: 319-386-0111
Install Custom Computer Systems
S.I.C.: 7371
Robert Staib *(Pres.)*

HP DIRECT
(Formerly Haynes & Pittenger Direct)
5561 West 74th St.
Indianapolis, IN 46268-4184
Tel.: 317-328-4650
Fax: 317-328-4646
Year Founded: 1984
Approx.Billings: $21,000,000
Emp.: 45
Direct Response Advertising
George Bouche *(Chm. Bd.)*
Robert W. Spangle *(Vice Chm.)*
Thomas J. Haynes *(Pres. & Chief Oper. Officer)*
David John *(Chief Fin. Officer)*
Thomas Ashley *(Chief Information Officer)*
Webber Lagrange *(Treas.)*
Jack Wilkes *(Counsel)*
Phil Onderdonk *(Sec.)*

Computer Systems/Hardware:
AS 400-IBM

H.P.H. INDUSTRIES LTD.
717 Forest Ave.
Lake Forest, IL 60045
Tel.: 708-295-6100
Fax: 708-295-9862
Approx.Sls.: $135,000,000
Emp.: 1,600
Holding Company; Manufacture Plastic Packaging
S.I.C.: 6719; 3291; 3086
Howard P. Hoeper *(Chm. Bd. & Pres.)*
Mike Anderson *(V.P.-Sls. & Mktg.)*
Jerry J. Corirossi *(V.P.-Fin. & Admin.)*
Principal(s):
Howard P. Hoeper

Outside Service Firm(s):

KPMG Peat Marwick*(Auditors)*
Peat Marwick Plaza, 303 E. Wacker Dr.
Chicago, IL 60601
Tel.: 312-938-1000

Security Pacific National Bank*(Major Banking Relationship)*
Chicago, IL

Subsidiary:

Packaging Resources, Inc. **(1)**
5566 New Vienna Rd.
New Vienna, OH 45159
Tel.: 513-987-3020
Plastic Containers & Enclosures
S.I.C.: 3089
Robert McCoy *(Gen. Mgr.)*

HPM CORPORATION
820 Marion Rd.
Mount Gilead, OH 43338
Tel.: 419-946-0222
Telex: 987426
Fax: 419-946-9621
Year Founded: 1877
Approx.Sls.: $100,000,000
Emp.: 850
Fiscal Year-end: 5/31/92
Export
Presses, Plastics Molding Machinery, Die Casting Machines, Extrusion Systems, Thermoformers
S.I.C.: 3542; 3544
R.T. Studer *(Pres.)*
W. Flickinger *(V.P.-Mfg.)*
W.K. Shepard *(V.P.-Sls.)*
W.C. Ahrens, Jr. *(Treas.)*
J.I. Griffey *(Dir.-Personnel)*

HPS, INC.
8020 Zionsville Rd.
Indianapolis, IN 46268
Mailing Address:
P.O. Box 68536
Indianapolis, IN 46268
Tel.: 317-875-9000 **IN**
Fax: 317-875-3910
Year Founded: 1939
Assets: $15,300,000
Liabilities: $11,400,000
Net Worth: $3,900,000
Sales Range: $60-79 Million
Emp.: 310
Fiscal Year-end: 9/30/90
Wholesale & Retail Printing, Photographic & Office Equipment & Supplies
S.I.C.: 3861
William A. Boncosky *(Pres.)*
David L. Bray *(Controller)*
Ronald A. Sharpe *(Treas.)*
Diana Puppin *(Dir.-Adv.)*
Mark O. Sullivan *(Dir.-EDP)*
Jeffery S. Wykoff *(Dir.-Pur.)*

No. of U.S. Offices: 11

Computer Systems/Hardware:
IBM AS 400

Outside Service Firm(s):

Geo. S. Olive & Company*(Auditors)*
Indianapolis, IN

H S DIE & ENGINEERING, INC.
0-215 Lake Michigan Dr., NW
Grand Rapids, MI 49504
Tel.: 616-453-5451
Fax: 616-453-7872
Emp.: 165
Special Dies, Tools, Jigs & Fixtures
S.I.C.: 3544
Harold Steele *(Pres.)*
Marcia Steele *(V.P. & Sec.)*
Tom Back *(Controller)*

Outside Service Firm(s):

Miller, Canfield, Padock & Stone*(Legal Firm)*
Grand Rapids, MI

HTB, INC.
900 N. Stiles
Oklahoma City, OK 73104-1845
Mailing Address:
P.O. Box 1845
Oklahoma City, OK 73101
Tel.: 405-239-4700
Fax: 405-239-4750
Year Founded: 1942
Approx.Sls.: $15,000,000
Emp.: 160
Fiscal Year-end: 12/31/91
Engineers, Architects, Planners
S.I.C.: 8711; 8712
Rex M. Ball *(Chm. Bd. & Chief Exec. Officer)*
Leonard F. Ball *(Sr. V.P., Gen. Counsel & Asst. Sec.)*
Wesley G. Britson *(Sr. V.P. & Mng. Principal-HTB/OKC)*
Frank W. Chitwood *(Sr. V.P., Asst. Sec. & Mng. Principal-HTB/Tulsa)*
Keith Hinchey *(Sr. V.P.)*
Douglas W. Hyde *(Sr. V.P., Asst. Sec. & Mng. Princpial-HTB/WDC)*
Larry J. Keller *(Sr. V.P.)*
Stanley R. Lewis *(Sr. V.P.)*
James L. Slade *(Sr. V.P.)*
Dennis Michael Arand *(V.P.)*
Susan Clark *(V.P., Treas. & Asst. Sec.)*
Scott Dedmon *(V.P.)*
Leon Glover *(V.P.)*
Leon M. Harris *(V.P.)*
David L. Huey *(V.P.)*
William R. Lawson *(V.P. & Asst. Sec.)*
George B. Lewis *(V.P.)*
Patrick J. McKee *(V.P.)*
Ed Riley *(V.P. & Asst. Sec.)*
Fred C. Seals, Jr. *(V.P.)*
James L. Slade *(V.P.)*
Kenneth R. Sullivan *(V.P.)*
Linda Duncan *(Sec.)*
Annese Bennett *(Asst. Sec.)*
Rosemary Hall *(Asst. Sec.)*

No. of U.S. Offices: 4

Outside Service Firm(s):

Luton & Co., Inc.*(Auditors)*
Oklahoma City, OK

Andrews Davis Legg Bixler Milsten & Price*(Legal Firm)*
500 W. Main
Oklahoma City, OK 73102
Tel.: 405-272-9241

Boatmen's First National Bank of Oklahoma*(Major Banking Relationship)*
P.O. Box 25189,
Oklahoma City, OK 73125

H W ELECTRONICS, INC.
6840 Hayvenhurst
Van Nuys, CA 91406
Tel.: 818-781-0300 **CA**
Fax: 818-781-0722
Year Founded: 1977
Approx.Sls.: $30,000,000
Emp.: 35
Wholesale Distributor & Retail Sales of Personal Computers; Business & Non-game & Game Software; Computers & Accessories, Personal & Home Entertainment; Computer Peripheral Equipment
S.I.C.: 5734; 5045
Terry Koosed *(Pres.)*
Gentille Koosed *(Treas.)*
Jay Consolati *(Sec.)*

H W Electronics, Inc.—(Continued)

Outside Service Firm(s):

BDO Seidman*(Auditors)*
1900 Avenue of the Stars, 11th Fl.
Los Angeles, CA 90067-6008
Tel.: 310-557-0300

Security Pacific National Bank*(Major Banking Relationship)*
Northridge, CA

HWH ARCHITECTS ENGINEERS PLANNERS INC.
1150 W. Third St.
Cleveland, OH 44113
Tel.: 216-623-0220 **OH**
Fax: 216-623-0238
Year Founded: 1908
Approx.Sls.: $10,900,000
Emp.: 120
Consulting Engineers, Architects & Planners
S.I.C.: 8711; 8712
Joseph Matts, Jr. *(Chm. Bd. & Pres.)*
Edward M. W. Chen *(V.P.)*
Jack L. Heideloff *(V.P.)*
Peter Jancan *(V.P.)*
Roger L. Knott *(V.P.)*
David L. Lehmer *(V.P.)*
Paul Martin, Jr. *(V.P.)*
G. Robert McCullough *(V.P.)*
Thomas D. Shinn *(V.P.)*
William T. Wells *(V.P.)*

No. of U.S. Offices: 1

Outside Service Firm(s):

Hausser & Taylor*(Auditors)*
Cleveland, OH

Arter & Hadden*(Legal Firm)*
1144 Union Commerce Bldg.,
Cleveland, OH 44115
Tel.: 216-696-1144

National City Bank*(Major Banking Relationship)*
P.O. Box 92301, Corp. Trust Dept.
Cleveland, OH 44101
Tel.: 216-575-2000

HAAS BROTHERS
2200 Jerrold Ave.
San Francisco, CA 94124
Tel.: 415-282-8585
Year Founded: 1851
Approx.Sls.: $10,000,000
Emp.: 7
Fiscal Year-end: 12/31/90
Wholesale Wines, Liquors, Bottles, Ceramics, Cyrus Noble Whiskey, Boord's Gin, Royal Gate Vodka
S.I.C.: 5182
E.R. Lilienthal *(Chm. Bd.)*
B.S. Burrows *(Pres.)*
Robert W. Schafer *(V.P.-Admin. & Fin.)*

Computer Systems/Hardware:
Digital

Subsidiary:

D & D Wholesale Liquors **(1)**
550 Evans Ave.
Reno, NV 89512
Tel.: 702-323-5135

THE HABAND CO.
265 N. 9th St.
Paterson, NJ 07530
Tel.: 201-942-2600 **NJ**
Fax: 201-942-3773
Fax: 201-942-1061
Year Founded: 1925
Sales Range: $100-499 Million
Mail Order Men's & Women's Wear
S.I.C.: 5961
Duke Habernickel *(Pres.)*
Anthony Del Gaudio *(Chief Fin. Officer)*
Dana Habernickel *(Dir.-Mktg.)*
Joan Heinricks *(Dir.-Adv. Space)*

No. of Mfg. Plants/Facilities: 5

Computer Systems/Hardware:
IBM

THE HABEGGER CORPORATION
4995 Winton Rd.
Cincinnati, OH 45232
Tel.: 513-681-6313 **OH**
Fax: 513-681-9892
Year Founded: 1952
Assets: $10,000,000
Liabilities: $4,000,000
Net Worth: $6,000,000
Approx.Sls.: $42,000,000
Emp.: 140
Fiscal Year-end: 12/31/91
Wholesale Distributor of Heating & Air Conditioning Equipment
S.I.C.: 5075
Fred Habegger *(Pres.)*
Thomas Habegger *(V.P.)*
James L. Habegger *(Sec.)*
Susanne Frey *(Treas.)*

No. of U.S. Offices: 6

Computer Systems/Hardware:
IBM System 36

Outside Service Firm(s):

Lindhorst & Dreidame*(Legal Firm)*
1700 Central Trust, 201 E. Fifth St.
Cincinnati, OH 45202
Tel.: 513-421-6630

Northside Bank*(Major Banking Relationship)*
Cincinnati, OH

THE ALLAN R. HACKEL ORGANIZATION
(d/b/a Advertising Agency Associates)
1330 Center St.
Newton Center, MA 02159
Tel.: 617-965-4400
Year Founded: 1959
Approx.Billings: $40,000,000
Emp.: 45
TV, Radio & Magazines; Media Buying Service
Allan Hackel *(Pres.)*
Paul St. Martin *(Chief Oper. Officer & Chief Fin. Officer)*
Herbert Cohen *(Gen. Counsel)*
Jodi Natali *(Treas.)*
James Brady *(Dir.-Mktg.)*

J. LEE HACKETT CO.
23550 Haggerty Rd.
Farmington, MI 48335
Tel.: 313-478-0200
Fax: 313-478-4730
Year Founded: 1923
Assets: $8,162,470
Liabilities: $5,732,732
Net Worth: $2,429,738
Approx.Sls.: $36,000,000
Emp.: 32
Fiscal Year-end: 8/31/90
Machine Tool Distributor
S.I.C.: 5084
J. Lee Juett *(Chm. Bd., Pres. & Chief Exec. Officer)*
John L. McCartney *(V.P.)*
Christopher G. Juett *(Mgr.-Sls.)*

No. of U.S. Offices: 4

Outside Service Firm(s):

Ernst & Young*(Auditors)*
One Detroit Center, 500 Woodward, Ste. 1700
Detroit, MI 48243
Tel.: 313-259-9600

Gromek, Bendure & Thomas*(Legal Firm)*
Detroit, MI

N.B.D. Bank, N.A.*(Major Banking Relationship)*
611 Woodward Ave.
Detroit, MI 48226
Tel.: 313-225-1122
Fax: 313-225-3420

Hackler Grain, Inc.
(Name Changed To Wheeler Bros. Grain Co.)

HACKNEY BROTHERS, INC.
301 N. Pender St.
Wilson, NC 27893
Mailing Address:
P.O. Box 2728,
Wilson, NC 27894-2728
Tel.: 919-237-8171
Tel.: 800-334-2296 (Outside NC)
Fax: 919-237-0305
Year Founded: 1854
Assets: $6,912,973
Liabilities: $1,236,228
Net Worth: $5,676,745
Sales Range: $10-19 Million
Emp.: 175
Fiscal Year-end: 11/30/91
Import Export
Mfr. Refrigerated Truck Bodies & Trailers, Refrigeration Systems, Ice Cream & Food Vending Carts
S.I.C.: 3713; 3715; 3585; 3711; 3589; 2599
Employee Matching Gifts Program: $1,000 Limit, Only to Qualified Educational Institutions
Thomas J. Hackney, Jr. *(Chm. Bd.)*
Robert H. Hackney *(Pres. & Chief Exec. Officer)*
Kenneth R. Hyde, Jr. *(Exec. V.P., Chief Opers. Officer & Treas.)*
T.F. Tinker *(V.P.-Opers. & Corp. Sec.)*
William L. Bryant *(Mgr.-Fin. Services)*
Ronald D. Byrd *(Mgr.-Personnel)*
David T. Seabaugh *(Mgr.-Engineering)*
Patricia H. Scott *(Mgr.-Mktg.)*
P.T. Scott *(Mgr.-Adv.)*
Harold Tharrington *(Pur. Agent)*
Principal(s):
Thomas J. Hackney, Jr.
Robert H. Hackney

No. of Mfg. Plants/Facilities: 1
No. of U.S. Offices: 1

Computer Systems/Hardware:
IBM AS 400

Outside Service Firm(s):

McGladrey & Pullen*(Auditors)*
Raleigh, NC

Liberty Mutual*(Commercial Insurance Carrier)*
Raleigh, NC

Womble, Carlyle, Sandridge & Rice*(Legal Firm)*
Raleigh, SC 27602

First Union National Bank*(Major Banking Relationship)*
CMG-5, Two First Union Center
Charlotte, NC 28288-1154
Tel.: 704-374-2698
Fax: 704-374-6987

THE H. T. HACKNEY CO.
502 S. Gay St.
Knoxville, TN 37901
Mailing Address:
P.O. Box 238
Knoxville, TN 37901
Tel.: 615-546-1291 **TN**
Fax: 615-546-1501
Year Founded: 1891
Approx.Sls.: $350,000,000
Emp.: 1,000
Fiscal Year-end: 3/31/90
Wholesale Grocery Distributor; Petroleum; Manufacture Table Tops & Industrial Equipment
S.I.C.: 5141; 6719; 5172; 5082; 5085; 2541
William B. Sansom *(Chm. Bd. & Chief Exec. Officer)*
B.E. France *(Pres., Chief Oper. Officer & Treas.)*
Mike Morton *(Chief Fin. Officer & V.P.)*
Leonard Robinett *(V.P.-Mngmt. Information Systems)*
B.M. Grinstead *(Asst. V.P. & Controller)*
Lauren Gass *(Sec.)*

Outside Service Firm(s):

Pugh & Co.*(Auditors)*
Knoxville, TN

Blue Cross & Blue Shield of Tennessee*(Group Insurer)*
Chattanooga, TN

Egerton, McAfee, Armistead, & Davis*(Legal Firm)*
Knoxville, TN

First Tennessee Bank, N.A.*(Major Banking Relationship)*
Knoxville, TN

Subsidiaries:

Appalachian Realty Co. **(1)**
P.O. Box 238
Knoxville, TN 37901
Tel.: 615-546-1291

Brink's, Inc. **(1)**
P.O. Box 238
Knoxville, TN 37901
Tel.: 615-546-1291
Wholesale Indus. Process Equip. & Supplies
S.I.C.: 5082; 5085

Volunteer Fabricators, Inc. **(1)**
P.O. Box 238
Knoxville, TN 37901
Tel.: 615-546-1291
Table Top Mfrs.
S.I.C.: 2541

HACKNEY & SONS, INC.
400 Hackney Ave.
Washington, NC 27889
Mailing Address:
P.O. Box 880
Washington, NC 27889
Tel.: 919-946-6521
Tel.: 800-763-0700 **NC**
Fax: 919-975-3274
Year Founded: 1941
Approx.Sls.: $35,000,000
Emp.: 320
Fiscal Year-end: 8/31/92
Import Export
Mfr. Truck Bodies & Trailers For The Beverage Industries & Emergency Service
S.I.C.: 3713; 3715
James A. Hackney III *(Chm. Bd.)*
Jay R. Troger *(Pres. & Chief Exec. Officer)*
R. Hodges Hackney *(Exec. V.P.)*
Rick Roll *(Exec. V.P.-Sls. & Mktg.)*
Raymond R. Bergevin *(V.P.-New Business Devel.)*
Steve H. Hill *(V.P.-Opers.)*
Ron Legere *(V.P.-Finance & Chief Fin. Officer)*
Jay Witte *(Dir.-Pur.)*
C.B. Cooper *(Mgr.-Warrant)*
Stuart Everett *(Mgr.-Data Processing)*
Bill Moore *(Mgr.-Customer Service)*
Yancey E. Warren *(Mgr.-Sls. Support)*

No. of Mfg. Plants/Facilities: 2
No. of U.S. Offices: 12
No. of Foreign Offices: 1

Computer Systems/Hardware:
IBM AS/400

Outside Service Firm(s):

Ernst & Young*(Auditors)*
P.O. Box 2171,
Raleigh, NC 27602

Pincus & Colnes*(Legal Firm)*
Charlotte, NC

Kansallis-Osake-Pankki*(Major Banking Relationship)*
New York, NY

HADDON CRAFTSMEN, INC.
1001 Wyoming Ave.
Scranton, PA 18509
Tel.: 717-348-9211 **PA**
Fax: 717-348-9266
Year Founded: 1903
Approx.Sls.: $60,000,000
Emp.: 1,000
Fiscal Year-end: 3/31/90
Import Export
Book Printing, Typesetting & Binding; Book Distributor; Complete Book Manufacturing
S.I.C.: 2731; 5192
Corporate Giving Program:
Employees Voluntary Contribution Fund of .4% of Gross Wages
Carl D. Toma *(Chm. Bd.)*
Thomas F. Sack *(Pres., Chief Exec. & Oper. Officer)*
Louis Auriemma *(Exec. V.P.)*
Bryan D. Richardson *(Sr. V.P. & Chief Fin. Officer)*
Robert A. Ciero *(V.P.-Printing)*
David Davis *(V.P.-Typesetting & Computers)*
Mary J. Decker *(V.P.-Dunmore Distribution Center)*
Andrew R. Teeple *(V.P.-Sls. & Mktg.)*
David D. Thomas *(V.P.-Bindery)*
Donald R. Vispi *(V.P.-Mfg. & Distr.)*
Michael J. Kenehan *(Controller)*
Timothy M. Davis *(Gen. Counsel & Sec.)*
George Blickens *(Dir.-Personnel)*
Thomas Gaynord *(Dir.-Pur.)*
Richard Koruszko *(Mgr.-Quality Control)*

Principal(s):
Thomas F. Sack
Louis Auriemma

No. of Mfg. Plants/Facilities: 5
No. of U.S. Offices: 5

Computer Systems/Hardware:
Atex

Outside Service Firm(s):

KPMG Peat Marwick*(Auditors)*
4905 Tildgman St.
Allentown, PA 18104
Tel.: 215-391-6380

Northeastern Bank of Pennsylvania*(Major Banking Relationship)*
Scranton, PA

Legg Mason Wood Walker*(Pension Manager)*
111 S. Calvert St.
Baltimore, MD 21203-1476

Haddon, Lynch & Baughman
(Name Changed To HLB Communications, Inc.)

HADEN, INC.
32200 N. Avis Dr.
Madison Heights, MI 48071
Tel.: 313-583-1900
Fax: 313-588-2551
Holding Company
S.I.C.: 6719; 3559; 3399
Arthur R. Geiger *(Chm. Bd.)*
Kenneth C. Dargatz *(Pres. & Chief Exec. Officer)*
Richard C. Johnston *(Sec. & Treas.)*

Outside Service Firm(s):

Coopers & Lybrand*(Auditors)*
400 Renaissance Center
Detroit, MI 48243
Tel.: 313-446-7100
Fax: 313-446-7117

Comerica Bank*(Major Banking Relationship)*
211 W. Fort St.
Detroit, MI 48226
Tel.: 313-222-3300

Subsidiaries:

Haden Equity, Ltd. **(1)**
32200 N. Avis Dr.
Madison Heights, MI 48071
Tel.: 313-583-1900
Approx.Sls.: $78,000,000
Emp.: 400
Richard C. Johnston *(Sec. & Treas.)*

Haden Investment, Ltd. **(1)**
32200 N. Avis Dr.
Madison Heights, MI 48071
Tel.: 313-583-1900
Approx.Sls.: $78,000,000
Emp.: 400
Metal Finishing Equipment For Plating, Machinery Installation
S.I.C.: 3559; 1796
Richard C. Johnston *(Sec. & Treas.)*

Haden Schweitzer Corporation **(1)**
32200 N. Avis Dr.
Madison Heights, MI 48071
Tel.: 313-583-1900
Metal Finishing Equipment for Plating, Machinery Installation
S.I.C.: 3559; 3399
Richard C. Johnston *(V.P., Sec. & Treas.)*

HAEGER INDUSTRIES, INC.
7 Maiden Lane
Dundee, IL 60118
Tel.: 708-426-3441
Fax: 708-426-8108
Year Founded: 1871
Emp.: 400
Export
Mfr. of Ceramic Gifts & Decorative Accessories; Haeger & Royal Haeger
S.I.C.: 3269
Alexandra H. Estes *(Chm. Bd. & Pres.)*
G.A. Salt *(Exec. V.P. & Gen. Mgr.)*
C.S. Zachrich *(Sec.)*
Russel R. Morehead *(Controller)*
Nevina M. Zarbock *(Mgr.-Adv.)*

No. of Mfg. Plants/Facilities: 2

Outside Service Firm(s):

Mueller & Co*(Auditors)*
Elgin, IL

Brady, McQueen, Martin, Collins & Jensen*(Legal Firm)*
Elgin, IL

First American Bank of Kane County*(Major Banking Relationship)*
Elgin, IL

Division:

Haeger Potteries of Macomb, Inc. **(1)**
411 Calhoun
Macomb, IL 61455
Tel.: 309-833-2171
Fax: 309-833-3860
Pottery
S.I.C.: 3269
A.H. Estes *(Pres.)*
G.A. Salt *(Exec. V.P.)*
L.R. Gillenwater *(V.P.)*

Subsidiary:

Haeger Potteries, Inc. **(1)**
7 Maiden Lane
Dundee, IL 60118
Tel.: 708-426-3033
Fax: 708-426-8108
Art Pottery
S.I.C.: 3269
Alexandra H. Estes *(Chm. Bd. & Pres.)*
G.A. Salt *(V.P. & G.M.)*
Russel R. Morehead *(Controller)*
Nevina Zarbock *(Mgr.-Adv.)*

BARRETT HAENTJENS & COMPANY
225-39 N. Cedar St.
Hazleton, PA 18201
Mailing Address:
P.O. Box 488
Hazleton, PA 18201
Tel.: 717-455-7711 **PA**
Fax: 717-459-2586
Year Founded: 1916
Assets: $18,263,000
Liabilities: $11,032,000
Net Worth: $7,231,000
Sales Range: $20-39 Million
Emp.: 350
Fiscal Year-end: 6/30/92
Import Export
Pumps & Pumping Equipment, Alloy Steel Castings
S.I.C.: 3561; 3325
Walter D. Haentjens *(Pres.)*
R.P. Haentjens *(Exec. V.P. & Treas.)*
Frances M. Sottile *(Sec.)*

Outside Service Firm(s):

Peoples First National Bank*(Major Banking Relationship)*
Hazleton, PA

HAGGAR APPAREL COMPANY
6113 Lemmon Ave.
Dallas, TX 75209
Tel.: 214-352-8481 **TX**
Fax: 214-956-0216
Year Founded: 1927
Sales Range: $100-499 Million
Import Export
Mfr. & Distribution of Apparel & Other Textile Products
S.I.C.: 5136; 2311; 2325; 2329
J.M. Haggar, Jr. *(Chm. Bd.)*
Joe Haggar III *(Pres. & Chief Exec. Officer)*
Ralph Beattie *(Exec. V.P. & Chief Fin. Officer)*
Frank Bracken *(Exec. V.P.-Mktg.)*
Milton Hickman *(Sr. V.P.-Specialty Label Div.)*
Tom Sample *(Sr. V.P. & Chief Information Officer MIS)*
Gary Swank *(Sr. V.P.-Opers.)*
George Greer *(V.P.-Human Resources)*
Peter Mitchell *(V.P.-Mktg. Communications)*
James Thompson *(V.P.-Natl. Sls.)*
Robert Qualls *(Treas.)*
Carlo Demarco *(Mgr.-Quality Control)*
Ronnie Scaggs *(Mgr.-Telecommunications)*
Shelly Van Deven *(Mgr.-Adv.)*

Computer Systems/Hardware:
IBM 3081

Outside Service Firm(s):

Ernst & Young*(Auditors)*
2121 San Jacinto, Ste. 500
Dallas, TX 75201
Tel.: 214-969-8000

Blue Cross & Blue Shield of Texas, Inc.*(Group Insurer)*
Dallas, TX

Baskin, Novakov & Thomas*(Legal Firm)*
Dallas, TX

HAGGEN'S, INC.
401 Harris Ave.
Bellingham, WA 98225
Tel.: 206-733-8720
Fax: 206-734-5848
Year Founded: 1936
Approx.Sls.: $120,000,000
Emp.: 700
Super Market Chain Stores With In Store Drug Stores
S.I.C.: 5411; 5912
Donald E. Haggen *(Chm. Bd. & Chief Exec. Officer)*
Richard R. Haggen *(Pres. & Chief Oper. Officer)*
Dale Henley *(Sr. V.P.-Fin. & Chief Fin. Officer)*
Larry Zieis *(Sr. V.P.-Mktg.)*

Outside Service Firm(s):

Ernst & Young*(Auditors)*
999 Third Av., Ste. 3500
Seattle, WA 98104
Tel.: 206-621-1800
Fax: 206-682-1234

Rainier National Bank*(Major Banking Relationship)*
Bellingham, WA

HAGIE MANUFACTURING CO.
721 Central Ave. West
Clarion, IA 50525
Mailing Address:
P.O. Box 273,
Clarion, IA 50525
Tel.: 515-532-2861
Tel.: 800-247-4885 **IA**
Fax: 515-532-3553
Year Founded: 1947
Approx.Sls.: $10,000,000
Emp.: 80
Fiscal Year-end: 12/31/91
Export
Mfr. of Special Products for Agriculture & Industry
S.I.C.: 3523
R.W. Hagie *(Chm. Bd.)*
John R. Hagie *(Pres.)*
David Duncalf *(Controller & Mgr.-Data Processing)*
Marlin Klehm *(Dir.-Pur.)*
Gaylen Kuperus *(Mgr.-Sls.)*
Jeff McOllough *(Mgr.-Adv.)*
Steve Mericle *(Mgr.-Mfg.)*

Principal(s):
R.W. Hagie

No. of Mfg. Plants/Facilities: 1
No. of U.S. Offices: 1

Computer Systems/Hardware:
IBM System 34

Outside Service Firm(s):

McGladrey & Pullen*(Auditors)*
Des Moines, IA

Copeland Insurance Agency, Inc.*(Commercial Insurance Carrier)*
Jefferson, IA

Brown, Winick, Graves, Donnelly, Baskerville & Schoenebaum*(Legal Firm)*
Two Ruan Center, 601 Locust, Ste. 1100
Des Moines, IA 50309
Tel.: 515-283-2076

Brenton Bank & Trust*(Major Banking Relationship)*
Clarion, IA

Principal Mutual Life Insurance Co.*(Pension Manager)*
711 High St.
Des Moines, IA 50309

Division:

Dodgen Feed Bodies **(1)**
721 Central Ave. West
Clarion, IA 50525
Mfr. Bulk Feed Bodies
S.I.C.: 3523

C.F. HAGLIN & SONS
4005 W. 65th St.
Minneapolis, MN 55435
Tel.: 612-920-6123 **MN**
Fax: 612-920-5318
Year Founded: 1881
Assets: $2,470,500
Liabilities: $1,176,000
Net Worth: $1,294,500
Approx.Sls.: $15,000,000

C.F. Haglin & Sons—(Continued)

Emp.: 60
Fiscal Year-end: 12/31/91
General Contractors; Nonresidential & Industrial Buildings & Warehouses
S.I.C.: 1542; 1541
Robert A. Roberts *(Pres. & Treas.)*
William Clynes *(V.P.-Engrng.)*
Tom Roberts *(V.P.-Mktg.)*
Doris A. Fritzen *(Controller & Sec.)*

Outside Service Firm(s):

Boulay, Heutmaker, Zibell & Co.*(Auditors)*
Edina, MN

Rode, Lucas & Schellhas*(Legal Firm)*
Edina, MN

First Southdale National Bank*(Major Banking Relationship)*
Edina, MN

J.R. HAHN CO., INC.
(d/b/a Hahn Systems)
2401 Production Dr.
Indianapolis, IN 46241
Mailing Address:
PO Box 42427,
Indianapolis, IN 46242-0427
Tel.: 317-243-3796 **IN**
Fax: 317-244-9079
Approx.Sls.: $17,000,000
Emp.: 79
Fiscal Year-end: 8/31/91
Pneumatic Stapling & Nailing Equipment; Carton Closing Equipment, Strapping, Glues & Adhesives
S.I.C.: 5039; 5085
Warren E. Hahn *(Chm. Bd.)*
George E. Hahn *(Pres.)*
Douglas E. Hahn *(V.P.-Mktg., Pur. & Adv.)*
David Hankins *(V.P.-Admin. & Sec.)*
Frank Harpold *(V.P.-Sls.)*
Hilda Wathen *(Dir.-Data Processing)*
Principal(s):
Warren E. Hahn
George E. Hahn

No. of U.S. Offices: 5

Computer Systems/Hardware:
Unisys

Outside Service Firm(s):

Crowe, Chizek & Co.*(Auditors)*
Indianapolis, IN

Ice, Miller, Donadio & Ryan*(Legal Firm)*
One American Square, Box 82001
Indianapolis, IN 46282
Tel.: 317-236-2219

INB National Bank*(Major Banking Relationship)*
One Indiana Sq.
Indianapolis, IN 46266
Tel.: 317-266-6000

W. L. HAILEY & COMPANY, INC.
2971 Kraft Dr.
Nashville, TN 37204
Mailing Address:
P.O. Box 40646
Nashville, TN 37204
Tel.: 615-255-3161 **TN**
Fax: 615-256-1316
Year Founded: 1925
Approx.Sls.: $30,000,000
Emp.: 250
Heavy Construction Contractors
S.I.C.: 1622; 1623; 1629
Lewis M. Steele *(Chm. Bd.)*
Edwin F. Jackson *(Assoc. Chm.)*
Edsel E. Bates *(Pres.)*
George D. Waller, III *(V.P. & Gen. Mgr.)*
Raymond E. Woodson *(V.P.)*
Thomas A. Battan *(Treas. & Comptroller)*
Rondall G. Woods *(Sec.)*

Computer Systems/Hardware:
IBM System 36

Outside Service Firm(s):

Cooper, Travis & Company*(Auditors)*
Nashville, TN

Third National Bank*(Major Banking Relationship)*
Nashville, TN

HAINES CITY CITRUS GROWERS ASSOCIATION
Railroad Ave.
Haines City, FL 33844
Mailing Address:
P.O. Box 337,
Haines City, FL 33845
Tel.: 813-422-1174
Fax: 813-422-3938
Year Founded: 1909
Assets: $7,000,000
Liabilities: $2,400,000
Net Worth: $4,600,000
Approx.Sls.: $14,500,000
Emp.: 600
Citrus Growers Cooperative; Fruit, Fruit Packing
S.I.C.: 0174; 0723; 5148
Irving Wheeler *(Pres.)*
Harold McTeer *(V.P.)*
H. R. Hamrick *(Sec., Treas. & Data Processing Mgr.)*
Robert C. Nettleton *(Gen. Counsel)*

Computer Systems/Hardware:
Datapoint

Outside Service Firm(s):

Bunting, Tripp & Ingley*(Auditors)*
Lake Wales, FL

NationsBank Florida*(Major Banking Relationship)*
St. Petersburg, FL

HAINES & CO., INC.
8050 Freedom Ave., N.W., Box #2117
North Canton, OH 44720
Tel.: 216-494-9111 **OH**
Fax: 216-494-6859
Year Founded: 1932
Sales Range: $20-39 Million
Emp.: 300
Fiscal Year-end: 12/31/90
Publisher Cross Reference & Tradename Directories; Mailing Lists
S.I.C.: 2741; 7331
W.K. Haines, Sr. *(Chm. Bd.)*
W.K. Haines, Jr. *(Pres.)*
R.W. Brannick *(V.P.-Admin.)*
James McGeorge *(V.P.)*
Jay Swallen *(Sec. & Treas.)*
Principal(s):
W.K. Haines, Sr.
W.K. Haines, Jr.

No. of U.S. Offices: 10

Computer Systems/Hardware:
IBM System 36

Outside Service Firm(s):

Swallen, Lawhun, Hubbard & Abraham, Inc.*(Auditors)*
Canton, OH

Society National Bank*(Major Banking Relationship)*
900 Euclid Ave., P.O. Box 6477
Cleveland, OH 44101-6477
Tel.: 216-737-5000
Fax: 216-566-8947

HAINES LUNDBERG WAEHLER
115 Fifth Ave.
New York, NY 10003
Tel.: 212-353-4600
Fax: 212-353-4666
Year Founded: 1885
Approx.Sls.: $23,000,000
Emp.: 210
Architects, Engineers, Planners, Interiors
S.I.C.: 8712; 8711; 8748
Robert A. Djerejian *(Sr. Mng. Partner)*
Theodore S. Hammer *(Sr. Mng. Partner)*
Leevi Kiil *(Sr. Mng. Partner)*
Martin D. Raab *(Sr. Mng. Partner)*
Richard T. Sparks *(Gen. Mgr.)*
Robert Brandt *(Partner)*
Seymour S. Fish *(Partner)*
Jay Fleishman *(Partner)*
John P. Gering *(Partner)*
Alan Kaplan *(Partner)*
Carl S. Muskat *(Partner)*
Carl W. Ordemann *(Partner)*
Stuart K. Pertz *(Partner)*
Ju-Chieh Ru *(Partner)*
Myron A. Schloss *(Partner)*
Stanley Stark *(Partner)*
Steven L. Viehl *(Partner)*
Edy B. Zingher *(Partner)*

Outside Service Firm(s):

David Berdon & Co.*(Auditors)*
415 Madison Ave.
New York, NY 10017
Tel.: 212-832-0400

Block, Powal, & Revilis*(Legal Firm)*
New York, NY

Le Patner, Gainen & Block*(Legal Firm)*
New York, NY

The Bank of New York*(Major Banking Relationship)*
Church Street Station, P.O. Box 11258
New York, NY 10286-1258
Tel.: 212-635-8133
Tel.: 800-524-4458
Fax: 212-635-8096

HAJOCA CORP.
127 Coulter Ave.
Ardmore, PA 19003
Tel.: 215-649-1430
Fax: 215-649-7258
Approx.Sls.: $180,000,000
Emp.: 800
Distributor Industrial Supplies; Plumbing & Heating Equipment
S.I.C.: 5074; 5085
Robert F. Parsons *(Pres. & Chief Oper. Officer)*
T.P. Callahan *(V.P.)*
Mike Plunkett *(Controller)*

Computer Systems/Hardware:
IBM

Outside Service Firm(s):

Ernst & Young*(Auditors)*
1800 John F. Kennedy Blvd.
Philadelphia, PA 19103-7499
Tel.: 215-864-3300

Mellon Bank, N.A.*(Major Banking Relationship)*
P.O. Box 444,
Pittsburgh, PA 15230
Tel.: 412-236-8000
Tel.: 1-800-451-7392
Fax: 412-236-8157

HALE-HALSELL COMPANY
9111 E. Pine
Tulsa, OK 74115
Mailing Address:
P.O. Box 582898
Tulsa, OK 74158
Tel.: 918-835-4484 **OK**
Fax: 918-834-1347
Year Founded: 1901
Assets: $68,761,000
Earnings: $1,687,000
Liabilities: $37,900,821
Net Worth: $30,860,179
Approx.Sls.: $375,600,000
Emp.: 4,922
Import Export
Wholesale Food Distributor
S.I.C.: 5141; 5411; 5142; 5147; 5148; 5143
Elmer Hale, Jr. *(Chm. Emeritus)*
Harrison Huls *(Chm. Bd.)*
Robert Hawk *(Pres. & Chief Exec. Officer)*
Bill Dufur *(V.P.-Transportation)*
Jim Lewis *(V.P., Chief Fin. Officer, Sec. & Treas.)*
Earl Mead, Jr. *(V.P.-Convenience Stores)*
Russell Jobe *(Controller)*
Jim Ryan *(Gen. Counsel)*
Paul Bradley *(Dir.-Human Resources)*
Joe Dickerson *(Dir.-Tech. Services)*
Joe Hoffman *(Dir.-Sls.)*
Wayne Gould *(Dir.-Pur.)*
Mark Long *(Dir.-Information Services)*
Fred Smith *(Dir.-Adv.)*
Buddy Stephens *(Dir.-Mktg.)*
Jim Scivally *(Gen. Mgr.)*
Rhonda Griffen *(Corp. Travel Planner)*

No. of Mfg. Plants/Facilities: 2

Computer Systems/Hardware:
IBM

Outside Service Firm(s):

KPMG Peat Marwick*(Auditors)*
One Williams Center, Ste. 1600
Tulsa, OK 74172

Conner & Winters*(Legal Firm)*
2400 First Natl. Tower
Tulsa, OK 74103
Tel.: 918-586-5683

Bank of Oklahoma*(Major Banking Relationship)*
One Williams Center
Tulsa, OK 74012
Tel.: 918-588-5100

Fourth National Bank & Trust Co.*(Major Banking Relationship)*
P.O. Box 2360,
Tulsa, OK 74101

Guaranty Bank & Trust Co.*(Major Banking Relationship)*
Tulsa, OK

Prudential Insurance Co. of America*(Pension Manager)*
751 Broad St.
Newark, NJ 07102-3777
Tel.: 201-802-6000

Branch:

Hale-Halsell Company **(1)**
P.O. Box 10
Durant, OK 74701
Tel.: 405-924-2800

Subsidiaries:

Arkansas Valley Distributing **(1)**
9111 E. Pine
Tulsa, OK 74115
Tel.: 918-835-4484
Emp.: 26
W.O. Smith *(Pres.)*

Curtis Equipment Co., Inc. **(1)**
6577 E. 40th St.
Tulsa, OK 74145
Tel.: 918-622-7390
Emp.: 70
Markets Restaurant Supplies & Equipment
S.I.C.: 5046
Dan Fulps *(Pres.)*

Fadler, Inc. **(1)**
6511 E. 44th St.
Tulsa, OK 74145
Tel.: 918-627-0770
Emp.: 80

Foodland, Inc. **(1)**
9111 E. Pine
Tulsa, OK 74115
Tel.: 918-835-4484
Emp.: 388
Robert Hawk *(Pres.)*

Foodtown, Inc. **(1)**
9111 E. Pine
Tulsa, OK 74115
Tel.: 918-835-4484
Benny Scilott *(Pres.)*

H.H. Foods, Inc. **(1)**
9111 E. Pine
Tulsa, OK 74115
Tel.: 918-835-4484
Emp.: 93

Git N Go, Inc. **(1)**
911 E. Pine
Tulsa, OK 74115
Tel.: 918-835-4484

Sipes Super Markets **(1)**
9111 E. Pine
Tulsa, OK 74115
Tel.: 918-835-4484
Emp.: 301

United Supermarkets **(1)**
P.O. Box 557
Altus, OK 73521
Tel.: 405-482-1414

Valu-Fare Foods, Inc. **(1)**
9111 E. Pine
Tulsa, OK 74115
Tel.: 918-835-4484
Retail Grocers; Supermarkets
S.I.C.: 5411
Bob Hawk *(Chief Oper. Officer)*

Valu-Foods, Inc. **(1)**
P.O. Box 582807
Tulsa, OK 74158-2807
Tel.: 918-835-4484
Wholesale Grocers
S.I.C.: 5141
Don Wiggley *(Pres.)*

THE C. P. HALL COMPANY
7300 S. Central Ave.
Chicago, IL 60638
Tel.: 312-767-4600
Fax: 708-458-0428
Year Founded: 1919
Sales Range: $80-99 Million
Emp.: 220
Fiscal Year-end: 9/30/90
Import Export
Specialty & Industrial Chemicals
S.I.C.: 2843; 2869
G.A. Vincent *(Chm. Bd., Pres., Chief Exec. Officer & Chief Oper. Officer)*
Robert C. Eitel *(V.P.-Oper.)*
James R. Klusendorf *(V.P. & Treas.)*
John J. Paro *(V.P.-Sls. & Mktg.)*
Robert A. De Prima *(Reg. Mgr.-Intl.)*
Steven Hopper *(Mgr.-Commercial Devel.)*
Kim Johnson *(Mgr.-Ind. Devel.)*
Thomas E. Miller *(Mgr.-Personnel)*
Richard J. Snyder *(Mgr.-Pur.)*
Robert J. Weiland *(Mgr.-Data Processing)*

Computer Systems/Hardware:
AS/400

Divisions:

The C.P. Hall Company **(1)**
P.O. Box 13303
Memphis, TN 38113
Tel.: 901-948-8663
Fax: 901-774-7241
Import Export
Computer Systems/Hardware:
AS-400
George Dozier *(Reg. Mgr.)*
Wendell Edwards *(Mgr.-Sls.)*
Edwina Staaten *(Matls. Mgr.)*

The C.P. Hall Company **(1)**
4460 Hudson Dr.
Stow, OH 44224
Tel.: 216-929-8311
Fax: 216-929-3616
Vincent Ross *(Reg. Mgr.)*
August Lendecke *(Mgr.-Sls.)*
Ron DeGrande *(Matls. Mgr.)*

The C.P. Hall Company **(1)**
444 Alaska Ave.
Torrance, CA 90503
Tel.: 310-320-2211
Fax: 310-618-0405
Donald Holstein *(Reg. Mgr.)*

The C.P. Hall Company **(1)**
7300 S. Central
Chicago, IL 60638
Tel.: 708-594-6000
Fax: 708-458-0428
Robert Walton *(Reg. Mgr.)*
Rick Snyder *(Matls. Mgr.)*

THE HALL CHINA COMPANY
Anna Ave.
East Liverpool, OH 43920
Mailing Address:
P.O. Box 989
East Liverpool, OH 43920
Tel.: 216-385-2900
Fax: 216-385-6185
Year Founded: 1903
Approx.Sls.: $12,000,000
Emp.: 250
Fiscal Year-end: 12/31/90
Fireproof Cooking China
S.I.C.: 3262
John C. Thompson *(Chief Exec. Officer)*
John G. Sayle *(Pres. & Treas.)*
J. Thomas Mayers *(V.P. & Sec.)*
James Clunk *(Mgr.-Sls.)*
J.J. Owen *(Mgr.-Adv.)*
J.M. Kachur *(Pur. Agent)*

HALL CONTRACTING CORP.
3800 Crittenden Dr.
Louisville, KY 40209
Mailing Address:
P.O. Box 37270
Louisville, KY 40233-7270 **KY**
Tel.: 502-367-6151
Fax: 502-361-5771
Year Founded: 1954
Assets: $15,000,000
Liabilities: $10,000,000
Net Worth: $5,000,000
Approx.Sls.: $50,000,000
Emp.: 550
Fiscal Year-end: 12/31/90
General Contractors Utilities, Pipelines, Bridges, Airports, Heavy Construction
S.I.C.: 1629; 1611; 1623
Kenneth E. Hall *(Chm. Bd.)*
K. Michael Hall *(Pres., Chief Exec. & Chief Oper. Officer)*
Jess M. Walters *(Exec. V.P.)*
John Van Dyke *(V.P.-Personnel)*
James E. Williams *(V.P.-Construction)*
Thomas Wood, Jr. *(V.P.-Estimating)*
Brian H. Loher *(Treas., Sec. & Dir.-Investor Rels.)*
Sandra Bruce *(Controller & Office Mgr.)*
Principal(s):
Kenneth E. Hall
K. Michael Hall

No. of Mfg. Plants/Facilities: 3
No. of U.S. Offices: 3

Outside Service Firm(s):

Deloitte & Touche*(Auditors)*
510 W. Broadway
Louisville, KY 40202
Tel.: 502-562-2000

CNA Insurance*(Commercial Insurance Carrier)*
New York, NY

Blue Cross & Blue Shield of Kentucky*(Group Insurer)*
9901 Linn Station Rd.
Louisville, KY 40223
Tel.: 502-426-3700

Greenebaum, Doll & McDonald*(Legal Firm)*
Louisville, KY

First National Bank of Louisville*(Major Banking Relationship)*
P.O. Box 36000,
Louisville, KY 40233

William M. Mercer Incorporated*(Pension Manager)*
Louisville, KY

HALL, HAERR, PETERSON & HARNEY, INC.
Knoxville Executive Plaza,
6907 N. Knoxville
Peoria, IL 61614
Tel.: 309-692-7011
Fax: 309-692-0934
Year Founded: 1952
Approx.Billings: $10,000,000
Emp.: 20
J. Philip Harney *(Chm. Bd.)*
Richard A. Hall *(Pres.)*
Lynn T. Truitt *(V.P., Controller)*
William Kamin *(V.P.)*

HALL SIGN, INC.
3000 W. 3rd St.
Bloomington, IN 47402
Mailing Address:
P.O. Box 515
Bloomington, IN 47402
Tel.: 812-332-9355
Tel.: 800-284-7446 **IN**
Fax: 812-332-9816
Year Founded: 1949
Sales Range: $10-19 Million
Emp.: 90
Export
Manufacture Traffic Signs
S.I.C.: 3993
Larry Hall *(Pres.)*
T. Montgomery Hopkins *(V.P.-Opers.)*
S.N. Chapman *(Mgr.-Sls. & Mktg.)*

Outside Service Firm(s):

Geo P. Adinanis*(Legal Firm)*
Indianapolis, IN

Bank One*(Major Banking Relationship)*
Bloomingon, IN

HALLIDIE MACHINERY COMPANY, INC.
2200 6th Ave., S.
Seattle, WA 98134
Tel.: 206-583-0600 **WA**
Fax: 206-624-7528
Year Founded: 1963
Approx.Sls.: $25,000,000
Emp.: 49
Wholesale Distribution of Machine Tools & Accessories
S.I.C.: 5084
Leonard A. Myhre *(Chm. Bd.)*
Larry E. Myhre *(Pres.)*
Warren Barlow *(V.P.)*
Jim Ellis *(V.P.)*
Lee Houghton *(V.P.)*
William Cavender *(Treas. & Sec.)*

Outside Service Firm(s):

Security Pacific National Bank*(Major Banking Relationship)*
Security Pacific Tower, T21-7,
Seattle, WA 98124
Tel.: 206-621-5920

HALLMARK ADVERTISING, INC.
Two Chatham Center
Pittsburgh, PA 15219
Tel.: 412-471-5300
Year Founded: 1965
Approx.Billings: $20,130,000
Emp.: 34
Marvin S. Jacobson *(Pres.)*
William Binstock *(Exec. V.P.)*
Louis Lasday *(Sr. V.P.)*
Theresa Allison *(Fin. V.P.)*
Phyllis Jacobson *(Treas.)*

HALLMARK CARDS, INC.
2501 McGee
Kansas City, MO 64108
Mailing Address:
P.O. Box 419580,
Kansas City, MO 64141-6580
Tel.: 816-274-5111 **MO**
Telex: 6841027 Hall UW
Fax: 816-274-5242
Year Founded: 1910
Approx.Sls.: $2,800,000,000
Emp.: 22,000
Fiscal Year-end: 12/31/91
Import Export
Greeting Cards, Stationery & Related Products; Hallmark Cards, Ambassador Cards
S.I.C.: 2678; 2771; 3999; 2679; 3952
Corporate Giving Program: Contribution Program Includes Arts & Humanities, Civic Organizations, Education & Social Welfare
Employee Matching Gifts Program: Matching Gifts to Education up to $6,000 Per Person Per Year, Subject to $2,000 Per Institution Maximum
Donald J. Hall *(Chm. Bd.)*
Irvine O. Hockaday, Jr. *(Pres. & Chief Exec. Officer)*
Lanny Julian *(Pres.-Ambassador Brand)*
Robert Firnhaber *(Pres.-Ambassador Cards & Grp. V.P.-Ambassador Brand)*
William Hall *(Pres.-Hall Family Foundations)*
Jim Toohey *(Pres.-Hallmark Intl.)*
Henry F. Frigon *(Exec. V.P.-Devel./Strategy & Chief Fin. Officer)*
Robert L. Stark *(Exec. V.P. & Pres.-Personnal Communications Grp.)*
Thomas Johnston *(Grp. V.P.-Hallmark Brand)*
Robert Kipp *(Grp. V.P.-Corp. Services & Pres.-Crown Ctr. Redevelopment Corp.)*
Charles W. Koester, Jr. *(Grp. V.P.-Admin.)*
Gray McMonigle *(Grp. V.P.-Opers.)*
Dave Case *(Div. V.P.-Mktg. Res.)*
Don Farquharson *(Div. V.P.-Prod. Discovery & Devel.)*
Charles W. Hucker *(Div. V.P.-Pub. Affairs & Communications)*
Brad R. Moore *(Div. V.P.-Adv. & Promo.)*
Laurie Beeson *(V.P.-Mktg.)*
John Collins *(V.P.-Mngmt. Information Systems)*
Charles J. Egan, Jr. *(V.P., Gen. Counsel & Sec.)*
Don Fletcher *(V.P.-Hallmark Brand Prod. Devel.)*
J.D. Goodwin *(V.P.-Mfg.)*
Lowell Mayone *(V.P.-Personnel & Services)*
Rod Sturgeon *(V.P.-Intl. Fin. & Plng.)*
Bruce Bentcover *(Treas.)*
Bob Benson *(Controller (SEG))*
Jack Gabriel *(Dir.-Employee Rels.)*
Jim Johnson *(Dir.-Data Center Opers.)*
John Losik *(Dir.-Facilities Services)*

Hallmark Cards, Inc.—(Continued)

Doug Browning *(Dir.-Benefit Trusts Admn.)*
Steve Doyal *(Mgr.-Corp. Media Rels.)*

No. of Mfg. Plants/Facilities: 11

Outside Service Firm(s):

KPMG Peat Marwick *(Auditors)*
1000 Walnut St.
Kansas City, MO 64106

United Missouri Bank *(Major Banking Relationship)*
Tenth & Grand
Kansas City, MO 64106
Tel.: 816-556-7000

Wilmington Trust Co. *(Pension Manager)*
Rodney Square North
Wilmington, DE 19890
Tel.: 302-651-1000

Division:

Ambassador Cards (1)
2501 McGee
Kansas City, MO 64108
Tel.: 816-274-5111
Fax: 816-274-7835
Approx.Sls.: $550,000,000
Emp.: 800
Fiscal Year-end: 12/31/91
Greeting Cards
S.I.C.: 2771
Donald J. Hall *(Chm. Bd.)*
Robert Firnhaber *(Pres. & Grp. V.P.-Ambassador Brand)*
Bill Stacy *(V.P.-Mktg.)*
Steve Doyal *(Dir.-Media Rels.)*

Subsidiaries:

Binney & Smith Inc. (1)
1100 Church Lane
Easton, PA 18042
Tel.: 215-253-6271 (100%)
Telex: 4761084
Fax: 212-250-5768
Approx.Sls.: $270,000,000
Emp.: 1,600
Fiscal Year-end: 12/31/91
Import Export
Crayola Crayons, Crayola Markers, Crayola Colored Pencils Crayola Chalks, Crayola Watercolors, Crayola Caddy, Crayola Art Workshop Kit, Crayola Creative Lettering Set; Designer Kit; Crayola Modeling Clay, Crayola Tempera Paint, Liquitex Acrylics, Oils and Watercolors, Liquitex Brushes, Crayola Coloring Books
S.I.C.: 3952; 3991; 3944; 2891
Richard S. Gurin *(Pres. & Chief Exec. Officer)*
Stan S. Strauss *(V.P. & Gen. Mgr.-Institutional Prods. Div.)*
Roger B. Cooley *(V.P. & Gen. Mgr.-Res. & Devel.)*
Thomas Muller *(V.P. & Gen. Mgr.-Consumer Prods. Div.)*
Graham Wyles *(V.P.-Intl. Div.)*
Neil A. Glickstein *(V.P.-Fin.)*
John Hasting *(V.P.-Mfg.)*
Drew W. Landis *(V.P.-Human Resources)*
Bruce Thompson *(Dir.-Mktg.)*
Dennis Malloy *(Dir.-Bus. Devel.)*

Divisions:

Crayola Products Div. (2)
1100 Church Lane
Easton, PA 18044
Tel.: 215-253-6271 (100%)
Emp.: 62
Mfr. of Crayons, Chalk, Water Colors, Clay, Tempera Paint
S.I.C.: 3952
Tom Muller *(V.P. & G.M.)*

Hallmark Art Products & International Div. (2)
PO Box 431, 1100 Church Lane
Easton, PA 18044
Tel.: 215-253-6271
Emp.: 40
Mfr of Artists Oils & Acrylic Colors, Mediums, Brushes & Water Colors
S.I.C.: 3952
Roger Cooley *(V.P. & G.M.)*

Hallmark Educational Products Div. (2)
1100 Church Lane
Easton, PA 18044
Tel.: 215-253-6271
Emp.: 40
Mfr. of Crayons, Chalk, Brushes, Water Colors, Clay, Tempura, Markers
S.I.C.: 3952
Stanley Strauss *(Vice Pres. & Gen. Mgr.)*

Crown Media Inc. (1)
One Galleria Tower, 13355 Noel Rd., Ste. 1500
Dallas, TX 75240
Tel.: 214-702-7380
Fax: 214-702-7382
Radio & Cable Television Interests
S.I.C.: 4832; 4841
Rod Thole *(Pres.)*

Subsidiary:

Crown Cable Inc. (2)
1 Galleria Tower, 13355 Noel Rd., Ste. 1500
Dallas, TX 75240
Tel.: 214-702-7380 (100%)
Cable TV Interests
S.I.C.: 4841
Rod Thole *(Pres.)*

Crown Center Redevelopment Corp. (1)
2440 Pershing Road, Ste. 500
Kansas City, MO 64108
Tel.: 816-274-4020 (100%)
Emp.: 115
Developer & Manager of Shopping & Office Complexes
S.I.C.: 6512
Robert Kipp *(Pres.)*

Graphics International Inc. (1)
P.O. Box 419566, 2501 McGee
Kansas City, MO 64141-6566
Tel.: 816-274-5761 (100%)
Emp.: 166
Importer of Affiliated Prods. for Sale to Retailers
S.I.C.: 5023; 5112; 5113
Thomas H. Johnston *(Pres.)*

Halls Merchandising Inc. (1)
200 E. 25th St.
Kansas City, MO 64108
Tel.: 816-274-8111 (100%)
Emp.: 328
Specialty Retailing
S.I.C.: 5399
Robert Leitstein *(Pres.)*

Litho-Krome Company (1)
1039 13th Street
Columbus, GA 31994
Tel.: 706-324-4211 (100%)
Emp.: 197
Commercial Lithography Services
S.I.C.: 2752
Lamar Powers *(Pres.)*

Signboard Hill Productions (1)
2501 McGee
Kansas City, MO 64108
Tel.: 816-274-5111
S.I.C.: 7312
Brad Moore *(Pres.)*

Univision Holdings, Inc. (1)
605 Third Ave., 12th Floor
New York, NY 10158-0180
Tel.: 212-455-5200
Spanish-Language Television Network & Group Of Spanish-Language Format Television Stations
S.I.C.: 4833
Ray Rodriguez *(Pres. & Chief Exec. Officer)*
George Blank *(Exec. V.P. & Chief Fin. Officer)*
Raul Torano *(Exec. V.P.)*
Andrew Goldman *(Sr. V.P.-Business Affairs)*
Dale Bills *(V.P.-Admin.)*
Guillermo Martinez *(V.P.-News Opers.)*
Tony Oquendo *(V.P.-Opers. & Technical Services)*
Peter Roslow *(V.P.-Sls. & Mktg.)*

Willitts Design (1)
1129 Industrial Ave.
Petaluma, CA 94952
Tel.: 707-778-7211
Designer, Importer & Marketer of Collectibles
S.I.C.: 5023
William Willitts *(Pres. & Chief Exec. Officer)*

Non-U.S. Holdings:

William E. Coutts, Co. Ltd. (1)
2 Hallcrown Place
Willowdale, ON M2J 1P6, Canada
Tel.: 416-492-1300
Telex: 389-069 66671
Mfr. of Greeting Cards, Party Goods
S.I.C.: 2771
John Kempster *(Pres.)*

Hallmark Cards Australia Ltd. (1)
611 Blackburn Rd. P.O. Box 140, Clayton, North Clayton, Victoria 2020, Australia
Tel.: 3 560 9033
Telex: 790-32780
Mfr. of Greeting Cards, Party Goods
S.I.C.: 2771

Hallmark Cards Ltd., European Div. (1)
Hallmark House Station Rd., Henley-on-Thames, Oxfordshire RG9 1LQ, United Kingdom
Tel.: 491-578383
Mfr. of Greeting Cards & Party Goods
S.I.C.: 2771

Hallmark Cards NZ Ltd. (1)
59 Mahunga Dr. Private Bag, Onehunga, Mangere, Auckland 6, New Zealand
Tel.: 9 644 469
Telex: 791 214 86
Mfr. of Greeting Cards & Party Goods
S.I.C.: 2771

Spanjersburg (1)
Capelle aan den Ijssel, Netherlands

HALOCARBON PRODUCTS CORP.
887 Kinderkamack Rd.
River Edge, NJ 07661
Tel.: 201-262-8899
Approx.Sls.: $25,100,000
Emp.: 105
Mfr. of Acid Resistant Lubricants
S.I.C.: 2992
Robert L. Ehrenfeld *(Pres.)*
L.L. Ferstandig *(V.P.)*
Elaine Reese *(Mgr.-Pur.)*

HALSEY DRUG CO., INC.
1827 Pacific St.
Brooklyn, NY 11233
Tel.: 718-467-7500
Year Founded: 1935
Earnings: $1,726,824
Approx.Sls.: $27,462,000
Emp.: 155
Fiscal Year-end: 12/31/91
Mfr. of Generic Drugs & Vitamins
S.I.C.: 2834; 2833
Alex Marcus *(Chm. Bd.)*
Seymour Marcus *(Vice Chm. & Treas.)*
Jay Marcus *(Pres.)*
Ken Handle *(Gen. Counsel)*
George Sloane *(Dir.-Tech.)*
Leonard Weiss *(Dir.-Admin.)*

HALSTEAD INDUSTRIES, INC.
300 N. Green St., Ste. 400
Greensboro, NC 27401
Tel.: 919-272-1966 **PA**
Fax: 919-272-6937
Year Founded: 1935
Approx.Sls.: $426,000,000
Emp.: 2,500
Fiscal Year-end: 12/31/90
Copper Tubing & Foam Rubber Prods.
S.I.C.: 3351; 3069
William B. Halstead *(Chief Oper. Officer)*
Frank H. Roland *(Pres.)*
John Fitzgerald *(Controller)*

No. of Mfg. Plants/Facilities: 7
No. of U.S. Offices: 2

Computer Systems/Hardware:
Digital

Outside Service Firm(s):

Coopers & Lybrand *(Auditors)*
600 Grant St., 35th Fl.
Pittsburgh, PA 15219
Tel.: 412-355-8000
Fax: 412-355-8089

Blue Cross of Western Pennsylvania *(Group Insurer)*
One Smithfield St.
Pittsburgh, PA 15222
Tel.: 1-800-242-6425

Dillon, McCandless & King *(Legal Firm)*
Butler, PA

Divisions:

Halstead Industrial Prods. Div. (1)
Hwy. 1
Wynne, AR 72396
Tel.: 501-238-3228
Mfr. Tube Kits & Cellular Rubber Prods.
S.I.C.: 3069
Charles Foriska *(Gen. Mgr.)*

Halstead Metal Prods. Div. (1)
Hwy. 311
Pine Hall, NC 27042
Tel.: 919-427-5111
Mfr. Copper Tubing
S.I.C.: 3351
Leroy Lintz *(Gen. Mgr.)*

HAMAMATSU CORP.
360 Foothill Rd.
Bridgewater, NJ 08807-0910
Mailing Address:
P.O. Box 6910,
Bridgewater, NJ 08807
Tel.: 908-231-0960
Fax: 908-231-1218
Approx.Sls.: $24,000,000
Emp.: 300
Fiscal Year-end: 9/30/90
Mfr. Photosensitive Devices & Special Lamps
S.I.C.: 3861
T. Hiruma *(Chm. Bd.)*
Julius Ralph Eno *(Pres.)*
Carol Simola *(V.P.-Admin.)*

HAMBURG BROTHERS INC.
40 24th Street
Pittsburgh, PA 15222
Tel.: 412-227-6200 **PA**
Fax: 412-227-6336
Year Founded: 1920
Approx.Sls.: $100,000,000
Emp.: 115
Fiscal Year-end: 12/31/90
Wholesale Consumer Electronics; Home Furnishings & Electrical Household Goods
S.I.C.: 5023
Jules Spokane *(Pres.)*
Mark Kreisler *(Sr. V.P.-Whirlpool Div.)*
Larry Levy *(Sr. V.P.-Electronics Div.)*
Larry Hamburg *(V.P.-New York Opers.)*
John Gemeinhart *(Controller)*
Richard T. Weaver *(Treas., Sec. & Chief Fin. Officer)*
Dennis Holzer *(Gen. Mgr.)*

No. of Mfg. Plants/Facilities: 5

Computer Systems/Hardware:
DEC VAX

Outside Service Firm(s):

Deloitte & Touche *(Auditors)*
2400 One PPG Place
Pittsburgh, PA 15222
Tel.: 412-281-2232

Employee Benefit Claims *(Group Insurer)*
Pittsburgh, PA

Marcus & Shapira*(Legal Firm)*
One Oxford Centre
Pittsburgh, PA 15219
Tel.: 412-471-3490

Pittsburgh National Bank*(Major Banking Relationship)*
Stock Transfer Dept., Fifth & Wood Streets
Pittsburgh, PA 15265

Pittsburgh National Bank*(Pension Manager)*
Stock Transfer Dept., Fifth & Wood Streets
Pittsburgh, PA 15265

Hameroff/Milenthal/Spence, Inc.

HAMEROFF/MILENTHAL/ SPENCE, INC.
One Columbus, 10 W. Broad St.
Columbus, OH 43215
Tel.: 614-221-7667 **OH**
Fax: 614-222-2596
Year Founded: 1955
Approx.Billings: $45,000,000
Emp.: 78
Fiscal Year-end: 9/30/91
Advertising Agency
S.I.C.: 7311
Corporate Giving Program: Annual Allocation with 75% to Designated Causes Including United Way, Jewish Federation, Ohio State University-School of Journalism Scholarship & Columbus College of Art & Design-Scholarship Program; 25% to Human Services & Cultural Organizations inwhich Employees are Active
David Milenthal *(Chm. Bd.)*
Alfred Cogossi *(Chief Fin. Officer)*
Paula Spence *(Pres.)*
Barry Mastrine *(Pres.-The Davon Res. Grp.)*
Richard K. Milenthal *(Exec. V.P.)*
Robert Gold *(V.P. & Gen. Mgr.)*
Bill Patterson *(V.P.-Corp. Communications)*
Lenere Shrieves *(V.P.-Agency Resources)*
Allan Franks *(Dir.-Environmental Pub. Rels.)*
Bob Tenenbaum *(Dir.-Pub. Rels.)*
Bobbi Abbruzzese *(Exec. Asst.)*
Peggy Heiss *(Supvr.-Word Processing)*
Jim Livecchi *(Dir.-Bus. Devel.)*

No. of Mfg. Plants/Facilities: 1
No. of U.S. Offices: 1

Computer Systems/Hardware:
IBM and MacIntosh

Outside Service Firm(s):

Ernst & Young*(Auditors)*
One Columbus, 10 W. Broad St.
Columbus, OH 43215
Tel.: 614-224-5678

Cincinnati Insurance Co.*(Commercial Insurance Carrier)*
Cincinnati, OH

Porter, Wright, Morris & Arthur*(Legal Firm)*
Huntington Center, 41 S. High St.
Columbus, OH 43215-3406
Tel.: 614-227-2000

The Huntington National Bank*(Major Banking Relationship)*
41 S. High St.
Columbus, OH 43216

The Huntington National Bank*(Pension Manager)*
41 S. High St.
Columbus, OH 43216

HAMILTON, CARVER & LEE, INC.
429 W. Superior St.
Chicago, IL 60614
Tel.: 312-642-1825
Year Founded: 1982
Approx.Billings: $73,000,000
Emp.: 85
Healthcare
James D. Lee *(Chm. Bd. & Pres.)*
Laurie A. Carver *(Exec. V.P., Creative Dir.)*
Dennis J. Hoppe *(V.P., Treas. & Plng.)*
Larry Iaquinto *(V.P., Intl. Bus.)*
Wayne Dunlop *(V.P.)*
Sherri Nemirow *(V.P., Human Resources)*
William McClure *(Gen. Counsel)*
John McNeany *(Controller)*
Lisa Fenger *(Librarian)*
Ken Ganzer *(Tech. Services Dir.)*
Robert Natonson, M.D. *(Medical Support Dir.)*
Alan Quarfoot, Ph.D. *(Sr. Medical Writer)*

Computer Systems/Hardware:
Novell Networks, DDI, MediaCheck

HAMILTON CO., INC.
P.O. Box 10030,
Reno, NV 89520-0012
Tel.: 702-858-3000
Tel.: 800-648-5950
Fax: 702-856-7259
Year Founded: 1953
Approx.Sls.: $25,000,000
Emp.: 400
Fiscal Year-end: 6/30/91
Import Export
Design & Manufacture of Laboratory Instruments & Supplies
S.I.C.: 3821; 3826
Steven Hamilton *(Pres.)*
John J. McCune *(Gen. Counsel)*
Charles DeGroff *(Dir.-Mfg.)*
Alan DiStefano *(Dir.-Mktg.)*
Richard Kirby *(Dir.-Fin.)*
Ken Lindner *(Dir.-Quality Control)*
Robert Scalese *(Dir.-Engrng.)*
Edie Harvey *(Mgr.-Personnel)*
Robert Lund *(Mgr.-Intl. Sls. & Mktg.)*
Corbin Peters *(Mgr.-Mngmt. Information Systems)*
Les Rice *(Mgr.-Production)*
Doug Wright *(Mgr.-Pur.)*

Computer Systems/Hardware:
DEC

Non-U.S. Holding:

Hamilton Bonaduz AG **(1)**
P.O. Box 26, CH-7402
Bonaduz, Switzerland
Tel.: 81 37 01 01 (100%)
Mfr. of Laboratory Instruments
S.I.C.: 3821; 3826
Max Waelchli *(Actg. Dir.)*

HAMILTON EQUIPMENT, INC.
567 S. Reading Rd.
Ephrata, PA 17522
Tel.: 717-733-7951 **PA**
Fax: 717-733-1783
Year Founded: 1975
Sales Range: $10-19 Million
Emp.: 80
Lawn, Garden & Industrial Machinery & Equipment; Agricultural Machinery; Paints
S.I.C.: 5083; 5198; 5084
Robert J. Hamilton Jr. *(Pres.)*
George W. Boyer *(Controller)*

Outside Service Firm(s):

Herbein & Co.*(Auditors)*
Reading, PA

Ephrata National Bank*(Major Banking Relationship)*
Ephrata, PA

HAMILTON MUTUAL INSURANCE COMPANY OF CINCINNATI
1520 Madison Rd.
Cincinnati, OH 45206
Tel.: 513-221-6010
Fax: 513-221-0412
Year Founded: 1858
Emp.: 87
Insurance Agents & Brokers Service
S.I.C.: 6411
Richard E. Felts *(Chm. Bd.)*
Jeffrey E. Felts *(Pres. & Chief Exec. Officer)*
William H. Ballmeyer *(V.P.-Plng. & Devel.)*
William R. Goedde *(V.P.-Mktg.)*
M. Brent Rouse *(Treas.)*

Outside Service Firm(s):

Star Bank*(Major Banking Relationship)*
425 Walnut Street
Cincinnati, OH 45202
Tel.: 513-632-4000

HAMILTON STORES, INC.
One Hamilton St.
West Yellowstone, MT 59758
Mailing Address:
P.O. Box 250
West Yellowstone, MT 59758
Tel.: 406-646-7325
Fax: 406-646-7323
Approx.Sls.: $14,000,000
Emp.: 25
General Country Stores
S.I.C.: 5399
Eleanor H. Povah *(Chm. Bd.)*
Trevor S. Povah *(Vice Chm.)*
Trevor H. Povah *(Pres.)*
Lynn Alpers *(V.P. & Controller)*
Patrick Povah *(V.P.)*
Stanley Rinehart *(V.P.)*
Peter B. Westnedge *(V.P.)*
Sandra Manger *(Sec.)*

Outside Service Firm(s):

Galusha, Higgins & Galusha*(Auditors)*
West Yellowstone, MT

First National Bank*(Major Banking Relationship)*
Livingston, MT

HAMILTON SWEENEY ADVERTISING, INC.
707 Sherman St.
Denver, CO 80203
Tel.: 303-837-0505
Fax: 303-837-0516
Year Founded: 1983
Approx.Billings: $12,500,000
Emp.: 21
Gen. & Minority Markets, Real Estate, Utilities & Business-to-Business Adv.
Sherman Hamilton *(Pres. & Chief Exec. Officer)*
Tom Schwing *(V.P.)*
Russell Gilmore *(Treas. & Controller)*

HAMLIN, INC.
612 E. Lake St.
Lake Mills, WI 53551
Tel.: 414-648-3000 **DE**
Fax: 414-648-3001
Year Founded: 1949
Approx.Sls.: $42,000,000
Emp.: 1,100
Fiscal Year-end: 5/31/91
Import Export
Mfr. Electronic Components
S.I.C.: 3679; 3825
Ronald T. Ferguson *(Chm. Bd.)*
Michael J. Fitzpatrick *(Pres.)*
Scott Ferguson *(V.P.-Mktg. & Sec.)*
Gerald Oesterreich *(V.P.-Fin.)*
Bradley Anderson *(Personnel Dir.)*
Dan Mabie *(Pur. Agent)*

Computer Systems/Hardware:
DEC System 5400; ROI Manage 2000

Non-U.S. Holdings:

Elec-Trol Mexico **(1)**
Prolong, Las Lomas Local 18 Las Brisas-Seccion, 1A-La Mesa,
Tijuana, B.C. Mexico
Tel.: 86-94-51 (100%)
Mfrs. Solid State Relays
S.I.C.: 3825
Roy T. Ferguson *(Gen. Mgr.)*

Hamlin Electronics Europe Ltd. **(1)**
Park Road
Diss, Norfolk IP22 3AY, United Kingdom

Hamlin Electronics GmbH **(1)**
6368 Bad Vilbel bei Friedberger Str. 124,
Frankfurt/Main, Germany

Hamlin S.A. de C.V. **(1)**
Calle 20 & Ave. 6
Agua Prieta, Son. Mexico

JERRY HAMM CHEVROLET INC.
2600 Phillips Hwy.
Jacksonville, FL 32207
Tel.: 904-396-1232 **FL**
Fax: 904-398-3032 x268
Year Founded: 1952
Approx.Sls.: $41,000,000
Emp.: 130
Automobile Dealership
S.I.C.: 5511
Jerry T. Hamm *(Pres.)*
R. Gerald Brewton *(Sec. & Treas.)*
Principal(s):
Jerry T. Hamm

Outside Service Firm(s):

Masten, Smith & Wisby*(Auditors)*
Jacksonville, FL

Danahoo, Danahoo, Wolf & Ball*(Legal Firm)*
Jacksonville, FL

First Union National Bank*(Major Banking Relationship)*
Jacksonville, FL

Hammacher Schlemmer

HAMMACHER, SCHLEMMER & CO., INC.
212 W. Superior
Chicago, IL 60610
Tel.: 312-664-8170
Fax: 312-664-8618
Year Founded: 1848
Approx.Sls.: $35,000,000
Emp.: 100
Fiscal Year-end: 2/ 1/92
Import Export
Retail Distributor of Housewares & Giftwares
S.I.C.: 5719; 5947; 5961
John R. MacArthur *(Chm. Bd.)*
Richard W. Tinberg *(Chief Exec. Officer)*
John L. Semmelhack *(Pres.)*
Denise Keane-Gillette *(V.P.-Mktg.)*
Irene Wilson *(V.P.-Adv.)*
Brian Hyzy *(Controller)*
Deborah Morales *(Mgr.-Pub. Rels.)*

Computer Systems/Hardware:
Altos 9062; Hewlett-Packard

Hammacher, Schlemmer & Co., Inc.—(Continued)

Outside Service Firm(s):

Deloitte & Touche*(Auditors)*
Two Prudential Plaza, 180 N. Stetson
Chicago, IL 60601
Tel.: 312-946-2039

Corroon & Black*(Group Insurer)*
Chicago, IL

HAMMEL, GREEN & ABRAHAMSON, INC.
1201 Harmon Place
Minneapolis, MN 55403
Tel.: 612-332-3944 **MN**
Fax: 612-332-9013
Year Founded: 1953
Approx.Sls.: $16,000,000
Emp.: 230
Architectural & Engineering Service; Interior Design
S.I.C.: 8712; 8711
Kurt E. Rogness *(Chief Exec. Officer)*
Roger D. Santelman *(Chief Oper. Officer)*
Loren Ahles *(1st V.P.)*
Jim Goulet *(2nd V.P.)*
Dennis D. Lanz *(V.P.-Mktg.)*
Daniel L. Avchen *(V.P.)*
Thomas F. Swearings *(Dir.-Fin. & Treas.)*
Ed Towey *(Sec.)*

Outside Service Firm(s):

McGladrey & Pullen*(Auditors)*
1800 Town Square, 445 Minnesota St.
St. Paul, MN 55101

First Bank Minneapolis*(Major Banking Relationship)*
Minneapolis, MN

THE HAMMERBLOW CORP.
1000 First St.
Wausau, WI 54401
Mailing Address:
P.O. Box 419,
Wausau, WI 54402-0419
Tel.: 715-842-0561
Fax: 715-842-5706
Year Founded: 1923
Approx.Sls.: $18,000,000
Emp.: 130
Fiscal Year-end: 11/30/90
Export
Trailer Axles, Couplers, Jacks & Other Trailer Parts
S.I.C.: 3569; 3714
Thomas Reinhart *(Chm. Bd.)*
Jack Olinger *(Exec. V.P.)*
Tom Snyder *(Chief Fin. Officer)*
Chris Heil *(Controller)*
Don Maul *(Dir.-Engrng.)*
Jeannette Kroll *(Dir.-Personnel)*
David R. Firle *(Mgr.-Sls. Services)*
Thomas M. Kniess *(Mktg. Specialist)*

J. L. HAMMETT COMPANY
Hammett Place
Braintree, MA 02184
Tel.: 617-848-1000
Fax: 617-843-4901
Approx.Sls.: $59,000,000
Emp.: 375
Retail School Supplies & Equipment
S.I.C.: 2531; 5943
Richmond Y. Holden, Sr. *(Chm. Bd.)*
Richmond Y. Holden, Jr. *(Pres.)*
Eugene R. Grant *(V.P.-Fin.)*
Herman W. Grip *(V.P.-Pur. & Distribution)*
Richard A. Krause *(V.P.-Retail Sls.)*
James A. Logie *(V.P.-Mktg.)*
Carl Olson *(V.P.-Admin. & Human Resources)*
Eric Small *(V.P.-Intl.)*
J. McGill *(Controller)*
Margaret Beckwith *(Dir.-Personnel)*
Lester G. Bartley *(Mgr.-Adv.)*
William G. Gillespie *(Mgr.-Mktg.)*
Lowell R. Watkins *(Mgr.-Data Processing)*

Outside Service Firm(s):

Deloitte & Touche*(Auditors)*
125 Summer St.
Boston, MA 02110
Tel.: 617-261-8000
Fax: 617-261-8111

Goodwin, Procter & Hoar*(Legal Firm)*
Exchange Place
Boston, MA 02109-2881
Tel.: 617-570-1000

First National Bank*(Major Banking Relationship)*
Boston, MA

HAMMOND FARRELL INC.
257 Park Ave. South
New York, NY 10010
Tel.: 212-995-5680
Fax: 212-995-5696
Year Founded: 1971
Approx.Billings: $19,400,000
Emp.: 20
Business-to-Business Adv.
Hugh J. Farrell *(Chief Exec. Officer & Creative Dir.)*
James Carter *(Vice Chm.)*
Jeff Kaumeyer *(Pres. & Chief Oper. Officer)*
Joseph Sraeel *(V.P.)*

HAMMOND LEAD PRODUCTS, INC.
5231 Hohman Ave.
Hammond, IN 46325
Mailing Address:
P.O. Box 6408
Hammond, IN 46325-6408
Tel.: 219-931-9360
Fax: 219-931-2140
Year Founded: 1930
Approx.Sls.: $60,000,000
Emp.: 150
Import Export
Mfr. of Lead Chemicals & No-Lead Pigments
S.I.C.: 2819; 2816
William P. Wilke IV *(Pres.)*
Stephen A. Bolanowski, Jr. *(V.P. & Mktg. Dir.)*
Charles T. Miller *(Treas.)*
Kenneth D. Reed *(Gen. Counsel)*

HAMPTON PRINT WORKS, INC.
2212 Buffalo Rd.
Johnson City, TN 37604
Tel.: 615-928-7247
Fax: 615-928-5663
Approx.Sls.: $44,000,000
Emp.: 135
Printing; Manmade Fiber & Broadwoven Fabrics; Womens, Childrens & Infants Swimsuits; Knit Fabrics
S.I.C.: 2262; 5137; 5131
Bruce Rabison *(Chm. Bd.)*
Buford J. Goldstein *(Pres.)*
Evelyn R. Rabison *(V.P.)*
Mary Jane Goldstein *(Sec.)*

Outside Service Firm(s):

Pugh & Co.*(Auditors)*
Knoxville, TN

Citizens Bank*(Major Banking Relationship)*
Elizabethton, TN

HAMPTON RESOURCES INC.
9400 S.W. Barnes Rd.
Portland, OR 97225
Tel.: 503-297-7691
Fax: 503-297-7691
Year Founded: 1942
Approx.Sls.: $250,000,000
Emp.: 450
Import Export
Lumber & Wood Products; Tree Farms
S.I.C.: 2421
John C. Hampton *(Chm. Bd., Pres. & Chief Exec. Officer)*

Computer Systems/Hardware:
IBM

Outside Service Firm(s):

Arthur Andersen & Co.*(Auditors)*
111 S.W. Columbia, Ste. 1400
Portland, OR 97201
Tel.: 503-226-1331

Spears, Lubersky, Lane, Powell*(Legal Firm)*
Portland, OR

U.S. National Bank*(Major Banking Relationship)*
309 S.W. Sixth Ave.
Portland, OR 97208
Tel.: 503-275-4942

Subsidiary:

Willamina Lumber Co. Inc. **(1)**
9400 S.W. Barnes Rd.
Portland, OR 97225
Tel.: 503-297-7691
Lumber & Wood Prods.
S.I.C.: 2421
John C. Hampton *(Chm. Bd. & Pres.)*

HANCOCK LUMBER, INC.
Rt. 121
Casco, ME 04015
Tel.: 207-627-4201 **ME**
Fax: 207-627-7041
Approx.Sls.: $40,000,000
Emp.: 250
Building Materials & Supplies; Wholesale & Retail; Eastern White Pine Lumber Milling
S.I.C.: 2426; 5031; 5211
K. David Hancock *(Chm. Bd.)*
Toby R. Hammond *(Pres.)*
Ralph Sama *(Sr. V.P.)*
Rick Merk *(Sr. V.P.)*
Ronald Wormwood *(Sr. V.P.)*
Douglas Hancock *(V.P.)*
Marc Beaudoin *(Sec. & Treas.)*

Outside Service Firm(s):

MacDonald, Page & Company*(Auditors)*
Portland, ME

Amerling & Burns*(Legal Firm)*
Portland, ME

HANCOCK PEANUT COMPANY
Hwy. 58 W. Bus
Courtland, VA 23837
Mailing Address:
P.O. Box 100,
Courtland, VA 23837
Tel.: 804-653-9351 **VA**
Fax: 804-653-2147
Year Founded: 1946
Approx.Sls.: $20,000,000
Emp.: 100
Producer Cleaned & Shelled Peanuts & Seed Peanuts
S.I.C.: 0173
Robert H. Pope *(Pres.)*
J. Mathews Pope *(V.P.)*
Mark H. Hodges *(Treas.)*
Principal(s):
Robert H. Pope
J. Mathews Pope

No. of Mfg. Plants/Facilities: 1
No. of U.S. Offices: 1

Computer Systems/Hardware:
Burroughs

Outside Service Firm(s):

Sovran Bank*(Major Banking Relationship)*
Sovran Center, 1111 E. Main St.
Richmond, VA 23219
Tel.: 804-788-2000

HANDEL & COMPANY, INC.
6900 Westfield Ave.
Pennsauken, NJ 08110
Tel.: 609-662-7901 **PA**
Fax: 609-662-7908
Year Founded: 1962
Approx.Sls.: $11,500,000
Emp.: 70
Fiscal Year-end: 7/31/91
Thermal Underwear
S.I.C.: 2322
Samuel Handel *(Pres.)*
Phyllis Tayler *(Chief Fin. Officer)*
George Handel *(Exec. V.P.)*

Outside Service Firm(s):

Kopple & Gottlieb*(Auditors)*
Philadelphia, PA

Cozen & O'Connor*(Legal Firm)*
Philadelphia, PA

Provident National Bank*(Major Banking Relationship)*
P.O. Box 7648
Philadelphia, PA 19101
Tel.: 215-585-5000

Division:

Handel & Company, Hantex Mills **(1)**
5019 Lamont Ave.
Temple, PA 19560
Tel.: 215-921-3576
Fax: 215-921-3530
Manufacturer of Thermal Underwear
S.I.C.: 2322
Jeffrey Levin *(Mgr.-Plant)*

HANDGARDS INC.
950 Skokie Blvd.
Northbrook, IL 60062
Tel.: 708-564-5870 **DE**
Fax: 708-564-5917
Year Founded: 1958
Approx.Sls.: $18,000,000
Emp.: 150
Fiscal Year-end: 12/31/91
Import Export
Mfr. & Distribute Disposable Plastic Products Including Gloves, Aprons, Bags, Bibs, Table Coverings & Shoe Covers
S.I.C.: 3089
Scotson Webbe *(Chm. Bd.)*
Douglas P. Marquis *(Pres. & Chief Oper. Officer)*
Mark Perkins *(Chief Fin. Officer)*
M.J. Foxx *(V.P. & Treas., Gen. Mgr. & Dir.-Pur.)*
Richard John Williams *(Legal Officer)*
Principal(s):
Scotson Webbe
Richard John Williams
S. Lindsay Webb

No. of Mfg. Plants/Facilities: 1
No. of U.S. Offices: 6

Computer Systems/Hardware:
IBM #36

Outside Service Firm(s):

Nussbarm, Schwartz & Torres, P.C.*(Auditors)*
El Paso, TX

Travelers Insurance Co.*(Group Insurer)*
El Paso, TX

Harris Trust & Savings Bank*(Investment Banker)*
111 W. Monroe St.
Chicago, IL 60690
Tel.: 312-461-2265
Tel.: 800-858-0840

Hlustik, Huizenga & Williams Ltd.*(Legal Firm)*
El Paso, TX

MBank Bassett, N.A.*(Major Banking Relationship)*
El Paso, TX

HANDLEY & MILLER, INC.
1712 N. Meridian St.
Indianapolis, IN 46202
Tel.: 317-927-5500
Fax: 317-927-5510
Year Founded: 1961
Approx.Billings: $11,500,000
Emp.: 20
Consumer Adv.
S.I.C.: 7311
Richard T. Kreusser *(Pres. & Chief Exec. Officer)*
Judi Kreusser *(Exec. V.P., Sec. & Dir.-Human Resources)*
Sam Davis *(V.P.-Acct. Services)*
Bob Finnegan *(V.P.-Bus. Devel.)*
Rick Ritter *(V.P. & Controller)*

Computer Systems/Hardware:
IBM

Outside Service Firm(s):

K. B. Parrish*(Auditors)*
Indianapolis, IN

Merchants National Bank & Trust Company of Indianapolis*(Major Banking Relationship)*
One Merchants Plaza, Ste. 901E
Indianapolis, IN 46255
Tel.: 317-267-7109

HANDLING SYSTEMS ENGINEERING
3000 W. 45th St.
Jacksonville, FL 32209
Tel.: 904-764-9793
Fax: 904-764-1079
Sales Range: $10-19 Million
Emp.: 20
Fiscal Year-end: 12/31/90
Retail Warehouse Equipment
S.I.C.: 3559
Roy Mohrman *(Chm. Bd., Pres. & Chief Exec. Officer)*
Wgonda Williams *(Treas. & Controller)*
Robert Stam *(Mgr.)*
Lou Mohrman *(Gen. Mgr.)*

Outside Service Firm(s):

Guardian Life Insurance Co.*(Group Insurer)*
New York, NY

Subsidiary:

Storage Systems Engineering **(1)**
3000 W. 45 St.
Jacksonville, FL 32209
Tel.: 904-764-9793

HANDY MANUFACTURING CO., INC.
337 Sherman Ave.
Newark, NJ 07114
Tel.: 201-242-1600
Fax: 201-623-5058
Approx.Sls.: $15,000,000
Emp.: 200
Store Fixtures
S.I.C.: 2542; 2541
Rayfield B. Kurland *(Chm. Bd.)*
Marc E. Kurland *(Pres.)*
Ross Cicaglao *(V.P.-Pur.)*
Richard M. Kurland *(V.P.-Mktg.)*

Outside Service Firm(s):

Broad National Bank*(Major Banking Relationship)*
Newark, NJ

Division:

Handy Store Fixtures, Inc. **(1)**
337 Sherman Ave.
Newark, NJ 07114
Tel.: 201-242-1600
Marc E. Kurland *(Pres.)*

HANDY WACKS CORPORATION
100 E. Averill, P.O. Box 26
Sparta, MI 49345
Tel.: 616-887-8268
Tel.: 800-445-4434 **MI**
Fax: 616-887-6110
Year Founded: 1935
Assets: $1,600,000
Net Worth: $1,600,000
Sales Range: $10-19 Million
Emp.: 40
Import Export
Waxed Paper Made From Purchased Material
S.I.C.: 2671
Marcia Fairchild *(Chm. Bd.)*
Henry B. Fairchild, III *(Pres.)*
Mike Gabriz *(Exec. V.P.-Sls.)*
Frances Bryant *(Gen. Mgr.)*
Mike Moberly *(Mgr.-Production)*
Principal(s):
Marcia Fairchild
Henry B. Fairchild, III

No. of Mfg. Plants/Facilities: 1
No. of U.S. Offices: 1
No. of Foreign Offices: 1

Computer Systems/Hardware:
IBM 36

Outside Service Firm(s):

BDO Seidman*(Auditors)*
99 Monroe Ave. NW, Ste. 800
Grand Rapids, MI 49503
Tel.: 616-774-7000
Fax: 616-451-2096

Olson Agency, Inc.*(Commercial Insurance Carrier)*
Grand Rapids, MI

Baxter & Associates*(Group Insurer)*
Grand Rapids, MI

Merrill Lynch*(Investment Banker)*
Grand Rapids, MI

Law, Weathers & Richardson*(Legal Firm)*
Grand Rapids, MI

Sparta State Bank*(Major Banking Relationship)*
Sparta, MI

HANEL LUMBER CO., INC.
4865 Hwy. 35
Hood River, OR 97031
Tel.: 503-354-1484 **OR**
Fax: 503-354-2472
Year Founded: 1943
Approx.Sls.: $40,000,000
Emp.: 300
Fiscal Year-end: 1/31/91
Export
General Sawmills & Planing Mills
S.I.C.: 2421
L. Sterling Hanel *(Pres.)*
William W. Hanel *(Treas.)*
Robert Hanel *(Sec.)*
Pat Ball *(Mgr.-Personnel)*
Joe Kochis *(Mgr.-Plant)*
Mike Mackin *(Mgr.-Sls.)*
Principal(s):
L. Sterling Hanel
Kathleen Hanel

No. of Mfg. Plants/Facilities: 2
No. of U.S. Offices: 2

Outside Service Firm(s):

Annala, Carey & Hull*(Legal Firm)*
Hood River, OR

Security Pacific National Bank*(Major Banking Relationship)*
Dallas, OR

HANES COMPANIES, INC.
2000 W. First St.
Winston-Salem, NC 27104
Mailing Address:
P.O. Box 202
Winston-Salem, NC 27102
Tel.: 919-777-3375
Fax: 919-724-1671
Approx.Sls.: $110,000,000
Emp.: 850
Holding Company; Processor & Converter of Textile Products
S.I.C.: 6719; 2261; 2262
Anton E. Schrafl *(Chm. Bd.)*
John B. Talbert, Jr. *(Pres.)*
Jerry W. Greene *(Sec. & Treas.)*

Outside Service Firm(s):

Ernst & Young*(Auditors)*
Wachovia Bldg., 301 N. Main, Ste. 200
Winston-Salem, NC 27111
Tel.: 919-725-0611
Fax: 919-725-4327

Womble, Carlyle, Sandridge & Rice*(Legal Firm)*
Wachovia Bank Bldg.
Winston Salem, NC 27101
Tel.: 919-725-1311

Wachovia Bank & Trust Co.*(Major Banking Relationship)*
P.O. Box 3001,
Winston-Salem, NC 27102
Tel.: 800-633-4236

HANKINS LUMBER COMPANY, INC.
P.O. Box 1397
Grenada, MS 38901-1397
Tel.: 601-226-2961 **MS**
Fax: 601-226-2961
Approx.Sls.: $57,000,000
Lumber; Rough Yellow Pine Dressed & Finished
S.I.C.: 5031
A. Burton Hankins *(Pres.)*
Albert Burton Hankins, Jr. *(V.P.)*
Charles Euerette Hankins *(V.P.)*
Lee Joseph Hankins *(V.P.)*
Robert Lewis Smith *(Treas., Sec. & Controller)*
Tillman Little *(Dir.-Sls.)*
Knox Penn *(Dir.-Sls.)*
Don Williams *(Dir.-Sls.)*
Steve Howell *(Mgr.-Sls.)*

Outside Service Firm(s):

Sunburst Bank*(Major Banking Relationship)*
Grenada, MS

HANNA CAR WASH INTERNATIONAL, INC.
2000 Hanna Dr.
Portland, OR 97222
Tel.: 503-659-0361
Tel.: 800-288-6927
Fax: 503-659-0631
Year Founded: 1964
Approx.Sls.: $18,000,000
Emp.: 125
Export
Automatic Car Wash Equipment
S.I.C.: 3589
Stuart Hall *(Pres.)*
David Williams *(Exec. V.P.)*
Ron Bottaro *(Mgr.-Major Accts.)*
Ray Graff *(Mgr.-Mfg.)*
Art Guariniello *(Mgr.-Domestic Mktg.)*
Ken Mickels *(Pur. Agent)*

No. of Mfg. Plants/Facilities: 5
No. of U.S. Offices: 5

Computer Systems/Hardware:
Unisys

HANNA CORPORATION
1765 N. Elston Ave.
Chicago, IL 60622
Tel.: 312-384-7000 **DE**
Fax: 312-384-5224
Earnings: $83,223,000
Approx.Sls.: $1,019,020,000
Emp.: 84
Fiscal Year-end: 12/31/90
Mfr. Pneumatic & Hydraulic Cylinders; Limit Switch Assemblies
S.I.C.: 3592; 3599
Robert Rakstang *(Pres.)*
Kenneth Sprague *(Mgr.-Gen. Sls.)*
Don Pappa *(Mgr.-Customer Sls. & Service)*

Computer Systems/Hardware:
Nixdorf 8890

Outside Service Firm(s):

Price Waterhouse*(Auditors)*
200 E. Randolph
Chicago, IL 60601
Tel.: 312-565-1500

Whyte & Hirschboeck, S.C.*(Legal Firm)*
2100 Marine Plaza
Milwaukee, WI 53202
Tel.: 414-271-8210

Unibank*(Major Banking Relationship)*
Chicago, IL

CLIFFORD B. HANNAY & SON INC.
(Hannay Reels)
600 E. Main St.
Westerlo, NY 12193
Tel.: 518-797-3791
Tel.: 800-REELING
Fax: 518-797-3259
Year Founded: 1933
Approx.Sls.: $20,000,000
Emp.: 151
Export
Mfr. of Reels to Handle Hose & Electric Cable
S.I.C.: 3569; 3499
George A. Hannay *(Chm. Bd.)*
Roger A. Hannay *(Pres. & Chief Exec. Officer)*
Robert D. Hannay *(Exec. V.P. & Chief Oper. Officer)*
Scott R. Hannay *(Dir.-Natl. Sls.)*
Edward Rash *(Dir.-Mktg. Communications)*
Dennis R. Blennis *(Mgr.-Mfg.)*
Roy Monkell *(Mgr.-Matl.)*
Richard L. Storm *(Mgr.-Credit)*

Computer Systems/Hardware:
Digital Micro Vax 3400

HANO BUSINESS FORMS, INC.
99 Guion St.
Springfield, MA 01104
Mailing Address:
P.O. Box 199,
Springfield, MA 01102
Tel.: 413-781-7800
Fax: 413-781-7808
Year Founded: 1888
Approx.Sls.: $26,000,000
Emp.: 400
Fiscal Year-end: 12/31/90
Record-Keeping Forms, Business Forms & Devices
S.I.C.: 2761
George Hano *(Chm. Bd.)*
Philip Hano *(Chief Exec. Officer)*
Michael J. Sullivan *(Pres.)*
Frank Hano *(V.P.)*
Philip Hano III *(V.P. & Sec.)*
Edwin Klemm *(Controller)*
William Bethel *(Mgr.-Personnel)*
Francis J. Fortier *(Mgr.-Distr. Sls.)*
Thomas Stepnowski *(Mgr.-Direct Sls.)*
Principal(s):
Philip Hano III
Frank Hano

Hano Business Forms, Inc.—(Continued)

Computer Systems/Hardware:
Prime 2755

Outside Service Firm(s):

Ernst & Young *(Auditors)*
1300 Huntington Bldg.
Cleveland, OH 44115
Tel.: 216-861-5000
Fax: 303-291-6234

BayBank Valley Trust Co. *(Major Banking Relationship)*
1500 Main St.
Springfield, MA 01101
Tel.: 413-781-7575

Divisions:

Hano Business Forms, Inc. **(1)**
P.O. Box 1159,
Conyers, GA 30207
Tel.: 404-929-1500
Fax: 404-929-1508
S.I.C.: 2761
Bud Fortier *(Plant Mgr.)*

Hano Business Forms, Inc. **(1)**
P.O. Box 278,
Mount Olive, IL 62069
Tel.: 217-999-2311
Fax: 217-999-6264
S.I.C.: 2761
Dave Fowler *(Plant Mgr.)*

HANOVER FOODS CORPORATION
P.O. Box 334
Hanover, PA 17331
Tel.: 717-632-6000
Fax: 717-632-6681
Year Founded: 1924
Approx.Sls.: $200,000,000
Emp.: 1,600
Fiscal Year-end: 3/31/91
Import Export
Processor of Canned & Frozen Foods
S.I.C.: 2099
John A. Warehime *(Chm. Bd. & Chief Exec. Officer)*
John E. Denton *(Pres.)*
Timothy Beard *(V.P.)*
Jack A. Brown *(V.P.-Fin.)*
Whitney Coombs *(V.P.-Mktg.)*
Warren Debnam *(V.P.-Mfg.)*
Gary T. Knisely *(V.P.-Admin., Sec. & Counsel)*
Michael Stick *(V.P.-Sls.)*
Alan T. Young *(V.P.-Opers.)*
Pietro Giraffa *(Comptroller)*
Michael Brookhart *(Dir.-Mktg.-Frozen Foods)*
Earl C. Erb *(Dir.-Technical Services)*
Mark Meabon *(Dir.-Pur.)*
Kenneth R. Bartosh *(Mgr.-Mfg.)*
Robert K. Biesecker *(Mgr.-Mngmt. Information Systems)*

Divisions:

Hanover Foods Corp. **(1)**
Plum & Liberty Streets
Lancaster, PA 17604
Tel.: 717-397-6141
Fax: 717-397-0233
S.I.C.: 2099

Hanover Foods Corp. **(1)**
Rt. 6 & Duck Creek Rd.
Clayton, DE 19938
Tel.: 302-653-9281
Jim Beamesderfer *(Gen. Mgr.)*

Myers Foods Company **(1)**
Kellers Church Rd.
Plumsteadville, PA 18949
Tel.: 215-766-8832
Fax: 215-766-2506
Approx.Sls.: $11,000,000
Emp.: 74
Fiscal Year-end: 3/31/91
Computer Systems/Hardware:
IBM PC XT
Myers Frozen Meat Pies, Entrees & Croquettes
S.I.C.: 2038; 5142

John Warehime *(Chm. Bd.)*
John Denton *(Pres.)*
Warren Debnam *(V.P.-Mfg.)*
Gary Kinsely *(V.P.-Admin.)*
Mike Stick *(V.P.-Sls.)*
Jack Brown *(Treas.)*
Pete Giraffa *(Controller)*
Whitney Coombs *(Dir.-Mktg.)*
Linda Nicholas *(Mgr.-Pur.)*
Oscar A. Tuason *(Mgr.-Mfg.)*

Subsidiary:

Alcosa/Sunwise **(1)**
7925 N.W. 12th St., Suite 318
Miami, FL 33126
Tel.: 305-591-1604
Fax: 305-591-2152
Frozen Foods, Food Processor
S.I.C.: 5142

A. L. HANSEN MFG. CO.
701 Pershing Rd.
Waukegan, IL 60085
Tel.: 708-244-8900
Fax: 708-244-7222
Year Founded: 1920
Approx.Sls.: $10,000,000
Emp.: 61
Fiscal Year-end: 6/30/92
Export
Hansen, Commercial Body & Industrial Hardware
S.I.C.: 3429
R.C. Hansen *(Pres.)*
Colt Fitzgerald *(Dir.-Sls.)*
Tom Dickleman *(Mktg. Admin.)*
Sheila Chappell *(Mgr.-Personnel)*
Lynn Kretsch *(Dir.-Pur.)*

HAPPY HOLIDAY TREE FARMS
3819 E. Sidney Rd.
Sheridan, MI 48884
Tel.: 517-261-4242
Fax: 517-261-4310
Year Founded: 1973
Sales Range: $10-19 Million
Emp.: 125
Fiscal Year-end: 6/30/90
Grow & Sell Christmas Trees
S.I.C.: 0831
Dick Gasaway *(Pres.)*
Jody Wilkes *(V.P.)*
Conrad Steinhart *(Treas. & Sec.)*

Principal(s):
Dick Gasaway
Conrad Steinhart

No. of U.S. Offices: 2

Outside Service Firm(s):

Richard Burke Co. *(Auditors)*
Greenville, MI

Peter Frye Associates *(Legal Firm)*
Greenville, MI

HARBERT CORPORATION
1 Riverchase Parkway S.
Birmingham, AL 35244
Mailing Address:
P.O. Box 1297
Birmingham, AL 35201
Tel.: 205-987-5500 **DE**
Telex: 59792
Telex: 596103
Fax: 205-987-5568
Year Founded: 1949
Sales Range: $100-499 Million
Emp.: 4,500
Holding Company; Through Subsidiaries Construct Bridges, Highways, Power & Industrial Plants, Pipelines & Commercial Buildings; Owns Natural Gas Transmission Pipelines; Retail Sales of Equipment; Manufactures Rotary Blast-Hole Drills; Develops & Owns Real Property; Operation & Maintenance; Exploration & Production of Oil & Gas; Overseas Construction
S.I.C.: 1611; 1622; 1541; 1629; 1623; 1389; 4922; 3532; 6552; 2911; 1382; 6799; 6719
John Murdoch Harbert III *(Chm. Bd.)*
Bill Lebold Harbert *(Vice Chm.)*
Raymond J. Harbert *(Pres. & Chief Exec. Officer)*
Barney Earles *(Pres.-Harbert Property)*
James O. Rein *(Sr. V.P.)*
Leonard R. Wohadlo *(Sr. V.P.)*
Howard E. Dyer-Smith *(V.P.)*
P. Solomon Lepp *(V.P.)*
Wayne B. Nelson *(V.P.)*
Swift C. Barnes *(Chief Fin. Officer)*
J. William Powers *(Corp. Sec. & Chief Admin. Officer)*

Computer Systems/Hardware:
Honeywell

Outside Service Firm(s):

Coopers & Lybrand *(Auditors)*
1901 6th Ave. North, Ste. 1600
Birmingham, AL 35203-2602

Blue Cross & Blue Shield of Alabama *(Group Insurer)*
450 Riverchase Pkwy. East
Birmingham, AL 35298
Tel.: 205-988-2245

Balch & Bingham *(Legal Firm)*
P.O. Box 306
Birmingham, AL 35201

AmSouth Bank N.A. *(Major Banking Relationship)*
P.O. Box 11426
Birmingham, AL 35202
Tel.: 205-326-5321

Continental Bank N. A. *(Major Banking Relationship)*
231 S. LaSalle St.
Chicago, IL 60697
Tel.: 312-828-2345
Tel.: 800-426-5754
Telex: 312-828-1783

SouthTrust Bank *(Major Banking Relationship)*
Birmingham, AL
Tel.: 205-254-5068

Apocalypse Corp. *(Pension Manager)*
Edina, MN

SouthTrust Bank *(Pension Manager)*
Birmingham, AL
Tel.: 205-254-5068

Stacey Braun Associates, Inc. *(Pension Manager)*
New York, NY

Trevor, Stewart, Burton & Jacobsen *(Pension Manager)*
New York, NY

HARBOR BANCORP
11 Golden Shore
Long Beach, CA 90802
Tel.: 310-491-1111 **CA**
Fax: 310-590-0264
Year Founded: 1982
Assets: $160,994,248
Earnings: $821,771
Liabilities: $147,863,085
Net Worth: $13,131,163
Approx.Income: $12,573,256
Fiscal Year-end: 12/31/91
Bank Holding Company
S.I.C.: 6712
James A. Willingham *(Chm. Bd. & Chief Exec. Officer)*
James H. Gray *(Pres. & Chief Exec. Officer)*
Melissa Lanfre *(V.P. & Chief Fin. Officer)*
Robert Turicchi *(V.P.)*

Outside Service Firm(s):

Ernst & Young *(Auditors)*
515 S. Flower St.
Los Angeles, CA 90071
Tel.: 213-621-1666

HARBOR FINANCIAL MORTGAGE CORP.
340 N. Sam Houston Pkwy. E., Ste. 100
Houston, TX 77060
Tel.: 713-931-1771
Approx.Sls.: $200,000,000
Emp.: 140
Fiscal Year-end: 9/30/91
Mortgage Banker
S.I.C.: 6162
Dick Gillen *(Chm. Bd., Pres. & Chief Exec. Officer)*
Tommy Orr *(Sr. V.P.)*
Steve Champagne *(Sr. V.P.)*
John Wright *(Chief Fin. Officer)*
Leon Jordan *(Treas. & Controller)*
Ann Frazee *(Dir.-Pur.)*
Bunny Gillen *(Mgr.-Personnel)*
Patty McMahon *(Mgr.-Data Processing)*
Scott Young *(Mgr.-Telecommunications)*
Linda Bramlett *(Mgr.-Quality Control)*
Karen Clayton *(Travel Planner)*

Computer Systems/Hardware:
IBM

Divisions:

Dungey & Associates **(1)**
340 N. Sam Houston Pkwy. E., Ste. 100
Houston, TX 77060
Tel.: 713-931-1771
S.I.C.: 6162

Harbor Financial Insurance Agency **(1)**
340 N. Sam Houston Pkwy. E., Ste. 100
Houston, TX 77060
Tel.: 713-931-1771
S.I.C.: 6162

Harbor Financial Property Management Co. **(1)**
340 N. Sam Houston Pkwy. E., Ste. 100
Houston, TX 77060
Tel.: 713-931-1771
S.I.C.: 6162

Harbor Financial Title Corp. **(1)**
340 N. Sam Houston Pkwy. E., Ste. 100
Houston, TX 77060
Tel.: 713-931-1771
S.I.C.: 6162

HARBOUR CONTRACTORS, INC.
22 E. Chicago Ave., Ste. 200
Naperville, IL 60540
Tel.: 708-717-4900
Fax: 708-717-0771
Year Founded: 1959
Approx.Sls.: $134,000,000
Emp.: 105
General Contractor
S.I.C.: 1522; 1541; 1542
I.C. Harbour *(Chm. Bd.)*
Patrick C. Harbour *(Pres.)*

Computer Systems/Hardware:
IBM System 36

Outside Service Firm(s):

Ernst & Young *(Auditors)*
233 S. Wacker Dr.
Chicago, IL 60606
Tel.: 312-368-1800
Fax: 312-645-3095

T. J. Adams & Associates *(Major Banking Relationship)*
Oak Brook, IL

HARBOUR GROUP LTD.
7701 Forsyth Blvd.
Clayton, MO 63105
Tel.: 314-727-5550 **DE**
Fax: 314-727-0941
Fax: 314-727-9912
Year Founded: 1976
Approx.Sls.: $500,000,000
Emp.: 4,600
Holding Company; Manufacturer of Expendable Cutting Tools, Medical Equipment, Industrial & Submersible Pumps, Master Alloys, Sealing Components, Molding of Plastics
S.I.C.: 6719; 3545; 3561; 3088; 3355; 3423; 2891; 3053; 3800
Sam Fox *(Chm. Bd. & Chief Exec. Officer)*
Donald Nickelson *(Vice Chm.)*
James C. Janning *(Pres. & Chief Oper. Officer)*
Samuel Hamacher *(Exec. V.P.)*
Peter S. Finley *(Sr. V.P.)*
Robert W. Hull *(Sr. V.P.)*
Peter S. Finley *(Mgr.)*

No. of Mfg. Plants/Facilities: 14
No. of U.S. Offices: 1

Outside Service Firm(s):

Price Waterhouse*(Auditors)*
One Boatmen's Plaza
St. Louis, MO 63101
Tel.: 314-425-0500

Dickstein, Shapiro & Morin*(Legal Firm)*
2101 L St. N.W.
Washington, DC 20037
Tel.: 202-785-9700

Bank of Boston*(Major Banking Relationship)*
Atlanta, GA

Subsidiaries:

Burks Prosser/Enpo Industries, Inc. **(1)**
1434 N. 22nd St.
Decatur, IL 62526
Tel.: 217-773-2442 (100%)
Fax: 217-429-0845
Mfr. of Centrifugal, Turbine & Submersible Pumps, Condensate Return & Boiler Feed Systems; Industrial & Submersible Pumps
S.I.C.: 3561
Paul G. Baldetti *(Pres.)*
Mike Koon *(V.P.-Fin.)*
Bill Loyd *(V.P.-Sls. & Mktg.)*

Burks Pumps, Inc. **(1)**
420 Third St.
Piqua, OH 45356-0603
Tel.: 513-773-2442
Fax: 513-773-2238
Approx.Sls.: $80,000,000
Emp.: 500
Fiscal Year-end: 12/31/91
Export
Mfr. of Burks Pumps & Water Systems; Submersible Pumps; Deep & Shallow Well Jet Pumps; Deep Well Multi Stage; Boiler Feed & Condensate Return Units; Turbine & Centrifugal Industrial Pumps
S.I.C.: 3561; 3559; 3589
P.G. Baldetti *(Pres.)*
C. Wayne Gillespey *(Sr. V.P.-Mfg.)*
Bill Loyd *(V.P.-Mktg. & Sls.)*
John Wichmann *(V.P.-Engrng.)*
M. Koon *(V.P.-Fin.)*
Ken McCabe *(Pur. Agent)*
Rob Baker *(Natl. Sls. Mgr.)*
Howard Binzer *(Mgr.-Mktg.)*

Subsidiaries:

AMW Industries Inc. **(2)**
P.O. Box 1364, 584 Commerce Rd.
Conway, AR 72032
Tel.: 501-329-9811
Fax: 501-329-9812
Emp.: 190
Mfg. Water System Pumps & Industrial Pumps
S.I.C.: 3594
Paul Baldetti *(Pres.)*
Wayne Gillespey *(V.P.-Mfg.)*
M. Koon *(V.P.-Fin.)*
Bill Loyd *(V.P.-Sales & Mktg.)*
Howard Binzer *(Mktg. Mgr.)*
Ken McCabe *(Pur. Mgr.)*

Barnes Pumps, Inc. **(2)**
1485 Lexington Ave.
Mansfield, OH 44907
Tel.: 419-774-1511
Fax: 419-774-1530
Mfg. of Barnes Submersible Non-Clog, Grinder, Effluent & Sewage Ejector Pumps; Crown Self-Priming Centrifugal & Trash Pumps & Packaged Lift Stations; Enpo Cutter Pumps, Vortex, Sewage Ejector & Effluent Pumps; Prosser Portable Submersible Dewatering Pumps
S.I.C.: 3561; 3589; 3559
P.G. Baldetti *(Pres.)*
Wayne Gillespey *(V.P.-Mfg.)*
M. Koon *(V.P.-Fin.)*
Bill Loyd *(V.P.-Sales & Mktg.)*
Dale Morris *(Sr. Applications Engr.)*
Howard Binzer *(Mktg. Mgr.)*
Bill Kabbaz *(Natl. Sls. Mgr.)*
Ken McCabe *(Purchasing Mgr.)*

Prosser/Enpo Industries **(2)**
420 Third St.
Piqua, OH 45356-0603
Tel.: 513-773-2442
Fax: 513-773-2238
Export
Mfg. of Sellers Rotating Cleaning Heads; Sellers Steam Injectors
S.I.C.: 3599
Paul Baldetti *(Pres.)*
Wayne Gillespey *(V.P.-Mfg.)*
M. Koon *(V.P.-Fin.)*
Bill Loyd *(V.P.-Sls. & Mktg.)*
John Wichmann *(Chief Engineer)*
Ken McCabe *(Pur. Mgr.)*
Howard Binzer *(Mktg. Mgr.)*

Carbide International Inc. **(1)**
5740 Tripp Ave.
Chicago, IL 60646
Tel.: 312-583-6362 (100%)
Fax: 312-583-8209
Mfr. of Expendable Cutting Tools
S.I.C.: 3545
Robert W. Britzke *(Pres.)*
Von Hood *(V.P.-Mfg.)*
Alan King *(V.P.-Sls. & Mktg.)*
Norm Williams *(V.P.-Admin.)*

Engineered Polymers Corporation **(1)**
1020 E. Maple Ave.
Mora, MN 55051
Tel.: 612-679-3232
Fax: 612-679-2323
Mfr. of Injection Moldings & Structural Foam Plastics
S.I.C.: 2821
Laird Mork *(V.P.-Opers.)*
Dale Harnish *(V.P.-Sls.)*
Charles Brown *(Controller)*

Greenfield Industries Inc. **(1)**
470 Old Evans Rd.
Evans, GA 30809
Tel.: 706-863-7708
Fax: 706-860-8559
Import Export
Mfr. of Taps, Dies, Arbors, Bits, Drills, Blades, Blanks, Centers, Holders, End Mills, Countersinks, Carbide, Stocks & Dies
S.I.C.: 3545; 3532; 3541
Paul W. Jones *(Pres.)*
Leo Starzec *(V.P.-Fin. & Admin.)*
Timothy Pletcher *(V.P.-Mfg.)*
Jim Poehling *(V.P.-Sls. & Mktg.)*
Brad Morgan *(Controller)*
George Blackburn *(Dir.-Sls.)*

JM Clipper Corporation d/b/a Acadia **(1)**
1420 Coulter Dr., N.W.
Roanoke, VA 24014
Tel.: 703-265-2700
Fax: 703-362-3095
Mfr. of Packing & Sealing Devices
S.I.C.: 3053
Patrick Malone *(Pres.)*
Doug Hahn *(V.P.-Fin.)*
Ronny Burden *(V.P.-Opers.)*
Bryan Collier *(V.P.-Sls.)*
William R. Schumann, Jr. *(V.P.-Sls. & Mktg.)*

KB Alloys, Inc. **(1)**
2917 Windmill Rd.
Sinking Spring, PA 19608
Tel.: 215-670-3350
Tel.: 800-523-8457
Fax: 215-670-3376
Export
Mfr. of Aluminum Master Alloys & Chemicals
S.I.C.: 3355
Robert Longenecker *(Pres.)*
Jerry E. Keenan *(V.P.-Fin.)*
Richard E. Malliris *(V.P.-Mfg.)*
William Lidman *(Dir.)*

Metal Cutting Tools Corp. **(1)**
21 Airport Dr.
Rockford, IL 61109
Tel.: 815-226-0650
Tel.: 800-435-0709
Fax: 815-226-0063
Mfr. of Mining Machinery; Metal Cutting Tools
S.I.C.: 3532; 3541; 3545
Richard Fratesi *(Pres.)*
Richard Ziegler *(Controller)*

Rogers Tool Works, Inc. **(1)**
205 N. 13th St.
Rogers, AR 72757-0009
Tel.: 501-636-1515
Fax: 501-631-7638
Mfr. of Mining Machinery; Machine Tools, Metal Cutting Tools
S.I.C.: 3532; 3541; 3545
Robert W. Britzke *(Pres.)*
Norm Williams *(V.P.-Fin. & Admin.)*
Alan King *(V.P.-Sls. & Mktg.)*
Von Hood *(V.P.-Carbide Production)*

Vermont Tap & Die Co. **(1)**
79 Main St.
Lyndonville, VT 05851
Tel.: 802-626-3331
Fax: 802-433-1235
Mfrs. & Markets of Indus. Taps & Dies & Twist Drills
S.I.C.: 3545
Ted Henderer *(Gen. Mgr.)*

HARBOUR INDUSTRIES, INC.
2075 Shelburne Rd.
Shelburne, VT 05482
Mailing Address:
P.O. Box 188
Shelburne, VT 05482
Tel.: 802-985-3311 **VT**
Fax: 802-985-9534
Year Founded: 1965
Approx.Sls.: $20,000,000
Emp.: 130
Fiscal Year-end: 10/31/91
Export
Insulating High Temperature Wire & Cable
S.I.C.: 3357
James C. Kenny *(Pres. & Chief Exec. Officer)*
John G. Heaslip *(Exec. V.P.)*
Albert T. Maxson *(V.P.-Fin. & Controller)*
R. Miller *(V.P.-Engrng.)*
Dennis Dodd *(V.P.-Mfg.)*
John Palasciaro *(V.P.-Sls. & Mktg.)*
Peter S. Kenny *(Mgr.-Natl. Sls.)*
Fay Howard *(Mgr.-Quality Control)*

Outside Service Firm(s):

Ernst & Young*(Auditors)*
Burlington, VT

Downs, Rachlin & Martin*(Legal Firm)*
P.O. Box 190
Burlington, VT 05402

State Street Bank & Trust Co.*(Major Banking Relationship)*
225 Franklin St.
Boston, MA 02101
Tel.: 617-328-5000

HARCO DRUG, INC.
3925 Rice Mine Rd., N.E.
Tuscaloosa, AL 35406
Tel.: 205-345-2400 **AL**
Fax: 205-759-2397
Year Founded: 1967
Approx.Sls.: $100,000,000
Emp.: 1,300
Drug Stores; Hospital Equipment & Supplies
S.I.C.: 5912; 5999
James I. Harrison, Jr. *(Pres.)*
John Campbell *(V.P.-Fin.)*
Jerry Thomas *(V.P.)*
Peggie T. Harrison *(Treas. & Sec.)*

Outside Service Firm(s):

Arthur Andersen & Co.*(Auditors)*
Birmingham, AL

Division:

Harco Total Care #101 **(1)**
3925 Rice Mine Rd., N.E.
Tuscaloosa, AL 35406
Tel.: 205-345-2400
Hospital Equipment & Supplies
S.I.C.: 5999

HARCO TECHNOLOGIES CORPORATION
1055 W. Smith Rd.
Medina, OH 44256
Tel.: 216-725-6681
Telex: 196184
Fax: 216-722-7654
Approx.Sls.: $30,000,000
Emp.: 300
Complete Cathodic Protection Engineering Services, Materials & Construction for Corrosion Control
S.I.C.: 3579
R. Langos *(Pres. & Treas.)*
Michael Baach *(V.P.-Mktg.)*
Dale Tschantz *(Dir.-Mktg.)*
S. Schauch *(Pur. Agent)*

THE HARDAWAY COMPANY
P.O. Box 1360
Columbus, GA 31993
Tel.: 706-322-3274
Fax: 706-322-7856
Sales Range: $100-499 Million
Emp.: 1,750
Highways, Bridges, Dams, Locks, Powerhouse Construction
S.I.C.: 1629
B.H. Hardaway III *(Chm. Bd.)*
Mason H. Lampton *(Pres.)*
R.A. Tillery *(V.P.-Opers.)*
B.J. Clay *(Treas.)*
F.J. Dodelin *(Sec.)*

Outside Service Firm(s):

Ernst & Young*(Auditors)*
One Columbus, 10 W. Broad St.
Columbus, OH 43215
Tel.: 614-224-5678

Davidson & Calhoun, P.C.*(Legal Firm)*
Columbus, GA

Columbus Bank & Trust Company*(Major Banking Relationship)*
Trust Dept., P.O. Box 120
Columbus, GA 31902
Tel.: 706-649-2311

HARDAWAY CONCRETE CO., INC.
2001 Taylor St.
Columbia, SC 29204
Mailing Address:
P.O. Box 4128,
Columbia, SC 29240
Tel.: 803-254-4350
Fax: 803-343-2408
Year Founded: 1968
Approx.Sls.: $20,000,000
Emp.: 140
Mfr. Ready-Mix Concrete
S.I.C.: 3273
G.M. Tate *(Pres.)*
Melissa Schumpert *(V.P. & Treas.)*
Richard Wells *(V.P.-Sls.)*
William Jackson *(V.P.-Prod. Opers.)*

Outside Service Firm(s):

Arthur Andersen & Co.*(Auditors)*
Columbia, SC

Citizens & Southern National Bank*(Major Banking Relationship)*
1801 Main St.
Columbia, SC 29201
Tel.: 803-765-8011

Hardaway Concrete Co., Inc.—(Continued)

Sinkler & Boyd*(Legal Firm)*
P.O. Box 1889,
Columbia, SC 29211

HARDAWAY CONSTRUCTION COMPANY, INC.
615 Main St.
Nashville, TN 37206
Tel.: 615-254-5461 **TN**
Telex: 62927795 (EASYLINK)
Fax: 615-254-4518
Year Founded: 1926
Sales Range: $60-79 Million
Emp.: 400
General Building Construction
S.I.C.: 1521; 1522; 1541
L. H. Hardaway, Jr. *(Chm. Bd.)*
Billy D. Grover *(Pres.)*
Kerry Sloan *(V.P.-Fin., Treas. & Chief Fin. Officer)*
Emmett Toombs *(V.P.-Admin.)*
Eddie Lambert *(Controller)*
Gayle Crabtree *(Dir.-Data Processing)*
George Thompson *(Dir.-Mktg.)*
Principal(s):
L. H. Hardaway, Jr.

No. of U.S. Offices: 1

Computer Systems/Hardware:
IBM System 38

Outside Service Firm(s):

Maggart & Welch*(Auditors)*
Nashville, TN

Aetna Life & Casualty*(Group Insurer)*
100 N. Riverside Plaza
Chicago, IL 60606

J. C. Bradford & Co., Inc.*(Investment Banker)*
Nashville, TN

Weldon B. White, Jr.*(Legal Firm)*
Nashville, TN

Commerce Union*(Major Banking Relationship)*
Nashville, TN

Nashville City Bank*(Major Banking Relationship)*
Nashville, TN

HARDEN FURNITURE COMPANY
1 Mill Pond Way
McConnellsville, NY 13401
Tel.: 315-245-1000
Fax: 315-245-2884
Year Founded: 1865
Approx.Sls.: $43,000,000
Emp.: 550
Fiscal Year-end: 12/31/91
Import Export
Solid Cherry, Solid Oak & Upholstered Household Furniture
S.I.C.: 2511
David E. Harden *(Chm.)*
Gordon W. Babcock *(Vice Chm.)*
Gregory Harden *(Chief Exec. Officer)*
Daniel Tartaglia *(V.P.-Admin.)*
Jack Gardner *(Mgr.-Sls.)*
Peter Raynsford *(Pur. Agent)*

Computer Systems/Hardware:
IBM System 36

Outside Service Firm(s):

Coopers & Lybrand*(Auditors)*
One Lincoln Center
Syracuse, NY 13202
Tel.: 315-474-8541
Fax: 315-474-0259

Bond, Schoeneck & King*(Legal Firm)*
One Lincoln Center
Syracuse, NY 13202
Tel.: 315-422-0121

Norstar Bank, N.A.*(Major Banking Relationship)*
Syracuse, NY

Subsidiary:

Harden Galleries **(1)**
1008 Baker Rd.
High Point, NC 27263
Tel.: 919-434-4116
Emp.: 35
Mfr. Upholstered Furniture
S.I.C.: 2511
Randy Hollar *(Mgr.-Plant)*

HARDEN INDUSTRIES, INC.
13915 S. Main St.
Los Angeles, CA 90061
Tel.: 310-532-7850 **CA**
Fax: 310-532-9699
Year Founded: 1982
Approx.Sls.: $28,000,000
Emp.: 320
Export
Mfr. of Metal & Plastic Faucets & Spigots
S.I.C.: 3432
Barbara I. Rodstein *(Pres.)*
Barry Saven *(V.P.)*

Outside Service Firm(s):

Imperial Bank*(Major Banking Relationship)*
Los Angeles, CA

HARDIE IRRIGATION-LANDSCAPE DIV.
(Div. of James Hardie Ltd.)
788 Fairview Dr.
Carson City, NV 89701
Tel.: 702-882-6786
Approx.Sls.: $55,000,000
Emp.: 1,114
Designs, Manufacturers & Markets Timers, Valves & Sprinkler Heads for Automatic & Drip Watering Systems Used in Residential & Light Commercial Lawn & Garden Applications
S.I.C.: 3625; 3494; 3089; 3569; 5191
R. Gleitsmann, Jr. *(Pres. & Chief Exec. Officer)*
Fred Peppe *(V.P.-Fin.)*

HARDIN CONSTRUCTION GROUP, INC.
1380 W. Paces Ferry Rd.
Atlanta, GA 30327
Tel.: 404-262-3700 **GA**
Fax: 404-264-3514
Year Founded: 1978
Assets: $64,000,000
Liabilities: $54,000,000
Net Worth: $10,000,000
Sales Range: $100-499 Million
Emp.: 500
Fiscal Year-end: 6/30/89
General Contractor Specializing in Commercial Construction
S.I.C.: 1542
Earl L. Shell *(Chm. Bd. & Chief Exec. Officer)*
Robert A. Smith *(Grp. Pres.)*
William A. Pinto *(Grp. Pres.)*
M. Brantley Barrow *(V.P., Fin. & Admin.)*
Jo Ann Weinberg *(Dir.-Personnel)*
Peggy Fuller Jackson *(Mgr.-Mktg. Services)*
Newton C. Smith *(Mgr.-Computer Services)*
Principal(s):
Allen S. Hardin
Earl L. Shell

No. of U.S. Offices: 10

Computer Systems/Hardware:
Wang VS 100

Outside Service Firm(s):

Arthur Andersen & Co.*(Auditors)*
133 Peachtree St., N.E.
Atlanta, GA 30303
Tel.: 404-658-1776

Aetna Life & Casualty*(Commercial Insurance Carrier)*
100 N. Riverside Plaza
Chicago, IL 60606

Alston & Bird*(Legal Firm)*
One Atlantic Center, 1201 West Peachtree St.
Atlanta, GA 30309-3424
Tel.: 404-881-7000

Smith & Fleming*(Legal Firm)*
Atlanta, GA

Bank South, N.A.*(Major Banking Relationship)*
P.O. Box 4387
Atlanta, GA 30302
Tel.: 404-529-4111

Trust Company Bank*(Major Banking Relationship)*
P.O. Box 4625
Atlanta, GA 30302
Tel.: 404-588-7711

Montag & Caldwell*(Pension Manager)*
Atlanta, GA

HARDINGE BROTHERS, INC.
P.O. Box 1507
Elmira, NY 14902-1507
Tel.: 607-734-2281
Fax: 607-734-3886
Year Founded: 1890
Earnings: $4,632,000
Approx.Sls.: $100,000,000
Emp.: 1,000
Fiscal Year-end: 12/31/91
Export
Manufacture & Distribution of Machine Tools
S.I.C.: 3541
R.E. Agan *(Pres. & Chief Exec. Officer)*
T.T. Connelly *(Exec. V.P.)*
J. Cordier *(V.P.)*
M.L. Gibson *(V.P. & Treas.)*
J. Krul *(V.P.-Res. & Devel.)*
R. Simmons *(Controller)*
W. Bobby *(Dir.-Pur.)*
C. O'Toole *(Dir.-Data Processing)*
C.O. Bombarger *(Mgr.-Adv.)*
R. Schwartz *(Mgr.-Personnel Training & Devel.)*
D. Tifft *(Mgr.-Personnel)*
J. Schiefen *(Corp. Travel Planner)*

Computer Systems/Hardware:
IBM & Prime

Non-U.S. Subsidiaries:

Canadian Hardinge Brothers Machine Tools Inc. **(1)**
415 Matheson Blvd. E.
Mississauga, ON L4Z 2H2, Canada
Tel.: 416-507-8550
Machine Tool Distributor
S.I.C.: 5084
Jim Carson *(Pres.)*

Hardinge Machine Tools, Ltd. **(1)**
Exeter, Devon United Kingdom EX2 8PN
Tel.: 0392 51431
Sls. of Industrial Machinery & Equipment
S.I.C.: 5084
Robert Duxbury *(Dir. & Chief Oper. Officer)*

HARDWARE WHOLESALERS, INC.
6502 Nelson Rd.
Fort Wayne, IN 46803
Mailing Address:
P.O. Box 868
Fort Wayne, IN 46801
Tel.: 219-749-8531 **IN**
Fax: 219-493-1245
Year Founded: 1945
Assets: $318,330,000
Liabilities: $200,000,000
Net Worth: $118,330,000
Approx.Sls.: $1,250,000,000
Emp.: 975
Fiscal Year-end: 6/30/91
Import
Jobber-Owned Co.; Distribute Lumber, Building Materials & Hardware to HWI Members
S.I.C.: 5072; 5064; 5074; 5099; 5039
Charlie Phillips *(Chm. Bd.)*
Mike McClelland *(Pres. & Chief Exec. Officer)*
Doug Dayton *(V.P.-Office Opers.)*
Dave Dietz *(V.P.-Sls. & Mktg.)*
George Mattes *(V.P.-Distr.)*
John Snider *(V.P.-Fin.)*
Ray Treen *(V.P.-Pur.-Bldg. Prods.)*
Ned Wolf *(V.P.-Pur.-Hardware)*
William Wannamaker *(Sec.)*
John Hammond *(Treas.)*
Larry Pensinger *(Dir.-Mktg.)*
Dan Federspiel *(Mgr.-Personnel)*

Outside Service Firm(s):

Krouse & Kern*(Auditors)*
Fort Wayne, IN

Lincoln National Life Insurance Co.*(Group Insurer)*
PO Box 208, 1300 S. Clinton
Fort Wayne, IN 46801
Tel.: 219-455-2926
Fax: 219-455-7619

Barnes & Thornburg*(Legal Firm)*
11 S. Meridian St.
Indianapolis, IN 46204
Tel.: 317-638-1313

Fort Wayne National Bank*(Major Banking Relationship)*
110 W. Berry St.
Fort Wayne, IN 46802
Tel.: 219-426-0555

Fort Wayne National Bank*(Pension Manager)*
110 W. Berry St.
Fort Wayne, IN 46802
Tel.: 219-426-0555

Subsidiary:

HWI Building Corp. **(1)**
6502 Nelson Rd.
Fort Wayne, IN 46803
Tel.: 219-749-8531

BRYAN HARDWICK ASSOCIATES
425 Via Corta
Palos Verdes Estates, CA 90274
Tel.: 310-375-2547
Fax: 310-375-3472
Year Founded: 1962
Approx.Billings: $10,000,000
Emp.: 15
Real Estate, Resorts, Sporting Goods & Financial Institutions
Bryan D. Hardwick, Jr. *(Pres.)*
Manny Greenfield *(V.P., Opers.)*
Jennifer Lyon *(Pub. Rels.)*

HARDWICK CLOTHES INC.
3800 Old Tasso Rd.
Cleveland, TN 37320
Mailing Address:
P.O. Box 2310,
Cleveland, TN 37320-2310
Tel.: 615-476-6534
Fax: 1-800-442-7394
Approx.Sls.: $25,000,000
Emp.: 650
Fiscal Year-end: 3/31/91
Men's & Ladies' Clothing, Suits, Sport Coats, Slacks, Shirts
S.I.C.: 2311; 2321; 2325; 2329; 2331; 2335; 2337; 2339
Wm. B. Foster, Jr. *(Chm. Bd.)*
Joe V. Williams III *(Pres. & Treas.)*
Tom Hopper *(Sec.)*
David Preis *(Dir.-Sls.-New York)*
Jim Park *(Mgr.-Sls.)*

Nancy Deakins *(Mgr.-Adv.)*
Bob Reffner *(Human Resources Exec.)*

HARDWOODS OF MICHIGAN, INC.
430 Division St.
Clinton, MI 49236
Tel.: 517-456-7431
Fax: 517-456-4931
Approx.Sls.: $23,000,000
Emp.: 180
Lumber Drying & Processing; Sawmill
S.I.C.: 2421; 2426
Richard L. Service *(Chm. Bd.)*
Jeffrey Hardcastle *(Pres.)*
Robert Vogel *(V.P.-Mktg.)*

Outside Service Firm(s):

Plante & Moran*(Auditors)*
Clinton, MI

Walker, Watts & Jackson*(Legal Firm)*
Adrian, MI

United Savings Bank*(Major Banking Relationship)*
Cheyenne, WY

HARGRO ENTERPRISES, INC.
One Landmark Square
Stamford, CT 06901
Tel.: 203-324-9707 **DE**
Fax: 203-964-0418
Year Founded: 1985
Assets: $190,000,000
Liabilities: $130,000,000
Net Worth: $60,000,000
Sales Range: $100-499 Million
Emp.: 1,500
Fiscal Year-end: 12/31/90
Export
Mfg. of Flexible Packaging Products, Computer Printer Supplies & Storage Products for Tape Cartridges
S.I.C.: 3955; 3861
Francis C. Oatway *(Pres. & Chief Exec. Officer)*
John B. Folts *(Exec. V.P., Sec. & Treas.)*
Jon E. Tropsa *(Controller)*
Principal(s):
Francis C. Oatway
John B. Folts

Outside Service Firm(s):

Deloitte & Touche*(Auditors)*
1600 Summer St.
Stamford, CT 06905-5121
Tel.: 203-351-4600

Skadden, Arps, Slate, Meagher, & Flom*(Legal Firm)*
153 E. 53rd St., One Citicorp Ctr.
New York, NY 10022
Tel.: 212-935-8000

Subsidiaries:

HP Packaging Holdings **(1)**
One Landmark Square
Stamford, CT 06901
Tel.: 203-324-9707
Fax: 203-964-0418
Sales Range: $60-79 Million
Emp.: 450
Flexible Packaging & Products
S.I.C.: 3086
John R. Woolford, Jr. *(Pres.)*

NER Holdings, Inc. **(1)**
One Landmark Square
Stamford, CT 06901
Tel.: 203-324-9707
Emp.: 710
Storage Products for Tape Cartridges
S.I.C.: 3577
Paul T. O'Neill *(Pres.)*

HARKER'S INC.
521 Eighth Ave. S.W.
Le Mars, IA 51031
Tel.: 712-546-8171
Fax: 712-546-3116
Year Founded: 1906
Approx.Sls.: $140,000,000
Emp.: 400
Fiscal Year-end: 9/30/92
Portion Controlled Frozen Foods
S.I.C.: 5142
Ron Geiger *(Pres. & Chief Exec. Officer)*
Mike Cranny *(V.P.-Mktg.)*

Computer Systems/Hardware:
IBM System AS 400

HARKINS BUILDERS, INC.
(Formerly Thomas P. Harkins, Inc.)
12301 Old Columbia Pike
Silver Spring, MD 20904
Tel.: 301-622-9000
Fax: 301-680-4299
Fax: 301-680-4290
Year Founded: 1965
Assets: $45,159,609
Liabilities: $35,117,312
Net Worth: $10,042,297
Approx.Sls.: $154,200,000
Emp.: 400
Fiscal Year-end: 4/30/90
Apartment & Industrial Buildings & Commercial Construction
S.I.C.: 1522; 1541; 1542
Thomas P. Harkins *(Chm. Bd. & Chief Exec. Officer)*
J.P. Blase Cooke *(Pres.)*
Theodore Nelson *(V.P.-Mktg. Devel.)*
Gary Garofalo *(Controller)*
Gladys Mesmer *(Employee Benefits Mgr.)*

Outside Service Firm(s):

Maryland National Bank*(Major Banking Relationship)*
Baltimore, MD 21202

Division:

Harkins Carpentry **(1)**
12301 Old Columbia Pike
Silver Spring, MD 20904
Tel.: 301-680-4300
Emp.: 100
Carpentry Subcontractor
S.I.C.: 1751
Bob Howes *(Pres.)*

HARLAN ELECTRIC CO.
24000 Telegraph Rd.
Southfield, MI 48034
Tel.: 313-353-8660 **MI**
Fax: 313-350-1341
Year Founded: 1940
Assets: $32,819,000
Liabilities: $21,637,000
Net Worth: $11,182,000
Approx.Sls.: $89,100,000
Emp.: 1,200
Fiscal Year-end: 9/30/90
Electrical Construction (Inside & Line); Fabrication & Erection of Piping Systems
S.I.C.: 1731; 1711; 3498
John M. Harlan *(Chm. Bd. & Pres.)*
G.W. Lowenstein *(Chief Exec. Officer)*
James F. Kimsey *(V.P.)*
Richard Miller *(V.P.-Construction)*
William R. Patterson *(V.P.)*
John W. Gelder *(Sec.)*
Carl Swenson *(Pur. Agent)*

Outside Service Firm(s):

Ernst & Young*(Auditors)*
One Detroit Center, 500 Woodward, Ste. 1700
Detroit, MI 48243
Tel.: 313-259-9600

Miller, Canfield, Paddock & Stone*(Legal Firm)*
150 W. Jefferson Ave.
Detroit, MI 48226
Tel.: 313-963-6420

Manufacturers National Bank N.A.*(Major Banking Relationship)*
38th Fl., 100 Renaissance Center
Detroit, MI 48243
Tel.: 313-222-4227

Subsidiaries:

Power Piping Company **(1)**
829 Beaver Ave.
Pittsburgh, PA 15233
Tel.: 412-323-6200
Pipe Fabricating
S.I.C.: 3498
William R. Patterson *(Pres.)*

Sturgeon Electric Company **(1)**
12150 E. 112th Ave.
Henderson, CO 80640
Tel.: 303-286-8000
Electrical Construction & High Lines
S.I.C.: 1731
James F. Kimsey *(Pres.)*

HARLEY ELLINGTON PIERCE YEE ASSOCIATES, INC.
Architecure Engineering Planning Interiors
26913 Northwestern Hwy., Ste. 200
Southfield, MI 48034
Mailing Address:
P.O. Box 5030
Southfield, MI 48086
Tel.: 313-262-1500 **MI**
Fax: 313-262-1515
Year Founded: 1908
Assets: $4,728,283
Liabilities: $2,555,870
Net Worth: $2,172,413
Approx.Sls.: $13,405,653
Emp.: 133
Fiscal Year-end: 12/31/91
Architectural Engineering & Planning
S.I.C.: 8711; 8712
John R. Lydic *(Sr. V.P., Dir.-Fin. & Controller)*
Dennis M. King *(Pres.)*
Donald K. Giroux *(Sr. V.P. & Dir.-Opers)*
Manfred Stryk *(Sr. V.P. & Dir.-Corp. Admin.)*
Ronald C. Morketter *(Sr. V.P.-Engrng. & Tech.)*
Harold F. VanDine *(Sr. V.P.-Architecture & Design)*
Keith S. Bauman *(V.P. & Dir.-Project Mngmt.)*
Anthony A. Foust *(V.P. & Dir.-Interior Architecture)*
Philip H. Granitz *(V.P. & Dir.-Electrical Engrng. & Computer Services)*
Barry N. Merenoff *(V.P. & Dir.-Pre-Design Services)*
John C. Hammer *(V.P.)*
David H. Lawrence *(V.P.)*
Fareed B. Rifat *(V.P.)*
Gary L. Skog *(V.P.)*
Dawn A. Black *(Mgr.-Mktg. Services)*
J. Robert D'Alessandro *(Project Mgr.)*
Barbara A. McGee *(Project Mgr.)*
Donald T. Root *(Project Mgr.)*
Jeffrey R. Zokas *(Project Mgr.)*
Samuel R. Bayne, Jr. *(Dir.-Design)*
Jack C. Goodnoe *(Dir.-Site Plng.)*
Gerd W. Hartung *(Dir.-Structural Engrng.)*
Robert J. Pesta *(Dir.-Mechanical Engrng.)*
Michael J. Proctor *(Dir.-Construction Admin.)*
Lawrence R. Chute *(Asst. Dir.-Structural Engrng.)*
Dale R. Clark *(Asst. Dir.-Mechanical Engrng.)*
Louis Hartman *(Asst. Dir.-Mechanical Engrng.)*

No. of U.S. Offices: 5
No. of Foreign Offices: 1

Computer Systems/Hardware:
CADD

Outside Service Firm(s):

Arthur Andersen & Co.*(Auditors)*
400 Renaissance Center
Detroit, MI 48243
Tel.: 313-259-8100

Garan, Lucow, Miller, Seward & Cooper*(Legal Firm)*
Detroit, MI

Comerica Bank*(Major Banking Relationship)*
211 W. Fort St.
Detroit, MI 48226
Tel.: 313-222-3300

HEPY Groups:

Burke, Bales & Mills/HEPY, Inc. **(1)**
111 N. Orange Ave., Ste. 650
Orlando, FL 32801
Tel.: 407-422-4747
Fax: 407-843-7728
Robert Burke *(Pres.)*

Commercial Design Architects/HEPY, Inc. **(1)**
4230 198th St., S.W.
Lynnwood, WA 98036
Tel.: 206-771-2300
Fax: 206-672-4244
Carl Pirscher *(Pres.)*

Fields & Devereaux/HEPY, Inc. **(1)**
116 N. Robertson Blvd., Ste. 802
Los Angeles, CA 90048
Tel.: 213-653-0160
Fax: 213-659-2167
Edwin Fields *(Pres.)*

KDA/HEPY, P.C. **(1)**
1201 18th St., Ste. 200
Denver, CO 80202
Tel.: 303-296-8556
Fax: 303-296-8555
William Dukes *(Pres.)*

Non-U.S. Holding:

Pierce Yee Associates, Ltd **(1)**
Windsor, ON Canada
Tel.: 313-262-1500

HARLEY INDUSTRIES, INC.
4504 E. 67th St., Suite 202
Tulsa, OK 74136
Mailing Address:
P.O. Box 470450
Tulsa, OK 74147
Tel.: 918-492-9706 **CA**
Fax: 918-481-1823
Year Founded: 1937
Approx.Sls.: $19,000,000
Emp.: 70
Fiscal Year-end: 10/31/90
Manufacturer & Distributor Engines, Pumps, Compressors & Generators, Fabricated Equipment Packages
S.I.C.: 5084; 3561; 3563; 3569
Martin Hubbard *(Chm. Bd.)*
Gene H. Maxon *(Pres., Chief Exec. & Chief Oper. Officer)*
Kirk Nellis *(Controller, Treas. & Sec.)*

No. of Mfg. Plants/Facilities: 8

Outside Service Firm(s):

Deloitte & Touche*(Auditors)*
One Williams Center, Ste. 2400
Tulsa, OK
Tel.: 918-586-8800

Rosenstein, Fist & Ringold*(Legal Firm)*
525 So. Main
Tulsa, OK 74103
Tel.: 918-585-9211

Bank of Oklahoma*(Major Banking Relationship)*
One Williams Center
Tulsa, OK 74012
Tel.: 918-588-5100

Harley Industries, Inc.—(Continued)

Subsidiaries:

Deluca Valve & Instrument Co. **(1)**
P.O. Box 11267
Columbia, SC 29211
Tel.: 803-799-4073
Fax: 803-799-1567
Emp.: 15
Distr. of Safety Relief Valves & Instrumentation
S.I.C.: 3491

Tulsa Gauge & Instrument Co. **(1)**
4445 South 91st
Tulsa, OK 74147
Tel.: 918-622-5061
Fax: 918-622-5762
Emp.: 30
Distr. Safety Relief Valves & Instrumentation
S.I.C.: 5085
Kenneth Grounds *(Gen. Mgr.)*

HARMESON MANUFACTURING COMPANY, INC.
509 W. Barner St.
Frankfort, IN 46041
Mailing Address:
P.O. Box 429
Frankfort, IN 46041
Tel.: 317-659-3388
Fax: 317-659-2956
Year Founded: 1961
Approx.Sls.: $12,000,000
Emp.: 250
Mfrs. Hardboard & Particle Board Parts For TV, Audio, Appliances, Sporting Goods, Toys, Furniture, Displays, Store Fixtures & the Sign Industry
S.I.C.: 2493
Peter Basquin *(Chm. Bd., Sec. & Treas.)*
John W. Kay *(Pres.)*
Dale Shaffer *(V.P.-Mfg.)*

Outside Service Firm(s):

Ent & Imler*(Auditors)*
Indianapolis, IN

Morrison, Robbins & Shaffer*(Legal Firm)*
Indianapolis, IN

Clinton County Bank & Trust*(Major Banking Relationship)*
Frankfort, IN

HARMON CITY, INC.
3540 S. 4000 West, Ste. 500
West Valley City, UT 84120
Tel.: 801-969-8261
Fax: 801-964-1299
Year Founded: 1938
Approx.Sls.: $165,000,000
Emp.: 1,500
Fiscal Year-end: 1/31/90
Retail Grocery
S.I.C.: 5411
Robert Morris *(Pres.)*
Don Carroll *(V.P.)*
Niels Pedersen *(Comptroller)*

Computer Systems/Hardware:
Prime

Outside Service Firm(s):

Arthur Andersen & Co.*(Auditors)*
36 South State St., Ste. 1600
Salt Lake City, UT 84111
Tel.: 801-533-0820
Fax: 801-534-0550

Nielsen & Senior*(Legal Firm)*
Salt Lake City, UT

North Carolina National Bank*(Major Banking Relationship)*
Raleigh, NC

HARMON SMITH INC.
801 West 47th St., Ste. 100
Kansas City, MO 64112-1298
Tel.: 816-756-0756
Fax: 816-756-0380
Year Founded: 1959
Approx.Billings: $16,400,000
Emp.: 22
Animal Healthcare, Business-to-Business, Leisure Products & Services
Austin Harmon *(Pres. & Chief Exec. Officer)*
Barbara Behner *(Chief Fin. Officer, Sec. & Treas.)*
Laurene Fanning *(Exec. Sec.)*
David Patzman *(Gen. Counsel)*
Mary McPherson *(Dir.-Admin.)*
Bruce Novotny *(Dir.-Video & Communications)*
R. Kelly Schwalbe *(Pub. Rels. Supvr.)*

HARMONY ENGINEERING CORPORATION
460 Hoover St., N.E.
Minneapolis, MN 55413
Tel.: 612-623-0510 **MN**
Fax: 612-623-4364
Year Founded: 1971
Approx.Sls.: $11,000,000
Emp.: 160
Precision Machine & Sheet Metal Shop
S.I.C.: 3599; 3444; 3679; 3728
Jim Nemec *(Pres.)*
Tom Haley *(V.P.-Opers.)*
Jim Krause *(V.P.-Fin.)*
Jon Bathke *(Mgr.-Pur.)*
George Hendren *(Mgr.-Sls.)*
Edward Kittelson *(Mgr.-Mktg.)*
Marylyn Manly *(Mgr.-Personnel)*
David Smith *(Mgr.-Quality Control)*

Computer Systems/Hardware:
IBM System 36

Outside Service Firm(s):

Brunelle & Associates*(Auditors)*
Minneapolis, MN

First Bank Minneapolis*(Major Banking Relationship)*
Minneapolis, MN

Harmony Grove Mills, Inc.
(See Listing Under R. B. Pamplin Corp.; Name Changed To Mount Vernon Mills, Inc.)

HARMONY HOUSE RECORDS & TAPES
1755 E. Maple
Troy, MI 48083-4287
Tel.: 313-524-2800
Fax: 313-524-1266
Emp.: 260
Retail Records & Tapes
S.I.C.: 5735
William C. Thom *(Pres.)*
Karen Cross *(V.P.-Human Resources)*
Charles Papke *(V.P.)*
Pat Welch *(Mgr.-Opers.)*

Outside Service Firm(s):

A.L. Cole & Associates*(Auditors)*
Royal Oak, MI

THE HARODITE FINISHING COMPANY INC.
66 South St.
North Dighton, MA 02764
Tel.: 508-824-6961
Fax: 508-880-0696
Year Founded: 1912
Approx.Sls.: $33,000,000
Emp.: 180
Import Export
Mfr. of Finished Textiles
S.I.C.: 2261; 2262
Michael P. Albert *(Chm. Bd. & Pres.)*
Joseph F. O'Neil *(Chief Fin. Officer & Controller)*
Rachel F. Albert *(Treas.)*
Ethel Buscemi *(Dir.-Purch.)*
Principal(s):
Michael P. Albert
Rachel F. Albert

No. of Mfg. Plants/Facilities: 2
No. of U.S. Offices: 4

Computer Systems/Hardware:
NCR

Outside Service Firm(s):

KPMG Peat Marwick*(Auditors)*
One Boston Place
Boston, MA 02108
Tel.: 617-723-7700

Ropes & Gray*(Legal Firm)*
One International Place
Boston, MA 02110
Tel.: 617-951-7000

First National Bank of Boston*(Major Banking Relationship)*
P.O. Box 644,
Boston, MA 02102-0644
Tel.: 617-575-2900
Fax: 617-575-2549

Subsidiaries:

Staflex Co. **(1)**
57 W. 38th St..
New York, NY 10018
Tel.: 212-764-8655
Fax: 212-764-8615
Emp.: 10
Import Export
Mfr. of Interlinings
S.I.C.: 2396
Robert Calice *(V.P.)*

Staflex/Harotex **(1)**
P.O. Box 1106
Taylors, SC 29687
Tel.: 803-268-0613
Emp.: 30
Mfr. of Interlinings & Converters
S.I.C.: 2396; 3621
Thomas Bridges *(Gen. Mgr.)*

HARPER BROS., INC.
14860 Six Mile Cypress Pkwy.
Fort Myers, FL 33912
Tel.: 813-481-2350 **FL**
Fax: 813-481-9131
Year Founded: 1957
Approx.Sls.: $36,000,000
Emp.: 350
Construction; Limerock Materials; Asphalt
S.I.C.: 1611; 1422; 1499; 1629
Daniel R. Harper *(Chm. Bd. & Pres.)*
Ronald E. Inge *(V.P.-Fin.)*
Quinton B. McNew *(V.P.)*
Denis J. Roza *(V.P.-Opers.)*
Anne M. Harper *(Treas.)*
Daniel S. Harper *(Sec.)*

Outside Service Firm(s):

Gilbert, Wallace & Stewart*(Auditors)*
Ft. Myers, FL

Henderson, Franklin, Starnes & Holt*(Legal Firm)*
Ft. Myers, FL

HARPER INDUSTRIES, INC.
350 Fifth Ave.
New York, NY 10118
Tel.: 212-971-9200 **NY**
Fax: 212-967-7319
Year Founded: 1946
Approx.Sls.: $50,000,000
Emp.: 700
Import
Mfr. of Mens' & Boys' Activewear & Swimwear
S.I.C.: 2321; 2329
Thomas S. Friedland *(Pres. & Chief Exec. Officer)*
Herbert J. Drucker *(V.P.-Fin.)*
Kenneth Danberg *(Exec. V.P.-Sls.)*
Laura S. Friedland *(V.P. & Sec.)*
Joseph Reyes *(Controller)*
Adele Oppenheimer *(Treas.)*
Sam Kim *(Mgr.-Data Processing)*
Ronald Cruz *(Mgr.-Import)*

Computer Systems/Hardware:
Wang VS 100

Outside Service Firm(s):

Buchbinder, Stein, Tunick & Platkin*(Auditors)*
One Pennsylvania Plaza
New York, NY 10119-0219

Kantor, Davidoff, Wolfe, Rabbino & Kass, P.C.*(Legal Firm)*
New York, NY

National Westminster Bank plc*(Major Banking Relationship)*
175 Water St.
New York, NY 10038-4924
Tel.: 212-602-3364

Divisions:

Harper Shirt Company **(1)**
350 Fifth Ave.
New York, NY 10118
Tel.: 212-971-9200
Mfr. of Knit Outerwear Shirts
S.I.C.: 2253
Thomas S. Friedland *(Pres. & Chief Exec. Officer)*
Herbert J. Drucker *(Chief Fin. Officer & V.P.)*
Kenneth Danberg *(Exec. V.P.-Sls.)*

Lucedale Sportswear Company **(1)**
350 Fifth Ave.
New York, NY
Thomas S. Friedland *(Chief Oper. Officer)*

Midland Shirt Company **(1)**
350 Fifth Ave.
New York, NY 10118
Tel.: 212-971-9200
Mfr. of Men's & Boys Dress Shirts
S.I.C.: 2329
Thomas S. Friedland *(Pres. & Chief Exec. Officer)*

HARP'S FOOD STORES, INC.
1004 S. Gutensohn Rd.
Springdale, AR 72764
Mailing Address:
P.O. Drawer 48
Springdale, AR 72764
Tel.: 501-751-7601 **AR**
Fax: 501-751-3625
Year Founded: 1930
Approx.Sls.: $190,000,000
Emp.: 1,700
Fiscal Year-end: 8/26/91
Retail Groceries; Wholesale Notions & Dry Goods
S.I.C.: 5411; 5131
Donald L. Harp *(Chm. Bd. & Pres.)*
Roger Collins *(V.P.-Fin. & Admin.)*
Bob Downum *(V.P.-Mktg. & Adv.)*
Harlon Earp *(V.P.-Human Resources)*
Gerald L. Harp *(V.P.-Opers., Sec. & Treas.)*
Ray Stuckey *(Controller)*
James J. Antz *(Dir.-Mngmt. Information Systems)*
Karen Ramsey *(Dir.-Pub. Rels.)*
Huey Couch *(Mgr.-Adv.)*

Computer Systems/Hardware:
IBM System 36

Outside Service Firm(s):

Arthur Andersen & Co.*(Auditors)*
111 Center St.
Little Rock, AR 72201

Nationwide Insurance*(Commercial Insurance Carrier)*
Memphis, TN

Cypert, Crouch, Clark & Harwell*(Legal Firm)*
Springdale, AR

First National Bank of Springdale*(Major Banking Relationship)*
Springdale, AR

HARRIET & HENDERSON YARNS, INC.
1724 Graham Ave.
Henderson, NC 27536
Mailing Address:
P.O. Box 789,
Henderson, NC 27536
Tel.: 919-430-5000
Fax: 919-438-3937
Year Founded: 1895
Assets: $80,500,000
Liabilities: $24,100,000
Net Worth: $56,400,000
Approx.Sls.: $200,000,000
Emp.: 1,800
Fiscal Year-end: 1/31/91
Export
Textile Mill Products; 100% Cotton Yarn, Poly/Cotton Blends, Acrylic/Cotton Yarn
S.I.C.: 2281
Employee Matching Gifts Program: Limited to Institutions of Higher Education
Marshall Y. Cooper, Jr. *(Pres., Chief Exec. Officer & Chm. Bd.)*
Tom R. Allen *(V.P.-Fin. & Treas.)*
S.W. Brummitt *(V.P.-Mfg.)*
James Chesnutt *(V.P.-Matls. Mngmt.)*
D.M. Durrett *(V.P.-Mktg.)*
Richard Linville *(V.P.-Personnel)*
C.G. Walker *(V.P.-Sls.)*

No. of Mfg. Plants/Facilities: 7
No. of U.S. Offices: 1

Computer Systems/Hardware:
IBM

Outside Service Firm(s):

McGladrey & Pullen*(Auditors)*
Drawer G-2, 230 N. Elm St.
Greensboro, NC 27402
Tel.: 919-273-4461

Protective Life Insurance*(Group Insurer)*
Box 11407,
Birmingham, AL 35246

Otterbourg, Steindler, Houston & Rosen*(Legal Firm)*
New York, NY

Zollicoffer & Zollicoffer*(Legal Firm)*
Henderson, NC

First Atlanta Bank*(Major Banking Relationship)*
Atlanta, GA

NationsBank Carolinas*(Major Banking Relationship)*
Henderson, NC

Southern National Bank*(Major Banking Relationship)*
South Pines, NC

Sovran Bank*(Major Banking Relationship)*
Sovran Center, 1111 E. Main St.
Richmond, VA 23219
Tel.: 804-788-2000

Wachovia Bank & Trust Co.*(Major Banking Relationship)*
P.O. Box 21048,
Greensboro, NC 27402

Southern National Bank*(Pension Manager)*
South Pines, NC

Sterling Capital Management Co.*(Pension Manager)*
1770 Independence Center
Charlotte, NC 28246
Tel.: 704-372-8670

Subsidiaries:

H&H International **(1)**
Box 789
Henderson, NC 27536
Tel.: 919-438-3101

Harriet & Henderson Cotton Co. **(1)**
1724 Graham Ave.
Henderson, NC 27536
Tel.: 919-430-5121

HARRINGTON & KING
5655 Fillmore St.
Chicago, IL 60644
Tel.: 312-626-1800
Tel.: 800-621-3869
Fax: 312-261-1686
Year Founded: 1883
Approx.Sls.: $19,000,000
Emp.: 175
Fiscal Year-end: 12/31/91
Export
Mfr. of Perforated Metal Sheets, Plates & Coils, Related Prods., Etc.
S.I.C.: 3469
Patrick S. Filter *(Chm. Bd.)*
Gordon E. Steil *(Pres. & Chief Exec. Officer)*
Thomas S. Moreley *(V.P.-Sls. & Mktg.)*
John Lovaas *(Exec. V.P. & Gen. Mgr.)*
William Jakosz *(V.P.-Mfg.)*
Mark E. Steil *(V.P.-Pur.)*
William Kelly *(Dir.-Quality Control)*
Randy Thompson *(Mgr.-Data Processing)*
Ernie Sobczak *(Mgr.-Engrng.)*

No. of Mfg. Plants/Facilities: 2
No. of U.S. Offices: 3

Computer Systems/Hardware:
Unisys

Outside Service Firm(s):

Miller-Cooper & Co., Ltd.*(Auditors)*
Chicago, IL

Alexander & Alexander*(Commercial Insurance Carrier)*
One Constitution Plaza
New York, NY 10036
Tel.: 617-241-9800

Carey, Filter, White & Boland*(Legal Firm)*
Chicago, IL

American National Bank*(Major Banking Relationship)*
Chicago, IL

Subsidiary:

Harrington & King, South, Inc. **(1)**
3939 Michigan Ave.
Cleveland, TN 37311
Tel.: 615-479-8691
Tel.: 800-251-6026
Emp.: 36
Perforated Materials
S.I.C.: 3469
A.H. Jenness *(V.P.-H&K South)*

HARRIS ADVERTISING, INC.
617 E. Huron
Ann Arbor, MI 48104
Tel.: 313-662-3442
Fax: 313-662-5913
Year Founded: 1978
Approx.Billings: $14,500,000
Emp.: 25
Janice Shukle *(Pres.)*
June Kirchgatter *(V.P.)*

HARRIS, BAIO & MCCULLOUGH INC.
520 S. Front St.
Philadelphia, PA 19147
Tel.: 215-440-9800
Fax: 215-440-9812
Year Founded: 1983
Approx.Billings: $22,457,601
Emp.: 22
Business-to-Business, Direct Response, Public Relations, Research & Promotion
George Harris *(Pres. & Chief Fin. Officer)*
Bob McCullough *(Exec. V.P., Sec. & Treas.)*
John Trumbore *(Sr. V.P., Mktg. Research)*
Jan Rotolo *(Controller)*

HARRIS DRURY COHEN

HARRIS DRURY COHEN
6360 N.W. 5th Way, Ste. 300
Fort Lauderdale, FL 33309
Tel.: 305-771-1800
Fax: 305-776-3301
Year Founded: 1980
Approx.Billings: $50,000,000
Emp.: 67
Fiscal Year-end: 12/31/89
Advertising Agency
S.I.C.: 7311
Stan Harris *(Pres. & Dir.-Creative)*
John R. Drury *(Chief Exec. Officer)*
Philip E. Cohen *(Chief Oper. Officer & Dir.-Client Services)*
Normand Tousignant *(Exec. V.P. & Controller)*
Lila Peralta *(Dir.-Communications)*
Martha Barrow *(Mgr.-EDP)*
Valerie Gautieri *(Mgr.-Office)*
Peggy Zbiegien *(Systems Analyst)*

No. of U.S. Offices: 1

Computer Systems/Hardware:
IBM System 36

Outside Service Firm(s):

Atkinson, Jenne, Diner, Stone & Cohen*(Legal Firm)*
Hollywood, FL

First Union National Bank*(Major Banking Relationship)*
100 N.E. 3rd Av.
Fort Lauderdale, FL 33301-1155
Tel.: 305-467-5531

Northern Trust Bank of Florida, N.A.*(Major Banking Relationship)*
700 Brickell Ave.
Miami, FL 33131
Tel.: 305-372-1000

HARRIS & DRUTT INC.
1520 Locust St.
Philadelphia, PA 19102
Tel.: 215-732-1106 **PA**
Fax: 215-735-8905
Year Founded: 1974
Approx.Billings: $11,115,000
Emp.: 8
Fiscal Year-end: 4/30/90
Broadcast & Media Buying Services
S.I.C.: 7319
William Drutt *(Pres., Chief Exec. Officer & Sec.)*
Diane Drutt *(V.P., Treas. & Media Dir.)*
Principal(s):
William Drutt

No. of Mfg. Plants/Facilities: 1
No. of U.S. Offices: 1

Computer Systems/Hardware:
NCR, IBM/PS2

Outside Service Firm(s):

Barbera & Shohm*(Auditors)*
Huntingdon Valley, PA

Mather & Co.*(Commercial Insurance Carrier)*
5th & Walnut
Philadelphia, PA

David Koss*(Legal Firm)*
Wynnewood, PA

Continental Bank, N.A.*(Major Banking Relationship)*
1500 Market St.
Philadelphia, PA 19102
Tel.: 215-564-7475

Savitz & Co.*(Pension Manager)*
1528 Walnut St.
Philadelphia, PA

HARRIS ENTERPRISES INC.
300 W. 2nd
Hutchinson, KS 67501
Mailing Address:
P.O. Box 190
Hutchinson, KS 67504
Tel.: 316-662-3311 **KS**
Fax: 316-662-4186
Sales Range: $40-59 Million
Emp.: 980
Holding Company for 10 Daily Newspapers & 11 Radio Stations
S.I.C.: 2711; 6719; 4832
Lloyd Ballhagen *(Pres. & Chief Exec. Officer)*
Bob Wells *(V.P.-Broadcasting)*
John G. Harris *(Treas. & Sec.)*
Arthur L. Fabrizius *(Controller)*
James Drake *(Bus. Mgr.)*
Mike Hurd *(Dir.-Plng.)*

Outside Service Firm(s):

Pierce, Faris, Cochran, Sutton*(Auditors)*
Hutchinson, KS

Blue Cross & Blue Shield of Kansas*(Group Insurer)*
1133 S.W. Topeka
Topeka, KS 66612

Security Benefit Life*(Group Insurer)*
Topeka, KS

Branine, Chalfant, Hill*(Legal Firm)*
Hutchinson, KS

First National Bank of Chicago*(Major Banking Relationship)*
One First National Plaza
Chicago, IL 60670
Tel.: 312-732-9781
Tel.: 312-732-4050
Fax: 312-732-4840
Fax: 312-732-3055

First National Bank Hutchinson*(Major Banking Relationship)*
Hutchinson, KS

Subsidiary:

Olathe Daily News **(1)**
514 S. Canvas Ave.
Olathe, KS 66061
Tel.: 913-764-2211
S.I.C.: 2711
Mike Hurd *(Editor-in-Chief)*

HARRIS FARMS, INC.
Rte. 1, Box 420
Coalinga, CA 93210
Tel.: 209-884-2477
Fax: 209-884-2267
Year Founded: 1937
Sales Range: $100-499 Million
Emp.: 1,500
Producer Crops & Livestock; Cattle Feeding & Slaughtering; Restaurant & Motel Owners & Operators
S.I.C.: 0212; 0131; 0175; 0191; 0272; 2011; 5812; 7011
John C. Harris *(Chm. Bd., Pres. & Chief Exec. Officer)*
David E. Wood *(Vice Chm. & Chief Oper. Officer)*
Jim Kelly *(V.P. & Controller)*
Donald Devine *(Chief Fin. Officer)*

Harris Farms, Inc.—(Continued)

Steve Renton *(Dir.-Personnel)*
Dave Dahlke *(Mgr.-Data Processing)*
Dick Lobmeyer *(Mgr.-Farm)*
Rod Radtke *(Mgr.-River Ranch)*

Outside Service Firm(s):

Coopers & Lybrand*(Auditors)*
2901 N. Central
Phoenix, AZ 85012

Frank B. Hall*(Group Insurer)*
Suite 400, 5260 N. Palm Ave.
Fresno, CA 93704
Tel.: 209-449-1900

Bank of America NT&SA*(Major Banking Relationship)*
Fresno, CA

Subsidiaries:

Harris Feeding Co. **(1)**
Rte. 1, Box 400
Coalinga, CA 93210
Tel.: 209-884-2435
Emp.: 175
David E. Wood *(Chief Exec. Officer)*

Harris Ranch Beef Co. **(1)**
P.O. Box 220,
Selma, CA 93662
Tel.: 209-233-4116
Beef Processing
S.I.C.: 2011
David Wood *(Pres. & Chief Exec. Officer)*

Harris Ranch Restaurant **(1)**
Rte. 1 Box 777, Interstate 5 & Hwy. 198
Coalinga, CA 93210
Tel.: 209-935-0717
S.I.C.: 5812
Steve Renton *(V.P. & Gen. Mgr.)*

Inn at Harris Ranch **(1)**
Rte. 1 Box 777, Interstate 5 & Hwy. 198
Coalinga, CA 93210
Tel.: 209-935-0717
S.I.C.: 7011
Steve Renton *(V.P. & Gen. Mgr.)*

HARRIS FORD, INC.
20006 64th Ave., W.
Lynnwood, WA 98036
Mailing Address:
P.O. Box 867
Lynnwood, WA 98046
Tel.: 206-774-4141 **WA**
Fax: 206-775-2587
Year Founded: 1956
Assets: $11,372,417
Liabilities: $9,796,338
Net Worth: $1,576,079
Approx.Sls.: $608,000,000
Emp.: 120
Fiscal Year-end: 12/31/90
Wholesale & Retail Automobiles & Trucks
S.I.C.: 5511; 5012
R.J. Ollinger *(Pres.)*
Rebecca Bright *(Exec. V.P.)*
Michelle Kristiansen *(Controller)*
Don Davis *(Mgr.-Sls.)*
Larry Stordahl *(Gen. Mgr.)*

Principal(s):
R.J. Ollinger

No. of Mfg. Plants/Facilities: 2

Computer Systems/Hardware:
COIN

Outside Service Firm(s):

Benson & McLaughlin*(Auditors)*
Seattle, WA

Seattle First National Bank*(Major Banking Relationship)*
701 Fifth Avenue
Seattle, WA 98104
Tel.: 206-358-3035

HARRIS-KAYOT, INC.
2801 W. State Blvd.
Fort Wayne, IN 46808
Tel.: 219-432-4555
Fax: 219-436-6907
Approx.Sls.: $21,000,000
Emp.: 325
Mfr. of Boats & Metal Finishing
S.I.C.: 3599; 3471; 3732
James R. Poiry *(Pres.)*
Don Benson *(V.P.-Pur.)*
Peter Gillon *(V.P.-Sls.)*
Jerome Ruda *(V.P.)*
Tom Wade *(V.P.-Mfg.)*
Robert Bellair *(Controller)*

Outside Service Firm(s):

Ernst & Young*(Auditors)*
2300 Fort Wayne Natl. Bank Bldg.
Fort Wayne, IN 46802

Holleran & Trexler*(Legal Firm)*
Ft. Wayne, IN

Fort Wayne National Bank*(Major Banking Relationship)*
110 W. Berry St.
Fort Wayne, IN 46802
Tel.: 219-426-0555

HARRIS AND LOVE, INC.
University Club Bldg., 136 E. South Temple, Ste. 1800
Salt Lake City, UT 84111
Tel.: 801-532-7333
Year Founded: 1938
Approx.Billings: $16,700,000
Emp.: 42
Robert G. Love *(Chm. Bd.)*
Donald G. Ware *(Pres.)*
Michael D. Gallivan *(Exec. V.P.)*
Dennis Guiver *(Sr. V.P.)*
Skip Branch *(V.P.)*
Richard B. Love *(V.P.)*
Charlie Seldin *(V.P.)*
Sam Tallerico, III *(V.P. & Controller)*
Gail Sanders *(Dir.-Pub. Rels.)*

HARRIS MECHANICAL CONTRACTING CO.
2300 Territorial Rd.
Saint Paul, MN 55114
Tel.: 612-643-6699 **MN**
Fax: 612-646-6800
Year Founded: 1954
Approx.Sls.: $56,000,000
Emp.: 250
Fiscal Year-end: 12/31/90
Mechanical Contractor
S.I.C.: 1711; 1623
Robert F. Hosch *(Chm. Bd. & Pres.)*
Jerry Crane *(V.P. & Controller)*
William Marshall *(V.P.)*
Gerald Mullenbach *(V.P. & Treas.)*
Kerby Olson *(V.P.)*
Dean Osland *(V.P. & Sec.)*
Jerome Sandin *(V.P.)*

Subsidiary:

Harris Waldinger, Inc. **(1)**
2300 Territorial Rd.
Saint Paul, MN 55114
Tel.: 612-646-2911
Emp.: 31
Sheet Metal Co.
S.I.C.: 3444
Randolph Stewart *(V.P. & Gen. Mgr.)*

HARRIS STEEL CO.
1223 S. 55th Ct.
Chicago, IL 60650
Tel.: 708-656-5500 **IL**
Fax: 708-656-5568
Year Founded: 1950
Approx.Sls.: $30,000,000
Emp.: 80
Marketing of Metal Products
S.I.C.: 5051
Thomas Eliasek *(Pres.)*
Bernie McCudden *(V.P.-Fin.)*
Ross Miller *(Treas. & Sec.)*
Jerry Bauer *(Mgr.-Pur.)*

Outside Service Firm(s):

American National Bank*(Major Banking Relationship)*
33 North LaSalle St.
Chicago, IL 60690
Tel.: 312-661-6967

HARRISON CONSTRUCTION CORP.
1000 N.W. 54th St.
Miami, FL 33127
Tel.: 305-757-0621
Fax: 305-759-4011
Approx.Sls.: $58,000,000
Emp.: 350
General Contractor Industrial & Commercial Buildings
S.I.C.: 1541; 1542
Rod E. Overholt *(Chm. Bd.)*
John C. Harrison, Jr. *(Pres.)*
Charlotte Y. Willis *(Controller)*
Jesus Fernandez *(Chief Engr. & Estimator)*

Outside Service Firm(s):

Berkowitz, Dick & Kaplan*(Auditors)*
Miami, FL

James E. Glass & Associates*(Legal Firm)*
Miami, FL

Plaza Bank of Miami*(Major Banking Relationship)*
Miami, FL

HARRISON PAINT CORPORATION
1329 Harrison Ave., S.W.
Canton, OH 44706
Mailing Address:
PO BOX 8470,
Canton, OH 44711
Tel.: 216-455-5125 **OH**
Fax: 216-454-1750
Year Founded: 1911
Sales Range: $20-39 Million
Emp.: 163
Fiscal Year-end: 11/31/91

Export
Paints & Allied Products
S.I.C.: 2851
Roger A. Walters *(Chm. Bd. & Pres.)*
Michael P. McCarthy *(Exec. V.P.)*
Edwin Gruenling *(V.P.-Mfg.)*
Andrew J. Evans *(Treas. & Sec.)*
Lester D. Boyd *(Controller & Mgr.-Office)*

Outside Service Firm(s):

Hall, Kistler*(Auditors)*
900 Central Trust Tower
Canton, OH 44702

Day, Ketterer, Raley, Wright & Rybolt*(Legal Firm)*
800 William R. Day Bldg., 121 Cleveland Ave. So.
Canton, OH 44702
Tel.: 216-455-0173

HARRISON, STAR, WIENER & BEITLER, INC.
16 W. 22nd St., 12th Fl.
New York, NY 10010
Tel.: 212-727-1330
Fax: 212-727-1342
Year Founded: 1987
Approx.Billings: $62,000,000
Emp.: 85
Healthcare
Thomas L. Harrison *(Pres.)*
John M. Sullivan *(Sr. V.P.-Fin.)*
Leonard Lustgarten *(Dir.-Medical)*

HARRISS & COVINGTON HOSIERY MILLS
2525 E. Green Dr.
High Point, NC 27260
Tel.: 919-882-6811 **NC**
Fax: 919-889-2412
Approx.Sls.: $10,000,000
Emp.: 225
Men's & Boys Hosiery
S.I.C.: 5136
Edward H. Covington *(Pres.)*
Darrell Frye *(V.P.-Fin. & Sec.)*
James Randle, Sr. *(V.P.-Sls.)*

Outside Service Firm(s):

Keziah, Gates & Samet*(Legal Firm)*
High Point, NC

High Point Bank & Trust Company*(Major Banking Relationship)*
High Point, NC

HARROP INDUSTRIES, INC.
3470 E. Fifth Ave.
Columbus, OH 43219
Tel.: 614-231-3621
Fax: 614-235-3699
Approx.Sls.: $10,000,000
Emp.: 90
Design & Construct Tunnel Kilns, Shuttle Kilns & Dryers for the Ceramic Industry. Complete Engineering Services for Feasability & Construction of Entire Plants. Manufacturer Modular Kilns & Furnaces & Thermal Analysis Testing Service Instruments, Material Testing Service
S.I.C.: 3567; 3821; 3826
James E. Houseman *(Pres. & Treas.)*
N.E. Bradstock *(Exec. V.P.-Sec.)*
D.A. O'Brian *(V.P.)*
J.H. Belger *(Mgr.-Sls.)*

HART CROWSER, INC.
1910 Fairview Ave. E.
Seattle, WA 98102
Tel.: 206-324-9530 **WA**
Fax: 206-328-5581
Year Founded: 1974
Sales Range: $20-39 Million
Emp.: 245
Fiscal Year-end: 6/30/91
Environmental Hazardous Waste Management, Hydrogeologic & Geotechnical Consulting, Underground Storage Tank Management, Property Assessments, Regulatory Assistance, Mobile Laboratory Analysis, Air & Water Quality Monitoring & Construction Management
S.I.C.: 8711; 8734; 8731
Ronald D. Hart *(Pres. & Treas.)*
John C. Crowser *(Chief Exec. Officer)*
David Eckberg *(Gen. Counsel & Sec.)*
Laurel Briskey *(Mgr.-Office)*
Paula Houston *(Mgr.-Human Resources)*
Sophia Smith *(Mgr.-Library & Information Systems)*
Carla Thompson *(Mgr.-Mktg. Services)*

Principal(s):
Ronald D. Hart
John C. Crowser
Garry Horvitz

No. of U.S. Offices: 7

Outside Service Firm(s):

West One Bank*(Major Banking Relationship)*
Fourth & Battery
Seattle, WA

Spectrum Pension Consultants*(Pension Manager)*
Tacoma, WA

HART ENGINEERING CORPORATION
29 Lark Industrial Pkwy.
Greenville, RI 02828
Tel.: 401-434-6700 RI
Fax: 401-949-5309
Year Founded: 1984
Approx.Sls.: $20,000,000
Emp.: 100
Mechanical Contractor
S.I.C.: 1711
C. Frank Rampone *(Pres.)*
David F. Rampone *(V.P.)*

Outside Service Firm(s):

Citizens Savings Bank*(Major Banking Relationship)*
Providence, RI

HART GRAPHICS INC.
8000 Shoal Creek Blvd.
Austin, TX 78758
Tel.: 512-454-4761
Fax: 512-467-4583
Approx.Sls.: $44,000,000
Emp.: 625
Lithographic Printing
S.I.C.: 2752
William L. Hart *(Chm. Bd. & Chief Exec. Officer)*
David Hart *(Pres.)*
Fred Cantu *(V.P.)*
Fred A. Colletta *(V.P.)*
Chris Hart *(V.P.-Mktg.)*
Brian K. Oetzel *(V.P.-Personnel)*
James L. Weatherby, Jr. *(V.P.)*
Britt Kauffman *(Treas.)*
Walter Picard *(Mgr.-Matls.)*

Outside Service Firm(s):

Grant Thornton*(Auditors)*
Austin, TX

McGinnis, Lochridge & Kilgore*(Legal Firm)*
Austin, TX

NationsBank Texas*(Major Banking Relationship)*
Austin, TX

Subsidiaries:

Hart Distribution Services **(1)**
3106 Longhorn Blvd.
Austin, TX 78759
Tel.: 512-834-6900

Hart Forms & Services **(1)**
11500 Metric Blvd., Ste. 300
Austin, TX 78758
Tel.: 512-339-3900
Jim Weatherby *(Pres.)*

HART SERVICES, INC.

101 N. Wacker Dr.
Chicago, IL 60606
Tel.: 312-372-6300
Fax: 312-444-2695
Year Founded: 1971
Approx.Billings: $15,000,000
Emp.: 32
Fashion Advertising; Sales Promotion & Public Relations
Frank A. Brenner *(Pres.)*
Irene O. Sawka *(V.P., Gen. Mgr.)*

HARTE-HANKS COMMUNICATIONS, INC.
Harte-Hanks Tower, 200
Concord Plaza Dr., Ste. 800
San Antonio, TX 78216
Mailing Address:
P.O. Box 269,
San Antonio, TX 78291
Tel.: 210-829-9000 DE
Fax: 210-829-9403
Year Founded: 1920
Assets: $527,000,000
Earnings: $38,000,000
Liabilities: $485,000,000
Net Worth: $42,000,000
Approx.Sls.: $420,000,000
Emp.: 6,000
Fiscal Year-end: 12/31/91
Newspaper Publishing, Printing, Television Broadcasting Advertising Publications, Direct Marketing & Data Processing Services
S.I.C.: 2711; 7331; 4833
Houston H. Harte *(Chm. Bd.)*
Larry Franklin *(Pres. & Chief Exec. Officer)*
Richard L. Ritchie *(Sr. V.P. & Chief Fin. Officer)*
Donald R. Crews *(Sr. V.P., Legal & Sec.)*
Harry J. Buckel *(Sr. V.P.)*
Michael J. Conly *(Sr. V.P.)*
Richard M. Hochhauser *(Sr. V.P.)*
Stephen W. Sullivan *(Sr. V.P.)*
Chalmers Williams *(Controller)*
Ann Downing *(Dir.-Corp. Communications)*
Carolyn Oatman *(Dir.-Information Services)*
Zada True-Courage *(Mgr.-Cash Mngmt.)*

Outside Service Firm(s):

Ernst & Young*(Auditors)*
1900 Frost Bank Tower, 100 W. Houston St.
San Antonio, TX 78205
Tel.: 210-228-9696
Fax: 210-554-0253

Liberty Mutual*(Commercial Insurance Carrier)*
175 Berkeley St.
Boston, MA

Aetna Life & Casualty*(Group Insurer)*
151 Farmington Avenue
Hartford, CT 06156
Tel.: 203-273-2128
Fax: 203-729-4295

Hughes & Luce*(Legal Firm)*
Bank One Center, 1717 Main St.
Dallas, TX 75202
Tel.: 214-651-0477

First National Bank of Chicago*(Major Banking Relationship)*
One First National Plaza
Chicago, IL 60670
Tel.: 312-732-9781
Tel.: 312-732-4050
Fax: 312-732-4840
Fax: 312-732-3055

NationsBank Texas*(Major Banking Relationship)*
901 Main St., 16th Fl.
Dallas, TX 75202
Tel.: 214-922-5000

Toronto Dominion Bank*(Major Banking Relationship)*
42 Wall St.
New York, NY 10005-1924
Tel.: 212-820-2160

Vaughan, Nelson & Hargrove*(Pension Manager)*
Houston, TX

Subsidiaries:

Advertising Distributors of Maryland, Inc. **(1)**
Lansdowne Industrial Pk., 100 Alco Pl.
Baltimore, MD 21227
Tel.: 410-247-0666 (100%)
Advertising Distribution
S.I.C.: 7331
Charles Dall'Acqua *(Pres.)*

Century Publications, Inc. **(1)**
Three Church St.
Winchester, MA 01890
Tel.: 617-729-8100
Newspaper, Publishing & Printing
S.I.C.: 2711
Asa Cole *(Publisher)*

Corpus Christi Caller-Times **(1)**
820 N. Lower Broadway
Corpus Christi, TX 78401
Tel.: 512-884-2011 (100%)
Publishing
S.I.C.: 2711
Stephen W. Sullivan *(Publisher)*

The Flyer Publishing Corp. **(1)**
P.O. Box 161900,
Miami, FL 33116
Tel.: 305-232-4115
Newspaper Publishing
S.I.C.: 2711
James Enright *(Pres.)*

Greater Houston Mailing Service, Inc. **(1)**
650 W. 6th St.
Houston, TX 77007
Tel.: 713-864-5666
Mailing Services
S.I.C.: 7331
Terry Ahrens *(Gen. Mgr.)*

Harte-Hanks Community Newspapers, Inc. **(1)**
c/o Plano Star Courier, P.O. Box 86248
Plano, TX 75086
Tel.: 214-424-6565
Newspaper Publishing
S.I.C.: 2711
Christian R. Schilt *(Pres.)*

Harte-Hanks Data Technologies **(1)**
25 Linnell Circle
Billerica, MA 01821
Tel.: 617-663-9955 (100%)
Computer Information System & Service Co.
S.I.C.: 7374
Thomas Swithenbank *(Pres.)*

Harte-Hanks Direct Mail/California **(1)**
2337 W. Commonwealth Ave.
Fullerton, CA 92633
Tel.: 714-738-5478
Mailing Services
S.I.C.: 7331
Ron Mastrianni *(Pres.)*

Harte-Hanks Graphics **(1)**
403 E. Ramsey, #104
San Antonio, TX 78216
Tel.: 210-525-8185
Pre-Press Graphics
S.I.C.: 7336
Kay Evans *(Pres. & Gen. Mgr.)*

Harte-Hanks Marketing Services **(1)**
65 Rte. 4
River Edge, NJ 07661
Tel.: 201-342-6400 (100%)
Research Marketing Services
S.I.C.: 7389
Charles Dall' Acqua *(Pres.)*

Harte-Hanks Television, Inc. (KENS-TV) **(1)**
5400 Fredricksburg Rd.
San Antonio, TX 78299
Tel.: 210-366-5000 (100%)
Broadcasting
S.I.C.: 4833
Michael J. Conly *(Pres. & Gen. Mgr.)*

Independent Publishing Company **(1)**
1000 Williamston Rd.
Anderson, SC 29621
Tel.: 803-224-4321 (100%)
Publishing
S.I.C.: 2711
Fred Foster *(Pres. & Publisher)*

Jordan Dennis Company, Inc. **(1)**
1010 W. Chestnut
Brockton, MA 02401
Tel.: 508-584-6000
Mailing Services
S.I.C.: 7331
Tim Young *(V.P. & Gen. Mgr.)*

Mid-America CDM, Inc. **(1)**
1329 Arlington St.
Cincinnati, OH 45225
Tel.: 513-542-7700
Advertising Distribution
S.I.C.: 7331
Ted Sherwin *(Pres.)*

The Middlesex News **(1)**
33 New York Ave.
Framingham, MA 01701
Tel.: 508-626-3800 (100%)
Publishing
S.I.C.: 2711
Bill R. Gulledge *(Publr.)*

PennySaver (Harte-Hanks California CDM, Inc.) **(1)**
P.O. Box 8900
Brea, CA 92622
Tel.: 714-996-8900
Publishing
S.I.C.: 2711
Peter Gorman *(Pres.)*

Pennysaver Publications, Inc. (The Shopper's Guide) **(1)**
1302 Ave. T.
Grand Prairie, TX 75050
Tel.: 214-641-7690 (100%)
Publishing
S.I.C.: 2711; 7331
Joe Saltamachio *(Gen. Mgr.)*

Potpourri (Harte-Hanks California CDM, Inc.) **(1)**
1350 Duane Ave.
Santa Clara, CA 95054
Tel.: 408-748-1360
Newspaper Publishing
S.I.C.: 2711
Hal Polak *(Pres.)*

Reporter Publishing Company **(1)**
N. First & Cypress
Abilene, TX 79604
Tel.: 915-673-4271 (100%)
Publishing
S.I.C.: 2711
Frank Puckett, Jr. *(Pres.)*
Andrew B. Shelton *(Publisher)*
Frank Puckett, Jr. *(Pres.)*

San Angelo Standard, Inc. **(1)**
34 W. Harris
San Angelo, TX 76903
Tel.: 915-653-1221 (100%)
Publishing
S.I.C.: 2711
Kevin J. Barry *(Publisher)*

Shopper's Guide, Inc. (Tucson Shopper) **(1)**
2915 E. Speedway
Tucson, AZ 85716
Tel.: 602-881-7423 (100%)
Publishing
S.I.C.: 2711; 7331
John Courtis *(Pres. & Gen. Mgr.)*

Times Publishing Company of Wichita Falls **(1)**
1301 Lamar
Wichita Falls, TX 76307
Tel.: 817-767-8341 (100%)
Newspaper Publishing
S.I.C.: 2711
James D. Lonergan *(Pres. & Publr.)*

Divisions:

Harte-Hanks Direct Marketing/Pennsylvania **(2)**
900 Rutter Ave.
Forty Fort, PA 18704
Tel.: 717-288-4557
S.I.C.: 7331
Norman Sallitt *(V.P. & Gen. Mgr.)*

Harte-Hanks Transportation Services **(2)**
1701 W. Hillsboro Blvd., Ste. 400
Deerfield Beach, FL 33442
Tel.: 305-429-3771 (100%)
Trucking
S.I.C.: 4213
David Chamberlain *(Pres.)*

Trademark Press, Inc. **(1)**
2346 Horne Rd.
Corpus Christi, TX 78415
Tel.: 512-854-4305 (100%)
Commercial Printing
S.I.C.: 2759
Grady Huges *(Mgr.-Opers.)*

THE HARTER GROUP
400 Prairie Ave.
Sturgis, MI 49091
Mailing Address:
P.O. Box 400,
Sturgis, MI 49091
Tel.: 616-651-3201
Tel.: 800-543-5449 **MI**
Fax: 616-651-6694
Year Founded: 1927
Approx.Sls.: $30,000,000
Emp.: 300
Fiscal Year-end: 12/31/92
Import Export
Mfr. Steel & Wood Office & Institutional Furniture, Office Partitions
S.I.C.: 2521; 2522; 2541; 2542
Evan C. Harter *(Chm. Bd.)*
Gary Gottschalk *(Pres. & Chief Exec. Officer)*
Carl Ceithaml *(Chief Fin. Officer)*
Peter Malcolm *(V.P.-Sls.)*
Jerry Mais *(V.P.-Mfg.)*
Dennis Sierens *(Controller)*
Anne Melchi *(Dir.-Personnel)*
Donald Hoffelder *(Dir.-Mngmt. Information Systems)*
John Gelvin *(Pur. Agent)*

No. of Mfg. Plants/Facilities: 4
No. of U.S. Offices: 5

Computer Systems/Hardware:
IBM AS400

Outside Service Firm(s):

Ernst & Young*(Auditors)*
1100 Old Kent Bank Bldg.
Kalamazoo, MI 49007
Tel.: 616-349-6671

Howard & Howard*(Legal Firm)*
400 Kalamazoo Bldg.
Kalamazoo, MI 49007
Tel.: 616-382-1483
Fax: 616-382-1568

Dann Brothers*(Commercial Insurance Carrier)*
Chicago, IL

First of America Bank*(Major Banking Relationship)*
Kalamazoo, MI

Division:

Harter Systems Div. **(1)**
11451 Harter Dr.
Middlebury, IN 46540
Tel.: 219-825-5871
Tel.: 800-543-5449
S.I.C.: 2541
Carl Bronkema *(Plant Mgr.)*
Jeanne Jacobson *(Mgr.-Mktg. Services)*

HARTFORD DISTRIBUTORS INC.
131 Chapel Rd.
Manchester, CT 06040
Tel.: 203-643-2337
Fax: 203-646-3780
Approx.Sls.: $51,000,000
Emp.: 140
Fiscal Year-end: 12/31/89
Wholesale Beer Distributor
S.I.C.: 5181
Jules A. Hollander *(Chm. Bd. & Treas.)*
Ross H. Hollander *(Pres.)*
Robert A. Hollander *(V.P.)*

Computer Systems/Hardware:
IBM-36

Outside Service Firm(s):

Coopers & Lybrand*(Auditors)*
280 Trumbull St.
Hartford, CT 06103

Aetna Life & Casualty*(Commercial Insurance Carrier)*
151 Farmington Avenue
Hartford, CT 06156
Tel.: 203-273-2128
Fax: 203-729-4295

Aetna Life & Casualty*(Group Insurer)*
151 Farmington Avenue
Hartford, CT 06156
Tel.: 203-273-2128
Fax: 203-729-4295

Connecticut Bank & Trust*(Major Banking Relationship)*
One Constitution Plaza,
Hartford, CT 06115

THE HARTWELL CORPORATION
900 S. Richfield Rd.
Placentia, CA 92670-6788
Tel.: 714-993-4200
Fax: 714-777-4031
Year Founded: 1939
Emp.: 420
Fiscal Year-end: 12/31/90
Export
Nylatch Plastic Fasteners, Micro Hinge, Dialatch Adjustable Container Latch, Lockwell Quick Release Pins, Rate-Chek Motion Dampeners, Aircraft Latches & Handle Accessories
S.I.C.: 5072; 3429; 3089
E. Hoogendijk *(Pres.)*
J.W. Chambers *(Sr. V.P.-Sls. & Mktg.)*
B.W. Henrichs *(Sr. V.P.-Engrng.)*

Division:

Hartwell Commercial Division **(1)**
620 S. Jefferson St., Unit A
Placentia, CA 92670-4783
Tel.: 714-993-2752
Fax: 714-777-4031
Emp.: 44
Plastic Molding, Design & Assembly; Sheet Metal Hinges & Latches
S.I.C.: 3089; 3444
E. Hoogendijk *(Pres.)*
Dana Heald *(V.P. & Gen. Mgr.)*

HARTZ GROUP
667 Madison Ave.
New York, NY 10021
Tel.: 212-308-3336
Nonresidential Buildings, Dog & Cat Food, & Manufacturing
S.I.C.: 6512; 2047; 3999
Leonard Stern *(Chm. Bd.)*
Curtis Schwartz *(Pres.)*

Subsidiaries:

Hartz Mountain Group **(1)**
700 Frank E. Roger Blvd.S.
Harrison, NJ 07029
Tel.: 201-485-5300
Dog & Cat Food & Pet Supplies
S.I.C.: 2047; 3089; 3231; 3499; 3999; 5199
Leonard Stern *(Chm.)*

Hartz Mountain Industries **(1)**
400 Plaza Dr.
Secaucus, NJ 07094-3688
Tel.: 201-348-1200
Nonresidential Buildings
S.I.C.: 6512

THE HARTZ MOUNTAIN CORP.
700 Frank E. Rodgers Blvd., S.
Harrison, NJ 07029
Tel.: 201-481-4800 **NJ**
Telex: 138997
Fax: 201-481-4800
Year Founded: 1926
Import
Pet Supplies & Accessories; Carpet Cleaning Supplies & Equipment Rentals, Pet Food
S.I.C.: 5149; 2842; 3999; 5199
Leonard N. Stern *(Chm. Bd. & Chief Exec. Officer)*
David D. Lovitz *(Pres. & Chief Oper. Officer)*
Curtis B. Schwartz *(Exec. V.P.-Fin.)*
William Salomon *(V.P. & Treas.)*
William Egan *(V.P. & Controller)*
James D. Proud *(Sr. V.P.-Sls. & Mktg.)*
Thomas E. Cognan *(V.P.-Sls)*
Leon Cooper *(V.P.-Opers.)*
Mark E. Johnson *(V.P.-Mktg.)*
Gilbert D. Kaye *(V.P.-Mfg.)*
Gerald S. Kirschbaum *(V.P. & Gen. Counsel)*
Annette Pazzani *(V.P.-Adv.)*
William Perlberg *(V.P.-Res. & Devel.)*
Walter J. Sesholtz *(V.P.-Pur.)*
F. Wechsler *(V.P.-Personnnel)*

HARTZELL CORPORATION
2515 Wabash Ave.
Saint Paul, MN 55114
Tel.: 612-642-2880
Fax: 612-642-1990
Year Founded: 1949
Approx.Sls.: $60,000,000
Emp.: 600
Manufacture Hardware, Storm & Screen Doors; Distribute Electronic Parts & Equipment
S.I.C.: 3089; 3369; 3429; 5064
Robert C. Hartzell *(Chm. Bd. & Pres.)*
Principal(s):
Robert C. Hartzell

No. of Mfg. Plants/Facilities: 4
No. of U.S. Offices: 15

Computer Systems/Hardware:
Hewlett-Packard 3000, B1955

Outside Service Firm(s):

Boulay, Heutmaker, Zibell & Co.*(Auditors)*
Edina, MN

Churchill Business*(Investment Banker)*
Minneapolis, MN

Maun & Simon*(Legal Firm)*
2300 World Trade Center, 30 E. 7th St.
St. Paul, MN 55101
Tel.: 612-229-2900

HARVARD INDUSTRIES, INC.
Central Avenue
Farmingdale, NJ 07727
Mailing Address:
P.O. Box 527,
Farmingdale, NJ 07727
Tel.: 908-938-9000 **DE**
Fax: 908-919-2531
Year Founded: 1932
Approx.Rev.: $800,000,000
Emp.: 6,700
Fiscal Year-end: 9/30/91
Mfrs. & Assembles O.E.M. Automotive Components, Office Chairs, Aerospace & Industrial Fastners, Aerospace & Automotive Equipment
S.I.C.: 2522; 3489; 3714; 3452
Dr. William D. Hurley *(Chm. Bd. & Chief Exec. Officer)*
Lee H. Runk *(Pres. & Chief Oper. Officer)*
J.J. Gagliardi *(V.P.-Fin. & Chief Fin. Officer)*
Jerome J. Lukas *(V.P.-Mktg.)*

Outside Service Firm(s):

KPMG Peat Marwick*(Auditors)*
One Boston Place
Boston, MA 02108
Tel.: 617-723-7700

Divisions:

Cast Products **(1)**
1999 Wildwood Ave.
Jackson, MI 49202
Tel.: 517-782-9421
Fax: 517-782-4478
Engine Cooling Fans, Window Assemblies, Oil Pumps & Water Pump Components; Malleable 3' Nodular Iron Castings, Aluminum, Magnesium & Zinc Die Castings
S.I.C.: 3714; 3322; 3363; 3364
David C. Stegemiller *(Pres.)*

Elastic Stop Nut **(1)**
2330 Vauxhall Rd.
Union, NJ 07083
Tel.: 908-686-6000
Fax: 908-964-3902
Approx.Sls.: $35,000,000
Emp.: 750
Fiscal Year-end: 9/30/90
Import Export
Mfr. of Elastic Stop Nut, Collarlok, Self-Locking Hex Nuts, ESlok, Self-Locking Two Way Hex Nut
S.I.C.: 3452
Terry Margolis *(Pres.)*
T. Bloom *(V.P.-Mktg. & Sls.)*
G. McCormick *(V.P.-Engrng.)*
R. Macre *(Controller)*
R. Laiken *(Mgr.-Info. Systems)*
David Fursman *(Dir.-Indus. Rels.)*

Harman Automotive **(1)**
27365 W. Eleven Mile Rd.
Southfield, MI 48034
Tel.: 313-827-2150
Fax: 313-827-2152
Mfr. of Outside Rear-View Mirrors for Automotive Vehicles
S.I.C.: 3714
Michael Leonard *(Pres.)*

Harvard Interiors Manufacturing Co. **(1)**
4321 Semple Ave.
Saint Louis, MO 63120
Tel.: 314-382-5590
Fax: 314-382-8102
Mfr. of Commercial & Restaurant Furniture; Office Chairs; Rocket Launchers
S.I.C.: 2522; 2542; 2599; 3489
Thomas Jenkins *(V.P.-Opers.)*

Kingston Warren **(1)**
27365 W. Eleven Mile Rd.
Southfield, MI 48034
Tel.: 313-827-2150
Fax: 313-827-2154
Automotive Door & Window Seals, Deck Lid & Hood-to-Cowl Seals
S.I.C.: 3053
Roger L. Burtraw *(Pres.)*
Brian Benninger *(V.P.-Sls. & Engrng.)*

Trim Trends **(1)**
1271 W. Maple Road
Clawson, MI 48017
Tel.: 313-435-4200
Fax: 313-435-9005
Decorative Trim, Door Frames, Door Intrusion Beams, Various Stampings & Roll-Formed Components
S.I.C.: 3465; 3442; 3499; 3469
Rex Carlile *(Pres.)*

HARVE BENARD LTD. MANUFACTURING
225 Meadowland Pkwy.
Secaucus, NJ 07096
Tel.: 201-319-0909
Fax: 201-865-7031
Sales Range: $40-59 Million
Emp.: 165
Ladies Coats, Suits, Sportswear, Dresses & Blouses; Men's Suits
S.I.C.: 2337; 2311; 2331; 2335
Bernard Holtzman *(Pres.)*
Morton Holtzman *(V.P., Sec. & Treas.)*

Outside Service Firm(s):

William Liebowitz*(Auditors)*
Brooklyn, NY

Phillips, Neizer, Benjamin, Krim & Ballon*(Legal Firm)*
40 W. 57th St.
New York, NY 10019
Tel.: 212-977-9700

Chemical Bank*(Major Banking Relationship)*
450 West 33rd St.
New York, NY 10001
Tel.: 212-613-7197
Fax: 212-947-7628

HARVEST STATES COOPERATIVES
1667 N. Snelling Ave.
Saint Paul, MN 55108
Tel.: 612-646-9433
Fax: 612-641-6579
Year Founded: 1936
Approx.Rev.: $3,073,000,000
Emp.: 2,800
Fiscal Year-end: 12/31/91
Export
Grain Marketing Cooperative; Export & Marketing Of Grains, Oil Seeds & Products
S.I.C.: 5153
Ed Ellison *(Chm. Bd.)*
Allan D. Hanson *(Pres. & Chief Exec. Officer)*
T.F. Baker *(Sr. V.P.-Fin., Treas. & Chief Fin. Officer)*
Harvey Kaner *(Sr. V.P. & Gen. Counsel)*
Michael Bergeland *(Grp. V.P.-Grain & Country Opers.)*
Al Andersan *(V.P.-Admin.)*
Gerald Redlin *(Corp. Sec.)*
Gregory Collier *(Dir.-Mngmt. Information Systems)*
Delmore Schmidt *(Dir.-Communications)*
Jennifer Olson-Goude *(Mgr.-Cash)*
Keith Walter *(Mgr.-Computer Opers.)*

Computer Systems/Hardware:
IBM 4381

Outside Service Firm(s):

Deloitte & Touche*(Auditors)*
1600 Landmark Towers, 345 St. Peter St.
St. Paul, MN 55102

Norwest Bank Minnesota, N.A.*(Major Banking Relationship)*
6th St. & Marquette Av.
Minneapolis, MN 55479
Tel.: 612-667-1234

Division:

Holsum Foods **(1)**
500 S. Prairie Ave.
Waukesha, WI 53186
Tel.: 414-544-4444
Fax: 414-548-5707
Approx.Sls.: $127,000,000
Emp.: 400
Fiscal Year-end: 12/31/90
Import
Computer Systems/Hardware:
IBM A/S 400
Soup Bases & Gravies, Preserves, Salad Dressings, Peanut Butter, Sauces, Syrup, Shortenings, Oils & Margarines, Spanish Olives, Green & Ripe, Mayonnaise
S.I.C.: 2033; 2035; 2099; 2062
Kevin Ruda *(Pres.)*
Gordon Maleu *(Sr. V.P.)*
Gregory L. Carlson *(V.P.-Fin.)*
Kirk Mellecker *(V.P.-Sls.)*
John Tuerff *(Dir.-Mktg.)*
David Boulay *(Dir.-Mktg.-Fats & Oils)*

J.H. HARVEY COMPANY
727 S. Davis St.
Nashville, GA 31639
Tel.: 912-686-7654 **GA**
Fax: 912-686-2927
Year Founded: 1950
Approx.Sls.: $180,000,000
Emp.: 2,000
Retail Supermarkets
S.I.C.: 5411
Joseph H. Harvey, Jr. *(Chm. Bd. & Chief Exec. Officer)*
Joseph H. Harvey III *(Pres. & Chief Oper. Officer)*
Altom Holloway *(V.P.-Real Estate & Devel.)*
Howard McLeod *(V.P.-Human Resources)*
Max M. Murphy *(V.P.-Sls.)*
Iris H. Smith *(V.P.-Consumer Affairs)*
Nancy J. Harvey *(Treas.)*
Elmer C. Keeffe *(Sec.)*
Benny Ensley *(Dir.-Data Processing)*
James Sutton *(Dir.-Pur.)*
Robert Heirs *(Mgr.-Mngmt. Information Systems)*

Outside Service Firm(s):

Arthur Andersen & Co.*(Auditors)*
Jacksonville, FL

King & Spalding*(Legal Firm)*
25 Park Place N.E.
Atlanta, GA 30303
Tel.: 404-572-4600

United Banking Company*(Major Banking Relationship)*
Nashville, GA

HARVEY CONSTRUCTION COMPANY, INC.
10 Harvey Rd.
Bedford, NH 03110
Tel.: 603-668-3100 **NH**
Fax: 603-668-0389
Year Founded: 1939
Approx.Sls.: $60,000,000
Emp.: 275
General Building Contractor & Industrial Buildings, Warehouses & Institutional Buildings
S.I.C.: 1541; 1542
Cornelius Allsopp, P.E. *(Pres. & Treas.)*
Conrad Jodoin *(V.P.)*
Arthur Lagios *(V.P.- Mktg.)*
John Zahr *(V.P.- Estimating)*
Robert Pedley *(Controller)*
Joseph Millimet *(Sec.)*
Claire Gaumont *(Admin. Asst.)*

Outside Service Firm(s):

Coopers & Lybrand*(Auditors)*
Manchester, NH

Devine, Millimet & Branch*(Legal Firm)*
Manchester, NH

Bank of New Hampshire*(Major Banking Relationship)*
Manchester, NH

SID HARVEY INC.
100 E. Mineola Ave.
Valley Stream, NY 11580
Tel.: 516-825-5654
Fax: 516-825-7254
Year Founded: 1930
Emp.: 900
Apparel & Other Textile Products; Fabricated Metal Products; Electric & Electronic Equipment
S.I.C.: 5075; 5052; 5065; 5136; 5137
Henry James Otto *(Pres. & Chief Fin. Officer)*
Ronald Stahl *(Treas.)*
Joseph Stoll *(Controller)*

No. of Mfg. Plants/Facilities: 2

Outside Service Firm(s):

Norman Keller*(Auditors)*
New York, NY

Empire Blue Cross & Blue Shield*(Group Insurer)*
New York, NY

Redmond & Pollio*(Legal Firm)*
Garden City, NY

The Bank of New York*(Major Banking Relationship)*
One Wall Street
New York, NY 10286
Tel.: 212-635-6805
Fax: 212-635-3201

Frank B. Hall*(Pension Manager)*
Akron, OH

HARVEY INDUSTRIES, INC.
43 Emerson Rd.
Waltham, MA 02154
Tel.: 617-899-3500
Fax: 617-899-2072
Approx.Sls.: $99,000,000
Emp.: 650
Roofing, Siding & Insulation, Metal Doors, Sash & Trim, Millwork
S.I.C.: 5033; 3442; 2431
Robert K. Morrison *(Chm. Bd.)*
Alan Marlow *(Pres. & Chief Oper. Officer)*
Glen Frederick *(Exec. V.P.)*
James E. Cronan *(Sr. V.P. & Chief Fin. Officer)*
Frances E. Martel *(Treas.)*
Robert N. Norris *(Sec.)*

Outside Service Firm(s):

Price Waterhouse*(Auditors)*
160 Federal St.
Boston, MA 02110
Tel.: 617-439-3308
Fax: 617-439-3308

Bay Bank*(Major Banking Relationship)*
Dedham, MA

HARWICK CHEMICAL CORP.
60 S. Seiberling St., P.O. Box 9360
Akron, OH 44305
Mailing Address:
P.O. Box 9360,
Akron, OH 44305-0360
Tel.: 216-798-9300
Telex: 810-431-2126
Year Founded: 1932
Approx.Sls.: $110,000,000
Emp.: 300
Fiscal Year-end: 12/31/91
Export
Chemicals
S.I.C.: 5169; 2865
R.T. Read *(Chm. Bd., Pres. & Chief Exec. Officer)*
E.M. Corbett, Jr. *(V.P.-Sls.)*
T.K. Goldsby *(V.P.-Mfg.)*
G.R. Hamrick, Jr. *(V.P.-Fin.)*
G.H. Proodian *(V.P.-Opers.)*
J.L. Slinger *(V.P.-Technical)*
R.C. Stambaugh *(V.P.-Business Devel.)*
E.E. Pouttu *(Controller)*
R.A. Chenoweth *(Sec. & Gen. Counsel)*
A.W. Fritts *(Dir.-Bus. Mfg.)*
D.K. Graber *(Dir.-Pur.)*

No. of Mfg. Plants/Facilities: 2
No. of U.S. Offices: 9

Outside Service Firm(s):

Ernst & Young*(Auditors)*
787 Seventh Ave.
New York, NY 10019
Tel.: 212-773-1243

Klais & Company*(Group Insurer)*
Akron, OH

Buckingham, Doolittle & Burroughs L.P.A.*(Legal Firm)*
50 S. Main St., P.O. Box 1500
Akron, OH 44309
Tel.: 216-376-5300

First National Bank of Ohio*(Major Banking Relationship)*
Akron, OH

Branches:

Harwick Chemical Corp. **(1)**
7225 Paramount Blvd.
Pico Rivera, CA 90660
Tel.: 310-723-9911
Fax: 310-948-2044
Machinery
S.I.C.: 5169
J. Marshall Dean, III *(V.P.-Los Angeles)*

Harwick Chemical Corp. **(1)**
1485 Bayshore Blvd.
San Francisco, CA 94124
Tel.: 415-467-0505
Fax: 415-467-0156
Chemicals & Allied Products
S.I.C.: 5169
H.C. Cavaness *(V.P.-San Francisco)*

Harwick Chemical Corp. **(1)**
800 Estes Ave.
Elk Grove Village, IL 60007
Tel.: 708-437-6560
Fax: 708-437-0191
Chemicals & Allied Products
S.I.C.: 5169
G.F. McGinnis *(V.P.-Chicago)*

Harwick Chemical Corp. **(1)**
5380 Peachtree Ind., Blvd., Ste. 210
Norcross, GA 30071
Tel.: 404-368-4033
Fax: 404-368-8962
Chemicals & Allied Products
S.I.C.: 5169
D.A. Stauber *(V.P.-Atlanta)*

Harwick Chemical Corp. **(1)**
8 Jewel Dr.
Wilmington, MA 01887
Tel.: 508-658-6710
Fax: 508-657-4112
Chemicals & Allied Products
S.I.C.: 5169
J.J. Buda *(V.P.-Boston)*

Harwick Chemical Corp. **(1)**
Box 5083, 88 Lakedale Dr.
Trenton, NJ 08638
Tel.: 609-599-2277
Fax: 609-599-9332
Chemical & Allied Products
S.I.C.: 5169
A.G. Martin *(V.P.-Trenton)*

Harwick Chemical Corp. **(1)**
4515 Poplar Ave.
Memphis, TN 38117
Tel.: 901-682-5653
Fax: 901-767-8711
Chemical & Allied Products
S.I.C.: 5169
W.B. Bearden *(V.P.-Memphis)*

Harwick Chemical Corp. **(1)**
1309 West 15th St., Ste. 302
Plano, TX 75075
Tel.: 214-422-0520
Fax: 214-424-4785
Chemicals & Allied Products
S.I.C.: 5169
R.G. Carter *(V.P.-Dallas)*
R.G. Carter *(V.P.-Dallas)*

Subsidiaries:

CMS Chemical Company **(1)**
P. O. Box 1008, 2151 Bartlett Rd.
Wynne, AR 72396
Tel.: 501-238-7931
Export
Chemicals & Allied Products
S.I.C.: 5169
Tom Breckenridge *(V.P. & Gen. Mgr.)*

Republic Chemical Company **(1)**
60 So. Seiberling St.
Akron, OH 44305
Tel.: 216-798-9300
Fax: 216-798-0214
Export
Chemical & Allied Products
S.I.C.: 5169
T.K. Goldsby *(V.P.-Mfg.)*

THE HARWOOD COMPANIES, INC.
1350 Ave. of the Americas
New York, NY 10019
Tel.: 212-397-6500
Fax: 212-397-6504
Sales Range: $20-39 Million
Emp.: 1,400
Fiscal Year-end: 12/31/91
Mfr. of Activewear, Robes, & Pajamas for Men & Children
S.I.C.: 2321; 2322; 2329; 2384
Michael Rothbaum *(Pres. & Chief Exec. Officer)*
Noel Dorf *(V.P.-Sls & Mktg.)*
Wendell Watkins *(V.P.-Mfg.)*
Donald Papiernick *(Treas. & Controller)*
Paul F. Myers *(Corp. Mgr.-Cash)*
Fran Schaller *(Mgr.-Office)*

No. of Mfg. Plants/Facilities: 2

The Harwood Companies, Inc.—(Continued)

Computer Systems/Hardware:
IBM

Outside Service Firm(s):

Ernst & Young*(Auditors)*
212 Locust St.
Harrisburg, PA 17101

Gelberg & Abrams*(Legal Firm)*
711 Third Ave.
New York, NY 10017

HARZA ENGINEERING CO.
Sears Tower, 233 S. Wacker Dr.
Chicago, IL 60606-6392
Tel.: 312-831-3000 **DE**
Telex: 25-3540
Cable: HARZENG CHICAGO
Fax: 312-831-3999
Year Founded: 1920
Approx.Sls.: $90,000,000
Emp.: 850
Fiscal Year-end: 12/31/90
Consulting Services in: Engineering, Agriculture, Ecology, Forestry, Recreation Planning, Hydrology Hydraulics, Geology and Hydrogeology
S.I.C.: 8711; 8712
Employee Matching Gifts Program: Matching Gifts of $10 to $100 by Regular, Full-Time Employees per Calendar Year to Educational Institutions
John A. Scoville *(Chm. Bd.)*
Walter J. Bogdovitz *(Pres.)*
Russell Roddy Jr. *(Sr. V.P.)*
Jon A. Veltrop *(Sr. V.P.)*
Roman Wengler *(Sr. V.P.)*
Lawrence S. Boval *(V.P.-Head Bus. Devel.)*
Vincent J. Zipparro *(V.P. & Chief Engineer)*
Leonard E. Zak *(V.P. & Gen. Counsel)*
Ernest R. Hoelterhoff *(Treas. & Chief Fin. Officer)*
Julieann Vukovich *(Mgr.-Human Resources)*
Daniel Poro *(Sec. Ret. Plan. Comm.)*

No. of U.S. Offices: 6
No. of Foreign Offices: 30

Computer Systems/Hardware:
Ardent Titan Supercomputer, Intergraph Unix CADD System, HP Laser Jet 2000 Printers, HP ScanJet Plus Scanner & IBM PCs

Outside Service Firm(s):

Arthur Andersen & Co.*(Auditors)*
33 W. Monroe St.
Chicago, IL 60603-4067
Tel.: 312-580-0033
Fax: 312-507-6748

Provident Life & Accident Insurance Co.*(Commercial Insurance Carrier)*
P.O. Box 12015
Chattanooga, TN 37401
Tel.: 615-755-7088

Provident Life & Accident Insurance Co.*(Group Insurer)*
P.O. Box 12015
Chattanooga, TN 37401
Tel.: 615-755-7088

McDermott, Will & Emery*(Legal Firm)*
111 W. Monroe
Chicago, IL 60603
Tel.: 312-372-2000

Continental Bank N. A.*(Major Banking Relationship)*
231 S. LaSalle St.
Chicago, IL 60697
Tel.: 312-828-2345
Tel.: 800-426-5754
Telex: 312-828-1783

The Northern Trust Co.*(Major Banking Relationship)*
50 S. LaSalle St.
Chicago, IL 60675
Tel.: 312-630-6000
Fax: 312-630-6516

American National Bank & Trust Company of Chicago*(Pension Manager)*
33 N. LaSalle St.
Chicago, IL 60602
Tel.: 312-661-5000
Fax: 312-661-6417

Dimensional Fund Advisors, Inc.*(Pension Manager)*
Chicago, IL

Harris Associates, L.P.*(Pension Manager)*
Two North LaSalle St.
Chicago, IL 60606-3790
Tel.: 312-621-0600

The Northern Trust Co.*(Pension Manager)*
50 S. LaSalle St.
Chicago, IL 60675
Tel.: 312-630-6000
Fax: 312-630-6516

Subsidiaries:

Harza Environmental Services, Inc. **(1)**
233 S. Wacker Dr.
Chicago, IL 60606-6392
Tel.: 312-831-3800 (100%)
Telex: 25-3540
Fax: 312-831-3999
Emp.: 38
Environmental Engineering, Waste Management, Hazardous Waste Management, Public Works
S.I.C.: 4953
Jitendra R. Ghia *(Pres.)*
James J. Hagan *(Dir.-Mktg.)*

Harza Northwest, Inc. **(1)**
P.O. Box C-96900
Bellevue, WA 98004
Tel.: 206-882-2455
Fax: 206-883-7555
Environmental Engineering
S.I.C.: 8712; 8711
James T. Passage *(Pres.)*

Stetson-Harza **(1)**
181 Genesee St.
Utica, NY 13501-2168
Tel.: 315-797-5800
Fax: 315-797-8143
Emp.: 240
S.I.C.: 8711; 8712
James H. Gwise *(Pres.)*

HASELOW & ASSOCIATES, INC.
5885 Landerbrook Dr.
Cleveland, OH 44124
Tel.: 216-446-1946
Fax: 216-446-9929
Year Founded: 1979
Approx.Billings: $10,600,000
Emp.: 21
Business-to-Business Advertising
John H. Haselow *(Pres.)*
Billie Tomoff *(V.P., Agency Opers. & Treas.)*
Scott Collins *(V.P., Pub. Rels.)*
Dennis Grantham *(Program Mgr.)*

HASKEL, INC.
100 E. Graham Pl.
Burbank, CA 91502
Tel.: 818-843-4000 **CA**
Fax: 818-841-4291
Sales Range: $20-39 Million
Emp.: 185
Export
Mfr. Air Driven Liquid Pumps, Air Amplifiers & Gas Boosters for the Production, Control & Storage of Extreme Hydraulic & Gas Pressures
S.I.C.: 3561
Fred J. Broderick *(Pres. & Chief Oper. Officer)*
Derrick Aldred *(Sr. V.P.-Standard Prods. Devel.)*
W.W. Bixby, Jr. *(Sr. V.P.-Mktg.)*
G. Freeman *(Sr. V.P.-Mfg.)*
J. Kelly *(Sr. V.P.-Special Prods. Devel.)*
H. Smith *(Sr. V.P.-Sls.)*
Genie Fuller *(Controller)*

No. of Mfg. Plants/Facilities: 2
No. of Foreign Offices: 1

Computer Systems/Hardware:
Hewlett-Packard 3000

Outside Service Firm(s):

Deloitte & Touche*(Auditors)*
21550 Oxnard St., Ste. 800
Woodland Hills, CA 91367-7100
Tel.: 818-593-4800
Fax: 818-347-4278

Goodson & Wachtel*(Legal Firm)*
Los Angeles, CA

Community Bank*(Major Banking Relationship)*
Burbank, CA

Non-U.S. Holding:

Haskel Energy Systems Ltd. **(1)**
North Hylton Rd.
Sunderland, Tyne & Wear SR53JD, United Kingdom
Tel.: 44 78 349 1212
Fax: 549 09 11
Mfrs. High Pressure Pumps, Gas Boosters & Related Access.
S.I.C.: 3561
R.M. Greaves *(Mng. Dir.)*

JOHN HASSALL, INC.
P.O. Box 698, Cantiague Rock Rd.
Westbury, NY 11590
Tel.: 516-334-6200
Fax: 516-222-1911
Year Founded: 1850
Approx.Sls.: $15,000,000
Emp.: 150
Fiscal Year-end: 12/31/90
Special Cold Forged Products & Fasteners
S.I.C.: 3429
Theodore B. Smith, Jr. *(Pres.)*
Walter J. Morley *(V.P.-Fin.)*
Alexander J. Smith *(V.P.)*
Theodore B. Smith, III *(Sec.)*
David Lax *(Mgr.-Natl. Sls.)*
Judith Rohde *(Mgr.-Adv.)*
Larry Dittmar *(Pur. Agent)*

Outside Service Firm(s):

KPMG Peat Marwick*(Auditors)*
345 Park Ave.
New York, NY 10154
Tel.: 212-758-9700
Fax: 212-872-3308

National Westminster Bank plc*(Major Banking Relationship)*
175 Water St.
New York, NY 10038-4924
Tel.: 212-602-3364

THE HASSINGER COMPANIES
300 Park Blvd., Ste. 515
Itasca, IL 60143
Tel.: 708-250-7878
Fax: 708-250-7465
Year Founded: 1949
Approx.Sls.: $80,000,000
Emp.: 210
Fiscal Year-end: 12/31/91
Land Development & Residential Construction
S.I.C.: 1522; 6552
Norman M. Hassinger, Jr. *(Chm. Bd., Pres., Chief Exec. & Chief Oper. Officer)*
William M. Laytin *(Sr. V.P. & Legal Counsel)*
Barbara Kininmoth *(V.P.-Corp. Communications)*
Richard Strahs *(Dir.-Data Processing)*

Principal(s):
Norman M. Hassinger, Jr.

Computer Systems/Hardware:
Sperry-Univac

Outside Service Firm(s):

Friedman, Eisenstein, Raemer & Schwartz*(Auditors)*
Chicago, IL

Commercial Union Insurance Co.*(Commercial Insurance Carrier)*
Oak Brook, IL

Great-West Life Assurance Co.*(Group Insurer)*
Columbus, OH

Gould & Ratner*(Legal Firm)*
222 N. LaSalle St.
Chicago, IL 60601
Tel.: 312-236-3003

LaSalle National Bank*(Major Banking Relationship)*
120 S. LaSalle St.
Chicago, IL 60603
Tel.: 312-781-8000

Subsidiaries:

Hoffman Homes, Inc. **(1)**
300 Park Blvd., Ste. 515
Itasca, IL 60143
Tel.: 708-250-7878
S.I.C.: 1522
William E. Griffin *(V.P.)*
Barbara Kininmonth *(V.P.-Mktg.)*

Illinois Home Mortgage Corp. **(1)**
300 Park Blvd.
Itasca, IL 60143
Tel.: 708-250-7878
S.I.C.: 6162
Kimberly Meek *(Gen. Mgr.)*

Portfolio Homes **(1)**
300 Park Blvd.
Itasca, IL 60143
Tel.: 708-250-7878
S.I.C.: 1522
John Dethmer *(V.P.)*

HASSLOCHER ENTERPRISES, INC., D/B/A FRONTIER ENTERPRISES
8520 Crownhill Blvd.
San Antonio, TX 78209
Tel.: 210-828-1493
Fax: 210-822-8606
Approx.Sls.: $35,000,000
Emp.: 1,100
Restaurant Operations
S.I.C.: 5812
Germano Hasslocher *(Pres.)*
Veva B. Hasslocher *(V.P.)*
Neal D. Miller *(V.P., Treas. & Sec.)*

Outside Service Firm(s):

Findling, Milan & Pyle*(Auditors)*
San Antonio, TX

NationsBank Texas*(Major Banking Relationship)*
San Antonio, TX

HASTINGS CO-OP CREAMERY COMPANY
1701 Vermillion St.
Hastings, MN 55033
Mailing Address:
P.O. Box 217
Hastings, MN 55033
Tel.: 612-437-9414
Fax: 612-437-3547
Approx.Sls.: $24,000,000
Emp.: 32
Process Fluid Milk & Retail Dairy Products
S.I.C.: 2026; 5451
Herb Peine *(Pres.)*
Kenneth Brown *(V.P.)*
John T. Cook *(Gen. Mgr.)*
Robert Winter *(Sec. & Treas.)*

Outside Service Firm(s):

Sands, Lee & Anderson*(Auditors)*
St. Paul, MN

Norwest Bank Minnesota, N.A.*(Major Banking Relationship)*
Hastings, MN

HATFIELD QUALITY MEATS, INC.
2700 Funks Rd.
Hatfield, PA 19440-2834
Tel.: 215-368-2500 **PA**
Fax: 215-362-1750
Year Founded: 1895
Approx.Sls.: $287,000,000
Emp.: 1,050
Fiscal Year-end: 4/30/91
Meat Packing
S.I.C.: 2011
Clair W. Clemens *(Pres. & Chief Exec. Officer)*
Kenneth Jones *(Exec. V.P., Chief Fin. Officer, Sec. & Treas.)*
Philip A. Clemens *(V.P.-Human Resources)*
David W. Budnick *(Controller)*
David C. Woelkers *(Dir.-Pur.)*

No. of Mfg. Plants/Facilities: 1
No. of U.S. Offices: 1

Outside Service Firm(s):

Price Waterhouse*(Auditors)*
30 S. 17th St.
Philadelphia, PA 19103
Tel.: 215-665-9500

Pennsylvania Blue Shield*(Group Insurer)*
Camp Hill, PA

Continental Bank, N.A.*(Investment Banker)*
Norristown, PA

Widmann, Siff & Co.*(Investment Banker)*
Narbeth, PA

Pearlstine/Salkin, Associates*(Legal Firm)*
Lansdale, PA

Continental Bank, N.A.*(Major Banking Relationship)*
Norristown, PA

HAUCK MFG. CO.
100 N. Harris St.
Cleona, PA 17042
Mailing Address:
P. O. Box 90
Lebanon, PA 17042
Tel.: 717-272-3051
Fax: 717-273-9882
Approx.Sls.: $15,000,000
Emp.: 142
Fiscal Year-end: 12/30/90
Export
Hauck Industrial Oil & Gas Burners & Equipment, Combustion Control Panels & Systems
S.I.C.: 3433; 3823; 3567
J.F. Kyne *(Pres.)*
N. Dieffenbach *(Exec. V.P.)*
Gene Winters *(Mgr.-Adv. Promo.)*
Michael Shay *(Mgr.-Field Sls.)*

Computer Systems/Hardware:
IBM System 38

HAUENSTEIN & BURMEISTER, INC.
2629 30th Ave., S.
Minneapolis, MN 55406
Tel.: 612-721-5031 **MN**
Fax: 612-728-2792
Emp.: 300
Mfr. of Elevators; Wholesale Distributor of Furniture & Electronic Parts Demountable Partitions & Acoustical & Electrical Work Installation
S.I.C.: 3534; 5021; 5065; 1742; 1731; 1799
Warren Hesselroth *(Pres.)*
G.F. McCulloch *(Exec. V.P.)*
Martin Beckman *(V.P. & Treas.)*
John Hammang *(V.P.)*

Outside Service Firm(s):

Deloitte & Touche*(Auditors)*
900 Pillsbury Ctr.
Minneapolis, MN 55402
Tel.: 612-332-2301
Fax: 612-375-5418

Gray, Plant, Mooty, Mooty & Bennett*(Legal Firm)*
3400 City Center, 33 So. 6th St.
Minneapolis, MN 55402
Tel.: 612-343-2800
Fax: 612-830-0270

Marquette Bank*(Major Banking Relationship)*
777 Marquette Ave.
Minneapolis, MN 55402
Tel.: 612-370-2182

THE HAUGHEY GROUP, INC.
313 Congress St.
Boston, MA 02210
Tel.: 617-439-0090
Fax: 617-439-4178
Year Founded: 1966
Approx.Billings: $18,000,000
Emp.: 35
Recruitment Advertising
Donald M. Shanbar *(Partner)*
Rhonda S. Hoffman *(Partner)*
Marlene R. Nussbaum *(Partner)*

HAVATAMPA INCORPORATED
3901 Riga Blvd.
Tampa, FL 33619
Mailing Address:
P.O. Box 1261,
Tampa, FL 33601
Tel.: 813-621-3535
Tel.: 800-237-2043 **FL**
Fax: 813-623-3923
Approx.Sls.: $40,000,000
Emp.: 200
Fiscal Year-end: 12/31/90
Manufactures Cigars
S.I.C.: 2121
Doyle E. Carlton *(Chm. Bd.)*
Thomas D. Arthur *(Pres.)*
W. Tommy Morgan III *(Exec. V.P.-Adv., Mktg. & Sls.)*
Robert Ennis *(Sr. V.P.-Mfg.)*
Jeff E. Freeman *(Sr. V.P.-Fin., Sec. & Treas.)*

No. of Mfg. Plants/Facilities: 3

Computer Systems/Hardware:
NCR Series 9800

Outside Service Firm(s):

Rex Meighen, CPA*(Auditors)*
Tampa, FL

First Florida Bank*(Major Banking Relationship)*
P.O. Box 31265,
Tampa, FL 33631-3265
Tel.: 813-224-1475

Subsidiaries:

Diamond Products Company **(1)**
3901 Riga Blvd.
Tampa, FL 33619
Tel.: 813-621-3535
Mfr. Health & Beauty Aids
S.I.C.: 2844

H.A.T. Holding Company **(1)**
3901 Riga Blvd.
Tampa, FL 33619
Tel.: 813-621-3535
Fax: 813-623-3923
Sales Range: $40-59 Million
Emp.: 400
Export
Computer Systems/Hardware:
NCR Series 85
Holding Company; Tobacco Products
S.I.C.: 6719
Doyle E. Carlton *(Chm. Bd.)*
Thomas D. Arthur *(Pres.)*
W. Tommy Morgan III *(Exec. V.P.-Adv., Mktg. & Sls.)*
Robert Ennis *(Sr. V.P.-Mfg.)*
Jeff E. Freeman *(Sr. V.P.-Fin., Sec. & Treas.)*

Phillies Cigar Company **(1)**
3901 Riga Blvd.
Tampa, FL 33619
Tel.: 813-621-3535
Export
Cigars
S.I.C.: 3999

HAVENS STEEL CO.
7219 E. 17th St.
Kansas City, MO 64126
Tel.: 816-231-5724
Fax: 816-241-0607
Year Founded: 1919
Approx.Sls.: $60,861,000
Emp.: 289
Structural Steel Fabrication & Erection
S.I.C.: 1791; 3441; 3443
Fred R. Havens *(Chm. Bd.)*
Robert D. Freeland *(Pres.)*
K.P. McCullough *(V.P.-Sls.)*
W.R. Richey *(V.P.-Engrng.)*
John Rogers *(V.P.-Fin.)*
Al Gebauer *(Mgr.-Pur.)*

Outside Service Firm(s):

KPMG Peat Marwick*(Auditors)*
1000 Walnut St.
Kansas City, MO 64106

Miller & Bash*(Legal Firm)*
Kansas City, MO

Commerce Bank of Kansas City*(Major Banking Relationship)*
10th & Walnut
Kansas City, MO 64141
Tel.: 816-234-2000
Fax: 816-234-2548

HAVILAND ENTERPRISES
421 Ann St., N.W.
Grand Rapids, MI 49504
Tel.: 616-361-6691
Fax: 616-361-9772
Year Founded: 1934
Approx.Sls.: $30,000,000
Emp.: 100
Fiscal Year-end: 11/30/91
Export
Mfr. & Distribution of Chemical Products for Home & Industry, ND-68, Ano Kleen, Havablack, Havabond, Havasol, Havastrip, Durachior
S.I.C.: 2812; 2834; 2841; 2842; 2899; 3821; 3826; 5084; 5085; 5169
M.M. Haviland *(Chm. Bd.)*
Robert McCoy *(Vice Chm.)*
E. Bernard Haviland *(Pres.-Haviland Products)*
R. Michael Haviland *(Pres.-Haviland Engrng.)*
H. Richard Garner *(Chief Exec. Officer)*
Robert Mastbergen *(V.P.)*
Carole Drudy *(Mgr.-Personnel)*
Eric Earl *(Mgr.-Sls. & Mkt. Research)*
Marie Haviland *(Mgr.-Adv.)*
Bruce Wiersma *(Mgr.-Data Processing)*
Doug Siegert *(Pur. Agent)*

Computer Systems/Hardware:
Unisys

Division:

Haviland-Kalamazoo **(1)**
2722 N. Burdick
Kalamazoo, MI 49007
Tel.: 616-342-9848
Fax: 616-342-0468
Manufacture & Distribute Specialty Chemicals
S.I.C.: 2899; 5169

HAVILAND/WILBUR-ELLIS AGRICULTURAL
4160 Ten Mile N. W.
Sparta, MI 49345
Tel.: 616-887-8333
Tel.: 800-677-6324
Tel.: 319-752-6324
Fax: 616-887-8644
Year Founded: 1950
Approx.Sls.: $15,000,000
Emp.: 40
Fiscal Year-end: 12/31/90
Agricultural Chemical Products
S.I.C.: 5191
K. Boyer *(Pres.)*
Ron Farrel *(V.P.)*
Robert Dow *(Controller)*
Robert Moellenbick *(Gen. Mgr.)*
Tom Mollan *(Pur.)*

GLENN O. HAWBAKER, INC.
325 W. Aaron Dr.
State College, PA 16803
Mailing Address:
P.O. Box 135
State College, PA 16804
Tel.: 814-237-1444
Fax: 814-237-5348
Assets: $3,200,000
Net Worth: $3,200,000
Sales Range: $20-39 Million
Emp.: 350
Crushed Stone & Paving Material
S.I.C.: 2951; 3295
Corporate Giving Program: Company Gives to the United Way & to Pennsylvania State University
Daniel P. Hawbaker *(Pres.)*
Alan Hawbaker *(Sec. & Treas.)*
Carmen S. Ametrano *(Controller)*

No. of Mfg. Plants/Facilities: 4
No. of U.S. Offices: 2

Computer Systems/Hardware:
Altos 2000

Outside Service Firm(s):

Stewart Greer & Company*(Auditors)*
Pittsburgh, PA

U.S.F. & G.*(Commercial Insurance Carrier)*
Stat College, PA

Mid-State Bank & Trust Co.*(Major Banking Relationship)*
State College, PA

Subsidiary:

Centre Lime & Stone Co., Inc. **(1)**
P.O. Box 130
Pleasant Gap, PA 16823
Tel.: 814-359-2773
Emp.: 110
Process Lime
S.I.C.: 2869
Terry J. Edwards *(Pres.)*

GERTRUDE HAWK CHOCOLATES, INC.
9 Keystone Industrial Park
Troop, PA 18512-1544
Tel.: 717-693-3158
Fax: 717-342-0266
Approx.Sls.: $13,000,000
Emp.: 225
Candy & Confectionery Products
S.I.C.: 2064
Elmer R. Hawk *(Pres.)*
David W. Hawk *(V.P.-Mfg.)*
Louise Hawk *(Sec. & Treas.)*

Gertrude Hawk Chocolates, Inc.—(Continued)

Allan Cornell *(Mgr.-Sls.)*
Janice Liddie *(Mgr.-Adv.)*
Lynn McDonald *(Mgr.-Personnel)*
Herbert Black *(Chief Engr.)*

Outside Service Firm(s):

Frank Merkel*(Auditors)*
Scranton, PA

Oliver, Price & Rhodes*(Legal Firm)*
Scranton, PA

First Eastern Bank N.A.*(Major Banking Relationship)*
Scranton, PA

HAWKEYE STEEL PRODUCTS, INC.
P.O. Box 2000,
Houghton, IA 52631
Tel.: 319-469-4141 **DE**
Telex: 379-1128 HAWKS
Fax: 319-469-4402
Year Founded: 1920
Approx.Sls.: $15,000,000
Emp.: 150
Import Export
Mfr. of Equipment & Systems for Livestock, Poultry & Grain Storage
S.I.C.: 3523
Thomas W. Wenstrand *(Co-Pres. & Sec.)*
Marvin Bricker *(Co-Pres. & Treas.)*
Bill Kullbom *(V.P.-Sls.)*
Principal(s):
Thomas W. Wenstrand
Marvin Bricker

No. of Mfg. Plants/Facilities: 1
No. of U.S. Offices: 5

Computer Systems/Hardware:
IBM System 38

Outside Service Firm(s):

Firstar Bank Cedar Rapids, N.A.*(Major Banking Relationship)*
222 Second Ave. S.E.
Cedar Rapids, IA 52406
Tel.: 319-398-4224

Subsidiary:

Brower Equipment **(1)**
Hwy. 16 West
Houghton, IA 52631
Tel.: 319-469-4141
Telex: 379-1128 HAWKS
Fax: 319-469-4402
Approx.Sls.: $3,000,000
Emp.: 30
Fiscal Year-end: 12/31/90
S.I.C.: 3523
Thomas W. Wenstrand *(Pres.)*
Santiago Sanchez *(Dir.-Adv.)*

HAWKINS MARKETS, INC.
2312 Akron Rd.
Wooster, OH 44691
Tel.: 216-264-8729 **OH**
Approx.Sls.: $79,000,000
Emp.: 570
Supermarket Chain
S.I.C.: 5411
O.E. Hawkins *(Pres.)*
Betty Hawkins *(V.P. & Sec.)*
Gregg Webb *(Treas.)*
Ford G. Ross *(Gen. Counsel)*
Principal(s):
O.E. Hawkins
Betty J. Hawkins

Outside Service Firm(s):

Frank, Seinger & Chaney, Inc.*(Auditors)*
Wooster, OH

Wayne County National Bank*(Major Banking Relationship)*
Wooster, OH

HAWLEY MARTIN PARTNERS, INC.
1703 N. Parham Rd.
Richmond, VA 23229-4606
Tel.: 804-285-4500
Fax: 804-288-4905
Year Founded: 1988
Approx.Billings: $25,000,000
Emp.: 41
David N. Martin *(Chm. Bd. & Dir.-Creative Plans)*
Stephen H. Martin *(Vice Chm. & Chief Exec. Officer)*
J.R. Hipple *(Pres.-Hawley Martin/ Hipple Pub. Rel.)*
Matt Smith *(Pres.-Creative Direct)*
Catherine R. Bendall *(Dir.-Strategic Plans)*

Computer Systems/Hardware:
IBM, Macintosh

HAWORTH GROUP INC.

HAWORTH GROUP INC.
6117 Blue Circle Dr.
Minnetonka, MN 55343
Tel.: 612-935-4454
Year Founded: 1970
Approx.Billings: $92,000,000
Emp.: 42
C. Dale Haworth *(Chm.)*
Claude Stevens *(Pres. & Chief Exec. Officer)*
Brenda Swanson *(Sr. V.P., Dir. Opers.)*
Glenn Smith *(Treasurer, Chief Fin. Officer)*
Dan Douville *(Plng. Supvr.)*
Eric Peterson *(Res. Mgr.)*

HAWORTH, INC.
One Haworth Center
Holland, MI 49423
Tel.: 616-393-3000
Tel.: 800-426-8562
Fax: 616-393-1570
Year Founded: 1948
Approx.Sls.: $600,000,000
Emp.: 4,500
Fiscal Year-end: 12/31/92
Import Export
Mfr. Office Furniture & Office Units
S.I.C.: 2521; 2522
G.W. Haworth *(Chm. Bd.)*
Richard G. Haworth *(Pres. & Chief Exec. Officer)*
Gerald B. Johanneson *(Chief Oper. Officer & Exec. V.P.)*
John Amell *(V.P.-Portfolio Opers.)*
John C. Berrett *(V.P.-Mktg.)*
Richard A. Berrett *(V.P.-Mfg. & Freestanding Opers.)*
Richard Codel *(V.P.-Intl.)*
Al Elders *(V.P.-Quality)*
Randall Evans *(V.P.-Human Resources)*
James J. Lehmann *(V.P.-Fin.)*
Dan Printz *(V.P.-Sls.)*
Craig Speck *(V.P.-Prod. Mktg. & Systems Opers.)*
Principal(s):
G.W. Haworth
Richard G. Haworth

No. of Mfg. Plants/Facilities: 11
No. of U.S. Offices: 27
No. of Foreign Offices: 9

Computer Systems/Hardware:
IBM Mainframe; IBM PC; Apple Macintosh

Outside Service Firm(s):

BDO Seidman*(Auditors)*
99 Monroe Ave. NW, Ste. 800
Grand Rapids, MI 49503
Tel.: 616-774-7000
Fax: 616-451-2096

Warner, Norcross & Judd*(Legal Firm)*
One Vandenberg Center
Grand Rapids, MI 49502
Tel.: 616-459-6121

First National Bank of Chicago*(Major Banking Relationship)*
One First National Plaza
Chicago, IL 60670
Tel.: 312-732-9781
Tel.: 312-732-4050
Fax: 312-732-4840
Fax: 312-732-3055

Subsidiaries:

Lunstead, A Haworth Portfolio Co. **(1)**
8655 S. 208th St.
Kent, WA 98031
Tel.: 206-872-8835
Fax: 206-395-3764
Export
Mfr. of Wood Office Furniture
S.I.C.: 2521
Robert Riley *(Gen. Mgr.)*

Mueller, A Haworth Portfolio Co. **(1)**
514 Fifth St., N.W.
Grand Rapids, MI 49504
Tel.: 616-451-2738
Approx.Sls.: $13,000,000
Emp.: 195
Mfr. of Contract Office Furniture, Desks, Credenzas, Seating & Tables
S.I.C.: 2521; 2522
Phil Vinnedge *(Gen. Mgr.)*

Myrtle, A Haworth Portfolio Co. **(1)**
801 Millis St.
High Point, NC 27261
Tel.: 919-885-4021
Tel.: 800-448-7177
Fax: 919-887-5233
Approx.Sls.: $25,000,000
Emp.: 265
Mfr. of Wood Office Furniture, Office & Lounge Seating
S.I.C.: 2521
Randy Harris *(Gen. Mgr.)*

Non-U.S. Holdings:

Comforto Group **(1)**
Bergstr. 1 4730
Ahlen, Germany
Tel.: 23 82 78 10 (100%)
Telex: 8 20 731
Approx.Sls.: $60,000,000
Emp.: 500
Mfr. of Office Seating
S.I.C.: 2522
Manfred von Prondzinski *(Chief Oper. Officer)*

Cortal-Seldex **(1)**
Mobiliario De Escritorio, SA 3751 Agueda,
Apartado 70, 3751 Aq,
Codex, Portugal
Tel.: 351-34-64-4102
Mfr. Wood & Metal Furniture

Haworth Ltd. **(1)**
33 Yonge Street
Toronto, ON M5E 1G4, Canada
Tel.: 416-363-0702 (100%)
Distribution & Sales of Office Systems
S.I.C.: 5021

Haworth U.K. Ltd. **(1)**
39 Charlton St.
London, NW1 1JE, United Kingdom
Tel.: 071-387-3164
Fax: 071-387-0525
Distribution & Sales of Office Systems
S.I.C.: 5021

Kinetics, Inc. **(1)**
110 Carrier Dr.
Rexdale, ON M9W 5R1, Canada
Tel.: 416-675-4300
Mfr. of Wood & Metal Furniture
S.I.C.: 2521; 2522
J.A. Amell *(Pres.)*

Mobilier International **(1)**
162 Blvd. Voltarre
Paris, France 75011
Tel.: 331-43-71-1211
Mfr. Wood & Metal Furniture

H.W. Schmidt GmbH **(1)**
Ahlen, Germany
Tel.: 02 382 781-0
Emp.: 500
Metal Office Furniture
S.I.C.: 2522

HAWS DRINKING FAUCET CO.
1435 Fourth St.
Berkeley, CA 94710
Mailing Address:
P.O. Box 1999
Berkeley, CA 94701
Tel.: 510-525-5801
Fax: 510-528-2812
Year Founded: 1909
Sales Range: $20-39 Million
Emp.: 100
Import Export
Drinking Fountains, Faucets, Eyewash & Eye Face Fountains, Electric Water Coolers, Portable Drinking Fountains, Emergency Drench Showers, Pantry Faucets & Dental Fountains
S.I.C.: 3431; 3432; 3494; 3843
Terry R. Haws *(Pres.)*
Michael H. Traynor *(Exec. V.P.)*
Patrick T. Kelly *(V.P.-Sls. & Mktg.)*
Walter Neuweiler *(V.P.-Fin.)*
Mat Stein *(Dir.-Engrng.)*
John Bronaugh *(Mgr.-Sls.)*
Bob Bowles *(Mgr.-Pur.)*

No. of Mfg. Plants/Facilities: 3
No. of U.S. Offices: 2
No. of Foreign Offices: 1

Computer Systems/Hardware:
NCR

Outside Service Firm(s):

Price Waterhouse*(Auditors)*
Orlando, FL

Crosby, Heafey, Roach & May*(Legal Firm)*
1939 Harrison
Oakland, CA 94612
Tel.: 510-834-4820

Bank of America NT&SA*(Major Banking Relationship)*
Oakland, CA

HAWTHORNE ADV., INC.

Colonial Penn Plaza, 19th & Market Sts.
Philadelphia, PA 19181
Tel.: 215-988-8000
Fax: 215-988-8163
Year Founded: 1958
Approx.Billings: $70,000,000
Emp.: 65
Insurance, Financial Direct Response Adv.
Bruce A. Finlayson *(V.P.-Mktg.)*
Kathleen Quinter *(Mgr.-Pur.)*

Computer Systems/Hardware:
IBM, NCR, Macintosh

HAWTHORNE COMMUNICATIONS, INC.
300 North 16th St.
Fairfield, IA 52556
Tel.: 515-472-3800
Year Founded: 1986$19,000,000
Emp.: 60
Direct Response & TV Commercials
Timothy R. Hawthorne *(Chm. Bd. & Pres.)*
Robert Moore *(Exec. V.P.)*
Gene Silverman *(V.P., Mktg.)*

HAWTHORNE CORP.
6543 Fain St.
Charleston, SC 29411
Mailing Address:
P.O. Box 61,000
Charleston, SC 29419
Tel.: 803-797-8484 **SC**
Fax: 803-797-5258
Year Founded: 1932
Approx.Sls.: $26,000,000
Emp.: 450
Gen. Aviation & Airline Servicing, Aircraft Sls., Indus. Distr. & Mfg., Govt. Technical Services Contracting; Fin. Services; Real Estate
S.I.C.: 4581; 5088; 6153
Vernon B. Strickland *(Chm. Bd.)*
T. Dean Harton *(Pres.)*
Bill Thrift *(V.P.)*
Cynthia A. Harton *(Sec.)*

No. of U.S. Offices: 19

Computer Systems/Hardware:
Wang

Outside Service Firm(s):

Finch, Hamilton, Oxner & Co.*(Auditors)*
Columbia, SC

R. N. Crawford, Co.*(Commercial Insurance Carrier)*
Columbia, NJ

Marsh & McLennan*(Commercial Insurance Carrier)*
1166 Avenue of the Americas
New York, NY 10036
Tel.: 212-345-6000
Fax: 212-345-3285

Marsh & McLennan*(Commercial Insurance Carrier)*
Columbia, SC

USAIG*(Group Insurer)*
New York, NY

Carlyle Group*(Investment Banker)*
Washington, DC

Vinson & Elkins*(Legal Firm)*
First City Natl. Bank Bldg.
Houston, TX 77001
Tel.: 713-651-2222

Citizens & Southern National Bank*(Major Banking Relationship)*
Charleston, SC

Subsidiaries:

Aircraft Insurance Agency **(1)**
6543 Fain St.
Charleston, SC 29411
Tel.: 803-797-8484
Aviation Insurance
S.I.C.: 6411
Bill Thrift *(V.P.)*

Atlantic National Corporation **(1)**
6543 Fain St.
Charleston, SC 29411
Tel.: 803-797-8484
Finance & Leasing
S.I.C.: 7359
Bill Thrift *(V.P.)*

Hawthorne Airport Services, Inc. **(1)**
6543 Fain St.
Charleston, SC 29411
Tel.: 803-797-8484
Airline Servicing
S.I.C.: 4581
Bill Thrift *(V.P.)*

Hawthorne Aviation **(1)**
6543 Fain St.
Charleston, SC 29411
Tel.: 803-797-8484
General Aviation
S.I.C.: 4581
Bill Thrift *(V.P.)*

Hawthorne Properties, Inc. **(1)**
6543 Fain St.
Charleston, SC 29411
Tel.: 803-797-8484
Real Estate
S.I.C.: 6552
Bill Thrift *(V.P.)*

Hawthorne Services, Inc. **(1)**
6543 Fain St.
Charleston, SC 29411
Tel.: 803-797-8484
Government Technical Service Contracting
S.I.C.: 4581
Bill Thrift *(V.P.)*

HAWTHORNE LIFT SYSTEMS
1044 W. Washington Ave.
Escondido, CA 92025
Mailing Address:
P.O. Box 121550
San Digeo, CA 92112
Tel.: 619-480-0277
Tel.: 800-289-8420 **CA**
Fax: 619-480-1184
Year Founded: 1963
Sales Range: $10-19 Million
Emp.: 60
Fiscal Year-end: 12/31/91
Import Export
Service For Fork Lifts
S.I.C.: 3531; 5084
Brian Hawthorne *(Pres. & Chief Exec. Officer)*
Gary Stark *(V.P.-Prod. Support)*

HAWTHORNE MACHINERY COMPANY
P.O. Box 708
San Diego, CA 92112
Tel.: 619-674-7000 **CA**
Fax: 619-674-7170
Year Founded: 1956
Assets: $65,000,000
Liabilities: $43,000,000
Net Worth: $22,000,000
Sales Range: $100-499 Million
Emp.: 420
Wholesale & Service Of Heavy Equipment
S.I.C.: 5084
James T. Hawthorne *(Pres.)*
Philip T. Nerhood *(Exec. V.P.)*
Tee K. Ness *(V.P.)*
Richard J. Moss *(Mgr.-Fin. & Treas.)*

Outside Service Firm(s):

KPMG Peat Marwick*(Auditors)*
750 B St.
San Diego, CA 92105
Tel.: 619-233-8000

Bank of America NT&SA*(Major Banking Relationship)*
San Diego, CA

Subsidiary:

Hawthorne Power Systems **(1)**
P.O. Box 708,
San Diego, CA 92112
Tel.: 619-674-7000
Bob Price *(Mgr.-Division)*

HAYES
HARWOOD
■ INTEGRATED MARKETING COMMUNICATIONS ■

HAYES/HARWOOD
234 Maple St., P.O. Box 179
Stowe, VT 05672
Tel.: 802-253-7141
Fax: 802-253-7140
Year Founded: 1980
Approx.Billings: $13,500,000
Emp.: 19
Packaged Goods, Travel & Tourism, Cooking Equipment & Health Insurance
Matthew Hayes *(Pres., Chief Exec. Officer & Treas.)*
Brian Harwood *(Exec. V.P. & Sec.)*
Charmane Raye *(Controller)*
Carole Whitaker *(Dir.-Pub. Rels.)*

C. I. HAYES, INC.
800 Wellington Ave.
Cranston, RI 02910
Tel.: 401-467-5200 **RI**
Fax: 401-467-2108
Year Founded: 1905
Approx.Sls.: $11,000,000
Emp.: 139
Fiscal Year-end: 12/31/90
Mfr. Electric Heat Treating Equip.
S.I.C.: 3567
Carl I. Hayes, Jr. *(Pres. & Treas.)*
Ronald C. Mowry *(Dir.-Sls.)*
Jacqueline Weintraub *(Dir.-Personnel)*
William E. Whitehead *(Dir.-Data Processing)*
Gary Nash *(Pur. Agent)*

No. of Mfg. Plants/Facilities: 1
No. of U.S. Offices: 2

Computer Systems/Hardware:
IBM System 36

Outside Service Firm(s):

Ward, Fisher & Co.*(Auditors)*
Providence, RI

Hinkley, Allen, Snyder & Comen*(Legal Firm)*
1500 Fleet Ctr.
Providence, RI 02903
Tel.: 401-274-2000

Fleet National Bank*(Major Banking Relationship)*
125 Dupont Dr.
Providence, RI 02907-3178
Tel.: 401-278-5335

HAYES MICROCOMPUTER PRODUCTS, INC.
5835 Peachtree Corners East
Norcross, GA 30092
Mailing Address:
P.O. Box 105203,
Atlanta, GA 30348
Tel.: 404-840-9200
Telex: 703500 HAYES USA
Fax: 404-441-1238
Year Founded: 1977
Sales Range: $100-499 Million
Emp.: 800
Export
Mfr. of Computer Communications Products
S.I.C.: 3661
Dennis C. Hayes *(Pres.)*
Margaret B. Ballard *(Dir.-Corp. Communications)*
Principal(s):
Dennis C. Hayes

No. of Mfg. Plants/Facilities: 2
No. of U.S. Offices: 6
No. of Foreign Offices: 4

Computer Systems/Hardware:
Modems, LANs, ISDN

Outside Service Firm(s):

NationsBank*(Major Banking Relationship)*
35 Broad St.
Atlanta, GA 30303
Tel.: 404-581-2121
Tel.: 800-848-8198

Subsidiaries:

Hayes Microcomputer Products, Inc. **(1)**
39/F Unit B. Manulife Tower, 169 Electric Rd.
North Point, Hong Kong
Tel.: 887 7548
Fax: 887 6836
Sales & Marketing Office
S.I.C.: 5065
Norman Lo *(Gen. Mgr.)*

Hayes Microcomputer Products (Canada) **(1)**
295 Philip St.
Waterloo, ON N2L 3W8, Canada
Tel.: 519-884-3141
Service Facility
S.I.C.: 7378
Ian Telford *(Chief Oper. Officer)*

Hayes Microcomputer Products Ltd. **(1)**
10 Roundwood Ave. Stockley Park, Uxbridge, Middlesex UB11 1AE, United Kingdom
Tel.: 81 848 1858
Fax: 81 848 0224
Sales & Marketing Office
S.I.C.: 5065
John Babb *(Gen. Mgr.)*

Practical Peripherals **(1)**
31245 La Baya Dr.
Westlake Village, CA 91362
Tel.: 818-706-0333
Communications Peripherals
S.I.C.: 3661

HAYES, SEAY, MATTERN & MATTERN, INC.
1315 Franklin Rd. S.W.
Roanoke, VA 24016
Mailing Address:
P.O. Box 13446
Roanoke, VA 24034
Tel.: 703-857-3100 **AL**
Fax: 703-857-3180
Year Founded: 1947
Assets: $6,306,000
Liabilities: $3,510,000
Net Worth: $2,796,000
Approx.Sls.: $20,000,000
Emp.: 305
Fiscal Year-end: 12/31/91
Architectural, Engineering & Planning Services
S.I.C.: 8711; 8712
H. Boyd Dickenson *(Chm. & Chief Exec. Officer)*
T. Howard Noel *(Pres. & Chief Oper. Officer)*
Cecil G. Doyle *(Exec. V.P. & Sec.)*
John P. Bradshaw *(Exec. V.P.)*
Stephen P. Clinton *(V.P.-Business Devel.)*
Timm Jamieson *(V.P.)*
Rick F. Beirne *(V.P.)*
David C. Hammond *(V.P.)*
Wendell R. Smith *(V.P.)*
Sam B. Wehrenberg *(Asst. V.P.)*

No. of U.S. Offices: 10

Outside Service Firm(s):

Spencer & Associates*(Auditors)*
Roanoke, VA

Woods, Rogers, Hazlegrove*(Legal Firm)*
Dominion Tower-Suite 1400, 10 S. Jefferson St..W.
Roanoke, VA 24004
Tel.: 703-983-7600
Fax: 703-983-7711

Dominion Bank*(Major Banking Relationship)*
P.O. Box 13327,
Roanoke, VA
Tel.: 703-563-7851
Fax: 703-563-7696

Hayes, Seay, Mattern & Mattern, Inc.—(Continued)

Branch:

Hayes, Seay Mattern & Mattern, Inc. (1)
900 Western America, Ste. 300
Mobile, AL 36691
Tel.: 205-343-9713
Engineering & Architectural Services
S.I.C.: 8711; 8712

HAYWIN TEXTILE PRODUCTS, INC.
106 Bayard St.
Brooklyn, NY 11222
Tel.: 718-384-0317 **NY**
Fax: 718-387-7179
Approx.Sls.: $13,000,000
Emp.: 20
Wholesale Distributor of Home Furnishings
S.I.C.: 5023
Alfred Haft *(Pres.)*
Julie Haft *(Sec. & Treas.)*

Outside Service Firm(s):

Paul B. Gottbetter*(Auditors)*
New York, NY

HAZEL BISHOP CORPORATION
910 Sylvan Ave.
Englewood Cliffs, NJ 07632
Tel.: 201-871-8773
Tel.: 800-424-7467
Fax: 201-871-0269
Year Founded: 1956
Emp.: 5
Import Export
Mfr. of Hazel Bishop Cosmetics
S.I.C.: 2844
Jack Rosen *(Chm., Pres., Chief Exec. & Chief Oper. Officer)*
Marc Birnbaum *(Exec. V.P.-Sls. & Mktg.)*
Jim Farmer *(Dir.-Pur.)*

Computer Systems/Hardware:
IBM

HAZEN PAPER COMPANY
Third Level Canal
Holyoke, MA 01040
Mailing Address:
P.O. Box 189,
Holyoke, MA 01041
Tel.: 413-538-8204
Fax: 413-533-1420
Year Founded: 1925
Approx.Sls.: $42,000,000
Emp.: 160
Import Export
Mfr. Converted Paper Packaging; Decorative Paper Wall Covering; Bookbinding Paper & Coated & Laminated Decorative Packaging Materials; Speciality Papers
S.I.C.: 3999
Robert Hazen *(Pres.)*
Thomas Hazen *(Chief Exec. Officer & Treas.)*
Edward J. Hollering *(V.P.-Mfg.)*
Steven J. Smith *(V.P.-Sls.)*
Clarke Lyon *(Gen. Counsel)*
Shirley I. Rossmeisl *(Controller)*
Timothy R. McDonald *(Dir.-Technology)*
Dennis Badger *(Mgr.-Data Processing)*
Judith Getto *(Mgr.-Sls.)*
Andrew J. Piecuch *(Mgr.-Prod.)*
Sarmento J. Silva *(Mgr.-Pur.)*
Charles A. Auclair *(Plant Engr.)*

No. of Mfg. Plants/Facilities: 1
No. of U.S. Offices: 1

Outside Service Firm(s):

Lester Harpern & Co.*(Auditors)*
Holyoke, MA

Lyon, Curley, Scully & Fitzpatrick*(Legal Firm)*
Holyoke, MA

Bank of Boston*(Major Banking Relationship)*
Springfield, MA

HAZEN & SAWYER
730 Broadway
New York, NY 10003
Tel.: 212-777-8400 **NY**
Fax: 212-614-9049
Year Founded: 1955
Approx.Sls.: $30,000,000
Emp.: 435
Civil Engineering
S.I.C.: 8711
Walter B. Sinnott *(Pres.)*
Robert E. Hagadorn *(Exec. V.P., Treas. & Sec.)*
Jerry Lastihenos *(Sr. V.P.)*
Peter Robinson *(Sr. V.P.)*
Gordon Ruggles *(Sr. V.P.)*
Dals Chaudhary *(V.P.)*
Alan Natter *(V.P.)*
David Walrath *(V.P.)*
Sheldon Yuan *(V.P.)*

Outside Service Firm(s):

Ronald P. McNavich*(Auditors)*
Rockville Center, NY

Manufacturers Hanover Trust Co.*(Major Banking Relationship)*
4 New York Plaza
New York, NY 10015
Tel.: 212-633-7938

HEAD SPORTS, INC.
4801 N. 63rd St.
Boulder, CO 80301
Tel.: 303-530-2000
Tel.: 800-874-3234
Fax: 303-530-2965
Year Founded: 1967
Approx.Sls.: $60,000,000
Emp.: 220
U.S. Distributor of HTM Sports Holding B.V. for Head, Tyrolia & Mares & SanMarco Brands - Tennis Racquets, Racquetball Racquets, Racquet Strings, Athletic Footwear & Ski Equipment
S.I.C.: 3949; 3149
Robert S. Puccini *(Pres. & Chief Exec. Officer)*
Steven Olson *(Treas.)*

HEADCO INDUSTRIES, INC.
(d/b/a Bearings Headquarters Co.)
2601 W. 16th St.
Broadview, IL 60153
Tel.: 708-681-4400
Fax: 708-681-4462
Year Founded: 1934
Approx.Sls.: $90,000,000
Emp.: 500
Fiscal Year-end: 10/31/91
Import Export
Bearing & Power Transmission Distributor with Specialized Job Shops Located Throughout the U.S.
S.I.C.: 5085; 5063
Frank Timble *(Chm. Bd.)*
James N. Timble *(Pres. & Chief Exec. Officer)*
Frank Volpentesta *(Chief Oper. Officer & Exec. V.P.)*
Michael J. Gricus *(Chief Fin. Officer & V.P.)*
Robert W. Singer *(Gen. Counsel)*
Karen Skinner *(Treas.)*

No. of Mfg. Plants/Facilities: 4
No. of U.S. Offices: 38

Computer Systems/Hardware:
Burroughs A10 H

Outside Service Firm(s):

Ernst & Young*(Auditors)*
233 S. Wacker Dr.
Chicago, IL 60606
Tel.: 312-368-1800
Fax: 312-645-3095

American Selfcare Corporation*(Group Insurer)*
Minneapolis, MN

LaSalle National Bank*(Major Banking Relationship)*
120 S. LaSalle St.
Chicago, IL 60603
Tel.: 312-781-8000

John Hancock Mutual Life Insurance Co.*(Pension Manager)*
John Hancock Place, P.O. Box 111
Boston, MA 02117

Subsidiaries:

Bronze Headquarters (1)
1022-30 Berea Rd.
Cleveland, OH 44102
Tel.: 612-651-3811
Manufacture Bushing, Sleeves & Flanges
S.I.C.: 3469

Gear Headquarters Inc. (1)
3012 S. 24th St.
Kansas City, KS 66101
Tel.: 913-831-1700
Mfr. Special Gears & Sprockets
S.I.C.: 3714; 3568

Headco Machine Works, Inc. (1)
Box 969, Main Street Rd.
Keokuk, IA 52632
Tel.: 319-524-1804
Mfr. Machine Parts
S.I.C.: 3469

Industrial Information Headquarters Co. (1)
2601 W. 16th St.
Broadview, IL 60153
Tel.: 708-681-4400
Publisher of Technical Manual
S.I.C.: 2731

HEADER PRODUCTS INC.
11850 S. Wayne Rd.
Romulus, MI 48174
Tel.: 313-941-2220
Fax: 313-941-2679
Approx.Sls.: $17,000,000
Emp.: 145
Mfr. Cold Headed Specials & Screw Machine Products
S.I.C.: 3451; 3547
Michael F. McManus, Jr. *(Pres.)*
Jon Van Buhler *(V.P.)*
Delta E. Smith *(Sec.)*

Outside Service Firm(s):

Godfrey Hamel & Co.*(Auditors)*
Detroit, MI

Manufacturers National Bank*(Major Banking Relationship)*
Romulus, MI

The Heaf Group
(Name Changed To Help Management Corporation)

J. H. HEAFNER CO. INC.
814 E. Main St.
Lincolnton, NC 28092
Tel.: 704-735-3003 **NC**
Fax: 704-735-0125
Year Founded: 1935
Approx.Sls.: $110,000,000
Emp.: 350
Distribute Rubber Tire Products
S.I.C.: 5014
Ann Heafner Gaither *(Chm. Bd., Pres. & Chief Exec. Officer)*
William H. Gaither *(Exec. V.P. & Chief Oper. Officer)*
Daniel Brown *(Sr. V.P.-Sls.)*
William Morrison *(Sr. V.P. & Treas.)*
Earl Martin *(V.P.)*
Michael Gaither *(Gen. Counsel)*
Ruth Beal *(Dir.-Personnel)*
A.M. Watson *(Dir.-Telecommunications)*

No. of Mfg. Plants/Facilities: 32

Outside Service Firm(s):

McGladrey & Pullen*(Auditors)*
Charlotte, NC

Isenhour, Gaither & Wood*(Legal Firm)*
Newton, NC

NationsBank Carolinas*(Major Banking Relationship)*
One NCNB Plaza T18-7
Charlotte, NC 28255

HEALTH CARE DISTRIBUTORS OF INDIANA, INC.
(Formerly South Bend Drug Co., Inc.)
4100 N. Technology Dr.
South Bend, IN 46628
Mailing Address:
P.O. Box 6009
South Bend, IN 46660
Tel.: 219-232-3303 **IN**
Fax: 219-287-2679
Year Founded: 1946
Approx.Sls.: $200,000,000
Emp.: 185
Fiscal Year-end: 12/31/89
Wholesaler of Drugs
S.I.C.: 5122; 5100
Michael Keiser *(Pres.)*
Irene Hudak *(Sec.)*
Nancy Darnell *(Treas.)*
Praful Raval *(Comptroller)*
Jim Kleinheinz *(Dir.-Sls.)*
Robert Koopman *(Dir.-Mdse.)*
Principal(s):
Michael Keiser

Outside Service Firm(s):

Thomas Westfall*(Auditors)*
South Bend, IN

Parker & Jaicome*(Legal Firm)*
South Bend, IN

Valley American*(Major Banking Relationship)*
South Bend, IN

HEALTH CARE LODGES
201 W. 8th St.
Coffeyville, KS 67337
Mailing Address:
P.O. Box 509
Coffeyville, KS 67337
Tel.: 316-251-6700
Tel.: 800-782-0120 **KS**
Fax: 316-251-6427
Year Founded: 1969
Assets: $31,562,482
Earnings: $545,036
Liabilities: $22,057,757
Net Worth: $9,504,725
Approx.Sls.: $51,601,000
Emp.: 2,700
Fiscal Year-end: 10/31/91
Oper. of Skilled-Care Nursing Homes
S.I.C.: 8051
S.A. Hann *(Chm. Bd. & Pres.)*
James H. Childers *(Sr. V.P.)*
Marianne Carey-Ranes *(Asst. Sec.)*
Garen Cox *(Gen. Counsel)*
Timothy R. Crowley *(Treas. & Sec.)*
Thomas C. Meeker *(Controller)*

Subsidiary:

Medicalodges, Inc. (1)
P.O. Box 509, 201 W. 8th St.
Coffeyville, KS 67337-0509
Tel.: 306-251-6700
Fax: 316-251-6427

Computer Systems/Hardware:
IBM System 36 286/386 PC
Larry Fischer *(Pres.)*
Stanley Herrenbruck *(Dir.-Pur.)*
Don Blythe *(Mgr.-Adv.)*

HEALTH MANAGEMENT SYSTEMS, INC.
401 Park Ave. S.
New York, NY 10016
Tel.: 212-685-4545 **NY**
Fax: 212-889-8776
Year Founded: 1974
Assets: $27,461,000
Liabilities: $28,720,000
Net Worth: $1,259,000
Sales Range: $20-39 Million
Fiscal Year-end: 12/31/91
Health Care Claim Processing & Reprocessing for State & Federal Agencies & Urban Hospitals
S.I.C.: 7374; 8062
Paul J. Kerz *(Chm. Bd., Pres. & Chief Exec. Officer)*
Robert M. Holster *(Exec. V.P.)*
Laurence P. Simon *(Sr. V.P.)*
Scott A. Remley *(V.P. & Chief Fin. Officer)*
Lewis D. Levetown *(V.P.-Human Resources)*
Mark D. Mandel *(V.P.-Mktg.)*
Stuart Rosen *(V.P.-Data Processing Opers.)*
Donald J. Staffa *(V.P.-California Opers.)*
Vincent Hartley *(Dir.-Pur.)*
Alexandra F. Holt *(Dir.-Corp. Communications & Training)*
Barbara A. Ely *(Corp. Travel Planner)*
Principal(s):
Paul J. Kerz
Laurence P. Simon

No. of U.S. Offices: 5

Computer Systems/Hardware:
IBM System 4381; DEC VAX 8350;AT & T 3B2 ; IBM PC

Outside Service Firm(s):

KPMG Peat Marwick*(Auditors)*
345 Park Ave.
New York, NY 10154
Tel.: 212-758-9700
Fax: 212-872-3308

Home Life Insurance Co.*(Commercial Insurance Carrier)*
P.O. Box 1326,
Newark, NJ

Home Life Insurance Co.*(Group Insurer)*
P.O. Box 1326,
Newark, NJ

Coleman & Rhine*(Legal Firm)*
New York, NY

Chase Manhattan Bank, N.A.*(Major Banking Relationship)*
One Chase Manhattan Plaza
New York, NY 10081
Tel.: 212-552-2222
Tel.: 800-526-0801
Fax: 212-552-7175

Chemical Banking Corp.*(Major Banking Relationship)*
277 Park Ave.
New York, NY 10041
Tel.: 212-310-6407
Fax: 212-310-4526

Addison Capital*(Pension Manager)*
Philadelphia, PA

Subsidiaries:

Accelerated Claims Processing, Inc. **(1)**
401 Park Ave. South
New York, NY 10016
Tel.: 212-685-4545
Fax: 212-889-8776
Emp.: 5
Hospital Accounts Receivable Management
S.I.C.: 6324
Donald J. Staffa *(Pres.)*
Paul J. Kerz *(Sec.)*
Laurence B. Simon *(Treas.)*

Quality Medical Adjudication, Inc. **(1)**
2897 Kilgore Rd.
Rancho Cordova, CA 95670
Tel.: 916-852-2500
Fax: 916-852-2669
Health Care Claim Processing for Hospitals
S.I.C.: 7374
Donald J. Staffa *(Chm.)*
Vincent McElroen *(Pres.)*
Robert Balthazor *(V.P.-Mktg.)*
Raresh Shivdasani *(Gen. Mgr.)*

HEALTH VITAMIN COMPANY, INC.
1060 Nepperhan Ave.
Yonkers, NY 10703
Tel.: 914-423-2900
Fax: 914-963-6001
Year Founded: 1973
Approx.Sls.: $24,000,000
Emp.: 160
Fiscal Year-end: 12/31/91
Import Export
Vitamins, Cosmetics, Healthfoods & Pharmaceuticals
Joseph Lewin *(Chm. Bd. & Pres.)*
Karen Linnington *(V.P.)*
Alan Miller *(V.P.-Mktg.)*
Chris Sasser *(Sec.)*
Douglas Auld *(Gen. Mgr.)*

BILL HEARD ENTERPRISES, INC.
2600 Cross Country Dr., Ste. 321
Columbus, GA 31906
Tel.: 706-561-6213 **GA**
Fax: 706-561-0258
Year Founded: 1983
Sales Range: $100-499 Million
Emp.: 1,000
Fiscal Year-end: 12/31/90
Retail Automobiles; Automobile & Truck Leasing; Nonresidential Building Operators
S.I.C.: 5511; 6512; 7513
William Heard, Jr. *(Pres.)*
Richard Young *(V.P. & Controller)*
Ronald A. Feldner *(Chief Fin. Officer)*

Outside Service Firm(s):

George B. Jones & Co.*(Auditors)*
Memphis, TN

Columbus Bank & Trust Company*(Major Banking Relationship)*
Trust Dept., P.O. Box 120
Columbus, GA 31902
Tel.: 706-649-2311

Subsidiaries:

Bill Heard Chevrolet Inc. **(1)**
3615 Manchester Expwy.
Columbus, GA 31908
Tel.: 706-322-8881
Approx.Sls.: $75,000,000
Emp.: 180
Retail New & Used Automobiles; Leasing
S.I.C.: 5511
William T. Heard, Jr. *(Pres.)*
Clinton G. Allen *(Sec. & Treas.)*

Bill Heard Leasing, Inc. **(1)**
1100 Martin Luther King Blvd.
Columbus, GA 31906
Tel.: 706-323-2429
Truck Leasing
S.I.C.: 7513
William T. Heard, Jr. *(Pres.)*
James R. Pearson *(V.P.)*
Clinton Allen *(Sec. & Treas.)*

THE HEARST CORPORATION
959 Eighth Ave.
New York, NY 10019
Tel.: 212-649-2000 **DE**
Year Founded: 1887
Sales Range: $1 Billion +
Emp.: 14,000
Publisher of Newspapers, Books & Magazines; Radio & Television Broadcasting; Hearst Entertainment; News & Features Syndicates; Cable Communications; Television Production & Distribution; Real Estate
S.I.C.: 2721; 4832; 4833; 2711; 2731; 5963; 6512; 4841; 6552; 6798
Randolph A. Hearst *(Chm. Bd.)*
W.R. Hearst, Jr. *(Chm.-Exec. Committee)*
Frank A. Bennack, Jr. *(Pres. & Chief Exec. Officer)*
Gilbert C. Maurer *(Chief Oper. Officer & Exec. V.P.)*
John G. Conomikes *(V.P. & Gen. Mgr.-Hearst Broadcasting)*
Robert J. Danzig *(V.P. & Gen. Mgr.-Hearst Newspapers)*
Peter J. DeMaria *(V.P. & Controller)*
Victor F. Ganzi *(V.P., Gen. Counsel & Sec.)*
J. Roger Grier *(V.P. & Grp. Exec.-Hearst Newspapers)*
Lee J. Guittar *(V.P. & Grp. Exec.-Hearst Newspapers)*
George R. Hearst, Jr. *(V.P.-Real Estate)*
Gordon L. Jones, Jr. *(V.P. & Grp. Head-Hearst Books/Business Publ.)*
Raymond E. Joslin *(V.P. & Grp. Head-Hearst Entertainment & Syndication)*
Joseph Kingsbury-Smith *(V.P. & Dir.-Corp. Activities, Washington D.C.)*
Edwin A. Lewis *(V.P. & Treas.)*
Bruce L. Paisner *(V.P. & Deputy Grp. Head-Hearst Entertainment & Syndication)*
Benson M. Srere *(V.P. & Exec. Asst. to Pres.)*
Joseph McDonald *(Dir.-Insurance)*
James F. O'Donnell *(Dir.-Corp. Communications)*
Edwin A. Rusgo *(Dir.-Employee Benefits)*
Fred I. Young *(Dir.-Brdcst. Opers.)*
Angelo Savino *(Mgr.-Cash)*

Computer Systems/Hardware:
IBM System 38 Model 40; IBM 4341 Model K02

Outside Service Firm(s):

Deloitte & Touche*(Auditors)*
1 World Trade Center
New York, NY 10048
Tel.: 212-669-5000

CIGNA*(Group Insurer)*
Plainville, CT

Empire Blue Cross & Blue Shield*(Group Insurer)*
New York, NY

William M. Mercer Incorporated*(Commercial Insurance Carrier)*
1166 Avenue of the Americas
New York, NY 10036
Tel.: 212-345-7444
Fax: 212-345-7414

Alliance Capital Management*(Pension Manager)*
1345 Avenue of the Americas
New York, NY 10017

Batterymarch Financial Management*(Pension Manager)*
600 Atlantic Ave.
Boston, MA 02210
Tel.: 617-973-9300

Lincoln Capital Management*(Pension Manager)*
200 South Wacker Dr.
Chicago, IL 60606
Tel.: 312-559-2880
Fax: 312-559-1837

Chemical Bank*(Pension Manager)*
450 West 33rd St.
New York, NY 10001
Tel.: 212-613-7197
Fax: 212-947-7628

Millikin National Bank of Decatur*(Pension Manager)*
Decatur, IL

Divisions:

Cal Graphics Division **(1)**
6370 Altura Blvd.
Buena Park, CA 90620
Tel.: 714-523-0324
Printers
S.I.C.: 2741
George W. Sjostrom *(Pres.)*

Hearst Books/Business Publishing Group **(1)**
959 Eighth Ave.
New York, NY 10019
Tel.: 212-649-2000
Publishers of Periodicals & Trade Books
S.I.C.: 2731; 2721
Howard Kaminsky *(Pres.-Trade Book Groups)*
Gordon L. Jones, Jr. *(V.P. & Grp. Head)*
Edward B. Hughes *(Grp. V.P.-Healthcare)*
Richard P. Malloch *(Gen. Mgr.)*

Division:

William Morrow & Co., Inc. **(2)**
1350 Ave. of the Americas
New York, NY 10016
Tel.: 212-261-6500
Tel.: 800-843-9389
Fax: 212-261-6595
Emp.: 180
Fiscal Year-end: 12/31/90
Book & Trade Paperback Publishers
S.I.C.: 2731
Allen Marchioni *(Chm. Bd., Pres. & Chief Exec. Officer)*
Susan C. Hirschman *(Sr. V.P. & Editor-in Chief-Greenwillow Books)*
Ann Bramson *(V.P. & Sr. Editor-Hearst Books)*
Lisa Drew *(V.P. & Sr. Editor-Adult Books)*
Maria Guarnaschelli *(V.P. & Sr. Editor-Adult Books)*
Susan Halligan *(V.P.-Adv. & Promo.)*
Jazan Higgins *(V.P. & Dir.-Children's Booking Mktg.)*
Harvey Hoffman *(V.P. & Dir.-Prod.)*
Paulette Kaufmann *(V.P. & Editor-in-Chief-Tambourine Books)*
Scott Manning *(V.P. & Dir.-Publicity)*
Lawrence Norton *(V.P.-Sls.)*
Susan Pearson *(V.P. & Editor-in-Chief-Lothrop, Lee & Shepard)*
Lisa Queen *(V.P. & Dir.-Subsidiary Rights)*
David Reuther *(V.P. & Editor-in-Chief-Morrow Jr. Books)*
Adrian Zackheim *(V.P. & Exec. Editor-Adult Books)*
Russell Biegel Jr. *(Controller)*
Brad Erlenbach *(Asst. Controller & Dir.-Acctg.)*
Paul Fornario *(Dir.-Opers.)*
Lenore Johnsen *(Dir.-Personnel)*
Nannette Hoeler *(Mgr.-Royalties)*
David Ekrem *(Corporate Librarian)*

Units:

Beech Tree Books **(3)**
1350 Ave. of the Americas
New York, NY 10019
Tel.: 212-262-6500
S.I.C.: 2731
Paulette Kaufman *(V.P. & Editor-in-Chief)*

Fielding Travel Books **(3)**
1350 Ave. of the Americas
New York, NY 10019
Tel.: 212-261-6500
Publishes Trade Paperback Informational Travel Titles
S.I.C.: 2731
Randy Ladenheim *(Sr. Editor)*

Greenwillow Books **(3)**
1350 Ave. of the Americas
New York, NY 10019
Tel.: 212-649-6500
Publishes Children's Picture Books & All Age Fiction
S.I.C.: 2731
Susan Hirschman *(Publisher)*

Hearst Marine Books **(3)**
1350 Ave. of the Americas
New York, NY 10019
Tel.: 212-649-6500
Publishes Hardcover & Paperback Books About Motor Boating, Sailing & the Sea
S.I.C.: 2731

The Hearst Corporation—(Continued)

Lothrop, Lee & Shepard Books (3)
1350 Ave. of the Americas
New York, NY 10019
Tel.: 212-261-6500
Publishes Children's Picture Books & Fiction Titles
S.I.C.: 2731

Morrow Junior Books (3)
1350 Ave. of the Americas
New York, NY 10019
Tel.: 212-261-6500
Publishes Hardcover Fiction & Non-Fiction Titles for Children
S.I.C.: 2721

Quill Trade Paperbacks (3)
105 Madison Ave.
New York, NY 10016
Tel.: 212-889-3050
Publishes Original & Reprint General Trade Paperback Titles
S.I.C.: 2731

Tambourine Books (3)
105 Madison Ave.
New York, NY 10016
Tel.: 212-889-3050
Publishes Hardcover Fiction & Non-Fiction Children's Books
S.I.C.: 2731
Paulette Kaufman *(V.P. & Editor-in-Chief)*

Operations:

First DataBank (2)
1111 Bayhill Dr.
San Bruno, CA 94066
Tel.: 415-588-5454
Emp.: 60
Electronic Publishing; Develops & Markets Pharmaceutical Drug Information
S.I.C.: 2721
Joseph L. Hirschmann *(Pres.)*
James L. Wilson *(Dir.-Mktg. & Sales)*

Healthcare Group (2)
60 E. 42nd St.
New York, NY 10165
Tel.: 212-682-3710
Periodicals
S.I.C.: 2721
Edward B. Hughes *(V.P.-Grp. Publisher)*

Publication:

American Druggist (3)
60 E. 42nd St.
New York, NY 10165
Tel.: 212-297-9600
Periodical
S.I.C.: 2721
Mark E. Altier *(Publisher)*

Hearst Book Group (2)
1350 Ave. of the Americas
New York, NY 10019
Tel.: 212-261-6500
Book & Trade Book Publishers
S.I.C.: 2731
Howard Kaminsky *(Chm. & Chief Exec. Officer)*
Gordon L. Jones, Jr. *(V.P. & Grp. Head)*
Philip D. Shalala *(Grp. V.P.-Hearst Business Publishing)*

Units:

Arbor House (3)
1350 Ave. of the Americas
New York, NY 10019
Tel.: 212-261-6500
Publishers: Fiction & Non-Fiction, Hardcover Trade Books
S.I.C.: 2731
James D. Landis *(Publisher)*

Avon Books (3)
1350 Ave. of the Americas
New York, NY 10019
Tel.: 212-261-6500
Softcover Mass Market & Tradebooks
S.I.C.: 2731
Carolyn Reidy *(Pres. & Publisher)*

Hearst Business Communications, Inc. (2)
645 Stewart Ave
Garden City, NY 11530
Tel.: 516-227-1300
Fax: 516-227-1901
Emp.: 115
Fiscal Year-end: 12/31/90
Export
Computer Systems/Hardware:
IBM AS/400
Publishes Business Information for the Electronics & Floor Covering Industry & Retirement Planning Materials
S.I.C.: 2721
William Baker *(V.P. & Gen. Mgr.)*
George Lahry *(Controller)*
Kathryn Chacana *(Dir.-Human Resources)*

Publications:

Electronic Engineers Master (3)
645 Stewart Ave.
Garden City, NY 11530
Tel.: 516-227-1300
Five Volume Catalog Specifying Information on a Spectrum of Component Parts & Products for Buyers & Designers in the Electronics Industry
S.I.C.: 2741

Electronic Products Magazine (3)
645 Stewart Ave.
New York, NY 11530
Tel.: 516-227-1300
Monthly Magazine Providing Electronic Engineers with Information on New Products & their Application
S.I.C.: 2721

Floor Covering Weekly (3)
555 W. 57th St.
New York, NY 10019
Tel.: 212-541-4080
Business Newspaper for Floor Covering Industry
S.I.C.: 2721
John P. McGrath *(Publisher)*

Integrated Circuits Master Catalog (3)
645 Stewart Ave.
Garden City, NY 11530
Tel.: 516-227-1300
Monthly Tabloid Covering General Machinery News
S.I.C.: 2741

Motor Crash Estimating Guide (3)
5600 Crooks Rd.
Troy, MI 48098
Tel.: 313-828-0000
Publishes Professional Manuals Estimating Automobile Collision Damage Repair Costs for Insurance Adjusters & Auto Body Shops
S.I.C.: 2741

National Auto Research (3)
P.O. Box 758, Hwy. 129 S. at Barrett Rd.
Gainesville, GA 30501
Tel.: 706-532-4111
Periodical
S.I.C.: 2721
C. Eugene McDonald *(Pres.)*

Hearst Professional Magazines, Inc. (2)
60 E. 42nd St.
New York, NY 10165
Tel.: 212-297-9600
Periodicals
S.I.C.: 2721

Publication:

Diversion (3)
60 E. 42nd St.
New York, NY 10165
Tel.: 212-297-9600
Periodical
S.I.C.: 2721
Thomas E. Duffy *(Publisher)*
Stephen Birnbaum *(Edit Dir.)*

Motor Publications (2)
645 Stewart Ave.
Garden City, NY 11530
Tel.: 516-227-1300
Periodical
S.I.C.: 2721; 2731
Philip D. Shalala *(Grp. V.P.)*

Operation:

Motor Consumer Books (3)
5600 Crooks Rd.
Troy, MI 48098
Tel.: 313-828-0000
Publications
S.I.C.: 2731
Philip D. Shalala *(Grp. V.P.-Business Publishing)*

Publication:

Motor Magazine (3)
645 Stewart Ave.
Garden City, NY 11530
Tel.: 516-227-1300
Periodical
S.I.C.: 2721
Philip D. Shalala *(Publisher)*

Retirement Advisors, Inc. (2)
105 Madison Ave.
New York, NY 10016
Tel.: 212-213-8711
Periodical
S.I.C.: 2721
Thomas A. Fowler *(Pres.)*

Sponsored Publications (2)
60 E. 42nd St.
New York, NY 10165
Tel.: 212-297-9600
S.I.C.: 2741
Edward B. Hughes *(Publisher)*

UTP (United Technical Publications) Division (2)
645 Stewart Ave.
Garden City, NY 11530
Tel.: 516-227-1300
Technical Publications
S.I.C.: 2731
William K. Baker *(V.P.)*

Wilmor Warehouse & Shipping Co., Inc. (2)
39 Plymouth St.
Fairfield, NJ 07006
Tel.: 201-227-7200
General Warehouse
S.I.C.: 4225
Allen A. Marchioni *(Pres.)*

Hearst Broadcasting Division (1)
959 Eighth Ave.
New York, NY 10019
Tel.: 212-649-2000
Radio & Television Broadcasting
S.I.C.: 4832; 4833
David J. Barrett *(V.P. & Deputy Gen. Mgr.-Radio)*
John G. Conomikes *(V.P. & Gen. Mgr.-Brdcst.)*
Fred I. Young *(Dir.-Broadcasting Opers.)*

Operations:

KMBC Division (2)
1049 Central St.
Kansas City, MO 64105
Tel.: 816-221-9999
Television Broadcasting
S.I.C.: 4833
Paul Dinovitz *(V.P. & Gen. Mgr.)*

TV Station:

KMBC-TV (3)
1049 Central St.
Kansas City, MO 64105
Tel.: 816-221-9999
Television Broadcasting
S.I.C.: 4833
Paul Dinovitz *(V.P. & Gen. Mgr.)*

WBAL Division (2)
3800 Hooper Ave.
Baltimore, MD 21211
Tel.: 410-467-3000
Radio & Television Broadcasting
S.I.C.: 4832; 4833

Radio & TV Stations:

WBAL-AM (3)
3800 Hooper Ave.
Baltimore, MD 21211
Tel.: 410-467-3000
Radio Broadcasting
S.I.C.: 4832
Edward C. Kiernan *(V.P. & Gen. Mgr.)*

WBAL-TV (3)
3800 Hooper Ave.
Baltimore, MD 21211
Tel.: 410-467-3000
Television Broadcasting
S.I.C.: 4833
Philip M. Stolz *(V.P. & Gen. Mgr.)*

WIYY-FM (3)
3800 Hooper Ave.
Baltimore, MD 21211
Tel.: 410-467-3000
Radio Broadcasting
S.I.C.: 4832
Edward C. Kiernan *(V.P. & Gen. Mgr.)*

WCVB Division (2)
5 TV Place, Needham Br.
Boston, MA 02192
Tel.: 617-449-0400
Television Broadcasting
S.I.C.: 4833
S. James Coppersmith *(V.P. & Gen. Mgr.)*

TV Station:

WCVB-TV (3)
5 TV Place, Needham Br.
Boston, MA 02192
Tel.: 617-449-0400
Television Broadcasting
S.I.C.: 4833
S. James Coppersmith *(Gen. Mgr.)*

WDTN Div. (2)
P.O. Box 741, 4595 S. Dixie Ave.
Dayton, OH 45401
Tel.: 513-293-2101
Television Broadcasting
S.I.C.: 4833
Cheryl Craigie-Parker *(V.P. & Gen. Mgr.)*

TV Station:

WDTN-TV (3)
P.O. Box 741, 4595 S. Dixie Ave.
Dayton, OH 45401
Tel.: 513-293-2101
Television Broadcasting
S.I.C.: 4833
Cheryl Craigie-Parker *(V.P. & Gen. Mgr.)*

WISN Division (2)
759 N. 19th St.
Milwaukee, WI 53233
Tel.: 414-342-8812
Radio & Television Broadcasting
S.I.C.: 4832; 4833

Radio & TV Stations:

WISN-AM (3)
759 N. 19th St.
Milwaukee, WI 53233
Tel.: 414-342-1111
Radio & Television Broadcasting
S.I.C.: 4832; 4833
Steven A. Downes *(V.P. & G.M.)*

WISN-TV (3)
759 N. 19th St.
Milwaukee, WI 53233
Tel.: 414-342-8812
Television Broadcasting
S.I.C.: 4833
Howard F. Ritchie, Jr. *(V.P. & Gen. Mgr.)*

WLTQ-FM (3)
759 N. 19th St.
Milwaukee, WI 53233
Tel.: 414-342-1111
Radio Broadcasting
S.I.C.: 4832
Steven A. Downes *(V.P. & Gen. Mgr.)*

WTAE Division (2)
400 Ardmore Blvd.
Pittsburgh, PA 15221
Tel.: 412-242-4300
Radio & Television Broadcasting
S.I.C.: 4832; 4833

Radio & TV Stations:

WHTX-FM (3)
400 Ardmore Blvd.
Pittsburgh, PA 15221
Tel.: 412-731-0996
Radio Broadcasting
S.I.C.: 4832
James Carter *(V.P. & Gen. Mgr.)*

WTAE-AM (3)
400 Ardmore Blvd.
Pittsburgh, PA 15221
Tel.: 412-731-1250
Radio Broadcasting
S.I.C.: 4832
James J. Carter *(V.P. & Gen. Mgr.)*

WTAE-TV (3)
400 Ardmore Blvd.
Pittsburgh, PA 15221
Tel.: 412-242-4300
Television Broadcasting
S.I.C.: 4833
James R. Hefner III *(V.P. & Gen. Mgr.)*

Hearst Enterprises Division (1)
224 W. 57th St.
New York, NY 10019
Tel.: 212-262-7855
Purchases Newsprint, Wire, etc. for Hearst Newspapers & Paper for Hearst Magazines
S.I.C.: 2711; 5113
Donald W. Hopkins *(V.P. & Gen. Mgr.)*

Hearst Entertainment (1)
235 E. 45th St.
New York, NY 10017
Tel.: 212-455-4000
Production & Distributor of Material for Television, Motion Pictures & Home Video Markets
S.I.C.: 7822
Bruce L. Paisner *(Chm. & Chief Exec. Officer)*
Gerald I. Isenberg *(Pres. & Chief Oper. Officer)*
Terry Botwick *(Pres.)*
Stephen L. Elsky *(V.P.-Fin. Plng.)*

Hearst Entertainment & Syndication (1)
959 Eighth Ave.
New York, NY 10019
Tel.: 212-649-2000
Cable Communications
S.I.C.: 4899
Raymond E. Joslin *(V.P. & Grp. Head)*
Bruce L. Paisner *(V.P. & Deputy Grp. Head)*

Operation:

Hearst Cablevision of California, Inc. (2)
2700 Scott Blvd.
Santa Clara, CA 95050
Tel.: 408-727-5295
Operates Cable TV Systems
S.I.C.: 4841
Raymond E. Joslin *(Pres.)*

Hearst Entertainment Productions, Inc. (1)
1640 S. Sepulveda Blvd.
Los Angeles, CA 90025
Tel.: 310-657-7502
Production of Material for TV, Motion Pictures
S.I.C.: 7812
Gerald I. Isenberg *(Co-Chm. & Chief Exec. Officer)*

Joint Ventures:

Arts & Entertainment Network (2)
235 E. 45th St.
New York, NY 10019
Tel.: 212-661-4500 (50%)
Jointly Owned by Hearst/ABC Video Services & RCA Cable, Inc.; Cable Programming
S.I.C.: 7812
Nickolas Davatzes *(Pres. & Chief Exec. Officer)*
Whitney Goit, II *(Exec. V.P.-Sls. & Mktg.)*
Seymour H. Lesser *(Exec. V.P., Chief Fin. & Chief Admin. Officer)*

Lifetime Television (2)
36-12 35th Ave.
Astoria, NY 11106
Tel.: 718-482-4125 (50%)
Jointly Owned by Hearst/ABC Video Services & Viacom Entertainment Services; Cable Television Network with Informational Programming about Lifestyles, Relationships, Personal Development & Health
S.I.C.: 4841
Thomas F. Burchill *(Pres. & Chief Exec. Officer)*
Kristin Dean FitzGerald *(Sr. V.P.-Sls.)*
Linda Fint *(V.P.-Reg. Sls.)*

Hearst Magazines Division (1)
959 Eighth Ave.
New York, NY 10019
Tel.: 212-649-2000
Publishes & Distributes Magazines & Books
S.I.C.: 2721; 2731
D. Claeys Bahrenburg *(Pres.)*
George Green *(Pres.-Intl.)*
K. Robert Brink *(Exec. V.P. & Grp. Publishing Dir.)*
Mark F. Miller *(Exec. V.P. & Gen. Mgr.)*
Daniel E. Zucchi *(Sr. V.P. & Dir.-Consumer Mktg.)*
Thomas Wolf *(Gen. Mgr.-Magazine Devel.)*
Daniel J. Coleman *(V.P. & Mgr.-Opers.)*
Frank Herrera *(V.P. & Dir.-Distr.)*
Eugene Ferrone *(Dir.-Circulation Plng.)*
James F. O'Donnell *(Dir.-Communications)*
Charlotte Veal *(Dir.-Pub. Rels.)*
Bertram M. Haber *(Pur. Agent)*
Richard E. Deems *(Consultant)*

Operations:

Communications Data Services, Inc. (2)
112 10th St.
Des Moines, IA 50309
Tel.: 515-247-7500
Provides Data Processing & Computer Services to the Communications Industry
S.I.C.: 7372
Donald F. Ross *(Pres.)*

Eastern News Distributors, Inc. (2)
250 W. 55th St.
New York, NY 10019
Tel.: 212-649-4484
Magazine Distribution
S.I.C.: 5192
Lisa Scott *(V.P. & Gen. Mgr.)*

International Circulation Distributors (2)
250 W. 55th St.
New York, NY 10019
Tel.: 212-649-2000
Magazine Distribution
S.I.C.: 5192
Frank E. Herrera *(Pres.)*

International Editions (2)
1775 Broadway
New York, NY 10019
Tel.: 212-649-2850
Periodical
S.I.C.: 2721
Kim St. Clair Bodden *(Mgr.)*

Periodical Publishers' Service Bureau, Inc. (2)
One N. Superior St.
Sandusky, OH 44870
Tel.: 419-626-0623
Installment Subscription Solicitors for Magazines & Books
S.I.C.: 5963
John P. Manion *(Chm.)*

Publications:

Colonial Homes (2)
1790 Broadway
New York, NY 10019
Tel.: 212-830-2900
Fax: 212-586-3455
Emp.: 27
Periodical
S.I.C.: 2721
Randolph A. Hearst *(Chm. Bd.)*
D. Claeys Bahrenburg *(Pres.-Hearst Magazines Division)*
Frank A. Bennack, Jr. *(Pres. & Chief Exec. Officer)*
Gilbert C. Maurer *(Chief Oper. Officer & Exec. V.P.)*
Stan Baker *(Chief Fin. Officer)*
K. Robert Brink *(Exec. V.P.)*
E. Michael Peterson *(V.P. & Publisher)*
Mark S. Hart *(Dir.-Adv.)*
Carol Springstun *(Dir.-Mktg.)*
Mary Perisco *(Mgr.-Bus.)*
Richard Beatty *(Editor)*
Jason Kontos *(Editor)*
Richard E. Deems *(Publ. Consultant)*

Cosmopolitan (2)
224 W. 57th St.
New York, NY 10019
Tel.: 212-649-2000
Fax: 212-265-1849
Approx.Sls.: $30,000,000
Emp.: 61
Periodical
S.I.C.: 2721
Seth Hoyt *(Pres. & Publr.)*
Helen Gurley Brown *(Editor-in-Chief)*
David Carey *(Dir.-Mktg. Services)*
Cindy Sperling *(Dir.-Adv.)*
Molly Schaefer *(Assoc. Publr.)*

Country Living (2)
224 W. 57th St.
New York, NY 10019
Tel.: 212-649-2000
Periodical with American Traditional Emphasis
S.I.C.: 2721
T.R. Shepard III *(Publisher)*
Anne Holton *(Assoc. Publisher)*
Barbara Germani *(Gen. Mgr.)*

Countryside (2)
1700 Broadway
New York, NY 10019
Tel.: 212-903-5000
Periodical
S.I.C.: 2721
Carol Sama Sheehan *(Editor)*
Chris Boskin *(Dir.-Adv.)*

Esquire (2)
1790 Broadway
New York, NY 10019
Tel.: 212-459-7500
Fax: 212-245-6533
Monthly Magazine Targeted to Males 25-44 Years Old
S.I.C.: 2721
Nancy Nadler LeWinter *(Publisher)*
Terry McDonell *(Editor-in-Chief)*

Good Housekeeping (2)
959 Eighth Ave.
New York, NY 10019
Tel.: 212-649-2000
Fax: 212-977-9824
Periodical
S.I.C.: 2721
John Mack Carter *(Editor-in-Chief)*
Alan M. Waxenberg *(V.P. & Publisher)*
John H. Grant, Jr. *(Assoc. Publisher & Dir.-Adv.)*
Sandra L. Spaeth *(Assoc. Publisher & Dir.-Mktg.)*
George Penz *(Mgr.-Natl. Adv.)*

Harper's Bazaar (2)
1700 Broadway
New York, NY 10019
Tel.: 212-903-5000
Periodical
S.I.C.: 2721
Carl Portale *(V.P. & Publisher)*
Jeannette Chang *(Assoc. Publisher)*
Elizabeth Tilberis *(Editor-in-Chief)*

Hearst Magazines Special Publications (2)
1700 Broadway
New York, NY 10019
Tel.: 212-903-5000
Fax: 212-262-9401
Comprised of House Beautiful's Building Manual, Home Remodeling & Decorating; Home Building; Country Living's Country Kitchens; Houses & Plans, Kitchens & Baths; HB Gardening & Outdoor Living; HB Houses & Plans; HB Home Decorating; HB Home Remodeling
S.I.C.: 2721
David J. Moore *(Publisher)*

House Beautiful (2)
1700 Broadway
New York, NY 10019
Tel.: 212-903-5000
Periodical
S.I.C.: 2721
Louis Gropp *(Editor-in-Chief)*
Carol Ference *(V.P. & Publr.)*
Reed Foster *(Dir.-Adv.)*
Paul Tsigrikes *(Dir.-Mktg.)*

Motor Boating & Sailing (2)
250 W. 55th St.
New York, NY 10019
Tel.: 212-649-4097
Fax: 212-489-9258
Publisher of Motor Boating & Sailing Magazine
S.I.C.: 2721
Peter Janssen *(Editor-in-Chief)*
Jay McGill *(V.P. & Publisher)*
Brian Doyle *(Assoc. Publisher)*
Suzanne Fields *(Assoc. Publisher)*
Peter McHeffey *(Dir.-Sls.)*
Michael L. Perrella *(Dir.-Mktg.)*
Thomas Herber *(Mgr.-Bus.)*

Popular Mechanics (2)
224 W. 57th St.
New York, NY 10019
Tel.: 212-649-3085
Fax: 212-586-5562
Emp.: 75
Periodical
S.I.C.: 2721
Joseph Oldham *(Editor-in-Chief)*
Robert Dillingham *(V.P. & Publr.)*
John Pagliaro *(Dir.-Adv.)*
Dorothy Nolan *(Mgr.-Classified Sls.)*

Redbook (2)
224 West 57th
New York, NY 10019
Tel.: 212-649-3331
Fax: 212-581-7605
Approx.Sls.: $53,000,000
Emp.: 130
Fiscal Year-end: 12/31/90
Periodical
S.I.C.: 2721
Corporate Giving Program: United Way
D. Claeys Bahrenburg *(Pres.-Hearst Magazine Div.)*
Ellen Levine *(Editor-in-Chief)*
Anthony Hoyt *(V.P. & Publr.)*
Sarah Scrymser *(Mng. Editor)*
Pat Keane *(Sr. Dir.-Mktg.)*
Reed Foster *(Dir.-Adv.)*
Mark Adeszko *(Mgr.-Adv.-Chicago)*
Jeff Hamill *(Mgr.-Adv.-New York)*
Diana Turner *(Mgr.-Los Angeles)*
Anita Umak *(Mgr.-San Francisco)*

Sports Afield (2)
250 W. 55th St.
New York, NY 10019
Tel.: 212-649-2000
Hunting & Fishing Magazines
S.I.C.: 2721
Jay P. McGill *(Publisher)*
Thomas F. Paugh *(Editor-in-Chief)*

Town & Country (2)
1700 Broadway
New York, NY 10019
Tel.: 212-903-5000
Fax: 212-765-8308
Fax: 212-307-5616
Fiscal Year-end: 12/31/90
Periodical
S.I.C.: 2721
David A. McCann *(V.P. & Publr.)*
John Cantrell *(Editor)*
William David *(Assoc. Publr. & Dir.-Adv.)*
Deborah Patton *(Dir.-Mktg.)*

Victoria (2)
224 W. 57th St.
New York, NY 10019
Tel.: 212-649-2000
Magazine
S.I.C.: 2721
Katherine W. Mountain *(Publ.)*
Nancy Lindemeyer *(Editor)*

Hearst Newspapers Division (1)
959 Eighth Ave.
New York, NY 10019
Tel.: 212-649-2000
Newspaper Publishing
S.I.C.: 2711
Robert J. Danzig *(V.P. & Gen. Mgr.)*
J. Roger Grier *(V.P.-Grp Exec.)*
Lee J. Guittar *(V.P.-Grp. Exec.)*
Joseph T. Lyons *(Publr. Emeritus)*
George Irish *(Grp. Publr.)*
Aubrey L. Webb *(Grp. Publr.)*

Operations:

Albany Times Union (2)
News Plaza, Box 15000
Albany, NY 12212
Tel.: 518-454-5694
Newspaper Publishers
S.I.C.: 2711
Timothy O. White *(V.P. & Publisher)*

Beaumont Enterprise (2)
380 Walnut Ave.
Beaumont, TX 77701
Tel.: 409-833-3311
Newspaper Publishers
S.I.C.: 2711
Aubrey Webb *(V.P. & Publisher)*

Capital Newspapers (2)
News Plaza, Box 15000
Albany, NY 12212
Tel.: 518-454-5694

The Hearst Corporation—(Continued)

Newspaper Publishing
S.I.C.: 2711
Joseph T. Lyons *(V.P. & Publisher)*

Edwardsville Intelligencer **(2)**
117 N. Second St.
Edwardsville, IL 62025
Tel.: 618-656-4700
Newspaper Publishing
S.I.C.: 2711
Bruce Coury *(V.P. & Publisher)*

Houston Chronicle **(2)**
801 Texas Ave.
Houston, TX 77002
Tel.: 713-220-7171
Daily & Sunday Newspaper
S.I.C.: 2711
R.J.V. Johnson *(Chm. & Publisher)*

Huron Daily Tribune **(2)**
211 N. Heisterman St.
Bad Axe, MI 48413
Tel.: 517-269-6461
Publishing
S.I.C.: 2711
H. Allen Wamsley *(V.P. & Publisher)*

Jasper News-Boy **(2)**
P.O. Box 1419, 302 N. Wheeler
Jasper, TX 75951
Tel.: 409-384-3441
Periodical
S.I.C.: 2711
C.M. Sam Yeary, Jr. *(V.P. & Publisher)*

Laredo Morning Times **(2)**
111 Esperanza Dr.
Laredo, TX 78041
Tel.: 210-723-2901
Newspaper Publishers
S.I.C.: 2711
William B. Green *(V.P. & Publisher)*

Midland Daily News **(2)**
124 S. McDonald St.
Midland, MI 48640
Tel.: 517-835-7171
Publishing
S.I.C.: 2711
Otto Wick, Jr. *(V.P. & Publisher)*

Midland Reporter-Telegram **(2)**
201 E. Illinois St.
Midland, TX 79701
Tel.: 915-682-5311
Newspaper Publishing
S.I.C.: 2711
Charles A. Spence *(V.P. & Publisher)*

Plainview Daily Herald **(2)**
820 Broadway
Plainview, TX 79072
Tel.: 806-293-1343
Newspaper Publishing
S.I.C.: 2711
Rollie D. Hyde *(V.P. & Publisher)*

San Antonio Light **(2)**
420 Broadway
San Antonio, TX 78205
Tel.: 210-271-2700
Fax: 210-271-2815
Emp.: 700
Fiscal Year-end: 12/31/91
Newspaper Publishing
S.I.C.: 2711
George Irish *(V.P. & Publisher)*
Larry R. Wynn *(V.P.-Gen. Mgr.)*
Ed Rademaekers *(Exec. Editor)*
Henrietta Hopper *(Dir.-Human Resources)*
Sergio Salinas *(Dir.-Adv. & Mktg.)*
Maria Elena Torralva *(Dir.-Community Rels.)*
Jeff Wendland *(Dir.-Display Adv.)*
B. Joe Vied *(Resident Controller)*
Paul Allison *(Mgr.-Bus. Services)*
Randall Brant *(Mgr.-Adv.,National/Zoned Prod.)*
Jerry Carpenter *(Mgr.-Computer Center)*
John Hetzler *(Mgr.-Retail Adv.)*
Robert S. Wilson *(Gen. Mgr.)*
Gilbert Alfaro *(Pur. Agent)*
Jeannette Kirby *(Editorial Librarian)*

San Francisco Examiner **(2)**
110 5th St.
San Francisco, CA 94103
Tel.: 415-777-2424
Newspaper Publishing; Jointly Owned by the San Francisco Chronicle
S.I.C.: 2711
Randolph A. Hearst *(Pres.)*
William R. Hearst, III *(V.P., Editor & Publisher)*

Seattle Post-Intelligencer **(2)**
101 Elliott Ave. W.
Seattle, WA 98119-4220
Tel.: 206-448-8000
Fax: 206-448-8165
Emp.: 180
Fiscal Year-end: 12/31/92
Newspaper Publishing; Owned by The Hearst Corporation; Printed, Sold & Distributed by Seattle Times Co.
S.I.C.: 2711
Virgil Fassio *(V.P. & Publisher)*
J.D. Alexander *(Exec. Editor)*
Kerry Slagle *(Mng. Editor)*
John Joly *(Dir.-Public Affairs)*
William R. Cobb *(Mgr.-Bus.)*

Hearst Real Estate Division **(1)**
1150 S. Olive St., Suite 2620
Los Angeles, CA 90015
Tel.: 213-749-1327
Renting, Buying, Selling, Managing & Appraising
S.I.C.: 6531
George R. Hearst, Jr. *(V.P.-Grp. Head)*

Operations:

Down East Timberlands Division **(2)**
23 1/2 E. Main St.
Machias, ME 04654
Tel.: 207-255-4732
Manages Woodlands in North Maine & New Brunswick, Canada
S.I.C.: 0811
Benson M. Srere *(V.P.)*

San Francisco Realties **(2)**
200 Hearst Bldg.
San Francisco, CA 94103
Tel.: 415-777-0600
S.I.C.: 6531

Sunical Land & Livestock Division **(2)**
200 Hearst Building
San Francisco, CA 94103
Tel.: 415-777-0600
Owns & Operates Ranch Properties & Timberlands in California
S.I.C.: 0811
Amory J. Cooke *(V.P. & Gen. Mgr.)*

Hesco Supply Co., Inc. **(1)**
959 Eighth Ave.
New York, NY 10019
Tel.: 212-649-2111
Publishing Equipment & Supplies
S.I.C.: 3555
Frank F. Roberts, Jr. *(Mgr.)*

King Features Syndicate Division **(1)**
235 E. 45th St.
New York, NY 10017
Tel.: 212-455-4000
Syndicates Features; Produces & Syndicates TV Programs; Produces Motion Picture Films
S.I.C.: 7812
Joseph F. D'Angelo *(Pres.)*
Bruce L. Paisner *(Exec. V.P.)*
James D. Head *(Exec. Editor)*

Operation:

Cowles Syndicate, Inc. **(2)**
235 E. 45th St.
New York, NY 10017
Tel.: 212-455-4000
Comics & Features
S.I.C.: 2741
Joseph F. D'Angelo *(Pres.)*

Non-U.S. Holding:

The National Magazine Company Ltd. **(1)**
72 Broadwick St.
London, W1V 2BP, United Kingdom
Tel.: 071-439 5000
Telex: 263879 natmag g
Fax: 071-437 6886
Emp.: 490
Magazine Publishing
S.I.C.: 2721
Beverlie Flower *(Dir.-Personnel)*
Stephen Hemsted *(Sec. & Dir.-Fin.)*
Terry Mansfield *(Mng. Dir.)*
David Sheilds *(Dir.-Grp. Mktg.)*

HEAT BATH PARK METALLURGICAL, INC.
107 Front St.
Indian Orchard, MA 01151
Mailing Address:
P.O. Box 2978,
Springfield, MA 01102
Tel.: 413-543-3381
Sales Range: $10-19 Million
Heating Devices
S.I.C.: 2819; 2822; 2899
Ernest Wallen *(Pres.)*

Subsidiary:

Heat Bath Park Metallurgical Products **(1)**
8074 Military Ave.
Detroit, MI 48204
Tel.: 313-895-7215
Import Export
Mfr. of Heat Treating Chemicals & Electroplating Compounds
S.I.C.: 2819; 2822; 2899

HEAT CONTROLLER, INC.
1900 Wellworth Ave.
Jackson, MI 49203
Mailing Address:
P.O. Box 1089,
Jackson, MI 49204
Tel.: 517-787-2100
Fax: 517-787-9341
Approx.Sls.: $50,000,000
Emp.: 100
Fiscal Year-end: 8/31/92
Export
Mfr. of Air Conditioning & Heating Equipment, Comfort-Aire; Century
S.I.C.: 3585
Warren E. Shoulders *(Pres.)*
J.A. Knight *(Chief Exec. Officer)*
Dave Duane *(Controller)*
Peter Gasparini *(Mgr.-Natl. Sls.)*
Dick Geisen *(Mgr.-Mfg.)*
Don Peck *(Mgr.-Natl. Sls.)*
John Rhoads *(Mgr.-Adv. & Pub. Rels.)*

HEATH CONSULTANTS INCORPORATED
100 Tosca Dr.
Stoughton, MA 02072
Mailing Address:
P.O. Box 9114
Stoughton, MA 02072-9114
Tel.: 617-344-1400
Tel.: 800-432-8487 **DE**
Fax: 617-341-4359
Year Founded: 1933
Assets: $6,000,000
Net Worth: $6,000,000
Approx.Sls.: $18,000,000
Emp.: 250
Export
Consulting Service To Gas, Oil, Water & Telephone Industry; Contract Locating & Leak Detection
S.I.C.: 3559; 3812; 3823; 3829; 7389; 8731; 8744
Milton W. Heath, Jr. *(Chm. Bd., Chief Exec. Officer & Treas.)*
Andre J. Massicott *(Pres. & Chief Oper. Officer)*
L. Elizabeth Johnson *(V.P.-Opers.)*
Normand D. Massicotte *(V.P.-Fin. & Admin.)*
Robert J. Perry *(V.P.-Mktg.)*
M. Vance Munro *(Sec.)*
David R. Bull *(Mgr.-Natl. Sls.)*
Daniel C. Hicks *(Mgr.-Market Devel.)*
James H. Nash *(Mgr.-Gen. Services)*
Frank Richardson *(Mgr.-Pur.)*
Stuart B. Eynon *(Legal Consultant)*

Principal(s):
Milton W. Heath, Jr.

No. of Mfg. Plants/Facilities: 1
No. of U.S. Offices: 7

Outside Service Firm(s):

Ernst & Young*(Auditors)*
200 Clarendon St., 46th Fl.
Boston, MA 02116
Tel.: 617-266-2000

Willis Corroon*(Commercial Insurance Carrier)*
301 Plus Park Blvd.
Nashville, TN 37217
Tel.: 615-367-9702

Gaston & Snow*(Legal Firm)*
One Federal St.
Boston, MA 02110
Tel.: 617-426-4600
Fax: 617-350-6146

Shawmut Bank*(Major Banking Relationship)*
Canton, MA

HEAVY MACHINES, INC.
4087 Viscount
Memphis, TN 38118
Tel.: 901-366-2200
Fax: 901-366-2206
Approx.Sls.: $30,000,000
Emp.: 140
Wholesale & Service Heavy Equipment Machines & Parts; Rebuild Electric Motor & Armature Services
S.I.C.: 5084; 7694
Rich Wilson Jr. *(Chm. Bd. & Pres.)*
Thomas A. Emerson *(Pres.-Mining Devel. & V.P.)*
Ted Bailey *(Chief Oper. Officer & V.P.)*
Lois R. Tribble *(V.P.-Fin.)*
Alan Mueser *(Treas.)*
Sylvia Armstrong *(Dir.-Human Resources)*

Outside Service Firm(s):

Whitehorn Tankersley*(Auditors)*
Memphis, TN

Charles M. Crump*(Legal Firm)*
Memphis, TN

Bank Of Boston*(Major Banking Relationship)*
Nashville, TN

HECK ENTERPRISES, INC.
5415 S. Choctaw
Baton Rouge, LA 70805
Tel.: 504-356-2481 **LA**
Fax: 504-356-2525
Approx.Sls.: $11,000,000
Emp.: 120
Mfr. of Ready-mixed Concrete; Gravel Mining; Common Sand Mining
S.I.C.: 3273; 1442
Raymond E. Heck *(Pres.)*
Wallace E. Heck, Jr. *(V.P.)*
Shirley A. Heck *(Sec.)*
Kathy Roy *(Controller)*

HECKETHORN MFG. COMPANY
(Div. Of 3900 Corp.)
2005 Forrest St.
Dyersburg, TN 38024
Mailing Address:
P.O. Box 310,
Dyersburg, TN 38025-0310
Tel.: 901-285-3310
Approx.Sls.: $30,000,000
Emp.: 398
Fiscal Year-end: 4/30/92
Export
Mfr. U-Bolts, Muffler Clamps
S.I.C.: 3542; 3423; 3449; 3429
G.J. Ostrom *(Pres. & Gen. Mgr.)*
Jerald Hamm *(V.P. & Dir.-Human Resources & Safety)*
Danny J. Whittle *(V.P.-Mfg., Quality Assurance & Asst. Gen. Mgr.)*
Ersley McLemore *(Dir.-Pur., Plng. & Inventory Control)*
James Dowell *(Mgr.-Office)*
W.J. Dowling *(Mgr.-Projects)*

Larry Tharpe *(Mgr.-Special Projects)*

Computer Systems/Hardware:
IBM

HEERY INTERNATIONAL, INC.
999 Peachtree St., NE
Atlanta, GA 30367
Tel.: 404-881-9880 **GA**
Fax: 404-875-1283
Year Founded: 1952
Approx.Sls.: $54,000,000
Emp.: 550
Fiscal Year-end: 12/31/92
Architecture, Engineering, Construction Management; Program Management; Interior Design; Graphic Design; Energy Management
S.I.C.: 8711; 8712; 8741
James J. Moynihan *(Pres. & Chief Exec. Officer)*
John P. Hill, Jr. *(Chief Fin. Officer)*
Joshua L. Brener *(Exec. V.P.)*
Victor L. Cohen *(Exec. V.P.-Admin.)*
Joseph M. Harris *(Exec. V.P.)*
Charles V. Raubacher *(Exec. V.P.)*
Frank Brewer *(Dir.-Computer Resources)*
David Johnson *(Dir.-Pur. & Telecommunications)*
Martha Pacini *(Dir.-Corp. Communications)*
Dan Wise *(Dir.-Human Resources)*
Richard Nikonovich-Kahn *(Legal Officer)*

Outside Service Firm(s):

Arthur Andersen & Co.*(Auditors)*
133 Peachtree Street N.E.
Atlanta, GA 30303
Tel.: 404-658-1776

Hicks, Maloof, & Campbell*(Legal Firm)*
101 Marietta Tower, Ste. 3401
Atlanta, GA 30335-5901

Trust Company Bank*(Major Banking Relationship)*
P.O. Box 4655,
Atlanta, GA 30302

HEHR INTERNATIONAL INC.
3333 Casitas Ave.
Los Angeles, CA 90039
Tel.: 213-663-1261
Fax: 213-663-2372
Approx.Sls.: $67,000,000
Emp.: 875
Fiscal Year-end: 8/31/90
Mfr. Windows & Accessories for Mobile Homes, Recreational Vehicles, Vans, Toppers, Buses & Boats
S.I.C.: 3442
Warren F. Jones *(Chm. Bd.)*
David Utick *(Pres. & Chief Exec.. Officer)*
Gene P. Bond *(V.P.-Matls.)*
Dick Negreu *(V.P.-Mktg.)*
Richard Stine *(Dir.-Sls.)*

HEICO INC.
4225 Naperville Rd., Ste. 200
Lisle, IL 60532
Tel.: 708-955-0220
Fax: 708-955-2230
Year Founded: 1979
Mfr. of Service Industry Machinery
S.I.C.: 3585; 3589
L. Edwin Donegan *(Chm. Bd.)*
Richard R. Dentner *(Pres.)*
Dan M. Schramm *(V.P.-Fin.)*
Fred Smith *(V.P.-Corp. Development)*

Outside Service Firm(s):

Arthur Andersen & Co.*(Auditors)*
33 W. Monroe St.
Chicago, IL 60603-4067
Tel.: 312-580-0033
Fax: 312-507-6748

First Wisconsin National Bank*(Major Banking Relationship)*
777 E. Wisconsin Ave.
Milwaukee, WI 53202
Tel.: 414-765-4321
Fax: 414-355-6903

Divisions:

Davis Walker Corp. **(1)**
5555 No. Irwindale Ave.
Irwindale, CA 91706
Tel.: 818-969-7651
Approx.Sls.: $125,000,000
Manufacturer of Wire & Wire Products
S.I.C.: 3496
Michael E. Yates *(Pres.)*
Steven Herrera *(V.P.-Fin.)*
James R. Pearsall *(V.P.-Mktg. & Sls.)*
Eddie D. McNew *(V.P.-Pur.)*
Hans G. Sidell *(V.P.-Mfg.)*

O'Brien Division **(1)**
P.O. Box 191
Mendota, IL 61342
Tel.: 815-539-7411
Sewer, Pipe Cleaning, Conduit Threading Equipment; Augers, Cables, Cutters, Continuous & Sectional Rods
S.I.C.: 3589

Davis Molding Co. **(1)**
350 Kehoe Blvd.
Carol Stream, IL 60187
S.I.C.: 5031

ALCO/Belgium Foundries **(1)**
1930 S. Fourth St.
Milwaukee, WI 53204
S.I.C.: 3325

Subsidiaries:

The Field Controls Company **(1)**
2308 Airport Rd.
Kinston, NC 28501
Tel.: 919-522-3031
Fax: 919-522-0214
Approx.Sls.: $8,000,000
Emp.: 80
Fiscal Year-end: 5/31/91
Export
Mfr. of Draft Regulators, Power Venters, Air-Boosters, Draft Inducers, Chimney Caps; Humidifiers
S.I.C.: 3823; 3585
Michael E. Heisley *(Pres.)*
Robert Bianchi *(Controller)*
Mac Fairclothe *(Dir.-Pur.)*

VIP Engineered Products, Inc. **(1)**
5501 W. Grand Ave.
Chicago, IL 60639
S.I.C.: 8711

Zalk Joseph Fabrications, Inc. **(1)**
400 Industrial Dr.
Staughton, WI 53589
S.I.C.: 8711

HEIDTMAN STEEL PRODUCTS, INC.
2401 Front St.
Toledo, OH 43605
Tel.: 419-691-4646
Fax: 419-698-1150
Approx.Sls.: $150,000,000
Emp.: 350
Shear, Slit & Roller Level Sheet Steel
S.I.C.: 3444; 3547
John C. Bates *(Pres.)*
Mark Ridenour *(Exec. V.P. & Treas.)*
W. DiNardo *(V.P.-Opers.)*
M. Kruse *(V.P.-Sls.)*
Carl Moore *(Mgr.-Sls.)*

Outside Service Firm(s):

Linda Shinkle*(Legal Firm)*
Toledo, OH

Fifth Third Bank*(Major Banking Relationship)*
Toledo, OH

HEIGHTS HEATING & COOLING
2005 Pontiac Rd.
Auburn Hills, MI 48326
Tel.: 313-373-5431
Fax: 313-373-4175
Approx.Sls.: $11,000,000
Emp.: 60
Mechanical Contractor
S.I.C.: 1711; 5075
Daniel J. Rollin *(Pres.)*
Gregory Giegler *(V.P.)*
James L. Giegler *(V.P.)*
Steven Rollin *(V.P.)*
Mary Jane Buchanan *(Sec. & Treas.)*

Outside Service Firm(s):

Runyan & Meiselbach*(Auditors)*
Detroit, MI

National Bank of Detroit*(Major Banking Relationship)*
Ann Arbor, MI

HEIL-BRICE RETAIL ADVERTISING
101 S. El Camino Real, Ste. 101
San Clemente, CA 92672
Tel.: 714-492-5101
Fax: 714-498-5437
Year Founded: 1982
Approx.Billings: $20,000,000
Emp.: 16
Supermarket Chains/Retail Adv.
Corporate Giving Program: Pro-Bono Work as Decided by All Staff in Monthly Meetings.
Hal Brice *(Pres.)*
Joni Brice *(Chief Exec. Officer)*
Vicki Scruggs *(V.P. & Dir.-Admin.)*
Ally Morris *(Dir.-Mktg.)*
Lisa Haynes *(Mgr.-Pub. Rels.)*
Seanapri Biggs *(Asst.-Mktg.)*
Nina Archbold *(Mgr.-Office)*

THE HEIL CO.
Eastgate Center
Chattanooga, TN 37411
Mailing Address:
P.O. Box 8676
Chattanooga, TN 37411
Tel.: 615-899-9100 **WI**
Fax: 615-855-3478
Year Founded: 1901
Sales Range: $100-499 Million
Emp.: 1,500
Fiscal Year-end: 10/31/90
Mfr. of Refuse Collection Equipment; Dump Bodies & Hoists; Trailerized Tanks; Plastic Refuse Containers
S.I.C.: 3089; 3443; 3536; 3713
Corporate Giving Program: 2% Club
Joseph F. Heil, Jr. *(Chm. Bd. & Chief Exec. Officer)*
Lawrence F. Gray *(Pres.)*
William H. Nehrkorn *(V.P., Sec. & Gen. Counsel)*
Norman F. Weinlein *(V.P.-Fin.)*
Gordon G. Smith *(Sr. V.P.-Mktg. & Sls.)*
Jerry Zanzig *(V.P.-Engrng.)*
Vicki Walker *(Controller)*
Richard J. Fridl *(Treas.)*
Jack Danner *(Mgr.-Personnel Training & Devel.)*

No. of Mfg. Plants/Facilities: 10
No. of U.S. Offices: 17
No. of Foreign Offices: 1

Computer Systems/Hardware:
Datapoint

Outside Service Firm(s):

Arthur Andersen & Co.*(Auditors)*
777 E. Wisconsin Ave., P.O. Box 1215
Milwaukee, WI 53202
Tel.: 414-271-5100
Fax: 414-283-3200

Corroon & Black*(Commercial Insurance Carrier)*
Milwaukee, WI

Provident Life & Accident Insurance Co.*(Group Insurer)*
230 West Monroe, Ste. 2520
Chicago, IL 60606
Tel.: 312-704-0220

Foley & Lardner*(Legal Firm)*
777 E. Wisconsin Ave.
Milwaukee, WI 53202
Tel.: 414-271-2400

First National Bank of Boston*(Major Banking Relationship)*
P.O. Box 644,
Boston, MA 02102-0644
Tel.: 617-575-2900
Fax: 617-575-2549

First Wisconsin National Bank*(Major Banking Relationship)*
777 E. Wisconsin Ave.
Milwaukee, WI 53202
Tel.: 414-765-4321
Fax: 414-355-6903

Fiduciary Management, Inc.*(Pension Manager)*
Madison, WI

First Wisconsin-Madison*(Pension Manager)*
Madison, WI

First Wisconsin Trust Company*(Pension Manager)*
Lewis Center, 615 E. Michigan Ave., 4th Fl.
Milwaukee, WI 53202
Tel.: 414-276-3737
Fax: 414-276-4226

Northwestern Mutual*(Pension Manager)*
Milwaukee, WI

Divisions:

Heil Bulk Trailer Co. **(1)**
3249 Hempland Rd.
Lancaster, PA 17604
Tel.: 717-397-7771
Truck & Bus Bodies
S.I.C.: 3713
Robert A. Foster *(Mgr.)*

Heil Bulk Trailer Co. **(1)**
P.O. Box 160,
Athens, TN 37303
Tel.: 615-745-5830
Truck & Bus Bodies
S.I.C.: 3713
Robert A. Foster *(Mgr.)*

Heil Bulk Trailer Div. **(1)**
P.O. Box 160,
Athens, TN 37303
Tel.: 615-745-5830
Truck & Bus Bodies
S.I.C.: 3713
Robert A. Foster *(V.P.-Sls.)*
Rick Connelly *(Chief Engineer)*
Bob Foster *(Plant Mgr.)*

Heil Refuse & Dump Body Co. **(1)**
P.O. Box 27,
Fort Payne, AL 35967
Tel.: 205-845-4912
Truck & Bus Bodies
S.I.C.: 3713
Glenn Chambers *(Mgr.)*

Heil Refuse & Dump Body Co. **(1)**
Hwy. 25 No.
Tishomingo, MS 38873
Tel.: 601-438-6361
Truck & Bus Bodies
S.I.C.: 3713
Glen W. Nelson *(Mgr.)*

Heil Solid Waste Div. **(1)**
P.O. Box 8676, Uptain Bldg., E,
Chattanooga, TN 37411
Tel.: 615-899-9100
Truck & Bus Bodies
S.I.C.: 3713
Lawrence Gray *(Pres.)*
Gordon Smith *(V.P.-Sls.)*
Jerald Zanzig *(Chief Engr.)*

The Heil Co.—(Continued)

Truck Equipment Div. (1)
Hwy. 25 N.
Tishomingo, MS 38873
Tel.: 601-438-7800
Truck & Bus Bodies
S.I.C.: 3713
Glenn Chambers *(Plant Mgr.)*
Don Kalberer *(Gen. Sls. Mgr.)*
Ronald Gerding *(Chief Engineer)*

Subsidiaries:

Heil Rotomold, Inc. (1)
108 E. Pioneer Rd.
Phoenix, AZ 85040
Tel.: 602-268-8688
Emp.: 62
Manufacture Rotomolded Plastic Refuse Containers & Custom Rotomolding
S.I.C.: 3089
Gerald Francisco *(Gen. Mgr.)*

Heil West, Inc. (1)
1450 N. First St.
Dixon, CA 95620
Tel.: 916-678-1961
Truck Bodies
S.I.C.: 3713
Tim Robinson *(Gen. Mgr.)*

Heil Steel Fabricating, Inc. (1)
d/b/a Euclid Body Co., 3121 Fruitland Av.
Los Angeles, CA
Tel.: 203-583-4845 (100%)
Truck Bodies
S.I.C.: 3713
Darrell Joel *(V.P.)*

Rapid Rail Systems (1)
2441 S. 40th St.
Phoenix, AZ 85034
Tel.: 602-470-1283
Truck & Bus Body
S.I.C.: 3713

Tank Service, Inc. (1)
P.O. Box 3386
Knoxville, TN 37917
S.I.C.: 3713
Wayne Thompson *(Pres. & Treas.)*
Gaylord Poeschl *(V.P. & Sec.)*

Divisions:

Heil Tank Service, Inc. (2)
P.O. Box 173-20,
Huntsville, TX 77340
Tel.: 713-295-8103
Truck & Bus Bodies
S.I.C.: 3713
Mike Berberich *(Mgr.)*

Heil Tank Services, Inc. (2)
P.O. Box 3386,
Knoxville, TN 37917
Truck & Bus Bodies
S.I.C.: 3713

Tesco (1)
2441 S. 40th St.
Phoenix, AZ 85034
Tel.: 602-437-3113
Mfr. of Truck Equipment
S.I.C.: 3713

Non-U.S. Holding:

Hillend Environmental Industry, Ltd. (1)
Hillend Industrial Estate
Dunfermline, KY11 5JW, United Kingdom
Tel.: Dalgety Bay 823625 (100%)
Approx.Sls.: $3,500,000
Emp.: 60
Manufacture of Refuse Bodies
S.I.C.: 3589
William W. McCracken *(Chief Oper. Officer)*

G. HEILEMAN BREWING CO., INC.
100 Harborview Plaza
La Crosse, WI 54601
Mailing Address:
P.O. Box 459,
La Crosse, WI 54602
Tel.: 608-785-1000 **WI**
Telex: 29-3414
Fax: 608-785-3795
Year Founded: 1853
Approx.Sls.: $830,000,000
Emp.: 2,200
Fiscal Year-end: 6/30/91
Import Export
Brewery; Air Transportation
S.I.C.: 2082; 4512; 5181
Thomas J. Rattigan *(Chm. Bd., Pres. & Chief Exec. Officer)*
Ian S. Crichton *(Sr. Exec. V.P.-Sls.)*
Robert W. D'Ornellas *(Exec. V.P.-Mktg.)*
Henry Gerfen *(Exec. V.P.-Mktg.)*
Michael B. Evans *(Exec. V.P. & Chief Admin. Officer)*
Daniel J. Schmid, Jr. *(Exec. V.P.-Fin., Treas. & Asst. Sec.)*
Jack Hanzlovic *(V.P.-Mktg.-West Region)*
Randy L. Hull *(V.P.-Sls. & Mktg. Admin.)*
David S. Mahoney *(V.P.-Sls.-West Region)*
Peter F. O'Sullivan *(V.P.-Pur. & Production Coordination)*
James L. Reynolds *(V.P.-Sls.-East Region)*
Paul Ricker *(V.P.-Information Systems)*
Wayne D. Ruppel *(V.P.-Quality Assurance)*
Randy J. Smith *(V.P., Gen. Counsel & Sec.)*
Foster Walton *(V.P.-Opers.)*
John L. Currie *(Controller)*
Jeff Scheel *(Dir.-Human Resources)*
Margie Neader *(Media Coord.)*
Jerry Collins *(Supvr.-Fin. Reporting)*
Stan Haas *(Asst. Sec.-East Region)*
John A. Massa *(Asst. Sec.)*

Subsidiary:

Heileman Air Services, Ltd. (1)
2709 Fanta Reed Rd.
La Crosse, WI 54601
Tel.: 608-784-5567 (100%)
Certified Air Transportation
S.I.C.: 4512; 4513
Jacob R. Gross *(Pres.)*

Manufacturing Plants:

Blitz-Weinhard Brewing (1)
1133 W. Burnside St.
Portland, OR 97209
Tel.: 503-222-4351
Fax: 503-222-1982
Emp.: 200
Mfr. of Blitz Beer
S.I.C.: 2082
Bruce Oshi *(Brewery Mgr.)*
Janis R. Yaun *(Mgr.-Admin.)*
Robert Weisskirchen *(Brewmaster)*
Gary Wegener *(Mgr.-Pkgng.)*
Eugene Clark *(Adv. Mgr.)*
Linda Barclay *(Adv.)*

G. Heileman Brewing Company, Inc. (1)
4501 Hollins Ferry Rd.
Baltimore, MD 21227
Tel.: 410-247-1600
Brewery
S.I.C.: 2082
John T. Gaustad *(Plant Mgr.)*
Robert T. Lathroum *(Mgr.-Admin.)*
John Houseman *(Brewmaster)*
Joseph Ponder *(Mgr.-Pkgng.)*

G. Heileman Brewing Co., Inc. (1)
100 Harborview Plaza
La Crosse, WI 54601
Tel.: 608-785-1000
Approx.Sls.: $1,341,549,000
Emp.: 3,117
Fiscal Year-end: 6/30/90
Brewery
S.I.C.: 2082; 2051; 2052
Ronald J. Fischer *(Plant Mgr.)*
Michael Newstrom *(Asst. Plant Mgr.)*
Terry Christopherson *(Grp. Mktg. Mgr.)*
Tan Lee *(Sls. Mgr.)*
John B. Snyder *(Brewmaster)*
Mark E. Aeling *(Mgr.-Admin.)*
Laverne R. Schol *(Mgr.-Pkgng.)*

Lone Star Brewing (1)
600 Lone Star Blvd.
San Antonio, TX 78204
Tel.: 210-226-8301
Approx.Sls.: $48,000,000
Emp.: 560
Lone Star, Buckhorn Beer, Lone Star Light Black Label, Black Label Light, Mickey's Malt Liquor, Colt 45 Malt Liquor, Heidelberg, Heidelberg Light, Stag, Stag Light, Blatz, Blatz Light, Wiedeman, Wiedeman Light, Red White & Blue, Red White & Blue Light
S.I.C.: 2082
Larry Thomas *(Dir-Brand Mngmt)*
Candyce Anderson *(Mgr.-Indus. Rels.)*
Rick Anderson *(Mgr.-Interim Plant)*
John H. Belter *(Mgr.-Admin.)*
Joe McFarland *(Mgr.-Pkgng.)*
Urbahn Phillips *(Mgr.-Quality Control)*
Michael J. Reilly *(Mgr.-Gen. Sls.)*
Vern Hophen *(Chief Engr.)*
Kenneth Lee *(Brewmaster)*
William W. Roth *(Military SM)*

Rainier Brewing Co. (1)
3100 Airport Way S.
Seattle, WA 98124
Tel.: 206-622-2600
Emp.: 350
Brewery
S.I.C.: 2082
Steven N. Sarich *(Brewery Mgr.)*
Jack Hanzlovic *(V.P.-Mktg.)*
Dave Mahoney *(V.P.-Sls.)*
Robert W. Magruder *(Brewmaster)*
John R. Davis *(Mgr.-Pkgng.)*
Carol Masnik *(Mgr.-Pub. Rels.)*
Barbara A. Stephens *(Mgr.-Admin.)*
Pat Siversten *(Mgr.-Personnel)*
Eugene Clark *(Dir.-Adv.)*
Linda Barclay *(Adv.)*

HEINEN'S INC.
20601 Aurora Rd.
Warrensville Heights, OH 44146
Tel.: 216-475-2300 **OH**
Fax: 216-475-5867
Year Founded: 1929
Approx.Sls.: $128,000,000
Emp.: 1,000
Retail Supermarkets
S.I.C.: 5411
John J. Heinen *(Pres. & Chief Exec. Officer)*
Thomas J. Heinen *(V.P.)*
Daniel Musil *(Controller)*
Al Mastny *(Dir.-Data Processing)*
Lawrence Ungar *(Mgr.-Adv.)*

Outside Service Firm(s):

Hill Stonestreet & Co.*(Auditors)*
Cleveland, OH

Thompson, Hine & Flory*(Legal Firm)*
1100 National City Bank Bldg.
Cleveland, OH 44114
Tel.: 216-566-5500

Society National Bank*(Major Banking Relationship)*
900 Euclid Ave., P.O. Box 6477
Cleveland, OH 44101-6477
Tel.: 216-737-5000
Fax: 216-566-8947

HEINTZELMAN'S TRUCK CENTER INC.
2424 John Young Pkwy.
Orlando, FL 32804
Tel.: 407-298-1000 **FL**
Fax: 407-293-5344
Approx.Sls.: $69,000,000
Emp.: 75
Export
New & Used Truck Dealership
S.I.C.: 5511
John Drakesmith *(Pres.)*
Margaret Drakesmith *(V.P.)*
Steven Drakesmith *(V.P.)*
Nancy Brown *(Treas. & Sec.)*

Outside Service Firm(s):

Corbett & Leukhoff*(Auditors)*
Countryside, IL

Southeast Bank, N.A.*(Major Banking Relationship)*
Orlando, FL

HELENA LABORATORIES CORPORATION
1530 Lindbergh
Beaumont, TX 77707
Mailing Address:
P.O. Box 752,
Beaumont, TX 77704-0752
Tel.: 409-842-3714 **TX**
Year Founded: 1966
Approx.Sls.: $50,000,000
Emp.: 600
Export
Mfr. of Surgical & Medical Instruments
S.I.C.: 3841
Tipton L. Golias *(Pres. & Chief Exec. Officer)*
O.H. Mayes *(V.P.)*
Noel Bartlett *(Treas.)*
Ann Golias *(Sec.)*

HELIKON FURNITURE CO., INC.
607 Norich Ave.
Taftville, CT 06380
Tel.: 203-886-2301
Telex: 966-463
Approx.Sls.: $17,000,000
Emp.: 380
Mfr. of Custom Executive Office Furniture
S.I.C.: 2511
Robert Domlesky *(Gen. Mgr.)*
Drew Gall *(Plant Mgr.)*
Rick Parkes *(Mgr.-Acctg. & Budgeting)*
Mark Stasko *(Mgr.-Natl. Sls.)*

HELLER BROS. PACKING CORP.
306 9th St.
Winter Garden, FL 34787
Mailing Address:
P.O. Box 770249
Winter Garden, FL 34777
Tel.: 407-656-2124 **FL**
Fax: 407-656-1751
Year Founded: 1939
Approx.Sls.: $35,000,000
Emp.: 1,000
Fiscal Year-end: 12/31/91
Export
Citrus Harvester & Packer
S.I.C.: 0174; 0723
James Heller *(Chm. Bd.)*
Harvey R. Heller *(Pres.)*
Harry Freitag *(Exec. V.P.)*
W.C. Adams *(Controller)*
Glenn Jackson *(Dir.-Real Estate)*
Robert Rath *(Dir.-Sls.)*

Computer Systems/Hardware:
IBM; ADDS; PC

Outside Service Firm(s):

Simasek & Whitley*(Auditors)*
Orlando, FL

HELLER INTERNATIONAL
500 W. Monroe
Chicago, IL 60661
Tel.: 312-441-7000
Approx.Rev.: $500,000,000
Emp.: 2,800
Commercial Finance Company
S.I.C.: 6036
Michael Blum *(Chm. Bd. & Pres.)*

HELLER SEASONINGS & INGREDIENTS, INC.
6363 W. 73rd St.
Bedford Park, IL 60638
Tel.: 312-581-6800 **IL**
Fax: 708-594-2342
Year Founded: 1893
Approx.Sls.: $24,000,000
Emp.: 190

Sorghum Syrups; For Sweetening; Seasonings; Dry Mixes
S.I.C.: 2099
John R. Heller *(Chm. Bd. & Pres.)*
Robert E. Ossmann *(Chief Fin. Officer, Treas. & Sec.)*
Roger A. Maehler *(Exec. V.P.)*
R. Coe Barnard *(V.P.)*
Muhammad Chaudry *(V.P.-Quality)*
Werner Goelz *(V.P.-Facilities)*
Roger Rave *(V.P.-Pur.)*
John Schaefer *(V.P.-Mfg.)*
Gary J. Zielinski *(V.P.-Sls. & Mktg.)*
Ronald James *(Dir.-Human Resources)*

Outside Service Firm(s):

Altschuler, Melvoin & Glasser*(Auditors)*
30 S. Wecker Dr.
Chicago, IL 60606
Tel.: 312-207-2800

Harris Trust & Savings Bank*(Major Banking Relationship)*
111 W. Monroe St.
Chicago, IL 60690
Tel.: 312-461-2265
Tel.: 800-858-0840

J. HELLMAN PRODUCE, INC.
1601 E. Olympic Blvd., Ste. 200
Los Angeles, CA 90021
Tel.: 213-243-9281 **CA**
Fax: 213-627-5300
Year Founded: 1956
Approx.Sls.: $17,000,000
Emp.: 40
Wholesale Distributor of Fresh, Vegetables & Frozen Fruits
S.I.C.: 5148; 5142
Bryce Hellman *(Pres.)*
Tracy Hellman *(Sec. & Treas.)*
Douglas Evavold *(Controller)*

Outside Service Firm(s):

Kellogg & Andelson*(Auditors)*
Los Angeles, CA

First Interstate Bank*(Major Banking Relationship)*
21021 Ventura Blvd.
Woodland Hills, CA 91364
Tel.: 818-992-7153

HELM, INC.
14310 Hamilton
Highland Park, MI 48203
Tel.: 313-865-5000
Fax: 313-865-5927
Approx.Sls.: $26,000,000
Emp.: 300
Bulk & Special Packaging, Storage & Shipping, Imprinting, Labeling, Data Processing Services
S.I.C.: 7389; 7374; 4225
John Poupore *(Chm. Bd., Co-Pres. & Chief Exec. Officer)*
Ralph Farabi *(Co-Pres. & Chief Oper. Officer)*
Frank Santo *(Pres.-Mktg.)*
Ron Rocheleau *(Exec. V.P.)*
Dennis Gusick *(V.P.-Fin., Treas. & Sec.)*

Outside Service Firm(s):

Plante & Moran*(Auditors)*
Southfield, MI

Freud, Markus, Slavin & Galgan*(Legal Firm)*
Detroit, MI

Michigan National Bank*(Major Banking Relationship)*
Detroit, MI

HELMICK CORPORATION
10th St. & Minor Ave.
Fairmont, WV 26554
Mailing Address:
P.O. Box 71
Fairmont, WV 26555-0071
Tel.: 304-366-3520
Year Founded: 1868
Emp.: 125
Import Export
Mfr. of Heavy Duty Equipment for Electric Utilities: High Alloy Iron Castings, Abrasive Pumps, Coal Pulverizer Parts, Power Plant Equipment, Boiler Tube Shielding & Boiler Equipment
S.I.C.: 3321
Louis G. Helmick *(Chm. Bd.)*
David G. Helmick *(Pres.)*
Louis G. Helmick III *(V.P. & Treas.)*
Bruce Gezon *(V.P.-Mktg.)*
Susan T. Helmick *(Sec.)*

Outside Service Firm(s):

Medwig, Labriola & Co.*(Auditors)*
Pittsburgh, PA

First National Bank*(Major Banking Relationship)*
Fairmont, WV

Gabler & Aloe, P.C.*(Legal Firm)*
Pittsburgh, PA

EDD HELMS ELECTRICAL CONTRACTING
17830 N.E. 5th Ave.
Miami, FL 33162
Tel.: 305-653-2520
Fax: 305-651-5527
Year Founded: 1975
Assets: $4,700,000
Liabilities: $2,400,000
Net Worth: $2,300,000
Sales Range: $10-19 Million
Emp.: 200
Electrical Contracting
S.I.C.: 1731
W. Edd Helms, Jr. *(Chm.)*
Carol A. Helms *(Pres.)*
Roberta Schuler *(Controller)*
Laz Schneider *(Gen. Counsel)*
Francisco Faraett *(Dir.-Data Processing & Mngmt. Information Systems)*
Principal(s):
W. Edd Helms, Jr.
Carol A. Helms

No. of Mfg. Plants/Facilities: 8
No. of U.S. Offices: 1

Computer Systems/Hardware:
Digital Equip. Systems PDP11/84X, RL02, & VT100; Fujitsa 134MB Winchester Drives

Outside Service Firm(s):

Dohan, Simon & Freedman CPA*(Auditors)*
Miami, FL

Aetna Life & Casualty*(Commercial Insurance Carrier)*
Coral Gables, FL

Siegfried, Kipnis, Rivera, Lerner & de LaTorre*(Legal Firm)*
Coral Gables, FL

Barnett Banks Trust Company, N.A.*(Major Banking Relationship)*
Palm Beach, FL

Pension Investors, Inc.*(Pension Manager)*
Miami, FL

Subsidiaries:

Edd Helms Electrical, Inc. **(1)**
17830 N.E. 5th Ave.
Miami, FL 33162
Tel.: 305-653-2520
S.I.C.: 1731
W. Edd Helms, Jr. *(Chief Oper. Officer)*

Edd Helms Electrical Service, Inc. **(1)**
17830 N.E. 5th Ave.
Miami, FL 33162
Tel.: 305-653-2520
S.I.C.: 1731
W. Edd Helms, Jr. *(Chief Oper. Officer)*

HELMSLEY ENTERPRISES, INC.
60 E. 42nd St.
New York, NY 10165
Tel.: 212-687-6400 **DE**
Fax: 212-880-0637
Approx.Sls.: $1,700,000,000
Emp.: 13,000
Fiscal Year-end: 12/31/90
Lodging, Restaurants, Food Service; Real Estate Development & Management
S.I.C.: 7011; 2099; 5812; 6531; 6552
Harry B. Helmsley *(Chm. Bd., Pres. & Chief Exec. Officer)*
William La Blina *(Sr. V.P.)*
Martin S. Stone *(Treas. & Sec.)*
Richard Taglianetti *(Controller)*
J. Voncina *(Mgr.-Personnel)*

Computer Systems/Hardware:
IBM 4381

Outside Service Firm(s):

Eisner & Lubin*(Auditors)*
New York, NY

Empire Blue Cross & Blue Shield*(Group Insurer)*
New York, NY

Metropolitan Life Insurance Co.*(Group Insurer)*
One Madison Ave.
New York, NY 10010-3690
Tel.: 215-578-9292

Chase Manhattan Bank, N.A.*(Major Banking Relationship)*
One Chase Manhattan Plaza
New York, NY 10081
Tel.: 212-552-2222
Tel.: 800-526-0801
Fax: 212-552-7175

Chemical Bank*(Major Banking Relationship)*
450 West 33rd St.
New York, NY 10001
Tel.: 212-613-7197
Fax: 212-947-7628

Subsidiaries:

Brown, Harris, Stevens, Inc. **(1)**
14 E. 47th St.
New York, NY 10017
Tel.: 212-697-8800 (100%)
Real Estate Brokerage
S.I.C.: 6531

Deco Purchasing Co. **(1)**
151 E. Washington
Orlando, FL 32801
Tel.: 407-841-3220
Purchasing
S.I.C.: 5141

Albert M. Greenfield & Company **(1)**
1880 JFK Blvd.
Philadelphia, PA 19103
Tel.: 215-569-8200 (100%)
Real Estate Brokerage
S.I.C.: 6531

Helmsley Hotels Inc. **(1)**
455 Madison Ave.
New York, NY 10022
Tel.: 212-860-1624 (100%)
Hotel Management
S.I.C.: 7011

Helmsley-Noyes Co., Inc. **(1)**
60 E. 42nd St.
New York, NY 10022
Tel.: 212-687-4200 (100%)
Real Estate Brokerage
S.I.C.: 6531

The Helmsley Palace Hotel **(1)**
455 Madison Ave.
New York, NY 10022
Tel.: 212-888-7000
Operates Hotel
S.I.C.: 7011
Leona Helmsley *(Pres.)*
Gerald M. Kadish *(Exec. V.P.)*

Helmsley-Spear Inc. **(1)**
60 E. 42nd St.
New York, NY 10165
Tel.: 212-687-6400
Emp.: 10,000
Restaurants, Real Estate, Hotels
S.I.C.: 7011; 2099; 5812; 6531
Harry B. Helmsley *(Pres. & Chief Exec. Officer)*
Greg Popkin *(V,P.-Corp. Admin. Plng.)*
William Lubliner *(Treas.)*
Richard Taglianetti *(Controller)*
Robert Lobman *(Dir.-Mngmt. Information Systems)*

Helmsley-Spear Conversion Sales Corp. **(1)**
140 E. 56th St.
New York, NY 10022
Tel.: 212-223-3631 (100%)
Real Estate Sls. Corp.
S.I.C.: 6531

National Realty Corp. **(1)**
305 W. 22nd St.
New York, NY 10011
Tel.: 212-989-0209 (100%)
Real Estate Brokerage
S.I.C.: 6531

Owners Maintenance Corp. **(1)**
420 Lexington Ave.
New York, NY 10170
Tel.: 212-986-0150 (100%)
Real Estate Services
S.I.C.: 6512

John J. Reynolds, Inc. **(1)**
685 5th Ave.
New York, NY 10022
Tel.: 212-355-7000 (100%)
Real Estate Brokerage
S.I.C.: 6531

Security Title & Guaranty Co. **(1)**
300 E. 40th
New York, NY 10016
Tel.: 212-661-5010 (100%)
Title Insurance
S.I.C.: 6361

HELP MANAGEMENT CORPORATION
6800 College Blvd., Suite 600
Overland Park, KS 66211
Tel.: 913-345-1300
Fax: 913-345-1770
Year Founded: 1977
Assets: $828,000,000
Earnings: $9,000,000
Liabilities: $677,000,000
Net Worth: $151,000,000
Approx.Rev.: $81,000,000
Emp.: 1,200
Fiscal Year-end: 9/30/89
Primary Guarantor of Student Loans
S.I.C.: 6163
Richard C. Hawk *(Chm. Bd. & Chief Exec. Officer)*
Bruce L. Olson *(Vice Chm. & Treas.)*

No. of U.S. Offices: 6

Computer Systems/Hardware:
IBM 300E

Outside Service Firm(s):

Aetna Life & Casualty*(Group Insurer)*
100 N. Riverside Plaza
Chicago, IL 60606

Help Management Corporation—(Continued)

Affiliates:

Help Service Corporation **(1)**
6800 College Blvd.
Overland Park, KS 66211
Tel.: 913-345-1300
Provides Data Processing & Support Services to Both Lenders & Guarantee Agencies
S.I.C.: 7374

Higher Education Assistance Foundation **(1)**
6800 College Blvd., Suite 600
Overland Park, KS 66211
Tel.: 913-345-1300
Student Loan Guarantor
S.I.C.: 6163

Higher Education Loan Program of Kansas **(1)**
6800 College Blvd., Suite 600
Overland Park, KS 66211
Tel.: 913-345-1300
Secures Student Loans
S.I.C.: 6163

Higher Education Loan Program of Washington, D.C. **(1)**
1800 K. St. N.W.
Washington, DC 20005
Tel.: 202-223-1360

Higher Education Loan Program of West Virginia **(1)**
830 Charleston Natl. Plaza
Charleston, WV 25301
Tel.: 304-343-0490
Guarantor of Student Loans
S.I.C.: 6163

JOAN & DAVID HELPERN, INC.
1935 Revere Beach Pkwy.
Everett, MA 02149
Tel.: 617-387-5005 **MA**
Fax: 617-389-8018
Year Founded: 1954
Approx.Sls.: $87,000,000
Emp.: 650
Retail Sales of Women's & Children's Shoes, Boots & Apparel Accessories
S.I.C.: 5661; 5632; 5139; 5137
David Helpern *(Chm. Bd.)*
Joan Helpern *(Pres.)*
Ron Cafarella *(V.P.-Fin.)*
Steven Fischman *(Sec.)*

Outside Service Firm(s):

KPMG Peat Marwick*(Auditors)*
One Boston Place
Boston, MA 02108
Tel.: 617-723-7700

State Street Bank & Trust Co.*(Major Banking Relationship)*
225 Franklin St.
Boston, MA 02101
Tel.: 617-786-3000

Subsidiary:

Joan & David, Inc. **(1)**
1935 Revere Beach Pkwy.
Everett, MA 02149
Tel.: 617-387-5005
Approx.Sls.: $54,000,000
Emp.: 23
Retail Sales of Women's & Children's Shoes, Boots & Clothing
S.I.C.: 5139; 5137
Joan Helpern *(Pres.)*
Ronald F. Cafarella *(Chief Fin. Officer)*
David M. Helpern *(Treas.)*
Steven F. Fischman *(Sec.)*

HELWIG CARBON PRODUCTS, INC.
8900 W. Tower Ave.
Milwaukee, WI 53224
Mailing Address:
P.O. Box 24400,
Milwaukee, WI 53224-0400
Tel.: 414-354-2411 **WI**
Fax: 414-354-2421
Year Founded: 1928
Approx.Sls.: $19,000,000
Emp.: 280
Fiscal Year-end: 10/31/91
Export
Manufacture Carbon Brushes, Mechanical Carbon Parts, Constant Pressure Brush Holders, Helwig Quick Disconnect Terminals (HQD)
S.I.C.: 3624
Corporate Giving Program: Member of Milwaukee Initative. Gives 4% of Pretax
J.C. Koenitzer *(Chm. Bd.)*
John E. Koenitzer *(Pres. & Chief Exec. Officer)*
N.T. Joers *(V.P.-Plant Opers.)*
Ken Kartman *(V.P. & Dir.-Adv.)*
J.D. Koenitzer *(V.P.-Engrng.)*
Ronald A. Carlson *(Sec. & Treas.)*
H.A. Kroening *(Dir.-Pur.)*
J.G. Koenitzer *(Mgr.-Sls.)*
Carol Schumann *(Mgr.-Export)*
Marjorie Hudson *(Exec. Sec.)*

No. of Mfg. Plants/Facilities: 1
No. of U.S. Offices: 1

Computer Systems/Hardware:
McDonnell Douglas Reality Model, Digital Equipment Corp, Vax 4000, Sun Sparc 1PX

Outside Service Firm(s):

Whyte & Hirschboeck, S.C.*(Legal Firm)*
111 E. Wisconsin Ave.
Milwaukee, WI 53202
Tel.: 414-271-8210

M & I Marshall & Ilsley Bank*(Major Banking Relationship)*
770 N. Water St.
Milwaukee, WI 53202
Tel.: 414-765-8700

HELZBERG'S DIAMOND SHOPS, INC.
1825 Swift Ave.
North Kansas City, MO 64116-3606
Tel.: 816-842-0479
Fax: 816-842-7780 ext. 214
Approx.Sls.: $35,000,000
Emp.: 1,300
Fiscal Year-end: 2/23/91
Retail Jewelry Stores
S.I.C.: 5944
Barnett C. Helzberg, Jr. *(Chm. Bd. & Chief Exec. Officer)*
J.W. Comment *(Pres. & Chief Oper. Officer)*
Marvin Beasley *(V.P.-Mdse.)*
John Goodman *(V.P.-Mktg.)*
L.E. Johnson *(V.P.-Real Estate)*
David C. Oshel *(V.P.-Fin.)*
Peg Billick *(Mgr.-Data Processing)*

Principal(s):
Barnett C. Helzberg, Jr.

Computer Systems/Hardware:
Qantel 285

Outside Service Firm(s):

Deloitte & Touche*(Auditors)*
1010 Grand Ave.
Kansas City, MO 64106-2232
Tel.: 816-474-6180

First National Bank of Kansas City*(Major Banking Relationship)*
10th & Baltimore
Kansas City, MO 64105
Tel.: 816-221-2800

United Missouri Bank of Kansas City, N.A.*(Major Banking Relationship)*
Securities Transfer Division, P.O. Box 410064
Kansas City, MO 64141-0064
Tel.: 816-556-7445

PAUL HEMMER CONSTRUCTION COMPANY
250 Grandview Dr.
Fort Mitchell, KY 41017
Tel.: 606-341-8300 **KY**
Fax: 606-341-6817
Year Founded: 1982
Approx.Sls.: $48,000,000
Emp.: 160
New Construction of Commercial, Industrial & Office Buildings
S.I.C.: 1542; 1541
Paul W. Hemmer, Sr. *(Chm. Bd.)*
Paul W. Hemmer, Jr. *(Pres. & Chief Exec. Officer)*
John F. Curtin *(V.P.-Sls.)*
William M. Hargis *(V.P.)*
John J. Hemmer *(V.P.-Devel.)*
Michael J. Hemmer *(V.P.-Engrng.)*
Barry G. Kienzle *(V.P.-Fin.)*
Donald M. Hemmer *(Treas. & Sec.)*

Outside Service Firm(s):

Ernst & Young*(Auditors)*
1300 Chiquita Center, 250 E. Fifth St.
Cincinnati, OH 45202
Tel.: 513-621-6454

INB National Bank*(Major Banking Relationship)*
One Indiana Sq.
Indianapolis, IN 46266
Tel.: 317-266-6000

HEMPT BROTHERS, INC.
205 Creek Rd.
Camp Hill, PA 17011
Tel.: 717-737-3411
Fax: 717-761-5019
Sales Range: $40-59 Million
Emp.: 400
Heavy Highway Construction; Road Building, Transit Mix Concrete, Limestone Quarries, Paving & Excavation, Grading, Asphalt Plants, Slag Process, Sand & Gravel Plants
S.I.C.: 1611; 1422; 2952; 3272; 3295
Max C. Hempt *(Chm. Bd.)*
George F. Hempt *(Pres.)*
Gerald L. Hempt *(Sec. & Treas.)*
Horace A. Johnson *(Gen. Counsel)*
Warren Kingsbury *(Chief Engr.)*
Harold Maxwell *(Mgr.-Sls.)*
Joseph Nokovich *(Mgr.-Matl.)*

Outside Service Firm(s):

KPMG Peat Marwick*(Auditors)*
P.O. Box 1190, 225 Market St., Ste. 300
Harrisburg, PA 17108-1190
Tel.: 717-238-7131

Johnson, Duffie, Stewart & Weidner*(Legal Firm)*
Lemoyne, PA

Dauphin Deposit Bank & Trust Co.*(Major Banking Relationship)*
213 Market St.
Harrisburg, PA 17101

HENCO, INC.
P.O. Box 547, Selmer Industrial Park
Selmer, TN 38375
Tel.: 901-645-3255 **TN**
Fax: 901-645-9700
Approx.Sls.: $36,000,000
Emp.: 525
Fiscal Year-end: 7/31/90
Import
Package Gourmet & Gift Items: Candy, Cookies, Cheese, Popcorn, Gift Wrap, Ribbon & Magazines
S.I.C.: 5149; 5145; 5199
Tom E. Hendrix *(Chm. Bd., Pres. & Chief Exec. Officer)*
N. David Landreth *(Pres.)*
Ralph Amos *(V.P.-Opers.)*
Bob Brooks *(V.P.-Sls.)*
George Donaldson *(V.P.-Admin.)*
Ardy McIntosh *(V.P.-Mktg.)*
Tom O'Neal *(V.P.-Personnel)*
George Donaldson *(Sec. & Treas.)*
Anita Graham *(Corp. Sec.)*
Jerry Eskridge *(Dir.-Data Processing)*
Jim Robison *(Dir.-Pur.)*
Robert Bedwell *(Mgr.-Quality Control)*
Robin Coleman *(Corp. Travel Planner)*

Principal(s):
Tom E. Hendrix
Sherry Hendrix

Outside Service Firm(s):

Price Waterhouse*(Auditors)*
One Commerce Square,
Memphis, TN 38103

Williams, Kirsch, Haskill Donalson*(Legal Firm)*
Memphis, TN

First American Bank, N.A.*(Major Banking Relationship)*
Jackson, TN

HENDERSON ADVERTISING, INC.

HENDERSON ADVERTISING, INC.
60 Pointe Circle
Greenville, SC 29615
Tel.: 803-271-6000 **SC**
Fax: 803-298-1280
Year Founded: 1946
Approx.Billings: $75,036,000
Emp.: 85
Fiscal Year-end: 12/31/89
Advertising Agency
S.I.C.: 7311
Ralph W. Callahan, Jr. *(Chm. Bd., Pres. & Chief Exec. Officer)*
John J. Kennedy Jr. *(Exec. V.P., Chief Fin. Officer)*
Dona Anderson *(V.P., Dir. Info. Services)*
Jeff Hare *(V.P., Admin.)*
JoAnne Pfister *(Dir., Personnel, Asst. Sec.)*

No. of U.S. Offices: 1

Computer Systems/Hardware:
IBM System 36

Outside Service Firm(s):

Elliott, Davis & Co.*(Auditors)*
Greenville, SC

Corroon & Black*(Commercial Insurance Carrier)*
P.O. Box 2007, 111 Williams St.
Greenville, SC 29602

Aetna Life & Casualty*(Group Insurer)*
425 Fifth Ave.
New York, NY 10018
Tel.: 212-512-0777

Brown & Hagins*(Legal Firm)*
Greenville, SC

South Carolina National Bank*(Major Banking Relationship)*
7515 Northside Dr.
Greenville, SC
Tel.: 803-577-8280

The Killen Group*(Pension Manager)*
Berwyn, PA

HENDERSON AUCTIONEERS
Highway 190
Livingston, LA 70754
Tel.: 504-686-2252
Fax: 504-686-7658
Year Founded: 1957
Approx.Sls.: $17,000,000
Emp.: 10
Auctioneering Service
S.I.C.: 7389
Marvin A. Henderson *(Pres.)*
Jeffery Henderson *(Sec. & Treas.)*

Outside Service Firm(s):

Central Underwriters*(Commercial Insurance Carrier)*
Baton Rouge, LA

Tuscaloosa Bank*(Major Banking Relationship)*
Denham Springs, LA

HENDERSON ELECTRIC CO., INC.
4502 Poplar Level Rd.
Louisville, KY 40213
Tel.: 502-452-6327
Fax: 502-452-1308
Year Founded: 1919
Approx.Sls.: $11,000,000
Emp.: 245
Electrical Contractors
S.I.C.: 1731
Rodney J. Henderson *(Chm. Bd.)*
Bruce M. Henderson *(Pres.)*
Mickey Masterson *(V.P.)*
Joe Pusateri *(V.P.)*
James Kean *(Comptroller & Treas.)*

Outside Service Firm(s):

Cotton & Allen*(Auditors)*
Louisville, KY

Middleton & Reutlinger*(Legal Firm)*
2500 Brown & Williamson Tower
Louisville, KY 40202
Tel.: 502-584-1135

Citizens Fidelity Bank & Trust Co.*(Major Banking Relationship)*
P.O. Box 33000-Citizens Plaza
Louisville, KY 40232
Tel.: 502-581-3381

JOSEPH J. HENDERSON & SON, INC.
4288 Grand Ave.
Gurnee, IL 60031
Mailing Address:
P.O. Box 9,
Gurnee, IL 60031
Tel.: 708-244-3222 IL
Fax: 708-244-9572
Year Founded: 1928
Assets: $12,035,567
Liabilities: $7,064,821
Net Worth: $4,970,746
Approx.Sls.: $33,000,000
Emp.: 130
Fiscal Year-end: 3/31/91
General Contractor, Waste Water & Sewage Treatment Plant Construction; New Construction of Office & Commercial Buildings
S.I.C.: 1629; 1542
Donald E. Henderson *(Pres.)*
Michael L. Henderson *(V.P.)*
Robert I. Bernhardt *(Treas.)*
Marilyn Henderson *(Sec.)*

Principal(s):
Donald E. Henderson
Marilyn Henderson

Outside Service Firm(s):

Clifton Gunderson & Co.*(Auditors)*
Waukegan, IL

Carl E. Mullen & Co.*(Commercial Insurance Carrier)*
Waukegan, IL

Financial Advisors*(Group Insurer)*
Franklin, IL

J. John Henderson*(Legal Firm)*
Waukegan, IL

Bank of Waukegan*(Major Banking Relationship)*
Waukegan, IL

HENDRICK MANAGEMENT CORPORATION
P.O. Box 18649, 6000 Monroe Rd., Ste. 100
Charlotte, NC 28218
Tel.: 704-568-5550
Fax: 704-535-5592
Year Founded: 1978
Sales Range: $500-999 Million
Emp.: 1,600
Holding Company for International Franchised Automobile Dealerships; Domestics, Imports & Motorspits (Nascar)
S.I.C.: 6719
J.R. Hendricks III *(Pres.)*
William Musgrave *(Exec. V.P.)*
James F. Huzl *(V.P.-Fin.)*
Principal(s):
J.R. Hendricks III

Outside Service Firm(s):

NationsBank Carolinas*(Major Banking Relationship)*
One NCNB Plaza T18-7
Charlotte, NC 28255

Subsidiaries:

Hendrick Imports **(1)**
6950 E. Independence Blvd.
Charlotte, NC 28212
Tel.: 704-535-0885
Retail New & Used Automobiles
S.I.C.: 5511
J.R. Hendrick III *(Pres.)*

Hendrick Motorsports **(1)**
5315 Stowe Lane
Harrisburg, NC 28075
Tel.: 704-455-3400
Fax: 704-455-3406
Builds & Maintains Race Cars
S.I.C.: 7948
J.R. Hendricks III *(Pres.)*
Jimmy Johnson *(Gen. Mgr.)*

LEON HENDRICKSON
(d/b/a Silver Towne Coin Shop)
RR #4 Old Union County Pike
Winchester, IN 47394
Tel.: 317-584-7481
Fax: 317-584-1246
Year Founded: 1960
Assets: $10,000,000
Liabilities: $5,000,000
Net Worth: $5,000,000
Approx.Sls.: $120,000,000
Emp.: 37
Fiscal Year-end: 12/31/89
Wholesale Jewelry; Retail Coins & Custom Minting; Investment Portfolios
S.I.C.: 5094; 5961; 6282
Stanley Hendrickson *(Controller)*
Principal(s):
Leon Hendrickson
David Hendrickson

Outside Service Firm(s):

Estep, Doctor & Drumm*(Auditors)*
Muncie, IN

HENKELS & MCCOY, INC.
985 Jolly Rd.
Blue Bell, PA 19422
Tel.: 215-283-7600
Year Founded: 1923
Approx.Sls.: $375,000,000
Emp.: 5,700
Fiscal Year-end: 9/30/91
Diversified Engineering, Management, Construction & Maintenance
S.I.C.: 1623; 1796; 8711; 4899
Paul M. Henkels *(Chm. Bd.)*
Kenneth L. Rose *(Pres. & Chief Exec. Officer)*
Bernard F. Hagan *(Chief Oper. Officer & Sr. V.P.)*
Richard Wright *(Chief Fin. Officer & V.P.)*
James F. Lafferty *(Sr. V.P.-Equipment)*
Joseph W. Munnis *(V.P.-Sls. & Mktg.)*
James E. O'Neill *(Treas.)*
Christine Crawford *(Sec. & Legal Officer)*
Joseph C. Barnett *(Dir.-Pur.)*
Vincent P.A. Benedict *(Dir.-Human Resources)*
Peggy Ruch *(Dir.-Data Processing)*
Robert Delark *(Credit & Collections)*

Computer Systems/Hardware:
Sperry System 80

Outside Service Firm(s):

Ernst & Young*(Auditors)*
1800 John F. Kennedy Blvd.
Philadelphia, PA 19103-7499
Tel.: 215-864-3300

Liberty Mutual*(Group Insurer)*
175 Berkeley St.
Boston, MA

Labrum-Doak*(Legal Firm)*
Philadelphia, PA

Meridian Bank*(Major Banking Relationship)*
One Meridian Plaza, 36th Fl.
Philadelphia, PA
Tel.: 215-854-3900

Subsidiaries:

Mako Construction Co. **(1)**
13338 E. Broad St., Rte. 16 P.O. Box A64
Pataskala, OH 43062
Tel.: 614-927-4205
Engineering, Management, Construction & Maintenance
S.I.C.: 1623; 1796; 8711

PCM Construction, Inc. **(1)**
c/o Brooklyn Navy Yard, Flushing Ave. & Cumberland St., Bldg. 27
Brooklyn, NY 11205
Tel.: 718-522-2570
S.I.C.: 1623

Worrad Services Inc. **(1)**
40 Federal Hill Rd.
Oxford, MA 01540
Tel.: 508-987-3977
S.I.C.: 1623

THE HENLEY GROUP, INC.
(Formerly Pnuemo Abex Holdings Co.)
Liberty Lane
Hampton, NH 03842
Tel.: 603-926-5911 DE
Fax: 603-929-2289
Year Founded: 1986
Assets: $3,160,000,000
Earnings: ($661,000,000)
Liabilities: $2,041,000,000
Net Worth: $1,119,000,000
Approx.Rev.: $704,000,000
Emp.: 10,300
Fiscal Year-end: 12/31/91
Import Export
Diversified Manufacturing Holding Co.; Aerospace Components, Laboratory Products
S.I.C.: 6719
Michael D. Dingman *(Chm. Bd. & Chief Exec. Officer)*
Paul M. Montrone *(Pres.)*
Robert J. Barone *(Mng. Dir.)*
Andrew M. Massimilla *(Mng. Dir.)*
Clifford T. Dirkes *(Mng. Dir.)*
Paul M. Meister *(Mng. Dir. & Chief Fin. Officer)*
Mark A. Underberg *(Mng. Dir., Sec. & Gen. Counsel)*

HENLEY PAPER COMPANY
8400 Triad Dr.
Greensboro, NC 27409
Mailing Address:
P.O. Box 20408
Greensboro, NC 27420
Tel.: 919-668-0081 NC
Fax: 919-668-3955
Year Founded: 1934
Approx.Sls.: $75,000,000
Emp.: 275
Import
Wholesale Distr. of Full Line Printing Papers, Packaging Materials & Other Paper & Paper Related Products
S.I.C.: 5111; 5113
A.B. Henley, Jr. *(Chm. Bd.)*
Nixon C. Henley *(Pres.)*
Charles G. Kennedy *(Treas.)*
D.S. Dudley *(Mgr.-Acctg.)*
F.T. Jenkins *(Mgr.-Employee Benefits)*
Principal(s):
A.B. Henley, Jr.
Nixon C. Henley

No. of Mfg. Plants/Facilities: 8
No. of U.S. Offices: 8

Computer Systems/Hardware:
Data General MV 15000

Outside Service Firm(s):

Provident Life & Accident Insurance Co.*(Group Insurer)*
P.O. Box 12015
Chattanooga, TN 37401
Tel.: 615-755-7088

Fisher, Fisher & Gayle*(Legal Firm)*
101 S. Main St.
High Point, NC 27261
Tel.: 919-883-9156

Wachovia Bank & Trust Co.*(Major Banking Relationship)*
P.O. Box 21048,
Greensboro, NC 27402

First Union National Bank*(Pension Manager)*
Shareholder Services Group, Two First Union Center, M-12
Charlotte, NC 28288-1154
Tel.: 704-383-5406
Tel.: 800-829-8432

THE HENNEGAN COMPANY
1001 Plum St.
Cincinnati, OH 45202
Tel.: 513-621-7300 OH
Fax: 513-421-6995
Year Founded: 1886
Assets: $22,200,000
Liabilities: $12,700,000
Net Worth: $9,500,000
Approx.Sls.: $45,000,000
Emp.: 346
Fiscal Year-end: 12/31/91
Import Export
Lithography & Letterpress Printing
S.I.C.: 2752
Robert B. Ott *(Chm. Bd.)*
Robert B. Ott, Jr. *(Pres.)*
Robert Dresmann *(Exec. V.P.-Admin.)*
Robert Haugom *(V.P.-Sls.)*
Kevin D. Ott *(Exec. V.P.)*
Donald C. Fleck *(V.P. & Controller)*
William Charles *(V.P.-Sls.)*
Dennis Purcell *(V.P.-Human Resources)*
William DeMarco *(V.P.-Prepress & Production)*
Roger Helms *(V.P.-Web Mfg.)*
Robert Meyer *(V.P.-Sheetfed Mfg.)*
Kenneth Tabet *(Dir.-Pur.)*
Nancy Jacobs *(Mgr.-Admin. Services)*
Principal(s):
Robert B. Ott

No. of Mfg. Plants/Facilities: 2
No. of U.S. Offices: 8

Computer Systems/Hardware:
IBM System 36

Outside Service Firm(s):

Arthur Andersen & Co.*(Auditors)*
425 Walnut St.
Cincinnati, OH 45202
Tel.: 513-381-6900

Thomas E. Wood*(Commercial Insurance Carrier)*
Cincinnati, OH

The Hennegan Company—(Continued)

Dinsmore & Shohl*(Legal Firm)*
2100 Fountain Square Plaza
Cincinnati, OH 45202-3172
Tel.: 513-977-8200

Star Bank*(Major Banking Relationship)*
425 Walnut Street
Cincinnati, OH 45202
Tel.: 513-632-4000

Star Bank*(Pension Manager)*
425 Walnut Street
Cincinnati, OH 45202
Tel.: 513-632-4000

HENNELLS, INC.
(Div. of C. M. Smillie & Co.)
1200 Woodward Hts.
Ferndale, MI 48220
Tel.: 313-544-3100
Fax: 313-545-1076
Approx.Sls.: $10,000,000
Emp.: 300
Plastics; Servaytor, Industrialvaytor, Bag-o-Matic, Convenience Cart & Bathmaster, Time Saver, Switch-Watch, Hydraulic & Air Fluid Power Prods.
S.I.C.: 3089
Charles M. Smillie III *(Chm. Bd. & Pres.)*
Paul Kulik *(Dir.-Sls., Mktg. & Adv.)*
George Morley *(Gen. Mgr.)*
Jack Nelson *(Pur. & Export Mgr.)*

HENRI'S FOOD PRODUCTS CO., INC.
2730 W. Silver Spring Dr.
Milwaukee, WI 53209
Tel.: 414-461-7760 **WI**
Fax: 414-461-1180
Year Founded: 1935
Sales Range: $20-39 Million
Emp.: 175
Salad Dressings
S.I.C.: 2035; 5149
Henrietta E. Mahler *(Chm. Bd. & Treas.)*
Herbert P. Mahler *(Pres.)*
Alexander Costigan *(Sr. V.P.)*
Jerome Boeselager *(V.P.-Opers.)*
Richard Rosenbaum *(V.P.-Fin.)*
Jenny Miklas *(Dir.-Personnel)*
Michael Russell *(Dir.-Mfg.)*
David Vollman *(Dir.-Data Processing)*
Deborah Westley *(Dir.-Pur.)*
John Brewster *(Mgr.-Mktg.)*

Computer Systems/Hardware:
IBM 400

Outside Service Firm(s):

Price Waterhouse*(Auditors)*
1500 Bank One Plaza, 100 E. Wisconsin Ave.
Milwaukee, WI 53202

Charne, Glassner*(Legal Firm)*
First Bank Bldg., Ste. 800, 211 W. Wisconsin Ave.
Milwaukee, WI 53203
Tel.: 414-273-2000

M & I Marshall & Ilsley Bank*(Major Banking Relationship)*
770 N. Water St.
Milwaukee, WI 53202
Tel.: 414-765-8700

E.P. HENRY CORPORATION
201 Park Ave.
Woodbury, NJ 08096
Mailing Address:
P.O. Box 615
Woodbury, NJ 08096
Tel.: 609-845-6200 **NJ**
Fax: 609-845-0023
Year Founded: 1913
Sales Range: $10-19 Million
Emp.: 120
Fiscal Year-end: 6/30/90
Import Export
Manufacture Concrete Products, Dealer Building Supplies; Manufacture Concrete Interlocking Paving Stones
S.I.C.: 3271; 1741; 5032
James C. Henry, Jr. *(Pres. & Chief Exec. Officer)*
J.C. Henry II *(Exec. V.P.)*
J.C. Henry III *(Exec. V.P..-Sls. & Mktg.)*
A. Shafer Henry *(Sr. V.P.)*
John M. Poignard *(V.P.-Opers. & Mfg. & Chief Oper. Officer)*
James S. Nash *(Treas., Chief Fin. Officer & Controller)*
Marianne W. Anzaldo *(Sec., Adv. & Chief Information Officer)*

Principal(s):
James C. Henry, Jr.
J.C. Henry II
A. Shafer Henry

No. of Mfg. Plants/Facilities: 2
No. of U.S. Offices: 3

Computer Systems/Hardware:
DEC

Outside Service Firm(s):

KPMG Peat Marwick*(Auditors)*
1600 Market St.
Philadelphia, PA 19103
Tel.: 215-299-3100

Archer & Greiner*(Legal Firm)*
Two Mellon Bank Center, Ste. 2200
Philadelphia, PA 19102

First & Peoples Bank*(Major Banking Relationship)*
Haddon, NJ

Division:

Paving Stone Div. **(1)**
201 Park Ave.
Woodbury, NJ 08096
Tel.: 609-845-6200
Emp.: 100
Paving Stone
S.I.C.: 3281
A. Shafer Henry *(V.P.)*

HENRYGILLSILVERMAN
ADVERTISING

HENRY GILL SILVERMAN ADVERTISING
1225 17th St., Ste. 2500
Denver, CO 80202
Tel.: 303-296-4100
Fax: 303-296-3410
Year Founded: 1977
Approx.Billings: $13,625,000
Emp.: 20
Consumer Products, Entertainment, Automotive, Travel & Tourism
David A. Henry *(Pres.)*

Computer Systems/Hardware:
AT&T, MacIntosh

HENRY RUSSELL BRUCE, INC.
1957 Blairs Ferry Rd. NE
Cedar Rapids, IA 52402
Tel.: 319-393-2656
Fax: 319-393-0283
Year Founded: 1973
Approx.Billings: $16,000,000
Emp.: 38
Business-to-Business & Consumer Adv.
Peter Langmack *(Pres. & New Bus. Contact)*
Joe Stambaugh *(Exec. V.P.)*
Mike Humbert *(V.P., Pub. Rels.)*
Randy Jacobs *(Sr. V.P., Quad City Mgr.)*
Jeri Zhorne *(V.P., Admin.)*

HENRYS, INC.
7700 E. Kellogg, Ste. 1201
Wichita, KS 67207
Mailing Address:
P.O. Box 789789
Wichita, KS 67278
Tel.: 316-687-7200
Fax: 316-688-9512
Year Founded: 1923
Approx.Sls.: $15,000,000
Emp.: 250
Retail Family Clothing, Shoes & Accessories Store
S.I.C.: 5651; 5661
David Goldschmidt *(Chm. Bd.)*
Patrick Neville *(Pres. & Chief Exec. Officer)*
Jan Brody *(V.P.-Fin.)*

Outside Service Firm(s):

Allen, Gibbs, Houlik*(Auditors)*
301 N. Main, Ste. 1700
Wichita, KS 67202
Tel.: 316-267-7231

Martin, Pringle, Davis, Oliver & Triplett*(Legal Firm)*
300 Page Ct., 220 W. Douglas
Wichita, KS 67202
Tel.: 316-265-9311

Union National Bank*(Major Banking Relationship)*
Wichita, KS

HENSEL PHELPS CONSTRUCTION CO.
420 Sixth Ave.
Greeley, CO 80632
Mailing Address:
P.O. Box 0
Greeley, CO 80632
Tel.: 303-352-6565 **DE**
Fax: 303-353-0517
Year Founded: 1937
Assets: $249,000,000
Liabilities: $218,000,000
Net Worth: $31,000,000
Approx.Sls.: $727,000,000
Emp.: 2,000
Fiscal Year-end: 5/31/92
General Contractor Engaging in Commercial, Institutional, Industrial & Heavy Construction
S.I.C.: 1541; 1542; 1611; 1629
Jerry L. Morgensen *(Pres.)*
Stephen J. Carrico *(V.P.)*
Eric Wilson *(V.P.)*
Principal(s):
Leonard Arnold
Robert Danials
Wayne Lindham
Jerry L. Morgensen
Ron Norby
Guy V. McNallie
Robert Pesalento
Eric Wilson

Computer Systems/Hardware:
IBM AS 400

Outside Service Firm(s):

Price Waterhouse*(Auditors)*
950 17th St., Ste. 2600
Denver, CO 80202
Tel.: 303-893-8100

Greeley National Bank*(Major Banking Relationship)*
Greeley, CO

HENSLEY & CO.
4201 N. 45th Ave.
Phoenix, AZ 85031
Tel.: 602-264-1635 **AZ**
Fax: 602-247-7094
Year Founded: 1954
Sales Range: $100-499 Million
Emp.: 100
Wholesale Beer
S.I.C.: 5181
James W. Hensley *(Pres.)*
Robert M. Delgado *(Exec. V.P.)*

Outside Service Firm(s):

Arthur Andersen & Co.*(Auditors)*
Phoenix, AZ

Valley National Bank*(Major Banking Relationship)*
241 North Central Ave., 11th Floor
Phoenix, AZ 85001

HER MAJESTY
(Div. of Heckler Mfg. & Investment Group, Inc.)
P.O. Box 9
Mauldin, SC 29662
Tel.: 803-288-5450
Approx.Sls.: $40,000,000
Emp.: 1,500
Mfr. of Her Majesty Girls Lingerie, Blouses, Sleepwear, Beachwear, Dresses, Jeans, Shirts, Playwear, Skirts; Cole of California for Her Majesty Swimwear & Sportswear
S.I.C.: 2389
John J. Heckler *(Pres.)*
Henry Eichenbaum *(Sr. V.P.-Sls.)*

HERBAL ENTERPRISES INC.
(d/b/a Right Ideas)
316 Hartford Rd.
Manchester, CT 06040
Tel.: 203-647-1492 **CT**
Fax: 203-647-8090
Approx.Sls.: $34,000,000
Emp.: 25
Wholesale Kitchen Cookware & Appliances, Jewelry, Hardware, Tools, Luggage & Giftware
S.I.C.: 5023; 5064; 5094; 5072; 5099
George Alexander *(Pres.)*
Terry Stada *(V.P. & Sec.)*

Outside Service Firm(s):

O'Connell & Co.*(Auditors)*
Manchester, CT

G. R. HERBERGER'S, INC.
600 Mall Germain
Saint Cloud, MN 56301
Mailing Address:
P.O. Box H-120
St. Cloud, MN 56302
Tel.: 612-251-5351 **DE**
Fax: 612-654-2200
Year Founded: 1927
Assets: $66,000,000
Liabilities: $42,000,000
Net Worth: $24,000,000
Approx.Sls.: $197,000,000
Emp.: 3,500
Fiscal Year-end: 2/ 2/91
Import
Retail Department Stores
S.I.C.: 5311
Robert J. Sullivan *(Chm. Bd. & Chief Exec. Officer)*
George B. Torrey *(Pres. & Chief Oper. Officer)*
Barry Ross *(Exec. V.P.)*
James M. Bouwkamp *(V.P.-Fin. & Opers.)*
Jack Gau *(Sec. & Treas.)*
Principal(s):
Employee Owned

No. of Mfg. Plants/Facilities: 34

Computer Systems/Hardware:
IBM

Outside Service Firm(s):

Arthur Andersen & Co.*(Auditors)*
45 S. 7th St.
Minneapolis, MN 55402

Briggs & Morgan*(Legal Firm)*
Minneapolis, MN

First Bank, N.A.*(Major Banking Relationship)*
First Bank Place
Minneapolis, MN 55480

First Bank, N.A.*(Pension Manager)*
First Bank Place
Minneapolis, MN 55480

HERCULES ENGINES, INC.
101 Eleventh, S.E.
Canton, OH 44707
Mailing Address:
P.O. Box 24101
Canton, OH 44701
Tel.: 216-454-5631 **OH**
Fax: 216-438-1313
Year Founded: 1915
Sales Range: $40-59 Million
Emp.: 350
Fiscal Year-end: 2/28/92
Import Export
Internal Combustion Engines-Gasoline, Diesel, LPG, Natural Gas
S.I.C.: 5084
Gary Smith *(Pres. & Chief Exec. Officer)*
Robert J. Holtgreive *(Sr. V.P.)*
John D. Dienes *(V.P.-Fin. & Admin.)*
Donald W. Hoisington *(V.P.-Intl. & Govt. Sls.)*
Roger Williams *(V.P.-Mfg.)*
Rod Baxter *(Dir.-Quality Assurance)*
Ron Bethel *(Dir.-Mfg.)*
Kim Boyer *(Dir.-Alternative Fueled Engines)*
Mike Ervin *(Dir.-Mktg. & Sls.)*

Outside Service Firm(s):

Ernst & Young*(Auditors)*
One Cascade Plaza
Akron, OH 44308

Society National Bank*(Major Banking Relationship)*
Canton, OH

HERCULES TIRE & RUBBER COMPANY
1300 Morrical Blvd.
Findlay, OH 45840
Tel.: 419-425-6400 **CT**
Fax: 419-425-6403
Year Founded: 1952
Approx.Sls.: $187,000,000
Emp.: 190
Fiscal Year-end: 10/31/92
Import Export
Mfr. Tread Rubber & Equipment; Custom-Mixing Rubber
S.I.C.: 3011; 5013; 3069
Robert Bogle *(Chm. Bd.)*
Craig E. Anderson *(Pres.)*
Steven Buck *(V.P. & Gen. Mgr.-Tires)*
John Kam *(V.P.-Export)*
Phillip Berra *(Treas.)*
Ralph Suville *(Controller)*
Ernie Ranallo *(Gen. Mgr.-West Coast)*
Paul Rinauro *(Gen. Mgr.-Retreading)*
M. Baddorf *(Dir.-Mktg.)*
R. Carr *(Dir.-Personnel)*
J. Hurt *(Dir.-Pur.)*

Principal(s):
Co-op Ownership

No. of Mfg. Plants/Facilities: 3
No. of U.S. Offices: 60
No. of Foreign Offices: 1

Computer Systems/Hardware:
J. Sellers/IBM

Outside Service Firm(s):

Price Waterhouse*(Auditors)*
One Seagate, Ste. 1800
Toledo, OH 43604
Tel.: 419-247-1800

Stradley, Ronon, Stevens & Young*(Legal Firm)*
2600 Commerce Sq.
Philadelphia, PA 19103
Tel.: 215-564-8000

Society National Bank*(Major Banking Relationship)*
Cleveland, OH

HERESITE PROTECTIVE COATINGS INC.
P.O. Box 250,
Manitowoc, WI 54221
Tel.: 414-684-6646
Tel.: 800-558-7747
Fax: 414-684-0110
Approx.Sls.: $15,000,000
Emp.: 100
Import Export
Mfr. of Corrosion Resistant Coatings & Paints
S.I.C.: 2851
G. Liban *(Chm. Bd. & Chief Exec. Officer)*
Tom L. Fritzke *(Pres.)*
A. Muchin *(Gen. Counsel)*
D. Schmidt *(Dir.-Sls. & Promotion)*

Computer Systems/Hardware:
EPSON-DOS

HERFF JONES INC.
4625 W. 62nd St.
Indianapolis, IN 46268
Mailing Address:
P.O. Box 68501
Indianapolis, IN 46268
Tel.: 317-297-3740 **IN**
Fax: 317-297-0599
Fax: 317-329-3308
Year Founded: 1920
Approx.Sls.: $200,000,000
Emp.: 3,000
Fiscal Year-end: 6/30/91
Scholastic-Related Graduation Products, Recognition/Motivational Awards, Photography, Multi-Media Instructional Programs
S.I.C.: 2759; 3499; 3961
A.J. Hackl *(Chm. Bd. & Chief Exec. Officer)*
David G. Daly *(Pres. & Chief Oper. Officer)*
James W. Hubbard *(Grp. V.P.)*
Dennis L. Maki *(Grp. V.P.)*
Boyd P. Boynton *(V.P. & Gen. Mgr.-Photography)*
Lawrence F. Fehr *(V.P., Controller & Sec.)*
Douglas F. Jewell *(V.P.-Scholastic Mktg.)*
Robert S. Potts *(V.P.-Yearbook Sls.)*
Joe Slaughter *(V.P.-Scholastic Sls.)*
David L. Van Bruaene *(V.P.-Jewelry Opers.)*
Christine Bachmann *(Co-Dir.-Human Resources)*
Michael S. Williams *(Co-Dir.-Human Resources)*

Fred Mayer *(Mgr.-Mngmt. Information Systems)*

Principal(s):
Employee-Owned

No. of Mfg. Plants/Facilities: 17
No. of U.S. Offices: 18
No. of Foreign Offices: 1

Computer Systems/Hardware:
Honeywell

HERLIN PRESS
475 Heffernan Dr.
West Haven, CT 06516
Mailing Address:
P.O. Box 427,
West Haven, CT 06516
Tel.: 203-934-6346 **CT**
Fax: 203-934-7057
Year Founded: 1935
Approx.Sls.: $10,500,000
Emp.: 106
Advertising & Commercial Printing
S.I.C.: 2752; 7311
Robert M. Herlin *(Chm. Bd. & Chief Exec. Officer)*
Chester R. Miller *(Pres.)*
Bert Bacon *(Exec. V.P.)*
Charles E. Skubas *(Chief Fin. Officer & Sec.)*

Outside Service Firm(s):

T.M. Byxbee Company*(Auditors)*
Hamden, CT

Connecticut Savings Bank*(Investment Banker)*
New Haven, CT

Pullman Comley Bradley & Reeves*(Legal Firm)*
Bridgeport, CT

Connecticut Savings Bank*(Major Banking Relationship)*
New Haven, CT

Subsidiary:

Ellison Graphics **(1)**
1400 Indiantown Rd.
Jupiter, FL 33468
Tel.: 407-746-9256
Emp.: 60
Commercial Printer & Lithographer
S.I.C.: 2752
Lloyd Ellison *(Pres.)*

HERMAN ASSOCIATES, INC.
488 Madison Ave.
New York, NY 10022
Tel.: 212-935-1730
Fax: 212-935-2834
Year Founded: 1973
Approx.Billings: $10,075,000
Emp.: 15
Travel & Tourism Adv., Transportation & Insurance
Stuart Herman *(Pres.)*
Paula Herman *(Chief Exec. Officer)*
Warren Goodwin *(Sr. V.P.)*
Pieter Meersschaert *(Dir.-Mktg. Services)*

Computer Systems/Hardware:
IBM, Ad-Aid

JOS. M. HERMAN SHOE CO.
One Sound Shore Dr.
Greenwich, CT 06830
Tel.: 203-625-2662
Approx.Sls.: $40,000,000
Emp.: 600
Manufacturer of Men's & Women's Work & Outdoor Shoes and Boots
S.I.C.: 3143
Tony DiPaolo *(Pres.)*
James Famulare *(V.P.-Sls.)*

HERMES AUTOMOTIVE MANUFACTURING CORP.
2703 23rd St.
Detroit, MI 48216
Tel.: 313-897-6395 **MI**
Fax: 313-897-1791
Approx.Sls.: $32,000,000
Emp.: 400
Iron & Steel Forgings for Automotive Parts
S.I.C.: 3714
John Sinanis *(Pres. & Chief Exec. Officer)*
Stylianos Sinanis *(V.P. & Treas.)*
Richard Horderecki *(Controller)*

Outside Service Firm(s):

Comerica Bank*(Major Banking Relationship)*
211 W. Fort St.
Detroit, MI 48226
Tel.: 313-222-3300

HERRING NEWMAN
414 Olive Way, Ste. 300
Seattle, WA 98101
Tel.: 206-343-9000
Fax: 206-447-2663
Year Founded: 1983
Approx.Billings: $35,000,000
Emp.: 55
Direct Response
Phil Herring *(Pres.)*
Chris Altwegg *(V.P. & Grp.-Dir.)*
Donna Herak *(Dir.-Opers.)*

HERSHEY CREAMERY COMPANY
301 S. Cameron
Harrisburg, PA 17101
Mailing Address:
P.O. Box 1821
Harrisburg, PA 17105
Tel.: 717-238-8134 **DE**
Fax: 717-233-7195
Sales Range: $10-19 Million
Emp.: 571
Fiscal Year-end: 12/31/91
Mfr. Ice Cream
S.I.C.: 2024
George H. Holder, Sr. *(Chm. Bd.)*
George Hugh Holder *(Pres.)*
Thomas M. Holder *(V.P.-Sls.)*
F.C. Nelson *(V.P. & Sec.)*
Thomas R. Ryan *(V.P.-Pur.)*
Virginia N. Westfall *(Treas.)*

No. of Mfg. Plants/Facilities: 1
No. of U.S. Offices: 1

Outside Service Firm(s):

KPMG Peat Marwick*(Auditors)*
P.O. Box 1190, 225 Market St., Ste. 300
Harrisburg, PA 17108-1190
Tel.: 717-238-7131

HESCO PARTS CORPORATION
10 Station Park
Louisville, KY 40210
Mailing Address:
P.O. Box 3008,
Louisville, KY 40201
Tel.: 502-589-9600
Approx.Sls.: $41,000,000
Emp.: 250
Authorized Ford Remanufacturer & Distributor of Engines, Transmissions & Component Parts
S.I.C.: 5013; 3694; 3714
Clyde F. Ensor, Sr. *(Chm. Bd. & Pres.)*
Barbara Sullivan *(Sec. & Treas.)*

Outside Service Firm(s):

Cotton & Allen*(Auditors)*
Louisville, KY

Hesco Parts Corporation—(Continued)

Citizens Fidelity Bank & Trust Co.*(Major Banking Relationship)*
P.O. Box 33000-Citizens Plaza
Louisville, KY 40232
Tel.: 502-581-3381

Subsidiary:

All-State Ford Truck Sales **(1)**
1357 Gardiner Lane
Louisville, KY 40232
Tel.: 502-459-0550
Retail Truck Dealership
S.I.C.: 5511
John Jackson *(Gen. Mgr.)*

HESS ENGINEERING INC.
191 Fir Road
Niles, MI 49120-9766
Tel.: 616-683-4182
Fax: 616-683-1775
Year Founded: 1976
Approx.Sls.: $16,300,000
Emp.: 160
Mfr. Auto Component Machines & Testing
S.I.C.: 3542; 3549; 3544
Johann T. Hess *(Chm. Bd.)*
Frederick Kucklick *(Pres.)*
Stephen M. Slavin *(Sec.)*

HEWITT-ROBINS CORP.
40 Fairfield Place
West Caldwell, NJ 07006
Tel.: 201-777-5500 **DE**
Twx: 710-989-7170
Fax: 201-777-1775
Year Founded: 1898
Approx.Sls.: $15,000,000
Emp.: 300
Import Export
Design & Manufacture Conveyer Belt Idlers; Crushing & Vibrating Equipment; Underground Mine Conveyors; Tuffguard Molded Polyurethane Products
S.I.C.: 2821; 3496; 3535
John Wrobel *(Pres.)*
W. Lagard *(Controller)*
A.J. Burzinski *(Dir.-Fin.)*
Chet Hempel *(Dir.-Data Processing)*
R.H. Staff *(Dir.-Mktg.)*

No. of Mfg. Plants/Facilities: 3
No. of U.S. Offices: 3
No. of Foreign Offices: 1

Computer Systems/Hardware:
IBM System 36; Four Phase Model 5, 000

Outside Service Firm(s):

Midlantic National Bank*(Major Banking Relationship)*
Bloomfield, NJ

Division:

Crushing & Screening Div. **(1)**
U.S. Hwy. 1 N.
Columbia, SC 29202
Tel.: 803-788-1424
S.I.C.: 3531; 3532; 1221
William Siegendorf *(Pres.)*

HEYMAN CORPORATION
6045 W. Howard St.
Niles, IL 60648
Tel.: 708-647-0909 **IL**
Fax: 708-647-1077
Fax: 708-647-1074
Year Founded: 1914
Approx.Sls.: $15,000,000
Emp.: 65
Fiscal Year-end: 12/31/90
Import Export
Mfr., Import & Distribute Women's, Men's & Children's Apparel, Accessories & Men's Underwear
S.I.C.: 5632; 2389; 5137; 5136
Leonard J. Heyman *(Chm. Bd., Pres., Chief Exec. & Chief Oper. Officer)*
Sam Mevorah *(Sr. V.P.)*
Lawrence S. Heyman *(V.P.)*
Michael J. Heyman *(V.P.)*
Seymour Brandin *(Chief Fin. Officer & Treas.)*
William Ruekberg *(Dir.-Data Processing)*

Computer Systems/Hardware:
Wang

Outside Service Firm(s):

Shepard Schwartz & Harris*(Auditors)*
Chicago, IL

PruCare*(Group Insurer)*
Chicago, IL

American National Bank & Trust Company of Chicago*(Major Banking Relationship)*
33 N. LaSalle St.
Chicago, IL 60602
Tel.: 312-661-5000
Fax: 312-661-6417

Divisions:

Oshkosh B'Gosh Hosiery Co. **(1)**
6045 W. Howard St.
Niles, IL 60648
Tel.: 708-647-0909
Oshkosh B'Gosh Socks for Children Only
S.I.C.: 5136; 5137
Michael Heyman *(Chief Oper. Officer)*

Sterling Hosiery Co. **(1)**
6045 W. Howard St.
Niles, IL 60648
Tel.: 708-647-0909
Approx.Sls.: $3,000,000
Emp.: 15
Mens', Womens' & Childrens' Hosiery & Related Mens' Items
S.I.C.: 2251

Tru-Fit Glove & Headwear Div. **(1)**
6045 W. Howard St.
Niles, IL 60648
Tel.: 708-647-0909
Fax: 708-647-1077
Approx.Sls.: $5,000,000
Emp.: 20
Mens', Womens' & Childrens' Gloves, Mittens, Scarves & Headwear
S.I.C.: 2339; 2369; 5136; 5137

HI NABOR SUPERMARKET INC.
7201 Winbourne Ave.
Baton Rouge, LA 70805
Tel.: 504-357-1448
Fax: 504-357-7109
Year Founded: 1963
Approx.Sls.: $23,000,000
Emp.: 160
Retail Groceries
S.I.C.: 5411
Samuel J. Crifasi *(Pres.)*
James Crifasi *(Sec. & Treas.)*

Outside Service Firm(s):

Hibernia National Bank*(Major Banking Relationship)*
Baton Rouge, LA

HIBBERT GROUP
P.O. Box 8116, 400 Pennington Ave.
Trenton, NJ 08650-0116
Tel.: 609-394-7500
Fax: 609-392-5946
Approx.Sls.: $24,000,000
Emp.: 450
Marketing Support Services
S.I.C.: 7331
Ted B. Brown *(Pres.)*
James Balara *(Sr. V.P.)*

Outside Service Firm(s):

Gushen & Moonin*(Auditors)*
Trenton, NJ

New Jersey National Bank*(Major Banking Relationship)*
Trenton, NJ

HICKERSON PHELPS KIRTLEY & ASSOCIATES
Two Pershing Square, 2300 Main St.
Kansas City, MO 64108
Tel.: 816-471-4000
Fax: 816-842-0274
Year Founded: 1978
Approx.Billings: $19,100,000
Emp.: 30
Ken Hickerson *(Chm.)*
Jon Phelps *(Pres. & Chief Exec. Officer)*
Jeff Kirtley *(Exec. V.P.)*
Linda Crawford *(Controller)*
John Ryan *(Yellow Pages)*

Computer Systems/Hardware:
Apple, MacIntosh; Local Network

HICKINBOTHAM BROS., LTD
635 S. Aurora St.
Stockton, CA 95203
Tel.: 209-942-4422 **CA**
Fax: 209-942-0347
Year Founded: 1852
Sales Range: $10-19 Million
Steel Service Center
S.I.C.: 5051
Ralph W. Hickinbotham *(Pres.)*
James R. Giles *(Chief Fin. Officer)*
Evelyn Oneto *(Sec.)*

Outside Service Firm(s):

Grant Thornton*(Auditors)*
Stockton, CA

Neumiller & Beardslee*(Legal Firm)*
Stockton, CA

Union Safe Deposit Bank*(Major Banking Relationship)*
Stockton, CA

Subsidiary:

Express Steel and Plastics **(1)**
809 So. Aurora St.
Stockton, CA 95203
Tel.: 209-465-5910
Emp.: 6
Steel Coil Processing
S.I.C.: 5051
J. Scott Patten *(Gen. Mgr.)*

HICKMAN WILLIAMS & CO. INC.
Chiquita Center, 250 E. 5th St., Ste. 1110
Cincinnati, OH 45202
Mailing Address:
P.O. Box 538
Cincinnati, OH 45201
Tel.: 513-621-1946
Fax: 513-621-0024
Year Founded: 1890
Assets: $30,000,000
Earnings: $1,500,000
Liabilities: $22,000,000
Net Worth: $8,000,000
Approx.Sls.: $150,000,000
Emp.: 140
Brokers of Coal, Coke & Other Products Used by the Foundry Industry; Coke Processing Plants
S.I.C.: 5052; 5085; 5051; 5199
Richard M. Frazier *(Acting Chm. Bd. & Pres.)*
Arthur L. Haack *(V.P., Sec. & Chief Fin. Officer)*
Jim Sanders *(Treas. & Asst. Sec.)*
Donn W. Bolce *(Controller)*
Principal(s):
Employee Owned

Computer Systems/Hardware:
Sperry System 80

Outside Service Firm(s):

Ernst & Young*(Auditors)*
1300 Chiquita Center, 250 E. Fifth St.
Cincinnati, OH 45202
Tel.: 513-621-6454

State Mutual Insurance Co.*(Group Insurer)*
Downers Grove, IL

Frost & Jacobs*(Legal Firm)*
2500 Central Trust Ctr.
Cincinnati, OH 45202
Tel.: 513-651-6800

Star Bank*(Major Banking Relationship)*
425 Walnut Street
Cincinnati, OH 45202
Tel.: 513-632-4000

Connecticut Mutual*(Pension Manager)*
Hartford, CT

HICKORY CONSTRUCTION COMPANY
1728 9th Ave., N.W.
Hickory, NC 28601
Tel.: 704-322-9234
Fax: 704-322-5138
Approx.Sls.: $23,000,000
Emp.: 150
Industrial Buildings & Warehouses; Commercial & Office Buildings; New Construction; Water Main Construction
S.I.C.: 1541; 1542; 1623
Charles W. Moss *(Pres.)*
Pat Day *(V.P.-Mktg.)*
P. Curt Eckard *(V.P.)*
David E. Looper *(V.P.)*
Jim Rowe *(V.P.)*
Larry Thorneburg *(V.P.)*
Alice Franklin *(Treas. & Sec.)*

Outside Service Firm(s):

Patrick, Harper & Dixon*(Legal Firm)*
Hickory, NC

Branch Banking & Trust*(Major Banking Relationship)*
Hickory, NC

HICKORY FARMS, INC.
1505 Holland Rd.
Maumee, OH 43537
Tel.: 419-893-7611
Fax: 419-893-0164
Approx.Rev.: $393,600,000
Emp.: 850
Fiscal Year-end: 12/31/90
Franchising Specialty Foods Stores; Cheeses, Smoked Meats, Crackers & Snacks, Gift Packages
S.I.C.: 5499; 5441; 6794
Thomas E. Frank *(Pres. & Chief Exec. Officer)*
Phil Burch *(Sr. V.P.-Retail Opers.)*
James Scheuer *(Sr. V.P. & Chief Fin. Officer)*
James E. Edwards *(V.P.-Leasing)*
Jack D. Bancer *(Dir.-Natl. Comml. Sls.)*
Rick Purdy *(Dir.-Design)*

Computer Systems/Hardware:
IBM

Outside Service Firm(s):

Price Waterhouse*(Auditors)*
One Seagate, Ste. 1800
Toledo, OH 43604
Tel.: 419-247-1800

The Huntington National Bank*(Major Banking Relationship)*
Maumee, OH

Subsidiary:

Catalogue Marketing, Inc. **(1)**
501 16th Ave., N.E.
Austin, MN 55912
Tel.: 507-437-5611
S.I.C.: 5399

Subsidiary:

Sunshine Shippers, Inc. **(2)**
2296 Senter Rd.
San Jose, CA
Tel.: 408-293-0441
S.I.C.: 5961

HICKORY PRINTING GROUP, INC.
542 Main Ave., S.E.
Hickory, NC 28602
Mailing Address:
P.O. Box 69
Hickory, NC 28603
Tel.: 704-322-3431 **NC**
Fax: 704-326-8901
Year Founded: 1917
Approx.Sls.: $30,000,000
Emp.: 320
Fiscal Year-end: 9/30/91
Commercial Printing, Business Forms & Packaging Printing
S.I.C.: 2752; 2657; 2761
Thomas W. Reese *(Chm. & Chief Exec. Officer)*
T. Darrell Smith *(Pres.)*
Doyle Little *(Pres.-Packaging Div.)*
Jeffrey A. Hale *(Exec. V.P. Admin. & Fin.)*
Lewis F. Setzer *(Sr. V.P.)*

No. of Mfg. Plants/Facilities: 5

HICKS OIL-HICKS GAS, INC.
U.S. 54 & 115
Roberts, IL 60962
Mailing Address:
P.O. Box 98
Roberts, IL 60962
Tel.: 217-395-2281 **IN**
Fax: 217-395-2572
Assets: $24,000,000
Liabilities: $13,000,000
Net Worth: $11,000,000
Approx.Sls.: $75,025,000
Emp.: 525
Fiscal Year-end: 6/30/90
Wholesale & Retail Gasoline
S.I.C.: 6719; 5171; 5541; 5984
Todd M. Coady *(Chm. Bd., Pres. & Chief Exec. Officer)*
Randy J. Spitz *(Treas., Sec. & Controller)*

Computer Systems/Hardware:
Burroughs

Outside Service Firm(s):

Michael L. Friese*(Auditors)*
Champaign, IL

Metropolitan Life Insurance Co.*(Group Insurer)*
One Madison Ave.
New York, NY 10010-3690
Tel.: 215-578-9292

Harris Trust & Savings Bank*(Major Banking Relationship)*
111 W. Monroe St.
Chicago, IL 60690
Tel.: 312-461-2265
Tel.: 800-858-0840

Subsidiary:

Rocket Supply Corp. **(1)**
U.S. 54 & 115
Roberts, IL 60962
Tel.: 217-395-2281

RONI HICKS & ASSOCIATES, INC.
1875 Third Ave.
San Diego, CA 92101
Tel.: 619-238-8787
Fax: 619-238-8660
Year Founded: 1979
Approx.Billings: $10,620,000
Emp.: 29
Real Estate, Financial, Healthcare, Hotels, Restaurants & Sporting Events
Roni Clemens *(Pres.)*
Lynn Chisnell *(Controller)*
Vicki Barrett *(Dir.-Personnel & Benefits)*
Cate Muldoon Roberts *(Dir.-Pub. Rels.)*
Mikki Symington *(Dir.-Pub. Affairs & Community Rels.)*

Computer Systems/Hardware:
MacIntosh, AT&T 3B2

THE HIEBING GROUP, INC.
802 E. Gorham St.
Madison, WI 53703
Tel.: 608-256-6357
Fax: 608-256-0693
Year Founded: 1981
Approx.Billings: $12,000,000
Emp.: 29
Consumer Adv. & Marketing
Roman G. Hiebing, Jr. *(Pres. & Mngmt. Dir.)*
Marion D. Michaels *(Treas.)*
Scott Cooper *(Sec.)*
Steve Krumrei *(Controller)*

IRA HIGDON GROCERY, INC.
Alton Hall Rd.
Cairo, GA 31728
Mailing Address:
P.O. Box 488
Cairo, GA 31728
Tel.: 912-377-1272 **GA**
Fax: 912-377-8756
Year Founded: 1972
Approx.Sls.: $65,000,000
Emp.: 80
Wholesale Grocers, General Line of Fresh, Frozen & Packaged Meats; Dairy Products, Except Dried or Canned
S.I.C.: 5141; 5147; 5142; 5143
Ira Higdon *(Pres.)*
Lawrence Higdon *(V.P. & Sec.)*

Outside Service Firm(s):

Guy & Guy*(Auditors)*
Thomasville, GA

Commercial Bank*(Major Banking Relationship)*
P.O. Box 710,
Thomasville, GA 31799
Tel.: 912-226-3535

HIGGINBOTHAM-BARTLETT CO.
8302 Indiana Ave.
Lubbock, TX 79423
Mailing Address:
P.O. Box 6880
Lubbock, TX 79493
Tel.: 806-793-8662 **TX**
Fax: 806-792-8089
Year Founded: 1916
Approx.Sls.: $16,000,000
Emp.: 125
Fiscal Year-end: 12/31/90
Retail Building Materials & Hardware; General Merchandise Stores
S.I.C.: 5211
J.L. Higginbotham *(Pres. & Chief Exec. Officer)*
Marvin L. Fraley *(V.P. & Gen. Mgr.)*
Carol S. Wood *(Treas., Sec., Controller & Chief Fin. Officer)*
R. Dean Null *(Dir.-Pur.)*

Computer Systems/Hardware:
Data General Desk Top 30

Outside Service Firm(s):

Davis & Clark*(Auditors)*
Dallas, TX

Connecticut General Life Insurance Co.*(Group Insurer)*
P.O. Box 2975,
Hartford, CT 06104
Tel.: 203-726-6000

McClesky, Harriger, Brazil & Graf*(Legal Firm)*
Lubbock, TX

American State Bank*(Major Banking Relationship)*
Lubbock, TX

Plains National Bank*(Major Banking Relationship)*
Lubbock, TX

J. E. HIGGINS LUMBER CO.
1485 Enea Ct., Ste. 1100
Concord, CA 94520
Mailing Address:
P.O. Box 4124
Concord, CA 94524
Tel.: 510-674-9300 **CA**
Fax: 510-674-9434
Year Founded: 1883
Approx.Sls.: $72,000,000
Emp.: 250
Fiscal Year-end: 12/31/91
Import
Wholesale Quality Hardwoods, Softwoods, Flooring & Related Forest Products
S.I.C.: 5031
Jonathan R. Long *(Pres. & Chief Fin. Officer)*
Harry S. Anthony *(Chief Exec. Officer)*
John C. Coates *(Exec. V.P.)*
Timothy N. Brown *(Corp. Counsel & Sec.)*
Michael Flener *(Controller)*
Sherry Perkins *(Dir.-Mktg.)*
Julie Commins *(Mgr.-Personnel)*
Ed Nagayama *(Mgr.-Accts.)*
Roxy Cummings *(Meeting/Travel Planner)*

No. of Mfg. Plants/Facilities: 14
No. of U.S. Offices: 14

Computer Systems/Hardware:
DEC

Outside Service Firm(s):

KPMG Peat Marwick*(Auditors)*
3 Embarcadero Center
San Francisco, CA 94111
Tel.: 415-951-0100
Fax: 415-397-1129

Insurance Services Co.*(Commercial Insurance Carrier)*
San Francisco, CA

Union Bank*(International Bank Affiliate)*
200 Pringle Ave.
Walnut Creek, CA 94596
Tel.: 510-947-2444

Travelers Insurance Co.*(Group Insurer)*
One Tower Square
Hartford, CT 06183-6130
Tel.: 203-277-4542
Fax: 203-277-5038

Wells Fargo Bank*(Investment Banker)*
420 Montgomery St.
San Francisco, CA 94104

Crosby, Heafey, Roach & May*(Legal Firm)*
1939 Harrison
Oakland, CA 94612
Tel.: 510-834-4820

Wells Fargo Bank*(Major Banking Relationship)*
San Francisco, CA

Wells Fargo Bank*(Major Banking Relationship)*
420 Montgomery St.
San Francisco, CA 94104

Wyatt Co.*(Pension Manager)*
345 California St.
San Francisco, CA 94104
Tel.: 415-986-6568

Divisions:

Golden State Flooring Company **(1)**
449 Littlefield Ave.
South San Francisco, CA 94080
Tel.: 415-872-0500
Flooring & Related Products
S.I.C.: 5031
Rick Coates *(Mgr.)*

Golden State Flooring Company **(1)**
1015 N. Market Blvd.
Sacramento, CA 95834
Tel.: 916-928-0400
Flooring & Related Products
S.I.C.: 5031
Lorenda Behrens *(Mgr.)*

HIGH INDUSTRIES INC.
1853 William Penn Way
Lancaster, PA 17605
Mailing Address:
P.O. Box 1526
Lancaster, PA 17603
Tel.: 717-293-4444 **PA**
Fax: 717-293-4452
Year Founded: 1931
Approx.Sls.: $240,000,000
Emp.: 2,000
Holding Company; Steel Fabrication & Erection, Cable Television, Concrete, Real Estate Development; Food Service, Employee Services, Hospitality Services, Management Consulting & Development
S.I.C.: 6719; 1791; 3272; 3441; 4841; 6552; 5812; 8741; 7011
S. Dale High *(Chm. Bd. & Pres.)*
Calvin G. High *(Sr. V.P.)*
Thomas C. Kile *(V.P.-Fin.)*
Walter J. Kissel *(V.P.-Admin.)*
Allon H. Lefever *(V.P.-Affiliated Cos.)*
Thomas R. Esposito *(Treas.)*
Betty J. Gerhart *(Sec.)*
James L. Linville *(Mgr.-Data Processing Services)*
Principal(s):
S. Dale High
Calvin G. High

No. of Mfg. Plants/Facilities: 6
No. of U.S. Offices: 4

Computer Systems/Hardware:
Data General

Outside Service Firm(s):

Arthur Andersen & Co.*(Auditors)*
Lancaster, PA

Appel & Yost*(Legal Firm)*
33 N. Duke St.
Lancaster, PA 17602
Tel.: 717-394-0521

Hamilton Bank*(Major Banking Relationship)*
Lancaster, PA

HIGH POINT FINANCIAL CORP.
Three Broad St.
Branchville, NJ 07826
Mailing Address:
P.O. Box 460,
Branchville, NJ 07826
Tel.: 201-948-3300
Fax: 201-948-3695
Year Founded: 1982
Assets: $253,259,000
Earnings: ($5,188,000)

High Point Financial Corp.—(Continued)

Liabilities: $244,151,000
Net Worth: $9,108,000
Approx.Income: $27,545,000
Emp.: 169
Fiscal Year-end: 12/31/91
Banking Services
S.I.C.: 6021; 6712
William A. Dolan II *(Chm. Bd.)*
Larry R. Condit *(Vice Chm.)*
Michael A. Dickerson *(Pres. & Chief Exec. Officer)*
Gregory W.A. Meehan *(V.P., Chief Fin. Officer & Treas.)*
Robert A. Vandenbergh *(Sec.)*
William J. McMillan *(Auditor)*

Computer Systems/Hardware:
Unisys

Banking Subsidiaries:

The National Bank of Sussex County **(1)**
3 Broad St.
Branchville, NJ 07826
Tel.: 201-948-3300 (100%%)
Emp.: 132
Banking Services
S.I.C.: 6021
Michael A. Dickerson *(Pres. & Chief Exec. Officer)*
Gregory W.A. Meehan *(Exec. V.P. & Chief Fin. Officer)*
Robert A. Vandenbergh *(Sr. V.P. & Chief Lending Officer)*
Fred Roberts *(Sr. V.P.)*
Nicholas Cioffi *(V.P.-Mortgages)*
Tammy I. Fielden *(V.P.-Loans)*
Michael Lippincott *(Asst. V.P.-Loans)*
Connie A. Jaeger *(Asst. V.P. & Human Resources Dir.)*
Lorraine Fasano *(Dir.-Mktg.)*
Rita A. Vander Wey *(Comptroller)*
Anna M. Harris *(Asst. Cashier)*
Cynthia M. San Phillip *(Asst. Cashier-Loans)*

Subsidiaries:

High Point Investment Advisory Services **(2)**
Three Broad St.
Branchville, NJ 07826
Tel.: 201-948-3300
Investment Advisory Services
S.I.C.: 6282

NBSC Investment Co. **(2)**
Three Broad St.
Branchville, NJ 07826
Tel.: 201-948-3300
Investments
S.I.C.: 6211

The Pocono Bank **(1)**
P.O. Box 1049,
Milford, PA 18337
Tel.: 717-296-5600
Emp.: 15
Banking Services
S.I.C.: 6021
Michael A. Dickerson *(Vice Chm., Pres. & Chief Exec. Officer)*
Elaine Filler *(V.P. & Treas.)*
David A. Krause *(V.P. & Sec.)*

HIGH POINT OIL CO.
3520 East 96th St., Ste. 10
Indianapolis, IN 46240
Tel.: 317-844-8886 **IN**
Fax: 317-844-0098
Approx.Sls.: $44,000,000
Emp.: 100
Petroleum Bulk Stations & Terminals; Retail Gasoline Service Stations
S.I.C.: 5171; 5541
Edwin D. Kelb *(Chm. Bd.)*
Don E. Kelb *(Pres.)*
Karl Kelb *(V.P.)*

Outside Service Firm(s):

Merchants National Bank & Trust Company of Indianapolis*(Major Banking Relationship)*
One Merchants Plaza, Ste. 901E
Indianapolis, IN 46255
Tel.: 317-267-7109

THE HIGHLAND GROUP

THE HIGHLAND GROUP, INC.
105 Woodrow Ave.
Southport, CT 06490
Tel.: 203-254-3505
Fax: 203-254-3066
Year Founded: 1979
Approx.Billings: $26,700,000
Emp.: 21
Fiscal Year-end: 2/28/89
Advertising Agency
S.I.C.: 7311
Frederick R. Tscheulin *(Chm. Bd., Pres. & Chief Exec. Officer)*
Richard J. Baker *(Exec. V.P., Treas.)*
Robert Heintz *(V.P.)*
Jack Drum *(Mgr., Pub. Rels.)*
Beth Ontra *(Human Resources)*

Computer Systems/Hardware:
IBM PC Network

Subsidiary:

Strategic Events Group **(1)**
105 Woodrow Ave.
Southport, CT 06490
Tel.: 203-254-3505
Fax: 203-254-3066

HIGHLAND MILLS INC.
340 E. 16th St.
Charlotte, NC 28233
Tel.: 704-375-3333
Mfr. Hosiery
S.I.C.: 2251; 2252
Saul Wojnowich *(Pres. & Chief Exec. Officer)*
Abraham Kaplan *(V.P.)*
Simon Wojnowich *(Treas.)*

Subsidiary:

Admiration Hosiery Mills, Inc. **(1)**
4210 Yancey Rd.
Charlotte, NC 28217
Tel.: 704-525-3162
Fax: 704-529-5107
Emp.: 168
Fiscal Year-end: 5/31/90
Computer Systems/Hardware:
IBM PC
Hosiery Mills
S.I.C.: 2251; 2252
Samuel Kaplan *(Pres., Chief Exec. Officer, Sec. & Dir.-Sls. & Pur.)*
Simon Wonowich *(V.P. & Chief Fin. Officer)*
Boris Wonowich *(Treas.)*
Mary Leslie *(Personnel Mgr.)*

HIGHLIGHTS FOR CHILDREN, INC.
2300 W. Fifth Ave.
Columbus, OH 43215
Mailing Address:
P.O. Box 269,
Columbus, OH 43216-0269
Tel.: 614-486-0631
Fax: 614-486-0762
Year Founded: 1946
Approx.Sls.: $60,000,000
Emp.: 500
Fiscal Year-end: 2/28/91
Magazine for Children, Educational Materials
S.I.C.: 2721
Richard H. Bell *(Chm. Bd.)*
Elmer Meider, Jr. *(Pres.)*
Garry C. Myers *(Chief Exec. Officer)*
William Hummel *(V.P.-Mktg.)*
John P. Marchak *(Dir.-Mktg. Admin.)*
Garry Brown *(Communications & Pub. Information Coord.)*

HILL-BEHAN LUMBER COMPANY
6515 Page Blvd.
Saint Louis, MO 63133
Tel.: 314-725-1111
Fax: 314-725-8460
Year Founded: 1912
Approx.Sls.: $85,000,000
Emp.: 725
Wholesale & Retail Lumber, Plywood, Hardware, Millwork, Industrial Supplies
S.I.C.: 5211; 5031; 5039; 5072; 5085
William L. Behan, Jr. *(Chm. Bd.)*
Lee A. Brandenburger *(Vice Chm.)*
Patrick J. Behan *(Pres. & Chief Oper. Officer)*
Gerald Koler *(Chief Fin. Officer)*
Donald R. Debrecht *(Sr. V.P., Treas. & Controller)*
David J. Matthews *(Sr. V.P.-Pur. & Gen. Mdse.)*
William L. Behan III *(V.P. & Sec.)*
Thomas H. Behan *(V.P.)*
Joseph A. Belcher *(V.P.)*
Roberta J. Gibson *(V.P.-Adv. & Pub. Rels.)*
Frank Hajek *(V.P.-Retail Sls.-Chicago Div.)*
S. T. Johnson *(V.P.-Security & Loss Prevention)*
Richard A. Miller *(V.P.-Retail Sls.-St. Louis Div.)*
George J. Schiller *(V.P.-Chicago Div.)*

Outside Service Firm(s):

Ernst & Young*(Auditors)*
701 Market St.
St. Louis, MO 63101
Tel.: 314-259-1000

HILL & GRIFFITH COMPANY
1262 State Ave.
Cincinnati, OH 45204
Tel.: 513-921-1075
Fax: 513-244-4199
Approx.Sls.: $20,000,000
Emp.: 90
Materials Processing; Sand Additives for Foundry Use
S.I.C.: 3295
David N. Greek *(Pres.)*
Jerry Agin *(V.P.-Sls.)*
Gary Follmer *(V.P.-Fin.)*
John Iglar *(V.P.)*
Dale Welsh *(Controller)*
Gary Miller *(Dir.-Pur.)*
Ray Sparks *(Plant Mgr.)*

HILL, HOLLIDAY, CONNORS, COSMOPULOS, INC.
John Hancock Tower, 200 Clarendon St.
Boston, MA 02116
Tel.: 617-437-1600 **MA**
Telex: 617-681-7519
Fax: 617-572-3534
Year Founded: 1968
Approx.Billings: $367,048,000
Emp.: 450
Fiscal Year-end: 4/30/91
Advertising Agency; Marketing Communications
S.I.C.: 7311
George J. Hill III *(Chm.)*
John M. Connors, Jr. *(Pres. & Chief Exec. Officer)*
Dick Pantano *(Vice Chm. & Co-Creative Dir.)*
Dr. Jack Sansolo *(Vice Chm. & Mktg./Corp. Devel.)*
Joseph Norberg *(Chief Fin. Officer & Treas.)*
Arthur Eisenbach *(Exec. V.P., Dir. Mktg./Media Services)*
John Mills *(Exec. V.P., Fin.)*
Margaret Fitzgerald *(Sr. V.P., Dir. Community Rels.)*
Mark Minkin *(Sr. V.P., New Bus.)*
Jorge Abellas-Martin *(V.P., Dir. MIS)*
Susan Chavez *(V.P., New Bus. Opers.)*
John Cormier *(V.P., Dir. Fin.)*
Joyce King *(V.P., Community Rels.)*
Sharon McDonald *(V.P., Bus. Affairs Dir.)*
Paula Polito *(V.P., Communications)*
Susan Roche *(V.P., Human Resources Dir.)*
Beth Sullivan *(V.P., Mktg. Res. & Plng. Dir.)*
Martha Tripp *(V.P., Plng.)*
Cindy Tungate *(V.P., Assoc. Res. Dir.)*
Betsy Wachtel *(V.P., Dir. Information Resources)*
John Vient *(Jr. Art Dir.)*

No. of U.S. Offices: 4
No. of Foreign Offices: 2

Computer Systems/Hardware:
Wang

Outside Service Firm(s):

Ernst & Young*(Auditors)*
200 Clarendon St., 46th Fl.
Boston, MA 02116
Tel.: 617-266-2000

Goodwin, Procter & Hoar*(Legal Firm)*
Exchange Place
Boston, MA 02109-2881
Tel.: 617-570-1000

Branches:

Hill, Holliday/Los Angeles **(1)**
4640 Admiralty Way, 9th Fl.
Marina Del Rey, CA 90292
Tel.: 213-822-7088
Fax: 213-574-0332/0299
Gene Cameron *(Pres./HHCC, Los Angeles)*
Dennis Farrington *(Sr. V.P., Dir. Reg. Mktg.)*
Marshall Rogers *(Sr. V.P., Dir. Mktg. Res. & Plng.)*
Terrence Sullivan *(Sr. V.P., Finance/ Admin.)*
Ed Collins *(V.P., Mgr. Reg. Field Opers.)*
Joanne Gordon *(V.P., Dir. Mktg./Res.)*
Kathleen Lundeen *(V.P., Dir. Human Resources)*
Velda Ruddock *(V.P., Information Services Mgr.)*

Hill, Holliday/New York **(1)**
885 Third Ave.
New York, NY 10022
Tel.: 212-753-1700
Telex: 212-697-8486
Fax: 212-759-0337

Non-U.S. Branches:

HHCC International, Inc. **(1)**
13/F Hop Hing Centre, 8-12 Hennessy Rd.
Wanchai, Hong Kong
Tel.: 5-865-5838
Telex: 73058
Fax: 5-861-2226
Approx.Billings: $7,700,000
Emp.: 32
Vivian Shum *(Mng. Dir.)*

Hill, Holliday/Toronto **(1)**
1133 Yonge St.
Toronto, ON M4T 2Z3, Canada
Tel.: 416-925-1944
Fax: 416-925-7837
Judy Paton *(Sr. V.P., Mng. Dir.)*

HILL INTERNATIONAL INC.
(Formerly Hill Group Inc.)
1 Leavitt Pkwy
Willingboro, NJ 08046
Mailing Address:
P.O. Box 397,
Willingboro, NJ 08046
Tel.: 609-871-5800 **DE**
Fax: 609-871-1261
Assets: $12,000,000
Earnings: $1,200,000
Liabilities: $7,000,000
Net Worth: $5,000,000
Approx.Sls.: $14,000,000
Emp.: 500
Construction Management Consultants, Interest in Construction Claims
S.I.C.: 8742

Irvin E. Richter *(Chm. Bd. & Chief Exec. Officer)*
Donal R. Kruver *(Pres.)*
James Cassano *(Treas. & Chief Fin. Officer)*
Jeanne Cook *(Gen. Counsel)*
Ronald F. Emma *(V.P.-Fin.)*

Computer Systems/Hardware:
Wang

Outside Service Firm(s):

Deloitte & Touche*(Auditors)*
1700 Market St.
Philadelphia, PA 19103
Tel.: 215-246-2322
Fax: 215-569-2441

Dechert, Price & Rhoads*(Legal Firm)*
4000 Bell Atlantic Tower, 1717 Arch St.
Philadelphia, PA 19103
Tel.: 215-994-4000
Tel.: 2000

First Fidelity Bank, N.A.*(Major Banking Relationship)*
Hackensack, NJ

First National State Bank of New Jersey*(Pension Manager)*
Hackensack, NJ

Subsidiary:

Gibbs & Hill, Inc. **(1)**
11 Penn Plaza
New York, NY 10001
Tel.: 212-760-4000
Irvin E. Richter *(Pres.)*

HILLERICH & BRADSBY CO., INC.
200 W. Broadway
Louisville, KY 40202
Mailing Address:
P.O. Box 35700
Louisville, KY 40232
Tel.: 502-585-5226
Fax: 502-585-1179
Year Founded: 1884
Approx.Sls.: $50,000,000
Emp.: 660
Manufacture Baseball & Softball Gloves & Bats, Golf Clubs, Hockey Sticks
S.I.C.: 3949
John A. Hillerich III *(Pres. & Chief Exec. Officer)*
Marty Archer *(V.P. & Gen. Mgr.-Athletic Goods Div.)*
Phil Armbruster *(V.P.-Mktg. Devel.)*
Rex Bradley *(V.P.-Amateur Bat Sls.)*
Tom Harris *(V.P.-Engrng.)*
Donald F. Hess *(V.P.-Pur.)*
Jerome D. Martin *(V.P. & Gen. Mgr.-Golf Div.)*
Michael McGrath *(V.P.-Intl. Mktg.)*
Richard G. Sawyer *(V.P.-Distr. Sls.)*
Bill B. Williams *(V.P.-Adv.)*
Harold Fisher *(Sec. & Treas.)*
William L. Johnson, Jr. *(Comptroller)*
Ronald L. Grubbs *(Mgr.-Data Processing)*

Outside Service Firm(s):

Coopers & Lybrand*(Auditors)*
Louisville, KY 46201

Middleton & Reutlinger*(Legal Firm)*
2500 Brown & Williamson Tower
Louisville, KY 40202
Tel.: 502-584-1135

First National Bank of Louisville*(Major Banking Relationship)*
P.O. Box 36000,
Louisville, KY 40233

HILLIARD CORPORATION
100 W. 4th St.
Elmira, NY 14901
Tel.: 607-733-7121 **NY**
Fax: 607-733-3009
Year Founded: 1905
Approx.Sls.: $20,000,000
Emp.: 264
Export
Mfr. of Clutches, Except Vehicular; Purification & Dust Collection Equipment
S.I.C.: 3568; 3564
N. Mooers Van Den Blink *(Chm. Bd., Chief Exec. Officer, & Treas.)*
Gerald F. Schichtel *(Pres. & Chief Oper. Officer)*
Gene Ebercht *(V.P.)*
Ralph H. Roberts, Jr. *(V.P.)*
Paul D. Webb *(V.P.)*
John R. Alexander *(Sec.)*
Michael Girardi *(Pur. Agent)*
R.D. Henry *(Mgr.-Prod. Control)*

Outside Service Firm(s):

Mengel, Metzer Barr & Co.*(Auditors)*
Rochester, NY

HILLMAN COMPANY
1900 Grant Bldg.
Pittsburgh, PA 15219
Tel.: 412-281-2620
Fax: 412-338-3529
Sales Range: $1 Billion + Diversified Investment Operations
S.I.C.: 6722
Henry Hillman *(Chm. Bd.)*
Carl Grefenstette *(Pres. & Chief Exec. Officer)*
Lawrence M. Wagner *(Chief Oper. Officer & Exec. V.P.)*
Coleman J. Benedict *(V.P.)*
J.R. Philp *(V.P.-Personnel & Admin.)*
Charles H. Bracken, Jr. *(Treas.)*
James E. Stoll *(Controller)*
H. Vaughan Blaxter III *(Gen. Counsel)*
Mark W. Cottrill *(Dir.-Mngmt. Information Systems)*
Michael S. Adamcyk *(Mgr.-Benefits & Pensions)*
Vicky J. Brilmyer *(Mgr.-Employee Relations)*
Reave J. Watkins *(Mgr.-Office)*

Computer Systems/Hardware:
Hewlett Packard

Outside Service Firm(s):

Pittsburgh National Bank*(Major Banking Relationship)*
Stock Transfer Dept., Fifth & Wood Streets
Pittsburgh, PA 15265

Subsidiary:

Richard Young Office Products, Inc. **(1)**
508 S. Military Trail
Deerfield Beach, FL 33442
Tel.: 305-426-8100
National Distributor of Computer Supplies & Accessories
S.I.C.: 5045
Richard P. Young *(Pres.)*
Crawford Paton *(V.P.-Opers.)*
Alice Chick *(V.P.-Fin. & Controller)*
Steve Green *(Dir.-Pur.)*

Hillsborough Holdings Corporation
(Name Changed To Walter Industries, Inc.)

HILLSIDE CAPITAL, INC.
405 Park Ave.
New York, NY 10022
Tel.: 212-935-6090
Fax: 212-759-4831
Year Founded: 1976
Approx.Sls.: $450,000,000
Emp.: 3,000
Sausage Casing, Food Packaging, Sheet Vinyl & Other Flooring Products
S.I.C.: 3086; 3089; 3996
John N. Irwin *(Mng. Dir.)*
Charles Straut *(Mng. Dir.)*

Outside Service Firm(s):

Chase Manhattan Bank, N.A.*(Major Banking Relationship)*
One Chase Manhattan Plaza
New York, NY 10081
Tel.: 212-552-2222
Tel.: 800-526-0801
Fax: 212-552-7175

Subsidiaries:

Hillside Industries, Inc. **(1)**
405 Park Ave.
New York, NY 10022
Tel.: 212-935-6090
Sausage Casing, Food Packaging, Sheet Vinyl & Other Flooring Products
S.I.C.: 3089; 3086; 3996
John Irwin *(V.P. & Mng. Dir.)*

Teepak, Inc. **(1)**
3 Westbrook Corporate Center
Westchester, IL 60154
Tel.: 708-409-3600
Telex: 708-409-3679
Approx.Sls.: $200,000,000
Emp.: 3,000
Fiscal Year-end: 9/30/90
Teepak Sausage Casings & Food Packaging
S.I.C.: 2013; 2099
J. Hermesdorf *(Pres. & Chief Exec. Officer)*
E.E. Badal *(Exec. V.P. & Gen. Mgr.-Cellulose Div.)*
R.D. Burtner *(V.P. & Dir.-N. American Opers.)*
F.N. Miller *(V.P. & Gen. Mgr.-Cora Div. & Dir.-Pur.)*
R.M. Rutan *(V.P.-Sls. & Mktg.)*
J. Fitzgerald *(Controller)*
R.D. Kelly *(Gen. Mgr.-Plastics)*
Frances Altman *(Mgr.-Pub. Rels.)*

Non-U.S. Holding:

Teepak, Inc., Zurich Branch **(1)**
P.O. Box 8025, Zahringerstrasse 32
Zurich, Switzerland
Tel.: 01/47 19 77
Telex: 816 366
Emp.: 5
Mktg. of Artificial Casings
S.I.C.: 5149
Francis A. Wouters *(Mng. Dir.)*

THE HILSINGER CORP.
33 W. Bacon St.
Plainville, MA 02762
Tel.: 508-699-4406
Telex: 951406 HILCO PLAE
Fax: 508-695-2742
Year Founded: 1956
Sales Range: $10-19 Million
Emp.: 150
Mfr. Optical Accessories
S.I.C.: 3851; 3999
Arthur R. Hilsinger, Jr. *(Chm. Bd., Pres. & Treas.)*
Fred M. Curtis *(Exec. V.P. & Sec.)*
Andrew E. Boyd *(V.P.-Mktg.)*
Norbert Demers *(V.P., Comptroller & Chief Fin. Officer)*

Principal(s):
Arthur R. Hilsinger, Jr.

Computer Systems/Hardware:
Wang

Outside Service Firm(s):

KPMG Peat Marwick*(Auditors)*
One Boston Place
Boston, MA 02108
Tel.: 617-723-7700

Ropes & Gray*(Legal Firm)*
One International Place
Boston, MA 02110
Tel.: 617-423-6100

First National Bank of Boston*(Major Banking Relationship)*
P.O. Box 644,
Boston, MA 02102-0644
Tel.: 617-575-2900
Fax: 617-575-2549

Division:

Eyecessories **(1)**
33 W. Bacon St.
Plainville, MA 02762
Tel.: 508-699-4406
Emp.: 340
Hilco Optical & Contact Lens Accessories for Consumer & Trade, Eyecessories
A.R. Hilsinger, Jr. *(Pres.)*
F.M. Curtis *(Exec. V.P.)*
E. Boyd *(V.P.-Mktg.)*
T. Rzemien *(Dir.-Mktg. Services)*

HINDERLITER INDUSTRIES, INC.
1600 Redbud Blvd., Ste. 301
McKinney, TX 75069
Tel.: 214-548-0797
Assets: $12,933,000
Earnings: ($7,863,000)
Liabilities: $8,589,000
Net Worth: $4,344,000
Approx.Sls.: $13,763,000
Fiscal Year-end: 6/30/90
Mfr. of Precision & Specialty Parts & Equipment for the Gas Transfer Industry & A Major Force in the Heat Treating Industry
S.I.C.: 3398; 4922
Richard Hughes *(Pres. & Chief Exec. Officer)*
Timothy Brasher *(V.P. & Chief Fin. Officer)*
Robert C. Diffenderfer *(V.P. & Devel.)*

Subsidiaries:

Hinderliter Heat Treating, Inc. **(1)**
3890 W. Northwest Hwy., Ste. 300
Dallas, TX 75220
Tel.: 214-352-8422
Heat Treatments
S.I.C.: 3398
John D. Hubbard *(Pres.)*

Scientific Corporation **(1)**
208 Rouse Rd.
Fort Pierce, FL 34946
Tel.: 407-464-8770
Mfr. High-Tech Mobile Systems & Prefabricated Enclosures for the Governmental Sector & for the High Technology Electronic Medical Industry
S.I.C.: 3663; 2451
Leslie P. Waller *(Pres.)*

HINIKER COMPANY
Rt. 5, Box 3407
Mankato, MN 56001
Tel.: 507-625-6621
Year Founded: 1967
Approx.Sls.: $16,000,000
Emp.: 200
Export
Mfr. of Farm Machinery & Equipment
S.I.C.: 3523
V. Stark *(Gen. Mgr.)*
D. McNea *(Chief Fin. Officer)*
V. Tomlonovic *(Dir.-Mktg.)*

Computer Systems/Hardware:
IBM

HINKLEY LIGHTING INC.
12600 Berea Rd.
Cleveland, OH 44111
Tel.: 216-671-3300
Year Founded: 1922
Approx.Sls.: $10,000,000
Emp.: 130
Import Export
Mfr. of Residential Lighting Fixtures
S.I.C.: 3645
Richard A. Wiedemer, Jr. *(Pres.)*
Richard A. Wiedemer, Sr. *(V.P. & Treas.)*
Art Crisfield *(Dir.-Engrng.)*
Mark Gardiner *(Dir.-Sls. & Mktg.)*
Henry Irizarry *(Dir.-Pur.)*
Ronald Chmielowiec *(Mgr.-Production)*

HIPPOCRATES PARTNERS
301 Howard St., 18th Fl.
San Francisco, CA 94105
Tel.: 415-512-9100
Year Founded: 1987
Approx.Sls.: $18,000,000
Emp.: 60
Fiscal Year-end: 12/31/92
Publishes Health & Medicine Magazines; Hippocrates Magazine for Physicians, Health Magazine for Consumers
S.I.C.: 2721
Eric Schrier *(Pres.)*
Allen Barr *(Chief Oper. Officer)*
William Kupper *(Assoc. Publr.)*
John P. Sheehy *(Gen. Mgr.)*

Division:

Midwest Division **(1)**
121 West Wacker Drive, Ste. 2016
Chicago, IL 60601
Tel.: 312-641-5667
Health & Medicine Publications
S.I.C.: 2721
Brenda Stone *(Mgr.)*

HIROSS INC.
2107 Liberty Dr.
Niagara Falls, NY 14304
Mailing Address:
P.O. Box 290 L.P.O.,
Niagara Falls, NY 14304
Tel.: 716-283-6464
Tel.: 1-800-388-3211 **NY**
Telex: 646305
Fax: 716-283-1911
Year Founded: 1976
Approx.Sls.: $20,000,000
Emp.: 200
Import Export
Mfr. Computer Room Air Conditioning Systems & Compressed Air & Gas Accessories
S.I.C.: 3679; 3585
Stephen Saldanha *(Chm. Bd.)*
Jack Wagner *(Pres. & Chief Exec. Officer)*
George V. Drennan *(V.P.-Sls. & Mktg.)*
Peter Grandits *(V.P.-Fin.)*
James Renda *(V.P.-Customer Support)*
Daniel Casper *(Dir.-Personnel)*
Pat Castillo *(Mgr.-Information Systems)*

No. of U.S. Offices: 1

Outside Service Firm(s):

Price Waterhouse*(Auditors)*
3600 Marine Midland Center
Buffalo, NY 14203
Tel.: 716-856-4650

Marine Midland Bank*(Major Banking Relationship)*
P.O. Box 803, 1 Marine Midland Center, 23rd Floor
Buffalo, NY 14203
Tel.: 716-841-2582

HIRSCHFELD, INC.
112 W. 29th St.
San Angelo, TX 76903
Tel.: 915-653-3211
Fax: 915-658-8469
Emp.: 225
Manufacture & Wholesale Fabricated Structural Steel
S.I.C.: 3441; 5051
David L. Hirschfeld *(Pres., Chief Exec. Officer & Treas.)*
Dennis C. Hirschfeld *(Exec. V.P. & Sec.)*

Outside Service Firm(s):

Larry Barnes*(Auditors)*
San Angelo, TX

Texas Commerce Bank*(Major Banking Relationship)*
San Angelo, CA

Subsidiary:

Hirschfeld Steel Company, Inc. **(1)**
112 W. 29th St.
San Angelo, TX 76903
Tel.: 915-653-3211
Fax: 332544
Approx.Sls.: $32,000,000
Emp.: 225
Fabricated Structural Metal & Metal Service Centers
S.I.C.: 3441; 5051
David L. Hirschfeld *(Chm. Bd. & Pres.)*
Dennis C. Hirschfeld *(V.P.-Engrng.)*
Danny S. Holtman *(Pur. Agent)*

HITCHCOCK CHAIR COMPANY LTD
13 Riverton Rd.
Riverton, CT 06065
Tel.: 203-379-8531
Fax: 203-738-1756
Approx.Sls.: $15,000,000
Emp.: 200
Early American Furniture
S.I.C.: 2512
Kenneth Bartle *(Pres.)*
Diane Anzellotti *(Chief Fin. Officer)*
Keith Heller *(Controller)*
Joan Arciero *(Dir.-Sls.)*
Margaret Bishop *(Dir.-Personnel)*
Keith Heller *(Mgr.-Credit)*
Carol Sterpka *(Pur. Agent)*

Outside Service Firm(s):

Price Waterhouse*(Auditors)*
One Financial Plaza
Hartford, CT 06103
Tel.: 203-240-2000

Connecticut Bank & Trust*(Major Banking Relationship)*
One Constitution Plaza,
Hartford, CT 06115

HITCHCOCK-FLEMING & ASSOCIATES, INC.
500 Wolf Ledges Pkwy.
Akron, OH 44311
Tel.: 216-376-2111
Fax: 216-376-2220
Fax: 216-996-7060
Year Founded: 1940
Approx.Billings: $28,200,000
Emp.: 53
R. Cyrus Hitchcock *(Pres. & New Bus. Contact)*
Stanley Buda *(Exec. V.P.)*
Jack S. DeLeo *(Sr. V.P.)*
Chuck Abraham *(V.P., Fin. Services)*
J. Patrick Kunklier *(Dir., Pub. Rels.)*

HITCHCOCK INDUSTRIES, INC.
8701 Harriet Ave. S.
Bloomington, MN 55420
Tel.: 612-881-1000
Telex: 29-0486
Fax: 612-887-7858
Year Founded: 1916
Approx.Sls.: $50,000,000
Emp.: 550
Fiscal Year-end: 12/31/88
Producer of Nonferrous Castings, Primarily for the Aerospace Market
S.I.C.: 3369; 3724
Gregory T. Hitchcock *(Chm. Bd.)*
Timothy R. Hitchcock *(Pres. & Chief Exec. Officer)*
Lawrence M. Martin *(V.P.-Mktg. & Sls.)*
Peter A. Redpath *(V.P.-Personnel)*
Michael C. Taggart *(V.P.-Fin.)*
Emogene Hitchcock *(Sec.)*
Principal(s):
Gregory T. Hitchcock
Timothy R. Hitchcock

No. of Mfg. Plants/Facilities: 2
No. of U.S. Offices: 4

Outside Service Firm(s):

Deloitte & Touche*(Auditors)*
900 Pillsbury Ctr.
Minneapolis, MN 55402
Tel.: 612-332-2301
Fax: 612-375-5418

Industrial Risk Insurers*(Commercial Insurance Carrier)*
Minneapolis, MN

St. Paul Insurance Companies*(Commercial Insurance Carrier)*
St.Paul, MN

Dorsey & Whitney*(Legal Firm)*
2200 First Bank Place East
Minneapolis, MN 55402

American National Bank & Trust of St. Paul*(Major Banking Relationship)*
Fifth & Minnesota Streets
St. Paul, MN 55101
Tel.: 612-298-6000

Investment Advisors Inc.*(Pension Manager)*
1100 Dain Tower, P.O. Box 357
Minneapolis, MN 55440

HITCHINER MANUFACTURING COMPANY, INC.
Elm St.
Milford, NH 03055
Mailing Address:
P.O. Box 2001,
Milford, NH 03055
Tel.: 603-673-1100
Fax: 603-673-7960
Approx.Sls.: $70,000,000
Emp.: 1,300
Fiscal Year-end: 12/31/90
Export
Investment Castings, Ferrous & Non-Ferrous
S.I.C.: 3369; 3364; 3365
John H. Morison *(Chm. Bd.)*
N. Babich *(Pres. & Chief Exec. Officer)*
Frederick Lofgren *(Chief Fin. Officer, Treas., Sec. & V.P.-Fin. & Admin.)*
John Morison III *(V.P.-Mktg. & Sls.)*
Darold A. Calderara *(Investor Mgr.)*
Edward H. Broad *(Dir.-Admin.)*
John McDonald *(Mgr.-Data Processing)*

Computer Systems/Hardware:
IBM PC XT

Outside Service Firm(s):

Arthur Andersen & Co.*(Auditors)*
One Intl. Place, 100 Oliver St.
Boston, MA 02110
Tel.: 617-330-4000
Fax: 617-439-9731

Insurance Company of North America*(Commercial Insurance Carrier)*
1600 Arch St.
Philadelphia, PA 19103
Tel.: 215-523-4000

McLane, Graf, Raulerson, & Middleton*(Legal Firm)*
Manchester, NH

First National Bank of Boston*(Major Banking Relationship)*
P.O. Box 644,
Boston, MA 02102-0644
Tel.: 617-575-2900
Fax: 617-575-2549

First National Bank of Boston*(Pension Manager)*
P.O. Box 644,
Boston, MA 02102-0644
Tel.: 617-575-2900
Fax: 617-575-2549

Division:

Hitchiner Mfg. Co., Inc. **(1)**
E. Terra & Cannonball Lane, P.O. Box 220
O'Fallon, MO 63366
Tel.: 314-272-6176
D. Kallery *(Gen. Mgr.)*

THE HIVELY AGENCY INC.
520 Post Oak Blvd., Ste. 800
Houston, TX 77027
Tel.: 713-961-2888
Fax: 713-961-5249
Year Founded: 1985
Approx.Billings: $14,100,000
Emp.: 23
Charles Hively *(Pres., Chief Exec. Officer & Creative Dir.)*
David Kuhlman *(Exec. V.P., Chief Oper. Officer & New Bus. Contact)*
Robert Zschunke *(V.P., Media & Mktg. Dir.)*
Arnold Brown *(Controller)*

HOBART BROTHERS CO.
Hobart Square, 600 W. Main
Troy, OH 45373
Tel.: 513-332-4000 **OH**
Telex: 28-2865
Fax: 513-332-4125
Year Founded: 1917
Assets: $160,000,000
Liabilities: $90,000,000
Net Worth: $70,000,000
Approx.Sls.: $300,000,000
Emp.: 2,500
Fiscal Year-end: 12/31/91
Import Export
Arc Welding Systems & Equipment, Industrial Battery Chargers, Aircraft Ground Power & Support Equipment, Arc Welding Filler Metals
S.I.C.: 3548; 3629; 3621
W.H. Hobart *(Chm. Bd., Pres., Chief Exec. & Chief Oper. Officer)*
P.C. Hobart *(Vice Chm.)*
Michael A. Wolf *(Pres. & Chief Oper. Officer)*
Terry Lefever *(Exec. V.P.-Welding Prods.)*
Conrad Schwab *(Sr. V.P. & Gen. Mgr.-Power Systems)*
Joseph Klotnia *(V.P.-Pur. & Transportation)*
Philip Monnin *(V.P. & Gen. Mgr.)*
Leonard Reardon *(V.P.-Fin. & Treas., Chief Fin. Officer)*
Robert White *(V.P.-Human Resources)*
R. Weber *(Controller)*
Richard Cultice *(Asst. Treas.)*
Russ Becker *(Dir.-Sls. & Mktg.)*
G.M. Nally *(Dir.-Communications)*
Pat Gonzalez *(Mgr.-Export)*
Richard C. Berry *(Legal Counsel)*

Outside Service Firm(s):

Ernst & Young*(Auditors)*
2300 Kettering Tower
Dayton, OH 45423
Tel.: 513-223-2000

Bricker & Eckler*(Legal Firm)*
100 E. Broad St.
Columbus, OH 43215
Tel.: 614-227-2300

The Huntington National Bank*(Major Banking Relationship)*
Dayton, OH

Non-U.S. Holding:

Hobart Brothers of Canada Ltd. **(1)**
P.O. Box 150,
Woodstock, ON Canada N4S 7W8
Tel.: 519-537-6291 (100%)
Mfr. Wire
S.I.C.: 3315
A. Gordon Stell *(Pres.)*

Subsidiaries:

HBC International Sales Corp. **(1)**
Hobart Square
Troy, OH 45373
Tel.: 513-332-4000 (100%)
Import Export
International Distributor of Welding Systems
S.I.C.: 5084

Hobart Tafa Technologies, Inc. **(1)**
146 Pembroke Rd.
Concord, NH 03301
Tel.: 603-224-9585
Manufacture of Arc Spray Systems for Thermal Coatings
S.I.C.: 3563

Tri-Mark Inc. **(1)**
8585 Industrial Park Dr.
Piqua, OH 45356
Tel.: 513-773-2010 (100%)
Manufacture Gas Shielded Flux Cored Electrodes for Semiautomatic, Automatic & Robotic Applications
S.I.C.: 3548
D. Stager *(Pres.)*

Wollard Airport Equipment Co. **(1)**
6950 N.W. 77th Ct.
Miami, FL 33122
Tel.: 305-592-5450
Manufacture of Aircraft Ground Support Equipment
S.I.C.: 3629
William Bliss *(Pres.)*

Worldwide Leasing **(1)**
Hobart Square
Troy, OH 45373
Tel.: 513-332-4318 (100%)
Rental of Equipment
S.I.C.: 7359
Leonard Reardon *(Chief Oper. Officer)*

HOBOKEN WOOD FLOORING CORPORATION
70 Demarest Dr.
Wayne, NJ 07470
Tel.: 201-694-2888
Tel.: 800-222-1068
Fax: 201-694-6885
Year Founded: 1923
Assets: $24,515,000
Liabilities: $19,374,000
Net Worth: $5,141,000
Approx.Sls.: $67,495,000
Emp.: 141
Fiscal Year-end: 12/31/90
Import Export
Wholesale Hardwood Flooring, Vinyl Tile, Resilient Sheet Goods & Ceramics; Installation Service
S.I.C.: 5031; 1752
John J. Sakosits *(Chm. Bd., Chief Exec. & Chief Oper. Officer)*
Mildred Sakosits *(Pres. & Sec.)*
Thomas Dougherty *(Chief Fin. Officer & V.P.)*
Ira Lefkowitz *(Exec. V.P.)*
Joel Lefkowitz *(Exec. V.P.)*
Michael Korris *(V.P.-Sls.)*
Roger Stohler *(Controller)*
Marty Ackerman *(Mgr.-Sls.)*
Larry Love *(Mgr.-Data Processing)*
Michael Corsetto *(Pur. Agent)*
Connie Marnin *(Corp. Travel Planner)*
Principal(s):
John J. Sakosits
Mildred Sakosits

Outside Service Firm(s):

Deloitte & Touche*(Auditors)*
51 John F. Kennedy Parkway
Short Hills, NJ 07078-2708
Tel.: 201-912-4000

EMAR Group, Inc.*(Group Insurer)*
354 Eisenhower Pkwy.
Livingston, NJ 07039
Tel.: 201-994-1313

Merrill Lynch*(Investment Banker)*
P.O. Box 20, World Trade Center
New York, NY 10281
Tel.: 212-449-4843

Orloff, Lowenbach, Stifelman & Siegel*(Legal Firm)*
Roseland, NJ

United Jersey Bank*(Major Banking Relationship)*
210 Main St.
Hackensack, NJ 07602
Tel.: 201-646-5000

Mazurek Associates*(Pension Manager)*
East Orange, NJ

Divisions:

Hoboken Floors-Adirondack Division **(1)**
1397 Broadway
Watervliet, NY 12189-3324

Hoboken Floors-A.S.T. Division **(1)**
1397 Broadway
Watervliet, NY 12189-3324

Hoboken Floors-Capitol Division **(1)**
c/o D&D Bldg., 979 3rd Ave.
New York, NY 10022

Hoboken Floors-Connecticut Div. **(1)**
290 Sylvan Lake Rd.
Oakville, CT 06779

Hoboken Floors-Eastern Flooring Division **(1)**
c/o D&D Bldg., 979 3rd Ave.
New York, NY 10022

Hoboken Floors-New England Division **(1)**
181 Campanelli Pkwy.
Stoughton, MA 07072-3703

HODSKINS SIMONE & SEARLS, INC.
225 Lytton Ave.
Palo Alto, CA 94301
Tel.: 415-327-3434
Fax: 415-327-3438
Year Founded: 1978
Approx.Billings: $17,000,000
Emp.: 25
High Tech Adv.
David Hodskins *(Pres.)*
David Searls *(V.P., Dir. Pub. Rels.)*
Carol Bailey *(Office Mgr.)*
Liliane Truong *(Acctg.)*

Computer Systems/Hardware:
Macintosh

HOECHST CERAMTEC NORTH AMERICA, INC.
171 Forbes Blvd.
Mansfield, MA 02048-1148
Tel.: 508-339-1911
Fax: 508-339-5099
Approx.Sls.: $150,000,000
Emp.: 2,200
Advanced Technical Ceramics, Including Substrates, Packages & Seals
S.I.C.: 3999
Edgar Lutz *(Chm. Bd.)*
James Di Sorbo *(Pres. & Chief Exec. Officer)*
Helga Mueller *(Controller & Personnel Mgr.)*
Walt Dollman *(Mgr.-Sls. N.A.)*

HOFFCO, INC.
358 N.W. F St.
Richmond, IN 47374
Tel.: 317-966-8161
Tel.: 800-999-8161
Telex: 20212 HOFFCO RIC
Fax: 317-935-2346
Year Founded: 1949
Approx.Sls.: $15,000,000
Emp.: 175
Hoffco; Gasoline Powered Portable Outdoor Power Clearing Equip.; Post Hole Drills; Portable Digger; Tiller/Cultivators & Shredder/Composter
S.I.C.: 3546; 3523; 3524; 3566; 3714
David J. Hoff *(Chm. Bd. & Chief Exec. Officer)*
Harold Hockersmith *(Pres. & Chief Oper. Officer)*
Arnold Boyd *(V.P.-Opers.)*
Ken Maurer *(V.P.-Admin. & Chief Fin. Officer)*
John D. Hedges *(Dir.-Mktg. & Sls.)*
Terry Devers *(Dir.-Pur.)*
Carol J. Smith *(Dir.-Adv. & Pub. Rels.)*
Joe McDonald *(Mgr.-Personnel)*

Division:

Comet Industries **(1)**
358 N.W. F St.
Richmond, IN 47374
Tel.: 317-966-8161
Tel.: 800-999-8161
Fax: 317-935-2346
Approx.Sls.: $15,000,000
Emp.: 175
Export
Automatic Centrifugal Clutches; Spring Clutches; Torque Converter Drive Systems; Clutch Brake Systems; Drive Train Components (Jackshafts, Sprockets, Brakes, Brake Bands, Disc Brakes, Brake Drums, Variators
David J. Hoff *(Chm. Bd. & Exec. V.P.)*
Harold Hockersmith *(Pres. & Chief Oper. Officer)*
Arnold Boyd *(V.P.-Opers.)*
Ken Maurer *(V.P.-Acct. & Chief Fin. Officer)*
Chuck Sieb *(Dir.-Comet Indus.)*
Carol J. Smith *(Dir.-Adv. & Pub. Rels.)*
Steve Hughes *(Mgr.-Comet O.E.M.)*
Robert Jensen *(Mgr.-Service)*
Joe McDonald *(Mgr.-Personnel)*

HOFFER PLASTICS CORPORATION
500 N. Collins St.
South Elgin, IL 60177
Tel.: 708-741-5740 **DE**
Fax: 708-741-3086
Approx.Sls.: $65,000,000
Emp.: 575
Injection Molding Of Plastics
S.I.C.: 3089
Robert A. Hoffer, Sr. *(Pres. & Chief Exec. Officer)*
Robert Hoffer, Jr. *(V.P.)*
William Hoffer *(V.P.-Sls.)*
Mary Eagin *(Treas.)*
Stanley L. Schambach *(Controller)*
Helen Hoffer *(Sec.)*

Outside Service Firm(s):

Borhart, Spellmeyer & Co.*(Auditors)*
Chicago, IL

NBD Larkin Bank*(Major Banking Relationship)*
Elgin, IL

HOFFMAN BROTHERS PACKING CO.
2731 S. Soto St.
Los Angeles, CA 90023
Tel.: 213-267-4600
Fax: 213-261-7350
Year Founded: 1946
Approx.Sls.: $85,000,000
Emp.: 250
Fiscal Year-end: 6/28/90
Meat Processors
S.I.C.: 2011
Julius Hoffman *(Pres.)*
Irwin Diamond *(Exec. V.P. & Sec.)*
Richard P. Creagh *(Controller, Treas. & Chief Fin. Officer)*

Computer Systems/Hardware:
Qantel 40

Outside Service Firm(s):

Arthur Andersen & Co.*(Auditors)*
633 W. Fifth St.
Los Angeles, CA 90071
Tel.: 213-614-6500

General American Life Insurance Co.*(Group Insurer)*
700 Market
Saint Louis, MO 63101
Tel.: 314-525-5458
Fax: 314-525-3677

Ball, Hunt, Hart, Brown & Baerwitz*(Legal Firm)*
Beverly Hills, CA

Bank of America NT&SA*(Major Banking Relationship)*
555 So. Flower St., 5th Fl.
Los Angeles, CA 90071
Tel.: 213-228-3526
Fax: 213-228-4062

Sanwa Bank California*(Pension Manager)*
601 S. Figueroa St.
Los Angeles, CA 90017
Tel.: 213-896-7000

HOFFMAN CORPORATION
1300 S.W. Sixth Ave.
Portland, OR 97201
Mailing Address:
P.O. Box 1300
Portland, OR 97207
Tel.: 503-221-8811
Fax: 503-221-8934
Approx.Sls.: $275,000,000
Emp.: 850
Fiscal Year-end: 9/30/91
Construction of Commercial & Industrial Buildings, High-Rise Office Buildings, Warehouses, Water & Waste Water Treatment Facilities, Educational Facilities
S.I.C.: 1542
Eric Hoffman *(Chm. Bd.)*
Cecil W. Drinkward *(Pres.)*
Wayne Drinkward *(V.P.)*
Dan Harmon *(V.P. & Sec.)*
J.W. Montee *(V.P.)*
Ed N. Newman *(V.P.)*
Richard L. Silliman *(V.P.)*
Darwin W. Purvis *(Treas.)*

No. of U.S. Offices: 4

Outside Service Firm(s):

Coopers & Lybrand*(Auditors)*
2700 First Interstate Tower, 1300 SW 5th Ave.
Portland, OR 97201

First Interstate Bank*(Major Banking Relationship)*
P.O. Box 3131,
Portland, OR 97208
Tel.: 503-220-4855
Fax: 503-225-7153

Subsidiaries:

Hoffman Construction Company of Alaska **(1)**
3201 C St., Ste. 610
Anchorage, AK 99503
Tel.: 907-561-5578
Construction Operations
S.I.C.: 1542

Hoffman Construction Company of California **(1)**
555 University Ave., Ste. 200
Sacramento, CA 95825
Tel.: 916-929-9158
Fax: 916-929-4960
Construction Operations
S.I.C.: 1542

Hoffman Construction Company of Oregon **(1)**
1300 S.W. Sixth Ave.
Portland, OR 97201
Tel.: 503-221-8811
Fax: 503-221-8934
Construction Operations
S.I.C.: 1542

Hoffman Corporation—(Continued)

Hoffman Construction Company of Washington **(1)**
Ste. 265, 135 Lake St. South
Kirkland, WA 98033
Tel.: 206-822-5655
Fax: 206-822-3970
Construction Operations
S.I.C.: 1542

Hoffman Mechanical Corporation **(1)**
1300 S.W. Sixth Ave.
Portland, OR 97201
Tel.: 503-221-8811
Fax: 503-221-8934
Construction Operations
S.I.C.: 1542

Ming Surveyors, Inc. **(1)**
1300 S.W. Sixth Ave.
Portland, OR 97201
Tel.: 503-221-8811
Construction Operations
S.I.C.: 1542

Hoffman Structures, Inc. **(1)**
1300 S.W. Sixth Ave.
Portland, OR 97201
Tel.: 503-221-8811
Construction Operations
S.I.C.: 1542

Precision Asbestos Abatement Company **(1)**
8025 N.E. Killingsworth
Portland, OR 97218
Tel.: 503-253-4827
Construction Operations
S.I.C.: 1542

Precision Construction Compan y **(1)**
8025 N.E. Killingsworth
Portland, OR 97218
Tel.: 503-253-4827
Construction Operations
S.I.C.: 1542

A. H. HOFFMAN, INC.
77 Cooper Ave.
Landisville, PA 17538
Tel.: 717-898-2461
Fax: 717-898-3190
Emp.: 60
Fiscal Year-end: 6/30/90
Package Fertilizer & Soil Conditioners; Potting Soils
S.I.C.: 2048
George Ewing, Jr. *(Pres.)*
John L. Noll *(V.P.-Opers.)*
Edmund Sajeski, Jr. *(Sec., Treas. & Controller)*
William Dittman *(Dir.-Sls. & Mktg.)*
Suzanne E. Smith *(Dir.-Human Resources)*

Computer Systems/Hardware:
Burroughs B-1855

Outside Service Firm(s):

Hamilton Bank*(Major Banking Relationship)*
Lancaster, PA

Subsidiary:

Hoffman Seeds, Inc. **(1)**
144 Main St.
Landisville, PA 17538
Tel.: 717-898-2261
Wholesaler of Agricultural Seeds
S.I.C.: 5191
David Longendecker *(Dir.-Opers.)*

HOFFMAN/LEWIS
1900 Embarcadero, 4th Fl.
Oakland, CA 94606
Tel.: 510-536-0500
Fax: 510-535-1441
Year Founded: 1985
Approx.Billings: $22,600,000
Emp.: 31
Bob Riddell *(V.P., Fin. & Opers.)*
Patti Dudgeon *(Exec. Producer)*
Karen Wood *(Mgr.-Admin.)*

Hoffman York & Compton

HOFFMAN YORK & COMPTON
Plaza East, 330 E. Kilbourn Ave.
Milwaukee, WI 53202
Tel.: 414-289-9700 **WI**
Fax: 414-289-0417
Year Founded: 1933
Approx.Billings: $49,600,500
Emp.: 66
Advertising Agency
S.I.C.: 7311
Gene Gilmartin *(Pres. & Chief Exec. Officer)*
Troy Peterson *(Dir., Mktg. Services)*
Walter J. Fiorentini *(Sr. V.P., Chief Fin. Officer)*

HOFFRITZ FOR CUTLERY
515 W. 24th St.
New York, NY 10011
Tel.: 212-924-7300
Tel.: 800-962-9699
Fax: 212-627-5952
Approx.Sls.: $10,000,000
Emp.: 400
Import
Cutlery, Personal Care Items, Housewares, Gifts, Weather Instruments, Optical Goods, Gadgets
S.I.C.: 5719; 5999
J. Leonard Silver *(Chm. Bd., Pres. & Personnel Training & Devel.)*
Joel Silver *(Vice Chm.)*
Allan P. Armbruster *(Chief Exec. Officer)*
Jay Doyle *(Chief Oper. Officer, Gen. Mgr., Mng. Dir. & Corp. Travel Planner)*
William Smith *(Chief Fin. Officer, Treas. & Controller)*
Mikki Castro *(Dir.-Mktg. & Mgr.-Adv.)*
Nancy Warman *(Dir.-Mktg. & Promotions)*
Mark Eskridge *(Dir.-Pur. & Mgr.-Sls. & Mdsg., Market Res.)*
Emily Mitchell *(Mgr.-Personnel)*
Janice Ambrose *(Govt. Affairs)*
Seymour Ossam *(Pur. Agent)*
MillieSandy *(Quality Control)*
Tim Kupetz *(Leasing)*

Computer Systems/Hardware:
Wang

Subsidiaries:

Cutlery World **(1)**
515 W. 24th St.
New York, NY 10011
Tel.: 212-924-7300
Tel.: 800-962-9699
S.I.C.: 5719; 5999

Hoffritz International **(1)**
515 W. 24th St.
New York, NY 10011
Tel.: 212-924-7300
S.I.C.: 5719; 5999
Alan Armburster *(Chief Oper. Officer)*
William Smith *(Chief Fin. Officer)*
Mikki Castro *(Dir.-Mktg. & Mgr.-Adv.)*
Mark Eskridge *(Dir.-Sls. & Pur.)*

HOFLEY MANUFACTURING COMPANY
22534 Groesbeck Hwy.
Warren, MI 48089
Tel.: 313-778-5444 **MI**
Fax: 313-778-1143
Year Founded: 1941
Approx.Sls.: $14,000,000
Emp.: 150
Export
Automotive Stampings; Metal Stampings
S.I.C.: 3465; 3469; 3548
Norman H. Hofley *(Pres.)*
T.M. Sayers *(V.P.)*
J. Mathias *(Controller)*
R. Barron *(Dir.-Quality Controller)*
D. Emerson *(Dir.-Data Processing)*
K. Goodell *(Dir.-Pur.)*
E. Hofley *(Mgr.-Matls.)*
C. Hofley *(Corp. Travel Planner)*

Principal(s):
Norman H. Hofley

No. of Mfg. Plants/Facilities: 2
No. of U.S. Offices: 1

Outside Service Firm(s):

CoAmerica Bank*(Major Banking Relationship)*
Detroit, MI

Subsidiary:

Electro-Spray Enameling **(1)**
22534 Groesbeck Hwy.
Warren, MI 48089-2644
Tel.: 313-776-4620
Electro-Static Spray Painting
S.I.C.: 2851

HOHNER/HSS INC.
Lakeridge Pk., Sycamore Dr.
Ashland, VA 23005
Mailing Address:
P.O. Box 15035
Richmond, VA 23227
Tel.: 804-550-2700
Fax: 804-550-2670
Year Founded: 1857
Approx.Sls.: $15,000,000
Emp.: 40
Fiscal Year-end: 3/31/91
Import Export
Harmonicas, Melodicas, Diatonic and Piano Accordions, Recorders, Instruments for Music Education, Percussion Instruments and Musical Accessories, Electric Guitars, Slingerland Drums, Amplifiers, Acoustic Guitars, Sabian Cymbals, Sonor Music Educational Instruments, Sonor Percussions
S.I.C.: 3931
Horst Mucha *(Pres.)*
Jack C. Kavoukian *(Dir.-Mktg. Communications & Adv.)*
Percy E. Pickral *(Controller)*

Computer Systems/Hardware:
NCR

HOLBROOK LUMBER COMPANY
70 Fuller Rd.
Albany, NY 12205
Mailing Address:
P.O. Box 5229,
Albany, NY 12205
Tel.: 518-489-4708 **NY**
Fax: 518-489-4781
Year Founded: 1910
Approx.Sls.: $31,000,000
Emp.: 10
Wholesale Lumber
S.I.C.: 5031
Paul R. Krihak *(Pres. & Treas.)*
Janet D. Caron *(V.P.)*
Charles N. Wysong *(V.P. & Sec.)*

Outside Service Firm(s):

Stulmacher, Kohn & Bailly*(Auditors)*
Albany, NY

Albany Savings Bank*(Major Banking Relationship)*
Albany, NY

HOLCOMB & HOKE MFG. COMPANY, INC.
1545 Van Buren
Indianapolis, IN 46203
Mailing Address:
P.O. Box A-33900
Indianapolis, IN 46203
Tel.: 317-784-2444 **IN**
Fax: 317-781-9164
Year Founded: 1913
Sales Range: $10-19 Million
Emp.: 150
Export
Manufacture Vinyl Covered & Wood Doors & Partitions, Folding Wood & Steel Operable Walls
S.I.C.: 2541; 2542; 3089
Charles P. Lesh *(Chm., Pres. & Treas.)*
Ward E. Sexson *(V.P.-Fin. & Sec.)*
Robert McCurdy *(Dir.-Engrng. & Sls.)*
June Scheuermann *(Dir.-Personnel)*
Melvin Woodard *(Dir.-Pur.)*
Dennis P. Jensen *(Plant Mgr.)*

Computer Systems/Hardware:
AT&T 3B2/400

Outside Service Firm(s):

Clifton Gunderson*(Auditors)*
Indianapolis, IN

Barnes & Thornburg*(Legal Firm)*
11 S. Meridian St.
Indianapolis, IN 46204
Tel.: 317-638-1313

Indiana National Bank*(Major Banking Relationship)*
Indianapolis, IN

HOLDER CORPORATION
333 Cumberland Cir., Ste. 400
Atlanta, GA 30339
Tel.: 404-988-3000 **DE**
Fax: 404-988-3265
Year Founded: 1960
Sales Range: $100-499 Million
Emp.: 551
Fiscal Year-end: 3/31/91
General Contractor & Commercial Buildings Management
S.I.C.: 1542; 6512
Robert M. Holder, Jr. *(Chm. Bd.)*
Thomas M. Holder *(Pres.)*
J.C. Pendrey, Jr. *(Sr. V.P., Chief Fin. Officer, Sec. & Treas.)*
H.S. Petres *(Chief Info. Officer)*
Lee Johnston *(V.P.-Human Resources)*
D.M. O'Haren *(Controller)*
J.J. Slattery, Jr. *(Dir.-Sls. & Mktg.)*

Principal(s):
Robert M. Holder, Jr.

No. of U.S. Offices: 2

Computer Systems/Hardware:
IBM PC

Outside Service Firm(s):

Arthur Andersen & Co.*(Auditors)*
Avenue des Arts 56 1040
Brussels, Belgium

Arthur Andersen & Co.*(Auditors)*
133 Peachtree St., N.E.
Atlanta, GA 30303
Tel.: 404-658-1776

King & Spalding*(Legal Firm)*
Trust Co. Tower
Atlanta, GA 30303
Tel.: 404-572-4600

First National Bank of Atlanta*(Major Banking Relationship)*
2 Peachtree Street N.W.
Atlanta, GA 30383

ED HOLDERNESS SUPPLIES
450 E. Irvington Rd.
Tucson, AZ 85714
Tel.: 602-889-1300
Fax: 602-294-1743
Year Founded: 1932
Sales Range: $20-39 Million
Emp.: 95
Wholesale Lumber
S.I.C.: 5031; 5039
T.R. Kenyon *(Pres.)*
V. Bruce Cobb *(V.P.)*

Computer Systems/Hardware:
Digital 1173 PDP

Outside Service Firm(s):

First Interstate Bank*(Major Banking Relationship)*
150 N. Stone
Tucson, AZ 85701
Tel.: 602-792-5385

HOLIDAY COMPANIES
4567 W. 80th St.
Minneapolis, MN 55437
Tel.: 612-830-8700
Fax: 612-830-8864
Year Founded: 1928
Approx.Sls.: $1,000,000,000
Emp.: 5,000
Fiscal Year-end: 12/31/91
Import
Wholesale & Retail Distribution of Food, Gas & Merchandise
S.I.C.: 5411; 5541; 5141
Donovan Erickson *(Pres. & Chief Exec. Officer)*
Richard Loughlin *(V.P.-Indus. Rels.)*
Arnold Mickelson *(V.P.-Fin. & Chief Fin. Officer)*
Dennis Lindahl *(Controller)*
Jerry Jensen *(Dir.-Real Estate)*

Computer Systems/Hardware:
IBM 3090

Outside Service Firm(s):

Arthur Andersen & Co.*(Auditors)*
45 S. 7th St.
Minneapolis, MN 55402

Travelers Insurance Co.*(Group Insurer)*
1 Tower Square
Hartford, CT 06183-2492
Tel.: 203-277-4542
Fax: 203-277-5038

Dorsey & Whitney*(Legal Firm)*
2200 First Bank Place East
Minneapolis, MN 55402
Tel.: 612-340-2600
Fax: 612-340-2600

First National Bank of Minneapolis*(Major Banking Relationship)*
Minneapolis, MN

Norwest Bank Minnesota, N.A.*(Major Banking Relationship)*
6th St. & Marquette Av.
Minneapolis, MN 55479
Tel.: 612-667-1234

Subsidiaries:

Fairway Foods, Inc. **(1)**
4567 W. 80th St.
Minneapolis, MN 55437
Tel.: 612-830-8700

Holiday Stations, Inc. **(1)**
4567 W. 80th St.
Minneapolis, MN 55437
Tel.: 612-830-8700

RON HOLLAND ADVERTISING INC.
39 E. 72nd St.
New York, NY 10021
Tel.: 212-517-5300
Fax: 212-517-5304
Approx.Billings: $24,000,000
Ron Holland *(Chm. Bd.)*

HOLLAND MARK MARTIN
174 Middlesex Tpke.
Burlington, MA 01803
Tel.: 617-270-3500
Fax: 617-221-0850
Year Founded: 1986
Approx.Billings: $10,000,000
Emp.: 128
Marketing Communications

Employee Matching Gifts Program:
Holland Mark Martin Matches Employee Contributions Made to the United Way
William H. Davis *(Pres. & Dir.-Quality)*
Christopher M. Colbert *(Exec. V.P. & New Bus. Contact)*
Vernon J. Tirey *(V.P.-Database Mktg.)*
William Higgins *(Sec. & Gen. Mgr.)*
Robert MacInnis *(Dir.-Tech. Services)*
Jennifer Montgomery *(Dir.-Human Resources)*
Melissa Yahia *(Dir.-Client Services)*
Jean E. Bradley *(Mgr.-Mktg. Communications)*
Jennifer Forsyth *(Admin. Asst.)*

A. J. HOLLANDER CO., INC.
257 Park Ave. S.
New York, NY 10010
Tel.: 212-353-8000
Fax: 212-353-8120
Fax: 212-353-8125
Year Founded: 1936
Approx.Sls.: $250,000,000
Emp.: 80
Fiscal Year-end: 2/28/90
Exports & Imports Hides, Skins, Leather
S.I.C.: 5159; 5199; 5099
Per M. Hollander *(Chm. Bd.)*
Roland C. Summer *(Pres.)*
David Saatchi *(V.P.-Sls.)*
Sidney Weingarten *(V.P. & Sec.)*
Howard Coanz *(Controller)*
Fritz Hollander *(Dir.-Intl. Sls.)*
Andrea H. Body *(Mgr.-Employee Benefits)*
Fairfax O'Riley *(Mgr.- Mngmt. Information Systems)*

Outside Service Firm(s):

Prudential Insurance Co. of America*(Group Insurer)*
Prudential Tower Suite 450, 800 Boylston St.
Boston, MA 02119

Chase Manhattan Bank, N.A.*(Major Banking Relationship)*
One Chase Manhattan Plaza
New York, NY 10081
Tel.: 212-552-2222

ROGER HOLLER CHEVROLET CO.
860 W. Fairbanks Ave.
Winter Park, FL 32789
Tel.: 407-645-1234 **FL**
Fax: 407-647-3582
Year Founded: 1938
Approx.Sls.: $88,400,000
Emp.: 210
Car & Truck Dealership
S.I.C.: 5511
Roger W. Holler, Jr. *(Pres.)*
Roger Holler III *(V.P.)*
Judy Holler *(Sec.)*
Dan Napoleon *(Sls. Mgr.-New Cars)*
Tom Glickson *(Sls. Mgr.-Used Cars)*
Jim Callan *(Service Dir.)*

Outside Service Firm(s):

Barnett Banks Trust Company, N.A.*(Major Banking Relationship)*
Orlando, FL

Sun Bank, N.A.*(Major Banking Relationship)*
200 S. Orange Ave., 8th Fl. SOAB
Orlando, FL
Tel.: 407-237-4141

JOHN R. HOLLINGSWORTH CO.
Nutt Rd. at French Creek
Phoenixville, PA 19460
Tel.: 215-933-8951
Fax: 215-935-0760
Sales Range: $20-39 Million
Emp.: 250
Mfr. of Motor Generators
S.I.C.: 3511
Vincent H. Tomei *(Chm. Bd.)*
Arthur Haggerty *(Pres.)*
Ray White *(Exec. V.P. & Sec.)*
John H. Beyer *(V.P.-Mktg.)*

Outside Service Firm(s):

William E. Howe & Co.*(Auditors)*
Philadelphia, PA

Kleinbard, Bell & Brecker*(Legal Firm)*
30 S. 17th St.
Philadelphia, PA 19103
Tel.: 215-568-2000

Fidelity Bank*(Major Banking Relationship)*
Broad & Walnut St.
Philadelphia, PA 19109

HOLLINGSWORTH OIL CO. INC.
1503 Memorial Blvd.
Springfield, TN 37172
Tel.: 615-242-8466
Fax: 615-384-5852
Year Founded: 1975
Sales Range: $20-39 Million
Emp.: 15
Wholesale Gasoline
S.I.C.: 5172
Ronnie Hollingsworth *(Pres.)*

Computer Systems/Hardware:
IBM PC 34

Outside Service Firm(s):

Robertson, Hughes & Christopher*(Auditors)*
Danville, KY

First American Bank, N.A.*(Major Banking Relationship)*
Nashville, TN

HOLLINGSWORTH & VOSE CO.
112 Washington St.
East Walpole, MA 02032
Tel.: 508-668-0295 **MA**
Fax: 508-668-6526
Year Founded: 1843
Approx.Sls.: $160,000,000
Emp.: 800
Fiscal Year-end: 12/31/90
Import Export
Mfr. of Technical & Industrial Paper
S.I.C.: 2621
Employee Matching Gifts Program:
Donations are Match to Maximum of $500
Gordon W. Moran *(Pres. & Chief Exec. Officer)*
Christopher L. Huntoon *(Chief Fin. Officer & Sr. V.P.-Fin.)*
Frank Gross *(Sr. V.P.-Admin. Services)*
Paul F. Ward *(Treas.)*
Barbara Beddingfield *(Controller)*
Steve B. Brooks *(Dir.-Pur.)*
T. Stehle *(Mgr.-Intl. Sls.)*

No. of Mfg. Plants/Facilities: 9
No. of Foreign Offices: 4

Computer Systems/Hardware:
Wang System 85; IBM Compatible Micro's, Networked

Outside Service Firm(s):

Ernst & Young*(Auditors)*
200 Clarendon St., 46th Fl.
Boston, MA 02116
Tel.: 617-266-2000

Travelers Insurance Co.*(Commercial Insurance Carrier)*
One Tower Square
Hartford, CT 06183-6130
Tel.: 203-277-4542
Fax: 203-277-5038

Blue Cross of Massachusetts, Inc.*(Group Insurer)*
Boston, MA

Nutter, McClennen & Fish*(Legal Firm)*
One International Place
Boston, MA 02210-2699
Tel.: 617-439-2000

Brown Brothers, Harriman & Co.*(Major Banking Relationship)*
Boston, MA

First National Bank of Boston*(Major Banking Relationship)*
P.O. Box 644,
Boston, MA 02102-0644
Tel.: 617-575-2900
Fax: 617-575-2549

First National Bank of Boston*(Pension Manager)*
P.O. Box 644,
Boston, MA 02102-0644
Tel.: 617-575-2900
Fax: 617-575-2549

Non-U.S. Holdings:

Bagnasco S.R.L. **(1)**
Via Molino, 87 12071
Bagnasco, Cuneo Italy
Tel.: 174 76333
Marketing & Sale of Paper
S.I.C.: 5113

Hollingsworth & Vose Co. U.K. Ltd. **(1)**
Postlip Mills Winchombe, Cheltenham, GL54 5BB, United Kingdom
Tel.: 0242 602227 (100%)
Marketing & Sale of Paper
S.I.C.: 5113
J. Fuller *(Mgr.)*

Hollingsworth & Vose Europe NV **(1)**
Woluwedal 12, Box 138 B-1940
Sint-Stevens-Woluwe, Belgium
Tel.: 2 720 55 34 (100%)
Marketing & Sale of Paper
S.I.C.: 5113

Hovomex S.A. de C.V. **(1)**
Ruben Dario #13, 6th Fl. Delegacion Miguel Hidalgo,
Mexico, D.F. 5, Mexico
Tel.: 52 5 545 3308 (100%)
Manufacture, Marketing & Sales of Technical Paper
S.I.C.: 2621; 5113

HOLLISTER ADVERTISING
121 Chanlon Rd.
New Providence, NJ 07974
Tel.: 908-441-2383
Year Founded: 1984
Approx.Billings: $10,000,000
Emp.: 10
Business-to-Business Adv.
Dean Hollister *(Pres. & Chief Exec. Officer)*
Steve Torpie *(Exec. V.P. & Controller)*

Computer Systems/Hardware:
Apple, MacIntosh, IBM

HOLLYMATIC CORPORATION
600 E. Plainfield Rd.
Countryside, IL 60525
Tel.: 708-579-3700 **IL**
Telex: 25-3092
Fax: 708-579-1057
Year Founded: 1948
Sales Range: $20-39 Million
Emp.: 80
Import Export
Mfr. Meat Portioning Machines, Meat Tenderizers, Automatic Meat Mixer/ Grinders, Patty Paper, Lubricants & Supplies, Sausage Stuffers, Vacuum Packaging Machines
S.I.C.: 3556; 2679
James D. Azzar *(Chm. Bd.)*
L. M. Reedy *(Pres.)*
Richard C. Wagner *(V.P.-Engrng. & Res. & Devel.)*
Victoria C. Morton *(Controller)*
Donald L. Berkey *(Mgr.-Mktg.)*
Rob Kovacik *(Mgr.-Customer Service)*
Marilyn Krische *(Mgr.-Human Resources)*
James R. Wacaser *(Mgr.-Mfg.)*
George Lee *(Pur. Agent)*

Computer Systems/Hardware:
IBM System 36

Outside Service Firm(s):

KPMG Peat Marwick*(Auditors)*
Peat Marwick Plaza, 303 E. Wacker Dr.
Chicago, IL 60601
Tel.: 312-938-1000

Sachnoff & Weaver*(Legal Firm)*
30 S. Wacker Dr.
Chicago, IL 60606
Tel.: 312-207-1000
Fax: 312-207-6400

American National Bank & Trust Company of Chicago*(Major Banking Relationship)*
33 N. LaSalle St.
Chicago, IL 60602
Tel.: 312-661-5000
Fax: 312-661-6417

HOLLY'S INC.
3033 Orchard Vista Dr. S.E., Ste. 306
Grand Rapids, MI 49546
Mailing Address:
P.O. Box 9260
Grand Rapids, MI 49509
Tel.: 616-949-8899
Fax: 616-452-7501
Approx.Sls.: $26,000,000
Emp.: 1,100
Restaurants & Motor Inns
S.I.C.: 5812; 7011
Jay Ahrens *(Chm. Bd., Pres. & Chief Exec. Officer)*
Ralph Wojtowicv *(Dir.-Mktg.)*

Subsidiary:

Fare Development Corp. **(1)**
255 Colrain St., S.W.
Grand Rapids, MI 49509
Tel.: 616-452-3181

HOLLYTEX CARPET MILLS, INC.
(Sub. of HMK Group Industries)
1251 S. Rockefeller
Ontario, CA 91761
Mailing Address:
P.O. Box 51472
Ontario, CA 91761
Tel.: 909-391-8100
Fax: 909-986-8089
Approx.Sls.: $70,000,000
Emp.: 1,200
Fiscal Year-end: 4/30/90
Mfr. of Residential & Commercial Carpeting
S.I.C.: 2273
Michael Kingele *(Pres.)*
Jack Wulz *(V.P.-Fin. & Admin.)*
Ron Threadgill *(V.P.-Mfg.)*
Dennis Whittle *(V.P.-Quality Assurance)*
Lorraine Humphrey *(V.P.-Sls. & Mktg.)*

Subsidiaries:

Hollytex Carpet Mills, Inc. **(1)**
1251 S. Rockefeller
Ontario, CA 91761
Tel.: 909-391-8100
Fax: 909-983-2699
Carpet Mill
S.I.C.: 2273

Hollytex Carpet Mills, Inc. **(1)**
505 N.E. 7th St.
Anadarko, OK 73005
Tel.: 405-247-6641
Fax: 405-247-7681
Carpet Mill
S.I.C.: 2273

HOLLYWOOD ALLOY CASTING COMPANY
2000 S. Santa Fe Ave.
Compton, CA 90221
Tel.: 310-537-7030
Fax: 310-537-7083
Sales Range: $10-19 Million
Emp.: 100
Manufacture Aluminum Castings
S.I.C.: 3363
James A. Reid *(Pres.)*
Michael Reid *(V.P.)*
Henry R. Machado *(Sec.)*

Principal(s):
James A. Reid

Outside Service Firm(s):

Paul Keil*(Auditors)*
Lomita, CA

Security Pacific National Bank*(Major Banking Relationship)*
61 Broadway, 14th Fl., Ste. 1412
New York, NY 10006

HOLLYWOOD PARK, INC.
1050 S. Prairie Ave.
Inglewood, CA 90306
Mailing Address:
P.O. Box 369,
Inglewood, CA 90306
Tel.: 310-419-1500
Earnings: $1,570,000
Approx.Rev.: $62,195,000
Fiscal Year-end: 12/31/91
Thoroughbred Horse Racing
S.I.C.: 7948
R. D. Hubbard *(Chm. Bd. & Chief Exec. Officer)*
Donald M. Robbins *(Pres.)*
Mike Finnigan *(Exec. V.P. & Chief Fin. Officer)*
Blake Cumbers *(V.P. & Dir.-Mktg.)*
Jack Disney *(Media Rels. Dir.)*

HOLMAN ENTERPRISES
7411 Maple Ave.
Pennsauken, NJ 08109
Tel.: 609-663-5200
Fax: 609-665-1419
Approx.Sls.: $700,000,000
Emp.: 2,000
New & Used Automobiles, Rebuilding Engines & Transmissions, Rent-a-Car Service, Truck Leasing Without Drivers
S.I.C.: 5511; 3714; 7514; 7513
Joseph S. Holman *(Chm. Bd.)*
J.W. Kolb *(Vice Chm.)*
H.H. Herrington *(V.P.)*
L.E. Parent *(V.P.)*
A.V. Andreola *(Sec.)*
Glenn Sanderson *(Treas.)*

HOLMES PROTECTION GROUP, INC.
(Formerly Holmes Protection)
440 Ninth Ave.
New York, NY 10001
Tel.: 212-760-0630 **DE**
Fax: 212-629-6763
Year Founded: 1858
Approx.Sls.: $60,000,000
Emp.: 759
Fiscal Year-end: 12/31/90
Installation and Monitoring of Burglar Alarms, Fire Alarms, Access Control and Closed Circuit Television Systems
S.I.C.: 7382
Sir Ian MacGregor *(Chm. Bd.)*
Eric F. Kohn *(Vice Chm. & Chief Exec. Officer)*
Keith Anderson *(Chief Fin. Officer)*
Richard Hickson *(Chief Oper. Officer, Sr. V.P. & Dir.)*
Glenn Riker *(Sr. V.P.-Human Resources & Sec.)*
Colin M. Deuchars *(V.P.)*

No. of U.S. Offices: 10
No. of Foreign Offices: 1

Outside Service Firm(s):

Arthur Andersen & Co.*(Auditors)*
1345 Ave. of the Americas
New York, NY 10105
Tel.: 212-708-4000

National Westminster Bank plc*(Major Banking Relationship)*
175 Water St.
New York, NY 10038-4924
Tel.: 212-602-3364

Divisions:

Holmes Protection of Long Island, Inc. **(1)**
Hicksville, NY
Raymond Keosayian *(Pres.)*

Holmes Protection of New Jersey, Inc. **(1)**
Edison, NJ
Joseph Riggio *(Pres.)*

Holmes Protection of New York, Incorporated **(1)**
New York, NY
Eugene Lestardo *(Pres.)*

Holmes Protection of Philadelphia, Inc. **(1)**
Philadelphia, PA
George McCafferty *(Pres.)*

HOLMES TUTTLE FORD, INC.
660 W. Auto Mall Dr.
Tucson, AZ 85705
Tel.: 602-292-3600 **AZ**
Fax: 602-887-2765
Year Founded: 1973
Approx.Sls.: $52,000,000
Emp.: 195
Retail Sales of New & Used Cars
S.I.C.: 5511
Frank L. McClure *(Pres.)*
Robert H. Tuttle *(Chief Exec. Officer)*
Stanley B. Newton *(V.P., Treas. & Sec.)*

Outside Service Firm(s):

Arizona Bank*(Major Banking Relationship)*
Phoenix, AZ

HOLMQUIST GRAIN & LUMBER CO.
200 N. Logan Ave.
Oakland, NE 68045-0127
Mailing Address:
P.O. Box 127,
Oakland, NE 68045
Tel.: 402-685-5641 **NE**
Year Founded: 1883
Approx.Sls.: $16,321,060
Emp.: 47
Fiscal Year-end: 3/31/92
Retail Grain- Corn, Soybeans, Oats; Feed, Petroleum & Building Materials
S.I.C.: 5211; 2048; 5541
Robert L. Peters *(Chm. Bd., Pres. & Chief Exec. Officer)*
Larry Larson *(Chief Fin. Officer, Treas., Sec. & Controller)*
Wayne Uman *(Mgr.-Data Processing)*

Principal(s):
Robert L. Peters
Mary Helen Peters

Computer Systems/Hardware:
Burroughs B90

Outside Service Firm(s):

Goracke & Wilcox*(Auditors)*
Omaha, NE

United States Life Insurance Co.*(Group Insurer)*
125 Maiden Lane
New York, NY 10038
Tel.: 212-709-6000
Fax: 212-709-8707

Robert L. Martin*(Legal Firm)*
Blair, NE

First National Bank of Lyons*(Major Banking Relationship)*
Lyons, NE

New York Life*(Pension Manager)*
51 Madison Ave.
New York, NY 10010
Tel.: 212-576-6367
Fax: 212-576-6630

WE MAKE FIRST IMPRESSIONS LAST
HOLOUBEK

HOLOUBEK INC.
W238 N1800 Rockwood Dr.
Waukesha, WI 53188
Tel.: 414-547-0500
Tel.: 800-558-0566 **WI**
Fax: 414-547-5847
Year Founded: 1962
Approx.Sls.: $10,000,000
Emp.: 160
Fiscal Year-end: 9/30/90
Manufacture & Wholesale Iron-On Heat Transfers; Manufacturer Boys' Clothing; Commercial & Textile Printing
S.I.C.: 2321; 2329; 2396; 2261; 2752
Verne R. Holoubek *(Pres.)*
Terri Holoubek *(Exec. V.P.)*
Jeff Witkowski *(V.P. & Gen. Mgr.)*
Ed Nelson *(Dir.-Pur.)*
Wade Avinger *(Mgr.-Sls.)*
Tony Martinello *(Mgr.-Premium Sls.)*

Principal(s):
Verne R. Holoubek

No. of Mfg. Plants/Facilities: 1
No. of U.S. Offices: 1

Computer Systems/Hardware:
IBM System 36; Macintosh

Outside Service Firm(s):

Associated Commerce Bank*(Major Banking Relationship)*
Milwaukee, WI

HOLSTEIN ASSOCIATION OF AMERICA
One Holstein Place
Brattleboro, VT 05301
Mailing Address:
P.O. Box 808,
Brattleboro, VT 05302-0808
Tel.: 802-254-4551
Fax: 802-254-8251
Year Founded: 1885
Approx.Sls.: $15,000,000
Emp.: 285
Fiscal Year-end: 12/31/90
Dairy Cattle Breed Assn.
S.I.C.: 0211
Stephen R. Kerr *(Chief Exec. Officer)*
Carl E. Butler *(Pres.)*
John P. Solz *(V.P.)*
Frederick Moriarity *(Treas.)*
Ben Coplan *(Dir.-Pub. Rels.)*

Subsidiary:

Holstein-Friesian Services, Inc. **(1)**
1 So. Main St.
Brattleboro, VT 05301
Tel.: 802-254-4551
Telex: 710-363-1871
Fax: 802-254-8251
Stephen R. Kerr *(Exec. V.P.)*
Fredrick Moriarty *(Treas.)*

CHARLES HOLSTON, INC.
P.O. Box 1014
Jennings, LA 70546
Tel.: 318-824-8184 **LA**
Fax: 318-824-7521
Year Founded: 1983
Sales Range: $10-19 Million
Emp.: 100
Oil Field Services
S.I.C.: 1382
Craig Holston *(Pres. & Chief Exec. Officer)*
Charles Holston *(Exec. V.P.)*
Rhonda Watkins *(Treas.)*
Cheryl Maggiore *(Corp. Sec.)*

Outside Service Firm(s):

Arthur Andersen & Co.*(Auditors)*
711 Louisiana St., Ste. 1300
Houston, TX 77002
Tel.: 713-237-2323

Vinson & Elkins*(Legal Firm)*
First City Natl. Bank Bldg.
Houston, TX 77001
Tel.: 713-651-2222

Jefferson Davis Bank*(Major Banking Relationship)*
Jennings, LA

Subsidiary:

Guillory Tank Truck Service **(1)**
Rte. 2 Box 710
Eunice, LA 70535
Tel.: 318-457-8121
Collection & Disposal of Refuse By Processing or Destruction
S.I.C.: 4953
Craig Holston *(Pres.)*

HOLSUM BAKERY, INC.
408 S. 23rd Ave.
Phoenix, AZ 85009
Tel.: 602-252-2351
Fax: 602-252-6506
Sales Range: $20-39 Million
Emp.: 350
Manufacture Bread, Buns & Rolls
S.I.C.: 2051
Ed Eisele *(Pres. & Chief Exec. Officer)*
Neil Bailey *(V.P.-Opers. & Engrng.)*
Betty Knopp *(Exec. Sec.)*
Jack Long *(Dir.-Sls.)*

Computer Systems/Hardware:
Nobell-Mini

Outside Service Firm(s):

Snell & Wilmer*(Legal Firm)*
3100 Valley Ctr.
Phoenix, AZ 85073
Tel.: 602-257-7211

First Interstate Bank*(Major Banking Relationship)*
P.O. Box 53441,
Phoenix, AZ 85072-3441
Tel.: 602-229-4049

HOLT HOSIERY MILLS, INC.
2119 W. Webb Ave.
Burlington, NC 27216
Mailing Address:
P.O. Box 1757
Burlington, NC 27217
Tel.: 919-227-1431 **NC**
Fax: 919-227-8614
Year Founded: 1947
Assets: $10,000,000
Liabilities: $8,000,000
Net Worth: $2,000,000
Approx.Sls.: $24,000,000
Emp.: 450
Fiscal Year-end: 6/30/91
Import Export
Women's Hosiery Except Socks
S.I.C.: 2251
Ralph M. Holt, Jr. *(Chm. Bd.)*
Terry L. Johnson *(Pres.)*
Ralph M. Holt, III *(V.P.-Mktg.)*
Philip H. Johnson *(V.P.-Admin. & Fin.)*
L.W. Mangum *(Controller)*
William Caviness *(Dir.-Quality Control)*
Allen McKimey *(Dir.-Mfg. Services)*
Doug Stephens *(Dir.-M.I.S.)*
Cyndy Matthews *(Mgr.-Human Resources)*

No. of Mfg. Plants/Facilities: 3
No. of U.S. Offices: 1

Computer Systems/Hardware:
IBM AS-400

Outside Service Firm(s):

McGladrey & Pullen*(Auditors)*
Burlington, IA

Brooks, Pierce, McLendon, Humphrey & Leonard*(Legal Firm)*
2000 Renaissance Plaza
Greensboro, NC 27402
Tel.: 919-373-8850

Wachovia Bank & Trust Co.*(Major Banking Relationship)*
Burlington, NC

HOLTON NAMIOTKA JONES, INC.
706 Ridge Pike
Lafayette Hill, PA 19444
Tel.: 215-825-7600
Fax: 215-825-7729
Year Founded: 1983
Approx.Billings: $13,000,000
Emp.: 15
John Holton *(Pres.)*

HOLY CROSS ELECTRIC ASSOCIATION
3799 Hwy. 82
Glenwood Springs, CO 81601
Tel.: 303-945-5491 **CO**
Fax: 030-945-4081
Year Founded: 1939
Approx.Sls.: $42,000,000
Emp.: 80
Co-Op; Distribution of Electric Power
S.I.C.: 4911
David Sage *(Pres.)*
Robert Mayne *(V.P.)*
Edward L. Grange *(Gen. Mgr.)*
Carter Jackson *(Treas.)*
George Leasch *(Sec.)*

HOLZER WATCH CO., INC.
501 Madison Ave.
New York, NY 10022
Tel.: 212-752-4848
Fax: 212-750-1275
Emp.: 50
Fiscal Year-end: 2/29/91
Distributor of Watches
S.I.C.: 5094
Julian Holzer *(Pres.)*
John E. Holzer *(Exec. V.P. & Adv. Dir.)*

Outside Service Firm(s):

Empire Blue Cross & Blue Shield*(Group Insurer)*
New York, NY

HOMAN LUMBER MART, INC.
1650 W. Lusher
Elkhart, IN 46517
Tel.: 219-293-6595 **IN**
Fax: 219-522-0338
Year Founded: 1951
Approx.Sls.: $13,000,000
Emp.: 65
Wholesale Distributor of Lumber & Other Building Materials
S.I.C.: 5211
Robert W. Homan *(Pres. & Treas.)*
Elizabeth Bowman *(Sec.)*

Outside Service Firm(s):

McGladrey & Pullen*(Auditors)*
Elkhart, IN

Charles Brodnik*(Legal Firm)*
Elkhart, IN

AmeriTrust National Bank*(Major Banking Relationship)*
Elkart, IN

HOME INNOVATIONS, INC.
295 Fifth Ave.
New York, NY 10016
Tel.: 212-686-2080
Fax: 212-779-0149
Draperies, Curtains, Bedspreads, Shower Curtains & Mattress Pads
S.I.C.: 2391; 2392
John Witkowski *(Pres.)*
Robert Fitch *(Chief Exec. Officer)*

Outside Service Firm(s):

Hertz, Herson & Company*(Auditors)*
New York, NY

Manufacturers Hanover Trust Co.*(Major Banking Relationship)*
4 New York Plaza
New York, NY 10015
Tel.: 212-422-3400

Subsidiaries:

R.A. Briggs & Co. **(1)**
650 N. Church St.
Lake Zurich, IL 60047
Tel.: 708-438-2345
Screen Printing Of Cotton Broadwoven Fabrics
S.I.C.: 2261
John Witowski *(Pres.)*

Home Curtain Corporation **(1)**
295 Fifth Ave.
New York, NY 10016
Tel.: 212-686-2080
Window Curtains Made From Purchased Materials; Plastic & Textile Draperies; Bedspreads & Bed Sets; Printing & Embossing On Plastic Fabric Articles
S.I.C.: 2391; 2392; 2396
John Witkowski *(Pres.)*

Home Innovations Bed Fashions **(1)**
295 Fifth Ave.
New York, NY 10016
Tel.: 212-686-2080
Manufacturer of Curtains & Drapes
S.I.C.: 2211; 2221
Robert Flynn *(Pres.)*

HOME INTERIORS & GIFTS, INC.
4550 Spring Valley Rd.
Dallas, TX 75244-3705
Tel.: 214-386-1000
Fax: 214-233-8825
Year Founded: 1957
Approx.Sls.: $400,000,000
Emp.: 1,150
Wholesale Decorative Accessories for Homes
S.I.C.: 5023
Donald J. Carter *(Pres., Treas. & Chief Exec. Officer)*
William J. Hendrix *(Chief Fin. Officer & V.P.-Fin.)*
Barbara Hammond *(Sr. V.P.-Sls.)*
Charles Daniel *(Mgr.-Data Processing)*
Principal(s):
Donald J. Carter

Computer Systems/Hardware:
NCR 8565

Outside Service Firm(s):

Judd, Thomas & Smith*(Auditors)*
Dallas, TX

Health Economics Corporation*(Group Insurer)*
1300 W. Mockingbird Lane
Dallas, TX 75247
Tel.: 214-905-4453

Bank One*(Investment Banker)*
P.O. Box 655415,
Dallas, TX 75265-5415
Tel.: 214-290-2000

Gardere & Wynne*(Legal Firm)*
3000 Thanksgiving Tower, 1601 Elm St.
Dallas, TX 75201-4761
Tel.: 214-999-3000

Bank One*(Major Banking Relationship)*
P.O. Box 655415,
Dallas, TX 75265-5415
Tel.: 214-290-2000

Subsidiary:

HI Service Enterprises, Inc. **(1)**
4550 Spring Valley Rd.
Dallas, TX 75234
Tel.: 214-386-1000 (100%)
William J. Hendrix *(Gen. Mgr.)*

HOME JUICE COMPANY
2000 N. 15th Ave.
Melrose Park, IL 60160-1473
Tel.: 708-345-3350 **IL**
Fax: 708-345-3361
Year Founded: 1946
Approx.Sls.: $55,000,000
Emp.: 200
Fiscal Year-end: 6/30/92
Bottler of Citrus Products
S.I.C.: 2033; 2086; 2087
Henry S. Lang *(Chm. Bd., Pres. & Chief Exec. Officer)*
Daniel J. Pallat *(Chief Fin. Officer, V.P., Treas. & Sec.)*
Frank J. Forstneger *(Controller)*
Alan Weinstein *(Mgr.-Data Processing)*

Computer Systems/Hardware:
IBM 4341

Outside Service Firm(s):

KPMG Peat Marwick*(Auditors)*
Peat Marwick Plaza, 303 E. Wacker Dr.
Chicago, IL 60601
Tel.: 312-938-1000

Employee Benefit Plan*(Group Insurer)*
Des Plaines, IL

Baker & McKenzie*(Legal Firm)*
One Prudential Plaza, 130 E. Randolph
Chicago, IL 60601-7026
Tel.: 312-861-8000

Home Juice Company—(Continued)

Midwest Bank*(Major Banking Relationship)*
Elmwood Park, IL

Subsidiaries:

Home Juice Co. of Florida **(1)**
2000 N. 15th Ave.
Melrose Park, IL 60160
Tel.: 708-345-3350

Tree Fresh Foods Corp. **(1)**
2000 N. 15th Ave.
Melrose Park, IL 60160
Tel.: 708-345-3350 (100%)

HOMELAND STORES, INC.
400 N.E. 36th St.
Oklahoma City, OK 73105
Mailing Address:
P.O. Box 25008,
Oklahoma City, OK 73125
Tel.: 405-557-5500 **DE**
Fax: 405-557-5600
Year Founded: 1987
Assets: $247,058,000
Liabilities: $234,564,000
Net Worth: $12,494,000
Approx.Sls.: $790,000,000
Emp.: 6,500
Grocery Store Chain
S.I.C.: 5411
Corporate Giving Program: United Way, Easter Seals
Max E. Raydon *(Pres. & Chief Exec. Officer)*
Don R. Taylor, Sr. *(Chief Fin. Officer, Treas. & Sec.)*
Jack M. Lotker *(Sr. V.P.-Natl. Sls.)*
Prentess Alletag *(V.P.-Human Resources)*
Creg Burns *(V.P.-Grocery Mktg. Opers.)*
Steve Mason *(V.P.-Retail Opers.)*
C.R. Misialek *(V.P.-Distr. Center & Transportation)*
Steve Slade *(V.P.-Mktg. Opers.)*
Jack Bateman *(Dir.-Plng.)*
Bill Rulla *(Dir.-Data Processing)*
Bill Sammons *(Dir.-Adv.)*
Lisa Sykes *(Dir.-Pub. Rels.)*

No. of Mfg. Plants/Facilities: 2
No. of U.S. Offices: 1

Outside Service Firm(s):

Coopers & Lybrand*(Auditors)*
Oklahoma City, OK

Crowe & Dunlevy*(Legal Firm)*
20 N. Broadway
Oklahoma City, OK 73102
Tel.: 405-232-0661
Tel.: 405-235-7700

Liberty National Bank & Trust Co.*(Major Banking Relationship)*
P.O. Box 25848,
Oklahoma City, OK 73125-0848
Tel.: 405-231-6000

HOMEMAKER SHOPS, INC.
25899 W. 12 Mile Rd.
Southfield, MI 48034
Tel.: 313-353-0404 **MI**
Fax: 313-353-8059
Year Founded: 1961
Approx.Sls.: $25,200,000
Emp.: 485
Retail Home Furnishings, Linens, Bed & Bath, Closet Shop, Housewares & Houshold Gifts
S.I.C.: 5719
Sidney Freedland *(Chm. Bd. & Pres.)*
Richard Weil *(Exec. V.P. & Gen. Mgr.)*
William Lang *(V.P. & Buyer)*
John Fields *(Controller)*
Phyllis Freedland *(Sec.)*
Dale Tonkovich *(Dir.-Data Processing)*

No. of U.S. Offices: 32

Outside Service Firm(s):

Coopers & Lybrand*(Auditors)*
400 Renaissance Center
Detroit, MI 48243
Tel.: 313-446-7100
Fax: 313-446-7117

Radner & Radner*(Legal Firm)*
Detroit, MI

First of America Bank*(Major Banking Relationship)*
Detroit, MI

Subsidiary:

Linens & More **(1)**
25889 W. 12 Mile Rd.
Southfield, MI 48034
Tel.: 313-353-0404 (100%)
Retail Home Furnishings, Linens, Bed & Bath, Closet Shop, Housewares & Household Gifts
S.I.C.: 5719
Richard Weil *(V.P. & Gen. Mgr.)*

HOMES BY DAVE BROWN
2164 E. Broadway, Ste. 300
Tempe, AZ 85282
Tel.: 602-921-1400
Fax: 602-921-0545
Year Founded: 1975
Emp.: 60
General Contractor Single-Family Residences
S.I.C.: 1521
Dave M. Brown *(Chm. Bd.)*
Walter W. Venberg *(Pres.)*
Jerome L. Joseph *(Sr. V.P.)*

Computer Systems/Hardware:
IBM

Outside Service Firm(s):

Blue Cross & Blue Shield of Arizona, Inc.*(Group Insurer)*
Phoenix, AZ

HOMES OF MERIT INC.
Bartow Air Base
Bartow, FL 33830
Mailing Address:
P.O. Box 1606
Bartow, FL 33830
Tel.: 813-533-0593
Fax: 813-533-0310
Year Founded: 1973
Approx.Sls.: $80,000,000
Emp.: 800
Export
Manufacture Mobile Homes & Real Estate Investors
S.I.C.: 2451; 6799
Charles E. Weeder *(Chm. Bd. & Chief Exec. Officer)*
Bill Harriss *(Pres.)*
Kevin Clancy *(V.P.-Sls. & Mktg.)*
Mark Weeder *(V.P.-Prod. Mktg.)*
David Amann *(Dir.-Fin.)*
William Masters *(Dir.-Engrng.)*
Michael Taylor *(Dir.-Personnel)*

No. of Mfg. Plants/Facilities: 6

Outside Service Firm(s):

Price Waterhouse*(Auditors)*
400 N. Ashley, Ste. 2800
Tampa, FL 33602
Tel.: 813-223-7577

Sun Bank, N.A.*(Major Banking Relationship)*
222 E. Robinson St., Ste. 350
Orlando, FL 32801

Olge & Waters*(Pension Manager)*
Clearwater, FL

HOMES & SON CONTRACTORS, INC.
(Formerly Homes & Son Construction Co.)
2950 W. Durango St.
Phoenix, AZ 85009
Tel.: 602-269-8301
Fax: 602-269-9362
Year Founded: 1946
Sales Range: $10-19 Million
Emp.: 75
Fiscal Year-end: 12/31/91
General Contractor Nonresidential & Industrial Buildings
S.I.C.: 1542; 1541
W.G. Homes *(Chm. Bd.)*
Pat Kuehner *(Pres.)*
Pat Homes *(V.P., Treas. & Sec.)*

Computer Systems/Hardware:
IBM PC

Outside Service Firm(s):

Blue Cross & Blue Shield of Arizona, Inc.*(Group Insurer)*
Phoenix, AZ

Thunderbird Bank*(Major Banking Relationship)*
Phoenix, AZ

HOMESTEAD HOUSE INC.
9410 Wadsworth Pkwy.
Broomfield, CO 80020
Tel.: 303-425-6544
Fax: 303-423-4917
Retail Furniture & Miscellaneous Home Furnishings
S.I.C.: 5712; 5719
David L. Smith *(Chm. Bd. & Owner)*
Alan Reinken *(Pres.)*
Charles R. Dahlman *(Exec. V.P.)*
Thomas A. Mauro *(V.P.)*

Computer Systems/Hardware:
Basic Four

Outside Service Firm(s):

Ernst & Young*(Auditors)*
4300 Republic Plaza
Denver, CO 80202
Tel.: 303-628-4406

Fairfield & Woods*(Legal Firm)*
Denver, CO

United Bank of Denver N.A.*(Major Banking Relationship)*
1740 Broadway
Denver, CO 80217
Tel.: 303-861-8811

Homestead Products
(Acquired by Seattle Lighting Fixture Co.)

HOMEWOOD CORPORATION
750 Northlawn Dr.
Columbus, OH 43214
Tel.: 614-451-9999 **OH**
Fax: 614-451-1197
Year Founded: 1964
Approx.Sls.: $34,000,000
Emp.: 50
Speculative Builders; Single Family Houses; Multi-Family Dwellings & Apartment Building Construction
S.I.C.: 1531; 1522
H. Bain *(Chm. Bd. & Pres.)*
Gary Klemek *(V.P.)*
James E. Frey *(Sec.)*

Outside Service Firm(s):

Deloitte & Touche*(Auditors)*
155 E. Broad St.
Columbus, OH 43215
Tel.: 614-221-1000
Fax: 614-229-4647

Murphey, Young & Smith*(Legal Firm)*
250 East Broad Street
Columbus, OH 43215

Tel.: 614-228-4371

BancOhio National Bank*(Major Banking Relationship)*
Columbus, OH

HONEYMEAD PRODUCTS CO.
2020 S. Riverfront Drive
Mankato, MN 56001
Mailing Address:
P.O. Box 3247
Mankato, MN 56002
Tel.: 507-625-7911
Fax: 507-345-2254
Year Founded: 1947
Approx.Sls.: $350,000,000
Emp.: 183
Fiscal Year-end: 5/31/90
Soybean Refiner; Savorysoy, Lustersoy, Clearsoy, Lamisoy, Honeysoy
S.I.C.: 5153
Merritt Petersen *(Grp. V.P.)*
Stanley Eichten *(V.P.)*
Larry M. Salzwedel *(V.P.-Admin.)*
Al Ambrose *(V.P.)*
Gaylen Ferley *(V.P.)*
James H. Amlie *(V.P.-Production)*

HONORBUILT INDUSTRIES, INC.
P.O. Box 266,
Minneapolis, KS 67467
Tel.: 913-392-2171
Tel.: 800-342-6234
Year Founded: 1990
Assets: $25,503,311
Earnings: ($100,127)
Liabilities: $19,825,525
Net Worth: $5,677,786
Approx.Sls.: $18,000,000
Emp.: 120
Fiscal Year-end: 12/31/91
Export
Mfr. of Recreational & Commercial Vehicles
S.I.C.: 3792; 3711
Robert L. Stewart *(Chm. Bd. & Pres.)*
Richard D. Muller *(V.P. & Treas.)*
Don Beran *(V.P.-Sls. & Mktg.)*
Kurt Myers *(Controller)*
Bob Barefield *(Gen. Counsel)*
Greg Stewart *(Sec.)*
Larry Nelson *(Mgr.-Personnel)*
Virginia Hoover *(Mgr.-Data Processing)*
Merlin Peterson *(Mgr.-Quality Control)*

Computer Systems/Hardware:
IBM System 36

HOOD & COMPANY
P.O. Box 485
Hamburg, PA 19526
Tel.: 215-562-3841
Year Founded: 1970
Approx.Sls.: $11,000,000
Emp.: 105
Import Export
Mfr. of Thermostatic Bimetal Strip & Parts
S.I.C.: 3499
Stanley M. Golemo, Jr. *(Chm. Bd. & Pres.)*
Anthony J. Izbicki *(V.P. & Sec.)*

HOOD CORPORATION
8201 S. Sorensen Ave.
Whittier, CA 90606
Tel.: 310-945-1411 **CA**
Fax: 213-945-6532
Year Founded: 1950
Approx.Sls.: $113,000,000
Emp.: 1,300
Pipeline Contractor
S.I.C.: 1623
M. Laulhere *(Pres.)*
M. Ewing *(V.P.)*
B. Svatos *(V.P.)*
Larry Laulhere *(Sec. & Treas.)*

Outside Service Firm(s):

Ernst & Young*(Auditors)*
515 S. Flower St.
Los Angeles, CA 90071
Tel.: 213-621-1666

Quinn, Kully & Morrow*(Legal Firm)*
Whittier, CA

Sanwa Bank*(Major Banking Relationship)*
601 S. Figueroa St.
Los Angeles, CA 90017
Tel.: 213-896-7817
Fax: 213-489-1977

Subsidiary:

Hood Communications, Inc. **(1)**
21496 Main St.
Grand Terrace, CA 92324
Tel.: 909-274-0577
Approx.Sls.: $35,000,000
Emp.: 350
Telephone & Communication Line Construction; Cable Television Line Construction
S.I.C.: 1623
Dan Grinder *(Pres. & Chief Exec. Officer)*
Elmer Bartz *(V.P.)*
Mark Cazee *(V.P.)*
Steve Cline *(V.P.)*
Bob Don *(V.P.)*
Scott Duncan *(V.P.)*
Jerry Jolley *(V.P.)*
Sandra Riely *(Sec. & Treas.)*

HOOF PRODUCTS COMPANY
4051 W. 51st St.
Chicago, IL 60632
Tel.: 312-767-6200
Fax: 312-767-9669
Year Founded: 1907
Approx.Sls.: $15,000,000
Emp.: 165
Fiscal Year-end: 12/31/90
Hoof Governors; Hydraulic Valves for Aircraft & Industrial; Silent Aluminum & Metal Timing Gears; Timing Chains; Sprockets & Oil Pumps
A. C. Hoof *(Pres. & Owner)*
Jerry Becker *(Controller)*
James Ketchmark *(Mgr.-Sls.)*

HOOGOVENS ALUMINUM CORP.
101 Venture Way
Secaucus, NJ 07094
Mailing Address:
P.O. Box 2127
Secaucus, NJ 07096
Tel.: 201-866-7776
Tel.: 800-631-3717 **DE**
Telex: 12-6786
Fax: 201-866-6146
Year Founded: 1971
Sales Range: $80-99 Million
Emp.: 52
Wholesale Distributor of Aluminum
S.I.C.: 5051
Hans VanDerven *(Chm. Bd.)*
Ronald Johnson *(Pres. & Chief Oper. Officer)*
Jerry Abrams *(Treas. & Chief Fin. Officer)*
Dorothy Johnson *(Controller)*
Jose Perez *(Chief Info. Officer & Dir.-Data Processing)*
James Cillo *(Dir.-Pur.)*
Robert Desberg *(Mgr.-Res. & Devel.)*

No. of U.S. Offices: 4

Computer Systems/Hardware:
IBM System AS 400

Outside Service Firm(s):

KPMG Peat Marwick*(Auditors)*
345 Park Ave.
New York, NY 10154
Tel.: 212-758-9700
Fax: 212-872-3308

Societe Generale*(International Bank Affiliate)*
50 Rockefeller Plaza
New York, NY 10020

European American Bank*(Major Banking Relationship)*
New York, NY

Guardian Life Insurance Co.*(Pension Manager)*
New York, NY

V. B. HOOK & CO., INC.
PO BOX 13503,
Columbia, SC 29201
Tel.: 803-799-0504 **SC**
Fax: 803-771-4618
Approx.Sls.: $23,000,000
Emp.: 80
Wholesale Fruits & Vegetables
S.I.C.: 5148
James B. Hook *(Pres.)*
Joseph P. Gates *(V.P.)*
Gary Martin Hook *(V.P.)*
Addie Joe Thomas *(Sec. & Treas.)*

Outside Service Firm(s):

Burkett, Burkett & Burkett*(Auditors)*
Columbia, SC

South Carolina National Bank*(Major Banking Relationship)*
700 Main St.
Columbia, SC 29201

J. G. HOOK, INC.
1300 Belmont Ave.
Philadelphia, PA 19104
Tel.: 215-477-9600 **PA**
Fax: 215-581-9574
Year Founded: 1974
Emp.: 550
Fiscal Year-end: 9/30/92
Import
Licensor for Women's, Children's, Men's Apparel & Home Furnishings
S.I.C.: 6794
Max L. Raab *(Chm. Bd. & Chief Exec. Officer)*
Gary A. Kane *(Pres. & Chief Oper. Officer)*
Steven Broder *(V.P.-Fin. & Admin.)*
Robert John Brecker, Esq. *(Corp. Counsel)*
Sid Manas *(Data Processing Dir.)*

No. of U.S. Offices: 2

Computer Systems/Hardware:
IBM AS400

Outside Service Firm(s):

BDO Seidman*(Auditors)*
Philadelphia, PA

Citizens & Southern Commercial Corp.*(Investment Banker)*
New York, NY

Kleinbard, Bell & Brecker*(Legal Firm)*
30 S. 17th St.
Philadelphia, PA 19103
Tel.: 215-568-2000

Citizens & Southern Commercial Corp.*(Major Banking Relationship)*
New York, NY

Philadelphia National Bank*(Major Banking Relationship)*
P.O. Box 13834, Broad & Chestnut Streets
Philadelphia, PA 19101-7618
Tel.: 215-973-8327

HOOKER FURNITURE CORPORATION
Hooker St., P.O. Box 4708
Martinsville, VA 24115
Tel.: 703-632-2133
Fax: 703-632-5240
Year Founded: 1924
Approx.Sls.: $75,000,000
Emp.: 1,100
Fiscal Year-end: 11/31/90
Import Export
Manufactures Bedroom Furniture, Wall Units, Desks, Occasional Tables, Curios
S.I.C.: 2511; 2519; 2522; 2541
J. Clyde Hooker, Jr. *(Chm. Bd. & Chief Exec. Officer)*
A. Frank Hooker, Jr. *(Pres. & Chief Oper. Officer)*
Larry Ryder *(Sr. V.P.-Fin. & Admin.)*
J.W. Roberts *(Sr. V.P.-Mktg.)*
Doug Williams *(Sr. V.P.-Mfg.)*
Ron Crews *(Pur. Agent)*

HOOKER INDUSTRIES
1024 W. Brooks St.
Ontario, CA 91762
Mailing Address:
P.O. Box 4030
Ontario, CA 91762
Tel.: 909-983-5871
Fax: 909-986-9860
Approx.Sls.: $12,000,000
Emp.: 350
Mfr. of High Performance Exhaust Systems Headers, Fiberglas Spoilers, Flares & Hood Scoops, Exhaust Accessories, Dual Exhaust Systems
S.I.C.: 3714; 3751; 2899
Gary R. Hooker *(Chm. Bd.)*
Dave Spangler *(Pres.)*
Diane M. Camp *(Dir.-Adv. & Pub. Rels.)*
Jim Hairston *(Dir.-Sls. & Mktg.)*

HOOVER GROUP, INC.
2001 Westside Pkwy., Ste. 155
Alpharetta, GA 30201
Tel.: 404-664-4047 **DE**
Fax: 404-664-2850
Year Founded: 1985
Assets: $91,076,000
Liabilities: $117,313,000
Net Worth: $26,237,000
Approx.Sls.: $77,746,000
Emp.: 800
Fiscal Year-end: 12/31/91
Import Export
Manufacturer Box Spring & Automotive Seating Components, Metal & Plastic Bulk Containers
S.I.C.: 3412; 3495
Larry D. Clay *(Pres. & Chief Exec. Officer)*
Rod Willnow *(Pres.& Gen. Mgr.-Matls. Handling Div.)*
John Horner *(V.P.-Sls.)*
Ray Jusak *(V.P.-Facilities & Environment)*
J. James Southard *(V.P., Controller & Treas.)*
John Kitchen *(Gen. Mgr.-Wire Prods. Div.)*

No. of Mfg. Plants/Facilities: 14

Computer Systems/Hardware:
Vamois

Outside Service Firm(s):

Ernst & Young*(Auditors)*
600 Peachtree St. N.E.
Atlanta, GA 30308
Tel.: 404-874-8300

Sonnenschien, Nath, & Rosenthal*(Legal Firm)*
Washington, DC

HOPE DESIGN GROUP
4520 Executive Dr., Ste. 300
San Diego, CA 92121
Tel.: 619-597-9400 **CA**
Fax: 619-233-4397
Year Founded: 1928
Sales Range: $10-19 Million
Emp.: 112
Architecture Engineering, Planners, Structural Engineering; Construction, Contract Administration, Development Service
S.I.C.: 8711; 8712
Corporate Giving Program: United Way
Frank L. Hope, Jr. *(Co-Chm.)*
Charles B. Hope *(Co-Chm.)*
Allen F. Flanders *(Pres. & Chief Exec. Officer)*
Theodre R. Brunich *(V.P. & Chief Fin. Officer)*
F. Leeland Hope *(Dir.-Mktg.)*
Leeland Hope *(Dir.-Bus. Devel.)*

No. of U.S. Offices: 1

Computer Systems/Hardware:
PC's, IBM Compatible, 15+ Workstations

Outside Service Firm(s):

Price Waterhouse*(Auditors)*
750 B St.
San Diego, CA 92101
Tel.: 619-231-9830

Gray, Cary, Ames & Frye*(Legal Firm)*
2100 Union Bank Bldg.
San Diego, CA 92101
Tel.: 619-699-2700

Security Pacific National Bank*(Major Banking Relationship)*
San Diego, CA

HOPE'S ARCHITECTURAL PRODUCTS INC.
84 Hopkins Ave.
Jamestown, NY 14701
Tel.: 716-665-5124
Fax: 716-665-3365
Year Founded: 1912
Approx.Sls.: $15,000,000
Emp.: 210
Fiscal Year-end: 6/30/91
Export
Steel & Aluminum Custom Windows
S.I.C.: 3442
Frank A. Farrell, Jr. *(Chm. Bd. & Pres.)*
S.C. Arvantinos *(V.P.)*
Richard E. Stawiarski *(Gen. Sls. Mgr.)*
Randall Manitta *(Adv. Mgr.)*

HOPKINSVILLE ELEVATOR COMPANY, INC.
Skyline Dr.
Hopkinsville, KY 42240
Mailing Address:
P.O. Box 767
Hopkinsville, KY 42240
Tel.: 502-886-5191 **KY**
Fax: 502-887-1608
Approx.Sls.: $36,000,000
Emp.: 29
Grain Elevators; Fertilizer & Fertilizer Materials; Field, Garden & Flower Seeds; Feed Co-Op
S.I.C.: 5153; 5191
Ronald N. Barry, Jr. *(Pres.)*
David B. Spain *(V.P.)*
G.R. Leenerts *(Gen. Mgr. & Treas.)*

HOPKINSVILLE MILLING CO.
2001 S. Walnut St.
Hopkinsville, KY 42240
Mailing Address:
P.O. Box 669
Hopkinsville, KY 42241
Tel.: 502-886-1231
Fax: 502-886-6407
Year Founded: 1874
Approx.Sls.: $14,000,000
Emp.: 66
Fiscal Year-end: 5/30/90
Sunflour Flour & Sunflower Corn Meal Mix; Grits
S.I.C.: 2041
Frank A. Yost *(Chm. Bd.)*
Haywood Strader *(Pres. & Chief Oper. Officer)*
Thos. H. Yates *(Sec. & Treas.)*
John Redmond *(Sls. Mgr.)*
Dorris Jones *(Plant Mgr.)*

HOPPER INC.
P.O. Box 2900
Bakersfield, CA 93303
Tel.: 805-861-7000 CA
Telex: 805-861-7117
Year Founded: 1927
Assets: $9,000,000
Liabilities: $6,500,000
Net Worth: $2,500,000
Approx.Sls.: $21,000,000
Emp.: 200
Fiscal Year-end: 5/31/91
Manufacture & Distribute Oil Field Equipment
S.I.C.: 3533; 3999; 5051; 7699
Victor D. Hopper *(Chm. Bd., Pres. & Chief Exec. Officer)*
Frank Hopper III *(Exec. V.P.)*
Claude Bradford *(Chief Oper. Officer)*
Harold Clifton *(Treas., Sec. & Chief Fin. Officer)*
Bruce Hodges *(Controller)*
Michael Foster *(Dir.-Pur.)*

Outside Service Firm(s):

Rohmiller, Brown & Rhodes*(Auditors)*
Bakersfield, CA

Guarantee Financial Services*(Group Insurer)*
Fresno, CA

Robinson, Palmer & Stanton*(Legal Firm)*
Bakersfield, CA

Security Pacific Business Center*(Major Banking Relationship)*
Pasadena, CA

HOPPLE PLASTICS, INC.
7430 Empire Dr.
Florence, KY 41042
Tel.: 606-283-1570 KY
Fax: 606-283-0061
Year Founded: 1958
Approx.Sls.: $20,000,000
Emp.: 250
Manufacturer of Plastic Packaging & Display Products
S.I.C.: 3081; 3089
Michael Evans *(Pres.)*
Anthony E. Blome *(Exec. V.P.)*
Robert T. Brady, Jr. *(Comptroller)*
Michael Dittrich *(Pur. Agent)*
Carl Vollmer *(Chief Engineer)*

Outside Service Firm(s):

Price Waterhouse*(Auditors)*
2200 Chemed Center, 255 E. 5th St.
Cincinnati, OH 45202-4798
Tel.: 513-621-1900

Star Bank*(Major Banking Relationship)*
425 Walnut Street
Cincinnati, OH 45202
Tel.: 513-632-4000

THOMAS R. HOPSON BROKER, INC.
P.O. Box 7295
Marietta, GA 30065
Tel.: 404-578-2400 GA
Fax: 404-578-2421
Year Founded: 1974
Approx.Sls.: $63,000,000
Emp.: 490
Fiscal Year-end: 10/31/91
Wholesale Millwork; Manufacture Wooden Doors, Windows & Sashes
S.I.C.: 2431; 5031
Thomas R. Hopson, Sr. *(Chm. Bd.)*
Steve M. Hopson *(Pres. & Chief Exec. Officer)*
Thomas R. Hopson, Jr. *(V.P.-Opers.)*
Kathleen Hopson Williams *(Sec.)*
Charles Van Peit *(Dir.-Sls.)*
Jackie Turner *(Dir.-Mktg.)*
Doug Chandler *(Dir.-Mfg.)*
Jay Chandler *(Dir.-Pur., Doors)*
Steve Holland *(Dir.-Pur., Stair Parts)*
Pamela Schulman *(Dir.-Human Resources)*
Jeff Arnold *(Dir.-Data Processing)*
Jack Baker *(Treas.)*

No. of Mfg. Plants/Facilities: 1
No. of U.S. Offices: 3

Outside Service Firm(s):

Arthur Andersen & Co.*(Auditors)*
Marietta, GA

First Union Commercial Credit*(Major Banking Relationship)*
Charlotte, NC

Little & Smith*(Commercial Insurance Carrier)*
Marietta, GA

Confederation Life Insurance Co.*(Group Insurer)*
P.O. Box 105103, 260 Interstate North
Atlanta, GA 30348
Tel.: 404-859-3300
Fax: 404-955-6170

Michael M. Smith*(Legal Firm)*
Atlanta, GA

HORIZON BANCORP
515 Franklin Square
Michigan City, IN 46360-3369
Tel.: 219-879-0211 IN
Fax: 219-873-2626
Assets: $361,858,000
Earnings: $2,278,000
Liabilities: $336,766,000
Net Worth: $25,092,000
Fiscal Year-end: 12/31/91
Bank Holding Company
S.I.C.: 6712
Larry E. Reed *(Chm. Bd. & Chief Exec. Officer)*
Robert C. Dabagia *(Pres. & Chief Admin. Officer)*
Thomas P. McCormick *(Exec. V.P. & Sec.)*
J. Michael Smith *(V.P. & Chief Fin. Officer)*
Leon A. Dargis *(Sr. V.P. & Chief Trust Officer)*

Subsidiary:

First Citizens Bank, N.A. **(1)**
515 Franklin Square
Michigan City, IN 46360-3369
Tel.: 219-879-0211 (100%)
Fax: 219-873-2626
National Bank
S.I.C.: 6021
Larry E. Reed *(Chm. Bd. & Chief Exec. Officer)*
Robert C. Dabagia *(Pres. & Chief Admin. Officer)*
Thomas P. McCormick *(Exec. V.P. & Sec.)*
J. Michael Smith *(V.P. & Treas.)*
David Rose *(V.P.-Fin.)*

HORIZON MEDIA, INC.
630 Third Ave.
New York, NY 10017
Tel.: 212-916-8600
Tel.: 800-633-4201 NY
Fax: 212-916-8685
Year Founded: 1989
Approx.Billings: $130,000,000
Emp.: 102
Media Buying Service, Specializing in Spot TV & Radio, Local Cable, Network, Syndication, National Cable, Print Negotiations, Startegic Planning, Marketing & Research Services
S.I.C.: 7311
Donald B. Miller *(Chm. Bd.)*
William A. Koenigsberg *(Pres. & Chief Exec. Officer)*
Jeremiah A. Riley *(Exec. V.P. & Chief Fin. Officer)*
John A. Dunning *(Grp. Sr. V.P.)*
Ruby Gottlieb *(V.P., Dir. Strategic Plng.)*
Nancy Peterson *(V.P., Dir.-Human Resources & Admin.)*
Gregory Hanna *(Controller)*
Alex Alcock *(Supvr.-Acct. Payable)*
Gail Bernstein *(Dir.-Local Cable)*
Kim Vassey *(Dir.-Radio Opers.)*
Ralph Spooner *(Mgr.-Opers.)*
Michael Aiello *(Credit Mgr.)*
Peggy Stephenson *(Asst. Mgr.-Billing)*
Mark Weigele *(Asst. Opers. Mgr.)*
Kim Krause *(Res. & Plng. Asst.)*
Dan Young *(Programmer)*

No. of U.S. Offices: 3

Outside Service Firm(s):

Arthur Andersen & Co.*(Auditors)*
1345 Ave. of the Americas
New York, NY 10105
Tel.: 212-708-4000

Massachusetts Mutual Life Insurance Co.*(Commercial Insurance Carrier)*
1295 State St.
Springfield, MA 01111
Tel.: 413-788-8411
Fax: 413-730-6144

Guardian Life Insurance Co.*(Group Insurer)*
New York, NY

Peter V. Wall*(Legal Firm)*
Greenwich, CT

Chemical Banking Corp.*(Major Banking Relationship)*
277 Park Ave.
New York, NY 10041
Tel.: 212-310-6407
Fax: 212-310-4526

Branches:

Horizon Media Inc. **(1)**
2320 Germantown Rd., S., Ste. 202
Germantown, TN 38138
Tel.: 901-753-0290
Fax: 901-753-0292
Edward F. Hartnett *(V.P., Mktg.)*

Horizon Media Inc. **(1)**
1801 Century Park East, Suite 1132
Los Angeles, CA 90067
Tel.: 310-282-0909
Fax: 310-277-9692
Nancy Kaye Swanson *(Exec. V.P. & Gen. Mgr.)*

Division:

Horizon Media Entertainment **(1)**
630 Third Ave.
New York, NY 10017
Tel.: 212-916-8600
Fax: 212-916-8685
Inventory Barter, Reciprocal Trade & Mdsg. Trade
Robert A. Roganti *(Pres.)*
William A. Koenigsberg *(Co-Chm.)*
Jeremiah A. Riley *(Co-Chm.)*
Carmine J. Cicchino *(Co-Chm.)*

HORIZON PAPER CO., INC.
230 Park Ave., Ste. 840
New York, NY 10169
Tel.: 212-682-5820
Fax: 212-986-0689
Approx.Sls.: $160,000,000
Emp.: 19
Printing Paper Sales
S.I.C.: 5111
Gerry L. Martin *(Pres. & Chief Oper. Officer)*
W.F. Johnston, Jr. *(Vice Chm.)*
Jeffery Hansen *(Chief Fin. Officer)*
Robert Obernier *(Exec. V.P.)*
Alan S. Guthrie *(Sr. V.P.)*

Outside Service Firm(s):

BDO Seidman*(Auditors)*
1430 Broadway
New York, NY
Tel.: 212-765-7500

Snitow & Pauley*(Legal Firm)*
New York, NY

Chemical Bank*(Major Banking Relationship)*
P.O. Box 24935, Church St. Station
New York, NY 10249-4935
Tel.: 212-613-7147
Fax: 212-971-3448

HORLICK LEVIN ADVERTISING INC.
11300 W. Olympic Blvd.
Los Angeles, CA 90064
Tel.: 310-473-6662
Fax: 310-473-2425
Year Founded: 1973
Approx.Billings: $22,480,000
Emp.: 15
Advertising Agency
S.I.C.: 7311
Ronald J. Levin *(Chm.)*
Dennis Horlick *(Pres. & Creative Dir.)*
Bebe Soto-Castroman *(Controller)*
Laney Gutstein *(Mgr.-Office)*

Principal(s):
Ronald J. Levin
Dennis Horlick

Computer Systems/Hardware:
Mac Network

HORN PACKAGING CORPORATION
11 Westford Rd.
Ayer, MA 01432
Tel.: 508-772-0290
Fax: 508-772-4611
Year Founded: 1944
Assets: $7,300,000
Liabilities: $2,100,000
Net Worth: $5,200,000
Approx.Sls.: $20,000,000
Emp.: 225
Corrugated Paperboard Boxes, Wooden Shipping Crates
S.I.C.: 2653; 2449
G. Arthur Horn *(Chm. Bd.)*
Robert H. Lang, Jr. *(Pres. & Chief Exec. Officer)*
John A. Haughn *(V.P.-Fin.)*
Paul Leonard *(V.P.-Mfg.)*
Violet F. Horn *(Sec.)*

Outside Service Firm(s):

Francis R. Zizza*(Auditors)*
Ayer, MA

Jager, Smith Stetler & Arta*(Legal Firm)*
Boston, MA

U.S. Trust Co.*(Major Banking Relationship)*
40 Court St.
Boston, MA 02108
Tel.: 617-726-7371
Fax: 617-726-7380

HORNADY MANUFACTURING COMPANY
Box 1848,
Grand Island, NE 68802
Approx.Sls.: $18,000,000
Emp.: 140
Export
Hornady Bullets
S.I.C.: 3482
S. Hornady *(Pres.)*
Doug Engh *(Dir.-Adv. & Pub. Rels.)*
Cyndi Flannigan *(Dir.-Sls.)*
Douglas Engh *(Mgr.-Adv.)*

Division:

Hornady Ammunition **(1)**
Grand Island, NE 68801
Tel.: 308-382-1390

HORNER RAUSCH COMPANY
968 Main St.
Nashville, TN 37206
Tel.: 615-226-0251
Year Founded: 1960
Approx.Sls.: $16,500,000
Emp.: 360
Fiscal Year-end: 12/31/90
27 Optical Retail Stores
S.I.C.: 5995
George Bandy *(Pres.)*
Glenna Fenn *(V.P.)*
Ann Harris *(Sec.)*
Mark Seurence *(Dir.-Mktg. & Mkt. Res.)*

HORSEHEAD INDUSTRIES, INC.
110 E. 59th St.
New York, NY 10022
Tel.: 212-527-3000 **DE**
Year Founded: 1981
Approx.Sls.: $600,000,000
Emp.: 1,500
Fiscal Year-end: 12/31/91
Holding Company; Producer of Zinc Metal, Zinc Oxide, Dust & Powders, Metal Powders & Zinc Alloys; Trader & Calciner of Petroleum Coke Worldwide; Producer of Graphite Electrodes for the Electric Arc Steel Industry; Recycles Industrial Waste Products
S.I.C.: 6719; 3624; 2999; 5172; 4953; 3399
William E. Flaherty *(Chm. Bd. & Chief Exec. Officer)*
David N. Judelson *(Vice Chm.)*
Dr. David O. Carpenter *(Pres.)*
William M. Flatley *(Sr. V.P. & Chief Fin. Officer)*
Peter Nelson *(V.P.-Corp. Plng.)*
Ronald J. Statile *(V.P. & Treas.)*

No. of Mfg. Plants/Facilities: 14
No. of Foreign Offices: 9

Outside Service Firm(s):

Ernst & Young*(Auditors)*
1800 John F. Kennedy Blvd.
Philadelphia, PA 19103-7499
Tel.: 215-864-3300

INA-CIGNA*(Commercial Insurance Carrier)*
Philadelphia, PA

Industrial Risk Insurers*(Commercial Insurance Carrier)*
85 Woodland St.
Hartford, CT 06102
Tel.: 203-520-7300

Aetna Life & Casualty*(Group Insurer)*
151 Farmington Avenue
Hartford, CT 06156
Tel.: 203-273-2128
Fax: 203-729-4295

Blue Cross of Western Pennsylvania*(Group Insurer)*
One Smithfield St.
Pittsburgh, PA 15222
Tel.: 1-800-242-6425

Equitable Life*(Group Insurer)*
New York, NY

Leboeuf, Lamb, Leiby, MacRae*(Legal Firm)*
140 Broadway
New York, NY 10005
Tel.: 212-269-1100

Chemical Bank*(Major Banking Relationship)*
450 West 33rd St.
New York, NY 10001
Tel.: 212-613-7197
Fax: 212-947-7628

Scarborough Capital Corp.*(Pension Manager)*
New York, NY

Division:

Zinc Corporation of America **(1)**
300 Frankfort Rd.
Monaca, PA 15061
Tel.: 412-774-1020
Emp.: 1,300
Producer of Zinc Oxide, Zinc Dust & Powder, Zinc Metal, Metal Powders & Zinc Alloys
S.I.C.: 2816
Gary A. Wickham *(Pres. & Chief Exec. Officer)*
Jerome Cline *(V.P.-Sls.)*

Subsidiaries:

Great Lakes Carbon Corp. **(1)**
320 Old Briarcliff Rd.
Briarcliff Manor, NY 10510
Tel.: 914-941-7800 (100%)
Emp.: 250
Produce & Distribute Petroleum Coke Products; Produce Graphite Electroder for the Electric Arc Steel Industry; Manufacture Specialty Graphite for Electronics, Aerospace & Composite Tooling
S.I.C.: 5172; 2911; 3295; 2999
William E. Flaherty *(Chm. Bd.)*
David O. Carpenter *(Pres.)*
James D. McKenzie *(Pres.-Petroleum Coke Grp.)*

Palmer Water Co. **(1)**
204 E. 39th St.
New York, NY 10016
Tel.: 212-972-2100 (100%)

Affiliate:

Horsehead Resource Development Company, Inc. **(1)**
613 3rd St.
Palmerton, PA 18071
Tel.: 215-826-8608 (45%)
Earnings: $5,968,000
Approx.Rev.: $71,104,000
Emp.: 545
Fiscal Year-end: 12/31/91
Specialized Hazardous Waste Recovery Services; Wholesale Products Produced from Scrap Materials
S.I.C.: 4953
James H. Davis *(Pres. & Chief Exec. Officer)*
William A. Smelas *(Exec. V.P.)*
Robert L. Hoguet *(Sr. V.P.-Fin.)*
Scott Moser *(V.P.-Sls.)*

Non-U.S. Holding:

Copetro, S.A. **(1)**
Bouchard 644 1106, Sigundo Piso,
Buenos Aires, Argentina (50%)
S.I.C.: 2999

HORTON HOMES, INC.
101 Industrial Blvd.
Eatonton, GA 31024
Tel.: 706-485-8506
Fax: 706-485-4446
Approx.Sls.: $93,000,000
Emp.: 600
Manufacture Mobiles Homes
S.I.C.: 2451
N.D. Horton, Jr. *(Pres.)*
Maude H. Hicks *(Sec. & Treas.)*
Steve Gregory *(Dir.-Pur.)*
Thomas Leach *(Dir.-Sls. & Mktg.)*
Carl Brorup *(Mgr.-Engrng.)*
R.W. Hicks *(Mgr.-Personnel)*
Steve Sinclair *(Mgr.-Data Processing)*

Outside Service Firm(s):

David Giddens*(Auditors)*
Eatonton, GA

Chamberlain Hendricks White Williams Houston*(Legal Firm)*
Eatonton, GA

HOST APPAREL, INC.
1359 Broadway
New York, NY 10018
Tel.: 212-695-5460 **NY**
Fax: 212-629-3965
Year Founded: 1959
Sales Range: $80-99 Million
Emp.: 650
Fiscal Year-end: 6/30/90
Import
Men's & Womens' Sleepwear
S.I.C.: 2322; 2341
Irving Cohen *(Chm. Bd.)*
Milton J. Margolis *(Vice Chm.)*
Howard Cohen *(Pres.)*
Steven Cohen *(Exec. V.P.)*
Robert H. Rosenblum *(Chief Fin. Officer)*
Principal(s):
Irving Cohen
Milton J. Margolis
Howard Cohen
Steven Cohen

No. of Mfg. Plants/Facilities: 10
No. of U.S. Offices: 1
No. of Foreign Offices: 1

Computer Systems/Hardware:
Wang

Outside Service Firm(s):

Buchbinder, Stein, Tunick & Platkin*(Auditors)*
One Pennsylvania Plaza
New York, NY 10119-0219

Kantor, Davidoff, Wolfe, Rabbino & Kass, P.C.*(Legal Firm)*
New York, NY

Bankers Trust Co.*(Major Banking Relationship)*
P.O. Box 9050, Church St. Station
New York, NY 10008
Tel.: 212-250-6037

Division:

Host for Her **(1)**
183 Madison Ave.
New York, NY 10016
Tel.: 212-482-3890
Manufacture Women's Sleepwear & Underwear
S.I.C.: 2341
Timothy Conney *(Pres.)*

Subsidiaries:

Dothan Underwear **(1)**
1359 Broadway
New York, NY 10118
Tel.: 212-564-6450
Fax: 212-695-0618
Manufacture Men's & Young Men's Shirts, Underwear & Gym Shorts
S.I.C.: 2321; 2322; 2329
Joel S. Scharf *(Gen. Mgr.)*
Douglas A. Wagner *(Controller)*
Lou Guadagho *(Pur. Agent)*

Pajama Craft, Inc. **(1)**
1359 Broadway
New York, NY 10018
Tel.: 212-594-6226
Men's & Women's Sleepwear
S.I.C.: 2341; 2322
Steve Gould *(Pres.)*

HOSTMARK MANAGEMENT GROUP
(Formerly The Management Group, Inc.)
1600 Golf Rd.
Rowing Meadows, IL 60008
Tel.: 708-439-8500
Fax: 708-439-8755
Year Founded: 1974
Approx.Sls.: $125,000,000
Emp.: 4,000
Hotel & Restaurant Developers & Management
S.I.C.: 7011; 6531
Stephen Narans *(Chm. Bd.)*
C.A. Cataldo *(Pres. & Chief Exec. Officer)*
Robert J. Cataldo *(Exec. V.P.-Opers.)*
Charles A. Gavzar *(Sr. V.P.-Fin.)*
Principal(s):
C.A. Cataldo
Robert J. Cataldo

Computer Systems/Hardware:
IBM PC

Outside Service Firm(s):

Phillip Rootberg*(Auditors)*
Chicago, IL

HOT SHOT DELIVERY INC.
701 Shepherd Dr.
Houston, TX 77007
Mailing Address:
P.O. Box 701189,
Houston, TX 77270
Tel.: 713-869-5525
Fax: 713-862-6354
Year Founded: 1978
Sales Range: $10-19 Million
Emp.: 35
Fiscal Year-end: 1/31/91
Delivery/Messenger Service in the Greater Houston Area
S.I.C.: 4214
Darrell Donaldson *(Pres., Chief Exec. & Fin. Officer)*

Computer Systems/Hardware:
Data General

Outside Service Firm(s):

G.I.C. Insurance*(Group Insurer)*
San Antonio, TX

NationsBank Texas*(Major Banking Relationship)*
Corporate Trust Department, 700 Louisiana St.
Houston, TX 77002
Tel.: 713-247-6000

THE HOTSY CORPORATION
21 Inverness Way E.
Englewood, CO 80112
Tel.: 303-792-5200
Tel.: 800-525-1976
Fax: 303-792-0547
Approx.Sls.: $18,000,000
Emp.: 200
Export
Manufactures High Pressure Cleaning Equipment & Related Chemicals
S.I.C.: 3699
Robert L. Cohen *(Pres. & Chief Exec. Officer)*
E. Lloyd Rizer *(Sr. V.P.-Fin.)*
Keith A. Price *(V.P.-Mktg.)*
Kurt Briggs *(V.P.-Pur.)*
Randy Mitchell *(Sec. & Treas.)*
Dave Stark *(Sr. Mgr.-Mktg.)*

Hottman Edwards

HOTTMAN EDWARDS
1003 N. Calvert St.
Baltimore, MD 21202
Tel.: 410-385-1443
Fax: 410-385-1446
Year Founded: 1971
Approx.Billings: $31,300,000
Emp.: 31
George D. Edwards, II *(Pres. & Chief Exec. Officer)*
William A. Hottman *(V.P., Treas.)*
Theresa Kozel *(Comptroller)*

HOUCHENS INDUSTRIES INC.
900 Church St.
Bowling Green, KY 42101
Tel.: 502-843-3252
Fax: 502-781-6377
Retail & Wholesale Grocers; 44 Grocery Stores
S.I.C.: 5141; 5411
Ruel Houchens *(Pres.)*

HOUCK INDUSTRIES, INC.
437 N. M St.
Tulare, CA 93274
Tel.: 209-688-2983
Fax: 209-688-0133
Emp.: 120
Builders & Cabinet Hardware
S.I.C.: 3429
Peter Houck *(Pres. & Chief Exec. Officer)*
Steve Hatcher *(Chief Fin. Officer)*
Judy Beckman *(Pur. Agent)*
Jim Ford *(Plant Supvr.)*

Outside Service Firm(s):

Ernst & Young*(Auditors)*
Fresno, CA

Wells Fargo Bank*(Major Banking Relationship)*
Tulare, CA

HOUGEN MANUFACTURING INC.
G5072 Corunna Rd.
Flint, MI 48532
Tel.: 313-732-5840
Fax: 313-732-3553
Year Founded: 1952
Approx.Sls.: $11,000,000
Emp.: 110
Mfr. of Drill Bits, Cutting Tools & Portable Hole-making Equipment
S.I.C.: 3545; 3546
Everett D. Hougen *(Chm. Bd.)*
Randall Hougen *(Pres. & Chief Exec. Officer)*
Therese Hougen *(V.P. & Sec.)*
Malcolm MacLean *(V.P.-Fin. & Admin.)*
Gerald Mueller *(Dir.-Engrng.)*
Sue Savage *(Dir.-Pur.)*

E. F. HOUGHTON & CO.
Madison & Van Buren
Valley Forge, PA 19482
Tel.: 215-666-4000 **PA**
Twx: 291-767-HOUG
Fax: 215-666-1376
Year Founded: 1865
Approx.Sls.: $183,000,000
Emp.: 350
Manufacture Specialty Chemicals used in Industrial Processing
S.I.C.: 2899; 2992
William F. MacDonald, Jr. *(Chm. Bd., Pres., Chief Exec. & Chief Oper. Officer)*
W.J. Pearcy *(V.P.-Sls.)*
Bruce Schuck *(V.P.-Production & Pur.)*
T.G. Kauffman *(V.P.-Mktg.)*
T.A. Williams *(V.P.-Sec. & Treas.)*
Richard Niwinski *(Controller)*
R.D. Geiselman *(Mgr.-Mktg. Services, Communications & Adv.)*
Chester Czulada *(Mgr.-Data Processing)*
Edward Schmidt *(Mgr.-Employee Rels.)*

No. of Mfg. Plants/Facilities: 6
No. of U.S. Offices: 9
No. of Foreign Offices: 28

Computer Systems/Hardware:
Digital Equipment

Outside Service Firm(s):

Deloitte & Touche*(Auditors)*
1700 Market St.
Philadelphia, PA 19103
Tel.: 215-246-2322
Fax: 215-569-2441

Morgan, Lewis & Bockius*(Legal Firm)*
2000 One Logan Square
Philadelphia, PA 19103
Tel.: 215-963-5000

Non-U.S. Holdings:

E. F. Houghton Co. of Canada Ltd. **(1)**
100 Symes Rd. P.O. Box 113, Station D, Toronto, ON M6P 3J5, Canada
Tel.: 416-763-4691 (100%)
Mfr. of Specialty Chemicals Used In Industrial Processing
S.I.C.: 2899
Frank Heath *(Pres.)*

Houghton-Benelux B.V. **(1)**
Mechelaarstraat 12 4903 RE
Oosterhout, NB Netherlands (100%)
Mfr. of Specialty Chemicals Used in Metal Processing
S.I.C.: 2899
Willy Moerdijk *(Chief Oper. Officer)*

E. F. Houghton do Brazil **(1)**
Cx Postal 107 Capuava Mava
Sao Paulo, S.P. Brazil
Tel.: 450-2133 (100%)
Mfr. of Specialty Chemicals Used in Metal Processing
S.I.C.: 2899
Claiton Scalea *(Dir.)*

Houghton Italia S.p.A. **(1)**
Casella Postale 669 1-16100
Genoa, Italy
Tel.: 581542-3 (100%)
Mfr. of Specialty Chemicals Used in Metal Processing
S.I.C.: 2899
Guido Galli *(Dir.)*

Houghton A.G. Switzerland **(1)**
Furstenlandstrasse 7 Postfach 1247, 9500 Bienne, 2, Switzerland
Tel.: 032-22-68-44 (100%)
Mfr. of Specialty Chemicals Used in Metal Processing
S.I.C.: 2899
K. Hani *(Mng. Dir.)*

Houghton Vaughn plc **(1)**
Legge St.
Birmingham, B47 EU, United Kingdom
Tel.: 021-359-6100 (100%)
Mfr. of Specialty Chemicals Used in Metal Processing
S.I.C.: 2899
Bryan Thomas *(Mng. Dir.)*

Produtec Houghton S.A. **(1)**
259 Rue Benoit-Mulsant Zac Nord Est., 69400
Villefranche-sur-Saone, France (100%)
Mfr. of Specialty Chemicals Used in Metal Processing
S.I.C.: 2899

HOUSE OF BIANCHI
293 A St.
Boston, MA 02210
Tel.: 617-482-5450 **MA**
Fax: 617-482-0216
Year Founded: 1953
Assets: $5,000,000
Liabilities: $2,400,000
Net Worth: $2,600,000
Approx.Sls.: $17,000,000
Emp.: 220
Fiscal Year-end: 6/30/92
Import Export
Mfr. of Bridal Gowns & Formal Gowns
S.I.C.: 2335; 2395
Joseph Massa *(Pres. & Gen. Mgr.)*
James Farrell *(V.P.)*
Joseph F. Shay *(Treas.)*
Brian Kelly *(Natl. Sls. Mgr.)*
George Bronstein *(Dir.-Pur.)*

No. of Mfg. Plants/Facilities: 1
No. of U.S. Offices: 6

Computer Systems/Hardware:
IBM System 36

Outside Service Firm(s):

Shawmut Bank*(Major Banking Relationship)*
1 Federal St.
Boston, MA 02110
Tel.: 617-292-3715

HOUSE OF PERFECTION, INC.
131 W. 33rd St.
New York, NY 10001
Tel.: 212-239-9780
Fax: 212-268-1431
Approx.Sls.: $23,000,000
Emp.: 800
Children's & Infants Slacks, Girls & Children's Play Suits, Childrens & Infants Skirts
S.I.C.: 2331; 2361; 2369
Gene Goldfarb *(Chm. Bd.)*
Ellen Goldfarb *(Pres.)*

Outside Service Firm(s):

BDO Seidman*(Auditors)*
1430 Broadway
New York, NY
Tel.: 212-765-7500

Chemical Banking Corp.*(Major Banking Relationship)*
277 Park Ave.
New York, NY 10041
Tel.: 212-310-6407
Fax: 212-310-4526

Subsidiary:

Capital City Manufacturing Company **(1)**
P.O. Box 1130
West Columbia, SC 29171
Tel.: 803-794-6850
Childrens & Infants Wear
S.I.C.: 2361
Johnnie Neese *(Controller)*
Robert Smith *(Plant Mgr.)*

HOUSE OF RAEFORD FARMS, INC.
520 E. Central Ave.
Raeford, NC 28376
Mailing Address:
P.O. Box 100
Raeford, NC 28376
Tel.: 919-875-5161
Fax: 919-875-8300
Year Founded: 1962
Approx.Sls.: $200,000,000
Emp.: 1,400
Export
Processor of Turkey & Chicken Products
S.I.C.: 2015
E. Marvin Johnson *(Pres.)*
Harold Brock *(V.P.)*
Brenda Branch *(Sec.)*
Allen Asbury *(Controller)*
Kenny Starling *(Dir.-Mktg.)*
Andy Spivey *(Mgr.-Sls.)*

Computer Systems/Hardware:
Wang

Outside Service Firm(s):

Cherry, Bekaert & Holland*(Auditors)*
Fayetteville, NC

Southern National Bank*(Major Banking Relationship)*
Winston-Salem, NC

HOUSE OF RONNIE, INC.
1333 Broadway, 2nd Fl.
New York, NY 10018
Tel.: 212-564-0900 **DE**
Fax: 212-643-9566
Approx.Sls.: $70,000,000
Emp.: 1,200
Fiscal Year-end: 6/30/91
Mfr. of Ladies' & Children's Clothing
S.I.C.: 2341; 5632
Irving Paparo *(Chm. Bd. & Pres.)*
Ralph Merola *(Exec. V.P.)*
Stanley Rappaport *(Exec. V.P.)*
Henry Rothman *(Sec.)*
Sidney Wagner *(Controller)*
Karen Blanding *(Dir.-Mngmt. Information Systems)*
Principal(s):
Irving Paparo
Stanley Rappaport

Computer Systems/Hardware:
IBM System 38

Outside Service Firm(s):

Rochland, Lipsky & Stoller*(Auditors)*
New York, NY

Empire Blue Cross & Blue Shield*(Group Insurer)*
New York, NY

Subsidiaries:

Bristol Lingerie **(1)**
203 Bob Morrison Blvd.
Bristol, VA 24201
Tel.: 703-669-7188
Mfr. of Women's Underwear
S.I.C.: 2341
Charles Walker *(Plant Mgr.)*

Denise Lingerie **(1)**
717 Rowland Dr.
Johnson City, TN 37601
Tel.: 615-928-8261
Sale of Women's Accessories
S.I.C.: 5632
Curtis Marshall *(Plant Mgr.)*

Sid Eagle Associates **(1)**
P.O. Box 308,
Dover, NC 28526
Tel.: 919-527-4635
Mfr. of Shirts & Jumpsuits for Women
S.I.C.: 2331; 2339

Jasper Textile **(1)**
Rte. 2, Box 35
Jasper, FL 32052
Tel.: 904-792-2562
Mfr. of Women's Underwear
S.I.C.: 2341
Bobby MacMillan *(Gen. Mgr.)*

Nashville Textile Corp. **(1)**
202 Industrial Park
Nashville, GA 31639
Tel.: 912-686-5581
Mfr. of Textile Goods
S.I.C.: 2299
Ronald Walker *(Plant Mgr.)*

HOUSTON EFFLER & PARTNERS
360 Newbury St.
Boston, MA 02115
Tel.: 617-267-5050
Fax: 617-267-6472
Year Founded: 1987
Approx.Billings: $74,000,000
Emp.: 80
Corporate Giving Program: Provide Adv. Services To One Non-Profit Organization Per Year At No Charge
Douglas Houston *(Chm. Bd. & Chief Exec. Officer)*
Donald Effler *(Pres.)*
Mark Richardson *(Exec. V.P., Dir. of Client Services)*
Robert N. Cauley, Jr. *(Sr. V.P., Treas.)*
Lisa Unsworth *(Sr. V.P., Mktg. Services Dir.)*

Computer Systems/Hardware:
Admark, Media Management Plus

HOUSTON FEARLESS 76 INC.
203 W. Artesia Blvd.
Compton, CA 90220-5550
Tel.: 310-605-0755
Twx: 910-346-6701
Fax: 310-608-1556
Approx.Sls.: $11,000,000
Emp.: 200
Fiscal Year-end: 12/31/90
Export
Mfr. Photographic Equip., Processors & Related Lab Accessories
S.I.C.: 3861
M.S. Lee *(Pres.)*
George M. Barr *(V.P.-Mktg.)*
Richard W. Geer *(V.P.-Opers.)*
Scott J. McCormac *(V.P.-Fin.)*

Outside Service Firm(s):

Union Bank*(Major Banking Relationship)*
3810 Wilshire Blvd.
Los Angeles, CA 90051
Tel.: 213-480-6500

HOUSTON FOODS COMPANY
4245 N. Knox Ave.
Chicago, IL 60641
Tel.: 312-777-2700 **IL**
Fax: 312-777-1680
Sales Range: $10-19 Million
Emp.: 200
Fiscal Year-end: 4/30/90
Distribute Prepackaged Food/Gift Assortments
S.I.C.: 5199; 2599
Joseph F. Vasselli *(Pres.)*
Gary D. Musick *(V.P.-Sls.)*
Robert C. Pesch *(V.P.-Opers. & Prod. Devel.)*
Bradley A. Schroeder *(V.P.-Fin.)*
Arthur Wlodarski *(V.P.-Pur.)*
Mindy Macius *(Dir.-Adv. & Pub. Rels.)*
Principal(s):
Joseph F. Vasselli
Gary D. Musick
Robert C. Pesch
Bradley A. Schroeder
Arthur Wlodarski
Mesirow Financial Corp.

Computer Systems/Hardware:
IBM

Outside Service Firm(s):

LaSalle National Bank*(Major Banking Relationship)*
120 S. LaSalle St.
Chicago, IL 60603
Tel.: 312-781-8000

THE DEE HOWARD COMPANY
9610 John Saunders Intl. Airport
San Antonio, TX 78216
Tel.: 210-828-1341
Fax: 210-821-4098
Approx.Sls.: $45,000,000
Emp.: 1,000
Manufacturer Jet Aircraft Modifications, Interiors & Thrust Reversers
S.I.C.: 3728; 3721
Luigi Fumagali *(Chm. Bd.)*
Matthew Donahue *(Pres.)*
Settimio Biondi *(Sr. V.P.-Fin.)*
Attilio Galasso *(V.P.-Engrng.)*
John Eranco *(V.P.-Opers.)*
Deanne Bridges *(Sec.)*
Principal(s):
Luigi Fumagali

Computer Systems/Hardware:
IBM Systems 36 & 34; Integraph CAD/CAM Terminals

Outside Service Firm(s):

Grant Thornton*(Auditors)*
San Antonio, TX

Fagan & Rigley, Inc.*(Legal Firm)*
San Antonio, TX

HOWARD INDUSTRIES, INC.
One North Dixie Hwy.
Milford, IL 60953
Tel.: 815-889-4105
Fax: 815-889-4313
Approx.Sls.: $30,000,000
Emp.: 500
Import Export
Motors, Fans, Blowers & Gearmotors
S.I.C.: 3566
Logan Delany, Jr. *(Chm. Bd.)*
Lee Perlman *(Vice Chm.)*
John Sandner *(Pres.)*
Bob Stanford *(Controller)*
Keith Breeling *(Chief Engr.)*
Hans Wolf *(Mgr.-Sls.)*

HOWARD MANUFACTURING
421 6th Ave. N.
Kent, WA 98032
Mailing Address:
P.O. BOx 1188
Kent, WA 98035
Tel.: 206-852-0640 **WA**
Fax: 206-854-0895
Year Founded: 1901
Emp.: 80
Import Export
Manufacture Wood, Aluminum & Fiberglass Ladders; Wood Arch Panels
S.I.C.: 2499
Charles Howard *(Pres.)*
Jim Howard *(V.P.-Sls.)*

No. of Mfg. Plants/Facilities: 5
No. of U.S. Offices: 5

Computer Systems/Hardware:
Basic 4

Outside Service Firm(s):

Shannon & Associates*(Auditors)*
Kent, WA

Graham & Dunn*(Legal Firm)*
1301 5th Ave., 34th Floor
Seattle, WA 98101
Tel.: 206-624-8300

HOWARD, MERRELL & PARTNERS, INC.
8521 Six Forks Rd.
Raleigh, NC 27615
Tel.: 919-848-2400
Year Founded: 1976
Approx.Billings: $39,763,000
Emp.: 61
J.T. Howard *(Chm.-Emeritus)*
W.M. Merrell *(Pres. & Chief Exec. Officer)*
G.H. Knutson *(Exec. V.P., Partner & Creative Dir.)*
R.L. Hoyt *(Exec. V.P., Partner & Acct. Services)*
C.A. Larsen, Jr. *(V.P., Dir. Bus. Devel.)*
M. Komives *(Dir., HM&P Consulting Group)*
B.I. Congleton *(V.P., Fin. Services)*
K. Crowder *(Studio Mgr., Dancing Bear Design Grp.)*
R.B. Hammer *(Office Services)*

HOWARD NEEDLES TAMMEN & BERGENDOFF
1201 Walnut, Ste. 700
Kansas City, MO 64106
Mailing Address:
P.O. Box 412197
Kansas City, MO 64141
Tel.: 816-472-1201
Fax: 816-472-4060
Year Founded: 1914
Approx.Sls.: $200,000,000
Emp.: 2,000
Engineering, Architectural & Planning Services
S.I.C.: 8711; 8712
Cary C. Goodman *(Chief Exec. Officer)*
Daniel J. Spigai *(Chief Exec. Officer)*
Robert S. Coma *(Chief Admin. Officer)*
Robert M. Berg *(Dir.-Human Resources)*
John L. Cotton *(Dir.-Mktg.)*
Michael P. Ingardia *(Dir.-Information Services)*
Kendall T. Lincoln *(Dir.-Fin. & Acctg.)*
Gary F. Link *(Dir.-Mktg. Services)*
Principal(s):
Robert S. Coma
John L. Cotton
Cary C. Goodman
Daniel J. Spigai

No. of U.S. Offices: 30

Subsidiary:

Thomas K. Dyer, Inc. **(1)**
1762 Massachusetts Ave.
Lexington, MA 02173
Tel.: 617-862-2075
Rail & Transit Engineering Consultants
S.I.C.: 8711
Charles L. O'Reilly *(Pres.)*

HOWARDS APPLIANCES, INC.
300 E. Valley Blvd.
San Gabriel, CA 91776
Tel.: 818-288-4010 **CA**
Fax: 818-573-2432
Year Founded: 1949
Sales Range: $20-39 Million
Emp.: 185
Major Electric Housold Appliances; Television Sets; Two-way, Citizen's Band, Weather, and Short-wave Radios
S.I.C.: 5722; 5731
Howard Roach *(Pres.)*
Robert Buchi *(V.P.)*
Carmeline Falabrino *(V.P.)*
John R. McLean *(V.P.)*
Michaeline Roach *(V.P.)*
Monica Roach *(V.P.)*
John Sherrill *(Treas. & Sec.)*

Outside Service Firm(s):

Security Pacific National Bank*(Major Banking Relationship)*
333 So. Hope
Los Angeles, CA 90071
Tel.: 213-613-6211

HOWDEN SIROCCO INC.
One Westinghouse Plaza
Hyde Park, MA 02136
Tel.: 617-361-3700
Year Founded: 1854
Approx.Sls.: $40,000,000
Emp.: 350
Fiscal Year-end: 4/30/90
Indus. Fans & Blowers, Heavy Duty & Mechanical Draft Fans, Axial Fans, Mechanical Dust Collectors, Variable Speed Fluid Drives, Bearings, Field Service
S.I.C.: 5084; 3634; 3564; 3566; 3562
J.L. Finn *(Pres.)*
Robin G. Fleming *(V.P.-Sls. & Mktg.)*
Edward Palmer *(V.P. Opers.)*
M.J. Magill *(V.P.-Engrng.)*
R. Taylor *(Pub. Rels. Mgr.)*
Kathy Bowie *(Mktg. Asst.)*

Division:

Sturtevant Div. **(1)**
One Westinghouse Plaza
Boston, MA 02136
Tel.: 617-361-3700
Approx.Sls.: $55,000,000
Emp.: 600
Industrial Ventilating & Exhaust Equip.; Process & Air Pollution Fans, Axial & Centrifugal; Electric Air Cleaners & Mechanical Draft Fans for Power Plants, Dampers, Silencers, Babbitted Sleeve Bearings, Field Service & Repairs
J.L. Finn *(Pres.)*
R.G. Fleming *(V.P.-Sls. & Mktg.)*
J. E. Dixon *(V.P.-Fin.)*
W.C. Higgins *(V.P.-Services)*

HOWE FURNITURE CORPORATION
12 Cambridge Dr.
Trumbull, CT 06611
Mailing Address:
P.O. Box 0386
Trumbull, CT 06611
Tel.: 203-374-7833
Tel.: 800-888-4693
Fax: 203-374-2287
Year Founded: 1928
Sales Range: $40-59 Million
Emp.: 165
Fiscal Year-end: 12/31/92
Export
Folding & Non-Folding Tables; Flip Top Tables; Computer Support Furniture; Training, Conference & Hospitality Tables
S.I.C.: 2521; 2522
Harold Howe, Jr. *(Chm. Bd., Chief Exec. Officer & Treas.)*
Eric Smith *(Pres. & Chief Oper. Officer)*
Gerald R. Taylor, Jr. *(Chief Fin. Officer & V.P.)*
George Esposito *(Dir.-Sls.)*
Walter Binck *(Mgr.-Customer Service)*
Scott Carey *(Mgr.-Mfg.)*
Joanne C. Island *(Mgr.-Mktg.)*
Paul Voland *(Mgr.-Natl. Accts.)*
Bryan Wilson *(Mgr.-Hospitality Sls. & Canada Sls.)*
John Wooding *(Mgr.-Credit)*
Lisa Ayr O'Connor *(Media Coord.)*

Outside Service Firm(s):

KPMG Peat Marwick*(Auditors)*
Stamford Square, 3001 Summer St.
Stamford, CT 06905
Tel.: 203-356-9800

City Trust*(Major Banking Relationship)*
Trumbull, CT

Subsidiary:

Hardwood Visuals **(1)**
5900 Main St. N.E.
Fridley, MN 55432
Tel.: 612-571-4521
Tel.: 800-634-9279
Fax: 612-571-2958
Export
Mfr. of Video Cabinets, Conference Tables, Credenzas, Lecturns & Visual Boards
S.I.C.: 2521
Ron Wells *(Pres.)*

E. W. HOWELL COMPANY, INC.
2 Seaview Blvd.
Port Washington, NY 11050
Tel.: 516-621-1100
Fax: 516-621-1192
Year Founded: 1963
Approx.Sls.: $130,000,000
Emp.: 1,600
Institutional, Commercial & Industrial Buildings Contractor
S.I.C.: 1541; 1542
Phillip Schiavone *(Pres. & Chief Exec. Officer)*
Alan Perlman *(Exec. V.P.)*

Outside Service Firm(s):

Arthur Andersen & Co.*(Auditors)*
Melville, NY

Jones, Day, Reavis & Pogue*(Legal Firm)*
599 Levington
New York, NY 10022

Chemical Bank*(Major Banking Relationship)*
395 North Service Rd.
Melville, NY 11747

HOWELL INSTRUMENTS CORP.
3479 W. Vickery Blvd.
Fort Worth, TX 76107
Tel.: 817-336-7411 **TX**
Telex: 758233
Fax: 817-336-7874
Year Founded: 1951
Assets: $13,096,739
Earnings: $810,324
Liabilities: $554,097
Net Worth: $12,542,642
Approx.Sls.: $13,628,698
Emp.: 116

Howell Instruments Corp.—(Continued)

Fiscal Year-end: 11/30/91
Mfr. of Electronics Equipment
S.I.C.: 3825
John S. Howell *(Chm. Bd., Pres. & Chief Exec. Officer)*
H.G. White *(V.P.-Fin.)*
John McMackin *(Gen. Counsel)*
Lonnie J. Thompson *(Controller)*
Bruce Pike *(Mgr.-Export)*
James L. Donawho *(Fin. Advisor)*
Corene Cloud *(Dir.-Personnel)*
Gary Gentry *(Dir.-Pur.)*
James Rhoades *(Dir.-Data Processing)*
William Howell *(V.P.-Mktg.)*

Computer Systems/Hardware:
IBM 4331

Outside Service Firm(s):

Aetna Life & Casualty*(Commercial Insurance Carrier)*
151 Farmington Avenue
Hartford, CT 06156
Tel.: 203-273-2128
Fax: 203-729-4295

Bank of Commerce*(Investment Banker)*
Ft. Worth, TX

Godfrey & Decker*(Legal Firm)*
3200 Continental Plaza
Ft. Worth, TX 76102
Tel.: 817-336-0361

Bank of Commerce*(Major Banking Relationship)*
Ft. Worth, TX

H. G. White*(Pension Manager)*
Ft. Worth, TX

Division:

Howell Exports **(1)**
3479 W. Vickery
Fort Worth, TX 76107
Tel.: 817-336-7411
Approx.Sls.: $3,000,000
Emp.: 5
Holding Company
S.I.C.: 6719
Bruce P. Pike *(Pres)*

HOWELL LABORATORIES, INC.
124 Harrison St.
Bridgton, ME 04009
Mailing Address:
P.O. Box 389
Bridgton, ME 04009
Tel.: 207-647-3327 **ME**
Fax: 207-647-8273
Assets: $4,300,000
Liabilities: $3,000,000
Net Worth: $1,300,000
Sales Range: $10-19 Million
Emp.: 70
Fiscal Year-end: 6/30/92
Import Export
Mfr. of Microwave & Radio Frequency Components; Transmitting & Communications Antennas; Electrical Equipment & Supplies
S.I.C.: 3679; 3663; 3699
Paul A. Wescott *(Pres.)*
D.S. Collins *(V.P.-Engrng.)*
Charles Peabody *(V.P.-Mktg.)*
Gary Somers *(V.P.-Mfg.)*
Carl Bishop *(Controller)*

Outside Service Firm(s):

Ernst & Young*(Auditors)*
Portland, ME

Pierce, Atwood, Scribner, Allen, Smith & Lancaster*(Legal Firm)*
Portland, ME

Casco Northern Bank*(Major Banking Relationship)*
1 Monument Square
Portland, ME 04104
Tel.: 207-774-8221

Fleet Bank*(Major Banking Relationship)*
Portland, ME

Subsidiary:

HLI Holdings, Inc. **(1)**
124 Harrison St.
Bridgton, ME 04009
Tel.: 207-647-3327
Fax: 207-647-8273
Real Estate Holding Co.
S.I.C.: 6719

HOWES LEATHER COMPANY, INC.
1 Batterymarch
Quincy, MA 02169
Tel.: 617-770-3900
Fax: 617-472-9042
Approx.Sls.: $60,000,000
Emp.: 402
Manufacture Sole Leather & Cut Stock
S.I.C.: 3111; 3131
James M. Fitzgibbons *(Chm. Bd.)*
Barry I. Getto *(Pres. & Chief Exec. Officer)*
Joseph P. McHugh *(V.P. & Treas.)*
Joseph J. Lyons, Jr. *(V.P.)*

Outside Service Firm(s):

Arthur Andersen & Co.*(Auditors)*
One Intl. Place, 100 Oliver St.
Boston, MA 02110
Tel.: 617-330-4000
Fax: 617-439-9731

Nutter, McClennen & Fish*(Legal Firm)*
One International Place
Boston, MA 02210-2699
Tel.: 617-439-2000

Bank of Boston*(Major Banking Relationship)*
Atlanta, GA

HOYT CORPORATION
251 Forge Rd.
Westport, MA 02790
Tel.: 508-636-8811
Fax: 508-636-2088
Year Founded: 1949
Approx.Sls.: $10,000,000
Emp.: 150
Export
Commercial Equipment & Machinery
S.I.C.: 3569; 3565
Virginia Hoyt Kurtz *(Pres.)*
Steve Rooney *(Exec. V.P.)*
Richard Krenmayer *(V.P.-Sls.)*
Derek W. Oakes *(V.P.-Indus. Div.)*
Jeannie Hoyt Olinger *(V.P.)*
Claire Wilcox *(Office Mgr.)*
Pat King *(Mgr.-Adv.)*

Computer Systems/Hardware:
IBM PC-XT

Outside Service Firm(s):

Lincoln National Life Insurance Co.*(Group Insurer)*
Lincoln, NE

State Street Bank & Trust Co.*(Major Banking Relationship)*
P.O. Box 366,
Boston, MA 02101
Tel.: 617-426-5523

THE HOYT GROUP
(Formerly The Hoyt Companies)
5453 W. 61st Pl.
Shawnee Mission, KS 66205
Tel.: 913-384-5700
Fax: 913-384-2367
Emp.: 200
Real Estate Investors, Brokers, Syndicators
S.I.C.: 6531
Bill Charcut *(V.P.)*
Kelly E. Smith *(Chief Fin. Officer)*
James Hoyt *(Gen. Partner)*

Computer Systems/Hardware:
IBM 6380

Outside Service Firm(s):

BDO Seidman*(Auditors)*
Kansas City, MO

Ernst & Young*(Auditors)*
One Kansas City Place, 1200 Main St.
Kansas City, MO 64105

United Missouri Bank*(Major Banking Relationship)*
Kansas City, MO

Subsidiaries:

EN-COM Properties, Inc. **(1)**
5453 W. 61st Pl.
Shawnee Mission, KS 66205
Tel.: 913-384-5700

Hoyt Securities, Inc. **(1)**
5453 W. 61st Pl.
Shawnee Mission, KS 66205
Tel.: 913-384-9056

RONALD HSU CONSTRUCTION
207 W. Hampton Ave.
Capitol Heights, MD 20743
Tel.: 301-350-3020 **DC**
Fax: 301-350-3609
Year Founded: 1976
Assets: $7,112,844
Earnings: $1,627,473
Liabilities: $4,158,747
Net Worth: $2,954,097
Approx.Sls.: $17,926,202
Emp.: 50
Fiscal Year-end: 6/30/90
General Construction Remodelling Renovation, Government & Commercial Contracts
S.I.C.: 1522
Ronald Hsu *(Chm. Bd.)*
Edward Kim *(Pres., Chief Oper. & Chief Exec. Officer)*
Mei Lee *(Treas., Controller & Chief Fin. Officer)*

Computer Systems/Hardware:
IBM PC; IBM System 36

Outside Service Firm(s):

The PMA Group*(Commercial Insurance Carrier)*
Baltimore, MD

Corcoran, Youngman & Rowe*(Legal Firm)*
Washington, DC

Maryland National Bank*(Major Banking Relationship)*
Largo, MD

HUB INC.
2146 Flintstone Dr.
Tucker, GA 30084
Mailing Address:
P.O. Box 125
Tucker, GA 30085-0125
Tel.: 404-934-3101
Tel.: 800-241-9460 **GA**
Fax: 404-934-6286
Year Founded: 1966
Approx.Sls.: $100,000,000
Emp.: 425
Fiscal Year-end: 2/28/91
Wholesale Pipe Valves & Fittings
S.I.C.: 5051; 5085
Ben H. Camp *(Chm. Bd. & Chief Exec. Officer)*
Barry S. Camp *(Pres.)*
J.M. Golden *(V.P.-Fin.)*
P.A. Knipper *(V.P.-Pur.)*
Michael Robertson *(V.P.-Human Resources)*
Brent Tippett *(Dir.-Data Processing)*
Principal(s):
Ben H. Camp
Barry S. Camp

No. of Mfg. Plants/Facilities: 23
No. of U.S. Offices: 22
No. of Foreign Offices: 1

Computer Systems/Hardware:
IBM

Outside Service Firm(s):

Bearden & Smith*(Auditors)*
Atlanta, GA

Trust Company Bank*(Investment Banker)*
P.O. Box 4625, 25 Park Place
Atlanta, GA 30302
Tel.: 404-588-7815

McCurdy Candler*(Legal Firm)*
Decatur, GA

Trust Company Bank*(Major Banking Relationship)*
Stock Trans. Dept. P.O.B. 4625, Trust Company of Georgia Bldg.
Atlanta, GA 30302
Tel.: 404-588-7831

HUBACHER CADILLAC INC.
#1 Cadillac Dr.
Sacramento, CA 95825
Tel.: 916-929-2777
Fax: 916-929-3641
Year Founded: 1980
Approx.Sls.: $38,000,000
Emp.: 80
Retail New & Used Automobiles
S.I.C.: 5511
Lee Castonguay *(Pres. & Gen. Mgr.)*

Outside Service Firm(s):

First Interstate Bank*(Major Banking Relationship)*
P.O. Box 3131,
Portland, OR 97208
Tel.: 503-220-4855
Fax: 503-225-7153

First Security National Bank & Trust*(Major Banking Relationship)*
San Francisco, CA

HUBBARD BROADCASTING, INC.
3415 University Ave.
Saint Paul, MN 55114
Tel.: 612-646-5555 **MN**
Fax: 612-642-4103
Year Founded: 1923
Emp.: 1,000
Fiscal Year-end: 6/30/91
Television & Radio Broadcasting; Hotels
S.I.C.: 7011; 4833; 4832
Stanley S. Hubbard *(Chm., Pres., & Chief Exec. Officer)*
John Mayasich *(Pres.-Radio Opers.)*
Gerald D. Deeney *(V.P., Chief Fin. Officer & Treas.)*
Harold Crump *(V.P. & Gen. Mgr.-KSTP-TV)*
Robert W. Hubbard *(V.P.)*
Stanley E. Hubbard II *(V.P.)*
Carlos W. Luis *(V.P.)*
Kathryn Hubbard Rominski *(Sec. & Dir.-Hubbard Foundation)*
Tom Newberry *(Controller)*
John McDonough *(Gen. Counsel)*
Bruce Hagerty *(Dir.-Pur.)*
Tom Hofkes *(Dir.-Data Processing)*

No. of U.S. Offices: 12

Computer Systems/Hardware:
IBM System 38

Outside Service Firm(s):

Ernst & Young*(Auditors)*
1300 Huntington Bldg.
Cleveland, OH 44115
Tel.: 216-861-5000
Fax: 303-291-6234

Fletcher, Heald & Hildreth*(Legal Firm)*
1225 Connecticut Ave., N.W.
Washington, DC 20036

Leonard, Street & Deinard*(Legal Firm)*
150 S. Fifth St., Ste. 2300
Minneapolis, MN 55402
Tel.: 612-335-1500

Division:

KSTP-TV **(1)**
3415 University Ave.
Saint Paul, MN 55114
Tel.: 612-646-5555
Fax: 612-642-4172
Emp.: 225
TV Station
S.I.C.: 4833
Stanley S. Hubbard *(Chm. Bd. & Chief Exec. Officer)*
Harold C. Crump *(Pres. & Gen. Mgr.)*
Dixie Hansen *(V.P. & Business Mgr.)*
Mendes Napoli *(V.P. & News Dir.)*
John Degan *(V.P. & Program Dir.)*
Karl Gensheimer *(V.P. & Dir.-Sls.)*
John McDonough *(Legal Counsel)*
Lori Shefa *(Dir.-Adv. & Promotion)*
Dayna Deutsch *(Dir.-Public Affairs)*
Bruce Hagerty *(Dir.-Pur.)*
Tom Hofkes *(Data Processing Mgr.)*

Subsidiaries:

CONUS Communication Company Limited Partnership **(1)**
3415 University Ave.
St. Paul, MN 55114
Tel.: 612-642-4645
Fax: 612-642-4680
Emp.: 12
News Gathering Services for Television
S.I.C.: 4899
Charles Dutcher *(V.P. & Gen. Mgr.)*

F & F Productions, Inc. **(1)**
9675 Fourth St. N.
St. Petersburg, FL 33702
Tel.: 813-576-7676 (80%)
Fax: 813-577-5011
Emp.: 27
Remote TV Broadcasting
S.I.C.: 4833
George Orgera *(Pres.)*
Bob Elsenstaedt *(Mgr.)*

Hubbard Communications **(1)**
9675 Fourth St. N.
St. Petersburg, FL 33702
Tel.: 813-572-7759 (80%)
Fax: 813-573-0314
Emp.: 3
Television Satellite Trucks
S.I.C.: 3669
George Orgera *(Pres.)*

KOB-TV, Inc. **(1)**
4 Broadcast Plaza S.W.
Albuquerque, NM 87103
Tel.: 505-243-4411 (100%)
Telex: 910 989 1682
Fax: 505-764-2456
Emp.: 112
TV Station
S.I.C.: 4833
Jerry Danziger *(Vice Chm.)*
Dave Herman *(Pres.)*

KSTP-AM, Inc. **(1)**
2792 Maplewood Dr.
Maplewood, MN 55109
Tel.: 612-481-9333 (100%)
Fax: 612-481-9324
Emp.: 44
AM Radio Station
S.I.C.: 4832
Virginia Morris *(V.P. & G.M.)*
Mike Boen *(Station & Sls. Mgr.)*

KSTP-FM, Inc. **(1)**
3415 University Ave.
St. Paul, MN 55114
Tel.: 612-646-5555 (100%)
Fax: 612-642-4142
Emp.: 29
FM Radio Station
S.I.C.: 4832
John Mayasich *(V.P. & G.M.)*
John Rohm *(Station Mgr. & Sls. Dir.)*

Pan American Ocean Resort Hotel **(1)**
17875 Collins Ave.
Miami Beach, FL 33154
Tel.: 305-932-1100 (100%)
Fax: 305-935-2769
Emp.: 100
Resort Motel
S.I.C.: 7011
Bruce Lange *(Mgr.)*

United States Satellite Broadcasting, Inc. **(1)**
3415 University Ave.
St. Paul, MN 55114
Tel.: 612-645-4500
Telex: 989092
Fax: 612-642-4103
Emp.: 8
Direct Broadcasting Satellite
S.I.C.: 4899
Stanley S. Hubbard *(Pres. & Chief Exec. Officer)*

Subsidiary:

WDIO-TV **(2)**
10 Observation Rd.
Duluth, MN 55811
Tel.: 218-727-6864
Emp.: 80
S.I.C.: 4833
George Couture *(Station & Sls. Mgr.)*

WTOG-TV, Inc. **(1)**
365 105th Terrace N.E.
St. Petersburg, FL 33716
Tel.: 813-576-4444 (100%)
Fax: 813-577-1806
Emp.: 66
TV Station
S.I.C.: 4833
Ed Aiken *(Gen. Mgr.)*
Mike Gehring *(Sls. Dir.)*

HUBBARD CONSTRUCTION CO.
1936 Lee Rd.
Winter Park, FL 32789
Mailing Address:
P.O. Box 547217
Orlando, FL 32854
Tel.: 407-645-5500
Fax: 407-623-3865
Year Founded: 1920
Approx.Sls.: $140,000,000
Emp.: 1,190
Fiscal Year-end: 12/31/90
Heavy Construction
S.I.C.: 1611; 1629; 1623
Jean Marc Allard *(Chm. Bd., Pres. & Chief Exec. Officer)*
Thomas Grimes *(V.P.-Data Processing)*
Ray Link *(V.P. & Chief Fin. Officer)*
Tom Rice *(V.P.-Opers.)*
Margaret Collins *(Dir.-Human Rels.)*

No. of Mfg. Plants/Facilities: 7
No. of U.S. Offices: 2

Computer Systems/Hardware:
IBM A/S 400

Outside Service Firm(s):

Arthur Andersen & Co.*(Auditors)*
200 S. Orange Ave., Ste. 2100
Orlando, FL 32801

CNA Insurance*(Commercial Insurance Carrier)*
CNA Plaza,
Chicago, IL 60685
Tel.: 312-822-5000

Aetna Life & Casualty*(Group Insurer)*
151 Farmington Avenue
Hartford, CT 06156
Tel.: 203-273-2128
Fax: 203-729-4295

Maguire, Voorhis & Wells*(Legal Firm)*
Two S. Orange Plz.
Orlando, FL 32801
Tel.: 407-843-4421

Sun Bank, N.A.*(Major Banking Relationship)*
200 S. Orange Ave.
Orlando, FL 32802
Tel.: 407-237-4899
Fax: 407-237-6704

Sun Bank, N.A.*(Pension Manager)*
200 S. Orange Ave.
Orlando, FL 32802
Tel.: 407-237-4899
Fax: 407-237-6704

Division:

Atlantic Coast Asphalt **(1)**
5154 Edwards St.
Jacksonville, FL 32205
Tel.: 904-786-1020

HUBBARD HALL INC.
563 S. Leonard St.
Waterbury, CT 06708
Mailing Address:
P.O. Box 790
Waterbury, CT 06725
Tel.: 203-756-5531
Tel.: 800-648-3412 CT
Fax: 203-756-9017
Year Founded: 1849
Sales Range: $20-39 Million
Emp.: 103
Fiscal Year-end: 9/31/91
Export
Metal Finishing & Industrial Chemicals
S.I.C.: 5169; 2812; 2819
Corporate Giving Program: United Way
Charles T. Kellogg *(Pres., Chief Exec. Officer & Treas.)*
A.N. Nardella *(Sr. V.P.-Distribution)*
Patrick Caruto *(V.P.-Rhode Island Div.)*
A.K. Skipp *(V.P.-Sls.)*
D. Stabile *(V.P.-Admin.)*
D. MacPartland *(Sec.)*
Molly Kellogg *(Dir.-Communications)*
Brent Burleson *(Gen. Mgr.-Southern Div.)*
Terry Post *(Mgr.-Mfg.)*
Principal(s):
Kellogg Family

No. of Mfg. Plants/Facilities: 2
No. of U.S. Offices: 4

Computer Systems/Hardware:
Data General

Outside Service Firm(s):

Lenkowski, Lonergan & Company*(Auditors)*
Waterbury, CT

Secor, Cassidy & McPartland*(Legal Firm)*
Waterbury, CT

Bank of Boston*(Major Banking Relationship)*
81 W. Main St.
Waterbury, CT 06702
Tel.: 203-574-7000

Division:

Mitchell-Bradford International **(1)**
563 S. Leonard St.
Waterbury, CT 06708
Tel.: 203-756-5521
Specialty Chemicals; Rust Inhibitors; Black Oxides
S.I.C.: 2819
Robert Farrell *(Gen. Mgr.)*

HUBBARD MILLING COMPANY
424 N. Riverfront Dr.
Mankato, MN 56002
Mailing Address:
P.O. Box 8500
Mankato, MN 56002-8500
Tel.: 507-388-9400 MN
Fax: 507-389-9427
Year Founded: 1878
Approx.Sls.: $300,000,000
Emp.: 1,200
Fiscal Year-end: 4/30/91
Export
Mfr. of Feed & Pet Food
S.I.C.: 2048; 2045; 2047
Richard P. Confer *(Pres. & Chief Exec. Officer)*
Ogden W. Confer *(Sr. V.P., Sec. & Chief Fin. Officer)*
Denis J. Daly *(Sr. V.P.)*
Gerald K. Corley *(V.P.)*
Paul Holzhueter *(V.P.)*
Timothy Violet *(V.P.-Legal)*
Harold Grems *(Dir.-Data Processing & Telecommunications)*
James Hoffman *(Dir.-Pur.)*
David T. Knutson *(Dir.-Personnel)*
Brian Mechler *(Mgr.-Mktg. Services)*

Computer Systems/Hardware:
Unisys Model 50

Outside Service Firm(s):

KPMG Peat Marwick*(Auditors)*
4200 Norwest Center, 90 S. 7th St.
Minneapolis, MN 55402
Tel.: 612-341-2222

Prudential Insurance Co. of America*(Group Insurer)*
751 Broad St.
Newark, NJ 07102-3777
Tel.: 201-802-6000

Faegre & Benson*(Legal Firm)*
2200 Norwest Ctr., 90 S. 7th St.
Minneapolis, MN 55402-3901
Tel.: 612-336-3000
Fax: 612-336-3026

First National Bank of Minneapolis*(Major Banking Relationship)*
Minneapolis, MN

Norwest Bank Minnesota, N.A.*(Major Banking Relationship)*
6th St. & Marquette Av.
Minneapolis, MN 55479
Tel.: 612-667-1234

Massachusetts Mutual Life Insurance Co.*(Pension Manager)*
1295 State Street
Springfield, MA 01111
Tel.: 413-788-8411

Prudential Insurance Co. of America*(Pension Manager)*
751 Broad St.
Newark, NJ 07102-3777
Tel.: 201-802-6000

Divisions:

Feed Div. **(1)**
P.O. Box 8500, 424 N. Riverfront Dr.
Mankato, MN 56002
Tel.: 507-625-1882
Prepared Feed
S.I.C.: 2048
G. Corley *(Chief Oper. Officer)*

Hubbard Petfood **(1)**
424 N. Riverfront Dr.
Mankato, MN 56002
Tel.: 507-625-1882
Manufacture Pet Food
S.I.C.: 2047
Paul Holzhueter *(Chief Oper. Officer)*

Hubbard West **(1)**
426 Omaha St.
Rapid City, SD 57709
Tel.: 605-342-6172
Flour
S.I.C.: 2041
Dennis Fredericksen *(Chief Oper. Officer)*

Schreiber Milling Co. **(1)**
8th & Mitchell Sts.
Saint Joseph, MO 64503
Tel.: 816-279-1631
Emp.: 75
Manufacture Pet Food & Dairy Feeds
S.I.C.: 2048; 2047
Robert Bucher *(Mgr.)*
Dwight Norris *(Sls. Mgr.)*

Hubbard Milling Company—(Continued)

Springfield Milling Corp. **(1)**
101 So. Cass St.
Springfield, MN 56087
Tel.: 507-723-4242
Feed Manufacturing
S.I.C.: 2048
Carl Todilben *(Chief Oper. Officer)*

Subsidiary:

Vigorena Feeds, Inc. **(1)**
P.O. Box 1205, West Hwy. #7
Storm Lake, IA 50588
Tel.: 712-732-4676 (100%)
Feed Manufacturing
S.I.C.: 2048
Russell Brugman *(Chief Oper. Officer)*

HUBBS IMPORTING CORP.
436 Old Hook Rd.
Emerson, NJ 07630
Tel.: 201-261-0033
Fax: 201-261-5630
Year Founded: 1953
Sales Range: $10-19 Million
Emp.: 37
Fiscal Year-end: 12/31/90
Import Export
Import, Export & Distribute Food & Confectionery Products; Merchandising & Product Licensing
S.I.C.: 5145; 5141; 9651
Kurt Rosenberg *(Chm. Bd.)*
Michael G. Rosenberg *(Pres.)*

Computer Systems/Hardware:
IBM

Division:

Vienna Biscuit Co. **(1)**
436 Old Hook Rd.
Emerson, NJ 07630
Tel.: 201-261-0033
Import Export
Kurt Rosenberg *(Chief Oper. Officer)*
Joe Edwards *(Dir.-Sls.)*
Michael Rosenberg *(Dir.-Mktg.)*

HUBER®

J.M. HUBER CORPORATION
333 Thornall St.
Edison, NJ 08818
Tel.: 908-549-8600 **NJ**
Fax: 908-549-0410
Year Founded: 1927
Assets: $741,000,000
Liabilities: $276,000,000
Net Worth: $465,000,000
Approx.Sls.: $874,000,000
Emp.: 5,306
Fiscal Year-end: 12/31/91
Import Export
Production of Crude Oil, Natural Gas, Kaolin Clay & Calcium Carbonate; Manufacture of Carbon, Black Printing Ink, Inorganic Chemicals, Pigments, Reconstituted Wood Products, Oil Field Equipment, Industrial Valves & Contract Electronics Manufacturing
S.I.C.: 1311; 3295; 2895; 2893; 2899; 2816; 3823; 3491; 3679
Employee Matching Gifts Program: Accredited Schools & Colleges; No Limitations
M.W. Huber *(Chm. Bd.)*
George Schenk *(Pres. & Chief Exec. Officer)*
W.J. Ryan *(Sr. V.P. & Chief Fin. Officer)*
E.L. Russell *(Grp. V.P. Human Res.)*
Oscar T. Scott IV *(Grp. V.P.)*
S.C. Danatos *(V.P.-Taxes)*
F.S. Gersten *(V.P. & Treas.)*
Brian M. Keidon *(V.P.-Corp. Devel.)*
M.I. Pearlman *(V.P.-Facilities)*
John Shiels *(V.P.-Information Services)*
Peter W. Tortorello *(V.P. & Controller)*
J.G. Webb *(V.P. & Gen. Counsel)*
Robin Wahl *(Mgr.-Treas. Services)*

No. of Mfg. Plants/Facilities: 35
No. of U.S. Offices: 11
No. of Foreign Offices: 4

Computer Systems/Hardware:
IBM

Outside Service Firm(s):

KPMG Peat Marwick*(Auditors)*
345 Park Ave.
New York, NY 10154
Tel.: 212-758-9700
Fax: 212-872-3308

Prudential Insurance Co. of America*(Group Insurer)*
751 Broad St.
Newark, NJ 07102-3777
Tel.: 201-802-6000

Chase Manhattan Bank, N.A.*(Major Banking Relationship)*
One Chase Manhattan Plaza
New York, NY 10081
Tel.: 212-552-2222
Tel.: 800-526-0801
Fax: 212-552-7175

Alliance Capital Management*(Pension Manager)*
1345 Avenue of the Americas
New York, NY 10017

Bankers Trust Co.*(Pension Manager)*
P.O. Box 9050, Church St. Station
New York, NY 10008
Tel.: 212-250-6037

Ferguson & Wellman*(Pension Manager)*
Washington, DC

GAMCO Investors, Inc.*(Pension Manager)*
655 Third Ave.
New York, NY 10017
Tel.: 212-972-6479
Fax: 212-557-1424

Scudder, Stevens & Clark*(Pension Manager)*
New York, NY

State Street Bank & Trust Co.*(Pension Manager)*
225 Franklin St.
Boston, MA 02101
Tel.: 617-654-3652

Divisions:

J.M. Huber, Calcium Carbonate Div. **(1)**
3150 Gardner Expwy.
Quincy, IL 62301
Tel.: 217-224-1100
Export
Industrial Fillers; Micro Nutrients for Feed
S.I.C.: 1422
R.B. Black *(V.P. & Gen. Mgr.)*
G.D. Anderson *(Controller)*
J.T. Hawk *(Dir.-Mktg.)*
D. Salisbury *(Pur. Agent)*
K. Goerlich *(Pur. Agent)*

J.M. Huber, Chemicals Division **(1)**
907 Revolution St.
Havre de Grace, MD 21078
Tel.: 301-939-3500
Export
Synthetic & Inorganic Pigments & Fillers
S.I.C.: 2816
S.K. Wason *(V.P.)*
L.J. Marrapodi *(Controller)*
T.J. Krieg *(Dir.-Sls.)*
J.E. Luppino *(Dir.-Pur.)*

J.M. Huber, Clay Div. **(1)**
One Huber Rd.
Macon, GA 31298
Tel.: 912-745-4751
Export
Kaolin Based Coatings; Filler Pigments
S.I.C.: 1455
J.J. Ferro *(V.P.)*
J.K. Bellnap *(V.P.-Mktg.)*
M.E. Cumpton *(Controller)*
S.H. Henderson *(Dir.-Pur.)*

J.M. Huber, Engineered Carbons Div. **(1)**
1110 Penn Ave.
Borger, TX 79007
Tel.: 806-274-6331
Export
Carbon Black
S.I.C.: 2895
J.L. Clem *(V.P.)*
K.E. Grodd *(V.P.-Mktg.)*
B.E. Burnham *(Controller)*
D. Cleveland *(Pur. Agent)*

J.M. Huber, Flow Control Div. **(1)**
14011 Park Ave., Ste. 201
Tomball, TX 77375
Tel.: 713-351-2222
Export
Oil Field Equipment; Industrial Flow Control Devices
S.I.C.: 3494
H.M. Hoff *(V.P.)*
D.P. Jatzlau *(Controller)*
S. Witte *(Mgr.-Mktg.)*
M. Plympton *(Mgr.-Mktg.)*
T. Clifton *(Pur. Agent)*

J.M. Huber, Oil & Gas Div. **(1)**
1900 West Loop So., Flrs. 16 & 17
Houston, TX 77027
Tel.: 713-871-4400
Export
Crude Oil; Natural Gas
S.I.C.: 1311
David B. Martin *(V.P.)*
H.L. Curtis *(V.P.-Mktg.)*
D.J. Sebastian *(Controller)*
R.D. Hanley *(Pur. Agent)*

J.M. Huber, Polymer Services Div. **(1)**
6522 Interstate Hwy. 10 W.
Orange, TX 77630
Tel.: 409-883-4331
Toll/Custom Plastics Compounding
S.I.C.: 2824
Donald E. Oakley *(V.P.)*
L.J. Fisher *(Controller)*
D.C. Cox *(Mgr.-Mktg.)*

J.M. Huber, Printing Ink Div. **(1)**
333 Thornall St.
Edison, NJ 08818
Tel.: 908-906-1760
News/Container Inks
S.I.C.: 2893
J.E. Coleman *(V.P.)*
J.A. Gamache *(Mgr.-Pur.)*
W.I. Roberts *(V.P.-Mktg.)*
J.M. Venditti *(Controller)*
F. Portaro *(Pur. Agent)*

J.M. Huber, Solem Div. **(1)**
4940 Peachtree Industrial Blvd.,Ste. 340
Norcross, GA 30071
Tel.: 404-441-1301
Import Export
Smoke Control Additives; High Brightness Pigments
S.I.C.: 2819
C.A. Snyder *(V.P.)*
D. Dubrow *(Controller)*
T.R. Cook *(Mgr.-Mktg.)*

J.M. Huber, Wood Products Div. **(1)**
Mallard Creek Ctr. III-Ste.175, 8604 Cliff Cameron Dr.
Charlotte, NC 28269
Tel.: 704-547-0671
Export
Timber; Oriented Strand Board
S.I.C.: 2493
R.J. Adams *(V.P.)*
G.M. Collins *(Controller)*
J.A. Rogalski *(Mgr.-Mktg.)*
W. Weatherhead *(Pur. Agent)*
R. Purvis *(Pur. Agent)*

Subsidiary:

AVEX Electronics, Inc. **(1)**
4807 Bradford Dr.
Huntsville, AL 35805
Tel.: 205-722-6000
Contract Electronics Manufacturing
S.I.C.: 3679
V.B. Ramsey *(Pres.)*
J.H. Fleddermann *(Controller)*
J.C. Roberts *(Pur. Agent)*

Non-U.S. Subsidiaries:

Avex Electronics Ltd. **(1)**
East Kilbride, United Kingdom

Avex Electronics Pte. Ltd. **(1)**
510 Thomson Rd. # 14-03
Singapore, Singapore
Tel.: 258 8055
Fax: 259 9827

Zlofin Oy **(1)**
Hamina, Finland

HUBERT COMPANY
9555 Dry Fork Rd.
Harrison, OH 45030
Tel.: 513-367-8600 **DE**
Fax: 513-367-8603
Year Founded: 1946
Approx.Sls.: $38,000,000
Emp.: 250
Wholesale Distribution of Store Fixture & Equipment For Supermarkets
S.I.C.: 5046
Edward Hubert *(Chm. Bd.)*
Howard Thomas *(Pres. & Chief Exec. Officer)*
George J. Hubert, Jr. *(V.P. & Sec.)*

Outside Service Firm(s):

Provident Bank*(Major Banking Relationship)*
One E. Fourth St.
Cincinnati, OH 45202
Tel.: 513-579-2731

THE HUBINGER COMPANY
(Member of Roquette Group)
P.O. Box 6647,
Keokuk, IA 52632
Tel.: 319-524-5757
Approx.Sls.: $200,000,000
Emp.: 470
Fiscal Year-end: 4/30/91
Export
Mfr. of Hi-Fructose Corn Syrup, Corn Syrup Solids, Corn Starch; Wet Corn Milling
S.I.C.: 2046
Bruce W. Brown *(Pres. & Chief Exec. Officer)*
W. Edwards *(V.P.-Pur.)*
K.W. Fink *(V.P.-Human Resources)*
Ivan Hasselbjocit *(V.P.-Fin.)*
J.F. Holsinger *(V.P.-Sls. & Mktg.)*
E.L. Karcher *(V.P.-Opers.)*
Kathy Eberline *(Gen. Mgr.-Mktg.)*

HUBLER CHEVROLET INC.
8220 S. U.S. 31
Indianapolis, IN 46227
Tel.: 317-882-4389 **IN**
Fax: 317-881-2954
Year Founded: 1961
Approx.Sls.: $64,600,000
Emp.: 172
Retail Automotive Sales & Service
S.I.C.: 5511
Howard Hubler *(Pres.)*
Rob Wilson *(Sec. & Treas.)*
Bob Day *(Mgr.-Sls.)*
Principal(s):
Howard Hubler
Bradley Hubler
John Hubler

HUDEPOHL-SCHOENLING BREWING COMPANY
1625 Central Pkwy.
Cincinnati, OH 45214
Tel.: 513-241-4344
Tel.: 515-721-7278=brewery
Fax: 513-241-2452
Sales Range: $20-39 Million
Emp.: 102
Beer Brewers
S.I.C.: 2082
Kenneth Lichtendahl *(Pres.)*

Charles Lichtendahl *(Exec. V.P.)*
Steve Reith *(Comptroller)*
Francie Patton *(Dir.-Pub. Rels.)*
John Toener *(Dir.-Personnel & Mgr.-Plant)*
Gerhard Erftenbeck *(Brewmaster)*

No. of Mfg. Plants/Facilities: 2
No. of U.S. Offices: 2

Computer Systems/Hardware:
IBM System 36

Outside Service Firm(s):

Ernst & Young*(Auditors)*
1300 Chiquita Center, 250 E. Fifth St.
Cincinnati, OH 45202
Tel.: 513-621-6454

Blue Cross & Blue Shield Association*(Group Insurer)*
Cincinnati, OH

Fidelity Fund*(Group Insurer)*
Newark, NJ

Star Bank*(Major Banking Relationship)*
425 Walnut Street
Cincinnati, OH 45202
Tel.: 513-632-4000

HUDSON & AFFILIATED CO.
4720 Rainbow Blvd.
Shawnee Mission, KS 66205
Tel.: 913-362-4000
Fax: 913-362-0937
Petroleum Refining; Automotive Dealer; Service Stations
S.I.C.: 2911; 5172; 5541
Thomas M. Raimo *(Pres. & Chief Exec. Officer)*
Joyce Cady *(V.P.)*
Frank Zimmerman *(Treas., Controller & Chief Fin. Officer)*

Computer Systems/Hardware:
IBM System 36

Outside Service Firm(s):

Blue Cross & Blue Shield of Kansas City*(Group Insurer)*
Kansas City, MO

H.D. HUDSON MANUFACTURING COMPANY
500 N. Michigan Ave.
Chicago, IL 60611
Tel.: 312-644-2830 **MN**
Year Founded: 1905
Emp.: 220
Mfr. of Agricultural Sprayers & Spraying Machines; Mechanical Dusters
S.I.C.: 3523
Robert C. Hudson, Jr. *(Pres. & Treas.)*
E.R. Sorenson *(Exec. V.P.)*
John C. Romans *(Sr. V.P. & Sec.)*
Jim Burke *(Chief Fin. Officer)*

Outside Service Firm(s):

Continental Bank N. A.*(Major Banking Relationship)*
231 S. LaSalle St.
Chicago, IL 60697
Tel.: 312-828-2345
Tel.: 800-426-5754
Telex: 312-828-1783

Subsidiary:

Green Garde **(1)**
500 N. Michigan Ave.
Chicago, IL 60611
Tel.: 312-644-2830
Tel.: 800-Lady-Bug
Fax: 312-644-7989
Emp.: 7
Import Export
Mfr. of Horticultural Products
S.I.C.: 3423; 2879
Gene Short *(Natl. Sls. Mgr.)*

JIM HUDSON, PONTIAC, OLDSMOBILE GMC
7201 Sumter Hwy.
Columbia, SC 29209
Tel.: 803-783-0110 **SC**
Fax: 803-695-2477
Approx.Sls.: $80,000,000
Emp.: 150
Retail Automobiles & Trucks
S.I.C.: 5511
James E. Hudson *(Pres.)*
Greg Richardson *(V.P.-Sls.)*
Donald W. Deese *(Sec. & Controller)*
Lorraine Lester *(Dir.-Fin.)*

Outside Service Firm(s):

C. C. McGregor & Co.*(Auditors)*
Columbia, SC

Callison, Tighe, Rush, Robinson*(Legal Firm)*
Columbia, SC

South Carolina National Bank*(Major Banking Relationship)*
Columbia, SC

Hudson Valley Apple Products Company
(See Jim Hudson, Pontiac, Oldsmobile GMC)

HUDSON VALLEY PAPER COMPANY
981 Broadway
Albany, NY 12201
Mailing Address:
PO Box 1988, 981 Broadway
Albany, NY 12201-1988
Tel.: 518-436-8481
Tel.: 518-471-5111
Fax: 518-455-8803
Year Founded: 1875
Sales Range: $20-39 Million
Emp.: 90
Fiscal Year-end: 12/31/91
Printing, Writing & Business Paper & Supplies
S.I.C.: 5111; 5112; 5113
Sydney T. Jones III *(Pres. & Treas.)*
Kurt Van Steemburg *(V.P.)*
Anthony Kugler *(Mgr.-Fin. & Corp. Sec.)*
Tom Kurtyka *(Mgr.-Warehouse Oper.)*
Joe Tierney *(Mgr.-Cust. Serv.)*
Dave Manoni *(Mgr.-Purch.)*
Donna Peffley *(Mgr.-Human Res.)*
John Haulik *(Mgr.-Credit)*

Outside Service Firm(s):

Bollam, Sheedy, Torani & Co.*(Auditors)*
Albany, NY

McNamee, Lochner, Titus & Williams*(Legal Firm)*
Albany, NY

Society National Bank*(Major Banking Relationship)*
900 Euclid Ave., P.O. Box 6477
Cleveland, OH 44101-6477
Tel.: 216-737-5000
Fax: 216-566-8947

Key Bank*(Major Banking Relationship)*
Albany, NY

HUDSON VALLEY TREE, INC.
840 Broadway
Newburgh, NY 12550
Tel.: 914-562-0070
Fax: 914-561-8029
Year Founded: 1982
Sales Range: $20-39 Million
Emp.: 1,000
Fiscal Year-end: 3/31/91
Import
Mfg. of Artificial Christmas Trees, Wreaths & Garlands
S.I.C.: 3999

Si Spiegel *(Pres.)*
Larry Squarci *(V.P.)*
Howard J. Weiss *(Gen. Counsel)*
Irwin Katz *(Dir.-Fin.)*
Sam Leone *(Dir.-Mfg.)*
Tamio Spiegel *(Mgr.-Natl. Sls.)*
Lorraine Squarci *(Mgr.-Pur.)*

No. of Mfg. Plants/Facilities: 2

Outside Service Firm(s):

Howard J. Weiss, CPA*(Auditors)*
Chappaqua, NY

Kemper Insurance*(Group Insurer)*
New York, NY

CNA Insurance*(Commercial Insurance Carrier)*
CNA Plaza,
Chicago, IL 60685
Tel.: 312-822-5000

USF & G*(Commercial Insurance Carrier)*
Baltimore, MD

Norstar Bank, N.A.*(Major Banking Relationship)*
Newburgh, NY

Norstar Employee Benefit Services, Inc.*(Major Banking Relationship)*
Albany, NY

BARRY HUEY, BULLOCK & COOK ADVERTISING, INC.
3800 Colonnade Pkwy., Ste. 400
Birmingham, AL 35243
Tel.: 205-969-3200
Fax: 205-969-3136
Year Founded: 1973
Approx.Billings: $12,500,000
Emp.: 28
Barry Huey *(Chm. Bd. & Chief Exec. Officer)*
Jess Bullock, III *(Vice Chm.)*
Ken W. Cook *(Pres. & Chief Oper. Officer)*
Brenda Huey *(Exec. V.P., Chief Fin. Officer)*
Vince Thompson *(V.P., Pub. Rels. Group)*
Marsha Thompson *(V.P., Acct. Service Admin.)*

S. E. HUFFMAN CORP.
1050 Huffman Way
Clover, SC 29710
Tel.: 803-222-4561 **SC**
Telex: 53-2735
Fax: 803-222-7599
Year Founded: 1961
Approx.Sls.: $22,000,000
Emp.: 145
Import Export
Manufacture Custom Tool & Cutter Grinders, Laser Drilling Machines & Waterjets
S.I.C.: 3546; 3541
Crandall Bowles *(Chm. Bd.)*
William Taylor *(Pres. & Chief Exec. Officer)*
Allen Turk *(Pres. & Chief Oper. Officer)*
Ernst Borchert *(V.P.-Advanced Engrng.)*
Frank Kellar *(Dir.-Engrng.)*
Alan Mandell *(V.P.-Sls. & Mktg.)*
Robert McBurney *(V.P.-Admin. & Controller)*
Thad Baird *(Dir.-Opers.)*

No. of Mfg. Plants/Facilities: 1
No. of U.S. Offices: 1
No. of Foreign Offices: 1

Computer Systems/Hardware:
IBM, Digital

Outside Service Firm(s):

Deloitte & Touche*(Auditors)*
2000 First Citizens Bank Plaza, 128 S. Tryon St.
Charlotte, NC 28202-5001
Tel.: 704-372-3560

Branch Banking & Trust Co.*(Major Banking Relationship)*
Gastonia, NC

HUFFMAN KOOS CO.
Route 4 & Main St.
River Edge, NJ 07661
Tel.: 201-343-4300
Fax: 201-343-0575
Earnings: $347,000
Approx.Sls.: $82,900,000
Emp.: 550
Fiscal Year-end: 1/31/92
Home Furnishings Store
S.I.C.: 5712
Fred Berk *(Pres., Chief Exec. & Chief Oper. Officer)*

NEIL HUFFMAN NISSAN INC.
(Formerly Neil Huffman Nissan-Volkswagen Inc.)
3922 Dutchmans Lane
Louisville, KY 40207
Tel.: 502-897-3151 **KY**
Fax: 502-897-0888
Sales Range: $20-39 Million
Emp.: 105
Automobile Dealerships
S.I.C.: 5511
Neil Huffman *(Pres. & Chief Oper. Officer)*
Ethel Huffman *(V.P.)*
Kip Huffman *(Sec. & Treas.)*

Subsidiaries:

Neil Huffman Volkswagon Mazda Suburu **(1)**
4926 Dixi Highway
Louisville, KY 40216
Tel.: 502-448-6666
Automobile Dealership
S.I.C.: 5511
Neil Huffman *(Pres.)*

Neil Huffman Chrysler Plymouth Dodge **(1)**
4126 Shelbyville Rd.
Louisville, KY 40207
Tel.: 502-897-0601
Automobile Dealership
S.I.C.: 5511
Neil Huffman *(Pres.)*

HUGHES
Advertising, Public Relations, Direct Marketing, Promotion.

HUGHES ADVERTISING INC.
130 S. Bemiston
Saint Louis, MO 63105
Tel.: 314-721-3400
Fax: 314-862-1616
Year Founded: 1977
Approx.Billings: $21,050,000
Emp.: 42
Jack A. Hughes *(Pres. & Treas.)*
Larry R. McLane *(Exec. V.P.)*
Henry George *(Sr. V.P., Retail Grp.)*
Walter L. Metcalfe, Jr. *(Sec.)*
Jan Sheehan *(Pub. Rels. Dir.)*
Ashley Slama *(Acctg. & Data Processing Mgr.)*

R. S. HUGHES CO., INC.
5303 San Fernando Rd., W.
Los Angeles, CA 90039
Tel.: 818-500-1221

R. S. Hughes Co., Inc.—(Continued)

Fax: 818-240-7016
Year Founded: 1954
Assets: $8,500,000
Earnings: $1,870,000
Net Worth: $8,500,000
Approx.Sls.: $45,000,000
Emp.: 200
Industrial Distributor of Adhesives, Tape & Safety Products
S.I.C.: 5169
Robert McCollum *(Chm. Bd. & Chief Exec. Officer)*
Rose Stone *(V.P. & Sec.)*

Computer Systems/Hardware:
IBM System 36

Outside Service Firm(s):

Arthur Andersen & Co.*(Auditors)*
633 W. Fifth St.
Los Angeles, CA 90071
Tel.: 213-614-6500

American General Life Insurance Co.*(Group Insurer)*
2727 Allen Pkwy.
Houston, TX 77019
Tel.: 713-522-1111

Security Pacific Corporation*(Investment Banker)*
Security Pacific Plaza
Los Angeles, CA 90071
Tel.: 213-345-6211
Fax: 213-625-0809

E.H. HUGHES COMPANY, INC.
340 Byrne Ave.
Louisville, KY 40217
Mailing Address:
P.O. Box 17552
Louisville, KY 40217
Tel.: 502-636-3411
Fax: 502-634-8809
Approx.Sls.: $60,000,000
Emp.: 569
General Contractor, Highway; Coal Mining; Asphalt
S.I.C.: 1221; 1499; 1622
George E. Hughes, Sr. *(Chm. Bd.)*
George E. Huges, Jr. *(Pres.)*
Grant Morton *(Sec. & Treas.)*

HERMAN HUGHES & SONS, INC.
900 N. Redwood Rd.
North Salt Lake, UT 84054
Tel.: 801-292-1411 **UT**
Fax: 801-295-0530
Emp.: 45
Commercial & Industrial Builders; Civil Engineering
S.I.C.: 1542
Glenn E. Hughes *(Pres.)*
Gary V. Smith *(Sec. & Treas.)*

Outside Service Firm(s):

Weeks & Patterson*(Legal Firm)*
Salt Lake City, UT

HUGHES MARKETS INC.
19005 Live Oak Ave.
Irwindale, CA 91706
Tel.: 818-856-6580
Fax: 213-227-6983
Year Founded: 1952
Approx.Sls.: $688,000,000
Emp.: 4,500
Grocery Stores
S.I.C.: 5411
Roger K. Hughes *(Chm. Bd.)*
Fred B. McLaren *(Pres.)*
Allen Brennan *(V.P.-Fin.)*
Harland L. Polk *(V.P.-Sls.)*
Paul Hughes *(Sec.)*
Jack Ackroyd *(Dir.-Adv.)*
Principal(s):
Roger K. Hughes

Computer Systems/Hardware:
IBM 4341

Outside Service Firm(s):

Arthur Andersen & Co.*(Auditors)*
633 W. Fifth St.
Los Angeles, CA 90071
Tel.: 213-614-6500

Willis & Urick*(Legal Firm)*
Los Angeles, CA

Union Bank*(Major Banking Relationship)*
Glendale, CA

Joint Venture:

Santee Dairies **(1)**
231 E. 23rd St.
Los Angeles, CA 90011
Tel.: 213-744-7000
Dairy & Specialty Food Products; Joint Venture of Stater Bros., Inc. & Hughes Markets Inc.
S.I.C.: 2026

HUGHES-TREITLER MANUFACTURING CORPORATION
300 Endo Blvd.
Garden City, NY 11530
Tel.: 516-832-8811 **NY**
Fax: 516-832-8054
Year Founded: 1949
Approx.Sls.: $22,000,000
Emp.: 210
Precision Sheet Metal Fabrications & Aluminum Dip Brazed Fabrications For Electronics & Aerospace Industries; Vacuum Brazing
S.I.C.: 3444; 3499; 3724; 3728; 3769
Harold R. Finkelstein *(Chm. Bd.)*
Martin Koeppel *(Chief Exec. Officer)*
Abe Weinstein *(Chief Fin. Officer & V.P.)*
Marc S. Finkelstein *(Pres.)*
Bernard Andrejkovics *(V.P. & Sec.)*
Morton Baine *(V.P.)*
John Cirillo *(V.P.-Engrng.)*
Anthony Salucci *(V.P.-Mfg.)*
James A. Smith *(V.P.-Materials)*

Outside Service Firm(s):

Siegel & Weill*(Auditors)*
New York, NY

Miller & McCarthy*(Legal Firm)*
Garden City, NY

The Bank of New York*(Major Banking Relationship)*
101 Barclay St.
New York, NY 10286
Tel.: 212-815-2000

HUITT-ZOLLARS, INC.
3131 McKinney Ave., Ste. 600
Dallas, TX 75204
Tel.: 214-871-3311 **TX**
Fax: 214-871-0757
Year Founded: 1975
Sales Range: $10-19 Million
Emp.: 125
Fiscal Year-end: 1/31/92
Engineering & Planning Services
S.I.C.: 8711
E. Larry Huitt *(Chm. Bd., Sec. & Treas.)*
Robert L. Zollars *(Pres. & Chief Oper. Officer)*
Aubrey Adcock *(Sr. V.P.)*
George V. Marks *(Sr. V.P.-Mktg.)*
Andrew C. Oakley *(Sr. V.P. & Dir.-Engrng.)*
Robert L. Phillips *(Sr. V.P.)*
Stephen E. Shepard *(Sr. V.P.-Special Projects)*

No. of U.S. Offices: 4

Computer Systems/Hardware:
DEC VAX 11/751; CADD

HULL CORPORATION
3535 Davisville Rd.
Hatboro, PA 19040
Tel.: 215-672-7800
Fax: 215-672-7807
Year Founded: 1954
Approx.Sls.: $15,000,000
Emp.: 100
Export
Mfr. of Plastic Molding Machinery; Freezing Drying Equipment & Systems
S.I.C.: 3559; 3565
Lewis Hull *(Chm. Bd.)*
John L. Hull *(Vice Chm.)*
C. Ted Lind *(V.P.-Sls. & Mktg.)*
John J. Kalata *(V.P.-Fin.)*
Bob Heacock *(V.P.-Mfg.)*

HULMAN & COMPANY
900 Wabash Ave.
Terre Haute, IN 47808
Mailing Address:
P. O. Box 150
Terre Haute, IN 47808
Tel.: 812-232-9446
Fax: 812-232-2397
Emp.: 165
Fiscal Year-end: 12/31/90
Wholesale Groceries & General Merchandise
S.I.C.: 5141; 5199; 2099
Mary H. George *(Pres.)*
Robert L. Hippleheuser *(V.P. & Gen. Mgr.-Baking Powder Div.)*
Margaret Burke *(Sec.)*

No. of Mfg. Plants/Facilities: 1
No. of U.S. Offices: 1

Computer Systems/Hardware:
IBM 4341

Outside Service Firm(s):

First National Bank of Terre Haute*(Major Banking Relationship)*
Terre Haute, IN

Division:

KC Foods **(1)**
900 Wabash Ave.
Terre Haude, IN 47808
Baking Powder
Robert Hipplehauser *(Gen. Mgr.)*

HULT FRITZ MATUSZAK & ASSOCIATES, INC.
245 N. E. Perry Ave.
Peoria, IL 61603
Tel.: 309-673-8191
Fax: 309-674-5530
Year Founded: 1956
Approx.Billings: $10,000,000
Emp.: 24
Mark Matuszak *(Pres.)*
Adam Sloan *(Exec. V.P.)*

HUMBOLDT EXPRESS, INC.
345 Hill Ave.
Nashville, TN 37210
Mailing Address:
P.O. Box 100906,
Nashville, TN 37224
Tel.: 615-242-5552
Tel.: 800-333-3010 **TN**
Fax: 615-726-1980
Year Founded: 1960
Assets: $9,412,716
Liabilities: $3,644,810
Net Worth: $5,767,906
Approx.Sls.: $34,000,000
Emp.: 300
Fiscal Year-end: 12/31/89
Export
Trucking, General Freight Carrier, General Commodity & Interstate Trucking
S.I.C.: 4212
Corporate Giving Program: Company gives to The United Way
David D. Dortch, Sr. *(Chm. Bd.)*
Patrick Sharbel *(Pres. & Chief Exec. Officer)*
William M. Drake *(V.P.-Opers.)*
Steve Franklin *(V.P.-Mktg.)*
Tim Seneker *(V.P.-Sls.)*
Ron Lowell *(Gen. Counsel)*
Ruth W. Dortch *(Sec.)*
Stanford Pritchett *(Controller)*
David W. Dortch *(Dir.-Pur.)*
Linda Nicholson *(Dir.-Quality Control)*
Stan Pritchett *(Dir.-Fin.)*
John Vahrenkamp *(Dir.-Human Resources)*
Debra Walker *(Dir.-Data Processing)*
Kathi Dewitt *(Mgr.-Mngmt. Information Systems)*
Principal(s):
David D. Dortch, Sr.
Rose Ann Baird
David W. Dortch
Beth Franklin

No. of U.S. Offices: 39

Computer Systems/Hardware:
IBM 38; IBM 36

Outside Service Firm(s):

Frank Nolan*(Auditors)*
Nashville, TN

Security Insurance*(Commercial Insurance Carrier)*
Nashville, TN

Third National Bank*(Investment Banker)*
201 4th Ave. No., Uptown Sta., Box 2844
Nashville, TN 37167
Tel.: 615-748-4742

Ron Lowell*(Legal Firm)*
Nashville, TN

Third National Bank*(Major Banking Relationship)*
Nashville, TN

Subsidiary:

Star Trasnportation, Inc. **(1)**
P.O. Box 100906,
Nashville, TN 37224
Tel.: 615-256-4336
Tel.: 800-333-3060
Emp.: 275
Irregular Toute Truck Load Carrier
S.I.C.: 4212
David W. Dortch *(Pres.)*
Beth Franklin *(V.P.)*
Jim Brower *(Mgr.-Opers.)*
Rick Johnson *(Gen. Mgr.)*

HUMISTON-KEELING, INC.
233 E. Erie St.
Chicago, IL 60611
Tel.: 312-943-6066 **IL**
Fax: 312-751-0473
Year Founded: 1884
Approx.Sls.: $785,000,000
Emp.: 185
Fiscal Year-end: 5/ 2/91
Distribution of Drugs & Toiletries
S.I.C.: 5122; 5100
Burton H. Olin *(Chm. Bd. & Chief Exec. Officer)*
Larry G. Olin *(Pres., Chief Oper. Officer & Treas.)*
Louis Genesen *(Chief Fin. Officer & V.P.)*
Linda O. Milberg *(V.P.)*
Bernard G. Sang *(Sec. & Gen. Counsel)*
Lawrence Zwrek *(Controller)*
Gary Gutierrez *(Mgr.-Data Processing)*
Charles Maloley *(Mgr.-Sls.)*
Richard Meserve *(Mgr.-Human Resources)*
Harry Myers *(Gen. Mgr.)*
Paul Van Stadt *(Mgr.-Pur.)*

No. of Mfg. Plants/Facilities: 1

Computer Systems/Hardware:
IBM

Outside Service Firm(s):

Altschuler, Melvoin & Glasser*(Auditors)*
30 S. Wecker Dr.
Chicago, IL 60606
Tel.: 312-207-2800

Affiliated Plan Services*(Group Insurer)*
Chicago, IL

Young, Hauslinger & Rosen*(Legal Firm)*
Chicago, IL

First Chicago Bank*(Major Banking Relationship)*
One First National Plaza
Chicago, IL 60670

Subsidiaries:

Response Systems, Inc. **(1)**
735 Wyenel Dr.
Elm Grove, WI 53122
Tel.: 414-785-7900 (100%)
Data Processing Services
S.I.C.: 7374
D. Huisman *(Chief Oper. Officer)*

Williams Drugs Distributors **(1)**
233 E. Erie St.
Chicago, IL 60611
Tel.: 312-943-6066
Fax: 312-751-0473
Distr. of Drugs & Sundries
S.I.C.: 5122; 5100
Linda Milberg *(Chief Exec. Officer)*

HUMPHREY PRODUCTS COMPANY
5070 E. N Ave.
Kalamazoo, MI 49001
Mailing Address:
P.O. Box 2008
Kalamazoo, MI 49003
Tel.: 616-381-5500
Fax: 616-381-4113
Year Founded: 1901
Sales Range: $20-39 Million
Emp.: 378
Export
Manufacture Pneumatic Valves & Cylinders & Actuators; Gas Lamps
S.I.C.: 3492; 3593; 3648
William H. Jackson *(Chm. Bd.)*
Randall M. Webber *(Pres.)*
Dale A. Dratt *(V.P.-Engrng.)*
Robert P. Humphrey *(V.P.-Mktg. & Sls.)*
Glenn Terborg *(Controller)*
Peter H. Jackson *(Sec. & Mgr.-Special Projects)*
David Blackburn *(Dir.-Quality)*
Don Hasselbring *(Dir.-Admin.)*
Patrick J. Aldworth *(Mgr.-Human Resources)*
Patricia Billingsley *(Mgr.-Data Processing)*
David Klien *(Mgr.-Res. & Devel.)*
Steven Mohney *(Mgr.-Mfg. Engrng.)*
Larry Myland *(Mgr.-Corp. Communications)*

No. of Mfg. Plants/Facilities: 1
No. of U.S. Offices: 1
No. of Foreign Offices: 1

Computer Systems/Hardware:
IBM AS 400

Outside Service Firm(s):

Ernst & Young*(Auditors)*
1100 Old Kent Bank Bldg.
Kalamazoo, MI 49007
Tel.: 616-349-6671

Gemrich, Moser, Dombrowski, Bowser & Fette*(Commercial Insurance Carrier)*
Kalamazoo, MI

First of America Bank*(Investment Banker)*
Kalamazoo, MI

Gemrich, Moser, Dombrowski, Bowser & Fette*(Legal Firm)*
Kalamazoo, MI

First of America Bank*(Major Banking Relationship)*
Kalamazoo, MI

First of America Bank*(Pension Manager)*
Kalamazoo, MI

Subsidiary:

South Haven Coil Inc. **(1)**
P.O. Box 409,
South Haven, MI 49090
Tel.: 616-637-5201
Fax: 616-637-4449
Import Export
Mfr. Electrical Coils & Electronic Components
S.I.C.: 3621; 3629
Virgil Brumbaugh *(Gen. Mgr.)*
Randall M. Webber *(Gen. Mgr.)*

Non-U.S. Holding:

Humphrey Fluid Power Ltd. **(1)**
570 Alden Road, Unit #10
Markham, ON L3R 6A8, Canada
Tel.: 416-479-3633
Fax: 416-479-3755
Distribution of Valves & Cylinders
S.I.C.: 5074
Robert A. Kirk *(V.P. & Gen. Mgr.)*
C. Craig Aspinall *(District Sls. Mgr.)*

HUMPHREYS PRICE/ COCHRAN & SANFORD ADVERTISING
(A Hill & Knowlton Associate)
5100 Poplar Ave., 14th Fl.
Memphis, TN 38137
Tel.: 901-761-1080
Fax: 901-761-3817
Year Founded: 1965
Approx.Billings: $16,000,000
Emp.: 20
General Advertising, Consumer, Industrial, Direct Marketing & Public Relations
M.S. "Buz" Price *(Chm. Bd. & Chief Exec. Officer)*
Anderson Humphreys *(Pres. & Exec. Dir.-Creative)*
Tami Williams *(Treas.)*
Curt Guenther *(V.P.-Pub. Rels.)*

HUNT BUILDING CORPORATION
4401 N. Mesa, Ste. 201
El Paso, TX 79902
Mailing Address:
P.O. Box 9368
El Paso, TX 79984
Tel.: 915-533-1122 **DE**
Fax: 915-533-1122
Year Founded: 1947
Approx.Sls.: $128,000,000
Emp.: 120
Fiscal Year-end: 12/31/90
Bldg. Contractors & Land Development
S.I.C.: 1522; 6552; 1521
W.L. Hunt *(Chm. Bd.)*
M.L. Hunt *(Pres. & Chief Exec. Officer)*
William C. Sander *(Exec. V.P., Sec. & Treas.)*
Tom Waggoner *(V.P.)*

CAROLINE HUNT TRUST ESTATE
200 Crescent Court, Ste. 300
Dallas, TX 75201
Tel.: 214-871-5700
Fax: 214-871-6464
Emp.: 1,800
Holding Company
S.I.C.: 6719; 1311; 6552
Donald W. Crisp *(Pres. & Chief Exec. Officer)*

Outside Service Firm(s):

InterFirst Bank*(Major Banking Relationship)*
P.O. Box 83000
Dallas, TX 75283
Tel.: 214-744-8000

Subsidiary:

Rosewood Corporation **(1)**
100 Crescent Court, Ste. 1700
Dallas, TX 75201
Tel.: 214-871-8400
Approx.Sls.: $250,000,000
Emp.: 1,200
Oil Producer, Real Estate Developer, Gas & Hotels
S.I.C.: 1311; 6531
Donald W. Crisp *(Pres. & Chief Exec. Officer)*

RODNEY HUNT COMPANY
46 Mill St.
Orange, MA 01364-1251
Tel.: 508-544-2511 **MA**
Fax: 508-544-7204
Year Founded: 1840
Sales Range: $20-39 Million
Emp.: 230
Fiscal Year-end: 12/31/91
Export
Water & Sewage Control Equipment, Gray Iron Castings
S.I.C.: 3441; 3321
Earl F. Harris *(Chm. Bd.)*
David F. Waskiewicz *(Pres.)*
Robert P. Collen *(V.P.-Personnel)*
Robert W. Henderson *(V.P.-Mktg.)*
William Staples *(V.P., Treas. & Controller)*
Martin Picard *(Dir.-Matls.)*

No. of Mfg. Plants/Facilities: 1

Computer Systems/Hardware:
IBM, DEC

Outside Service Firm(s):

Arthur Andersen & Co.*(Auditors)*
One Intl. Place, 100 Oliver St.
Boston, MA 02110
Tel.: 617-330-4000
Fax: 617-439-9731

THE HUNT CORPORATION
2450 S. Tibbs Ave.
Indianapolis, IN 46241
Mailing Address:
P.O. Box 128,
Indianapolis, IN 46206
Tel.: 317-241-0761 **IN**
Fax: 317-243-3461
Year Founded: 1974
Assets: $118,735,000
Liabilities: $84,710,000
Net Worth: $34,025,000
Approx.Sls.: $450,000,000
Emp.: 3,200
Fiscal Year-end: 12/31/89
General Construction Contractors & Construction Managers
S.I.C.: 1541; 1611; 8741
Robert C. Hunt *(Chm. Bd. & Chief Exec. Officer)*
Bruce Bennett *(Pres.)*
Mack Furlow *(Sr. V.P. & Chief Fin. Officer)*
Ronald Schuster *(V.P. & Controller)*
Donald Rothenberger *(Mgr.-Data Processing)*

Principal(s):
Robert C. Hunt

Computer Systems/Hardware:
IBM System 36

Outside Service Firm(s):

Dutton & Overman*(Legal Firm)*
710 Century Building, 36 S. Pennsylvania St.
Indianapolis, IN 46204
Tel.: 317-633-4000

Bank One, Indianapolis, N.A.*(Major Banking Relationship)*
111 Monument Circle, Ste. 1611
Indianapolis, IN 46204-1611
Tel.: 317-321-8110

Bank One, Indianapolis, N.A.*(Pension Manager)*
111 Monument Circle, Ste. 1611
Indianapolis, IN 46204-1611
Tel.: 317-321-8110

Subsidiaries:

Avery Mays Construction Co. **(1)**
P.O. Box 35612,
Dallas, TX 75235
Tel.: 214-350-7991
General Building Contractor; Construction Manager
S.I.C.: 1541; 8742
D.L. Williams *(Pres.)*

Huber, Hunt & Nichols, Inc. **(1)**
P.O. Box 128,
Indianapolis, IN 46206
Tel.: 317-241-6301
General Building Contractor; Construction Manager
S.I.C.: 1541; 8742
B.W. Bennett *(Pres.)*

The Hunt Paving Company, Inc. **(1)**
P.O. Box 128,
Indianapolis, IN 46206
Tel.: 317-243-3551
Concrete Paving Contractor
S.I.C.: 1611
T.J. McNelis *(V.P.)*

HuntCor Inc. **(1)**
426 N. 44th St., Ste. 410
Phoenix, AZ 85008
Tel.: 602-225-9500
General Building Contractor; Construction Manager
S.I.C.: 1541; 8742
R.G. Hunt *(Pres.)*

HUNT OIL COMPANY
Fountain Place, 1445 Ross at Field
Dallas, TX 75202-2785
Tel.: 214-978-8000 **DE**
Telex: 6718141 HCCOMCTR
Fax: 214-978-8888
Fax: 214-855-5217
Year Founded: 1934
Approx.Sls.: $900,000,000
Emp.: 1,900
Domestic & Foreign Oil & Gas Exploration & Production; Refining, Marketing & & Transportation; Agriculture Products
S.I.C.: 1311; 2911; 0191; 0212; 1382
Ray L. Hunt *(Chm. Bd. & Chief Exec. Officer)*
Gary T. Hurford *(Pres.)*
C.E. Cornutt *(Exec. V.P. & Chief Fin. Officer)*
James B. Jennings *(Exec. V.P.)*
Jan D. Maycock *(Sr. V.P.-Intl. Exploration)*
Thomas E. Neurer *(Sr. V.P.-Admin.)*
Carl Boetticher *(V.P.-Tax)*
Ted D. Autrey *(V.P.-North American Production)*
C.F. Brady *(V.P. & Treas.)*
Arie C. Britt *(V.P.-Gas Mktg.)*
Michael M. Cobb *(V.P.)*
E. Anthony Copp *(V.P.-Fin.)*
P.E. Jones *(V.P. & Controller)*
Charles A. Mills *(V.P.-Human Resources)*
James C. Oberwetter *(V.P.-Public & Govt. Affairs)*
R. Casey Olson *(V.P.-Energy Ventures)*
Max A. Perkins *(V.P.-North American Exploration)*
Thomas J. Reed *(V.P.)*

Hunt Oil Company—(Continued)

John R. Scott *(V.P., Sec. & Gen. Counsel)*
John W. Thompson *(V.P.-Safety & Environmental Affairs)*

No. of Mfg. Plants/Facilities: 1
No. of Foreign Offices: 2

Computer Systems/Hardware:
IBM 3081

Outside Service Firm(s):

KPMG Peat Marwick*(Auditors)*
1601 Elm St., Ste. 1600
Dallas, TX 75201
Tel.: 214-754-2000
Fax: 214-754-2297

Johnson & Swanson*(Legal Firm)*
100 Founders Sq., 900 Jackson St.
Dallas, TX 75202
Tel.: 214-977-9000

Shank, Irwin, Conant, Liphsy & Casterline*(Legal Firm)*
Dallas, TX

North American Exploration Group:

Offices:

Hunt Oil Lafayette Land Office **(1)**
Bldg. 14, 106 Oil Center Dr., Ste. 103
Lafayette, LA 70508
Tel.: 318-232-7095
Fax: 318-232-2443
Oil & Gas Services
S.I.C.: 1389
David Brooks *(Landman)*
Rusty Peyton *(Landman)*
Peter Sogard *(Landman)*

Hunt Oil Shreveport Land Office **(1)**
Ste. 502, 400 Travis St.
Shreveport, LA 71101-3113
Tel.: 318-227-1562
Fax: 318-425-8310
Oil & Gas Services
S.I.C.: 1389
W.A. Hearne *(Landman)*

Hunt Oil Southwestern Office **(1)**
1204 Wilco Bldg., 415 W. Wall St.
Midland, TX 79702
Tel.: 915-684-8093
Fax: 915-684-7157
Oil & Gas Services
S.I.C.: 1389
Temple Pyle *(Coord., West Texas Opers.)*

Non-U.S. Division:

Hunt Oil Canadian Division Office **(1)**
1450-801 6th Ave., S.W.
Calgary, AB T2P 3W2, Canada
Tel.: 403-269-3400
Fax: 403-266-4042
Oil & Gas Exploration & Production
S.I.C.: 1382; 1311
Russ Nawolsky *(Div. Mgr.)*
Wayne Moses *(Div. Landman)*

Divisions:

Hunt Oil Central Exploration Division **(1)**
Fountain Place, 1445 Ross at Field
Dallas, TX 75202-2785
Tel.: 214-978-8000
Fax: 214-978-8888
Fax: 214-855-5217
Oil & Gas Exploration
S.I.C.: 1382
Dale Hostenske *(Div. Mgr.)*
William Rex *(Div. Landman)*
Carl Nail *(Landman)*
Less Cantrell *(Landman)*
Mike Shaw *(Landman)*

Hunt Oil Gulf Coast Exploration Division **(1)**
Brookhollow Central Three, 2950 North Loop W., Ste. 900
Houston, TX 77092
Tel.: 713-681-9742
Fax: 713-681-5054
Oil & Gas Exploration
S.I.C.: 1382
Art Link *(Div. Mgr.)*
Wayne Adams *(District Landman)*

North American Production Group:

Plant:

Hunt Oil Fairway Gas Plant **(1)**
P.O. Box 144,
Poynor, TX 75782
Tel.: 214-876-2591
Fax: 214-876-2188
Gas Exploration & Production
S.I.C.: 1311; 1382
Jerry Kroll *(Plant Mgr.)*

Districts:

Fairway District **(1)**
P.O. Box 138,
Poynor, TX 75782
Tel.: 214-876-2227
Fax: 214-876-2188
Oil & Gas Exploration & Production
S.I.C.: 1311; 1382
Mike Houston *(Coord.-East Texas Opers.)*

Hunt Oil Cotton Valley District **(1)**
P.O. Box 38,
Cotton Valley, LA 71018-0038
Tel.: 318-832-4265
Fax: 318-832-4367
Oil & Gas Exploration & Production
S.I.C.: 1382; 1311
Danny Ford *(Coord.-North Louisiana Opers.)*

Hunt Oil Gulf Coast District **(1)**
P.O. Box 727
Scott, LA 70583
Tel.: 318-896-8431
Fax: 318-896-5794
Oil & Gas Exploration & Production
S.I.C.: 1311; 1382
Fred Richards *(Coord.-Gulf Coast Opers.)*

International Exploration Group:

Office:

Hunt Oil International Exploration-Fountain Place **(1)**
1445 Ross at Field
Dallas, TX 75202-2785
Tel.: 214-978-8000
Fax: 214-978-8888
Fax: 214-855-5217
Oil & Gas Exploration
S.I.C.: 1382
James B. Jennings *(Exec. V.P.)*
Chris Stone *(Exec. Mgr., Europe, Africa, Asia)*
Robert H. Garrett *(Exec. Mgr., South & Central America)*
Gayeon Haigood *(Exec. Mgr., Yemen, Ethiopia)*
Ian D. Maycock *(Sr. V.P.)*

Non-U.S. Office:

Hunt Oil International Exploration-London Office **(1)**
William Blake House, 8 Marshall St.
London, W1V 1LP, United Kingdom
Tel.: 011-4471-287-1275
Telex: 851-28556 HUNTOC G
Fax: 011-4471-287-7187
Oil & Gas Exploration
S.I.C.: 1382
James Webb *(Pres.)*

International Production Group:

Office:

Hunt Oil International Production-Fountain Place **(1)**
1445 Ross at Field
Dallas, TX 75202-2785
Tel.: 214-978-8000
Fax: 214-978-8888
Fax: 214-855-5217
Oil & Gas Production
S.I.C.: 1311
Michael M. Cobb *(V.P.)*
William J. Furr *(V.P.-YHOC Production)*

Subsidiary:

Hunt Refining Company **(1)**
1855 Fairlawn Rd.
Tuscaloosa, TX 25401
Tel.: 205-391-3300
Cyrus E. Webb *(Pres.)*

HUNTCO INC.
14323 S. Outer Forty Dr.
Chesterfield, MO 63017
Tel.: 314-878-0155
Fax: 314-878-4537
Holding Company
S.I.C.: 6719
B.D. Hunter *(Chm. Bd.)*
Robert J. Marischen *(Pres.)*

Outside Service Firm(s):

Price Waterhouse*(Auditors)*
One Boatmen's Plaza
St. Louis, MO 63101
Tel.: 314-425-0500

Mercantile Bank St. Louis*(Major Banking Relationship)*
P.O. Box 321
St. Louis, MO 63166
Tel.: 314-425-2755

Subsidiaries:

Amedco Health Care, Inc. **(1)**
401 S. Outer Service Rd.
Wright City, MO 63390
Tel.: 314-745-3173 (100%)
Health Care Facilities
S.I.C.: 5047
Robert J. Kotarba *(Pres.)*

Huntco Acquisitions Holdings, Inc. **(1)**
14323 S. Outer Forty Dr.
Chesterfield, MO 63017
Tel.: 314-878-0155 (100%)
Holding Company
S.I.C.: 6719; 6799
Robert J. Marischen *(Pres.)*

Huntco Health Care Co. **(1)**
14323 S. Outer Forty Dr.
Chesterfield, MO 63017
Tel.: 314-576-5101 (100%)
Design & Equiping Services for Health Care Facilities
S.I.C.: 8712; 5047; 3089; 1542
Robert H. Fox, Jr. *(Pres.)*

Huntco Steel Co. **(1)**
1200 E. Woodhurst, Bldg. J
Springfield, MO 65804
Tel.: 417-881-6697 (100%)
Manufacture Casket Components from Raw Steel
S.I.C.: 2599
Terry K. Heinz *(Pres.)*

Midwest Products, Inc. **(1)**
R.R.#1, Box 417
Strafford, MO 65757
Tel.: 417-736-2163 (100%)
Emp.: 50
Portable Air Tanks & Air Receivers
S.I.C.: 3563
David Martin *(Pres.)*

Overhill Mfg., Inc. **(1)**
2502 W. Lawton St.
South Bend, IN 46628
Tel.: 219-232-5220 (100%)
Emp.: 40
Manufacture Air Brake Tanks
S.I.C.: 3563
William Welsch *(Pres.)*

Professional Securities Corp. **(1)**
575 Hillcrest E.
Lake Quivera, KS 66106
Tel.: 913-631-4464 (100%)
Financing & Leasing Services to Manufacturing, Commercial, Institutional & Health Care Enterprises
S.I.C.: 6159; 7359
Robert H. Fox, Jr. *(Pres.)*

Universal Flowers, Inc. **(1)**
1300 W. Poplar
Springfield, MO 65808
Tel.: 417-866-6660 (100%)
Emp.: 100
Import & Manufacture Artificial Silk Flowers
S.I.C.: 3999; 5193
Roy E. Teters *(Pres.)*

HUNTER CONTRACTING COMPANY
701 N. Cooper Rd.
Gilbert, AZ 85234
Mailing Address:
P.O. Box 900
Gilbert, AZ 85234
Tel.: 602-892-0521 **AZ**
Fax: 602-892-4932
Year Founded: 1961
Assets: $9,874,133
Liabilities: $1,547,265
Net Worth: $8,326,868
Approx.Sls.: $20,000,000
Emp.: 160
General Highway, Street & Engineering Contracting
S.I.C.: 1611
Corporate Giving Program: Requirements by Board of Directors; No Limitations
Armando Taddei *(Chm. Bd., Pres. & Treas.)*
Steve Padilla *(Sr. V.P.-Data Processing & Engrng.)*
Mirian H. Taddei *(Sec.)*
Jack Klausner *(Gen. Counsel)*
Gary Davis *(Controller)*
Tom Sorenson *(Chief Estimator)*
Mary Tucker *(Office Mgr.)*
Principal(s):
Armando Taddei
Mirian H. Taddei

Computer Systems/Hardware:
NCR

Outside Service Firm(s):

DeMarcus & Associates*(Auditors)*
Phoenix, AZ

Passey Bona*(Commercial Insurance Carrier)*
Mesa, AZ

Buch & Cracciolo*(Legal Firm)*
Phoenix, AZ

Citibank N.A.*(Major Banking Relationship)*
Phoenix, AZ

HUNTER CORP.
6000 Southport Rd.
Portage, IN 46368
Tel.: 219-762-0200
Fax: 219-762-9294
Year Founded: 1909
Approx.Sls.: $86,000,000
Emp.: 1,500
General Contractor Heavy Industrial Construction
S.I.C.: 1629; 1731; 1791; 1796
Chester Jones *(Pres. & Chief Exec. Officer)*
Jerry P. Oshinski *(Exec. V.P., Treas. & Sec.)*
Ken Selman *(V.P.)*

Outside Service Firm(s):

KPMG Peat Marwick*(Auditors)*
Peat Marwick Plaza, 303 E. Wacker Dr.
Chicago, IL 60601
Tel.: 312-938-1000

Sherfsky, Saitlin & Froelich*(Legal Firm)*
Chicago, IL

HUNTER ENGINEERING CO., INC.
(Sub. of Fata European Group S.r.l.)
1455 Columbia
Riverside, CA 92507
Mailing Address:
P.O. Box 5677
Riverside, CA 92507
Tel.: 909-683-4010
Fax: 909-369-6833
Approx.Sls.: $30,000,000

Emp.: 265
Fiscal Year-end: 12/31/90
Aluminum & Zinc Producing; Aluminum, Zinc & Steel Processing Equipment
S.I.C.: 3339; 3334; 3547
Curt Braun *(Pres.)*
Sam Sankaran *(V.P.-Engrng.)*
Raymond Sanchez *(Controller, Treas. & Asst. Sec.)*

Computer Systems/Hardware:
IBM System 3

Outside Service Firm(s):

Inland Health*(Group Insurer)*
San Bernardino, CA

Pacific Care*(Group Insurer)*
Anaheim, CA

First Interstate Bank of California, N.A.*(Major Banking Relationship)*
P.O. Box 3667,
Los Angeles, CA 90051
Tel.: 213-614-4000

HUNTER MARINE CORPORATION
Rte. 441
Alachua, FL 32615
Mailing Address:
P.O. Box 1030
Alachua, FL 32615
Tel.: 904-462-3077
Fax: 904-462-4077
Approx.Sls.: $36,000,000
Emp.: 300
Fiscal Year-end: 12/31/90
Sail Boats
S.I.C.: 3732; 5091
Warren R. Luhrs *(Chm.)*
Charles Spires *(Chief Exec. Officer)*
Dick Ash *(Pres.)*
Bob Defilipo *(Dir.-Pur.)*
Stephen Cutsforth *(Adv. Mgr.)*

HUNTSINGER & JEFFER
809 Brook Hill Circle
Richmond, VA 23227
Tel.: 804-266-2499
Year Founded: 1964
Approx.Billings: $20,200,000
Emp.: 26
Direct Response
Jerald E. Huntsinger *(Chm. & Founder)*
Donald P. Jeffer *(Pres.)*
Paul Braeckmans *(Exec. V.P., Gen. Mgr.)*
Vicki Lester *(Dir., Bus. Devel.)*
Joy Kaulfers-Beggs *(Dir., List Brokerage)*
Meghan McGreevy *(Dir., Telemarketing)*
Beth McCray *(Pub. Rels. & Acct. Mgr.)*

HUNTSMAN CHEMICAL CORPORATION
2000 Eagle Gate Tower
Salt Lake City, UT 84111
Tel.: 801-536-1500 **UT**
Telex: 759496
Fax: 801-536-1581
Year Founded: 1982
Approx.Sls.: $1,460,000,000
Emp.: 1,300
Fiscal Year-end: 12/31/90
Mfr. Polystyrene Resins
S.I.C.: 2821
Jon M. Huntsman *(Chm. Bd. & Chief Exec. Officer)*
Ronald A. Rasband *(Pres. & Chief Oper. Officer)*
Mark Bruner *(Pres. & Gen. Mgr.-Polystyrene Div.)*
Philip Jacobs *(Sr. V.P. & Gen. Mgr.-Research)*
Jim Kimball *(Mgr.-Mktg.)*
Brent Turkington *(Sr. V.P.-Pur., Styrene Monomer SLs.)*
Rick Durham *(Sr. V.P.-Devel.)*
Winston H. Connor *(V.P.-Human Resources)*
Redge L. Cook *(Dir.-Mngmt. Information Systems)*
Jenny Stephenson *(Dir.-Mktg.)*

No. of Mfg. Plants/Facilities: 12
No. of U.S. Offices: 12

Computer Systems/Hardware:
IBM

Subsidiaries:

Co-Ex Plastics, Inc. **(1)**
851 Garrett Pkwy.
Lewisburg, TN 37091
Tel.: 615-359-7815
Mfr. of Plastics
S.I.C.: 2821; 3081; 3089
John L. Coyle *(Pres.)*

Wingfoot Films Corporation **(2)**
P.O. Box 98, Garfield Ave., N.W.
Carrollton, OH 44615
Tel.: 216-627-2111 (100%)
Emp.: 200
Mfr. of Film Products
S.I.C.: 3089
John L. Coyle *(Pres. & Chief Exec. Officer)*
Don Wolfe *(V.P.-Mfg.)*
C.E. Monaco *(Controller)*
Doug Vucovich *(Mgr.-Gen. Mktg. & Sls.)*
Lyn Wood *(Pur. Agent)*

HUNTTING ELEVATOR CO.
109 N. Main St.
Austin, MN 55912
Mailing Address:
P.O. Box 99
Austin, MN 55912
Tel.: 507-433-3476 **SD**
Fax: 507-433-5139
Year Founded: 1860
Approx.Sls.: $85,000,000
Emp.: 110
Fertilizer & Grain Business
S.I.C.: 5153; 5191
J.G. Huntting, Jr. *(Chief Exec. & Chief Fin. Officer)*
James Heimark *(Pres.)*
James Wermerskirchen *(Sec. & Treas.)*

Outside Service Firm(s):

Bowlby, Anfinson, Crandall & Haedt, Inc.*(Auditors)*
Austin, MN

First Bank of Austin*(Major Banking Relationship)*
Austin, MN

First National Bank of Minneapolis*(Major Banking Relationship)*
Minneapolis, MN

MIKE DAUGHERTY'S HURLING CHEVROLET, INC.
(Formerly Frank Hurling Chevrolet, Inc.)
2449 Fulton Ave.
Sacramento, CA 95825
Tel.: 916-482-1600 **DE**
Fax: 916-482-1662
Approx.Sls.: $80,000,000
Emp.: 215
Fiscal Year-end: 12/31/88
Retail Automobiles & Recreational Vehicles
S.I.C.: 5511; 5561
Mike Daugherty *(Pres.)*
Steve Downing *(Gen. Mgr.)*
Jeanann Seyle *(Sec. & Treas.)*
Neil Watson *(Controller)*
Ali Bonhoff *(Mgr.-Personnel)*
Valerie Gullarian *(Mgr.-Office)*

Outside Service Firm(s):

Donald J. Licker Legal Firm*(Legal Firm)*
Sacramento, CA

Bank of America NT&SA*(Major Banking Relationship)*
Sacramento, CA

HURON VALLEY STEEL CORP.
41000 Huron River Dr.
Belleville, MI 48111
Tel.: 313-697-3400 **MI**
Fax: 313-697-5970
Approx.Sls.: $40,000,000
Emp.: 200
Processing of Steel & Nonferrous Metals
S.I.C.: 3312; 3341
Leonard Fritz *(Pres.)*
William Rees *(Sr. V.P.)*
Mark Gafney *(Controller)*

Outside Service Firm(s):

Coopers & Lybrand*(Auditors)*
400 Renaissance Center
Detroit, MI 48243
Tel.: 313-446-7100
Fax: 313-446-7117

Karbel, Rothstein, Stuart & Wallace*(Legal Firm)*
Southfield, MI

Michigan National Bank*(Major Banking Relationship)*
Clawson, MI

HUSSEY CORPORATION
Dyer St.
North Berwick, ME 03906
Tel.: 207-676-2271
Fax: 207-676-9031
Year Founded: 1835
Approx.Sls.: $50,000,000
Emp.: 425
Fiscal Year-end: 3/31/90
Import Export
Manufacture of Roll-Out Gym Seats, Auditorium & Stadium Chairs, Telescopic Bleachers & Platforms
S.I.C.: 2531; 3949
Philip W. Hussey, Jr. *(Pres. & Chief Exec. Officer)*
Peter A. Hussey *(Exec. V.P.)*
Steven Kolkhorst *(V.P., Sec. & Treas.)*

No. of Mfg. Plants/Facilities: 4
No. of U.S. Offices: 5
No. of Foreign Offices: 3

Outside Service Firm(s):

Coopers & Lybrand*(Auditors)*
Portland, ME

Preti, Flaherty & Beliveau*(Legal Firm)*
Portland, ME

Shawmut Bank*(Major Banking Relationship)*
Portland, ME

Subsidiaries:

Hussey Plastics Co. **(1)**
65 Middlesex Rd.
Tyngsboro, MA 01879
Tel.: 508-649-7345

Hussey Seating Company **(1)**
Dyer St.
North Berwick, ME 03906
Tel.: 207-676-2271
Approx.Sls.: $47,000,000
Emp.: 400
Fiscal Year-end: 3/31/91
Import Export
Computer Systems/Hardware:
NCR
Gym Seating, Auditorium & Theatre Seating, Telescopic Platform Seating, Stadium & Arena Seating
S.I.C.: 2531
P.W. Hussey, Jr. *(Pres.)*
P.A. Hussey *(Exec. V.P.)*
Steve Kolkorst *(V.P.-Fin.)*
Tim Hussey *(V.P.-Telescopic Seating Grp.)*
Gary Merrill *(V.P.-Chair Grp.)*
Curtis Mildner *(V.P.-Mktg.)*
Julian Pinkos *(V.P.-Human Resources)*
Peter Gagnon *(V.P.-Mngmt. Information System)*
Roger Lowell *(V.P.-Pur.)*

Non-U.S. Subsidiaries:

Hussey Seating Co. (Canada) Ltd. **(1)**
20 Torlake Crescent
Toronto, ON M82 1B3, Canada

Hussey Seating Systems (Europe) Ltd. **(1)**
Astmoor Industrial Estate, 37 Arkwright Rd., Runcorn, Cheshire WA7 1NU, United Kingdom

HUTCHENS INDUSTRIES INC.
215 N. Patterson
Springfield, MO 65802-2206
Mailing Address:
P.O. Box 1427
Springfield, MO 65801-1427
Tel.: 417-862-5012
Tel.: 800-654-8824
Fax: 417-862-2317
Year Founded: 1951
Approx.Sls.: $50,000,000
Emp.: 700
Fiscal Year-end: 12/31/90
Export
Suspension Systems & Sliding Subframes for Trailers & Trucks; Custom Steel Fabrication; Stampings & Castings
S.I.C.: 3325
Jeff Hutchens *(Pres.)*
Fred R. Rosenberger *(V.P.-Fin.)*
Mike White *(V.P.-Sls. & Mktg.)*
Jim Cantrell *(V.P.-Pur.)*
Russ Brazeal *(V.P.-Engrng.)*
Louis King *(Adv. Mgr.)*

Computer Systems/Hardware:
IBM

Divisions:

Mans-Steel Div. **(1)**
P.O. Box 137
Mansfield, MO 65704
Tel.: 417-924-3274
Fax: 417-924-8778
Export
Chuck Brazeal *(V.P.-Mfg.)*
Delbert Cantrell *(Plant Mgr.)*

Mans-Steel Foundry **(1)**
P.O. Box 137
Mansfield, MO 65704
Export
Chuck Brazeal *(V.P.-Mfg.)*
Joe Neal *(Plant Mgr.)*

Steel Processors Div. **(1)**
P.O. Box 496
Seymour, MO 65746
Tel.: 417-935-2276
Fax: 417-935-2932
Export
Chuck Brazeal *(V.P.-Mfg.)*
Dale Green *(Plant Mgr.)*

HUTCHINS MANUFACTURING COMPANY
49 N. Lotus Ave.
Pasadena, CA 91107
Tel.: 818-792-8211
Fax: 818-792-8574
Year Founded: 1950
Emp.: 51
Hand & Air Powered Sanders
S.I.C.: 3546
Alma A. Hutchins *(Pres.)*
Alme J. Hutchins *(V.P.)*

Outside Service Firm(s):

McCulgan & Vanni*(Legal Firm)*
Pasadena, CA

Hutchins Manufacturing Company—(Continued)

Community Bank*(Major Banking Relationship)*
Pasadena, CA

CHUCK HUTTON CHEVROLET COMPANY
2471 Mt. Moriah
Memphis, TN 38115
Tel.: 901-365-9700
Fax: 901-795-1579
Approx.Sls.: $60,000,000
Emp.: 300
Retail Chevrolet Dealer
S.I.C.: 5511
Charles R. Hutton *(Pres.)*
Richard Carney *(Treas.)*
Nell Wood *(Sec.)*

Outside Service Firm(s):

George B. Jones & Co.*(Auditors)*
Memphis, TN

Evans, Petree, Cobb, Edwards*(Legal Firm)*
Memphis, TN

First American Bank, N.A.*(Major Banking Relationship)*
McLean, VA

HVIDE SHIPPING, INC.
2200 Eller Dr.
Fort Lauderdale, FL 33316
Mailing Address:
P.O. Box 13038
Ft. Lauderdale, FL 33316
Tel.: 305-523-2200
Fax: 305-527-1772
Year Founded: 1958
Approx.Sls.: $265,000,000
Emp.: 189
Fiscal Year-end: 12/31/90
Chartering of Commercial Boats & Marine Towing
S.I.C.: 4492
Hans J. Hvide *(Chm. Bd.)*
J. Erik Hvide *(Pres.)*
Gene Douglas *(V.P.-Legal & Admin.)*
Gerry Farmer *(V.P.-Fin.)*
Anders Hvide *(V.P.-Mktg.)*
Robert A. Santos *(V.P.)*
Eugene Sweeney *(V.P.)*
Ron Ross *(Dir.-Pur.)*
Gary Vail *(Dir.-Human Resources)*

No. of U.S. Offices: 4

Outside Service Firm(s):

Ernst & Young*(Auditors)*
Fort Lauderdale, FL

Massachusetts Mutual Life Insurance Co.*(Group Insurer)*
Ft. Lauderdale, FL

California Federal Bank*(Major Banking Relationship)*
Ft. Lauderdale, FL

HY-VEE FOOD STORES INCORPORATED
1801 Oceola Ave.
Chariton, IA 50049
Tel.: 515-774-2121
Fax: 515-774-7210
Approx.Sls.: $1,200,000,000
Emp.: 14,000
Retail Food & Drug Stores
S.I.C.: 5411; 5912; 5112; 5141
Ronald Pearson *(Chm. Bd., Pres. & Chief Exec. Officer)*
Mike Wheeler *(Chief Fin. Officer, V.P. & Treas.)*
Richard Mitchell *(Chief Admin. Officer & Sr. V.P.)*
John Briggs *(V.P., Sec. & Controller)*
Dennis Ausenhus *(Asst. V.P.-Real Estate)*
Ron Waldbillig *(Asst. V.P.-Mngmt. Information Systems)*
Denny Bisgard *(Dir.-Data Processing)*
Dan Luger *(Dir.-Office Admin.)*

Computer Systems/Hardware:
IBM 4381 & IBM 4341

Outside Service Firm(s):

McGladrey & Pullen*(Auditors)*
Des Moines, IA

The Principal Financial Group*(Group Insurer)*
Des Moines, IA

Myer's Law Offices*(Legal Firm)*
Chariton, IA

National Bank & Trust*(Major Banking Relationship)*
Chariton, IA

HYDE MANUFACTURING CO.
54 Eastford Rd.
Southbridge, MA 01550
Tel.: 508-764-4344
Fax: 508-765-5250
Year Founded: 1875
Approx.Sls.: $29,000,000
Emp.: 307
Fiscal Year-end: 12/28/90
Industrial Hand & Machine Knives, Putty Knives & Scrapers; Dry Wall Joint Knives; Paint, Razor Blade & Wood Scrapers; Fix-Up Tools; Painting Aids; Wallpapering Tools; Wallpaper Removers; Paperhanging Outfits; Floor, Tile & Carpet Tools; Butcher & Chef Knives
S.I.C.: 3423; 3421
Robert U. Clemence *(Chm. Bd.)*
Richard B. Hardy *(Pres., Chief Exec. & Chief Oper. Officer)*
Richard R. Clemence *(Exec. V.P.-Mfg.)*
Ralph G. Lawrence *(Sr. V.P.-Sls. & Mktg.)*
Joseph Zalieckas *(Treas.)*
Ronald P. Carlson *(Controller)*
R.S. List *(Mgr.-Trade Sls.)*
Donald P. Cummings *(Dir.-Mktg.)*
Allan Baker *(Dir.-Pur.)*

Computer Systems/Hardware:
IBM System 38

Outside Service Firm(s):

Love, Bollus & Rogers, CPA*(Auditors)*
Worcester, MA

Mechanics Bank*(Major Banking Relationship)*
Worcester, MA

Subsidiaries:

Beaut-Ease Corporation **(1)**
5401 W. 65th St.
Bedford Park, IL 60638
Tel.: 708-252-2500
Import & Distribute Hand Tools & Painters Accessories

Gutmann Cutlery, Inc. **(1)**
120 S. Columbus Ave.
Mount Vernon, NY 10553
Tel.: 914-699-4044
Fax: 914-699-4217
Approx.Sls.: $14,000,000
Emp.: 50
Wholesale Sporting & Recreational Goods & Supplies; Cutlery; Toys & Hobby Goods
S.I.C.: 3421; 5072; 3949
E. Richard Gerety *(Pres.)*

Russell Harrington Cutlery Inc. **(1)**
44 Green River St.
Southbridge, MA 01550
Tel.: 508-765-0201
Fax: 508-764-2897
Approx.Sls.: $20,000,000
Emp.: 280
Fiscal Year-end: 12/00/92
Import Export
Computer Systems/Hardware:
IBM System 38
Professional & Industrial Cutlery
S.I.C.: 3421
R.B. Hardy *(Chm. Bd.)*
Edmond A. Neal, Jr. *(Pres. & Gen. Mgr.)*
Charles H. Eden *(V.P.-Sls.)*
N. William Pioppi *(V.P.)*
Raymond C. Rohr *(Treas.)*
David Picard *(Dir.-Pur.)*

Wilson Machine Knife Co., Inc. **(1)**
Louisa Viens Dr.
Dayville, CT 06241
Tel.: 203-774-1978
Fax: 203-774-1058
Manufacturer of Cutting Knives For Textile Industry
S.I.C.: 3421
Richard Clemence *(Pres.)*
Ronald Carlson *(Controller)*
William Fletcher *(Sls. Mgr.)*

HYDRAULICS INTERNATIONAL, INC.
9000 Mason Ave.
Chatsworth, CA 91311
Tel.: 818-998-1231
Fax: 818-709-3862
Approx.Sls.: $11,000,000
Emp.: 220
Ground Support Parts & Equipment
S.I.C.: 3728
Nicky Ghaemmaghami *(Pres.)*
Linda Ghaemmaghami *(V.P.)*
Robert T. Moore *(V.P.-Engrng.)*
Jeff Riley *(Gen. Mgr.)*
J. Ulberg *(Mgr.-Pur.)*

Outside Service Firm(s):

Henri Plat*(Auditors)*
Chatsworth, CA

Transworld Bank*(Major Banking Relationship)*
Chatsworth, CA

HYDRIL COMPANY
3300 N. Sam Houston Pkwy., East
Houston, TX 77032-3411
Mailing Address:
P.O. Box 60458
Houston, TX 77205-0458
Tel.: 713-449-2000
Telex: 168905
Fax: 713-985-3457
Year Founded: 1933
Approx.Sls.: $150,000,000
Emp.: 1,000
Fiscal Year-end: 12/31/91
Export
Mfr. & Sale of Oilfield Equip.
S.I.C.: 3533; 3061; 3494; 3825; 3829
Lynn L. Leigh *(Pres.)*
Gary Kirsch *(Dir.-Mktg.)*

Computer Systems/Hardware:
Various

Divisions:

Hydril Company **(1)**
714 W. Olympic Blvd.
Los Angeles, CA 90015
Tel.: 213-749-4180
Telex: 275349
Fax: 213-748-0506
Approx.Sls.: $115,000,000
Emp.: 1,000
Computer Systems/Hardware:
IBM System 38; Hewlett-Packard 3000/48
Manufacture Oil Field Specialty Equipment
S.I.C.: 1389; 3411; 3412; 3443; 3449; 3533
Richard C. Seaver *(Chm. Bd.)*
Lynn Leigh *(Pres.)*
John Hall *(V.P. & Sec.)*
Larry Wilber *(Controller)*
Dennis Winter *(Treas.)*

Hydril Production Technology Div. **(1)**
P.O. Box 721560
Houston, TX 77272
Tel.: 713-777-5361
Charles Peterman *(Gen. Mgr.)*

Hydril Rubber Opers. **(1)**
18000 E. Tex Frwy.
Humble, TX 77347-1888
Tel.: 713-446-0041
Mfr. Industrial Rubber Products for Oil Field Industry
S.I.C.: 3061
Doug Carlson *(Dir.)*

HYDRITE CHEMICAL COMPANY
300 N. Patrick Blvd.
Brookfield, WI 53045
Mailing Address:
P.O. Drawer 0948,
Brookfield, WI 53008-0948
Tel.: 414-792-1450
Fax: 414-792-8721
Approx.Sls.: $75,000,000
Emp.: 350
Chlorine; Metal Plating; Tanning: Solvents; Phosphoric Acid
S.I.C.: 2812; 2819; 2874; 2899; 3471
John A. Honkamp *(Pres.)*
Paul F. Honkamp *(Exec. V.P.)*
Mark Laehr *(V.P.-Corp. Resources)*
Robert Adams *(Dir.-Specialty Sls.)*
Avis Browne *(Dir.-Pur.)*
David Miller *(Dir.-Fin. & Acctg.)*
Donna Weinstock *(Dir.-Distr. Sls.)*

Outside Service Firm(s):

Ernst & Young*(Auditors)*
111 E. Kilbourn Ave., Ste. 900
Milwaukee, WI 53202
Tel.: 414-273-5900

HYDRO GROUP, INC.
1011 Rte. 22 W
Bridgewater, NJ 08807
Tel.: 908-704-8880 **NY**
Fax: 908-725-5467
Year Founded: 1922
Assets: $13,446,775
Liabilities: $9,395,562
Net Worth: $4,051,213
Approx.Sls.: $41,356,470
Emp.: 325
Fiscal Year-end: 12/31/90
Mfr. of Water Treatment Equipment; Water Well Drilling
S.I.C.: 3449; 1781
R. Charles *(Chm. Bd. & Pres.)*
W.B. Armstrong *(V.P.)*
J.L. Gagnassola *(V.P.)*
G.M. Stahlman *(V.P. & Gen. Mgr.)*
Dave Ward, Sr. *(V.P.)*
W. Takacs *(Treas.)*
M.A. Locher *(Sec.)*

No. of Mfg. Plants/Facilities: 8
No. of U.S. Offices: 7

Outside Service Firm(s):

Frank S. Mannuzza*(Auditors)*
Clark, NJ

Connell, Foley & Geiser*(Legal Firm)*
Roseland, NJ

First Fidelity Bank*(Major Banking Relationship)*
Morristown, NJ

United Jersey Bank/Central N.A.*(Major Banking Relationship)*
Somerset, NJ

Subsidiary:

Ground Water Associates, Inc. **(1)**
1011 Rte. 22 W.
Bridgewater, NJ 08807
Tel.: 908-563-0775
Emp.: 21
Hydrogeological Consultants
S.I.C.: 8711
Dave G. Ward, Sr. *(Pres.)*

HYDRO/KIRBY AGRI SERVICE, INC.
(Formerly R/K Agri Services, Inc.)
500 Running Pump Rd.
Lancaster, PA 17603
Mailing Address:
P.O. Box 6277
Lancaster, PA 17603
Tel.: 717-299-2541
Tel.: 800-745-7524 **PA**
Fax: 717-293-9306
Year Founded: 1992
Sales Range: $20-39 Million
Import Export
Wholesale Fertilizer & Agricultural Chemicals
S.I.C.: 5191
Carroll R. Kirby *(Pres.)*
Principal(s):
Carroll R. Kirby

No. of Mfg. Plants/Facilities: 9
No. of U.S. Offices: 9

Computer Systems/Hardware:
IBM

HYDRO-MILL CO.
9301 Mason Ave.
Chatsworth, CA 91311
Tel.: 213-873-4161
Fax: 818-341-7159
Year Founded: 1955
Approx.Sls.: $36,000,000
Emp.: 360
Job Machine Shop For Aircraft Parts
S.I.C.: 3728; 3599
Heidi C. Dunn *(Vice Chm.)*
J. Anthony Baird *(Pres.)*
Robert Perry *(V.P. & Gen. Mgr.)*
Ramon A. Ordonez *(Controller)*
Patricia R. Caine *(Mgr.-Cost Acctng.)*
Karin Lenander *(Mgr.-Engrng.)*
Jim Madden *(Mgr.-Quality Control)*

Outside Service Firm(s):

Wells Fargo Bank*(Major Banking Relationship)*
333 S. Grand
Los Angeles, CA 90071
Tel.: 213-253-6836

HYER INDUSTRIES INC./ THAYER SCALE
Route 139
Pembroke, MA 02359
Tel.: 617-826-8101
Fax: 617-826-7944
Approx.Sls.: $12,000,000
Emp.: 120
Export
Weight Feeders, Loss-in-Weight Feeders, Belt Scales, Bridge Breakers, Bin Flow Aid Devices
S.I.C.: 3545
Frank S. Hyer *(Pres.)*
Charles Wesley *(V.P.-Sls. & Mktg.)*
Kristin Scharf *(Sls. Mgr.)*
Lou Sawyer *(Pur. Agent)*

HYGEIA DAIRY CO., INC.
720 S. "F" St.
Harlingen, TX 78550
Mailing Address:
P.O. Box 751,
Harlington, TX 78551
Tel.: 210-423-2050
Fax: 210-423-3092
Year Founded: 1927
Approx.Sls.: $70,000,000
Emp.: 525
Fiscal Year-end: 9/30/91
Food Products; Dairy Products
S.I.C.: 2026; 2021; 2024
H. Lee Richards *(Chm. Bd. & Chief Exec. Officer)*
Don Smith *(Pres.)*
Wayne Townsend *(Chief Fin. Officer & Controller)*
Doug Purl *(V.P.)*
Carol Law *(Treas.)*
Jerry Schussler *(Dir.-Personnel)*
Don Shelton *(Dir.-Data Processing)*

Computer Systems/Hardware:
Hewlett-Packard 3000 Series 48

Outside Service Firm(s):

Deloitte & Touche*(Auditors)*
700 N. St. Mary's, Suite 1100
San Antonio, TX 78205-3589
Tel.: 210-224-1041

Pilot Life*(Group Insurer)*
Greensboro, NC

Gibben & Gibben*(Legal Firm)*
Harlingen, TX

Texas Commerce Bank*(Major Banking Relationship)*
Brownsville, TX

Massachusetts Mutual Life Insurance Co.*(Pension Manager)*
1295 State Street
Springfield, MA 01111
Tel.: 413-788-8411

William M. Mercer Incorporated*(Pension Manager)*
San Antonio, TX

Texas Commerce Bank*(Pension Manager)*
Brownsville, TX

HYGRADE METAL MOULDING MFG. CORP.
540 Smith St.
Farmingdale, NY 11735
Tel.: 516-293-8797
Year Founded: 1961
Approx.Sls.: $10,000,000
Emp.: 73
Mfr. of Roll Formed Metal Shapes, Spacer Tubing for Insulated Glass
S.I.C.: 3356
Richard Cole *(Pres.)*
Mark Zimmerman *(V.P.)*
Ann Cole *(Treas.)*
Marion Stern *(Sec.)*

HYMAN FREIGHTWAYS INC.
5267 Program Ave.
Moundsview, MN 55112
Tel.: 612-784-5030
Fax: 612-645-0381
Fax: 612-785-6390
Approx.Sls.: $62,500,000
Holding Company; Motor Common Carrier
S.I.C.: 6719; 4213
Eugene Pikovsky *(Chm. & Chief Exec. Officerr)*
Peter Jones *(Pres.)*
Peter Martin *(Exec. V.P.)*
Ron Peters *(V.P.-Mktg.)*
Scott Pikovsky *(V.P.)*
Principal(s):
Eugene Pikovsky

Outside Service Firm(s):

Deloitte & Touche*(Auditors)*
1600 Landmark Towers, 345 St. Peter St.
St. Paul, MN 55102

HYNES INDUSTRIES INC.
3760 Oakwood Ave.
Youngstown, OH 44509
Mailing Address:
P.O. Box 2459,
Youngstown, OH 44509
Tel.: 216-799-3221
Tel.: 800-321-9257 **OH**
Fax: 216-799-9098
Year Founded: 1925
Approx.Sls.: $29,000,000
Emp.: 200
Export
Steel Service Center; Manufacturer of Roll Rormed Shapes, Flat & Shaped Wire, Slotted Steel Angles
S.I.C.: 3316; 3496; 3429
William W. Bresnahan *(Chm. Bd.)*
William J. Bresnahan *(Pres.)*
Ted Clarke *(Chief Fin. Officer, Treas. & Controller)*
Patrick Bresnahan *(Dir.-Data Processing)*
James E. Kearns *(Dir.-Personnel)*
Richard S. Evans *(Mgr.-Pur.)*

Computer Systems/Hardware:
IBM System 36

Outside Service Firm(s):

Ernst & Young*(Auditors)*
Bank One Bldg., Ste. 809
Youngstown, OH 44503
Tel.: 216-743-1124
Fax: 216-743-2966

Mahoning National Bank*(Major Banking Relationship)*
Youngstown, OH

Pittsburgh National Bank*(Major Banking Relationship)*
Stock Transfer Dept., Fifth & Wood Streets
Pittsburgh, PA 15265

Pittsburgh National Bank*(Pension Manager)*
Stock Transfer Dept., Fifth & Wood Streets
Pittsburgh, PA 15265

HYPERTRONICS CORPORATION
16 Brent Dr.
Hudson, MA 01749
Tel.: 508-568-0451
Tel.: 800-225-9228 **MA**
Fax: 508-568-0680
Year Founded: 1970
Sales Range: $10-19 Million
Emp.: 150
Import Export
Electric & Electronic Connectors
S.I.C.: 3678
Richard T. Downey *(Pres.)*
C. Beradinelli *(Exec. V.P.)*
G. Dawson *(Dir.-Engrng.)*
J. Kelley *(Dir.-Admin.)*
E. Dalrymple *(Mgr.-Sls.)*
J. Harris *(Pur. Agent)*

No. of Mfg. Plants/Facilities: 1
No. of U.S. Offices: 1

HYPLAINS DRESSED BEEF, INC.
2000 E. Trail
Dodge City, KS 67801
Mailing Address:
P.O. Box 539,
Dodge City, KS 67801
Tel.: 316-227-7135 **KS**
Fax: 316-225-6413
Year Founded: 1962
Approx.Sls.: $412,000,000
Emp.: 315
Fiscal Year-end: 1/ 2/90
Meat Packing
S.I.C.: 2011
John Miller *(Pres.)*
Lowell Zoet *(Gen. Mgr.)*
Rod Schoonover *(Controller)*
Nancy Guthrey *(Dir.-Personnel)*
Ron Lewis *(Dir.-Pur.)*

No. of Mfg. Plants/Facilities: 1
No. of U.S. Offices: 1

Computer Systems/Hardware:
IBM System 36

Outside Service Firm(s):

Allen, Gibbs, Houlik*(Auditors)*
301 N. Main, Ste. 1700
Wichita, KS 67202
Tel.: 316-267-7231

Home Life Insurance Co.*(Commercial Insurance Carrier)*
Dodge City, KS

Mangan, Dalton, Trenkle, Rebein & Doll*(Legal Firm)*
Dodge City, KS

Wells Fargo Bank*(Major Banking Relationship)*
Denver, CO

HYPRO CORPORATION
375 Fifth Ave. N.W.
New Brighton, MN 55112
Tel.: 612-633-9300
Telex: 4310109
Fax: 612-633-6864
Year Founded: 1947
Emp.: 125
Fiscal Year-end: 9/30/91
Import Export
Mfg. of Pumps & Accessories for Agricultural, Pressure Cleaning & Fire Protection Markets
S.I.C.: 3561
W. Ted Dudley *(Pres.)*
Mark Boggess *(Chief Fin. Officer)*
John Goode *(V.P.-Opers.)*
Stephen Meydell *(V.P.-Pur.)*
R.E. Neitzel *(V.P.-Sls.)*
Steve Dickhaus *(Controller)*
Myrna Press *(Sec.)*
Kathy Hult *(Mgr.-Mktg. Plng.)*
Deb LaDue *(Mgr.-Mngmt. Information Systems)*
Deb North *(Mgr.-Intl.)*
June Nusz *(Mgr.-Communications)*
Dale Sharp *(Mgr.-Quality Control)*

No. of Mfg. Plants/Facilities: 2

Outside Service Firm(s):

Deloitte & Touche*(Auditors)*
900 Pillsbury Ctr.
Minneapolis, MN 55402
Tel.: 612-332-2301
Fax: 612-375-5418

Fredrikson & Byron, P.A.*(Legal Firm)*
1100 International Center, 900 Second Av. South
Minneapolis, MN 53402-3397
Tel.: 612-349-6265

Norwest Bank Minnesota, N.A.*(Major Banking Relationship)*
St. Paul, MN

Division:

Sherwood Co. **(1)**
6331 E. Jefferson Ave.
Detroit, MI 48207
Tel.: 313-259-2095
Manufacture of Pumps for Marine & Industrial Applications
S.I.C.: 3561
David Thompson *(Gen. Mgr.)*

HYSPAN PRECISION PRODUCTS, INC.
1685 Brandywine Ave.
Chula Vista, CA 91911
Tel.: 619-421-1355
Fax: 619-421-1702
Approx.Sls.: $15,500,000
Emp.: 250
Export
Iron Or Steel Expansion Joints; Wire Braid
S.I.C.: 3441; 3496
Donald R. Heye *(Pres.)*
Frank Hervey, Jr. *(Mgr.-Mktg.)*
Douglas Hardison *(Dir.-Production)*

Outside Service Firm(s):

First Interstate Bank*(Major Banking Relationship)*
San Diego, CA

I SKI SKI GOGGLES
(Div. of Advanced Sports Optics)
1935 Tubeway
City of Commerce, CA 90040
Tel.: 213-724-0262
Fax: 213-721-6962
Year Founded: 1962
Approx.Sls.: $25,000,000
Fiscal Year-end: 6/30/90
Mfr. Ski Glasses & Sunglasses
S.I.C.: 3851
Lee Hines *(Pres. & Chief Exec. Officer)*
Donald F. Allen, Jr. *(Sr. V.P.)*
Jeff Halpern *(V.P.)*
Robert Jones *(Chief Fin. Officer)*
Julie Chapman *(Controller)*
Heidi Hoffner *(Dir.-Mktg.)*

IA CONSTRUCTION CORP.
Rte. 202, P.O. Box 8
Concordville, PA 19331
Tel.: 215-459-3136
Tel.: 800-338-9108 **PA**
Fax: 215-459-2086
Year Founded: 1924
Assets: $51,165,125
Liabilities: $25,469,161
Net Worth: $25,695,964
Approx.Sls.: $110,000,000
Emp.: 800
Fiscal Year-end: 12/31/89
Heavy & Highway Construction; Bituminous Concrete Paving Materials
S.I.C.: 1611; 1629; 2951
Michel Roullet *(Chm. Bd.)*
George Searle *(Pres. & Chief Exec. Officer)*
Frank Albero *(V.P.-Fin.)*
Laurent J. Lavigne *(V.P.)*
Harry W. Merz, Jr. *(V.P.)*
Henri Molleron *(V.P.)*
James Kutys *(Sec., Treas. & Controller)*
Juanita Dye *(Dir.-Data Processing)*

No. of U.S. Offices: 26

Computer Systems/Hardware:
IBM 38

Outside Service Firm(s):

Deloitte & Touche*(Auditors)*
1700 Market St.
Philadelphia, PA 19103
Tel.: 215-246-2322
Fax: 215-569-2441

Stradley, Ronon, Stevens & Young*(Legal Firm)*
2600 Commerce Sq.
Philadelphia, PA 19103
Tel.: 215-564-8000

Dauphin Deposit Bank & Trust Co.*(Major Banking Relationship)*
213 Market St.
Harrisburg, PA 17101

IA CORP.
1301 Harbor Bay Parkway
Alameda, CA 94501-6541
Tel.: 415-769-5400
Telex: 336440
Telecopier: 415-521-5499
Systems for Automated Document, IPnformation, and Distribution Management, Inspection and Process Control
S.I.C.: 7373

I B DIFFUSION, LP
350 N. Orleans, Ste. 170
Chicago, IL 60654
Tel.: 312-836-4477
Fax: 312-222-0039
Year Founded: 1986
Approx.Sls.: $75,000,000
Emp.: 300
Wholesale Distributor of Women's Clothing
S.I.C.: 5137
Ronald Schmidt *(Pres. & Chief Exec. Officer)*
John Rogers *(Chief Fin. Officer)*
Art Goodman *(V.P.)*
Gail Johnson *(V.P.)*
Bill Martin *(V.P.)*

Outside Service Firm(s):

The Hong Kong & Shanghai Bank*(Major Banking Relationship)*
Chicago, IL

IBM FOODS
(d/b/a Overhill Farms)
506 S. Isis Ave.
Inglewood, CA 90301
Tel.: 310-641-3680
Fax: 310-645-3911
Approx.Sls.: $82,000,000
Emp.: 850
Poultry Slaughtered & Dressed; Frozen Specialities
S.I.C.: 2038; 2015
Maurice H. Gettleman *(Chm. Bd. & Pres.)*
Edward Marek *(V.P.-Fin.)*
Karl Schlabach *(V.P.-Sls.)*
Raymond Goodman *(Mgr.-Data Processing)*
Joyce Yamamoto *(Supvr.-Acctng.)*

Outside Service Firm(s):

Herbert S. Belinsky*(Auditors)*
Los Angeles, CA

City National Bank*(Major Banking Relationship)*
8525 W. Pico Blvd.
Los Angeles, CA 90035
Tel.: 310-550-5690

IBT, INC.
P.O. Box 2982
Shawnee Mission, KS 66201
Tel.: 913-677-3151
Fax: 913-677-3752
Year Founded: 1949
Approx.Sls.: $90,000,000
Emp.: 435
Distribution of Industrial Parts & Supplies
S.I.C.: 5085
Forrest R. Cloud *(Chm. Bd.)*
Stephen R. Cloud *(Pres. & Chief Exec. Officer)*
Wayne L. Shields *(Chief Fin. Officer & Treas.)*
Larry Brand *(V.P.-Oper.)*
Robert Saling *(Controller)*
Gary Hense *(Dir.-Training)*
Principal(s):
Forrest R. Cloud
Stephen R. Cloud

Outside Service Firm(s):

Ernst & Young*(Auditors)*
Kansas City, KS

Hartford Life Insurance Co.*(Commercial Insurance Carrier)*
Hartford, CT 06104-2999

Shughart, Thomson & Kilroy*(Legal Firm)*
Kansas City, MO

Mercantile National Bank of Kansas City*(Major Banking Relationship)*
Kansas City, KS

Subsidiary:

Sunrise Industrial Automation & Design **(1)**
P.O. Box 2982
Shawnee Mission, KS 66201
Tel.: 913-677-3151
Emp.: 18
Industrial Computer Automation & Design
S.I.C.: 5085
Bob Sherwood *(Gen. Mgr.)*

I.C. SYSTEM, INC.
444 E. Hwy. 96
Vadnais Heights, MN 55127
Mailing Address:
P.O. Box 64444
St. Paul, MN 55164-0444
Tel.: 612-483-8201
Tel.: 800-443-4123 **MN**
Fax: 612-481-6411
Year Founded: 1938
Approx.Sls.: $37,000,000
Emp.: 520
Collection Agency & Direct Mail Advertising Service
S.I.C.: 7322; 7331
Ruth Johnson *(Chm. Bd. & Chief Exec. Officer)*
John Erickson *(Pres.)*
Max E. Hill *(Chief Fin. Officer, V.P.-Fin. & Sec.)*
Patrice Scheiber *(Sr. V.P.-Opers.)*
Robert Jordan *(V.P.-Sls.)*
Dieter Pape *(V.P.-CSD)*

Outside Service Firm(s):

McGladrey & Pullen*(Auditors)*
Minneapolis, MN

First National Bank of St. Paul*(Major Banking Relationship)*
St. Paul, MN

ICC INDUSTRIES, INC.
720 Fifth Ave.
New York, NY 10019
Tel.: 212-903-1700 **NY**
Fax: 212-903-1794
Assets: $200,000,000
Net Worth: $200,000,000
Approx.Sls.: $420,000,000
Emp.: 2,000
Fiscal Year-end: 12/31/90
Trading Company for Mfrs. of Chemicals, Generic Pharmaceuticals, Plastics, Flavors & Fragrances
S.I.C.: 6799; 2869; 2844; 2834; 2821; 3081
Dr. John J. Farber *(Chm. Bd.)*
John Oram *(Pres.)*
Susan A. Binder *(V.P. & Treas.)*
Paul Falick *(V.P. & Gen. Counsel)*
Frances Foti *(Sec. & Dir.-Personnel)*

Outside Service Firm(s):

KPMG Peat Marwick*(Auditors)*
345 Park Ave.
New York, NY 10154
Tel.: 212-758-9700
Fax: 212-872-3308

Connecticut General Life Insurance Co.*(Group Insurer)*
195 Broadway, 12th floor
New York, NY 10017
Tel.: 212-618-5500

Webster & Sheffield*(Legal Firm)*
One Rockefeller Plaza
New York, NY 10004-2594
Tel.: 212-957-9800

Swiss Bank Corp.*(Major Banking Relationship)*
Box 395, Church St. Station
New York, NY 10008
Tel.: 212-574-3000

Hewitt & Associates*(Pension Manager)*
40 Highland Ave.
Rowayton, CT 06853
Tel.: 203-852-1100
Fax: 203-853-2224

Subsidiaries:

Dover Chemical Corp. **(1)**
P.O. Box 40, 15th & Davis Sts.
Dover, OH 44622
Tel.: 216-343-7711 (100%)
Approx.Sls.: $16,000,000
Emp.: 120
Chemicals
S.I.C.: 2819; 2869
Joseph Monaco *(Chief Oper. Officer)*

I.C.C. Trading, Inc. **(1)**
720 5th Ave.
New York, NY 10019
Tel.: 212-903-1700 (100%)
Emp.: 100
Robert Podewils *(Chief Oper. Officer)*

Primex Plastics Corp. **(1)**
65 River Drive
Garfield, NJ 07026
Tel.: 201-470-8000 (100%)
Approx.Sls.: $50,000,000
Emp.: 325
Rigid Plastic Sheet
S.I.C.: 2821
Paul Bertsch *(Exec. V.P.)*

Plants:

Primex Plastics Corp. **(2)**
65 River Dr.
Garfield, NJ 07026
Tel.: 201-470-8000 (100%)
S.I.C.: 2821
Paul Bertsch *(Chief Opr. Officer)*

Primex Plastics Corp. **(2)**
1409 E. Watsoncenter Rd.
Carson, CA 90745
Tel.: 213-775-4181
S.I.C.: 2821
Murray Aibinder *(Chief Opr. Officer)*

Primex Plastics Corp. **(2)**
1235 North F St.
Richmond, IN 47374
Tel.: 317-966-7774
S.I.C.: 2821
Paul Bertsch *(Chief Opr. Officer)*

Primex Plastics Corp. **(2)**
Rte. #2 Old Oakwood Rd.
Oakwood, GA 30566
Tel.: 706-534-0223
S.I.C.: 2821
Paul Bertsch *(Chief Opr. Officer)*

Non-U.S. Holdings:

Electrochemical Industries (Frutarom) Ltd. **(1)**
P.O. Box 1929
Haifa, 31000, Israel
Tel.: 972-04-91-22-31 (60%)
Earnings: $12,913,000
Approx.Rev.: $247,208,000
Fiscal Year-end: 12/31/90
Chloride, Caustic Soda, Indus. Chemicals, PVC, Flavors & Fragrances, Spices
S.I.C.: 2812; 2819; 2087

Fallek Chemical Company (UK) Ltd. **(1)**
57-61 West Wycombe Rd.
High Wycombe, Buck HP11 2LR, United Kingdom
Tel.: 44-494-450411
S.I.C.: 5169

Fallek Chemical Corp. **(1)**
Teisen Kandabashi Bldg., 3rd Floor 1-27, Kanda Nishiki-cho, Chiyoda-ku, Tokyo, Japan
Tel.: 03-3291-4107

Fallek Chemical S.A. **(1)**
Ave. Franklyn Roosevelt 81 1050
Brussels, Belgium
Tel.: 32-2-6400155
S.I.C.: 5169

ICC Chemical (UK) Limited **(1)**
7, Prebendal Ct., Oxford Rd.
Aylesbury, Bucks HP19 3EY, United Kingdom
Tel.: 44-296-393999

ICC Comercio e Industria Ltds. **(1)**
Alameda Lorena 1304-14 Andar Conjuntos, 1406, A 1408, 01424
Sao Paulo, SP 01424, Brazil
Tel.: 55-11-8812522 (100%)
Chemical, Pharmaceutical
S.I.C.: 5169; 2834

ICC Handels AG **(1)**
Chamerstr. 12 C/POB 611, 6301 Bellerive, Zug, Switzerland
Tel.: 41-42-218044 (100%)

Chemicals, Pharmaceuticals
S.I.C.: 5169; 2834

ICC (Hong Kong) Ltd. **(1)**
20 th Flr., Universal House, 229-230
Gloucester Rd.
Causeway Bay, Hong Kong
Tel.: 852-5-75099 (100%)
Chemicals
S.I.C.: 5169

ICC Iberica S.A. **(1)**
Paseo de la Castellana 115
Madrid, 28046, Spain
Tel.: 34-1-4553186 (100%)

ICC Industries, B.V. **(1)**
Amteldijk 166, P.O. Box 7000 1007 MA
Amsterdam, Netherlands
Tel.: 31-20-448888 (100%)
Chemicals
S.I.C.: 5169

ICC (Israel) Chemicals Ltd. **(1)**
135 Dizengoff St.
Tel Aviv, 53461, Israel
Tel.: 3-910296 (100%)

ICC Italia S.R.L. **(1)**
Via Cardano 8 I-20124
Milan, Italy
Tel.: 39-2-6701406 (100%)

ICC Trading (Taiwan) Ltd. **(1)**
6th Fl. No. 8 Lane 22 Chi Lin Rd. POB 1369,
Taipei, Taiwan
Tel.: 886-2-5627131 (100%)

Intertec Limited **(1)**
20th. Flr., Universal House, 229-230
Gloucester Rd.
Causeway Bay, Hong Kong

Intertec Limited **(1)**
7 Premendal Ct., Oxford Rd.
Aylesbury, Bucks HP19 3EY, United Kingdom
Tel.: 44-296-393999
S.I.C.: 5169

ICE COMMUNICATIONS, INC.
2290 East Ave.
Rochester, NY 14610
Tel.: 716-244-5400
Fax: 716-244-0628
Year Founded: 1983
Approx.Billings: $24,000,000
Emp.: 51
Full Service Marketing Communications
Francis J. Cosentino *(Pres. & Chief Exec. Officer)*
John Connelly *(Exec. V.P. & Dir-Creative/Writer)*
Mike Fountain *(Exec. V.P. & Dir.-Creative)*
George H. Klemann *(Exec. V.P.-Fin.)*
Marcia A. Ilardo *(V.P.-Fin. & Dir.-Human Resources)*
Barbara Laughton *(V.P. & Dir.-Pub. Rels.)*
Margo Ellis *(Coord.-Admin.)*
Betty Lou Hope *(Asst.-Admin. & Human Resources)*
Paul Mittak *(Billing Coord.)*
Dee Pelow *(Computer Graphics Specialist)*
Eileen Rhodes *(Sr. Coord.-Admin.)*
Erika Seiffer *(Accounts Payable)*
Char Semrau *(Asst. Controller)*

Computer Systems/Hardware:
Macintosh; Qume; Media Management Plus

ICM INDUSTRIES, INC.
122 S. Michigan Ave., Ste. 1700
Chicago, IL 60603
Tel.: 312-939-5008 DE
Fax: 312-939-4985
Year Founded: 1985
Approx.Sls.: $300,200,000
Emp.: 3,486
Fiscal Year-end: 12/31/90
Export
Holding Company; Manufacture Hydraulics & Material Handling Equipment; Aluminum Die Castings
S.I.C.: 6719; 3399; 3569; 3593; 3714
Corporate Giving Program: United Way
Jack D. Rutherford *(Chm. & Chief Exec. Officer)*
David T. Shelby *(Pres.)*
Raymond A. Imp *(V.P.-Fin. & Chief Fin. Officer)*
Anthony Parrottino *(V.P.-Quality)*
Ry Smith *(Mgr.-Tax & Acctg.)*
Marge Illich *(Admin. Asst.)*
Kelly Carter *(Admin. Asst.)*

Principal(s):
Jack D. Rutherford
David T. Shelby

No. of Mfg. Plants/Facilities: 16
No. of U.S. Offices: 16

Computer Systems/Hardware:
IBM PC-XT

Outside Service Firm(s):

Deloitte & Touche*(Auditors)*
Two Prudential Plaza, 180 N. Stetson
Chicago, IL 60601
Tel.: 312-946-2039

Marsh & McLennan*(Commercial Insurance Carrier)*
500 W. Monroe
Chicago, IL 60661
Tel.: 312-627-6000
Fax: 312-627-6242

Mutual Health Services*(Group Insurer)*
P.O. Box 94601,
Cleveland, OH 44101-1900

Bankers Trust Co.*(Investment Banker)*
233 S. Wacker Dr., Ste. 5200
Chicago, IL 60606

Laser, Schostok, Kolman & Frank*(Legal Firm)*
30 N. La Salle St., Suite 2500
Chicago, IL 60602
Tel.: 312-641-1300

Citibank N.A.*(Major Banking Relationship)*
Corporate Trust Services, 399 Park Ave.
New York, NY 10043
Tel.: 212-559-1605

Subsidiaries:

Doehler-Jarvis **(1)**
5400 N. Detroit Ave.
Toledo, OH 43612
Tel.: 419-470-8020
Fax: 419-470-8185
Emp.: 2,122
Aluminum Foundry Castings
S.I.C.: 3363
George H. Wells *(Pres. & Chief Exec. Officer)*
Robert R. Fulton *(Exec. V.P. & Chief Oper. Officer)*
Raymond E. Konczal *(V.P. & Controller)*
John E. James *(V.P.-Mktg. & Sls.)*
David Adkins *(Dir.-Pur.)*

Ferralloy **(1)**
Becks Mill Rd.
Salem, IN 47167
Tel.: 812-883-3381

The Gradall Co. **(1)**
406 Mill Ave.
New Philadelphia, OH 44663
Tel.: 216-339-2211 (100%)
Fax: 216-339-5224
Approx.Sls.: $58,000,000
Emp.: 621
Mfr. of Hydraulic Boom Excavators & Rough Terrain Material Handlers
S.I.C.: 3492
Barry J. Phillips *(Pres.)*
David Williams *(V.P.-Sls.)*
Jack Dooling *(Chief Fin. Officer)*
Junior Evans *(Mgr.-Pur.)*

Hydreco **(1)**
1885 Tobacco Rd.
Augusta, GA 30906
Tel.: 706-790-6800
Approx.Sls.: $14,900,000
Hydraulic Valves, Gear Pumps & Motors, Piston Pumps, Filters & Systems for Construction, Farm & Materials Handling Machinery
S.I.C.: 3492; 3594; 3561; 3714
G.L. Rice *(Pres.)*
D.A. Fuller *(V.P.-Fin.)*
Don Brockmeyer *(V.P.-Mktg. & Engrng.)*
Larry McCord *(Pur. Agent)*
John Millichamp *(Dir.-Matl. Control)*
Joe Kenworthy *(Master Scheduler)*

ICM Investment Co. **(1)**
122 So. Michigan Ave., Ste. 1700
Chicago, IL 60603
Tel.: 312-939-5008 (100%)
Holding Company
S.I.C.: 6719

IFP Hydraulics Inc. **(1)**
3412 No. River Road
Franklin Park, IL 60131
Tel.: 708-678-5795 (100%)
Approx.Sls.: $5,900,000
Emp.: 37
Hydraulic Valves & Precision Machining
S.I.C.: 3511
Roy Corrigan *(Pres.)*
Donald Pillsbury *(Controller)*
Eileen Raymond *(Matl. Control Supvr.)*

Iowa Industrial Hydraulics, Inc. **(1)**
Industrial Park Rd.
Pocahontas, IA 50574
Tel.: 712-335-3311 (100%)
Approx.Sls.: $20,000,000
Manufacture Hydraulic Cylinders
S.I.C.: 3593
Mike Dahl *(Pres.)*
Robert Hoover *(V.P.-Mktg. & Sls.)*
John Williams *(Controller)*
Dean Ewoldt *(Matl. Mgr.)*

Magna-Pow'r Inc. **(1)**
3412 N. River Road
Franklin Park, IL 60131
Tel.: 708-678-5795
Tel.: 312-625-2190 (100%)
Fax: 708-678-5799
Approx.Sls.: $50,000,000
Emp.: 374
Fiscal Year-end: 12/31/90
Hydraulic Motors
S.I.C.: 3511
Walter P. Wasylowsky *(Pres.)*
George Aravosis *(Sr. V.P.-Mktg. & Engrng.)*
D. Kluver *(V.P. & Chief Fin. Officer)*

Plants:

Doehler-Jarvis Plant **(1)**
Rufe Taylor Rd.
Greeneville, TN 37743
Tel.: 615-639-1155
Thomas E. Toothman *(V.P.-Opers.)*

Doehler-Jarvis Plant **(1)**
400 Old Reading Pike
Stowe, PA 19464
Tel.: 215-327-5400
Steve Yodoff *(V.P.-Opers.)*

Doehler-Jarvis Plant **(1)**
2019 Ford Rd.
Sheffield, AL 35660
Tel.: 205-381-0182
Thomas E. Toothman *(V.P.-Opers.)*

Doehler-Jarvis Plant **(1)**
1945 Smead Ave.
Toledo, OH 43691
Tel.: 419-470-8020
Ken Schutle *(V.P.-Opers.)*

IDAB INTERNATIONAL INCORPORATED
One Enterprise Pkwy., Ste. 300
Hampton, VA 23666
Tel.: 804-825-2260
Fax: 804-825-9307
Approx.Sls.: $60,000,000
Emp.: 500
Export
Robotics; Material Handling Systems & Equipment Manufacturer; Mailroom Systems & Equipment for the Newspaper Industry
S.I.C.: 3537
Ole B. Rygh *(Pres. & Chief Exec. Officer)*
Gary Duffield *(Exec. V.P. & Gen. Mgr.-Mailroom Div.)*
Jaimie Kirkwood *(V.P. & Treas.)*
Paul Roche *(V.P. & Gen. Mgr.-Matl. Handling Div.)*
Pat Lynch *(V.P.-Sls. & Mktg.)*
Linda Boatright *(Mgr.-Personnel)*
Fred Wolf *(Mgr.-Mktg.)*
Terry Bradford *(Mgr.-Exports)*
Carin Cowell *(Coord.-Communications)*

Outside Service Firm(s):

Deloitte & Touche*(Auditors)*
100 S.E. 2nd St.
Miami, FL 33131-2135
Tel.: 305-538-4141

Walton, Lantaff, Schroeder & Carson*(Legal Firm)*
Miami, FL

Sun Bank, N.A.*(Major Banking Relationship)*
Miami, FL 33131

Non-U.S. Subsidiaries:

IDAB Wamac AB **(1)**
Box 189, S-575
Eksjo, 22, Sweden
Tel.: 381 159 20
Manufacturer of Mailroom Equipment Used for the Newspaper Industry
S.I.C.: 3599; 3559
Ralf Backman *(Mng. Dir.)*

IDAB Wamac Pacific **(1)**
Trinity House, Stes. 1703-1704, 165-171 Wanchai Rd.
Hong Kong, Hong Kong
Tel.: 852-893-9255
Fax: 852-893-0715
Henry Barman *(Mng. Dir.)*

Non-U.S. Holding:

IDAB WAMAC Pacific Limited **(1)**
Trinity House, 165-171 Wanchai Road
Suites 1703-1704,
Hong Kong, Hong Kong
Tel.: 852-893-9255
Fax: 852-893-0715
Mfr. of Mailroom Equipment Used for the Newspaper Industry
S.I.C.: 3559
Henry Barman *(Mng. Dir.)*

IDC SERVICES, INC.
303 East Ohio Street
Chicago, IL 60611
Tel.: 312-943-7500 IL
Fax: 312-670-3529
Year Founded: 1961
Assets: $61,982,566
Liabilities: $46,322,743
Net Worth: $15,659,823
Approx.Rev.: $42,125,000
Emp.: 475
Fiscal Year-end: 12/31/89
Provides Financially-Oriented Administration & Information Systems & Services, Market Research Services to the Advertising & Entertainment Industries; Provider of Advertising & Entertainment Industry Payroll Processing & Casting Services in Connection with the Production of Commercials & Motion Pictures & a Provider of Electronic, Communications-Based Market Research Services
S.I.C.: 7319; 8741; 7389; 7819; 8721; 8743
Kenneth Gorman *(Chm. Bd.)*
Donald S. Crossett *(Pres. & Chief Exec. Officer)*
Paul McDonald *(Sr. V.P. & Chief Information Officer)*
Carl Beatty *(V.P.-Data Processing)*

IDC Services, Inc.—(Continued)

Michael B. Krueger *(Controller & Asst. Sec.)*

Outside Service Firm(s):

Arthur Andersen & Co.*(Auditors)*
33 W. Monroe St.
Chicago, IL 60603-4067
Tel.: 312-580-0033
Fax: 312-507-6748

Skadden, Arps, Slate, Meagher, & Flom*(Legal Firm)*
New York, NY

American National Bank & Trust Company of Chicago*(Major Banking Relationship)*
33 N. LaSalle St.
Chicago, IL 60602
Tel.: 312-661-5000
Fax: 312-661-6417

Divisions:

BCI Talent Payments **(1)**
79 Fifth Avenue
New York, NY 10003
Tel.: 212-243-2224 (100%)
Dave Alen *(Chief Exec. Officer)*

PowerForce Company, Inc. **(1)**
79 Fifth Ave.
New York, NY 10003
Tel.: 212-741-7777
Payroll Service & Sales Merchandisers
S.I.C.: 8741
Dave Allen *(Chief Exec. Officer)*

Talent & Residuals, Inc. **(1)**
79 Fifth Ave.
New York, NY 10003
Tel.: 212-741-7777
Payroll Service
S.I.C.: 8741
Dave Allen *(Chief Oper. Officer)*

Subsidiaries:

ASI Market Research, Inc. **(1)**
2600 W. Olive Ave.
Burbank, CA 91505
Tel.: 818-843-4400 (100%)
Emp.: 150
Market Analysis
S.I.C.: 8732
Gerald C. Lukeman *(Pres.)*

ASI Market Research, Inc. **(1)**
79 Fifth Avenue
New York, NY 10003
Tel.: 212-807-9393
Market Analysis
S.I.C.: 8732

Entertainment Partners **(1)**
2600 W. Olive St.
Burbank, CA 91505
Tel.: 818-569-5100 (100%)
Payroll Service
S.I.C.: 8721
Howard Siegel *(Sr. V.P.)*
Eric Capoorosso *(V.P.)*

PowerForce Company, Inc. **(1)**
303 E. Ohio St., 25th Fl.
Chicago, IL 60611
Tel.: 312-943-7500 (100%)
Payroll Service & Part-Time Sales Merchandisers
S.I.C.: 8721
Donald Crossett *(Acting Pres.)*
Wayne McClay *(V.P.-Sls.)*

Production Payments, Inc. **(1)**
2600 W. Olive St.
Burbank, CA 91505
Tel.: 818-569-5100 (100%)
Payroll Service
S.I.C.: 8721
Howard Siegel *(Sr. V.P.)*
Eric Capoorosso *(V.P.)*

Talent & Residuals, Inc. **(1)**
2600 W. Olive Ave.
Burbank, CA 91505
Tel.: 818-569-5100 (100%)
Payroll Service
S.I.C.: 8721
David Allen *(Chief Oper. Officer)*
Howard Seigel *(Sr. V.P.)*

I D E CORPORATION
29 Dumham Rd.
Billerica, MA 01821
Tel.: 508-663-6878
Fax: 508-663-8851
Approx.Sls.: $300,000,000
Emp.: 1,650
Mfr. of Computer Peripheral Equipment
S.I.C.: 3577
Gautom Gupta *(Pres.)*

Outside Service Firm(s):

First National Bank of Boston*(Auditors)*
P.O. Box 644,
Boston, MA 02102-0644
Tel.: 617-575-2900
Fax: 617-575-2549

Subsidiaries:

I D E Associates **(1)**
29 Dumham Rd.
Billerica, MA 01821
Tel.: 508-663-6878
Mfr. of Computer Peripheral Equipment
S.I.C.: 3577
Gautam Gupta *(Pres.)*
Dave Page *(V.P.-Opers.)*
Edward Marohn *(Chief Fin. Officer)*
Nora Feldman *(Dir.-Mktg.)*
David Hunter *(Chief Engr.)*

Idea Courier, Inc. **(1)**
1515 W. 14th St.
Tempe, AZ 85281
Tel.: 601-894-7000
Mfr. of Computer Peripheral Equipment; Computer Peripheral Equipment Rental & Leasing; Personal Computers
S.I.C.: 3577; 7377; 3571
Gautam Gupta *(Pres.)*

THE IDI GROUP COMPANIES
901 N. Stuart St.
Arlington, VA 22203
Tel.: 703-558-7300 **VA**
Fax: 703-558-7377
Year Founded: 1975
Approx.Sls.: $50,000,000
Emp.: 55
Fiscal Year-end: 12/31/91
Import Export
Real Estate Developer; Condominium & Commercial Buildings Operator
S.I.C.: 6512; 6514; 6552
Giuseppe Cecchi *(Pres. & Chief Exec. Officer)*
Thomas Rackowski *(V.P. & Controller)*
R. Leon McFillen *(V.P.)*
Richard Grizzard *(V.P.)*
Fred Togni *(V.P.)*
Norman Dreyfuss *(V.P.)*
Jesse Lee *(Chief Fin. Officer)*
Joseph Molina *(Gen. Counsel)*
John Heller *(Dir.-Opers.)*
Carlo Baietti *(Mgr.-Sls.)*

Outside Service Firm(s):

KPMG Peat Marwick*(Auditors)*
2001 M St., N.W.
Washington, DC 20036
Tel.: 202-467-3800

Hazel & Thomas, PC*(Legal Firm)*
Washington, DC
Tel.: 202-659-7000

IDM CONTROLS
6116 Milwee St.
Houston, TX 77092
Tel.: 713-681-6942
Fax: 713-681-2712
Emp.: 61
Motor Control Systems, Sales & Service
S.I.C.: 5084
Norman S. Myers *(Pres., Treas., Chief Exec. & Fin. Officers)*
David Huntington *(V.P.)*
Rod Reyes *(Controller)*

Computer Systems/Hardware:
Altos

Outside Service Firm(s):

Boelkel, Cabaniss & Co.*(Auditors)*
Houston, TX

Blue Cross & Blue Shield of Texas, Inc.*(Group Insurer)*
Dallas, TX

Crain & Caton*(Legal Firm)*
Houston, TX

Texas Commerce Bank*(Major Banking Relationship)*
600 Travis Street, Suite 1150
Houston, TX 77002
Tel.: 713-236-4865

Subsidiary:

IDM Equipment Company **(1)**
11616 Galayda Rd.
Houston, TX 77086
Tel.: 713-447-2731
Doug Piper *(Mgr.-Fin.)*

IGA, INC. (INDEPENDENT GROCERS ALLIANCE)
8725 W. Higgins
Chicago, IL 60631
Tel.: 312-693-4520
Fax: 312-693-1271
Year Founded: 1926
Approx.Sls.: $25,000,000
Emp.: 35
Fiscal Year-end: 12/31/90
Food Products
S.I.C.: 5084
Corporate Giving Program: Contribute *& Support Special Olympics*
Thomas S. Haggai *(Chm. Bd. & Chief Exec. Officer)*
William S. Kies *(Pres. & Chief Oper. Officer)*
John Baloun *(Controller)*
Ronald R. Burkhart *(V.P.-Communications)*
Mary Castro *(V.P.-Insurance)*

ILC INDUSTRIES, INC.
105 Wilbur Pl.
Bohemia, NY 11716
Tel.: 516-567-5600 **DE**
Fax: 516-563-5204
Year Founded: 1966
Assets: $96,000,000
Liabilities: $74,000,000
Net Worth: $22,000,000
Approx.Sls.: $114,900,000
Emp.: 1,560
Fiscal Year-end: 12/31/91
Import Export
Electronics, Solid State & Hybrid Data Converters, Computer Interface, Transformers; Aerostats Protective Equipment & Garments for Industrial, Military & Space Application
S.I.C.: 3674
Leonard C. Lane *(Chm. Bd. & Chief Exec. Officer)*
Clifford Lane *(Pres. & Chief Oper. Officer)*
Kenneth J. Sheedy *(V.P.-Fin.)*
Arlene Lane Fisher *(Sec.)*

No. of Foreign Offices: 5

Outside Service Firm(s):

Arthur Andersen & Co.*(Auditors)*
200 Broadhollow Road
Melville, NY 11747

Barclays Bank plc*(Major Banking Relationship)*
Jericho, NY

Subsidiaries:

ILC Data Device **(1)**
105 Wilbur Pl.
Bohemia, NY 11716
Tel.: 516-567-5600
Micro Electronic Components
S.I.C.: 3674
Clifford Lane *(Pres.)*
Kenneth J. Sheedy *(V.P.-Fin.)*

ILC Dover, Inc. **(1)**
Harrington-Frederica Rd.
Frederica, DE 19946
Tel.: 302-335-3911
Space & Environmental Protective Products
S.I.C.: 3999
Homer D. Reihm *(Pres.)*
Carl Zlock *(V.P.-Fin.)*

THE ISI MANUFACTURING, INC.
31915 Groesbeck Hwy.
Fraser, MI 48026
Mailing Address:
P.O. Box 220
Fraser, MI 48026
Tel.: 313-294-9500 **MI**
Fax: 313-294-9772
Fax: 313-294-8373
Year Founded: 1958
Assets: $50,000,000
Liabilities: $12,000,000
Net Worth: $38,000,000
Approx.Sls.: $70,000,000
Emp.: 400
Fiscal Year-end: 12/31/91
Export
Manufacture Automated Systems & Parts, Clamps, Fluid Power Products
S.I.C.: 3559; 3429; 3545; 3541; 3542
L. Douglas Blatt *(Pres. & Chief Exec. Officer)*
John A. Blatt *(Vice Chm.)*
T. Szydlowski *(Chief Exec. Officer)*
David Crorey *(Exec. V.P.-Sls. & Mktg.)*
Clifford Stanton *(V.P.-Fin.)*
Marilyn Woods *(Sec.)*
Michael Hudson *(Dir.-Info. Systems)*
Joseph Wilseck *(Dir.-Human Resources)*
Dennis Buch *(Pur. Agent)*

No. of Mfg. Plants/Facilities: 4
No. of Foreign Offices: 2

Outside Service Firm(s):

Follmer, Rudzewicz & Co.*(Auditors)*
Southfield, MI

Michael Biber*(Legal Firm)*
Farmington Hills, MI

Comerica Bank*(Major Banking Relationship)*
211 W. Fort St.
Detroit, MI 48226
Tel.: 313-222-3300

Subsidiaries:

Automation Products Group **(1)**
44831 Groesbeck
Mount Clemens, MI 48043
Tel.: 313-463-3000
John A. Blatt *(Pres.)*

ISI FLuid Power, Inc. **(1)**
P.O. BOx 400
Fraser, MI 48026
Charles Stahl *(Pres.)*

ISI Robotics I **(1)**
31915 Groesbeck Hwy.
Fraser, MI 48026
Tel.: 313-294-9500
L.D. Blatt *(Pres.)*

ISI Robotics II **(1)**
6100 Titan Dr.
Anchorville, MI 48004
Tel.: 313-725-2500
John A. Blatt *(Pres.)*

Pinckney Molded Plastics **(1)**
3970 Parsons
Howell, MI 48843
Tel.: 517-546-9900
Wayne Humphrey *(Plant Mgr.)*

ITA GROUP
4800 Westown Pkwy., Suite 300
West Des Moines, IA 50265
Tel.: 515-224-3400
Fax: 515-224-3589
Approx.Sls.: $50,000,000
Emp.: 120
Full Service Travel Incentive Corp.
R.W. Berg *(Chm. Bd.)*
Steven G. Chapman *(Pres.)*
J.E. Trabert *(Chief Exec. Officer)*
Richard Rue *(Sr. V.P. & Chief Fin. Officer)*
Mary Bussone *(V.P.-Opers.)*
Tom Mahoney *(V.P.-Mktg.)*
Rick Lotich *(V.P.-Sls.)*

ITI MARKETING SERVICES INC

ITI MARKETING SERVICES, INC.
7415 Dodge St.
Omaha, NE 68114
Tel.: 402-393-8000
Tel.: 800-562-5000 DE
Fax: 402-393-2635
Year Founded: 1986
Approx.Sls.: $65,000,000
Emp.: 4,000
Telemarketing Services
S.I.C.: 7389
Steven A. Idelman *(Chm. Bd.)*
Brent J. Welch *(Pres.)*
Sheri Idelman *(Chief Oper. Officer)*
W.B. Belew, Jr. *(Chief Fin. Officer)*
Kathryn A. Ekeler *(Legal Counsel)*
Matthew R. McKain *(V.P.-Fin.)*
Barry Siff *(V.P.-Human Resources)*
Vern Snider *(V.P.-Information Services)*
Jeff Symon *(V.P.-Mktg.)*
Principal(s):
Steven A. Idelman
Sheri Idelman

Outside Service Firm(s):

Arthur Andersen & Co.*(Auditors)*
1700 Farnam
Omaha, NE 68102
Tel.: 402-348-0123

Continental Bank, N.A.*(Major Banking Relationship)*
30 N. LaSalle St.
Chicago, IL 60693

Subsidiaries:

ITI Marketing Services, Inc., Inbound **(1)**
531 N. Wayne Ave.
Cincinnati, OH 45215
Tel.: 513-563-8666
Tel.: 800-543-8666
Telemarketing Company
S.I.C.: 7389
Sheri Idelman *(Chief Oper. Officer)*

ITI Marketing Services, Inc., Outbound **(1)**
7415 Dodge St.
Omaha, NE 08114
Tel.: 402-393-8000
Tel.: 800-562-5000
Telemarketing Company
S.I.C.: 7389
Lester Wells *(Chief Oper. Officer)*
Tom Cunnigham *(V.P.-Sls.)*

IAMS COMPANY
7250 Poe Ave.
Dayton, OH 45414
Tel.: 513-898-7387
Fax: 513-898-2408
Approx.Sls.: $50,000,000
Emp.: 270
Manufacturer of Pet Food
S.I.C.: 2047
Clay Mathile *(Chm. Bd. & Chief Exec. Officer)*
Tom Madeod *(Pres. & Chief Oper. Officer)*
Robert Meyer *(V.P.-Fin.)*
Steve Bobowski *(V.P.-Mktg.)*

ICAHN & CO., INC.
100 S. Bedford Rd.
Mount Kisco, NY 10549
Tel.: 914-242-4000
Fax: 914-242-4097
Year Founded: 1968
Emp.: 35
Fiscal Year-end: 12/31/91
Securities Dealer
S.I.C.: 6211
Carl C. Icahn *(Chm. Bd. & Chief Exec. Officer)*
Alfred D. Kingsley *(Sr. V.P.)*
Richard T. Buonato *(V.P. & Controller)*
Gary K. Duberstein *(V.P. & Gen. Counsel)*
Joseph Freilich *(Treas. & Sec.)*

Subsidiaries:

ACF Industries, Inc. **(1)**
3301 Rider Trail So.
Earth City, MO 63045
Tel.: 314-344-4500
Telex: 447691
Assets: $1,988,285,000
Earnings: $15,355,000
Liabilities: $1,869,021,000
Net Worth: $119,264,000
Approx.Rev.: $669,591,000
Emp.: 1,950
Fiscal Year-end: 12/31/90
Computer Systems/Hardware:
IBM 4381
Manufacture Railroad Equipment; Railroad Car Leasing
S.I.C.: 3743; 4741
Carl C. Icahn *(Chm. Bd.)*
Alfred D. Kingsley *(Vice Chm.)*
James J. Unger *(Pres.)*
Roger D. Wynkoop *(Exec. V.P.)*
Donald E. Reese *(Sr. V.P.-Mfg.)*
James C. Bates *(V.P. & Chief Fin. Officer)*
Carl D. Eckhoff *(V.P.-Taxes)*
William L. Finn *(V.P.-Fleet Opers. & Gen. Mgr.-New Business Group)*
George E. Sullivan *(V.P.-Sls. & Leasing)*
David R. Sutliff *(V.P.-Engrng.)*
Robert J. Mitchell *(Treas. & Asst. Sec.)*
Umesh Choksi *(Asst. Treas.)*
Janet A. Kniffen *(Asst. Sec.)*
R. Kase *(Dir.-Employee Benefits)*
Brian Evdoe *(Dir.-Adv.)*
Gary G. Rager *(Personnel Dir.)*
Larry R. Stewart *(Dir.-Pur.)*

Trans World Airlines, Inc. **(1)**
100 S. Bedford Rd.
Mount Kisco, NY 10549
Tel.: 914-242-3000
Fax: 914-242-3000
Assets: $4,107,656,000
Earnings: $249,743,000
Liabilities: $4,138,911,000
Net Worth: $31,255,000
Approx.Rev.: $4,361,145,000
Emp.: 30,819
Fiscal Year-end: 12/31/90
Air Transportation of Passengers & Cargo
S.I.C.: 4512
Carl C. Icahn *(Chm. Bd. & Chief Exec. Officer)*
Al Kingsley *(Vice Chm.)*
J. William Hoar *(Exec. V.P.)*
Glenn R. Zander *(Chief Oper. Officer)*
Robin Wilson *(Chief Oper. Officer)*
Charles Adams *(Sr. V.P.-Intl. Div.)*
Mark Buckstein *(Sr. V.P.-External Affairs & Gen. Counsel)*
Harry T. Chandis *(Sr. V.P.-Mktg.)*
Chuck Thibideau *(Sr. V.P.-Employee Rels.)*
Ronald E. Reynolds *(Sr. V.P.-Flight Opers.)*
Harold First *(V.P. & Chief Fin. Officer)*
Edgar R. Ashburn *(V.P. & Controller)*
L. Clark Billie *(V.P.-Engrng. & Opers. Control)*
C. Gary Bowring *(V.P.-Engrng. & Quality Assurance)*
Barbara Colwell *(V.P.-Business Mktg.)*
John C. Crowe *(V.P.-Opers. Admin.)*
John A. Jessup *(V.P.-Matls. Mngmt. & Contract Services)*
Arthur N. Knudsen *(V.P.-Properties & Facilities)*
John M. Krause *(V.P.-Inflight Services)*
Sheldon J. Kravitz *(V.P.-Adv. & Consumer Mktg.)*
J.J. McCarthy *(V.P.-Maintenance Oper.)*
Joseph F. Nemecek *(V.P.-Ground Oper. Support)*
J. Robert O'Neill *(V.P.-Scheduling)*
Robert C. Osborne *(V.P.-Health & Mkt. Devel.)*
John S. Sheldon *(V.P.-Sls.)*
Steven J. Slade *(V.P.-Govt. Affairs)*
Stephen M. Souza *(V.P. & Asst. Treas.)*
Marsha A. Hewitt *(Sec. & Assoc. Gen. Counsel)*
Robert J. Mitchell *(Treas.)*
Jim Faulkner *(Dir.-Public Rels.)*
Frank Brander *(Dir.-Business Mktg.)*
Theresa DeGiuli *(Dir.-Adv.)*
Margaret McKinley *(Mgr.-Adv.)*
Diane Barkoe *(Adv. Supvr.)*

ICELAND SEAFOOD CORPORATION
1250 Sate Hill Rd.
Camp Hill, PA 17011
Tel.: 717-761-2600
Tel.: 800-448-3848
Fax: 717-761-1613
Approx.Sls.: $130,000,000
Emp.: 400
Frozen Packaged Seafood
S.I.C.: 2092
M.G. Fridgeirsson *(Pres.)*
M.L. Finkelstein *(Exec. V.P.)*

ICELANDAIR
21 Penn Plaza
New York, NY 10001
Tel.: 212-967-8888
Telex: 4970657
Fax: 212-330-1456
Year Founded: 1937
Approx.Sls.: $75,000,000
Emp.: 200
Fiscal Year-end: 12/31/90
International Air Transportation
S.I.C.: 4512; 4522
Hordur Sigurgeston *(Chm. Bd.)*
Sigurdur Helgason *(Pres. & Chief Exec. Officer)*
Petur Eiriksson *(Sr. V.P.-Mktg.)*
Sigfus Erlingsson *(V.P.-Americas)*
William Connors *(Pub. Rels. Dir.)*

ICICLE SEAFOODS, INC.
4019 21st Ave. West
Seattle, WA 98199
Mailing Address:
P.O. Box 79003
Seattle, WA 98119
Tel.: 206-282-0988
Fax: 206-282-7222
Year Founded: 1965
Approx.Sls.: $191,000,000
Emp.: 275
Markets & Processes Seafood; Canned Seafood Products
S.I.C.: 2091
Robert M. Thorstenson *(Chm. Bd.)*
Robert Brophy *(Pres.)*
Ralph G. Hoard *(Exec. V.P.)*
Don M. Giles *(V.P.-Prod. Opers.)*
Larry D. Hill *(V.P.-Canned Sls.)*
Mark S. Sandvik *(V.P.-Frozen Sls.)*
Ken Franick *(Dir.-Surimi Sls.)*
Larry Rafferty *(Dir.-Data Processing)*
Julie Aydelotte *(Mgr.-Human Resources)*
Reed Smith *(Natl. Sls. Mgr.)*
Karen Budnick *(Mgr.-Admin.)*

Outside Service Firm(s):

Moss Adams*(Auditors)*
1001 4th Ave., Ste. 2900
Seattle, WA 98154-1106
Tel.: 206-223-1820

Graham & Dunn*(Legal Firm)*
1301 5th Ave., 34th Floor
Seattle, WA 98101
Tel.: 206-624-8300

Security Pacific National Bank*(Major Banking Relationship)*
Security Pacific Tower, T21-7,
Seattle, WA 98124
Tel.: 206-621-5920

IDAHO FOREST INDUSTRY, INC.
2850 Seltice Way
Coeur D'Alene, ID 83816
Tel.: 208-765-1414 ID
Fax: 208-765-5045
Year Founded: 1968
Approx.Sls.: $86,000,000
Emp.: 450
General Sawmills & Planing Mills
S.I.C.: 2421
R.J. DeArmond *(Chm. Bd.)*
William T. Richards *(Pres.)*
Richard L. DeArmond *(Sr. V.P.)*
Jim English *(V.P.)*
D.J. Jeffrey *(V.P.-Fin. & Treas.)*
R.W. Weiss *(Sec.)*
D.K. Frank *(Dir.-Personnel)*

Outside Service Firm(s):

BDO Seidman*(Auditors)*
Portland, OR

United States National Bank of Oregon*(Major Banking Relationship)*
P.O. Box 3850,
Portland, OR 97208
Tel.: 503-275-6111

IDAHO LOTTERY
1199 Shoreline Lane
Boise, ID 83702
Mailing Address:
P.O. Box 6537,
Boise, ID 83707
Tel.: 208-334-2600
Fax: 908-334-2610
Year Founded: 1989
Approx.Sls.: $52,000,000
Emp.: 46
Fiscal Year-end: 6/30/91
State Lottery
S.I.C.: 7999
Wally Hedrick *(Dir.)*
Bob Cooper *(Deputy Dir.-Mktg. & Information)*

IDAHO SUPREME COMPANY
614 E. 800 N. St.
Firth, ID 83236
Mailing Address:
P.O. Box 246
Firth, ID 83236
Tel.: 208-346-6841 ID
Fax: 208-346-4104
Year Founded: 1966
Approx.Sls.: $32,000,000
Emp.: 150
Fiscal Year-end: 8/31/89
Export
Potato Processor & Fresh Pack
S.I.C.: 0134; 2034
Wilford Chapman *(Chm. Bd. & Pres.)*
Wayne Allen *(V.P.-Sls. & Mktg. & Sec.)*
Paul Byington *(V.P.-Fin.)*
Steve Prescott *(Controller)*
Vondel Chapman *(Dir.-Pur.)*
Wade Chapman *(Dir.-Data Processing)*
Gil Dayley *(Dir.-Quality Control)*
Kevin Hardy *(Mgr.-Personnel)*
Larry Haws *(Mgr.-Retail Sls.)*
Pam Volk *(Mgr.-Human Resources)*

Computer Systems/Hardware:
IBM Compatible Leading Edge

Outside Service Firm(s):

Rudd, DaBell & Call*(Auditors)*
Idaho Falls, ID

Peterson, Moss & Olson*(Legal Firm)*
Idaho Falls, ID

Idaho First National*(Major Banking Relationship)*
Blackfoot, ID

IDAHOAN FOODS
One Potato Place
Lewisville, ID 83431
Mailing Address:
P.O. Box 130
Lewisville, ID 83431
Tel.: 208-754-4665
Fax: 208-754-0094
Approx.Sls.: $86,000,000
Emp.: 600
Manufacture Dehydrated Potatoes
S.I.C.: 2034
Gale W. Clement *(Chm. Bd. & Pres.)*
Norman Hart *(Exec. V.P.)*
Todd Clement *(V.P. & Dir.-Data Processing)*
Hal Christensen *(Dir.-Mktg.)*
Rodney K. Roberts *(Dir.Personnel.)*

Outside Service Firm(s):

Galusha, Higgins & Galusha*(Auditors)*
Idaho Falls, ID

Valley Bank*(Major Banking Relationship)*
Rexburg, ID

IDEA ENGINEERING & FABRICATING
13881 Elmira Rd.
Detroit, MI 48227
Tel.: 313-834-8000
Fax: 313-834-8756
Approx.Sls.: $50,000,000
Emp.: 200
Conveyors & Conveying Equipment; Cranes, Industrial Plant; Structural Steel Erection; Fabricated Structural Metal
S.I.C.: 3535; 3536; 1791; 3441
Joseph R. Dunville *(Chm. Bd., Pres., & Chief Exec. Officer)*
Richard D. Barnhill *(Chief Fin. Officer, Treas. & Sec.)*

IDEA MAN, INC.
1945 S. La Cienega Blvd.
Los Angeles, CA 90034
Tel.: 213-870-0700
Fax: 213-870-0524
Year Founded: 1971
Approx.Sls.: $22,600,000
Emp.: 120
Fiscal Year-end: 12/31/91
Import
Sales Promotion Firm; Specialty Advertising Distribution
S.I.C.: 5199
Robert Waldorf *(Chm. Bd. & Pres.)*
James Buescher *(Chief Oper. Officer)*
Marvin Baida *(V.P.-Sls.)*
Campbell Brown *(V.P.)*
Les Morris *(V.P.)*
Toby Waldorf *(Treas. & Corp. Sec.)*
Lynn Baum *(Controllor & Mgr.-Acct.)*
Robert Faux *(Dir.-Pur.)*
Susan Malone *(Mgr.-Admin.)*
Principal(s):
Robert Waldorf

No. of Mfg. Plants/Facilities: 9

Computer Systems/Hardware:
Micro-Data CPU; ADDS Terminals; IBM PC

Outside Service Firm(s):

BDO Seidman*(Auditors)*
1900 Avenue of the Stars, 11th Fl.
Los Angeles, CA 90067-6008
Tel.: 310-557-0300

Corletto & Ackerman*(Legal Firm)*
Encino, CA

First Interstate Bank of California, N.A.*(Major Banking Relationship)*
P.O. Box 3667,
Los Angeles, CA 90051
Tel.: 213-614-4000

IDEAL CHEMICAL & SUPPLY COMPANY
4025 Air Park St.
Memphis, TN 38118
Tel.: 901-363-7720 **TN**
Fax: 901-366-0864
Year Founded: 1932
Approx.Sls.: $15,000,000
Emp.: 76
Wholesale Distribution of Industrial Chemicals
S.I.C.: 5169
Sam Block, Sr. *(Chm. Bd.)*
Sam Block, Jr. *(Pres.)*
Peter Brim *(V.P.)*
Daniel Richards *(Chief Fin. Officer)*
Marx J. Borod *(Sec.)*

Outside Service Firm(s):

KPMG Peat Marwick*(Auditors)*
4200 Norwest Center, 90 S. 7th St.
Minneapolis, MN 55402
Tel.: 612-341-2222

IDEAL FORGING CORPORATION
167 Center St.
Southington, CT 06489
Tel.: 203-621-0133
Fax: 203-621-7550
Approx.Sls.: $15,000,000
Emp.: 170
Commercial Forgings & Stainless Steel Flanges
S.I.C.: 3462; 3494
Michael J. Simone *(Chm. Bd.)*
James Simone, Jr. *(Pres.)*
Victor W. D'Amato *(Exec. V.P.)*
John A. Susco *(Sec. & Treas.)*

Outside Service Firm(s):

Edward Greenberg & Co.*(Auditors)*
New Haven, CT

Connecticut Bank & Trust*(Major Banking Relationship)*
One Constitution Plaza,
Hartford, CT 06115

IDEAL INDUSTRIES, INC.
1000 Park Ave.
Sycamore, IL 60178
Tel.: 815-895-5181 **DE**
Fax: 815-895-9470
Year Founded: 1916
Approx.Sls.: $50,000,000
Emp.: 600
Export
Manufacture Electrician's Tools & Supplies
S.I.C.: 3643; 3644
D.W. Juday *(Chm. Bd.)*
P.V. Nall *(Pres.)*
J.P. Benisek *(V.P.-Human Resources)*
G.D. Hollister *(V.P.-Mktg.)*
P.L. Sawyer *(V.P.-Engrng.)*
R. Snow *(V.P.-Mfg.)*
Joe DiCianni *(Dir.-Data Processing)*
L.P. Jones *(Dir.-Intl. Mktg.)*
James Pfotenhauer *(Dir.-Fin.)*
R.C. Bukowsky *(Natl. Sls. Mgr.)*
D.M. Urbaniec *(Mgr.-Mktg. Communications)*
Terry A. Duchaine *(Mktg. Communications Specialist)*

Outside Service Firm(s):

Coopers & Lybrand*(Auditors)*
6000 E. State St.
Rockford, IL 61108
Tel.: 815-394-0300

McDermott, Will & Emery*(Legal Firm)*
227 W. Monroe St.
Chicago, IL 60606-5096
Tel.: 312-372-2000

The Northern Trust Co.*(Major Banking Relationship)*
50 S. LaSalle St.
Chicago, IL 60675
Tel.: 312-630-6000
Fax: 312-630-6516

Subsidiary:

Buchanan Construction Products, Inc. **(1)**
Hackettstown Commerce Park, 101 Bilby Rd.
Hackettstown, NJ 07840
Tel.: 908-850-5200
Manufacture Electrical Connectors
S.I.C.: 3643
J. Tony Mitchell *(Pres.)*

IDEAL MACARONI COMPANY
26001 Richmond Rd.
Bedford Heights, OH 44146
Tel.: 216-292-7272
Fax: 216-292-2967
Approx.Sls.: $10,000,000
Emp.: 50
Fiscal Year-end: 9/30/91
Ippolitos Ideal Macaroni & Spaghetti
S.I.C.: 3556
Pat Ippolito *(Pres.)*

IDEAL POOL CORP.
(Sub. of Ideal Leisure Products)
3955 N. Peachtree Rd.
Atlanta, GA 30341
Tel.: 404-455-1800
Fax: 404-986-6462
Approx.Sls.: $10,000,000
Emp.: 25
Fiscal Year-end: 2/28/91
Mfr. Vinyl-Lined Pools & Components
S.I.C.: 1799; 5999; 3312
Steven L. Renda *(Chm. Bd., Pres. & Chief Exec. Officer)*
Duane B. Jackson *(Exec. V.P. & Sr. Legal Counsel)*
Paul Johnston *(V.P.)*
Bob Hudson *(Gen. Mgr.)*

Division:

Pool World, Inc. **(1)**
3955 N. Peachtree Rd
Atlanta, GA 30341
Tel.: 404-458-6621

Affiliate:

Atlanta Southeastern Development Corp. **(1)**
3955 No. Peachtree Rd.
Atlanta, GA 30341
Tel.: 404-457-1311

IGLOO CORPORATION
1001 W. Sam Houston Pkwy., N.
Houston, TX 77043
Mailing Address:
P.O. Box 19322
Houston, TX 77224-9322
Tel.: 713-461-5955
Telex: 77-5331
Fax: 713-465-2009
Year Founded: 1947
Approx.Sls.: $150,000,000
Emp.: 900
Fiscal Year-end: 9/30/91
Import Export
Portable Water Coolers & Picnic Chests, Heavy-Duty Utility Containers
S.I.C.: 3085; 2821; 2891; 3585; 3086; 3089
Jonathan H. Godshall *(Pres.)*
Sam Davis *(V.P.-Fin.)*
Harry Marcionetti *(V.P.-Opers.)*
Jon Jones *(V.P.-Distr. & Customer Services)*
Lee Stranathan *(V.P.-Mktg.)*
John K. Worrell *(V.P.-Sls.)*
Mark Zehnder *(Mgr.-Pur.)*

Outside Service Firm(s):

Price Waterhouse*(Auditors)*
1201 Louisiana, Ste. 2900
Houston, TX 77002
Tel.: 713-654-4100

Security Pacific National Bank*(Major Banking Relationship)*
Chicago, IL

ILLINOIS AUTO ELECTRIC CO.
656 County Line Rd.
Elmhurst, IL 60126
Tel.: 708-833-4300 **IL**
Fax: 708-832-6104
Approx.Sls.: $40,000,000
Emp.: 180
Export
Diesel Fuel System Rebuilding; Air-Cooled Engines & Parts; Non-Automotive Engine Repair & Replacement; Motor Vehicle Supplies & New Parts; Lawn & Garden Machinery & Equipment
S.I.C.: 3519; 5084; 7699; 5013; 5083
Robert L. Sirotek *(Chm. Bd.)*
H. Bruce Sirotek *(Pres.)*
Jonathan R. Sirotek *(Grp. V.P.)*
R. Gordon Sirotek *(Grp. V.P.)*
Richard A. Johnson *(V.P.-Fin.)*
Bill Fritz *(V.P.-Sls. & Mktg.)*
Norman Schmitt *(Mgr.-Pur.)*
Principal(s):
Robert L. Sirotek
H. Bruce Sirotek
Jonathan R. Sirotek
R. Gordon Sirotek

No. of Mfg. Plants/Facilities: 8

Outside Service Firm(s):

Crowe Chizek*(Auditors)*
Chicago, IL

Seigan & Weisman*(Legal Firm)*
Chicago, IL

LaSalle National Bank*(Major Banking Relationship)*
135 S. LaSalle St.
Chicago, IL 60603
Tel.: 312-443-2440
Fax: 312-443-2819

Divisions:

Illinois Auto Central Div. **(1)**
4750 S. Central
Chicago, IL 60638
Tel.: 708-563-2700
Refrigeration Repair Service; Truck Engine Repair Except Industrial
S.I.C.: 7623; 7538
R. Gordon Sirotek *(V.P.)*
David A. Swanson *(Gen. Mgr.)*

Illinios Auto Electric Midwest Engine Warehouse Div. **(1)**
515 Roman Rd.
Elmhurst, IL 60126
Tel.: 708-833-1200
Air-cooled Engines & Parts
S.I.C.: 3519
Jonathan Sirotek *(V.P.)*
Mark A. McCormick *(Gen. Mgr.-Sls.)*

ILLINOIS CEREAL MILLS, INC.
P.O. Box 550, 616 S. Jefferson Ave.
Paris, IL 61944
Tel.: 217-465-5331 **DE**
Fax: 217-463-1644
Year Founded: 1933
Approx.Sls.: $135,000,000
Emp.: 240
Fiscal Year-end: 9/30/91
Export
Milling Dry Corn
S.I.C.: 2041
Joseph W. Hasler *(Pres. & Chief Exec. Officer)*
T. Alan Russell *(Exec. V.P., Sec. & Treas.)*
J. Monroe Hall *(Asst. to Pres.)*
Stephen W. Eitel *(Sr. V.P.)*
James B. Buchanan *(V.P.-Grain)*
Bruce Smith *(Treas.)*
Kenneth Hamilton *(Controller)*
Charles Barnes *(Dir.-Labor Rels.)*
Jim Edmonds *(Dir.-Tech. & Engrng.)*
Jerry Egan *(Dir.-Pur.)*

Harry Frost *(Dir.-Quality Control)*
Mike Smith *(Dir.-Res. & Devel.)*
Chris Eldredge *(Mgr.-Prods.)*
Richard German *(Mgr.-Data Processing)*
Stephanie Gosnell *(Mgr.-Export)*
Richard McFarland *(Mgr.-Traffic; Trucks & Rail)*

No. of Mfg. Plants/Facilities: 2

Computer Systems/Hardware:
Unisys

Outside Service Firm(s):

Arthur Andersen & Co.*(Auditors)*
111 Monument Circle
Indianapolis, IN 46204
Tel.: 317-634-3210

Wausau Insurance Companies*(Group Insurer)*
Paris, IL

Massey, Anderson & Gibson*(Legal Firm)*
Paris, IL

Harris Trust & Savings Bank*(Major Banking Relationship)*
111 W. Monroe St.
Chicago, IL 60690
Tel.: 312-461-2265
Tel.: 800-858-0840

ILLINOIS CONSOLIDATED TELEPHONE CO.
121 S. 17th St.
Mattoon, IL 61938
Tel.: 217-235-3311 **IL**
Telex: 217-234-9934
Year Founded: 1894
Assets: $96,786,000
Earnings: $7,136,000
Liabilities: $49,391,000
Net Worth: $47,395,000
Approx.Sls.: $56,600,000
Emp.: 702
Fiscal Year-end: 12/31/91
Telephone Communications System
S.I.C.: 4813
Richard A. Lumpkin *(Chm. Bd. & Chief Exec. Officer)*
R.J. Currey *(Pres. & Chief Oper. Officer)*
R.D. Arnold *(V.P.)*
D.L. Erickson *(V.P.-Opers.)*
G.B. Glisan *(V.P.-Mktg. & Plng.)*
J.L. Patrick *(V.P. & Controller)*
P.L. Rossiter *(Sec.)*
S.L. Grissom *(Treas.)*
Kevin R. Ferguson *(Asst. Treas.)*
P.C. Barr *(Dir.-Pub. Rels.)*

No. of U.S. Offices: 1

Outside Service Firm(s):

Arthur Andersen & Co.*(Auditors)*
33 W. Monroe St.
Chicago, IL 60603-4067
Tel.: 312-580-0033
Fax: 312-507-6748

Commercial Union Insurance Co.*(Commercial Insurance Carrier)*
Boston, MA

St. Paul Insurance of Illinois*(Commercial Insurance Carrier)*
Chicago, IL

Aetna Life & Casualty*(Group Insurer)*
100 N. Riverside Plaza
Chicago, IL 60606

Blue Cross & Blue Shield of Illinois*(Group Insurer)*
100 Tower Drive
Burr Ridge, IL 60521
Tel.: 708-323-3666

HMO Illinois*(Group Insurer)*
Chicago, IL

Personal Care HMO*(Group Insurer)*
Champaign, IL

Kidder, Peabody & Co.*(Investment Banker)*
125 South Wacker
Chicago, IL

Schiff, Hardin & Waite*(Legal Firm)*
7200 Sears Tower, 233 S. Wacker Dr.
Chicago, IL 60606
Tel.: 312-876-1000

Harris Trust & Savings Bank*(Major Banking Relationship)*
111 W. Monroe St.
Chicago, IL 60690
Tel.: 312-461-2265
Tel.: 800-858-0840

The Burridge Group*(Pension Manager)*
115 South LaSalle St.
Chicago, IL 60603

Chicago Asset Management Co.*(Pension Manager)*
11 S. LaSalle
Chicago, IL 60603

Monetta Financial Services, Inc.*(Pension Manager)*
Wheaton, IL

Harris Trust & Savings Bank*(Pension Manager)*
111 W. Monroe St.
Chicago, IL 60690
Tel.: 312-461-2265
Tel.: 800-858-0840

The Prudential Asset Management Company*(Pension Manager)*
71 Hanover Rd.
Florham Park, NJ 07932

Affiliates:

Central Communications Company **(1)**
121 S. 17th St.
Mattoon, IL 61938
Tel.: 217-235-3311
Installation / Maintenence of Telecommunications Equipment
S.I.C.: 1731

Consolidated Communications Directories, Inc. **(1)**
121 S. 17th St.
Mattoon, IL 61938
Tel.: 217-235-3311
Emp.: 181
Telephone Directory Provider
S.I.C.: 2759

Consolidated Communications Mobile Services, Inc. **(1)**
121 S. 17th St.
Mattoon, IL 61938
Tel.: 217-235-3311
Emp.: 10
Provider of One-Way Pager Service
S.I.C.: 3663

Consolidated Communications Operator Services, Inc. **(1)**
121 S. 17th St.
Mattoon, IL 61938
Tel.: 217-235-3311
Emp.: 89
Provider of Alternate Operator Services

Consolidated Communications Public Services, Inc. **(1)**
121 S. 17 St.
Mattoon, IL 61938
Tel.: 217-235-3311
Emp.: 16

Consolidated Network, Inc. **(1)**
121 S. 17th St.
Mattoon, IL 61938
Tel.: 217-235-3311
Emp.: 82

Consolidated Telemarketing America, Inc. **(1)**
121 S. 17th St.
Mattoon, IL 61938
Tel.: 217-235-3311
Emp.: 20

ILLINOIS HYDRAULIC CONSTRUCTION COMPANY
1797 La Fox St.
South Elgin, IL 60177
Mailing Address:
P.O. Box 545,
Elgin, IL 60121
Tel.: 708-742-1516 **DE**
Fax: 708-742-6610
Year Founded: 1906
Approx.Sls.: $24,000,000
Emp.: 152
Fiscal Year-end: 4/30/91
Water & Sewage Treatment Plants, Construction & Commercial, Industrial & Institutional Building, Contractor & Underground Pipe Installation, Underground Utility Construction
S.I.C.: 1629; 1542; 1541; 1623
Thomas S. Rakow *(Pres., Chief Exec. Officer & Treas.)*
May T. Rakow *(Sr. V.P.-Personnel & Sec.)*
Donald J. Kumorek *(Dir.-Data Processing)*
Principal(s):
Thomas S. Rakow
May T. Rakow

No. of Mfg. Plants/Facilities: 1
No. of U.S. Offices: 1

Computer Systems/Hardware:
GEAC Systems/Motorola 84203

Outside Service Firm(s):

Crowe, Chizek & Co.*(Auditors)*
P.O. Box 3687,
Oak Brook, IL 60822
Tel.: 708-954-7408
Fax: 708-799-1299

Assurance Agency*(Commercial Insurance Carrier)*
114 N Arlington Hghts. Rd.
Arlington Heights, IL 60004

AGC Group Health*(Group Insurance Broker/Consult)*
1028 S. Second St.
Springfield, IL 62705

Unum Life Insurance Company*(Group Insurance Broker/Consult)*
3525 Piedmont Rd., N.E.
Atlanta, GA 30305

Brady, McQueen, Martin, Collins & Jensen*(Legal Firm)*
Elgin, IL

AVM Financial Services*(Pension Manager)*
Elgin, IL

ILLINOIS RANGE COMPANY
708 W. Central Rd.
Mount Prospect, IL 60056
Tel.: 708-253-4950
Fax: 708-253-5080
Year Founded: 1922
Approx.Sls.: $54,000,000
Emp.: 350
Export
Commercial Food Service Equipment
S.I.C.: 3556
E.T. Krakowiak *(Chm. Bd.)*
Donald C. Brokaw *(Pres.)*
E.M. Krysa *(Exec. V.P.)*
D. Last *(Dir.-Personnel)*
R. Cabak *(Mgr.-Engr.)*
E. Schultz *(Mgr.-Data Processing)*

Outside Service Firm(s):

McClure, Inserra & Company*(Auditors)*
Arlington Heights, IL

American National Bank & Trust Company of Chicago*(Major Banking Relationship)*
33 N. LaSalle St.
Chicago, IL 60602
Tel.: 312-661-5000
Fax: 312-661-6417

ILLINOIS STATE LOTTERY
201 E. Madison
Springfield, IL 62702
Tel.: 217-524-5156
Fax; 217-524-5235
Year Founded: 1974
Approx.Sls.: $1,636,000,000
Emp.: 320
Fiscal Year-end: 6/30/92
State Lottery
S.I.C.: 7999
Desiree Rogers *(Dir.)*
Sam Owen *(Deputy Dir.-Admin.)*
Lois Shelton *(Deputy Dir. Mktg. & Sls.)*
David Mizeur *(Deputy Dir.-Audit & Fin.)*
Guy Lahr *(Gen. Counsel)*

Subsidiary:

Illinois State Lottery **(1)**
676 N. St. Clair
Chicago, IL 60611
Tel.: 312-793-3026
Fax: 312-951-7204
S.I.C.: 7999

JOHN ILTIS ASSOCIATES
680 N. Lake Shore Dr.
Chicago, IL 60611
Tel.: 312-337-6012
Fax: 312-337-1258
Year Founded: 1977
Approx.Billings: $12,350,000
Emp.: 18
Entertainment Adv. & Pub. Rels.
John F. Iltis *(Pres.)*
Mary Kay Kammer *(V.P., Adv. & Admin.)*

Computer Systems/Hardware:
Macintosh, IBM

Image Dynamics, Incorporated
1101 N. Calvert Street
Baltimore, Maryland 21202

IMAGE DYNAMICS, INCORPORATED
1101 N. Calvert Street
Baltimore, MD 21202
Tel.: 301-539-7730
Fax: 301-752-7182
Year Founded: 1966
Approx.Billings: $21,500,000
Emp.: 26
Healthcare, Tourism, Manufacturing, Retail Advertising & Business to Business Real Estate
Corporate Giving Program: Standard Contributions Given to Arts, Cultural & Educational Programs & The US Olympic Committee
Phyllis B. Brotman *(Pres., Chief Exec. Officer & New Bus. Contact)*
Barbara Brotman Kaylor *(Exec. V.P., Adv.)*
David Imre *(Sr. V.P., Pub. Rels.)*
Linda Rutkowski *(V.P., Admin.)*
David Gasper *(V.P., Comptroller)*
David Williams *(Mktg.)*
Carolyn Brown *(Pub. Rels.)*

Computer Systems/Hardware:
Novel Network, Word Perfect, Lotus, Higgons, Macintosh, IBM

IMPERIA BROS., INC.
57 Canal Rd.
Pelham Manor, NY 10803
Tel.: 914-738-0900 **NY**
Fax: 914-738-2494
Year Founded: 1959
Approx.Sls.: $17,000,000

Imperia Bros., Inc.—(Continued)

Emp.: 75
Mfr. of Concrete & Lightweight Blocks, Mason & Building Materials; Retail Home Center
S.I.C.: 5211; 3271
Enio Imperia *(Pres.)*
Salvatore P. Ferrotti *(V.P.)*
Vito Iannuzzi *(Controller)*
Joseph Imperia *(Sec. & Treas.)*
Jay Crystal *(Mgr.-Pub. Rels.)*
Gerald T. Ferrotti *(Mgr.-Pur.)*
Steven P. Ferrotti *(Mgr.-Home Center)*
Andy Leverson *(Mgr.-Adv.)*

Outside Service Firm(s):

L. H. Frishkoff & Co.*(Auditors)*
New York, NY

Pitassy & Leslie, P.C.*(Legal Firm)*
New York, NY

The Bank of New York*(Major Banking Relationship)*
1290 Avenue of the Americas
New York, NY 10104

IMPERIAL, INC.
789 Packer Dr.
Green Bay, WI 54304
Tel.: 414-494-7474
Fax: 414-494-3212
Approx.Sls.: $30,000,000
Service Trucking Industry; Small Maintenance Parts
S.I.C.: 5084
Donald J. Long *(Chm. Bd. & Chief Exec. Officer)*
John D. McDowell *(Pres.)*

Outside Service Firm(s):

Trawbridge, Planert & Schaefer*(Legal Firm)*
Greenbay, WI

Associated Kellogg*(Major Banking Relationship)*
Green Bay, WI

IMPERIAL LITHO/GRAPHICS, INC.
210 S. 4th Ave.
Phoenix, AZ 85003
Tel.: 602-257-8500
Tel.: 800-745-4846 **AZ**
Fax: 602-495-2544
Year Founded: 1958
Approx.Sls.: $20,000,000
Emp.: 200
Fiscal Year-end: 12/31/91
Lithographic Printing, Typesetting, Graphic Arts & Visuals & Mailing Service
S.I.C.: 2752; 2791; 7331
Jerry Wisotsky *(Chm. Bd., Sec. & Treas.)*
Malcolm Marr *(Pres.)*
Bernard Goldstein *(V.P.-Fin.)*
Lee Zierton *(Mgr.-Sls. & Mktg.)*

Outside Service Firm(s):

Schulman Klock*(Auditors)*
Phoenix, AZ

Citibank N.A.*(Major Banking Relationship)*
Phoenix, AZ

IMPERIAL MANUFACTURING COMPANY
11 W. Butler
Memphis, TN 38103
Mailing Address:
P.O. Box 650,
Memphis, TN 38101
Tel.: 601-781-1151 **TN**
Fax: 601-781-1609
Year Founded: 1965
Sales Range: $10-19 Million
Emp.: 190
Fiscal Year-end: 3/31/90
Import Export
Metal & Wood Dining Furniture
S.I.C.: 2511; 2514
Joe Magdovitz *(Chm. Bd., Sec. & Treas.)*
Earl Magdovitz *(Pres.)*
Paul Frankel *(Dir.-Mfg.)*
Morris Marcus *(Dir.-Opers.)*
Joe Key *(Mgr.-Data Processing)*

Outside Service Firm(s):

BDO Seidman*(Auditors)*
Miami, FL

Heiskell, Donelson, Bearman, Adams, Williams & Kirsch*(Legal Firm)*
165 Madison Ave.
Memphis, TN 38103
Tel.: 901-526-2000

United American Bank*(Major Banking Relationship)*
Memphis, TN

IMPERIAL PEARL COMPANY, INC.
25 Manton Ave.
Providence, RI 02909
Tel.: 401-331-5873 **RI**
Fax: 401-751-4630
Year Founded: 1986
Approx.Sls.: $30,000,000
Emp.: 500
Export
Mfr. of Artificial Pearls & Costume Jewelry Including Precious Metal & Semiprecious Stones
S.I.C.: 3911
Robert Marsello *(Pres.)*
Robert Nohejl *(V.P.-Fin. & Sec.)*
Arthur C. Kreuter *(V.P.)*
Donald Sarasin *(Mgr.-Personnel)*
Ernest Decesare *(Plant Mgr.)*

IMPERIAL POOLS, INC.
33 Wade Rd.
Latham, NY 12110
Tel.: 518-786-1200
Fax: 518-786-0954
Approx.Sls.: $11,000,000
Emp.: 125
Mfr. of Plastics & Steel Fabrications
S.I.C.: 3441
John M. Maiuccoro *(Pres. & Treas.)*
William Churchman *(V.P.-Fin. & Admin.)*
Gary Maiuccoro *(Dir.-Sls. & Mktg.)*
Wes Verbraska *(Pur. Agent)*

Outside Service Firm(s):

Norstar Bank, N.A.*(Major Banking Relationship)*
Latham, NY

IMPERIAL SCHRADE CORP.
99 Madison Ave., Ste.1500
New York, NY 10016
Tel.: 212-889-5700 **DE**
Fax: 212-779-7699
Approx.Sls.: $75,000,000
Emp.: 2,500
Mfr. of Cutlery
S.I.C.: 3421; 3914
Albert Baer *(Chm. Bd. & Chief Exec. Officer)*
Walter A. Gardiner *(Pres.)*
David Swinden *(Exec. V.P.)*
John M. Jenkins *(V.P.-Sls.)*
James H. Stathis *(Gen. Sls. Mgr.)*

No. of U.S. Offices: 3
No. of Foreign Offices: 3

Computer Systems/Hardware:
IBM

Outside Service Firm(s):

Goldstein, Golub, Kessler & Co.*(Auditors)*
New York, NY

Wagner, Davis & Gold*(Legal Firm)*
New York, NY

Philadelphia National Bank*(Major Banking Relationship)*
5th & Market Sts.
Philadelphia, PA 19101
Tel.: 215-629-3100
Fax: 215-834-2069

Division:

Imperial Schrade Corp. **(1)**
Route 209 North
Ellenville, NY 12428
Tel.: 914-647-7600
Tel.: 800-2-SCHRADE
Fax: 914-647-8701
Emp.: 500
Import Export
Manufacture Pocket & Hunting Knives
S.I.C.: 3421
Albert M. Baer *(Chm. Bd.)*
Walter A. Gardiner *(Pres.)*
David A. Swinden *(Exec. Pres.)*
Tom Burrows *(Creative Dir.-Housewares)*
James J. Economos *(V.P.-Opers.)*
Faith Supple *(Dir.-Human Resources)*

Non-U.S. Holdings:

Imperial Schrade (Europe) G.m.b.H. **(1)**
Cologne, Germany
Marketing, Warehousing & Distribution
S.I.C.: 5072

Imperial Stag Ltd. **(1)**
Listowel, Ireland
Manufacture Cutlery
S.I.C.: 3421

IMPO GLAZTILE
7600 County Line Rd., Unit 1
Burr Ridge, IL 60521
Tel.: 708-655-4676
Fax: 708-655-4696
Approx.Sls.: $10,000,000
Emp.: 65
Distr. of Ceramic Tile
S.I.C.: 5039
James G. Drechsel *(Pres.)*
Richard J. Deutsch *(V.P.-Adv. & Sls.)*

IMPRINT PRODUCTS, L.P.
70 Randall Ave.
Rockville Centre, NY 11570
Mailing Address:
P.O. Box 357
Valley Stream, NY 11582
Tel.: 516-536-6360 **NY**
Fax: 516-536-1802
Year Founded: 1964
Approx.Sls.: $15,000,000
Emp.: 125
Fiscal Year-end: 12/31/90
Personalized Stationery Items
S.I.C.: 5961; 2678
William Mooar *(Chm. Bd.)*
James M. Ryan *(Pres.)*
Nancy Gagliano *(Controller)*
Christina Seery *(Dir.-Mfg. & Pur.)*
Catherine M. Ryan *(Dir.-Adv.)*
Loretta Carhart *(Dir.-Human Resources)*
Tina Seery *(Mgr.-Opers. & Pur.)*
John McGlynn *(Dir.-Data Processing)*

Computer Systems/Hardware:
Radio Shack CCS; Cromemco 3

Outside Service Firm(s):

Deloitte & Touche*(Auditors)*
1 World Trade Center
New York, NY 10048
Tel.: 212-669-5000

Hartford Life Insurance Co.*(Group Insurer)*
Hartford, CT 06104-2999

Kaye, Scholer, Fierman, Hays & Handler*(Legal Firm)*
New York, NY

National Westminster Bank plc*(Major Banking Relationship)*
100 Jericho Quadrangle
Jericho, NY 11753

THE IN-HOUSE AGENCY
331 Park Ave.
Weehawken, NJ 07087
Tel.: 201-867-0010
Fax: 201-867-7106
Year Founded: 1981
Approx.Billings: $10,000,000
Emp.: 15
Package Goods
W. Douglas MacGibbon *(Pres., Treas. & Dir.-Creative)*
Edward J. Daley *(Exec. V.P.)*
Robert C. Hamlin *(Exec. V.P.)*
Robert M. Webb *(Exec. V.P.)*

IN-N-OUT BURGERS
13502 E. Virginia
Baldwin Park, CA 91706
Tel.: 818-338-5587
Year Founded: 1948
Approx.Sls.: $90,000,000
Emp.: 1,785
Hamburger Chain
S.I.C.: 5812
R.A. Snyder *(Pres.)*
Philip R. West *(Exec. V.P.-Admin.)*
Ken Iriart *(V.P.-Personnel)*
E.L. Snyder *(Treas. & Sec.)*
Kathleen Kelley *(Public Relations Rep.)*

INDECK POWER EQUIPMENT COMPANY
1111 S. Willis
Wheeling, IL 60090
Tel.: 708-541-8300 **IL**
Fax: 708-541-9984
Approx.Sls.: $24,000,000
Emp.: 50
Wholesale Distributor of Power Plant Machinery; Diesel Engines & Parts; Industrial Power Boilers; Equipment Rental & Leasing
S.I.C.: 5084; 5074; 7359
Gerald Forsythe *(Chm. Bd., Pres. & Chief Exec. Officer)*
James Forsythe *(V.P.)*
Lawrence A. Lagowski *(V.P. & Chief Fin. Officer)*
Harry Von Beetz *(Pur. Agent)*

Outside Service Firm(s):

BDO Seidman*(Auditors)*
111 E. Wacker Dr.
Chicago, IL 60601

NBD Park Ridge*(Major Banking Relationship)*
Park Ridge, IL

Subsidiary:

Indeck Energy Services, Inc. **(1)**
1130 Lake Cook Rd.
Buffalo Grove, IL 60089
Tel.: 708-520-3212
Engineering Services
S.I.C.: 8711
Russ Lindsay *(Pres.)*

INDEPENDENT CAN COMPANY
1300 Brass Mill Rd.
Belcamp, MD 21017
Tel.: 410-272-0090
Fax: 301-273-7500
Year Founded: 1929
Approx.Sls.: $15,000,000
Emp.: 97
Import Export
Mfr. of Custom Cans
S.I.C.: 3411
Douglas Huether *(Pres.)*
Richard Huether *(Treas.)*
George R. McClelland *(Sec.)*

Subsidiary:

Western Specialty Container **(1)**
17955 E. Ajax Circle
City of Industry, CA 91748
Tel.: 818-912-8600
Export
Distr. of Decorative Tins
S.I.C.: 5051
John Thompson *(Chief Exec. Officer)*

INDEPENDENT INSURANCE AGENTS OF AMERICA
127 S. Peyton St.
Alexandria, VA 22314
Tel.: 703-683-4422
Fax: 703-683-7556
Approx.Sls.: $12,000,000
Emp.: 65
Promotion
S.I.C.: 8611
R.C. Riley *(Pres.)*
Jeffery M. Yates *(Exec. V.P. & Gen. Counsel)*
C. Courtney Wood *(Sr. V.P.)*
Russ Burnett *(V.P. & Chief Fin. Officer)*
Howard B. Gaylor *(V.P.)*

Division:

Independent Insurance Agents and Brokers of California **(1)**
101 Market St., Ste. 702
San Francisco, CA 94105
Tel.: 415-957-1212
Fax: 415-541-9184
Approx.Sls.: $4,000,000
Emp.: 23
Fiscal Year-end: 8/31/92
Computer Systems/Hardware:
HP 3000
Insurance & Related Services Offered by Independent Insurance Agents in California
S.I.C.: 6411
Anthony J. DiBuduo *(Pres.)*
Jerry W. O'Kane *(Exec. V.P. & Chief Exec. Officer)*
Glema Androus *(V.P.)*
James T. Hamilton *(Sec. & Treas.)*

INDEPENDENT METALS
N115 W18945 Edison Dr.
Germantown, WI 53022-0247
Mailing Address:
P.O. Box 247
Germantown, WI 53022
Tel.: 414-255-4444
Tel.: 800-558-8567 **WI**
Fax: 414-255-2989
Year Founded: 1982
Sales Range: $80-99 Million
Emp.: 120
Import
Metals Distributor/Service Center Specializing In Aluminum, Stainless Steel, Brass & Copper Products
S.I.C.: 5051
Barry C. Quinnies *(Pres. & Chief Exec. Officer)*
Lee E. Feiereisen *(V.P.-Sls.)*
Ronald Seiser *(Chief Fin. Officer & Dir.-Opers.)*
Judith A. Bullock *(Controller)*
Sandra J. Beckwith *(Mgr.-Human Resources)*
David G. Horwich *(Mgr.-Pur.)*
Gavin L. Quinnies *(Mgr.-Quality Assurance)*
Michael P. Evans *(Computer Programmer)*
Phyllis Wenhart *(Corp. Travel Planner)*
Principal(s):
Barry C. Quinnies

No. of Mfg. Plants/Facilities: 2
No. of U.S. Offices: 1

Computer Systems/Hardware:
IBM

Outside Service Firm(s):

Ernst & Young*(Auditors)*
111 E. Kilbourn Ave., Ste. 900
Milwaukee, WI 53202
Tel.: 414-273-5900

Liberty Mutual*(Group Insurer)*
Milwaukee, WI

Michael, Best & Friedrich*(Legal Firm)*
100 East Wisconsin Avenue
Milwaukee, WI 53202
Tel.: 414-271-6560

Bank One Milwaukee, N.A.*(Major Banking Relationship)*
111 E. Wisconsin Ave.
Milwaukee, WI
Tel.: 414-765-3000

Bank One Milwaukee, N.A.*(Pension Manager)*
111 E. Wisconsin Ave.
Milwaukee, WI
Tel.: 414-765-3000

Division:

Independent Metals **(1)**
5701 International Pkwy.
New Hope, MN 55426-3097
Tel.: 612-537-2110
Tel.: 800-762-5550
Emp.: 9
Office & Warehouse
S.I.C.: 5051

INDEPENDENT PUBLICATIONS, INC.
945 Haverford Rd.
Bryn Mawr, PA 19010
Tel.: 215-527-6330
Fax: 215-527-0338
Year Founded: 1975
Approx.Sls.: $29,000,000
Emp.: 500
Newspaper Publishing; Electronic Publishing of Newsletters; Music & Sound Distribution Service
S.I.C.: 2711; 7389
William L. McLean, III *(Chm. Bd. & Pres.)*
John H. Buhsmer *(V.P.)*
William E. Strasburg *(V.P. & Treas.)*

Outside Service Firm(s):

Morgan, Lewis & Bockius*(Legal Firm)*
2000 One Logan Square
Philadelphia, PA 19103
Tel.: 215-963-5000

Philadelphia National Bank*(Major Banking Relationship)*
5th & Market Sts.
Philadelphia, PA 19101
Tel.: 215-629-3100
Fax: 215-834-2069

Subsidiary:

Finger Lakes Printing Company **(1)**
218 Genesee St.
Geneva, NY 14456
Tel.: 315-789-3333
Newspaper Publishing
S.I.C.: 2711
George Park *(Publisher)*

INDIAN HEAD INDUSTRIES INC.
26899 Northwestern Hwy., Ste. 400
Southfield, MI 48034
Tel.: 313-353-8960
Fax: 313-353-4512
Approx.Sls.: $100,000,000
Emp.: 650
Import Export
Mfr. Auto Interior Trim, Marine Trim & Gaskets, Truck Spring Brakes
S.I.C.: 3714
Ronald I. Parker *(Chm. Bd., Pres. & Chief Exec. Officer)*
Charles Johnson *(V.P.-Pur.)*
Robert Nesler *(V.P.-DG Trim)*
Rebecca Phillips *(V.P.-Communications & Bus. Devel.)*
Brian Schrandt *(V.P.-Detroit Gasket)*
Elaine Tschirhart *(V.P.-Human Resources)*
Fred Folson *(Controller)*
Principal(s):
Ronald I. Parker
John Goense
Robert Nesler
Brian Schrandt

No. of Mfg. Plants/Facilities: 6
No. of U.S. Offices: 1

Outside Service Firm(s):

Ernst & Young*(Auditors)*
One Detroit Center, 500 Woodward, Ste. 1700
Detroit, MI 48243
Tel.: 313-259-9600

Manufacturers National Bank N.A.*(Major Banking Relationship)*
38th Fl., 100 Renaissance Center
Detroit, MI 48243
Tel.: 313-222-4227

Subsidiaries:

DG Trim Products Div. **(1)**
26899 Northwestern Hwy., Ste. 400
Southfield, MI 48034
Tel.: 313-353-8960
Manufacture Trim Products
S.I.C.: 3714
Robert Nesler *(V.P.)*

Indian Head Gasket Div.-Detroit **(1)**
26899 Northwestern Hwy., Ste. 400
Southfield, MI 48034
Tel.: 313-353-8960
Manufacture of Gaskets
S.I.C.: 3053
Brian Schrandt *(V.P.)*

MGM Brakes Div. **(1)**
26899 Northwestern Hwy., Ste. 400
Southfield, MI 48034
Tel.: 313-353-8960
Manufacture Brakes & Brake Parts
S.I.C.: 3714
Ron Parker *(Pres.)*

INDIANA RECORDS MANAGERS
6971 Hillsdale Ct.
Indianapolis, IN 46250
Tel.: 317-842-5580
Fax: 317-576-6290
Sales Range: $10-19 Million
Emp.: 18
Distribute Office Equipment, Supplies & Systems
S.I.C.: 5943; 5045; 5112
Douglas J. McPhail *(Pres., Chief Exec. & Fin. Officer & Treas.)*

Outside Service Firm(s):

Ernst & Young*(Auditors)*
One Indiana Square, Ste. 3400
Indianapolis, IN 46204
Tel.: 317-236-1100

Subsidiary:

Productive Business Interiors **(1)**
6971 Hillsdale Ct.
Indianapolis, IN 46250
Tel.: 317-842-5580 (100%)
Douglas J. McPhail *(Pres.)*

INDRESCO, INC.
2121 San Jacino St., Ste. 2500
Dallas, TX 75201
Tel.: 214-953-4500
Mfr. of Construction Equipment
S.I.C.: 3531; 3532
Ralph Ytterberg *(Chm. Bd. & Chief Exec. Officer)*
Yazan N. Sharif *(Pres.)*
Jean Gleason *(Exec. V.P.-Admin.)*

Divisions:

Harbison-Walker Refractories **(1)**
One Gateway Center
Pittsburgh, PA 15222
Tel.: 412-562-6200 (100%)
Fax: 412-562-6209
Mfr. of Refractory Products
S.I.C.: 3255
Y.N. Sharif *(Pres.)*

Jeffrey Division **(1)**
274 E. First Ave.
Columbus, OH 43201
Tel.: 614-297-3123
Fax: 614-297-3666
Mfr. of Heavy Underground Mining Machinery
S.I.C.: 3532
W. Fife *(V.P.-Engrng.)*
W. Graessle *(V.P.-Mktg.)*
E. W. Miskinis *(V.P.-Human Resources)*
W. Burtch *(V.P. & Controller)*
R. Zwick *(V.P.-Mfg.)*

Industrial Tools Div. **(1)**
7007 Pinemont
Houston, TX 77040
Tel.: 713-462-4521 (100%)
Fax: 713-460-7077
Mfr. of Air Tools
S.I.C.: 3546
T.R. Hurst *(Pres.)*

Komatsu Dresser Company **(1)**
200 Tri-State International
Lincolnshire, IL 60069
Tel.: 708-831-6700 (50%)
Fax: 708-831-7200
Approx.Sls.: $1,500,000
Emp.: 5,000
Fiscal Year-end: 9/31/91
Importer & Manufacturer of Heavy-Duty Construction Equipment; (Joint Venture of Komatsu Ltd. & Dresser Industries, Inc.)
S.I.C.: 5082; 5084; 3531
Arlie Tucker *(Chief Exec. Officer)*
Masahiro Sakane *(Pres. & Chief Oper. Officer)*
Ken Nakamura *(V.P.-Mktg. Admin.)*
Karl Hoshino *(V.P.-Prod. Mktg.)*
Dave Grezelak *(V.P.-Mktg.)*
Ed McCord *(V.P. Engrng. & Mfg.)*
Gary Aubrey *(V.P.-Human Resources)*
Earl Weed *(V.P.-Total Quality)*
Steve Day *(V.P.-Parts, Opers. & Sls.)*
Howard Nagaike *(Treas.)*
Robert Benson *(Controller)*
Tom McGonigle *(Dir.-Mktg. Services)*
W. Charaf *(Dir.-Intl. Accounts)*
Herman Voth *(Dir.-Natl. Accts.)*
John Sido *(Mgr.-Prod. Mktg.-Crawlers, Loaders & Trucks)*
Doug Gunn *(Mgr.-Prod. Mktg.-Excavators)*
Les Scott *(Mgr.-Sls. Training)*
Alfred Bru *(Mgr.-Adv. & Pub. Rels.)*

Division:

Haulpak Division, Komatsu Dresser Company **(2)**
2300 N.E. Adams St.
Peoria, IL 61639
Tel.: 309-672-7000
Approx.Sls.: $220,000,000
Emp.: 835
Mfr. of Earthmoving, Construction & Mining Equip., Haulpak Off-Highway Trucks & Hydrair II Truck Suspension System & Aftermarket Parts
S.I.C.: 3531; 3532; 3711; 3714
A.G. Tucker *(Pres.)*
R.L. Brenkman *(V.P.-Sls.)*
J.J. Poupard *(V.P. & Controller)*
H. Collins *(V.P.-Mfg.)*
M.C. Neul *(V.P.-Engrng.)*

Marion Power Shovel Division **(1)**
617 W. Center St.
Marion, OH 43302
Tel.: 614-383-5211
Fax: 614-383-5211 Ext. 2181
Emp.: 1,500
Mfr. of Draglines, Shovels & Drills
S.I.C.: 3531
D.R. Stout *(Pres.)*
W. D. Carter *(VP-Mktg)*
L. E. Schaffer *(VP-Sls)*
P. J. Gilewicz *(Mktg Service Mgr)*

Valve and Controls Division **(1)**
10077 Grogan's Mill Rd., Ste. 500
The Woodlands, TX 77380
Tel.: 713-367-5741
Fax: 713-363-8244
Mfr. of Valves
S.I.C.: 3494
M.J. Kammerer *(Pres.)*

INDUSTRIAL ACOUSTICS COMPANY, INC.
1160 Commerce Ave.
Bronx, NY 10462
Tel.: 718-931-8000

Industrial Acoustics Company, Inc.—(Continued)

Telex: 212-863-1138
Year Founded: 1949
Assets: $68,980,530
Earnings: $3,694,338
Liabilities: $30,472,551
Net Worth: $38,507,979
Approx.Sls.: $80,993,000
Emp.: 900
Fiscal Year-end: 12/31/90
Noise Control Equipment
S.I.C.: 3275; 3296; 3446
Martin Hirschorn *(Pres.)*
Frederic M. Oran *(Exec. V.P.)*
John M. Handley *(Sr. V.P.-Mkt. Devel.)*
Arnold W. Kanarek *(Sr. V.P. & Sec.)*
Jasjit T. Ahluvalia *(V.P.-Mngmt. Information Systems)*
Robert Bertrand *(V.P.-Fin.)*
Robert J. Buelow *(V.P.-Architectural)*
David A. Collings *(V.P.-Res. & Devel.)*
Peter Kohner *(V.P.-Mfg.)*
Morton I. Schiff *(V.P.-Special Prod.)*
Robert A. Schmidt *(V.P.-Air Conditioning)*
Robert E. Schmidt *(V.P.-Indus. Prod.)*
Ellis Singer *(V.P.-Medical/Life Sciences)*
Seymour Wasserman *(V.P.-Engrng. Services)*
Patrick J. Waters *(V.P.-Pur.)*
Neville N. Rosemin *(Controller)*
Zachary Jaquett *(Dir.-Communications)*
Raymond E. Svana *(Dir.-Personnel)*

Subsidiary:

Industrial Acoustics Company S.C. Inc. **(1)**
P.O. Box 579,
Moncks Corner, SC 29461
Tel.: 803-761-6430
Mfr. of Heavy-Duty Aviation & Gas Turbine Products
S.I.C.: 3511
Edward B. Saxton *(V.P.-Mfg.)*

Non-U.S. Holdings:

Industrial Acoustics Company, Ltd. **(1)**
Central Trading Estate
Staines, Middlesex TW18 4XB, United Kingdom
Tel.: 0784-56251
Telex: 25518 IACLTD G
Acoustical Treatment & Noise Control
S.I.C.: 3296
George J. Sotos *(Joint Mng. Dir.)*
George Dawson *(Joint Mng. Dir. & Dir.-Aviation & Engrng.)*
Derek Percy *(Dir.-Sls.)*
David Reynard *(Commercial Dir.)*
Peter Gelstharp *(Treas.)*
Colin Bayman *(Assoc. Dir.-Aviation)*
Geoff Crowhurst *(Assoc. Dir.-Bldg. Services)*
Geoff Howse *(Assoc. Dir.-Engrng.)*
Clive Urquhart *(Assoc. Dir.-Mfg.)*
Simon White *(Dir.-Mktg.)*

Industrial Acoustics Company GmbH **(1)**
4055
Niederkruchten, Germany
Tel.: 02 163/84 31-23
Sales & Service
S.I.C.: 5033
Heinz Mueller *(Mng. Dir.)*

Intra-Acoustics Company, Ltd. **(1)**
600 Rene-Lavesgne Blvd. W., Ste 800
Montreal, PQ H3B 4V6, Canada
Tel.: 514-954-1811
Sales & Distr.
S.I.C.: 5033
Donald Aitkens *(Mgr.)*

INDUSTRIAL CERAMICS, INC.
Porcelain Park
Derry, PA 15627
Tel.: 412-539-6300
Fax: 412-539-6295
Sales Range: $20-39 Million
Emp.: 350
Mfr. of Porcelain Insulators
S.I.C.: 3264
Howard S. Jacobs *(Chm. Bd.)*
Lewis Miller *(Pres. & Chief Exec. Officer)*
James Conrad *(V.P.-Mktg.)*
Barry Hartmann *(V.P.-Human Resources)*
A.M. Kairys *(Chief Fin. Officer)*
David Lockwood *(Mgr.-Engrng.)*

Outside Service Firm(s):

Grant Thornton*(Auditors)*
605 Third Ave.
New York, NY 10158
Tel.: 212-599-0100
Fax: 212-370-4520

Spengler, Carlson, Gubar, Brodsky & Frischling*(Legal Firm)*
280 Park Ave.
New York, NY 10017
Tel.: 212-682-4444

Marine Midland Bank*(Major Banking Relationship)*
P.O. Box 803, 1 Marine Midland Center, 23rd Floor
Buffalo, NY 14203
Tel.: 716-841-2582

Plant:

Industrial Ceramics, Inc. **(1)**
674 E. Main St.
Lima, NY 14485
Tel.: 716-624-1110
Mfr. of Porcelain Insulators
S.I.C.: 3264
Lewis Miller *(Pres.)*

Industrial Chemical Laboratories, Inc.
(See Listing Under Rochester Midland Corporation; Name Changed To Rochester-Midland, ICL)

INDUSTRIAL COATINGS GROUP, INC.
2141 S. Jefferson St.
Chicago, IL 60616
Tel.: 312-421-4030 **DE**
Fax: 312-226-2634
Year Founded: 1897
Approx.Sls.: $60,000,000
Emp.: 320
Fiscal Year-end: 12/31/91
Export
Manufacture Industrial Fabrics & Polyethylene Films
S.I.C.: 2295
John P. Clark *(Pres. & Chief Exec. Officer)*
Thomas J. Lavelle *(Exec. V.P. & Chief Oper. Officer)*
David R. Meyers *(V.P.-Opers.)*
Rolf Hennington *(V.P.-Sls. & Mktg.)*
W. Wilson Troutman *(Controller & Asst. Treas.)*
Robert J. Stucker *(Sec.)*
George Pentaris *(Dir.-Admin. Services & Asst. Sec.)*
Richard F. Smock *(Dir.-Corp. Communications)*

Computer Systems/Hardware:
Bull DPS-6/6935

Outside Service Firm(s):

Arthur Andersen & Co.*(Auditors)*
33 W. Monroe St.
Chicago, IL 60603-4067
Tel.: 312-580-0033
Fax: 312-507-6748

Vedder, Price, Kaufman & Kammholz*(Legal Firm)*
115 S. La Salle
Chicago, IL 60603
Tel.: 312-781-2200

Harris Trust & Savings Bank*(Major Banking Relationship)*
111 W. Monroe St.
Chicago, IL 60690
Tel.: 312-461-2265
Tel.: 800-858-0840

Divisions:

Industrial Coatings Group (Sales Office) **(1)**
220 Broad St.
Kingsport, TN 37660
Tel.: 615-247-2131
Tel.: 800-251-7520
Tel.: 800-251-7528
Telex: 55-3241
Fax: 615-247-2134
Export
William Dooley *(Mgr.-Customer Service)*
L. Michael Holt *(Mgr.-Book Products)*
James Whalen *(Mgr.-Industrial Products)*

Phillips-Joanna, Inc. **(1)**
P.O. Box 425
Ladd, IL 61329
Tel.: 815-894-2331
Fax: 815-894-3387
Export
S.I.C.: 3081
Tom Malpass *(Gen. Mgr.)*
Dick Hauck *(Mgr.-Sls., Ribbon Film)*
Robert Sabdo *(Sls. Rep.)*

INDUSTRIAL CONTRACTORS, INC.
1330 W. Broadway
Idaho Falls, ID 83402
Mailing Address:
P.O. Box 51920
Idaho Falls, ID 83405
Tel.: 208-522-6745 **ID**
Fax: 208-529-5360
Year Founded: 1957
Approx.Sls.: $14,000,000
Emp.: 50
Mechanical Contractor; Fabricated Pipe & Fittings
S.I.C.: 1711; 3498
Orvil J. Hendrickson *(V.P. & Sec.)*
Briggs Minor *(Pur. Agent)*

Outside Service Firm(s):

Bank of Commerce*(Major Banking Relationship)*
Idaho Falls, ID

INDUSTRIAL DIELECTRICS, INC.
407 S. 7th St.
Noblesville, IN 46060
Mailing Address:
P.O. Box 357
Noblesville, IN 46060
Tel.: 317-773-1766 **IN**
Fax: 317-773-3877
Year Founded: 1966
Approx.Sls.: $20,000,000
Emp.: 170
Fiscal Year-end: 6/30/92
Import Export
Electrical Insulators & Insulation Materials
S.I.C.: 3644
John K. Merrell *(Pres., Chief Exec. Officer & Chief Oper. Officer)*
Jon W. Coleman *(V.P.-Personnel Training & Devel.)*
William Funke *(V.P.-Tech. & Engrng.)*
Laurence R. Henss *(V.P., Treas. & Controller)*
Paul Rhodes *(V.P.-Mktg.)*
Donald K. Steele *(V.P.-Sls. & Sec.)*
Gary Zion *(Mgr.-Quality Control)*

No. of Mfg. Plants/Facilities: 3
No. of U.S. Offices: 3
No. of Foreign Offices: 1

Outside Service Firm(s):

Rider, Hinshaw & Associates*(Auditors)*
Noblesville, IN

Campbell, Kyle & Profitt*(Legal Firm)*
Noblesville, IN

The Huntington National Bank of IN*(Major Banking Relationship)*
Noblesville, IN

INDUSTRIAL ELECTRONIC ENGINEERS, INC.
7740 Lemone Ave.
Van Nuys, CA 91405
Tel.: 818-787-0311
Year Founded: 1947
Approx.Sls.: $29,000,000
Emp.: 250
Graphic Displays, Except Graphic Terminals; Computer Keyboards, Office Machines; Incandescent Lamps & Related Supplies
S.I.C.: 3577; 3575; 5063
Patrick J. McEvoy *(Pres.)*
Richard Pleasant *(Exec. V.P.)*
Geri Seeger *(Mgr.-Human Resources)*

INDUSTRIAL GENERAL CORPORATION
Olive & Taylor Sts.
Elyria, OH 44035
Tel.: 216-323-3136
Fax: 216-323-4017
Assets: $111,584,000
Earnings: $5,751,000
Net Worth: $111,584,000
Approx.Sls.: $165,943,000
Emp.: 2,360
Sub-Fractional Horsepower Motors, Plastic Components, Special Machinery, Automated Material-Handling Systems, Solid Waste Shredders
S.I.C.: 3082; 3462; 3463; 3465; 3469; 3531
Eli S. Jacobs *(Chm. Bd.)*
James M. Lyman *(Pres. & Chief Exec. Officer)*
George Uveges *(Chief Fin. Officer)*
Lawrence M. Fell *(Sec. & Gen. Counsel)*

Computer Systems/Hardware:
IBM System 38

Outside Service Firm(s):

Ernst & Young*(Auditors)*
1300 Huntington Bldg.
Cleveland, OH 44115
Tel.: 216-861-5000

Travelers Insurance Co.*(Group Insurer)*
1 Tower Square
Hartford, CT 06183-2492
Tel.: 203-277-4542
Fax: 203-277-5038

National City Bank*(Major Banking Relationship)*
P.O. Box 92301, Ninth & Euclid Avenues
Cleveland, OH 44193

INDUSTRIAL METALS OF THE SOUTH
401 N. Roman St.
New Orleans, LA 70112
Mailing Address:
P.O. Box 10507,
New Orleans, LA 70181
Tel.: 504-586-9191 **LA**
Fax: 504-528-1041
Approx.Sls.: $14,000,000
Emp.: 22
Aluminum Bars, Rods, Ingots, Sheets, Pipes, Plates; Copper; Steel
S.I.C.: 5051
John J. Gelpi *(Pres.)*
Ray Peters *(V.P.)*
Marilyn Hutter *(Treas.)*
John J. Gelpi, III *(Sec.)*

Outside Service Firm(s):

Paul A. Woessner*(Auditors)*
New Orleans, LA

First National Bank*(Major Banking Relationship)*
New Orleans, LA

INDUSTRIAL RUBBER PRODUCTS COMPANY
815 Court St.
Charleston, WV 25301
Tel.: 304-344-1791
Tel.: 800-624-1791 **WV**
Fax: 304-343-1670
Year Founded: 1937
Approx.Sls.: $25,000,000
Emp.: 115
Export
Wholesale Distribution of Rubber Goods; Mechanical Power Transmission Equipment & Apparatus
S.I.C.: 5085
Robert C. White *(Pres. & Chief Exec. Officer)*
B.H. Basham *(V.P. & Sec.)*
David Brucker *(Controller)*

Outside Service Firm(s):

William R. Breese*(Auditors)*
South Charleston, WV

INDUSTRIAL STEEL & WIRE COMPANY
1901 N. Narragansett Ave.
Chicago, IL 60639
Tel.: 312-804-0404
Fax: 312-804-0408
Year Founded: 1986
Approx.Sls.: $26,000,000
Emp.: 40
Metal Service Centers For The Marketing Of Metal
S.I.C.: 5051
Ralph D. Furlong *(Pres.)*
M. Zemick *(Exec. V.P.-Sls. & Mktg.)*

Outside Service Firm(s):

Huntington National Bank*(Major Banking Relationship)*
Cleveland, OH

INDUSTRIAL TOWEL & UNIFORM
2700 S. 160th St.
New Berlin, WI 53151
Tel.: 414-782-1950 **WI**
Fax: 414-782-1802
Year Founded: 1965
Approx.Sls.: $19,000,000
Emp.: 320
Wiping Towel & Work Clothing Supply; Laundered Mat & Rug Supply; Janitors' Supplies
S.I.C.: 7218; 5087
George L. Leef *(Chm. Bd. & Chief Exec. Officer)*
James M. Leef *(Pres.)*
David Leef *(V.P.)*
Ruth L. Leef *(Treas. & Sec.)*
Ann Leef *(Dir.-Personnel)*

Outside Service Firm(s):

Feld Schumacher & Co.*(Auditors)*
Milwaukee, WI

Marshall & Ilsley Trust Company*(Major Banking Relationship)*
770 N. Water St.
Milwaukee, WI

INDUSTRIAL WIRE PRODUCTS CORPORATION
3880 W. Valley Blvd.
Pomona, CA 91769
Mailing Address:
P.O. Box 1710
Pomona, CA 91769-1710
Tel.: 909-595-6617
Tel.: 800-255-6944
Tel.: 800-284-9473 **CA**
Fax: 909-595-0439
Year Founded: 1943
Approx.Sls.: $60,000,000
Emp.: 280
Fiscal Year-end: 9/30/90
Import Export
Manufacture Steel Wire
S.I.C.: 3315
Marshall R. Bull *(Chm. Bd. & Pres.)*
Richard Miale *(V.P.-Sls.)*
John Ternus *(V.P.-Mfg.)*
Bruce Yost *(V.P.-Pur.)*
John Bradshaw *(Gen. Counsel)*
Patrick Prestosa *(Controller)*
Marty Boxer *(Dir.-Data Processing)*
Principal(s):
Marshall R. Bull

No. of Mfg. Plants/Facilities: 3
No. of U.S. Offices: 1

Computer Systems/Hardware:
Hewlett Packard

Outside Service Firm(s):

Deloitte & Touche*(Auditors)*
Pomona, CA

First Interstate Bank*(Major Banking Relationship)*
City of Industry, CA

Subsidiaries:

Fundamental Management, Inc. **(1)**
3880 W. Valley Blvd.
Pomona, CA 91769
Tel.: 909-595-7511
Holding Company; Purchasing for Subsidiaries
S.I.C.: 6719; 8741
Marshall R. Bull *(Pres.)*

Industrial Alloys, Inc. **(1)**
3880 W. Valley Blvd.
Pomona, CA 91769
Tel.: 909-594-7511
Fax: 909-595-0439
Approx.Sls.: $17,000,000
Emp.: 75
Wire Drawing Mill
S.I.C.: 3357
Marshall R. Bull *(Pres.)*

Industrial Wire Products **(1)**
12459 Arrow Rd.
Rancho Cucamonga, CA 91730
Tel.: 310-945-3556
Manufacture Steel Wire Products
S.I.C.: 3315
Tom Weber *(Plant Mgr.)*

INFINITY BROADCASTING CORPORATION
600 Madison Ave.
New York, NY 10022
Tel.: 212-750-6400
Fax: 212-888-2958
Earnings: ($6,006,000)
Approx.Rev.: $117,959,000
Emp.: 378
Fiscal Year-end: 12/31/91
Radio Broadcasting
S.I.C.: 4832
G. Carrus *(Co.-Chm. & Treas.)*
M.A. Wiener *(Co.-Chm. Bd. & Sec.)*
Mel Karmazin *(Pres. & Chief Exec. Officer)*
Farid Suleman *(Chief Fin. Officer & V.P.-Fin.)*

Outside Service Firm(s):

KPMG Peat Marwick*(Auditors)*
345 Park Ave.
New York, NY 10154
Tel.: 212-758-9700
Fax: 212-872-3308

Debevoise & Plimpton*(Legal Firm)*
875 Third Ave.
New York, NY 10022
Tel.: 212-909-6000

Chase Manhattan Bank, N.A.*(Major Banking Relationship)*
One Chase Manhattan Plaza
New York, NY 10081
Tel.: 212-552-2222
Tel.: 800-526-0801
Fax: 212-552-7175

INFORMATION BUILDERS
1250 Broadway
New York, NY 10001
Tel.: 212-736-4433
Tel.: 800-969-4636
Fax: 212-564-1726
Year Founded: 1975
Approx.Sls.: $202,000,000
Emp.: 1,600
Fiscal Year-end: 12/31/92
Export
Manufacture Computer Software
S.I.C.: 7372
Gerald D. Cohen *(Pres.)*
Tim Benthall *(V.P.-Intl.)*
David Kemler *(V.P.-Sls. & Mktg.)*
Harry J. Lerner *(V.P. & Controller)*
Peter Mittelman *(V.P.)*
Martin Slagowitz *(V.P.)*
Alex Plavocos *(Dir.-Mktg.)*
Lila Goldberg *(Mgr.-Human Resources)*
William Madaras *(Mgr.-Pub. Rels.)*
Linda J. Meister *(Mgr.-Mktg. Communications)*
Judy Rattner *(Pub. Rels. Specialist)*

No. of U.S. Offices: 20
No. of Foreign Offices: 40

Computer Systems/Hardware:
IBM Mainframe, AS/400, DEC/VAX; Wang; UNIX, TANDEM, Hewlett-Packard, PCs, LANs, Apple & Macintosh

Outside Service Firm(s):

Deloitte & Touche*(Auditors)*
1 World Trade Center
New York, NY 10048
Tel.: 212-669-5000

Empire Blue Cross & Blue Shield*(Group Insurer)*
New York, NY

Kassel, Neuwirth & Geiger*(Legal Firm)*
New York, NY

Citibank N.A.*(Major Banking Relationship)*
Corporate Trust Services, 399 Park Ave.
New York, NY 10043
Tel.: 212-559-1605

Subsidiary:

Level Five Research Inc. **(1)**
503 5th Ave.
Indialantic, FL 32903
Tel.: 800-444-4303
Export
Software Development
S.I.C.: 7371

INFORMATION SYSTEMS & NETWORK CORPORATION
10411 Motor City Dr.
Bethesda, MD 20817
Tel.: 301-469-0400 **MD**
Fax: 301-469-7726
Year Founded: 1980
Approx.Sls.: $42,000,000
Emp.: 456
Fiscal Year-end: 9/30/91
Export
Telecommunications Engineering Systems
S.I.C.: 7372
Roma Malkani *(Pres. & Chief Exec. Officer)*
Vera Chawla *(Exec. V.P.)*
Herb Rubinstein *(Corp. V.P.)*
Frank Ortonic *(V.P.-Mktg.)*
Jim Wroth *(V.P.-Washington Region)*
Susan Dawson *(Sec. & Dir.-Admin.)*
Rick Dorn *(Dir.-Pur.)*
Les Klingensmith *(Dir.-Personnel)*
Allie Shaw *(Dir.-Mngmt. Information Systems)*
Jack Gould *(Corp. Librarian)*
Kay Hall *(Corp. Travel Planner)*
Ron Winkler *(Legal Officer)*
Principal(s):
Roma Malkani

No. of U.S. Offices: 10

Computer Systems/Hardware:
Wang

Outside Service Firm(s):

Coopers & Lybrand*(Auditors)*
Washington, DC

Joseph McCartin Insurance*(Commercial Insurance Carrier)*
College Park, MD

Lincoln National Life Insurance Co.*(Group Insurer)*
Bethesda, MD

Shearson Lehman Brothers, Inc.*(Investment Banker)*
Boston, MA

Shea & Gardner*(Legal Firm)*
Washington, DC

Sovran Bank*(Major Banking Relationship)*
Washington, DC

Shea & Gardner*(Pension Manager)*
Washington, DC

INFOTEC DEVELOPMENT, INC.
3611 S. Harbor Blvd., Ste. 260
Santa Ana, CA 92704
Tel.: 714-549-0460 **CA**
Fax: 714-549-9683
Year Founded: 1979
Approx.Sls.: $68,000,000
Emp.: 700
Fiscal Year-end: 9/30/88
Space Systems
S.I.C.: 3577; 3761; 3812; 8731
J. Fernando Niebla *(Chm. Bd. & Chief Exec. Officer)*
Joseph Soulia *(Pres.)*
Harry Rector *(V.P.-Fin.)*
J.D. Wells *(Controller)*
Mas Takeuchi *(Dir.-Fin.)*
Marilyn Walsh *(Dir.-Mngmt. Information Services)*
Ron Candelaria *(Mgr.-Benefits Admin.)*

No. of U.S. Offices: 12

Computer Systems/Hardware:
IBM System 36

Outside Service Firm(s):

KPMG Peat Marwick*(Auditors)*
Center Tower, 650 Town Center Drive
Costa Mesa, CA 92626
Tel.: 714-850-4300

Cigna*(Group Insurer)*
Glendale, CA

Bank of America NT&SA*(Major Banking Relationship)*
Costa Mesa, CA

INGALLS, QUINN & JOHNSON
855 Boylston St.
Boston, MA 02116
Tel.: 617-954-1000
Fax: 617-536-6119
Year Founded: 1911
Approx.Billings: $130,000,000
Emp.: 210
Advertising
S.I.C.: 7311
Richard C. Garrison *(Chm. & Chief Exec. Officer)*
Peter W. Evans *(Vice Chm., Chief Fin. Officer)*
Vin Cipolla *(Pres.)*

Ingalls, Quinn & Johnson—(Continued)

Edwin P. Carboni *(Exec. V.P., Gen. Mgr.)*
Barbara Harkins *(Sr. V.P., Controller)*
Peter Cohen *(Sr. V.P., Pub. Rels.)*
Suzanne McCarthy *(V.P., Bus. Devel.)*
David McLaughlin *(V.P., Recruitment & Yellow Pages)*

Computer Systems/Hardware:
MacIntosh, NEC

INGERSOLL ENGINEERS INC.
1021 N. Mulford Rd.
Rockford, IL 61107
Tel.: 815-395-6440 **DE**
Fax: 815-395-6452
Year Founded: 1963
Approx.Sls.: $10,000,000
Emp.: 200
Fiscal Year-end: 12/31/91
Consulting Services for Manufacturing Management
S.I.C.: 8742
Robert L. Callahan *(Pres.)*
Frank J. Darazsdi *(Sr. Partner)*
Crispin R.W. Brown *(Sr. Partner)*

No. of U.S. Offices: 3
No. of Foreign Offices: 10

Outside Service Firm(s):

KPMG Peat Marwick*(Auditors)*
Rockford, IL

Thomas Hinshaw Culbertson*(Legal Firm)*
Rockford, IL

LaSalle National Bank*(Major Banking Relationship)*
120 S. LaSalle St.
Chicago, IL 60603
Tel.: 312-781-8000

Divisions:

Ingersoll Engineers **(1)**
535 Middlefield Rd., Ste. 280
Menlo Park, CA 94025
Tel.: 415-324-1384
Consulting Services
S.I.C.: 8711; 8742
Crispin R.W. Brown *(Gen. Mgr.)*

Ingersoll Engineers **(1)**
39500 14 Mile Rd., Ste. 207
Walled Lake, MI 48390
Tel.: 313-661-8686
Consulting Services
S.I.C.: 8742; 8711
Richard T. Smith *(Gen. Mgr.)*

Ingersoll Engineers **(1)**
88 E. Main St., Ste. 334
Mendham, NJ 07945
Tel.: 201-543-9030
Consulting Services
S.I.C.: 8742; 8711
Frank J. Darazsdi *(Gen. Mgr.)*

Affiliated Companies:

Ingersoll Engineers Limited **(1)**
Bourton Hall, Bourton on Dunsmore
Rugby, Warwickshire CV23 9SD, United Kingdom
Tel.: 0926-427088
Consulting Services
S.I.C.: 8742
Brian Small *(Mng. Dir.)*

Ingersoll Engineers S.A. **(1)**
Le Concorde, 2, Ave. Zanaroli 74600
Seynod,
Annecy, France
Tel.: 50 45 43 66
Consulting Services
S.I.C.: 8742
Maurice Iacovella *(Dir.)*

Subsidiary:

Ingersoll Engineers **(2)**
Strada Anulare-Torre 10 20090 San Felice,
Segrate, Italy
Tel.: 02-70 30 03 50
Consulting Services
S.I.C.: 8742
Maurice Iacovella *(Dir.)*

Ingersoll Engineers GmbH **(1)**
Niederkasseler Lohweg 8 4000
Dusseldorf, 11 Germany
Tel.: 0211/59 60 61
Consulting Services
S.I.C.: 8742
Bodo Holz *(Dir.)*

Ingersoll Engineers Pty. Ltd. **(1)**
47 Neridah St., Ste. 39
Chatswood, N.S.W. 2067, Australia
Tel.: 02 419-6977
Consulting Services
S.I.C.: 8742
Colin Ashman *(Dir.)*

Ingersoll Engineers Pty. Ltd. **(1)**
Hawthorn, Victoria Australia
Tel.: 03 811-9918
Consulting Services
S.I.C.: 8742
Colin Ashman *(Dir.)*

INGERSOLL INTERNATIONAL INC.
707 Fulton Ave.
Rockford, IL 61103
Tel.: 815-987-6000 **IL**
Telex: 257427
Fax: 815-987-6725
Year Founded: 1978
Approx.Sls.: $500,000,000
Emp.: 5,000
Manufacturer of Special Machine Tools
S.I.C.: 3541; 6719
Edson I. Gaylord *(Chm. Bd. & Chief Exec. Officer)*
Mary Lewis *(Mgr.-Mktg. Communications)*

Outside Service Firm(s):

Coopers & Lybrand*(Auditors)*
6000 E. State St.
Rockford, IL 61108
Tel.: 815-394-0300

McDermott, Will & Emery*(Legal Firm)*
Rockford, IL

Continental Bank N. A.*(Major Banking Relationship)*
231 S. LaSalle St.
Chicago, IL 60697
Tel.: 312-828-2345
Tel.: 800-426-5754
Telex: 312-828-1783

Amcore Bank*(Pension Manager)*
Rockford, IL

Subsidiaries:

Ingersoll Bohle Ingersoll GmbH Inc. **(1)**
1303 Eddy Ave.
Rockford, IL 61103
Tel.: 815-654-5830
Telex: 257427
Fax: 815-654-5804

Ingersoll CM Systems Inc. **(1)**
3505 Centennial Dr.
Midland, MI 48640
Tel.: 517-496-2656
Fax: 517-496-3554

Ingersoll Cutting Tool Co. **(1)**
505 Fulton Ave.
Rockford, IL 61103
Tel.: 815-987-6600
Telex: 257427
Fax: 815-987-6968
S.I.C.: 3545

Ingersoll GmbH Inc. **(1)**
1303 Eddy Ave.
Rockford, IL 61103
Tel.: 815-654-5830
Telex: 257427
Fax: 815-654-5804

The Ingersoll Milling Machine Co. **(1)**
707 Fulton Ave.
Rockford, IL 61103
Tel.: 815-987-6000 (100%)
Telex: 257427
Fax: 815-987-6725
Approx.Sls.: $200,000,000
Emp.: 1,700
Development, Manufacture & Sale of Special Machine Tools & Integrated Manufacturing Systems for All Heavy Industry Including Automotive, Aircraft & Defense
S.I.C.: 3541; 3569
Fred Wilson *(Pres.)*
William J. Shannon *(V.P.-Fin.)*
Robert Boehler *(V.P.-Mfg.)*
Brian P. Howard *(V.P.-Human Resources)*
Mary Lewis *(Mgr.-Mktg. Communications)*
John McVay *(Pur. Agent)*

Waldrich Coburg Ingersoll GmbH Inc. **(1)**
1302 Eddy Ave.
Rockford, IL 61103
Tel.: 815-654-5830
Telex: 257427
Fax: 815-654-5804

Waldrich Siegen Ingersoll GmbH Inc. **(1)**
1303 Eddy Ave.
Rockford, IL 61103
Tel.: 815-654-5830
Telex: 257427
Fax: 815-654-5804

Ingersoll Milling Machine Co. **(2)**
Timberland Office Park, 5455 Corporate Dr., Ste. 200
Troy, MI 48098
Tel.: 313-641-5995
Fax: 313-641-1876

Divisions:

Customer Services Div. **(2)**
1301 Eddy Ave.
Rockford, IL 61101
Tel.: 815-987-6491
Rebuilding & Upgrading of Machine Tools
S.I.C.: 7389

Heavy Machinery Div. **(2)**
707 Fulton Ave.
Rockford, IL 61103
Tel.: 815-987-6000
Portal-Type Adjustable Rail & Fixed Rail Milling Machines & Other Machining Systems
S.I.C.: 3541

Production Machinery Div. **(2)**
707 Fulton Ave.
Rockford, IL 61103
Tel.: 815-987-6000
Special Design Automated Production Systems, Free Transfer Lines, Palletized Transfer Lines, Head Exchange Systems, Rotary Transfer Machines, Shuttle Machines, Flexible Machining Systems, Stand-Alone Machines
S.I.C.: 3541

Non-U.S. Holdings:

Bohle Werkzeugmaschinen GmbH **(1)**
Postfach 150141 D-4800,
Bielefeld, 15, Germany
Tel.: 05206 6030
Telex: 932782
Fax: 05206 603163

Ingersoll Maschinen und Werkzeuge GmbH **(1)**
P.O. Box 1140, D-5909
Burbach, Germany
Tel.: 02736 481
Telex: 0875715
Fax: 0276 48244
Design & Manufacture Cutting Tools & Electrical Discharge Machines (EDM), Abraders, Thread Whirling Systems & Tool Grinders
S.I.C.: 3545; 3541; 3549; 8711
Helmut Belz *(Mng. Dir)*

Ingersoll Milling Machines Overseas Ltd. **(1)**
4 Scotia Close
Brackmills, Northampton NN4 OHR, United Kingdom
Tel.: 011-44 604 7-66411
Telex: 312298 INGMIL G
Fax: 011-44 604 7-66821

Waldrich Coburg Werkzeugmaschinenfabrik GmbH **(1)**
Postfach 3253 D-8630,
Coburg, Germany
Tel.: 05961 651
Telex: 0663225
Fax: 09561 60500

Waldrich Siegen Werkzeugmaschinen GmbH **(1)**
Postfach 1320 D-5909,
Burbach, Germany
Tel.: 02736 40-0
Telex: 872849
Fax: 02736 40559

INGLES MARKETS, INC.
Hwy. 70, P.O. Box 6676
Asheville, NC 28816
Tel.: 704-669-2941
Fax: 704-669-5159
Earnings: $10,745,000
Approx.Sls.: $1,044,452,000
Emp.: 5,209
Fiscal Year-end: 9/30/91
Own & Operate Grocery Stores; Manages Nonresidential Buildings; Sells Milk, Bottled & Canned Soft Drinks, Carbonated Waters
S.I.C.: 5411; 5149; 6512
R.P. Ingle *(Chm. & Chief Exec. Officer)*
L.C. Laney *(Pres. & Chief Oper. Officer)*
Jack Ferguson *(V.P. & Chief Fin. Officer)*
V.C. Fisher *(V.P.)*
J.T. Outlaw, Jr. *(V.P.)*
S.G. Slade *(V.P.)*
Ken Jarvis *(Mgr.-Adv.)*

INGRAM INDUSTRIES INC.
One Belle Meade Place, 4400 Harding Rd.
Nashville, TN 37202
Mailing Address:
P.O. Box 23049
Nashville, TN 37202
Tel.: 615-298-8200
Fax: 615-298-8242
Year Founded: 1978
Approx.Sls.: $3,421,000,000
Emp.: 7,200
Inland Water Transport; Distribution of Consumer Products, Software, Texts, Coal; Insurance; Manufacture Gas/Oil Wellheads
S.I.C.: 4449; 5199; 6411
E. Bronson Ingram *(Pres. & Chief Exec. Officer)*
Chris Homrich *(Asst. Treas.-Intl.)*
Marilyn Seagraves *(Asst. Treas.-Cash Mgmt.)*
Philip Maurice Pfeffer *(Exec. V.P.)*
Roy E. Claverie *(Sr. V.P.)*
James Anderson *(V.P. & Gen. Counsel)*
Michael Grainger *(V.P. & Controller)*
Michael Head *(V.P.-Human Resources)*
Thomas L. Lunn *(V.P. & Treas.)*
David Sampsell *(V.P.-Corp. Plng. & Devel.)*
Ann B. Ewers *(Dir.-Employee Benefits)*
Martha Ingram *(Dir.-Pub. Affairs)*
Allen Scott *(Dir.-Employee Rels.)*
Joyce Redden *(Corp. Communications Coord.)*

Outside Service Firm(s):

Price Waterhouse*(Auditors)*
4400 Harding Rd.
Nashville, TN 37205
Tel.: 615-292-5000

Bass, Berry & Sims*(Legal Firm)*
27th Fl., First American Ctr.
Nashville, TN 37238
Tel.: 615-244-5370

NationsBank*(Major Banking Relationship)*
Nashville, TN

Sovran Bank*(Major Banking Relationship)*
One Commerce Place M-B
Nashville, TN 37219
Tel.: 615-749-4113

Divisions:

Ingram Barge Company **(1)**
One Belle Meade Place, 4400 Harding Rd.
Nashville, TN 37205
Tel.: 615-298-8200
Marine Barge Towing
S.I.C.: 4492
Neil N. Diehl *(Chm. Bd. Emeritus)*
Lester E. Sutton *(Pres.)*
Craig Philip *(Chief Oper. Officer & Sr. V.P.)*
Allen Oldham *(V.P. & Controller)*
Dan T. Martin *(V.P.-Sls. & Customer Service Dry Bulk)*
J.A. Tinkey *(V.P.-Opers.)*
O.H. Ingram, II *(Asst. V.P.-Liquid Sls. & Customer Service)*
P.B. Shah *(Asst. V.P.-Mngmt. Information Systems & Strategic Plng.)*

Ingram Book Company **(1)**
1125 Heil Quaker Blvd.
La Vergne, TN 37086
Tel.: 615-793-5000
General Trade Books, Textbooks
S.I.C.: 5192
Lee Synott *(Chm. Bd., Pres. & Chief Exec. Officer)*
S.J. Mason *(Vice Chm.)*
M.F. Lovett *(Chief Fin. Officer & Sr. V.P.)*
S.R. Flaster *(Sr. V.P.-Sls.)*
S.W. Little *(Sr. V.P.-Book Prod. Group)*
W.H. Pickler, III *(Sr. V.P.-Mngmt. Information Systems)*
L.G. Russell *(Sr. V.P.-Opers.)*
S.R. Taylor *(Sr. V.P.-Distribution)*

Ingram Coal Company **(1)**
One Belle Meade Place, 4400 Harding Rd.
Nashville, TN 37205
Tel.: 615-298-8200
Sales of Coal From Producers To Industrial & Utility Customers
S.I.C.: 5989
Roy E. Claverie *(Pres.)*

Ingram Entertainment Inc. **(1)**
1123 Heil Quaker Blvd.
La Vergne, TN 37086-7006
Tel.: 615-793-5000
Prerecorded Video Cassette Products
S.I.C.: 5045
John Taylor *(Pres. & Chief Exec. Officer)*
Vern Fross *(Sr. V.P.-Sls. & Mktg.)*
Marty Jorgensen *(V.P.-Mktg.)*
Frank Mattson *(V.P.-Distr. & Strategic Plng.)*
Mark Ramer *(V.P.-Mngmt. Information Systems)*
C.W. Weaver *(V.P.-Opers.)*
Bob Webb *(V.P.-Field Opers.)*
Carol Wiel *(V.P.-Adv.)*

Subsidiary:

Commtron Corporation **(2)**
7900 Hickman Rd.
Des Moines, IA 50322
Tel.: 515-226-3000 (80%)
Earnings: $7,682,000
Approx.Sls.: $527,641,000
Fiscal Year-end: 8/31/91
Wholesale Electronics
S.I.C.: 5045
Robert E. Martini *(Vice Chm. & Pres.)*

Ingram Library Services, Inc. **(1)**
1125 Heil Quaker Blvd.
La Vergne, TN 37086
Tel.: 615-793-5000
Distributor of Audio & Video Cassettes To Libraries
S.I.C.: 5099
Steven J. Mason *(Pres.)*
L.C. Price *(V.P. & Gen. Mgr.)*

Ingram Materials Co. **(1)**
10 Fatherland St.
Nashville, TN 37213
Tel.: 615-256-0263
Emp.: 60
Water Transportation & Wholesale Sand
S.I.C.: 4489; 5032
Charles J. Sanders, III *(Chief Oper. Officer & V.P.)*
Elaine Flick *(Controller)*

Ingram Merchandising Service Inc. **(1)**
1125 Heil Quaker Blvd.
La Vergne, TN 37086
Tel.: 615-793-5000
Merchandising & Rack Jobbing Services For Mass Merchants, Department, Grocery, Drug, Video & Computer Stores
S.I.C.: 4225
Ray Capp *(Pres.)*
Ron Peek *(Sr. V.:-Opers.)*
Chris Tate *(Asst. Controller)*

Ingram Periodicals Inc. **(1)**
1117 Heil Quaker Blvd.
La Vergne, TN 37086-7000
Tel.: 615-793-5000
Distributor of Periodicals
S.I.C.: 4226
Marlene Scott *(Pres.)*

Ingram Production Company **(1)**
One Belle Meade Place, 4400 Harding Rd.
Nashville, TN 37205
Tel.: 615-298-8200
Oil Production
S.I.C.: 1629
Roy E. Claverie *(Pres.)*

Publisher Resources Inc. **(1)**
1125 Heil Quaker Blvd.
La Vergne, TN 37086
Tel.: 615-793-5000
Wholesale Distrubtion, Warehousing, Order Fulfillment, Inventory Control and Order Processing To Credit Management, Royalty Accounting & Customer Service
S.I.C.: 4225
Thomas Scott *(Pres.)*

Tennessee Book Company **(1)**
1109 Heil Quaker Blvd.
La Vergne, TN 37086-9962
Tel.: 615-793-5000
Textbook & Workbook Depository For Tenessee's School Systems
S.I.C.: 4225
Charles Marshall *(Pres.)*

Tennessee Insurance Co. **(1)**
633 Thompson Ln.
Nashville, TN 37204
Tel.: 615-242-1961
Insurance for Property, Liability & Marine Risks
S.I.C.: 6321
Roy E. Claverie *(Chm. Bd.)*
Drew S. Barkley *(Pres.)*

Subsidiaries:

Ingram Cactus Co. **(1)**
One Greenway Plaza, Ste. 200
Houston, TX 77046
Tel.: 713-871-2300
Approx.Sls.: $139,000,000
Emp.: 360
Wellhead Equipment & Related Valves
S.I.C.: 3533
Scott Bender *(Pres.)*
Joel Bender *(V.P.-Opers.)*
D.A. Salcich *(V.P.-Fin.)*

Ingram Distribution Group Inc. **(1)**
1125 Heil Quaker Blvd.
La Vergne, TN 37086
Tel.: 615-793-5000
Approx.Sls.: $300,000,000
Emp.: 1,000
General Trade Books & Textbooks; Microcomputer Software; Prerecorded Video Cassette Products
S.I.C.: 5192; 5045; 7822
M.F. Lovett *(Chief Fin. Officer & V.P.)*
L.A. Lacey, Jr. *(Sr. V.P.)*
J.L. Taylor *(Sr. V.P.)*
Lee Synott *(Sr. V.P.)*

Ingram Micro Inc. **(1)**
1600 E. St. Andrw Pl.
Santa Ana, CA 92799-5125
Tel.: 714-566-1000
Fax: 714-549-0634
Assets: $39,642,000
Earnings: $8,256,000
Liabilities: $16,604,000
Net Worth: $23,038,000
Approx.Sls.: $553,403,000
Emp.: 250
Wholesale Distributor of Computer Hardware, Software, Peripherals & Accessories
S.I.C.: 5045
L.A. Lacy, Jr. *(Chm. Bd. & Chief Exec. Officer)*
D.R. Dukes *(Pres. & Chief Oper. Officer)*
R.K. Hardaway *(Chief Fin. Officer & Sr. V.P.)*
Sanat Dutta *(Sr. V.P.-Opers.)*
J.M. Kelly *(Sr. V.P.-Mngmt. Information Services)*
D.W. Rutledge *(Sr. V.P.-Admin.)*
Jim Wittry *(Sr. V.P.-Sls.)*
Bruce Martin *(V.P.-Pur. & Prods.)*

Permanent General Companies **(1)**
633 Thompson Lane
Nashville, TN 37204
Tel.: 615-242-1961
Insurance Agents, Brokers & Service
S.I.C.: 6411
Roy E. Claverie *(Chm. Bd.)*
Drew S. Barkley *(Pres.)*

INGRAM PAPER COMPANY
17411 Valley Blvd.
City of Industry, CA 91744
Mailing Address:
P.O. Box 60003
City of Industry, CA 91716
Tel.: 818-854-5400
Fax: 818-854-5449
Year Founded: 1923
Assets: $28,950,000
Net Worth: $28,950,000
Approx.Sls.: $133,000,000
Emp.: 340
Distribute Wholesale Paper Products
S.I.C.: 5111; 5085
John C. Ingram *(Chm. Bd.)*
Donald C. Ingram *(Pres. & Chief Exec. Officer)*
James G. Ingram *(Chief Fin. Officer & V.P.)*
John M. Ingram *(Exec. V.P.)*
David M. Ingram *(V.P.)*
Donald C. Ingram, Jr. *(V.P.)*
Everett F. Sanborn *(V.P.)*
Robert Wedehase *(V.P.)*
Dean Melnick *(Dir.-Personnel)*
Paul Tidball *(Mgr.-Data Processing)*

No. of Mfg. Plants/Facilities: 5
No. of U.S. Offices: 5

Computer Systems/Hardware:
ICL

Outside Service Firm(s):

KPMG Peat Marwick*(Auditors)*
725 S. Figueroa St.
Los Angeles, CA 90017
Tel.: 213-972-4000

Fireman's Fund Insurance Co.*(Commercial Insurance Carrier)*
San Francisco, CA

Pettit & Martin*(Legal Firm)*
Los Angeles, CA

Bank of America NT&SA*(Major Banking Relationship)*
201 Mission St.
San Francisco, CA 94105
Tel.: 415-624-2484

Bank of Hawaii*(Major Banking Relationship)*
Honolulu, HI

Wells Fargo Bank*(Pension Manager)*
420 Montgomery St.
San Francisco, CA 94104

INGRID-SEVKO, INC.
1419 Lake Cook Rd., Ste. 210
Deerfield, IL 60015
Tel.: 708-940-8788
Fax: 708-940-1252
Approx.Sls.: $30,000,000
Emp.: 150
Fiscal Year-end: 6/30/91
Food Containers, Microwave Oven Ware, Heatware, Horticulture, Housewares
S.I.C.: 3411; 2656; 3229; 3089
Larry Mosely *(Pres.)*
Edward W. Elhott, Jr. *(Chief Oper. Officer)*
Mary Jo Keller *(Dir.-Personnel)*
Anita Held *(Mgr.-Mktg.)*

Outside Service Firm(s):

Manufacturers National Bank N.A.*(Major Banking Relationship)*
38th Fl., 100 Renaissance Center
Detroit, MI 48243
Tel.: 313-222-4227

Sevco, Inc. **(1)**
100 Mechanic St.
Momence, IL 60954
Tel.: 815-472-2454
Fax: 815-472-4615
Injection Molded Finished Plastic Products
S.I.C.: 3089
John Handler *(Asst. to Pres.)*

INJECTION FOOTWEAR CORP.
8730 N.W. 36th Ave.
Miami, FL 33147
Tel.: 305-696-4611
Fax: 305-696-0018
Approx.Sls.: $28,000,000
Emp.: 700
Manufacture Shoes
S.I.C.: 3131; 3143; 3144
Alberto Barrocas *(Pres. & Treas.)*
Charles Barrocas *(Exec. V.P.)*
Jacob Barrocas *(V.P.-Mfg.)*
Jose E. Barrocas *(V.P.-Mktg.)*
Julio Magrisso *(V.P.-Fin. & Controller)*
Maria Gallo *(Dir.-Personnel)*

Outside Service Firm(s):

Deloitte & Touche*(Auditors)*
100 S.E. 2nd St.
Miami, FL 33131-2135
Tel.: 305-538-4141

Davis & Feig*(Legal Firm)*
Miami, FL

City Savings of Atlanta*(Major Banking Relationship)*
Atlanta, GA

INJECTRON CORPORATION
1000 S. Second St.
Plainfield, NJ 07063
Mailing Address:
P.O. Box 3012
Plainfield, NJ 07063
Tel.: 908-753-1990
Fax: 908-753-8537
Year Founded: 1959
Sales Range: $10-19 Million
Emp.: 300
Custom Injection Moldings
S.I.C.: 3089
Louis M. Pollak *(Pres.)*
Diane Mazur *(Controller)*
Mary Bolivar *(Dir.-Personnel)*

No. of Mfg. Plants/Facilities: 1
No. of U.S. Offices: 1

Outside Service Firm(s):

Rosenberg, Druker & Co.*(Auditors)*
Somerville, NJ

Ozzard Wharton*(Legal Firm)*
Sommerville, NJ

United Jersey Bank*(Major Banking Relationship)*
Westfield, NJ

INKEL CORP.
14830 Alondra Blvd.
La Mirada, CA 90638
Tel.: 714-521-6100
Wholesale Household Appliances
S.I.C.: 5064
Y.K. Cho *(Chm. Bd.)*
Larry Lammis *(Pres.)*

Inkel Corp.—(Continued)

Subsidiaries:

Inkel Technology **(1)**
4181 Business Center Dr.
Fremont, CA 94538-6355
Tel.: 510-623-8900
S.I.C.: 3571; 3674
John Kim *(Pres.)*

Sherwood Corporation **(1)**
4181 Business Center Dr.
Fremont, CA 94538-6355
Tel.: 510-623-8900
Twx: 910-338-0387
Fax: 510-623-8945
Assets: $4,420,000
Liabilities: $1,946,000
Net Worth: $2,474,000
Approx.Sls.: $25,000,000
Emp.: 250
Fiscal Year-end: 9/30/90
Computer Systems/Hardware:
Maxicom 230
Mfr. Computers
S.I.C.: 3571
Y.K. Cho *(Chm.)*
Larry Lummis *(Pres.)*
H. Kim *(Controller)*

INLAND ASSOCIATES
15021 W. 117th St.
Olathe, KS 66061
Mailing Address:
P.O. Box 940,
Olathe, KS 66062
Tel.: 913-764-7977 **KS**
Year Founded: 1970
Assets: $6,000,000
Liabilities: $2,400,000
Net Worth: $3,600,000
Sales Range: $20-39 Million
Emp.: 40
Distribution of Computer Peripherals
S.I.C.: 5045
Don C. Omer *(Pres.)*
Chuck Floyd *(Chief Fin. Officer)*
Anita Lickteig *(Dir.-Personnel)*
Peggy Meader *(Mgr.-Opers.)*
Principal(s):
Don C. Omer

No. of U.S. Offices: 6

Computer Systems/Hardware:
Digital Equipment

Outside Service Firm(s):

KPMG Peat Marwick*(Auditors)*
1000 Walnut St.
Kansas City, MO 64106

Commercial Union Insurance Co.*(Commercial Insurance Carrier)*
Boston, MA

Haas & Wilkerson*(Group Insurer)*
Kansas City, MO

H. B. Oppenheimer & Co.*(Investment Banker)*
Kansas City, MO

Stinson, Mag & Fizzell*(Legal Firm)*
2100 Charter Bank Ctr.
Kansas City, MO 64105

Bank IV*(Major Banking Relationship)*
Olathe, KS

De Mars Pension*(Pension Manager)*
Overland Park, KS

THE INLAND GROUP, INC.
2901 Butterfield Rd.
Oak Brook, IL 60521
Tel.: 708-218-8000
Tel.: 800-828-8999 **DE**
Fax: 708-218-4935
Year Founded: 1967
Approx.Sls.: $630,600,000
Emp.: 800
Fiscal Year-end: 6/30/92
Real Estate, Brokerage, Financing, Property Management, Syndication & Development
S.I.C.: 6513; 6531
Daniel L. Goodwin *(Chm. Bd. & Chief Exec. Officer)*
G. Joseph Cosenza *(Vice Chm.)*
Robert H. Baum *(Vice Chm. & Gen. Counsel)*
R. Kurt Huddleston *(Pres.-Inland Computer Services, Inc.)*
Norm Treonis *(Pres.-Inland Property Management Group, Inc.)*
Alan F. Kremin *(Treas.)*
Bella P. Zielinski *(Dir.-Mktg. Communications)*
Norma Pearch *(Dir.-Human Resources)*
Anne Halston *(Mgr.-Res. & Communications)*
Principal(s):
Daniel L. Goodwin
G. Joseph Cosenza
Robert H. Baum
Robert D. Parks

Computer Systems/Hardware:
DEC VAX's, IBM Compatible PC's

INLAND PRINTING CO., INC.
2009 W. Ave. S.
La Crosse, WI 54601
Tel.: 608-788-5800 **WI**
Fax: 608-787-5870
Year Founded: 1944
Approx.Sls.: $23,000,000
Emp.: 175
Offset Commercial Lithography, Rotogravure Printing
S.I.C.: 2752; 2754
Jack Glendenning *(Pres.)*
Greg Prairie *(V.P. & Chief Fin. Officer)*
Loren Dieckrager *(V.P. & Controller)*
Frank Barry *(V.P.-Sls. & Mktg.)*
John Gates *(V.P.-Opers.)*

Outside Service Firm(s):

First National Bank*(Major Banking Relationship)*
LaCrosse, WI

Norwest Bank Minnesota, N.A.*(Major Banking Relationship)*
La Crosse, WI

INLANDER-STEINDLER PAPER
850 Forest Edge Dr.
Vernon Hills, IL 60061-3105
Tel.: 708-913-9500 **IL**
Fax: 708-913-9522
Year Founded: 1887
Approx.Sls.: $73,000,000
Emp.: 200
Fiscal Year-end: 9/30/90
Wholesale Distributor of Industrial Paper & Printing Supplies
S.I.C.: 5113; 5111; 5085; 5169
Thomas I. Altholz *(Pres. & Chief Oper. Officer)*
Ronald G. Hilton *(Corp. Treas. & Sec.)*
Richard A. Mignano *(Exec. V.P.)*
Joseph Kowalczyk *(Dir.-Information Systems)*

Computer Systems/Hardware:
Digital

Outside Service Firm(s):

Coopers & Lybrand*(Auditors)*
203 N. LaSalle St.
Chicago, IL 60601
Tel.: 312-701-5500

The Home Indemnity Company*(Commercial Insurance Carrier)*
Manchester, NY

Altheimer & Gray*(Legal Firm)*
10 S. Wacker Dr.
Chicago, IL 60606
Tel.: 312-715-4000

Continental Bank N. A.*(Major Banking Relationship)*
231 S. LaSalle St.
Chicago, IL 60697
Tel.: 312-828-2345
Tel.: 800-426-5754
Telex: 312-828-1783

Continental Illinois*(Major Banking Relationship)*
231 So. LaSalle St.
Chicago, IL
Tel.: 312-828-2345

INMAN CONSTRUCTION CORPORATION
5100 Poplar Ave., Ste. 1210
Memphis, TN 38137
Tel.: 901-682-4100
Fax: 901-526-1627
Year Founded: 1970
Sales Range: $40-59 Million
Emp.: 75
Commercial & Industrial Building Contractor
S.I.C.: 1541; 1542
Frank Inman, Jr. *(Chm. Bd.)*
George W. Inman *(Pres.)*
Paul N. Akin *(Sr. V.P.)*
H.T. Graddy *(Sr. V.P.)*
Gary W. Moore *(Controller)*

Outside Service Firm(s):

Watkins, Watkins & Keenan*(Auditors)*
Memphis, TN

First Tennessee Bank, N.A.*(Major Banking Relationship)*
P.O. Box 84
Memphis, TN 38101-0034
Tel.: 901-523-4541

Sovran Bank*(Major Banking Relationship)*
Collierville, TN

INMAN MILLS
P.O. Box 207
Inman, SC 29349
Tel.: 803-472-2121
Fax: 803-472-9674
Year Founded: 1902
Sales Range: $100-499 Million
Emp.: 1,500
Manufacture Cotton Textiles & Blends
S.I.C.: 2211
W. Marshall Chapman *(Chm. Bd. & Chief Exec. Officer)*
Robert H. Chapman, III *(Pres.)*
John F. Renfro, Jr. *(V.P.)*
Howard L. Price *(V.P.)*
George A. Abbott *(V.P.)*
Patricia Bird *(Sec.)*
James C. Pace, Jr. *(Controller)*
Roy E. Metcalf *(Dir.-Data Processing)*

Outside Service Firm(s):

George G. Scott & Co.*(Auditors)*
Charlotte, SC

NationsBank South Carolina*(Major Banking Relationship)*
Columbia, SC

PAUL INMAN ASSOCIATES INC.
30095 Northwestern Hwy.
Farmington Hills, MI 48334
Tel.: 313-626-8300 **MI**
Fax: 313-626-6893
Year Founded: 1954
Sales Range: $100-499 Million
Emp.: 310
Fiscal Year-end: 9/30/91
Food Brokers & Manufacturers Representatives
S.I.C.: 5141
Paul Inman *(Chm. Bd.)*
Gerald Inman *(Pres. & Chief Exec. Officer)*
Ronald Fairchild *(Chief Oper. Officer & Dir.-Grovery Distribution)*
E. Malcolm York *(Chief Fin. Officer & Exec. V.P.)*
Phillip Fischioni *(Exec. V.P. & Corp. Dir.-Mktg.)*
Kenneth Elwert *(Sr. V.P.-Data Processing)*
Joseph C. Rimarcik *(Sr. V.P.-Accounting & Admin.)*
Stephen K. Valentine, Jr. *(Gen. Counsel)*
Cherie Jerue *(Mgr.-Personnel)*
Principal(s):
Employee Owned

No. of U.S. Offices: 6

Computer Systems/Hardware:
IBM A/S 400

Outside Service Firm(s):

Plante & Moran*(Auditors)*
Detroit, MI

Midwest Benefits*(Group Insurer)*
Detroit, MI

Valentine Assoc.*(Legal Firm)*
West Bloomfield, MI

Manufacturers National Bank N.A.*(Major Banking Relationship)*
38th Fl., 100 Renaissance Center
Detroit, MI 48243
Tel.: 313-222-4227

Investment Management Services*(Pension Manager)*
Birmingham, MI

INNER SECRETS, INC.
1500 Hudson St.
Hoboken, NJ 07030
Tel.: 201-963-0800
Fax: 201-963-1296
Approx.Sls.: $14,000,000
Emp.: 350
Corsets, Brassieres & Allied Garments
S.I.C.: 2342
Morton Sloan *(Chm. Bd.)*
Bernard Lorn *(Pres.)*
Jack Phekkekara *(Controller)*
Irving L. Gartenberg *(Gen. Counsel)*

Outside Service Firm(s):

Konigberg, Wolf & Co.*(Auditors)*
New York, NY

National Westminster Bank plc*(Major Banking Relationship)*
Astor Plaza, 1515 Broadway
New York, NY 10036

INNOVATIVE PLASTICS CORPORATION
400 Rte. 303
Orangeburg, NY 10962
Tel.: 914-359-7500 **NY**
Fax: 914-359-0237
Year Founded: 1982
Approx.Sls.: $15,000,000
Emp.: 250
Mfr. of Plastic Packaging
S.I.C.: 3086
Judith Hershaft *(Pres.)*
Steve Hershaft *(V.P.)*
Bud Macfarlane *(V.P.-Sls. & Mktg.)*
Janice Asaro *(Dir.-Personnel)*

Outside Service Firm(s):

Grossman, Brozman & Agrin*(Auditors)*
New York, NY

Connecticut Bank & Trust*(Major Banking Relationship)*
One Constitution Plaza,
Hartford, CT 06115

INPUT
1280 Villa St.
Mountain View, CA 94041
Tel.: 415-961-3300 **CA**
Fax: 415-961-3966
Year Founded: 1977
Approx.Sls.: $7,000,000
Emp.: 75
Fiscal Year-end: 12/31/91
Export
Marketing, Research & Management Consulting Firm for the Computer & Telecommunications Industries
S.I.C.: 7374; 8742
Peter A. Cunningham *(Chm. Bd., Pres. & Chief Exec. Officer)*
Patricia Cunningham *(V.P., Chief Fin. Officer , & Sec.)*
Tom O'Flaherty *(V.P.)*
J.P. Richards *(V.P.)*
Christopher Smith *(V.P.-Sls. & Mktg.)*
Denny Wayson *(V.P.)*
Sheila Collins *(Controller)*

No. of Mfg. Plants/Facilities: 7
No. of U.S. Offices: 3
No. of Foreign Offices: 4

Outside Service Firm(s):

Ernst & Young*(Auditors)*
660 Hansen Way
Palo Alto, CA 94304
Tel.: 415-496-1600

Sedgwick James*(Commercial Insurance Carrier)*
1290 Avenue of the Americas
New York, NY 10104
Tel.: 212-830-1000

Silicon Valley Bank*(Major Banking Relationship)*
San Jose, CA

Subsidiary:

INPUT, Inc. **(1)**
Vienna, VA
S.I.C.: 7374; 8742

Non-U.S. Holdings:

INPUT, K.K. **(1)**
Tokoyo, Japan
S.I.C.: 7374; 8742

INPUT, Ltd. **(1)**
London, England United Kingdom
S.I.C.: 7374; 8742

INPUT, SARL **(1)**
Paris, France
S.I.C.: 7374; 8742

INSIGNIA FINANCIAL GROUP, INC.
1 Insignia Place
Greenville, SC 29602
Mailing Address:
P.O. Box 1089,
Greenville, SC 29602
Tel.: 803-239-1000
Fax: 803-239-1096
Year Founded: 1990
Assets: $25,405,000
Earnings: ($11,681,000)
Liabilities: $51,607,000
Net Worth: $26,202,000
Approx.Rev.: $16,285,000
Emp.: 1,800
Fiscal Year-end: 12/31/90
Property Management
S.I.C.: 6531
Andrew L. Farkas *(Chm. & Chief Exec. Officer)*
Carol D. Vinson *(Pres. & Chief Oper. Officer)*
William N. Page *(Mng. Dir.-Admin. & Sec.)*
James A. Aston *(Mng. Dir.-Investment Banking & Treas.)*
Albert H. Gossett *(V.P. & Chief Information Officer)*
Scott T. Hocking *(V.P. & Chief Fin. Officer)*

Subsidiaries:

Am Real Corp. **(1)**
P.O. Box 1089,
Greenville, SC 29602
Property Mngmt.
S.I.C.: 6531

Insignia Management Group **(1)**
1 Insignia Place
Greenville, SC 29602
S.I.C.: 6531
Tom Shuler *(Pres.)*

Insignia Mortgage & Investment Corp. **(1)**
100 Ashford Center North, Ste. 440
Atlanta, GA 30338
S.I.C.: 6531
John Beam *(Pres.)*

INSILCO CORPORATION
300 N. Marienfeld, Ste. 400
Midland, TX 79701
Mailing Address:
P.O. Box 1919,
Midland, TX 79702
Tel.: 915-684-4411 **CT**
Fax: 915-688-7327
Holding Company
S.I.C.: 6719; 2452; 3356; 3357
Joel L. Reed *(Pres. & Chief Exec. Officer)*
J. Randal Greaves *(Exec. V.P. & Chief Fin. Officer)*
Les Jacobs *(Dir.-Human Resources)*
Grant Billingsley *(Mgr.-Pub. Affairs)*
Kathy Holt *(Cash Mgr.)*

Divisions:

Basic Industries **(1)**
1275 Old Hwy. 8
New Brighton, MN 55112
Tel.: 612-636-6300
Precision Metal & Plastic Parts for Computer Manufacturers
S.I.C.: 3599
Virg J. Paulson *(Pres.)*

Computer Circuitry Group **(1)**
Riverbiran Bldg., Ste. 307, 4709 Creekstone Dr.
Morrisville, NC 27560
Tel.: 919-941-5550
Cable Assemblies & Wire Harnesses for Electronic Equipment Manufacturers; Interconnect Cable for Mainframe Computers
S.I.C.: 3577
Peter J. Meehan *(Pres.)*

Curtis Manufacturing Company, Inc. **(1)**
30 Fitzgerald Dr.
Jaffrey, NH 03452
Tel.: 603-532-4123
Manufactures Computer & Electronic Equipment Accesories
S.I.C.: 3577
Thomas W. Judd *(Pres.)*

Escod Industries **(1)**
P.O. Box 12138,
Research Triangle Park, NC 27709
Tel.: 919-549-9502
Electronic Components, Wiring Harnesses & Assemblies
Peter J. Meehan *(Pres.)*

Rolodex Corp. **(1)**
245 Secaucus Rd.
Secaucus, NJ 07094
Tel.: 201-348-3939
Desktop Rotary Files
S.I.C.: 3499
Donald H. Gels *(Pres.)*

Signal Transformer Co., Inc. **(1)**
500 Bayview Ave.
Inwood, NY 11696
Tel.: 516-239-5777
Emp.: 396
Mfr. & Sale of Transformers for High-Tech Industries
S.I.C.: 3612
Hugh R. Arnold *(Pres.)*

Sinclair Paint Co. **(1)**
6100 S. Garfield Ave.
Los Angeles, CA 90040
Tel.: 213-268-2511
Paint
S.I.C.: 2851
Robert M. Sinclair *(Pres.)*

Thermal Components, Inc. **(1)**
2760 Gunter Park, West, P.O. Box 3253
Montgomery, AL 36193
Tel.: 205-277-1810
Mfr. of Heat Exchange Products for Automotive Industry
S.I.C.: 3714
C. Bari Saunders *(Pres.)*

Subsidiaries:

Dac Easy, Inc. **(1)**
17950 Preston Road, Ste. 800
Dallas, TX 75252
Tel.: 214-248-0205
Tel.: 800-877-8088
Fax: 214-250-3752
Approx.Sls.: $18,000,000
Emp.: 135
Fiscal Year-end: 12/31/90
Manufacture Software
S.I.C.: 7372
Kevin Howe *(Pres.)*
Lee Jones *(V.P.-Admin.)*
Charlie Kilpatrick *(V.P.-Sls.)*
Allen Walker *(V.P.-Customer Services)*
Cheryl Hammer *(Dir.-Mktg.)*
Susan Morrow *(Dir.-Communications)*

Steel Parts Corp. **(1)**
Berryman Pike
Tipton, IN 46072
Tel.: 317-675-2191 (100%)
Automotive Stampings
S.I.C.: 3465
Barry W. Clark *(Pres. & Chief Exec. Officer)*

Stewart Connector Systems, Inc. **(1)**
R.D.2, P.O. Box 2020,
Glen Rock, PA 17327
Tel.: 717-235-7512
Mfr. of Printed Circuit Board Connectors & Modular Plugs & Connectors
S.I.C.: 3678
Robert Brennan *(Pres.)*

Stewart Stamping Corp. **(1)**
630 Central Park Ave.
Yonkers, NY 10704
Tel.: 914-965-0816
Specialized Wiring Harnesses, Coaxial Cable & Cable Assemblies for Computer Industry
S.I.C.: 3577
Fred Afragola *(Pres.)*

Taylor Publishing Co. **(1)**
1550 W. Mockingbird Ln.
Dallas, TX 75235
Tel.: 214-637-2800 (100%)
Yearbook Printing
S.I.C.: 2741
Frank Perliski *(Pres.)*

Valentec International Corp. **(1)**
3190 Pullman Lane
Costa Mesa, CA 92626
Tel.: 714-540-0128
Emp.: 965
Manufacture Small Arms Ammunition; Screw Machine Products
S.I.C.: 3451; 3482
Robert Zummo *(Pres.)*

Valentec International Corp. **(1)**
1901 N. Ft. Meyer Dr., Ste. 1016
Arlington, VA 22209
Tel.: 703-841-1021
General Defense Contractors
Robert Zummo *(Pres.)*

THE INSTANT WEB COMPANIES
7951 Powers Blvd.
Chanhassen, MN 55317
Tel.: 612-474-0961 **MN**
Fax: 612-474-6467
Year Founded: 1968
Approx.Sls.: $80,000,000
Emp.: 1,200
Commercial Printing; Manufacture Envelopes; Direct Mail Advertising Services; Mailing & Lettershop; Plastic Cards
S.I.C.: 2752; 2677; 7331; 2759
E. Jerome Carlson *(Pres. & Chief Exec. Officer)*
David Gardella *(Pres.-The Instant Web Companies)*
H. Bill Carlson *(Chief Fin. Officer)*
Ronald M. Kaufenberg *(V.P.-Sls.)*
Melissa Jo Halvorson *(Sec.)*

No. of Mfg. Plants/Facilities: 4
No. of U.S. Offices: 5

Subsidiaries:

Instant Web, Inc. **(1)**
7951 Powers Blvd.
Chanhassen, MN 55317
Tel.: 612-474-0961
Bradley H. Bloss *(Exec. V.P.)*
David E. High *(Mgr.-Acct. Service)*

United Mailing, Inc. **(1)**
1001 Park Rd.
Chanhassen, MN 55317
Tel.: 612-474-4182
James R. Rice *(Exec. V.P.)*
Phyllis McPhillips *(Mgr.-Acct. Services)*

Victory Envelope, Inc. **(1)**
1000 Park Rd.
Chanhassen, MN 55317
Tel.: 612-474-3264
Thomas A. Cristelli *(Exec. V.P.)*

INSTITUTIONAL FINANCING SERVICES
5100 Park Rd.
Benicia, CA 94510
Tel.: 707-746-7600 **CA**
Fax: 707-746-7611
Year Founded: 1981
Sales Range: $40-59 Million
Emp.: 600
Fiscal Year-end: 6/30/92
Import Export
Supply Products for Sale by Non-Profit Organizations
S.I.C.: 7389

Institutional Financing Services—(Continued)

Mike Rippey *(Chm. Bd.)*
Peter Raisbeck *(Pres. & Chief Exec. Officer)*
John Harbottle *(Chief Fin. Officer & V.P. Fin.)*
J. Cascino *(Sr. V.P.-Sls.)*
J. Benson *(V.P.-Opers. & Mngmt. Information Systems)*
Nancy Eubel *(Controllor)*
Bob Spector *(Dir.-MIS)*

No. of Mfg. Plants/Facilities: 1
No. of U.S. Offices: 1
No. of Foreign Offices: 3

Computer Systems/Hardware:
Hewlett-Packard Model 3000

Outside Service Firm(s):

Deloitte & Touche*(Auditors)*
50 Fremont St.
San Francisco, CA 94105-2230
Tel.: 415-393-4300
Fax: 415-227-0452

Brobeck, Phleger & Harrison*(Legal Firm)*
Spear St. Tower, One Market Plaza
San Francisco, CA 94105
Tel.: 415-442-0900

The Bank of California, N.A.*(Major Banking Relationship)*
Oakland, CA

INSTRUMENT SPECIALTIES COMPANY
Rt. 611 & Broad St.
Delaware Water Gap, PA 18327
Mailing Address:
P.O. Box A
Delaware Water Gap, PA 18327
Tel.: 717-424-8510 **NJ**
Fax: 717-424-6213
Year Founded: 1938
Approx.Sls.: $25,000,000
Emp.: 350
Fiscal Year-end: 12/31/91
Export
Stamping Metal For The Trade
S.I.C.: 3469
Employee Matching Gifts Program: Instrument Specialties Matches Employee Gifts to Approved Universities, Colleges & Junior Colleges up to $250 per Participant per Calendar Year
William C. Carson *(Chm. Bd. & Chief Exec. Officer)*
Frank Rushen *(Pres.)*
Richard Anderson *(V.P. & Chief Fin. Officer)*
Thys Rienstra *(V.P.-Sls.)*
Maurice Della Vecchia *(V.P.-Engineering Tech. Services)*
Bill McCloskey *(Mgr.-New Bus. Devel.)*
Stephanie Arnold *(Mgr.-Adv.)*
Sherwood Gum *(Mgr.-Pur.)*
Susan Toleno *(Mgr.-Personnel)*
Rebecca Connor *(Mgr.-Data Processing)*
Pete Brockway *(Mgr.-Quality Control)*

No. of Mfg. Plants/Facilities: 3
No. of U.S. Offices: 2
No. of Foreign Offices: 1

Computer Systems/Hardware:
MAI Basic Four

Outside Service Firm(s):

Arthur Andersen & Co.*(Auditors)*
P.O. Box 221, 101 Eisenhower Pkwy.
Roseland, NJ 07068
Tel.: 201-403-6100
Fax: 201-403-0579

Philadelphia National Bank*(Major Banking Relationship)*
P.O. Box 13834, Broad & Chestnut Streets
Philadelphia, PA 19101-7618
Tel.: 215-973-8327

Divisions:

Instrument Specialties - Western Division **(1)**
505 Porter Way
Placentia, CA 92670
Tel.: 714-579-7100
Emp.: 25
Mfg. of EMI Shielding & Custom Stampings
S.I.C.: 3469
James F. Walsh *(Div. Mgr.)*
William Carson *(Admin. Mgr.)*

Instrument Specialties Europe, S.A. - European Division **(1)**
3 Avenue Du Progres B4432
Alleur, Belgium
Tel.: 32 41 46 4862
Emp.: 10
Distribution/Value Added Operations
S.I.C.: 7373
Phillipe Lamboray *(Managing Dir.)*

INSTRUMENTARIUM IMAGING, INC.
300 W. Edgerton Ave.
Milwaukee, WI 53207
Tel.: 414-747-1030
Tel.: 800-558-6120
Fax: 414-481-8665
Approx.Sls.: $20,000,000
Emp.: 32
Fiscal Year-end: 12/31/91
Import
Marketing of X-Ray & MRI Equipment
S.I.C.: 5047
Ed Barker *(Pres.)*
Sue Mitch *(Controller)*
Mike Silver *(V.P.-MRI Div.)*
Ed Barker *(V.P.-X-Ray Div.)*
Gerry Buss *(Dir.-Regulatory Affairs & Quality Assurance)*
Kathy Nightingale *(Dir.-Mammography Mktg.)*
William Conn *(MRI Mktg. Mgr.)*
Jackie Balh *(Pur. Mgr.)*

INSULATING MATERIALS, INC.
One Campbell Rd.
Schenectady, NY 12306
Tel.: 518-395-3300
Electrical Insulators and Insulating Materials
S.I.C.: 3644
Gary Bivona *(Pres.)*

Subsidiary:

Acme Chemicals & Insulation Co. **(1)**
166 Chapel St.
New Haven, CT 06505
Tel.: 203-562-2171
Emp.: 72
Epoxy Formulation; Coated Materials
S.I.C.: 2295; 2821
Richard Van Horn *(Div. Pres.)*

INSURANCE CORP. OF AMERICA
4295 San Felipe
Houston, TX 77027
Mailing Address:
P.O. Box 56308
Houston, TX 77256-6308
Tel.: 713-871-8100
Tel.: 800-899-2356
Fax: 713-871-8218
Approx.Sls.: $45,000,000
Emp.: 60
Fiscal Year-end: 12/31/90
Property & Casualty Carrier Specializing in Medical Liability Insurance
S.I.C.: 6351; 6331; 6321
James N. Augustine *(Chm. Bd. & Chief Exec. Officer)*
Willard E. Shuman *(Pres. & Chief Oper. Officer)*
Louis M. Guzick *(Chief Fin. Officer & Sr. V.P.)*
Cynthia Barlow *(Sr. V.P.-Underwriting & Sec.)*
Robert J. Hallmark *(Sr. V.P.-Claims & Gen. Counsel)*
Kay H. Houston *(V.P.-Mktg. Services)*
Stephen D. Richards *(V.P.-Claims)*
Linda Knighton *(Dir.-Personnel)*

Computer Systems/Hardware:
IBM System 38

Outside Service Firm(s):

First Houston Bank*(Major Banking Relationship)*
Houston, TX

Texas Commerce Bank*(Major Banking Relationship)*
600 Travis Street, Suite 1150
Houston, TX 77002
Tel.: 713-236-4865

INSURANCE MANAGEMENT ASSOCIATES
250 N. Water, Suite 600
Wichita, KS 67202
Tel.: 316-267-9221
Fax: 316-266-6254
Year Founded: 1974
Approx.Sls.: $10,000,000
Emp.: 175
Insurance Agency
S.I.C.: 6411
Joe Moddrell, Jr. *(Chm. Bd.)*
Joseph C. Lukens II *(Pres.)*
W.C. Cohen, Jr. *(Chief Exec. Officer)*
Kathy Burnett *(Mgr.-Personnel)*

No. of U.S. Offices: 3

Outside Service Firm(s):

KPMG Peat Marwick*(Auditors)*
Wichita, KS

Foulston & Siefkin*(Legal Firm)*
700 Fourth Financial Center
Wichita, KS 67202
Tel.: 316-267-6371

Emprise Bank*(Major Banking Relationship)*
P.O. Box 2970,
Wichita, KS 67201
Tel.: 316-269-7400

INTECH ADVANCED ANALOG
(Formerly Advanced Analog)
2270 Martin Ave.
Santa Clara, CA 95050
Tel.: 408-988-4930
Fax: 408-988-2702
Year Founded: 1969
Approx.Sls.: $20,000,000
Emp.: 180
Fiscal Year-end: 3/31/91
Import Export
Mfr. Electronic Function Modules, Data Conversion, Data Acquisition, OP Amps, Non-Linear Amps, Custom Modular & Hybrid Circuits
S.I.C.: 3674; 3679
Leroy M. Buckler *(Chm. Bd.)*
W.E. Kaelin *(V.P. & G.M.-Communications Div.)*
Sharon Allen Smith *(Dir.-Personnel)*
Jim Gobin *(Dir.-Mfg.)*
Mike Sullivan *(Dir.-Sls.)*

Computer Systems/Hardware:
IBM

INTEGRA TECHNOLOGIES CORP.
132 Calvary St.
Waltham, MA 02154
Tel.: 617-899-0012
Fax: 617-891-8940
Approx.Sls.: $10,000,000
Emp.: 140
Mfr. Computer Peripheral Products Computer-Link
S.I.C.: 3577
E.P. Brandeis *(Chief Exec. Officer)*
D. Goldman *(V.P.-New Technology)*
R.D. Blackburn *(V.P.-Mktg.)*
J. Power *(Chief Fin. Officer)*
M. Ready *(Pur. Agent)*

INTEGRAL SYSTEMS
Tishman Bldg., 2185 N. California Blvd.
Walnut Creek, CA 94596
Tel.: 510-939-3916
Tel.: 800-346-4002 **DE**
Fax: 510-946-4891
Year Founded: 1972
Assets: $50,137,000
Earnings: $116,000
Liabilities: $30,713,000
Net Worth: $19,424,000
Approx.Sls.: $58,053,000
Emp.: 447
Fiscal Year-end: 3/31/91
Export
Sales & Development of Human Resource & Financial Manufacturing & Distribution Systems Applications; Computer Software Distributor; Related Professional Services-Consulting, Custom Modification, Training; Maintenance
S.I.C.: 7372; 7379
L. George Klaus *(Chm. Bd., Pres. & Chief Exec. Officer)*
Thomas L. Gough *(Pres. & Chief Oper. Officer)*
James A. Clark *(Chief Fin. Officer & Treas.)*
David A. Kadish *(Sec. & Gen. Counsel)*
Daniel V. Callahan *(V.P.-Sls.)*
Kevin Lynch *(V.P.-Eastern Sls. Opers.)*
David Potts *(V.P.-Western Sls. Opers.)*
Charles Snyder *(V.P.-Midrange)*
Louis A. Wright *(V.P.-Product Devel.)*
Kara Brand *(Dir.-Plng. & Reporting)*
Katherine Boshkoff *(Dir.-Mktg.)*
Sandra Nakaji *(Dir.-Human Res.)*
Peter Gonzalves *(Mgr.-Leasing)*
James Hardy *(Mgr.-Data Center)*
Lisa Urbina *(Supvr.-Pur.)*
Peter Gonzalves *(Supvr.-Facility)*
Efren F. De Los Angeles *(Fin. Analyst)*

No. of U.S. Offices: 9
No. of Foreign Offices: 2

Computer Systems/Hardware:
IBMS Systems 38-5381, 4341-12 & 4381

Outside Service Firm(s):

KPMG Peat Marwick*(Auditors)*
3 Embarcadero Center
San Francisco, CA 94111
Tel.: 415-951-0100
Fax: 415-397-1129

Massie & Beck*(Commercial Insurance Carrier)*
675 Ygnacio Valley Rd., Ste. A 200
Walnut Creek, CA 94596

General American Life Insurance Co.*(Group Insurer)*
44 Montgomery St., Ste. 2270
San Francisco, CA 94102

Morgan Stanley & Co.*(Investment Banker)*
555 California St.
San Francisco, CA 94104

Heller, Ehrman, White & McAuliffe*(Legal Firm)*
525 University Ave.
Palo Alto, CA 94301
Tel.: 415-326-7600

Silicon Valley Bank*(Major Banking Relationship)*
3000 Lakeside Dr.
Santa Clara, CA 95054

Great-West Life Assurance Co.*(Pension Manager)*
8505 East Orchard Rd.
Englewood, CO 8011
Tel.: 800-537-2033

Subsidiaries:

Integral Systems, Inc. **(1)**
1279 Oakmead Pkwy.
Sunnyvale, CA 94086
Tel.: 408-730-0100
Fax: 408-736-6322
Assets: $14,803,000
Earnings: $2,069,000
Liabilities: $4,000,000
Net Worth: $10,803,000
Approx.Sls.: $16,205,000
Emp.: 400
Fiscal Year-end: 12/31/89
Computer Systems/Hardware:
IBM 4381
Develops & Markets Software Products
S.I.C.: 7372; 7379; 5045
Brian Aspland *(Chm. Bd., Pres. & Chief Exec. Officer)*
Albert Duffield *(Chief Oper. Officer)*
Paul Salsgiver *(Exec. V.P.-Support & Dir.-Devel.)*
Joseph Girata *(Chief Fin. Officer)*
Michael Kaiser *(Dir.-Res.)*
Peter Akraboff *(Mgr.-Data Processing)*
Charles Jolly *(Mgr.-Information Systems)*
Windy Vanwinkle *(Mgr.-Sls.)*
Barbie Jackson *(Mgr.-Telecommunications)*
Lynn Harris *(Mgr.-Pur.)*
Joan Costello *(Meetings Planner)*

Integral Systems **(1)**
1000 Park Forty Plaza, Ste. 500
Durham, NC 27713
Tel.: 919-544-5008
Fax: 919-549-5394
Emp.: 30
Sales & Development of Financial & Human Resource Applications for IBM Midrange Computers
S.I.C.: 7372

Integral Systems **(1)**
39555 Orchard Hill Pl., Ste. 160
Novi, MI 48375
Tel.: 313-380-0600
Fax: 313-380--646
Emp.: 60
Sales & Development of Manufacturing & Distribution Application for IBM Midrange Computers
S.I.C.: 5045

INTEGRATEC
3003 Chamblee Tucker Rd.
Atlanta, GA 30341
Tel.: 404-936-1000
Fax: 404-936-1060
Emp.: 850
Financial Service Company
S.I.C.: 6153; 8721
Donald K. Griffen *(Pres. & Chief Exec. Officer)*
Mike Fletcher *(Chief Oper. Officer)*
Barbara Lee *(V.P.-Human Resources)*

No. of U.S. Offices: 5

Outside Service Firm(s):

Deloitte & Touche*(Auditors)*
100 Peachtree St., Ste. 1700
Atlanta, GA 30303-1943
Tel.: 404-220-1500
Fax: 404-220-1583

King & Spalding*(Legal Firm)*
Trust Co. Tower
Atlanta, GA 30303
Tel.: 404-572-4600

INTEGRATED ENERGY CONTROLS CORP.
5150 W. 76th St.
Minneapolis, MN 55439
Tel.: 612-831-8242 **MN**
Fax: 612-831-8243
Year Founded: 1979
Sales Range: $10-19 Million
Emp.: 10
Fiscal Year-end: 12/31/91
Export
Building Automation, Energy Management
S.I.C.: 3823
Byron Westphal *(Chm. Bd., Pres. & Chief Exec. Officer)*
Bruce Anderson *(Exec. V.P., Treas. & Dir.-Mfg. & Quality Control)*
Jeanette Daniel *(Dir.-Admin. & Opers. & Pur.)*
Dave Strong *(Dir.-Sls. & Mktg.)*
Bob Korpotich *(Dir.-Res. & Devel.)*

Principal(s):
Byron Westphal
Bruce Anderson

No. of Mfg. Plants/Facilities: 1
No. of U.S. Offices: 1

Computer Systems/Hardware:
Stearns; IBM/Novell Network; Intel

Integrated Financial Solutions
(See Listing Under Western & Southern Life Insurance Co., Name Changed To IFS Systems, Inc.)

INTEGRATED RESOURCES, INC.
(Filed Chapter 11 Bankruptcy on Feb. 13, 1990)
10 Union Square East
New York, NY 10003
Tel.: 212-353-7000 **DE**
Year Founded: 1969
Assets: $6,252,514,000
Earnings: $49,161,000
Liabilities: $5,732,248,000
Net Worth: $520,266,000
Approx.Rev.: $1,500,494,000
Emp.: 3,200
Fiscal Year-end: 12/31/89
Insurance, Real Estate & Financial Services
S.I.C.: 6211; 6311; 6411; 6531; 6799
Frank W. Geller *(Chm. Bd. & Chief Exec. Officer)*
Jay D. Chazanoff *(Sr. Exec. V.P. & Chief Oper. Officer)*
John Grippo *(Exec. V.P. & Chief Fin. Officer)*
Stephanie Cuskley *(Exec. V.P.)*
Donald Lassoff *(Exec. V.P.)*
Stephen A. Mintz *(Exec. V.P.)*
Ewald M. Karbiner *(V.P.)*

Subsidiaries:

Dascit/White & Winston, Inc. **(1)**
136 Madison Ave., 12th Flr.
New York, NY 10016
Tel.: 212-689-6100 (100%)
Life Insurance Agency
S.I.C.: 6411
William P. White *(Chm.)*

Integrated Acquisition, Inc. **(1)**
666 Third Ave.
New York, NY 10017
Tel.: 212-551-6000
Buying & Selling Comml. & Residential Property
S.I.C.: 6531
Richard H. Ader *(Sr. Exec. V.P.)*

Integrated Benefit Systems **(1)**
Bldg. D, 3933 Spice Wood Springs Rd.
Austin, TX 78759
Tel.: 512-338-0137
Life Insurance Agency
S.I.C.: 6411
Coy W. Streetman, Jr. *(Pres.)*

Integrated Financial **(1)**
16530 Ventura Blvd., Ste. 500
Encino, CA 91436
Tel.: 213-872-0555 (100%)
Financial Planning & Investments; Offices in Newport Beach, San Diego & Northern CA
S.I.C.: 6289
Howard M. Koff *(Chm. Bd. & Chief Exec. Officer)*

Integrated Funding, Inc. **(1)**
10 Union Square East
New York, NY 10003
Tel.: 212-353-7000 (100%)
Loans to Multi-Family Housing Projects
S.I.C.: 6162
Arthur Habighorst *(Pres.)*

Integrated Resources Asset Management Corp. **(1)**
666 Third Ave.
New York, NY 10017
Tel.: 212-551-6000 (100%)
Mngmt. of Individual, Corp. Foundation & Retirement Plan Portfolios
S.I.C.: 6371
Harvey P. Eisen *(Pres.)*

Integrated Resources Capital Services, Inc. **(1)**
10 Union Square East
New York, NY 10003
Tel.: 212-353-7000 (100%)
Securities Mktg.
S.I.C.: 6211
Gregory Brakovich *(Pres.)*

Integrated Resources Equipment Group, Inc. **(1)**
733 Third Ave.
New York, NY 10017
Tel.: 212-551-5000 (100%)
Equipment Leasing; Offices in San Francisco, CA, Chicago, IL& New York, N.Y.
S.I.C.: 7359
Donald Lassoff *(Pres.)*

Integrated Resources Equity Corp. **(1)**
10 Union Square East
New York, NY 10003
Tel.: 212-353-7000 (100%)
Security Broker & Dealer; Office in Englewood, CO. & Branch Offices in 50 States
S.I.C.: 6211
Arthur H. Goldberg *(Pres.)*

Integrated Resources International, Ltd. **(1)**
733 Third Ave.
New York, NY 10017
Tel.: 212-551-5522
Mkts. Prods. to the Military
Charlynn Goins *(Exec. V.P.)*

Integrated Resources Life Insurance Co. **(1)**
P.O. Box 65180, 2337 Westown Pkwy.
West Des Moines, IA 50265
Tel.: 515-223-3000
Life Insurance Brokers
S.I.C.: 6411
Garry J. Leavell *(Sr. V.P.)*

Integrated Resources Marketing, Inc. **(1)**
10 Union Square East
New York, NY 10003
Tel.: 212-353-7000 (100%)
Security Broker & Dealer
S.I.C.: 6211
Creighton Lacey-Baker *(Pres.)*

Resources Funding Corp. **(1)**
666 Third Ave.
New York, NY 10029
Tel.: 212-551-6123
Mortgage Banking & Lender
S.I.C.: 6163
Arthur Habighorst *(Pres.)*

Resources Life Insurance Co. **(1)**
One Bridge Plaza
Fort Lee, NJ 07024
Tel.: 201-461-0606
Life Insurance Agency
S.I.C.: 6311
Sanford Merkin *(Pres.)*

Resources Property Management Corp. **(1)**
800 Second Ave., 9th Fl.
New York, NY 10017
Tel.: 212-878-9500 (100%)
Property Mngmt.
S.I.C.: 6531
Abraham Gelber *(Pres.)*

Resources Real Estate Finance Group, Inc. **(1)**
666 Third Ave.
New York, NY 10017
Tel.: 212-551-6612
Mortgage Lending
S.I.C.: 6163
Herbert Liechtung *(Pres.)*

The Selmer Co. **(1)**
P.O. Box 310,
Elkhart, IN 46515
Tel.: 219-522-1675 (100%)
Fax: 219-522-0334
Approx.Sls.: $46,000,000
Emp.: 1,100
Mfr. Musical Instruments
S.I.C.: 3931
Thomas Burzycki *(Pres.)*
P.A. Ryan, Jr. *(Exec. V.P.)*
Ralph Garrow *(V.P.-Fin.)*
W.P. Elliott *(V.P.-Sls.)*
Louie Heerwagen *(V.P.-Mfg.)*
Stan Garber *(Mktg. Mgr.-Brass & Woodwinds)*
R.S. Johnson *(Mktg. Mgr.-Strings)*
J.A. Catalano *(Mktg. Mgr.-Percussion)*
Paul Mock *(Public Rels. Mgr.)*

United Resources Insurance Services, Inc. **(1)**
23879 Madison St.
Torrance, CA 90505
Tel.: 310-373-0531 (100%)
Pension & Retirement Plans & Related Services
S.I.C.: 6411
Phillip Mortimer *(Pres.)*

Underwriters Service Agency, Inc. **(1)**
P.O. Box 100,
West Hartford, CT 06107
Tel.: 203-249-1000 (100%)
Life Insurance Brokers; Offices in Houston, TX., & Lexington, MA
S.I.C.: 6411
Theodore Kaplan *(Pres.)*

Underwriters Service Agency, Inc. **(1)**
420 Bedford St., Ste.150
Lexington, MA 02173
Tel.: 617-862-0300 (100%)
Insurance Brokers; Office in Houston, TX
S.I.C.: 6411
Wilbur Bullen *(Pres.)*

Non-U.S. Holdings:

Integrated Resources Insurance & Investment Services, Ltd. **(1)**
Ste. 2109 Edinburgh Towers The Landmark Central,
Hong Kong, Hong Kong (100%)
Securities Mktg.
S.I.C.: 6211

Integrated Resources (Japan), Inc. **(1)**
710 Sunkaido Bldg. 1-9-13 Akasaka, Minato-ku,
Tokyo, 107, Japan
Securities Mktg.
S.I.C.: 6211

INTEGRATED SYSTEMS ANALYSTS, INC.
2800 Shirlington Rd., Ste. 1100
Arlington, VA 22206
Tel.: 703-824-0700 **VA**
Fax: 703-379-6321
Year Founded: 1981
Approx.Sls.: $41,100,000
Emp.: 557
Fiscal Year-end: 12/31/90
Systems Engineering; Information Systems Services, Corrosion Engineering
S.I.C.: 8711; 3761; 3571
C. Michael Gooden *(Chm. Bd. & Pres.)*
Larry Herrman *(Chief Oper. Officer)*
C. Scott Thorell *(Sr. V.P.)*

No. of U.S. Offices: 9

Outside Service Firm(s):

Aronson, Fetridge, Weigle & Stern*(Auditors)*
Rockville, MD

Venable, Baetjer & Howard*(Legal Firm)*
McLean, VA

Signet Bank*(Major Banking Relationship)*
McLean, VA

INTELLIGENT CONTROLS INC.
6825 216th St. S.W.
Lynnwood, WA 98066
Mailing Address:
P.O. Box 1194
Lynwood, WA 98036
Tel.: 206-771-8107
Tel.: 800-842-0221 **WA**
Fax: 206-775-1641
Year Founded: 1982
Emp.: 30
Fiscal Year-end: 6/30/91
Export
Mfr. Bar Code Reading Equipment & Accessories
S.I.C.: 3577
Robert Percival *(Pres.)*
Jeffrey R. Kruse *(Exec. V.P. & Controller)*
Sylvia Percival *(Treas.)*
Trudy Francis *(Asst. Controller)*

No. of Mfg. Plants/Facilities: 1
No. of U.S. Offices: 1
No. of Foreign Offices: 1

Computer Systems/Hardware:
IBM

Outside Service Firm(s):

KPMG Peat Marwick*(Auditors)*
3100 Two Union Square, 601 Union St., Ste. 3100
Seattle, WA 98101
Tel.: 206-292-1500

Perkins, Coie*(Legal Firm)*
Washington Mutual Tower, 1201 3rd Ave., 40th Flr.
Seattle, WA 98101-3099
Tel.: 206-583-8888
Fax: 206-583-8500

Seafirst Bank*(Major Banking Relationship)*
Seattle, WA

Standard Chartered Bank*(Major Banking Relationship)*
Seattle, WA

Division:

ID Solutions **(1)**
6825 216th St. S.W.
Lynnwood, WA 98036
Tel.: 206-775-2320
Export
Computer Systems/Hardware:
IBM
Mfr. of Bar Code Reading Equipment & Accessories
S.I.C.: 3577
Jeff Kruse *(V.P.)*

INTERBATH, INC.
427 N. Baldwin Park Blvd.
City of Industry, CA 91746
Tel.: 818-369-1841
Tel.: 800-423-9485
Fax: 818-961-3534
Year Founded: 1971
Approx.Sls.: $20,000,000
Emp.: 150
Fiscal Year-end: 12/31/90
Export
Mfg. & Distribution of Bathroom Related Products; Elite, Great Vibrations, Ondine X90
S.I.C.: 3432
Claus D. Zieger *(Pres. & Treas.)*
Juscy Zieger *(V.P. & Sec.)*
Scott Staff *(Reg. Mgr.)*
Karan Jain *(Controller)*
Catherine Condon *(Dir.-Oper.)*
Mutsumi Gregg *(Dir.-Adv.)*
Ari Zieger *(Mgr.-Sls.)*
Monette Moore *(Admin. Asst.)*

Ondine Div. **(1)**
427 N. Baldwin Park Blvd
City of Industry, CA 91746
Tel.: 818-369-1841
Fax: 818-369-3316
Export
Claus Zieger *(Pres.)*

Draw Co. **(1)**
427 N. Baldwin Park Blvd.
City of Industry, CA 91746
Tel.: 818-369-3739
Claus Zieger *(Pres.)*

Great Vibrations Div. **(1)**
427 N. Baldwin Park Blvd.
City of Industry, CA 91746
Tel.: 818-369-1841
Claus Zieger *(Pres.)*

INTERCOLE, INC.
2833 Chestnut St.
Washington, PA 15301
Mailing Address:
P.O. Box 762
Washington, PA 15301
Tel.: 412-222-7060 **CA**
Fax: 412-222-6420
Approx.Sls.: $115,000,000
Emp.: 595
Fiscal Year-end: 7/31/90
Manufacture Electronic Wire & Tire Molds
S.I.C.: 3544; 3357
Bryan C. Cressey *(Chm. Bd.)*
Paul Olson *(Pres.)*
Kent Hale *(V.P. & Sec.)*
Steve Blair *(Dir.-Admin.)*

No. of Mfg. Plants/Facilities: 4

Computer Systems/Hardware:
IBM

Outside Service Firm(s):

Arthur Andersen & Co.*(Auditors)*
633 W. Fifth St.
Los Angeles, CA 90071
Tel.: 213-614-6500

Connecticut General Life Insurance Co.*(Group Insurer)*
P.O. Box 2975,
Hartford, CT 06104
Tel.: 203-726-6000

Gibson, Dunn & Crutcher*(Legal Firm)*
333 S. Grand Ave.
Los Angeles, CA 90067
Tel.: 310-552-8500
Fax: 310-277-5827

Bank of America NT&SA*(Major Banking Relationship)*
555 So. Flower St., 5th Fl.
Los Angeles, CA 90071
Tel.: 213-228-3526
Fax: 213-228-4062

Chemical Bank*(Major Banking Relationship)*
450 West 33rd St.
New York, NY 10001
Tel.: 212-613-7197
Fax: 212-947-7628

INTERCOMMUNICATIONS INC.
(d/b/a InterCom)
620 Newport Center Dr.
Newport Beach, CA 92660
Tel.: 714-644-7520
Fax: 714-640-5739
Year Founded: 1984
Approx.Billings: $22,000,000
Emp.: 35
Real Estate, Resort Devel., Travel & Leisure Time Industries
Toni Alexander *(Pres.)*
Bill Strateman *(Pres.-InterSport)*
Pat Cherpeski *(V.P., Admin.)*

INTERCOUNTY TITLE CO. OF ILLINOIS
120 W. Madison
Chicago, IL 60602
Tel.: 312-977-2600 **IL**
Fax: 312-977-2643
Emp.: 300
Real Estate Title Insurance
S.I.C.: 6361
Jack L. Hargrove *(Chm. Bd.)*
Laurence Capriotti *(Pres. & Chief Exec. Officer)*
Mike Hermes *(Dir.-Personnel)*
Susan Peloza *(Dir.-Mktg.)*

Computer Systems/Hardware:
DEC

Outside Service Firm(s):

Ernest & Whitney*(Auditors)*
Chicago, IL

LaSalle National Bank*(Major Banking Relationship)*
120 S. LaSalle St.
Chicago, IL 60603
Tel.: 312-781-8000

INTERFACE ELECTRONICS CORPORATION
228 South St.
Hopkinton, MA 01748
Tel.: 508-435-0100
Fax: 508-435-6516
Sales Range: $10-19 Million
Emp.: 35
Distributor of Semiconductors, Microprocessors, Resistor Networks, Capacitors
S.I.C.: 3674; 3675
Joseph F. Oliveri *(Pres.)*
Brian M. Perry *(Chief Fin. Officer & Treas.)*
James T. Barhite *(V.P.-Sls. & Mktg.)*
Dana Mathews *(Dir.-Mktg.)*
Mark Tully *(Dir.-Data Processing)*
Jack Grider *(Plant Mgr.)*

Outside Service Firm(s):

Harold Wald Company*(Auditors)*
Boston, MA

Perry & O'Brien*(Legal Firm)*
Boston, MA

Milford National Bank*(Major Banking Relationship)*
Milford, MA

INTERFORM CORPORATION
Mayview & Scott Rds.
Bridgeville, PA 15017
Mailing Address:
P.O. Box A
Bridgeville, PA 15017
Tel.: 412-221-3300 **PA**
Fax: 412-221-8937
Year Founded: 1962
Sales Range: $40-59 Million
Emp.: 350
Export
Manifold Business Forms; Commercial Letterpresses & Offset Printing
S.I.C.: 2752; 2761
Corporate Giving Program: United Way
Ronald H. Scott *(Chm. Bd. & Chief Exec. Officer)*
Duncan Fraser *(Pres.)*
Ronald T. Anthony *(Chief Oper. Officer & Exec. V.P.)*
Thomas A. Tadda *(Chief Fin. Officer & V.P.-Fin.)*
Ted Nowleau *(Chief Information Officer-Mngmt. Information Systems)*
Gerald Bayne *(V.P.-Mfg.)*
Cliff Bright *(Controller)*
Robert M. Brown *(Gen. Counsel)*
Robert Sanford *(Corp. Sec.)*
Joseph Bak *(Dir.-Sls. & Service)*
Clyde House *(Dir.-Data Processing)*
Dennis Banks *(Mgr.-Distribution Sls.)*
Cheryl Kuchera *(Mgr.-Quality Control)*
Jay Larocca *(Mgr.-Personnel)*
Richard McMavish *(Mgr.-Pur.)*

No. of Mfg. Plants/Facilities: 2
No. of U.S. Offices: 3

Computer Systems/Hardware:
DEC/VAX

Outside Service Firm(s):

Deloitte & Touche*(Auditors)*
2400 One PPG Place
Pittsburgh, PA 15222
Tel.: 412-281-2232

Eckert, Seamans, Cherin & Mellott*(Legal Firm)*
600 Grant St., 42nd Fl.
Pittsburgh, PA 15219
Tel.: 412-566-6000

Pittsburgh National Bank*(Major Banking Relationship)*
5th Ave. & Wood St.
Pittsburgh, PA 15222
Tel.: 412-355-3000

INTERLAKEN CAPITAL, INC.
(Formerly Finevest Services)
165 Mason St.
Greenwich, CT 06830
Tel.: 203-629-8750 **DE**
Fax: 203-629-8554
Year Founded: 1980
Approx.Sls.: $1,800,000,000
Emp.: 12,000
Diversified Holding Company
S.I.C.: 6719
William Berkley *(Pres.)*
A.M. Bursky *(Mng. Dir.)*
S.M. Cunningham *(Mng. Dir.)*
Catherine James *(Mng. Dir.)*
R.V. Mendelsohn *(Mng. Dir.)*
Josh Polan *(Mng. Dir.)*
J.V. Simon *(Mng. Dir.)*

Outside Service Firm(s):

Deloitte & Touche*(Auditors)*
1 World Trade Center
New York, NY 10048
Tel.: 212-669-5000

KPMG Peat Marwick*(Auditors)*
345 Park Ave.
New York, NY 10154
Tel.: 212-758-9700
Fax: 212-872-3308

Willkie, Farr & Gallagher*(Legal Firm)*
One City Corp. Ctr.
New York, NY 10017
Tel.: 212-935-8000

Subsidiary:

Northfield Cheese Co. **(1)**
375 Chestnut St.
Norwood, NJ 07648
Tel.: 201-767-8010
Manufacture Cheese
S.I.C.: 2022
R.H. Danenberg *(Pres.)*

INTERLOCK INDUSTRIES, INC.
10300 Linn Station Rd., Ste. 200
Louisville, KY 40223
Tel.: 502-426-5215 **KY**
Fax: 502-423-8618
Year Founded: 1982
Assets: $63,000,000
Liabilities: $48,000,000
Net Worth: $15,000,000
Sales Range: $100-499 Million
Emp.: 810
Fiscal Year-end: 2/28/91
Import Export
Holding Company
S.I.C.: 6719
Donald G. McClinton *(Co-Chm. Bd.)*
J. Leo Mackin *(Co-Chm. Bd.)*

No. of Mfg. Plants/Facilities: 17
No. of U.S. Offices: 1

Subsidiaries:

The Louisville Transportation Company **(1)**
10300 Lynn Station Rd., Ste. 200
Louisville, KY 40223
Tel.: 502-426-5215

Operates Taxicab Companies; Tour Bus & Limousine Services; Driver Training; Package Delivery Services
S.I.C.: 4121; 4119; 4215; 8249

Metal Sales Manufacturing Corporation **(1)**
4001 Produce Rd.
Louisville, KY 40218
Tel.: 502-969-9318
Manufacture Steel Siding, Roofing Components & Related Accessories
S.I.C.: 3444

Ohio Valley Aluminum Company **(1)**
1100 Industrial Park
Shelbyville, KY 40065
Tel.: 502-633-2783
Recycles Scrap; Manufacture Aluminum Extrusions
S.I.C.: 3354; 5093

Thorobred Containers Incorporated **(1)**
1400 Southwestern Pkwy.
Louisville, KY 40201
Tel.: 502-776-2451
Manufacture Corrugated Containers
S.I.C.: 2653

INTERMATIC INC.
Intermatic Plaza
Spring Grove, IL 60081
Tel.: 815-675-2321 DE
Fax: 815-675-2112
Year Founded: 1891
Assets: $59,866,000
Liabilities: $18,816,000
Net Worth: $41,050,000
Sales Range: $100-499 Million
Emp.: 1,100
Fiscal Year-end: 12/31/90
Import Export
Mfr. Time Switches, Portable Timers, Clock-Type Motors, Photo Controls, Outdoor Lighting, Surge Suppressors, Pool & SPA Controls
S.I.C.: 3645; 3625; 3823; 3824; 3621
Douglas M. Kinney *(Chm. Bd.)*
Leon E. Vinyard *(Pres. & Chief Exec. Officer)*
Robert C. Bedford *(V.P.-Sls.)*
Jim Bohn *(V.P.-Fin.)*
Edward F. Condon, Jr. *(V.P.-Engrng.)*
Donald J. Ferguson *(V.P.-Mktg.)*
Burt Mall *(V.P.-Mngmt. Information Systems)*
William E. Morrison *(V.P.-Admin.)*
Arvind A. Patel *(V.P.-Mfg.)*
Norm Joyce *(Controller)*
Linnea T. Bruin *(Dir.-Employee Rels.)*
Arthur Schuenemann *(Dir.-Pur.)*
Hank Miller *(Mgr.-Adv.)*
Principal(s):
Leon E. Vinyard
Walter D. Scott
Joan K. Seppala
Barbara K. Sweet
Leon E. Vinyard

No. of Mfg. Plants/Facilities: 3
No. of U.S. Offices: 6

Computer Systems/Hardware:
DEC VAX

Outside Service Firm(s):

Altschuler, Melvoin & Glasser*(Auditors)*
30 S. Wecker Dr.
Chicago, IL 60606
Tel.: 312-207-2800

Self Insured Services*(Group Insurer)*
Chicago, IL

Schiff, Hardin & Waite*(Legal Firm)*
7200 Sears Tower, 233 S. Wacker Dr.
Chicago, IL 60606
Tel.: 312-876-1000

The Northern Trust Co.*(Major Banking Relationship)*
50 S. LaSalle St.
Chicago, IL 60675
Tel.: 312-630-6000
Fax: 312-630-6516

INTERMOUNTAIN FARMERS ASSOCIATION
1147 W. 2100 S.
Salt Lake City, UT 84119
Mailing Address:
P.O. Box 30168,
Salt Lake City, UT 84130
Tel.: 801-972-2122
Fax: 801-972-2186
Year Founded: 1923
Approx.Sls.: $81,000,000
Emp.: 400
Fiscal Year-end: 6/30/91
Farmers Cooperative; Feed & Farm Supplies & IFA Cooperator; Retail Seeds & Chemicals
S.I.C.: 5191
Claude Rowley *(Chm. Bd.)*
Cletus Hamilton *(Vice Chm.)*
Robert W. Turley *(Pres. & Chief Exec. Officer)*
Gary K. Arbon *(V.P.-Sls.)*
Fred E. Brunner *(V.P.-Fin.)*
Spence Lloyd *(V.P.-Opers.)*
Steve Palmer *(V.P.-Mktg.)*
Helen P. Miller *(Sec.)*
Stan Ronna *(Dir.-Govt. Affairs)*
Ken Sorensen *(Dir.-Pur.)*
Les Spencer *(Mgr.-Adv.)*

Outside Service Firm(s):

Suniville, Griffin & Smith*(Auditors)*
Salt Lake City, UT

Jones, Waldo, Holbrook & McDonough*(Legal Firm)*
1500 First Interstate Plaza, 170 South Main St.
Salt Lake City, UT 84101
Tel.: 801-521-3200

National Bank for Cooperatives*(Major Banking Relationship)*
Sacramento, CA

INTERMOUNTAIN INDUSTRIES, INC.
555 S. Cole Rd.
Boise, ID 83709
Mailing Address:
P.O. Box 7608,
Boise, ID 83707
Tel.: 208-377-6000 ID
Fax: 208-377-6097
Year Founded: 1950
Approx.Sls.: $170,000,000
Emp.: 287
Fiscal Year-end: 9/30/91
Holding Company; Natural Gas Distribution; National Gas Aggregating
S.I.C.: 4924; 1311; 6719
Corporate Giving Program: Private Charitable Foundation--Contributes to Non-Profit Charitable, Civic & Education Programs
Employee Matching Gifts Program: Employee Matching Funds--Co. Foundation Matches 50% of Employee Contribution with a Minimum of $25.00--Maximum $500. Foundation--Will Make $100 Grant to an Eligible Organization Where an Employee Has Volunteered 60 or More Hours During a Year
Richard Hokin *(Chm. Bd.)*
William C. Glynn *(Pres.)*
Jeffrey K. Lebens *(V.P., Treas. & Chief Fin. Officer)*
Rudolph Rosemann *(V.P.)*
Eugene C. Thomas *(Sec. & Gen. Counsel)*

Outside Service Firm(s):

Arthur Andersen & Co.*(Auditors)*
999 Main St.
Boise, ID 83702

Moffatt, Thomas, Barrett, Rock & Fields*(Legal Firm)*
911 W. Idaho St., Ste. 300
Boise, ID 83701

First Security Bank, N.A.*(Major Banking Relationship)*
P.O. Box 2618,
Boise, ID 83701
Tel.: 208-338-2032

Subsidiaries:

IGI Resources, Inc. **(1)**
300 Mallard Dr., Ste. 350
Boise, ID 83706
Tel.: 208-345-6623 (100%)
Fax: 208-345-8743
Approx.Sls.: $84,000,000
Emp.: 7
Natural Gas Marketing
S.I.C.: 4924
Richard Hokin *(Chm. Bd.)*
William C. Glynn *(Pres.)*
Randy Schultz *(Exec. V.P. & Chief Oper. Officer)*
Jeffrey K. Lebens *(V.P., Treas. & Chief Fin. Officer)*

Intermountain Gas Co. **(1)**
555 S. Cole Rd.
Boise, ID 83709
Tel.: 208-377-6000 (100%)
Fax: 208-377-6097
Approx.Sls.: $86,000,000
Emp.: 280
Natural Gas Distribution
S.I.C.: 4924
Richard Hokin *(Chm. Bd.)*
William C. Glynn *(Pres.)*
N.C. Hedemark *(Exec. V.P.)*
Jeffrey K. Lebens *(Sr. V.P.-Fin., Admin. & Treas.)*
Phillip Bordeaux *(V.P.-Mktg.)*
James G. Derricolt *(V.P.-Opers.)*
Jamex E. Ware *(V.P.-Admin.)*
R.L. Worthan *(V.P.-Reg. & Resource Plng.)*

INTERNATIONAL AIRLINE SUPPORT GROUP, INC.
8095 N.W. 64th St.
Miami, FL 33166
Tel.: 305-593-2658 DE
Fax: 305-593-1751
Year Founded: 1989
Assets: $14,139,069
Earnings: $1,412,065
Liabilities: $9,609,959
Net Worth: $4,529,110
Approx.Sls.: $21,551,041
Fiscal Year-end: 5/31/91
Acquisition & Sale of Used Parts & Equipment for Commercial Aircraft; Aircraft Leasing
S.I.C.: 5088; 7359
Richard Wellman *(Chm. Bd. & Chief Exec. Officer)*
Dennis Young *(Pres.)*
William Hartman *(Chief Fin. Officer)*
Lex Dyer III *(Exec. V.P.-Capital Mkts.)*
Bernard Foster *(V.P.-Opers.)*
Lynda Wellman *(Sec./Treas.)*
Cliff Scheurich *(Dir.-Sales)*

Outside Service Firm(s):

Grant Thornton*(Auditors)*
1221 Brickell Ave.
Miami, FL 33131-3216
Tel.: 305-764-1235

Subsidiaries:

Aircraft Support Group, Inc. **(1)**
8095 N.W. 64th St.
Miami, FL 33166
Tel.: 305-597-0120 (100%)
Acquisition & Sales of Used Parts & Equipment for Commercial Aircraft
S.I.C.: 5088

Barnstorm Aviation **(1)**
6915 N.W. 43rd St.
Miami, FL 33166
Tel.: 305-593-2658 (100%)
Aircraft Leasing
S.I.C.: 7359

Non-U.S. Holding:

Wildcat Ltd. **(1)** (100%)
Limerick, Ireland
Aircraft Leasing
S.I.C.: 7359

Joint Venture (Non-U.S.):

Seven Seas Leasing **(1)**
Shannon, Ireland (50%)
Aircraft Leasing
S.I.C.: 7359

THE INTERNATIONAL BOILER WORKS COMPANY
460 Birch St.
East Stroudsburg, PA 18301
Mailing Address:
P.O. Box 498,
East Stroudsburg, PA 18301
Tel.: 305-558-5225
Telex: EASYLINK 62954120
Fax: 717-424-0356
Year Founded: 1886
Approx.Sls.: $10,000,000
Emp.: 14
Fiscal Year-end: 12/31/90
Products: Boilers-Steam Heating & Power; Thermal Liquid Heaters; High Temp Water Generators; Heat Recovery
S.I.C.: 3433
Jeffrey A. Beals *(Pres.)*

INTERNATIONAL BUSINESS INTERIORS INC.
770 N. Halstead St.
Chicago, IL 60622
Tel.: 708-298-2140
Fax: 708-298-2120
Approx.Sls.: $49,500,000
Emp.: 195
Office Furniture Dealer
S.I.C.: 5021
Robert C. Warner *(Chm. Bd.)*
Margaret A. Dennis *(Vice Chm.)*
Alan Molsbee *(Pres.)*
Donald A. Dahl *(Sr. V.P. & Sec.)*
Joseph R. Siemianowski *(V.P. & Mgr.-Sls.)*
Jeffrey D. Warner *(V.P. & Controller)*

Computer Systems/Hardware:
Prime; DEC

Outside Service Firm(s):

Deloitte & Touche*(Auditors)*
Two Prudential Plaza, 180 N. Stetson
Chicago, IL 60601
Tel.: 312-946-2039

Pedersen & Houpt*(Legal Firm)*
180 N. LaSalle, Ste. 3400
Chicago, IL 60601

American National Bank & Trust Company of Chicago*(Major Banking Relationship)*
33 N. LaSalle St.
Chicago, IL 60602
Tel.: 312-661-5000
Fax: 312-661-6417

INTERNATIONAL CHEESE COMPANY LIMITED PARTNERSHIP
Main Street
Hinesburg, VT 05461
Mailing Address:
P.O. Box 9
Hinesburg, VT 05461
Tel.: 802-482-2121
Approx.Sls.: $60,000,000
Emp.: 125
Cheese Manufacturer
S.I.C.: 2022
C. Dean Metropoulos *(Pres.)*
Evan D. Metropoulos *(Chief Exec. Officer)*
Ernie Sencal *(Pur. Dir.)*
Jack Wells *(Personnel Dir.)*

Outside Service Firm(s):

Urbach, Kohn & Werling*(Auditors)*
Burlington, VT

International Cheese Company Limited Partnership—(Continued)

Langrock, Sperry Parker & Wool*(Legal Firm)*
Burlington, VT

State Street Bank & Trust Co.*(Major Banking Relationship)*
225 Franklin St.
Boston, MA 02110
Tel.: 617-985-8179
Fax: 617-985-9722

International Cheese Company, Inc. **(1)**
Main Street
Hinesburg, VT
Cheese Manufacturer
S.I.C.: 2033

Branch Cheese Company, Inc. **(1)**
3826 Branch River Rd.
Branch, WI 54203
Tel.: 414-684-0121
Approx.Sls.: $15,000,000
Emp.: 150
Processor of Assorted Cheeses
S.I.C.: 2022
Lorenz H. Raeder *(Pres.)*
Ken Beghart *(V.P. & G.M.)*
Dale Ducat *(Controller)*
Ray Chapman *(Natl. Sls. Mgr.)*

INTERNATIONAL CHEMICAL COMPANY
1887 E. 71st St.
Tulsa, OK 74136
Tel.: 918-496-7711
Fax: 918-492-1719
Approx.Sls.: $148,000,000
Emp.: 25
Wholesale Chemical Fertilizer & Coal
S.I.C.: 5052; 5191
John R. Arend *(Chm. Bd. & Chief Exec. Officer)*
Wallace J. Wells *(Pres.)*
Albert A. Colby, Jr. *(V.P. & Treas.)*
Gene Graves *(V.P.-Fin.)*
Patricia Arend *(Sec.)*
Betty Coatney *(Dir.-Personnel)*

Outside Service Firm(s):

Arthur Andersen & Co.*(Auditors)*
1 Williams Center, Suite 1900,
Tulsa, OK 74172

Credit Agricole*(Major Banking Relationship)*
Chicago, IL

INTERNATIONAL COLD STORAGE CO., INC.
P.O. Box 425,
Andover, KS 67002
Year Founded: 1952
Approx.Sls.: $13,000,000
Emp.: 140
Mfr. of Refrigerated Storage Freezers & Coolers
S.I.C.: 3585
Deane Stevens *(Chm. Bd.)*
Frank D. Stevens *(Pres.)*
Jim McClure *(V.P.-Sls. & Mfg.)*
Robert O. Large *(V.P.-Fin., Sec. & Treas.)*
Robert Hall *(Gen. Counsel)*

International Communications Group, Inc.

INTERNATIONAL COMMUNICATIONS GROUP, INC.
1925 Century Park East, Ste. 1850
Los Angeles, CA 90067
Tel.: 310-557-2585
Fax: 310-557-3009
Year Founded: 1979
Approx.Billings: $192,000,000
Emp.: 87
Andrew D.W. Butcher *(Pres., Chief Exec. Officer)*
Bruce D. Milner *(Exec. V.P.)*
John F. Record *(Sr. V.P. & Treas.)*
Charlie Steffey *(Pres., Yellow Pages)*
Edith K. Whaley *(V.P.)*
Bill Frash *(V.P., Bus. Devel.)*
Roger A. Schaffner *(V.P., Mktg.)*
Barbara Israel *(V.P.)*
Rosa G. Sarrano *(Mgr., Special Markets)*
May Iles *(Special Asst. To Pres.)*
Paula Heffner *(Data Processing Supvr.)*

Computer Systems/Hardware:
IBM

INTERNATIONAL COMPONENTS CORPORATION
105 Maxess Rd.
Melville, NY 11747
Tel.: 516-293-1500
Fax: 516-293-4983
Year Founded: 1949
Emp.: 50

Import Export
Electronic Parts & Equipment
S.I.C.: 5065
Mortimer Grossman *(Pres.)*
Irwin Friedman *(Exec. V.P.)*
Fredric Grossman *(V.P.)*
Harvey Grossman *(V.P.)*
Florence Tochterman *(Controller)*

Outside Service Firm(s):

Chase Manhattan Bank, N.A.*(Major Banking Relationship)*
One Chase Manhattan Plaza
New York, NY 10081
Tel.: 212-552-2222
Tel.: 800-526-0801
Fax: 212-552-7175

INTERNATIONAL DATA GROUP
One Exeter Plaza
Boston, MA 02116-2851
Tel.: 617-534-1200
Fax: 617-262-2300
Year Founded: 1966
Approx.Sls.: $320,000,000
Emp.: 2,800
Periodicals Publishing & Printing; Management Consulting & Public Relations Services; Amusement & Recreation Services; Promo. of Trade Shows; Market Research
S.I.C.: 2721; 8742; 7999; 7389; 8732
Patrick J. McGovern *(Chm. Bd.)*
Walter Boyd *(Pres.)*
William P. Murphy *(Exec. V.P.-Fin.)*
Ted Bloom *(V.P. & Controller)*

Principal(s):
Patrick J. McGovern

Computer Systems/Hardware:
IBM 4340

Outside Service Firm(s):

Deloitte & Touche*(Auditors)*
125 Summer St.
Boston, MA 02110
Tel.: 617-261-8000
Fax: 617-261-8111

State Mutual Life Assurance Co. of America*(Group Insurer)*
Framington, MA

Foley, Hoag & Eliot*(Legal Firm)*
One Post Office Square
Boston, MA 02210
Tel.: 617-482-1390

First National Bank of Boston*(Major Banking Relationship)*
P.O. Box 644,
Boston, MA 02102-0644
Tel.: 617-575-2900
Fax: 617-575-2549

Subsidiaries:

IDG Communications **(1)**
One Exeter Plaza
Boston, MA 02116
Tel.: 617-534-1200
Fax: 617-262-2300

U.S. Branches:

A+ Publishing **(2)**
80 Elm St.
Peterborough, NH 03458
Tel.: 603-924-0100 (100%)
Fax: 603-924-9384
S.I.C.: 2721

B C Publishing **(2)**
80 Elm St.
Peterborough, NH 03458
Tel.: 603-924-0100 (100%)
Fax: 603-924-9384
S.I.C.: 2721

CIO Publishing Corp. **(2)**
492 Old Connecticut Path
Framingham, MA 01701
Tel.: 508-872-8200 (100%)
Fax: 508-872-0618
S.I.C.: 2721

CW Publishing, Inc. **(2)**
375 Cochituate Rd.
Framingham, MA 01701
Tel.: 508-879-0700
Fax: 508-872-8564
Approx.Sls.: $70,000,000
Emp.: 180
Fiscal Year-end: 9/30/90
Magazine Publisher
S.I.C.: 2721
Val Landi *(Sr. V.P.)*
Matthew Smith *(Sr. V.P. & Chief Fin. Officer)*
John Corrigan *(V.P.-Classified Adv.)*

Computer Buying Publishing, Inc. **(2)**
401 Edgewate Pl., 6th Fl.
Wakefield, MA 01880
Tel.: 617-246-3800 (100%)
Fax: 617-246-8280
S.I.C.: 2721

Digital News Publishing Company, Inc. **(2)**
33 West St.
Boston, MA 02111
Tel.: 617-482-8470 (100%)
Fax: 617-426-4456
S.I.C.: 2721

Electronic News Publishing **(2)**
488 Madison Ave., 6th Fl.
New York, NY 10022
Tel.: 212-909-5916 (100%)
Fax: 212-326-6989
S.I.C.: 2721

FCW Publishing Corp. **(2)**
3110 Fairview Park Dr., Ste. 1040
Falls Church, VA 22042
Tel.: 703-876-5100 (100%)
Fax: 703-876-5126
S.I.C.: 2721

GamePro **(2)**
2421 Broadway, Ste. 200
Redwood City, CA 94063
Tel.: 415-363-5200 (100%)
Fax: 415-364-3905
S.I.C.: 2721

IDG Books Worldwide **(2)**
155 Bovet Rd., Ste. 730
San Mateo, CA 94402
Tel.: 415-358-1250 (100%)
Fax: 415-358-1260
S.I.C.: 2731

IDG Communications List Services **(2)**
P.O. Box 9151, 4 Chrysler Rd.
Natick, MA 01760
Tel.: 509-879-0700 (100%)
Fax: 508-653-6155

IDG International News Group **(2)**
41 West St., 8th Fl.
Boston, MA 02111
Tel.: 617-423-9030 (100%)
Fax: 617-423-0712

IDG Communications Research **(2)**
4 Chrysler Rd.
Natick, MA 01760
Tel.: 508-820-2525 (100%)
Fax: 508-653-6155

Infoworld Publishing, Inc. **(2)**
155 Bovet Rd., Ste. 800
San Mateo, CA 94402
Tel.: 415-572-7341 (100%)
Fax: 415-312-0558
S.I.C.: 2721

Integrated Media, Inc. **(2)**
501 2nd St.
San Francisco, CA 94402
Tel.: 415-243-0600 (100%)
Fax: 415-442-1891
S.I.C.: 2721

International Marketing Services **(2)**
187 Oaks Rd.
Framingham, MA 01701
Tel.: 508-879-0700 (100%)
Telex: 9102502620
Fax: 508-820-1639
S.I.C.: 8742

Lotus Publishing Corporation **(2)**
55 Cambridge Pkwy.
Cambridge, MA 02142
Tel.: 617-577-8500
Fax: 617-225-6845
Approx.Sls.: $10,000,000
Emp.: 45
Publishes Lotus, a Monthly Magazine for Microcomputer Users
S.I.C.: 2721
James Manzi *(Pres. & Chief Exec. Officer)*
Robert Weiler *(Sr. V.P.-Mktg. & Sls.)*
Rick Faulk *(V.P.)*
Elisabeth Folsom *(Assoc. Publisher-Circulation)*
Ralph M. Hodgson *(Dir.-Mktg.)*
Mary Ellen Bittel *(Dir.-Prod.)*
Sydney Turner *(Mgr.-Adv.)*

Macworld **(2)**
501 2nd St.
San Francisco, CA 94107
Tel.: 415-243-0505 (100%)
Fax: 415-442-0766
S.I.C.: 2721

MPC World **(2)**
524 2nd St.
San Francisco, CA 94107
Tel.: 415-281-6850 (100%)
Fax: 415-281-3915
S.I.C.: 2721

Network World, Inc. **(2)**
161 Worcester Rd., 5th Fl.
Framingham, MA 01701
Tel.: 508-875-6400 (100%)
Fax: 508-879-3167
S.I.C.: 2721

PC World (2)
501 2nd St.
San Francisco, CA 94107
Tel.: 415-243-0500 (100%)
Fax: 415-442-1891
S.I.C.: 2721

Techmedia (2)
80 Elm St.
Peterborough, NH 03458
Tel.: 603-924-0100 (100%)
Fax: 603-924-9384

Non-U.S. Branches:

Asia Computerworld (2)
701-4-Kam Chung Bldg., 54 Jaffe Rd.
Wanchai, Hong Kong
Tel.: 011-852-5-861-3238
Fax: 011-852-5-861-0953

Asia Computerworld Communications (2)
#04-07 Pkwy. Builder's Ctr., No. 1 Marine Parade Central
Singapore, 1544, Singapore
Tel.: 011-65-345-8383
Telex: (786) RS37003 (COMWOR)
Fax: 011-65-345-7097

CW Communicacaciones S/A (2)
Av Belgrano 406-Piso 9 CP-1092,
Buenos Aires, Argentina
Tel.: 011-541-342-5583
Telex: 39022644 (BAZAN AR)
Fax: 39022644

CW/Communications AB (2)
Sodra Hamnvagen 22 S-115 78,
Stockholm, Sweden
Tel.: 011-46-8-667-9180
Fax: 011-46-8-665-3132

CW Publikationen AG (2)
Witkonerstrasse no.15 P.O. Box 253, CH-8030,
Zurich, Switzerland
Tel.: 011-41-1-55-1077
Telex: (845) 8160 (CWVICH)
Fax: 011-41-1-55-1135

China Computerworld (2)
74 Lu Gu Rd. P.O. Box 750,
Beijing, 100039, People's Republic of China
Tel.: 011-861-810-044
Telex: (716) 222214 (CCW CN)
Fax: 011-861-821-7869

Compu News Publishing (2)
Fatima Court Ltd., Argwings Kodaheck P.O. Box 67335,
Nairobi, Kenya
Tel.: 0112545672777
Fax: 0112522566412

Computerworld de Brazil (2)
Praca Floriano 19/26 andar CEP: 20031,
Rio de Janeiro, RJ Brazil
Tel.: 011-55-21-240-8225
Telex: (391) 213838 (WORD BR)
Fax: 011-55-21-240-7759

Computerworld-Columbia (2)
Transversal 23 No. 58-28
Bogota, D.E. Colombia
Tel.: 011-57-1-310-0199
Fax: 011-57-1-211-6848

Hi Tech Information Inc. (2)
3rd Fl., Bo-Lim Bldg., 411-16 Do Kok Dong Kangnam-Ku,
Seoul, Korea
Tel.: 011-82-578-8031/46
Fax: 011-82-579-8035/46

IDG Communications (2)
Verlag AG, Rheinstrasse 26/28 P.O. Box 40 04 29, 8000,
Munich, 40, Germany
Tel.: 011-49-89-3-60860
Telex: (851) 5215350 (COMW D)
Fax: 011-49-89-3-6086257

IDG Communications, Inc. (2)
11F No. 137, Fu Hsin S. Rd., Sec 1
Taipei, Taiwan 10639
Tel.: 011-886-2-776-4553
Fax: 011-886-2-777-5339

IDG Communications, S.A. (2)
Rafael Calvo 18,4B,
Madrid, 28010, Spain
Tel.: 011-34-1-319-4014
Telex: (831) 45522 (GW E)
Fax: 011-34-1-319-6104

IDG Communications France (2)
Immeuble La Fayette 2, Place des Vosges,
Paris, Cedex 65-92501, France
Tel.: 011-33-49-04-79-00
Telex: 613 234 (F)
Fax: 011-33-1-49-04-78-00

IDG Communications Ltd. (2)
99 Gray's Inn Rd.
London, WC1X 8UT, United Kingdom
Tel.: 252 (831-9%)
Fax: 011-44-71-405-2347

IDG Communications PTY Ltd. (2)
37-43 Alexander St.
Crows Nest, NSW 2065, Australia
Tel.: 011-612-439-5133
Telex: 790AA74752
Fax: 011-612-439-5512

IDG Communications Italia srl (2)
Via Mecenate 30/14,
Milan, 20138, Italy
Tel.: 011-39-2-5801-1660
Fax: 011-39-2-5801-1670

IDG Communications/Japan (2)
Kioicho TBR Bldg., 5-7, Kojimachi Chiyoda ku,
Tokyo, Japan 102
Tel.: 011-81-33-222-6411
Telex: (781) 2524217
Fax: 011-81-33-222-6566

IDG Communications Nederland BV (2)
Schipholweg 1 P.O. Box 5446, 2034 LS,
Haarlem, Netherlands
Tel.: 011-31-23-366814
Fax: 011-31-23-366184

IDG Communications Ltd. (2)
2nd Fl., 15 Augustus Ter. P.O. Box 6813, Wellesley St.,
Parnell, Auckland New Zealand
Tel.: 011-64-9-779-902
Fax: 011-64-9-774-604

IDG Communications Norge AS (2)
Hovinveien 43, P.O. Box 2862, 0608, Toyen,
Oslo, 0576, Norway
Tel.: 011-47-2-688090
Telex: 856 76476 (CWNOR N)
Fax: 011-47-2-571888

IDG Communications Verlagsges.mbH (2)
Zieglergasse 6 A-1070
Vienna, Austria
Tel.: 011-43-1-523-1631-0
Telex: (847) 115-542
Fax: 011-43-1-523-0508-33

IDG Communications (W. Africa) Ltd. (2)
Mars House, Plot 43b, First Ave.
Festac Town, Lagos Nigeria
Tel.: 011-234-1-883-585
Fax: 011-234-1-883-585

IDG Communicaciones C.A. (2)
Torre Maracaibo, Piso 10 Oficina H Av. Libertador,
Caracas, Venezuela
Tel.: 011-58-2-727630
Fax: 011-58-2-274970

IDG Communicaciones S.A. de C.V. (2)
Gonzalez de Cossio #334
Col. del Valle, Mexico 03100
Tel.: 011-52-5-669-4454
Telex: (383) 1771300 (ACHAME)
Fax: 011-52-669-1140

IDG Czechoslovakia (2)
Luzna 2 160 00,
Prague, 6, Czechoslovakia
Tel.: 011-42-2-36-51
Fax: 011-42-2-34-78-81

IDG Denmark A/S (2)
Krumtappen 4 DK-2500,
Valby, Denmark
Tel.: 011-45-36-442800
Telex: (855) 31566 (CW DAN)
Fax: 011-45-36-442033

IDG High Tech Company (2)
Rm. 821, 15 Fuxing Rd.
Beijing, 100038, People's Republic of China
Tel.: 011-861-801-5544
Telex: (716) 20079
Fax: 011-861-801-4073

IDG Magyaroszagi Laplado Kft. (2)
P.O. Box 386, 30-32, Gellerthegy utca,
Budapest, H-1536 Hungary
Tel.: 011-361-156-9122
Fax: 011-361-202-5565

IDG (Malaysia) Sdn Bhd (2)
38-3B Jalan Pandan 3/2 55100, Pandan Jaya,
Kuala Lumpa, Malaysia
Tel.: 011-60-3-983-4482
Fax: 011-60-983-4750

IDG Poland S.A. (2)
ut. Tytoniowa 20 04-228,
Warsaw, Poland
Tel.: 011-48-22-15-2045
Tel.: 011-48-39-12-1390
Telex: 824 203 (labor pl)
Fax: 011-48-22-15-4495

IDG-Technika Communications, Ltd. (2)
1, Slaveikov Sq. 1000
Sofia, Bulgaria
Tel.: 011-359-2-874-869
Fax: 011-359-2-802-652

IDG/UFT (2)
Eski Osmanli Sk, Dilan Sitesi A Blok 8/11,
Istanbul, Mecidiyekoy Turkey
Tel.: 011-904-174-7527
Fax: 011-904-174-9766

Information Computer Enterprise (2)
Prospekt Mira 187-98-22, VDNH, Pavillion #4 129223,
Moscow, Russia
Tel.: 011-709-5-187-8868
Telex: 414 819 (BSTP)
Fax: 011-709-5-187-8830

Laurentian Technomedia Inc. (2)
501 Oakdale Rd.
Downsview, ON M3N 1W7, Canada
Tel.: 416-746-7630
Fax: 416-746-1420

Media Transia India Ltd. (2)
103 Anand Lok
New Delhi, India 110049
Tel.: 011-91-544-0110
Fax: 011-91-11-643-2950

Media Transia Thailand Ltd. (2)
14th Fl. Orakaarn Bldg., 26 Chidlom Rd. Ploenchit,
Bangkok, Thailand 10330
Tel.: 011-66-2-251-9905
Fax: 011-66-2-253-5335

Moj Mikro (2)
Titova 35 61000,
Ljubljana, Yugoslavia
Tel.: 011-38-61-319-798
Telex: 31255 (YUDELO)
Fax: 011-38-61-302-339

People and Computers (2)
64 Pinkster St. P.O. Box 61116,
Tel Aviv, Israel 11616
Tel.: 011-9723-295-145
Fax: 011-9723-295-144

Publicaciones en Computacion Ltda. (2)
Pedro de Valdivia 2103,
Santiago, Chile
Tel.: 011-56-2-204-7677
Telex: (392) 340260
Fax: 011-56-2-204-7245

WS Publishing Company, Inc. (2)
7/F Sedcco 1 Bldg., Rada St. Legaspi Village,
Metro Manila, Makati Philippines
Tel.: 011-632-812-8397
Fax: 011-632-817-6430

H.A. Samouhos Pub. Ltd. (2)
3-5, Stiron Str. GR-157, 71, Zografou,
Athens, Greece
Tel.: 011-301-771-3666
Telex: 215578 (ABNA GR)
Fax: 011-301-770-4475

Servicios Expeciales de Edicion (2)
El Comercio, Jr. Miro Quesada 247-702
Lima, 1, Peru
Tel.: 011-51-14-281-061
Fax: 011-51-14-272-843

Stinta & Technica S.A. (2)
Plata Pressi Libere no. 1 79781,
Bucharest, 1, Romania
Tel.: 011-40-0-17-7244
Fax: 011-40-0-17-5833

OY Talentum Ab (2)
Ratavartjankatu 2 SF-00520,
Helsinki, Finland
Tel.: 011-358-0-148-801
Telex: (857) 123629 (TALEN SF)
Fax: 011-358-0-145-109

Waffai & Associates (2)
23 Shehab St., Ste. 402
Mohamdessen, Giza Cairo Egypt
Tel.: 011-20-2-344-8668
Fax: 011-20-2-347-0118

International Data Corp. (1)
5 Speen St.
Framingham, MA 01701
Tel.: 617-872-8200 (100%)
Publishes Technical Information
S.I.C.: 2721; 8742; 7999
Walter Boyd *(Pres.)*

Branches:

IDC Irvine (2)
18008 Sky Park Circle, Ste. 145
Irvine, CA 92714
Tel.: 714-250-1960 (100%)
Fax: 714-250-4881
S.I.C.: 2721

IDC New Jersey (2)
120 Wood Ave. S., Ste. 300
Iselin, NJ 08830
Tel.: 908-632-9222 (100%)
Fax: 908-321-6562

IDC Texas (2)
Shepard Mountain Exec. Suites, 6043 W. Courtyard Dr., Ste. 305
Austin, TX 78730
Tel.: 512-338-2404
Fax: 512-338-2408

IDC Virginia (2)
8300 Boone Blvd., Ste. 500
Vienna, VA 22182
Tel.: 703-848-9217
Fax: 703-356-5884

IDC West (2)
2083 Landings Dr.
Mountain View, CA 94043
Tel.: 415-691-0500
Fax: 415-691-0525

Non-U.S. Branches:

IDC Argentina (2)
CW Communications S/A Belgrano 406 -, CP 1092, Piso 9,
Buenos Aires, Argentina
Tel.: 011-54-134-5583
Fax: 011-54-1-331-7372

IDC Australia (2)
56 Berry St.
North Sydney, NSW 2060 Australia
Tel.: 011-61-2-922-5300
Fax: 011-61-2-957-2330

International Data Group—(Continued)

IDC Austria **(2)**
c/o Loisel, Spiel, Zach Consulting Erwin Spiel A-1040 Mayerhofgasse-6,
Vienna, Austria
Tel.: 011-43-222-50-50-900
Telex: 847-133030
Fax: 011-43-222-50-50912

IDC Beijing **(2)**
c/o IDG High Tech Co., 15 Fuxing Rd., Room 821
Beijing, 100038 People's Republic of China
Tel.: 011-861-801-5544
Fax: 011-861-801-4073

IDC Brazil **(2)**
Computerword do Brazil Ltda, Praca Floriano 19 26 andar 20.031,
Rio de Janeiro, RJ Brazil
Tel.: 011-55-21-240-8225
Fax: 011-55-21-240-7759

IDC Canada **(2)**
36 Toronto St., 9th Fl.
Toronto, ON M5C 2C5, Canada
Tel.: 416-369-0033
Fax: 416-369-0419

IDC China/Hong Kong Ltd. **(2)**
12/F, Seabird House, 22 Wyndham St.
Central, Hong Kong
Tel.: 011-852-845-6588
Fax: 011-852-845-9228

IDC Deutschland GmbH **(2)**
Westerbachstr. 23A D-6242
Kronberg, Ts. 1 Germany
Tel.: 011-49-6173-7098-0
Telex: 841-4072894
Fax: 011-49-6173-7098-30

IDC European Research Center **(2)**
2 Bath Rd. Chiswick,
London, W4 1LN, United Kingdom
Tel.: 011-44-81-995-8082
Fax: 011-44-81-995-2172

IDC Finland **(2)**
John Stenbergin Ranta 2 SF-00530
Helsinki, Finland
Tel.: 011-358-0-701-6377
Fax: 011-358-0-701-6801

IDC France **(2)**
12 Avenue George V 75008
Paris, France
Tel.: 011-33-1-4-7230021
Telex: 842-620174
Fax: 011-33-1-4-7207190

IDC Greece **(2)**
Strategic International Ltd., 8 Isiodou St. 106 74
Athens, Greece
Tel.: 011-301-7224531
Fax: 011-301-7224531

IDC Hungary **(2)**
P.O. Box 55, H-1364
Budapest, Hungary
Tel.: 011-361-252-8830
Telex: 22-6307 (CWI H)
Fax: 011-361-252-8830

IDC India **(2)**
D-74 Panchsheel Enclave
New Delhi, 110 017, India
Tel.: 011-91-11-643-5999
Telex: 953-031-71344
Fax: 011-91-11-644-7032

IDC Italia S.r.l. **(2)**
ViaR. Pitteri 110 20134,
Milan, Italy
Tel.: 011-39-2-58011660
Fax: 011-39-2-58011670

IDC Japan **(2)**
4-7, 1 Chome Kudankita, Chiyoda-ku,
Tokyo, 102, Japan
Tel.: 011-81-3-3264-3179
Telex: 781-25906
Fax: 011-81-3-3264-3150

IDC Korea, Inc. **(2)**
3/F Shin Bong Bldg., 835-6, Yeuksam-Dong
Seoul, Kangnam-Ku Korea
Tel.: 011(82)-2-555-6030
Fax: 011-(82)-555-5347

IDC Mexico **(2)**
Select, S.A. de C.V., Av. Nuevo Leon No. 54,Desp. 501 Col. Hipodromo Condesa, C.P.06100,
Mexico City, D.F., Mexico
Tel.: 011-525-256-0981
Fax: 011-525-553-4641

IDC Nederland **(2)**
A. Fokkerweg 1059 CM,
Amsterdam, Netherlands
Tel.: 011-31-20-6692721
Fax: 011-31-20-6175566

IDC New Zealand **(2)**
31 Ganges Rd.
Wellington, Khandallah New Zealand
Tel.: 011-64-44-791-989
Fax: 011-64-44-793-707

IDC Norge **(2)**
Baerumsveien 385 P.O. Box 171, N-1346,
Gjettum, Norway
Tel.: 011-47-2-547141
Fax: 011-47-2-542401

IDC Poland **(2)**
ul. Dluga 16 00-238,
Warsaw, Poland
Tel.: 011-(48) 2-6359434
Fax: 011-48-63-52-44-2

IDC Russia **(2)**
Prospekt Mira, VDNH, Pav. 4, Room 105-107
Moscow, 129223, Russia
Tel.: 011-709-5-187-9889
Fax: 011-709-5-187-8830

IDC Scandinavia A/S **(2)**
Aldersrogade 3A DK-2100,
Copenhagen, Denmark
Tel.: 011-45-31-186344
Fax: 011-45-31-184448

IDC Singapore **(2)**
62 Queen St.
Bugis Village, Singapore 0718
Tel.: 331-0804

IDC Spain **(2)**
Rafael Calvo 18 20B 28010,
Madrid, Spain
Tel.: 011-34-1-410-4282
Fax: 011-34-1-410-4416

IDC Sweden **(2)**
Torsnaegatan 4 P.O. Box 1096, 164 21,
Kista, Sweden
Tel.: 011-46-8-751-041
Fax: 011-46-8-750 58 88

IDC Switzerland **(2)**
Rhypark-Rheinweg 4 P.O. Box 368, CH-8201,
Schaffhausen, Switzerland
Tel.: 011-41-53-24 21 23
Fax: 011-41-53-24 73 64

IDC Taiwan **(2)**
3F-5 No. 201 Fu Hsin N. Rd.
Taipai, Taiwan R.O.C.
Tel.: 011-886-2-7170868
Fax: 011-886-2-7171251

IDC Thailand **(2)**
c/o A.R. Business Consultants, CCT Building, 8th Fl. 109 Surawong Rd.,
Bangkok, 10500, Thailand
Tel.: 011-662-236-2902
Fax: 011-662-236-2900

IDC United Kingdom **(2)**
2 Bath Rd.
London, Chiswick W4 1LN, England
Tel.: 011-44-81-995-8082
Fax: 011-44-81-995-1090
Fax: 011-44-81-7470212

IDC Venezuela **(2)**
Torre Maracaibo, Piso 10, Oficina H, Av. Libertador
Caracas, Venezuela
Tel.: 011-58-2-72-76-30
Fax: 011-58-2-72-49-70

Information Strategies Group **(2)**
800 Tower Crescent Dr., Ste. 1180
Vienna, VA 22180
Tel.: 703-893-0833
Fax: 703-893-3129

LINK Resources **(2)**
79 Fifth Ave.
New York, NY 10003
Tel.: 212-627-1500
Fax: 212-620-3099

Technology Investment Strategies Corp. **(2)**
Five Speen St.
Framingham, MA 01701
Tel.: 508-875-5000
Fax: 508-572-8186

World Expo Corporation **(1)**
P.O. Box 9107, 111 Speen St.
Framingham, MA 01701-9107
Tel.: 508-879-6700
Fax: 508-872-8237
Organizes Trade Shows
S.I.C.: 7389

Non-U.S. Branches:

IDG/World Expo Corporation **(2)**
Ichibancho First Bldg., 3F, 15-1 Ichibancho Chiyoda-ku,
Tokyo, 102, Japan
Tel.: 011-81-3-5276-3751
Fax: 011-81-3-5276-3752

World Expo Corporation **(2)**
37-43 Alexander St.
Crows Nest, NSW 2065, Australia
Tel.: 011-612-439-5133
Fax: 011-612-439-5512

World Expo Corporation **(2)**
99 Gray's Inn Rd.
London, WC1X 8UT, United Kingdom
Tel.: 011-44-71-831-9252
Fax: 011-44-71-405-2347

World Expo Corporation **(2)**
Karl-Theodor-Strasse 91 D-8000,
Munich, 40, Germany
Tel.: 011-49-89-360-86-208
Fax: 011-49-89-360-86-262

World Expo Corporation **(2)**
5A, rue de Bailliage 78000
Versailles, France
Tel.: 011-33-1-39-02-1000
Fax: 011-33-1-39-02-0999

World Expo Corporation **(2)**
701-4 Kam Chung Bldg., 54 Jaffe Rd.
Hong Kong, Wanchai Hong Kong
Tel.: 011-852-5-866-9876
Fax: 011-852-5-527-8657

INTERNATIONAL DESIGNER ACCESSORIES, INC.
(Formerly Baronet Corp.)
375 County Ave.
Secaucus, NJ 07096
Tel.: 201-864-2175
Fax: 201-864-0225
Approx.Sls.: $15,000,000
Emp.: 200
Mfr. Small Leather Goods & Handbags
S.I.C.: 3171; 3172
Rex M. Sano *(Pres.)*
Mark Sevelovitz *(V.P.-Fin. & Admin.)*
Fred Williams *(V.P.-Prod. Devel.)*
Susan Aitken *(Pur. Agent)*

INTERNATIONAL GEAR CORPORATION
23555 Euclid Ave.
Cleveland, OH 44117
Tel.: 216-692-4327
Fax: 216-692-5428
Year Founded: 1988
Approx.Sls.: $20,000,000
Emp.: 200
Fiscal Year-end: 11/30/90
Export
Mfr. of Precision Gearing & Helicopter Transmissions
S.I.C.: 3728; 3724
George Radu *(Pres.)*
Woodrow Haddix *(Opers. Mgr.)*
Geoff Masters *(Mgr.-Mfg. & Engrng.)*
E. Charles Ulle *(Product Mgr.)*

Computer Systems/Hardware:
Hewlett-Packard 3000 570

INTERNATIONAL JENSEN INC.
25 Tri-state Intl. Office Center
Lincolnshire, IL 60069
Tel.: 708-317-3700
Year Founded: 1927
Emp.: 1,500
Fiscal Year-end: 2/28/91
Import Export
Car Stereo Speakers, Cassette Receivers, Equalizers, Amplifiers; Home Hi-Fi Speaker Systems
S.I.C.: 3651
Robert Shaw *(Pres.)*
Larry Bentley *(V.P.-Human Resources)*
Donald Cowie *(V.P.-Fin.)*
Roger Heuberger *(V.P.-Mktg.)*
David Marinello *(V.P.-Sls. & Mktg.-Branded Prods.)*
John Moss *(V.P.-Operations)*
George Pariza *(V.P.-Plng. & Prod. Devel.)*
James Sula *(Controller)*
Thomas Bihun *(Dir.-MIS)*
Laurie Farrell *(Mgr.-Pub. Rels.)*

Divisions:

Advent Loudspeakers **(1)**
25 Tri-State International Office Center
Lincolnshire, IL 60069
Tel.: 708-317-3700
Mktg. & Sls. of Advent Loudspeakers
S.I.C.: 5064
Robert O'Connor *(Dir.-Sls.)*

Phase Linear **(1)**
25 Tri-State Intl. Office Center
Lincolnshire, IL 60069
Tel.: 708-317-3700 (100%)
Fax: 708-317-3826
Car Stereo Speakers & Electronics
S.I.C.: 3651
Ken Linde *(Sls. Dir.)*

Subsidiaries:

Acoustic Research **(1)**
330 Turnpike St.
Canton, MA 02021
Tel.: 617-821-2300 (100%)
Fax: 617-784-4102
Emp.: 100
Export
Acoustic Suspension Speaker Systems & Turntables
S.I.C.: 3651
Robert Thompson *(V.P.-Opers.)*
Pat Mazzone *(Sr. Buyer)*
Ed Ferrara *(Dir.-Opers.)*
Michael Bartlett *(Dir.-Mktg.)*
Elliot Schwartz *(Mgr.-Sls.)*
Barbara Silva *(Asst. Pur. Agent)*

Now Hear This (NHT) **(1)**
537 Stone Rd., Ste. E
Benicia, CA 94510
Tel.: 707-747-0151 (100%)
Fax: 707-747-0169
Mfr. Home Audio Loudspeakers
S.I.C.: 3651
Chris Byrne *(Gen. Mgr.)*

INTERNATIONAL MANAGEMENT GROUP (IMG)
One Erieview Plaza, Ste. 1300
Cleveland, OH 44114
Tel.: 216-522-1200 OH
Twx: 980-144

Fax: 216-522-1145
Year Founded: 1960
Approx.Billings: $300,000,000
Emp.: 1,000
Sports & Leisure Mktg. & Sales Promotion
S.I.C.: 8741
Mark H. McCormack *(Chm. Bd., Pres. & Chief Exec. Officer)*
H. Kent Stanner *(Sr. V.P.)*
Susan Doughit *(Office Mgr.)*

No. of U.S. Offices: 40

Outside Service Firm(s):

National City Bank*(Major Banking Relationship)*
P.O. Box 92301, Corp. Trust Dept.
Cleveland, OH 44101
Tel.: 216-575-2000

Branch:

International Management Group (IMG) **(1)**
22 East 71st St.
New York, NY 10021
Tel.: 212-772-8900
Fax: 212-772-2617
Marjorie Caruso *(Gen. Mgr.)*

INTERNATIONAL MARINE HOLDINGS, INC.
48 Signal Rd.
Stamford, CT 06902
Tel.: 203-357-9899
Fax: 203-358-0748
Year Founded: 1974
Assets: $260,000,000
Liabilities: $170,000,000
Net Worth: $90,000,000
Approx.Sls.: $230,000,000
Fiscal Year-end: 12/31/91
Import Export
Marine Accessories; Navigation Equipment & Supplies, Aluminum Extruded Products, Marine Hardware, Nautical Instruments, Nautical & Navigational Instrument Repair
S.I.C.: 5088; 3354; 3429; 3812; 7699
John E.D. Grunow, Jr. *(Chm. Bd. & Chief Exec. Officer)*
Michael F. Stauff *(V.P.-Fin. & Chief Fin. Officer)*
Russell N. Spector *(Asst. Treas.)*

No. of Mfg. Plants/Facilities: 4
No. of U.S. Offices: 6
No. of Foreign Offices: 12

Computer Systems/Hardware:
NCR/ADDS

Outside Service Firm(s):

Deloitte & Touche*(Auditors)*
New Haven, CT

Johnson & Higgins*(Group Insurer)*
125 Broad St.
New York, NY 10004-2424
Tel.: 212-574-7000
Fax: 212-574-8988

Haythe & Curley*(Legal Firm)*
237 Park Ave.
New York, NY 10017
Tel.: 212-880-6000

Mellon Bank, N.A.*(Major Banking Relationship)*
New York, NY

New England Mutual Life Insurance Co.*(Pension Manager)*
Boston, MA

Non-U.S. Holding:

Benjamin Priest Ltd. **(1)**
Priest House, Priest St. Cradley Heath, Warley, West Midlands B64 6JW, United Kingdom
Tel.: 0384 66501
Approx.Sls.: $180,000,000
Emp.: 1,900
Manufacturer of Marine Equipment
S.I.C.: 3812
John Hugget *(Mng. Dir.)*

INTERNATIONAL MICROCIRCUITS, INC.
525 Los Coches St.
Milpitas, CA 95035
Tel.: 408-263-6300 **CA**
Fax: 408-263-6571
Year Founded: 1972
Sales Range: $10-19 Million
Emp.: 50
Mfr. Semi-Conductors & Defense Related Equipment
S.I.C.: 3674
Frank T. Deverse *(Chm. Bd., Pres., Chief Exec. Officer & Treas.)*
Charlie Stimson *(Chief Fin. Officer)*
Orhan Tozun *(V.P.-Mktg., Sls. & Engrng.)*
Elisa Kung *(Controller)*

Computer Systems/Hardware:
DEC VAX; Apollo

Outside Service Firm(s):

KPMG Peat Marwick*(Auditors)*
3 Embarcadero Center
San Francisco, CA 94111
Tel.: 415-951-0100
Fax: 415-397-1129

Financial Guardian*(Group Insurer)*
San Jose, CA

Anthony Santucci, Esq.*(Legal Firm)*
Santa Clara, CA

Union Bank*(Major Banking Relationship)*
San Jose, CA

Non-U.S. Holding:

Profile Intl. Microcircuits, Ltd. **(1)**
Brooks House, Alencon Link
Basingstoke, Hampshire RG21 1RG, United Kingdom
Tel.: 256 54 017 (100%)

INTERNATIONAL PERMALITE, INC.
300 N. Haven Ave.
Ontario, CA 91761
Tel.: 909-983-9591
Fax: 909-391-2666
Approx.Sls.: $75,000,000
Emp.: 300
Fiscal Year-end: 1/31/91
Roof Insulation Boards, Roof Membranes
S.I.C.: 2493
James J. Carcich *(Pres.)*
Bartley E. Rodgensack *(V.P.-Mktg.)*
Jack Masheech *(Mgr.-Pur.)*

INTERNATIONAL SEAWAY TRADING CORPORATION
6680 Beta Drive
Mayfield Village, OH 44143
Tel.: 216-446-1000 **OH**
Fax: 216-446-1018
Year Founded: 1956
Assets: $9,925,000
Liabilities: $8,343,000
Net Worth: $1,582,000
Approx.Sls.: $20,000,000
Emp.: 32
Fiscal Year-end: 12/31/90
Import
Importer of Athletic Footwear; Cold Weather Footware, Leather & Synthetic Sandals
S.I.C.: 5139
Harvey Gerdy *(Chm. Bd., Pres. & Chief Exec. Officer)*
Arnold J. Spitz *(Exec. V.P., Sec. & Treas.)*
Lawrence J. Satz *(V.P.-Sls.)*
Joel Sedley *(V.P.)*
Michael Wolf *(V.P. & Dir.-Sls. & Mdsg.)*
Frederick W. Romick *(Dir.-Fin. & Controller)*
James Budzick *(Mgr.-Prod. Devel.)*
Alice Kendall *(Admin. Asst.)*

Outside Service Firm(s):

Coopers & Lybrand*(Auditors)*
1500 One Cleveland Center, 1375 East 9th Street
Cleveland, OH 44114
Tel.: 216-241-4380
Fax: 216-575-0170

Benesch, Friedlander, Coplan & Aronoff*(Legal Firm)*
1100 Citizens Bldg.
Cleveland, OH 44114
Tel.: 216-363-4500

Society National Bank*(Major Banking Relationship)*
Cleveland, OH

INTERNATIONAL SHOE MACHINE CORP.
Simon & Ledge Sts.
Nashua, NH 03060
Tel.: 603-883-550 **MA**
Fax: 603-882-7560
Year Founded: 1971
Approx.Sls.: $34,000,000
Emp.: 350
Mfr. of Shoe Making & Repairing Machinery & Digital, Analog or Hybid Computers; Wholesale Distributor of Adhesives, Tape & Plasters
S.I.C.: 3559; 5085; 3571
Jacob S. Kamborian *(Pres.)*
Michael M. Becka *(Exec. V.P. & Gen. Mgr.)*
V.E. Santilli *(V.P.-Sls.)*
John H. Morton *(Sec.)*

Outside Service Firm(s):

Bank of New England*(Major Banking Relationship)*
28 State Street
Boston, MA 02109
Tel.: 617-742-4000

Subsidiary:

Fasfax Corporation **(1)**
Simon & Ledge Sts.
Nashua, NH 03060
Tel.: 603-883-5500
Approx.Sls.: $26,000,000
Emp.: 210
Mfr. of Electronic Computers For Restaurant Industry
S.I.C.: 3571
Charles Lee *(Pres.)*
James Henderson *(Dir.-Sls. & Mktg.)*

INTERNATIONAL SYSTEMS & CONTROLS CORP.
2727 Allen Pkwy.
Houston, TX 77019
Mailing Address:
P.O. Box 2589
Houston, TX 77252
Tel.: 713-526-5461 **DE**
Approx.Sls.: $15,833,000
Emp.: 200
Holding Company; Principal Markets in Chemical Industry; Fibreboard
S.I.C.: 6719
Dr. Robert S. Medina *(Chm. Bd.)*
J.D. Kenneally *(Pres.)*
K.L. Albracht *(Chief Fin. Officer & V.P.)*
P.D. Fowler *(Sec.)*

Outside Service Firm(s):

Arthur Andersen & Co.*(Auditors)*
711 Louisiana, Ste. 1300
Houston, TX 77002-2323
Tel.: 713-237-2793

Subsidiary:

BS & B Safety Systems **(1)**
P.O. Box 470590
Tulsa, OK 74147-0590
Tel.: 918-492-5732
Manufacture & Distribute Burglar Alarms
S.I.C.: 3669
A. R. Huse *(Pres.)*

INTERPLAST UNIVERSAL INDUSTRIES, INC.
199 Garibaldi Ave.
Lodi, NJ 07644
Tel.: 201-471-4100 **NY**
Fax: 201-471-4931
Year Founded: 1936
Approx.Sls.: $11,000,000
Emp.: 90
Mfr. of Resin or Plastic Coated Fabrics
S.I.C.: 2295
David L. Goldman *(Pres.)*
Ashok Betra *(Sr. V.P.-Fin.)*
Ovidio Fontana *(Dir.-Personnel)*

Outside Service Firm(s):

Gaines Fox & Co.*(Auditors)*
New York, NY

First Fidelity Bank*(Major Banking Relationship)*
765 Broad Street
Newark, NJ 07101

INTERPLASTIC CORP.
1225 Wolters Blvd.
Saint Paul, MN 55110-5145
Tel.: 612-481-6860
Fax: 612-481-9834
Year Founded: 1962
Approx.Sls.: $90,000,000
Emp.: 225
Fiscal Year-end: 12/31/90
Import Export
Synthetic Resins & Companion Items & Sheet Molding Compound
S.I.C.: 2821; 3089
James D. Wallenfelsz *(Pres.)*
M.J. Brost *(V.P.-Fin.)*
R.A. DeRoma *(V.P.)*
Ray Eustace *(V.P.-IDG)*
William Sofko *(V.P.-Gel Coat Div.)*
Ivan Levy *(Gen. Counsel)*
David Engelsgaard *(Controller)*
Robert Hoffman *(Dir.-mfg.)*
Lee Hagelee *(Tech. Dir.)*
R.T. McCabe *(Dir.-Mktg.)*
Bob Capes *(Mgr. Data Processing)*
Peter DiPietro *(Natl. Sls. Mgr.)*
Sharon Fisk *(Mgr.-Pur.)*

Computer Systems/Hardware:
Hewlett-Packard

Outside Service Firm(s):

Arthur Andersen & Co.*(Auditors)*
45 S. 7th St.
Minneapolis, MN 55402

First Bank Minneapolis*(Major Banking Relationship)*
P.O. Box A700, 120 S. Sixth St.
Minneapolis, MN 55480
Tel.: 612-370-4141

Divisions:

Interplastic Commercial Resins Division **(1)**
2015 N.E. Broadway
Minneapolis, MN 55413
Tel.: 612-481-6860
Fax: 612-331-4235
Import Export
Computer Systems/Hardware:
Hewlett-Packard
Mfr.

Interplastic Corporation **(1)**
Hunt St. Mid-America Industrial Park
Pryor, OK 74361
Tel.: 918-825-2756
Fax: 918-825-4157
Import Export
Computer Systems/Hardware:
Hewlett-Packard
Manufacture Plastic Resins
S.I.C.: 2821
Benny Williams *(Gen. Mgr.)*

Interplastic Corp.—(Continued)

Interplastic Distribution Group **(1)**
10940 Laureate Dr.,Ste.8250
San Antonio, TX 78249
Tel.: 210-697-3366
Fax: 210-697-3123
Export
Computer Systems/Hardware:
Hewlett-Packard
Manufacture & Distribute Products To Reinforce Fiberglass Industry
S.I.C.: 2821; 5162
R.R. Eustace *(Gen. Mgr.)*

Interplastic Molding Products Div. **(1)**
1545 S. Olive St.
South Bend, IN 46619
Tel.: 219-234-1105
Fax: 219-234-6686
Bulk & Sheet Molding Compound
S.I.C.: 2821; 3087
Jack Allessandra *(V.P. & Gen. Mgr.)*

INTERROYAL CORPORATION
151 Struthers
Warren, PA 16365
Tel.: 814-723-3900 **DE**
Fax: 814-723-7872
Approx.Sls.: $15,000,000
Emp.: 200
Manufacture Steel Industrial & Institutional Storage Products
S.I.C.: 2542
Alexander A. Dadourian *(Chm. Bd.)*
Haig R. Dadourian *(Pres.)*
Poozant Piranian *(Treas.)*
Salvatore M. Sica *(Sec. & Gen. Counsel)*
John LaMancuso *(Mgr.-Sls./Distr.)*

Computer Systems/Hardware:
IBM

Outside Service Firm(s):

KPMG Peat Marwick*(Auditors)*
345 Park Ave.
New York, NY 10154
Tel.: 212-758-9700
Fax: 212-872-3308

Marine Bank*(Major Banking Relationship)*
New York, NY

Division:

Interroyal Storage Products Div. **(1)**
P.O. Box 428, Struthers St.
Warren, PA 16365
Tel.: 814-723-3900
Steel Shelving & Shop Equipment Sales
S.I.C.: 5072

INTERSTATE COMMODITIES INC.
7 Madison St.
Troy, NY 12181
Tel.: 518-272-7212
Fax: 518-272-7299
Approx.Sls.: $90,000,000
Emp.: 8
Wholesale Feed Ingredients & Grains
S.I.C.: 5153; 5191
V.A. Oberting, Jr. *(Pres.)*
Gary Oberting *(Exec. V.P.)*
Laurie Alessi *(Treas.)*

Outside Service Firm(s):

Bollam, Sheedy, Torani & Co.*(Auditors)*
Albany, NY

Cooper, Erving, Nolan & Heller*(Legal Firm)*
Albany, NY

Key Bank*(Major Banking Relationship)*
Albany, NY

INTERSTATE DISTRIBUTOR COMPANY
11707 21st Ave. S.
Tacoma, WA 98444
Mailing Address:
P.O. Box 45999,
Tacoma, WA 98445-0999
Tel.: 206-537-9455
Approx.Sls.: $65,000,000
Emp.: 650
Interstate Trucking
S.I.C.: 4213
Gary R. McLean *(Chm. Bd. & Pres.)*
George N. Payne *(Exec. V.P. & Chief Fin. Officer)*
Terry S. McLean *(V.P.)*
Douglas C. McLean *(Treas.)*
Rodney A. McLean *(Sec.)*

Outside Service Firm(s):

Ernst & Young*(Auditors)*
Tacoma, WA

Puget Sound National Bank*(Major Banking Relationship)*
P.O. Box 11500
Tacoma, WA 98411
Tel.: 206-383-2871

INTERSTATE DISTRIBUTORS INC.
4101 Blue Ridge Industrial Pkwy.
Norcross, GA 30071
Tel.: 404-476-0103
Fax: 404-497-1681
Sales Range: $100-499 Million
Emp.: 465
Distribution to Fast Food Industries
S.I.C.: 5141
Tom Willingham *(Pres. & Chief Exec. Officer)*
William D. Bartels *(V.P.-Fin.)*
Dave Brininger *(V.P.-Pur.)*
Nelson Gale *(V.P.-Mtkg. & Sls.)*
Dave Kuntz *(V.P. & Chief Oper. Officer)*
August Wingo *(V.P.-MIS)*
Mick Becker *(Controller)*
Ted Leseniak *(Gen Mgr.-Atlanta Opers.)*

Outside Service Firm(s):

Ernst & Young*(Auditors)*
600 Peachtree St. N.E.
Atlanta, GA 30308
Tel.: 404-874-8300

Kilpatrick & Cody*(Legal Firm)*
3100 Equitable Bldg., 100 Peachtree St. N.W.
Atlanta, GA 30343
Tel.: 404-572-6500

Security Pacific National Bank*(Major Banking Relationship)*
Dallas, TX

INTERSTATE DRUG EXCHANGE, INC.
1500 New Horizons Blvd.
Amityville, NY 11701
Tel.: 516-957-8300
Fax: 516-957-1678
Approx.Sls.: $50,000,000
Emp.: 138
Wholesaler of Drugs, Drug Proprietaries & Druggist Sundries, Professional Equipment & Supplies
S.I.C.: 5122; 5100
Rose Sandler *(Chm. Bd.)*
Ernest Sandler *(Pres. & Chief Exec. Officer)*
Peter McCann *(V.P. & Sec.)*
F. Salit *(Pur. Agent)*

Outside Service Firm(s):

Margulis, Hyams & Chaifetz*(Auditors)*
Mincola, NY

Hall, Dickler, Lawler, Kent & Friedman*(Legal Firm)*
460 Park Ave.
New York, NY 10017
Tel.: 212-838-4600

Bank Leumi le-Israel B.M.*(Major Banking Relationship)*
New York, NY

INTERSTATE ELECTRIC SUPPLY COMPANY, INC.
14110G Sullyfield Circle
Chantilly, VA 22021
Tel.: 703-631-2500
Fax: 703-378-3557
Year Founded: 1963
Approx.Sls.: $46,500,000
Emp.: 170
Wholesale Electrical Apparatus & Equipment
S.I.C.: 5063
Francis J. Carr *(Pres. & Chief Oper. Officer)*
Noel W. Baker *(V.P.-Pur. Opers.)*
Michael C. Vincent *(V.P.-Sls. & Mktg.)*

Outside Service Firm(s):

Murry, Johnson & White*(Auditors)*
Arlington, VA

Ronald Tydings*(Legal Firm)*
Fairfax, VA

Sovran Bank*(Major Banking Relationship)*
12th & Main Sts.
Richmond, VA 23208
Tel.: 804-344-1359

INTERSTATE PAYCO SEED COMPANY
1215 Prairie Pkwy.
West Fargo, ND 58078
Mailing Address:
P.O. Box 338
West Fargo, ND 58078
Tel.: 701-282-7338
Emp.: 60
Hybrid Seed Corn
S.I.C.: 0115
Bruce Hovland *(Pres. & Gen. Mgr.)*
Monty Routledge *(Controller)*
Jerry Scott *(Mgr.-District Sls.)*
Shirley Bachmeier *(Adv. Mgr.)*

INTERSTATE PRODUCERS LIVESTOCK ASSOCIATION
1705 W. Luthy
Peoria, IL 61615
Tel.: 309-691-5360 **IL**
Approx.Sls.: $242,000,000
Emp.: 260
Fiscal Year-end: 3/31/92
Wholesale Trade & Marketing-Livestock; Membership Organization
S.I.C.: 5154; 8611
Ken Riskedal *(Pres.)*
Edward J. Strasma *(Exec. V.P., Chief Fin. Officer & Controller)*
Merton Pond *(Treas.)*
Wheeler McDougal *(Mgr.-Data Processing)*

Computer Systems/Hardware:
IBM System 38

Outside Service Firm(s):

KPMG Peat Marwick*(Auditors)*
Decatur, IL

Country Companies*(Group Insurer)*
Bloomington, IL

Co-Bank St. Louis Region*(Major Banking Relationship)*
1415 Olive St.
St. Louis, MO 63166

Illinois Farm Bureau*(Pension Manager)*
Bloomington, IL

INTERSTATE RESOURCES, INC.
1800 N. Kent St., #1200
Rosslyn, VA 22209
Tel.: 703-243-3355
Telex: 214315
Fax: 703-243-4681
Year Founded: 1982
Assets: $116,408,254
Liabilities: $65,068,851
Net Worth: $51,339,403
Sales Range: $100-499 Million
Emp.: 800
Fiscal Year-end: 12/31/90
Export
Manufacturing of Kraft Linerboard, Medium Board, Corrugated Shipping Containers & Timber & Lumber Buying Agent
S.I.C.: 2631; 2653
George N. Frem *(Chm. Bd. & Chief Exec. Office)*
Antoine N. Frem *(Vice Chm.)*
Fares F. Korkmaz *(Pres.)*
Alfred J. Perry *(V.P.-Sls. & Mktg.)*
Basile H. Zaloum *(V.P.-Human Resources)*
Ramez G. Skaff *(Sec. & Treas.)*
Principal(s):
George N. Frem
Antoine N. Frem

No. of Mfg. Plants/Facilities: 5
No. of U.S. Offices: 6

Computer Systems/Hardware:
IBM PC's; Harry Rhode System; IBM System 36

Outside Service Firm(s):

Deloitte & Touche*(Auditors)*
1900 M St. N.W., 4th Fl.
Washington, DC 20036

Johnson Higgins*(Group Insurance Broker/Consult)*
Washington, DC

Morgan Stanley & Co.*(Investment Banker)*
Washington, DC

Talbot & Gallagher*(Legal Firm)*
McLean, VA

Maryland National Bank*(Major Banking Relationship)*
Rockville, MD

Merrill Lynch*(Pension Manager)*
Morristown, NJ

Subsidiaries:

Interstate Container Corporation **(1)**
Industrial Ave. E.
Lowell, MA 01853
Tel.: 508-458-4555
Fax: 508-458-4445
Corrugated Shipping Containers
S.I.C.: 2653
Mike Ustick *(Mgr.)*

Interstate Container Corporation **(1)**
Grace & Meade Sts.
Reading, PA 19611
Tel.: 215-376-7123
Fax: 215-376-0350
Corrugated Shipping Containers & Medium Board
S.I.C.: 2653; 2631
Tom Grace *(Mgr.)*
Charles Feghali *(Mgr.)*

Interstate Paper Corporation **(1)**
One Interstate Rd.
Riceboro, GA 31323
Tel.: 912-884-3371
Fax: 912-884-3498
Kraft Linerboard
S.I.C.: 2631
Dean Barger *(Mgr.)*

Marsh Lumber Company **(1)**
2 Interstate Rd.
Riceboro, GA 31323
Tel.: 912-884-3410

INTERSTATE STEEL SUPPLY CO.
1800 E. Byberry Rd.
Philadelphia, PA 19116
Tel.: 215-673-0300
Fax: 215-969-0334
Year Founded: 1949
Approx.Sls.: $36,000,000
Emp.: 102
Fiscal Year-end: 12/31/91
Import Export
Steel Distribution
S.I.C.: 5051
Arnold W. Bradburd *(Chm. Bd., Pres. & Chief Exec. Officer)*
Joseph V. Vesci *(Chief Fin. Officer)*
Donald S. Everett *(V.P.-Pur.)*
David R. Riley *(V.P.-Sls.)*
William A. Sarle *(V.P.)*
Milton D. Abowitz *(Gen. Counsel)*
John C. Magasko *(Controller)*

Computer Systems/Hardware:
Hewlett Packard 3000/70

Division:

Interstate Steel Supply Co. of Maryland **(1)**
1600 Cherry Hill Rd.
Baltimore, MD 21230-0165
Tel.: 410-752-6900
Fax: 410-752-3087
Import Export
Computer Systems/Hardware:
Hewlett Packard 3000/70
S.I.C.: 5051
Charles VanLanen *(Mgr.-Reg. Sls.)*

INTERSTATE VAN LINES, INC.
5801 Rolling Rd.
Springfield, VA 22152
Tel.: 703-569-2121
Tel.: 800-336-4533 **VA**
Fax: 703-569-3006
Year Founded: 1943
Assets: $11,385,958
Liabilities: $2,500,000
Net Worth: $8,885,958
Sales Range: $20-39 Million
Emp.: 250
Fiscal Year-end: 12/31/91
Local, Long Distance & International Household Goods Carrier; Storage Facilities
S.I.C.: 4212; 4213; 4214
Arthur E. Morrissette *(Pres.)*
Arthur Morrissette, Jr. *(Exec. V.P.)*
Anthony F. Baracat *(V.P.-Sls.)*

Outside Service Firm(s):

Matthews, Carter & Boyce*(Auditors)*
Fairfax, VA

NationsBank*(Major Banking Relationship)*
4th Fl. Pavillon, 1111 E. Main St.
Richmond, VA
Tel.: 804-788-2551

INTERTRADE INDUSTRIES
15301 Transistor Ln.
Huntington Beach, CA 92649
Tel.: 714-894-5566
Fax: 714-894-3927
Earnings: $300,000
Emp.: 60
Manufacture Marine Equipment
S.I.C.: 3089; 3731; 3732
Luke Wyckaerk *(Chm. Bd., Pres. & Chief Exec. Officer)*
Veronica M. Wyckaerk *(Chief Fin. Officer & Treas.)*
Joe McGuire *(Chief Acctg. Mgr.)*

Computer Systems/Hardware:
IBM PC-XT

Outside Service Firm(s):

Liberty Mutual*(Group Insurer)*
175 Berkeley St.
Boston, MA

Bank of America NT&SA*(Investment Banker)*
Newport Beach, CA

Donovan Forrester*(Legal Firm)*
Newport Beach, CA

Bank of America NT&SA*(Major Banking Relationship)*
Newport Beach, CA

Subsidiaries:

Cercom Technologies, Inc. **(1)**
15301 Transistor Ln.
Huntington Beach, CA 92649
Tel.: 714-894-5566
Tooling

Comtool Technologies **(1)**
15301 Transistor Ln.
Huntington Beach, CA 92649
Tel.: 714-894-5566
Tooling

INTEX CHEMICAL INC.
(Div. of EZE Products, Inc.)
High Tee Court
Greer, SC 29650
Mailing Address:
P.O. Box 5744
Greenville, SC 29606
Tel.: 803-877-5747
Fax: 803-232-8192
Year Founded: 1971
Approx.Sls.: $30,000,000
Emp.: 250
Fiscal Year-end: 12/31/91
Export
Mfr. Cleaners, Polishes & Specialty Chemicals
S.I.C.: 2899; 2842
J. Carroll Rushing *(Pres.)*
George Campbell *(Gen. Mgr.)*
Janet LaGore *(Dir.-Pur.)*

INTREPID CORP.
11925 W. Carmen Ave.
Milwaukee, WI 53225
Tel.: 414-358-3666 **WI**
Fax: 414-353-2426
Approx.Sls.: $240,000,000
Emp.: 900
Wholesale Heating, Air Conditioning & Refrigeration Equipment & Supplies, Electrical Appliances, Televisions & Radios, Farm Machinery & Equipment; Manufacture Bicycles & Parts
S.I.C.: 5075; 5078; 5064; 5083; 3751
Richard A. Burke *(Pres.)*
Joseph Siefkes *(V.P.)*

Outside Service Firm(s):

Deloitte & Touche*(Auditors)*
250 E. Wisconsin Ave.
Milwaukee, WI 53202-4283
Tel.: 414-271-3000

Subsidiary:

Trek Bicycle Corporation **(1)**
801 W. Madison St.
Waterloo, WI 53594
Tel.: 414-478-2191
Approx.Sls.: $75,000,000
Emp.: 425
Wholesale Distributor of Bicycles, Parts & Accessories
S.I.C.: 3751; 5091
Richard A. Burke *(Pres.)*
Thomas Albers *(Exec. V.P.)*
John Burke *(V.P.-Sls. & Mktg.)*

INTREPID ENTERPRISES, INC.
1848 Industrial Blvd.
Harvey, LA 70058
Tel.: 504-348-2861
Twx: 460236
Fax: 504-340-7018
Approx.Sls.: $35,000,000
Emp.: 400
Stone Contractor; Wholesale Construction Materials
S.I.C.: 1771; 5039
H. Prestenburg, Jr. *(Pres.)*
John L. Blanda *(Exec. V.P.-Engrng.)*
Richard DiLorenzo *(V.P.-Construction)*
Marlon Landry *(V.P.-Mktg. & Estimating)*
Gasper K. Naquin *(Sec. & Treas.)*

Outside Service Firm(s):

Paul A. Ferrara*(Auditors)*
Harvey, LA

Victor Stillwell*(Legal Firm)*
New Orleans, LA

First NBC*(Major Banking Relationship)*
210 Baronne St.
New Orleans, LA 70112
Tel.: 504-561-1371

INVERNESS CORP.
17-10 Willow St.
Fair Lawn, NJ 07410
Tel.: 201-794-3400
Fax: 201-794-6814
Year Founded: 1975
Approx.Sls.: $30,000,000
Emp.: 200
Manufacture & Wholesale Cosmetic & Jewelry Products
S.I.C.: 2844; 3961; 5094; 5122
Samuel J. Mann *(Pres. & Chief Exec. Officer)*
Arthur Valentine *(V.P.-Intl. Div.)*
Jayne A. Turpin *(Controller)*
Gail Ribas *(Dir.-Creative Services)*
Anthony J. Vlahides *(Dir.-Intl. Div.)*
Arthur Perrone *(Mgr.-Natl. Sls.)*

Computer Systems/Hardware:
Data General Nova 4X

Outside Service Firm(s):

Gikow, Bierman & Talesnick*(Auditors)*
Millburn, NJ

Midlantic National Bank*(Major Banking Relationship)*
One Engle Street
Englewood, NJ 07631
Tel.: 201-894-5021

Invest West Financial Corporation
(Acquired by Pacifica Real Estate Group)

INVESTOR'S MANAGEMENT CORP.
5151 Glenwood Ave.
Raleigh, NC 27612
Mailing Address:
P.O. Box 29502,
Raleigh, NC 27626
Tel.: 919-781-9310
Fax: 919-881-4485
Year Founded: 1973
Earnings: $6,500,000
Approx.Sls.: $410,000,000
Emp.: 19,000
Chain of Steak Houses
S.I.C.: 5812
James H. Maynard *(Chm. Bd., Chief Exec. Officer & Treas.)*
Richard A. Urquhart III *(V.P.-Fin.)*
Gene Amen *(V.P.)*
John M. Day *(V.P.)*
Jim McWhorter *(V.P.)*
Sampson Sterling *(V.P.)*
John McCormick *(Corp. Sec.)*

Computer Systems/Hardware:
IBM System 38

Outside Service Firm(s):

KPMG Peat Marwick*(Auditors)*
3100 Smoketree Court
Raleigh, NC 27629
Tel.: 919-872-3600
Fax: 919-790-9731

Massachusetts Mutual Life Insurance Co.*(Group Insurer)*
Boston, MA

Shaw, Pittman, Potts & Trowbridge*(Legal Firm)*
2300 N St. N.W.
Washington, DC 20037
Tel.: 202-663-8000

Branch Banking & Trust Co.*(Major Banking Relationship)*
Raleigh, NC

NationsBank Carolinas*(Major Banking Relationship)*
One NCNB Plaza T18-7
Charlotte, NC 28255

Subsidiaries:

Oh! Brian's Rip Roarin' Ribs **(1)**
P.O. Box 29511
Raleigh, NC 27626
Tel.: 919-781-0308

Sunbelt Lodging Development Co. **(1)**
5151 Glenwood Ave.
Raleigh, NC 27612
Tel.: 919-781-9310
Operates Days Inn Hotels
S.I.C.: 7011

INVETECH CO.
1400 Howard St.
Detroit, MI 48216
Tel.: 313-963-6011
Fax: 313-963-5427
Year Founded: 1917
Approx.Sls.: $206,000,000
Emp.: 992
Fiscal Year-end: 12/31/91
Export
Ball & Roller Bearings; Power Transmissions & Other Industrial Products
S.I.C.: 5085; 7389
E. Joseph Moore *(Chm. Bd. Emeritus)*
J. Michael Moore *(Chm. Bd. & Chief Exec. Officer)*
James T. Moore II *(Pres. & Chief Oper. Officer)*
Steven P. Mellos *(Chief Fin. Officer, V.P. & Treas.)*
Thomas Jeffery *(V.P.-Opers.)*
Bill Purser *(V.P.-Sls.)*
Robert L. Zeirstra *(V.P.)*
Steve Laten *(Controller)*
Ann Meiggs *(Dir.-Employee Benefits)*
Lali Zoke *(Dir.-Management Information Systems)*

Computer Systems/Hardware:
IBM System 3090

Outside Service Firm(s):

Deloitte & Touche*(Auditors)*
200 Renaissance Center, 16th Fl.
Detroit, MI 48243
Tel.: 313-396-3000
Fax: 313-259-8087

Blue Cross & Blue Shield Association*(Group Insurer)*
Detroit, MI

Oppenheimer & Co., Inc.*(Investment Banker)*
New York, NY

Miller, Canfield, Paddock & Stone*(Legal Firm)*
150 W. Jefferson Ave.
Detroit, MI 48226
Tel.: 313-963-6420

Comerica Bank*(Major Banking Relationship)*
211 W. Fort St.
Detroit, MI 48226
Tel.: 313-222-3300

National Bank of Detroit*(Major Banking Relationship)*
611 Woodward
Detroit, MI 48226
Tel.: 313-225-1000

Invetech Co.—(Continued)

United Bank of Denver*(Major Banking Relationship)*
Denver, CO

Subsidiaries:

American Bearing & Power **(1)**
1400 Howard St.
Detroit, MI 48216
Tel.: 313-963-6011

En-Pak, Inc. **(1)**
1400 Howard St.
Detroit, MI 48216
Tel.: 313-963-6011

Moore Bearing Co. **(1)**
1400 Howard St.
Detroit, MI 48216
Tel.: 313-963-6011

Tri-State Development Co. **(1)**
1400 Howard St.
Detroit, MI 48216
Tel.: 313-963-6011

INVINCIBLE METAL FURNITURE CO.
842 S. 26th St.
Manitowoc, WI 54220
Mailing Address:
P.O. Box 607
Manitowoc, WI 54220
Tel.: 414-682-4601
Tel.: 800-558-4417 (Orders)
Fax: 414-682-7316
Year Founded: 1913
Approx.Sls.: $15,000,000
Emp.: 295
Import Export
Steel Office Furniture
S.I.C.: 2522; 5044
John A. Schuette *(Pres.)*
Tim Schuette *(Exec. V.P.)*
Robert L. Eaton *(Sec. & Treas.)*
Charles A. Teteak *(Pur. Agent)*

IOWA LOTTERY
2015 Grand Ave.
Des Moines, IA 50312
Tel.: 515-281-7900
Fax: 515-281-7882
Year Founded: 1985
Approx.Rev.: $169,000,000
Emp.: 125
Fiscal Year-end: 6/30/91
State Lottery of Iowa; Instant Tickets, Pull-Tabs, Iowa Lotto & Lotto America
S.I.C.: 7999
Emma Chance *(Chm. Bd.)*
Gary Hughes *(Vice Chm.)*
Sherie Barnett *(Legal Counsel)*
Steve King *(Dir.-Acctg.)*
Harry Braafhart *(Dir.-Security)*
Doug Orr *(Dir.-Mktg. & Sls.)*
Cindy Cameron Combs *(Dir.-Mktg.)*
Tammy Watson *(Dir.-Pur.)*
Bev Opie *(Adv. Mgr.)*
Karen Langbein *(Promotion Mgr.)*
Joe Harding *(Mgr.-Instant Ticket)*
Margaret Pierce *(Mgr.-Data Processing)*
Bret Voorhees *(Communications Coord.)*
Dr. Edward J. Stanek *(Commissioner)*
Nichola Schissel *(Asst. Commissioner)*

IOWA PAINT MFG. COMPANY, INC.
17th St. & Grand Ave.
Des Moines, IA 50309
Mailing Address:
P.O. Box 1417,
Des Moines, IA 50305
Tel.: 515-283-1501
Tel.: 800-283-1933
Fax: 515-283-1470
Year Founded: 1933
Approx.Sls.: $30,000,000
Emp.: 200
Fiscal Year-end: 9/30/90
Manufacture Paint & Lacquers
S.I.C.: 2851
Harold A. Goldman *(Chm. Bd.)*
Thomas Goldman *(Pres.)*
A. Martin Hermann *(V.P.-Fin.)*
Carroll Anderson *(Treas.)*

Computer Systems/Hardware:
Honeywell

Outside Service Firm(s):

KPMG Peat Marwick*(Auditors)*
2500 Ruan Center
Des Moines, IA 50309
Tel.: 515-288-7465

Belin, Harris & Lamson*(Legal Firm)*
Des Moines, IA

Bankers Trust Co.*(Major Banking Relationship)*
Des Moines, IA

IRELAND COFFEE TEA, INC.
#8 Canale Dr.
Pleasantville, NJ 08232
Mailing Address:
P.O. Box 1103,
Pleasantville, NJ 08232
Tel.: 609-646-7200
Fax: 609-646-8606
Year Founded: 1917
Approx.Sls.: $15,000,000
Emp.: 85
Market & Manufacture Fresh Roasted Ground Coffee & Tea
S.I.C.: 5149; 2095
William Schroeder *(Chm. Bd. & Chief Exec. Officer)*
John Siracuss, Jr. *(Vice Chm.)*
John Lee, Jr. *(Pres. & Treas.)*
Bob Mussbaun *(V.P.-Sls. & Mktg.)*
Raymond Smith *(V.P.-Opers.)*
Deccie Bryte *(Sec.)*
Dave Politt *(Dir.-Pur.)*
Rick Smith *(Dir.-Bus. Devel.)*

Computer Systems/Hardware:
Digital; Vax

Outside Service Firm(s):

Stanley, Joseph & Company*(Auditors)*
Upper Darby, PA

Levine, Staller, Sklar, Chan & Brodsky*(Legal Firm)*
Pleasantville, NJ

National Westminster Bank plc*(Major Banking Relationship)*
P.O. Box 960,
Jersey City, NJ 07303
Tel.: 201-547-7000

Subsidiaries:

Ireland Gourmet Shop **(1)**
P.O. Box 45,
Atlantic City, NJ 08401
Tel.: 800-443-9675
Sell Coffee, Tea & Gourmet Items
S.I.C.: 5812; 5149
John J. Lee Jr. *(Pres.)*
Raymond Smith *(V.P.)*
Patricia Lee *(Gourmet Shop Mgr.)*

The Lenson Corporation **(1)**
Offshore Commercial Park, 8 Canale Dr.
Pleasantville, NJ 08232
Tel.: 609-646-7200
Tel.: 800-220-5147
Fax: 609-646-8606
Approx.Sls.: $7,000,000
Emp.: 20
Co-Pack & Contract Packaging of Private Label Coffee
S.I.C.: 2095
John Lee, Jr. *(Pres.)*
William Schroeder *(Chief Exec. Officer)*
Robert Nussbaum *(V.P.-Sls. & Mktg.)*

IROQUOIS DIE & MFG. CO.
24400 Hoover
Warren, MI 48089
Tel.: 313-756-6920 **MI**
Fax: 313-756-8793
Year Founded: 1964
Approx.Sls.: $50,000,000
Emp.: 180
Import Export
Heavy Metal Stampings for Automotive OEM & Aftermarket
S.I.C.: 3465
Rudolf Eschbach *(Pres.)*
Leo Deutschmann *(V.P.)*
Reinhard Eschbach *(Sec.)*
Gary Laine *(Controller)*

Outside Service Firm(s):

Amerisure Companies*(Group Insurer)*
Farmington Hills, MI

Blue Cross & Blue Shield of Michigan*(Group Insurer)*
Detroit, MI

IRVINE COMPANY
550 Newport Center Dr.
Newport Beach, CA 92660
Mailing Address:
P.O. Box I
NewportBeach, CA 92658-8904
Tel.: 714-720-2000
Fax: 714-720-3422
Approx.Sls.: $540,000,000
Emp.: 300
Home Building; Real Estate Agent & Broker; Cable Television Services; Agricultural Products
S.I.C.: 6552; 0191; 0174; 1521; 6531; 4899
Donald Bren *(Chm. Bd.)*
Ray Watson *(Vice Chm. Bd.)*
John Martin *(V.P.-Residential Mktg.)*
Richard Moran *(V.P.-Treas.)*
Dawn McCormick *(Dir.-Corp. Communications)*

Computer Systems/Hardware:
IBM System 38

Outside Service Firm(s):

Wells Fargo Bank*(Major Banking Relationship)*
420 Montgomery St.
San Francisco, CA 94104

Subsidiary:

Irvine World News Newspaper Company **(1)**
2712 McGraw Ave.
Irvine, CA 92714
Tel.: 714-261-2401
Brien Manning *(Publisher)*

ISEMOTO CONTRACTING CO. LTD.
648 Piilani St.
Hilo, HI 96720
Mailing Address:
P.O. Box 4669,
Hilo, HI 96720
Tel.: 808-935-7194 **HI**
Fax: 808-961-6417
Year Founded: 1926
Assets: $16,400,000
Liabilities: $9,600,000
Net Worth: $6,800,000
Approx.Sls.: $35,000,000
Emp.: 175
Fiscal Year-end: 12/13/91
Earthmoving, Land Clearing & Trenching Contractor; Industrial Buildings Construction, Renovation & Remodeling; Warehouse Construction, Renovation & Repair; Shopping Center Construction
S.I.C.: 1629; 1541; 1542
Corporate Giving Program: Local charities-subject to annual profit volume.
Larry Isemoto *(Chief Exec. Officer)*
Toshito Isemoto *(Pres.)*
Lester Sakamoto *(Controller)*
Leslie Isemoto *(Sec.)*

Outside Service Firm(s):

Deloitte & Touche*(Auditors)*
Hilo, HI

King & Neal*(Commercial Insurance Carrier)*
1164 Bishop St., Ste. 1710
Honolulu, HI

First Hawaiian Bank*(Major Banking Relationship)*
1205 Kilauea Ave.
Hilo, HI 96720

ISFEL COMPANY, INC.
900 Hart
Rahway, NJ 07065
Tel.: 908-382-3100
Fax: 908-382-6343
Approx.Sls.: $55,000,000
Emp.: 73
Mfg. of Children's Clothing
S.I.C.: 2369; 2361
Joseph Feldman *(Pres. & Chief Exec. Officer)*
J. Blumenfrucht *(V.P. & Chief Fin. Officer)*
J. Rottenberg *(V.P.-Mfg.)*
Shirley Feldman *(Sec. & Treas.)*
Robert Lerman *(Controller)*
L. Danziger *(Dir.-Pur.)*
H. Daum *(Dir.-Data Processing)*
R. Gaber *(Dir.-Personnel)*
J. Gorsd *(Chief Engr.)*

Outside Service Firm(s):

Rashba & Polkart*(Auditors)*
New York, NY

E.J. Greenwald*(Legal Firm)*
Brooklyn, NY

Bankers Trust Co.*(Major Banking Relationship)*
P.O. Box 9050, Church St. Station
New York, NY 10008
Tel.: 212-250-6037

ISLAND LINCOLN-MERCURY
1850 E. Merritt Island Causeway
Merritt Island, FL 32952
Tel.: 407-452-9220
Car Dealership
S.I.C.: 5511
Michael Lister *(Gen. Mgr.)*

ITALIA/GAL ADVERTISING
5750 Wilshire Blvd., Ste. 480
Los Angeles, CA 90036
Tel.: 213-934-7711
Fax: 213-934-7733
Year Founded: 1983
Approx.Billings: $37,750,000
Emp.: 30
Kenneth Gal *(Chm., Chief Exec. Officer)*
Carmen Italia *(Pres. & Creative Dir.)*
Monica Hecht *(Office Mgr.)*

ITHACA INDUSTRIES INC.
Hwy. 268 W.
Wilkesboro, NC 28697
Mailing Address:
P.O. Box 620
Wilkesboro, NC 28697
Tel.: 919-667-5231
Fax: 919-667-4052
Approx.Sls.: $50,000,000
Emp.: 700
Manufacture Ladies', Men's & Children's Hosiery & Socks
S.I.C.: 2251; 2252
Nick Wehrmann *(Chm. Bd.)*
Jim Waller *(Chief Exec. Officer)*
Larry Krause *(Chief Fin. Officer)*

Outside Service Firm(s):

KPMG Peat Marwick *(Auditors)*
Two First Union Center
Charlotte, NC
Tel.: 704-335-5300

ITRAN CORPORATION
670 N. Commercial St.
Manchester, NH 03101-1147
Tel.: 603-669-6332 **DE**
Fax: 603-669-2369
Year Founded: 1983
Sales Range: $20-39 Million
Emp.: 60
Import Export
Manufacture Computer Vision Systems
S.I.C.: 3577

John C. Pemble *(Pres. & Chief Exec. Officer)*
Ken Garofano *(V.P. & Chief Oper. Officer)*
Roger Kuhn *(V.P.-Fin.)*
William Riley *(V.P.-Engrng.)*
Brian St. Pierre *(Dir.-Sls.)*
Kinloch Grewar *(Dir.-Distr.)*
R. Allen Burns *(Mgr.-Mktg.)*

No. of Mfg. Plants/Facilities: 1
No. of U.S. Offices: 5
No. of Foreign Offices: 1

Outside Service Firm(s):

Arthur Andersen & Co. *(Auditors)*
One Intl. Place, 100 Oliver St.
Boston, MA 02110
Tel.: 617-330-4000
Fax: 617-439-9731

Bank of New England *(Major Banking Relationship)*
28 State Street
Boston, MA 02109
Tel.: 617-742-4000

Foley, Hoag & Eliot *(Legal Firm)*
One Post Office Square
Boston, MA 02210
Tel.: 617-482-1390

H. B. IVES
(A Harrow Company)
62 Barnes Park North
Wallingford, CT 06492
Mailing Address:
P.O. Box 5035,
Wallingford, CT 06492
Tel.: 203-294-4837
Year Founded: 1876
Approx.Sls.: $45,000,000
Emp.: 450
Fiscal Year-end: 11/30/90
Hardware Mfr.
S.I.C.: 3429
Robert Hoagland *(Pres.)*
Roby Briggs *(V.P.-Sls.)*
James Casey *(Controller)*

IVEX PACKAGING CORPORATION
(Formerly Ivex Corporation)
100 Tri-State Dr., Suite 200
Lincolnshire, IL 60069
Tel.: 708-945-9100 **TX**
Fax: 708-945-9184
Approx.Sls.: $400,000,000
Emp.: 2,200
Holding Company; Manufacture Paper & Plastic Packaging Products
S.I.C.: 6719; 2673; 2674; 2676; 2677; 2678; 2679; 3089
George V. Bayly *(Pres. & Chief Exec. Officer)*
Frank V. Tannura *(Chief Fin. Officer)*
Roger Kurinsky *(V.P.-Mktg.)*
Jerry Lawrence *(V.P.-Human Resources)*
Douglas Patterson *(V.P.-Legal)*
Tom Riordan *(V.P.-Mfg.)*
Rick Cote *(Treas.)*
Jim Slamp *(Controller)*
John Corrigan *(Asst. Controller)*
Larinda Clark *(Dir.-Bus. Devel.)*
Rick Kerr *(Dir.-Pur.)*
Marie Montroy *(Dir.-Human Resources)*
Dan Vice *(Dir.-Environmental Affairs and Materials)*
John Cahill *(Mgr.-Gen. Accounting)*
Maria Cassidy *(Mgr.-Admin.)*
Rob Pfunder, Jr. *(Mgr.-MIS)*
Larry Adeleye *(Sr. Fin. Analyst)*
Bernie Bolte *(Applications Analyst)*
Nancy Braatz *(Fin. Reporting Accountant)*
Anne Greenhill *(Mktg. Asst.)*
Kim Hix *(Payroll/Accounts Payable Coord.)*
Kathy Jarvis *(Mktg. Analyst)*
Tricia Kelly *(Treasury Analyst)*
Janet Sandstrom *(Benefits Specialist)*

No. of Mfg. Plants/Facilities: 19
No. of Foreign Offices: 3

Outside Service Firm(s):

Andrews & Kurth *(Legal Firm)*
4200 Texas Commerce Tower
Houston, TX 77002
Tel.: 713-220-4200

Harris Trust & Savings Bank *(Major Banking Relationship)*
111 W. Monroe St.
Chicago, IL 60690
Tel.: 312-461-2265
Tel.: 800-858-0840

Divisions:

Ivex Packaging Corporation-Food Packaging Division **(1)**
100 Tri-State Drive, Suite 200
Lincolnshire, IL 60069
Tel.: 708-945-9100
Fax: 708-945-9184
Tim Carrigan *(V.P.-Sls.)*
Darwin Groesbeck *(V.P.-Food Packaging)*
Tom Noonan *(Div. Controller)*
Gene Gentili *(Dir.-Sls. Foodservice Natl. Accounts)*
Bob Nyborg *(Dir.-Natl. Accounts Bakery & Confectionery)*

Plants:

Ivex Packaging Corporation-Engineering Group **(2)**
P.O. Box 399, 221 E. Greenwood
Grant Park, IL 60940
Tel.: 815-465-2002
Fax: 815-465-2024
Jim Timmer *(Mgr.-Engrng. Opers.)*
Hollis Habeger *(Mgr.-Prod. Devel.)*
John Ulcej *(Engr.-Process Devel.)*
Neil Wingate *(Mgr.-Tooling)*

Ivex Packaging Corporation-Floral and Nursery Products **(2)**
P.O. Box 518, 221 E. Greenwood
Grant Park, IL 60940
Tel.: 815-465-2092
Tel.: 800-473-4730
Fax: 800-473-5552
Steve Lefebvre *(Mgr.-Gen.)*
Jim Bachmann *(Mgr.-Sls.)*
Ron Gutowski *(Mgr.-Gen. Accounting)*

Ivex Packaging Corporation-Grant Park **(2)**
P.O. Box G, 304 North E. Main St.
Grant Park, IL 60940
Tel.: 815-465-2115
Fax: 815-465-2543
Joe Desiderio *(Mgr.-Opers.)*
Steve Indrelunas *(Mgr.-Plant)*
Frank McCabe *(Mgr.-Natl. Accounts Central)*
Wayne McKay *(Mgr.-Distr.)*
Brett York *(Mgr.-Reg. Sls. Central)*
Mary Porter *(Controller)*

Ivex Packaging Corporation-Grove City **(2)**
P.O. Box 1128, 600 Barkeyville Rd.
Grove City, PA 16127
Tel.: 412-458-1800
Fax: 412-458-1612
Jim Bondurant *(Mgr.-Opers.)*
Sean Condon *(Mgr.-Industrial Sls.)*
Bill DeVries *(Mgr.-Natl. Accounts Bakery & Confectionery)*
Bill Ebeck *(Mgr.-Reg. Sls. & Mktg.)*
Brian Sullivan *(Mgr.-Mkt. Devel. Mdse Prods.)*
John Godlove *(Controller)*

Ivex Packaging Corporation-Madison **(2)**
P.O. Box 508,
Madison, GA 30650
Tel.: 404-342-4500
Fax: 404-342-0757
Joe White *(Mgr.-Opers.)*
Mike Newman *(Mgr.-Plant)*
Dan Marra *(Mgr.-Reg. Sls. Mgr. Southeast)*
Brian Miller *(Controller)*

Ivex Packaging Corporation-Visalia **(2)**
7101 Avenue 304
Visalia, CA 93291
Tel.: 209-651-2126
Fax: 209-651-1050
Jim McCarty *(Mgr.-Opers.)*
Dan Ashley *(Mgr.-Industrial Prods. Sls.)*
Ed Byrne *(Mgr.-Natl. Accounts Western)*
Bill Davis *(Mgr.-Reg. Sls. Western)*
Gary Hagar *(Controller)*

Unit:

Bestpak, Inc. **(2)**
P.O. Box 1128, 600 Barkeyville Rd.
Grove City, PA 16127
Tel.: 412-458-5615
Fax: 412-458-1612
Mike Wennemer *(Mgr.-Sls.)*

Ivex Packaging Corporation-Industrial Products Division **(1)**
55 Tower Rd.
Newton, MA 02164
Tel.: 617-527-4980
Fax: 617-244-2051
Fax: 617-964-4669
Patrick Farrell *(V.P. & Gen. Mgr.)*
Lee McGuiness *(V.P.-Merchant Sls.)*
Paul Fournier *(Controller)*
Dan Mirski *(Division Controller)*
Paul Fortin *(Dir.-Mfg. Engrng.)*
Rich Korane *(Dir.-Technical)*
John Cavanagh *(Mgr.-Mktg. Masking Prods.)*
Pat Scanlon *(Mgr.-Sls. East)*
Bill Tripp *(Mgr.-Opers.)*

Units:

Ivex Packaging Corporation-Bridgeview **(2)**
8100 S. 77th Ave.
Bridgeview, IL 60455
Tel.: 708-458-8084
Fax: 708-458-8099
Kyle Behringer *(V.P.-Industrial Prods. Sls.)*
Ed Keyes *(Mgr.-Opers.)*

Ivex Packaging Corporation-Hillside **(2)**
50 S. Mannheim Rd.
Hillside, IL 60172
Tel.: 708-547-2400
Fax: 708-547-0361
Ed Keyes *(Mgr.-Opers.)*
Joanne Slonski *(Division Mgr.-Customer Service)*
Cynthia Brooks *(Mgr.-Customer Service)*
Dave Lutz *(Mgr.-Industrial Prods. Sls.)*
Jack Rettker *(Mgr.-Natl. Accounts (Food))*
Bob Jacob *(Controller)*

Ivex Packaging Corporation-Troy **(2)**
421 S. Union St.
Troy, OH 45373
Tel.: 513-335-5611
Fax: 513-339-9223
Dale Mahon *(Dir.-Mktg. (Coated Prods.))*
John Cousins *(Mgr.-Natl. Sls. Specialty Printing)*
Pat Geron *(Mgr.-Natl. Accounts Specialty Prods.)*
Bob Matz *(Mgr.-Opers.)*
Tim Schenck *(Controller)*

Ivex Packaging Corporation-Polymerization and Extrusion Division **(1)**
P.O. Box 658, 666 Dietrich Ave.
Hazleton, PA 18201
Tel.: 717-455-2022
Eugene Whitacre *(V.P.-Polymerization and Extrusion)*
John Maxwell *(V.P.-Sls. & Mktg.)*
Gene Caboner *(Division Controller)*
Mike Bower *(Mgr.-Res. & Devel.)*
Joe Gelgot *(Mgr.-P&E Division Engrng.)*

Plants:

Ivex Packaging Corporation-Avenel **(2)**
30 Production Way
Avenel, NJ 07001
Tel.: 908-388-2300
Fax: 908-388-1133
Ludwig Piehler *(Sr. Opers. Mgr.)*

Ivex Packaging Corporation-Manteno **(2)**
1050 Sycamore Rd.
Manteno, IL 60950
Tel.: 815-468-8300
Fax: 815-468-8322
Mark Ballard *(Mgr.-Opers.)*

Ivex Packaging Corporation-Mill Division **(1)**
P.O. Box 685, 292 Logan Ave.
Joliet, IL 60434
Tel.: 815-740-6421
Fax: 815-722-3884
Lew Brown *(V.P. & Gen. Mgr.)*
Tom Ellsworth *(V.P.-Mfg. & Fin.)*
John Kaniuga *(Mgr.-Information Systems)*
Ken Meyer *(Mgr.-Sls.)*
Martin Smith *(Mgr.-Prod. Devel.)*
Tony Ugone *(Sr. Accountant)*

Plants:

IPMC, Inc.-Detroit **(2)**
9125 W. Jefferson
Detroit, MI 48209
Tel.: 313-842-0042
Fax: 312-842-1055
Jim Painter *(V.P. & Mill Mgr.)*
Doug Murray *(Mill Controller)*
Kris Brady *(Mgr.-Pur.)*
Darrel Dick *(Mgr.-Engrng.)*
Dave Fleet *(Mgr.-Sls.)*
Lou Sturm *(Mgr.-Technical)*

Ivex Packaging Corporation-Chagrin Falls **(2)**
P.O. Box 300, 218 Cleveland St.
Chagrin Falls, OH 44022
Tel.: 216-247-5530
Fax: 216-247-3924
Paper Mill
S.I.C.: 2621
Kirk Olsen *(Mill Mgr.)*
Dan Davis *(Mill Engr.)*
Darlene Jacobson *(Mill Controller)*

Ivex Packaging Corporation-Joliet **(2)**
P.O. Box 685, 292 Logan Ave.
Joliet, IL 60434
Tel.: 312-242-3850
Fax: 815-740-6481
Dick LeGrand *(Mill Mgr.)*
Bob Baitinger *(Mgr.-Production & Scheduler)*
Joe Pomykala *(Mgr.-Customer Service)*
Ron Evans *(Mill Engr.)*
Cliff Kohler *(Plant Controller)*

Ivex Packaging Corporation-Peoria **(2)**
P.O. Box 1820, Foot of Sloan St.
Peoria, IL 61656
Tel.: 309-686-3830
Fax: 309-686-0324
Denny Potts *(Mill Mgr.)*
Chuck Erwin *(Mill Accountant)*
Larry Rohman *(Mill Division Engr.)*

Non-U.S. Division:

Ivex Packaging Corporation-Canadian Region **(1)**
40 Butterick Rd.
Toronto, Ontario Canada M8W 3Z8
Tel.: 416-259-4231
Tel.: 416-259-4234
Fax: 416-259-6521
Bob Wedgbury *(V.P. & Canadian Reg. Mgr.)*
David Brown *(Controller-Canada)*
Maureen Clark *(Mgr.-Admin.)*
Jim Graham *(Mgr.-Production)*
Dave Nicholishen *(Mgr.-Sls. & Mktg.)*
Bob Nurse *(Mgr.-New Prod. Devel.)*
Terry Sharon *(Mgr.-Opers.)*

Plants:

Ivex Packaging Corporation-Keele Street **(2)**
500 Keele St., Unit 306
Toronto, Ontario Canada M6N 3C9
Tel.: 416-766-3017
Fax: 416-766-5770

Ivex Packaging Corporation—(Continued)

Gary Lane *(Mgr.-Distr. & Customer Service)*
Bob Lafferty *(Shipping Supervisor)*

Ivex Packaging Corporation-Longueuil **(2)**
2355 Rue De La Province
Longueuil, Quebec Canada J4G 1G3
Tel.: 514-679-4750
Fax: 514-679-6400
Fred Blersch *(Mgr.-Plastic Prods.)*
Suzanne Bouchard *(Mgr.-Office)*

FRANK IX & SONS, INC.
469 7th Ave., 11th Fl.
New York, NY 10018
Tel.: 212-239-4480
Fax: 718-268-0795
Sales Range: $80-99 Million
Emp.: 650
Broad Woven Fabrics
S.I.C.: 2211
Paul Tikkanen *(Pres.)*
F.M. Dimartini *(V.P.-Prod. Devel, Raw Matls. & Pur.)*
Peter Formosa *(V.P.-Mktg.)*
John Todd *(V.P.-Mfg.)*
Frank Inzitari *(Controller)*

Outside Service Firm(s):

Skwiersky, Alpert & Bressler*(Auditors)*
New York, NY

Hahn & Hessen*(Legal Firm)*
350 Fifth Ave., Ste. 3700
New York, NY 10118
Tel.: 212-736-1000

First Union National Bank of North Carolina*(Major Banking Relationship)*
Securities Transfer Dept., First Union Plaza (CMG 5)
Charlotte, NC 28288
Tel.: 704-374-2064
Fax: 704-374-6987

J. CREW GROUP, INC.
625 6th Ave.
New York, NY 10011
Tel.: 212-886-2500
Fax: 212-886-2666
Assets: $142,000,000
Liabilities: $108,000,000
Net Worth: $34,000,000
Approx.Sls.: $384,000,000
Emp.: 3,200
Fiscal Year-end: 2/ 1/91
Import
Catalog Mail Order; Popular Club Plan, J. Crew, Clifford & Wills
S.I.C.: 5961
Arthur Cinader *(Chm. Bd.)*
Arnold Cohen *(Pres.)*
Keith Monda *(Exec. V.P.)*
Michael P. McHugh *(V.P., Chief Fin. Officer)*
Joseph Del Gaudio *(V.P.-Mngmt. Information Systems)*
Robert Paris *(V.P.-Opers.)*
Nicholas Lamberti *(Controller)*
Adrian Perkov *(Dir.-New Mkt. Devel.)*

Outside Service Firm(s):

Deloitte & Touche*(Auditors)*
1 World Trade Center
New York, NY 10048
Tel.: 212-669-5000

Herzfeld & Rubin*(Legal Firm)*
40 Wall St.
New York, NY 10005
Tel.: 212-344-0680

J. & W. SELIGMAN & COMPANY
130 Liberty St.
New York, NY 10006
Tel.: 212-488-0200
Fax: 212-488-0846
Emp.: 300
Investment Managers & Advisors
S.I.C.: 6211
William C. Morris *(Chm. Bd. & Pres.)*
Michael J. Del Priore *(Sr. V.P. & Mng. Dir.)*

Outside Service Firm(s):

Price Waterhouse*(Auditors)*
153 E. 53rd St., 44th Fl.
New York, NY 10022
Tel.: 212-371-2000

Cravath, Swaine & Moore*(Legal Firm)*
Worldwide Plaza, 825 8th Ave.
New York, NY 10019
Tel.: 212-474 1000
Fax: 201-474-3700

J B LABS, INC.
130 Central
Holland, MI 49423
Tel.: 616-396-3221
Fax: 616-396-6499
Approx.Sls.: $18,000,000
Emp.: 88
Mfr. of Medicinals & Botanicals; Vitamin, Nutrient & Hematinic Preparations For Human Use
S.I.C.: 2833; 2834
William L. Baker, Jr. *(Pres.)*
Frank Lamb *(Exec. V.P.-Fin.)*
Patrick Micula *(V.P.-Opers.)*

Outside Service Firm(s):

FMB First Michigan Bank*(Major Banking Relationship)*
Zeeland, MI

JCI DATA PROCESSING, INC.
501 Delran Pkwy.
Delran, NJ 08075
Tel.: 609-461-2000
Fax: 609-764-7157
Year Founded: 1958
Approx.Sls.: $14,000,000
Emp.: 500
Fiscal Year-end: 12/31/92
Computer Service to Magazine Publishers, Circulation Fulfillment, Postal Presort, Reader Service Processing, Payroll Processing, Accounts Receivable, Class Action Administration Service, Direct Mail, Merge/Purge, Personalization & LED Laser Printing
S.I.C.: 7371; 7374; 7375; 7379
Victor L. Johnson *(Pres.)*
Raymond Liscik *(V.P.-Adv., Mktg., Sls. & Pub. Rels.)*
Saul Lapp *(V.P.-Fin.)*

Computer Systems/Hardware:
IBM Mainframe

JFC INC.
309 Lincoln Ave. S.E.
Saint Cloud, MN 56304
Mailing Address:
P.O. Box 1106
St. Cloud, MN 56302
Tel.: 612-251-3570
Tel.: 800-328-2814
Fax: 612-259-7373
Year Founded: 1926
Assets: $35,000,000
Net Worth: $35,000,000
Approx.Sls.: $85,000,000
Emp.: 1100
Fiscal Year-end: 9/30/92
Import Export
Holding Company; Poultry Broiler, Hatchery & Processing
S.I.C.: 6719; 0254; 0251; 0252
Donald P. Helgeson *(Chm. Bd.)*
Michael Helgeson *(V.P.)*
Stephen Jurek *(Treas.)*
Diane Erickson *(Controller)*

Outside Service Firm(s):

Schecter, Dokken, Kantor, Andrews & Selcer LTD*(Auditors)*
Minneapolis, MN

First American National Bank*(Major Banking Relationship)*
Saint Cloud, MN

Subsidiaries:

Gold'n Plump, Inc. **(1)**
309 Lincoln Ave., S.E.
Saint Cloud, MN 56302
Tel.: 612-251-3570
Poultry Broilers, Hatchery & Processing
S.I.C.: 0251; 0252; 0254
Donald P. Helgeson *(Pres.)*
Steve Jurek *(Chief Fin. Officer)*

Jack Frost, Inc. **(1)**
309 Lincoln Ave., S.E.
Saint Cloud, MN 56304
Tel.: 612-251-3570
Processing of Chickens
S.I.C.: 2015
Donald P. Helgeson *(Pres.)*

J.F.P. & ASSOCIATES OF FLORIDA, INC.
201 W. First St.
Sanford, FL 32771
Tel.: 407-321-7003
Fax: 407-330-9886
Year Founded: 1946
Approx.Billings: $10,000,000
Emp.: 5
Jeno F. Paulucci *(Chm. Bd.)*
Michael J. Paulucci *(Vice Chm.)*
James J. Tills *(Pres.)*

J H COLLECTIBLES
200 W. Vogel
Milwaukee, WI 53207
Tel.: 414-744-5080 **WI**
Telex: 910-262-3060
Fax: 414-747-7439
Year Founded: 1945
Assets: $60,420,341
Liabilities: $34,611,623
Net Worth: $25,808,718
Approx.Sls.: $175,000,000
Emp.: 800
Fiscal Year-end: 12/31/91
Import Export
Manufacture Junior & Misses Sportswear
S.I.C.: 2331; 2339
Kenneth Ross *(Chm. & Chief Exec. Officer)*
Bruce Ross *(Pres.)*
Normand Neal *(Exec. V.P.-Sls. & Mktg.)*
David Hirsch *(Exec. V.P.-Mfg.)*
Brian Tinant *(Exec. V.P.- Oper.)*
Kristine Amborn *(V.P. & Controller)*
Michael Best *(V.P. & Chief Fin. Officer)*
Patrick Johnson *(V.P.-Data Processing)*
Richard Korman *(V.P.-Merchandising)*
John Larkin *(V.P.-Mfg.)*
Robert Watchmaker *(V.P.-Plng.)*
Audrey Ross *(Treas.)*
Georgia Schuette *(Dir.-Personnel)*
Frank Lombardi *(Mgr.-Quality Control)*
Isabel Sellers *(Mgr.-Adv.)*
Mary Sedlacek *(Mgr.-Pur.)*
Mary Wingenter *(Mgr.-Import)*
Principal(s):
Kenneth Ross
Bruce Ross
Audrey Ross

No. of Mfg. Plants/Facilities: 2
No. of U.S. Offices: 8
No. of Foreign Offices: 1

Computer Systems/Hardware:
Hewlett Packard

Outside Service Firm(s):

Deloitte & Touche*(Auditors)*
250 E. Wisconsin Ave.
Milwaukee, WI 53202-4283
Tel.: 414-271-3000

Godfrey & Kahn*(Legal Firm)*
780 N. Water St.
Milwaukee, WI 53202
Tel.: 414-273-3500
Fax: 414-273-5198

First Bank Milwaukee*(Major Banking Relationship)*
201 W. Wisconsin Ave.
Milwaukee, WI 53259
Tel.: 414-278-6000

JM FAMILY ENTERPRISES INC.
100 NW 12th Ave.
Deerfield Beach, FL 33443
Mailing Address:
P.O. Box 1160
Deerfield Beach, FL 33443
Tel.: 305-429-2000
Sales Range: $1 Billion +
Emp.: 2,300
Automobile Distributorship
S.I.C.: 5012
Corporate Giving Program: Supports Organizations That Focus On Youths & Educational Efforts In Communities In Which The Company's Corporate Officer Are Located
James M. Moran *(Chm. Bd.)*
Patricia Moran *(Pres. & Chief Exec. Officer)*
Casey Ginnel *(Chief Fin. Officer)*
John McNally *(Exec. V.P.)*
James M. Moran, Jr. *(Exec. V.P.-Mktg.)*
Lawrence Rich *(Exec. V.P.)*
William Donahoe *(V.P.-Govt. Affairs)*
Rhonda Gallaspy *(V.P.-Human Resources)*
Debbie Mason *(V.P.-Corp. Communications)*
Tucker Allen *(Treas.)*
Andra Smith *(Controller)*
Taylor Ward *(Sec.)*
Principal(s):
James M. Moran
Arlene McNally
John McNally
James M. Moran, Jr.
Jan Moran
Patricia Moran

Outside Service Firm(s):

Arthur Andersen & Co.*(Auditors)*
2100 One Biscayne Tower
Miami, FL 33131
Tel.: 305-374-3700

JMB REALTY CORPORATION
900 N. Michigan Ave.
Chicago, IL 60611
Tel.: 312-440-4800
Fax: 312-415-2310
Approx.Sls.: $1,500,000,000
Emp.: 1,400
Real Estate Investment Firm, Syndicator, Developer
S.I.C.: 6798; 6552
Neil G. Bluhm *(Pres.)*
Jerry Claeys *(Exec. V.P.)*
Bruce W. Duncan *(Exec. V.P.)*
Doug Cameron *(Exec. V.P.)*
Burton E. Glazov *(Exec. V.P.)*
John G. Schreiber *(Exec. V.P.)*
Gary V. Chensoff *(Sr. V.P.)*
Mike Hertzberg *(Sr. V.P.)*
John Tuney *(Sr. V.P.)*
Howard Kogen *(V.P. & Treas.)*
Stuart C. Nathan *(V.P.)*
Mary Farrell *(Dir.-Corp. Communication)*

Outside Service Firm(s):

KPMG Peat Marwick*(Auditors)*
Peat Marwick Plaza, 303 E. Wacker Dr.
Chicago, IL 60601
Tel.: 312-938-1000

Mayer, Brown & Platt*(Legal Firm)*
190 S. LaSalle St., Ste. 3900
Chicago, IL 60603
Tel.: 312-782-0600

Continental Bank N. A.*(Major Banking Relationship)*
231 S. LaSalle St.
Chicago, IL 60697

Tel.: 312-828-2345
Tel.: 800-426-5754
Telex: 312-828-1783

Subsidiaries:

Amfac, Inc. **(1)**
900 N. Michigan Ave., # 2800
Chicago, IL 60611
Tel.: 312-915-2400
Assets: $1,078,308,000
Earnings: $17,912,000
Liabilities: $666,715,000
Net Worth: $411,593,000
Approx.Rev.: $2,195,062,000
Emp.: 18,000
Wholesale Distribution; Food Processing; Hotels & Resorts; Retailing; Agriculture & Property
S.I.C.: 0133; 7221; 0131; 6141; 2061; 5211; 2399
Judd Malkin *(Chm. Bd.)*
Neil Bluhm *(Pres.)*
Robert Chapman *(Exec. V.P.)*
Mary Farrel *(V.P.-Corp. Communications)*

Groups:

Amfac Distribution Corporation **(2)**
81 Blue Ravine Rd.
Folsom, CA 95630
Tel.: 916-985-5000 (100%)
Approx.Rev.: $1,100,000,000
Emp.: 2,010
Wholesale Distr. of Pharmaceutical, Veterinary, Electrical, Plumbing, Heating, Air Conditioning, Hardware & Industrial Supplies
S.I.C.: 5122; 5044; 5074; 5072; 5100
Ronald H. Dykehouse *(Pres.)*
Armando B. Flores *(Sr. V.P.-Admin.)*

Division:

Amfac Health Care **(3)**
81 Blue Ravine Rd.
Folsom, CA 95630
Tel.: 916-985-5000
Approx.Rev.: $744,100,000
Wholesale Distribution of Pharmaceuticals
S.I.C.: 5122; 5100
Melburn G. Whitmire *(Pres.)*
Gary E. Close *(Exec. V.P.-Opers.)*
Steven J. Divine *(V.P.-Mktg.)*

Amfac Foods, Inc. **(2)**
6600 S.W. Hampton St.
Portland, OR 97223
Tel.: 503-620-3720 (100%)
Approx.Rev.: $516,600,000
Emp.: 6,280
Frozen Food Processors
S.I.C.: 2037; 2092
Ronald H. Dykehouse *(Pres.)*

Subsidiaries:

AFI Export, Inc. **(3)**
6600 S.W. Hampton Street
Portland, OR 97223
Tel.: 503-620-3720
Domestic International Sales Corporation
S.I.C.: 6799
Ronald H. Dykehouse *(Pres.)*

Amfac Amycel, Inc. **(3)**
P.O. Box 1260,
San Juan Bautista, CA 95045
Tel.: 408-623-4586 (100%)
Production, Distr. & Sale of Mushroom Spawn
S.I.C.: 0182
John S. Henningsen *(Pres.)*

Monterey Mushrooms, Inc. **(3)**
P.O. Box 1990,
Santa Cruz, CA 95061
Tel.: 408-475-1955 (100%)
Growing & Processing Mushrooms
S.I.C.: 0182
John S. Henningsen *(Pres.)*

Amfac/JMB Hawaii, Inc. **(2)**
700 Bishop Street
Honolulu, HI 96813
Tel.: 808-945-8286
Approx.Rev.: $138,600,000
Emp.: 2,500
Property Investment & Participation in Agricultural Activities
S.I.C.: 6519; 6552
Richard L. Griffith *(Chm.)*
Roderick T. Wilson *(Pres.)*
John W. Bauroth *(Exec. V.P.)*

Subsidiaries:

Amfac Financial Inc. **(3)**
700 Bishop St.
Honolulu, HI 96813
Tel.: 808-945-8296 (100%)
Coord. of Financial & Devel. Activities
S.I.C.: 6552

Subsidiaries:

Amfac Development Corp. **(4)**
700 Bishop St.
Honolulu, HI 96813
Tel.: 808-945-8296 (100%)
Real Estate Devel.
S.I.C.: 6552

API, Inc. **(4)**
700 Bishop St.
Honolulu, HI 96813
Tel.: 808-945-8296 (100%)
Property Devel.
S.I.C.: 6552

Metropolitan Arizona Corporation **(4)**
700 Bishop St.
Honolulu, HI 96813
Tel.: 808-945-8286 (100%)
Real Estate Devel.
S.I.C.: 6552

Subsidiary:

Casa Grande West Water Company, Inc. **(5)**
700 Bishop St.
Honolulu, HI 96813
Tel.: 808-945-8144 (100%)
Oper. of Water Co.
S.I.C.: 4941

Amfac Property Development Corp. **(3)**
700 Bishop St.
Honolulu, HI 96802
Tel.: 808-945-8296 (100%)
Real Estate Devel.
S.I.C.: 6552
R. Brian Tsujimura *(Pres.)*

Amfac Property Investment Corp. **(3)**
2530 Kekaa Dr.
Lahaina, HI 96761
Tel.: 808-667-7411 (100%)
Property Investment
S.I.C.: 6799
D. H. Gleason *(Pres.)*

Subsidiary:

Kaanapali Water Corporation **(4)**
2530 Kekaa Dr.
Lahaina, HI 96761
Tel.: 808-667-7411 (100%)
Oper. of Water Co.
S.I.C.: 4941
D. H. Gleason *(Pres.)*

Amfac Sugar and Agribusiness, Inc. **(3)**
P.O. Box 3230
Honolulu, HI 96801
Tel.: 808-945-8245
Participation in Sugar and Other Agricultural Activities
S.I.C.: 5149; 5159
Lawrence P. Perry *(Pres.)*

Subsidiary:

Amfac Agribusiness, Inc. **(4)**
700 Bishop St.
Honolulu, HI 96813
Tel.: 808-945-8141 (100%)
Diversified Agriculture
S.I.C.: 9641
Dennis Y. Teranishi *(Pres.)*

American Factors Assoc. Australia Pty., Ltd. **(3)**
700 Bishop St.
Honolulu, HI 96813
Tel.: 808-945-8276 (100%)
Devel. of Agricultural Lands in Australia
S.I.C.: 6552
Blake Senior *(Mng. Dir.)*

Amfac Garden Hawaii **(3)**
P.O. Box 537,
Waipahu, HI 96797
Tel.: 808-945-8498
Growing Tropical Foliage
S.I.C.: 0181
Susan Matsushima *(Pres.)*

Amfac Tropical Products **(3)**
P.O. Box 210,
Keaau, HI 96749
Tel.: 808-966-7435
Growing & Processing Papaya & Other Tropical Fruit Products
S.I.C.: 0179
Dennis Y. Teranishi *(Pres.)*

Amfac Energy, Inc. **(3)**
700 Bishop St.
Honolulu, HI 96813
Tel.: 808-945-8154 (100%)
Devel., Production, Mktg. of Energy, Energy Products & By-Products
Paul S. Sakuda *(Pres.)*

Subsidiaries:

Oahu Waste Energy Recovery, Inc. **(4)**
700 Bishop Street
Honolulu, HI 98601
Tel.: 808-945-8154
Development, Production & Marketing of Energy & Energy Related Products & By-Products
S.I.C.: 5093
George E. St John *(Pres.)*

Kekaha Sugar Company, Limited **(4)**
P. O. Box AA
Kekaha, HI 96752
Tel.: 808-337-1472 (100%)
Grower & Processor of Sugarcane
S.I.C.: 2061
Lindsay A. Faye, Jr. *(Pres. & Mgr.)*

The Lihue Plantation Company, Limited **(3)**
P.O. Box 751,
Lihue, HI 96766
Tel.: 808-245-7325 (100%)
Grower & Processor of Sugarcane
S.I.C.: 2061
Hiroshi Kawazoe *(Pres. & Mgr.)*

Division:

Kauai Sugar Storage Co. **(4)**
P.O. Box 1743,
Lihue, HI 96766
Tel.: 808-245-2142
Storage & Delivery of Bulk Sugar Molasses
S.I.C.: 2061
Hiroshi Kawazoe *(Pres.)*

Subsidiary:

H. Hackfeld & Co. Ltd. **(4)**
P.O. Box 751
Lihue, HI 96766
Tel.: 808-245-7325 (100%)
Accumulation & Distribution of Irrigation & Indus. Water
S.I.C.: 4941
Hiroshi Kawazoe *(Pres.)*

Oahu Sugar Company, Limited **(3)**
P. O. Box O
Waipahu, HI 96797
Tel.: 808-677-3577 (100%)
Grower & Processor of Sugarcane
S.I.C.: 0133
W. D. Balfour, Jr. *(Pres. & Mgr.)*

Subsidiary:

Waiahole Irrigation Co., Ltd. **(4)**
P. O. Box O
Waipahu, HI 96797
Tel.: 808-677-3577 (100%)
Distributing Irrigation Water
S.I.C.: 4971
W. D. Balfour, Jr. *(Pres. & Mgr.)*

Pioneer Mill Company, Ltd. **(3)**
P. O. Box 727
Lahaina, HI 96761
Tel.: 808-661-0592 (100%)
Emp.: 133
Grower & Processor of Sugarcane
S.I.C.: 2061
John C. Hance *(Pres. & Mgr.)*

Puna Sugar Co., Ltd. **(3)**
P. O. Box 210
Keaau, HI 96749
Tel.: 808-966-9242 (100%)
Inactive
S.I.C.: 0133
W. D. Balfour, Jr. *(Pres. & Mgr.)*

Amfac Resorts, Inc. **(2)**
5200 E. Cortland Blvd., Ste. A-16
Flagstaff, AZ 86004
Tel.: 602-527-2100 (100%)
Approx.Rev.: $32,800,000
Emp.: 2,312
Hotel, Restaurant & Resort Opers.
S.I.C.: 6513
Richard A. Naille, II *(Chm. & Chief Exec. Officer)*

Subsidiary:

Fred Harvey Transportation Company **(3)**
5200 E. Cortland Blvd.
Flagstaff, AZ 86001
Tel.: 602-527-2100 (100%)
Transportation Services at Grand Canyon; Gas Stations & Visitor Concessions
S.I.C.: 5541; 5947
Richard A. Naille, II *(Pres.)*

Amfac Retail Corp. **(2)**
Ala Moana Pacific Center, 1585 Kapiolani Blvd.
Honolulu, HI 96815
Tel.: 808-945-5505 (100%)
Approx.Rev.: $283,500,000
Emp.: 3,290
Retail Merchandising
S.I.C.: 6719
Donald C. Onasch *(Pres.)*

Subsidiaries:

Baydale, Inc. **(3)**
Ala Moana Pacific Center, 1585 Kapiolani Blvd.
Honolulu, HI 96815
Tel.: 808-945-5505 (100%)
Donald C. Onasch *(Pres.)*

Amfac Nurseries Cole, Inc. **(3)**
44 Montgomery St.
San Francisco, CA 94120
Tel.: 415-772-3564 (100%)
Inactive
S.I.C.: 0181
Thomas L. Braje *(Pres.)*

Amfac Silverado Corp. **(3)**
5200 E. Cortland Blvd.
Flagstaff, AZ 86001
Tel.: 602-527-2100 (100%)
Real Estate Developer
S.I.C.: 6552
Richard A. Naille II *(Pres.)*

Hawaiian Discovery Tours, Inc. **(3)**
5200 E. Cortland Blvd.
Flagstaff, AZ 86001
Tel.: 602-527-2100
Inactive
S.I.C.: 4724
Richard A. Naille, II *(Pres.)*

Island Holidays, Ltd. **(3)**
5200 E. Cortland Blvd.
Flagstaff, AZ 86004
Tel.: 602-527-2100 (100%)
Hotel, Resort & Travel Operations
S.I.C.: 7011
Richard A. Naille, II *(Pres.)*

Subsidiary:

Poipu Waste Water Corporation **(4)**
5200 E. Cortland Blvd.
Flagstaff, AZ 86001
Tel.: 602-527-2100 (100%)
S.I.C.: 9511
Richard A. Naille, II *(Pres.)*

Liberty House, Inc. **(3)**
Ala Moana Pacific Center, P.O. Box 2690
Honolulu, HI 96845
Tel.: 808-941-2345 (100%)
Approx.Sls.: $28,100,000
Retail Mdsg.
S.I.C.: 5311
Donald C. Onasch *(Pres.)*

Division:

Liberty House **(4)**
Ala Moana Shopping Center
Honolulu, HI 96803
Tel.: 808-941-2345

JMB Realty Corporation—(Continued)

Retail Mdsg.
S.I.C.: 5311
Donald C. Onasch *(Pres.)*

Arvida **(1)**
7900 Glades Road
Boca Raton, FL 33434
Tel.: 407-479-1100
Approx.Sls.: $300,000,000
Emp.: 3,300
Community Development; Resort Management
S.I.C.: 6552
Roger M. Hall *(Chm. Bd.)*
Ernest M. Miller, Jr. *(Pres.)*
A. L. Sacks *(Exec. V.P.)*
Barbara Sullivan *(Dir. Mktg. Services)*

J.M.P. BAKERY CO., INC.
508 Junius St.
Brooklyn, NY 11212
Tel.: 718-272-5400 **NY**
Fax: 718-272-5427
Year Founded: 1977
Approx.Sls.: $15,000,000
Emp.: 230
Import
Mfr. Italian Bread & Kaiser Rolls
S.I.C.: 2051
Joseph P. Palagonia *(Pres.)*
Chris Palagonia *(Exec. V.P.)*
Anthony Palagonia *(V.P.-Admin.)*
Joseph A. Palagonia *(V.P.-Sls.)*
Frances Palagonia *(Sec.)*
Anil Patel *(Controller)*
Richard Palagonia *(Gen. Mgr.)*
Joesph Barrise *(Dir.-Sls.)*

Outside Service Firm(s):

B. Chipelene*(Auditors)*
Hempstead, NY

Ross, Suchoff & Taroff*(Legal Firm)*
Brooklyn, NY

Chemical Bank*(Major Banking Relationship)*
Westbury, NY

J P FOODSERVICE, INC.
7250 Parkway Dr.
Hanover, MD 21076
Tel.: 410-712-7111 **DE**
Fax: 410-712-4591
Year Founded: 1989
Approx.Sls.: $1,000,000,000
Emp.: 2,400
Groceries & Related Products; Industrial & Personal Service Paper Restaurant Equipment & Supplies; Janitors' Supplies
S.I.C.: 5149; 5113; 5046; 5087
Jim Miller *(Pres. & Chief Exec. Officer)*
Lewis Hay *(Chief Oper. & Chief Fin. Officer)*
Mark Kaiser *(V.P.-Sls. & Mktg. Services)*
Daniel Berliant *(V.P.)*
James Boretos *(V.P.)*
George Megas *(Controller)*

Division:

Monarch Div. **(1)**
7250 Parkway Dr.
Hanover, MD 21076
Tel.: 410-712-7111
Packaged Frozen Foods
S.I.C.: 5142
Jim Miller *(Pres.)*

JPM COMPANY
Rte. 15
Lewisburg, PA 17837
Tel.: 717-524-8200
Fax: 717-524-8181
Year Founded: 1949
Sales Range: $20-39 Million
Emp.: 500
Fiscal Year-end: 9/30/91
Mfr. Wire Assemblies & Harnesses
S.I.C.: 3679
John H. Mathias *(Chm. Bd. & Chief Exec. Officer)*
James P. Mathias *(Pres.)*
John Spangler *(Chief Fin. Officer)*
Charles Kinney *(Dir.-Materials)*
Robert Langton *(Dir.-Quality Assurance)*
Susan K. Mathias *(Dir.-Human Resources)*

No. of Mfg. Plants/Facilities: 3

Computer Systems/Hardware:
IBM

Outside Service Firm(s):

Dreese, Gerhart & Associates*(Auditors)*
Mifflinburg, PA

PMA*(Commercial Insurance Carrier)*
Philadelphia, PA

McQuaide, Blasko, Schwartz, Fleming & Faulkner*(Legal Firm)*
State College, PA

Commonwealth Bank & Trust Co.*(Major Banking Relationship)*
Williamsport, PA

National Retirement Plan Services*(Pension Manager)*
State College, PA

Subsidiary:

The JPM Company of South Carolina, Inc. **(1)**
Route 321
Winnsboro, SC 29180
Tel.: 803-635-6464
Fax: 803-635-3411
Emp.: 215
Mfg. Wire and Cable Assemblies
S.I.C.: 3679
W.H. Brakefield *(V.P. & Plant Mgr.)*

JPS TEXTILE GROUP, INC.
555 N. Pleasantburg Dr., Ste. 202
Greenville, SC 29607
Tel.: 803-271-9919
Fax: 803-271-9939
Approx.Sls.: $800,000,000
Emp.: 9,200
Broadwoven Fabric Mills, Cotton; Apparel & Outerwear Fabrics, Upholstery, Tapestry Fabrics, Fiberglass Fabrics, Automotive Fabrics, Manmade Fiber, Elastic Fabrics
S.I.C.: 2211; 2221
Steven M. Friedman *(Chm. Bd. & Chief Exec. Officer)*
Jerry E. Hunter *(Pres.)*
William H. Gray *(Exec. V.P.-Opers.)*
David H. Taylor *(Exec. V.P.-Fin. & Sec.)*
Monnie Broome *(V.P.-Human Resources)*

Outside Service Firm(s):

NationsBank South Carolina*(Major Banking Relationship)*
Columbia, SC

Subsidiaries:

JPS Automotive **(1)**
29 Stevens St.
Greenville, SC 29605
Tel.: 803-239-2320
S.I.C.: 2221
Robert P. Parks *(Pres.)*

JPS Carpet Corp. **(1)**
P.O. Box A, Hwy. 5
Aberdeen, NC 28315
Tel.: 919-944-2371
S.I.C.: 2281
Paul B. Comiskey *(Chief Oper. Officer)*

JPS Converter & Industrial Corp. **(1)**
33 Stevens St.
Greenville, SC 29605
Tel.: 803-239-4991
Emp.: 4,000
Broadwoven Fabric Mills, Manmade Yarn, Spinning Mills
S.I.C.: 2221; 2281
J.M. Ward *(Chief Oper. Officer)*
Wilford Stowe *(Controller & Sec.)*

JPS Elastomerics Corp. **(1)**
395 Pleasant St.
Northampton, MA 01060
Tel.: 413-586-8750
Fax: 413-584-6348
Approx.Sls.: $100,000,000
Emp.: 550
Mfr. of Calendered & Extruded Elastomeric Products including Natural & Synthetic Rubber & Polyurethane
S.I.C.: 3069; 2241
Lewis M. Coco *(Pres.)*
John Mitchell *(V.P. & Gen. Mgr.-Rubber Prods. Grp.)*
Bruce Wilby *(V.P. & Gen. Mgr.-Construction Prods. Grp.)*
Richard Mario *(Controller)*
Rob Nicoll *(Dir.-Mktg. Communications)*

J & R FILM COMPANY
1135 N. Masnfield
Los Angeles, CA 90038
Tel.: 213-467-3107 **CA**
Fax: 213-466-2201
Sales Range: $10-19 Million
Emp.: 120
Export
Motion Picture Film Editing Equipment & Supplies
S.I.C.: 3861
Joseph Paskal *(Pres.)*
Jim Reichow *(Exec. V.P.)*
Ron Powell *(V.P.-Sls. & Mktg.)*
Betty Paskal *(Sec.)*
Marv Paskal *(Pur. Agent)*

Outside Service Firm(s):

Bank of America NT&SA*(Major Banking Relationship)*
P.O. Box 37002,
San Francisco, CA 94137
Tel.: 415-624-2486

Subsidiary:

Magnasync Moviola Corporation **(1)**
1135 Mansfield Ave.
Hollywood, CA 90038
Tel.: 213-962-0382
Fax: 213-962-8601
Communications Logging Equipment
S.I.C.: 3651; 3861
Joseph Paskal *(Pres.)*
Brett Juris *(Chief Oper. Officer)*
Carl S. Nelson, Jr. *(V.P.-Engrng.)*
Randy Paskal *(V.P.-Mfg.)*
Sally Morrow *(Dir.-Pur.)*

JRN, INC.
201 W. 7th St.
Columbia, TN 38401
Mailing Address:
P.O. Box 1257,
Columbia, TN 38401
Tel.: 615-381-3000 **TN**
Fax: 615-381-1543
Year Founded: 1970
Assets: $53,748,000
Liabilities: $42,557,000
Net Worth: $11,191,000
Approx.Sls.: $59,472,000
Emp.: 1,700
Fiscal Year-end: 12/31/91
Owns & Operates Some Kentucky Fried Chicken Restaurants, James K. Polk Motel
S.I.C.: 5812; 7011
Corporate Giving Program: March of Dimes
John R. Neal *(Chm. Bd. & Pres.)*
Walter A. Lowe *(V.P. & Treas.)*
David G. Neal *(V.P.-Opers.)*
James W. Walsh *(Controller)*
Wally Hebert *(Mgr.-Adv. & Sls. Promo.)*
Debbie Follis *(Mgr.-Data Processing)*
Patrick Smith *(Mgr.-Employee Benefits)*
Steve Dearing *(Mgr.-Real Estate)*
Principal(s):
John R. Neal

No. of U.S. Offices: 1

Computer Systems/Hardware:
Intel File Server; LAN with Advanced Logic R esearch File Server; Compaq PC & Adv. Logic Research PC's

Outside Service Firm(s):

Marlin & Edmondson CPA'S*(Auditors)*
Nashville, TN

Liberty Mutual*(Commercial Insurance Carrier)*
Nashville, TN

Alexander & Alexander*(Commercial Insurance Carrier)*
3319 West End Ave.
Nashville, TN 37202
Tel.: 615-383-9539

RIC Administrators Inc.*(Group Insurer)*
Worthington, OH

Wyatt, Tarrant, Combs, Gilbert & Milom*(Legal Firm)*
Nashville, TN

Wyatt, Tarrant, Combs, Gilbert & Milom*(Legal Firm)*
28th Fl., Citizens Plaza
Louisville, KY 40202
Tel.: 502-589-5235

Third National Bank*(Major Banking Relationship)*
Nashville, TN

JS&A ADVERTISING
3350 Palms Centre Dr.
Las Vegas, NV 89113
Tel.: 702-798-9000
Year Founded: 1965
Approx.Billings: $10,000,000
Emp.: 10
Mail Order Adv.
Joseph Sugarman *(Chm., Creative & Mktg. Dir.)*
Mary Stanke *(Pres. & Sec.)*

JS&A GROUP, INC.
3350 Palms Ctr. Dr.
Las Vegas, NV 89103
Tel.: 702-597-2000
Fax: 702-597-2002
Year Founded: 1971
Approx.Sls.: $25,000,000
Emp.: 50
National Mktg. Organization
S.I.C.: 7389
Joseph Sugarman *(Chm. Bd.)*
Mary Stanke *(Pres.)*
Wendy Sugarman *(Treas.)*
George Gerstman *(Legal Officer)*

Outside Service Firm(s):

Bell, Boyd & Lloyd*(Legal Firm)*
Three First National Plaza
Chicago, IL 60602
Tel.: 312-372-1121

Glenview State Bank*(Major Banking Relationship)*
Glenview, IL

JWG ASSOCIATES
888 Worcester Rd.
Wellesley, MA 02181
Tel.: 617-235-6800
Year Founded: 1979
Approx.Billings: $18,000,000
Emp.: 50
James W. Goldman *(Pres.)*

JWK INTERNATIONAL CORP.
Ste. 1000, 7617 Little River Turnpike
Annandale, VA 22003
Tel.: 703-750-0500 **VA**
Fax: 703-256-1986
Year Founded: 1973

Sales Range: $10-19 Million
Emp.: 300
Fiscal Year-end: 12/31/89
Export
Research & Development; Social & Economic Program Planning
S.I.C.: 8999
Dr. Jay W. Khim *(Chm. Bd., Pres. & Chief Exec. Officer)*
Millie Khim *(Treas.)*

Computer Systems/Hardware:
IBM PC

Outside Service Firm(s):

Coopers & Lybrand*(Auditors)*
Washington, DC

Blue Cross & Blue Shield of Virginia*(Group Insurer)*
2015 Staples Mill Rd.
Richmond, VA 23230
Tel.: 804-359-7000
Fax: 804-354-7397

Signet Bank*(Major Banking Relationship)*
McLean, VA

JABIL CIRCUIT INC.
(Formerly Jabil Circuit Company)
10800 Roosevelt Blvd.
Saint Petersburg, FL 33716
Tel.: 813-577-9749
Fax: 813-577-3926
Approx.Sls.: $57,000,000
Emp.: 540
Manufacture Circuit Boards
S.I.C.: 3679
William Morean *(Chief Exec. Officer)*
Tom Sansone *(Pres.)*
Tim Main *(V.P.-Bus. Devel.)*
Nolan Holzapfel *(Dir.-Pur.)*
Ronald J. Rapp *(Treas.)*

Outside Service Firm(s):

KPMG Peat Marwick*(Auditors)*
St. Petersburg, FL

Barnett Banks Trust Company, N.A.*(Major Banking Relationship)*
St. Petersburg, FL

Jac Pac Food Sales
(See Granite State Packing Co. Listing)

JACKES-EVANS MFG. CO.
(Sub. of GSW Inc., GSW Bldg. Prods. Div., Hamilton, ON)
4427 Geraldine Ave.
Saint Louis, MO 63115
Tel.: 314-385-4132
Fax: 314-385-0802
Approx.Sls.: $18,000,000
Emp.: 250
St. Louis Blue Stove Pipe & Accessories; Class A Stove Pipe; Fireplace & BBQ Accessories
S.I.C.: 3444; 3433; 3429
Edward Sepanik *(Pres.)*
Bob Winkler *(V.P.-Sls.)*
Joan Daab *(Mktg. Coord.)*

JACKSON HOLE SKI RESORT
7658 N. Teewinot, Chairlift Rd.
Teton Village, WY 83025
Mailing Address:
P.O. Box 290,
Teton Village, WY 83025
Tel.: 307-733-2292
Fax: 307-733-2660
Year Founded: 1963
Approx.Sls.: $10,500,000
Emp.: 90
Fiscal Year-end: 9/30/91
Winter & Summer Resort
S.I.C.: 7011
Paul McCollister *(Chm. Bd., Pres. & Chief Exec. Officer)*
Michael McCollister *(V.P.-Opers.)*
Holly McCollister *(V.P. & Personnel Dir.)*
Harry Baxter *(V.P. & Dir.-Public Rels.)*
Barb Fields *(Treas. & Dir.-Accounting)*
Steve Duerr *(Gen. Counsel)*
Kari Gemmel *(Mktg. & Intl. Sls. Dir.)*
Bill Lewkowitz *(Natl. Sls. Dir.)*
Richard Ray *(Mgr.-Data Processing)*

Computer Systems/Hardware:
MacIntosh

JACKSON MILLS, INC.
One Railroad St.
Wellford, SC 29385
Mailing Address:
P.O. Box 219
Wellford, SC 29385
Tel.: 803-439-3011 **DE**
Fax: 803-439-3011, Ext. 272
Approx.Sls.: $56,000,000
Emp.: 890
Fiscal Year-end: 9/30/92
Cotton, Cotton & Polyester Broad Woven Fabrics; Yarn; Manufacturer for Griege Fabrics for Home Furnishings and Apparel
S.I.C.: 2211; 2221
George E. Stone *(Chm.)*
G.C. Harris, Jr. *(Pres. & Chief Exec. Officer)*
Arnie Applebaum *(V.P. & Sec.)*
James W. Walch, III *(V.P.-Sls.)*
Richard Clayton *(V.P.)*

No. of Mfg. Plants/Facilities: 2
No. of U.S. Offices: 3

Outside Service Firm(s):

Ernst & Young*(Auditors)*
C & S Bank Tower, Two Shelter Centre, Ste. 800
Greenville, SC 29603

Nelson Mullins Riley & Scarborough*(Legal Firm)*
301 N. Main Street
Greenville, SC 29601

Trust Company Bank*(Major Banking Relationship)*
Stock Trans. Dept. P.O.B. 4625, Trust Company of Georgia Bldg.
Atlanta, GA 30302
Tel.: 404-588-7831

JACKSON PACKING CO. INC.
P.O. Box 113
Jackson, MS 39205
Tel.: 601-355-8351
Fax: 601-355-7026
Approx.Sls.: $1,000,000,000
Emp.: 300
Meat Processors
S.I.C.: 2011
H.S. Clark *(Pres. & Chief Exec. Officer)*

No. of Mfg. Plants/Facilities: 1

Computer Systems/Hardware:
IBM

Outside Service Firm(s):

KPMG Peat Marwick*(Auditors)*
One Jackson Place,
Jackson, MS 39201
Tel.: 601-354-3701
Fax: 601-354-3745

Blue Cross & Blue Shield of Mississippi, Inc.*(Group Insurer)*
P.O. Box 1043
Jackson, MS 39215
Tel.: 601-932-3704

Wells, Moore, Simmons & Neeld*(Legal Firm)*
P.O. Box 1970, 1300 Deposit Guarantee Plaza
Jackson, MS 39215-1970
Tel.: 601-354-5400

Deposit Guaranty National Bank*(Major Banking Relationship)*
One Deposit Guaranty Plaza,
Jackson, MS 39201

JACKSON PAPER COMPANY
197 N. Gallatin St.
Jackson, MS 39207
Tel.: 601-352-0837 **MS**
Year Founded: 1921
Approx.Sls.: $26,000,000
Emp.: 130
Wholesale Distributor of Fine Paper; Paper & Products, Wrapping or Course; Janitorial Supplies
S.I.C.: 5111; 5113; 5087
James P. Archer *(Chm. Bd.)*
Charles W. Baker *(Pres. & Chief Exec. Officer)*
B.J. Graves *(Exec. V.P.)*
James Thompson *(Exec. V.P.)*
Frank Cupit *(V.P.)*
Tommy Galyean *(V.P.)*

Outside Service Firm(s):

KPMG Peat Marwick*(Auditors)*
One Jackson Place,
Jackson, MS 39201
Tel.: 601-354-3701
Fax: 601-354-3745

Deposit Guaranty National Bank*(Major Banking Relationship)*
One Deposit Guaranty Plaza,
Jackson, MS 39201

Trustmark Bank*(Major Banking Relationship)*
PO Box 291,
Jackson, MS 39205

Subsidiaries:

Newell Paper Co. of Columbus **(1)**
1616 7th Ave., S.
Volumnud, MO 39708
Tel.: 601-327-1467
Wholesale Distributor of Fine Paper; Paper & Products, Wrapping or Coarse; Janitorial Supplies
S.I.C.: 5111; 5113; 5087
James Thompson *(Pres.)*

Newell Paper Co. of Meridian **(1)**
2502 Front St.
Meridian, MS 39302
Tel.: 601-693-1783
Wholesale Distributor of Fine Paper; Paper & Products, Wrapping or Coarse; Janitorial Supplies
S.I.C.: 5111; 5113; 5087
Tommy Galyean *(Gen. Mgr.)*

JACKSON PRODUCTS CORP.
15365 Hwy. 22
Lexington, TN 38351
Tel.: 901-968-5753
Approx.Sls.: $20,000,000
Emp.: 30
Fiscal Year-end: 9/30/90
Restaurant Equip.
S.I.C.: 3589
Terry Crouch *(Pres.)*
Martin Schenk *(V.P.-Sls. & Mktg.)*

JACMAR COMPANIES, INC.
2200 W. Valley Blvd.
Alhambra, CA 91803
Tel.: 818-576-0737
Fax: 818-458-9224
Approx.Sls.: $40,000,000
Emp.: 25
Fiscal Year-end: 10/31/90
Franchising of Shakey's Restaurants in Los Angeles Area; Wholesale Food Service Distr.; Uniforms & Aprons
S.I.C.: 5812; 6794; 2337; 2326; 2399
William H. Tilley *(Pres. & Owner)*
Robert R. Hill *(Exec. V.P.)*
Jim Dal Pozzo *(Chief Fin. Officer)*
Frank Visvikis *(Gen. Mgr.)*
Stacey Comstock *(Dir.-Mktg.)*

Subsidiaries:

Design USA **(1)**
2200 W. Valley Blvd.
Alhambra, CA 91803
Tel.: 818-570-1960
Fax: 818-458-9224
Uniforms & Aprons
S.I.C.: 2326; 2337; 2399
Joe Wilson *(Gen. Mgr.)*

Jacmar Development Corp. **(1)**
2200 W. Valley Blvd.
Alhambra, CA 91803
Tel.: 818-570-1960
Fax: 818-458-9224

JACOBS & GERBER, INC.
731 N. Fairfax
Los Angeles, CA 90046
Tel.: 213-655-4082
Year Founded: 1974
Approx.Billings: $25,000,000
Emp.: 32
Broadcast And Entertainment Advertising And Promotion
Albert Litewka *(Pres. & Chief Exec. Officer)*
Barbara Breest *(V.P., Fin. & Admin.)*
Susan Kantor *(V.P., Client Services)*

JAC JACOBSEN INDUSTRIES, INC.
67 Holly Hill Ln.
Greenwich, CT 06830
Mailing Address:
P.O. Box 4207
Greenwich, CT 06830
Tel.: 203-869-9330 **NY**
Fax: 203-869-9537
Year Founded: 1938
Approx.Rev.: $85,000,000
Emp.: 1,000
Fiscal Year-end: 12/31/90
Mfr. of Lighting Fixtures
S.I.C.: 3645; 3646
Robert N. Haidinger *(Chm. Bd., Pres. & Chief Exec. Officer)*
Charles J. Florio *(V.P. & Controller)*
Harry J. Keenan *(V.P.-Human Resources)*
C. Joseph Incrocci *(V.P.)*
Martin T. Tell *(Chief Fin. Officer & Treas.)*
Donald A. Herner *(Gen. Counsel & Sec.)*
Stephanie Reiss *(Dir.-Personnel)*

No. of Mfg. Plants/Facilities: 13
No. of U.S. Offices: 12

Outside Service Firm(s):

Deloitte & Touche*(Auditors)*
1600 Summer St.
Stamford, CT 06905-5121
Tel.: 203-351-4600

Metropolitan Life Insurance Co.*(Commercial Insurance Carrier)*
One Madison Ave.
New York, NY 10010-3690
Tel.: 215-578-9292

Metropolitan Life Insurance Co.*(Group Insurer)*
One Madison Ave.
New York, NY 10010-3690
Tel.: 215-578-9292

DNC America Banking Corp.*(International Bank Affiliate)*
600 Fifth Ave.
New York, NY 10020
Tel.: 212-315-6500
Fax: 212-307-1589

Anderson, Kill, Olick & Oshinsky*(Legal Firm)*
New York, NY

J. Henry Schroder Bank & Trust Co.*(Major Banking Relationship)*
One State St.
New York, NY 10015
Tel.: 212-269-6500

Jac Jacobsen Industries, Inc.—(Continued)

Connecticut National Bank*(Major Banking Relationship)*
777 Main St.
Hartford, CT 06115
Tel.: 203-728-2000

George Buck Associates*(Pension Manager)*
Two Pennsylvania Plaza
New York, NY 10001
Tel.: 212-330-1050

Subsidiaries:

Alkco Lighting Company **(1)**
11500 W. Melrose Ave.
Franklin Park, IL 60131
Tel.: 708-451-0700 (100%)
Fax: 708-451-7512
Mfr. of Lighting Fixtures
S.I.C.: 3646
C. Joseph Incrocci *(V.P. & Gen. Mgr.)*

Burton Medical Products Corporation **(1)**
7922 Haskell Ave.
Van Nuys, CA 91406
Tel.: 818-989-4700 (100%)
Fax: 818-989-3250
Mfr. of Lighting Fixtures for Medical Lighting Market
S.I.C.: 3646
Robert Christianson *(V.P. & Gen. Mgr.)*

Guth Lighting Company **(1)**
2615 Washington Blvd.
Saint Louis, MO 63103
Tel.: 314-533-3200 (100%)
Fax: 314-533-9127
Emp.: 100
Fiscal Year-end: 1/30/91
Import Export
Mfr. of Lighting Fixtures
S.I.C.: 3646
C. Joseph Incrocci *(Acting Gen. Mgr.)*
Sue Pries *(Controller)*
Craig Brauks *(Mgr.-Mfg.)*
Walter B. Coleman *(Dir.-Sls.)*

High-Lites, Inc. **(1)**
2142 Thomaston Ave.
Waterbury, CT 06704
Tel.: 203-575-2044
Fax: 203-574-3289
Mfr. of Lighting Fixtures
S.I.C.: 3646; 3645
Charles J. Florio *(Acting V.P. & Gen. Mgr.)*

MWC Lighting Systems, Inc. **(1)**
10870 Kalama River Rd.
Fountain Valley, CA 92708
Tel.: 714-962-2286 (100%)
Fax: 714-964-2502
Emp.: 34
Mfr. of Commercial & Industrial Lighting Systems
S.I.C.: 3645; 3646

Nessen Lamps **(1)**
36 Midland Ave.
Port Chester, NY 10573
Tel.: 914-934-1300
Fax: 914-934-8052
Mfr. of Lighting Fixtures
S.I.C.: 3645
Robert N. Haidinger, Jr. *(V.P. & Gen. Mgr.)*

Quality Lighting, Inc. **(1)**
11530 Melrose Ave.
Franklin Park, IL 60131
Tel.: 708-451-0040
Fax: 708-451-6768
Mfr. of Lighting Fixtures
S.I.C.: 3645; 3646
Perry Romano *(V.P. & Gen. Mgr.)*

South Coast Lighting Systems **(1)**
2200 S. Anne St.
Santa Ana, CA 92704
Tel.: 714-549-9765 (100%)
Fax: 714-662-4515
Mfr. of Lighting Fixtures
S.I.C.: 3646
Gerald Overheu *(V.P. & Gen. Mgr.)*

Specialty Lighting **(1)**
Washburn Switch Rd.
Shelby, NC 28151
Tel.: 704-482-3416
Fax: 704-484-0818
Mfr. of Lighting Fixtures
S.I.C.: 3645; 3646
H. Manfred Schellpfeffer *(V.P. & Gen. Mgr.)*

Troy/Trak Lighting, Inc. **(1)**
14625 E. Clark Ave.
City of Industry, CA 91746
Tel.: 818-336-4511 (100%)
Fax: 818-330-4266
Emp.: 275
Mfr. of Residential & Commercial Track Lighting
S.I.C.: 3645; 3646
Todd Langner *(V.P. & Gen. Mgr.)*

JACOBSEN MANUFACTURING, INC.
901 Fourth St., N.
Safety Harbor, FL 34695
Tel.: 813-726-1138 **FL**
Fax: 813-726-7019
Year Founded: 1975
Approx.Sls.: $31,000,000
Emp.: 165
Mfr. of Mobile Homes, Except Recreational
S.I.C.: 2451
William R. Jacobsen *(Pres.)*
Sid Boughton *(Sec.)*
Mik Trevino *(Dir.-Engrng.)*
Dennis Schrader *(Gen. Mgr.)*
Mike Davis *(Pur. Agent)*

Outside Service Firm(s):

Gregory, Sharer & Stuart*(Auditors)*
Tampa, FL

Sun Bank, N.A.*(Major Banking Relationship)*
Tampa, FL

JACOBSON ROST, INC.
529 Ontario Ave.
Sheboygan, WI 53081
Mailing Address:
P.O. Box 1027,
Sheboygan, WI 53082
Tel.: 414-458-3541
Tel.: 800-468-7355
Year Founded: 1956
Approx.Billings: $25,000,000
Emp.: 65
Business-to-Business, Food & Packaged Goods
Tryg Jacobson *(Chm. Bd.)*
Jon Rost *(Pres.)*
Matt Schultz *(Dir. of Pub. Rels.)*
Paula Zenk *(Office Mgr.)*

Computer Systems/Hardware:
Macintosh

JACQUES MORET, INC.
1350 Broadway
New York, NY 10018
Tel.: 212-736-0041
Fax: 212-714-0031
Year Founded: 1975
Approx.Sls.: $80,000,000
Emp.: 85
Import Export
Mfr. Women's Sports Apparel
S.I.C.: 2331; 2339; 5137; 2369
Ralph Harary *(Chm. Bd.)*
Joe Harary *(Pres.)*
Alan Shapiro *(V.P.-Adv. & Mktg.)*
Irwin Luxenberg *(Controller)*
Leslie Sexer *(Dir.-Pub. Rels.)*

Computer Systems/Hardware:
UNIX

CHARLES JACQUIN ET CIE, INC.
2633 Trenton Ave.
Philadelphia, PA 19125
Tel.: 215-425-9300
Fax: 215-425-9438
Year Founded: 1884
Approx.Sls.: $100,000,000
Emp.: 275
Fiscal Year-end: 9/30/90
Mfr. & Importer of Liquors & Wines
S.I.C.: 2084; 2085; 5182
Norton J. Cooper *(Pres. & Chief Exec. Officer)*
Kevin O'Brian *(V.P.-Mktg.)*
Paul Stefan *(V.P.)*
Conrad Ekart *(Chief Fin. Officer)*
William Heinz *(Pur. Agent & Plant Mgr.)*

Principal(s):
Norton J. Cooper

Computer Systems/Hardware:
DEC VAX 11/750

Outside Service Firm(s):

BDO Seidman*(Auditors)*
Philadelphia, PA

Schnader, Harrison, Segal & Lewis*(Legal Firm)*
1600 Market Street
Philadelphia, PA 19103
Tel.: 215-751-2000

Fidelity Bank*(Major Banking Relationship)*
Broad & Walnut St.
Philadelphia, PA 19109

Subsidiary:

Saxony Distillers Et Cie, Inc. **(1)**
2633 Trenton Ave.
Philadelphia, PA 19125
Tel.: 215-425-9300
S.I.C.: 2084; 2085

don jagoda associates, inc.

DON JAGODA ASSOCIATES, INC.
100 Marcus Dr.
Melville, NY 11747
Tel.: 516-454-1800
Fax: 516-454-1833
Year Founded: 1962
Approx.Billings: $15,000,000
Emp.: 125
Development & Implementation of Sls. Promo. Programs, Sweepstakes, Incentives, Games, Group Travel, Refunds, POS, Collateral, Fulfillment & Entertainment Mktg.
Don Jagoda *(Pres.)*
Syd Jagoda *(Exec. V.P.)*
Leonard Daykin *(Sr. V.P.)*
Bruce Hollander *(Sr. V.P.)*
John Zamoiski *(Sr. V.P.)*
Chris Bragas *(V.P., Fin.)*
Jack Burlick *(V.P.)*
Steve Caputo *(V.P.)*
Marvin Racer *(V.P., Pur.)*
Tammy Weiler *(Dir., Travel Services)*

JAMECO INDUSTRIES, INC.
248 Wyandanch Ave.
Wyandanch, NY 11798
Tel.: 516-643-5300
Fax: 516-643-5305
Year Founded: 1931
Approx.Sls.: $42,000,000
Emp.: 300
Import Export
Mfr. & Distributor of Miscellaneous Plumbing Products
S.I.C.: 3432; 5074
Harry Lipman *(Chm. Bd. & Chief Exec. Officer)*
Michael Lipman *(Pres. & Chief Oper. Officer)*
Sidney Greenberg *(Sr. V.P.-Sls.)*
G. Lewin *(Sr. V.P.-Mktg.)*
Terry Entrekin *(V.P.-Sls.)*
Joel Sandberg *(V.P, Sec., Fin. & Personnel)*

Outside Service Firm(s):

KPMG Peat Marwick*(Auditors)*
1 Jericho Plaza
Jericho, NY 11753
Tel.: 516-822-9100

Salamon, Gruber & Blaymore*(Legal Firm)*
New York, NY

Marine Midland Bank*(Major Banking Relationship)*
Melville, NY

JAMES BUILDING CORPORATION
1535 Lake Cook Rd., Ste. 302
Northbrook, IL 60062
Tel.: 708-564-7720
Fax: 708-564-5175
Emp.: 300
Real Estate Investment & Development
S.I.C.: 6552; 6531; 6798
Edward R. James *(Pres.)*
Jerry S. James *(V.P.)*

Computer Systems/Hardware:
Microdata

Outside Service Firm(s):

Philip Rootberg*(Auditors)*
Chicago, IL

American National Bank & Trust Company of Chicago*(Major Banking Relationship)*
33 N. LaSalle St.
Chicago, IL 60602
Tel.: 312-661-5000
Fax: 312-661-6417

JAMES CHEVROLET INC.
35500 S. Gratiot
Mount Clemens, MI 48043
Tel.: 313-791-1010
Fax: 313-791-0834
Approx.Sls.: $47,500,000
Emp.: 69
Automobile Dealership
S.I.C.: 5511
James F. Causley, Jr. *(Pres.)*
James A. Weiss *(Sec. & Treas.)*
Dick Milne *(Sls. Mgr.-New Cars)*

T.L. JAMES & COMPANY
106 West Mississippi Ave.
Ruston, LA 71270
Mailing Address:
P.O. Box 1260
Ruston, LA 71273-1260
Tel.: 318-255-7912 **LA**
Fax: 318-255-3129
Year Founded: 1926
Sales Range: $100-499 Million
Emp.: 2,500
Fiscal Year-end: 12/31/90
Construction & Forestry Production
S.I.C.: 0851; 1629
G.W. James, Jr. *(Chm. Bd.)*
William J. Dessy *(Vice Chm., Pres. & Chief Exec. Officer)*
Lance F. Bosfflub *(Chief Fin. Officer)*
Jimmy Love *(Sr. V.P. & Sec.)*
Thomas James Folk, Jr. *(Group V.P.)*
L.A. Hubert, Jr. *(Group V.P.)*
Paul E. Hurley *(Group V.P.)*
George W. James, III *(Group V.P.)*
Thomas Lewis Love *(V.P.)*
W.T. Westbrook *(V.P.)*
Glenn Echols *(V.P.-Admin. Services)*
Thomas E. Brantley *(V.P.-Fin. & Acctng.)*
Felton W. Barlow *(Treas.)*
Rickey Hickman *(Controller)*
Freddie J. Baragona, Jr. *(Mgr.-Payroll & Employee Benefits)*

No. of U.S. Offices: 15

Computer Systems/Hardware:
IBM AS/400

Outside Service Firm(s):

Arthur Andersen & Co.*(Auditors)*
201 St. Charles Ave., Ste. 4500
New Orleans, LA 70170

Aetna Life & Casualty*(Group Insurer)*
151 Farmington Avenue
Hartford, CT 06156
Tel.: 203-273-2128
Fax: 203-729-4295

Dawkins, Coyle & Carter*(Legal Firm)*
Ruston, LA

Jones Walker*(Legal Firm)*
New Orleans, LA

NationsBank Texas*(Major Banking Relationship)*
1707 Pacific St.
Dallas, TX 75201
Tel.: 214-922-5000

Commercial National Bank*(Pension Manager)*
Shreveport, LA

Lincoln National Corporation*(Pension Manager)*
P.O. Box 2249
Fort Wayne, IN 46801

ROBERT JAMES SALES INC.
269 Hinman Ave.
Buffalo, NY 14216
Mailing Address:
P.O. Box 1672,
Buffalo, NY 14216
Tel.: 716-874-6300
Fax: 716-874-6308
Year Founded: 1972
Sales Range: $20-39 Million
Emp.: 135
Fiscal Year-end: 12/31/90
Distr. Stainless Steel Pipe, Valves & Fittings; Mfr. Sanitary Pipe Fittings
S.I.C.: 5051; 3494
Robert Glidden *(Chm. Bd.)*
James Bokor *(Pres.)*
William Barto *(V.P.-Sls.)*
Robert D. Glidden, Jr. *(V.P.-Fin. & Treas.)*
James Schmit *(Sec.)*
John McKenna *(Controller)*
Frank Lazzaro *(Gen. Mgr.)*
Jonathan Duffett *(Dir.-Data Processing)*
Bill Franz *(Dir.-Pur.)*
Terry Smith *(Dir.-Sls.)*
James Bokor, Jr. *(Mgr.-Quality Assurance)*
Principal(s):
James Bokor
Robert D. Glidden, Jr.

No. of Mfg. Plants/Facilities: 7
No. of U.S. Offices: 7

Computer Systems/Hardware:
IBM System 36

Outside Service Firm(s):

KPMG Peat Marwick*(Auditors)*
Buffalo, NY

Matthews, Bartlett & Dedecker*(Commercial Insurance Carrier)*
Buffalo, NY

Lawrence Healthcare*(Group Insurer)*
Schenectady, NY

Damon & Morey*(Legal Firm)*
1000 Cathedral Plaza
Buffalo, NY
Tel.: 716-856-5500
Fax: 716-856-5510

Northeast Consulting*(Pension Manager)*
11 Commerce Dr.
Cranford, NJ 07016
Tel.: 908-709-1600
Fax: 908-709-1615

TOM JAMES COMPANY
690 E. Lamar Blvd., Ste. 350
Arlington, TX 76011
Tel.: 817-548-7198
Fax: 817-548-5793
Year Founded: 1967
Approx.Sls.: $65,000,000
Emp.: 1,200
Mfr. & Retail Stores For Men's & Boys Clothing
S.I.C.: 5611; 2311
James McEachern *(Chm. Bd. & Chief Exec. Officer)*
Robert Sherrer *(Pres.)*
Phil Williams *(Controller)*
James Woodard *(Treas.)*

Subsidiary:

Tom James Of Atlanta, Inc. **(1)**
2800 N. Druid Hills Rd.
Atlanta, GA 30329
Tel.: 404-636-0900
Approx.Sls.: $2,000,000
Emp.: 32
Retail Store For Men's & Boys Clothing
S.I.C.: 5611
Spencer Hays *(Chm. Bd.)*
James McEachern *(Chief Exec. Officer)*
Robert Sherrer *(Pres.)*
Dorothy Fudge *(Treas. & Sec.)*

JAMISON BEDDING, INC.
Highway 31
Franklin, TN 37064
Mailing Address:
P.O. Box 518,
Franklin, TN 37065
Tel.: 615-794-1883
Fax: 615-794-2254
Year Founded: 1883
Approx.Sls.: $25,000,000
Emp.: 300
Fiscal Year-end: 12/31/90
Mfr. Bedding & Upholstered Furniture
S.I.C.: 2515; 2512
Frank Gorell *(Pres.)*
Thomas Wade *(Exec. V.P.)*

JAMISON, CAWDREY, BENJAMIN
130 Sutter St.
San Francisco, CA 94104
Tel.: 415-398-2848
Fax: 415-394-6974
Year Founded: 1982
Approx.Billings: $19,000,000
Emp.: 30
Retail, Franchise, Business-to-Business, Financial
David Jamison *(Pres.)*
Gary Benjamin *(Exec. V.P.)*
Marc Cawdrey *(Exec. V.P.)*

Computer Systems/Hardware:
Apple

JAMISON DOOR COMPANY
P.O. Box 70
Hagerstown, MD 21741-0070
Tel.: 301-733-3100
Fax: 301-791-7339
Year Founded: 1906
Sales Range: $10-19 Million
Export
Mfr. of Cold Storage, Sound Reduction & Other Specialty Engineered Doors
S.I.C.: 3442
John Vincent Jamison III *(Chm. Bd.)*
Roland F. Smith *(Pres. & Chief Exec. Officer)*
George Hamilton *(Mgr.-Adv.)*
Tom Johnson *(Mgr.-Plant)*
Robert L. Ruby *(Pur. Agent)*

Outside Service Firm(s):

Deloitte & Touche*(Auditors)*
1100 Mercantile Bank Bldg., 2 Hopkins Plaza
Baltimore, MD 21201
Tel.: 410-576-6700

Urner, Narin, Barton & Williams*(Legal Firm)*
Hagerstown, MD

First National Bank of Maryland*(Major Banking Relationship)*
Hagerstown, MD

JAMISON PLASTIC CORPORATION
5001 Crackersport Rd.
Allentown, PA 18104
Tel.: 215-391-1400
Fax: 215-391-1414
Approx.Sls.: $12,000,000
Emp.: 150
Injection Molded Plastic Products
S.I.C.: 3089
J. Bonifazio *(Chief Exec. Officer)*
Marc Solda *(Pres. & Treas.)*
Arthur Murphy *(Controller)*
Charles Stanko *(Gen. Mgr.)*
Cesar Solda *(Pur. Agent)*

Outside Service Firm(s):

Olvany, Eisner & Donnelly*(Legal Firm)*
New York, NY

Meridian Bank*(Major Banking Relationship)*
Allentown, PA

JAN-CO., INC.
35 Sockanosset Cross Rd.
Cranston, RI 02920
Tel.: 401-946-4000 **RI**
Fax: 401-946-4392
Year Founded: 1969
Approx.Sls.: $65,000,000
Emp.: 2,000
Sells Franchises For Fast Food Restaurant Chains
S.I.C.: 6794
Nicholas Janikies *(Pres.)*
Leslely S. Rich *(V.P.-Admin.)*
Cynthia Janikies *(Controller)*
Margaret R. Janikies *(Treas.)*

JANDY INDUSTRIES
21 Pimentel Ct.
Novato, CA 94948-6101
Mailing Address:
P.O. Box 6101,
Novato, CA 94948-6101
Tel.: 415-382-8220
Tel.: 800-227-1442 **CA**
Fax: 415-382-0820
Fax: 415-382-3091(Purchasing)
Year Founded: 1958
Assets: $6,000,000
Liabilities: $1,000,000
Net Worth: $5,000,000
Approx.Sls.: $13,000,000
Emp.: 80
Fiscal Year-end: 12/31/90
Import Export
Mfr. Service Industry Machines
S.I.C.: 3589
Andrew L. Pansini *(Chm. Bd.)*
Andrew A. Pansini *(Pres.)*
Vance Gillette *(Exec. V.P.)*
Tom Bale *(V.P.-Fin.)*
David Pansini *(Treas. & Sec.)*
Ken Jones *(Gen. Counsel)*
John Goldstein *(Dir.-Mktg.)*
Gene Lawler *(Dir.-Mfg.)*
Sue Paterson *(Dir.-Pur.)*
Robert Gould *(Mgr.-Engrng.)*
Dan Jostedt *(Mgr.-Sls.)*
Mary Nastasuk *(Mgr.-Personnel)*
Principal(s):
Andrew L. Pansini
Andrew A. Pansini

No. of Mfg. Plants/Facilities: 1
No. of U.S. Offices: 1

Computer Systems/Hardware:
AS 400

Outside Service Firm(s):

BDO Seidman*(Auditors)*
San Francisco, CA

Fred S. James*(Commercial Insurance Carrier)*
Portland, OR

Aetna Life & Casualty*(Group Insurer)*
151 Farmington Avenue
Hartford, CT 06156
Tel.: 203-273-2128
Fax: 203-729-4295

Feldman, Waldman & Kline*(Legal Firm)*
San Francisco, CA

Wells Fargo Bank*(Major Banking Relationship)*
420 Montgomery St.
San Francisco, CA 94104

The Principal Financial Group*(Pension Manager)*
711 High St.
Des Moines, IA 50309
Tel.: 515-247-4593
Tel.: 800-543-4015

JANI KING INTERNATIONAL, INC.
4950 Keller Springs, Ste. 190
Dallas, TX 75248
Tel.: 214-991-0900
Tel.: 800-552-5264
Fax: 214-239-7706
Year Founded: 1969
Approx.Sls.: $55,000,000
Emp.: 400
Maintenance
S.I.C.: 7349
Jim Cavanaugh *(Pres.)*
James A. Cavanaugh, Sr. *(Pres.-Jani-King Leasing, Inc.)*
Jerry Crawford *(Pres.-Jani-King Franchising, Inc.)*

Outside Service Firm(s):

Scott Bryan & Co.*(Auditors)*
Dallas, TX

Frontier Bank*(Major Banking Relationship)*
La Palma, CA

North Dallas Bank & Trust*(Major Banking Relationship)*
Dallas, TX

Subsidiaries:

Jani King of California, Inc. **(1)**
1 Centerpointe Dr., Ste. 330
La Palma, CA 90623
Tel.: 213-921-5413
Jim Cavanaugh *(Chm. Bd.)*
Gene Nunn *(Pres.)*
Jeff Freeman *(V.P.)*
Richard Robison *(V.P.)*

Jani King, Inc. **(1)**
4950 Keller Springs
Dallas, TX 75248
Tel.: 214-991-0900
Tel.: 800-552-5264
Maintenance
S.I.C.: 7349
Ted Hirst *(Pres.)*

JANIK & ASSOCIATES, INC.
Ste. 610, 1901 Ave. of The Stars
Los Angeles, CA 90067
Tel.: 310-552-8281
Fax: 310-552-7867
Year Founded: 1979
Approx.Billings: $20,000,000
Emp.: 7
Richard A. Janik *(Pres. & Chief Exec. Officer)*
Julie Manton *(Billing Supvr., Traffic Mgr. & Admin. Asst.)*

JANLYNN CORPORATION
34 Front St.
Indian Orchard, MA 01151
Tel.: 413-543-3091
Fax: 800-526-5966
Approx.Sls.: $10,000,000
Emp.: 100
Fiscal Year-end: 12/31/90
Mfr. Needlecraft, Stitchery Kits & Related Access.
S.I.C.: 3944
Edward F. Kozub *(Pres.)*
Norman B. Wagner *(Gen. Counsel)*
Nancy Joyce *(Mgr.-Admin.)*
John F. Kozub *(Mgr.-Sls.)*
Robert S. Kozub *(Mgr.-Plant)*

JAPAN TRAVEL BUREAU INTERNATIONAL, INC.
One Rockefeller Plaza, Ste. 1250
New York, NY 10020
Tel.: 212-247-2583
Fax: 212-265-7234
Year Founded: 1960
Approx.Sls.: $1,000,000,000
Emp.: 1,400
Fiscal Year-end: 3/31/92
Package, Convention, Group & Individual Tours
S.I.C.: 4725
Shunichi Oyama *(Pres.)*
Hironori Honsho *(V.P.)*
Takato Ayabe *(Controller)*
Koichi Fukuroe *(Gen. Mgr.-Wholesale)*
Kazuo Hirai *(Mgr.-Mktg. & Plng.)*
E. Sakashita *(Mgr.-Admin.)*

Outside Service Firm(s):

KPMG Peat Marwick*(Auditors)*
345 Park Ave.
New York, NY 10154
Tel.: 212-758-9700
Fax: 212-872-3308

Bank of Tokyo*(Major Banking Relationship)*
New York, NY

JAPS-OLSON COMPANY
30 N. 31st Ave.
Minneapolis, MN 55411-1694
Tel.: 612-522-4461
Tel.: 800-548-2897 **MN**
Fax: 612-522-3837
Year Founded: 1907
Approx.Sls.: $47,000,000
Emp.: 350
Fiscal Year-end: 12/31/90
Printing, Packaging & Mailing
S.I.C.: 2752; 2759; 7389
William N. Beddor *(Chm. Bd.)*
Robert E. Murphy *(Pres.)*

Principal(s):
William N. Beddor
Robert E. Murphy

No. of Mfg. Plants/Facilities: 2
No. of U.S. Offices: 1

Outside Service Firm(s):

House, Nezerka & Froelich*(Auditors)*
Minneapolis, MN

National City Bank*(Major Banking Relationship)*
Rome, GA

JARCHEM INDUSTRIES, INC.
40 Ball St.
Newark, NJ 07105
Tel.: 201-344-0600 **NJ**
Fax: 201-344-5743
Sales Range: $10-19 Million
Emp.: 42
Import Export
Mfr. of Pharmaceutical Preservatives & Acetate Salts for Food, Textile, Photographic & Chemical Processing Industries
S.I.C.: 2899
Arnold Stern *(Pres.)*
Julius N. Bauer *(V.P.-Opers.)*
Robert Honig *(V.P.)*
Stephen Winer *(Gen. Mgr.)*

Outside Service Firm(s):

Seymour Kriegsman & Co.*(Auditors)*
New York, NY

Cuccio & Cuccio*(Legal Firm)*
Hackensack, NJ

National Westminster Bank plc*(Major Banking Relationship)*
One Exchange Place
Jersey City, NJ 07303
Tel.: 201-547-7000

Division:

Jarchem Specialty Chemical Division **(1)**
40 Ball St.
Newark, NJ 07105
Tel.: 201-344-0600
Imports Specialty Alcohols, Monomers & other Specialty Chemicals
S.I.C.: 5169
Arnold Stern *(Pres.)*

THE JASON GROUP, INC.
788 Morris-Essex Turnpike
Short Hills, NJ 07078
Tel.: 201-379-3535
Fax: 201-379-1921
Year Founded: 1979
Approx.Billings: $16,970,000
Emp.: 10
Business-to-Business & Consumer Advertising
Art Sasso *(Pres. & Dir.-Creative)*
Claire Sasso *(V.P. & Sec.)*
Dave Manahan *(Dir.-Pub. Rels.)*

Computer Systems/Hardware:
IBM

JASON INDUSTRIAL, INC.
340 Kaplan Dr.
Fairfield, NJ 07004
Tel.: 201-227-4904
Fax: 201-227-1651
Sales Range: $10-19 Million
Emp.: 100
Import Export
V Belting, Rubber & Plastic Hoses, Couplings & Rubber Flooring
S.I.C.: 3052; 3069; 3429
Jacques Cohenca *(Pres.)*
Philip Cohenca *(Exec. V.P.)*
Edward Menashe *(V.P.)*
Albert Nacawa *(V.P.)*
Robert Sutter *(V.P.)*

Outside Service Firm(s):

Max Rothenberg*(Auditors)*
New York, NY

Midlantic National Bank*(Major Banking Relationship)*
P.O. Box 600
Edison, NJ 08818
Tel.: 908-321-8400

JASPER COUNTY FARM BUREAU CO-OP ASSOCIATION, INC.
Hwy. 231, P.O. Box 238
Rensselaer, IN 47978
Tel.: 219-866-7131
Tel.: 800-828-7516 **IN**
Fax: 219-866-7490
Year Founded: 1927
Assets: $22,155,542
Earnings: $1,149,514
Liabilities: $10,538,123
Net Worth: $11,617,419
Approx.Sls.: $60,471,899
Emp.: 120
Fiscal Year-end: 7/31/91
Retail Agriculture Supply & Grain Marketing Co-op, Bulk Fuels-Gas, Diesel, Fuel Oil, LP Gas, Fertilizer, Chemicals, Seed, Feed, Grain Marketing
S.I.C.: 5984; 5211; 5999
William F. Ramey *(Chm. Bd.)*
Donald L. Misch *(Chief Exec. Officer & Gen. Mgr.)*
Kevin P. Benner *(Controller, Sec. & Treas.)*

Principal(s):
William F. Ramey
John Taylor

No. of Mfg. Plants/Facilities: 17
No. of U.S. Offices: 17

Computer Systems/Hardware:
IBM System 36

Outside Service Firm(s):

Michael R. Lafferty*(Auditors)*
Morgantown, IN

Daseke Insurance*(Group Insurer)*
Indianapolis, IN

Farm Bureau Insurance*(Group Insurer)*
Rensselear, IN

Blaney, Nesbitt, Casey & Walton*(Legal Firm)*
Rensselear, IN

CoBank-National Bank for Cooperatives*(Major Banking Relationship)*
Louisville, KY

First American Bank, N.A.*(Major Banking Relationship)*
Rensselear, IN

Subsidiary:

Double D Fertilizer **(1)**
R.R.I. Box 2
Wolcott, IN 47995
Tel.: 219-279-2114
Distributor Of Dry & Liquid Fertilizer
S.I.C.: 2873
Chuck Schuetti *(Gen. Mgr.)*

Jay
INCORPORATED
THE COMMUNICATIONS COMPANY

JAY INCORPORATED
170 Linden Oaks
Rochester, NY 14625
Tel.: 716-454-2650
Tel.: 800-836-6800
Year Founded: 1973
Approx.Billings: $24,000,000
Emp.: 24
In-House Television, Radio, Music & Video Production & Retail Adv.
Corporate Giving Program: United Way Campaign Program
Ferdinand J. Smith, III *(Chm. Bd., Pres., Chief Exec. Officer, Creative Dir.)*
Gregory W. Smith *(Exec. V.P., Chief Oper. Officer)*
Lesley T. Foy *(V.P.)*
Louis G. Deutsch *(Chief Fin. Officer & Human Resources)*
Marie Smith *(Corp. Sec., Office Mgr.)*
John Ark *(Gen. Counsel)*
Paula Howk *(Dir., Pub. Rels.)*
Mariann McCormick *(Dir., Mktg. & Market Res.)*
Guy S. Smith *(Pub. Rels. & Acct. Exec.)*

Computer Systems/Hardware:
Unisys 5050 Mainframe, IBM P.C. Network System, Novell Network, Apple P.C.

JAY INSTRUMENT & SPECIALTY CO.
555 N. Wayne Ave.
Cincinnati, OH 45215
Tel.: 513-733-5200
Fax: 513-733-5207
Approx.Sls.: $25,000,000
Emp.: 300
Distribute Measurement Instruments
S.I.C.: 3823; 5084; 3822
Dwight Leimer *(Pres.)*

Outside Service Firm(s):

J.D. Cloud & Co.*(Auditors)*
Cincinnati, OH
Tel.: 513-621-1188

Society National Bank*(Major Banking Relationship)*
900 Euclid Ave., P.O. Box 6477
Cleveland, OH 44101-6477
Tel.: 216-737-5000
Fax: 216-566-8947

JAYCO INC.
58075 State Rd. 13 S.
Middlebury, IN 46540
Mailing Address:
P.O. Box 460
Middlebury, IN 46540
Tel.: 219-825-5861 **IN**
Fax: 219-825-7354
Year Founded: 1968
Assets: $24,000,000
Net Worth: $24,000,000
Approx.Sls.: $100,000,000
Emp.: 750
Fiscal Year-end: 8/31/91
Export
Mfr. Recreational Vehicles
S.I.C.: 3711
Bertha Bontrager *(Chm. Bd.)*
Allen Yoder, Jr. *(Pres.)*
Kent A. Yoder *(Chief Fin. Officer)*
Wilbur Bontrager *(Exec. V.P.)*
Bernard Lambright *(Sr. V.P.)*
Paul C. Geczy *(V.P.-Human Resources)*
Chuck McKimmey *(V.P.-Sls. & Mktg.)*
Ed Farmwald *(Dir.-Pur.)*
Greg Stutsman *(Dir.-Data Processing)*

Computer Systems/Hardware:
IBM System AS/400

Outside Service Firm(s):

McGladrey & Pullen*(Auditors)*
Minneapolis, MN

Midwest Commerce Insurance*(Commercial Insurance Carrier)*
Elkhart, IN

Warrick, Weaver, Boyn*(Legal Firm)*
Midwest Commerce Bldg., 121 W. Franklin St.
Elkhart, IN 46516

Midwest Commerce Banking Co.*(Major Banking Relationship)*
Elkhart, IN

Midwest Commerce Banking Co.*(Pension Manager)*
Elkhart, IN 46516
Tel.: 219-294-6621

Subsidiary:

JET, Inc. **(1)**
P.O. Box 460
Middlebury, IN 46540
Tel.: 219-825-5861
Emp.: 60

JAYDON INCORPORATED
7800 14th St. West
Rock Island, IL 61201
Tel.: 309-787-4492
Fax: 309-787-4335
Approx.Sls.: $65,000,000
Emp.: 500
Distributor of Health & Beauty Aids, Housewares, School Supplies, Soft Goods, Pet Supplies
S.I.C.: 5122; 5092; 5099; 5199; 5100
Jay M. Gellerman *(Pres. & Treas.)*
R. James McCaughey *(Exec. V.P.-Sls.)*
James Tansey *(Comptroller)*
Michael Fenley *(Mgr.-Adv.)*
James Kohley *(Mgr.-Opers.)*

Outside Service Firm(s):

Portes, Sharp, Herbat & Kravets*(Legal Firm)*
Rock Island, IL

First National Bank Of The Quad Cities*(Major Banking Relationship)*
Rock Island, IL

THE JAYDOR CORPORATION
16 Bleeker St.
Millburn, NJ 07041
Tel.: 201-379-1234
Fax: 201-379-1913
Year Founded: 1933
Approx.Sls.: $100,000,000
Emp.: 350
Import
Wholesale Wines & Liquors; Specialty Foods & Beverages
S.I.C.: 5182; 4212; 4225
Barry S. Silverman *(Chm. Bd.)*
Michael D. Silverman *(Pres.)*
Craig M. Hazan *(Chief Fin. Officer & Controller)*
Louis T. DeMarino *(Sr. V.P.-Sls. & Mktg.)*
Stuart M. Balter *(V.P.-Trade Rels.)*
Ronald B. Garnett *(V.P. & Dir.-Opers.)*
Frank Genovese *(V.P. & Gen. Sls. Mgr.)*
Jeffrey J. Silverman *(V.P. & Mgr.-Opers.)*
Harry Patetta *(Dir.-Mngmt. Information Services)*
Jerome Blumberg *(Treas.)*

Computer Systems/Hardware:
IBM 4300

Outside Service Firm(s):

KPMG Peat Marwick*(Auditors)*
Roseland, NJ

Barry Evenchick*(Legal Firm)*
Livingston, NJ

First Fidelity Bank, N.A.*(Major Banking Relationship)*
Millburn, NJ

United Jersey Bank*(Major Banking Relationship)*
Hasbrouck Heights, NJ

Neuberger & Berman Pension Management, Inc.*(Pension Manager)*
522 Fifth Ave.
New York, NY 10036

JAYME

THE JAYME ORGANIZATION, INC.
One Corporate Exchange,
25825 Science Park Dr.
Cleveland, OH 44122
Tel.: 216-831-0110
Fax: 216-464-2308
Year Founded: 1947
Approx.Billings: $37,095,297
Emp.: 64
Edward D. Young *(Hon. Chm.)*
George N. Havens *(Chm, Emeritus)*
James K. DeVoe *(Chm. Bd., Chief Exec. Officer)*
Cathy A. Pokorny *(Vice Chm.)*
Mark C. Nylander *(Pres.-PROCONSUL)*
Kim F. Zarney *(Pres.-The Boardroom)*
Joe Winklmann *(Pres.-Market-Zing)*
Lawrence R. Kavanaugh *(Exec. V.P., Gen. Mgr.-Jayme Advertising)*
Judith A. Feniger *(Sr. V.P.-PROCONSUL)*
Michael S. Paulus *(Sr. V.P.-Jayme Advertising)*
Diane Pucko *(V.P.-ProConsul)*
Allen B. Straka *(V.P., Chief Fin. Officer)*
Joanne Gonzalez *(Treas.)*

J. M. JAYSON & CO., INC.
2350 North Forest
Getsville, NY 14068
Tel.: 716-636-9090 **NY**
Fax: 716-636-0466
Assets: $3,485,202
Liabilities: $1,484,717
Net Worth: $2,000,485
Sales Range: $80-99 Million
Emp.: 250
Fiscal Year-end: 12/31/90
Real Estate Investors & Syndicators
S.I.C.: 6531
Corporate Giving Program: United Way
Joseph M. Jayson *(Chm. Bd. & Chief Exec. Officer)*
Randy C. Anger *(Pres.)*
Richard Pyzikiewicz *(V.P.-Acquisitions)*
Judith P. Jayson *(Dir.-Mktg.)*
Principal(s):
Joseph M. Jayson

Computer Systems/Hardware:
Wang VS 500

Outside Service Firm(s):

Deloitte & Touche*(Auditors)*
50 Fountain Plaza
Buffalo, NY 14202
Tel.: 716-843-7200

Goldome Federal Savings Bank*(Investment Banker)*
Buffalo, NY

Empire of America*(Major Banking Relationship)*
Buffalo, NY

JAZZ HOLDING CORPORATION
4505 Bandini Blvd.
Vernon, CA 90040
Tel.: 213-747-8466 **DE**
Fax: 213-749-2555
Year Founded: 1987
Approx.Sls.: $85,000,000
Emp.: 225
Mfr. of Women's Dresses
S.I.C.: 2335
Barry Sacks *(Chm. Bd.)*

Outside Service Firm(s):

Weber, Lipshie & Co.*(Auditors)*
Los Angeles, CA

Subsidiary:

Chorus Line, Inc. **(1)**
4505 Bandini Blvd.
Vernon, CA 90040
Tel.: 213-747-8466
Mfr. of Women's, Juniors & Missess Dresses
S.I.C.: 2335
Mark Steinman *(Pres.)*
Jay Balaban *(Treas. & Sec.)*

JAZZERCISE, INC.
2808 Roosevelt St.
Carlsbad, CA 92008
Tel.: 619-434-2101
Fax: 619-434-8958
Year Founded: 1969
Approx.Sls.: $16,000,000
Emp.: 110
Fiscal Year-end: 6/30/91
Exercise Programs Franchisor; Retail Dancewear, Diet Program
S.I.C.: 7991; 5699
Judi Missett *(Pres. & Chief Exec. Officer)*
Robin Wilkins *(Chief Fin. Officer)*
Margaret P. Stanton-Riesgo *(Exec. V.P. & Copr. Sec.)*
Sharon Biddle *(V.P.-Mktg.)*
Jan Kinney *(V.P.-Opers.)*
Jayne Ridge *(Dir.-Human Resources)*

Outside Service Firm(s):

KPMG Peat Marwick*(Auditors)*
750 B St.
San Diego, CA 92105
Tel.: 619-233-8000

Michael Wischkaemper*(Legal Firm)*
Carlsbad, CA

Wells Fargo Bank*(Major Banking Relationship)*
Carlsbad, CA

JEFFERSON CHEVROLET CO.
2130 E. Jefferson
Detroit, MI 48207
Tel.: 313-259-1200
Fax: 313-259-5597
Approx.Sls.: $25,300,000
Emp.: 92
New & Used Automobiles & Trucks
S.I.C.: 5511
Raymond R. Tessmer *(Pres.)*
Jerry DeWaele *(Gen. Mgr.)*
James P. Tellier *(Sec. & Treas.)*
Joel Theut *(Mgr.-New Car Sls.)*

Division:

Jefferson Chevrolet **(1)**
15175 E. Jefferson
Grosse Point Park, MI 48230
Tel.: 313-821-2000
John Cook *(Gen. Mgr.)*

JEFFREY BUICK-NISSAN INC.
30800 Gratiot
Roseville, MI 48066
Tel.: 313-296-1300
Fax: 313-296-1512
Year Founded: 1983
Approx.Sls.: $38,800,000
Emp.: 125
Fiscal Year-end: 12/31/90
Automobile Dealership
S.I.C.: 5511
Jeffrey L. Tamaroff *(Pres.)*
William H. Hoffman *(Sec. & Treas.)*
Roger Lau *(Gen. Mgr.-New Cars)*
Rick Szmigiel *(Nissan Sls. Mgr.-New Cars)*
Mike Scenga *(Asst. Sls. Mgr.-Buick)*

Outside Service Firm(s):

Doeren & Mayhew*(Auditors)*
Troy, MI

The Dickerson Group*(Legal Firm)*
Southfield, MI

JEFFREY MICHAEL
533 Sixth St. South
Kirkland, WA 98033
Tel.: 206-827-7997
Fax: 206-827-3850
Sales Range: $10-19 Million
Emp.: 300
Fiscal Year-end: 12/31/88
Retailer of Mens Apparel
S.I.C.: 5611
Jeff Brotman *(Chm. Bd.)*
Craig Richards *(Pres., Chief Oper. Officer & Treas.)*

Computer Systems/Hardware:
IBM PC-AT

Outside Service Firm(s):

King County Medical Blue Shield*(Group Insurer)*
P.O. Box 21267
Seattle, WA 98111
Tel.: 206-464-3958
Fax: 206-622-7959

Seattle First National Bank*(Major Banking Relationship)*
701 Fifth Avenue
Seattle, WA 98104
Tel.: 206-358-3035

THE JEL SERT CO.
Rt. 59 & Conde St.
West Chicago, IL 60185
Mailing Address:
P.O. Box 261,
West Chicago, IL 60186
Tel.: 708-231-7590
Fax: 708-231-3993
Year Founded: 1926
Approx.Sls.: $60,000,000
Emp.: 450
Export
Manufacturer of Frozen Desserts & Flavorings
S.I.C.: 2038; 2087
Joan M. Wegner *(Chm. Bd.)*
Charles T. Wegner IV *(Pres. & Chief Oper. Officer)*
Mark Benrus *(Controller)*
Wayne Keating *(Dir.-Data Processing)*
Ken Wegner *(Dir.-Pur.)*
Terry Hagy *(Mgr.-Natl. Sls.)*
W. Meisenheimer *(Distr. Mgr.-Sls.)*
Jack Dolan *(Div. Mgr.-Sls.)*
Mack King *(Div. Mgr.-Sls.)*
Gary La Dolche *(Div. Mgr.-Sls.)*
Andy Marck *(Div. Mgr.-Sls.)*
Robert Prentice *(Div. Mgr.-Sls.)*
David Russell *(Div. Mgr.-Sls.)*
John Wegner *(Div. Mgr.-Sls.)*
F. Gonzalez *(Mgr.-Export)*

Computer Systems/Hardware:
IBM PC-XT

Outside Service Firm(s):

Baker & McKenzie*(Legal Firm)*
Citicorp Plaza, 36th Fl., 725 S. Figuerua St.
Los Angeles, CA 90017
Tel.: 213-892-7300

Jack Beem*(Legal Firm)*
Chicago, IL

The Northern Trust Co.*(Major Banking Relationship)*
30 S. LaSalle St.
Chicago, IL 60675
Tel.: 312-630-6000

JELD-WEN, INC.
3303 Lakeport Blvd.
Klamath Falls, OR 97601
Tel.: 503-882-3451
Fax: 503-884-2231
Approx.Sls.: $250,000,000
Emp.: 3,500

Jeld-Wen, Inc.—(Continued)

Millwork; Wood Door Frames, Windows, Doors; Sawmills & Planing Mills; Metal Doors, Sash & Trim; Wood Pallets
S.I.C.: 2431; 2421; 3442; 3089; 2448
Richard Wendt *(Chm. Bd.)*
Roderick Wendt *(Pres. & Treas.)*
Larry Wetter *(Exec. V.P.)*
William B. Early *(V.P. & Asst. Sec.)*
Theodore Schnomeier *(V.P. & Asst. Sec.)*
Gary Florence *(Controller)*

Outside Service Firm(s):

In-House*(Auditors)*

First Interstate Bank*(Major Banking Relationship)*
P.O. Box 53441,
Phoenix, AZ 85072-3441
Tel.: 602-229-4049

Subsidiaries:

Frank Paxton Company **(1)**
6311 St. John Ave.
Kansas City, MO 64123
Tel.: 816-483-3007
Assets: $61,662,583
Earnings: $3,275,108
Liabilities: $14,844,702
Net Worth: $46,817,881
Approx.Sls.: $107,661,757
Emp.: 560
Fiscal Year-end: 3/31/90
Import
Computer Systems/Hardware:
IBM System 36
Lumber
S.I.C.: 5031; 5211; 5084
Richard Wendt *(Chm. Bd.)*
Donald C. Moreland *(Pres. & Chief Exec. Officer)*
Roger W. Davis *(Pres.)*
Craig R. Ramsey *(Exec. V.P.)*
Roy Jackson *(V.P.)*
Rosemary Plum *(Corp. Sec.)*
Jerry Underwood *(Comptroller)*

Subsidiaries:

Graves-Humphreys Company **(2)**
5320 Peter Creek Rd.
Roanoke, VA 24033
Tel.: 703-343-8011
Fax: 703-343-0911
Approx.Sls.: $10,000,000
Emp.: 30
Distr. of Industrial Arts & Vocational & Technical Educational Tools, Equip. & Supplies; Distrs. School Athletic Supplies
S.I.C.: 5049; 5084
Frances R. Yates *(V.P. & Gen. Mgr.)*
George Sink *(Asst. Sec.)*
Shirley Fletcher *(Asst. Sec.)*

Paxton Beautiful Woods **(2)**
14200 Chef Menteur Hwy.
New Orleans, LA 70189
Tel.: 504-254-1550
Fax: 504-835-5804
Hardwood Distr. Center
S.I.C.: 5031
Jerry Thompson *(Gen. Mgr.)*
Wayne Fritz *(Chief Oper. Officer)*

Paxton Beautiful Woods **(2)**
1105 Sixth Avenue
Carrollton, TX 75006
Tel.: 214-245-1192
Distribution Warehouse
S.I.C.: 5031

Frank Paxton Lumber Company **(2)**
4837 Jackson St., Box 16343
Denver, CO 80216
Tel.: 303-399-6810
Fax: 303-321-4766
S.I.C.: 5031
Jack Egan *(Chief Oper. Officer)*

Frank Paxton Lumber Company **(2)**
5701 W. 66th St.
Chicago, IL 60638
Tel.: 312-767-1207
Fax: 312-458-6016
S.I.C.: 5031
Mike King *(Mgr.)*

Frank Paxton Lumber Company **(2)**
1400 Market Street
Des Moines, IA 50303
Tel.: 515-283-2131
Fax: 515-244-4225
S.I.C.: 5031
Gordon Suckow *(Mgr.)*

Frank Paxton Lumber Company **(2)**
4990 South Crittenden Drive
Louisville, KY 40233
Tel.: 502-361-7131
Fax: 502-361-9869
Lumber Processing
S.I.C.: 2421
Gregg Gauthier *(Mgr.)*

Frank Paxton Lumber Company **(2)**
7455 Dawson, Box 43334
Cincinnati, OH 45243
Tel.: 513-984-8200
Fax: 513-984-9060
Distribution Warehouse
S.I.C.: 5031
Jerry Thompson *(Chief Oper. Officer)*

Frank Paxton Lumber Company **(2)**
1815 S. Agnew, Box 82215
Oklahoma City, OK 73148
Tel.: 405-235-4411
Fax: 405-236-0350
Distribution Warehouse
S.I.C.: 5031
Jim Kahler *(Chief Oper. Officer)*

Frank Paxton Lumber Company **(2)**
6311 St. John Ave.
Kansas City, MO 64123
Tel.: 816-483-7000
Fax: 816-241-5110
Distribution Warehouse
S.I.C.: 5031
Jerry Fuller *(Chief Oper. Officer)*

Frank Paxton Lumber Company **(2)**
1909 Bellamah N.W., P.O. Box. 25152
Albuquerque, NM 87125
Tel.: 505-243-7891
Fax: 505-242-3783
Distribution Warehouse
S.I.C.: 5031
Alan Crownover *(Mgr.)*

Frank Paxton Lumber Company **(2)**
2900 Bryan Ave., Box 1225
Fort Worth, TX 76101
Tel.: 817-924-2224
Fax: 817-926-3135
Distribution Warehouse
S.I.C.: 5031
Brad Jones *(Mgr.)*

Frank Paxton Lumber Company **(2)**
5420 S. 99th E. Ave.
Tulsa, OK 74145
Tel.: 918-665-2411
S.I.C.: 5031
Wes McCormick *(Chief Oper. Officer)*

Paxton Properties, Inc. **(2)**
6311 St. John Ave.
Kansas City, MO 64123
Tel.: 816-483-3007 (100%)
Approx.Rev.: $1,426,341
Real Estate Company
S.I.C.: 6552
Roy Jackson *(Chief Oper. Officer)*

Twin Y Corporation **(1)**
2526 N. Western
Plymouth, IN 46563
Tel.: 219-936-2183
Fax: 219-936-7433
Mfr. of Wood Doors
S.I.C.: 2431
Bill Early *(V.P.)*

JELMAR COMPANY
6600 N. Lincoln Ave.
Lincolnwood, IL 60645
Tel.: 708-675-8400
Fax: 708-675-1708
Approx.Sls.: $12,000,000
Emp.: 12
Fiscal Year-end: 2/28/91
Export
Tarnx Tarnish Remover
S.I.C.: 2842
Manny Gutterman *(Chm. Bd.)*
Arthur Gutterman *(Pres., Chief Oper. & Chief Exec. Officer)*
Steven Gutterman *(Exec. V.P.)*
Richard Drnec *(V.P.)*

Computer Systems/Hardware:
AST PC, Network, Compaq - AS1

JEMISON, INC.
35 Union Ave., Ste. 200
Memphis, TN 38103
Tel.: 901-526-1211 **FL**
Fax: 901-525-7641
Year Founded: 1956
Assets: $6,621,743
Liabilities: $1,371,262
Net Worth: $5,250,481
Sales Range: $10-19 Million
Emp.: 188
Real Estate Holding Company
S.I.C.: 6531; 6719
Frank Z. Jemison, Sr. *(Chm. Bd.)*
Frank Z. Jemison, Jr. *(Pres., Chief Exec. & Chief Oper. Officer)*
Michael Johnson *(Chief Fin. Officer)*
Ruby T. Bennett *(Corp. Sec.)*
William H. Lawson, Jr. *(Gen. Counsel)*

Computer Systems/Hardware:
IBM System 36

Outside Service Firm(s):

Ernst & Young*(Auditors)*
1400 One Commerce Sq.
Memphis, TN 38103

Aetna Life & Casualty*(Group Insurer)*
Memphis, TN

Fireman's Fund Insurance Co.*(Group Insurer)*
New York, NY

Lexington Insurance Co.*(Group Insurer)*
New York, NY

Bogatin, Lawson & Chiapella*(Legal Firm)*
860 Ridgelake Blvd., Ste. 360
Memphis, TN 38120
Tel.: 901-767-1234

First Tennessee Bank, N.A.*(Major Banking Relationship)*
Memphis, TN

Massachusetts Mutual Life Insurance Co.*(Pension Manager)*
1295 State Street
Springfield, MA 01111
Tel.: 413-788-8411

Subsidiary:

Alco Properties, Inc. **(1)**
35 Union Ave., Ste. 200
Memphis, TN 38103
Tel.: 901-526-1211 (100%)
Emp.: 3
Real Estate Agents & Managers
S.I.C.: 6552; 6531
Frank Z. Jemison, Jr. *(Pres.)*
Michael Johnson *(Treas.)*

Subsidiary:

Alco Management, Inc. **(2)**
35 Union Ave., Ste. 200
Memphis, TN 38103
Tel.: 901-526-1211 (100%)
Fax: 901-525-7641
Emp.: 185
Real Estate Agents & Managers
S.I.C.: 6531
Frank Z. Jemison, Jr. *(Pres. & Chief Exec. Officer)*
Michael Johnson *(V.P.-Fin. & Treas.)*
George C. Caruso *(Chief Oper. Officer)*

JENKINS SPIRITS CORP. LTD.
21 S. Perimeter Rd.
Londonderry, NH 03053
Mailing Address:
P.O. Box 6128
Manchester, NH 03108
Tel.: 603-623-3231
Approx.Sls.: $18,000,000
Emp.: 50
Manufactures Jenkins Reddy Made Prepared Cocktails & Other Liquors
S.I.C.: 2085
Bertram R. Silver *(Pres.)*

JENNIFER CONVERTIBLES INC.
331 Rt. 4
Paramus, NJ 07652
Tel.: 201-343-1610
Approx.Sls.: $29,091,000
Sells Sofabeds, Sofas & Cocktail Tables
S.I.C.: 5712
Harley J. Greenfield *(Chm., Pres. & Chief Exec. Officer)*
Adam Falchook *(V.P. & Treas.)*
Kenneth Koch *(Sec.)*
Lisa Schwartz *(Dir.-Adv.)*

JENNIFER DALE, INC.
180 Madison Ave., 19th Fl.
New York, NY 10016
Tel.: 212-532-5522
Fax: 212-545-1795
Approx.Sls.: $37,000,000
Emp.: 500
Nightwear; Nightgowns, Negligees & Pajamas
S.I.C.: 2254
Marvin Tolkin *(Pres.)*
Larry Tolkin *(V.P.-Sls.)*
David Tolkin *(Dir.-Sls., Import & Export)*
Scott MacKenzie *(Mgr.-Natl. Sls.)*

Outside Service Firm(s):

Eisner & Lubin*(Auditors)*
New York, NY

Manufacturers Hanover Trust Co.*(Major Banking Relationship)*
4 New York Plaza
New York, NY 10015

JENSEN ELECTRIC COMPANY
140 Jensen St.
Reno, NV 89502
Tel.: 702-322-3100 **NV**
Fax: 702-322-5249
Year Founded: 1968
Approx.Sls.: $10,000,000
Emp.: 125
Manufacture Commercial, Industrial & Institutional Electrical/Electronic Control & Building Automation Systems; Sales, Service & Contract Installation Of Proprietary Systems
S.I.C.: 1731; 1623; 3625; 3646; 3669; 3613
Diane P. Jensen *(Chm. Bd.)*
Gary A. Jensen *(Pres. & Sec.)*
Elizabeth D. Jensen *(V.P. & Chief Exec. Officer)*
Harold Arnott *(Controller)*
D.M. Jensen *(Sec. & Treas.)*
Chris Jensen *(Mgr.-Sls. & Mktg.)*
Principal(s):
Gary A. Jensen
Elizabeth D. Jensen

No. of Mfg. Plants/Facilities: 1
No. of U.S. Offices: 3

Computer Systems/Hardware:
IBM

Outside Service Firm(s):

Ken Keneran*(Auditors)*
Reno, NV

Chubb Group*(Commercial Insurance Carrier)*
Walnut Creek, CA

Royal Insurance Co.*(Group Insurer)*
Reno, NV

Vargas & Bartlett*(Legal Firm)*
201 W. Liberty St., Ste. 300
Reno, NV 89504

Tel.: 702-786-5000

First Interstate Bank*(Major Banking Relationship)*
Reno, NV

Valley Bank of Nevada*(Major Banking Relationship)*
Reno, NV

Jensen Electric Pension Trust*(Pension Manager)*
Reno, NV

IRVING F. JENSEN CO., INC.
2220 Hawkeye Dr.
Sioux City, IA 51102
Mailing Address:
P.O. Box 1618
Sioux City, IA 51102
Tel.: 712-252-1891 **IA**
Fax: 712-252-4850
Year Founded: 1898
Sales Range: $40-59 Million
Emp.: 225
Fiscal Year-end: 3/31/91
Street & Highway Construction
S.I.C.: 1622
Irving F. Jensen, Jr. *(Chm., Treas. & Sec.)*
Colin C. Jensen *(Pres.)*
Erik M. Jensen *(Exec. V.P.)*

Principal(s):
Colin C. Jensen
Erik M. Jensen

Computer Systems/Hardware:
IBM

Outside Service Firm(s):

Nichols, Rise & Co.*(Auditors)*
Sioux City, IA

Robert Eidsmoe*(Legal Firm)*
Sioux City, IA

Security National Bank*(Major Banking Relationship)*
Sioux City, IA

JEPSON-MURRAY ADVERTISING
(Div. of AVISO, Inc.)
1116 N. Washington Ave.
Lansing, MI 48906
Tel.: 517-374-8500
Fax: 517-374-8556
Year Founded: 1943
Approx.Billings: $15,000,000
Emp.: 40
Philip E. Rosenberger *(Pres.)*
Terri Austin *(Office Mgr.)*

JERELL, INC.
1431 Regal Row
Dallas, TX 75247
Tel.: 214-637-5300
Tel.: 800-727-5815 **TX**
Fax: 214-637-4205
Approx.Sls.: $55,000,000
Emp.: 390
Fiscal Year-end: 10/31/90
Mfr. Women's Apparel
S.I.C.: 2335; 2331; 5137
Ed Vierling *(Pres.)*
Leroy Spencer *(Sr. V.P.-Fin.)*
Norman Cohn *(V.P.-Piece Goods)*
David W. Dailey *(V.P.-Mngmt. Information Systems)*
Sam Klapholz *(V.P.-Sls.)*
Mary Manwarring *(V.P.-Design Mktg.)*

Outside Service Firm(s):

Philip Vogel & Co.*(Auditors)*
Dallas, TX

Comerica Bank*(Major Banking Relationship)*
Dallas, TX

JERGENS INC.
19520 Nottingham Rd.
Cleveland, OH 44110
Tel.: 216-486-2100
Fax: 216-481-6193
Year Founded: 1942
Approx.Sls.: $14,000,000
Emp.: 156
Fixturing & Tooling
S.I.C.: 3544
Jack H. Schron, Sr. *(Chm. Bd.)*
Jack H. Schron, Jr. *(Pres.)*
Joseph Ignat *(V.P.)*
Morton E. O'Ryan *(V.P.)*
Courtney Schron *(V.P.)*
Sue Evans *(Sec.)*

Principal(s):
Jack H. Schron, Sr.
Sue Evans
Jack H. Schron, Jr.

Outside Service Firm(s):

Arthur Andersen & Co.*(Auditors)*
1717 E. 9th St.
Cleveland, OH 44114
Tel.: 216-781-2140
Fax: 216-781-3683

Baker & Hostetler*(Legal Firm)*
3200 National City Center
Cleveland, OH 44114
Tel.: 216-621-0200
Fax: 216-696-0740

Society National Bank*(Major Banking Relationship)*
900 Euclid Ave., P.O. Box 6477
Cleveland, OH 44101-6477
Tel.: 216-737-5000
Fax: 216-566-8947

JERNBERG INDUSTRIES, INC.
328 W. 40th Place
Chicago, IL 60609
Tel.: 312-268-3004 **IL**
Fax: 708-268-3220
Year Founded: 1985
Approx.Sls.: $100,000,000
Emp.: 520
Mfr. of Iron & Steel Forgings; Nonferrous Forgings
S.I.C.: 3462; 3463
M.L. Eldon Wheeler *(Chm. Bd. & Chief Exec. Officer)*
R. Thomas Beecham *(Pres. & Chief Oper. Officer)*
John Everly *(V.P.)*
William Gilfune *(V.P.-Engrng.)*
Thomas McDonald *(Chief Fin. Officer & Treas.)*
Howard Campbell *(Chief Engr.)*

Outside Service Firm(s):

Ernst & Young*(Auditors)*
233 S. Wacker Dr.
Chicago, IL 60606
Tel.: 312-368-1800
Fax: 312-645-3095

American National Bank & Trust Company of Chicago*(Major Banking Relationship)*
33 N. LaSalle St.
Chicago, IL 60602
Tel.: 312-661-5000
Fax: 312-661-6417

Division:

Component Machining Div. **(1)**
1901 S. Meyers Rd., Ste. 340
Lombard, IL 60148
Tel.: 708-495-0619
Cams, Machine Tool Accessories
S.I.C.: 3545
R. Thomas Beecham *(Pres. & Chief Oper. Officer)*

Plant:

Jernberg Industries **(2)**
1901 S. Meyers Rd., Ste. 340
Lombard, IL 60148
Tel.: 708-495-0619

JEROME-DUNCAN FORD
8000 Ford Country Ln.
Sterling Heights, MI 48314
Mailing Address:
P.O. Box 100
Sterling Heights, MI 48314
Tel.: 313-268-7500 **MI**
Fax: 213-268-1790
Year Founded: 1956
Assets: $9,415,080
Liabilities: $8,745,641
Net Worth: $669,439
Approx.Sls.: $64,000,000
Emp.: 180
Fiscal Year-end: 6/30/91
Retail & Leasing of Cars & Trucks, Parts & Service
S.I.C.: 5511; 7515; 7513
Richard J. Duncan *(Chm. Bd.)*
Gail Duncan-Campagne *(Pres.)*
Diane L. Kitts *(V.P. & Controller)*

Principal(s):
Richard J. Duncan
Gail Duncan-Campagne

Outside Service Firm(s):

National Bank of Detroit*(Major Banking Relationship)*
611 Woodward
Detroit, MI 48226
Tel.: 313-225-1000

JEROME FOODS INC.
34 N. 7th St.
Barron, WI 54812
Tel.: 715-537-3131
Fax: 715-537-9685
Emp.: 2,000
Processor of Turkey Products
S.I.C.: 2015
Wallace H. Jerome *(Chm. Bd.)*
Jerome K. Jerome *(Pres. & Chief Exec. Officer)*
Larry J. Jarvela *(V.P.-Fin. & Treas.)*
Richard L. Pajula *(V.P.-Opers.)*
William Kelly *(Chief Engr.)*
Tyrone Lipp *(Mgr.-Data Processing)*

Computer Systems/Hardware:
IBM

Outside Service Firm(s):

Arthur Andersen & Co.*(Auditors)*
45 S. 7th St.
Minneapolis, MN 55402

Fredrikson & Byron, P.A.*(Legal Firm)*
1100 International Centre, 900 2nd Ave. S.
Minneapolis, MN 55402
Tel.: 612-347-7000

First National Bank of The Lakes*(Major Banking Relationship)*
Barron, WI

JERSEY PRINTING COMPANY, INC.
111 Linnet St.
Bayonne, NJ 07002
Tel.: 201-436-4200 **NJ**
Fax: 201-436-9248
Year Founded: 1940
Sales Range: $10-19 Million
Emp.: 140
Commercial & Publication Offset Printing
S.I.C.: 2752
Arthur Shlossman *(Pres. & Chief Exec. Officer)*
Lloyd Goldberg *(Exec. V.P.-Opers. & Personnel)*

Outside Service Firm(s):

Mortenson, Fleming, Grizzetti & Boiko*(Auditors)*
340 North Ave.
Cranford, NJ 07016

Nathan Fishman*(Legal Firm)*
Union, NJ

JESCO, INC.
7175 Cahill Rd.
Minneapolis, MN 55439
Tel.: 612-944-7700 **MN**
Fax: 612-944-7711
Year Founded: 1949
Approx.Sls.: $24,000,000
Emp.: 150
Masonry & Concrete Work
S.I.C.: 1741; 1771
Chester R. Sazenski *(Chm. Bd. & Chief Exec. Officer)*
Jim Sazenski *(Pres.)*
David Olson *(V.P.-Treas., Sec. & Data Processing)*

Outside Service Firm(s):

Charles Bailey & Co.*(Auditors)*
Minneapolis, MN

Coleman, Hull & Van Vliet*(Legal Firm)*
Edine, MN

First Bank, N.A.*(Major Banking Relationship)*
Bloomington, MN

JET SPRAY CORP.
825 University Ave.
Norwood, MA 02062
Tel.: 617-769-7500
Tel.: 800-538-2677 **MA**
Fax: 617-769-2368
Year Founded: 1954
Assets: $8,175,450
Liabilities: $3,363,149
Net Worth: $4,812,301
Approx.Sls.: $20,000,000
Emp.: 200
Fiscal Year-end: 12/31/91
Export
Mfr. of Beverage Dispensers
S.I.C.: 3585
Leonard J. Jacobs *(Chm. Bd., Pres. & Chief Exec. Officer)*
Michael J. Russell *(V.P.-Fin)*
Morris Goldings *(Sec. & Gen. Counsel)*
Manfred Bayer *(Dir.-Intl. Sls.)*
Timothy Donlon *(Dir.-Domestic Sls.)*
Sandra Micelotti *(Dir.-Personnel)*
Greg Oden *(Dir.-Data Processing)*
Gary Sardynski *(Dir.-Engrng.)*
Charles McGloin *(Mgr.-Pur.)*

Principal(s):
Leonard J. Jacobs

No. of Mfg. Plants/Facilities: 1
No. of U.S. Offices: 1
No. of Foreign Offices: 2

Computer Systems/Hardware:
IBM AS 400

Outside Service Firm(s):

Kaitz, Levine & Ilacqua*(Auditors)*
Boston, MA

MacIntyre, Fay & Thayer*(Commercial Insurance Carrier)*
Newton, MA

Employee Benefit Administrators*(Group Insurer)*
Hampton Fall, NH

Mahoney, Hawkes & Goldings*(Legal Firm)*
Boston, MA

U.S. Trust Co.*(Major Banking Relationship)*
40 Court St.
Boston, MA 02108
Tel.: 617-726-7371
Fax: 617-726-7380

Subsidiary:

Jet Spray International **(1)**
825 University Ave.
Norwood, MA 02062
Tel.: 617-769-7500
S.I.C.: 3585

JEWELERS MUTUAL INSURANCE COMPANY
24 Jewelers Park Dr.
Neenah, WI 54957-0468
Mailing Address:
P.O. Box 468,
Neenah, WI 54957-0468
Tel.: 414-725-4326
Tel.: 800-558-6411 **WI**
Fax: 414-725-9401
Year Founded: 1913
Assets: $49,662,813
Liabilities: $25,138,702
Net Worth: $24,524,111
Approx.Sls.: $35,221,111
Emp.: 132
Fiscal Year-end: 12/31/91
Insurance Company
S.I.C.: 6331
Richard M. Kern *(Chm. Bd.)*
Ronald R. Harder *(Pres. & Chief Exec. Officer)*
William W. McGinnis *(Exec. V.P.-Opers.)*
James P. Jordan *(V.P.-Mktg.)*
Lee Zuberbier *(V.P.-Information Services)*
William P. Herrbold *(V.P.-Claims)*
Gary L. Draheim *(V.P.-Underwriting)*
Robert Torgerson *(Gen. Counsel)*
Jed A. Block *(Dir.-Communications & Sec.)*
William J. Stoegbauer *(Treas.)*
Connie Rank *(Mgr.-Human Resources)*

Principal(s):
Mutual Company-The Policyholders

No. of U.S. Offices: 1

Computer Systems/Hardware:
IBM AS/400

Outside Service Firm(s):

Ernst & Young*(Auditors)*
111 E. Kilbourn Ave., Ste. 900
Milwaukee, WI 53202
Tel.: 414-273-5900

Associated Bank*(Major Banking Relationship)*
Neenah, WI

JEWELL BUILDING SYSTEMS
P.O. Box 397
Dallas, NC 28034
Tel.: 704-922-8652 **NC**
Fax: 704-922-3237
Year Founded: 1977
Emp.: 48
Licensor, Manufacturer, Exporter & Distributor of Light Gauge Steel Buildings
S.I.C.: 3448; 5039
Everett G. Jewell *(Chm. Bd., Pres., Chief Exec. Officer & Treas.)*
C. Thomas Scott *(V.P.-Sls.)*

Computer Systems/Hardware:
IBM

Outside Service Firm(s):

Cherry, Bekaert & Holland*(Auditors)*
Charlotte, NC

Cameron Brown*(Commercial Insurance Carrier)*
Charlotte, NC

Performance Inc.*(Group Insurer)*
Charlotte, NC

Garland & Wren*(Legal Firm)*
Gastonia, NC

NationsBank Carolinas*(Major Banking Relationship)*
Gastonia, NC

Subsidiary:

First Choice Homes **(1)**
Hwy. 321 North, P.O. Box 375
Dallas, NC 28034
Tel.: 704-922-8652
Emp.: 20
Mfr. of Pre-Engineered Single Family & Multi-Family Residences
S.I.C.: 1521; 1522
Everett G. Jewell *(Chief Oper. Officer)*

JEWELL INSTRUMENTS, INC.
Grenier Industrial Air Park, 850 Perimeter Rd.
Manchester, NH 03103
Mailing Address:
P.O. Box 4038
Manchester, NH 03108
Tel.: 603-669-6400
Tel.: 800-227-5955 **DE**
Fax: 603-669-5962
Year Founded: 1936
Sales Range: $10-19 Million
Emp.: 140
Panel Meters, Temperature Controls, Avionics Products, Prime Flight Instruments
S.I.C.: 3812; 3823; 3825
Gerald R. Allard *(Chm. Bd.)*
John R. Allard *(Pres. & Chief Exec. Officer)*
Don Dandurand *(V.P. & Treas.)*
Edward J. Mosher *(V.P.-Opers.)*
James C. Folk *(V.P.-Mktg. & Sls.)*
Nancy Berry *(Controller)*

Principal(s):
Gerald R. Allard
Younes Nazarian
Raymond Torbati

No. of Mfg. Plants/Facilities: 1
No. of U.S. Offices: 1

Computer Systems/Hardware:
C. Itoh

Outside Service Firm(s):

Howe, Riley & Howe*(Auditors)*
Manchester, NH

Lion Associates, Paul Revere*(Group Insurer)*
Manchester, NH

McLane, Graf, Raulerson, & Middleton*(Legal Firm)*
Manchester, NH

Fleet Bank-NH*(Major Banking Relationship)*
Indian Head Plaza
Nashua, NH 03060
Tel.: 603-594-5000

JEWELMONT CORPORATION
800 Boone Ave., N.
Minneapolis, MN 55427
Tel.: 612-546-3800
Fax: 612-546-2957
Year Founded: 1933
Approx.Sls.: $34,000,000
Emp.: 250
Mfr. & Distributor of Jewelry, Watches & Parts
S.I.C.: 3911; 5094
Robert K. Leeds *(Chm. Bd. & Pres.)*
Robert J. Leeds *(V.P.-Admin.)*
Scott Dressen *(Chief Fin. Officer)*
Teresa Leeds *(Treas.)*

Outside Service Firm(s):

KPMG Peat Marwick*(Auditors)*
4200 Norwest Center, 90 S. 7th St.
Minneapolis, MN 55402
Tel.: 612-341-2222

Norwest Bank Minnesota, N.A.*(Major Banking Relationship)*
6th St. & Marquette Av.
Minneapolis, MN 55479
Tel.: 612-667-1234

JIMLAR CORPORATION
160 Great Neck Rd.
Great Neck, NY 11021
Tel.: 516-829-1717
Fax: 516-829-2970
Year Founded: 1956
Sales Range: $100-499 Million
Emp.: 100
Importer & Wholesaler of Shoes
S.I.C.: 5139
James Tarica *(Pres.)*
Laurence Tarica *(Exec. V.P. & Sec.)*

No. of U.S. Offices: 1
No. of Foreign Offices: 4

Outside Service Firm(s):

Goldstein, Golub, Kessler & Co.*(Auditors)*
New York, NY

Tannenbaum Dubin & Robinson*(Legal Firm)*
1400 Broadway
New York, NY 10001
Tel.: 212-687-3470

Irving Trust Co.*(Major Banking Relationship)*
New York, NY

JITNEY-JUNGLE STORES OF AMERICA, INC.
453 N. Mill St.
Jackson, MS 39202
Mailing Address:
P.O. Box 3409
Jackson, MS 39207
Tel.: 601-948-0361
Fax: 601-352-0483
Assets: $223,932,000
Earnings: $9,065,000
Liabilities: $97,799,000
Net Worth: $126,133,000
Approx.Sls.: $1,044,000,000
Emp.: 9 000
Fiscal Year-end: 5/ 2/92
Food Stores
S.I.C.: 5411
W. H. Holman, Jr. *(Chm. Bd., Pres. & Chief Exec. & Oper. Officers)*
Roger P. Friou *(Vice Chm. & Chief Fin. Officer)*
Claude W. Duvall *(Exec. V.P.)*
David K. Essary *(Exec. V.P.)*
W.H. Holman III *(Sr. V.P.-Mktg.)*
Ralph C. Humphreys *(Sr. V.P.-Store Oper.)*
Jerry L. Jones *(Sr. V.P.-Human Res.)*
Roger Parks *(Sr. V.P.-MIS)*
Clyde D. Staley *(V.P.)*
Bishop Wallace *(V.P.-Adv.)*
A.Q. Winstead *(V.P.-Grocery)*
David R. Black *(Controller & Treas.)*

No. of Mfg. Plants/Facilities: 60

Computer Systems/Hardware:
IBM ES 9000

Outside Service Firm(s):

Deloitte & Touche*(Auditors)*
Jackson, MS

Pan-American Life Insurance Company*(Group Insurance Broker/ Consult)*
601 Poydras St.
New Orleans, LA 70130
Tel.: 504-566-1300
Fax: 504-566-3459

Deposit Guaranty National Bank*(Major Banking Relationship)*
One Deposit Guaranty Plaza,
Jackson, MS 39201

Deposit Guaranty National Bank*(Pension Manager)*
One Deposit Guaranty Plaza,
Jackson, MS 39201

Subsidiaries:

Florida Jitney Jungle Stores, Inc. **(1)**
453 N. Mill St.
Jackson, MS 39207
Tel.: 601-948-0361
Food Stores
S.I.C.: 5411

Foodway, Inc. **(1)**
210 Highway N. (Europa Shopping Center)
Europa, MS 39744
Tel.: 601-258-7666
Grocery Store
S.I.C.: 5411

Interstate Jitney Jungle Stores, Inc. **(1)**
1306 Woodward Ave. (Shoals Plaza)
Muscle Shoals, AL 35660
Tel.: 205-383-5466
Grocery Stores
S.I.C.: 5411

Jitney Jungle Wholesale Co., Inc. **(1)**
453 N. Mill St.
Jackson, MS 39202
Tel.: 601-948-0361
S.I.C.: 5141

CURT G. JOA, INC.
P.O. Box 903, Crocker Ave.
Sheboygan Falls, WI 53085-0903
Tel.: 414-467-6136
Fax: 414-467-2924
Year Founded: 1932
Sales Range: $20-39 Million
Emp.: 255
Mfr. Paper Converting Machinery
S.I.C.: 3554
Curt G. Joa *(Chm. Bd.)*
Martha F. Joa *(Pres.)*
Timothy Kenney *(V.P.)*
Herbert E. Bickelhaupt *(Treas.)*
Lou Suprise *(Asst. Treas.)*
Curt G. Joa, III *(Dir.-Data Processing)*
Jeffrey J. Radder *(Dir.-Personnel)*
Donald W. Lammers *(Gen. Mgr.)*
Duane A. Stevens *(Pur. Agent)*

Principal(s):
Curt G. Joa
Martha F. Joa

No. of Mfg. Plants/Facilities: 4
No. of U.S. Offices: 5
No. of Foreign Offices: 1

Computer Systems/Hardware:
EMS

Outside Service Firm(s):

Kuehl & Company*(Auditors)*
Menomonee Falls, WI

Aetna Life & Casualty*(Commercial Insurance Carrier)*
Milwaukee, WI

Wausau Insurance*(Group Insurer)*
2000 Westwood Dr.
Wausau, WI 54401-7881
Tel.: 715-842-6902
Fax: 715-847-8534

Foley & Lardner*(Legal Firm)*
777 E. Wisconsin Ave.
Milwaukee, WI 53202
Tel.: 414-271-2400

First Wisconsin National Bank*(Major Banking Relationship)*
Sheboygan, WI

M & I Marshall & Ilsley Bank*(Major Banking Relationship)*
770 N. Water St.
Milwaukee, WI 53202
Tel.: 414-765-8700

CIGNA*(Pension Manager)*
Hartford, CT
Tel.: 203-726-6000

JOAN FABRICS CORP.
100 Vesper Executive Pk.
Tyngsboro, MA 01879
Tel.: 508-649-5626
Fax: 508-649-9142
Sales Range: $40-59 Million
Emp.: 1,300
Mfr. Upholstery Fabrics
S.I.C.: 2231
Elkin McCallum *(Pres. & Chief Exec. Officer)*
Richard Alden *(Chief Fin. Officer & Exec. V.P.)*
Penny Richards *(Chief Oper. Officer & Exec. V.P.)*
Charles G. Burke *(Sr. V.P.-Admin., Treas., & Asst. Sec.)*
Robert Check *(V.P.-Sls. Auto Div.)*
Richard Coombes *(V.P.-Engrng. Services)*
Bob Daros *(V.P.-Mfg. Information Systems)*
Thomas E. McCall *(V.P.-Auto Quality Assurance)*
Jay Orlin *(Sec.)*

Computer Systems/Hardware:
IBM System 38

Outside Service Firm(s):

KPMG Peat Marwick*(Auditors)*
600 Fleet Center
Providence, RI 02903
Tel.: 401-421-6600

Goulston & Storrs*(Legal Firm)*
131 State St.
Boston, MA 02109
Tel.: 617-742-1950

Rhode Island Hospital Trust National Bank*(Major Banking Relationship)*
Providence, RI

G. JOANNOU CYCLE CO. INC.
151 Ludlow Ave.
Northvale, NJ 07647
Tel.: 201-768-9050
Approx.Sls.: $14,000,000
Emp.: 100
Mfr. of Bicycles
S.I.C.: 3751
Madeline Joannou *(Chief Exec. Officer)*
Cindy Joannou *(Shipping Mgr.)*

JOCKEY INTERNATIONAL, INC.
2300 60th
Kenosha, WI 53140
Tel.: 414-658-8111
Fax: 414-658-0036
Year Founded: 1876
Approx.Sls.: $300,000,000
Emp.: 4,000

Export
Mfr. of Jockey Men's & Boy's Underwear & Sleepwear; Hosiery & Sportswear; Jockey For Her Underwear & Sleepwear
S.I.C.: 2322; 2254; 2341; 5136
Donna Wolf Steigerwaldt *(Chm. & Chief Exec. Officer)*
Paul E. Sebastian *(Sr. Exec. V.P.-Fin. & Sec.)*
Arthur F. DeCesaro, Jr. *(Exec. V.P.-Mktg.& Nat'l. Sls.)*
Fred W. Holmes *(Sr. V.P.-Mfg.)*
Gayle Compton Huff *(V.P.-Adv.)*
Frank Armistead *(V.P.-Opers.)*
John H. Casey *(V.P.-Human Resources)*
Paul J. Yoo *(V.P.-Fin. & Treas.)*
Anne Arbus *(V.P.-Taxes)*
Peter J. Hannes *(V.P.-Special Mkts.)*
Earl Winkelman *(V.P., Gen. Counsel & Asst. Sec.)*
Ed Emma *(Dir.-Sportswear & Jockey Men's Wear)*

Computer Systems/Hardware:
IBM System 34

Outside Service Firm(s):

Deloitte & Touche*(Auditors)*
250 E. Wisconsin Ave.
Milwaukee, WI 53202-4283
Tel.: 414-271-3000

M & I Marshall & Ilsley Bank*(Major Banking Relationship)*
770 N. Water St.
Milwaukee, WI 53202
Tel.: 414-765-8700

JOFCO INC.
13th & Vine St.
Jasper, IN 47547-0071
Mailing Address:
P.O. Box 71,
Jasper, IN 47547-0071
Tel.: 812-482-5154
Tel.: 800-235-6326
Fax: 812-634-2392
Year Founded: 1922
Sales Range: $20-39 Million
Emp.: 425
Mfr. Wooden Office Furniture & Seating
S.I.C.: 2521
Joe Steurer *(Chm. & Chief Exec. Officer)*
Bill Rubino *(Pres.)*
Jerry Olinger *(V.P.-Mktg.)*
Gregory W. Sturm *(V.P. & Treas.)*
Fred Dupps *(Dir.-Pur.)*
Stan Englert *(Dir.-Mktg. & Sls.)*
Lee Kraft Jr. *(Mgr.-Quality Control)*
Gene Luebbehusen *(Mgr.-Mktg. Services)*
Stan Englert *(Mgr.-Reg. Sls.)*
Matt Latimer *(Mgr.-Human Resources)*
Jerry Olinger *(Mgr.-Mfg.)*

No. of Mfg. Plants/Facilities: 2
No. of U.S. Offices: 1

Computer Systems/Hardware:
Honeywell

Outside Service Firm(s):

Buechlein & Brough*(Auditors)*
Jasper, IN

Forrest Sherer Agency*(Commercial Insurance Carrier)*
Terre Haute, IN

Sturm, Smith & Webster*(Legal Firm)*
Vincennes, IN

German American Bank*(Major Banking Relationship)*
Jasper, IN

The Principal Financial Group*(Pension Manager)*
711 High St.
Des Moines, IA 50309
Tel.: 515-247-4593
Tel.: 800-543-4015

JOFFKO INTERNATIONAL
8038 El Rio
Houston, TX 77054
Tel.: 713-644-3888
Telex: 794366 JOFFKO INC HOU
Fax: 713-644-3015
Year Founded: 1980
Assets: $2,915,534
Liabilities: $643,854
Net Worth: $2,271,680
Sales Range: $10-19 Million
Emp.: 8
Fiscal Year-end: 4/15/92
Export
Design & Build for the Commercial, Industrial & Petrochemical Industries; Plant Maintenance & Procurement Services
S.I.C.: 8711; 8712; 8741; 7349; 1541
Achilles Kozakis *(Chm. Bd. & Mng. Dir.)*
A.A. Joffrion *(Pres.)*
Foster Carter *(Chief Fin. Officer)*
Jamie Baker *(Gen. Counsel)*
Vaso Papandrianos *(Sec.)*
Thomas Kozakis *(Mgr.-Admin.)*
Julio Elayada *(Consultant)*
Principal(s):
Achilles Kozakis
A.A. Joffrion

No. of U.S. Offices: 1
No. of Foreign Offices: 3

Computer Systems/Hardware:
TRS-80 II

Outside Service Firm(s):

Melton & Melton*(Auditors)*
Houston, TX

First Meridian*(Commercial Insurance Carrier)*
Houston, TX

Barclays Bank plc*(International Bank Affiliate)*
Saint Helier, Jersey Channel Islands

China Banking Corporation*(International Bank Affiliate)*
Makati,
Metro Manila, Philippines

Baker & Botts*(Legal Firm)*
3000 One Shell Plaza
Houston, TX 77002
Tel.: 713-229-1789

First City National Bank*(Major Banking Relationship)*
Houston, TX

Texas Commerce Bank*(Major Banking Relationship)*
600 Travis Street, Suite 1150
Houston, TX 77002
Tel.: 713-236-4865

Subsidiaries:

Joffko Cameroon Corporation **(1)**
6815-A Lindbergh St.
Houston, TX 77087
Tel.: 713-644-3888

SadCo Ltd. **(1)**
76 Hill Ln.,
Southhampton, SO1 5BA, United Kingdom
Emp.: 6
Design & Build; Procurement & Maintenence Services
S.I.C.: 8711; 8712; 8741; 7349; 1541
Duncan Sharp-Smith *(Dir.)*

Joffko Philippines, Inc. **(1)**
11 Emerald Dr. Ortigas Greenheights, Rizal, Tatay Philippines
Tel.: 632 665 4050
Emp.: 6
Architecture, Engrng., Construction, Procurement Services & Construction Mngmt.
S.I.C.: 8711; 8712; 8741
Frank Escobar *(Chm. & Gen. Mgr.)*

JOHANSON MANUFACTURING CORPORATION
400 Rockaway Valley Rd.
Boonton, NJ 07005
Tel.: 201-334-2676
Fax: 201-334-2954
Approx.Sls.: $13,000,000
Emp.: 200
Import Export
Precision Variable Capacitors & Microwave Tuning Elements Utilizing Air, Sapphire, Quartz & Ceramic Dielectrics; Phase-Trim & Tunable Back Shorts Microwave Components
S.I.C.: 3675; 3679
Edna L. Johanson *(Chm. Bd.)*
Nancy Krawczyk *(Pres.)*
Walter Hutton *(V.P.-Opers.)*
Tom W. Rowan, Jr. *(V.P.-Sls. & Mktg.)*

Outside Service Firm(s):

Leshner, Franchino & Co.*(Auditors)*
Parsippany, NJ

Hannoch, Weisman, Stern, Besser, Berkowitz & Kinne*(Legal Firm)*
Union, NJ

United Jersey Bank*(Major Banking Relationship)*
Boonton, NJ

JOHN HANCOCK MUTUAL LIFE INSURANCE COMPANY
John Hancock Place, 200 Clarendon St.
Boston, MA 02117
Mailing Address:
P.O. Box 111
Boston, MA 02117 **MA**
Tel.: 617-572-6000
Fax: 617-572-6639
Year Founded: 1862
Assets: $36,220,199,822
Liabilities: $34,640,106,933
Net Worth: $1,580,092,889
Approx.Premiums: $6,825,000,000
Emp.: 15,200
Fiscal Year-end: 12/31/91
Individual Life, Group & Personal Health Insurance and Specialty Investment Products
S.I.C.: 6311; 6411; 6321
Employee Matching Gifts Program: Gifts Are Matched at .5:1 Up to $1, 500 Per Employee; Minimum Gift is $25
Stephen L. Brown *(Chm. Bd. & Chief Exec. Officer)*
Foster L. Aborn *(Vice Chm.)*
William L. Boyan, Jr. *(Pres. & Chief Oper. Officer)*
Thomas E. Moloney *(Chief Fin. Officer)*
David F. D'Alessandro *(Sr. Exec. V.P.-Retail Sector)*
George F. Miller *(Sr. Exec. V.P.-Business Insurance Sector)*
Diane M. Capstaff *(Exec. V.P.-Corp. Sector)*
William E. Caufield *(Sr. V.P.-Grp. Benefit Opers.)*
Derek Chilvers *(Sr. V.P.-Intl.)*
Nathaniel S. Coolidge *(Sr. V.P.-Bonds & Fin.)*
Edward P. Dowd *(Sr. V.P.-Mortgage Investments)*
William R. Gordon *(Sr. V.P.-Agricultural Investment)*
Raeburn B. Hathaway, Jr. *(Sr. V.P. & Sec.)*
Frank S. Irish *(Sr. V.P. & Corp. Actuary-Corp. Actuarial Services)*
Joel Y. Kamer *(Sr. V.P.-Retail Distr. Fin. Services)*
Jeanne M. Livermore *(Sr. V.P.-Ctr. for Quality Control)*
John T. Longmoore *(Sr. V.P.-Group Pensions)*
Robert A. Marra *(Sr. V.P.-Retail Mktg. & Prod. Devel.)*
Michael B. O'Toole *(Sr. V.P.-Retail Information Services)*
Henry D. Shaw *(Sr. V.P.-Individual Insurance Prods.)*
Barry L. Shemin *(Sr. V.P.-Retirement Security)*
Richard P. Caliri *(V.P.-Grp. Opers.)*
John T. Farady *(V.P. & Treas.)*
Osbert M. Hood *(V.P. & Controller)*
Judith Markland *(V.P.-Group Pension)*
David L. Murphy, Jr. *(V.P.-Retail Human Resources)*
Page Palmer *(V.P.-Human Resources)*
Diane B. Smigel *(V.P.-Corp. Information Services)*
Ronald A. Smith *(V.P.-Information Processing)*
Richard S. Scipione *(Gen. Counsel)*
Patricia C. Bond *(Gen. Dir.-Adv.)*
Frederick W. McManus *(Gen. Dir.-Meeting Mngmt. & Travel)*
Robert S. Paster *(Gen. Dir.-Corp. Fin. Analysis)*

John Hancock Mutual Life Insurance Company—(Continued)

James H. Young *(Gen. Dir.-Office of the Sec.)*
Les Hemmings *(Dir.-Human Resources Training)*
Allen Hymovitz *(Dir.-Benefit Admin.)*
Stephen F. Kelley *(Dir.-Telecommunications)*
William J. McDevitt *(Dir.-Pur.)*
Harold F. Portle *(Dir.-Bldg. Leasing)*
Dale L. Kutz *(Sr. Assoc. Controller)*
Barry Sanborn *(Asst. Sec.)*
Amy Wang *(Mgr.-Corp. Library)*

Computer Systems/Hardware:
IBM 3480

Outside Service Firm(s):

Ernst & Young*(Auditors)*
200 Clarendon St., 46th Fl.
Boston, MA 02116
Tel.: 617-266-2000

First National Bank of Boston*(Major Banking Relationship)*
P.O. Box 644,
Boston, MA 02102-0644
Tel.: 617-575-2900
Fax: 617-575-2549

Subsidiaries:

Independence Investment Associates, Inc. **(1)**
One Liberty Square
Boston, MA 02109
Tel.: 617-292-8701 (100%)
Approx.Sls.: $7,929,306
Emp.: 42
Investment Services
S.I.C.: 6282
Lewis J. Kleinrock *(Pres. & Chief Exec. Officer)*
William C. Fletcher *(Exec. V.P.)*
Vincent B. Burns *(Sr. V.P.)*

John Hancock Freedom Securities Corporation **(1)**
One Beacon St., 4th Fl.
Boston, MA 02108
Tel.: 617-572-6000 (100%)
Approx.Sls.: $225,066,664
Emp.: 2,044
Holding Company
S.I.C.: 6719
John Goldsmith *(Chm. & Chief Exec. Officer)*
Richard K. Howe *(Gen. Counsel)*

John Hancock Mutual Funds **(1)**
101 Huntington Ave.
Boston, MA 0219907603
Tel.: 617-375-1500 (100%)
Mutal Fund Management
S.I.C.: 6211
David King *(Pres.)*

John Hancock Subsidiaries, Inc. **(1)**
John Hancock Pl.
Boston, MA 02117
Tel.: 617-572-6000 (100%)
Approx.Sls.: $966,153,313
Emp.: 4,740
Holding Co.
S.I.C.: 6719
William L. Boyan *(Pres.)*

Subsidiaries:

Cost Care, Inc. **(2)**
7711 Center Ave., Ste. 100
Huntington Beach, CA 92647
Tel.: 714-895-1520
Utilization Review Manangement Firm
S.I.C.: 6722; 6726
Lawrence Goelman *(Pres.)*
David Ackley *(V.P.)*
Ray Foose *(V.P.)*

First Signature Bank & Trust Co. **(2)**
190 Commerce Way
Portsmouth, NH 03801
Tel.: 603-433-3700 (100%)
Approx.Sls.: $1,413,621
Emp.: 24
Consumer Bank
S.I.C.: 6022
James W. McLaughlin *(Pres. & Chief Exec. Officer)*
Anne M. McDonley *(V.P. & Treas.)*

John Hancock Advisers, Inc. **(2)**
101 Huntington Ave.
Boston, MA 02199
Tel.: 617-375-1900 (100%)
Approx.Sls.: $58,439,981
Emp.: 186
Investment Adviser
S.I.C.: 6282
Edward J. Boudreau *(Chm. Bd., Pres. & Chief Exec. Officer)*
James B. Little *(Sr. V.P. & Chief Fin. Officer)*
Robert H. Watts *(Sr. V.P.)*

Subsidiary:

John Hancock Distributors, Inc. **(3)**
101 Huntington Ave.
Boston, MA 02199
Tel.: 617-375-1900 (100%)
Approx.Sls.: $942,894,897
Emp.: 125
Broker-Dealer
S.I.C.: 6211
Robert Watts *(Pres. & Chief Exec. Officer)*

John Hancock Capital Growth Management, Inc. **(2)**
1140 Taylor St.
San Francisco, CA 94108
Tel.: 415-775-9400 (100%)
Approx.Sls.: $1,206,095
Emp.: 6
Dexter B. Dawes *(Mng. Dir.)*
Lambert C. Thom *(Mng. Dir.)*
Deane K. Reade *(Mng. Dir.)*

John Hancock Capital Corporation **(2)**
John Hancock Place
Boston, MA 02117
Tel.: 617-572-1779 (100%)
Approx.Sls.: $22,294,121
Provides Access to the Foreign and Domestic Commercial Paper & Debt Markets for the John Hancock Complex
S.I.C.: 7389
Karen E. Liukkonen *(Pres.)*
Henry J. Desautel *(V.P.)*
James E. Cruickshank *(Treas.)*

John Hancock HealthPlans, Inc. **(2)**
1585 Paoli Pike
West Chester, PA 19380
Tel.: 215-344-7780 (100%)
Approx.Sls.: $62,041,667
Emp.: 418
Data Processing & Systems Analysis Services for Health Care Providers; Health Maintenance Organizations
S.I.C.: 7374; 6324
Stephen L. Brown *(Chm. Bd. & Chief Exec. Officer)*
William L. Boyan *(Pres.)*
Thomas E. Moloney *(Chief Fin. Officer)*

John Hancock Networking Insurance Agency **(2)**
John Hancock Place
Boston, MA 02117
Tel.: 617-572-9656 (100%)
Approx.Sls.: $2,490,397
Emp.: 18
Develops & Markets Financial Products
S.I.C.: 7389
Paul D. LaFleur *(Pres.)*
Robert W. Krempa *(V.P. & Treas.)*
J. Edward Anguish *(V.P. & Treas.)*

John Hancock Leasing Corporation **(2)**
John Hancock Pl.
Boston, MA 02117
Tel.: 617-572-4700 (100%)
Approx.Sls.: $20,094,178
Emp.: 57
Financial Services
S.I.C.: 6159
Theodore J. Rogenski *(Pres. & Chief Exec. Officer)*
John M. Butler *(Sr. V.P. & Treas.)*
Gerard P. Kelly *(Sr. V.P.-Mktg.)*
Alan R. Seghezzi *(V.P. & Gen. Counsel)*

John Hancock Property and Casualty Holding Co. **(2)**
John Hancock Pl.
Boston, MA 02117
Tel.: 617-375-3000 (100%)
Approx.Sls.: $557,844,405
Emp.: 1,790
Insurance and Reinsurance, Property & Casualty Risks
S.I.C.: 6411
William L. Boyan *(Chm.)*
Larry O'Connor *(Pres. & Chief Exec. Officer)*
Michael J. McSally *(Sr. V.P. & Chief Oper. Officer)*
Paul L. Sweeney *(Sr. V.P. & Treas.)*

Hancock Realty Investors, Inc. **(2)**
200 Berkely St., 19th Fl.
Boston, MA 02117
Tel.: 617-572-3804 (100%)
Approx.Sls.: $56,198
Emp.: 36
Serves as a General Partner of a Limited Partnership for Institutional Investors
S.I.C.: 6411
Steven E. Wheeler *(Chm. & Chief Exec. Officer)*

John Hancock Realty Services Corp. **(2)**
One Exeter Plaza, 14th Fl., 699 Boylston St.
Boston, MA 02116
Tel.: 617-424-8100 (100%)
Approx.Sls.: $10,788,579
Emp.: 67
Holding Company for Real Estate Investments
S.I.C.: 6552; 6719
Donald N. Brown *(Pres.)*

John Hancock Venture Capital Management, Inc. **(2)**
One Financial Ctr., 39th Floor
Boston, MA 02111
Tel.: 617-350-4002 (100%)
Approx.Sls.: $6,199,285
Emp.: 21
Venture Capital Investors
S.I.C.: 6282
Edward W. Kane *(Mng. Dir.)*
D. Brooks Zug *(Mng. Dir.)*

Profesco Corporation **(2)**
John Hancock Place
Boston, MA 02117
Tel.: 617-572-5110 (100%)
Approx.Sls.: $3,542,414
Emp.: 30
Assist Members of Professions with Personal Financial Objectives
S.I.C.: 8742
Joseph W. Buckley, Jr. *(Pres. & Chief Exec. Officer)*

Professional Economic Services, Inc. **(2)**
John Hancock Place
Boston, MA 02117
Tel.: 617-421-6572 (100%)
S.I.C.: 8748
Joseph W. Buckley, Jr. *(Pres. & Chief Exec. Officer)*

John Hancock Variable Life Insurance Co. **(1)**
John Hancock Place
Boston, MA 02117
Tel.: 617-572-5600 (100%)
Approx.Premiums: $397,000,000
Emp.: 25
S.I.C.: 6311
Henry D. Shaw *(Pres.)*
Patrick F. Smith *(V.P & Controller)*
Ronald C. Horton *(V.P.-Mktg.)*

Unigard Security Insurance Co. **(1)**
15805 N.E. 24th St.
Bellevue, WA 98008
Tel.: 206-641-4321
Fax: 206-644-2994
Assets: $584,130,229
Liabilities: $470,634,760
Net Worth: $113,495,469
Approx.Sls.: $202,000,000
Emp.: 800
Fiscal Year-end: 12/31/90
Computer Systems/Hardware:
IBM 3081
Insurance
S.I.C.: 6331
Corporate Giving Program: Subject to Modest Budget Based on Income and Previous Year's Budget
Employee Matching Gift Program: $25 to $300 Match to Colleges or Universities; 50% Match to Employee Contribution to Annual United Way Drive
Laurence P. O'Connor *(Chm. Bd. & Chief Exec. Officer)*
Donald K. Shanks *(Pres. & Chief Oper. Officer)*
D.E. Abbrederis *(Sr. V.P. & Chief Fin. Officer)*
M.J. Pagano *(Sr. V.P.-Reinsurance Assumed)*
J.L. Epler *(V.P. & Controller)*
Paul Neuss *(V.P.-Data Processing)*
Francis P. Hogan *(V.P.-Commercial Lines)*
James C. Lett *(V.P.-Regional)*
Brian Upton-Rowley *(Asst. V.P.-Mktg. & Prod. Devel.)*
Doyle Hargis *(Asst. V.P.-Pur. & Leasing)*
T.R. Olson *(Treas.)*
H.R. McGough *(Gen. Counsel & Sec.)*
Ann Chapin *(Mgr.-Human Resources)*
Pat Palmer *(Mgr.-Personnel Training & Devel.)*
Patricia A. Barone *(Asst. Sec.)*

Subsidiaries:

Unigard Indemnity Co. **(2)**
3515 Glenwood Ave.
Raleigh, NC 27612
Tel.: 919-787-2412 (100%)
Fax: 919-781-0533
Approx.Sls.: $11,000,000
Insurance
S.I.C.: 6331
Laurence P. O'Connor *(Chm. Bd. & Chief Exec. Officer)*
Donald K. Shanks *(Pres. & Chief Oper. Officer)*
D.E. Abbrederis *(Sr. V.P. & Chief Fin. Officer)*
J.L. Epler *(V.P. & Controller)*
Francis P. Hogan *(V.P.-Mktg.)*
T.R. Olson *(Treas.)*
H.R. McGough *(Gen. Counsel & Sec.)*

Unigard Insurance Co. **(2)**
1215 Fourth Ave.
Seattle, WA 98161
Tel.: 206-641-4321 (100%)
Fax: 206-644-2994
Approx.Sls.: $53,000,000
Insurance
S.I.C.: 6331
Laurence P. O'Connor *(Chm. Bd. & Chief Exec. Officer)*
Donald K. Shanks *(Pres. & Chief Oper. Officer)*
D.E. Abbrederis *(Sr. V.P. & Chief Fin. Officer)*
J.L. Epler *(V.P. & Controller)*
Francis P. Hogan *(V.P.-Mktg.)*
T.R. Olson *(Treas.)*
H.R. McGough *(Gen. Counsel & Sec.)*

Unigard Service Corp. **(2)**
1215 Fourth Ave.
Seattle, WA 98161
Tel.: 206-641-4321 (100%)
Fax: 714-963-9468
Approx.Sls.: $2,248,197
Premium Financing
S.I.C.: 6411
Laurence P. O'Connor *(Chm. Bd. & Chief Exec. Officer)*
Donald K. Shanks *(Pres. & Chief Oper. Officer)*
D.E. Abbrederis *(Sr. V.P. & Chief Fin. Officer)*
R.E. Torobin *(V.P. & G.M.)*
J.L. Epler *(V.P. & Controller)*
T.R. Olson *(Treas.)*
H.R. McGough *(Sec.)*

Non-U.S. Holdings:

John Hancock Advisers International, Ltd. **(1)**
34 Dover St.
London, W1X 3RA, United Kingdom
Tel.: 071-4140131 (100%)
Mutual Fund Company
S.I.C.: 6722
John Wills *(V.P.)*

John Hancock Insurance Company of Bermuda Ltd. **(1)**
Clarendon House, Church St.
Hamilton, 5-31, Bermuda
Tel.: (809-29) 5-1422 (100%)
Approx.Sls.: $8,500,000
Reisurance
S.I.C.: 6411
Paul L. Sweeney *(Pres.)*
Robert S. McMann *(V.P. & Treas.)*

John Hancock Intl. Services S.A. **(1)**
Avenue des Arts 44, BTE. 4
Brussels, 1040, Belgium (99.9%)
Emp.: 8
Coordinates Associate Insurer Activities
S.I.C.: 8742
Derek Chilvers *(Chm.)*

John Hancock Servicos Internacionais S/C., Ltda. **(1)**
Ave. Ipiranga 324 Building C Edifico Inv , 01046
Sao Paulo, Brazil (99.9%)
Serves International Group Program Clients in South America
S.I.C.: 8742
Derek Chilvers *(Mng. Dir.-Quota Holder)*

Maritime Life Assurance Co. **(1)**
2701 Dutch Village Rd. P.O. Box 1030, Halifax, NS Canada B3J 2X5
Tel.: (902) 455-0481 (99.7%)
Approx.Sls.: $421,000,000
Emp.: 500
Life Insurance Coverage for Canadian Markets
S.I.C.: 6311; 6321
J. Dickson Crawford *(Pres. & Chief Exec. Officer)*

JOHNNY APPLESEED'S, INC.
30 Tozer Road
Beverly, MA 01915
Tel.: 508-922-2040 **MA**
Fax: 508-922-7001
Year Founded: 1946
Approx.Sls.: $40,000,000
Emp.: 500
Fiscal Year-end: 6/30/91
Mail Order Apparel & Gifts
S.I.C.: 5961
H.A. Billeter *(Pres. & Chief Exec. Officer)*
Dana Pappas *(Controller)*
Brian Haley *(Dir.-Mktg.)*
Craig Smith *(Dir.-Human Resources)*

No. of Mfg. Plants/Facilities: 14

Computer Systems/Hardware:
IBM AS/400 IBM S/38

Outside Service Firm(s):

Arthur Andersen & Co.*(Auditors)*
One Intl. Place, 100 Oliver St.
Boston, MA 02110
Tel.: 617-330-4000
Fax: 617-439-9731

Peabody & Arnold*(Legal Firm)*
50 Rowes Wharf
Boston, MA 02110
Tel.: 617-292-3474

Shawmut Bank*(Major Banking Relationship)*
Salem, MA

JOHNSON ACOUSTICAL & SUPPLY CO.
2001 N.W. 19th Ave.
Portland, OR 97209
Tel.: 503-226-2100 **OR**
Fax: 503-226-2104
Year Founded: 1948
Approx.Sls.: $14,000,000
Emp.: 120
Contract & Distribute Interior Building Systems & Products
S.I.C.: 1799; 1742; 5039; 5085
David O. Johnson *(Chm. & Chief Exec. Officer)*
Karl E. Nulton *(Pres.)*
Vernell E. Moodhe *(Chief Fin. Officer)*
Joe Davenport *(V.P.-Supply)*
Darrell G. Martin *(V.P.-Construction & Production)*

No. of U.S. Offices: 1

Computer Systems/Hardware:
Bidtek

Outside Service Firm(s):

Blue Cross & Blue Shield of Oregon*(Group Insurer)*
Portland, OR

Lindsay, Hart, Neil & Weigler*(Legal Firm)*
Portland, OR

First Interstate Bank*(Major Banking Relationship)*
P.O. Box 3131,
Portland, OR 97208
Tel.: 503-220-4855
Fax: 503-225-7153

AL JOHNSON CONSTRUCTION CO.
3209 W. 76th St.
Minneapolis, MN 55435
Tel.: 612-831-8151
Fax: 612-893-9215
Year Founded: 1928
Approx.Sls.: $61,000,000
Emp.: 425
Heavy Industrial Construction: Tunnels, Marine Projects, Paving
S.I.C.: 1541; 1611; 1622; 1629
Tom R. Gessner *(Chm. Bd.)*
D.A. Johnson *(Pres.)*
A.R. Rund *(V.P.-Equip.)*
R.T. Taylor *(V.P., Sec. & Asst. Treas.)*
M.D. Wolf *(Treas.)*
G.F. Bruggeman *(Asst. Sec.)*

Computer Systems/Hardware:
IBM System 36

Outside Service Firm(s):

Deloitte & Touche*(Auditors)*
900 Pillsbury Ctr.
Minneapolis, MN 55402
Tel.: 612-332-2301
Fax: 612-375-5418

Faegre & Benson*(Legal Firm)*
2200 Norwest Ctr., 90 S. 7th St.
Minneapolis, MN 55402-3901
Tel.: 612-336-3000
Fax: 612-336-3026

Norwest Bank of Minneapolis N.A.*(Major Banking Relationship)*
P.O. Box 738, 161 N. Concord Exchange
So. St. Paul, MN 55075-0738
Tel.: 612-450-4064
Fax: 612-450-4078

JOHNSON BROS. CORP.
Hwy. 22 So.
Litchfield, MN 55355
Mailing Address:
P.O. Box 1002
Litchfield, MN 55355
Tel.: 612-693-2871 **MN**
Fax: 612-693-9192
Year Founded: 1930
Approx.Sls.: $100,000,000
Emp.: 1000
Fiscal Year-end: 3/31/90
Import Export
Heavy Construction; Power Plants, Materials Handling Facilities, Highways, Bridges, Underground Utilities, Treatment Facilities
S.I.C.: 1629; 1622; 1623
Richard W. Johnson *(Pres. & Chief Exec. Officer)*
Walter D. Johnson *(Exec. V.P., Chief Fin. Officer & Sec.)*
Kenneth O. Hafner *(Sr. V.P.)*
A.A. Sehlin *(Sr. V.P.-Structures)*
Carl Baumgartner *(V.P.)*
Bradley E. Eilertson *(V.P.)*
James R. Florey *(V.P.-Data Processing)*
Steven P. Jackson *(V.P.)*
Philip R. Johnson *(V.P.)*
Merlyn D. Lokken *(V.P.)*
Jack McCreery *(V.P.)*
Joseph H. Michels *(V.P.)*
Michael C. Swanson *(V.P.)*
Ronald L. Johnson *(Treas.)*
Ted Durkee *(Controller)*
Principal(s):
Richard W. Johnson
Walter D. Johnson
Philip R. Johnson

No. of U.S. Offices: 6

Computer Systems/Hardware:
AS 400

Outside Service Firm(s):

Virchow, Krause, Helgeson & Company*(Auditors)*
Minneapolis, MN

Reliance National*(Commercial Insurance Carrier)*
77 Water St.
New York, NY 10005
Tel.: 212-858-6323
Fax: 212-858-3612

Norwest Bank Minnesota, N.A.*(International Bank Affiliate)*
6th St. & Marquette Av.
Minneapolis, MN 55479
Tel.: 612-667-1234

Dorsey & Whitney*(Legal Firm)*
2200 First Bank Place East
Minneapolis, MN 55402

Norwest Bank Minnesota, N.A.*(Major Banking Relationship)*
6th St. & Marquette Av.
Minneapolis, MN 55479
Tel.: 612-667-1234

Subsidiary:

Indeco, Inc. **(1)**
630 E. River Dr.
Bettendorf, IA 52722
Tel.: 319-359-5451
Fax: 319-359-4318
Specialty Engineering
S.I.C.: 8712
Paul H. Schwartz *(Pres.)*

C. S. JOHNSON CO.
502 S. Kenwood
Champaign, IL 61821
Mailing Address:
P.O. Box 3067
Champaign, IL 61821
Tel.: 217-356-3781
Telex: 404-312 JO-CHN
Fax: 217-356-3786
Year Founded: 1928
Approx.Sls.: $10,000,000
Emp.: 60
Fiscal Year-end: 10/31/90
Export
Mobile & Stationary Concrete Batching Plants & Concrete Mixers
S.I.C.: 3531; 3535
Alex Balc, Jr. *(Chm. Bd.)*
Allen R. Seeland *(Pres.)*
John W. Mortimer *(V.P.)*

Computer Systems/Hardware:
VAN

THE JOHN JOHNSON CO.
1481 14th St.
Detroit, MI 48216
Tel.: 313-496-0600 **MI**
Fax: 313-496-0252
Approx.Sls.: $10,000,000
Emp.: 100
Fiscal Year-end: 8/31/91
Import Export
Manufacture Awnings, Tarpaulins, Cargo Covers, Drop Cloths, Canvas Specialties
S.I.C.: 2394; 5131
Charles A. Keersmaeker *(Pres.)*
Richard H. Dancy, Jr. *(V.P. & Treas.)*
Robert B. Dancy *(V.P.)*
Debbie Ficarra *(Sec.)*
Principal(s):
Richard H. Dancy, Sr.

Outside Service Firm(s):

Collis, Kopmeyer & Co., P.C.*(Auditors)*
Birmingham, MI

Comerica Bank*(Major Banking Relationship)*
211 W. Fort St.
Detroit, MI 48226
Tel.: 313-222-3300

RICK JOHNSON & COMPANY, INC.
6100 Indian School Rd., NE
Albuquerque, NM 87110
Mailing Address:
P.O. Box 4770,
Albuquerque, NM 87196
Year Founded: 1977
Approx.Billings: $14,000,000
Emp.: 40
Eric D. Johnson *(Chm. Bd., Chief Exec. Officer)*
Deborah U. Johnson *(Pres.)*
Gail Vavruska *(V.P., Corp. Treas.)*
Lin Clark *(Asst. V.P. & Gen. Mgr., Recruitment)*
Aimee Martin *(Dir., Pub. Rels.)*

Computer Systems/Hardware:
PSS-Ad Unit, Unisys

G. E. JOHNSON CONSTRUCTION CO., INC.
310 S. 14th St.
Colorado Springs, CO 80904
Mailing Address:
P.O. Box 2139
Colorado Springs, CO 80901
Tel.: 719-473-5321 **CO**
Fax: 719-473-5324
Year Founded: 1967
Approx.Sls.: $108,100,000
Emp.: 450
Fiscal Year-end: 9/30/91
General Contractor & Construction Manager
S.I.C.: 1542
Gilbert E. Johnson *(Pres. & Treas.)*
Gerald C. Snyder *(Exec. V.P.)*
Bill G. Brown *(V.P.-Estimating & Sec.)*
Phil Harris *(V.P.-Opers.)*
David E. Alberts *(Controller)*
Principal(s):
Gilbert E. Johnson

Outside Service Firm(s):

Martin, Vejvoda & Associates*(Auditors)*
Denver, CO

St. Paul Fire & Marine Insurance Co.*(Commercial Insurance Carrier)*
385 Washington St.
St. Paul, MN 55102
Tel.: 612-221-7911

Sparks, Dix & Enoch*(Legal Firm)*
Colorado Springs, CO

Affiliated National Bank of Colorado*(Major Banking Relationship)*
Colorado Springs, CO

First National Bank of Colorado Springs*(Major Banking Relationship)*
Colorado Springs, CO

THE JOHNSON CORPORATION
805 Wood St
Three Rivers, MI 49093
Tel.: 616-278-1715 **MI**
Telex: 022-4457
Fax: 616-279-5980
Year Founded: 1933
Approx.Sls.: $35,000,000
Emp.: 130
Fiscal Year-end: 6/30/90
Mfr. Rotary Joints, Syphons, Condensate Systems, Cylinder & Solenoid Valves, Vacuum Breakers, Separators, After-Coolers
S.I.C.: 3494; 3569
Roger D. Wiedenbeck *(Chm. Bd. & Pres.)*
Bruce B. Monroe *(Vice Chm. & V.P.-Mktg.)*
James Dechnik *(V.P.-Fin. & Sec.)*
Thomas O. Monroe, Jr. *(V.P.-Intl. Sls.)*
Daniel Berkey *(Mgr.-Data Processing)*
Craig Garrison *(Pur. Agent)*

The Johnson Corporation—(Continued)

No. of Mfg. Plants/Facilities: 3
No. of Foreign Offices: 7

Computer Systems/Hardware:
IBM System 38

Outside Service Firm(s):

Grant Thornton*(Auditors)*
700 One Prudential Plaza, 130 East Randolph St.
Chicago, IL 60601
Tel.: 312-856-0200
Fax: 312-565-4719

Goedert & Huntington*(Legal Firm)*
Three Rivers, MI

First National Bank of Three Rivers*(Major Banking Relationship)*
Three Rivers, MI

Subsidiary:

Specialty Castings **(1)**
211 Mill St., P.O. Box 129
Springport, MI 49284
Tel.: 517-857-3660
Emp.: 128
Foundry Grey Iron & Ductile Iron
S.I.C.: 3321

JOHNSON COUNTY FARM BUREAU CO-OP
755 Hamilton Ave.
Franklin, IN 46131
Tel.: 317-736-5131
Fax: 317-736-6170
Assets: $3,000,000
Earnings: $200,000
Net Worth: $3,000,000
Approx.Sls.: $17,000,000
Emp.: 28
Agricultural Production-Crops; Agricultural Services; Membership Organization
S.I.C.: 5153; 5191
James Black *(Chm. Bd. & Pres.)*
Keith Cochran *(Chief Exec. & Chief Fin. Officer)*
Richard Henderson *(Treas.)*

Computer Systems/Hardware:
IBM 3741

Outside Service Firm(s):

Indianapolis Farm Co-op Assn.*(Auditors)*
Indianapolis, IN

Farm Bureau Insurance*(Group Insurer)*
Indianapolis, IN

Geffe & Rogers*(Legal Firm)*
Franklin, IN

Franklin Bank*(Major Banking Relationship)*
Franklin, IN

E.F. JOHNSON COMPANY
11095 Viking Dr., Ste. 220
Eden Prarie, MN 55344
Mailing Address:
P.O. Box 59089,
Minneapolis, MN 55459
Tel.: 612-943-5500
Tel.: 800-328-3911 Ext. 6380
Telex: 933008
Fax: 612-943-5656
Year Founded: 1923
Earnings: $1,200,000
Approx.Sls.: $85,800,000
Emp.: 1,100
Fiscal Year-end: 12/31/91
Import Export
Mfr. of Mobile Communications Equipment & Electronic Components
S.I.C.: 3663; 3674; 3679; 3678
J.D. Somrock *(Pres. & Chief Exec. Officer)*
Kathleen P. Pepski *(Chief Fin. Officer & V.P.-Fin.)*
R.E. Cavins *(Sr. V.P.-Opers.)*
J.M. Eastman *(V.P.-Human Resources)*
Ernest J. Glass, Jr. *(V.P.-Component & Custom Prods.)*
J.D. Goodman *(V.P.-Mktg.)*
Frederick G. Hamer *(V.P.-Sls. & Distr.)*
Scott R. Bocklund *(Controller)*
Bert Erickson *(Mgr.-Mktg. Communications)*

JOHNSON & HIGGINS
125 Broad St.
New York, NY 10004
Tel.: 212-574-7000 **NJ**
Year Founded: 1845
Sales Range: $500-999 Million
Emp.: 8,200
Insurance & Risk Management & Consultants; Pension Consultants & Actuaries
S.I.C.: 6411
David A. Olsen *(Chm., Pres., Chief Exec. & Chief Oper. Officer)*
Kenneth A. Hecken *(Vice Chm.)*
Richard E. Meyer *(Exec. V.P.)*
Richard Nielsen *(Exec. V.P.)*
Raymond C. Brooks *(Sr. V.P.)*
James Delaney *(Sr. V.P.)*
James Readon *(Sr. V.P.)*
Karen Stein-Townsend *(Sr. V.P.)*
Margo R. Bowden *(V.P.-Pub. Rels.)*
Marie Gorey *(V.P.)*
Fred Kingsbury *(V.P.)*
Jane Krumrine *(V.P.-Corp. Communications)*
Joseph D. Roxe *(Chief Fin. Officer)*
Gardner M. Mundy *(Gen. Counsel & Sec.)*

Principal(s):
David A. Olsen

No. of U.S. Offices: 70
No. of Foreign Offices: 49

Computer Systems/Hardware:
IBM System 36; Boeing

Subsidiary:

Foster & Higgins, Inc. **(1)**
125 Broad St.
New York, NY 10004
Tel.: 212-574-9000
Employee Benefits Consulting Co.
S.I.C.: 8631
John Feldtmose *(Pres.)*

BERNARD JOHNSON INCORPORATED
3000 Wilcrest, Ste. 200
Houston, TX 77042
Tel.: 713-977-7411
Fax: 713-977-4781
Approx.Sls.: $25,000,000
Emp.: 150
Architecture, Engineering, Design
S.I.C.: 8711; 8712
Edward Davis *(Pres.)*
Bob Cheshire *(Sr. V.P.)*
Ray Martin *(Sr. V.P.)*
Franklin Moon *(Sr. V.P.)*
David C. Blaschke *(Dir.-Personnel)*

No. of U.S. Offices: 4

Computer Systems/Hardware:
DEC; Intergraph CADD System

Outside Service Firm(s):

Arthur Andersen & Co.*(Auditors)*
711 Louisiana, Ste. 1300
Houston, TX 77002-2323
Tel.: 713-237-2793

Texas Commerce Bank*(Major Banking Relationship)*
600 Travis Street, Suite 1150
Houston, TX 77002
Tel.: 713-236-4865

THE JOHNSON INDUSTRIES CORP.
605 Miami St.
Urbana, OH 43078
Tel.: 513-652-2181
Fax: 513-653-8352
Approx.Sls.: $20,000,000
Emp.: 325
Mfr. Air & Vacuum Reservoirs; Plastic & Fabricated Metal Products
S.I.C.: 3585; 3089; 3469
Thomas B. Johnson *(Chm. & Pres.)*
Robert Hilgendorf *(V.P. & Chief Oper. Officer)*
Daniel Veligan *(V.P.-Fin., Sec. & Treas.)*

Principal(s):
Thomas B. Johnson
Dorothy T. Johnson

Computer Systems/Hardware:
IBM PC

Outside Service Firm(s):

Ernst & Young*(Auditors)*
2300 Kettering Tower
Dayton, OH 45423
Tel.: 513-223-2000

Boehm, Rance, Pritchett, Brantner & Robison*(Legal Firm)*
Dayton, OH

Citizens National Bank of Urbana*(Major Banking Relationship)*
Urbana, OH

LEGRAND JOHNSON CONSTRUCTION CO.
1000 S. Main
Logan, UT 84323-0248
Mailing Address:
P.O. Box 248
Logan, UT 84321
Tel.: 801-752-2000 **UT**
Fax: 801-752-2968
Year Founded: 1934
Approx.Sls.: $27,000,000
Emp.: 150
Fiscal Year-end: 4/30/92
Heavy & Highway Construction; Quarrying & Mining; Asphalt Paving; Ready Mix Concrete
S.I.C.: 1611; 3273
LaRee K. Johnson *(Chm. Bd.)*
Janice J. Sackett *(Pres.)*
Larry L. Jardine *(Exec. V.P.)*
Richard Sackett *(Sr. V.P.)*
Sydney J. Sackett *(Treas.)*
Robert Jardine *(Dir.-Data Processing)*
Don Hancey *(Sec.)*

Principal(s):
LaRee K. Johnson
Janice J. Sackett

No. of Mfg. Plants/Facilities: 5

Outside Service Firm(s):

KPMG Peat Marwick*(Auditors)*
60 E. South Temple, Ste. 900
Salt Lake City, UT 84111
Tel.: 801-328-3000
Fax: 801-237-1552

Preston & Chambers*(Legal Firm)*
Logan, UT

First Interstate Bank*(Major Banking Relationship)*
2nd South & Main
Salt Lake City, UT 84101

Subsidiary:

Southern Paving Co. **(1)**
5101 E. Old Airport Rd.
Moab, UT 84532
Tel.: 801-259-5809
Sand, Gravel, & Asphalt Paving
S.I.C.: 1611
Brenda Stock *(Chief Oper. Officer)*

JOHNSON NEWSPAPER CORPORATION
260 Washington St.
Watertown, NY 13601
Tel.: 315-782-1000
Fax: 315-782-2337
Sales Range: $20-39 Million
Emp.: 270
Newspaper Publishing
S.I.C.: 2711
John B. Johnson *(Pres., Editor & Treas.)*
Catherine C. Johnson *(V.P. & Sec.)*
Kenneth Holloway *(Gen. Mgr.)*
Loren W. Walts *(Comptroller)*
Robert Cornell *(Dir.-Adv.)*

Principal(s):
John B. Johnson
Catherine C. Johnson

Computer Systems/Hardware:
Systems Integrators; IBM

Outside Service Firm(s):

Key Bank*(Major Banking Relationship)*
Watertown, NY

W.B. JOHNSON PROPERTY, INC.
3414 Peachtree Rd., Ste. 300
Atlanta, GA 30326
Tel.: 404-237-5500
Fax: 404-233-1745
Approx.Sls.: $350,000,000
Emp.: 7,500
Hotels, Cocktail Lounges & Restaurants
S.I.C.: 7011; 5813; 5812
William B. Johnson *(Chm. Bd. & Chief Exec. Officer)*
Larry Martindale *(Vice Chm.)*
Horst Schulze *(Pres. & Chief Oper. Officer)*
Jack J. Faussemagne *(Treas.)*
Rufus A. Chambers *(Sec.)*
Karon Cullen *(Dir.-Corp. Communications)*

Subsidiary:

Ritz-Carlton Hotel Company **(1)**
3414 Peachtree Rd., Ste. 300
Atlanta, GA 30326
Tel.: 404-237-5500
Emp.: 11,500
Hotel
S.I.C.: 7011
W.B. Johnson *(Chm. Bd. & Chief Exec. Officer)*
Horst Schulze *(Pres.)*
Richard Stevens *(Chief Fin. Officer)*

JOHNSON PUBLISHING COMPANY, INC.
820 S. Michigan Ave.
Chicago, IL 60605
Tel.: 312-322-9200
Fax: 312-322-0918
Year Founded: 1942
Approx.Sls.: $261,300,000
Emp.: 1,828
Fiscal Year-end: 12/31/91
Publishers of Ebony, Jet, & EM Magazines; Book Publishers; Radio Broadcasting; Television Production; Manufacture Cosmetics
S.I.C.: 2721; 2844; 4832; 4833
John H. Johnson *(Chm. Bd. & Chief Exec. Officer)*
Linda Johnson Rice *(Pres. & Chief Oper. Officer)*
H. John Alex *(V.P. & Western Adv. Dir.)*
James Beifuss *(V.P. & Dir.-Data Processing)*
Dennis H. Boston *(V.P. & Midwest Adv. Dir.)*
Robert H. Fentress *(V.P. & Circulation Mgr.)*
June A. Rhinehart *(V.P. & Gen. Counsel)*
Eunice W. Johnson *(Treas. & Sec.)*

Principal(s):
John H. Johnson

Computer Systems/Hardware:
IBM 370 Model 138

Outside Service Firm(s):

Supreme Life Insurance Co. of America*(Group Insurer)*
Chicago, IL

Subsidiaries:

Ebony Fashions **(1)**
820 S. Michigan Ave.
Chicago, IL 60605
Tel.: 312-322-0918

Fashion Fair Cosmetics **(1)**
820 S. Michigan Ave
Chicago, IL 60605
Tel.: 312-322-9444
Emp.: 150
Mfr. Cosmetics
S.I.C.: 2844
John H. Johnson *(Chm. Bd. & Chief Exec. Officer)*
Linda Johnson Rice *(Pres.)*
J. Lance Clarke *(Sr. V.P. & Gen. Mgr.)*
Michael Bellamy *(V.P.-Sls.)*
Marilyn Bynum *(Pur. Agent)*

Supreme Beauty Products **(1)**
820 S. Michigan Ave.
Chicago, IL 60605
Tel.: 312-322-9400

WJPC Radio Station **(1)**
820 S. Michigan Ave
Chicago, IL 60605
Tel.: 312-322-9400

WLNR Radio Station **(1)**
820 S. Michigan Ave.
Chicago, IL 60605
Tel.: 312-322-0918

WLOU Radio Station **(1)**
2549 So. 3rd St.
Louisville, KY 40208
Tel.: 502-636-3535

JOHNSON & QUIN, INC.
7460 N. Lehigh
Niles, IL 60648
Tel.: 708-647-6900
Fax: 708-647-6949
Approx.Sls.: $23,000,000
Emp.: 185
Specialty Forms; Printing & Laser Imaging; Personalized Direct Mail
S.I.C.: 2752; 2761; 7331
David R. Henkel *(Chm. Bd. & Pres.)*
Kathleen A. Veatch *(V.P.-Opers.)*
Donald Danner *(V.P.-Finance)*

Outside Service Firm(s):

Price Waterhouse*(Auditors)*
200 E. Randolph
Chicago, IL 60601
Tel.: 312-565-1500

First American Bank, N.A.*(Major Banking Relationship)*
Skokie, IL

S. C. JOHNSON & SON, INC.
1525 Howe St.
Racine, WI 53403
Tel.: 414-631-2000 **WI**
Telex: 264429 JON WAX RCN
Fax: 414-631-2133
Year Founded: 1886
Approx.Sls.: $2,500,000,000
Emp.: 12,500
Fiscal Year-end: 6/30/90

Import Export
Mfr. Laundry Aids, Cleaners, Air Fresheners, Wax Products, Insecticides & Personal Care Products; Insurance & Venture Capital
S.I.C.: 2842; 2879; 2841; 2844; 6722; 5122; 6531
Samuel C. Johnson *(Chm. Bd.)*
Richard M. Carpenter *(Pres. & Chief Exec. Officer)*
David H. Cool *(Exec. V.P.)*
George W. Delp *(Exec. V.P.-U.S. Consumer Prods.)*
William D. George, Jr. *(Exec. V.P. & Chief Oper. Officer-Worldwide Consumer Prods.)*
Larry K. Switzer *(Sr. V.P. & Chief Fin. Officer)*
Laurance T. Burden *(Sr. V.P. & Chief Information Officer)*
James F. DiMarco *(Sr. V.P.-Worldwide Consumer Prods., Res.)*
Laurence R. Newman *(Sr. V.P.-Worldwide Service Businesses & Corp. Devel.)*
Robert C. Hart *(Sr. V.P., Sec. & Gen. Counsel)*
C.J. Taylor *(V.P. & Controller)*
Harold J. Wilhelmsen *(V.P. & Controller, Intl.)*
Larry L. Beebe *(V.P.-U.S. Consumer Prods. Sls.)*
Dr. Roger H. Grothaus *(V.P.-Scientific Support & Govt. Affairs)*
M. Garvin Shankster *(V.P. & Chief Human Resources Officer)*
Gayle P. Kosterman *(V.P.-Human Resources-U.S. Consumer Prods.)*
W. Lee McCollum *(V.P.-North American Sanitation Services & Pres.-PRISM)*
Barry P. Harris *(V.P.-Dir.-Mktg.-Corporate New Prods. & Tech.)*
Edwin R. Rossini *(V.P.-Deputy Gen. Counsel & Asst. Sec.)*
John D. Crabb *(V.P.-Reg. Dir., Cons. Prods.-Pacific/Far East)*
Richard A. Dow *(V.P.-Reg. Dir., Commercial Prods.- Americas)*
William J. Freund *(V.P.-Global Specialty Chemicals)*
David C. Henry *(V.P.-Customer Service & Logistics Mngmt.)*
Gerald K. Konz *(V.P.-Corp. Taxes)*
Scott P. Kramer *(V.P.-Worldwide Human Resources Support)*
Nico J. Meiland *(V.P.-Mfg., U.S.)*
Gianni C. Montezemolo *(V.P.-New Markets)*
Neal R. Nottleson *(V.P.-Fin.-U.S. Consumer Prods.)*
Robert E. Olivero *(V.P.-Worldwide Home Care & Worldwide Labs.)*
William D. Perez *(V.P.-Home Care Bus., U.S. Consumer Prods.)*
Beth M. Pritchard *(V.P.-Gen. Mgr.-Insect Control Bus., U.S. Consumer Prods.)*
Andrew W. Schultz *(V.P.-Research & Devel.-Worldwide Innochem)*
Victor A. Thomas *(V.P.-Reg. Dir.-Cons. Prods.-Africa & Near East)*
Patricia Penman *(Adv. Services Mgr.)*
James R. Russell *(Dir.-Employees Benefits)*
James J. Chwala *(Dir.-Cash Mngmt.)*
Richard M. Spinks *(Dir.-Corp. Pub. Affairs)*
T. Michael Parker *(Dir.-Meeting Planning)*
Edward C. Furey *(Dir.-Materials Mngmt.)*
James P. May *(Corp. Pub. Rels. Mgr.)*
Cynthia Georgeson *(Environmental Communications Mgr.)*

No. of Mfg. Plants/Facilities: 1
No. of U.S. Offices: 21
No. of Foreign Offices: 46

Computer Systems/Hardware:
IBM 3083

Outside Service Firm(s):

Coopers & Lybrand*(Auditors)*
203 N. LaSalle St.
Chicago, IL 60601
Tel.: 312-701-5500

Provident Life & Accident Insurance Co.*(Group Insurer)*
P.O. Box 12015
Chattanooga, TN 37401
Tel.: 615-755-7088

Morgan Stanley & Co.*(Investment Banker)*
1251 Avenue of the Americas
New York, NY 10020
Tel.: 212-703-8447
Fax: 212-703-6476

Shearson Lehman Brothers, Inc.*(Investment Banker)*
World Financial Center
New York, NY 10285
Tel.: 212-298-2000

Kirkland & Ellis*(Legal Firm)*
200 E. Randolph Dr.
Chicago, IL 60601
Tel.: 312-861-2000
Fax: 312-861-2200

Bank of America, N.T. & S.A.*(Major Banking Relationship)*
P.O. Box 37002,
San Francisco, CA 94137

Chemical Banking Corp.*(Major Banking Relationship)*
277 Park Ave.
New York, NY 10041
Tel.: 212-310-6407
Fax: 212-310-4526

Citibank N.A.*(Major Banking Relationship)*
Corporate Trust Services, 399 Park Ave.
New York, NY 10043
Tel.: 212-559-1605

First National Bank of Chicago*(Major Banking Relationship)*
One First National Plaza
Chicago, IL 60670
Tel.: 312-732-9781
Tel.: 312-732-4050
Fax: 312-732-4840
Fax: 312-732-3055

Aetna Life & Casualty*(Pension Manager)*
151 Farmington Avenue
Hartford, CT 06156
Tel.: 203-273-2128
Fax: 203-729-4295

Equitable Life*(Pension Manager)*
1221 Ave. of the Americas
New York, NY 10022
Tel.: 212-382-8038
Fax: 212-382-8089

IDS Advisory Group*(Pension Manager)*
Minneapolis, MN

Subsidiaries:

Johnson Venture Capital, Inc. **(1)**
1525 Howe St.
Racine, WI 53403
Tel.: 414-631-2000
Venture Capital Investments
S.I.C.: 6799
Arthur DelVesco *(Gen. Partner)*
S. Curtis Johnson III *(Gen. Partner)*

Johnson Wax Development Corp. **(1)**
4041 N. Main St.
Racine, WI 53402
Tel.: 414-631-2331
Real Estate
S.I.C.: 6531
Paul J. Cody *(Chief Oper. Officer)*

Micro-Gen Equipment Corp. **(1)**
10700 Sentinel Dr.
San Antonio, TX 78217
Tel.: 210-654-8570
Mfr. Foggers for Pest Control
S.I.C.: 3559

Rydelle Laboratories **(1)**
1525 Howe St.
Racine, WI 53403
Tel.: 414-631-2000
Approx.Sls.: $52,000,000
Emp.: 30
Distr. & Mktg. of Over-the-Counter Drugs, Soaps & Druggists' Sundries
S.I.C.: 5122; 5100

Prism Integrated Sanitation Management, Inc. **(1)**
8300 Executive Center Dr., 4th Fl.
Miami, FL 33166-4680
Tel.: 305-592-6312
Emp.: 1,200
Fiscal Year-end: 6/30/90
Provides Pest Elimination Services Primarily To Restaurants & Hotels; Hood & Duct Cleaning; Exhaust Filter Exchange
S.I.C.: 7342; 2842; 2841
Larry Newman *(Chm. Bd. & Chief Exec. Officer)*
Larry Bittinger *(Pres. & Chief Oper. Officer)*
Dennis Pearce *(V.P.-Fin.)*
Richard R. Mason *(Dir.-Mktg.)*

Non-U.S. Holdings:

Ceras Johnson de Portugal, Lda. **(1)**
Rua Maestro Raul Portela, 1
Lagoa, Portugal
Tel.: 243-6661
Emp.: 90
Consumer & Commercial Prods.
S.I.C.: 2841; 2842; 2899
G. R. Paine *(Gen. Manager)*

Ceras Johnson Ltda. **(1)**
Via 8, No. 505, Jacarepagua Postal 2757, 22700
Rio de Janeiro, Brazil
Tel.: (021) 342-4455
Telex: (021) 23.618
Emp.: 497
Mfr. Home Care Products: Air Fresheners, Floor Waxes/Cleaners, All Purpose Cleaners, Toilet Care Products, Furniture Polishes; Laundry Care Products; Consumer Automotive Products: Waxes, Polishes, Additives; Insecticides
S.I.C.: 2841; 2842; 2879
Ronald William Gordon Miles *(Pres. & Gen. Mgr.)*
Steven Pease *(Chief Fin. Officer & Fin. Dir.)*
Charles Lewis Colman *(Dir.-Mktg.)*
Paulo de Souza Bello *(Dir.-Sls.)*
Antonio Carlos Laet *(Dir.-Innochem)*
Edgar Polhmann *(Mfg. Dir.)*
Jane Assis *(Personnel Dir.)*

Johnson Company, Ltd. **(1)**
Ninomiya P.O. Box 7 Kanagawa-ku,
Yokohama, 259-01, Japan
Tel.: 0463-72-2111
Telex: 3882-441 JONWAX J
Fax: 0463-72-3127
Approx.Sls.: $30,000,000,000
Emp.: 629
Consumer & Commercial Prods.
S.I.C.: 2841; 2842; 2899
Takao Honda *(Pres.)*
F. Mikuriya *(Gen. Mgr.)*
Kazuo Kohda *(Mng. Dir.-Consumer Business)*
Morio Nishikawa *(Mktg. Mgr.-Consumer Prods.)*

La Johnson Francaise S.A. **(1)**
B.P. 606 95004
Cergy Pontoise, France
Tel.: 464-92-92
Emp.: 393
Consumer & Commercial Prods.
S.I.C.: 2841; 2842; 2899
B. J. Dezaly *(Gen. Manager)*

P.T. S.C. Johnson & Son (Indonesia) Ltd. **(1)**
P.O. Box 41/JNG
Jakarta, Indonesia
Tel.: 481408
Emp.: 110
Consumer Prods.
S.I.C.: 2841; 2842; 2899
A. A. Gde. Agung *(Gen. Manager)*

S. C. Johnson & Son de Argentina S.A.I.C. **(1)**
Av. Marquez 2249 Casilla de Correo 4747,
1000 Correo Central,
Buenos Aires, Argentina
Tel.: 769-0012
Telex: 26229 jhnsn ar
Approx.Sls.: $50,000,000

S. C. Johnson & Son, Inc.—(Continued)

Emp.: 439
Consumer & Commercial Prods.
S.I.C.: 2841; 2842; 2899
Alejandro Martinez de Hoz *(Gen. Mgr.)*
Santiago Chouhy *(Dir.-Mktg.)*

S. C. Johnson & Son Colombiana S.A. **(1)**
Apartado Aereo 29632
Bogota, D.E. Colombia
Tel.: 275-13-28
Emp.: 77
Consumer & Commercial Prods.
S.I.C.: 2841; 2842; 2899
C. F. Silva *(Gen. Manager)*

S. C. Johnson & Son (Hellas) E.P.E. **(1)**
210 Messogion Ave., Holargos
Athens, Greece
Emp.: 98
Consumer & Commercial Prods.
S.I.C.: 2841; 2842; 2899
M. Pagidas *(Gen. Mgr.)*

S. C. Johnson & Son, Limited **(1)**
1 Webster St.
Brantford, ON M3T 5R1, Canada
Tel.: 519-756-7900
Emp.: 385
Consumer & Commercial Products
S.I.C.: 2841; 2842; 2899
Dermot G. Kelly *(Gen. Mgr.)*
James Malliet *(V.P.-Fin.)*
J.C. Brooks *(V.P.-Information Services)*

S. C. Johnson & Son, Inc. **(1)**
Mcc P.O. Box 505,
Manila, Philippines
Tel.: 63 85-59-51
Emp.: 156
Consumer & Commercial Prods.
S.I.C.: 2841; 2842; 2899
E. A. Rialp *(Gen. Mgr.)*

S. C. Johnson & Son, Ltd. **(1)**
P.O. Box 11-1140
Bangkok, Thailand
Tel.: 392-4017
Emp.: 53
Consumer & Commercial Prods.
S.I.C.: 2841; 2842; 2899
F.F. Guerra, III *(Gen. Mgr.)*

S. C. Johnson & Son Pte. Limited **(1)**
23, Playfair Road
Singapore, 13, Singapore
Tel.: 283-1334
Emp.: 40
Consumer & Commercial Prods.
S.I.C.: 2841; 2842; 2899
K. C. Ow *(Gen. Mgr.)*

S. C. Johnson & Son Pty. Ltd. **(1)**
P.O. Box 277
Milsons Point, N.S.W. 2061, Australia
Tel.: 923-7111
Emp.: 234
Consumer & Commercial Prods.
S.I.C.: 2841; 2842; 2899
W. J. Walley *(Gen. Mgr.)*

S. C. Johnson & Son, S.A. de C.V. **(1)**
Poniente 140 No. 717 Col. Industrial Va,
Azcapotzalco, 02300, Mexico
Tel.: 905-567-6922
Emp.: 405
Consumer & Commercial Prods.
S.I.C.: 2841; 2842; 2899
I. Febles *(Gen. Mgr.)*

S. C. Johnson & Son of South Africa (Pty.) Ltd. **(1)**
Private Bag XOB
Fairland, 2030, South Africa
Tel.: 678-5412
Emp.: 168
Consumer & Commercial Prods.
S.I.C.: 2841; 2842; 2899
G. S. Cooper *(Gen. Manager)*

S. C. Johnson & Son Taiwan Ltd. **(1)**
P.O. Box 87-300
Taipei, Taiwan
Tel.: 760-2211
Emp.: 53
Consumer & Commercial Prods.
S.I.C.: 2841; 2842; 2899
M.K. Hu *(Gen. Mng.)*

S. C. Johnson & Son de Venezuela, C.A. **(1)**
Apartado 70.041
Caracas, 1071-A, Venezuela
Tel.: 91-6011
Emp.: 237
Consumer & Commercial Prods.
S.I.C.: 2841; 2842; 2899
J.M. Shepherd *(Gen. Mgr.)*

S. C. Johnson Company Limited **(1)**
Margarita House, 15 Themistocles Dervis
Nicosia, Cyprus
Tel.: 57711
Emp.: 29
Consumer & Commercial Prods.
J.A. Langdell *(Gen. Mgr.)*

S. C. Johnson de Centroamerica S.A. **(1)**
Apartado Postal #4971
San Jose, Costa Rica
Tel.: 32-07-66
Emp.: 41
Consumer & Commercial Prods.
S.I.C.: 2841; 2842; 2899
L. M. Bolton *(Gen. Manager)*

S. C. Johnson, Ltd. **(1)**
P.O. Box 98450 Tsimshatsui Post Office,
Kowloon, Hong Kong
Tel.: K-7226261
Emp.: 112
Consumer & Commercial Prods.
S.I.C.: 2841; 2842; 2899
D. J. Chapman *(Gen. Manager)*

S. C. Johnson Kiev Corp. **(1)** (100%)
Kiev, Ukraine
Mfr. of Detergents, Household Cleaners & Shampoo
S.I.C.: 2841; 2844
James M. Shepherd *(Gen. Mgr.)*

Johnson Wax AG **(1)**
CH-8104
Weiningen, ZH Switzerland
Tel.: 41-1-750-2233
Emp.: 53
Consumer & Commercial Prods.
S.I.C.: 2841; 2842; 2899
Markus Kesselring *(Gen. Manager)*

Johnson Wax A/S **(1)**
Midtager 18 DK2600
Glostrup, Denmark
Tel.: 296 32 00
Emp.: 32
Consumer & Commercial Prods.
S.I.C.: 2841; 2842; 2899
S. H. Kirk *(Gen. Manager)*

Johnson Wax (Egypt) **(1)**
c/o J. Wax Africa & Near East, Milton Park
Stroude Road,
Egham, Surrey TW 20 9UH, United Kingdom
Tel.: 78434333
Emp.: 72
Consumer & Commercial Prods.
S.I.C.: 2841; 2842; 2899
M. E. Elhalwagy *(Gen. Manager)*

Johnson Wax GmbH **(1)**
Postfach 1355, 5657
Haan, 1, Germany
Emp.: 141
Consumer & Commercial Prods.
S.I.C.: 2841; 2842; 2899
J. Schlebrowski *(Gen. Mgr.)*

Johnson Wax (Ireland) Limited **(1)**
Robinhood Industrial Estate Clondakin Co.,
Dublin, Ireland
Tel.: 507798
Emp.: 31
Consumer & Commercial Prods.
S.I.C.: 2841; 2842; 2899
John Molan *(Gen. Mgr.)*

Johnson Wax Limited **(1)**
Frimley Green
Camberley, Surrey GU16 5AJ, United Kingdom
Tel.: 276-63456
Emp.: 401
Consumer & Commercial Prods.
S.I.C.: 2841; 2842; 2899
Richard E. Posey *(Gen. Mgr.)*
Barry H. Aiken *(Dir.-Human Res. & Public Affairs)*

Johnson Wax Morocco S.A. **(1)**
3 rue Jabal Boubilane, Bourgogne
Casablanca, 01, Morocco
Tel.: 367094
Emp.: 12
Consumer Prods.
S.I.C.: 2841; 2842; 2899
S. Mansour *(Gen. Mgr.)*

Johnson Wax Nederland B.V. **(1)**
P.O. Box 22 3640 AA
Mijdrecht, Netherlands
Tel.: 2679-3800
Emp.: 67
Consumer & Commercial Prods.
S.I.C.: 2841; 2842; 2899
A. van der Vaart *(Gen. Mgr.)*

Johnson Wax New Zealand Ltd. **(1)**
Private Bag, One hunga
Auckland, 6, New Zealand
Tel.: 661-259
Emp.: 135
Consumer & Commercial Prods.
S.I.C.: 2841; 2842; 2899
G. L. Konarske *(Gen. Mgr.)*

Johnson Wax Nigeria Limited **(1)**
Plot 5, Block H, Isolo Industrial Estate
Ikeja, Nigeria
Tel.: 845397
Emp.: 156
Consumer Prods.
S.I.C.: 2841; 2842; 2899
B. Fowode *(Gen. Mgr.)*

Johnson Wax S.p.A. **(1)**
P.le M. M. Burke 1/3 Casella Postale No. 18, 20020
Arese, Milan Italy
Tel.: 02-93371
Fax: 9384665
Emp.: 201
Consumer & Commercial Prods.
S.I.C.: 2841; 2842; 2899
F. Meroni *(Gen. Mgr.)*

N.V. Johnson Wax Belgium S.A. **(1)**
Noordkustlaan 16 (B) 1702
Groot-Bijgaarden, Belgium
Tel.: 2-467-5211
Telex: 25202 johbru b
Fax: 02/466 86 14
Approx.Sls.: $49,635,000
Emp.: 66
Fiscal Year-end: 6/30/90
Consumer & Commercial Prods.
S.I.C.: 2841; 2842; 2899
F. Louvrier *(Sales Dir.-Consumer Prods.)*
V. Vrancken *(Fin. & Admin. Mgr.)*

Johnson's Wax (East Africa) Ltd. **(1)**
Lunga Lunga Road P.O. Box 18373,
Nairobi, Kenya
Tel.: 557400
Emp.: 56
Consumer Products
C.J. Hoare *(Gen. Mgr.)*
Stephen G. Bannell *(Reg. Controller)*

Johnson's Wax Espanola, S.A. **(1)**
Calle Orense 4-6.a
Madrid, 20, Spain
Emp.: 324
Consumer & Commercial Prods.
S.I.C.: 2841; 2842; 2899
P.R. McCready *(Gen. Mng.)*

Johnson's Wax, Ges. M.B.H. **(1)**
P.O. Box 39 A-1222
Vienna, Austria
Tel.: 4289111
Emp.: 28
Consumer & Commercial Prods.
S.I.C.: 2841; 2842; 2899
E. F. Chladek *(Gen. Manager)*

Johnson's Wax Ltd. **(1)**
P.O. Box 5249
Accra, Ghana
Tel.: Accra 75235
Emp.: 49
Consumer Prods.
S.I.C.: 2841; 2842; 2899
S. Yeboeh *(Gen. Mgr.)*

Johnsonwax del Ecuador S.A. **(1)**
P.O. Box 874
Guayaquil, Ecuador
Tel.: 352-349
Emp.: 29
Consumer & Commercial Prods.
S.I.C.: 2841; 2842; 2899
J. M. Marzo *(Gen. Manager)*

Korea Johnson Co., Ltd. **(1)**
Sungdong P.O. Box 39
Seoul, Korea
Tel.: 544-2101
Emp.: 80
Consumer & Commercial Prods.
S.I.C.: 2841; 2842; 2899
P. A. Mathias *(Gen. Manager)*

Modern Home Care Products Pvt. Ltd. **(1)**
No. 4 Community Centre New Friends Colo,
New Delhi, 110065, India
Tel.: 636387
Emp.: 5
Consumer Prods.
S.I.C.: 2841; 2842; 2899
C.D. Sharma *(Gen. Mgr.)*

Norsk Johnson's Wax A/S **(1)**
Postboks 34 N-1481
Hagan, Norway
Tel.: 02-77-84-10
Emp.: 43
Consumer & Commercial Prods.
S.I.C.: 2841; 2842; 2899
K. I. Saelid *(Gen. Manager)*

Quimica S.C. Johnson & Son Chilena S.A.C.I. **(1)**
Casilla 35-D
Vina del Mar, Chile
Tel.: 974521
Emp.: 94
Consumer & Commercial Prods.
S.I.C.: 2841; 2842; 2899
A. Martinez de Hoz *(Gen. Manager)*

Svenska Johnson's Vax AB **(1)**
Postbox 28 S-183 21
Stockholm, Sweden
Tel.: TABY 1 758-0150
Emp.: 59
Consumer & Commercial Prods.
S.I.C.: 2841; 2842; 2899
A. Graffner *(Gen. Mgr.)*

JOHNSON STORAGE & MOVING COMPANY
221 Broadway
Denver, CO 80203
Tel.: 303-722-2855
Fax: 303-698-0512
Year Founded: 1900
Sales Range: $20-39 Million
Emp.: 400
Moving & Storage Company
S.I.C.: 4213; 4214
Ralph D. Johnson *(Pres.)*
Jim Johnson *(Exec. V.P.)*
Mark Johnson *(Exec. V.P.)*

No. of U.S. Offices: 11

Computer Systems/Hardware:
ADDS

Outside Service Firm(s):

Coopers & Lybrand*(Auditors)*
370 17th St., Ste. 3300
Denver, CO 80202
Tel.: 303-573-2800

Subsidiary:

Security Van Line, Inc. **(1)**
100 W. Airline Hwy.
Kenner, LA 70062
Tel.: 504-468-7711
Fax: 504-464-1818
Approx.Sls.: $10,250,000
Emp.: 150
Fiscal Year-end: 12/31/91
Household Goods Transport; Local Furniture Moving & Storage
S.I.C.: 4213; 4214

Affiliated Facilities:

Johnson Storage & Moving, Aurora (1)
5050 Havana
Aurora, CO 80239
Tel.: 303-373-0770
Tel.: 800-395-0770
Fax: 303-373-0778
S.I.C.: 4213; 4214

Johnson Storage & Moving, Boulder/Longmont (1)
900 S. Sunset St.
Longmont, CO 80501
Tel.: 303-561-0430
Tel.: 800-934-MOVE
Tel.: 303-443-MOVE
Fax: 303-447-9745
S.I.C.: 4213; 4214

Johnson Storage & Moving, Cheyenne (1)
204 N. American Rd.
Cheyenne, WY 82001
Tel.: 307-778-MOVE
Tel.: 800-568-MOVE
Fax: 307-632-2209
S.I.C.: 4213; 4214

Johnson Storage & Moving, Cleburne (1)
117 E. Industrial Blvd.
Cleburne, TX 76031
Tel.: 817-641-6624
Tel.: 800-288-6624
Fax: 817-641-6625
S.I.C.: 4213; 4214

Johnson Storage & Moving, Colorado Springs (1)
4226 N. Sinton Rd.
Colorado Springs, CO 80907
Tel.: 719-598-MOVE
Tel.: 800-947-MOVE
Fax: 719-598-1415
S.I.C.: 4213; 4214

Johnson Storage & Moving, Denver (1)
P.O. Box 9188,
Denver, CO 80209-0188
Tel.: 303-778-MOVE
Tel.: 800-289-MOVE
Fax: 303-689-0512
S.I.C.: 4213; 4214

Johnson Storage & Moving, Englewood (1)
6989 S. Jordan Rd.
Englewood, CO 80112
Tel.: 303-690-0666
Tel.: 800-385-0026
Fax: 303-690-0451
S.I.C.: 4213; 4214

Johnson Storage & Moving, San Diego (1)
12225 Kirkham Rd., Ste. 400
Poway, CA 92064
Tel.: 619-488-9292
Tel.: 800-234-1515
Tel.: 619-234-9292
Fax: 619-488-7138
S.I.C.: 4213; 4214

Johnson Storage & Moving, Santa Fe (1)
Rte. 20, Box 2911, (Corner of Airport Rd. & Colony Dr.)
Santa Fe, NM 87501
Tel.: 505-473-3576
Tel.: 800-876-MOVE
Fax: 505-473-3991
S.I.C.: 4213; 4214

Security Facility:

Johnson Moving & Storage, New Orleans (1)
100 W. Airline Hwy.
Kenner, LA 70062
Tel.: 504-468-7711
Tel.: 800-999-0725
Fax: 504-464-1818

JOHNSON SUPPLY & EQUIPMENT CORP.
10151 Stella Link
Houston, TX 77025
Tel.: 713-661-6666
Fax: 713-661-3684
Emp.: 180
Wholesaler Compressors, Controls, Tubing, Fittings, Misc. Parts & Supplies for Refrigeration, Air Conditioning & Heating
S.I.C.: 5078; 5064; 5065; 5075; 5085
Robert E. Uehlinger *(Pres.)*
Carl I. Johnson, Jr. *(Exec. V.P.)*
Dennis D. Waitschies *(V.P.-Fin.)*
Ruby T. Hall *(Pur. Agent)*
Gwen Shulte *(Mgr.-Credit)*

Computer Systems/Hardware:
NCR 9050

Outside Service Firm(s):

Ernst & Young*(Auditors)*
1 Houston Ctr., 1200 McKinney
Houston, TX 77002
Tel.: 713-750-1500

Franklin, Kelly, Graham & Kilbugh*(Legal Firm)*
Houston, TX

Texas Commerce Bank*(Major Banking Relationship)*
600 Travis Street, Suite 1150
Houston, TX 77002
Tel.: 713-236-4865

JOHNSON & TOWERS, INC.
2021 Briggs Rd.
Mount Laurel, NJ 08054
Tel.: 609-234-6990 **PA**
Twx: 6853047
Fax: 609-234-3635
Assets: $29,595,065
Liabilities: $19,365,261
Net Worth: $10,229,804
Approx.Sls.: $50,000,000
Emp.: 125
Fiscal Year-end: 12/31/91
Export
Manufacture & Wholesale Diesel Engines, Transportation Equipment & Supplies
S.I.C.: 3519; 5088
Walter F. Johnson, Jr. *(Pres.)*
Peter M. Johnson *(Chief Oper. Officer & V.P.)*
Albert Harris *(V.P.-Mktg. & Sls.)*
David Johnson *(Controller)*
Warren Carrieri *(Dir.-Engrng.)*
Richard Toone *(Mgr.-Opers.)*
John Wolfinger *(Pur. Agent)*

Outside Service Firm(s):

Grant Thornton*(Auditors)*
2000 Market St.
Philadelphia, PA 19101

Pluese & Libotz*(Legal Firm)*
Cherry Hill, NJ

Provident National Bank*(Major Banking Relationship)*
P.O. Box 7648
Philadelphia, PA 19101
Tel.: 215-585-5000

JOHNSONVILLE FOODS, INC.
950 Woodlake Rd.
Kohler, WI 53044
Mailing Address:
P.O. Box 786
Sheboygan, WI 53082-0786
Tel.: 414-459-6800
Fax: 414-459-7824
Emp.: 500
Mfr. Sausage
S.I.C.: 2013
Ralph F. Stayer *(Chm. Bd.)*
Ralph C. Stayer *(Pres. & Chief Exec. Officer)*
Alice Stayer *(V.P., Sec. & Treas.)*
Robert H. Salzwedel *(Dir.-Fin.)*
Mark Fischer *(Dir.-Creative Services)*

Outside Service Firm(s):

Security First National Bank*(Major Banking Relationship)*
Sheboygan Falls, WI

Subsidiaries:

Johnsonville Sausage, Inc. (1)
County Trunk J
Sheboygan Falls, WI 53085
Tel.: 414-467-2641
Sausage Maker
S.I.C.: 2013
Michael J. Roller *(Pres.)*

Perri Sausage, Inc. (1)
P.O. Box 8327
New Haven, CT 06530
Tel.: 203-469-1374
Approx.Sls.: $18,000,000
Emp.: 130
Sausage Products
S.I.C.: 2013
Ralph Stayer *(Chm. Bd.)*
Frank Perri *(Pres.)*

ERNEST S. JOHNSTON ADVERTISING, INC.
1156 15th St., NW
Washington, DC 20005
Tel.: 202-223-3660
Fax: 202-857-7863
Year Founded: 1947
Approx.Billings: $15,000,000
Emp.: 21
Entertainment, Travel, Resort, Financial & Real Estate Adv.
Ernest S. Johnston *(Chm.)*
Ernest S. Johnston III *(Pres.)*
Thom Thore *(V.P.)*
James McHale *(V.P.)*
Helen Kalbaugh *(Office Mgr.)*

FRED B. JOHNSTON COMPANY, INC.
300 E. Boundry Rd.
Chapin, SC 29036
Mailing Address:
P.O. Box 280,
Chapin, SC 29036
Tel.: 803-345-5481
Fax: 803-345-5512
Approx.Sls.: $12,500,000
Emp.: 135
Import Export
Import Silk Screen Printing Equipment & Export Graphics
S.I.C.: 3552
Corporate Giving Program: Supports Education Related Projects
Fred B. Johnston, II *(Pres. & Chief Exec. Officer)*
James E. Patterson *(Exec. V.P. & Gen. Mgr.)*
Jim Johnston *(V.P.-Pur.)*
Evelyn Johnston *(Sec.)*
Bob Underwood *(Controller)*
Principal(s):
Fred B. Johnston, II
Jim Johnston
Bette Johnson
Barbara DeVoire

No. of Mfg. Plants/Facilities: 1
No. of U.S. Offices: 1

Computer Systems/Hardware:
IBM System 36 with RPGII Software

Outside Service Firm(s):

Ernst & Young*(Auditors)*
P.O. Box 627, 1611 Devonshire Dr.
Columbia, SC 20202
Tel.: 803-254-4700
Fax: 803-252-4090

NationsBank South Carolina*(Major Banking Relationship)*
Columbia, SC

Division:

Weisz Graphics (1)
300 E. Boundry Rd.
Chapin, SC 29036
Tel.: 803-345-5481
Fred B. Johnston, II *(Pres.)*

JOHNSTON, LEMON & CO. INC.
1101 Vermont Ave., N.W.
Washington, DC 20005
Tel.: 202-842-5500
Fax: 202-842-5531
Approx.Sls.: $27,200,000
Emp.: 300
Underwriters, Dealers in Corpate Municipal Securities, Industry Revenue Bonds & Mutual Fund Shares, Brokers in Stocks & Bonds, Business Managers
S.I.C.: 6211; 6726; 8742
James H. Lemon, Jr. *(Chm. Bd. & Chief Exec. Officer)*
Thomas T. Wallace *(Pres.)*
Kenneth I. Miller *(Chief Fin. Officer, Treas. & Sr. V.P.)*
Bernard J. Nees *(Exec. V.P.)*
Ralph S. Richard *(Exec. V.P.)*
David H. Davis *(Sr. V.P.)*
James R. Kleeblatt *(Sr. V.P.)*
Harry J. Lister *(Sr. V.P.)*
Carroll W. Owens, Jr. *(Sr. V.P.)*
Patrick C. Ryan *(Sr. V.P.)*
Principal(s):
James H. Lemon, Jr.

Computer Systems/Hardware:
IBM

Outside Service Firm(s):

Arthur Andersen & Co.*(Auditors)*
1666 K Street, N.W.
Washington, DC 20006

Reed, Smith, Shaw & McClay*(Legal Firm)*
Mellon Square, P.O. Box 2009
Pittsburgh, PA 15230
Tel.: 412-288-3131
Fax: 412-288-3063

Riggs National Bank of Washington, D.C.*(Major Banking Relationship)*
P.O. Box 96206, 1120 Vermont Ave. N.W.
Washington, DC 20090-6206
Tel.: 202-835-4082

JOHNSTOWN CORPORATION
545 Central Ave.
Johnstown, PA 15902
Tel.: 814-535-9000 **PA**
Fax: 814-536-0868
Year Founded: 1984
Assets: $32,000,000
Liabilities: $25,000,000
Net Worth: $7,000,000
Approx.Sls.: $40,000,000
Emp.: 420
Fiscal Year-end: 12/31/91
Export
Manufacture Specialty Steel
S.I.C.: 3321; 3325
Corporate Giving Program: The Corporate Giving Budget is Established at the Beginning of the Year; Individual Requests are Decided Upon When the Request is Made. The Corporate Budget is Total Amount, Not an Amount for each Specific Request.
Robert Funk *(Chm. Bd. & Chief Exec. Officer)*
John E. Sheehan *(Vice Chm.)*
Ian Sadler *(Chief Oper. Officer)*
Carol Warner *(Chief Fin. Officer)*
David Culp *(Chief Information Officer)*
Richard Evans *(V.P.-Sls.)*
Mary I. Diehl *(Sec.)*

No. of Mfg. Plants/Facilities: 1
No. of U.S. Offices: 1

Johnstown Corporation—(Continued)

Outside Service Firm(s):

Barnes, Saly & Company*(Auditors)*
1 Atlee St.
Johnstown, PA 15905

Johnstown Bank & Trust Company*(Major Banking Relationship)*
532 - 534 Main St.
Johnstown, PA 15901

JOHNSTOWN KNITTING MILL CO.
309 W. Montgomery St.
Johnstown, NY 12095
Tel.: 518-762-3156
Fax: 518-762-4293
Year Founded: 1905
Approx.Sls.: $20,000,000
Emp.: 500
Manufacture Underwear, Sportswear, Athletic Clothing, Sleepwear, Sweatshirts & Fleece Active Wear
S.I.C.: 2254; 2253
Clark Easterly *(Chm. Bd.)*
Thomas B. Easterly *(Pres.)*
Virginia Easterly *(V.P.)*
William Easterly *(V.P.-Cloth, Bleach & Dyeing Sls.)*
Erich Mooradian *(V.P.-Sls.)*
Clark Easterly, Jr. *(Treas.)*
Debra Sullivan *(Controller)*
Principal(s):
Clark Easterly
Thomas B. Easterly
Virginia Easterly

Outside Service Firm(s):

Stulmaker, Roach, Dorfman & Co.*(Auditors)*
Johnstown, NY

First American Bank, N.A.*(Major Banking Relationship)*
Johnstown, NY

JOINER ROWLAND SERIO KOEPPEL
2305 Cedar Springs, Ste. 450
Dallas, TX 75201
Tel.: 214-871-2305
Fax: 214-963-0396
Year Founded: 1985
Approx.Billings: $16,945,000
Emp.: 26
Jay B. Serio *(Pres. & New Bus. Contact)*
Perry Radoff *(Chief Fin. Officer)*
Peter S. Koeppel *(Exec. V.P., Mktg. Dir.)*
Chip Rowland *(Treas., Media Dir.)*
Caren Jellison *(Asst. Acct. Planner)*
Brenda Martinek *(Asst. Bkpr.)*
Janet Tuthill *(Controller)*
Debbie Edgren *(Office Mgr.)*

Computer Systems/Hardware:
MacIntosh, IBM

THE JOLT COMPANY
130 Linden Oakes Dr., Ste. C
Rochester, NY 14625
Mailing Address:
P.O. Box 25107,
Rochester, NY 14625
Tel.: 716-381-3560
Fax: 716-381-3560
Year Founded: 1985
Emp.: 14
Export
Mfg. & Distribution of Soft Drink Syrups
S.I.C.: 2086; 5149
C.J. Rapp *(Pres.)*
Jim Beauchamp *(V.P.)*
Donna Bartoo *(Office Mgr.)*
Bob Di Pasca *(N.E. Sls. Mgr.)*
Chuck Robb *(Reg. Mktg. Mgr.)*
Brian Creary *(Reg. Mktg. Mgr.)*
Scott Pressler *(Reg. Mktg. Mgr.)*
Jim Eggebrecht *(Reg. Mktg. Mgr.)*

Computer Systems/Hardware:
Twin, Libra, Multi-mate 2

Outside Service Firm(s):

Mengel, Metzer Barr & Co.*(Auditors)*
Rochester, NY

The Central Trust Company, N.A.*(Major Banking Relationship)*
44 Exchange St.
Rochester, NY 14692

JOMAC, INC.
863 Easton Rd.
Warrington, PA 18976
Tel.: 215-343-0800
Fax: 215-343-0912
Year Founded: 1938
Approx.Sls.: $30,000,000
Emp.: 399
Fiscal Year-end: 7/31/91
Import Export
Mfr. of Jomac Work Gloves & Knit Specialties, PVC Protective Clothing & Coated Gloves, Seamless Dampener Materials for Graphic Arts, Ryno Rollers, Printing Rollers, Industrial Rubber Rolls
S.I.C.: 3069; 2259; 2381
William J. Grundy *(Chm. Bd.)*
William S. Colehower *(Pres.)*
Scott Lynch *(Mktg. Mgr.)*
James J. Podall *(Sales-Mgr.)*

Non-U.S. Holding:

Barry Manufacturing Company Ltd. (BEMAC) **(1)**
P.O. Box 360,
Beebe, PQ J1B 1E0, Canada

JONATHAN MANUFACTURING CORP.
1101 S. Acacia Ave.
Fullerton, CA 92631
Tel.: 714-526-4651 **DE**
Fax: 714-773-5582
Year Founded: 1956
Approx.Sls.: $23,000,000
Emp.: 300
Fiscal Year-end: 12/31/90
Export
Mfr. Ball Bearing Slide Mechanisms; Door & Chassis Slides for the Military
S.I.C.: 3499; 3463; 3562
R.L. Burch *(Chm. Bd. & Pres.)*
W.W. Wachtel *(Exec. V.P.)*
Norman Peterson *(V.P. & Comptroller)*
M. Glastetter *(Chief Engineer)*
W. Landry *(Pur. Agent)*

No. of U.S. Offices: 1

Computer Systems/Hardware:
IBM System 36

Outside Service Firm(s):

Security Pacific National Bank*(International Bank Affiliate)*
Newport Beach, CA

Gibson, Dunn & Crutcher*(Legal Firm)*
800 Newport Center Dr.
Newport Beach, CA 92660
Tel.: 714-451-3800

Irell & Manella*(Legal Firm)*
840 Newport Center Dr., Ste. 500
Newport Beach, CA 92660-6324
Tel.: 714-760-0991

JONBIL INC.
Hwy. 785 Industrial Ave.
Chase City, VA 23924
Mailing Address:
P.O. Box 37
Chase City, VA 23924
Tel.: 804-372-3181
Fax: 804-372-1113
Approx.Sls.: $25,000,000
Emp.: 750
Manufacture Jeans
S.I.C.: 2325; 2339
Herbert Winkler *(Pres.)*
William J. Bank *(Chief Exec. Officer)*
Marty Carter *(Chief Engineer)*
Thomas C. Smith *(Exec. V.P.-Fin.)*
Esther K. Bank *(V.P.)*
Jack Albertson *(Sec.)*
Gloria Bolick *(Mgr.-Data Processing)*
Principal(s):
Herbert Winkler

Computer Systems/Hardware:
IBM

Outside Service Firm(s):

Ernst & Young*(Auditors)*
P.O. Box 2171,
Raleigh, NC 27602

Hashmall, Sheer, Bank & Geist*(Legal Firm)*
Chase City, VA

SouthTrust Bank*(Major Banking Relationship)*
Birmingham, AL
Tel.: 205-254-5068

JONES, ANASTASI & BIRCHFIELD
6065 Frantz Rd.
Dublin, OH 43017
Tel.: 614-764-1274
Fax: 614-764-1531
Year Founded: 1945
Approx.Billings: $13,240,000
Emp.: 12
Advertising Agency
S.I.C.: 7311
H. Douglas Jones *(Pres.)*
Joseph A. Anastasi *(Exec. V.P., Creative Dir.)*
Cynthia Birchfield *(Sr. V.P., Acct. Exec.)*
Principal(s):
H. Douglas Jones
Joseph A. Anastasi

Computer Systems/Hardware:
IBM PC

JONES APPAREL GROUP, INC.
250 Rittenhouse Circle
Bristol, PA 19007
Tel.: 215-785-4000
Assets: $128,712,000
Earnings: $30,763,000
Liabilities: $42,909,000
Net Worth: $85,803,000
Approx.Sls.: $334,066,000
Emp.: 1,000
Fiscal Year-end: 12/31/91
Mfr. of Women's Apparel; Shorts, Suits, Pants, Skirts, Coats, Sweaters, Shirts & Dresses for Women, Accessories; Jones New York Div. Ladies' Knit Skirts, Pants, Suits, Coats, Pant Suits, Shirts, Dresses, Blazers
S.I.C.: 2331; 2335; 2337; 2339
Sidney Kimmel *(Chm. Bd. & Chief Exec. Officer)*
Herbert J. Goodfriend *(Vice Chm.)*
Andrew Grossman *(Pres.)*
Wesley Card *(Chief Fin. Officer)*
Irwin Samelman *(Exec. V.P.-Mktg.)*
Gary Klocek *(Controller)*
Chuck Hostetler *(Dir.-Mngmt. Information Systems)*
Sharon O'Grady *(Dir.-Indus. Rels.)*

Divisions:

Christian Dior **(1)**
250 Rittenhouse Circle
Bristol, PA 19007
Tel.: 215-785-4000
Mfr. of Women's Apparel
S.I.C.: 2331; 2339

JNY **(1)**
250 Rittenhouse Circle
Bristol, PA 19007
Tel.: 215-785-4000
Mfr. of Women's Apparel
S.I.C.: 2331; 2335; 2337; 2339

Jones Investment Co., Inc. **(1)**
300 Delaware Ave., Ste. 534
Wilmington, DE 19801
Tel.: 302-427-5747

Jones Holding Corporation **(1)**
300 Delaware Ave.
Wilmington, DE 19801
Tel.: 302-427-5747

Joneswear **(1)**
250 Rittenhouse Circle
Bristol, PA 19007
Tel.: 215-785-4000
Mfr. of Women's Apparel
S.I.C.: 2331; 2335; 2337

Rena Rowan for Saville **(1)**
250 Rittenhouse Circle
Bristol, PA 19007
Tel.: 215-785-4000
Mfr. of Women's Apparel
S.I.C.: 2331; 2335; 2339

Saville **(1)**
250 Rittenhouse Circle
Bristol, PA 19007
Tel.: 215-788-0272
Mfr. of Women's Suits
S.I.C.: 2337

Non-U.S. Holdings:

Jones Apparel Group, Inc. Canada **(1)**
55 St. Regis Crescent North
Downsview, ON M3J 1Y9, Canada
Tel.: 416-635-7111
Distr. of Women's Apparel
S.I.C.: 5137

Jones International Ltd. **(1)**
Unit 804-6, Tower 1, Cheung Sha Wan Plaza, 833 Cheung Sha Wan Road, Kowloon, Hong Kong
Tel.: 744-1000

JONES BLAIR COMPANY
2728 Empire Central
Dallas, TX 75235
Mailing Address:
P.O. Box 35286
Dallas, TX 75235
Tel.: 214-353-1600
Fax: 214-350-7624
Year Founded: 1928
Approx.Sls.: $90,000,000
Emp.: 600
Fiscal Year-end: 12/31/90
Export
Protective & Decorative Coatings, Resins, Elastomeric Coatings & Waterproofing
S.I.C.: 2851; 2821
Richard W. Blair, Jr. *(Chm. Bd.)*
Paul D. Dague *(Pres.)*
Richard A. Nayes *(Exec. V.P.)*
Paul Fredrickson *(Opers.)*
Michael Flanigan *(Treas. & Comptroller)*
Robert Asbill *(Mgr.-Sls.)*
Carlos Dorris *(Mgr.-Govt. Affairs)*
Will Dryden *(Mgr.-Gen. Sls.)*
Ann Dryer *(Mgr.-Adv.)*
Betty Dunn *(Mgr.-Personnel)*
Chuck Edwards *(Mgr.-Sls.)*
Lloyd Peck *(Mgr.-Gen. Sls.)*
John Smith *(Mgr.-Data Processing)*
Richard Rick *(Engrng.)*
Dick Cannon *(Technical Dir.)*
Manuel Lopez *(Quality Control)*
William Yeargan *(Pur. Agent)*

Outside Service Firm(s):

Locke, Purnell, Rain, Harrell*(Legal Firm)*
Republic Natl. Bank Tower, Ste. 4200
Dallas, TX 75201

Tel.: 214-742-1021

Texas Commerce Bank*(Major Banking Relationship)*
2200 Ross Ave.
Dallas, TX 75266

Divisions:

The Gilman Company **(1)**
801 Riverfront Pkwy.
Chattanooga, TN 37401
Tel.: 615-756-5185
Approx.Sls.: $38,000,000
Emp.: 200
Chemical Coating
S.I.C.: 2899
R.A. Nayes *(Pres.)*
Dan Hamblen *(Controller)*
Richard Vogel *(Dir.-Res. & Devel.)*
Betty Dieter *(Pur. Dir.)*
H.T. Tonkin *(Gen. Mgr.)*
Rick Schmertzler *(Mgr.-Mfg.)*
Susan Humphreys *(Sec.)*
Gerry Davis *(Personnel Mgr.)*

The Neogard Corporation **(1)**
2732 Empire Central
Dallas, TX 75235
Tel.: 214-353-1600
Export
Mfr. Paints & Coatings
S.I.C.: 2851

Texas Resin **(1)**
2728 Empire Central
Dallas, TX 75235
Tel.: 214-353-1698
Mfr. of Paints, Enamels, Resins, Varnishes
S.I.C.: 2851; 2821

Subsidiary:

Jones Blair Energy, Inc. **(1)**
P.O. Box 35286
Dallas, TX 75235
Tel.: 214-353-1600
Paint Manufacturing Co.
S.I.C.: 2851

CAROLINE JONES
ADVERTISING, INC.

CAROLINE JONES ADVERTISING, INC.
1290 Ave. of the Americas
New York, NY 10104
Tel.: 212-262-8181
Fax: 212-333-4208
Year Founded: 1987
Approx.Billings: $14,450,000
Emp.: 25
Ethnic Adv.
Caroline R. Jones *(Pres. & Creative Dir.)*
Floydetta M. McAfee *(V.P., Pub. Rels. Dir.)*
Dinah Robinson *(V.P., Dir. Mktg. Services)*
Yolanda Caraway *(Dir., Special Events)*

JONES CHEMICALS, INC.
80 Munson St.
Le Roy, NY 14482
Tel.: 716-768-6281
Fax: 716-768-2632
Approx.Sls.: $100,000,000
Emp.: 750
Sol Brand Chemicals
S.I.C.: 2812; 2819
R.B. Jones *(Chm. Bd. & Chief Exec. Officer)*
Jeffrey Jones *(Pres. & Chief Oper. Officer)*
Vito Pricola *(Chief Fin. Officer)*
K. Richard Brumber *(Sec.)*
Steve Roberts *(Asst. to Pres.)*
Jim Chappel *(Pur. Agent)*

Computer Systems/Hardware:
DEC VAX

Outside Service Firm(s):

Deloitte & Touche*(Auditors)*
One Lincoln First Square
Rochester, NY 14604
Tel.: 716-232-1200

Travelers Insurance Co.*(Group Insurer)*
1 Tower Square
Hartford, CT 06183-2492
Tel.: 203-277-4542
Fax: 203-277-5038

Norstar Bank, N.A.*(Major Banking Relationship)*
Rochester, NY

Subsidiary:

Jones Chemicals, Inc. **(1)**
100 Sunny Sol Blvd.
Caledonia, NY 14423
Tel.: 716-538-2311
Fax: 716-538-2316
Manufacturer of Chemicals
S.I.C.: 2812; 2819
Jay Wells *(Gen. Mgr.)*
Gerald Gardner *(Mgr.-Opers.)*

EDWARD D. JONES & CO.
201 Progress Pkwy.
Maryland Heights, MO 63043
Tel.: 314-851-2000
Fax: 314-851-3789
Year Founded: 1871
Approx.Sls.: $500,000,000
Emp.: 4,300
Fiscal Year-end: 12/31/91
Securities Brokerage Firm with 1,936 Offices
S.I.C.: 6159; 6211
John W. Bachmann *(Mng. Principal)*
Edward Soule *(Principal & Chief Fin. Officer)*
Lawrence R. Sobol *(Principal & Gen. Counsel)*
William H. Broderick III *(Principal-Syndicate Dept.)*
Daniel A. Burkhardt *(Principal-Corp. Debt & Equity Offerings)*
James Harrod *(Principal-Sls. Training)*
Douglas E. Hill *(Principal-Mktg.)*
Rich Malone *(Principal-Data Processing)*
Robert Pearce *(Principal-Human Resources)*
Darryl Pope *(Principal-Opers.)*
Ray Robbins *(Principal-Quality Control)*
Spencer B. Burke *(Principal-Public Fin.)*
Merry L. Mosbacher *(Principal-Investment Banking)*
Colleen Geraty *(Mgr.-Adv.)*
Mary Beth Heying *(Mgr.-Pub. Rels.)*
Brad Frick *(Mgr.-Travel)*

Computer Systems/Hardware:
IBM

JONES COMPANY, INC.
102 Lee Ave.
Waycross, GA 31501
Tel.: 912-283-1661
Fax: 912-285-5610
Year Founded: 1982
Approx.Sls.: $200,000,000
Emp.: 1150
Fiscal Year-end: 12/31/92
Gasoline Service Stations;Automobile Dealership;Grocery Warehouse;Convenience Store Chain;Petrolem Wholesale;Lessors of Real Estate
S.I.C.: 5541; 5411; 6519; 5172
James C. Jones, Jr. *(Chm. Bd. & Chief Exec. Officer)*
James A. Walker, Jr. *(Pres.)*
Patrick Jones *(V.P.-Mktg.)*
Phil Wysong *(V.P.-Treas. & Sec.)*

Principal(s):
James C. Jones, Jr.

Outside Service Firm(s):

Barnett Banks Trust Company, N.A.*(Major Banking Relationship)*
9000 Southside Blvd., P.O. Box 40200
Jacksonville, FL 32202-0200
Tel.: 904-464-2802

Subsidiaries:

Kwickie/Flash Foods, Inc. **(1)**
102 Lee Ave.
Waycross, GA 31501
Tel.: 912-283-1661
Retail Groceries; Gasoline Service Stations; Lessors Of Real Estate Property
S.I.C.: 5411; 5541; 6519
James A. Walker, Jr. *(Pres.)*

Fuel South Inc. **(1)**
102 Lee Ave.
Waycross, GA 31501
James A. Walker Jr. *(Pres.)*

Bacon Grocery Co., Inc. **(1)**
102 Lee Ave.
Waycross, GA 31501

BIG J Super Stores, Inc. **(1)**
102 Lee Ave.
Waycross, GA 31501

Walter-Jones Cheverolet-Buick-Oldsmobile **(1)**
102 Lee Ave.
Waycross, GA 31501

JONES DAIRY FARM
Jones Ave.
Fort Atkinson, WI 53538
Tel.: 414-563-2431 **WI**
Fax: 414-563-6801
Year Founded: 1906
Sales Range: $40-59 Million
Emp.: 365
Fiscal Year-end: 9/31/90
Export
Meat Products
S.I.C.: 2011; 2013; 2077
M.C. Jones *(Pres.)*
Edward C. Jones *(Exec. V.P. & Chief Oper. Officer)*
Alan P. Jones, Jr. *(V.P., Chief Fin. Officer & Treas.)*
Frances Paddock Highsmith *(V.P.-Consumer Affairs)*
Steve E. Wholihan *(V.P.-Sls. & Mktg.)*
Loren Gray *(Controller)*
D.J. Donaldson *(Sec.)*
Todd Berry *(Dir.-Mktg.)*
Barry Hoops *(Dir.-Personnel)*
David Klevgaard *(Dir.-Data Processing)*
John Sherman *(Mgr.-Mfg.)*

No. of Mfg. Plants/Facilities: 2
No. of U.S. Offices: 2

Computer Systems/Hardware:
MAI Basic 4; IBM

Outside Service Firm(s):

KPMG Peat Marwick*(Auditors)*
777 E. Wisconsin Ave.
Milwaukee, WI 53202
Tel.: 414-276-4200

Aetna Life & Casualty*(Group Insurer)*
100 N. Riverside Plaza
Chicago, IL 60606

Foley & Lardner*(Legal Firm)*
777 E. Wisconsin Ave.
Milwaukee, WI 53202
Tel.: 414-271-2400

Subsidiary:

Ralph & Paul Adams, Inc. **(1)**
Market St. & Railroad Ave.
Bridgeville, DE 19933
Tel.: 302-337-8208
Fax: 302-337-3275
Processors Of Scrapple
S.I.C.: 2013
Dick Hedl *(Gen. Mgr.)*

JONES, DAY, REAVIS & POGUE
North Point, 901 Lakeside Ave.
Cleveland, OH 44114
Tel.: 216-586-3939
Fax: 216-579-0212
Year Founded: 1893
Approx.Sls.: $108,000,000
Emp.: 1,470
Law Firm
S.I.C.: 8111
Richard W. Pogue *(Mng. Partner)*
Girard E. Boudreau *(Reg. Mng. Partner-Washington, S.E. Region)*
James L. Baumoel *(Reg. Mng. Partner-California)*
Dennis W. LaBarre *(Reg. Mng. Partner-Intl.)*
Joe Sims *(Grp. Coordinator-Govt. Regulations)*
Patrick F. McCartan *(Grp. Coordinator-Litigation)*
Francis P. Hubach, Jr. *(Grp. Coordinator-Real Estate)*
James T. O'Hara *(Grp. Coordinator-Tax)*

No. of U.S. Offices: 5

Computer Systems/Hardware:
Wang

JONES INTERNATIONAL LTD.
9697 E. Mineral Ave.
Englewood, CO 80112
Tel.: 303-792-9191
Year Founded: 1969
Approx.Rev.: $119,000,000
Holding Co.; Cable Television Services
S.I.C.: 6719; 4841
Glenn R. Jones *(Chm. Bd., Pres., Chief Exec. Officer & Sole Stockholder)*
Carl E. Vogel *(V.P.-Fin.)*
Elizabeth M. Steele *(V.P. & Gen. Counsel)*

Outside Service Firm(s):

Arthur Andersen & Co.*(Auditors)*
One Intl. Place, 100 Oliver St.
Boston, MA 02110
Tel.: 617-330-4000
Fax: 617-439-9731

Davis, Graham & Stubbs*(Legal Firm)*
370 Seventeenth St., Ste. 4700
Denver, CO 80202
Tel.: 303-892-9400

Subsidiaries:

Jones Information Management, Inc. **(1)**
9697 E. Mineral Ave.
Englewood, CO 80112
Tel.: 303-792-9191 (100%)
Information Mngmt. & Data Processing Services
S.I.C.: 7374

Jones Properties, Inc. **(1)**
9697 E. Mineral Ave.
Englewood, CO 80112
Tel.: 303-792-9191 (100%)
Management of Co. Properties
S.I.C.: 6512

Jones Spacelink, Ltd. **(1)**
9697 E. Mineral Ave.
Englewood, CO 80112
Tel.: 303-792-9191 (93%)
Assets: $319,116,000
Earnings: ($21,776,000)
Liabilities: $292,990,000
Net Worth: $26,126,000
Approx.Rev.: $118,621,000
Fiscal Year-end: 5/31/91
Cable Television Services
S.I.C.: 4841
Glenn R. Jones *(Chm., Pres. & Chief Exec. Officer)*
Gregory J. Liptak *(Grp. V.P.-Opers.)*
Carl E. Vogel *(Grp. V.P.)*
Ruth E. Warren *(V.P.-Opers.)*
Kevin P. Coyle *(Treas.)*
Elizabeth M. Steele *(Corp. Sec.)*

Jones International Ltd.—(Continued)

Cynthia L. Swartz *(Mgr.-Corp. Communications)*

Subsidiary:

Jones Intercable, Inc. **(2)**
9697 E. Mineral Ave.
Englewood, CO 80112
Tel.: 303-792-9191 (75%)
Cable TV Services
S.I.C.: 4841
Gregory J. Liptak *(Pres.)*
Bob Luff *(Grp. V.P.-Tech.)*
J. Rodney Dyer *(V.P.-Taxation)*

R. A. JONES & CO. INC.
2701 Crescent Springs Rd.
Covington, KY 41017
Mailing Address:
P.O. Box 485
Cincinnati, OH 45201
Tel.: 606-341-0400
Fax: 606-341-0519
Year Founded: 1905
Assets: $36,976,784
Liabilities: $9,994,249
Net Worth: $26,982,535
Approx.Sls.: $53,080,110
Emp.: 525
Export
Mfr. Cartoning Machinery, Case Packers, Pouchmaking & Filling Machinery
S.I.C.: 3559
Corporate Giving Program: Through R.A. Jones Foundation.
Arthur E. Motch, Jr. *(Chm. Bd.)*
A.W. Koehlinger *(Pres. & Chief Exec. Officer)*
David W. Motch *(Exec. V.P.)*
D.C. Amann *(V.P.-Human Resources)*
William R. Dossenbach *(V.P.-Fin. & Chief Fin. Officer)*
Paul Grimes *(V.P.-Mfg.)*
S.R. Knapp *(V.P.-Sls. & Mktg.)*
E.W. Scarpa *(V.P. Prod. Dev.)*
J.W. Craig *(Dir.-Plng. & Devel.)*
Eugene C. Dirr *(Mgr.-Pur.)*
Don Flory *(Mgr.-Mktg. Services)*
John Headley *(Mgr.-Market Research)*

Outside Service Firm(s):

KPMG Peat Marwick*(Auditors)*
1600 Central Trust Ctr., 201 East Fifth St.
Cincinnati, OH 45202
Tel.: 513-421-6430

Taft, Stettinius & Hollister*(Legal Firm)*
First Natl. Bank Center
Cincinnati, OH 45202
Tel.: 513-381-2838

Citizens National Bank of Covington*(Major Banking Relationship)*
Covington, KY

JONES & THOMAS, INC.
300 W. Main St.
Decatur, IL 62522
Tel.: 217-423-1889
Fax: 217-425-0680
Year Founded: 1980
Approx.Billings: $20,000,000
Emp.: 20
Agricultural, Industrial & Business-to-Business Adv.
Phil Jones *(Pres.)*
Gerald Jacks *(V.P., Bus. Devel.)*

JORDACHE ADVERTISING

226 West 37th St.
New York, NY 10018
Tel.: 212-643-8400
Year Founded: 1980
Approx.Billings: $20,000,000
Emp.: 4
Creative, Media Buying & Mktg.
Jerry Taylor *(V.P. & Dir.-Adv. & Mktg.)*

JORDACHE ENTERPRISES, INC.
226 W. 37th St.
New York, NY 10018
Tel.: 212-643-8400
Fax: 212-643-8508
Sales Range: $100-499 Million
Emp.: 300
Wholesale Jeans, Athletic Wear & Sportswear
S.I.C.: 2325; 2329; 2339; 5136; 5137
Joseph Nakash *(Chm. Bd. & Pres.)*
Avi Nakash *(Exec. V.P.)*
Al Goldberg *(Sr. V.P.)*
Liz Berlinger *(V.P.-Sls.)*
Jerry Taylor *(V.P. & Dir.-Adv. & Publicity)*
Ralph Nakash *(Treas. & Sec.)*
Randy Chudnow *(Controller)*
Linda Feinman *(Mgr.-Personnel)*
Rose Smith *(Mgr.-Import)*

Outside Service Firm(s):

Connecticut General Life Insurance Co.*(Group Insurer)*
P.O. Box 2975,
Hartford, CT 06104
Tel.: 203-726-6000

JORDAN ASSOCIATES
1000 W. Wilshire
Oklahoma City, OK 73116
Mailing Address:
P.O. Box 14005,
Oklahoma City, OK 73113
Tel.: 405-840-3201
Fax: 405-840-4149
Year Founded: 1961
Approx.Billings: $21,900,000
Emp.: 50
Warren K. Jordan *(Chm. Bd. & Chief Exec. Officer)*
Jeanette L. Gamba *(Pres. & Sec.)*
Sue Dimond *(Controller)*
Ann Adams *(Dir.-Pub. Rels.)*
Barbara Murcer *(Mgr.-Office)*

JORDAN COMPANY
315 Park Ave., S.
New York, NY 10010
Tel.: 212-460-1920
Fax: 212-477-2461
Year Founded: 1982
Investment Bankers; Venture Capital Companies
S.I.C.: 6211; 6799

Subsidiaries:

American Safety Razor Company **(1)**
Razor Blade Lane
Verona, VA 24482
Tel.: 703-248-8000
Fax: 703-248-0522
Approx.Sls.: $100,000,000
Emp.: 680
Fiscal Year-end: 12/31/90
Computer Systems/Hardware:
IBM
Mfr. of Shaving, Industrial & Surgical Blades; Soap & Shampoo
S.I.C.: 3421; 2844; 3841
Tom Quinn *(Chm. Bd.)*
William C. Weathersby *(Pres.)*
Joseph Hackett *(V.P.-Mktg. & Sls.)*
Emerson Dietz *(Admin.-Personnel)*

Archibald Candy Company **(1)**
1137 W. Jackson
Chicago, IL 60607
Tel.: 312-243-2700
Fax: 312-243-3921
Approx.Sls.: $80,000,000
Emp.: 2,000
Fiscal Year-end: 8/31/91
Computer Systems/Hardware:
IBM System AS/400
Manufacture Candies
S.I.C.: 2064; 5441
Thomas Quinn *(Chm. Bd.)*
John D. Thorne *(Pres.)*
Richard Peritz *(Chief Exec. Officer)*
Alan W. Petrik *(Chief Oper. Officer)*

Subsidiary:

Fannie May Candy Shops, Inc. **(2)**
1137 W. Jackson
Chicago, IL 60607
Tel.: 312-243-3921
Approx.Sls.: $25,000,000
Emp.: 300
Candy Mfr. & Retailer
S.I.C.: 2064; 5441
Charles B. Morrow *(Pres.)*
Michael W. Hennessy *(Chief Oper. Officer)*
Thomas R. Arenth *(V.P.-East Coast Sls.)*
Jack C. Barber *(V.P.-Midwest Retail Sls.)*
Charles E. Toole *(V.P.-Whlse. Sls.)*
Trevor C. Davies *(V.P.-Internal Audit & Taxes)*
Sharon L. Gunia *(V.P.-Mngmt. Information Systems)*
James H. Jones *(Treas.)*
Gina Pieroni *(Dir.-Personnel)*

Ardell Industries inc. **(1)**
555 Lehigh Ave.
Union, NJ 07083
Tel.: 908-687-5900
Fax: 908-687-3341
Approx.Sls.: $14,000,000
Emp.: 197
Fiscal Year-end: 12/31/90
Computer Systems/Hardware:
IBM System 38
Mfr. Knives Blades, Scrapers, Hand Tools & Drywall Tools
S.I.C.: 3421; 3423
Wayne Boylan *(Plant Mgr.)*
Pat Cosgrove *(V.P. & Pur. Agent)*
Edward Gauntt *(Controller)*

Subsidiary:

Hewitt Soap Co. **(2)**
333 Linden Ave.
Dayton, OH 45403
Tel.: 513-253-1151 (100%)
Emp.: 250
Mfr. of Soap & Shampoo
S.I.C.: 2844
Bruce L. Stichter *(Pres.)*

JORDAN INDUSTRIES, INC.
1751 Lake Cook Rd., Ste. 550
Deerfield, IL 60015
Tel.: 708-945-5591
Year Founded: 1988
Approx.Rev.: $325,000,000
Emp.: 6,000
Fiscal Year-end: 12/31/90
Holding Company
S.I.C.: 6719
John W. Jordan II *(Chm. Bd. & Chief Exec. Officer)*
Thomas H. Quinn *(Pres. & Chief Oper. Officer)*
Jonathan F. Boucher *(Chief Fin. Officer)*
Joseph Secker *(V.P.-Fin.)*
Thomas Spielberger *(Controller)*
G. Robert Fisher *(Legal Counsel)*
Principal(s):
John W. Jordan II
Thomas H. Quinn

No. of Mfg. Plants/Facilities: 39
No. of U.S. Offices: 16
No. of Foreign Offices: 2

Outside Service Firm(s):

Ernst & Young*(Auditors)*
Lisle, IL

Smith, Gill, Fisher & Butts*(Legal Firm)*
One Kansas City Place, 35th Fl, 1200 Main St.
Kansas City, MO 64105
Tel.: 816-474-7400

Subsidiary:

JII/Sales Promotion Associates, Inc. **(1)**
545 Walnut St.
Coshocton, OH 43812
Tel.: 614-622-4422
Fax: 614-622-5868
Approx.Sls.: $67,000,000
Emp.: 650
Fiscal Year-end: 12/31/90
Computer Systems/Hardware:
IBM AS/400
Designs & Produces Calendars & Advertising Specialties; School Book Memories
S.I.C.: 2741; 7319
James D. Jung *(Pres.)*
J. Phillip Casey *(V.P.-Mktg. & Sls.)*
Daniel C. Harms *(V.P.-Fin.)*
James F. Huntington *(V.P.-Admin.)*
James M. Trzop *(V.P.-Mfg.)*
Norman Strayer *(Controller)*
Curt W. Derby *(Mgr.-Prod. Devel.)*
Michael A. Swope *(Mgr.-Mngmt. Information Systems)*
James Yarrington *(Mgr.-Mktg.)*
Beth Saylor *(Promo. Coord.)*

JORDAN, MCGRATH, CASE & TAYLOR INC.
445 Park Ave.
New York, NY 10022
Tel.: 212-326-9100
Fax: 212-308-4984
Year Founded: 1980
Approx.Billings: $370,000,000
Emp.: 313
Advertising Agency
S.I.C.: 7311
James Jordan *(Chm. Bd.)*
Gene Case *(Vice Chm.)*
Henry Seiden *(Vice Chm.)*
John L. Taylor *(Vice Chm.)*
Patrick J. McGrath *(Pres.)*
Stephen Badenhop *(Exec. V.P.-Acct. Services)*
Alice Bond *(Exec. V.P.-Acct. Services)*
Tom Finneran *(Exec. V.P.-Fin. Services)*
Bruce Guidotti *(Exec. V.P.-Acct. Services)*
Mark Itkowitz *(Exec. V.P. & Dir.-Creative)*
Alex Ross *(Exec. V.P.-Creative Services)*
Ilon Specht *(Exec. V.P. & Dir.-Creative)*
Donald Weir *(Exec. V.P.-Acct. Services)*
Rosalie Fasano *(V.P. & Gen. Mgr.-Acctg.)*

Computer Systems/Hardware:
IBM System One

Outside Service Firm(s):

Richard Eisner*(Auditors)*
New York, NY

Aetna Life & Casualty*(Group Insurer)*
151 Farmington Avenue
Hartford, CT 06156
Tel.: 203-273-2128
Fax: 203-729-4295

Davis & Gilbert*(Legal Firm)*
850 Third Ave.
New York, NY 10022
Tel.: 212-326-1300

Midlantic National Bank*(Major Banking Relationship)*
Iselin, NJ

Branches:

JMCT/Direct **(1)**
445 Park Ave.
New York, NY 10022
Tel.: 212-326-9600
Fax: 212-326-9298
Karen Hochman *(Pres.)*

JMCT Health **(1)**
445 Park Ave.
New York, NY 10022
Tel.: 212-326-9126
Stephen Kling *(Pres. & Creative Dir.)*

JMCT Publicidad **(1)**
445 Park Ave.
New York, NY 10022
Tel.: 212-326-9126
Don Weir *(Chm.)*
Marta Ferreira-Pero *(Pres.)*

Subsidiary:

Stawasz Public Relations **(1)**
445 Park Ave.
New York, NY 10022
Tel.: 212-326-9800
Emp.: 8
Cherie Stawasz *(Pres.)*
Susan Wolfson *(Sr. V.P.)*
Christiana Sutor *(V.P.)*
Julie Demlow *(V.P.)*

JORDAN MOTORS, INC.
609 E. Jefferson
Mishawaka, IN 46545
Tel.: 219-259-1981 **IN**
Fax: 219-255-0984
Approx.Sls.: $300,000,000
Emp.: 200
New & Used Automobiles
S.I.C.: 5511
Jordan H. Kapson *(Chm. Bd.)*
Craig Kapson *(Pres.)*
Betty Kapson *(Sec. & Tres.)*

Outside Service Firm(s):

1st Source Bank*(Major Banking Relationship)*
P.O. Box 1602, 100 N. Michigan
South Bend, IN 46634
Tel.: 219-236-2000
Fax: 219-235-2765

JORDAN TAMRAZ CARUSO
ADVERTISING, INC.
1419 N. Wells Street
Chicago, Illinois 60610-1395
312 951-2000

JORDAN TAMRAZ CARUSO ADVERTISING, INC.
1419 N. Wells St.
Chicago, IL 60610-1395
Tel.: 312-951-2000
Fax: 312-951-8475
Year Founded: 1968
Approx.Billings: $40,557,900
Emp.: 75
Full Service Advertising Agency
S.I.C.: 7311
Joseph A. Caruso *(Pres.)*
Charles A. Jordan *(V.P. & Sec.)*
Anthony M. Sokolowski *(Controller)*
Kevan L. Gaug *(Dir.-Bus. Devel.-Dealer Grps.)*
Al Richman *(Mgr.-Automotive Div.)*

JORDAN'S MEATS
38 India
Portland, ME 04112
Mailing Address:
P.O. Box 588,
Portland, ME 04112
Tel.: 207-772-5411 **ME**
Fax: 207-772-4814
Year Founded: 1927
Assets: $226,000,000
Earnings: $125,014
Liabilities: $17,160,000
Net Worth: $208,840,000
Approx.Sls.: $125,000,000
Emp.: 525
Fiscal Year-end: 12/31/91
Processor & Wholesaler of Meats & Meat Products, Groceries & Associated Products
S.I.C.: 5147; 2013; 5142; 5148; 5141
Joseph C. Jordan *(Chm. Bd. & Chief Exec. Officer)*
Joseph G. Kelley, Jr. *(Pres., Treas. & Chief Fin. Officer)*
Bruce Dunphey *(V.P. & Plant Mgr.)*
Joanne Favreau *(Controller)*
Ginger Kilgore *(Dir.-Personnel)*
Terry Wood *(Supvr.)*

No. of Mfg. Plants/Facilities: 5

Computer Systems/Hardware:
IBM Systems 36

Outside Service Firm(s):

KPMG Peat Marwick*(Auditors)*
100 Middle St. Plaza
Portland, ME

KPMG Peat Marwick*(Auditors)*
1211 S.W. Fifth Ave.
Portland, OR 97204

Maine Health Plan*(Group Insurance Broker/Consult)*
Suite 5, 778 Main St.
S. Portland, ME 04106

Jensen Baird Gardner & Henry*(Legal Firm)*
P.O. Box 4510,
Portland, ME 04112
Tel.: 207-775-7271

Continental Bank N. A.*(Major Banking Relationship)*
231 S. LaSalle St.
Chicago, IL 60697
Tel.: 312-828-2345
Tel.: 800-426-5754
Telex: 312-828-1783

Key Bank*(Major Banking Relationship)*
Portland, ME

Divisions:

Jordan's Foods-Bangor Division **(1)**
216 Thatcher St.
Bangor, ME 04401
Tel.: 207-945-5646
Emp.: 100
Wholesale Trade-Food & Associated Products
S.I.C.: 5141; 5142; 5147; 5148; 5113; 2013; 5144; 2015
Frederick A. Rice *(Pres.)*
Joseph F. Jordan *(V.P. & Plant Mgr.)*

Jordan's Foods-Caribou Division **(1)**
Bennett Dr.
Caribou, ME 04736
Tel.: 207-498-3827
Wholesale Trade-Food & Associated Products
S.I.C.: 5141; 5142; 5147; 5148; 5113; 2011; 2013
Dick Franck *(Sls. Mgr.)*

Jordan's Foods-Colchester Division **(1)**
Hercules Dr., P.O. Box 70
Colchester, VT 05446
Tel.: 802-655-2226
Emp.: 80
Fruits, Fresh Vegetables, Fresh Meats, Groceries, Frozen Goods, Industrial & Personal Service Paper
S.I.C.: 5148; 5147; 5141; 5142; 5113
Rosalie Patten *(Gen. Mgr.)*

Jordan's Foods-Fairfield Division **(1)**
14 Davis St.
Fairfield, ME 04937
Tel.: 207-453-9711
Wholesale Food Distributor
S.I.C.: 5141; 5142; 5147; 5148; 5113
Steve Strout *(Gen. Mgr.)*

Jordan's Foods-Westbrook Division **(1)**
Thomas Dr.
Westbrook, ME 04092
Tel.: 207-871-0700
Emp.: 125
Wholesale Trade-Food & Associated Products
S.I.C.: 2011; 2013; 2015; 5147; 5141; 5142; 5148; 5113
Richard A. Giles *(Pres.)*

Joseph Kirschner Co. **(1)**
Riverside Dr.
Augusta, ME
Tel.: 207-623-3544
Meat Processor
S.I.C.: 2013
Robert Bertoncini *(Gen. Mgr.)*

JORDON COMMERCIAL REFRIGERATOR CO.
2200 Kennedy
Philadelphia, PA 19137
Tel.: 215-535-8301
Tel.: 800-523-0171
Fax: 215-289-1597
Year Founded: 1899
Approx.Sls.: $10,000,000
Emp.: 130
Fiscal Year-end: 12/30/90

Export
Commercial Freezers & Refrigerators
S.I.C.: 3556; 5078
William Fogel *(Pres.)*
Gene E. Sterner *(Sec. & Treas.)*
Walt Freiling *(Dir.-Sls. & Mktg.)*

EARLE M. JORGENSEN COMPANY
3050 E. Birch
Brea, CA 92621
Tel.: 714-579-8823 **DE**
Fax: 714-579-3789
Year Founded: 1924
Assets: $541,628,000
Earnings: $13,275,000
Liabilities: $432,540,000
Net Worth: $109,088,000
Approx.Sls.: $850,000,000
Emp.: 2,400
Fiscal Year-end: 3/31/92

Export
Distribution of Steel & Aluminum
S.I.C.: 5051
Earle M. Jorgensen *(Chm. Bd.)*
Neven Hulsey *(Pres. & Chief Exec. Officer)*
Lonnie R. Terry *(Chief Oper. Officer & Exec. V.P.)*
William E. Dale *(Chief Fin. Officer & V.P.)*
Graham P. Kilsby *(Chief Information Officer & V.P.)*
Randall J. Haas *(V.P.-Human Resources & Admin.)*
James E. Lawrence *(V.P.-Corp. Communications)*
John W. Ruck *(V.P.-Plng.)*
Al Walker *(V.P.-Opers.)*
Ray M. Endsley *(Mgr.-Gen. Credit)*

Computer Systems/Hardware:
DEC

Outside Service Firm(s):

Ernst & Young*(Auditors)*
515 S. Flower St.
Los Angeles, CA 90071
Tel.: 213-621-1666

Bank of America*(Major Banking Relationship)*
701 S. Western Ave.
Los Angeles, CA 91201

Divisions:

Jorgensen Steel & Aluminum **(1)**
3050 E. Birch St.
Brea, CA 92621
Tel.: 714-579-8823
Fax: 714-577-3789
Distribution of Aluminum, Steel & Brass Rods, Beams, Plates, Bars & Sheet Metal
S.I.C.: 5051
George Von Arx *(Pres.)*
Alexander Walker *(V.P.-Opers.)*

Service Centers:

Jorgensen Steel & Aluminum/Baltimore **(2)**
7463 New Ridge Rd.
Hanover, MD 21076
Tel.: 410-850-4444
Fax: 301-850-5636
Distribution of Steel, Aluminum & Brass Bars, Plates, Beams, Rods & Sheet Metal
S.I.C.: 5051

Jorgensen Steel & Aluminum/Birmingham **(2)**
200 Kilsby Circle
Bessemer, AL 35023
Tel.: 205-426-6061
Fax: 205-424-7483
Distribution of Steel, Aluminum & Brass Rods, Beams, Plates, Bars & Sheet Metal
S.I.C.: 5051

Jorgensen Steel & Aluminum/Boston **(2)**
59 South St.
Hopkinton, MA 01748
Tel.: 508-435-6854
Fax: 508-435-2520
Distribution of Steel, Aluminum & Brass Rods, Beams, Plates, Bars & Sheet Metal
S.I.C.: 5051

Jorgensen Steel & Aluminum/Buffalo **(2)**
1275 Sheridan Dr.
Tonawanda, NY 14150
Tel.: 716-876-4700
Fax: 716-876-1252
Distribution of Steel, Aluminum & Brass Rods, Beams, Plates, Bars & Sheet Metal
S.I.C.: 5051

Jorgensen Steel & Aluminum/Charlotte **(2)**
3731-I Woodpark Blvd.
Charlotte, NC 28206
Tel.: 704-596-6116
Fax: 704-596-2774
Distribution of Steel, Aluminum & Brass Rods, Beams, Plates, Bars & Sheet Metal
S.I.C.: 5051

Jorgensen Steel & Aluminum/Chicago **(2)**
1900 Mitchell Blvd.
Schaumburg, IL 60193
Tel.: 708-307-6100
Fax: 708-307-6114
Distribution of Steel, Aluminum & Brass Rods, Beams, Plates, Bars & Sheet Metal
S.I.C.: 5051

Jorgensen Steel & Aluminum/Cincinnati **(2)**
601 Redna Terrace
Cincinnati, OH 45215
Tel.: 513-771-3223
Fax: 513-771-6734
Distribution of Steel, Aluminum & Brass Rods, Beams, Plates, Bars & Sheet Metal
S.I.C.: 5051

Jorgensen Steel & Aluminum Cleveland **(2)**
26400 Richmond Rd.
Cleveland, OH 44146
Tel.: 216-292-5555
Fax: 216-292-3037
Distribution of Steel, Aluminum & BrassRods, Beams, Plates, Bars & Sheet Metal
S.I.C.: 5051

Jorgensen Steel & Aluminum/Dallas **(2)**
2030 W. Commerce St.
Dallas, TX 75208
Tel.: 214-741-1761
Fax: 214-263-6513
Distribution of Steel, Aluminum & Brass Rods, Beams, Plates, Bars & Sheet Metal
S.I.C.: 5051

Jorgensen Steel & Aluminum/Dayton **(2)**
2531 Needmore Rd.
Dayton, OH 45414
Tel.: 513-276-5961
Fax: 513-276-5620
Distribution of Steel, Aluminum & Brass Rods, Beams, Plates, Bars & Sheet Metal
S.I.C.: 5051

Jorgensen Steel & Aluminum/Denver **(2)**
6050 Downing St.
Denver, CO 80216
Tel.: 303-287-0381
Fax: 303-288-0512
Distribution of Steel, Aluminum & Brass Rods, Beams, Plates, Bars & Sheet Metal
S.I.C.: 5051

Earle M. Jorgensen Company—(Continued)

Jorgensen Steel & Aluminum/Detroit (2)
13200 W. Eight Mile Rd.
Detroit, MI 48237
Tel.: 313-547-9000
Fax: 313-548-9442
Distribution of Steel, Aluminum & Brass Products
S.I.C.: 5051

Jorgensen Steel & Aluminum/ Hartford (2)
1060 Silas Deane Hwy.
Wethersfield, CT 06109
Tel.: 203-529-6861
Fax: 203-563-1445
Distribution of Steel, Aluminum & Brass Rods, Beams, Plates, Bars & Sheet Metal
S.I.C.: 5051

Jorgensen Steel & Aluminum/ Honolulu (2)
91-104 Kalaeloa Blvd.
Ewa Beach, HI 96707
Tel.: 808-682-2020
Fax: 808-682-4978
Service Center; Mfr. of Metal Culvert, Metal Roofing & Siding, Galvanizing
S.I.C.: 5051; 3444; 3479

Jorgensen Steel & Aluminum/ Houston (2)
5311 Clinton Dr.
Houston, TX 77020
Tel.: 713-672-1621
Fax: 713-672-0528
Distribution of Steel, Aluminum & Brass Products
S.I.C.: 5051

Jorgensen Steel & Aluminum/ Indianapolis (2)
8604 Allisonville Rd., Ste. 105
Indianapolis, IN 46250
Tel.: 317-841-0033
Fax: 317-841-0893
Distribution of Steel, Aluminum& Brass Products
S.I.C.: 5051

Jorgensen Steel & Aluminum/Kansas City (2)
1701 W. 25th
Kansas City, MO 64108
Tel.: 816-842-7300
Fax: 816-283-3843
Distribution of Steel, Aluminum & Brass Products
S.I.C.: 5051

Jorgensen Steel & Aluminum/Los Angeles (2)
10650 Alameda St.
Lynwood, CA 90262
Tel.: 213-567-1122
Fax: 213-567-9300
Distribution of Steel, Aluminum & Brass Products
S.I.C.: 5051

Jorgensen Steel & Aluminum/ Minneapolis (2)
1775 101st Ave. N.E.
Blaine, MN 55434
Tel.: 612-784-5000
Fax: 612-784-2645
Distribution of Steel, Aluminum & Brass Products
S.I.C.: 5051

Jorgensen Steel & Aluminum/ Oakland (2)
1699 W. Grand Ave.
Oakland, CA 94607
Tel.: 510-835-8222
Fax: 510-834-1446
Distribution of Steel, Aluminum & BrassProducts
S.I.C.: 5051

Jorgensen Steel & Aluminum/ Philadelphia (2)
58 Cabot Blvd.
Langhorne, PA 19047
Tel.: 215-949-2850
Fax: 215-949-1937
Distribution of Steel, Aluminum & Brass Products
S.I.C.: 5051

Jorgensen Steel & Aluminum/ Phoenix (2)
5445 W. Madison
Phoenix, AZ 85043
Tel.: 602-272-0461
Fax: 602-278-1007
Distrution of Steel, Aluminum & Brass Products
S.I.C.: 5051

Jorgensen Steel & Aluminum/St. Louis (2)
3701 Rider Trail S.
Earth City, MO 63045
Tel.: 314-291-6080
Fax: 314-291-5935
Distribution of Steel, Aluminum & Brass Products
S.I.C.: 5051

Jorgensen Steel & Aluminum/Seattle (2)
5964 Sixth Ave. S.
Seattle, WA 98108
Tel.: 206-762-4400
Fax: 206-763-7589
Distribution of Steel, Aluminum & Brass Products
S.I.C.: 5051

Jorgensen Steel & Aluminum/Tulsa (2)
7311 E. Pine St.
Tulsa, OK 74115
Tel.: 918-835-1511
Fax: 918-836-2909
Distribution of Steel, Aluminum & BrassProducts
S.I.C.: 5051

Kilsby-Roberts (1)
3050 Birch St.
Brea, CA 92621
Tel.: 714-579-8823
Fax: 714-577-3789
Distribution of Steel, Aluminum & Brass Products
S.I.C.: 5051
Terry Wilson *(Pres.)*
Fred Parker *(V.P.-European Opers.)*
Terry Van Winkle *(V.P.-Admin.)*

Service Centers:

Kilsby-Roberts/Baltimore (2)
7463 New Ridge Rd.
Hanover, MD 21076
Tel.: 410-850-4472
Fax: 410-850-5078
Distribution of Steel, Aluminum, Carbon & Alloy Tubing
S.I.C.: 5051

Kilsby-Roberts/Birmingham (2)
200 Kilsby Circle
Bessemer, AL 35023
Tel.: 205-426-6061
Fax: 205-424-7483
Distribution of Steel, Aluminum, Carbon & Alloy Tubing
S.I.C.: 5051

Kilsby-Roberts/Boston (2)
59 South St.
Hopkinton, MA 01748
Tel.: 508-435-6854
Fax: 508-435-2520
Distribution of Metal Tubing
S.I.C.: 5051

Kilsby-Roberts/Charlotte (2)
4015 Westinghouse Blvd.
Charlotte, NC 28273
Tel.: 704-588-3001
Fax: 704-588-6659
Distribution of Metal Tubing
S.I.C.: 5051

Kilsby-Roberts/Chicago (2)
2401 25th Ave.
Franklin Park, IL 60131
Tel.: 708-455-6400
Fax: 708-455-3309
Distribution of Metal Tubing
S.I.C.: 5051

Kilsby-Roberts/Cleveland (2)
2060 Enterprise Pkwy.
Twinsburg, OH 44087
Tel.: 216-425-4911
Fax: 216-425-3329
Distribution of Metal Tubing
S.I.C.: 5051

Kilsby-Roberts/Dallas (2)
2200 W. Marshall Dr.
Grand Prairie, TX 75051
Tel.: 214-647-1717
Fax: 214-660-1180
Distribution of Metal Tubing
S.I.C.: 5051

Kilsby-Roberts/Davenport (2)
3116 W. 73rd St.
Davenport, IA 52806
Tel.: 319-386-3200
Fax: 319-386-6455
Distribution of Metal Tubing
S.I.C.: 5051

Kilsby-Roberts/Denver (2)
3737 Troy St.
Denver, CO 80239
Tel.: 303-371-7600
Fax: 303-373-5343
Distribution of Metal Tubing
S.I.C.: 5051

Kilsby-Roberts/Detroit (2)
23680 Research Dr.
Farmington, MI 48335
Tel.: 313-477-1400
Fax: 313-477-0611
Distribution of Metal Tubing
S.I.C.: 5051

Kilsby-Roberts/Hayward (2)
31100 Weigman Rd.
Hayward, CA 94544
Tel.: 510-487-2700
Fax: 510-487-5513
Distribution of Metal Tubing
S.I.C.: 5051

Kilsby-Roberts/Houston (2)
4404 Windfern Rd.
Houston, TX 77041
Tel.: 713-460-4140
Fax: 713-460-8532
Distribution of Metal Tubing
S.I.C.: 5051

Kilsby-Roberts/Indianapolis (2)
2300 S. Tibbs Ave.
Indianapolis, IN 46241
Tel.: 317-241-8251
Fax: 317-248-1438
Distribution of Metal Tubing
S.I.C.: 5051

Kilsby-Roberts/Kansas City (2)
1800 N. Universal Ave.
Kansas City, MO 64120
Tel.: 816-483-4140
Fax: 816-241-1020
Distribution of Metal Tubing
S.I.C.: 5051

Kilsby-Roberts/Little Rock (2)
5207 Scott Hamilton Dr.
Little Rock, AR 72209
Tel.: 501-568-4371
Fax: 501-568-4371
Distribution Of Metal Tubing
S.I.C.: 5051

Kilsby-Roberts/Los Angeles (2)
3700 S. Capital Ave.
City of Industry, CA 91749
Tel.: 310-699-9961
Fax: 310-695-0430
Distribution of Metal Tubing
S.I.C.: 5051

Kilsby-Roberts/Memphis (2)
1340 Channel Ave.
Memphis, TN 38113
Tel.: 901-948-1284
Fax: 901-947-4785
Distribution Of Metal Tubing
S.I.C.: 5051

Kilsby-Roberts/Milwaukee (2)
11610 W. North Ave.
Wauwatosa, WI 53226
Tel.: 414-771-2550
Fax: 414-771-0312
Distribution of Metal Tubing
S.I.C.: 5051

Kilsby-Roberts/Philadelphia (2)
58 Cabot Blvd.
Langhorne, PA 19047
Tel.: 215-945-7665
Fax: 215-945-4255
Distribution of Metal Tubing
S.I.C.: 5051

Kilsby-Roberts/Portland (2)
6650 N. Ensign St.
Portland, OR 97217
Tel.: 503-283-2251
Fax: 503-283-1108
Distribution of Metal Tubing
S.I.C.: 5051

Kilsby-Roberts/St. Louis (2)
4735 LeBourget Dr.
Saint Louis, MO 63134
Tel.: 314-427-5100
Fax: 314-427-8767
Distribution of Metal Tubing
S.I.C.: 5051

Kilsby-Roberts/Seattle (2)
22011 76th Ave. S.
Kent, WA 98032
Tel.: 206-872-0100
Fax: 206-872-8552
Distribution of Metal Tubing
S.I.C.: 5051

Kilsby-Roberts/Tulsa (2)
3116 E. 31st St. N.
Tulsa, OK 74110
Tel.: 918-835-7070
Fax: 918-835-9748
Distribution of Metal Tubing
S.I.C.: 5051

Kilsby-Roberts/Twin Cities (2)
1034 Gemini Rd.
Eagan, MN 55121
Tel.: 612-454-6250
Fax: 612-454-0546
Distribution Of Metal Tubing
S.I.C.: 5051

Kilsby-Roberts Cutting Center/ Indianapolis (2)
2233 S.W. St.
Indianapolis, IN 46225
Tel.: 317-783-3299
Fax: 317-788-0753
S.I.C.: 5051

Kilsby-Roberts Cutting Center/ Honing/Tulsa (2)
2522 N. Columbia Pl.
Tulsa, OK 74110
Tel.: 918-836-7666
Fax: 918-832-9946
S.I.C.: 5051

Kilsby-Roberts Honing/Blue Island (2)
2850 W. 139th St.
Blue Island, IL 60406
Tel.: 708-371-9666
Fax: 708-371-9769
S.I.C.: 5051

Non-U.S. Subsidiaries:

Kilsby-Jorgensen Steel & Aluminum Inc. (1)
1255 Ave. Laplace St. Vincent DePaul, Laval, PQ H7C 2N6, Canada
Tel.: 514-328-2507
Fax: 514-661-0422
Norman LaBrecque *(Dir.)*

Kilsby-Jorgensen Steel & Aluminum Inc. (1)
1666 Shawson Drive East
Mississauga, ON L4W 1N7, Canada
Tel.: 416-564-0866
Fax: 416-564-1921
Jean-Guy Leduc *(Dir.)*
Frank Travetto *(Corp.)*

Kilsby-Jorgensen Steel & Aluminum SA de CV (1)
Parque Industrial El Cerillo, Avenida El Cerillo #6
Lerma, CP52000, Mexico
Tel.: 011 527-285-0188
Jim Miller *(Dir.)*

Kilsby-Jorgensen Steel & Aluminum Ltd. **(1)**
Units 7-9 Provincial Park, Nether Lane
Sheffield, Ecclesfield S30 3XT, United Kingdom
Tel.: 011 44-742-577577
Fax: 011 44-742-570639

JOSAM COMPANY
P.O. Box T-525 W. U.S. 20
Michigan City, IN 46360
Tel.: 219-872-5531
Fax: 219-874-9539
Approx.Sls.: $20,000,000
Emp.: 50
Fiscal Year-end: 12/31/90
Josam Plumbing Drainage Specialties
S.I.C.: 3432; 3431; 3494; 3714
Caswell F. Holloway, Jr. *(Chm. Bd.)*
Stephen J. Holloway *(Vice Chm.)*
Barry J. Hodgekins *(Pres.)*
Deborah S. Hartnett *(V.P.-Admin. & Adv. Mgr.)*
Arthur M. Podgorski *(V.P. & Gen. Mgr.)*

Outside Service Firm(s):

Coplan & Arnoff*(Legal Firm)*
Michigan City, IN

First Citizens Bank & Trust Co.*(Major Banking Relationship)*
Michigan City, IN

Division:

Richmond Foundry and Manufacturing Co. **(1)**
3514 Mayland Ct.
Richmond, VA 23233
Tel.: 804-266-4244
Fax: 804-266-4246
Donna Heishman *(Gen. Mgr.)*

JOSEPH, LITTLEJOHN & LEVY
126 E. 56th St.
New York, NY 10022
Tel.: 212-644-8666
Fax: 212-644-2707
Investment Company
S.I.C.: 6282
Peter Joseph *(Partner)*
Angus Littlejohn *(Partner)*
Paul Levy *(Partner)*

Subsidiary:

Cancer Industries **(1)**
126 E. 56th St.
New York, NY 10022
Tel.: 212-644-8666

Subsidiary:

Golding Industries **(2)**
One Park Ave.
New York, NY 10016
Tel.: 212-696-7000
Fax: 212-696-7031
Mfr. Printed Mattress Ticking; Prints & Finishes; Fabric For Home Furnishings
S.I.C.: 2211
Henry W. Golding *(Pres. & Chief Exec. Officer)*

J. JOSEPHSON, INC.
20 Horizon Blvd.
South Hackensack, NJ 07606
Tel.: 201-440-7000
Fax: 201-440-7109
Sales Range: $20-39 Million
Emp.: 200
Mfr. of Vinyl Wall Coverings
S.I.C.: 2295
Mark Goodman *(Pres.)*
Gilbert Goodman *(Chief Exec. Officer)*
John Fitzgerald *(Exec. V.P.)*
Jeff Rogers *(V.P.-Sls.)*

JOSEPHSON INTERNATIONAL INC.
40 W. 57th St
New York, NY 10019
Tel.: 212-556-5600 **DE**
Fax: 212-556-5665
Sales Range: $100-499 Million
Emp.: 400
Fiscal Year-end: 6/30/90
Theatrical & Literary Talent Agency; TV Production
S.I.C.: 7922; 7812
Marvin Josephson *(Chm. Bd., Pres. & Chief Exec. Officer)*
Ralph S. Mann *(Vice Chm.)*
Michael Cooperman *(Chief Fin. Officer, V.P. & Treas.)*
Wayne Kabak *(Legal Officer)*
Ronald Peters *(Sec.)*
Katharine Kenyon *(Dir.-Fin. Analysis)*

Outside Service Firm(s):

Price Waterhouse*(Auditors)*
153 E. 53rd St., 44th Fl.
New York, NY 10022
Tel.: 212-371-2000

Chase Manhattan Bank, N.A.*(Major Banking Relationship)*
One Chase Manhattan Plaza
New York, NY 10081
Tel.: 212-552-2222
Tel.: 800-526-0801
Fax: 212-552-7175

Subsidiaries:

ICM Artists, Ltd. **(1)**
40 W. 57th St.
New York, NY 10019
Tel.: 212-556-5600 (100%)
Management Company Representing Artists in Classical Music & Dance Fields
S.I.C.: 7922
Lee Lamont *(Chief Oper. Officer)*

International Creative Management, Inc. **(1)**
40 W. 57th St.
New York, NY 10019
Tel.: 212-556-5600 (100%)
Talent Agency
S.I.C.: 7922; 7389
Jeff Berg *(Chm. Bd. & Chief Exec. Officer)*
James Wiatt *(Pres.)*

Branch Office:

International Creative Management, Inc. **(2)**
8899 Beverly Blvd.
Los Angeles, CA 90048
Tel.: 310-550-4000
Talent Agency
S.I.C.: 7389; 7922
Jeff Berg *(Chm. Bd. & Chief Exec. Officer)*
James Wiatt *(Pres.)*

Robert Keeshan Associates, Inc. **(1)**
40 W. 57th St.
New York, NY 10019
Tel.: 212-556-5714 (100%)
Production of "Captain Kangaroo" Children's Television Program
S.I.C.: 7812
Robert J. Keeshan *(Pres.)*

Non-U.S. Holdings:

Duncan Heath Associates **(1)**
162/170 Wardour St.
London, W1N 9HE, United Kingdom
Tel.: 071 439-1471
Talent Agency
S.I.C.: 7389; 7922

International Creative Management Ltd. **(1)**
388/396 Oxford St.
London, W1N 9HE, United Kingdom
Tel.: 071-629-8080 (100%)
Talent Agency
S.I.C.: 7389; 7922

JOURNAL COMMUNICATIONS INC.
333 W. State St.
Milwaukee, WI 53201
Mailing Address:
P.O. Box 661,
Milwaukee, WI 53201-0661
Tel.: 414-224-2000 **WI**
Fax: 414-224-2599
Year Founded: 1882
Earnings: $40,626,000
Approx.Sls.: $465,982,000
Emp.: 4,300
Fiscal Year-end: 12/31/91
Communications Company; Publications, Broadcasting, Printing & Telecommunications
S.I.C.: 6719; 4899; 2752; 2711; 4832; 4833
Corporate Giving Program: Company Gives to United Way, Social Welfare Agencies, Cultural Institutions & Educational Institutions in Milwaukee & Wisconsin
Thomas J. McCollow *(Chm. Bd., Pres. & Chief Exec. Officer)*
Robert A. Kahlor *(Pres.)*
Steven J. Smith *(Exec. V.P.)*
Peter P. Jarzembinski *(V.P.-Fin. & Chief Fin. Officer)*
William Lutzen *(Controller)*
Robert Dye *(V.P.-Communications)*
Paul Kritzer *(Legal Officer & Corp. Sec.)*

Computer Systems/Hardware:
Burroughs 2900

Outside Service Firm(s):

Ernst & Young*(Auditors)*
111 E. Kilbourn Ave., Ste. 900
Milwaukee, WI 53202
Tel.: 414-273-5900

Foley & Lardner*(Legal Firm)*
777 E. Wisconsin Ave.
Milwaukee, WI 53202
Tel.: 414-271-2400

First Wisconsin National Bank*(Major Banking Relationship)*
777 E. Wisconsin Ave.
Milwaukee, WI 53202
Tel.: 414-765-4321
Fax: 414-355-6903

M & I Marshall & Isley Bank*(Pension Manager)*
Milwaukee, WI

Division:

MRC Telecommunications Inc. **(1)**
918 N. 4th St.
Milwaukee, WI 53203
Tel.: 414-224-2059
Approx.Sls.: $15,398,000
Emp.: 123
Telecommunications
S.I.C.: 8999; 4899
John Patterson *(Pres.)*

Subsidiary:

Norlight **(2)**
579 D'Onofrio Dr.
Madison, WI
Tel.: 608-833-8332
Telecommunications
S.I.C.: 4899; 8999

Subsidiaries:

ADD, Inc. **(1)**
P.O. Box 267,
Waupaca, WI 54981
Tel.: 715-258-8450 (80%)
Approx.Sls.: $41,234,000
Emp.: 517
Publishers-Shoppers
S.I.C.: 2721
Thomas Karavakis *(Pres.)*
James Garsombke *(V.P. & Controller)*

Hometown Publications **(1)**
P.O. Box 298,
Trumbull, CT 06611
Tel.: 203-268-6234 (100%)
Emp.: 22
Publishers of Weekly Newspapers
S.I.C.: 2711
Ben Gumm *(Publisher)*

Journal/Sentinel Inc. **(1)**
333 W. State St.
Milwaukee, WI 53201
Tel.: 414-224-2000 (100%)
Approx.Sls.: $188,250,000
Emp.: 1,565
Publrs. of The Milwaukee Journal & Milwaukee Sentinel Newspaper
S.I.C.: 2711
Robert Wills *(Pres.)*
Beverly Klein *(Sr. V.P.-Mktg.)*
Todd Adams *(V.P. & Controller)*
Ben Kordus *(V.P.-Adv.)*

Subsidiaries:

The Milwaukee Journal **(2)**
333 W. State St.
Milwaukee, WI 53203
Tel.: 414-224-2000
Fax: 414-224-2469
Emp.: 1,565
Computer Systems/Hardware:
Burroughs
Newspaper
S.I.C.: 2711
Thomas J. McCollow *(Chm. Bd.-Journal Communications)*
Robert A. Kahlor *(Vice Chm.)*
Robert Wills *(Pres.)*
Kenneth Adams *(Sr. V.P.)*
Sig Gissler *(Sr. V.P.)*
Beverly A. Klein *(Sr. V.P.-Mktg.)*
Todd Adams *(V.P. & Controller)*
Roger Brinkmeier *(V.P.)*
James Clark *(V.P.-Circulation)*
Ben Kordus *(V.P.-Adv.)*
Richard A. Williams *(V.P.-Employee Rels.)*
Scott Bong *(Mgr.-Gen. Adv.)*
Carlyn Ziarek *(Mgr.-Adv.-Retail)*
Harvey Schaefer *(Mgr.-Adv.-Classified)*
Robert Schwartz *(Mgr.-Adv.)*

Milwaukee Sentinel **(2)**
918 N. 4th St.
Milwaukee, WI 53203
Tel.: 414-224-2000
Fax: 414-224-2049
Emp.: 1,500
Fiscal Year-end: 12/31/90
Computer Systems/Hardware:
Burroughs
Newspaper
S.I.C.: 2711
Robert A. Kahlor *(Chm. Bd.-Journal Communications)*
Robert Wills *(Pres.)*
Kenneth Adams *(Sr. V.P.-Printing Opers.)*
Beverly Klein *(Sr. V.P.-Mktg.)*
Todd Adams *(V.P. & Controller)*
James Clark *(V.P.-Circulation)*
Jack Koller *(V.P.-Bus. Devel.)*
Ben Kordus *(V.P.-Adv.)*
Keith Spore *(V.P. & Editor)*
Richard Williams *(V.P.-Employee Rels.)*
Harvey Schaefer *(Mgr.-Adv.-Classified)*
Robert Schwartz *(Mgr.-Adv.-Retail)*
Carlyn Ziarek *(Mgr.-Gen. Adv.)*

Perry Printing Corp. **(1)**
575 W. Madison St.
Waterloo, WI 53594
Tel.: 414-478-3551 (100%)
Approx.Sls.: $167,371,000
Emp.: 1,600
Printing Co.
S.I.C.: 2752
Craig A. Hutchison *(Pres.)*
Paul Bonaivto *(Controller)*

Branches:

Perry/Baraboo **(2)**
1300 Sauk Ave.
Baraboo, WI 53913
Tel.: 608-356-7787
Emp.: 120
Printing Co.
S.I.C.: 2752
Ralph Duley *(Gen. Mgr.)*

Perry/Milwaukee **(2)**
5100 W. Brown Deer Rd.
Milwaukee, WI 53223
Tel.: 414-354-5100
Emp.: 203
Printing Co.
S.I.C.: 2752
James Edkoldt *(Chief Oper. Officer)*

Journal Communications Inc.—(Continued)

Perry/Norway **(2)**
512 9th Ave.
Norway, MI 49870
Tel.: 715-251-4540
Emp.: 160
Printing Co.
S.I.C.: 2752

Label Products & Design Division **(2)**
1836 Sal St.
Green Bay, WI 54308
Tel.: 414-468-8808
Approx.Sls.: $7,000,000
Emp.: 80
Commercial Printing
S.I.C.: 2752
Mike Beno *(Pres.)*
Terri Pawer *(Comptroller)*
Todd G. Fellbaum *(Dir.-Mktg.)*
Paul Pasowicz *(Plant Mgr.)*

WTMJ, Inc. **(1)**
720 E. Capitol Dr.
Milwaukee, WI 53212
Tel.: 414-332-9611 (100%)
Approx.Sls.: $52,088,000
Emp.: 360
Broadcasting-Radio & Television
S.I.C.: 4833; 4832
Douglas G. Kiel *(Pres.)*
Ron Kurtis *(Controller)*

Divisions:

KTNV-TV **(2)**
3355 Valley View Blvd.
Las Vegas, NV 89102
Tel.: 702-876-1313
Television Broadcasting
S.I.C.: 4833
Jim Behling *(Gen. Mgr.)*
Gary Plumlee *(Gen. Sls. Mgr.)*

WIFC-FM **(2)**
602 Jefferson St.
Wausau, WI 54401
Tel.: 715-842-1672
Programmed for Young Adults
S.I.C.: 4832
David J. Armstrong *(V.P. & Gen. Mgr.)*
Tom Chapman *(Gen. Sls. Mgr.)*
Roger Eisenman *(Natl. Sls. Mgr.)*

WSAU-AM **(2)**
602 Jefferson St.
Wausau, WI 54401
Tel.: 715-842-1672
Programmed for Adult General Interest
S.I.C.: 4832
David J. Armstrong *(V.P. & Gen. Mgr.)*
Tom Chapman *(Gen. Sls. Mgr.)*
Roger Eisenman *(Natl. Sls. Mgr.)*

WSYM-TV **(2)**
600 W. St. Joseph St.
Lansing, MI 48933
Tel.: 517-484-7747 (100%)
S.I.C.: 4833
Peter Bannister *(V.P. & Gen. Mgr.)*

JOURNAL REGISTER COMPANY
50 W. State St., 12th Fl.
Trenton, NJ 08608
Tel.: 609-396-2200
Fax: 609-396-2292
Year Founded: 1983
Sales Range: $10-19 Million
Emp.: 2,500
Fiscal Year-end: 12/31/90
Newspaper Publishing
S.I.C.: 2711
Robert M. Jelenic *(Pres. & Chief Exec. Officer)*
Jean B. Clifton *(Exec. V.P. & Chief Fin. Officer)*
Alan J. Leslie *(Sr. V.P.-Fin.)*
John G. Walsh *(V.P.-Opers. & Circulation Dir.)*
Richard C. Ottensmeyer *(Controller)*
David B. Bonfield *(Adv. Dir.)*
Allen J. Mailman *(Dir.-Information Services)*

No. of Mfg. Plants/Facilities: 20
No. of U.S. Offices: 16

Computer Systems/Hardware:
IBM

Outside Service Firm(s):

Ernst & Young*(Auditors)*
202 Carnegie Center
Princeton, NJ 08640
Tel.: 609-243-0303
Fax: 609-243-9322

Subsidiary:

Capitol City Publishing Co., Inc. **(1)**
600 Perry St.
Trenton, NJ 08638
Tel.: 609-989-8602
Newpaper Publishers
S.I.C.: 2711
H.L. Schwartz III *(Publr.)*

Unit:

The Trentonian **(2)**
600 Perry St.
Trenton, NJ 08602
Tel.: 609-989-7800
Daily Newspaper
S.I.C.: 2711
H.L. Schwartz, III *(Publr.)*

JOYCE INTERNATIONAL, INC.
114 5th Ave., 4th Fl.
New York, NY 10011
Tel.: 212-463-9044
Fax: 212-463-8920
Approx.Sls.: $336,000,000
Emp.: 4,192
Distribute Office Products, Manufacture Office Furniture
S.I.C.: 2522; 5021
G. Lynn Shostack *(Chm. Bd. & Pres.)*
Larry Fensterstock *(Controller)*
Lynn Sochon *(Dir.-Personnel)*

Computer Systems/Hardware:
Data Point 8600, 3800 & 6000; IBM: Burroughs

Divisions:

Cole Business Furniture **(1)**
640 Whiteford Rd.
York, PA 17405
Tel.: 717-854-1545
Office Furniture & Systems
S.I.C.: 5021
Richard D. Tierney *(Pres.)*
Peter Beier *(V.P.-Mktg. & Sls.)*
Michael Tarren *(V.P.-Fin.)*
Thomas O'Malley *(V.P.-Indus. Rels.)*
Thomas S. Bird, Jr. *(Dir.-Communications)*

Lehigh-Leopold **(1)**
2825 Mt. Pleasant St.
Burlington, IA 52601
Tel.: 319-753-2271
Fax: 319-752-0358
Approx.Sls.: $10,000,000
Emp.: 150
Fiscal Year-end: 7/31/90
Wooden & Upholstered Office Furniture
S.I.C.: 2522
R. Lyons *(Pres.)*
L.B. Boughtman *(Exec. V.P.)*
Don Dixon *(Personnel Dir.)*
L. Scheiderman *(Pur. Dir.)*

LOPC **(1)**
812 Moorefield PK. Dr.
Richmond, VA 23222
Tel.: 804-320-2800
Office Supplies & Furniture
S.I.C.: 5021

Streater Store Fixtures Div. **(1)**
411 S. 1st Ave.
Albert Lea, MN 56007
Tel.: 507-373-0611
Store Planning Consultation, Including Design, Fixture Installation & Financing for Chain & Department Stores
S.I.C.: 8711

Non-U.S. Holding:

Atal SA **(1)**
7 rue Mariott 75017
Paris, France
Tel.: 331 387 8000
Mfr. of Furniture
S.I.C.: 2522
Roger Janin *(Pres. & Dir. General)*

JUDD'S INCORPORATED
1500 Eckington Pl. N.E.
Washington, DC 20002
Tel.: 202-635-1200
Fax: 202-636-9509
Year Founded: 1868
Approx.Sls.: $90,746,000
Emp.: 1,265
Commercial, Magazine, Book Printing; Book Binding
S.I.C.: 2752; 2732
James W. Shields *(Chm. Bd.)*
Thomas A. Manning *(Pres.)*
John Anderson *(Sr. V.P.)*
John J. Broderick *(V.P., Sec. & Treas.)*
John R. Thomas *(Controller)*
Thomas Michaels *(Corp. Services Mngmt.)*

Computer Systems/Hardware:
IBM

Outside Service Firm(s):

Stoy Maloney & Co.*(Auditors)*
Bethesda, MD

Sanders, Schnabel & Brandenberg*(Legal Firm)*
Washington, DC

Maryland National Bank*(Major Banking Relationship)*
Baltimore, MD 21202

Subsidiaries:

Mount Jackson Press, Inc. **(1)**
1868 Judd's Dr.
Mount Jackson, VA 22842
Tel.: 703-477-3000
S.I.C.: 2752
Willis S. Georgia *(V.P. & G.M.)*

Port City Press, Inc. **(1)**
1323 Greenwood Rd.
Pikesville, MD 21208
Tel.: 410-486-3000
S.I.C.: 2752
Thomas A. Manning *(Pres.)*

Shenandoah Valley Press, Inc. **(1)**
P.O. Box 777, Route 55E
Strasburg, VA 22657
Tel.: 703-465-3731
S.I.C.: 2752
Wilson K. Rembold *(V.P. & Gen Mgr.)*

JUDSON-ATKINSON CANDIES, INC.
831 S. Flores
San Antonio, TX 78204
Mailing Address:
P.O. Box 830046,
San Antonio, TX 78283-0046
Tel.: 210-227-5201
Fax: 210-222-8498
Year Founded: 1899
Approx.Sls.: $14,000,000
Emp.: 110
Fiscal Year-end: 12/31/90
Mfr. Candies
S.I.C.: 2064
Basil Atkinson *(Pres.)*
Amy Voltz *(V.P.-Pur.)*
Mark Love *(V.P.-Opers.)*
Patricia Scrivner *(Controller)*
Steve Voltz *(Sls. Mgr.)*

JUDY BOND, INC.
330 W. 34th St.
New York, NY 10001
Tel.: 212-868-4800
Fax: 212-239-0925
Approx.Sls.: $50,000,000
Emp.: 1,200
Mfr. of Judy Bond Blouses
S.I.C.: 2331
Robert Postal *(Chm. Bd.)*
Andrew Postal *(Pres.)*
Elaine Postal *(Exec. V.P.)*
Neil Ronga *(Controller)*

Outside Service Firm(s):

Berenson, Berenson, Adler & Co.*(Auditors)*
New York, NY

Division:

Brewton Fashions Div. **(1)**
330 W. 34th St.
New York, NY 10001
Tel.: 212-868-4800
Women's Ready-to-wear Apparel
S.I.C.: 2331

JACQUES JUGEAT, INC.
225 5th Ave.
New York, NY 10010
Tel.: 212-684-6760
Year Founded: 1954
Approx.Sls.: $19,282,000
Emp.: 24
Fiscal Year-end: 12/31/90
Import
Distributors of French Crystal & Porcelain
S.I.C.: 5023
Lloyd J. Glasgow *(Pres.)*
Francis Soichet *(Exec. V.P.)*
John Bridgewater *(Dir.-Opers.)*
Polly R. Winograd *(Dir.-Communications)*
Christian Scelles *(Mgr.-Sls.)*

Juhl
MARKETING COMMUNICATIONS

JUHL MARKETING COMMUNICATIONS
3930 Edison Lakes Pkwy.
Mishawaka, IN 46545
Tel.: 219-271-5621
Year Founded: 1945
Approx.Billings: $24,000,000
Emp.: 59
Howard Blackwood *(Chm. Bd.)*
Bruce Cashbaugh *(Pres.)*
George Anderson *(Chief Fin. Officer & V.P.)*
Steve Patton *(Exec. V.P.)*
Michele Morgan *(Sr. V.P.)*
Ralph Sullivan *(Sr. V.P.-Personnel Training & Devel.)*
Mike Cottingham *(V.P.)*
Maggie Smith *(V.P. & Dir.-Pub. Rels.)*
Cindy Hammel *(Sec. & Travel Planner)*
Diane Stellingwerf *(Dir.-Human Resources)*

JUNIATA OFFICE SUPPLIES
1554 Valley View Blvd.
Altoona, PA 16602
Tel.: 814-944-7291 **PA**
Year Founded: 1978
Sales Range: $10-19 Million
Emp.: 12
Sale & Service of Office Supplies, Furniture, Office Machines, Computers, Copiers, Typewriters
S.I.C.: 5943
James C. Ellis *(Pres.)*
J. P. Haupt *(Corp. Sec., Treas. & Chief Fin. & Exec. Officer)*

Computer Systems/Hardware:
NCR PC 4; Apple; IBM Compatibles

Outside Service Firm(s):

Central Bank*(Major Banking Relationship)*
Hollidaysburg, PA

Guy Landolfi *(Auditors)*
Altoona, PA

JUNIOR GALLERY LTD.
512 7th Ave.
New York, NY 10018
Tel.: 212-764-3707
Twx: 424235
Fax: 212-391-0379
Emp.: 350
Manufacture Womens & Junior Outerwear
S.I.C.: 2339
Nathan Hirsch *(Pres. & Chief Exec. Officer)*
Harvey Bernstein *(Chief Fin. Officer)*
Patrick Delisi *(Controller)*
Martin Oshrin *(Sec. & Treas.)*

Outside Service Firm(s):

Mahoney Cohen & Co., P.C. *(Auditors)*
New York, NY

Feltman, Karesh, Major & Farbman *(Legal Firm)*
New York, NY

Republic National Bank *(Major Banking Relationship)*
355 Lexington Ave.
New York, NY 10017
Tel.: 212-573-5514

JUPITER INDUSTRIES, INC.
919 N. Michigan Ave., Ste. 1500
Chicago, IL 60611
Tel.: 312-642-6000
Fax: 312-642-2316
Year Founded: 1906
Assets: $234,561,000
Earnings: $30,880,000
Liabilities: $165,479,000
Net Worth: $69,082,000
Approx.Sls.: $475,544,000
Emp.: 5,000
Fiscal Year-end: 12/31/91
Holding Company for Transportation Services, Real Estate & Construction
S.I.C.: 6719
Edward W. Ross *(Vice Chm.)*
C.H. Jamison *(Pres.)*
George E. Murphy *(Chief Fin. Officer & V.P.)*
Philip Rootberg *(Sr. V.P.-Corp. Devel.)*
Robert Berliner *(Corp. Sec.)*
John Starcevich *(Treas.)*
Linda Koh *(Controller)*

Outside Service Firm(s):

Coopers & Lybrand *(Auditors)*
203 N. LaSalle St.
Chicago, IL 60601
Tel.: 312-701-5500

Connecticut General Life Insurance Co. *(Group Insurer)*
Chicago, IL

Jenner & Block *(Legal Firm)*
One IBM Plaza
Chicago, IL 60611
Tel.: 312-222-9350

Division:

Colony Press Inc. **(1)**
707 Skokie Blvd.
Northbrook, IL 60062
Tel.: 708-272-4141 (100%)
Direct Response Advertising
S.I.C.: 7331
Jerry Margolis *(Pres.)*
Jeffery Sedlack *(Chief Fin. Officer)*

Subsidiary:

The Jupiter Corporation **(1)**
919 N. Michigan Ave.
Chicago, IL 60611
Tel.: 312-642-6000
Assets: $220,900,000
Earnings: $29,433,000
Liabilities: $159,662,000
Net Worth: $61,238,000
Approx.Sls.: $472,773,000
Fiscal Year-end: 12/31/91
Import Export
Diversified Holding Co.; Oil & Gas; Real Estate; Transportation Services; Construction; Manufacturing & Specialized Engineering
S.I.C.: 4213; 7331; 1711; 1521; 1321; 4231; 6552; 6719; 8711
Jerrold Wexler *(Chm. Bd.)*
Edward W. Ross *(Pres.)*
C.H. Jamison *(Sr. V.P.)*
George E. Murphy *(V.P. & Treas.)*
Ira A. Kipnis *(V.P. & Sec.)*
Philip Rootberg *(V.P.-Corp. Devel.)*
John Starcevich *(Controller)*

Subsidiaries:

Celebrity Boats, Inc. **(2)**
451 Illinois St.
Benton, IL
Tel.: 618-439-9444
Export
Robert Anderson *(Pres.)*
Steve Pease *(V.P.)*
Lynn Stone *(Controller)*

Crown Coat, Inc. **(2)**
700 Wealthy St., S.W.
Grand Rapids, MI 49501
Tel.: 616-451-0784
Richard Oechler *(Pres.)*
Gayle Brown *(Controller)*

Crown Store Equipment **(2)**
8200 Central Ave.
Toledo, OH
C.H. Jamison *(Pres.)*

Elgin National Industries, Inc. **(2)**
120 S. Riverside Plaza
Chicago, IL 60606
Tel.: 312-454-1900 (100%)
Telex: 324372
Fax: 312-726-2872
Approx.Sls.: $167,166
Emp.: 1,500
Engrng., Mfg. & Installation for Coal & Mineral Industry
S.I.C.: 8711; 3532
Richard G. Miller, Jr. *(Chm. Bd.)*
Fred C. Schulte *(Pres. & Chief Exec. Officer)*
Wayne Conner *(Chief Fin. Officer)*
Harry Chase *(V.P.-Fin., Treas. & Admin.)*
Charles Hall *(V.P.)*
Lynn Batory *(Controller)*
Marge Egger *(Mgr.)*

Divisions:

American Fasteners **(3)**
1919 W. 19th St.
Broadview, IL 60153
Tel.: 708-681-1820
Distributor of Packaged Threaded Products
S.I.C.: 3452; 5072
Joseph R. Kuchar *(Pres.)*

Centrifugal & Mechanical Industries **(3)**
146 President St.
Saint Louis, MO 63118
Tel.: 314-894-1711
Telex: 477256 CMI STL
Fax: 314-894-7867
Emp.: 72
Export
Computer Systems/Hardware:
IBM System 36
Design, Mfr. & Sls. of Centrifuges for Coal Indus.
S.I.C.: 3569; 3559
Jack Hurley *(Pres. & Chief Exec. Officer)*
H.E. Derton *(Exec. V.P.)*
Ted Iwasyszyn *(V.P.-Sls.-West)*
C.H. Henderson *(V.P.-Sls.-East)*
Kenneth K. Geldmacher *(Treas. & Controller)*
A. Buddy Sebastiao *(Mgr.-Mktg. & Intl. Sls.)*
Dianna Batha *(Pur. Agent)*

Plant:

Centrifugal & Mechanical Industries, Inc. **(4)**
146 President St.
Saint Louis, MO 63118
Tel.: 314-776-2848
S.I.C.: 3569
Winifred Hurley *(Chief Oper. Officer)*

Chandler Products, Inc. **(3)**
1491 Chardon Rd.
Cleveland, OH 44117
Tel.: 216-481-4400
Mfr. Specialty Engineered Fasteners for Internal Combustions Engines
S.I.C.: 3714; 3452
James C. Hanson *(Pres.)*

Cornell Manufacturing Company **(3)**
25 Ramland Rd.
Orangeburg, NY 10962
Tel.: 914-365-0400
Mfr. Fasteners
S.I.C.: 3452
Louis S. Schnur *(Pres.)*

Ohio Rod Products Company, Inc. **(3)**
P.O. Box 416,
Versailles, IN 47042
Tel.: 812-689-6565
Mfrs. & Distr. Threaded Rods & Long Bolts
S.I.C.: 3452
Charles D. Hall *(Pres.)*

Subsidiaries:

Clinch River Corp. **(3)**
Rt. 6, P.O. Box 60
Tazewell, VA 24651
Tel.: 703-988-2548 (100%)
Emp.: 32
Repair & Mfr. of Light Mining Machinery & Equip.
S.I.C.: 3532
William Wampler *(Pres.)*

Langley & Morgan Corp. **(3)**
P.O. Box 777,
Harlan, KY 40831
Tel.: 606-573-3665 (100%)
Emp.: 35
Constructs Coal Preparation Plants
S.I.C.: 1542
Roger Rowland *(Pres.)*

Mining Controls, Inc. **(3)**
P.O. Box 1141,
Beckley, WV 25801
Tel.: 304-252-6243 (100%)
Emp.: 64
Mfg. Electric Controls for Coal & Mineral Indus.
S.I.C.: 3825
Randall Hurst *(Pres.)*

Norris Screen & Mfg., Inc. **(3)**
614 South Wickham Avenue
Princeton, WV 24740
Tel.: 304-487-2478 (100%)
Emp.: 20
Mfr. of Screen Cloth for Vibrating Screens & Centrifuges
S.I.C.: 3532
Hollis Tabor *(Pres. & Gen. Mgr.)*

Roberts & Schaefer Co. **(3)**
120 S. Riverside Plaza
Chicago, IL 60606
Tel.: 312-236-7292 (100%)
Emp.: 144
Constructs Coal & Mineral Benefication Plants & Material Handling Facilities; Provides Engrng. & Construction Srvs. for Mining & Construction Indus.
S.I.C.: 8711
Richard G. Miller, Jr. *(Pres.)*

Subsidiaries:

ENI Engineering Company **(4)**
339 Haymaker Rd.
Monroeville, PA 15146
Tel.: 412-373-8020
Mfr. Engrng. & Construction of Coal Drying Systems
S.I.C.: 3567
Dominick C. Sisti *(Pres.)*

Roberts & Schaeffer Company-Salt Lake City **(4)**
1405 W. 2200 S.
Salt Lake City, UT 84119
Tel.: 801-973-7787
S.I.C.: 8711
Earl C. Antonson *(Sr. V.P.)*

Tabor Machine Co. **(3)**
P.O. Box 3037,
Bluefield, WV 24701
Tel.: 304-327-2431 (100%)
Emp.: 57
Mfr. of Vibrating Separating Screens
S.I.C.: 3532
Lindy Tabor *(Pres.)*

Thompson-Starrett Construction Company, Inc. **(3)**
120 S. Riverside Plaza
Chicago, IL 60606
Tel.: 312-930-9856
General Construction & Engrng. Services
S.I.C.: 8711; 1541
Bill S. Taylor *(Pres.)*

Economy Mechanical Industries, Inc. **(2)**
77 S. Wheeling
Wheeling, IL 60090
Tel.: 708-541-8700 (100%)
Plumbing, Heating Contracting Services
S.I.C.: 1711
Roland Besserud *(Pres.)*
Sue Lehde *(Chief Fin. Officer)*

The Robert Irsay Company **(2)**
8130 N. St. Louis Ave.
Skokie, IL 60076
Tel.: 708-674-8500 (100%)
Design, Engrng. & Construction of Air Handling & Air Conditioning Removal Systems; Sheet Metal Contractor & Clean Room Construction
S.I.C.: 1711; 3585; 1541
Donald G. Lewis *(Chief Oper. Officer)*
George E. Murphy *(Chief Fin. Officer)*

Jupiter Corp. Transportation System **(2)**
4314 39th Ave.
Kenosha, WI 53140
Dennis Troha *(Pres.)*
Mark Portman *(Chief Fin. Officer)*

Subsidiaries:

Boat Transit, Inc. **(3)**
1343 Logan Ave.
Costa Mesa, CA 92626
Tel.: 714-546-7172 (100%)
Transportation of Boats Thru-Out 48 States
S.I.C.: 5091; 4731
C.H. Jamison *(Chief Oper. Officer)*
Dennis Troha *(Pres.)*
Mark Portman *(Chief Fin. Officer)*

Cabell Construction Company **(3)**
120 S. Riverside Plaza
Chicago, IL 60606
Tel.: 312-236-7292

Dallas & Mavis Forwarding Co., Inc. (D & M) **(3)**
4314 39th Ave.
Kenosha, WI 53140
Tel.: 800-558-3271 (100%)
Trucking Services
S.I.C.: 4213
Dennis Troha *(Pres.)*
Mark Portman *(Chief Fin. Officer)*

Jupiter Transportation Corp. **(3)**
4314 39th Ave.
Kenosha, WI 53140
Tel.: 414-658-4833 (100%)
Trucking Transportation Services
S.I.C.: 4213
Dennis Troha *(Pres.)*
Mark Portman *(Chief Fin. Officer)*

Jupiter Energy Corp. **(2)**
919 N. Michigan Ave.
Chicago, IL 60611
Tel.: 312-642-6000 (100%)
Production & Processing Oil & Gas
S.I.C.: 1311
George E. Murphy *(Chief Oper. Officer)*

G.C. Thorsen, Inc. **(2)**
1801 Morgan St.
Rockford, IL 61102
Tel.: 815-968-9661
Tel.: 800-435-2931
Telex: 383956
Fax: 815-968-9731
Approx.Sls.: $40,000,000
Emp.: 200
Import
Mfr. Electronic Supplies
S.I.C.: 3546; 3679
Charles Hall *(Chief Oper. Officer)*
Robert Fierce *(Chief Fin. Officer)*
Alan Walter *(V.P.-Mktg.)*
Brad Corbin *(V.P.-Sls.)*
Al Andreini *(Gen. Mgr.)*

Jupiter Industries, Inc.—(Continued)

Bob Weber *(Natl. Sls. Mgr.-Hand Tools/ Automotive)*
Kevin Rossdeutcher *(Natl. Sls. Mgr.-Consumer Elec. Prods.)*
Vic Giovingo *(Natl. Sls. Mgr.-Electronic Distr.)*
Scott Pyle *(Natl. Sls. Mgr.-Hand Tools/ Hardware)*
Jeff Champion *(Product Mgr.)*
Bruce Martin *(Mgr.-Personnel)*

JUST BORN, INC.
1300 Stefko Blvd.
Bethlehem, PA 18017
Mailing Address:
P.O. Box 1158
Bethlehem, PA 18016
Tel.: 215-867-7568
Approx.Sls.: $48,000,000
Emp.: 250
Fiscal Year-end: 6/30/91
Candy Manufacturer
S.I.C.: 2064
Ross J. Born *(Co-Pres.)*
David N. Shaffer *(Co-Pres.)*
Kenneth Evans *(Chief Fin. Officer)*
Jack M. Shaffer *(Treas.)*
Peter Goold *(Dir.-Mktg. & Sls.)*
Burt Schaffer *(Dir.-Opers.)*
William Sommers *(Dir.-Technical Services)*
Peter Ford *(Mgr.-Pur.)*
Dan Grant *(Mgr.-Natl. Sls.)*
Lew Horvath *(Plant Mgr.)*
Eric Yaindl *(Mgr.-Engrng.)*

Principal(s):

Outside Service Firm(s):

KPMG Peat Marwick*(Auditors)*
4905 Tildgman St.
Allentown, PA 18104
Tel.: 215-391-6380

M. Scoblionko*(Legal Firm)*
Allentown, PA

First Valley Bank*(Major Banking Relationship)*
Bethlehem, PA

Division:

Just Born, Inc. **(1)**
1300 Stefko Blvd.
Bethlehem, PA 18017
Tel.: 215-867-7568
Fax: 215-543-4981
Approx.Sls.: $10,000,000
Emp.: 50
Fiscal Year-end: 6/30/91
Marshmallow Specialties
S.I.C.: 2064
Ross J. Born *(Co-Pres.)*
David N. Shaffer *(Co-Pres.)*
Kenneth Evons *(Chief Fin. Officer)*
Jack M. Shaffer *(Treas.)*
Peter Gould *(Dir.-Mktg. & Sls.)*
Peter Ford *(Mgr.-Pur.)*
Dan Grant *(Mgr.-Natl. Sls.)*
Burt Shaffer *(Mgr.-Opers.)*

JUST PANTS
3525 W. Peterson Ave., Ste. 10
Chicago, IL 60659-3312
Tel.: 312-588-8900 **IL**
Approx.Sls.: $44,000,000
Emp.: 800
Fiscal Year-end: 11/30/90
135 Retail Jeans & Tops Stores, Located Throughout U.S.
S.I.C.: 5651
Louis Brien *(Chief Exec. Officer)*
John Schliessmann *(Controller)*
Henry Levin *(Legal Officer)*
Rick Jouza *(Dir.-Personnel & Pur. Agent)*
Bernie Bloomenkranz *(Dir.-Franchise Devel.)*

Outside Service Firm(s):

Caldwell Coren & Co., Ltd.*(Auditors)*
Downers Grove, IL

Rudnick & Wolfe*(Legal Firm)*
203 N. LaSalle St.
Chicago, IL 60602
Tel.: 312-368-4000

Pathway Financial*(Major Banking Relationship)*
99 W. Washington St.
Chicago, IL 60602
Tel.: 312-346-4200

JUSTISS OIL CO., INC.
Hwy. 84 E.
Jena, LA 71342
Mailing Address:
P.O. Box 1385,
Jena, LA 71342
Tel.: 318-992-4111 **LA**
Fax: 318-992-4111
Year Founded: 1946
Assets: $38,000,000
Earnings: ($522,000)
Liabilities: $6,000,000
Net Worth: $32,000,000
Approx.Sls.: $30,000,000
Emp.: 300
Fiscal Year-end: 11/30/89
Oil & Gas Extraction; Fabricated Metal Prods.
S.I.C.: 1381; 1311; 3443; 1629
James F. Justiss, Jr. *(Chm. Bd., Pres. & Chief Exec. Officer)*
Robert L. Wood *(Treas., Sec. & Chief Fin. Officer)*
Ray G. Thompson *(Mgr.-Employee Rels.)*

Principal(s):
James F. Justiss, Jr.

No. of Mfg. Plants/Facilities: 2
No. of U.S. Offices: 2

Computer Systems/Hardware:
IBM System 36

Outside Service Firm(s):

Payne, Moore & Herrington*(Auditors)*
Alexandria, LA

Lloyds Bank Plc*(Commercial Insurance Carrier)*
London, United Kingdom

Aetna Life & Casualty*(Group Insurer)*
151 Farmington Avenue
Hartford, CT 06156
Tel.: 203-273-2128
Fax: 203-729-4295

Hibernia National Bank*(Investment Banker)*
New Orleans, LA

Gaharan & Wilson*(Legal Firm)*
Jena, LA

Hibernia National Bank*(Major Banking Relationship)*
New Orleans, LA

JUSTRITE MANUFACTURING COMPANY
2454 Dempster St.
Des Plaines, IL 60016
Tel.: 708-298-9250
Tel.: 800-798-9250
Fax: 708-298-3429
Year Founded: 1907
Emp.: 110
Export
Mfr. Safety & Oil Waste Cans, Safety Cabinets & Tanks, Portable Electric Lights & Lanterns, Carbide Lamps
S.I.C.: 3411; 3648; 3641
C.L. Barancik *(Chm. Bd.)*
John Rowe *(Pres.)*
John W. Ozag *(Treas.)*
James Rackley *(Controller)*
Allyn C. Buric *(Dir.-Natl. Sls.)*
Kenneth W. Furtsh *(Dir.-Mktg.)*

Computer Systems/Hardware:
IBM System AS 400

Outside Service Firm(s):

Coopers & Lybrand*(Auditors)*
203 N. LaSalle St.
Chicago, IL 60601
Tel.: 312-701-5500

Altheimer & Gray*(Legal Firm)*
10 S. Wacker Dr.
Chicago, IL 60606
Tel.: 312-715-4000

American National Bank & Trust Co.*(Major Banking Relationship)*
Chicago, IL

American National Bank & Trust Company of Chicago*(Major Banking Relationship)*
33 N. LaSalle St.
Chicago, IL 60602
Tel.: 312-661-5000
Fax: 312-661-6417

Division:

Justrite Mfg. Co. **(1)**
W. Rte. 121
Mattoon, IL 61938
Tel.: 217-234-7486
Fax: 217-234-7632
Manufacturers of Safety Equipment for Handling Flammable Liquids
S.I.C.: 3599
Davies Wakefield *(V.P. & G.M.)*

K & G OF WISCONSIN, INC.
2203 W. Wisconsin Ave.
Milwaukee, WI 53233
Mailing Address:
P.O. Box 1155
Milwaukee, WI 53201
Tel.: 414-933-3123 **WI**
Fax: 414-931-1552
Approx.Sls.: $18,000,000
Emp.: 120
Mechanical Contractor
S.I.C.: 1711
Kenneth M. Coffman *(Chm. Bd.)*
Gregory M. Coffman *(Pres.)*
William S. Pickett *(V.P.-Fin. & Sec.)*
James Westcot *(V.P.)*

Outside Service Firm(s):

Reinhart, Boerner, Van Deuren, Norris & Rieselbach, S.C.*(Legal Firm)*
1000 N. Water St., Ste. 2100
Milwaukee, WI 53202
Tel.: 414-298-1000

Subsidiary:

Downey, Inc. **(1)**
2203 W. Michigan St.
Milwaukee, WI 53233
Tel.: 414-933-3123
Mechanical Contractor
S.I.C.: 1711
Kenneth M. Coffman *(Chm. Bd.)*
Gregory M. Coffman *(Pres.)*
William S. Pickett *(V.P.-Fin. & Sec.)*
James A. Westcot *(V.P.)*

K & R DELIVERY, INC.
15 W. 460 Frontrage Rd.
Hinsdale, IL 60521
Tel.: 708-323-3230 **IL**
Fax: 708-323-3890
Year Founded: 1939
Assets: $17,000,000
Liabilities: $3,000,000
Net Worth: $14,000,000
Approx.Sls.: $30,000,000
Emp.: 350
Fiscal Year-end: 12/31/91
Trucking; Truck Rental
S.I.C.: 4212; 4213; 4214; 7513
David M. Gerstein *(Chief Exec. Officer)*
Lawrence A. Klong *(Pres.)*
David Eggleston *(Exec. V.P. & Gen. Mgr.)*
Dan Sutton *(V.P.-Admin.)*
Tom Toten *(Controller)*
Mike Kramer *(Dir.-Data Processing)*
Paul Morris *(Dir.-Maintenance)*
Tony Joyce *(Mgr.-Sls.)*
Jef Epstein *(Dock Supt.)*

Principal(s):
David M. Gerstein
Lawrence A. Klong

No. of Mfg. Plants/Facilities: 6

Computer Systems/Hardware:
Hewlett Packard

Outside Service Firm(s):

Ernst & Young*(Auditors)*
233 S. Wacker Dr.
Chicago, IL 60606
Tel.: 312-368-1800
Fax: 312-645-3095

Liberty Mutual*(Group Insurer)*
Chicago, IL

Cole Taylor/Bank of Yorktown*(Investment Banker)*
Lombard, IL

Laser, Schostok, Kolman & Frank*(Legal Firm)*
30 N. La Salle St., Suite 2500
Chicago, IL 60602
Tel.: 312-641-1300

Cole Taylor Bank*(Major Banking Relationship)*
Chicago, IL

Subsidiary:

K & R Rentals, Inc. **(1)**
15 W. 460 Frontrage Rd.
Hinsdale, IL 60521
Tel.: 708-323-3230
Fax: 708-323-3890
Emp.: 5
Common Carrier
S.I.C.: 4212
Jim Halloran *(Dir.-Personnel)*

K-III COMMUNICATIONS CORPORATION
(Formerly K-III Holdings)
(Sub. of Films for The Humanities, Inc.)
717 5th Ave., 22nd Fl.
New York, NY 10022
Tel.: 212-745-0100
Fax: 212-745-0199
Year Founded: 1989
Approx.Sls.: $950,000,000
Emp.: 3,500
Fiscal Year-end: 12/31/90
Holding Company; Publisher of Magazines & Newsletters for the Ground, Sea Transportation & Electrical Industries, Horse Racing, Television, Railroad Guides, Truck & Freight Schedules, Adult & Juvenile Books & Book Clubs & Development & Sales of Encyclopedias, Consumer Magazines, Health Care Booklets & Educational Films
S.I.C.: 2721; 2731; 6719; 2711
William F. Reilly *(Chm. Bd.)*
Beverly Chell *(Vice Chm.)*
Charles G. McCurdy *(Pres.)*
Douglas P. Miscoll *(V.P.-Fin.)*
Curtis A. Thompson *(V.P.-Operational Finance & Controller)*

No. of U.S. Offices: 15
No. of Foreign Offices: 2

Outside Service Firm(s):

Deloitte & Touche*(Auditors)*
1 World Trade Center
New York, NY 10048
Tel.: 212-669-5000

Bankers Trust Co.*(Major Banking Relationship)*
P.O. Box 318, Church St. Station
New York, NY 10008
Tel.: 212-454-2212
Fax: 212-454-2783

Operating Companies:

Daily Racing Form, Inc. **(1)**
10 Lake Dr.
Hightstown, NJ 08520
Tel.: 609-448-9100
Fax: 609-443-6091
Horse Racing Publication
S.I.C.: 2711
William F. Reilly *(Chm. Bd.)*
Jack Farnsworth *(Pres. & Chief Exec. Officer)*
William H. Williams *(Publisher)*
George Bernet *(Editor)*
Michael Carvalhido *(Dir.-Finance)*
James E. Rinehimer *(Eastern Circulation Dir.)*
Katherine Wilkins *(Mktg. Mgr.)*
Richard Witt *(Eastern Adv. Dir.)*

Divisions:

Daily Racing Form, Inc. Pacific **(2)**
170 S. Bimini Pl.
Los Angeles, CA 90004
Tel.: 213-387-5131 (100%)
Fax: 213-389-5730
Approx.Sls.: $58,000,000
Emp.: 700
Satellite Printing Operation
S.I.C.: 2711
Jack Farnsworth *(Pres. & Chief Oper. Officer)*
Michael Carvalhido *(Dir.-Finance)*
Katherine Wilkins *(Mktg. Mgr.)*
Bill Allen *(Western Circulation Mgr.)*
Ellen Hilts-Gossett *(Western Dir.-Adv.)*
William Dow *(Gen. Mgr.)*

Daily Racing Form, Inc. (Midwest) **(2)**
1301 N. Elston Ave.
Chicago, IL 60622
Tel.: 312-227-3000
Fax: 312-276-5889
Satellite Printing Operation
S.I.C.: 2759
Jack Farnsworth *(Pres. & Chief Oper. Officer)*
Mike Carvalhido *(Dir.-Finance)*
Stanley Shulman *(Gen. Mgr.)*
Gary Salis *(Circulation Mgr.)*
Midge Koontz *(Mgr.-Midwestern Adv. Dept.)*
Katherine Wilkins *(Mgr.-Mktg.)*

Daily Racing Form, Inc. (Northwest) **(2)**
12559 26th St., N.E.
Seattle, WA 98125
Tel.: 206-365-9300
Satellite Printing Operation
S.I.C.: 2759
Jack Farnsworth *(Pres. & Chief Oper. Officer)*
Michael Carvalhido *(Dir.-Finance)*
Katherine Wilkins *(Mktg. Mgr.)*
Philip Fitterer *(Gen. Mgr.)*

Funk & Wagnalls Corp. **(1)**
One Intl. Blvd., Ste. 444
Mahwah, NJ 07430
Tel.: 201-529-6900
Development & Sale of Encyclopedias & other Publications through Supermarkets
S.I.C.: 2731; 5192
George Philips *(Pres.)*
Robert Jackson *(V.P. & Treas.)*
Sally Mitchell *(V.P.-Opers.)*
Leon Bran *(Sr. Editor)*
Betsy Sherer *(Dir.-Mktg.)*
W. Scott Iacone *(Dir.-Adv. & Promo.)*
Sally McCravey *(Dir.-Mfg.)*

Intertec Publishing **(1)**
9221 Quivira Rd.
Overland Park, KS 66215
Tel.: 913-888-4664
Publishers of: 27 Trade Magazines Serving Automotive, Engineering, Telecommunications, and Horticulture Industries
S.I.C.: 2721
Robert J. Hancock *(Pres. & Gen. Mgr.)*
Bob Moraczewski *(Grp. V.P.)*
Cam Bishop *(Grp. V.P.)*
Eric Jacobson *(Grp. V.P.)*
Ron Wall *(Grp. V.P.)*
Bill Wiesner *(Grp. V.P.)*
Raymond Maloney *(V.P.-Fin.)*
Nancy R. Diebel *(V.P.-Opers.)*

Subsidiaries:

Intertec Publishing Corp. **(2)**
5072 W. Chester Pike
Edgemont, PA 19028
Tel.: 215-359-1249
Fax: 215-359-9379
Emp.: 20
Publisher of Transmission & Distribution International Magazine
S.I.C.: 2721; 5192
Barry H. LeCerf *(Publisher)*
Elgin G. Enabnit, Jr. *(Editorial Dir. & Assoc. Publisher)*
Joanne Romanek *(Mktg. Services Mgr.)*

Pacific Shipper, Inc. **(2)**
562 Mission St.
San Francisco, CA 94105
Tel.: 415-546-3946
Publisher of Weekly Business Information For Manufacturing Traffic Managers, Freight Forwarders & Custom House Brokers
S.I.C.: 2711

Ward's Communications, Inc. **(2)**
28 W. Adams
Detroit, MI 48226
Tel.: 313-962-4433
Publisher of Ward's Auto World and Other Publications for the Automotive Industry
S.I.C.: 2721
Roger K. Powers *(Publr.)*

K-III Magazines Corporation **(1)**
755 Second Ave.
New York, NY 10022
Tel.: 212-880-0700
Publishers of Special Interest Magazines
S.I.C.: 2721
Harry A. McQuillen *(Pres. & Chief Exec. Officer)*
Christina B. Wagner *(V.P. & Chief Fin. Officer)*

Subsidiaries:

Automobile Magazine **(2)**
120 E. Liberty
Ann Arbor, MI 48104
Tel.: 313-994-3500
Consumer Magazine, Featuring Entertaining & Informative Articles
S.I.C.: 2721
David E. Davis, Jr. *(Publication Dir.)*
Terry Russel *(Publr.)*
Kevin Smith *(Editor)*

European Travel & Life **(2)**
122 E. 42nd St.
New York, NY 10168
Tel.: 212-949-3500
Lifestyle Magazine Covering European Travel, Fashion, Society, Real Estate & Cuisine
S.I.C.: 2721
David Breul *(Editor-in-Chief)*
Carl Portale *(Publr.)*

New Woman Magazine **(2)**
215 Lexington Ave.
New York, NY 10016
Tel.: 212-685-4790
Magazine Geared for Young, Employed Women; Featuring Articles on Self-Improvement
S.I.C.: 2721
Janis Grossman *(Publisher)*
Gay Bryant *(Editor-in-Chief)*
Laura Cherensky *(Adv. Dir.)*

New York Magazine Company **(2)**
755 Second Ave.
New York, NY 10017
Tel.: 212-880-0700
Fax: 212-972-2185
Emp.: 165
Fiscal Year-end: 12/31/91
Periodical Publishing
S.I.C.: 2721
Edward Kosner *(Pres. & Editor)*
Richard Kinsler *(Publisher)*
Betsy Cronen *(Bus. Dir.)*
Beverly Allen *(Mktg. Dir.)*

Premiere Magazine **(2)**
2 Park Ave., 4th Fl.
New York, NY 10016
Tel.: 212-725-3437 (50%)
S.I.C.: 2721
Peter Eldredge *(Publisher)*
Susan Lyne *(Publr.)*

Seventeen Magazine **(2)**
850 Third Ave.
New York, NY 10022
Tel.: 212-759-8100
Monthly Publication for Young Women
S.I.C.: 2721
William F. Reilly *(Chm.)*
Charles G. McCurdy *(Vice Chm.)*
Beverly C. Chell *(Vice Chm.)*
Harry A. McQuillen *(Pres.)*
Janice Grossman *(Publisher)*
Midge Richardson *(Editor-in-Chief)*
Mary Anne Vallis *(Controller)*
Amy R. Chargin *(Assoc. Publr.)*
Diane Arlotta *(Dir.-Adv. Production)*
Lynne Berentson *(Dir.-Mktg.)*
Lori Fromm *(Mgr.-Sls. Devel.)*

Soap Opera Digest **(2)**
888 7th Ave., 38th Fl.
New York, NY 10106
Tel.: 212-332-0252
Fax: 212-332-0252
Approx.Sls.: $35,000,000
Emp.: 35
Computer Systems/Hardware:
ADP
Magazine Publisher
S.I.C.: 2721
William F. Reilly *(Chm. Bd.)*
Janice Grossman *(Group Publisher)*
Linda Vaughn *(Publisher)*
Dave DelGaiso *(Controller)*
Howard Halligan *(Asst. Controller)*
Brian Beckwith *(Dir.-Circulation)*
Lori Nash *(Dir.-Adv.)*
Susan Mansfield *(Adv. Coord.)*

Sports Travel **(2)**
500 Plaza Drive
Secaucus, NJ 07096
Tel.: 201-902-1900
Ed McNeill *(Publisher)*
Rich O'Connor *(Editor-in-Chief)*

Sportswear International **(2)**
438 West 37th St.
New York, NY 10018
Tel.: 212-563-3470
Trade Fashion Publication
S.I.C.: 2721
Michael Belluomo *(Editor & Associate Publisher)*

Star Magazine **(2)**
660 White Plains Rd.
Tarrytown, NY 10591
Tel.: 914-332-5000
Magazine Publishing
S.I.C.: 2721
Elaine Shindler *(Publr.)*
Dick Kaplan *(Editor)*

K-III Information **(1)**
424 W. 33rd St.
New York, NY 10001
Tel.: 212-714-3100
Publishes Railroad Guides, Truck & Freight Schedules
S.I.C.: 2721
Jack Farnsworth *(Pres.)*
Susan Frederick *(V.P.-Special Mkts.)*
Alan Glass *(Grp. Publr.)*
John Nolan *(V.P.-Fin.)*

Field Publications **(1)**
245 Long Hill Rd.
Middletown, CT 06457
Tel.: 203-638-2400
Publr. Classroom Periodicals, Encyclopedias & Other Supplementary Educational Products: Books & Other Educational & Entertainment Products for Juvenile & Special Interest Clubs
S.I.C.: 2721; 2731; 2741
Robert Quigley *(Pres.)*

Krames Communications **(1)**
1100 Grundy Lane
San Bruno, CA 94066
Tel.: 415-742-5400
Publisher of Magzines for Hospital and Health Industries
Richard Levett *(Sr. V.P. & Acting Pres.)*

Newbridge Communications **(1)**
333 E. 38th St., 10 Fl.
New York, NY 10016
Tel.: 212-455-5000
Mail Order Book Clubs
S.I.C.: 2731
Peter J. Quandt *(Pres.)*
Sam Bell *(Sr. V.P.-Fin. & Chief Fin. Officer)*
Peter Bergen *(Sr. V.P.-Mktg.)*
Paul Granville *(Sr. V.P.-Mkt. Plng. & Admin.)*
Dennis Chua *(V.P.-Fin.)*
Bob Warner *(V.P. & Controller)*
Elizabeth Cater *(V.P. & Editor-in-Chief)*
Rich Kelley *(V.P. & Dir.-Scientific & Professional Programs)*
Derek Reicherter *(V.P.-Mktg. Plng.)*

Newfield Publications **(1)**
245 Long Hill Rd.
Middletown, CT 06457
Tel.: 203-638-2400
Mail Order Children & Adult Book Clubs
S.I.C.: 2721; 2731
Robert Quigley *(Pres.)*

Weekly Reader Corp. **(1)**
245 Long Hill Rd.
Middletown, CT 06457
Tel.: 203-638-2400
Tel.: 800-999-7100 (100%)
Fax: 203-638-2788
Supplementary Educational Materials for the School Market
S.I.C.: 2721
Peter J. Quandt *(Pres.)*
Richard LeBrasseur *(Exec. V.P.)*

Non-U.S. Holding:

Daily Racing Form, Inc. (Toronto) **(1)**
245 Carlaw Ave.
Toronto, ON M4M 2S7, Canada
Tel.: 416-465-5487
Printing of Racing Information
S.I.C.: 2759
James Rogers *(Gen. Mgr.)*

K & B, INC.
1055 St. Charles Pl.
New Orleans, LA 71030
Tel.: 504-586-1234 **LA**
Fax: 504-585-4482
Year Founded: 1905
Approx.Sls.: $450,000,000
Emp.: 4,000
Fiscal Year-end: 9/30/90
Import
Chain of Drug Stores; 173 U.S. Stores
S.I.C.: 5912
Sydney J. Besthoff III *(Chief Exec. Officer)*
James J. LeBlanc *(Pres. & Chief Oper. Officer)*
Ron Dyer *(V.P.-Admin. & Treas.)*
Lance Clark *(V.P.-Mktg.)*
Thomas E. Heifner *(V.P.-Devel.)*
Maury Midlo *(V.P.-Adv.)*
Rodger W. Baumgarten *(Dir.-Personnel)*
Virginia F. Besthoff *(Dir.-Real Estate)*
Gerard Lagarde *(Dir.-Office Systems & Procedures)*

Computer Systems/Hardware:
IBM System 4341

Outside Service Firm(s):

Arthur Andersen & Co.*(Auditors)*
201 St. Charles Ave., Ste. 4500
New Orleans, LA 70170

Montgomery, Barnett, Brown & Read*(Legal Firm)*
New Orleans, LA

First National Bank of Commerce*(Major Banking Relationship)*
New Orleans, LA

Group Insurance Service Center*(Pension Manager)*
Marshfield, MA

KCL CORPORATION
Hodell & Prospect Sts.
Shelbyville, IN 46176
Tel.: 317-392-2521
Fax: 317-392-4772
Approx.Sls.: $25,000,000
Emp.: 400
Flexible Packaging; Packaging Machinery; Paper; Film & Foil Products
S.I.C.: 2671; 3353; 3565
D. Billings Swain *(Chm. Bd.)*
Robert C. Stolmeier *(Pres.)*
Roy Hanson *(V.P.)*
Ronald G. Thieman *(Treas.)*
Paulette Gardiner *(Dir.-Personnel)*
Judy Douglas *(Pur. Agent)*

KCL Corporation—(Continued)

Tom McAdams *(Dir.-Mngmt. Info. System)*
Bob Crouch *(Mgr.-Mfg.)*
Merrill Stillabower *(Mgr.-Mfg.)*
Richard Zurich *(Mgr.-Sls.)*

No. of Mfg. Plants/Facilities: 3
No. of U.S. Offices: 4
No. of Foreign Offices: 1

Outside Service Firm(s):

Ernst & Young*(Auditors)*
One Indiana Square, Ste. 3400
Indianapolis, IN 46204
Tel.: 317-236-1100

White & Raub*(Legal Firm)*
Shelbyville, IN

Bank One, Indianapolis, N.A.*(Major Banking Relationship)*
111 Monument Circle, Ste. 1611
Indianapolis, IN 46204-1611
Tel.: 317-321-8110

KCS ENERGY INC.
(Formerly KCS Group, Inc.)
379 Thornall St.
Edison, NJ 08837
Tel.: 908-632-1770 **DE**
Fax: 908-603-8960
Assets: $60,499,000
Earnings: $2,495,000
Liabilities: $34,798,000
Net Worth: $25,701,000
Approx.Rev.: $98,946,000
Emp.: 68
Fiscal Year-end: 9/30/90
Integrated Energy Company Engaged in Oil & Gas Exploration & Production, Natural Gas Transportation, Natural Gas Marketing & Energy Services
S.I.C.: 1382; 1311; 4924
Stuart B. Kean *(Chm. Bd.)*
James W. Christmas *(Pres. & Chief Exec. Officer)*
Henry A. Jurand *(V.P.-Corp. Plng. & Devel. & Sec.)*

K-D LAMP COMPANY
1910 Elm
Cincinnati, OH 45210
Tel.: 513-621-4211
Fax: 513-621-6088
Year Founded: 1914
Approx.Sls.: $19,000,000
Emp.: 235
Fiscal Year-end: 12/31/90
Import Export
Mfr. Truck Lighting & Mirrors
S.I.C.: 3231; 3647
Andrew L. Stone *(Chm. Bd., Pres. & Chief Exec. Officer)*
Richard Ward *(V.P.)*
Craig Stone *(Grp. V.P.)*
Michael Kessler *(Controller)*
Ron Sparks *(Sls. Mgr.)*
S. Mosey *(Natl. Sls. Mgr.)*
Frank Leurch *(Mgr.-Personnel)*
Don Frederick *(Mgr.-Mfg.)*
Charles Manning *(Pur. Agent)*

KDI CORPORATION
5721 Dragon Way
Cincinnati, OH 45227
Tel.: 513-272-1421 **DE**
Fax: 513-527-5038
Year Founded: 1956
Assets: $183,447,393
Liabilities: $101,479,322
Net Worth: $81,968,071
Approx.Sls.: $315,000,000
Emp.: 3,913
Fiscal Year-end: 12/31/90
Holding Co.; Mfr. & Sales of Swimming Pools & Related Items; Variety Technical Prods. & Components; Distrs. of Indus. Chemicals & Gases, Scientific Apparatus & Motion Picture Films
S.I.C.: 6719; 1799; 2892; 3678; 7822
Eugene A. Cafiero *(Chm. Bd., Pres., Chief Exec. & Oper. Officer)*
P. Roger Byer *(V.P.-Fin. & Treas.)*
David A. Conway *(V.P.-Admin.)*
Bruce Crowley *(V.P.-Mktg.)*
Kevan K. Langner *(Legal Officer)*
Bill Pinkerton *(Sls. & Adv. Mgr.)*

Outside Service Firm(s):

In-House*(Legal Firm)*

Chemical Bank*(Major Banking Relationship)*
450 West 33rd St.
New York, NY 10001
Tel.: 212-613-7197
Fax: 212-947-7628

Manufacturing Cos.-Components:

Subsidiaries:

KDI Electro-Tec Corp. **(1)**
1600 N. Main St.
Blacksburg, VA 24060
Tel.: 703-552-2111 (100%)
Emp.: 325
Mfr. Slip Rings, Brush Blocks, Capsule Access., etc.
S.I.C.: 3679; 3577
Harold D. Hankins *(Pres.)*

KDI Electronics **(1)**
60 S. Jefferson Rd.
Whippany, NJ 07981
Tel.: 201-887-8100 (100%)
Emp.: 280
Mfr. Resistors
S.I.C.: 3679
Douglas K. McConnell *(Pres.)*

Subsidiaries:

KDI American Products, Inc. **(2)**
10951 W. Los Angeles Ave.
Moorpark, CA 93021
Tel.: 805-523-2400 (100%)
Emp.: 225
Mfr. Swimming Pool Prods.
S.I.C.: 3949
Frederick O. Wagner *(Pres.)*

KDI Paragon, Inc. **(2)**
12 Paulding St.
Pleasantville, NY 10570
Tel.: 914-769-6221
Emp.: 36
Mfr. Swimming Pool Equip.
S.I.C.: 3589; 3444
Philip Sperber *(Chief Opr. Officer)*

KDI Sylvan Pools, Inc. **(2)**
P.O. Box 1449
Doylestown, PA 18901
Emp.: 400
Mfr. Concrete Swimming Pools & Equipment
S.I.C.: 1799
Raymond Calvitti *(Pres. & Chief Exec. Officer)*
Ronald Zaberer *(V.P.-Fin.)*
Debbie Wade *(Adv. Administrator)*

Subsidiary:

Sylvan Pools of Arizona, Inc. **(3)**
2210 E. Indian School Rd.
Phoenix, AZ 85016
Tel.: 602-264-4921 (100%)
Emp.: 35
Sells & Constructs Swimming Pools
S.I.C.: 1799
Hermann Gerbracht *(V.P.)*

Masterite Industries, Inc. **(1)**
2841 Lomita Blvd.
Torrance, CA 90505
Tel.: 310-534-0962 (100%)
Emp.: 260
Mfr. Electrical Inter-Connecting Devices
S.I.C.: 3678
Gordon Olson *(Pres.)*

RFI Corp. **(1)**
100 Pine Aire Dr.
Bay Shore, NY 11706
Tel.: 516-231-6400 (100%)
Emp.: 230
Design & Mfr. RF Interference Filters
S.I.C.: 3675
Mervin H. First *(Pres.)*

Sylvan Pools of Texas, Inc. **(1)**
11306 LBJ Freeway
Dallas, TX 75238
Tel.: 214-343-3338 (100%)
Emp.: 15
Sells & Constructs Swimming Pools
S.I.C.: 1799
Scott Quisling *(V.P.)*

Sylvan Pools of Texas, Inc. **(1)**
7613 H Katy Fwy.
Houston, TX 77024
Tel.: 713-688-1290
Emp.: 13
Sells & Constructs Swimming Pools
S.I.C.: 1799
Vernon L. Quisling *(Pres.)*

Manufacturing Cos.-Technical Products:

Subsidiaries:

KDI Precision Products, Inc. **(1)**
3975 McMann Rd.
Cincinnati, OH 45245
Tel.: 513-943-2000 (100%)
Emp.: 520
Products for Aerospace & Ordinance
S.I.C.: 3489
Mark E. Clark *(Pres.)*

Martin Electronics, Inc. **(1)**
Rte. 1, P.O. Box 500
Perry, FL 32347
Tel.: 904-584-2634 (100%)
Emp.: 250
Grenade Component Parts, etc.
S.I.C.: 2892
Roy B. York *(Pres.)*

Manufacturing & Services Cos.-Custom Specifications

Subsidiaries:

Electronic Plating Service, Inc. **(1)**
13021 S. Budlong Ave.
Gardena, CA 90247
Tel.: 213-321-5747 (100%)
Emp.: 80
Precious Metal Plating
S.I.C.: 3471
Ronald Novkov *(Pres.)*

Precise Metals & Plastics, Inc. **(1)**
501 Mosside Blvd.
East McKeesport, PA 15035
Tel.: 412-823-2100 (100%)
Emp.: 400
Plastic Injection Molders
S.I.C.: 3089
Paul E. Finer *(Pres.)*

University Casework Systems, Inc. **(1)**
2718 Pershing Ave.
Memphis, TN 38112
Tel.: 901-458-2775 (100%)
Emp.: 60
Institutional, Commercial & Architectural Woodwork
S.I.C.: 1799
Earl N. Whitehead *(Pres.)*

Non-Manufacturing Companies:

Subsidiaries:

HVC/Daly Company **(1)**
4600 Dues Dr.
Cincinnati, OH 45246
Tel.: 513-874-9261 (100%)
Emp.: 145
Chemical Distr.
S.I.C.: 5169
Dean R. Gaudin *(Pres.)*

Modern Talking Picture Service, Inc. **(1)**
5000 Park St. N.
Saint Petersburg, FL 33709
Tel.: 813-541-7571 (100%)
Emp.: 300
Distr. Motion Pictures
S.I.C.: 7822
G. C. Kater *(Pres.)*

K-J DISTRIBUTORS, INC.
(d/b/a/ Shamrock Distributing Co.)
5061 N. 51st Ave.
Glendale, AZ 85301
Tel.: 602-842-8000 **AZ**
Fax: 602-269-8602
Sales Range: $40-59 Million
Emp.: 150
Wholesale Beer
S.I.C.: 5181
Patrick Harris *(Pres.)*
Michael Harris *(Sr. V.P.)*
Cynthia Harris Dunham *(Owner, Treas. & Sec.)*
Principal(s):
Patrick Harris
Michael Harris
Cynthia Harris Dunham

Computer Systems/Hardware:
IBM System 36

Outside Service Firm(s):

Olan Bassar Barrows*(Auditors)*
Phoenix, AZ

Provident Life & Accident Insurance Co.*(Group Insurer)*
1951 W. Camelback Rd.
Phoenix, AZ 85015
Tel.: 800-237-1870
Fax: 602-433-6663

Valley National Bank*(Major Banking Relationship)*
241 North Central Ave., 11th Floor
Phoenix, AZ 85001

KOA HOLDINGS
100 Park Ave.
New York, NY 10017
Tel.: 212-370-1110
Fax: 212-692-9749
Air Carrier, Scheduled; Campgrounds; Commercial Printing; Franchises; Equipment Rental & Leasing
S.I.C.: 6719; 4513; 7033; 2752; 6794; 7359
Oscar L. Tang *(Chm. & Pres.)*
Lorraine Hysler *(Sec.)*
Peter Frelinghuysen *(Legal Counsel)*

Outside Service Firm(s):

KPMG Peat Marwick*(Auditors)*
1000 1st. Interstate Center, 401 N. 31st. St.
Billings, MT 59103

The Bank of New York*(Major Banking Relationship)*
One Wall Street
New York, NY 10286
Tel.: 212-635-6805
Fax: 212-635-3201

Morris & McVeigh*(Legal Firm)*
New York, NY

Subsidiaries:

Canyon Capital Inc. **(1)**
24012 Calle de la Plata, Ste. 310
Laguna Hills, CA 92653
Tel.: 714-458-7900 (100%)
Equipment Leasing
S.I.C.: 7359
Thomas O'Connor *(Pres.)*

Comprehensive Business Services Inc. **(1)**
1925 Palomar Oaks Way #105
Carlsbad, CA 92008
Tel.: 619-431-2150
Fax: 610-431-2156
Approx.Sls.: $45,000,000
Emp.: 180
Fiscal Year-end: 1/31/91
Computer Systems/Hardware:
Datapoint; Hewlett-Packard; IBM
Set-Up & Sale of Accounting Practices
S.I.C.: 8721; 6794
Don F. Lowe *(Chm. Bd.)*
C. Robert Wissler *(Pres. & Chief Oper. Officer)*
Allan Fera *(V.P.-Fin. & Admin.)*
Chuck White *(V.P.-Mktg.)*
Robert A. Kotz *(V.P.-Franchise Services)*
Peter Kijac *(V.P.-Data Processing)*

Robert S. Anderson *(V.P.)*

Division:

Mid Pacific Air **(2)**
P.O. Box 2835
West Lafayette, IN 47906
Tel.: 317-743-2085
Cargo Air Services
S.I.C.: 4513
Michael English *(V.P. & G.M.)*

Subsidiary:

West Advertising/Public Relations, Inc. **(3)**
Transwestern 3 Bldg., 4th Fl.,
Billings, MT 59103
Tel.: 406-248-7444 (100%)
Advertising & Public Relations
S.I.C.: 7311
Ray Todd *(V.P. & Gen. Mgr.)*

Kampgrounds of America, Inc. **(1)**
Transwestern 3 Bldg., 4th Fl.
Billings, MT 59103
Tel.: 406-248-7444
Fax: 406-248-7414
Approx.Sls.: $18,600,000
Emp.: 258
Computer Systems/Hardware:
IBM System 38
Campgrounds
S.I.C.: 7033
Arthur M. Peterson *(Pres.)*
Kent Zimmerman *(V.P.-Mktg.)*
Dave Nusbaum *(V.P.-Adv. & Pub. Rels. & Dir.-Mktg.)*
Dave Johnson *(V.P.-Sls.)*
Harry Cuff *(Treas.)*
Pat Giblin *(Legal Officer)*
Kurt Klaas *(Dir.-Pur.)*

Mid Pacific Air Corporation **(1)**
100 Park Ave.
New York, NY 10017
Tel.: 212-370-1110 (100%)
Cargo Airline
S.I.C.: 4513
Mark Leinger *(Chief Oper. Officer)*

Sir Speedy, Inc. **(1)**
23131 Verdugo Dr.
Laguna Hills, CA 92653
Tel.: 714-472-0330
Fax: 714-458-1297
Approx.Sls.: $336,000,000
Emp.: 70
Franchisor of Printing Centers
S.I.C.: 5999; 7334
Don F. Lowe *(Pres. & Chief Exec. Officer)*
Dan Beck *(Grp. V.P.-Franchise Services)*
Catherine Monson *(Grp. V.P.-Mktg. & Training)*
Ken Ross *(Grp. V.P.-System Devel.)*
Dave Collins *(V.P.-Franchise Sls.)*
Dan Conger *(V.P.-Fin. & Admin.)*
Janet Martin *(Gen. Counsel)*
Kathy McGlamery *(Controller)*
Gibson MacDonald *(Adv. Coord.)*
Michele Kimberlin *(Mktg. Services Mgr.)*
Chuck Lennon *(Adv. Mgr.)*
Bill McCue *(Pub. Rels. Mgr.)*
Kathleen Bass *(Corp. Librarian)*
Marci Hanover *(Corp. Travel Planner)*

Non-U.S. Holding:

Kampgrounds of America (Canada) Ltd. **(1)**
6-A Tilbury Court
Brampton, ON L6T 4T9, Canada
Tel.: 416-453-7080 (100%)
Campgrounds
S.I.C.: 7033
Arthur M. Peterson *(Pres.)*

KPMG PEAT MARWICK
345 Park Ave.
New York, NY 10154
Tel.: 212-758-9700
Fax: 212-758-9819
Year Founded: 1897
Approx.Sls.: $1,350,000,000
Emp.: 18,500
Accounting & Consulting Firm
S.I.C.: 8721
Jon C. Madonna *(Chm. & Chief Exec. Officer)*
Joseph E. Heintz *(Partner & Dir.-Fin. & Admin.)*
Bernard J. Malano *(Partner & Dir.-Human Resources)*
Bruce Curry *(Dir.-Computer Resources)*
John A. Higgins *(Dir.-Pub. Rels.)*

No. of U.S. Offices: 136
No. of Foreign Offices: 265

Computer Systems/Hardware:
IBM 3081 Mainframe

Outside Service Firm(s):

KPMG Peat Marwick*(Auditors)*
Level 8, 161 Collins St.
Melbourne, 3000, Australia
Tel.: 613-288-5603

Equitable Life*(Group Insurer)*
1221 Ave. of the Americas
New York, NY 10022
Tel.: 212-382-8038
Fax: 212-382-8089

KSG INC.
115 Grimes Dr.
Guntersville, AL 35976
Tel.: 205-582-0691 **AL**
Fax: 205-582-1163
Sales Range: $10-19 Million
Emp.: 180
Manufacture Industrial Protective Clothing for Use in Hazardous Material Handling, Clean Rooms
S.I.C.: 2329; 2339; 6719
George Kappler *(Chm., Pres. & Chief Exec. Officer)*
Don Kelly *(Chief Fin. Officer & Treas.)*
Beth Garrett *(Dir.-Adv.)*
John Langley *(Dir.-Res. & Devel.)*
Randal Vaughn *(Dir.-Pur.)*
Principal(s):
George Kappler

No. of Mfg. Plants/Facilities: 3
No. of U.S. Offices: 1
No. of Foreign Offices: 1

Computer Systems/Hardware:
IBM System 34

Outside Service Firm(s):

Woodward & Nolen*(Auditors)*
Albertville, AL

American National Bank & Trust Company of Chattanooga*(Major Banking Relationship)*
736 Market St.
Chattanooga, TN 37402
Tel.: 615-757-3011

Subsidiaries:

Kappler, Inc. **(1)**
70 Grimes St.
Guntersville, AL 35976
Tel.: 205-582-2195 (100%)
Mfrs. Full Line of Industrial Protective Apparel
S.I.C.: 2329; 2339
John Petrey *(Pres.)*

Kappler Europe, Ltd. **(1)**
Kappler Close
Netherfield, Nottingham NG4 2PP, United Kingdom
Tel.: 602-61-81-82
Protective Clothing Manufacturer
S.I.C.: 2385
John Petrey *(Pres.)*

KSK COMMUNICATIONS, LTD.
8618 Westwood Center Dr., Ste. 400
Vienna, VA 22182-2280
Tel.: 703-734-1880
Fax: 703-821-2756
Year Founded: 1983
Approx.Billings: $25,000,000
Emp.: 39
Business-to-Business, High Technology, Marketing, Advertising & Public Relations
Corporate Giving Program: Pro Bono Work for Local Non-Profit Civic & Professional Organizations
Karen S. Kennedy *(Chm. Bd., Pres., Treas. & New Bus. Contact)*
Karen Kazmark *(V.P., Investor & Pub. Rels.)*
Lu Chiang *(V.P., Fin.)*

Computer Systems/Hardware:
NCR Tower, IBM, Apple LAN

KYB CORPORATION OF AMERICA
901 Oak Creek Drive
Lombard, IL 60148
Tel.: 708-620-5555
Telex: 25-4394
Fax: 708-620-8133
Year Founded: 1974
Approx.Sls.: $28,000,000
Emp.: 34
Fiscal Year-end: 3/31/91
Import
Automotive Shock Absorbers; Industrial Hydraulic Motors & Components
S.I.C.: 3714
Takashi Sanada *(Pres.)*
Gail Rose *(V.P.-Admin.)*
M. Casper *(V.P.-Fluid Power)*
A. L. Tiffany *(V.P.-Sls. & Mktg.)*
S. Kamimura *(Sec.)*
O. Kunihara *(Treas.)*
Betty Olson *(Data Processing Supervisor)*

Computer Systems/Hardware:
IBM AS400

Division:

KYB Corp. of America **(1)**
6601 Darin Way
Cypress, CA 90630
Tel.: 714-897-9005
Fax: 714-891-4728
Import
Computer Systems/Hardware:
MAI Basic 4
Warehouse Distr. of Motor Vehicle Parts to West Coast Region
S.I.C.: 5013
Joseph Ratliff *(Dir.-Distribution)*

Subsidiary:

KYB Industries Inc. **(1)**
1860 Northwood Plaza
Franklin, IN 46131
Tel.: 317-736-7774
Fax: 317-736-4618
Computer Systems/Hardware:
IBM AS400
Mfr. of Struts & Shock Absorbers
S.I.C.: 3714

THE KAEMPFER COMPANY, INVESTMENT BUILDERS
1150 18th St., N.W., Ste. 1000
Washington, DC 20036
Tel.: 202-331-4300
Fax: 202-331-4313
Year Founded: 1977
Approx.Sls.: $150,000,000
Emp.: 100
Real Estate Development & Investment Company
S.I.C.: 6552; 6798
J.W. Kaempfer, Jr. *(Pres.)*
John Nicolosi *(Exec. V.P.-Construction)*
Julia J. Calabrese *(Sr. V.P.-Property Mngmt.)*
Steve Levin *(Sr. V.P. & Gen. Counsel)*
Principal(s):
J.W. Kaempfer, Jr.

No. of U.S. Offices: 2

Computer Systems/Hardware:
Prime Minicomputer

Outside Service Firm(s):

Beers & Cutler*(Auditors)*
Washington, DC

Dunnells, Duvall, Bennett & Porter*(Legal Firm)*
Washington, DC

Subsidiary:

Barnes, Morris, Pardoe & Foster Management Services **(1)**
1150 18th St., N.W., Ste. 1000
Washington, DC 20036
Tel.: 202-331-4300
Julia J. Calabrese *(Chief Oper. Officer)*

KAEPA INC.
5410 Kaepa Ct.
San Antonio, TX 78218
Tel.: 210-661-7463
Fax: 210-661-7630
Approx.Sls.: $50,000,000
Emp.: 43
Fiscal Year-end: 12/31/90
Markets Athletic Footwear
S.I.C.: 5139
Frank Legacki *(Pres.)*
Paul Tschoepe *(V.P.-Fin.)*
Katie Hoffner *(Dir.-Mktg. & Intl. Opers.)*
John Atkinson *(Mgr.-Natl. Sls.)*

KAHLER FRIENDT & PARTNERS, INC.
2405 South 130th Circle
Omaha, NE 68144-5908
Tel.: 402-334-6900
Fax: 402-334-7517
Year Founded: 1991
Approx.Billings: $20,000,000
Emp.: 42
Jeff Kahler *(Chm. Bd.)*
Glenn Friendt *(Pres. & Chief Exec. Officer)*
Linda Morse *(Sr. V.P., Controller)*
Dave Robertson *(Dir. Pub. Rels.)*

Computer Systems/Hardware:
Apple; Macintosh; IBM

ALBERT KAHN ASSOCIATES, INC.
Albert Kahn Bldg., 7430 Second Ave.
Detroit, MI 48202-2798
Tel.: 313-871-8500
Fax: 313-871-8539
Year Founded: 1895
Approx.Sls.: $20,000,000
Emp.: 265
Architechtural & Engineering Services
S.I.C.: 8712; 8711
Edgar E. Parks *(Chm. Bd. & Chief Exec. Officer)*
Gordon V.R. Holness *(Pres.)*
Robert L. Eck *(Exec. V.P.)*
George M. Barbu *(V.P.)*
William L. Demiene *(V.P.)*
John E. Enkemann, Jr. *(V.P.)*
Marvin D. Keefover *(V.P.)*
Robert J. Mauck *(V.P.)*
David G. Reeve *(V.P.)*
Henry L. Ritter *(V.P.)*
Charles T. Robinson *(V.P.)*
Stephen Q. Whitney *(V.P. & Sec.)*
Robert A. Paulsen *(Mgr.-Mktg.)*

Outside Service Firm(s):

Arthur Andersen & Co.*(Auditors)*
400 Renaissance Center
Detroit, MI 48243
Tel.: 313-259-8100

Butzel, Keidan, Simon, Myers & Graham*(Legal Firm)*
2490 First National Bldg.
Detroit, MI 48226

Albert Kahn Associates, Inc.—(Continued)

Tel.: 313-961-7900

N.B.D. Bank, N.A.*(Major Banking Relationship)*
611 Woodward Ave.
Detroit, MI 48226
Tel.: 313-225-1122
Fax: 313-225-3420

M. B. KAHN CONSTRUCTION CO., INC.
Hwy. 555, Flintlake Rd.
Columbia, SC 29202
Mailing Address:
P.O. Box 1179,
Columbia, SC 29202
Tel.: 803-736-2950 **SC**
Fax: 803-736-5833
Year Founded: 1927
Assets: $34,277,690
Liabilities: $21,573,232
Net Worth: $12,704,458
Approx.Sls.: $245,000,000
Emp.: 575
Fiscal Year-end: 12/31/91
General Building Contractors
S.I.C.: 1629; 1522; 1541; 1542; 8741
Alan Kahn *(Chm. Bd.)*
Ronald L. McCall *(Vice Chm., Chief Exec. Officer, Chief Fin. Officer & Treas.)*
Bill Neely *(Pres. & Chief Oper. Officer)*
Wayne Brewer *(V.P.-Kahn Corp. Div.)*
Buzz Fleming *(V.P.-Sls.)*
H. "Sandy" Frazier *(V.P.-Frazier Div.)*
Bill Myers *(V.P.-N. Carolina Div)*
Mike Nevitt *(V.P.-M.B. Kahn Div.)*
Rick Ott *(V.P.-Construction Mngmt.)*
Al Ruble *(V.P.-Argo & Public Div.)*
Robert Synnett *(V.P.-Human Resources & Personnel Training & Devel.)*
Mike Hayes *(Controller & Dir.-Data Processing)*
Al Adams *(Corp. Sec. & V.P.-Adams Div.)*
Ronald L. McCall *(Dir.-Merger/ Acquisiton)*

Principal(s):
Alan Kahn
Ronald L. McCall
Bill Neely

No. of U.S. Offices: 8

Computer Systems/Hardware:
IBM 545 System 38

Outside Service Firm(s):

J. W. Hunt & Co.*(Auditors)*
Middleburg Office Park, 1607 St. Julian Place
Columbia, SC 29202
Tel.: 803-254-8196

Aetna Life & Casualty*(Group Insurer)*
151 Farmington Avenue
Hartford, CT 06156
Tel.: 203-273-2128
Fax: 203-729-4295

General American Life Insurance Co.*(Group Insurer)*
700 Market
Saint Louis, MO 63101
Tel.: 314-525-5458
Fax: 314-525-3677

The Quinn Firm*(Legal Firm)*
Columbia, SC

Citizens & Southern National Bank*(Major Banking Relationship)*
Columbia, SC

Equitable Life*(Pension Manager)*
1221 Ave. of the Americas
New York, NY 10022
Tel.: 212-382-8038
Fax: 212-382-8089

KAIBAB INDUSTRIES
4602 E. Thomas Rd.
Phoenix, AZ 85018
Mailing Address:
P.O. Box 52111,
Phoenix, AZ 85072
Tel.: 602-840-5555 **AZ**
Fax: 602-952-6963
Year Founded: 1951
Assets: $55,000,000
Liabilities: $36,000,000
Net Worth: $19,000,000
Approx.Sls.: $160,000,000
Emp.: 900
Fiscal Year-end: 9/30/90
Manufacture Wood Products; Wholesale Lumber, Petroleum & Sheet Metal
S.I.C.: 2421; 5031; 5051; 5172
A. Milton Whiting *(Chm. Bd. & Chief Exec. Officer)*
R. Bruce Whiting *(Pres. & Chief Oper. Officer)*
Don Olsen *(Pres.-Forest Prods.)*
William M. Cassel *(Pres.-Kaibab Petroleum Co.)*
Duane Simmons *(V.P.-Plng.)*
Richard A. Fletcher *(V.P.-Fin.)*
Victoria Hauser *(Dir.-M.I.S.)*
Delbert Tingey *(Dir.-Benefits)*
Lyn Glenn *(Dir.-Communications)*

Computer Systems/Hardware:
IBM System 36; Hewlett-Packard

Outside Service Firm(s):

Arthur Andersen & Co.*(Auditors)*
Phoenix, AZ

Jennings, Strouss & Salmon*(Legal Firm)*
2 N. Central, Ste. 1600
Phoenix, AZ 85004
Tel.: 602-942-8659

Security Pacific Bank Arizona*(Major Banking Relationship)*
Phoenix, AZ

Divisions:

Forest Products Division **(1)**
4602 E. Thomas Rd.
Phoenix, AZ 85018
Tel.: 602-840-5555
Fax: 602-952-6963
Approx.Sls.: $46,450,000
Emp.: 750
Manufacture Lumber
S.I.C.: 5031
Don Olson *(Exec. V.P.)*

Petroleum Division **(1)**
4602 E. Thomas Rd.
Phoenix, AZ 85018
Tel.: 602-840-5555
Fax: 602-952-6963
Approx.Sls.: $103,880,000
Emp.: 200
Wholesale & Retail Petroleum Marketing
S.I.C.: 2911
William M. Cassel *(Exec. V.P.)*

Subsidiary:

Kaibab Metals, Inc. **(1)**
4602 E. Thomas Rd.
Phoenix, AZ 85018
Tel.: 602-840-5555 (100%)
Fax: 602-952-6963
Approx.Sls.: $21,000,000
Emp.: 116
Sheet Metal
S.I.C.: 5051
W. Brent Taylor *(Pres.)*

KAISER AEROSPACE & ELECTRONICS CORP.
950 Tower Lane, Ste. 800
Foster City, CA 94404
Tel.: 415-349-7400
Fax: 415-349-8284
Sales Range: $100-499 Million
Emp.: 2,000
Fiscal Year-end: 12/31/91
Defense Contractors; Aircraft & Component Parts & Electronic Displays
S.I.C.: 3728; 3663; 3769
H.J. Smead *(Chm. Bd., Pres., Chief Exec. & Chief Fin. Officer & Sec.)*
Ed Durbin *(Sr. V.P.)*
John E. Chapin *(Controller)*
Barry Burlingame *(Dir.-Human Resources)*

Computer Systems/Hardware:
Hewlett-Packard 3000/68; IBM 4341

Outside Service Firm(s):

Ernst & Young*(Auditors)*
555 California St., Ste. 3000
San Francisco, CA 94104
Tel.: 415-951-3000

Equitable Life*(Group Insurer)*
1221 Ave. of the Americas
New York, NY 10022
Tel.: 212-382-8038
Fax: 212-382-8089

Kidder, Peabody & Co.*(Investment Banker)*
10 Hanover Square
New York, NY 10005
Tel.: 212-510-3000

Collette & Erickson*(Legal Firm)*
San Francisco, CA

Bank of America, N.T. & S.A.*(Major Banking Relationship)*
P.O. Box 37002,
San Francisco, CA 94137

Atalanta/Sosnoff Capital Corp.*(Pension Manager)*
New York, NY

Dean Investment Assocs.*(Pension Manager)*
Dayton, OH

Founders Capital Management*(Pension Manager)*
Denver, CO

Siebel Capital Management Co.*(Pension Manager)*
Larkspur, CA

Subsidiaries:

Polhemus Inc. **(1)**
1 Hercules Dr.
Colchester, VT 05446
Tel.: 802-655-3159
Machine & Other Job Shop Work
S.I.C.: 3599
Phil Cooper *(Pres.)*

Votaw Precision Technologies **(1)**
13153 Lakeland Rd.
Santa Fe Springs, CA 90670
Tel.: 310-944-0661
Fax: 310-944-0675
Approx.Sls.: $20,000,000
Emp.: 150
Machine & Other Job Shop Work
S.I.C.: 3599
James Barnes *(Pres.)*

KAISER FOUNDATION HEALTH & HOSPITALS GROUP
1 Kaiser Plaza
Oakland, CA 94612
Tel.: 510-271-5910
Fax: 510-271-6495
Year Founded: 1945
Approx.Rev.: $8,400,000,000
Health & Medical Service Plans
S.I.C.: 6324
James Vohs *(Chm. Bd.)*
Dr. David Lawrence *(Chief Exec. Officer)*
Wayne Moon *(Pres. & Chief Oper. Officer)*
Mark Hellender *(V.P.-Sls. & Mktg.)*

Regions:

Kaiser Permanente, Northern California Region **(1)**
1950 Franklin St.
Oakland, CA 94612
Tel.: 510-987-3165
Health Maintenance Organization
S.I.C.: 6324
Jerry Fleming *(Health Plan Mgr.)*

Kaiser Permanente, Southern California Division **(1)**
393 E. Walnut St.
Pasadena, CA 91188
Tel.: 818-405-3026
HMO Plan
S.I.C.: 6324
L. Jerome Ashford *(Health Plan Mgr.)*

Kaiser Permanente, Colorado Division **(1)**
10350 E. Dakota Ave.
Denver, CO 80231-1314
Tel.: 303-344-7740
HMO Plan
S.I.C.: 6324
Steve Tomme *(Health Plan Mgr.)*

Kaiser Permanente, Georgia Division **(1)**
3355 Lenox Rd., NE, Ste. 1000
Atlanta, GA 30326
Tel.: 404-233-0555
HMO Plan
S.I.C.: 6324
Ronald Hostettler *(Health Plan Mgr.)*

Kaiser Permanente, Hawaii Division **(1)**
711 Kapiolani Blvd.
Honolulu, HI 96813
Tel.: 808-529-5241
HMO Plan
S.I.C.: 6324
David Dunlap *(Health Plan Mgr.)*

Kaiser Permanente, Kansas/Missouri Division **(1)**
10561 Barkley
Overland Park, KS 66212
Tel.: 913-469-5853
HMO Plan
S.I.C.: 6324
Dotti Dam *(Health Plan Mgr.)*

Kaiser Permanente, Mid-Atlantic States Division **(1)**
4200 Wisconsin Ave., NW, Ste. 300
Washington, DC 20016
Tel.: 202-364-3434
HMO Plan
S.I.C.: 6324
Robert Essink *(Health Plan Mgr.)*

Kaiser Permanente, North Carolina Division **(1)**
3120 Highwoods Blvd.
Raleigh, NC 27604-1018
Tel.: 919-878-9870
HMO Plan
S.I.C.: 6324
Anna M. Lore *(Health Plan Mgr.)*

Kaiser Permanente, Northeast Division **(1)**
76 Batterson Park Rd.
Farmington, CT 06034-4011
Tel.: 203-678-6000
HMO Plan
S.I.C.: 6324
William Kramer *(Health Plan Mgr.)*

Kaiser Permanente, Northwest Division **(1)**
3600 N. Interstate Ave.
Portland, OR 97227-1191
Tel.: 503-721-4600
HMO Plan
S.I.C.: 6324
Denise Honzel *(Health Plan Mgr.)*

Kaiser Permanente, Ohio Division **(1)**
North Point Tower, Ste. 1200, 1001 Lakeside Ave.
Cleveland, OH 44114
Tel.: 216-621-5600
HMO Plan
S.I.C.: 6324
Robert Baker *(Health Plan Mgr.)*

Kaiser Permanente, Texas Division (1)
12720 Hillcrest Rd., Ste. 600
Dallas, TX 75230
Tel.: 214-458-5055
HMO Plan
S.I.C.: 6324
John Pinkney *(Health Plan Mgr.)*

KAISER MCEUEN INC.
1631 Pontius Ave.
Los Angeles, CA 90025
Tel.: 310-479-8999
Fax: 310-479-8006
Year Founded: 1970
Approx.Billings: $13,500,000
Emp.: 26
Advertising Agency
S.I.C.: 7311
Michael Kaiser *(Chm. & Chief Exec. Officer)*
Thomas McEuen *(Pres. & New Bus. Contact)*

Computer Systems/Hardware:
Data General; Word Perfect System; Advanced Data System

Outside Service Firm(s):

State Farm Insurance*(Group Insurer)*
Bloomington, IL

Segal & Klar*(Legal Firm)*
Century City, CA

Santa Monica Savings*(Major Banking Relationship)*
Santa Monica, CA

KAISER TOBACCO COMPANY, INC.
415 E. Oak St.
New Albany, IN 47150
Mailing Address:
P.O. Box 1115,
New Albany, IN 47150-1115
Tel.: 812-945-2651 **IN**
Fax: 812-949-5353
Year Founded: 1956
Approx.Sls.: $13,000,000
Emp.: 29
Wholesale Distribution of Tobacco & Tobacco Products; Confectionery; Paper & Disposable Plastic Bags; Wrapppng or Coarse Paper & Products; Tobacco Stores & Stands
S.I.C.: 5194; 5145; 5113; 5993
John R. Kaiser *(Pres.)*
Louis A. Kaiser *(V.P.)*
George E. Kaiser *(Sec.)*

Outside Service Firm(s):

First National Bank*(Major Banking Relationship)*
Louisville, KY

KALAMAZOO HOLDINGS, INC.
3713 W. Main St.
Kalamazoo, MI 49007
Mailing Address:
P.O. Box 511,
Kalamazoo, MI 49005
Tel.: 616-349-9711
Fax: 616-382-3060
Holding Company
S.I.C.: 6719
Paul Todd, Jr. *(Pres.)*
Gary Hainrihar *(V.P.-Intl.)*
Howard D. Cripps *(V.P.-Sls.)*
George Todd *(V.P.-Mfg.)*
Donn Baird *(Treas.)*

Outside Service Firm(s):

Ernst & Young*(Auditors)*
1100 Old Kent Bank Bldg.
Kalamazoo, MI 49007
Tel.: 616-349-6671

First American Bank, N.A.*(Major Banking Relationship)*
Kalamazoo, MI

Subsidiary:

Kalsec, Inc. (1)
3713 W. Main St.
Kalamazoo, MI 49007
Tel.: 616-349-9711
Approx.Sls.: $12,000,000
Emp.: 115
Food Flavors & Natural Colors, Hop Extractives
S.I.C.: 2087; 5199
Paul Todd, Jr. *(Pres.)*
Howard D. Cripps *(V.P.-Sls.)*
George Todd *(V.P.-Comml.)*
Donn Baird *(Treas.)*

KALAMAZOO LABEL CO.
321 W. Ransom St.
Kalamazoo, MI 49007
Tel.: 616-381-5820
Tel.: 800-321-0076
Fax: 616-381-0533
Year Founded: 1906
Approx.Sls.: $17,000,000
Emp.: 165
Fiscal Year-end: 12/31/91
Export
Kalco, Kal-Namel, Kal-Foil, Kalco-Stik & Kal-Gum Paper Labels
S.I.C.: 2672
Jack L. Page *(Chm. Bd.)*
James D. English *(Pres.)*
V.J. Page *(Sec. & Treas.)*
Doug Severns *(Natl. Sls. Mgr.)*
Richard Martin *(Plant Supt.)*
Principal(s):
Jack L. Page
James D. English

No. of Mfg. Plants/Facilities: 3
No. of U.S. Offices: 5

Computer Systems/Hardware:
IBM Model 36

Outside Service Firm(s):

Plante & Moran*(Auditors)*
815 Kalamazoo Bldg.
Kalamazoo, MI 49007
Tel.: 616-385-1858

Early, Lennon, Peters & Crocker*(Legal Firm)*
Kalamazoo, MI

CoAmerica Bank*(Major Banking Relationship)*
Kalamazoo, MI

Affiliate:

Sterling Color Process (1)
8184 Broadmoor Ave. S.E.
Caledonia, MI 49316
Tel.: 616-891-1700
Printer of Cut & Stack Litho Labels
S.I.C.: 2752
Alan Tran Jr. *(Gen. Mgr.)*

KALAS MANUFACTURING, INC.
25 Main St.
Denver, PA 17517
Mailing Address:
P.O. Box 328,
Denver, PA 17517-0328
Tel.: 215-267-5575 **PA**
Fax: 215-267-4248
Wiredrawing and Insulating
S.I.C.: 3357
Walter A. Cubberly *(Chm. Bd. & Treas.)*
Richard P. Witwer *(Pres.)*
Paul Witwer *(Chief Exec. Officer)*
Owen Hart *(Sec.)*
Jon J. Wiig *(Mgr.-Sls.)*

Outside Service Firm(s):

Jacobson & Co.*(Auditors)*
Norristown, PA

Barley, Snyder, Cooper & Barber*(Legal Firm)*
Lancaster, PA

KALB VOORHIS & CO.
27 William St., 3rd Fl.
New York, NY 10005
Tel.: 212-804-0200
Fax: 212-269-4199
Year Founded: 1946
Assets: $139,900,000
Liabilities: $104,800,000
Net Worth: $35,100,000
Sales Range: $10-19 Million
Emp.: 80
Fiscal Year-end: 9/30/90
Securities Broker & Dealer
S.I.C.: 6211
Kenneth A. Hipkins *(Partner)*
Mark R. Feller *(Partner)*
Fred Bensinger *(Partner)*
Peter Dunn *(Partner)*
Robert G. Guttenstein *(Partner)*
Neil F. Hayes *(Partner)*
William H. Herrman *(Partner)*
William W. Prager, Jr. *(Partner)*
Mark S. Criscitello *(Partner)*
Wayne Wu *(Partner)*
Neil B. Rindlaub *(Partner)*

Outside Service Firm(s):

Price Waterhouse*(Auditors)*
153 E. 53rd St., 44th Fl.
New York, NY 10022
Tel.: 212-371-2000

Morgan, Lewis & Bockius*(Legal Firm)*
1800 M St. N.W.
Washington, DC 20036
Tel.: 202-467-7000

KALIN ENTERPRISES, INC.
5252 S. Tamiami Trail
Sarasota, FL 34231
Tel.: 813-924-1271 **FL**
Fax: 813-923-0045
Year Founded: 1950
Approx.Sls.: $12,000,000
Emp.: 85
Fiscal Year-end: 12/31/91
Furniture Stores, Women's Ready-to-wear Apparel, Bankers & Correspondents
S.I.C.: 5712; 5621; 6162
Edward L. Kalin *(Pres.)*
Jeffrey M. Kalin *(V.P.)*
Phyllis K. Kessler *(Chief Fin. Officer)*
Alyce Kalin *(Sec.)*

Outside Service Firm(s):

Lloyd K. Duncan*(Auditors)*
Sarasota, FL

Nicholas & Cannon*(Commercial Insurance Carrier)*
Sarasota, FL

Abel, Band, Brown, Russell, Collier, Petchford & Gordon*(Legal Firm)*
Sarasota, FL

KALMBACH PUBLISHING CO.
21027 Crossroads Circle
Milwaukee, WI 53187
Mailing Address:
P.O. Box 1612,
Milwaukee, WI 53187
Tel.: 414-796-8776
Tel.: 800-558-1544
Fax: 414-796-0126
Approx.Sls.: $32,000,000
Emp.: 200
Fiscal Year-end: 8/31/92
Publishers: Consumer Specialty Periodicals, Hard & Soft Cover Books; Model Railroader Magazine; Trains Magazine; Classic Toy Trains Magazine; Collecting Toys Magazine; Creative Prod. Magazine; EARTH Magazine; Fine Scale Modeler Magazine; Astronomy Magazine; Model Retailer Magazine; Nutshell News Magazine; Miniatures Showcase Magazine; Magazine Distributors
S.I.C.: 2721
Walter J. Mundschau *(Pres.)*
Robert A. Maas *(V.P.-Sls. & Mktg.)*
Gerald Boettcher *(V.P.-Fin.)*
Robert L. Hayden *(V.P.-Editorial)*
Russell Larson *(V.P.-Editorial)*
Connie Bradley *(V.P.-Human Resourses)*
Charles Post *(Dir.-Circulation)*
Daniel R. Lance *(Dir.-Adv. Sls.)*

M. KAMENSTEIN, INC.
190 E. Post Rd.
White Plains, NY 10601
Tel.: 914-948-2290
Telex: 137013
Fax: 914-997-0373
Approx.Sls.: $30,000,000
Manufactures, Imports & Markets Wood, Plastic & Porcelain-enamel-on-steel Household & Office Products
S.I.C.: 2541; 2519
David R. Kamenstein *(Chm. Bd. & Chief Exec. Officer)*
Peter D. Kamenstein *(Vice Chm., Pres. & Chief Oper. Officer)*
Robert Varakian *(Sr. V.P.-Sls. & Mktg.)*
Arman Figueras *(V.P., Western Region)*
Brian Simmons *(V.P. & Sec.)*
Thomas LaRosa *(Dir.-Mfg., Spice Opers.)*
Mark Girouard *(Mgr.-Distribution)*
Celena Vitalo *(Mgr.-Natl. Sls.)*

Outside Service Firm(s):

Ernst & Young*(Auditors)*
787 Seventh Ave.
New York, NY 10019
Tel.: 212-773-1243

Schnader, Harrison, Segal & Lewis*(Legal Firm)*
330 Madison Ave.
New York, NY 10017
Tel.: 212-973-8000

Republic National Bank*(Major Banking Relationship)*
355 Lexington Ave.
New York, NY 10017
Tel.: 212-573-5514

Branches:

M. Kamenstein, Inc. (1)
4966 El Camino Real, Ste. 118
Los Altos, CA 94022
Tel.: 415-964-7453
Armand Figueras *(V.P.)*

Kamenstein Europe, Ltd. (1)
Sentinel House, 4 Queen Sq.
Bistol, BS1 4JQ, United Kingdom
Tel.: 44 272 255028
Stuart Harding *(Dir.)*

KAMSTRA

KAMSTRA COMMUNICATIONS, INC.
370 Selby Ave., Ste. 300
Saint Paul, MN 55102-1880
Tel.: 612-228-1419
Fax: 612-224-9837
Year Founded: 1963
Approx.Billings: $27,000,000
Emp.: 53
K.M. Kamstra *(Chm. & Chief Exec. Officer)*
D.A. Buresh *(Pres.)*
J. Stanton *(V.P., Pub. Rels.)*

KANAWHA STEEL & EQUIPMENT CO.
Edens Fork Rd. & I-77 Jct.
Charleston, WV 25312
Mailing Address:
P.O. Box 3203
Charleston, WV 25332
Tel.: 304-343-8801 **WV**
Fax: 304-343-8801, Ext. 133
Year Founded: 1948
Approx.Sls.: $16,000,000
Emp.: 90
Wholesale Distribution of Industrial Machine Parts
S.I.C.: 5084
Tom L. Horn, Jr. *(Pres. & Chief Exec. Officer)*
Marcella Barnett *(Sr. V.P.)*
Ray Hart *(Controller)*
Ann B. Horn *(Sec.)*

Outside Service Firm(s):

United National Bank*(Major Banking Relationship)*
Parkersburg, WV

SAM KANE BEEF PROCESSORS, INC.
P.O. Box 9254,
Corpus Christi, TX 78469
Tel.: 512-241-5000
Fax: 512-242-2999
Approx.Sls.: $225,000,000
Emp.: 450
Beef Processors
S.I.C.: 2013; 5147
Sam Kane *(Chm. Bd., Chief Exec. & Chief Fin. Officer)*
Bernard Kane *(Vice Chm.)*
Jerry Kane *(Pres.)*
Jesse Lieberman *(Sr. V.P.-Opers.)*
Esther Kane *(V.P.)*
Harold Kane *(V.P.)*
Harold Alberts *(Sec.)*
Aranka Kane *(Treas.)*

Computer Systems/Hardware:
IBM System 36

Outside Service Firm(s):

Collier, Johnson & Woods*(Auditors)*
Corpus Christi, TX

Merrill Lynch*(Pension Manager)*
Corpus Christi, TX

KANE-MILLER CORP.
555 White Plains Rd.
Tarrytown, NY 10591
Tel.: 914-631-6900 **DE**
Fax: 914-631-4707
Year Founded: 1920
Assets: $130,000,000
Liabilities: $56,000,000
Net Worth: $74,000,000
Approx.Sls.: $235,000,000
Emp.: 750
Fiscal Year-end: 12/31/91
Food Processing
S.I.C.: 2011; 2077; 2079; 2099
Daniel Kane *(Chm. Emeritus)*
Stanley B. Kane *(Chm. & Sec.)*
Harold Oelbaum *(Pres.)*
M.J. Raffia *(V.P.-Fin.)*
Max Lucash *(Asst. Treas.)*

Outside Service Firm(s):

Deloitte & Touche*(Auditors)*
1600 Summer St.
Stamford, CT 06905-5121
Tel.: 203-351-4600

Kemper Insurance*(Commercial Insurance Carrier)*
Long Grove, IL 60049-0001

Aetna Life & Casualty*(Group Insurer)*
151 Farmington Avenue
Hartford, CT 06156
Tel.: 203-273-2128
Fax: 203-729-4295

Chadbourne & Parke*(Legal Firm)*
30 Rockefeller Plaza
New York, NY 10112
Tel.: 212-408-5100

The Bank of New York*(Major Banking Relationship)*
One Wall Street
New York, NY 10286
Tel.: 212-635-6805
Fax: 212-635-3201

Subsidiaries:

The American Meat Packing Corp. **(1)**
3946 S. Normal Ave.
Chicago, IL 60609
Tel.: 312-538-7000 (100%)
Approx.Sls.: $89,000,000
Emp.: 319
Slaughters, Bones & Fabricates Hogs
S.I.C.: 2011
Carl Herrman *(Pres.)*

HRR Enterprises, Inc. **(1)**
2129 W. Pershing Rd.
Chicago, IL 60609
Tel.: 312-376-7735 (100%)
Rendering Plant
S.I.C.: 2077
W.G. Tarpley *(Pres.)*

Pip Printing **(1)**
27001 Agoura Rd.
Agoura Hills, CA 91301
Tel.: 818-880-3800 (80%)
Fax: 818-880-3840
Assets: $80,048,000
Earnings: $78,000
Liabilities: $56,305,000
Net Worth: $23,743,000
Approx.Sls.: $265,024,000
Emp.: 75
Fiscal Year-end: 12/31/90
Business Printing Franchises; 1,110 Locations in 49 States, United Kingdom, Canada
S.I.C.: 2759
Corporate Giving Program: Supports National Center for Missing & Exploited Children
Betsy Burton *(Chm. Bd. & Chief Exec. Officer)*
Dave Schofield *(Sr. V.P.-Opers. & Chief Oper. Officer)*
L. Anthony Rubin *(V.P. & Gen. Counsel)*
Carol LaPorta *(Sr. V.P.-Mktg.)*
David Smith *(V.P.-Fin.)*
Fenton Markevich *(Controller)*
Chuck Carr *(Dir.-Mktg.)*
Tom Patterson *(Mgr.-Mktg.)*
Susan Falck *(Mgr.-Pub. Rels.)*

Subsidiary:

PIP Capital Inc. **(2)**
27001 Agoura Rd.
Agoura Hills, CA 91301
Tel.: 818-880-3840
Approx.Sls.: $229,391,000
Emp.: 120
Business Printing Franchise; Business Forms, Color Printing & High-Speed Duplicating
S.I.C.: 2752; 2759; 2761; 7334

Sunnyland Refining Co., Inc. **(1)**
3330 10th Ave.
Birmingham, AL 35234
Tel.: 205-251-7253 (100%)
Approx.Sls.: $60,000,000
Emp.: 240
Export
Mfg. Margarine, Shortening & Peanut Butter
S.I.C.: 2079; 2099
Thomas F. Pinzino *(Pres.)*
William F. McDonald *(Exec. V.P.)*
Robert T. Smith *(V.P.-Opers.)*
Richard Spivey *(Controller)*

KANEX
3121 Bridge Ave.
Cleveland, OH 44113
Tel.: 216-281-3150
Fax: 216-281-6233
Approx.Sls.: $10,000,000
Emp.: 80
Office Automation Dealer
S.I.C.: 7379
Horzt Lorenz *(Chm. Bd.)*
Ron Bell *(Pres.)*
Brad Lebovitz *(Chief Oper. Officer & Chief Fin. Officer)*
Ron Davis *(Dir.-Sls.)*
Principal(s):
Horzt Lorenz
John Elgin

Computer Systems/Hardware:
IBM System 34

Outside Service Firm(s):

Cuini & Panici*(Auditors)*
Cleveland, OH

KANGAROOS, USA INC.
1809 Clarkson Rd.
Chesterfield, MO 63017
Tel.: 314-532-3357
Fax: 314-532-4967
Year Founded: 1967
Approx.Sls.: $80,000,000
Fiscal Year-end: 2/28/91
Mfr. & Distributor Of Athletic & Leisure Footwear
S.I.C.: 3021; 3144; 3149; 5139
Donald A. Simon *(Chm. Bd.)*
Jerome B. Richter *(Vice Chm. & Pres.)*
D. Sanders *(Exec. V.P.)*
Tim Dwyer *(Controller)*
Principal(s):
Jerome B. Richter

Computer Systems/Hardware:
Wang VS 100

Outside Service Firm(s):

Ernst & Young*(Auditors)*
701 Market St.
St. Louis, MO 63101
Tel.: 314-259-1000

Peper, Martin, Jensen, Maichel & Hetlage*(Legal Firm)*
720 Olive St.
St. Louis, MO 63101
Tel.: 314-421-3850

Division:

Trans World Shoe Import Co., Inc. **(1)**
1809 Clarkson Rd.
Chesterfield, MO 63017
Tel.: 314-532-3357
Mfr. Athletic & Leisure Footwear
S.I.C.: 3021; 3144; 3149; 5139; 3143
Donald A. Simon *(Chm. Bd.)*
Jerome B. Richter *(Pres.)*
William J. Sanders *(Exec. V.P.)*

KANSAS CITY CHIEFS FOOTBALL CLUB
One Arrowhead Drive
Kansas City, MO 64129
Tel.: 816-924-9300
Fax: 816-923-5281
Year Founded: 1960
Approx.Sls.: $50,000,000
Emp.: 180
Fiscal Year-end: 1/31/91
NFL Football Club
S.I.C.: 7997
Lamar Hunt *(Owner)*
Jack Steadman *(Chm. Bd.)*
Carl Peterson *(Pres. & Gen. Mgr.)*
Tim Connolly *(V.P.-Admin.)*
Dale Young *(Treas.)*
Jim Seigfreid *(Sec.)*
Jeff Klein *(Dir.-Stadium Opers.)*
Dennis Watley *(Dir.-Sls. & Promo.)*
Bob Moore *(Dir.-Pub. Rels.)*

Kansas State Network, Inc.
(Company Acquired by SJL Broadcast Management Corp.; Name Changed to SJL of Kansas Corp.)

KAPLAN ELECTRONICS
1700 RT. 23 N
Wayne, NJ 07470
Tel.: 201-694-8600
Fax: 201-694-8873
Sales Range: $60-79 Million
Emp.: 1,300
Holding Company
S.I.C.: 6719
James Kaplan *(Pres.)*
C.E. Brino *(V.P.-Fin.)*
Principal(s):
James Kaplan

Computer Systems/Hardware:
DEC with Ultimate 2000

Subsidiary:

Cornell Dubilier Electronics **(1)**
1700 Rt. 23 N.
Wayne, NJ 07470
Tel.: 201-694-8600
Fax: 201-694-8873
Approx.Sls.: $30,000,000
Emp.: 1,000
Fiscal Year-end: 8/31/90
Manufacture Capacitors, Relays, Filters & Electro-Mechanical Modules
S.I.C.: 3675; 3625; 3613
James Kaplan *(Pres.)*
E. Brino *(V.P.-Fin.)*
Anthony Cavuto *(V.P.-Sls.)*

Kaprielian/O'Leary

KAPRIELIAN/O'LEARY
99 Madison Ave.
New York, NY 10016
Tel.: 212-696-1300
Fax: 212-696-4651
Year Founded: 1980
Approx.Billings: $25,000,000
Emp.: 40
Walter Kaprielian *(Chm. & Creative Dir.)*
John Koutsantanou *(Vice Chm. & Chief Fin. Officer)*
Alice O'Leary *(Pres. & Chief Exec. Officer)*
Florence Tischler *(Exec. V.P.)*
Carolyn Aldrick *(V.P., Office Mgr.)*
Victoria Phair *(V.P., Opers. Dir.)*
Georgia Ramondi *(V.P., Bus. Devel. Dir.)*

KARAKAS, VANSICKLE OUELLETTE ADVERTISING & PUBLIC RELATIONS
200 SW Market St., Ste. 1400
Portland, OR 97201
Tel.: 503-221-1551
Year Founded: 1983
Approx.Billings: $27,000,000
Emp.: 49
High Technology Adv. & Pub. Rels.
Steve Karakas *(Pres. & Adv. Dir.)*
Will Anderson *(Exec. V.P.)*
Marge Breya *(V.P., Pub. Rels.)*
Chuck Nobles *(V.P., Adv.)*
Peter Wendel *(V.P., Opers.)*
Pierre Ouellette *(Sec. & Dir. Creative Services)*
Sharon VanSickle *(Treas. & Dir. Pub. Rels.)*
Gordon Sorensen *(Direct Mktg.)*

KARGES FURNITURE COMPANY
1501 W. Maryland
Evansville, IN 47710
Mailing Address:
P.O. Box 6517,
Evansville, IN 47719
Tel.: 812-425-2291
Fax: 812-425-4016
Approx.Sls.: $10,000,000
Emp.: 100
Import Export

Mfr. of Fine Furniture
S.I.C.: 2511
Edwin Karges *(Chm. Bd. & Pres.)*
Joan Rogier *(V.P.)*
Donna Gault *(Controller)*
Glenn Farabee *(Plant Mgr.)*
Juanita Chattin *(Admin. Asst.)*

KARLER PACKING COMPANY, INC.
9111 Broadway, S.E.
Albuquerque, NM 87103
Tel.: 505-877-3550 **NM**
Fax: 505-877-3550, Ext. 63
Approx.Sls.: $30,000,000
Emp.: 160
Livestock Showing Services
S.I.C.: 0751
Jess Karler *(Pres.)*
Henry Karler *(Exec. V.P.)*
Mike Karler *(V.P.)*

Outside Service Firm(s):

First National Bank Albuquerque*(Major Banking Relationship)*
40 First Plaza
Albuquerque, NM 87102
Tel.: 505-765-4190

KARNAK CORPORATION
330 Central Ave.
Clark, NJ 07066
Tel.: 908-388-0300
Fax: 908-388-9422
Year Founded: 1933
Approx.Sls.: $20,000,000
Emp.: 70
Export
Asphalt Roofing Fabrics & Coatings
S.I.C.: 2952
William Jelin *(Pres.)*
Joseph P. Toto *(Controller)*
Jerry Mills *(Dir.-Mktg.)*
Jill Marcus *(Mgr.-Personnel)*
Arthur Purdy *(Mgr.-Sls.)*
Fred Mansfield *(Pur. Agent)*

Outside Service Firm(s):

J. H. Cohn & Co.*(Auditors)*
75 Eisenhower Pkwy.
Roseland, NJ 07068-1697
Tel.: 201-228-3500

Rubin, Baum, Levin, Constant & Friedman*(Legal Firm)*
645 Fifth Ave.
New York, NY 10022
Tel.: 212-759-2700

Summit Trust*(Major Banking Relationship)*
Summit, NJ

L. KARP & SONS, INC.
1301 Estes Ave.
Elk Grove Village, IL 60007
Tel.: 708-593-5700 **DE**
Year Founded: 1914
Approx.Sls.: $115,000,000
Emp.: 450
Baking Supplies, Syrups & Ice Cream Supplies
S.I.C.: 2087; 2099; 2062
Jack L. Karp *(Pres.)*
E. Day *(V.P.-Minnesota)*
W. Goldman *(V.P.-Fin.)*
W. Rock *(V.P.-Milwaukee)*
D. Snyder *(V.P.-Sls.)*
Jack Waldron *(V.P.-Boston)*
E. Karp *(Treas.)*
S. Hochberg *(Sec.)*
Principal(s):
Jack L. Karp

Outside Service Firm(s):

BDO Seidman*(Auditors)*
111 E. Wacker Dr.
Chicago, IL 60601

Altheimer & Gray*(Legal Firm)*
10 S. Wacker Dr.
Chicago, IL 60606
Tel.: 312-715-4000

American National Bank & Trust Company of Chicago*(Major Banking Relationship)*
33 N. LaSalle St.
Chicago, IL 60602
Tel.: 312-661-5000
Fax: 312-661-6417

KARSH & HAGAN, INC.
5500 Greenwood Plaza Blvd.
Englewood, CO 80111-2106
Mailing Address:
P.O. Box 6581,
Englewood, CO 80155-6581
Tel.: 303-770-8088
Fax: 303-770-8410
Year Founded: 1977
Approx.Billings: $42,569,000
Emp.: 60
Phil Karsh *(Co-Chm. & Chief Exec. Officer)*
Tom Hagan *(Co-Chm. & Chief Exec. Officer)*
Pasquale Marranzino, Jr. *(Pres.)*
Keith Roberts *(V.P., Controller)*
Barbara Williams *(V.P., Admin.)*
Diane Willmann *(Gen. Mgr.-K&H Services)*
Charles Russell *(Gen. Mgr. & Pub. Rels.)*

Computer Systems/Hardware:
DOS, Apple

PING®

KARSTEN MANUFACTURING CORPORATION
2201 W. Desert Cove
Phoenix, AZ 85029
Mailing Address:
P.O. Box 9990
Phoenix, AZ 85068
Tel.: 602-870-5000
Fax: 602-997-6256
Sales Range: $100-499 Million
Emp.: 2,000
Fiscal Year-end: 6/30/92
Export
Mfrs. of Golf Irons, Woods, Putters, Bags, Carry Bags, Wood Covers, Balls, Shirts, Sweaters
S.I.C.: 3949; 2321; 2329; 2339; 3364; 3369; 3398
Karsten Solheim *(Pres.)*
George Drewry *(Chief Fin. Officer)*
Louise Solheim *(Exec. V.P.)*
Allan Solheim *(V.P.)*
John Solheim *(V.P.)*
Louis Solheim *(V.P.)*
Robert L. Cantin *(Dir.-Communications)*
Dan Shoenhair *(Dir.-Mktg.)*
Jack Mundy *(Mgr.-Bus.)*
Mary Perez *(Adv. Coord.)*

Outside Service Firm(s):

Abold Privee & Associates*(Auditors)*
Phoenix, AZ

First Interstate Bank*(Major Banking Relationship)*
P.O. Box 53441,
Phoenix, AZ 85072-3441
Tel.: 602-229-4049

Divisions:

Maximet **(1)**
5925 W. Monroe
Phoenix, AZ 85043
Tel.: 602-272-3241
Fax: 602-272-0500
Mfr. of Ferrous & Non-Ferrous Components & Assemblies Requiring Some Form of Brazing or Metal Joining
S.I.C.: 3499; 3369
Rick Heppler *(Gen. Mgr.)*

Sonee Heat Treating **(1)**
3900 N. 31st Ave.
Phoenix, AZ 85017
Tel.: 602-277-4757
Fax: 602-230-7811
Thermal Processing of All Metals & Alloys for Aerospace, Defense & Commercial Applications
S.I.C.: 3398
Ed Ryan *(Gen. Mgr.)*

Subsidiaries:

Dolphin, Inc. **(1)**
740 S. 59th Ave
Phoenix, AZ 85005
Tel.: 602-272-6747 (100%)
Fax: 602-233-9570
Mfr. of Investment Castings
S.I.C.: 3364
George Ball *(Gen. Mgr.)*

Karsten Engineering Corp. **(1)**
2201 W. Desert Cove
Phoenix, AZ 85029
Tel.: 602-870-5600 (100%)
Fax: 602-944-6286
Numerically Controlled Machine Work
S.I.C.: 3541
Robert Shaw *(Gen. Mgr.)*

THE KARTRIDG PAK CO.
807 W. Kimberly Rd.
Davenport, IA 52806
Mailing Address:
P.O. Box 3848
Davenport, IA 52808
Tel.: 319-391-1100
Fax: 319-391-4951
Approx.Sls.: $25,000,000
Emp.: 210
Fiscal Year-end: 10/31/90
Aerosol Filling Machinery, Meat Processing & Fat Testing Machinery, Tortilla Folders, Flexible Packaging & Filling Machines
S.I.C.: 3565; 3823
Barry Shoulders *(Pres. & Chief Exec. Officer)*
H.J. Sievers *(Gen. Mgr.-Food Div.)*

M.W. KASCH COMPANY
5401 W. Donges Bay Rd.
Mequon, WI 53092
Tel.: 414-242-5000 **WI**
Fax: 414-242-9345
Year Founded: 1934
Approx.Sls.: $86,000,000
Emp.: 195
Fiscal Year-end: 2/28/92
Import
Wholesale Toys, Hobbies, Sporting Goods, Stationery & School Supplies
S.I.C.: 5091; 5092
Jeffrey C. Kasch *(Pres.)*
James A. Kasch *(Exec. V.P.)*
Bill Skebba, Jr. *(V.P.-Sls.)*
Ken Sobkoviak *(V.P.-Fin.)*
Myron Weinbach *(V.P.-Pur.)*
John Brah *(Mgr.-Adv.)*

Outside Service Firm(s):

Ernst & Young*(Auditors)*
111 E. Kilbourn Ave., Ste. 900
Milwaukee, WI 53202
Tel.: 414-273-5900

Godfrey & Kahn*(Legal Firm)*
780 N. Water St.
Milwaukee, WI 53202
Tel.: 414-273-3500
Fax: 414-273-5198

First Bank Milwaukee*(Major Banking Relationship)*
201 W. Wisconsin Ave.
Milwaukee, WI 53259
Tel.: 414-278-6000

KASH N KARRY FOOD STORES, INC.
6422 Harney Rd.
Tampa, FL 33610
Tel.: 813-621-0200
Fax: 813-621-0293
Year Founded: 1988
Approx.Sls.: $1,000,000,000
Emp.: 12,000
Supermarket Chain; Liquor & Drug Stores
S.I.C.: 5411; 5921; 5912
Ronald Floto *(Pres.)*
Raymond P. Springer *(Exec. V.P.-Admin.)*
Thomas A. Whipple *(Exec. V.P.-Mktg.)*
Richard D. Coleman *(V.P., Controller & Sec.)*

KASLE STEEL CORPORATION
4343 Wyoming
Dearborn, MI 48126
Mailing Address:
P.O. Box 33536
Detroit, MI 48232
Tel.: 313-943-2500 **MI**
Fax: 313-943-2597
Year Founded: 1935
Assets: $56,665,000
Liabilities: $45,886,000
Net Worth: $10,779,000
Approx.Sls.: $184,000,000
Emp.: 350
Steel & Service Center, Processing Center
S.I.C.: 5051
Leonard Kasle *(Chm. Bd. & Chief Exec. Officer)*
Ben Jones *(Vice Chm., Treas. & Chief Fin. Officer)*
Roger Kasle *(Pres.)*
Michael Ulewicz *(Chief Oper. Officer)*
Stephen Kasle *(Sec.)*
David Bolio *(Dir.-Fin.)*
Joseph Bowman *(Dir.-Data Processing)*
Reg Campbell *(Dir.-Mktg.)*
Michael Vaterasian *(Dir.-Personnel)*
Ron White *(Dir.-Pur.)*

No. of Mfg. Plants/Facilities: 3
No. of U.S. Offices: 2
No. of Foreign Offices: 1

Computer Systems/Hardware:
Digital VT 220

Outside Service Firm(s):

Arthur Andersen & Co.*(Auditors)*
400 Renaissance Center
Detroit, MI 48243
Tel.: 313-259-8100

Blue Cross & Blue Shield Association*(Group Insurer)*
233 N. Michigan Ave.
Chicago, IL 60601

Butzel, Keidan, Simon, Myers & Graham*(Legal Firm)*
2490 First National Bldg.
Detroit, MI 48226
Tel.: 313-961-7900

Manufacturers National Bank N.A.*(Major Banking Relationship)*
38th Fl., 100 Renaissance Center
Detroit, MI 48243
Tel.: 313-222-4227

Connecticut General Life Insurance Co.*(Pension Manager)*
P.O. Box 2975,
Hartford, CT 06104
Tel.: 203-726-6000

KASPAR WIRE WORKS, INC.
Hwy. 95 N.
Shiner, TX 77984
Mailing Address:
P.O. Box 667,
Shiner, TX 77984
Tel.: 512-594-3327

Kaspar Wire Works, Inc.—(Continued)

Fax: 512-594-3311
Approx.Sls.: $22,000,000
Emp.: 430
Coin-Operated Newspaper Racks & Wire Fabricated Products
S.I.C.: 3581; 3496
Don G. Kaspar *(Chm. Bd. & Pres.)*
Norman Kaiser *(Controller)*
Brian Helweg *(Mgr.-Wire Prod. Sls.)*
David C. Kaspar *(Mgr.-Rack & Wire Prod. Sls.)*
Dan A. Price *(Dir.-Personnel)*
Leroy Kloese *(Pur. Agent)*
Dan A. Kaspar *(Prod. Mgr.)*

Outside Service Firm(s):

Ernst & Young*(Auditors)*
1900 Frost Bank Tower, 100 W. Houston St.
San Antonio, TX 78205
Tel.: 210-228-9696
Fax: 210-554-0253

First National Bank of Shiner*(Major Banking Relationship)*
Shiner, TX

KASPER MACHINE COMPANY
29275 Stephenson Hwy.
Madison Heights, MI 48071
Mailing Address:
P.O. Box 228
Madison Heights, MI 48071
Tel.: 313-547-3150 **MI**
Fax: 313-547-1293
Year Founded: 1942
Approx.Sls.: $18,000,000
Emp.: 110
Export
Precision Boring & Turning Machines, C.N.C.-Hyd.-Mech., Horizontal & Vertical Single & Multi Spindle
S.I.C.: 3541; 3545
Arthur J. LeMire *(Pres.)*
Jack P. Accardo *(V.P. & Chief Fin. Officer, Treas. & Sec.)*
Robert P. Jones *(Gen. Mgr.)*
Douglas R. Myers *(Chief Engineer)*
Norman Lewis *(Mgr.-Sls.)*
Tom E. Ditto *(Pur. Agent)*

Outside Service Firm(s):

Zabel, Quall & Ryan*(Legal Firm)*
Birmingham, MI

National Bank of Detroit*(Major Banking Relationship)*
P.O. Box 222,
Detroit, MI 48232
Tel.: 313-225-3423
Fax: 313-225-3420

Subsidiary:

Knurlet Tool Co. **(1)**
24807 Romano
Warren, MI 48091
Tel.: 313-756-6360
Emp.: 30
Mfg. of Precision Tooling Details & Prototype
S.I.C.: 3541
Gordon Ziemianski *(Mgr.)*
William Crisp *(Sls. Mgr.)*

KASSEL & ZOLL PROVISIONS, INC.
1455 Willow St.
Chicago, IL 60622
Tel.: 312-252-3900 **IL**
Fax: 312-252-4062
Approx.Sls.: $40,000,000
Emp.: 120
Fresh Meats; Poultry Products
S.I.C.: 5147; 5144
Lawrence Zoll *(Pres.)*
Richard Zielinski *(V.P.)*
Steven Zoll *(Sec.)*

Outside Service Firm(s):

Ralph Bell*(Auditors)*
Northbrook, IL

Popower & Company*(Legal Firm)*
Chicago, IL

American National Bank & Trust Company of Chicago*(Major Banking Relationship)*
33 N. LaSalle St.
Chicago, IL 60602
Tel.: 312-661-5000
Fax: 312-661-6417

KATSIN/LOEB ADVERTISING
1050 Battery St., 1st Fl.
San Francisco, CA 94111
Tel.: 415-399-9960
Year Founded: 1989
Approx.Billings: $21,194,000
Emp.: 24
Gen. Packaged Goods, Telecommunications, Healthcare, Hotel, Travel, Leisure, Utilities & Broadcast
Jef Loeb *(Chm. Bd.)*
Daniel H. Katsin *(Pres. & New Bus. Contact)*
Donna Fabianac *(Chief Fin. Officer)*

KASTLE SYSTEMS, INC.
1501 Wilson Blvd.
Arlington, VA 22209
Tel.: 703-528-8800
Tel.: 800-448-3722 **DE**
Fax: 703-528-2103
Year Founded: 1971
Assets: $6,008,000
Liabilities: $2,148,000
Net Worth: $3,860,000
Approx.Sls.: $15,000,000
Emp.: 225
Fiscal Year-end: 12/31/91
Export
Central Station Security; Access Control Systems; Software for Process Control
S.I.C.: 7382
A. Gene Samburg *(Chm. Bd., Pres. & Chief Exec. Officer)*
William V. Dietrich *(Exec. V.P.)*
Alfred Lee Wilder *(Exec. V.P.)*
Mickela D. Gay *(V.P.-Opers. & Sec.)*
T. Michael Shortal *(V.P.-Mktg.)*
Herman J. Sines *(V.P.-Installation & Service)*
Lewis Cohen *(Treas. & Controller)*
Charles Gray *(Dir.-Pur.)*

No. of U.S. Offices: 6
No. of Foreign Offices: 1

Computer Systems/Hardware:
Digital Equipment; IBM / PC's

Outside Service Firm(s):

Grant Thornton*(Auditors)*
Washington, DC 20090

Patterson/Smith Associates*(Commercial Insurance Carrier)*
Falls Church, VA

New York Life*(Group Insurer)*
New York, NY

Zuckerman, Spaeder, Goldstein, Taylor & Kolker*(Legal Firm)*
Washington, DC

Signet Bank*(Major Banking Relationship)*
McLean, VA

Signet Bank*(Pension Manager)*
McLean, VA

KATZ COMMUNICATIONS, INC.
One Dag Hammarskjold Plaza
New York, NY 10017
Tel.: 212-572-5500 **DE**
Fax: 212-751-1910
Year Founded: 1888
Approx.Sls.: $1,600,000,000
Emp.: 1,500
Fiscal Year-end: 12/31/90
National Advertising Representatives For Television & Radio
S.I.C.: 7313
James L. Greenwald *(Chm. Bd.)*
Peter Goulazian *(Pres. & Chief Exec. Officer)*
Paul Belitz *(Pres.-Media Data Div.)*
Ken Swetz *(Pres.-Katz Radio Grp.)*
Harvey Fenster *(Sr. V.P. & Chief Fin. Officer)*
Arnold Sheiffer *(Sr. V.P. & Chief Oper. Officer)*
Lucille Luongo *(Sr. V.P.-Corp. Communications)*
Maria-Luis Busi *(V.P. & Controller)*
Carol Rosen *(V.P.-Pur., Facilities Plng. & Office Services)*
Nancy Williams *(V.P.-Personnel)*
Marie Lequillow *(Mgr.-Employee Benefits)*
Brian Watson *(Mgr.-Corp. Benefits)*
Andy Weinberg *(Mgr.-Client Acctg.)*

Outside Service Firm(s):

Arthur Andersen & Co.*(Auditors)*
1345 Ave. of the Americas
New York, NY 10105
Tel.: 212-708-4000

Alexander & Alexander*(Commercial Insurance Carrier)*
1 Huntington Quad
Melville, NY

Battle, Fowler, Jaffin & Kheel*(Legal Firm)*
280 Park Ave.
New York, NY 10017
Tel.: 212-949-8300

Chase Manhattan Bank, N.A.*(Major Banking Relationship)*
One Chase Manhattan Plaza
New York, NY 10081
Tel.: 212-552-2222
Tel.: 800-526-0801
Fax: 212-552-7175

National Westminster Bank plc*(Major Banking Relationship)*
175 Water St.
New York, NY 10038-4924
Tel.: 212-602-3364

Television Group:

Subsidiaries:

Katz American Television **(1)**
One Dag Hammarskjold Plaza
New York, NY 10017
Tel.: 212-572-5500 (100%)
Fax: 212-572-8021
Television & National Representative Firm
S.I.C.: 7313
Jim Joyella *(Pres.)*

Katz Continental Television **(1)**
One Dag Hammarskjold Plaza
New York, NY 10017
Tel.: 212-572-5500 (100%)
Fax: 212-572-8022
Television Advertising Representative
S.I.C.: 7313
Jack Higgins *(Pres.)*

Katz Independent Television **(1)**
One Dag Hammarskjold Plaza
New York, NY 10017
Tel.: 212-572-5500 (100%)
Fax: 212-572-9786
Television Advertising Representative
S.I.C.: 7313
Marty Ozer *(Pres.)*

Radio Group:

Subsidiaries:

Banner Radio **(1)**
One Dag Hammarskjold Plaza
New York, NY 10017
Tel.: 212-572-5500 (100%)
Fax: 212-572-8020
Radio Advertising Representative
S.I.C.: 7313
Charlie Colombo *(Pres.)*

Christal Radio **(1)**
One Dag Hammarskjold Plaza
New York, NY 10017
Tel.: 212-688-4414 (100%)
Fax: 212-572-8177
Radio Advertising Representative
S.I.C.: 7313
Bill Fortenbaugh *(Pres.)*

Eastman Radio, Inc. **(1)**
1 Dag Hammarskjold Plaza
New York, NY 10017
Tel.: 212-572-5500
Tel.: 212-572-9206 (100%)
Fax: 212-572-9217
Radio Advertising Sales Representative
S.I.C.: 7313
Carl Butrum *(Pres.)*

Katz Hispanic Radio Sales **(1)**
One Dag Hammarskjold Plaza
New York, NY 10017
Tel.: 212-572-5500 (100%)
Fax: 212-572-9831
Radio Advertising Representative
S.I.C.: 7313

Katz Radio **(1)**
One Dag Hammarskjold Plaza
New York, NY 10017
Tel.: 212-572-5500 (100%)
Fax: 212-572-9831
Radio Advertising Representative
S.I.C.: 7313
Robert McCurdy *(Pres.)*

KATZ, INC.
214 6th St.
Honesdale, PA 18431
Tel.: 717-253-2544
Fax: 717-253-2590
Approx.Sls.: $26,000,000
Emp.: 600
Women's & Children's Undergarments
S.I.C.: 2341
Robert W. Katz, Jr. *(Pres.)*
James E. Katz *(Exec. V.P.)*
Mariam Katz *(Sr. V.P.)*

Outside Service Firm(s):

Parente, Randolph, Orlando, Carey & Associates*(Auditors)*
46 Public Square
Wilkes-Barre, PA 18701-2681
Tel.: 717-820-0100
Fax: 717-824-9865

Rosenn, Jenkins & Greenwald*(Legal Firm)*
Scranton, PA

First Eastern Bank N.A.*(Major Banking Relationship)*
Scranton, PA

KAUFFMAN PRODUCTS, INC.
1092 Third Ave., S.W.
Carmel, IN 46032
Tel.: 317-844-3337
Fax: 317-848-3696
Approx.Sls.: $12,000,000
Emp.: 105
Mfr. of Automotive Stampings; Appliance Parts; Enameled Porcelain
S.I.C.: 3465; 3469
Reese Kauffman *(Pres.)*
Robert D. Tansey *(Sr. V.P.-Admin.)*
Robert Davis *(V.P.-Mfg.)*
James Douglas *(V.P.-Sls.)*
Mitch Morgan *(V.P.-Opers.)*
Joe Bartemus *(Gen. Mgr.)*

Outside Service Firm(s):

Roy J. Pile & Co.*(Auditors)*
Indianapolis, IN

INB National Bank*(Major Banking Relationship)*
One Indiana Sq.
Indianapolis, IN 46266
Tel.: 317-266-6000

KAUFFMAN STEWART ADVERTISING

KAUFFMAN STEWART ADVERTISING
890 Butler Square West, 100
North 6th St.
Minneapolis, MN 55403
Tel.: 612-339-7614
Year Founded: 1984
Approx.Billings: $15,000,000
Emp.: 28
Consumer & Business to Business Adv.
Jeff Wright *(Pres.)*

KAUKAUNA CHEESE
Hwy. 00, Little Chute Indus. Park
Little Chute, WI 54140
Mailing Address:
P.O. Box 1974,
Kaukauna, WI 54130
Tel.: 414-788-3524
Fax: 414-788-9725
Approx.Sls.: $60,000,000
Emp.: 200
Fiscal Year-end: 11/28/90
Kaukauna Cheese
S.I.C.: 2022
Robert Gilbert *(Pres.)*
Hans C. Wurster *(Exec. V.P.-Mktg. & Sls.)*
A. Patz *(V.P.-Fin.)*
D. Peterson *(V.P.-Sls.)*
JoAnn Lauterborn *(Mgr.-Special Sls. Accts.)*

Computer Systems/Hardware:
NCR

Outside Service Firm(s):

Arthur Andersen & Co.*(Auditors)*
777 E. Wisconsin Ave., P.O. Box 1215
Milwaukee, WI 53202
Tel.: 414-271-5100
Fax: 414-283-3200

KAYE INSTRUMENTS, INC.
15 De Angelo Dr.
Bedford, MA 01730
Tel.: 617-275-0300 **MA**
Fax: 617-275-9024
Year Founded: 1959
Assets: $5,942,325
Liabilities: $4,196,377
Net Worth: $1,745,948
Approx.Sls.: $13,119,255
Emp.: 105
Fiscal Year-end: 12/29/91
Export
Mfr. & Sales of Data Acquisition & Process Monitoring Systems
S.I.C.: 3823; 7379
Thomas R. Liebermann *(Chm Bd., Pres, & Chief Oper. Officer)*
Dr. Robert E. Goldschmidt *(V.P.-Engrng.)*
Kenneth B. Hurley *(V.P.-Mktg. & Sls.)*
Joseph J. DePino *(V.P.-Opers.)*
Steven Dasaro *(V.P.-Fin. & Admin.)*
Goran Bringert *(Dir.-Intl. Sls.)*
Kenneth Appel *(Dir.-Mktg.)*
Donna M. Boston *(Mgr.-Pur.)*
Carolyn K. Madsen *(Mgr.-Human Resources)*
Fred Reed *(Mgr.-Mngmt. Information Systems)*
Janet West *(Mgr.-Quality Assurance)*
Stephen Donaghey *(Mgr.-Materials)*

No. of Mfg. Plants/Facilities: 1
No. of U.S. Offices: 1
No. of Foreign Offices: 1

Computer Systems/Hardware:
IBM System 38

Outside Service Firm(s):

Coopers & Lybrand*(Auditors)*
1 Post Office Square
Boston, MA 02110
Tel.: 617-574-5000
Fax: 617-345-0398

Corroon & Black*(Commercial Insurance Carrier)*
Rochester, NH

Sullivan & Worcester*(Legal Firm)*
One Post Office Square
Boston, MA 02109
Tel.: 617-338-2800

U.S. Trust Co.*(Major Banking Relationship)*
40 Court St.
Boston, MA 02108
Tel.: 617-726-7371
Fax: 617-726-7380

KAYEM FOODS, INC.
75 Arlington St.
Chelsea, MA 02150
Mailing Address:
P.O. Box 490 A
Chelsea, MA 02150
Tel.: 617-889-1605
Fax: 617-889-5931
Year Founded: 1909
Approx.Sls.: $80,000,000
Emp.: 260
Sausage Processor
S.I.C.: 2013
Frank V. Monkiewicz *(Chm. Bd.)*
Ray C. Monkiewicz *(Pres.)*
William Colcord *(Treas.)*
Edward Blonchette *(V.P.-Opers.)*
Stephen Mosher *(V.P.-Fin.)*
Joel Palmer *(Mgr.-Adv.)*
Carl Colson *(Pur. Agent)*
Principal(s):
Ray C. Monkiewicz

No. of Mfg. Plants/Facilities: 1
No. of U.S. Offices: 4

Computer Systems/Hardware:
Honeywell

Outside Service Firm(s):

Morgan & Morgan*(Auditors)*
Boston, MA

Adams & Blinn*(Legal Firm)*
Chelsea, MA

Shawmut Bank*(Major Banking Relationship)*
One Federal St.
Boston, MA 02211
Tel.: 617-292-2969
Fax: 617-292-4417

KAZ, INC.
10 Columbus Circle, Ste. 1620
New York, NY 10019
Tel.: 212-586-1630
Tel.: 800-241-1131 **NY**
Fax: 212-265-9248
Year Founded: 1956
Approx.Sls.: $20,000,000
Emp.: 200
Fiscal Year-end: 4/30/91
Import Export
Mfr. of Electric Vaporizers, Electric Heating Pads, Private-label Heating Products, Electric Humidifiers, Home Steam Bath & Sauna, Heating Caps
S.I.C.: 3634; 2834; 3842
Lawrence Katzman *(Chm. Bd. & Chief Exec. Officer)*
Richard Katzman *(Pres.)*
Martin A. Cohen *(Dir.-Mktg.)*
Harry Ehrlich *(Dir.-Engrng.)*
Leonard Lang *(Dir.-Personnel & Controller)*
Tom Cappadona *(Mgr.-Mfg.)*
Ira Kantrowitz *(Mgr.-Adv.)*

Outside Service Firm(s):

Weiner & Co.*(Auditors)*
New York, NY

Norstar Bank, N.A.*(Major Banking Relationship)*
New York, NY

P.J. KEATING COMPANY
Reservoir Rd.
Lunenburg, MA 01462
Mailing Address:
P.O. Box 367,
Fitchburg, MA 01420
Tel.: 508-582-9931
Fax: 508-582-7130
Approx.Sls.: $40,000,000
Emp.: 100
Manufacturer Ready Mixed Concrete & Asphalt Mixtures; Wholesale Sand, Gravel, Trap Rock & Crushed Stone; Highway & Street Paving Construction
S.I.C.: 1611; 2951; 3273; 5039
P. Warren Keating *(Chm. Bd.)*
Robert P. Keating *(Pres.)*
John J. Keating *(V.P.-Sls., Mktg. & Fin.)*
John A. Delrossi *(Controller)*
Paul J. Keating, II *(Dir.-Sls. & Mktg. & Treas.)*

Outside Service Firm(s):

William S. Reagan & Company*(Auditors)*
Fitchburg, MA

Mintz, Levin, Cohn, Ferris, Glovsky & Popeo, P.C.*(Legal Firm)*
One Financial Center
Boston, MA 02111
Tel.: 617-542-2241

State Bank*(Major Banking Relationship)*
Albany, NY

Subsidiaries:

Keating Materials Corporation **(1)**
2140 Bridge St.
Dracut, MA 01826
Tel.: 508-454-7878
Approx.Sls.: $7,000,000
Emp.: 20
Mfr. Bituminous Concrete & Crushed Stone
S.I.C.: 2951
Paul J. Keating *(Chief Exec. Officer)*

Worlite Corporation **(1)**
628 Saratoga St.
Cohoes, NY 12047
Tel.: 518-235-0401
Emp.: 40
Mfr. Lightweight Aggregate
S.I.C.: 3255
Paul J. Keating *(Pres.)*

DANIEL J. KEATING CO.
812 Lancaster Ave.
Villanova, PA 19085
Tel.: 215-527-4100 **PA**
Fax: 215-527-0894
Approx.Sls.: $100,000,000
Emp.: 65
Construction Manager, General Building Contractor & Developer
S.I.C.: 1541; 1542; 8741
Daniel J. Keating, Jr. *(Chm. Bd., Pres. & Chief Exec. Officer)*
Daniel J. Keating, III *(Chief Oper. Officer)*
Joseph J. Maloney *(Treas. & Sec.)*
Principal(s):
Daniel J. Keating, Jr.
Daniel J. Keating, III

Computer Systems/Hardware:
IBM PC

Outside Service Firm(s):

Shoriak & Kiely*(Auditors)*
Wynnewood, PA

Blue Cross of Greater Philadelphia*(Group Insurer)*
Philadelphia, PA

Jacoby, Donner & Jacoby*(Legal Firm)*
Wayne, PA

CoreStates First Pennsylvania Bank, N.A.*(Major Banking Relationship)*
Philadelphia, PA

Division:

Daniel J. Keating Construction Co. **(1)**
812 Lancaster Ave.
Villanova, PA 19085
Tel.: 215-527-4100
Fax: 215-527-0894
Construction Company
S.I.C.: 1541; 1542
Daniel J. Keating III *(Pres.)*

KECO INDUSTRY, INC.
7375 Industrial Rd.
Florence, KY 41042
Tel.: 606-525-2102 **OH**
Fax: 606-525-6667
Year Founded: 1942
Approx.Sls.: $21,000,000
Emp.: 300
Export
Mfr. of Air Conditioning & Heating Equipment
S.I.C.: 3585
George W. Andrews *(Chm. Bd. & Pres.)*

Outside Service Firm(s):

Fifth Third Bank*(Major Banking Relationship)*
Florence, KY

Division:

Keco Aerospace Ground Equipment Div. **(1)**
7375 Industrial Rd.
Florence, KY 41042
Tel.: 606-525-2102
Mfr. of Show, Display & Refrigerated Cabinets; Aircraft Parts & Equipment
S.I.C.: 3585

KEEN COMPRESSED GAS CO., INC.
101 Rogers Rd.
Wilmington, DE 19801
Mailing Address:
P.O. Box 407,
Wilmington, DE 19899
Tel.: 302-594-4557 **DE**
Fax: 302-594-4560
Year Founded: 1919
Approx.Sls.: $13,000,000
Emp.: 100
Wholesale Distributor of Compressed & Liquified Gases; Welding Supplies; Bottle Propane Gas
S.I.C.: 5169; 5085; 5984
J. Merrill Keen *(Pres.)*
David Haas *(Treas.)*
Ruth Lloyd *(Sec.)*

Outside Service Firm(s):

Donsek S. Emenheiser*(Auditors)*
Wilmington, DE

Delaware Trust*(Major Banking Relationship)*
Wilmington, DE

Divisions:

Keen Propane Division **(1)**
4061 New Castle Ave.
New Castle, DE 19720-1492
Tel.: 302-594-4565
S.I.C.: 1321

Keen Compressed Gas Co., Inc.—(Continued)

Keen Welding Division **(1)**
4063 New Castle Ave.
New Castle, DE 19720-1492
Tel.: 302-594-4547
S.I.C.: 5084

KEENELAND ASSOC., INC.
4201 Versailles Rd.
Lexington, KY 40510
Mailing Address:
P.O. Box 1690,
Lexington, KY 40592
Tel.: 606-254-3412
Tel.: 800-456-3412
Fax: 606-288-4348
Year Founded: 1936
Approx.Sls.: $300,000,000
Emp.: 115
Fiscal Year-end: 6/30/91
Export
Racing & Selling of Thoroughbred Horses
S.I.C.: 7948
James E. Bassett III *(Chm. Bd.)*
William C. Greely *(Pres. & Chief Exec. Officer)*
R. James Williams *(Dir.-Publicity)*

KEENERS, INC.
2900 4th Ave., S.
Seattle, WA 98124
Tel.: 206-628-4811
Fax: 206-628-4836
Year Founded: 1942
Approx.Sls.: $45,000,000
Emp.: 110
Wholesale Meat, Poultry & Frozen Foods; K & N Meats
S.I.C.: 5147; 5144; 5142; 5146; 5141
Wayne Keener *(Chief Exec. Officer)*
Eugene Orrico *(Pres.)*
Principal(s):
Wayne Keener
Eugene Orrico

Outside Service Firm(s):

Dodd, Wing & Company*(Auditors)*
Kirkland, WA

Hatch & Leslie*(Legal Firm)*
Seattle, WA

First Interstate Bank of Washington, N.A.*(Major Banking Relationship)*
P.O. Box 21927, 999 Third Ave.
Seattle, WA 98111
Tel.: 206-292-3522
Tel.: 800-522-6645

KEENEY MANUFACTURING CO.
1170 Main St.
Newington, CT 06111
Tel.: 203-666-3342
Fax: 203-665-0374
Year Founded: 1923
Approx.Sls.: $23,000,000
Emp.: 300
Fiscal Year-end: 12/31/91
Import Export
Mfr. of Plumbers' Brass Goods, Floor & Ceiling Steel Plates Valves, Injection-Molded Plastic Plumbing Goods
S.I.C.: 3432; 3089; 3312; 3494
Stuart Holden, Jr. *(Pres.)*
Kenneth L. Collett *(Controller)*
Carole Lipka *(Dir.-Mktg.)*
David Laflame *(Mgr.-Pur.)*

Outside Service Firm(s):

Arthur Andersen & Co.*(Auditors)*
One Financial Plaza
Hartford, CT 06103
Tel.: 203-280-0649
Fax: 203-280-0898

KEHNE ELECTRIC COMPANY, INC.
670 Vandelia St.
Saint Paul, MN 55114
Tel.: 612-645-5781
Fax: 612-649-3516
Approx.Sls.: $10,000,000
Emp.: 60
Electrical & Mechanical Contracting
S.I.C.: 1731; 1711
Richard M. Kehne *(Chm. Bd. & Pres.)*
Charles Ford *(Exec. V.P.)*
Roma V. Kehne *(Sec.)*
Principal(s):
Richard M. Kehne

Computer Systems/Hardware:
IBM

Outside Service Firm(s):

Ernst & Young*(Auditors)*
1400 Pillsbury Center
Minneapolis, MN 55402
Tel.: 612-343-1000

Felhaber, Larson, Fenlon & Vogt*(Legal Firm)*
222 S. Ninth St., Ste. 1935
Minneapolis, MN 55402
Tel.: 612-339-6321
Fax: 612-339-4714

First Bank Security*(Major Banking Relationship)*
St. Paul, MN

KEILER & COMPANY
304 Main St.
Farmington, CT 06032-2957
Tel.: 203-677-8821
Fax: 203-676-8164
Year Founded: 1973
Approx.Billings: $56,000,000
Emp.: 75
Advertising (Print & Broadcast; Business-to-Business and Consumer), Design (Collateral, Direct Marketing, Packaging, Sales Promotion), Public Relations Consulting
Richard W. Keiler *(Pres.)*
Ken Donoghue *(Dir.-Pub. Rels.)*
Bill Smith *(Dir.-Consulting Services)*
Doug Webster *(Dir.-Communications)*

Computer Systems/Hardware:
IBM AS400, Ethernet Network

KEIPER RECARO, INC.
905 W. Maple Rd.
Clawson, MI 48017
Tel.: 313-288-6800
Tel.: 800-873-2276
Fax: 313-288-0811
Year Founded: 1977
Approx.Sls.: $20,000,000
Emp.: 157
Fiscal Year-end: 12/31/90
Export
Mfr. Automotive Components & Seats
S.I.C.: 3714; 2531
D. Simon *(Chm. Bd.)*
Hans Milobinski *(Pres.)*
Joe Peters *(Controller)*
Becky McDonald *(Dir.-Sls.)*
Brad Allen *(Mgr.-Mktg.)*

BEN E. KEITH COMPANY
600 E. 9th & Pecan Sts.
Fort Worth, TX 76102
Mailing Address:
P.O. Box 2628
Fort Worth, TX 76113
Tel.: 817-332-9171 **TX**
Fax: 817-338-1701
Year Founded: 1906
Assets: $80,000,000
Liabilities: $27,000,000
Net Worth: $53,000,000
Approx.Sls.: $350,000,000
Emp.: 1,350
Fiscal Year-end: 6/30/90
Wholesale Frozen Foods, Fresh Fruits & Vegetables, Beer & Ale
S.I.C.: 5148; 5142; 5181
Robert Hallam *(Chm. Bd. & Chief Exec. Officer)*
Howard Hallam *(Pres. & Chief Oper. Officer)*
Mel Cockrell *(Chief Fin. Officer, Treas., Controller & Sec.)*
Robert Scoggins *(Mgr.-Employee Benefits)*
Tom Watson *(Mgr.-Data Processing)*

Computer Systems/Hardware:
IBM 4181

Outside Service Firm(s):

Ernst & Young*(Auditors)*
500 Throckmorton St.
Fort Worth, TX 76102
Tel.: 817-335-1900
Fax: 817-335-2728

Massachusetts Mutual Life Insurance Co.*(Group Insurer)*
Boston, MA

Team Bank*(Investment Banker)*
P.O. Box 2604,
Fort Worth, TX 76113
Tel.: 817-884-4614

Team Bank*(Major Banking Relationship)*
P.O. Box 2604,
Fort Worth, TX 76113
Tel.: 817-884-4614

Team Bank*(Pension Manager)*
P.O. Box 2604,
Fort Worth, TX 76113
Tel.: 817-884-4614

Subsidiaries:

CMD-Keith Co. **(1)**
P.O. Box 2628
Fort Worth, TX 76113
Tel.: 817-332-9171 (100%)
S.I.C.: 5142; 5148; 5181

Ben E. Keith Co. of Oklahoma **(1)**
P.O. Box 2628
Fort Worth, TX 76102
Tel.: 817-332-9171 (100%)
S.I.C.: 5142; 5148; 5181

Pan Handle Fruit Co. **(1)**
P.O. Box 2628
Fort Worth, TX 76113
Tel.: 817-332-9171 (100%)

GEO. E. KEITH COMPANY
31 Perkins St.
Bridgewater, MA 02324
Tel.: 508-697-6104
Tel.: 800-227-1298
Fax: 508-697-7998
Year Founded: 1758
Approx.Sls.: $15,000,000
Emp.: 250
Fiscal Year-end: 1/31/91
Export
Walk-Over, John E. Lucey, Keith Highlander Shoes for Men; Klev-Bro, Walk-Over Shoes for Women
S.I.C.: 5139
John Thorbeck *(Chief Exec. Officer & Pres.)*
Jeff Webber *(V.P. & Chief Fin. Officer)*
David Harrington *(Dir.-Opers.)*
Gary Schanil *(Dir.-Sls.)*
Jennifer Berry *(Mktg. Coordinator)*
Donald Peterson *(Factory Superintendent)*

Computer Systems/Hardware:
MAI

Division:

Walk-Over Shoes **(1)**
31 Perkins St.
Bridgewater, MA 02324
Tel.: 508-697-6104
S.I.C.: 5139

J. J. KELLER & ASSOCIATES, INC.
3003 W. Breezewood Lane
Neenah, WI 54957-0368
Mailing Address:
P.O. Box 368,
Neenah, WI 54957-0368
Tel.: 414-722-2848
Tel.: 800-558-5011
Fax: 414-727-7526
Year Founded: 1953
Approx.Sls.: $65,000,000
Emp.: 600
Fiscal Year-end: 4/30/91
Export
Technical Publishers & Regulatory Services Serving Transportation, Distribution & Chemical Process Industries
S.I.C.: 2741
John J. Keller *(Chm. Bd.)*
Robert L. Keller *(Pres. & Chief Exec. Officer)*
James J. Keller *(Chief Oper. Officer & Exec. V.P.)*
Ronald M. Phillips *(V.P.-Fin., Treas. & Sec.)*
Mark Tremble *(Dir.-Sls.)*
Tom Wildermuth *(Sr. Mgr.-Adv. & Promo.)*
David R. Ellis *(Mgr.-Bus. Devel.)*
Robert Fox *(Mgr.- Res. & Devel.)*
Michael P. Kenney *(Sr. Supvr.-Mktg. Communications)*

KELLER CONSTRUCTION COMPANY LTD.
9950 E. Baldwin Pl.
El Monte, CA 91731
Tel.: 818-443-6633 **CA**
Fax: 818-448-3101
Year Founded: 1966
Assets: $8,000,000
Net Worth: $8,000,000
Approx.Sls.: $57,000,000
Emp.: 41
General Contractor; New Construction of Office & Industrial Buildings
S.I.C.: 1542; 1541
Paul Keller *(Pres.)*
Thomas Keeton *(Chief Oper. Officer)*
Steve Perzyna *(Controller)*
Stephen Converse *(Dir.-Mktg.)*
Robert Stoge *(Dir.-Pur.)*

Principal(s):
Paul Keller
Thomas Keeton
Stephen Converse
Robert Stoge

Outside Service Firm(s):

Wells Fargo Bank*(Major Banking Relationship)*
9000 Flair
El Monte, CA

KELLER CRESCENT CO.
1100 E. Louisiana St.
Evansville, IN 47711
Mailing Address:
P.O. Box 3,
Evansville, IN 47701
Tel.: 812-464-2461
Tel.: 800-457-3837 **IN**
Fax: 812-426-7601
Year Founded: 1885
Approx.Billings: $121,411,000
Emp.: 550
Fiscal Year-end: 12/31/91
Advertising Agency
S.I.C.: 7311
Corporate Giving Program: Contact Company Directly for Details
Thomas M. Smythe *(Chm Bd. & Pres.)*
Robert E. Hampel *(Sr. Exec. Chief Fin. Officer, Treas. & Sec.)*
F.A. Samuelson *(Exec. V.P.-Creative Services)*
Dellas Graham *(Exec. V.P.-Production & Opers. Services)*
Fred Kitch *(Exec. V.P.)*
Richard Wittgen *(V.P.-Mngmt. Supvr.)*
Don Minton *(V.P.-Mngmt. Supvr.)*
Hank Zunk *(V.P.-Mngmt. Supvr.)*
Miles Jackson *(V.P.-Mngmt. Supvr.)*
Mike Mayers *(V.P.-Mngmt. Supvr.)*
Frank Ferrara *(V.P.-Mngmt. Supvr.)*
Ronald Edwards *(V.P.-Mngmt. Supvr.)*
Bob Ubelhor *(V.P.-Graphics & A/V Services)*
Jim Weitzel *(V.P.-Media, Research & Plng.)*
Howard Mitchell *(V.P.-Public Rels.)*
Pam Bailey *(V.P.-Media Dir.)*
Allen Mounts *(V.P.-Human Resources)*
Joe Gelarden *(Purchasing Supvr.)*
Principal(s):
Thomas M. Smythe
Robert E. Hampel
F.A. Samuelson
Fred Kitch
Mark A. Gustafson

No. of Mfg. Plants/Facilities: 3
No. of U.S. Offices: 3

Computer Systems/Hardware:
IBM, MacIntosh

Outside Service Firm(s):

Ernst & Young*(Auditors)*
One Indiana Square, Ste. 3400
Indianapolis, IN 46204
Tel.: 317-236-1100

Kahn, Dees, Donovan & Kahn*(Legal Firm)*
Fort Branch, IN

Branches:

Keller-Crescent Co. **(1)**
1100 E. Louisiana St., P.O. Box 3
Evansville, IN 47701
Tel.: 812-464-2461
Approx.Billings: $96,061,000
Emp.: 550
Thomas Smythe *(Pres.)*
Robert Hampel *(Sr. Exec. V.P., Fin.)*
Fred Kitch *(Exec. V.P.)*
Jim Weitzel *(V.P., Media, Market Research & Pub. Rels)*
Allen Mounts *(V.P., Human Resources)*
Howard Mitchell *(V.P., Pub. Rels.)*
Jerry Kunze *(V.P., Sls. Promo.)*
Sharon Wood *(Yellow Pages Supvr.)*
Joe Gelarden *(Pur. Supvr.)*

Keller Crescent Co. **(1)**
102 Decker Court, Suite 100
Irving, Las Colinas, TX 75062
Tel.: 214-541-0700
Approx.Billings: $25,350,000
Emp.: 30
Computer Systems/Hardware:
IBM 36, MacIntosh, Personal Computers
Business/Consumer Services, Entertainment, Pharmaceuticals/Health Care, Telecommunications, Travel/Hotels/Airlines, Apparel
Thomas M. O'Connor *(Mng. Dir.)*
Cindy DeMent *(Controller)*
Jerriann Crawford *(Dir.-Pub. Rels.)*
Sue Harper *(Mgr.-Office)*

THE KELLER MANUFACTURING CO., INC.
Cedar & Water St.
Corydon, IN 47112
Mailing Address:
P.O. Box 8,
Corydon, IN 47112
Tel.: 812-738-2222
Fax: 812-738-7382
Year Founded: 1895
Approx.Sls.: $32,000,000
Emp.: 600
Fiscal Year-end: 12/31/91
Export
Solid Wood Bedroom & Dining Room Furniture
S.I.C.: 2511
William H. Keller *(Chm. Bd.)*
Robert Byrd *(Pres. & Chief Exec. Officer)*
John Hoback *(V.P.-Mfg.)*
Chris Kulwicki *(V.P.-Mktg.)*
Marvin Miller *(V.P.-Engrng. & Sec.)*
Steve Robertson *(V.P.-Mktg.)*
Danny Utz *(V.P.-Fin. & Treas.)*
Thelma Crosier *(Mgr.-Export)*
Dennis Leffler *(Mgr.-Personnel)*
Paul Kitterman *(Pur. Agent)*

Computer Systems/Hardware:
IBM

KELLER MOTOR CAR COMPANY, INC.
1111 Troy-Schenectady Rd.
Latham, NY 12110
Tel.: 518-785-4154
Fax: 518-785-4190
Emp.: 130
Retail Automobiles
S.I.C.: 5511
Alexander Keeler *(Pres. & Treas.)*
Geanne Austin *(V.P. & Sec.)*
Roy C. Sutton *(V.P.)*

Outside Service Firm(s):

Key Bank*(Major Banking Relationship)*
Albany, NY

KELLEY & WALLWORK INC.
The Milk Exchange, 177 Milk St.
Boston, MA 02109-3410
Tel.: 617-542-2100
Fax: 617-542-1700
Year Founded: 1982
Approx.Billings: $18,500,000
Emp.: 12
Consumer Brands, Banking/Financial Services, Recreation/Sports Marketing
Glenn Kelley *(Pres.)*
Joy Bergman *(V.P., Fin. & Admin.)*

KELLEY BEAN CO., INC.
Bean Blvd.
Morrill, NE 69358
Mailing Address:
P.O. Box 457,
Morrill, NE 69358
Tel.: 308-247-2101
Fax: 308-247-2213
Year Founded: 1970
Approx.Sls.: $70,000,000
Emp.: 200
Fiscal Year-end: 6/30/91
Export
Processor & Wholesaler of Agricultural Products; Dry Edible Beans
S.I.C.: 5153
Gary L. Kelley *(Chm. Bd., Pres. & Chief Exec. Officer)*
G. Lee Glenn *(Chief Fin. Officer, V.P. & Treas.)*
Robert L. Kelley *(Exec. V.P. & Sec.)*

Computer Systems/Hardware:
NCR 9300

Outside Service Firm(s):

Grant Thornton*(Auditors)*
Lincoln, NE

Keith Miller*(Legal Firm)*
Omaha, NE

First State Bank*(Major Banking Relationship)*
Scottsbluff, NE

Sharp, Ross, Browning*(Pension Manager)*
Omaha, NE

KELLIHER/SAMETS MARKETING COMMUNICATIONS
130-138 S. Willard St.
Burlington, VT 05401
Tel.: 802-862-8261
Year Founded: 1977
Approx.Billings: $10,000,000
Emp.: 24
Strategic Marketing, Direct Marketing, Advertising, Public Relations, Marketing Research
Linda Kelliher *(Pres. & Dir.-Creative)*
Tim Volk *(Sr. V.P. & Dir.-Mktg. Services)*
Maureen Cross *(Dir.-Fin.)*
Jeffrey Wakefield *(Dir.-Pub. Rels.)*
Sally Weary *(Dir.-Plng. & Mktg. Res.)*

KELLY MICHENER INC.
416-418 W. Marion St.
Lancaster, PA 17603
Mailing Address:
P.O. Box 959,
Lancaster, PA 17603
Tel.: 717-393-9776
Fax: 717-393-0443
Year Founded: 1950
Approx.Billings: $22,000,000
Emp.: 30
Robert L. Kelly *(Pres. & Chief Exec. Officer)*
Gregory D. Purcell *(Exec. V.P. & Dir.-Opers.)*
Warren W. Ashburn *(Sr. V.P. & Dir.-Mktg.)*
Maria G. Kelly *(Controller)*
Jan Griesemar *(Dir.-Pub. Rels.)*
Gale McComsey *(Dir.-Acctg.)*

Computer Systems/Hardware:
IBM System 36; IBM PC's; Apple Macintosh Quadra 900 & Mac II ci

KELLY-MOORE PAINT COMPANY, INC.
987 Commercial St.
San Carlos, CA 94070
Mailing Address:
P.O. Box 3016,
San Carlos, CA 94070
Tel.: 415-592-8337
Tel.: 800-874-4436 **CA**
Fax: 415-591-5084
Year Founded: 1946
Assets: $169,336,916
Liabilities: $22,165,214
Net Worth: $147,171,702
Approx.Sls.: $191,814,000
Emp.: 1,559
Fiscal Year-end: 12/31/90
Import Export
Paints & Paint Sundries
S.I.C.: 2851; 5198; 5231
Corporate Giving Program: Donates paint to organizations which house mentally retarded or homeless persons
William E. Moore *(Chm. Bd.)*
Joseph P. Cristiano *(Pres. & Chief Exec. Officer)*
John W. Bacigalupo *(Chief Exec. Officer)*
Dante Andaya *(Corp. Controller)*
Ted Andreatta *(V.P.-Property Admin.)*
Verian Carey *(V.P.-Sls.)*
Herbert R. Giffins *(V.P.-Paint Store Opers.)*
George C. Hunt *(V.P.-Tech.)*
Patrick T. McDonald *(V.P.-Internal Auditing & Loss Prevention)*
Douglas W. Merrill *(V.P.-Mfg. Opers.)*
Calvin Chun *(Coordinator-Regulatory & Production)*
Bill Berry *(Mgr.-Store Plng. & Mdsg.)*
John Brundage *(Mgr.-Information Systems)*
Jim Livermore *(Mgr.-Personnel Training & Devel.)*
Tim O'Reilly *(Mgr.-Sundry Pur.)*
Betsy Peterkin *(Mgr.-Corp. Personnel)*
Principal(s):
William E. Moore

No. of Mfg. Plants/Facilities: 2

Outside Service Firm(s):

Ernst & Young*(Auditors)*
55 Almaden Blvd.
San Jose, CA 95115
Tel.: 408-947-5476
Fax: 408-294-2744

Ropers, Majeski, Kohn, Bentley, Wagner & Kane*(Legal Firm)*
San Jose, CA

Sanwa Bank*(Major Banking Relationship)*
San Jose, CA

KELLY, SCOTT AND MADISON, INC.

KELLY, SCOTT AND MADISON, INC.
35 E. Wacker Dr., Ste. 1150
Chicago, IL 60601
Tel.: 312-977-0772
Fax: 312-977-0874
Year Founded: 1966
Approx.Billings: $33,200,000
Emp.: 33
Comprehensive Media Management Services
Leonard Cohen *(Pres. & Chief Exec. Officer)*
Herb Isaacs *(Exec. V.P.)*
Joann Trotta *(V.P., Admin. & Station Rels.)*
Joanne Evans *(V.P., Plng. & Client Services)*
Alan Schlossberg *(V.P., Media Devel.)*
Jerry Shneider *(Treas. & Controller)*
Donald Groski *(Asst. Controller)*
Cate Schmid *(Billing Supvr.)*

Computer Systems/Hardware:
Telmar Micronet II; ABS Spot 36

KELSEY CONSTRUCTION, INC.
306 E. Princeton St.
Orlando, FL 32804
Tel.: 407-898-4101 **FL**

Kelsey Construction, Inc.—(Continued)

Fax: 407-898-1444
Year Founded: 1934
Assets: $3,469,144
Liabilities: $1,637,258
Net Worth: $1,831,886
Approx.Sls.: $34,000,000
Emp.: 75
Fiscal Year-end: 7/31/90
Commercial & Industrial Construction Contractor
S.I.C.: 1542; 1541; 8741
Eugene W. Kelsey III *(Chm. Bd.)*
Robert E. Kelsey *(Pres.)*
Michael Kelsey *(V.P.)*
Mike Smith *(Sec. & Treas.)*
Suzanne Popaditch *(Dir.-Personnel)*

Computer Systems/Hardware:
IBM

Subsidiary:

Kelsey Development **(1)**
306 E. Princeton St.
Orlando, FL 32804
Tel.: 407-898-4101

KELSO-BURNETT COMPANY
5200 Newport Dr.
Rolling Meadows, IL 60008
Tel.: 708-259-9720
Fax: 708-259-0839
Approx.Sls.: $37,000,000
Emp.: 300
Electrical Contractor
S.I.C.: 1731; 3613
Terry Butz *(Pres.)*
J.R. Kostek *(V.P., Sec. & Treas.)*
J.J. Madden *(V.P.)*
Donald J. Plefka *(V.P.)*
Gary Niederkorn *(Gen. Mgr.)*

Outside Service Firm(s):

William Engelter*(Auditors)*
Chicago, IL

Gorham, Metge, Bowman & Hourigan*(Legal Firm)*
Chicago, IL

Lakeside Bank*(Major Banking Relationship)*
Chicago, IL

Branches:

Kelso-Burnett Chicago Branch **(1)**
223 W. Jackson Blvd.
Chicago, IL 60606
Tel.: 312-922-2610
Electrical Contractor
S.I.C.: 1731
James R. Chorley *(Mgr.)*

Kelso-Burnett Rockford Branch **(1)**
4611 Stenstrom Rd.
Rockford, IL 61109
Tel.: 815-874-6311
Electrical Contractor
S.I.C.: 1731
J. Nichols *(Mgr.)*

Kelso-Burnett Zion Branch **(1)**
3063 Sheridan
Zion, IL 60099
Tel.: 708-746-2300
Electrical Contractor
S.I.C.: 1731
Tom Hegel *(V.P. & Gen. Mgr.)*

KELSO OIL COMPANY
641 Atlantic Ave.
Knoxville, TN 37912
Tel.: 615-525-7125
Fax: 615-546-3531
Retail Service Stations; Oil & Gas Exploration
S.I.C.: 1382; 5541
Herman E. Gettlefinger *(Pres.)*

Outside Service Firm(s):

Pickering, Hensley, Pickering*(Auditors)*
Knoxville, TN

First Tennessee Bank, N.A.*(Major Banking Relationship)*
Knoxville, TN

Subsidiary:

Pride Oil Co., Inc. **(1)**
5414 Clinton Hwy.
Knoxville, TN 37912
Tel.: 615-687-4682
Retail Service Stations; Oil & Gas Exploration
S.I.C.: 1382; 5541
Andrew J. Gettlefinger *(Chm. Bd., Pres. & Chief Exec. Officer)*
Herman E. Gettlefinger *(Chief Fin. Officer, Treas. & Sec.)*
Hugh T. Stooksbury *(Controller)*

KEMMERER BOTTLING GROUP INC.
777 Joyce Rd.
Joliet, IL 60436
Tel.: 815-741-7777
Fax: 815-741-9083
Approx.Sls.: $220,000,000
Emp.: 1,100
Mfr. Carbonated Beverages
S.I.C.: 2086
Tim Healy *(Pres. & Chief Oper. Officer)*
Bill Schumacher *(Sr. V.P. & Chief Fin. Officer)*
Ron Stanley *(Sr. V.P.-Sls.)*
Brian Landers *(V.P.-Fin.)*
Nile Wendorf *(Sr. V.P.-Bus. Devel.)*
Bill Scott *(V.P.-Mktg.)*

Computer Systems/Hardware:
IBM System 38

Outside Service Firm(s):

Joseph Decosimo & Co.*(Auditors)*
Tallan Building, Ste. 1100, Two Union Square
Chattanooga, TN 37402
Tel.: 615-756-7100

Seyfarth, Shaw, Fairweather & Geraldson*(Legal Firm)*
55 E. Monroe
Chicago, IL 60606
Tel.: 312-346-8000

First Chicago Bank*(Major Banking Relationship)*
One First National Plaza
Chicago, IL 60670

KEN-MAC METAL, INC.
17901 Englewood Dr.
Cleveland, OH 44130
Tel.: 216-234-7500
Fax: 216-234-4459
Approx.Sls.: $100,000,000
Emp.: 85
Aluminum & Stainless Metals Service Center; Metal Processing & Distribution
S.I.C.: 3471; 5051
Edward S. Young *(Chm. Bd.)*
Robert D. McMahon *(Vice Chm.)*
Larry E. Parsons *(Pres.)*
Charles Emrick *(V.P. & Sec.)*
Edward Murray *(Treas.)*
Scott Seabeck *(Production Mgr.)*

KENDALE INDUSTRIES, INC.
7600 Hub Parkway
Valley View, OH 44215
Tel.: 216-524-5400
Fax: 216-524-6750
Year Founded: 1960
Approx.Sls.: $20,000,000
Emp.: 180
Export
Mfr. of Metal Stampings, Washers & Semi-Precision Ball Bearings
S.I.C.: 3469; 3562
Dale K. Honroth *(Pres. & Chief Exec. Officer)*
James Herbst *(Exec. V.P.)*
Jim Albertonni *(V.P.-Pur.)*
Larry McLaughlin *(V.P.-Sls.)*
John Naylor *(Sec.)*
Dennis Vail *(Comptroller)*
John Slusarick *(Dir.-Mktg.)*
Ron Koeppen *(Mgr.-Sls.)*

Computer Systems/Hardware:
McDonnell Douglas

KENDALL HEALTHCARE PRODUCTS CO.
15 Hampshire St.
Mansfield, MA 02048
Tel.: 508-261-8000 **DE**
Fax: 508-261-8145
Year Founded: 1903
Approx.Sls.: $687,500,000
Emp.: 8,700
Fiscal Year-end: 12/31/90
Mfr. of Surgical Dressings, Hospital Products, Kerlix Surgical Dressings, T.E.D. Surgical Stockings, Tensor Elastic Bandages, Webcol Pads, Polyken Pipeline Coating Systems, Medical & Industrial Tapes
S.I.C.: 3841; 2843; 3842; 3861; 3800; 3080
Richard A. Gilleland *(Chm. Bd., Pres. & Chief Exec. Officer)*
Richard D. Meelia *(Pres.-Domestic Group)*
Alexander R. Castaldi *(Sr. V.P.-Fin. & Chief Fin. Officer)*
James S. Bacciocco *(Treas.)*
Kenneth H. Titlebaum *(Controller)*
Richard Brown *(Mgr.-Leasing)*
Moses Elias *(Mgr.-Intl. Fin.)*
J. Esposito *(Mgr.-Employee Benefit)*
Debbie McDermott *(Adv. Coord.)*

Outside Service Firm(s):

Coopers & Lybrand*(Auditors)*
P.O. Box 538, 800 Akron Centre Plaza
Akron, OH 44308

Aetna Life & Casualty*(Group Insurer)*
151 Farmington Avenue
Hartford, CT 06156
Tel.: 203-273-2128
Fax: 203-729-4295

Bank of Boston*(Major Banking Relationship)*
Atlanta, GA

Manufacturers Hanover Trust Co.*(Major Banking Relationship)*
40 Wall St.
New York, NY 10005
Tel.: 212-623-4444

NationsBank Texas*(Major Banking Relationship)*
901 Main St., 16th Fl.
Dallas, TX 75202
Tel.: 214-922-5000

BEA Associates, Inc.*(Pension Manager)*
One Citicorp Center, 153 East 53rd St.
New York, NY 10022
Tel.: 212-832-2626
Fax: 212-751-2470

Subsidiaries:

Kendall-Futuro Company **(1)**
1 Riverfront Place, Ste. 900
Newport, KY 41071
Tel.: 606-655-3400
Tel.: 800-933-0210 (100%)
Fax: 606-655-3690
Approx.Sls.: $120,000,000
Emp.: 700
Fiscal Year-end: 12/31/90
Computer Systems/Hardware:
IBM AS/400/MAPICS
Mfr. & Sale of Elastic Braces, Supporters, Convalescent Wheelchairs & Crutches, Graduated Compression Stockings, Curity Brand Wound Care & Incontinence Products, Home Diagnostic Devices; Curity First Aid Line
S.I.C.: 3842; 3800
Peter Stratton *(Pres.)*
Steven Steigelman *(V.P.-Fin. & Admin.)*
Paul C. Amatangelo *(V.P.-Mktg.)*
Steve W. Barnhart *(V.P.-Opers.)*
Edward A. Pierami *(V.P.-Sls.)*
M.J. Lewis *(Controller)*
Mary E. Zalla *(Mktg. Services Mgr.)*

Kendall Healthcare Products Company **(1)**
One Mansfield Corp. Center, 15 Hampshire St.
Mansfield, MA 02048
Tel.: 508-261-8000
Mfr. of Wound Care, Urological, Critical Care, Patient Care & Diagnostic Products
S.I.C.: 3841; 3842; 3800
Richard D. Meelia *(Pres.)*

Polyken Technologies **(1)**
690 Canton St.
Westwood, MA 02090
Tel.: 617-320-1000
Mfr. of Adhesive Products, Specialized Wetting Agents & Tapes for the Removal of Asbestos
S.I.C.: 2891; 2899; 2672
Edward N. Miner *(Pres.)*

Non-U.S. Holdings:

Kendall Australia Pty. Ltd. **(1)**
82 Waterloo Rd.
North Ryde, N.S.W. 2113, Australia (100%)
Sls. of Surgical Dressings, Bandages & other Medical Supplies
S.I.C.: 5122; 5100
R. Silberbauer *(Chief Oper. Officer)*

Kendall Canada Ltd. **(1)**
1100 Curity Ave.
Peterborough, ON K9J 6Z6, Canada
Tel.: 416-288-1020 (100%)
Mfr. of Hospital & Surgical Supplies
S.I.C.: 3841; 3842; 3800
W.S.B. Francis *(Pres.)*

The Kendall Co. **(1)**
15 rue Marcelin Berthelot 92167
Antony, Cedex France (100%)
Sls. of Surgical Dressings, Bandages & other Medical Supplies
S.I.C.: 5122; 5100
B. Combe *(Chief Oper. Officer)*

The Kendall Co. (UK) Ltd. **(1)**
Colgate Palmolive House, 76 Oxford St.
London, W1A 1EN, United Kingdom
Tel.: 071-637 9664 (100%)
Telex: 8811882 PALMOL G
Fax: 071-580 1615
Mfr. & Sls. of Surgical Dressings, Bandages & other Medical Supplies
S.I.C.: 5122; 3842; 5100; 3800
D. Imperiali *(Chief Oper. Officer)*

Kendall de Mexico S.A. de D.V. **(1)**
Poniente 44, No. 3401 Col. San Salvador Xochimanca,
Mexico, D.F. 02870, Mexico (100%)
Sls. of Surgical Dressings, Bandages & other Medical Supplies
S.I.C.: 5122
H. Ortega *(Chief Oper. Officer)*

Kendall GmbH **(1)**
Raffineriestrasse 8 8428
Neustadt, Do Germany (100%)
Sls. of Surgical Dressings, Bandages & other Medical Supplies
S.I.C.: 5122
E. Welker *(Chief Oper. Officer)*

Kendall S.A. **(1)**
Calle Ricardo Arias #22 Campo Alegre,
P.O. Box 3289,
Panama, 4, Panama
Sls. of Surgical Dressings, Bandages & other Medical Supplies
S.I.C.: 5122; 5100
P. Rodriquez *(Chief Oper. Officer)*

Kendall Singapore **(1)**
Unit 03-39, Paramount Hotel Shopping 30 East Coast Rd.,
Singapore, Ctr. 1542, Singapore (100%)
Sls. of Surgical Dressings, Bandages & other Medical Supplies
S.I.C.: 5122; 5100
G. Ong *(Chief Oper. Officer)*

Kendall Thailand **(1)**
19 off Suthornkosa Rd.
Bangkok, Thailand (100%)

Sls. of Surgical Dressings, Bandages & other Medical Supplies
S.I.C.: 5122; 5100
L. Tejayan *(Chief Oper. Officer)*

KENNEDY ASSOCIATES
951 E. Byrd St., Ste.710
Richmond, VA 23219
Tel.: 804-648-7622
Year Founded: 1974
Sales Range: $10-19 Million
Emp.: 28
Export
Supplies Business Applications for a Variety of Minicomputers
S.I.C.: 7372; 7371
Tom Kennedy *(Pres.)*

No. of Mfg. Plants/Facilities: 1
No. of U.S. Offices: 4

Computer Systems/Hardware:
Wang, Digital, IBM, Apple MacIntosh SE

Division:

APPX Software **(1)**
951 E. Byrd St., Ste. 710
Richmond, VA 23219
Tel.: 804-643-2779
Software Applications for Minicomputers
S.I.C.: 7372
Tom Kennedy *(Pres.)*

KENNEDY MANUFACTURING COMPANY
520 E. Sycamore St.
Van Wert, OH 45891
Mailing Address:
P.O. Box 151,
Vanwert, OH 45891
Tel.: 419-238-2442
Fax: 419-238-5644
Approx.Sls.: $29,000,000
Emp.: 350
Export
Manufactures Kennedy Tool Boxes, Chests, Roller Cabinets, Work Benches
S.I.C.: 3469; 2599
Roger K. Thompson *(Pres.)*
David Thompson *(V.P.-Admin. Opers. & Treas.)*
Karl Wermer *(V.P.-Opers.)*
H.A. Zoeller *(V.P.-Sls.)*
Dennis C. Warnecke *(Treas.)*
Jim Kennedy *(Dir.-Personnel)*
John Aycock *(Mgr.-Export)*
Larry Dineen *(Mgr.-Natl. Sls.)*
Marge Linser *(Mgr.-Pur.)*
Carol Proffitt *(Mgr.-Sls. Opers.)*

Outside Service Firm(s):

Price Waterhouse*(Auditors)*
One Seagate, Ste. 1800
Toledo, OH 43604
Tel.: 419-247-1800

Markhon Industries, Inc **(1)**
200 Bond St.
Wabash, IN 46992
Tel.: 219-563-2161
Approx.Sls.: $10,000,000
Emp.: 200
Mfr. of Cabinetry for the Data Processing & Electronic Industries
S.I.C.: 3449
Frank Gallup *(Pres.)*
John Philippsen *(V.P.-Fin.)*

KENNEDY VALVE
1021 E. Water St.
Elmira, NY 14901
Mailing Address:
P.O. Box 931
Elmira, NY 14902-0931
Tel.: 607-734-2211
Fax: 607-734-3288
Approx.Sls.: $55,000,000
Emp.: 800
Mfr. of Valves & Fire Hydrants
S.I.C.: 3494; 3491
Ray Schofield *(Gen. Mgr.)*
Tim Decker *(Pur. Mgr.)*

KENNEY MANUFACTURING COMPANY
1000 Jefferson Blvd.
Warwick, RI 02886
Tel.: 401-739-2200
Fax: 401-821-5430
Approx.Sls.: $110,000,000
Emp.: 1,000
Fiscal Year-end: 12/31/90
Mfr. of Drapery Hardware, Window Shades, Venetian & Roll-Up Blinds
S.I.C.: 2591
G. Dickson Kenney *(Pres. & Chief Exec. Officer)*
J. Pacermo *(Sr. V.P.-Fin.)*
Milton C. Gupton *(V.P.-Sls.)*
Leslie Kenney *(V.P.-Matls.)*
William D. Kenney *(V.P.-Mktg.)*
Larry L. Nielsen *(V.P.-Distr.)*
W. Pfeil *(V.P.-Mktg.)*
Edward Poirier *(Dir.-Indus. Rels.)*
W. Biron *(Mgr.-Matls.)*

Outside Service Firm(s):

Ernst & Young*(Auditors)*
One Old Stone Square
Providence, RI 02903
Tel.: 401-331-7000

Hinkley, Allen, Snyder & Comen*(Legal Firm)*
1500 Fleet Ctr.
Providence, RI 02903
Tel.: 401-274-2000

Fleet National Bank*(Major Banking Relationship)*
125 Dupont Dr.
Providence, RI 02907-3178
Tel.: 401-278-5335

KENNINGTON LTD., INC.
3209 Humboldt St.
Los Angeles, CA 90031
Tel.: 213-225-1655 **CA**
Fax: 213-225-3235
Approx.Sls.: $30,000,000
Emp.: 40
Men's, Boys' & Youths' Shirts
S.I.C.: 2321
Stanley Tendler *(Chm. Bd. & Chief Exec. Officer)*
Leon J. Condon *(Pres., Chief Oper. Officer & Treas.)*
Kathleen A. Hayes *(Controller)*
Jerome Janger *(Sec. & Legal)*

Computer Systems/Hardware:
IBM

Outside Service Firm(s):

Joseph Herbert & Co.*(Auditors)*
Beverly Hills, CA

Jerome Janger, A Professional Corp.*(Legal Firm)*
1800 Century Park East, Ste. 1150
Los Angeles, CA 90067
Tel.: 310-557-1155

Union Bank*(Major Banking Relationship)*
445 S. Figueroa St.
Los Angeles, CA 90071
Tel.: 213-236-5076

Subsidiaries:

Com Corp Factors, Inc. **(1)**
3209 Humboldt St.
Los Angeles, CA 90031
Tel.: 213-225-8422 (100%)
Emp.: 80
Men's & Boys' Shirts
S.I.C.: 2321
Kathleen A. Hayes *(Pres.)*

Kennington Properties, Inc. **(1)**
1800 Century Park E., Ste. 1150
Los Angeles, CA 90067
Tel.: 310-557-1155 (100%)
Emp.: 11
Real Estate
S.I.C.: 6552
Jerome Janger *(Pres.)*
Kathleen A. Hayes *(Sec. & Treas.)*

Stanleigh International, Inc. **(1)**
3209 Humboldt St.
Los Angeles, CA 90031
Tel.: 213-225-8422 (100%)
Emp.: 20
Men's & Boys' Sportshirt & Sweater Mfr.; Buying Office for Kennington
S.I.C.: 2321
Leon J. Condon *(Pres.)*

THE KENT MANUFACTURING CO.
Hwy. 183
Pickens, SC 29671
Mailing Address:
P.O. Box 67,
Pickens, SC 29671
Tel.: 803-878-6367 **PA**
Telex: 5106018663
Fax: 803-878-2723
Year Founded: 1843
Assets: $15,240,409
Liabilities: $5,126,260
Net Worth: $10,114,149
Approx.Sls.: $15,849,140
Emp.: 150
Fiscal Year-end: 12/28/91
Import Export
Manufacturer of Yarn
S.I.C.: 2281; 2282
Warren T. Kent *(Chm. & Chief Exec. Officer)*
Mark B. Kent *(Pres. & Chief Opers. Officer)*
William C. Bagwell *(V.P. & Dir.-Mfg. & Pur.)*
John A. MacGregor, Jr. *(V.P.-Sls. & Mktg.)*
Augustus S. Ballard *(Sec.)*
Jack T. Campbell *(Treas., Asst. Sec. & Chief Fin. Officer)*
Principal(s):
Warren T. Kent

No. of Mfg. Plants/Facilities: 1
No. of U.S. Offices: 1

Computer Systems/Hardware:
Wang VS 65; PC's

Outside Service Firm(s):

Ernst & Young*(Auditors)*
C & S Bank Tower, Two Shelter Centre, Ste. 800
Greenville, SC 29603

Marsh & McLennan*(Commercial Insurance Carrier)*
Greenville, SC

Blue Cross & Blue Shield of South Carolina*(Group Insurer)*
1517 Laurel St.
Columbia, SC 29201

Pepper, Hamilton & Scheetz*(Legal Firm)*
123 S. Broad
Philadelphia, PA 19109
Tel.: 215-893-3000

South Carolina National Bank*(Major Banking Relationship)*
Pickens, SC

KENTILE FLOORS INC.
Kentile Rd.
South Plainfield, NJ 07080
Tel.: 908-757-3000
Fax: 908-757-8953
Year Founded: 1899
Emp.: 600
Import Export
Mfr. Resilient Flooring
S.I.C.: 3996; 3082
Andrew G. Kennedy *(Chm. & Pres.)*
Carl Schwarz *(Exec. V.P. & Chief Exec. Officer)*
W. Mailler *(Chief Fin. Officer & V.P.)*
R.J. Hennessey *(V.P.-Sls. & Mktg.)*
P. Weimar *(V.P.-Quality Control)*
J. Schoefield *(Exec. Grp. Dir.)*
Greg Miller *(Controller)*
Gerry Dolce *(Dir.-Mngmt. Information Systems)*
Wayne Porter *(Dir.-Pur.)*
Tom Cerchiaro *(V.P.-Mfg.)*
G. Marsh *(Mgr.-Sls. Admin.)*

No. of Mfg. Plants/Facilities: 2

Computer Systems/Hardware:
IBM System 38

Outside Service Firm(s):

James D. Miller & Co.*(Auditors)*
New York, NY

CIGNA*(Group Insurer)*
175 Water St.
New York, NY 10038-4980
Tel.: 212-701-0200
Fax: 212-701-0450

Metropolitan Life Insurance Co.*(Group Insurer)*
One Madison Ave.
New York, NY 10010-3690
Tel.: 215-578-9292

Lord, Day & Lord, Barrett Smith*(Legal Firm)*
1675 Broadway
New York, NY 10019
Tel.: 212-969-6000
Fax: 212-969-6100

National Westminster Bank plc*(Major Banking Relationship)*
Astor Plaza, 1515 Broadway
New York, NY 10036

Manufacturers Hanover Trust Co.*(Pension Manager)*
270 Park Ave.
New York, NY 10017
Tel.: 212-286-3229

KENTUCKY DEPARTMENT OF TRAVEL DEVELOPMENT
500 Mero St., Room 2200
Frankfort, KY 40601-1974
Tel.: 502-564-4930
Approx.Sls.: $5,000,000,000
Emp.: 40
Fiscal Year-end: 6/30/90
Advertising, Travel Promotion, Tourism Mktg. Research & Business Devel.
S.I.C.: 4725; 8743
Daniel Bennett *(Dir.-Mktg. & Adv.)*
Don Peck *(Asst. Dir.-Tourism Services)*
Robin Phillips *(Matching Funds)*

KENTUCKY INDIANA LUMBER CO. INC.
227 E. Lee St.
Louisville, KY 40208
Mailing Address:
P.O. Box 2289
Louisville, KY 40201-2289
Tel.: 502-637-1401 **KY**
Fax: 502-637-6801
Sales Range: $20-39 Million
Emp.: 200
Wholesale Lumber, Millwork & Building Materials
S.I.C.: 5031
Walter Freeman *(Pres.)*
Ron Mason *(Exec. V.P.)*
Doris L. Matthis *(Sec. & Treas.)*
Ken Alderson *(Dir.-Adv.)*

No. of Mfg. Plants/Facilities: 5
No. of U.S. Offices: 3

Outside Service Firm(s):

Cox, Oldham & Bartlett*(Auditors)*
Louisville, KY

First National Bank of Louisville*(Major Banking Relationship)*
P.O. Box 36000,
Louisville, KY 40233

Kentucky Indiana Lumber Co. Inc.—(Continued)

Branches:

Kentucky Indiana Lumber Co. **(1)**
1700 N. Kentucky
Evansville, IN 47711
Tel.: 812-464-2428
S.I.C.: 5031

Kentucky Indiana Lumber Co. **(1)**
P.O. Box 5506,
Lexington, KY 40555
Tel.: 606-268-0953
S.I.C.: 5031

KENTUCKY MANUFACTURING CO.
2601 S. 3rd St.
Louisville, KY 40208
Mailing Address:
P.O. Box 17185
Louisville, KY 40217
Tel.: 502-637-2551 **KY**
Fax: 502-635-1314
Year Founded: 1936
Approx.Sls.: $38,000,000
Emp.: 400
Manufacture Commercial Truck Trailers & Truck Bodies
S.I.C.: 3715; 3713
Robert C. Tway, Jr. *(Chm. Bd.)*
Robert C. Tway III *(Pres. & Chief Exec. Officer)*
Glenn Dobrick *(Exec. V.P.)*
Larry Hartog *(V.P. & Treas.)*
Margaret Guilford *(Sec.)*

Outside Service Firm(s):

Deloitte & Touche*(Auditors)*
510 W. Broadway
Louisville, KY 40202
Tel.: 502-562-2000

First National Bank of Louisville*(Major Banking Relationship)*
P.O. Box 36000,
Louisville, KY 40233

KENWAL PRODUCTS CORP.
9301 Central Ave.
Detroit, MI 48204
Tel.: 313-933-4362
Fax: 313-933-1281
Approx.Sls.: $130,000,000
Emp.: 150
Steel Service Center
S.I.C.: 5051
Kenneth Eisenberg *(Pres.)*
Tom Popma *(Controller)*

Computer Systems/Hardware:
Data General

Outside Service Firm(s):

Coopers & Lybrand*(Auditors)*
400 Renaissance Center
Detroit, MI 48243
Tel.: 313-446-7100
Fax: 313-446-7117

Blue Cross & Blue Shield of Michigan*(Group Insurer)*
Detroit, MI

Manufacturers National Bank N.A.*(Investment Banker)*
38th Fl., 100 Renaissance Center
Detroit, MI 48243
Tel.: 313-222-4227

Manufacturers National Bank N.A.*(Major Banking Relationship)*
38th Fl., 100 Renaissance Center
Detroit, MI 48243
Tel.: 313-222-4227

Kenwood Dealer Group, Inc.
(See Kenwal Products Corp.)

KENWORTH OF INDIANAPOLIS INC.
2929 S. Holt Rd.
Indianapolis, IN 46241
Mailing Address:
P.O. Box 42607,
Indianapolis, IN 46242-0607
Tel.: 317-247-8421 **IN**
Twx: 810-341-3338
Fax: 317-241-5742
Year Founded: 1965
Assets: $44,100,000
Liabilities: $36,400,000
Net Worth: $7,700,000
Approx.Sls.: $54,800,000
Emp.: 185
Fiscal Year-end: 12/31/92
Retail & Service New & Used Heavy-Duty Kenworth Trucks; Leasing Franchise
S.I.C.: 5511; 7538; 7513
Eldon D. Palmer *(Pres. & Chief Exec. Officer)*
Jeffrey Curry *(Chief Fin. Officer)*
Elaine Palmer *(Sec.)*

Outside Service Firm(s):

Ernst & Young*(Auditors)*
One Indiana Square, Ste. 3400
Indianapolis, IN 46204
Tel.: 317-236-1100

Forbes, Kias & Pennamped*(Legal Firm)*
Indianapolis, IN

Merchants National Bank & Trust Company of Indianapolis*(Major Banking Relationship)*
One Merchants Plaza, Ste. 901E
Indianapolis, IN 46255
Tel.: 317-267-7109

KERN INDUSTRIES
13000 E. Temple Ave.
City of Industry, CA 91749-1207
Mailing Address:
P.O. Box 1207,
City of Industry, CA 91749
Tel.: 818-369-5111
Fax: 818-330-6772
Year Founded: 1982
Approx.Sls.: $125,000,000
Emp.: 70
Mfr. Steel Cans & Broker Tomato Products
S.I.C.: 3411; 5149
Principal(s):
Richard C. Kern
Jay Kern

Outside Service Firm(s):

Deloitte & Touche*(Auditors)*
21550 Oxnard St., Ste. 800
Woodland Hills, CA 91367-7100
Tel.: 818-593-4800
Fax: 818-347-4278

Wells Fargo Bank*(Major Banking Relationship)*
Alameda, CA

KERN'S BAKERIES, INCORPORATED
2110 Chapman Hwy.
Knoxville, TN 37920
Tel.: 615-573-1941
Approx.Sls.: $75,000,000
Emp.: 1,200
Wholesale Bread, Rolls & Cake
S.I.C.: 5149
William Schwartz *(Pres.)*
Mike Kendrick *(Controller)*
Pam Kennedy *(Dir.-Personnel)*
Jim Blevins *(Mgr.-Product)*
Keith Cantwell *(Mgr.-Sls.)*
Jim Mathis *(Mgr.-Data Processing)*
David Reno *(Mgr.-Mktg.)*
Robert Rice *(Mgr.-Sls.)*

KEROFF & ROSENBERG ADVERTISING INC.
444 N. Wabash
Chicago, IL 60611
Tel.: 312-321-9000 **IL**
Fax: 312-321-1736
Year Founded: 1972
Approx.Billings: $42,000,000
Emp.: 64
Advertising Agency
S.I.C.: 7311
Henry Hechtman *(Sr. V.P. & Dir.-Creative)*
Michael Swidler *(Sr. V.P. & Dir.-Client Services)*
Mary Jo Montana *(V.P.-Admin. & Human Rels.)*
Barbara Siegel *(Dir.-Fin.)*

No. of U.S. Offices: 1

Computer Systems/Hardware:
Unisys+, Apple

Outside Service Firm(s):

Michigan Avenue National Bank*(Major Banking Relationship)*
Chicago, IL

KERRISON DRY GOODS COMPANY, INC.
260 King St.
Charleston, SC 29401
Tel.: 803-722-4011 **SC**
Fax: 803-722-4045
Year Founded: 1830
Assets: $8,800,000
Liabilities: $2,860,000
Net Worth: $5,940,000
Sales Range: $10-19 Million
Emp.: 250
Fiscal Year-end: 1/31/91
Import
Non-Discount Department Stores; Property Operation
S.I.C.: 5311; 6512
Edwin Poulnot, III *(Pres.)*
Dale Widman *(Exec. V.P.)*
Gene Riggs *(V.P.)*
Carol Kirchner *(Mgr.-Acctng.)*

Outside Service Firm(s):

J. W. Hunt & Co.*(Auditors)*
Middleburg Office Park, 1607 St. Julian Place
Columbia, SC 29202
Tel.: 803-254-8196

South Carolina National Bank*(Major Banking Relationship)*
Charleston, SC

KERVICK ENTERPRISES, INC.
40 Rockdale St.
Worcester, MA 01606
Tel.: 508-853-4500
Fax: 508-853-2753
Approx.Sls.: $29,000,000
Emp.: 325
Iron & Steel Forgings; Nonferrous Forgings; Commercial Printing Offset; Alloy Steel Castings
S.I.C.: 3462; 3463; 2752; 3325; 3369
Paul J. Kervick *(Chm. Bd.)*
Robert N. Kervick *(Vice Chm.)*
Robert B. Kervick *(Pres.)*
Kevin M. Kervick *(Exec. V.P.)*
Joe Dyros *(Treas.)*
Salvatore Emma, Jr. *(Controller)*
E. Colby Cameron *(Sec.)*

Outside Service Firm(s):

Batchelor, Dennis & Frechette*(Auditors)*
Providence, MA

Edwards & Angell*(Legal Firm)*
2700 Hospital Trust Twr.
Providence, RI 02903
Tel.: 401-274-9200

First National Bank of Boston*(Major Banking Relationship)*
150 Royall St.
Canton, MA 02021
Tel.: 617-575-2900
Tel.: 800-442-2001

H. KESSLER & COMPANY
87 Peachtree St., S.W.
Atlanta, GA 30303
Tel.: 404-523-0531
Fax: 404-681-0320
Year Founded: 1937
Department Store Chain
S.I.C.: 5311

Outside Service Firm(s):

Deloitte & Touche*(Auditors)*
100 Peachtree St., Ste. 1700
Atlanta, GA 30303-1943
Tel.: 404-220-1500
Fax: 404-220-1583

Branches:

H. Kessler & Company **(1)**
2044 Campbellton Rd. S.W.
Atlanta, GA 30303
Tel.: 404-753-1616
S.I.C.: 5311

H. Kessler & Company **(1)**
2014 Candler Rd.
Decatur, GA 30034
Tel.: 404-284-6411
S.I.C.: 5311

H. Kessler & Company **(1)**
228 Broad St.
Rome, GA 30161
Tel.: 706-291-7580
S.I.C.: 5311

KESTERSON FOOD COMPANY, INC.
211 Hwy. 69 N.
Paris, TN 38242
Tel.: 901-642-5031
Tel.: 800-627-8303
Fax: 901-642-7804
Year Founded: 1963
Sales Range: $40-59 Million
Emp.: 125
Fiscal Year-end: 6/30/91
Frozen Meat, Packaged Poultry, Frozen & Packaged Seafoods, Groceries & Related Products, Green or Roasted Coffee, Tea, Canned Goods, Janitors Supplies
S.I.C.: 5142; 5146; 5149; 5087
Tommy Kesterson *(Chm. Bd. & Pres.)*
Danny Kesterson *(Exec. V.P.-Sls. & Mktg.)*
Jimmy Kiser *(V.P.-Fin.)*
Johnny Petrie *(V.P.-Natl. Accts.)*
Mark Thompson *(Dir.-Personnel)*
David Lowe *(Mgr.-Sls.)*
Anita Peale *(Mgr.-Data Processing)*
Janice Chapman *(Sls. Coord.)*

No. of Mfg. Plants/Facilities: 1
No. of U.S. Offices: 1

Computer Systems/Hardware:
IBM AS/36

Outside Service Firm(s):

Deloitte & Touche*(Auditors)*
Memphis, TN

Nationwide Insurance*(Commercial Insurance Carrier)*
Memphis, TN

American National Insurance Company*(Group Insurer)*
Galveston, TX

Greer & Greer*(Legal Firm)*
Paris, TN 38242

LaSalle National Bank*(Major Banking Relationship)*
135 S. LaSalle St.
Chicago, IL 60690
Tel.: 312-443-2000

First Tennessee Bank, N.A.*(Pension Manager)*
P.O. Box 84
Memphis, TN 38101-0034
Tel.: 901-523-4541

KETCHUM COMMUNICATIONS INC.
6 PPG Place
Pittsburgh, PA 15222
Tel.: 412-456-3500 PA
Fax: 412-456-3834
Year Founded: 1923
Approx.Billings: $1,030,356,000
Emp.: 1,182
Advertising Agency
S.I.C.: 7311
Paul H. Alvarez *(Chm. Bd., Pres. & Chief Exec. Officer)*
Edward L. Graf *(Vice Chm. & Chief Fin. Officer)*
William Cameron *(Sr. V.P., Treas.)*
Ronald Cruikshank *(Sr. V.P., Gen. Counsel)*
Susan Engle *(Sr. V.P., Corp. Human Resources/Facilities)*
Daniel R. Madia *(Sr. V.P., Asst. to the Pres.)*
Charles Southworth *(Sr. V.P., Dir. Information Services)*
Michael J. Kaczmarski *(Sr. V.P., Controller)*

Computer Systems/Hardware:
Donovan Data Systems, ROSS Financial, IDC/Vanguard, DEC, Wang, IBM

Outside Service Firm(s):

Deloitte & Touche*(Auditors)*
2400 One PPG Place
Pittsburgh, PA 15222
Tel.: 412-281-2232

PNC Financial*(Investment Banker)*
Philadelphia, PA

Buchanan, Ingersoll p.c.*(Legal Firm)*
600 Grant St., 57th Flr.
Pittsburgh, PA 15219
Tel.: 412-562-8800

Pittsburgh National Bank*(Major Banking Relationship)*
Stock Transfer Dept., Fifth & Wood Streets
Pittsburgh, PA 15265

Branches:

Braun/Ketchum Public Relations (1)
3580 Wilshire Blvd., Ste. 1520
Los Angeles, CA 90010
Tel.: 213-385-3481
Fax: 213-385-1980
Lawrence Fisher *(Pres. & Dir.)*
Doug Jeffe *(Exec. V.P.)*

Braun/Ketchum Public Relations (1)
915 L. St., Ste. 1435
Sacramento, CA 95814
Tel.: 916-442-1913
Fax: 916-442-5001
T. Tony Quinn *(V.P., Grp. Mgr.)*

Ketchum Advertising/Chicago (1)
111 N. Canal St., Ste. 1150
Chicago, IL 60606-7272
Tel.: 312-715-9200
Fax: 312-902-1758
Tim Dorgan *(Pres.)*

Ketchum Advertising/Los Angeles (1)
11755 Wilshire Blvd., Ste. 1900
Los Angeles, CA 90025
Tel.: 310-444-5000
Fax: 213-477-3118
J. Craig Mathiesen *(Pres.)*
Tim Hart *(Exec. V.P., Chief Oper. Officer)*
Steve Beaumont *(Exec. V.P., Creative Dir.)*
Bill Stenton *(Sr. V.P., Co-Creative Dir.)*
Cherie Crane *(Sr. V.P., Dir., Plng. & Opers.)*

Ketchum Advertising/New York (1)
220 East 42nd St.
New York, NY 10017
Tel.: 212-907-9300
Fax: 212-907-9364
Steve Penchina *(Chm. & Exec. Creative Dir.)*
William Perkins *(Pres.)*
Gerald Cutler *(Exec. V.P., Dir.-Plng. & Opers.)*

Ketchum Advertising/Philadelphia (1)
Bell Atlantic Tower, 1717 Arch St., Ste. 3300
Philadelphia, PA 19103-2786
Tel.: 215-656-8000
Fax: 215-656-8038
Samuel Rand *(Pres.)*
Frederick R. Siegel *(Exec. V.P., Exec. Creative Dir.)*
Charles Housam *(Sr. V.P., Dir.-Plng. & Opers.)*

Ketchum Advertising/Pittsburgh (1)
Six PPG Place
Pittsburgh, PA 15222
Tel.: 412-456-3500
Jan Hedquist *(Pres.)*
S. Christopher Labash *(Exec. V.P., Exec. Creative Dir.)*
James Ficco *(Exec. V.P., Chief Oper. Officer)*
David Egan *(Sr. V.P., Dir. Client Services)*
Jean-Anne Matter *(Sr. V.P., Dir. Mktg. & Res.)*

Ketchum Advertising/San Francisco (1)
55 Union St.
San Francisco, CA 94111
Tel.: 415-984-6100
Fax: 415-982-5861
Dianne Snedaker *(Pres.)*
Lynn Upshaw *(Exec. V.P., Chief Oper. Officer)*
Robert Johnson *(Sr. V.P., Gen. Mgr., KM&S)*
Jerry Hamilton *(Sr. V.P., Dir., Mktg. Services)*

Ketchum Advertising/USA (1)
55 Union St.
San Francisco, CA 94111
Tel.: 415-984-6100
Fax: 415-982-5861

Ketchum Advertising/USA (1)
220 E. 42nd St.
New York, NY 10017
Tel.: 212-907-9300
Fax: 212-907-9364
Robert W. Kroyer *(Pres.)*
James K. Larkin *(Exec. V.P., Dir. U.S. Opers.)*
Robert Childs *(V.P., Systems & Tech.)*

Ketchum Directory Advertising/Chicago (1)
111 N. Canal St., Ste. 1150
Chicago, IL 60606
Tel.: 312-715-9320
Fax: 312-902-1758
John Jospeh *(Sr. V.P., Dir.)*

Ketchum Directory Advertising/Executive (1)
1133 Ave. of the Americas
New York, NY 10036
Tel.: 212-536-8800
Fax: 212-398-0387
Rick Barry , Sr. *(Sr. V.P. & Dir.)*

Ketchum Directory Advertising/Los Angeles (1)
11755 Wilshire Blvd., Ste. 1900
Los Angeles, CA 90025
Tel.: 310-444-5000
Fax: 213-477-3118
Nancy Roth *(Sr. V.P., Reg. Mgr.)*
Valeri Ann Young *(V.P., Bus. Devel.)*

Ketchum Directory Advertising/Louisville (1)
Summit I, 4350 Brownsboro Rd., Ste. 302
Louisville, KY 40207-1679
Tel.: 502-894-3220
Fax: 502-894-3255
Jim Broome *(Sr. V.P., Reg. Mgr.)*
Nancy Milliken *(V.P., Bus. Devel.)*

Ketchum Directory Advertising/Pittsburgh (1)
Six PPG Place
Pittsburgh, PA 15222
Tel.: 412-456-3500
Fax: 412-456-3834
Blanche McGuire *(Sr. V.P., Res. Mgr.)*
Pat Brandy *(V.P., Bus. Devel.)*
Dorothy Talkington *(V.P., Natl. Opers.)*

Ketchum Directory Advertising/San Francisco (1)
55 Union St.
San Francisco, CA 94111
Tel.: 415-984-6000
Fax: 415-984-6387
Gretchen Taylor *(V.P.)*

Ketchum Directory Advertising/USA (1)
11755 Wilshire Blvd., Ste. 1900
Los Angeles, CA 90025
Tel.: 310-444-5000
Fax: 213-477-8370
Steven Troy *(Pres.)*
Rick McFadden *(V.P., Dir.-Opers. & Planning)*

Ketchum International Inc. (1)
Six PPG Place
Pittsburgh, PA 15222
Tel.: 412-456-3693
Telex: 199120 (KMG UT)
Cable: Ketchumads, Pittsburgh
Fax: 412-456-3700
Jan Hedquist *(Mng. Dir.)*

Ketchum Public Relations/Corporate (1)
1133 Ave. of The Americas
New York, NY 10036
Tel.: 212-536-8800
Fax: 212-398-0387
David R. Drobis *(Chm. & Chief Exec. Officer)*
Raymond L. Kotcher *(Pres. & Chief Oper. Officer)*
John L. Paluszek *(Pres., Pub. Affairs)*

Ketchum Public Relations/Atlanta (1)
First Union Plaza, 999 Peachtree St., N.E., Ste. 1850
Atlanta, GA 30309
Tel.: 404-873-1711
Fax: 404-873-2044
Jane Shivers *(Exec. V.P., Dir.)*
Michael Turnbull *(V.P., Assoc. Dir.)*

Ketchum Public Relations/Chicago (1)
142 E. Ontario St.
Chicago, IL 60611
Tel.: 312-266-4550
Fax: 312-266-4564
Judith Rich *(Exec. V.P., Exec. Dir. & Creative Services-USA)*
Keith Burton *(Sr. V.P., Dir.)*
Steve Singerman *(Sr. V.P., Assoc. Dir.)*

Ketchum Public Relations/New York (1)
1133 Ave. of the Americas
New York, NY 10036
Tel.: 212-536-8800
Fax: 212-398-0387
Robert C. Feldman *(Exec. V.P., Dir.)*
Robert Flaherty *(Sr. V.P., Assoc. Dir.)*

Ketchum Public Relations/Philadelphia (1)
Bell Atlantic Tower, 1717 Arch St., Ste. 3300
Philadelphia, PA 19103-2786
Tel.: 215-656-8000
Fax: 215-656-8042
Barry Brinster *(Exec. V.P., Dir.)*

Ketchum Public Relations/Pittsburgh (1)
Six PPG Place
Pittsburgh, PA 15222
Tel.: 412-456-3500
Fax: 412-456-3834
Lawrence R. Werner *(Exec. V.P., Dir.)*
Robert J. Aiello *(Sr. V.P., Assoc. Dir.)*
Michael Kelly *(Sr. V.P., Assoc. Dir.)*
Kay Cushing *(Sr. V.P., Grp. Mgr.)*

Ketchum Public Relations/San Francisco (1)
55 Union St.
San Francisco, CA 94111
Tel.: 415-984-6100
Fax: 415-984-6387
Allen Miller *(Exec. V.P., Dir.)*
James Caudill *(Sr. V.P., Assoc. Dir.)*
Betsy Gullickson *(Sr. V.P., Assoc. Dir.)*

Ketchum Public Relations/Washington, DC (1)
1201 Connecticut Ave., N.W., Ste. 300
Washington, DC 20036
Tel.: 202-835-8800
Fax: 202-835-8879
Lorraine Thelian *(Exec. V.P.)*

Subsidiaries:

Botto, Roessner, Horne & Messinger, Inc. (1)
1133 Ave. of the Americas, 44th Fl.
New York, NY 10036
Tel.: 212-556-2000
Fax: 212-869-1295
Approx.Billings: $47,600,000
Emp.: 53
Healthcare Advertising & Promotion
S.I.C.: 7311
Robert J. Botto *(Pres.)*
Herbert J. Messinger *(Exec. V.P., Agency Opers.)*

DiFranza Williamson, Inc. (1)
16 West 22nd St.
New York, NY 10010
Tel.: 212-463-8302
Fax: 212-463-9346
Sales Promotion
S.I.C.: 7311
Elizabeth Powers-Trupp *(Sr. V.P., Mng. Dir.)*

Non-U.S. Branches:

IG Conseil S.A. (1)
55 Rue de la Federation 75015
Paris, France
Tel.: 1-45667045
Fax: 1-43065235
Public Relations
Anne Fournier *(Chm.)*
Jean-Charles Riberat *(Chief Exec. Officer)*

Ketchum Werbeagentur GmbH (1)
Alexander-Diehl-Str. 2a Postfach 1920, 6500
Mainz, 26, Germany
Tel.: 31-80160
Fax: 31-801614
Public Relations

Komplettburo GmbH, Internationale Kommunikation (1)
Flemingstr. 15 8000
Munich, 81, Germany
Tel.: 089-928020
Telex: 5216059
Fax: 089-9280280
Approx.Billings: $3,500,000
Emp.: 47
Full Service Specializing in Food, Public Affairs, Corporate Public Relations, Environment
Freya Kohler *(Chief Exec. Officer)*
Sabine Stadel-Strauch *(Mng. Dir.)*
Barbara Stieghan *(Mng. Dir.)*

CIA Ketchum (1)
6, Rue Deodat de Severac 75017
Paris, France
Tel.: 1-47540381
Fax: 1-47633569
Public Relations
Gerard Commerot *(Pres.)*

Ketchum Advertising Singapore (1)
5 & 7 Halifax Rd.
Singapore, 0922, Singapore
Tel.: 65-2963813
Telex: RS29196 (TCR)
Fax: 65-2972340
Approx.Billings: $11,700,000
Emp.: 31
Ad Agency
S.I.C.: 7311
Garry Abbott *(Mng. Dir. & Creative Dir.)*
Lena Ong Guek Hiang *(Gen. Mgr.)*
Rebecca Koh *(Fin. Mgr.)*

Ketchum Public Relations PLC **(1)**
5 Langley St.
London, WC2H 9JA, United Kingdom
Tel.: 071-3793404
Fax: 071-2408311
Approx.Billings: $5,000,000
Emp.: 30
Public Relations
Chris O'Donoghue *(Mng. Dir.)*
Pamela Poe *(Mng. Dir.)*

R.P. Partners SRL **(1)**
Via Lentasio 9 20122
Milan, Italy
Tel.: 2-58303530
Fax: 2-58303356
Approx.Billings: $2,937,621,700
Emp.: 18
Press Relations, Financial Relations, Corporate Communication, Scientific Relations, Product Publicity
Fausto Carnevali *(Pres.)*
Nicoletta Cerana *(Chief Exec. Officer)*
Mirka Giacoletto Papas *(Exec. V.P.)*

Stringer Veroni Ketchum **(1)**
160 Bedford Rd., Ste. 307
Toronto, ON M5R 2K9, Canada
Tel.: 416-975-0011
Fax: 416-975-3990
Public Relations
Clive Veroni *(Pres.)*

Non-U.S. Holdings:

Ketchum Advertising (Japan) Ltd. **(1)**
Plus One Bldg., 2-16-4 Azabu Juban
Minato-Ku,
Tokyo, 106, Japan
Tel.: 03-37696060
Telex: J23298
Fax: 03-37699886
Approx.Billings: $213,000,000
Emp.: 26
Consumer Advertising
Thomas J. Smith *(Chm. Bd.)*
Michael Rosenberg *(Pres.)*

KETCHUM, INC.
Ketchum Center, 1030 5th Ave.
Pittsburgh, PA 15219
Tel.: 412-281-1481
Tel.: 800-242-9688
Year Founded: 1919
Approx.Sls.: $12,000,000
Emp.: 150
Fund Raising Counsel
S.I.C.: 7389
Robert L. Thompson *(Chm. & Chief Exec. Officer)*
Robert E. Carter *(Pres.)*
Fred E. Beeson *(Sr. V.P.)*
David A. Norris *(Sr. V.P.)*
Elliott S. Oshry *(Sr. V.P.)*
Charles E. Trimble *(Exec. V.P.)*
George W. Rooney, Jr. *(V.P.-Fin.)*
Bob McCully *(Dir.-Communications)*

KETTENBURG MARINE CORPORATION
2810 Carleton St.
San Diego, CA 92106
Mailing Address:
P.O. Box 6448,
San Diego, CA 92106
Tel.: 619-224-8211
Tel.: 800-234-8211 **DE**
Fax: 619-221-7559
Year Founded: 1918
Approx.Sls.: $20,000,000
Emp.: 200
Fiscal Year-end: 10/31/90
Export
Retail & Wholesale of Marine Hardware; Ship & Boat Repair
S.I.C.: 3429; 3731; 3732; 5088; 5551
Jane T. Fetter *(Chm. Bd. & Sec.)*
Thompson Fetter *(Pres. & Chief Exec. Officer)*
Roger Bowman *(V.P.-Opers.)*
Karen Forbes *(V.P.-Fin. & Treas.)*
Jay Sanders *(V.P.-Sls.)*
Mary Darrow *(Dir.-Data Processing)*
Margaret Fetter *(Dir.-Plng. & Devel.)*
Kris Hayes *(Dir.-Human Resources)*
James Tinsky *(Dir.-Mktg. & Sls. Promo.)*
Jeffrey Cummins *(Mgr.-Export Sls.)*
Ignacio Saldana *(Mgr.-Latin American Sls.)*
William Dosta *(Buyer)*
Principal(s):
Jane T. Fetter
Thompson Fetter

Computer Systems/Hardware:
Qantel

Outside Service Firm(s):

Considine & Considine*(Auditors)*
San Diego, CA

Sedgwick James*(Commercial Insurance Carrier)*
San Diego, CA

Sedgwick James*(Group Insurer)*
San Diego, CA

Security Pacific National Bank*(International Bank Affiliate)*
San Diego, CA

Mitchell, Keeney, Barry & Pike*(Legal Firm)*
San Diego, CA

Security Pacific National Bank*(Major Banking Relationship)*
San Diego, CA

Divisions:

Kettenburg Marine/Dana Point **(1)**
34467 Golden Lantern
Dana Point, CA 92629
Tel.: 714-496-3640
Emp.: 4
S.I.C.: 3429
Charlene Weiss *(Gen. Mgr.)*

Kettenburg Marine/Newport Beach Retail **(1)**
2700-B West Coast Hwy.
Newport Beach, CA 92663
Tel.: 714-722-2700
Tel.: 800-288-2730
Fax: 714-722-2729
Emp.: 12
Retail of Marine Hardware; Electronics & Accessories
S.I.C.: 5088
Rebecca Dailey *(Gen. Mgr.)*

Kettenburg Marine/Newport Engines **(1)**
2633 W. Coast Hwy.
Newport Beach, CA 92663
Tel.: 714-722-2730
Tel.: 800-288-2730
Fax: 714-722-2769
Emp.: 4
Retail, Wholesale & Distribution of Marine Engines
S.I.C.: 5088
George Sears *(Gen. Mgr.)*

Kettenburg Marine **(1)**
3010 Carleton St.
San Diego, CA 92106
Tel.: 619-221-7400
Tel.: 800-234-8211
Fax: 619-221-7439
Marine Hardware Wholesale & Retail; Electronics, Engines & Accessories
S.I.C.: 5088
Roger Bowman *(Gen. Mgr.)*

Kettenburg Marine **(1)**
2810 Carleton St.
San Diego, CA 92106
Tel.: 619-221-7560
Tel.: 800-234-8211
Fax: 619-221-7439
Boat & Yacht Repair
S.I.C.: 3732
Karl Adriany *(Gen. Mgr.)*

KETTERING ADVERTISING DISPLAY CO.
570 Sylvan Ave.
Englewood Cliffs, NJ 07632
Tel.: 201-569-9100 **DE**
Fax: 201-569-8948
Assets: $12,000,000
Liabilities: $6,000,000
Net Worth: $6,000,000
Approx.Sls.: $50,000,000
Emp.: 300
Fiscal Year-end: 4/30/90
Point of Purchase Displays
S.I.C.: 3993
Philip Marks *(Chm. Bd.)*
Steven L. Marks *(Pres. & Chief Exec. Officer)*
Len Lipsky *(Chief Opers. Officer)*
John Sprague *(Sr. V.P.-Sls.)*
N.R. Johnson *(V.P.-Mktg. & Sls.)*
Joseph Witt *(V.P. & Controller)*

Outside Service Firm(s):

Deloitte & Touche*(Auditors)*
411 Hackensack Ave.
Hackensack, NJ 07601-6367
Tel.: 201-646-7700

Lym, Hoens, Abeises, Conant & Davis*(Legal Firm)*
Englewood Cliffs, NJ

First Fidelity Bank, N.A.*(Major Banking Relationship)*
Englewood Cliffs, NJ

KETTLE RESTAURANTS
3131 Argonne
Houston, TX 77098
Tel.: 713-524-3464
Fax: 713-524-0943
Year Founded: 1961
Approx.Sls.: $47,000,000
Emp.: 1,700
Restaurants
S.I.C.: 5812
Danny M. Chambers *(Chm. Bd.)*
Harry L. Chambers, Sr. *(Pres. & Chief Exec. Officer)*
Donald A. Theesfeld *(Exec. V.P.-Sls. & Mktg.)*
Katherine G. Craine *(V.P. & Gen. Counsel)*
Berthyl Embry *(V.P. & Restaurant Supvr.)*
Calvin Doyle Smith *(V.P.-Fin. & Treas.)*
Jessie Tabor *(V.P.-Admin. & Sec.)*
Carlette Woods *(V.P. & Controller)*

KETTLER BROTHERS, INC.
9426 Stewartown Rd.
Montgomery Village, MD 20879
Tel.: 301-948-4000
Fax: 301-963-7074
Year Founded: 1952
Approx.Sls.: $32,578,960
Emp.: 105
Fiscal Year-end: 12/31/90
Operative Builder General Single Family House Residential & Nonresidential Building; Contractor Agents Brokers & Managers
S.I.C.: 1522; 1531; 6531
Clarence E. Kettler *(Pres.)*
Paul W. Barrick *(Chief Fin. Officer)*
James M. Kettler *(Exec. V.P. & Gen. Mgr.)*
Edward Desimon *(Sr. V.P., Land Devel.)*

Outside Service Firm(s):

Bond Beebe Muckelbauer & Barton*(Auditors)*
Washington, DC

Melrod, Redman, Gartland*(Legal Firm)*
1801 K St., N.W., Ste. 1100
Washington, DC 20006
Tel.: 202-822-5300

Riggs National Bank of Washington, D.C.*(Major Banking Relationship)*
P.O. Box 96206, 1120 Vermont Ave. N.W.
Washington, DC 20090-6206
Tel.: 202-835-4082

Subsidiary:

Hidden Valley Resort **(1)**
One Craighead Dr.
Hidden Valley, PA 15502
Tel.: 814-443-6454
Tel.: 800-458-0175
Resort Housing, Conference, Golf, Skiing, etc.
S.I.C.: 7011
James B. Coulter *(Mng. Dir.)*
Paul W. Barrick *(Chief Fin. Officer)*
Terry L Babb *(Sec.)*

KEY CADILLAC, INC.
6825 York Ave. S.
Edina, MN 55435
Tel.: 612-920-4300 **MN**
Fax: 612-920-4321
Year Founded: 1973
Approx.Sls.: $47,000,000
Emp.: 89
Retail Sales & Service of New & Used Automobiles
S.I.C.: 5511
Adam Stanzak *(Pres.)*
Ken Greening *(V.P.-Opers.)*
Dennis A. Burg *(V.P.)*
Pam Thompson *(Treas. & Sec.)*
Jim Hill *(Dir.-Pur.)*

Outside Service Firm(s):

Larsen, Allen, Weishair & Co.*(Auditors)*
St. Louis Park, MN

Larkin, Hoffman Daily & Lindgren*(Legal Firm)*
Edina, MN

Century Bank*(Major Banking Relationship)*
Eden Prairie, MN

KEY CONTAINER CORPORATION
21 Campbell St.
Pawtucket, RI 02862
Tel.: 401-723-2000
Fax: 401-725-5980
Approx.Sls.: $19,000,000
Emp.: 170
Corrugated Shipping Containers
S.I.C.: 2631; 2653
David Strauce *(Chm. Bd. & Pres.)*
Richard Strause *(Chief Exec. Officer)*
Tom Pruneau *(V.P. & Plant Mgr.)*

Outside Service Firm(s):

Max M. Gold*(Auditors)*
New York, NY

Winograd, Shine & Zacks*(Legal Firm)*
Providence, RI

Rhode Island Hospital Trust National Bank*(Major Banking Relationship)*
Providence, RI

KEY FOOD STORES CO-OPERATIVE, INC.
8925 Ave. D
Brooklyn, NY 11236
Tel.: 718-451-1000
Fax: 718-629-0962
Approx.Sls.: $660,000,000
Emp.: 400
Fiscal Year-end: 4/30/91
Wholesale Food Co-operative
S.I.C.: 5141
Sheldon Geller *(Chm. Bd.)*
Lawrence Mandell *(Pres.)*
Allen Newman *(Chief Exec. Officer)*
Jules Levine *(V.P.)*
Walter Czajka *(Controller)*
Samuel Kristal *(Treas.)*
Joseph Binder *(Sec.)*
Robert Cavanagh *(Dir.-Mngmt. Information Systems)*

No. of Mfg. Plants/Facilities: 150

Computer Systems/Hardware:
IBM 4361

Outside Service Firm(s):

Miller Ellin & Co.*(Auditors)*
New York, NY

Empire Blue Cross & Blue Shield*(Group Insurer)*
New York, NY

Warshaw, Burstein, Cohen, Schlesinger & Kuh*(Legal Firm)*
55 Fifth Ave.
New York, NY 10017

Chemical Bank*(Major Banking Relationship)*
450 West 33rd St.
New York, NY 10001
Tel.: 212-613-7197
Fax: 212-947-7628

KEY HANDLING SYSTEMS, INC.
210 S. Newman St.
Hackensack, NJ 07601
Tel.: 201-342-6223
Fax: 201-342-4095
Sales Range: $10-19 Million
Emp.: 70
Conveyors, Monorails, Lift Tables
S.I.C.: 3535; 3536
Charles Van Melis *(Pres.)*
William Stefan *(Exec. V.P.)*
John McKenzie *(Sr. V.P. & Chief Engr.)*
Ralph Cooper *(V.P.-Rail Engrng.)*
Fred Macholt *(V.P.-Mfg.)*
William McCandless *(V.P.-Sls.)*
Ray Mendoza *(V.P.-Natl. Accounts)*
Ed Zakrzewski *(V.P.-P.O. Sls.)*
Gil Meierhans *(Controller)*

Outside Service Firm(s):

Joseph Miranda & Associates*(Auditors)*
New York, NY

Richard Davidoff*(Legal Firm)*
New York, NY

National Community Bank*(Major Banking Relationship)*
Ridgefield, NJ

KEY INDUSTRIES, INC.
523 E. Wall
Fort Scott, KS 66701
Mailing Address:
P.O. Box 389
Fort Scott, KS 66701
Tel.: 316-223-2000
Tel.: 800-835-0365 **KS**
Fax: 316-223-5822
Year Founded: 1908
Assets: $14,212,265
Liabilities: $2,861,625
Net Worth: $11,350,640
Approx.Sls.: $33,376,943
Emp.: 650
Fiscal Year-end: 12/28/91
Import Export
Mfr. Overalls, Work Clothes, Jeans
S.I.C.: 2326
William K. Pollock *(Chm. Bd. & Chief Exec. Officer)*
Wayne Baumgarner *(V.P.-Sls.-Eastern Grp.)*
Gary Bukowski *(V.P.-Fin., Controller & Sec.)*
Michael Hahn *(V.P.-Sls.-Western Grp.)*
Joy O'Neal *(V.P. & Treas.)*
Robert Stone *(V.P.-Opers.)*
Susan Tassi *(Dir.-Adv.)*

No. of Mfg. Plants/Facilities: 6

Outside Service Firm(s):

Diehl, Fletcher, Banwart & Bolton*(Auditors)*
Fort Scott, KS

Hoskins, King, McGannon, Hahn & Hurwitz*(Legal Firm)*
Commerce Bank Bldg., 922 Walnut, Ste. 1100
Kansas City, MO 64106
Tel.: 816-221-2416

Commerce Bank of Kansas City*(Major Banking Relationship)*
10th & Walnut
Kansas City, MO 64141
Tel.: 816-234-2000
Fax: 816-234-2548

KEY MANUFACTURING GROUP, INC.
3200 W. 14 Mile Rd.
Royal Oak, MI 48073
Tel.: 313-280-0880 **MI**
Fax: 313-355-2015
Approx.Sls.: $25,000,000
Emp.: 200
Metal Nuts & Bolts
S.I.C.: 3452
Joel D. Tauber *(Chm. Bd.)*
John A. Toth *(Pres.)*
Gary M. Winkler *(V.P. & Chief Fin. Officer)*
Kenneth A. Dishell *(V.P.)*

Outside Service Firm(s):

Coopers & Lybrand*(Auditors)*
400 Renaissance Center
Detroit, MI 48243
Tel.: 313-446-7100
Fax: 313-446-7117

Comerica Bank*(Major Banking Relationship)*
211 W. Fort St.
Detroit, MI 48226
Tel.: 313-222-3300

Subsidiary:

Industrial & Automotive Fasteners **(1)**
3200 W. 14 Mile Rd.
Royal Oak, MI 48073
Tel.: 313-280-0880
S.I.C.: 3452

KEY PLASTICS, INC.
39325 Plymouth Rd., Ste. 201
Livonia, MI 48150
Tel.: 313-462-2322
Fax: 313-462-2395
Approx.Sls.: $53,000,000
Emp.: 600
Mfr. Plastic Parts For Automobiles
S.I.C.: 3081
George Mars *(Pres.)*
David C. Benoit *(Exec. V.P.)*

Outside Service Firm(s):

Manufacturers National Bank N.A.*(Major Banking Relationship)*
38th Fl., 100 Renaissance Center
Detroit, MI 48243
Tel.: 313-222-4227

Division:

Superior Division of Key Plastics **(1)**
Box 160, Rd. 1
Felton, PA 17322-0160
Tel.: 717-244-5557
George Mars *(Pres.)*

KEYES COMPANY
100 N. Biscayne Blvd., 19th Fl.
Miami, FL 33132
Tel.: 305-371-3592
Fax: 305-358-6394
Approx.Sls.: $53,000,000
Emp.: 238
Real Estate Investment, Syndication, Development
S.I.C.: 6552
Ted Pappas *(Chm. Bd.)*
Fred Stanton Smith *(Vice Chm.-New Acquisitions, Expansions & Mngmt.)*
Michael Pappas *(Pres.)*
Marie Pappas *(V.P.)*
Timothy D. Pappas *(V.P.)*

Computer Systems/Hardware:
IBM

Subsidiaries:

Keyes Investments **(1)**
100 No. Biscayne Blvd., 19th Fl.
Miami, FL 33132
Tel.: 305-371-3592
S.I.C.: 6798
Ken Pappas *(Pres.)*

Keyes Management **(1)**
100 No. Biscayne Blvd.
Miami, FL 33132
Tel.: 305-371-3592
S.I.C.: 6722

KEYES MARTIN

KEYES MARTIN
841 Mountain Ave.
Springfield, NJ 07081
Tel.: 201-376-7300
Fax: 201-376-8921
Year Founded: 1946
Approx.Billings: $63,000,000
Emp.: 55
Advertising, Public Relations, Promotions & Direct Mail
Dan Gaby *(Chm. & Chief Exec. Officer)*
Linda Mezo *(Pres. & Chief Oper. Officer)*
Edward F. Stukane *(Exec. V.P.)*
Robert Williams *(Sr. V.P., Chief Fin. Officer)*

KEYES MOTORS, INC.
5855 Van Nuys Blvd.
Van Nuys, CA 91401
Tel.: 818-782-1120
Fax: 818-907-440
Year Founded: 1960
Approx.Sls.: $122,000,000
Emp.: 325
Retail Sales of New & Used Automobiles
S.I.C.: 5511
Howard Keys *(Pres.)*
Larry Abramson *(V.P. & Treas.)*

No. of U.S. Offices: 8

KEYMARK CORPORATION
Rte. 334, Cayadutta St.
Fonda, NY 12068
Tel.: 518-853-3421
Fax: 518-853-3299
Approx.Sls.: $42,000,000
Emp.: 500
Aluminum Extrusions
S.I.C.: 3354; 3442
William L. Keller, III *(Pres.)*
Jack Bethel *(V.P.)*
Gus Bratsis *(V.P.-Engrng.)*
Bob Channell *(V.P.-Mfg.)*
Olga Keller *(V.P.)*

Outside Service Firm(s):

Edgar Leonhardt*(Legal Firm)*
Fonda, NY

Subsidiary:

Kasson & Keller **(1)**
Rte 334, Cayadutta St.
Fonda, NY 12068
Tel.: 518-853-3421
S.I.C.: 3442

KEYSOR CENTURY CORPORATION
26000 Springbrook Ave.
Saugus, CA 91350
Tel.: 805-259-2360
Fax: 805-259-7937
Approx.Sls.: $35,000,000
Emp.: 220
Poly Vinyl Chloride Resins & Compounds; Phonograph Records, Bottles, Profile & Injection Moulding
S.I.C.: 2821; 3087; 3089; 3652; 3085
James B. Keysor *(Chm. Bd.)*
Howard Hill *(Pres.)*
Kenneth Law *(V.P.)*
Everett Scott *(V.P.)*
Wayne Packer *(Controller)*

Outside Service Firm(s):

Price Waterhouse*(Auditors)*
400 S. Hope St.
Los Angeles, CA 90071-2889
Tel.: 213-236-3000

Gibson, Dunn & Crutcher*(Legal Firm)*
333 S. Grand Ave.
Los Angeles, CA 90067
Tel.: 310-552-8500
Fax: 310-277-5827

Wells Fargo Bank*(Major Banking Relationship)*
333 S. Grand
Los Angeles, CA 90071
Tel.: 213-253-6836

KEYSTONE AUTOMOTIVE INDUSTRIES, INC.
700 E. Bonita Ave.
Pomona, CA 91767
Tel.: 909-624-8041
Tel.: 909-621-2926 **CA**
Fax: 909-624-9136
Year Founded: 1947
Approx.Sls.: $73,000,000
Emp.: 525
Import
Mfr. of Automotive Crash Parts & Bumpers; Auto Parts Locations
S.I.C.: 3714
Virgil K. Benton *(Chm. Bd.)*
Virgil Benton II *(Vice Chm. & Treas.)*
Charles J. Hogarty *(Pres.)*
Al Ronco *(Chief Oper. Officer, Exec. V.P., & Sec.)*
Robert L. Blanton *(V.P.-Fin. & Asst. Treas.)*
Larry Bussard *(Dir.-Natl. Branch Computer Opers.)*
Lisa Glenn *(Dir.- Import)*
Scott Hadden *(Dir.-Purch.)*
Christopher Northup *(Dir.-Mktg.)*
Evelyn Pippen *(Dir.- Benefits)*
Art Lowe *(Coordr.-Admin. Training)*
Rick Livermore *(Sr. Staff Accountant)*

Outside Service Firm(s):

Ernst & Young*(Auditors)*
515 S. Flower St.
Los Angeles, CA 90071
Tel.: 213-621-1666

Union Bank*(Major Banking Relationship)*
City of Industry, CA

Branches:

Keystone Automotive Industries, Inc. - Ontario **(1)**
610 East State St.
Ontario, CA 91761
Tel.: 909-986-4586
Fax: 909-986-5643
Leo Sweeney *(Gen. Mgr.)*

Keystone Automotive Industries, Inc. - San Diego **(1)**
11 30th Street
San Diego, CA 92102
Tel.: 619-232-7555
Fax: 619-232-3712
Virgil Benton II *(Gen. Mgr.)*

Keystone Automotive Industries, Inc. - Chicago **(1)**
3301 West 47th Place
Chicago, IL 60632
Tel.: 312-927-9600
Fax: 312-927-9376
Ted Geinosky *(Gen. Mgr.)*
Joe Fandl *(Sls. Mgr.)*

Keystone Automotive Industries, Inc.—(Continued)

Keystone Automotive Industries, Inc. - Roseville **(1)**
2980 N. Cleveland Ave.
Roseville, MN 55113
Tel.: 612-636-4040
Fax: 619-636-8810
Pat Parchem *(Gen. Mgr.)*

Keystone Automotive Industries, Inc. - St. Louis **(1)**
3615 Forest Park Blvd.
Saint Louis, MO 63108
Tel.: 314-371-2983
Fax: 314-371-2848
Michael J. Diggs *(Gen. Mgr.)*

Keystone Automotive Industries, Inc. - Brooklyn Hts. **(1)**
1277 East Schaaf Rd.
Brooklyn Heights Village, OH 44131
Tel.: 216-398-7788
Fax: 216-398-6445
Mike Gittings *(Gen. Mgr.)*

Keystone Automotive Industries, Inc. - Newark **(1)**
24 Legal Street
Newark, NJ 07114
Tel.: 201-824-8381
Fax: 201-824-0529
John Ronco *(Gen. Mgr.)*
Victor Villalta *(Mgr.-Production)*

Keystone Automotive Industries, Inc. - Palmyra **(1)**
P.O. Box 52, Market at Jefferson Street
Palmyra, NJ 08065
Tel.: 609-829-4700
Fax: 609-829-4700
Joe Mizzi *(Gen. Mgr.)*

Keystone Automotive Industries, Inc. - Linthicum **(1)**
822 Central Ave.
Linthicum Heights, MD 21090
Tel.: 410-636-4600
Fax: 410-636-4701
Dan Morrissey *(Gen. Mgr.)*
Lowell Bell *(Mgr.-Sls.)*
Ted Smith *(Mgr.-Service)*
Al Tribbitt *(Mgr.-Production)*

Keystone Automotive Industries, Inc. - Bethlehem **(1)**
R.D. #3, Route 378
Bethlehem, PA 18015
Tel.: 215-865-5553
Fax: 215-865-2722
Dennis Kolumber *(Gen. Mgr.)*

Keystone Automotive Industries, Inc. - York **(1)**
1000 Roosevelt Ave.
York, PA 17404
Tel.: 717-843-8927
Fax: 717-845-1042
Fred Schmidt *(Gen. Mgr.)*

Keystone Automotive Industries, Inc. - Milford **(1)**
125 Furniture Row
Milford, CT 06460
Tel.: 203-878-5550
Fax: 203-877-2404
Tony Ratzing *(Gen. Mgr.)*

Keystone Automotive Industries, Inc. - W. Palm **(1)**
940 West 13th St.
West Palm Beach, FL 33404
Tel.: 407-845-3700
Fax: 407-845-3785
John Arenovski *(Gen. Mgr.)*

Keystone Automotive Industries, Inc. - Dallas **(1)**
4949 Sharp St., Suite 104
Dallas, TX 75247
Tel.: 214-634-0161
Fax: 214-905-0867
Wayne Spence *(Gen. Mgr.)*

Keystone Automotive Industries, Inc. - Newburgh **(1)**
5 Jeanne Dr.
Newburgh, NY 12550
Tel.: 914-566-0900
Fax: 914-566-0992
Denis Flannigan *(Gen. Mgr.)*

Keystone Automotive Industries, Inc. - Albany **(1)**
1 Selina Drive
Albany, NY 12205
Tel.: 518-452-7730
Fax: 518-452-7855
Gary Thompson *(Gen. Mgr.)*

Keystone Automotive Industries, Inc.- Tijuana **(1)**
Paseo Reforma #123 Fracc. Urias, LaMesa,
Tijuana, Mexico
Tel.: 11-52-66 89-34-40
Rene Armando Lafon *(Gen. Mgr.)*

Keystone Automotive Industries, Inc.- Louisville **(1)**
1214 Spring Street
New Albany, IN 47150
Tel.: 812-948-2329
Fax: 812-948-2330
Gene Williams *(Gen. Mgr.)*

Keystone Automotive Industries, Inc.- Little Rock **(1)**
6100 Forbing Rd.
Little Rock, AR 72219
Tel.: 501-562-7157
Fax: 501-562-2569
Sam Bates *(Gen. Mgr.)*

Keystone Automotive Industries, Inc.- Jackson **(1)**
325 S. Farish St.
Jackson, MS 39201
Tel.: 601-355-9544
Fax: 601-353-1855
Sara Crosby *(Gen. Mgr.)*

Keystone Automotive Industries, Inc.- Huntsville **(1)**
617 Meridian
Huntsville, AL 35801
Tel.: 205-533-1050
Fax: 205-536-3394
Sue Cartier *(Gen Mgr.)*

Keystone Automotive Industries, Inc.- Macon **(1)**
895 Third Street
Macon, GA 31201
Fax: 912-745-5790
Bill Smith *(Gen. Mgr.)*

Keystone Automotive Industries, Inc- Jacksonville **(1)**
4227 Clinton Ave.
Jacksonville, FL 32207
Tel.: 904-730-7501
Fax: 904-730-2106
Matthew McGill *(Gen. Mgr.)*

Keystone Automotive Industries, Inc.- Orlando **(1)**
Suite D2, 3320 Vineland Rd.
Orlando, FL 32811
Tel.: 407-425-7531
Fax: 407-425-5907
Al Ortiz *(Gen. Mgr.)*

Keystone Buffalo Warehouse - Buffalo **(1)**
485 Ludwig Ave.
Buffalo, NY 14227
Tel.: 716-894-6262
Fax: 716-894-8269
Jim Grawe *(Gen. Mgr.)*

Keystone Crash Parts Mart - Old Forge **(1)**
433 Lawrence St.
Old Forge, PA 18518
Tel.: 717-457-6464
Fax: 717-457-6957
Frank Scavo *(Gen. Mgr.)*

Keystone Crash Parts Mart - West Springfield **(1)**
93 Craig Drive
West Springfield, MA 01089
Tel.: 413-731-7863
Fax: 413-731-7505
Doug Roberts *(Operating Mgr.)*

Keystone Crash Parts Mart - Indianapolis **(1)**
4145 N. Keystone Ave.
Indianapolis, IN 46205
Tel.: 317-545-2145
Fax: 317-547-7024
Mary Taylor *(Operating Mgr.)*

Keystone Crash Parts Mart - North Syracuse **(1)**
731 W. Genessee St.
Syracuse, NY 13204
Tel.: 315-478-6011
Fax: 315-478-1404
Roger Giuseppetti II *(Operating Mgr.)*

Keystone Crash Parts Mart - Rochester **(1)**
961 Lyell Ave.
Rochester, NY 14606
Tel.: 716-458-0850
Fax: 716-458-0048
Richard Lanich *(Operating Mgr.)*

Keystone Crash Parts Mart - Bedford **(1)**
548 Donald St., Unit 7
Bedford, NH 03102
Tel.: 603-626-4400
Fax: 603-626-4404
Jeff Smith *(Gen. Mgr.)*

Keystone Crash Parts Mart - Wilmington **(1)**
214 East Lea Blvd.
Wilmington, DE 19802
Tel.: 302-764-8010
Fax: 302-764-8033
Marty Grzybowski *(Gen. Mgr.)*

Keystone Master Warehouse - Chicago **(1)**
3327 West 47th Place
Chicago, IL 60632
Tel.: 312-523-0096
Fax: 312-523-0392
Greg Behncke *(Gen. Mgr.)*

Keystone Midwest Warehouse - Chicago **(1)**
3301 West 47th Place
Chicago, IL 60632
Tel.: 312-523-0354
Fax: 312-523-2385
Ivan Cofre *(Gen. Mgr.)*

Keystone New England Warehouse - Norwood **(1)**
117 Lenox St.
Norwood, MA 02062
Tel.: 617-551-0556
Fax: 617-762-7590
Mike Koren *(Gen. Mgr.)*
William Powers *(Mgr.- Warehouse Opers.)*
Brian Duffy *(Mgr.-Sls.)*
Lawrence Barnes *(Mgr.- Depot)*

Keystone Northeast Warehouse - Bethlehem **(1)**
R.D. #3, Route 378
Bethlehem, PA 18015
Tel.: 215-866-0313
Fax: 215-868-5544
Doug Hurley *(Gen. Mgr.)*
Ron Kutos *(Asst. Mgr.)*

Keystone Northern California Warehouse - Benicia **(1)**
3919 Oregon St.
Benicia, CA 94510
Tel.: 707-745-6911
Fax: 707-745-6917
Pete Gonsalves *(Gen. Mgr.)*

Keystone Recycling Center - Chicago **(1)**
3327 West 47th Place
Chicago, IL 60632
Tel.: 312-523-0096
Fax: 312-523-0392
Greg Behneke *(Gen. Mgr.)*

Keystone Southern Warehouse - Atlanta **(1)**
777 A Wharton Dr.
Atlanta, GA 30336
Tel.: 404-691-6930
Fax: 404-691-4005
John Meyne *(Gen. Mgr.)*

KEYSTONE CARBON COMPANY
1935 State St.
Saint Marys, PA 15857-0313
Tel.: 814-781-1591
Telex: 91-4517
Fax: 814-781-7648
Year Founded: 1927
Approx.Sls.: $105,000,000
Emp.: 1,500
Fiscal Year-end: 12/31/90
Export
Powder Metal Parts, NTC and PTC Thermistors
S.I.C.: 3399; 3823
Richard Reuscher *(Pres.)*
Eugene H. Gleixner *(V.P.-Engrng. Res.)*
Robert B. Reuscher *(V.P.-Opers.)*
Everett D. Shea, Jr. *(V.P.-Mktg. & Sls.)*
Conrad J. Kogovsek *(Treas.)*
William Reuscher *(Sec.)*
M.F. Nissel *(Mgr.-Sls.)*
Thomas H. Wright *(Mgr.-Pur.)*

Outside Service Firm(s):

Mellon Financial Services*(Major Banking Relationship)*
Four Station Square, Third Floor
Pittsburgh, PA 15219-1173
Tel.: 412-566-1313

Divisions:

P/M Bearing Div. **(1)**
Sunbeam Indus. Park
Cherryville, NC 28021
Tel.: 704-435-4036
Fax: 704-435-8132
Mfr. of Bearings
S.I.C.: 3568
Dick Buchhait *(Gen. Mgr.)*

P/M Structural Parts Div. **(1)**
2100 Advance Ave.
Columbus, OH 43207
Tel.: 614-443-9488
Fax: 614-445-6363
S.I.C.: 3399
Tom Gaul *(Gen. Mgr.)*

PTC Thermistor Div. **(1)**
Drawer 1
Mount Jewett, PA 16704
Tel.: 814-778-9941
Mfr. of Electronic Devices (PTC)
S.I.C.: 3823
Tom Muroski *(Gen. Mgr.)*

Joint Venture:

TRW-Keystone Powder Metal Products Co. **(1)**
Sunbeam Industrial Park
Cherryville, NC 28021
Tel.: 704-435-4036
Fax: 704-435-8132
Joint Venture of Keystone Carbon & TRW, Inc.; Mfr. of Valve Seats
S.I.C.: 3592
Dick Buchhalt *(Gen. Mgr.)*

KEYSTONE COFFEE
3870 Charter Park Dr.
San Jose, CA 95136
Tel.: 408-998-2221
Fax: 408-286-7054
Approx.Sls.: $21,000,000
Emp.: 55
Fiscal Year-end: 12/31/90
Wholesale Institutional Supplier of Coffee
S.I.C.: 5149
Tim Wright *(Pres.)*
Kim Moore *(Gen. Mgr.)*

KEYSTONE FOODS CORPORATION
401 City Ave., Ste. 800
Bala-Cynwyd, PA 19004
Tel.: 215-667-6700
Fax: 215-667-1460
Approx.Sls.: $700,000,000
Emp.: 1,400
Produces Cryogenically Frozed 100% Pure Beef Hamburger Patties; Poultry Products; Distributes Food & Operating Supplies To Fast Food Restaurants
S.I.C.: 2013; 2038; 5113; 5142; 5144
Herbert Lotman *(Chm. Bd.)*
Steve Calvert *(Pres.)*
Hector A. Coats *(Sr. V.P.)*
Jack Conway *(Sr. V.P. & Controller)*
Edward L. Silverberg *(Sr. V.P.)*
John Grabowski *(V.P.)*

Outside Service Firm(s):

Ernst & Young*(Auditors)*
1800 John F. Kennedy Blvd.
Philadelphia, PA 19103-7499
Tel.: 215-864-3300

Pelino & Lentz, P.C.*(Legal Firm)*
Packard Bldg.
Philadelphia, PA 19102
Tel.: 215-665-1540

CoreStates First Pennsylvania Bank, N.A.*(Major Banking Relationship)*
Center Sq. West Tower, 15th & Market Streets
Philadelphia, PA 19101

Subsidiary:

M & M Restaurant Supply **(1)**
3581 Dayton Park Dr.
Dayton, OH 45414
Tel.: 513-233-6502
Fax: 513-233-7458
Wholesale Groceries
S.I.C.: 5141
Herb Lotman *(Pres.)*
Jules Freeze *(Gen. Mgr.)*

KEYWELL CORPORATION
(Formerly Samuel G. Keywell Company)
3075 Lonyo St.
Detroit, MI 48209
Tel.: 313-841-6800
Fax: 313-841-3843
Holding Company
S.I.C.: 6719
Joel D. Tauber *(Chm. Bd.)*
Richard Odle *(Pres.)*
Jack Forebaugh *(Sr. V.P.)*
Barry Hunter *(Sr. V.P.)*
Mark Lozier *(Sr. V.P.)*
Arnold Plante *(Sr. V.P.)*
Michael Rosenberg *(Sr. V.P.)*
Daniel Weinstein *(Sr. V.P.)*

Outside Service Firm(s):

Ameritrust Company, N.A.*(Major Banking Relationship)*
Ashtabula, OH

Subsidiary:

Samuel G. Keywell Co. **(1)**
7600 Rolling Mill Rd.
Baltimore, MD 21224
Tel.: 410-282-9500
Fax: 410-282-9752
Approx.Sls.: $118,000,000
Emp.: 313
Wholesale Scrap Metals
S.I.C.: 5093
Morton B. Plant *(Pres.)*
Arnold I. Plant *(V.P.)*

Samuel G. Keywell Co. **(1)**
890 Noble Dr.
West Mifflin, PA 15122
Tel.: 412-462-5555
S.I.C.: 5093
Richard Odle *(Pres.)*

Samuel G. Keywell Co. **(1)**
11900 S. Cottage Grove Ave.
Chicago, IL 60628
Tel.: 312-660-2060
S.I.C.: 5093
Michael Rosenberg *(Sr. V.P.)*

KIDVERTISER
270 Lafayette St.
New York, NY 10012
Tel.: 212-966-2345
Fax: 212-966-2770
Year Founded: 1989
Approx.Billings: $10,500,000
Emp.: 8
Children's & Family Directed Prods.
Deyna Vesey *(Co-Pres., Creative Dir. & New Bus. Contact)*
Diane Simon *(Gen. Mgr., Traffic)*
Gail Lee *(Fin.)*

Computer Systems/Hardware:
Macintosh

PETER KIEWIT SONS INC.
1000 Kiewit Plaza
Omaha, NE 68131
Tel.: 402-342-2052 **DE**
Fax: 402-271-2829
Year Founded: 1884
Approx.Rev.: $3,356,000,000
Emp.: 43,600
Fiscal Year-end: 12/30/91
Holding Company; Construction Contracting, Mining
S.I.C.: 1541; 1611; 1622; 1623; 1221; 1241; 1081; 1542; 1629; 6719; 1222
Walter Scott, Jr. *(Chm. Bd. & Pres.)*
William L. Grewcock *(Vice Chm.)*
Donald L. Sturm *(Vice Chm.)*
Charles H. Campbell *(Exec. V.P.)*
Robert E. Julian *(V.P.-Fin. & Admin.)*
James O. Spitzenberger *(V.P.)*
Kenneth E. Stinson *(V.P.)*
Thomas C. Stortz *(V.P.-Real Estate)*
Raul Pupo *(V.P.-Mgmnt. Info. Systems)*
Frank Yelick *(V.P. & Controller)*
George F. Heiden *(V.P. & Gen. Counsel)*
Brad Chapman *(Dir.-Human Resources Devel.)*
Steven C. Beyer *(Pur. Agent)*

No. of Mfg. Plants/Facilities: 150
No. of U.S. Offices: 50
No. of Foreign Offices: 25

Computer Systems/Hardware:
IBM 383 BX-2

Outside Service Firm(s):

KPMG Peat Marwick*(Auditors)*
Two Central Park Plaza,
Omaha, NE 68102
Tel.: 402-348-1450

Aetna Life & Casualty*(Group Insurer)*
151 Farmington Avenue
Hartford, CT 06156
Tel.: 203-273-2128
Fax: 203-729-4295

Goldman, Sachs & Co.*(Investment Banker)*
85 Broad St.
New York, NY 10004
Tel.: 212-902-1000
Fax: 212-902-4451

Salomon Brothers*(Investment Banker)*
7 World Trade Center
New York, NY 10048
Tel.: 212-783-7000

First Chicago Shareholder Services Trust Co.*(Major Banking Relationship)*
153 West 51st St.
New York, NY 10019
Tel.: 212-791-6422
Fax: 212-385-9798

FirsTier Bank*(Major Banking Relationship)*
Omaha, NE

United Benefit Life*(Pension Manager)*
Omaha, NE

Subsidiaries:

Kiewit Construction Group, Inc. **(1)**
1000 Kiewit Plaza
Omaha, NE 68131
Tel.: 402-342-2052 (100%)
Construction Contracting
S.I.C.: 1541; 1542; 1611; 1622; 1623; 1629
William Grewcock *(Chief Oper. Officer)*

Kiewit Mining Group, Inc. **(1)**
1000 Kiewit Plaza
Omaha, NE 68131
Tel.: 402-342-2052 (100%)
Bituminous Coal, Metals & Minerals Mining
S.I.C.: 1221; 1222; 1241; 1081
William Grewcock *(Chm.)*

KIFUKI U.S.A. CO., INC.
15547 First St.
Irwindale, CA 91706

Subsidiary:

Henningsen Foods, Inc. **(1)**
2 Corporate Park Dr.
White Plains, NY 10604
Tel.: 914-694-1000
Fax: 914-694-1221
Approx.Sls.: $40,000,000
Emp.: 260
Export
Computer Systems/Hardware:
IBM System 36
Dehydrated Food Products; Custom Dehydration
S.I.C.: 2015; 2034
Victor W. Henningsen, Jr. *(Chm.)*
Gilbert B. Eckhoff *(Pres. & Chief Exec. Officer)*
William E. Dumke *(V.P.-Fin. & Chief Fin. Officer)*
Michael H. Cruger *(V.P.-Oper. & Controller)*
Christopher K. Henningsen *(V.P.-Sls.)*
Michael Nolan *(V.P.)*
Masami Ohi *(V.P.-Corp. Plng.)*
Michael R. Paturzo *(Treas. & Sec.)*
Barbara Liberatore *(Mgr.-Data Processing)*
Dale L. Petersen *(Pur. Agent)*

Division:

Henningsen Foods, Inc. **(2)**
14334 Industrial Rd.
Omaha, NE 68137
Tel.: 402-330-2500
District Sales Offices
S.I.C.: 5144; 5149
Gary D. Lorimar *(V.P.-Engrg.)*
John Toney *(V.P.-Research)*

Plant:

Henningsen Foods, Inc. **(2)**
325 3rd St.
David City, NE 68632
Tel.: 402-367-3141
Dehydrated Food Products; Also Located at Norfolk & Ravenna, NE; Waalwijk, The Netherlands
S.I.C.: 2015; 2034
Jim Rountree *(Gen. Mgr.)*

Non-U.S. Subsidiaries:

Henningsen Foods Ltd. **(2)**
"Lumeah" Perranwell Station Nr. Truro, Cornwall, TR3 7NJ, United Kingdom
Tel.: 0872-862070
Emp.: 2
Liaison Customer Service
S.I.C.: 7389
Roy Dick *(Chief Oper. Officer)*

Henningsen Nederland B.V. **(2)**
Slvisweg 20 5145 PE,
Waalwijk, Netherlands
Tel.: 04160-50333 (75%)
Approx.Sls.: $3,500,000
Emp.: 12
Dehydrated Meat Prods.
S.I.C.: 2013
Albert van de Donck *(Mng. Dir.)*

Q.P. Corporation **(2)**
Tokyo, Japan

Joint Venture:

Henningsen-Van den Burg **(2)**
Slvisweg 20 5145 PE,
Waalwijk, Netherlands
Tel.: 04160-37911 (50%)
Telex: 2017
Approx.Sls.: $5,000,000
Emp.: 15
Joint Venture with Van den Burg Erprodukten B.V.; Process Powdered Egg Products
S.I.C.: 2015
Bert Wouters *(Mng. Dir.)*

L. ROBERT KIMBALL & ASSOCIATES
615 W. Highland Ave.
Ebensburg, PA 15931
Tel.: 814-472-7700
Fax: 814-472-7712
Year Founded: 1953
Approx.Sls.: $30,000,000
Emp.: 550
Engineering, Architecture, Automated Design, Data Processing, Mapping, Photogrammetry, Surveying, Earth & Foundation Drilling, Environmental & Soils Testing, Automated Property Valuation
S.I.C.: 8711; 8712; 8713; 6531; 1499
L. Robert Kimball *(Pres. & Treas.)*
Gerard L. Delahanty *(Pres.-Horsham Div.)*
R. Jeffrey Kimball *(Exec. V.P.)*
Csaba S. Balazs *(Sr. V.P.-Architecture)*
Richard E. Genday *(Sr. V.P.-Engrng. Grp.)*
James T. Hockensmith *(Sr. V.P.-Environmental Services)*
John R. Kimball *(Sr. V.P.-Mktg.)*
James L. Morgan *(Sr. V.P.-Surveying & Mapping)*
G. William Myers *(Sr. V.P. & Legal Counsel)*
Daniel S. Gilligan *(V.P.-Pennsylvania)*
R. Handler *(V.P.-Mass Appraisal)*
James A. Haney, Jr. *(V.P.-Program Management)*
Richard L. Heaton *(V.P.-Communications)*
Gerald A. Kabala *(V.P.-N. Carolina)*
Joseph F. Moon, Jr. *(V.P.-Pittsburgh Div.)*
John C. Pierchoski *(V.P.-Structures & Hydraulics)*
Raymond F. Kuzemchak *(Controller)*
K. Maul *(Dir.-Personnel)*

No. of U.S. Offices: 9

Outside Service Firm(s):

Deloitte & Touche*(Auditors)*
2400 One PPG Place
Pittsburgh, PA 15222
Tel.: 412-281-2232

Equibank*(Major Banking Relationship)*
Two Oliver Plz.
Pittsburgh, PA 15222
Tel.: 412-288-5000

KIMRAY, INC.
52 N.W. 42nd
Oklahoma City, OK 73118
Mailing Address:
P.O. Box 18255
Oklahoma City, OK 73154
Tel.: 405-525-6601 **OK**
Fax: 405-525-7520
Year Founded: 1948
Approx.Sls.: $25,000,000
Emp.: 250
Export
Mfr. of Oil Field Machinery & Equipment; Gray Iron Castings; Ductile Iron Castings
S.I.C.: 3533; 3321
Garman O. Kimmell *(Pres.)*
Thomas A. Hill *(Exec. V.P.)*
Larry McAtee *(Treas.)*
Tom McCormick *(Mgr.-Mktg.)*

Kimray, Inc.—(Continued)

Outside Service Firm(s):

Bank of Oklahoma*(Major Banking Relationship)*
201 Robert S. Kerr Ave.
Oklahoma City, OK 73102
Tel.: 918-588-6000

KIMSTOCK, INC.
2200 S. Yale St.
Santa Ana, CA 92704
Tel.: 714-546-6850 **CA**
Fax: 714-557-7592
Year Founded: 1957
Approx.Sls.: $35,000,000
Emp.: 450
Fiberglass Tubs, Showers, Doors, Mirrors & Spas
S.I.C.: 3088; 3089; 3231
Arthur W. Fuzak *(Pres.)*
Roger Lynch *(Exec. V.P.)*
Gloria McMillan *(V.P.-Sls. & Mktg.)*
David Miller *(Pur. Agent)*

No. of Mfg. Plants/Facilities: 3
No. of U.S. Offices: 3

Outside Service Firm(s):

Arthur Andersen & Co.*(Auditors)*
18500 Von Karman Ave., Ste. 1100
Irvine, CA 92715
Tel.: 714-757-3100

Security Pacific National Bank*(Major Banking Relationship)*
Santa Ana, CA

Division:

Kimglass Division **(1)**
2200 S. Yale St.
Santa Ana, CA 92704
Tel.: 714-546-6850
Mfr. Fiberglass & Acrylic Tubs & Enclosures
S.I.C.: 3088
Roland Sundquist *(Gen. Mgr.)*

Subsidiary:

Kimstock Inc. **(1)**
20th & Michigan Ave.
Cleveland, TN 37311
Tel.: 615-476-6632

KINDEL FURNITURE COMPANY
100 Garden S.E.
Grand Rapids, MI 49507
Mailing Address:
P.O. Box 2047
Grand Rapids, MI 49501
Tel.: 616-243-3676
Fax: 616-243-6248
Sales Range: $10-19 Million
Emp.: 240
Manufacture Traditional Bedroom & Dining Room Furniture; Upholstered Furniture
S.I.C.: 2511; 2512
Robert S. Fogarty, Jr. *(Chm. Bd. & Pres.)*
Jon P. Graber *(Exec. V.P.)*
John W. Fisher *(V.P.)*
Bob Colleen *(Dir.-Adv. Design)*

Computer Systems/Hardware:
IBM

Outside Service Firm(s):

Great-West Life Assurance Co.*(Group Insurer)*
8505 East Orchard Rd.
Englewood, CO 8011
Tel.: 800-537-2033

Old Kent Bank*(Major Banking Relationship)*
Grand Rapids, MI

KINETIC SYSTEMS CORPORATION
11 Maryknoll Dr.
Lockport, IL 60441
Tel.: 815-838-0005
Tel.: 800-DATA-NOW
Telex: 910-638-2831
Fax: 815-838-4424
Year Founded: 1970
Approx.Sls.: $11,000,000
Emp.: 120
Fiscal Year-end: 9/30/91
Export
Manufactures Electronic Data Acquisition & Process Control Systems
S.I.C.: 3823; 3577
James M. Stephenson, Jr. *(Chm. Bd. & Pres.)*
Robert F. Filotto *(Chief Oper. Officer, V.P., & Controller)*
Robert T. Cleary *(Exec. V.P.)*
Wilmer C. Martin *(V.P.-Prod. & Opers. & Real Estate Officer)*
Roderick H. Wischermann *(V.P.-Mktg. & Intl.)*
Norman Ellison *(Dir.-Sls.)*
C.L. Thomas *(Dir.-Data Processing)*

No. of Mfg. Plants/Facilities: 2
No. of U.S. Offices: 4
No. of Foreign Offices: 2

Computer Systems/Hardware:
Digital, H-P, Concurrent, IBM PC, Convex

Outside Service Firm(s):

McGladrey & Pullen*(Auditors)*
Joliet, IL

Baker & McKenzie*(Legal Firm)*
One Prudential Plaza, 130 E. Randolph
Chicago, IL 60601-7026
Tel.: 312-861-8000

LaSalle National Bank*(Major Banking Relationship)*
135 S. LaSalle St.
Chicago, IL 60603
Tel.: 312-443-2440
Fax: 312-443-2819

Subsidiary:

Phoenix Data Incorporated **(1)**
3384 W. Osborn Rd.
Phoenix, AZ 85017
Tel.: 602-278-8528
Fax: 602-278-8679
Approx.Sls.: $4,000,000
Emp.: 50
Mfr. Electronics, High Speed Data Acquisition Systems
S.I.C.: 3823
Lloyd Kaiser *(Pres.)*
Chris Kokias *(V.P.-Mktg.)*
H. Mills *(Pur. Agent)*

VICTOR KING ADVERTISING

1000 Centerville Turnpike
Virginia Beach, VA 23463
Tel.: 804-523-7000
Fax: 804-523-7851
Year Founded: 1972
Approx.Billings: $22,563,000
Emp.: 40
David Hummel *(Pres.)*
Van Mylar *(Syndication Mgr.)*
Maria McMillan *(Acct. Expeditor)*
Janie Creech *(Data Coord.)*

KING BEAR ENTERPRISES, INC.
1390 Jerusalem Ave.
North Merrick, NY 11566
Tel.: 516-483-3500
Approx.Sls.: $10,200,000
Emp.: 14
Auto Franchise & Warehouse; Franchise Co. Selling Franchises
S.I.C.: 6794
Jerry Kolopsky *(Chm. Bd., Pres. & Adv. Dir.)*
A. L. Blaker *(Sec., Treas. & Mktg. Dir.)*

Subsidiary:

King Bear Auto Centers **(1)**
4603 Manhattan Beach Blvd.
Lawndale, CA 90260
Tel.: 310-643-7100

THE KING COMPANY
1001 21st Ave., N. W
Owatonna, MN 55060
Mailing Address:
P.O. Box 287
Owatonna, MN 55060
Tel.: 507-451-3770
Fax: 507-455-7400
Approx.Sls.: $17,500,000
Emp.: 250
Fiscal Year-end: 4/30/91
King Ventilating, Heating, Drying Equipment, King Air Kurtains, King Refrigerated Air Systems, Plate Fin Coils, Custom HVAC
S.I.C.: 3564; 3433; 3552
Jerry Jungquist *(Acting Pres. & Chief Exec. Officer)*

KING FUELS INC.
(Formerly King Service Inc.)
Foot Of Main St.
Troy, NY 12181
Mailing Address:
P.O. Box 838,
Troy, NY 12180
Tel.: 518-274-4200
Fax: 518-274-0582
Approx.Sls.: $56,000,000
Emp.: 275
Wholesale & Retail Fuel Oil, Gasoline & Diesel Oil; Burner Services; Retail Groceries
S.I.C.: 5172; 5411; 5541; 5983; 7699
Edwin D. King *(Pres.)*
Everett G. King *(V.P.)*
Lawrence E. King *(Treas.)*
Richard B. Slote *(Sec.)*

KING GROUP, INC.
1139 Pennway Circle
Fenton, MI 48430
Mailing Address:
P.O. Box 169,
Fenton, MI 48430
Tel.: 313-629-5464 **MI**
Fax: 313-663-4264
Approx.Sls.: $45,000,000
Emp.: 100
Wholesale Tobacco & Confectioneries; Retail Gifts, Novelties; Computer Related Services
S.I.C.: 5122; 7379; 5947
Jack Sharpe *(Pres.)*
Richard Augustyn *(V.P.-Mktg. & Sls.)*
Leslie George, Sr. *(V.P.)*
Leslie George, Jr. *(Treas. & Sec.)*
Principal(s):
Leslie George, Sr.
Jack Sharpe

No. of Mfg. Plants/Facilities: 2

Computer Systems/Hardware:
Texas Instruments; IBM

Outside Service Firm(s):

Blue Cross & Blue Shield of Michigan*(Group Insurer)*
Detroit, MI

Divisions:

Distributor Concepts **(1)**
2460 S. Industrial Highway
Ann Arbor, MI 48104
Tel.: 313-663-4214
Computer Software
S.I.C.: 7372
Leslie George, Jr. *(Chief Exec. Officer)*

King Michigan Sundries Div. **(1)**
1139 Fenway Circle
Fenton, MI 48430
Tel.: 313-629-5464
Candy, Tobacco & Sundry Wholesale Distribution
S.I.C.: 5122; 5145; 5194
Jack Sharpe *(Gen. Mgr.)*

KING INDUSTRIES, INC.
Science Rd.
Norwalk, CT 06852
Tel.: 203-866-5551
Fax: 203-866-0425
Sales Range: $20-39 Million
Emp.: 135
Rubber, Plasticizers, Corrosion Inhibitors For Chemical Specialties, Industrial Lubricants & Rust Preventives, Paint & Coatings Additives
S.I.C.: 2869; 2851; 2899; 2992
Richard S. King *(Pres.)*
Edward Cherenson *(V.P.-Engrng.)*
Lawrence Gallager *(V.P.-Res. & Devel.)*
William O. King *(Treas.)*
Lavinia K. King *(Sec.)*

Outside Service Firm(s):

W.H. Parr & Company*(Auditors)*
Darien, CT

Union Trust*(Major Banking Relationship)*
637 West Avenue
Norwalk, CT 06856

KING KOIL LICENSING COMPANY INC.
770 Transfer Rd., Ste. 13
Saint Paul, MN 55114
Tel.: 612-646-6882
Fax: 612-646-8864
Approx.Sls.: $80,000,000
Emp.: 20
King Koil Mattresses & Box Springs
S.I.C.: 2515
Ernest L. Friedman *(Pres.)*
Mary Ann Iversen *(Dir.-Mktg. & Adv.)*
Paul K. Sullivan, Jr. *(Mgr.-Natl. Sls.)*

KING KULLEN GROCERY CO., INC.
1194 Prospect Ave.
Westbury, NY 11590
Tel.: 516-333-7100 **NY**
Fax: 516-333-7929
Year Founded: 1930
Assets: $83,861,000
Liabilities: $48,333,000
Net Worth: $35,528,000
Approx.Sls.: $700,000,000
Emp.: 4,500
Fiscal Year-end: 9/27/91
Operates 47 King Kullen Grocery Stores in NY
S.I.C.: 5411
John B. Cullen *(Chm. Bd. & Chief Exec. Officer)*
Bernard Kennedy *(Pres. & Chief Oper. Officer)*
J. Donald Kennedy *(Chief Fin. Officer, V.P.-Fin. & Admin.)*
Jack R. Muratori *(Exec. V.P. & Sec.)*
Rudolph Becht *(V.P.-Sls. & Mdsg.)*
Brian C. Cullen *(V.P.-Leasing)*
Thomas K. Cullen *(V.P.-Govt. & Industry Rels.)*
Joseph Eck *(Treas. & Controller)*
Bernard P. Kennedy *(Gen. Counsel)*
James A. Cullen, Jr. *(Dir.-Real Estate)*
Fran Holmann *(Dir.-Adv.)*
William Leghecza *(Dir.-Data Processing)*
Thomas Nagel *(Dir.-Personnel & Labor Rels.)*
Josephine Bourke *(Mgr.-Office)*

Computer Systems/Hardware:
IBM 4341

Outside Service Firm(s):

Grant Thornton*(Auditors)*
605 Third Ave.
New York, NY 10158
Tel.: 212-599-0100
Fax: 212-370-4520

KING LOUIE INTERNATIONAL, INC.
13500 15th St.
Grandview, MO 64030
Tel.: 816-765-5212
Fax: 816-765-3228
Approx.Sls.: $22,000,000
Emp.: 800
Mfr. Bowling Shirts, Athletic Jackets, Baseball Caps, Other Athletic Apparel
S.I.C.: 2321; 2329; 2331; 2337; 2339; 2353
Robert Palan *(Pres. & Chief Exec. Officer)*
David Lindsay *(V.P.-Mfg.)*
John Payne *(V.P.-Fin.)*
Michael D. Robinson *(V.P. & Sec.)*
Gary Ruhnke *(Dir.-Adv.)*
Nancy Vellinga *(Mgr.-Adv.)*

Computer Systems/Hardware:
Qantel

Outside Service Firm(s):

A. Sheiffer & Co.*(Auditors)*
Westbury, NY

Spencer, Fane, Britt & Browne*(Legal Firm)*
106 W. 14th
Kansas City, MO 64105
Tel.: 816-474-8100

Commercial National Bank of Kansas City*(Major Banking Relationship)*
Kansas City, MO

Mid American Bank & Trust Co.*(Major Banking Relationship)*
Kansas City, MO

KING MILLING COMPANY
115 Broadway
Lowell, MI 49331
Tel.: 616-897-9264 **MI**
Fax: 616-897-4350
Year Founded: 1890
Approx.Sls.: $20,000,000
Emp.: 45
Milling of Wheat Flour
S.I.C.: 2041
King Doyle *(Pres.)*
Roland M. Doyle *(Sr. V.P.-Mfg.)*
Brian Doyle *(V.P., Gen. Mgr, Treas. & Dir.-Sls.)*
James M. Doyle *(V.P.-Grain)*
Donald Osterhouse *(Sec. & Gen. Counsel)*

Outside Service Firm(s):

BDO Seidman*(Auditors)*
99 Monroe Ave. NW, Ste. 800
Grand Rapids, MI 49503
Tel.: 616-774-7000
Fax: 616-451-2096

FMB State Savings Bank*(Major Banking Relationship)*
Lowell, MI

KING PRIME, INC.
P.O. Box 4484
Morgantown, WV 26505
Tel.: 304-599-6253 **WV**
Fax: 304-291-3089
Year Founded: 1978
Approx.Sls.: $12,000,000
Emp.: 55
Wholesale Distribution of Cured or Smoked Meats
S.I.C.: 5147
William C. Brewer *(Pres.)*
Martin Derrico *(Sec.)*

Outside Service Firm(s):

First Bank of Morgantown*(Major Banking Relationship)*
Morgantown, WV

KING & PRINCE SEAFOOD CORPORATION
100 Lanier Blvd.
Brunswick, GA 31520
Mailing Address:
P.O. Box 899,
Brunswick, GA 31521
Tel.: 912-265-5155 (In GA)
Tel.: 800-841-0205 (Outside GA)
Fax: 912-264-4812
Approx.Sls.: $75,000,000
Emp.: 800
Fiscal Year-end: 12/31/90
Import Export
Mfr. of Frozen & Processed Seafood Products
S.I.C.: 5142
J. Roy Duggan *(Chm. Bd.)*
Bob Brubaker *(Pres.)*
Earl Swicord *(Sr. V.P.)*
Dr. Domy Broce *(V.P.-Tech. Services)*
Jim Jarus *(V.P.-Food Service Sls.)*
Richard Lyons *(V.P.-Procurement)*
Hugh Paladino *(V.P.-Mfg.)*
Dennis Sullivan *(V.P.-Fin.)*
John Williams *(V.P.-Mktg.)*
John Adams *(Mgr.-S.E. Distr. Sls.)*
Rich Armstrong *(Mgr.-Natl. Sls.)*
Colonel J. Gaddy *(Mgr.-Data Processing)*
R. Pruett *(Mgr.-Admin. Sls.)*
David Trent *(Mgr.-Human Resouces)*
Don Black *(Chief Engr.)*
Howard Browning *(Pur. Agent)*

Outside Service Firm(s):

KPMG Peat Marwick*(Auditors)*
Brunswick, GA

Gilbert, Whittle, Harrell, Scarlett & Skelton*(Legal Firm)*
Brunswick, GA

Barnett Bank*(Major Banking Relationship)*
Brunswick, GA

KING WIRE & CABLE CORPORATION
179-45 110th Ave.
Jamaica, NY 11433
Tel.: 718-657-4422 **NY**
Fax: 718-739-0027
Year Founded: 1971
Approx.Sls.: $49,000,000
Emp.: 160
Wholesale Distribution of Wire & Cable
S.I.C.: 5063
Robert Dorfman *(Pres.)*
Martin C. Newman *(Exec. V.P.)*
Henry Zeinger *(Treas. & Sec.)*

Outside Service Firm(s):

Goldstein, Goldman, Kessler & Underberg*(Auditors)*
Rochester, NY

Citibank N.A.*(Major Banking Relationship)*
Syosset, NY

KINGFISHER CO-OP ELEVATOR ASSOCIATION
1 Co-Op Way
Kingfisher, OK 73750
Tel.: 405-375-5900 **OK**
Fax: 405-375-5732
Year Founded: 1934
Approx.Sls.: $10,000,000
Emp.: 25
Feed Grain Elevators; Field, Garden & Flower Seeds; Fertilizer & Fertilizer Materials
S.I.C.: 5153; 5191
Perry Castonguay *(Pres.)*
Dennis Smith *(V.P.)*
Doug Fisher *(Gen. Mgr.)*

Outside Service Firm(s):

Kingfisher Bank & Trust Co.*(Major Banking Relationship)*
Kingfisher, OK

E. B. KINGMAN COMPANY
96 Exchange St.
Leominster, MA 01453
Mailing Address:
P. O. Box 208
Leominster, MA 01453
Tel.: 508-534-4996
Fax: 508-537-9120
Approx.Sls.: $15,500,000
Emp.: 250
Fiscal Year-end: 9/30/90
Custom Injected Molded Plastics
S.I.C.: 3089
Samuel Phillips *(Exec. V.P. & Gen. Mgr.)*
J. Joseph Lee *(Mgr.-Opers.)*
Wayne Powers *(Pur. Agent)*
David Burney *(Personnel Mgr.)*

KINGS TOYOTA SUZUKI
(Formerly Kenwood Dealer Group, Inc.)
9500 Kings Automall Rd.
Cincinnati, OH 45249
Tel.: 513-683-5440 **DE**
Fax: 513-683-5244
Sales Range: $60-79 Million
Emp.: 185
Auto Sales, Service & Leasing; Owns & Operates Kenwood Lincoln Mercury, Kings Toyota, Kenmont Dodge, Montgomery Jeep/Eagle, Kings Suzuki, Kings Dodge Dealerships
S.I.C.: 5511; 7514; 7515
Robert C. Reichert *(Pres.)*
G.M. Carmichael *(V.P.)*
J.J. Meirose *(V.P.)*
J.A. Weiss *(V.P.)*
R.K. Whitton *(V.P.)*

Outside Service Firm(s):

Provident Bank*(Major Banking Relationship)*
One East Fourth St.
Cincinnati, OH 45202
Tel.: 513-579-2732

KINGSBRIDGE MEDIA & MARKETING, INC.
6835 Valjean Ave.
Van Nuys, CA 91406
Tel.: 818-989-5760
Twx: 910-495-1793
Fax: 818-989-3850
Year Founded: 1974
Approx.Billings: $11,000,000
Emp.: 20
Retail Television
Frank Robinson *(Pres.)*
Glenda Bogart *(Controller)*

KINGSBURY CORPORATION
80 Laurel St.
Keene, NH 03431
Mailing Address:
P.O. Box 2020
Keene, NH 03431
Tel.: 603-352-5212 **DE**
Telex: RCA 287317
Fax: 603-352-8789
Year Founded: 1928
Assets: $55,000,000
Net Worth: $55,000,000
Approx.Sls.: $100,000,000
Emp.: 450
Fiscal Year-end: 10/ 2/92
Export
Manufacture & Marketing of Special Purpose Machinery
S.I.C.: 3541; 3569; 3559; 3549
Employee Matching Gifts Program: Company Will Match up to $500 Per Employee, Per Institution each Year to a University
Walter Burkart *(Chm. Bd.)*
James L. Koontz *(Pres. & Chief Exec. Officer)*
Richard Whipple *(Exec. V.P.)*
John S. Cookson *(V.P.-Fin., Treas., Chief Fin. Officer, Sec. & Dir.-Investor Rels.)*
Neil P. Coughlin *(V.P.-Sls. & Mktg.)*
Clifford Emery *(V.P. & Gen. Mgr.-Assembly Mktg. Div.)*
James E. O'Neil, Jr. *(V.P.-Mfg.)*
Richard N. Hoehn *(Asst. Sec.)*
Peter F. Mangan *(Controller)*
Peter Gammans *(Dir.-Res. & Devel.)*
William Henderson *(Dir.-Pur.)*
Duncan Stewart *(Dir.-Intl. Sls.)*
Ralph G. Worden *(Dir.-Personnel Training & Devel.)*
Norman Glover *(Mgr.-Customer Service)*
Randolphe G. Lavigne *(Mgr.-Sls. Proposals)*
David N. Spring *(Mgr.-Info. Systems, Corp. Video Systems & Telecommunications)*
Dianne Tisdale *(Exec. Asst. & Travel Coord.)*
Robert Van Valzah *(Mgr.-Adv.)*

No. of Mfg. Plants/Facilities: 4
No. of U.S. Offices: 4
No. of Foreign Offices: 1

Computer Systems/Hardware:
IBM

Outside Service Firm(s):

Ernst & Young*(Auditors)*
2 Wall St.
Manchester, NH
Tel.: 603-625-9601

Rollins Burdick Hunter*(Commercial Insurance Carrier)*
75 Park Plaza
Boston, MA 02116
Tel.: 617-482-9700

Safeco Insurance Co. of America*(Group Insurer)*
Seattle, WA

State Street Bank & Trust Co.*(Investment Banker)*
P.O. Box 366,
Boston, MA 02101
Tel.: 617-426-5523

Choate, Hall & Stewart*(Legal Firm)*
Exchange Place, 53 State St.
Boston, MA 02109
Tel.: 617-227-5020

Citibank N.A.*(Major Banking Relationship)*
Corporate Trust Services, 399 Park Ave.
New York, NY 10043
Tel.: 212-559-1605

N.B.D. Bank, N.A.*(Major Banking Relationship)*
611 Woodward Ave.
Detroit, MI 48226
Tel.: 313-225-1122
Fax: 313-225-3420

State Street Bank & Trust Co.*(Major Banking Relationship)*
P.O. Box 366,
Boston, MA 02101
Tel.: 617-426-5523

Essex Invest. Mgmt. Co.*(Pension Manager)*
Boston, MA

Travelers Insurance Co.*(Pension Manager)*
1 Tower Square
Hartford, CT 06183
Tel.: 203-222-7821
Fax: 203-222-7813

Kingsbury Corporation—(Continued)

Divisions:

Kingsbury Assembly Machine Div. (1)
80 Laurel St.
Keene, NH 03431-2059
Tel.: 603-352-5212
Telex: RCA 287317
Fax: 603-357-2275
Export
Multiple Station Automated, Assembly, Testing Systems
S.I.C.: 3549; 3559; 3569
Clifford D. Emery *(V.P. & G.M.)*
David L. Newton *(Mgr.-Engrng.)*
Peter Austin *(Mgr.-Sls. & Mktg.)*

Kingsbury Machining Center, Div. (1)
80 Laurel St.
Keene, NH 03431-2059
Tel.: 603-352-5212
Telex: RCA 287317
Fax: 603-352-8789
Mfr. CNCY Vertical Machining Centers Bridge Type
S.I.C.: 3541

Kingtool Division (1)
80 Laurel St.
Keene, NH 03431-2059
Tel.: 603-352-5212
Telex: RCA 287317
Export
Remanufacturing of Kingsbury Components & Machinery
S.I.C.: 3541; 3569; 3559; 3549

The Vertical Turning Systems Div. (1)
P.O. Box 2020
Keene, NH 03431
Tel.: 603-352-5212
Metal Working Machines
S.I.C.: 3541
Frederic Way *(V.P.)*

Subsidiaries:

Kingsbury Service Corp. (1)
80 Laurel St., P.O. Box 2020
Keene, NH 03431
Tel.: 603-352-5212
S.I.C.: 7699

Kingsbury World Sales (1)
80 Laurel St., P.O. Box 2020
Keene, NH 03431
Tel.: 603-352-5212
S.I.C.: 5084

Non-U.S. Holdings:

Kingsbury Canada, Inc. (1)
3385 Mainway Dr.
Burlington, ON L7M 1A6, Canada
Tel.: 416-335-6000
Emp.: 300
Mfr. Auto-Body Machinery & Assembly Equipment, including Robotics
S.I.C.: 3549
Richard Hammett *(Pres.)*

KINGSBURY, INC.
10385 Drummond Rd.
Philadelphia, PA 19154
Tel.: 215-824-4000 **DE**
Fax: 215-824-4999
Sales Range: $20-39 Million
Emp.: 250
Export
Thrust Bearings & Related Parts
S.I.C.: 3568
George A. Olsen *(Pres. & Chief Exec. Officer)*
W.S. Chambers *(V.P.-Engrng.)*
Richard S. Gregory *(V.P. & Gen. Mgr.)*
Hewitt Heiserman *(V.P., Treas. & Sec.)*
James R. Prairie *(V.P.-Sls.)*
T.W. Wagner *(V.P.-Mfg.)*

No. of Mfg. Plants/Facilities: 2

Outside Service Firm(s):

Carl J. Santoro & Co.*(Auditors)*
Conshohocken, PA

Stradley, Ronon, Stevens & Young*(Legal Firm)*
2600 Commerce Sq.
Philadelphia, PA 19103
Tel.: 215-564-8000

Philadelphia National Bank*(Major Banking Relationship)*
Philadelphia, PA

KINGSDOWN, INC.
126 West Holt St.
Mebane, NC 27302
Mailing Address:
P.O. Box 388
Mebane, NC 27302
Tel.: 919-563-3531
Fax: 919-563-6730
Year Founded: 1904
Approx.Sls.: $39,000,000
Emp.: 280
Fiscal Year-end: 12/31/91
Export
Kingsdown Matresses: Sleep Sofas Mattresses
S.I.C.: 5021
W. Eric Hinshaw *(Pres.)*
George T. McLamb *(Exec. V.P., Treas. & Chief Fin. Officer)*
Thomas I. McLean *(V.P.-Mktg. & Research)*
William Fulp *(V.P.-Mfg.)*
Kirt Basinger *(V.P.-Sls.)*
Art Bourne *(V.P.-Sls./National Acct.)*
Pat Flippin *(Plant Mgr.)*

KINGSLEY MACHINE CO.
850 Cahuenga Blvd.
Hollywood, CA 90038
Tel.: 213-469-7243
Fax: 213-895-0728
Year Founded: 1930
Emp.: 92
Fiscal Year-end: 8/31/90
Export
Monogramming & Wire Marking Machines
S.I.C.: 3544; 3549; 3555
Michael J. Rawson *(Pres.)*
Norman Friedman *(Sr. V.P.)*
Patty Meier *(Dir.-Personnel)*
Christina Owen *(Mgr.-Adv.)*

Computer Systems/Hardware:
NCR

Outside Service Firm(s):

Anson & Spiegel*(Auditors)*
Los Angeles, CA

KINGSWOOD ADVERTISING, INC.
Cricket Terrace Center
Ardmore, PA 19003
Tel.: 215-896-9260
Tel.: 800-950-3902
Year Founded: 1974
Approx.Billings: $27,500,000
Emp.: 49
Anthony J. Parrotto *(Chm.)*
Richard Moore *(Pres. & Chief Exec. Officer)*
John J. Tucker *(Sr. V.P.)*

KINKO'S CORPORATION
225 W. Stanley Ave.
Ventura, CA 93001
Tel.: 805-652-4000
Fax: 805-652-4142
Year Founded: 1969
Approx.Sls.: $44,000,000
Emp.: 900
Provides Photocopying, Duplicating & Printing Services
S.I.C.: 7334
Paul Orfalea *(Chm. Bd.)*
James Warren *(Pres.)*

KINNEY SYSTEM, INC.
60 Madison Ave., 7th Fl.
New York, NY 10010
Tel.: 212-889-4444
Year Founded: 1945
Sales Range: $100-499 Million
Emp.: 2,500
Parking Lots & Garages
S.I.C.: 7521
Lewis Katz *(Pres. & Chief Exec. Officer)*
Daniel J. Stark *(Exec. V.P.)*
Shelley Boxer *(Exec. V.P. & Chief Fin. Officer)*
Robert A. Rapuano *(V.P. & Corp. Counsel)*

No. of U.S. Offices: 6

Outside Service Firm(s):

Arthur Andersen & Co.*(Auditors)*
1345 Ave. of the Americas
New York, NY 10105
Tel.: 212-708-4000

Chemical Bank*(Major Banking Relationship)*
450 West 33rd St.
New York, NY 10001
Tel.: 212-613-7197
Fax: 212-947-7628

THE KIPLINGER WASHINGTON EDITORS, INC.
1729 H St., N.W
Washington, DC 20006
Tel.: 202-887-6400 **DE**
Fax: 202-833-2431
Year Founded: 1923
Approx.Sls.: $64,000,000
Emp.: 450
Fiscal Year-end: 12/31/90
Publishing - Newsletters & Magazines.
S.I.C.: 2721; 2752
Austin H. Kiplinger *(Chm. Bd.)*
James O. Mayo *(Vice Chm. & Sec.)*
Knight A. Kiplinger *(Pres.)*
Todd L. Kiplinger *(V.P.-Investments)*
Edward R. Sheppard *(V.P.-Opers. & Admin.)*
Corbin M. Wilkes *(V.P.-Fin. & Treas.)*
Tom Eggleston *(Dir.-Circulation)*
Nancy Fisher *(Dir.-Personnel)*
Liz Reilly *(Dir.-Communications)*
Stephen J. Broderick *(Mgr.-Real Estate)*
David Daugherty *(Mgr.-Pension Admin.)*
Anne Wilcox *(Mgr.-Pur.)*
Principal(s):
Austin H. Kiplinger
Knight A. Kiplinger
Todd L. Kiplinger

Outside Service Firm(s):

Councilor, Buchanan & Mitchell*(Auditors)*
Washington, DC

Sanders, Schnabel & Brandenberg*(Legal Firm)*
Washington, DC

Riggs National Bank of Washington, D.C.*(Major Banking Relationship)*
P.O. Box 96206, 1120 Vermont Ave. N.W.
Washington, DC 20090-6206
Tel.: 202-835-4082

Glickenhaus & Co.*(Pension Manager)*
6 East 43rd Street
New York, NY 10017-4641
Tel.: 212-953-7800
Fax: 212-687-9255

Divisions:

Kiplinger Editors (1)
3401 East West Hwy.
Hyattsville, MD 20782
S.I.C.: 2721
Jo Ann Farrell *(Personnel Dir.)*

Kiplinger's Personal Finance Magazine (1)
1729 H St., N.W
Washington, DC 20006
Tel.: 202-887-6400
Fax: 202-331-1206
Emp.: 35
Magazine Publisher
S.I.C.: 2721
Austin H. Kiplinger *(Pres.)*
Knight A. Kiplinger *(Publisher & Editor-in-Chief)*
Theodore J. Miller *(Editor)*
Liz Reilly *(Dir.-Communications)*
Carol Le Petere *(Dir.-Sls.)*

Subsidiaries:

Editors Press, Inc. (1)
3401 East West Hwy.
Hyattsville, MD 20782
Tel.: 202-853-4900
Approx.Sls.: $35,000,000
Emp.: 235
Printing & Binding (Lithography & Rotary Presses)
S.I.C.: 2752; 2789
Kenneth King *(Pres.)*

Fairview Properties, Inc. (1)
1729 H St., N.W.
Washington, DC 20006
Tel.: 202-887-6400

Magazine Services Inc. (1)
15 W. 44th St.
New York, NY 10036
Tel.: 212-398-6320
John T. Abbott *(Pres.)*

Outlook, Incorporated (1)
28 Tidewaters Rd., Henlopen Acres
Rehoboth Beach, DE 19971
Tel.: 302-227-6382

KIPP GROUP
930 Wanamaker Ave.
Ontario, CA 91761
Tel.: 909-983-8081
Fax: 909-983-4393
Approx.Sls.: $12,000,000
Emp.: 135
Manufacture Special Dies & Tools, Die Sets, Jig Fixtures, Industrial Molds, Miscellaneous Plastics Products & Medical Components
S.I.C.: 3544; 3841
Principal(s):
David Kipp
James Kipp

Outside Service Firm(s):

Singer, Lewak, Greenbaum & Goldstein*(Auditors)*
Ontario, CA

First Trust & Savings Bank*(Major Banking Relationship)*
Ontario, CA

KIRBY BUILDING SYSTEMS, INC.
555 Marriott Dr., Ste. 800
Nashville, TN 37210
Mailing Address:
P.O. Box 390,
Portland, TN 37148
Tel.: 615-889-0020 **TN**
Fax: 800-872-6551
Year Founded: 1985
Approx.Sls.: $42,000,000
Emp.: 300
Export
Mfr. & Wholesaler of Pre-Fabricated Buildings
S.I.C.: 3448
George F. King *(Chm. Bd., Pres. & Chief Exec. Officer)*
R.W. Osgood *(Sr. V.P.)*
R.H. Price *(Sr. V.P.)*
Lewis Ellis *(V.P.-Data Processing)*
Jay Pence *(V.P.-Pur.)*
Yates Wright *(V.P.-Sls. & Mktg.)*
Charles Wilcox *(Dir.-Personnel)*

Sharon H. Howard *(Mgr.-Mktg. Services)*
Principal(s):
George F. King

No. of Mfg. Plants/Facilities: 1
No. of U.S. Offices: 15

Computer Systems/Hardware:
Digital

Outside Service Firm(s):

Ernst & Young*(Auditors)*
200 One Commerce Place
Nashville, TN 37239

Willis Corroon*(Commercial Insurance Carrier)*
301 Plus Park Blvd.
Nashville, TN 37217
Tel.: 615-367-9702

Pilot Life*(Group Insurer)*
Nashville, TN

J. C. Bradford & Co., Inc.*(Investment Banker)*
Nashville, TN

Farris, Warfield & Kanaday*(Legal Firm)*
Third Natl. Financial Ctr., 424 Church St., Ste. 1900
Nashville, TN 37219
Tel.: 615-244-5200
Fax: 615-726-3185

WILLIAM J. KIRCHER & ASSOCIATES
1101 14th St., NW, Ste. 900
Washington, DC 20005
Tel.: 202-371-0700
Fax: 202-371-0706
Year Founded: 1963
Approx.Billings: $32,000,000
Emp.: 25
Association Mktg., Trade Shows, Corporate Communications
William J. Kircher *(Chm. Bd., Pres., Creative Dir. & Acct. Supvr.)*
Robert R. Kircher *(Exec. V.P.)*
Robert F. James *(Gen. Mgr.)*

THE KIRK & BLUM MFG. CO.
3120 Forrer St.
Cincinnati, OH 45209
Tel.: 513-351-1400
Fax: 513-351-5475
Approx.Sls.: $47,000,000
Emp.: 600
Manufacture Dust & Fume Control Systems, Industrial Drying & Baking Ovens, Sheet Metal & Steel Plate Fabrication
S.I.C.: 3444; 3441; 3564; 3567
Richard J. Blum *(Pres.)*
L.J. Blum *(V.P.-Production)*
L.B. Kallmeyer *(Treas.)*
R.E. Fibbe *(Sec. & Pur. Agent)*
L.J. Bertoli *(Mgr.-Sls.)*
J.H. Cloran *(Mgr.-Bus. Devel.)*

Computer Systems/Hardware:
Honeywell

Outside Service Firm(s):

Deloitte & Touche*(Auditors)*
Chiquita Center, 250 E. 5th St., Ste. 1900
Cincinnati, OH 45202
Tel.: 513-784-7100

Fifth Third Bank*(Major Banking Relationship)*
Corporate Trust Services, 38 Fountain Square Plaza
Cincinnati, OH 45263

KIRK & MATZ LTD.
95 Golden Hill Rd.
Danbury, CT 06811
Mailing Address:
P.O. Box 68,
Danbury, CT 06813
Tel.: 203-743-4401
Fax: 203-794-1215
Emp.: 25
Manufacturer, Distributor & Importer Cast Brass, Brass Holloware & Silverplated Flatware & Holloware
S.I.C.: 3914
V. Matz *(Pres.)*
M. Grube *(Mgr.-Adv.)*

Computer Systems/Hardware:
Fujitsu

Outside Service Firm(s):

Larson, Durgy & Mellelo*(Auditors)*
Danbury, CT

KIRK-MAYER, INC.
11801 Mississippi Ave.
Los Angeles, CA 90025
Tel.: 310-272-6131 **CA**
Fax: 310-479-7223
Year Founded: 1941
Approx.Sls.: $130,000,000
Emp.: 3,250
Fiscal Year-end: 12/31/91
Engineering & Architecture
S.I.C.: 8711; 8712
Thomas L. Kirk *(Chm. Bd. & Pres. & Chief Exec. Office)*
Michael J. Gordon *(Pres.-KMI Services)*
Bernard Van Rijn *(Chief Fin. Officer, Treas. & Sec.)*
Robert Kiddoo *(Exec. V.P.)*
Carman J. Chapman *(V.P.-Opers.)*
Principal(s):
Thomas L. Kirk

Outside Service Firm(s):

Arthur Andersen & Co.*(Auditors)*
633 W. Fifth St.
Los Angeles, CA 90071
Tel.: 213-614-6500

Bank of America*(Major Banking Relationship)*
701 S. Western Ave.
Los Angeles, CA 91201

KIRKWOOD INDUSTRIES, INC.
4855 W. 130th St.
Cleveland, OH 44135
Tel.: 216-267-6200
Fax: 216-362-3804
Year Founded: 1944
Emp.: 1,298
Export
Manufactures Commutators, Mica Sheet & Plate Products, Carbon Brushes & Contacts Plating, Radio Frequency Instruments & Components
S.I.C.: 3621; 3624; 3299; 3679
Richard W. Klym *(Pres. & Chief Exec. Officer)*
Tom Bauer *(V.P.-Sls.)*
Gregory M. Ensign *(V.P., Sec. & Gen. Counsel)*
L. Thomas Koechley *(Controller)*
Gerard J. Joyce *(Dir.-Human Resources)*
Robert Hynick *(Mgr.-Mngmt. Information Systems)*
Carolyn V. Keller *(Benefits Admin.)*
Janet Kelly *(Pur. Agent)*
Mary Beth Hennessy *(Exec. Asst.)*

Computer Systems/Hardware:
IBM 3800

Outside Service Firm(s):

Price Waterhouse*(Auditors)*
BP America Bldg., 200 Public Square, 27th Floor
Cleveland, OH 44114-2301
Tel.: 216-781-3700

Continental Insurance*(Commercial Insurance Carrier)*
180 Maiden Lane
New York, NY

Kemper Insurance*(Commercial Insurance Carrier)*
Long Grove, IL 60049-0001

CNA Insurance*(Group Insurer)*
Hartford, CT

Calfee, Halter & Griswold*(Legal Firm)*
800 Superior Ave., Ste. 1800
Cleveland, OH 44115-2688
Tel.: 216-622-8200
Fax: 216-241-0816

National City Bank*(Major Banking Relationship)*
P.O. Box 92301, Corp. Trust Dept.
Cleveland, OH 44101
Tel.: 216-575-2000

Society National Bank*(Major Banking Relationship)*
800 Superior Ave.
Cleveland, OH 44114
Tel.: 216-689-5931
Fax: 216-689-3814

New England Mutual Life Insurance Co.*(Pension Manager)*
Boston, MA

Union Mutual Life Insurance Co.*(Pension Manager)*
Portland, ME

Subsidiaries:

Keystone Brush & Contact Co. **(1)**
440 Burgin Danville Rd., P.O. Box 478
Burgin, KY 40310
Tel.: 606-748-5287

Kirkwood Carbon **(1)**
4855 W. 130th St.
Cleveland, OH 44135
Tel.: 216-267-6200

Kirkwood Commutator **(1)**
4855 W. 130th St.
Cleveland, OH 44135
Tel.: 216-267-6200

Kirkwood Foreign Sales Corp. **(1)**
4855 W. 130th St.
Cleveland, OH 44135
Tel.: 216-267-6200

Midwest Mica **(1)**
4855 W. 130th St.
Cleveland, OH 44135
Tel.: 216-267-6200

Toledo Commutator Co. **(1)**
1101 Chestnut
Owosso, MI 48867
Tel.: 517-725-8192
Approx.Sls.: $15,000,000
Emp.: 250
Commutators for Electrical Machinery, Slip Rings, Brush Springs
S.I.C.: 3679
Richard W. Klym *(Pres.)*
J.M. Bruff *(Personnel Mgr.)*
Paul Hanson *(Pur. Agent)*

MORRIS KIRSCHMAN & COMPANY, INC.
5050 Almonaster
New Orleans, LA 70177
Mailing Address:
P.O. Box 3038,
New Orleans, LA 70177
Tel.: 504-947-6673
Fax: 504-942-9468
Approx.Sls.: $30,000,000
Emp.: 220
Retail Furniture, Household Furnishings & Appliances
S.I.C.: 5712; 5722
Victor F. Kirschman *(Chm. Bd.)*
Arnold Kirschman *(Pres.)*
F.L. Benjamin *(V.P.-Pur., Opers., Personnel & Data Processing)*

Outside Service Firm(s):

Bourgeois, Bennett & Thokey*(Auditors)*
New Orleans, LA

Lemie, Kelleher, Kohlmeyer & Matthews*(Legal Firm)*
New Orleans, LA

Whitney National Bank of New Orleans*(Major Banking Relationship)*
P.O. Box 61260
New Orleans, LA 70161
Tel.: 504-586-7422

KIRSHENBAUM & BOND
145 Ave. of the Americas
New York, NY 10013
Tel.: 212-633-0080
Fax: 212-463-8643
Year Founded: 1987
Approx.Billings: $100,000,000
Emp.: 87
Jonathan Bond *(Pres.)*
Michael Rowland *(Sr. V.P. & Supvr.-Mngmt.)*
Nigel Carr *(Dir.-Brand Planning)*
Kerry Ernst *(Dir.-Fin.)*

J. I. KISLAK INC.
7900 Miami Lakes Dr.
Miami Lakes, FL 33016
Mailing Address:
P.O. Box 025409
Miami Lakes, FL 33102
Tel.: 305-364-4100 **FL**
Fax: 305-364-4174
Year Founded: 1906
Approx.Rev.: $40,000,000
Emp.: 725
Holding Company; Mortgage Banker, Loan Brokers, Real Estate Managers & Brokers, Insurance Agency
S.I.C.: 6719; 6162; 6163; 6531; 6411
Jay I. Kislak *(Chm. Bd., Pres. & Chief Exec. Officer)*
Willard B. Soper, II *(Chief Oper. Officer)*
Marvin Schwartzbard *(Exec. V.P.)*
Doris Christie *(Exec. V.P.)*
Jim Gross *(Sr. V.P. & Chief Fin. Officer)*
Eduardo Alvarez *(Sr. V.P. & Dir. Data Processing)*
David Roberts *(Sr. V.P.-Mngmt. Information Services)*
Linda F. Basilick *(Sr. V.P.-Mktg.)*
Howard Brafman *(Gen. Counsel)*
Dwight Smith *(Dir.-Personnel)*

Outside Service Firm(s):

KPMG Peat Marwick*(Auditors)*
One Biscayne Tower, 2 South Biscayne Blvd., Ste.2900
Miami, FL 33131

Greenberg, Traurig, Hoffman, Lipoff, Rosen & Quentel, P.A.*(Legal Firm)*
1221 Brickell Ave.
Miami, FL 33131
Tel.: 305-579-0500

Southeast Bank, N.A.*(Major Banking Relationship)*
One Southeast Financial Center
Miami, FL 33131

Subsidiaries:

J. I. Kislak Agency, Inc. **(1)**
1000 Rt. 9
Woodbridge, NJ 07095
Tel.: 908-750-3000

J. I. Kislak Mortgage Corporation **(1)**
7900 Miami Lakes Dr.
Miami Lakes, FL 33016
Tel.: 305-364-4100

J. I. Mortgage Service Corporation **(1)**
7900 Miami Lakes Dr.
Miami Lakes, FL 33102
Tel.: 305-364-4100

The Kislak Company, Inc. **(1)**
1000 Rt. 9
Woodbridge, NJ 07095
Tel.: 908-750-3000

KISSIMMEE TOYOTA INC.
2535 N. Orange Blossom Trail
Kissimmee, FL 34744
Tel.: 407-870-5511 **FL**
Fax: 407-843-2110
Year Founded: 1980
Approx.Sls.: $30,000,000
Emp.: 60
Automobile Dealership
S.I.C.: 5511
John H. Russell *(Pres.)*
John B. Russell *(Exec. V.P.)*
Terry A. Neff *(Controller)*
James Barber *(Mgr.-New Car Sls.)*
Ken Monhollen *(Mgr.-Service)*
Doug Savage *(Mgr.-Used Car Sls.)*

Outside Service Firm(s):

Barnett Banks Trust Company, N.A.*(Major Banking Relationship)*
Orlando, FL

First Florida Bank*(Major Banking Relationship)*
Orlando, FL

A. C. KISSLING, INC.
140 E. Richmond St.
Philadelphia, PA 19125
Tel.: 215-423-4700
Fax: 215-425-0525
Approx.Sls.: $13,500,000
Emp.: 60
Fiscal Year-end: 12/31/90
Kisslings Sauerkraut; Meats
S.I.C.: 2033; 2035; 2013; 5147
Richard W. Kissling, Sr. *(Pres.)*
Richard W. Kissling, Jr. *(Plant Mgr.)*
Mark Kissling *(Asst. Plant Mgr.)*

KITCHELL CORPORATION
1707 East Highland, Ste. 100
Phoenix, AZ 85016
Tel.: 602-264-4411 **AZ**
Fax: 602-264-6133
Year Founded: 1962
Assets: $55,000,000
Liabilities: $41,000,000
Net Worth: $14,000,000
Approx.Sls.: $148,000,000
Emp.: 285
Fiscal Year-end: 12/31/91
Management Holding Company; Construction & Real Estate Development; Construction Management Services; Program & Project Management for the Public Sector
S.I.C.: 1542; 1541; 6552; 6719; 8741; 8742
Samuel F. Kitchell *(Chm. Bd.)*
William C. Schubert *(Pres., Treas., & Chief Exec. Officer)*
Gregory P. Denk *(Exec. V.P.)*
Vince Alfaro *(V.P.-Legal)*
Donna Lorch *(V.P.-Computer Services)*
Joseph J. Quigley *(V.P.-Fin. & Chief Fin. Officer)*
Joan Korljan *(Sec.)*
Barbara Bean *(Dir.-Communications)*
Kay Ellis *(Dir.-Human Resources)*
Dave Lindstrom *(Dir.-Training & Education)*
Principal(s):
Samuel F. Kitchell
William C. Schubert

No. of U.S. Offices: 4

Computer Systems/Hardware:
Digital Vax Network

Outside Service Firm(s):

Arthur Andersen & Co.*(Auditors)*
Phoenix, AZ

St. Paul Fire & Marine Insurance Co.*(Commercial Insurance Carrier)*
385 Washington St.
St. Paul, MN 55102
Tel.: 612-221-7911

Federal Insurance Co.*(Group Insurer)*
Los Angeles, CA

Northwestern National Life*(Group Insurer)*
20 Washington Ave. S.
Minneapolis, MN 55401

Goldman, Sachs & Co.*(Investment Banker)*
4900 Sears Tower, 53rd Flr.
Chicago, IL 60606
Tel.: 312-655-4600
Fax: 312-655-4556

Carson, Messinger, Elliott, Laughlin & Ragan*(Legal Firm)*
Phoenix, AZ

Bank of America*(Major Banking Relationship)*
Los Angeles, CA

Subsidiaries:

Kitchell CEM, Inc. **(1)**
1707 E. Highland, Ste. 280
Phoenix, AZ 85016
Tel.: 602-266-1970
Program, Project & Construction Management Services to Federal, State, Local & Quasi-Public Agencies
S.I.C.: 8741; 8742
Gregory P. Denk *(Pres. Chief Exec. Officer & Chief Oper. Officer)*

Kitchell Contractors, Inc. of Arizona **(1)**
1006 So. 24th St.
Phoenix, AZ 85034
Tel.: 602-275-7541
Construction Management & General Contracting Firm Operating in the Western United States with the Exception of California
S.I.C.: 1541; 8741
Mark J. Pendleton *(Pres.)*

Kitchell Contractors, Inc. **(1)**
26 Executive Park, Suite 100
Irvine, CA 92714
Tel.: 714-261-1227
Construction Management & General Contracting Operating in California
S.I.C.: 1541; 8741
James W. Howard *(Pres.)*

Kitchell Development Company **(1)**
1707 E. Highland, Ste. 100
Phoenix, AZ 85016
Tel.: 602-264-4411
Real Estate Development
S.I.C.: 6552
Charles A. Byxbee *(Pres.)*

KITCHEN KOMPACT, INC.
KK Plaza
Jeffersonville, IN 47130
Mailing Address:
P.O. Box 868
Jeffersonville, IN 47131
Tel.: 812-282-6681
Fax: 812-282-7880
Year Founded: 1937
Approx.Sls.: $50,000,000
Emp.: 300
Fiscal Year-end: 4/30/91
Mfr. of Kitchen Cabinets
S.I.C.: 2511
W. Dwight Gahm *(Chm. Bd., Pres. & Chief Exec. Officer)*
Theodore J. Duerr, Jr. *(V.P.-Pur.)*
Walter D. Gahm, Jr. *(V.P. & Treas.)*
Robert G. Wilson *(Controller)*
Fielden Woodward *(Sec.)*
Gordon Gahm *(Dir.-Sls.)*

Outside Service Firm(s):

Coopers & Lybrand*(Auditors)*
Louisville, KY 46201

Woodward, Hobson & Fulton*(Legal Firm)*
Louisville, KY

First National Bank of Louisville*(Major Banking Relationship)*
P.O. Box 36000,
Louisville, KY 40233

KITCHENS OF THE OCEAN, INC.
104 S.E. 5th Ct.
Deerfield Beach, FL 33441
Tel.: 305-421-2192 **FL**
Fax: 305-421-5207
Year Founded: 1972
Approx.Sls.: $40,000,000
Emp.: 200
Preparing of Fresh, Raw, Cooked or Frozen Shrimp
S.I.C.: 2092
Albert F. Margus *(Chief Exec. Officer)*
Brad Margus *(Pres.)*

Outside Service Firm(s):

Barnett Bank N.A.*(Major Banking Relationship)*
Hollywood, FL

KLAPMEIER MANAGEMENT COMPANY
811 E. Maple
Mora, MN 55051
Tel.: 612-679-3811
Fax: 612-679-3820
Year Founded: 1954
Approx.Sls.: $15,000,000
Emp.: 120
Fiscal Year-end: 7/31/90
Holding Company, Manufacture Boats
S.I.C.: 6719; 3732
James Klapmeier *(Pres.)*
Lowell Larson *(Exec. V.P.)*

Outside Service Firm(s):

Rider, Bennett, Egan & Arundel*(Legal Firm)*
900 First Natl. Bank Bldg.
Minneapolis, MN 55402
Tel.: 612-340-7951

First Bank of St. Paul*(Major Banking Relationship)*
Minneapolis, MN

Subsidiary:

Bluewater Marine Inc. **(1)**
811 E. Maple
Mora, MN 55051
Tel.: 612-679-3811
Approx.Sls.: $12,000,000
Emp.: 120
Manufacture Fiberglass Yachts & Cruisers
S.I.C.: 3732
James Klapmeier *(Pres.)*

KLAUS RADIO INC.
8400 N. Allen Rd.
Peoria, IL 61615
Tel.: 309-691-4840
Fax: 309-693-1724
Year Founded: 1919
Sales Range: $40-59 Million
Emp.: 120
Fiscal Year-end: 5/31/92
Wholesale Consumer Electronics, Industrial Electronics & Parts, Major Appliances, High Tech Electronics & Indus. Parts
S.I.C.: 5064; 5065
Robert Klaus *(Pres. & Chief Exec. Officer)*
Ronald Henderson *(Controller & Chief Fin. Officer)*
Bernie Sieks *(Dir.-Computer Services)*

Outside Service Firm(s):

KPMG Peat Marwick*(Auditors)*
Peoria, IL

Jefferson National Bank*(Investment Banker)*
Peoria, IL

Sutkowski & Washkuhn*(Legal Firm)*
Jefferson Bank Bldg., Ste. 505, 123 S.W. Adams St.
Peoria, IL 61602
Tel.: 309-673-4500

Davenport Bank & Trust Co.*(Major Banking Relationship)*
Davenport, IA

Jefferson National Bank*(Major Banking Relationship)*
Peoria, IL

Jefferson National Bank*(Pension Manager)*
Peoria, IL

KLAUSSNER CORPORATION
Lewallen St.
Asheboro, NC 27203
Mailing Address:
P.O. Box 220
Asherboro, NC 27203
Tel.: 919-625-6174 **DE**
Fax: 919-626-0905
Emp.: 4,000
Upholstered Household Furniture
S.I.C.: 2512
Hans Klaussner *(Chm. Bd.)*
J.B. Davis *(Pres.)*
Ben Frazier *(Exec. V.P.)*
Leo Peraldo *(V.P.-Fin., Treas. & Sec.)*

Outside Service Firm(s):

Chase Manhattan Bank, N.A.*(Major Banking Relationship)*
One Chase Manhattan Plaza
New York, NY 10081
Tel.: 212-552-2222
Tel.: 800-526-0801
Fax: 212-552-7175

Wachovia Bank & Trust Co.*(Major Banking Relationship)*
Asherboro, NC

Subsidiary:

Klaussner Furniture Industry **(1)**
Lewallen St.
Asheboro, NC 27203
Approx.Sls.: $250,000,000
Emp.: 3,400
Upholstered Household Furniture; Wood Office Furniture
S.I.C.: 2512; 2521
Hans Klaussner *(Chm. Bd.)*
J.B. Davis *(Pres.)*
Ben Frazier *(Exec. V.P.)*
Leo Peraldo *(V.P.-Fin., Treas. & Sec.)*
Edward Kinney *(V.P.-Mktg.)*
Jerry Bullins *(V.P.-Sls.)*
Peter Brisley *(Controller)*
Mark Walker *(Dir.-Personnel)*

KLEAR KNIT INC.
510 Sunset Dr.
Clover, SC 29710
Tel.: 803-222-3011 **SC**
Fax: 803-222-7003
Approx.Sls.: $40,000,000
Emp.: 1,300
Manufacture Men's Knitwear
S.I.C.: 2321
Ulf Boshamer *(Pres.)*
Lawrence S. Lau *(V.P. & Controller)*

Outside Service Firm(s):

Brittain, Gilbert & Associates*(Auditors)*
Charlotte, NC

Fleming, Robinson, Bradshaw & Hinson, P.A.*(Legal Firm)*
First Union Plz.
Charlotte, NC 28801
Tel.: 704-377-2536

South Carolina National Bank*(Major Banking Relationship)*
700 Main St.
Columbia, SC 29201

KLECO CORP.
10147 Brecksville Rd.
Brecksville, OH 44141
Tel.: 216-526-0142
Fax: 216-526-9765
Year Founded: 1926
Emp.: 300

Manufacture Original Equipment & Replacement Parts for Military Vehicles & Custom-Made Commercial Elevator Cabs; Repair of Jet Engine Components
S.I.C.: 3714; 3534; 3728
Walter S. Klevay, Sr. *(Chm. & Chief Exec. Officer)*

Computer Systems/Hardware:
Hewlett-Packard

Subsidiary:

Aviation Product Support Inc. **(1)**
7600 Tyler Blvd.
Mentor, OH 44060-4853
Tel.: 216-951-1133
S.I.C.: 4581

Subsidiary:

Aero-Finish Inc. **(2)**
1815 Blaze Nemeth Rd.
Painsville, OH 44077-4715
Tel.: 216-357-9135
S.I.C.: 3471

KLEER PAK CORPORATION
1411 N. Vine St.
Berwick, PA 18603
Mailing Address:
P.O. Box 218,
Berwick, PA 18603
Tel.: 717-752-2735 **PA**
Fax: 717-752-2483
Approx.Sls.: $15,000,000
Emp.: 70
Import
Manufacture & Sell Flexible Plastic Packaging; Plastic Bags, Polyethylene & Polypropylene
S.I.C.: 3089; 5162
Andrew Krupsha *(Chm. Bd. & Pres.)*
J.K. Slyman *(Controller)*
Principal(s):
Andrew Krupsha

Outside Service Firm(s):

Parente, Randolph, Orlando, Carey & Associates*(Auditors)*
46 Public Square
Wilkes-Barre, PA 18701-2681
Tel.: 717-820-0100
Fax: 717-824-9865

Meridian Bank*(Major Banking Relationship)*
Reading, PA

KLEIN ADVERTISING INC.
1888 Century Park East, Ste. 1104
Los Angeles, CA 90067-1725
Tel.: 310-556-0500
Fax: 310-556-0949
Year Founded: 1970
Approx.Billings: $10,000,000
Emp.: 12
John Steven Klein *(Pres.)*
John E. Gunn *(V.P.)*

JOHN KLEIN & ASSOC., INC.
20700 Miles Ave.
Cleveland, OH 44128
Tel.: 216-587-3070
Fax: 216-587-4625
Year Founded: 1971
Approx.Billings: $22,750,000
Emp.: 54
Database Marketing, Direct Mail, Intergrated Marketing
John I. Klein *(Pres. & New Bus. Contact)*
Dan Klein *(V.P., Data Processing)*
David Koch *(V.P., Database Mgr.)*
Beverlee Fertig *(Office Mgr.)*

Computer Systems/Hardware:
McDonnell Douglas Pick System

CALVIN KLEIN, INC.
205 W. 39th St.
New York, NY 10018
Tel.: 212-719-2600 **NY**
Assets: $144,802,000
Earnings: $11,923,000
Liabilities: $123,898,000
Net Worth: $20,904,000
Approx.Sls.: $218,100,000
Emp.: 1,600
Fiscal Year-end: 12/30/90
Import Export
Men's & Ladies' Fashions
S.I.C.: 2337; 2321; 2325
Barry K. Schwartz *(Chm. Bd. & Chief Oper. Officer)*
Calvin Klein *(Pres. & Chief Exec. Officer)*
John K. Kabay *(Sr. V.P., Chief Fin. Officer & Treas.)*
Joel I. Semel *(Controller)*
Robert DiPaola *(Gen. Counsel)*
James H. Coe *(Dir.-Human Resources)*
Sam Deutschen *(Dir.-Data Processing)*
Neil Kraft *(Dir.-Adv. & Creative Services)*
Patricia Durkin *(Mgr.-Adv.)*
Paul Wilmot *(Mgr.-Pub Rels.)*

No. of Mfg. Plants/Facilities: 3
No. of U.S. Offices: 10

Computer Systems/Hardware:
IBM AS 400

Outside Service Firm(s):

Ernst & Young*(Auditors)*
787 Seventh Ave.
New York, NY 10019
Tel.: 212-773-1243

Central Bank*(Investment Banker)*
Hackensack, NJ

Manufacturers Hanover Trust Co.*(Major Banking Relationship)*
New York, NY

Rubin, Rubin & DiPaola*(Legal Firm)*
375 Park Ave.
New York, NY 10022
Tel.: 212-759-4530

Division:

Calvin Klein Sport **(1)**
205 W. 39th St.
New York, NY 10018
Tel.: 212-575-0800
Manufacture Calvin Klein Jeans & Tops for Men & Women
S.I.C.: 2325; 2339; 2321; 2331; 2322
Andrew Rosen *(Pres.)*
Connye D'Agosta *(V.P.-Employee Benefits & Personnel Admin.)*

Subsidiary:

Calvin Klein Sport, Inc. **(1)**
205 W. 39th St.
New York, NY 10018
Tel.: 212-719-2600 (100%)
Sale of Apparel under Trademark "Calvin Klein" Pursuant to License from Company, Including Men's, Women's & Boy's Jeans & Related Items
S.I.C.: 5137; 5136
Andrew Rosen *(Pres.)*

KLEIN TOOLS INC.
7200 McCormick Blvd.
Skokie, IL 60076
Mailing Address:
P.O. Box 599033
Chicago, IL 60659-9033
Tel.: 708-677-9500 **DE**
Fax: 708-677-4476
Year Founded: 1857
Approx.Sls.: $100,000,000
Emp.: 1,000
Fiscal Year-end: 12/31/91
Import Export
Mfr. of Hand Tools; Occupational Protective Equipment; Leather & Canvas Bags & Pouches; Specialty Chemicals; Splicing Tents
S.I.C.: 2394; 3151; 3421; 3423; 3425; 3429; 3531; 3199
Michael S. Klein *(Chm. Bd. & Chief Exec. Officer)*
Richard T. Klein, Jr. *(Pres. & Chief Oper. Officer)*
Mathias A. Klein III *(Exec. V.P.)*
Charles R. Hain *(Sr. V.P.-Fin.)*
Donald P. Phillips *(Sr. V.P.-Sls. & Mktg.)*
Thomas R. Klein *(V.P.-Matls. Mgmnt.)*
Michael J. Loftus *(V.P.-Mktg.)*
Scott Siler *(Dir.-Quality Assurance)*
Principal(s):
Michael S. Klein

No. of Mfg. Plants/Facilities: 7

Outside Service Firm(s):

Arthur Andersen & Co.*(Auditors)*
33 W. Monroe St.
Chicago, IL 60603-4067
Tel.: 312-580-0033
Fax: 312-507-6748

Keck, Mahin, Cate & Koehler*(Legal Firm)*
8300 Sears Tower, 233 S. Wacker Dr.
Chicago, IL 60606
Tel.: 312-876-3400

LaSalle National Bank*(Major Banking Relationship)*
135 S. LaSalle St., Rm.260
Chicago, IL 60603

Non-U.S. Holding:

Herramientas Klein S.A. de C.V. **(1)**
Avenida 1 No. 3, Parque Indus. Cartagena
Edo de Tultitlan,
Mexico, Mexico
Tel.: 52 5-781-6289 (49%)
Emp.: 300
Hand Tools & Safety Equip.
S.I.C.: 3423
Ricardo Lujambio *(Pres)*

KLEINSCHMIDT INC.
450 Lake-Cook Rd.
Deerfield, IL 60015-4973
Tel.: 708-945-1000 **IL**
Fax: 708-945-4619
Sales Range: $10-19 Million
Emp.: 37
Tandem Computer Software, General Purpose Tandem Software Services; Electronic Data Interchange & Equipment
S.I.C.: 3571; 3577; 3663; 7372; 7379
Harry S. Gaples *(Pres.)*
D. Myers *(V.P.-Mktg.)*
David A. Bath *(V.P. & Controller)*
Joseph W. Fay *(V.P.-CLM)*
Robert J. Schmidt *(V.P.-Software)*
R. Wyzukovicz *(V.P.-Customer Service)*
Principal(s):
Harry S. Gaples

No. of Mfg. Plants/Facilities: 1

Computer Systems/Hardware:
Tandem

KLEMTNER ADVERTISING INC.
375 Hudson St.
New York, NY 10014-3620
Tel.: 212-463-3400
Fax: 212-463-3541
Year Founded: 1944
Approx.Billings: $190,000,000
Emp.: 160
Medical & Health Care Adv.
S.I.C.: 7311
Albert P. Molinaro, Jr. *(Chm.-Emeritus)*
Gavin A. Scotti *(Pres. & Chief Exec. Officer)*
R. Jay Conlan *(Exec. V.P., Dir. Strategic Plng.)*
Robert Brilliant *(Exec. V.P., Fin. & Admin.)*
George Constantinoff *(Exec. V.P., Dir. Scientific & Medical Affairs)*
Douglas A. Bruce *(Sr. V.P., Dir. Consumer HealthCare Grp.)*
Richard A. Nuzzo *(Pres.-Comtact Corp.)*

KLINE IRON & STEEL CO., INC.
P.O. Box 1013,
Columbia, SC 36645
Tel.: 803-251-8000
Fax: 803-251-8080
Approx.Sls.: $32,000,000
Emp.: 260
Fabricated Structural Steel; Construction Of Radio & Television Towers; Steel Service Center
S.I.C.: 3441; 5051
Bernard H. Kline *(Chm. Bd.)*
Jerome C. Kline *(Pres.)*
John Jones *(Controller)*

Computer Systems/Hardware:
Hewlett-Packard

Outside Service Firm(s):

Derrick, Stubbs & Stith*(Auditors)*
Columbia, SC

Barnes, Alford, Stork & Johnson*(Legal Firm)*
Columbia, SC

Citizens & Southern National Bank*(Major Banking Relationship)*
Columbia, SC

GEORGETTE KLINGER, INC.
501 Madison Ave.
New York, NY 10022
Tel.: 212-838-7080
Fax: 212-754-2520
Year Founded: 1940
Approx.Sls.: $20,000,000
Emp.: 300
Fiscal Year-end: 9/30/90
Skin & Hair Care Products & Cosmetics; Full Service Salons
S.I.C.: 2844; 7991
Georgette Klinger *(Chm. Bd.)*
Arthur T. Minson *(Chief Oper. Officer & Gen. Mgr.)*
Kathryn Klinger *(Pres.)*
Peter Morris *(Controller)*
Phyllis Apostole *(Mgr.-Mktg.)*

Computer Systems/Hardware:
IBM PC

Outside Service Firm(s):

KPMG Peat Marwick*(Auditors)*
345 Park Ave.
New York, NY 10154
Tel.: 212-758-9700
Fax: 212-872-3308

Weil, Gotshal & Manges*(Legal Firm)*
767 5th Ave.
New York, NY 10153
Tel.: 212-310-8000

KLIPSCH & ASSOCIATES INC.
Rte. 4, Oakhaven Rd.
Hope, AR 71801
Mailing Address:
P.O. Box 688
Hope, AR 71801
Tel.: 501-777-6751 **AR**
Fax: 501-777-6753
Year Founded: 1948
Approx.Sls.: $25,000,000
Emp.: 200
Fiscal Year-end: 3/31/90
Import Export
Manufacturer of Loudspeakers
S.I.C.: 3651
Fred S. Klipsch *(Chm. Bd. & Pres.)*
Walt Byington *(Exec. V.P.)*
Jack W. Fountain *(V.P.-Intl. Sls.)*

Klipsch & Associates Inc.—(Continued)

Tammy Smith *(V.P.-Fin.)*
George Barckley *(Dir.-Data Processing)*
Jerry Carlew *(Dir.-Pur.)*

No. of Mfg. Plants/Facilities: 1
No. of U.S. Offices: 1

Computer Systems/Hardware:
3-Com, Wyse, Toshiba, Hewlett Packard

Outside Service Firm(s):

Ernst & Young*(Auditors)*
425 W. Capitol, Ste. 3600
Little Rock, AR 72201
Tel.: 501-372-5443
Fax: 501-372-6288

First National Bank of Hope*(Major Banking Relationship)*
Hope, AR

KLOSTERMAN'S BAKING COMPANY
4760 Paddock Rd.
Cincinnati, OH 45229
Tel.: 513-242-1004
Approx.Sls.: $60,000,000
Emp.: 775
Bakery: Bread & Pastries
S.I.C.: 2051
Kenneth Klosterman *(Chm. Bd.)*
Ken Klosterman Jr. *(Pres.)*
Tom Knabb *(V.P.-Fin.)*
Mike Outlaw *(V.P.-Opers.)*
Dennis Wiltshire *(V.P.-Sls.)*

KLUENER PACKING COMPANY
2842 Massachusetts Ave.
Cincinnati, OH 45225
Tel.: 513-681-2850 **OH**
Fax: 513-681-1206
Year Founded: 1895
Sales Range: $80-99 Million
Emp.: 93
Import
Distribute Cheese, Fish, Beef, Pork & Poultry; Cattle Slaughtering
S.I.C.: 5147; 5143; 5144; 5154
James A. Kluener, Sr. *(Chm. Bd. & Pres.)*
Leo R. Verst *(V.P.-Pur.)*
Jim Jaeger *(Mgr.-Sls.)*
William Taulbee *(Treas.)*
Thomas A. Diehl *(Mgr.-Livestock & Beef Opers.)*
James A. Kluener, Jr. *(Human Resources Dir.)*
Principal(s):
James A. Kluener, Sr.

No. of Mfg. Plants/Facilities: 2

Computer Systems/Hardware:
NCR Model 9300

Outside Service Firm(s):

Deloitte & Touche*(Auditors)*
Chiquita Center, 250 E. 5th St., Ste. 1900
Cincinnati, OH 45202
Tel.: 513-784-7100

Art Hauser Ins. Co.*(Group Insurer)*
Cincinnati, OH

Frost & Jacobs*(Legal Firm)*
2500 Central Trust Ctr.
Cincinnati, OH 45202
Tel.: 513-651-6800

Fifth Third Bank*(Major Banking Relationship)*
Corporate Trust Services, 38 Fountain Square Plaza
Cincinnati, OH 45263

Subsidiary:

Kluener Foods Co. **(1)**
113 Circle Freeway Dr.
Cincinnati, OH 45246
Tel.: 513-874-9960
Emp.: 40
Food Distributors to Hotels, Restaurants & Institutions (H.R.I. Market)
S.I.C.: 5141
James A. Kluener, Sr. *(Pres.)*
Kenneth Kluener *(Exec. V.P.)*
Steve Larkin *(V.P.-Mktg. & Sls. Mgr.)*

KNAPE & KNAPE
3131 McKinney, Ste. 800
Dallas, TX 75204
Tel.: 214-871-2461
Year Founded: 1985
Approx.Billings: $16,000,000
Emp.: 20
Susan Knape *(Pres.)*
Anthony Knape *(Chief Exec. Officer)*
Steven Silvers *(V.P., Pub. Rels.)*

THE KNAPHEIDE MFG. CO.
436 S. 6th
Quincy, IL 62301
Mailing Address:
P.O. Box C140
Quincy, IL 62306-2140
Tel.: 217-222-7131
Fax: 217-222-5939
Year Founded: 1848
Sales Range: $20-39 Million
Emp.: 300
Fiscal Year-end: 12/31/90
Mfr. Truck Bodies: Hoist, Grain & Livestock Truck Bodies, Contractor Bodies, Custom Engineered Bodies
S.I.C.: 3731; 5084; 3625; 3537
H. W. Knapheide III *(Pres.)*
Gerry Korb *(V.P.-Opers.)*
Arthur Cox *(Sec. & Treas.)*
Steve Bybee *(Dir.-Sls. & Mktg.)*
Gail Helkey *(Mgr.-Personnel)*

Principal(s):
H. W. Knapheide III

Computer Systems/Hardware:
IBM System 38

Outside Service Firm(s):

Connecticut General Life Insurance Co.*(Group Insurer)*
P.O. Box 2975,
Hartford, CT 06104
Tel.: 203-726-6000

Boatmen's Trust Company*(Major Banking Relationship)*
100 North Broadway
St. Louis, MO 63102
Tel.: 314-466-2469

Mercantile Commerce Trust*(Major Banking Relationship)*
Saint Louis, MO

KNAPP COMMUNICATIONS CORPORATION
5900 Wilshire Blvd.
Los Angeles, CA 90036
Tel.: 213-965-3400
Fax: 310-937-5643
Year Founded: 1965
Approx.Sls.: $100,000,000
Emp.: 210
Fiscal Year-end: 1/31/91
Publishers Of Architectural Digest, Bon Appetit, The Knapp Press
S.I.C.: 2721
Cleon T. Knapp *(Chm. Bd. & Pres.)*
Thomas P. Losee, Jr. *(Sr. V.P. & Publishing Dir.)*
Paige Rense *(Sr. V.P. & Editor-in-Chief)*
Paul H. Hayase *(Sr. V.P. & Gen. Counsel)*
John F. Jastrem *(Sr. V.P. & Chief Fin. Officer)*
Douglas A. Waugaman *(V.P.-Fin.)*
Victor S. Rappa *(V.P.-Tax)*
Elizabeth W. Knapp *(Sec.)*

Outside Service Firm(s):

Security Pacific National Bank*(Major Banking Relationship)*
Corp. Trust Admin., Box 30376
Los Angeles, CA 90030
Tel.: 213-613-6211

Subsidiaries:

Architectural Digest **(1)**
5900 Wilshire Blvd.
Los Angeles, CA 90036
Tel.: 213-937-4740
Fax: 213-937-5643
Emp.: 300
Architectural Digest Magazine
S.I.C.: 2721
Cleon T. Knapp *(Chm. & Chief Exec. Officer)*
Paige Rense *(Sr. V.P. & Editor-in-Chief)*
Tom Losee *(Sr. V.P. & Publishing Dir.)*
Patrick R. Casey *(Sr. V.P.-Opers.)*
R. Jeffrey Petersen *(V.P. & Publr.)*
Lee Anne Taylor *(Adv. Mgr.)*
Carla Johnson *(Circulation Dir.)*

Bon Appetit Magazine **(1)**
5900 Wilshire Blvd.
Los Angeles, CA 90036
Tel.: 213-965-3600
Fax: 213-930-2369
Approx.Sls.: $45,000,000
Emp.: 85
Fiscal Year-end: 1/31/91
Computer Systems/Hardware:
Wang; IBM; Novel Lans
Food & Entertaining Magazine
S.I.C.: 2741
Cleon T. Knapp *(Chm. & Chief Exec. Officer)*
Martha S. Murray *(Publisher)*
William J. Garry *(Editor-in-Chief)*
Raymond J. Sachs *(Sr. V.P. & G.M.)*
Tom Losee *(Sr. V.P. & Publishing Dir.)*
John Jastren *(Chief Fin. Officer)*
Paul Hayase *(Gen. Counsel)*
Lynne G. Berentson *(Mktg. Dir.)*
Douglas N. Roeder *(Adv. Dir.)*
Nancy B. Van Ness *(Dir.-Opers.)*

Wood Knapp & Co., Inc. **(1)**
5900 Wilshire Blvd.
Los Angeles, CA 90036
Tel.: 213-937-5486
Fax: 213-937-5643
Publisher
S.I.C.: 2721
Betsy Wood Knapp *(Pres. & Chief Exec. Officer)*

KNAPP SHOES INC.
One Knapp Centre
Brockton, MA 02401
Tel.: 508-588-9000 **MA**
Fax: 508-583-7578
Year Founded: 1920
Approx.Sls.: $40,000,000
Emp.: 600
Import
Men & Women's Shoes, Rugged Active Wear & Work Wear for Men & Women
S.I.C.: 2329; 3144; 3143; 2321; 2325
John J. Schlueter *(Chm. Bd. & Chief Exec. Officer)*
Gary Holter *(Chief Oper. Officer & Exec. V.P.)*
M. Morin *(V.P. & Controller)*
Terry DeArruda *(Mgr.-Adv. & Promo.)*
Principal(s):
John J. Schlueter

No. of Mfg. Plants/Facilities: 1
No. of U.S. Offices: 125

Computer Systems/Hardware:
IBM 4381

Outside Service Firm(s):

Ernst & Young*(Auditors)*
200 Clarendon St., 46th Fl.
Boston, MA 02116
Tel.: 617-266-2000

Sonnenschein, Nath & Rosenthal*(Legal Firm)*
8000 Sears Tower
Chicago, IL 60606
Tel.: 312-876-8000
Fax: 312-876-7934

Shawmut Bank*(Major Banking Relationship)*
1 Federal St.
Boston, MA 02110
Tel.: 617-292-3715

KNAR GOLD & SILVER EXCHANGE
640 S. Hill St., Ste. 241
Los Angeles, CA 90014
Tel.: 213-622-5627
Fax: 213-622-2078
Year Founded: 1985
Precious Metals
S.I.C.: 5094
Aram Kouleyan *(Owner)*

Outside Service Firm(s):

Alex Dunetz*(Auditors)*
Los Angeles, CA

Bank of America NT&SA*(Major Banking Relationship)*
555 S. Flower St.
Los Angeles, CA 90071
Tel.: 213-228-3868

E.W. KNAUSS & SON, INC.
625 E. Broad St.
Quakertown, PA 18951
Tel.: 215-536-4220
Fax: 215-536-1129
Approx.Sls.: $12,000,000
Emp.: 70
Manufacture Dried Beef
S.I.C.: 2013
Donald T. Knauss *(Chm. Bd. & Chief Exec. Officer)*
E. William Knauss *(Pres., Chief Oper. Officer & Treas.)*
Donald O. Merkef *(V.P., Sec. & Dir.-Pur. & Data Processing)*
Richard K. Hartan *(Mgr.-Sls., Mktg. & Adv.)*

Outside Service Firm(s):

Isdaner & Company*(Auditors)*
Bala Cynwyd, PA

Klehr, Harrison, Harvey, Branzburg, Ellers & Weir*(Legal Firm)*
Philadelphia, PA

Bucks County Bank & Trust Company*(Major Banking Relationship)*
Perkasie, PA

KNIGHT EQUIPMENT CORP.
2945 Airway Ave.
Costa Mesa, CA 92627
Mailing Address:
P.O. Box 1378
Costa Mesa, CA 92626
Tel.: 714-557-5400
Tel.: 800-854-3764 **CA**
Fax: 714-557-0527
Year Founded: 1972
Assets: $12,000,000
Liabilities: $8,000,000
Net Worth: $4,000,000
Sales Range: $10-19 Million
Emp.: 100
Fiscal Year-end: 10/31/90
Export
Manufacture Electronic Pumps, Dishwashing Machines
S.I.C.: 3569; 3589
William K. Russell *(Chm. Bd.)*
Paul Beldham *(Chief Oper. Officer)*
Chuck Sarno *(Treas.)*
Roy June *(Gen. Counsel)*
Mary Rose Skolyan *(Corp. Sec.)*

No. of Mfg. Plants/Facilities: 2
No. of U.S. Offices: 2
No. of Foreign Offices: 2

Computer Systems/Hardware:
MAI Basic Four

Outside Service Firm(s):

Deloitte & Touche*(Auditors)*
Newport Beach, CA

John Burnham & Co.*(Commercial Insurance Carrier)*
Costa Mesa, CA

Commercial Bankers Life*(Group Insurer)*
Newport Beach, CA

Roy June, Esq.*(Legal Firm)*
Costa Mesa, CA

Wells Fargo Bank*(Major Banking Relationship)*
420 Montgomery St.
San Francisco, CA 94104

LESTER B. KNIGHT & ASSOCIATES, INC.
549 W. Randolph St.
Chicago, IL 60661
Tel.: 312-346-2100 **DE**
Telex: 25-4622
Fax: 312-648-1085
Approx.Sls.: $54,000,000
Emp.: 410
International Management Consultants, Architects, Engineers & Planners
S.I.C.: 8742; 8711; 8712
DeForest P. Davis, Jr. *(Chm. Bd. & Chief Exec. Officer)*
Stephen C. Mitchell *(Pres. & Chief Oper. Officer)*
Charles E. Fausel *(Exec. V.P.)*
Donald S. Hitchcock *(Exec. V.P.)*
Erhard Wendling *(Exec. V.P.)*
William J. Poad *(Sr. V.P.)*
A. Freimanis *(V.P.)*
James A. Turner *(V.P. & Dir.-Human Resources)*
Margaret A. Fraser *(Sec.)*
Robert D. Webb *(Controller & Asst. Sec.)*

No. of U.S. Offices: 4
No. of Foreign Offices: 20

Outside Service Firm(s):

Arthur Andersen & Co.*(Auditors)*
33 W. Monroe St.
Chicago, IL 60603-4067
Tel.: 312-580-0033
Fax: 312-507-6748

Fireman's Fund Insurance Co.*(Group Insurer)*
San Francisco, CA

DPIC Companies*(Group Insurer)*
P.O. Box DPIC
Monterey, CA 93942
Tel.: 408-649-5522

McDermott, Will & Emery*(Legal Firm)*
227 W. Monroe St.
Chicago, IL 60606-5096
Tel.: 312-372-2000

American National Bank & Trust Company of Chicago*(Major Banking Relationship)*
33 N. LaSalle St.
Chicago, IL 60602
Tel.: 312-661-5000
Fax: 312-661-6417

Subsidiaries:

Keller & Gannon **(1)**
1453 Mission St.
San Francisco, CA 94103
Tel.: 415-621-1199
Consulting Engineering/Architects
S.I.C.: 8712
Thomas M. Reinarts *(Chief Exec. Officer)*
Robert A. Falciani *(Exec. V.P.)*
Alan E. Smith *(Sr. V.P.)*
John W. Granicher *(Sr. V.P. & Sec. & Treas.)*

Knight Architects Engineers Planners, Inc. **(1)**
549 W. Randolph St.
Chicago, IL 60661
Tel.: 312-346-2300
Architects, Engineers and Planners
S.I.C.: 8712
Donald S. Hitchcock *(Chm. & Chief Exec. Officer)*
DeForest P. Davis, Jr. *(Vice Chm.)*
Stephen C. Mitchell *(Vice Chm.)*
Robert L. Barnes *(Pres. & Chief Oper. Officer)*
Dominick J. Gatto *(Exec. V.P.)*
Robert H. Mellott *(Exec. V.P.)*
Sid A. Gaswhala *(Sr. V.P.)*
Warren J. Hendrickson *(Sr. V.P.)*
Richard M. Lemons *(Sr. V.P.)*
William J. Poad *(Sr. V.P.)*
Dirk Van Erp *(Sr. V.P.)*
Robert D. Webb *(Sr. V.P. & Treas.)*
GaryL. Bollier *(V.P.)*
Alvis Freimanis *(V.P.)*
Kurt E. Johnson *(V.P.)*
Christopher S. Rauch *(V.P.)*
Gene Schnair *(V.P.)*
James A. Turner *(V.P.)*
Ronald S. Walkington *(V.P.)*
Susan E. Ford *(Sec.)*

Lester B. Knight Cast Metals, Inc. **(1)**
549 W. Randolph St.
Chicago, IL 60661
Tel.: 312-346-2100
Management/Engineering Consulting
S.I.C.: 8712
Joseph R. Ponteri *(Pres. & Chief Exec. Officer)*
David O. Kennedy *(Sr. V.P.)*
Robert D. Webb *(Sec.)*

Knight/Emerson Consulting, Inc. **(1)**
549 W. Randolph St.
Chicago, IL 60661
Tel.: 312-346-3653
Management Consulting
S.I.C.: 8711
Leon G. Hoyt *(Chm. & Chief Exec. Officer)*
Robert E. Sabath *(Pres. & Chief Oper. Officer)*
Clifford D. Earls *(Sr. V.P.)*
Donald H. Nyman *(V.P.)*
Randy Podany *(V.P.)*
Carol A. Piacenti *(Sec.)*
Robert D. Webb *(Treas.)*

Knight Management Consulting, Inc. **(1)**
549 w. Randolph St.
Chicago, IL 60661
Tel.: 312-346-2100
Management Consulting
S.I.C.: 8742
DeForest P. Davis, Jr. *(Chm.)*
Robert E. Sabath *(Pres.)*
Clifford D. Earls *(V.P.)*
Randy Podany *(V.P.)*
Beverly L. Russell *(Sec.)*
Robert D. Webb *(Treas.)*

Knight PMD, Inc. **(1)**
P.O. Box 187,
Barrington, IL 60011
Tel.: 708-381-6793
Food Industry Management Consulting
S.I.C.: 8742
Robert Sabath *(Chm.)*
Leslie G. Behrend *(Pres.)*
Robert D. Webb *(Sec. & Treas.)*

Non-U.S. Holdings:

Knight Korea **(1)**
7th Fl., Hanhyo Bldg., 34-2, Youido-dong, Yongdungpo-gu
Seoul, Korea
Tel.: 02783-8537
Telex: LBKKOR K27193
Architechtural Services
S.I.C.: 8712
Dirk van Erp *(Contact in U.S.)*

Knight Wendling AG **(1)**
Forrlibuckstrasse 66 P.O. Box 490, CH-8037
Zurich, Switzerland
Tel.: 01/272 2922
Telex: 822 691
Fax: 01 44 74 11
Mngmt. Consultants, Executive Search, Foundry Consulting
S.I.C.: 8741
DeForest P. Davis, Jr. *(Chm.)*
Erhard Wendling *(Chief Exec. Officer)*
Kurt Stahlin *(Chief Fin. Officer)*
Dr. Jutta Seibold-Dietl *(Treas.)*

Knight Wendling Ltd. **(1)**
13-14, Cornwall Terrace
London, NW1 4QP, United Kingdom
Tel.: 071-486-7711
Telex: 268662 KNIGHT G
Mngmt. Services
S.I.C.: 8741

KNIGHTBRIDGE PARTNERS
225 W. Washington, Ste. 2150
Chicago, IL 60606
Tel.: 312-641-2700
Fax: 312-782-7623
Holding Company
S.I.C.: 6719
David Lipson *(Pres.)*

Subsidiaries:

Golden Cat Corporation **(1)**
348 S. Columbia St.
South Bend, IN 46601
Tel.: 219-234-8191
Fax: 219-232-2934
Approx.Sls.: $170,000,000
Emp.: 700
Fiscal Year-end: 6/30/91
Mfr. Cat Box Filler; Processors of Absorbent Clays
S.I.C.: 3295
Frank Krum *(Pres. & Chief Exec. Officer)*
Phil Smith *(Pres.)*
Guy Harper *(Pres.-Mfg. Div.)*
Dave Tooker *(Exec. V.P.-Sls. & Mktg.)*
James A. Dinges *(V.P.-Fin.)*
Tom Ramey *(V.P.-Mktg.)*
Harvey Ross *(V.P.-Specialty Sls.)*

Golden Cat Corporation **(1)**
P.O. Box 1086
Cape Girardeau, MO 63701
Tel.: 314-334-6618
S.I.C.: 3295

Knoll International Holdings, Inc.
(Name Changed to 21 International Holdings, Inc.)

KNOTH & MEADS COMPANY
401 West A St., 11th Fl.
San Diego, CA 92101
Tel.: 619-234-6001
Fax: 619-234-6074
Year Founded: 1958
Approx.Billings: $14,620,000
Emp.: 25
Advertising Agency
S.I.C.: 7311
Richard Meads *(Chm. & Chief Exec. Officer)*
Richard Knoth *(Vice Chm. & Chief Fin. Officer)*
Gary Meads *(Pres. & Chief Oper. Officer)*
Richard Zamora *(Dir.-Fin.)*

No. of U.S. Offices: 1

Computer Systems/Hardware:
IBM 23; Zenith

Outside Service Firm(s):

Richard Blum, CPA*(Auditors)*
San Diego, CA

Miller, Boyko & Bell*(Legal Firm)*
San Diego, CA

Bank of San Diego*(Major Banking Relationship)*
San Diego, CA

KNOTT'S BERRY FARM
8039 Beach Blvd.
Buena Park, CA 90620
Tel.: 714-827-1776
Fax: 714-220-5124
Year Founded: 1922
Sales Range: $100-499 Million
Emp.: 4,000
Amusement Park, Food Prods.
S.I.C.: 7996; 5812; 5399; 5149; 2033
Terry Van Gorder *(Pres. & Chief Exec. Officer)*
Gerald Elmer *(V.P.-Fin.)*
Larry D. Frack *(V.P.-Maintenance & Construction)*
James Hancock *(V.P.-Mktg.)*
Joseph Meck *(V.P.-Opers. & Entertainment)*
Andy Rich *(V.P.-Human Resources)*
James Troge *(V.P.-Food Service)*

No. of Mfg. Plants/Facilities: 1
No. of U.S. Offices: 2

Computer Systems/Hardware:
IBM System 38

Outside Service Firm(s):

Deloitte & Touche*(Auditors)*
Newport Beach, CA

Massachusetts Mutual Life Insurance Co.*(Group Insurer)*
1295 State St.
Springfield, MA 01111
Tel.: 413-788-8411
Fax: 413-730-6144

Gibson, Dunn & Crutcher*(Legal Firm)*
800 Newport Center Dr.
Newport Beach, CA 92660
Tel.: 714-451-3800

Security Pacific Corporation*(Major Banking Relationship)*
Security Pacific Plaza
Los Angeles, CA 90071
Tel.: 213-345-6211
Fax: 213-625-0809

Subsidiary:

KBF Foods Division **(1)**
200 Boysenberry Lane
Placentia, CA 92670
Tel.: 714-579-2400 (100%)
Fax: 714-579-2490
Emp.: 200
Jellies, Jams, Preserves, Salad Dressings, Sauces & Syrups
S.I.C.: 2033; 5149
Ron Bennett *(V.P. & Gen. Mgr.)*
Erwin Hettervik *(V.P.-Mfg. Opers.)*
Ralph Clark *(Controller)*
Cindy Gevorkian *(Mgr.-Mktg.)*

KNOUSE FOODS INC.
800 Peach Glen/Idaville Rd.
Peach Glen, PA 17375-0001
Tel.: 717-677-8181
Fax: 717-677-7069
Year Founded: 1949
Approx.Sls.: $200,000,000
Emp.: 2,000
Fiscal Year-end: 6/30/91
Export
Apple Products, Cherries, Fruit Pie Fillings, Peaches & Vinegar
S.I.C.: 2033; 2099
D.L. Carey *(Pres.)*
R.W. Esser *(V.P.-Sls.)*
K.E. Guise *(V.P. & Gen. Mgr.)*
Paul G. Haller *(V.P.-Opers.)*
John A. Leeti *(V.P. & Treas.)*
M. Everett Weiser *(V.P.)*
Robert Weary *(Dir.-Human Res.)*
Kay S. Rentzel *(Adv. & Program Co-Ordinator)*
Principal(s):
D.L. Carey

Computer Systems/Hardware:
Sperry System 80 Model 20

Outside Service Firm(s):

KPMG Peat Marwick*(Auditors)*
Buffalo, NY

CoBank-National Bank for Cooperatives*(Major Banking Relationship)*
Baltimore, MD

KNOWLES ELECTRONICS, INC.
1151 Maplewood Dr.
Itasca, IL 60143
Tel.: 708-455-3600
Year Founded: 1955
Sales Range: $20-39 Million
Emp.: 425

Knowles Electronics, Inc.—(Continued)

Mfr. of Sub-Miniature Acoustic Transducers
S.I.C.: 3651
Nancy W. Knowles *(Chm.-Emeritus)*
Reginald G. Garratt *(Pres. & Chief Oper. Officer)*
Richard W. Lane *(V.P.-Indus. Rels.)*
Harold Jones *(V.P.-Mfg.)*
John W. Hupp *(Sec.)*

Computer Systems/Hardware:
DEC 785

Outside Service Firm(s):

Ernst & Young*(Auditors)*
233 S. Wacker Dr.
Chicago, IL 60606
Tel.: 312-368-1800
Fax: 312-645-3095

Aetna Life & Casualty*(Group Insurer)*
100 N. Riverside Plaza
Chicago, IL 60606

Anchor HMO*(Group Insurer)*
Chicago, IL

HMO Illinois*(Group Insurer)*
Chicago, IL

Defrees & Fiske*(Legal Firm)*
Chicago, IL

Continental Bank N. A.*(Major Banking Relationship)*
231 S. LaSalle St.
Chicago, IL 60697
Tel.: 312-828-2345
Tel.: 800-426-5754
Telex: 312-828-1783

Subsidiary:

Synchro-Start Products, Inc. **(1)**
6250 Howard St.
Niles, IL 60714
Tel.: 708-967-7730
Fax: 708-967-7832
Emp.: 150
Fiscal Year-end: 6/30/91
Computer Systems/Hardware:
Hewlett-Packard
Mechanical Speed Switches, Electronic Speed Switches, D.C. Solenoids, Signal Generators, Electronic Engine Protective Systems
S.I.C.: 3613
Jay L. Geldmacher *(V.P. & Gen. Mgr.)*
Ted Staniec *(V.P.-Mfg.)*
Paul F. Dolinar *(V.P.-Mktg.)*
Ronald Izydorek *(Controller)*
Ken Ryl *(Mgr.-Natl. Sls.)*
Marc Gordon *(Mgr.-Quality Control)*
Suzanne Harris *(Media/Adv. Coord.)*
Ann Fleming *(Mgr.-Personnel)*

KNOX INTERNATIONAL CORP.
505 Market St., Seventh Fl.
Knoxville, TN 37902
Tel.: 615-521-5669 **DE**
Fax: 615-521-4189
Year Founded: 1988
Approx.Sls.: $100,000,000
Emp.: 20
Fiscal Year-end: 2/28/91
Import
Direct Mktg. of Consumer Products & Services
S.I.C.: 5961
Robert Van Camp *(Chm. Bd.)*
Iain Macfarlane *(Pres. & Chief Exec. Officer)*
William M. Kunkel *(Sr. V.P. & Chief Fin. Officer)*
Elwood G. Forsythe *(Sr. V.P. & Chief Information Officer)*
George McMillan *(Sr. V.P.-Opers.)*
Dale Fujimoto *(V.P.-Sls. & Mktg.)*
Thomas Campbell *(V.P.-Mktg. & Sls.)*
W. Thomas Stumb *(Treas.)*
Kevin Norwood *(Sec. & Gen. Counsel)*

Subsidiaries:

Michigan Bulb Company **(1)**
1950 Waldorf N.W.
Grand Rapids, MI 49550
Tel.: 616-453-5401
Fax: 616-453-3560
Sales Range: $60-79 Million
Emp.: 150
Garden Stock By Mail
S.I.C.: 5261; 5961
Iain MacFarlane *(Chm. & Chief Exec. Officer)*
William Kunkel *(Sr. V.P. & Chief Fin. Officer)*
Dale Fujimoto *(V.P.-Mktg.)*
W. Thomas Stumb *(Treas.)*
Kevin Norwood *(Sec.)*
Jerry Kremer *(Pur. Mgr.)*
John Huitsing *(Controller & Dir.-Fin.)*

Weinstock's Flowers & Gifts **(1)**
5290 Roswell Rd., NW
Atlanta, GA 30342
Tel.: 404-255-1611
Fax: 404-255-7309
Approx.Sls.: $2,000,000
Emp.: 20
Retail Flowers & Gifts
S.I.C.: 5193
Iain Macfarlane *(Pres. & Chief Exec. Officer)*
William Kunkel *(Sr. V.P. & Chief Fin. Officer)*
Thomas E. Campbell *(V.P.-Mktg. Mgr.)*
Kevin Norwood *(Sec.)*

Weinstock's Florist Inc. **(1)**
5290 Roswell Rd.
Atlanta, GA 30342
Tel.: 404-255-1611
Fax: 404-255-1611
Iain MacFarlane *(Pres.)*

Non-U.S. Subsidiary:

Rockwood Gardens, Ltd. **(1)**
501 Harris St.
Rockwood, ON N0B 2K0, Canada
Tel.: 519-586-9539 (100%)
Fax: 519-856-2361
Emp.: 80
Direct. Mktg. of Nursery Products
S.I.C.: 5261; 5961
Iain Macfarlane *(Chm. & Chief Exec. Officer)*
William Kunkel *(Chief Fin. Officer)*
W. Thomas Stumb *(Treas.)*
John F.T. Warren *(Sec.)*

KNOX OIL OF TEXAS INC.
4835 LBJ Fwy., Ste. 800
Dallas, TX 75244
Tel.: 214-960-9663 **DE**
Fax: 214-458-1361
Approx.Sls.: $160,000,000
Emp.: 150
Petroleum Production & Mktg.
S.I.C.: 1311; 5172
Charles E. Knox, Jr. *(Chm. Bd. & Chief Exec. Officer)*
Richard Knox *(Exec. V.P., Sec. & Treas.)*
Lawner L. Knox *(Exec. V.P.)*
Robert Knox *(Exec. V.P.)*

Outside Service Firm(s):

Cornwell & Co.*(Auditors)*
Dallas, TX

KNUTSON CONSTRUCTION CO.
5500 Wayzata Blvd., Ste. 300
Minneapolis, MN 55416-1216
Tel.: 612-546-1400
Fax: 612-546-2226
Year Founded: 1911
Approx.Sls.: $110,000,000
Emp.: 500
Gen. Bldg. Contractors; Heavy Construction Contractors
S.I.C.: 1542; 1629
John Curry *(Pres.)*
Steven Curry *(V.P.)*
Michael Armato *(Chief Fin. Officer)*

Computer Systems/Hardware:
IBM

Outside Service Firm(s):

McGladrey & Pullen*(Auditors)*
1800 Town Square, 445 Minnesota St.
St. Paul, MN 55101

St. Paul Fire & Marine Insurance Co.*(Commercial Insurance Carrier)*
385 Washington St.
St. Paul, MN 55102
Tel.: 612-221-7911

Lincoln National Corporation*(Group Insurer)*
P.O. Box 2249
Fort Wayne, IN 46801

Fabyanske, Svoboda, Westra & Davis*(Legal Firm)*
1210 Minnesota World Trade Ctr, 30 E. 7th St.
St. Paul, MN 55101
Tel.: 612-228-0115
Fax: 612-228-0734

First Bank*(Major Banking Relationship)*
601 2nd Ave. S.
Minneapolis, MN 55402-4302
Tel.: 612-973-0586
Fax: 612-973-0828

THE KOBACKER COMPANY & AFFILIATES
P.O. Box 16751, 6606 Tussing Rd.
Columbus, OH 43068
Mailing Address:
P.O. Box 16751,
Columbus, OH 43216-6751
Tel.: 614-863-7400 **OH**
Fax: 614-575-7285
Approx.Sls.: $365,000,000
Emp.: 5,400
Fiscal Year-end: 1/31/91
780 Retail Shoe Stores Located Throughout U.S.
S.I.C.: 5661
Arthur J. Kobacker *(Chm. Bd. & Chief Exec. Officer)*
Alfred J. Kobacker *(Pres.)*
Dennis Bailen *(Pres.-Adv.)*
William Pavony *(Exec. V.P.-Admin. & Treas.)*
Anthony Matteo *(Sr. V.P.)*
Michael Allen *(V.P.-Human Resources)*
Robert J. Cepanec *(V.P.-Warehouse & Trans.)*
John E. Lattanzio *(V.P.)*
Thomas W. Osborn *(V.P.-Mngmt. Information Systems)*
Peter Struzzi *(V.P. & Controller)*
Timothy C. Robinson *(Asst. Treas.)*

No. of Mfg. Plants/Facilities: 4
No. of U.S. Offices: 3

Outside Service Firm(s):

Price Waterhouse*(Auditors)*
41 South High Street
Columbus, OH 43215

Marshall, Melhorn, Cole, Hummer & Spitzer*(Legal Firm)*
Fourteenth Fl., National Bank Bldg.
Toledo, OH 43604
Tel.: 419-243-4200

The Huntington National Bank*(Major Banking Relationship)*
41 S. High St.
Columbus, OH 43216

Subsidiary:

Picway Shoe Stores **(1)**
6606 Tussing Rd.
Columbus, OH 43216-6751
Tel.: 614-863-7400
Retail Family Shoe Stores
S.I.C.: 5661

Affiliates:

Gussini Shoe Stores **(1)**
6606 Tussing Rd.
Columbus, OH 43216-6751
Tel.: 614-863-7400
Retail Family Shoe Stores
S.I.C.: 5661

Kathe-K Shoe Stores **(1)**
6606 Tussing Rd.
Columbus, OH 43216-6751
Tel.: 614-863-7400
Retail Family Shoe Stores
S.I.C.: 5661

Patrini Shoe Stores **(1)**
6606 Tussing Rd.
Columbus, OH 43216-6751
Tel.: 614-863-7400
Retail Family Shoe Stores
S.I.C.: 5661

The Shoe Works Shoe Stores, Inc. **(1)**
6606 Tussing Rd.
Columbus, OH 43216-6751
Tel.: 614-863-7400
Retail Family Shoe Stores
S.I.C.: 5661

KOBRA INTERNATIONAL LTD
525 7th Ave., 20th Fl.
New York, NY 10018
Tel.: 212-719-9200 **NY**
Fax: 212-391-4327
Year Founded: 1982
Assets: $6,000,000
Liabilities: $3,000,000
Net Worth: $3,000,000
Approx.Sls.: $25,000,000
Emp.: 50
Fiscal Year-end: 12/31/90
Import Export
Ensemble Dresses, Blouses, Shirts, Slacks; Men's Wear
S.I.C.: 2335; 2331; 2337; 2339; 2321; 2325
B. Brad Konheim *(Pres. & Chief Exec. Officer)*
Nicole Miller *(Exec. V.P.)*
Estelle Rose *(Chief Fin. Officer)*
Colleen Konheim *(Sec.)*
Lisa Lemery *(Dir.-Sls.)*
Judy Scarpulla *(Mgr.-Sls.)*

No. of Mfg. Plants/Facilities: 8
No. of U.S. Offices: 2
No. of Foreign Offices: 1

Computer Systems/Hardware:
IBM AS/36

Outside Service Firm(s):

Mahoney Cohen & Co., P.C.*(Auditors)*
New York, NY

Feigen, Post & Holm*(Legal Firm)*
950 3rd Ave.
New York, NY

Chemical Banking Corp.*(Major Banking Relationship)*
277 Park Ave.
New York, NY 10041
Tel.: 212-310-6407
Fax: 212-310-4526

KOCH ENGINEERING COMPANY, INC.
(Knight Div.)
171 Kelly Ave.
Akron, OH 44306
Mailing Address:
P.O. Box 109
Akron, OH 44309
Tel.: 216-724-1277
Tel.: 800-562-4364
Telex: 986371
Fax: 216-724-6503
Year Founded: 1910
Approx.Sls.: $10,000,000
Emp.: 50
Fiscal Year-end: 12/31/91
Export
Mfr. of Chemical Equip., Acid Proof & Corrosion Proof Materials; Knight-Ware, Permanite, Pyroflex & Resibond
S.I.C.: 3559

Verne Griffith *(Pres.)*
Chuck Crowe *(V.P. & Gen. Mgr.)*
Keith Klaasen *(Controller)*
Jenni Herndon *(Adv. Dir.)*
Michael Davids *(Natl. Sls. & Mktg. Mgr.)*

Computer Systems/Hardware:
AST

GEORGE KOCH SONS, INC.
10 S. 11th Ave.
Evansville, IN 47744
Tel.: 816-465-9600 **IN**
Fax: 812-465-9724
Year Founded: 1873
Assets: $109,000,000
Liabilities: $24,000,000
Net Worth: $85,000,000
Approx.Sls.: $210,000,000
Emp.: 1,500
Fiscal Year-end: 12/31/91
Export
Mfr. Industrial Paint Finishing Systems, Indus. Ovens, Conveyors, Spray Booths, Portable Offices, Water Chillers, Refrigeration Systems
S.I.C.: 3567; 3535; 3559; 3449; 3444; 3443; 5075; 3561; 3585
Robert L. Koch II *(Pres. & Chief Exec. Officer)*
James H. Muehlbauer *(Exec. V.P. & Sec.)*
James C. Oskins *(Controller)*
Helen Deig *(Dir.-Purch.)*
Susan E. Parsons *(Dir.-Specialist)*
James Russell *(Dir.- Materials)*
Phil Williams *(Mgr.-Intl. Sls.)*
Sam Woehler *(Mgr.-Production)*

Principal(s):
Robert L. Koch II

No. of Mfg. Plants/Facilities: 5
No. of Foreign Offices: 1

Computer Systems/Hardware:
IBM System 38

Outside Service Firm(s):

Harding, Shymanski & Co.*(Auditors)*
Evansville, IN

Citizens National Bank*(Major Banking Relationship)*
20 NW Third St.
Evansville, IN 47739-0001
Tel.: 812-464-3400

Citizens National Bank*(Pension Manager)*
20 NW Third St.
Evansville, IN 47739-0001
Tel.: 812-464-3400

Subsidiaries:

Brake Supply Co. **(1)**
4001 Vogel Rd.
Evansville, IN 47715
Tel.: 812-479-6881
S.I.C.: 3559

Gibbs Diecasting Aluminum Corp. **(1)**
369 Community Dr.
Henderson, KY 42420
Tel.: 502-827-1801
Manufacturers Custom Aluminum Die Castings
S.I.C.: 3363
Robert L. Koch, II *(Chm. Bd. & Chief Exec. Officer)*
Nick Gibbs *(Pres.)*
William Baxter *(V.P.-Fin.)*
Don Crump *(Mgr.-Purch.)*

Uniseal, Inc. **(1)**
1800 W. Maryland St.
Evansville, IN 47712
Tel.: 812-425-1361
Manufactures Sealants & Adhesives
S.I.C.: 2891
Randall Zahn *(Pres.)*
Jack Zahn *(Treas.)*

KOCH INDUSTRIES, INCORPORATED
411 E. 37th St. No.
Wichita, KS 67220
Mailing Address:
P.O. Box 2256,
Wichita, KS 67201
Tel.: 316-832-5500 **KS**
Fax: 316-832-5860
Year Founded: 1942
Approx.Sls.: $13,000,000,000
Emp.: 7,000
Oil & Gas Producer; Crude Oil & Natural Gas Refining & Transportation by Pipeline
S.I.C.: 2911; 5171; 4613; 3089; 4612; 1311
Charles G. Koch *(Chm. Bd. & Chief Exec. Officer)*
Sterling V. Varner *(Vice Chm.)*
William W. Hanna *(Pres. & Chief Oper. Officer)*
Allen Caldwell *(Exec. V.P., Sec. & Gen. Counsel)*
F. Lynn Markel *(Exec. V.P.-Fin. & Chief Fin. Officer)*
Paul W. Brooks *(V.P.-Plng. & Devel.)*
C.J. Nelson *(Treas.)*
Dale Ballew *(Dir.-Personnel)*
Brad Hall *(Chief Information Officer)*
Allan Davis *(Mgr.-Information Svcs.)*

Computer Systems/Hardware:
Burroughs A15; IBM System 34

Outside Service Firm(s):

KPMG Peat Marwick*(Auditors)*
Wichita, KS

First Chicago Shareholder Services Trust Co.*(Major Banking Relationship)*
153 West 51st St.
New York, NY 10019
Tel.: 212-791-6422
Fax: 212-385-9798

Aetna Life & Casualty*(Group Insurer)*
151 Farmington Avenue
Hartford, CT 06156
Tel.: 203-273-2128
Fax: 203-729-4295

Mellon Bank*(Investment Banker)*
San Francisco, CA

Subsidiaries:

Koch Engineering Co., Inc. **(1)**
4111 E. 37th St., N.
Wichita, KS 67204
Tel.: 316-832-5110 (100%)
Mfr. Process Equip. Primarily for Fluid Separation; Mass Transfer Equip.
S.I.C.: 3599; 3443
John Van Gelder *(Pres.)*

Subsidiary:

John Zink Co. **(2)**
11920 E. Apache
Tulsa, OK 74116
Tel.: 918-234-1800
Fax: 918-234-2700
Approx.Sls.: $100,000,000
Emp.: 1,000
Fiscal Year-end: 12/31/91
Export
Mfr. Industrial Burners, Flares, Pollution Control Systems, Boilers, Vapor Recovery Systems, Incinerators, Process Control Systems, Hydro-Sonic Scrubber Systems
S.I.C.: 3433; 3443; 3567; 3823; 4953
Earl Schmell *(Pres.)*
Robert L. Rawlings *(V.P.-Sls. & Mktg.)*
William Hermann *(Mktg. Dir.)*
Bob Murry *(Pur. Dir.)*
Jack Carter *(Personnel Dir.)*
Jennifer Herndon *(Communications Dir.)*

Koch Membrane Systems **(1)**
850 Main St.
Wilmington, MA 01887
Tel.: 617-657-4250 (100%)
Mfr. Filtering Equip.
S.I.C.: 3569
William Ekyamp *(Pres.)*

Koch Refining Company **(1)**
P.O. Box 2302
Wichita, KS 67201
Tel.: 316-832-5500
Gasoline, Distillate Fuel Oils, Residual Fuel Oils, Coke, Sulphur, Road Oils & Asphalt
S.I.C.: 2911; 2899; 3312
B. A. Paulson *(Pres.)*

KOCH SUPPLIES INC.
1411 W. 29th St.
Kansas City, MO 64108
Tel.: 816-753-2150
Telex: 42264
Fax: 816-561-3286
Year Founded: 1883
Approx.Sls.: $40,000,000
Emp.: 140
Import Export
Mfg./ Distributor of Packaging Machines, Machinery Equipment & Supplies for Meat Handling, Commercial Kitchens, Sausage Makers, Locker Plants, Food Retailers, Laboratories, Automated Production Lines
S.I.C.: 5084
Lawrence D. Starr *(Pres.)*
John Starr *(Chief Oper. Officer)*
Robert Fillmore *(V.P.-Processing)*
Akhil Gupta *(V.P.-Corp. Plng.)*
Howard E. Meyer *(V.P. & Treas.)*
Bruce Sterling *(V.P.-Facilities)*
David L. Summers *(V.P.-Telemarketing)*
Reese Naftel *(Mgr.-Adv.)*

Outside Service Firm(s):

Arthur Andersen & Co.*(Auditors)*
1500 Commerce Tower, 911 Main St.
Kansas City, MO 64105
Tel.: 816-221-4200
Fax: 816-221-7693

Smith, Gill, Fisher & Butts*(Legal Firm)*
One Kansas City Place, 35th Fl, 1200 Main St.
Kansas City, MO 64105
Tel.: 816-474-7400

Boatmen's Trust Company*(Major Banking Relationship)*
100 North Broadway
St. Louis, MO 63102
Tel.: 314-466-2469

KOCOLENE OIL CORP.
1725 E. Tipton St.
Seymour, IN 47274
Mailing Address:
P.O. Box 448
Seymour, IN 47274
Tel.: 812-522-2224
Fax: 812-522-6264
Year Founded: 1973
Approx.Sls.: $94,100,000
Emp.: 250
Retail Petroleum Products
S.I.C.: 5541
Robert Myers *(Chm. Bd.)*
Gary F. Myers *(Pres.)*
Robert L. Prather *(Exec. V.P., Sec. & Treas.)*

KOEHLER MANUFACTURING COMPANY
123 Felton St.
Marlborough, MA 01752
Tel.: 508-485-1000
Tel.: 800-456-2200
Telex: 94 8400
Fax: 508-485-1004
Year Founded: 1921
Approx.Sls.: $12,000,000
Emp.: 150
Fiscal Year-end: 12/31/90
Import Export
Mfr. of Cap Lamps, Hand Lanterns, Rechargeable Lights & Flashlights, Vehicle-Mounted Battery Chargers, AC/DC Converters & Battery Testers
S.I.C.: 3648

M.W. Powning *(Chm. & Chief Exec. Officer)*
R.L. Mitchell *(Pres.)*
J.E. Gulliksen *(V.P.-Mktg.)*
J.M. Rilla *(V.P.-Fin. & Admin.)*
Frederick A. Coe, Jr. *(Mgr.-Natl. Sls.)*
C.F. Daly *(Mgr.-Engrng.)*
L.J. Moody *(Mgr.-Mfg.)*
P.M. Morcone *(Mgr.-Human Resources)*
Melanie L. Goddard *(Coord.-Mktg.)*

Computer Systems/Hardware:
NCR

KOH-I-NOOR, INC.
100 North St.
Bloomsbury, NJ 08804
Mailing Address:
P.O. Box 2028
Lehigh Valley, PA 18001
Tel.: 908-479-4124
Fax: 201-479-4285
Year Founded: 1790
Approx.Sls.: $30,000,000
Emp.: 500
Import Export
Rapidograph Technical Pens, Montblanc Fountain Pens, Pelikan Drawing Inks & Artist Materials
S.I.C.: 3951; 3952
Fred Clauser *(Pres.)*
Richard L. Mattes *(V.P.-Mktg.)*
Edward A. Murray *(V.P.-Sls. & Mktg.)*
Vincent A. Trippy *(Dir.-Adv.)*

Division:

Cosmolab Div. **(1)**
Lewisburg, TN 37091
Tel.: 615-359-6253
Mfr. of Cosmetic Pencils, Powder & Other Cosmetic Prods.
S.I.C.: 2844
Robert Lasater *(Pres.)*

KOHLER COMPANY
444 Highland Dr.
Kohler, WI 53044
Tel.: 414-457-4441 **WI**
Telex: 269558
Fax: 414-457-1271
Year Founded: 1873
Sales Range: $500-999 Million
Emp.: 13,500
Fiscal Year-end: 12/31/90
Import Export
Cast Iron & Vitreous China; Fiberglass Reinforced Plastic Sheet Molded Compound & Acrylic Plumbing Fixtures & Fittings, Faucets, Air-Cooled Engines, Generators & Specialty Products; Environmental Enclosures; Owns Furniture Businesses; Hospitality & Real Estate Businesses
S.I.C.: 3432; 3261; 3519; 7011; 6531; 3089; 3321; 3613; 3621; 7992; 7997
Corporate Giving Program:
Corporated Giving is Generally Community & Employee Focused in Areas Where Company Has Manufacturing Facilities
Herbert V. Kohler, Jr. *(Chm. Bd., Pres., Chief Oper. & Chief Exec. Officer)*
Sam H. Davis *(Vice Chm.)*
Frank J. Feraco *(Pres.-Sterling Plumbing Group)*
George R. Tiedens *(Grp. V.P.-Power Systems)*
Natalie A. Black *(V.P. & Gen. Counsel)*
K.W. Conger *(V.P.-Human Resources)*
Joseph W. Harbrecht *(V.P.-Plumbing & Specialty Prods.-No. America)*
John W. Lillesand *(V.P.-Tech. Services)*
Richard A. Wells *(V.P.-Fin.)*
Jeffrey P. Cheney *(Treas.)*
W.J. Drew *(Sec.)*
Clyde W. Kometer *(Controller)*
J. Morris Elliott *(Dir.-Pur.)*

Kohler Company—(Continued)

Carol E. Erwin *(Dir.-Public Affairs)*
Rachel Kohler *(Dir.-Plng. & Devel.)*
Mark Vogel *(Dir.-Adv.)*
Arlyn Engman *(Mgr.-Telecommunications)*
Peter J. Fetterer *(Mgr.-Media & Civic Services)*
Noel E. Fredrickson *(Mgr.-Data Processing Opers.)*

No. of Mfg. Plants/Facilities: 3
No. of U.S. Offices: 16
No. of Foreign Offices: 3

Computer Systems/Hardware:
IBM 308X COBOL

Outside Service Firm(s):

Ernst & Young*(Auditors)*
233 S. Wacker Dr.
Chicago, IL 60606
Tel.: 312-368-1800
Fax: 312-645-3095

John Hancock Mutual Life Insurance Co.*(Group Insurer)*
John Hancock Place, P.O. Box 111
Boston, MA 02117

Quarles & Brady*(Legal Firm)*
411 E. Wisconsin Av.
Milwaukee, WI 53202
Tel.: 414-277-5000

Bank of America, N.T. & S.A.*(Major Banking Relationship)*
P.O. Box 37002,
San Francisco, CA 94137

Citibank N.A.*(Major Banking Relationship)*
Corporate Trust Services, 399 Park Ave.
New York, NY 10043
Tel.: 212-559-1605

Continental Bank N. A.*(Major Banking Relationship)*
231 S. LaSalle St.
Chicago, IL 60697
Tel.: 312-828-2345
Tel.: 800-426-5754
Telex: 312-828-1783

First Wisconsin National Bank*(Major Banking Relationship)*
Sheboygan, WI

NationsBank Texas*(Major Banking Relationship)*
901 Main St., 16th Fl.
Dallas, TX 75202
Tel.: 214-922-5000

John Hancock Mutual Life Insurance Co.*(Pension Manager)*
John Hancock Place, P.O. Box 111
Boston, MA 02117

Subsidiaries:

Baker Knapp & Tubbs Inc. **(1)**
1661 Monroe Ave. N.W.
Grand Rapids, MI 49505
Tel.: 616-361-7321 (100%)
Emp.: 1,390
Manufacturing of Traditional & Contemporary Furniture
S.I.C.: 2512; 2521; 2511
Roderick G. Kreitzer *(Pres. & Chief Exec. Officer)*
Vince Creadon *(Sr. V.P.-Sls. & Mktg.)*
Thomas J. O'Connell *(V.P.-Fin.)*
Philip Van Suilichem *(Dir.-Adv.)*
Donald S. Milton *(Dir.-Matls.)*

Kallista, Inc. **(1)**
1658, 2701 Merced St.
San Leandro, CA 94577
Tel.: 510-895-6400
Mfr. of Whirlpool Baths, Metallic & Ceramic Lavs., Faucets & Bath Accessories
S.I.C.: 3842; 3431; 3432; 3261

Kohler Co. (SC) **(1)**
P.O. Box 1987,
Spartanburg, SC 29304
Tel.: 803-582-3401
Emp.: 700
Vitreous China & Fiberglass Reinforced Plastic Plumbing Fixtures
S.I.C.: 3261
John M. Kohler, Jr. *(Mgr.)*

Kohler Co. (TX) **(1)**
P.O. Box 1709,
Brownwood, TX 76801
Tel.: 915-643-2661
Emp.: 870
Vitreous China & Acrylic Plumbing & Leisure Prods.
S.I.C.: 3261
Robert Bagwell *(Mgr.)*

Ann Sacks Tile & Stone, Inc. **(1)**
535 N.E. 28th Ave.
Portland, OR 97232
Tel.: 503-231-7558
Ceramic Tile, Marble & Stone
S.I.C.: 3253; 5032
Timothy J. Mullally *(Chm. Bd.)*

The Sterling Group **(1)**
1730 Remington Rd.
Schaumburg, IL 60195
Tel.: 708-843-5420 (100%)
Emp.: 1520
Plumbing Faucets & Fittings
S.I.C.: 3432; 3431; 3089
William Boyd *(Chief Oper. Officer)*

Sterling Plumbing Group, Inc. **(1)**
1375 Remington Rd.
Schaumburg, IL 60195
Tel.: 708-843-5400 (100%)
Telex: 280-142
Fax: 708-843-5411
Approx.Sls.: $10,000,000
Emp.: 990
Import Export
Mfr. of Plumbing Fixtures
S.I.C.: 3432
William W. Boyd *(Chmn. Bd. & Pres.)*
Mark S. Arnold *(V.P., Chief Fin. Officer & Controller)*
J.P. McClone *(Dir.-Mktg.)*

Plants:

Sterling Faucet Co. **(2)**
P. O. Box 427, South Oklahoma St.
Sheridan, AR 72150
Tel.: 501-942-2111 (100%)
Emp.: 300
Mfrs. Plumbing Fittings & Trim
S.I.C.: 3432
David C. Brown *(Plant Mgr.)*

Sterling Faucet Co. **(2)**
P. O. Box 798, Route 7 East
Morgantown, WV 26505
Tel.: 304-292-6393 (100%)
Emp.: 700
Mfrs. Plumbing Fitting & Trim
S.I.C.: 3432
Richard Grosshuesch *(Plant Mgr.)*

Non-U.S. Holdings:

Compagnie Internationale Des Produits Sanitaires (CIPS) Jacob Delafon **(1)**
51 Rue Du Commandant Rolland 93350 Le Jrourget,
Paris, France
Tel.: 33-14-027-5300 (100%)
Fax: 33-14-804-9882
Emp.: 2,000
Full-Line Plumbing Prods. Mfr.--Vitreous China, Enameled Cast Iron, Stainless Steel & Acrylic Plumbing Fixtures, Brass Faucets & Vanity Cabinets
S.I.C.: 3432; 3261; 3088
Steven E. Malm *(Pres.)*

Kohler de Mexico, S.A. de C.V. **(1)**
Calle Norte 45 No. 766 Fraccio Namiento Ind. Vallego, Codigo postal 2300,
Mexico, D.F. 15, Mexico
Tel.: 905-587-3656 (100%)
Telex: 269688
Fax: 414-459-1570
Emp.: 250
Mfr. Engines
S.I.C.: 3621; 3519
A.A. Soules *(Mng. Dir.)*

Kohler Japan K.K. **(1)**
3-19-23 Minami-Azabu Minanto-Ku,
Tokyo, T-106, Japan
Tel.: 81-3-440-4440
Telex: 269558
Emp.: 22
Plumbing Prods. Sls. & Showroom
S.I.C.: 5074
Kenneth G. Boston *(Pres.)*

Kohler Japan K.K. **(1)**
3-19-23 Minami Azabu Minato-ku,
Tokyo, T-106, Japan
Tel.: 03-3440-4440 (100%)
Fax: 3-440-2727
Emp.: 25
Sls. & Distr. of Kohler Plumbing Prods.
S.I.C.: 5074
Toru Nakamuru *(Gen. Mgr.)*

Kohler Ltd. **(1)**
RR3, C-1 Palisades
Armstrong, BC VOE 1BO, Canada
Tel.: 604-546-3196
Emp.: 90
Fiberglass Reinforced Plastic & Plumbing Fixtures
S.I.C.: 3088
Donald J. Matheson *(Gen. Mgr.)*

Kohler Ltd. **(1)**
805 Education Rd.
Cornwall, ON Canada K6H 6C7
Tel.: 613-933-4520 (100%)
Fax: 613-938-4945
Emp.: 140
Manufacture Of Acrylic & Fiberglass Plumbing Products
S.I.C.: 3088
Philip Koechlein *(Plant Mgr.)*

Kohler Ltd. **(1)**
195 The West Mall
Etobicoke, ON M9C 5K1, Canada
Tel.: 416-626-8256 (100%)
Fax: 416-626-8698
Emp.: 25
Sls. of Acrylic & Fibreglass Plumbing Prods.
S.I.C.: 5074
Mike Roy *(Dir.-Sls. & Mktg.)*

Kohler Ltd. **(1)**
4150 Spallumcheed Road Spallumcheed Ind. Pk,
Armstrong, B.C. V0E 1B0, Canada
Tel.: 604-546-3196
Fax: 604-546-8677
S.I.C.: 3089
Thomas Pinkney *(Plant Mgr.)*

KOHM ASSOCIATES, INC.
496 Kinderkamack Rd.
Oradell, NJ 07649
Tel.: 201-265-6550
Year Founded: 1961
Approx.Billings: $19,000,000
Emp.: 24
Corporate Positioning
William Kohm *(Chm. Bd.)*
James McQueeny *(Pres.)*
Gary Davis *(Exec. V.P., Adv. & Gen. Mgr.)*
Marie Smith *(Sec.)*

KOKOMO GRAIN CO., INC.
1002 W. Morgan St.
Kokomo, IN 46901
Mailing Address:
P.O. Box 745
Kokomo, IN 46903
Tel.: 317-457-7536 **IN**
Fax: 317-456-1207
Year Founded: 1950
Approx.Sls.: $72,300,000
Emp.: 80
Grain Elevator
S.I.C.: 5153
Raymond L. Ortman *(Pres.)*
Elizabeth J. Ortman *(Treas. & Sec.)*

Principal(s):
Ortman Family

Outside Service Firm(s):

Crowe, Chizek & Co.*(Auditors)*
South Bend, IN

INB National Bank*(Major Banking Relationship)*
One Indiana Sq.
Indianapolis, IN 46266
Tel.: 317-266-6000

KOKOMO SANITARY POTTERY CORP.
4656 West Touhy Avenue
Chicago, IL 60646
Tel.: 708-675-6570
Fax: 1-800-5-GERBER
Year Founded: 1933
Approx.Sls.: $80,000,000
Emp.: 750
Fiscal Year-end: 11/30/91
Export
Mfr. of Vitreous China Plumbing Fixtures
S.I.C.: 3261
Harriet G. Lewis *(Chm. Bd.)*
Jack Hanlon *(Pres. & Chief Oper. Officer)*
Alan G. Lewis *(Chief Exec. Officer)*
Robert C. Luker *(Chief Fin. Officer & V.P.)*
Jon Deiter *(Controller)*
Ila J. Lewis *(Treas.)*
Daryl E. Gerber *(Sec.)*
Douglas Elias *(Mgr.-Data Processing)*

KOKOMO SPRING COMPANY, INC.
329 E. Firmin St.
Kokomo, IN 46902
Tel.: 317-459-5156
Fax: 317-459-4567
Year Founded: 1910
Approx.Sls.: $12,000,000
Emp.: 140
Fiscal Year-end: 12/31/91
Mechanical Coil Springs & Fabricated Wire Products
S.I.C.: 3495
Bob Balcerzak *(Pres.)*
John Armstead *(Mgr.-Quality Control)*
Gary Chivellit *(Mgr.-Mfg.)*
Bill Getner *(Mgr.-Mktg.)*
Dave McPike *(Mgr.-Sls.)*

Outside Service Firm(s):

Ernst & Young*(Auditors)*
One Indiana Square, Ste. 3400
Indianapolis, IN 46204
Tel.: 317-236-1100

Union Bank*(Major Banking Relationship)*
Indianapolis, IN

KOKOSING CONSTRUCTION COMPANY, INC.
17531 Waterford Rd.
Fredericktown, OH 43019
Tel.: 614-694-6315 **OH**
Fax: 614-694-1481
Year Founded: 1951
Assets: $72,722,736
Liabilities: $58,031,827
Net Worth: $14,690,909
Approx.Sls.: $188,000,000
Emp.: 1,000
Fiscal Year-end: 3/31/92
General Contractor: Highway, Heavy Construction & Utilities
S.I.C.: 1541; 1542; 1611; 1623; 1622
William Brian Burgett *(Pres.)*
Daniel W. Walker *(Sr. V.P.)*
William Barth Burgett *(V.P.-Equipment)*
Daniel J. Compston *(V.P.-Hwy. & Heavy Construction)*
Valerie Matusik *(V.P.-Pub. Rels.)*
John Neighbors *(V.P.-Opers.)*
John Rigo *(V.P.-Engrng.)*
Marsha Rinehart *(V.P.-Human Resources)*
Michael Rohal *(V.P.-Asphalt)*
Dennis Tuttle *(V.P.-Estimating)*
James Geiser *(Controller)*
Ron Cochran *(Dir.-Mktg.)*
Dan Orr *(Mgr.-Data Processing)*

No. of U.S. Offices: 2

Computer Systems/Hardware:
IBM AS/400

Outside Service Firm(s):

Coopers & Lybrand*(Auditors)*
100 E. Broad St.
Columbus, OH 43215

William Heichel*(Legal Firm)*
Mansfield, OH

National City Bank*(Major Banking Relationship)*
P.O. Box 92301, Corp. Trust Dept.
Cleveland, OH 44101
Tel.: 216-575-2000

Subsidiaries:

Kokosing Materials, Inc. **(1)**
P.O. Box 334,
Fredericktown, OH 43109
Tel.: 614-694-6315
Asphalt
S.I.C.: 3531
Wayne Brassell *(Pres.)*

McGraw/Kokosing, Inc. **(1)**
P.O. Box 370,
Middletown, OH 45042
Tel.: 513-422-4521
Emp.: 300
Steel Mill Maintenance, Heavy Industrial
S.I.C.: 3325
Lee Warner *(V.P.)*

Olen Corporation **(1)**
4755 S. High St.
Columbus, OH 43207
Tel.: 614-491-1515
Aggregate Plant
S.I.C.: 5032
Wayne Rayburn *(Pres.)*
April Bobo *(Sec. & Controller)*

KOLD KIST BRANDS, INC.
P.O. Box 91-1228,
Los Angeles, CA 90091
Mailing Address:
P.O. Box 91-1228,
Los Angeles, CA 90091-1228
Year Founded: 1939
Approx.Sls.: $20,000,000
Emp.: 180
Fiscal Year-end: 9/30/90
Kold Kist Prepared Frozen Entrees, Retail & Institutional; Kold Kist Frozen Italian Entrees, Jimi's, Tio Rito & Granada, Frozen Mexican Foods, Retail & Institutional
S.I.C.: 2038; 5421
Roger Peters *(Pres. & Chief Exec. Officer)*
Dahl Cosey *(V.P.-Mfg.)*
Sako Aryan *(Controller)*
Douglas Werner *(Dir.-Sls.)*

Outside Service Firm(s):

Costillo & Ebenhoch*(Auditors)*
Santa Monica, CA

Gold, Marks, Ring & Pepper*(Legal Firm)*
Los Angeles, CA

Security Pacific National Bank*(Major Banking Relationship)*
P.O. Box 60228, Terminal Annex,
Los Angeles, CA 90060
Tel.: 213-580-2829

KOLESAR & HARTWELL INC.
1201 Marquette Ave.
Minneapolis, MN 55403
Tel.: 612-343-0418
Year Founded: 1970
Approx.Billings: $18,700,000
Emp.: 30
Travel, Financial Services, Sporting Goods & Consumer Durables
Doug Sietsema *(Pres. & Chief Exec. Officer)*
Jay Gould *(V.P., Bus. Devel. & Media)*
John Clay *(V.P.)*
Bob Sievers *(V.P.)*
Paula Nelson *(Treas.)*

Computer Systems/Hardware:
US West

KOLL CO.
4343 Von Karmen Ave.
Newport Beach, CA 92660
Tel.: 714-833-3030 **CA**
Fax: 714-833-9750
Year Founded: 1962
Approx.Sls.: $725,000,000
Emp.: 1,050
Real Estate Developer; General Contractor Non-Residential Buildings
S.I.C.: 6552; 1542
Donald M. Koll *(Chm. Bd. & Chief Exec. Officer)*
Ray Wirta *(Pres. & Chief Oper. Officer)*
John L. Wills *(Pres.-Construction Services Grp.)*
Lawrence Kellner *(Chief Fin. Officer)*
Lynda Lane *(Sr. V.P.-Admin. Corp. Communications)*
Liz Hallin *(V.P.-Human Resources)*
Principal(s):
Donald M. Koll

No. of U.S. Offices: 12

Computer Systems/Hardware:
NCR

Outside Service Firm(s):

Allen, Matkins, Leck, Gamble & Mallory*(Legal Firm)*
515 So. Figueroa St., Eighth Fl.
Los Angeles, CA 90071

Wells Fargo Bank*(Major Banking Relationship)*
420 Montgomery St.
San Francisco, CA 94104

KOLLER ENTERPRISES, INC.
1400 S. Hwy. 141
Fenton, MO 63026
Tel.: 314-343-9220 **MO**
Fax: 314-343-1034
Year Founded: 1941
Approx.Sls.: $21,000,000
Emp.: 160
Import Export
Injection Molded Finished Plastic Products; Vacuum Plating of Plastics; Louvres
S.I.C.: 3089; 3471
Alois J. Koller, Sr. *(Chm. Bd.)*
Alois J. Koller, Jr. *(Pres.)*
Marie Koller *(Treas. & Sec.)*

Outside Service Firm(s):

Gus V. Keller & Co.*(Auditors)*
St. Louis, MO

John Howard*(Legal Firm)*
Hillsboro, MO

Chippewa First Financial Bank*(Major Banking Relationship)*
St. Louis, MO

Division:

Paramount Metalizing Div. **(1)**
1008 W. North Service Rd.
Sullivan, MO 63080
Tel.: 314-468-3181
Emp.: 12
Vacuum Metallizing of Plastic & Metal Articles
S.I.C.: 3471
Bill Lopez *(Gen. Mgr.)*

JOHN F. KOLODY INC.
Central Westchester Bus. Pk.,
100 Exec. Blvd.
Ossining, NY 10562
Tel.: 914-762-0300
Fax: 914-762-3608
Year Founded: 1980
Approx.Billings: $16,000,000
Emp.: 12
John F. Kolody *(Pres. & Dir.-Creative)*

Sophia Braun *(Mgr.-Fin.)*

KOLON, BITTKER & DESMOND, INC.
Ameritech Publishing Bldg.,
100 E. Big Beaver, Ste. 1000
Troy, MI 48083
Tel.: 313-524-2500
Fax: 313-524-2527
Year Founded: 1966
Approx.Billings: $40,100,000
Emp.: 55
Advertising Agency
S.I.C.: 7311
John S. Kolon *(Pres.)*
Tim Brown *(Sr. V.P.-Fin. & Admin.)*
Rebecca McLennan *(Dir.-Pub. Rels.)*
Marlene Stone *(Dir.-Res.)*

No. of U.S. Offices: 1

Outside Service Firm(s):

Price Waterhouse*(Auditors)*
200 Renaissance Center, Ste. 3900
Detroit, MI 48243

Miro, Miro & Weiner*(Legal Firm)*
500 N. Woodward Ave., Ste. 100
Bloomfield Hills, MI 48013
Tel.: 313-646-2400

CHARLES KOMAR & SONS, INC.
16 E. 34th St., 10th Fl.
New York, NY 10016
Tel.: 212-725-1500
Fax: 212-889-1408
Sales Range: $20-39 Million
Emp.: 900
Women's Lingerie, Robes, Shifts, Housecoats & Nightwear
S.I.C.: 2341; 2253; 2254
Charles E. Komar *(Pres. & Chief Exec. Officer)*
David L. Komar *(Exec. V.P.)*
Charles J. Stempler *(Exec. V.P.)*

Outside Service Firm(s):

Sanford E. Moore & Co.*(Auditors)*
New York, NY

KOMBI, LTD.
102 Great Hill Rd.
Naugatuck, CT 06770
Tel.: 203-723-7441
Tel.: 800-243-6117
Telex: 996-418
Fax: 203-723-4980
Year Founded: 1969
Approx.Sls.: $15,000,000
Emp.: 25
Fiscal Year-end: 1/31/93
Import Export
Mfr. Hunting, Fishing & Ski Gloves; Thermal Underwear & Socks & Turtlenecks
S.I.C.: 3949; 2322
Danny Gold *(Pres.)*
Joseph Grandieri *(Gen. Mgr.)*
Edward Pascal *(Managing Partner, V.P. & Corp. Sec.)*
Carol Small *(Credit Mgr.)*

Computer Systems/Hardware:
Data General

KOMLINE-SANDERSON ENGINEERING CORP.
12 Holland Ave.
Peapack, NJ 07977
Tel.: 908-234-1000
Fax: 908-234-9487
Year Founded: 1946
Approx.Sls.: $30,000,000
Emp.: 250
Import Export

Mfr. Liquid-Solids Separation Equip., Pumps, Drying Equip. & Incineration Systems
S.I.C.: 3569; 3559; 3561; 3567; 3586; 3433
Elizabeth M. Komline *(Vice Chm.)*
Russel M. Komline *(Pres.)*
Robert Blickens *(V.P.-Fin., Treas. & Comptroller)*
James A. Louden *(V.P.-Sls.)*

KOOL SEAL, INC.
1499 Enterprise Pkwy.
Twinsburg, OH 44087
Tel.: 216-425-4717
Fax: 216-425-9778
Approx.Sls.: $10,000,000
Emp.: 30
Mfr. of Protective Roof Coatings and Sealants
S.I.C.: 2952; 2851
Steve Hudak *(Pres.)*
Sherry Lehnert *(Mgr.-Sls.)*
William Scott *(Mgr.-Sls.)*

KOOLVENT ALUMINUM PRODUCTS, INC.
1417 McLaughlin Rd.
Pittsburgh, PA 15241
Tel.: 412-257-2400
Fax: 412-257-2424
Approx.Sls.: $18,000,000
Emp.: 450
Manufacture Aluminum, Roofing & Sheet Metal Works; Custom Make & Mfg. Windows & Doors
S.I.C.: 1761; 3353
Gary Iskra *(Pres. & Chief Exec. Officer)*
Mel J. Feinberg *(Sr. V.P.)*
Clark Burget *(V.P.-Mfg.)*
Alexander H. Koontz *(Controller)*

Outside Service Firm(s):

Deloitte & Touche*(Auditors)*
2400 One PPG Place
Pittsburgh, PA 15222
Tel.: 412-281-2232

Houston Harbaugh*(Legal Firm)*
Pittsburgh, PA

Union National Bank*(Major Banking Relationship)*
Pittsburgh, PA

PERRY H. KOPLIK & SONS
505 Park Ave.
New York, NY 10022
Tel.: 212-752-2288
Brokers for Pulp & Paper Products
S.I.C.: 5113; 2679
Michael Koplik *(Pres.)*

J. KORBER & COMPANY
2311 Vassar N.E.
Albuquerque, NM 87107
Mailing Address:
P.O. Box 30548
Albuquerque, NM 87190
Tel.: 505-884-4652 **NM**
Fax: 505-884-4681
Year Founded: 1885
Approx.Sls.: $20,000,000
Emp.: 100
Wholesale Distributor & Retail Sales of Automotive Supplies & Parts
S.I.C.: 5013; 5531
Al Korber *(Pres.)*
Judy Elstner *(Exec. V.P.)*
Mike Hostzeller *(V.P.-Auto Parts)*
Libby Korber *(Controller, Treas. & Sec.)*

Outside Service Firm(s):

Sutin, Thayer & Browne*(Legal Firm)*
P.O. Box 1945, First Plz.
Albuquerque, NM 87103
Tel.: 505-842-8200

J. Korber & Company—(Continued)

Bank of Las Vegas*(Major Banking Relationship)*
Las Vegas, NV

KORES NORDIC USA CORP.
2745 W. 5th North St.
Summerville, SC 29483
Tel.: 803-871-6084
Year Founded: 1979
Approx.Sls.: $15,000,000
Emp.: 200
Import Export
Mfr. of Word & Data Processing Equipment
S.I.C.: 3955; 2678
J.J. O'Connor *(Chief Exec. Officer)*
Melvin Goldman *(Pres.)*
Michael Derum *(V.P.-Sls.)*
Edward Tassin *(V.P.-Mfg.)*
William Hartzell *(V.P.-Fin.)*
H. Vroon *(Dir.-Mktg.)*

KORET OF CALIFORNIA
611 Mission St.
San Francisco, CA 94105
Tel.: 415-957-2000
Fax: 415-957-2039
Emp.: 1,200
Mfr. & Retail Women's Wear
S.I.C.: 5921
Steven Rudin *(Pres.)*

Outside Service Firm(s):

KPMG Peat Marwick*(Auditors)*
3 Embarcadero Center
San Francisco, CA 94111
Tel.: 415-951-0100
Fax: 415-397-1129

Bankers Trust Co.*(Major Banking Relationship)*
280 Park Ave.
New York, NY 10017
Tel.: 212-454-2647

Wells Fargo Bank*(Major Banking Relationship)*
420 Montgomery St.
San Francisco, CA 94104

Morrison & Foerster*(Legal Firm)*
345 California St.
San Francisco, CA 94104
Tel.: 415-677-7000

Subsidiaries:

Koret of California **(1)**
595 Market St., 15th Fl.
San Francisco, CA 94105
Tel.: 415-957-2000

KORET GIVENCHY
136 Madison Ave.
New York, NY 10016
Tel.: 212-683-8544
Fax: 212-686-1027
Year Founded: 1929
Approx.Sls.: $13,500,000
Emp.: 250
Fiscal Year-end: 12/31/90
Mfr. & Distribution of Women's Handbags, Luggage, Personal Leather Goods, Manicure Sets, Clocks, Lighters, Keyrings
S.I.C.: 3161; 3171; 3172; 3199
Michael Gordon *(Pres. & Treas.)*
Harold Feigelson *(V.P.-Sls.)*
Thomas Tillander *(V.P. & Sec.)*

Outside Service Firm(s):

Reminick, Arron & Company*(Auditors)*
New York, NY

National Westminster Bank plc*(Major Banking Relationship)*
Astor Plaza, 1515 Broadway
New York, NY 10036

KOREY, KAY & PARTNERS

KOREY, KAY & PARTNERS
130 Fifth Ave.
New York, NY 10011
Tel.: 212-620-4300
Fax: 212-620-7149, 7055
Year Founded: 1982
Approx.Billings: $62,500,425
Emp.: 49
Allen Kay *(Chm. Bd. & Chief Creative Officer)*
Steve Fajen *(Exec. V.P., Dir. Media & Mktg. Services)*
Milda Misevicius *(Exec. V.P., Dir. New Bus. Devel.)*
David S. Harris *(Sr. V.P., Dir. Fin.)*
Cindy Rosenfeld *(V.P., Dir. Human Resources)*

Computer Systems/Hardware:
MacIntosh, Wang

KORMAN CO.
Two Neshaminy Interplex
Trevose, PA 19047
Mailing Address:
P.O. Box 2000,
Trevose, PA 19047
Tel.: 215-245-0700
Telex: 510-667-1508-TREV
Emp.: 320
Residential, Commercial & Industrial Devel. & Mngmt. Company
S.I.C.: 1611; 1531; 6552; 6531
Berton E. Korman *(Partner)*
Leonard I. Korman *(Partner)*
Steven H. Korman *(Partner)*
Michael M. Struglia *(Controller)*
Jeanne Landgraf *(Asst. Treas.)*

Outside Service Firm(s):

Price Waterhouse*(Auditors)*
30 S. 17th St.
Philadelphia, PA 19103
Tel.: 215-665-9500

Mellon Bank, N.A.*(Major Banking Relationship)*
P.O. Box 444,
Pittsburgh, PA 15230
Tel.: 412-236-8000
Tel.: 1-800-451-7392
Fax: 412-236-8157

Philadelphia National Bank*(Major Banking Relationship)*
P.O. Box 13834, Broad & Chestnut Streets
Philadelphia, PA 19101-7618
Tel.: 215-973-8327

Pilot Life*(Group Insurer)*
Greensboro, NC

Wolf, Block, Schorr & Solis-Cohen*(Legal Firm)*
Packard Bldg.
Philadelphia, PA 19102
Tel.: 215-977-2000

Mellon Bank, N.A.*(Pension Manager)*
P.O. Box 444,
Pittsburgh, PA 15230
Tel.: 412-236-8000
Tel.: 1-800-451-7392
Fax: 412-236-8157

KORN/FERRY INTERNATIONAL
1800 Century Park East, #900
Los Angeles, CA 90067
Tel.: 310-552-1834 **CA**
Fax: 310-553-6452
Year Founded: 1969
Assets: $55,064,000
Liabilities: $34,013,000
Net Worth: $21,051,000
Approx.Rev.: $100,000,000
Emp.: 537
Fiscal Year-end: 4/30/92
Executive Search Service
S.I.C.: 7361
Richard M. Ferry *(Chm. Bd., Pres. & Chief Exec. Officer)*
Peter L. Dunn *(V.P.-Admin., Gen. Counsel & Sec.)*
Norman A. Glick *(V.P.-Fin.)*
Dennis Harris *(V.P. & Controller)*
Richard A. Testa *(V.P.-Mngmt. Information Systems)*
Robert Woodrum *(V.P.-Pub. Rels. & Dir.-Media)*

No. of Mfg. Plants/Facilities: 17
No. of U.S. Offices: 25

Outside Service Firm(s):

Arthur Andersen & Co.*(Auditors)*
633 W. Fifth St.
Los Angeles, CA 90071
Tel.: 213-614-6500

O'Melveny & Myers*(Legal Firm)*
400 S. Hope St.
Los Angeles, CA 90071
Tel.: 213-669-6000

First Business Bank*(Major Banking Relationship)*
Los Angeles, CA

Subsidiaries:

Korn/Ferry International **(1)**
303 Peachtree St., N.E., Ste. 1600
Atlanta, GA 30303
Tel.: 404-577-7542
Fax: 404-584-9781
Alan Neely *(Office Mgr.)*

Korn/Ferry International **(1)**
101 Federal St., 24th Fl.
Boston, MA 02110
Tel.: 617-345-0200
Fax: 617-345-0544
John Sullivan *(Office Mgr.)*

Korn/Ferry International **(1)**
120 South Riverside Plaza, Ste. 918
Chicago, IL 60606
Tel.: 312-726-1841
Fax: 312-726-2836
Michael D. Boxberger *(Mng. Dir.-N. America)*
Paul Flask *(Office Mgr.)*

Korn/Ferry International **(1)**
Eaton Center, 1111 Superior Ave., Ste. 1300
Cleveland, OH 44114
Tel.: 216-861-5656
Fax: 216-861-5987
James Herget *(Office Mgr.)*

Korn/Ferry International **(1)**
3950 Lincoln Plaza, 500 North Akard St.
Dallas, TX 75201
Tel.: 214-954-1834
Fax: 214-954-1849
Richard Hardison *(Office Mgr.)*

Korn/Ferry International **(1)**
81 Wethersfield Ave.
Hartford, CT 06114
Tel.: 203-727-0721
Fax: 203-727-1081
Howard Nitschke *(Office Mgr.)*

Korn/Ferry International **(1)**
1100 Milam Bldg., Ste. 3400
Houston, TX 77002
Tel.: 713-651-1834
Fax: 713-651-0848
Jack Baber *(Office Mgr.)*

Korn/Ferry International **(1)**
100 East Wardlow
Long Beach, CA 90807
Tel.: 310-595-1101
Fax: 310-427-4225
Jane Hurd *(Office Mgr.)*

Korn/Ferry International **(1)**
601 S. Figueroa, Ste. 1900
Los Angeles, CA 90017
Tel.: 213-624-6600
Fax: 213-617-0688
Pete Kelly *(Office Mgr.)*

Korn/Ferry International **(1)**
1800 Century Park East, Ste. 900
Los Angeles, CA 90067
Tel.: 310-552-1834
Fax: 310-554-6452

Korn/Ferry International **(1)**
2508 IDS Center, 80 S. Eigth St.
Minneapolis, MN 55402
Tel.: 612-333-1834
Fax: 612-333-8971
Allan Raymond *(Office Mgr.)*

Korn/Ferry International **(1)**
1300 Dove St., Ste. 300
Newport Beach, CA 92600
Tel.: 714-851-1834
Fax: 714-833-7608
Elliot Gordon *(Office Mgr.)*

Korn/Ferry International **(1)**
237 Park Ave.
New York, NY 10017
Tel.: 212-687-1834
Fax: 212-986-5684
John Bassler *(Office Mgr.)*

Korn/Ferry International **(1)**
Embarcadero Corporate Center, 2483 E. Bayshore Rd., Ste. 101
Palo Alto, CA 94303
Tel.: 415-856-2611
Fax: 415-856-3682

Korn/Ferry International **(1)**
The Transamerica Pyramid, 600 Montgomery St., 31st Fl.
San Francisco, CA 94111
Tel.: 415-956-1834
Fax: 415-956-1988
Ted Ward *(Office Mgr.)*

Korn/Ferry International **(1)**
1201 Third Ave., Ste. 2120
Seattle, WA 98101
Tel.: 206-621-1834
Fax: 206-682-9491
Ed Blecksmith *(Office Mgr.)*

Korn/Ferry International **(1)**
One Landmark Square
Stamford, CT 06901
Tel.: 203-359-3350
Cable: 203-327-2044
Duke Foster *(Office Mgr.)*

Korn/Ferry International **(1)**
Presidential Plaza, 900 19th St., N.W.
Washington, DC 20006
Tel.: 202-822-9444
Fax: 202-822-8127
Ron Walker *(Office Mgr.)*

Korn/Ferry International **(1)**
431 Ponce de Leon Ave., Ste. 1508
San Juan, PR 00917
Tel.: 809-250-0707
William O'Connor *(Office Mgr.)*

Korn/Ferry Organizational Consulting **(1)**
75 Federal St.
Boston, MA 02110
Tel.: 617-423-9364
Fax: 617-423-9371
Deborah Cornwall *(Office Mgr.)*

Strategic Compensation Associates **(1)**
644 S. Figueroa St., 2nd Fl.
Los Angeles, CA 90017
Tel.: 213-488-8570
Fax: 213-489-2144

Non-U.S. Holdings:

Korn/Ferry International **(1)**
Strawinskylaan 545 1077 xx,
Amsterdam, Netherlands
Tel.: 31-20-664-13-01
Telecopier: 31-20-675-02-05
Hans Lap *(Office Mgr.)*

Korn/Ferry International (1)
12th Fl. Rajapark Bldg., 163 Soi Asoke (21)
Sukhumvit Rd.,
Bangkok, 10110, Thailand
Tel.: 66-2-2589040
Telex: 81182 TH
Telecopier: 66-2-2589039

Korn/Ferry International (1)
523, Avenue Louise B - 1050,
Brussels, Belgium
Tel.: 32-2-640-3240
Telex: (846) 24390
Telecopier: 32-2-640-8382
Jean-Marie Van den Borre *(Office Mgr.)*

Korn/Ferry International (1)
1-3 Rakoczi u. 1088,
Budapest, Hungary
Tel.: 36-1-266-0027
Tel.: 36-1-266-1178
Tel.: 36-1-266-7558
Telecopier: 36-1-266-0026
Tibor Voros *(Office Mgr.)*

Korn/Ferry International (1)
Avenida Quintana 585 1129, Piso 6,
Buenos Aires, Argentina
Tel.: 541-804-0046
Telecopier: 541-804-7568
Alejandro Cirone *(Office Mgr.)*

Korn/Ferry International (1)
Caracas, Venezuela
Tel.: 58-2-263-0256
Telecopier: 58-2-261-1784
Roy Caple *(Area Mgr.)*
Marjorie Kean *(Office Mgr.)*

Korn/Ferry International (1)
Edivicio Progapanda Sancho, Oficina 803
Calle 98 #9-03,
Bogota, Colombia
Tel.: 571 2184539
Tel.: 571 2184934
Tel.: 571 6170125
Telecopier: 571 6170124

Korn/Ferry International (1)
Lyoner Strasse 15, ATRICOM, 6000
Frankfurt am Main 71
Frankfurt, Germany
Tel.: 49-69-669-0170
Telecopier: 49-69-66-90-1766
Axel Motlik *(Office Mgr.)*

Korn/Ferry International (1)
61 Rue du Rhone 1204,
Geneva, Switzerland
Tel.: 41-22-310-2071
Telecopier: 41-22-311-7829
Heinrich Eichenberger *(Office Mgr.)*

Korn/Ferry International (1)
808 Gloucester Tower The Landmark,
Hong Kong, Hong Kong
Tel.: 852-521-5457
Telex: (780) 66343
Telecopier: 852-810-1632
Peter Tan *(Office Mgr.)*

Korn/Ferry International (1)
6th Fl., UBN Tower, 10 Jalan P. Ramlee
Letter Box #33,
Kuala Lumpur, 50250, Malasia
Tel.: 60-3-238-1655
Telecopier: 60-3-238-8276
Anne Venus *(Office Mgr.)*

Korn/Ferry International (1)
Pepys House, 12 Buckingham St.
London, WC2N 6DF, United Kingdom
Tel.: 44-71-930-4334
Telex: (851) 914860
Telecopier: 44-71-930-8085
Ed Kelley *(Office Mgr.)*

Korn/Ferry International (1)
Calle Felipe IV, #9
Madrid, #14, Spain
Tel.: 34-1-532-8624
Telex: (8310) 49062
Telecopier: 34-1-531-2038
Artemio Hernandez *(Office Mgr.)*

Korn/Ferry International (1)
Level 42, 80 Collins St. Nauru House,
Melbourne, Victoria 3000, Australia
Tel.: 61-3-654-4588
Telecopier: 61-3-650-9161

Korn/Ferry International (1)
Montes Urales 641, Lomas De Chapultepec
Delegacion Miguel Hidalgo, 11000,
Mexico, D.F., Mexico
Tel.: 52-5-202-0046
Telex: (383) 1771951
Telecopier: (525) 202-4469
Telecopier: (525) 202-4469
Horacio McCoy *(Office Mgr.)*

Korn/Ferry International (1)
Piazzetta M. Bossi, 1 20121,
Milan, Italy
Tel.: 392-7202-2550
Telecopier: 392-7202-2611
Raimondo Nider *(Office Mgr.)*

Korn/Ferry International (1)
Daniel Zambrano 525 Co. Chepe Vera,
Monterrey, N.L. Mexico
Tel.: 52-83-484-355
Telex: (383) 1771951
Telecopier: 52-83-337-362
Juan Llaguno *(Office Mgr.)*

Korn/Ferry International (1)
30 Avenue George V
Paris, France
Tel.: 33-14-720-3500
Telex: (842) 615217
Telecopier: 33-14-720-1106
Jean Batsere *(Office Mgr.)*

Korn/Ferry International (1)
Via Nicolo' Tartaglia, 11 00197,
Rome, Italy
Tel.: 396-858-7090
Telecopier: 396-807-3380
Daniel De Luca *(Office Mgr.)*

Korn/Ferry International (1)
Avenida Indianapolis 80 04062
Sao Paulo, Brazil
Tel.: 55-11-549-7133
Telecopier: 55-11-575-0959
Paul Levison *(Office Mgr.)*
David Ivy *(Office Mgr.)*

Korn/Ferry International (1)
29-05 Shell Tower, 50 Raffles Pl.
Singapore, Singapore 0104
Tel.: 65-224-3111
Telecopier: 65-224-3384
Young Kuan Sing *(Office Mgr.)*

Korn/Ferry International (1)
11th Fl., Kyle House, 31 Macquarie Pl.
Sydney, New South Wales 2000, Australia
Tel.: 61-2-247-7941
Telecopier: 61-2-251-2043

Korn/Ferry International (1)
AIU Bldg. 7th Fl., 1-3 Marunounchi 1-
Chrome Chiyoda-Ku,
Tokyo, 100, Japan
Tel.: 81-33-211-6851
Telex: (781) 23745
Telecopier: 81-33-216-1300
John Harlow *(Office Mgr.)*

Korn/Ferry International (1)
Scotia Plaza, 40 King Street West, Ste.
1814 P.O. Box 118,
Toronto, Ontario M5H 3Y2, Canada
Tel.: 416-366-1300
Telecopier: 416-366-0623

Korn/Ferry International (1)
C.F. Meyer - Strasse 14 8002,
Zurich, Switzerland
Tel.: 41-1-281-0100
Telecopier: 41-1-281-0944
Heinrich Eichenberger *(Office Mgr.)*

KOVA FERTILIZER INC.
1330 North Anderson St.
Greensburg, IN 47240
Tel.: 812-663-5081 **IN**
Fax: 812-663-5370
Year Founded: 1935
Approx.Sls.: $90,000,000
Emp.: 40
Fiscal Year-end: 9/30/90
Wholesale Fertilizers & Agricultural Chemicals
S.I.C.: 5191
Richard C. Reed *(Chm Bd. & Pres.)*
Brad Reed *(Chief Oper. Officer, Sec. & Treas.)*
Brian Reed *(Dir.-Personnel)*
Todd Reed *(Dir.-Pur.)*
Principal(s):
Reed Family

Outside Service Firm(s):

Dunbar, Cook Shepard*(Auditors)*
Indianapolis, IN

INB National Bank*(Major Banking Relationship)*
One Indiana Sq.
Indianapolis, IN 46266
Tel.: 317-266-6000

GEORGE KOVACS LIGHTING, INC.
67-25 Otto Rd.
Glendale, NY 11385
Tel.: 718-628-5201
Fax: 718-628-5212
Year Founded: 1954
Approx.Sls.: $25,000,000
Emp.: 200
Import Export
Manufacturer & Retailer of Lighting Fixtures
S.I.C.: 3645
George Kovacs *(Pres.)*
Morris Bennett *(V.P.-Mfg.)*
Richard Donnelly *(Controller)*
Mary Rohan *(Dir.-Pub. Rels.)*

No. of Mfg. Plants/Facilities: 2
No. of U.S. Offices: 2

Outside Service Firm(s):

Schwartz, Franzman, Suchman & Company*(Auditors)*
New York, NY

Israel Discount Bank Of New York*(Major Banking Relationship)*
New York, NY

KOWALSKI SAUSAGE CO., INC.
2270 Holbrook Ave.
Hamtramck, MI 48212
Tel.: 313-873-8200
Fax: 313-873-8206
Approx.Sls.: $20,000,000
Emp.: 225
Fiscal Year-end: 12/31/90
Sausages, Hams, Bacon & Luncheon Meats
S.I.C.: 2011; 2013; 5421
Audrey Kowalski *(Pres. & Chief Exec. Officer)*
Michael Kowalski *(V.P.)*
Ulrich Eggert *(Treas.)*
Linda Kowalski *(Sec.)*
Brian Bushy *(Reg. Mgr.-Sls.)*
Daniel Doyle *(Gen. Mgr.-Sls.)*

Outside Service Firm(s):

KPMG Peat Marwick*(Auditors)*
Suite 1200, 150 W. Jefferson
Detroit, MI 48226

Cross Wrock*(Legal Firm)*
Detroit, MI

Peoples State Bank*(Major Banking Relationship)*
Detroit, MI

KRACO ENTERPRISES, INC.
505 E. Euclid Ave.
Compton, CA 90224
Tel.: 310-639-0666
Tel.: 800-678-1910
Fax: 310-603-2260
Year Founded: 1955
Approx.Sls.: $150,000,000
Emp.: 500
Import Export
Car Stereo Players, Speakers & Antennas, Carpeted, Rubber & Vinyl Automotive Car Mats, Car Security Systems; Manufacturer of Citizens Band Radios; Mobile Security System, Radar Dectectors, Audio Amplifier, Auto Sound Packages
S.I.C.: 3651; 3069; 3089; 3669; 3663; 3714
Maurice H. Kraines *(Chm. Bd.)*
Lawrence M. Kraines *(Pres.)*
Robert R. Brocoff *(Sr. V.P.-Fin.)*
Terrence Conley *(Sr. V.P.)*
Kent Friend *(Sr. V.P.-Sls. & Mktg.)*
Steve Kraines *(Sr. V.P.-Sls.)*
Clara Krotzer *(V.P.-Admin.)*
Allen McCreight *(Dir.-Mktg.)*
Tim Best *(Mgr.-Pur.)*

Outside Service Firm(s):

KPMG Peat Marwick*(Auditors)*
Beverly Hills, CA

City National Bank*(Major Banking Relationship)*
120 S. Spalding Dr.
Beverly Hills, CA 90213
Tel.: 310-550-5821

KRAFT HARDWARE, INC.
306 E. 61st St.
New York, NY 10021
Tel.: 212-838-2214
Fax: 212-644-9254
Approx.Sls.: $10,000,000
Emp.: 50
Mfr. of Brass Cabinet & Door Hardware, Bathroom Accessories
S.I.C.: 3429
Stan Saperstein *(Pres.)*
Carol Saperstein *(Sec.)*

WARD KRAFT, INC.
2401 S. Cooper St.
Fort Scott, KS 66701
Mailing Address:
P.O. Box 938,
Fort Scott, KS 66701-0938
Tel.: 316-223-5500
Fax: 316-223-2706
Approx.Sls.: $18,000,000
Emp.: 250
Manufacture Manifold Business Forms & Labels
S.I.C.: 2761
Harold E. Kraft *(Chm. Bd. & Chief Exec. Officer)*
Roger Kraft *(Pres.)*
Mel Anderson *(V.P.-Fin.)*
Daryl Roller *(V.P.-Natl. Sls.)*
Larry Lane *(Gen. Mgr.)*

Outside Service Firm(s):

Diehl, Fletcher, Banwart & Bolton*(Auditors)*
Fort Scott, KS

Wheeler & Mitchelson*(Legal Firm)*
Pittsburgh, PA

Security State Bank*(Major Banking Relationship)*
Fort Scott, KS

KRAGIE/NEWELL
2633 Fleur Drive
Des Moines, IA 50321
Tel.: 515-288-7910
Year Founded: 1977
Approx.Billings: $35,000,000
Emp.: 76
Local Market Impact Services
Jack Kragie *(Chm. Bd.)*
Liz Newell *(Pres. & Chief Exec. Officer)*
Michelle Diehl *(Exec. V.P. & Chief Oper. Officer)*
J. Glasnapp *(Exec. V.P.)*
Roger Grote *(Exec. V.P.)*
Scott Stines *(V.P., Data Base Mktg.)*
Sara Maltby *(Dir.-Pub. Rels.)*
Jill Taylor *(Dir.-Research)*

KRANCO, INC.
10543 Fisher Rd.
Houston, TX 77041
Tel.: 713-466-7541
Fax: 713-466-6515
Approx.Sls.: $35,000,000
Emp.: 236
Cranes; Industrial Plant
S.I.C.: 3536
James P. Shanahan *(Pres. & Chief Exec. Officer)*
Larry Park *(Exec. V.P. & Gen. Mgr.-Opers.)*
Fred Delmastro *(V.P.-Engrng.)*
Joe Shaughnessy *(V.P.-Service Opers.)*
Steven Philips *(Dir.-Fin.)*
Ray Bauer *(Chief Engr.)*

Outside Service Firm(s):

Coopers & Lybrand*(Auditors)*
1100 Louisiana, Ste. 4100
Houston, TX 77002
Tel.: 713-757-5200
Fax: 713-757-5249

First Interstate Bank*(Major Banking Relationship)*
First Interstate Plaza
Houston, TX 77210
Tel.: 713-224-6611

Division:

Euclid Crane Division **(1)**
1365 Chardon Rd.
Cleveland, OH 44117
Tel.: 216-692-0470
Cranes
S.I.C.: 3536
Bruce Heon *(Mgr.)*

KRANSCO
160 Pacific Ave., Ste. 200
San Francisco, CA 94111
Mailing Address:
P.O. Box 884866,
San Francisco, CA 94188-4866
Tel.: 415-433-9350
Fax: 415-989-7180
Emp.: 1,500
Water Recreational Products, Body Surf Products, Floating Lounges, Pool Games & Water Ski Knee Boards, Flying Discs, Exercise Hoops, Footbags, Tubes, Children's Ride Ons
S.I.C.: 3949; 5091
John G. Bowes *(Chm. Bd.)*
John N. Rosekrans, Jr. *(Pres.)*
E. Alexander Glover *(Sr. V.P.-Mktg., Res. & Devel.)*
Glenn J. Gross *(Sr. V.P.-Sls.)*
Doug Tinker *(Sr. V.P.-Fin.)*
William C. Herman *(V.P.-Mktg.)*

Divisions:

Power Wheels, Inc. **(1)**
3405 Meyer Rd.
Ft. Wayne, IN 46896
Tel.: 219-424-1400
Battery Operated Ride-on Toys

Wham-O Div. of Kransco **(1)**
835 E. Elmonte Blvd.
San Gabriel, CA 91778
Tel.: 818-287-9681
Emp.: 120
Frisbee Brand Flying Disc, Monster-Zillion Bubbles Fluid, Superelasticbubbleplastic Plastic For Creating Multi Colored Balloons, Hula Hoop, Super Ball, Fun Fountain Water Toy, Trac-Ball, Willy Water Bug Water Toy, Magic Sand Toy
S.I.C.: 5945
John Rosekrans *(Pres.)*
John Harbottle *(Controller)*

KRASDALE FOODS INC.
400 Food Ctr. Dr.
Bronx, NY 10474
Tel.: 718-378-1100
Fax: 718-328-7302
Year Founded: 1905
Approx.Sls.: $369,000,000
Emp.: 525
Fiscal Year-end: 12/31/90
Wholesale Grocery Distributor
S.I.C.: 5141
Charles A. Krasne *(Pres. & Chief Exec. Officer)*
Brian Cassidy *(Chief Fin. Officer)*
Ubaldo Sorrentino *(V.P.-Fin. & Treas.)*
George Mitschele *(Controller)*
Sigmound Balka *(Gen. Counsel)*
Steve Laskowitz *(Dir.-Mngmt. Information Systems)*
John Mascis *(Dir.-Mngmt. Information Systems)*
Ralph Zampini *(Dir.-Personnel)*

Computer Systems/Hardware:
Wang

Outside Service Firm(s):

Mann, Judd, Landau*(Auditors)*
New York, NY
Tel.: 212-661-5500

Empire Blue Cross & Blue Shield*(Group Insurer)*
New York, NY

Bankers Trust Co.*(Investment Banker)*
P.O. Box 318, Church St. Station
New York, NY 10008
Tel.: 212-454-2212
Fax: 212-454-2783

Chase Manhattan Bank, N.A.*(Investment Banker)*
One Chase Manhattan Plaza
New York, NY 10081
Tel.: 212-552-2222
Tel.: 800-526-0801
Fax: 212-552-7175

Chemical Bank*(Investment Banker)*
450 West 33rd St.
New York, NY 10001
Tel.: 212-613-7197
Fax: 212-947-7628

Chase Manhattan Bank, N.A.*(Major Banking Relationship)*
One Chase Manhattan Plaza
New York, NY 10081
Tel.: 212-552-2222
Tel.: 800-526-0801
Fax: 212-552-7175

Chemical Bank*(Major Banking Relationship)*
450 West 33rd St.
New York, NY 10001
Tel.: 212-613-7197
Fax: 212-947-7628

Chemical Banking Corp.*(Major Banking Relationship)*
277 Park Ave.
New York, NY 10041
Tel.: 212-310-6407
Fax: 212-310-4526

Citibank N.A.*(Major Banking Relationship)*
Corporate Trust Services, 399 Park Ave.
New York, NY 10043
Tel.: 212-559-1605

KRAUS-ANDERSON, INC.
523 S. 8th St.
Minneapolis, MN 55404
Tel.: 612-332-1241 **MN**
Fax: 612-332-8940
Year Founded: 1937
Approx.Sls.: $425,000,000
Emp.: 1,000
Fiscal Year-end: 12/31/91
General Building Contractors; Heavy Construction Contractors; Real Estate Development
S.I.C.: 1522; 6531
Lloyd Engelsma *(Chm. Bd. & Chief Exec. Officer)*
Burton F. Dahlberg *(Pres.)*
Bruce W. Engelsma *(V.P. & Chief Fin. Officer)*
Tom Dunleavy *(Controller)*
Jon Sarff *(Gen. Counsel)*
Janice R. Goebel *(Sec.)*
Andy Duda *(Dir.-Personnel)*
Margaret Meyer *(Dir.-Art)*
Julie Belden *(Mgr.-Data Processing)*

Outside Service Firm(s):

KPMG Peat Marwick*(Auditors)*
4200 Norwest Center, 90 S. 7th St.
Minneapolis, MN 55402
Tel.: 612-341-2222

Independent Administration Company*(Group Insurer)*
Minnetonka, MN

First Bank Minneapolis*(Major Banking Relationship)*
120 S. Sixth St.
Minneapolis, MN 55480
Tel.: 612-370-4141

Marquette Bank, N.A.*(Major Banking Relationship)*
Sixth & Marquette
Minneapolis, MN 55402
Tel.: 612-341-5651

Subsidiaries:

Kraus-Anderson Construction **(1)**
523 S. 8th St.
Minneapolis, MN 55404
Tel.: 612-332-7281
S.I.C.: 1522; 1622
Bill Jaeger *(Pres.)*
Jerry Dreis *(V.P.-Fin. & Admin.)*

Kraus-Anderson Mortgage Co. **(1)**
523 S. 8th St.
Minneapolis, MN 55404
Tel.: 612-332-1241
S.I.C.: 6162
Carl Carlson *(V.P.)*

Kraus-Anderson Realty Co. **(1)**
523 S. 8th St.
Minneapolis, MN 55404
Tel.: 612-332-1241
S.I.C.: 6531
Burt Dahlberg *(Pres.)*

KRAUSE, NADUREK & EICKMEYER
(Formerly Krause & Young)
501 Elm St., Ste. 300, LB6
Dallas, TX 75202
Tel.: 214-741-7500
Fax: 214-747-3831
Year Founded: 1979
Approx.Billings: $14,800,000
Emp.: 18
Hospitality, Sports Mktg., Telecommunications & Retail
Jim Krause *(Dir. Client Services & New Bus. Contact)*
Jo Davis *(Controller)*

KRAUSE PLOW CORP.
305 S. Monroe St.
Hutchinson, KS 67501
Mailing Address:
P.O. Box 2707,
Hutchinson, KS 67504-2707
Tel.: 316-663-6161
Fax: 316-663-6943
Year Founded: 1916
Approx.Sls.: $35,000,000
Emp.: 300
Fiscal Year-end: 6/30/92
Export
Farm Equipment Disc Harrows, Chisel Plows, Field Cultivators, Grain Drills & Trash Compaction Equipment
S.I.C.: 3523; 3531; 3589
Steve Krause *(Pres.)*
William S. Southern, Jr. *(Exec. V.P.)*
Gayle Buri *(V.P.-Sls.)*

Computer Systems/Hardware:
HP, IBM, APPLE

KRAUSE'S SOFA FACTORY, INC.
200 N. Berry St.
Brea, CA 92621
Tel.: 714-990-3100
Fax: 714-964-6195
Year Founded: 1973
Approx.Sls.: $80,000,000
Emp.: 1,200
Manufacturer of Sofas
S.I.C.: 5021
Michael Gibbons *(Pres.)*
Mark Gill *(Chief Fin. Officer)*
Steve Burgess *(Sr. V.P.-Retail Sls.)*
Bill Gamble *(V.P.-Adv.)*
Ubaldo Salcedo *(V.P.-Mfg.)*

KREHER STEEL COMPANY, INC.
1550 N. 25th Ave.
Melrose Park, IL 60160
Tel.: 708-345-8180 **NY**
Fax: 708-345-8180
Year Founded: 1978
Approx.Sls.: $55,000,000
Emp.: 62
Import Export
Marketing of Steel
S.I.C.: 5051
Thomas W. Kreher *(Pres.)*
Joseph Druzak *(V.P.)*
William Thompson *(V.P.-Sls.)*
Allen Lazar *(Controller)*
Janit Kreher *(Sec.)*

KREONITE, INC.
715 E. 10th St.
Wichita, KS 67214
Mailing Address:
P.O. Box 2099
Wichita, KS 67201
Tel.: 316-263-1111
Fax: 316-263-6829
Year Founded: 1955
Approx.Sls.: $19,000,000
Emp.: 325
Manufacture Photo Equipment
S.I.C.: 3861
William K. Oetting *(Pres.)*
Larry W. Burd *(Sr. V.P.)*
Carl D. Best *(V.P.-Fin.)*
Dean Lott *(V.P.-N.A. Sls.)*

Outside Service Firm(s):

Fleeson, Gooing, Coulson & Kitch*(Legal Firm)*
Wichita, KS

KREPS-WISE ASSOCIATES
1608 Menard
Saint Louis, MO 63104
Tel.: 314-436-4719
Fax: 314-436-4877
Year Founded: 1979
Approx.Billings: $19,000,000
Emp.: 16
Sales Promotion, Advertising & Packaging Design
Dennis J. Kreps *(Chm. Bd., Pres. & Dir.-Creative)*
Michelle R. Wise *(Exec. V.P.)*
James L. Perabo *(V.P., Dir.-Mktg. & New Bus. Contact)*

Computer Systems/Hardware:
ISIS, Macintosh, IBM

KRESSER/CRAIG

KRESSER/CRAIG
2501 Colorado Ave., 2nd Fl.
Santa Monica, CA 90404-3585
Tel.: 310-315-3000
Fax: 310-315-3005
Year Founded: 1976

Approx.Billings: $74,344,472
Emp.: 75
General Advertising
S.I.C.: 7311
Bob Kresser *(Chm. & Chief Exec. Officer)*
Jean Craig *(Pres. & Exec. Creative Dir.)*
Monty McKinney *(Vice Chm.)*
Yushi Ebihara *(Exec. V.P., Chief Oper. Officer)*
Paul Anton *(Exec. V.P., Mngmt. Supvr.)*
Joh Koppel *(V.P., Fin. & Admin.)*
Jim Sala *(Dir.-Reg. Mktg.)*

LEONARD KREUSCH, INC.
1 Caesar Place
Moonachie, NJ 07074
Mailing Address:
P. O. Box 0822
Carlstadt, NJ 07072
Tel.: 201-935-4550 **NJ**
Fax: 201-935-7234
Year Founded: 1950
Approx.Sls.: $30,000,000
Emp.: 47
Import Export
Wine & Distilled Alcohol Importer
S.I.C.: 5182
Paul P. Kreusch *(Pres. & Chief Exec. Officer)*
Leonard Kreusch III *(V.P. & Gen. Mgr.)*
Rolf O. Theuerkauf *(V.P.)*
Anita E. Kreusch *(Sec.)*
Principal(s):
Paul P. Kreusch

No. of Mfg. Plants/Facilities: 1
No. of U.S. Offices: 2
No. of Foreign Offices: 1

Subsidiary:

LKI **(1)**
495 S. Broadway
Yonkers, NY 10705
Tel.: 212-925-4512
Import Export
S.I.C.: 5182

Non-U.S. Holding:

Leonard Kreusch GmBH & Co. **(1)**
Martinerfeld 61 5500
Trier, Germany
Tel.: 0651-827030
Fax: 0651-800627
Import Export

KRIER FOODS, INC.
4555 W. Schroeder Dr., Ste. 190
Brown Deer, WI 53223
Tel.: 414-355-5400 **WI**
Fax: 414-355-5577
Year Founded: 1913
Assets: $8,500,000
Liabilities: $2,250,000
Net Worth: $6,250,000
Approx.Sls.: $20,000,000
Emp.: 50
Fiscal Year-end: 3/31/91
Import
Mfr. of Fruit Juices & Nonalocholic Carbonated Beverages
S.I.C.: 2086
B. Bruce Krier *(Chm. Bd. & Pres.)*
Thomas Bretza *(Exec. V.P.-Fin. & Treas.)*
Steve Ihrake *(Dir.-Pur.)*

No. of Mfg. Plants/Facilities: 1
No. of U.S. Offices: 1

Computer Systems/Hardware:
IBM 36

Outside Service Firm(s):

Arthur Andersen & Co.*(Auditors)*
777 E. Wisconsin Ave., P.O. Box 1215
Milwaukee, WI 53202
Tel.: 414-271-5100
Fax: 414-283-3200

Marshall & Ilsley Trust Company*(Major Banking Relationship)*
770 N. Water St.
Milwaukee, WI

Plant:

Krier Foods **(1)**
520 Wolf Rd.
Random Lake, WI 53075
Tel.: 414-994-2469
Fruit Juices & Vegetables Packed In Cans & Jars; Nonalcoholic Carbonated Beverages In Bottles & Cans
S.I.C.: 2086
Robert Younglove *(Mgr.)*

KROCH'S & BRENTANO'S, INC.
29 S. Wabash Ave.
Chicago, IL 60603
Tel.: 312-332-7500
Fax: 312-332-6074
Year Founded: 1907
Approx.Sls.: $40,000,000
Emp.: 750
Retail Book Stores
S.I.C.: 5942
Carl A. Kroch *(Chm. Bd.)*
William Rickman *(Pres.)*
Ray Carroll *(Sr. V.P.)*
Phillip Jackson *(V.P.-Opers.)*
Doris Laufer *(V.P.-Mktg.)*
Harlan Smith *(V.P.-Pur.)*
William Yeung *(Sec. & Treas.)*

Outside Service Firm(s):

Blackman Kallick Bartelstein*(Auditors)*
300 Riverside Plaza
Chicago, IL 60606
Tel.: 312-207-1040

Lewis, Overbeck & Furman*(Legal Firm)*
Chicago, IL

Boulevard Bank*(Major Banking Relationship)*
410 N. Michigan Ave.
Chicago, IL 60611
Tel.: 312-836-6500

KROEHLER FURNITURE MANUFACTURING COMPANY, INC.
1800 Conover Blvd.
Conover, NC 28613
Mailing Address:
P.O. Box 1178,
Conover, NC 28613
Tel.: 704-459-9865
Fax: 704-459-9869
Emp.: 150
Manufacturer Upholstered Living Room & Den Furniture, Contemporary, Traditional & Early American; Sleepers & Occasional Chairs
S.I.C.: 2512
Jerome Schottenstein *(Chm. Bd. & Pres.)*
Saul Schottenstein *(Sec.)*
Robert Annas *(Gen. Mgr.)*
Wade Austin *(Mgr.-Plant)*

No. of Mfg. Plants/Facilities: 2

Outside Service Firm(s):

Phillip Willeke Inc.*(Auditors)*
Conover, NC

First Citizens Bank & Trust Company*(Major Banking Relationship)*
Conover, NC

KROH OPERATING L.P.
4550 W. 109th St., Ste. 220
Overland Park, KS 66211
Tel.: 800-831-1332
Fax: 913-345-8222
Year Founded: 1988
Emp.: 12
Fiscal Year-end: 12/31/91
Real Estate Investment Firm
S.I.C.: 6552
Greg Galvin *(Chief Oper. Officer)*
Marci Berry *(Controller)*

No. of U.S. Offices: 3

Computer Systems/Hardware:
IBM System 38

Subsidiary:

Pathmark Development Group **(1)**
4550 W. 109th St, Ste. 220
Overland Park, KS 66211
Tel.: 913-345-0535
Tel.: 800-831-1332
Leasing & Property Management

KROMMENHOEK MCKEOWN ASSOCIATES
1515 Morena Blvd.
San Diego, CA 92110
Tel.: 619-276-7710 **CA**
Fax: 619-276-7715
Year Founded: 1973
Sales Range: $10-19 Million
Emp.: 35
Fiscal Year-end: 5/31/91
Architectural Services
S.I.C.: 8712
William Krommenhoek *(Chief Exec. Officer)*
John M. McKeown *(Pres.)*
Donna Krommenhoek *(V.P. & Sec.)*
Principal(s):
William Krommenhoek
John M. McKeown

No. of U.S. Offices: 1

KRUSE HARDWARE COMPANY
4275 Thunderbird Lane
Fairfield, OH 45014
Tel.: 513-860-3600 **OH**
Fax: 513-860-3639
Approx.Sls.: $33,000,000
Emp.: 175
Hardware; Lawn & Garden Machinery & Equipment; Home Furnishings; Athletic Goods; Industrial Fasteners; Nuts, Bolts & Screws; Industrial Brushes; Industrial Fittings; Hand & Power Tools
S.I.C.: 5072; 5083; 5023; 5091; 5085; 5251
George D. Hovekamp, Sr. *(Chm. Bd.)*
Stanley Groene *(Pres.)*
George D. Hovekamp, Jr. *(V.P.)*
Allan Vogeter *(Sec.)*

Outside Service Firm(s):

Grant Thornton*(Auditors)*
1600 Atrium One
Cincinnati, OH 45202
Tel.: 513-762-5000

Frost & Jacobs*(Legal Firm)*
2500 Central Trust Ctr.
Cincinnati, OH 45202
Tel.: 513-651-6800

The Central Trust Company, N.A.*(Major Banking Relationship)*
201 E. Fifth
Cincinnati, OH 45202
Tel.: 513-651-8255

KRUSE INTERNATIONAL
5400 CR 11-A at 69
Auburn, IN 46706
Mailing Address:
P.O. Box 190
Auburn, IN 46706
Tel.: 219-925-5600 **IN**
Fax: 219-925-5467
Approx.Sls.: $350,000,000
Emp.: 37
Fiscal Year-end: 12/31/90
Auction Company; Collector Cars & Real Estate, Mobile Homes & Collectibles
S.I.C.: 6531; 7389
Mitchell Kruse *(Pres., Chief Exec. Officer & Auctioneer)*
Michael A. Butler *(Chief Oper. Officer & Exec. V.P.)*
Dean V. Kruse *(Dir.-Sls. & Auctioneer)*
Danette Fitzgerald *(Mgr.-Adv.)*
Roberta Wurm *(Coord.-Adv.)*
Principal(s):
Mitchell Kruse

No. of Mfg. Plants/Facilities: 35
No. of Foreign Offices: 2

Computer Systems/Hardware:
Northstar

Outside Service Firm(s):

All Risk Insurance*(Group Insurer)*
Fort Wayne, IN

Kruse & Kruse*(Legal Firm)*
Auburn, IN

Auburn State Bank*(Major Banking Relationship)*
Auburn, IN

KRYSTAL COMPANY
Krystal Bldg., One Union Sq.
Chattanooga, TN 37402
Tel.: 615-757-1550
Fax: 615-757-1590
Year Founded: 1932
Approx.Sls.: $200,000,000
Emp.: 9,000
Fiscal Year-end: 12/31/91
Operates Fast Food Restaurants
S.I.C.: 5812
Corporate Giving Program: Children's Miracle Network
R.B. Davenport III *(Chm.-Exec. Comm.)*
C.D. Long *(Chm. Bd. & Chief Exec. Officer)*
R.B. Davenport IV *(Pres. & Chief Oper. Officer)*
C.B. Scearce *(Chief Fin. Officer, V.P., Sec. & Controller)*
M. Bass *(V.P.-Admin.)*
D. Beairsto *(V.P.-Data Processing)*
Bruce Bloom *(V.P.-Franchising)*
J.W. Compton *(V.P.-Human Resources)*
P. Frankenberg *(V.P.-Product Devel.)*
Phil McNeely *(V.P.-Real Estate)*
Thomas Whitley *(V.P.-Mktg.)*
Carla Koeffler *(Dir.-Adv. & Sls. Promo.)*
Principal(s):
Krystal Shares, Inc.

No. of U.S. Offices: 240

Computer Systems/Hardware:
IBM

Outside Service Firm(s):

Arthur Andersen & Co.*(Auditors)*
734 Market St.
Chattanooga, TN 37402
Tel.: 615-756-5000
Fax: 615-265-3869

Miller & Martin*(Legal Firm)*
Chattanooga, TN

Krystal Company—(Continued)

First Tennessee Bank, N.A.*(Major Banking Relationship)*
701 Market St.
Chattanooga, TN 37402

KUHLMAN, INC.
N57 WI 3666 Reichert Ave.
Menomonee Falls, WI 53051
Tel.: 414-781-9202 **WI**
Fax: 414-781-7531
Year Founded: 1957
Approx.Sls.: $12,000,000
Emp.: 150
Refrigeration Contractor
S.I.C.: 1711
Harvey G. Kuhlman *(Chm. Bd.)*
Ronald Kuhlman *(Pres.)*
Dale Kuhlman *(V.P.)*
Ryan Kuhlman *(Sec.)*

Outside Service Firm(s):

Wayne Pipkorn, Inc.*(Auditors)*
Milwaukee, WI

M & I Northern Bank*(Major Banking Relationship)*
Brookfield, WI

KUHN & WITTENBORN, INC.
2405 Grand Ave., Ste. 600
Kansas City, MO 64108
Tel.: 816-471-7888
Fax: 816-471-7530
Year Founded: 1978
Approx.Billings: $23,000,000
Emp.: 45
Dale Wittenborn *(Co-Chm. Bd.)*
Richard S. Kuhn *(Co-Chm. Bd.)*
John P. Blanck *(Controller)*
Becky Rusk *(Dir.-Pub. Rels.)*

KUKLA PRESS, INC.
855 Morse Ave.
Elk Grove Village, IL 60007
Tel.: 708-593-1090 **DE**
Fax: 708-593-0406
Year Founded: 1964
Approx.Sls.: $42,000,000
Emp.: 140
Fiscal Year-end: 3/31/92
Commercial Printing
S.I.C.: 2752
Stanley J. Kukla *(Chm. Bd. & Chief Exec. Officer)*
Robert J. Kukla *(Pres. & Chief Oper. Officer)*
Frank Schellinger *(Chief Fin. Officer)*

Outside Service Firm(s):

Reuben & Proctor*(Legal Firm)*
19 S. LaSalle St.
Chicago, IL 60603
Tel.: 312-558-5500

Lake Shore National Bank*(Major Banking Relationship)*
605 N. Michigan Ave.
Chicago, IL 60611
Tel.: 312-787-1900

KULITE SEMICONDUCTOR PRODUCTS, INC.
One Willow Tree Rd.
Leonia, NJ 07605
Tel.: 201-461-0900 **NJ**
Fax: 201-461-0990
Year Founded: 1959
Approx.Sls.: $25,000,000
Emp.: 350
Mfr. of Pressure Tranducers, Accelerometers; Strain Gages; Solid State
S.I.C.: 3829; 3674
Anthony D. Kurtz *(Pres.)*
Amnon Brosh *(Sr. V.P.)*
John Hayer *(Sr. V.P.)*
Ronald Moores *(Sr. V.P.)*
Charles Gravel *(V.P.)*
Timothy A. Nunn *(V.P.)*
Michael Eckstein *(Controller)*
Stephen Kurtz *(Sec. & Treas.)*
Robert Gardner *(Pur. Agent)*

Outside Service Firm(s):

Rosenberg, Rosenberg, Barr & Weinberg*(Auditors)*
Morristown, NJ

Hannoch, Weisman, Stern, Besser, Berkowitz & Kinne*(Legal Firm)*
Union, NJ

Manufacturers Hanover Trust Co.*(Major Banking Relationship)*
Morristown, NJ

KUNZLER & COMPANY, INC.
640-662 Manor St.
Lancaster, PA 17603
Mailing Address:
P.O. Box 4747,
Lancaster, PA 17604
Tel.: 717-299-6301
Fax: 717-299-5956
Approx.Sls.: $52,000,000
Emp.: 180
Sausage, Bolognas & Smoked Meats
S.I.C.: 2013
Christian C. Kunzler, Jr. *(Chm. Bd. & Pres.)*
Christian C. Kunzler, III *(V.P.)*
Robert V. Zigmundt *(Sec. & Treas.)*
Robert W. Stover *(Mgr.-Sls.)*

Outside Service Firm(s):

Kuntz, Lesher, Siergist & Martini*(Auditors)*
Lancaster, PA

Tryon, Friedman & Espenshade*(Legal Firm)*
Lancaster, PA

Fulton Bank*(Major Banking Relationship)*
110 Penn Sq.
Lancaster, PA 17602
Tel.: 717-291-2411

KUONI TRAVEL, INC.
11 E. 44th St.
New York, NY 10017
Tel.: 212-687-7190
Fax: 212-986-4158
Emp.: 10
International Tour Operators
S.I.C.: 4724
Casper Kranenburg *(Gen. Mgr.)*

KUPPER PARKER COMMUNICATIONS INC.
(Acct. Service Office)
6900 Delmar Blvd.
Saint Louis, MO 63130
Tel.: 314-727-4000
Fax: 314-727-3034
Year Founded: 1992
Approx.Billings: $50,000,000
Emp.: 67
Automobile Dealers, Brdcst. Stations, Sports & Entertainment, Business-to-Business Sales & Direct Mktg., Health Care Mktg.
Bruce D. Kupper *(Mng. Partner)*
Larry L. Parker *(Mng. Partner)*
Peter A.M. Charlton *(Partner, Creative Dir.)*
Susan M. Christensen *(Pres., Direct Mktg. Sub.)*
Ian N. Cohen *(Partner, Acct. Services)*
Mary L. DeHahn *(Partner, Production & Pub. Rels.)*
Alan L. Epstein *(Partner, Media Services)*
Steve J. Grzyb *(Partner, Brdcst. Consulting)*
James H. Taylor, Jr. *(Partner, Chief Fin. Officer)*

Computer Systems/Hardware:
IBM compatible DOS System, Apple Macintosh

KURDZIEL INDUSTRIES, INC.
Co-America Bank Building, 801 W. Norton Ave., Ste. 300
Muskegon, MI 49441
Tel.: 616-739-4349
Fax: 616-739-8418
Year Founded: 1938
Approx.Sls.: $38,000,000
Emp.: 270
Fiscal Year-end: 12/31/91
Gray Iron Counterweight Castings
S.I.C.: 3321
Joseph Kurdziel *(Chm. Bd. & Pres.)*
Douglas G. Platt *(Chief Fin. Officer)*
Walter J. Kurdziel *(Exec. V.P.-Production)*
Theodore Kurdziel *(V.P.-Prod. & Treas.)*
Glen Leckie *(V.P.-Opers.)*
Constance Kurdziel *(Sec.)*
Scott Pranger *(Mgr.-Sls.)*
Principal(s):
Joseph Kurdziel
Walter J. Kurdziel
Theodore Kurdziel

No. of Mfg. Plants/Facilities: 3

Computer Systems/Hardware:
AS/400

Outside Service Firm(s):

BDO Seidman*(Auditors)*
801 W. Norton
Muskegon, MI 49441
Tel.: 616-739-9441

NBD Bank, N.A.*(Major Banking Relationship)*
611 Woodward Ave.
Detroit, MI 48226
Tel.: 313-225-1122

Culver, Lague & McNally*(Legal Firm)*
P.O. Box 389,
Muskegon, MI 49443

Subsidiaries:

Britt Industries, Inc. **(1)**
525 Enterprise Dr.
Wauseon, OH 43567
Tel.: 419-337-6000 (100%)
Processor
S.I.C.: 3321

Kurdziel Iron of Rothbury **(1)**
2625 Winston Rd.
Rothbury, MI 49452
Tel.: 616-893-1415 (100%)
Foundry
S.I.C.: 3321

Kurdziel Iron of Wauseon **(1)**
820 W. Leggett
Wauseon, OH 43567
Tel.: 419-335-4544 (100%)
Foundry
S.I.C.: 3321

KURFEES COATINGS, INC.
201 E. Market St.
Louisville, KY 40202
Tel.: 502-584-0151
Tel.: 800-626-6147 **KY**
Fax: 502-584-0151, Ext. 240
Emp.: 90
Mfr. of Paints & Allied Products
S.I.C.: 2851
Joseph Whittenberg *(Pres. & Chief Exec. Officer)*
John C. Ballard *(V.P.-Opers.)*
Logan C. Lang *(V.P.)*

Outside Service Firm(s):

Cotton & Allen*(Auditors)*
Louisville, KY

Ewen, McKenzie & Peden*(Legal Firm)*
650 Strauss Bldg.
Louisville, KY 40202
Tel.: 502-589-1110

Citizens Fidelity Bank & Trust Co.*(Major Banking Relationship)*
P.O. Box 33000-Citizens Plaza
Louisville, KY 40232
Tel.: 502-581-3381

KURT MANUFACTURING CO. INC.
5280 Main St. N.E.
Fridley, MN 55421
Tel.: 612-572-1500 **MN**
Fax: 612-572-9878
Year Founded: 1946
Approx.Sls.: $125,000,000
Emp.: 1,100
Import Export
Precision Machine Shop; Fabricated Metal Products; Machine Tools & Accessories, Measuring Devices
S.I.C.: 3499; 3545; 3451; 3625; 3823
William G. Kuban *(Pres., Chief Exec. Officer & Treas.)*
Steve Carlsen *(V.P.-Mfg.)*
Roger DeLacey *(V.P.-Fin.)*
Merle Griffith *(V.P.-Admin.)*
Roland Schmidt *(V.P.-Quality Control)*
Kern Walker *(V.P.-Human Resources)*
Richard Wallin *(V.P.-Sls.)*
Ingo Wolfe *(V.P.-Engrng.)*
John Kvidera *(Dir.-Pur.)*
Susan Supina *(Mgr.-Mktg.)*

No. of Mfg. Plants/Facilities: 7
No. of U.S. Offices: 7

Computer Systems/Hardware:
DEC VAX

Outside Service Firm(s):

Grant Thornton*(Auditors)*
500 Pillsbury Center
Minneapolis, MN 55402-1459

Subsidiary:

Strite-Anderson Die Castings **(1)**
7585 Hwy. 65 N.E.
Fridley, MN 55432
Tel.: 612-572-4650
Precision Shop
S.I.C.: 3599
Lowell Timmersman *(Plant Mgr.)*

KURTZ BROS., INC.
P.O. Box 392, 4th & Reeds St.
Clearfield, PA 16830
Tel.: 814-765-6561
Fax: 814-765-5332
Approx.Sls.: $19,000,000
Emp.: 200
Manufacture & Distribute Stationers Printers, Lithographers & School Supplies
S.I.C.: 2621; 2678; 2752; 5111; 5112
Robert M. Kurtz, Jr. *(Pres.)*
James H. Liu *(V.P.-Opers.)*
Ron L. Turner *(V.P.-Mktg.)*
Robert C. Volovic *(V.P. & Treas.)*
David Kurtz *(Dir.-Special Projects)*

Outside Service Firm(s):

Young, Oakes, Brown & Co.*(Auditors)*
Altoona, PA

Belin, Belin & Naddeo*(Legal Firm)*
Clearfield, PA

Clearfield Bank & Trust Co.*(Major Banking Relationship)*
Clearfield, PA

KURTZMAN/SLAVIN/LINDA, INC.
One Northfield Plaza
Northfield, IL 60093
Tel.: 708-501-5009
Fax: 708-501-5088
Year Founded: 1989
Approx.Billings: $15,000,000
Emp.: 20
Adv., Communications Design, Direct Mktg. & Pub. Rels.
Allan Kurtzman *(Pres.)*
Barry Slavin *(Treas.)*
Gerald Linda *(Sec., Dir. Client & Mktg. Services)*
Lorrine Littwin *(V.P., Fin. & Admin.)*
Robert Simak *(Dir.-Sls.)*
Charles Kazarian *(Dir.-Pur.)*
Paul Twombly *(Dir.-Mktg.)*
Mark Czopek *(Mgr.-Adv.)*
Rita Hofer *(Mgr.-Personnel)*

Computer Systems/Hardware:
IBM/Adman, Macintosh
IBM

Kwickie Food Stores Inc.
(See Listing Under Jones Company, Inc.; Name Changed To Kwickie/Flash Foods, Inc.)

KWIK-KOPY CORP.
One Kwik-Kopy Lane
Cypress, TX 77429
Mailing Address:
P.O. Box 777
Cypress, TX 77429
Tel.: 713-373-3535
Fax: 713-373-4450
Approx.Sls.: $180,000,000
Emp.: 110
Fiscal Year-end: 12/31/89
Franchiser of Instant Printing Centers & Wholesale Thermography Centers
S.I.C.: 2759; 2754; 2752
F.C. Hadfield *(Chm. Bd.)*
Steve Hammerstein *(Pres.)*
LaDonna Meadows *(Exec. V.P.)*
R.W. Harrison *(Exec. V.P.)*
Janice Meador *(V.P.-Corp. Services & Personnel Dir.)*
Al Alverson *(Mgr.-Adv.)*

Subsidiary:

Demand Graphics Research **(1)**
P.O. Box 777
Cypress, TX 77429
Tel.: 713-373-3535
Research on Instant Printing Equip.

KYANITE MINING CORPORATION
Hwy. 15 S.
Dillwyn, VA 23936
Tel.: 804-983-2043
Fax: 804-983-3579
Approx.Sls.: $12,000,000
Emp.: 180
Virginia Blue Crystal Kyanite, Raw and Calcined (Mullite)
S.I.C.: 1099
Gene Dixon, Jr. *(Pres.)*
Billy R. Coleman *(V.P.-Production)*
Carroll Kay *(V.P.-Sls., Adv. & Traffic)*
George V. Conner, Jr. *(Treas.)*
T. H. Dunnavant *(Sec.)*
T. Shelton *(Pur. Agent)*

L&J TECHNOLOGIES
(Formerly GPE Controls)
6511 Oakton
Morton Grove, IL 60053
Tel.: 708-966-4000
Telex: 21016 GPELNJ VR
Fax: 708-966-9331
Year Founded: 1978
Approx.Sls.: $17,000,000
Emp.: 200
Fiscal Year-end: 12/30/90
Export
GPE Controls, Shand & Jurs Control Systems for Metals, Petroleum & Material Industries; L & J Engineering
S.I.C.: 3625
J.M. Fausel *(V.P. & Gen. Mgr.)*

L & L NURSERY SUPPLY, INC.
5350 G St.
Chino, CA 91710
Tel.: 909-591-0461
Fax: 909-591-3280
Approx.Sls.: $48,000,000
Emp.: 300
Manufacturer of Wooden Nursery Supplies & Soil Products
S.I.C.: 2449; 5191; 5199
Denis Valois *(Pres.)*
Doug Cater *(V.P.)*
Ken Mathews *(Mgr.-Sls.)*

Outside Service Firm(s):

Bowen McBeth Inc.*(Auditors)*
Pomona, CA

Bank of America NT&SA*(Major Banking Relationship)*
Chino, CA

Division:

L & L Plant Soil Division **(1)**
2507 Frank Albert Rd., Ste. 130
Fife, WA 98424
Tel.: 206-922-7714
Denis Valois *(Pres.)*

L & L OIL COMPANY, INC.
3421 N. Causway Blvd., Ste. 502
Metairie, LA 70002
Mailing Address:
P.O. Box 6984
Metairie, LA 70009
Tel.: 504-832-8600
Fax: 504-832-8620
Approx.Sls.: $110,000,000
Emp.: 150
Export
Wholesale Petroleum Products & Lubricants
S.I.C.: 5172
Frank L. Levy *(Pres. & Chief Exec. Officer)*
Richard D. Childers *(Chief Fin. Officer & V.P.)*
Jerry R. Blake *(V.P.-Sls.)*

Outside Service Firm(s):

Kushner, LaGraize & Moore*(Auditors)*
New Orleans, LA

William M. Lucas, Jr.*(Legal Firm)*
New Orleans, LA

Commerce Corporation*(Major Banking Relationship)*
New Orleans, LA

L & R COMMUNICATIONS, LIMITED
2301 Bridgeport Dr.
Sioux City, IA 51111
Mailing Address:
P.O. Box 3807,
Sioux City, IA 51112
Tel.: 712-252-4101
Fax: 712-252-2803
Year Founded: 1980
Approx.Sls.: $40,000,000
Emp.: 220
Export
Construction of Telecommunications Transmitting Towers
S.I.C.: 1623
John Miller *(Pres.)*
Kenneth P. Fentress *(Treas. & Sec.)*
Dennis Harward *(Mgr.-Western Reg. Sls.)*

L&R MANUFACTURING CO.
577 Elm St.
Kearny, NJ 07032
Tel.: 201-991-5330
Tel.: 800-572-5326
Fax: 201-991-5870
Year Founded: 1930
Approx.Sls.: $10,000,000
Emp.: 200
Import Export
Ellanar Silver Polish Jewelry Cleaner, L & R Ultrasonic & Mechanical Watch Cleaning Machines & Solutions, L & R Dental Ultrasonic Equipment, Industrial, Mechanical & Ultrasonic Cleaning Equipment & Chemicals; Optical Ultrasonic Equipment, Lapidary Products
S.I.C.: 2842; 3699; 3843; 3915
James J. Lazarus *(Pres.)*
David Romanok *(Exec. V.P.)*
John Nordstedt *(Dir.-Opers.)*
Robert Lazarus *(Mgr.-Adv.)*
Paul McNichol *(Mgr.-Sls.)*
Robert H. Shiff *(Mgr.-Mktg.)*
Pat Marshall *(Head Engr.)*
Gene Varani *(Pur. Agent)*

LB INDUSTRIES INC.
1401 Shoreline Dr.
Boise, ID 83701
Tel.: 208-345-7515 ID
Telex: 150059
Fax: 208-345-7028
Approx.Sls.: $241,000,000
Emp.: 180
Holding Company; Wholesale & Retail Automobiles; Rental & Leasing, Subdividers & Developers of Nonresidential Buildings
S.I.C.: 5012; 5511; 7514; 2451; 6552; 6512; 6719; 7515
Larry B. Barnes *(Chm. Bd.)*
Joe Davis *(Pres.)*
Mike Taylor *(V.P.)*

Computer Systems/Hardware:
IBM

Outside Service Firm(s):

Grant Thornton*(Auditors)*
Boise, ID

The Bank of California, N.A.*(Major Banking Relationship)*
400 California
San Francisco, CA 94104
Tel.: 415-765-0400

Division:

Oil & Gas Division **(1)**
12200 E. Briarwood
Englewood, CO 80112
Tel.: 303-790-8340
Oil & Gas Exploration Servies
S.I.C.: 1382
Charles Williams *(Pres.)*

LDI, LTD.
251 N. Illinois St., Ste. 1800
Indianapolis, IN 46204
Tel.: 317-237-2251 IN
Fax: 317-237-2280
Assets: $141,024,000
Liabilities: $41,182,000
Net Worth: $99,842,000
Approx.Sls.: $35,000,000
Emp.: 598
Mfr. Wooden Doors
S.I.C.: 2431; 3751; 7999
Andre B. Lacy *(Chm., Pres. & Chief Exec. Officer)*
William J. Fennessy *(V.P.-Fin. & Treas.)*
Margot L. Eccles *(V.P. & Sec.)*
Robert A. Nickell *(V.P.)*
Dale D. Tucker *(V.P.)*
Walter S. Wiseman *(V.P.)*
Robert H. Reynolds *(Sec.)*
Marcus Chandler *(Asst. Sec.)*

No. of Mfg. Plants/Facilities: 4

Computer Systems/Hardware:
IBM System 36

Outside Service Firm(s):

Coopers & Lybrand*(Auditors)*
2900 One American Square, Box 82002
Indianapolis, IN 46282
Tel.: 317-639-4161

Barnes & Thornburg*(Legal Firm)*
11 S. Meridian St.
Indianapolis, IN 46204
Tel.: 317-638-1313

Merchants National Bank & Trust Company of Indianapolis*(Major Banking Relationship)*
One Merchants Plaza, Ste. 901E
Indianapolis, IN 46255
Tel.: 317-267-7109

Subsidiaries:

Major Video Concepts, Inc. **(1)**
8399 Zionsville Rd.
Indianapolis, IN 46268
Tel.: 317-875-8000
S.I.C.: 7999
Walter S. Wiseman *(Pres.)*

Tucker-Rocky Distributing **(1)**
1775 Hurd Dr.
Irving, TX 75038
Tel.: 214-580-0555
Distribution Service for Motorcycle Aftermarket Parts & Accessories
S.I.C.: 3751
Bob Nickell *(Pres.)*

LFC HOLDING CORPORATION
6111 Broken Sound Pkwy. N.W.
Boca Raton, FL 33487
Tel.: 407-994-6006 FL
Fax: 407-994-5197
Year Founded: 1985
Assets: $459,555,000
Earnings: ($1,376,000)
Liabilities: $573,361,000
Net Worth: $113,806,000
Approx.Sls.: $892,657,000
Emp.: 6,100
Fiscal Year-end: 3/31/92
Holding Co.
S.I.C.: 6719; 5712
Robert M. Elliott *(Chm. Bd. & Chief Exec. Officer)*
George H. Bradley *(Pres.)*
Patrick J. Nolan *(Sr. V.P., Chief Fin. Officer & Treas.)*
Edward Zimmer *(Sr. V.P., Sec. & Gen. Counsel)*
Lawrence R. McDevitt *(V.P. & Controller)*

Outside Service Firm(s):

Arthur Andersen & Co.*(Auditors)*
1601 Market St.
Philadelphia, PA 19103
Tel.: 215-241-7300

Wells Fargo Bank*(Major Banking Relationship)*
420 Montgomery St.
San Francisco, CA 94104

Subsidiary:

Levitz Furniture Corporation **(1)**
6111 Broken Sound Pkwy., N.W.
Boca Raton, FL 33436
Tel.: 407-994-6006 (100%)
Assets: $459,555,000
Earnings: ($1,376,000)
Liabilities: $573,361,000
Net Worth: $113,806,000
Approx.Sls.: $892,657,000
Emp.: 5,947
Fiscal Year-end: 3/31/92
117 Retail Furniture Stores Located in 25 States
S.I.C.: 5712
Robert M. Elliott *(Chm. Bd. & Chief Exec. Officer)*
George H. Bradley *(Pres.)*
Jack J. Brehm *(Sr. V.P.-Mktg.)*
Patrick J. Nolan *(Sr. V.P. & Treas.)*
Edward Zimmer *(Sr. V.P., Sec. & Gen. Counsel)*
Frank W. Bonheim *(V.P.-Personnel)*

LFC Holding Corporation—(Continued)

Eleanor P. Eckardt *(V.P.-Consumer Rels.)*
Robert E. Gorden *(V.P.-Adv. & Sls. Promo.)*
Larry McDevitt *(V.P. & Controller)*
Richard Mazzoni, Jr. *(V.P.-Mngmt. Information Systems)*
J. Thomas Pipkin *(V.P.-Opers.)*

Subsidiary:

Levitz Credit Corporation **(2)**
6111 Broken Sound Parkway, N.W.
Boca Raton, FL 33487
Tel.: 407-994-6006 (100%)
Assets: $2,678,000
Liabilities: $2,563,000
Net Worth: $115,000
Approx.Rev.: $10,790,000
Fiscal Year-end: 3/31/90
Financial Services
S.I.C.: 6159

THE LINC GROUP, INC.
303 E. Wacker Dr., Ste. 1000
Chicago, IL 60601
Tel.: 312-946-1000
Tel.: 800-669-5462 DE
Fax: 312-938-4290
Year Founded: 1975
Assets: $226,000,000
Earnings: $2,100,000
Liabilities: $172,000,000
Net Worth: $54,000,000
Approx.Rev.: $45,000,000
Emp.: 338
Fiscal Year-end: 12/31/90

Export
Lessor of Medical, Computer, Communications & High Technology Systems
S.I.C.: 7359
Martin E. Zimmerman *(Pres. & Chief Exec. Officer)*
Paul E. Watkins *(Chief Fin. Officer)*
Vincent T. Jaewinski *(Sr. V.P.-External Affairs)*
Allen P. Palles *(Sr. V.P., Chief Oper. Officer & Gen. Counsel)*
Mitchel D. Weiss *(Sr. V.P.-Opers.)*
Joseph Hohmann *(V.P. & Asst. Gen. Counsel)*
Peter Lorio *(V.P.-Vendor Programs & Natl Accts.)*
Pat Rice *(V.P.-Corporate Devel.)*
John Snead *(V.P.-Mngmt. Info. Systems)*
Joseph Metro *(Treas.)*
Thomas R. Ehmann *(Controller)*
Orlando Holway *(Mgr.-International Sls.)*
Lauren Nannini *(Sr. Personnel Admin.)*
Michelle Ventress *(Asst. Gen. Counsel)*

Subsidiaries:

LINC Capital Corporation **(1)**
303 E. Wacker Dr.
Chicago, IL 60601
Tel.: 312-946-1000
S.I.C.: 7352
Paul Keplen *(Pres.)*

LINC Capital Management **(1)**
303 E. Wacker Dr.
Chicago, IL 60601
Tel.: 312-946-1000
S.I.C.: 7352
Mark Broussard *(Pres.)*

LINC Equipment Services **(1)**
550 Bond St.
Lincolnshire, IL 60069
Tel.: 800-221-LINC
S.I.C.: 7352
William E. King *(Pres.)*

LINC Management Services **(1)**
303 E. Wacker Dr.
Chicago, IL 60601
Tel.: 312-946-1000
S.I.C.: 7352

LINC Medical Imaging **(1)**
3991 MacArthur Blvd., Ste. 310
Newport Beach, CA 92660
Tel.: 714-852-1155
S.I.C.: 7352
Lou Spidalette *(Pres.)*

LINC Quantum Analytics **(1)**
363-D Vintage Park Dr.
Foster City, CA 94404
Tel.: 415-570-5656
S.I.C.: 7352
Burt Lang *(Pres.)*

LINC Scientific Leasing Inc. **(1)**
303 E. Wacker Dr.
Chicago, IL 60601
Tel.: 312-946-1000 (100%)
Medical Instrument Leasing
S.I.C.: 7352
Terrence J. Quinn *(Pres. & Chief Exec. Officer)*

L.L. BEAN, INC.
Casco St.
Freeport, ME 04033
Tel.: 207-865-4761
Fax: 207-865-6738
Approx.Sls.: $597,000,000
Emp.: 3,300
Fiscal Year-end: 2/28/91
Catalog & Mail Order, Outdoor Sports Clothes Specialists; Men's & Women's Active Leisurewear & Equipment
S.I.C.: 5941; 5611; 5621; 5661; 5961; 3143
L.A. Gorman *(Pres.)*
Scott Howard *(Sr. V.P.-Opers.)*
Norman A. Poole *(Sr. V.P.-Fin. & Treas.)*
Austin Farrar *(V.P.-Human Resources)*
Horace Gower *(V.P.-Information Systems)*
Edward Howell *(V.P.-Prod. Devel.)*
Christopher McCormick *(V.P.-Adv. & Direct Mktg.)*
Lee Surace *(V.P. & Controller)*
Rodie Lloyd *(Mgr.-Pub. Rels.)*
Ken Paille' *(Mgr.-Mktg. Res.)*
Zane O. Shatzer *(Mgr.-Adv.)*

Computer Systems/Hardware:
IBM

Outside Service Firm(s):

Coopers & Lybrand*(Auditors)*
Portland, ME

Protection Mutual*(Commercial Insurance Carrier)*
Boston, MA

Liberty Mutual*(Group Insurer)*
Portland, ME

Kidder, Peabody & Co.*(Investment Banker)*
10 Hanover Square
New York, NY 10005
Tel.: 212-510-3000

Brann & Issacson*(Legal Firm)*
Lewiston, ME

Maine National Bank*(Major Banking Relationship)*
Augusta, ME

Frontier Capital Management Company*(Pension Manager)*
Boston, MA
Tel.: 617-261-0777
Fax: 617-261-0684

Gardner, Preston & Moss, Inc.*(Pension Manager)*
Boston, MA

LNR COMMUNICATIONS
180 Marcus Blvd.
Hauppauge, NY 11788
Tel.: 516-273-7111
Fax: 516-273-7119
Year Founded: 1971
Approx.Sls.: $25,000,000
Emp.: 250
Low Noise Amplifiers, Satellite Earth Station Equipment, Receivers & Exciters for Data, Message, Video
S.I.C.: 3663
Sy Okwit *(Pres.)*
Frank Arams *(Exec. V.P.)*
Larry Fodrowski *(V.P.-Fin.)*
O.J. Hanas *(V.P.-Advanced Tech. Prods. Div.)*
Herman Okean *(V.P.-Gov. Prods. Div.)*
Ed Salamone *(V.P.-Admin.)*

LPL TECHNOLOGIES, INC.
358 Hall Ave.
Wallingford, CT 06492-0384
Tel.: 203-265-8600 DE
Fax: 203-265-8628
Mfr. of Coaxial Cable; Metallic Wire Used For Communication Transmission; Designs & Manufactures Microwave Transmission Assemblies & Specially Engineered Cables
S.I.C.: 3356; 3355; 3399
Lawrence J. DeGeorge *(Chm. Bd., Pres. & Chief Exec. Officer)*
Edward G. Jepsen *(Exec. V.P., Chief Fin. Officer & Controller)*
Timothy F. Cohane *(V.P.)*
John P. Forde *(V.P.)*
Edward C. Wetmore *(Sec. & Gen. Counsel)*
James P. Rogers *(Treas.)*

Outside Service Firm(s):

Price Waterhouse*(Auditors)*
One Financial Plaza
Hartford, CT 06103
Tel.: 203-240-2000

Bankers Trust Co.*(Major Banking Relationship)*
P.O. Box 9050, Church St. Station
New York, NY 10008
Tel.: 212-250-6037

Winthrop, Stimson, Putnam & Roberts*(Legal Firm)*
One Battery Park Plaza
New York, NY 10004
Tel.: 212-943-0700

Subsidiaries:

Amphenol Corporation **(1)**
358 Hall Ave.
Wallingford, CT 06492
Tel.: 203-265-8900
Fax: 203-265-8516
Assets: $197,522,000
Earnings: ($12,095,000)
Liabilities: $123,504,000
Net Worth: $74,018,000
Approx.Sls.: $420,913,000
Emp.: 8,300
Fiscal Year-end: 12/31/90
Manufactures Electrical, Electronic & Fiber Optic Interconnections Including Fiber Optic Components, Associated Cable, Accessories & Assemblies
S.I.C.: 3678
Martin H. Loeffler *(Pres.)*
Allan S. Dickson *(V.P.-Mktg.)*
Brandon Barnwell *(V.P.-European Opers.)*
Stanley Aris *(Controller)*

Subsidiary:

Pyle Inc. **(2)**
1334 N. Kostner Ave.
Chicago, IL 60651
Tel.: 312-342-6300 (100%)
Fax: 312-342-0872
Electrical Connectors
S.I.C.: 3678
John Journalist *(Gen. Mgr.)*
R.M. Hansen *(V.P.-Mktg. & Sls.)*
J. Jamatka *(V.P.-Engrng.)*
D.R. Ross *(V.P. & Controller)*
C. Skobel *(Dir.-Pur.)*
T.M. Muellner *(Dir.-Adv.)*
M. Carroccia *(Natl. Sls. Dir.)*

Times Fiber Communications, Inc. **(1)**
358 Hall Ave.
Wallingford, CT 06492
Tel.: 203-265-8500
Fax: 203-265-8422
Approx.Sls.: $124,405,000
Emp.: 400
Fiscal Year-end: 12/31/90
Mfr. Coaxial Cable
S.I.C.: 3357
L. DeGeorge *(Chm. Bd. & Chief Exec. Officer)*
John P. Forde *(Pres. & Chief Oper. Officer)*
Edward Jepsen *(Exec. V.P. & Chief Fin. Officer)*
James Rogers *(Treas.)*
Timothy Cohane *(Sec.)*
Edward Wetmore *(Gen. Counsel)*

LWMCK CORPORATION
2301 S. Banker St.
Effingham, IL 62401
Tel.: 217-347-2210
S.I.C.: 2452
L.W. McKenzie, Jr. *(Pres.)*

Subsidiary:

National Building Systems **(1)**
2301 S. Banker
Effingham, IL 62401
Tel.: 217-347-2210
Mfr. of Prefabricated Homes
S.I.C.: 2452

LA BELLE INDUSTRIES, INC.
510 S. Worthington
Oconomowoc, WI 53066
Tel.: 414-567-9101
Telex: 910-260-1438
Fax: 414-567-4047
Year Founded: 1946
Approx.Sls.: $12,000,000
Emp.: 135

Import Export
Noise Measuring & Analysis Instrumentation, Electronic Programmable Signs, Contract Metal Stamping & Contract Electronic Assembly, System Device for the Hearing Impaired
S.I.C.: 3469; 3669; 3829; 3825
Robert Wurm *(Chm. Bd. & Chief Exec. Officer)*
Duane Kobs *(Chief Oper. Officer)*
Ken Kraft *(Exec. V.P.)*
Dan Heerey *(Chief Fin. Officer)*
Bill Hughes *(Sls. & Mktg. Mgr.)*
Glenn Schulz *(Div. Mgr.)*

Computer Systems/Hardware:
IBM AS 400

Division:

Quest Electronics Div. **(1)**
510 S. Worthington
Oconomowoc, WI 53066
Tel.: 414-567-9157
Fax: 414-567-4047
Import Export
Computer Systems/Hardware:
IBM AS 400
S.I.C.: 3825; 3829
Paul James *(Gen. Mgr.)*

LA-CO INDUSTRIES, INC.
250 N. Washtenaw Ave.
Chicago, IL 60612
Tel.: 312-826-1700
Fax: 312-826-7130
Approx.Sls.: $25,000,000
Emp.: 99

Export
Mfr. Thread & Gasket Compounds; Slic-Tite Paste; Stik, Thread Tape & Cord; Thread & Gasket Compound; Sealants & Fluxes, Pipe Thread Compounds, Silver Solder Flux; Aluminum Soldering Fluxes; Acid Brushes & Daubers
S.I.C.: 2899
Don Lytton *(Pres.)*
Dan Kleiman *(V.P.)*
R.F. Begani *(Mgr.-Export)*
Thomas Rynberg *(Mgr.-Mktg.)*
Dennis Mitzner *(Pur. Agent)*

LA COMPUTER CENTER
17013 Hawthorne Blvd.
Lawndale, CA 90260
Tel.: 310-542-3501
Year Founded: 1987
Approx.Sls.: $48,000,000
Emp.: 35
Wholesale Distribution of Computers; Retail Computer & Software Stores
S.I.C.: 5045; 5734
Robert Neman *(Pres.)*
Hersel Neman *(V.P.)*

LA FRANCE CORPORATION
8425 Executive Dr.
Philadelphia, PA 19153
Tel.: 215-365-8000
Tel.: 800-220-9800
Fax: 215-365-4420
Year Founded: 1946
Approx.Sls.: $27,000,000
Emp.: 382
Import Export
Mfr. of Custom, Decorative, Zinc Die Cast & Injection Molded Name Plates
S.I.C.: 3364; 3993
Joseph A. Teti, Jr. *(Chm. Bd.)*
Jerrold Helbein *(Pres.)*
Brian McHenry *(V.P.-Sls. & Mktg.)*
Peter Peroni *(V.P.-Engrng.)*
Robert Helmig *(Controller)*
George Barrar *(Gen. Mgr.)*
Jack Flood *(Mgr.-Pur.)*
A. Pandoli *(Mgr.-Quality Control)*

No. of Mfg. Plants/Facilities: 4
No. of U.S. Offices: 3
No. of Foreign Offices: 2

Computer Systems/Hardware:
IBM System 38

Outside Service Firm(s):

Deloitte & Touche*(Auditors)*
1700 Market St.
Philadelphia, PA 19103
Tel.: 215-246-2322
Fax: 215-569-2441

Continental Bank, N.A.*(Major Banking Relationship)*
Norristown, PA

Division:

United States Name Plate **(1)**
Enterprise & Executive
Philadelphia, PA 19153
Tel.: 215-365-8000
Signs & Advertising Specialties; Injection Molding of Plastic
S.I.C.: 3993; 3364
Robert Helmig *(V.P. & Chief Oper. Officer)*

LA MARCHE MFG. CO.
106 Bradrock Dr.
Des Plaines, IL 60018
Tel.: 708-299-1188
Fax: 708-299-3061
Year Founded: 1945
Approx.Sls.: $14,000,000
Emp.: 200
Fiscal Year-end: 5/31/91
Mfr. of Industrial & Utility Battery Chargers, DC Power Systems, Power Supplies, DC to AC Inverters; LaMarche, Consta-Volt Chargers, Uninterruptible Power Systems
S.I.C.: 3629; 3679
John Walsh *(Pres.)*
John Kalmuck *(V.P.-Sls. & Mktg.)*
Michael Britton *(Pur. Agent)*

LA MESA R V CENTER, INC.
7601 Alvarado Rd.
La Mesa, CA 92044
Tel.: 619-462-5660
Fax: 619-461-2260
Year Founded: 1972
Approx.Sls.: $35,000,000
Emp.: 150
Motor Homes, Recreational Vehicles, Campers, Parts & Service
S.I.C.: 5561; 7538
James R. Kimbrell *(Pres. & Chief Exec. Officer)*

Outside Service Firm(s):

Luce, Forward, Hamilton & Scripps*(Legal Firm)*
One American Plaza, 600 West Broadway, Ste. 2600
San Diego, CA 92101
Tel.: 619-236-1414

Union Bank*(Major Banking Relationship)*
8155 Mercury Ct., P.O. Box 2529
San Diego, CA 92112

LA PREFERIDA, INC.
3400 W. 35th St.
Chicago, IL 60632
Tel.: 312-254-7200
Telex: 25-3149
Cable: PRE-TROPIC
Fax: 312-254-8546
Approx.Sls.: $42,000,000
Emp.: 300
Mfr. & Distr. of Mexican, Cuban & Puerto Rican Foods
S.I.C.: 2032; 5149
Ralph Steinbarth *(Pres.)*
Emil Smider *(Exec. V.P.-Bus. Devel.)*
Bob Gouwens *(V.P.-Sls.)*
David Steinbarth *(V.P.-Adv. & Mktg.)*
Richard Steinbarth *(V.P.-Pur.)*
John Badke *(Dir.-Logistics)*

LA REINA, INC.
316 N. Ford Blvd.
Los Angeles, CA 90022
Tel.: 213-268-2791
Fax: 213-265-4295
Year Founded: 1958
Approx.Sls.: $55,000,000
Emp.: 600
Export
Manufacture Flour Tortillas
S.I.C.: 2099
Mauro Robles *(Chm. Bd. & Pres.)*
Ricardo Robles *(Chief Fin. Officer)*
Estela Robles *(Sec. & Treas.)*
Jose Luis *(Dir.-Human Resources & Mktg.)*

LA ROSA'S, INC.
2334 Boudinot
Cincinnati, OH 45238
Tel.: 513-347-5660
Year Founded: 1954
Approx.Sls.: $30,000,000
Emp.: 312
Grocery Stores; Pizzeria Chain; Italian Restaurants
S.I.C.: 5411; 5812; 6794
Donald S. La Rosa *(Chm. Bd.)*
Michael La Rosa *(Pres.)*
T.D. Hughes *(Chief Exec. & Chief Fin. Officer)*
Stewart Smetts *(Dir.-Mktg.)*

LA SALLE COUNTY FARM SUPPLY
(Farmer Owned Cooperative)
3107 N. Illinois Rte. 23
Ottawa, IL 61350
Tel.: 815-434-0131
Assets: $7,400,000
Earnings: $289,000
Net Worth: $7,400,000
Approx.Sls.: $36,197,000
Emp.: 53
Fiscal Year-end: 8/31/91
Retail Farm Supplier; Petroleum Feed Fertilizer; Agricultural Chemicals; Liquified Petroleum; Grain Elevator
S.I.C.: 5171; 5191; 5984; 4221; 5153
Gordon Jamieson *(Pres.)*
Robert Schwarz *(Chief Fin. Officer & Controller)*
Walter Bernard *(Treas.)*

Computer Systems/Hardware:
Honeywell Equipment

Outside Service Firm(s):

Illinois Agricultural Auditing*(Auditors)*
Bloomington, IL

Country Companies*(Group Insurer)*
Bloomington, IL

First American Bank, N.A.*(Investment Banker)*
Dundee, IL

First National Bank Ottawa*(Major Banking Relationship)*
Ottawa, IL

Country Companies*(Pension Manager)*
Bloomington, IL

LA VICTORIA FOODS, INC.
240 S. 6th Ave.
City of Industry, CA 91746
Mailing Address:
P.O. Box 3884,
City of Industry, CA 91744
Tel.: 818-333-0787
Fax: 818-333-5057
Year Founded: 1917
Emp.: 600
Mfr. of Mexican Salsa & Sauces
S.I.C.: 2033
Robert C. Tanklage *(Pres.)*
Russell N. Frank *(Sr. V.P.-Natl. Accounts)*
Ernest Johnson *(Sr. V.P. & Sec.)*
Frank Yorio *(Sr. V.P.-Mktg. & Sls.)*
Glen Leonard *(V.P.-Retail Sls.)*
Arthur Leatherman *(V.P.-Plant Oper.)*
James Lee *(Chief Fin. Officer)*
Carolyn Johnson *(Treas.)*
Dennis Mari *(Dir.-Pur.)*
M. Lyn Kelly *(Mgr.-Personnel)*
Rhaun Turner *(Technical Dir.)*

Outside Service Firm(s):

Union Bank*(Major Banking Relationship)*
City of Industry, CA

LABARGE PIPE & STEEL COMPANY
901 N. 10th St.
Saint Louis, MO 63101
Tel.: 314-231-3400
Telex: 910-761-1159
Assets: $16,400,000
Liabilities: $14,000,000
Net Worth: $2,400,000
Approx.Sls.: $55,000,000
Emp.: 200
Warehousing & Distribution of Carbon Steel Pipe & Tubing
S.I.C.: 5051
Pierre LaBarge III *(Chm. Bd. & Pres.)*
Richard A. Bauman *(Exec. V.P.-Fin. & Admin.)*
Raymond D. Benner *(V.P.-Mngmt. Information Systems)*
Robert L. Gilleland *(V.P.-Sls. & Adv. Dir.)*
Principal(s):
Richard A. Bauman
Pierre LaBarge III

Computer Systems/Hardware:
IBM 4381

Outside Service Firm(s):

KPMG Peat Marwick*(Auditors)*
1010 Market St.
Saint Louis, MO 63101
Tel.: 314-444-1400

Boatmen's Trust Company*(Major Banking Relationship)*
100 North Broadway
St. Louis, MO 63102
Tel.: 314-466-2469

Blain Braswell*(Group Insurer)*
St. Louis, MO

Bryan, Cave, McPheeters & McRoberts*(Legal Firm)*
One Metropolitan Sq.
St. Louis, MO 63102
Tel.: 314-259-2000

LABEL-AIRE INC.
550 Burning Tree Rd.
Fullerton, CA 92633
Tel.: 714-441-0700 **DE**
Fax: 714-994-1152
Year Founded: 1976
Approx.Sls.: $15,000,000
Emp.: 110
Fiscal Year-end: 12/31/91
Export
Mfr. High-Speed Label Applicating Equipment
S.I.C.: 3565
Garrison W. Brinton *(Chm. Bd.)*
Richard W. Riley *(Pres.)*
Robert MacMillan *(V.P.-Oper.)*
Paul Martinez *(V.P.-Sls. & Mktg.)*
G.W. Brinton *(Treas.)*
George Allen *(Dir.-Technical Services)*
Stella Rodriguez *(Dir.-Personnel)*
Fran Older *(Mgr.-Adv.)*
William Riley *(Mgr.-Materials)*
Dennis W. Harwood *(Legal Officer)*
Principal(s):
Garrison W. Brinton
Richard W. Riley

No. of Mfg. Plants/Facilities: 1

Computer Systems/Hardware:
Qantel

Outside Service Firm(s):

Deloitte & Touche*(Auditors)*
Newport Beach, CA

Harwood, Atkinson & Meindl*(Legal Firm)*
Newport Beach, CA

The Bank of California, N.A.*(Major Banking Relationship)*
Newport Beach, CA

LABELON CORPORATION
10 Chapin St.
Canandaigua, NY 14424
Tel.: 716-394-6220
Tel.: 800-428-5566
Fax: 716-394-3154
Year Founded: 1946
Approx.Sls.: $20,000,000
Emp.: 400
Fiscal Year-end: 9/30/91
Import Export
Mfr. Office Prods.
S.I.C.: 3579; 2672; 2899
William Irwin *(Pres.)*
E. Billings Brewster *(Chief Exec. Officer)*
Warren Hookway *(Exec. V.P.-Mfg.)*
Gregg Gittens *(V.P.-Sls. & Mktg.)*
David Baker *(Mgr.-Personnel)*
Deb Boughton *(Mgr.-Mktg.)*

LABORATORY SUPPLY COMPANY, INC.
4444 Park Blvd.
Louisville, KY 40209
Mailing Address:
P.O. Box 17009,
Louisville, KY 40217-0009
Tel.: 502-363-1891
Tel.: 800-888-5227 **KY**
Fax: 502-364-1609
Year Founded: 1972
Assets: $5,000,000
Net Worth: $5,000,000
Approx.Sls.: $30,000,000
Emp.: 140
Fiscal Year-end: 4/30/91
Wholesale Laboratory & Medical Supplies; Instrumentation & Service
S.I.C.: 5047

Laboratory Supply Company, Inc.—(Continued)

Charles E. Davis, Sr. *(Chm. Bd. & Pres.)*
Charles E. Davis, Jr. *(Sec. & Treas.)*
Linda Craig *(Dir.-Personnel)*
Roger K. Steele *(Dir.-Mtkg.)*
Noble Hickerson, Jr. *(Mgr.-Pur.)*

Principal(s):
Charles E. Davis, Sr.

No. of Mfg. Plants/Facilities: 7
No. of U.S. Offices: 7

Outside Service Firm(s):

Deloitte & Touche*(Auditors)*
510 W. Broadway
Louisville, KY 40202
Tel.: 502-562-2000

Liberty Mutual*(Group Insurer)*
Louisville, KY 40232

Ogden Associates, Inc.*(Investment Banker)*
Louisville, KY

Friedman & Robinson*(Legal Firm)*
1000 Republic Bldg.
Louisville, KY 40202

First National Bank of Louisville*(Major Banking Relationship)*
P.O. Box 36000,
Louisville, KY 40233

Branches:

LABSCO **(1)**
7721 Records St.
Indianapolis, IN 46226
Tel.: 317-546-6872
Tel.: 800-888-1200
Fax: 317-547-6705
Emp.: 12
Sls. of Laboratory Supplies
S.I.C.: 5047
Charles L. Lancaster *(Branch Mgr.)*

Laboratory Supply Company **(1)**
1009A N.E. Jib Ct.
Lees Summit, MO 64064
Tel.: 816-795-1140
Tel.: 800-666-1140
Fax: 816-795-1144
Emp.: 9
Sls. of Laboratory Supplies
S.I.C.: 5047
Dick Matchael *(Branch Mgr.)*

Laboratory Supply Company **(1)**
6390 N.E. 14th St.
Des Moines, IA 50313
Tel.: 515-289-1065
Tel.: 800-888-2300
Fax: 515-289-1744
Emp.: 8
Sls. of Laboratory Supplies
S.I.C.: 5047
Charles Davis *(Pres.)*
Ray Nelson *(Branch Mgr.)*

Laboratory Supply Company **(1)**
723 N. Ann Arbor
Oklahoma City, OK 73127
Tel.: 405-947-5895
Tel.: 800-888-2500
Fax: 405-946-1031
Emp.: 18
Sls. of Laboratory Supplies
S.I.C.: 5047
Mike Minden *(Branch Mgr.)*

Laboratory Supply Company **(1)**
112 Griffith Plaza Dr.
Winston-Salem, NC 27103
Tel.: 919-768-5648
Tel.: 800-888-9004
Fax: 919-768-3176
Emp.: 11
Sls. of Laboratory Supplies
S.I.C.: 5047
Calvin Nichols *(Branch Mgr.)*

Laboratory Supply Company **(1)**
336 Wilhagen Rd.
Nashville, TN 37217
Tel.: 615-361-8501
Tel.: 800-759-8830
Fax: 615-367-0652
Emp.: 12
Sls. of Laboratory Supplies
S.I.C.: 5047
Roger Steele *(Branch Mgr.)*

LACKMAN FOOD SERVICE
303 Crossways Park Dr.
Woodbury, NY 11797
Tel.: 516-364-2300
Fax: 516-364-9788
Year Founded: 1967
Sales Range: $40-59 Million
Emp.: 1,200
Fiscal Year-end: 6/30/90
Food Service Contractor
S.I.C.: 5141
Corporate Giving Program: United Wayves to Uni
Thomas F. Lackman *(Chm. Bd. & Pres.)*
Gil Velazquez *(Exec. V.P.)*
Peter Alessio *(V.P.-Opers.)*
Michael Mines *(V.P.-Fin.)*
Pat Baker *(Asst. V.P.-Human Resources)*
Marcia Pearl *(Dir.-Pur.)*

Principal(s):
Thomas F. Lackman

Computer Systems/Hardware:
IBM System 36

Outside Service Firm(s):

Albrecht, Viggiano & Zurich*(Auditors)*
New York, NY

New York Life*(Group Insurer)*
New York, NY

LADDIN & COMPANY, INC.
2 Park Ave.
New York, NY 10016
Tel.: 212-532-4381
Fax: 212-689-4888
Year Founded: 1962
Approx.Billings: $11,100,000
Emp.: 15
Communications, Direct Response, Chemical & Industrial, Business-to-Business, Consumer, Fashion, Financial Services, Photography, Publishing, Media, Spirits & Retail Adv.
Paul Laddin *(Pres.)*
Don Aaronson *(Exec. V.P.)*
Stan Pearlman *(Pres.-Kenmar Sls./Promo. Div.)*
Howard Laddin *(Sec., Treas.)*

LADY MARLENE SALES CORP.
183 Madison Ave.
New York, NY 10016
Mailing Address:
20-20 129th Ave.
College Point, NY 11356
Tel.: 212-889-6200
Fax: 212-725-7248
Approx.Sls.: $10,500,000
Emp.: 100

Import Export
Lady Marlene Brassieres, Girdles, Body Briefs
S.I.C.: 2342
Ezra Dayan *(Pres.)*
Jim Burkoff *(V.P.-Mktg.)*
Bernard Dayan *(Gen. Mgr. & Sls. Mgr.)*

RAY LAETHEM PONTIAC GMC TRUCK CO.
17677 Mack Ave.
Detroit, MI 48224
Tel.: 313-886-1700
Fax: 313-886-1721
Approx.Sls.: $42,900,000
Emp.: 85
Automobile & Truck Dealership
S.I.C.: 5511
Ray Laethem *(Pres.)*
Philip Castiglione *(Sec. & Treas.)*

Outside Service Firm(s):

N.B.D. Bank, N.A.*(Major Banking Relationship)*
611 Woodward Ave.
Detroit, MI 48226
Tel.: 313-225-1122
Fax: 313-225-3420

LAFAYETTE MANUFACTURING, INC.
3440 Enterprise Ave.
Hayward, CA 94545
Tel.: 510-785-5280
Fax: 510-887-2724
Approx.Sls.: $15,000,000
Emp.: 70
Fiscal Year-end: 9/30/92
Manufacture & Install Architectural Precast Concrete
S.I.C.: 3531
Maurice Lafayette, Jr. *(Pres. & Chief Exec. Officer)*
Walt Birdsall *(V.P.-Fin. & Gen. Mgr.)*
Edward S. Knowles *(V.P.-Opers.)*
Adele Schou *(Treas.)*

Computer Systems/Hardware:
IBM, Wang

Outside Service Firm(s):

Moss Adams*(Auditors)*
San Francisco, CA

Miller, Morton, Caillat & Nevis*(Legal Firm)*
San Jose, CA

Bay Bank of Commerce*(Major Banking Relationship)*
San Leandro, CA

Joel Cherande Financial Service*(Pension Manager)*
Chestnut Hill, MA

LAFAYETTE STEEL CO.
3600 N. Military St.
Detroit, MI 48210
Tel.: 313-894-4552
Fax: 313-894-7930
Approx.Sls.: $115,900,000
Emp.: 178
Flatroll Steel Warehouse & Processor
S.I.C.: 5051
Suren Hovespian *(Chm. Bd. & Pres.)*
Bill Corbett *(V.P.-Fin.)*
Dan Zemon *(V.P. & Gen. Mgr.)*

LAIDLAW CORPORATION
6625 N. Scottsdale Rd.
Scottsdale, AZ 85250
Tel.: 602-951-0003 **IL**
Year Founded: 1917
Approx.Sls.: $42,000,000
Emp.: 400
Fiscal Year-end: 9/30/91

Import Export
Flyswatters, Garment Hangers, Springs
S.I.C.: 3496; 3999
John S. Mueller *(Chm. & Chief Exec. Officer)*
Curtis Livermore *(Chief Opers. Officer)*
John Grootveld *(V.P.-Fin.)*
Brent N. McWilliams *(V.P.-Sls.)*
Kathy Priebe *(Corp. Sec.)*

Principal(s):
John S. Mueller

Computer Systems/Hardware:
IBM 36

Outside Service Firm(s):

Arthur Andersen & Co.*(Auditors)*
Phoenix, AZ

Sutkowski & Washkuhn*(Legal Firm)*
Phoenix, AZ

First Interstate Bank*(Major Banking Relationship)*
P.O. Box 53441,
Phoenix, AZ 85072-3441
Tel.: 602-229-4049

LAIRD & COMPANY
1 Laird Rd.
Scobeyville, NJ 07724
Tel.: 908-542-0312 **NJ**
Fax: 908-542-2244
Year Founded: 1780
Approx.Sls.: $40,000,000
Emp.: 70
Fiscal Year-end: 12/31/91

Import Export
Manufacture Liquor & Wine
S.I.C.: 2085; 2084; 5182
Larrie W. Laird *(Pres.)*
Peter D. Howell *(V.P.-Bus. Unit.)*
Gary W. Krause *(V.P.-Sls.)*
John E. Laird III *(V.P.-Admin.)*
F. Gary Stover *(Treas.)*
M.L. Laird *(Sec.)*
Catherine Schlipf *(Asst. Sec.)*
Thomas Alberico *(Mgr.-Import)*
Janice Custer *(Mgr.-Plant)*
Lisa Laird *(Mgr.-Bus. Unit Sls.)*
Chris Armstrong *(Chief Engineer)*
Robert Reed *(Chief Accountant)*

Computer Systems/Hardware:
Data General

Outside Service Firm(s):

Leskowicz, Brower & Driver*(Auditors)*
New York, NY

McOmber & McOmber*(Legal Firm)*
Red Bank, NJ

Midlantic National Bank*(Major Banking Relationship)*
Neptune, NJ

Division:

Kasser/Laird Distilling Co. **(1)**
419 Sargon Way, Unit 8
Horsham, PA 19044
Tel.: 215-443-0305
Fax: 215-443-8904
Import Export
Computer Systems/Hardware:
Data General
Liquor Brokers
S.I.C.: 2085
Gary W. Krause *(Pres.)*

THE LAITRAM CORPORATION
220 Laitram Lane
Harahan, LA 70123
Mailing Address:
P.O. Box 50699,
New Orleans, LA 70150
Tel.: 504-733-6000 **LA**
Fax: 504-733-2143
Year Founded: 1949
Sales Range: $20-39 Million
Emp.: 450
Fiscal Year-end: 3/31/91

Export
Shrimp Processing Machinery, Plastic Modular Conveyor Belting, Sensing Devices & Related Equipment for Navigation, Oceanography & Seismography, Magnetic Compasses, Alternating Metal & Wood Stairtreads
S.I.C.: 3535; 3556; 3559; 3812; 3829
Jay Lapeyre, Jr. *(Chm. & Pres.)*
Lawrence P. Oertling *(Chief Fin. Officer)*
Timothy J. Christiansen *(Controller)*
Barry LaCour *(Gen. Counsel)*
Ted Baer *(Chief Info. Officer)*
Jim Evans *(Mgr.-Human Resources)*

Principal(s):
Jay Lapeyre, Jr.

Computer Systems/Hardware:
IBM AS 400

Outside Service Firm(s):

KPMG Peat Marwick*(Auditors)*
One Shell Center, Ste. 3500
New Orleans, LA 70139

Whitney National Bank of New Orleans*(Major Banking Relationship)*
P.O. Box 61260
New Orleans, LA 70161
Tel.: 504-586-7422

Subsidiaries:

Digicourse, Inc. **(1)**
5200 Toler St.
Harahan, LA 70123
Tel.: 504-733-6061 (100%)
Fax: 504-734-8627
Approx.Sls.: $2,500,000
Emp.: 55
Remote Reading Digital Magnetic Compasses, Adaptable to Peripheral Electronic Devices, Depth Sensors & Related Equip.
S.I.C.: 3812
J.M. Lapeyre, Jr. *(Pres.)*
Roy Kelm *(V.P. & Gen. Mgr.)*

Intralox, Inc. **(1)**
201 Laitram Lane
Harahan, LA 70123
Tel.: 504-733-0463
Tel.: 800-535-8848 (100%)
Telex: 6821268
Fax: 504-733-0063
Emp.: 190
Export
Conveyor Belting & Accessories
S.I.C.: 3535
J.M. Lapeyre, Jr. *(Chm. & Pres.)*
Ted Boer *(Chief Info. Officer)*
Lawrence P. Oertling *(Chief Fin. Officer)*
Timothy J. Christiansen *(Controller)*
Barry LaCour *(Gen. Counsel)*
Anita Koek *(Mgr.-Media Buying & Pub. Rels.)*
Frank J. Profumo *(Mgr.-Adv.)*

Laitram Machinery Inc. **(1)**
220 Laitram Lane
Harahan, LA 70123
Tel.: 504-733-6000 (100%)
Fax: 504-733-2143
Mfg. Shrimp Processing Equip.
S.I.C.: 3559

Lapeyre Stair, Inc. **(1)**
220 Laitram Lane
Harahan, LA 70123
Tel.: 504-733-6009 (100%)
Fax: 504-733-4393
Alternating Tread Stair
S.I.C.: 3446
J.M. Lapeyre, Jr. *(Pres.)*
Bob Larson *(Sls. Dir.)*

Non-U.S. Holdings:

Intralox A/S **(1)**
Egholmvej 3, 9800
Hjorring, Denmark
Tel.: 98 90 08 77 (100%)
Fax: 98 90 07 91
Mfr. of Conveyor Belting
S.I.C.: 3052; 3535
Joe Gianfalla *(Mktg. Mgr.)*

Intralox A/S **(1)**
8, Strandvagen 29b 312 61
Mellbystrand, Sweden
Tel.: 0430-273 75
Fax: 0430-278 10
S.I.C.: 3052; 3535

Intralox A/S **(1)**
P.B. 40 3484
Holmsbu, Norway
Tel.: 03-793612
Fax: 03-793611
S.I.C.: 3052; 3535

Intralox European **(1)**
Postbus 23280, Lemeterbergweg 36D 1100 DT,
Amsterdam, Z.O, Netherlands
Tel.: 055-221012
Fax: 055-215632
S.I.C.: 3052; 3535

Intralox, Inc. GmbH **(1)**
Heinrich-Hertz-Strasse 44 4006
Erkrath, Germany
Tel.: 49-211-25-3091
Tel.: 0130-81-0448 (100%)
Fax: 49-211 20 80 84
Mfr. of Conveyor Belting
S.I.C.: 3052; 3535

Intralox Italia s.r.l. **(1)**
Via Y Gagarin 42100
Reggio Emilia, Italy
Tel.: 0522-360 300
Fax: 0522-360 235
S.I.C.: 3052; 3535

Intralox Ltd. **(1)**
Building 69, Third Ave., Pensnett Trading Estate
Kingswinford, West Midlands DY6 7PP, United Kingdom
Tel.: 0384-291052
Fax: 0384-291684
S.I.C.: 3052; 3535

Lake Charles American Press
(See Shearman Corporation Listing)

LAKE COUNTY PRESS
98 Noll St.
Waukegan, IL 60085
Tel.: 708-336-4333
Fax: 708-336-5840
Approx.Sls.: $12,000,000
Emp.: 130
Offset & Letterpress Printing
S.I.C.: 2752
William Clay *(Chm. Bd.)*
Ralph Johnson *(Pres.)*

Outside Service Firm(s):

McGladrey & Pullen*(Auditors)*
Chicago, IL

LAKE ERIE ELECTRIC, INC.
25730 First St.
Westlake, OH 44145
Mailing Address:
P.O. Box 450859
Westlake, OH 44145
Tel.: 216-835-5565 OH
Fax: 216-835-5688
Approx.Sls.: $30,000,000
Emp.: 500
Fiscal Year-end: 12/31/91
Engineering & Electrical Construction Services & Contracting
S.I.C.: 1731; 8711
John S. Corogin *(Chm. Bd., Sec. & Treas.)*
Peter J. Corogin *(Pres.)*
Dennis Tarnay *(Chief Fin. Officer & Treas.)*
Robert Boucherle *(V.P.)*
Evan Kargiotis *(V.P.)*

Computer Systems/Hardware:
IBM-System 36

Outside Service Firm(s):

KPMG Peat Marwick*(Auditors)*
1500 National City Center
Cleveland, OH 44114
Tel.: 216-696-9100

Group America*(Group Insurer)*
Cleveland, OH

Calfee, Halter & Griswold*(Legal Firm)*
800 Superior Ave., Ste. 1800
Cleveland, OH 44115-2688
Tel.: 216-622-8200
Fax: 216-241-0816

Wickens, Herzer & Panza*(Legal Firm)*
Lorain, OH
Tel.: 216-246-5268

Bank One*(Major Banking Relationship)*
Cleveland, OH

LAKE REGION MANUFACTURING COMPANY, INC.
340 Lake Hazeltine Dr.
Chaska, MN 55318
Tel.: 612-448-5111 MN
Fax: 612-448-3441
Year Founded: 1947
Approx.Sls.: $33,000,000
Emp.: 600

Export
Mfr. of Medical Devices for Diagnostic Use
S.I.C.: 3841
Gary Melton *(Chief Fin. Officer)*
Joseph J. Fleischhacker, Sr. *(Pres.)*
Joe F. Fleischhacker, Jr. *(V.P.-Res. & Devel.)*
Mark Fleischhacker *(V.P.-Mfg.)*
V.M. Fleischhacker *(Treas.)*
Katherine S. Roehl *(Sec.)*
John Van Etta *(Dir.-Human Resources)*
Paul Kohl *(Mgr.-Plant)*

Outside Service Firm(s):

W.F. Denny & Co.*(Auditors)*
Excelsior, MN

LAKESIDE FOODS, INC.
(Formerly Lakeside Packing Company)
PO Box 1327, 508 Jay St.
Manitowoc, WI 54220
Tel.: 414-684-3356
Fax: 414-684-8217
Year Founded: 1887
Sales Range: $100-499 Million
Emp.: 1000
Fiscal Year-end: 4/30/92
Manufacture Canned & Frozen Vegetables & Meats
S.I.C.: 2033; 2013; 2037
J. Douglas Quick *(Pres. & Chief Exec. Officer)*
Daniel Cavanaugh *(V.P.-Oper.)*
Jeffrey Lund *(V.P.-Process & Food Sls.)*
Russell J. Schmidt *(V.P.-Admin. & Fin.)*
David Yanda *(V.P.-Frozen Food Sls.)*
David Aggen *(Dir.-Quality Control)*
Jamar Ferguson *(Dir.-Customer Serv.)*
Barbara Nundahl *(Dir.-Data Processing)*
Thomas E. Reilly *(Dir.-Human Resources)*
Gordon Schaefer *(Dir.-Business Devel.)*

Outside Service Firm(s):

KPMG Peat Marwick*(Auditors)*
777 E. Wisconsin Ave.
Milwaukee, WI 53202
Tel.: 414-276-4200

Nash, Spindler, Dean & Grimstad*(Legal Firm)*
926 S. 8th St.
Manitowoc, WI 54220
Tel.: 414-684-3321

First Wisconsin National Bank*(Major Banking Relationship)*
777 E. Wisconsin Ave.
Milwaukee, WI 53202
Tel.: 414-765-4321
Fax: 414-355-6903

Subsidiary:

Oceana Foods **(1)**
PO Box 156, 97 W. 2nd Street
Shelby, MI 49455
Tel.: 616-861-2141
Emp.: 100
Fruit Processor
S.I.C.: 0723
J. Douglas Quick *(Pres. & Chief Exec. Officer)*

LAKESIDE INDUSTRIES
7735 178th Place NE
Redmond, WA 98052
Mailing Address:
P.O. Box 1379,
Bellevue, WA 98009
Tel.: 206-641-4600
Fax: 206-869-2249
Year Founded: 1972
Approx.Sls.: $75,000,000
Emp.: 500
Highway & Street Construction Contractors
S.I.C.: 1611
Rhoady R. Lee, Jr. *(Chm. Bd. & Chief Exec. Officer)*
Larry Darnell *(Pres.)*
Rhoady R. Lee, Sr. *(Sr. V.P.)*
Tim Lee *(V.P.)*
Robert Sturgis *(V.P.-Sls.)*
Jeanne Marie Lee *(Sec. & Treas.)*
Henry R. Waggoner *(Controller & Asst. Sec.)*

Principal(s):
Rhoady R. Lee, Jr.

Outside Service Firm(s):

Deloitte & Touche*(Auditors)*
700 Fifth Ave., Suite 4500
Seattle, WA 98104-5044
Tel.: 206-292-1800

Short, Cressman & Burgess*(Legal Firm)*
Seattle, WA

Seafirst Bank*(Major Banking Relationship)*
Columbia-SeaFirst Center, 701 5th Ave., 11th Flr.
Seattle, WA 98124
Tel.: 206-358-3039
Fax: 206-358-3113

LAKESIDE REFINING CO. INC.
21700 Northwestern Hwy., Ste. 1160
Southfield, MI 48075
Tel.: 313-559-1800
Fax: 313-559-1861
Approx.Sls.: $200,000,000
Emp.: 50
Petroleum Refining
S.I.C.: 2911
Marvin H. Fleischman *(Pres., Chief Exec. & Chief Fin. Officer)*
Willis Pergiga *(V.P.)*
Steven Robinson *(Sec.)*
Naweed Rana *(Dir.-Mngmt. Information Systems)*

Computer Systems/Hardware:
Burroughs

Outside Service Firm(s):

Price Waterhouse*(Auditors)*
200 Renaissance Center, Ste. 3900
Detroit, MI 48243

Michigan Mutual Insurance Co.*(Group Insurer)*
Columbus, OH

Butzel Long*(Legal Firm)*
Madden Bldg., 150 W. Jefferson, Ste. 900
Detroit, MI 48226-4430
Tel.: 313-225-7000
Fax: 313-225-7080

Manufacturers National Bank N.A.*(Major Banking Relationship)*
38th Fl., 100 Renaissance Center
Detroit, MI 48243
Tel.: 313-222-4227

Subsidiaries:

Crystal Refining **(1)**
21700 Northwest Hwy.
Southfield, MI 48075
Tel.: 313-559-1800

Lakeside Refining Co. Inc.—(Continued)

Joy Service **(1)**
21700 Northwest Hwy.
Southfield, MI 48075
Tel.: 313-559-1800

Peerless Distributing Co. **(1)**
21700 Northwest Hwy.
Southfield, MI 48075
Tel.: 313-559-1800

Petroleum Specialties **(1)**
21700 Northwest Hwy.
Southfield, MI 48075
Tel.: 313-559-1800

LAKEWOOD ENGINEERING & MANUFACTURING CO.
501 N. Sacramento Blvd.
Chicago, IL 60612
Tel.: 312-722-4300
Fax: 312-722-5346
Approx.Sls.: $40,000,000
Emp.: 350
Manufacture Ventilating Fans & Equipment, Ball Bearing Swivels, Metal Specialty Products
S.I.C.: 3564
Carl W. Krauss *(Chm. Bd.)*
Christine L. Krauss *(Exec. V.P. & Sec.)*
Carl R. Krauss *(Pres.)*
Principal(s):
Carl W. Krauss

Computer Systems/Hardware:
Burroughs 83

Outside Service Firm(s):

Ernst & Young*(Auditors)*
233 S. Wacker Dr.
Chicago, IL 60606
Tel.: 312-368-1800
Fax: 312-645-3095

American National Bank & Trust Co.*(Major Banking Relationship)*
Chicago, IL

Continental Bank N. A.*(Major Banking Relationship)*
231 S. LaSalle St.
Chicago, IL 60697
Tel.: 312-828-2345
Tel.: 800-426-5754
Telex: 312-828-1783

LAKIN GENERAL CORPORATION
2044 N. Dominick St.
Chicago, IL 60614
Tel.: 312-871-6360
Fax: 312-871-6675
Emp.: 250
Manufacturer of Rubber Products; Seals; Steel & Rubber Rolls
S.I.C.: 2891; 3069
Louis Lakin *(Pres.)*
Ken Lakin *(Exec. V.P.)*
Dan Lakin *(V.P.)*
Rob Grammer *(Controller)*

Outside Service Firm(s):

Landgren & Associates*(Auditors)*
Chicago, IL

American National Bank*(Major Banking Relationship)*
33 North LaSalle St.
Chicago, IL 60690
Tel.: 312-661-6967

LAMAR CORPORATION
5551 Corporate Blvd.
Baton Rouge, LA 70808
Tel.: 504-926-1000
Fax: 504-923-0698
Year Founded: 1902
Approx.Sls.: $75,000,000
Emp.: 600
Real Estate Owner, Manager & Outdoor Advertising
S.I.C.: 6531
Kevin Reilly, Jr. *(Pres. & Chief Exec. Officer)*
Keith Istre *(V.P.-Fin.)*
Charles W. Lamar, III *(Sec.)*
Keith A. Istre *(Treas.)*

Lamar Life Corporation
(Name Changed to Capitol Street Corp.)

LAMARCA GROUP INC.
640 Fifth Ave.
New York, NY 10019
Tel.: 212-265-5200 **NY**
Fax: 212-265-2626
Year Founded: 1975
Assets: $4,041,000
Earnings: $2,300,000
Net Worth: $4,041,000
Sales Range: $60-79 Million
Emp.: 35
Fiscal Year-end: 5/31/88
Advertising, Media & Marketing Services
S.I.C.: 7311; 7319; 8743
James LaMarca *(Chm. Bd., Pres. & Chief Exec. Officer)*
Al DiPietro *(Chief Fin. Officer & Sr. V.P.)*
Joseph A. Kelly *(Sr. V.P.)*
David Wheeler *(Sr. V.P.)*
Anthony Curto *(Treas. & Sec.)*
Mary Durant *(Controller)*

Computer Systems/Hardware:
Wang VS65

Outside Service Firm(s):

Robert J. Eckhart*(Auditors)*
New York, NY

Guardian Life Insurance Co.*(Group Insurer)*
New York, NY

Merrill Lynch*(Investment Banker)*
North Tower, 28th Fl., 4 World Financial Center
New York, NY 10281-1200
Tel.: 212-449-1000

Meyer, Suozzi, English & Klein*(Legal Firm)*
Long Island, NY

The Bank of New York*(Major Banking Relationship)*
One Wall Street
New York, NY 10286
Tel.: 212-635-6805
Fax: 212-635-3201

Subsidiaries:

LaMarca Direct Marketing **(1)**
640 Fifth Ave.
New York, NY 10019
Tel.: 212-265-5200
Fax: 212-265-2626
Emp.: 25
Direct Marketing & Direct Response Adv.
James LaMarca *(Chm. Bd & Pres.)*
Stevens P. Jackson *(Sr. V.P.-Direct Mktg.)*
David Wheeler *(Sr. V.P.-Mktg.)*
Al DiPietro *(V.P.-Fin.)*
Anthony Curto *(Sec. & Treas.)*

The Radio Group **(1)**
640 Fifth Ave.
New York, NY 10019
Tel.: 212-265-5200 (100%)
Emp.: 6
Radio Commercial & Program Production
S.I.C.: 8743
Ed Bearon *(Chief Oper. Officer)*
Al DiPietro *(Chief Fin. Officer)*

LAMASTER FARMER, ET AL
430 First Ave. North, Ste. 500
Minneapolis, MN 55401
Tel.: 612-334-3232
Year Founded: 1987
Approx.Billings: $16,000,000
Emp.: 16
Consumer Goods Adv. & Mktg.
James W. Farmer *(Pres.)*
Mike O'Connor *(Dir.-Direct Mktg.)*
Tom Chapman *(Dir.-Acct. Planning)*
Jim Mackin *(Gen. Mgr.)*

LAMB ENGINEERING & CONSTRUCTION CO.
125 Walton Ave.
Salt Lake City, UT 84115
Tel.: 801-486-2317 **UT**
Fax: 801-486-2322
Year Founded: 1976
Assets: $2,931,847
Liabilities: $904,753
Net Worth: $2,027,094
Sales Range: $10-19 Million
Emp.: 100
Fiscal Year-end: 7/31/90
Construction of Heavy Industrial Facilities
S.I.C.: 1629; 1623; 1541
Michael R. Lamb *(Pres. & Mgr.-Construction)*
James R. Lamb *(Exec. V.P.)*
Janice B. Lamb *(Sec. & Treas.)*
Craig V. Mills *(Controller & Dir.-Data Processing)*
Alfred Abram *(Dir.-Pur.)*
Fred Mills *(Dir.-Sls.)*
Legrand R. Lamb *(Mgr.-Construction)*
Joel McRae *(Mgr.-Sls.)*
Principal(s):
Michael R. Lamb
James R. Lamb

No. of Mfg. Plants/Facilities: 1
No. of U.S. Offices: 1

Computer Systems/Hardware:
Promation

Outside Service Firm(s):

Wisan & Smith*(Auditors)*
Salt Lake City, UT

Blue Cross & Blue Shield of Utah*(Group Insurer)*
Salt Lake City, UT

Royal Insurance Co.*(Commercial Insurance Carrier)*
Salt Lake City, UT

Watkiss & Campbell*(Legal Firm)*
Salt Lake City, UT

Key Bank*(Major Banking Relationship)*
Salt Lake City, UT

Subsidiary:

Lamb Leasing & Lamb Brothers General **(1)**
125 Walton Ave.
Salt Lake City, UT 84115
Tel.: 801-486-2317
Emp.: 64

ROBERT E. LAMB, INC.
939 Jefferson Ave., P.O. Box 821
Valley Forge, PA 19482
Tel.: 215-666-9200 **PA**
Fax: 215-666-6040
Year Founded: 1917
Approx.Sls.: $16,000,000
Emp.: 50
Design & Build Industrial Facilities & Office Buildings
S.I.C.: 1541; 1542; 8742; 8711; 8712
Robert E. Lamb II *(Pres.)*
John J. Peterman *(V.P.-Construction)*
Joseph A. Shatt *(V.P.-Sls.)*
Joseph M. Sterchak *(V.P. & Gen. Mgr.)*
Peter G. Vreeland *(V.P.-Plng.)*
Barbara Bailey *(Mgr.-Mktg./Communications)*
Principal(s):
Robert E. Lamb II

No. of U.S. Offices: 1

Computer Systems/Hardware:
Wang/IBM PC

Outside Service Firm(s):

Kimmel, Lorah & Associates*(Auditors)*
Valley Forge, PA

Morgan, Lewis & Bockius*(Legal Firm)*
2000 One Logan Square
Philadelphia, PA 19103-6993
Tel.: 215-963-5000
Fax: 215-963-5299

Fidelity Bank*(Major Banking Relationship)*
Broad & Walnut St.
Philadelphia, PA 19109

TONY LAMBERT COMPANY
1407 Broadway
New York, NY 10018
Tel.: 212-391-1700
Fax: 212-719-4097
Sales Range: $10-19 Million
Emp.: 40
Mfr. of Wigs & Sweaters
S.I.C.: 3999; 2253; 2329
B.P. Hopp *(Pres.)*
M.J. Grebler *(Exec. V.P.)*

Outside Service Firm(s):

Seidman & Seidman*(Auditors)*
New York, NY

Tanen & Tanen*(Legal Firm)*
New York, NY

Mellon Bank, N.A.*(Major Banking Relationship)*
New York, NY

LAMBESIS COMMUNICATIONS
11770 Bernardo Plaza Ct., Ste. 308
San Diego, CA 92128
Tel.: 619-451-0242
Year Founded: 1985
Approx.Billings: $12,000,000
Emp.: 14
Nicholas Lambesis *(Pres. & Chief Exec. Officer)*
Vicki Lambesis *(Chief Fin. Officer)*
Ann Hirou *(Dir., Mktg.)*

Computer Systems/Hardware:
MacIntosh

LAMINAIRE CORPORATION
960 E. Hazelwood Ave.
Rahway, NJ 07065
Tel.: 908-381-8200
Tel.: 800-777-4500 **NJ**
Fax: 908-381-4091
Year Founded: 1964
Approx.Sls.: $10,000,000
Emp.: 110
Import Export
Mfr. of Clean Room Equipment & Supplies; Subcontract Electronic Assembly
S.I.C.: 3599; 1731; 2842; 3679
Charles J. Garay *(Chm. Bd. & Pres.)*
Gerald E. Reilly *(V.P. & Controller)*
Elena Colucci *(Treas.)*
Marie Garay *(Sec.)*
A. Garay *(Mgr.-Div.-Electronics)*
O. McClelland *(Mgr.-Mfg.-Clean Room)*
E. Monteleone *(Mgr.-Office Services)*
Mary Peerboom *(Mgr.-Personnel)*
Andrew Serenyi *(Mgr.-Mktg.)*

Computer Systems/Hardware:
ALTOS

LAMP POST FRANCHISE CORPORATION
3002 Dow, Ste. 320
Tustin, CA 92680
Tel.: 714-731-6171 **CA**

Fax: 714-731-0951
Year Founded: 1967
Assets: $4,174,790
Liabilities: $409,950
Net Worth: $3,764,840
Approx.Sls.: $36,000,000
Emp.: 1,300
Fiscal Year-end: 9/30/90
Chain of 68 Restaurants
S.I.C.: 5812
Angelo Barro *(Founder)*
Tom Barro *(Pres.)*
Dan Barro *(V.P. & Corp. Sec.)*
Kim Eastin *(Dir.-Mktg.)*
Marsha Lima *(Dir.-Data Processing & Franchising)*
Principal(s):
Tom Barro

No. of Mfg. Plants/Facilities: 65
No. of U.S. Offices: 1

Computer Systems/Hardware:
IBM

Outside Service Firm(s):

Gerald Bobrosky*(Auditors)*
Lakewood, CA

Golden Eagle*(Commercial Insurance Carrier)*
San Diego, CA

Golden Eagle*(Group Insurer)*
San Diego, CA

Baldikoski, Charles & Kane*(Legal Firm)*
Newport Beach, CA

The Bank of Orange County*(Major Banking Relationship)*
Fountain Valley, CA

LAMPERT YARDS, INC.
1850 Como Ave.
Saint Paul, MN 55108
Mailing Address:
P.O. Box 64076
St. Paul, MN 55164
Tel.: 612-645-8155
Sales Range: $10-19 Million
Fiscal Year-end: 12/31/91
Sale of Lumber, Millwork & Other Building Materials, Hardware, Paints, Glass & Wallpaper
S.I.C.: 5211; 5231
John L. Fesler *(Chm. Bd.)*
Robert T. Ungerman *(Pres.)*
Fred L. Chown *(V.P.-Sls.)*
Daniel L. Fesler *(V.P. & Sec.)*
J. Cooper Blaxton *(Treas.)*
Victoria L. Burt *(Asst. Sec.)*
Donald Bratton *(Dir.-Pur.)*

Computer Systems/Hardware:
Computer Systems Dynamic

Outside Service Firm(s):

McGladrey & Pullen*(Auditors)*
1800 Town Square, 445 Minnesota St.
St. Paul, MN 55101

Briggs & Morgan*(Legal Firm)*
Minneapolis, MN

American National Bank & Trust of St. Paul*(Major Banking Relationship)*
Fifth & Minnesota Streets
St. Paul, MN 55101
Tel.: 612-298-6000

LAN-CHILE AIRLINES
9700 So. Dixie Highway
Miami, FL 33156
Tel.: 305-670-1961
Fax: 305-670-9553
Approx.Sls.: $40,000,000
Emp.: 128
Airline Travel & Cargo Carriers
S.I.C.: 4512; 4491
George Edelmann *(Gen. Mgr.-North America)*
Mary Calderon *(Administrative Asst.)*

LAN-O-SHEEN, INC.
289 5th St. E., Ste. 210
Saint Paul, MN 55101
Tel.: 612-293-0522
Tel.: 800-728-3475 **MN**
Fax: 612-293-0602
Emp.: 3
Marketing & Sales of Lan-O-Sheen, Lan-O-Soft & Lan-O-Wipe Products
S.I.C.: 5169
William A. Mears *(Pres.)*
Lyle Ross *(Controller)*
Dee Boulais *(Mgr.-Sls. & Service)*

Outside Service Firm(s):

Oppenheimer, Wolff & Donnelly*(Legal Firm)*
332 Minnesota St.
St. Paul, MN 55101
Tel.: 612-227-7271

Norwest Bank Minnesota, N.A.*(Major Banking Relationship)*
P.O. Box 738, 161 N. Concord Exchange
St. Paul, MN 55075-0738
Tel.: 612-450-4064

LANCASTER HOST RESORT
2300 Lincoln Hwy. E.
Lancaster, PA 17602
Tel.: 717-299-5500
Tel.: 800-233-0121
Fax: 717-295-5112
Year Founded: 1966
Approx.Sls.: $15,000,000
Emp.: 300
Fiscal Year-end: 12/31/90
Luxury Resorts & Inns
S.I.C.: 7011
Bob Gansfuss *(Gen. Mgr.)*
Jim LaBadie *(Dir.-Sls. & Mktg.)*

LANCASTER MALLEABLE CASTINGS COMPANY
1170 Lititz Ave.
Lancaster, PA 17601
Tel.: 717-295-8200
Fax: 717-295-8204
Year Founded: 1910
Sales Range: $10-19 Million
Emp.: 325

Export
Malleable Iron Castings
S.I.C.: 3322
Robert Hess *(Chm. Bd. & Pres.)*
Jere R. Duke *(V.P.)*
Charles Hobday *(V.P.)*
E.B. Zimmerman *(Pur. Agent)*
Franklyn A. Cover *(Chief Engineer)*
John L. Witwer, Jr. *(Dir.-Personnel)*
Larry Boozer *(Mgr.-Mktg. & Sls.)*
Russell W. Reitler *(Mgr.-Mfg.)*

Outside Service Firm(s):

Trout, Ebersole & Groff*(Auditors)*
Lancaster, PA

Fulton Bank*(Major Banking Relationship)*
110 Penn Sq.
Lancaster, PA 17602
Tel.: 717-291-2411

LANCE CAMPER MANUFACTURING CORPORATION
10234 Glenoaks Blvd.
Pacoima, CA 91331
Tel.: 818-897-3155
Fax: 818-890-1645
Approx.Sls.: $135,000,000
Emp.: 180
Manufacture & Retail Campers
S.I.C.: 3792; 5561
Jack Cole *(Pres.)*
Jeff Souleles *(V.P.)*
Sharon Murphy *(Controller)*

Outside Service Firm(s):

Arthur Guglielmi*(Auditors)*
Los Angeles, CA

American Pacific State Bank*(Major Banking Relationship)*
North Hollywood, CA

LAND N SEA, INC.
1370 Broadway, 9th Fl.
New York, NY 10018
Tel.: 212-244-1010 **NY**
Fax: 212-244-1081
Year Founded: 1958
Approx.Sls.: $100,000,000
Emp.: 160
Fiscal Year-end: 12/31/91
Mfr. of Women's, Juniors, Girls, Children's & Infants Blouses Made From Purchased Material
S.I.C.: 2331; 2361
Seymour Sobel *(Chm. Bd.)*
Robert Sobel *(Pres.)*

Outside Service Firm(s):

Chase Manhattan Bank, N.A.*(Major Banking Relationship)*
One Chase Manhattan Plaza
New York, NY 10081
Tel.: 212-552-2222
Tel.: 800-526-0801
Fax: 212-552-7175

LAND O'LAKES, INC.
4001 Lexington Ave. N.
Arden Hills, MN 55126
Mailing Address:
P.O. Box 116,
Minneapolis, MN 55440
Tel.: 612-481-2222 **MN**
Telex: 910-563-3663
Fax: 612-481-2022
Year Founded: 1921
Assets: $822,945,000
Earnings: $53,771,000
Liabilities: $523,124,000
Net Worth: $299,821,000
Approx.Sls.: $2,458,074,000
Emp.: 5,000
Fiscal Year-end: 12/31/91

Export
Food Processing & Marketing; Farm Supplies
S.I.C.: 5191; 5149; 2024; 2026; 2021; 2022; 5143
Stan Zylstra *(Chm. Bd.)*
Jack Gherty *(Pres. & Chief Exec. Officer)*
Dick Fogg *(Grp. V.P.-Dairy Foods)*
Duane Halverson *(Grp. V.P.-Agricultural Services)*
Ron Ostby *(Grp. V.P. & Chief Fin. Officer)*
Martha Cashman *(V.P.-Intl.)*
Fred Fezatte *(V.P.-Pur.)*
Dave Gray *(V.P.-Sls., Dairy Food)*
Dan Hanson *(V.P.-Plng.)*
David Hettinga *(V.P.-Res. & Devel.)*
Jack Martin *(V.P.-Human Resources)*
John Rebane *(V.P. & Gen. Counsel)*
Thomas Verdoorn *(V.P. & Controller)*
Mark Wilberts *(V.P.-Information Systems)*
John Siegmund *(Sec.)*
Bruce Charon *(Dir.-Leasing)*
Mike Driscoll *(Dir.-Mngmt. Devel.)*
Dan Knutson *(Dir.-Finance)*
Terry Koves *(Dir.-Employee Benefits)*
Bruce Lach *(Dir.-Telecommunications)*
Terry Nagle *(Dir.-Communications)*
Donna Koenig *(Corp. Librarian)*

No. of Mfg. Plants/Facilities: 30
No. of Foreign Offices: 1

Computer Systems/Hardware:
IBM 3090-20E

Outside Service Firm(s):

KPMG Peat Marwick*(Auditors)*
4200 Norwest Center, 90 S. 7th St.
Minneapolis, MN 55402
Tel.: 612-341-2222

MSI*(Group Insurer)*
Minneapolis, MN

Doherty, Rumble & Butler*(Legal Firm)*
2800 Minnesota World Trade Center
St. Paul, MN 55101-4999
Tel.: 612-291-9333

Norwest Bank Minnesota, N.A.*(Major Banking Relationship)*
6th St. & Marquette Ave.
Minneapolis, MN 55479-0065
Tel.: 612-667-8101

Saint Paul Bank for Cooperatives*(Major Banking Relationship)*
Saint Paul, MN

Divisions:

Cenex/Land O'Lakes, Inc. **(1)**
P.O. Box 64089
Saint Paul, MN 55164
Tel.: 612-451-5151 (50%)
Telex: 297-060
Fax: 612-451-5568
Assets: $606,016,000
Earnings: $12,060,000
Liabilities: $320,677,000
Net Worth: $285,339,000
Emp.: 700
Computer Systems/Hardware:
Hewlett Packard 922 & 955; IBM 3084QX
Plant Foods & Chemicals
S.I.C.: 2873; 2874
Noel Estenson *(Pres. & Chief Exec. Officer-Cenex Inc.)*
John Gherty *(Pres. & Chief Exec. Officer-Land O'Lakes Inc.)*
Al Giese *(V.P.-Agronomy & Food)*
Dave Johnson *(V.P. & Chief Oper. Officer)*
Joel Koonce *(V.P.-Fin. & Chief Fin. Officer)*
Paul Rhein *(V.P.-Agronomy Chemicals)*
Stan Marquart *(Dir.-Sls.)*
Frank Bezdizek *(Mgr.-Adv.)*
Annette Degnan *(Mgr.-Adv.)*

Food Ingredients **(1)**
P.O. Box 116
Minneapolis, MN 55440
Tel.: 612-481-2222
Mike Fronk *(V.P.)*
Gary Zinter *(Controller)*

Lake to Lake Dairy **(1)**
1125 8th St.
Kiel, WI 53042
Tel.: 414-894-2615 (100%)
Fax: 414-894-2615
Approx.Sls.: $150,000,000
Emp.: 225
National Champion Dairy Products, USDA "AA" Cheddar Cheese
S.I.C.: 5143
Laurie Kull *(V.P. & Chief Oper. Officer)*
Don Meyer *(Controller)*
Nadine Miller *(Pub. Rels. Mgr.)*
Ron Schaller *(Sls. Mgr.-Bulk Cheeses)*
Francis J. Cobian *(Production Dir.)*
Cathy Shimon *(Pur. Agent)*

Land O'Lakes, Inc., Agricultural Services Div. **(1)**
P.O. Box 64089
Saint Paul, MN 55164
Tel.: 612-451-5151
Approx.Sls.: $1,047,618,186
Emp.: 1,600
Sale of Farm Supplies
S.I.C.: 5191
Duane Halverson *(Grp. V.P.-Agricultural Services)*
Charles Schmidt *(V.P.-Feed)*
Dave Seehusen *(V.P.-Seed)*
Gary Moore *(Controller-Feed)*
Dave Bowser *(Controller-Seed)*
Frank Bezdicek *(Mgr.-Adv.)*
Peter S. Janzen *(Assoc. Counsel)*

Land O'Lakes International Div. **(1)**
P.O. Box 116
Minneapolis, MN 55440
Tel.: 612-481-2222
Emp.: 10
Mktg. & Distr. of Dairy Products
S.I.C.: 5149
Martha Cashman *(V.P.-International)*
Sally Collins *(Controller)*

Land O'Lakes Seed Division **(1)**
2827 8th Ave. S.
Fort Dodge, IA 50501
Tel.: 515-955-0129

Land O'Lakes, Inc.—(Continued)

Division:

Wilson Seeds Inc. **(2)**
P.O. Box 391,
Harlan, IA 51537
Tel.: 712-755-3841

Ventures Group **(1)**
P.O. Box 116
Minneapolis, MN 55440
Tel.: 612-481-2222
Martha Cashman *(V.P.)*
Sally Collins *(Controller)*

Subsidiaries:

Alex Fries **(1)**
1000 Redna Terrace
Cincinnati, OH 45215

B&E Grain Company **(1)**
310 S. Third St.
Saint Joseph, MO 64501

Country Lake Foods, Inc. **(1)**
2 Appletree Square
Saint Paul, MN 55164
Tel.: 612-851-1260
Fax: 612-851-1272
Approx.Sls.: $189,000,000
Emp.: 720
Mfr. Dairy Products; Fluid Milk, Ice Cream & Frozen Desserts
S.I.C.: 2026
Thomas N. Packard *(Pres. & Chief Exec. Officer)*
Roland J. Dant *(V.P.-Opers.)*
Timothy I. Martin *(V.P. & Chief Fin. Officer)*
David G. Schwain *(V.P.-Mktg.)*

Indiana Seed Co., Inc. **(1)**
P.O. Box 440,
Noblesville, IN 46060

Land O'Lakes Farm Centers **(1)**
4001 Lexington Ave.
Arden Hills, MN 55126

Land O'Lakes Finance Co. **(1)**

Land O'Lakes International Development Corp. **(1)**
P.O. Box 116,
Minneapolis, MN 55112

Procor Technologies **(1)**
4001 Lexington Ave.
Arden Hills, MN 55126

Research Seeds, Inc. **(1)**
310 S. Third St.
Saint Joseph, MO 64501

Scott Farm Seed Co. **(1)**
50-56 Mill St.
Mechanicsburg, OH 43044

Union Seed Co. **(1)**
4 9th Ave. South
Nampa, ID 83651

LANE PRESS, INC.
1000 Hinesburg Rd.
South Burlington, VT 05403
Mailing Address:
P.O. Box 130
Burlington, VT 05402
Tel.: 802-863-5555
Twx: 469134
Fax: 802-865-2470
Approx.Sls.: $34,000,000
Emp.: 325
Fiscal Year-end: 6/30/92
Publication Printers
S.I.C.: 2752
Dan P. Drumheller *(Chm. Bd.)*
Phillip M. Drumheller *(Pres.)*
Robert J. Francis *(Sr. V.P.-Sls.)*
William A. Meador *(V.P.-Mktg.)*
Terry McDonnell *(Treas.)*

Outside Service Firm(s):

Deloitte & Touche*(Auditors)*
Anaheim, CA

Pierson, Affolter & Wadhams*(Legal Firm)*
Burlington, VT

Chittenden Bank*(Major Banking Relationship)*
Burlington, VT

Vermont National Bank*(Major Banking Relationship)*
100 Main St.
Brattleboro, VT
Tel.: 802-257-7151

LANDAU BUILDING CO.
9855 Rinaman Rd.
Wexford, PA 15090
Tel.: 412-935-8800
Fax: 412-935-6510
Year Founded: 1881
Approx.Sls.: $20,000,000
Emp.: 70
Fiscal Year-end: 10/31/91
General Building Contractors
S.I.C.: 1541
Roy Landau *(Chm. Bd., Pres. & Chief Exec. & Chief Fin. Officer)*
Thomas A. Landau *(V.P.)*
Edward E. Hughes III *(Treas.)*
Richard Pavelik *(Controller)*
Jeffrey C. Landau *(Sec.)*

Computer Systems/Hardware:
Compaq PC

Outside Service Firm(s):

Sobel Bosco*(Auditors)*
Pittsburgh, PA

Nernberg & Laffey*(Legal Firm)*
Pittsburgh, PA

Mellon Bank N.A.*(Major Banking Relationship)*
1 Mellon Center
Pittsburgh, PA 15258

LANDAU & HEYMAN INC.
180 N. LaSalle, Suite 3000
Chicago, IL 60601
Tel.: 312-372-3133
Fax: 312-372-0633
Year Founded: 1933
Emp.: 250
Real Estate Investment & Devel.; Broker
S.I.C.: 6552; 6153
Phillip Schonberger *(Chm. Bd.)*
Patrick B. O'Leary *(Pres.)*
Gerry Curciarello *(Chief Fin. Officer)*
Martin Levy *(Exec. V.P.)*
James Roche *(V.P. & Dir.-Leasing)*
Edmund Sadleir *(V.P.-Devel. & Construction)*
Arlene Richman *(Gen. Counsel)*
Stephanie L. Hall *(Dir.-Mktg.)*

LANDMARK COMMUNICATIONS, INC.
150 W. Brambleton Ave.
Norfolk, VA 23510
Tel.: 804-446-2000 VA
Telex: 804-446-2489
Year Founded: 1932
Approx.Sls.: $425,000,000
Emp.: 5,000
Fiscal Year-end: 12/31/90
Import
Newspaper Publishing; Television & Radio Broadcasting & Cable Programming; Specialty Periodical Publishing
S.I.C.: 2711; 2721; 4832; 4833; 4841
Frank Batten *(Chm. Bd.)*
Richard F. Barry III *(Vice Chm.)*
John O. Wynne *(Pres.)*
Louis F. Ryan *(Exec. V.P. & Gen. Counsel)*
Kevin Senie *(Exec. V.P. & Chief Fin. Officer)*
Donald H. Patterson, Jr. *(Exec. V.P.)*
Richard F. Spears *(V.P.-New Ventures)*
James D. Wagner *(V.P. & Treas.)*
Becky Powhatan *(V.P. & Corp. Counsel)*
John F. Estes *(V.P.-Fin.)*
Paul E. Rose *(V.P.)*
Colleen Pittman *(Controller)*
Susan Smith *(Sec.)*
Bruce Bradley *(Dir.-Adv.)*
Charlie Hill *(Mgr.-Employment & Benefits Admin.)*

Computer Systems/Hardware:
IBM System 4341-Grp. 12

Outside Service Firm(s):

Price Waterhouse*(Auditors)*
3110 Fairview Drive #300
Falls Church, VA 22042

Aetna Life & Casualty*(Group Insurer)*
151 Farmington Avenue
Hartford, CT 06156
Tel.: 203-273-2128
Fax: 203-729-4295

Morgan Stanley & Co.*(Investment Banker)*
1251 Avenue of the Americas
New York, NY 10020
Tel.: 212-703-8447
Fax: 212-703-6476

Kaufman & Canoles*(Legal Firm)*
One Commercial Place
Norfolk, VA 23510

Crestar Bank*(Major Banking Relationship)*
P.O. Box 2642,
Norfolk, VA 23514
Tel.: 804-624-5507
Fax: 804-624-5538

Sovran Bank*(Major Banking Relationship)*
Norfolk, VA

Aetna Life & Casualty*(Pension Manager)*
151 Farmington Avenue
Hartford, CT 06156
Tel.: 203-273-2128
Fax: 203-729-4295

Delaware Investment Advisors*(Pension Manager)*
One Commerce Square
Philadelphia, PA 19103

Dreman Value Management Inc.*(Pension Manager)*
New York, NY

Kurtz Capital Management*(Pension Manager)*
Livingston, NJ

T. Rowe Price Associates*(Pension Manager)*
100 E. Pratt St.
Baltimore, MD 21202
Tel.: 410-547-2000
Fax: 410-659-0965

Sovran Bank*(Pension Manager)*
One Commercial Place
Norfolk, VA
Tel.: 804-441-4849
Fax: 804-624-2965

Divisions:

Broadcast and Video Enterprises Div. **(1)**
150 W. Brambleton Ave.
Norfolk, VA 23501
Tel.: 804-446-2000
Video Programming & Related Enterprises
S.I.C.: 4899
Michael J. Eckert *(Pres.)*
Richard A. Fraim *(V.P.)*
Patrick C. Clark *(V.P.)*

Subsidiaries:

KLAS-TV **(2)**
P.O. Box 15047, 3228 Channel 8 Dr.
Las Vegas, NV 89114
Tel.: 702-733-8850
Television Broadcasting Station
S.I.C.: 4833
Richard A. Fraim *(V.P. & Gen. Mgr.)*

The Travel Channel **(2)**
2690 Cumberland Pkwy.
Atlanta, GA 30339
Tel.: 404-801-2400
Fax: 404-801-2441
Cable Network
S.I.C.: 4841
Michael Eckert *(Chief Exec. Officer)*
E. Roger Williams *(Pres.)*
Dana Michaelis *(V.P.-Affiliated Sls.)*
Doris Shannon-Yancy *(V.P.-Human Resources)*
Norman Zeller *(V.P.-Natl. Adv. Sls. Mgr.)*

The Weather Channel **(2)**
2600 Cumberland Pkwy.
Atlanta, GA 30339
Tel.: 404-434-6800
Fax: 404-801-2130
Emp.: 240
Computer Systems/Hardware:
DEC 4200
Cable Television Channel Broadcasting Live Continuous Weather Coverage
S.I.C.: 4841
John O. Wynne *(Chm. Bd.)*
Michael J. Eckert *(Chief Exec. Officer)*
Paul FitzPatrick *(Pres. & Chief Oper. Officer)*
Stan Hunter *(Sr. V.P.-Programming & Opers.)*
Pat Clark *(Sr. V.P.-Fin. & Admin.)*
Raymond P. Ban *(V.P.-Opers.)*
Alan Galumbeck *(V.P.-New Technologies)*
Frank Garland *(V.P.-Adv. Sls.)*
Michael Lerner *(V.P.-Adv. & Promo.)*
Mark McKeen *(V.P.-Engrng.)*
Rebecca Ruthven *(V.P.-Affiliate Sls.)*
Doris Shannon-Yancey *(V.P.-Human Resources)*
Charleen Carl *(Dir.-Adv. Services)*
Cindy Andreu *(Controller)*
Janice Bozzi *(Mgr.-Database Opers.)*
Kathleen Lane *(Mgr.-Pub. Rels.)*

Advertising Sales Offices:

The Weather Channel, Inc.-New York Sales Office **(3)**
780 Third Ave.
New York, NY 10017
Tel.: 212-308-3055
Advertising Sales Office for the Weather Channel
S.I.C.: 7313
Edward Byrnes *(Eastern Div. Adv. Sls. Mgr.)*

The Weather Channel, Inc.-Chicago Sales Office **(3)**
435 N. Michigan Ave.
Chicago, IL 60611
Tel.: 312-644-0570
Advertising Sales Office for the Weather Channel
S.I.C.: 7313
Frank Garland *(Central/Western Div. Adv. Sls. mgr.)*
Robert Mahon *(Central Reg. Adv. Sls. Mgr.)*

The Weather Channel, Inc.-Detroit Sales Office **(3)**
25689 Kelly Road, Ste. D
Roseville, MI 48066
Tel.: 313-777-0970
Advertising Sales Office for the Weather Channel
S.I.C.: 7313
Norm Zeller *(East-Central Div. Adv. Sls. Office)*

The Weather Channel, Inc.-Los Angeles Sales Office **(3)**
1925 Century Park East, Ste. 830
Los Angeles, CA 90067
Tel.: 213-785-0511
Advertising Sales Office for the Weather Channel
S.I.C.: 7313
Mary Hogan *(Western Div. Affiliate Sls. Dir.)*
Daniel A. Mohler *(Western Region Adv. Sls. Mgr.)*

The Weather Channel, Inc.-Atlanta Sales Office **(3)**
2600 Cumberland Pkwy.
Atlanta, GA 30339
Tel.: 404-434-6800
Advertising Sales Office for the Weather Channel
S.I.C.: 7313
Larry McHugh *(Southern Reg. Adv. Sls. Mgr.)*
Tamra Cantore *(Eastern Div. Affiliate Sls. Dir.)*

WLTY-FM **(2)**
720 Boush St.
Norfolk, VA 23510
Tel.: 804-446-2700
Radio Broadcasting Station
S.I.C.: 4832
Ronald Reeger *(V.P. & Gen. Mgr.)*
Deborah Donour *(Gen. Sls. Mgr.)*

WTAR-AM **(2)**
720 Boush St.
Norfolk, VA 23510
Tel.: 804-446-2700
S.I.C.: 4832
Ronald Reeger *(V.P. & Gen. Mgr.)*
Deborah Donour *(Gen. Sls. Mgr.)*

Greensboro News & Record **(1)**
200 E. Market St., P.O. Box 20848
Greensboro, NC 27420
Tel.: 919-373-7000
Daily Newspaper Publisher; Contract Printing
S.I.C.: 2711; 2752
Carl W. Mangum, Jr. *(Pres. & Publisher)*
Ben J. Bowers *(V.P. & Exec. Editor)*
Mark Fentross *(Controller)*
Joe Antle *(Dir.-Adv.)*

Landmark Community Newspapers, Inc. **(1)**
P.O. Box 549,
Shelbyville, KY 40065
Tel.: 502-633-4334
Newpaper Publishers; Publishers of Dailies, Tri-Weeklies, Semi-Weeklies, Weeklies, Shoppers & Specialty Publications
S.I.C.: 2711
Larry R. Coffey *(Pres. & Treas.)*
Larry Paden *(V.P. & Gen. Mgr.)*
Max Heath *(V.P. & Exec. Editor)*
Randall Mast *(V.P.-Production)*
Gary Miller *(Controller)*
Bonnie Gray *(Dir.-Adv.)*
Patricia T. Darby *(Dir.-Human Resources)*

Specialty Publications:

Baltimore Book **(2)**
P.O. Box 346,
Westminster, MD 21157
Tel.: 301-875-5400
Real Estate Listing Newspaper for the Baltimore Area
S.I.C.: 2711
Greg Linard *(Gen. Mgr.)*

Homes of York-Adams County **(2)**
P.O. Box 346,
Westminster, MD 21157
Tel.: 301-875-5400
Real Estate Listing Newspaper for York & Adams Counties in Pennsylvania
S.I.C.: 2711
Greg Linard *(Gen. Mgr.)*

Central Maryland Homes **(2)**
P.O. Box 346
Westminster, MD 21157
Tel.: 301-875-5400
Real Estate Listing Newspaper for the Central Maryland Area
S.I.C.: 2711
Greg Linard *(Gen. Mgr.)*

Century 21 Homes Magazine-York, PA **(2)**
P.O. Box 346
Westminster, MD 21157
Tel.: 301-875-5400
Real Estate Listing Newspaper for the York, PA Area
S.I.C.: 2711
Greg Linard *(Gen. Mgr.)*

Commercial Real Estate **(2)**
P.O. Box 346
Westminster, MD 21157
Tel.: 301-875-5400
Commercial Real Estate Listing Newspaper
S.I.C.: 2711
Barbara Brown *(Publshr. & Editor)*

Dailies:

Carroll County Times **(2)**
P.O. Box 346, 201 Railroad Ave.
Westminster, MD 21157
Tel.: 410-875-5400 (100%)
Daily Newspaper Covering Carroll County, MD
S.I.C.: 2711
Daniel Barkin *(Publisher)*

Los Alamos Monitor **(2)**
P.O. Box 1268,
Los Alamos, NM 87544
Tel.: 505-662-4185 (100%)
Daily Newspaper Covering Los Alamos, NM
S.I.C.: 2711
Evelyn Vigil *(Editor & Publshr.)*

News-Enterprise **(2)**
P.O. Box 430, 408 W. Dixie Dr.
Elizabethtown, KY 42701
Tel.: 502-769-2312 (100%)
Daily Newspaper
S.I.C.: 2711
Mike Anders *(Publisher)*

Citrus County Chronicle **(2)**
P.O. Box 1899, 130 Heights Ave.
Inverness, FL 32650
Tel.: 904-726-1441 (100%)
Newspapers
S.I.C.: 2711
Gary Manning *(Gen. Mgr.)*

Tri-Weeklies:

The Gazette **(2)**
108 W.Stuart Dr.
Galax, VA 24333
Tel.: 703-236-5178 (100%)
Tri-Weekly Newspaper
S.I.C.: 2711
Chuck Burress *(Gen. Mgr.)*

Kentucky Standard **(2)**
P.O. Box 639
Bardstown, KY 40004
Tel.: 502-348-9003
Tri-Weekley Newspaper
S.I.C.: 2711
Steve Lowery *(Publisher)*

The Lancaster News **(2)**
P.O. Box 640, 701 N. White St.
Lancaster, SC 29720
Tel.: 803-283-1133
Tri-Weekly Newspaper
S.I.C.: 2711
Van King *(Reg. V.P. & Publr.)*

Roane County News **(2)**
P.O. Box 610, 204 Franklin St.
Kingston, TN 37763
Tel.: 615-376-3481
Tri-Weekly Newspaper
S.I.C.: 2711
Doug Morris *(Publr.)*

Semi-Weeklies:

The News **(2)**
537 Main St.
Tell City, IN 47586
Tel.: 812-547-3424 (100%)
Semi-Weekly Newspaper
S.I.C.: 2711
Linda Stewart-Bolin *(Gen. Mgr.)*

Central Kentucky News-Journal **(2)**
P.O. Box 279, 428 Woodlawn
Campbellsville, KY 42718
Tel.: 502-465-8111 (100%)
Semi-Weekly Newspaper
S.I.C.: 2711
Richard RoBards *(Mng. Editor)*

New Albany Gazette **(2)**
P.O. Box 300, 713 Carter Ave.
New Albany, MS 38652
Tel.: 601-534-6321 (100%)
Semi-Weekly Newspaper
S.I.C.: 2711
Brian Roy *(Gen. Mgr.)*

The Sentinel-News **(2)**
P.O. Box 399, 702 Washington St.
Shelbyville, KY 40066
Tel.: 502-633-2526 (100%)
Semi-Weekly Newpaper Covering the Shelbyville, KY Area
S.I.C.: 2711
James L. Edelen *(Publisher)*

Vandalia Leader-Union **(2)**
229 So. Fifth St.
Vandalia, IL 62471
Tel.: 618-283-3374
Semi-Weekly Newspaper Covering the Vandalia, IL Area
S.I.C.: 2711
David R. Bell *(Editor/Gen. Mgr.)*

Chester News and Reporter **(2)**
P.O. Box 250, 104 York St.
Chester, SC 29706
Tel.: 803-385-3177
Semi-Weekley Newspaper Covering the Chester,SC Area
S.I.C.: 2711
James McKeown, Sr. *(Publisher)*

Pioneer News **(2)**
P.O. Box 98
Shepherdsville, KY 40165
Tel.: 502-955-9701
Semi-Weekly Newspaper Covering the Shepherdsville, KY Area
S.I.C.: 2711
Peter Mio *(Gen. Mgr.)*

Weeklies:

The Anderson News **(2)**
133 So. Main St.
Lawrenceburg, KY 40342
Tel.: 502-839-6906
Weekly Newspaper Covering the Lawrenceburg, KY Area
S.I.C.: 2711
Don White *(Mng. Editor)*

Bedford Bulletin **(2)**
P.O. Box 331
Bedford, VA 24523
Tel.: 703-586-8612
Weekly Newspaper Covering the Bedford, VA Area
S.I.C.: 2711
Jeanette Richardson *(Gen. Mgr.)*

The Casey County News **(2)**
P.O. Box 40,
Liberty, KY 42539
Tel.: 606-787-7171
Weekly Newspaper Covering the Casey County, KY Area
S.I.C.: 2711
Randall Vaught *(Gen. Mgr.)*

Cynthiana Democrat **(2)**
P.O. Box 160, Webster at Springdale
Cynthiana, KY 41031
Tel.: 606-234-1035 (100%)
Weekly Newspaper Covering the Cynthiana, KY Area
S.I.C.: 2711
George W. Jacobs *(Gen. Mgr.)*

Grant County News **(2)**
P.O. Box 247
Williamstown, KY 41097
Tel.: 606-824-3343
Weekly Newspaper Covering the Grant County, KY Area
S.I.C.: 2711
Ken Stone *(Gen. Mgr.)*

Harriman Record **(2)**
P.O. Box 261, 510 Devonia St.
Harriman, TN 37748
Tel.: 615-882-1313
Weekly Newspaper Covering the Harriman, TN Area
S.I.C.: 2711
Doug Morris *(Publisher)*

Henry County Local **(2)**
P.O. Box 209
New Castle, KY 40050
Tel.: 502-845-2858
Weekly Newspaper Covering the Henry County, KY Area
S.I.C.: 2711
Mary Carol Tingle *(Mgr.)*

The Journal-Democrat **(2)**
P.O. Box 6
Rockport, IN 47635
Tel.: 812-649-9196
Weekly Newspaper Covering the Rockport, IN Area
S.I.C.: 2711
George Gabehart *(Gen. Mgr.)*

The Lebanon Enterprise **(2)**
119 So. Proctor Knott Ave.
Lebanon, KY 40033
Tel.: 502-692-6026
Weekly Newspaper Covering the Lebanon, KY Area
S.I.C.: 2711
John Bramel *(Publisher)*

Morgan County News **(2)**
P.O. Box 346, Cumberland St.
Wartburg, TN 37887
Tel.: 615-346-6225
Weekly Newspaper Covering the Morgan County, TN Area
S.I.C.: 2711
Doug Morris *(Gen. Mgr.)*

Mount Vernon Democrat **(2)**
430 Main St.
Mount Vernon, IN 47620
Tel.: 812-838-4811
Weekly Newspaper Covering the Mount Vernon, IN Area
S.I.C.: 2711
Tim Rutherford *(Gen. Mgr.)*

The News-Democrat **(2)**
422 Main St.
Carrollton, KY 41008
Tel.: 502-732-4261
Weekly Newspaper Covering the Carrollton, KY Area
S.I.C.: 2711
Debbie Wright *(Gen. Mgr.)*

The Oldham Era **(2)**
204 S. First St.
La Grange, KY 40031
Tel.: 502-222-7183 (100%)
Weekly Newspaper covering the La Grange, KY Area
S.I.C.: 2711
Dorothy Abernathy *(Publisher)*

Opinion-Tribune **(2)**
116 So. Walnut St.
Glenwood, IA 51534
Tel.: 712-527-3191
Weekly Newspaper Covering the Glenwood, IA Area
S.I.C.: 2711
Lois Helms *(Gen. Mgr.)*

Red Oak Express **(2)**
P.O. Box 377, 2012 Commerce Dr.
Red Oak, IA 51566
Tel.: 712-623-2566 (100%)
Weekly Newspaper Covering the Red Oak, IA Area
S.I.C.: 2711
Ronald G. Anderson *(Publisher)*

Rockwood Times **(2)**
P.O. Box 297, 325 N. Kingston Ave.
Rockwood, TN 37854
Tel.: 615-354-9162
Weekly Newspaper Covering the Rockwood, TN Area
S.I.C.: 2711
Doug Morris *(Publisher)*

Spencer Magnet **(2)**
P.O. Box 219
Taylorsville, KY 40071
Tel.: 502-477-2239
Weekly Newspaper Covering the Taylorsville, KY Area
S.I.C.: 2711
Jennifer Brislin *(Gen. Mgr.)*

The Springfield Sun **(2)**
P.O. Box 31,
Springfield, KY 40069
Tel.: 606-336-7718
Weekly Newspaper Covering the Springfield, KY Area
S.I.C.: 2711
George Gabehart *(Mng. Editor)*

Landmark Communications, Inc.—(Continued)

Sumter County Times **(2)**
303 E. McCollum Ave.
Bushnell, FL 33513
Tel.: 904-793-2161
Weekly Newspaper Covering the Bushnell, FL & Sumter County Area
S.I.C.: 2711
Bob Reichman *(Gen. Mgr.)*

The Trimble Banner-Democrat **(2)**
P.O. Box 68
Bedford, KY 40006
Tel.: 502-255-3205
Weekly Newspaper Covering the Bedford, KY Area
S.I.C.: 2711
Dorothy L. Abernathy *(Publisher)*

Landmark Special Publications **(1)**
149 Business Park Dr.
Virginia Beach, VA 23462
Tel.: 804-490-8123
Publishes Free-Distribution Newsprint Magazines Covering Leisure-Time Activities
S.I.C.: 2721
Conrad M. Hall *(Pres.)*
George Brooks *(V.P. & Gen. Mgr.)*

Times-World Corporation **(1)**
P.O. Box 2491, 201 Campbell Ave. S.W.
Roanoke, VA 24010
Tel.: 703-981-3100
Publishers of The Roanoke Times & World News, Serving Roanoke, Salem, New River & Southwestern Virginia
S.I.C.: 2711
Walter Rugaber *(Pres. & Publisher)*
Forrest M. Landon *(V.P. & Exec. Editor)*
Judith Perfater *(V.P. & Adv. Dir.)*
Carl Wright *(Treas.)*
William K. Warren, Jr. *(Mng. Editor)*
R. Vincent Reynolds *(Dir.-Prod.)*
C. Vaughn Porter *(Mgr.-Personnel)*

The Virginian-Pilot and The Ledger Star **(1)**
150 W. Brambleton Ave.
Norfolk, VA 23510
Tel.: 804-446-2000
Publishers of The Virginian-Pilot and The Ledger-Star Newspapers, Serving the South Hampton Roads Area, Norfolk, Chesapeake, Portsmouth, Suffolk & Virginia Beach & Southeastern Virginia & Northeastern North Carolina
S.I.C.: 2711
Frank Batten Jr. *(Pres. & Publisher)*
Sandra M. Rowe *(V.P. & Exec. Editor)*
R. Bruce Bradley *(V.P. & Adv. Dir.)*
Robin Saul *(V.P. & Prod. Dir.)*
Carolyn S. Wood *(V.P.)*
Norman T. Matthews *(V.P.)*
James Raper *(Mng. Editor)*
Kay McGraw *(Dir.-Human Resources)*

Subsidiaries:

Autonet, Inc. **(2)**
150 West Brambleton Ave.
Norfolk, VA 23510
Tel.: 804-446-2980
Multiple Listing Service for the Sale of Motor Vehicles
S.I.C.: 2741

Commonwealth Printing Company **(2)**
150 W. Brambleton Ave.
Norfolk, VA 23510
Tel.: 804-499-3818
Comml. Printing & Total Market Distr. Company
S.I.C.: 2752; 2759
Richard F. Berry, III *(Pres.)*

Commonwealth Building Company **(2)**
150 W. Brambleton Ave.
Norfolk, VA 23510
Tel.: 804-855-2769
Real Estate Holding Company for Virginia Pilot/Ledger Star Properties
S.I.C.: 6719

Commonwealth Direct Marketing **(2)**
150 W. Brambleton Ave.
Norfolk, VA 23510
Tel.: 804-446-2959
Direct Marketing Services Company Providing Mail & Alternate Delivery Services
S.I.C.: 7331

Chicago **(2)**
414 N. Orleans, Ste. 800
Chicago, IL 60610
Tel.: 312-222-8999
Fax: 312-222-0699
Sales Range: $10-19 Million
Emp.: 56
Fiscal Year-end: 12/31/91
Computer Systems/Hardware:
NCR-IBM-MacIntosh-Fujitsu
Consumer Publication for the City of Chicago
S.I.C.: 2721
Richard F. Spears *(Pres.)*
Heidi Schultz *(Publisher)*
John Carroll *(Assoc. Publr. & Adv. Dir.)*
Joanne Trestrail *(Mng. Editor)*
Richard Babcock *(Editor)*
Thomas Baliga *(Controller)*
Linda Hanson *(Mgr.-Admin.)*
Karen Hayes *(Mktg. Coord.)*

The Californian **(1)**
P.O. Box 1565, 1000 Pioneer Way
El Cajon, CA 92022
Tel.: 619-442-4404 (90%)
Daily Newspaper
S.I.C.: 2711
Paul Zindell *(Pres. & Publshr.)*

Units:

Antiques & Collectibles **(2)**
1000 Pioneer Way
El Cajon, CA 92022
Tel.: 619-442-4404
S.I.C.: 2711
Maxine Ritter *(Sls. Mgr.)*

Senior World (California) **(2)**
1000 Pioneer Way
El Cajon, CA 92022
Tel.: 619-442-4404
S.I.C.: 2711
David Reese *(Gen. Mgr.)*

Community Times Extra **(1)**
11502 Reisterstown Rd.
Reisterstown, MD 21136
Tel.: 410-356-2030
Newspaper
S.I.C.: 2711
Greg Linard *(Editor)*

Affiliate:

Capital-Gazette Communications, Inc. **(1)**
213 West St.
Annapolis, MD 21401
Tel.: 410-268-5000 (49.9%)
Newspapers
S.I.C.: 2711
Philip Merrill *(Pres. & Treas.)*
Eleanor Merrill *(Exec. V.P.)*
George Cruz *(Bus. Mgr.)*
Fred P. Glennie *(Sec. & Controller)*

LANDMARK HOTEL CORPORATION

1200 Executive Dr.
Topeka, KS 60615
Mailing Address:
P.O. Box 4526,
Topeka, KS 66604
Tel.: 913-272-7500 **KS**
Fax: 913-272-0433
Year Founded: 1982
Approx.Sls.: $60,000,000
Emp.: 2,000
Hotels
S.I.C.: 5812; 7011
Gary H. Keller *(Chm. Bd. & Pres.)*
Linda L. Siecrist *(Sr. V.P., Sec. & Treas.)*
Donald E. Redford *(Sr. V.P.-Opers.)*
James E. Steele *(Sr. V.P. & Controller)*

Outside Service Firm(s):

Braunsdorf, Carlson & Clinkenbeard*(Auditors)*
990 S.W. Fairlawn
Topeka, KS 66606

Insurance Management Associates*(Commercial Insurance Carrier)*
1631 S.W. Topeka
Topeka, KS 66612

Blue Cross & Blue Shield of Kansas*(Group Insurer)*
1133 S.W. Topeka
Topeka, KS 66612

Commerce Bank & Trust*(Investment Banker)*
Topeka, KS

Commerce Bank & Trust*(Major Banking Relationship)*
Topeka, KS

E. B. LANE & ASSOCIATES, INC.

733 W. McDowell
Phoenix, AZ 85007
Tel.: 602-258-5263
Fax: 602-257-8128
Year Founded: 1961
Approx.Billings: $15,300,000
Emp.: 25
Edward B. Lane *(Chm. & Chief Exec. Officer)*
Beau Lane *(Pres.)*
Diane Lane *(Pub. Rels. Dir.)*
Diane Fitch *(Acctg. Mgr.)*

THE LANE CONSTRUCTION CORP.

965 E. Main St.
Meriden, CT 06450
Tel.: 203-235-3351
Fax: 203-237-4260
Approx.Sls.: $160,000,000
Emp.: 1,500
Heavy Construction
S.I.C.: 1622; 1623; 1629; 1611
Byron Westmore *(Pres.)*
R.D. Stapleton *(Exec. V.P.-Fin. & Admin., Sec. & Gen. Counsel)*
Jayne M. Pitts *(Treas.)*
Vincent Caiola *(Controller)*
Fred Kells Murphy *(Mgr.-Data Processing)*

Computer Systems/Hardware:
IBM System 38

Outside Service Firm(s):

Liberty Mutual*(Commercial Insurance Carrier)*
Boston, MA

Empire Blue Cross & Blue Shield*(Group Insurer)*
New York, NY

Connecticut National Bank*(Investment Banker)*
777 Main St.
Hartford, CT 06115
Tel.: 203-728-2000

Connecticut National Bank*(Major Banking Relationship)*
777 Main St.
Hartford, CT 06115
Tel.: 203-728-2000

Connecticut National Bank*(Pension Manager)*
777 Main St.
Hartford, CT 06115
Tel.: 203-728-2000

Gardner, Preston & Moss, Inc.*(Pension Manager)*
Boston, MA

LANE INDUSTRIES, INC.

(Formerly General Binding Corporation)
One Lane Center, 1200 Shermer Rd.
Northbrook, IL 60062
Tel.: 708-498-6789 **DE**
Fax: 708-498-2104
Year Founded: 1969
Assets: $390,000,000
Liabilities: $285,000,000
Net Worth: $105,000,000
Approx.Sls.: $352,000,000
Emp.: 40
Fiscal Year-end: 12/31/91
Holding Co.; Lodging, Ranching, Manufacturing of Office Products, and Radio Broadcasting Stations
S.I.C.: 6719; 6091; 7011; 0212; 3579; 4832
William N. Lane III *(Chm. Bd., Pres. & Chief Exec. Officer)*
Thomas Kalebic *(Exec. V.P. & Chief Oper. Officer)*
Forrest M. Schneider *(Sr. V.P. & Chief Fin. Officer)*
Stephen D. Daniels *(V.P. & Treas.)*
Richard R. Fabbrini *(V.P.-Fin.)*
Robert J. Stucker *(Corp. Sec.)*
William M. Keating *(Controller)*
Arthur Shiller *(Gen. Counsel)*
Richard M. Smith *(Asst. Treas.)*

Computer Systems/Hardware:
IBM

Outside Service Firm(s):

Arthur Andersen & Co.*(Auditors)*
33 W. Monroe St.
Chicago, IL 60603-4067
Tel.: 312-580-0033
Fax: 312-507-6748

Credit Suisse*(International Bank Affiliate)*
200 E. Randolph
Chicago, IL

American National Bank & Trust Company of Chicago*(Major Banking Relationship)*
33 N. LaSalle St.
Chicago, IL 60602
Tel.: 312-661-5000
Fax: 312-661-6417

American National Bank & Trust Co.*(Major Banking Relationship)*
Chicago, IL

First National Bank of Chicago*(Major Banking Relationship)*
One First National Plaza
Chicago, IL 60670
Tel.: 312-732-9781
Tel.: 312-732-4050
Fax: 312-732-4840
Fax: 312-732-3055

Harris Trust & Savings Bank*(Major Banking Relationship)*
111 W. Monroe St.
Chicago, IL 60690
Tel.: 312-461-2265
Tel.: 800-858-0840

Irving Trust Co.*(Major Banking Relationship)*
Chicago, IL

National Bank of Detroit*(Major Banking Relationship)*
611 Woodward
Detroit, MI 48226
Tel.: 313-225-1000

Subsidiaries:

General Binding Corporation **(1)**
One GBC Plaza
Northbrook, IL 60062
Tel.: 708-272-3700
Tel.: 800-DIAL-GBC (80%)
Telex: 254264 (Domestic)
Fax: 708-272-1389

Assets: $173,437,000
Earnings: $12,599,000
Liabilities: $68,903,000
Net Worth: $104,534,000
Approx.Sls.: $311,199,000
Emp.: 3,207
Fiscal Year-end: 12/31/91
Export
Designs, Manufactures & Distributes Business Machines & Related Supplies for Binding, Laminating & Shredding
S.I.C.: 3579; 3554; 2782; 7389
Corporate Giving Program: Requests are Considered On Individual Merits
William N. Lane III *(Chm. Bd.)*
Warren Rothwell *(Chm.-Exec. Committee)*
Rudolph Grua *(Pres. & Chief Exec. Officer)*
Elliott L. Smith *(Exec. V.P.)*
Walter M. Hebb *(Sr. V.P.-Office Products Group)*
John G. Lindroth *(Sr. V.P.-Domestic Sls.)*
Govi C. Reddy *(Sr. V.P. & Pres.-Film Prod. Div.)*
Thomas F. Gueth *(V.P.-Res. & Devel.)*
John A. Janes *(V.P. & Pres.-USRB)*
Joseph J. LaPorte *(V.P.-Corp. Rels.)*
Theodore Manakas *(V.P.-Intl. Div.)*
Edward J. McNulty *(V.P. & Chief Fin. Officer)*
Steven Rubin *(V.P., Sec. & Gen. Counsel)*
Charles Shattuck *(V.P.-Office Products Grp.)*
Paul E. Wiedlin *(V.P.-Mfg.)*
Robert F. Neuschel *(Staff V.P.-Direct Mktg.)*
Eero Turen *(Staff V.P.-Corp. Information systems)*
Terrence Krush *(Treas.)*
William Hefferman *(Controller)*
Kay Bowman *(Asst. Corp. Treas.)*
S. Folkes *(Dir.-Mktg. Communications)*
Gary Smith *(Dir.-Human Resources)*
J. Groner *(Mgr.-Communications)*
Elaine DuPlessis *(Pension Administrator)*
Mildred Mastro *(Training & Dev. Admin.)*

Divisions:

General Binding Corporation **(2)**
21039 N. 27th Ave.
Phoenix, AZ 85027
Tel.: 602-869-8100
Emp.: 91
Mfr. of Business Supplies
S.I.C.: 2782
Patrick Shyan *(Plant Mgr.)*

Lane Graphics Products Div. **(2)**
P.O. Box 215
Amelia, VA 23007
Tel.: 804-561-2531
Emp.: 94
Bookbinding
S.I.C.: 2789
Jim Vance *(Plant Mgr.)*

Lane Film Products Division **(2)**
712 Winthrop
Addison, IL 60101
Tel.: 708-543-7100
Laminating Process
S.I.C.: 3089
Govi C. Reddy *(Sr. V.P. & Pres.-Film Prod. Div.)*

VeloBind, Inc. **(2)**
1135 Skokie Blvd.
Northbrook, IL 60062-4100
Tel.: 708-272-3700
Assets: $26,218,000
Earnings: $35,000
Liabilities: $4,102,000
Net Worth: $22,116,000
Approx.Sls.: $44,041,000
Emp.: 305
Fiscal Year-end: 12/31/90
Mfg. Equip. & Supplies for Use in Binding Soft Cover Documents & Library Quality Hard Cover Books
S.I.C.: 3999; 3579
Rudolph Grua *(Pres. & Chief Exec. Officer)*

Branches:

VeloBind, Inc. **(3)**
1255 Corporate Ctr. Dr.
Monterey Park, CA 91754
Tel.: 213-269-9511
Mktg. & Sls.
S.I.C.: 5044

VeloBind, Inc. **(3)**
One E. Erie St.
Chicago, IL 60611
Tel.: 312-280-4702
Mktg. & Sls.
S.I.C.: 5044

VeloBind, Inc. **(3)**
275 Wyman St.
Waltham, MA 02154
Tel.: 617-890-6780
Mktg. & Sls.
S.I.C.: 5044

VeloBind, Inc. **(3)**
6 East 43rd St.
New York, NY 10017
Tel.: 212-972-2400
Mktg. & Sls.
S.I.C.: 5044

VeloBind, Inc. **(3)**
2 Elm St.
Conshohocken, PA 19428
Tel.: 215-667-8151
Mktg. & Sls.
S.I.C.: 5044

VeloBind, Inc. **(3)**
1840 Wilson Blvd., #200
Arlington, VA 22201
Tel.: 703-243-8400
Mktg. & Sls.
S.I.C.: 5044

Manufacturing and Distribution Centers:

VeloBind, Inc. **(3)**
1960 Old Cuthbert Rd.
Cherry Hill, NJ 08034
Tel.: 609-428-5660
Mfr. of Equipment & Supplies for Use in Binding Soft Cover Documents & Library-Quality Hard Cover Books
S.I.C.: 3999; 3579; 5044

VeloBind-Reno Division **(3)**
850 Spice Island
Sparks, NV 89431
Tel.: 702-331-3222
Mfr. & Distr. of Binding Equipment
S.I.C.: 3999; 3579; 5044

Subsidiaries:

Loose Leaf Metals Company Inc. **(2)**
6800 Arsenal
Saint Louis, MO 63139
Tel.: 314-645-7880 (100%)
Approx.Sls.: $21,000,000
Emp.: 119
Mfrs. of Metal Devices for Loose Leaf Binders
S.I.C.: 2782

U.S. Ring Binder Corp. **(2)**
429 Church St.
New Bedford, MA 02745
Tel.: 508-998-1181 (100%)
Fax: 508-998-5168
Emp.: 154
Mfr. Metal Devices for Loose Leaf Binders
S.I.C.: 2782

Lane Broadcasting, Inc. **(1)**
One Lane Center, 1200 Shermer Rd.
Northbrook, IL 60062
Tel.: 708-498-6789

Lane Hotels, Inc. **(1)**
1200 Shermer Rd.
Northbrook, IL 60062
Tel.: 708-498-6789 (100%)
Fax: 708-498-2104
Owns & Manages Five Hotels Totaling 1433 Rooms & Four Unaffiliated Hotels Totaling 1,204 Rooms
S.I.C.: 7011
John Rijos *(Pres.)*

Lane Properties, Inc. **(1)**
Northbrook, IL

LANE LIMITED
2280 Mountain Industrial Blvd.
Tucker, GA 30084
Tel.: 404-934-8540
Tel.: 800-221-4134
Fax: 404-938-9473
Year Founded: 1890
Approx.Sls.: $40,000,000
Emp.: 200
Fiscal Year-end: 3/31/91
Produces Pipe Tobaccos, Loose Leaf Chewing Tobacco, Cigars, Pipes, Accessories & Butane Fuel
S.I.C.: 2121; 2131; 3999; 2899
David Michod *(Chm. Bd. & Chief Exec. Officer)*
George McGrath *(V.P.-Fin.)*
William E. Welch *(V.P.-Mfg.)*
Sidney C. Wooten, Jr. *(V.P.-Mktg. & Sls.)*
Brian G. Dewey *(Dir.-Mktg.)*
Joe Rowe *(Dir.-Natl. Sls.)*
Alex R. Mroz *(Mgr.-Natl. Key Accts.)*

C.J. LANGENFELDER & SON, INC.
8427 Pulaski Hwy.
Baltimore, MD 21237
Mailing Address:
P.O. Box 9606
Baltimore, MD 21237
Tel.: 410-682-2000
Fax: 410-391-4367
Year Founded: 1925
Assets: $41,500,000
Liabilities: $7,750,000
Net Worth: $33,750,000
Sales Range: $100-499 Million
Emp.: 425
Fiscal Year-end: 12/31/90
Road, Heavy Highway, Bridge & Airport Contractor
S.I.C.: 1611; 1622; 1629
Charles Scheeler *(Pres.)*
Kenneth C. Lundeen *(Exec. V.P.)*
John B. Baker *(V.P.)*
William E. Gable *(V.P.)*
William E. Hazlehurst *(V.P.)*
Mark M. Stokes *(V.P.)*

Computer Systems/Hardware:
IBM C-MAS

Outside Service Firm(s):

George Brown Associates*(Auditors)*
Baltimore, MD

Alexander & Alexander*(Commercial Insurance Carrier)*
P.O. Box 73223
Baltimore, MD 21273
Tel.: 310-547-2800

Blue Cross & Blue Shield of Maryland, Inc.*(Group Insurer)*
10455 Mill Run Circle
Owings Mills, MD 2117-5559

Smith, Somerville & Case*(Legal Firm)*
301 Light St.
Baltimore, MD 21202
Tel.: 410-727-1164

Maryland National Bank*(Major Banking Relationship)*
2 N. Charles St.
Baltimore, MD 21202

Security Trust Co.*(Pension Manager)*
B & O Bldg., 2 N. Charles St., 5th Fl.
Baltimore, MD 21202
Tel.: 410-244-6565
Tel.: 800-537-5485

DAVID LANGER & CO., INC.
6430 Sunset Blvd., Suite 105
Hollywood, CA 90028
Mailing Address:
P.O. Box 2080,
Beverly Hills, CA 90213 **CA**
Tel.: 213-466-2225
Fax: 213-466-7327
Year Founded: 1964
Assets: $2,420,488
Liabilities: $126,908
Net Worth: $2,293,580
Approx.Sls.: $21,000,000
Emp.: 27
Fiscal Year-end: 12/31/89
Import
Wholesale Distributor of Electronic Components & Computer Peripherals
S.I.C.: 5065; 5045
David Langer *(Pres., Chief Exec. & Chief Oper. Officer & Treas.)*
J. Meng *(Chief Fin. Officer)*
Fred Stern *(Legal Officer)*
Principal(s):
David Langer
J. Meng
Fred Stern

No. of U.S. Offices: 3
No. of Foreign Offices: 2

Computer Systems/Hardware:
IBM

Outside Service Firm(s):

Ernst & Young*(Auditors)*
515 S. Flower St.
Los Angeles, CA 90071
Tel.: 213-621-1666

Blue Shield of California*(Group Insurer)*
San Francisco, CA

Union Bank*(Investment Banker)*
445 S. Figueroa St.
Los Angeles, CA 90071
Tel.: 213-236-5076

HAL LANGERMAN CO.
25 Norristown Rd.
Blue Bell, PA 19422
Tel.: 215-646-5939
Year Founded: 1981
Approx.Billings: $16,318,160
Emp.: 10
Direct Response
Doris Tustin *(Pres.)*

LANGSTON COMPANIES
3294 Poplar Ave.
Memphis, TN 38111
Tel.: 901-454-1100
Fax: 901-454-1110
Year Founded: 1946
Approx.Sls.: $50,000,000
Emp.: 425
Fiscal Year-end: 11/30/91
Import Export
Mfr. of Multiwall Paper Bags, Woven Polypropylene Bags, Burlap & Cotton Bags,Velated Bagging & Packaging Products
S.I.C.: 2393; 2621; 5199
Robert E. Langston *(Pres.)*
William Barden *(V.P.-Fin. & Admin.)*
Dudley I. Langston *(Dir.-Pur., Personnel, Fin. & Sec.)*

Computer Systems/Hardware:
AT&T

Outside Service Firm(s):

Pannell Kerr & Foster*(Auditors)*
Memphis, TN

Dowden & Monroe*(Legal Firm)*
Memphis, TN

First Tennessee Bank, N.A.*(Major Banking Relationship)*
Memphis, TN

LANMAN & KEMP-BARCLAY CO. INC.
25 Woodland Ave.
Westwood, NJ 07675
Tel.: 201-666-4990
Tel.: 800-848-5047
Telex: 642807
Fax: 201-666-5836
Year Founded: 1808
Approx.Sls.: $15,000,000
Emp.: 60
Export
Murray & Lanman's Florida Water Cologne & Soap, Barry's Tricopherous Hair Tonic, Barry's V.I.P. Hair Color Restorer, Reuter's Soap, Sandalo & Pachuli Soap, Rose Cologne & Orange Blossom Cologne
S.I.C.: 2834
Edith P. Kemp *(Pres.)*

Lanman & Kemp-Barclay Co. Inc.—(Continued)

Emilio J. Ciciola *(Exec. V.P. & Sec.)*
John F. Samayoa *(Exec. V.P.-Mktg. Mgr. & Treas.)*

LANSDALE, CARR & BAUM
17662 Armstrong Ave.
Irvine, CA 92714
Tel.: 714-250-3303
Fax: 714-261-5473
Year Founded: 1939
Approx.Billings: $10,000,000
Emp.: 8
Macy Baum *(Pres.)*

LANTECH INC.
11000 Bluegrass Pkwy.
Louisville, KY 40299
Tel.: 502-267-4200 **KY**
Fax: 502-266-5031
Approx.Sls.: $32,000,000
Emp.: 270
Export
Manufacture & Distribute Materials Handling & Packaging Systems, Stretch Wrap Equipment
S.I.C.: 3569; 5084; 5085; 5162
Patrick R. Lancaster, III *(Pres. & Chief Exec. Officer)*
William G. Lancaster *(Exec. V.P.)*
Mike Balough *(V.P.-Corp. Opers.)*
John Fain *(V.P.-Research & Devel.)*
Bill Kugler *(V.P.-Customs)*
Jerry Todd *(Dir.-Res. & Devel.)*

Outside Service Firm(s):

Ernst & Young*(Auditors)*
1000 Brown & Williamson Tower
Louisville, KY 40202
Tel.: 502-585-1400

Hirn, Reed, Harper & Eisinger*(Legal Firm)*
Louisville, KY

First National Bank of Louisville*(Major Banking Relationship)*
P.O. Box 36000,
Louisville, KY 40233

LANTZSCH-ANDREAS ENTERPRISES, INC.
8545 Leesburg Pike
Vienna, VA 22182
Tel.: 703-442-8200
Fax: 703-356-3328
Year Founded: 1979
Assets: $12,965,853
Liabilities: $10,100,527
Net Worth: $2,865,326
Approx.Sls.: $76,075,409
Emp.: 136
Fiscal Year-end: 12/31/90
Retail Auto Dealer
S.I.C.: 5511
George C. Andreas *(Chm. Bd. & Pres.)*
Ursula E. Andreas *(Exec. V.P.)*
Margarete G. Lantzsch *(Exec. V.P.)*
Nikitas C. Manitsas *(Exec. V.P.)*
Gilbert Hofheimer *(V.P. & Gen. Mgr.)*
Principal(s):
George C. Andreas
Ursula E. Andreas
Christopher M. Andreas
Michael A. Andreas

Computer Systems/Hardware:
ADP & IBM

Outside Service Firm(s):

Price Waterhouse*(Auditors)*
1801 K. Street, N.W.
Washington, DC 20006
Tel.: 202-296-0800

Kenneth H. Michael Insurance Co.*(Commercial Insurance Carrier)*
Riverdale, MD 20737

Automotive Trade Assn. Capital Area*(Group Insurer)*
Rockville, MD 20855

Miles & Stockbridge*(Legal Firm)*
10 Light St.
Baltimore, MD 21202
Tel.: 410-727-6464

Chevy Chase F.S.B.*(Major Banking Relationship)*
Bethesda, MD

Riggs National Bank of Washington, D.C.*(Major Banking Relationship)*
P.O. Box 96206, 1120 Vermont Ave. N.W.
Washington, DC 20090-6206
Tel.: 202-835-4082

Riggs National Bank of Washington, D.C.*(Pension Manager)*
P.O. Box 96206, 1120 Vermont Ave. N.W.
Washington, DC 20090-6206
Tel.: 202-835-4082

Subsidiaries:

Andreas Galleries, Inc. **(1)**
8545 Leesburg Pike
Vienna, VA 22182
Tel.: 703-337-2000
Art Gallery
S.I.C.: 8412
Gilbert Hofheimer *(V.P. & Gen. Mgr.)*

Capital Funding Co. **(1)**
8545 Leesburg Pike
Vienna, VA 22182
Tel.: 703-442-8200
Automotive Leasing
S.I.C.: 7515
Gilbert Hofheimer *(V.P. & Gen. Mgr.)*

H.B.L., Inc. **(1)**
8545 Leesburg Pike
Vienna, VA 22182
Tel.: 703-442-8200
Mercedes Dealership
S.I.C.: 5511
Gilbert Hofheimer *(V.P. & Gen. Mgr.)*

LANZ, INC.
8680 Hayden Pl.
Culver City, CA 90232
Mailing Address:
P.O. Box 3600,
Culver City, CA 90232
Tel.: 310-558-0200
Tel.: 800-421-0731 **CA**
Fax: 310-558-0342
Year Founded: 1938
Approx.Sls.: $47,000,000
Emp.: 300
Fiscal Year-end: 12/31/91
Export
Mfr. of Women's Dresses, Blouses, Skirts, Beachwear, Coats, Accessories & Sleepwear
S.I.C.: 2335; 2337; 2339
Werner G. Scharff *(Chm. Bd. & Pres.)*
Robert Laret *(Chief Fin. Officer)*
Robert Fiddler *(Exec. V.P.)*
Christopher Scharff *(V.P. & Dir.-Mktg.)*
Charles Guggenheimer *(Mgr.-Natl. Sls.)*
Principal(s):
Werner G. Scharff
Alexis G. Scharff
Peter Scharff

Outside Service Firm(s):

Deloitte & Touche*(Auditors)*
1000 Wilshire Blvd.
Los Angeles, CA 90017-2472
Tel.: 213-688-0800
Fax: 213-688-0100

Union Bank*(Major Banking Relationship)*
3810 Wilshire Blvd.
Los Angeles, CA 90051
Tel.: 213-480-6500

Minton, Minton & Rand*(Legal Firm)*
Los Angeles, CA

LAPHAM-HICKEY STEEL CORP.
5500 W. 73rd St.
Chicago, IL 60638
Tel.: 708-496-6111
Fax: 708-496-8504/708-496-1177
Emp.: 300
Fiscal Year-end: 12/31/90
Specialty Steel Service Center
S.I.C.: 5051
William M. Hickey *(Pres. & Chief Exec. Officer)*
R. A. Vikander *(Chief Fin. Officer, V.P. & Treas.)*
Warren J. Rusgis *(Exec. V.P.)*
Jeff Hubson *(V.P.)*
Gary Frelan *(Controller)*
Robert Carlisle *(Mgr.-Info. Systems)*
Richard A. Battles *(Gen. Sls. Mgr.)*

Outside Service Firm(s):

Ernst & Young*(Auditors)*
233 S. Wacker Dr.
Chicago, IL 60606
Tel.: 312-368-1800
Fax: 312-645-3095

McBride, Baker & Coles*(Legal Firm)*
500 W. Madison St., 40th Fl.
Chicago, IL 60606
Tel.: 312-715-5700

Harris Trust & Savings Bank*(Major Banking Relationship)*
111 W. Monroe St.
Chicago, IL 60690
Tel.: 312-461-2265
Tel.: 800-858-0840

Massachusetts Mutual Life Insurance Co.*(Pension Manager)*
1295 State Street
Springfield, MA 01111
Tel.: 413-788-8411

Travelers Insurance Co.*(Pension Manager)*
1 Tower Square
Hartford, CT 06183
Tel.: 203-222-7821
Fax: 203-222-7813

Division:

Clifford Metal **(1)**
200 Cortiss St.
Providence, RI 02904
Tel.: 401-861-4100
Approx.Sls.: $23,000,000
Emp.: 80
Metals Service Centers & Offices
S.I.C.: 5051
Michael B. Lawlor *(Pres.)*
Walter Kerttula *(Gen. Mgr.)*
Joe Salum *(Dir.-Opers.)*
Ann Lablond *(Dir.-Fin.)*
Debbie Farias *(Mgr.-Pur.)*
Walter Van Sickle *(Inside Sls. Mgr.)*
Terri Porter *(Office Mgr.)*

Subsidiaries:

Lapham-Hickey Steel Corp. (MO) **(1)**
500 S. Spring Ave.
St. Louis, MO 63110
Tel.: 314-535-8200

Lapham Hickey Steel (WI) **(1)**
2585 W. 20th Ave.
Oshkosh, WI 54903
Tel.: 414-233-8502

LAPPIN ELECTRIC COMPANY
1300 N. 4th St.
Milwaukee, WI 53212
Mailing Address:
P.O. Box 354
Milwaukee, WI 53212
Tel.: 414-276-7878 **WI**
Fax: 414-276-1482
Year Founded: 1919
Approx.Sls.: $47,000,000
Emp.: 190
Wholesale Distribution & Retail Sales of Electrical Apparatus & Equipment; Lighting Fixtures
S.I.C.: 5063; 5719
Gerald D. Lappin *(Chm. Bd.)*
R. Todd Lappin *(Pres.)*
Gerald H. Robbins *(Exec. V.P.)*
Christopher Florentino *(V.P.)*
Richard D. Lappin *(V.P.)*
Allen Onopa *(V.P.-Indus.)*
James Schweke *(V.P.)*
James D. Wilson *(V.P.-Sls.)*
Robert Bartzen *(Sec.)*

Outside Service Firm(s):

Sattell, Johnson & Appel*(Auditors)*
Milwaukee, WI

Lloyd S. Jacbson*(Legal Firm)*
Milwaukee, WI

Associated Commerce Bank*(Major Banking Relationship)*
Milwaukee, WI

LARAMIE TIRE DISTRIBUTORS INC.
700 Markley St.
Norristown, PA 19404
Mailing Address:
P.O. Box 28
Norristown, PA 19404-0028
Tel.: 215-275-6480
Tel.: 800-523-0430 **PA**
Fax: 215-275-3980
Year Founded: 1970
Approx.Sls.: $74,000,000
Emp.: 100
Fiscal Year-end: 12/31/91
Export
Distribute Tires & Auto Parts
S.I.C.: 5014; 5013
Wayne Reichman *(Pres.)*
Regina Harris *(Dir.-Intl. Sls.)*

Outside Service Firm(s):

Bush, Levine & Ticosky*(Auditors)*
Huntington Valley, PA

Solomon Berschler*(Legal Firm)*
Philadelphia, PA

Continental Bank N. A.*(Major Banking Relationship)*
231 S. LaSalle St.
Chicago, IL 60697
Tel.: 312-828-2345
Tel.: 800-426-5754
Telex: 312-828-1783

LOU LARICHE CHEVROLET-SUBARU INC.
40875 Plymouth Rd.
Plymouth, MI 48170
Tel.: 313-453-4600 **DE**
Fax: 313-455-2570
Year Founded: 1968
Approx.Sls.: $26,000,000
Emp.: 75
Fiscal Year-end: 6/30/91
Automobile Dealership
S.I.C.: 5511
Louis LaRiche *(Pres.)*
Sharon Pratt *(Sec. & Treas.)*
Tony Wasil *(Mgr.-Sls.)*
Ronald Chaudoin *(Gen. Mgr.)*

LARIO OIL & GAS COMPANY
301 S. Market
Wichita, KS 67202
Tel.: 316-265-5611
Fax: 316-265-5610
Year Founded: 1927
Sales Range: $20-39 Million
Emp.: 70
Fiscal Year-end: 12/31/91
Oil Production
S.I.C.: 1311
Patrick E. O'Shaughnessy *(Chm. Bd. & Chief Exec. Officer)*
Marvin E. Kraft *(Pres.)*
Gerald E. O'Shaughnessy *(V.P. & Sec.)*
Michael W. O'Shaughnessy *(V.P.)*
Leroy Orth *(Controller)*

Outside Service Firm(s):

KPMG Peat Marwick*(Auditors)*
Wichita, KS

Bank IV*(Major Banking Relationship)*
P.O. Box 1122,
Wichita, KS 67201
Tel.: 316-261-4304

Subsidiary:

Lario Enterprises, Inc. **(1)**
301 S. Market
Wichita, KS 67202
Tel.: 316-265-5611
Emp.: 24
Housing Rental
S.I.C.: 6514
Gerald O'Shaughnessy *(Pres.)*
P. O'Shaughnessy *(V.P. & Sec.)*
Virginia Morgan *(Asst. Sec.)*

LARKEN INC.
3330 Southgate Ct. S.W.
Cedar Rapids, IA 52404
Mailing Address:
P.O. Box 1808
Cedar Rapids, IA 52406
Tel.: 319-366-8201 **IA**
Fax: 319-362-5663
Year Founded: 1967
Approx.Sls.: $200,000,000
Emp.: 6,000
Motel & Restaurant Operations
S.I.C.: 7011; 5812
Larry Cahill *(Pres. & Treas.)*
Kenneth Cahill *(V.P. & Sec.)*
John Swanson *(Dir.-Adv. & Pub. Rels.)*

Principal(s):
Larry Cahill
Kenneth Cahill

Computer Systems/Hardware:
IBM

Outside Service Firm(s):

Ernst & Young*(Auditors)*
Cedar Rapids, IA

Stewart Devore, Jr.*(Legal Firm)*
Arlington, TX

Firstar Bank Cedar Rapids, N.A.*(Major Banking Relationship)*
222 Second Ave. S.E.
Cedar Rapids, IA 52406
Tel.: 319-398-4224

LARKIN·MEEDER & SCHWEIDEL INC.

LARKIN MEEDER & SCHWEIDEL
7800 Stemmons Frwy., Ste. 770
Dallas, TX 75247
Tel.: 214-688-7070
Year Founded: 1982
Approx.Billings: $50,000,000
Emp.: 45
Consumer & Business-to-Business Adv.
Carl Larkin *(Chm. Bd., Pres. & New Bus. Contact)*
Bruce Anderson *(Exec. V.P., Gen. Mgr. & Dir.-Acct Services)*
Bill Meeder *(Exec. V.P.)*
Lee Andrews *(V.P.-Grp. Supvr.)*
Charles Hodges *(V.P./Pub. Rels.)*
Michael Leonard *(V.P., Mktg. Services)*
Gary Strange *(V.P.)*

Computer Systems/Hardware:
Macintosh Network

LAROCHE HOLDINGS, INC.
1100 Johnson Ferry Rd.
Atlanta, GA 30342
Tel.: 404-851-0300 **DE**
Fax: 404-851-0476
Year Founded: 1986
Sales Range: $100-499 Million
Fiscal Year-end: 2/28/92
Holding Company
S.I.C.: 6719
C. Max Henderson *(Chm. Bd. & Chief Exec. Officer)*
Walter Laroche *(Pres.)*
Felix J. Prinzo *(Sr. V.P. & Chief Fin. Officer)*
Harvey R. Linder *(V.P., Sec. & Gen. Counsel)*
N.A. DiCrescenzo *(Corp. Dir.-Human Resources)*
Barry Morton *(Mgr.-Systems & Programming)*

Principal(s):
C. Max Henderson
Felix J. Prinzo
Johnnie Lou LaRoche

No. of Mfg. Plants/Facilities: 40
No. of U.S. Offices: 6

Outside Service Firm(s):

Ernst & Young*(Auditors)*
600 Peachtree St. N.E.
Atlanta, GA 30308
Tel.: 404-874-8300

Northwestern National Life*(Commercial Insurance Carrier)*
20 Washington Ave. S.
Minneapolis, MN 55401

Stamford Atlanta Capital Corp.*(Investment Banker)*
Atlanta, GA

Jones, Day, Reavis & Pogue*(Legal Firm)*
3300 First Atlanta Tower
Atlanta, GA 30383
Tel.: 404-581-8000

Bankers Trust Co.*(Major Banking Relationship)*
130 Liberty St., 20th Fl.
New York, NY 10006
Tel.: 212-250-2737

The Principal Financial Group*(Pension Manager)*
Des Moines, IA

Subsidiaries:

LaRoche Chemicals Inc. **(1)**
Airline Hwy.
Baton Rouge, LA 70805
Tel.: 504-356-8406
Fax: 504-356-8556
Approx.Sls.: $216,000,000
Emp.: 600
Manufacture Chemicals
C. Max Henderson *(Chm. Bd. & Chief Exec. Officer)*
R.L. Jeansonne *(Chief Oper. Officer)*
Felix J. Prinzo *(Sr. V.P. & Chief Fin. Officer)*
Harvey R. Linder *(Gen. Counsel)*

LaRoche Industries Inc. **(1)**
1100 Johnson Ferry Rd.
Atlanta, GA 30342
Tel.: 404-851-0300
Fax: 404-851-0476
Manufacture Nitrogenous Chemicals Fertilizers
S.I.C.: 2813; 2873; 2892
C. Max Henderson *(Chm. Bd. & Chief Exec. Officer)*

LARRYS, INC.
2020 Schoonover Rd.
Gillette, WY 82716
Tel.: 307-682-5394
Fax: 307-686-6523
Emp.: 80
Sewer Line & Water Main Construction; Plumbing Contractors; Warm Air Heating & Air Conditioning Contractor; Bridge & Viaduct Construction
S.I.C.: 1623; 1711; 1622
Lawrence F. Suchor *(Pres.)*
Joe Suchor *(V.P.)*
Leo Suchor *(Sec. & Treas.)*

Outside Service Firm(s):

Stanley Wolfe*(Legal Firm)*
Gillette, WY

First Interstate Bank*(Major Banking Relationship)*
Gillette, WY

Larsam Incorporated
(Name Changed to Sebastian & Cooke)

LARSEN COLBY ADVERTISING
5657 Wilshire Blvd., 5th Fl.
Los Angeles, CA 90036
Tel.: 213-931-0009
Fax: 213-930-2835
Year Founded: 1984
Approx.Billings: $42,000,000
Emp.: 32
Rick Colby *(Pres. & Creative Dir.)*
Marlene Handler *(Controller)*

JACK LENOR LARSEN, INC.
41 E. 11th St.
New York, NY 10003
Tel.: 212-674-3993
Fax: 212-674-1403
Year Founded: 1953
Approx.Sls.: $12,000,000
Emp.: 75
Import Export
Woven Drapery Material & Upholstery Fabrics, Carpets & Office Furniture
S.I.C.: 5131; 5023; 5021
Jack Lenor Larsen *(Chm. Bd.)*
Frank Huggins *(Pres.)*
G. Cerf *(V.P.-Mktg.)*
E. Karanauskas *(V.P.-Sls.)*
K. Tokar *(V.P.-Opers.)*
Susan Lehrmitt *(Treas.)*

AL LARSON BOAT SHOP, INC.
1046 S. Seaside Ave.
Terminal Island, CA 90731
Tel.: 213-514-4100
Fax: 213-831-4912
Year Founded: 1903
Approx.Sls.: $10,000,000
Emp.: 110
Boat Repair & Marine Operator
S.I.C.: 3731; 4493
Gloria Wall *(Pres.)*
Gene Crvarich *(V.P., Sec. & Treas.)*
Michael Iacomo *(V.P.)*
George Wall *(V.P.)*
John L. Wall *(V.P.)*
Jack Fischer *(Pur. Agent)*

Outside Service Firm(s):

Farmers & Merchants Bank*(Major Banking Relationship)*
Long Beach, CA

J.H. LARSON ELECTRICAL COMPANY
700 Colorado Ave., S.
Golden Valley, MN 55416
Tel.: 612-545-1717 **WI**
Year Founded: 1931
Approx.Sls.: $35,000,000
Emp.: 130
Wholesale Distribution of Electrical & Plumbing Supplies
S.I.C.: 5063; 5074
Charles E. Pahl *(Pres. & Chief Exec. Officer)*
Larry Soukup *(Controller)*
Edward Chesen *(Mgr.-Opers.)*

Outside Service Firm(s):

McGladrey & Pullen*(Auditors)*
Minneapolis, MN

Wagner, Johnson & Falconer*(Legal Firm)*
Minneapolis, MN

Marquette Bank*(Major Banking Relationship)*
777 Marquette Ave.
Minneapolis, MN 55402
Tel.: 612-370-2182

LARSON MANUFACTURING COMPANY
2333 Eastbrook Dr.
Brookings, SD 57006
Tel.: 605-692-6115
Fax: 605-692-4791
Approx.Sls.: $30,000,000
Emp.: 150
Fiscal Year-end: 12/31/91
Mfr. of Aluminum Storm Doors
S.I.C.: 3442
Dale Larson *(Pres.)*
Bill Hay *(V.P.-Sls.)*
Patricia Larson *(Treas.)*
Joyce Kruger *(Corp. Acctg.)*
Glenn Keufchel *(Dir.-Opers.)*
Al Lee *(Dir.-Engrng.)*
Ron Hovland *(Mgr.-Data Processing)*
Dave Morgan *(Mgr.-Production)*
Gary Isenberg *(Pur. Agent)*

Outside Service Firm(s):

Grant Thornton*(Auditors)*
500 Pillsbury Center
Minneapolis, MN 55402-1459

McCann, Martin & McCann*(Legal Firm)*
Brookings, SD

First National Bank*(Major Banking Relationship)*
Brookings, SD

LARWIN COMPANY
16255 Ventura Blvd., Ste. 900
Encino, CA 91436
Tel.: 818-986-8890 **CA**
Fax: 818-784-2891
Year Founded: 1978
Approx.Sls.: $44,000,000
Emp.: 80
Construction of Single Family Homes
S.I.C.: 1521
Michael I. Keston *(Pres.)*
Ron Juskiewicz *(V.P.-Fin.)*
Charles Preston *(V.P. & Sec.)*
Monty Polson, Sr. *(V.P.)*

Outside Service Firm(s):

Greenstein, Block Fishman & Gavey*(Auditors)*
Los Angeles, CA

Security Pacific National Bank*(Major Banking Relationship)*
Los Angeles, CA

LAS VEGAS SUN, INC.
800 S. Valley View
Las Vegas, NV 89107
Mailing Address:
P.O. Box 4275,
Las Vegas, NV 89127
Tel.: 702-385-3111 **NV**
Fax: 702-383-7264
Year Founded: 1950
Approx.Sls.: $22,000,000
Emp.: 300
Fiscal Year-end: 12/31/90
Newspaper
S.I.C.: 2711
Mike O'Callaghan *(Chm. Bd.)*
Brian L. Greenspun *(Pres.)*
David Greenspun *(V.P.)*
Barbara Greenspun *(Publr. & Treas.)*
Ruthe Deskin *(Exec. Asst. to the Publr.)*

Las Vegas Sun, Inc.—(Continued)

Jack Harpster *(Dir.-Adv.)*
Jim McGlasson *(Gen. Mgr.)*

Outside Service Firm(s):

McGladrey & Pullen*(Auditors)*
300 S. Fourth St., Ste. 900
Las Vegas, NV 89101
Tel.: 702-386-5800

Valley Bank of Nevada*(Major Banking Relationship)*
300 S. 4th St.
Las Vegas, NV 89101
Tel.: 312-732-4000

LASALLE-DEITCH CO., INC.
640 Industrial Pkwy.
Elkhart, IN 46515
Mailing Address:
P.O. Box 2347
Elkhart, IN 46515
Tel.: 219-294-2661 **IN**
Fax: 219-294-2266
Year Founded: 1961
Approx.Sls.: $115,000,000
Emp.: 500
Fiscal Year-end: 12/31/90
Import Export
Distributor of Carpet, Vinyl Flooring & Furniture
S.I.C.: 5021; 5023
Corporate Giving Program: United Way
Joseph N. Ellis *(Chm. Bd.)*
A. Clark Peters *(Pres. & Chief Exec. Officer)*
Donald L. Bobay *(V.P.-Fin. & Admin.)*
Tom Hall *(Legal Officer)*

Principal(s):
A. Clark Peters

Computer Systems/Hardware:
IBM 4361

Outside Service Firm(s):

May, Oberfell & Lorber*(Legal Firm)*
South Bend, IN

Midwest Commerce Banking Co.*(Major Banking Relationship)*
Elkhart, IN

Division:

LaSalle Lighting **(1)**
2111 E. Industrial Pkwy.
Elkhart, IN 46514
Tel.: 219-294-5511

LASALLE PARTNERS
(Formerly LaSalle Street Partners)
11 S. LaSalle St.
Chicago, IL 60603
Tel.: 312-782-5800
Fax: 312-782-4339
Year Founded: 1968
Emp.: 700
Fiscal Year-end: 12/31/90
Corporate Real Estate Services
S.I.C.: 6531
Corporate Giving Program: Contact Company Directly for Details
Employee Matching Gifts Program: Contact Company Directly for Details
C. Gary Gerst *(Co-Chm.)*
Stuart L. Scott *(Co-Chm.)*
Gretchen F. Needham *(Sr. V.P.-Communications)*
Jeffrey H. Olian *(Gen. Counsel)*

No. of U.S. Offices: 33
No. of Foreign Offices: 2

Computer Systems/Hardware:
IBM

LASER POWER CORPORATION
12777 High Bluff Dr.
San Diego, CA 92130
Tel.: 619-755-0700 **DE**
Fax: 619-259-0956
Year Founded: 1979
Approx.Sls.: $12,000,000
Emp.: 120
Optical Elements & Assemblies, Except Opthalmic
S.I.C.: 3827
Dr. Glenn Sherman *(Chm. Bd. & Chief Exec. Officer)*
Dr. Douglas Tanimoto *(Pres. & Chief Oper. Officer)*

Outside Service Firm(s):

Ernst & Young*(Auditors)*
501 W. Broadway, Ste. 1200
San Diego, CA 92101

Wells Fargo Bank*(Major Banking Relationship)*
San Diego, CA

LASER PRECISION CORP.

109 N. Genesee St.
Utica, NY 13502
Tel.: 315-797-4449
Fax: 315-758-4038
Earnings: ($251,000)
Approx.Rev.: $22,479,000
Fiscal Year-end: 12/31/90
Robert Ostrander *(Adv. Mgr.)*

LASKEY ASSOCIATES
39210 State St.
Fremont, CA 94538
Tel.: 510-794-7901
Fax: 510-794-8803
Sales Range: $100-499 Million
Emp.: 3
Commercial Real Estate Broker, Real Estate Investments
S.I.C.: 6531; 6798
John L. Laskey *(Pres.)*
David A. Richards *(Associate)*
Principal(s):
John L. Laskey

Computer Systems/Hardware:
IBM PC

Outside Service Firm(s):

Hart, Byars, Eng, Cambe & O'Connor*(Auditors)*
Palo Alto, CA

Charles Chase*(Legal Firm)*
Foster City, CA

Bank of America NT&SA*(Major Banking Relationship)*
San Jose, CA

LASKO METAL PRODUCTS, INC.
820 Lincoln Ave.
West Chester, PA 19380
Tel.: 215-692-7400
Fax: 215-696-4648
Year Founded: 1947
Approx.Sls.: $100,000,000
Emp.: 1,300
Import Export
Mfr. of Electrical Household Appliances
S.I.C.: 3634
Oscar Lasko *(Pres.)*
Edward McAssey *(Exec. V.P.)*
Michael Boneck *(Pur. Agent)*
Bernard Eisman *(Mgr.-Personnel)*
Principal(s):
Oscar Lasko

No. of Mfg. Plants/Facilities: 6
No. of U.S. Offices: 5
No. of Foreign Offices: 1

Outside Service Firm(s):

KPMG Peat Marwick*(Auditors)*
1600 Market St.
Philadelphia, PA 19103
Tel.: 215-299-3100

Pelino & Lentz, P.C.*(Legal Firm)*
Packard Bldg.
Philadelphia, PA 19102
Tel.: 215-665-1540

Philadelphia National Bank*(Major Banking Relationship)*
5th & Market Sts.
Philadelphia, PA 19101
Tel.: 215-629-3100
Fax: 215-834-2069

LASKY COMPANY
67 E. Willow St.
Millburn, NJ 07041
Tel.: 201-376-9200
Fax: 201-376-3832
Year Founded: 1917
Approx.Sls.: $56,000,000
Emp.: 320
Web & Sheetfed Color Lithography: General Commercial, Advertising, Sales Promotion, Annual Reports
S.I.C.: 2752
Sherwood A. Barnhard *(Chm. Bd.)*
S.J. Weissman *(Vice Chm.)*
Ronald H. Barnhard *(Pres.)*
Albert J. Yonadi *(Exec. V.P.)*
Principal(s):
Sherwood A. Barnhard
S.J. Weissman

Outside Service Firm(s):

J. H. Cohn & Co.*(Auditors)*
Livingston, NJ

Orloff, Lowenbach, Stifelman & Siegel*(Legal Firm)*
Milburn, NJ

LASTING PRODUCTS, INC.
2115 W. Valley View
Dallas, TX 75234
Tel.: 214-247-9696 **TX**
Fax: 214-247-8540
Year Founded: 1968
Sales Range: $20-39 Million
Emp.: 175
Kitchen, Bathroom & Household Ware; Wood; Metal Household Articles Giftware, Brass Goods; Woven Wire Products; Pottery Household Articles
S.I.C.: 2499; 3499; 3496; 3269
Oscar Blonkenmeyer Jr. *(Pres.)*
Harold L. Blonkenmeyer *(V.P.)*
Gerald G. Blonkenmeyer *(Treas. & Sec.)*
Robert W. Griffin *(Gen. Mgr.)*
Larry Pryor *(Mgr.-Plant)*
Lynn Titus *(Pur. Agent)*

THE LATHROP COMPANY
1220 Dussel Dr.
Toledo, OH 43537
Mailing Address:
P.O. Box 772,
Toledo, OH 43697
Tel.: 419-893-7000
Fax: 419-893-1741
Year Founded: 1896
Assets: $22,284,309
Liabilities: $14,457,467
Net Worth: $7,826,842
Approx.Sls.: $99,912,256
Emp.: 400
Fiscal Year-end: 12/31/91
Contractors-Construction Mgr. & Pre-Engineered Butler Bldgs.; Equipment Installation & Rigging
S.I.C.: 1541; 1542
R. L. Maxwell *(Pres. & Chief Exec. Officer)*
W.S. Robinson *(Chief Fin. Officer & Treas.)*
J.D. Cocboth *(Exec. V.P.)*
R.L. Lee *(V.P.-Adv.)*
Mark Kusner *(Controller)*
Joseph Vumbacco *(Gen. Counsel & Sec.)*
Richard E. Lee *(Dir.-Mktg.)*
JoLaine Riffle *(Dir.-Communications)*
Marsha Gallagher *(Mgr.-Data Processing)*
Robert C. Riddle *(Mgr.-Admin.)*
Tom Bigler *(Yard Supvsr.)*
Principal(s):
R. L. Maxwell

No. of Mfg. Plants/Facilities: 1
No. of U.S. Offices: 4

Computer Systems/Hardware:
Burroughs; IBM

LAUBECK CORPORATION/ CROSS
166 Dundaff St.
Carbondale, PA 18407
Mailing Address:
P.O. Drawer 507,
Carbondale, PA 18407
Tel.: 717-282-4344
Tel.: 800-872-7373 **PA**
Fax: 717-282-4627
Approx.Sls.: $18,000,000
Emp.: 140
Fiscal Year-end: 12/31/90
Import Export
Manufacture Screens; Plastic, Rubber, Polyurethane & Perforated Metal, Hardboard, Paper
S.I.C.: 3499; 2821
F. Warner *(Pres.)*
Jim Carlson *(Exec. V.P.)*
Robert Wallis *(V.P.-Sls.)*
L. Warner *(Sec.)*
Dallas Miller *(Controller)*
D. Novitsky *(Dir.-Engrng.)*
Sherman Mead *(Mgr.-Natl. Sls.)*
J. Jerin *(Pur. Agent)*

No. of Mfg. Plants/Facilities: 3
No. of U.S. Offices: 3

Computer Systems/Hardware:
IBM

Outside Service Firm(s):

Coopers & Lybrand*(Auditors)*
2400 Eleven Penn Center
Philadelphia, PA 19103-2962
Tel.: 215-963-8000

Divisions:

Beckley Perforating Co. **(1)**
60 Brown Ave.
Springfield, NJ 07081
Tel.: 201-467-3500
Tel.: 800-526-4249
Manufacture of Perforated Metal, Hardboard & PaperProducts
S.I.C.: 3499
Fred Warner *(Pres.)*

Laubeck Corporation, Beckley Division **(1)**
60 Brown Ave.
Springfield, NJ 07081
Tel.: 201-467-3500
Tel.: 800-526-4249
Sales & Marketing of Perforated Steel
S.I.C.: 5051
David Babetski *(Gen. Mgr.)*

Laubeck Corporation, Laubenstein Division **(1)**
418 S. Hoffman Blvd.
Ashland, PA 17921
Tel.: 717-875-2151
Metal Perforating
S.I.C.: 3443
Fred Warner *(Gen. Mgr.)*

LAUERER MARKIN GIBBS, INC.

LAUERER MARKIN GIBBS, INC.
1725 Indian Wood Circle
Maumee, OH 43537
Tel.: 419-893-2500
Fax: 419-893-1050
Year Founded: 1968
Approx.Billings: $34,000,000
Emp.: 58
Advertising Agency
S.I.C.: 7311
William R. Markin *(Chm. & Chief Exec. Officer)*
Kenneth G. Lauerer *(Pres. & Chief Oper. Officer)*
Donald G. Pennell *(Controller)*
Robert Lubell *(Dir.- Support Services)*
Jill Barry *(Admin. Asst.)*

Branch:

Lauerer Markin Gibbs Public Relations Group **(1)**
1725 Indian Wood Circle
Maumee, OH 43537
Tel.: 419-893-2500
Vitamite
Anne Roman *(Sr. Pub. Rels. Counsel)*

THE HOMER LAUGHLIN CHINA COMPANY
Harrison St.
Newell, WV 26050
Tel.: 304-387-1300
Tel.: 800-452-4462
Year Founded: 1871
Approx.Sls.: $25,000,000
Emp.: 800
Fiscal Year-end: 12/31/90
Export
Mfr. of Vitreous China
S.I.C.: 3262
Marcus Aaron II *(Pres.)*
J.M. Wells III *(Exec. V.P. & Gen. Mgr.)*
Jon Bentley *(V.P.)*
Ray Keefer *(Sls. Mgr.)*
O. Sirianni *(Pur. Agent)*

Computer Systems/Hardware:
AS 400

LAUNEY, HACHMANN & HARRIS, INC.
866 3rd Ave.
New York, NY 10022
Tel.: 212-605-4700
Fax: 212-605-4810
Year Founded: 1965
Approx.Billings: $15,089,900
Emp.: 12
Textiles, Apparel & Home Furnishings, Trademark Protection, Particpation Sports
Robert E. Launey *(Pres.)*
Marc Rutman *(V.P., Pub. Rels.)*

LAVELLE AIRCRAFT COMPANY
275 Geiger Rd.
Philadelphia, PA 19115
Tel.: 215-673-7700 **PA**
Fax: 215-673-8964
Year Founded: 1940
Approx.Sls.: $13,000,000
Emp.: 160
Fiscal Year-end: 12/31/89
Sheet Metal Weldments & Assemblies For Space Vehicles, Missiles, Jet Engines, Air Frames & Electronic Systems
S.I.C.: 3724; 3764
Paul DiJulius *(Chm. Bd.)*
John Thach *(Pres.)*
Carmine J. DeLiberato *(Dir.-Mktg. & Sls.)*
Timothy Hedgepath *(Dir.-Fin.)*
Joseph Spitz *(Dir.-Engrng. & Mfg.)*
Anita Meinzer *(Mgr.-Human Resources)*
Principal(s):
Paul DiJulius

No. of Mfg. Plants/Facilities: 1
No. of U.S. Offices: 1

Computer Systems/Hardware:
Hewlett Packard 3000

Outside Service Firm(s):

Morris J. Cohen & Co.*(Auditors)*
Philadelphia, PA

Bank, Minehart & DeAngelo*(Legal Firm)*
Philadelphia, PA

Continental Bank, N.A.*(Major Banking Relationship)*
1500 Market St.
Philadelphia, PA 19102
Tel.: 215-564-7475

LAVELLE INDUSTRIES INC.
665 McHenry St.
Burlington, WI 53105
Tel.: 414-763-2434 **WI**
Fax: 414-763-5607
Year Founded: 1912
Sales Range: $10-19 Million
Emp.: 150
Export
Korky Flapper Tank Balls for Toilet Tanks
S.I.C.: 3069
Rhonda L. Sullivan *(Pres.)*
Tracy Roberts *(V.P.-Fin.)*
Paul J. Sullivan *(V.P.-Sls. & Mktg.)*
Dana McSweeney *(Mgr.-Adv.)*

No. of Mfg. Plants/Facilities: 1
No. of U.S. Offices: 2

Computer Systems/Hardware:
NCR/ADDS 6000

Outside Service Firm(s):

Price Waterhouse*(Auditors)*
200 E. Randolph
Chicago, IL 60601
Tel.: 312-565-1500

Employer's Health Insurance*(Group Insurer)*
Green Bay, WI

Freeborn & Peters*(Legal Firm)*
11 S. LaSalle St.
Chicago, IL 60603
Tel.: 312-750-9500

LaSalle National Bank*(Major Banking Relationship)*
135 S. LaSalle St., Rm.260
Chicago, IL 60603

LAVERDIERE'S ENTERPRISES
Benton Ave.
Winslow, ME 04901
Mailing Address:
P.O. Box 1014
Waterville, ME 04903
Tel.: 207-873-1151 **ME**
Fax: 207-872-2977
Year Founded: 1923
Approx.Sls.: $90,000,000
Emp.: 1,400
Variety Stores; Drug Stores
S.I.C.: 5331; 5912
Stephen Laverdiere *(Pres. & Chief Exec. Officer)*
John McDonald *(Chief Fin. Officer & V.P.)*
Donald Deschane *(Sr. V.P.-Store Opers.)*
Bruce Carrier *(V.P. & Corp. Counsel)*
Robert Marden *(Sec.)*

Outside Service Firm(s):

KPMG Peat Marwick*(Auditors)*
1211 S.W. Fifth Ave.
Portland, OR 97204

Marine National Bank*(Major Banking Relationship)*
Portland, ME

LAVIDGE & ASSOCIATES INC.
Bearden Park Circle
Knoxville, TN 37919
Tel.: 615-584-6121
Fax: 615-584-6756
Year Founded: 1950
Approx.Billings: $10,000,000
Emp.: 20
Arthur W. Lavidge *(Pres. & Treas.)*
Hal Ernest *(Exec. V.P.)*
Lyle Lavidge *(V.P.)*
Joyce McElyea *(V.P. & Office Mgr.)*
Townes Osborn *(V.P.-Pub. Rels.)*

THE LAW COMPANY, INC.
345 Riverview
Wichita, KS 67203
Tel.: 316-268-0200
Fax: 316-268-0210
Year Founded: 1959
Approx.Sls.: $60,000,000
Emp.: 125
Retail Building Contractors
S.I.C.: 1522; 1542
Richard Kerschen *(Chm. Bd., Pres. & Chief Exec. Officer)*
Marc A. Porter *(Chief Fin. Officer, V.P. & Treas.)*
George C. Bolton *(Sr. V.P. & Dir.-Pur. & Sls.)*
Larry L. Will *(Controller)*
Rose Rausch *(Dir.-Personnel)*

Outside Service Firm(s):

Grant Thornton*(Auditors)*
800 Fourth Financial Center
Wichita, KS 67202

Fleeson, Gooing, Coulson & Kitch*(Legal Firm)*
Wichita, KS

Kansas State Bank & Trust Co.*(Major Banking Relationship)*
Wichita, KS
Tel.: 316-266-6600

LAW ENGINEERING, INC.
1000 Abernathy Rd., N.E.
Atlanta, GA 30328
Mailing Address:
P.O. Box 888013
Atlanta, GA 30356
Tel.: 404-396-8000 **GA**
Fax: 404-391-0291
Year Founded: 1946
Emp.: 1,550
Professional Consulting Engineers, Materials & Testing Laboratory
S.I.C.: 8711; 8734; 8748
Walter T. Kiser *(Chm. Bd. & Chief Exec. Officer)*
James I. Dangar *(Pres.)*
Wilbur C. Greer *(Sr. V.P.)*
Thomas C. Hunter *(Sr. V.P.)*
James G. LaBastie *(Sr. V.P.)*
E.W. Lingo *(Sr. V.P.-Engrng.)*
Clay E. Sams *(V.P.)*

Outside Service Firm(s):

Trust Company Bank*(Major Banking Relationship)*
P.O. Box 4655,
Atlanta, GA 30302

Division:

Law Co. Scroop Inc. **(1)**
1000 Abernathy Rd., N.E.
Atlanta, GA 30328
Tel.: 404-396-8000

LAWLER-HAVENS INC.
700 Bond Court Bldg., 1300 E. Ninth St.
Cleveland, OH 44114
Tel.: 216-621-2407 **OH**
Fax: 216-621-4972
Year Founded: 1922
S.I.C.: 8711; 4941; 4953
John P. Lawler, P.E. *(Chm. Bd.)*
Gary M. Siegel, P.E. *(Pres.)*
Lawrence J. Papes, P.E. *(Div. V.P.)*
Michael J. Skelly, P.E. *(Div. V.P.)*
James P. Harris, P.E. *(V.P.-Devel.)*
Peter M. McGroddy, P.E. *(V.P.)*

Divisions:

Havens & Emerson, Inc. **(1)**
700 Bond Court Bldg., 1300 E. Ninth St.
Cleveland, OH 44114
Tel.: 216-621-2407
Fax: 216-621-4972
Sales Range: $10-19 Million
Emp.: 210
Environmental Engineering Services Including Water Resources, Wastewater Treatment, Industrial Wastes, Sludge Management, Sewage & Drainage, Hazardous Waste Management, Environmental Planning, Solid Wastes Management, Program Management & Funding & Rates
S.I.C.: 8711; 4941; 4953

Subsidiary:

Anderson-Parrish Associates, Inc. **(2)**
Paragon Crossing Bldg., 11300 4th St., North, Suite 100
St. Petersburg, FL 33716
Tel.: 813-578-2357
Emp.: 25
Architects, Engineers
S.I.C.: 8711; 8712
James P. Harris *(Pres.)*

Lawler, Matusky & Skelly Engineers **(1)**
One Blue Hill Plaza
Pearl River, NY 10965
Tel.: 914-735-8300
Fax: 914-735-7466
Sales Range: $10-19 Million
Emp.: 160
Environmental Science & Engineering Services
S.I.C.: 8711

JACK LAWLOR ADVERTISING, INC.
777 Walnut St.
Pasadena, CA 91101
Tel.: 818-449-0021
Year Founded: 1955
Approx.Billings: $21,190,000
Emp.: 16
Consumer Products
Dean F. Dudley *(Co-Chm.)*
Eldon W. Gottschalk *(Co-Chm., Sec. & Treas.)*
Dennis Haig *(Radio & TV Production Dir.)*

LAWNWARE PRODUCTS, INC.
8220 N. Austin
Morton Grove, IL 60053
Tel.: 708-966-3400 **IL**
Fax: 708-966-8421
Approx.Sls.: $19,000,000
Emp.: 200
Mfr. of Garden, Patio, Walkway & Yard Electric Lighting Fixtures; Plastic Flower Pots; Garden Furniture
S.I.C.: 3645; 3089; 2519
Leo P. Niemiec *(Pres. & Chief Exec. Officer)*
Jeffery L. Niemiec *(V.P.)*

Outside Service Firm(s):

Robert Callero*(Auditors)*
Morton Grove, IL

Glenview State Bank*(Major Banking Relationship)*
Glenview, IL

THE F. D. LAWRENCE ELECTRIC CO.
3450 Beekman St.
Cincinnati, OH 45223
Tel.: 513-542-1100 **OH**
Fax: 513-542-2422
Year Founded: 1904
Sales Range: $40-59 Million
Emp.: 90
Fiscal Year-end: 12/31/91
Wholesale Distributor of Electrical Supplies & Equipment
S.I.C.: 5063
Dennis P. O'Leary *(Chm. Bd. & Pres.)*
Alan M. Faulhaber *(Exec. V.P.)*
Richard G. Krueger *(V.P.)*
Gerald T. Menke *(Treas. & Sec.)*
Gregory A. Kelly *(Pur. Agent)*
Patrick Retherford *(Mgr.-Data Processing)*

Principal(s):

No. of Mfg. Plants/Facilities: 4
No. of U.S. Offices: 3

Computer Systems/Hardware:
IBM AS/400

Outside Service Firm(s):

Louis F. Schott & Co.*(Auditors)*
Cincinnati, OH

Blue Cross & Blue Shield in Southwest Ohio*(Group Insurer)*
Cincinnati, OH

Graydon, Head & Ritchey*(Legal Firm)*
1900 Fifth Third Center
Cincinnati, OH 45202
Tel.: 513-621-6464

Fifth Third Bank*(Major Banking Relationship)*
Corporate Trust Services, 38 Fountain Square Plaza
Cincinnati, OH 45263

Fifth Third Bank*(Pension Manager)*
Corporate Trust Services, 38 Fountain Square Plaza
Cincinnati, OH 45263

LAWRENCE GROUP, INC.
108 Union St.
Schenectady, NY 12305-1788
Tel.: 518-370-1720
Tel.: 800-456-1720
Fax: 518-370-4426
Emp.: 1,008
Holding Company
S.I.C.: 6719
Albert W. Lawrence *(Chm.)*
Lawrence A. Shore *(Pres.)*
David C. Lawrence *(V.P.)*
Elizabeth A. Lawrence *(V.P.)*
Janet H. Lawrence *(V.P.)*
Albert W. Lawrence *(Treas.)*
Barbara C. Lawrence *(Sec.)*
Wolfgang J. Reimer, Esq. *(Asst. Sec.)*

Subsidiaries:

Lawrence Agency Corporation **(1)**
108 Union St.
Schnectady, NY 12305-1788
Tel.: 518-370-1720
Tel.: 800-456-1720 (100%)
Fax: 518-370-4426
Emp.: 612
Insurance Brokers
S.I.C.: 6411
Albert W. Lawrence *(Chm.)*
William J. Mather *(Pres. & Chief Exec. Officer)*
Susan Gager *(Controller)*
Joyce Morris *(V.P.-MIS)*

Subsidiaries:

Adapt, Inc. **(2)**
Hartford Plaza
Hartford, CT 06105
Tel.: 203-547-4855
Emp.: 75
Insurance Agents, Brokers & Service
S.I.C.: 6411

Subsidiaries:

Lundberg and Associates **(3)**
265 W. Bullard, Ste. 101
Fresno, CA 93704-1706
Tel.: 209-432-1800
Fax: 209-436-2500
Emp.: 35
Insurance Agents, Brokers & Service
S.I.C.: 6411
Brian Gorham *(Pres.)*

Robson, Cavignac & Associates **(3)**
1230 Columbia St., Ste. 400
San Diego, CA 92101-3528
Tel.: 619-235-6301
Fax: 619-233-0340
Emp.: 35
Insurance Agents, Brokers & Service
S.I.C.: 6411
John C. Harper *(Dir.)*
James Reynolds *(Dir.)*
Richard Thompson *(Dir.)*

A.W. Lawrence & Company, Inc. **(2)**
108 Union St.
Schenectady, NY 12305-1788
Tel.: 518-370-1720
Fax: 518-370-4426
Insurance Agents, Brokers & Services
S.I.C.: 6411
Gary L. Keehfus *(Pres.)*
Thomas M. Hali *(V.P.)*
Gerald Lumley *(V.P.)*
Horace VanVoast, III *(V.P.)*
Helen A. Whimple *(V.P.)*

Lawrence Healthcare Administrative Services **(2)**
3000 Troy-Schenectady Rd.
Schenectady, NY 12309-1614
Tel.: 518-783-1801
Tel.: 800-833-3650
Fax: 518-785-3017
Employee Benefits Administrator for Insured & Self-Insured Plans
S.I.C.: 6411

Lawrence United Corp. **(2)**
1222 Troy-Schnectady Rd.
Schenectady, NY 12309-1719
Tel.: 518-785-3284
Insurance Brokerage
S.I.C.: 6411
William J. Mather *(Pres.)*
Douglas E. Cotterill *(V.P.)*
Robert P.B. Kidd *(V.P.)*
Robert W. Melsom *(V.P.)*

Lawrence General Corporation **(1)**
108 Union St.
Schnectady, NY 12305-1788
Tel.: 518-370-1720
Tel.: 800-456-1720
Fax: 518-370-4426
Non-insurance Operations Providing Support to Lawrence Group, Inc.
Kenneth McPartlin *(Pres.)*

Subsidiaries:

Fitts-Lawrence, Inc. **(2)**
106 Erie Blvd.
Schnectady, NY 12305-2203
Tel.: 518-370-4457
Fax: 518-370-0305
Communications Arts Company; Advertising, Printing, Graphics, Mailing Services
S.I.C.: 7311; 2759; 7331
Joseph M. McGinnis *(Pres.)*
Mary E. Siegel *(V.P.)*

Logic World, Inc. **(2)**
2716 Albany St.
Schenectady, NY 12304-1891
Tel.: 518-370-2624
Fax: 518-393-3651
Administrative Support, Data Entry Services & Personal Computer Support Services
S.I.C.: 7374
Kenneth McPartlin *(Pres.)*
Joyce E. Morris *(Gen. Mgr.)*

Lawrence Insurance Group, Inc. **(1)**
500 5th Ave.
New York, NY 10110-0002
Tel.: 212-944-8242
Tel.: 800-241-0888 (100%)
Fax: 212-944-8328
Assets: $254,023,000
Earnings: $7,200
Liabilities: $188,219,088
Net Worth: $65,803,912
Approx.Sls.: $118,324,000
Emp.: 246
Fiscal Year-end: 12/31/91
Computer Systems/Hardware:
AS/400
Underwriting Company: Property/Casualty; Accident/Health Insurance and Assumes Reinsurance from Other Insurers.
S.I.C.: 6719; 6331; 6321
Corporate Giving Program: All Requests are Reviewed by a Contributions Committee
Albert W. Lawrence *(Chm. Bd.)*
F. Herbert Brantlinger *(Pres. & Chief Exec. Officer)*
Benjamin Rosenberg *(V.P. & Gen. Counsel)*
Barbara Dunbar *(V.P.-Training)*
Carmel T. Roberson *(V.P.-Employee Relations)*
Barbara C. Lawrence *(Sec.)*
Lawrence A. Shore *(Treas.)*
Gail A. Reynolds *(Mgr.-Investor & Public Relations)*

Subsidiaries:

United Community Insurance Co. **(2)**
33 Elk Street
Albany, NY 12207-2199
Tel.: 518-465-0457 (100%)
Approx.Sls.: $78,556,000
Emp.: 190
Fiscal Year-end: 12/31/91
Personal & Commercial Lines Property & Casualty Insurance
S.I.C.: 6331
Albert W. Lawrence *(Chm.)*
Edward V. Kovalefsky *(V.P. & Chm.)*
F. Herbert Brantlinger *(Pres. & Chief Exec. Officer)*
Benjamin Rosenberg, Esq. *(Exec. V.P., Gen. Counsel & Asst. Sec.)*
John A. Culley *(V.P.-Claims)*
Rita Harfield *(V.P.-Speciality Underwriting)*
Janet H. Lawrence *(V.P.-Product Devel.)*
John R. Tomassi *(V.P.-Underwriting)*
Barbara C. Lawrence *(Sec.)*
Lawrence A. Shore *(Treas.)*

United Republic Reinsurance Company **(2)**
5718 Westheimer, Ste. 1310
Houston, TX 77057-5732
Tel.: 713-975-6810 (100%)
Approx.Sls.: $34,092,000
Emp.: 14
Fiscal Year-end: 12/31/91
Property & Casualty Reinsurance
S.I.C.: 6331
Lawrence A. Shore *(Pres. & Chief Exec. Officer)*
Benjamin Rosenberg, Esq. *(V.P. & Gen. Counsel)*
Kevin L. Preston *(Treas.)*

Subsidiaries:

Global Insurance Company **(3)**
5718 Westheimer, Ste. 1310
Houston, TX 77057-5732
Tel.: 713-975-6810
Fax: 713-975-7421
Property/Casualty Underwriter
William J. Mather *(Pres.)*
Gary L. Keehfus *(Exec. V.P.)*
Benjamin Rosenberg, Esq. *(V.P. & Gen. Counsel)*
Lowry D. Vaughn *(V.P.)*
Peter A. Ramaglia *(Controller)*
Bruce S. Wise *(Sec. & Treas.)*
Norma R. Bailey *(Asst. Sec.)*
F. Herbert Brantlinger *(Asst. Treas.)*
Edward W. Kovalefsky *(Asst. Treas.)*

Senate Insurance Company **(3)**
108 Union St.
Schenectady, NY 12305-1788
Tel.: 518-370-1720
Tel.: 800-456-1720 (100%)
Fax: 518-370-4426
Approx.Sls.: $5,724,000
Fiscal Year-end: 12/31/91
Accident & Health Insurance
S.I.C.: 6321
William Mather *(Pres.)*

Subsidiary:

Commercial Resource Insurance Co. **(4)**
234 N. Central Ave.
Phoenix, AZ 85004
Tel.: 602-464-1784
Assumed Reinsurance: Credit Life
S.I.C.: 6411
William Mather *(Pres.)*

Lawrence Management Group, Inc. **(1)**
33 Elk St.
Albany, NY 12207-2199
Tel.: 518-465-0457
Tel.: 800-833-0059
Fax: 518-465-1773
Albert W. Lawrence *(Chm.)*
Lawrence A. Shore *(Pres.)*
Wayne Diesel *(Chief Fin. Officer)*
Barbara B. Dunbar *(V.P.-Training)*
Gary G. Fryer *(V.P.)*
Carmel T. Roberson *(V.P.-Employee Rels. & Benefits)*
Gail A. Reynolds *(Mgr.-Pub. Rels., Investor Rels. & Adv.)*
Albert Kilts *(Internal Auditor)*

Lawrence Risk Services Corporation **(1)**
106A Erie Blvd.
Schenectady, NY 12305-2203
Tel.: 518-370-4400
Tel.: 800-283-7475
Fax: 518-370-0305
Loss Control Services
S.I.C.: 6411
Dr. Richard Shands *(Pres.)*

North American Safety Program Administrators **(1)**
1222 Troy Rd.
Schenectady, NY 12309-1719
Tel.: 518-785-3284
Tel.: 800-342-2025
Fax: 518-785-4015
School & Municipal Insurance Services
S.I.C.: 6331
Dr. Richard Shands *(Pres.)*
Henry J. Muller *(Exec. V.P.)*

LAWRENCE METAL PRODUCTS, INC.
260 Spur Dr., S.
Bay Shore, NY 11706
Mailing Address:
P.O. Box 400-M
Bay Shore, NY 11706
Tel.: 516-666-0300
Tel.: 800-441-0019
Fax: 516-666-0336
Year Founded: 1881
Approx.Sls.: $10,000,000
Emp.: 125
Export
Posts, Ropes, Railings, Metal Specialties
S.I.C.: 3446
Steve Lawrence *(Pres.)*
Sam Goldman *(V.P.)*
Lou Rabeno *(Mgr.-Mktg.)*

LAWRENCE PAPER COMPANY
2801 Lakeview Rd.
Lawrence, KS 66044
Mailing Address:
P.O. Box 887
Lawrence, KS 66044
Tel.: 913-843-8111
Approx.Sls.: $22,000,000
Emp.: 300
Fiscal Year-end: 12/31/90
Special Corrugated Boxes & Thermoformed Packaging
S.I.C.: 2653
Alan Hill *(Pres.)*
Mike Sullivan *(V.P.-Sls. & Mgr.-Adv.)*
Justin Hill, Jr. *(Sec. & Treas.)*
Martin Ward *(Pur. Agent)*

LAWRENCE PUMPS, INC.
371 Market St.
Lawrence, MA 01843
Tel.: 508-682-5248
Fax: 508-975-4291
Year Founded: 1935
Approx.Sls.: $19,000,000
Emp.: 145
Export
Mfr. of Centrifugal Pumps For Industrial Applications
S.I.C.: 3561
Victor J. Mill, Jr. *(Chm. Bd.)*
Victor J. Mill, III *(Pres. & Treas.)*

Walde Arndt *(Chief Oper. Officer)*
Judy Ouellette *(Mgr.-Human Resources)*
Craig Owen *(Pur. Agent)*

Outside Service Firm(s):

Shawmut Bank*(Major Banking Relationship)*
Lawrence, MA

LAWRENCE & SCHILLER, INC.
3932 S. Willow Ave.
Sioux Falls, SD 57105
Tel.: 605-338-8000
Fax: 605-338-8892
Year Founded: 1976
Approx.Billings: $10,000,000
Emp.: 40
Agriculture, Medical Services, Fitness Industry (Retail & Mfg.)
Paul Schiller *(Pres.)*
Craig Lawrence *(V.P., Sec. & Treas.)*
Karla Haugan *(Comptroller)*

Computer Systems/Hardware:
IBM, Macintosh

LAWRY'S RESTAURANTS, INC.
2950 Los Feliz Blvd., Ste. 204
Los Angeles, CA 90039
Tel.: 213-660-2720 **CA**
Fax: 213-660-8144
Year Founded: 1937
Sales Range: $20-39 Million
Emp.: 460
Restaurants
S.I.C.: 5812
Richard N. Frank *(Chm. & Chief Exec. Officer)*
Richard R. Frank *(Pres.)*
Arthur Wynne *(Sr. V.P.)*
Ralph Frank, Jr. *(V.P.)*
Lorraine F. Petitfils *(V.P.)*
David E. Stockman *(V.P.-Opers.)*
Anna M. Martorelli *(Treas.)*
Carolyn M. White *(Dir.-Personnel)*
Cece J. Eckert *(Mgr.-Mktg. & Food Standards)*

No. of Mfg. Plants/Facilities: 5

Computer Systems/Hardware:
IBM

Outside Service Firm(s):

PKF*(Auditors)*
Los Angeles, CA

Blue Cross of California*(Group Insurer)*
2101 Western St.
Oakland, CA 94659
Tel.: 800-645-3000

Massachusetts Mutual Life Insurance Co.*(Group Insurer)*
Boston, MA

First Interstate Bank of California, N.A.*(Major Banking Relationship)*
P.O. Box 3667,
Los Angeles, CA 90051
Tel.: 213-614-4000

Subsidiaries:

Five Crowns **(1)**
3801 E. Coast Hwy.
Corona del Mar, CA 92625
Tel.: 714-760-0331
Fax: 714-760-3987
S.I.C.: 5812

Lawry's The Prime Rib **(1)**
100 E. Ontario St.
Chicago, IL 60611
Tel.: 312-787-5000
S.I.C.: 5812

Lawry's The Prime Rib **(1)**
55 N. La Cienega Blvd.
Beverly Hills, CA 90211
Tel.: 310-652-2827
Fax: 310-657-5463
S.I.C.: 5812

Lawry's The Prime Rib **(1)**
3008 Maple Ave.
Dallas, TX 75201
Tel.: 214-521-7777
Fax: 214-880-7427
S.I.C.: 5812

Tam O'Shanter Inn **(1)**
2980 Los Feliz Blvd.
Los Angeles, CA 90039
Tel.: 213-664-0228
S.I.C.: 5812

LAWSON ASSOCIATES INC.
1300 Godward St.
Minneapolis, MN 55413
Tel.: 612-379-2633
Tel.: 800-477-1357 **MN**
Fax: 612-379-7141
Year Founded: 1975
Assets: $13,376,000
Earnings: $341,000
Liabilities: $9,366,000
Net Worth: $4,010,000
Approx.Sls.: $31,300,000
Emp.: 403
Fiscal Year-end: 5/31/91
Export
Integrated Software Distributor
S.I.C.: 7372
H. Richard Lawson *(Chm. Bd.)*
Kenneth Holec *(Pres. & Chief Exec. Officer)*
M. E. Milbrandt *(Chief Oper. Officer)*
Ken Behrendt *(Chief Fin. Officer, V.P.-Fin. & Controller)*
John J. Cerullo *(V.P.-IBM Mid-Range)*
Daniel Metzger *(V.P.-Mktg.)*
M.E. Milbrandt *(V.P.-Software Div.)*
Kathi Potter *(Dir.-Human Resources)*
W.L. Lawson *(Mgr.-Prod. Environmental)*
Sue Weinacht *(Mktg. Coordinator)*

No. of U.S. Offices: 8
No. of Foreign Offices: 1

Computer Systems/Hardware:
Burroughs A3; IBM AS/400; IBM Mainframe;Unisys A Series

Outside Service Firm(s):

Deloitte & Touche*(Auditors)*
900 Pillsbury Ctr.
Minneapolis, MN 55402
Tel.: 612-332-2301
Fax: 612-375-5418

Med Centers Health Plan*(Group Insurer)*
Minneapolis, MN

Physicians Health Plan*(Group Insurer)*
Minneapolis, MN

Popham, Haik, Schnobrich Ltd.*(Legal Firm)*
Minneapolis, MN

Norwest Bank Minnesota, N.A.*(Major Banking Relationship)*
6th St. & Marquette Av.
Minneapolis, MN 55479
Tel.: 612-667-1234

LAWSON MECHANICAL CONTRACTORS
6090 S. Watt Ave.
Sacramento, CA 95829
Mailing Address:
P.O. Box 15224,
Sacramento, CA 95851
Tel.: 916-381-5000
Fax: 916-381-5073
Year Founded: 1947
Approx.Sls.: $22,000,000
Emp.: 200
Plumbing, Heating & Air Conditioning, Mechanical & Industrial Buildings & Warehouses, General Contractors
S.I.C.: 1541; 1711
Rodney Lawson *(Pres., Chief Oper. Officer & Chief Exec. Officer)*
Rodney Barbour *(Chief Fin. Officer & Gen. Counsel)*
Donald Gibbs *(V.P.-Sls. & Mktg.)*
Archie Lawson *(V.P.-Admin.)*
Jack Jensen *(Dir.-Pur.)*
Principal(s):
Rodney Lawson
Archie Lawson

Outside Service Firm(s):

Glentzler & Dunnigan*(Auditors)*
Sacramento, CA

The Bank of California, N.A.*(Major Banking Relationship)*
400 California
San Francisco, CA 94104
Tel.: 415-765-0400

LAY PACKING COMPANY INC.
P.O. Box 2447
Knoxville, TN 37901
Tel.: 615-546-2511 **TN**
Fax: 615-546-2130
Year Founded: 1920
Approx.Sls.: $51,000,000
Emp.: 270
Fiscal Year-end: 12/31/91
Regional Full Line Meat Processor
S.I.C.: 2011
Joe L. Lay, Jr. *(Chm. Bd., Pres. & Chief Exec. Officer)*
Ken Lay *(Chief Oper. Officer & Sec.)*
F. Edwin Lay, Jr. *(Chief Fin. Officer & Treas.)*
Charles W. Hurst *(V.P.-Sls. & Mktg.)*
Ed Tankersley *(V.P.-Personnel)*
Ruble Smith *(Dir.-Engrng.)*
Tom Bragg *(Mgr.-Mngmt. Information Systems)*
Jay Burgin *(Mgr.-Adv.)*

No. of Mfg. Plants/Facilities: 3

Computer Systems/Hardware:
Cado

Outside Service Firm(s):

Cherry, BeKaert & Holland*(Auditors)*
Knoxville, TN

Corroon & Black*(Commercial Insurance Carrier)*
Knoxville, TN

Gentry, Tipton, Kizer & Little*(Legal Firm)*
Knoxville, TN

First Tennessee Bank, N.A.*(Major Banking Relationship)*
Knoxville, TN

First Tennessee Bank, N.A.*(Pension Manager)*
Knoxville, TN

LAYMAN CANDY COMPANY, INC.
1637 E. Main St.
Salem, VA 24153
Mailing Address:
P.O. Box 1015
Salem, VA 24153
Tel.: 703-986-0123
Year Founded: 1948
Approx.Sls.: $24,000,000
Emp.: 35
Fiscal Year-end: 6/30/92
Wholesale Distributor of Tobacco & Tobacco Products & Confectionery
S.I.C.: 5194; 5145
Wm. D. Layman *(Chm. Bd.)*
Juanita L. Neely *(Pres.)*
Glen Bowe *(V.P.)*
Judy Ross *(Sec. & Treas.)*

Outside Service Firm(s):

Salyer, Garber & Co.*(Auditors)*
Richmond, VA

Signet Bank*(Major Banking Relationship)*
7 N. 8th St.
Richmond, VA 23219
Tel.: 804-747-2000

LAZY DAYS R V CENTER, INC.
11028 N. Florida Ave.
Tampa, FL 33612
Tel.: 813-933-7613
Tel.: 800-626-7800 **FL**
Fax: 813-931-7839
Year Founded: 1976
Approx.Sls.: $60,000,000
Emp.: 117
Retail Sales of Motor Homes; Recreational Vehicle Parts & Accessories; Travel Trailers
S.I.C.: 5561
H.K. Wallace *(Pres.)*
Donald W. Wallace *(V.P. & Sec.)*
Chuck Thibault *(Controller)*

Outside Service Firm(s):

Hanna LeMar & Co.*(Auditors)*
Tampa, FL

Barnett Banks Trust Company, N.A.*(Major Banking Relationship)*
Tampa, FL

LEACH CORPORATION
6900 Orangethorpe Ave.
Buena Park, CA 90622-5032
Mailing Address:
P.O. Box 5032,
Buena Park, CA 90622-5032
Tel.: 714-739-0770
Fax: 714-739-1713
Year Founded: 1919
Emp.: 750
Fiscal Year-end: 6/30/91
Export
Mfr. Electronic & Electromechanical Components & Subsystems
S.I.C.: 3679; 3674; 3629
Larry L. Parker *(Pres. & Chief Exec. Officer)*
Evan Clements *(V.P.-Res. & Devel.)*
Robert E. Collins *(V.P. & Chief Fin. Officer)*
Tina Doty *(V.P.-Quality Control)*
Al Firebaugh *(V.P. & Gen. Mgr.)*
Ron Zimmerman *(V.P.-Sls. & Mktg.)*
Jim Owens *(Dir.-Human Rels.)*
Paul Rohr *(Dir.-Field Sls.)*
David Abend *(Mgr.-Mktg. Services)*

LEACH & GARNER COMPANY
57 John L. Dietsch Sq.
North Attleboro, MA 02760
Tel.: 508-695-7800
Tel.: 800-525-1092
Fax: 508-699-5947
Jewelry Findings & Precious Metals
S.I.C.: 3356; 3339; 3341; 3914; 3915
Philip F. Leach *(Chm. Bd.)*
Edwin F. Leach, II *(Pres.)*
Mark R. Buckley *(Chief Fin. Officer)*
P.B. Smith *(Gen. Counsel)*

Outside Service Firm(s):

Ernst & Young*(Auditors)*
One Old Stone Square
Providence, RI 02903
Tel.: 401-331-7000

LEADER FEDERAL BANK FOR SAVINGS
158 Madison Ave.
Memphis, TN 38103
Tel.: 901-578-2000 **TN**
Fax: 901-524-5715
Year Founded: 1928
Emp.: 850

Leader Federal Bank For Savings—(Continued)

Federal Savings Bank; Machinery & Equipment Financial Leasing; Small Business Investment Companies; Subdividers & Developers; Real Estate Appraiser; Operative Builders; Mortgage Brokers, Using Own Money
S.I.C.: 6035; 6159; 6552; 6531; 1531; 6162
Edgar H. Bailey *(Chm. Bd. & Pres.)*
Ronald Stimpson *(Chief Fin. Officer & Exec. V.P.)*
Kirk Bailey *(Exec. V.P.)*
Will E. May *(Exec. V.P.)*
Frederick H. Romine *(Sr. V.P.)*
Steve Shaner *(V.P.)*

Outside Service Firm(s):

KPMG Peat Marwick*(Auditors)*
Memphis, TN
Tel.: 901-725-3131

Subsidiaries:

Leader Leasing, Inc. **(1)**
158 Madison Ave.
Memphis, TN 38103
Tel.: 901-578-2021
Approx.Sls.: $3,000,000
Emp.: 5
Medical Equipment Rental & Leasing; Computer Peripheral Rental & Leasing
S.I.C.: 7359; 7352; 7377
Dan H. Waters *(Pres.)*

Leader Services, Inc. **(1)**
158 Madison Ave.
Memphis, TN 38103
Tel.: 901-578-2000
Emp.: 15
Insurance Company
S.I.C.: 6411
Joe H. Davis, Jr. *(Pres.)*

LEADER INSTRUMENTS CORPORATION
380 Oser Ave.
Hauppauge, NY 11788
Tel.: 516-231-6900
Fax: 516-231-5295
Year Founded: 1969
Approx.Sls.: $13,000,000
Emp.: 38
Fiscal Year-end: 12/31/91
Wholesale Electrical Test Equipment
S.I.C.: 5063
S. Ohmatsu *(Chm. Bd.)*
S. Hirota *(Pres.)*
Reiko Kuroda *(Chief Fin. Officer)*
Robert Sparks *(Dir.-Sls.)*

LEAR SIEGLER DIVERSIFIED HOLDINGS CORP.
(A Co. of Forstmann Little & Co.)
220 S. Orange Ave.
Livingston, NJ 07039
Tel.: 201-535-9522 **DE**
Fax: 201-535-9837
Assets: $1,490,317,000
Earnings: $55,510,000
Liabilities: $848,118,000
Net Worth: $642,199,000
Approx.Sls.: $600,000,000
Emp.: 5,000
Holding Company
S.I.C.: 6719
William J. Turner *(Chm. Bd., Pres. & Chief Exec. Officer)*
Henry S. Lager *(V.P.-Human Resources)*
Jim Mattews *(V.P. & Gen. Counsel)*

Computer Systems/Hardware:
IBM PC XT

Outside Service Firm(s):

Price Waterhouse*(Auditors)*
400 S. Hope St.
Los Angeles, CA 90071-2889
Tel.: 213-236-3000

Security Pacific Corporation*(Major Banking Relationship)*
Security Pacific Plaza
Los Angeles, CA 90071
Tel.: 213-345-6211
Fax: 213-625-0809

Divisions:

Lear Siegler Hawaiian Properties Div. **(1)**
Amfac Bldg., 700 Bishop St., Ste. 1112
Honolulu, HI 96813
Tel.: 808-521-8781
Emp.: 14
Development of LSI Property in Hawaii
S.I.C.: 6552
Charles K. Hamane *(Pres.)*

Lear Siegler Telecommunications Div. **(1)**
714 N. Brookhurst
Anaheim, CA 92803
Tel.: 714-774-1010
Emp.: 222
Mfr. of Commercial Telephone Products & Specialized Electronic Equipment & Components
S.I.C.: 3669
Joseph W. Back *(Pres.)*
F. Timothy Trujillo *(Dir.-Personnel)*

Subsidiaries:

Anchorlok Corp. **(1)**
2910 E. Ana
Compton, CA 90221
Tel.: 310-537-6710
Emp.: 360
Mfr. of Parking & Emergency Spring Brakes & Air Dryers for Heavy Duty Trucks & Trailers
S.I.C.: 3714
Gordon L. Gibson *(Pres.)*
Leonard Cowles *(Dir.-Indus. Rels.)*

LSI Truck Products Corp.-Neway/ Anchor Lock **(1)**
1950 Industrial Blvd.
Muskegon, MI 49442
Tel.: 616-773-3271
Fax: 616-766-3893
Approx.Sls.: $100,000,000
Emp.: 400
Fiscal Year-end: 6/30/90
Mfr. of Air & Mechanical Suspension Systems for Medium & Heavy-Duty Trucks
S.I.C.: 3714
Jack Smith *(Pres.)*
Barbara DeBruyn *(Controller)*
John W. Conley *(Dir.-WW Sls. & Services)*
Gary J. Schultz *(Dir.-Mktg.)*
Carl Goeb *(Mgr.-Mktg. Services)*
Kenneth Locascio *(Mgr.-Natl. Sls.)*

Lear Siegler Accurate Corp. **(1)**
4370 Jutland Dr.
San Diego, CA 92117
Tel.: 619-273-1212 (100%)
Emp.: 144
Mfr. of Extruded & Molded Rubber & Plastic Parts
S.I.C.: 3069
Gordon L. Gibson *(Pres.)*

Lear Siegler Measurement Controls Corp. **(1)**
74 Inverness Dr. E.
Englewood, CO 80112
Tel.: 303-792-3300
Emp.: 121
Mfr. & Marketing of Energy Monitoring & Process Control Instruments
S.I.C.: 3823
Homer S. Hoard *(Pres.)*

Lear Siegler Plastics Corp. **(1)**
236 W. Clark St.
Mendon, MI 49072
Tel.: 616-496-2215
Emp.: 334
Mfr. of Plastic Parts for Aerospace & Industrial Markets
S.I.C.: 3089
Richard C. Donovan *(Pres.)*
Dale C. Yost *(Pur. Dir.)*
George R. Barrie *(Personnel Dir.)*

Lear Siegler Seating Corp. **(1)**
21557 Telegraph Rd.
Southfield, MI 48034
Tel.: 313-746-1500
Mfr. & Designers of Automotive Seating
S.I.C.: 3714
R. Rossiter *(Pres.)*
R. Williams *(V.P.-Intl. Mktg.)*

Lear Siegler Seymour Corp. **(1)**
885 N. Chestnut St., P.O. Box 408
Seymour, IN 47274
Tel.: 812-522-5130
Emp.: 248
Mfr. of Bed Frames & Home Laundry Equipment
S.I.C.: 2514
Norman R. Proulx *(Pres. & Chief Exec. Officer)*
Dennis E. Renschler *(Data Processing Dir.)*
John K. Ortlieb *(Personnel Dir.)*

Safelite Autoglass **(1)**
245 N. Waco
Wichita, KS 67201
Tel.: 316-267-4000
Emp.: 1,700
Mfr. of Replacement Glass for Vehicles, Industrial & Architectural Applications
S.I.C.: 1793
Ernest Malbin *(Pres.)*
Dick Krant *(Exec. V.P.)*
Donald E. Hartig *(V.P. & Controller)*
Frank J. Vedock *(V.P.-Information Systems)*
Charles C. Parks *(V.P.-Mfg.)*
Robert L. Courtney *(V.P.-Indus. Rels.)*
Matt Knoblauch *(Mgr.-Adv.)*

Non-U.S. Holdings:

Bangor Punta Overseas, S.A. **(1)**
5 Rue Saint-Ours CH-1205
Geneva, Switzerland
Tel.: (022) 29 98 11 (100%)
Intl. Sales
S.I.C.: 5091
Harold Ehrenstrom *(Pres.)*

Bangor Punta do Brazil Ltda. **(1)**
Sao Paulo, Brazil (99.9%)
Mfr. of Boats
S.I.C.: 3732

Central de Industrias, S.A. **(1)**
Minerva 104-602 Colonia Florida, Deleg. 001030
Mexico, D.F. Mexico
Tel.: 905-524-5012 (40%)
Mfr. of Vehicle Seats & Seat Assemblies; Door Panels, Folding Furniture, Furniture & Bedding Springs
S.I.C.: 2515; 2531
Henry Gerard *(Chm.)*

Certified Div. **(1)**
1000 Martin Grove Rd.
Rexdale, ON M9W 4V9, Canada
Tel.: 416-249-8381
Emp.: 1,000
Mfr. of Replacement Auto & Truck Disc & Drum Brake Linings & Parts
S.I.C.: 3714
James R. Schmelzer *(Pres.)*

Jeanneau Constructions Nautiques S.A. **(1)**
Boite Postal 83 85500
Les Herbiers, France
Tel.: (33.51) 91 06 10 (95%)
Mfr. of Sail, Power, Fishing, Canal & Work Boats; Small Four-Wheel, Two-Seat Vehicle for Local Transportation
S.I.C.: 3732
Harold N. Ehrenstrom *(Pres.)*

Lear Siegler Industries Ltd., Gen. Seating Div. **(1)**
530 Manitou Dr. P.O. Box 758,
Kitchener, ON N2G 4C2, Canada
Tel.: 519-893-6500 (100%)
Emp.: 1,000
Mfr. of Automotive Seating & Stampings; Automotive Furniture
S.I.C.: 2531
William R. Douglas *(V.P. Canadian Opers.)*

Mariner Constructors Nauticas, S.A. **(1)**
Porto Alegre, Brazil (100%)
Mfr. of Sailboats; Foreign Holding of Bangor Punto Corp.
S.I.C.: 3732

Steinheil-Lear Siegler AG **(1)**
Osterfeldstrasse 82 8045
Ismaning, Germany
Tel.: 089 96970 (100%)
Emp.: 500
Mfr. of Precision Optics, Gyros, Stabilization & Servo Systems, CRT Trace Recording Cameras, Pumps & Actuators
S.I.C.: 3829; 3812

LEATHER CENTER, INC.
2724 Realty Rd.
Carrollton, TX 75006
Tel.: 214-418-0073 **DE**
Fax: 214-416-3022
Year Founded: 1982
Approx.Sls.: $54,000,000
Emp.: 426
Fiscal Year-end: 2/28/91
Mfr. & Retail Leather Furniture
S.I.C.: 2512; 2519
Kent Bouldin *(Pres.)*
George Borck *(Exec. V.P.-Mktg.)*
Juan Leon *(Exec. V.P.-Mfg.)*
Fernando Sanchez *(Exec. V.P.-Fin. & Admin.)*
Tim Merritt *(V.P.-Adv.)*
Dennis Dorsey *(Controller)*

Principal(s):
Kent Bouldin
George Borck
Juan Leon
Fernando Sanchez

No. of Mfg. Plants/Facilities: 1
No. of U.S. Offices: 27

Computer Systems/Hardware:
IBM AS400

Outside Service Firm(s):

Arthur Andersen & Co.*(Auditors)*
901 Main St., Ste. 5600
Dallas, TX 75202
Tel.: 214-741-8300

LEATHER WAREHOUSE, INC.
33 Rte. 17th S.
East Rutherford, NJ 07073
Tel.: 201-933-5153
Fax: 201-933-5152
Approx.Sls.: $10,000,000
Emp.: 100
Manufacturer & Importer of Sheepskin, Leather & Suede Coats & Accessories
S.I.C.: 2386
Alvin Margulies *(Pres.)*
Joan Margulies *(Sec.)*

Outside Service Firm(s):

Goldstein, Golub, Kessler & Co.*(Auditors)*
New York, NY

National Westminster Bank plc*(Major Banking Relationship)*
Astor Plaza, 1515 Broadway
New York, NY 10036

LEATHERS BEST
(Formerly L B International, Inc.)
30 Hub Dr.
Melville, NY 11747
Tel.: 516-420-8844
Fax: 516-420-8986
Emp.: 75
Leather Importer
S.I.C.: 3111
David Finkelstein *(Pres.)*
Marshall Lelchuk *(Exec. V.P.)*

Outside Service Firm(s):

David L. Lieb & Company*(Auditors)*
New York, NY

Chase Manhattan Bank, N.A.*(Major Banking Relationship)*
One Chase Manhattan Plaza
New York, NY 10081
Tel.: 212-552-2222
Tel.: 800-526-0801
Fax: 212-552-7175

THE LEAVELL COMPANY
4401 N. Mesa, Ste. 200
El Paso, TX 79902
Tel.: 915-533-9511
Assets: $13,366,000
Earnings: $2,897,000
Net Worth: $13,366,000
Approx.Sls.: $5,820,000
Emp.: 16
Fiscal Year-end: 3/31/87
Real Estate Devel. & Mngmt.; Oil, Gas & Other Investments
S.I.C.: 6552; 6519; 6799; 6792
Charles H. Leavell *(Chm. Bd.)*
C. J. Roberts, Jr. *(Pres., Chief Oper. Officer & Treas.)*
Harry W. Buckley *(V.P.)*
William H. Scott *(V.P., Sec. & Controller)*

Outside Service Firm(s):

L. Edward Wheeler*(Auditors)*
El Paso, TX

Cowen & Co.*(Investment Banker)*
Houston, TX

Goldman, Sachs & Co.*(Investment Banker)*
Dallas, TX

Morgan Stanley & Co.*(Investment Banker)*
555 California St.
San Francisco, CA 94104

Kemp, Smith, Duncan & Hammond*(Legal Firm)*
2000 MBank Plaza
El Paso, TX 79901
Tel.: 915-533-4424

MBank El Paso*(Major Banking Relationship)*
El Paso, TX

Subsidiary:

Leavell Mineral Resources, Inc. **(1)**
4401 No. Mesa, Ste. 200
El Paso, TX 79902
Tel.: 915-533-9511 (100%)

LEBANON CHEMICAL CORP.
1600 E. Cumberland St.
Lebanon, PA 17042
Mailing Address:
P.O. Box 180
Lebanon, PA 17042
Tel.: 717-273-1685
Fax: 717-273-9466
Approx.Sls.: $90,000,000
Emp.: 350
Fiscal Year-end: 10/27/92
Mfr. Agricul. Chemicals & Fertilizer
S.I.C.: 2873; 2874; 2875; 2879
Vernon Bishop *(Chm. Bd., Pres. & Chief Exec. Officer)*
Kendall Tomlinson *(Sr. V.P. & Chief Oper. Officer)*
Katherine Bishop *(V.P.)*
Frank Fischer *(Dir.-Data Processing)*
Amelia Eisenhower *(Mgr.-Adv.)*
Principal(s):
Vernon Bishop

Computer Systems/Hardware:
IBM System 38

Outside Service Firm(s):

KPMG Peat Marwick*(Auditors)*
P.O. Box 1190, 225 Market St., Ste. 300
Harrisburg, PA 17108-1190
Tel.: 717-238-7131

Pennsylvania Blue Shield*(Group Insurer)*
Camp Hill, PA

McNee's, Wallace, & Nurick*(Legal Firm)*
100 Pine St.
Harrisburg, PA 17108-1166

CoreStates First Pennsylvania Bank, N.A.*(Major Banking Relationship)*
Center Sq. West Tower, 15th & Market Streets
Philadelphia, PA 19101

CoreStates First Pennsylvania Bank, N.A.*(Pension Manager)*
Philadelphia, PA

Subsidiaries:

Greenview Garden Supply **(1)**
Rte. 422 East
Lebanon, PA 17042
Tel.: 717-273-8103

Lebanon Total Turf Care **(1)**
Rte. 422 East
Lebanon, PA 17042
Tel.: 717-273-1685
Paul G. Mengle *(Gen. Mgr.)*

LEBHAR-FRIEDMAN, INC.
425 Park Ave.
New York, NY 10022
Tel.: 212-756-5000
Tel.: 800-756-5000
Fax: 212-838-9487
Year Founded: 1925
Approx.Sls.: $65,000,000
Emp.: 350
Fiscal Year-end: 12/31/91
Publishers of Magazines, Newspapers & Books; Drug Store News, Apparel Merchandising, Discount Store News, Nation's Restaurant News, National Home Center News, Chain Store Age Executive, Accounting Today, Business Guides, Inc., Mail & Marketing Resources, Inside Retailing; Food Merchandising, Home Market Trends, Supermarket Meadquarters Quarterly
S.I.C.: 2721; 2711; 7383
J. Roger Friedman *(Pres.)*
Daniel J. Mills *(Chief Fin. Officer & V.P.)*
Harold Estes *(V.P.-Admin.)*
John M. Murro *(V.P.-Human Resources)*
Joel Safer *(Controller)*

Computer Systems/Hardware:
IBM

Outside Service Firm(s):

Deloitte & Touche*(Auditors)*
1 World Trade Center
New York, NY 10048
Tel.: 212-669-5000

Manufacturers Hanover Trust Co.*(Major Banking Relationship)*
4 New York Plaza
New York, NY 10015
Tel.: 212-623-3165

Subsidiary:

Business Guides Inc. **(1)**
3922 Coconut Palm Dr.
Tampa, FL 33619
Tel.: 813-664-6700
Publishing
S.I.C.: 2721
John O'Brien *(Publisher)*

G. LEBLANC CORPORATION
7001 Leblanc Blvd.
Kenosha, WI 53141-1415
Tel.: 414-658-1644
Tel.: 800-558-9421
Telex: 264443
Fax: 414-658-2824
Year Founded: 1946
Approx.Sls.: $25,000,000
Emp.: 400
Import Export
Mfr. & Marketing of Musical Instruments
S.I.C.: 5736; 3931; 3161; 5099
Vito Pascucci *(Chm. Bd.)*
Leon Pascucci *(Pres.)*
John Musselman *(Exec. V.P.)*
Ron Griggs *(V.P.-Sls.)*
Joe Kunzman *(V.P. & Treas.)*
Sally Jewell *(Dir.-Quality Control)*
Mike Johnson *(Dir.-Communications)*
Celeste Akright *(Mgr.-Personnel)*
John Hauter *(Mgr.-Adv.)*
Charlotte Kelps *(Mgr.-Pur.)*
Joe Shore *(Mgr.-Data Processing)*

Computer Systems/Hardware:
IBM System 38

Subsidiaries:

Frank Holton Co. **(1)**
320 N. Church St.
Elkhorn, WI 53121
Tel.: 414-723-2220
Mfr. of Musical Instruments
S.I.C.: 3931
Vito Pascucci *(Pres.)*
Paul Revord *(V.P.)*

Leblanc Case Co. **(1)**
320 1/2 N. Church St.
Elkhorn, WI 53121
Tel.: 414-723-4234
Mfr. of Musical Instrument Accessories
S.I.C.: 3931
Ralph Zumpano, Jr. *(Mgr.)*

Martin Band Instrument Co. **(1)**
9002 Sheridan Rd
Kenosha, WI 53140
Tel.: 414-694-8000
Mfr. of Musical Instruments
S.I.C.: 3931
Angelo Battellini *(Mgr.)*
Ralph Zumpano, Sr. *(V.P.)*

Non-U.S. Holding:

G. Leblanc **(1)**
403 Rue de Pyrenees
Paris, 75020, France
Mfr. of Musical Instruments
S.I.C.: 3931; 3161; 5099

LECHMERE, INC.
275 Wildwood St.
Woburn, MA 01801
Tel.: 617-935-8320 **MA**
Fax: 617-935-2980
Year Founded: 1945
Approx.Sls.: $672,000,000
Emp.: 4,500
Fiscal Year-end: 1/31/92
Discount & Hard Goods Store
S.I.C.: 5311; 5722
Corporate Giving Program:
Contributions to Programs Dealing with Substance Abuse Prevention & Professional Arts for Youth; Limited to Lechmere Communities Only
J. Kent Flummerfelt *(Pres., Chief Exec. Officer & Chm.)*
James M. Tomaszewski *(Exec. V.P.-Retail Opers.)*
Howard L. Benidt *(Sr. V.P.-Adv. & Sls. Promo.)*
Paul H. Chaddock *(Sr. V.P.-Human Resources)*
Mike London *(Sr. V.P. & Gen. Mktg. Mgr.)*
Robert Trabucco *(Sr. V.P., Chief Fin. Officer, & Treas.)*
Elaine Ricci *(Dir.-External Rels.)*

LEDONNE, WILNER & WEINER, INC.
1500 Broadway, Ste. 902
New York, NY 10036
Tel.: 212-764-5200
Fax: 212-764-7064
Year Founded: 1991
Approx.Billings: $10,000,000
Emp.: 15
Theatrical Advertising & Entertainment
S.I.C.: 7311
Peter LeDonne *(Pres.)*
Jon Wilner *(Exec. V.P.)*
Jim Weiner *(Exec. V.P.)*
Frank Verlizzo *(Sr. V.P., Art Dir.)*
Dante Mele *(V.P.)*
Scott Wolson *(V.P.)*

LEE COMPANY
2 Pettipaug Rd.
Westbrook, CT 06498
Mailing Address:
P.O. Box 424
Westbrook, CT 06498
Tel.: 203-399-6281
Fax: 203-399-7058
Year Founded: 1949
Approx.Sls.: $44,000,000
Emp.: 545
Fiscal Year-end: 10/31/91
Export
Mfr. of Miniature Hydraulic Inserts & Electro-Fluidic Systems
S.I.C.: 3728; 3724
Leighton Lee II *(Chm. Bd.)*
Leighton Lee III *(Pres.)*
Eugene Lohrs *(Exec. V.P.)*
Nathan Beale *(V.P.-Mfg.)*
J.A. Stamos *(V.P.-Sls.)*
Howard G. Tuttle *(Treas.)*
William G. Crocker *(Mgr.-Pur.)*
John Kingsbury *(Mgr.-Adv.)*

Computer Systems/Hardware:
IBM PC/MAC

Outside Service Firm(s):

Coopers & Lybrand*(Auditors)*
280 Trumbull St.
Hartford, CT 06103

Connecticut Bank & Trust*(Major Banking Relationship)*
One Constitution Plaza,
Hartford, CT 06115

Non-U.S. Holdings:

Lee Hydraulische Miniaturkomponenten **(1)**
Rebstocker Str. 33-39 6000
Frankfurt/Main, 19, Germany
Tel.: 01149695076111
Mfr. of Airplane Parts
S.I.C.: 3728; 3724

Lee Products Ltd. **(1)**
Chalfont St. Peter Gerrard's,
Cross, Buckinghamshire SL9 9SU, United Kingdom
Tel.: 0753 886664
Mfr. of Airplane Parts
S.I.C.: 3728; 3724

LEE GROCERY COMPANY
3200-3220 Hewitt Ave.
Everett, WA 98206
Mailing Address:
P.O. Box 630,
Everett, WA 98206
Tel.: 206-259-2145
Fax: 206-259-1766
Year Founded: 1900
Approx.Sls.: $63,000,000
Emp.: 64
Wholesale Tobacco Products, Groceries & Frozen Foods
S.I.C.: 5141; 5142; 5194
William Lee *(Pres.)*
Leslie Lee *(V.P.)*
Donald Miller *(Treas. & Sec.)*
Ron Verhage *(Controller)*
Gary Anderson *(Gen. Mgr.)*
Robert Greer *(Mgr.-Sls. & Mdsg.)*
Andrew Springer *(Mgr.-Intl.)*
Wes Huffman *(Pur. Agent)*
Principal(s):
Lee Family

Outside Service Firm(s):

Hanson, McLaughlin & Onstad*(Auditors)*
Edmonds, WA

U.S. Bank of Washington*(Major Banking Relationship)*
Everett, WA

LEE-MOORE OIL CO., INC.
1807 Douglas Dr.
Sanford, NC 27331
Mailing Address:
P.O. Drawer 9
Sanford, NC 27331
Tel.: 919-775-2301 **NC**
Fax: 919-774-6463
Year Founded: 1937
Assets: $19,804,412
Liabilities: $8,394,239
Net Worth: $11,410,173
Approx.Sls.: $40,000,000
Emp.: 20
Wholesale Gasoline & Diesel Fuels
S.I.C.: 5172
Truby G. Proctor, Jr. *(Chm. Bd.)*
Kirk J. Bradley *(Pres.)*
Pattie L. Gaster *(V.P.-Fin. & Treas.)*
Barbara T. Maddox *(Sec.)*

Outside Service Firm(s):

Deloitte & Touche*(Auditors)*
Lenoir, NC

Dixon, Odom & Co.*(Auditors)*
Sanford, NC

Branch Banking & Trust Co.*(Major Banking Relationship)*
Sanford, NC

LEE MYLES ASSOCIATES CORPORATION
25 E. Spring Valley Ave.
Maywood, NJ 07607
Tel.: 201-843-3200
Fax: 201-843-7706
Year Founded: 1947
Approx.Sls.: $35,000,000
Emp.: 18
Fiscal Year-end: 12/31/90
Franchising; Lee Myles Transmissions
S.I.C.: 6794; 7537
Sally A. Guido *(Pres.)*
Roy Biagi *(V.P.)*
Silvio Sartori *(Treas.)*
Craig Ells *(Gen. Counsel)*
Theodore Ells *(Corp. Sec.)*

Computer Systems/Hardware:
IBM 360

LEE NATIONAL CORPORATION
645 Fifth Ave., 8th Fl.
New York, NY 10022
Tel.: 212-848-9800 **NY**
Fax: 212-355-5056
Year Founded: 1978
Approx.Sls.: $100,000,000
Emp.: 130
Real Estate, Financial & Investment Services
S.I.C.: 6552; 6799
Alvin Dworman *(Chm. Bd. & Pres.)*
Mark Krugman *(Chief Fin. Officer, V.P. & Treas.)*
Shepard Forest *(V.P.)*
Martin Kimelman *(V.P. & Sec.)*
Russell F. Blake, Jr. *(Controller)*

Outside Service Firm(s):

Ernst & Young*(Auditors)*
787 Seventh Ave.
New York, NY 10019
Tel.: 212-773-1243

Chemical Bank*(Major Banking Relationship)*
450 W. 33rd St., 15th Fl.
New York, NY 10001
Tel.: 212-613-7202
Tel.: 800-647-4273

LEE & RILEY, INC.
1221 Nicollet Mall
Minneapolis, MN 55403
Tel.: 612-332-5242
Fax: 612-647-0322
Year Founded: 1984
Approx.Billings: $10,000,000
Emp.: 20
Micromarketing, Intl. Communications
Richard A. Lee *(Pres.)*
Ricardo Vahejos *(Dir., Intl. Communications)*

LEEWARDS CREATIVE CRAFTS, INC.
1200 St. Charles St.
Elgin, IL 60120
Tel.: 708-888-5800 **DE**
Fax: 708-888-5719
Year Founded: 1945
Earnings: $27,000
Approx.Sls.: $160,000,000
Emp.: 2300
Fiscal Year-end: 1/31/91
Import
Retail Yarn, Needlework, Art Crafts, Home Decor
S.I.C.: 5949; 5945; 5719
Corporate Giving Program: United Way
John A. Popple *(Chm. Bd., Pres. & Chief Exec. Officer)*
David E. Bolen *(Chief Oper. Officer)*
Robert Evans *(V.P.-Mngmt. Information Systems)*
Gail Frauenhoffer *(V.P.-Human Resources)*
Chris Holland *(V.P. & Controller)*
Kimberly Lee *(V.P. & Mgr.-Mdse. Div.)*
Barry Schwaab *(V.P.-Real Estate)*
Martin L. Kresge *(Dir.-Adv. & Sls. Promo.)*
Maureen McStay *(Pur. Agent)*
Principal(s):
John A. Popple
David E. Bolen

Outside Service Firm(s):

Deloitte & Touche*(Auditors)*
Two Prudential Plaza, 180 N. Stetson
Chicago, IL 60601
Tel.: 312-946-2039

Prudential-Bache*(Investment Banker)*
9 West 57th St.
New York, NY 10019
Tel.: 212-415-5800
Fax: 212-415-5885

First National Bank of Elgin*(Major Banking Relationship)*
Elgin, IL

CARLOS R. LEFFLER INC.
225 E. Main St.
Richland, PA 17087
Mailing Address:
P.O. Box 278
Richland, PA 17087
Tel.: 717-866-2105
Fax: 717-866-7291
Year Founded: 1941
Approx.Sls.: $440,000,000
Emp.: 300
Wholesale Petroleum Products, Tires & Tubes; Retail Fuel
S.I.C.: 5171; 5014; 5983
Carlos R. Leffler *(Pres.)*
Robert Blecker *(Exec. V.P.)*
John Byler *(Exec. V.P. & Sec.)*
Patrick Castagna *(Exec. V.P.)*
Ralph Sheetz *(Sr. V.P.)*
Mike Bollinger *(V.P.-Transportation)*
Glenda Greiner *(V.P.)*
Paul Wheaton *(V.P.-Propane Sls.)*
Timothy Steinrock *(Comptroller)*
Georgiana E. Leffler *(Treas.)*
Principal(s):
Carlos R. Leffler

Computer Systems/Hardware:
Digital

Outside Service Firm(s):

John Good Associates*(Auditors)*
Richland, PA

Hamilton Bank*(Major Banking Relationship)*
Richland, PA

LEFRAK ORGANIZATION INC.
97-77 Queens Blvd.
Rego Park, NY 11374
Tel.: 718-459-9021
Fax: 718-897-0688
Emp.: 12,000
Real Estate Builder & Developer
S.I.C.: 6552
Samuel J. LeFrak *(Chm. Bd.)*
Richard S. LeFrak *(Pres.)*
Edward Cortese *(Sr. V.P.-Mktg. & Pub. Rels.)*
Arthur Klein *(V.P.)*
Gerald Weinstein *(V.P.-Treas.)*
Howard Boris *(Gen. Counsel)*

Computer Systems/Hardware:
NCR Criterion

Outside Service Firm(s):

Lewis Goldberg*(Auditors)*
New York, NY

Chemical Banking Corp.*(Major Banking Relationship)*
277 Park Ave.
New York, NY 10041
Tel.: 212-310-6407
Fax: 212-310-4526

AL PAUL LEFTON CO., INC.
Rohm & Haas Bldg., Independence Mall West
Philadelphia, PA 19106
Tel.: 215-923-9600
Fax: 215-351-4298
Year Founded: 1928
Approx.Billings: $85,000,000
Emp.: 135
Advertising Agency
S.I.C.: 7311
Al Paul Lefton, Jr. *(Pres. & Chief Exec. Officer)*
Raymond Scanlon *(Chief Fin. Officer & V.P.)*
John Evans *(Sr. V.P.)*
Michael Heffner *(Sr. V.P.-Pub. Rels.)*
Erwin Goldberg *(V.P. & Mgr.-Lefton Direct)*
John Orr *(V.P. & Mgr.-Pub. Rels.)*
Maggy Magee *(Dir.-Admin. Services)*
John C. McKinley *(Mgr.-Opers.)*

Computer Systems/Hardware:
IBM Mainframe; IBM Compatible PC's; MacIntosh

Branch:

Al Paul Lefton Co., Inc., Public Relations **(1)**
Rohm and Haas Bldg., Independence Mall West
Philadelphia, PA 19106
Tel.: 215-923-9600
Fax: 215-351-4299
Approx.Billings: $10,800,000
Emp.: 15
Computer Systems/Hardware:
IBM Compatible PC's
Public Relations
S.I.C.: 8743
John Evans *(Sr. V.P.)*
Michael Heffner *(Sr. V.P., Pub. Rel.)*
John Orr *(V.P. & Mgr., Pub. Rel. Dept.)*

A.C. LEGG PACKING COMPANY, INC.
2319 First Ave., N.
Birmingham, AL 35203
Tel.: 205-324-3451 **AL**
Fax: 205-324-5971
Approx.Sls.: $10,000,000
Emp.: 70
Mfr. of Dry Mixes & Seasonings For The Food Industry
S.I.C.: 2099
Kathryn M. Purvis *(Chm. Bd.)*
J.E. Purvis *(Pres. & Treas.)*
Sandra K. Purvis *(Exec. V.P. & Sec.)*

Outside Service Firm(s):

Benefield & Borland*(Auditors)*
Birmingham, AL

GEO. H. LEHLEITNER & CO., INC.
301 Plantation Rd.
Harahan, LA 70123
Mailing Address:
P.O. BOx 23707
New Orleans, LA 70183
Tel.: 504-734-0530
Fax: 504-734-0530 Ext. 162
Sales Range: $40-59 Million
Emp.: 191
Wholesale Appliances, Floor Coverings
S.I.C.: 5023; 5064
Thomas P. Hoy *(Pres. & Chief Exec. Officer)*
George E. Dumun, Jr. *(Exec. V.P.)*
Donald R. Pettavino *(V.P. & Mgr. Carpet Dept.)*
Merlin J. Remmers *(V.P.-Personnel)*
W.C. Rosenmeier, Jr. *(Sec. & Treas.)*

Outside Service Firm(s):

Pepperman, Embaulas & Schwartz*(Auditors)*
New Orleans, LA

Whitney National Bank of New Orleans*(Major Banking Relationship)*
P.O. Box 61260,
New Orleans, LA 70161

LEICHTUNG, INC.
4944 Commerce Pkwy.
Cleveland, OH 44128
Tel.: 216-831-6191 **OH**
Fax: 216-831-4026
Year Founded: 1974
Approx.Sls.: $30,000,000
Emp.: 140
Import
Retail Mail Order Wood Working Tools, Hardware & Specialty Consumer Products
S.I.C.: 5961
Coy Clement *(Pres. & Chief Exec. Officer)*
John Lazarc *(Chief Fin. Officer & V.P.-Fin.)*
Paul Collander *(V.P.-Adv.)*
Ken Ellingsen *(V.P.-Mdse.)*
Sharon Kives *(Mgr.-Human Resources)*
Mike Steffen *(Mgr.-Data Processing)*

No. of U.S. Offices: 1

Computer Systems/Hardware:
Hewlett-Packard

Outside Service Firm(s):

Arthur Andersen & Co.*(Auditors)*
1717 E. 9th St.
Cleveland, OH 44114
Tel.: 216-781-2140
Fax: 216-781-3683

Liberty Mutual*(Commercial Insurance Carrier)*
175 Berkeley St.
Boston, MA

Blue Cross & Blue Shield of Northern Ohio*(Group Insurer)*
2060 E. 9th St.
Cleveland, OH 44115
Tel.: 216-687-7000

Society National Bank*(Major Banking Relationship)*
800 Superior Ave.
Cleveland, OH 44114
Tel.: 216-689-5931
Fax: 216-689-3814

Subsidiary:

DRI Industries **(1)**
4944 Commerce Pkwy.
Cleveland, OH 44128
Tel.: 216-831-6191

Retail Mail Order Wood Working Tools
S.I.C.: 5961
Coy Clement *(Pres. & Chief Exec. Officer)*

LENAC, WARFORD, STONE, INC.
4701 Teller Ave.
Newport Beach, CA 92660
Tel.: 714-833-8435
Fax: 714-833-8463
Year Founded: 1973
Approx.Billings: $14,200,000
Emp.: 18
Full Service Adv., Pub. Rels., Sls. Promo. & Packaging
Ralph Z. Lenac *(Pres.)*
David Warford *(V.P., Sec. & Treas.)*
David Burkhart *(Pub. Rels. Supvr.)*
Erin Davern *(Pub. Rels., Acct Exec.)*

Computer Systems/Hardware:
IBM

LENAPE FORGE, INC.
1280 Lenape Rd.
West Chester, PA 19382
Tel.: 215-793-1500
Fax: 215-793-3240
Emp.: 100
Mfr. of Custom Forgings, Ferrous & Aluminum & Pressure Vessel Connections, Nuclear
S.I.C.: 3462; 3443; 3463
Frank S. Krempa *(Pres.)*
Peter D. Horvat *(V.P., Sec. & Treas.)*
William D. Cummings *(Dir.-Engrng. & Estimating)*
Robert Friederick *(Mgr.-Quality Control)*
Richard Grieb *(Mgr.-Opers.)*

Outside Service Firm(s):

Elko, Fischer, McCabe & Rudman*(Auditors)*
999 West Chester Rd.
West Chester, PA
Tel.: 215-431-1003

MacElree, Harvey, Gallagher & Featherman*(Legal Firm)*
West Chester, PA

LENNOX INTERNATIONAL INC.
2100 Lake Park Blvd.
Richardson, TX 75080
Mailing Address:
P.O. Box 799900,
Dallas, TX 75379-9900
Tel.: 214-497-5000
Telex: 4630018 LENOXINTL RCHN
Fax: 214-497-5299
Year Founded: 1895
Sales Range: $1 Billion +
Emp.: 8,000
Export
Holding Company; Heating & Air Conditioning Products for Residential & Commercial Applications
S.I.C.: 3585; 6719
John W. Norris, Jr. *(Chm. Bd. & Chief Exec. Officer)*
Richard W. Booth *(Exec. V.P. & Sec.)*
Clyde Wyant *(Exec. V.P.-Fin. & Treas.)*
David J. Chase *(V.P.-Govt. & Pub. Rels.)*
Carl Edwards Jr. *(V.P. & Gen. Counsel)*

No. of Mfg. Plants/Facilities: 12
No. of U.S. Offices: 52
No. of Foreign Offices: 10

Computer Systems/Hardware:
IBM 3083

Outside Service Firm(s):

Coopers & Lybrand*(Auditors)*
1999 Bryan St., Ste. 3000
Dallas, TX 75201
Tel.: 214-754-5000

The Northern Trust Co.*(Investment Banker)*
50 S. LaSalle St.
Chicago, IL 60675
Tel.: 312-630-6000
Fax: 312-630-6516

The Northern Trust Co.*(Major Banking Relationship)*
50 S. LaSalle St.
Chicago, IL 60675
Tel.: 312-630-6000
Fax: 312-630-6516

The Northern Trust Co.*(Pension Manager)*
50 S. LaSalle St.
Chicago, IL 60675
Tel.: 312-630-6000
Fax: 312-630-6516

Travelers Insurance Co.*(Pension Manager)*
1 Tower Square
Hartford, CT 06183
Tel.: 203-222-7821
Fax: 203-222-7813

Divisions:

Lennox Industries Inc. **(1)**
2100 Lake Park Blvd.
Richardson, TX 75080
Tel.: 214-497-5000 (100%)
Emp.: 6,500
Manufacture Air Conditioning Equipment
S.I.C.: 3585
Don W. Munson *(Pres. & Chief Oper. Officer)*

Lennox Industries Inc.-Copper Tube Div. **(1)**
5007 Hazel Jones Rd.
Bossier City, LA 71111
Tel.: 318-747-4950
Copper Tubing
S.I.C.: 3351

Lennox Industries Inc.-Eastern Div. **(1)**
P.O. Box 1319,
Columbus, OH 43216
Tel.: 614-421-6000
S.I.C.: 3585
Robert W. Caster *(V.P. & Gen. Mgr.)*

Lennox Industries, Inc.-Midwest Div. **(1)**
P.O. Box 250,
Marshalltown, IA 50158
Tel.: 515-754-4011
S.I.C.: 3585
T.R. Thompson *(V.P. & Gen. Mgr.)*

Lennox Industries Inc.-Southeast Div. **(1)**
P.O. Box 170255,
Atlanta, GA 30317
Tel.: 404-377-5511
S.I.C.: 3585
Jim Damiani *(V.P. & Gen. Mgr.)*

Lennox Industries-Southwest Div. **(1)**
P.O. Box 161038,
Fort Worth, TX 76161
Tel.: 817-831-0931
S.I.C.: 3585
Tom Morton *(V.P. & Gen. Mgr.)*

Lennox Industries Inc.-Western Div. **(1)**
P.O. Box 13017-C,
Sacramento, CA 95813
Tel.: 916-361-2000
S.I.C.: 3585
Jack Enright *(V.P. & Gen. Mgr.)*

Subsidiaries:

Armstrong Air Conditioning Inc. **(1)**
421 Monroe St.
Bellville, OH 44813
Tel.: 419-483-4840
Manufacture Heating & Air Conditioning Equipment
S.I.C.: 3585
Robert Johnson *(Pres. & Chief Oper. Officer)*

Heatcraft, Inc. **(1)**
4900 Lewis Rd.
Stone Mountain, GA 30083
Tel.: 404-939-4450
Approx.Sls.: $35,000,000
Emp.: 260
Manufacturer of Refrigeration Equipment
S.I.C.: 3585
Ed French *(V.P. & Gen. Mgr.)*
Tom Slade *(V.P.-Mfg.)*
Dale Huffman *(Controller)*
Jeff Almond *(Dir.-Adv. & Mktg.)*
Vern Laird *(Pur. Dir.)*
Bob McDonough *(Sls. Mgr.)*
Lynda P. Skiff *(Mktg. Analyst)*

Heatcraft Inc. **(1)**
Hwy. 51 South
Grenada, MS 38901
Tel.: 601-226-3421
Fax: 601-226-3421, Ext. 288
Manufactures Furnaces
S.I.C.: 5075; 3694

Heatcraft Inc. **(1)**
Hwy. 51 S.
Grenada, MS 38901
Tel.: 601-226-3421
Manufacture Heating Elements
S.I.C.: 3694

Divisions:

Heatcraft Refrigeration Products Division **(2)**
602 Sunnyvale Dr.
Wilmington, NC 28403
Tel.: 919-791-8510
Manufacture Refrigeration Equipment
S.I.C.: 3585

Larkin, Inc. **(2)**
P.O. Box 1699
Atlanta, GA 30371
Tel.: 404-939-4450
Approx.Sls.: $35,000,000
Emp.: 260
Mfr. Refrigeration Equipment
S.I.C.: 3585
Charles Dawson *(Pres.)*
Tom Slade *(V.P.-Mfg.)*
Dale Huffman *(Controller)*
Jeff Almond *(Dir.-Adv. & Mktg.)*
Bob McDonough *(Sls. Mgr.)*
Lynda P. Skiff *(Mktg. Analyst)*
Vern Laird *(Pur. Dir.)*

Non-U.S. Holdings:

Lennox Industries (Canada) Ltd. **(1)**
3916-70th Ave., S.E., P.O. Box 5460
Station A,
Calgary, AB T2H 1X8, Canada
Tel.: 403-279-8072
Heat & Air Conditioning Prods.
S.I.C.: 3433; 3585
Robert Caster *(Pres. & Chief Exec. Officer)*

Lennox Industries (Canada) Ltd. **(1)**
400 Norris Glen Rd.
Etobicoke, ON M9C 1H5, Canada
Tel.: 416-621-9302
Fax: 416-621-6303
Heat & Air Conditioning Products
S.I.C.: 3585
Robert Caster *(Pres. & Chief Exec. Officer)*

S. R. LEON COMPANY, INC.
29 W. Main St.
Oyster Bay, NY 11771
Tel.: 516-922-0031
Year Founded: 1929
Approx.Billings: $21,370,000
Emp.: 17
Direct Response
Thomas Leon *(Pres., Chief Exec. Officer & Creative Dir.)*
Daniel S. Leon *(Sr. V.P., Client Services)*
Susan Koennecke *(Comptroller)*
Teresa O'Connel *(Talent Payment Coord.)*

Computer Systems/Hardware:
Epson, Lotus, Wordperfect

LEON-FERENBACH COMPANY
95 River St.
Hoboken, NJ 07030
Mailing Address:
P.O. Box 610,
Hoboken, NJ 07030
Tel.: 201-963-3800 **TN**
Year Founded: 1909
Approx.Sls.: $20,000,000
Emp.: 350
Export
Manufacturer of Filament Yarns
S.I.C.: 2282
Richard S. Ferenbach *(Pres.)*

Outside Service Firm(s):

Hertz, Herson & Company*(Auditors)*
New York, NY

Cole & Deitz*(Legal Firm)*
New York, NY

Mountain Empire Bank*(Major Banking Relationship)*
New York, NY

HAROLD LEONARD & COMPANY, INC.
600 Green Lane
Union, NJ 07083
Mailing Address:
P.O. Box 3127
Union, NJ 07083
Tel.: 908-289-1000
Fax: 908-289-3186
Approx.Sls.: $20,000,000
Emp.: 60
Fiscal Year-end: 12/31/91
Wholesale Restaurant Supplies
S.I.C.: 5046
Frank W. Marcus *(Pres.)*
Jesse Gross *(Exec. V.P.)*
Carl Marcus *(V.P.)*
Harriet Marcus *(Sec. & Treas.)*
Martin Corbett *(Mgr.-Sls. & Adv.)*
Graziano Marchi *(Mgr.-Mktg.)*
Suqi Gu *(Pur. Agent)*

Outside Service Firm(s):

M.R. Weiser & Co.*(Auditors)*
New York, NY

Phillips, Nizer, Benjamin, Krim & Ballon*(Legal Firm)*
40 W. 57th St.
New York, NY 10019
Tel.: 212-977-9700

The Bank of New York*(Major Banking Relationship)*
One Wall Street
New York, NY 10286
Tel.: 212-635-6805
Fax: 212-635-3201

LEONARD & HARRAL PACKING CO.
122 Woodhull
San Antonio, TX 78214
Mailing Address:
P.O. Box 14514
San Antonio, TX 78214
Tel.: 210-924-4403 **TX**
Fax: 210-532-3399
Approx.Sls.: $167,000,000
Emp.: 600
Wholesale Meats & Meat Packing
S.I.C.: 5147; 2011
K. E. Leonard *(Pres. & Chief Exec. Officer)*
Rodney Spencer *(Exec. V.P.)*
Terry Black *(V.P.)*
David Scott *(V.P.-Sls.)*

Computer Systems/Hardware:
IBM System 34

Outside Service Firm(s):

Deloitte & Touche*(Auditors)*
1400 Lincoln Plaza, LB-4
Dallas, TX 75201-3302
Tel.: 214-220-8000

Leonard & Harral Packing Co.—(Continued)

Haynes & Boone*(Legal Firm)*
San Antonio, TX

National Bank of Commerce*(Major Banking Relationship)*
San Antonio, TX

CHARLES LEONARD, INC.
79-11 Cooper Ave.
Glendale, NY 11385
Tel.: 718-894-4851
Fax: 718-326-4347
Sales Range: $20-39 Million
Emp.: 100
Mfr. of Office Supply Accessories; Loose Leaf Metals & Accessories
S.I.C.: 2782; 3499; 5112
Charles L. Hirsch *(Chm. Bd.)*
David J. Hirsch *(Exec. V.P.)*
Ken Sherman *(Exec. V.P.)*

Subsidiary:

Charles Leonard Western, Inc. **(1)**
13617 S. St. Andrew Pl.
Gardena, CA 90249
Tel.: 213-770-4062
Approx.Sls.: $6,000,000
Emp.: 15
Mfr. of Binder Boards
S.I.C.: 2361
Ken Sherman *(Chief Oper. Officer)*

LEONARD MONAHAN LUBARS & KELLY
127 Dorrance St.
Providence, RI 02903
Tel.: 401-277-9020
Fax: 401-273-4491
Year Founded: 1978
Approx.Billings: $35,000,000
Emp.: 67
Bruce N. Leonard *(Chm. & Chief Exec. Officer)*
Tom Monahan *(Pres.)*
Susan Cashen *(V.P., Pub. Rels. Dir.)*
Gail Moore *(V.P., Fin. & Admin.)*

LEONARD WHOLESALE, INC.
1050 Sherman Ave.
Elizabeth, NJ 07208-6008
Mailing Address:
P.O. Box 6008
Elizabeth, NJ 07207
Tel.: 908-289-6600 **NJ**
Fax: 908-289-9418
Year Founded: 1946
Approx.Sls.: $40,000,000
Emp.: 50
Fiscal Year-end: 11/30/92
Import
Wholesale of Health & Beauty Aids; Promotional Groceries; Cosmetic Fragrances
S.I.C.: 5122; 5141
Marc Beckoff *(Chief Fin. Officer)*
Lawrence Wolf *(Pres., Chief Exec. Officer, Sec. & Treas.)*
Kevin M. Wolf *(Exec. V.P.)*
Mitch Kobran *(V.P.-Sls.)*
Jerry Militano *(V.P.-Pur.)*
Principal(s):
Lawrence Wolf

No. of Mfg. Plants/Facilities: 1

Computer Systems/Hardware:
Wang

L'ERMITAGE HOTELS
8440 Sunset Blvd.
West Hollywood, CA 90069
Tel.: 213-650-1199 **CA**
Telex: 559501 LEHG CORP
Fax: 213-656-3706
Year Founded: 1976
Approx.Sls.: $20,000,000
Emp.: 1,000
Build, Manage, Service & Maintain Luxury All-Suite Hotels
S.I.C.: 7011
Severyn Ashkenazy *(Pres.)*
Bob Schofield *(Chief Fin. Officer)*
Arnold Ashkenazy *(Sr. V.P.)*
Gary W. Nielson *(V.P.)*
Mark Muratori *(Controller)*
Stephen Weaver *(Gen. Counsel)*
Steven Barnes *(Dir.-Sls.)*
Monica Erne *(Dir.-Adv. & Media)*
Paul Racz *(Dir.-Data Processing)*
Ilse Spivack *(Dir.-Personnel)*
Candy Guresky *(Corp. Pur.)*

LESHNER MILLS. INC.
1010 Eaton Ave.
Hamilton, OH 45013
Mailing Address:
P.O. Box 179
Hamilton, OH 45012
Tel.: 513-868-3500 **OH**
Fax: 513-868-0731
Year Founded: 1947
Approx.Sls.: $70,000,000
Emp.: 490
Manufacture Towels, Washcloths, Tablecloths, Napkins & Related Textile Products
S.I.C.: 2823; 2211; 2241; 2299; 2392
Mark Petricoff *(Pres.)*
David Mizrachi *(V.P.-Institutional Sls.)*
Alan Selig *(V.P.-Sls.)*
Richard Sander *(Treas.)*

Computer Systems/Hardware:
IBM System 38

Outside Service Firm(s):

Deloitte & Touche*(Auditors)*
Chiquita Center, 250 E. 5th St., Ste. 1900
Cincinnati, OH 45202
Tel.: 513-784-7100

Star Bank*(Major Banking Relationship)*
425 Walnut Street
Cincinnati, OH 45202
Tel.: 513-632-4000

LESLIE ADVERTISING

LESLIE ADVERTISING
874 S. Pleasantburg Dr.
Greenville, SC 29607
Mailing Address:
P.O. Box 6168,
Greenville, SC 29606
Tel.: 803-271-8340 **SC**
Fax: 803-271-7481
Year Founded: 1959
Assets: $4,126,894
Liabilities: $3,812,959
Net Worth: $313,935
Approx.Billings: $31,055,000
Emp.: 59
Fiscal Year-end: 3/31/92
Advertising Agency
S.I.C.: 7311
Employee Matching Gifts Program:
Employer Matches 25% of Employee Contribution Up to 4% of Compensation
E. Dean Anderson *(Chm. Bd. & Chief Exec. Officer)*
Carlos Jimenez *(Pres., Chief Oper. Officer & Dir.-Creative)*
Dave Chesson *(Exec. V.P.-Opers. & Sec.)*
W. Crayton Mauldin *(Sr. V.P. & Controller)*
Neil Bloomfield *(V.P.)*
Barry Garrison *(V.P. & Dir.-Strategic Plng.)*
Terry McDermott *(V.P.)*
Gail Wilson *(Mgr.-Data Processing)*

No. of U.S. Offices: 1

Computer Systems/Hardware:
MAI Basic Four

Outside Service Firm(s):

Elliott, Davis & Co.*(Auditors)*
Greenville, SC

American Economy Insurance*(Commercial Insurance Carrier)*
Indianapolis, IN

Self-Insured*(Group Insurer)*

Dan A. Collins*(Legal Firm)*
Greenville, SC

United Carolina Bank*(Major Banking Relationship)*
Greenville, SC

United Carolina Bank*(Pension Manager)*
Greenville, SC

Branch:

Leslie Public Relations **(1)**
874 S. Pleasantburg Dr.
Greenville, SC 29607
Tel.: 803-271-8340
Vicki Dixon *(Acct. Exec.)*

LESON CHEVROLET COMPANY, INC.
1501 Westbank Expwy.
Harvey, LA 70058
Tel.: 504-366-4381
Fax: 504-366-4381 Ext. 91
Approx.Sls.: $25,000,000
Emp.: 101
Retail New & Used Automobiles
S.I.C.: 5511
Donald Trapp *(Pres.)*
Jan Stipelcovich *(Gen. Mgr.)*
Principal(s):

Outside Service Firm(s):

Whitney National Bank of New Orleans*(Major Banking Relationship)*
P.O. Box 61260
New Orleans, LA 70161
Tel.: 504-586-7422

J.L. LESTER & SON, INC.
326 S. Marble St.
Rockmart, GA 30153
Mailing Address:
P.O. Box 549
Rockmart, GA 30153
Tel.: 404-684-6524
Tel.: 404-688-7744 **GA**
Fax: 706-684-5062
Year Founded: 1926
Approx.Sls.: $75,000,000
Emp.: 140
Import Export
Wholesale Groceries
S.I.C.: 5141
Raymond R. Lester *(Pres.)*
Nelle Lester *(Exec. V.P.)*
Roger Hubbard *(Controller)*
Mary T. Simon *(Treas. & Dir.-Personnel)*
James L. Lester III *(Sec. & Gen. Mgr.)*
Ron Crumley *(Dir.-Pur.)*
Brad Helsey *(Dir.-Mktg. & Adv.)*
Larry Sherman *(Dir.-Data Processing)*
Jerry Wilson *(Dir.-Grocery Sls.)*
Sam Lindsey *(Mgr.-Mktg.)*
Jerry Wilson *(Mgr.-Sls.)*
Sue Weaver *(Corp. Travel Planner)*
Ron Crumley *(Head Buyer)*

No. of Mfg. Plants/Facilities: 1
No. of U.S. Offices: 1

Computer Systems/Hardware:
RISC 6000 IBM ADVANTAGE-SOFTWARE

Outside Service Firm(s):

Jones & Kolb*(Auditors)*
Rockmart, GA

Merritt E M*(Commercial Insurance Carrier)*
Rockmart, GA

Daniel B. Simon III*(Legal Firm)*
Rockmart, GA

LETICA CORPORATION
1700 W. Hamlin Rd.
Rochester Hills, MI 48309
Tel.: 313-652-0557
Fax: 313-652-0577
Approx.Sls.: $65,000,000
Emp.: 1,00
Manufacturer of Miscellaneous Plastics Products
S.I.C.: 3089
Illija Letica *(Pres. & Chief Exec. Officer)*
Mara Letica *(Gen. Counsel)*
Gudrun Letica *(Sec. & Treas.)*

Outside Service Firm(s):

Danielson, Schultz, & Co.*(Auditors)*
Lansing, MI

LETTS INDUSTRIES, INC.
1111 Bellevue Ave.
Detroit, MI 48207
Tel.: 313-579-1100
Fax: 313-579-2379
Approx.Sls.: $59,000,000
Emp.: 340
Manufacture Auto Components; Distribute Crawler Tractor Replacement Parts
S.I.C.: 3462; 3463; 3465; 5082; 5084
Charles E. Letts, Jr. *(Pres. & Chief Exec. Officer)*
Edwin R. Clarke *(Chief Fin. Officer, Treas. & Sec.)*

Outside Service Firm(s):

Price Waterhouse*(Auditors)*
200 Renaissance Center, Ste. 3900
Detroit, MI 48243

N.B.D. Bank, N.A.*(Major Banking Relationship)*
611 Woodward Ave.
Detroit, MI 48226
Tel.: 313-225-1122
Fax: 313-225-3420

Division:

Letts Industries, Pioneer Div. **(1)**
One Industrial Dr.
Pioneer, OH 43554
Tel.: 419-737-2373
Automotive Forging
S.I.C.: 3463
Roger A. Ohman, Jr. *(Gen. Mgr.)*

LETTUCE ENTERTAIN YOU ENTERPRISES, INC.
5419 N. Sheridan Rd.
Chicago, IL 60640
Tel.: 312-878-7340 **DE**
Fax: 312-878-7667
Approx.Sls.: $91,000,000
Emp.: 2,750
Fiscal Year-end: 12/31/90
Restaurants & Night Clubs
S.I.C.: 5812; 5813
Richard Melman *(Pres.)*
Charles L. Haskell *(Exec. V.P.-Fin. & Legal)*
Fred Joast *(Exec. V.P.-Opers.)*
Bob Wattel *(Exec. V.P.-Pur. & Opers.)*
Joseph E. Lanuti *(V.P.-Fin. & Treas.)*
Susie Southgate-Fox *(V.P.-Human Resources)*
Mary Pat Sullivan *(Dir.-Mktg.)*
Janet Kerrigan *(Mgr.-Pub. Rels.)*
Principal(s):
Richard Melman
Charles L. Haskell

Computer Systems/Hardware:
Microdata 9000; Fortune 3216

Outside Service Firm(s):

Blackman Kallick Bartelstein*(Auditors)*
300 Riverside Plaza
Chicago, IL 60606
Tel.: 312-207-1040

Jenner & Block*(Commercial Insurance Carrier)*
One IBM Plaza
Chicago, IL 60611
Tel.: 312-222-9350

Fireman's Fund Indemnity Corporation*(Group Insurer)*
35 Waterview Blvd., 4th Fl.
Parsippany, NJ 07054
Tel.: 201-299-2989

Continental Bank N. A.*(Major Banking Relationship)*
231 S. LaSalle St.
Chicago, IL 60697
Tel.: 312-828-2345
Tel.: 800-426-5754
Telex: 312-828-1783

Restaurants:

Ambria **(1)**
2300 Lincoln Park W.
Chicago, IL 60614
Tel.: 312-472-0076
Fax: 312-472-9077
Gabino Sotelino *(V.P.-Opers.)*

Avanzare **(1)**
161 E. Huron
Chicago, IL 60611
Tel.: 312-337-8056
Fax: 312-337-5296
Howard Katz *(V.P.-Opers.)*

Big Bowl Cafe **(1)**
159.5 W. Erie St.
Chicago, IL 60610
Tel.: 312-787-8269

Blue Crab Lounge **(1)**
21 E. Hubbard
Chicago, IL 60611
Tel.: 312-527-2722 (100%)
Restaurant
S.I.C.: 5812
Kevin Brown *(Chief Oper. Officer)*

Bones/Lincolnwood **(1)**
7110 N. Lincoln Ave.
Lincolnwood, IL 60646
Tel.: 708-677-3350
Restaurant
S.I.C.: 5812
Jimmy Banakis *(V.P.-Opers.)*

Bub City Crabshack & Bar-B-Q **(1)**
901 W. Weed St.
Chicago, IL 60622
Tel.: 312-266-1200
Restaurant
S.I.C.: 5812
Jimmy Binakis *(V.P.-Opers.)*
Bob Vick *(V.P.-Opers.)*

Cafe Ba-Ba-Reeba **(1)**
2024 N. Halsted
Chicago, IL 60614
Tel.: 312-935-5000 (100%)
Restaurant
S.I.C.: 5812
Gabino Sotelino *(V.P.-Opers.)*

P. J. Clarke's **(1)**
1204 No. State Pkwy.
Chicago, IL 60610
Tel.: 312-664-1650
Restaurant
S.I.C.: 5812
Mark Tormey *(V.P.-Opers.)*

Corner Bakery **(1)**
516 N. Clark St.
Chicago, IL 60610
Tel.: 312-644-8100

Don and Charlie's **(1)**
7501 E. Camelback Rd.
Scottsdale, AZ 85251
Tel.: 602-990-0900
Restaurant
S.I.C.: 5812
Don Carson *(Mng. Partner)*

Ed Debevic's **(1)**
660 Lake Cook Rd.
Deerfield, IL 60015
Tel.: 708-945-3242
Restaurant
S.I.C.: 5812

Ed Debevic's **(1)**
134 N. Lacienga
Beverly Hills, CA 90211
Tel.: 310-659-1952
Restaurant
S.I.C.: 5812

Ed Debevic's of Arizona **(1)**
2102 E. Highland
Phoenix, AZ 85016
Tel.: 602-956-2760
Restaurant
S.I.C.: 5812

Ed Debevic's/Short Orders Deluxe/ Phoenix **(1)**
2102 E. Highland
Phoenix, AZ 85016
Tel.: 602-956-2760
S.I.C.: 5812
Gerard Centioli *(V.P.-Opers.)*

Ed Debevic's/Short Orders Deluxe/ Torrance **(1)**
23705 Hawthorne Blvd.
Torrance, CA 90505
Tel.: 310-378-5454
S.I.C.: 5812
Gerard Centioli *(V.P.-Opers.)*

Ed's Deerfield **(1)**
660 Lake Cook Rd.
Deerfield, IL 60015
Tel.: 708-945-3242
Fax: 708-948-0343
Gerard Centioli *(V.P.-Opers.)*

The Eccentric/Big Bowl **(1)**
159 W. Erie
Chicago, IL 60611
Tel.: 312-787-8390
Tel.: 312-787-8297
Fax: 312-787-8190
Kevin Brown *(V.P.-Opers.)*

Everest **(1)**
One Financial Place, 440 S. LaSalle, 40th Fl.
Chicago, IL 60605
Tel.: 312-663-8920
Fax: 312-663-8817

Gino's East/Rolling Meadows **(1)**
Paddock Shopping Center, 1321 W. Golf Rd.
Rolling Meadows, IL 60008
Tel.: 708-935-5000
Italian Restaurant
S.I.C.: 5812
Jimmy Banakis *(V.P.-Opers.)*

R.J. Grunts/Chicago **(1)**
2056 Lincoln Park West
Chicago, IL 60614
Tel.: 312-929-5363
Restaurant
S.I.C.: 5812
Jimmy Banakis *(V.P.-Opers.)*

Hat Dance **(1)**
325 W. Huron
Chicago, IL 60610
Tel.: 312-649-0066
Restaurant
S.I.C.: 5812
John Buchanan *(V.P.-Opers.)*

Maggiano's Little Italy **(1)**
516 N. Clark St.
Chicago, IL 60610
Tel.: 312-644-7700
Fax: 312-644-1077
Frank Conaty *(Gen. Mgr.)*
Mark Tormey *(V.P.-Opers.)*

The Original A-1 **(1)**
401 E. Illinois
Chicago, IL 60611
Tel.: 312-644-0300
Fax: 312-644-0437
John Buchanan *(V.P.-Opers.)*

Papoulis Greek Taverna **(1)**
620 N. State
Chicago, IL 60610
Tel.: 312-642-8450
Greek Theme Restaurant
S.I.C.: 5812

Paragus **(1)**
620 N. State St.
Chicago, IL 60610
Tel.: 312-642-8450
Fax: 312-943-7629
Yorgo Koutsogiorgas *(Gen. Mgr.)*
David Wolfgram *(V.P.-Opers.)*

The Pump Room **(1)**
The Ambassador East, 1301 N. State Parkway
Chicago, IL 60610
Tel.: 312-266-0360
Restaurant
S.I.C.: 5812; 5813
Mark K. Tormey *(V.P.-Opers.)*
David Wolfgram *(V.P.-Opers.)*

Savoy Bar and Grill **(1)**
One Financial Plaza, 44 So. LaSalle, 2nd Fl.
Chicago, IL 60605
Tel.: 312-663-8800
Restaurant
S.I.C.: 5812
Mark Torney *(V.P.-Opers.)*

Scoozi **(1)**
410 W. Huron
Chicago, IL 60610
Tel.: 312-943-5900
Restaurant
S.I.C.: 5812
Steve Ottmann *(V.P.-Opers.)*

Shaw's Crab House/Chicago **(1)**
21 E. Hubbard
Chicago, IL 60610
Tel.: 312-527-2722 (100%)
Restaurant
S.I.C.: 5812
Kevin Brown *(V.P.-Opers.)*
Steve LaHaie *(V.P.-Opers.)*

Shaw's Deerfield **(1)**
660 Lake Cook Rd.
Deerfield, IL 60015
Tel.: 708-948-1020
Fax: 708-948-0343
Kevin Brown *(V.P.-Opers.)*

Tuchetti **(1)**
2135 E. Camelback Rd.
Phoenix, AZ 85016
Tel.: 602-957-0222
Fax: 602-381-1950
Steve Ottoman *(V.P.-Opers.)*

Tucci Benucch **(1)**
900 Michigan N.
Chicago, IL 60611
Tel.: 312-266-2500
Restaurant
S.I.C.: 5812
Howard Katz *(V.P.-Opers.)*
Steve Ottmann *(V.P.-Opers.)*

Tucci Milan **(1)**
6 W. Hubbard
Chicago, IL 60610
Tel.: 312-222-0044
Fax: 312-222-9269

Un Grand Cafe' **(1)**
2300 Lincoln Park West
Chicago, IL 60614
Tel.: 312-348-8886 (100%)
Restaurant
S.I.C.: 5812
Gabino Sotelino *(V.P.-Opers.)*

LETVEN-DICCICCO, INC.
Horsham Business Ctr., 455 Business Ctr. Dr.
Horsham, PA 19044
Tel.: 215-957-0300
Year Founded: 1968
Approx.Billings: $18,660,000
Emp.: 30
Food, Personal Computer & Software, Consumer Prods., Financial, High Technology
Edward Letven *(Chm. & Chief Exec. Officer)*
Michael Diccicco *(Pres.)*
Richard Battista *(Exec. V.P.)*
Bernice Slosburg *(Sr. V.P.)*
Donna Belardi *(V.P., Controller)*
Richard Krone *(V.P., Direct Mktg.)*

Computer Systems/Hardware:
Advantage Software Systems, Desktop Publishing Network.

LEUPOLD & STEVENS, INC.
600 N.W. Meadow Dr.
Beaverton, OR 97006
Mailing Address:
P.O. Box 688
Beaverton, OR 97075
Tel.: 503-646-9171 **OR**
Telex: 15-1227
Fax: 503-526-1455
Year Founded: 1907
Approx.Sls.: $51,000,000
Emp.: 435
Fiscal Year-end: 12/31/91

Import Export
Mfr. of Scopes & Mounts, Water Level Recorders, Hydrologic Instruments
S.I.C.: 3827; 3824; 3829
Werner K. Wildauer *(Chm. Bd. & Pres.)*
Daniel W. Wisdom *(Exec. V.P. & Chief Oper. Officer)*
Michael J. Kontich *(Chief Fin. Officer & Treas.)*
Wendell Neumeyer *(V.P.-Engrng.)*
Ray Oeltjen *(V.P.-Mktg.)*
William T. Owen *(V.P.-Mfg.)*
James W. Gilles *(Mgr.-Human Resources)*
Ray Kelly *(Sr. Buyer)*
Nikki Poersch *(Asst. to Pres.)*
Denise Gentry *(Sls. Asst.)*
Shelby Davis *(Mktg. Services Coord.)*

Principal(s):
Ruth Leupold
R.J. Stevens

No. of Mfg. Plants/Facilities: 1
No. of U.S. Offices: 1

Computer Systems/Hardware:
Honeywell

Outside Service Firm(s):

Price Waterhouse*(Auditors)*
1221 S.W. Morrison, Suite 1800
Portland, OR 97204
Tel.: 503-224-9040

Alexander & Alexander*(Group Insurer)*
Portland, OR

Blue Cross & Blue Shield of Oregon*(Group Insurer)*
Portland, OR

Stoel, Rives, Boley, Jones & Grey*(Legal Firm)*
900 S.W. Fifth Ave.
Portland, OR 97204
Tel.: 503-224-3381

Leupold & Stevens, Inc.—(Continued)

Key Bank*(Major Banking Relationship)*
1211 S.W. Fifth Ave., Suite 300
Portland, OR 97205
Tel.: 503-790-7500

Security Pacific Oregon*(Major Banking Relationship)*
Portland, OR

Security Pacific National Bank*(Pension Manager)*
1301 Fifth Ave.
Seattle, WA 98101
Tel.: 206-621-4530

LEVEL EXPORT SALES CORP.
1460 Broadway
New York, NY 10036
Tel.: 212-354-2600
Telex: 232305
Fax: 212-302-8421
Year Founded: 1940
Approx.Sls.: $35,000,000
Emp.: 11
Fiscal Year-end: 12/31/91
Export
Textile Export
S.I.C.: 5131
Isaac A. Levy *(Chm. Bd.)*
Nessim Levy *(Pres. & Chief Exec. Officer)*
Allan Levy *(V.P., Controller, Sec. & Data Processing Dir.)*
Principal(s):
Isaac A. Levy
Nessim Levy
Allan Levy

No. of U.S. Offices: 1

Computer Systems/Hardware:
Compaq

Outside Service Firm(s):

Arthur Andersen & Co.*(Auditors)*
1345 Ave. of the Americas
New York, NY 10105
Tel.: 212-708-4000

F. J. Wilkes*(Commercial Insurance Carrier)*
New York, NY

Fried, Frank, Harris, Shriver & Jacobson*(Legal Firm)*
1 New York Plaza
New York, NY 10004
Tel.: 212-820-8000

Citibank N.A.*(Major Banking Relationship)*
399 Park Ave.
New York, NY 10043
Tel.: 212-559-1000
Tel.: 800-248-4636

LEVENSON & HILL, INC.
5215 N. O'Connor, Ste. 1100
Irving, TX 75039
Mailing Address:
P.O. Box 619507,
Dallas/Fort Worth Airport, TX 75261
Tel.: 214-556-0944
Fax: 214-556-0667
Year Founded: 1984
Approx.Billings: $43,271,319
Emp.: 70
William L. Hill *(Chm. Bd. & Exec. Dir.-Creative)*
Barbara L. Levenson *(Pres. & Chief Exec. Officer)*
Stanley R. Levenson *(Chief Exec. Officer & Dir.-Pub. Rels.)*
Faithe Nicholson *(Chief Acctg. Officer)*
Rob McEnany *(Exec. V.P.)*
Cindy Leak Evans *(V.P. & Supvr.-Accts.)*
Jean Peterman *(V.P. & Mgr.-Print Production)*
Dixie Pineda *(V.P.-Pub. Rels.)*
Michael W. Lehman *(Dir.-Media Plng. & Res.)*
Louis Tridico *(Gen. Mgr.-Creative Dept.)*

KENNETH LEVENTHAL & COMPANY
2049 Century Park East
Los Angeles, CA 90067
Tel.: 310-277-0880
Fax: 310-284-7970
Year Founded: 1949
Sales Range: $100-499 Million
Emp.: 950
Fiscal Year-end: 9/30/92
Consulting & CPA Firm
S.I.C.: 8748; 8721
Kenneth Leventhal *(Chm. Bd.)*
Stan Ross *(Mng. Partner)*
Marvin Goldman *(Dir.-Natl. Acctg. & Auditing)*
Jack Oldham *(Dir.-Natl. Tax Services)*
James Strother *(Legal Officer)*

No. of U.S. Offices: 12

Computer Systems/Hardware:
IBM; Compaq PC

Outside Service Firm(s):

Aetna Life & Casualty*(Group Insurer)*
Boston, MA

Bank of America NT&SA*(Major Banking Relationship)*
555 So. Flower St., 5th Fl.
Los Angeles, CA 90071
Tel.: 213-228-3526
Fax: 213-228-4062

LEVI STRAUSS & CO.
1155 Battery St.
San Francisco, CA 94111
Mailing Address:
P.O. Box 7215,
San Francisco, CA 94120
Tel.: 415-544-6000 **DE**
Fax: 415-544-3939
Year Founded: 1850
Assets: $2,633,400,000
Earnings: $356,700,000
Liabilities: $558,300,000
Net Worth: $2,075,100,000
Approx.Sls.: $4,902,900,000
Emp.: 30,000
Fiscal Year-end: 11/30/91
Import Export
Mfr. of Men's & Women's Apparel
S.I.C.: 2339; 2326; 2325; 2329
Robert D. Haas *(Chm. Bd. & Chief Exec. Officer)*
Thomas W. Tusher *(Pres. & Chief Oper. Officer)*
Pete Jacobi *(Pres.-Global Souring)*
Bob Rockey *(Pres.-U.S. Mktg. Div.)*
Lee C. Smith *(Pres.-Levi Strauss Intl.)*
Thomas J. Bauch *(Sr. V.P. & Gen. Counsel)*
Donna Goya *(Sr. V.P.-Human Resources)*
George James *(Sr. V.P. & Chief Fin. Officer)*
Jim Chriss *(V.P.-Mktg.-Women's Wear)*
Robert H. Dunn *(V.P.-Corp. Communications & Community Affairs)*
Alan Gregson *(V.P.-Fin.)*
Joseph Maurer *(V.P. & Treas.)*
Bill Eaton *(Chief Information Officer)*
Maureen Moriarty *(Dir.-Consumer Mktg.)*
Michael Schultz *(Mgr.)*
Reese Smith *(Mgr.-Employee Benefits)*

Outside Service Firm(s):

Arthur Andersen & Co.*(Auditors)*
Spear Street Tower, One Market Plaza, Ste. 3500
San Francisco, CA 94105
Tel.: 415-546-8200

Richard N. Goldman & Co.*(Commercial Insurance Carrier)*
San Francisco, CA

Aetna Life & Casualty*(Group Insurer)*
151 Farmington Avenue
Hartford, CT 06156
Tel.: 203-273-2128
Fax: 203-729-4295

Heller, Ehrman, White & McAuliffe*(Legal Firm)*
525 University Ave.
Palo Alto, CA 94301
Tel.: 415-326-7600

Crocker National Bank*(Major Banking Relationship)*
Crocker Center-West Tower
San Francisco, CA 94104
Tel.: 415-983-2000

Wells Fargo Bank*(Pension Manager)*
420 Montgomery St.
San Francisco, CA 94104

Division:

The Jeans Company **(1)**
Levi's Plz., 1155 Battery St.
San Francisco, CA 94111
Tel.: 415-544-6000
S.I.C.: 2325
Peter L. Thigpen *(Pres.)*

Subsidiaries:

Levi Strauss Sportswear **(1)**
1155 Battery St.
San Francisco, CA 94111
Tel.: 415-544-6000
Mfr. of Men's & Women's Sportswear & Women's Jeans
S.I.C.: 2325; 2329; 2339
Leo P. Isotalo *(Pres.)*

Division:

Menswear Div. **(2)**
Levi's Plz., 1155 Battery St.
San Francisco, CA 94111
Tel.: 415-544-6000
Manufacture of Menswear
S.I.C.: 2325; 2329; 2321
Harry Cohn *(Pres.)*

Plant:

Levi Strauss, Jeanswear Div. **(3)**
5800 Old Hwy. 90
San Antonio, TX 78227
Tel.: 210-673-5570
Emp.: 1,000
Manufacture of Jeans
S.I.C.: 2325
B. Morris *(Plant Mgr.)*

Battery St. Enterprises, Running Gear Div. **(1)**
2400 Central Ave., Ste. L
Boulder, CO 80301
Tel.: 303-449-9045
Approx.Sls.: $4,000,000
Emp.: 17
Mfr. Running Apparel
S.I.C.: 2329; 2339
Frank C. Shorter *(Chm.)*
Tim Cronin *(Pres.)*
Joan Lowe *(Controller)*
Ron Addison *(Natl. Sls. Mgr.)*
Mary Cronin *(Adv. Mgr.)*
Larry Crabb *(Mdsg. & Pur. Mgr.)*

Levi Strauss Employee Purchase Plan, Inc. **(1)**
1611 Third Creek Rd.
Knoxville, TN 37921
Tel.: 615-637-3731
S.I.C.: 5611
Donna J. Goya *(Dir.)*

Levi Strauss International **(1)**
1155 Battery St.
San Francisco, CA 94111
Tel.: 415-544-6000 (100%)
S.I.C.: 5136
Lee C. Smith *(Pres.)*

Non-U.S. Holdings:

Levi Strauss (Australia) Pty. Ltd. **(1)**
41 McLaren St.
North Sydney, N.S.W. 2060, Australia
Tel.: 2 922-5588 (100%)
Apparel Mfr.
S.I.C.: 2325; 2326; 2329; 2339
Barry Shafran *(Gen. Mgr.)*

Levi Strauss Belgium, S.A. **(1)**
Brussels Intl. Trade Mart Sq., Atomium
Avignon 272
Brussels, Belgium
Tel.: 2 479-18-15 (100%)
Manufacture of Apparel
S.I.C.: 2325; 2326; 2329; 2339
J. Hubregtse *(Gen. Mgr.)*

Levi Strauss & Co. (Canada), Inc. **(1)**
80 Allstate Pkwy.
Markham, ON L3R 8X6, Canada
Tel.: 416 470 2777 (100%)
Fax: 416-470-4517
Emp.: 2,200
Fiscal Year-end: 11/30/89
Manufacture of Apparel
S.I.C.: 2325; 2326; 2329; 2339
John V. DeShano *(Pres.)*
John Chappell *(V.P.-Mktg.)*
Dan O'Neill *(Treas.)*
Carlo Tucci *(Sales Dir.)*
Bernard Gorecki *(Adv. & Promo. Mgr.)*
Luann MacDonald *(Mgr.-Human Resources)*

Plants:

Levi Strauss & Co. (Canada), Inc. **(2)**
563 Barton St. East
Stoney Creek, ON L8G 3X5, Canada
Tel.: 416-643-4143
Manufacture of Apparel
S.I.C.: 2325; 2326; 2329; 2339
Maurice Polidori *(Plant Mgr.)*

Levi Strauss & Co. (Canada), Inc. **(2)**
700 Education Rd.
Cornwall, ON K6H 6B8, Canada
Tel.: 613-933-8800
Manufacture of Apparel
S.I.C.: 2325; 2326; 2339; 2329
Paul Barker *(Plant Mgr.)*

Levi Strauss & Co. (Canada), Inc. **(2)**
10660-85th St.
Edmonton, AB T5H 1N1, Canada
Tel.: 403-422-4181
Manufacture of Apparel
S.I.C.: 2325; 2326; 2329; 2339
Jean Binette *(Plant Mgr.)*

Levi Strauss & Co. (Canada), Inc. **(2)**
7080 Eastern Rd.
Brantford, ON N3T 5Y6, Canada
Tel.: 519-756-8770
Manufacture of Apparel
S.I.C.: 2325; 2326; 2329; 2339
Dennis Zukowsky *(Plant Mgr.)*

Levi Strauss & Co. (Canada), Inc. **(2)**
90 Clairiville Dr.
Rexdale, ON S9W 5Y1, Canada
Tel.: 416-675-1222
Distribution Center Apparel
S.I.C.: 5136; 5137
Gordon Shank *(V.P.-Mktg.)*

Levi Strauss & Co. (Europe) S.A. **(1)**
489 Ave. Louise B-1050
Brussels, Belgium
Tel.: 2 648-6045 (100%)
Manufacture of Apparel
S.I.C.: 2325; 2326; 2329; 2339
Pete Jacobi *(Pres.-Euro Grp.)*

Levi Strauss de Espana, S.A. **(1)**
2Y4 Planta 20, Torre Catalvnya
Barcelona, 14, Spain
Tel.: 3-423-1551 (100%)
Manufacture of Apparel
S.I.C.: 2325; 2326; 2329; 2339
Magin Marti *(Gen. Mgr.)*

Levi Strauss Eximco (Ltd.) **(1)**
Fl. 13-Mandarin Plaza Tower A, 14 Science Museum Rd.
Kowloon, Hong Kong (100%)
Manufacture of Apparel
S.I.C.: 2325; 2326; 2329; 2339
Peter Thewlis *(Gen. Mgr.)*

Levi Strauss (Far East), Ltd. **(1)**
9F, Hong Kong Spinners Indus. Bldg.
Kowloon, Hong Kong
Tel.: 3-7429211 (100%)
Manufacture of Apparel
S.I.C.: 2325; 2326; 2329; 2339
Len Bennett *(Gen. Mgr.)*

Levi Strauss France, S.A. **(1)**
6 Avenue du Pacifique 91944
Les Ulis, France
Tel.: 20 56-88-65 (100%)
Telex: 601 897
Fax: 64 46 54 78
Emp.: 100
Fiscal Year-end: 11/30/90
Manufacture of Apparel
S.I.C.: 2325; 2326; 2329; 2339
Jacques Berard *(Gen. Mgr.)*
T. Kran *(Mktg. Dir.)*

Levi Strauss (Geneva) S.A. **(1)**
World Trade Center CH-1215 Geneva 15-Airport,
Geneva, Switzerland (100%)
Manufacture of Apparel
S.I.C.: 2325; 2326; 2329; 2339
Felix Sulzberger *(Gen. Mgr.)*

Levi Strauss Germany G.m.b.H. **(1)**
Rembrucker Strasse 21-25 Postfach 1260, 6056
Heusenstamm, Germany
Tel.: 6104-601/1 (100%)
Manufacture of Apparel
S.I.C.: 2325; 2326; 2329; 2339
Rolf Schumann *(Gen. Mgr.)*

Levi Strauss Italia, S.p.A. **(1)**
Via Serbelloni 2022
Milan, Italy
Tel.: 2 70-92-81 (100%)
Manufacture of Apparel
S.I.C.: 2325; 2326; 2329; 2339
Tullio Portone *(Gen. Mgr.)*

Levi Strauss Japan K.K. **(1)**
1-30 Minami Aoyama 3-chome Minato-Ku,
Tokyo, 107, Japan
Tel.: 03-3478-7521 (100%)
Manufacture of Apparel
S.I.C.: 2325; 2326; 2329; 2339

Levi Strauss (Malaysia) Sdn. Bhd. **(1)**
78/78A Lorong Selamat
Penang, Malaysia
Tel.: 28545 (100%)
Manufacture of Apparel
S.I.C.: 2325; 2326; 2329; 2339
Len Bennett *(Gen. Mgr.)*

Levi Strauss de Mexico, S.A. de C.V. **(1)**
Horacio 1844, 4th Fl., Col. Polanco
Reforma 1150
Mexico, D.F. Mexico
Tel.: 905-202-1851 (100%)
Manufacture of Apparel
S.I.C.: 2325; 2326; 2329; 2339
Adolfo Moreno *(Gen. Mgr.)*

Levi Strauss Nederland B.V. **(1)**
Schurenbergweg 6 1105 AR
Amsterdam, Netherlands
Tel.: 20-5633633 (100%)
Telex: 16315
Fax: 20 964263
Manufacture of Apparel
S.I.C.: 2325; 2326; 2329; 2339
A. Melafair *(Gen. Mgr.)*

Levi Strauss (New Zealand) Ltd. **(1)**
22 Heather St. Parnell,
Auckland, 1, New Zealand
Tel.: 6 9 30-319 (100%)
Fax: 373-999
Approx.Sls.: $12,000,000
Emp.: 35
Manufacture of Apparel
S.I.C.: 2325; 2326; 2329; 2339
Jann Westfall *(Gen. Mgr.)*
Dianne Hansen *(Mktg. Mgr.)*

Levi Strauss Norway, A/S **(1)**
Marcus Thrangest 2
Oslo, Norway
Tel.: 2-350504 (100%)
Manufacture of Apparel
S.I.C.: 2325; 2326; 2329; 2339
B. Aas-Engelstad *(Reg. Mgr.)*

Levi Strauss (Philippines) Inc. **(1)**
2264 Pasong Tamo Extn. Rizal,
Manila, Philippines
Tel.: 2-82-29-91 (100%)
Manufacture of Apparel
S.I.C.: 2325; 2326; 2329; 2339
Mike Lam *(Gen. Mgr.)*

Levi Strauss (Suisse) S.A. **(1)**
Rte. de la Pierre 1024
Ecublens, VD Switzerland
Tel.: 21-35-63-63 (100%)
Wholesale of Apparel
S.I.C.: 5136; 5137
Rolf Schumann *(Gen. Mgr.)*

Levi Strauss (U.K.) Ltd. **(1)**
Levi's house, Moulton Park
Northampton, NN3 1QG, United Kingdom
Tel.: 081-908-3141 (100%)
Manufacture of Apparel
S.I.C.: 2325; 2326; 2329; 2339
Jack Gerrish *(Gen. Mgr.)*

Suomen Levi Strauss Oy **(1)**
Iso Roobertinkatu 43 00120
Helsinki, 12, Finland (100%)
Manufacture of Apparel
S.I.C.: 2329; 2325; 2339; 2326
Bjorn Aas-Engelstad *(Reg. Mgr.)*

Zenith Intl. Insurance Ltd. **(1)**
Cedar Park Center Bldg. Cedar Ave.
Hamilton, 5, Bermuda (100%)
Insurance Co.
S.I.C.: 6411

LEVITON MFG. CO., INC.
59-25 Little Neck Pkwy.
Little Neck, NY 11362
Tel.: 718-229-4040
Fax: 718-631-6549
Approx.Sls.: $60,000,000
Emp.: 4,500
Primary Metal Industries; Electric & Electronic Equip.; Trucking & Warehousing
S.I.C.: 3643; 3537
J. Amsterdam *(Chm. Bd.)*
H. Leviton *(Pres.)*
Thomas A. Blumberg *(Grp. V.P.-Mktg. & Sls.)*
D. Hendler *(Grp. V.P.-Distr.)*
Edwin Kanner *(Grp. V.P.-Wire & Cable)*
J. Pearse *(Grp. V.P.-Engrng.)*
Steve Sokolow *(Grp. V.P.-Admin.)*
Ralph DeBiasi *(V.P.-Fin.)*
Tibor Gerstl *(V.P.-Mktg. Communications)*
H. Kram *(V.P.-Opers.)*
Ronald J. Landisi *(V.P.-Elect. Distr. & Dir.-Mktg.)*
James B. Rosenwald *(V.P.-OEM Mktg. & Dir.-Sls.)*
Murray Strouber *(V.P.-Consumer Mktg. & Dir.-Sls.)*
Anthony J. Valone *(V.P.-Pur.)*
Mark Baydarian *(Controller)*
Charles Haber *(Dir.-Art)*
Kenneth Miller *(Dir.-Personnel)*
Frances Kroshinsky *(Mgr.-Mktg., Export Div.)*
Carol Lynch *(Mgr.-Mktg. Communications, Consumer Prods.)*
Mario Mattich *(Mgr.-Pub. Rels.)*
Charlotte Nash *(Mgr.-Trade Shows & Mktg. Communications-OEM)*
James Sherman *(Mgr.-Mktg. Communications, Electrical Distr.)*

Computer Systems/Hardware:
IBM 3090-200

Outside Service Firm(s):

Empire Blue Cross & Blue Shield*(Group Insurer)*
New York, NY

New York Life*(Group Insurer)*
New York, NY

Connecticut Mutual*(Pension Manager)*
Hartford, CT

Subsidiaries:

American Insulated Wire Corp. **(1)**
36 Freeman St.
Pawtucket, RI 02862
Tel.: 401-726-0700 (100%)
Fax: 401-723-1420
Mfr. of Specialty Wire & Cable for Industry & Utilities
S.I.C.: 3315
Edwin Kanner *(Pres.)*

Cable Electric Products, Inc. **(1)**
234 Daboll St.
Providence, RI 02907
Tel.: 401-781-5400 (100%)
Approx.Sls.: $18,000,000
Emp.: 300
Fiscal Year-end: 6/30/91
Import Export
Mfr. Electric & Electronic Specialty Prods.; Infra-Red Devices; Surge Control Devices; Outlet Strips (Multi-Outlet); Radio Frequency Products
S.I.C.: 3634; 3641; 3644; 3645; 3679
Fred W. Schwartz *(Pres.)*
J. Tracy *(Natl. Sls. Mgr.)*
Don B. Fournier *(Dir.-Mktg.)*
E. Guertin *(Pur. Agent)*
P. Hoffman *(Personnel Mgr.)*

Pacific Electricord Co. **(1)**
747 W. Redondo Beach Blvd.
Gardena, CA 90247
Tel.: 310-532-6600 (100%)
Electric Cords
S.I.C.: 3643
Edwin Kanner *(Pres.)*

Non-U.S. Holdings:

Levimex de Baja California S.A. de C.V. **(1)**
Blvd. Los Insurgentes 20004 Parque Industrial,
Tijuana, Mexico
Tel.: 25-17-96
Manufacture of Transformers
S.I.C.: 3643

Manufacture Leviton du Canada **(1)**
165 Hymus Blvd.
Pointe Claire, PQ H9R 1G2, Canada
Tel.: 514-954-1840 (100%)
Mfrs. Electric Wiring Devices
S.I.C.: 3643
Stephen Sokolow *(Pres. & Chief of Opers.-Canada)*

LEVLAD, INC.
9183-5 Kelvin Ave.
Chatsworth, CA 91311
Tel.: 818-882-2951
Tel.: 800-327-2012
Fax: 818-341-3840
Year Founded: 1974
Approx.Sls.: $10,000,000
Emp.: 100
Export
Mfr. of Cosmetics; Nature's Gate, Promotional Prods., Aloegen Skin & Hair Care Prods.
S.I.C.: 2844
Leo Weinstein *(Pres.)*
Walter Weinstein *(Exec. V.P.)*
Steven Biroczky *(V.P. & Gen. Mgr.)*
Richard Peck *(V.P.-Sls. & Mktg.)*
H. E. Williams *(Controller)*
Mary Anders *(Dir.-Sls.)*
Murray Bason *(Dir.-Pur.)*
Mardell Masters *(Pur. Agent)*

LEVLANE ADVERTISING, INC.
One Belmont Ave.
Bala-Cynwyd, PA 19004
Tel.: 215-667-7313
Fax: 215-667-3176
Year Founded: 1984
Approx.Billings: $16,600,000
Emp.: 43
David Alan Lane *(Pres.)*
Michael Buckland *(Sr. V.P.)*
Anne B. Inman *(V.P., Pub. Rels. Services)*
Cara Levinson *(Mgr.-Mktg. Services)*

THE LEVOLOR CORPORATION
595 Lawrence Expwy.
Sunnyvale, CA 94086
Tel.: 408-245-4000
Fax: 408-245-3105
Year Founded: 1914
Approx.Sls.: $200,000,000
Emp.: 1,800
Mfr. Blinds & Component Blinds
S.I.C.: 2591
Thomas Mullaney *(Chm. Bd.)*
Richard W. Egan *(Pres. & Chief Exec. Officer)*
Phil Koen *(Chief Fin. Officer)*
Don Hinshaw *(V.P.-Mktg. & Sls.)*
R. Pearson *(V.P.-Mfg.)*
Sandee Young *(V.P.-Design)*
Tina Glover *(Dir.-Mktg.)*
Jim Peekey *(Mgr.-Human Resources)*

Computer Systems/Hardware:
Data General 23

Outside Service Firm(s):

Chase Manhattan Bank, N.A.*(Major Banking Relationship)*
One Chase Manhattan Plaza
New York, NY 10081
Tel.: 212-552-2222
Tel.: 800-526-0801
Fax: 212-552-7175

LEVONIAN BROTHERS INC.
27 River St.
Troy, NY 12180
Mailing Address:
P.O. Box 629
Troy, NY 12180
Tel.: 518-274-3610
Tel.: 800-338-0970 NY
Fax: 518-274-0098
Year Founded: 1947
Approx.Sls.: $32,000,000
Emp.: 65
Fiscal Year-end: 12/31/91
Producer & Distributor Of Meat Products
S.I.C.: 5147; 2013
Elia Y. Levonian *(Chm. Bd.)*
Ralph Darian *(Pres., Chief Exex. & Chief Fin. Officer)*
Gregory L. Nazarian *(Treas.)*
Robert G. Nazarian *(Corp. Sec.)*
Tom Haggerty *(Controller)*
James McCormick *(Plant Mgr.)*

No. of Mfg. Plants/Facilities: 1
No. of U.S. Offices: 1

Computer Systems/Hardware:
IBM 3100

Outside Service Firm(s):

Union National Bank*(Major Banking Relationship)*
Troy, NY

A. LEVY & J. ZENTNER CO.
P.O. Box 292307
Sacramento, CA 95829
Tel.: 916-381-7100
Fax: 916-381-8276
Year Founded: 1907
Approx.Sls.: $110,000,000
Emp.: 500
Fiscal Year-end: 12/31/91
Distribute Fresh Fruit, Produce & Beer; Exporting Citrus & Car Lot; Distribute Fresh Fruit & Produce
S.I.C.: 5148; 5181; 5182
G. N. Thomas *(Chm. Bd., Pres., Chief Exec. Officer, Chief Fin. Officer & Treas.)*
Chester Shiu *(Vice Chm.)*
Edward A. Melia *(Sec.)*
Gabrele West *(Controller)*

A. Levy & J. Zentner Co.—(Continued)

No. of Mfg. Plants/Facilities: 3

Computer Systems/Hardware:
IBM System 38

Outside Service Firm(s):

KPMG Peat Marwick*(Auditors)*
2495 Natomas Park Dr., Ste. 600
Sacramento, CA 95833-2936

Marsh & McLennan*(Commercial Insurance Carrier)*
Sacramento, CA

Safeco Insurance Co. of America*(Group Insurer)*
Seattle, WA

Boutin, Lassner, Gibson & Delehant*(Legal Firm)*
Sacramento, CA

Imperial Bank*(Major Banking Relationship)*
Los Angeles, CA

NORMAN LEVY ASSOCIATES, INC.
21415 Civic Center Dr.
Southfield, MI 48076
Tel.: 313-353-8640
Fax: 313-353-1442
Year Founded: 1952
Approx.Sls.: $85,000,000
Emp.: 50
Fiscal Year-end: 4/30/91
Auctioneers/Liquidators/Appraisers
S.I.C.: 7389
Lew Nucian *(Chief Exec. Officer)*
Robert Levy *(Pres. & Chief Oper. Officer)*
Richard Brodie *(V.P.)*
Richard Nucian *(V.P.)*
Marsha Fales *(Dir.-Media)*

Computer Systems/Hardware:
DEC; Macintosh

Division:

Norman Levy Associates, Inc. **(1)**
Ten Post Office Sq., Ste. 600 S
Boston, MA 02109
Tel.: 617-457-5705
Fax: 617-457-5700
Auctioneers/Liquidators/Appraisers
S.I.C.: 7389

JACK LEVY ASSOCIATES
1 E. Erie
Chicago, IL 60611
Tel.: 312-337-7800
Fax: 312-337-1677
Year Founded: 1973
Approx.Billings: $68,724,400
Emp.: 80
Jack Levy *(Pres.)*
Barbara H. Podkul *(Sr. V.P., Fin. & Opers.)*
Denise Kaufmann *(Dir.-Pub. Rels.)*
Diane Briscoe *(Mgr.-Brdcst. Bus. Affairs)*

THE CHARLES LEVY COMPANY
1200 N. North Branch St.
Chicago, IL 60622
Tel.: 312-440-4400 **DE**
Fax: 312-440-4434
Year Founded: 1893
Assets: $116,000,000
Liabilities: $102,048,000
Net Worth: $13,952,000
Approx.Sls.: $306,000,000
Emp.: 2,000
Fiscal Year-end: 3/31/92
Wholesale Distributor of Information & Home Entertainment Products-Magazines, Books, Videos, Laser Disc, Music; Transportation Services
S.I.C.: 5112; 5192; 7822
Corporate Giving Program: Restricted *to Geographical Areas in Which the* Company is Located; Contributions Not Made to Religious Groups, Fraternal Organizations, Private Foundations, or Political Purposes; Eligibility Requires IRS Determination Status
Employee Matching Gifts Program: Resticted to Full Time Employees With One Year Service; Qualification Limited to Organizations Recognized by IRS as a Public Charity Operating in Social Service, Literacy Areas, as well as Public Television & Radio; for Each Dollar Contributed- Company Matches Up to Annual Total of $1500.00 per Employee
Barbara L. Kipper *(Chm. Bd.)*
Carol G. Kloster *(Pres. & Chief Exec. Officer)*
Robert Schmidt *(Sr. V.P. & Chief Fin. Officer)*
James E. Bonning *(V.P.-Data Processing)*
Judy Cotton *(V.P.-Sls. & Mktg.)*
Mary Donnellon *(V.P. & Gen. Mgr.)*
Dave Gutman *(V.P. & Controller)*
Frances Lefkow *(V.P.-Human Resources)*
Tom Strelka *(V.P.-Opers.)*
Principal(s):
Barbara L. Kipper
Carol G. Kloster
Herbert Fried
Ruth Levy

No. of Mfg. Plants/Facilities: 13
No. of U.S. Offices: 14

Computer Systems/Hardware:
IBM

Outside Service Firm(s):

Checkers, Simon & Rosner*(Auditors)*
Chicago, IL

Sonnenschein, Nath & Rosenthal*(Legal Firm)*
8000 Sears Tower
Chicago, IL 60606
Tel.: 312-876-8057

Continental Bank Corporation*(Major Banking Relationship)*
231 S. LaSalle St.
Chicago, IL 60697
Tel.: 312-828-2345
Telex: 25-3412
Fax: 312-828-3820

Subsidiaries:

Central Illinois Periodicals, Inc. **(1)**
PO BOX 3757,
Bloomington, IL 61702

D & D Newspaper Circulators, Inc. **(1)**
1200 N. North Branch Street
Chicago, IL 60622

Levy Home Entertainment **(1)**
4201 N. Raymond Dr.
Hillside, IL 60102

Charles Levy Transportation Co. **(1)**
1200 N. North Branch Street
Chicago, IL 60162

Levy United News **(1)**
850 E. Luzerne St.
Philadelphia, PA 19124

Norbran Leasing **(1)**
1200 N. North Branch Street
Chicago, IL 60622

EDWARD C. LEVY CO., INC.
8800 Dix Ave.
Detroit, MI 48209
Tel.: 313-843-7200 **MI**
Fax: 313-843-8940
Year Founded: 1918
Approx.Sls.: $250,000,000
Emp.: 1,800
Fiscal Year-end: 12/31/91
Import Export
Mfr. Slag Aggregates, Burned Lime, Asphalt Mixtures, Ready-Mix Concrete, Sand & Gravel, Crushed Stones & Steel Mill Processing Services
S.I.C.: 3274; 2951; 3273; 1611; 1442
Edward C. Levy, Jr. *(Pres. & Treas.)*
Robert Lemke *(Pres.-Colorado & Arizona Group)*
Frank Lesters *(Pres.-Indiana Group)*
J. J. Broderick *(V.P.)*
Robert Carson *(V.P.)*
Robert Flucker *(V.P. & Controller)*
S. Evan Weiner *(V.P.)*
Paul Deller *(Dir.-Pur.)*
Principal(s):
Edward C. Levy, Jr.

Computer Systems/Hardware:
IBM System 38

Outside Service Firm(s):

Coopers & Lybrand*(Auditors)*
400 Renaissance Center
Detroit, MI 48243
Tel.: 313-446-7100
Fax: 313-446-7117

Honigman, Miller, Schwartz & Cohn*(Legal Firm)*
2290 First National Bldg.
Detroit, MI 48226
Tel.: 313-256-7800

JACOB LEVY & BROS., INC.
1126 W. Breckenridge St.
Louisville, KY 40210
Tel.: 502-583-5341
Fax: 502-583-5348
Approx.Sls.: $25,000,000
Emp.: 225
Retailer of Lumber & Other Building Materials
S.I.C.: 5211
Philip J. Levy *(Pres.)*
William G. Levy *(V.P.)*
Lewis Opper *(Treas. & Sec.)*

Outside Service Firm(s):

Youngblood, Burton & Dicken*(Auditors)*
Louisville, KY

Liberty National Bank & Trust Co.*(Major Banking Relationship)*
Louisville, KY

Morris, Garlove, Waterman & Johnson*(Legal Firm)*
Louisville, KY

THE LEVY ORGANIZATION
980 N. Michigan Ave.
Chicago, IL 60611
Tel.: 312-664-8200
Fax: 312-280-2739
Year Founded: 1976
Approx.Rev.: $100,000,000
Emp.: 3,000
Real Estate Operations; Restaurants; Newstands
S.I.C.: 5812; 6552; 5994
Lawrence F. Levy *(Chm. Bd.)*
Mark Levy *(Vice Chm.)*
Bill Post *(Pres.)*
Robert Seiffert *(Sr. V.P. & Chief Fin. Officer)*
Carol Cohen *(Sr. V.P.)*
John Swanson *(Sr. V.P.)*
Carol Geis *(V.P.-Mktg.)*
Larry Steinberg *(V.P.-Human Resources)*
Andrew Lansing *(Gen. Counsel)*
Amy Schroeder *(Treas.)*
Carol Drew *(Dir.-Sls.)*
Lisa Howard *(Dir.-Pur.)*
Lynne Goldman *(Mktg. Coord.)*

Subsidiaries:

Eastern Lobby Shops **(1)**
980 N. Michigan Ave., Ste. 400
Chicago, IL 60611
Tel.: 312-664-8200
Newstands
S.I.C.: 5994

Levy Real Estate Partners **(1)**
980 N. Michigan Ave., Ste. 400
Chicago, IL 60611
Tel.: 312-664-8200
S.I.C.: 6552
Lawrence J. Levy *(Chm. Bd.)*
Roger Peck *(Sr. V.P.-Devel.)*
Jeffrey Barron *(Sr. V.P.)*

Levy Restaurants **(1)**
980 N. Michigan Ave., Ste. 400
Chicago, IL 60611
Tel.: 312-664-8200
S.I.C.: 5812
William Post *(Pres.)*
Carol Cohen *(Sr. V.P.)*
John Swanson *(Sr. V.P.)*

LEVY SECURITY CONSULTANTS, LIMITED
55 W. Superior St.
Chicago, IL 60610
Tel.: 312-649-9204
Fax: 312-787-0697
Year Founded: 1976
Sales Range: $10-19 Million
Emp.: 400
Security & Loss Prevention Consulting Services
S.I.C.: 7382
Barry W. Levy *(Chm. Bd., Chief Exec. Officer & Communications Dir.)*
D.G. Levy *(Exec. V.P.)*
Randy J. Bell *(Sr. V.P. & Controller)*
David P. Bergisma *(Sr. V.P.-Opers.)*
David A. Schlack *(Legal Officer)*
Ann M. Pratt *(Dir.-Human Resources)*
Principal(s):
Barry W. Levy

No. of U.S. Offices: 2

Computer Systems/Hardware:
Compaq

B. LEVY & SONS
700 North-South Rd.
Scranton, PA 18504
Tel.: 717-346-4601
Fax: 717-969-6193
Year Founded: 1888
Approx.Sls.: $20,000,000
Emp.: 50
Fiscal Year-end: 12/31/91
Importer & Distr. Shoes
S.I.C.: 5139
F. Levy *(Exec. V.P.-Fin.)*
R. Levy *(Exec. V.P.-Sls. & Mdsg.)*
Clyde Craft *(Mgr.-Adv.)*
Glenn Estes *(Mgr.)*
Principal(s):
Benjamin Levy
Bernard Levy

Computer Systems/Hardware:
Unisys 5055

LEWIS ADVERTISING AGENCY
17 Academy
Newark, NJ 07102
Tel.: 201-642-4800
Fax: 201-642-8948
Year Founded: 1935
Approx.Billings: $12,000,000
Emp.: 30
Fred H. Lewis *(Pres. & Treas.)*
Bonney Young *(Exec. V.P.)*
John Ward *(V.P.)*

DONALD D. LEWIS ADVERTISING
405 Riverside Dr.
Burbank, CA 91506
Tel.: 818-841-4070

Fax: 818-841-0694
Year Founded: 1965
Approx.Billings: $35,000,000
Emp.: 27
Retail & Direct Response Adv.
Donald D. Lewis *(Pres. & Chief Exec. Officer)*
William Merriman *(V.P., Fin. & Chief Fin. Officer)*

LEWIS ADVERTISING, INC.
1050 Country Club Dr.
Rocky Mount, NC 27804
Mailing Address:
P.O. Drawer L,
Rocky Mount, NC 27804
Tel.: 919-443-5131
Fax: 919-443-9340
Year Founded: 1969
Approx.Billings: $30,000,000
Emp.: 54
Gene L. Lewis *(Chm.)*
Donald H. Williams, Jr. *(Pres.)*
Sandra Parker *(Sr. V.P., Controller)*
Alberta L. Jones *(Asst. V.P., Asst. to Chm.)*
Joann Zalusky *(Asst. V.P., Client Support Services)*

LEWIS BROTHERS BAKERIES, INC.
500 North Fulton Avenue
Evansville, IN 47710
Tel.: 812-425-4642
Fax: 812-425-7609
Year Founded: 1925
Approx.Sls.: $110,000,000
Emp.: 1,200
Fiscal Year-end: 12/30/91
Manufactures & Distributes Baked Products
S.I.C.: 2051; 5149
R. Jack Lewis, Sr. *(Chm. Bd.)*
R. Jack Lewis, Jr. *(Pres. & Chief Exec. Officer)*
Rodger L. Lesh *(Chief Fin. Officer, V.P. & Treas.)*
Ann Greenfield *(V.P.-Human Resources)*
Jeffery Sankovitch *(Sec.)*
E.R. Whitman *(Dir.-Pur.)*
Dan Coyle *(Mgr.-Data Processing)*
Principal(s):
Lewis Family

Computer Systems/Hardware:
Honeywell

Outside Service Firm(s):

Tillinghast, Nelson & Warren*(Auditors)*
St. Louis, MO

Liberty Mutual*(Commercial Insurance Carrier)*
Boston, MA

Old National Bank in Evansville*(Major Banking Relationship)*
P.O. Box 718, 420 Main St.
Evansville, IN 47705
Tel.: 812-464-1200

Subsidiaries:

Holsum of Fort Wayne, Inc. **(1)**
156 E. Murray
Fort Wayne, IN 46858
Tel.: 219-456-2130
S.I.C.: 2051

Division:

Bonnie Baking Co. **(2)**
800 Boyd Blvd.
La Porte, IN 46350
Tel.: 219-362-4561

Lewis Bros. Bakeries **(1)**
RR 1
Anna, IL 62906
Tel.: 618-833-5185
S.I.C.: 2051

Lewis Bros. Bakeries (MO) **(1)**
504 Kendall
Sikeston, MO 63801
Tel.: 314-471-1650
S.I.C.: 2051

Lewis Bros. Bakeries (TN) **(1)**
847 Scott Dr.
Murfreesboro, TN 37133
Tel.: 615-893-6041
S.I.C.: 2051

Lewis Vincennes, Inc. **(1)**
3114 Old Decker Rd.
Vincennes, IN 47591
Tel.: 812-886-6533

LEWIS, CLARK & GRAHAM
230 Peachtree St. N.W., Ste. 400
Atlanta, GA 30303
Tel.: 404-221-0700
Year Founded: 1984
Approx.Billings: $13,000,000
Emp.: 17
Edwin Clark *(Chm. & Chief Exec. Officer)*
Stacey Graham *(Pres. & Chief Oper. Officer)*

LEWIS & COKER SUPER MARKETS
12561 Memorial Dr.
Houston, TX 77024
Mailing Address:
P.O. Box 79770,
Houston, TX 77279-9770
Tel.: 713-973-9400
Approx.Sls.: $12,500,000
Emp.: 52
Fiscal Year-end: 7/31/92
Food Stores
S.I.C.: 5411
Eugene Lewis *(Pres.)*

Computer Systems/Hardware:
PC

Outside Service Firm(s):

Pannell, Kerr, Forster*(Auditors)*
Houston, TX

Compass Bank*(Major Banking Relationship)*
Houston, TX

LEWIS COMMUNICATIONS, INC.
1668 Government St.
Mobile, AL 36604
Mailing Address:
P.O. Box 6829,
Mobile, AL 36660-0829
Tel.: 205-476-2507
Fax: 205-470-9658
Year Founded: 1951
Approx.Billings: $15,400,000
Emp.: 35
John H. Lewis, Jr. *(Chm. Bd. & Pres.)*
Emil T. Graf, III *(Pres.-Mobile Office)*
Larry D. Norris *(Pres.-Birmingham)*
David W. Nichol *(V.P., Pub. Rels.)*
Carol T. Sealy *(Sec. & Treas.)*
Dixie Steelreath *(Bookkeeper)*

LEWIS DRUG, INC.
2701 S. Minnesota, Ste. 1
Sioux Falls, SD 57105
Tel.: 605-333-2800
Fax: 605-333-2876
Approx.Sls.: $36,000,000
Drugs & Mass Merchandising
S.I.C.: 5912; 5311; 5399
Mark E. Griffin *(Chm. Bd., Pres. & Chief Exec. Officer)*
Michael Bender *(Treas., Controller & Chief Accountant)*
John McDowell *(Sec.)*
Gene Elrod *(Dir.-Personnel)*
Joan Fickbolm *(Mgr.-Adv.)*
Kevin Reilly *(Mgr.-Data Processing)*

Outside Service Firm(s):

Henry Scholten & Co.*(Auditors)*
Sioux Falls, SD

Boyce, Murphy, McDowell & Greenfield*(Legal Firm)*
Sioux Falls, SD

Norwest Bank Minneosta, N.A.*(Major Banking Relationship)*
Sioux Falls, SD

LEWIS & GACE, INC.
1 Bridge Plaza
Fort Lee, NJ 07024
Tel.: 201-461-9600
Year Founded: 1988
Approx.Billings: $83,000,000
Emp.: 76
Health Care/Pharmaceuticals
Clive Lewis *(Chm. & Chief Exec. Officer)*
Francis Gace *(Pres. & Chief Oper. Officer)*
Stephen King *(Exec. V.P., Creative Services)*
Peter Noto *(Exec. V.P., Creative Services (DTC))*
Michael Reid *(Exec. V.P., Creative Services (DTC))*
Martin Shanahan *(Exec. V.P., Chief Fin. Officer)*
Larry Stoll *(Exec. V.P., Client Services)*
Patrick Crowley *(Sr. V.P., Strategic Mktg., Media Grp. & New Bus. Contact)*
Ed Gillespie *(V.P., Dir.-Human Resources)*
Dan Reinhardt *(Strategic Mktg. Assoc.)*

LEWIS HOMES MANAGEMENT CORP.
1156 North Mountain Avenue
Upland, CA 91786
Mailing Address:
P.O. Box 670
Upland, CA 91785-0670
Tel.: 909-985-0971
Fax: 909-949-6700
Year Founded: 1957
Assets: $650,000,000
Liabilities: $400,000,000
Net Worth: $250,000,000
Approx.Sls.: $500,000,000
Emp.: 700
Fiscal Year-end: 12/31/91
Real Estate Developers
S.I.C.: 1531
Ralph M. Lewis *(Chm. Bd.)*
Richard A. Lewis *(Pres. & Chief Exec. Officer)*
Robert E. Lewis *(Pres. NV Opers. & Exec. V.P.)*
John M. Goodman *(Chief Exec. Officer)*
Goldy S. Lewis *(Exec. V.P.)*
Randall W. Lewis *(Exec. V.P.)*
Roger G. Lewis *(Exec. V.P.)*
Dennis A. Alekel *(Sr. V.P. & Gen. Counsel)*
Hubert Scheffy, Jr. *(V.P. & Controller)*
James R. Price *(Treas.)*

Computer Systems/Hardware:
IBM AS/400

Outside Service Firm(s):

Kenneth Leventhal & Co.*(Auditors)*
Century City, CA

Blue Cross of New York*(Group Insurer)*
New York, NY

First Interstate Bank*(Major Banking Relationship)*
Pomona, CA

First Interstate Bank*(Major Banking Relationship)*
P.O. Box 98511,
Las Vegas, NV 89193-8511

Wells Fargo Bank*(Major Banking Relationship)*
420 Montgomery St.
San Francisco, CA 94104

Affiliates:

Lewis Building Co., Inc. **(1)**
5420 S. Polaris, P.O. Box 19297
Las Vegas, NV 89132
Tel.: 702-736-8960

Lewis Construction Co., Inc. **(1)**
1156 N. Mountain Ave.
Upland, CA 91786
Tel.: 909-985-0971

Lewis Development Co. **(1)**
1156 N. Mountain Ave.
Upland, CA 91786
Tel.: 909-985-0971

Lewis Homes Of California **(1)**
1156 N. Mountain Ave.
Upland, CA 91786
Tel.: 909-985-0971

Lewis Homes Of Nevada **(1)**
3325 Ali Baba Lane
Las Vegas, NV 89132
Tel.: 702-736-8960

Republic Sales Co., Inc. **(1)**
1156 N. Mountain Ave.
Upland, CA 91786
Tel.: 909-985-0971

Western Land Properties **(1)**
1156 N. Mountain Ave.
Upland, CA 91786
Tel.: 909-985-0971

Western Supply Corp. **(1)**
1156 N. Mountain Ave.
Upland, CA 91786
Tel.: 909-985-0971

LEXINGTON CO-OP OIL CO.
P.O. Box A
Lexington, NE 68850
Tel.: 308-324-5539 **NE**
Fax: 308-324-3459
Year Founded: 1926
Approx.Sls.: $12,000,000
Emp.: 48
Wholesale Distribution of Fertilizer & Fertilizer Materials & Feeds & Petroleum Products
S.I.C.: 5191; 5172
Don Anthony *(Pres.)*
Gail Hall *(Gen. Mgr.)*
Robert Caraway *(Sec.)*

Outside Service Firm(s):

McDermott & Miller*(Auditors)*
McCook, NE

Lexington State Bank*(Major Banking Relationship)*
Lexington, NE

LEXMARK INTERNATIONAL, INC.
55 Railroad Ave.
Greenwich, CT 06836
Tel.: 203-629-6700
Fax: 203-629-6724
Year Founded: 1991
Approx.Sls.: $2,000,000,000
Emp.: 5,000
Mfr. & Sale of IBM Laser Printers, Typing Systems, Keyboards & Related Supplies, 10%-Owned by IBM
S.I.C.: 3577; 3579
Marvin L. Mann *(Chm. & Chief Exec. Officer)*

Lexmark International, Inc.—(Continued)

Achim Knust *(V.P. & Chief Fin. Officer)*
Doug LeGrande *(V.P.-U.S. Sls.)*
William Whalley *(Communications Consultant)*

Manufacturing & Development:

Lexmark International, Inc. **(1)**
740 New Circle Rd.
Lexington, KY 40511
Tel.: 606-232-3934
Emp.: 3,000
Mfr. of Lexmark IBM Typewriter, Printer & Keyboard Products, Supplies
S.I.C.: 3577; 3579; 3955
Joan Blomberg *(Dir.-Comms.)*

Lexmark International, Inc. **(1)**
6300 Diagonal Highway
Boulder, CO 80301
Tel.: 303-924-9197
Emp.: 250
Mfr. of Printer Supplies, Toners, Fuser Rolls, Photoconductors & Developers
S.I.C.: 3861
Howard Anderson *(Supplies Product Mgr.)*

Branches:

Lexmark International, Inc. **(1)**
1701 Golf Rd., Tower Two, 2nd Fl.
Rolling Meadows, IL 60008
Tel.: 708-981-6417
Mktg. & Sales of IBM Printers, Typewriters, Keyboards, Supplies
S.I.C.: 5045; 5044; 5043
William Burnette *(Mgr.)*

Lexmark International, Inc. **(1)**
P.O. Box 2868
Greenwich, CT 06835-2868
Tel.: 203-629-6759
Mktg. & Sales of IBM Printers, Typewriters, Keyboards, Supplies
S.I.C.: 5045; 5043
Peter Delle Donne *(Mgr.)*

Lexmark International, Inc. **(1)**
1603 LBJ Freeway, 3rd Fl.
Dallas, TX 75234
Tel.: 214-888-4965
Mktg. & Sales of IBM Printers, Typewriters, Keyboards & Supplies
S.I.C.: 5045; 5044; 5043
Reed Farley *(Mgr.)*

Lexmark International, Inc. **(1)**
1201 W. Peachtree St. N.E., 24th Fl.
Atlanta, GA 30367
Tel.: 404-877-6101
Tel.: 404-877-4592
Mktg. & Sales of IBM Printers, Typewriters, Keyboards & Supplies
S.I.C.: 5045; 5044; 5043
Robert Kendrick *(Mgr.)*

Lexmark International, Inc. **(1)**
425 Market St., 6th Fl.
San Francisco, CA 94105
Tel.: 415-545-5879
Mktg. & Sales of IBM Printers, Typewriters, Keyboards & Supplies
S.I.C.: 5043; 5044
James Lucas *(Mgr.)*

Non-U.S. Holdings:

Lexmark Australia **(1)**
Level 4, Bldg. 2, 20 Bridge St.
Pymble, N.S.W. 2037, Australia
Tel.: 02 481-1204
Mktg. & Sales of IBM Printers, Typewriters, Keyboards & Supplies
S.I.C.: 5045; 5044; 5043
Michael O'Halloran *(Mgr.)*

Lexmark Canada Inc. **(1)**
105 Moatfield Dr. Dept. 500,
North York, ON M3B 3L9, Canada
Tel.: 416-443-4995 (100%)
Mfr. of Ribbons for Printers, Typewriters
S.I.C.: 3955
Eamon Ryan *(Pres.)*
Sandy Corlett *(V.P.-Mktg.)*

Lexmark France **(1)**
Tour Pascal la Defense 7 SND Cedex, F-92075
Paris la Defense, France
Tel.: 01-4767-7755
Mfr. of Ribbons, Toners & Laser Printer Cartridges at Boigny; European Support Center
S.I.C.: 3955; 3861
Minika Veiser *(Mgr.)*

W.S. LIBBEY COMPANY
401 Dearborn St.
Great Falls, SC 29055
Mailing Address:
P.O. Box 148,
Great Falls, SC 29055
Tel.: 803-482-6688
Fax: 803-482-6655
Approx.Sls.: $14,000,000
Emp.: 230
Woven & Nonwoven Industrial Fire Retardant Fabrics, Drapery Fabric, Vertical Blinds
S.I.C.: 2281; 2211; 2295; 2297; 2591
Armand Favreau *(Pres.)*
James Bell *(V.P.-Fin.)*
Peter Bennett *(Gen. Counsel)*
Macklin Grider *(Plant Mgr.)*

Outside Service Firm(s):

Barry, Dunn, McNeil & Parker*(Auditors)*
Portland, ME

Peoples Heritage Savings Bank*(Major Banking Relationship)*
Portland, ME

LIBCO CORPORATION
737 N. Michigan Ave., Ste. 1200
Chicago, IL 60611
Tel.: 312-751-2990 DE
Fax: 312-751-2913
Approx.Sls.: $50,000,000
Emp.: 500
Holding Co.
S.I.C.: 6719; 7359
Clyde W. Engel *(Chm. Bd. & Pres.)*
Phil Robinson *(Controller)*

Subsidiary:

Telco Capital Corp. **(1)**
737 N. Michigan, Ste. 1200
Chicago, IL 60611
Tel.: 312-751-2990 (65%)
Approx.Sls.: $10,000,000
Emp.: 30
Medical Equipment Leasing
S.I.C.: 7359
Clyde W. Engel *(Chief Oper. Officer)*

Subsidiary:

Indiana Financial Investors, Inc. **(2)**
737 N. Michigan Ave., Ste. 1200
Chicago, IL 60611
Tel.: 312-751-2990 (54%)
Assets: $13,366,127
Earnings: $288,191
Liabilities: $679,411
Net Worth: $12,686,716
Approx.Rev.: $842,110
Fiscal Year-end: 6/30/91
Real Estate Investment Co.
S.I.C.: 6798
Clyde Wm. Engle *(Chm. Bd.)*
Richard H. Kendall *(Pres. & Treas.)*
Eugene L. Henderson *(Sec.)*

LIBERTY GLASS COMPANY
1000 N. Mission
Sapulpa, OK 74066
Tel.: 918-224-1440
Approx.Sls.: $60,000,000
Emp.: 400
Fiscal Year-end: 12/31/90
Glass Beverage, Bottles
S.I.C.: 5085
Fulton Collins *(Chm. & Chief Exec. Officer)*
Jim Bolin *(Pres. & Chief Oper. Officer)*
Ralph Moore *(Dir.-Human Resources)*

LIBERTY MILITARY SALES CO.
10550 Rockley Road, Ste. 120
Houston, TX 77099
Tel.: 713-561-2600
Fax: 713-561-2628
Year Founded: 1981
Approx.Sls.: $19,610,000
Emp.: 50
Fiscal Year-end: 12/31/91
Retail Stereos & Appliances
S.I.C.: 5731
John Buckles *(Pres.)*

LIBERTY MUTUAL INSURANCE CO.
175 Berkeley St.
Boston, MA 02117
Tel.: 617-357-9500 MA
Fax: 617-426-3221
Assets: $18,947,422,000
Earnings: $149,211,000
Liabilities: $16,100,730,000
Net Worth: $2,846,692,000
Approx.Sls.: $6,434,427,000
Emp.: 20,000
Fiscal Year-end: 12/31/91
Fire, Marine & Casualty Insurance
S.I.C.: 6331
Gary L. Countryman *(Chm. & Chief Exec. Officer)*
Edmund F. Kelly *(Pres. & Chief Oper. Officer)*
Robert H. Gruhl *(Chief Fin. Officer, Sr. V.P. & Treas.)*
A. Alexander Fontanes *(Chief Investment Officer & Sr. V.P.)*
John B. Conners *(Exec. V.P.)*
Gary Lia *(Exec. V.P.)*
Therese A. Maloney *(Exec. V.P.)*
Maryann P. Burke *(Sr. V.P.-Data Processing & Corp. Research)*
Christopher C. Mansfield *(Sr. V.P. & Gen. Counsel)*
Thomas J. Driscoll *(V.P.-Gov't Affair)*
Helen Sayles *(V.P. & Mgr.-Human Resources)*
Whitney C. Lancaster *(Asst. V.P. & Mgr.-Adv. & Pub. Rels.)*
Stephen W. Keene *(Sec.)*
David Connelly *(Mgr.-Gen. Services)*
Anthony Cirignano *(Mgr.)*
Douglas L. Anderson *(Mgr.-Real Estate)*

No. of U.S. Offices: 300

Computer Systems/Hardware:
IBM 3090, 3081 & 3083 Mainframes Supported by System 3380 Disc Drives and VAX

Outside Service Firm(s):

KPMG Peat Marwick*(Auditors)*
One Boston Place
Boston, MA 02108
Tel.: 617-723-7700

Liberty Mutual*(Group Insurer)*
175 Berkeley St.
Boston, MA

Shawmut Bank*(Major Banking Relationship)*
1 Federal St.
Boston, MA 02110
Tel.: 617-292-3715

Subsidiaries:

Helmsman Management Services, Inc. **(1)**
175 Berkeley St.
Boston, MA 02117
Tel.: 617-357-9500 (100%)
Services for Self-Insured Companies
S.I.C.: 6411

Liberty Financial Companies **(1)**
600 Atlantic Ave.
Boston, MA 02210
Tel.: 617-722-6050
Tel.: 800-433-3399 (100%)
Security Broker/Dealer
S.I.C.: 6211
Kenneth Leibler *(Pres.)*

Subsidiary:

Liberty Distributors Inc. **(2)**
600 Atlantic Ave.
Boston, MA 02210
Tel.: 617-722-6050 (100%)
Securities Brokers/Dealers, Underwriter of Mutual Funds
S.I.C.: 6211
Ralph E. Nixon *(Joint Mng. Dir.)*
Allen Merritt *(Joint Mng. Dir.)*

Liberty Mutual Fire Insurance Co. **(1)**
175 Berkeley St.
Boston, MA 02117
Tel.: 617-357-9500 (100%)
Casualty Insurance
S.I.C.: 6331
G.L. Countryman *(Chm.)*
E.F. Kelly *(Pres. & Chief Oper. Officer)*

Subsidiaries:

Liberty Life Assurance Company of Boston **(2)**
175 Berkeley St.
Boston, MA 02117
Tel.: 617-357-9000 (100%)
Fax: 617-357-9500
Emp.: 637
Life Insurance
S.I.C.: 6311
Stuart L. Lerner *(Pres. & Chief Admin. Officer)*

Liberty Northwest Insurance Corp. **(2)**
825 N.E. Multnomah St.
Portland, OR 97232
Tel.: 503-239-5800 (100%)
Emp.: 504
Casualty Insurance
S.I.C.: 6331
Charles B. Gill, Jr. *(Pres.)*
John R. Galbraith *(Sr. V.P. & Chief Fin. Officer)*
David A. Davidson *(Sr. V.P. & Sec.)*

LIBERTY TOOL CORPORATION
350 Buell Rd.
Rochester, NY 14624
Mailing Address:
P.O. Box 22785
Rochester, NY 14692
Tel.: 716-328-6060
Fax: 716-328-6835
Year Founded: 1922
Approx.Sls.: $10,000,000
Emp.: 145
Fiscal Year-end: 12/31/90
Special Machinery & Molds, Tools, Gauges, Jigs, Fixtures
S.I.C.: 5084; 3829
Karl Fuchs *(Chief Exec. Officer)*
Bryan Hickman *(Pres.)*
Michael Dickinson *(V.P.-Engrng.)*
James Nieboer *(V.P.-Fin.)*
Douglas K. Woods *(V.P.-Sls.)*
Paula Billmon *(Mgr.-Mktg. & Sls. Support)*
Dick Deisenroth *(Engr.)*

LIBERTYVILLE LINCOLN-MERCURY SALES, INC.
941 S. Milwaukee Ave.
Libertyville, IL 60048
Tel.: 708-367-1700 DE
Fax: 708-816-7527
Year Founded: 1981
Approx.Sls.: $173,000,000
Emp.: 100
Fiscal Year-end: 12/31/91
Automobile Sales & Rental
S.I.C.: 5511; 7514
Julius Marks, Jr. *(Pres.)*
Karen L. Casey *(Sec. & Treas.)*

Subsidiary:

Classic Chevrolet **(1)**
425 N. Green Bay Rd.
Waukegan, IL 60085
Tel.: 708-336-4300
Automobile Rental
S.I.C.: 5511
Dan Kern *(Gen. Mgr.)*
Patricia Kluck *(Chief Fin. Officer)*

LIDA ADVERTISING COMPANY
393 N. McLean Blvd.
Wichita, KS 67203
Tel.: 316-263-1029
Fax: 316-263-0493
Year Founded: 1979
Approx.Billings: $15,000,000
Robert S. Lida *(Pres.)*
Roger Shurtz *(V.P.-Opers.)*
Rebecca Nelson *(Dir.-Pub. Rels.)*

LIEBERMAN-APPALUCCI
4635 Crackersport Rd.
Allentown, PA 18104
Tel.: 215-395-7111
Fax: 215-395-8027
Year Founded: 1954
Approx.Billings: $17,000,000
Emp.: 35
Joseph L. Appalucci *(Chm. & Chief Exec. Officer)*
Mark T. Lieberman *(Pres. & Chief Oper. Officer)*
Michael J. Lieberman *(Exec. V.P., Bus. Devel.)*
Richard L. Frick *(Sr. V.P., Fin.)*

LIFE LINE NUTRITIONALS, INC.
3317 Arden Rd.
Hayward, CA 94545
Mailing Address:
P.O. Box 56865
Hayward, CA 94545
Tel.: 510-782-8622
Fax: 510-782-3127
Year Founded: 1974
Assets: $5,000,000
Liabilities: $3,300,000
Net Worth: $1,700,000
Sales Range: $10-19 Million
Emp.: 75
Fiscal Year-end: 9/30/92
Export
Mfr. of Vitamins & Over-the-Counter Pharmaceuticals
S.I.C.: 2834
Dan Varella *(Pres.)*
Linda Whetson *(Chief Fin. Officer & Controller)*
Kim Flynn *(Dir.-Personnel)*
Mysti Knox *(Dir.-Export)*
Jane Morhouse *(Dir.-Adv.)*
Rich Sims *(Dir.-Mktg.)*
Steve Varella *(Dir.-Mfg.)*

Computer Systems/Hardware:
McDonnell-Douglas Spirit

Outside Service Firm(s):

Chubb Group*(Commercial Insurance Carrier)*
Two Embarcadero Center, Ste. 900
San Francisco, CA 94111

Shartsis, Friese & Ginsburg*(Legal Firm)*
255 California St.
San Francisco, CA 94111
Tel.: 415-421-6500

Union Bank*(Major Banking Relationship)*
200 Pringle Ave.
Walnut Creek, CA 94596
Tel.: 510-947-2444

LIFETIME DOORS INC.
30700 Northwestern Hwy.
Farmington Hills, MI 48334
Tel.: 313-851-7700
Fax: 313-851-8534
Approx.Sls.: $77,000,000
Emp.: 1,000
Manufacture Residential & Commercial Doors
S.I.C.: 2431
William B. Gilbert *(Chm. Bd. & Pres.)*
James Mitchell *(V.P.-Admin.)*

No. of Mfg. Plants/Facilities: 10

No. of U.S. Offices: 10

Outside Service Firm(s):

Kleiman, Carney & Greenbaum*(Auditors)*
Farmington Hills, MI

Manufacturers National Bank N.A.*(Major Banking Relationship)*
38th Fl., 100 Renaissance Center
Detroit, MI 48243
Tel.: 313-222-4227

LIFETOUCH, INC.
7831 Glenroy Rd.
Bloomington, MN 55439
Tel.: 612-893-0500 **MN**
Fax: 612-832-4557
Year Founded: 1936
Approx.Sls.: $300,000,000
Emp.: 5,000
Fiscal Year-end: 6/30/91
Photographic Studios
S.I.C.: 7221
Richard P. Erickson *(Chm. Bd. & Chief Exec. Officer)*
David D. Koentopf *(Pres. & Chief Oper. Officer)*
Gary Goerner *(V.P.-Prod.)*
Mark Kilchenman *(V.P.-School Grp.)*
Paul D. Milne *(V.P.-Mngmt. Information Systems)*
Randy Pladson *(V.P.-Fin.)*
Robert H. Treuchel *(V.P.-Admin.)*
Richard Eng *(Treas.)*
Principal(s):
Employee-Owned

No. of Mfg. Plants/Facilities: 6

Outside Service Firm(s):

Norwest Bank Minnesota, N.A.*(Major Banking Relationship)*
6th St. & Marquette Av.
Minneapolis, MN 55479
Tel.: 612-667-1234

Subsidiaries:

Lifetouch National School Studios Inc. **(1)**
7800 Picture Dr.
Minneapolis, MN 55439
Tel.: 612-835-3400
S.I.C.: 7221
David D. Koentopf *(Pres. & Chief Exec. Officer)*

Lifetouch Portrait Studios Inc. **(1)**
7831 Glenroy Rd.
Bloomington, MN 55437
Tel.: 612-893-0500
S.I.C.: 7221
David D. Koentopf *(Pres. & Chief Exec. Officer)*

Lifetouch Publishing Inc. **(1)**
400 Paramount Plaza, 7831 Glenroy Rd.
Minneapolis, MN 55435
Tel.: 612-893-0500
Publish Yearbooks
S.I.C.: 2741
David D. Koentopf *(Pres. & Chief Exec. Officer)*

Lifetouch Senior Portraits Inc. **(1)**
7831 Glenroy Rd.
Bloomington, MN 55439
Tel.: 612-832-4389
S.I.C.: 7221
Koentopf, David D. *(Pres. & Chief Exec. Officer)*

Lifetouch Video Creations, Inc. **(1)**
7831 Glenroy Rd.
Bloomington, MN 55439
Tel.: 612-893-0500
Video Yearbooks
S.I.C.: 7221
David D. Koentopf *(Pres. & Chief Exec. Officer)*

Max Ward-Delmar Studios **(1)**
2210 Paramont Ave.
Chesapeake, VA 23320
Tel.: 804-420-7780
Fax: 804-420-7804
Individual Portrait & Yearbook Requirements For Public & Private Schools
S.I.C.: 7221
Robert M. Hendrickson *(Chief Oper. Officer)*

Potrait Industries Corporation **(1)**
2210 Paramont Ave.
Chesapeake, VA 23320
Tel.: 804-420-7790
Fax: 804-420-7804
Photographic Portrait Business
S.I.C.: 7221
James W. Saine *(Pres. & Chief Oper. Officer)*
Charles G. Bingenheimer, Jr. *(V.P.-Fin.)*
Robert M. Hendrickson *(V.P.-Mfg.)*
Pamela J. Leadbetter *(V.P.-Mktg.)*

LIFT-ALL CO., INC.
102 S. Heintzelman St.
Manheim, PA 17545
Tel.: 717-665-6821 **PA**
Emp.: 165
Lifting and Swing Wire Fasteners
S.I.C.: 3496
Jeffery M. Klibert *(Pres. & Chief Exec. Officer)*
Robert E. Doster *(Treas. & Sec.)*
Jeffery R. Kauffman *(Asst. Treas. & Asst. Sec.)*
John D. Roberts *(V.P.-Sls.)*
Steven S. Kleavert *(Mgr.-Plant)*
J. Martin Rankin *(Pur. Agent)*

Outside Service Firm(s):

Charles T. Anton*(Auditors)*
Philadelphia, PA

Barley, Snyder, Cooper & Barber*(Legal Firm)*
Lancaster, PA

Fulton Bank*(Major Banking Relationship)*
110 Penn Sq.
Lancaster, PA 17602
Tel.: 717-291-2411

LIGGETT·STASHOWER

LIGGETT-STASHOWER, INC.
1228 Euclid Ave.
Cleveland, OH 44115
Tel.: 216-348-8500
Fax: 216-861-1284
Year Founded: 1987
Approx.Billings: $72,400,000
Emp.: 130
Consumer/Business-to-Business Adv., Direct Mktg., Public Relations, Yellow Pages Adv. & Recruitment Adv.
David L. Stashower *(Chm. & Chief Exec. Officer)*
Thomas S. Case *(Vice Chm., Chief Creative Dir.)*
Edmund M. Kagy *(Vice Chm., Graphics Arts Div.)*
C. Henry Foltz *(Pres. & Chief Oper. Officer)*
Thomas A. Moore *(Exec. V.P., Dir. Mktg. Services)*
John R. Ballantyne *(Sr. V.P.)*
Sylvia Morrison *(V.P., Direct Response Mktg. Gen. Mgr.)*
David Slavick *(V.P., Dir. Mktg. & Media Planning)*
James W. Upson *(V.P., Treas.)*
John Duddy *(Gen. Mgr., Directory Services Grp.)*
Traci Rath-Kanuch *(Mgr., Liggett-Stashower Recruitment Services)*
Nancy M. Disbrow *(Personnel Admin.)*

LIGHTS OF AMERICA, INC.
611 Reyes Dr.
Walnut, CA 91789
Tel.: 909-594-7883
Fax: 909-598-5931
Year Founded: 1978
Approx.Sls.: $50,000,000
Emp.: 400
Mfr. of Fluorescent Lighting Products; Security Motion Devices
S.I.C.: 3645
Usman U. Vakil *(Chm. Bd., Pres. & Treas.)*
Farooq U. Vakil *(Exec. V.P. & Sec.)*
Abubakar U. Vakil *(V.P.-Research & Devel.)*
Ishaq U. Vakil *(V.P.-Sls.)*
Iqbal U. Vakil *(V.P.-Pur.)*

Outside Service Firm(s):

Manatt, Phelps, Phillips & Kantor*(Legal Firm)*
11355 W. Olympic Blvd.
Los Angeles, CA 90067
Tel.: 310-312-4000

The Bank of California, N.A.*(Major Banking Relationship)*
400 California
San Francisco, CA 94104
Tel.: 415-765-0400

THE CHAS. H. LILLY CO.
7737 N. E. Killingsworth
Portland, OR 97218
Tel.: 503-256-4600
Approx.Sls.: $32,000,000
Emp.: 135
Fiscal Year-end: 10/31/92
Mfr. of Home & Garden Fertilizer & Chemicals, Pkgng. Flower & Vegetable Seed
S.I.C.: 2874
F.L. Trullinger *(Pres.)*
Robert Griffith *(V.P., Sec. & Treas.)*
Vaughn Myers *(V.P.-Fin.)*
Walt Griffith *(V.P.-Mktg.)*
Larry Miller *(Dir.-Sls.)*

Computer Systems/Hardware:
IBM

LINBECK CORP.
3810 W. Alabama
Houston, TX 77027
Mailing Address:
P.O. Box 22500
Houston, TX 77227
Tel.: 713-621-2350 **TX**
Fax: 713-840-7525
Approx.Sls.: $125,000,000
Emp.: 180
Fiscal Year-end: 3/31/92
General Contractor; Commercial & Industrial Buildings, Warehouses, Concrete Work
S.I.C.: 1542; 1541; 1771
Corporate Giving Program:
Contributes to the Linbeck Foundation
Employee Matching Gifts Program:
Limited primarily to University matching gifts
Leo E. Linbeck, Jr. *(Chm. Bd. & Chief Exec. Officer)*
Peter G. Doyle *(Chief Fin. Officer & Exec. V.P.)*
Glenn D. Graff *(Exec. V.P.-Fin.)*
Nancy L. Breland *(Sec.)*
Principal(s):
Leo E. Linbeck, Jr.
Patricia Doyle
Suzanne Reynolds

Computer Systems/Hardware:
IBM/MAC

Outside Service Firm(s):

Deloitte & Touche*(Auditors)*
333 Clay St., Ste. 2300
Houston, TX 77002
Tel.: 713-756-2000

LINCOLN ELECTRIC SYSTEMS
1040 O St.
Lincoln, NE 68508
Mailing Address:
P.O. Box 80869,
Lincoln, NE 68501
Tel.: 402-475-4211

Lincoln Electric Systems—(Continued)

Assets: $421,500,000
Liabilities: $30,785,000
Net Worth: $390,715,000
Approx.Sls.: $106,835,000
Emp.: 400
Fiscal Year-end: 12/31/90
Electric Utility
S.I.C.: 4911
Robert L. Tyler *(Chm. Bd.)*
Keith C. Brown *(Chief Fin. Officer)*
Oscar A. Sandberg *(Sec.)*
William Cortney *(Dir.-Pur.)*
Debbra Hoy *(Dir.-Human Resources)*

LINCOLN INDUSTRIES
4700 S. 19th St.
Lincoln, NE 68512
Mailing Address:
P.O. Box 80529
Lincoln, NE 68501
Tel.: 402-421-7300
Tel.: 800-548-3221
Fax: 402-421-0507
Emp.: 800
Lessor of Gas, Mineral Rights & Railroad Equipment; Grain Wholesaler; Cattle Ranching; Wholesale & Retail Textbooks
S.I.C.: 0212; 4741; 5199; 5942; 6519
George A. Lincoln *(Chm. Bd. & Pres.)*
Bill C. Macy *(Exec. V.P.)*
Ardean Arndt *(V.P. & Sec.)*
Larry Rempe *(V.P.-Info. Systems)*

No. of U.S. Offices: 7

Computer Systems/Hardware:
IBM 4341

Outside Service Firm(s):

Arthur Andersen & Co.*(Auditors)*
1500 Commerce Tower, 911 Main St.
Kansas City, MO 64105
Tel.: 816-221-4200
Fax: 816-221-7693

First National Bank & Trust Co.*(Major Banking Relationship)*
Lincoln, NE

Subsidiaries:

Nebraska Book Co. **(1)**
4700 S. 19th
Lincoln, NE 68512
Tel.: 402-421-7300
Wholesale & Retail Textbooks
S.I.C.: 5192; 5942
Mark Oppegard *(Pres.)*

25 Corporation **(1)**
4700 S. 19th
Lincoln, NE 68512
Tel.: 402-421-7300
George Lincoln *(Chief Oper. Officer)*

LINCOLN PROPERTY COMPANY
500 N. Akard
Dallas, TX 75201
Tel.: 214-740-3300
Fax: 214-740-3313
Year Founded: 1965
Sales Range: $100-499 Million
Emp.: 4,000
Land Subdividers & Developers; Apartment Building Operators; Real Estate Managers; Commercial & Industrial Building Operation; Financial Management For Business; Adminstrative Management
S.I.C.: 6552; 6512
A. Mack Pogue *(Chm. Bd., Pres. & Chief Exec. Officer)*
Ken E. Mooter *(Exec. V.P.-Fin.)*
W. Mark Wallis *(Exec. V.P. & Chief Fin. Officer)*
Jeff Courtwright *(Sr. V.P.-Leasing)*
Ed Mace *(V.P.-Intl. Fin.)*
Connie Rutledge *(V.P. & Corp. Controller)*
Preston Butcher *(Reg. Partner)*
Tim Byrne *(Reg. Partner)*
Bill Duvall *(Reg. Partner)*
Marshall Tycher *(Reg. Partner)*
Mike Loftis *(Dir.-Mktg.)*
Debi Davis *(Mgr.-Personnel Training)*
Steve Fallon *(Mgr.-Employee Benefits)*
Marsha Spring *(Mgr.-Corp. Adv.)*
Leigh Ann Everett *(Corp. Travel Coordinator)*

Outside Service Firm(s):

Ernst & Young*(Auditors)*
2121 San Jacinto, Ste. 500
Dallas, TX 75201
Tel.: 214-969-8000

Texas Commerce Bank*(Major Banking Relationship)*
2200 Ross Ave.
Dallas, TX 75266

Branches:

Lincoln Property Company CSE, Inc. **(1)**
500 N. Akard, Ste. 3300
Dallas, TX 75201
Tel.: 214-740-3300
Approx.Sls.: $89,000,000
Emp.: 700
General Construction Contractors For Industrial Buildings & Warehouses
S.I.C.: 1541
Mack Pogue *(Chm. Bd.)*
William C. Duvall *(Pres.)*
Ken Mooter *(Sr. V.P.)*

Lincoln Property Co., Northern California **(1)**
101 Lincoln Center Dr.
Foster City, CA 94404
Tel.: 415-571-2250
Emp.: 1,500
Commercial, Office Buildings & Multi-family Dwellings New Construction; Commercial, Industrial Building & Apartment Building Operators
S.I.C.: 1542; 1522; 6512; 6513
Mack Pogue *(Chm. Bd.)*
C. Preston Butcher *(Pres. & Chief Exec. Officer)*
Gary Rossi *(Sr. V.P.-Fin. & Admin.)*

LINCOLN PROVISION COMPANY, INC.
824 W. 38th Place
Chicago, IL 60609
Tel.: 312-254-2400 **IL**
Year Founded: 1985
Approx.Sls.: $65,000,000
Emp.: 90
Wholesale Distributor of Meat & Meat Products
S.I.C.: 5147
Jim J. Stevens *(Pres.)*
Jim J. Stevens, Jr. *(Treas. & Sec.)*

Outside Service Firm(s):

Marquette National Bank*(Major Banking Relationship)*
Chicago, IL

LINDER & ASSOCIATES, INC.
840 N. Main
Wichita, KS 67203
Tel.: 316-265-6691 **KS**
Fax: 316-265-0674
Approx.Sls.: $10,000,000
Emp.: 95
General Electrical Contractor
S.I.C.: 1731
James L. Linder *(Pres.)*
Allan Linder *(Exec. V.P.)*
Delmar D. Klocke *(Sr. V.P.)*
Kaye Hall *(Sec.)*

Outside Service Firm(s):

Allen, Gibbs, Houlik*(Auditors)*
301 N. Main, Ste. 1700
Wichita, KS 67202
Tel.: 316-267-7231

Adams, Jones, Robinson & Malone*(Legal Firm)*
Wichita, KS

First National Bank of Wichita*(Major Banking Relationship)*
Box One
Wichita, KS 67201
Tel.: 316-268-1201

LINDSAY MANUFACTURING INC.
Bldg. 3, Darr Industrial Park
Ponca City, OK 74601
Tel.: 405-762-2457
Fax: 405-762-9547
Year Founded: 1956
Emp.: 80
Import Export
Built-In Central Vacuum Systems: Residential, Commercial & Industrial
S.I.C.: 3635; 3589
Winston S. Lindsay III *(Chm. Bd. & Chief Exec. Officer)*
Edward W. Lindsay, Jr. *(Pres.)*
Edward W. Lindsay, Sr. *(V.P.)*
Paul J. Seeley *(Treas., Sec. & Controller)*

Outside Service Firm(s):

Deloitte & Touche*(Auditors)*
One Williams Center, Ste. 2400
Tulsa, OK
Tel.: 918-586-8800

Security Bank & Trust Co.*(Major Banking Relationship)*
Southgate, MI

LINDSAY OLIVE GROWERS
650 W. Tulare Rd.
Lindsay, CA 93247
Mailing Address:
P.O. Box 278
Lindsay, CA 93247
Tel.: 209-562-5121
Approx.Sls.: $55,000,000
Emp.: 500
Import
Cooperative Mktg. Assn. of Olive Growers; Lindsay, Valencia, Charles Hill, Orinda, Wyandotte, San Fernando Valley, Aunt Penny's Sauces
S.I.C.: 8611; 0179
Greg Childress *(Chm. Bd.)*
Robert Hardin *(Vice Chm.)*
Robert D. Rossio *(Pres. & Chief Exec. Officer)*
Jerry C. Sullivan *(V.P.-Opers.)*
Eric M. Boyle *(Sr. V.P.-Intl. Sls. & Mktg.)*
J.B. Earle *(Sec.)*
Rod Vieira *(Controller)*
Stan Carlson *(Field Opers.)*
Richard W. Vorreyer *(Dir.-Indus. Rels.)*
Grant Wagner *(Dir.-Sls.)*
Nancy Williams *(Exec. Sec.)*

Division:

Lindsay International **(1)**
650 W. Tulare Rd.
Lindsay, CA 93247
Tel.: 209-562-5121
Fax: 209-562-1620
Approx.Sls.: $55,000,000
Emp.: 250
Fiscal Year-end: 8/31/90
Lindsay Olives, Onions, Aunt Penny Sauces
S.I.C.: 2033
Robert D. Rossio *(Pres.)*
Eric M. Boyle *(V.P.-Intl. Sls.)*
Bill Osterbauer *(Controller)*
Jim Earle *(Sec. & Distr. Mgr.)*
Fred J. Hobscheid *(Sls. Mgr.-Natl. Food Service)*
Grant Wagner *(Prod. Mgr.)*

LINDSAY, STONE & BRIGGS ADVERTISING, INC.
100 State St.
Madison, WI 53703
Tel.: 608-251-7070
Fax: 608-251-8989
Year Founded: 1978
Approx.Billings: $11,600,000
Emp.: 22
Packaged Goods, Sporting Goods, Travel, Leisure & Hospitality
Marsha Lindsay *(Pres. & Chief Exec. Officer)*
Richard Stone *(Exec. V.P., Chief Oper. Officer)*
Howard Cosgrove *(V.P., Pub. Rels.)*
Pam Koch *(Controller)*

Computer Systems/Hardware:
IBM

LINEAR DYNAMICS INC.
400 Lanidex Plaza
Parsippany, NJ 07054
Tel.: 201-884-0300
Fax: 201-884-9407
Approx.Sls.: $35,000,000
Emp.: 150
Matls. & Equip. for Hwy. Marking
S.I.C.: 3272; 3251; 1422; 1611; 2851; 2891; 3713; 3827
William L. Henry III *(Pres.)*
Carl Fry *(V.P.)*
Karen H. Henry *(Dir.-Mktg. & Adv.)*

LINETT & HARRISON
306 Main St.
Millburn, NJ 07041
Tel.: 201-912-8800
Fax: 201-912-8806
Year Founded: 1989
Approx.Billings: $19,000,000
Emp.: 15
Advertising, Direct Marketing, Sales Promotion & Public Relations
Caryl Linett *(Pres. & Creative Dir.)*
Barbara Haas *(Controller)*

O.P. LINK HANDLE COMPANY
P.O. Box 350
Salem, IN 47167-0350
Tel.: 812-883-2981
Tel.: 800-992-9171 **IN**
Fax: 812-883-1672
Sales Range: $20-39 Million
Emp.: 415
Fiscal Year-end: 5/31/91
Export
Wood Tool Handles
S.I.C.: 2499
Norman Link *(Chm. Bd. & Chief Exec. Officer)*
Perry Link *(Pres.)*
Bonnie Davis *(Sec. & Treas.)*
Mike McCarty *(Dir.-Mktg.)*
Lowell Little *(Gen. Mgr.)*
Pauline Stephens *(Corporate Travel Planner)*

Outside Service Firm(s):

Henderman & Company*(Auditors)*
Louisville, KY

Ogden, Newell & Welch*(Legal Firm)*
1200 One Riverfront Plaza
Louisville, KY 40270
Tel.: 502-582-1601

National Bank*(Major Banking Relationship)*
Philadelphia, PA

Divisions:

Bruner-Ivory Handle Company **(1)**
P.O. Box 647
Hope, AR 71801
Tel.: 501-777-2304
Wood Tool Handles
S.I.C.: 2499
Perry Link *(Pres.)*

Sequatchie Handle Works, Inc. **(1)**
P.O. Box 140
Sequatchie, TN 37374
Tel.: 615-942-5901
Wood Tool Handles
S.I.C.: 2499
Perry Link *(Pres.)*

Turner, Day & Woolworth Handle Corp. **(1)**
P.O. Box 322
Crossville, TN 38555
Tel.: 615-484-8491
Emp.: 75
Wood Tool Handles
S.I.C.: 2499
Perry Link *(Pres.)*

LINKOUS CONSTRUCTION COMPANY, INC.
6075 Poplar, Ste. 202
Memphis, TN 38119
Tel.: 901-767-7373
Fax: 901-767-4704
Year Founded: 1983
Approx.Sls.: $45,000,000
Emp.: 75
Commercial & Industrial Building Contractor
S.I.C.: 1541; 1542; 1521
R.E. Linkous *(Pres. & Chief Exec. Officer)*
Michael Brewer *(Exec. V.P.)*
Clare Linkous *(Treas. & Sec.)*

Outside Service Firm(s):

National Bank of Commerce*(Major Banking Relationship)*
Memphis, TN

LINN PRODUCTS, INC.
1700 E. Packard Hwy.
Charlotte, MI 48813
Tel.: 517-543-1820
Fax: 517-543-3520
Year Founded: 1979
Assets: $1,471,501
Liabilities: $1,080,555
Net Worth: $390,946
Sales Range: $10-19 Million
Emp.: 48
Fiscal Year-end: 12/31/91
Extrude & Fabricate Aluminum
S.I.C.: 3334; 3354; 3429; 3444; 3471
Randy Linn *(Pres.)*
Charlotte Grimwood *(Controller)*
Kelly Custer *(Mgr.-Sls.)*
Gregory Shaver *(Gen. Mgr.)*

Principal(s):
Randy Linn

No. of Mfg. Plants/Facilities: 1

Computer Systems/Hardware:
Pick

Outside Service Firm(s):

Coplin & Baughman Accounting*(Auditors)*
Eaton Rapids, MI

Hall & Kennedy, Inc.*(Group Insurer)*
Lansing, MI

Foster, Swift, Collins & Smith*(Legal Firm)*
Lansing, MI

First America Bank*(Major Banking Relationship)*
East Lansing, MI

LINOTYPE-HELL COMPANY
425 Oser Ave.
Hauppauge, NY 11788
Tel.: 516-434-2000
Fax: 516-434-2748
Year Founded: 1886
Sales Range: $100-499 Million
Emp.: 900
Manufacturer & Distributor of Typsetting Systems
S.I.C.: 3555; 5044
David Dinin *(Pres.)*
James Klauber *(V.P.-Sls.)*
Gus Keysor *(Gen. Counsel)*
Joel Kurtz *(Dir.-Fin.)*
Thomas Edwards *(Mgr.-Mktg. Services)*
Vickie Matus *(Mgr.-Market Research)*

No. of Mfg. Plants/Facilities: 1
No. of U.S. Offices: 20
No. of Foreign Offices: 4

LINZER PRODUCTS CORP.
13330 37th Ave.
Flushing, NY 11354
Mailing Address:
P.O. Box 5466
Flusing, NY 11354
Tel.: 718-961-0900
Tel.: 800-221-0787 **NY**
Fax: 718-358-0551
Year Founded: 1892
Approx.Sls.: $30,000,000
Emp.: 300
Fiscal Year-end: 12/31/91
Import Export
Paint Brushes, Rollers & Pad Painters
S.I.C.: 3991
Morton A. Linzer *(Pres. & Treas.)*
Alan Benson *(Chief Exec. Officer & V.P.)*
Sidney Zichlin *(Chief Oper. Officer & V.P.)*
Mark Saji *(Chief Fin. Officer & V.P.)*
Brent Swenson *(Exec. V.P. & V.P. Sls.)*
Sam Ruffo *(V.P. Sls.)*
Gerry Nitzberg *(Controllor)*

No. of Mfg. Plants/Facilities: 3
No. of U.S. Offices: 2

Outside Service Firm(s):

KPMG Peat Marwick*(Auditors)*
345 Park Ave.
New York, NY 10154
Tel.: 212-758-9700
Fax: 212-872-3308

Laventhall & Zicklin*(Legal Firm)*
New York, NY

Manufacturers Hanover Trust Co.*(Major Banking Relationship)*
4 New York Plaza
New York, NY 10015
Tel.: 212-623-4444

LION BROTHERS COMPANY, INC.
10246 Registertown Rd.
Owings Mills, MD 21117
Tel.: 410-363-1000
Tel.: 800-365-6543
Fax: 410-363-0181
Year Founded: 1899
Approx.Sls.: $15,000,000
Emp.: 368
Fiscal Year-end: 12/31/90
Import Export
Mfr. of Embroidered Emblems & Caps
S.I.C.: 2395
Susan Ganz *(Pres.)*
Gordon Jenkins *(V.P.)*
Charisse Wernecke *(V.P.-Fin.)*
Tony Dale *(Dir.-Sls. & Admin.)*

Computer Systems/Hardware:
Mapex

Outside Service Firm(s):

Arthur Anderson & Co.*(Auditors)*
Baltimore, MD

Maryland National Bank*(Major Banking Relationship)*
2 N. Charles St.
Baltimore, MD 21201

THE LION, INC. (GIBBONS-STEGMAIER BREWERY)
700 N. Pennsylvania Ave., Box GS
Wilkes-Barre, PA 18703
Tel.: 717-823-8801
Fax: 717-823-6686
Approx.Sls.: $15,000,000
Emp.: 150
Fiscal Year-end: 12/31/90
Stegmaier Gold Medal Beer, Ale, Porter, Bock Beer; Gibbons Premium Beer & Ale; Bartels Pure Beer; Liebotschoner Cream Ale; Esslinger Premium Beer, Steg Light Low Calorie Beer, Lionshead Deluxe Pilsener Beer, 1857 Lager, 1857 Light, 1857 Dry, 1857 Porter
S.I.C.: 2082
William Smulowitz *(Chm., Pres. & Chief Exec. Officer)*
Robert Covert *(V.P.-Logistics & Mngmt. Inventory)*
Guy Hanger *(V.P.-Production)*
David Finn *(V.P.-Pkgng.)*
Phil Leinhart *(Brewmaster)*
Joseph Federicci *(Controller)*
Allan Kluger *(Gen. Counsel)*
Walter Ciolek *(Sec.)*
Leo Orlandini *(Mgr.-Quality Assurance)*

LIONEL TRAINS, INC.
50625 Richard W. Blvd.
Chesterfield, MI 48051-2493
Tel.: 313-949-4100 **MI**
Fax: 313-949-3273
Approx.Sls.: $55,000,000
Emp.: 700
Fiscal Year-end: 12/31/90
Import Export
Mfr. Lionel Model Electric Trains & Accessories
S.I.C.: 3944
Richard P. Kughn *(Chm. Bd. & Chief Exec. Officer)*
Nicholas J. DeGrazia *(Pres. & Chief Oper. Officer)*
Patrice M. Bogden *(V.P.-Human Resources)*
Mark Gordon *(V.P.-Mktg. & Sls.)*
Gene Kutcher *(V.P.)*
Charles Rataj *(V.P.-Fin.)*
Sherrie Weitzman *(Dir.-Mktg. Services)*

Principal(s):
Richard P. Kughn
Nicholas J. DeGrazia
Gary A. Kughn

No. of Mfg. Plants/Facilities: 2
No. of U.S. Offices: 2

Computer Systems/Hardware:
IBM System 38

Outside Service Firm(s):

Plante & Moran*(Auditors)*
Detroit, MI

Honigman, Miller, Schwartz & Cohn*(Legal Firm)*
2290 First National Bldg.
Detroit, MI 48226
Tel.: 313-256-7800

Manufacturers National Bank N.A.*(Major Banking Relationship)*
38th Fl., 100 Renaissance Center
Detroit, MI 48243
Tel.: 313-222-4227

LIPMAN, RICHMOND, GREENE
470 Park Ave. South
New York, NY 10016
Tel.: 212-684-1100
Fax: 212-684-5387
Year Founded: 1943
Approx.Billings: $18,000,000
Emp.: 35
Full Service Diversified Accounts., Consumer & Trade
Robert S. Lipman *(Pres.)*
Donna Lipman *(Exec. V.P.)*
Richard Lipman *(Exec. V.P.)*
David Lipman *(Exec. V.P.)*
Chuck Auerbach *(Sr. V.P.)*
Marcia Ben-Eli *(Sr. V.P.)*
Richard Brauner *(Sr. V.P.)*
Alvin George *(Sr. V.P.)*
Saul Ginsberg *(Sr. V.P.)*
Peter Santi *(Sr. V.P.)*
Joyce Silverman *(Sr. V.P.)*
Matthew Forbes *(Sr. V.P., Assoc. Creative Dir.)*

LIQUID CONTROLS CORPORATION
105 Albrecht Dr.
Lake Bluff, IL 60064
Tel.: 708-295-1050
Fax: 708-689-8090
Approx.Sls.: $20,000,000
Emp.: 105
Export
Mfr. Positive Displacement Flow Meters & Accessories
S.I.C.: 3823
Fred G. Wacker, Jr. *(Chm. Bd.)*
Fred G. Wacker, III *(Pres.)*
Douglas Beattie *(V.P.-Mktg.)*
W. Kolb *(V.P.-Engrng.)*
Robert Traettino *(V.P.-Quality)*
Daniel Drury *(Treas. & Controller)*
Mel Hankel *(Chief Engineer)*
Susan Koesser *(Mgr.-Human Resources)*
Royal Wollberg *(Natl. Sls. Mgr.)*

Outside Service Firm(s):

Bansley & Keiner*(Auditors)*
Chicago, IL

Gardner, Carton & Douglas*(Legal Firm)*
321 N. Clark St., Ste. 3400
Chicago, IL 60610
Tel.: 312-644-3000

Lakeshore National Bank*(Major Banking Relationship)*
Chicago, IL

LIST INDUSTRIES, INC.
401 N.W. 12th Ave.
Deerfield Beach, FL 33442
Tel.: 305-429-9155 **IL**
Fax: 305-428-3843
Year Founded: 1953
Approx.Sls.: $17,000,000
Emp.: 180
Export
Mfr. of Lockers, Except Wood
S.I.C.: 2542
Herbert A. List, Jr. *(Pres.)*
David J. List *(Treas.)*
Alice McKenny *(Sec.)*

Outside Service Firm(s):

McGladrey & Pullen*(Auditors)*
Chicago, IL

LITECONTROL CORPORATION
100 Hawks Ave.
Hanson, MA 02341
Tel.: 617-294-0100
Fax: 617-293-2849
Approx.Sls.: $20,000,000
Emp.: 180
Manufacturer of Architecural Fluorescent Lighting
S.I.C.: 3646; 3634
Robert Danforth *(Pres.)*

Litecontrol Corporation—(Continued)

Richard Smith *(V.P.-Engrng.)*
Veda Clark *(V.P.-Mktg. & Sls.)*
William Butler *(Treas.)*
Michael Kelly *(Pur. Agent)*

Outside Service Firm(s):

Gerald T. Reilly & Co.*(Auditors)*
Milton, MA

Ropes & Gray*(Legal Firm)*
One International Place
Boston, MA 02110
Tel.: 617-423-6100

Brown Brothers, Harriman & Co.*(Major Banking Relationship)*
59 Wall St.
New York, NY 10005-2818
Tel.: 212-493-8029

LITHOGRAPH PRINTING COMPANY, INC.
4222 Pilot Dr.
Memphis, TN 38118
Tel.: 901-365-7100
Fax: 901-795-7815
Year Founded: 1947
Approx.Sls.: $16,000,000
Emp.: 142
Fiscal Year-end: 12/31/91
Lithography
S.I.C.: 2752
Walter P. McMullen, Sr. *(Chm. Bd. & Chief Exec. Officer)*
Herbert H. Akers *(Vice Chm.)*
Perkins Cochran *(Pres.)*
Phil Smythe *(V.P.-Mfg.)*
Phyllis A. Leoncavallo *(Mgr.-Personnel)*
Principal(s):
Walter P. McMullen, Sr.
Herbert H. Akers

No. of Mfg. Plants/Facilities: 1
No. of U.S. Offices: 1

Outside Service Firm(s):

Richard Armour*(Auditors)*
Memphis, TN

Bogatin, Lawson & Chiapella*(Legal Firm)*
Memphis, TN

First Tennessee Bank, N.A.*(Major Banking Relationship)*
P.O. Box 101
Memphis, TN 38101
Tel.: 901-523-4555

LITHOGRAPHIX, INC.
13500 S. Figueroa St.
Los Angeles, CA 90061
Tel.: 213-770-1000
Tel.: 800-848-2449 **CA**
Fax: 213-770-1731
Year Founded: 1954
Approx.Sls.: $22,500,000
Emp.: 135
Fiscal Year-end: 8/31/90
Lithographic Printing
S.I.C.: 2752
Herbert Zebrack *(Pres.)*
Melvin Grossman *(V.P., Sec. & Treas.)*
Victor Wolfe *(Controller)*

No. of Mfg. Plants/Facilities: 1
No. of U.S. Offices: 1

Outside Service Firm(s):

Utica Mutual Insurance*(Commercial Insurance Carrier)*
Utica, NY

CIGNA*(Group Insurer)*
Los Angeles, CA

First Interstate Bank of California, N.A.*(Major Banking Relationship)*
P.O. Box 3667,
Los Angeles, CA 90051
Tel.: 213-614-4000

LITHOTYPE COMPANY, INC.
333 Pt. San Bruno Blvd.
South San Francisco, CA 94080
Mailing Address:
P.O. Box 2885,
South San Francisco, CA 94083
Tel.: 415-871-1750
Fax: 415-871-0714
Year Founded: 1932
Approx.Sls.: $16,000,000
Emp.: 42
Fiscal Year-end: 12/31/90
Import Export
Lithographic Printing in Flexible Packaging
S.I.C.: 2752
I.F. Sewell *(Chm. Bd.)*
Chris Sewell *(Pres.)*
Lynn Davis *(V.P.-Sls., Mktg., Pur. & Mfg.)*
Linda Sartori *(Treas. & Dir.-Data Processing)*
Principal(s):
I.F. Sewell

Outside Service Firm(s):

Dwight Allen*(Auditors)*
San Francisco, CA

Severson Werson*(Legal Firm)*
San Francisco, CA

Wells Fargo Bank*(Major Banking Relationship)*
420 Montgomery St.
San Francisco, CA 94104

RONALD LITOFF, LTD.
49 W. 45th St.
New York, NY 10036
Tel.: 212-719-1444
Fax: 212-382-1624
Approx.Sls.: $19,000,000
Emp.: 75
Jewelry, Precious Metal
S.I.C.: 3911
Ronald Litoff *(Pres.)*
Carol Litoff *(Treas. & Sec.)*

LITTELFUSE, INC.
800 E. Northwest Hwy.
Des Plaines, IL 60016
Tel.: 708-824-1188
Fax: 708-824-3024
Year Founded: 1927
Emp.: 1,700
Export
Mfr. of Littelfuse Fuses, Fuseholders, Switches, Circuit Breakers, Relays, Indicator Lights
S.I.C.: 3679; 3613; 3632; 3714; 3677
Howard Witt *(Pres.)*
James Brace *(V.P.-Treasurer & CFO)*
Scott Nease *(V.P.-Corp. Controller)*
David Krueger *(V.P.-Engineering)*
William Barron *(V.P.-Sls. & Mktg.)*
Lloyd Turner *(V.P.-Opers.)*
Kenneth Audino *(V.P.-Reliability & Qual. Assurance)*
Milan Bagel *(Sls. Mgr.-Electronics)*
D. Ferbert *(Sls. Mgr.-Power Fuse)*
L. Altmayer *(Sls. Mgr.-Automotive Aftermarket)*
Ad Hazinga *(Sls. Mgr.-Automotive OE)*
Arthur Skwerski *(Adv. Mgr.)*
Dan Sundt *(Pur. Mgr.)*

Non-U.S. Holdings:

Littelfuse Ltd. **(1)**
34-36 Hutton Close Crowther District 3, Durham, Tyne & Wear NE 38 OAH, United Kingdom
Tel.: 091 4162479 (100%)
Telex: 537095 LTFUSE G
Mfr. of Fuse Devices
S.I.C.: 3613
Kenneth Audino *(Chief Oper. Officer)*

Littelfuse S.A. de C.V. **(1)**
Piedras Negras, Coahuila 20966, Mexico
Tel.: 23549 (100%)
Telex: 383 37233
Mfr. of Fuse Devices
S.I.C.: 3613
Munsey Fender *(Gen. Mgr.)*

Littelfuse B.V. **(1)**
Kanonstraat 36 3531 BM
Utrecht, Netherlands
Tel.: 030-937347 (100%)
Telex: 47655 LFTRA NC
Assembly of Fuse Devices
S.I.C.: 3613
Kenneth Audino *(Chief Oper. Officer)*

Littelfuse AG **(1)**
Rebgasse 40 2540
Grenchen, Switzerland
Tel.: 065-529931 (100%)
Telex: 934830 LFTR CH
Sales of Fuse Devices
S.I.C.: 5063
Rudolf Roth *(Plant Mgr.)*

LITTFIN LUMBER COMPANY
555 Baker Ave.
Winsted, MN 55395
Tel.: 612-485-3861 **MN**
Fax: 612-473-1245
Year Founded: 1962
Approx.Sls.: $15,000,000
Emp.: 60
Fiscal Year-end: 12/31/91
Mfr. of Wooden Roof & Floor Trusses
S.I.C.: 2439
John A. Littfin *(Pres.)*
Steve Laxen *(Dir.-Fin. & Data Processing)*
Jack Littfin *(Mgr.-Mktg. & Pur.)*

Outside Service Firm(s):

Larson, Allen, Weishair & Co.*(Auditors)*
Minneapolis, MN

Thies & Long*(Legal Firm)*
Glencoe, MN

Norwest Bank Minnesota, N.A.*(Major Banking Relationship)*
P.O. Box 2900, Loop Station
Minneapolis, MN 55402
Tel.: 612-372-8114

LITTLE CAESAR ENTERPRISES, INC.
2211 Woodward Ave.
Detroit, MI 48201-3400
Tel.: 313-983-6000 **MI**
Fax: 313-983-6494
Year Founded: 1959
Approx.Sls.: $1,725,000,000
Emp.: 75,000
Fiscal Year-end: 12/31/91
Take-Out Pizzeria
S.I.C.: 5812; 5141; 5046; 6794
Michael Ilitch *(Chm. Bd. & Pres.)*
Charles Jones *(Vice Chm.)*
David Deal *(Sr. Exec. V.P.)*
Denise Ilitch Lites *(Sr. Exec. V.P.)*
Robert Mazziotti *(Reg. V.P.-Franchise Sls.)*
Al Thompson *(Reg. V.P.)*
Susan Sherbow *(V.P.-Corp. Communications)*
Marian Ilitch *(Sec. & Treas.)*
Timothy Burke *(Dir.-Adv.)*
Principal(s):
Michael Ilitch
Marian Ilitch

Subsidiary:

Blue Line Distributing **(1)**
24120 Haggerty Rd.
Farmington Hills, MI 48024
Tel.: 313-478-6200
Fax: 313-478-2390
Distr. of Little Caesars Prods. to Franchised & Company-Owned Locations
S.I.C.: 5149

ARTHUR D. LITTLE, INC.
25 Acorn Park
Cambridge, MA 02140-2390
Tel.: 617-864-5770 **MA**
Fax: 617-661-5830
Year Founded: 1886
Approx.Rev.: $360,000,000
Emp.: 2,500
Fiscal Year-end: 12/31/91
Industrial Research, Product Development, Environmental, Health and Safety Consulting, Management Consulting Services
S.I.C.: 8731; 8742
Corporate Giving Program:
Contributions Supporting Educational & Research Programs in the Areas of Science & Technology, as well as to Human Service Organizations
John F. Magee *(Chm. Bd.)*
Charles R. LaMantia *(Pres. & Chief Exec. Officer)*
Jeffrey W. Traenkle *(Chief Fin. Officer)*
Samuel J. Gallo *(Sr. V.P., Sec. & Gen. Counsel)*
Ashok S. Kalelkar *(Sr. V.P. & Grp. Officer)*
P.R. Nayak *(Sr. V.P. & Dir.-Mktg.)*
Lewis Rambo *(Sr. V.P.-Personnel)*
Harland A. Riker, Jr. *(Sr. V.P. & Grp. Officer)*
Alfred E. Wechsler *(Sr. V.P. & Chief Professional Officer)*
D. Elliott Wilbur *(Sr. V.P.)*
Stephen R. Lorentzen *(V.P.-Information Systems)*
Patrick A. Pollino *(V.P.-Corp. Communications)*
George S. Sacerdote *(V.P.)*
John F. Burns *(Controller & Principal Acctg. Officer)*
Jose S. Bairos *(Pur. Mgr.)*
Karl Fagens *(Office Mgr.)*
Victoria J. Arnold *(Mgr.-Corp. Mktg.)*

Outside Service Firm(s):

Deloitte & Touche*(Auditors)*
125 Summer St.
Boston, MA 02110
Tel.: 617-261-8000
Fax: 617-261-8111

Blue Shield of Massachusetts, Inc.*(Commercial Insurance Carrier)*
Boston, MA

Powers & Hall Professional Corp.*(Legal Firm)*
100 Franklin St.
Boston, MA 02110

First National Bank of Boston*(Major Banking Relationship)*
150 Royall St.
Canton, MA 02021
Tel.: 617-575-2900
Tel.: 800-442-2001

BEA Associates, Inc.*(Pension Manager)*
One Citicorp Center, 153 East 53rd St.
New York, NY 10022
Tel.: 212-832-2626
Fax: 212-751-2470

Chase Investors Management Corporation*(Pension Manager)*
New York, NY

Division:

Arthur D. Little Program Systems Management Co. **(1)**
Acorn Park
Cambridge, MA 02140
Tel.: 617-864-5770
Project Management Services
S.I.C.: 8741
Dennis C. Smith *(Pres.)*

Subsidiaries:

ADL Management Education Institute, Inc. **(1)**
Acorn Park
Cambridge, MA 02140
Tel.: 617-864-5657 (100%)

Accredited Masters Degree Granting Graduate School in Management
S.I.C.: 8221
Kenneth L. Hoadley *(Dean)*

Arthur D. Little Enterprises, Inc. **(1)**
Acorn Park
Cambridge, MA 02140
Tel.: 617-864-5770
Invention & Equity Management Services
S.I.C.: 8741
Bernard J. Lacomis *(Pres. & Chief Exec. Officer)*

Non-U.S. Holdings:

Cambridge Consultants Limited **(1)**
Science Park,Milton Rd.
Cambridge, CB4 4DW, United Kingdom
Tel.: (44-223) 420024 (92%)
Telex: 81481 CCL G
Research & Consulting
S.I.C.: 8731
Harland A. Riker Jr. *(Chm.)*
J. Paul Auton *(Mng. Dir.)*
Mark F. Pettit *(Sec)*

Arthur D. Little of Canada Ltd. **(1)**
67 Yonge St., Ste. 400
Toronto, ON M5E 1J8, Canada
Tel.: 416-361-1051 (100%)
Telex: 06-218190 ADL of CDA
Management Consulting
S.I.C.: 8742
Ashok S. Kacelkar *(Pres.)*
Frederick T. McElligott *(Treas.)*
Samuel J. Gallo *(Sec.)*

Arthur D. Little S.R.C. **(1)**
General Peron 40A 28020
Madrid, Spain
Tel.: (34-1) 597-3375 (100%)
Telex: 49102 ADLI
Management Consulting Services
S.I.C.: 8742
Javier Baixas *(Mng. Dir.)*

Arthur D. Little Far East, Inc. **(1)**
152 Bearch Rd., #13-06/08 Gateway East
Singapore, 0718, Singapore
Tel.: 297 2306
Tel.: 297 2300 (100%)
Fax: 292 7631
Management Consulting
S.I.C.: 8742
Dermot J. McMeekin *(Pres.)*
Peter J. Connell *(V.P.)*
Frederick T. McElligott *(Treas.)*
Samuel J. Gallo *(Sec.)*

Arthur D. Little Intl., Inc. **(1)**
230 Rue du Faubourg, Saint Honore 75008
Paris, France
Tel.: 45-63-14-59 (100%)
Telex: 642583 D LITTLE
Management Consulting
S.I.C.: 8742
Jean-Luc Fallou *(Mng. Dir.)*

Arthur D. Little Intl., Inc. **(1)**
2 Blvd. de la Woluwe B-1150
Brussels, Belgium
Tel.: 32 2 762-0285 (100%)
Telex: 22812 LITTLE B
Fax: 32 2 762 0758
Management Consulting Services
S.I.C.: 8742
Maurice Olivier *(Mng. Dir.)*

Arthur D. Little Intl., Inc. **(1)**
Via Serbelloni 4 20122,
Milan, Italy
Tel.: (39-2) 7601-5046
Telex: 326506 LITTLE I
Management Consulting
S.I.C.: 8742
Claude P. Arragon *(Mng. Dir.)*

Arthur D. Little Intl., Inc. **(1)**
World Trade Center, Strawinskylaan 621
1077-XX
Amsterdam, Netherlands
Tel.: (31-20) 5711-011
Telex: 12808
Management Consulting
S.I.C.: 8742
L. Martin van der Mandele *(Mng. Dir.)*

Arthur D. Little Intl., Inc. **(1)**
Gustav-Stresemann-Ring 1 D-6200,
Wiesbaden, Germany
Tel.: 6121 71480 (100%)
Telex: 4186310 ADLI D
Management Consulting
S.I.C.: 8742
Michael Mollenhauer *(Mng. Dir.)*

Arthur D. Little Intl., Inc. **(1)**
Stepanska 65 Roh Vaclavskeho Namesti-2,
Prague, 1, Czechoslovakia
Tel.: 42-2-2353258
Pedro A. Pick *(Mng. Dir.)*

Arthur D. Little Intl., Inc. **(1)**
Level 23 Grosvenor Place, 225 George St.
Sydney, NSW 2000, Australia
Tel.: 61-2-247-9955
Fax: 6102-247-3985
Management Consulting
S.I.C.: 8742
Arthur A. Owen *(Mng. Dir.)*

Arthur D. Little (Japan), Inc. **(1)**
Fukide #2 Bldg.,4-1-13 Toranomon Minato-ku,
Tokyo, 105, Japan
Tel.: 03-3436-2196 (100%)
Telex: 2426640 ADLJ J
Management Consulting Services
S.I.C.: 8742
Yoshimichi Yamashita *(Pres.)*

Arthur D. Little Limitada **(1)**
Avenida Brigadeiro Faria Lima 2003 Jardim Paulistano, 19 Andur, 01451 Conjunto 1901,
Sao Paulo, Brazil
Tel.: (55-11) 814-8144 (100%)
Telex: 1131347 ADLLBR
Management Consulting Services
S.I.C.: 8742
Moyses Gedanke *(Mng. Dir.)*

Arthur D. Little Ltd. **(1)**
Berkeley Square House, Berkeley Square
London, W1X 6EY, United Kingdom
Tel.: 071-409-2277 (100%)
Telex: 261109 LITTLE G
Management Consulting & Energy Economics Operations
S.I.C.: 8742
Tim Simpson *(Mng. Dir.)*

Arthur D. Little Mexicana, S.A. de C.V. **(1)**
Av. Sinola No. 149-10 Piso, Col. Roma 06700,
Mexico, D.F. Mexico
Tel.: 52-5-525-1484
Telex: 01772517 ADL WME
Management Consulting, 49% owned by Arthur D. Little International, Inc.,; 51% Owned by Other Mexican-Related Interests
S.I.C.: 8742
Roberto E. Batres *(Pres.)*
Julio C. Trevino *(Sec.)*

LITTLE LADY FOODS, INC.
2323 Pratt Blvd.
Elk Grove Village, IL 60007
Tel.: 708-806-1440
Year Founded: 1985
Approx.Sls.: $10,000,000
Emp.: 110
Fiscal Year-end: 12/31/91
Import Export
Mfr. Frozen Pizza & Private Label Pizzas
S.I.C.: 2038
John T. Geocaris *(Pres.)*
Roger Williams *(Chief Fin. Officer)*
Dan Geocaris *(V.P.-Custom Products)*
Mike Eisel *(Controller & Mgr.-Pur.)*
Richard Madsen *(Dir.-Sls.)*

LITTLEFORD DAY, TAYLOR-STILES DIVISION
(Formerly J. H. Day Company)
(Div. of Littleford Day Inc.)
7451 Empire Dr.
Florence, KY 41042
Tel.: 606-525-7600
Telex: 214684
Fax: 606-525-1446
Year Founded: 1887
Approx.Sls.: $15,000,000
Emp.: 200
Export
Size Reduction Equipment For the Process Industries Rotary Cutters, Guillotines, Dicing Cutters, Pelletizers, Bale Openers
S.I.C.: 3559; 3599
Donald Steedman *(Chm. Bd. & Pres.)*
Jai K.L. Bajaj *(Bus. Mgr.)*

Computer Systems/Hardware:
IBM

LITTLETON COIN CO., INC.
253 Union St
Littleton, NH 03561
Tel.: 603-444-5386 **NH**
Fax: 603-444-0121
Year Founded: 1945
Emp.: 135
Mail Order Coins For Collectors
S.I.C.: 5961
Maynard Sundman *(Founder)*
David M. Sundman *(Pres.)*
Michael Morelli *(Chief Oper. Officer)*
Edward Hennessey *(Chief Fin. Officer)*
Milton Bratz *(Dir.-Personnel)*
Paul Charlton *(Dir.-Mktg.)*
Terri Fillion *(Mgr.-Adv.)*

Computer Systems/Hardware:
IBM AS/400

Outside Service Firm(s):

Blue Cross & Blue Shield Association*(Group Insurer)*
Littleton, NH

R. Shillaber*(Legal Firm)*
Rochester, NH

Dartmouth National Bank*(Major Banking Relationship)*
Littleton, NH

Savers Bank*(Major Banking Relationship)*
Littleton, NH
Tel.: 603-444-5321

Subsidiary:

Mystic Stamp Company **(1)**
24 Mill St.
Camden, NY 13316
Tel.: 315-245-2690
Emp.: 50
Mail Order Stamps for Collectors
S.I.C.: 5961
Donald Sundman *(Pres.)*
Mark Fox *(Gen. Mgr.)*

LIVERNOIS ENGINEERING COMPANY
25315 Keen
Dearborn, MI 48124
Tel.: 313-278-0200 **MI**
Fax: 313-278-5992
Year Founded: 1949
Approx.Sls.: $35,000,000
Emp.: 450
Export
Manufacture of Heat Exchangers Equipment; Engineering & Tooling Services; Prototype Vehicle Development Services, Nitrogen Die Cylinder Systems, CAD/CAM, Die Automation Systems
S.I.C.: 8711; 8712; 3443
Bernard J. Wallis *(Chm. Bd.)*
Norma Wallis *(Pres. & Chief Exec. Officer)*
Sabation Bianchi *(V.P.-Opers.)*
Edmund Haslem *(V.P.-Fin.)*
Cynthia Haslem *(Sec.)*
I. Shiffman *(Mgr.-Data Processing)*

Outside Service Firm(s):

Grant Thornton*(Auditors)*
Dearborn, MI

Commercial Underwriters*(Group Insurer)*
Dearborn, MI

Manufacturers National Bank*(Major Banking Relationship)*
Dearborn, MI

Merrill Lynch*(Pension Manager)*
Southfield, MI

Subsidiary:

Livernois Vehicle Co. **(1)**
25241 Trowbridge St.
Dearborn, MI 48124
Tel.: 313-278-3970
Prototype & Vehicle Development
S.I.C.: 8711

Livingston

LIVINGSTON & COMPANY
800 Fifth Ave.
Seattle, WA 98104
Tel.: 206-382-5500
Fax: 206-622-4532
Year Founded: 1974
Approx.Billings: $75,000,000
Emp.: 50
Advertising Agency
S.I.C.: 7311
Roger Livingston *(Pres. & Chief Exec. Officer)*
Glenna Mileson *(V.P. & Chief Fin. Officer)*
Jeff Timmons *(Dir.-Data Processing)*
Patrick Doody *(Gen. Mgr.)*
Linda Lester *(Office Mgr.)*

Computer Systems/Hardware:
Macintosh

Branches:

Livingston & Company **(1)**
250 Sutter St.
San Francisco, CA 94108
Tel.: 415-397-5525
Fax: 415-397-9776
Barbara Wingate *(V.P., Dir. Acct. Plng.)*

Livingston + Keye **(1)**
901 Abbot Kinney Blvd.
Venice, CA 90291
Tel.: 213-396-2225
Fax: 213-450-6133
Paul Keye *(Chm. & Exec. Creative Dir.)*
Roger Livingston *(Pres. & Chief Exec. Officer)*
Glenna Carter *(Office Mgr.)*

LLOYD CONTROLS, INC.
21414 66th Ave., W.
Mountlake Terrace, WA 98043
Tel.: 206-775-1561
Fax: 206-778-9040
Year Founded: 1961
Emp.: 65
Export
Manufacture Custom Electrical/ Electronic & Computer Control
S.I.C.: 3823; 3577
Harold E. Lloyd *(Chm. Bd.)*
Harold S. Lloyd *(Pres.)*
Robert G. Hurst *(V.P. & Gen. Mgr.)*
Robert D. Dzurick *(Sec.)*
Jim Woods *(Pur. Agent)*

No. of Mfg. Plants/Facilities: 2
No. of U.S. Offices: 3

Outside Service Firm(s):

KPMG Peat Marwick*(Auditors)*
3100 Two Union Square, 601 Union St., Ste. 3100
Seattle, WA 98101
Tel.: 206-292-1500

Lloyd Controls, Inc.—(Continued)

Seafirst Bank*(Major Banking Relationship)*
Columbia-SeaFirst Center, 701 5th Ave., 11th Flr.
Seattle, WA 98124
Tel.: 206-358-3039
Fax: 206-358-3113

Division:

Lloyd Electric Apparatus Co. **(1)**
7126 W. Marginal Way, S.W.
Seattle, WA 98106
Tel.: 206-762-7773
Electric Apparatus Repair
S.I.C.: 3577
Robert G. Hurst *(V.P. & Gen. Mgr.)*

LLOYD PROPERTIES
12400 Wilshire Blvd., Ste. 1180
Los Angeles, CA 90025
Tel.: 213-207-9479
Approx.Sls.: $32,000,000
Emp.: 210
Fiscal Year-end: 12/31/90
Oil & Gas Extraction; Real Estate Development & Mngmt.
S.I.C.: 1311; 6531; 6552
Larry C. Bucher *(Pres.)*
Francis J. Cribbs *(Exec. V.P., Chief Fin. Officer & Treas.)*

Outside Service Firm(s):

Deloitte & Touche*(Auditors)*
1000 Wilshire Blvd.
Los Angeles, CA 90017-2472
Tel.: 213-688-0800
Fax: 213-688-0100

The Principal Financial Group*(Pension Manager)*
711 High St.
Des Moines, IA 50309
Tel.: 515-247-4593
Tel.: 800-543-4015

LOBDELL-EMERY MANUFACTURING COMPANY
P.O. Box 129, 1325 E. Superior St.
Alma, MI 48801-0129
Tel.: 517-463-3151
Fax: 517-463-2833
Manufacture Auto Parts
S.I.C.: 3465
John F. Hiemenz *(Chm. Bd.)*
D. Kennedy Fesenmyer *(Pres. & Chief Exec. Officer)*
Charles L. Dardas *(Exec. V.P.)*
Michael E. Regina *(Exec. V.P.-Opers.)*
William Hollabaugh *(V.P.-Mfg.)*
James V. Finkbeiner *(Sec.)*

LOCKARD CONSTRUCTION, INC.
901 Black Hawk Rd.
Waterloo, IA 50701
Mailing Address:
P.O. Box 2220
Waterloo, IA 50704
Tel.: 319-235-9391 **IA**
Fax: 319-235-9744
Assets: $1,700,000
Net Worth: $1,700,000
Approx.Sls.: $32,000,000
Emp.: 70
Fiscal Year-end: 12/31/91
New Construction of Commercial, Office & Industrial Buildings
S.I.C.: 1541
Wendell Lockard *(Chm. Bd.)*
Ken Lockard *(Pres.)*
David Peters *(Exec. V.P.)*
Terry Miller *(V.P. & Estimator)*
Gary Sevey *(Treas.)*
Mildred Rekward *(Sec.)*

Outside Service Firm(s):

McGladrey & Pullen*(Auditors)*
Waterloo, IA

Beecher, Rathert, Field, Fister, Walker & Morris*(Legal Firm)*
Waterloo, IA

National Bank of Waterloo*(Major Banking Relationship)*
Trust Department, P.O. Box 5300
Waterloo, IA 50704

LOCKHART CADILLAC INC.
5550 N. Keystone Ave.
Indianapolis, IN 46220
Tel.: 317-253-1551 **IN**
Fax: 317-254-6428
Year Founded: 1973
Approx.Sls.: $39,327,000
Emp.: 82
Retail Automotive Sales & Service
S.I.C.: 5511
Freda L. Lockhart *(Pres. & Chief Exec. Officer)*
Lynn Kimmel *(V.P.)*
Gregory M. Lockhart *(V.P.-Sls.)*
Thomas W. Hanlin *(Controller)*

Outside Service Firm(s):

George S. Olive & Co.*(Auditors)*
201 N. Illinois St.
Indianapolis, IN 46204

Klineman, Rose, Wolf & Wallack*(Legal Firm)*
Indianapolis, IN

Merchants National Bank & Trust Company of Indianapolis*(Major Banking Relationship)*
One Merchants Plaza, Ste. 901E
Indianapolis, IN 46255
Tel.: 317-267-7109

Subsidiary:

Saturn of Indianapolis **(1)**
5333 Pike Plaza Rd.
Indianapolis, IN 46254
Tel.: 317-293-1551
Emp.: 36
Retail Automobile Dealership
S.I.C.: 5511
Freda L. Lockhart *(Pres.)*
Lynn B. Kimmel *(V.P.)*
G. Marc Lockhart *(V.P.)*
Thomas W. Hanlin *(Controller)*
Charles G. Kimmel *(Gen. Mgr.)*

Lockhart&Pettus
ADVERTISING•PUBLIC RELATIONS

LOCKHART & PETTUS, INC.
79 Fifth Ave.
New York, NY 10003
Tel.: 212-633-2800
Fax: 212-633-2983
Year Founded: 1977
Approx.Billings: $30,000,000
Emp.: 30
Fiscal Year-end: 2/28/92
Advertising Agency Specializing In Marketing & Communications Programs Geared To The Black Consumer
S.I.C.: 7311
Keith E. Lockhart *(Pres.)*
Robert A. McVeigh *(Chief Fin. Officer & Sr. V.P.)*
Theodore D. Pettus *(Exec. V.P.)*
Chris Roman *(Mgr.-Office)*
Principal(s):
Keith E. Lockhart
Theodore D. Pettus

LOCKS ADVERTISING AGENCY
222 S. Second St.
East Northport, NY 11731
Tel.: 516-368-8000
Tel.: 800-736-3976
Year Founded: 1968
Approx.Billings: $14,963,273
Emp.: 28
Automotive, Fast Food, Professional Sports, Sweepstakes, Sales Promo. & Trade Show Participation
Clifford K. Locks *(Pres.)*
John Orlow *(V.P.-Mktg.)*

Computer Systems/Hardware:
IBM-386 with Lasermaster

LOCKWOOD CORPORATION
E. Hwy. 92
Gering, NE 69341
Mailing Address:
P.O. Box 160,
Gering, NE 69341
Tel.: 308-436-5051 **DE**
Fax: 308-436-5732
Year Founded: 1935
Sales Range: $20-39 Million
Emp.: 450
Fiscal Year-end: 6/30/92
Import Export
Mfr. of Specialized Farm Equipment; Hoists, Pivot Irrigation Systems
S.I.C.: 3523; 3713; 3531
Terry McCall *(Chm. Bd.)*
Bruce Wood *(Pres. & Chief Exec. Officer)*
Robert Lewis *(Chief Fin. Officer, V.P. & Sec.)*
Dean Edwards *(V.P.-Irrigation Sls.)*
Bruce Fisher *(V.P.-Ag. Sls.)*
Joe Schon *(V.P.-Sls.)*
John Bushore *(Dir.-Human Resources)*
Roy Dugan *(Mgr.-Quality Control)*
Jim Grewe *(Mgr.-Intl.)*
Bob Jacobson *(Mgr.-Engrng.)*
Nancy Kerr *(Mgr.-Data Processing)*
Randy Markheim *(Mgr.-Pur.)*

Computer Systems/Hardware:
Hewlett-Packard 949

Outside Service Firm(s):

Deloitte & Touche*(Auditors)*
1040 NBC Center
Lincoln, NE 68508

Jardine Insurance*(Commercial Insurance Carrier)*
Kansas City, MO

Wisconsin Area Health Fund*(Group Insurer)*
Madison, WI

Sherman & Howard*(Legal Firm)*
633 17th St., Ste. 2900
Denver, CO 80202

Scottsbluff National Bank & Trust*(Major Banking Relationship)*
Scottsbluff, NE

Division:

Perfection Company **(1)**
Hwy. 92 E, Box 160
Gering, NE 69341
Tel.: 308-436-5051
Emp.: 500
Military Div. Producing Dump Bodies, Steel Dump Bodies,
S.I.C.: 3713
Rob Lewis *(Chief Oper. Officer)*
Micki Schwartzkopf *(Mgr.-Parts Sls.)*

LOCUS COMPUTING CORP.
9800 La Cienega Blvd.
Inglewood, CA 90301-4440
Tel.: 310-670-6500 **CA**
Fax: 310-670-2980
Year Founded: 1982
Emp.: 275
Fiscal Year-end: 1/31/91
Computer Software Development
S.I.C.: 7372
Gerald J. Popek *(Chm. Bd.)*
Martin C. Waters *(Pres. & Chief Exec. Officer)*
Elaine Bailey *(V.P.-Sls.)*
Robin Wallich *(V.P.-Mktg.)*
Kirby Sechovek *(V.P.-Human Resources)*
Samuel Auriemma *(Chief Fin. Officer)*
Randy Snelling *(Controller)*

No. of U.S. Offices: 5
No. of Foreign Offices: 1

Computer Systems/Hardware:
Arete System; AT&T 3B2, 3B15 & 6300; DEC VAX; IBM PC; MicroVax; Motorola S8000S; NCR; Ridge

Outside Service Firm(s):

Arthur Andersen & Co.*(Auditors)*
633 W. Fifth St.
Los Angeles, CA 90071
Tel.: 213-614-6500

Chubb Group*(Commercial Insurance Carrier)*
P.O. Box 1615,
Warren, NJ 07061
Tel.: 201-580-2000

LODAL, INC.
East Blvd.
Kingsford, MI 49802
Mailing Address:
P.O. Box 2315
Kingsford, MI 49802
Tel.: 906-779-1700
Fax: 906-779-1160
Approx.Sls.: $20,000,000
Emp.: 200
Fiscal Year-end: 5/31/92
Refuse Collection Vehicles & Equipment
S.I.C.: 3711; 3599
John Giuliani *(Treas. & Sec.)*
Randy Brisson *(Chief Engr.)*
Peter Ryan *(Gen. Counsel)*
Jeff Waller *(Pur. Agent)*

Outside Service Firm(s):

Fleury, Singer & Co.*(Auditors)*
Iron Mountain, MI

First Wisconsin National Bank*(Major Banking Relationship)*
Sheboygan, WI

LOEBER MOTORS, INC.
1111 N. Clark St.
Chicago, IL 60610
Tel.: 312-944-0500
Fax: 312-944-0907
Approx.Rev.: $70,000,000
Emp.: 110
Fiscal Year-end: 12/31/91
New & Used Automobiles
S.I.C.: 5511
George Loeber *(Pres.)*
Paul Loeber *(Sec. & Treas.)*

Outside Service Firm(s):

Robert B. Flink & Company*(Auditors)*
Chicago, IL

Boulevard Bank*(Major Banking Relationship)*
410 N. Michigan Ave.
Chicago, IL 60611
Tel.: 312-836-6500

Colonial Bank & Trust Co.*(Major Banking Relationship)*
Chicago, IL

LOEFFLER KETCHUM MOUNTJOY
7401 Carmel Exec. Park Dr.
Charlotte, NC 28226
Tel.: 704-542-8131

Fax: 704-541-9930
Year Founded: 1981
Approx.Billings: $22,000,000
Emp.: 43
William G. Loeffler *(Chm. & Treas.)*
John W. Ketchum *(Pres.)*
James W. Mountjoy *(Exec. V.P., Creative Dir.)*
Patty Reuss *(V.P., Media)*
Harry Hoover *(Dir. Pub. Rels.)*
Nancy Forman *(Acctg. Mgr.)*

Computer Systems/Hardware:
MAC, IBM

LOEHMANN'S, INC.
2500 Halsey St.
Bronx, NY 10461
Tel.: 718-409-2000
Fax: 718-518-2766
Year Founded: 1921
Approx.Sls.: $400,000,000
Emp.: 3,000
Fiscal Year-end: 2/ 2/91
Retail Women's Apparel Stores
S.I.C.: 5311
Philip Kaplan *(Chm. Bd.)*
Robert Friedman *(Pres. & Chief Exec. Officer)*
George J. Nadel *(Sr. V.P.)*

LOFT'S SEEDS, INC.
Chimney Rock Rd.
Bound Brook, NJ 08805
Tel.: 908-356-8700
Fax: 908-356-5607
Approx.Sls.: $35,000,000
Emp.: 150
Mfr. of Grass Seed, Fertilizer, Lawn Chemicals & Insecticides
S.I.C.: 2875; 2879
John D. Loft *(Chm. Bd. & Pres.)*
Dennis Smaldone *(Comptroller & Asst. Sec.)*
Donna Moskal *(Coord.-Sls.)*

LOGAN & KANAWHA COAL CO.
8044 Montgomery Rd., Ste. 157
Cincinnati, OH 45236
Tel.: 513-891-8333 **OH**
Fax: 513-891-8808
Year Founded: 1913
Sales Range: $100-499 Million
Emp.: 8
Export
Coal Processing & Distribution
S.I.C.: 1241; 5052; 1221; 1222
Kenneth Meyer *(Pres.)*
J.W. Reinhart *(Controller & Asst. Treas.)*
Ron Haley *(Mgr.-Opers.)*
Steven Weber *(Mgr.-Sls.)*

No. of Mfg. Plants/Facilities: 1

Computer Systems/Hardware:
IBM System 38

Outside Service Firm(s):

Brammel & Ackley*(Auditors)*
Erlanger, KY

Wend Grove Taylor*(Group Insurer)*
Mobile, AL

Star Bank*(Investment Banker)*
425 Walnut Street
Cincinnati, OH 45202
Tel.: 513-632-4000

Cors & Bassett*(Legal Firm)*
Cincinnati, OH

Provident National Bank*(Major Banking Relationship)*
4140 Hamilton Ave.
Cincinnati, OH
Tel.: 513-681-3900

Star Bank*(Pension Manager)*
425 Walnut Street
Cincinnati, OH 45202
Tel.: 513-632-4000

Subsidiary:

Guyan Corp. **(1)**
8044 Montgomery Ste. 157
Cincinnati, OH 45236
Tel.: 513-891-8333
Holding Company
S.I.C.: 6719
Kenneth A. Meyer *(Pres.)*
James Reinhart *(V.P.-Fin.)*

LOGGHE STAMPING COMPANY
16711 13 Mile Rd.
Fraser, MI 48026
Tel.: 313-293-2250 **MI**
Fax: 313-293-7202
Year Founded: 1946
Approx.Sls.: $19,000,000
Emp.: 55
Fiscal Year-end: 12/31/90
Export
Automobile Body Parts, Stamped Metal, Moldings & Trim
S.I.C.: 3465
Eugene A. Logghe *(Pres.)*
Ronald M. Logghe *(V.P. & Sec.)*
Karen Young *(Controller)*
Howard Dearing *(Dir.-Engrng. & Tech. Services)*
Richard Gallagher *(Dir.-Personnel Training & Devel.)*
Tom Neill *(Dir.-Quality Control)*
William A. Sroka *(Mgr.-Sls.)*
John Logghe *(Pur. Agent)*

No. of U.S. Offices: 1

Outside Service Firm(s):

State Bank*(Major Banking Relationship)*
Fraser, MI

LOGISTIX
48021 Warm Springs Blvd.
Fremont, CA 94539
Tel.: 510-656-8000 **CA**
Fax: 510-438-9486
Year Founded: 1980
Approx.Sls.: $34,000,000
Emp.: 156
Contract Manufacturer In Computer & Related Industries, Printing Of Technical Manuals, Software Duplication, Assembly & Fulfillment
S.I.C.: 7372
Stephen G. Weinstein *(Pres.)*
Marta Weinstein *(Exec. V.P.)*
Daniel G. DePalma *(Sr. V.P.-Opers.)*
Frank J. Schneider *(V.P.-Fin.)*

No. of Mfg. Plants/Facilities: 2

Outside Service Firm(s):

Deloitte & Touche*(Auditors)*
60 S. Market St., Ste. 800
San Jose, CA 95113-2303
Tel.: 408-998-7111
Fax: 408-298-5782

Plaza Bank of Commerce*(Major Banking Relationship)*
Sunnyvale, CA

LOHMEYER SIMPSON COMMUNICATIONS, INC

LOHMEYER SIMPSON COMMUNICATIONS, INC.
14 Pine St.
Morristown, NJ 07960
Tel.: 201-267-0400
Fax: 201-984-9050
Year Founded: 1979
Approx.Billings: $15,000,000
Emp.: 18
Industrial, Consumer Advertising, Sales Promotion, Business to Business
Richard J. Lohmeyer *(Pres.)*
Donna A. Ely *(Pres.-DAE Assoc. Div.)*
Peter Adler *(V.P.)*
Donna Lohmeyer *(V.P., Mktg. Services)*
Katrina Holhauser *(Office Mgr.)*

Computer Systems/Hardware:
Admark-Data General

LOIS/USA

LOIS/USA
40 West 57th St.
New York, NY 10019
Tel.: 212-373-4700
Fax: 212-586-9472
Approx.Billings: $266,000,000
Emp.: 187
S.I.C.: 7311
George Lois *(Chm. & Chief Exec. Officer)*
Theodore D. Veru *(Co-Chm. & Chief Oper. Officer)*

LOMBARD COMPANY
4245 W. 123rd. St.
Alsip, IL 60658
Tel.: 708-389-1060
Fax: 708-389-7120
Approx.Sls.: $38,000,000
Emp.: 110
General Contractor
S.I.C.: 1521; 1522; 1541; 1542
George E. Lombard *(Pres. & Chief Exec. Officer)*
Principal(s):
George E. Lombard

Computer Systems/Hardware:
IBM

Outside Service Firm(s):

Peter Shannon*(Auditors)*
Hinsdale, IL

Michigan Avenue National Bank*(Major Banking Relationship)*
Chicago, IL

LOMBARD LINCOLN-MERCURY & LEASING, INC.
500 E. Roosevelt Rd.
Lombard, IL 60148
Tel.: 708-495-2500 **IL**
Year Founded: 1981
Emp.: 63
New & Used Automobiles
S.I.C.: 5511
Larry Sherman *(Pres.)*
Thomas Jones *(V.P.)*
Dorothy Mueller *(Sec. & Treas.)*

Outside Service Firm(s):

Clifton Gunderson*(Auditors)*
Oak Brook, IL

Kenneth May*(Legal Firm)*
Clarendon Hills, IL

LOMBARDI FOODSERVICE, INC.
(Formerly Lombardi Food Co.)
2465 23 Mile Rd.
Utica, MI 48316
Mailing Address:
P.O. Box 189008,
Utica, MI 48318-9008
Tel.: 313-254-3550 **MI**
Fax: 313-254-3963
Approx.Sls.: $32,000,000
Emp.: 80
Restaurant & Institutional Food-Service Products & Equipment Distributor
S.I.C.: 5141; 5142; 5113; 5046
Dennis J. Foley *(Pres.)*
Ronald A. Foley *(V.P.)*
Edward J. Caram *(Treas.)*

Outside Service Firm(s):

Parker, Wittus & Co.*(Auditors)*
Southfield, MI

N.B.D. Bank, N.A.*(Major Banking Relationship)*
611 Woodward Ave.
Detroit, MI 48226
Tel.: 313-225-1122
Fax: 313-225-3420

LONDON LITHO ALUMINUM CO., INC.
7100 N. Lawndale
Lincolnwood, IL 60645
Tel.: 708-679-4600
Fax: 708-679-6453
Sales Range: $60-79 Million
Emp.: 100
Distributor of Plates, Chemicals, Film & Equipment, Graphic Arts Materials & Equipment, Rebuilding & Service, Sack Electronic Pre-Press Equipment
S.I.C.: 5065; 3553; 3861; 5043; 5051; 5169; 5199
Melvyn London *(Chm. Bd.)*
Eric London *(Pres.)*
Edith London *(Sec.)*

Outside Service Firm(s):

Goldenberg & Barasch*(Auditors)*
Northbrook, IL

Tenney & Bentley*(Legal Firm)*
111 W. Washington, Ste. 1900
Chicago, IL 60602
Tel.: 312-407-7800

Standard Chartered Bank*(Major Banking Relationship)*
33 W. Monroe
Chicago, IL 60603
Tel.: 312-726-3300
Fax: 312-372-5694

LONDONTOWN HOLDINGS CORPORATION
Londontown Blvd.
Eldersburg, MD 21784
Tel.: 410-795-5900 **DE**
Fax: 410-549-2395
Year Founded: 1988
Approx.Sls.: $265,000,000
Emp.: 3,000
Holding Company; Raincoats, Men's & Boy's Tailored Suit-type Jackets; Men's & Boy's Leather & Sheep-lined Jackets; Knit Sweaters & Sweater Coats
S.I.C.: 2385; 2311; 2386; 2253; 6719
Mark H. Lieberman *(Pres.)*
Ed Frey *(Exec. V.P.-Opers.)*
Zachary C. Goldman *(Exec. V.P., Treas. & Sec.)*
Douglas C. Hillman *(Exec. V.P.)*

Outside Service Firm(s):

KPMG Peat Marwick*(Auditors)*
111 S. Calvert St.
Baltimore, MD 21202
Tel.: 410-783-8300

Londontown Holdings Corporation—(Continued)

Maryland National Bank *(Major Banking Relationship)*
Baltimore, MD 21202

Division:

Knitwear Division **(1)**
Londontown Blvd.
Eldersburg, MD 21784
Tel.: 410-795-5900
Knit Outerwear Mills
S.I.C.: 2253
Mark H. Lieberman *(Pres.)*

Subsidiaries:

Londontown Corporation **(1)**
1332 Londontown Blvd.
Eldersburg, MD 21784
Tel.: 410-795-5900
Emp.: 3,000
Mfr. of Raincoats; Untailored Women's, Misses & Juniors Jackets; Men's & Boys Tailored Suit-type Jackets; Knit Sweaters & Sweater Coats; Leather & Sheep-lined Coats; Copyright Buying & Licensing
S.I.C.: 2385; 2339; 2311; 2253; 2386; 6794
Mark H. Lieberman *(Pres.)*
Edward L. Frey *(Exec. V.P.-Opers.)*
Douglas C. Hillman *(Exec. V.P.-Mktg. & Sls.)*
Zachary C. Goldman *(V.P., Chief Fin. Officer & Sec.)*
Louis G. McComas *(V.P. & Treas.)*
John P. Clark *(V.P. & Controller)*

Star Sportswear Manufacturing **(1)**
Londontown Blvd.
Eldersburg, MD 21784
Tel.: 410-795-5900
Leather Coats; Rainwear
S.I.C.: 5136; 5137; 2385
Mark H. Lieberman *(Pres.)*

LONE STAR CADILLAC CO.
11501 E. Northwest Hwy.
Dallas, TX 75218
Tel.: 214-348-2211 **TX**
Fax: 214-553-2491
Approx.Sls.: $47,000,000
Emp.: 100
Automobile Sales & Leasing
S.I.C.: 5511; 7514; 7515
Lee De Sanders *(Pres.)*
Delvis A. Hall *(V.P., Treas., Sec. & Gen. Mgr.)*

Computer Systems/Hardware:
ADP

Outside Service Firm(s):

Ernst & Young *(Auditors)*
2121 San Jacinto, Ste. 500
Dallas, TX 75201
Tel.: 214-969-8000

Cain & Magee *(Legal Firm)*
1717 Main Street, Ste. 3310
Dallas, TX 75201

NationsBank Texas *(Major Banking Relationship)*
901 Main St., 16th Fl.
Dallas, TX 75202
Tel.: 214-922-5000

LONE STAR CORRUGATED CONTAINER CORPORATION
(d/b/a Dixie Reel Co.)
P.O. Box 157357
Irving, TX 75015
Tel.: 214-579-1551 **TX**
Fax: 214-554-6081
Year Founded: 1959
Assets: $10,500,000
Liabilities: $5,800,000
Net Worth: $4,700,000
Approx.Sls.: $25,000,000
Emp.: 170
Fiscal Year-end: 12/31/90
Manufacture & Whole Corrugated Shipping Containers
S.I.C.: 2653; 4213; 5113
John McLeod *(Chm. Bd.)*
Jerry Hardison *(Pres.)*
John McLeod, Jr. *(V.P. & Chief Fin. Officer)*
Tom Turrentine *(V.P.-Sls.)*
Lorene Cash *(Controller)*
Edward Resh *(Dir.-Mktg.)*

Computer Systems/Hardware:
DEC

Outside Service Firm(s):

Elms Ferris Co. *(Auditors)*
Dallas, TX

NationsBank Texas *(Major Banking Relationship)*
P.O. Box 831402,
Dallas, TX 75283-1402
Tel.: 214-508-0877
Tel.: 800-583-6877

THE LONG & FOSTER COMPANIES, INC.
11351 Random Hills Rd.
Fairfax, VA 22030
Tel.: 703-359-1500
Fax: 703-591-6978
Year Founded: 1968
Assets: $34,652,000
Liabilities: $9,700,000
Net Worth: $24,952,000
Approx.Sls.: $165,000,000
Emp.: 747
Fiscal Year-end: 4/30/90
Real Estate Brokers
S.I.C.: 6531
P. Wesley Foster, Jr. *(Pres.)*
George T. Eastment, III *(Sr. V.P.)*
William Fore *(V.P.-Fin.)*
June Martello *(Controller)*
Ed Sears *(Mgr.-Mktg.)*

Outside Service Firm(s):

Price Waterhouse *(Auditors)*
1801 K. Street, N.W.
Washington, DC 20006
Tel.: 202-296-0800

Arent, Fox, Kintner, Plotkin & Kahn *(Legal Firm)*
1815 H St. N.W.
Washington, DC 20006
Tel.: 202-857-6000

Signet Bank *(Major Banking Relationship)*
McLean, VA

Subsidiary:

The Long & Foster Real Estate, Inc. **(1)**
11351 Random Hills Rd.
Fairfax, VA 22030
Tel.: 703-359-1500
Approx.Sls.: $112,000,000
Emp.: 706
Residential & Commercial Real Estate Brokers & Property Managers
S.I.C.: 6531
P. Wesley Foster, Jr. *(Pres.)*
George T. Eastment, III *(Sr. V.P.)*
Jack Queen *(V.P.)*
William R. Fore *(V.P.)*
Betty F. Foster *(Treas.)*

LONG ISLAND WATER CORPORATION
733 Sunrise Hwy.
Lynbrook, NY 11563
Tel.: 516-593-1000
Year Founded: 1884
Approx.Sls.: $29,000,000
Emp.: 149
Public Water Utility
S.I.C.: 4941
C.A. Buescher *(Chm. Bd.)*
Loues Mirando *(Pres. & Gen. Mgr.)*
Thomas Whiteside, Jr. *(V.P.)*
Philip Peters *(Treas.)*
Thomas Huber *(Comptroller)*
Gloria Jean Penza *(Dir.-Information)*

LONG MFG. NC, INC.
111 Fairview St.
Tarboro, NC 27886
Mailing Address:
P.O. Box 1139,
Tarboro, NC 27886
Tel.: 919-823-4151
Tel.: 800-334-5622 **NC**
Telex: 510-929-0695
Fax: 919-823-4151 x274
Year Founded: 1946
Assets: $28,000,000
Earnings: $7,200,000
Liabilities: $13,800,000
Net Worth: $14,200,000
Approx.Sls.: $28,000,000
Emp.: 350
Fiscal Year-end: 10/31/91
Import Export
Mfr. of Farm Machinery & Equipment, Woodburning Stoves
S.I.C.: 3433; 3523; 5083
Antonio C. Alvarez *(Chm. Bd.)*
David G. Walsh *(Pres.)*
James H. Long *(Exec. V.P. & Chief Oper. Officer)*
Thurman Kirkland *(V.P.-Sls. & Mktg.)*
Alton H. Cobb, Jr. *(Chief Fin. Officer)*
Moore Van Allen *(Gen. Counsel)*
David Walls *(Gen. Counsel)*
Paul Harrell, Jr. *(Sec. & Treas.)*
Tommy Furlough *(Dir.-Res. & Devel.)*
George Johnson *(Dir.-Pur.)*
Dennis Bell *(Service Mgr.)*
Faye Britt *(Mgr.-Personnel)*
Larry Cox *(Mgr.-Data Processing)*
George Whitehurst *(Mgr.-Quality Control)*
Sue Joines *(Acting Mgr.-Corp. Travel Planner)*
Robert Rosen Kotter *(Environment/ Natural Resources)*

No. of Mfg. Plants/Facilities: 1
No. of U.S. Offices: 1

Computer Systems/Hardware:
IBM 4331-2

Outside Service Firm(s):

D H & S *(Auditors)*
Raleigh, NC

Blue Cross & Blue Shield of North Carolina *(Group Insurer)*
Durham, NC

General American Life Insurance Co. *(Pension Manager)*
700 Market
Saint Louis, MO 63101
Tel.: 314-525-5458
Fax: 314-525-3677

Moore & Van Allen *(Legal Firm)*
Charlotte, NC

Subsidiary:

Long Equipment Co. **(1)**
1201 Northern Blvd.
Tarboro, NC 27886
Tel.: 919-823-1163 (100%)
Fax: 919-823-4157
Approx.Sls.: $1,000,000
Emp.: 7
S.I.C.: 5083
Thurman Kirkland *(V.P.-Sls. & Mktg.)*
Alton H. Cobb, Jr. *(Chief Fin. Officer)*
George Johnson *(Dir.-Pur.)*

W. E. LONG COMPANY
300 W. Washington St.
Chicago, IL 60606
Tel.: 312-726-4606
Fax: 312-726-4525
Approx.Sls.: $44,300,000
Emp.: 55
Independent Bakers' Cooperative
S.I.C.: 2051
B. Forrest *(Pres.)*

Computer Systems/Hardware:
IBM Systems 34 & 36

Outside Service Firm(s):

Lincoln National Life Insurance Co. *(Group Insurer)*
PO Box 208, 1300 S. Clinton
Fort Wayne, IN 46801
Tel.: 219-455-2926
Fax: 219-455-7619

The Northern Trust Co. *(Major Banking Relationship)*
50 S. LaSalle St.
Chicago, IL 60675
Tel.: 312-630-6000
Fax: 312-630-6516

LONGYEAR COMPANY
(Sub. of Boart International Limited, South Africa)
2340 West 1700 South
Salt Lake City, UT 84104
Mailing Address:
P.O. Box 27314
Salt Lake City, UT 84127
Tel.: 801-972-6430
Tel.: 800-453-8740 **MN**
Fax: 801-977-3374
Year Founded: 1891
Assets: $148,000,000
Liabilities: $61,000,000
Net Worth: $87,000,000
Approx.Sls.: $240,000,000
Emp.: 2,005
Fiscal Year-end: 12/31/91
Import Export
Mfr. of Diamond Drills & Equipment; Diamond Drilling Contractors
S.I.C.: 1481; 3532
Corporate Giving Program: Reviewed by Contributions Committee
Hilton Davies *(Chm. Bd.)*
M.H. Moore *(Pres. & Chief Exec. Officer)*
R.E. Swayne *(V.P. & Gen. Mgr.-U.S. Opers.)*
Hugh G. Judge *(Treas.)*
Robert L. Martin *(Sec. & Controller)*
Ken L. Seamon *(Dir.-Personnel)*
George Burnhart *(Mgr.-Natl. Mktg.)*
Jim Watts *(Plant Mgr.)*

Outside Service Firm(s):

Ernst & Young *(Auditors)*
50 S. Main, Ste. 1400
Salt Lake City, UT 84144
Tel.: 801-538-2500

Lindquist & Vennum *(Legal Firm)*
4200 IDS Center, 80 South 8th St.
Minneapolis, MN 55402
Tel.: 612-371-3211

First National Bank of Minneapolis *(Major Banking Relationship)*
Minneapolis, MN

Non-U.S. Holdings:

Longyear (Australia) Pty. Ltd. **(1)**
919-929 Marion Rd.
Mitchell Park, South Australia 5043, Australia
Tel.: 618-296-6022
Third Party Contract Drilling; Mfr. & Mktg. of Diamond Core Drilling Equipment
S.I.C.: 1481; 3532
Des Bland *(Mgr.)*

Longyear Canada Inc. **(1)**
P.O. Box 330
North Bay, ON P1B 8H6, Canada
Tel.: 705-474-2800
Third Party Contract Drilling; Mfr. & Mktg. of Diamond Core Drilling Equipment
S.I.C.: 1799; 3532
Reg McCarthy *(Chief Oper. Officer)*

Longyear Centroamericana S.A. **(1)**
Apartado Postal 5235
San Jose, Costa Rica
Tel.: 011-506-353103
Mfr. & Mktg. of Diamond Core Drilling Equipment
S.I.C.: 3532

Carlos R. Molina *(Chief Oper. Officer)*

Longyear Chile Ltda. **(1)**
Las Dalias 2900 (Macul) Casilla 15118
Nunoa,
Santiago, Chile
Tel.: 221-5588
Mfr. & Mktg. of Diamond Core Drilling Equipment
S.I.C.: 3532
Romeo Brouillette *(Chief Oper. Officer)*

Longyear de Mexico S.A. de C.V. **(1)**
Apartado Postal 325 Tlalnepantla, Edo. de Mexico, 54080
Mexico, D.F. Mexico
Tel.: 905-394-7177
Mfr. & Mktg. of Diamond Bit Drills & Equipment
S.I.C.: 3532
Alberto Pardo *(Chief Oper. Officer)*

Longyear Deutschland GmbH **(1)**
Graffring 1 Postfach 460, 3100
Celle, Germany
Tel.: 49-5141-81071
Mfr. & Mktg. Diamond Core Drills & Mining Equipment
S.I.C.: 3532
Piet Ginter *(Chief Oper. Officer)*

Longyear Diamond Prods. (Philippines) Inc. **(1)**
M.P.C., P.O. Box 308, 3117 Makati,
Metro Manila, Philippines
Tel.: 632-88-9804
Mktg. of Diamond Core Mining Drills
S.I.C.: 5082
Jose E. Ignacio *(Chief Oper. Officer)*

Longyear France **(1)**
20, Ave Vladimir Komarov 78190
Trappes, France
Tel.: 3313-051-6117
Mktg. of Diamond Core Mining Drills
S.I.C.: 5082
Christian Peyre *(Chief Oper. Officer)*

Longyear Iberica S.A. **(1)**
Avda de los Metales, S-N Leganes
Madrid, Spain
Tel.: 341-6940011
Mfr. & Mktg. of Diamond Core Mining Drills
S.I.C.: 3532
Jose-Ignacio Recoder *(Chief Oper. Officer)*

Longyear (Nederland) B.V. **(1)**
P.O. Box 56, Nijverheidsweg 47 4870 AB
Etten-Leur, Netherlands
Tel.: 311-60834250
Mktg. of Diamond Core Drilling Equipment
S.I.C.: 5082
F. Van Den Berg *(Chief Oper. Officer)*

Longyear New Zealand Ltd. **(1)**
P.O. Box 43-030 Mangere
Auckland, New Zealand
Tel.: 649-275-4049
Mktg. of Diamond Core Drilling Equipment
S.I.C.: 5082
Barry Hogan *(Chief Oper. Officer)*

Longyear U.K. Ltd. **(1)**
Littlemoor Eckington S31 9EF
Sheffield, United Kingdom
Tel.: 44-246-435601
Mktg. of Diamond Core Drills
S.I.C.: 5082

LOOMIS BROTHERS, INC.
1619 F. Ave., N.E.
Cedar Rapids, IA 52406
Mailing Address:
P.O. Box608
Cedar Rapids, IA 52406
Tel.: 319-366-7193 **IA**
Fax: 319-366-7197
Year Founded: 1960
Emp.: 35
New Construction of Commercial & Office Buildings; Renovation & Repair
S.I.C.: 1542
Charles E. Loomis, Jr. *(Pres.)*
David Loomis *(V.P.)*
Lois Loomis *(Treas.)*
James Loomis *(Asst. Sec.)*

Outside Service Firm(s):

Firstar Bank Cedar Rapids, N.A.*(Major Banking Relationship)*
222 Second Ave. S.E.
Cedar Rapids, IA 52406
Tel.: 319-398-4224

LOOS & CO., INC.
Rte. 101 & 169
Pomfret, CT 06258
Tel.: 203-928-7981
Fax: 203-928-6167
Year Founded: 1961
Approx.Sls.: $16,000,000
Emp.: 150
Fiscal Year-end: 8/31/90
Mfr. of Mechanical Steel Cable, Cable Assemblies, Tools & Hardware, Plastic Jacketed Cable & Stainless Steel Wire
S.I.C.: 3315; 3423
A.W. Loos *(Chm. Bd.)*
Richard Griswold *(V.P. & Treas.)*
Tony Carminati *(Mgr.-Matls.)*
Allen Joaskela *(Mgr.-Opers.)*

Outside Service Firm(s):

Rhode Island Hospital Trust National Bank*(Major Banking Relationship)*
Providence, RI

Division:

Cableware Technology Div. **(1)**
900 Industrial Blvd.
Naples, FL 33942
Tel.: 813-643-5667
Fax: 813-643-4558
Mfr. of Aircraft Fittings
S.I.C.: 3728
Tony Naines *(V.P. & Gen. Mgr.)*
Donna Naines *(V.P.-Admin.)*

LORBER INDUSTRIES OF CALIFORNIA
17908 S. Figueroa
Gardena, CA 90248
Tel.: 213-321-8450
Fax: 213-538-1286
Approx.Sls.: $32,000,000
Emp.: 450
Knitting, Dyeing & Finishing, Rotary Screen Printing, Textile Fabrics, Transfer Paper
S.I.C.: 2257; 2261; 2262; 2281; 2672
Arnold Lorber *(Pres.)*
Bob Dalziel *(V.P.)*
Anita Lorber *(Head Designer)*

Outside Service Firm(s):

Weber, Lipshie & Co.*(Auditors)*
Los Angeles, CA

Levy & Norminton*(Legal Firm)*
Los Angeles, CA

Union Bank*(Major Banking Relationship)*
Beverly Hills, CA

LORD CORPORATION
2000 W. Grandview Blvd.
Erie, PA 16514-0038
Mailing Address:
P.O. Box 10038
Erie, PA 16514
Tel.: 814-868-0924 **PA**
Telex: 291935
Fax: 814-864-3452
Year Founded: 1924
Assets: $188,000,000
Liabilities: $105,000,000
Net Worth: $83,000,000
Approx.Sls.: $243,433,000
Emp.: 2,222
Fiscal Year-end: 12/31/91
Import Export
Manufactures Bonded Rubber Products; Manufactures & Markets Paints, Adhesives & Sealants, Industrial Organic Chemicals, Plastic Products
S.I.C.: 2851; 2891; 2869; 3089; 3069
Donald M. Alstadt *(Chm. Bd.)*
A. James Freeman *(Vice Chm. & Chief Exec. Officer)*
Robert C. Busch *(V.P.-Human Resources)*
Thomas A. Cole *(V.P.-Aerospace Prods. Div.)*
Dr. David L. Lewis *(V.P.-Corp. Research)*
Thomas J. Loftus *(V.P. & Gen. Mgr.-Industrial Products Div.)*
William R. Ludwig *(V.P.-Quality & Info. Systems)*
Richard L. Russell *(V.P. & Chief Fin. Officer)*
James W. Wright *(V.P.-Legal Affairs & Sec.)*
R.E. Alexander *(Mgr.-Mktg. Services)*
Paul J. Ditmore *(Mgr.-Information Services)*
D.W. Saurer *(Mgr.-Public Rels.)*
Ruth A. Shindledecker *(Mgr.-Employee Benefit Admin.)*
B.Q. Whitehair *(Mgr.-Adv. & Mktg. Communications)*
P.A. Gaston *(Mktg. Service Rep.)*

Computer Systems/Hardware:
Univac 1100 & 72

Outside Service Firm(s):

Coopers & Lybrand*(Auditors)*
600 Grant St., 35th Fl.
Pittsburgh, PA 15219
Tel.: 412-355-8000
Fax: 412-355-8089

Penn Bank of Erie*(Major Banking Relationship)*
Erie, PA

Divisions:

Lord Corporation, Aerospace Products Division **(1)**
1635 W. 12th St.
Erie, PA 16514
Tel.: 814-455-6191
Fax: 814-454-7446
Mfrs. of Vibration, Shock, Noise Control Mounting Systems, Elastomeric Bearings, Rubber-Bonded-To-Metal Products, O-Rings & Precision Molded Products
S.I.C.: 3089; 3069
Thomas A. Cole *(V.P. & Gen. Mgr.)*

Lord Corporation, Chemical Products Division **(1)**
P.O. Box 10038, 2000 W. Grandview Blvd.
Erie, PA 16514
Tel.: 814-868-3611
Adhesives Coatings Chemical Specialties; Plant Located at Saegertown, PA
S.I.C.: 2891
C.J. Hora *(V.P. & Gen. Mgr.)*

Divisions:

Lord Corp., Elastomer Products **(2)**
2000 W. Grandview Blvd.
Erie, PA 16514
Tel.: 814-868-3611
S.I.C.: 2821
A.J. Ciampa *(Business Mgr.)*

Lord Corp., Industrial Adhesives & Coatings Div. **(2)**
2000 W. Grandview Blvd.
Erie, PA 16514
Tel.: 814-868-3611
S.I.C.: 2891
J.A. Graham *(Business Mgr.)*

Lord Corp., Industrial Products Div. **(1)**
1952 W. Grandview Blvd.
Erie, PA 16514-10040
Tel.: 814-868-5424
INdustrial Products
S.I.C.: 3599
T.J. Loftus *(V.P. & Gen. Mgr.)*

Subsidiary:

Lord Research Corporation **(1)**
407-T Gregson Dr.
Cary, NC 27511
Tel.: 919-469-2500
Research Facility
S.I.C.: 8734
D.L. Lewis *(V.P.)*

Non-U.S. Holdings:

Lord Corp. (U.K.) Ltd. **(1)**
Lyon Motorway Estate Barton Dock Rd.
Stretford, Manchester M32 0ZH, United Kingdom
Tel.: 61 865-8048 (100%)
Telex: HUGMAN 665701
Fax: 61-865-0096
Mfr. of Paints, Adhesives & Sealants, Plastic Products
S.I.C.: 2851; 2891; 3089

Lord Far East, Inc. **(1)**
2F, Yoyogi Center Bldg. 57-1 Yoyogi, 1-chome, Shibuya-ku,
Tokyo, 151, Japan
Tel.: 3378-9011 (100%)
Telex: 781 252 37
Fax: 3378-9739
Mfr. of Paints, Adhesives & Sealants, Industrial Organic Chemicals, Plastic Products
S.I.C.: 2851; 2891; 2869; 3089

Lord Industrial Ltda. **(1)**
Caixa Postal 31 CEP 13200
Sao Paulo, Brazil
Tel.: 258-1122 (100%)
Telex: 391-36339; 524126 LIKI
Fax: 11 436 3581
Mfr. of Paints, Adhesives & Sealants, Industrial Organic Chemicals, Plastic Products, Rubber Products
S.I.C.: 2851; 2891; 2869; 3069; 3089

Joint Venture:

Lord Korea Ltd. **(1)**
C.P.O. Box No. 10156
Seoul, Korea
Tel.: 734-9690
Tel.: 734-9691 (75%)
Telex: 787-26526 SEWONCO K
Joint Venture of Parent Co.; Mfr. of Adhesives & Sealants, Industrial Organic Chemicals, Paints
S.I.C.: 2891; 2869; 2851
H.M. Choi *(Chief Oper. Officer)*

LORD, SULLIVAN & YODER, INC. ADVERTISING
250 Old Wilson Bridge Rd.
Columbus, OH 43085-0800
Tel.: 614-846-8500
Fax: 614-846-2679
Year Founded: 1965
Approx.Billings: $36,000,000
Emp.: 75
Advertising Agency
S.I.C.: 7311
Robert E. Sullivan *(Chm. & Chief Exec. Officer)*
Robert D. Ackerman *(Pres. & Chief Oper. Officer)*
Robert L. Bender *(Exec. V.P. & Treas.)*
Raymond S. Caruso *(Exec. V.P.)*
Gary E. Armstrong *(Sr. V.P. & Dir.-Mktg.)*
Nancy P. Barr *(Sr. V.P. & Dir.-Client Services)*
John Brinkerhoff *(Sr. V.P. & Dir.-Creative)*
C. Douglas Fisher *(Sr. V.P. & Dir.-Creative)*
John C. Walkenhorst *(Sr. V.P.-Fin.)*
John C. Bartram *(Sec.)*
Brad M. McCurdy *(Mgr.-Data Processing)*

Lord, Sullivan & Yoder, Inc. Advertising—(Continued)

No. of U.S. Offices: 1

Computer Systems/Hardware:
IBM AS/400

Outside Service Firm(s):

KPMG Peat Marwick *(Auditors)*
Two Nationwide Plaza
Columbus, OH 43215
Tel.: 614-249-2300

Bartram & Bartram *(Legal Firm)*
Marion, OH

BancOhio National Bank *(Major Banking Relationship)*
Columbus, OH

Branch:

Lord, Sullivan & Yoder/Public Relations **(1)**
P.O. Box 800, 250 Old Wilson Bridge Rd.
Columbus, OH 43085
Tel.: 614-846-7777
Fax: 614-846-2679
Emp.: 14
Public Relations Counsel
S.I.C.: 8743
Neil R. Mortine *(V.P., Dir. Pub. Rels.)*
Russ Birkos *(Asst. Dir.)*
Kym Carr *(Asst. Dir.)*

LCN

LORSCH CREATIVE NETWORK
5950 Wilshire Blvd., 2nd Fl.
Los Angeles, CA 90036
Tel.: 213-930-2260
Fax: 213-931-5582
Year Founded: 1976
Approx.Billings: $34,000,000
Emp.: 23
Advertising Agency
S.I.C.: 7311
Robert H. Lorsch *(Chm. Bd.)*
Robert Wolpert *(Chief Fin. Officer)*
Pamela Allen *(Dir.-Admin.)*
William Fenske *(Dir.-Pur.)*

Outside Service Firm(s):

Howard Greene *(Auditors)*
Los Angeles, CA

Wells Fargo Bank *(Major Banking Relationship)*
420 Montgomery St.
San Francisco, CA 94104

LORTZ DIRECT MARKETING INC.
11316 "P" St.
Omaha, NE 68137
Tel.: 402-331-5740
Year Founded: 1982
Approx.Billings: $15,000,860
Emp.: 19
Direct Response Adv.
Gary Lortz *(Pres. & New Bus. Contact)*
Nadine Lortz *(Treas.)*
Mara Orsi *(Controller)*

THE LORVIC CORP.
8810 Frost Ave.
St. Louis, MO 63134
Tel.: 314-524-7444 **MO**
Fax: 314-524-7446
Year Founded: 1954
Emp.: 24
Fiscal Year-end: 3/31/90
Import Export
Maker of Dental Supplies
S.I.C.: 3843
Kathryn S. Nemanick *(Chm. Bd.)*
Richard C. Nemanick *(Pres.)*
Arthur J. Scherle *(Sec. & Treas.)*
Dr. F. Lochner *(Mgr.-Quality Control)*
K. Vandy *(Mgr.-Production)*

Computer Systems/Hardware:
Compaq

Outside Service Firm(s):

Simpson, Thacher & Bartlett *(Legal Firm)*
425 Lexington Ave
New York, NY 10017
Tel.: 212-455-2000
Fax: 212-455-2502

Manufacturers National Bank N.A. *(Major Banking Relationship)*
38th Fl., 100 Renaissance Center
Detroit, MI 48243
Tel.: 313-222-4227

LOS ALAMOS TECHNICAL ASSOCIATES, INC.
1650 Trinity Dr.
Los Alamos, NM 87544
Tel.: 505-662-9080 **NM**
Fax: 505-662-1725
Year Founded: 1976
Sales Range: $10-19 Million
Emp.: 264
Professional, Scientific & Engineering Services
S.I.C.: 8711
L.P. Reinig *(Chm. Bd. & Pres.)*
E.M. Cole *(Dept. Mgr.-Environment Safety)*
W.M. Robson *(Contract Mgr.)*
D.B. Geran *(Mgr.-Personnel)*
Principal(s):
L.P. Reinig

No. of U.S. Offices: 5

Computer Systems/Hardware:
Prime; AT&T

Outside Service Firm(s):

KPMG Peat Marwick *(Auditors)*
Two Park Square, 6565 Americas Pkwy., N.E., Ste. 700
Albuquerque, NM 87110
Tel.: 505-884-3939
Fax: 505-884-8348

Los Alamos National Bank *(Major Banking Relationship)*
Los Alamos, NM

LOS ANGELES SMOKING CURING COMPANY
778 Kohler St.
Los Angeles, CA 90021
Mailing Address:
P.O. Box 21938,
Los Angles, CA 90021
Tel.: 213-622-0724 **CA**
Fax: 213-614-8857
Year Founded: 1921
Approx.Sls.: $30,000,000
Emp.: 170
Import Export
Smoked & Cured Fish
S.I.C.: 2091
Louis Vitale *(Pres.)*
Keith Fogel *(Mgr.-Plant)*
Jim Fielding *(Mgr.-Plant)*
Alicia Lopez *(Mgr.- Quality Control)*
Rose Garbarini *(Sec.)*
Principal(s):
Louis Vitale
Rose Garbarini
Louisa Vitale

No. of Mfg. Plants/Facilities: 1
No. of U.S. Offices: 1

Computer Systems/Hardware:
Hewlett Packard

Outside Service Firm(s):

Bank of America NT&SA *(Major Banking Relationship)*
City of Industry, CA

LOST ARROW CORPORATION
259 W. Santa Clara
Ventura, CA 93001
Mailing Address:
P.O. Box 150
Ventura, CA 93002
Tel.: 805-643-8616
Telex: 69-1729
Fax: 805-653-6355
Year Founded: 1957
Approx.Sls.: $20,000,000
Emp.: 500
Fiscal Year-end: 4/30/92
Mfr. & Distr. Outdoor Clothing
S.I.C.: 2329; 5136; 5137
Corporate Giving Program: 10% of Pretax Profits Go To Environmental Groups
Employee Matching Gifts Program: United Way
Kris McDivitt *(Pres. & Chief Exec. Officer)*
Alison May *(Chief Fin. Officer)*
Scott Campbell *(Controller)*
Kathy Bremer *(Dir.-Data Processing)*
Megan Montgomery *(Dir.-Pub. Rels.)*
Teri Wolfe *(Dir.-Personnel)*
Mike Harrelson *(Mgr.-Pub. Rels.)*
Geffrey Cline *(Legal Officer)*
Principal(s):
Yvon Chouinard
Melinda Chouinard

No. of U.S. Offices: 1

Computer Systems/Hardware:
IBM Systems 36 & 38

Outside Service Firm(s):

Moss Adams *(Auditors)*
Los Angeles, CA

Kalmarble Insurance *(Commercial Insurance Carrier)*
Santa Barbara, CA

Union Bank *(Major Banking Relationship)*
Oxnard, CA

LOSURDO FOODS, INC.
20 Owens Rd.
Hackensack, NJ 07601
Tel.: 201-343-6680
Fax: 201-343-8078
Approx.Sls.: $25,000,000
Emp.: 85
Fiscal Year-end: 12/31/91
General Grocery Line Distributors; Mfrs. Pickles, Sauces & Salad Dressings, Natural & Processed Cheese, Prepared Pizza Dough
S.I.C.: 5141; 2035; 2022; 2041
Michael Losurdo *(Pres.)*
Michael Losurdo, Jr. *(Exec. V.P.)*
Mark Losurdo *(Exec. V.P.)*
Maria Losurdo *(Treas.)*
Mary Losurdo *(Sec.)*

Outside Service Firm(s):

National Community Bank *(Major Banking Relationship)*
Jefferson, NJ

L·M·P·M

LOTAS MINARD PATTON MCIVER
152 West 57th St.
New York, NY 10019
Tel.: 212-333-5676
Fax: 212-333-5018
Year Founded: 1986
Approx.Billings: $90,000,000
Emp.: 51
Michael Macchio *(Talent)*
Ed Hackimer *(Comptroller)*
Rosa Amelia Lawrence *(Admin. Dir.)*

LOUIS LONDON ADVERTISING & SALES PROMOTION
408 N. Euclid Ave.
Saint Louis, MO 63108
Tel.: 314-367-4100
Fax: 314-367-1987
Year Founded: 1984
Approx.Billings: $24,000,000
Emp.: 42
Adv., Sales Promotion & Mktg. Communications
Mark Shapiro *(Pres. & New Bus. Contact)*
Jerry Best *(Chief Fin. Officer)*

Computer Systems/Hardware:
MacIntosh, Financial-IBM DOS

LOUISIANA UTILITIES SUPPLY COMPANY
2056 Sorrel
Baton Rouge, LA 70802
Tel.: 504-383-8916
Fax: 504-387-5256
Year Founded: 1976
Approx.Sls.: $16,000,000
Emp.: 33
Wholesale Municipal Water Works Supplies
S.I.C.: 5051
Hilmer C. Hultgren *(Pres.)*
Carter Parker *(Treas. & Sec.)*

Outside Service Firm(s):

Thomas, Wilson & Ragua *(Auditors)*
Baton Rouge, LA

Andy Broussard Legal Firm *(Legal Firm)*
Baton Rouge, LA

Guaranty Bank & Trust *(Major Banking Relationship)*
Baton Rouge, LA

LOUISVILLE BEDDING COMPANY
10400 Bunsen Way
Louisville, KY 40299
Tel.: 502-491-3370
Year Founded: 1889
Approx.Sls.: $91,000,000
Emp.: 800
Mfr. of Mattress Pads, Bedspreads, Quilts, Comforters, Dust Ruffles, Tablecloths, Napkins, Placemats etc.
S.I.C.: 2221; 2392
John M. Minihan *(Pres. & Chief Exec. Officer)*
Kenneth A. King *(Exec. V.P.)*
Charles J. Lohman *(Sr. V.P.-Pur.)*
Ronald A. Benson *(V.P.-Mktg.)*
Christian F. Rapp *(V.P.-Fin. & Sec.)*

LOUISVILLE SCRAP MATERIAL CO., INC.
301 E. Main St.
Louisville, KY 40202
Tel.: 502-589-9171 **KY**
Fax: 502-589-8188
Year Founded: 1913
Sales Range: $40-59 Million
Emp.: 200
Fiscal Year-end: 12/31/90
Export
Scrap Metal Processing; Rail Car Dismantling & Modification
S.I.C.: 4789; 3499
David S. Blue *(Pres. & Chief Exec. Officer)*
Bruce Hall *(V.P.)*
Douglas C. Smith *(V.P.)*
Principal(s):
David S. Blue

No. of Mfg. Plants/Facilities: 4

Computer Systems/Hardware:
IBM S/36

Outside Service Firm(s):

Deloitte & Touche*(Auditors)*
510 W. Broadway
Louisville, KY 40202
Tel.: 502-562-2000

CNA Insurance*(Group Insurer)*
Louisville, KY

Liberty National Bank & Trust Co.*(Major Banking Relationship)*
416 W. Jefferson St.
Louisville, KY 40202
Tel.: 502-566-2000

Liberty National Bank & Trust Co.*(Pension Manager)*
416 W. Jefferson St.
Louisville, KY 40202
Tel.: 502-566-2000

LOVE BOX COMPANY, INC.
700 E. 37th St. N.
Wichita, KS 67219
Tel.: 316-838-0851
Fax: 316-838-0851 Ext. 270
Year Founded: 1954
Approx.Sls.: $60,000,000
Emp.: 600
Fiscal Year-end: 9/30/92
Mfr. Corrugated Boxes & Wood Pallets
S.I.C.: 2448; 2653
Robert D. Love *(Pres.)*
Philip Elder *(V.P.-Mfg.)*
Randolph D. Love, Sr. *(V.P.-Sls.)*
Barry Tinius *(Treas. & Sec.)*
Robert W. Love *(Dir.-Admin.)*

Outside Service Firm(s):

Peterson, Peterson & Goss*(Auditors)*
Wichita, KS

Martin Churchill*(Legal Firm)*
Wichita, KS

First National Bank of Tulsa*(Major Banking Relationship)*
P.O. Box One
Tulsa, OK 74193

LOVE MORTGAGE COMPANY
Exec. Office Bldg., 515 Olive Street, Ste. 1400
St. Louis, MO 63101
Tel.: 314-621-1200
Fax: 314-621-7360
Emp.: 285
Real Estate Investors & Brokers
S.I.C.: 6798; 6531
Laurence A. Schiffer *(Pres.)*
Gloria Clement *(Chief Fin. Officer)*
Jolene Keel *(Dir.-Personnel)*

Computer Systems/Hardware:
Plexus

Outside Service Firm(s):

Ernst & Young*(Auditors)*
701 Market St.
St. Louis, MO 63101
Tel.: 314-259-1000

Brian Cave McPheeters & McRoberts*(Legal Firm)*
St. Louis, MO

LOVEJOY INC.
2655 Wisconsin Ave.
Downers Grove, IL 60515-4299
Tel.: 708-852-0500
Telex: 4330208
Fax: 708-852-2120
Year Founded: 1900
Approx.Sls.: $21,000,000
Emp.: 200
Fiscal Year-end: 12/31/90
Import Export
Manufactures Power Transmission Equipment
S.I.C.: 3568
Michael W. Hennessy *(Pres.)*
Thomas Brininger *(Chief Fin. Officer)*
James A. Minton *(V.P.-Sls.)*
Michael Cobb *(Mgr.-Adv.)*

Computer Systems/Hardware:
IBM AS400

LOVE'S ENTERPRISES, INC.
3195-C Airport Loop Dr., Ste. B
Costa Mesa, CA 92626
Tel.: 714-435-3550
Fax: 714-837-2469
Year Founded: 1950
Approx.Sls.: $30,000,000
Emp.: 5
Franchised Restaurants
S.I.C.: 5812
Ron Mesker *(Pres.)*
Steve Ousdahl *(Dir.-Opers. & Admin.)*

T. A. LOVING COMPANY
400 Patetown Rd.
Goldsboro, NC 27530
Mailing Address:
P.O. Drawer 919
Goldsboro, NC 27530
Tel.: 919-734-8400 **NC**
Fax: 919-736-2148
Fax: 919-731-7538
Year Founded: 1926
Approx.Sls.: $60,000,000
Emp.: 350
General Contractor Building, Highway, Bridge & Utility Construction
S.I.C.: 1542; 1611; 1629; 1622
R.A. Bryan, Jr. *(Chm. Bd. & Chief Exec. Officer)*
Samuel P. Hunter *(Pres.)*
William P. Franklin *(Exec. V.P.-Bldg. Div.)*
Steve Bryan *(V.P.-Mktg.)*
George E. Hart *(V.P.-Bldg. Div.)*
C. Banks McNairy, III *(V.P.-Bldg. Div.)*
Donald Robinson *(V.P.-Utilities Div.)*
Benton Satterfield *(V.P.-Bldg. Div.)*
James J. Smith *(V.P.-Utilities Div.)*
Giles Trimble *(V.P.-Bridge Div.)*
Wilson Twiford *(V.P.-Bridge Div.)*
Richard Ingram *(Treas. & Sec.)*

Outside Service Firm(s):

KPMG Peat Marwick*(Auditors)*
3100 Smoketree Court
Raleigh, NC 27629
Tel.: 919-872-3600
Fax: 919-790-9731

Poyner & Spruill*(Legal Firm)*
Raleigh, NC

First Union National Bank*(Major Banking Relationship)*
Goldsboro, NC

THE LOWE GROUP
1345 Ave. of the Americas
New York, NY 10105
Tel.: 212-708-8899
Fax: 212-708-8550
Year Founded: 1981
Approx.Billings: $1,800,000,000
Advertising Agency
S.I.C.: 7311
Frank Lowe *(Chm.)*
Joseph Gilbride *(Exec. V.P., Chief Fin. Officer)*
Lucinda Holmes *(Exec. V.P., Gen. Mgr.)*
Lester A. Delano *(Exec. Dir.)*

Non-U.S. Holdings:

AdPlus GmbH **(1)**
Hamburger Allee 45, 6000
Frankfurt/Main, 90, Germany
Tel.: 69-794040
Fax: 69-79404155
Advertising
S.I.C.: 7311
Hans-Joachim Drenk *(Mng. Dir.)*

Deacon Day Advertising and The McLauchlan Group **(1)**
20 Richmond St. E.,
Toronto, ON M5C 2R9, Canada
Tel.: 416-362-8600
Fax: 416-362-5669
Full Service Advertising
S.I.C.: 7311
Cal McLauchlan *(Chm.-The McLauchlan Group)*
David Deacon *(Pres. & Chief Exec. Officer)*
Peter Johnson *(Chief Fin. Officer)*

Gariboldi Parisi Verga/Interad **(1)**
P. Le Biancamano 8 20121
Milan, Italy
Tel.: 2-6595156
Fax: 2-290 10206
Advertising
S.I.C.: 7311
Emanuele Pirella *(Pres.)*
Agostino Bordignon *(Chief Fin. Officer)*

Hager Gesellschaft **(1)**
Seilerstatte 13 1015
Vienna, Austria
Tel.: 1-5126666
Fax: 1-5125469
Ad Agency
S.I.C.: 7311
Theodore Mautner Markhof *(Chief Exec.)*

Lowe & Associes **(1)**
96, av. du General Leclerc 92514
Boulogne, Billancourt Cedex France
Tel.: 46-047272
Fax: 46-047273
Advertising
S.I.C.: 7311
Jean-Paul Lichtenberg *(Pres. & Creative Dir.)*

Lowe Communication Group **(1)**
402, Av. de Tervuren 1150
Brussels, Belgium
Tel.: 02-7710120
Fax: 02-7628683
Approx.Billings: $81,314,590
Emp.: 2
Ad Agency
S.I.C.: 7311
Georges Lafleur *(Chm. & Chief Exec.)*
Herve van Ypersele *(Mng. Dir.)*

Lowe FMS **(1)**
Tambre 33 28002
Madrid, Spain
Tel.: 1-411-3003
Fax: 1-562-9071
Advertising Agency
S.I.C.: 7311
Adolfo Castro *(Chief Exec. Officer)*
Urs Frick *(Gen. Mgr.)*

The Lowe Group **(1)**
Bowater House, 68-114 Knightsbridge
London, SW1X 7LT, United Kingdom
Tel.: 071-225 3434
Fax: 071-584-0336
Approx.Billings: $1,800,000,000
Advertising Agency
S.I.C.: 7311
Frank Lowe *(Chm.)*
Lucinda Holmes *(Exec. V.P., Gen. Mgr.)*
Geoff Howard-Spink *(Dir. of Strategic Plng.)*
Chris Morley *(Gen. Mgr.-Europe)*
Irving Samwell *(Vice Chm.-Europe)*
Neil McNab *(Vice Chm.-Europe)*

Lowe Howard-Spink Limited **(1)**
Bowater House, 68-114 Knightsbridge
London, SW1X 7LT, United Kingdom
Tel.: 071-5845033
Telex: 25109
Fax: 071-5849557
Approx.Billings: $497,500,000
Emp.: 267
Computer Systems/Hardware:
Donovan, Apple Macintosh
Full Service Advertising
S.I.C.: 7311
Adrian Holmes *(Chm.)*
David Wheldon *(Mng. Dir.)*
Richard Jameson *(Fin. Dir.)*

Lowe Kuiper & Schouten B.V. **(1)**
Koningslaan 42 1075 AE
Amsterdam, Netherlands
Tel.: 020-6642737
Fax: 020-6643230
Approx.Billings: $40,000,000
Emp.: 35
Full Service Advertising
S.I.C.: 7311
Jack Schouten *(Mng. Dir.)*
R.A.H. Fiolet *(Controller)*

Lowe Luerzer GmbH **(1)**
Hamburger Allee 45 6000
Frankfurt/Main, 90, Germany
Tel.: 69-794040
Fax: 69-771091
Computer Systems/Hardware:
Novell, Kienzle
Advertising
S.I.C.: 7311
Heimar Schroter *(Mng. Dir.)*
Bill Murphy *(Chief Exec.)*
Jorg F. Troester *(Mng. Dir.)*
Hans Grimm *(Chief Fin. Officer)*

Lowe Luerzer GmbH **(1)**
Heinrichstr. 85 Postfach 8013, 4000
Dusseldorf, Germany
Tel.: 211-62190
Fax: 211-6219130
Advertising
S.I.C.: 7311
Hans-Theo Muller-Schildt *(Mng. Dir.)*
Dieter Hainski *(Fin. Mgr.)*

Lowe MBAC **(1)**
Paseo de los Tilos, 3-9 08034
Barcelona, Spain
Tel.: 3-280-3355
Fax: 3-205-6214
Advertising
S.I.C.: 7311
Adolfo Castro *(Chief Exec. Officer)*
Paco Montalvo *(Exec. V.P.)*
Iuma Duran *(Admin. Dir.)*

Lowe Troost S.A. **(1)**
402 av. de Tervuren 1150
Brussels, Belgium
Tel.: 2-7710120
Fax: 2-7628683
Approx.Billings: $70,000,000
Emp.: 62
Advertising, Direct Marketing
S.I.C.: 7311
Georges Lafleur *(Pres. & Chief Exec. Officer)*
Pierre Rousseau *(Gen. Mgr.)*
Eliane Landeut *(Corp. Sec.)*
Gerard Severs *(Chief Fin. Officer)*
Najad Menouar *(Pub. Rels. Dir.)*

Pirella Goettsche Lowe S.p.A. **(1)**
P. Le Biancamano 8 20121
Milan, Italy
Tel.: 2-290281
Fax: 2-6597722
Approx.Billings: $117,688,200
Emp.: 118
Full Service Advertising
S.I.C.: 7311
Emanuele Pirella *(Pres.)*
Michael Goettsche *(V.P.)*
Arrigo Frisoni *(Gen. Mgr.)*
Franco Bertolini *(Vice Gen. Mgr.)*

Pirella Goettsche Lowe S.p.A. **(1)**
Via Aventina 7 00153
Rome, Italy
Tel.: 6-5745631
Fax: 6-574-3930
Emp.: 10
Advertising
S.I.C.: 7311
Giorgio Gramazio *(Gen. Mgr.)*

LOWELL PACKING COMPANY
P.O. Box 220
Fitzgerald, GA 31750
Tel.: 912-423-2051 **GA**
Fax: 912-443-6601
Year Founded: 0095
Approx.Sls.: $16,000,000
Emp.: 95
Meat Packing Plants
S.I.C.: 2011
Lowell M. Dowing, Sr. *(Pres.)*
Lowell Morris Downing, Jr. *(V.P.)*
Jim Davis *(Exec. V.P.)*
Geraldine D. Bryant *(Treas. & Sec.)*
Principal(s):
Lowell M. Dowing, Sr.
Lowell Morris Downing, Jr.
D.S. Downing

No. of Mfg. Plants/Facilities: 1
No. of U.S. Offices: 1

Lowell Packing Company—(Continued)

Outside Service Firm(s):

George Pennington*(Auditors)*
Fitzgerald, GA

Bank of Fitzgerald*(Major Banking Relationship)*
Fitzgerald, GA

LOXCREEN COMPANY
1630 Old Dunbar Rd.
West Columbia, SC 29169
Mailing Address:
P.O. Box 4004
West Columbia, SC 29171
Tel.: 803-822-8200 **GA**
Fax: 803-822-8547
Year Founded: 1946
Assets: $22,000,000
Liabilities: $6,000,000
Net Worth: $16,000,000
Sales Range: $40-59 Million
Fiscal Year-end: 12/31/91
Mfr. Aluminum & Vinyl Extrusion Fabricated Building Products
S.I.C.: 3354; 3442
John W. Parrish *(Chm. Bd. & Pres.)*
Terrell E. Stutts *(Exec. V.P.)*
G. R. Drafts *(V.P.-Sls.)*
Thomas J. Moseley *(V.P.-Acctg. & Sec.)*
Charles C. Rone, Jr. *(V.P.-Fin. & Treas.)*

No. of Mfg. Plants/Facilities: 4
No. of U.S. Offices: 11

Computer Systems/Hardware:
NCR Criterion

Outside Service Firm(s):

J. W. Hunt & Co.*(Auditors)*
Middleburg Office Park, 1607 St. Julian Place
Columbia, SC 29202
Tel.: 803-254-8196

Sutherland, Asbill & Brennan*(Legal Firm)*
999 Peachtree St.
Atlanta, GA 30309
Tel.: 404-658-8700

Trust Company Bank*(Major Banking Relationship)*
P.O. Box 4625
Atlanta, GA 30302
Tel.: 404-588-7711

LOZIER CORPORATION
6336 Pershing Dr.
Omaha, NE 68110
Mailing Address:
P.O. Box 188,
Omaha, NE 68101-0188
Tel.: 402-457-8000 **NE**
Fax: 402-457-8338
Assets: $103,049,735
Earnings: $32,000,000
Net Worth: $103,049,735
Approx.Sls.: $178,009,062
Emp.: 1,800
Fiscal Year-end: 1/28/91
Mfr. & Sales of Store Fixtures & Storage Systems
S.I.C.: 2541; 2542
Allan Lozier *(Chief Exec. Officer)*
John Paben *(Pres.)*
Monty Allgood *(V.P.-Indus. Rels.)*
Sheri L. Andrews *(V.P. & Treas.)*
Jim Arvin *(V.P.-Opers.)*
Bob Braun *(V.P.)*
Dick Dyer *(V.P.-Engrng.)*
Mark Kleinsmith *(V.P.-Fin.)*
Wayne Moeller *(V.P.-Sls. & Mktg.)*
James E. Sedlacek *(V.P.-Mfg.)*
Don Shoemaker *(V.P.-Sls.)*
Vickey Thayer *(V.P.-Human Resources)*

Computer Systems/Hardware:
IBM 4381

Outside Service Firm(s):

Deloitte & Touche*(Auditors)*
2000 First National Center
Omaha, NE 68102
Tel.: 402-346-7788

Liberty Mutual*(Commercial Insurance Carrier)*
Boston, MA

United of Omaha*(Group Insurer)*
Mutual of Omaha Plaza
Omaha, NE 68175
Tel.: 800-327-8871

First National Bank of Omaha*(Major Banking Relationship)*
One First National Center
Omaha, NE 68102

The Principal Financial Group*(Pension Manager)*
711 High St.
Des Moines, IA 50309
Tel.: 515-247-4593
Tel.: 800-543-4015

Subsidiaries:

Lozier Corporation, AFI Division **(1)**
1625 Schifferdecker
Joplin, MO 64801
Tel.: 417-781-1611
Fax: 417-781-1611, Ext. 233
Approx.Sls.: $12,000,000
Emp.: 160
Metal Store Fixtures
S.I.C.: 2541; 2542
Bob Matteo *(Gen. Mgr.)*

Lozier Store Fixtures, Inc. **(1)**
6336 Pershing Dr.
Omaha, NE 68110
Tel.: 402-457-8000
Approx.Sls.: $180,000,000
Emp.: 150
Sales of Store Fixtures
S.I.C.: 2542; 2541; 5046
John M. Paben *(Exec. V.P. & Gen. Mgr.)*
Wayne A. Moeller *(V.P.-Sls. & Mktg.)*

LUBECON SYSTEMS, INC.
(Formerly LubeCon Maintenance Systems, Inc.)
6735 W. 64th St.
Fremont, MI 49412-0589
Mailing Address:
P.O. Box 589,
Fremont, MI 49412-0589
Tel.: 616-924-0653
Tel.: 800-LUBECON
Fax: 616-924-6147
Year Founded: 1975
Sales Range: $10-19 Million
Emp.: 75
Fiscal Year-end: 3/31/92
Export
Mfr. Of Automatic Lubricating Systems For Conveyors, Robotics; Mfr. of Dry-film Lubricants, Gear Oil, Heavy Duty Greases; Mfr. Of Hand Held Grease Guns, Transfer Pumps & Sprayers
S.I.C.: 2992; 3569
L.G. Myers *(Pres., Chief Exec. Officer & Admin. Dir.)*
H.J. Myers *(Chief Fin. Officer)*
Bernie Boersma *(Mgr.-Natl. Sls. & Export)*
Susan Canfield *(Mgr.-Sls. Coord. & Adv.)*
Principal(s):
L.G. Myers
Bernie Boersma

No. of Mfg. Plants/Facilities: 2
No. of U.S. Offices: 1
No. of Foreign Offices: 1

LUBRICATION ENGINEERS, INC.
3851 Airport Frwy.
Fort Worth, TX 76111
Tel.: 817-834-6321
Emp.: 325
Oils & Greases, Blending & Compounding
S.I.C.: 2992
Joseph C. Valentine *(Chm. Bd., Pres. & Chief Exec. Officer)*
Charles L. Brandt *(Exec. V.P.-Admin. & Sec.)*
Donald F. King, Jr. *(V.P.)*

Outside Service Firm(s):

M Bank*(Major Banking Relationship)*
Fort Worth, TX

LUCKY FRUIT & PRODUCE, INC.
2630 5th St.
Sacramento, CA 95818
Tel.: 916-446-7621
Fax: 916-446-4157
Year Founded: 1970
Approx.Sls.: $25,000,000
Emp.: 87
Wholesale Fruit & Produce
S.I.C.: 5148
Emery Mitchell *(Pres.)*
Ted Kitada *(V.P.)*
Dean FOng *(Sec. & Treas.)*

Outside Service Firm(s):

Merrill Lynch*(Investment Banker)*
Sacramento, CA

LUCKY WINNER, INC.
525 Seventh Ave.
New York, NY 10018
Tel.: 212-354-9464 **NY**
Fax: 212-354-4199
Year Founded: 1973
Approx.Sls.: $18,000,000
Emp.: 216
Mfr. of Women's & Misses' Blouses & Shirts
S.I.C.: 2339; 2331
Marco Yeshoua *(Chm. Bd.)*
Jack Yeshoua *(Pres.)*
Valentine Yeshoua *(V.P. & Sec.)*
Peter Roth *(Gen. Counsel)*

Outside Service Firm(s):

BDO Seidman*(Auditors)*
1430 Broadway
New York, NY
Tel.: 212-765-7500

National Westminster Bank plc*(Major Banking Relationship)*
Astor Plaza, 1515 Broadway
New York, NY 10036

LUDINGTON NEWS CO. INC.
1600 E. Grand Blvd.
Detroit, MI 48211-3195
Tel.: 313-925-7600 **MI**
Fax: 313-922-3909
Year Founded: 1921
Approx.Sls.: $80,000,000
Emp.: 350
Fiscal Year-end: 12/31/90
Books & Magazine Sales & Distribution
S.I.C.: 5192
Ivan Ludington, Jr. *(Chm Bd. & Chief Exec. Officer)*
David Ludington *(Pres. & Chief Oper. Officer)*
William F. Penz *(Exec. V.P. & Treas.)*
Dana Ludington *(V.P.-Mktg.)*
James Miller *(Sec.)*
Tom Singstock *(Dir.-Personnel)*
Jeff Wardford *(Dir.-Mktg.)*
Principal(s):
Ivan Ludington, Jr.

Computer Systems/Hardware:
Wang

Outside Service Firm(s):

Ernst & Young*(Auditors)*
One Detroit Center, 500 Woodward, Ste. 1700
Detroit, MI 48243
Tel.: 313-259-9600

Mason-McBride*(Commercial Insurance Carrier)*
Troy, MI

Keller, Thoma, Schwarze, Schwarze, Dubay & Katz*(Legal Firm)*
Detroit, MI

National Bank of Detroit*(Major Banking Relationship)*
P.O. Box 751-A
Detroit, MI 48232
Tel.: 313-225-1000

LUDLOW COMPOSITES CORPORATION
2100 Commerce Dr.
Fremont, OH 43420
Tel.: 419-332-5531
Tel.: 800-628-5463
Approx.Sls.: $15,000,000
Emp.: 150
Export
Mfr. of Carpet-Topped Vinyl-Backed Floor Mats, Latex & Sponge Vinyl Products
S.I.C.: 2295
Robert J. Moram *(Pres. & Chief Exec. Officer)*
James Norris *(V.P.-Opers.)*
Arnold Boedeker *(V.P. & Controller)*
D.E. Bertsch *(Dir.-Personnel)*
R.S. Hartman *(Dir.-Pur.)*
D.H. Knoblauch *(Mgr.-Central Reg. Sls.)*
Daniel M. Laity *(Mgr.-Mktg. Services)*
Tom Schreiner *(Mgr.-Midwestern & N.E. Reg. Sls.)*

LUDLOW TEXTILES CO., INC.
State Street
Ludlow, MA 01056
Tel.: 413-583-5051 **MA**
Fax: 413-589-1415
Sales Range: $10-19 Million
Emp.: 100
Import Export
Mfr. of Synthetic & Natural Threads & Twines
S.I.C.: 2284; 2298
Robert H. Welsh *(Chm. Bd. & Chief Exec. Officer)*
Martin A. Lower *(Pres. & Treas.)*

Outside Service Firm(s):

Ernst & Young*(Auditors)*
200 Clarendon St., 46th Fl.
Boston, MA 02116
Tel.: 617-266-2000

Ropes & Gray*(Legal Firm)*
One International Place
Boston, MA 02110
Tel.: 617-423-6100

Shawmut Bank*(Major Banking Relationship)*
Springfield, MA

LUGBILL BROTHERS, INC.
1396 S. Defiance
Archbold, OH 43502
Mailing Address:
P.O. Box 198,
Archbold, OH 43502
Tel.: 419-445-0815
Fax: 419-445-0260
Approx.Sls.: $11,000,000
Emp.: 100
Fiscal Year-end: 3/31/92
Home Building Supply; Hardware & Lumber
S.I.C.: 5072; 5211
Charles Lugbill *(Chm. Bd. & Pres.)*
Marvin Nafziger *(Exec. V.P.)*
Karlen Wyse *(V.P.)*
Jerry Lugbill *(Treas. & Sec.)*

Outside Service Firm(s):

Bock, Korsnack & Hinds, Inc.*(Auditors)*
Maumee, OH

Plassman, Rupp, Hensal & Short*(Legal Firm)*
Archbold, OH

Farmers & Merchants State Bank*(Major Banking Relationship)*
Archbold, OH

LUKENHEIMER CO.
Beekman & Waverly St.
Cincinnati, OH 45214
Mailing Address:
P.O. Box 145487
Cincinnati, OH 45214
Tel.: 513-921-3400
Fax: 513-244-5224
Approx.Sls.: $30,000,000
Emp.: 50
Fiscal Year-end: 10/31/90
Bronze-Iron-Steel-Ball-Butterfly-Valves; Lubricators & Engrng. Devices; Automated Fluid Control Systems; Power Actuated Valves
S.I.C.: 3491; 3492; 3569
Dr. Bernard DeSilva *(Pres.)*
Guenter Pansch *(Gen. Mgr.-Sls.)*

Division:

Lukenheimer Co.-Energo Valves **(1)**
P.O. Box 14249,
Cincinnati, OH 45250
Kruno Rojaica *(Pres.)*
Larry Baldwin *(Controller)*

LUMAS REALTY, INC.
11035 S.W. 156th Pl.
Miami, FL 33189
Tel.: 305-596-2626 **FL**
Fax: 305-274-2686
Year Founded: 1972
Approx.Sls.: $42,000,000
Emp.: 30
Fiscal Year-end: 6/30/92
Residential Real Estate Agents & Brokers
S.I.C.: 6552
Antonio A. Sarmiento *(Chm. Bd., Pres. & Sec.)*

No. of U.S. Offices: 1

Outside Service Firm(s):

Luis M. de los Santos*(Auditors)*
Miami, FL

Liberty Mutual*(Commercial Insurance Carrier)*
Ft. Lauderdale, FL

Ocean Bank*(International Bank Affiliate)*
Miami, FL

Ocean Bank*(Major Banking Relationship)*
Miami, FL

LUMBER SYSTEMS, INC.
600 S.E. Maritime Way, Ste. #100
Vancouver, WA 98661
Mailing Address:
P.O. Box 61686
Vancouver, WA 98666-1686
Tel.: 206-693-8800
Fax: 206-693-3488
Approx.Sls.: $20,000,000
Emp.: 100
Export
Manufacture Sawmill Equipment
S.I.C.: 3553
Robert C. Jackson *(Pres.)*
Donald E. Turner *(Exec. V.P.-Sls.)*
Laurie McAlpine *(Comptroller)*
Al Gasunas *(Gen. Mgr.-Fabrication)*
Carl Cramer *(Pur. Agent)*
Ed Ritola *(Chief Engineer)*

Computer Systems/Hardware:
Wang 2200

Outside Service Firm(s):

KPMG Peat Marwick*(Auditors)*
1211 S.W. Fifth Ave.
Portland, OR 97204

Lindsay, Hart, Neil & Weigler*(Legal Firm)*
Portland, OR

Oregon Bank*(Major Banking Relationship)*
Portland, OR

LUMBERMENS MERCHANDISING CORPORATION
137 W. Wayne Ave.
Wayne, PA 19087
Tel.: 215-293-7000
Fax: 215-293-7098
Year Founded: 1935
Sales Range: $1 Billion +
Emp.: 185
Fiscal Year-end: 9/30/92
Cooperative; Wholesale Building Materials & Lumber
S.I.C.: 5031; 5039
Anthony J. DeCarlo *(Pres. & Chief Exec. Officer)*
J.V. Reznor *(V.P.-Dealer Relations)*
John Rohanna *(Sec. & Treas.)*

Outside Service Firm(s):

KPMG Peat Marwick*(Auditors)*
1600 Market St.
Philadelphia, PA 19103
Tel.: 215-299-3100

Saul, Ewing, Remick & Saul*(Legal Firm)*
Philadelphia, PA

Mellon Bank, N.A.*(Major Banking Relationship)*
P.O. Box 444,
Pittsburgh, PA 15230
Tel.: 412-236-8000
Tel.: 1-800-451-7392
Fax: 412-236-8157

LUMCO INDUSTRIES, INC.
3812 Old York Rd.
Philadelphia, PA 19140
Tel.: 215-225-4050
Fax: 215-229-2351
Year Founded: 1920
Approx.Sls.: $16,000,000
Emp.: 90
Wholesale Lumber & Building Materials
S.I.C.: 5031
Jules R. Aronson *(Pres.)*
David Aronson *(Exec. V.P.-Sls. & Pur.)*
Robert DiSpaldo *(V.P.)*
Warren J. Mazzochetta *(Asst. V.P.-Opers.)*
Jerome W. Ralph *(Asst. V.P.-Personnel)*
Marvin G. Ralph *(Sec. & Treas.)*

Outside Service Firm(s):

Stein, Goldberg & Co.*(Auditors)*
Philadelphia, PA

Burton Stein*(Legal Firm)*
Philadelphia, PA

Philadelphia National Bank*(Major Banking Relationship)*
2240 Butler Pike, Ste. 300
Plymouth Meeting, PA

LUNDIA DIV. OF MII, INC.
600 Capitol Way
Jacksonville, IL 62650
Tel.: 217-243-8585
Fax: 800-869-9663
Approx.Sls.: $20,000,000
Emp.: 150
Mfr. Filing & Storage Shelving Systems
S.I.C.: 2541; 2542
William Hunt *(Chief Exec. Officer)*
Gary Frye *(V.P. & Gen. Mgr.)*
Jeff DeGeal *(Mgr.-Adv.)*

LUNDY CONSTRUCTION CO., INC.
Arch St. & Reach Rd.
Williamsport, PA 17701
Mailing Address:
P.O. Box 3276
Williamsport, PA 17701
Tel.: 717-323-8451
Fax: 717-323-8535
Year Founded: 1933
Approx.Sls.: $12,000,000
Emp.: 75
Prefabricated Metal Industrial Buildings
S.I.C.: 3448
Richard Lundy, Jr. *(Pres.)*
Frank Lundy, II *(V.P. & Chief Engr.)*
George Wilson *(Gen. Mgr.)*
Douglas Keiper *(Mgr.-Sls.)*

Outside Service Firm(s):

Commonwealth Bank & Trust Co.*(Major Banking Relationship)*
Williamsport, PA

LUNDY PACKING CO. INC.
P.O. Box 49
Clinton, NC 28328
Tel.: 919-592-2104
Fax: 919-592-7411
Year Founded: 1950
Approx.Sls.: $250,000,000
Emp.: 750
Process & Package Pork Prods.
S.I.C.: 2011
Annabelle L. Fetterman *(Chm. Bd. & Chief Exec. Officer)*
Lewis M. Fetterman, Jr. *(Pres. & Chief Exec. Officer)*
Molly Held *(Sr. V.P.-Admin.)*

Computer Systems/Hardware:
Hewlett-Packard

Outside Service Firm(s):

KPMG Peat Marwick*(Auditors)*
3100 Smoketree Court
Raleigh, NC 27629
Tel.: 919-872-3600
Fax: 919-790-9731

Spuill & Pointer*(Legal Firm)*
Raleigh, NC

Subsidiary:

Tomahawk Farms, Inc. **(1)**
603 S. Wilson Ave.
Dunn, NC 28334
Tel.: 919-392-3155
Processes Country Ham
S.I.C.: 2011
Lewis M. Fetterman *(Pres.)*

Lunt Silversmiths
(See Rogers, Lunt & Bowlen Co. Listing)

LUNTZ CORPORATION
237 Tuscarawas St., E.
Canton, OH 44702
Mailing Address:
P.O. Box 21070
Canton, OH 44701
Tel.: 216-455-0211 **OH**
Fax: 216-455-2801
Year Founded: 1918
Approx.Sls.: $100,000,000
Emp.: 250
Fiscal Year-end: 12/31/91
Wholesale Scrap Metal
S.I.C.: 5093
John Luntz *(Chm. Bd.)*
Andrew Luntz *(Pres.)*
Andrew M. Luntz *(Chief Oper. Officer)*
Gregory W. Luntz *(Chief Fin. Officer & Treas.)*
Timothy Pucky *(Controller)*
Rodger Beitler *(Corp. Office Mgr.)*

No. of Mfg. Plants/Facilities: 7
No. of U.S. Offices: 7

Computer Systems/Hardware:
Point 4-Mark 12

Outside Service Firm(s):

Ernst & Young*(Auditors)*
One Cascade Plaza
Akron, OH 44308

Krugliak, Wilkins, Griffith, Dougherty*(Legal Firm)*
Canton, OH

The Central Trust Company, N.A.*(Major Banking Relationship)*
Canton, OH

Community Mutual*(Major Banking Relationship)*
Canton, OH

Society National Bank*(Major Banking Relationship)*
800 Superior Ave.
Cleveland, OH 44114
Tel.: 216-689-5931
Fax: 216-689-3814

The Central Trust Company, N.A.*(Pension Manager)*
Canton, OH

The Central Trust Company, N.A.*(Pension Manager)*
Cincinnati, OH
Tel.: 513-651-8896

JIM LUPIENT ENTERPRISES
7100 Wayzata Blvd.
Golden Valley, MN 55426
Tel.: 612-546-2222 **MN**
Fax: 612-546-9579
Year Founded: 1969
Approx.Sls.: $350,000,000
Emp.: 250
Automobile Dealerships
S.I.C.: 5511
James W. Lupient *(Pres. & Treas.)*
Julie Pearson *(Sec.)*
Robert P. Banse *(Chief Fin. Officer)*

No. of Mfg. Plants/Facilities: 8

THE LUSK COMPANY
17550 Gillette Ave.
Irvine, CA 92714
Mailing Address:
P.O. Box C 19560,
Irvine, CA 92713
Tel.: 714-757-6000
Fax: 714-261-1324
Approx.Sls.: $487,000,000
Emp.: 750
Holding Company; Real Estate Development
S.I.C.: 6719; 6552
John D. Lusk *(Chm. Bd.)*
William D. Lusk *(Vice Chm.)*
Donovan D. Huennekens *(Pres.)*
Donald D. Steffensen *(Exec. V.P.)*
Richard Deihl *(V.P. & Sec.)*
Carlos B. Quinn *(V.P.)*
W. Kent Weathers *(Treas.)*
Marty Reinfried *(Mgr.-Adv.)*

Outside Service Firm(s):

Arthur Andersen & Co.*(Auditors)*
Costa Mesa, CA

Security Pacific National Bank*(Major Banking Relationship)*
Whittier, CA

The Lusk Company—(Continued)

Subsidiary:

Lusk Interiors, Inc. **(1)**
17550 Gillette Ave.
Irvine, CA 92713
Tel.: 714-757-6200
Emp.: 63
Retail Furniture, Floor Covering, Drapery, Curtains, Upholstery & Miscellaneous Home Furnishings
S.I.C.: 5712; 5713; 5714; 5719
Nancy Lusk *(Pres.)*
John D. Lusk *(V.P.)*
William D. Lusk *(V.P.)*
Donovan D. Huenneken *(Sec.)*
W. Kent Weathers *(Treas.)*

LUSKEYS WESTERN STORES, INC.
101 N. Houston
Fort Worth, TX 76102-2080
Tel.: 817-335-5833 **TX**
Fax: 817-332-7206
Year Founded: 1919
Approx.Sls.: $12,000,000
Emp.: 100
Fiscal Year-end: 1/31/92
Retailer of Western Apparel
S.I.C.: 5699
Louis Luskey *(Chm. Bd. & Pres.)*
Alvin (Butch) Luskey *(Pres.)*
Edward Luskey *(V.P.-Opers.)*
Alvin Leon Luskey *(Sec.)*
David Luskey *(Mgr.-Mail Order)*

Outside Service Firm(s):

Coopers & Lybrand*(Auditors)*
301 Commerce, Suite 1900
Fort Worth, TX 76102
Tel.: 817-332-2243

Gilbert & Colvin*(Legal Firm)*
Fort Worth, TX

Texas Commerce Bank*(Major Banking Relationship)*
Fort Worth, TX

LUSTINE OLDSMOBILE & BUICK, INC.
5323 Baltimore Ave.
Hyattsville, MD 20781
Tel.: 301-277-2000
Fax: 301-277-7509
Year Founded: 1923
Approx.Sls.: $50,000,000
Emp.: 145
Automobiles, Auto Parts & Service
S.I.C.: 5511; 5531
Burton Lustine *(Chm.)*
L.M. Kairys *(Pres.)*

Outside Service Firm(s):

Caplan, Wechsler & Selzen*(Legal Firm)*
Bethesda, MD

Citizen Bank*(Major Banking Relationship)*
Bethesda, MD

LUTHERAN BROTHERHOOD
625 4th Ave. S.
Minneapolis, MN 55415
Tel.: 612-340-7000 **MN**
Fax: 612-340-8389
Year Founded: 1917
Sales Range: $500-999 Million
Emp.: 1,000
Fiscal Year-end: 12/31/91
Fraternal Benefit Society; Life, Disability Income Insurance; Universal Life, Mutual Funds, Variable Universal Life & Variable Annuities
S.I.C.: 6411; 6311
Corporate Giving Program: Fraternal (Charitable & Benevolent) Allocations: $47,000,000; Corporate Social Responsibility: $935,000
Employee Matching Gifts Program: Matches Gifts from $25.00-$100.00 to Lutheran Grade Schools, High Schools, Colleges & Seminaries
Clair E. Stommen *(Chm. Bd.)*
Robert P. Gandrud *(Pres. & Chief Exec. Officer)*
Bruce J. Nicholson *(Chief Fin. Officer & Exec. V.P.)*
Rolf F. Bjelland *(Exec. V.P.-Investment Mngmt.)*
Paul R. Ramseth *(Exec. V.P.-Member Services)*
William H. Reichwald *(Exec. V.P.-Mktg.)*
Harlan J. Hogsven *(Sr. V.P.-Human Resources)*
David J. Larson *(Sr. V.P., Sec. & Gen. Counsel)*
Edward A. Lindell *(Sr. V.P.-External Affairs)*
Richard K. Lund *(Sr. V.P.-Corp. Admin.)*
Edwin Pfursich *(Sr. V.P.-Agencies)*
Jerald Sourdiff *(Sr. V.P. & Controller)*
Michael E. Loken *(V.P.-Mngmt. Information Services)*
Dennis Peterson *(V.P.-Fraternal)*
Anita J.T. Young *(V.P. & Treas.)*
Steven Bak *(Asst. V.P.-Compensation & Benefits)*
Kay Owen *(Asst. V.P.-Human Resource Devel.)*
James Fromm *(Mgr.-Pur. & Inventory Control)*
Richard Hagen *(Mgr.-Communications Services)*
Marilyn Thompson *(Librarian)*
Turi Whiting *(Foundation Admin.)*

Computer Systems/Hardware:
IBM

Outside Service Firm(s):

Price Waterhouse*(Auditors)*
3100 Multifoods Tower, 33 S. Sixth St.
Minneapolis, MN 55402

Best & Flanagan*(Legal Firm)*
3500 IDS Ctr.
Minneapolis, MN 55402
Tel.: 612-339-7121

State Street Bank & Trust Co.*(Major Banking Relationship)*
P.O. Box 366,
Boston, MA 02101
Tel.: 617-426-5523

Subsidiaries:

Lutheran Brotherhood Family for Mutual Funds **(1)**
625 4th Ave. S.
Minneapolis, MN 55415
Tel.: 612-340-7000

Lutheran Brotherhood Financial Corporation **(1)**
625 4th Ave. S.
Minneapolis, MN 55415
Tel.: 612-340-7000

Lutheran Brotherhood Foundation **(1)**
625 4th Ave. S.
Minneapolis, MN 55415
Tel.: 612-340-7000

Lutheran Brotherhood Real Estate Products Company **(1)**
625 4th Ave. S.
Minneapolis, MN 55415
Tel.: 612-340-7000

Lutheran Brotherhood Research Corp. **(1)**
625 4th Ave. S.
Minneapolis, MN 55145
Tel.: 612-340-7000

Lutheran Brotherhood Securities Corp. **(1)**
625 4th Ave. S.
Minneapolis, MN 55415
Tel.: 612-340-7000

Lutheran Brotherhood Variable Insurance Products Company **(1)**
625 4th Ave. S.
Minneapolis, MN 55415
Tel.: 612-340-7000

LYKE CORPORATION
(d/b/a Ripon Community Printers)
656 Douglas St.
Ripon, WI 54971
Mailing Address:
P.O. Box 6,
Ripon, WI 54971
Tel.: 414-748-3136 **WI**
Fax: 414-748-3741
Year Founded: 1962
Assets: $9,000,000
Liabilities: $5,000,000
Net Worth: $4,000,000
Approx.Sls.: $24,000,000
Emp.: 300
Fiscal Year-end: 12/31/91
Offset Printing & Newspaper Publishing
S.I.C.: 2752; 2711
Corporate Giving Program: United Way-Matches 50% of Employee's Contributions
A. Douglas Lyke *(Pres.)*
Audrey R. Lyke *(Chief Fin. Officer & Treas.)*
Dave Gray *(Exec. V.P.)*
H. Andersen Lyke *(Controller)*
Sara Meyer *(Dir.-Pur.)*
Diane Shady *(Dir.-Human Resources)*
Tom Welk *(Dir.-Sls. & Mktg.)*

No. of Mfg. Plants/Facilities: 1
No. of U.S. Offices: 1

Computer Systems/Hardware:
IBM Compatible

Outside Service Firm(s):

Marousek Inc.*(Auditors)*
Oshkosh, WI

Quarles & Brady*(Legal Firm)*
411 E. Wisconsin Av.
Milwaukee, WI 53202
Tel.: 414-277-5000

Valley National Bank*(Major Banking Relationship)*
Ripon, WI

LYKES BROTHERS INC. OF FLORIDA
211 Madison St.
Tampa, FL 33602
Mailing Address:
P.O. Box 1690,
Tampa, FL 33601
Tel.: 813-223-3981
Fax: 813-273-5493
Approx.Sls.: $850,000,000
Emp.: 3,000
Agricul. Production-Crops; Metal Mining; Wholesale Trade-Agricul. Prods.
S.I.C.: 0721; 1099
Thompson L. Rankin *(Chm., Pres. & Chief Exec. Officer)*
Bill Bailey *(Chief Fin. Officer)*
David R. Schindler *(Treas.)*

Computer Systems/Hardware:
IBM Series 1, PCs

Outside Service Firm(s):

Price Waterhouse*(Auditors)*
400 N. Ashley, Ste. 2800
Tampa, FL 33602
Tel.: 813-223-7577

Continental Insurance*(Commercial Insurance Carrier)*
180 Maiden Lane
New York, NY

Aetna Life & Casualty*(Group Insurer)*
151 Farmington Avenue
Hartford, CT 06156
Tel.: 203-273-2128
Fax: 203-729-4295

Hartford Life Insurance Co.*(Group Insurer)*
Hartford, CT 06104-2999

Paine Webber*(Investment Banker)*
1285 Ave. of the Americas
New York, NY 10019
Tel.: 212-713-2000
Fax: 212-713-3010

MacFarlane, Ferguson, Allison & Kelly*(Legal Firm)*
512 No. Florida Ave.
Tampa, FL 33602
Tel.: 813-223-2411

Chemical Banking Corp.*(Major Banking Relationship)*
277 Park Ave.
New York, NY 10041
Tel.: 212-310-6407
Fax: 212-310-4526

Wachovia Bank & Trust Co.*(Major Banking Relationship)*
P.O. Box 3001,
Winston-Salem, NC 27102
Tel.: 800-633-4236

Chemical Banking Corp.*(Pension Manager)*
277 Park Ave.
New York, NY 10041
Tel.: 212-310-6407
Fax: 212-310-4526

John Hancock Mutual Life Insurance Co.*(Pension Manager)*
John Hancock Place, P.O. Box 111
Boston, MA 02117

Division:

Lykes Dispenser Div. **(1)**
40047 Hwy. 45 E.
Zephyrhills, FL 33540
Tel.: 813-788-5581

Subsidiary:

Multi-Line Can Co. **(1)**
P.O. Box 1194,
Dade City, FL 33526
Tel.: 904-567-5211

LYKES BROS. STEAMSHIP CO., INC.
(Sub. of Interocean Steamship Corp.)
Lykes Center, 300 Poydras St.
New Orleans, LA 70130
Mailing Address:
P.O. Box 50998
New Orleans, LA 70150
Tel.: 504-523-6611
Fax: 504-528-1365
Year Founded: 1900
Sales Range: $100-499 Million
Emp.: 1,000
Ocean Freight Transportation
S.I.C.: 4412
W. James Amoss, Jr. *(Chm. Bd. & Chief Exec. Officer)*
E.F. McCormick *(Pres. & Chief Oper. Officer)*
F. Lee Betz *(Sr. V.P.-Latin American Div.)*
William V. Brierre *(Sr. V.P.-Washington)*
Mac G. Bulloch, Jr. *(Sr. V.P.-Conventional Services)*
Roger L. Clark *(Sr. V.P.-Mediterranean Services)*
Carl J. Horn *(Sr. V.P.-Sls.)*
Ralph W. Kreuger *(Sr. V.P.-Opers.)*
Joseph T. Lykes III *(Sr. V.P.-Strategic Plng. & Analysis)*
Robert T. Martinez *(Sr. V.P.-Intermodal)*
James R. Wachtel *(Sr. V.P.-Atlantic)*
George P. Buchert, Jr. *(V.P.-Voyage Reporting)*

James H.F. Crosby *(V.P.-Intermodal Equip.)*
John R. Hulcher III *(V.P.-Mediterranean)*
Barton W.B. Jahncke *(V.P.-Corp. Accts.)*
Paul C. Lightband *(V.P.-North Europe)*
R.E. Manchester *(V.P.-Plng. & Analysis)*
John F. Ohman *(V.P.-Vessel Engrng., Maint. & Repair)*
John T. Scardasis *(V.P.-West Gulf)*
Gregory L. Stangel *(V.P.-Mid-Atlantic)*
T.F. Summers *(V.P. & Treas.)*
Allen C. Taylor *(V.P.-Labor Rels. & Human Resources)*
Allen G. Tomek *(V.P. & Controller)*
Robert V. Whittaker III *(V.P.-Conventional Services)*
G.B. Wiggins *(Asst. V.P.-Information Systems)*
M.L. Vooss *(Dir.-Adv. & Corp. Rels.)*
Pamela Fritch *(Mgr.-Employee Benefits & Compensation)*

Outside Service Firm(s):

Ernst & Young*(Auditors)*
4200 One Shell Square, 701 Poydras St.
New Orleans, LA 70139
Tel.: 504-581-4200

Subsidiary:

Lykes Lines Agency, Inc. **(1)**
300 Poydras St.
New Orleans, LA 70130
Tel.: 504-523-6611
Telex: 6821271 LIKES NLN
Fax: 504-528-1271
Ocean Transportation
S.I.C.: 4412

LYKES ENERGY, INC.
111 Madison St.
Tampa, FL 33602
Tel.: 813-273-0074
Fax: 813-272-0061
Emp.: 955
Natural Gas Distribution; Gas Household Appliances; Bottled Propane Gas
S.I.C.: 4924; 5722; 5984
Thompson L. Rankin *(Chm. Bd. & Chief Exec. Officer)*
John A. Brabson, Jr. *(Pres.)*
Jack E. Uhl *(V.P.-Fin.)*
M. Lee Young *(V.P.-Opers., S. Florida Divisions)*
Bill Shelton *(Mgr.-Communication)*

Outside Service Firm(s):

Price Waterhouse*(Auditors)*
400 N. Ashley, Ste. 2800
Tampa, FL 33602
Tel.: 813-223-7577

First Florida Bank*(Major Banking Relationship)*
P.O. Box 31265,
Tampa, FL 33631-3265
Tel.: 813-224-1475

Subsidiary:

Peoples Gas System, Inc. **(1)**
111 Madison St.
Tampa, FL 33602
Tel.: 813-273-0074
Fax: 813-223-4627
Approx.Sls.: $200,000,000
Emp.: 950
Natural Gas Utility
S.I.C.: 4924
John Brabson *(Chm. Bd., Pres. & Chief Exec. Officer)*
Jack Uhl *(Exec. V.P.-Fin. & Admin.)*
C.H. Montague *(Sr. V.P.)*
B.T. Bailey *(V.P. & Controller)*
Gerald Cox *(V.P.-Tech. Services)*
Dan Pountney *(V.P.-Mktg.)*
Frank Sivard *(V.P.-Acctng.)*
E. Elliott White *(V.P.-Plng. & Devel.)*
Michael Barney *(Dir.-Pur.)*
Robert Gadsen *(Dir.-MIS)*
Charles R. Gandy *(Dir.-Taxation & Regulatory Research)*

JOHN R. LYMAN COMPANY
60 Depot St.
Chicopee, MA 01013
Mailing Address:
P.O. Box 157,
Chicopee, MA 01014
Tel.: 413-598-8344
Tel.: 800-628-9260 **MA**
Fax: 413-592-4112
Year Founded: 1908
Approx.Sls.: $15,000,000
Emp.: 100
Import Export
Polishing Cloths; Wiping Materials
S.I.C.: 2392
Edward S. Wright *(Pres.)*
William Wright *(V.P.)*
Jean C. Wright *(Treas.)*
William McCormick *(Officer Mgr.)*

No. of Mfg. Plants/Facilities: 1
No. of U.S. Offices: 1

Computer Systems/Hardware:
IBM 36

Outside Service Firm(s):

James Slawsky*(Auditors)*
Springfield, MA

Travelers Insurance Co.*(Commercial Insurance Carrier)*
1 Tower Square
Hartford, CT 06183-2492
Tel.: 203-277-4542
Fax: 203-277-5038

Travelers Insurance Co.*(Group Insurer)*
P.O. Box 1711,
Stamford, CT 06920

BayBank Valley Trust Company*(Major Banking Relationship)*
Springfield, MA

Subsidiary:

Lym-Tech Scientific **(1)**
P.O. Box 157,
Chicopee, MA 01014
Tel.: 413-592-4111
Tel.: 800-628-8606
Edward S. Wright *(Pres.)*

LYMAN LUMBER COMPANY
P.O. Box 40, 300 Morse Ave.
Excelsior, MN 55331
Tel.: 612-474-0844 **MN**
Fax: 612-474-0910
Year Founded: 1897
Approx.Sls.: $84,000,000
Emp.: 475
Fiscal Year-end: 12/31/90
Retail Lumber & Building Materials
S.I.C.: 5211
Thomas P. Lowe *(Pres.)*
James Hurd *(Exec. V.P.)*
John D. Gilpin *(Sr. V.P.)*
Brian Balcer *(Controller)*

Computer Systems/Hardware:
DEC VAX

Outside Service Firm(s):

Deloitte & Touche*(Auditors)*
900 Pillsbury Ctr.
Minneapolis, MN 55402
Tel.: 612-332-2301
Fax: 612-375-5418

Dorsey & Whitney*(Legal Firm)*
2200 First Bank Place East
Minneapolis, MN 55402
Tel.: 612-340-2600
Fax: 612-340-2600

LYNDEN INCORPORATED
18000 Pacific Hwy. So., Ste. 800
Seattle, WA 98188
Mailing Address:
P.O. Box 3757,
Seattle, WA 98124
Tel.: 206-241-8778 **WA**
Fax: 206-243-8415
Year Founded: 1947
Transportation Holding Company
S.I.C.: 6719; 4424; 4213
Henry Jansen *(Chm. Bd.)*
James H. Jansen *(Pres., Chief Exec. & Oper. Officer)*
Richard A. Korpela *(Sr. V.P., Sec. & Treas.)*
Patricia L. Blagg *(Pur. Dir.)*
Nancy Wittenberg *(Data Processing Dir.)*
John K. Woodruff *(Ins. Admin.)*
Christel Holm *(Fin. Analyst)*
Diane Chervinak *(Sec.)*

Outside Service Firm(s):

Deloitte & Touche*(Auditors)*
700 Fifth Ave., Suite 4500
Seattle, WA 98104-5044
Tel.: 206-292-1800

Great-West Life Assurance Co.*(Group Insurer)*
8505 East Orchard Rd.
Englewood, CO 8011
Tel.: 800-537-2033

Standard Life Insurance Co.*(Group Insurer)*
Portland, OR

Bogle & Gates*(Legal Firm)*
Two Union Square, 601 Union St.
Seattle, WA 98101-2322
Tel.: 206-682-5151

Rainier National Bank*(Major Banking Relationship)*
Seattle, WA

Bankers Life & Casualty*(Pension Manager)*
Des Moines, IA

Subsidiaries:

Alaska Marine Lines, Inc. **(1)**
5615 W. Marginal Way, S.W.
Seattle, WA 98106
Tel.: 206-763-4244 (100%)
Fax: 206-764-5782
Emp.: 52
Marine Transportation
S.I.C.: 4424
William E. Troy *(Chief Oper. Officer)*

Alaska-West Express, Inc. **(1)**
660 Ocean Dock Rd.
Anchorage, AK 99501
Tel.: 907-279-9515 (100%)
Fax: 907-272-8152
Emp.: 12
Intercity Hauling, General Freight
S.I.C.: 4213
Mark Anderson *(Chief Oper. Officer)*

Arctic Packaging & Logistics Inc. **(1)**
P.O. Box 3757
Seattle, WA 98124
Tel.: 206-241-8778 (100%)
David W. Haugen *(Chief Opr. Officer)*

Bering Marine Corporation **(1)**
P.O. Box 3757
Seattle, WA 98124
Tel.: 206-241-8778 (100%%)
Fax: 206-243-8415
Towing & Tugboat Service
S.I.C.: 4492
Guy Jansen *(Chief Oper. Officer)*

Bowhead Equipment Company **(1)**
P.O. Box 3757
Seattle, WA 98124
Tel.: 206-767-3226 (100%)
Fax: 206-764-5782
Motor Vehicle Dealer; Equipment Rental & Leasing Service
S.I.C.: 7359
Robert C. Miller *(Chief Oper. Officer)*

Douglas Management Company **(1)**
P.O. Box 3757,
Seattle, WA 98124
Tel.: 206-241-8778 (100%)
Fax: 206-243-8415
Commercial Property Mngmnt.
S.I.C.: 6519
Christel Holm *(Chief Oper. Officer)*

Knik Construction Co., Inc. **(1)**
P. O. Box 3757
Seattle, WA 98124
Tel.: 206-241-5465 (100%)
Fax: 206-243-8415
Emp.: 10
Gen. Construction Contracting
S.I.C.: 1629
Steve Jansen *(Chief Oper. Officer)*

LTI, Inc. **(1)**
P.O. Box 433
Lynden, WA 98264
Tel.: 206-354-2101 (100%)
Fax: 206-354-3571
Emp.: 30
Trucking, Except Local
S.I.C.: 4213
Henry Jansen *(Chief Oper. Officer)*

Division:

Milky Way, Inc. **(2)**
1602-A Rudkin Road
Yakima, WA 98901
Tel.: 509-575-0039 (100%)
Emp.: 40
Bulk Milk Hauling
S.I.C.: 4213
Don Guthrie *(Chief Opr. Officer)*

Lynden Air Freight, Inc. **(1)**
411 First Ave. S., #655
Seattle, WA 98104
Tel.: 206-447-4300 (100%)
Fax: 206-447-4360
Emp.: 58
Air Freight Forwarding
S.I.C.: 4731
D. W. Patrick *(Chief Oper. Officer)*

Lynden Financial Services, Inc. **(1)**
P.O, Box 3757
Seattle, WA 98124
Tel.: 206-241-8778 (100%)
Fax: 206-243-8415
Short Term Business Credit
S.I.C.: 6153
Kitty Samuel *(Chief Oper. Officer)*

Lynden Forwarding, Inc. **(1)**
411 First Ave. S., #655
Seattle, WA 98104
Tel.: 206-447-4300 (100%)
Fax: 206-447-4360
Emp.: 2
Freight Forwarding
S.I.C.: 4731
D. W. Patrick *(Chief Oper. Officer)*

Lynden Transport, Inc. **(1)**
6250 S. 228th
Kent, WA 98032
Tel.: 206-575-9575 (100%)
Fax: 206-395-3241
Emp.: 300
Interstate Hauling; General Freight
S.I.C.: 4213
David B. Neely *(Chief Oper. Officer)*

Dairy Express, Inc. **(1)**
6337-A N.E. 112th Ave.
Portland, OR 97220
Tel.: 503-256-4811 (100%)
Fax: 503-257-3112
Bulk Milk Hauling
S.I.C.: 4213
Bob Griggs *(Chief Oper. Officer)*

Lynden Logistics, Inc. **(1)**
P.O. Box 3757
Seattle, WA 98124
Tel.: 206-241-8778
Fax: 206-243-8415
Project Management
S.I.C.: 8741
Jon Burdick *(Chief Oper. Officer)*

Lynden Incorporated—(Continued)

Non-U.S. Holdings:

Canadian Lynden Transport Ltd. **(1)**
10004 29A Avenue
Edmonton, AB Canada T6N 1A8
Tel.: 403-463-6914 (100%)
Emp.: 5
Intercity Hauling, General Freight
S.I.C.: 4213
David B. Neely *(Pres.)*

Yukon Alaska Transport Ltd. **(1)**
P.O. Box 5240,
Whitehorse, YK X1A 4Z1, Canada
Intercity Transport
S.I.C.: 4213

LYON CONKLIN & COMPANY
Race & McComas Sts.
Baltimore, MD 21230
Tel.: 410-752-6800
Fax: 410-752-3201
Approx.Sls.: $45,000,000
Emp.: 125
Wholesale Sheet Metal, Roofing, Heating & Air Conditioning Supplies, Conductor, Pipe & Eave Trough
S.I.C.: 5051; 3498; 5033; 5075
Richard J. Powers *(Chm. Bd.)*
Ronald E. Walker *(Pres. & Sec.)*
Dave Boggs *(Sr. V.P.)*
R.D. Bossle *(Treas.)*

Outside Service Firm(s):

C. W. Amos & Co.*(Auditors)*
2 N. Charles St.
Baltimore, MD 21201
Tel.: 410-727-5341

Weinberg & Green*(Legal Firm)*
100 S. Charles St.
Baltimore, MD 21202
Tel.: 410-332-8795

First National Bank of Maryland*(Major Banking Relationship)*
25 S. Charles St.
Baltimore, MD 21201
Tel.: 410-244-4025

LYON COUNTY CO-OP OIL CO.
1100 East Main
Marshall, MN 56258
Tel.: 507-532-9686
Assets: $1,250,000
Earnings: $56,000
Net Worth: $1,250,000
Approx.Sls.: $13,000,000
Emp.: 29
Fiscal Year-end: 11/30/90
Retailer of Petroleum & Refined Fuels
S.I.C.: 5171; 5983
Floyd Wild *(Pres.)*
Willard Engel *(Gen. Mgr.)*
Kathy Pollock *(Office Mgr.)*
Richard Richards *(Dir.-Employee Benefits)*

LYON METAL PRODUCTS, INC.
420 N. Main
Montgomery, IL 60538
Mailing Address:
P.O. Box 671,
Aurora, IL 60507
Tel.: 708-892-8941
Tel.: 800-323-0082
Tel.: 800-323-0096 **DE**
Fax: 800-367-6681
Year Founded: 1901
Assets: $34,631,804
Liabilities: $19,770,000
Net Worth: $14,861,804
Approx.Sls.: $80,000,000
Emp.: 700
Fiscal Year-end: 12/31/90
Import Export
Steel Shelving, Lockers, Cabinets, Benches
S.I.C.: 2542; 2541; 2599
Corporate Giving Program: United Way
R. Peter Washington *(Chm. Bd. & Chief Exec. Officer)*
W. Gerard Gosselin *(Pres.)*
Keith Shadek *(Exec. V.P.)*
Donald E. Anderson *(V.P.-Human Resources)*
Douglas M. Harrison *(V.P.-Fin., Chief Fin. Officer & Treas.)*
Frank J. Butler *(Controller & Chief Info. Officer)*
D.A. Thanepohn *(Sec.)*
William J. Fick *(Creative Dir.)*
Robert Bell *(Mgr.-Mktg.)*
D.L. Ammons *(Mgr.-Pur.)*
Jerry Wiebusch *(Mgr.-Natl. Sls.)*

No. of Mfg. Plants/Facilities: 4

Computer Systems/Hardware:
IBM System 38

Outside Service Firm(s):

Coopers & Lybrand*(Auditors)*
203 N. LaSalle St.
Chicago, IL 60601
Tel.: 312-701-5500

The Merchants National Bank of Aurora*(Major Banking Relationship)*
Aurora, IL

Kemper Insurance*(Commercial Insurance Carrier)*
Long Grove, IL 60049-0001

NationsBank*(Investment Banker)*
35 Broad St.
Atlanta, GA 30303
Tel.: 404-581-2121
Tel.: 800-848-8198

Metropolitan Life Insurance Co.*(Group Insurer)*
One Madison Ave.
New York, NY 10010-3690
Tel.: 215-578-9292

Griffin & Fadden Ltd.*(Legal Firm)*
Chicago, IL

First Chicago Investment Advisors*(Pension Manager)*
Chicago, IL

First National Bank of Chicago*(Pension Manager)*
One First National Plaza
Chicago, IL 60670
Tel.: 312-732-9781
Tel.: 312-732-4050
Fax: 312-732-4840
Fax: 312-732-3055

Division:

Paltier Div. **(1)**
1701 Kentucky St.
Michigan City, IN 46360
Tel.: 219-872-7238
Emp.: 59
Mfr. of Warehouse Shelving
S.I.C.: 2542
Glenn H. Clark *(Plant Mgr.)*

Subsidiary:

Sycamore Systems, Inc. **(1)**
449 N. California St.
Sycamore, IL 60178
Tel.: 815-895-8322
Mfr. of Steel Shelving Warehouse Shelving
S.I.C.: 2542
R. Richard Bedard *(Pres.)*
Jim Navota *(Dir.-Mktg.)*

WILLIAM LYON COMPANY
4490 Von Karman
Newport Beach, CA 92660
Mailing Address:
P.O. Box 7520,
Newport Beach, CA 92658-7520
Tel.: 714-833-3600
Fax: 714-476-8604
Approx.Sls.: $692,000,000
Emp.: 850
Home Builder
S.I.C.: 1531
William Lyon *(Chm. Bd.)*
Dick J. Randall *(Pres.)*
Paul Pfeiffer *(V.P.)*
Richard Frankel *(Sec.)*
Richard Robinson *(Treas.)*
Principal(s):
William Lyon

Outside Service Firm(s):

Kenneth Leventhal & Co.*(Auditors)*
Los Angeles, CA

LYON'S RESTAURANTS, INC.
1165 Triton Dr.
Foster City, CA 94404
Tel.: 415-349-5966
Tel.: 800-827-5966
Fax: 415-573-7743
Year Founded: 1988
Approx.Sls.: $120,000,000
Emp.: 4000
Fiscal Year-end: 6/31/91
Family Coffee Shop Restaurants in CA, OR & NV
S.I.C.: 5812
Thomas S. Glikbarg *(Chm., Pres. & Chief Exec. Officer)*
William R. Pope *(Sr. V.P.-Fin./Plng.)*
Bruce Shirck *(Sr. V.P.-Opers.)*
Jon Greenawalt *(V.P.-Sls. & Mktg.)*
Arden Howell *(V.P.-Human Resources)*
Jon Olson *(V.P.-Pur. & Food Devel.)*
Mike Simonson *(V.P.-Real Estate)*
Tim Bohan *(Dir.-Property)*
Jerry Borgman *(Treas. & Controller)*
Mike Corioso *(Dir.-Opers.)*
Jim Donovan *(Dir.-Opers.)*
Valerie Hunt *(Dir.-Mktg.)*

Computer Systems/Hardware:
IBM 36 Mainframe

Outside Service Firm(s):

First Interstate Bank*(Major Banking Relationship)*
Foster City, CA

LYTRON INCORPORATED
Dragon Court
Woburn, MA 01801
Tel.: 617-933-7300
Fax: 617-935-4529
Year Founded: 1958
Approx.Sls.: $11,000,000
Emp.: 70
Fiscal Year-end: 10/31/92
Export
Mfr. Heat Exchangers
S.I.C.: 3443
Charles Carswell *(Pres.)*
Woodrow Curtis *(V.P. & Gen. Mgr.)*
Daniel De Freitas *(Mgr.-Adv. & Mktg.)*
Dick Svenson *(Mgr.-Pur.)*

Subsidiary:

Alpha United **(1)**
1301 E. El Segundo Blvd.
El Segundo, CA 90245
Tel.: 310-322-9570

M & C SPECIALTIES COMPANY
90 James Way
Southampton, PA 18966
Tel.: 215-322-1620 **PA**
Fax: 215-322-1620
Year Founded: 1946
Approx.Sls.: $18,000,000
Emp.: 140
Import Export
Converter/Distributor of Pressure Sensitive Tapes
S.I.C.: 5113; 3069; 3999
Francis Rauch *(Chm. Bd. & Pres.)*
Donald Rauch *(Exec. V.P.)*
Daniel Cistone *(V.P.-Fin. & Admin., Sec. & Dir.-Real Estate)*
James Rauch *(V.P.-Western Opers.)*
Kathleen Taylor *(Gen. Mgr.-MtC Remco Tape Products)*
Dave Cornelison *(Mgr.-Mktg. & Natl. Sls.)*
Mike Boyle *(Dir.-Mfg.)*

No. of Mfg. Plants/Facilities: 2

Outside Service Firm(s):

Gross & Co.*(Auditors)*
Huntington Valley, PA

Schubert, Bellwoar, Mallon & Walheim*(Legal Firm)*
Philadelphia, PA

Continental Bank, N.A.*(Major Banking Relationship)*
1500 Market St.
Philadelphia, PA 19102
Tel.: 215-564-7475

Subsidiary:

MtC Remco Tape Products Co. **(1)**
5547 Vineland Ave.
North Hollywood, CA 91601
Tel.: 213-877-0436
Tel.: 800-544-1864
Emp.: 19
Converter/Distributor of Pressure Sensitive Tapes
S.I.C.: 5113; 3069
Kathy Taylor *(Gen. Mgr.)*
Daniel Cistone *(Treas.)*
James Rauch *(Dir.-Western Sls.)*

M&H ADVERTISING
1128 Harmon Place, Ste. 200
Minneapolis, MN 55403
Tel.: 612-339-2991
Fax: 612-349-6220
Year Founded: 1982
Approx.Billings: $16,000,000
Emp.: 14
Consumer Adv./Packaged Goods/Food
Ron Harvieux *(Pres. & Chief Exec. Officer)*

Computer Systems/Hardware:
IBM, PS2, Novell Network

M & T INCORPORATED
15115 Southwest Sequoia Pkwy., #200
Portland, OR 97224
Tel.: 503-624-6300 **CA**
Fax: 503-624-7755
Year Founded: 1933
Sales Range: $20-39 Million
Emp.: 115
Real Estate
S.I.C.: 6552
Peter F. Bechen *(Chm. Bd., Pres. & Chief Oper. Officer)*
Timothy F. Freeman *(V.P.)*
David W. Ramus *(V.P., Controller, Treas. & Chief Fin. Officer)*
Christopher Clegg *(Sec.)*

Outside Service Firm(s):

Deloitte & Touche*(Auditors)*
50 Fremont St.
San Francisco, CA 94105-2230
Tel.: 415-393-4300
Fax: 415-227-0452

Pillsbury, Madison & Sutro*(Legal Firm)*
235 Montgomery St.
San Francisco, CA 94104
Tel.: 415-983-1000

Bank of America, N.T. & S.A.*(Major Banking Relationship)*
P.O. Box 37002,
San Francisco, CA 94137

First Trust Company, Inc.*(Pension Manager)*
Denver, CO

M&W GEAR COMPANY
1020 S. Sangamon Ave.
Gibson City, IL 60936
Tel.: 217-784-4261
Fax: 217-784-4326
Year Founded: 1949
Approx.Sls.: $20,000,000
Emp.: 200
Fiscal Year-end: 12/31/91
M & W Products; PTO Dynamometers, Diesel Turbo-Chargers, 300 & 525 Bush Grain Boxes, Running Gears, Dual Wheels, Rotary Hoes, Round Balers, Conservation Tillage Systems
S.I.C.: 3523; 3829; 3714
William B. Ertel *(Pres.)*
Rick Ertel *(V.P.-Mfg.)*
Harry B. Rakers *(V.P.-Fin.)*
John Smith *(V.P.-Sls. & Mktg.)*
Mike Grubich *(Controller)*
Loran Boppart *(Chief Engineer-Res. & Devel.)*
Jerry Boyum *(Dir.-Pur.)*
James Forney *(Dir.-Quality Control)*
Mike Cornwell *(Adv. Mgr.)*
Don Bielfeldt *(Mgr.-Personnel)*
Errol Rotman *(Mgr.-Data Processing)*

MADD
Mothers Against Drunk Driving

Tel.: 214-744-6233
Tel.: 800-GET-MADD
Fax: 214-869-2206
Fax: 214-869-2207
Year Founded: 1980
Emp.: 360
Fiscal Year-end: 6/30/91
Non-Profit Organization
S.I.C.: 8699
James R. Morris *(Chm. Bd. & Chief Exec. Officer)*
Milo Kirk *(Pres.)*
Robert J. King *(Exec. Dir. & Chief Oper. Officer)*
Katherine Prescott *(V.P.-Chapter Issues)*
Sandy Freeman *(V.P.-Victim Issues)*
Dorothy Taylor *(Sec.)*
M. Joseph McHugh *(Treas.)*
Jean Folwell *(Chief Fin. Officer & Asst. Treas.)*
Linda Braswell *(Asst. Sec.)*
Katherine Durante *(Asst. Sec.)*
Dean Wilkerson *(Asst. Sec.)*
Andy Briscoe *(Dir.-Natl. Pub. Affairs)*

M-B COMPANY INC. OF WISCONSIN
1200 So. Park St.
Chilton, WI 53014
Tel.: 414-849-2313
Tel.: 800-558-5800
Fax: 414-849-2109
Year Founded: 1907
Approx.Sls.: $15,000,000
Emp.: 90
Fiscal Year-end: 12/31/90
Export
Mfr. of Municipal Sweeping & Striping Equip. & Indus. Equip.
T.J. Cosgrove *(Pres.)*
Steve Muellenbach *(V.P. & Gen. Mgr.-Pavement Marking)*
Tom Umlauf *(Gen. Mgr.-Special Products)*

MBI INC.
47 Richards Ave.
Norwalk, CT 06856
Tel.: 203-853-2000
Fax: 203-853-0647
Emp.: 700
Import
Marketing for Fine Collectibles
S.I.C.: 6719; 5961
Theodore R. Stanley *(Pres.)*
Warren J. Strausser *(V.P.)*
Roy S. Pfeil *(Dir.-Jewelry Div.)*
Steve Gordon *(Dir.-Postal Commemoratives)*
Robert Gabler *(Dir.-New Products)*
David S. Ward *(Dir.-Books)*
Peter Maglathlin *(Dir.-Danbury Mint)*
Karl Nelson *(Program Mgr.)*

Divisions:

Danbury Mint **(1)**
47 Richards Ave.
Norwalk, CT 06857
Tel.: 203-853-2000
Fax: 203-853-0647
Retail-by-Mail Marketing of Fine Collectibles
S.I.C.: 5961
Peter Maglathlin *(Dir.)*
Richard Hebert *(Opers. Mgr.)*
Tom Reese *(Accts. Mgr.)*
Rolf Linder *(Program Mgr.)*

Easton Press Books **(1)**
677 Connecticut Ave.
Norwalk, CT 06854
Tel.: 203-866-0101
Retail of Books by Mail
S.I.C.: 5961; 5192
Eric Stones *(Dir.)*

Easton Press Videos **(1)**
677 Connecticut Ave.
Norwalk, CT 06854
Tel.: 203-866-0101
Retail-by-Mail of Video Tapes
S.I.C.: 5961; 5735
James Lee *(Dir.)*

Hamilton Collection **(1)**
677 Connecticut Ave.
Norwalk, CT 06854
Tel.: 203-866-0101
Retail-by-Mail Collectibles; Books, Watches, Videos, Thimbles
S.I.C.: 5961
David Ward *(Chief Oper. Officer)*

Postal Commemorative Society Collection **(1)**
47 Richards Avenue
Norwalk, CT 06856
Tel.: 203-853-2000
Retail-by-Mail Postal Commemorative Stamps
S.I.C.: 5961
Karl Nelson *(Dir.)*

Thimble Collectors Club Collections **(1)**
677 Connecticut Ave.
Norwalk, CT 06854
Tel.: 203-866-0101
Retail-by-Mail of Collectibles
S.I.C.: 5961
Tim Kochuba *(Dir.)*

MBS HOLDING, INC.
3403 E. Abram
Arlington, TX 76010
Mailing Address:
P.O. Box 398
Arlington, TX 76004-0398
Tel.: 817-640-1234 **TX**
Fax: 817-649-2560
Holding Company; Wholesale Distributor of Lumber, Rough, Dressed & Finsihed, Brick, Stone & Related Materials
S.I.C.: 5031; 5032; 6719
Cecil W. Mayfield *(Chm. Bd.)*
Jack S. Lewis *(Pres.)*

Outside Service Firm(s):

CoAmerica Bank*(Major Banking Relationship)*
Fort Worth, TX

Subsidiary:

Mayfield Building Supply Co. **(1)**
3403 E. Abram
Arlington, TX 76010
Tel.: 817-640-1234
Approx.Sls.: $20,000,000
Emp.: 110
Wholesale Distributor of Lumber, Rough Dressed & Finished; Doors & Windows
S.I.C.: 5031
Cecil W. Mayfield *(Chm. Bd.)*
Jack S. Lewis *(Pres.)*
James Wallace *(Exec. V.P.)*
Gail Brown *(Sec. & Treas.)*

MBT ASSOCIATES, INC.
539 Bryant St.
San Francisco, CA 94107
Tel.: 415-896-0800 **CA**
Telex: 38-2685
Fax: 415-495-5237
Year Founded: 1954
Sales Range: $10-19 Million
Emp.: 50
Fiscal Year-end: 10/31/91
Architects
S.I.C.: 8712
Frank Tomsick *(Chm. & Chief Exec. Officer)*
Michael Hearn *(Pres.)*
Andrea Jacoby *(Chief Fin. Officer)*
Peter S. Hockaday *(Sr. V.P.)*
Alan Williams *(Sr. V.P.)*
D. Tom Ayers *(V.P.)*
John J. Damonte, Jr. *(V.P.)*
David Lindemulder *(V.P.-Mktg.)*
Tully Shelley, III *(V.P.)*
Robert Yee *(V.P.)*
Carolyn Holtz *(Office Mgr.)*
Principal(s):
Frank Tomsick
Michael Hearn
Peter S. Hockaday
Alan Williams
D. Tom Ayers
John J. Damonte, Jr.
Tully Shelley, III
Robert Yee

No. of U.S. Offices: 1

Computer Systems/Hardware:
ISI CAD System 25 & CADVANCE; IBM PC Word Processing

Outside Service Firm(s):

Chernin & Company*(Auditors)*
San Francisco, CA

Aetna Life & Casualty*(Group Insurer)*
100 N. Riverside Plaza
Chicago, IL 60606

Buffington & Konigsberg*(Legal Firm)*
San Francisco, CA

Union Bank*(Major Banking Relationship)*
San Francisco, CA

Employee Benefit Plan*(Pension Manager)*
San Francisco, CA

MCC GROUP, INC.
3001 17th St.
Metairie, LA 70002
Tel.: 504-833-8291
Fax: 504-831-4760
Approx.Sls.: $28,000,000
Emp.: 185
Construction Company
S.I.C.: 1542
Fred N. Estopinal, Jr. *(Chm. Bd.)*
Joseph A. Jaeger *(Pres.)*
Paul E. Coe, Jr. *(Sr. V.P.)*
Charles W. Cassreino *(Treas.)*
Scuddy F. Fontenelle, Jr. *(Sec.)*

Outside Service Firm(s):

Little & Metzger*(Legal Firm)*
Metairie, LA

Whitney National Bank of New Orleans*(Major Banking Relationship)*
P.O. Box 61260
New Orleans, LA 70161
Tel.: 504-586-7422

MCC, INC.
(Marketing Communications Corporation, Inc.)
P.O. Box 651, 45 Main St.
Essex, CT 06426
Tel.: 203-767-7010
Year Founded: 1990
Approx.Billings: $17,500,000
Emp.: 8
Consumer Marketing, Advertising, Sales Promotion & Media Merchandising; Specialties Include Beverages, Financial, Health Care, Gaming & Outdoors
Jeffrey Maher *(Pres. & Chief Exec. Officer)*
Ray Maher *(Exec. V.P., Creative Dir. & Sec.)*
William G. Keim *(Sr. V.P., CLient Services)*
Stephanie Arbige *(Dir., Pub. Rels.)*

Computer Systems/Hardware:
Macintosh

MCM ENTERPRISES, INC.
510 S. Oak St.
Crawfordsville, IN 47933
Tel.: 317-362-2200
Holding Company
S.I.C.: 6719
Edwin Marberg *(Pres., Chief Exec. Officer & Treas.)*

Outside Service Firm(s):

George S. Olive & Co.*(Auditors)*
201 N. Illinois St.
Indianapolis, IN 46204

Reiling, Teder & Withers*(Legal Firm)*
Lafayette, IN

AmiTrust Company, N.A.*(Major Banking Relationship)*
Indianapolis, IN

Divisions:

Chicago Steel & Wire **(1)**
10257 S. Torrence Ave.
Chicago, IL 60617
Tel.: 312-768-2140
Fax: 312-768-6535
S.I.C.: 3315

Mid-State Wire Company **(1)**
510 S. Oak
Crawfordsville, IN 47933
Tel.: 317-362-2200
Fax: 317-362-4143
S.I.C.: 3315
Mary Barker *(Admin. Sec.)*

Wilson Steel & Wire **(1)**
4840 S. Western Ave.
Chicago, IL 60609
Tel.: 312-523-1221
Fax: 312-523-8336
S.I.C.: 3315

MCRB SERVICE BUREAU, INC.
11633 Victory Blvd.
North Hollywood, CA 91609
Tel.: 818-509-1790
Fax: 818-980-6453
Year Founded: 1978
Approx.Sls.: $12,000,000
Emp.: 200
Fiscal Year-end: 12/31/91
IBM Mainframe Data Processing and Programming, Merge/Purge, Data Conversion, Data Input, Computer Letters, Fulfillment, Order Entry, Remittance Processing
S.I.C.: 7379
Jarvis J. Slade *(Chm. Bd.)*
Richard Yung *(Pres.)*
Stephen L. Allen *(Exec. V.P.)*
Chris Henderson *(V.P.-Fulfillment Services)*
Dan Javage *(V.P.-Fin.)*
Gary Morgan *(V.P.-Systems & Programming)*

MCRB Service Bureau, Inc.—(Continued)

Max H. Schulze *(V.P., Sec., Treas. & Gen. Counsel)*
Rick Sirak *(V.P.-Mktg.)*

Divisions:

MCRB Fulfillment Co. **(1)**
7447 Candlewood Rd.
Hanover, MD 21076
Tel.: 410-850-5885
Fax: 410-684-2930
Eastern Fulfillment Service Center
S.I.C.: 7379

MCRB Fulfillment Co. **(1)**
21330 Superior St.
Chatsworth, CA 91311
Tel.: 818-407-4300
Fax: 818-882-0359
Western Fulfillment Services Center
S.I.C.: 7379

M.E.D. COMMUNICATIONS
Aspen Corporate Park Two,
1460 Rte. 9 North
Woodbridge, NJ 07095
Tel.: 908-636-6600
Telex: 325780
Fax: 908-636-5634
Year Founded: 1974
Approx.Billings: $103,000,000
Emp.: 100
Health Care Advertising
Robert Portman, Ph.D. *(Chm.)*
William H. Schermund *(Pres.)*
David Casey *(Chief Fin. Officer & Sr. V.P.)*
Paula Davis, Ph.D. *(Sr. V.P.-Scientific Services)*
Skip Hurley *(Sr. V.P.-Computer Graphic Services)*
Alan Rezza *(Sr. V.P. & Dir.-Client Services)*
Helene Schwartz *(Sr. V.P.-Human Resources)*
Carl McMackin *(V.P.-Mktg. Res.)*

MEPC AMERICAN PROPERTIES INCORPORATED
15303 Dallas Pkwy., Ste. 400
Dallas, TX 75248
Tel.: 214-980-5000
Fax: 214-980-5092
Emp.: 140
Real Estate Investment Firm
S.I.C.: 6552
David Gruber *(Pres.)*
Peter Johnson *(Sr. V.P.)*
Jim Fant *(V.P.)*

MFA OIL COMPANY
Ray Young Dr.
Columbia, MO 65201
Mailing Address:
P.O. Box 519
Columbia, MO 65205
Tel.: 314-442-0321
Fax: 314-876-0321
Year Founded: 1929
Approx.Sls.: $181,000,000
Emp.: 1,000
Fiscal Year-end: 8/31/90
Motor Oils, Grease, Light Oils, Gasoline, Propane Gas
S.I.C.: 2911; 2992; 1321
Fred Grohn *(Chm. Bd.)*
J. Clint Hinds *(Vice Chm.)*
Dale Creach *(Pres. & Chief Oper. Officer)*
Ron Benne *(V.P.-Admin.)*
Ken Caspall *(V.P.-Sls.)*
Jerome Taylor *(V.P.-Supply & Distr.)*
Larry Marshall *(Sec. & Gen. Counsel)*
Larry Ficke *(Dir.-Fin. Services)*
John Kruse *(Dir.-Fin.)*
Dean Lakin *(Dir.-Product & Environmental Services)*
Frank McCarty *(Mgr.-Data Processing)*
Jim Rausch *(Mgr.-Mngmt. Information Systems)*
Diane L. Searcy *(Asst. to the Pres.)*

Computer Systems/Hardware:
IBM

MFA INCORPORATED
615 Locust
Columbia, MO 65201
Tel.: 314-874-5111 **MO**
Fax: 314-876-5423
Year Founded: 1927
Assets: $210,000,000
Earnings: $5,100,000
Liabilities: $143,600,000
Net Worth: $66,400,000
Approx.Sls.: $465,000,000
Emp.: 1,200
Fiscal Year-end: 6/30/91
Farm Cooperative; Manufacture & Marketing Animal Feeds, Plant Food, Hybrid Seeds; Marketing Farm Supply Equipment & Grain
S.I.C.: 2048; 2047; 0723; 2873; 2874; 5153; 5159; 5169; 5191; 5261; 5399
Bud L. Frew *(Pres. & Chief Exec Officer)*
Robert Rothwell *(Sr. V.P.-Fin.)*
Janice Shuerman *(V.P.-Admin. & Personnel)*
Allen Floyd *(Controller)*
Mary F. Gonnerman *(Sec.)*
Wayne Hoecker *(Gen. Counsel)*
Tom Montgomery *(Dir.-Adv.)*
Gene Walker *(Dir.-Information Systems)*

No. of Mfg. Plants/Facilities: 11
No. of U.S. Offices: 120

Computer Systems/Hardware:
IBM System 4341 VM VSE

Outside Service Firm(s):

Deloitte & Touche*(Auditors)*
1010 Grand Ave.
Kansas City, MO 64106-2232
Tel.: 816-474-6180

Equitable Life*(Group Insurer)*
Pittsburgh, PA

Gage & Tucker*(Legal Firm)*
2345 Grand Ave., 28th Fl.
Kansas City, MO 64108
Tel.: 816-292-2000

Co-Bank St. Louis Region*(Major Banking Relationship)*
1415 Olive St.
St. Louis, MO 63166

Mercantile Trust Co., N.A.*(Pension Manager)*
St. Louis, MO

Reimer & Koger Assocs.*(Pension Manager)*
Mission, KS

MGR EQUIPMENT CORP.
22 Gates Ave.
Inwood, NY 11696
Tel.: 516-239-3030
Fax: 516-239-3602
Emp.: 38
Mfr. Ice, Refrigeration & Air Conditioning Equip.
S.I.C.: 3585
Gerald Ross *(Pres., Chief Exec. & Chief Fin. Officer & Treas.)*
George Mauder *(V.P.)*

Outside Service Firm(s):

European American Bank*(Major Banking Relationship)*
New York, NY

MHB INC.
1207 Almond St.
Williamsport, PA 17701
Tel.: 717-323-3761 **PA**
Fax: 717-323-6823
Year Founded: 1974
Sales Range: $20-39 Million
Emp.: 40
Smoked Meats from Purchased Meats
S.I.C.: 2013
Morton D. Harrison *(Pres.)*
David S. Harrison *(V.P.)*
Arthur Harrison *(Treas.)*
Mitchell Harrsion *(Sec.)*

Outside Service Firm(s):

Northern Central Bank*(Major Banking Relationship)*
102 W. 4th St.
Williamsport, PA 17701
Tel.: 717-326-2611

MI FUND INCORPORATED
1384 Broadway
New York, NY 10018
Tel.: 212-398-0728 **NY**
Fax: 212-827-0176
Year Founded: 1947
Assets: $30,049,092
Earnings: $2,665,455
Net Worth: $30,049,092
Fiscal Year-end: 12/31/91
Regulates Investments (Closed-End Mutual Funds)
S.I.C.: 6726
Steven Meltzer *(Chm. Bd. & Pres.)*
Juliette Meltzer *(V.P.)*
Harvey Silverman *(Sec., Treas., Controller & Dir.-Mngmt. Information Systems)*
Richard Derzaw *(Gen. Counsel)*

M K DIAMOND PRODUCTS, INC.
1315 Storm Parkway
Torrance, CA 90501-2803
Mailing Address:
P.O. Box 2803
Torrance, CA 90509
Tel.: 310-784-2800
Fax: 310-539-5158
Year Founded: 1860
Approx.Sls.: $23,000,000
Emp.: 71
Manufacture Diamond Cutting Wheels & Saws
S.I.C.: 3545
Robert J. Delahaut *(Pres.)*
Richard J. Rice *(V.P.)*

Outside Service Firm(s):

Ernst & Young*(Auditors)*
515 S. Flower St.
Los Angeles, CA 90071
Tel.: 213-621-1666

Bank of America NT&SA*(Major Banking Relationship)*
City of Industry, CA

M M SYSTEMS CORPORATION
4520 Elmdale Dr.
Tucker, GA 30085
Mailing Address:
P.O. Box 0326
Tucker, GA 30085
Tel.: 404-938-7570 **GA**
Fax: 404-939-3006
Sales Range: $10-19 Million
Emp.: 105
Fiscal Year-end: 12/31/91
Export
Metal Facia Roofing Systems & Related Accessories, Distribute Architectural Pre-Painted Aluminum & Steel Sheet & Plaster/Dry-Wall Moldings, Expansion Joint Assemblies
S.I.C.: 3444; 5033; 5051
Julian J. Attaway *(Pres.)*
R.W. Driggers *(Exec. V.P.)*
William C. Minton *(V.P.-Opers.)*
Michael C. Timma *(V.P.-Fin., Sec. & Treas.)*
Michael H. Attaway *(Asst. Treas.)*
R.M. Gentle *(Mgr.-Matls.)*
Principal(s):
Julian J. Attaway
Michael H. Attaway
J. Mark Attaway
J. Paul Attaway
P. Faith Attaway

No. of Mfg. Plants/Facilities: 2

Outside Service Firm(s):

Windham, Brannon & Co.*(Auditors)*
Atlanta, GA

Parker, Johnson, Cook & Dunlevie*(Legal Firm)*
Atlanta, GA

Citizens & Southern National Bank*(Major Banking Relationship)*
Tucker, GA

NationsBank*(Major Banking Relationship)*
Tucker, GA

Branch:

M M Systems Corporation **(1)**
2985 West Whitton Ave.
Phoenix, AZ 85009
Tel.: 602-254-9747
Metal Facia Roofing Systems & Related Accessories, Distribute Architectural Pre-Painted Aluminum & Steel Sheet & Plaster/Dry-Wall Moldings, Expansion Joint Assemblies
S.I.C.: 3444; 5033; 5051
J. Paul Attaway *(Gen. Mgr.)*

M M I COMPANIES, INC.
540 Lake Cook Rd.
Deerfield, IL 60015
Tel.: 708-940-7550 **DE**
Fax: 708-940-2372
Emp.: 145
Full Service Insurance Company
S.I.C.: 6331; 6311
Anthony J. Perry *(Chm. Bd.)*
B. Frederick Becker *(Pres. & Chief Exec. Officer)*
John Groskopt *(Sr. V.P.)*
Arthur D. Holley *(Sr. V.P.)*
James E. DeWald *(V.P.)*
Peter Gunder *(Treas.)*
Richard Seeligman *(Sec.)*

Outside Service Firm(s):

Ernst & Young*(Auditors)*
233 S. Wacker Dr.
Chicago, IL 60606
Tel.: 312-368-1800
Fax: 312-645-3095

Katten, Muchin & Zavis*(Legal Firm)*
525 W. Monroe St., Ste. 1600
Chicago, IL 60661-3693
Tel.: 312-902-5200

M M M SALES, INC.
(d/b/a Mulligan Sales)
14214 Lomitas Ave
City of Industry, CA 91746
Mailing Address:
P.O. Box 90008
City of Industry, CA 91715
Tel.: 818-968-9621
Fax: 818-369-8452
Year Founded: 1966
Assets: $12,000,000
Liabilities: $10,000,000
Net Worth: $2,000,000
Approx.Sls.: $241,000,000
Emp.: 23
Fiscal Year-end: 3/31/91
Import Export
Wholesale Distributor of a General Line of Dairy Products
S.I.C.: 5141
James Mulligan *(Pres.)*
Jeffrey Mulligan *(V.P.)*
Gene Tanzey *(Treas.)*
Principal(s):
James Mulligan
Lois F. Mulligan

No. of U.S. Offices: 1

Computer Systems/Hardware:
IBM

Outside Service Firm(s):

First Interstate Bank*(Major Banking Relationship)*
Covina, CA

MNP CORP.
44225 Utica Rd.
Utica, MI 48317
Mailing Address:
P.O. Box 189002,
Utica, MI 48318-9002
Tel.: 313-254-1320 **MI**
Fax: 313-781-4888
Year Founded: 1970
Assets: $43,833,415
Liabilities: $36,815,394
Net Worth: $7,018,021
Approx.Sls.: $80,000,000
Emp.: 400
Fiscal Year-end: 11/30/90

Import Export
Manufacture Fasteners, Screws & Washers; Steel Service Center
S.I.C.: 3452; 5051
Larry S. Berman *(Chm. Bd.)*
Robert Baur *(Pres.)*
David N. Cronovich *(V.P.-Auto. & OEM Sls.)*
Floyd E. Cushman *(V.P.-Steel & Wire Processing)*
William A. Drypen *(V.P.-Steel & Wire Sls.)*
Tom Klein *(V.P.-Mfg.)*
Craig L. Stormer *(V.P.-Fin.)*
Christopher Wackrow *(V.P.-Quality Assurance & Prod. Reliability)*
Andrew S. Ciecko *(Dir.-Pur.)*
Erich Hatlen *(Dir.-Human Resources)*
Ronald West *(Dir.-Info. Systems)*
Jerry S. Chapman *(Gen. Mgr.-Distribution Sls.)*

No. of Mfg. Plants/Facilities: 4
No. of U.S. Offices: 4

Computer Systems/Hardware:
DEC

Outside Service Firm(s):

Kleiman, Carney & Greenbaum*(Auditors)*
Farmington Hills, MI

Jacob & Weingarten*(Legal Firm)*
Troy, MI

Harris Trust & Savings Bank*(Major Banking Relationship)*
111 W. Monroe St.
Chicago, IL 60690
Tel.: 312-461-2265
Tel.: 800-858-0840

NBD Bank, N.A.*(Major Banking Relationship)*
P.O. Box 222,
Detroit, MI 48232
Tel.: 313-225-1122

MPD, INC.
316 E. 9th St.
Owensboro, KY 42303
Tel.: 502-685-6200
Fax: 502-685-6399
Manufacture Microwave Components
S.I.C.: 3679
Gary Braswell *(Pres. & Chief Exec. Officer)*
Gordon Sides *(Treas.)*
Bob White *(Dir.-Prisms & Engrng.)*
Mary Perigo *(Controller)*

Outside Service Firm(s):

INB National Bank*(Major Banking Relationship)*
One Indiana Sq.
Indianapolis, IN 46266
Tel.: 317-266-6000

Subsidiary:

MPH & CMI **(1)**
316 E. 9th St.
Owensboro, KY 42301
Tel.: 502-685-6545
Fax: 502-685-6268
Manufactures Alcohol Breath Analyzers & Speed Radar Guns
S.I.C.: 3669; 3823

MPO VIDEOTRONICS, INC.
619 W. 54th St.
New York, NY 10019
Tel.: 212-708-0550 **NY**
Fax: 212-397-0866
Year Founded: 1947
Earnings: $1,969,850
Approx.Sls.: $51,000,000
Emp.: 321
Fiscal Year-end: 12/31/90

Import Export
Television Commercial Distr.; Mfr., Sales & Leasing of Video & Projector Equipment; Sls. & Distr. of Equestrian Equipment & Apparel
S.I.C.: 5064; 7822; 7359; 5091; 5136; 5137; 3861
Larry Kaiser *(Pres.)*
Charles A. Ahto *(Exec. V.P. & Sec.)*
Julius Barron *(V.P.)*
R.M. Martinelli *(Treas. & Controller)*
Michael Albanese *(Dir.-Data Processing)*
Gerald P. Beiser *(Mgr.-Credit & Collections)*

No. of Mfg. Plants/Facilities: 1
No. of U.S. Offices: 6

Computer Systems/Hardware:
Honeywell Level 66

Outside Service Firm(s):

Awchin Black Awchin*(Auditors)*
New York, NY

National Westminster Bank USA*(Investment Banker)*
175 Water St.
New York, NY 10038
Tel.: 212-602-4000
Fax: 212-602-2279

National Westminster Bank USA*(International Bank Affiliate)*
175 Water St.
New York, NY 10038
Tel.: 212-602-4000
Fax: 212-602-2279

Barish, Grook, Friend & Friedman*(Legal Firm)*
New York, NY

National Westminster Bank USA*(Major Banking Relationship)*
175 Water St.
New York, NY 10038
Tel.: 212-602-4000
Fax: 212-602-2279

Benefit Consultants*(Pension Manager)*
Philadelphia, PA

Divisions:

MPO Videotronics **(1)**
2580 Turquoise Circle
Newbury Park, CA 91320
Tel.: 805-499-8513
Fax: 850-499-8206
Mfr. of Motion Picture & Still Projectors
S.I.C.: 3861
Larry Kaiser *(Pres.)*

MPO Videotronics **(1)**
131 Mitchell Ct., Ste. C-10
Addison, IL 60101
Tel.: 708-629-1099
Fax: 708-629-0758
Sls. of Motion Picture & Video Equip.
S.I.C.: 5043; 5064
Larry Kaiser *(Pres.)*

Miller Harness, Inc. **(1)**
235 Murray Hill Pkwy.
East Rutherford, NJ 07070
Tel.: 201-460-1200
Sls. & Distr. of Equestrian Equip. & Apparel
S.I.C.: 5941; 5091
Larry Kaiser *(Pres.)*

POP TV **(1)**
4040 SE International Way, Ste. E104
Portland, OR 97222
Tel.: 503-659-9868
Fax: 503-659-9727
Rental of Video, Motion Picture & Still Picture Projection Equip.
S.I.C.: 7359
Larry Kaiser *(Pres.)*

TFI (Tape Films Inc.) **(1)**
619 West 54th St.
New York, NY 10019
Tel.: 212-708-0550
Television Commercial Distr.
S.I.C.: 7822
Larry Kaiser *(Pres.)*

MSC INDUSTRIAL SUPPLY CO.
151 Sunnyside Blvd.
Plainview, NY 11803
Tel.: 516-349-7100
Tel.: 800-645-7270
Tel.: 800-255-5067
Fax: 516-349-0625
Year Founded: 1941
Sales Range: $100-499 Million
Emp.: 600
International Distributor of Industrial Tools, Machinery & Supplies
S.I.C.: 5085
Sidney Jacobson *(Chm. Bd.)*
Mitchell Jacobson *(Pres. & Chief Exec. Officer)*
James Schroeder *(Exec. V.P.)*
Thomas Eccleston *(V.P.)*
Barbara Schwartz *(V.P.-Human Resources)*
David Gillies *(Dir.-MIS)*
Jean Haas *(Dir.-Mktg.)*
Principal(s):
Sidney Jacobson
Mitchell Jacobson

No. of Mfg. Plants/Facilities: 20
No. of U.S. Offices: 20

Computer Systems/Hardware:
IBM AS/400

MSD, INC.
(Formerly Nytronics Components Group, Inc.)
700 Orange St.
Darlington, SC 29532
Tel.: 803-393-5421
Fax: 803-393-4123
Year Founded: 1947
Approx.Sls.: $16,000,000
Emp.: 497
Fiscal Year-end: 12/31/90
Mfr. Electronic Components for. Indus. Equip., Aircraft, Automotive, Computers, Communication Equip. Etc.
S.I.C.: 5065
James Steinbach *(Pres.)*
M.W. Windham *(V.P.-Mktg.)*
Norm Dionne *(Pur. Agent)*

Subsidiary:

Struthers-Dunn Inc. **(1)**
512 Lambs Rd.
Pitman, NJ 08071
Tel.: 609-589-7500
Fax: 609-589-2619
Emp.: 500
Fiscal Year-end: 12/31/90
Mfr. Electrical Relays, Timers, Solid-State Modules & Motor Controls, Solid-State Programmable Controllers, Welding Controls and Special Systems
S.I.C.: 3625; 3674
Ernie J. Johnson *(Pres.)*
Robert Jackson *(Exec. V.P.)*
Brad Bassi *(V.P.-Mktg.)*
Mark Jenofsky *(V.P. & Treas.)*
Hil Lurie *(Chief Fin. Officer)*
Robert Spence *(Dir.-Quality Control)*
Ed Hanker, Jr. *(Dir.-Engrng.)*
Dave Conrad *(Mgr.-Data Processing)*
Ida Saul *(Mgr.-Human Resources)*

MSI INSURANCE COMPANIES
Two Pine Tree Dr.
Arden Hills, MN 55112-3793
Mailing Address:
P.O. Box 64035
St. Paul, MN 55164
Tel.: 612-631-7000 **MN**
Fax: 612-631-7294
Year Founded: 1933
Assets: $755,551,000
Liabilities: $656,696,000
Net Worth: $98,855,000
Approx.Sls.: $192,711,001
Emp.: 600
Fiscal Year-end: 12/31/91

Import Export
All Lines of Insurance
S.I.C.: 6411; 6311; 6321; 6331; 6351; 6361
Corporate Giving Program: To Cooperatives & Cooperative-Related & to Community 501 (c) 3 Organizations
Employee Matching Gifts Program: $50 to $1,000 Annually to a Four Year Degree-Granting College or University, Graduate School, Junior or Two-Year College
Bruce Anderson *(Chm. Bd.)*
Donald Armstrong *(Vice Chm.)*
James F. Van Houten *(Pres. & Chief Exec. Officer)*
Alan P. Blackwell *(V.P. & Chief Life Actuary)*
Robert Gaecke *(V.P. & Gen. Mgr. Life/Health Opers.)*
Donald M. Gray *(V.P. & Controller)*
J. Randal Powers *(V.P.-Mktg. & Agency Sls.)*
Charles W. Quandt *(V.P.-& Gen.Mgr. Property/Casualty Opers.)*
Stephen L. Rohde *(V.P.-Fin. & Treas.)*
Thomas R. Schori *(V.P.-Mkt. Plng.)*
Randall Stoneking *(V.P.-Agribusiness Sls.)*
Jerome L. Sychowski *(V.P.-Admin.)*
Chester A. Zinn, Jr. *(V.P., Sec. & Gen. Counsel)*
Hicri Koroglu *(Dir.-Tech. Services)*
James Melchoir *(Dir.-Agency Sls.)*
Gilbert F. Wenzel *(Dir.-Human Resources)*
Rod Schnuckle *(Dir.-Data Center)*
Joni Barg *(Mgr.-Pur.)*
Terry Higgins *(Mgr.-Telecommunications)*
Bill Rustad *(Fleet Admin.)*
Pat Ryan Greene *(Sr. Pub. Rels. Specialist)*
Michelle Johnson *(Sls. Communication Specialist)*
Lori Werner *(Sls. Communication Specialist)*

Computer Systems/Hardware:
HDS EX-30

Outside Service Firm(s):

KPMG Peat Marwick*(Auditors)*
1600 Meritor Tower, 444 Cedar St.
St. Paul, MN 55102

Mutual Service Life Insurance Co.*(Group Insurer)*
Arden Hills, MN

Doherty, Rumble & Butler*(Legal Firm)*
2800 Minnesota World Trade Center
St. Paul, MN 55101-4999
Tel.: 612-291-9333

Norwest Bank Minnesota, N.A.*(Major Banking Relationship)*
St. Paul, MN

MSI SERVICES, INC.
1015 18th St., N.W., Ste. 800
Washington, DC 20036
Tel.: 202-659-2262
Fax: 202-659-1392
Year Founded: 1976
Approx.Sls.: $17,000,000
Emp.: 200
Furnishes Business Consulting Services To Large & Small Corporations
S.I.C.: 8742; 8748
Winston Childs *(Pres.)*
Dick Backus *(V.P.)*

Outside Service Firm(s):

Bert W. Smith, Jr. & Co.*(Auditors)*
Washington, DC

MTD PRODUCTS, INC.
5965 Grafton Rd.
Valley City, OH 44280
Mailing Address:
P.O. Box 368022
Cleveland, OH 44136
Tel.: 216-225-2600
Fax: 216-273-4617
Year Founded: 1932
Sales Range: $500-999 Million
Emp.: 5,500
Fiscal Year-end: 7/31/90
Mfr. of Lawn Mowers, Lawn & Garden Tractors, Garden Tillers, Snow Blowers, Automotive Supplies
S.I.C.: 3524; 3429; 3423; 3645
Curtis E. Moll *(Chm. Bd. & Chief Exec. Officer)*
David Campbell *(Pres.)*
Michael Murray *(V.P.-Employee Benefits)*
Chris Obey *(Dir.-Mtkg.)*

Computer Systems/Hardware:
IBM System 38

Outside Service Firm(s):

Price Waterhouse*(Auditors)*
BP America Bldg., 200 Public Square, 27th Floor
Cleveland, OH 44114-2301
Tel.: 216-781-3700

Continental Bank N. A.*(Major Banking Relationship)*
231 S. LaSalle St.
Chicago, IL 60697
Tel.: 312-828-2345
Tel.: 800-426-5754
Telex: 312-828-1783

First National Bank of Boston*(Major Banking Relationship)*
P.O. Box 644,
Boston, MA 02102-0644
Tel.: 617-575-2900
Fax: 617-575-2549

National City Bank*(Major Banking Relationship)*
P.O. Box 92301, Corp. Trust Dept.
Cleveland, OH 44101
Tel.: 216-575-2000

Society National Bank*(Major Banking Relationship)*
800 Superior Ave.
Cleveland, OH 44114
Tel.: 216-689-5931
Fax: 216-689-3814

Subsidiary:

Aircap Industries Corp. **(1)**
Hwy. 45 S.
Verona, MS 38879
Tel.: 601-566-2332
Approx.Sls.: $115,000,000
Emp.: 1,200
Fiscal Year-end: 12/31/91
Outdoor Power Equipment; Mastercut Electric Lawn Mowers; Aircap Snow Throwers
S.I.C.: 3524; 5261
Ted Moll *(Pres.)*
Bill Docherty *(V.P.-Sls.)*
Mike Fitzpatrick *(Controller)*
Chris Obey *(Dir.-Mktg.)*

Non-U.S. Holding:

MTD Products Limited **(1)**
97 Kent St.
Kitchener, ON N2G 4J1, Canada
Tel.: 519-579-5500
Manufacture Lawn Mowers & Automotive Stampings
S.I.C.: 3524; 3469
John Vingoe *(Chm.)*
John Hohmeier *(Pres.)*
David J. Hessler *(Sec. & Treas.)*
G.L. McNaughton *(Controller)*
Robert Adams *(Dir.-Personnel)*
John C. Hohmeier *(Dir.-Mfg.)*
Harold Smith *(Dir.-Sls. & Mktg.)*
Ken Thorn *(Mgr.-Consumer Products Mfg.)*

MTI VACATIONS, INC.
1220 Kensington
Oak Brook, IL 60521
Tel.: 708-990-8028
Fax: 708-990-3353
Year Founded: 1972
Approx.Sls.: $110,000,000
Emp.: 450
Wholesale Travel & Telemarketing Services
S.I.C.: 4725
James F. Miller *(Chm. Bd.)*
James E. Noyes *(Pres.)*
Frank S. Silzer *(V.P. & Controller)*
Randy Christensen *(V.P.-Hawaii Opers.)*
Brenda Mocny *(V.P.-Opers. & Mngmt. Information Services)*
Robert Pancoast *(V.P.-Mktg.)*
Art Reilly *(V.P.-Sls.)*
Mark Rittmanic *(V.P.-New Bus. Devel.)*

Outside Service Firm(s):

Deloitte & Touche*(Auditors)*
Two Prudential Plaza, 180 N. Stetson
Chicago, IL 60601
Tel.: 312-946-2039

Cowan & Minetz*(Legal Firm)*
Chicago, IL

Continental Bank N. A.*(Major Banking Relationship)*
231 S. LaSalle St.
Chicago, IL 60697
Tel.: 312-828-2345
Tel.: 800-426-5754
Telex: 312-828-1783

Division:

Trase-Miller **(1)**
1220 Kensington
Oak Brook, IL 60521
Tel.: 708-990-8028
Travel Technology Services
S.I.C.: 4725
Mark Rittmanic *(Exec. V.P. & Gen. Mgr.)*

MTS, INC.
2500 Del Monte St., Bldg. C
West Sacramento, CA 95611
Tel.: 916-373-2500
S.I.C.: 5735; 5942
Russell M. Solomon *(Pres. & Chief Exec. Officer)*

Subsidiaries:

Pulse Magazine **(1)**
2500 DelMonte St.
West Sacramento, CA 95691
Tel.: 916-373-2500
S.I.C.: 2721
Russell M. Solomon *(Pres. & Chief Exec. Officer)*

Tower Records **(1)**
2500 Del Monte Ave.
West Sacramento, CA 95691
Tel.: 916-373-2500
Fax: 916-373-2534
Sales Range: $500-999 Million
Import Export
Retail Record Stores
S.I.C.: 5735
Russ Solomon *(Pres.)*
Walter Martin *(Exec. V.P.)*
Stan Goman *(Sr. V.P.-Sls.)*
Mike Solomon *(Sr. V.P.-Legal)*
Chris Hopson *(V.P.-Adv.)*

Dee Searson *(V.P.-Fin.)*

MAACO ENTERPRISES INC.
381 Brooks Rd.
King of Prussia, PA 19406
Tel.: 215-265-6606
Year Founded: 1972
Approx.Sls.: $275,000,000
Emp.: 150
Fiscal Year-end: 10/31/90
Auto Painting & Collision Repair
S.I.C.: 7532
Anthony A. Martino *(Chm. Bd. & Pres.)*
William D. McKaig *(Treas. & Sec.)*
Eileen Moran *(Adv. Dir.)*

MAC PAPERS, INC.
3300 Phillips Hwy.
Jacksonville, FL 32207
Mailing Address:
P.O. Box 5369
Jacksonville, FL 32247
Tel.: 904-348-3300 **FL**
Fax: 904-348-3340
Year Founded: 1964
Approx.Sls.: $200,000,000
Emp.: 480
Fiscal Year-end: 12/31/91
Wholesale Paper Products
S.I.C.: 5111
Thomas R. McGehee *(Co-Chm Bd. & Chief Exec. Officer)*
Frank S. McGehee *(Co-Chm. Bd.)*
F. Sutton McGehee *(Pres.)*
Raymond A. Patterson *(Chief Fin. Officer)*
David S. McGehee *(Exec. V.P.)*
Thomas R. McGehee, Jr. *(V.P.)*
Jerry Shane *(V.P.-Pur.)*
J. W. Dupree, Jr. *(Treas.)*
Walter Gordon *(Controller)*
Guy Fisher *(Dir.-Real Estate)*
Roger Gadd *(Dir.-Data Processing)*
Principal(s):
Thomas R. McGehee
Frank S. McGehee

No. of Mfg. Plants/Facilities: 11
No. of U.S. Offices: 14

Computer Systems/Hardware:
Burroughs A-3

Outside Service Firm(s):

Deloitte & Touche*(Auditors)*
Jacksonville, FL

Martin, Ade, Birchfield & Johnston*(Legal Firm)*
Jacksonville, FL

First Union National Bank*(Major Banking Relationship)*
Jacksonville, FL

Florida Union National Bank*(Major Banking Relationship)*
Jacksonville, FL

Sun Bank, N.A.*(Major Banking Relationship)*
Jacksonville, FL

MACANDREWS & FORBES HOLDINGS INC.
36 E. 63rd St.
New York, NY 10021
Tel.: 212-688-9000 **NY**
Fax: 212-421-1643
Year Founded: 1983
Assets: $321,790,000
Earnings: $82,550,000
Net Worth: $321,790,000
Approx.Sls.: $2,440,000,000
Emp.: 28,000
Licorice Extract; Film Processing; Cosmetics, Fragrances, Beauty Care & Treatment, Health Care Prods.; Banking
S.I.C.: 2087; 2844; 7384; 2834; 6036
Ronald O. Perelman *(Chm. Bd. & Chief Exec. Officer)*
Howard Gittis *(Vice Chm.)*
Donald G. Drapkin *(Vice Chm.)*
Bruce Slovin *(Pres.)*
Fred L. Tepperman *(Exec. V.P. & Chief Fin. Officer)*
James T. Conroy *(Sr. V.P.-Corp. Affairs)*
Richard E. Halperin *(Sr. V.P.)*
Todd J. Slotkin *(Sr. V.P.)*
Norman J. Ginstling *(V.P. & Dir.-Taxes)*

Outside Service Firm(s):

Coopers & Lybrand*(Auditors)*
1301 Avenue of The Americas
New York, NY 10019
Tel.: 212-536-2000

Skadden, Arps, Slate, Meagher & Flom*(Legal Firm)*
Los Angeles, CA

Divisions:

Associated Group **(1)**
P.O. Box 1762
Wichita, KS 67201
Tel.: 316-261-3211
Clair E. McCurdy *(Gen. Mgr.)*

Boam Chemicals Co., Inc. **(1)**
3rd St. & Jefferson Ave.
Camden, NJ 08104
Tel.: 609-964-8840
Chemicals
S.I.C.: 5169
Lachlan McLean *(Pres.)*

Boam Produce (Overseas) Ltd. **(1)**
3rd St. & Jefferson Ave.
Camden, NJ 08104
Tel.: 609-964-8840
Flavoring Extracts & Flavoring Syrups
S.I.C.: 2087
Selina Sherman *(Dir.)*

MacAndrews & Forbes Co. **(1)**
3rd St. & Jefferson Ave.
Camden, NJ 08104
Tel.: 609-964-8840
Fax: 609-964-6029
Approx.Sls.: $55,600,000
Emp.: 225
Fiscal Year-end: 12/31/90
Right Dress Garden Products, Licorice & Chemicals
S.I.C.: 2087
Meyer Laskin *(Pres. & Chief Oper. Officer)*
Irwin Engelman *(Exec. V.P. & Chief Fin. Officer)*
S.J. Taub *(Sr. V.P.-Mfg.)*
P.W. Grace *(V.P. & Controller)*
William J. Green *(V.P.-Govt. Rels.)*
Barry F. Schwartz *(V.P. & Chief Counsel-Litigation)*
R. Whitman *(V.P.-Sls.)*
John Karpinski *(Mgr.-Indus. Rels.)*
Bill Haney *(Pur. Agent)*

MacAndrews & Forbes Ltd. **(1)**
3rd St. & Jefferson Ave.
Camden, NJ 08104
Tel.: 609-964-8840
Flavorings
S.I.C.: 2087
Leonard Groom *(Mng. Dir.)*

Maf Cote Specialties Co., Inc. **(1)**
3rd St. & Jefferson Ave.
Camden, NJ 08104
Tel.: 609-964-8840
Coating Paperboards
S.I.C.: 2671
Roy Weidman *(Gen. Mgr.)*

Master Skiis **(1)**
4590 Pell Dr.
Sacramento, CA 95838
Tel.: 916-920-3993
S.I.C.: 3949
Kris LaPoint *(Gen. Mgr.)*

M.F. Neal & Co.,Inc. **(1)**
1900 E. Franklin St.
Richmond, VA 23219
Tel.: 804-648-5891
Mfr. Flavors
S.I.C.: 2087
L. Schantz *(Gen. Mgr.)*

Winros, Inc. **(1)**
250 San Francisco St.
Old San Juan, PR 00902
Distribution
Enrique Ferreiro *(Pres.)*

Subsidiaries:

The Coleman Company, Inc. **(1)**
250 N. St. Francis St.
Wichita, KS 67202
Tel.: 316-261-3211
Fax: 316-261-3400
Assets: $330,372,000
Earnings: $14,380,000
Liabilities: $231,947,000
Net Worth: $98,425,000
Approx.Rev.: $352,949,000
Emp.: 2,513
Fiscal Year-end: 12/31/91
Import Export
Computer Systems/Hardware:
IBM
Outdoor Recreation Products; Heating & Air Conditioning Equip. for Manufactured & Site-Built Housing & A/C for RV's
S.I.C.: 3949; 3634; 3585; 5064; 3792; 3799; 3484
Lawrence M. Jones *(Chm. & Chief Exec. Oficer)*
Bob Ring *(Pres. & Chief Oper. Officer)*
George Mileusnic *(Sr. V.P. & Chief Fin. Officer)*
Ronald J. Nold *(Sr. V.P.-Opers.)*
Larry Sanford *(Sr. V.P.-Legal)*
Charles Ogden *(Sr. V.P.-Sls.)*
David Stearns *(Sr. V.P.-Mktg.)*
J. Richard Crist *(V.P.-Field Sls.)*
Michael S. Hawes *(V.P.-Fin. & Treas.)*
Charles B. McIlwaine *(V.P.-Communications)*
J. Michael Murray *(V.P.-Int'l Opers.)*
John P. Rukavina *(V.P.-Sales)*
William H. Sanders *(V.P.-Customer Service)*
Bob Sharp *(V.P.-Textiles)*
Lynn E. Feldkemp *(Controller)*
Tim Cotter *(Dir.-Human Resources)*

Groups:

Coleman International Operation **(2)**
2111 E. 37th St. No.
Wichita, KS 67219
Tel.: 316-261-3211
Approx.Sls.: $69,100,000
Emp.: 48
Mfr. & Sls. of Products Manufactured in U.S., Canada, Australia, W. Germany & France
S.I.C.: 3949
Richard Conarroe *(Mgr.-Sls. & Mktg. Devel.)*

Coleman Outdoor Products **(2)**
250 N. St. Francis Ave.
Wichita, KS 67202
Tel.: 316-261-3211
Approx.Sls.: $174,800,000
Emp.: 1,319
Import Export
Lanterns, Campstoves, Catalytic Heaters, Coolers, Jugs, Tents, Sleeping Bags, Fuel, Camping Accessories, 12-volt Air Inflators, Peak 1 Backpacking Equip., Canoes
S.I.C.: 2394; 3089; 3648
Bob Ring *(Pres.)*
Larry Jones *(Chief Oper. Officer)*
George Mileusnie *(Chief Fin. Officer)*
Brad Bartlett *(Dir.-Mktg. & Adv.)*
Charles Ogden *(Dir.-Sls.)*

Plants:

The Coleman Company **(3)**
766 Hwy. 306
New Braunfels, TX 78130
Tel.: 210-625-6943
Mfrs. Canoes, Coolers & Acces.
S.I.C.: 3732; 3086
Randy Kuntz *(Plant Mgr.)*

The Coleman Company **(3)**
P.O. Box 1119, Hwy. 341
Lake City, SC 29560
Tel.: 803-394-8893
Mfrs. Tents, Sleeping Bags
S.I.C.: 2394; 2399
Howard Peterson *(Plant Mgr.)*

The Coleman Company **(3)**
597 N. 1500 West
Cedar City, UT 84720
Tel.: 801-586-9437
Mfrs. Tents, Sleeping Bags
S.I.C.: 2394; 2399
Terry Wilson *(Plant Mgr.)*

Coleman Water Recreation Operations **(2)**
4925 E. Oceanside Blvd.
Oceanside, CA 92056
Tel.: 619-758-9100
Approx.Sls.: $97,700,000
Skis, Boats, Spas & Diving Equip.
S.I.C.: 3949; 3732
Jerry M. Moyer *(Sr. V.P. & Gen. Mgr.)*

Subsidiaries:

Coleman Spas, Inc. **(3)**
25805 So. Arizona Ave.
Chandler, AZ 85248
Tel.: 602-895-0598
Fax: 602-895-7849
Emp.: 100
Mfrs. Hot Tubs, Saunas, Spatubs & Acrylic Spas
S.I.C.: 3088; 2452; 5091
James Weber *(Pres.)*
Kent Crudup *(V.P.-Fin.)*
Vern Sandlin *(V.P.-Opers.)*
Dick Smith *(Dir.-Sls.)*

MasterCraft Boat Company **(3)**
Route 9
Maryville, TN 37801
Tel.: 615-983-2178
Emp.: 105
Mfg. & Sales of Ski Boats & Skis
S.I.C.: 3949
Chuck West *(Gen. Mgr.)*

O'Brien International, Inc. **(3)**
14615 N.E. 91st
Redmond, WA 98052
Tel.: 206-885-5900 (100%)
Emp.: 108
Mfr. & Sls. of Slalom Skis, Sailboards & Access.
S.I.C.: 3949
Walt Hare *(Gen. Mgr.)*

Skeeter Products, Inc. **(3)**
1 Skeeter Road
Kilgore, TX 75662
Tel.: 903-984-0541
Emp.: 150
Mfr. & Sales of Bass Fishing Boats
S.I.C.: 3949
Mike Allbritton *(Gen. Mgr.)*

SoniForm, Inc. **(3)**
1908 Friendship Drive
El Cajon, CA 92020
Tel.: 619-562-3681
Emp.: 70
Mfr. of Bouyancy Vest for Scuba Diving
S.I.C.: 3949
Lanny Cruse *(V.P. & Gen. Mgr.)*

Subsidiary:

Crosman Corporation **(2)**
Rts. 5 & 20
East Bloomfield, NY 14443
Tel.: 716-657-6161 (100%)
Emp.: 303
Fiscal Year-end: 12/31/89
Mfr. & Sls. of Compressed Air & CO-2 Guns, Pellets & Accessories, Archery Accessories
S.I.C.: 3484; 3949
Sheldon Coleman *(Chm. Bd.)*
Jim Feimster *(Pres.)*
Daniel Roberts *(V.P.-Mktg. & Sls.)*
Margaret Murray *(Dir.-Adv. & Pub. Rels.)*
Bob Ramsay *(Prod. Mgr.)*
Tom Campbell *(Prod. Mgr.)*
Barbara Schubert *(Pur. Agent)*

Non-U.S. Holdings:

Australian Coleman, Inc. **(2)**
5 Hallstrom Place
Wetherill Park, N.S.W. 2164, Australia
Tel.: 02-604-9444 (100%)
Distr. of Coolers
S.I.C.: 5091; 5078

The Canadian Coleman Co., Ltd. **(2)**
15 N. Queen St.
Toronto, ON M8Z 2C6, Canada
Tel.: 416-252-6161 (100%)
Telex: 06-967720
Fax: 416-252-9476
Approx.Sls.: $19,100,000
Emp.: 250
Manufacturing & Sales of Lanterns, Camp Stoves, Jugs, Coolers, Compressed Air & CO2 Guns, Pellets & Accessories; Canoes
S.I.C.: 3089; 3648; 3429; 3484; 3631
A.R. Smith *(V.P.-Mfg.)*
L. Grozelle *(Natl. Sales Dir.-Group I)*
H. Ryan *(Pur. Dir.)*
D. King *(Personnel Dir.)*

Coast Catamaran France **(2)**
Le Viet, Route de Pierrefeu 83400
Hyeres, France (100%)
Mfr. Boats
S.I.C.: 3732; 3089

Coleman Evcon Supply Limited **(2)**
3115 Peppermill Court, Unit #3
Mississauga, ON L5L 4X5, Canada
Tel.: 416-569-9111
Distr.of Sporting Goods
S.I.C.: 5091
Tony Corrillo *(Sls. Dir.)*

Coleman (Deutschland) GmbH **(2)**
Inheiden Ezetilstrasse D-6303
Hungen, 3, Germany (100%)
Approx.Sls.: $5,000,000
Mfr. Soft-sided, Insulated Prods. for Camping
S.I.C.: 2394

Coleman Japan Ltd. **(2)**
5th Flr., Eight Bldg., 4-5-9, Hachobori Chuo-ku,
Tokyo, 104, Japan
Tel.: 03 3553 5941 (100%)
Fax: 03 3552-2040
Distr.of Camping Equipment
S.I.C.: 5091; 5078

Coleman U.K., Inc. **(2)**
Unit 2, Parish Wharf Estate, Harbour Roa
Bristol, BS20 9DA, United Kingdom (100%)
Distr.
S.I.C.: 5091; 5078

MacAndrews & Forbes Group, Inc. **(1)**
36 E. 63rd St.
New York, NY 10021
Tel.: 212-688-9000
Holding Company
S.I.C.: 6719

Revlon Group Inc. **(1)**
21 E. 63rd St.
New York, NY 10021
Tel.: 212-593-4300
Fax: 212-572-8400
Approx.Rev.: $1,800,000,000
Emp.: 7,000
Fiscal Year-end: 12/31/91
Holding Company
S.I.C.: 6719
Ronald Perelman *(Chm. & Chief Exec. Officer)*
Howard Gittis *(Vice Chm.)*
Donald Drapkin *(Vice Chm.)*
Sol Levine *(Pres.)*
Annette Golden *(Exec. V.P.)*
Richard Tarlow *(Exec. V.P.-Adv.)*
George W. Feld *(V.P.-Adv. Services)*
James T. Conroy *(V.P.-Public Affairs)*
Anthony Cozzolino *(V.P.-Media & Budget)*

Divisions:

Technicolor Professional Film Div. **(2)**
4050 Lankershim Blvd.
North Hollywood, CA 91608
Tel.: 310-769-8500
Worldwide Color Processing & Special Services For Motion Pictures & TV

Technicolor Videocassette Inc. **(2)**
4050 Lankershim Blvd.
North Hollywood, CA 91608
Tel.: 310-769-8500

Subsidiaries:

Almay, Inc. **(2)**
625 Madison Ave.
New York, NY 10022
Tel.: 212-527-4000 (100%)
Fax: 212-750-0630
Mfr. & Distr. Cosmetics
S.I.C.: 2844; 5122
Michael M. Hammond *(Pres.)*
Cynthia Stremba *(V.P.-Mktg.)*

Bill Blass, Inc. **(2)**
625 Madison Ave.
New York, NY 10022
Tel.: 212-527-5000 (100%)
Mfr. of Beauty Care Products
S.I.C.: 2844
Lawrence Wechsler *(Pres.)*

Carrington Parfums Ltd. **(2)**
767 Fifth Ave.
New York, NY 10153
Tel.: 212-572-5000 (100%)
Manufacture & Distribute Fragrances & Toiletries
S.I.C.: 2844
Sol Levine *(Pres.)*

Charles of the Ritz Group Ltd. **(2)**
625 Madison Ave.
New York, NY 10022
Tel.: 212-527-4000 (100%)
Fax: 212-527-4420
Manufacture & Distribute Cosmetics, Fragrances, Toiletries & Healthcare Products
S.I.C.: 2844; 5122
Michael T. Gannaway *(Pres.-Fragrance Grp.)*
Stanley B. Dessen *(V.P.)*
Lynn Krominga *(V.P.-Law)*
Frederick W. McNabb, Jr. *(V.P. & Asst. Sec.)*
Wade H. Nichols III *(V.P. & Sec.)*
Tedd Thomas *(V.P.-Mktg.)*
Frank Zappetti *(V.P.-Acctg. & Opers. Services)*

Alexandra De Markoff, Ltd. **(2)**
625 Madison Ave.
New York, NY 10022
Tel.: 212-527-4000 (100%)
Mfr. & Distr. of Cosmetics, Skincare & Fragrances
S.I.C.: 2844; 5122
Michael M. Hammond *(Pres.-Revlon-N. Amer.)*
Walter Klingman *(Exec. V.P.)*
Bruce Slovin *(Sr. V.P.)*
Wendy Banks *(V.P.-Mktg.)*

D.V.F. Inc. **(2)**
625 Madison Ave.
New York, NY 10022
Tel.: 212-527-4000 (100%)
Distribute Beauty Products
S.I.C.: 5122
Robert M. Cankes *(V.P. & Gen. Mgr.)*
William H. Frank *(V.P. & Treas.)*

Fila Fitness Ltd. **(2)**
767 Fifth Ave.
New York, NY 10153
Tel.: 212-572-5000 (100%)
Distr. of Beauty Products
S.I.C.: 5122
Sol Levine *(Pres.)*

General Wig Manufacturers, Inc. **(2)**
13982 N.W. 58th Ct.
Miami Lakes, FL 33014
Tel.: 305-823-0600 (100%)
Manufacture & Sale Wigs & Hairpieces
S.I.C.: 3999
Alan M. Smiley *(Pres.)*

Marvel Entertainment Group **(2)**
387 Park Ave. S.
New York, NY 10016
Tel.: 212-696-0808
S.I.C.: 2721
Terry Stewart *(Pres.)*
Joseph Calamari *(Exec. V.P.)*
Barry Kaplan *(Exec. V.P.)*

Subsidiaries:

Asher Candy Company **(3)**
1815 Gilford Ave.
New Hyde Park, NY 11040
Tel.: 516-437-1900
Candy Canes & Other Boiled Candy; Trading Cards
S.I.C.: 2064; 2759
James Spampinato *(Pres.)*

Fleer Corporation **(3)**
Executive Plaza, Ste. 300, 1120 Rte. 73
Mount Laurel, NJ 08054
Tel.: 609-231-6250
Earnings: $23,395,000
Approx.Sls.: $161,641,000
Emp.: 350
Fiscal Year-end: 12/31/91
Gum & Candy Products, Trading Cards, Stickers & Novelties
S.I.C.: 2064; 2067; 2759
Paul Mullan *(Chm. Bd. & Chief Exec. Officer)*
Vince Murray *(Pres. & Chief Oper. Officer)*

MacAndrews & Forbes Holdings Inc.—(Continued)

John J. Roarty *(V.P.-Sls.)*
T.G. Leonard *(V.P.-Fleer Intl.)*
Oscar Hauer *(V.P.-Pur.)*
Jeff Massin *(V.P.-Mktg.)*
Greg Kilson *(Chief Fin. Officer)*
Michael G. Wolverton *(Dir.-Personnel)*
Tom Giglio *(Dir.-Adv. & Promo.)*
Tom Ryder *(Sls. Dir.)*
Ron Elias *(Quality Control Supvr.)*

National Health Laboratories Inc. **(2)**
7590 Fay Ave.
La Jolla, CA 92037
Tel.: 619-454-3314 (40%)
Earnings: $82,600,000
Approx.Sls.: $501,900,000
Fiscal Year-end: 12/31/90
Clinical Diagnostic Laboratories
S.I.C.: 8071
Robert Draper *(Pres. & Chief Exec. Officer)*

Norell Perfumes, Inc. **(2)**
767 Fifth Ave.
New York, NY 10153
Tel.: 212-572-5000 (100%)
Beauty Care Products
S.I.C.: 2844
Lawrence Wechsler *(Pres.)*

Prestige Fragrance & Cosmetics, Inc. **(2)**
767 Fifth Ave.
New York, NY 10153
Tel.: 212-572-5000 (100%)
Retailer of Beauty Products
S.I.C.: 5122
Sol Levine *(Pres.)*
Carol Shaughnessy *(V.P. & G.M.)*

Prestige Perfumes Ltd. **(2)**
767 Fifth Ave.
New York, NY 10153
Tel.: 212-572-5000 (100%)
Distr. of Beauty Products
S.I.C.: 5122
Sol Levine *(Pres.)*

Prestige Fragrances, Ltd. **(2)**
625 Madison Ave., 4th Fl.
New York, NY 10022
Tel.: 212-527-4000 (100%)
Distribute Beauty Products
S.I.C.: 5122
Sol Levine *(Pres.)*
Gerald M. Lausin *(Exec. V.P.)*

Revlon Commissary Sales, Inc. **(2)**
767 Fifth Ave.
New York, NY 10153
Tel.: 212-572-5000 (100%)
Sells Retail Beauty Products to Commissaries
S.I.C.: 5122
Richard H. Metzler *(Pres.)*

Revlon Government Sales, Inc. **(2)**
767 Fifth Ave.
New York, NY 10153
Tel.: 212-572-5000 (100%)
Sells Retail Beauty Products to Military Exchanges
S.I.C.: 5122
Richard H. Metzler *(Pres.)*

Revlon, Inc. **(2)**
625 Madison Ave.
New York, NY 10022
Tel.: 212-527-4000
Assets: $3,219,765,000
Liabilities: $2,178,746,000
Net Worth: $1,041,019,000
Approx.Sls.: $1,611,281,000
Emp.: 26,500
Fiscal Year-end: 12/31/90
Mfr. of Cosmetics & Fragrances
S.I.C.: 6211; 2834; 2844; 3421; 8071
Ronald O. Perelman *(Chm. Bd. & Chief Exec. Officer)*
Bruce Slovin *(Chm.-Exec. Committee)*
Howard Gittis *(Vice Chm.)*
Jerry W. Levin *(Pres. & Chief Exec. Officer)*
Michael M. Hammond *(Pres.-Revlon N. Amer.)*
William J. Fox *(Exec. V.P. & Chief Fin. Officer)*
Stanley B. Dessen *(Sr. V.P.-Taxation)*
Ronald H. Dunbar *(Sr. V.P.-Human Resources)*
Daniel Moriarty *(Sr. V.P.-Pub. Rels.)*
Wade H. Nichols III *(Sr. V.P. & Gen. Counsel)*
Edward F. Skeffington, Jr. *(Sr. V.P. & Controller)*
Carl J. Deddens *(V.P. & Treas.)*
Glenn P. Dickes *(V.P. & Asst. Sec.)*
George W. Feld *(V.P.-Adv. Services)*
Lynn Krominga *(V.P.-Law)*
Cecil Canale *(V.P.-Mktg.-Fragrances)*
Steve Costa *(V.P.-Mktg.-Cosmetics & Treatment)*
Alida Curcio *(V.P.-Mktg.-Toiletries)*

Revlon International Corporation **(2)**
767 Fifth Ave.
New York, NY 10153
Tel.: 212-572-5000 (100%)
Wholesale Distr. of Beauty Products
S.I.C.: 5122
Paul J. Block *(Pres.)*
Annette M. McEvey *(Sr. V.P.-Mktg.)*

Revlon (Puerto Rico), Inc. **(2)**
Calle A. esq. C., Urb. Ind. Dr. Mario Julia
Caparra, PR 00926 (100%)
Distribute Beauty Products
S.I.C.: 5122
Sol Levine *(Pres.)*

Revlon-Realistic Professional Products, Inc. **(2)**
625 Madison Ave.
New York, NY 10022
Tel.: 212-527-4000 (100%)
Fax: 212-408-8062
Approx.Sls.: $275,000,000
Emp.: 2,000
Fiscal Year-end: 12/31/90
Professional Cosmetic & Hair Products
S.I.C.: 2844
Irving J. Bottner *(Pres. & Chief Oper. Officer)*
Louis J. Roppolo *(Sr. V.P.-Mktg.)*
Norman Kagan *(Sr. V.P.-Sls.)*
Thomas S. Lacy *(V.P.-Opers.)*
Andrew Roberts *(V.P.-Adv.)*
Ira Bassen *(Dir.-Adv.)*
Barbara Evans *(Asst. Mgr.-Copy)*

Revlon Research Center, Inc. **(2)**
Rt. #27 & Talmadge Rd.
Edison, NJ 08817
Tel.: 908-287-1400 (100%)
Beauty Care Research & Development
S.I.C.: 8731
Sol Levine *(Chm.)*
George Fiato *(Pres.)*

Revlon Service, Inc. **(2)**
767 Fifth Ave.
New York, NY 10153
Tel.: 212-572-5000 (100%)
Beauty Care
S.I.C.: 2844
John Bulzacchelli *(Pres.)*

Charles Revson, Inc. **(2)**
767 Fifth Ave.
New York, NY 10153
Tel.: 212-527-4000 (100%)
Beauty Care Products
S.I.C.: 2844

Ritz Corporation **(2)**
767 Fifth Ave.
New York, NY 10153
Tel.: 212-572-5000
Sol Levine *(Pres.)*

Roux Laboratories, Inc. **(2)**
3733 University Blvd. W.
Jacksonville, FL 32217
Tel.: 904-731-3050 (100%)
Emp.: 320
Manufacture Beauty Care & Treatment Products for Professional & Retail Use
S.I.C.: 2844
Irving J. Bottner *(Chm.)*
Norman Kagan *(Pres.)*
Louis Roppolo *(V.P.-Mktg.)*

Non U.S. Holding:

Revlon S.p.A. **(2)**
Rome, Italy (100%)
Sub. of Revlon Intl. Corp.
S.I.C.: 5122

Non-U.S. Joint Venture:

Industrias Kolmex, S.A. **(2)**
Calle del Rio No.u
Naucalpan de Juarez, Estado de Mexico
53370, Mexico (49%)
Joint Venture, Mfr. Lanterns, Life Vest, Tents, Jugs & Related
S.I.C.: 3648; 2394; 3585

MACCABEES MUTUAL LIFE INSURANCE
25800 Northwestern Hwy.
Southfield, MI 48037
Tel.: 313-357-4800
Approx.Sls.: $65,000,000
Emp.: 600
Life, Health Insurance
S.I.C.: 6411
J.L. Pallone *(Chm. Bd.)*
Robert Ferguson *(Pres.)*
William Paxton *(Sr. V.P.-Grp. Sls.)*
Gail Brooks *(Dir.-Employee Rels.)*

MACCO CONSTRUCTORS, INC.
P.O. Box 257, 14409
Paramount Blvd.
Paramount, CA 90723-3418
Tel.: 213-630-5801 DE
Fax: 213-633-1370
Year Founded: 1929
Approx.Sls.: $100,000,000
Emp.: 700
Gen. Contractor for Commercial, Industrial, Office & Institutional Bldgs.; Pipeline Contractor Including Gas Distribution & Transmission, Underground Power & Communication, Refined Products, Crude Oil & Water Transmission; Pile Driving Contractor & Mfg. of Prestressed Concrete Piling
S.I.C.: 1623; 1542; 1522; 1541; 1629; 1771; 1799
William McCune *(Chm. Bd.)*
Warren R. Strong *(Chief Exec. Officer, Chief Oper. Officer, & Pres.)*
Vincent J. Dinkler *(Sr. V.P.)*
Robert A. Parker *(Sr. V.P.)*
Thomas A. Stocksdale *(Sr. V.P.)*
John E. Clement *(V.P.)*
David C. Elmore *(V.P.)*
John W. Fredenburg *(V.P.)*
Stephen A. Hay *(V.P.)*
William B. Sparks *(V.P., Sec. & Treas.)*
Robert Glidewell *(Mgr.-Fin. Services & Admin.)*
Theodore C. Anderson *(Asst. Sec.)*

No. of Mfg. Plants/Facilities: 6
No. of U.S. Offices: 1

Outside Service Firm(s):

Bank of America NT&SA*(Major Banking Relationship)*
Downey, CA

MACDANIELS, HENRY & SPROUL, INC.
930 Montgomery St.
San Francisco, CA 94133
Tel.: 415-981-2250
Fax: 415-981-0164
Year Founded: 1989
Approx.Billings: $15,500,000
Emp.: 14
Advertising, Public Relations, Sales Promotion & Direct Marketing Services
John Scott MacDaniels *(Chief Exec. Officer & Creative Dir.)*
Thomas E. Henry *(Chief Oper. Officer)*
Robert G. Sproul *(Gen. Mgr.)*
Marilyn Hunt *(Fin. Mgr.)*
Charles Seifert *(Pub. Rels. Dir.)*

Computer Systems/Hardware:
Admark Agency System, Data General Network, IBM PC's, Macintosh PC's

THE MACERICH CO.
233 Wilshire Blvd., Ste. 700
Santa Monica, CA 90401
Tel.: 310-394-6911
Telex: 310-395-2791
Fax: 310-395-2791
Year Founded: 1964
Emp.: 650
Real Estate Development; Shopping Center Owner & Manager
S.I.C.: 6552; 6513
Mace Siegel *(Pres.)*
Dana K. Anderson *(Exec. V.P.)*
Arthur Coppola *(Exec. V.P.)*
Dane Smith *(Sr. V.P.)*
Edward Coppola *(Sr. V.P.)*

No. of U.S. Offices: 5

MACHADO & CO. INC.
20 Exchange Pl., 52nd fl.
New York, NY 10005
Tel.: 212-797-5260
Fax: 212-514-6590
Assets: $4,930,000
Net Worth: $4,930,000
Approx.Sls.: $81,860,000
Emp.: 30
Coffee & Cocoa Importers
S.I.C.: 5149
Daniel Barnett *(Pres.)*
William F. Moreno *(Treas.)*
Jerome Crown *(Controller)*
Tom Shea *(Asst. V.P.)*

Outside Service Firm(s):

Royal Insurance Co.*(Commercial Insurance Carrier)*
New York, NY

Bankers Trust Co.*(Major Banking Relationship)*
P.O. Box 318, Church St. Station
New York, NY 10008
Tel.: 212-454-2212
Fax: 212-454-2783

Brown Brothers, Harriman & Co.*(Major Banking Relationship)*
59 Wall St.
New York, NY 10005-2818
Tel.: 212-493-8029

GUS MACHADO ENTERPRISES
1200 W. 49th St.
Hialeah, FL 33012
Tel.: 305-822-3211 FL
Fax: 305-825-7063
Approx.Sls.: $137,000,000
Emp.: 283
Retail New & Used Automobiles
S.I.C.: 5511
Gus Machado *(Pres. & Chief Exec. Officer)*
Victor Benitez *(V.P., Gen. Mgr. & Mgr.-Sls.)*
George Koenning *(Controller)*
Jose Granados *(Mgr.-New Cars)*
Armando Portillo *(Mgr.-Fin.)*
Principal(s):
Gus Machado

Computer Systems/Hardware:
Automatic Data Processing

Outside Service Firm(s):

Mario Toca*(Auditors)*
Miami, FL

Universal Underwriters Insurance Co.*(Commercial Insurance Carrier)*
Maitland, FL

South Floria Auto Dealers Trust*(Group Insurer)*
Orlando, FL

Schwartz & Nash*(Legal Firm)*
Miami, FL

Consolidated Bank*(Major Banking Relationship)*
Hialeah, FL

MACHINING ENTERPRISES INC.
11400 Toepfer
Warren, MI 48089
Tel.: 313-755-3180
Fax: 313-759-3540
Approx.Sls.: $80,000,000

Emp.: 500
Production of Machined Castings & Assemblies
S.I.C.: 3499; 3429; 3449; 3451
Ronald F. Scott *(Pres.)*
Larry Long *(Comptroller)*

Outside Service Firm(s):

Ernst & Young*(Auditors)*
One Detroit Center, 500 Woodward, Ste. 1700
Detroit, MI 48243
Tel.: 313-259-9600

Miller, Canfield, Paddock & Stone*(Legal Firm)*
150 W. Jefferson Ave.
Detroit, MI 48226
Tel.: 313-963-6420

National Bank of Detroit*(Major Banking Relationship)*
611 Woodward
Detroit, MI 48226
Tel.: 313-225-1000

MACK MOLDING COMPANY
East Arlington Rd.
Arlington, VT 05250
Tel.: 802-375-2511
Fax: 802-375-9419
Approx.Sls.: $84,000,000
Emp.: 460
Custom Molded Plastics
S.I.C.: 3089
Donald S. Kendall III *(Chm. Bd. & Pres.)*
Raymond E. Burns *(V.P.-Sls.)*
William H. Cooley *(V.P.-Mfg.)*
Stephen D. Mellin *(V.P.-Res. & Devel.)*
Thomas M. Gaylord *(Sec. & Treas.)*
John H. Williams *(Gen. Counsel)*
Bruce Bixler *(Mgr.-Matls.)*

Outside Service Firm(s):

Merchants Bank of Boston*(Major Banking Relationship)*
Boston, MA

MACK PRINTING COMPANY
1991 Northampton St.
Easton, PA 18042
Tel.: 215-258-9111
Fax: 215-250-7310
Year Founded: 1901
Approx.Sls.: $48,500,000
Emp.: 700
Offset Printing of Magazines & Catalogs; Publishing
S.I.C.: 2752; 2741; 2759
Paul F. Mack *(Pres.)*
Robert A. Sadler *(Exec. V.P.)*
Emerson H. Heilman *(V.P.-Admin. & Sec.)*

Principal(s):
Paul F. Mack

Outside Service Firm(s):

Ernst & Young*(Auditors)*
1800 John F. Kennedy Blvd.
Philadelphia, PA 19103-7499
Tel.: 215-864-3300

Drinker, Biddle & Reath*(Legal Firm)*
1000 Westlakes Dr., Ste. 300
Berwyn, PA 19312
Tel.: 215-993-2200
Fax: 215-993-8585

Meridian Bank*(Major Banking Relationship)*
Easton, PA

Divisions:

Mack Printing Co. Inc. **(1)**
34 N. Crystal St.
East Stroudsburg, PA 18301
Tel.: 717-421-9033
Offset Printing
S.I.C.: 2752
John Schivek *(Chief Oper. Officer)*

Subsidiary:

Monroe Printing Company **(2)**
34 N. Crystal St.
East Stroudsburg, PA 18301
Tel.: 717-421-9033
Fax: 717-421-5929
Magazine, Journal & Commercial Printing
S.I.C.: 2721; 2752
Paul F. Mack *(Chm. Bd.)*
Robert A. Sadler *(Pres.)*
Emerson H. Heilman *(V.P. & Sec.)*
Mary Brogan *(Treas.)*

Mack Publishing Co. **(1)**
1991 Northampton St.
Easton, PA 18042
Tel.: 215-258-9111

Subsidiary:

Science Press **(1)**
300 W. Chestnut
Ephrata, PA 17522
Tel.: 717-738-9300
Medical Journals; Financial Publications & General Commercial Printing
S.I.C.: 2731; 2759
Paul Knox *(Chief Oper. Officer)*

MACKINNON-PARKER, INC.
4750 W. Bancroft St.
Toledo, OH 43615
Tel.: 419-535-3100 **OH**
Fax: 419-535-1263
Year Founded: 1921
Approx.Sls.: $40,000,000
Emp.: 150
General Construction; Construction Managers
S.I.C.: 1541; 1542; 1629; 8741
B.L. Parker *(Chm. Bd.)*
Thomas L. Parker *(Pres. & Treas.)*
Pamela Pitzen *(V.P.)*

Principal(s):
B.L. Parker
Thomas L. Parker

Outside Service Firm(s):

Deloitte & Touche*(Auditors)*
Toledo, OH

Shumaker, Loop & Kendrick*(Legal Firm)*
1000 Jackson St.
Toledo, OH 43624
Tel.: 419-241-9000

First National Bank of Toledo*(Major Banking Relationship)*
Toledo, OH

MACKLANBURG-DUNCAN CO.
4041 N. Santa Fe
Oklahoma City, OK 73118
Mailing Address:
P. O. Box 25188
Oklahoma City, OK 73125
Tel.: 405-525-6363
Tel.: 800-678-3572 **OK**
Fax: 405-557-3541
Year Founded: 1920
Assets: $75,000,000
Liabilities: $27,000,000
Net Worth: $48,000,000
Approx.Sls.: $141,000,000
Emp.: 1,200
Fiscal Year-end: 12/31/91
Import Export
Manufactures Building Supplies
S.I.C.: 3429
Nona Jean Hulsey *(Chm. Emeritus)*
Richard L. Gaugler *(Chm. Bd.)*
Michael S. Samis *(Pres. & Chief Exec. Officer)*
Pat Flores *(Exec. V.P. & Dir.-Mfg.)*
Edward LeBlanc *(Exec. V.P.)*
Don Horan *(Sr. V.P.-Fin., Chief Fin. Officer, Sec. & Treas.)*
Vernon MacKenzie *(Sr. V.P.-Admin. & Dir.-Human Resources, Personnel Training)*
Charles Hopper *(V.P.-Pur.)*
Don Owens *(V.P.-Admin. Services)*
Daniel Sharp *(V.P.-Information Services & Dir.-Data Processing)*
Pat Avery *(Controller)*
Charles Goforth *(Controller)*
Mark Skinner *(Controller)*
Jack Bennett *(Dir.-Quality Control & Res. & Devel.)*
Larry Bost *(Dir.-Sls.)*
Darwin Frankum *(Dir.-Sls. & Mktg.)*
Leroy Haefner *(Dir.-Res. & Devel. & Tech. & Engrng.)*
Darrell Hart *(Dir.-Pur. & Traffic)*
Chuck Hopper *(Dir.-Pur.)*
Jim Lodge *(Dir.-Quality Control)*
David Lyon *(Dir.-Mktg.)*
William O'Hare *(Dir.-Sls.)*
Loren Plotkin *(Dir.-Res. & Devel., Mktg. & Art)*
Harold Smith *(Dir.-Tech. & Engrng.)*
George Stockham *(Dir.-Mfg. & Quality Control)*
Clarence Bruce *(Mgr.-Personnel Training & Devel.)*
James Landess *(Mgr.-Intl. Sls.)*
Debra Nemlowill *(Mgr.-Telecommunications)*
Sue Robinett *(Mgr.-Pension Admin.)*
Nancy Whitley *(Corp. Travel Planner)*

Principal(s):
Nona Jean Hulsey

No. of Mfg. Plants/Facilities: 7
No. of U.S. Offices: 7

Computer Systems/Hardware:
Sequent, Honeywell DPS 8, Oracle

Outside Service Firm(s):

Arthur Andersen & Co.*(Auditors)*
20 W. Broadway, Ste. 1200
Oklahoma City, OK 73109
Tel.: 405-236-1491

United States Fidelity & Guaranty Co.*(Commercial Insurance Carrier)*
100 Light Street
Baltimore, MD 21202
Tel.: 301-547-3000

Member Services Administrators*(Group Insurer)*
Tulsa, OK

McKinney, Stringer, Webster*(Legal Firm)*
Oklahoma City, OK

Liberty National Bank & Trust Co.*(Major Banking Relationship)*
P.O. Box 25848,
Oklahoma City, OK 73125-0848
Tel.: 800-395-2662

Liberty National Bank & Trust Co.*(Pension Manager)*
P.O. Box 25848,
Oklahoma City, OK 73125-0848
Tel.: 800-395-2662

Division:

Ames Division **(1)**
Drawer A
Gainesville, GA 30503
Tel.: 404-241-0528
S.I.C.: 3429

Subsidiaries:

Macklanburg-Duncan Co. of California, Inc. **(1)**
15257 Proctor Ave.
City of Industry, CA 91745
Tel.: 818-333-4578
Emp.: 50
Mfr. of Adhesives
S.I.C.: 2891

Ultra Industries, Inc. **(1)**
777 Monterey Pass Rd.
Monterey Park, CA 91754
Tel.: 213-260-7330
Mouldings & Trim
S.I.C.: 3442
Grant Palenske *(Gen. Mgr.)*

MACLEAN-FOGG CO.
1000 Allanson Rd.
Mundelein, IL 60060
Tel.: 708-566-0010 **DE**
Fax: 708-949-0285
Year Founded: 1925
Approx.Sls.: $115,000,000
Emp.: 1,000
Manufacture of Fasteners & Assemblies, Drive Train Components & Connectors for Wire & Cable
S.I.C.: 3089; 3452; 3462; 3643; 3644; 3714
Barry L. MacLean *(Chm., Pres., Chief Exec. & Chief Oper. Officer)*
Patrick M. O'Connor *(Chief Fin. Officer & V.P.)*
Emil Hlinsky *(V.P.-Engrng.)*
Dennis Keesey *(V.P.)*
David Trendler *(V.P. & Gen. Mgr.)*
Michael Brennolt *(Mgr.-Systems Information)*

Principal(s):
Barry L. MacLean

No. of Mfg. Plants/Facilities: 10
No. of U.S. Offices: 11
No. of Foreign Offices: 2

Computer Systems/Hardware:
IBM System 41 & 43, Hewlett Packard & Xerox P.C.

Outside Service Firm(s):

Coopers & Lybrand*(Auditors)*
203 N. LaSalle St.
Chicago, IL 60601
Tel.: 312-701-5500

Rollins Burdick Hunter*(Group Insurer)*
123 No. Wacker
Chicago, IL 60606
Tel.: 312-701-4000

Continental Bank N. A.*(International Bank Affiliate)*
231 S. LaSalle St.
Chicago, IL 60697
Tel.: 312-828-2345
Tel.: 800-426-5754
Telex: 312-828-1783

Continental Bank N. A.*(Investment Banker)*
231 S. LaSalle St.
Chicago, IL 60697
Tel.: 312-828-2345
Tel.: 800-426-5754
Telex: 312-828-1783

Hopkins & Sutter*(Legal Firm)*
Three First Natl. Plaza
Chicago, IL 60602
Tel.: 312-558-6600

McDermott, Will & Emery*(Legal Firm)*
227 W. Monroe St.
Chicago, IL 60606-5096
Tel.: 312-372-2000

Divisions:

Polymer Technologies **(1)**
369 N. Newcomb St.
Whitewater, WI 53190
Tel.: 414-473-7800
Fax: 414-473-7829
S.I.C.: 3842

Reliable Power Products **(1)**
11411 Addison St.
Franklin Park, IL 60131
Tel.: 708-455-0014
Fax: 708-455-0029
Mfr. Metal & Plastic Parts
S.I.C.: 3644
Walter Dockus *(Gen. Mgr.)*

Stamptech **(1)**
5600 Wilson Rd.
Richmond, IL 60071
Tel.: 815-678-4566
S.I.C.: 3452

Maclean-Fogg Co.—(Continued)

Subsidiaries:

MacLean Molded Products, Inc. **(1)**
410 Mercantile Court
Wheeling, IL 60090
Tel.: 708-541-1616
Fax: 708-541-5849
Approx.Sls.: $9,000,000
Emp.: 65
Fiscal Year-end: 12/31/90
Mfr. of Custom Molded Plastic Components; Compression, Transfer & Injection, Thermoset
S.I.C.: 3089
Michael Fallaw *(Gen. Mgr.)*
Bernadette Fallaw *(Office Mgr.)*

Metform, Inc. **(1)**
2551 Wacker Rd.
Savanna, IL 61074
Tel.: 815-273-2201
Fax: 815-273-7837
Mfr. Metal & Plastic Parts for Auto & Truck, Power & Telecommunications & Health Care Industries
S.I.C.: 3452

Reliable/Bethea Power Products Inc. **(1)**
3098 Highway 31, S.
Pelham, AL 35124
Tel.: 205-663-0765
Fax: 205-663-2406
Electrical Components
S.I.C.: 3644

MACNAMARA, KLEIN & SOLIN INC.
150 Fifth Ave.
New York, NY 10011
Tel.: 212-206-8484
Fax: 212-463-7405
Year Founded: 1981
Approx.Billings: $61,500,000
Emp.: 38
Fiscal Year-end: 12/31/91
Advertising Agency
S.I.C.: 7311
Donald M. Klein *(Chm. Bd. & Creative Dir.)*
Frank W. MacNamara *(Vice Chm., Dir., Media & Communications)*
Darrol B. Solin *(Pres. & Chief Exec. Officer)*
Mary-Ann Lambert *(Sr. V.P.)*
John Scott *(Sr. V.P.)*
Tom Arnold *(V.P.)*

Computer Systems/Hardware:
Apple

Outside Service Firm(s):

Fred Atkins*(Auditors)*
New York, NY

Travelers Insurance Co.*(Group Insurer)*
80 John St.
New York, NY 10038
Tel.: 212-574-2536
Fax: 212-574-2545

U.S. Trust Co.*(Investment Banker)*
114 W. 47th St.
New York, NY 10036
Tel.: 212-852-1946

Schoeman, Marsh, Updike*(Legal Firm)*
New York, NY

Citibank N.A.*(Major Banking Relationship)*
Corporate Trust Services, 399 Park Ave.
New York, NY 10043
Tel.: 212-559-1605

MACNAUGHTON EINSON GRAPHICS
20-10 Maple Ave.
Fair Lawn, NJ 07410
Tel.: 201-423-1900
Fax: 201-423-3823
Emp.: 350
Commercial Lithographic Printing
S.I.C.: 2752
Albert Merson *(Chm. Bd.)*
Robert C. Quain *(Pres.)*

Outside Service Firm(s):

Abraham Soloman & Company*(Auditors)*
New York, NY

Rosen & Reade*(Legal Firm)*
666 5th Ave.
New York, NY 10019
Tel.: 212-581-1100

Chemical Bank*(Major Banking Relationship)*
Hawthorne, NJ

Division:

Command Web Offset Co. **(1)**
100 Castle R.
Secaucus, NJ 07094
Tel.: 201-863-8100
Offset Printing
S.I.C.: 2752
Andrew Merson *(Pres.)*

MACRISTY INDUSTRIES, INC.
206 Newington Ave.
New Britain, CT 06051
Tel.: 203-225-4637 **CT**
Fax: 203-229-4328
Approx.Sls.: $20,000,000
Emp.: 350
Tube Fabricating; Nickel Foil; Plastic Plumbing Fixture Fittings Assembly; Room & Wall Heaters; Real Estate Agent
S.I.C.: 3498; 3497; 3432; 3433; 6531; 4226
J. Bruce Barlow *(Pres.)*
Ellen Macristy *(V.P.)*
Carol Ann Barlow *(Sec. & Treas.)*

Outside Service Firm(s):

Weinstein, Schwartz & Pinkus*(Auditors)*
Bloomfield, CT

Eisenberg, Anderson, Michalik & Lynch*(Legal Firm)*
New Britain, CT

United Bank*(Major Banking Relationship)*
New Britain, CT

MACRO COMPUTER PRODUCTS INC.
2523 Product Court
Rochester Hills, MI 48309
Tel.: 313-853-5353
Tel.: 800-447-3823 **MI**
Fax: 313-853-2484
Year Founded: 1981
Sales Range: $10-19 Million
Emp.: 71
Computer Sales & Leasing; Software Publishing & Sales
S.I.C.: 5045; 7372; 7377
David Shellenbarger *(Chm. Bd. & Pres.)*
Terry Cornwell *(V.P.)*
James Western *(V.P.)*
Bruce Ferguson *(Treas.)*
Garth Gilboe *(Dir.-Leasing)*
Principal(s):
David Shellenbarger
James Western
Terry Cornwell
William Binder

No. of Mfg. Plants/Facilities: 2
No. of U.S. Offices: 12

Computer Systems/Hardware:
Unisys A-4, V340, IBM AS/400

Outside Service Firm(s):

Deloitte & Touche*(Auditors)*
200 Renaissance Center, 16th Fl.
Detroit, MI 48243
Tel.: 313-396-3000
Fax: 313-259-8087

Travelers Insurance Co.*(Commercial Insurance Carrier)*
1 Tower Square
Hartford, CT 06183-2492
Tel.: 203-277-4542
Fax: 203-277-5038

National Bank of Detroit*(Major Banking Relationship)*
611 Woodward Ave.
Detroit, MI 48226

Macrodyne Industries, Inc.
(Name Changed to Phoenix International, Inc.)

MACROMEDIA INC.
150 River Street
Hackensack, NJ 07601
Tel.: 201-646-4000 **NJ**
Fax: 201-646-4310
Year Founded: 1921
Approx.Sls.: $148,492,000
Emp.: 1,596
Fiscal Year-end: 12/28/91
Import
Owns & Operates Newspapers & Television Stations
S.I.C.: 2711; 4833
Malcolm A. Borg *(Chm. Bd. & Pres.)*
Sandra A. Borg *(Vice Chm. & Asst. Sec.)*
Charles W. Gibney *(Sr. V.P. & Chief Fin. Officer)*
Charles A. Agemian *(Treas.)*
Melissa Ludlum *(Sec.)*

Outside Service Firm(s):

Arthur Andersen & Co.*(Auditors)*
101 Eisenhower Pkwy.
Roseland, NJ 07068
Tel.: 201-403-6100

Liberty Mutual*(Commercial Insurance Carrier)*
175 Berkeley St.
Boston, MA

Ballard, Spahr, Andrews & Ingersoll*(Legal Firm)*
1735 Market St., 51st Fl.
Philadelphia, PA 19103-7599
Tel.: 215-665-8500

First Fidelity Bank, N.A.*(Major Banking Relationship)*
Paramus, NJ

United Jersey Bank*(Major Banking Relationship)*
Hackensack, NJ

Subsidiaries:

Bergen Record Corp. **(1)**
150 River St.
Hackensack, NJ 07601
Tel.: 201-646-4000

Gateway Communications **(1)**
150 River St.
Hackensack, NJ 07601
Tel.: 201-646-4000
Earnings: $1,001,000
Fiscal Year-end: 12/28/91

Gremac Inc. **(1)**
150 River St.
Hackensack, NJ 07601
Tel.: 201-646-4000

Macromedia Leasing **(1)**
150 River St.
Hackensack, NJ 07601
Tel.: 201-646-4000

Macromedia Publishing Inc. **(1)**
150 River St.
Hackensack, NJ 07601
Tel.: 201-646-4000

Magna Media Advertising **(1)**
150 River St.
Hackensack, NJ 07601
Tel.: 201-646-4000

MACTAVISH MACHINE MANUFACTURING COMPANY
9001 Hermitage Rd.
Richmond, VA 23228
Tel.: 804-264-6109 **VA**
Fax: 804-262-4118
Year Founded: 1985
Approx.Sls.: $12,000,000
Emp.: 42

Export
Mfr. of Tobacco Products Machinery
S.I.C.: 3559
Sam Levy *(Chief Exec. Officer)*
Ray Amato *(Controller)*

Outside Service Firm(s):

Ernst & Young*(Auditors)*
One James Center, 901 E. Cary St.,Ste. 1000
Richmond, VA 23219
Tel.: 804-780-0010

Sovran Bank*(Major Banking Relationship)*
Sovran Center, 1111 E. Main St.
Richmond, VA 23219
Tel.: 804-788-2000

R. H. MACY & CO., INC.
151 W. 34th St.
New York, NY 10001
Tel.: 212-695-4400 **NY**
Fax: 212-629-6814
Assets: $4,797,699,000
Earnings: ($150,000,000)
Liabilities: $5,547,950,000
Net Worth: $750,251,000
Approx.Sls.: $6,762,000,000
Emp.: 76,000
Fiscal Year-end: 8/ 3/91
Operates 147 Dept. Stores in 18 States & 2 Shopping Centers, 105 Specialty Stores
S.I.C.: 5311
Myron E. Ullman III *(Co-Chm. & Co-Chief Exec. Officer)*
Mark S. Handler *(Co-Chm. & Co-Chief Exec. Officer)*
Howard Adler *(Sr. V.P.-Sls. Promo. & Mktg.)*
S. Lester Block *(Sr. V.P.-Govt. Rels. & Labor Counsel)*
A. David Brown *(Sr. V.P.-Human Resources)*
Herbert M. Hellman *(Sr. V.P. & Gen. Counsel)*
Nat Kurtz *(Sr. V.P.-Taxes)*
Gertrude G. Michelson *(Sr. V.P.-External Affairs)*
Edward Morenberg *(Sr. V.P.-Store Plng., Constr. & Admin.)*
Michael W. Steman *(Sr. V.P.-Store Plng.)*
Richard A. Wall *(Sr. V.P.-Special Projects)*
Diane P. Baker *(Sr. V.P.-Fin. & Chief Fin. & Info. Officer)*
Jay Carothers *(Sr. V.P.-Buying)*
Diane P. Barcer *(Sr. V.P.-Fin.)*
Donald Eugene *(Sr. V.P. & Sec.)*
James O. York *(Pres. & Chief Exec. Officer-R H Macy Properties)*
Harvey Samuelson *(V.P.-Real Estate)*
Barbara Levy *(Grp V.P.-Stores)*
Irving Haber *(V.P.-Legal)*
James D. Wiese *(V.P.-Legal)*
Joy Levien *(V.P.-Legal)*
David C. Stopsky *(V.P.-Legal)*
Kennard N. Hirsch *(V.P.-Taxes)*
Philipp J. Beisel *(V.P.-Information)*
Elias S. Gottlieb *(V.P.-Research)*
Lawrence Soifer *(V.P.-Legal)*
Art Burac *(V.P.-Real Estate)*
Bradley Chafetz *(Councillor-Corp. Fin.)*

Outside Service Firm(s):

Deloitte & Touche*(Auditors)*
1 World Trade Center
New York, NY 10048
Tel.: 212-669-5000

Division:

Bullock's **(1)**
800 S. Hope St.
Los Angeles, CA 90017
Tel.: 213-612-5000
Tel.: 415-954-6000 (Adv.)
Fax: 213-612-5160
Approx.Sls.: $751,800,000
Fiscal Year-end: 12/31/90
Department Store
S.I.C.: 5311
Myron E. Ullman III *(Co-Chm. Bd. & Co-Chief Exec. Officer)*
Mark S. Handler *(Co-Chm. Bd. & Co-Chief Exec. Officer)*
Jeffrey Rusinow *(Sr. V.P.-Gen. Mdsg. Mgr.)*
Greg Hribar *(Sr. V.P.-Adv.)*
Duane Johnson *(Sr. V.P.-Personnel)*
William Sumner *(V.P.-Mngmt. Info. Systems)*

Subsidiaries:

Bay Fair Shopping Ctr. **(1)**
15555 E. 14th St.
San Leandro, CA 94578
Tel.: 510-353-3333 (100%)
S.I.C.: 6512

Brunswick Square **(1)**
Rte. 18
East Brunswick, NJ 08816
Tel.: 908-238-1400 (50%)
S.I.C.: 6512

Columbia Mall **(1)**
3604 Memorial Dr.
Decatur, GA 30032
Tel.: 404-284-7612 (100%)
S.I.C.: 6512

The Garden State Plaza Corp. **(1)**
Rte. 4 & State Hwy. No. 17
Paramus, NJ 07652
Tel.: 201-843-3690 (100%)
S.I.C.: 6512

Kings Plaza Shopping Ctr. & Marina **(1)**
5400 Ave. U
Brooklyn, NY 11234
Tel.: 212-253-3100 (50%)
S.I.C.: 6512

Macy Credit Corp. **(1)**
61 Myrtle St.
Cranford, NJ 07016
Tel.: 908-272-0444 (100%)
Business Credit Institution
S.I.C.: 6153
Jack Hanson *(Pres.)*

I. Magnin & Co. **(1)**
135 Stockton St.
San Francisco, CA 94108
Tel.: 415-362-2100 (100%)
Fax: 415-543-6985
Approx.Sls.: $317,100,000
Emp.: 3,800
Specialty Dept. Store
S.I.C.: 5311
Joseph Cicio *(Chm. Bd. & Chief Exec. Officer)*
Paul Fitzpatrick *(Sr. V.P.)*
Judie Rice *(Sr. V.P. & Store Mgr.)*
A. Sullivan *(Sr. V.P.-Fin.)*
Wilmer Weiss *(Sr. V.P.-Adv.)*
Pauline Roothmann *(V.P.-Personnel)*

Mission Shopping Ctr. **(1)**
Roe Blvd. & Johnson Dr.
Mission, KS 66222
Tel.: 913-262-3000 (100%)
S.I.C.: 6512

New Park Mall **(1)**
200 New Park Mall
Newark, CA 94560
Tel.: 510-794-5522 (50%)
S.I.C.: 6512

Quaker Bridge Mall **(1)**
400 Quaker Bridge Mall
Lawrenceville, NJ 08648
Tel.: 609-799-8000 (50%)
S.I.C.: 6512

Sunnyvale Towncenter **(1)**
200 W. Washington Ave.
Sunnyvale, CA 94086
Tel.: 408-245-3270 (50%)
S.I.C.: 6512

South Shore Mall **(1)**
1653B Sunrise Hwy.
Bay Shore, NY 11706
Tel.: 516-665-8600 (100%)
S.I.C.: 6512

Valley Fair Shopping Ctr. **(1)**
2801 Stevens Creek Rd.
San Jose, CA 95128
Tel.: 408-248-3333 (100%)
S.I.C.: 6512

THE MAD BUTCHER, INC.
2001 W. Fifth
Pine Bluff, AR 71613
Mailing Address:
P.O. Box 1020
Pine Bluff, AR 71613
Tel.: 501-535-6356 **AR**
Fax: 501-535-4039
Year Founded: 1955
Approx.Sls.: $56,000,000
Emp.: 550
Fiscal Year-end: 7/28/90
Wholesale & Retail Groceries, Meats, Produce
S.I.C.: 5421; 5411
George A. Lea, Jr. *(Chm. Bd., Pres. & Chief Exec. Officer)*
Clarence Evans *(Chief Oper. Officer & Exec. V.P.-Personal Training & Devel.)*
Ron Cantrell *(Chief Fin. Officer, Exec. V.P. & Controller)*
Roger Burks *(Sr. V.P.-Mdsg. & Pur.)*
Gerald Goshien *(V.P.-Meat Mktg.)*
Ann Garrett *(Sec.)*
Chris Bradley *(Mgr.-Data Processing)*

Outside Service Firm(s):

Baird, Kurtz & Dobson*(Auditors)*
Little Rock, AR

Ramsay, Cox, Lile, Bridgforth, Gilbert, Harrelson & Starling*(Legal Firm)*
Pine Bluff, AR

Simmons First National Bank of Pine Bluff*(Major Banking Relationship)*
Pine Bluff, AR

MADER CONSTRUCTION GROUP INC.
970 Bullis Rd.
Elma, NY 14059
Mailing Address:
P.O. Box 420,
Elma, NY 14059-0420
Tel.: 716-655-3400 **NY**
Fax: 716-655-4427
Year Founded: 1961
Approx.Sls.: $52,700,000
Emp.: 500
Fiscal Year-end: 12/31/91
Commercial Interior Construction
S.I.C.: 1742
James Biddle, Sr. *(Pres. & Chief Exec. Officer)*
Robert Giannelli *(Dir.-Pur.)*
Harold Keller *(Dir.-Engrng. Opers.)*
William Milliman *(Dir.-Fin.)*

Outside Service Firm(s):

KPMG Peat Marwick*(Auditors)*
700 Empire Tower
Buffalo, NY 14202-3786
Tel.: 716-854-1830
Fax: 716-856-8063

Duke, Holzman, Yaeger & Radlin*(Legal Firm)*
Buffalo, NY

Fleet Bank*(Major Banking Relationship)*
Deer Park, NY 14202

MADIGAN BROTHERS, INC.
7440 W. Central Ave.
River Forest, IL 60305
Tel.: 708-771-7400 **IL**
Fax: 708-771-2647
Approx.Sls.: $75,000,000
Emp.: 750
Family Clothing Stores
S.I.C.: 5651
Joseph D. Madigan, Jr. *(Chm. Bd.)*
Henry H. Hubbard, III *(Pres. & Chief Exec. Officer)*
Julie Weldon *(V.P.)*
Carol M. Madigan *(Sec.)*

Outside Service Firm(s):

Selden Fox & Associates*(Auditors)*
Oak Brook, IL

Harris Trust & Savings Bank*(Major Banking Relationship)*
111 W. Monroe St.
Chicago, IL 60690
Tel.: 312-461-2265
Tel.: 800-858-0840

MADISON DAIRY PRODUCE COMPANY
1002 E. Washington Ave.
Madison, WI 53703
Mailing Address:
P.O. Box 389,
Madison, WI 53701
Tel.: 608-256-5561
Fax: 608-256-5561
Year Founded: 1906
Approx.Sls.: $105,000,000
Emp.: 35
Dairy Products; Butter, Margarine
S.I.C.: 2021; 2079
Frederick C. Steinhauer *(Chm. Bd. & Pres.)*
Chuck Steinhauer *(Exec. V.P.)*
Gary Steinhauer *(Sec. & Treas.)*

Outside Service Firm(s):

Suby, Von Haden & Associates*(Auditors)*
Madison, WI

Murphy & Desmond*(Legal Firm)*
Madison, WI

Valley National Bank*(Major Banking Relationship)*
Middleton, WI

MADISON ELECTRIC CO.
6000 Woodward Ave.
Detroit, MI 48202
Tel.: 313-875-1560 **MI**
Fax: 313-875-3331
Year Founded: 1914
Approx.Sls.: $48,500,000
Emp.: 212
Fiscal Year-end: 12/31/91
Wholesale Electrical Supplies
S.I.C.: 5063
Joseph Schnider *(Pres.)*
Benjamin Rosenthal *(Sec. & Treas.)*
Scott Leemastes *(V.P.)*
Richard Soneklar *(V.P.)*

No. of U.S. Offices: 10

Computer Systems/Hardware:
IBM 4341

Outside Service Firm(s):

Rosenbloom, Rosenbloom & Lameti*(Auditors)*
Southfield, MI

Comerica Bank*(Major Banking Relationship)*
211 W. Fort St.
Detroit, MI 48226
Tel.: 313-222-3300

Prudential-Bache*(Pension Manager)*
Boston, MA

MADISON GRAHAM COLORGRAPHICS, INC.
150 N. Myers St.
Los Angeles, CA 90033
Tel.: 213-261-7171
Fax: 213-267-4302
Year Founded: 1953
Approx.Sls.: $50,000,000
Emp.: 300
Offset Commercial Printing; Graphic Arts & Related Design
S.I.C.: 2752; 7336
Harold N. Madison *(Chm. Bd.)*
Chris Madison *(Pres.)*
Judy Updegraff *(V.P. & Chief Fin. Officer)*
Arthur Bell *(V.P. & Sec.)*

Outside Service Firm(s):

Wells Fargo Bank*(Major Banking Relationship)*
333 S. Grand
Los Angeles, CA 90071
Tel.: 213-253-6836

MADISON GROCERY CO., INC.
U.S. Hwy. 25 S.
Richmond, KY 40475
Tel.: 606-623-2416 **KY**
Approx.Sls.: $23,000,000
Emp.: 55
Wholesale Distributor of General Line of Groceries
S.I.C.: 5141; 5142; 5072
Maurice W. Baker *(Pres. & Chief Exec. Officer)*
J.L. Lewis *(V.P.)*
Teresa Hager *(Treas.)*
Marty Baker *(Sec.)*

Outside Service Firm(s):

Citizens Fidelity Bank & Trust Co.*(Major Banking Relationship)*
Richmond, KY

MAECORP INC.
155 N. Wacker Dr., Ste. 400
Chicago, IL 60606
Tel.: 312-372-3300 **DE**
Fax: 312-853-4050
Year Founded: 1986
Approx.Sls.: $19,000,000
Emp.: 151
Hazardous Waste Management; Asbestos Management Services
S.I.C.: 4953
G. Vern Diedrick *(Chm. Bd., Chief Exec. Officer, & Pres.)*
Jerry Cioci *(Chief Fin. Officer & Corp. Sec.)*
Cathy Zator *(Controller)*
Terry Fish *(Dir.-Pur.)*
Steven Przyhylowski *(Dir.-Data Processing)*
Donna M. Manak *(Mgr.-Human Resources)*

No. of Mfg. Plants/Facilities: 5

Outside Service Firm(s):

Grant Thornton*(Auditors)*
700 One Prudential Plaza, 130 East Randolph St.
Chicago, IL 60601
Tel.: 312-856-0200
Fax: 312-565-4719

Boulevard Bank*(Major Banking Relationship)*
410 N. Michigan Ave.
Chicago, IL 60611
Tel.: 312-836-6500

MAESCHER INDUSTRIES, INC.
2106 Florence Ave.
Cincinnati, OH 45206
Mailing Address:
P.O. Box 6098
Cincinnati, OH 45206
Tel.: 513-751-3200 **OH**

Maescher Industries, Inc.—(Continued)

Fax: 513-751-0253
Year Founded: 1893
Assets: $16,365,000
Liabilities: $12,550,000
Net Worth: $3,815,000
Sales Range: $60-79 Million
Emp.: 160
Fiscal Year-end: 12/31/91
General Contractor; Construction Management
S.I.C.: 1541; 1542; 1629; 1771; 1794
E. Grant Hesser *(Chm. Bd.)*
Harold M. Allen *(Vice Chm.)*
Grant V. Hesser *(Pres. & Chief Exec. Officer)*
D.W. Barker *(Treas. & Chief Fin. Officer)*
Michael J. Cook *(Mgr.-Data Processing)*

No. of U.S. Offices: 4

Computer Systems/Hardware:
IBM System AS400

Outside Service Firm(s):

Schiff Kreidler-Shell, Inc.*(Commercial Insurance Carrier)*
Cincinnatti, OH

Frost & Jacobs*(Legal Firm)*
2500 Central Trust Ctr.
Cincinnati, OH 45202
Tel.: 513-651-6800

Fifth Third Bank*(Major Banking Relationship)*
Corporate Trust Services, 38 Fountain Square Plaza
Cincinnati, OH 45263

Subsidiaries:

Chas. V. Maescher & Co., Inc. **(1)**
2106 Florence Ave.
Cincinnati, OH 45206
Tel.: 513-751-3200
Emp.: 40
Roger M. Baldwin *(Pres.)*
Thomas E. Toman *(V.P.)*

Maescher Construction Co. **(1)**
500 Reading Rd.
Cincinnati, OH 45206
Tel.: 513-651-5770
Robert G. Compton *(Pres.)*

Matrix Building Co., Inc. **(1)**
1650 Russell St.
Covington, KY 41011
Tel.: 606-261-9551
Emp.: 40
R. Stephen Steltenkamp *(Pres.)*
David E. Ollerich *(V.P.)*

THE MAGEE CARPET COMPANY
(Affil. of Magee Industrial Enterprises, Inc.)
480 W. Fifth
Bloomsburg, PA 17815
Tel.: 717-784-4100
Fax: 717-784-4100 ext. 318
Approx.Sls.: $80,000,000
Emp.: 750
Fiscal Year-end: 12/31/91
Automobile Carpet
S.I.C.: 2273
James A. Magee *(Pres.)*
Mike Katerman *(V.P.)*
Jeffrey Lewis *(V.P.-Automotive Div.)*
Kenneth Nadel *(V.P.-Fin.)*
Steven Diacont *(Dir.-Personnel)*

MAGHIELSE TOOL CORPORATION
731 Broadway, N.W.
Grand Rapids, MI 49504
Mailing Address:
P.O. Box 2387
Grand Rapids, MI 49504
Tel.: 616-459-8285
Fax: 616-459-8292
Year Founded: 1977
Approx.Sls.: $12,000,000
Emp.: 140
Mfr. of Metal Stamping Dies, Jigs & Fixtures
S.I.C.: 3544
Craig Maghielse *(Chm. Bd., Pres. & Chief Exec. Officer)*
Ed Baker *(V.P.-Fin. & Admin.)*
E. Metzler *(V.P.-Sls.)*
Jim Williams *(Pur. Agent)*

Outside Service Firm(s):

BDO Seidman*(Auditors)*
99 Monroe Ave. NW, Ste. 800
Grand Rapids, MI 49503
Tel.: 616-774-7000
Fax: 616-451-2096

Varnum, Riddering, Schmidt & Howlett*(Legal Firm)*
666 Old Kent Bldg.
Grand Rapids, MI 49502
Tel.: 616-459-4186
Fax: 616-459-8468

Old Kent Bank*(Major Banking Relationship)*
Grand Rapids, MI

MAGIC PAN INTERNATIONAL INC.
(Sub. of Bay Bottlers Ltd., A Holding Co.)
818 Burlway Rd.
Burlingame, CA 94010
Tel.: 415-340-9800 **CA**
Fax: 415-340-8698
Year Founded: 1976
Approx.Sls.: $60,000,000
Emp.: 2,000
Chain of 65 Restaurants
S.I.C.: 5812
Charles Patel Sr. *(Chm. Bd.)*
Charles Patel, Jr. *(Vice Chm. & Chief Exec. Officer)*
Michael Patel *(Pres.)*
Eleanor Falcon *(Chief Fin. Officer & V.P.-Fin.)*

Outside Service Firm(s):

Security Pacific National Bank*(Major Banking Relationship)*
San Francisco, CA

MAGIC VALLEY FOODS, INC.
Hwy. 24 & Hwy. 25
Rupert, ID 83350
Mailing Address:
P.O. Box 475
Ruport, ID 83350
Tel.: 208-436-3126
Fax: 208-436-4542
Year Founded: 1966
Approx.Sls.: $10,000,000
Emp.: 200
Export
Dried & Dehydrated Potato Products; Frozen Potatoes; Hash Browns
S.I.C.: 2034; 0134; 2037
Roger Jones *(Pres.)*
William F. Schow *(V.P.)*
Dorothy Jones *(Sec.)*

Outside Service Firm(s):

Reincke & Mayes*(Auditors)*
Ruport, ID

Goodman & Duff*(Legal Firm)*
Bosie, ID

Key Bank*(Major Banking Relationship)*
Bosie, ID

MAGICSILK, INC.
15150 Stateline Dr.
Charlotte, NC 28273
Tel.: 704-588-4499
Fax: 704-588-8944
Year Founded: 1975
Approx.Sls.: $25,000,000
Emp.: 60
Fiscal Year-end: 12/30/90
Import
Mfr., Importer & Distributor of Magicsilk & Karisma Flowers; Botanix Permanent Plants, Christmas Trees, Ornaments, Garlands, Wreaths, Planters & Novelties
S.I.C.: 3999; 5199
Pete Condict *(Pres.)*

Computer Systems/Hardware:
Wang & Macintoch

Outside Service Firm(s):

Bank of New York*(Major Banking Relationship)*
90 Washington St.
New York, NY 10015

MAGLA PRODUCTS
700 Shunpike Rd.
Chatham, NJ 07928-2199
Tel.: 201-377-0500
Fax: 201-377-6900
Emp.: 1000
Magla Ironing Board Covers, Pads, Sponges, Scrubbers, Laundry Access., Easy Wipes, Rubber Gloves, Fabric Softener Sheets, Table Top Ironing Boards, Full-Size Ironing Tables, Wiping Cloths
S.I.C.: 2392; 3089; 3069; 3431
Herbert Glatt *(Pres.)*
Jordan Glatt *(V.P.)*
Mitchell S. Glatt *(V.P.)*

Outside Service Firm(s):

J.H. Cohn & Company*(Auditors)*
75 Eisenhower Pkwy.
Roseland, NJ 07068-1697
Tel.: 201-228-3500

MAGLINE, INC.
503 S. Mercer St.
Pinconning, MI 48650
Tel.: 517-879-2411
Tel.: 800-624-5463 **MI**
Fax: 517-879-5399
Approx.Sls.: $10,000,000
Emp.: 300
Mfr. Dockboards, Ramps, 2 & 4-Wheel Trucks, Light Metal Fabrications
S.I.C.: 3448; 3715
D. Brian Law *(Pres.)*
Mike Kirby *(V.P.-Mktg.)*
Harry Davidson *(Mgr.-Sls. North America)*
Amy Henderson *(Mktg. Coord.)*

Computer Systems/Hardware:
NCR 8430

Outside Service Firm(s):

Schilling, Werner & Brilinsky*(Auditors)*
Bay City, MI

Law, Weathers & Richardson*(Legal Firm)*
Grand Rapids, MI

MAGNECO/METREL, INC.
223 Interstate Rd.
Addison, IL 60101
Tel.: 708-543-6660
Fax: 708-543-1479
Approx.Sls.: $31,000,000
Emp.: 230
Refactory Clay Products; Ceramics For The Steel Industry
S.I.C.: 3297; 3299
Charles W. Connors *(Chief Exec. Officer & Sec.)*
Chester L. Connors *(Pres. & Treas.)*

Outside Service Firm(s):

Pierce, Riesbeck & Associates*(Auditors)*
Burr Ridge, IL

LaSalle National Bank*(Major Banking Relationship)*
135 S. La Salle St.
Chicago, IL 60690

Plants:

Magneco, Inc. **(1)**
206 Factory Rd.
Addison, IL 60101
Tel.: 708-543-6660
Ceramics For The Steel Industry
S.I.C.: 3297
Chester L. Connors *(Pres.)*

Metrel, Inc. **(1)**
P.O. Box 176
Negley, OH 44441
Tel.: 216-426-9468
Refractory Clay Products
S.I.C.: 3299
Chester L. Connors *(Pres.)*

MAGNETIC ANALYSIS CORP.
535 S. 4th Ave.
Mount Vernon, NY 10550
Tel.: 914-699-9450
Fax: 914-699-9837
Year Founded: 1928
Approx.Sls.: $10,000,000
Emp.: 150
Export
Mfr. of Electro-Magnetic Testing Equipment & Ultrasonic Instrumentation
S.I.C.: 3825; 3829
Margaret Z. Gould *(Chm. Bd.)*
William S. Gould, III *(Pres.)*
Paul Bebick *(V.P.-Engrng.)*
F.E. Bryant *(V.P.-Field Services)*
Donald Bugden *(V.P.-Mktg.)*
Ed Ryan *(Controller)*
Paul Levine *(Treas.)*
Lucia Heubel *(Dir.-Pur.)*
Joseph Demaio *(Mgr.-Adv.)*

Outside Service Firm(s):

KPMG Peat Marwick*(Auditors)*
Mount Vernon, NY

Chemical Bank*(Major Banking Relationship)*
Mount Vernon, NY

MAGNETIC DATA, INC.
6754 Shady Oak Rd.
Eden Prairie, MN 55344
Tel.: 612-941-0453 **MN**
Fax: 612-941-0951
Year Founded: 1988
Approx.Sls.: $15,000,000
Emp.: 160
Mfr. of Process Control Instruments
S.I.C.: 3823
James P. Legus *(Chm. Bd. & Chief Exec. Officer)*
Ronald Schauer *(Pres.)*
Lee B. Lewis *(V.P.)*
Rodney E. Nelson *(V.P.-Mktg. & Sls.)*
Howard D. Oney *(V.P.-Mfg.)*
William L. Wilder *(V.P.-Engrng.)*
Rich Hegstrand *(Controller)*

Outside Service Firm(s):

Coopers & Lybrand*(Auditors)*
1000 TCF Bldg.
Minneapolis, MN 55402
Tel.: 612-293-2929
Fax: 612-370-9395

Faegre & Benson*(Legal Firm)*
2200 Norwest Ctr., 90 S. 7th St.
Minneapolis, MN 55402-3901
Tel.: 612-336-3000

The First Bank of Minneapolis*(Major Banking Relationship)*
P.O. Box A 799
Minneapolis, MN 55480
Tel.: 612-370-4606

Division:

Sun Maintenance Work Station Div. **(1)**
6754 Shady Oak Rd.
Eden Prairie, MN 55344
Tel.: 612-941-0453
Rodney E. Nelson *(V.P.)*

MAGNETIC TECHNOLOGIES CORPORATION
770 Linden Ave.
Rochester, NY 14625
Tel.: 716-385-8711 **DE**
Assets: $6,052,459
Earnings: $171,593
Liabilities: $4,124,663
Net Worth: $1,927,796
Approx.Sls.: $14,675,000
Emp.: 70
Fiscal Year-end: 7/31/92
Develop, Manufacture & Assemble Precision Magnetic, Electronic & Mechanical Devices Comprise Subassemblies of Copiers, Laser Printers & Page Printers; Engineering Design Service
S.I.C.: 3577; 3579; 8711
Isadore Diamond *(Chm. Bd., Treas. & Chief Fin. & Chief Acctg. Officer)*
Gordon H. McNeil *(Pres. & Chief Exec. Officer)*
Sal Latone *(Exec. V.P.)*
Ihor Jejna *(V.P.-Quality Assurance)*
Nancy Williams *(V.P.-Mfg. & Matls.)*

MAGNETROL INTERNATIONAL
5300 Belmont Rd.
Downers Grove, IL 60515
Tel.: 708-969-4000
Tel.: 800-MAG-TROL
Fax: 708-969-9489
Year Founded: 1932
Approx.Sls.: $25,000,000
Emp.: 200
Fiscal Year-end: 12/31/90
Level & Flow Instrumentation
S.I.C.: 3823
Victor Shoaff *(Dir.-Sls. & Mktg.)*

MAGNOLIA HI-FI, INC.
3701 7th Ave., S.
Seattle, WA 98134
Tel.: 206-623-7872
Fax: 206-621-9277
Year Founded: 1970
Approx.Sls.: $80,000,000
Emp.: 300
Fiscal Year-end: 12/31/89
Retail Stereophonic Video Equipment & Car Steros
S.I.C.: 5731
Leonard M. Tweten *(Chm. Bd.)*
James Tweten *(Pres.)*
Tom Conrad *(V.P.-Opers.)*
Dave Kaplan *(V.P.-Pur.)*
Ginger Shorey *(Sec. & Treas.)*
Kurt Frost *(Controller)*
Stephen John *(Mgr.-Gen. Sls.)*

Principal(s):
Leonard M. Tweten
James Tweten
Tweten Family

Outside Service Firm(s):

KPMG Peat Marwick*(Auditors)*
3100 Two Union Square, 601 Union St., Ste. 3100
Seattle, WA 98101
Tel.: 206-292-1500

MAGUIRE GROUP INC.
225 Foxborough Blvd.
Foxboro, MA 02035
Tel.: 508-543-1700 **DE**
Fax: 508-543-5157
Year Founded: 1938
Approx.Sls.: $35,000,000
Emp.: 425
Engineering, Architectural & Planning Services, Hazardous Waste, Resource Recovery, Recycling, Construction Engineering Services, Program Management
S.I.C.: 6531; 8712
Richard J. Repeta *(Pres.)*
Raymond T. Bush *(Sr. V.P. & Chief Fin. Officer)*
Victor V. Calabretta *(Sr. V.P. & Northeast Opers. Mgr.)*
James B. Fritz *(Sr. V.P. & Metro Reg. Opers. Mgr.)*
Mary G. Rendini *(Sr. V.P. & Human Resources Dir.)*
William H. Yost *(Treas. & Controller)*
John T. Coffey, Jr. *(Sec. & Gen. Counsel)*
Alan Dyer *(Mgr.-Data Processing)*
Sherrill Papallia *(Mgr.-Employee Benefits, Training & Devel.)*

Principal(s):
Richard J. Repeta
Raymond T. Bush
Mary G. Rendini

No. of Mfg. Plants/Facilities: 8
No. of U.S. Offices: 8

Computer Systems/Hardware:
IBM; Hewlett Packard

Outside Service Firm(s):

KPMG Peat Marwick*(Auditors)*
600 Fleet Center
Providence, RI 02903
Tel.: 401-421-6600

Provident Life & Accident Insurance Co.*(Group Insurer)*
P.O. Box 12015
Chattanooga, TN 37401
Tel.: 615-755-7088

Fleet National Bank*(Investment Banker)*
Corporate Trust Department, 125 Dupont Dr.
Providence, RI 02907
Tel.: 401-278-5400

Coffey & Martinelli*(Legal Firm)*
Providence, RI

Fleet National Bank*(Major Banking Relationship)*
125 Dupont Dr.
Providence, RI 02907-3178
Tel.: 401-278-5335

Fleet National Bank*(Pension Manager)*
125 Dupont Dr.
Providence, RI 02907-3178
Tel.: 401-278-5335

Subsidiary:

Maguire Group Architects, Inc. **(1)**
One Court St.
New Britain, CT 06051
Tel.: 203-224-9141
Emp.: 10
Architectural Services
S.I.C.: 8712
Peter Morrison *(Pres.)*

MAGUIRE OIL CO.
4000 Renaissance Tower, 1201 Elm St.
Dallas, TX 75270
Tel.: 214-741-5137 **TX**
Fax: 214-712-8005
Year Founded: 1969
Sales Range: $10-19 Million
Emp.: 34
Fiscal Year-end: 12/31/91
Oil Exploration & Development
S.I.C.: 1311; 1382; 1381
Employee Matching Gifts Program: Board of Directors Determines Total Company Matching Amount Each Year Which is Divided Proportionately by the Participating Employee's Contributions
Cary M. Maguire *(Pres.)*
C.T. Jackson *(V.P. & Chief Fin. Officer)*
W.T. Patterson *(V.P.)*
J.R. Way *(V.P.)*
V.P. Collier *(Asst. V.P.)*
Rick Lewis *(Controller)*
Myron A. Methvin *(Mgr.-Taxes)*
Kenoth H. Flournoy *(Mgr.-Prod. Engrng.)*
W.M. Frew *(Mgr.-Exploration)*
S.R. Cox *(Mgr.-Individual & Trust Acctg.)*
E.R. Denniston *(Mgr.-Lease Records)*
V.L. Snider *(Office Mgr.)*

Principal(s):
Cary M. Maguire

No. of U.S. Offices: 1

Outside Service Firm(s):

Arthur Andersen & Co.*(Auditors)*
901 Main St., Ste. 5600
Dallas, TX 75202
Tel.: 214-741-8300

Vial, Hamilton, Koch & Knox*(Legal Firm)*
Dallas, TX

NationsBank Texas*(Major Banking Relationship)*
P.O. Box 2964,
Dallas, TX 75221

MAGUIRE THOMAS PARTNERS
355 S. Grande Ave., Ste. 4500
Los Angeles, CA 90071
Tel.: 213-626-3300
Fax: 213-687-4753
Year Founded: 1965
Sales Range: $1 Billion +
Emp.: 180
Real Estate Investor, Developer, Syndicator
S.I.C.: 6531; 6552
Tom Allen *(Mng. Partner)*
Michael Croft *(Mng. Partner)*
Robert F. Maguire, III *(Mng. Partner)*
James A. Thomas *(Mng. Partner)*
Edward D. Fox, Jr. *(Sr. Partner)*
Richard I. Gilchrist *(Sr. Partner)*
Nelson C. Rising *(Sr. Partner)*
John Cope *(Partner)*
Kim K. Keller *(Partner)*

Principal(s):
Robert F. Maguire, III
James A. Thomas

Outside Service Firm(s):

Arthur Andersen & Co.*(Auditors)*
Costa Mesa, CA

MAHARAM FABRIC CORPORATION
45 Rasons Ct.
Hauppauge, NY 11788
Mailing Address:
P.O. Box 6900,
Hauppauge, NY 11788
Tel.: 516-582-3434
Fax: 516-582-1026
Fax: 516-582-3612
Year Founded: 1951
Approx.Sls.: $60,500,000
Emp.: 300
Wholesale Textile Converters
S.I.C.: 5131
Donald Maharam *(Pres.)*
Michael Belasky *(Exec. V.P.-Fin. & Personnel)*
Paul Wyckoff *(Exec. V.P.-Sls. & Mktg.)*

No. of U.S. Offices: 30

Outside Service Firm(s):

Richard Eisner*(Auditors)*
New York, NY

Herrick, Feinstein*(Legal Firm)*
2 Park Ave.
New York, NY 10016
Tel.: 212-684-1400

The Bank of New York*(Major Banking Relationship)*
One Wall Street
New York, NY 10286
Tel.: 212-635-6805
Fax: 212-635-3201

MAIDENFORM, INC.
90 Park Ave., 38th Fl.
New York, NY 10016
Tel.: 212-953-1400 **NY**
Fax: 212-983-5834
Year Founded: 1922
Approx.Sls.: $200,000,000
Emp.: 5,000
Mfr. Intimate Apparel
S.I.C.: 2342; 2341
Elizabeth J. Coleman *(Chm.)*
Robert A. Brawer *(Pres. & Chief Exec. Officer)*
David C. Masket *(Exec. V.P. & Chief Oper. Officer)*
Ira Glazer *(Sr. V.P.-Fin. & Treas.)*
Abraham P. Kanner *(Sr. V.P.-Corp. Affairs)*
Steven N. Masket *(Sr. V.P. & Gen. Counsel)*
James Mogan *(Sr. V.P.-Sls. & Mdsg.)*
Jerry Rodman *(Sr. V.P.-Mfg.)*
Marilyn Bane *(V.P.-Adv.)*
Irwin Bernstein *(V.P.-Plng. & Admin.)*
Ron Koeserich *(Asst. V.P. & Controller)*
Robert Romph *(Dir.-Training & Devel.)*
Rhonda Cohen *(Dir.-Art)*

Computer Systems/Hardware:
IBM 4341

Outside Service Firm(s):

Ernst & Young*(Auditors)*
787 Seventh Ave.
New York, NY 10019
Tel.: 212-773-1243

Aetna Life & Casualty*(Group Insurer)*
151 Farmington Avenue
Hartford, CT 06156
Tel.: 203-273-2128
Fax: 203-729-4295

Arnold & Porter*(Legal Firm)*
1200 New Hampshire Ave. NW
Washington, DC 20036
Tel.: 202-872-6700

Chase Manhattan Bank, N.A.*(Major Banking Relationship)*
G.P.O. Box 1990,
San Juan, PR 00936
Tel.: 809-753-3625

Citibank N.A.*(Major Banking Relationship)*
Corporate Trust Services, 399 Park Ave.
New York, NY 10043
Tel.: 212-559-1605

Irving Trust Co.*(Major Banking Relationship)*
New York, NY

Philadelphia National Bank*(Major Banking Relationship)*
P.O. Box 13834, Broad & Chestnut Streets
Philadelphia, PA 19101-7618
Tel.: 215-973-8327

Grantham, Mayo, Van Otterloo & Co.*(Pension Manager)*
40 Rowes Wharf, 4th Fl.
Boston, MA 02110
Tel.: 617-330-7500
Fax: 617-261-0438

Rothschild Asset Management*(Pension Manager)*
New York, NY

Subsidiary:

True Form Intimate Apparel **(1)**
16 E. 40th St.
New York, NY 10016
Tel.: 212-684-6641
Fax: 212-889-9109
Sales Range: $10-19 Million
Emp.: 500

Maidenform, Inc.—(Continued)

Foundation Garments
S.I.C.: 2342

MAIN BROTHERS OIL COMPANY, INC.
P.O. Box 11029
Albany, NY 12211
Tel.: 518-438-7856
Fax: 518-438-5991
Approx.Sls.: $35,000,000
Emp.: 102
Wholesale & Retail Petroleum Products; Wholesale Heating Equipment & Business Services; Special Trade Construction
S.I.C.: 5172; 5983; 1799
Richard Burke *(Pres.)*
Ronald Von Ronne *(V.P.)*
Carl Taub *(Controller)*

Outside Service Firm(s):

Alexander W. Cruden*(Auditors)*
Albany, NY

Matthew Mataraso*(Legal Firm)*
Albany, NY

Norstar Bank, N.A.*(Major Banking Relationship)*
Albany, NY

MAINE POTATO GROWERS, INC.
56 Parsons St.
Presque Isle, ME 04769
Mailing Address:
P.O. Box 271,
Presque Isle, ME 04769
Tel.: 207-764-3131 **ME**
Fax: 207-764-8450
Year Founded: 1932
Assets: $16,000,000
Liabilities: $10,000,000
Net Worth: $6,000,000
Approx.Sls.: $56,000,000
Emp.: 160
Fiscal Year-end: 6/30/90
Paper & Burlap Bags, Oats, Potatoes, Farm Machinery, Agricultural Chemicals, Building Supplies, Livestock Feed, Petroleum Supplies
S.I.C.: 2674; 0119; 0134; 2393; 5031; 5039; 5144; 5148; 5153; 5171; 5172; 5191
Gregory H. Smith *(Chm. Bd. & Pres.)*
Carl Louley *(V.P.)*
Gerald D. Sytsema *(Gen. Mgr. & Treas.)*
Ramona C. Alley *(Controller)*
Lester Hersey *(Mgr.-Mfg.)*
Raymond Kilcollins *(Mgr.-Mktg.)*

Outside Service Firm(s):

Chester Kearny Co.*(Auditors)*
Presque Isle, ME

Phillips, Olore, Presque, Isle & Dunlovey*(Legal Firm)*
Portland, ME

MAINE PRINTING & BUSINESS FORMS CO.
P.O. Box 3878,
Portland, ME 04104
Tel.: 207-775-2216 **ME**
Fax: 207-774-2865
Approx.Sls.: $18,000,000
Emp.: 210
Printing Of Business Forms & Wholesale Distributor Of Envelopes
S.I.C.: 2752; 5112
Robert F. Willis *(Pres. & Chief Exec. Officer)*
Sumner Burnstein *(Sec.)*
Rita S. Willis *(Treas.)*

Outside Service Firm(s):

Tofias, Fleishman, Shapiro & Co.*(Auditors)*
Portland, OR

MAINE STATE LOTTERY COMMISSION
State House Station #30, 219 Capitol St.
Augusta, ME 04333
Tel.: 207-289-6700
Fax: 207-624-6733
Approx.Sls.: $96,000,000
Emp.: 43
Fiscal Year-end: 6/30/91
State Lottery
S.I.C.: 7999
Wallace Soule, Jr. *(Dir.)*
Pamela Coutts *(Deputy Dir.-Fin.)*

MAJESTIC MOLDED PRODUCTS, INC.
4333 Veterans Memorial Hwy.
Holbrook, NY 11741
Tel.: 516-588-7200
Fax: 516-588-9146
Year Founded: 1945
Sales Range: $10-19 Million
Emp.: 100
Mfr. Custom Injection Molder
S.I.C.: 3089
Craig K. Harding *(Chm. Bd. & Pres.)*
Tom Elznic *(Chief Fin. Officer & Controller)*
Glenn Davis *(Gen. Mgr.)*

Outside Service Firm(s):

Ernst & Young*(Auditors)*
787 Seventh Ave.
New York, NY 10019
Tel.: 212-773-1243

European American Bank*(Major Banking Relationship)*
New York, NY

MAKERS OF KAL, INC.
6415 DeSoto Ave.
Woodland Hills, CA 91367
Mailing Address:
P.O. Box 4023
Woodland Hills, CA 91365
Tel.: 818-340-3035
Fax: 818-702-9956
Year Founded: 1932
Emp.: 95
Mfr. of Nutritional Supplements
S.I.C.: 2099
Stephen N. Weldon *(Pres.)*
Dennis R. Clark *(V.P.-Fin.)*
Bill Logan *(V.P.-Sls.)*

Outside Service Firm(s):

BDO Seidman*(Auditors)*
Beverly Hills, CA

Frank, Greenberg & Simone*(Legal Firm)*
Beverly Hills, CA

California First Bank*(Major Banking Relationship)*
Beverly Hills, CA

MAKI CORPORATION
160 Mass Ave.
Lunenburg, MA 01462
Tel.: 508-343-7422
Fax: 508-345-8351
Approx.Sls.: $17,000,000
Emp.: 90
Lumber & Other Building Materials; Lumber, Plywood & Millwork; Paint, Glass & Wallpaper; Metal Screen Doors, Aluminum Extruded Products
S.I.C.: 5211; 5031; 5231; 3442; 3354
Glen Maki *(Pres.)*
Principal(s):
Glen Maki
Theresa Maki
Walter Maki

Outside Service Firm(s):

Mercadante & Mercadante*(Auditors)*
Fitchburg, MA

Edwin E. Kaarela*(Legal Firm)*
Fitchburg, MA

Shawmut Bank*(Major Banking Relationship)*
446 Main St.
Worcester, MA 01608

Subsidiary:

Maki Home Center, Inc. **(1)**
160 Mass Ave.
Lunenburg, MA 01462
Tel.: 508-343-7422
Lumber & Other Building Materials; Plywood & Millwork; Paint, Glass & Wallpaper; Metal Screen Doors; Aluminum Extruded Products
S.I.C.: 5211; 5031; 5231; 3442; 3354
Glen Maki *(Pres.)*

MALCO PRODUCTS, INC.
361 Fairview Ave.
Barberton, OH 44203
Mailing Address:
P. O. Box 892
Barberton, OH 44203
Tel.: 216-753-0361
Tel.: 800-253-2526
Fax: 216-753-2025
Year Founded: 1953
Approx.Sls.: $30,000,000
Emp.: 210
Fiscal Year-end: 6/30/92
Import Export
Malco Automotive Chemical Specialties, Industrial & Household Chemicals; Bowlene, Climalene, Old Blue & Whiz
S.I.C.: 2841; 2842
Stuart Glauberman *(Pres.)*
Jay D. Glauberman *(V.P.)*
Dominick DeMasi *(V.P.-Fin. & Admin.)*
Allan Bartholomew *(Natl. Sls. Mgr.-Non Foods Div.)*
Louis Petit *(Natl. Sls. Mgr.-Grocery Div.)*
John Ginley *(Sls. Mgr.-Malco Automotive Div.)*
Rod McGregor *(Mgr.-Mktg.)*
Jack White *(Div. Mgr.-Janitorial & Industrial)*
Joel Pochron *(Dir.-Tech.)*
William Wallace *(Dir.-Pur.)*

Division:

Whiz Automotive Chemicals Div. **(1)**
361 Fairview Ave.
Barberton, OH 44203
Tel.: 216-753-0361
Tel.: 800-253-2526
Fax: 216-753-2025
Import Export
Allan Bartholomew *(Sls. Mgr.)*

MALDEN MILLS INDUSTRIES, INC.
46 Stafford St.
Lawrence, MA 01841
Tel.: 508-685-6341
Fax: 508-975-2595
Approx.Sls.: $125,000,000
Emp.: 1,500
Manufacture Apparel & Upholstery Fabrics
S.I.C.: 2221; 2253; 5131
Aaron Feuerstein *(Pres. & Chief Exec. Officer)*
Wes Rydin *(V.P. & Chief Fin. Officer)*
Albert J. Baroni *(Controller)*
Michael Reeve *(Asst. Treas.)*
Al Kraunellis *(Dir.-Personnel)*
Jeff Weiss *(Dir.-Pur.)*

Computer Systems/Hardware:
Burroughs 3800; Hewlett-Packard 3000

Outside Service Firm(s):

Blue Cross of Massachusetts, Inc.*(Group Insurer)*
Boston, MA

Connecticut General Life Insurance Co.*(Group Insurer)*
P.O. Box 2975,
Hartford, CT 06104
Tel.: 203-726-6000

Goulston & Storrs*(Legal Firm)*
131 State St.
Boston, MA 02109
Tel.: 617-742-1950

First National Bank of Boston*(Major Banking Relationship)*
P.O. Box 644,
Boston, MA 02102-0644
Tel.: 617-575-2900
Fax: 617-575-2549

Prudential Insurance Co. of America*(Pension Manager)*
751 Broad St.
Newark, NJ 07102-3777
Tel.: 201-802-6000

MALESON NAYLOR
10220 S. Dolfield Rd.
Owings Mills, MD 21117
Tel.: 410-363-4480
Year Founded: 1972
Approx.Billings: $10,700,000
Emp.: 10
Howard S. Maleson *(Chm. Bd.)*
James Naylor, Jr. *(Pres.)*
Barry Spector *(Exec. V.P., Mktg.)*
Dolores Mazzarella *(Opers. Mgr.)*

MALIBU GRAND PRIX CORPORATION
7301 Topanga Canyon Blvd.
Canoga Park, CA 91303
Tel.: 818-887-6900
Fax: 818-704-0249
Year Founded: 1974
Approx.Sls.: $30,000,000
Emp.: 1,500
Fiscal Year-end: 12/31/90
Recreational Amusement & Consumer Racing Centers
S.I.C.: 7948; 7997; 7991
Ira L. Young *(Chm. Bd.)*
Don Parmiter *(Pres.)*
Jeffrey Kahn *(Chief Fin. Officer)*
William Patterson *(Exec. V.P.)*
Rich Wheeler *(Reg. V.P.-Opers.)*
Lance Ingmanson *(Dir.-Sls. & Mktg.)*

Outside Service Firm(s):

Coopers & Lybrand*(Auditors)*
350 S. Grand Ave.
Los Angeles, CA 90071
Tel.: 213-481-1000
Fax: 213-482-6440

Union Bank*(Major Banking Relationship)*
445 S. Figueroa St.
Los Angeles, CA 90071
Tel.: 213-236-5076

MALLERY LUMBER CORP.
Star Rte., Box #1
Emporium, PA 15834
Tel.: 814-486-3764
Fax: 814-486-3392
Year Founded: 1952
Approx.Sls.: $10,000,000
Emp.: 125
Export
Rough Cut Hardwood Lumber, Pallet Stock, Wood Chips & Sawdust
S.I.C.: 2421; 2435; 2499
George Mee *(Chm. & Pres.)*
John L. Mallery *(V.P. & Plant Mgr.)*
John Rogers *(Treas. & Controller)*
Gary Dubler *(Mgr.-Sls.)*

No. of Mfg. Plants/Facilities: 2

Outside Service Firm(s):

Price Waterhouse*(Auditors)*
600 Grant St., Ste. 4400
Pittsburgh, PA 15219
Tel.: 412-355-6000
Fax: 412-391-0609

Ball & McDonough*(Legal Firm)*
Binghampton, NY

Marine Bank*(Major Banking Relationship)*
Erie, PA

Subsidiary:

Mallery Lumber Corp.-NY **(1)**
36 Labarr
Hancock, NY 13783
Tel.: 607-637-2236 (100%)
Emp.: 30
Rough Cut Hardwood Lumber, Pallet Stock, Wood Chips & Sawdust
S.I.C.: 2421; 2435; 2499
George Mer *(Pres. & Chief Exec. Officer)*

MALLET & CO.
Arch Street Extension
Carnegie, PA 15106
Mailing Address:
P.O. Box 474
Carnegie, PA 15106
Tel.: 412-276-9000
Fax: 412-276-9002
Year Founded: 1939
Approx.Sls.: $25,000,000
Emp.: 90
Mfr. Edible Fats, Salad Oils, Baking Pan Oils & Releasers, Shortening & Bakery Equip.
S.I.C.: 2074; 2075; 2076; 2079; 3556
Robert I. Mallet *(Pres.)*
A.E. Margolis *(Exec. V.P.)*
Jeff Reichel *(Sls. Mgr.)*
Anita Dufalla *(Adv. Consultant)*
Mary Nicholson *(Indus. Mktg. Specialist)*

Outside Service Firm(s):

Pittsburgh National Bank*(Major Banking Relationship)*
5th Ave. & Wood St.
Pittsburgh, PA 15222
Tel.: 412-355-3000

MALLORY, INC.
550 Mallory Way
Carson City, NV 89701
Tel.: 702-882-6600
Fax: 702-887-4326
Year Founded: 1932
Approx.Sls.: $10,000,000
Emp.: 200
Fiscal Year-end: 12/31/90
Mfr. of Automotive High Performance Ignition Products
S.I.C.: 3612; 3825; 3694; 3822
Gregg Koehlein *(Pres., Chief Exec. Officer, Plant & Mfg. Mgr.)*
Robert Wyman, Jr. *(Mgr.-Adv., Mktg., Sls. & Sls. Promo.)*
Becki Teague *(Personnel Mgr.)*
Susan Dalluhn *(Controller)*
Linda Lee *(Pur. Agent)*

MALLOY LITHOGRAPHING INC.
5411 Jackson Rd.
Ann Arbor, MI 48106
Mailing Address:
P.O. Box 1124
Ann Arbor, MI 48106
Tel.: 313-665-6113 **MI**
Fax: 313-665-2326
Approx.Sls.: $30,400,000
Emp.: 345
Fiscal Year-end: 10/31/91
Book Printing
S.I.C.: 2732
Herbert H. Upton, Jr. *(Pres.)*
Ben Mattison *(V.P. & Treas.)*
William L. Upton *(V.P.)*
Robert Scheible *(V.P.)*
Gabriel Watts *(V.P.)*
Leonard McCalla *(Sec.)*
Joseph H. Upton *(Asst. Sls. Mgr.)*
Don Jones *(Dir.-Pur.)*
James Mitchell *(Dir.-Personnel)*
Don Jones *(Dir.-Data Processing)*
No. of Mfg. Plants/Facilities: 1
No. of U.S. Offices: 1

Computer Systems/Hardware:
Data General

Outside Service Firm(s):

Bredernitz, Wagner & Co.*(Auditors)*
Howell, MI

Miller, Canfield, Paddock & Stone*(Legal Firm)*
Ann Arbor, MI

N.B.D. Bank, N.A.*(Major Banking Relationship)*
611 Woodward Ave.
Detroit, MI 48226
Tel.: 313-225-1122
Fax: 313-225-3420

MALONE ADVERTISING, INC.
209 S. Main St.
Akron, OH 44308
Tel.: 216-376-6148
Tel.: 800-468-6148
Fax: 216-253-1218
Year Founded: 1943
Approx.Billings: $70,000,000
Emp.: 100+
Integrated Marketing
H.P. Stitzlein *(Chm.)*
F. Bidwell *(Pres.)*
B.L. Malone *(Chief Exec. Officer)*

MALT-O-MEAL COMPANY
80 S. 8th St., Ste. 2600
Minneapolis, MN 55402-2297
Tel.: 612-338-8551 **MN**
Year Founded: 1919
Approx.Sls.: $100,000,000
Emp.: 450
Fiscal Year-end: 12/31/91
Malt-o-Meal Hot Wheat Cereal; Toasty-O's Toasted Oat Cereal; Malt-O-Meal, Puffed Wheat & Rice; Toasted Oat Cereal; Sugar Puffs Wheat Cereal, Corn Flakes, Raisin Bran, Crispy Rice, Sugar Frosted Flakes, 40% Bran Flakes; Branded & Private Label Cereals, Fruit-Flavored Toasty O's, Honey & Nut Coated Toasty O's
S.I.C.: 2043
John W. Lettmann *(Pres.)*
Donavon Pautzke *(Sr. V.P.)*
John Stull *(V.P.-Mfg.)*
Gordy Robertson *(Controller)*
Diane Dietz *(Mgr.-Mkgt.)*
Sally Literski *(Mgr.-Mktg.)*
Julie Smith *(Admin. Asst.)*

Computer Systems/Hardware:
IBM System 36

Outside Service Firm(s):

Johnson, West & Co.*(Auditors)*
St. Paul, MN

First National Bank of Minneapolis*(Major Banking Relationship)*
P.O. Box A799
Minneapolis, MN 55480
Tel.: 612-370-4606

Manufacturing Site:

Malt-O-Meal Co. **(1)**
701 W. Fifth St.
Northfield, MN 55057
Tel.: 507-645-6681
Cereal
S.I.C.: 2043

MAMA TISH'S ITALIAN SPECIALTIES
4800 S. Central Ave.
Chicago, IL 60638
Tel.: 708-458-7900
Year Founded: 1989
Approx.Sls.: $15,000,000
Export
Marketer of Italian Ices
S.I.C.: 5143
Andrew Zahn *(Pres.)*
Fergal Mulchrone *(Exec. V.P.)*

MAN-GILL CHEMICAL COMPANY
23000 St. Clair Ave.
Cleveland, OH 44117
Tel.: 216-486-5300
Fax: 216-486-1214
Approx.Sls.: $35,000,000
Emp.: 200
Fiscal Year-end: 6/30/91
Industrial Cleaning Compounds & Machines
S.I.C.: 2842; 3589
Jack Kohl *(Pres.)*
Mike Clark *(V.P.-Sls.)*
P. Kit Donaldson *(Dir.-Mktg.)*

MANAGEMENT DYNAMICS
121 Chanlon Rd.
New Providence, NJ 07974
Tel.: 908-464-6800
Fax: 908-771-7704
Year Founded: 1981
Approx.Rev.: $15,000,000
Emp.: 20
Management Consulting Services
S.I.C.: 8742; 8748; 8741
Owen O'Donnell *(Pres. & Chief Exec. Officer)*
George Aygard *(Sr. Exec. V.P.-Sls.)*
Nicholas Whitney *(Exec. V.P. & Chief Oper. Officer)*
Lyle E. Cornwall *(Exec. V.P. & Chief Fin. Officer)*
Terence Duncan *(Sr. V.P.-Mktg.)*
Julia Axelrode *(V.P.-Human Resources)*
Daryle Driver *(V.P.-Matls. Mngmnt.)*
Stewart Lemoyne *(Sec. & Gen. Counsel)*
Daneen Brown *(Dir.-Adv.)*
Carroll Priest *(Dir.-Mngmt. Information Services)*

Principal(s):
Owen O'Donnell

No. of U.S. Offices: 2

Computer Systems/Hardware:
MAI Basic 4 Model 8030

Outside Service Firm(s):

Ernst & Young*(Auditors)*
233 S. Wacker Dr.
Chicago, IL 60606
Tel.: 312-368-1800
Fax: 312-645-3095

Ernst & Young*(Auditors)*
787 Seventh Ave.
New York, NY 10019
Tel.: 212-773-1243

The Management Group
(See Management Dynamics)

MANCHESTER TANK & EQUIPMENT COMPANY
2880 Norton Ave.
Lynwood, CA 90262
Tel.: 213-979-4188 **CA**
Fax: 213-979-5343
Approx.Sls.: $90,000,000
Emp.: 850
Import Export
Fuel Tanks, Metal Plate
S.I.C.: 3443
Darrel Reifschneider *(Chm. Bd. & Chief Exec. Officer)*
Larry Corn *(V.P.-Fin. & Budgeting)*
John Breckenridge *(Gen. Counsel)*

Outside Service Firm(s):

Muller, King & Mathys*(Auditors)*
South Gate, CA

B.T. MANCINI CO., INC.
876 So. Milpitas Blvd.
Milpitas, CA 95035
Mailing Address:
P.O. Box 361930,
Milpitas, CA 95036-1930
Tel.: 408-942-7900 **CA**
Fax: 408-945-1360
Year Founded: 1964
Approx.Sls.: $34,000,000
Emp.: 200
Fiscal Year-end: 1/31/90
Import
Metal Decking & Siding Contractors; Flooring Contractors; Office Partition Contractors; Access Floor Clean Room Contractors
S.I.C.: 1761; 1751
Brooks T. Mancini *(Pres. & Treas.)*
Skip Mancini *(V.P.)*
Steve Murphy *(V.P.)*
David Roddick *(V.P.)*

No. of Mfg. Plants/Facilities: 2

Outside Service Firm(s):

Brooks, Stednitz & Rhodes*(Auditors)*
San Jose, CA

Miller, Morton, Caillat & Nevis*(Legal Firm)*
San Jose, CA

Wells Fargo Bank*(Major Banking Relationship)*
420 Montgomery St.
San Francisco, CA 94104

MANDELBAUM MOONEY ASHLEY
111 Maiden Lane
San Francisco, CA 94108
Tel.: 415-781-2100
Fax: 415-781-3220
Year Founded: 1988
Approx.Billings: $25,000,000
Emp.: 15
Cathi Mooney *(Chm. Bd., Creative Dir.)*
Ken Mandelbaum *(Chief Exec. Officer)*
L. Michael Goefft *(Pres.)*

Computer Systems/Hardware:
Macintosh

MANESS INDUSTRIES, INC.
1101 E. Spring St.
Long Beach, CA 90806
Tel.: 310-595-4555 **CA**
Fax: 310-424-4062
Year Founded: 1964
Sales Range: $20-39 Million
Emp.: 275
Heavy Construction Equipment Rental; Excavation Work; Welding on Site; Hazardous Waste Transport
S.I.C.: 7353; 1794; 1799
Kenneth P. Maness, Sr. *(Pres.)*
Calvin Leong *(Exec. V.P.)*

Outside Service Firm(s):

BankAmerica Corp.*(Major Banking Relationship)*
Anaheim, CA

MANHATTAN BUILDING COMPANIES
111 W. 5th St., Ste. 1000
Tulsa, OK 74103-4235
Tel.: 918-583-6900
Fax: 918-592-4334
Emp.: 600

Manhattan Building Companies—(Continued)

Holding Company; Industrial, Commercial & Institutional Building Contractor, Aerospace Components, Lumber & Building Materials
S.I.C.: 6719; 1541; 1542; 3728; 2431; 5211
L.F. Rooney, III *(Pres.)*
Michael Loinette *(V.P.-Estimating)*
Greg McCrocklin *(V.P.-Mktg.)*
Timothy Rooney *(V.P.)*
Ron Stoots *(V.P. & Treas.)*

Outside Service Firm(s):

Ernst & Young*(Auditors)*
4300 One William's Ctr.
Tulsa, OK 74142
Tel.: 918-560-3600
Fax: 918-560-3691

Texas Commerce Bank*(Major Banking Relationship)*
717 Travis St.
Houston, TX 77002
Tel.: 713-236-4636
Fax: 713-236-5476

Liddell, Sapp, Zivley, Hill & LaBoon, L.L.P.*(Legal Firm)*
3400 Texas Commerce Tower
Houston, TX 77002
Tel.: 713-223-4151

Subsidiary:

Manhattan Construction Company **(1)**
111 W. 5th St., Ste. 1000
Tulsa, OK 74103-4235
Tel.: 918-583-6900
Approx.Sls.: $115,000,000
Emp.: 600
Industrial, Commercial & Institutional Building Contractor
S.I.C.: 1541; 1542
L.F. Ronney, III *(Chm. Bd. & Chief Exec. Officer)*

MANHATTAN STORE INTERIORS, INC.
17 Moultrie St.
Brooklyn, NY 11222
Mailing Address:
P.O. Box 229001
New York, NY 11222
Tel.: 718-389-4493 **NY**
Fax: 718-389-6431
Sales Range: $10-19 Million
Emp.: 120
Export
Store Fixtures
S.I.C.: 2541; 2542
Alvin Katz *(Pres.)*
S. Katz *(Sec. & Treas.)*

Outside Service Firm(s):

Conrad Homler*(Auditors)*
Great Neck, NY

Kazdin, Weinstein & Bier*(Legal Firm)*
2 Pennsylvania Ave.
New York, NY 10121
Tel.: 212-567-4272

National Westminster Bank plc*(Major Banking Relationship)*
Astor Plaza, 1515 Broadway
New York, NY 10036

MANKE LUMBER COMPANY, INC.
1717 Marine View Dr.
Tacoma, WA 98422
Tel.: 206-572-6252
Fax: 206-383-2489
Approx.Sls.: $25,000,000
Emp.: 300
Rough & Surfaced Wood Treating Logs & Lumber
S.I.C.: 2411; 2491
Charles Manke *(Pres.)*
James Manke *(Treas.)*
J. Randal Jordan *(Controller)*
Virgil Manke *(Sec.)*

Outside Service Firm(s):

Knight, Vale & Gregory*(Auditors)*
Tacoma, WA

Security Pacific National Bank*(Major Banking Relationship)*
Tacoma, WA

MANNA PRO CORPORATION
7711 Carondelet, Ste. 800
Saint Louis, MO 63105
Tel.: 314-746-1700 **CA**
Fax: 314-746-1799
Year Founded: 1930
Assets: $30,311,726
Liabilities: $23,865,764
Net Worth: $6,445,962
Sales Range: $80-99 Million
Emp.: 450
Fiscal Year-end: 1/31/92
Export
Manufacture & Distribute Animal Feeds
S.I.C.: 2048; 2047
Lawrence Chapman *(Pres. & Chief Exec. Officer)*
John D. Minard *(V.P., Controller & Chief Fin. Officer)*
David Johnston *(Dir.-Mngmt. Information Systems)*

No. of Mfg. Plants/Facilities: 9

Outside Service Firm(s):

Price Waterhouse*(Auditors)*
One Boatmen's Plaza
St. Louis, MO 63101
Tel.: 314-425-0500

Alexander & Alexander*(Commercial Insurance Carrier)*
1000 Walnut
Kansas City, MO 64105

Northwestern National Life*(Group Insurer)*
Kansas City, MO

Armstrong, Teasdale, Schlafly, Davis & Dicus*(Legal Firm)*
One Metropolitan Square
St. Louis, MO 63102
Tel.: 314-621-5065
Fax: 314-621-5065

Mercantile Bank*(Major Banking Relationship)*
Saint Louis, MO

Boatmen's Trust Company*(Pension Manager)*
100 North Broadway
St. Louis, MO 63102
Tel.: 314-466-2469

Limited Partnership:

Manna Pro Partner L.P. (Limited Partnership) **(1)**
4545 Madison St.
Denver, CO 80216
Tel.: 303-296-8668
Emp.: 75
Mfg. & Distribute Animal Feeds
S.I.C.: 2047; 2048
Buck Markley *(Gen. Mgr.)*
Glen Shelhause *(Controller)*
Tom Knopf *(Sls. Mgr.)*

MANNA PRO PARTNERS
4545 Madison St.
Denver, CO 80216
Tel.: 303-296-8668
Fax: 303-292-9120
Approx.Sls.: $15,000,000
Emp.: 60
A Partnership of Wholesale Grain Farm Supplies
S.I.C.: 2048; 4221; 5153; 5191
Buck Markley *(Gen. Mgr.)*
Glenn Schelhaas *(Controller)*

Outside Service Firm(s):

Price Waterhouse*(Auditors)*
950 17th St., Ste. 2600
Denver, CO 80202
Tel.: 303-893-8100

Colorado National Bank N.E.*(Major Banking Relationship)*
Denver, CO

Division:

Farmers Marketing Association **(1)**
4545 Madison St.
Denver, CO 80216
Tel.: 303-296-8668
Fax: 303-392-9120
A Partnership of Wholesale Grain Farm Supplies
S.I.C.: 2048; 4221; 5153; 5191
John Ehler *(Chm. Bd.)*
Gene Beville *(Chief Exec. Officer)*

MANNING EQUIPMENT, INC.
12000 Westport Rd.
Louisville, KY 40223
Mailing Address:
P.O. Box 23229
Louisville, KY 40223
Tel.: 502-426-5210
Fax: 502-426-5213
Approx.Sls.: $10,000,000
Emp.: 166
Wholesale Truck Bodies, Equipment & Supplies
S.I.C.: 5013
J. William Manning, Sr. *(Chm. Bd. & Chief Exec. Officer)*
M.J. Stich *(Gen. Mgr.)*
Tom Tanselle *(Dir.-Pur.)*
Mindy Manning *(Mgr.-Adv.)*
Randy Sirko *(Mgr.-Sls.)*

No. of Mfg. Plants/Facilities: 5

Outside Service Firm(s):

William S. Wetterer & Co.*(Auditors)*
Louisville, KY

First National Bank of Louisville*(Major Banking Relationship)*
P.O. Box 36000,
Louisville, KY 40233

MANNING & LEWIS ENGINEERING CO.
675 Rahway Ave.
Union, NJ 07083
Tel.: 908-687-2400
Year Founded: 1937
Approx.Sls.: $10,000,000
Emp.: 90
Export
Shell and Tube Heat Exchangers
S.I.C.: 3443; 3559
Richard J. Owens *(Pres. & Chief Exec. Officer)*
Glenn Mumma *(Controller)*
V. Iannuzzi *(Natl. Sls. Mgr.)*
Pat Dillner *(Pur. Agent)*

MANNINGTON MILLS, INC.
Mannington Mills Rd.
Salem, NJ 08079
Mailing Address:
P.O. Box 30,
Salem, NJ 08079
Tel.: 609-935-3000
Fax: 609-339-5910
Emp.: 700
Mfr. Wood, Ceramic & Resilient Sheet Vinyl Floor Coverings
S.I.C.: 3996
R. Scott Smith *(Chm. & Chief Exec. Officer)*
Gary Anderson *(V.P.-Sls.)*
Francis J. Norris *(Treas. & Sec.)*
Louise Griggs *(Mktg. Coord.)*

Computer Systems/Hardware:
IBM

Outside Service Firm(s):

KPMG Peat Marwick*(Auditors)*
1600 Market St.
Philadelphia, PA 19103
Tel.: 215-299-3100

Weinberg & Green*(Legal Firm)*
100 S. Charles St.
Baltimore, MD 21202
Tel.: 410-332-8795

Midlantic National Bank*(Major Banking Relationship)*
Metro Park Plaza,
Edison, NJ 08818
Tel.: 908-321-8000

Divisions:

Mannington Ceramic Tile **(1)**
20 Victor St.
Lexington, NC 27293
Tel.: 704-249-3931
Fax: 704-249-8928
Emp.: 555
Manufactures Ceramic Tile
S.I.C.: 3253
Al Cox *(Pres.)*
Roy Gorton *(Exec. V.P.)*
Allen Robertson *(V.P.-Sls.)*
Richard L. Thomas *(Treas. & Sec.)*
Roy Berrier *(Personnel Dir.)*
Bill Leatherman *(Pur. Agent)*

Mannington Wood Floors **(1)**
1327 Lincoln Dr.
High Point, NC 27260-9945
Tel.: 919-884-5600
Fax: 919-884-8171
Emp.: 150
Export
Manufactures Wood Floors
S.I.C.: 3996
Dan Harper *(Pres.)*
John Patterson *(V.P.-Sls. & Mktg.)*
Joel Martin *(Dir.-Mktg.)*

Subsidiaries:

Mannington Carpet Corp. **(1)**
P.O. Box 281,
Calhoun, GA 30701
Tel.: 609-629-7301

Mannington Ceramic Tile **(1)**
Victor St.
Lexington, NC 27293

Mannington Resilient Floors **(1)**
Mannington Mills Rd.
Salem, NJ 08079
Tel.: 609-935-3000
Emp.: 700
Resilient Flooring
S.I.C.: 2426
M. Bruce Jones *(Pres.)*
Keith Campbell *(Exec. V.P.)*
R.W. Russell *(V.P.-Mktg.)*
Louise Griggs *(Mktg. Coord.)*

Wellco Carpet Corp. **(1)**
Box 281
Calhoun, GA 30701
Tel.: 609-629-7301

MANOSTAT CORPORATION
519 Eighth Ave.
New York, NY 10018
Tel.: 212-594-6262 **NY**
Fax: 212-629-0483
Year Founded: 1955
Sales Range: $10-19 Million
Emp.: 28
Fiscal Year-end: 4/30/91
Import Export
Mfr. Laboratory Instruments
S.I.C.: 3841
R.E. Bader *(Pres.)*
Amanda Bader *(V.P.)*
Roberta Brill *(Dir.-Personnel)*
Reva Alpert *(Mgr.-Direct Sls.)*
Andy Ginsberg *(Pur. Agent)*

Computer Systems/Hardware:
MAI Basic 4

Outside Service Firm(s):

Anchin, Block & Anchin*(Auditors)*
1375 Broadway
New York, NY 10018

First American Bank, N.A.*(Major Banking Relationship)*
New York, NY

MANSFIELD OIL COMPANY
1025 Airport Pkwy. SW
Gainesville, GA 30505-0198
Tel.: 706-532-7571
Fax: 706-535-0127
Approx.Sls.: $250,000,000
Emp.: 52
Wholesale & Retail Petroleum
S.I.C.: 5171; 5541
John E. Mansfield, Sr. *(Chm. Bd.)*
Michael F. Mansfield *(Pres.)*

Outside Service Firm(s):

Smith & Howard*(Auditors)*
Atlanta, GA

Whelchel, Dunlap & Gigniliatt*(Legal Firm)*
Gainsville, GA

MANUFACTURERS CONSOLIDATION SERVICE
187 W. Industrial Ave.
Memphis, TN 38109
Tel.: 901-942-1551 **TN**
Fax: 901-948-2726
Year Founded: 1968
Approx.Sls.: $96,000,000
Emp.: 120
Freight Consolidation; Local Trucking Without Storage
S.I.C.: 4731; 4212
Rick Rodell *(Pres. & Chief Exec. Officer)*
C.O. Turner, III *(Sec. & Treas.)*

Outside Service Firm(s):

Denny A. Vaughn*(Auditors)*
Memphis, TN

Community Bank*(Major Banking Relationship)*
Germantown, TN

MANUFACTURERS' NEWS, INC.
1633 Central St.
Evanston, IL 60201
Tel.: 708-864-7000 **IL**
Fax: 708-332-1100
Year Founded: 1912
Sales Range: $10-19 Million
Emp.: 70
Fiscal Year-end: 12/31/91
Import Export
Publisher of Industrial Directories; Supplier of Industrial Information on Diskettes, Tape & Lists
S.I.C.: 2741
Howard S. Dubin *(Pres.)*
Thomas G. Dubin *(Exec. V.P.)*
Marc Pickel *(V.P.-Systems)*
Louise West *(V.P.-Editorial)*
Phillip Brown *(Gen. Mgr.)*

No. of Mfg. Plants/Facilities: 1
No. of U.S. Offices: 1

Computer Systems/Hardware:
Qantel, Everex, MacIntosh

Outside Service Firm(s):

Katch, Tyson & Co.*(Auditors)*
Northfield, IL

Much, Shelist, Freed, Denenberg, Ament & Eiger*(Legal Firm)*
Chicago, IL

Bank One*(Major Banking Relationship)*
Evanston, IL

Lake Shore National Bank*(Major Banking Relationship)*
605 N. Michigan Ave.
Chicago, IL 60611
Tel.: 312-787-1900

Subsidiary:

Industrial Bookstore **(1)**
1633 Central St.
Evanston, IL 60201
Tel.: 708-864-7000
Retail Bookstore
S.I.C.: 5961

MANUFACTURERS PRODUCTS COMPANY
26020 Sherwood Ave.
Warren, MI 48091
Tel.: 313-961-4034 **MI**
Fax: 313-755-2187
Year Founded: 1949
Approx.Sls.: $25,000,000
Emp.: 140
Export
Mfr. of Automotive Stampings & Assemblies
S.I.C.: 3465
Wesley C. Fredericks, Jr. *(Pres. & Chief Oper. Officer)*
Matthew S. Galvez *(Chief Fin. Officer)*
Jerry D. Holley *(V.P. & Gen. Mgr.)*
Maroun Tabet *(V.P.-Sls.)*
James B. Weber *(Mgr.-Sls.)*
Terri Irvine *(Controller)*
Principal(s):
Wesley C. Fredericks, Jr.
Matthew S. Galvez

No. of Mfg. Plants/Facilities: 1
No. of U.S. Offices: 1

Outside Service Firm(s):

Cominskey, Bobrowski & Quellette*(Auditors)*
Troy, MI

Dykema, Gossett*(Legal Firm)*
Troy, MI

National Bank of Detroit*(Major Banking Relationship)*
Warren, MI

MANUFACTURERS TECHNOLOGIES, INC.
59 Interstate Dr.
West Springfield, MA 01089
Tel.: 413-733-1972
Fax: 413-739-9250
Year Founded: 1983
Emp.: 20
Export
Mfr. Computer Software
S.I.C.: 7372
Thomas Charkiewicz *(Pres.)*
Nancy Charkiewicz *(Chief Fin. Officer & Controller)*
Rene Laviolette *(Sr. V.P.-Product Devel.)*
Robert W. Rossow *(V.P.-Sls. & Mktg.)*

Computer Systems/Hardware:
IBM PC's & PS/2

MAPLEHURST FARMS, INC.
3745 Farnsworth St.
Indianapolis, IN 46241
Tel.: 317-244-2481
Fax: 317-240-5940
Year Founded: 1921
Approx.Sls.: $65,000,000
Emp.: 300
Produce & Distribute Milk, Ice Cream, Cultured Dairy Products
S.I.C.: 2026; 2022; 2024; 5143
Howard Mills, Jr. *(Chm. Bd. & Chief Exec. Officer)*
Ralph Dischler *(Pres.)*
Phil Littell *(V.P.-Fin.)*
Bill Truesdale *(V.P.-Sls.)*

Outside Service Firm(s):

Henderson, Daily, Withrow & DeVoe*(Legal Firm)*
Indianapolis, IN

MAR-JAC INC.
P.O. Box 1017
Gainesville, GA 30503
Tel.: 706-536-0561
Fax: 706-531-5015
Approx.Sls.: $59,000,000
Emp.: 650
Poultry Processor
S.I.C.: 2015
Jamal Al-Barzinji *(Pres.)*
Doug Karns *(V.P.)*
MaHmud Mohamed *(V.P.-Fin.)*
Randy Bruce *(Controller)*
Pete Martin *(Plant Mgr.)*

Outside Service Firm(s):

Frost & Co.*(Auditors)*
Gainesville, GA

Gainesville Bank & Trust*(Major Banking Relationship)*
Gainesville, GA

Subsidiaries:

Mar-Jac Farms, Inc. **(1)**
Hwy. 52
Lula, GA 30501
Tel.: 706-536-0561
Emp.: 70
Poultry Hatchery & Local Hauling
S.I.C.: 0254; 4212
Jamal Al-Barzinji *(Pres.)*
MaHmud D. Mahamed *(Fin. Dir.)*

Mar-Jac Processing, Inc. **(1)**
Airport Circle, Aviation Blvd.
Gainesville, GA 30501
Tel.: 706-532-0456
Approx.Sls.: $28,000,000
Emp.: 450
Poultry Processor
S.I.C.: 2015
Jamal Al-Barzinji *(Pres.)*
Dr. Hisham Al-Talib *(Sec.)*
Dr. Yaqub Marza *(Treas.)*
MaHmud Mohamed *(Fin. Dir.)*

MAR-MAC MANUFACTURING COMPANY, INC.
Highway One, N.
McBee, SC 29101
Mailing Address:
P.O. Box 278
McBee, SC 29101
Tel.: 803-335-8211 **SC**
Fax: 803-335-8599
Year Founded: 1953
Sales Range: $10-19 Million
Emp.: 250
Export
Disposable Garments & Accessories
S.I.C.: 2389
John S. McLeod, Sr. *(Pres.)*
J. Ray Hemby *(V.P.-Mfg.)*
John S. McLeod, Jr. *(V.P.-Mktg.)*
Fran Masters *(Dir.-Pur.)*
Rebecca M. Davis *(Mgr.-Personnel)*
Belle Lovelace *(Treas. & Sec.)*
Principal(s):
John S. McLeod, Sr.
John S. McLeod, Jr.

No. of Mfg. Plants/Facilities: 3
No. of U.S. Offices: 1

Outside Service Firm(s):

Arthur Andersen & Co.*(Auditors)*
Columbia, SC

Liberty Mutual*(Commercial Insurance Carrier)*
Columbia, SC

Jefferson Pilot*(Group Insurance Broker/Consult)*
P.O. Box 20727
Greensboro, NC 27420
Tel.: 919-691-4324

Citizens & Southern National Bank*(Major Banking Relationship)*
Camden, SC

NationsBank of South Carolina*(Major Banking Relationship)*
Camden, SC

Shearson Lehman*(Pension Manager)*
Charlotte, NC

Mays, Foster, Booth & Gunter*(Legal Firm)*
Columbia, SC

MARATHON CHEESE CORP.
304 East St.
Marathon, WI 54448
Mailing Address:
P.O. Box 185,
Marathon, WI 54448
Tel.: 715-443-2211 **WI**
Year Founded: 1954
Sales Range: $100-499 Million
Emp.: 950
Cheese & Cheese Packaging
S.I.C.: 2022
Raymond Goldbath *(Chm. Bd. & Chief Exec. Officer)*
Donald Menzer *(Pres.)*
Norbert Schumacher *(Sr. V.P., Controller & Chief Fin. Officer)*
Kenneth Jilidian *(V.P.)*
Duane Handrick *(Dir.-Data Processing)*
David Tylinski *(Dir.-Personnel)*

Computer Systems/Hardware:
Wang

Outside Service Firm(s):

Mabie Assocs.*(Auditors)*
Stevens Pt., WI

Wausau Insurance*(Group Insurer)*
2000 Westwood Dr.
Wausau, WI 54401-7881
Tel.: 715-842-6902
Fax: 715-847-8534

M & I Marshall & Ilsley Bank*(Major Banking Relationship)*
770 N. Water St.
Milwaukee, WI 53202
Tel.: 414-765-8700

MARATHON ELECTRIC MANUFACTURING CORP.
100 E. Randolph
Wausau, WI 54401
Mailing Address:
P.O. Box 8003
Wausau, WI 54402-8003
Tel.: 715-675-3311 **WI**
Telex: 260175 ME WAS
Fax: 715-675-6361
Year Founded: 1913
Fiscal Year-end: 12/31/91
Import Export
Manufacture Electric Motors, Generators & Wiring Devices
S.I.C.: 3621; 3643
H.R. Baker *(Pres. & Chief Exec. Officer)*
Bill D. Dodson *(V.P.-Fin., Services & Treas.)*
David Eisenreich *(V.P.-Admin.)*
Ray C. Kacvinsky *(V.P.-Mktg. & Sls.)*
Marvin Lilley *(V.P.-Matls.)*
Hugh Reardon *(V.P.-Quality Assurance)*
Gary Schurter *(V.P.-Engrng.)*
T. Campbell Walton *(V.P.-Mfg.)*
S.W. Orr, Jr. *(Sec.)*
William Boos *(Dir.-Mngmt. Information Systems)*

Computer Systems/Hardware:
IBM AS/400

Outside Service Firm(s):

Wipfli, Ullrich, Bertelson*(Auditors)*
P.O. Box 8010,
Wausau, WI 54402-8010

Marathon Electric Manufacturing Corp.—(Continued)

Wausau Insurance*(Group Insurer)*
2000 Westwood Dr.
Wausau, WI 54401-7881
Tel.: 715-842-6902
Fax: 715-847-8534

M & I Marshall & Ilsley Bank*(Investment Banker)*
770 N. Water St.
Milwaukee, WI 53202
Tel.: 414-765-8700

Smith Barney, Harris Upham & Company, Inc.*(Investment Banker)*
1345 Avenue of the Americas
New York, NY
Tel.: 212-698-6559
Fax: 212-698-5735

Foley & Lardner*(Legal Firm)*
777 E. Wisconsin Ave.
Milwaukee, WI 53202
Tel.: 414-271-2400

First American Bank, N.A.*(Major Banking Relationship)*
Wausau, WI

M & I Marshall & Ilsley Bank*(Major Banking Relationship)*
770 N. Water St.
Milwaukee, WI 53202
Tel.: 414-765-8700

Aetna Life & Casualty*(Pension Manager)*
151 Farmington Avenue
Hartford, CT 06156
Tel.: 203-273-2128
Fax: 203-729-4295

M & I Marshall & Isley Bank*(Pension Manager)*
Milwaukee, WI

Northern Capital Management, Inc.*(Pension Manager)*
6510 Grand Teton Plaza, Suite 412
Madison, WI
Tel.: 608-829-2990

Subsidiaries:

Lima Electric Co., Inc. **(1)**
200 E. Chapman Rd.
Lima, OH 45802
Tel.: 419-227-7327 (100%)
Fax: 419-227-9926
Emp.: 100
S.I.C.: 3621

Marathon Special Prods. **(1)**
13300 Van Camp Rd.
Bowling Green, OH 43402
Tel.: 419-352-8441 (100%)
Fax: 419-352-0875
Emp.: 120
S.I.C.: 3643

MARC advertising

MARC ADVERTISING
Four Station Square
Pittsburgh, PA 15219
Tel.: 412-562-2000
Fax: 412-562-2022
Year Founded: 1955
Approx.Billings: $63,000,000
Emp.: 99
Louis J. Cardamone *(Chm.)*
Anthony L. Bucci *(Pres. & Chief Exec. Officer)*
Norbert J. Sieber *(Exec. V.P., Gen. Mgr.)*
Stuart M. Zolot *(Sr. V.P., Chief Fin. Officer)*

MARCAL PAPER MILLS, INC.
One Market St.
Elmwood Park, NJ 07407
Tel.: 201-796-4000
Fax: 201-796-0470
Year Founded: 1932
Approx.Sls.: $200,000,000
Emp.: 1,200
Fiscal Year-end: 4/30/90
Import Export
Manufacture Tissue Paper & Paper Products for Consumer & Institutional Use
S.I.C.: 2621; 2679
Robert L. Marcalus Sr. *(Chm. Bd. & Chief Exec. Officer)*
Nicholas R. Marcalus *(Pres. & Chief Oper. Officer)*
Chester Grygorcewicz *(Sr. V.P. & Controller)*
Michael C. Mazzarino *(Sr. V.P.-Fin. & Treas.)*
Nat Argento *(V.P.-Trade Rels.)*
Joseph Elvin *(V.P.-Pur.)*
Edward Jacod *(V.P.-Converting)*
Florence Noren *(Sec.)*
Joseph Calao *(Dir.-Data Processing)*
Jim Cobern *(Dir.-Human Resources)*

Computer Systems/Hardware:
IBM

Outside Service Firm(s):

KPMG Peat Marwick*(Auditors)*
150 John F. Kennedy Pkwy.
Short Hills, NJ 07078
Tel.: 201-467-9650

Prudential Insurance Co. of America*(Group Insurer)*
751 Broad St.
Newark, NJ 07102-3777
Tel.: 201-802-6000

Schumann, Hession, Kennelly & Dorment*(Legal Firm)*
30 Montgomery St.
Jersey City, NJ 07302
Tel.: 201-434-2000

Manufacturers Hanover Trust Co.*(Major Banking Relationship)*
270 Park Ave.
New York, NY 10017
Tel.: 212-286-3229

Midlantic National Bank*(Major Banking Relationship)*
Metro Park Plaza,
Edison, NJ 08818
Tel.: 908-321-8000

MARCH MANUFACTURING INC.
1819 Pickwick Ave.
Glenview, IL 60025
Tel.: 708-729-5300 **DE**
Fax: 708-729-7062
Year Founded: 1954
Assets: $14,600,000
Liabilities: $1,219,500
Net Worth: $13,380,500
Approx.Sls.: $18,000,000
Emp.: 127
Fiscal Year-end: 9/30/91
Import Export
Manufacture of March Pumps, Chemical, Hydronic, Condensate, Epoxy Clad Submersible & Air Cooled Centrifugal Pumps, Positive Displacement
S.I.C.: 3561
F.N. Zimmermann *(Chm. Bd. & Pres.)*
W.K. Zimmermann *(Treas. & Sec.)*
Richard Myers *(Dir.-Pur.)*
Tony Toma *(Dir.-Sls.)*

No. of Mfg. Plants/Facilities: 1
No. of U.S. Offices: 5
No. of Foreign Offices: 1

Outside Service Firm(s):

Egan & Egan*(Auditors)*
Ste. 1901, 200 W. Adams St.
Chicago, IL 60606

Vedder, Price, Kaufman & Kammholz*(Legal Firm)*
115 S. La Salle
Chicago, IL 60603
Tel.: 312-781-2200

Banc One*(Major Banking Relationship)*
Evanston, IL

MARCO COLOR LABS, INC.
12410 Wilkie Ave.
Hawthorne, CA 90250
Tel.: 213-756-8113
Fax: 213-756-9053
Approx.Sls.: $15,000,000
Emp.: 25
Plating & Polishing, Plastic Products
S.I.C.: 3471; 5162
Al Marin *(Pres.)*
Randy Treadaway *(V.P.)*

Outside Service Firm(s):

MetroBank*(Major Banking Relationship)*
Torrance, CA

MARCUS ADVERTISING, INC.
25700 Science Park Dr.
Cleveland, OH 44122
Tel.: 216-292-4700
Fax: 216-831-6189
Year Founded: 1946
Approx.Billings: $39,200,000
Emp.: 68
Donald H. Marcus *(Chm. & Chief Exec. Officer)*
Harvey Scholnick *(Pres. & Chief Oper. Officer)*
Donald A. Campbell *(Exec. V.P.)*
William Greenwald *(Exec. V.P.)*
Harlan Miller *(Sr. V.P.)*
James W. Reed *(Sr. V.P.)*
Howard Zoss *(Sr. V.P.)*
John Coe *(V.P., Gen. Mgr. & Direct Mktg.)*

MARCUS BROTHERS TEXTILES, INC.
1460 Broadway
New York, NY 10036
Tel.: 212-354-8700
Fax: 212-819-1986
Emp.: 130
Cotton & Cotton Blends, Woven & Knit Textile Converter
S.I.C.: 5131
Samuel Marcus *(Chm. Bd.)*
Martin Marcus *(Pres.)*
Steven Wachsman *(Exec. V.P.)*
Arthur Marcus *(V.P. & Sec.)*
Jeff Most *(Controller)*
Jay Marcus *(Mgr.-Data Processing)*
Larry Krell *(Pur. Agent)*

Outside Service Firm(s):

Sisner & Lublin*(Auditors)*
New York, NY

Proskauer, Rose, Goetz & Mendelsohn*(Legal Firm)*
1585 Broadway
New York, NY 10036
Tel.: 212-969-3000

Citibank N.A.*(Major Banking Relationship)*
Corporate Trust Services, 399 Park Ave.
New York, NY 10043
Tel.: 212-559-1605

MARDEN-KANE, INC.
410 Lakeville Rd.
Lake Success, NY 11042
Tel.: 516-326-3666
Fax: 516-326-3679
Year Founded: 1955
Approx.Billings: $18,000,000
Emp.: 36
Sales Promotion, Sweepstakes, Contests, Games, Incentive Programs, Refund Offers, Fulfillment & Tie-Ins
Gibby Kane *(Chm. Bd. & Pres.)*
Robert Bell *(Exec. V.P.)*
Paul Goldman *(Exec. V.P.)*
Alan Richter *(Sr. V.P., Fin.)*
Rose Chiechi *(V.P.)*
John Slattery *(V.P.)*

MARGEOTES FERTITTA & WEISS, INC.
411 Lafayette St.
New York, NY 10003
Tel.: 212-979-6600
Fax: 212-475-3932
Year Founded: 1973
Approx.Billings: $107,000,000
Emp.: 97
Advertising Agency
S.I.C.: 7311
George A. Fertitta *(Pres. & Chief Oper. Officer)*
Paul Mendela *(Chief Fin. Officer & Corp. Sec.)*
Paul Donaher *(Dir.-Strategic Plng.)*

Outside Service Firm(s):

David Wiener & Co.*(Auditors)*
Englewood Cliffs, NJ

Davis & Gilbert*(Legal Firm)*
850 Third Ave.
New York, NY 10022
Tel.: 212-326-1300

Morgan Guaranty Trust Company of New York*(Major Banking Relationship)*
23 Wall St.
New York, NY 10015
Tel.: 212-483-2323

MARGO NURSERY FARMS, INC.
19995 S.W. 194th Ave.
Miami, FL 33187
Mailing Address:
P.O. Box 427
Miami, FL 33170
Tel.: 305-255-0550
Tel.: 800-327-3252 **FL**
Fax: 305-255-6329
Year Founded: 1981
Assets: $12,500,000
Earnings: $214,000
Liabilities: $7,800,000
Net Worth: $4,700,000
Approx.Sls.: $8,500,000
Emp.: 450
Fiscal Year-end: 12/31/90
Import Export
Wholesale Nursery Stock; Growing of Tropical Foliage, Landscape Contracting
S.I.C.: 0181; 5199
Michael J. Spector *(Chm. Bd. & Pres., & Chief Exec. Officer)*
James F. Brenner *(V.P. & Chief Fin. Officer)*
Bill Fradera *(V.P. & G.M.)*
Margaret D. Spector *(Sec.)*

Computer Systems/Hardware:
DEC Microvax 3300

Subsidiary:

Margo Farms Del Caribe, Inc. **(1)**
P.O. Box 706,
Dorado, PR 00646
Nursery Stocks
S.I.C.: 0181
Michael J. Spector *(Pres.)*
Rene Llerandi *(V.P.-Sls.)*

Non-U.S. Subsidiaries:

Cariplant S.A. (1)
Av. Abraham Lincoln Edificio Alico, 4th Fl., Santo Domingo, Dominican Republic
Tel.: 809-533-6136 (100%)
Telex: 4275 CARI DR
Fax: 809-535-4313
Growing of Tropic Plants
S.I.C.: 0181
Byron Smalley *(Pres.)*

Margo Imports B.V. (1)
Corelli 14 2671 XC
Naaldwijk, Netherlands
Tel.: 1740 26385 (100%)
Fax: 1740 29070
Import of Nursery Stock
S.I.C.: 5199
Johan Dijkxhoorn *(Mng. Dir.)*

MARINE CONSTRUCTION & DESIGN CO.
2300 W. Commodore Way
Seattle, WA 98199
Tel.: 206-285-3200 **WA**
Telex: 160587 MARCO UT
Fax: 206-283-4731
Year Founded: 1953
Sales Range: $80-99 Million
Emp.: 1,000
Fiscal Year-end: 8/31/90
Import Export
Build & Service Fishing Vessels; Manufacture Marine Machinery & Pollution Control Equipment; Owns, Operates & Manufactures Fishing & Fish Processing Vessels
S.I.C.: 3731; 0912
Peter G. Schmidt *(Pres. & Chief Exec. Officer)*
H. Allen Fernstrom *(Exec. V.P. & Chief Oper. Officer)*
Charles R. Hart *(Sr. V.P.-Intl. Opers.)*
Robert T. McMahon *(V.P.-Shipyard Opers.)*
Michael V. Romig *(V.P. & Chief Fin. Officer)*
Lawrence R. King *(Controller)*
Richard O. Rentel *(Dir.-Pur.)*
David Row *(Dir.-Data Processing)*
Henry T. Schlapp *(Dir.-Personnel)*
Principal(s):
Peter G. Schmidt

Subsidiaries:

Campbell Industries, Inc. (1)
P.O. Box 1870, Harbor Dr. & 8th Ave.
San Diego, CA 92112
Tel.: 619-233-7115 (100%)
Ship Bldg. & Repair
S.I.C.: 3731
Robert F. Allen *(Pres.)*

Marco Marine San Diego (1)
P.O. Box 1870,
San Diego, CA 92112
Tel.: 619-239-2245 (100%)
Sales & Service, Marine Machinery & Electronics
S.I.C.: 5088
C. R. Hart *(Chief Oper. Officer)*

Marco Seattle, Inc. (1)
2300 W. Commodore Way
Seattle, WA 98199
Tel.: 206-285-3200 (100%)
Design & Construction of Commercial & Fishing Vessels; Mfr. of Marine Machinery; Oil Skimming Vessels; Export Supplier of Marine Matls. & Equip.
S.I.C.: 3731
P.G. Schmidt *(Chief Exec. Officer)*
H. Allen Fernstrom *(Exec. V.P. & Chief Oper. Officer)*

MARINE TRANSPORT LINES, INC.
150 Meadowland Pkwy.
Secaucus, NJ 07096-1550
Tel.: 201-330-0200
Telex: 12220
Twx: 710-581-6260
Cable: Matraline Seca
Fax: 201-330-7791
Year Founded: 1816
Assets: $157,380,000
Earnings: $5,428,000
Liabilities: $113,046,000
Net Worth: $44,334,000
Approx.Rev.: $121,710,000
Fiscal Year-end: 12/31/90
Owns & Operates Ocean-Going & Short-Sea Vessels Engaged In The Transportation Of Bulk Commodities In Domestic & International Trades; Crude Oil, Clean Petroleum Product, Chemical, Dry Bulk & Pure Car Carriers
S.I.C.: 4412; 4424
Richard T. duMoulin *(Chm., Pres. & Chief Exec. Officer)*
Mark Filanowski *(Sr. V.P. & Chief Fin. Officer)*
Joseph G. Drescher *(V.P.-Opers.)*
Peter N. Popov *(V.P., Gen. Counsel & Sec.)*
Carl W. Rumpp *(Controller)*

Outside Service Firm(s):

Deloitte & Touche*(Auditors)*
1 World Trade Center
New York, NY 10048
Tel.: 212-669-5000

Irving Trust Co.*(Major Banking Relationship)*
New York, NY

MARINE TRAVELIFT, INC.
49 E. Yew St.
Sturgeon Bay, WI 54235
Mailing Address:
P.O. Box 66,
Sturgeon Bay, WI 54235
Tel.: 414-743-6202
Fax: 414-743-1522
Year Founded: 1975
Approx.Sls.: $30,000,000
Emp.: 320
Fiscal Year-end: 12/31/91
Import Export
Mfr. of Marine Hoists, Boat Lifts & Marine Fork Lifts
S.I.C.: 3441; 3536; 3537
Gerald P. Lamer *(Pres.)*
Steve Krueger *(V.P.-Fin.)*
Allan J. Lamer *(V.P.-Sls.)*
Larry Rader *(Sec. & Gen. Counsel)*
John Kacmarynski *(Dir.-Sls.)*
Robert Papke *(Dir.-Personnel)*
Jim Waples *(Dir.-Intl. Sls.)*
Tom Feider *(Mgr.-Engrng.)*
Jim Kintopf *(Supvr.-Pur.)*

Subsidiaries:

Kewaunee Engineering Corp. (1)
520 N. Main St.
Kewaunee, WI 52416
Tel.: 414-388-2000
Approx.Sls.: $18,000,000
Emp.: 230
Import
Mfr. of Construction Machinery
S.I.C.: 3531; 3441
Gerald Lamer *(Pres.)*
Steve Krueger *(V.P.-Fin.)*
Allan Lamer *(V.P.-Mktg. & Adv. Mgr.)*
John Kacmarynski *(Dir.-Sls.)*

MTI Leasing, Ltd. (1)
49 E. Yew St.
Sturgeon Bay, WI 54235
Tel.: 414-743-6202
Rental & Leasing of Boat Handling Equipment
S.I.C.: 4499
Gerald Lamer *(Pres.)*
Steve Krueger *(V.P.)*
Allan Lamer *(V.P.-Mktg.)*
John Kacmarynski *(Dir.-Sls.)*
Jim Kintopf *(Supvr.-Pur.)*

Shuttlelift, Inc. (1)
49 E. Yew St.
Sturgeon Bay, WI 54235
Tel.: 414-743-6202
Fax: 414-743-1522
Import Export
Mfr. of Cranes & Hoists
S.I.C.: 3536
Gerald Lamer *(Pres.)*
Allan Lamer *(V.P.-Mktg. & Adv. Mgr.)*
John Kacmarynski *(Dir.-Sls.)*
Jim Kintopf *(Supvr.-Pur.)*

MARINE WORLD AFRICA USA
Marine World Pkwy.
Vallejo, CA 94589
Tel.: 707-644-4000
Fax: 707-644-0241
Year Founded: 1968
Approx.Sls.: $26,000,000
Emp.: 1,200
Fiscal Year-end: 12/31/90
Nonprofit Theme Park; Marine & Land Animals, Water Ski Show
S.I.C.: 7996
Terry A. Curtola, Jr. *(Chm. Bd.)*
Michael B. Demetrios *(Pres.)*
John E. Corcoran *(Exec. V.P. & Gen. Mgr.)*
Phillip E. Ensor *(Exec. V.P.-Fin. & Admin.)*
Michael B. Gallagher *(Exec. V.P.-Mktg.)*
Steve Ramirez *(V.P.-Foods & Games)*
Scott Yoder *(V.P.-Opers.)*
Joyce Erickson *(Controller)*
Chris Baldwin *(Dir.-Devel.)*
Mollie English *(Dir.-Sls.)*
Pat Foster-Turley *(Dir.-Conservation, Research & Devel.)*
Mary J. O'Herron *(Dir.-Pub. Rels.)*
Lisa Rodriguez *(Dir.-Personnel)*
Jane L. Johnson *(Mgr.-Sls. Promo.)*

MARINETTE MARINE CORPORATION
1600 Ely St.
Marinette, WI 54143-0198
Tel.: 715-735-9341
Fax: 715-735-3516
Year Founded: 1942
Approx.Sls.: $75,000,000
Emp.: 500
Export
Ships; Boats; Combat Vehicles
S.I.C.: 3731; 3732
Roger H. Derusha *(Chm. Bd.)*
Daniel L. Gulling *(Pres. & Chief Exec. Officer)*
Bernard Bentgen *(V.P.-Oper.)*
Tom Cook *(Controller)*
Bob Cassibry *(Mgr.-Contracts)*

Outside Service Firm(s):

Deloitte & Touche*(Auditors)*
Two Prudential Plaza, 180 N. Stetson
Chicago, IL 60601
Tel.: 312-946-2039

Sidley & Austin*(Legal Firm)*
One First National Plaza, 42nd Fl.
Chicago, IL 60603
Tel.: 312-853-7000
Fax: 312-853-7036

MARIS, WEST & BAKER, INC.
5120 Galaxie Dr.
Jackson, MS 39206
Mailing Address:
P.O. Box 12426,
Jackson, MS 39236-2426
Tel.: 601-362-6306
Fax: 601-981-1902
Year Founded: 1970
Approx.Billings: $16,000,000
Emp.: 31
Ken Sandridge *(Pres.)*
Larry Painter *(Sr. V.P., Pub. Rels.)*
Mike Booth *(V.P., Fin.)*
Sutton Marks *(Consultant)*

MARISA CHRISTINA INC.
1410 Broadway
New York, NY 10018
Tel.: 212-221-5770
Fax: 212-921-7632
Approx.Sls.: $25,000,000
Emp.: 45
Importers of Ladies Sweaters; Marisa Christina Knits
S.I.C.: 5137; 2339
Mike Lerner *(Pres.)*
Elliot R. Epstein *(Exec. V.P.-Adv., Mktg. & Mdsg.)*
Margie Conigliaro *(V.P.-Admin. & Production)*
Christine Murphy *(Controller)*

MARITZ INC.
1375 N. Highway Dr.
Fenton, MO 63099
Tel.: 314-827-4000 **MO**
Fax: 314-827-3700
Year Founded: 1894
Earnings: $15,000,000
Approx.Sls.: $1,300,000,000
Emp.: 5,200
Fiscal Year-end: 3/31/92
Motivation & Training Programs, Group & Business Travel, Marketing Research, Sales & Business Meetings
S.I.C.: 8741; 8999; 4729; 8742; 7389; 7812
Employee Matching Gifts Program: Matching Gifts to Accredited Schools, Arts & Cultural Organizations
William E. Maritz *(Chm. Bd. & Chief Exec. Officer)*
N.L. Schwesig *(Pres.)*
David L. Fleisher *(Sr. Exec. V.P. & Chief Fin. Officer)*
Jeffrey Reinberg *(Sr. Exec. V.P.-Admin.)*
Henry Stolar *(Sr. V.P. & Gen. Counsel)*
Duane D. Christensen *(Sr. V.P.-Corp. Communications)*
Terry Goring *(V.P.-Personnel)*
Dan Westrich *(V.P.-Mngmt. Information Systems)*
Thomas Crank *(Dir.-Pur.)*

No. of U.S. Offices: 135
No. of Foreign Offices: 8

Computer Systems/Hardware:
IBM

Outside Service Firm(s):

Deloitte & Touche*(Auditors)*
One City Centre
St. Louis, MO 63101
Tel.: 314-342-4900
Fax: 314-342-1100

Boatmen's Trust Company*(Major Banking Relationship)*
100 North Broadway
St. Louis, MO 63102
Tel.: 314-466-2469

Boatmen's Trust Company*(Pension Manager)*
100 North Broadway
St. Louis, MO 63102
Tel.: 314-466-2469

Subsidiaries:

Maritz Communications Co. (1)
1315 N. Highway Dr.
Fenton, MO 63099
Tel.: 314-827-4000 (100%)
Fax: 314-827-1739
Approx.Sls.: $90,000,000
Emp.: 300
Fiscal Year-end: 3/31/91
Business Meetings, AV Production, Training Materials
S.I.C.: 7812
Don Ferman *(V.P.-Mktg.)*
Fred Howell *(V.P. & Controller)*
Mark Cohen *(V.P. & Eastern Area Gen. Mgr.)*
Mike Craven *(V.P. & Detroit Area Gen. Mgr.)*
Kevin Quigley *(V.P. & Western Area Gen. Mgr.)*
Terry Hobbs *(V.P. & Central Area Gen. Mgr.)*
Mark Tucker *(V.P. & Dir.-Performance Training)*
Paul Eades *(Dir.-Human Resources)*

Maritz Marketing Research, Inc. (1)
1385 N. Highway Dr.
Fenton, MO 63026
Tel.: 314-827-4000 (100%)
Research Services
S.I.C.: 8748

Maritz Inc.—(Continued)

William H. Lewellen *(Pres.)*

Maritz Performance Improvement Company (1)
1400 S. Highway Dr.
Fenton, MO 63026
Tel.: 314-827-4000 (100%)
Sales Motivation Programs
S.I.C.: 7389
Richard T. Hurley *(Pres.)*

Maritz Travel Co. (1)
1395 N. Highway Dr.
Fenton, MO 63026
Tel.: 314-827-4000 (100%)
Incentive & Business Travel
S.I.C.: 4724; 4725
Robert K. Swearingen *(Pres.)*

Non-U.S. Holding:

Maritz Limited (1)
Dean Street
Marlow, Buckinghamshire SL7 3JJ, United Kingdom
Tel.: 6284-6011
Motivation & Training Programs
S.I.C.: 8742; 8999
Brian Alexander *(Grp. Chm.)*

MARK ANDY, INC.
18081 Chesterfield Airport Rd.
Chesterfield, MO 63005
Mailing Address:
P.O. Box 1023
Chesterfield, MO 63006
Tel.: 314-532-4433
Fax: 314-532-1510
Year Founded: 1946
Approx.Sls.: $30,000,000
Emp.: 300
Export
Mfr. Rotary Printing & Die-Cutting Machines, Label Converting Equip.
S.I.C.: 3555; 3554; 3569
Mark Andrews, Jr. *(Chm. Bd.)*
John Eulich *(Pres.)*
Dale Bunnell *(V.P.-Sls.)*
Mike Howard *(Controller)*
April Wamser *(Dir.-Personnel)*
Pat Scott *(Mgr.-Pur.)*
Principal(s):
Mark Andrews, Jr.

No. of Mfg. Plants/Facilities: 3

Outside Service Firm(s):

Grace & Co.*(Auditors)*
St. Louis, MO

Schramm & Pines*(Legal Firm)*
St. Louis, MO

Boatmen's Trust Company*(Major Banking Relationship)*
100 North Broadway
St. Louis, MO 63102
Tel.: 314-466-2469

MARK CHEVROLET INC.
33200 Michigan Ave.
Wayne, MI 48184
Tel.: 313-722-9100
Fax: 313-722-4498
Approx.Sls.: $27,700,000
Emp.: 79
Automobile Dealership
S.I.C.: 5511
Charles Cabana *(Pres.)*
Linda Romano *(Controller)*
Bill Cabana *(Mgr.-New Car Sls.)*
Principal(s):
Charles Cabana
Bill Cabana

MARK FABRICKS, INC.
1555 Newton St.
Los Angeles, CA 90021
Tel.: 213-748-5274 **CA**
Fax: 213-748-3264
Year Founded: 1981
Approx.Sls.: $120,000,000
Emp.: 40
Wholesale Distributor of Textile Converters
S.I.C.: 5131
Mark Walzman *(Pres.)*
Ira Kipnis *(Chief Fin. Officer)*
Howard Deutchman *(V.P., Sec. & Treas.)*
Saul Bennett *(Controller)*

Outside Service Firm(s):

Weber, Lipshie & Co.*(Auditors)*
Los Angeles, CA

Barclays Bank*(Major Banking Relationship)*
Los Angeles, CA

MARK LIGHTING FIXTURE CO., INC.
25 Knickerbocker Rd.
Moonachie, NJ 07074
Tel.: 201-939-0880
Fax: 201-939-1094
Approx.Sls.: $10,750,000
Emp.: 70
Fiscal Year-end: 12/31/90
Export
Commercial Lighting Fixtures
S.I.C.: 3646
Carl Coppola *(Pres. & Sec.)*
Robert J. Hausler *(V.P.-Sls. & Mktg.)*
Roselaine Fernino *(Controller)*
Benjamin Bucaro *(Mgr.-Prod.)*
George Miller *(Mgr.-Sls.)*
William Vida *(Mgr.-Engrng.)*
Rudolph Vleck *(Mgr.-Pur.)*

No. of Mfg. Plants/Facilities: 1
No. of U.S. Offices: 1

Outside Service Firm(s):

Sax, Macy, Fromm & Company*(Auditors)*
Clifton, NJ

Orloff, Lowenbach, Stifelman & Siegel*(Legal Firm)*
Roseland, NJ

Chemical Bank*(Major Banking Relationship)*
Paramus, NJ

MARK MACHINE INC.
(Formerly HMC Corporation)
912 Antelope Rd.
White City, OR 97503
Mailing Address:
P.O. Box 2614
White City, OR 97503
Tel.: 503-826-8900
Fax: 503-826-8989
Year Founded: 1974
Approx.Sls.: $30,000,000
Emp.: 150
Fiscal Year-end: 9/30/90
Mfr. Lawn Equip.
S.I.C.: 3423; 3524
Thomas Bilinovich *(Pres.)*

No. of Mfg. Plants/Facilities: 1
No. of U.S. Offices: 1
No. of Foreign Offices: 1

Computer Systems/Hardware:
MAI Basic Four

Outside Service Firm(s):

Deloitte & Touche*(Auditors)*
1000 Wilshire Blvd.
Los Angeles, CA 90017-2472
Tel.: 213-688-0800
Fax: 213-688-0100

Security Pacific Business Credit*(Major Banking Relationship)*
Pasadena, CA

MARK III INDUSTRIES
5401 N.W. 44th Ave.
Ocala, FL 32675
Mailing Address:
P.O. Box 2525,
Ocala, FL 32678
Tel.: 904-732-5878 **FL**
Fax: 904-351-1017
Year Founded: 1978
Approx.Sls.: $450,000,000
Emp.: 1,700
Export
Van Conversions
S.I.C.: 3792
Roy T. Boyd, III *(Chm. Bd. & Chief Exec. Officer)*
Charles E. Dorrity *(Pres.)*
Glen Cordrey *(V.P.)*
Joe Krim Sr. *(V.P.)*
Greg Lance *(V.P.-Sls.)*
Bobby Pilarczy *(V.P.)*
Carl Raschke *(Treas.)*
Hans Tansler III *(Gen. Counsel)*
Sally Boyd *(Sec.)*
Robert Cahill *(Dir.-Human Resources)*
Cindy Thomas *(Dir.-Data Processing)*
Bubba Yongue *(Dir.-Research & Devel.)*

No. of Mfg. Plants/Facilities: 1
No. of U.S. Offices: 1

Computer Systems/Hardware:
Hewlett Packard-Growth Poer Software

Outside Service Firm(s):

Marsh & McLennan*(Group Insurer)*
Jacksonville, FL
Tel.: 904-398-2311

Barnett Bank*(Major Banking Relationship)*
Ocala, FL

MARKAIR, INC.
P.O. Box 196769
Anchorage, AK 99519-6769
Tel.: 907-243-1414
Tel.: 800-426-6784
Tel.: 800-478-0800
Telex: 09025274 MARKAIR AHG
Fax: 907-248-6943
Year Founded: 1947
Approx.Sls.: $160,000,000
Emp.: 1,000
Fiscal Year-end: 12/31/90
Holding Company; Subsidiaries Operate Fields of Air Transportation (Cargo & Passenger), Oil & Gas Drilling, Real Estate
S.I.C.: 4512; 1381; 6531; 6719
Neil G. Bergt *(Chm. Bd. & Chief Exec. Officer)*
Steven L. Hartung *(Chief Fin. Officer & V.P.)*
Mike Bergt *(Pres.)*
Judy Bandel *(Controller)*
Steve Williams *(Gen. Counsel)*
Mac Ferguson *(Dir.-Pur.)*
Leslye Langla *(Dir.-Sls. & Mktg.)*
Dusty Rhodes *(Dir.-Human Resources)*

Computer Systems/Hardware:
Tandem TNX-2

Outside Service Firm(s):

KPMG Peat Marwick*(Auditors)*
Anchorage, AK

Metropolitan Life Insurance Co.*(Group Insurer)*
One Madison Ave.
New York, NY 10010-3690
Tel.: 215-578-9292

Charles E. Cole*(Legal Firm)*
Fairbanks, AK

First National Bank of Chicago*(Major Banking Relationship)*
One First National Plaza
Chicago, IL 60670
Tel.: 312-732-9781
Tel.: 312-732-4050
Fax: 312-732-4840
Fax: 312-732-3055

Norwest Bank Minnesota, N.A.*(Major Banking Relationship)*
6th St. & Marquette Av.
Minneapolis, MN 55479
Tel.: 612-667-1234

Seattle First National Bank*(Major Banking Relationship)*
701 Fifth Avenue
Seattle, WA 98104
Tel.: 206-358-3035

Subsidiaries:

Arctic Alaska Drilling (1)
P.O. Box 6769
Anchorage, AK 99502
Tel.: 907-243-1414
Oil & Gas Drilling
S.I.C.: 1381

Markair Express (1)
P.O. Box 196769
Anchorage, AK 99519-6769
Tel.: 907-243-1414
Tel.: 800-426-6784
Fax: 907-243-8897
Air Transportation
S.I.C.: 4512
Mike Bergt *(Pres. & Chief Exec. Officer)*

MARKDATA INC.
Markdata Plaza
Pittston, PA 18640
Mailing Address:
P.O. Box 765
Pittston, PA 18640
Tel.: 717-654-2406 **PA**
Fax: 717-655-0144
Year Founded: 1977
Assets: $10,500,000
Liabilities: $3,700,000
Net Worth: $6,800,000
Sales Range: $10-19 Million
Emp.: 150
Export
Mail Marketing
S.I.C.: 5961
Thomas Joseph *(Chm., Pres. & Chief Exec. Officer)*
Ronald Ackourey *(Mgr.-Opers.)*
George Saban *(Mgr.-Opers.)*
Principal(s):
Thomas Joseph

No. of Mfg. Plants/Facilities: 1
No. of U.S. Offices: 2

Computer Systems/Hardware:
Prime

Outside Service Firm(s):

Parente, Randolph, Orlando, Carey & Associates*(Auditors)*
46 Public Square
Wilkes-Barre, PA 18701-2681
Tel.: 717-820-0100
Fax: 717-824-9865

Snyder & Clemente*(Auditors)*
Kingston, PA 18704

First Eastern Bank N.A.*(Investment Banker)*
11 West Market St.
Wilkes-Barre, PA 18768
Tel.: 717-826-4603

MARKEM CORPORATION
150 Congress St.
Keene, NH 03431
Tel.: 603-352-1130
Tel.: 800-462-7536
Telex: RCA 216470
Fax: 603-357-5871
Year Founded: 1911
Approx.Sls.: $150,000,000

Emp.: 1,400
Fiscal Year-end: 12/31/90
Import Export
Mfr. In-House Printing Systems & Supplies
S.I.C.: 3559; 2893
Joseph A. Baute *(Chm. Bd. & Chief Exec. Officer)*
Thomas Putnam *(Pres.)*
Richard Church *(V.P.-Opers.)*
Frank Plummer *(V.P. & Sec.)*
James Putnam *(V.P. & Gen Mgr.)*
Spencer Struble *(V.P. & Div. Mgr.-Supplies)*
Steve Gallant *(Controller)*
Benjamin Nelson *(Dir.-Indus. Mkt. Rels.)*
Dave Hill *(Mgr.-Personnel)*
John MacAllister *(Mgr.-Adv.)*

Computer Systems/Hardware:
AS 400

Outside Service Firm(s):

Arthur Andersen & Co.*(Auditors)*
One Intl. Place, 100 Oliver St.
Boston, MA 02110
Tel.: 617-330-4000
Fax: 617-439-9731

Industrial Risk Insurers*(Commercial Insurance Carrier)*
Hartford, CT

Group Insurance Service Center*(Group Insurer)*
Marshfield, MA

Gaston & Snow*(Legal Firm)*
One Federal St.
Boston, MA 02110
Tel.: 617-426-4600
Fax: 617-350-6146

First National Bank of Boston*(Major Banking Relationship)*
P.O. Box 644,
Boston, MA 02102-0644
Tel.: 617-575-2900
Fax: 617-575-2549

John Hancock Mutual Life Insurance Co.*(Pension Manager)*
John Hancock Place, P.O. Box 111
Boston, MA 02117

MARKET DEVELOPMENT GROUP, INC.
1053 Maitland Center Common
Maitland, FL 32751
Tel.: 407-875-1770
Fax: 407-875-1580
Year Founded: 1980
Approx.Billings: $20,000,000
Emp.: 45
Hospitality & Real Estate
Drew J. Cherner *(Pres.)*
Pamela Mosley *(V.P., Opers.)*
Karmen Hagen *(V.P., Hospitality Div.)*

Computer Systems/Hardware:
IBM, Macintosh

MARKET DEVELOPMENT GROUP INC.
1200 Potomac St., N.W.
Washington, DC 20007
Tel.: 202-298-8030
Fax: 202-342-2039
Year Founded: 1978
Approx.Billings: $10,000,000
Emp.: 20
Direct Marketing
W. Michael Gretschel *(Pres.)*
John Alahouzos, Jr. *(Exec. V.P.)*
C. Ann Papp *(V.P.)*

MARKETING ALTERNATIVES, INC.
3721 Ventura Dr., Ste. 180
Arlington Heights, IL 60004
Tel.: 708-253-1410
Fax: 708-253-2232
Year Founded: 1983
Approx.Billings: $20,000,000
Emp.: 23
Home Products
Gary Stanko *(Pres., Chief Exec. Officer)*
Thomas M. Behan *(V.P.)*
John M. Wallseck *(V.P.)*
Debra Dlugatch *(Controller)*

MARKETING COMMUNICATIONS
10605 W. 84th Terrace
Lenexa, KS 66214
Tel.: 913-492-1575 **MO**
Fax: 913-492-9812
Year Founded: 1969
Assets: $3,321,000
Liabilities: $1,280,000
Net Worth: $2,041,000
Sales Range: $10-19 Million
Emp.: 90
Fiscal Year-end: 12/31/90
Direct Mail Marketing Sevices
S.I.C.: 5961; 7331
Bob White *(Pres. & Chief Exec. Officer)*
John O'Connor *(Chief Fin. Officer & Controller)*
Robert W. Norman *(V.P. & Dir.-Opers.)*
Mike Rose *(V.P.)*
Principal(s):
Bob White
Mike Rose
Larry Hawks

No. of Mfg. Plants/Facilities: 1
No. of U.S. Offices: 3

Computer Systems/Hardware:
IBM 4341 & System 36

Outside Service Firm(s):

Coopers & Lybrand*(Auditors)*
Kansas City, MO

Blue Cross & Blue Shield of Kansas City*(Commercial Insurance Carrier)*
Kansas City, MO

Shughart, Thomson & Kilroy*(Legal Firm)*
Kansas City, MO

United Missouri Bank*(Major Banking Relationship)*
10th & Grand
Kansas City, MO 64106
Tel.: 816-860-7000
Fax: 800-892-2944

TMC
THE MARKETING CONTINUUM INC

THE MARKETING CONTINUUM, INC.
4311 Oak Lawn Ave., Ste. 600
Dallas, TX 75219
Tel.: 214-855-0080
Fax: 214-528-8203
Year Founded: 1984
Approx.Billings: $16,000,000
Emp.: 22
Beverages, Package Goods & Fast Food, Business to Business
Roberta A. Merkel *(Chief Exec. Officer)*
David T. Mullen *(Pres. & New Bus. Contact)*
Odell A. Scott *(Exec. V.P.)*

MARKETING CORP. OF AMERICA
285 Riverside Ave.
Westport, CT 06880
Tel.: 203-222-1000
Fax: 203-222-6536
Year Founded: 1971
Approx.Sls.: $165,000,000
Emp.: 2,000
Fiscal Year-end: 6/30/90
Consumer Marketing Service
S.I.C.: 8742; 7311; 5199; 5812; 6512
James R. McManus *(Chm. Bd., Pres. & Chief Exec. Officer)*
Edmund R. McGill *(V.P. & Chief Fin. Officer)*
Brian C. Bedford *(Controller)*
John F. Muskus *(Corp. Sec.)*
Patrick M. Ryan *(Mgr.-Real Estate)*

Computer Systems/Hardware:
Wang VS300, VS100, VS65 & VS15

Outside Service Firm(s):

Price Waterhouse*(Auditors)*
300 Atlantic St.
Stamford, CT 06904

Aetna Life & Casualty*(Commercial Insurance Carrier)*
151 Farmington Avenue
Hartford, CT 06156
Tel.: 203-273-2128
Fax: 203-729-4295

Levett, Rockwood & Sanders*(Legal Firm)*
Westport, CT

MARKETING DISPLAYS INTERNATIONAL, INC.
38271 W. 12 Mile Rd.
Farmington Hills, MI 48331
Tel.: 313-553-1900 **MI**
Fax: 313-488-5700
Year Founded: 1965
Sales Range: $10-19 Million
Emp.: 150
Mfr. of Point of Purchase Displays, Lightboxes, Poster Frames; Literature Racks; Price Signs; Curb Displays; Traffic Control Products
S.I.C.: 3993; 2542
Robert Sarkisian *(Pres.)*
Colleen M. Spencer *(Controller)*
Travis Dunbar *(Mgr.-Opers.)*
Brian Manwaring *(Mgr.-Mktg.)*
Gary Rigby *(Mgr.-Natl. Sls.)*
Robert West *(Pur. Agent)*

Outside Service Firm(s):

Mathews, Nightingdale, Reich & Scott, P.C.*(Auditors)*
Birmingham, MI

Comerica Bank*(Major Banking Relationship)*
211 W. Fort St.
Detroit, MI 48226
Tel.: 313-222-3300

MARKETING MAGIC INC.
4801 S. University Dr., Ste. 201W
Fort Lauderdale, FL 33328
Tel.: 305-434-2330
Fax: 305-434-7594
Year Founded: 1981
Approx.Billings: $20,000,000
Emp.: 30
Retail, Travel & Leisure, Automotive, Restaurant, Radio & TV Stations Promo.
Jon J. Mark *(Chm. Bd.)*
Robert Rose *(Pres. & New Bus. Contact)*
Tom Baroni *(Exec. V.P., Creative Services)*
Carol Mark *(Sec., Treas., Sr. Art Dir.)*
Lisa Del Pozzo *(Dir.-Pub. Rels.)*

MARKETING RESOURCES OF AMERICA, INC.
10551 Barkley
Overland Park, KS 66212
Tel.: 913-648-8333
Fax: 913-648-5024
Year Founded: 1981
Approx.Billings: $57,900,000
Emp.: 110
Automotive & Heavy Duty Industry; Retirement Community Development Industry
Frank G. Weyforth, Jr. *(Chm. Bd., Chief Exec. Officer & Pres.)*
Tom Clevinger *(Sr. V.P., Gen. Mgr.)*
Bill Moser *(Sr. V.P., Vehicle Systems)*
Rick Skaggs *(Sr. V.P., Fin. & Admin.)*
Tommy Wealand *(Sr. V.P., Gen. Mgr.)*
Deanea Boydston *(Controller)*
Bob Inderman *(Dir.-Pub. Rels.)*

MARKETING SERVICES UNLTD.
(House Agency)
W220 N507 Springdale Rd.
Waukesha, WI 53187
Mailing Address:
P.O. Box 1647,
Waukesha, WI 53187
Tel.: 414-542-6060
Fax: 414-542-4258
Year Founded: 1973
Approx.Billings: $10,000,000
Durable Medical Equip.
Mary Kallenbach *(Mktg. Mgr.)*

MARKETING SUPPORT, INCORPORATED
303 E. Wacker Dr., Ste. 711
Chicago, IL 60601
Tel.: 312-565-0044
Fax: 312-819-3666
Year Founded: 1962
Approx.Billings: $38,000,000
Emp.: 65
David L. Weiner *(Pres.)*
Jane Storey *(Exec. V.P.)*
Brian Arnold *(V.P.)*
John Edlemann *(V.P.)*
Steve Farkos *(V.P., Opers.)*
Dennis Janssen *(V.P.)*
Howard Levitetz *(V.P.)*
Frank Morosky *(V.P.)*
Andrew J. Pongress *(V.P.)*
Tom Tully *(V.P.)*
Jo-Ann Balasko *(Controller)*

MARKIN TUBING, INC.
Pearl Creek Rd.
Wyoming, NY 14591
Mailing Address:
P.O. Box 242
Wyoming, NY 14591
Tel.: 716-495-6211
Fax: 716-495-6482
Sales Range: $10-19 Million
Emp.: 120
Mfr. of Cold Rolled Electrical Welded Mechanical Steel Tubing
S.I.C.: 3317; 3313
Barton Dambra *(Pres. & Chief Exec. Officer)*
Arthur Smith *(V.P.-Sls.)*

Markin Tubing, Inc.—(Continued)

Peter Lignos *(Chief Engr.)*

Outside Service Firm(s):

Ernst & Young*(Auditors)*
1400 Key Tower - 50 Fountain Plaza
Buffalo, NY
Tel.: 716-843-5000
Fax: 716-847-6949

Mousaw, Vigdor, Reeves, Heilbronner & Kroll*(Legal Firm)*
600 First Federal Plaza
Rochester, NY 14614
Tel.: 716-325-2500

Marine Midland Bank*(Major Banking Relationship)*
P.O. Box 803, 1 Marine Midland Center, 23rd Floor
Buffalo, NY 14203
Tel.: 716-841-2582

MARKWOOD INC.
667 W. Ward Ave.
High Point, NC 27261
Mailing Address:
P.O. Box 2448
High Point, NC 27261
Tel.: 919-889-6944 NC
Fax: 919-886-4996
Approx.Sls.: $55,000,000
Emp.: 750
Fiscal Year-end: 9/31/89
Manufacture Upholstered Furniture; Distribute Piece Goods
S.I.C.: 2512
S.C. Lee *(Chm. Bd.)*
Jack Cochran *(Pres.)*
Dave Simpson *(Mgr.-Sls.)*

No. of Mfg. Plants/Facilities: 7

Outside Service Firm(s):

BDO Seidman*(Auditors)*
High Point, NC

Parker, Poe, Adams & Bernstein*(Legal Firm)*
2600 Charlotte Plaza
Charlotte, NC 28244
Tel.: 704-372-9000

First Union National Bank of North Carolina*(Major Banking Relationship)*
Stock Transfer Dept., First Union Plz.
Charlotte, NC 28288
Tel.: 704-374-6161
Fax: 704-374-6987

Subsidiaries:

Stanton Cooper **(1)**
667 W. Ward Ave.
High Point, NC 27261
Tel.: 919-841-4900
Manufacture Sofas, Loveseats & Chairs
S.I.C.: 2512
Jack Cochran *(Pres.)*

Woodmark Originals **(1)**
1920 Jarrell Ave.
High Point, NC 27261
Tel.: 919-889-6944
Manufacture Chairs
S.I.C.: 2512
Jack Cochran *(Pres.)*

THE MARLEY COMPANY
1900 Shawnee Mission Pkwy.
Mission Woods, KS 66205
Mailing Address:
P.O. Box 2965,
Shawnee Mission, KS 66201
Tel.: 913-362-5440 DE
Fax: 913-432-1451
Year Founded: 1922
Assets: $359,000,000
Earnings: $14,618,000
Liabilities: $319,000,000
Net Worth: $40,000,000
Approx.Sls.: $621,465,000
Emp.: 4,700
Fiscal Year-end: 4/30/92
Import Export
Mfr. of Water Cooling Towers; Residential & Commercial Boilers; Electric Resistance Heaters; Water Well Drilling & Supplies; Pumps & Heat Exchangers
S.I.C.: 1781; 3433; 3444; 3561; 3589; 3443
Corporate Giving Program: Written Proposals Required; Giving Limited Primarily to Areas Where Company Has Facilities and/or Employees
Employee Matching Gifts Program: Matches Employee Gift Between $25 - $500 to Four-Year College or Universityy
R.J. Dineen *(Pres. & Chief Exec. Officer)*
Errol P. Mitlyng *(Sr. V.P.-Fin., Treas. & Chief Fin. Officer)*
Robert F. Wrobel *(Sr. V.P., Gen. Counsel & Chief Admin. Officer)*
N.E. Holmes *(V.P. & Controller)*
Robert A. Pitcel *(V.P.-Taxes)*
T.L. Potter *(V.P.-Benefits Admin.)*
Timothy J. Verhagen *(V.P.-Human Resources & Assoc. Gen. Counsel)*
K.B. Magill *(Gen. Counsel)*
Steve Menaugh *(Dir.-Corp. Communications)*

No. of Mfg. Plants/Facilities: 12

Computer Systems/Hardware:
IBM 4381

Outside Service Firm(s):

Deloitte & Touche*(Auditors)*
Mission, KS

Hartford Life Insurance Co.*(Commercial Insurance Carrier)*
Hartford, CT 06104-2999

Equilor*(Group Insurer)*
Chicago, IL

Continental Bank N. A.*(Major Banking Relationship)*
231 S. LaSalle St.
Chicago, IL 60697
Tel.: 312-828-2345
Tel.: 800-426-5754
Telex: 312-828-1783

Bankers Trust Co.*(Major Banking Relationship)*
P.O. Box 318, Church St. Station
New York, NY 10008
Tel.: 212-454-2212
Fax: 212-454-2783

Bankers Trust Co.*(Pension Manager)*
P.O. Box 318, Church St. Station
New York, NY 10008
Tel.: 212-454-2212
Fax: 212-454-2783

Davis, Weaver & Mendel, Inc.*(Pension Manager)*
Atlanta, GA

Equitable Real Estate Investment Managment Inc.*(Pension Manager)*
3414 Peachtree Rd. N.E.
Atlanta, GA 30326-1162

Loomis, Sayles & Co., Inc.*(Pension Manager)*
3 First National Plaza, Suite 5450
Chicago, IL
Tel.: 312-346-9750

Thomson, Horstmann & Bryant*(Pension Manager)*
New York, NY

Divisions:

Layne & Bowler **(1)**
1993 Chelsea Ave.
Memphis, TN 38108
Tel.: 901-725-6300
Fax: 901-725-6314
Emp.: 250
Mfr. of Pumping Equipment
S.I.C.: 3561
R.E. Goodwill, Jr. *(Pres.)*
D. Mungle *(V.P.-Fin.)*
G. Richert *(V.P.-Sls. & Mktg.)*
T. Brenton *(V.P.-Mfg.)*
F. King *(Pur. Agent)*

Marley Electric Heating Co. **(1)**
470 Beauty Spot Rd. E.
Bennettsville, SC 29512
Tel.: 803-479-4006
Emp.: 365
S.I.C.: 3433
Dennis Porzio *(Pres.)*

Marley Pump Co. **(1)**
5800 Foxridge Dr.
Mission, KS 66202
Tel.: 913-831-5700
Fax: 913-831-5145
Sales Range: $20-39 Million
Fiscal Year-end: 4/30/92
Export
Mfr. of Pumps & Pumping Equipment
S.I.C.: 3561
Robert L. Beeson *(Pres.)*
Al Davis *(V.P. & Controller)*
Assad Sobky *(V.P.-Intl. Opers.)*
Allen Van Riper *(Mgr.-Natl. Sls.)*

Weil-McLain **(1)**
Blaine St.
Michigan City, IN 46360
Tel.: 219-879-6561
Fax: 219-879-4025
Emp.: 750
Residential & Commercial Heating Boilers
S.I.C.: 3433
B.A. Radi *(Pres.)*
W.L. Jackson *(Exec. V.P.)*
E.W. Johann *(V.P.-Mktg. & Engrng.)*
J.M. Goodall *(Adv. Mgr.)*
Larry Norlington *(Pur. Agent)*

Subsidiaries:

Engineers & Fabricators Co. **(1)**
3501 W. 11th St.
Houston, TX 77008
Tel.: 713-869-3461 (100%)
Fax: 713-869-8088
Emp.: 200
Mfr. of Shell & Tube Heat Exchangers
S.I.C.: 3443
Harold L. Sides *(Pres.)*

Layne-Western Co., Inc. **(1)**
1900 Shawnee Mission Pkwy.
Mission Woods, KS 66205
Tel.: 913-362-0510
Fax: 913-362-0133
Approx.Sls.: $128,400,000
Emp.: 1,500
Drillingof Water Wells
S.I.C.: 1781
Robert C. Dymond *(Pres.)*

The Marley Cooling Tower Co. **(1)**
5800 Foxridge Dr.
Mission, KS 66202
Tel.: 913-362-1818
Fax: 913-362-3610
Emp.: 900
Mfr. of Cooling Towers
S.I.C.: 3443
Thomas P. Kroehle *(Pres.)*

Division:

Recold, Inc. **(2)**
550 W. Mercury Ln.
Brea, CA 92621
Tel.: 714-529-6080
Fax: 714-529-6733
Mfr. of Cooling Towers
S.I.C.: 3443
Dave Wilkerson *(Pres.)*

THE MARLIN COMPANY
1200 E. Woodhurst Dr., Bldg. V
Springfield, MO 65804
Tel.: 417-887-7446
Fax: 417-887-3643
Year Founded: 1985
Approx.Billings: $11,400,000
Emp.: 24
Dennis K. Martin *(Pres.)*
Thomas R. Kujawa *(Mktg. Services Mgr.)*

ED MARLING STORES, INC.
2950 McClure Rd.
Topeka, KS 66614
Tel.: 913-273-6970 KS
Fax: 913-273-6208
Approx.Sls.: $13,000,000
Emp.: 100
Furntiure Stores; Two-way, Citizens' Band, Weather & Shortwave Radios; Television Sets; Major Electric Household Appliances
S.I.C.: 5712; 5731; 5722
Mark E. Marling *(Chm. Bd. & Pres.)*
Mary A. Frazen *(Exec. V.P., Sec. & Treas.)*
Jon Anderson *(V.P.)*
Michael Dunn *(V.P.)*

Outside Service Firm(s):

Mize Houser Mehlinger & Kimes*(Auditors)*
Topeka, KS

Schroeder, Henry, Groff & Coffman*(Legal Firm)*
Topeka, KS

MARLOW INDUSTRIES
10451 Vista Park Rd.
Dallas, TX 75238
Tel.: 214-340-4900
Fax: 214-341-5212
Year Founded: 1973
Approx.Rev.: $12,000,000
Emp.: 160
Thermoelectric Coolers, Cooling Systems & Controllers
S.I.C.: 3625
Raymond Marlow *(Pres.)*
John L. Nelson *(V.P.-Sls. & Mktg.)*
Ed Burke *(Asst. V.P.-Assembly)*
Robbie Peck *(Controller)*

Outside Service Firm(s):

Arthur Andersen & Co.*(Auditors)*
901 Main St., Ste. 5600
Dallas, TX 75202
Tel.: 214-741-8300

Doke & Riley*(Legal Firm)*
1717 Main St.
Dallas, TX 75201
Tel.: 214-746-5700

MARMAC CORPORATION
P.O. Box 1825,
Parkersburg, WV 26102
Tel.: 304-485-4494
Marine Leasing
James T. Wakley *(Chm. Bd.)*
Mark C. Kury *(Pres.)*
Francis C. McCusker *(Chief Fin. Officer)*

Subsidiaries:

Colonial Millwork, Inc. **(1)**
P.O. Box 436,
Beverley, WV 25653
Tel.: 304-636-9338
Mfr. & Distributor of Wood Products
James T. Wakley *(Pres.)*

Mongold Lumber Co. **(1)**
Rte. 1, Box 6,
Elkins, WV 26241
Tel.: 304-636-2081
Mfr. & Distributor of Wood Products
Max Armentrout *(Pres.)*

Preferred Millwork, Inc. **(1)**
980 Hawthorne Lane
West Chicago, IL 60185
Tel.: 708-293-4406
Wood Product Distributor
Michael R. Turner *(Chief Oper. Officer)*

L. J. Smith, Inc. **(1)**
35280 Scio-Bowerston Rd.
Bowerston, OH 44695
Tel.: 614-269-2221 (100%)
Fax: 614-269-9047
Approx.Sls.: $35,000,000
Emp.: 200
Manufactures Wooden Stair Parts & Custom Stairs
S.I.C.: 2431
Dwain Hicks *(Pres.)*
Jay A. Harstine *(Controller)*

THE MARMON GROUP, INC.
(Formerly Marmon Holdings, Inc.)
225 W. Washington St.
Chicago, IL 60606
Tel.: 312-372-9500 **DE**
Telex: 253112
Fax: 312-845-5305
Year Founded: 1953
Earnings: $125,100,000
Approx.Sls.: $3,900,000,000
Emp.: 26,705
Fiscal Year-end: 12/31/90
Diversified Holding Company; Manufacture & Marketing Operations: Industrial Materials & Components, Automotive, Building & Consumer Products, Systems & Equipment, Rail Transportation & Maintenance Equipment, Water & Industrial Fluids Treatment Systems; Industrial & Commercial Services: Full-Service Leasing of Railway Tank & Freight Cars, Consumer Credit & Telecommunications Services
S.I.C.: 3199; 3841; 3493; 3432; 3354; 3714; 2381; 6719; 4741; 5051; 7359; 3452; 3672; 3494; 3523; 3711; 3715; 3351
Jay A. Pritzker *(Chm. Bd.)*
Robert A. Pritzker *(Pres. & Chief Exec. Officer)*
Robert C. Gluth *(Chief Fin. Officer)*
Timothy P. Dimond *(Dir.-Fin. Reporting)*

Computer Systems/Hardware:
IBM PC

Outside Service Firm(s):

Ernst & Young*(Auditors)*
233 S. Wacker Dr.
Chicago, IL 60606
Tel.: 312-368-1800
Fax: 312-645-3095

Continental Bank N. A.*(Major Banking Relationship)*
231 S. LaSalle St.
Chicago, IL 60697
Tel.: 312-828-2345
Tel.: 800-426-5754
Telex: 312-828-1783

Subsidiaries:

Marmon Corporation **(1)**
225 W. Washington St.
Chicago, IL 60606
Tel.: 312-372-9500
Fax: 312-845-5305
Manufacture General Industrial Products; Copper, Brass, Aluminum, Iron, Steel & Tubular Products; Automotive Products; Coal Mining & Mining Equipment; Building Products & Store Fixtures
S.I.C.: 3351; 3463; 3321; 3325; 3714; 1222
Jay A. Pritzker *(Chm. Bd.)*
Robert A. Pritzker *(Pres. & Chief Oper. Officer)*
R.C. Gluth *(Exec. V.P.)*
Sidney H. Bonser *(Exec. V.P.)*
Gerald T. Shannon *(Sr. V.P.)*
R.W. Webb *(V.P. & Sec.)*
N.C. Gustafson *(V.P.-Taxes)*
D.W. Pethick *(V.P.)*

Subsidiaries:

Accutronics, Inc. **(2)**
225 N. First St.
Cary, IL 60013
Tel.: 708-639-2102
Fax: 708-639-8838
Printed Circuit Boards, Metal Stampings
S.I.C.: 3672
Milan S. Mortimer *(Pres. & Gen. Mgr.)*

Aluminum Forge Company **(2)**
502 E. Alton St.
Santa Ana, CA 92707
Tel.: 714-549-4075
Fax: 714-545-8286
Precision & Conventional Aluminum Forgings for Aerospace Vehicles Airframes, Hydraulic Systems, Computers, Medical Equipment & Other Applications
S.I.C.: 3463; 3721; 3761; 3728; 3764; 3769
James C. McGovern *(Pres.)*

Amarillo Gear Company **(2)**
P.O. Box 1789,
Amarillo, TX 79105
Tel.: 806-622-1273
Fax: 806-622-3258
Right-Angle Gear Drives for Pumps, Cooling Tower Fans & Other Industrial Applications; Large Spiral Bevel Gear Sets
S.I.C.: 3566
B.D. Pyeatt *(Pres. & Gen. Mgr.)*

Anderson Copper & Brass Company **(2)**
3800 W. 127th St.
Alsip, IL 60658
Tel.: 708-597-8656
Fax: 312-597-8656
Brass Fittings & Valves for Use With Copper & Plastic Tubing in the Transmission of Fluids, Air & Other Gases
S.I.C.: 3432; 3494
Richard Boyer *(Pres.)*

Cerro Copper Products Co. **(2)**
Hwy. 3, Mississippi Ave.
Sauget, IL 62201
Tel.: 618-337-6000
Fax: 618-332-9402
Emp.: 1,000
Export
Computer Systems/Hardware:
IBM Compatible
Electrolytic Copper Refining; Copper Plumbing, Refrigeration & Industrial Tubing.
S.I.C.: 3331; 3351
H.L. Schweich *(Pres. & Gen. Mgr.)*
Frank Murphy *(V.P.-Sls. & Mktg.)*
Paul Tandler *(V.P.-Mfg.)*
James R. Matcuk *(V.P., Controller & Treas.)*
Don Stickler *(Dir. of Sls.-Plumbing & Refrigeration)*
David Durham *(Dir.-Pur.)*
Royce Huffman *(Mgr.-Mktg. Communications)*
Al Finkelstein *(Mgr.-Human Resources)*
Don Zagari *(Mgr.-Personnel)*
Lorraine Cange *(Mktg. Asst.)*
Lewis C. Smith *(Natl. Sls. Mgr.-Industrial Tubing)*

Cerro Metal Products Company **(2)**
P.O. Box 388,
Bellefonte, PA 16823
Tel.: 814-355-6217
Fax: 814-355-6299
Brass Mill Products & Fabricated Parts; Low-Melt Alloy Products
S.I.C.: 3432
D.A. Gardiner *(Pres. & Gen. Mgr.)*

Cerro Sales Corporation **(2)**
540 Madison Ave.
New York, NY 10022
Tel.: 212-888-2100
Fax: 212-759-4611
International Metals Trading & Marketing
S.I.C.: 5051
Jaime Claro *(Pres.)*

Cerro Wire & Cable Co., Inc. **(2)**
P.O. Box 1049
Hartselle, AL 35640
Tel.: 205-773-2522
Fax: 205-773-5849
Building Wire & Cable, Power Cable
S.I.C.: 3351
Michael P. Hartley *(V.P. & Gen. Mgr.)*

L. A. Darling Company **(2)**
P.O. Box 970,
Paragould, AR 72450
Tel.: 501-239-9564
Fixtures for General Merchandise, Variety, Discount, Specialty & Department Stores; Shelving & Integrated Modular Merchandising Systems; Point of Purchase Displays
S.I.C.: 2542
Kent E. Toomey *(Pres. & Gen. Mgr.)*

Fenestra Corporation **(2)**
P.O. Box 8189,
Erie, PA 16505
Tel.: 814-838-2001
Fax: 814-883-2009
Approx.Sls.: $29,800,000
Emp.: 410
Mfr. of Standard, Custom-Built Residential & Specialty Steel Doors & Frames
S.I.C.: 3442
R.A. Pritzker *(Pres.)*
R.C. Gluth *(V.P. & Treas.)*
Jerome Hughes *(V.P. & Gen. Mgr.)*
R.W. Webb *(Sec. & Gen. Counsel)*
Richard Rectenwald *(Sls. Mgr.)*

Fontaine International, Inc. **(2)**
125 Cleage Dr.
Birmingham, AL 35217
Tel.: 205-853-8837
Fax: 205-854-3790
Fontaine "Fifth Wheels" (Tractor-Trailer Couplers); Dump Bodies & Hydraulic Hoists; Bulk Feed Bodies & Trailers; Lime & Fertilizer Spreaders, Salt Spreaders for Ice Control; Flatbed & Special Heavy-Duty Trailers
S.I.C.: 3715; 3711; 3523
Kelly Dier *(Pres.)*

Division:

Marmon-Herrington Company **(3)**
2000 Plantside Dr.
Louisville, KY 40299
Tel.: 502-491-0727
Fax: 502-491-2274
Approx.Sls.: $8,000,000
Emp.: 20
Remanufacturers of Ford, GMC, Chevrolet & Dodge Chassis & Manufacturers of Special Purpose Vehicles
S.I.C.: 5521; 3799
Robert Gimbel *(Gen. Mgr.)*
William Riley *(Gen. Sls. Mgr.)*
J. Johnson *(Chief Prod. Engr.)*

Subsidiary:

Fontaine Modification/Components Company **(3)**
P.O. Box 24475
Louisville, KY 40224
Tel.: 502-499-5601
Fax: 502-491-0086
Sales & Installation of Truck Equipment; Conversions of Medium & Heavy Duty Trucks to Marmon-Herrington All-Wheel Drive
S.I.C.: 5012
C. Granville Dennison, Jr. *(Pres.)*

Long-Airdox Company **(2)**
227 W. Maple Ave.
Oak Hill, WV 25901
Tel.: 304-469-3301
Fax: 304-469-4178
Mining Equipment: Belt & Chain Conveyor Systems; Underground & Open Pit Mining Haulage Systems; Face Drills, Feeder Breakers; Longwall Systems; Utility Vehicles; Carbide Bits; Augers; Ladco Bulk-Breaking Systems; Coal Preparation Plants & Material-Handling Systems
S.I.C.: 3532; 3535
W.E. Meador *(Pres. & Gen. Mgr.)*
Art Shaffer *(Adv. Mgr.)*

The Marmon Group, Inc. **(2)**
225 W. Washington St.
Chicago, IL 60606
Tel.: 312-372-9500
S.I.C.: 3589
Jay Pritkzer *(Chm. Bd.)*
Robert Pritkzer *(Pres.)*
Robert Gluth *(Exec. V.P.)*
Robert Webb *(Sec.)*

Marmon/Keystone Corp. **(2)**
P.O. Box 992
Butler, PA 16001
Tel.: 412-283-3000
Fax: 412-283-0558
Market & Distribute Tubular Products
S.I.C.: 5051
Norman E. Gottschalk, Jr. *(Pres.)*

Meyer Material Company **(2)**
580 Wolf Rd.
Des Plaines, IL 60017
Tel.: 708-824-4111
Fax: 708-824-7382
Ready-Mixed Concrete & Related Construction Materials & Services
S.I.C.: 3273
Merlin Wille *(Gen. Mgr.)*

Micro-Aire Surgical Instruments, Inc. **(2)**
24971 Ave. Stanford
Valencia, CA 91355
Tel.: 805-295-1020
Fax: 805-295-1064
Mfr. of Pneumatic & Electric Surgical Instruments
S.I.C.: 3841; 3845
Judy Lindstrom *(V.P. & Gen. Mgr.)*
Carolyn Carlson *(Controller)*
Jack Hogan *(Reg. Sls. Mgr.)*
Dave Forrest *(Reg. Sls. Mgr.)*
Joan Kennedy *(Reg. Sls. Mgr.)*
Ellen K. Repar *(Mktg. Sls. Mgr.)*
Frank Murphy *(Intl. Mktg. Mgr.)*

Penn Aluminum International **(2)**
P.O. Box 531,
Murphysboro, IL 62966
Precision Extruded & Drawn Aluminum Tube, Rigid Conduit & Shapes
S.I.C.: 3354
Charles Parke *(Pres. & Gen. Mgr.)*

Penn Pocahontas Coal Company **(2)**
Rte. 219, P.O. Box 248
Garrett, PA 15542
Tel.: 814-267-4635
Coal
S.I.C.: 1241
Daniel N. McLaughlin *(Pres.)*

Perfection Hy-Test Company **(2)**
1943-C Hoffmeyer Rd.
Florence, SC 29501
Tel.: 803-665-5543
Fax: 803-662-1984
Emp.: 350
Replacement Automotive Transmission Gears, Clutch Plates; Timing Chains, Sprockets & Gears; Ring Gears & Pinions; Remanufactured Automotive Parts
S.I.C.: 3714
J.H. Peacock *(Pres. & Gen. Mgr.)*
Richard W. Price *(Mktg. Mgr.)*
Kay Weinberg *(Customer Service Mgr.)*

Divisions:

Perfection-Hy-Test Rebuilding Div. **(3)**
306 Juneau
Purcell, OK 73080
Tel.: 405-527-5653
Fax: 405-527-7444
S.I.C.: 3714

Perfection-Hy-Test Rebuilding Div. **(3)**
426 Maple St.
Graham, NC 27253
Tel.: 919-226-5501
Fax: 919-227-0295
S.I.C.: 3714

The Rockbestos Company **(2)**
285 Nicolle St.
New Haven, CT 06511
Tel.: 203-772-2250
Fax: 203-787-5941
Special-Purpose Electrical Wire & Cable Resistant to Heat, Fire, Corrosion, Radiation, Chemicals & Other Hazards
S.I.C.: 3351
Stanley J. Bond *(Pres.)*

Triangle Auto Spring Company **(2)**
P.O. Box 425, Maloney Rd.
Du Bois, PA 15801
Tel.: 814-375-7211
Fax: 814-371-4495
Flat Leaf Springs, Threaded Rods, U-Bolts & Chassis Parts for Truck & Trailer Aftermarket; Marketing Chassis Parts
S.I.C.: 3714; 3452
J. Deardorff *(Pres. & Gen. Mgr.)*

The Colson Group, Inc. **(1)**
225 W. Washington St.
Chicago, IL 60606
Tel.: 312-372-9500
Industrial, Institutional Casters, Wheels & Rubber Bumpers
S.I.C.: 3429
Edward F. Gill, Jr. *(V.P. & Gen. Mgr.)*

Subsidiaries:

Colson Equipment, Inc. **(2)**
P. O. Box 1000,
Caruthersville, MO 63830
Tel.: 314-333-2070
Fax: 314-333-5859
Mobile Material-Handling Systems for Hospitals, Department Stores, Hotels & Industry; Wheel Chairs; Stretchers, & Operating Room Equipment
S.I.C.: 3496
Brad Enslin *(V.P. & Gen. Mgr.)*

Non-U.S. Holding:

Colson Transportwielen B.V. **(3)**
P.O. Box 421,
Veenendaal, Netherlands
Mfg. of Casten

The Marmon Group, Inc.—(Continued)

Colson Caster Corporation **(2)**
3700 Airport Rd.
Jonesboro, AR 72401
Tel.: 501-932-4501
Tel.: 800-643-5515
Fax: 800-356-6708
Emp.: 350
Export
Industrial & Institutional Casters, Wheels & Rubber Bumpers
S.I.C.: 3429
Edward F. Gill, Jr. *(V.P. & Gen. Mgr.)*
Darrell Pickney *(Personnel Dir.)*
Cary Gillespie *(Mktg. Mgr.)*
Robert Glenn *(Gen. Sls. Mgr.)*

G L Sub Company **(1)**
39 S. La Salle St.
Chicago, IL 60603
Tel.: 312-372-9500
Railroad Car Rental; Manufacture Fabricated Plate Work, Bolts, Nuts, Screws, Rivets & Washers; Consumer Credit & Mercantile Reporting Agencies; Adjustment & Collection Agencies; Subdividers & Developers
S.I.C.: 3443; 4741; 3452; 7322; 6553
Robert A. Pritzker *(Pres.)*

Subsidiary:

Marmon Industrial Corporation **(2)**
225 W. Washington St.
Chicago, IL 60606
Tel.: 312-372-9500
Approx.Sls.: $1,385,157,000
Fiscal Year-end: 12/31/89
Manufacture & Rent Railroad Equipment; Manufacture Water Treatment Equipment, Fasteners & Controls; Rental & Leasing Services
S.I.C.: 3743; 4741; 3589; 3452; 3625
Jay A. Pritzker *(Chm. Bd.)*
Robert A. Pritzker *(Pres. & Chief Exec. Officer)*

Subsidiaries:

Atlas Bolt & Screw Company **(3)**
1628 Troy Rd.
Ashland, OH 44805
Tel.: 419-289-6171
Emp.: 160
Steel Fasteners for Manufacturers of Metal Buildings, Rigid Board Roof Insulation, Automotive Products, Appliances & Electrical Equipment
S.I.C.: 3452
Robert W. Moore *(V.P. & Gen. Mgr.)*

Data Preference, Inc. **(3)**
1950 Elkhorn Court
San Mateo, CA 94403
Tel.: 415-574-4424
Rental, Leasing & Sale of All Purpose Electronic Test Equipment
S.I.C.: 7359; 7377
Crista L. Martyr *(Pres. & Gen. Mgr.)*

Eco Water Systems, Inc. **(3)**
P.O. Box 64420,
Saint Paul, MN 55164
Tel.: 612-739-5330
Fax: 612-739-4547
S.I.C.: 3589
Edward J. Fierko *(Pres. & Gen. Mgr.)*

Subsidiary:

Ecodyne Water Systems, Inc. **(4)**
P.O. Box 64420,
Saint Paul, MN 55164
Tel.: 612-739-5330
Fax: 612-739-4547
Lindsay, Miracle Water & Servisoft Residential, Institutional & Industrial Water Treatment Equipment & Systems; Mec-O-Matic Chemical Solution Feeders; Skid-Mounted Industrial Water & Waste-Water Treatment Systems
S.I.C.: 4971; 3443; 3589
Edward J. Fierko *(Pres. & Gen. Mgr.)*

Subsidiary:

EvsWater Industrial Systems **(5)**
500 N Verity Pkwy.
Middletown, OH 45042
Tel.: 513-423-9421
Emp.: 52
Residential, Institutional & Light & Medium Industrial Water Treatment Equip. & Systems
S.I.C.: 4971; 3589
Robert J. Wimmer *(Pres.)*
J.C. Shoemacher *(Dir.-Mktg.)*
S. Davis *(Dir.-Mfg.)*
A. Lorenz *(Natl. Sls. Mgr.)*

Ecodyne MRM, Inc. **(3)**
607 First St., SW
Massillon, OH 44646
Tel.: 216-832-5091
Emp.: 60
Large, Custom-Engineered, Industrial Air-Cooled Heat Exchangers; Finned Tubing, & Related Heat Transfer Products
S.I.C.: 3443
J. William Holsinger *(Pres.)*

The Getz Corporation **(3)**
150 Post St.
San Francisco, CA 94108
Tel.: 415-772-5500
Fax: 415-772-5659
Emp.: 1,700
International Marketing Distributor; Commercial, Industrial, Travel & Manufacturing Services
S.I.C.: 4724
Robert E. Brindley *(Pres.)*

The Graver Company **(3)**
2720 U.S. Hwy 22
Union, NJ 07083
Tel.: 908-964-0768
Fax: 908-964-7770
Emp.: 275
Industrial & Utility Water & Wastewater Treatment Equipment Systems
S.I.C.: 4971; 3589
Leonard Limon *(Pres.)*

Divisions:

The Graver Chemical Div. **(4)**
2720 U.S. Hwy 20
Union, NJ 07083
Tel.: 908-964-0768
Proprietary Filter Precoats of Powered Ion Exchange Resins, Other Materials; Speciality Bead Ion Exchange Resins & Filter Elements
S.I.C.: 2295
Rex D'Agostino *(Pres.)*

Graver Water Division **(4)**
2720 U.S. Hwy 22
Union, NJ 07083
Tel.: 908-964-2400
Industrial & Utility Water & Wastewater Treatment Equipment & Systems
S.I.C.: 4971
Leonard Limon *(Pres.)*

Unitech Division **(4)**
2720 U.S. Hwy 22
Union, NJ 07083
Tel.: 908-964-2400
Evaporators, Crystallizers & Other Solids-Concentrating Equipment & Systems
S.I.C.: 4971
A. Roland Flores *(V.P. & Gen. Mgr.)*

Leasametric, Inc. **(3)**
1164 Triton Dr.
Foster City, CA 94404
Tel.: 415-574-4441
Emp.: 480
Rental, Leasing & Sale of General Purpose Electronic Test Equipment, Computer Terminals, Telecommunications Test Equipment, Microprocessor Test & Development Systems
S.I.C.: 7377; 5065; 7359
Marshall A. Hart *(Pres. & Gen. Mgr.)*

New Century Freight Traffic Association, Inc. **(3)**
600 W. Jackson Blvd.
Chicago, IL 60606
Tel.: 312-236-8436
Emp.: 60
Auditing of Freight Bills for Shippers, Other Modes of Transportation; Recovery of Overcharges
S.I.C.: 8721
Greg Kozik *(V.P. & Gen. Mgr.)*

Rochester Instruments Systems, Inc. **(3)**
255 N. Union St.
Rochester, NY 14605
Tel.: 716-263-7700
Fax: 716-262-4777
Emp.: 500
Electronic Monitoring Instruments & Systems for Process & Power Industry Equipment Manufacturers & Users
S.I.C.: 3825
Edward Dohring *(Pres. & Gen. Mgr.)*

Solidstate Controls, Inc. **(3)**
875 Dearborn Dr., P.O. Box 1216
Columbus, OH 43085
Tel.: 614-846-7500
Fax: 614-885-3990
Emp.: 170
High-Performance Single & Three-Phase Uninterruptible Electrical Power Systems
S.I.C.: 3612; 3629

Trans Union Corp. **(3)**
111 W. Jackson
Chicago, IL 60604
Tel.: 312-431-0144
Fax: 312-431-5023
Emp.: 1,500
Consumer Credit Reports, Automated Services for Retailers, Banks & Other Credit Granters
S.I.C.: 7323
Harry Gambill *(Pres.)*

Union Tank Car Company **(3)**
111 W. Jackson
Chicago, IL 60604
Tel.: 312-431-3111
Fax: 312-431-5003
Emp.: 1,220
Manufacture Railway Tank Cars for Lease or Sale; Full-Service Leasing of Tank & Freight Cars to Shippers of Liquids, Compressed Gases & Dry Bulk Products in U.S. & Mexico; Lease Fleet
S.I.C.: 3743; 4741
Sidney Bonser *(Pres.)*

WCTU Railway Company **(3)**
111 W. Jackson Blvd.
Chicago, IL 60604
Tel.: 312-431-5001
Railcar Switching Services
S.I.C.: 4013
William Snelglove *(Mgr.-Opers.)*

Miles Metal Company **(1)**
540 Madison Ave.
New York, NY 10022
Tel.: 212-303-9100
Fax: 212-759-4611
World-Wide Traders in Metals & Ores
S.I.C.: 5051
Robert Joblove *(Pres.)*

Wells Lamont **(1)**
6640 W. Touhy Ave.
Niles, IL 60174
Tel.: 708-647-8200
Fax: 708-647-6943
Approx.Sls.: $165,000,000
Emp.: 1,600
Fiscal Year-end: 12/31/91
Import Export
Gloves for Work, Factory, Gardening, Sports, Dress, Casual & Speciality Uses; Athletic & Work Hosiery; Contract Leather Tanning
S.I.C.: 2381; 3111
Lloyd F. Rogers *(Pres. & Chief Exec. Officer)*
Terry Brooks *(V.P.-Distr.)*
O.B. Gilbertson *(V.P.-Mktg.)*
W.J. Leiser *(V.P.-Procurement & Intl. Opers.)*
D. F. Rehm *(V.P.-Fin.)*
R.K. Chesler *(Mgr.-Mktg. Communications)*

Non-U.S. Holdings:

Compania Minera Raura S.A. **(1)**
P.O. Box 876
Lima, 100, Peru
Tel.: 28-3625 (51.59%)
Mining Of Copper & Silver Concentrates
S.I.C.: 1021; 1044

Indeco Peruana S.A. **(1)**
P.O. Box 785
Lima, 100, Peru
Tel.: 52-0978 (76%)
Copper Wire, Copper & Aluminum Cable For Bldg. Power, Telephone & Other Indus.
S.I.C.: 3351

Industrias Metalicas Sud Americanas Ltda. (IMSA) **(1)**
Medellin, Colombia
Casters; Institutional & Industrial Trucks; Contract Fabricating & Fire Protection
S.I.C.: 3429; 3537

Jamesway Co. **(1)**
756 Bishop St. North
Cambridge, ON N3H 4S4, Canada
Tel.: 519-653-6264
Poultry Incubator-Hatcher Systems
S.I.C.: 3523

Kangol Ltd. **(1)**
Cleator Mill.,
Cleator, Cumbria CA23 3DJ, United Kingdom
Tel.: 0946 810312
Telex: 64162 KANGOL G
Fax: 0946 811186
Men's and Women's Fashion & Uniform Headwear
S.I.C.: 2353

Marmon/Keystone Canada-Montreal **(1)**
290 Chemin du Tremblay
Boucherville, J4B 5X9 Canada
Tel.: 514-527-9153
Mktg. & Distribution of Tubular Products
S.I.C.: 5051

Marmon/Keystone Canada-Toronto **(1)**
1200 Heritage Road
Burlington, ON M9P 3S6, Canada
Tel.: 416-335-8827
Mktg. & Distribution of Tubular Products
S.I.C.: 5051

McRobert Springs Co. **(1)**
575 Conestoga Blvd.
Cambridge, ON N1R 7P5, Canada
Tel.: 519-740-0400
Emp.: 125
Flat-Leaf Automotive Springs; Truck Spring Replacement Parts; Service
S.I.C.: 3495

Pikrose & Co., Ltd. **(1)**
Delta Works Audenshaw,
Manchester, M34 5HS, United Kingdom
Tel.: 061-370-1368
Emp.: 190
Haulages Winches And Hoists; Transportation Systems for Men and Materials in Mining; Non-explosive Blasting Systems For Construction And Demolition
S.I.C.: 3531

Procor Engineering Ltd. **(1)**
Wakefield, United Kingdom
Emp.: 240
Design, Fabrication & Assembly of Road Tankers, Semi-Trailers, Rail, Tank, Hopper & Specialized Freight Cars
S.I.C.: 3743; 3715

Procor LPG Storage Division **(1)**
734 7th ave. S.W. Suite 1200,
Calgary, AB P2P 3P9, Canada
Tel.: 403-264-1773
Emp.: 27
Underground Cavern Leasing for Storage of Liquid Petroleum Gas & Products
S.I.C.: 4922; 4226; 5044

Procor Rail Car Division **(1)**
2001 Speers Rd.
Oakville, ON L6J 5E1, Canada
Tel.: 416-827 4111
Emp.: 815
Rail Tank Car & Hopper Car Manufacture
S.I.C.: 3743; 3443

Procor Sulphur Services Division **(1)**
310 Southport Bldg., 1033 Southport Rd. S.W.
Calgary, AB T2W 3X6, Canada
Tel.: 403-253-5969
Emp.: 260
Contract processing of Sulphur Into Granules & Slates; Modular Construction of Sulphur Processing Plants
S.I.C.: 1622

Procrane Inc. **(1)**
2440 76th Ave.
Edmonton, AB T6C 4J4, Canada
Tel.: 403-440-4455
Emp.: 260
Rental of Cranes for Construction
S.I.C.: 7359

Rail Car Services Ltd. **(1)**
350 Bourneville Ln.
Bourneville, Birmingham B3O 1QZ, United Kingdom
Tel.: 021-475 5151
Telex: 338 758 RAILCA G
Emp.: 340
Rail Car Management; Repair & Maintenance Services
S.I.C.: 3743; 3621

Robertson-Whitehouse **(1)**
97 Bronte St.
Milton, ON L9T 2N8, Canada
Tel.: 416-878-2861
Emp.: 300
Standard & Special Steel, Stainless & Non-Ferrous Industrial Fasteners
S.I.C.: 3965

MARONTATE & CO.
2701 University Dr., 5th Fl.
Auburn Hills, MI 48326
Tel.: 313-373-1700
Fax: 313-373-3137
Year Founded: 1977
Approx.Billings: $10,686,000
Emp.: 19
Michael Marontate *(Pres.)*
Felix Malinowski *(V.P.-Pub. Rels.)*
Tony Moceri *(V.P.-Print Adv.)*
John Cook *(Treas.)*
Denise Campbell *(Controller)*
Barbara Korneder *(Dir.-Telecommunications & Librarian)*

MAROTTA SCIENTIFIC CONTROLS, INC.
78 Boonton Ave.
Montville, NJ 07045
Tel.: 201-334-7800
Fax: 201-334-1219
Approx.Sls.: $22,500,000
Emp.: 270
Mfr. of Solenoid Valves & Regulators, Relief & Check Valves, Electronic Control Devices, Flow Control Devices
S.I.C.: 3491; 3494; 3823; 3825
Thomas S. Marotta *(Chm. Bd. & Pres.)*
Richard D. Lander *(Exec. V.P. & Chief Oper. Officer)*
William T. Browne, Jr. *(Sr. V.P.-Mktg. & Sls.)*
Richard Collins *(V.P.-Engrng.)*
Robert F. Dathe *(V.P.-Fin.)*
S. Robert Smolen *(V.P.-Mfg.)*
George Johnson *(Mgr.-Pur.)*
Robert W. Nunamann *(Mgr.-Marine Sls.)*
Thomas C. Rogers *(Mgr.-New Prod. Sls.)*

Outside Service Firm(s):

Price Waterhouse*(Auditors)*
4 Headquarters Plaza North, 9th Fl.
Morristown, NJ 07962
Tel.: 201-540-8980

Lum, Hoens, Conant & Danzis*(Legal Firm)*
Roseland, NJ

Chemical Bank*(Major Banking Relationship)*
Morristown, NJ

MARQUARDT & ROCHE INC.
600 Summer St.
Stamford, CT 06901
Tel.: 203-327-0890 **CT**
Fax: 203-353-8487
Year Founded: 1970
Approx.Billings: $33,000,000
Emp.: 40
Advertising Agency
S.I.C.: 7311
James Marquardt *(Pres.)*
Allan Clamage *(V.P.)*
Howard Meditz *(V.P.)*
George Pryde *(V.P.)*
Frank Ruggiero *(V.P., Fin.)*
Susan Richman *(Supvr., Direct Mktg.)*

Computer Systems/Hardware:
Applied Digital Data Systems

Outside Service Firm(s):

Blum, Shapiro & Co.*(Auditors)*
West Hartford, CT

Murphy & Murphy*(Commercial Insurance Carrier)*
Norwalk, CT

American Association of Advertising Agencies Insurance Trust*(Group Insurer)*
New York, NY

Hall, Dickler, Lawler, Kent & Friedman*(Legal Firm)*
460 Park Ave.
New York, NY 10017
Tel.: 212-838-4600

A.A.A.A.*(Pension Manager)*
New York, NY

MARQUETTE COPPERSMITHING CO., INC.
P.O. Box 4584
Philadelphia, PA 19131
Tel.: 215-877-9362 **PA**
Fax: 215-877-4433
Year Founded: 1888
Sales Range: $20-39 Million
Emp.: 110
Fiscal Year-end: 8/31/91
Import Export
Packless Corrugated Expansion Joints For Power & Process Pipe Lines, Related Pipe Fittings, Bellows Assemblies, Flexible Metal Tubing
S.I.C.: 3053; 3498
Dr. Chester M. Heller, Sr. *(Chm. Bd., Pres. & Chief Exec. Officer)*
C.M. Heller, Jr. *(Vice Chm. & Treas.)*
Andrew T. Heller *(Exec. V.P.)*
Cyrus Heller *(V.P.-Pur.)*
Thelma T. Heller *(Corp. Sec.)*
Rodney D. Heller *(Comptroller)*
Robert L. Barrett *(Prod. Engineer)*
Robert Pritsker *(Dir.-Personnel & Prod. Mgr.)*
Ed Burns *(Mgr.-Import/Export)*
John Eldridge *(Mgr.-Adv.)*
Robert Kee *(Mgr.-Works)*
Robert Pressley *(Mgr.-Sls.)*
Lisa W. Marinucci *(Sec.)*
Principal(s):
Dr. Chester M. Heller, Sr.
C.M. Heller, Jr.
Andrew T. Heller
Cyrus Heller
Thelma T. Heller
Rodney D. Heller
Lisa W. Marinucci

No. of Mfg. Plants/Facilities: 3
No. of U.S. Offices: 30
No. of Foreign Offices: 3

Computer Systems/Hardware:
IBM

Outside Service Firm(s):

I. Perrick Company*(Auditors)*
Philadelphia, PA

Divisions:

Manufacturing Div. **(1)**
P.O. Box 4584,
Philadelphia, PA 19131
Tel.: 215-877-9362
Fax: 215-877-4433
Emp.: 22
Manufacture of Pipe Fittings
S.I.C.: 3498
Dr. Chester M. Heller, Sr. *(Pres.)*

Piping Design Div. **(1)**
P.O. Box 4584,
Philadelphia, PA 19131
Tel.: 215-877-9362
Fax: 215-877-4433
Emp.: 51
Piping Design
S.I.C.: 3498
Dr. Chester M. Heller, Sr. *(Pres.)*

MARRINER MARKETING COMMUNICATIONS, INC.
10221 Wincopin Circle, Ste. 300
Columbia, MD 21044
Tel.: 410-715-1500
Year Founded: 1989
Approx.Billings: $14,000,000
Emp.: 13
E. Randolph Marriner *(Pres., Chief Exec. Officer)*
Kenneth Hatter *(Chief Oper. Officer, Sr. V.P. & New Bus. Contact)*
Mary E. Marriner *(Exec. V.P. & Treas.)*
Ray M. Marriner *(Exec. V.P., Sec. & New Bus. Contact)*

MARS ADVERTISING CO.
24209 Northwestern Hwy.
Southfield, MI 48075
Tel.: 313-354-9760
Tel.: 800-521-9317
Fax: 313-354-0412
Year Founded: 1973
Approx.Billings: $50,420,875
Emp.: 73
Marilyn Barnett *(Pres.)*
Ken Barnett *(Exec. V.P., Gen. Mgr.)*
John Tierney *(1st Sr. V.P.)*
Carol Butash *(V.P., Comptroller)*
Kay Scheidt *(Dir., Brand Mktg.)*

MARS, INCORPORATED
6885 Elm St.
McLean, VA 22101
Tel.: 703-821-4900 **DE**
Fax: 703-448-9678
Year Founded: 1920
Approx.Sls.: $11,000,000,000
Emp.: 22,000
Mfr. Chocolate Candy, Rice, Dog & Cat Foods
S.I.C.: 2044; 2047; 2064; 2066
Forrest E. Mars, Jr. *(Chm. Bd. & Co-Pres.)*
John F. Mars *(Co-Pres. & Chief Exec. Officer)*
Thomas Armstrong *(Pres.-Kal-Kan Foods)*
William Hellegas *(Pres.-M&M Mars Div.)*
Randy Webb *(Pres.-Uncle Ben's Inc.)*
Hans Fiuczynski *(Dir.-External Rels.)*

Outside Service Firm(s):

Alliance Capital Management*(Pension Manager)*
1345 Avenue of the Americas
New York, NY 10017

Harris Trust & Savings Bank*(Pension Manager)*
111 W. Monroe St.
Chicago, IL 60690
Tel.: 312-461-2265
Tel.: 800-858-0840

Jennison Assoc. Capital Corp.*(Pension Manager)*
466 Lexington Ave.
New York, NY 10071
Tel.: 212-421-1000

Neuberger & Berman Pension Management, Inc.*(Pension Manager)*
522 Fifth Ave.
New York, NY 10036

Oppenheimer Capital Corp.*(Pension Manager)*
Oppenheimer Tower, World Financial Ctr.
New York, NY 10281
Tel.: 212-667-7500

Travelers Insurance Co.*(Pension Manager)*
1 Tower Square
Hartford, CT 06183
Tel.: 203-222-7821
Fax: 203-222-7813

Division:

M&M/Mars **(1)**
High St.
Hackettstown, NJ 07840
Tel.: 908-852-1000
Fax: 908-850-2624
Candies
S.I.C.: 2064; 2066
William B. Hellegas *(Pres.)*
Mary Ann Donovan *(V.P.-Mktg.)*
Whitney Hill *(Trade Rels. Dir.)*

Subsidiaries:

Dove International, Inc. **(1)**
660 W. 79th St.
Burr Ridge, IL 60521
Tel.: 708-850-9898
Fax: 708-850-9021
Approx.Sls.: $200,000,000
Mfr. of Hand-Dipped Chocolate Ice Cream Bars
S.I.C.: 2024
Michael Stefano *(Pres.)*
Rick Stolman *(V.P.)*
John Herr *(Mgr.-Human Resources)*

Kal Kan Foods, Inc. **(1)**
3250 E. 44th St.
Vernon, CA 90058
Tel.: 213-587-2727
Fax: 213-586-8347
S.I.C.: 2047
Michael Murphy *(Pres.)*
Vreij Kolandjian *(V.P.-Mktg.)*
Robert Kozlowicz *(V.P.-Sls.)*
M. Coleman *(V.P.-Personnel)*
Alice Ragenovich *(Mgr.-Pub. Rels.)*

Uncle Ben's, Inc. **(1)**
5721 Harvey Wilson Dr.
Houston, TX 77020
Tel.: 713-674-9484
Fax: 713-670-2227
Emp.: 500
Rice
S.I.C.: 2044
James R. Webb *(Pres.)*
James C. Harding *(V.P.-Human Resources)*
Michael Owen *(Dir.-Mktg.-Grocery Prods.)*

Non-U.S. Holdings:

Dove Europe **(1)**
Strasbourg, France
Ice Cream Products
S.I.C.: 2024
Andrew Tempest *(Bus. Devel. Dir.)*

Effems AG **(1)**
Hertizentrum 6 CH-6300
Zug, 3, Switzerland
Tel.: 042 22 55 88
Telex: 868793
Fax: 042 22 34 50
Trading Company, Food & Pet Food
S.I.C.: 5141; 5149

Mars Confectionery **(1)**
Dundee Rd. Trading Estate,
Slough, SL1 4JX, United Kingdom
Tel.: 0753 550055
Telex: 848253
Fax: 0753-550111
Emp.: 2,300
Confections
S.I.C.: 2064
Kay Randall *(External Rels.)*

Mars, Incorporated—(Continued)

Master Foods **(1)**
Hansa Road
Kings Lynn, Norfolk PE30 4JE, United Kingdom
Tel.: 0553 692222
Emp.: 400
Confectionery
S.I.C.: 2064; 2066
A.P. Hallatt *(Mng. Dir.)*
Michael Toms *(Catering Sls. & Dir.-Mktg.)*
Terry Riley *(Dir.-Retail Sls.)*
Ian Ding *(Mgr.-Intl. Mktg.)*

Master Foods AB **(1)**
Box 4138 S-20312
Malmo, Sweden
Tel.: 040 350600
Mktg. of Confections
S.I.C.: 5145

Master Foods Austria GmbH **(1)**
Eisenstaederstr. 80 DA-7091
Breitenbrunn, Austria
Tel.: 02683/5248-0
Mktg. of Confections
S.I.C.: 5145

Master Foods NV **(1)**
100 Boulevard Du Souverain D-1170
Brussels, Belgium
Tel.: 02-674-9211
Confectionery
S.I.C.: 2064

Masterfoods Ltd. **(1)**
728 Harcourt St.
Dublin, 2, Ireland
Tel.: 353-1-784955
Emp.: 950
Confectionery
S.I.C.: 2064
Ciron Murphy *(Gen. Mgr.)*

Masterfoods Oy **(1)**
Lonnrotinkatu 18A 00120
Helsinki, Finland
Tel.: 3580-7016900
Telex: 857-121146
Confectionery
S.I.C.: 2064
Riitta-Leena Lindstrom *(Mktg Dir)*
Anna Hannikainen *(Mktg. Mgr.)*

Mars Petfoods (UNISABI) **(1)**
Boite Postale No. 7 45550
Saint-Denis, del l'Hotel France
Tel.: 33-38-59-61-61
Pet Food
S.I.C.: 2047

Mars Confectionery **(1)**
33 Chemin de la Sandlach 67501
Haguenau, France
Tel.: 33-88-736400
Confectionery
S.I.C.: 2064; 2066
Claudine Kintz *(Mktg.)*

MARS SUPER MARKETS, INC.
7183 Holabird Ave.
Baltimore, MD 21222
Tel.: 410-282-2100
Approx.Sls.: $160,000,000
Emp.: 975
Supermarkets
S.I.C.: 5411
Angelo N. D'Anna *(Pres.)*
Carmen V. D'Anna *(Exec. V.P.)*
Samuel J. Cox *(V.P. & Treas.)*
Anthony S. D'Anna *(V.P. & Sec.)*

Outside Service Firm(s):

Ernst & Young*(Auditors)*
1 N. Charles St.
Baltimore, MD 21201
Tel.: 410-539-7940
Fax: 410-783-3832

Weinberg & Green*(Legal Firm)*
100 S. Charles St.
Baltimore, MD 21202
Tel.: 410-332-8795

Maryland National Bank*(Major Banking Relationship)*
Baltimore, MD 21202

MARSH FURNITURE COMPANY
1001 S. Centennial St.
High Point, NC 27260
Tel.: 919-884-7363 **NC**
Fax: 919-884-0883
Year Founded: 1906
Approx.Sls.: $34,000,000
Emp.: 510
Mfr. of Wood Kitchen Cabinets
S.I.C.: 2434
George M. Marsh *(Chm. Bd.)*
G. Reid Marsh, III *(Pres.)*
Laverene Ard *(V.P.)*
James P. Marsh *(V.P.)*
Howard Whitford *(V.P.)*
Phil Kusiak *(Treas. & Sec.)*

Outside Service Firm(s):

McGladrey & Pullen*(Auditors)*
High Point, NC

NCNB National Bank Of North Carolina*(Major Banking Relationship)*
High Point, NC

MARSHALL & WILLIAMS CO.
301 Airport Rd.
Greenville, SC 29607
Tel.: 803-232-7468
Fax: 803-240-2810
Approx.Sls.: $17,000,000
Emp.: 225
Manufacture Textile & Plastics Working Machinery
S.I.C.: 3552; 3559
Frederick Hyatt *(Chm. Bd.)*
Stuart R. McDonald *(Pres., Chief Exec. Officer & Treas.)*
Joseph S. Fulmer *(V.P.-Sls.)*
Lloyd V. MacPherson *(V.P.)*
James C. Scott *(V.P.)*
Glenda Winchester *(Controller)*

Outside Service Firm(s):

Ernst & Young*(Auditors)*
C & S Bank Tower, Two Shelter Centre, Ste. 800
Greenville, SC 29603

James Baldwin*(Legal Firm)*
Greenville, SC

Greenville National Bank*(Major Banking Relationship)*
Greenville, SC
Tel.: 803-240-6156

South Carolina National Bank*(Major Banking Relationship)*
7515 Northside Dr.
Greenville, SC
Tel.: 803-577-8280

R. J. MARSHALL CO.
26776 W. 12 Mile Rd.
Southfield, MI 48034
Tel.: 313-353-4100 **MI**
Fax: 313-948-6460
Year Founded: 1978
Approx.Sls.: $10,000,000
Emp.: 35
Fiscal Year-end: 10/31/88
Manufacture & Distribute Industrial Minerals & Chemicals
S.I.C.: 2833
R J. Marshall *(Pres.)*
Joan Marshall *(V.P. & Treas.)*
Dan Mahlmeister *(Gen. Mgr.)*
Mardelle Poozai *(Mgr.-Data Processing)*

No. of Mfg. Plants/Facilities: 4

Computer Systems/Hardware:
Data General

Outside Service Firm(s):

Plante & Moran*(Auditors)*
Detroit, MI

Central Benefits*(Group Insurer)*
Columbus, OH

Miller, Canfield, Paddock & Stone*(Legal Firm)*
150 W. Jefferson Ave.
Detroit, MI 48226
Tel.: 313-963-6420

Comerica Bank*(Major Banking Relationship)*
Detroit, MI

MARSHALL CONTRACTORS INC.
75 Newman Ave.
Rumford, RI 02916
Tel.: 401-438-3500 **RI**
Fax: 401-438-3500, Ext. 123
Year Founded: 1963
Approx.Sls.: $350,000,000
Emp.: 235
Commercial & Industrial Construction; General Contractor
S.I.C.: 1542; 1541
John L. Marshall III *(Pres.)*
Robert McNamara *(Exec. V.P.)*
S. James Busam *(V.P.-Business Devel.)*
David Corbett *(V.P.-Fin.)*
Lawrence Jamison *(V.P.-Admin.)*
Joananne Marshall *(V.P. & Sec.)*

No. of U.S. Offices: 1

Computer Systems/Hardware:
IBM System 38

Outside Service Firm(s):

Deloitte & Touche*(Auditors)*
125 Summer St.
Boston, MA 02110
Tel.: 617-261-8000
Fax: 617-261-8111

Fleet National Bank*(Major Banking Relationship)*
125 Dupont Dr.
Providence, RI 02907-3178
Tel.: 401-278-5335

Marshall
Jaccoma
Mitchell
ADVERTISING

MARSHALL JACCOMA MITCHELL ADVERTISING
41 Madison Ave.
New York, NY 10010
Tel.: 212-683-0001
Fax: 212-683-2634
Year Founded: 1978
Approx.Billings: $60,000,000
Emp.: 53
George E. Jaccoma *(Chm. Bd.)*
R.B. Mitchell *(Pres., Chief Exec. Officer)*
Pat Schwedler *(V.P., Controller)*

MARSTRAT, INC.

125 S. Franklin St.
Chicago, IL 60606
Tel.: 312-606-5820
Fax: 312-606-5566
Year Founded: 1976
Approx.Billings: $10,000,000
Emp.: 46
Dennis P. Ford *(Pres.)*
A.D. Raponi *(Mgr., Adv. Services)*

ALBERT C. MARTIN & ASSOCIATES
811 W. Seventh St.
Los Angeles, CA 90017
Tel.: 213-683-1900
Fax: 213-614-6002
Year Founded: 1906
Approx.Sls.: $10,000,000
Emp.: 87
Architecture & Engineering, Land Planning Interior Design & Graphics; Computer Applications Engineered In Seismic Analysis & Energy Optimization
S.I.C.: 8712; 6552; 7336; 7379; 7389; 8711; 8713; 8748
Albert C. Martin *(Partner)*
Christopher C. Martin *(Partner)*
David C. Martin *(Partner)*
J. Edward Martin *(Partner)*
Oliver Santos *(Controller)*
Robert W. Braunschweiger *(Gen. Mgr.)*
Daniel F. Jacobs *(Dir.-Sls. & Mktg.)*

Outside Service Firm(s):

KPMG Peat Marwick*(Auditors)*
725 S. Figueroa St.
Los Angeles, CA 90017
Tel.: 213-972-4000

Latham & Watkins*(Legal Firm)*
633 West Fifth St.
Los Angeles, CA 90071
Tel.: 213-485-1234
Fax: 213-643-9086

Bank of America NT&SA*(Major Banking Relationship)*
555 So. Flower St.
Los Angeles, CA 90071
Tel.: 213-228-3868

MARTIN & BAYLEY INC.
Hwy. 1 S., P.O. Box 385
Carmi, IL 62821
Tel.: 618-382-2334 **IL**
Fax: 618-382-8956
Approx.Sls.: $170,000,000
Emp.: 1,350
Retail Groceries
S.I.C.: 5148
Bob Martin *(Chm. Bd.)*
Frank Bayley *(Vice Chm.)*
Ed Smith *(Treas. & Sec.)*

Computer Systems/Hardware:
IBM

Outside Service Firm(s):

Bartz, Postl & Associates*(Auditors)*
Milwaukee, WI

Ted Van Winkle*(Legal Firm)*
McLeansboro, IL

Peoples Bank*(Major Banking Relationship)*
Paducah, KY

MARTIN & BENEDICT INC.
1250 6th St., Ste. 200
Santa Monica, CA 90401
Tel.: 310-451-5894
Year Founded: 1975
Approx.Billings: $22,000,000
Emp.: 20
Entertainment & Political Adv.
Jack Fiman *(Chm. Bd. & Pres.)*

MARTIN, COLE, DANDO & ROBERTSON
5100 Wheelis St., Ste. 200
Memphis, TN 38117
Tel.: 901-761-0911 **TN**
Fax: 901-761-1054
Year Founded: 1981
Approx.Sls.: $36,000,000
Emp.: 100
New Commercial, Office & Institiutional Buildings & Warehouse Construction
S.I.C.: 1542; 1541
David Martin *(Chief Exec. Officer)*
David C. Gando *(Pres.)*

MARTIN DOOR MFG., INC.
2828 S. 900 W.
Salt Lake City, UT 84119
Mailing Address:
P.O. Box 27437,
Salt Lake City, UT 84127
Tel.: 801-973-9310
Tel.: 800-688-8182
Fax: 801-977-4222
Approx.Sls.: $13,000,000
Emp.: 70
Import Export
Mfr. of Steel, Sectional Overhead Garage Doors & Electric Openers
S.I.C.: 3442; 3699
David O. Martin *(Chm. Bd.)*
Kenneth D. Martin *(Pres.)*
Larry Martin *(V.P.)*
Virginia H. Martin *(Sec. & Treas.)*
Loren D. Martin *(Gen. Counsel)*

MARTIN EXPLORATION MANAGEMENT COMPANY
4501 W. 127th St.
Alsip, IL 60658
Mailing Address:
P.O. Box 298
Blue Island, IL 60406
Tel.: 708-385-6500 **CO**
Fax: 708-385-6598
Year Founded: 1985
Assets: $47,000,000
Liabilities: $19,000,000
Net Worth: $28,000,000
Approx.Sls.: $20,000,000
Emp.: 50
Fiscal Year-end: 4/30/92
Petroleum Exploration
S.I.C.: 1311
Carl C. Greer *(Pres.)*
Thomas A. Floyd *(Sr. V.P.-Fin., Treas. & Admin.)*
Calvin Cahill *(V.P.-Exploration)*
Emile Garneau *(V.P.-Fin.)*
Harry Vasels *(V.P.-Project Control & Devel.)*
Ronald Brand *(Controller)*
Stephen McLaughlin *(Sec. & Gen. Counsel)*

Principal(s):
Carl C. Greer

No. of U.S. Offices: 2

Computer Systems/Hardware:
IBM System 36

Outside Service Firm(s):

Deloitte & Touche*(Auditors)*
Two Prudential Plaza, 180 N. Stetson
Chicago, IL 60601
Tel.: 312-946-2039

Sedgwick James*(Commercial Insurance Carrier)*
1290 Avenue of the Americas
New York, NY 10104
Tel.: 212-830-1000

Kirkland & Ellis*(Legal Firm)*
200 E. Randolph Dr.
Chicago, IL 60601
Tel.: 312-861-2000
Fax: 312-861-2200

Wildman, Harrold, Allen, Dixon & Smith*(Legal Firm)*
One Rockefeller Plaza, Ste. 900
New York, NY 10029

Continental Bank N. A.*(Major Banking Relationship)*
231 S. LaSalle St.
Chicago, IL 60697
Tel.: 312-828-2345
Tel.: 800-426-5754
Telex: 312-828-1783

The Northern Trust Co.*(Major Banking Relationship)*
50 S. LaSalle St.
Chicago, IL 60675
Tel.: 312-630-6000
Fax: 312-630-6516

Connecticut General Life Insurance Co.*(Pension Manager)*
Chicago, IL

Subsidiary:

Illinois Limited Partnership **(1)**
4501 W. 127th Street
Alsip, IL 60658
Retail Service Stations & Convenience Stores & Wholesaling Refined Petroleum Products
S.I.C.: 5411; 5541; 5172
Carl Greer *(Pres.)*
Thomas A. Floyd *(Sr. V.P. Fin.)*
J. Kirkland Greer III *(Sr. V.P.-Retail & Whls. Mktg.)*

MARTIN FOREST INDUSTRIES
P.O. Box 159
Healdsburg, CA 95448
Tel.: 707-433-2500 **CA**
Fax: 707-433-0188
Year Founded: 1979
Sales Range: $20-39 Million
Emp.: 26
Wholesale Lumber Brokers
S.I.C.: 0851
Corporate Giving Program: Company Will Match Gifts by Employees on the Basis of 3-Years Employment
Gordon Martin *(Chm. Bd., Pres. & Chief Exec. Officer)*
James R. Bucheister *(Chief Fin. Officer)*
Terri Martin *(Treas. & Sec.)*
Les Le Gaux *(Mgr.-Sls.)*
Beverley Taylor *(Office Mgr.)*
Bob Haas *(Pur. Agent)*

Principal(s):
Gordon Martin

Computer Systems/Hardware:
Compaq Desk-Pro PC

Outside Service Firm(s):

Kempkey Insurance Services*(Commercial Insurance Carrier)*
Napa, CA

North Coast Builders Exchange*(Group Insurer)*
Santa Rosa, CA

O'Brien, Sawyer, Waters & Davis*(Legal Firm)*
Santa Rosa, CA

LaSalle National Bank*(Major Banking Relationship)*
Santa Rosa, CA

William Hutchinson Investment Counselor & Portfolio Mgr.*(Pension Manager)*
Santa Rosa, CA

MARTIN GAS CORPORATION
101 E. Sabine
Kilgore, TX 75662
Mailing Address:
P.O. Box 191
Kilgore, TX 75662
Tel.: 903-983-1551 **TX**
Fax: 903-983-2326
Approx.Sls.: $210,000,000
Emp.: 500
Fiscal Year-end: 6/30/89
Distribute Natural Gas
S.I.C.: 5172; 5169
Ruben S. Martin, III *(Chm. Bd. & Pres.)*
R.S. Martin, Jr. *(Chief Exec. Officer)*
D.R. Neumeyer *(V.P.-Opers.)*
Wesley M. Skelton *(Treas.)*

Outside Service Firm(s):

KPMG Peat Marwick*(Auditors)*
1900 Comml. Natl.Tower, 333 Texas St.
Shreveport, LA 71101
Tel.: 318-227-8800

Bear Stearns & Co.*(Investment Banker)*
Dallas, TX

Thompson & Knight*(Legal Firm)*
3300 First City Center
Dallas, TX 75201
Tel.: 214-969-1700

First City Bank of Houston*(Major Banking Relationship)*
1301 Fannin, 21st Fl.
Houston, TX 77002
Tel.: 713-658-7705
Fax: 601-335-2903

MARTIN INDUSTRIES (AL)
301 E. Tennessee
Florence, AL 35630
Mailing Address:
P.O. Box 128,
Florence, AL 35631
Tel.: 205-767-0330
Fax: 205-767-0341
Year Founded: 1905
Approx.Sls.: $55,000,000
Emp.: 2,000
Fiscal Year-end: 11/30/90
Mfr. Heating Equip. & Fireplaces; Stoves, Dehumidifiers, Heat Pumps & Water Coolers
S.I.C.: 3567; 3585; 3272; 3589; 3634
B.C. Hughey *(Pres.)*
Jack Townsend *(V.P.-Sls. & Mktg.)*
Louis Martin *(V.P.-Engrng.)*
Russell Todd *(V.P.-Mfg.)*
Jim Truitt *(Treas. & Sec.)*
Lee Smart *(Dir.-Adv., Pub. Rels. & Mktg. Services)*
Phil Williams *(Pur. Agent)*

J.B. MARTIN COMPANY
10 E. 53rd St., Ste. 3100
New York, NY 10022
Tel.: 212-421-2020
Fax: 212-421-1460
Emp.: 425
Manufacture & Distribute Velvet Material
S.I.C.: 2221
Paul G. Charbin *(Chm. Bd.)*
Loic De Kertanguy *(Pres.)*
X. Anton *(V.P.)*
B. Blanc *(V.P.)*
James Donovan *(V.P. & Controller)*
Minos Samoladas *(V.P.)*
A.E. Taylor *(V.P.-Fin.)*

MARTIN PAINT STORES
182-20 Liberty Ave.
Jamaica, NY 11432
Tel.: 718-454-5100
Fax: 718-454-3830
Approx.Sls.: $50,000,000
Emp.: 500
Import
Home Decorating Centers
S.I.C.: 5231; 2851; 6719
Robert Glick *(Pres. & Chief Exec. Officer)*
Gerald Gutterson *(Chief Fin. Officer, Treas. & Sec.)*
Martin Pepkin *(Exec. V.P. & Dir.-Pur.)*
M. Morowitz *(Controller)*
Ronald Smith *(Dir.-Personnel)*
Joe Keane *(Mgr.-Data Processing)*

Computer Systems/Hardware:
IBM PC

Outside Service Firm(s):

Grant Thornton*(Auditors)*
605 Third Ave.
New York, NY 10158
Tel.: 212-599-0100
Fax: 212-370-4520

Halland Agency*(Group Insurer)*
Jericho, NY

Summit, Solomon & Feldesman*(Legal Firm)*
445 Park Ave.
New York, NY 10022
Tel.: 212-702-2200

Chemical Bank*(Major Banking Relationship)*
450 West 33rd St.
New York, NY 10001
Tel.: 212-613-7197
Fax: 212-947-7628

Chemical Bank*(Pension Manager)*
450 West 33rd St.
New York, NY 10001
Tel.: 212-613-7197
Fax: 212-947-7628

MARTIN SPROCKET & GEAR, INC.
3100 Sprocket Dr.
Arlington, TX 76015
Mailing Address:
P.O. Box 91588,
Arlington, TX 76015
Tel.: 817-465-6377 **TX**
Fax: 817-465-2401
Year Founded: 1951
Emp.: 1,500
Export
Manufacture Roller Chain Sprockets & Gears, Screw Conveyors & Bucket Elevators; V-belt Sheaves & Hand Tools
S.I.C.: 3535; 3566; 3568
Joe R. Martin *(Chm. Bd. & Pres.)*
Emory Fletcher *(V.P. & Treas.)*
B.G. Howard *(V.P.)*
James L. Johnson *(V.P.-Sls.)*
Gary C. Martin *(V.P. & Sec.)*
M.E. Martin *(V.P.)*
L. Thomas Melton *(V.P.)*
Russell H. Thompson *(V.P.)*

No. of Mfg. Plants/Facilities: 5

Outside Service Firm(s):

Weaver & Tidwell*(Auditors)*
Fort Worth, TX

Godfrey & Decker*(Legal Firm)*
Fort Worth, TX

MARTIN UNIVERSAL DESIGN, INC.
(Formerly Martin Group, Inc.)
4444 Lawton Ave.
Westland, MI 48208
Tel.: 313-895-0700
Tel.: 800-366-7337
Fax: 313-895-0709
Year Founded: 1947
Approx.Sls.: $23,000,000
Emp.: 210
Import Export
Manufactures, Imports & Distributes Drafting, Engineering, Graphic & Artist Materials; Furniture & Equipment, Office Furniture & School Supplies
S.I.C.: 3829; 7336
Michael Gorak *(Pres.)*
Dennis R. Kapp *(Chief Exec. Officer)*
Bob Hautamaki *(Chief Fin. Officer)*
David Wood *(Gen. Counsel)*
Joe Augustyne *(Dir.-Pur.)*
Daran Bair *(Dir.-Sls. & Mktg.)*
Steve Pavlichek *(Dir.-Data Processing)*

No. of Mfg. Plants/Facilities: 1
No. of U.S. Offices: 4

Outside Service Firm(s):

Doeren & Mayhew*(Auditors)*
Troy, MI

Midwest Benefits*(Group Insurer)*
Suite 3000, 2205 W. 12 Mile Rd.
Southfield, MI 48034-8339
Tel.: 313-351-0200

Martin Universal Design, Inc.—(Continued)

Wood & Wood*(Legal Firm)*
Farmington Hills, MI

Manufacturers National Bank N.A.*(Major Banking Relationship)*
38th Fl., 100 Renaissance Center
Detroit, MI 48243
Tel.: 313-222-4227

Subsidiaries:

Martin F. Weber Company **(1)**
2727 Southampton
Philadelphia, PA 19154
Tel.: 215-677-5600
Fax: 215-677-3336
Approx.Sls.: $7,000,000
Emp.: 50
Import
Computer Systems/Hardware:
Basic Four Sorbus
Mfr. Art Matls.
S.I.C.: 5199
Dennis Kapp *(Chm.)*
Michael Gorak *(Pres.)*
Robert Hautamaki *(Chief Fin. Officer)*
Edward J. Flax *(V.P.-Mfg. & Opers.)*
Alan Cooper *(Natl. Sls. Mgr.)*
Alan Brown *(Pur. Agent)*

Martin/Universal Industries **(1)**
1561 N. Bonnie Beach
Los Angeles, CA 90063
Tel.: 213-269-2117
Fax: 213-269-8920

MARTINS ABBATOIR & WHOLESALE MEATS INC.
Hwy. 13
Godwin, NC 28344
Tel.: 919-567-6102 **NC**
Fax: 919-567-5241
Year Founded: 1955
Approx.Sls.: $71,000,000
Emp.: 110
Fiscal Year-end: 9/30/91
Export
Meat Packing & Processing; Distribution of Beef By-Products
S.I.C.: 2011
Carlton Martin *(Pres.)*
Lynell Martin *(Treas. & Sec.)*
Richard Bullard *(Dir.-Personnel)*
W.C. Martin, Jr. *(Dir.-Pur.)*
W.R. Shatterly *(Dir.-Data Processing)*
W.A. Bullard, Jr. *(Mgr.-Plant)*

Outside Service Firm(s):

William T. Allen*(Auditors)*
Fayetteville, NC

Branch Banking & Trust Co.*(Major Banking Relationship)*
Fayetteville, NC

MARTINY & COMPANY
8150 Corporate Park Dr.
Cincinnati, OH 45242
Tel.: 513-489-4600
Fax: 513-489-4788
Year Founded: 1981
Approx.Billings: $12,500,000
Emp.: 31
Business-to-Business & Consumer Adv.
Kim R. Martiny *(Chm. Bd., Pres. & Chief Exec. Officer)*
Bob Hermann *(V.P., Mktg.)*
Penny Cappel *(V.P., Opers.)*
Sandy Deogracias *(V.P., Pub. Rels.)*
Lynn Martiny *(Sec. & Treas.)*

Computer Systems/Hardware:
NCR, MacIntosh

MARTRADE LTD.
13705 Milroy Place
Santa Fe Springs, CA 90670
Tel.: 310-926-6636 **MN**
Telex: 3718924
Fax: 310-926-0134
Year Founded: 1985
Approx.Sls.: $30,000,000
Emp.: 24
Fiscal Year-end: 6/30/90
Trading, Processing, Storage & Transportation of Animal Feed, Agricultural Products & By-products; Grain Business Consulting; Import & Export Grain Sales; Trading In Sugar Beets By-products, Molasses, Pulp, Hay & Straw; Transportation Of Asphalt Road Materials, Agricultural Truck & Tractor Operations; Hammermill & Custom Grain Grinding; Trading In Juice Concentrates, Oils, Essences & Juices For Flavor
S.I.C.: 5153; 2048; 2087; 4221; 4226; 4731; 6221; 8741
William A. Martindale *(Chm. Bd., Pres. & Chief Exec. Officer)*
Michael Birnbryer *(Dir.-Export)*
Patricia Thompson *(Dir.-Personnel)*
Principal(s):
William A. Martindale

No. of Mfg. Plants/Facilities: 3
No. of U.S. Offices: 4
No. of Foreign Offices: 1

Computer Systems/Hardware:
IBM PC

Outside Service Firm(s):

Lindquist & Vennum*(Legal Firm)*
4200 IDS Center, 80 South 8th St.
Minneapolis, MN 55402
Tel.: 612-371-3211

First Bank Minneapolis*(Major Banking Relationship)*
Minneapolis, MN

Subsidiary:

Yellowstone Transportation Service, Inc. **(1)**
13705 Milroy Pl.
Santa Fe Springs, CA 90670
Tel.: 310-926-6636
Fax: 310-926-0134
Emp.: 8
Trade & Storage of Sugar Beet By-Prods.; Storage of Other Liquids; Storage & Transportation of Asphalt Road Materials
S.I.C.: 4221; 4214; 3523
Leroy Iversen *(Chief Oper. Officer)*

Martz&Wadas

MARTZ & WADAS
8700 E. Via de Ventura, Ste. 301
Scottsdale, AZ 85258
Tel.: 602-998-3154
Fax: 602-998-7985
Year Founded: 1980
Approx.Billings: $10,210,520
Emp.: 25
Hitech, Real Estate, Manufacturing, Retail, Consumer & Pub. Rels.
Corporate Giving Program: Participate *in Local Civic & Charitable* Organizations Donating Services & Materials.
Carrie Martz *(Chm. Bd. & Pres.)*
Alicia Wadas *(Exec. V.P. & Sec.)*
Barbara Starley *(Controller & Dir.-Personnel)*
Missy Lagomarsino *(Dir.-Pub. Rels.)*

Computer Systems/Hardware:
IBM, MacIntosh

MARUCHAN INC.
(Sub. of Toyo Suisan Kaisha, Ltd., Japan)
1902 Deere Ave.
Irvine, CA 92714
Tel.: 714-261-6525
Fax: 714-250-4945
Approx.Sls.: $50,000,000
Emp.: 240
Fiscal Year-end: 3/31/91
Mfr. Dehydrated Instant Noodle Soups & Won Ton Soup & Related Products
S.I.C.: 2034
Don R. Muche *(Natl. Sls. Mgr.)*

MARVAL INDUSTRIES, INC.
315 Hoyt Ave.
Mamaroneck, NY 10543
Tel.: 914-381-2400 **NY**
Fax: 914-381-2259
Year Founded: 1956
Sales Range: $10-19 Million
Emp.: 50
Fiscal Year-end: 10/31/90
Export
Plastic Materials, Synthetic Resins, Color Concentrates, Dry Color
S.I.C.: 2821; 2865
Alan K. Zimmerman *(Pres.)*
Emil Kocur *(V.P.)*
Thomas A. Zimmerman *(V.P.)*
Joyce I. Zimmerman *(Sec. & Treas.)*

No. of Mfg. Plants/Facilities: 1
No. of U.S. Offices: 1

Computer Systems/Hardware:
Unisys-Datalogic Software

Outside Service Firm(s):

Band, Rosenbaum & Martin*(Auditors)*
New Rochelle, NY

National Westminster Bank plc*(Major Banking Relationship)*
Astor Plaza, 1515 Broadway
New York, NY 10036

MARVIN ENGINEERING COMPANY, INC.
260 W. Beach Ave.
Inglewood, CA 90302
Tel.: 213-678-1281 **CA**
Fax: 213-673-9472
Year Founded: 1963
Approx.Sls.: $53,000,000
Emp.: 420
Machine Shop, Jobbing & Repair
S.I.C.: 3599
Marvin Gussman *(Pres.)*
Jerry Friedman *(Exec. V.P., Treas. & Sec.)*
Chuck Wright *(V.P.)*
Bill Lane *(Controller)*
Jim Fish *(Gen. Mgr.)*

Outside Service Firm(s):

Richard Berger*(Legal Firm)*
Encino, CA

MARVIN LUMBER & CEDAR COMPANY
Hwy. #11
Warroad, MN 56763
Mailing Address:
P.O. Box 100
Warroad, MN 56753
Tel.: 218-386-1430
Fax: 218-386-2925
Year Founded: 1904
Approx.Sls.: $250,000,000
Emp.: 3,000
Fiscal Year-end: 11/30/91
Mfr. Wood Window Units & Stock Millwork; Retail Lumber, Marine Prods.
S.I.C.: 2431; 5211; 5251; 5999; 8999
William S. Marvin *(Chm. Bd.)*
John W. Marvin *(Vice Chm.)*
Frank R. Marvin *(Pres.)*
Jake Marvin *(Chief Fin. Officer)*
Elliot J. Larson *(Controller)*
Duane Fausher *(Dir.-Personnel)*
Gerald Krahn *(Dir.-Pur.)*
Duff Marshall *(Mgr.-Sls., Mktg. & Adv.)*
George G. Marvin, III *(Plant Mgr.)*

No. of Mfg. Plants/Facilities: 3

Outside Service Firm(s):

Johnson, Cohler & Co., Ltd.*(Auditors)*
South St. Paul, MN

Felhaber, Larson, Fenlon & Vogt*(Legal Firm)*
222 S. Ninth St., Ste. 1935
Minneapolis, MN 55402
Tel.: 612-339-6321
Fax: 612-339-4714

American National Bank & Trust of St. Paul*(Major Banking Relationship)*
Fifth & Minnesota Streets
St. Paul, MN 55101
Tel.: 612-298-6000

GILDA MARX INC.
(Formerly Gilda Marx Industries, Inc.)
11755 Exposition Blvd.
Los Angeles, CA 90064
Tel.: 310-473-0872
Fax: 310-473-6695
Year Founded: 1977
Approx.Sls.: $28,000,000
Emp.: 150
Mfr. of Women's, Misses & Juniors Bathing Suits & Women's Sportswear
S.I.C.: 2339
Mitchell Guzik *(Pres.)*
Gilda Marx *(Co-Chief Exec. Officer)*
Robert Marx *(Co-Chief Exec. Officer)*
Ronald Ozur *(Chief Fin. Officer)*

Outside Service Firm(s):

Community Bank*(Major Banking Relationship)*
Pasadena, CA

MARX/KNOLL, DENIGHT & DODGE, INC.
1230 S.W. First Ave.
Portland, OR 97204
Tel.: 503-226-2867
Fax: 503-273-8007
Year Founded: 1952
Approx.Billings: $12,000,000
Emp.: 17
Financial, Wood Prods., Utilities, Service Indus., Tourism, Automotive, Food & Outdoor, Medical-Dental
Robert Knoll *(Pres.)*
Patricia Green *(Controller)*

MARY KAY CORPORATION
8787 Stemmons Freeway
Dallas, TX 75247
Tel.: 214-630-8787
Cosmetics & Toiletries Holding Company
S.I.C.: 6719; 2844; 5963
Richard R. Rogers *(Chm. Bd., Pres. & Chief Exec. Officer)*
John P. Rochon *(Vice Chm. & Chief Fin. Officer)*
Lawrence G. Cox *(Exec. V.P.)*

Outside Service Firm(s):

Locke, Purnell, Rain, Harrell*(Legal Firm)*
First Republic Bank Center, 3600 Tower II
Dallas, TX 75201-3989
Tel.: 214-754-7400

Subsidiary:

Mary Kay Cosmetics Inc. **(1)**
8787 Stemmons Freeway
Dallas, TX 75247
Tel.: 214-630-8787
Fax: 214-638-4755
Assets: $261,564,000
Earnings: $21,165,000
Liabilities: $189,132,000
Net Worth: $72,432,000
Approx.Sls.: $500,000,000
Emp.: 1,700
Fiscal Year-end: 12/31/90
Computer Systems/Hardware:
IBM System 34 & 36
Cosmetics & Toiletries
S.I.C.: 2844; 5963
Richard R. Rogers *(Chm. & Chief Exec. Officer)*

Richard C. Bartlett *(Pres. & Chief Oper. Officer)*
Gerald M. Allen *(Pres.-Intl. Div.)*
John Rochon *(Chief Exec. Officer)*
Tim Byrd *(Chief Fin. Officer)*
Lawrence Cox *(Exec. V.P. & Chief Fin. Officer)*
Larry Harley *(Exec. V.P.-Distr. Group)*
Patrick Howard *(Exec. V.P.-Mfg. Grp.)*
Barbara Beasley *(Sr. V.P.-Sls. Group)*
Curran Dandurand *(Sr. V.P.-Mktg.)*
R. Bradley Glendening *(Sr. V.P., Gen. Counsel & Sec.)*
Lowrance Hodge *(Sr. V.P.-Mfg. Opers. & Engrng.)*
Bruce Wilke *(Sr. V.P.-Distribution Opers.)*
Dale Alexander *(V.P.-Sls. Training)*
Amy DiGeso *(V.P.-Human Resources)*
Gary Bishop *(V.P. & Chief Information Officer)*
Tom Chowning *(V.P.-Southwest Reg. Dist.)*
Dennis Greaney *(V.P.-Matl. Control)*
Thad Hogan *(V.P.-Intl. Mfg.)*
Sepp A. Kortschak *(V.P.-Quality Assurance & Regulatory Affairs)*
Michael Lunceford *(V.P.-Corp. Affairs)*
John McCook *(V.P.-Res. & Devel.)*
Virgil Pulliam *(V.P.-Legal Affairs)*
Ron Smith *(V.P.-Intl. Opers.)*
Walter Trapp *(V.P.-Treas.)*
Don Wagner *(V.P.-Corp. Distr.)*
Sharon M. Drobeck *(Controller)*
Randall Graham *(Coord.-Mktg. Publicity)*
Myra O. Barker, Ph.D. *(Chief Scientific Officer)*
Gary Jinks *(Natl. Dir.-Sls. Devel.)*
Terry Jackson *(Asst. Treas.)*

Branches:

Mary Kay Cosmetics, Inc. **(2)**
3500 Hyland
Costa Mesa, CA 92626
Tel.: 714-546-3500
Cosmetics
S.I.C.: 2844

Mary Kay Cosmetics, Inc. **(2)**
1651 Montreal Circle
Tucker, GA 30084
Tel.: 404-934-2920
Cosmetics
S.I.C.: 2844

Mary Kay Cosmetics, Inc. **(2)**
800 W. Thorndale
Itasca, IL 60143
Tel.: 708-773-2840
S.I.C.: 2844

Mary Kay Cosmetics, Inc. **(2)**
313 Pierce St., CN6702
Somerset, NJ 08873
Tel.: 908-563-9100
Cosmetics
S.I.C.: 2844

Mary Kay Cosmetics, Inc. **(2)**
1421 Patton Place
Carrollton, TX 75005
Tel.: 214-446-1221
Cosmetics
S.I.C.: 2844

Subsidiaries:

Business Travel Management, Inc. **(2)**
8777 Stemmons Fwy.
Dallas, TX 75247
Tel.: 214-631-8777 (100%)
S.I.C.: 4729

Richmont Corporation **(2)**
Dallas, TX

Non-U.S. Holdings:

Mary Kay Cosmeticos de Mexico Pty., S.A. de C.V. **(2)**
Zaragoza 1300 Sur Edificio Kalos Mezzannine,
Monterrey, N.L. 64000, Mexico (100%)
Mfr. of Cosmetics
S.I.C.: 2844
Jorge Moeller *(Pres.)*

Mary Kay Cosmetics, GMBH **(2)**
Fraunhoferstr 10 8033
Munich, Martinsreid Germany
Tel.: 011-498-985-76001 (100%)
Telex: 8415215749MKCD
Approx.Sls.: $1,210,000
Emp.: 7
Cosmetics
S.I.C.: 5963

Mary Kay Cosmetics Ltd. **(2)**
5600 Ambler Dr.
Mississauga, ON Canada L4W 2K9
Tel.: 416-624-5600 (100%)
Telex: 3896960415
Approx.Sls.: $13,000,000
Emp.: 95
Cosmetics
Ray Patrick *(V.P.)*

Mary Kay Cosmetics Pty. Ltd. **(2)**
551 Burwood Hwy.
Knoxfield, Victoria 3180, Australia
Tel.: 613-221-6244 (100%)
Telex: 79036486
Approx.Sls.: $9,494,000
Emp.: 30
Cosmetics
S.I.C.: 5963
Ian Ross *(Mng. Dir.)*

Mary Kay Cosmetics, S.A. **(2)**
Corrientes 345 3 Piso, 1005
Buenos Aires, Argentina
Tel.: 541-313-2088 (100%)
Telex: 390-25063
Approx.Sls.: $3,638,000
Emp.: 59
Cosmetics
Gerardo Segura *(Pres.)*

MARYLAND PAPER BOX COMPANY
4545 Annapolis Rd.
Baltimore, MD 21227
Tel.: 410-789-1700
Fax: 410-789-5937
Approx.Sls.: $19,000,000
Emp.: 350
Manufacturer Folding Cartons & Folding Paper Boxes, Printed Papers; Manufacture & Retail Paper Bags
S.I.C.: 2657; 2674; 5943
Malcolm Mahr *(Chm. Bd.)*
Michael Mahr *(Pres.)*
Art Perrier *(Exec. V.P., Treas. & Sec.)*
Janice Middleton *(Controller)*
Principal(s):
Malcolm Mahr
Michael Mahr
Art Perrier

Outside Service Firm(s):

W. S. B. Wolper*(Auditors)*
Baltimore, MD

Fedder & Garten*(Legal Firm)*
Baltimore, MD

Union Trust*(Major Banking Relationship)*
Baltimore, MD

MARYLAND PLASTICS, INC.
251 E. Central Ave.
Federalsburg, MD 21632
Tel.: 410-754-5566
Fax: 410-754-8882
Approx.Sls.: $25,000,000
Emp.: 325
Fiscal Year-end: 10/31/90
Custom Molded Products, Plastic Cutlery & Plastic Laboratory Equip.
S.I.C.: 3089
Allen Penrod *(Pres.)*
Charles Butler *(Mgr.-Sls.-Custom)*
George Nicoletos *(Mgr.-Sls.-Cutlery & Scientific)*
George E. Weeks *(Mgr.-Personnel)*

MARYLAND STATE LOTTERY
6776 Reistertown Rd., Ste. 204
Baltimore, MD 21215
Tel.: 410-764-5700
Year Founded: 1973
Approx.Sls.: $852,000,000
Emp.: 119
Fiscal Year-end: 6/30/91
State Lottery
S.I.C.: 9311
William F. Rochford *(Dir.)*
Carroll H. Hynson *(Deputy Dir.-Public Affairs)*
Martin R. Goldman *(Deputy Dir.-Mktg.)*
Thomas Skarzynski *(Adv. Mgr.)*

Computer Systems/Hardware:
GTECH

MARYLAND VIRGINIA MILK PRODUCERS ASSOCIATION, INC.
1985 Isaac Newton Square
Reston, VA 22090
Tel.: 703-742-6800
Fax: 703-742-7459
Year Founded: 1920
Approx.Sls.: $280,000,000
Emp.: 250
Cooperative; Producer & Wholesaler Raw Milk for Processing, Ice Cream Mix, Skim Powder, Butter, Fluid Milk Products
S.I.C.: 2026; 2021; 2023; 2024; 5143; 5451
Russell S. Wachter *(Pres.)*
John D. Hardesty *(1st V.P.)*
Robert E. Vaughn *(Treas., Sec. & Gen. Mgr.)*
Margorie Braun *(Controller)*

Computer Systems/Hardware:
IBM System 36

Outside Service Firm(s):

Price Waterhouse*(Auditors)*
1801 K. Street, N.W.
Washington, DC 20006
Tel.: 202-296-0800

National Savings & Trust*(Investment Banker)*
15th New York Ave.
Washington, DC 20006
Tel.: 202-383-8000

Edward L. Merrigan*(Legal Firm)*
Washington, DC

National Savings & Trust*(Major Banking Relationship)*
15th New York Ave.
Washington, DC 20006
Tel.: 202-383-8000

MASEK DISTRIBUTING INC.
1100 Rundell Rd.
Gering, NE 69341
Mailing Address:
PO BOX 130,
Gering, NE 69341
Tel.: 308-436-2100 **DE**
Fax: 308-436-2800
Year Founded: 1930
Assets: $7,500,000
Liabilities: $5,000,000
Net Worth: $2,500,000
Approx.Sls.: $35,000,000
Emp.: 60
Fiscal Year-end: 9/30/91
Import
Wholesale Motorcycles; Outboard Motor Boats; Trailers, Parts & Accessories; Golf Carts, New & Used; Lawn & Garden Equipment; Chainsaws, Etc.; Major Appliances, Refrigerators, Room Air Conditioners, Freezers, Ranges, Etc.; Televisions, VCR's & Audio Equipment; Small Engine Parts & Turf Equipment Such as Large Mowers & Utility Trucks
S.I.C.: 5012; 5013; 5088; 5078; 5083; 5084; 5722
Fred F. Masek *(Chm. Bd.)*
Joseph P. Masek *(Pres.)*
Roger Garwood *(V.P.)*
Randy K. Hays *(Sec., Controller, & Treas.)*
Principal(s):
Fred F. Masek

No. of Mfg. Plants/Facilities: 2
No. of U.S. Offices: 2

Computer Systems/Hardware:
IBM AS/400

Outside Service Firm(s):

Schafer, Blundell & Groeuke*(Auditors)*
Scotts Bluff, NC

Aetna Life & Casualty*(Commercial Insurance Carrier)*
Coral Gables, FL

Blue Cross & Blue Shield of Nevada*(Group Insurer)*
Reno, NV

Simmons, Olsen & Ediger*(Legal Firm)*
Scottsbluff, NE

Norwest Bank*(Major Banking Relationship)*
Denver, CO

FirsTier Bank*(Major Banking Relationship)*
Gering, NE

First Interstate Bank*(Pension Manager)*
Casper, WY

MASHBURN CONSTRUCTION COMPANY
1404 Laurel St.
Columbia, SC 29201
Tel.: 803-256-6080
Fax: 803-779-6202
Approx.Sls.: $14,000,000
Emp.: 75
Commercial Building Contractor
S.I.C.: 1542
Harry L. Mashburn *(Pres. & Treas.)*
Jane C. Andrews *(V.P.-Admin.)*
Lynn M. Shelay *(V.P.-Opers.)*

Outside Service Firm(s):

Arthur Andersen & Co.*(Auditors)*
Columbia, SC

South Carolina National Bank*(Major Banking Relationship)*
Columbia, SC

MASLAND INDUSTRIES
50 Spring Rd.
Carlisle, PA 17013
Mailing Address:
P.O. Box 40,
Carlisle, PA 17013
Tel.: 717-249-1866
Fax: 717-249-1228
Year Founded: 1866
Approx.Sls.: $300,000,000
Emp.: 2,400
Export
Mfr. Automotive Components; Interior Trim Parts; Floor Systems; Hoodliners
S.I.C.: 2273; 2396
William J. Branch, Jr. *(Pres. & Chief Exec. Officer)*
James P. Sheya *(V.P.-Mktg. & Sls.)*
Larry Owen *(V.P.-Opers.)*
Richard G. Sears *(V.P.-Employee Rels.)*
Richard E. Krout *(V.P.-Procurement & Supply)*

Masland Industries—(Continued)

Daniel Perkins *(Chief Fin. Officer)*
James D. Allgyer *(Controller)*
Donald M. Makie *(Dir.-Quality Assurance)*

MASON COMPANY
2355 Harrodsburg Rd.
Lexington, KY 40504
Tel.: 606-223-2277 **DE**
Mfr. of Large-Scale Ammunition, Electronics; Computer Software; Engineering Services
S.I.C.: 3483; 3672; 7372; 7371; 8711; 6719
Robert B. Jewell *(Chm. Bd.)*
D.E. Heffelbower *(Pres.)*
W.R. Lickert *(Treas. & Sec.)*

Outside Service Firm(s):

First Security National Bank & Trust Co.*(Major Banking Relationship)*
One First Security Plaza,
Lexington, KY 40507
Tel.: 606-231-1000

Subsidiaries:

Benchmark Security Inc. **(1)**
2355 Harrodsburg Rd.
Lexington, KY 40504
Tel.: 606-223-2277
David Humbert *(Mgr.)*

Mason Hanger-Silas Mason Co. **(1)**
2355 Harrodsburg Rd.
Lexington, KY 40504
Tel.: 606-233-2277 (100%)
Mfr. of Large-Scale Ammunition, Electronics; Software; Building Services; Engineering
S.I.C.: 3483; 3672; 7372; 7389; 8711; 7349
Robert B. Jewell *(Chm. Bd.)*
D.E. Heffelberger *(Pres.)*

Subsidiaries:

DWC Computer Solutions Inc. **(2)**
2355 Harrodsburg Rd.
Lexington, KY 40504
Tel.: 606-223-2316 (100%)
Computer Software
S.I.C.: 7372; 7371
Barbara H. Dotson *(Pres.)*

Mason & Hanger Engineering Inc. **(2)**
2355 Harrodsburg Rd.
Lexington, KY 40504-3363
Tel.: 606-223-4773 (100%)
Architectural Engineering
S.I.C.: 8711; 8712
James W. Wilson III *(Pres.)*

Mason & Hanger National Inc. **(2)**
2227 Drake Ave., Ste. 10D
Huntsville, AL 35805
Tel.: 205-881-2728 (100%)
Civil Engineering
S.I.C.: 8711
Edward Snow *(Pres.)*

Mason & Hanger Services Inc. **(2)**
P.O. Box 668, Langley Air Force Base
Hampton, VA 23665
Tel.: 804-864-1327 (100%)
Building Maintenance Services
S.I.C.: 7349
John Hill *(Pres.)*

Mason Technologies Inc. **(2)**
Stinnis Space Center, MS 39529-7099
Tel.: 601-689-8000 (100%)
Mfr. of Artillery Shells; Company Now Dormant
S.I.C.: 3483
Richard Augur *(Pres.)*

Versatech Engineering **(1)**
835 Porter Pl.
Lexington, KY 40504
Tel.: 606-233-1808
Robotics Engineering
S.I.C.: 8711
Louis Reives *(Pres.)*

MASON DISTRIBUTORS, INC.
5105 N.W. 159th St.
Hialeah, FL 33014
Tel.: 305-624-5557
Fax: 800-328-3944
Emp.: 170
Wholesaler of Generic Drugs & Vitamins
S.I.C.: 5122; 5100
Carlos Rodriguez *(Pres.)*
Caridad Gonzalez *(V.P.)*
Ray Padilla *(V.P.-Opers.)*
Juana Rodriguez *(Treas.)*

Outside Service Firm(s):

Republic National Bank*(Major Banking Relationship)*
Hialeah, FL

MASON & MADISON, INC.
23 Amity Rd.
New Haven, CT 06524
Tel.: 203-393-1101
Fax: 203-393-2813
Year Founded: 1951
Approx.Billings: $22,000,000
Emp.: 38
Charles T. Mason, Jr. *(Chm. Bd. & Pres.)*
Judy Smith *(V.P., Fin.)*
Jim Frawley *(V.P., Pub. Rels. Dir.)*

MASON OIL COMPANY
117 W. Jackson St.
Ione, CA 95640
Tel.: 209-274-2470
Approx.Sls.: $350,000,000
Emp.: 31
Fiscal Year-end: 12/31/89
Oil Distribution
S.I.C.: 5172
David D. S. Mason *(Pres., Chief Exec. Officer, Chief Fin. Officer & Treas.)*
David R. Mason, Jr. *(V.P. & Sec.)*
Linda Upton *(Mgr.-Mngmt. Information Systems)*

Computer Systems/Hardware:
Vector

MASON SHOE MFG. CO.
1251 First Ave.
Chippewa Falls, WI 54729
Tel.: 715-723-1871
Tel.: 800-826-7030
Fax: 715-723-2169
Year Founded: 1904
Sales Range: $20-39 Million
Emp.: 750
Import
Mfr. of Men's & Women's Shoes
S.I.C.: 3143; 3144; 3021
William M. Scobie *(Chm. Bd., Chief Exec. & Legal Officer)*
John Lubs *(Pres. & Chief Oper. Officer)*
Dale J. Cayo *(Sr. V.P.)*
David Ball *(V.P.-Mfg.)*
Roy Mayberry, Jr. *(V.P.-Data Processing)*
Robert J. Allen *(Treas. & Sec.)*
Richard Johnson *(Dir.-Human Resources)*
Herb Steinmetz *(Dir.-Adv.)*
Principal(s):
William M. Scobie

No. of Mfg. Plants/Facilities: 1
No. of U.S. Offices: 1

Computer Systems/Hardware:
IBM 4341

Outside Service Firm(s):

Wipfli, Ullrich, Bertleson*(Auditors)*
Eau Claire, WI

Wiley, Rasmus, Colbert, Cray & Norseng*(Legal Firm)*
Chippewa Falls, WI

Northwestern Bank*(Major Banking Relationship)*
Chippewa Falls, WI

Subsidiaries:

F & F Shoe Company **(1)**
Palmer & Williams St.
Chippewa Falls, WI 54729
Tel.: 715-723-1871
Mfr. Men's Shoes
S.I.C.: 3143

Wissota Trader Ltd. **(1)**
1313 First Ave.
Chippewa Falls, WI 54729
Tel.: 715-723-6496
Mail-Order Clothing
S.I.C.: 5961

Wissota Trader & B.A. Mason **(1)**
1313 First Ave.
Chippewa Falls, WI 54729
Tel.: 715-723-1871
Fax: 715-723-2169
Import
William M. Scobie *(Chm. Bd., Chief Exec. & Legal Officer)*
John Lubs *(Pres. & Chief Oper. Officer)*
Roy Mayberry, Jr. *(V.P.- Data. Proc.)*
David Ball *(V.P.-Mfg.)*
Robert J. Allen *(Sec. & Treas.)*
Herb Steinmetz *(Dir.-Adv.)*
Richard Johnson *(Dir.-Human Resources)*

MASSACHUSETTS ENVELOPE CO.
30 Cobble Hill Rd.
Somerville, MA 02143
Tel.: 617-623-8000
Fax: 617-623-8058
Emp.: 100
Envelopes, Forms & Labels
S.I.C.: 2677; 2678; 2679
Steven Grossman *(Pres.)*
Michael Flynn *(V.P.)*
Robert Ruechford *(V.P.)*
Louis Stader *(V.P.)*
Henry Ward *(V.P.)*
Edgar Grossman *(Treas.)*
Edward D. Fox *(Controller)*

Outside Service Firm(s):

Parent, McLaughlin & Nagle*(Auditors)*
Boston, MA

Palmer & Dodge*(Legal Firm)*
One Beacon St.
Boston, MA 02108
Tel.: 617-573-0100

First National Bank of Boston*(Major Banking Relationship)*
150 Royall St.
Canton, MA 02021
Tel.: 617-575-2900
Tel.: 800-442-2001

MASSACHUSETTS MUTUAL LIFE INSURANCE CO.
1295 State St.
Springfield, MA 01111
Tel.: 413-788-8411 **MA**
Fax: 413-730-6005
Year Founded: 1851
Assets: $29,290,591,225
Liabilities: $27,931,333,728
Net Worth: $1,359,257,497
Sales Range: $1 Billion +
Emp.: 11,000
Fiscal Year-end: 12/31/91
Life Insurance
S.I.C.: 6311; 6321
Corporate Giving Program: Company Concentrates its Charitable Contributions Mostly in the Home Office Community, Along with Selective Projects on a National/ Regional Level, as they Support Corporate Goals
Employee Matching Gifts Program: Full Time Home Office Associates With at Least One Year of Service are Eligible to Participate; Eligible Institutions Include Four-Year Colleges, Graduate Schools or Junior Colleges, & the American College; Institutions Must be Regionally Accredited & Tax Exemptpt
William J. Clark *(Chm. Bd.)*
Thomas B. Wheeler *(Pres. & Chief Exec. Officer)*
Richard G. Dooley *(Exec. V.P. & Chief Investment Officer)*
Warren R. Wise *(Exec. V.P. & Gen. Counsel)*
Lawrence L. Grypp *(Exec. V.P.)*
James E. Miller *(Exec. V.P.)*
John M. Naughton *(Exec. V.P.)*
John J. Pajak *(Exec. V.P.)*
Gary E. Wendlandt *(Exec. V.P.)*
Lawrence V. Burkett, Jr. *(Sr. V.P. & Deputy Gen. Counsel)*
Michael D. Hays *(Sr. V.P. & Actuary)*
Anthony Van Werkhooven *(Sr. V.P. & Actuary)*
Paul D. Adornato *(Sr. V.P.)*
William J. Burton *(Sr. V.P.)*
Donald D. Cameron *(Sr. V.P.)*
Kenneth D. Cardwell *(Sr. V.P.)*
Barry Gottehrer *(Sr. V.P.)*
Stephen A. Hawkins *(Sr. V.P.)*
Dennis L. Reyhons *(Sr. V.P.)*
Peter J. Vogian *(Sr. V.P.)*
Daniel J. Fitzgerald *(Sr. V.P. & Actuary)*
Kenneth L. Hargreaves *(Sr. V.P.)*
Peter Daboul *(Sr. V.P.)*
Donald P. Paczkowski *(Sr. V.P.)*
John J. Libera *(Sr. V.P.)*
William T. McElmurray *(Sr. V.P.)*
James C. McKeon *(Sr. V.P.)*
Colin Collins *(V.P.-Pur.)*
Eustis Walcott *(V.P.-Corp. Communications & Grants Contact)*
Peter A. Feige *(V.P.-Employee Benefits)*
Susan Alfano *(V.P.-Human Resources)*
Thomas J. Finnegan, Jr. *(V.P. & Sec.)*
Allan B. Bixby *(Jr. V.P. & Treas.)*

No. of U.S. Offices: 700

Computer Systems/Hardware:
IBM PC 5150; Amdahl 5860, 5880

Outside Service Firm(s):

Coopers & Lybrand*(Auditors)*
2300 Bay Bank Tower, 1500 Main St.
Springfield, MA 01101
Tel.: 413-781-7200

Shawmut First Bank & Trust Company*(Major Banking Relationship)*
127 State St.
Springfield, MA 01103
Tel.: 413-737-4321

Member Companies:

MML Bay State Life Insurance Company **(1)**
1295 State St.
Springfield, MA 01111
Tel.: 413-788-8411 (100%)
Approx.Sls.: $34,913,600
Life, Accident & Health Insurance
S.I.C.: 6311; 6321
Daniel J. Fitzgerald *(Pres.)*

MML Investors Services, Inc. **(1)**
One Financial Plaza, 1350 Main St.
Springfield, MA 01103
Tel.: 413-737-8400 (100%)
Broker-Dealer
S.I.C.: 6211
Kenneth M. Rickson *(Pres.)*

MML Pension Insurance Company **(1)**
1295 State St.
Springfield, MA 01111
Tel.: 413-788-8411 (100%)
Approx.Sls.: $39,637,695
Life Insurance
S.I.C.: 6311; 6321
Daniel J. Fitzgerald *(Pres.)*

MML Series Investment Fund **(1)**
1295 State St.
Springfield, MA 01111
Tel.: 413-788-8411 (100%)

Approx.Sls.: $63,000,000
Investment Company
S.I.C.: 6211
Gary E. Wendlandt *(Pres.)*

MassMutual Holding Company **(1)**
1295 State St.
Springfield, MA 01111
Tel.: 413-788-8411 (100%)
Holding Company for Real Estate Corporations
S.I.C.: 6719

Subsidiaries:

MML Real Estate Corporation **(2)**
1295 State Street
Springfield, MA 01111
Tel.: 413-788-8411 (100%)
Real Estate Management
S.I.C.: 6531
Kenneth L. Hargreaves *(Pres.)*

MML Realty Management Corp. **(2)**
1295 State St.
Springfield, MA 01111
Tel.: 413-788-8411 (100%)
Emp.: 132
Real Estate Management
S.I.C.: 6531

Oppenheimer Management Corp. **(1)**
2 World Trade Center, 34th Fl.
New York, NY 10048
Tel.: 212-323-0200
Fax: 212-323-0558
Approx.Rev.: $900,000,000
Emp.: 150
Fiscal Year-end: 12/30/91
Investment Management
S.I.C.: 6282
Jon A. Fossel *(Chm. Bd. & Chief Exec. Officer)*
Bridget Macaskill *(Pres. & Chief Oper. Officer)*
Robert G. Galli *(Exec. V.P.-Legal)*
James S. McClure *(Exec. V.P.-Portfolio)*
Tim Pitts *(Exec. V.P.)*
Loretta McCarthy *(Sr. V.P.-Mktg. & Communications)*
Robert Zack *(V.P.)*
Kenneth E. Eich *(Chief Fin. Officer)*
George Bowen *(Treas.)*
Katherine P. Feld *(Sec.)*
Rob Densen *(Dir.-Pub. Affairs)*

Subsidiaries:

Centennial Capital Corporation **(2)**
One New York Plaza
New York, NY 10004
Tel.: 212-825-4000 (47.5%)
Fund Management
S.I.C.: 6282

Oppenheimer Asset Management Corp. **(2)**
3410 S. Galena St.
Denver, CO 80231
Tel.: 303-671-3200
Investment Adviser
S.I.C.: 6282
Jon Fossel *(Pres.)*

MASSACHUSETTS STATE LOTTERY
15 Rockdale St.
Braintree, MA 02184
Tel.: 617-849-5555
Fax: 617-849-5546
Year Founded: 1972
Approx.Sls.: $1,600,000,000
Emp.: 525
Fiscal Year-end: 6/30/91
State Lottery Commision
S.I.C.: 7999
Eric M. Turner *(Exec. Dir.)*
Louis Totino *(Dir.-Mktg.)*
Frank R. Ciota *(Mgr.-Adv.)*
Frances McDonnell *(Mgr.-Pub. Rels.)*

DON MASSEY CADILLAC INC.
40475 Ann Arbor Rd.
Plymouth, MI 48170
Tel.: 313-453-7500 **MI**
Fax: 313-453-7500, Ext. 299
Approx.Sls.: $300,000,000
Emp.: 126
Automobile Dealership
S.I.C.: 5511
Donald E. Massey *(Pres. & Chief Exec. Officer)*
John D. Sills *(V.P. & Gen. Counsel)*
Barbara A. Kucka *(Chief Fin. Officer)*
Karen Tibus *(Sec.)*

No. of U.S. Offices: 11

Outside Service Firm(s):

Deloitte & Touche*(Auditors)*
200 Renaissance Center, 16th Fl.
Detroit, MI 48243
Tel.: 313-396-3000
Fax: 313-259-8087

Sills, Hemming, Law*(Legal Firm)*
Bloomfield Hills, MI 48304

National Bank of Detroit*(Major Banking Relationship)*
611 Woodward
Detroit, MI 48226
Tel.: 313-225-1000

Subsidiaries:

Capitol Cadillac, Corp. **(1)**
5901 S. Pennsylvania Ave.
Lansing, MI 48911
Tel.: 517-393-5600 (100%)
Fax: 517-393-1746
Emp.: 57
Automobile Dealership
S.I.C.: 5511

Don Massey Buick, Inc. **(1)**
9701 E. Arapahoe Rd.
Englewood, CO 80112
Tel.: 303-799-1157 (100%)
Fax: 303-790-4565
Emp.: 28
Automobile Dealership
S.I.C.: 5511

Don Massey Cadillac, Inc. **(1)**
9400 E. Arapahoe Rd.
Englewood, CO 80112
Tel.: 303-799-1110 (100%)
Fax: 303-799-1843
Emp.: 64
Automobile Dealership
S.I.C.: 5511

Massey Cadillac, Inc. **(1)**
4241 N. John Young Pkwy.
Orlando, FL 32804
Tel.: 407-299-6161
Fax: 407-290-0028
Approx.Sls.: $43,000,000
Emp.: 150
Computer Systems/Hardware:
IBM
Cadillac Automobile Sales & Service
S.I.C.: 5511
Donald E. Massey *(Pres.)*
Charlotte R. Harris *(Controller)*
John Roettger *(Gen. Mgr.)*
John Thornton *(Dir.-Service)*

Massey Cadillac, Inc. **(1)**
2177 Covington Pike
Memphis, TN 38128
Tel.: 901-373-7373 (100%)
Fax: 901-373-3194
Emp.: 61
Automobile Dealership
S.I.C.: 5511

Saturn of Plymouth **(1)**
4301 Massey Dr.
Plymouth, MI 48170
Tel.: 313-453-7890 (100%)
Fax: 313-453-7993
Emp.: 26
Automobile Dealership
S.I.C.: 5511

Affiliates:

Arnold Palmer Cadillac Inc. **(1)**
501 S. Caldwell St.
Charlotte, NC 28202
Tel.: 704-376-9181
Fax: 704-377-5762
Emp.: 124

Cave City Chevrolet **(1)**
I-65 & Highway 90 East
Cave City, KY
Tel.: 502-773-3174
Fax: 502-773-4610
Emp.: 20

Crest Cadillac, Inc. **(1)**
2121 Metro Center Pkwy.
Nashville, TN 37228
Tel.: 615-242-4242
Fax: 615-254-9331
Emp.: 96

Nugget Motors **(1)**
116 E. Main St.
Quincy, CA 93971
Tel.: 916-283-0600
Emp.: 20

MASSMAN CONSTRUCTION COMPANY
8901 State Line Rd.
Kansas City, MO 64114
Tel.: 816-523-1000
Fax: 816-333-2109
Year Founded: 1916
Approx.Sls.: $45,000,000
Emp.: 300
General Contractor; Heavy Construction, Bridges, Tunnels, Elevated Highways, Industrial Buildings
S.I.C.: 1542; 1629
Henry J. Massman IV *(Pres.)*
F. Keith Jacobson *(V.P.)*
Herbert W. Martin *(V.P. & Controller)*
Henry B. McCoy *(V.P.)*
Paul C. Schnoebelen, Jr. *(V.P.)*
Joseph T. Kopp *(Treas. & Sec.)*
L.C. Schlumpberger *(Mgr.-Equip.)*
Rob Devore *(Pur. Agent)*
Principal(s):
Henry J. Massman IV

Computer Systems/Hardware:
IBM System 34; IBM PC's

Outside Service Firm(s):

Ernst & Young*(Auditors)*
One Kansas City Place, 1200 Main St.
Kansas City, MO 64105

Security National Bank*(Major Banking Relationship)*
Kansas City, MO

MASTER APPLIANCE CORP.
2420 18th St.
Racine, WI 53403
Mailing Address:
P.O. Box 68
Racine, WI 53401
Tel.: 414-633-7791 **WI**
Telex: 269-505
Fax: 414-633-9745
Year Founded: 1958
Sales Range: $10-19 Million
Emp.: 65
Import Export
Designs & Manufactures Heat Tools for the Industry
S.I.C.: 3559
Alvera Radwill *(Chm. Bd., Chief Fin. Officer & Treas.)*
Scott Radwill *(Pres., Chief Exec. & Chief Oper. Officer-Export)*
Linda Radwill *(V.P., Mgr.-Mktg. & Sec.)*
Joe Knors *(Mgr.-Personnel, Office & Credit)*
Dan Naughton *(Mgr.-Pur.)*
Don Royer *(Natl. Sls. Mgr.)*
Mary Sorenson *(Mgr.- Production)*
Dick Urbush *(Mgr.-Product Design & Devel.)*
Erin-Robyn Jericho *(Dir-Telecomm. & Coord Spec. Projects)*
Principal(s):
Alvera Radwill
Scott Radwill
Linda Radwill
Arthur Radwill

No. of Mfg. Plants/Facilities: 1
No. of U.S. Offices: 1

Computer Systems/Hardware:
Compaq, Wang

Outside Service Firm(s):

Sturbin & Stone*(Auditors)*
Racine, WI

Bank One*(Major Banking Relationship)*
Racine, WI

MASTER COLLECTORS INC.
5883 Glenridge Dr., Ste. 260
Atlanta, GA 30328
Tel.: 404-843-9400 **DE**
Fax: 404-252-0089
Year Founded: 1968
Emp.: 310
Full Service Licensed & Bonded Collection Agency
S.I.C.: 7322
James G. Bailey *(Chm.)*
Dennis M. Cunningham *(Pres.)*
Carl Harkleroad *(V.P.-Data Processing)*
William J. Strang *(V.P.)*
William T. Stewart *(Controller)*
Richard H. Cerny *(Dir.-Reg. Mktg.)*
Carl Harkleroad *(Dir.-Data Processing)*
Paul D. Kearns *(Gen. Mgr.)*

Outside Service Firm(s):

Arthur Andersen & Co.*(Auditors)*
133 Peachtree St., N.E.
Atlanta, GA 30303
Tel.: 404-658-1776

NationsBank*(Major Banking Relationship)*
35 Broad St.
Atlanta, GA 30303
Tel.: 404-581-2121
Tel.: 800-848-8198

MASTER INDUSTRIES CORP.
350 Fifth Ave.
New York, NY 10118
Tel.: 212-760-9200 **NY**
Year Founded: 1915
Approx.Sls.: $50,000,000
Emp.: 1,500
Mfr. Boy's & Men's Slacks, Jeans & Shorts; Ladies' Jeans & Slacks
S.I.C.: 2325; 2339
Norman Bernard *(Chm. Bd. & Chief Exec. Officer)*
Albert S. Mushkin *(Pres. & Chief Oper. Officer)*
Donald Eisenberg *(Treas.)*
Mark Baron *(Controller)*
Principal(s):
Norman Bernard
Albert S. Mushkin

No. of Mfg. Plants/Facilities: 4
No. of U.S. Offices: 1

Computer Systems/Hardware:
IBM System 38

Outside Service Firm(s):

Weinick, Sanders & Co.*(Auditors)*
New York, NY

Blumenkrantz, Klepper & Wilkins*(Commercial Insurance Carrier)*
New York, NY

Ladenburg, Thalmann & Co.*(Investment Banker)*
New York, NY

Blindman, Vram, Bordelon & Swords*(Legal Firm)*
New York, NY

Chemical Bank*(Major Banking Relationship)*
450 West 33rd St.
New York, NY 10001
Tel.: 212-613-7197
Fax: 212-947-7628

Master Industries Corp.—(Continued)

Chemical Banking Corp.*(Major Banking Relationship)*
277 Park Ave.
New York, NY 10041
Tel.: 212-310-6407
Fax: 212-310-4526

Subsidiary:

Master Trouser/ Master Apparel/ Botany 500 Slacks Ltd. **(1)**
350 Fifth Ave.
New York, NY 10118
Tel.: 212-760-9200
Emp.: 1000
Mfg. of Slacks & Jeans
S.I.C.: 2325
Albert S. Mushkin *(Chief Oper. Officer)*

MASTER MOLDED PRODUCTS CORPORATION
1000 Davis Rd.
Elgin, IL 60123
Tel.: 708-695-9700
Fax: 708-695-9707
Year Founded: 1946
Approx.Sls.: $13,000,000
Emp.: 145
Export
Custom Thermoplastic Molders
S.I.C.: 3089
Martin Weinhart *(Chm. Bd., Chief Exec. Officer & Treas.)*
James J. Weinhart *(Pres.)*
John M. Weinhart *(V.P.)*
Frances Patrasso *(Sec.)*
John Hinner *(Dir.-Sls. & Mktg.)*
Don Ortberg *(Mgr.-Opers.)*

Outside Service Firm(s):

Mid-City National Bank of Chicago*(Major Banking Relationship)*
Chicago, IL

MASTERCARD INTERNATIONAL, INC.
888 Seventh Ave.
New York, NY 10106
Tel.: 212-649-4600
Fax: 212-649-5043
Year Founded: 1966
Approx.Sls.: $200,000,000,000
Emp.: 1,100
Fiscal Year-end: 12/31/91
Licensor of MasterCard Trademarks to Financial Institutions
S.I.C.: 6153
Alan G. McNally *(Chm. Bd.)*
Alex W. Hart *(Pres. & Chief Exec. Officer)*
William T. Sandalls *(Chief Oper. Officer)*
Edward Brode *(Chief Fin. Officer)*
James A. Cassin *(Pres.-Asia/Pacific Region)*
Peter S.P. Dimsey *(Pres.-U.S. Region)*
James W. John *(Exec. V.P.)*
John O. Smith *(Exec. V.P.-Debit Card Services)*
Philip Verdi *(Exec. V.P.-Electronic Services)*
Robert M. Frechette *(Sr. V.P.-Merchant Acceptance)*
Robert Norton *(Sr. V.P. & Gen. Counsel)*
Albert Prendergast *(Sr. V.P.-Human Resources)*
Richard Woods *(Sr. V.P. & Dir.-Pub. Rels.)*
James Desrosier *(V.P.-Adv.)*

Divisions:

Mastercard International, Inc. **(1)**
Four Ohio Dr.
Lake Success, NY 11042
Tel.: 516-574-4400 (100%)
Licensor of MasterCard Trademarks to Financial Institutions
S.I.C.: 6153

MasterCard International, Inc. **(1)**
12115 Lackland Rd.
Saint Louis, MO 63146
Tel.: 314-275-6100 (100%)
S.I.C.: 6153

Subsidiary:

Cirrus System, Inc. **(1)**
One Westbrook Corp. Center, Ste. 700
Westchester, IL 60154
Tel.: 708-449-4000
Fax: 708-965-9165
Emp.: 25
Automated Teller Machines
S.I.C.: 6099
G. Henry Mundt III *(Pres. & Chief Exec. Officer)*
Stephen VanFleet *(Sr. V.P.-Systems & Opers.)*
Caroline Raeder *(Dir.-Communications)*
Linda Snelgrove *(Mktg. Coord.)*

MASTERCRAFT FURNITURE CORP.
1111 N. 13th St.
Omaha, NE 68102
Tel.: 402-345-8550
Fax: 402-345-3717
Approx.Sls.: $12,000,000
Emp.: 280
Fiscal Year-end: 12/31/89
Mfr. Upholstered Furniture
S.I.C.: 2514
Julius Katzman *(Chm. Bd.)*
Maurice Katzman *(Pres.)*
Michael Katzman *(V.P.-Mktg. & Sls.)*

MASTERS INC.
7891 Beechcraft Ave.
Gaithersburg, MD 20879
Tel.: 301-948-8950 MD
Fax: 301-258-7368
Year Founded: 1986
Assets: $9,423,957
Liabilities: $6,120,837
Net Worth: $3,303,120
Approx.Sls.: $28,000,000
Emp.: 300
Fiscal Year-end: 12/31/89
Mechanical Contractor
S.I.C.: 1711
Ronald D. Bryant *(Pres.)*
William D. Duval *(V.P. & Treas.)*
John Burke *(Dir.-Pur.)*
Janis Reyes *(Dir.-Human Resources)*
Principal(s):
Ronald D. Bryant

Computer Systems/Hardware:
MAI Basic-4

Outside Service Firm(s):

Deloitte & Touche*(Auditors)*
1900 M St. N.W., 4th Fl.
Washington, DC 20036

Liberty Mutual*(Commercial Insurance Carrier)*
6101 Executive Blvd.
Rockville, MD 20852

Northwestern National Life Insurance Company*(Group Insurer)*
7701 Greenbelt Rd., Ste. 501
Greenbelt, MD 20770

Willoner, Calabrese & Rosen, P.A.*(Legal Firm)*
4603 Calvert Rd.
College Park, MD 20740

MASTERS, INC.
725 Summa Ave.
Westbury, NY 11590
Tel.: 516-997-8000 NY
Fax: 516-997-8562
Year Founded: 1937
Assets: $42,432,623
Earnings: ($3,169,085)
Liabilities: $20,946,102
Net Worth: $21,486,521
Approx.Sls.: $108,666,873
Emp.: 1,400
Fiscal Year-end: 2/ 3/91
Import
Retail Discounters
S.I.C.: 5311
Louis Biblowitz *(Chm. Bd.)*
Max Biblowitz *(Vice Chm.)*
Joshua Biblowitz *(Pres. & Chief Oper. Officer)*
Jerome Zelin *(Exec. V.P.)*
Robert Gordonson *(Treas. & Chief Fin. Officer)*
Jerome Becker *(Controller)*
Joseph Greenspan *(Sec.)*
James Alterbaum *(Gen. Counsel)*
Frank Papia *(Data Processing Dir.)*
Sam Horowitz *(Adv. Mgr.)*

Computer Systems/Hardware:
IBM 4381

Outside Service Firm(s):

Janover, Rubinroit & Co.*(Auditors)*
New York, NY

Chemical Bank*(Major Banking Relationship)*
Westbury, NY

Parker, Chapin, Flattau & Klimpl*(Legal Firm)*
1211 Ave. of the Americas
New York, NY 10036
Tel.: 212-704-6012
Fax: 212-704-6283

Divisions:

Central Textile Div. **(1)**
725 Summa Ave.
Westbury, NY 11590
Tel.: 516-997-8000
Retail Dept. Stores
S.I.C.: 5311
Joshua Biblowitz *(Pres.)*

Lady Rose Div. **(1)**
725 Summa Ave.
Westbury, NY 11590
Tel.: 516-997-8000
Retail Dept. Store
S.I.C.: 5311
Joshua Biblowitz *(Pres.)*

Lord Bibb Div. **(1)**
725 Summa Ave.
Westbury, NY 11590
Tel.: 516-997-8000
S.I.C.: 5311
Joshua Biblowitz *(Pres.)*

Susan Terry Div. **(1)**
725 Summa Ave.
Westbury, NY 11590
Tel.: 516-997-8000
Retail Dept. Stores
S.I.C.: 5311
Joshua Biblowitz *(Pres.)*

MASTERSON ROTHBERG ADVERTISING
342 Madison Ave.
New York, NY 10173
Tel.: 212-808-0100
Fax: 212-867-9329
Year Founded: 1988
Approx.Billings: $30,000,000
Emp.: 22
Joan O. Rothberg *(Chm. Bd., Chief Exec. Officer & New Bus. Contact)*
Peggy Bell Masterson *(Pres. & Creative Dir.)*
Patricia B. Hamway *(Opers. Mgr.)*

MATECO ELECTRONICS CORP.
2375 Flatbush Ave.
Brooklyn, NY 11234
Tel.: 718-338-8555 NY
Fax: 718-253-1509
Year Founded: 1951
Approx.Sls.: $30,000,000
Fiscal Year-end: 12/31/90
Television & Hi-Fi Components; Car Stereos; Portable Radios & Tape Recorders, Video Components
S.I.C.: 3629; 3651
Martin Gutenplan *(Pres.)*
Stella Austi *(V.P.-Pur.)*
Principal(s):
Martin Gutenplan

No. of U.S. Offices: 1

Computer Systems/Hardware:
Qantal

Divisions:

Rabson's **(1)**
119 W. 57th St.
New York, NY 10019
Tel.: Tel.: 212-217-0070
Retail
S.I.C.: 3629; 3651

Stereo Corp. of America **(1)**
2375 Flatbush Ave.
Brooklyn, NY 11234
Tel.: Tel.: 212-338-8555
Retail
S.I.C.: 3629; 3651

Stereo Warehouse Inc. **(1)**
2375 Flatbush Ave.
Brooklyn, NY 11234
Tel.: Tel.: 212-338-8555
Retail
S.I.C.: 3629; 3651

CURTIS MATHES CORPORATION
1 Curtis Mathes Pkwy.
Athens, TX 75751
Mailing Address:
P.O. Box 223607,
Dallas, TX 75222
Tel.: 903-675-2292 DE
Fax: 903-675-2843
Year Founded: 1957
Approx.Sls.: $400,000,000
Emp.: 300
Fiscal Year-end: 3/31/91
Retailer/Franchisor of Televisions, Stereos, Tape Combination Units, Stereo Components, Video Tape Recorders, Projection TVs & Other Electronic Home Entertainment Products
S.I.C.: 3651; 5731
Gary Whitaker *(Chm., Pres. & Chief Exec. Officer)*
James L. Jenkins *(Exec. V.P.-Retail Sls. & Mktg.)*
Horace Kelton *(Exec. V.P.-Opers.)*
Dan Moore *(V.P., Sec. & Gen. Counsel)*
Thomas E. Palley *(Chief Fin. Officer)*
Fred Lawrence *(Controller)*
Lance Peck *(Dir.-Natl. Adv.)*

Computer Systems/Hardware:
IBM System 38

Outside Service Firm(s):

Price Waterhouse*(Auditors)*
100 Cumberland Circle, Ste. 1400
Atlanta, GA 30339

Team Bank*(Major Banking Relationship)*
P.O. Box 2604,
Fort Worth, TX 76113
Tel.: 817-884-4614

MATHEWS & BOUCHER
1950 Brighton-Henrietta Town Line Rd.
Rochester, NY 14623
Tel.: 716-424-2790
Fax: 716-424-2798
Year Founded: 1890
Sales Range: $20-39 Million
Emp.: 86
Wholesale Sporting Goods
Richard H. Howk *(Chm. Bd. & Pres.)*
F. Parker Sterner *(V.P.-Natl. Sls.)*
Richard B. Malcolm *(Chief Fin. Officer)*

MATHIEU CORPORATION
Five Mathews Ave.
Riverdale, NJ 07457
Tel.: 201-838-0660
Fax: 201-838-2994
Sales Range: $40-59 Million
Emp.: 75
Packaging, Blending & Distribution Of Industrial & Specialty Chemicals
S.I.C.: 2819; 2869; 5169
C.H. Bendheim *(Chm. Bd.)*
P.E. Bendheim *(Pres.)*
Jeffrey V. Scocchio *(Chief Fin. Officer)*
Richard Goodson *(Gen. Mgr.)*

Outside Service Firm(s):

Ernst & Young*(Auditors)*
Park 80 West - Plaza One
Saddle Brook, NJ 07662

Lasser, Hochman, Marcus, Guryan & Kuskin*(Legal Firm)*
Roseland, NJ

First Fidelity Bank, N.A.*(Major Banking Relationship)*
Saddle Brook, NJ

MATHIEU, DONOVAN & ASSOCIATES, INC.
77 Ward St.
Montgomery, NY 12549
Tel.: 914-457-5100
Fax: 914-457-1077
Year Founded: 1984
Approx.Billings: $15,000,000
Emp.: 8
A.H. Pete Mathieu *(Chm. Bd. & Creative Dir.)*
Barbara Mathieu *(V.P., Chief Fin. Officer)*
Karen Naef *(Office Mgr.)*

MATRIX ESSENTIALS, INC.
30601 Carter St.
Solon, OH 44139
Tel.: 216-248-3700
Fax: 216-248-1433
Approx.Sls.: $30,000,000
Emp.: 200
Mfg. of Hair Care Products
S.I.C.: 2844
Arnold Miller *(Pres.)*
Sydell Miller *(Exec. V.P.)*
David Cook *(V.P.-Fin.)*
Kim Chapman *(Mgr.-Pub. Rels.)*

Outside Service Firm(s):

City National Bank*(Major Banking Relationship)*
Cleveland, OH

THE F. X. MATT BREWING CO.
811 Edward
Utica, NY 13502
Tel.: 315-732-3181
Year Founded: 1888
Approx.Sls.: $20,000,000
Emp.: 100
Fiscal Year-end: 12/31/90
Export
Produces Matt's Premium & Light Beer, Utica Club Beer, Ale & Light, Maximus Super, Fort Schuyler Beer, FX Matt's Traditional Holiday Amber Beer, Saranac 1888 All Malt Liquor
S.I.C.: 2082
F.X. Matt, II *(Chm. Bd.)*
Nicholas O. Matt *(Pres)*
Robert Cooley *(Comptroller)*
Alfred D. Matt *(Mgr.-Mktg.)*
Robert D. Kelly *(Mgr.-Sls.)*

MATTHEWS INTERNATIONAL CORP.
6117 Broad St.
Pittsburgh, PA 15206
Mailing Address:
P.O. Box 4999,
Pittsburgh, PA 15206
Tel.: 412-665-8200 **PA**
Fax: 412-363-3281
Assets: $69,000,000
Liabilities: $20,000,000
Net Worth: $49,000,000
Approx.Sls.: $120,000,000
Emp.: 1,300
Manufactures Industrial Marking Products, Bronze, Aluminum & Plastic Tablets, Signs & Memorials, Rubber Printing Plates, Rubber Stamps & Projects, Machinery for Product Identification & Cutting Dies
S.I.C.: 2893; 3069; 3281; 3366; 3559; 5084; 3544
W.M. Hauber *(Chm. Bd., Pres. & Chief Exec. Officer)*
R.T. Busteed *(V.P.)*
David J. DeCarlo *(V.P.)*
T.N. Kennedy *(V.P. & Treas.)*
James L. Parker *(V.P., Gen. Counsel & Sec.)*
Edward Stewart *(Dir.-Mngmt. Information Systems)*
Robert O. Read *(Mgr.-Plng. & Human Resources)*

Computer Systems/Hardware:
IBM 4361

Outside Service Firm(s):

Coopers & Lybrand*(Auditors)*
600 Grant St., 35th Fl.
Pittsburgh, PA 15219
Tel.: 412-355-8000
Fax: 412-355-8089

Blue Cross of Western Pennsylvania*(Group Insurer)*
One Smithfield St.
Pittsburgh, PA 15222
Tel.: 1-800-242-6425

Reed, Smith, Shaw & McClay*(Legal Firm)*
Mellon Square, P.O. Box 2009
Pittsburgh, PA 15230
Tel.: 412-288-3131
Fax: 412-288-3063

Divisions:

Identification Systems Div. **(1)**
1315 W. Liberty Ave.
Pittsburgh, PA 15226
Tel.: 412-344-4200
Grave Memorialization
S.I.C.: 3366
D.J. DeCarlo *(V.P.)*

Plants:

Identification Systems **(2)**
P.O. Box N,
Sun City, CA 92586
Tel.: 909-657-3174
S.I.C.: 3366
E. Dvorak *(Plant Mgr.)*

Identification Systems **(2)**
501 Lincoln St.
Searcy, AR 72143
Tel.: 501-268-3504
S.I.C.: 3366
James E. Russell *(Plant Mgr.)*

Identification Systems **(2)**
25 Chestnut St.
Seneca Falls, NY 13148
Tel.: 315-568-9835
S.I.C.: 3366
R. Sandroni *(Plant Mgr.)*

Matthews International Marking Systems Div. **(1)**
6515 Penn Ave.
Pittsburgh, PA 15206
Tel.: 412-362-6500
Stamping Products
S.I.C.: 3559
R.T. Busteed *(V.P. & Div. Mgr.)*

Matthews Intl. Corp.-Graphic Systems Div. **(1)**
1910 Cochran Rd.
Pittsburgh, PA 15220
Tel.: 412-665-2588
S.I.C.: 3069
G.D. Barefoot *(Div. Mgr.)*

Plants:

Graphic Systems **(2)**
5555 Fresca Dr.
La Palma, CA 90624
Tel.: 714-523-5511
S.I.C.: 3069
George Shumaker *(Plant Mgr.)*

Graphic Systems **(2)**
3435 N. Kimball Ave.
Chicago, IL 60618
Tel.: 312-539-7000
S.I.C.: 3069
Joseph P. Pacella *(Plant Mgr.)*

Graphic Systems **(2)**
1303 Logan Circle, N.W.
Atlanta, GA 30318
Tel.: 404-355-3255
S.I.C.: 3069
Malcom Paxton *(Plant Mgr.)*

Graphic Systems **(2)**
10866 Indian Head Ind. Blvd.
Saint Louis, MO 63106
Tel.: 314-423-9800
S.I.C.: 3069
Don Mahlin *(Plant Mgr.)*

Graphic Systems **(2)**
3 Brooks Dr.
Braintree, MA 02184
Tel.: 617-848-8220
S.I.C.: 3069
Bruce Chilcoat *(Plant Mgr.)*

Matthews International Memorial Division **(1)**
1315 W. Liberty Ave.
Pittsburgh, PA 15226
Tel.: 412-344-4200
S.I.C.: 3366
D.J. DeCarlo *(V.P. & Div. Mgr.)*

Subsidiary:

Matthews Intl. Trading Corp. **(1)**
1050 Brinton Rd.
Pittsburgh, PA 15221
Tel.: 412-241-0500
Export of Industrial Printing Prods.
S.I.C.: 5084
F.J. Sarknas *(Mgr.)*

Non-U.S. Holding:

Matthews Canada Ltd. **(1)**
5051 North Service Rd.
Burlington, ON L7L 5H6, Canada
Tel.: 416-336-1100 (100%)
Manufactures Industrial Marking Devices
S.I.C.: 3953

MATTISON MACHINE WORKS
545 Blackhawk Park Ave.
Rockford, IL 61101
Tel.: 815-962-5521 **IL**
Fax: 815-962-5568
Year Founded: 1896
Assets: $16,000,000
Liabilities: $6,000,000
Net Worth: $10,000,000
Sales Range: $20-39 Million
Emp.: 325
Fiscal Year-end: 10/31/91
Import Export
Mfr. Woodworking, Metalworking-Production Rotary & Horizontal Surface Grinders, Double Disc Grinders & Slideway Grinders & Special Machinery & Machine Tools, Magnetic & Vacuum Holding Devices
S.I.C.: 3546; 3553; 3541
Corporate Giving Program: Mattison Foundation
Employee Matching Gifts Program: Company Will Match Up To $5, 000.00.
A.M. Mattison *(Pres.)*
Paul Fleischer *(V.P.-Mfg. & Engrng.)*
P.L. Mattison, Jr. *(V.P. & Sec.)*
Samuel Overton *(Controller)*
Greg Champion *(Dir.-Mktg.)*
Principal(s):
A.M. Mattison
P.L. Mattison, Jr.

No. of Mfg. Plants/Facilities: 2
No. of U.S. Offices: 1
No. of Foreign Offices: 2

Computer Systems/Hardware:
IBM

Outside Service Firm(s):

Coopers & Lybrand*(Auditors)*
6000 E. State St.
Rockford, IL 61108
Tel.: 815-394-0300

Connolly & Oliver*(Legal Firm)*
Rockford, IL

Amcore Bank*(Major Banking Relationship)*
Rockford, IL

Joint Venture:

Koyo-Mattison **(1)**
34, 2-Chome Minami-uematsu Cho,
Yao City, Osaka 582, Japan
Emp.: 350
Mfr. Machinery
S.I.C.: 3541

MAUI DIVERS OF HAWAII, LTD.
1520 Liona St.
Honolulu, HI 96814
Tel.: 808-946-7979 **HI**
Fax: 808-946-0406
Approx.Sls.: $16,000,000
Emp.: 256
Export
Holding Company
S.I.C.: 6719
Corporate Giving Program: United Way; Employee Contributions are Matched on a 1 to 1 Basis up to a Pre-Determined Amount
Keith B. Hudson *(Chm. Bd.)*
Clifford D. Slater *(Pres.)*
Robert M. Taylor *(Exec. V.P. & Sec.)*
Gilbert Higuera *(V.P.-Whlse. Sls.)*
Sandra Arntzen *(V.P.-Retail Sls.)*
Carl P. Marsh *(V.P.-Mfg. & Pur.)*

Outside Service Firm(s):

Price Waterhouse*(Auditors)*
Honolulu, HI

Ashford & Wriston*(Legal Firm)*
Honolulu, HI

First Hawaiian Bank*(Major Banking Relationship)*
165 South King St.
Honolulu, HI 96813
Tel.: 808-525-5876
Fax: 808-525-5791

MAUI VARIETIES, LTD.
7192 Kalanianaole Hwy.
Honolulu, HI 96825
Tel.: 808-395-9431
Fax: 808-396-0132
Approx.Sls.: $19,000,000
Emp.: 200
Holding Company For Variety Stores, Real Estate Investments
S.I.C.: 6719; 5331; 6531
Tadami Kamitaki *(Pres.)*
Charles Mizoguchi *(V.P.)*
Paul Mizoguchi *(Treas.)*
Wayne Kamitaki *(Sec.)*
Principal(s):
Tadami Kamitaki

Outside Service Firm(s):

KPMG Peat Marwick*(Auditors)*
P.O. Box 4150,
Honolulu, HI 76812
Tel.: 808-531-7286

Maui Varieties, Ltd.—(Continued)

Fax: 808-541-9321

Chun, Kerr & Dodd*(Legal Firm)*
Honolulu, HI

Bank of Hawaii*(Major Banking Relationship)*
Honolulu, HI

MAUNEY HOSIERY MILLS, INC.
20 Pine St.
Kings Mountain, NC 28086
Mailing Address:
P.O. Box 1279
Kings Mountain, NC 28086
Tel.: 704-739-3621 **NC**
Fax: 704-734-0608
Year Founded: 1939
Assets: $5,741,860
Liabilities: $2,924,872
Net Worth: $2,816,988
Approx.Sls.: $15,144,000
Emp.: 325
Fiscal Year-end: 12/31/91
Export
Mfr. of Men's, Women's, Boy's & Girls Socks
S.I.C.: 2252
William K. Mauney, Jr. *(Chm. Bd.)*
Charles F. Mauney *(Exec. V.P. & Chief Oper. Officer)*
William K. Mauney III *(Pres.)*
Ransom A. Carpenter *(Treas. & Controller)*
Eddie Mauney *(Dir.-Pur.)*
Becky Pruitt *(Dir.-Data Processing)*
David B. Faunce *(Gen. Mgr.)*
Elizabeth Rayfield *(Mgr.-Personnel)*
Principal(s):
William K. Mauney, Jr.
Charles F. Mauney
William K. Mauney III

No. of Mfg. Plants/Facilities: 1
No. of U.S. Offices: 1

Computer Systems/Hardware:
IBM

Outside Service Firm(s):

Collins & Wilson*(Auditors)*
Gastonia, NC

Franklin Brown Co.*(Commercial Insurance Carrier)*
Charlotte, NC

Fringe Benefit Review, Inc.*(Group Insurer)*
Charlotte, NC

First Citizens Bank & Trust Co.*(International Bank Affiliate)*
Kings Mountain, NC

Branch Banking & Trust Co.*(Investment Banker)*
200 S. Tryon Street
Charlotte, NC 28202
Tel.: 704-342-7039
Fax: 704-342-7048

First Citizens Bank & Trust Co.*(Investment Banker)*
Kings Mountain, NC

Parker, Poe, Adams & Bernstein*(Legal Firm)*
Charlotte, NC

First Citizens Bank & Trust Co.*(Major Banking Relationship)*
Kings Mountain, NC

Lincoln National Life Insurance Co.*(Pension Manager)*
Fort Wayne, IN

MAUREY MANUFACTURING CORP.
2907 S. Wabash Ave.
Chicago, IL 60616
Tel.: 312-326-6550
Fax: 312-225-3812
Year Founded: 1917
Approx.Sls.: $12,000,000
Emp.: 200
Manufacturer V-Belt Pulleys
S.I.C.: 3429
Joseph E. Maurey *(Chm. Bd. & Pres.)*
Chuck Lloyd *(V.P.-Sls.)*
Principal(s):
Joseph E. Maurey

Outside Service Firm(s):

Strauss, Snider, Siegel & White*(Auditors)*
Chicago, IL

Tews, Theisen & Theisen*(Legal Firm)*
Chicago, IL

American National Bank & Trust Company of Chicago*(Major Banking Relationship)*
33 N. LaSalle St.
Chicago, IL 60602
Tel.: 312-661-5000
Fax: 312-661-6417

MAURICE ELECTRIC SUPPLY COMPANY
500 Penn St., N.E.
Washington, DC 20002
Tel.: 202-675-9400 **DE**
Fax: 202-543-3315
Approx.Sls.: $62,000,000
Emp.: 153
Electrical Supplies; Hardware Stores
S.I.C.: 5063; 5251
Bernard S. Green *(Pres.)*
Faye Green *(V.P.)*
Muriel Kogod *(V.P.)*
Robert Clark *(Controller)*
Marvin Kogod *(Treas. & Sec.)*

Outside Service Firm(s):

Stoy Maloney & Co.*(Auditors)*
Bethesda, MD

Signet Bank*(Major Banking Relationship)*
Arlington, VA

Division:

Maurexco Exporters **(1)**
13 C St., Ste. D
Laurel, MD 20707
Tel.: 410-792-8030
Mechanical & Electrical Architectural Supplies
S.I.C.: 5999
Thomas M. Hutchias *(Mgr.)*

THE MAURIN-ODGEN COMPANIES
460 Broadway St.
New Orleans, LA 70118
Tel.: 504-866-9757 **LA**
Fax: 504-866-9065
Year Founded: 1975
Sales Range: $10-19 Million
Emp.: 85
Real Estate Developer, Management & Brokerage
S.I.C.: 6552; 6531
Roger H. Ogden *(Chm. Bd.)*
James E. Maurin *(Pres.)*
Grady K. Brame *(Chief Fin. Officer)*
Gerald E. Songy *(Exec. V.P.)*
Michael Saucier *(V.P.-Project Mngmt.)*
Principal(s):
Roger H. Ogden
James E. Maurin
Gerald E. Songy

No. of Mfg. Plants/Facilities: 39
No. of U.S. Offices: 6

Subsidiaries:

Maurin-Ogden Management Corporation **(1)**
615 Baronne St., Ste. 100
New Orleans, LA 70113
Tel.: 504-523-4481
Emp.: 25
Real Estate Management
S.I.C.: 6531
Martin A. Mayer *(Pres.)*
Jeff Marshall *(Chief Fin. Officer)*

Stirling Properties, Inc. **(1)**
615 Baronne St., Ste. 100
New Orleans, LA 70113
Tel.: 504-523-4481
Real Estate Operations
S.I.C.: 6531
Lewis W. Stirling *(Pres.)*

MAUTZ PAINT COMPANY
939 E. Washington Ave.
Madison, WI 53703
Mailing Address:
P.O. Box 7068
Madison, WI 53707
Tel.: 608-255-1661
Fax: 608-255-4342
Year Founded: 1922
Sales Range: $20-39 Million
Emp.: 225
Fiscal Year-end: 11/30/90
Manufacture Paints & Varnishes; Wholesale & Retail Paint Supplies & Wallpaper; Retail Floor Coverings, Draperies & Furniture
S.I.C.: 2851; 5198; 5231; 5713; 5714
Bernhard F. Mautz, Jr. *(Pres.)*
Dan Drury *(V.P.-Opers.)*
Robert J. Gurske *(V.P.-Fin.)*
Louise U. Mautz *(Sec.)*
Mark Buehl *(Mgr.-Data Processing)*
Robert Christy *(Mgr.-Sls.)*
Robert Regenberg *(Mgr.-Sls. Promo.)*
Principal(s):
Bernhard F. Mautz, Jr.

Computer Systems/Hardware:
Honeywell

Outside Service Firm(s):

Grant Thornton*(Auditors)*
Madison, WI

Stroud & Stroud*(Legal Firm)*
Madison, WI

First Wisconsin National Bank*(Major Banking Relationship)*
Madison, WI

MAVERIK COUNTRY STORES, INC.
P.O. Box 457
Afton, WY 83110
Tel.: 307-886-3861 **WY**
Fax: 307-886-3832
Year Founded: 1935
Assets: $31,204,251
Liabilities: $11,085,086
Net Worth: $20,119,165
Sales Range: $100-499 Million
Emp.: 1,000
Fiscal Year-end: 3/31/91
Convenience Stores; Retail Gasoline & Groceries
S.I.C.: 5411; 5541
William Call *(Chm., Pres. & Chief Exec. Officer)*
Val Call *(V.P., Sec. & Treas.)*
Richard J. Marshall *(V.P.-Opers. & Legal Counsel)*
Stanford Fluckiger *(Dir.-Data Processing)*
Dan Murray *(Dir.-Real Estate)*
Terry Pippin *(Dir.-Mktg. & Pur.)*
Joe Shaw *(Dir.-Adv.)*
Michael Call *(Controller)*
Principal(s):
William Call
Val Call
Richard J. Marshall

No. of U.S. Offices: 2

Computer Systems/Hardware:
IBM

Outside Service Firm(s):

Price Waterhouse*(Auditors)*
Salt Lake City, UT

Blue Cross & Blue Shield of Utah*(Group Insurer)*
Salt Lake City, UT

Ronald C. Barker*(Legal Firm)*
Salt Lake City, UT

Zions First National Bank*(Major Banking Relationship)*
P.O. Box 30880
Salt Lake City, UT 84130
Tel.: 801-524-4624
Fax: 801-533-0464

Piper, Jaffray & Hopwood, Inc.*(Pension Manager)*
Salt Lake City, UT

MAXCOR MANUFACTURING, INC.
4230 N. Nevada St.
Colorado Springs, CO 80907
Mailing Address:
P.O. Box 7228
Colorado Springs, CO 80933
Tel.: 719-598-4606 **CO**
Fax: 719-548-1319
Year Founded: 1981
Approx.Sls.: $25,000,000
Emp.: 300
Mfr. of Metal Machine Bases, Custom Machinery; Stamping Metal For The Trade; Tempering of Metal; Plating of Metals or Formed Products
S.I.C.: 3499; 3469; 3398; 3471
Ron Marold *(Pres.)*
Bob Werschky *(V.P. & Treas.)*
Don Werschky *(V.P. & Sec.)*
Jack Head *(V.P.)*

Outside Service Firm(s):

United Bank of Colorado Springs, N.A.*(Major Banking Relationship)*
Colorado Springs, CO

MARY MAXIM, INC.
2001 Holland Ave.
Port Huron, MI 48060
Mailing Address:
P.O. Box 5019,
Port Huron, MI 48061-5019
Tel.: 313-987-2000
Tel.: 800-962-9504
Fax: 313-987-5056
Year Founded: 1952
Approx.Sls.: $30,000,000
Emp.: 150
Fiscal Year-end: 12/31/90
Export
Mail Order Yarns, Fabrics, Stitchery, Hobbycrafts
S.I.C.: 5961
Willard M. McPhedrain *(Pres.)*
Robert McManaman *(V.P.-Mktg. & Mdsg.)*
Larry L. McPhedrain *(V.P.-Opers.)*
Dick Ward *(Controller)*
Chuck Cowley *(Mgr.-Plant)*
Donna Hietikko *(Mgr.-Personnel)*
Joyce Minis *(Mgr.-Retail)*
Orville Smith *(Mgr.-Data Processing)*
Audrey Conrad *(Pur. Agent)*
Principal(s):
W.M. McPhedrain Family

No. of Foreign Offices: 1

Outside Service Firm(s):

Grant & Silverman*(Auditors)*
Southfield, MI

NBD Bank, N.A.*(Major Banking Relationship)*
Port Huron, MI

Davidson, Staiger, Adair & Hill*(Legal Firm)*
901 Huron Ave.
Port Huron, MI 48060

Non-U.S. Subsidiary:

Mary Maxim, Ltd. **(1)**
75 Scott Ave,
Paris, ON N3L 3G5, Canada

THE MAXIMA CORPORATION
4200 Parliament Place, Ste. 300
Lanham, MD 20706
Tel.: 301-459-2000
Fax: 301-459-2003
Year Founded: 1978
Assets: $24,434,000
Liabilities: $19,222,000
Net Worth: $5,212,000
Approx.Sls.: $58,000,000
Emp.: 1,000
Fiscal Year-end: 9/30/89
Integrated Information Management Services & Products Company that Provides Systems Engineering & Integration, Facilities & Management Information Resources Management, Scientific & Health Support Services; Computer Products & Services
S.I.C.: 8731; 7376; 7379; 8711
Joshua I. Smith *(Chm. Bd. & Chief Exec. Officer)*
Major L. Clark, III *(V.P.-Human Resources & Admin.)*
Tom Downey *(Treas.)*
Gary R. Franklin *(Corp. Counsel)*

No. of U.S. Offices: 46

Outside Service Firm(s):

Deloitte & Touche*(Auditors)*
1900 M St. N.W., 4th Fl.
Washington, DC 20036

Chubb Group*(Commercial Insurance Carrier)*
P.O. Box 1615,
Warren, NJ 07061
Tel.: 201-580-2000

Chubb Group*(Group Insurer)*
P.O. Box 1615,
Warren, NJ 07061
Tel.: 201-580-2000

Sovran Bank*(Major Banking Relationship)*
Rockville, MD

Subsidiaries:

Maintain **(1)**
1611 Sulphur Spring Rd., Stes. 111 & 118
Baltimore, MD 21227
Tel.: 301-621-1178
Emp.: 9
Computer Hardware Maintenance & Services, Primarily IBM Mainframe
S.I.C.: 7379
Major L. Clark, II *(V.P.-Human Resources & Admin.)*

Maxima Business Systems **(1)**
2101 E. Jefferson St.
Rockville, MD 20872
Tel.: 410-770-7500
Emp.: 21
Microcomputer Hardware & Software Sales, Systems Integration, Computer-Aided Design, Computer Publishing Capabilities, Custom Software Design, "Value-Added" Services
S.I.C.: 7379
Major L. Clark, III *(V.P.-Human Resources & Admin.)*

Maxima Computer Systems Corp. **(1)**
14741 Governor Oden Bowie Dr., Rm. L128
Upper Marlboro, MD 20772
Tel.: 301-952-3160
Emp.: 73
Computer Information Mngmt. Servies Focusing on State & Local Government Facilities Mngmt. Type Applications
S.I.C.: 7376; 7379
Major L. Clark, III *(V.P.-Human Resources & Admin.)*

Maxima Data Systems **(1)**
2101 E. Jefferson St.
Rockville, MD 20852
Tel.: 410-230-2000
Emp.: 7
Contract Computer Programming, Systems Intergration & Software Engineering Services for Commercial, State & Local Government Clients
S.I.C.: 7379
Major L. Clark, III *(V.P.-Human Res. & Admin.)*

MAXINE OF HOLLYWOOD, INC.
2424 E. 28th St.
Los Angeles, CA 90058
Tel.: 213-749-8391
Fax: 213-588-0466
Approx.Sls.: $15,000,000
Emp.: 50
Women's, Misses' & Juniors' Bathing Suits
S.I.C.: 2339
Harvey Cooper *(Pres.)*
Minnie Robinson *(V.P.)*
Maxine Cooper *(Sec. & Treas.)*

Outside Service Firm(s):

Heller & Broida*(Auditors)*
Los Angeles, CA

Tyre, Kamins, Katz & Granof*(Legal Firm)*
Century City, CA

Bank of America NT&SA*(Major Banking Relationship)*
555 So. Flower St.
Los Angeles, CA 90071
Tel.: 213-683-3868

MAXITROL CO.
23555 Telegraph Rd.
Southfield, MI 48037
Mailing Address:
P.O. Box 2230,
Southfield, MI 48037
Tel.: 313-356-1400
Fax: 313-356-0829
Year Founded: 1946
Approx.Sls.: $14,000,000
Emp.: 250
Manufacturer Pressure & Temperature Controls for the Gas Appliance & Equipment, Industry & Emergency Safety Valves
S.I.C.: 3822; 3829
Frank Kern, Jr. *(Chm. Bd.)*
H. J. Schlachter *(Pres. & Chief Exec. Officer)*
Frank Kern, III *(Exec. V.P.)*
John McHale *(V.P.-Sls.)*
M.J. Kozma *(Treas. & Controller)*
Charles Stang, Jr. *(Dir.-Pur.)*

No. of Mfg. Plants/Facilities: 3
No. of U.S. Offices: 1
No. of Foreign Offices: 1

Computer Systems/Hardware:
Digital; DEC

Outside Service Firm(s):

Arthur Andersen & Co.*(Auditors)*
400 Renaissance Center
Detroit, MI 48243
Tel.: 313-259-8100

Dykema, Gossett*(Legal Firm)*
400 Renaissance Ctr., 35th Fl.
Detroit, MI 48243
Tel.: 313-568-6800

National Bank of Royal Oak*(Major Banking Relationship)*
Royal Oak, MI

MAXON CORPORATION
201 E. 18th St.
Muncie, IN 47302-4124
Mailing Address:
P.O. Box 2068,
Muncie, IN 47307-0068
Tel.: 317-284-3304 **IN**
Fax: 317-286-8394
Year Founded: 1916
Sales Range: $20-39 Million
Emp.: 430
Fiscal Year-end: 12/31/91
Export
Mfr. Industrial Combustion Equipment & Valves
S.I.C.: 3433; 3494
Corporate Giving Program: Funds Provided through the Maxon Charitable Foundation
Harry R. Maxon III *(Chm. Bd.)*
Robert M. Smitson *(Pres. & Chief Exec. Officer)*
C.N. Hetrick *(Exec. V.P.)*
Theodore R. Wanthal *(V.P.-Sls.)*
Robert G. Syring *(V.P.-Engrng.)*
James C. Smith *(V.P.-Business Devel.)*
Mark J. Vanderstelt *(Chief Fin. Officer & Treas.)*
Russell Anderson *(Asst. V.P.-Admin.)*
William P. Coppin *(Asst. V.P.-Res. & Devel.)*
Robert F. Beavers *(Sec.)*
Terry J. Clark *(Controller)*
E. Kay Place *(Dir.-Personnel)*

Computer Systems/Hardware:
IBM System AS 400

Outside Service Firm(s):

George S. Olive & Co.*(Auditors)*
Indianapolis, IN

Merchants National Bank*(Major Banking Relationship)*
Muncie, IN

Non-U.S. Holdings:

Maxon Combustion Systems, Ltd. **(1)**
Chantry House High Street
Coleshill, Birmingham B46 3BP, United Kingdom
Tel.: 0675-64334 (100%)
Telex: 841-0724384
Emp.: 7
Mktg. & Sales
S.I.C.: 5074

Maxon GmbH **(1)**
Neiderlassung Stuttgart Gottlieb-Daimler-Strasse, 17, D-7053
Kernen/Stuttgart, Germany
Tel.: 07151 420 51 (100%)
Telex: 841-0724384
Emp.: 7
Mktg. & Sales
S.I.C.: 5074

Maxon GmbH **(1)**
Ruttenscheider Platz 3 D-4300
Essen, 1 Germany
Tel.: 0201/779017
Telex: 857-1493
Emp.: 10
Mktg. & Sales
S.I.C.: 5074

N.V. Maxon International S.A. **(1)**
Groningensingel 1 6835 EA
Arnhem, Netherlands
Tel.: (085) 21 11 12
Telex: 45512
Emp.: 6
Mktg. & Sales
S.I.C.: 5074

N.V. Maxon International S.A. **(1)**
Luchthavenlaan 16 1800
Vilvoorde, Belgium
Tel.: (02) 25-41-35 (100%)
Telex: 45512
Emp.: 100
Mfg. of Combustion Equip. & Valves
S.I.C.: 3433; 3494
Jan Berben *(Mng. Dir.)*
Omer Rayen *(Admin. Mgr.)*
Daniel Heroes *(Sales Mgr.)*

Maxon S.A.R.L. **(1)**
Avenue Du Parc 5 Le Campus, 95033
Cergy Pontoise, Cedex France
Tel.: 1-30739696
Telex: 609259
Emp.: 13
Mktg. & Sales
S.I.C.: 5074

Joint Venture:

C.I.C.S.A. **(1)**
Rosas Moreno No. 60 06470 Col. San Rafael,
Mexico, D.F. Mexico
Tel.: 566-3365 (49%)
Emp.: 30
Mfr., Marketing, Sales & Service
S.I.C.: 3433; 3494
Lino Rangel Escalera *(Gen. Mgr.)*
Arturo Sevilla *(Asst. Gen. Mgr.)*
Adan Benitez *(Dir.-Sls. Fin.)*
Guillermo Olvera *(Mgr.-Fin.)*
Carlos Silva *(Mgr.-Tech.)*

THE MAY APPAREL GROUP, INC.
Interstate 85
Mebane, NC 27302
Mailing Address:
P.O. Box 190
Mebane, NC 27302
Tel.: 919-563-5521
Fax: 919-563-3475
Approx.Sls.: $10,000,000
Emp.: 300
Manufacturer Children's Clothes
S.I.C.: 2361
John May *(Chm. Bd.)*
Henry L. May *(Pres.)*
James T. May *(V.P.)*
Vicky Paterline *(Controller)*

Principal(s):
John May
Henry L. May

Computer Systems/Hardware:
IBM

Outside Service Firm(s):

Apple, Bell, Johnson & Co.*(Auditors)*
Burlington, NC

BB&T Bank*(Major Banking Relationship)*
Greensboro, NC

GEORGE S. MAY INTERNATIONAL COMPANY
303 S. Northwest Hwy.
Park Ridge, IL 60068-4265
Tel.: 708-825-8806
Tel.: 800-999-3020 **DE**
Fax: 708-825-7937
Year Founded: 1925
Approx.Sls.: $50,000,000
Emp.: 750
Fiscal Year-end: 12/31/91
Import Export
Management Consultants Primarily for Medium & Small-Sized Businesses
S.I.C.: 8742; 7389
Donald J. Fletcher *(Pres.)*
Dorothy May Campbell *(V.P.)*
Jean May Rech *(V.P.)*
John E. McArdle *(V.P.-Communications)*
Roy S. Matthews *(V.P.-Fin. & Treas.)*
Daniel J. Dunaway *(Controller)*
Dominick P. Latigo *(Dir.-Sls., U.S. & Canada)*
Patricia Kralik *(Dir.-Pur.)*
Joy A. McGuirl *(Dir.-Personnel)*
James V. Stefanelli *(Dir.-Data Processing)*
Norman Aamlie *(Dir.-Telecommunications)*

Computer Systems/Hardware:
Hewlett Packard 3000

Outside Service Firm(s):

KPMG Peat Marwick*(Auditors)*
Peat Marwick Plaza, 303 E. Wacker Dr.
Chicago, IL 60601
Tel.: 312-938-1000

George S. May International Company—(Continued)

Schiff, Hardin & Waite*(Legal Firm)*
7200 Sears Tower, 233 S. Wacker Dr.
Chicago, IL 60606
Tel.: 312-876-1000

American National Bank & Trust Co.*(Major Banking Relationship)*
Chicago, IL

American National Bank & Trust Company of Chicago*(Major Banking Relationship)*
33 N. LaSalle St.
Chicago, IL 60602
Tel.: 312-661-5000
Fax: 312-661-6417

Subsidiary:

George S. May Intl. Co. **(1)**
230 Twin Dolphin Dr., Ste. A
Redwood City, CA 94065
Tel.: 415-593-9500
Israel Kushnir *(Mng. Dir.)*

Non-U.S. Holdings:

George S. May Canada, Ltd. **(1)**
615 Rene Levesque Blvd. W., Ste. 1100
Montreal, PQ H3B 1P5, Canada
Tel.: 514-879-9250 (100%)
Approx.Sls.: $4,100,000
Emp.: 90
Management Consulting
S.I.C.: 8742
Donald J. Fletcher *(Pres.)*

George S. May International, S.P.A. **(1)**
Centro Direzionale Colleoni Paluzzo
Orionez, 200 Agrate Brianza,
Milan, Italy
Tel.: 650221 (100%)
Approx.Sls.: $7,500,000
Emp.: 150
Management Consulting
S.I.C.: 8742
Ronald Dysvick *(Mng. Dir.)*

EARL MAY SEED & NURSERY L.P.
208 N. Elm St.
Shenandoah, IA 51603
Mailing Address:
P. O. Box 500
Shenandoah, IA 51603
Tel.: 712-246-1020
Approx.Sls.: $40,000,000
Emp.: 750
Import
Seeds, Nursery Stock & Garden Centers
S.I.C.: 5193; 5261
Bill Shaw *(Chief Exec. Officer)*
Bill LeVere *(Adv. Mgr.)*

Computer Systems/Hardware:
IBM AS/400

MAY & SPEH, INC.
1501 Opus Place
Downers Grove, IL 60515
Tel.: 708-964-1501
Fax: 708-964-0340
Approx.Sls.: $35,000,000
Emp.: 220
Complete Data Processing Services; Facility Mngmt. Systems, Procedures, Programming, Remote Computing, Custom Software Key Entry, Computer Processing, Direct Mktg. Services, Database Management Services, Data Enhancement Services
S.I.C.: 7374; 8744; 7379; 7331; 2791; 7371; 7373; 7375; 7376
Albert J. Speh, Jr. *(Chm. Bd. & Pres.)*
Charles Zayed *(Chief Exec. Officer)*
Willard Engel *(Chief Fin. Officer)*

May & Speh Direct **(1)**
1501 Opus Place
Downers Grove, IL 60515
Tel.: 708-964-1501
Direct Marketing Information Services
S.I.C.: 7331

MAYER BERKSHIRE CORPORATION
25 Edison Dr.
Wayne, NJ 07470
Tel.: 201-696-6200
Fax: 201-696-6203
Sales Range: $10-19 Million
Emp.: 70
Hosiery, Panty Hose, Underwear & Related Apparel
S.I.C.: 2251; 2252; 2254
Cyrus Mayer *(Pres.)*
Chester Mayer *(Exec. V.P.)*
Michael Mayer *(Exec. V.P.)*
Kathy Mayer *(V.P.)*
Slyvia Mayer *(Sec. & Treas.)*

Outside Service Firm(s):

Anchin, Block & Anchin*(Auditors)*
1375 Broadway
New York, NY 10018

Lowenstein, Sandler, Kohl, Fisher & Boylan*(Legal Firm)*
65 Livingston Ave.
Roseland, NJ 07068
Tel.: 908-992-8700

Merchants Bank*(Major Banking Relationship)*
New York, NY

Valley National Bank*(Major Banking Relationship)*
Wayne, NJ

MAYER MYERS PAPER COMPANY
1769 Latham St.
Memphis, TN 38101
Mailing Address:
P.O. Box 410
Memphis, TN 38101
Tel.: 901-948-5631
Tel.: 800-766-1466 **TN**
Fax: 901-774-7482
Year Founded: 1919
Approx.Sls.: $15,000,000
Emp.: 70
Import Export
Wholesaler Packaging Materials & Equipment, Sanitary Papers, Printing Papers, School Supplies, Janitorial Supplies, Food Disposables
S.I.C.: 5113
Malcolm Levi, Sr. *(Chm. Bd.)*
Kenneth Levi *(Pres.)*
Louis Byall *(Exec. V.P.)*
Malcolm Levi, Jr. *(Sr. V.P.)*
E. Brooks Lammey *(V.P.)*
Harry Prest *(V.P.)*
Principal(s):
Malcolm Levi, Sr.
Kenneth Levi

Outside Service Firm(s):

James A. Matthews & Co.*(Auditors)*
Memphis, TN

Bogatin, Lawson & Chiapella*(Legal Firm)*
860 Ridgelake Blvd., Ste. 360
Memphis, TN 38120
Tel.: 901-767-1234

National Bank of Commerce*(Major Banking Relationship)*
Memphis, TN

PETER A. MAYER ADVERTISING, INC.
324 Camp St.
New Orleans, LA 70130
Tel.: 504-581-7191
Fax: 504-581-3009
Year Founded: 1967
Approx.Billings: $20,000,000
Emp.: 39
Full Service Agency
Peter A. Mayer *(Chm.)*
Mark A. Mayer *(Pres.)*
Frank Montagnino *(Exec. V.P.)*
Mark Romig *(Pub. Rels. & Acct. Supvr.)*
Jan Pitesa *(Controller)*

Computer Systems/Hardware:
Media Mngmt. Plus

Mayfair Infants Wear
(See Tawil Associates Inc. Listing)

MAYFAIR MILLS, INC.
1885 Hayne St.
Arcadia, SC 29320
Tel.: 803-576-2610 **SC**
Fax: 803-576-6741
Year Founded: 1934
Sales Range: $100-499 Million
Emp.: 2,200
Fiscal Year-end: 10/30/90
Manufacturer of Premium Print Cloths, Broad Cloths, Blended Fabrics, Pocketings & Sheetings
S.I.C.: 2211; 2221
Frederick B. Dent *(Chm. Bd.)*
Frederick B. Dent, Jr. *(Pres.)*
L.O. Bragg *(V.P.)*
Ben F. Hagood, Jr. *(V.P.)*
Kenneth Hayes *(V.P.)*
Charles Skelton *(V.P.)*
H.D. Towles *(Sec.)*
Cecil Hutcherson *(Controller)*
Paul Dorman *(Dir.-Personnel)*
Connie Wells *(Mgr.-Pur.)*

No. of Mfg. Plants/Facilities: 6

Computer Systems/Hardware:
Honeywell Bull

Outside Service Firm(s):

Deloitte & Touche*(Auditors)*
1200 NCNB Plaza, 7 N. Laurens St.
Greenville, SC 29601
Tel.: 803-242-3640

South Carolina National Bank*(Major Banking Relationship)*
7515 Northside Dr.
Greenville, SC
Tel.: 803-577-8280

MAYFAIR SUPER MARKETS, INC.
681 Newark Ave.
Elizabeth, NJ 07208
Tel.: 908-352-6400 **DE**
Fax: 908-352-0103
Assets: $140,000,000
Earnings: $12,013,000
Liabilities: $100,000,000
Net Worth: $40,000,000
Approx.Sls.: $575,000,000
Emp.: 5,000
Fiscal Year-end: 9/30/90
41 Supermarkets Located in New Jersey
S.I.C.: 5411
Stanley P. Kaufelt *(Chm. Bd., Pres. & Chief Exec. Officer)*
Frank Curci *(Sr. V.P.-Fin.)*
Jacqueline Keller *(Sr. V.P.-Mktg. & Communications)*
John Kovaleski *(Dir.-Personnel)*
Susan Petrillo *(Dir.-Mgmt. Information Systems)*
Florence Kaufelt *(Sec.)*
Michelle Maselli *(Mgr.-Consumer Affairs)*

Outside Service Firm(s):

Greenbaum, Rowe, Smith, Ravin, Davis & Bergstein*(Legal Firm)*
Metro Corporate Campus 1, P.O. Box 5600
Woodbridge, NJ 07095
Tel.: 908-549-5600

The Bank of New York*(Major Banking Relationship)*
One Wall Street
New York, NY 10286
Tel.: 212-635-6805
Fax: 212-635-3201

MAYFLOWER TRANSIT, INC.
9998 N. Michigan Rd.
Carmel, IN 46032
Mailing Address:
P. O. Box 107,
Indianapolis, IN 46206
Tel.: 317-875-1000 **IN**
Fax: 317-875-2214
Year Founded: 1927
Assets: $160,903,000
Liabilities: $116,567,000
Net Worth: $44,336,000
Approx.Rev.: $421,349,000
Emp.: 1,400
Fiscal Year-end: 12/31/91
International, Interstate & Local Trucking & Warehousing
S.I.C.: 4213; 4225; 4214
Michael L. Smith *(Chm. Bd. & Chief Exec. Officer)*
Patrick F. Carr *(Pres. & Chief Oper. Officer)*
Donald K. Sears *(Exec. V.P.-Opers. & Sls.)*
Ronald W. Martin *(Sr. V.P. & Chief Fin. Officer)*
Simon Morse *(Sr. V.P. & Chief Information Officer)*
Dennis C. Norman *(Sr. V.P. & Chief Fin. Officer)*
Robert H. Irvin *(Sr. V.P. & Gen. Counsel)*
Charles Berning *(V.P.-Tech. & Prod. Services)*
Larry W. Dodge *(V.P. & Treas.)*
Lynn Smith *(V.P.-Communication & Adv.)*
Janet Allaby *(Controller)*

Outside Service Firm(s):

Ernst & Young*(Auditors)*
One Indiana Square, Ste. 3400
Indianapolis, IN 46204
Tel.: 317-236-1100

The Indiana National Bank*(Major Banking Relationship)*
One Indiana Sq.
Indianapolis, IN 46266
Tel.: 317-266-6000

Subsidiaries:

Mayflower Transit, Inc. **(1)**
9998 N. Michigan Rd.
Carmel, IN 46032
Tel.: 317-875-1000 (100%)
Fax: 317-875-2040
Approx.Sls.: $355,599,000
Emp.: 751
Fiscal Year-end: 12/31/91
Interstate Motor Carrier
S.I.C.: 4213; 4214
Michael L. Smith *(Chm., Pres. & Chief Exec. Officer)*
Pat Carr *(Pres. & Chief Exec. Officer)*
Ronald Martin *(Sr. V.P. & Chief Fin. Officer)*

Subsidiaries:

Advantage Moving & Storage Co., Inc. **(2)**
9998 N. Michigan Rd.
Carmel, IN 46032
Tel.: 317-875-1967 (100%%)
Local Moving & Storage
S.I.C.: 4213; 4214
Dennis C. Norman *(Pres.)*
Ronald W. Martin *(Chief Fin. Officer)*

Hogan Transfer & Storage Corporation, Inc. **(2)**
825 E. St. Clair
Indianapolis, IN 46202
Tel.: 317-639-9583 (100%)
Local Moving & Storage
S.I.C.: 4214; 4213
Dennis C. Norman *(Pres.)*

Smith's Moving & Storage Corp. **(2)**
611 S. Pickett
Alexandria, VA 22304
Tel.: 703-370-8300 (100%)
Local Moving & Storage
S.I.C.: 4214
Dennis C. Norman *(Pres.)*

American Transfer & Storage Co. **(1)**
2605 LBJ Fwy.
Dallas, TX 75234
Tel.: 214-620-2665 (100%)
Moving & Storage of Household Goods
S.I.C.: 4214; 4226
Dennis C. Norman *(Pres.)*

Crest-Mayflower International, Inc. **(1)**
9998 N. Michigan Rd.
Carmel, IN 46032
Tel.: 317-875-1283 (100%)
Freight Forwarder
S.I.C.: 4731
Michael L. Smith *(Chm. Bd.)*

Elder Moving & Storage Co. **(1)**
561 Stevens St.
Jacksonville, FL 32205
Tel.: 904-781-7920 (100%)
Local Moving & Storage
S.I.C.: 4214
Dennis C. Norman *(Pres.)*

Gentry Insurance Agency, Inc. **(1)**
9998 N. Michigan Rd.
Carmel, IN 46032
Tel.: 317-875-1054 (100%)
Insurance Agency
S.I.C.: 6411
Michael L. Smith *(Chm. Bd. & Chief Exec. Officer)*

Dobson Moving & Storage, Inc. **(1)**
9998 N. Michigan Rd.
Carmel, IN 46032
Tel.: 317-875-1000 (100%)
Local Moving & Storage
S.I.C.: 4214
Dennis C. Norman *(Pres.)*

Mayflower of Texas **(1)**
2605 LBJ Freeway
Dallas, TX 75234
Tel.: 214-241-3581 (100%)
S.I.C.: 4214
Dennis C. Norman *(Pres.)*

Mayflower Motor Coach, Inc. **(1)**
9998 N. Michigan Rd.
Carmel, IN 46032
Tel.: 317-875-1000 (100%)
Long-Distance Passenger Bus Opers.
S.I.C.: 4131
Donald K. Sears *(Pres.)*

Transport Service of Indiana, Inc. **(1)**
9998 N. Michigan Rd.
Carmel, IN 46032
Tel.: 317-875-1695 (100%)
Supplier of Fuel & Transportation Access & Moving Equip.
S.I.C.: 5541; 5251
Donald K. Sears *(Pres.)*

Wald Moving and Storage Services, Inc. **(1)**
5205 S. Rice Ave.
Houston, TX 77001
Tel.: 713-666-2121 (100%)
S.I.C.: 4214
Dennis C. Norman *(Pres.)*

Subsidiary:

Corpus Christi Transfer Company **(2)**
900 N. Staples St.
Corpus Christi, TX 78401
Tel.: 512-883-4391 (100%)
S.I.C.: 4213; 4214
Dennis C. Norman *(Pres.)*

Affiliate:

Mayflower Contract Services, Inc. **(1)**
5360 College Blvd.
Overland Park, KS 66211 (100%)
School Bus Opers. & Sales
S.I.C.: 5012; 4151
Michael Smith *(Pres.)*

Subsidiary:

Allied Bus Sales, Inc. **(2)**
17327 So. Hwy. 71
Belton, MO 64012
Tel.: 816-331-9600 (100%)
School Bus Sales
S.I.C.: 5012
Michael Smith *(Pres.)*

MAYNARD STEEL CASTING COMPANY
2856 S. 27th St.
Milwaukee, WI 53234
Tel.: 414-645-0440
Fax: 414-645-7378
Approx.Sls.: $20,000,000
Emp.: 400
Manufacture Steel Castings for Power Shovel & Road Building, Auto & Metal Working
S.I.C.: 3325
Edmund D. Wabiszewski *(Pres.)*
Eugene O'Kelly *(V.P.-Human Resources)*
Rudy Pacioni *(V.P.-Sls.)*
Robert Phill *(V.P.-Fin.)*
Mike Klammert *(Dir.-Personnel)*
Edmund E. Wabiszewski, Jr. *(Plant Mgr. & Pur. Mgr.)*

Principal(s):
Edmund D. Wabiszewski

Outside Service Firm(s):

Meier, Clancy, George & Co.*(Auditors)*
Milwaukee, WI

McDermott, Will & Emery*(Legal Firm)*
227 W. Monroe St.
Chicago, IL 60606-5096
Tel.: 312-372-2000

Heritage Bank*(Major Banking Relationship)*
2323 N. Mayfair Rd.
Milwaukee, WI 53226
Tel.: 414-771-8100

MAYS CHEMICAL COMPANY
7760 E. 89th St.
Indianapolis, IN 46256
Mailing Address:
P.O. Box 50915,
Indianapolis, IN 42650-0915
Tel.: 317-842-8722 **IN**
Fax: 317-576-9630
Fax: 317-845-8410
Year Founded: 1980
Approx.Sls.: $50,000,000
Emp.: 60
Fiscal Year-end: 12/31/90
Distributor Industrial Chemicals
S.I.C.: 5169
William Mays *(Chm. Bd. & Pres.)*
Ted Mays *(V.P.-Personnel)*
Mark Miller *(V.P.-Opers.)*
John Thompson *(V.P.-Sls. & Mktg.)*
Wilmer A. West *(V.P. & Controller)*

Principal(s):
William Mays

No. of Mfg. Plants/Facilities: 3
No. of U.S. Offices: 3

Computer Systems/Hardware:
IBM System AS 400 & PC's

Outside Service Firm(s):

Price Waterhouse*(Auditors)*
300 N. Meridian
Indianapolis, IN 46204
Tel.: 317-632-8361

INB National Bank*(Major Banking Relationship)*
One Indiana Sq.
Indianapolis, IN 46266
Tel.: 317-266-6000

Kemper Insurance*(Group Insurer)*
Long Grove, IL 60049-0001

Liberty Mutual*(Group Insurer)*
175 Berkeley St.
Boston, MA

Massachusetts Mutual Life Insurance Co.*(Group Insurer)*
1295 State Street
Springfield, MA 01111
Tel.: 413-788-8411

Barnes & Thornburg*(Legal Firm)*
11 S. Meridian St.
Indianapolis, IN 46204
Tel.: 317-638-1313

Equitable Financial Companies*(Pension Manager)*
Indianapolis, IN

Division:

United Chemical Products **(1)**
1650 Luett St.
Indianapolis, IN 46222
Tel.: 317-634-8820
Distributor of Industrial Chemicals
S.I.C.: 5169
William G. Mays *(Chief Oper. Officer)*

MAYVILLE ENGINEERING CO., INC.
715 South St.
Mayville, WI 53050
Tel.: 414-387-4500 **WI**
Fax: 414-387-2682
Year Founded: 1946
Assets: $23,500,000
Liabilities: $7,000,000
Net Worth: $16,500,000
Approx.Sls.: $44,000,000
Emp.: 430
Fiscal Year-end: 5/31/91
Export
Metal Stamping, Fabrications & Assemblies, Shotshell, Reloaders, Aerialwork Platforms
S.I.C.: 3469; 3537
Employee Matching Gifts Program: United Way
Ted J. Bachhuber *(Chm. Bd.)*
Carl Bachhuber *(Pres.)*
Robert Bachhuber *(V.P.-MEC)*
Dave Pasbrig *(V.P.-Personnel)*
Robert Wild *(V.P.-Mktg.)*
Glen V. Helmbrecht *(Chief Fin. Officer & Sec.)*
Joe Cheesebro *(Dir.-Pur.)*
Duwayne Kuenzi *(Dir.-Data Processing)*
Jim Sokoly *(Mgr.-Sls.)*
Tom Leigl *(Mktg. Coord.)*

Principal(s):
Ted J. Bachhuber
Carl Bachhuber
Robert Bachhuber

No. of U.S. Offices: 1

Computer Systems/Hardware:
HP 3000, System 70

Outside Service Firm(s):

Jannsen & Co.*(Auditors)*
Milwaukee, WI

Edgarton, Ondrasek, Hobbs, Petak & Massey*(Legal Firm)*
Fond Du Lac, WI

M & I Marshall & Ilsley Bank*(Major Banking Relationship)*
770 N. Water St.
Milwaukee, WI 53202
Tel.: 414-765-8700

Emjay Corp.*(Pension Manager)*
Milwaukee, WI

MAYWOOD, INC.
900 E. Second
Amarillo, TX 79120
Mailing Address:
P.O. Box 30550
Amarillo, TX 79120
Tel.: 806-374-2835
Fax: 806-373-6235
Year Founded: 1954
Sales Range: $40-59 Million
Emp.: 700
Manufacture Wood Products: Louvered & Panel Doors, Louvered Shutters, Bifolds & Wood Patio Doors, Exterior Doors
S.I.C.: 2431
John C. Maynard *(Pres.)*
Chuck Taylor *(Chief Fin. Officer & Controller)*
Tom Maynard *(V.P.-Production)*
Bobby Sidman *(Dir.-Personnel)*
Jim Dutton *(Mgr.-Data Processing)*
Jerry Cogburn *(Pur. Agent)*

Principal(s):
John C. Maynard

Outside Service Firm(s):

KPMG Peat Marwick*(Auditors)*
600 First National Pl. II
Amarillo, TX 79101
Tel.: 806-373-6661

Underwood, Wilson, Sutton, Berry, Stein & Johnson*(Legal Firm)*
Amarillo, TX

First National Bank of Amarillo*(Major Banking Relationship)*
Amarillo, TX

Mazda Distributors Great Lakes
(See Transnational Motors Inc. Listing)

MAZE NAILS
100 Church St.
Peru, IL 61354
Mailing Address:
P.O. Box 449,
Peru, IL 61354
Tel.: 815-223-8290
Tel.: 800-435-5949
Fax: 815-223-7585
Approx.Sls.: $10,000,000
Emp.: 100
Export
Mfr. Specialty Nails
S.I.C.: 3315
Peter G. Loveland *(Pres., Treas. & Gen. Counsel)*
George H. Maze *(V.P. & Sec.)*
Eldon Radtke *(Comptroller)*
Doug Whitefield *(Dir.-Personnel)*
Roelif M. Loveland *(Mgr.-Adv.)*
Charles Swanson *(Product Mgr.)*
Jerome J. Kobold *(Pur. Agent)*

Subsidiary:

Independent Nail Company **(1)**
106 Hale St.
Bridgewater, MA 02324
Tel.: 800-443-1966
S.I.C.: 3315
Bob Fisher *(Gen. Mgr.)*

MAZO LERCH COMPANY, INC.
4720 Eisenhower Ave.
Alexandria, VA 22304
Tel.: 703-370-5900 **DE**
Year Founded: 1927
Approx.Sls.: $80,000,000
Emp.: 250
Food Service Distributor
S.I.C.: 5141
Howard D. Lerch, Sr. *(Pres.)*
Howard D. Lerch, Jr. *(V.P.)*
Robert J. Lerch *(V.P.)*
William N. Lerch *(V.P.)*
Allan MacArther *(Controller)*

Principal(s):
Howard D. Lerch, Sr.

No. of Mfg. Plants/Facilities: 3

Outside Service Firm(s):

BDO Seidman*(Auditors)*
Washington, DC

First American Bank, N.A.*(Major Banking Relationship)*
Washington, DC

MCADAMS, RICHMAN & ONG, INC.
15 N. Presidential Blvd.
Bala-Cynwyd, PA 19004
Tel.: 215-667-8900 **PA**
Fax: 215-667-0694
Year Founded: 1976
Approx.Billings: $48,500,000
Emp.: 45
Fiscal Year-end: 9/30/89
Advertising, Sales Promotion, Corporate Design & Public Relations
S.I.C.: 7311
Brian McAdams *(Chm. Bd.)*
Frank Mercurio *(Chief Oper. Officer & Exec. V.P.)*
Richard Booth *(Chief Fin. Officer & Exec. V.P.)*

No. of U.S. Offices: 1

Computer Systems/Hardware:
IBM, Apple

Outside Service Firm(s):

Ernst & Young*(Auditors)*
1800 John F. Kennedy Blvd.
Philadelphia, PA 19103-7499
Tel.: 215-864-3300

Provident Life & Accident Insurance Co.*(Commercial Insurance Carrier)*
Philadelphia, PA

Morgan, Lewis & Bockius*(Legal Firm)*
123 So. Broad St.
Philadelphia, PA 19109
Tel.: 215-875-2500

Fidelity Bank*(Major Banking Relationship)*
Broad & Walnut St.
Philadelphia, PA 19109

Richard Booth*(Pension Manager)*
Philadelphia, PA

WILLIAM DOUGLAS MCADAMS INC.
1740 Broadway
New York, NY 10019
Tel.: 212-698-4000
Year Founded: 1926
Approx.Billings: $176,900,000
Emp.: 221
Pharmaceuticals & Healthcare Adv.
Irwin C. Gerson *(Chm. & Chief Exec. Officer)*
Thomas Lom *(Pres.)*
George Carteris *(Chief Fin. Officer & V.P.)*
Howard Mandelbaum *(Exec. V.P.)*
Ronald J. Vignone *(Exec. V.P.)*
Sue Foreman *(Sr. V.P., Creative Dir./ Consumer Products)*
Paul Hansen *(Sr. V.P., Mngmt. Supvr.)*
Kevin McShane *(Sr. V.P., Creative Dir./Copy)*
Barnett Mennen, M.D. *(Sr. V.P., Medical & Mktg. Dir.)*
Donald Morgan *(Sr. V.P., Acct. Group Supvr.)*
Peter Parks *(Sr. V.P., Pres.-Helix Div.)*
John Puglisi *(Sr. V.P., Mngmt. Supvr.)*
Janice Radam *(Sr. V.P., Media Dir.)*
Bill Robertson *(Sr. V.P., Acct. Grp. Supvr.)*
Ronald Souza *(Sr. V.P., Bus. Devel.)*
Beverly Simons *(Sr. V.P., Pres.-McAdams PR)*
William J. Young *(Sr. V.P., Human Resources Dir.)*
David Zackson, M.D. *(Sr. V.P., Medical Dir.)*
John Avery *(V.P., Copy)*
Lee Grissom *(V.P., Client Acctg.)*
Marlene Molinoff *(V.P., Copy)*
Joanne Peppard *(V.P., Copy Dir.-Helix Div.)*
Robert Dempsey *(Pres.-Triclinica Communications)*
Bill Firing *(Mgr., Information Services)*
Molly Garfin *(Mgr., Library Services)*
Mark Stahl *(Mgr., Computer Design)*

MCAFEE CONSOLIDATED INC.
840 E. Southern
Mesa, AZ 85204
Tel.: 602-964-1751 **AZ**
Fax: 602-964-6066
Year Founded: 1948
Sales Range: $20-39 Million
Emp.: 195
General Contractor, Utility Pipeline Construction
S.I.C.: 1521; 1541; 1542; 1623
Roy E. McAfee *(Chm. Bd.)*
Charles McAfee *(Pres.)*

Computer Systems/Hardware:
MAI Basic Four; IBM PC

Outside Service Firm(s):

KPMG Peat Marwick*(Auditors)*
2020 No. Central Ave.
Phoenix, AZ 85004
Tel.: 602-253-2000

First Interstate Bank*(Major Banking Relationship)*
P.O. Box 53441,
Phoenix, AZ 85072-3441
Tel.: 602-229-4049

MCANALLY ENTERPRISES, INC.
12215 7th St.
Yucaipa, CA 92399
Mailing Address:
P.O. Box 1129,
Yucaipa, CA 92399
Tel.: 909-797-0144
Tel.: 800-726-2002 **CA**
Fax: 909-790-1736
Year Founded: 1939
Approx.Sls.: $50,000,000
Emp.: 450
Fiscal Year-end: 12/31/91
Export
Production of Chicken Eggs
S.I.C.: 0252
N.A. McAnally *(Chm. Bd. & Chief Fin. Officer)*
Carlton R. Lofgren *(Pres.)*
Frank R. Campbell *(V.P.-Prod.)*
Charles S. Chao *(V.P.-Feed Div.)*
Wayne F. Morgan *(V.P.-New Mexico Div.)*
James V. Wyatt *(V.P.-Opers.)*
John D. Brennan *(Controller)*
Raye M. Lofgren *(Corp. Sec.)*
James Selzler *(Mgr.-Sls. & Mktg.)*
Herbert F. Barber *(Dir.-Pur.)*
Cathy M. Murray *(Dir.-Personnel/ Insurance)*

No. of Mfg. Plants/Facilities: 6
No. of U.S. Offices: 3

Computer Systems/Hardware:
IBM AS/400-C20

Outside Service Firm(s):

Price Waterhouse*(Auditors)*
3403 Tenth St., Ste. 800
Riverside, CA 92501

McCAFFERY & RATNER INC.

MCCAFFERY & RATNER, INC.
370 Lexington Ave.
New York, NY 10017
Tel.: 212-661-8940
Fax: 212-490-1923
Year Founded: 1983
Approx.Billings: $24,500,000
Emp.: 27
Advertising Agency
S.I.C.: 7311
S. Ratner *(Chm. Bd. & Dir-Acct. Services)*
W. McCaffery *(Pres. & Dir.-Creative Services)*
D. Hooper *(Exec. V.P. & Dir.-Mktg.)*

No. of U.S. Offices: 1

Computer Systems/Hardware:
IBM

Outside Service Firm(s):

Chemical Bank*(Major Banking Relationship)*
277 Park Ave.
New York, NY 10172
Tel.: 212-310-6161

McCAFFREY AND McCALL
575 Lexington Avenue, New York, NY 10022

MCCAFFREY AND MCCALL
575 Lexington Ave.
New York, NY 10022
Tel.: 212-350-1000
Tel.: 800-777-1011
Fax: 212-355-0224
Year Founded: 1962
Approx.Billings: $175,000,000
Emp.: 265
Michael B. Robertson *(Chm., Chief Exec. Officer & Chief Creative Dir.)*
Daniel S. Reid *(Pres., Chief Oper. Officer)*
Robert M. Henry *(Vice Chm., Chief Fin. Officer)*
Bruce McCall *(Vice Chm., Creative Dir.)*
Burtis C. Flounders *(Exec. V.P., Mngmt. Supvr.)*
Theodore Pettus *(Exec. V.P., Creative Dir.)*
Alan C. Herzog *(Exec. V.P., Assoc. Creative Dir.)*
Bernard J. Long *(Exec. V.P., Mngmt. Supvr.)*
William A. Metzger *(Exec. V.P., Mngmt. Supvr.)*
Lynnda Pollio *(Exec. V.P., Corp. Devel.)*
Herbert W. Warden *(Exec. V.P., Mngmt. Supvr.)*
H. Thomas Wilson *(Exec. V.P., Media Dir.)*
Vicki Blucher *(Sr. V.P., Dir., Brdcst. Production)*
Ilene Danuff *(Sr. V.P., Grp. Media Dir.)*

MCCAIN CITRUS INC.
1821 S. Kilbourn
Chicago, IL 60623
Tel.: 312-762-9000
Fax: 312-762-3537
Year Founded: 1985
Approx.Sls.: $210,000,000
Emp.: 300
Fiscal Year-end: 7/31/91
Import
Juice Processor & Packages of Frozen Concentrate & Aseptic Juices & Drinks
S.I.C.: 2037
Richard Lan *(Pres.)*
S. Wayne Hanscom *(V.P.-Fin.)*
Don Raezler *(V.P.-Opers.)*
Dan Curtin *(V.P.-Sls.)*
Nicholas Andrus *(V.P.-Mktg.)*
Jim Karlovitz *(Controller)*
David Bliss *(Plant Mgr.)*

MCCAIN MANUFACTURING CORP.
6200 W. 60th St.
Chicago, IL 60638
Tel.: 312-586-6200
Fax: 312-586-6210
Year Founded: 1926
Emp.: 200
Bookbinding, Magazine Binding & Newspaper Stuffing Machinery
S.I.C.: 3555
William B. McCain *(Chm. Bd.)*
John S. Iverson *(Pres.)*
George Higgins *(V.P.-Sls.)*
Victor Krzyzanski *(V.P.-Sls.)*
Ronald Weller *(V.P.-Engrng.)*
Don Dicchetti *(Asst. Intl. Sls. Mgr.)*
Laurel McCain *(Mktg. Coordinator)*

Computer Systems/Hardware:
IBM

Outside Service Firm(s):

Grant Thornton*(Auditors)*
700 One Prudential Plaza, 130 East Randolph St.
Chicago, IL 60601
Tel.: 312-856-0200
Fax: 312-565-4719

The Travelers*(Group Insurer)*
P.O. Box 2911,
Overland Park, KS 66201-1311

Lakeshore National Bank*(Major Banking Relationship)*
Chicago, IL

MCCALL OIL & CHEMICAL CORP.
808 S.W. 15th Ave.
Portland, OR 97205
Tel.: 503-228-2600 **WA**
Fax: 503-221-5752
Year Founded: 1939
Assets: $19,103,000
Earnings: $506,000
Liabilities: $8,410,000
Net Worth: $10,693,000
Approx.Sls.: $64,319,000
Emp.: 80
Fiscal Year-end: 3/31/92
Wholesale Petroleum Products, Including Bulk Stations & Terminals, Chemical & Allied Products; Heating Oil Dealers; Manufacture Specialty Chemicals
S.I.C.: 5171; 5172; 5989
W. Calder McCall *(Chm. Bd.)*
Robert H. McCall *(Pres. & Chief Exec. Officer)*
Frank Moore *(Exec. V.P. & Chief Oper. Officer)*
D.A. Kieffer *(V.P.-Fin., Sec. & Treas.)*
Cheryl Summers *(Controller & Asst. Sec.)*

No. of U.S. Offices: 1

Computer Systems/Hardware:
Digital Equipment

Outside Service Firm(s):

Arthur Andersen & Co.*(Auditors)*
111 S.W. Columbia, Ste. 1400
Portland, OR 97201
Tel.: 503-226-1331

Tonkon, Torp, Galen, Marmaduke & Booth*(Legal Firm)*
1600 Pioneer Tower, 888 S.W. Fifth Ave.
Portland, OR 97204
Tel.: 503-221-1440

First Interstate Bank*(Major Banking Relationship)*
P.O. Box 3131,
Portland, OR 97208
Tel.: 503-220-4855
Fax: 503-225-7153

First Interstate Bank*(Pension Manager)*
P.O. Box 3131,
Portland, OR 97208
Tel.: 503-220-4855
Fax: 503-225-7153

Seafirst Bank*(Pension Manager)*
Columbia-SeaFirst Center, 701 5th Ave., 11th Flr.
Seattle, WA 98124
Tel.: 206-358-3039

Fax: 206-358-3113

Subsidiaries:

GWC Properties, Inc. **(1)**
808 S.W. 15th Ave.
Portland, OR 97205
Tel.: 503-228-2600
Fax: 503-221-5752
S.I.C.: 6531
W.C. McCall *(Chm.)*
R.H. McCall *(Pres.)*
D.A. Kieffer *(Sec./Treas.)*

McCall Oil Real Estate Corporation **(1)**
808 S.W. 15th Ave.
Portland, OR 97205
Tel.: 503-288-2600
Fax: 503-221-5752
S.I.C.: 6531
W.C. McCall *(Chm. Bd.)*
R.H. McCall *(Pres. & Chief Exec. Officer)*
D.A. Kieffer *(Sec. & Treas.)*

McCall Properties, Inc. **(1)**
808 S.W. 15th Ave.
Portland, OR 97205
Tel.: 503-228-2600 (100%)
Fax: 503-221-5752
Investment Real Estate Operation
S.I.C.: 6798
W.C. McCall *(Chm.)*
R.H. McCall *(Pres.)*
D.A. Kieffer *(Sec./Treas.)*

MCCARTHY BUILDING COMPANIES
1341 N. Rock Hill Rd.
Saint Louis, MO 63124
Tel.: 314-968-3300
Fax: 314-968-4502
Year Founded: 1864
Approx.Sls.: $610,000,000
Emp.: 2,000
Holding Company; Industrial & Commercial Construction Management & General Contracting
S.I.C.: 6719; 1541; 1542; 8741
Michael M. McCarthy *(Chm. Bd.)*
Timothy R. McCarthy *(Vice Chm.)*
Roger H. Burnet *(Pres.)*
George Scherer *(Chief Fin. Officer & Controller)*
Richard Vandegrift *(Exec. V.P.)*
Francis F. McCarthy *(Sr. V.P.)*
Jack Soderholm *(V.P.-Admin. Support)*
James Staskiel *(V.P., Legal Counsel & Sec.)*
Principal(s):
Michael M. McCarthy

Computer Systems/Hardware:
IBM System 38

Outside Service Firm(s):

Deloitte & Touche*(Auditors)*
One City Centre
St. Louis, MO 63101
Tel.: 314-342-4900
Fax: 314-342-1100

Mercantile Commerce Trust*(Major Banking Relationship)*
Saint Louis, MO

Subsidiary:

McCarthy Brothers Co. **(1)**
1341 N. Rock Hill Rd.
Saint Louis, MO 63124
Tel.: 314-968-3300
Management Consulting & Public Relations Services; Nonresidential & Industrial Building & Warehouse General Contractors
S.I.C.: 8742; 1542; 1541
Roger H. Burnet *(Pres. & Chief Oper. Officer)*

MCCARTY FARMS
P.O. Box 366
Magee, MS 39111
Tel.: 601-849-3351 **MS**
Fax: 601-849-4835
Year Founded: 1948
Approx.Sls.: $265,000,000
Emp.: 3,670
Fiscal Year-end: 12/31/91
Export
Processor & Wholesaler Broiler, Fryer & Further Processed Chicken Products
S.I.C.: 0251; 0254; 2015; 5144
Corporate Giving Program: At the Discretion of the Chairman
H.F. McCarty, Jr. *(Chm. Bd.)*
John R. McCarty *(Pres., Chief Exec. Officer & Chief Fin. Officer)*
Tommy Bass *(V.P.-Sls.-Farms)*
Stewart Bridgforth *(V.P.-Mktg.)*
Bill Darling *(V.P.-Sls.-Foods)*
Richard Venable *(V.P.-Admin.)*
Marsha McCarty Wells *(Treas.)*
Doris V. Tullos *(Sec.)*
Rodney Edwards *(Controller)*
Thomas Bounds *(Dir.-Mngmt. Information Systems)*
Donn Paul *(Dir.-Personnel Admin.)*
Jim Bush *(Mgr.-Telecommunications)*

No. of Mfg. Plants/Facilities: 6
No. of U.S. Offices: 1

Computer Systems/Hardware:
Data General

Outside Service Firm(s):

Price Waterhouse*(Auditors)*
One Commerce Square,
Memphis, TN 38103

Ross-King Walker*(Commercial Insurance Carrier)*
P.O. Box 15069,
Hattiesburg, MS 39404
Tel.: 601-544-3300

Blue Cross & Blue Shield of Mississippi, Inc.*(Group Insurer)*
P.O. Box 1043
Jackson, MS 39215
Tel.: 601-932-3704

Knight & Knight*(Legal Firm)*
P.O. Box 662,
Jackson, MS 39205
Tel.: 601-948-5605

Trustmark National Bank*(Major Banking Relationship)*
248 E. Capital
Jackson, MS 39201

Wells Fargo Nikko Investment Advisors*(Pension Manager)*
45 Fremont St., 16th Fl.
San Francisco, CA 94105
Tel.: 415-597-2000
Fax: 415-597-2199

Subsidiaries:

McCarty Foods, Inc. **(1)**
P.O. Box 2718, I-55 South
Jackson, MS 39207
Tel.: 601-371-2700
Fax: 601-372-0748
Further Processing of Chicken Products
S.I.C.: 5144
Gene McDonald *(V.P. & Gen. Mgr.)*
Bill Darling *(V.P.-Sls.)*

McCarty Processors, Inc. **(1)**
238 Wilmington St.
Jackson, MS 39207
Tel.: 601-372-7441
S.I.C.: 5144
Joe McGinty *(V.P. & Gen. Mgr.)*
Tommy Bass *(V.P.-Sls.)*

MCCLAIN FINLON ADVERTISING
1331 17th St., Ste. 200
Denver, CO 80202
Tel.: 303-292-5650
Year Founded: 1982
Approx.Billings: $10,000,000
Emp.: 18
Cathey M. Finlon *(Pres., Treas. & New Bus. Contact)*
Shay Lindemann *(Gen. Mgr.)*

MCCOMMUNICATIONS INC.
13140 Coit Rd., Ste. 515
Dallas, TX 75240
Tel.: 214-480-8383
Year Founded: 1986
Approx.Billings: $11,300,000
Emp.: 15
High Tech Adv.
Mike Crawford *(Chm. Bd. & Pres.)*
Deanna Casey *(Office Coord.)*
Debra Caston *(Treas. & Media Buyer)*
Kristine Ryan *(Pub. Rels. Specialist)*
Mary Nell Westbrook *(Dir.-Pub. Rels.)*

MCCONNAUGHY STEIN SCHMIDT BROWN
North Pier, 401 E. Illinois St., Ste. 500
Chicago, IL 60611
Tel.: 312-321-8000
Fax: 312-321-8008
Year Founded: 1986
Approx.Billings: $50,000,000
Emp.: 45
Tom McConnaughy *(Chm. & Chief Exec. Officer)*
William E. Stein *(Pres. & Chief Oper. Officer)*
Jeremy Brown *(Vice Chm.)*
Geoff Kehoe *(Mng. Dir.)*
Judy Peyton *(Dir. Acct. Plng.)*

MCCONNELL AUTOMOTIVE
3150 Dauphin St.
Mobile, AL 36606
Tel.: 205-476-4141 **DE**
Fax: 205-476-4157
Year Founded: 1971
Approx.Sls.: $36,000,000
Emp.: 80
Retail Sales of New & Used Automobiles
S.I.C.: 5511
James V. McConnell, Jr. *(Pres.)*
Ray Zakutney *(Treas. & Sec.)*

Outside Service Firm(s):

SouthTrust Bank of Mobile*(Major Banking Relationship)*
Mobile, AL

MCCONNELL CABINETS, INC.
3017 N. Rumford
El Monte, CA 91732
Tel.: 213-283-8488
Tel.: 818-444-2653 **CA**
Fax: 818-443-5420
Year Founded: 1944
Approx.Sls.: $22,000,000
Emp.: 250
Fiscal Year-end: 9/30/91
Import
Manufacture Wood Built-In Cabinets
S.I.C.: 2434
William R. McConnell *(Chm. Bd. & Pres.)*
W.S. McConnell *(V.P.-Admin.)*
H.B. Sarrail *(V.P.-Production)*
J.L. Sarrail *(Sec. & Treas.)*

No. of Mfg. Plants/Facilities: 2

Outside Service Firm(s):

Nitchman & Co.*(Auditors)*
Santa Monica, CA

Liberty Mutual*(Commercial Insurance Carrier)*
Los Angeles, CA

Sheppard, Mullin, Richter & Hampton*(Legal Firm)*
333 S. Hope Street, 48th Fl.
Los Angeles, CA 90071

First Interstate Bank*(Major Banking Relationship)*
El Monte, CA

Subsidiary:

Costal Wood Products, Inc. **(1)**
13110 Louden Lane
City of Industry, CA
Tel.: 818-333-1104
Emp.: 42
Laminated Panels
S.I.C.: 3083
W.S. McConnell *(Pres.)*
Robert Rogers *(Gen. Mgr.)*

J.H. MCCORMICK, INC.
2507 Empire Ave.
Burbank, CA 91504
Tel.: 818-843-2010 **CA**
Fax: 818-842-9909
Year Founded: 1914
Approx.Sls.: $105,000,000
Emp.: 120
New Construction of Commercial & Office Buildings, Industrial Buildings & Warehouses
S.I.C.: 1542; 1541
Jack McCormick *(Pres.)*
Gary McCormick *(Exec. V.P.)*
Robert McCormick *(V.P.)*
Steven McCormick *(Controller)*
Gerald McCormick *(Treas.)*

Outside Service Firm(s):

Bank of America NT&SA*(Major Banking Relationship)*
701 S. Western Ave.
Glendale, CA 91201
Tel.: 818-507-2830

MCCORMICK PAINT WORKS COMPANY
2355 Lewis Ave.
Rockville, MD 20851
Tel.: 301-770-3235 **MD**
Fax: 301-770-9814
Approx.Sls.: $18,000,000
Emp.: 140
Manufacture Paint & Architectural Coatings
S.I.C.: 2851
T.P. McCormick *(Pres.)*
Yamna M. Stanger *(Chief Fin. Officer)*
G. Allison *(Exec. V.P.)*
James E. Booth *(V.P.-Sls.)*

No. of Mfg. Plants/Facilities: 2

Outside Service Firm(s):

Wilkerson & Zapp*(Legal Firm)*
Hyattsville, MD

Maryland National Bank*(Major Banking Relationship)*
Rockville, MD

MCCOURT LABEL CO.
20 Egbert Lane
Lewis Run, PA 16738
Mailing Address:
P.O. Box 157
Bradford, PA 16701
Tel.: 814-362-3851
Fax: 814-362-4156
Year Founded: 1896
Approx.Sls.: $11,000,000
Emp.: 99
Fiscal Year-end: 12/31/90
Import Export
Mfr. of Pressure Sensitive Labels, Bar Code Labels, Pharmacy, Roll & Cut Labels, Gummed Labels, Drum & Pail Labels
S.I.C.: 2672
John C. Egbert *(Pres. & Chief Exec. Officer)*

McCourt Label Co.—(Continued)

Louis V. Luzzi *(V.P.)*
Randy Bittinger *(Chief Oper. Officer)*
Robert L. Thompson *(Controller)*
Henry B. Hulings *(Pur. Agent)*
Jane Luzzi *(Mgr.-Personnel)*
Denise Strouse *(Mgr.-Sls.)*

Computer Systems/Hardware:
IBM System 36, PC's & Macintosh

McCracken Brooks

MCCRACKEN BROOKS COMMUNICATIONS, INC.
8400 Normandale Lake Blvd., Ste. 375
Minneapolis, MN 55437
Tel.: 612-921-8400
Fax: 612-921-8477
Year Founded: 1966
Approx.Billings: $30,015,000
Emp.: 51
Behavioral Mktg.
A. Keith McCracken *(Pres. & Chief Exec. Officer)*
Karl Kaufmann *(Sr. V.P., Client Devel.)*
John Harmon *(V.P., Controller)*

MCCRORY CONSTRUCTION CO., INC.
1280 Assembly St.
Columbia, SC 29201
Tel.: 803-799-8100 **SC**
Fax: 803-254-9800
Year Founded: 1918
Approx.Sls.: $38,000,000
Emp.: 135
General Contractor Commercial & Industrial Buildings
S.I.C.: 1542; 1541
James T. Tharp *(Chm. Bd. & Pres.)*
Clarence A. Richards *(Exec. V.P.)*
Del A. Rosebrock *(V.P.-Fin. & Admin.)*
Dennis G. Shealy *(V.P.-Bus. Devel.)*
Danny Mercer *(Dir.-Personnel & Safety)*

Outside Service Firm(s):

J. W. Hunt & Co.*(Auditors)*
Middleburg Office Park, 1607 St. Julian Place
Columbia, SC 29202
Tel.: 803-254-8196

Setzler, Chewning & Scott*(Legal Firm)*
West Columbia, SC

South Carolina National Bank*(Major Banking Relationship)*
Columbia, SC

MCCURDY & CO., INC.
Midtown Plaza, 285 Main St., E.
Rochester, NY 14645
Tel.: 716-232-1000
Fax: 716-546-0136
Year Founded: 1901
Sales Range: $60-79 Million
Emp.: 1,500
Retail & Specialty Department Stores
S.I.C.: 5311
Gilbert G. McCurdy *(Chm. Bd.)*
Ken McCurdy *(Pres. & Chief Exec. Officer)*
Sidney Rosenbloom *(V.P., Chief Fin. Officer & Treas.)*
Larry Hinkle *(V.P.)*
Dennis Meeh *(Dir.-Mngmt. Information Systems)*

Computer Systems/Hardware:
IBM Systems 38 & 370

Outside Service Firm(s):

Price Waterhouse*(Auditors)*
153 E. 53rd St., 44th Fl.
New York, NY 10022
Tel.: 212-371-2000

Blue Cross of the Rochester Area*(Group Insurer)*
Rochester, NY

McDonald Davis & Associates

MCDONALD DAVIS & ASSOCIATES, INC.
250 W. Coventry Ct.
Milwaukee, WI 53217
Tel.: 414-228-1990
Fax: 414-228-7561
Year Founded: 1963
Approx.Billings: $55,500,000
Emp.: 85
Retail, Legal, Consumer, Healthcare & Entertainment
Richard E. McDonald *(Pres. & Chief Exec. Officer)*
James Locatelli *(Exec. V.P.)*
Jim Cattanach *(V.P.)*
Chuck Schiller *(V.P., Creative Dir.)*
Thomas A. Altenburg *(V.P.)*
Luan Laev *(V.P.)*
Lynn Margason *(V.P.)*
Stan Merriman *(V.P.)*
Larry Swanlund *(V.P.)*
Joel English *(Dir., Mktg. Services)*
Eric McDonald *(Dir., Alternative Mktg. Communications)*
Mitchel Winter *(Controller)*

Computer Systems/Hardware:
IBM, Macintosh

MCDONALD EQUIPMENT CO.
37200 Vine St.
Willoughby, OH 44094
Mailing Address:
P.O. Box 810
Willoughby, OH 44094
Tel.: 216-951-8222 **OH**
Fax: 216-951-2089
Year Founded: 1968
Assets: $10,230,660
Liabilities: $2,733,498
Net Worth: $7,497,162
Approx.Sls.: $43,500,000
Emp.: 78
Fiscal Year-end: 10/31/91
Distribute Engines & Engine Generators
S.I.C.: 5063
Charles R. McDonald *(Chm., Pres. & Chief Exec. Officer)*
Scott McDonald *(Chief Oper. Officer)*
Sylvia Sullivan *(Chief Fin. Officer)*
Charles McDonald, Jr. *(Exec. V.P.)*
Theodore Saltz *(Sec.)*
Tami Weisbarth *(Mgr.-Mngmt. Information Systems)*

Principal(s):
Charles R. McDonald

No. of U.S. Offices: 3

Computer Systems/Hardware:
Ultimate (Honeywell Level 6)

Outside Service Firm(s):

Page Saltz & Shamis*(Auditors)*
Beachwood, OH

Lincoln National Life Insurance Co.*(Group Insurer)*
PO Box 208, 1300 S. Clinton
Fort Wayne, IN 46801
Tel.: 219-455-2926
Fax: 219-455-7619

Weston, Hurd, Fallon & Paisley*(Legal Firm)*
Cleveland, OH

Society National Bank*(Major Banking Relationship)*
900 Euclid Ave., P.O. Box 6477
Cleveland, OH 44101-6477
Tel.: 216-737-5000
Fax: 216-566-8947

American States Insurance Co.*(Pension Manager)*
500 N. Meridian St.
Indianapolis, IN 46204-1275
Tel.: 317-262-6262
Fax: 317-262-6290

Subsidiary:

McDonald Equipment Co.-IN **(1)**
5005 W. 106th St.
Zionsville, IN 46077
Tel.: 317-873-5005
Emp.: 23
Distr. Engines & Engine Generators
S.I.C.: 5063
Darlene Guzman *(Gen. Mgr.)*

A. Y. MCDONALD INDUSTRIES, INC.
4800 Chavenelle Rd.
Dubuque, IA 52002
Mailing Address:
P.O. Box 508
Dubuque, IA 52004-0508
Tel.: 319-583-7311
Fax: 319-588-0720
Year Founded: 1856
Approx.Sls.: $120,000,000
Emp.: 686
Fiscal Year-end: 12/31/91
Import Export
Mfr. Pumps & Water Systems, Well Supplies, Plumbing Brass, Water Works Brass, High Pressure Iron & Brass Gas Valves, Gas & Water Service Valves & Fittings, Meter Setting Devices, Bulk Oil & Gasoline Valves, Wholesale Plumbing, Heating, Cooling, Light Fixtures, Kitchen Cabinets, Industrial Products, Electrical
S.I.C.: 3432; 3494; 3561; 3645; 3646; 5074; 5075
J.M. McDonald III *(Chm. Bd., Pres. & Chief Exec. Officer)*
M.B. McDonald *(Sr. V.P. & Corp. Sec.)*
L.J. Sherman *(Sr. V.P.-Corp. Finance)*

Subsidiaries:

A. Y. McDonald Mfg. Co. **(1)**
4800 Chavenelle Rd., P.O. Box 508
Dubuque, IA 52004-0508
Tel.: 319-583-7311
Telex: 43-9020 AYMCD DUQU
Cable: AYMCD DUBUQUE, IOWA U.S.A
Fax: 319-588-0720
Import Export
Mfr. Pumps & Water Systems, Well Supplies, Plumbing Brass, Water Works Brass, High Pressure Iron & Brass Gas Valves, Gas & Water Service Valves & Fittings, Meter Setting Devices, Bulk Oil & Gasoline Valves
S.I.C.: 3494; 3432; 3561
R.D. McDonald *(Chm. Bd., Pres. & Chief Exec. Officer)*

A. Y. McDonald Supply Co. Inc. **(1)**
4800 Chavenelle Rd.
Dubuque, IA 52002
Tel.: 319-583-7311
Fax: 319-583-0031
Wholesale Plumbing, Heating, Cooling, Light Fixtures, Kitchen Cabinets, Industrial & Electrical Products
S.I.C.: 3645; 3646; 5074; 5075
W.A. Knapp *(Pres. & Chief Exec. Officer)*

A.Y.M. Inc. **(1)**
So. Clinton & 17th Ave. W.
Albia, IA 52531
Tel.: 515-932-7841
Fax: 515-932-5129
Mfr. Gas Valves & Meter Setters
S.I.C.: 3494; 3432
R.D. McDonald *(Chm. Bd., Pres. & Chief Exec. Officer)*

Brock-McVey Company **(1)**
1100 Brock-McVey Dr.
Lexington, KY 40555
Tel.: 606-255-1412
Fax: 606-233-4387
Approx.Sls.: $90,000,000
Emp.: 700
Wholesale Plumbing, Heating, Cooling, Light Fixtures, Kitchen Cabinets, Industrial Products, Electrical
S.I.C.: 3645; 3646; 5074; 5075
J.M. McDonald III *(Chm. Bd., Pres., Treas. & Chief Exec. Officer)*
R.T. Curry *(V.P.)*
S.J. Ales *(Sec. & Controller)*
Carl Thomason *(Sls. Mgr.)*

MCDOUGAL, LITTELL & COMPANY
1560 Sherman Ave.
Evanston, IL 60201
Mailing Address:
P.O. Box 1667
Evanston, IL 60204
Tel.: 708-869-2300 **DE**
Fax: 708-869-0841
Year Founded: 1969
Approx.Sls.: $70,000,000
Emp.: 300
Fiscal Year-end: 10/31/92
Export
Textbook Publisher
S.I.C.: 2731
Julie McGee *(Pres. & Editor-In-Chief)*
Alfred L. McDougal *(Chief Exec. Officer)*
Nancy A. Lauter *(Sr. V.P.-Mkt. Devel. & Intl. Sls.)*
Richard D. Wild *(Sr. V.P.-Fin. & Opers.)*
Rita Schaefer *(V.P.-Sls.)*
Lesa Scott *(V.P.-Mktg.)*
Susan Lindahl *(Controller & Asst. Treas.)*
Susan Fowler *(Dir.-Mngmt. Information Systems)*
Kathleen Mattox *(Dir.-Personnel)*
David A. Pieklo *(Mgr.-Adv. & Sls. Promotion)*
Anne Ruffell *(Office Mgr.)*
David White *(Corp. Librarian)*

Principal(s):
Alfred L. McDougal

No. of U.S. Offices: 6

Computer Systems/Hardware:
Wang VS 300

Outside Service Firm(s):

Union Mutual Life Insurance Co.*(Group Insurer)*
Portland, ME

Gass & Lewis*(Legal Firm)*
Chicago, IL

Katten, Muchin & Zavis*(Legal Firm)*
525 W. Monroe St., Ste. 1600
Chicago, IL 60661-3693
Tel.: 312-902-5200

McDermott, Will & Emery*(Legal Firm)*
111 W. Monroe St.
Chicago, IL 60611
Tel.: 312-372-2000

Harris Trust & Savings Bank*(Major Banking Relationship)*
111 W. Monroe St.
Chicago, IL 60690
Tel.: 312-461-2265
Tel.: 800-858-0840

McDougall

MCDOUGALL ASSOCIATES, INC.
17 Centennial Dr.
Peabody, MA 01960
Tel.: 508-532-6500
Fax: 508-532-6276
Year Founded: 1968
Approx.Billings: $40,000,000
Emp.: 41
Advertising, Public Relations, Strategic Market Planning, Complete Communications Programs & Promotions Serving Many Fortune 100 Companies Nationally & Internationally
Michael J. McDougall *(Chm. Bd.)*
Daniel R. McDougall *(Pres.)*
Philip H. Hureau *(Exec. V.P., Treas.)*
Sue McGovern *(Pub. Rels. Dir.)*
Alex Lippish *(Photographer)*

MCFARLAND & DRIER, INC.
Rivergate West, 99 S.E. 5th St.
Miami, FL 33131
Tel.: 305-358-0108
Fax: 305-358-8430
Year Founded: 1979
Approx.Billings: $43,000,000
Emp.: 47
Advertising Agency
S.I.C.: 7311
William C. McFarland *(Chm. Bd. & Treas.)*
William E. Drier *(Pres. & Exec. Creative Dir.)*
John Arnholt *(Sr. V.P., Chief Fin. Officer)*

Computer Systems/Hardware:
IBM

Subsidiary:

McFarland & Drier International **(1)**
One Television Plaza, Ste. 300, 171 Quisquya St.
San Juan, PR 00919
Advertising Agency
S.I.C.: 7311
Guillermo Ramis *(Pres.)*

MCFARLING FOODS, INC.
333 W. 14th St.
Indianapolis, IN 46208
Tel.: 317-635-2633
Year Founded: 1948
Approx.Sls.: $50,000,000
Emp.: 140
Wholesale Grocer for Restaurants & Institutional Markets
S.I.C.: 5141
James W. McFarling *(Chm. Bd.)*
Donald P. McFarling *(Pres. & Chief Exec. Officer)*
Robert E. McFarling *(V.P.-Sls. & Treas.)*

Principal(s):
McFarling Family

Outside Service Firm(s):

Ernst & Young*(Auditors)*
One Indiana Square, Ste. 3400
Indianapolis, IN 46204
Tel.: 317-236-1100

Bank One, Indianapolis, N.A.*(Major Banking Relationship)*
111 Monument Circle, Ste. 1611
Indianapolis, IN 46204-1611
Tel.: 317-321-8110

MCGAW, INC.
2525 McGaw Ave.
Irvine, CA 92714
Mailing Address:
P.O. Box 19791,
Irvine, CA 92713-9791
Tel.: 714-660-2000
Sales Range: $100-499 Million
IV Suppliers to Hospitals; Generic Injectable Drugs
S.I.C.: 2834
James Sweeney *(Pres.)*
Robert Krist *(V.P.-Fin.)*
Don Cook *(V.P.-Mktg.)*
Don Emmel *(Plant Mgr.)*

MCGEAN-ROHCO, INC.
2910 Harvard Avenue
Cleveland, OH 44105-3010
Tel.: 216-441-4900
Tel.: 800-932-7006
Fax: 216-441-1377
Year Founded: 1929
Approx.Sls.: $55,000,000
Emp.: 235
Mfr. of Industrial & Proprietory Chemicals
S.I.C.: 2899; 2819; 3339
Dickson L. Whitney, Sr. *(Chm. Bd.)*
Klaus Romer *(Pres. & Chief Exec. Officer)*
James E. Vamos *(Sr. V.P.-Real Estate)*
James A. Lucas *(V.P. & Gen. Counsel)*
Kerry H. May *(V.P.-Fin.)*
Dickson L. Whitney, Jr. *(V.P.-Intl. Div.)*
Willie R. Smith *(V.P.-Cee Bee Div.)*
Robert J. Erwin *(V.P. & Gen. Mgr.-Rohco Div.)*
Lawrence N. Murray *(Gen. Mgr.-McGean Div.)*
Robert A. DeMell *(Natl. Mktg. Mgr.)*

MCGUFFEY'S RESTAURANTS, INC.
13 Kenilworth Knoll
Asheville, NC 28805
Tel.: 704-252-3300
Fax: 704-254-3907
Approx.Sls.: $15,000,000
Emp.: 500
Fiscal Year-end: 12/31/90
Theme Restaurant
S.I.C.: 5812
Keith Dunn *(Pres.)*
Michael Brandson *(V.P.-Human Resources)*
Richard Laibson *(V.P.-Opers.)*
Alan Laibson *(Controller)*
Don Finlayson *(Pur. Dir.)*

JAMES MCHUGH CONSTRUCTION CO.
2222 S. Indiana Ave.
Chicago, IL 60616
Tel.: 312-842-8400
Fax: 312-842-3989
Approx.Sls.: $250,000,000
Emp.: 500
General Building Contractor
S.I.C.: 1542; 1522; 1622; 1629
James P. McHugh *(Pres. & Chief Exec. Officer)*
Patrick Seery *(Chief Fin. Officer, Treas. & Controller)*
James LaRocque *(Gen. Counsel & Sec.)*
Patricia McHugh *(Dir.-Mktg.)*
Mike Meagher *(Mgr.-Bus. Devel.)*
Richard Snyder *(Mgr.-Data Processing)*

Computer Systems/Hardware:
McDonnell Douglas 9240

Outside Service Firm(s):

Peter Shannon*(Auditors)*
Hinsdale, IL

Rollins Burdick Hunter*(Commercial Insurance Carrier)*
123 No. Wacker
Chicago, IL 60606
Tel.: 312-701-4000

Benefit Trust & Life*(Group Insurer)*
Chicago, IL

Peterson & Houpt*(Legal Firm)*
Chicago, IL

American National Bank*(Major Banking Relationship)*
33 North LaSalle St.
Chicago, IL 60690
Tel.: 312-661-6967

MCILHENNY COMPANY
Avery Island, LA 70513
Tel.: 318-365-8173 **ME**
Fax: 318-369-6326
Year Founded: 1868
Emp.: 160
Export
Manufacture Tabasco Brand Products
S.I.C.: 2032; 2033
Edward M. Simmons *(Pres.)*
E.P. Terrell III *(Exec. V.P. & Treas.)*
Richard G. Dunn *(V.P.-Sls. & Mktg.)*
Cecil Hymel, Sr. *(V.P.-Admin.)*
Paul C.P. McIlhenny *(V.P. & Sec.)*
Carlos E. Malespin *(V.P.-Intl.)*
Lisa Bell *(Dir.-Data Processing)*

No. of Mfg. Plants/Facilities: 1
No. of U.S. Offices: 1
No. of Foreign Offices: 1

Computer Systems/Hardware:
R & D Systems

Outside Service Firm(s):

KPMG Peat Marwick*(Auditors)*
One Shell Center, Ste. 3500
New Orleans, LA 70139

First National Bank Of Commerce*(Major Banking Relationship)*
New Orleans, LA

Pan American Life*(Group Insurer)*
New Orleans, LA

Bank of Nova Scotia*(International Bank Affiliate)*
Charlotte Amalie, Virgin Islands

B. F. Trappey's Sons, Inc. **(1)**
900 E. Main St.
New Iberia, LA 70560
Tel.: 318-365-8281
Fax: 318-369-7342
Approx.Sls.: $33,000,000
Emp.: 250
Fiscal Year-end: 11/30/90
Mfr. of Pickled Peppers & Pepper Sauce
S.I.C.: 2035
Edward M. Simmons *(Chm. Bd. & Pres.)*
Eddie Terrell *(Sec. & Treas.)*
Rick Dunn *(Dir.-Adv. & Mktg.)*

Subsidiaries:

McIlhenny Resources **(1)**
Avery Island, LA 70513
Tel.: 318-365-8173
Emp.: 150

J. GIBSON MCILVAIN CO.
P.O. Box 222
White Marsh, MD 21162
Tel.: 301-335-9600 **MD**
Fax: 301-335-3574
Year Founded: 1798
Assets: $12,000,000
Liabilities: $7,700,000
Net Worth: $4,300,000
Approx.Sls.: $23,000,000
Emp.: 90
Fiscal Year-end: 10/31/92
Import Export
Wholesale Distributor of Hardwoods & Softwoods Planing Mill & Dry Kilns; Domestic & Imported Lumber
S.I.C.: 5031; 2421; 5039
J. Gibson McIlvain, III *(Pres.)*
David C. Bell *(Sr. V.P.-Sls.)*
William E. Glenn, Jr. *(V.P.-Pur.)*
Scott A. McAllister *(V.P. & Controller)*
Robert L. Watters *(Treas.)*
Philip C. Herr *(Sec.)*

No. of Mfg. Plants/Facilities: 2
No. of U.S. Offices: 2

Outside Service Firm(s):

C. W. Amos & Co.*(Auditors)*
2 N. Charles St.
Baltimore, MD 21201
Tel.: 410-727-5341

Herr, Potts & Herr*(Legal Firm)*
Baltimore, MD

Provident National Bank*(Major Banking Relationship)*
Baltimore, MD

MCINERNEY INC.
14100 W. Eight Mile Rd.
Oak Park, MI 48237
Tel.: 313-398-8200 **DE**
Fax: 313-398-4289
Approx.Sls.: $159,000,000
Emp.: 438
Automobile Dealership
S.I.C.: 5511
Martin J. McInerney *(Pres.)*
John J. McInerney *(V.P.-Sls. & Mktg.)*
Maryellen Sherwood *(Treas.)*

Outside Service Firm(s):

Vincent Gilleo*(Legal Firm)*
Troy, MI

Manufacturers National Bank N.A.*(Major Banking Relationship)*
38th Fl., 100 Renaissance Center
Detroit, MI 48243
Tel.: 313-222-4227

MCINERNEY-MILLER BROTHERS INC.
2001 Brewster St.
Detroit, MI 48207
Tel.: 313-833-4800 **MI**
Fax: 313-833-8634
Approx.Sls.: $37,000,000
Emp.: 100
Wholesale Poultry Products, Fresh Meats & Seafood, Frozen Foods
S.I.C.: 5144; 5142; 5146; 5147
Max Miller *(Chm. Bd. & Treas.)*
David Miller *(Pres.)*
Glenn Lee *(V.P.)*
Richard Miller *(V.P.-Fin. & Chief Fin. Officer)*

Outside Service Firm(s):

Mellen, Seal & Pivoz*(Auditors)*
Birmingham, MI

Liberty State Bank*(Major Banking Relationship)*
Troy, MI

MCINNES STEEL COMPANY
441 E. Main St.
Corry, PA 16407
Tel.: 814-664-9664
Tel.: 800-458-0571 **PA**
Fax: 814-664-9452
Year Founded: 1895
Approx.Sls.: $42,000,000
Emp.: 300
Fiscal Year-end: 12/31/90
Import Export
Mfr. of Nuclear, Aircraft, Alloy, Carbon, Stainless Steel Forgings
S.I.C.: 3462; 3364; 3363

McInnes Steel Company—(Continued)

Employee Matching Gifts Program: Contributions to Qualified College or University on a Half Dollar Amount to $500.00 Maximum
Stephen J. Mahoney *(Pres. & Chief Exec. Officer)*
Frank K. Smith *(Exec. V.P.)*
Anthony A. Montani *(V.P.-Sls. & Mktg.)*
Timothy Hunter *(Treas.)*
J. Earle Bliley *(Sec.)*
Tom McMullin *(Gen. Sls. Mgr.)*
Dominic Andriachi *(Dir.-Metallurgy)*
Walter E. Bowen *(Mgr.-Matls.)*
Richard Skalos *(Mgr.-Plant)*
Dave Turner *(Mgr.-Quality Control)*
Joe Zallik *(Mgr.-Data Processing)*

Principal(s):
ESOP 56%

No. of Mfg. Plants/Facilities: 4

Outside Service Firm(s):

Ernst & Young*(Auditors)*
100 State St., Ste. 200
Erie, PA 16507
Tel.: 814-454-2453

MacDonald, Illig, Jones & Britton*(Legal Firm)*
600 First Natl. Bank Bldg.
Erie, PA 16501
Tel.: 814-453-4691

Marine Bank*(Major Banking Relationship)*
Erie, PA

Division:

McInnes Rolled Rings **(1)**
1533 E. 12th St.
Erie, PA 16511
Robert Shephard *(Plant Mgr.)*

Subsidiary:

Erie Bronze & Aluminum Co. **(1)**
6300 West Ridge Rd.
Erie, PA 16505
Tel.: 814-838-8602
Fax: 814-838-8917
Import Export
Mfr. of Steel Forgings & Non-Ferrous Castings
S.I.C.: 3364; 3363; 3325
Kevin O'Connell *(Mgr.-Plant)*

MCJUNKIN CORPORATION
835 Hillcrest Dr.
Charleston, WV 25311
Tel.: 304-348-5211
Fax: 304-348-4922
Assets: $109,000,000
Net Worth: $109,000,000
Approx.Sls.: $250,000,000
Emp.: 1,400
Distribution of Metal Products; Trucking & Warehousing; Supplier of Pipes, Valves & Fittings
S.I.C.: 5085; 5084; 5199; 5051; 5063
Henry B. Wehrle, Jr. *(Chm. Bd. & Chief Exec. Officer)*
Henry B. Wehrle III *(Pres. & Chief Oper. Officer)*
Michael H. Wehrle *(Chief Fin. Officer & Treas.)*
S.D. Wehrle *(Sr. V.P.-Sls.)*
James F. Underhill *(Controller)*
William E. Board *(Dir.-Personnel)*
H.R. Hill *(Dir.-Mngmt. Information Systems)*
Paul A. Buechler *(Mgr.-Fin.)*

Computer Systems/Hardware:
IBM 4341 Model 2

Outside Service Firm(s):

Ernst & Young*(Auditors)*
787 Seventh Ave.
New York, NY 10019
Tel.: 212-773-1243

First Chicago Shareholder Services Trust Co.*(Major Banking Relationship)*
153 West 51st St.
New York, NY 10019
Tel.: 212-791-6422
Fax: 212-385-9798

Pittsburgh National Bank*(Major Banking Relationship)*
Stock Transfer Dept., Fifth & Wood Streets
Pittsburgh, PA 15265

Sovran Bank*(Major Banking Relationship)*
Sovran Center, 1111 E. Main St.
Richmond, VA 23219
Tel.: 804-788-2000

Lazard Freres & Co.*(Pension Manager)*
One Rockefeller Plaza
New York, NY 10020
Tel.: 212-632-6442
Fax: 212-373-4430

MCKEAN OLDSMOBILE COMPANY
5001 Liberty Ave.
Pittsburgh, PA 15224
Tel.: 412-683-3800
Fax: 412-622-8796
Emp.: 120
Oldsmoblile/Honda/GMC; Retail New & Used Automobiles, Service & Parts
S.I.C.: 5511
Brad McKean *(Pres.)*
Alec McKean *(V.P.)*
Steven Walker *(Controller)*

Outside Service Firm(s):

Chamberlin & Company*(Auditors)*
Pittsburgh, PA

Brennan Robins & Daley*(Legal Firm)*
Pittsburgh, PA

Mellon Bank, N.A.*(Major Banking Relationship)*
P.O. Box 444,
Pittsburgh, PA 15230
Tel.: 412-236-8000
Tel.: 1-800-451-7392
Fax: 412-236-8157

MCKEE BAKING CO., INC.
P.O. Box 750
Collegedale, TN 37315-0750
Tel.: 615-238-7111
Year Founded: 1934
Approx.Sls.: $440,000,000
Emp.: 3,700
Bakery Prods.
S.I.C.: 2051; 2052
O. D. McKee *(Chm. Bd.)*
R. Ellsworth McKee *(Pres. & Chief Exec. Officer)*
Jack C. McKee *(Exec. V.P. & Chief Oper. Officer)*
Barry Patterson *(Chief Fin. Officer & Treas.)*
Glenn Fuller *(V.P. & Sec.)*

Computer Systems/Hardware:
Sperry Univac 1160

MCKEE DOOR, INC.
85 Hankes Ave.
Aurora, IL 60505
Mailing Address:
P.O. Box 1930
Aurora, IL 60507
Tel.: 708-897-9600
Fax: 708-896-7154
Approx.Sls.: $40,000,000
Emp.: 200
Fiscal Year-end: 7/31/90
Export
Garage & Commerical Doors & Electric Door & Gate Openers
S.I.C.: 3442; 3699
E.R. Smidt *(Pres.)*
John McKee *(V.P.-Retail)*
Pat Hunter *(Dir.-Engrng.)*
Ray Pozezinski *(Dir.-Fin.)*
David E. Duffy *(Dir.-Adv. & Pur.)*
Larry Murphy *(Dir.-Inside Sls.)*

Computer Systems/Hardware:
IBM System 38

MCKEE FOODS CORPORATION
10000 McKee Rd.
Collegedale, TN 37315
Mailing Address:
P.O. Box 750,
Collegedale, TN 37315
Tel.: 615-238-7111
Fax: 615-238-7170
Year Founded: 1934
Approx.Sls.: $480,000,000
Emp.: 3,700
Bakers of Cakes & Cookies
S.I.C.: 2051; 2052
O.D. McKee *(Chm. Bd.)*
Ellsworth McKee *(Pres. & Chief Exec. Officer)*
Jack C. McKee *(Exec. V.P. & Chief Oper. Officer)*
John A. Phillips *(Sr. V.P.)*
Eddie Avant *(V.P.-Engrng.)*
Glenn Fuller *(V.P. & Sec.)*
Charles Wilson *(V.P.-Prod.)*
Barry Patterson *(Treas.)*

Principal(s):
O.D. McKee
Ellsworth McKee
Jack C. McKee

No. of Mfg. Plants/Facilities: 3

Outside Service Firm(s):

Claimfacts*(Group Insurer)*
Collegedale, TN

Pioneer Bank*(Major Banking Relationship)*
Collegedale, TN

Subsidiary:

Sovex Natural Foods **(1)**
P.O. Box 310
Collegedale, TN 37315
Tel.: 615-396-3145
Natural Foods
S.I.C.: 2041
Glenn Fuller *(Pres.)*

MCKELLAR DEVELOPERS OF LA JOLLA
5151 Shoreham, Suite 200
San Diego, CA 92122
Tel.: 619-587-1355 **CA**
Fax: 619-587-0315
William F. Miller *(Pres.)*
Christopher S. McKellar *(Chief Exec. Officer)*
Christopher M. Judson *(Chief Fin. Officer)*

Outside Service Firm(s):

Price Waterhouse*(Auditors)*
750 B St.
San Diego, CA 92101
Tel.: 619-231-9830

JOHN MCKENZIE PACKING CO., INC.
160 Flynn Ave.
Burlington, VT 05401
Tel.: 802-864-4585
Fax: 802-862-1602
Approx.Sls.: $18,000,000
Emp.: 60
Sausage Products: Smoked Hams, Bacon & Processed Meats
S.I.C.: 2013
Mary Alice McKenzie *(Pres.)*
Mark Dubie *(V.P.-Opers.)*
Arlene Torre *(V.P.-Fin.)*
Thomas J. Kenney *(Gen. Counsel)*
Gregg Rouille *(Mgr.-Sls.)*

Outside Service Firm(s):

KPMG Peat Marwick*(Auditors)*
Burlington Business Ctr. II, 77 S. Bedford St.
Burlington, MA 01803

The Merchants Bank*(Major Banking Relationship)*
Burlington, VT

MCKENZIE TANK LINES, INC.
122 Apple Yard Dr.
Tallahassee, FL 32304
Tel.: 904-576-1221
Fax: 904-574-2351
Approx.Sls.: $48,000,000
Emp.: 800
Liquid Petroleum Transport; Automotive Tires; Truck Leasing Without Driver; Lessors Of Piers & Docks; Real Estate Lessors
S.I.C.: 4213; 5531; 7513; 6512; 6519
W. Guy McKenzie, Sr. *(Chm. Bd.)*
W. Guy McKenzie, Jr. *(Chief Exec. Officer)*
Pat Patterson *(Pres.)*
Joseph Audie *(V.P.-Fin.)*
William M. Smith *(Treas.)*
Aubrey Blount *(Controller)*

Outside Service Firm(s):

Barnett Banks Trust Company, N.A.*(Major Banking Relationship)*
Tallahassee, FL

MCKINLAY & PARTNERS, INC.
The Grist Mill, 75 West St.
Simsbury, CT 06070
Mailing Address:
P.O. Box 157,
Simsbury, CT 06070
Tel.: 203-651-0971
Fax: 203-651-4708
Year Founded: 1981
Approx.Billings: $14,000,000
Emp.: 15
Douglas R. McKinlay *(Pres.)*

McKinney Inc.
Advertising & Public Relations

MCKINNEY INC. ADVERTISING & PUBLIC RELATIONS
One Curtis Center, One Independence Square West
Philadelphia, PA 19106
Tel.: 215-922-2635
Fax: 215-922-7353
Year Founded: 1936
Approx.Billings: $26,714,000
Frank W. Callahan *(Pres. & Chief Exec. Officer)*
Helen P. Fanning *(V.P., Fin.)*

MCKINNEY & SILVER
333 Fayetteville Mall
Raleigh, NC 27601
Tel.: 919-828-0691
Fax: 919-821-6452
Year Founded: 1969
Approx.Billings: $90,750,246
Emp.: 95

Robert C. Doherty *(Pres. & Chief Exec. Officer)*
L. Lloyd Jacobs *(Exec. V.P.)*
Toni Jordan *(Sr. V.P., Controller)*

MCKINNON BRIDGE CO.
205 Eddy Ln.
Franklin, TN 37064
Tel.: 615-794-2552
Fax: 615-794-6939
Year Founded: 1966
Approx.Sls.: $24,000,000
Emp.: 120
Bridge Construction
S.I.C.: 1622
T. Benson McKinnon *(Pres. & Chief Exec. Officer)*
Principal(s):
T. Benson McKinnon

Computer Systems/Hardware:
IBM

Outside Service Firm(s):

Blue Cross & Blue Shield of Tennessee*(Group Insurer)*
Chattanooga, TN

MCKINSEY & COMPANY, INC.
55 E. 52nd St.
New York, NY 10022
Tel.: 212-446-7000 **NY**
Approx.Sls.: $900,000,000
Emp.: 5,000
Fiscal Year-end: 12/31/91
Management Consultants
S.I.C.: 8742
Frederick Gluck *(Mng. Dir.)*
James W. Wu *(Treas.)*
Virginia L. Molino *(Gen. Counsel)*
Randi E. Zeller *(Assoc. Gen. Counsel)*
Gregory P. Ho *(Dir. Fin. Plng.)*
James E. Farrell *(Dir.-Benefits Plng.)*
William L. Matassoni *(Dir.-Communications)*
Richard H. Moskowitz *(Dir.-MGM Investment Programs)*
James L. Rogers *(Dir.-Fin.)*
Arthur Williams, III *(Dir.-PSRP Investment Programs)*

No. of U.S. Offices: 14
No. of Foreign Offices: 34

Computer Systems/Hardware:
IBM 3812

Outside Service Firm(s):

Arthur Andersen & Co.*(Auditors)*
1345 Ave. of the Americas
New York, NY 10105
Tel.: 212-708-4000

Metropolitan Life Insurance Co.*(Group Insurer)*
Tampa, FL

Chase Manhattan Bank, N.A.*(Major Banking Relationship)*
One Chase Manhattan Plaza
New York, NY 10081
Tel.: 212-552-2222
Tel.: 800-526-0801
Fax: 212-552-7175

First Chicago Shareholder Services Trust Co.*(Major Banking Relationship)*
153 West 51st St.
New York, NY 10019
Tel.: 212-791-6422
Fax: 212-385-9798

MCKONE & CO., INC.
1900 Westridge Dr.
Irving, TX 75038
Tel.: 214-550-7433
Fax: 214-550-7443
Year Founded: 1977
Approx.Billings: $20,000,000
Emp.: 28
Peter J. McKone *(Pres.)*
Jim Martin *(Sr. V.P., Acct. Services)*
Sheila Durante *(V.P. Pub. Rels.)*
Larry Hanlon *(V.P. Direct Response)*
Al Belota *(Controller)*

MCLAUGHLIN GORMLEY KING COMPANY
8810 10th Ave. N.
Minneapolis, MN 55427
Tel.: 612-544-0341
Fax: 612-544-6437
Year Founded: 1902
Sales Range: $20-39 Million
Emp.: 60
Fiscal Year-end: 9/30/90
Import Export
Pesticides & Insecticides
S.I.C.: 2879
W.D. Gullickson *(Chm. Bd.)*
W.D. Gullickson, Jr. *(Pres. & Chief Exec. Officer)*
K. Neu *(Treas.)*
T.D. Lloyd *(Dir.-Sls.)*
B. Ward *(Mgr.-Pur.)*

No. of Mfg. Plants/Facilities: 2
No. of U.S. Offices: 2

Computer Systems/Hardware:
Microdata

Outside Service Firm(s):

Deloitte & Touche*(Auditors)*
900 Pillsbury Ctr.
Minneapolis, MN 55402
Tel.: 612-332-2301
Fax: 612-375-5418

Dorsey & Whitney*(Legal Firm)*
2200 First Bank Place East
Minneapolis, MN 55402

First National Bank of Minneapolis*(Major Banking Relationship)*
Minneapolis, MN

Subsidiaries:

A. E. Development Corp. **(1)**
8810 10th Ave. North
Minneapolis, MN 55427
Tel.: 612-544-0341

Insect Control & Research Corp. **(1)**
1330 Dillon Heights Ave.
Baltimore, MD 21228
Tel.: 301-747-4500
Pesticides & Insecticides
S.I.C.: 2879
Marvin Bertsch *(Gen. Mgr.)*

New England Research, Inc. **(1)**
100 Grove St.
Worcester, MA 01605
Tel.: 508-752-0346
Dr. Paul Erickson *(Pres.)*

MCLAUGHLIN INDUSTRIAL DISTRIBUTORS, INC.
7141 Paramount Blvd.
Pico Rivera, CA 90660
Tel.: 310-723-2411
Fax: 310-948-4448
Approx.Sls.: $13,000,000
Emp.: 60
Abrasives, Precision & Hand Cutting Tools; Drills & Files
S.I.C.: 5072
E.H. McLaughlin, Jr. *(Chm. Bd.)*
Harry Y. McLaughlin *(Pres.)*
E.H. McLaughlin, III *(Exec. V.P., Treas. & Asst. Sec.)*
Ray Wilson *(Pur. Agent)*

Outside Service Firm(s):

Deloitte & Touche*(Auditors)*
1000 Wilshire Blvd.
Los Angeles, CA 90017-2472
Tel.: 213-688-0800
Fax: 213-688-0100

First Interstate Bank of California, N.A.*(Major Banking Relationship)*
P.O. Box 3667,
Los Angeles, CA 90051
Tel.: 213-614-4000

MCLAUGHLIN MFG. COMPANY
2006 Perimeter Rd.
Greenville, SC 29605
Tel.: 803-277-5870
Tel.: 800-435-9340 **DE**
Fax: 803-235-9661
Year Founded: 1921
Sales Range: $10-19 Million
Emp.: 61
Fiscal Year-end: 12/31/90
Import Export
Horizontal Drilling Tools for Mining & Earth Drilling Industries
S.I.C.: 3532
Paul Barker *(Chm. Bd.)*
Bill Gilman *(Pres. & Chief Oper. Officer)*
Dave J. Gasmovic *(Exec. V.P. & Mgr.-Natl. Sls.)*
Lance Snyder *(Controller)*
Ron Cheers *(Dir.-Tech. Engrng.)*
Judy Hiller *(Buyer)*
Principal(s):
Paul Barker

No. of Mfg. Plants/Facilities: 1
No. of U.S. Offices: 2

Computer Systems/Hardware:
IBM System 36

Outside Service Firm(s):

KPMG Peat Marwick*(Auditors)*
One Shelter Place, Box 10529
Greenville, SC 29603

Rollins Burdick Hunter*(Commercial Insurance Carrier)*
Winston-Salem, NC

Blue Cross & Blue Shield of South Carolina*(Group Insurer)*
1517 Laurel St.
Columbia, SC 29201

NationsBank Carolinas*(Major Banking Relationship)*
7 N. Laurens St.
Greenville, SC 29601
Tel.: 803-271-5600

MCLEAN ENTERPRISES, INC.
2610 N. Glenstone
Springfield, MO 65803
Tel.: 417-864-0711
Fax: 417-864-0725
Year Founded: 1951
Sales Range: $40-59 Million
Emp.: 100
Motor Lodges, Restaurants, Construction, Agriculture, Meat Packing & Real Estate Development
S.I.C.: 7011; 2011; 5812; 6552
Lee McLean, Jr. *(Pres.)*
Joe Watkins *(V.P. & Controller)*
Principal(s):
Lee McLean, Jr.
Joe Watkins

Computer Systems/Hardware:
IBM System 36

Outside Service Firm(s):

House, Park & Company*(Auditors)*
Springfield, MO

Great Southern Bank*(Major Banking Relationship)*
Kansas City, MO

MCLEAN-THOMAS INC.
266 Broadway
Buffalo, NY 14204
Tel.: 716-852-2531 **NY**
Fax: 716-852-1957
Year Founded: 1942
Approx.Sls.: $10,700,000
Emp.: 35
Wholesale Building Materials.
S.I.C.: 5031; 5032; 5033; 5039
James A. McLean, Jr. *(Pres.)*
Judith Snyder *(Sec.)*

Outside Service Firm(s):

Seligman, Sunshine & Co.*(Auditors)*
Amherst, NY

Goldman, Costa & Getman*(Legal Firm)*
Buffalo, NY

Marine Midland Bank*(Major Banking Relationship)*
P.O. Box 803, 1 Marine Midland Center, 23rd Floor
Buffalo, NY 14203
Tel.: 716-841-2582

MCLOUTH STEEL
1650 W. Jefferson Ave.
Trenton, MI 48183
Tel.: 313-285-1200 **MI**
Fax: 313-246-4059
Year Founded: 1988
Approx.Sls.: $490,000,000
Emp.: 1,650
Fiscal Year-end: 12/31/90
Import Export
Steel Production
S.I.C.: 3312; 3316
Robert D. McBride *(Pres. & Chief Exec. Officer)*
James S. Adams *(V.P.-Opers.)*
Dave Davison *(V.P.-Pur.)*
Thomas J. Mavor *(V.P.-Fin. & Chief Fin. Officer)*
Joseph F. Schatt *(V.P.-Human Resources)*
Thomas G. Whittingham *(V.P.-Sls.)*
Larry L. Filippine *(Treas.)*

No. of Mfg. Plants/Facilities: 2
No. of U.S. Offices: 1

Computer Systems/Hardware:
Hitachi EX25

Outside Service Firm(s):

Ernst & Young*(Auditors)*
One Detroit Center, 500 Woodward, Ste. 1700
Detroit, MI 48243
Tel.: 313-259-9600

National Bank of Detroit*(Major Banking Relationship)*
300 S. Livernois
Detroit, MI 48232
Tel.: 313-225-1122

MCMASTER CARR SUPPLY CO. INC.
(Sub. of Europa-Norway)
600 County Line
Elmhurst, IL 60126
Mailing Address:
P.O. Box 4355
Chicago, IL 60680
Tel.: 708-834-9600
Fax: 708-834-9427
Approx.Sls.: $37,000,000
Emp.: 350
Retail & Mail Order Supplier Industrial Machines & Equipment
S.I.C.: 5961; 5085; 5084
Robert Delaney *(Chm. Bd.)*
R.J. Franklin *(Pres. & Chief Fin. Officer)*

Computer Systems/Hardware:
IBM 3831

Outside Service Firm(s):

Provident Life & Accident Insurance Co.*(Group Insurer)*
Des Moines, IA

Harris Trust & Savings Bank*(Major Banking Relationship)*
111 W. Monroe St.
Chicago, IL 60690
Tel.: 312-461-2265
Tel.: 800-858-0840

MCNALLY INDUSTRIES, INC.
216 S. Pine St.
Grantsburg, WI 54840
Mailing Address:
P.O. Box 21009
Grantsburg, WI 54840
Tel.: 715-463-5311 **WI**
Fax: 715-463-5261
Approx.Sls.: $12,000,000
Emp.: 120
Export
Mfr. of Precision Machined Parts; Assemblies; Gear Pumps
S.I.C.: 3499; 3561
Albert Scheideler *(Pres. & Chief Exec. Officer)*
Don Erickson *(V.P.-Mktg.)*
Herbert Josephson *(V.P.-Adv. & Mfg.)*
Paul Lombardi *(V.P.-Contract & Tech. Oper.)*
Dianne Farrell *(Sec. & Controller)*

Outside Service Firm(s):

Ernst & Young*(Auditors)*
1400 Pillsbury Center
Minneapolis, MN 55402
Tel.: 612-343-1000

Faegre & Benson*(Legal Firm)*
2200 Norwest Ctr., 90 S. 7th St.
Minneapolis, MN 55402-3901
Tel.: 612-336-3000
Fax: 612-336-3026

First Wisconsin Bank of Grantsburg*(Major Banking Relationship)*
Grantsburg, WI

MCNALLY WELLMAN COMPANY
4800 Grand Ave.
Pittsburgh, PA 15225
Mailing Address:
P.O. Drawer D
Pittsburg, KS 66762
Tel.: 412-269-5000
Fax: 316-231-4373
Year Founded: 1889
Approx.Sls.: $50,000,000
Emp.: 200
Fiscal Year-end: 12/31/90
Manufactures Coal Washeries & Preparation Machinery
S.I.C.: 3532
Raymond Koper *(V.P. & Gen. Mgr.)*
Roy Behling *(V.P.-Sls. & Mktg.)*
John A. Hredzak *(Mgr.-Mktg. Services)*

Outside Service Firm(s):

Baird, Kurtz & Dobson*(Auditors)*
1st National Bank Building
Joplin, MO
Tel.: 417-624-1065

Wilbert & Towner*(Legal Firm)*
Kansas City, MO

Commerce Bank of Kansas City*(Major Banking Relationship)*
10th & Walnut
Kansas City, MO 64141
Tel.: 816-234-2000
Fax: 816-234-2548

Divisions:

McNally Pittsburg Mfg. Corp. **(1)**
P. O. Box 228
Wellston, OH 45692
C. F. Milliken *(V.P. & Gen. Mgr.)*

McNally Wellman Kansas Div. **(1)**
P. O. Drawer D
Pittsburg, KS 66762
Lyle H. Laughlin *(V.P. & Gen. Mgr.)*

Stephens-Adamson **(1)**
4800 Grand Ave.
Pittsburgh, PA 15225
Tel.: 412-269-5010
Fax: 412-269-5070
Approx.Sls.: $15,000,000
Emp.: 20
Specialized Machinery for Bulk Material Handling; Plant Located in Clarksdale, MS
S.I.C.: 3535
R.M. Koper *(V.P. & Gen. Mgr.)*
D.M. Basler *(Mgr.-Engineered Prods.)*
John A. Hredzak *(Mgr.-Mktg. Services)*

Subsidiary:

Kennedy Van Saun Corp. **(1)**
2 Beaver St.
Danville, PA 17821
Tel.: 717-275-3050
R. F. Wesner *(Pres.)*

MCNAMARA PONTIAC INC.
1010 W. Colonial Dr.
Orlando, FL 32804
Tel.: 407-849-0610 **FL**
Fax: 407-843-9164
Year Founded: 1961
Approx.Sls.: $65,000,000
Emp.: 100
Automobile Dealership
S.I.C.: 5511
Dennis C. McNamara, Sr. *(Pres.)*
Dennis Hadd *(V.P. & Gen. Sls. Mgr.)*
Hal B. McNamara *(V.P.-Opers.)*
Willie K. McInvale, Jr. *(Sec. & Treas.)*
Richard E. Rekoff *(Dir.-Service)*
Ron Cuddeback *(Mgr.-Sls./New Cars)*
Doug Goodwin *(Mgr.-Sls./New Cars)*
Rickey Jorgensen *(Mgr.-Sls./New Cars)*
Bob Kamauff *(Mgr.-Sls./Used Cars)*

Outside Service Firm(s):

KPMG Peat Marwick*(Auditors)*
P.O. Box 3031, 111 N. Orange Ave., Suite 1600
Orlando, FL 32802
Tel.: 407-423-3426

Barnett Banks Trust Company, N.A.*(Major Banking Relationship)*
Orlando, FL

MCNAUGHTON & GUNN, INC.
960 Woodland Dr.
Saline, MI 48176
Mailing Address:
P.O. Box 10
Saline, MI 48176
Tel.: 313-429-5411 **MI**
Fax: 313-429-4033
Year Founded: 1975
Assets: $10,700,000
Liabilities: $7,500,000
Net Worth: $3,200,000
Approx.Sls.: $24,000,000
Emp.: 255
Fiscal Year-end: 12/31/91
Book Printing
S.I.C.: 2732
Robert L. McNaughton *(Pres.)*
Dorothy Hart *(V.P.-Fin. & Admin.)*
Jack Briegel *(V.P.)*
Julie McFarland *(Controller)*
Ronald A. Mazzola *(Exec. Dir.-Mktg. & Sls.)*
James Clark *(Dir.-Quality Control)*
James Gilbertson *(Dir.-Mfg.)*
Tim Turton *(Dir.-Pur.)*
Rick Welch *(Dir.-Human Resources)*
Principal(s):
Robert L. McNaughton
Dorothy Hart
Jack Briegel

No. of Mfg. Plants/Facilities: 1

Outside Service Firm(s):

Elser & Briggs*(Auditors)*
Saline, MI

Manufacturers Bank of Saline*(Major Banking Relationship)*
Saline, MI

MCNAUGHTON-MCKAY ELECTRIC CO.
1357 E. Lincoln Ave.
Madison Heights, MI 48071
Tel.: 313-399-7500 **MI**
Fax: 313-399-6828
Approx.Sls.: $124,000,000
Emp.: 146
Wholesale Industrial Electrical Supplies & Equipment.
S.I.C.: 5063
William H. Bull *(Pres., Chief Exec. Officer & Treas.)*
David Beattie *(V.P.-Sls. & Mktg.)*
George L. Bull *(V.P.)*
John MacDonald *(V.P.-Opers.)*
John R. McNaughton, Jr. *(V.P.)*
James Jackson *(Sec.)*
Michael T. Jenkins *(Dir.-Data Processing)*

Outside Service Firm(s):

KPMG Peat Marwick*(Auditors)*
Suite 1200, 150 W. Jefferson
Detroit, MI 48226

Hill, Lewis, Goodrich & Tait*(Legal Firm)*
100 Renaissance Center, Ste. 3000
Detroit, MI 48243
Tel.: 313-259-3232

Manufacturers National Bank N.A.*(Major Banking Relationship)*
38th Fl., 100 Renaissance Center
Detroit, MI 48243
Tel.: 313-222-4227

MCNEEL INTERNATIONAL CORP.
5401 West Kennedy Blvd., Ste. 751
Tampa, FL 33609
Tel.: 813-286-8680
Telex: 52-889
Fax: 813-286-1535
Year Founded: 1963
Assets: $42,000,000
Liabilities: $21,000,000
Net Worth: $21,000,000
Approx.Sls.: $48,000,000
Fiscal Year-end: 12/31/91
Export
Mfrs. of Lighting Fixtures & Systems
S.I.C.: 3081
Van L. McNeel *(Chm. Bd. & Chief Exec. Officer)*
Rene M. Wood *(V.P.-Fin. & Sec.)*
Clayton W. McNeel *(V.P.-Corp. Devel.)*
William J. Klerk *(Controller)*

Subsidiaries:

Envirocon International Corp. **(1)**
Lincoln Center, 5401 West Kennedy Blvd., Ste. 751
Tampa, FL 33609
Tel.: 813-287-2102 (100%)
Asbestos Abatement Services
S.I.C.: 7389
Van McNeel *(Pres.)*

Affiliate:

BNZ Materials, Inc. **(1)**
2501 South Raritan St.
Englewood, CO 80110
Tel.: 303-922-4562 (25%)
Mfrs. of Firebricks, Refractory & Other Industrial Products
S.I.C.: 3083
John Fischer *(Pres.)*

Non-U.S. Holdings:

Olefinas, S.A. **(1)**
Guatemala City, Guatemala (100%)
Mfrs. Twine, Rope, Packaging Films, Labeling, Mulch Film & Greenhouse Film for use in Agriculture & Industry
S.I.C.: 3081

Holophane, S.A. de C.V. **(1)**
Mexico, Mexico
Mfrs. of Commercial Lighting Systems & Fixtures
S.I.C.: 3646

Polymer, S.A. **(1)**
Cartagena, Colombia (50%)
Mfrs. Of Specialty Industrial & Agricultural Plastic Products
S.I.C.: 3081

MCNEIL & NRM., INC.
(Formerly McNeil Akron Inc.)
96 E. Crosier St.
Akron, OH 44311
Tel.: 216-253-2525
Tel.: 800-669-2525
Telex: 98-6482
Fax: 216-253-5612
Approx.Sls.: $20,000,000
Emp.: 200
Fiscal Year-end: 12/31/90
Export
Mfrs. of Bag-O-Matic Tire Curing Presses; Bladder & Tube Presses, General Rubber Goods Presses, Tube Splicers; Mill Calendars, Extruders, High Intensity Mixers, Injection Molding Machines; Rotational Molding Machines; Latex & Vinyl Dip Lines; Plastic Extrusion Equip.
S.I.C.: 3542
Paul Yared *(Pres. & Chief Exec. Officer)*
Al Melek *(Exec. V.P.)*
Ray Keller *(V.P.-Fin.)*
Bernard Lesneski *(V.P.-Engrng. & Mktg.)*
Joan McCormick *(V.P.-Tire Equipment Sls.)*
Dick Immel *(V.P.-Opers.)*
Albert Chaovi *(Admin.)*
Karen Minor *(Exec. Sec.)*
Joe Siegfried *(Mgr.-Accounting)*
Kurt Kyle *(Sls. & Mktg. Coord.)*
Richard Fair *(Sls. Mgr.-Rotolast)*
Glenn Davy *(Mgr.-Spare Parts)*
Dennis Paradise *(Sls. Mgr.-Extrusion, Polymer Div.)*
Les Heinrich *(Mgr.-Pur.)*

Computer Systems/Hardware:
NCR

MCNEILUS COMPANIES
Hwy. #14 East
Dodge Center, MN 55927
Tel.: 507-374-6321
Fax: 507-374-6306
Emp.: 400
Construction & Oil Lease, Construction Equipment & Manufacture Concrete
S.I.C.: 3531; 3533; 3273; 5531
Garwin McNeilus *(Chm. Bd.)*
Denzil McNeilus *(Pres.)*
Brandon McNeilus *(V.P.)*
Thomas Winkels *(Sec. & Treas.)*

Outside Service Firm(s):

Blue Ball National Bank*(Major Banking Relationship)*
Blue Ball, PA

Branch:

McNeilus Companies **(1)**
Hemlock Rd.
Morgantown, PA 19543
Tel.: 215-286-0400
Manufacture Mixer Trucks
James Johnston *(Gen. Mgr.)*

MCORP
1717 Main, Ste. 3100
Dallas, TX 75201
Tel.: 214-939-5800
Earnings: $14,930,000
Fiscal Year-end: 12/31/90
Bank Holding Co.
S.I.C.: 6021; 6719; 6022
Peter Bartholow *(Chm. Bd., Pres. & Chief Oper. Officer)*

Mack Goforth *(Chief Fin. Officer)*
Michael D. Magill *(Sec.)*
James Taylor *(Dir.-Human Resources)*
Kenneth Shaver *(Asst. Sec.)*

Subsidiaries:

Mercantile Bank **(1)**
835 East Levee, P.O. Box 2219
Brownsville, TX 78520
Tel.: 210-546-2421 (100%)
Approx.Sls.: $46,219,000
Emp.: 184
Banking
S.I.C.: 6021

MBank New Braunfels **(1)**
451 Main Plaza
New Braunfels, TX 78130
Tel.: 210-625-8501 (100%)
Approx.Sls.: $8,593,000
Emp.: 44
Banking
S.I.C.: 6022
Joe T. Seibold *(Chm. & Chief Exec. Officer)*

MCRAE'S, INC.
McRae's Executive Plaza
Jackson, MS 39209
Mailing Address:
P.O. Box 20080
Jackson, MS 39209
Tel.: 601-968-4400
Fax: 601-968-5320
Approx.Sls.: $120,000,000
Emp.: 7,000
Fiscal Year-end: 12/31/90
Department Stores
S.I.C.: 5311
Richard McRae, Sr. *(Chm. Bd.)*
Richard McRae, Jr. *(Pres. & Chief Exec. Officer)*
Skip Scheimantle *(Dir.-Human Resources)*
Bubba Carter *(Dir.-Adv.)*

Computer Systems/Hardware:
IBM 4381

Outside Service Firm(s):

Ernst & Young*(Auditors)*
188 E. Capital St., Ste. 400
Jackson, MI 39201-2157
Tel.: 601-948-6600

Blue Cross & Blue Shield of Mississippi, Inc.*(Group Insurer)*
P.O. Box 1043
Jackson, MS 39215
Tel.: 601-932-3704

MCSWAIN CARPETS INC.
4730 Glendale-Milford Rd.
Cincinnati, OH 45242
Tel.: 513-554-1600 **OH**
Fax: 513-554-0411
Year Founded: 1968
Approx.Sls.: $25,500,000
Emp.: 150
Retail & Wholesale Carpeting & Flooring
S.I.C.: 5713; 5023
Ronald McSwain *(Pres.)*
Jim Leamer *(Exec. V.P. & Chief Oper. Officer)*
Thomas Pawley *(V.P. & Controller)*
Chris Gewehr *(V.P. & Dir.-Adv.)*

Outside Service Firm(s):

Barnes, Dennig & Co.*(Auditors)*
Cincinnati, OH

Katz, Teller, Brant & Hild*(Legal Firm)*
Cincinnati, OH

Fifth Third Bank*(Major Banking Relationship)*
Corporate Trust Services, 38 Fountain Square Plaza
Cincinnati, OH 45263

MCWANE, INC.
23 Inverness Center Pkwy.
Birmingham, AL 35242
Mailing Address:
P.O. Box 43327
Birmingham, AL 35243
Tel.: 205-991-9888
Fax: 205-995-1941
Year Founded: 1948
Approx.Sls.: $415,000,000
Emp.: 3,675
Pipe Manufacturer
S.I.C.: 3321; 3312; 3322; 6311; 6321; 6331
James R. McWane *(Chm. Bd.)*
John J. McMahon *(Pres.)*
Ronald O. Travis *(V.P. & Chief Fin. Officer)*
Jan Ehrhardt *(Sec.)*
Glenda Burson *(Treas.)*
Charles Nowlin *(Controller)*

Computer Systems/Hardware:
IBM PC

Outside Service Firm(s):

Coopers & Lybrand*(Auditors)*
1901 6th Ave. North, Ste. 1600
Birmingham, AL 35203-2602

Blue Cross & Blue Shield of Alabama*(Group Insurer)*
450 Riverchase Pkwy. East
Birmingham, AL 35298
Tel.: 205-988-2245

Maynard, Cooper, Frierson & Gale*(Legal Firm)*
Birmingham, AL

Subsidiaries:

Clow Corporation **(1)**
23 Inverness Center Pkwy.
Birmingham, AL 35243
Tel.: 205-991-9888 (100%)
Mfr. Pipe
S.I.C.: 3321; 3494
James R. McWane *(Chm. Bd.)*
John J. McMahon Jr. *(Pres. & Chief Exec. Officer)*
Ronald O. Travis *(Sr. V.P.-Fin.)*
Jan Ehrhard *(Sec.)*
Larry Brown *(Personnel Dir.)*

Division:

Clow Valve Div. **(2)**
So. 2nd St.
Oskaloosa, IA 52577
Tel.: 515-673-8611
Waterworks Valves & Fire Hydrants
S.I.C.: 3494; 3589
Roger Nelson *(V.P. & Gen. Mgr.)*

Subsidiary:

Clow Water Systems Corp. **(2)**
2021 Midwest Rd., Ste. 301
Oak Brook, IL 60521
Tel.: 708-932-2300
Cast Iron Pressure Pipe & Fittings
S.I.C.: 3321; 3494
John L. Kelly *(Pres.)*
Robert Phelps *(V.P.)*

Plant:

Clow Water Systems Corp. **(3)**
P.O. Box 479, So. 6th St.
Coshocton, OH 43812
Tel.: 614-622-6651
Pipe Mfg. Plant
S.I.C.: 3321
Jack Kanuckel *(V.P. & Gen. Mgr.)*

McWane Cast Iron Pipe Co. **(1)**
P.O. Box 607,
Birmingham, AL 35201
Tel.: 205-322-3521
Pipe Manufacturer
S.I.C.: 3317
Mac Luna *(V.P. & Mgr.)*

MCWILLIAMS FORGE CO.
Franklin Ave.
Rockaway, NJ 07866
Tel.: 201-627-0200
Fax: 201-625-9316
Year Founded: 1880
Sales Range: $10-19 Million
Emp.: 133

Export
Open & Closed Die Forgings For Aircraft Missiles, Space Applications & Nuclear; General Forgings
S.I.C.: 3462; 3463; 3728
Alexander M. McWilliams *(Pres.)*
Timothy C. McWilliams *(Exec. V.P.)*
Peter V. McWilliams *(V.P. & Gen. Mgr.)*
Scott G. McWilliams *(V.P.-Mktg.)*
Timothy F. McBride, III *(Controller)*
Richard D. Brusco *(Dir.-Quality Engrng.)*
Marion J. McWilliams *(Dir.-Human Resources)*
Gary A. McWilliams *(Mgr.-Sls.)*
Sigrid Hennings *(Wage & Benefits Admin.)*
John Sutherland *(Procurement Agent)*

Principal(s):
Alexander M. McWilliams
Timothy C. McWilliams

No. of Mfg. Plants/Facilities: 1
No. of U.S. Offices: 1

Outside Service Firm(s):

Smolin, Lupin & Co.*(Auditors)*
West Orange, NJ

Courter, Kobert, Lauffer, Purcell & Cohen, P.C.*(Legal Firm)*
Morristown, NJ

Midlantic National Bank/South*(Major Banking Relationship)*
Rockaway, NJ

MEADE GROUP, INC.
130 Kercheval
Detroit, MI 48236
Tel.: 313-726-7990
Fax: 313-726-7979
Approx.Sls.: $120,000,000
Emp.: 575
Retail New & Used Automobiles
S.I.C.: 5511
Kenneth Meade *(Pres.)*
Charles R. Riley *(V.P.-Sls. & Mktg.)*
Jean Mott *(Controller)*
John F. Youngblood *(Sec.)*

Outside Service Firm(s):

Czapal & Kaiser*(Auditors)*
Mount Clemens, MI

Abbott, Nichalson, Quilter, Esshaki & Youngblood*(Legal Firm)*
Detroit, MI

Michigan National Bank*(Major Banking Relationship)*
Detroit, MI

MEADE ULLMAN ADVERTISING & PUBLIC RELATIONS
30851 Agoura Rd., Ste. 102
Agoura Hills, CA 91301
Tel.: 818-889-2973
Fax: 818-889-8231
Year Founded: 1978
Approx.Billings: $12,000,000
Emp.: 15
Full Service AgencySpecializing in Market Research, StrategyDevelopment, Advertising, Design, Collaterals, In-House Production, Media, Trade Promotion and Event Marketing
Robert Stewart *(Pres. & Partner)*
Sterling Meade *(Partner)*
David Ullman *(Partner)*

MEADOWCRAFT, INC.
1401 Meadowcraft Rd.
Birmingham, AL 35215
Mailing Address:
P.O. Box 1357
Birmingham, AL 35201
Tel.: 205-853-2220
Fax: 205-854-4054
Approx.Sls.: $68,000,000
Emp.: 750
Fiscal Year-end: 5/30/92
Mfr. Wrought-Iron & Metal Casual Furniture
S.I.C.: 2514
S. Robert Blount *(Chm.)*
William McCanna *(Pres.)*
Steven C. Braswell *(V.P.-Fin. & Chief Fin. Officer)*
David Maunus *(V.P.-Mfg.)*
Rory Renmert *(V.P.-Sls. (Specialty Mkt.))*
Tim Leroy *(V.P.-Sls. (Mass Mkt.))*
Larry York *(V.P.-Human Resources)*
Rory Rehmert *(V.P.-Mktg.)*

No. of Mfg. Plants/Facilities: 3

Computer Systems/Hardware:
Wang

rg meadows inc
MARKETING AND SALES PROMOTION SPECIALISTS

R.G. MEADOWS, INC.
310 East Shore Rd.
Great Neck, NY 11023
Tel.: 516-829-4404
Fax: 516-829-4377
Year Founded: 1972
Approx.Billings: $25,000,000
Emp.: 30
Sales Promotion & Marketing
Guy F. Allen *(Chm. Bd. & Pres.)*
Paul Amershadian *(Sr. V.P.)*
Sally Weiss *(Sr. V.P., Pub. Rels. Dir.)*
Susan March *(Dir.-Admin. & Opers.)*
Stacy O'Connor *(Dir.-Res. & Devel.)*
Eileen Sci *(Mgr.-Data Processing)*

MEADVILLE FORGING CO.
P.O. Box 459-D
Meadville, PA 16335
Tel.: 814-724-1280
Fax: 814-333-4657
Year Founded: 1955
Approx.Sls.: $40,000,000
Emp.: 270

Import Export
Commercial & Closed Die Forgings
S.I.C.: 3462; 3423
John Keller *(Chm. & Treas.)*
James R. Martin *(Pres.)*
George Sieg *(Controller)*
Tom McGinnis *(Gen. Mgr.-Sls.)*
Tim Graham *(Mgr. Sls.-Auto.)*
Wilma Boyle *(Dir.-Pur.)*
Dennis Gregory *(Dir.-Engrng.)*

DON MEALEY CHEVROLET INC.
3707 W. Colonial Dr.
Orlando, FL 32808
Tel.: 407-295-7000 **FL**
Fax: 407-291-2054
Year Founded: 1974
Approx.Sls.: $68,000,000
Emp.: 171
Automobile Dealership
S.I.C.: 5511
Donald Mealey *(Pres.)*
Kevin Mealey *(Gen. Mgr.)*

Don Mealey Chevrolet Inc.—(Continued)

Outside Service Firm(s):

Deloitte & Touche*(Auditors)*
200 S. Orange Ave., Ste. 1800
Orlando, FL 32801
Tel.: 407-246-8200
Fax: 407-422-0936

Peirsol, Burroughs, Grimm, Bennett*(Legal Firm)*
Orlando, FL

Sun Bank, N.A.*(Major Banking Relationship)*
200 S. Orange Ave., 8th Fl. SOAB
Orlando, FL
Tel.: 407-237-4141

MEARS TRANSPORTATION GROUP
324 W. Gore St.
Orlando, FL 32806
Tel.: 407-422-4561 FL
Fax: 407-422-6923
Assets: $9,600,000
Liabilities: $7,000,000
Net Worth: $2,600,000
Approx.Sls.: $25,000,000
Emp.: 500
Fiscal Year-end: 12/31/89
Owner & Operation of Taxi, Limousine & Shuttle Services
S.I.C.: 4121; 4119; 4215
Paul S. Mears, Sr. *(Chm. Bd.)*
Paul S. Mears, Jr. *(Pres.)*
Robert A. Searcy *(Exec. V.P.-Opers.)*
James Mears *(Sr. V.P.)*
Charles E. Carns, Jr. *(V.P., Treas. & Chief Fin. Officer)*
Judy Haley *(Controller)*
Bret Voisin *(Dir.-Sls. & Mktg.)*

Outside Service Firm(s):

Ernst & Young*(Auditors)*
390 N. Orange Ave., Ste. 1700
Orlando, FL 32801
Tel.: 407-872-6600

Sun Trust*(Major Banking Relationship)*
Orlando, FL

MEASURED MARKETING SERVICES
12800 Culver Blvd.
Los Angeles, CA 90066
Tel.: 310-823-5755
Fax: 213-823-1272
Year Founded: 1953
Approx.Sls.: $40,000,000
Emp.: 400
Advertising Novelties, Direct Mail Advertising Services, Advertising Specialties
S.I.C.: 3993; 7331; 5199
Jack Nadel *(Chm. Bd. & Pres.)*
Robert W. Buckingham *(V.P.)*
Harold Holland *(V.P.)*
Martin Nadel *(Sec.)*

Outside Service Firm(s):

Levine, Cooper, Spiegel & Co.*(Auditors)*
Los Angeles, CA

Union Bank*(Major Banking Relationship)*
Lincoln, NE

Divisions:

M M S Design **(1)**
7775 Healdsburg Ave.
Sebastopol, CA 95472
Tel.: 707-829-2277
Commercial Art & Graphic Design
S.I.C.: 7336
Toby Cowan *(Pres.)*

Jack Nadel, Inc. Div. **(1)**
9950 W. Jefferson Blvd.
Culver City, CA 90232
Tel.: 310-836-1050
Advertising Specialties
S.I.C.: 5199
Jack Nadel *(Pres.)*

MECHANICAL HEAT & COLD, INC.
24535 Hallwood Ct.
Farmington, MI 48335
Tel.: 313-471-0600 MI
Fax: 313-471-2630
Year Founded: 1965
Approx.Sls.: $22,000,000
Emp.: 175
Mechanical Contractor
S.I.C.: 1711
Ed Sici *(Pres.)*
Tim Flynn *(V.P.)*
Douglas A. Hoerner *(Treas.)*

Outside Service Firm(s):

Moore & Moore*(Auditors)*
Detroit, MI

National Bank of Detroit*(Major Banking Relationship)*
611 Woodward Ave.
Detroit, MI 48226

MECO CORPORATION
1500 Industrial Rd.
Greeneville, TN 37743
Tel.: 615-639-1171
Fax: 615-639-2570
Year Founded: 1959
Approx.Sls.: $95,000,000
Emp.: 700
Fiscal Year-end: 6/30/91
Import Export
Outdoor Charcoal Grills, Metal Folding Furniture
S.I.C.: 2514; 3631
Jerald K. Jaynes *(Chm. Bd.)*
Gary Landes *(Pres.)*
Martin H. Hund *(Controller)*
Dominick Jackson *(Mgr.-Personnel)*
Rex Arrington *(Mgr.-Data Processing)*
James Ellenburg *(Mgr.-Quality Control)*
Bob Gass *(Pur. Agent)*

Computer Systems/Hardware:
IBM AS/400

MED-LAB SUPPLY COMPANY, INC.
923 N.W. 27th Ave.
Miami, FL 33125
Tel.: 305-642-5144
Year Founded: 1965
Approx.Sls.: $12,000,000
Emp.: 50
Sls. & Srvc. of Electromedical Equip.
S.I.C.: 5047; 7629
Gonzalo E. Diaz *(Pres.)*
Saul Diaz *(V.P. & Sec.)*
Gonzalo A. Diaz *(V.P. & Treas.)*
Agustin Diaz *(V.P.)*

Outside Service Firm(s):

Shutts & Bowen*(Legal Firm)*
201 S. Biscayne Blvd., 1500 Miami Center
Miami, FL 33131

MEDIA AMERICA CORP.
(Formerly Arizona Television, KTVK Channel 3)
3435 N. 16th St.,
Phoenix, AZ 85016
Mailing Address:
P.O. Box 5068
Phoenix, AZ 85010
Tel.: 602-266-5691 AZ
Fax: 602-263-3377
Sales Range: $20-39 Million
Emp.: 202
Television Broadcasting
S.I.C.: 4833; 4832; 2731
Jewell M. Lewis *(Chm.)*
Delbert R. Lewis *(Pres.)*
James Galvin *(Dir.-Adv. & Mktg. & Mgr.-Sls.)*
Bill Lawrence *(Dir.-Engrng.)*
James Tuton *(Dir.-Data Processing)*

Computer Systems/Hardware:
IBM System 38

Outside Service Firm(s):

Winston & Strawn*(Legal Firm)*
Phoenix, AZ

First Interstate Bank*(Major Banking Relationship)*
P.O. Box 53441,
Phoenix, AZ 85072-3441
Tel.: 602-229-4049

Divisions:

KEZ **(1)**
5555 N. 7th Ave., Ste. B-300
Phoenix, AZ 85013
Tel.: 602-263-0100
Radio Broadcasting
S.I.C.: 4832
Win Holder *(Gen. Mgr.)*

Phoenix Magazine **(1)**
5555 N. 7th Ave., Ste. B-200
Phoenix, AZ 85013
Tel.: 602-207-3750
Fax: 602-207-3777
Publisher of Guide to Local Entertainment Social Events
S.I.C.: 2731
Richard Vonier *(Editor & Publr.)*

Subsidiary:

Desert Production Services **(1)**
2235 W. Alice
Phoenix, AZ 85021
Tel.: 602-263-3977
Television Programming
S.I.C.: 7922
Bill Lewis *(Gen. Mgr.)*

MEDIA BUYING SERVICES INTL. INC.
104 Fifth Ave.
New York, NY 10111
Tel.: 212-206-0600
Fax: 212-206-0613
Year Founded: 1968
Approx.Billings: $150,000,000
Emp.: 40
Media Strategy & Buying
Matthew C. Bryant *(Pres.-USA)*
Helane Naiman *(Brdcst. Media Mgr.)*
Joe Scangamor *(Chief Fin. Officer)*
Skip Pollard *(Plng. Dir.)*
Carmelita Longo *(Billings Supvr.)*

MEDIA CONCEPTS CORPORATION
25 N. Main St.
Assonet, MA 02702
Tel.: 508-644-3131
Fax: 508-644-5201
Year Founded: 1969
Approx.Billings: $13,800,000
Emp.: 15
High Tech & Consumer Adv.
Paul H. Beaulieu *(Pres. & Creative Dir.)*
Bruce D. White *(Exec. V.P., Treas.)*

MEDIA LOGIC, INC.
1520 Central Ave.
Albany, NY 12205
Tel.: 518-456-3015
Fax: 518-456-4279
Year Founded: 1984
Approx.Billings: $40,000,000
Emp.: 45
Retail, Industrial & Educational Adv.
David M. Schultz *(Pres.)*
Suzanne Gunther *(Dir., New Bus. Devel.)*
Lisa Rudgers *(Pub. Rels. Dir.)*

Computer Systems/Hardware:
Novell, Macintosh

MEDIA MANAGEMENT ASSOCIATES
1 Parker Plaza
Fort Lee, NJ 07024
Tel.: 201-592-7320
Fax: 201-944-3111
Year Founded: 1985
Approx.Billings: $17,475,600
Emp.: 9
Marketing & Media Placement
John Gaskell *(Pres.)*
Susan Laskey *(Exec. V.P.)*
Mary Loncharich *(V.P., Strategic Plng.)*
Sandy Gray *(V.P.)*
Mary Mantineo *(Comptroller)*
Rick Kober *(Media Biller)*

MEDIA PLUS
1818 Westlake Ave., N., Ste. 114
Seattle, WA
Tel.: 206-282-5677
Fax: 206-284-4862
Year Founded: 1983
Approx.Billings: $10,500,000
Emp.: 5
Media Consulting, Plng. & Buying
Kathy Neukirchen *(Pres.)*
Lani Jacobsen *(V.P.)*
Karen Cavit *(Office Mgr.)*

MEDIA POWER, INC.
5009 Monroe Rd.
Charlotte, NC 28205
Tel.: 704-567-1000
Fax: 704-567-8193
Year Founded: 1985
Approx.Billings: $12,800,000
Emp.: 14
Media Planning & Buying
Judith Kaufman *(Pres.)*
Barbara Goldstein *(Exec. V.P., Treas.)*
Ronald P. Kaufman *(Exec. V.P., Sec.)*

MEDIA PRINTING CORPORATION
8050 N.W. 74th Ave.
Miami, FL 33166
Tel.: 305-888-1300 FL
Fax: 305-888-8542
Year Founded: 1972
Approx.Sls.: $20,500,000
Emp.: 140
Lithographic Commercial Printing
S.I.C.: 2752
John Grubman *(Pres.)*
John Checchia *(V.P., Treas., & Mgr.-Personnel & Data Processing)*

Outside Service Firm(s):

Southeast Bank, N.A.*(Major Banking Relationship)*
1 Southeast Financial Center
Miami, FL 33131
Tel.: 305-666-5656

M S I
MEDIA STORE INC

MEDIA STORE INC.
220 East 42nd St.
New York, NY 10017
Tel.: 212-972-4477
Year Founded: 1987
Approx.Billings: $38,500,000
Emp.: 20
Cable Television Buying
John P. Kramer *(Pres. & New Bus. Contact)*
Robert Hew *(V.P., Fin.)*
Rachel Lellio *(V.P., Controller)*
Elizabeth Tushaj *(Opers. Mgr.)*

MEDIA THAT WORKS
455 Delta Ave.
Cincinnati, OH 45226
Tel.: 513-871-7779
Tel.: 800-688-7779
Fax: 513-871-1804
Year Founded: 1985
Approx.Billings: $92,500,000
Emp.: 65
Media Strategic Planning, Placement, Post-Analysis, Promotions, Consulting & Auditing Services
William C. Price *(Principal)*
Mary Beth Price *(Pres.)*
Lynne C. Veil *(Exec. V.P.)*
Eileen B. Weinert *(Sr. V.P.)*
Barb W. McGrath *(V.P.)*
Susan E. Bentzinger *(V.P.)*
Michael T. Kiley *(Chief Fin. Officer)*

Computer Systems/Hardware:
IBM AS/400

MEDIACOMP, INC.
One West Loop S., Ste. 720
Houston, TX 77027
Tel.: 713-621-1071
Fax: 713-621-8427
Year Founded: 1955
Approx.Sls.: $10,000,000
Emp.: 11
Fiscal Year-end: 7/31/90
Developers & Marketers of Media Optimization Software to Advertisers, Advertising Agencies & Media Services
S.I.C.: 7371; 7372
Sylvan L. Brown *(Chm. Bd., Pres. & Chief Exec. Officer)*
Jerry R. Storseth *(Chief Oper. Officer & Mktg. Dir.)*
Francis Foytek *(Treas.)*

Computer Systems/Hardware:
IBM-Compatible PCs & Network

Mediacomp Media Management Services **(1)**
One West Loop S., Ste. 720
Houston, TX 77027
Tel.: 713-621-1071
Fax: 713-621-8427
Computer Systems/Hardware:
IBMCompatible
Plans & Buys Media for National, Regional & Local Clients
S.I.C.: 7319
Sylvan L. Brown *(Pres.)*
Jerry R. Storseth *(Dir.-Mktg.)*

MEDIANEWS GROUP INC.
Loop Centeral One, 4888 Loop Central Dr., Ste. 525
Houston, TX 77081
Tel.: 713-840-5165
Fax: 713-840-6997
Year Founded: 1984
Approx.Sls.: $600,000,000
Emp.: 6,000
Publishes 17 Daily & 58 Non-Daily Newspapers Nationwide
S.I.C.: 2711
Richard B. Scudder *(Chm. Bd.)*
William Dean Singleton *(Vice Chm. & Chief Exec. Officer)*
E. Michael Fluker *(Exec. V.P. & Chief Fin. Officer)*
Walter L. Holt, Jr. *(V.P.)*
Nicholas L. Lebra, Jr. *(V.P. & Dir.-Human Resources)*
Anthony F. Tierno *(V.P.-Opers.)*
Charlie Eickenhorst *(Dir.-Tax)*
Kurt Hannigan *(Dir.-Mngmt. Information Systems)*
Joseph Lodovic *(Treas.)*
Patricia Robinson *(Sec.)*
Principal(s):
Richard B. Scudder
William Dean Singleton

Computer Systems/Hardware:
IBM

Subsidiary:

MediaNews Group, Eastern Operations **(1)**
309 So. Broad St.
Woodbury, NJ 08096
Tel.: 609-845-3300
Headquarters; Newspaper Publishing
S.I.C.: 8741; 2711
Anthony F. Tierno *(V.P.-Opers.)*

MEDIATEX COMMUNICATIONS CORPORATION
P. O. Box 1569
Austin, TX 78767
Tel.: 512-320-6900
Year Founded: 1973
Sales Range: $20-39 Million
Emp.: 115
Magazine Publishing; Texas Monthly
S.I.C.: 2721
Michael R. Levy *(Chm. & Pres.)*
Stephen A. Childs *(V.P.-Devel.)*
Greg Curtis *(V.P.-Editorial)*
Marsha Weir Cook *(Treas. & Sec.)*

Subsidiary:

Texas Monthly, Inc. **(1)**
P.O. Box 1569
Austin, TX 78767
Tel.: 512-476-7085
S.I.C.: 2721
Stephen A. Childs *(Pres.)*
Michael R. Levy *(Publisher)*

MEDICAL ANALYSIS SYSTEMS INC.
542 Flynn Rd.
Camarillo, CA 93010
Tel.: 805-987-7891 CA
Fax: 805-987-6498
Year Founded: 1974
Approx.Sls.: $15,000,000
Emp.: 72
Fiscal Year-end: 3/31/92
Export
Mfr. of Diagnostics
S.I.C.: 2835
Ivan Modrovich *(Chm. Bd.)*
E.G. Slautterback *(Pres.)*
Keith R. Gold *(V.P.-Mktg.)*

Computer Systems/Hardware:
Hewlett Packard

MEDICAL LABORATORY AUTOMATION, INC.
270 Marble Ave.
Pleasantville, NY 10570
Tel.: 914-747-3020
Tel.: 800-431-1720
Telex: 710-562-0117
Cable: 22
Fax: 914-747-0498
Year Founded: 1962
Approx.Sls.: $50,000,000
Emp.: 400
Fiscal Year-end: 11/31/91
Export
Manufacture Medical Laboratory Equipment,including Coagulation Analyzers & Liquid Handling Devices
S.I.C.: 3821
Emil A. Scordato *(Chm. & Chief Exec. Officer)*
Richard E. Scordato *(Pres.)*
E. Stuart Clymer *(V.P.-Fin.)*
Jack Campbell *(V.P.-Mfg.)*
Niall D. Bowman *(V.P.-Engrng.)*
Jerome Berkman *(Sec.)*
Sharon Tucker *(Controller)*
Richard L. Minnihan *(Dir.-Mktg.)*
Joe McKenna *(Dir.-Personnel)*
Edward Kozel *(Mgr.-Mktg.)*
Michael Carrubba *(Mgr.-Technical Services)*
R. Alison Leavitt *(Mktg.-Communications)*

Outside Service Firm(s):

Deloitte & Touche*(Auditors)*
1600 Summer St.
Stamford, CT 06905-5121
Tel.: 203-351-4600

Day, Berry & Howard*(Legal Firm)*
Stamford, CT

Chemical Banking Corp.*(Major Banking Relationship)*
277 Park Ave.
New York, NY 10041
Tel.: 212-310-6407
Fax: 212-310-4526

Division:

Technology for Medicine, Inc. **(1)**
270 Marble Ave.
Picasantville, NY 10570
Tel.: 914-747-3020
Fax: 914-747-0498
Manufacture Specimen Collection & Transport Systems
Charles Saunders *(Pres.)*

THE MEDICAL PROTECTIVE COMPANY
5814 Reed Rd.
Fort Wayne, IN 46835
Mailing Address:
P.O. Box 15021
Fort Wayne, IN 46885
Tel.: 219-485-9622
Fax: 219-486-0415
Year Founded: 1899
Approx.Sls.: $119,000,000
Emp.: 200
General Liability Insurance
S.I.C.: 6351; 6331
Dale F. Doehrman *(Chm. Bd. & Chief Exec. Officer)*
Robert Gibson *(Pres. & Chief Oper. Officer)*
Dan Landrigan *(V.P. & Treas.)*
Dave Treacy *(Controller)*

Outside Service Firm(s):

Ernst & Young*(Auditors)*
2300 Fort Wayne Natl. Bank Bldg.
Fort Wayne, IN 46802

Lincoln National Life Insurance Co.*(Major Banking Relationship)*
Fort Wayne, IN

MEDICO INDUSTRIES, INC.
1500 Hwy. 315
Wilkes-Barre, PA 18711
Tel.: 717-825-7711
Tel.: 800-633-0027
Fax: 717-824-1169
Year Founded: 1937
Approx.Sls.: $10,000,000
Emp.: 175
Export
Manufacturer of Custom Metal Parts, Defense Ammunition; Hot Cup Cold Extrusion, High Production Turning; Distributor of Construction & Industry Equipment
S.I.C.: 3451; 3499; 5082; 5084; 3482
Thomas Medico *(Pres.)*
Lawrence Medico *(Treas.)*
Len Taretto *(Controller)*
Cataldo Medico *(Sec.)*
Anthony Denisco *(Mgr.-Rental)*
William Vinsko *(Mgr.-Sls.)*
Carmen Uritz *(Electrical Engr.)*

No. of Mfg. Plants/Facilities: 1
No. of U.S. Offices: 2

Outside Service Firm(s):

Parente, Randolph, Orlando, Carey & Associates*(Auditors)*
46 Public Square
Wilkes-Barre, PA 18701-2681
Tel.: 717-820-0100
Fax: 717-824-9865

Merchants Bank, North*(Major Banking Relationship)*
Wilkes-Barre, PA

Subsidiary:

Action Lift **(1)**
1500 Hwy. 315
Wilkes-Barre, PA 18711
Emp.: 25
Sales & Service of Rental Material Handling Equipment
S.I.C.: 5082
William Medico *(Pres.)*
Len Tarreto *(Controller)*
Bernard Toma *(Dir.-Mktg.)*
Joe Mescavage *(Gen. Mgr.)*

MEDIEVAL DINNER & TOURNAMENT, INC.
7662 Beach Blvd.
Buena Park, CA 90622
Mailing Address:
P.O. Box 5670
Buena Park, CA 90622
Tel.: 714-562-0220 CA
Fax: 714-523-8360
Year Founded: 1986
Sales Range: $40-59 Million
Emp.: 300
Fiscal Year-end: 12/31/90
Import
Restaurant & Entertainment with a Medieval Theme; Facilities in Buena Park CA, Kissimmee FL, The Meadowlands NJ & Schaumburg IL, Dallas TX; Opened June 1992
S.I.C.: 5812
Kenneth H. Kim *(Chm., Pres., Chief Exec. Officer, Corp. Sec. & Treas.)*
Jose Sans *(Exec. V.P.)*
Charles C. Bellows *(Sr. V.P.-Mktg. & Sls.)*
Antonio Alcina *(V.P.)*
Eric Chiusulo *(V.P.)*
MaryAnn Powell *(V.P.-Communications)*
Ron Yeakley *(Mgr.-Adv.)*

Medieval Dinner & Tournament, Inc.—(Continued)

Outside Service Firm(s):

Coopers & Lybrand *(Auditors)*
350 S. Grand Ave.
Los Angeles, CA 90071
Tel.: 213-481-1000
Fax: 213-482-6440

State Bank of South Australia *(Major Banking Relationship)*
Los Angeles, CA

THE MEDISCUS GROUP
6900 Aragon Circle
Buena Park, CA 90620
Tel.: 714-522-2408
Fax: 714-994-2491
Approx.Sls.: $65,000,000
Emp.: 400
Fiscal Year-end: 12/31/90
Rental of Hospital Beds
S.I.C.: 7359; 7352
Richard Bear *(Pres.)*

MEDLINE INDUSTRIES, INC.
One Medline Place
Mundelein, IL 60060
Tel.: 708-949-5500 **IL**
Fax: 708-949-3126
Approx.Sls.: $274,000,000
Emp.: 2,000
Fiscal Year-end: 3/31/91
Mfr. of Health Care Products, Textiles, Plastic Disposable Items; Plan & Design Health Care Institutions
S.I.C.: 3089; 3842; 8711; 3800
James S. Mills *(Chm. Bd. & Chief Exec. Officer)*
John Mills *(Pres. & Chief Oper. Officer)*
Frank Resnick *(Chief Fin. Officer)*
Ed Becker *(V.P.-Information Services)*
C. Larkin *(V.P.-Sls.)*
Thomas Pawlick *(Dir.-Mktg. Communications)*

Computer Systems/Hardware:
IBM Systems 36 & 32, IBM 4341, Series 1, PC

Outside Service Firm(s):

Coopers & Lybrand *(Auditors)*
203 N. LaSalle St.
Chicago, IL 60601
Tel.: 312-701-5500

American National Bank & Trust Company of Chicago *(Major Banking Relationship)*
33 N. LaSalle St.
Chicago, IL 60602
Tel.: 312-661-5000
Fax: 312-661-6417

Divisions:

Accucare Div. **(1)**
One Medline Place
Mundelein, IL 60060
Tel.: 708-949-5500
Medical Supplies
S.I.C.: 5049
Johnathan Brown *(Pres.)*

Disposamed Div. **(1)**
One Medline Place
Mundelein, IL 60060
Tel.: 708-949-5500
Medical Supplies
S.I.C.: 5049
William Sanders *(Pres.)*

Dynacor Div. **(1)**
One Medline Place
Mundelein, IL 60060
Tel.: 708-949-5500
Medical Supplies
S.I.C.: 5049
Charles Mills *(Pres.)*

Medcrest Div. **(1)**
One Medline Place
Mundelein, IL 60060
Tel.: 708-949-5500
Fax: 708-949-3126
Wholesale Distr. of Medical Supplies
S.I.C.: 5047
John Mills *(Pres. & Chief Exec. Officer)*

Medecore Div. **(1)**
One Medline Place
Mundelein, IL 60060
Tel.: 708-949-3006
Fax: 708-949-3116
Approx.Sls.: $25,000,000
Import Export
Wholesale Distr. of Medical Supplies
S.I.C.: 5047
Norman Raven *(Pres.)*
Marvin Wein *(V.P.-Opers.)*
Gary Few *(V.P.-Sls.)*

Medline Skin Care Div. **(1)**
One Medline Place
Mundelein, IL 60060
Tel.: 708-949-5500
Skin Care Prods.
S.I.C.: 2844
William Sanders *(Pres.)*

MEDRAD, INC.
271 Kappa Dr.
Pittsburgh, PA 15238
Tel.: 412-967-9700
Tel.: 800-633-7231
Fax: 412-967-9028
Year Founded: 1968
Approx.Sls.: $60,000,000
Emp.: 650
Import Export
Mfr. of Medical & Surgical Instruments
S.I.C.: 3841
John L. Laubach *(Chm. Bd. & Sec.)*
Thomas H. Witmer *(Pres. & Chief Exec. Officer)*
A.K. Grob *(Exec. V.P.-Opers.)*
John P. Friel *(V.P.-Sls. & Mktg.)*
R.M. Evans *(V.P.-Sls. & Service)*
E.W. Graham *(V.P.-Mfg.)*
J.R. Graham *(V.P.-Quality & Reg. Services)*
J.B. Havrilla *(V.P.-Research & Devel.)*
David Kent *(Mgr.-Mktg. Support Services)*

Outside Service Firm(s):

Deloitte & Touche *(Auditors)*
2400 One PPG Place
Pittsburgh, PA 15222
Tel.: 412-281-2232

Laubach, Fulton, Jeselnik & Delaney *(Legal Firm)*
Pittsburgh, PA

Pittsburgh National Bank *(Major Banking Relationship)*
Stock Transfer Dept., Fifth & Wood Streets
Pittsburgh, PA 15265

MEDTECH LABORATORIES, INC.
3510 N. Lake Creek Dr.
Jackson, WY 83001
Mailing Address:
P.O. Box 1108
Jackson, WY 83001
Tel.: 307-733-1680
Fax: 307-733-0393
Year Founded: 1973
Emp.: 20
Fiscal Year-end: 3/31/91
Mfr. of Pharmaceuticals & Health & Beauty Aids
S.I.C.: 2834
A.H. Peralta-Ramos *(Pres.)*
W.D. Weiss *(Chief Exec. Officer)*
D.L. Auslander *(V.P.-Sls. & Mktg.)*
Glenn E. Ross *(V.P.-Sls.)*
C.J. Schmidlapp III *(V.P.-Pur.)*
Dale M. Johnson *(Controller)*
Mary L. Hughes *(Sec.)*

Division:

Medtech Laboratories, Inc. **(1)**
2444 Morris Ave.
Union, NJ 07083
Tel.: 908-686-2777
Mfr. & Distr. of Pharmaceuticals & Beauty Aids
S.I.C.: 2834; 5122; 2844

MEEHAN TOOKER
55 Madison Circle Dr.
East Rutherford, NJ 07073
Tel.: 201-933-9600
Fax: 201-933-8322
Year Founded: 1986
Approx.Sls.: $100,000,000
Emp.: 500
Commercial Printers
S.I.C.: 2759
Michael D. Voss *(Chm. Bd. & Chief Exec. Officer)*
Tom Simunek *(Pres.)*
Tom Murphy *(Exec. V.P.-Sls. & Mktg.)*
Al Starzyk *(Mgr.-Natl. Sls.)*
Alan Concha *(Chief Fin. Officer)*
Jo Ann Claccum *(Gen. Counsel)*
Linda Scarry *(Mgr.-Human Resources)*
Principal(s):
Michael D. Voss

Subsidiaries:

Drucker Printing **(1)**
325 Cantor Ave.
Linden, NJ 07036
Tel.: 908-862-3370
Printers
S.I.C.: 2759
Bill Drucker *(Chm. Bd.)*

Elmira Litho **(1)**
C St., Bldg. J, Center At Horsehead
Elmira, NY 14903
Tel.: 607-796-2772
Printers
S.I.C.: 2759
Mike Peterson *(Gen. Mgr.)*

MEENAN OIL CO. LIMITED PARTNERSHIP
(Formerly Meenan Oil Co.)
6800 Jericho Turnpike
Syosset, NY 11791
Tel.: 516-364-9030 **DE**
Fax: 516-364-9171
Year Founded: 1933
Assets: $58,000,000
Net Worth: $58,000,000
Approx.Sls.: $300,000,000
Emp.: 750
Fiscal Year-end: 6/30/91
Retail & Wholesale Petroleum Products
S.I.C.: 5983; 5172
Stanley R. Orczyk *(Chm. & Chief Oper. Officer)*
Paul A. Vermylen, Jr. *(Pres., Treas. & Sec.)*
Richard Zaweski *(Controller)*

Computer Systems/Hardware:
ITT

Outside Service Firm(s):

KPMG Peat Marwick *(Auditors)*
345 Park Ave.
New York, NY 10154
Tel.: 212-758-9700
Fax: 212-872-3308

Connecticut General Life Insurance Co. *(Group Insurer)*
P.O. Box 2975,
Hartford, CT 06104
Tel.: 203-726-6000

Hartford Life Insurance Co. *(Commercial Insurance Carrier)*
Hartford, CT 06104-2999

Simpson, Thacher & Bartlett *(Legal Firm)*
425 Lexington Ave.
New York, NY 10017
Tel.: 212-455-2000

Chemical Banking Corp. *(Major Banking Relationship)*
277 Park Ave.
New York, NY 10041
Tel.: 212-310-6407
Fax: 212-310-4526

Fidelity Bank *(Major Banking Relationship)*
Broad & Walnut St.
Philadelphia, PA 19109

Manufacturers Hanover Trust Co. *(Major Banking Relationship)*
270 Park Ave.
New York, NY 10017
Tel.: 212-286-3229

Mutual of New York *(Pension Manager)*
New York, NY

Divisions:

Christy Halsey Oil Co. **(1)**
65 Maple Ave.
Chester, NJ 07930
Tel.: 908-879-5411
Emp.: 14
Home Heating Oil & Service
S.I.C.: 5983
Henry Palmer *(Gen. Mgr.)*

Meenan LI Div. **(1)**
3020 Burns Ave.
Wantagh, NY 11793
Tel.: 516-783-1000
Emp.: 256
Home Heating Oil & Service; Home Reinsulation & Oil Burner Installations
S.I.C.: 5983; 5074
Eugene Walsh *(Gen. Mgr.)*

Meenan Oil Div. **(1)**
108 W. Main St.
Clinton, NJ 08809
Tel.: 908-735-5158
Emp.: 14
Home Heating Oil & Service
S.I.C.: 5983
Henry Palmer *(Gen. Mgr.)*

Meenan Oil Pennsylvania Div. **(1)**
113 Main St.
Tullytown, PA 19007
Tel.: 215-943-3500
Emp.: 142
Home Heating Oil & Service; Home Reinsulation, Burner Sales & Solar Heating
S.I.C.: 5983; 5074
John Kuebler *(Gen. Mgr.)*

Subsidiaries:

Burke Fuel & Heating Co. **(1)**
475 Commerce St.
Hawthorne, NY 10532
Tel.: 914-769-5050 (100%)
Emp.: 75
Home Heating Oil & Service
S.I.C.: 5983
Dan Donovan *(Gen. Mgr.)*

Effron Fuel Oil Co., Inc. **(1)**
154 Garden Street
Poughkeepsie, NY 12682
Tel.: 914-452-2600 (100%)
Emp.: 76
Home Heating Oil & Service
S.I.C.: 5983
Jeff Hitchings *(Gen. Mgr.)*

Young Supply Co. **(1)**
8301 Lansdowne Ave.
Upper Darby, PA 19082
Tel.: 215-789-4200 (100%)
Approx.Sls.: $15,800,000
Emp.: 166
Home Heating Oil & Service
S.I.C.: 5983
Barry Radcliff *(Gen. Mgr.)*

MEER CORPORATION
9500 Railroad Ave.
North Bergen, NJ 07047
Tel.: 201-861-9500
Fax: 891-861-9267
Year Founded: 1926
Approx.Sls.: $27,000,000
Emp.: 200

Import Export
Botanicals, Water Soluble Gums, Flavors, Oleoresins Enhancers, Extracts, Oils
S.I.C.: 2834; 2087; 2099
Richard H. Meer *(Chm. Bd. & Chief Exec. Officer)*
E. Harvey Meer *(Pres., Chief Oper. Officer & Treas.)*
R.J. Nikula Jr. *(V.P.-Sls.)*
Michael Coombs *(Controller)*
William Broth *(Dir.-Mfg.)*
Richard San Martin *(Dir.-Sls. & Mktg.)*
Herb Schultz *(Dir.-Tech.)*

Outside Service Firm(s):

Leventhal, Zupnick, Berg & Co.*(Auditors)*
New York, NY

NatWest*(Major Banking Relationship)*
New York, NY

MEGAPULSE, INC.
8 Preston Ct.
Bedford, MA 01730
Tel.: 617-275-2010
Fax: 617-275-9636
Emp.: 40
Import Export
Mfr. of Electronic Aids To Navigation; Transmitters & Receivers
S.I.C.: 3812
Paul Johnannessen *(Chm. Bd. & Pres.)*
Edward L. McGann *(V.P.)*
Edwin Larsen *(Comptroller)*

No. of Mfg. Plants/Facilities: 1
No. of U.S. Offices: 1

Computer Systems/Hardware:
Digital VAX

Outside Service Firm(s):

Arthur Andersen & Co.*(Auditors)*
One Intl. Place, 100 Oliver St.
Boston, MA 02110
Tel.: 617-330-4000
Fax: 617-439-9731

First National Bank*(Major Banking Relationship)*
Boston, MA

MEGAS BEAUTY AIDS, INC.
15501 Industrial Pkwy.
Cleveland, OH 44135
Tel.: 216-676-6400 **OH**
Year Founded: 1976
Sales Range: $20-39 Million
Emp.: 250
Mfr. of Health & Beauty Aids-Cotton Balls, Swabs, Tissues, Foot Insoles
S.I.C.: 2676; 2844; 3842; 3800
Robert Bender *(Chm. Bd., Pres. & Chief Exec. Officer)*
F. Michael Demeter *(V.P.-Opers.)*
Bob Logan *(V.P.-Sls.)*
Gerry Trafis *(V.P.-Fin.)*
Tom Derr *(Dir.-Mktg.)*
Kevin Pace *(Dir.-Pur.)*

No. of Mfg. Plants/Facilities: 1
No. of U.S. Offices: 1

Computer Systems/Hardware:
IBM System 36

Outside Service Firm(s):

The Central Trust Company, N.A.*(Investment Banker)*
Canton, OH

JOSHUA MEIER CORP.
7401 West Side Ave.
North Bergen, NJ 07047
Tel.: 201-869-8200
Tel.: 800-526-7131
Fax: 201-869-0034
Approx.Sls.: $25,000,000
Emp.: 250
Fiscal Year-end: 12/31/90
Import Export
Manufacturing Office Supplies; V.P.D. Binders, Easels, Photo Albums, Sheet Protectors & Plastic Specialties; Spel-Binder, Flip-File, Grip-Strip, Visi/Belle, Execu-Line, Maga- Seen, Have-Desk-Will-Travel, Space-Case, Insta-Magic, Album-Unlimited, Skan-A- Page, Slide-Sho, Stik-Eese, Stikit-All, Renaissance, Clkassic, Silverline, Indexable Business Card Files, Boardroom Report Covers, Menu Covers, Diplom
S.I.C.: 2782; 3089
Alfred Magid *(Pres.)*
John Gregory *(Controller)*
David Brous *(Dir.-Mktg.)*
Frank Clement *(Mgr.-Natl. Sls.)*

MEIER METAL SERVICE CENTERS, INC.
1471 E. Nine Mile Rd.
Hazel Park, MI 48030
Tel.: 313-398-1900
Fax: 313-398-0852
Emp.: 124
Copper Sheets, Plates, Bars, Rods, Pipes; Aluminum Bars, Rods Ingots, Sheets, Pipes, Plates; Non-ferrous Metal Sheets, Bars & Rods
S.I.C.: 5051
William J. Targett *(Pres. & Chief Exec. Officer)*
William J. Devanney *(V.P., Sec. & Treas.)*
Robert F. Kirk *(V.P. & Gen. Mgr.)*
Laurence C. Sauers *(V.P. & Gen. Mgr.)*

Outside Service Firm(s):

Manufacturers National Bank N.A.*(Major Banking Relationship)*
38th Fl., 100 Renaissance Center
Detroit, MI 48243
Tel.: 313-222-4227

MEIJER, INC.
2929 Walker Ave. N.W.
Grand Rapids, MI 49504
Tel.: 616-453-6711
Fax: 616-453-6067
Approx.Sls.: $2,000,000,000
Emp.: 19,000
Fiscal Year-end: 1/31/91
69 Hypermarkets; 2 General Merchandise Stores
S.I.C.: 5399; 5411
Doug Meijer *(Co-Chm.)*
Hank Meijer *(Co-Chm.)*
Earl Holton *(Pres.)*
Paul Boyer *(Sr. V.P. Property & Distr.)*
Jack Koetje *(Sr. V.P.-Retail Opers.)*
Charles Hemmerflag *(V.P. & Controller)*
Fred L. Kistler *(V.P. & Treas.)*
Fritz D. Kolk *(V.P.-Fin. & Chief Fin. Officer)*
Dave Paasche *(V.P.-Information Systems)*
Gordon Ondersma *(V.P. & Dir.-Adv.)*
Windell Ray *(V.P.-Personnel)*
Robert Riley *(V.P. & Gen. Counsel)*
Jennifer Downs *(Dir.-Pub. Consumer Affairs)*

No. of U.S. Offices: 4

Computer Systems/Hardware:
IBM System 3975

Outside Service Firm(s):

Arthur Andersen & Co.*(Auditors)*
Grand Rapids, MI

Miller, Johnson, Snell & Cummisky*(Legal Firm)*
Grand Rapids, MI

Michigan National Bank*(Major Banking Relationship)*
77 Monroe Center
Grand Rapids, MI 49501
Tel.: 616-451-7600

MELARD MANUFACTURING CORPORATION
153 Linden St.
Passaic, NJ 07055
Tel.: 201-472-8888
Fax: 201-472-5274
Year Founded: 1948
Approx.Sls.: $50,000,000
Emp.: 500
Fiscal Year-end: 8/31/91
Import Export
Manufacturer of Plumbing, Household, Energy Saving & Floor Protection Products; Bathroom Accessories
S.I.C.: 3432; 3088
Sidney J. Shames *(Chm. Bd., Pres., CEO, COO, CFO & Treas.)*
Harold Shames *(Exec. V.P. & Sec.)*
R. Green *(Controller)*
Michael Duggan *(Exec. V.P.-Sls.)*
John Logan *(V.P.-Mfg.)*
Ira Berkowitz *(V.P.-Pur.)*
William Sicheri *(Prod. Mgr.)*
Samuel Paris *(Plant Mgr.)*

Computer Systems/Hardware:
IBM

Outside Service Firm(s):

J.H. Cohn & Company*(Auditors)*
75 Eisenhower Pkwy.
Roseland, NJ 07068-1697
Tel.: 201-228-3500

Orloff, Lowenbach, Stifelman & Siegel*(Legal Firm)*
Roseland, NJ

National Westminster Bank plc*(Major Banking Relationship)*
Astor Plaza, 1515 Broadway
New York, NY 10036

Subsidiary:

Melard Plastics Inc. **(1)**
153 Linden St.
Passaic, NJ 07055
Tel.: 201-472-8888
Emp.: 50
DIY Home Products, Bathroom Accessories; Towel Bars, Recessed Soap Dishes, Tumbler & Toothbrush Holders, etc.
S.I.C.: 3088; 3431
Sidney J. Shames *(Chm. Bd. & Pres.)*
Harold Shames *(Exec. V.P.- Mktg. & Sls.)*
Ira Berowitz *(V.P.-Pur.)*
Dave Trojan *(Mgr.)*

MELDRUM & FEWSMITH COMMUNICATIONS INC.
1350 Euclid Ave.
Cleveland, OH 44115
Tel.: 216-241-2141 **OH**
Telex: 701199
Fax: 216-241-3929
Year Founded: 1930
Approx.Billings: $116,211,000
Emp.: 175
Fiscal Year-end: 12/31/91
Advertising Agency
S.I.C.: 7311
Chris N. Perry *(Chm. Bd. & Chief Exec. Officer)*
Jeffrey H. Bryden *(Vice Chm. & Chief Oper. Officer)*
Robert P. Huddilston *(Chief Fin. Officer & Exec. V.P.)*
Charles T. Hurley *(Sr. V.P. & Controller)*
Linda Gajevski *(V.P.-Bus. Devel. & Publ. Rels.)*
Ronald A. Kalish *(V.P. & Mgr.-Office Services)*

No. of U.S. Offices: 4

Computer Systems/Hardware:
HP 3000

Outside Service Firm(s):

Deloitte & Touche*(Auditors)*
1717 East Ninth St.
Cleveland, OH 44114
Tel.: 216-589-1300

Calfee, Halter & Griswold*(Legal Firm)*
800 Superior Ave., Ste. 1800
Cleveland, OH 44115-2688
Tel.: 216-622-8200
Fax: 216-241-0816

The Huntington National Bank*(Major Banking Relationship)*
E. 9th at Euclid
Cleveland, OH 44114

Branches:

Meldrum & Fewsmith Advertising Inc. **(1)**
1350 Euclid Ave.
Cleveland, OH 44115
Tel.: 216-241-2141
Telex: 701199
Fax: 216-241-3929
Chris N. Perry *(Chm., Chief Exec. Officer & Exec. Creative Dir.)*
Robert Iredell, IV *(Vice Chm.)*
William C. Waldman *(Pres.)*
Bruce S. Childers *(Exec. V.P., Mktg. Services)*
William J. Brown *(V.P., Dir. Mktg.)*
Donna I. Post *(V.P., Opers. Admin.)*
Guy L. Shirk *(V.P., Grp. Supvr.)*
James Wojtkun *(V.P., Grp. Supvr.)*

Meldrum & Fewsmith Advertising Inc. **(1)**
37 W. Broad St., Ste. 480
Columbus, OH 43215
Tel.: 614-224-5222
Fax: 614-224-7007
Andrew R. Chiodo *(Mgr.)*

Meldrum & Fewsmith Yellow Pages Inc. **(1)**
1350 Euclid Ave.
Cleveland, OH 44115
Tel.: 216-241-2141
Fax: 216-566-0552
Bruce S. Childers *(Chm., Chief Exec. Officer)*
David O. Bowling *(Pres.)*

Excel Media Services Inc. **(1)**
1350 Euclid Ave.
Cleveland, OH 44115
Tel.: 216-241-2141
Fax: 216-241-8275
Bruce S. Childers *(Chm., Chief Exec. Officer)*
Patrick J. McDonough *(Pres.)*

Arocom Direct, Inc. **(1)**
1350 Euclid Ave.
Cleveland, OH 44115
Tel.: 216-696-9660
Fax: 216-479-2439
Leo J. LeFort *(Chm., Chief Exec. Officer)*
J. Keith Sutton *(Pres.)*

Arocom Marketing Group, Inc. **(1)**
1350 Euclid Ave.
Cleveland, OH 44115
Tel.: 216-696-9660
Fax: 216-479-2437
Leo J. LeFort *(Chm., Chief Exec. Officer)*
Michael J. Atwell *(Exec. V.P., Creative Dir.)*

Arocom Marketing Group, Inc. **(1)**
425 Jefferson Ave., Ste. 808
Toledo, OH 43604
Tel.: 419-241-9151
Fax: 419-241-5306
Mary G. Reinbolt *(Gen. Mgr.)*

Arocom Marketing Group, Inc. **(1)**
935 West Chestnut St.
Chicago, IL 60622
Tel.: 312-226-2699
Fax: 312-226-2363
Jeffrey A. Durski *(Gen. Mgr.)*

MELE MANUFACTURING CO., INC.
1712 Erie St.
Utica, NY 13503
Mailing Address:
P.O. Box 538
Utica, NY 13503
Tel.: 315-733-4600
Tel.: 800-635-6353
Fax: 315-733-3183
Year Founded: 1912
Emp.: 450
Fiscal Year-end: 6/30/91
Import Export
Manufactures Jewel Boxes, Musical & Nonmusical
S.I.C.: 3999
Edward V. Mele *(Chm. Bd.)*
Michael Valentine *(Pres.)*
Joseph E. Mele *(V.P.)*
Thomas J. Kinney *(Controller)*
Kevin J. Siembab *(Mgr.-Sls. & Mktg.)*
Joe Kiggins *(Pur. Agent)*

Computer Systems/Hardware:
IBM

MELLON CORPORATION
351 W. 35th St.
New York, NY 10001
Tel.: 212-563-5278
Fax: 212-967-5875
Sales Range: $20-39 Million
Emp.: 50
Carbon Paper, Apparel Paper, Textile Supplies, Bar Coding Inks & Ribbons
S.I.C.: 2299; 2679; 2893; 3955
J. Weston *(Pres.)*
S. Stevens *(V.P.)*
B. Jeffries *(Treas.)*
A. Alyn, Jr. *(Mgr.-Sls.)*
R. Scott *(Pur. Agent)*

Outside Service Firm(s):

Cooper & Dunham*(Legal Firm)*
New York, NY

European American Bank*(Major Banking Relationship)*
New York, NY

H.B. MELLOTT ESTATE, INC.
328 N. Second St.
McConnellsburg, PA 17233
Tel.: 717-485-3171
Fax: 717-485-5973
Sales Range: $10-19 Million
Emp.: 100
Crushed Limestone, Ready Mix Concrete, Custom Portable Crushing
S.I.C.: 1422; 3273
Forrest R. Mellott *(Pres.)*
Paul C. Mellott *(Chief Exec. Officer)*
Paul C. Mellott Jr. *(Exec. V.P.)*

Outside Service Firm(s):

Smith, Elliott, Kearns & Co.*(Auditors)*
Hagerstown, MD

First National Bank*(Major Banking Relationship)*
McConnellsburg, PA

MELLOY BROS. ENTERPRISES
7707 Lomas N.E.
Albuquerque, NM 87110
Tel.: 505-265-8721 **NM**
Fax: 505-268-0124
Emp.: 300
Investment Holding Company; New & Used Automobiles & Pickups
S.I.C.: 6719; 5511
Robert E. Melloy *(Pres.)*
Patrick C. Melloy *(V.P., Sec. & Treas.)*

Outside Service Firm(s):

Valley National Bank*(Major Banking Relationship)*
Valley Center
Phoenix, AZ 85001
Tel.: 602-261-2900

Subsidiary:

Melloy Nissan **(1)**
7707 Lomas N.E.
Albuquerque, NM 87110
Tel.: 505-265-8721
New & Used Automobiles & Pickups
S.I.C.: 5511
Robert Melloy *(Pres.)*
Patrick Melloy *(Sec. & Treas.)*

MELODY FOODS, INC.
30777 Northwestern Hwy.
Farmington Hills, MI 48334
Tel.: 313-851-6990 **MI**
Fax: 313-851-9551
Year Founded: 1950
Assets: $31,633,742
Liabilities: $23,181,709
Net Worth: $8,452,033
Approx.Sls.: $106,888,000
Emp.: 312
Fiscal Year-end: 3/31/91
Processor & Wholesale Distributor of Dairy Products
S.I.C.: 2026; 2024; 5143
Sharkey T. George *(Chm. Bd.)*
Michael J. George *(Pres. & Chief Exec. Officer)*
Frederick J. Abraham *(Exec. V.P. & Chief Oper. Officer)*
William J. Fowler *(V.P.-Fin.)*
Stephen M. George *(V.P.-Mktg.-Ice Cream Div.)*
Rodney M. George *(V.P.-Mktg.)*
Robert George *(V.P.-Sls.)*
Maurice P. Geromette *(V.P.-Opers.)*
Philip Sattler *(V.P.-Information Systems)*
Thomas A. George *(Sec. & Treas.)*

Outside Service Firm(s):

Geller, Herbach, Shapero*(Auditors)*
Southfield, MI

Carson, Fischer & Potts*(Legal Firm)*
Birmingham, MI

Michigan National Bank*(Major Banking Relationship)*
Southfield, MI

Subsidiaries:

Lansing Dairy, Inc. **(1)**
2224 W. Willow
Lansing, MI 48917
Tel.: 517-485-7263
Fluid Milk
S.I.C.: 5143
Bruce BeVier *(Plant Mgr.)*

Pioneer Snacks **(1)**
3111 Industrial Rd.
Livonia, MI 48150
Tel.: 313-525-4000
Wholesale Distributor of Meat & Cheese Snacks
S.I.C.: 5142; 5143
Robert George *(Pres.)*

MEMBERS ONLY BY EUROPE CRAFT
441 Fifth Ave., 7th Fl.
New York, NY 10016
Tel.: 212-686-5050
Approx.Sls.: $90,000,000
Emp.: 150
Mfr. & Importers of Men's Outerwear & Sportswear
S.I.C.: 2329; 5136
Herbert Goldsmith *(Pres.)*
Michelle Goldsmith *(Dir.-Mktg. Services)*

MEMPHIS GROUP, INC.
3900 Willow Lake Blvd.
Memphis, TN 38118
Tel.: 901-362-8600 **TN**
Fax: 901-365-1482
Year Founded: 1971
Approx.Sls.: $32,000,000
Emp.: 100
Wholesale Distributor of Aircraft Engines & Engine Parts; Aircraft Equipment & Supplies; Aircraft Electrical Equipment Repair
S.I.C.: 5088; 7629
John A. Williams *(Pres.)*
John M. Temple *(Exec. V.P.)*
Carolyn Williams *(Sec.)*

Outside Service Firm(s):

Sovran Bank*(Major Banking Relationship)*
Memphis, TN

MEMPHIS LIGHT, GAS & WATER
220 S. Main St.
Memphis, TN 38103
Mailing Address:
P.O. Box 430
Memphis, TN 38101-0403
Tel.: 901-528-4736
Fax: 901-528-4086
Year Founded: 1939
Approx.Sls.: $806,741,000
Emp.: 2,910
Fiscal Year-end: 12/31/90
Public Utility
S.I.C.: 8611
James McWillie *(Chm.-Bd. Commissioners)*
Elsie Boaz *(Vice Chm.)*
William Crawford *(Pres. & Chief Exec. Officer)*
Paul S. Harris *(Sr. V.P.-Opers. & Fin.)*
Joyce Blackman *(Sr. V.P.-Admin. Support)*
Ken Cole *(V.P.-Public Affairs)*
Curtis L. Dillihunt *(V.P.-Customer Service & Mktg.)*
Sandy Novick *(V.P.-Opers.)*
Paula Payne *(V.P.-Support Services)*
Peggy Prater-Harvey *(V.P.-Human Resources)*
Larry Thompson *(V.P.-Construction & Maintenance)*
Herman Morris *(Gen. Counsel)*
Michael L. Magness *(Mgr.-Personnel)*
John A. Fite *(Mgr.-Internal Audit)*
Thomas McCormack *(Mgr.-Pur. & Stores)*
Ted Reynolds *(Mgr.-Mngmt. Information Services)*
Carolyn Turman *(Mgr.-Training & Devel.)*
Gene McKnatt *(Supvr.-Telecommunications Engrng.)*
Mark Heuberger *(Supvr.-Communications)*

MEMPHIS PUBLISHING COMPANY
495 Union Ave.
Memphis, TN 38101
Tel.: 901-529-2211
Fax: 901-529-2362
Year Founded: 1840
Emp.: 1,150
Publishes The Commercial Appeal Newspaper
S.I.C.: 2711
Joseph R. Williams *(Gen. Mgr.)*
Lionel Linder *(Editor)*
Ken McNamee *(Controller)*
Warren Funk *(Dir.-Personnel)*
Lester Gingold *(Dir.-Major Accts.)*
Tom Harrison *(Dir.-Circulation)*
Jim Hamilton *(Dir.-Production & Mngmt. Information Systems)*
Richard Remmert *(Dir.-Adv.)*
David Swearingen *(Dir.-Mktg.)*
Robbie Jones *(Mgr.-Pur.)*
Bill Joyner *(Mgr.-Display Adv.)*
Mike Stanley *(Mgr.-Classified Adv.)*

Outside Service Firm(s):

Baker & Hostetler*(Auditors)*
Memphis, TN

Deloitte & Touche*(Auditors)*
Memphis, TN

Union Planters National Bank*(Major Banking Relationship)*
Memphis, TN

MENARD ELECTRIC COOPERATIVE
122 S. 6th St.
Petersburg, IL 62675
Mailing Address:
P.O. Box 279,
Petersburg, IL 62675
Tel.: 217-632-7746 **IL**
Fax: 217-632-2578
Year Founded: 1936
Assets: $21,986,461
Liabilities: $14,523,469
Net Worth: $7,462,992
Approx.Sls.: $12,905,556
Emp.: 38
Fiscal Year-end: 12/31/91
Distributor of Electric Energy
S.I.C.: 4911
Warren D. Goetsch *(Pres.)*
Caroll F. Cline *(V.P.)*
Dorland W. Smith *(Gen. Mgr.)*
Robert I. Brauer *(Treas.)*
Meredith Worner *(Sec.)*
David H. Crosnoe *(Systems Engr.)*
Wayne E. Jones *(Office Mgr.)*
Earl L. Pillsbury *(Special Services Coord.)*

Computer Systems/Hardware:
Digital

Outside Service Firm(s):

R. L. Quint*(Auditors)*
Mission, KS

Grosboll, Becker, Tice, Alverez & Smith*(Legal Firm)*
122 S. 6th St.
Petersburg, IL

National Bank of Petersburg*(Major Banking Relationship)*
Petersburg, IL

MENASHA CORPORATION
1645 Bergstrom Rd.
Neenah, WI 54957-0818
Mailing Address:
P.O. Box 367,
Neenah, WI 54957-0367
Tel.: 414-751-1000
Fax: 414-751-1236
Year Founded: 1849
Assets: $381,000,000
Liabilities: $137,000,000
Net Worth: $244,000,000
Approx.Sls.: $613,000,000
Emp.: 4,000
Fiscal Year-end: 12/31/90
Import Export
Manufacturer of Corrugated Containers, Wood Fiber, Paper board, Timber, Plastics, Product Identification Items; Commercial Printing
S.I.C.: 0811; 2631; 2679; 2411; 3089; 2653; 2752; 2754; 2759
Corporate Giving Program: Company Funded Menasha Corporation Foundation
Employee Matching Gifts Program: Matching Gifts to Private Colleges & Universities
D. C. Shepard *(Chm. Bd.)*
Walter H. Drew *(Pres. & Chief Exec. Officer)*
William C. Griffith *(V.P. & Chief Fin. Officer)*
James J. Sarosiek *(V.P., Gen. Counsel & Sec.)*
Donald Riviere *(V.P.-Mktg. & Plng.)*
David Rust *(V.P.-Human Resources)*

Daniel Ankeney *(Treas.)*
Ken J. Bonkoski *(Controller)*
Steven H. Kromholtz *(Corp. Grants Contact)*
Roger Ackerman *(Pur. Dir.)*
Dennis Biederman *(Mgr.-Mngmt. Information Systems)*
Raymond Roth *(Insurance Mgr.)*

No. of Mfg. Plants/Facilities: 49
No. of Foreign Offices: 2

Computer Systems/Hardware:
Burroughs

Outside Service Firm(s):

Arthur Andersen & Co.*(Auditors)*
777 E. Wisconsin Ave., P.O. Box 1215
Milwaukee, WI 53202
Tel.: 414-271-5100
Fax: 414-283-3200

Aetna Life & Casualty*(Group Insurer)*
151 Farmington Avenue
Hartford, CT 06156
Tel.: 203-273-2128
Fax: 203-729-4295

First Wisconsin National Bank*(Major Banking Relationship)*
777 E. Wisconsin Ave.
Milwaukee, WI 53202
Tel.: 414-765-4321
Fax: 414-355-6903

First Chicago Shareholder Services Trust Co.*(Pension Manager)*
153 West 51st St.
New York, NY 10019
Tel.: 212-791-6422
Fax: 212-385-9798

The Principal Financial Group*(Pension Manager)*
711 High St.
Des Moines, IA 50309
Tel.: 515-247-4593
Tel.: 800-543-4015

Subsidiaries:

Menasha Development Corporation **(1)**
P.O. Box 367
Neenah, WI 54957-0367
Tel.: 414-751-1000

Menasha Foreign Sales Corporation **(1)**
P.O. Box 367
Neenah, WI 54957-0367
Tel.: 414-751-1000 (100%)

Menasha Transport Inc. **(1)**
P.O. Box 367
Neenah, WI 54957-0367
Tel.: 414-751-1000 (100%)

MENDELSOHN/ZIEN ADVERTISING, INC.
Westwood Gateway, 11111 Santa Monica Blvd., Ste. 2250
Los Angeles, CA 90025-3356
Tel.: 310-824-1990
Fax: 310-208-6521
Year Founded: 1984
Approx.Billings: $12,300,000
Emp.: 12
Consumer Products
Richard Zien *(Pres.)*
Linda Krakowsky *(V.P., Acct. Dir.)*

Computer Systems/Hardware:
MacIntosh

A. W. MENDENHALL CO., INC.
2301 Lunt Ave.
Elk Grove Village, IL 60007
Tel.: 708-952-9000
Fax: 708-952-9016
Year Founded: 1917
Approx.Sls.: $75,000,000
Emp.: 144
Redistributor & Mfr.'s Rep for Paper, Plastic Aluminum & Allied Prods. For Sale To the Wholesale Trade
S.I.C.: 5111; 5162; 5051
Hal Wolken *(Pres. & Chief Exec. Officer)*
Joseph Vlach *(V.P.-Admin.)*

Computer Systems/Hardware:
IBM System 36

Subsidiary:

Bleyco Paper Co. of Michigan **(1)**
951 Front St.
Burr Oak, MI 49030
Tel.: 616-489-5061
S.I.C.: 5111

MENDENHALL & LEISTRA
60 Monroe Center N.W., Ste. 1100
Grand Rapids, MI 49503
Tel.: 616-451-2632
Fax: 616-451-2176
Year Founded: 1976
Approx.Billings: $15,000,000
Emp.: 21
William Mendenhall *(Chm.)*
Wayne Leistra *(Pres.)*
Sonya DeWitt *(Fin.)*

MENNEN MEDICAL INC.
10123 Main St.
Clarence, NY 14031
Tel.: 716-759-6921 **NY**
Fax: 716-759-2816
Year Founded: 1963
Approx.Sls.: $32,000,000
Emp.: 330
Import Export
Mfr. of Medical Patient Monitoring Systems
S.I.C.: 3841; 3845
Dr. Ehud Geller *(Chm. & Chief Exec. Officer)*
Herbert Mennen *(Pres.)*
Moshe Barone *(V.P.-Sls. & Mktg.)*
Yossi Elaz *(V.P.-Engrng.)*
Joseph Faraci *(Dir.-Fin.)*

No. of Mfg. Plants/Facilities: 2
No. of Foreign Offices: 4

Outside Service Firm(s):

Coopers & Lybrand*(Auditors)*
Buffalo, NY

Saperston & Day, P.C.*(Legal Firm)*
1500 Liberty Bank Bldg.
Buffalo, NY 14202
Tel.: 716-856-5400

Marine Midland Bank*(Major Banking Relationship)*
P.O. Box 803, 1 Marine Midland Center, 23rd Floor
Buffalo, NY 14203
Tel.: 716-841-2582

MENU FOODS, INC.
(Formerly Cadillac Pet Foods, Inc.)
9130 Griffith Morgan Lane
Pennsauken, NJ 08110
Tel.: 609-662-7412
Fax: 609-662-4673
Year Founded: 1940
Approx.Sls.: $18,000,000
Emp.: 120
Import Export
Cadillac Dog & Cat Foods
S.I.C.: 2047
Donald Green *(Chm. Bd. & Sr. V.P. & Gen. Mgr.)*
Robert W. Bras *(Pres.)*
Douglas Havlam *(Chief Exec. Officer)*
John J. Dobbins *(V.P.-Sls.)*
Nick Iwanisziw *(V.P.-Mfg.)*
George Rittner *(Sec.)*
Dennis Ryan *(Controller)*

MERCER TRANSPORTATION CO.
1128 W. Main St.
Louisville, KY 40203
Tel.: 502-584-2301 **KY**
Fax: 502-584-2301, Ext. 422
Year Founded: 1977
Approx.Sls.: $100,000,000
Emp.: 141
Long-Haul Trucking Operating Irregular Routes
S.I.C.: 4213
William G. Howard *(Chm. Bd.)*
James L. Stone *(Pres.)*
John Sallot *(V.P.-Mktg. & Sls.)*
Annie W. Howard *(Sec. & Treas.)*
F.C. Bird *(Mgr.-Freight Opers.)*

No. of U.S. Offices: 50

Outside Service Firm(s):

Strothman & Co.*(Auditors)*
Louisville, KY

Citizens Fidelity Bank & Trust Co.*(Major Banking Relationship)*
P.O. Box 33000-Citizens Plaza
Louisville, KY 40232
Tel.: 502-581-3381

MERCHANDISING EQUIPMENT GROUP
3025 W. Salt Creek Ln.
Arlington Heights, IL 60005
Tel.: 708-398-3338
Approx.Sls.: $55,000,000
Emp.: 900
Mfr. of Production Metal Store Fixtures; Mfr. & Designer of Wood Store Fixtures, Display Equip., Storage Shelving Systems, Pharmacy Equip.
S.I.C.: 2541; 2542
William D. Davis *(Pres. & Chief Exec. Officer)*
Bernard Camarda *(V.P.-Sls. & Mktg.)*
Garry G. Chamberlain *(V.P.-Mfg.)*
Thomas L. Phillips *(Natl. Sls. Mgr.-Chain Sls.)*
Mike Owens *(Mgr.-Western Div.)*
Bob Reidy *(Mgr.-Eastern Div.)*
Robert W. Anderson *(Plant Mgr.)*

Groups:

Merchandising Equipment Group **(1)**
3025 W. Salt Creek Lane
Arlington Heights, IL 60005
Tel.: 708-398-2400

Merchandising Equipment Group, National Marketing **(1)**
3025 W. Salt Creek Lane
Arlington Heights, IL 60005
Tel.: 708-398-3338
William D. Davis *(Sr. V.P.-Mktg.)*

MERCHANT CAPITAL GROUP LTD
135 S. LaSalle Street Ste. 1030
Chicago, IL 60603
Tel.: 312-419-4700 **DE**
Fax: 312-419-4754
Approx.Sls.: $46,000,000
Emp.: 350
Overhead Metal Garage Doors; Silk Screen Imprinted Apparel; Sportswear (T-Shirts, Fleece) For Men Women, & Children
S.I.C.: 3442; 2321; 2325; 2331; 2339; 2396
Eugene C. Cashman *(Chm. Bd.)*
Charles R. O'Hara *(V.P.)*
Richard W. Vetter *(V.P.)*
Eugene J. Berens *(Treas.)*
Randy Evangelidis *(Corp. Sec.)*

No. of Mfg. Plants/Facilities: 5
No. of U.S. Offices: 4

Outside Service Firm(s):

Querry & Harrow Ltd.*(Legal Firm)*
35th Fl., 135 LaSalle St.
Chicago, IL 60603

Ernst & Young*(Auditors)*
233 S. Wacker Dr.
Chicago, IL 60606
Tel.: 312-368-1800
Fax: 312-645-3095

Continental Bank, N.A.*(Major Banking Relationship)*
30 N. LaSalle St.
Chicago, IL 60693

Subsidiaries:

General American Door Company **(1)**
5050 Base Line Rd.
Montgomery, IL 60538
Tel.: 708-859-3000
Fax: 708-859-8122
Emp.: 250
Overhead Garage Doors; Metal Siding
S.I.C.: 3442; 3444
Joseph C. Kee *(Chm. Bd. & Pres.)*
Ronald D. Brazener *(V.P. & Chief Fin. Officer)*
Ted Billman *(V.P.-Sls.)*
Larry Herker *(V.P.& Mktg.)*
Charles R. O'Hara *(V.P.)*
Robert Pfennig *(V.P.-Opers.)*
Michael Adam *(Pur. Agent)*

LSJ Sportswear Inc. **(1)**
P.O. Box 528, 54 Golf Car Rd.
Deerfield, WI 53531
Tel.: 608-764-5425
Fax: 608-764-5159
Emp.: 40
Silk-Screen Imprinted T-Shirts& Fleece; Sportswear Men, Women, & Children
S.I.C.: 2321; 2325; 2331; 2339; 2396
Stephen E. Smith *(Chm. Bd. & Pres.)*
Charles R. O'Hara *(V.P.)*
Stewart P. Ramsey *(Treas. & Sec.)*

Merchants Distributors, Inc.
(Acquired by Alex Lee, Inc.)

MERCHANTS PUBLISHING CO.
(d/b/a Universal Litho)
3500 Sprinkle Rd.
Kalamazoo, MI 49002
Tel.: 616-342-7457 **MI**
Fax: 616-345-6999
Approx.Sls.: $13,000,000
Mfr. of Label Printing & General Commercial Lithography
S.I.C.: 2752
Mark Jack Fleming *(Chm. Bd., Pres. & Chief Exec. Officer)*
Rodney Woodworth *(Chief Fin. Officer)*

MERCHANTS RENT A CAR, INC.
1278 Hooksett Rd.
Hooksett, NH 03106
Mailing Address:
P.O. Box 395,
Hooksett, NH 03106
Tel.: 603-669-4100 **NH**
Fax: 603-622-3895
Year Founded: 1962
Assets: $45,934,813
Liabilities: $34,870,383
Net Worth: $11,064,430
Approx.Sls.: $88,000,000
Emp.: 200
Fiscal Year-end: 6/30/88
Leasing & Rental Of Vehicles, Car Sales
S.I.C.: 5511; 7514; 7515
Bernice Singer *(Pres.)*
Stephen H. Singer *(Exec. V.P.)*
Alan Singer *(V.P.)*
Jeffrey Singer *(V.P.)*
Gary J. Singer *(V.P.)*
Michael H. Sydney *(V.P.)*
Robert Singer *(V.P.)*
Robert Movine *(Controller)*
Jeffrey Levine *(Gen. Counsel)*

Merchants Rent A Car, Inc.—(Continued)

Outside Service Firm(s):

Nathan Wechsler & Company*(Auditors)*
Concord, NH

Jeffery Levine Esq.*(Legal Firm)*
Hooksett, NH

First New Hampshire Bank*(Major Banking Relationship)*
Manchester, NH

MERCHANTS TRUCK LINE, INC.
125 Snyder St.
New Albany, MS 38652
Tel.: 601-534-7655
Fax: 601-534-2945
Approx.Sls.: $26,000,000
Emp.: 500
Long Distance Trucking
S.I.C.: 4213
Gene Tate *(Pres.)*
Chuck Clowdis *(V.P.-Sls. & Opers.)*
James E. Roberson *(Sec. & Treas.)*

Outside Service Firm(s):

Peoples Bank & Trust Company*(Major Banking Relationship)*
Tupelo, MS

MERCURY COMPUTER SYSTEMS, INC.
600 Suffolk St.
Lowell, MA 01854
Tel.: 508-458-3100
Fax: 508-458-9580
Year Founded: 1983
Assets: $12,214,000
Liabilities: $10,353,000
Net Worth: $1,861,000
Sales Range: $40-59 Million
Emp.: 130
Fiscal Year-end: 6/30/91
Export
Special Purpose Computing Systems for Numerically Intensive Applications
S.I.C.: 3577
Jay Bertelli *(Chm. Bd., Pres. & Chief Exec. Officer)*
John I. Anderson *(V.P.-Fin. & Admin.)*
David Bertelli *(V.P.-Human Resources)*
Robert Frisch *(V.P.)*
John Nitzsche *(V.P.-Hardware Engrng.)*
Robert Siegel *(V.P.-Software Engrng.)*
Es Marcato *(Dir.-Business Devel.)*
Graham Smith *(Dir.-Intl. Sls.)*
Linda Vasquez *(Mgr.-Pur.)*

Outside Service Firm(s):

Coopers & Lybrand*(Auditors)*
1 Post Office Square
Boston, MA 02110
Tel.: 617-574-5000
Fax: 617-345-0398

Hutchins & Wheeler*(Legal Firm)*
101 Federal St.
Boston, MA 02110
Tel.: 617-725-1500

Bay Bank Middlesex*(Major Banking Relationship)*
Burlington, MA

MERCURY DISTRIBUTING CO., INC.
9600 Lurline Ave.
Chatsworth, CA 91311
Tel.: 818-998-1811
Fax: 818-998-4286
Year Founded: 1944
Approx.Sls.: $34,500,000
Emp.: 130
Wholesale Beauty Supplies, Drug Sundries & Cosmetic Accessories
S.I.C.: 5122; 5087
Edward Nave *(Chm. Bd.)*
Michael Nave *(Pres.)*
Larry Jaffee *(V.P.-Fin.)*

Outside Service Firm(s):

Ernst & Young*(Auditors)*
515 S. Flower St.
Los Angeles, CA 90071
Tel.: 213-621-1666

Union Bank*(Major Banking Relationship)*
North Hollywood, CA

Meridian
COMMUNICATIONS

MERIDIAN COMMUNICATIONS
444 E. Main, Ste. 200
Lexington, KY 40507
Tel.: 606-252-3350
Tel.: 800-366-4426
Fax: 606-254-5511
Year Founded: 1975
Approx.Billings: $17,500,000
Emp.: 46
Business-to-Business & Retail Adv.; Public Relations/Special Events; Production Oriented
Mary Ellen Slone *(Pres.)*
Don Van Erden *(Sr. V.P., Mktg.)*
Jim Gleason *(V.P., Communications)*

Computer Systems/Hardware:
IBM, MacIntosh, Adman

MERIDIAN INDUSTRIES, INC.
100 E. Wisconsin, Ste. 2750
Milwaukee, WI 53202
Tel.: 414-224-0610 WI
Fax: 414-224-9544
Year Founded: 1944
Approx.Sls.: $120,000,000
Emp.: 900
Fiscal Year-end: 10/31/91
Import
Mfr. of Cosmetic Applicators, Dairy Filters, Medical Products, Polyurethane Products; Contract Manufacturing & Packaging; Textile Converting & Combining of Shoe Fabrics, Custom Bleaching, Dyeing & Finishing of Natural & Synthetic Yarns & Cotton Fabrics
S.I.C.: 2231; 2261; 2295; 2834; 3069; 3842; 3070; 3800
Bruce E. Pindyck *(Chm. Bd. & Chief Exec. Officer)*
Gerald P. Teske *(Exec. V.P. & Treas.)*
Mary E. Pindyck *(V.P. & Asst. Sec.)*
Richard H. Miller *(Sec.)*

No. of Mfg. Plants/Facilities: 10

Outside Service Firm(s):

Arthur Andersen & Co.*(Auditors)*
777 E. Wisconsin Ave., P.O. Box 1215
Milwaukee, WI 53202
Tel.: 414-271-5100
Fax: 414-283-3200

First Wisconsin National Bank*(Major Banking Relationship)*
777 E. Wisconsin Ave.
Milwaukee, WI 53202
Tel.: 414-765-4321
Fax: 414-355-6903

Foley & Lardner*(Legal Firm)*
777 E. Wisconsin Ave.
Milwaukee, WI 53202
Tel.: 414-271-2400

Division:

Belmont Dyers Company **(1)**
10 Linestowe Dr.
Belmont, NC 28012
Tel.: 704-825-4242
Yarn Purchasing & Dyeing
S.I.C.: 2231
Clint Simpkins *(Pres.)*

MERIDIAN TECHNOLOGY LEASING SERVICES
570 Lake Cook Rd.
Deerfield, IL 60015
Tel.: 708-940-1200
Tel.: 800-426-3090 IL
Fax: 708-940-8062
Year Founded: 1979
Approx.Sls.: $477,000,000
Emp.: 280
Fiscal Year-end: 6/30/92
Import Export
Computers, Telecommunications & Other Capital Equipment Leasing
S.I.C.: 6159; 7377
Patrice Courbey *(Chm. Bd. & Pres.)*
Ian Pye *(Chief Fin. Officer)*
John Peck, Jr. *(Exec. V.P.-Sls., Telemarketing & Opers.)*
Michael Brannan *(V.P. & Treas.)*
Keith Olenek *(V.P.-Sls-National Accts.)*
Denis Pepin *(V.P.-Sls., Western Div.)*
Martin Robins *(V.P. & Gen. Counsel)*
Dan Zuppardo *(V.P.-Sls., Eastern Div.)*
Jim Leman *(Dir.-Sls. & Mktg.)*

No. of U.S. Offices: 21

Computer Systems/Hardware:
DEC VAX, IBM-Compatible PC's

MERITCARE, INC.
One PPG Place, Ste. 2260
Pittsburgh, PA 15222
Tel.: 412-391-4469 DE
Fax: 412-391-6382
Year Founded: 1986
Assets: $39,000,000
Liabilities: $29,000,000
Net Worth: $10,000,000
Sales Range: $20-39 Million
Emp.: 4,700
Own & Operate Long-Term Care Facilities
S.I.C.: 8059; 8051
Thomas Konig *(Pres. & Chief Exec. Officer)*
Jan Beresford *(Chief Oper. Officer)*
James Wilkinsom *(Chief Fin. Officer & Gen. Counsel)*
Frank E. Wyman *(Data Processing Dir.)*

No. of Mfg. Plants/Facilities: 25
No. of U.S. Offices: 5

Computer Systems/Hardware:
Care Computer Systems

Outside Service Firm(s):

Ernst & Young*(Auditors)*
2000 Pittsburgh Natl. Bldg.
Pittsburgh, PA 15222
Tel.: 412-644-7800
Fax: 412-644-7419

Johnson & Higgins*(Commercial Insurance Carrier)*
Pittsburgh, PA

Paine Webber*(Investment Banker)*
1285 Ave. of the Americas
New York, NY 10019
Tel.: 212-713-2000
Fax: 212-713-3010

Equicor*(Group Insurer)*
New York, NY

Buchanan, Ingersoll p.c.*(Legal Firm)*
600 Grant St., 57th Flr.
Pittsburgh, PA 15219
Tel.: 412-562-8800

Pittsburgh National Bank*(Major Banking Relationship)*
Stock Transfer Dept., Fifth & Wood Streets
Pittsburgh, PA 15265

Subsidiaries:

Carriage House Manor **(1)**
901 Ernston Rd.
South Amboy, NJ 08879
Tel.: 908-721-8200 (100%)
Nursing Home
S.I.C.: 8059
Nicholas Dubner *(Admin.)*

Carriage House Manor **(1)**
245 E. Wilshire
Fullerton, CA 92632
Tel.: 714-871-6020 (100%)
Nursing Home
S.I.C.: 8059
Carol DeMarco *(Admin.)*

Majestic Pines Care Center **(1)**
1628 "B" St.
Hayward, CA 94541
Tel.: 510-582-4636 (100%)
Nursing Home
S.I.C.: 8059
Mary Ann Reynolds *(Admin.)*

Parkmont Nursing Home **(1)**
2400 Parkside Dr.
Fremont, CA 94536
Tel.: 415-793-7222 (100%)
Nursing Home
S.I.C.: 8059
Imogene Ellwinger *(Admin.)*

Twin Palms Care Center **(1)**
11900 E. Artesia Blvd.
Artesia, CA 90701
Tel.: 310-865-0271 (100%)
Nursing Home
S.I.C.: 8059
Catherine M. Eichberg *(Admin.)*

Valley Manor Care **(1)**
3806 Clayton Rd.
Concord, CA 94521
Tel.: 415-689-2266 (100%)
Nursing Home
S.I.C.: 8059
Vicki Johnson *(Admin.)*

MERLE NORMAN COSMETICS, INC.
9130 Bellanca Ave.
Los Angeles, CA 90045
Tel.: 310-641-3000 CA
Fax: 310-641-7144
Year Founded: 1930
Assets: $74,000,000
Earnings: $9,700,000
Net Worth: $74,000,000
Approx.Sls.: $95,000,000
Emp.: 850
Fiscal Year-end: 12/31/90
Mfr. Cosmetics
S.I.C.: 2844
J.B. Nethercutt *(Chm. Bd. & Chief Exec. Officer)*
Gary Hollister *(Pres.)*
Robert Dressler *(Exec. V.P.)*
Dick Nolind *(Exec. V.P.)*
Marvin Landon *(V.P.-Personnel)*
Thomas Smith *(V.P.-Pur.)*
William Miller *(Controller & Treas.)*
Arthur O. Armstrong *(Admin. Officer & Sec.)*
Tony Barrett *(Dir.-Information Systems)*
James Bridgeman *(Dir.-Data Processing)*
Brian Talbott *(Dir.-Prods.)*

Computer Systems/Hardware:
IBM 4341

Outside Service Firm(s):

Deloitte & Touche*(Auditors)*
21550 Oxnard St., Ste. 800
Woodland Hills, CA 91367-7100
Tel.: 818-593-4800
Fax: 818-347-4278

Equitable Real Estate Investment Managment Inc.*(Group Insurer)*
3414 Peachtree Rd. N.E.
Atlanta, GA 30326-1162

Armstrong, Hendler & Hirsch*(Legal Firm)*
1888 Century Park East
Los Angeles, CA 90067
Tel.: 310-553-0305

Union Bank*(Major Banking Relationship)*
445 S. Figueroa St.
Los Angeles, CA 90071
Tel.: 213-236-5076

MERLING, MARX & SEIDMAN, INC.
440 Park Ave. South
New York, NY 10016
Tel.: 212-683-2100
Tel.: 800-696-4795
Year Founded: 1964
Approx.Billings: $15,800,000
Emp.: 55
Arthur A. Marx *(Pres. & Chief Exec. Officer)*
Sheldon H. Marx *(Exec. V.P.)*
Jeanette Kelley *(V.P., Mktg. Medical Grp.)*
Christine Shom *(Controller)*
Carmen Costa *(Exec. Mgr.)*

STAN MERRITT INC./ ADVERTISING
369 Lexington Ave.
New York, NY 10017
Tel.: 212-867-4650
Fax: 212-983-5832
Year Founded: 1971
Approx.Billings: $29,000,000
Emp.: 16
Advertising Agency
S.I.C.: 7311
Jeffrey W. Clapp, Jr. *(Chm. & New Bus. Contact)*
Stanley S. Merritt *(Pres. & Chief Exec. Officer)*
Lynne King *(Exec. V.P.)*
Bernard Ackerman *(Gen. Counsel)*

No. of U.S. Offices: 2

Branch:

Stan Merritt Inc./Advertising **(1)**
2400 E. Devon Ave.
Des Plaines, IL 60018
Tel.: 708-390-8880

MERSMAN FURNITURE
500 W. Wayne St.
Celina, OH 45822
Tel.: 419-586-2351
Year Founded: 1897
Approx.Sls.: $10,000,000
Emp.: 150
Fiscal Year-end: 12/31/90
Tables, Bookcases, Desks & Other Living Room Furniture
S.I.C.: 2511
James W. Simons *(Pres.)*
James Jones *(Sr. V.P.-Sls. & Mktg.)*
Terry Johnson *(Controller)*
Gene Brunswick *(Dir.-Data Processing)*
Monty Hathaway *(Dir.-Pur.)*
Carey Simons *(Mgr.-Personnel)*
Bob Linn *(Mgr.-Mfg.)*
Gene Reichert *(Pur. Agent)*

MESA CITRUS GROWERS
254 W. Broadway
Mesa, AZ 85210
Tel.: 602-964-8615 **AZ**
Fax: 602-834-0764
Approx.Sls.: $10,000,000
Emp.: 25
Fruit Crops Market Preparation Services
S.I.C.: 0723
Jim Mast *(Gen. Mgr.)*
Gerald Hirsch *(Mgr.-Office)*

Outside Service Firm(s):

Valley National Bank*(Major Banking Relationship)*
Mesa, AZ

MESIROW FINANCIAL
350 N. Clark St.
Chicago, IL 60610
Tel.: 312-670-6000 **DE**
Fax: 312-670-6257
Year Founded: 1937
Approx.Sls.: $59,000,000
Emp.: 368
Fiscal Year-end: 3/31/91
Financial Services Company
S.I.C.: 6211; 6282; 6798; 6799
Lester A. Morris *(Chm. Bd.)*
James C. Tyree *(Chief Exec. Officer)*
Eve Slusarczyk *(Chief Fin. Officer)*
Julie VanderWeele *(Sr. V.P.-Mktg.)*
Dale Swanson *(V.P.-Human Resources)*
Ruth C. Hannenberg *(Sec. & Legal Officer)*
Lawrence Williams *(Dir.-Data Processing)*

Computer Systems/Hardware:
IBM

Outside Service Firm(s):

Coopers & Lybrand*(Auditors)*
203 N. LaSalle St.
Chicago, IL 60601
Tel.: 312-701-5500

Goldberg, Kohn, Bell, Black & Rosenbloom*(Legal Firm)*
55 E. Monroe
Chicago, IL 60603
Tel.: 312-332-2177
Fax: 312-332-2196

First National Bank of Chicago*(Major Banking Relationship)*
One First National Plaza
Chicago, IL 60670
Tel.: 312-732-9781
Tel.: 312-732-4050
Fax: 312-732-4840
Fax: 312-732-3055

MESSENGER CORPORATION
110 S. 41st Ave.
Phoenix, AZ 85009
Tel.: 602-272-2944 **AZ**
Fax: 602-352-2335
Year Founded: 1969
Approx.Sls.: $16,000,000
Emp.: 150
Commercial Printing; Lithographic; Graphic Arts & Related Design
S.I.C.: 2752; 7336
William C. Hammer *(Chm. Bd.)*
Joseph J. Marici *(Pres.)*
Larry Hurst *(Chief Fin. Officer)*

Outside Service Firm(s):

Valley National Bank*(Major Banking Relationship)*
3636 N. Central Av.
Phoenix, AZ 85038
Tel.: 602-261-1313

FRANK MESSER & SONS CONSTRUCTION CO.
(Sub. of Frank Messer & Sons Inc.-A Holding Co.)
4612 Paddock Rd.
Cincinnati, OH 45229
Tel.: 513-242-1541
Fax: 513-242-6467
Year Founded: 1932
Sales Range: $100-499 Million
General Construction & Construction Management of Commercial, Industrial, Medical, Retail Facilities, including Power Generation Facilities
S.I.C.: 1541; 1542
Alfred C. Berndsen *(Chm. Bd.)*
Peter S. Strange *(Pres.)*
Kathleen C. Daly *(Treas. & Sec.)*
Joseph D. Glassmeyer, Jr. *(Dir.-Safety)*
Thomas M. Keckeis *(V.P.)*
Edward H. Miller *(V.P.-Bus. Devel.)*
Bernard P. Suer *(V.P.)*

No. of U.S. Offices: 1

Computer Systems/Hardware:
Data General

Outside Service Firm(s):

Arthur Andersen & Co.*(Auditors)*
425 Walnut St.
Cincinnati, OH 45202
Tel.: 513-381-6900

United States Fidelity & Guaranty Co.*(Commercial Insurance Carrier)*
100 Light Street
Baltimore, MD 21202
Tel.: 301-547-3000

Taft, Stettinius & Hollister*(Legal Firm)*
First Natl. Bank Center
Cincinnati, OH 45202
Tel.: 513-381-2838

Star Bank*(Major Banking Relationship)*
425 Walnut Street
Cincinnati, OH 45202
Tel.: 513-632-4000

METABO CORPORATION
1231 Wilson Dr.
West Chester, PA 19380
Tel.: 215-436-5900
Fax: 215-436-9072
Approx.Sls.: $20,000,000
Emp.: 60
Mfr. of Industrial Hand Tools
S.I.C.: 3546; 3291
John Ham *(Exec. V.P. & Gen. Mgr.)*
David Smith *(V.P.-Sls. & Mktg.)*
Dave Johnson *(Controller)*
Gary S. Young *(Gen. Counsel)*

METAL MASTERS FOODSERVICE EQUIPMENT
655 Glenwood Ave., W.
Smyrna, DE 19977
Tel.: 302-653-3000 **MD**
Fax: 302-653-2065
Year Founded: 1978
Approx.Sls.: $30,000,000
Emp.: 400
Export
Mfr. of Stainless Steel Ware
S.I.C.: 3914
Larry N. McAllister *(Pres.)*
Randolph Fox *(V.P.-Fin., Treas. & Sec.)*
Gary Griffith *(V.P.-Engrng.)*
Scott Pelton *(V.P.-Mktg.)*
Julius Tilley *(V.P.-Mfg.)*
Glenn Hitchens *(Gen. Counsel)*
Robin C. Dickerson *(Mgr.-Pur.)*
Robin Dickerson *(Pur. Agent)*

Outside Service Firm(s):

Law, Casson & Co.*(Auditors)*
Dover, DE

METAL SEAL & PRODUCTS, INC.
4323 Hamann Pkwy.
Willoughby, OH 44094
Tel.: 216-946-8500 **OH**
Fax: 216-953-4984
Year Founded: 1953
Approx.Sls.: $23,000,000
Emp.: 230
Export
Mfr. of Screw Machine Products
S.I.C.: 3451
Edmund B. Diemer *(Pres. & Treas.)*
William T. Caine *(Exec. V.P.)*
Irving Diemer, Jr. *(V.P. & Sec.)*
Terry Reagan *(Controller)*
Linda Shaffer *(Dir.-Human Res.)*
Russell B. Diemer *(Mgr.-Plant)*
Alan Pirnat *(Mgr.-Sls.)*
David N. Saletrik *(Mgr.-Quality Control)*

No. of Mfg. Plants/Facilities: 4

Computer Systems/Hardware:
IBM3600

Outside Service Firm(s):

Swearingen & Swearingen*(Auditors)*
Cleveland, OH

National City Bank*(Major Banking Relationship)*
P.O. Box 92301, Corp. Trust Dept.
Cleveland, OH 44101
Tel.: 216-575-2000

METAL TRADES, INC.
4194 Hwy. 165
Hollywood, SC 29449
Tel.: 803-889-6441 **SC**
Fax: 803-889-6592
Approx.Sls.: $19,000,000
Emp.: 300
Building & Repairing Of Combat Vessels, Crew Boats, Dredges & Troop Transport Vessels; Jobbing & Repair Of Machine Shops
S.I.C.: 3731; 3599
James E. Corbin, Jr. *(Chm. Bd.)*
R.B. Corbin *(Pres.)*
Michael D. Roland *(Exec. V.P.)*
William D. Corbin *(Asst. V.P.)*
Richard F. Corbin *(Sec. & Treas.)*
James E. Corbin, III *(Pur. Agent)*

Outside Service Firm(s):

Gamble Givens & Moody*(Auditors)*
Charleston, SC

Bachman S. Smith, III*(Legal Firm)*
Charleston, SC

NationsBank South Carolina*(Major Banking Relationship)*
Charleston, SC

THE METAL WARE CORP.
1700 Monroe St.
Two Rivers, WI 54241
Mailing Address:
P.O. Box 237
Two Rivers, WI 54241
Tel.: 414-793-1368
Fax: 414-793-1086
Year Founded: 1920
Approx.Sls.: $12,000,000
Emp.: 100
Fiscal Year-end: 3/31/91
Import Export
Mfr. Home Electrical Appliances
S.I.C.: 3634
Wesley C. Drumm *(Chm. Bd., Pres. & Treas.)*
Robin Anderson *(V.P.-Sls. & Mktg.)*
Herbert Bunke *(V.P.-Mfg.)*
Richard B. Ott *(V.P.-Engineering)*
Victor F. Trastek *(V.P.-Adv. & Sls.)*
Linda L. Youngchild *(Corp. Sec. & Asst. Treas.)*
Gene Braun *(Mgr.-Personnel)*
Curtis W. Drumm *(Pur. Agent)*

No. of Mfg. Plants/Facilities: 1
No. of U.S. Offices: 1

Computer Systems/Hardware:
IBM

Outside Service Firm(s):

Conley, McDonald, & Co.*(Auditors)*
Milwaukee, WI

Liberty Life Assurance Co.*(Commercial Insurance Carrier)*
Dover, NH

Liberty Life Assurance Co.*(Group Insurer)*
Dover, NH

The Metal Ware Corp.—(Continued)

First Bank, N.A.*(Major Banking Relationship)*
201 W. Wisconsin Ave.
Milwaukee, WI 53259-1000
Tel.: 414-227-5474

Subsidiaries:

Aristo Manufacturing Co. **(1)**
1704 Monroe St.
Two Rivers, WI 54241
Tel.: 414-793-1000
Emp.: 3
Computer Systems/Hardware:
IBM System 36
Injection & Compression Molding of Thermoplastic
S.I.C.: 3089
Donald Paulus *(Gen. Mgr.)*

Monarch Ware, Inc. **(1)**
340 N. Water St.
Algoma, WI 54201
Tel.: 414-487-5236
Fax: 414-487-5239
Emp.: 75
Fiscal Year-end: 3/31/91
Metal Stamping; Porcelain Enameling
S.I.C.: 3469; 3479
W.C. Drumm *(Pres.)*
John Berner *(V.P.-Admin.)*
James J. Polzin *(V.P.-Mfg.)*
Victor Trastek *(V.P.-Adv. & Sls.)*
Robert Klein *(Natl. Sls. Mgr.)*

METALCENTER, INC.
12034 Greenstone Avenue
Santa Fe Springs, CA 90670
Tel.: 310-944-3322
Fax: 310-944-1346
Year Founded: 1986
Assets: $30,000,000
Liabilities: $22,000,000
Net Worth: $8,000,000
Sales Range: $80-99 Million
Emp.: 110
Distribute Stainless & Silicon Steel & Aluminum
S.I.C.: 5199
Joe D. Crider *(Chm. Bd. & Chief Exec. Officer)*
William Gimbel *(Vice Chm.)*
George J. Heuser *(Pres. & Chief Oper. Officer)*
David Hannah *(Chief Fin. Officer)*
Bettie Littell *(Sec. & Treas.)*
David Harridine *(Mgr.-Mktg.)*

No. of Mfg. Plants/Facilities: 1
No. of U.S. Offices: 1

Computer Systems/Hardware:
IBM

METALLOY CORPORATION
103 W. Main St.
Hudson, MI 49247
Tel.: 517-448-2521
Fax: 517-448-7156
Year Founded: 1945
Approx.Sls.: $45,000,000
Emp.: 500
Aluminum Die-castings
S.I.C.: 3363
David N. Berlin *(Chm. Bd. & Pres.)*
Philip A. Long *(V.P.-Mfg.)*
Robert Cavanaugh *(V.P.-Fin.)*
James K. Whitehouse *(Sec.)*
Roland Holmes *(Pur. Agent)*
Ken J. Smith *(Dir.-Engrng.)*

No. of Mfg. Plants/Facilities: 5

Outside Service Firm(s):

Ernst & Young*(Auditors)*
One Detroit Center, 500 Woodward, Ste. 1700
Detroit, MI 48243
Tel.: 313-259-9600

Manufacturers National Bank N.A.*(Major Banking Relationship)*
38th Fl., 100 Renaissance Center
Detroit, MI 48243
Tel.: 313-222-4227

METALLURG, INC.
25 E. 39th St.
New York, NY 10016
Tel.: 212-686-4010
Fax: 212-658-6280
Year Founded: 1947
Approx.Sls.: $600,000,000
Emp.: 2,800
Mfr. of Ferrous Alloys, Ores & Minerals, Aluminum Master Alloys
S.I.C.: 3313; 1061
Michael Standen *(Chm., Pres. & Chief Exec. Officer)*
Steven N. Rappaport *(Exec. V.P.)*
Michael A. Banks *(V.P.-Admin.)*
George J. Udcoff *(V.P.-Fin.)*
Michael A. Finn *(Sec.)*
Charles J. Jones *(Treas.)*
Principal(s):
Michael Standen
Charles J. Jones

No. of Mfg. Plants/Facilities: 7
No. of U.S. Offices: 6
No. of Foreign Offices: 12

Computer Systems/Hardware:
IBM System 36

Outside Service Firm(s):

Deloitte & Touche*(Auditors)*
1 World Trade Center
New York, NY 10048
Tel.: 212-669-5000

Hartman & Craven*(Legal Firm)*
460 Park Ave.
New York, NY 10022
Tel.: 212-753-7500

Subsidiaries:

Shieldalloy Metallurgical Corportation **(1)**
P.O. Box 768
Newfield, NJ 08344
Tel.: 609-692-4200
Telex: 510-687-8918
Telecopier: 609-692-4017
Dr. W. Fergus Porter *(Pres.)*

Frankel Metal Company **(1)**
19300 Filer Ave.
Detroit, MI 48234
Tel.: 313-366-5300
Telex: 23 0654 FRANKALLOY-DET
Fax: 313-366-5305
Kenneth I. MacLeod *(Pres.)*

Non-U.S. Holdings:

AB Ferrolegeringar **(1)**
Box 7163 S-103 88
Stockholm, Sweden
Tel.: 8 23 51 30 (100%)
Telex: 19122
Telecopier: 8-796-0636
Mfr. of Ferrous Alloys
S.I.C.: 3313
Bo Thunborg *(Mng. Dir.)*

Brandau y Compania S.A. **(1)**
Emillo Vargas, 15, 1 C 28043
Madrid, Spain
Tel.: 1 519 4728
Telex: 27 485 bracoe
Telecopier: 1 519 4694
Mfr. of Ferrous Alloys
S.I.C.: 3313
Hans Reich *(Dir.)*

Ferrolegeringar AG **(1)**
Zuerichstrasse 131 CH-8600
Dubendorf, Switzerland
Tel.: 1 801 6565 (100%)
Telex: 817 101
Telecopier: 1 801 0403
Emp.: 26
Sales of Electrometallurical Products, Except Steel
S.I.C.: 5051
A. Merk *(Mng. Dir.)*

Gesellschaft fur Elektrometallurgie m.b.H. **(1)**
Postfach 3520, 4000
Dusseldorf, 1, Germany
Tel.: 211-68830 (100%)
Telex: 858 6875
Telecopier: 211-688-3380
Dr. Olaf Kraus *(Mng. Dir.)*

London & Scandinavian Metallurgical Co. Limited **(1)**
45 Wimbledon Hill Road
London, SW19 7LZ, United Kingdom
Tel.: 81-947 1221 (100%)
Telex: 929830
Telecopier: 81 947-2966
Mfr. of Metallurgical Products
S.I.C.: 3313
Alan D. Ewart *(Joint Mng. Dir.)*
Dr. James Pearson *(Joint Mng. Dir.)*

Metalchimica srl **(1)**
Via San Pio V, 36 10125
Turino, Italy
Tel.: 11 669 2057
Telex: 221331
Telecopier: 11 669 8116
Mfr. of Metallurgical Products
S.I.C.: 3313
Vincenzo Fontana *(Mng. Dir.)*

Metallurg (Canada) Limited **(1)**
2700 Matheson Blvd. E.
Mississauga, ON L4W 4V9, Canada
Tel.: 416 238 1130 (100%)
Telex: 06 217582
Telecopier: 416 238 1333
Import of Alloys
S.I.C.: 3313
H. Nils Schooley *(Pres.)*

Metallurg Mexico, S.A. de CV **(1)**
Eucken 16-302 Colonia Anzures,
Mexico, D.F. 11590, Mexico
Tel.: 5 254 6986 (100%)
Telex: 1763016
Telecopier: 5 531 3362
Mfr. of Electrometallurgical Products
S.I.C.: 3313
Carlos Nunez *(Gen. Mgr.)*

Metallurg do Brazil Ltda. **(1)**
Rua Geraldo Flausino Gomes, 85-3 andar
Brooklin Novo - Ed. Tapajos, CEP: 04575
Sao Paulo, SP, Brazil
Tel.: 11 530 1682 (100%)
Telex: 53997
Telecopier: 11 535 5246
Mfr. of Metallurgical Products
S.I.C.: 3313
Erundino Diniz *(Pres.)*

Metallurg (Far East) Limited **(1)**
P.O. Box 5221, Tokyo Int. 10031
Tokyo, Japan
Tel.: 3-3591-0431 (100%)
Telex: Gelomet J 22772
Telecopier: 3-35 919060
Mfr. of Metallurgical Products
S.I.C.: 3313
Wolfgang Schedelbauer *(Mng. Dir.)*

The Aluminum Powder Company **(1)**
Forge Lane Minworth,
Sutton Coldfield, West Midlands B76 8AF, United Kingdom
Tel.: 21-351-4686
Fax: 21-351-7604
S.I.C.: 3313

Turk Maadin Sirketi A.S. **(1)**
Kemeralti Cad. 24/4 Karakoy Ticaret Merkizi,
Istanbul, Turkey
Tel.: 1-249-7700 (100%)
Telex: 25180
Telecopier: 1-249-2952
Mfr. of Ferrous Alloys
S.I.C.: 3313
Melih Turhan *(Joint Mng. Dir.)*
Selahattin Aydiner *(Joint Mng. Dir.)*

Subsidiary:

Elektrowerk Weisweiler GmbH **(2)**
Durener Strasse Postfach 7209, D-5180
Eschweiler, Weisweiler Germany
Tel.: 2403-6460
Telex: 832193
Fax: 2403-646222
Mfr. of Electrometallurgical Products
S.I.C.: 3313

Plant:

London & Scandinavian Metallurgical Co. Ltd. **(2)**
Fullerton Road
Rotherham, South Yorkshire S60 1DL, United Kingdom
Tel.: 709 828500
Telex: 54581 lsmrhm g
Fax: 709-828367
Mfr. of Metallurgical Products
S.I.C.: 3313

METALTECH, INC.
206 Prospect Ave.
Kirkwood, MO 63122
Tel.: 314-965-4550
Fax: 314-965-4234
Emp.: 13
Manufacture Rain Carrying Products, Gutters
S.I.C.: 3444
Everett E. Stout *(Pres., Chief Exec. Officer, Chief Fin. Officer & Controller)*
Judith Stout *(Treas.)*

Outside Service Firm(s):

Mary Park C.P.A.*(Auditors)*
St. Louis, MO

Cass Bank*(Investment Banker)*
St. Louis, MO

John Gray*(Legal Firm)*
St. Louis, MO

Cass Bank*(Major Banking Relationship)*
St. Louis, MO

METPAC, LTD.
875 Waimanu St., Suite 102
Honolulu, HI 96813
Tel.: 808-537-2991
Fax: 808-524-1748
Year Founded: 1974
Fiscal Year-end: 6/30/91
Medical Equipment
S.I.C.: 5047
P. Reed Maurer *(Chm. Bd., Chief Exec. Officer & Pres.)*

Outside Service Firm(s):

Ernst & Young*(Auditors)*
Pouahi Tower, Ste. 2400, 1001 Bishop St.
Honolulu, HI 96813
Tel.: 808-531-2037

Izaki, Devens, Lo & Youth*(Legal Firm)*
Honolulu, HI

Central Pacific Bank*(Major Banking Relationship)*
Honolulu, HI

First Hawaiian Bank*(Major Banking Relationship)*
165 South King St.
Honolulu, HI 96813
Tel.: 808-525-5876
Fax: 808-525-5791

Subsidiary:

Galaxy Business Products **(1)**
875 Waimanu St., Ste.102
Honolulu, HI 96813
Tel.: 808-537-2991
Fax: 808-524-1748
Sells Office Products Commercial Accounts; Medical Supplies & Diagnostics; Medical Waste Treatment & Sterilization
S.I.C.: 5021; 5045; 5112
P. Reed Mauren *(Chm. Bd., Pres., & Gen. Mgr.)*
J. Signori *(Chief Fin. Officer & Treas.)*
Russell Saito *(Gen. Counsel)*
R. Dement *(Dir.-Pur.)*

METPAR CORPORATION
95 State St.
Westbury, NY 11590
Tel.: 516-333-2600

Fax: 516-333-2618
Year Founded: 1952
Approx.Sls.: $12,000,000
Emp.: 120
Import Export
Mfr. of Toilet, Shower & Dressing Compartments
S.I.C.: 2542; 2821; 3431
John Fallarino *(Pres.)*
Robert Berman *(Sec. & Treas.)*

METRIC & MULTISTANDARD COMPONENTS
120 Old Saw Mill River Rd.
Hawthorne, NY 10532
Tel.: 914-769-5020 **NY**
Fax: 914-769-5049
Year Founded: 1963
Approx.Sls.: $12,000,000
Emp.: 98
Wholesale Distribution of Fasteners, Industrial Nuts, Bolts & Screws; Hand Tools; Machinists Precision Measuring Tools
S.I.C.: 5085; 5072; 5084
Joseph Voves *(Pres.)*
Alois Hacaj *(V.P.)*
Ivo Peske *(Gen. Mgr.)*
Milian Peske *(Treas. & Sec.)*

Outside Service Firm(s):

Primoff, Tarshis, Weisen & Co.*(Auditors)*
114 Old Country Rd.
Mineola, NY 11501

Bank of New York*(Major Banking Relationship)*
90 Washington St.
New York, NY 10015

METRO FOODS, INC.
3657 Old Getwell Rd.
Memphis, TN 38118
Tel.: 901-365-6420 **TN**
Fax: 901-362-1166
Year Founded: 1980
Approx.Sls.: $32,000,000
Emp.: 40
Wholesale Distribution of Meats; Live, Fresh Dressed or Frozen Unpackaged Poultry; Butter; Cheese
S.I.C.: 5147; 5144; 5143
Thomas F. Mattingly *(Chm. Bd. & Pres.)*
Thomas M. Mattingly *(Exec. V.P.)*
Barbara A. Mattingly *(Treas. & Sec.)*
John Ryder *(Gen. Counsel)*
K. Doodson *(Mgr.-Sls. & Mktg.)*

Outside Service Firm(s):

John Warpole*(Auditors)*
Memphis, TN

First American National Bank*(Major Banking Relationship)*
Nashville, TN

METRO FORD INC.
9000 N.W. 7th Ave.
Miami, FL 33150
Tel.: 305-751-9711 **DE**
Fax: 301-751-9111, Ext. 230
Year Founded: 1983
Assets: $8,040,257
Liabilities: $4,990,761
Net Worth: $3,049,496
Approx.Sls.: $34,883,449
Emp.: 99
Fiscal Year-end: 12/31/91
Export
Retail New & Used Automobiles
S.I.C.: 5511
Lombardo Perez *(Chm. Bd., Pres. & Chief Oper. Officer)*
Lombardo Perez, Jr. *(V.P.)*
Esther Manso *(Comptroller, Sec. & Treas.)*
Principal(s):
Lombardo Perez

No. of Mfg. Plants/Facilities: 1

No. of U.S. Offices: 1

Computer Systems/Hardware:
Texas Instrument

Outside Service Firm(s):

Morrison, Brown, Argiz & Co.*(Auditors)*
Miami, FL

O.H. Carter Insurance*(Commercial Insurance Carrier)*
Tampa, FL

CareFlorida*(Group Insurer)*
Miami, FL

Barnett Banks Trust Company, N.A.*(International Bank Affiliate)*
Miami, FL

Southeast Bank, N.A.*(Investment Banker)*
One Southeast Financial Center
Miami, FL 33131

Quniton, Lummus, Dunwody & Adams*(Legal Firm)*
Miami, FL

Barnett Banks Trust Company, N.A.*(Major Banking Relationship)*
Miami, FL

METRO FORD SALES, INC.
3601 State St.
Schenectady, NY 12304
Tel.: 518-382-1010
Fax: 518-382-1019
Approx.Sls.: $45,000,000
Emp.: 115
Retail New & Used Automobiles
S.I.C.: 5511
Leonard Dariano *(Pres.)*
David Dariano *(Gen. Mgr.)*

METRO INFORMATION SERVICES
607 Lynnhaven Pkwy.
Virginia Beach, VA 23452
Mailing Address:
P.O. Box 8888
Virginia Beach, VA 23450
Tel.: 804-486-1900 **VA**
Year Founded: 1979
Approx.Sls.: $33,500,000
Emp.: 571
Fiscal Year-end: 12/31/91
Computer Systems Analysis, Design & Implementation
S.I.C.: 7389
Corporate Giving Program: United Way
John H. Fain *(Chm., Pres., Chief Exec. & Chief Oper. Officer)*
Steven A. Lurus *(Chief Fin. Officer & Dir.-Fin., Treas.)*
Terry Lyon *(Controller)*
Marilyn Moschel *(Dir.-Human Resources)*
Lawrence Whitley *(Dir.-Information Services)*
Principal(s):
John H. Fain

No. of U.S. Offices: 14

Computer Systems/Hardware:
Wang VS 5000; IBM PC

Outside Service Firm(s):

Robert M. Salter*(Auditors)*
Virginia Beach, VA

Clark & Stant*(Legal Firm)*
Virginia Beach, VA

Crestar Bank*(Major Banking Relationship)*
P.O. Box 2642,
Norfolk, VA 23514
Tel.: 804-624-5507
Fax: 804-624-5538

NationsBank*(Major Banking Relationship)*
Virginia Beach, VA

METRO LABEL CORP.
3525 Asset
Garland, TX 75042
Mailing Address:
P.O. Box 550129,
Dallas, TX 75355-0129
Tel.: 214-343-8686
Commercial Printing
S.I.C.: 2759
Jerry Abbot *(Pres.)*
Patricia Abbot *(Treas. & Sec.)*

Subsidiary:

Metro Label Corp. **(1)**
357 Cortlandt St.
Belleville, NJ 07109
Tel.: 201-759-5500
Fax: 201-759-0551
Approx.Sls.: $12,000,000
Emp.: 136
Computer Systems/Hardware:
Datapoint
Commercial Printing
S.I.C.: 2759; 2672; 3993
Jerry Abbot *(Pres.)*

METROLOGIC INSTRUMENTS, INC.
Coles Rd., Rte. 42
Blackwood, NJ 08012
Mailing Address:
P.O. Box 307
Bellmawr, NJ 08099
Tel.: 609-228-8886
Fax: 609-228-6673
Year Founded: 1968
Approx.Sls.: $16,000,000
Emp.: 185
Fiscal Year-end: 12/31/91
Export
Mfr. Laser Bar Code Scanners, Data Collectors
S.I.C.: 3577
C. Harry Knowles *(Pres. & Chief Exec. Officer)*
Janet Knowles *(V.P.-Admin. & Dir.-Pur.)*
Dale Fischer *(Dir.-Intl. Sls. & Mktg.)*
John Jankowski *(Dir.-Quality Control)*
Nick Martino *(Mgr.-Natl. Sls.)*
William Smeader *(Mgr.-Mfg.)*
Betty Williams *(Mgr.-Public Rels.)*
Mel Fiehler *(Data Processing)*
Pam Farrell *(Admin. Asst.)*
Chic Naylor *(Chief Engr.)*

Divisions:

Metrologic Instruments-Midwest **(1)**
8745 Waumegah Lake Rd.
Clarkston, MI 48348
Tel.: 313-625-1100
Fax: 313-625-9451
Export
S.I.C.: 3829

Metrologic Instruments-Northeast **(1)**
301 Daniel Webster Hwy.
Thornton's Landing, Merrimack, NH 03054
Tel.: 603-424-1755
Fax: 603-424-6711
Export
S.I.C.: 3829

Metrologic Instruments-Western Region **(1)**
19171 Red Bluff Dr.
Trabuco Canyon, CA 92679
Tel.: 714-858-0456
Fax: 714-589-0666
Export
S.I.C.: 3829

METROMEDIA COMPANY
1 Meadowlands Plaza
East Rutherford, NJ 07073
Tel.: 201-804-6400
Year Founded: 1986
General Partnership
S.I.C.: 6719
John W. Kluge *(Chm. & Pres.)*
Stuart Subotnick *(Exec. V.P.)*
Robert Maresca *(Sr. V.P. & Treas.)*
Arnold Wadler *(Sr. V.P., Gen. Counsel & Sec.)*

Outside Service Firm(s):

KPMG Peat Marwick*(Auditors)*
4905 Tildgman St.
Allentown, PA 18104
Tel.: 215-391-6380

John Hancock Mutual Life Insurance Co.*(Group Insurer)*
John Hancock Place, P.O. Box 111
Boston, MA 02117

Zurich American Insurance Co.*(Group Insurer)*
New York, NY

Paul, Weiss, Rifkind, Wharton & Garrison*(Legal Firm)*
345 Park Ave.
New York, NY 10022
Tel.: 212-644-8000

The Bank of New York*(Major Banking Relationship)*
One Wall Street
New York, NY 10286
Tel.: 212-635-6805
Fax: 212-635-3201

Chemical Bank*(Major Banking Relationship)*
450 West 33rd St.
New York, NY 10001
Tel.: 212-613-7197
Fax: 212-947-7628

Batterymarch Financial Management*(Pension Manager)*
600 Atlantic Ave.
Boston, MA 02210
Tel.: 617-973-9300

Neuberger & Berman Pension Management, Inc.*(Pension Manager)*
605 Third Ave.
New York, NY 10158-3698
Tel.: 212-476-9000
Fax: 212-476-5610

Subsidiaries:

METPON **(1)**
1 Harmon Plaza
Secaucus, NJ 07096
Tel.: 201-348-3244 (100%)
Holding Company
S.I.C.: 6719
John W. Kluge *(Chm. & Pres.)*
Stuart Subotnick *(Exec. V.P.)*

Subsidiary:

PON Holding Corp. **(2)**
P.O. Box 578
Vandalia, OH 45377
Tel.: 513-454-2400 (100%)
Holding Company
S.I.C.: 6719
John W. Kluge *(Chm.)*
Stuart Subotnick *(Vice Chm.)*

Subsidiary:

Ponderosa, Inc. **(3)**
Dayton International Airport, Terminal Drive
Vandalia, OH 45377
Tel.: 513-454-2400
Telex: 288060
Fax: 513-454-2647
Assets: $382,688,000
Earnings: $1,860,000
Liabilities: $362,506,000
Net Worth: $20,182,000
Approx.Rev.: $493,661,000
Emp.: 23,000
Fiscal Year-end: 2/29/91
Computer Systems/Hardware:
IBM 3083-J
Operate & Franchise Steakhouse Restaurants
S.I.C.: 5812; 6794
John W. Kluge *(Chm. Bd.)*
Stuart Subotnick *(Vice Chm.)*
J. Michael Jenkins *(Pres. & Chief Exec. Officer)*
Mike Woodhouse *(Exec. V.P. & Chief Fin. Officer)*
Robert J. Harig *(Sr. V.P.-Human Resources)*

Metromedia Company—(Continued)

John R. Mohr *(Sr. V.P., Gen. Counsel & Sec.)*
Ed Greene *(V.P.-Pur.)*
Bob Hoffman *(V.P.-Opers. & Franchising)*
Robert V. Mare *(V.P.-Opers. & Unit Devel.)*
Mike Mathane *(V.P.-Information Services)*
James J. Rieger *(V.P. & Controller)*
William K. White *(V.P. & Dir.-Fin. Plng. & Asst. Treas.)*
Diana S. Wynne *(V.P.-Internal Audit)*
Susan Lloyd *(Dir.-Cash Mgmnt.)*
Donna McCarty *(Dir.-Employee Benefits)*
Joe O'Mara *(Dir.-Real Estate)*
Margaret Nelson *(Mgr.-Communications)*

Subsidiaries:

Casa Lupita Restaurants, Inc. **(4)**
P.O. Box 578,
Dayton, OH 45401
Tel.: 513-454-2400 (100%)
Approx.Sls.: $39,281,000
Emp.: 2,500
Franchisor of Mexican Restaurants
S.I.C.: 5812

ESI Meats, Inc. **(4)**
605 Kesco Dr., P.O. Box 157
Bristol, IN 46507
Tel.: 219-848-7661 (100%)
Approx.Sls.: $157,237,000
Emp.: 500
Processing & Distribute Meat & Other Products
S.I.C.: 2013
Anthony R. Brinkman *(V.P. & Gen. Mgr.)*

Ponderosa Financial Corporation **(4)**
Dayton International Airport, Terminal Dr.
Vandalia, OH 45377
Tel.: 513-454-2400 (100%)
Financing Services for Franchisees
S.I.C.: 6159

Ponderosa International Development, Inc. **(4)**
P.O. Box 578,
Dayton, OH 45401
Tel.: 513-454-2400 (100%)
Patent Owners & Lessors
S.I.C.: 6794

Ponlupa Restaurant Financing, Inc. **(4)**
Dayton International Airport, Terminal Dr.
Vandalia, OH 45377
Tel.: 513-454-2400 (100%)
Financing Services for Franchises
S.I.C.: 6159

METSA, Inc. **(1)**
1 Harmon Plaza
Secaucus, NJ 07096
Tel.: 201-348-3244 (100%)
Holding Co.
S.I.C.: 6719
John W. Kluge *(Chm.)*

Subsidiary:

Bonanza Restaurants **(2)**
8080 N. Central Expy., Ste. 500
Dallas, TX 75206
Tel.: 214-891-8400
Approx.Sls.: $560,000,000
Emp.: 80
Family Restaurants
S.I.C.: 5812
C. Jeffrey Rogers *(Pres.)*
Michael Jenkins *(Exec. V.P. & Gen. Mgr.)*
Ronald W. Parker *(Sr. V.P.-Franchise Opers.)*
Lane Schmiesing *(Sr. V.P.-Mktg.)*
Amy Thompson *(Mktg. Services)*

Metromedia Communication Corp. **(1)**
1 Meadowlands Place
East Rutherford, NJ 07073
Tel.: 201-804-6400 (100%)
Long Distance Telephone Company
S.I.C.: 4813
Howard Finklestein *(Pres.)*

Metromedia Steakhouses, Inc. **(1)**
Terminal Dr.
Vandalia, OH 45377
Tel.: 513-454-2400
Fax: 513-454-2633
Steak House Managers
S.I.C.: 5812
John Klugy *(Chm. Bd.)*
Michael S. Kaufman *(Pres.)*
Michael Woodhouse *(Exec. V.P. & Chief Fin. Officer)*
Howard Terry *(Dir.-Mktg.)*
Larry White *(Treas.)*

METRON STEEL CORP.
12900 S. Metron Dr.
Chicago, IL 60633
Tel.: 312-646-4000
Tel.: 800-638-7661
Fax: 312-646-4102
Year Founded: 1951
Approx.Sls.: $120,000,000
Emp.: 175
Primary Metal Industries; Metal Service Center
S.I.C.: 5051
Edward C. Nemergut *(Sr. V.P.-Fin.)*
Richard E. O'Toole *(V.P. & Gen. Mgr.)*
Richard Swanson *(Controller)*
Jim Barnthouse *(Dir.-Admin.)*
William G. Crowley *(Dir.-Sls.)*
Ben Tinsley *(Dir.-Opers.)*
Tom V. Zager *(Mgr.-Sls. & Mktg.)*

Computer Systems/Hardware:
IBM System 36

Outside Service Firm(s):

Price Waterhouse*(Auditors)*
200 E. Randolph
Chicago, IL 60601
Tel.: 312-565-1500

Kemper Insurance*(Commercial Insurance Carrier)*
Long Grove, IL 60049-0001

Williams, Mannos, Rutstein, Goldfarb & Sharp*(Legal Firm)*
Chicago, IL

LaSalle National Bank*(Major Banking Relationship)*
135 S. LaSalle St., Rm.260
Chicago, IL 60603

LaSalle National Bank*(Pension Manager)*
135 S. LaSalle St., Rm.260
Chicago, IL 60603

METROPOLITAN LIFE INSURANCE CO.
1 Madison Ave.
New York, NY 10010-3690
Tel.: 212-578-2211 NY
Fax: 212-578-3320
Year Founded: 1868
Assets: $103,228,000,000
Liabilities: $98,922,000,000
Net Worth: $4,306,000,000
Approx.Rev.: $39,500,000,000
Emp.: 32,839
Fiscal Year-end: 12/31/91
Insurance
S.I.C.: 6512; 6531; 6311; 6321; 6324; 6371; 6411

Robert G. Schwartz *(Chm. Bd., Pres. & Chief Exec. Officer)*
Philip Briggs *(Vice Chm.)*
Ted Athanassiades *(Sr. Exec. V.P.-Pensions)*
Robert E. Chappell, Jr. *(Sr. Exec. V.P. & Chief Fin. Officer)*
Harry P. Kamen *(Sr. Exec. V.P.-Professional Service Opers.)*
Stewart G. Nagler *(Sr. Exec. V.P.-Insurance Opers.)*
Gerald Clark *(Exec. V.P.-Corp. Investments)*
Glen E. Coverdale *(Exec. V.P.-Corp. Quality & Planning)*
Robert J. Crimmins *(Exec. V.P.-Personal Insurance)*
John D. Moynahan, Jr. *(Exec. V.P.-Group Insurance)*
William G. Poortvliet *(Exec. V.P.-International Operations)*
Catherine A. Rein *(Exec. V.P.-Corp. Services)*
Richard M. Blackwell *(Sr. V.P. & Gen. Counsel)*
Bruce J. Goodman *(Sr. V.P. & Chief Info. Officer)*
Fred P. Hauser *(Sr. V.P. & Controller)*
Jeffrey J. Hodgman *(Sr. V.P.-Corp. Plng.)*
Vincent P. Reusing *(Sr. V.P.-External Rels.)*
Arthur G. Typermass *(Sr. V.P. & Treas.)*
Bruce A. Feller *(V.P.-Pur.)*
Sibyl Jacobson *(V.P. & Corp. Grants Contact)*
Anne E. Hayden *(V.P.-Human Resources)*
Daniel P. Kaidan *(V.P.-Mktg.)*
Nicholas D. Latrenta *(V.P. & Sec.)*
Susan H. Berger *(Asst. V.P.-Recruiting, Training & Devel.)*
David Janelli *(Asst. V.P.-Corp. Travel Planner)*
Mary M. LoSardo *(Asst. V.P.-Corp. Quality)*
Robert B. Weinstein *(Asst. V.P.-Adv.)*
Dorothy R. Kelly *(Dir.-Employee Communications)*
T.W. McGarvey *(Dir.-Leasing)*
Barbara Willis *(Dir.-Communications Program)*
Marianne Stolp *(Corp. Librarian)*

No. of U.S. Offices: 477

Computer Systems/Hardware:
IBM Systems 3081, 3033, 3083 & 4341

Outside Service Firm(s):

Deloitte & Touche*(Auditors)*
1 World Trade Center
New York, NY 10048
Tel.: 212-669-5000

Chase Manhattan Bank, N.A.*(Major Banking Relationship)*
One Chase Manhattan Plaza
New York, NY 10081
Tel.: 212-552-2222
Tel.: 800-526-0801
Fax: 212-552-7175

Subsidiaries:

Century 21 Real Estate Corp. **(1)**
2601 S.E. Main St.
Irvine, CA 92713
Tel.: 714-553-2100 (100%)
Approx.Sls.: $86,827,000
Emp.: 154
Computer Systems/Hardware:
Honeywell
Real Estate
S.I.C.: 6794; 6531
Richard J. Loughlin *(Pres. & Chief Exec. Officer)*
Gary Cooper *(Exec. V.P.)*
Robert Hutchinson *(Exec. V.P.)*
W. Robert Penner *(Sr. V.P., Chief Fin. Officer & Asst. Treas.)*
John Moravek *(Sr. V.P. & Gen. Counsel)*
Bruce J. Oseland *(Sr. V.P.-Mktg.)*
Marty Rueter *(V.P.-Reg. Devel.)*
Monte Helme *(V.P.-Pub. Info.)*
Dennis Haroun *(Dir.-Adv.)*

Corporate Health Strategies, Inc. **(1)**
276 Post Rd., West
Westport, CT 06880
Tel.: 203-454-6100 (100%)
Fax: 203-454-6110
Emp.: 92
Health Care Data Analysis
S.I.C.: 7374
Dennis K. Dang *(Chm. Bd.)*
Leon I. Hyman *(Pres. & Chief Oper. Officer)*
Alex Hutchinson *(V.P.-Mktg.)*

Cross & Brown Company **(1)**
522 Fifth Ave.
New York, NY 10036
Tel.: 212-840-3200 (100%)
Emp.: 229
Real Estate Managers
S.I.C.: 6531
Glen E. Coverdale *(Chm. Bd. & Chief Exec. Officer)*
William A. Reilly *(V.P. & Treas.)*

MetLife Capital Corporation **(1)**
10900 N. E. 8th St., Ste. 1300
Bellevue, WA 98004
Tel.: 206-451-0090 (100%)
Fax: 206-451-2719
Approx.Sls.: $1,000,000,000
Approx.Assets: $3,000,000,000
Emp.: 281
General Equipment Leasing
S.I.C.: 7379
John C. Morrison, Jr. *(Chm. & Chief Exec. Officer)*
John R. Cornwall *(Pres. & Chief Oper. Officer)*
Timothy L. Johnson *(V.P. & Mktg. Dir.)*

MetLife Capital Credit Corp. **(1)**
P.O. Box 601, 10 Stamford Forum
Stamford, CT 06904
Tel.: 203-328-2700 (100%)
Fax: 203-328-2809
Emp.: 64
Small Business Credit Institution & Equipment Rental & Leasing Services
S.I.C.: 6159; 7359
John C. Morrison, Jr. *(Chm. Bd.)*
John R. Cornwall *(Pres. & Chief Exec. Officer)*
John L. Guadagno, Jr. *(Exec. V.P.-Fin.)*
John F. Spain *(Sr. V.P.-Sls.)*

MetLife-State Street Investment Services, Inc. **(1)**
One Financial Center
Boston, MA 02111-2690
Tel.: 617-348-2000 (100%)
Emp.: 76
Mutual Funds
S.I.C.: 6722
David P. McLean *(Pres.)*

Metropolitan Insurance & Annuity Co. **(1)**
One Madison Ave.
New York, NY 10010
Tel.: 212-578-2211 (100%)
Approx.Sls.: $605,000,000
Life Insurance
S.I.C.: 6311
Stewart G. Nagler *(Chm. Bd.)*
Robert J. Crimmins *(Pres. & Chief Exec. Officer)*
J. Edmond Diver *(V.P. & Treas.)*

Metropolitan Property & Casualty Insurance Co.(Met P&C) **(1)**
700 Quaker Lane
Warwick, RI 02887
Tel.: 401-827-2400
Tel.: 800-422-4272 (100%)
Fax: 401-827-2674
Approx.Sls.: $700,000,000
Emp.: 2,915
Automobile & Homeowner's Insurance
S.I.C.: 6331
Stewart G. Nagler *(Chm. Bd.)*
Daniel J. Cavanagh *(Pres.)*
Francis S. Porterfield *(V.P.-Mktg.)*
John J. McSweeney *(Treas.)*

Metropolitan Tower Life Insurance Co. **(1)**
One Madison Ave.
New York, NY 10010
Tel.: 212-578-6862 (100%)
Approx.Sls.: $11,000,000
Life Insurance
S.I.C.: 6311
Stewart G. Nagler *(Chm. Bd.)*
Robert J. Crimmins *(Pres. & Chief Exec. Officer)*
J. Edmond Diver *(V.P. & Treas.)*

State Street Research & Management Company **(1)**
One Financial Ctr.,30th Fl.
Boston, MA 02111
Tel.: 617-482-3920 (100%)
Emp.: 218
Investment Advisor & Manager
S.I.C.: 6282
Robert F. Verni *(Chm. Bd. & Chief Exec. Officer)*
William P. Rich *(Pres. & Chief Oper. Officer)*
John D. Phillips, Jr. *(Exec. V.P. & Chief Investment Officer-Equities)*

Affiliates:

Farmers National Company **(1)**
11516 Nichols St.
Omaha, NE 68154-4427
Tel.: 402-496-3276
Farm Management and Land Sale
S.I.C.: 0762
Leo T. Rasmussen *(Chm.)*
Richard C. Hahn *(Pres. & Chief Exec. Officer)*

MetLife Funding Co. **(1)**
Citicorp Center, 1200 Smith St.
Houston, TX 77002
Tel.: 713-951-0940
Financing & Investment
S.I.C.: 6159
Arthur G. Typermass *(Chm.)*
Richard E. McElrath *(Pres.)*

MetLife HealthCare Management Corp. **(1)**
14500 S. Forty Rd.
St. Louis, MO 63017-5736
Tel.: 314-469-9900
S.I.C.: 6321
John D. Moynahan *(Chm.)*
Robert A. Chernow *(Pres. & Chief Exec. Officer)*

MetLife Securities, Inc. **(1)**
One Madison Ave.
New York, NY 10010
Tel.: 212-578-2211
Financing & Investment
S.I.C.: 6159
George B. Trotta *(Chm.)*

MetLife Security Insurance Company of Louisiana **(1)**
650 Poydras St.
New Orleans, LA 70130-6101
Tel.: 504-833-8225
Insurance
S.I.C.: 6311
Ted Athanassiades *(Pres. & Chief Exec. Officer)*

Metmor Financial, Inc. **(1)**
9225 Indian Creek Parkway
Overland Park, KS 66210
Tel.: 913-661-0555
Mortgage Banker for Residential and Commercial Property
S.I.C.: 6162
Glen E. Coverdale *(Chm.)*
Jerold K. Hoerner *(Pres. & Chief Exec. Officer)*

Metric Realty, Inc. **(1)**
950 Tower Lane
Foster City, CA 94404
Tel.: 415-378-7000
Real Estate Investment Co.
S.I.C.: 6159
W. Patrick McDowell *(Pres. & Chief Exec. Officer)*

Texas Life Insurance Company **(1)**
Texas Center, 900 Washington Ave.
Waco, TX 76701
Tel.: 817-752-6521
Insurance
S.I.C.: 6311
Stewart G, Nagler *(Chm.)*
John D. Mayfield III *(Pres. & Chief Exec. Officer)*

Non-U.S. Holdings:

Albany Life Assurance Company Limited **(1)**
Station House, 3 Darkes Lane
Potters Bar, Hertfordshire EN6 1AJ, United Kingdom
Tel.: 44-707-42311 (100%)
Telex: 44-707-51275
Emp.: 1,398
Sell Variable Life Insurance and Pension Products in the United Kingdom
S.I.C.: 6311
Ralph Sepel *(Mng. Dir.)*
The Honorable Lord Aberdare *(Mng. Dir.)*

Metropolitan Life Holdings, Ltd. **(1)**
99 Bank St.
Ottawa, ON k1P 5A3, Canada
Tel.: 613-560-7446
Health Care Holding Co.
S.I.C.: 6719
William G. Poortvliet *(Chm.)*
John H. Tweedie *(Pres. & Chief Exec. officer)*

Metropolitan Life Insurance Company of Canada **(1)**
99 Bank St.
Ottawa, ON K1P 5A3, Canada
Tel.: 613-560-7919
Sells Nonparticipating Life Insurance, Annuities & Other Life Products
S.I.C.: 6311
Albert E. Bates *(Pres. & Chief Exec. Officer)*

Metropolitan Trust Company of Canada **(1)**
6 Crescent Rd.
Toronto, ON M4W 3K9, Canada
Tel.: 416-967-0880
Provides Personal Banking Services, Money Market Investments, Mutual Funds & Mortgages
S.I.C.: 6091
Paul G. Haggis *(Pres.)*

Morguard Investments Limited, Toronto **(1)**
6 Crescent Rd.
Toronto, ON M4W 3K9, Canada
Tel.: 416-967-0880
Develops & Operates Income-Producing Properties for Institutional Investors
S.I.C.: 6162
Antony A. Stephens *(Chm. & Pres. and Chief Exec. Office)*

GFM International Investors, Limited **(1)**
11th Fl., Orion House, 5 Upper, St. Martins Lane
London, WC2H 9EA, United Kingdom
Tel.: 011-4471-957-9000
International Advisory Firm Providing Investment Products & Services for American Institutional Investors, Particularly American Pension Funds
S.I.C.: 6162
Stephen Bamford *(Chief Exec. Officer)*

MetLife (UK) Limited **(1)**
Metropolitan House, Drake Lane
Potters Bar, Hertfordshire EN6 IAJ, United Kingdom
Coordinates MetLife's Diversification & Expansion in the United Kingdom
The Rt. Hon. Lord Aberdare *(Chm.)*

ACFC Corporate Finance Limited **(1)**
Station House, 3 Darkes Lake
Potters Bar, Hertfordshire EN6 1AJ, United Kingdom
Provides Commercial Financing to Small & Medium Sized U.K. Companies
S.I.C.: 6282

Santander Met., S.A. Madrid **(2)**
Paseo De La Castellana 95
Madrid, SP 28046, Spain
A Corporate Joint Venture with Banco Santander; Coordinates MetLife's Business in the Spanish Insurance & Pension Markets
S.I.C.: 6371; 6411
Matias Rodriguez Inciarte *(Chm.)*

Metropolitan Insurance and Annuity Company, Taiwan Branch **(1)**
11th Floor, 85 Jen Ai Road, Sec. 4
Taipei, 10649, Taiwan
Tel.: 2-741-7810
Telex: 886-2-741-7810
Emp.: 448
Markets Insurance Products in Taiwan
S.I.C.: 6321
Harry C. Hsiang *(Gen. Mgr.)*

Seguros Gensis, SA **(1)**
Paseo de la Castellana 95, 28046
Madrid, Spain
Tel.: 34-1-597-2943
Telex: 34-1-597-1248
Emp.: 176
Sells Insurance and Pension Products in Spain
S.I.C.: 6311; 6371
Jose Maria Dot *(Mng. Dir.)*

Joint Venture:

Kolon-Met Life Insurance Company Limited **(1)**
Ms. Bldg. 6-7 Fl., 53-1 Myung-Dong 1 Ga Jung-Ku,
Seoul, 100-021, Korea
Tel.: 82-2-773-8888
Telex: 82-2-774-8273
Approx.Rev.: $2,000,000,000
Emp.: 1,996
Joint Venture with Kolon group; Sells Insurance and Pension Products
S.I.C.: 6311
Jae-Ku Wooh *(Pres.)*

METROPOLITAN PROPERTIES INC.
1476 Davenport
Cleveland, OH 44114
Tel.: 216-696-6343 **OH**
Fax: 216-696-2060
Year Founded: 1972
Emp.: 75
Acquisitions & Operations of Parking Facilities; Commercial Real Estate Development & Investment
S.I.C.: 7521; 6799; 6552
Elias Kassouf *(Chm. Bd.)*
James Kassouf *(Pres., Chief Exec. Officer & Treas.)*

Computer Systems/Hardware:
Kaypro; IBM PC-XT

Outside Service Firm(s):

Transamerica Occidental Insurance Co.*(Group Insurer)*
P.O. Box 30253,
Los Angeles, CA 90099

Midwest Bank*(Major Banking Relationship)*
Cleveland, OH

Subsidiary:

Metro Parking Systems **(1)**
1476 Davenport
Cleveland, OH 44114
Tel.: 216-696-6343
Acquires Parking Facilities & Downtown Bldgs. & Properties
S.I.C.: 6519; 6552

METROPOLITAN SUNDAY NEWSPAPERS, INC.
260 Madison Ave.
New York, NY 10016
Tel.: 212-689-8200
Fax: 212-779-9795
Year Founded: 1932
Approx.Sls.: $50,000,000
Emp.: 100
Newspaper Published Magazines & Comics
S.I.C.: 2711; 2721; 2741
Carmen Willix *(Pres. & Chief Exec. Officer)*
Anthony J. Martone *(V.P.-Fin. & Admin.)*
Louis Spino *(V.P.-Mktg.)*
Michael Baratoff *(Adv. Dir.-Eastern)*
Ken Tarzon *(Chicago Mgr.)*
Don Jumisco *(Detroit Mgr.)*

Computer Systems/Hardware:
AS 400

Subsidiaries:

Metro-Puck Comics Network **(1)**
260 Madison Ave.
New York, NY 10016
Tel.: 212-689-8200
Fax: 212-779-9795
Approx.Sls.: $6,000,000
Emp.: 55
Fiscal Year-end: 12/31/90
Newspaper Published Sunday Comics Sections
S.I.C.: 2721
Carmen Willix *(Pres. & Chief Exec. Officer)*
Anthony J. Martone *(V.P.-Fin. & Admin.)*
Richard Splittorf *(V.P.-Sls.)*
Louis Spino *(V.P. & Mktg. Dir.)*
Phyllis Cavaliere *(Dir.-Eastern Adv.)*
Ken Tarzon *(Mgr.-Chicago)*
Don Jumisco *(Mgr.-Detroit)*

Sunday Magazine Network **(1)**
260 Madison Ave.
New York, NY 10016
Tel.: 212-689-8200
Fax: 212-779-9795
Approx.Sls.: $35,000,000
Emp.: 55
Fiscal Year-end: 12/31/89
Computer Systems/Hardware:
AS 400
S.I.C.: 2741
Carmen Willix *(Pres. & Chief Exec. Officer)*
Anthony J. Martone *(V.P.-Fin. & Admin.)*
Louis Spino *(V.P. & Mktg. Dir.)*
Michael Baratoff *(Dir.-Eastern Adv.)*
Kenneth Tarzon *(Mgr.-Chicago)*
Donald Jumisco *(Mgr.-Detroit)*

METROPOLITAN TRANSPORTATION AUTHORITY
347 Madison Ave.
New York, NY 10017
Tel.: 212-878-7000
Fax: 212-878-7398
Emp.: 64,119
Public Transportation
S.I.C.: 4111
Peter E. Stangl *(Chm. & Chief Exec. Officer)*
Daniel T. Scannell *(1st Vice Chm.)*
Mortimer L. Downey III *(Exec. Dir. & Chief Fin. Officer)*
Robert Bergen *(Gen. Counsel)*
John Cunningham *(Press Sec.)*
Bernard E. Cohen *(Dir.-Policy & Plng.)*
Alicia Martinez *(Dir.-Mktg. & Corp. Communications)*
Henry Rissmeyer *(Chief-Mktg. & Adv. Services)*

Operating Agencies:

The Long Island Rail Road Co. **(1)**
Jamaica Station
Jamaica, NY 11435
Tel.: 718-990-7400
Fax: 718-990-8212
Emp.: 6,200
Local Railroad Company
S.I.C.: 4111
Charles W. Hoppe *(Pres.)*
Daniel G. Cleary *(V.P.-Opers.)*
John C. Bennett *(V.P.-Plng., Mktg. & Mngmt. System)*
Brian P. Dolan *(Exec. Dir.-Pub. Affairs)*
Jack Larsen *(Exec. Dir.-Human Res. & Organization)*
Donald P. Malone *(Mgr.-Publications)*
Thomas Taranto *(Gen. Counsel)*

Manhattan and Bronx Surface Transit Operating Authority **(1)**
370 Jay St.
Brooklyn, NY 11201
Tel.: 718-330-3000
S.I.C.: 4111
Alan F. Kiepper *(Pres.)*

Metro-North Commuter Railroad Company **(1)**
347 Madison Ave.
New York, NY 10017
Tel.: 212-340-3000
S.I.C.: 4111
Donald E. Nelson *(Pres.)*

Metropolitan Suburban Bus Authority **(1)**
700 Commercial Ave.
Garden City, NY 11530
Tel.: 516-542-0100
S.I.C.: 4111
L.A. Kimball *(Gen. Mgr.)*

New York City Transit Authority **(1)**
370 Jay St.
Brooklyn, NY 11201
Tel.: 718-330-3000
S.I.C.: 4111
Alan F. Kiepper *(Pres.)*

Triborough Bridge & Tunnel Authority **(1)**
Randall's Island
New York, NY 10035
Tel.: 212-360-3100
S.I.C.: 4785; 4111
Michael C. Ascher *(Pres.)*

MEXICAN INDUSTRIES IN MICHIGAN
1616 Howard
Detroit, MI 48216
Tel.: 313-963-6115
Fax: 313-963-6217
Year Founded: 1979
Approx.Sls.: $20,700,000
Emp.: 130

Mexican Industries in Michigan—(Continued)

Manufacture Automotive Trim
S.I.C.: 2396
Henry J. Aguirre *(Pres. & Treas.)*
John Livingstone *(Controller)*

MEYER BROADCASTING COMPANY
200 Fourth St. N.
Bismarck, ND 58501
Mailing Address:
P.O. Box 1738,
Bismark, ND 58501
Tel.: 701-255-5757
Fax: 701-255-4921
Year Founded: 1930
Assets: $49,947,277
Liabilities: $4,635,334
Net Worth: $45,311,943
Approx.Sls.: $15,000,000
Emp.: 250
Fiscal Year-end: 12/31/91
AM & FM Radio Station Operations; Television Broadcasting
S.I.C.: 4832; 4833
Marietta Meyer Ekberg *(Chm. Bd.)*
Judith Ekberg Johnson *(Pres. & Chief Exec. Officer)*
Edward J. Kautzman *(Treas.)*

Outside Service Firm(s):

Eide, Helmeke & Co.*(Auditors)*
Moorhead, MN

Pearce & Durick*(Legal Firm)*
Bismarck, ND

First National Bank & Trust Co. Of Bismarck*(Major Banking Relationship)*
Bismarck, ND

MEYER JEWELERS
20500 Eureka Rd., Ste. 200
Taylor, MI 48180
Tel.: 313-283-0900 **MI**
Fax: 313-285-8097
Approx.Sls.: $35,000,000
Emp.: 300
Jewelry Stores
S.I.C.: 5944
Gary Mohr *(V.P.-Admin.)*
Joseph Munoz *(V.P.-Human Resources)*

Outside Service Firm(s):

Grant Thornton*(Auditors)*
Southfield, MI

Comerica Bank*(Major Banking Relationship)*
211 W. Fort St.
Detroit, MI 48226
Tel.: 313-222-3300

MEYER & WALLIS, INC.
111 E. Kilbourn Ave., Ste. 1000
Milwaukee, WI 53202
Tel.: 414-224-0212 **WI**
Fax: 414-224-0420
Year Founded: 1967
Assets: $1,622,000
Liabilities: $1,047,000
Net Worth: $575,000
Approx.Billings: $16,300,000
Emp.: 22
Retail, Consumer, & Food Advertising
S.I.C.: 7311
Robert L. Meyer *(Pres.)*
Neal Bardele *(V.P.- Dir. Acct. & Mktg. Services)*
Fran Weber *(V.P.- Fin. Services)*
Bob Bourgeois *(Dir.- Pub. Rels.)*

No. of U.S. Offices: 1

Computer Systems/Hardware:
IBM, Adman

Outside Service Firm(s):

Vrakas Blum*(Auditors)*
Brookfield, WI

Frank B. Hall*(Commercial Insurance Carrier)*
Milwaukee, WI

Wisconsin Health Organization*(Group Insurer)*
Milwaukee, WI

Aul, McKoy, Aschenbrener & Dean*(Legal Firm)*
Milwaukee, WI

M & I Marshall & Ilsley Bank*(Major Banking Relationship)*
770 N. Water St.
Milwaukee, WI 53202
Tel.: 414-765-8700

Emjay Corp.*(Pension Manager)*
Milwaukee, WI

Subsidiary:

Media Management **(1)**
Ste. 1000, 111 E. Kilbourn Ave.
Milwaukee, WI 53202
Tel.: 414-224-0767
Emp.: 3
Janet Ebert *(Gen. Mgr.)*

THE MEYERCORD COMPANY
365 E. North Ave.
Carol Stream, IL 60188
Tel.: 708-682-6200
Tel.: 800-223-6923
Telex: 244543
Fax: 708-682-6345
Year Founded: 1896
Sales Range: $20-39 Million
Emp.: 200
Manufacture Applied Transfer Systems for Advertising, Identification, Instruction & Decoration; Mechanical Application Systems for Ceramic & Non-Ceramic Products; Pressure Sensitive, High Tensile Strength Vinyl Films, Vinyl Inks & Application Tape
S.I.C.: 3269; 3953; 2672; 2752
Dennis McDonald *(Chm. Bd.)*
M.C. Miller *(V.P.-Revenue Div.)*
J.S. O'Briskie *(V.P.-Printed Prods. Grp.)*
J. Galloni *(Sls. Mgr.-Printed Prods. Grp.)*
Frank Jancewicz *(Pur. Agent)*

Outside Service Firm(s):

Arthur Andersen & Co.*(Auditors)*
33 W. Monroe St.
Chicago, IL 60603-4067
Tel.: 312-580-0033
Fax: 312-507-6748

Chadwell, Kayser, Ltd.*(Legal Firm)*
35 West Wacker Dr., Ste. 3300
Chicago, IL 60601-1698
Tel.: 312-419-7500

Harris Trust & Savings Bank*(Major Banking Relationship)*
111 W. Monroe St.
Chicago, IL 60690
Tel.: 312-461-2265
Tel.: 800-858-0840

GERHARDT F. MEYNE CO.
(Sub. of Bulley & Andrews Co.)
345 N. Canal St.
Chicago, IL 60606
Tel.: 312-207-2100 **DE**
Fax: 312-207-0488
Approx.Sls.: $30,000,000
Emp.: 250
General Contractor
S.I.C.: 1629
Jack H. Bornhoeft *(Pres.)*
Stephen Bing *(V.P.)*
Rick Van Pelt *(V.P.)*

Computer Systems/Hardware:
IBM System 36

Outside Service Firm(s):

Blackman Kallick Bartelstein*(Auditors)*
300 Riverside Plaza
Chicago, IL 60606
Tel.: 312-207-1040

American National Bank & Trust Company of Chicago*(Major Banking Relationship)*
33 N. LaSalle St.
Chicago, IL 60602
Tel.: 312-661-5000
Fax: 312-661-6417

Defrees & Fiske*(Legal Firm)*
Chicago, IL

MEYOCKS BENKSTEIN ASSOCIATES
100 Court Ave., Ste. 303
Des Moines, IA 50309
Tel.: 515-246-1800
Tel.: 800-475-1611
Year Founded: 1989
Approx.Billings: $11,800,000
Emp.: 29
Agricultural Communications
Richard Meyocks *(Pres. & Chief Exec. Officer)*
Ken Benkstein *(Exec. V.P. & Pub. Rels. Dir.)*
J. Doug Mertz, II *(V.P., Sec. & Media Dir.)*
John Lambert *(V.P.)*
Bruce Larson *(Treas.)*
Kim Smythe *(Media Buyer)*

Computer Systems/Hardware:
IBM Compatible-Novell Network

MI-JACK PRODUCTS, INC.
3111 W. 167th St.
Hazel Crest, IL 60429
Tel.: 708-596-5200 **IL**
Fax: 708-596-7461
Year Founded: 1955
Sales Range: $80-99 Million
Emp.: 1,000

Import Export
Manufacture & Distribute Construction & Material Handling Equipment
S.I.C.: 5084; 3531; 3536; 5082; 7353; 8711; 8712
John J. Lanigan, Sr. *(Chm. Bd. & Pres.)*
John J. Lanigan, Jr. *(Pres.)*
Michael Lanigan *(Exec. V.P.-Sls.)*
John J. Boquist *(V.P. & Controller)*
Harry Engnell *(V.P.-Opers.)*
Henry B. Gurion *(V.P. & Corp. Counsel)*
Daniel P. Heraty *(V.P.-Travelift Sls.)*
Patrick Lanigan *(V.P.-Indus. Sls.)*
William J. Lanigan *(V.P.-Regional Services)*
R.E. Newhall *(V.P. & Treas.)*
Harvey W. Schmidt *(V.P.-Mfg.)*
Thomas Stangl *(V.P.-Railroad Terminal Opers.)*
Raymond Tippit *(V.P.-Natl. Railroad Sls.)*
S. Ira Miller *(Gen. Counsel)*
John Wepfer *(Dir.-Data Processing)*

No. of U.S. Offices: 6

Computer Systems/Hardware:
Honeywell

Outside Service Firm(s):

Bansley & Kiener*(Auditors)*
Chicago, IL

LaSalle National Bank*(Major Banking Relationship)*
135 S. LaSalle St., Rm.260
Chicago, IL 60603

THE MIAMI MARGARINE CO.
5226 Vine St.
Cincinnati, OH 45217
Tel.: 513-242-2310
Fax: 513-242-2310, Ext. 213
Approx.Sls.: $50,000,000
Emp.: 160

Export
Manufacture & Distribute Margarine, Salad Dressing, Shortening
S.I.C.: 2079; 5149; 5411
James K. Heidrich, Jr. *(Chm. Bd., Pres. & Chief Exec. Officer)*
James L. Day *(Chief Fin. Officer & Controller)*
Kevin McDole *(Natl. Sls. Mgr.)*
R.A. Kolkmeyer *(Mgr.-Mktg.)*
David Fisher *(Pur. Agent)*

Computer Systems/Hardware:
IBM

Outside Service Firm(s):

Andrew, Littner, Mancini & Vogel*(Auditors)*
Cincinnati, OH

Graydon, Head & Ritchey*(Legal Firm)*
1900 Fifth Third Center
Cincinnati, OH 45202
Tel.: 513-621-6464

The Central Trust Company, N.A.*(Major Banking Relationship)*
Cincinnati, OH
Tel.: 513-651-8896

MIAMI SYSTEMS CORPORATION
10150 Alliance Rd.
Cincinnati, OH 45242
Tel.: 513-793-0110
Fax: 513-793-2974
Year Founded: 1926
Sales Range: $60-79 Million
Emp.: 650
Computer Forms, Unit Sets & Register Forms
S.I.C.: 2761
Samuel L. Peters *(Pres.)*
Fay Olsen *(V.P.-Admin.)*
Henry Peters *(V.P.-Mktg.)*
Jack Pulskamp *(Controller)*

Outside Service Firm(s):

Mathews, Negatingdale & Reich*(Auditors)*
Cincinnati, OH

Fifth Third Bank*(Major Banking Relationship)*
Corporate Trust Services, 38 Fountain Square Plaza
Cincinnati, OH 45263

Subsidiary:

Uforma Shelby Business Forms **(1)**
40 High School Ave.
Shelby, OH 44875
Tel.: 419-342-3515
Approx.Sls.: $28,000,000
Emp.: 450
Manufacture Business Forms
S.I.C.: 2761
Samuel L. Peters *(Pres.)*
Timothy Downie *(V.P.-Customer Service)*
William J. Butler *(Sec.)*

MICHAEL, BOLGER, REINSCHMIEDT, KING (MBRK)
(Formerly Michael & Partners)
3110 Webb Ave.
Dallas, TX 75205
Tel.: 214-520-1200
Fax: 214-520-0364/522-5550
Fax: 214-520-0685
Year Founded: 1983
Approx.Billings: $25,000,000
Emp.: 45
Consumer Adv.
S.I.C.: 4512
George Michael *(Principal)*

Tom Bolger *(Principal/Mktg. Services)*
Monica Haskins Jorns *(V.P.-Finance)*
Marilyn Pippin *(V.P., Pub. Rels.)*

Computer Systems/Hardware:
Unix Enviro, MacIntosh

MICHAEL BUSINESS MACHINES CORPORATION
3290 Ashley Phosphate Rd.
North Charleston, SC 29418
Tel.: 803-552-2700
Tel.: 800-223-2508
Fax: 803-552-2974
Year Founded: 1936
Sales Range: $10-19 Million
Emp.: 50
Fiscal Year-end: 10/31/91

Import Export
Mfr. Paper Shredders & Paper Balers
S.I.C.: 3579
Wolfgang Priester *(Chm. Bd.)*
William Golde *(Pres.)*
Tom Gallagher *(V.P.-Sls.)*
Norma Crawford *(Controller)*
Mike Venitelli *(Natl. Sls. Mgr.)*
Holly Wilson *(Adv. Mgr.)*

Computer Systems/Hardware:
ADP

Outside Service Firm(s):

Prudential Insurance Co. of America*(Group Insurer)*
751 Broad St.
Newark, NJ 07102-3777
Tel.: 201-802-6000

DAVID MICHAEL & CO. INC.
10801 Decatur Rd.
Philadelphia, PA 19154
Tel.: 215-632-3100
Fax: 215-637-3920
Year Founded: 1896
Sales Range: $10-19 Million
Emp.: 100
Manufacture Flavorings for Processed Food Industry
S.I.C.: 2087; 2099
Edward W. Rosenbaum *(Chm. Bd. & Chief Exec. Officer)*
Skip Rosskam III *(Pres. & Chief Oper. Officer)*
George Rosskam *(Exec. V.P.-Oper.)*
Steve Rosskam *(Exec. V.P.-Sls. & Mktg.)*
Robert A. Schmidt *(V.P.-West Coast)*
Kurt L. Schoen *(V.P.-Res.)*
Jedd B. Stillman *(Treas. & Dir.-Personnel)*
Stuart Rosenbaum *(Dir.-Pur.)*
Ken Dorsey *(Mgr.-Prod.)*

Computer Systems/Hardware:
IBM

Outside Service Firm(s):

Blank, Rome, Comisky & McCauley*(Legal Firm)*
Four Penn Center Plaza
Philadelphia, PA 19103
Tel.: 215-209-3700

Philadelphia National Bank*(Major Banking Relationship)*
P.O. Box 13834, Broad & Chestnut Streets
Philadelphia, PA 19101-7618
Tel.: 215-973-8327

MICHAEL FOODS, INC.
5353 Wayzata Blvd.
Minneapolis, MN 55416
Tel.: 612-546-1500
Earnings: $19,667,000
Approx.Sls.: $454,735,000
Emp.: 520
Fiscal Year-end: 12/31/91
Mfr. Refrigerated Dairy Prods. & Potato Products-Frozen & Non-Frozen, Fresh & Frozen Egg Products
S.I.C.: 2026; 2021; 2022; 2023; 2024; 2038; 2099; 5411
Richard G. Olson *(Pres.)*
Jeffrey M. Shapiro *(Exec. V.P.)*
Kevin s. Murphy *(Sec. & Treas.)*
John D. Reedy *(Chief Fin. Officer)*

MICHAEL'S DEVELOPMENT COMPANY
1 Stow Rd.
Marlton, NJ 08053
Mailing Address:
P.O. Box 994
Marlton, NJ 08053
Tel.: 609-596-3008
Fax: 609-596-6093
Emp.: 575
Developer & Syndicator
S.I.C.: 6531; 6552
Michael J. Levitt *(Pres.)*
James V. Bleil *(V.P.-Mktg.)*
Robert J. Greer *(V.P.)*
Anne Lindgren *(V.P.)*
Frank J. Nash *(V.P.)*

Computer Systems/Hardware:
IBM

Outside Service Firm(s):

Continental Bank N. A.*(Major Banking Relationship)*
231 S. LaSalle St.
Chicago, IL 60697
Tel.: 312-828-2345
Tel.: 800-426-5754
Telex: 312-828-1783

MICHAELS GROUP INC.
6 Century Hill Dr.
Latham, NY 12110
Tel.: 518-783-9641 **NY**
Fax: 518-783-0930
Year Founded: 1981
Assets: $20,000,000
Liabilities: $12,200,000
Net Worth: $7,800,000
Approx.Sls.: $38,800,000
Emp.: 50
Fiscal Year-end: 12/31/89
Single Family Homes, Townhouses & Condos Contractor
S.I.C.: 1521
J. David Michaels *(Chm. Bd. & Pres.)*
John H. Michaels *(V.P.)*
James Braman *(Legal Officer)*

Principal(s):
John H. Michaels

No. of U.S. Offices: 1

Computer Systems/Hardware:
Wang Mini Model 2200; IBM & Compatible Personal Computers

Outside Service Firm(s):

KPMG Peat Marwick*(Auditors)*
74 N. Pearl St.
Albany, NY 12207
Tel.: 518-455-8809

Hanover Insurance Co.*(Commercial Insurance Carrier)*
Albany, NY

United Community Insurance Group*(Commercial Insurance Carrier)*
Albany, NY

Blue Shield of Northeastern New York, Inc.*(Group Insurer)*
Albany, NY

Guardian Life Insurance Co.*(Group Insurer)*
Albany, NY

Tobin & Dempf*(Legal Firm)*
Albany, NY

First of Glens Falls*(Major Banking Relationship)*
Glens Falls, NY

Key Bank*(Major Banking Relationship)*
Albany, NY

Marine Midland Bank*(Major Banking Relationship)*
Syracuse, NY

Ellsworth Amidon*(Pension Manager)*
Albany, NY

MICHIGAN BLUEBERRY GROWERS ASSN.
(d/b/a MBG Marketing)
P.O. Box B,
Grand Junction, MI 49056
Tel.: 616-434-6791
Fax: 616-434-6779
Year Founded: 1934
Approx.Sls.: $31,000,000
Emp.: 60

Import Export
Great Lakes Blueberry Preserves & Frozen Blueberries
S.I.C.: 0171
Charles Dailey *(Pres.)*
John Shelford *(Gen. Mgr.)*
Lorrie Ford Merker *(Treas.)*
Rodney Cook *(Dir.-Opers.)*
Michael Klackle *(Dir.-Fresh Sls.)*
Lynn Hawkinson *(Mgr.-Sls. Promo.)*

Computer Systems/Hardware:
DEC

MICHIGAN MILK PRODUCERS ASSOCIATION
41310 Bridge St.
Novi, MI 48375
Tel.: 313-474-6672
Fax: 313-474-0924
Year Founded: 1919
Approx.Sls.: $409,000,000
Emp.: 250
Fiscal Year-end: 9/30/90
Dairy Cooperative; Milk Processing & Marketing
S.I.C.: 2026; 5143; 8611
Elwood Kirkpatrick *(Pres.)*
Remus Rigg *(V.P.)*
Velmar Green *(Treas.)*
Paul Jermanus *(Controller)*
Walt Wosje *(Sec. & Gen. Mgr.)*
Sheila Burkhardt *(Dir.-Member Rels.)*
John Dilland *(Dir.-Fin. & Asst. Treas.)*
Patricia Hebert *(Dir.-Human Resources)*
Greg Schulkey *(Mgr.-Data Processing)*
Laura Child *(Member Communications Coord.)*

Computer Systems/Hardware:
Burroughs; Macintosh

Outside Service Firm(s):

Deloitte & Touche*(Auditors)*
200 Renaissance Center, 16th Fl.
Detroit, MI 48243
Tel.: 313-396-3000
Fax: 313-259-8087

Blue Cross & Blue Shield of Michigan*(Group Insurer)*
Detroit, MI

Foster, Swift, Collins & Smith*(Legal Firm)*
Lansing, MI

National Bank of Detroit*(Major Banking Relationship)*
611 Woodward
Detroit, MI 48226
Tel.: 313-225-1000

AFA Financial*(Pension Manager)*
Cleveland, OH

NWQ Investment Management*(Pension Manager)*
655 S. Hope St.
Los Angeles, CA
Tel.: 213-624-6700
Fax: 213-689-4757

Division:

Michigan Milk Products Div. **(1)**
1336 E. Maumee St.
Adrian, MI 49221
Tel.: 517-265-6184

MICHIGAN STATE LOTTERY BUREAU
101 E. Hillsdale
Lansing, MI 48913
Mailing Address:
P.O. Box 30023
Lansing, MI 48909
Tel.: 517-335-5600
Fax: 517-335-5685
Approx.Sls.: $886,000,000
Emp.: 200
Fiscal Year-end: 3/31/91
State Lottery Games
S.I.C.: 7999
Jerry R. Crandall *(Commissioner)*
Jack Schaffer *(Chief Deputy Commissioner)*
Scott Matteson *(Deputy Commissioner-Admin.)*
James Kipp *(Deputy Commissioner-Opers.)*
Thomas Egan *(Deputy Commissioner-Mktg.)*
Libbie Ballard *(Exec. Asst.)*

Division:

Charitable Gaming Div. **(1)**
6545 Mercantile Way
Lansing, MI 48909
Tel.: 517-887-6850
S.I.C.: 7999

MICHIGAN TRACTOR AND MACHINERY CO.
(d/b/a Michigan Cat)
24800 Novi Rd.
Novi, MI 48375
Mailing Address:
P.O. Box 918
Novi, MI 48050
Tel.: 313-349-4800 **MI**
Fax: 313-349-4800
Year Founded: 1943
Assets: $100,000,000
Liabilities: $75,000,000
Net Worth: $25,000,000
Approx.Sls.: $155,000,000
Emp.: 400
Fiscal Year-end: 12/31/90
Sales & Service of Construction & Mining Equipment.
S.I.C.: 5082
Jerrold M. Jung *(Pres.)*
Bob White *(Exec. V.P.-Opers.)*
Jerrold A. Frost *(Staff V.P.-Mktg. Services)*
W.E. Creel *(Treas. & Sec.)*

Outside Service Firm(s):

Plante & Moran*(Auditors)*
Southfield, MI

Butzel Long*(Legal Firm)*
Madden Bldg., 150 W. Jefferson, Ste. 900
Detroit, MI 48226-4430
Tel.: 313-225-7000
Fax: 313-225-7080

National Bank of Detroit*(Major Banking Relationship)*
611 Woodward
Detroit, MI 48226
Tel.: 313-225-1000

MICHIGAN WHEEL CORPORATION
1501 Buchanan, S.W.
Grand Rapids, MI 49507
Tel.: 616-452-6941
Fax: 616-247-0227
Year Founded: 1903
Approx.Sls.: $30,000,000
Emp.: 250
Export
Manufacture Inboard & Outboard Boat Propellers; Industrial Agitating & Mixing Propellers
S.I.C.: 3366; 3599
Charles Robins *(Chm. Bd.)*
Stan Heide *(Pres. & Chief Exec. Officer)*
Tom Siler *(V.P.-Fin. & Treas.)*
Marty Ronis *(V.P.-Mktg.)*
D.W. Seitz *(Mgr.-Credit)*
William Herrick *(Dir.-Mktg. Svcs.)*
John Baar *(Dir.-Human Resources)*
Elane Cannady *(Pur. Agent)*

No. of Mfg. Plants/Facilities: 1
No. of U.S. Offices: 1
No. of Foreign Offices: 1

Computer Systems/Hardware:
IBM

Outside Service Firm(s):

Crowe, Chizek & Co.*(Auditors)*
Grand Rapids, MI

Union Bank*(Major Banking Relationship)*
200 Ottawa NW
Grand Rapids, MI 49503
Tel.: 616-451-7000

MICO, INC.
6790 Commercial Dr.
Springfield, VA 22151
Tel.: 703-256-6400 **VA**
Fax: 703-750-9061
Approx.Sls.: $46,000,000
Emp.: 250
Holding Company; Kitchen Cabinets; Hardware For Building Industrial
S.I.C.: 5031; 5072; 6512; 5719
O. Ashby Reardon, Jr. *(Chm. Bd.)*
Andy Ellis *(Pres.)*

Outside Service Firm(s):

Bruner, Kane & McCarthy*(Auditors)*
Alexandria, VA

Stirtz, Bernards & Company*(Auditors)*
7200 Metro Blvd.
Edina, MN 55435

Crestar Bank*(Major Banking Relationship)*
P.O. Box 26665,
Richmond, VA 23261
Tel.: 804-782-5995

Schwalb, Donnenfeld, Bray & Silbert*(Legal Firm)*
Washington, DC

Subsidiaries:

Valley National Bank*(Major Banking Relationship)*
North Mankato, MN

Robinson Export-Import Corporation **(1)**
6790 Commercial Dr.
Springfield, VA 22151
Tel.: 703-256-6400
Approx.Sls.: $41,000,000
Emp.: 183
Hardboard Kitchen Cabinets; Plumbing
S.I.C.: 5031; 5074
H. Hammond Snyder *(Chm. Bd.)*
O. Ashby Reardon *(Vice Chm. Bd.)*
William A. Ellis *(Pres.)*
Richard Maresco *(Sr. V.P.)*
Daniel R. Riso *(Sr. V.P.)*

Division:

Rudolph & West **(1)**
6728 Industrial Rd.
Springfield, VA 22151
Tel.: 703-750-3514
Hardware
S.I.C.: 5072
H. Hammond Snyder *(Pres.)*

Mico West **(1)**
701 E. Francis St.
Ontario, CA 91761
Tel.: 909-947-9058
Mfg. Hydraulic Brake Systems & Components, Including Brake Locks, Multiple Disc Brakes, Brake Activators & Brake Cylinders
S.I.C.: 3714
Mark McGrath *(Chief Oper. Officer)*

MICO INC.
1911 Lee Blvd.
North Mankato, MN 56003
Tel.: 507-625-6426 **MN**
Fax: 507-625-3212
Year Founded: 1946
Assets: $11,876,882
Liabilities: $1,308,887
Net Worth: $10,567,995
Approx.Sls.: $22,000,000
Emp.: 250
Export
Mfr. Hydraulic Brake Systems & Components, Including Brake Locks, Multiple Disc Brakes, Brake Actuators & Brake Cylinders
S.I.C.: 3714
G.J. McGrath *(Chm. Bd. & Pres.)*
Brent P. McGrath *(Chief Fin. Officer, Treas. & Sec.)*
Daniel S. McGrath *(V.P.-Sls.)*
Katie Wilaby *(Controller)*
Tod Tillman *(Dir.-Res. & Devel.)*
Michael Danberry *(Plant Mgr.)*
Tim McCall *(Mgr.-Intl. Sls.)*
William Vagts *(Mgr.-Adv. & Art)*
Tim Loe *(Pur. Agent)*
Principal(s):
G.J. McGrath
Brent P. McGrath
Daniel S. McGrath

No. of Mfg. Plants/Facilities: 2
No. of U.S. Offices: 2

Computer Systems/Hardware:
NCR

MICOM COMMUNICATIONS CORP.
4100 Los Angeles Ave.
Simi Valley, CA 93063
Tel.: 805-583-8600
Tel.: 800-642-6687 **CA**
Telex: 687-497
Fax: 805-583-1997
Year Founded: 1973
Assets: $223,206,000
Liabilities: $48,605,000
Net Worth: $174,601,000
Sales Range: $60-79 Million
Emp.: 375
Fiscal Year-end: 3/31/93
Export
Mfr. of Data Communications Equipment
S.I.C.: 3577
Barry Phelps *(Chm. & Chief Exec. Officer)*
Gilbert Cabral *(Pres. & Chief Exec. Officer)*
Dwight Olson *(V.P.-Opers.)*
John Rouse *(V.P.-Worldwide Sls. & Mktg.)*
Fran Good *(Chief Fin. Officer)*
Jim Kinnebrew *(Asst. V.P.-Domestic Sls.)*
Bill Dilfer *(Dir.-Mktg.)*
Jack Eberts *(Dir.-Production Opers.)*
Betty Harper *(Dir.-Employee Benefits)*
Susan Mason *(Dir.)*
Dick Ballagh *(Mgr.-Human Resources)*
Richard Borden *(Mgr.-Mktg. Communications)*
Lawrence Ellis *(Mgr.-Cash)*

No. of Mfg. Plants/Facilities: 2
No. of U.S. Offices: 12
No. of Foreign Offices: 55

Computer Systems/Hardware:
IBM, Hewlett-Packard, DEC

Outside Service Firm(s):

Arthur Andersen & Co.*(Auditors)*
1500 Commerce Tower, 911 Main St.
Kansas City, MO 64105
Tel.: 816-221-4200
Fax: 816-221-7693

Bank of America NT&SA*(Major Banking Relationship)*
555 S. Flower St., 5th Fl.
Los Angeles, CA 90071
Tel.: 213-228-3868

Plant:

Black Box Corporation **(1)**
Mayview Road at Park Drive
Lawrence, PA 15055
Tel.: 412-746-5500 (100%)
Mfr. of Data Communications Accessories
S.I.C.: 3577
Eugene R. Yost *(Pres.)*

Subsidiaries:

Black Box Corporation **(1)**
P.O. Box 12800,
Lawrence, PA 15055
Tel.: 412-746-5500 (100%)
Fax: 412-476-0746
Approx.Sls.: $65,000,000
Emp.: 421
Mfr. of Data Communications Accessories
S.I.C.: 3577
Eugene R. Yost *(Pres.)*
Peter Highberg *(V.P.-Sls. & Mktg.)*
Kenneth C. Shaw *(V.P.-Engrng.)*
Anna Baird *(Controller)*
David R. Hughes *(Gen. Counsel)*
Kathy Bullions *(Mgr.-Pur.)*
Dan Dougherty *(Dir.-Personnel)*

MICOM Caribe, Inc. **(1)**
Vicks Merrel Drive, Lotio
Cayey, PR 00633
Tel.: 809-738-4221 (100%)
Emp.: 233
Mfr. of Data Communications Equipment
S.I.C.: 3577
Thomas Moschetti *(Gen. Mgr.)*

Non-U.S. Holding:

MICOM Communications Corp. **(1)**
Wier Bank, Bray-on-Thames Near Maidenhead 5L62ED, Berkshire United Kingdom
Tel.: 44 628 770011
Fax: 44 628 770701
Mfr. of Data Communications Equipment
S.I.C.: 3577
Ken Burrough *(Asst. V.P.-Intl. Sls.)*
Richard Borden *(Mgr.-Pub. Rels.)*

The Micor Center
(See Micro Electronics Listing)

MICRO COMPONENT TECHNOLOGY INC.
3850 N. Victoria St.
Saint Paul, MN 55126
Mailing Address:
P.O. Box 64013
St. Paul, MN 55164
Tel.: 612-482-5100
Tel.: 800-628-1628 **DE**
Fax: 612-482-6492
Year Founded: 1972
Approx.Sls.: $57,400,000
Emp.: 620
Fiscal Year-end: 6/30/92
Import Export
Manufacture Test Equipment, Package Inspection & Handling Machinery, Automation Equipment
S.I.C.: 3825; 3699
Gunther Schaaf *(Chm. Bd.)*
D.J. Hill *(Pres. & Chief Exec. Officer)*
Raeanne Keefe *(V.P. Admin./Opers.)*
Russ Smith *(V.P.-Mfg.)*
Steve Turner *(V.P.-Sls. & Mktg.)*
John Matsushima *(Chief Fin. Officer)*
Phil DeCaro *(Gen. Counsel)*
Tom Doyle *(Dir.-Data Processing)*
Mark Godfrey *(Dir.-Mktg.)*
Kathleen Higgins *(Dir.-Import/Export)*
Mike Corrazzo *(Mgr.-Pur.)*
Jo Ebertowski *(Mgr.-Human Resources)*
Laura Miraglio *(Mgr.-Meetings Planning)*
Chet Breiholtz *(Corp. Travel Planner)*

No. of Mfg. Plants/Facilities: 3
No. of U.S. Offices: 5

Outside Service Firm(s):

Price Waterhouse*(Auditors)*
3100 Multifoods Tower, 33 S. Sixth St.
Minneapolis, MN 55402

First Bank, N.A.*(Major Banking Relationship)*
First Bank Place
Minneapolis, MN 55480

Subsidiary:

ITS: Intertrade Scientific, Inc. **(1)**
176 Bolton Rd.
Vernon, CT 06066
Tel.: 203-871-0401
Emp.: 30
Joe Landry *(Chief Fin. Officer)*
Joe Mahar *(Dir.-Sls.)*

MICRO ELECTRONICS
(d/b/a The Micro Center)
1555 W. Lane Ave.
Columbus, OH 43221
Tel.: 614-481-8041
Fax: 614-481-4439
Year Founded: 1980
Sales Range: $20-39 Million
Emp.: 250
Micro-Computer Dept. Store
S.I.C.: 5734
John Baker *(Pres.)*

Computer Systems/Hardware:
IBM PC

MICRO-MET L CORP.
3419 Roosevelt Ave.
Indianapolis, IN 46218
Tel.: 317-543-5980 **IN**
Fax: 317-543-5986
Year Founded: 1964
Approx.Sls.: $11,000,000
Emp.: 75
Manufacture Accessories for Commercial Heating & Air Conditioning Companies
S.I.C.: 3496; 5075
Gerald Shultz *(Chm. Bd., Pres. & Chief Exec. Officer)*
James Lindgren *(Chief Oper. Officer & V.P.-Opers.)*
Ann Wolf *(Controller)*
Principal(s):
Gerald Shultz

No. of Mfg. Plants/Facilities: 1
No. of U.S. Offices: 1

Computer Systems/Hardware:
PC-Various

Outside Service Firm(s):

Ernst & Young*(Auditors)*
One Indiana Square, Ste. 3400
Indianapolis, IN 46204
Tel.: 317-236-1100

Hartford Life Insurance Co.*(Group Insurer)*
Hartford, CT 06104-2999

Thomas Fitzpatrick*(Legal Firm)*
Chicago, IL

Standard Chartered Bank*(Major Banking Relationship)*
33 W. Monroe
Chicago, IL 60603
Tel.: 312-726-3300
Fax: 312-372-5694

MICROBAND COMPANIES, INC.
286 Eldridge Rd.
Fairfield, NJ 07004
Tel.: 201-227-8700 **DE**
Fax: 201-227-2612
Year Founded: 1985
Approx.Sls.: $18,000,000
Emp.: 120
Fiscal Year-end: 12/31/91
Import Export
Cable Television Services; Subscription Television Services
S.I.C.: 4841
J. Patrick Dugan *(Pres. & Chief Exec. Officer)*
William K. Hoffman *(Sr. V.P. & Gen. Counsel)*
Alfred A. Dalimonte *(Sr. V.P.)*
Mary Ellen Bauman *(V.P.-Fin. & Chief Fin. Officer)*
Mike Abramson *(Treas.)*
Larry Morgan *(Dir.-Opers.)*
Gary Lindeman *(Dir.-Mktg. & Sls.)*
Lloyd McWhorter *(Dir.-Customer Service)*
Irene Regan *(Dir.-Data Processing)*
Michelle Zimmerman *(Dir.-Human Resources)*
Jim Baumann *(Asst. V.P.)*
Jim Carlino *(Mgr.-Sls.)*

Outside Service Firm(s):

Chase Manhattan Bank, N.A.*(Major Banking Relationship)*
One Chase Manhattan Plaza
New York, NY 10081
Tel.: 212-552-2222
Tel.: 800-526-0801
Fax: 212-552-7175

MICRODOT, INC.
10 S. LaSalle St.
Chicago, IL 60603
Mailing Address:
P.O. Box 3001
Fullerton, CA 92634-3001
Tel.: 312-899-1925
Fax: 312-899-9041
Year Founded: 1983
Approx.Sls.: $100,000,000
Emp.: 1,100
Export
Corporate Headquarters; Mfr. of Industrial Components
S.I.C.: 3452; 3499; 3679; 3699
Richard P. Strubel *(Pres. & Chief Exec. Officer)*
Dianne Blanco *(Exec. V.P.)*
David A. Werner *(Chief Fin. Officer & V.P.)*
Terry Grundman *(Sec.)*
Violeta B. Rotz *(Asst. Treas.)*
Joseph Blombers *(Dir.-Human Resources)*
Principal(s):
Richard P. Strubel

No. of Mfg. Plants/Facilities: 20
No. of U.S. Offices: 25
No. of Foreign Offices: 2

Computer Systems/Hardware:
IBM System 5150, IBM PC

Outside Service Firm(s):

Arthur Andersen & Co.*(Auditors)*
33 W. Monroe St.
Chicago, IL 60603-4067
Tel.: 312-580-0033
Fax: 312-507-6748

Mayer, Brown & Platt*(Legal Firm)*
190 S. LaSalle St., Ste. 3900
Chicago, IL 60603
Tel.: 312-782-0600

Divisions:

Connector Industries of America **(1)**
10340 Julian Dr.
Cincinnati, OH 45246
Tel.: 513-772-3680
Fax: 513-772-3688
Mfr. of Hermetically Sealed Connectors
S.I.C.: 3679
Dale Haney *(Chief Oper. Officer)*

Industrial Fastening Systems Group **(1)**
433 Stephenson Hwy.
Troy, MI 48084
Tel.: 313-583-1000

Malco Microdot **(1)**
201 Progress Dr.
Montgomeryville, PA 18936
Tel.: 215-699-5373
Fax: 215-699-5536
Mike Schmell *(Chief Oper. Officer)*

Microdot Inserts **(1)**
190 W. Crowther
Placentia, CA 92670
Tel.: 714-524-5854
Fax: 714-524-5346
Emp.: 200
Mfr. of Inserts for Aerospace & Aircraft Industries
S.I.C.: 3724
Patti Stubban *(Gen. Mgr.)*
Terry Keenahan *(Mgr.-Mktg.)*

Poly-Seal Div. **(1)**
1754 W. 500 So.
Salt Lake City, UT 84101
Tel.: 801-973-9171

Selastomer Div. **(1)**
23800 Research Dr.
Farmington, MI 48024
Tel.: 313-477-6100

Valley Mould Div. **(1)**
P. O. Box 10
Hubbard, OH 44425
Tel.: 216-534-1195

Group:

Microdot Aerospace Fastening Systems Group **(1)**
800 South State College Blvd.
Fullerton, CA 92634-3001
Tel.: 714-871-1550
Fax: 714-680-0175
Mfr. of Industrial Components
S.I.C.: 3069; 3089; 3452; 3469; 3499; 3679; 3699
Jordan Law *(Grp. Pres. & Gen. Mgr.)*
Robert Beers *(V.P.-Sls. & Mktg.)*
Joe Blomberg *(V.P.-Personnel)*
David Werner *(V.P., Chief Fin. & Chief Information Officer)*
Imre Berecz *(Dir.-Research & Devel.)*
Clay Glessner *(Dir.-Environment/Natural Resources)*
George Uhrich *(Dir.-Taxes)*
Craig Brown *(Mgr.-Tech. Services)*
Tom Flecky *(Mgr.-Personnel Training & Devel.)*
Sue Hay *(Mgr.-Pur.)*
Rosemary Kuczer *(Mgr.-Data Processing)*
Gabor Lingauer *(Mgr.-Printing)*
Margaret Morales *(Mgr.-Employee Benefits)*
Herb Sorensen *(Mgr.-Quality Control)*
Tamira Smith *(Corp. Librarian)*
Gail A. Carr *(Coord.-Mktg. Service)*

Non-U.S. Holding:

Microdot Aerospace Limited **(1)**
Blackthorne Road Colnbrook,
Slough, SL3 OAG, United Kingdom
Tel.: 753 683256
Fax: 0753 684893
Mfg., Sls. & Mktg. of Metal Fasteners for the Aerospace Industry
S.I.C.: 3429; 5088; 3728
Joseph Varholick *(Mng. Dir.)*
R.M. Bale *(Mgr.-Fin.)*

MICRODYNAMICS, INC.
10461 Brockwood Rd.
Dallas, TX 75238
Tel.: 214-343-1170
Fax: 214-503-8571
Approx.Sls.: $18,000,000
Emp.: 150
Manufacture Computer CADD Systems
S.I.C.: 7372
C. Ron Martell *(Chm. Bd. & Pres.)*
Ray Cotten *(V.P.-Mktg.)*
Ed Dealey *(V.P.-Fin.)*
Elmer N. Leslie *(V.P.-Opers.)*
Debbie Garrett *(Dir.-Human Resources)*

Outside Service Firm(s):

Ernst & Young*(Auditors)*
2121 San Jacinto, Ste. 500
Dallas, TX 75201
Tel.: 214-969-8000

Texas Commerce Bank*(Major Banking Relationship)*
2200 Ross Ave.
Dallas, TX 75266

MICROFLECT COMPANY, INC.
3575 25th St., S.E.
Salem, OR 97302
Mailing Address:
P.O. Box 12985
Salem, OR 97309-0985
Tel.: 503-363-9267 **OR**
Fax: 503-363-4613
Year Founded: 1956
Assets: $8,000,000
Liabilities: $2,000,000
Net Worth: $6,000,000
Approx.Sls.: $20,000,000
Emp.: 153
Fiscal Year-end: 12/31/91
Import Export
Microwave Communication Equipment; Grating, Open Steel Flooring; Industrial Fasteners; Nuts, Bolts Screws
S.I.C.: 3663; 5085
James S. Kreitzberg *(Chm. Bd.)*
Richard A. Kreitzberg *(Pres. & Chief Exec. Officer)*
Edwin E. Stahl *(Controller)*
John J. Kranitz *(Mgr.-Mktg.)*
Michael Kreitzberg *(Pur. Agent)*
Robert R. Callaway *(Chief Engr.)*
Richard T. Semke *(Plant Supvr.)*

No. of Mfg. Plants/Facilities: 1
No. of U.S. Offices: 1

Computer Systems/Hardware:
HP 3000

Outside Service Firm(s):

Commercial Bank*(Major Banking Relationship)*
Salem, OR 97309
Tel.: 503-399-2900

Bullivant, Houser, Bailey, Pendergrass & Hoffman*(Legal Firm)*
Portland, OR

MICRON SEPARATIONS, INC.
135 Flanders Rd.
Westborough, MA 01581
Mailing Address:
P.O. Box 1046,
Westborough, MA 01581
Tel.: 508-366-8212
Tel.: 800-444-8212
Year Founded: 1982
Approx.Sls.: $10,000,000
Emp.: 50
Fiscal Year-end: 10/31/92
Export
Develops, Manufactures & Markets a Wide Range of Filters, Filtration Devices, Hybridization & Diagnostic Membranes for the Laboratory, Research, Medical Electronic & Beverage Markets
S.I.C.: 3826
John Greenwood *(Pres.)*
David Hann *(V.P.-Mktg. & Sls.)*
Steven Johnson *(V.P.-Research & Devel.)*

MICROPHASE CORPORATION
587 Connecticut Ave.
Norwalk, CT 06854
Mailing Address:
P.O. Box 960
Norwalk, CT 06856-0960
Tel.: 203-866-8000
Fax: 203-853-3304
Fax: 203-857-0915
Approx.Sls.: $13,000,000
Emp.: 130
Microwave Components & Sub-Systems
S.I.C.: 3679
Necdet Ergul *(Pres.)*
Joseph F. Chiappetta *(V.P.-Video Circuits Grp.)*
Leon Gauthier *(V.P.-Fin. & Treas.)*
Floyd Parin *(V.P.-Mktg.)*
Selim Temel *(Sec.)*
Sonia Kowalkowski *(Pur. Agent)*

Outside Service Firm(s):

Ernst & Young*(Auditors)*
One North Broadway
White Plains, NY 10601
Tel.: 914-761-7888

Cohen & Wolf*(Legal Firm)*
Bridgeport, CT

Chase Manhattan Bank, N.A.*(Major Banking Relationship)*
Bridgeport, CT

MICROPUMP CORPORATION
1402 N.E. 136th Ave.
Vancouver, WA 98684
Tel.: 206-253-2008 **CA**
Fax: 415-680-0754
Year Founded: 1960
Approx.Sls.: $16,000,000
Emp.: 110
Pumps & Pumping Equipment
S.I.C.: 3561
Wayne Ross *(Pres.)*
R. Mullaney *(V.P.)*
Tom Hinrichs *(Controller)*

Outside Service Firm(s):

First Interstate Bank*(Major Banking Relationship)*
Concord, CA

Subsidiary:

Micropump **(1)**
1990 Olivera Rd.
Concord, CA 94520
Tel.: 510-689-6000
Fax: 510-680-0754
Emp.: 110
Pumps & Pumping Equipment
S.I.C.: 3561
Wayne Ross *(Pres.)*
R. Mullaney *(V.P.)*
Tom Hinrichs *(Controller)*

MICROWAVE NETWORKS INCORPORATED
10795 Rockley Rd.
Houston, TX 77099
Tel.: 713-495-7123
Fax: 713-879-4728
Year Founded: 1982
Approx.Sls.: $20,000,000
Emp.: 160
Fiscal Year-end: 6/30/91
Export
Mfr. Short-Haul Microwave Radio Equip.
S.I.C.: 3669
Arthur Epley *(Pres.)*
Walter Lammert *(Exec. V.P.)*
Bruce Jenning *(V.P.-Intl. Bus. Contact)*
Bill Kiuenta *(Controller)*
Mark Feller *(Dir.-Quality Control)*
Bruce Weaver *(Dir.-Pur.)*
Milton Lutz *(Mgr.-Adv.)*

Computer Systems/Hardware:
Microwave Radio

MID-AM BUILDING SUPPLY, INC.
100 W. Sparks
Moberly, MO 65270
Tel.: 816-263-2140

Mid-Am Building Supply, Inc.—(Continued)

Fax: 816-263-7892
Year Founded: 1967
Approx.Sls.: $40,000,000
Emp.: 100
Rough, Dressed & Finished Lumber
S.I.C.: 5031
Joseph I. Knaebel *(Pres.)*
Joseph F. Knaebel *(V.P.)*
Richard L. Knaebel *(Treas.)*
R. Elliott *(Sec.)*

Outside Service Firm(s):

John H. Koffman, Inc.*(Auditors)*
Moberly, MO

Citibank*(Major Banking Relationship)*
Moberly, MO

MID-AMERICA DAIRYMEN, INC.
3253 E. Chestnut Expwy.
Springfield, MO 65802
Tel.: 417-865-7100
Fax: 417-865-1093
Year Founded: 1968
Earnings: $8,306,000
Approx.Sls.: $1,344,280,000
Emp.: 4,100
Fiscal Year-end: 12/31/91
Manufacture & Market Butter, Cheese, Condensed, Evaporated & Fluid Milk
S.I.C.: 2021; 2022; 2023; 2026; 5143
Ivan Stickler *(Pres.)*
Gary Hanman *(Chief Exec. Officer)*
Larry Claypool *(Sr. V.P.-Research & Quality Control)*
Bill Blakeslee *(Corp. V.P.- Mktg. & Plng.)*
Gerald Bos *(Corp. V.P.-Acctg. & Fin. & Asst. Treas.)*
David Parrish *(Corp. V.P.-Member Rels. & Admin.)*
Ray Silvey *(Corp. V.P.-Human Resources)*
Lonni Spurgeon *(V.P.-Refrigerated Dairy Prods.)*
Arlen Schwinke *(Treas.)*
Michael Kuechle *(Sec.)*
Marti Burnett *(Controller)*
Les Long *(Dir.-Pension Admin.)*
Leroy Robertson *(Mgr.-Data Processing)*

Principal(s):
Ivan Stickler
Gary Hanman

No. of Mfg. Plants/Facilities: 30

Computer Systems/Hardware:
IBM 4381

Outside Service Firm(s):

Deloitte & Touche*(Auditors)*
1010 Grand Ave.
Kansas City, MO 64106-2232
Tel.: 816-474-6180

Co-Bank St. Louis Region*(Investment Banker)*
1415 Olive St.
St. Louis, MO 63166

Gage & Tucker*(Legal Firm)*
2345 Grand Ave., 28th Fl.
Kansas City, MO 64108
Tel.: 816-292-2000

MID AMERICA INTERNATIONAL TRUCKS, INC.
1750 E. Brooks Rd.
Memphis, TN 38116
Tel.: 901-345-6275 **DE**
Fax: 901-396-3746
Year Founded: 1982
Approx.Sls.: $38,000,000
Emp.: 100
Fiscal Year-end: 10/31/91
Wholesale Distribution of New & Used Pickups, Commercial Trucks, Truck Equipment & Parts; Truck Engine Repair, Except Industrial; Truck Leasing Without Drivers
S.I.C.: 5511; 5012; 5531; 7538
Richard C. Sweebe *(Pres.)*
John T. Brannen *(Treas. & Sec.)*

Outside Service Firm(s):

National Bank of Commerce*(Major Banking Relationship)*
Memphis, TN

Divisions:

Idealease of Memphis **(1)**
3340 Pearson Rd.
Memphis, TN
Emp.: 15

MID AMERICA STEEL, INC.
92 N. P Ave.
Fargo, ND 58102
Tel.: 701-232-8831
Fax: 701-280-0103
Sales Range: $10-19 Million
Emp.: 150
Structural Steel Fabrication & Bulk Storage
S.I.C.: 3441; 3443; 3523
Edward A. Simonson *(Chm. Bd.)*
Don Clark *(Pres. & Chief Exec. Officer)*
Roger Hentges *(V.P.-Sls.)*
James Kerting *(V.P.)*
George Cook *(Treas.)*
Everett A. Martin *(Sec.)*

Outside Service Firm(s):

Eide Helmeke & Co.*(Auditors)*
500 Dakota Bank Building
Fargo, ND 58102

Norwest Bank of North Dakota, N.A.*(Major Banking Relationship)*
Fargo, ND

Mid Continent Cabinetry, Inc.
(Name Changed To Norcraft Companies, Inc.)

MID-CONTINENT SCREW PRODUCTS CO.
3701 W. Lunt
Lincolnwood, IL 60645
Tel.: 708-679-3737
Telex: 724379
Fax: 708-470-9220
Year Founded: 1952
Approx.Sls.: $15,000,000
Emp.: 135
Fiscal Year-end: 7/31/90
Export
Mfr. & Distributor Industrial Fasteners: Screws, Nuts, Bolts & Washers. Fasten-Pak; Band-A-Tape; Extru-Lok; Ultra-Gard; Extru-Plas
S.I.C.: 5072; 3452
N.C. Couzin *(Pres.)*
J.E. Hirsch *(Exec. V.P. & Treas.)*
Mark S. Couzin *(V.P. & Dir.-Sls.)*
Richard Burkhart *(Comptroller)*
G. Brandon *(Mgr.-Quality Control)*
T. Chustak *(Mgr.-Prod.)*
D. MacGirr *(Mgr.-Plant)*
M. Rodriguez *(Pur. Agent)*

Subsidiary:

Abacus Packaging Corp. **(1)**
3701 W. Lunt
Lincolnwood, IL 60645
Tel.: 708-679-3737
Fax: 708-470-09220

MID-KANSAS CO-OP ASSOCIATION
307 W. Cole
Moundridge, KS 67107
Mailing Address:
P.O. Box D
Moundridge, KS 67107
Tel.: 316-345-6328 **KS**
Fax: 316-345-6330
Year Founded: 1965
Assets: $9,848,911
Earnings: $562,088
Liabilities: $5,329,189
Net Worth: $4,519,722
Approx.Sls.: $32,985,130
Emp.: 75
Fiscal Year-end: 2/28/92
Oper. Grain Elevator; Feed & Fertilizer Retailer; Oper. Service Station
S.I.C.: 2048; 4221; 5541
John Ratzlaff *(Pres.)*
Robert Nattier *(Chief Oper. Officer, Chief Fin. Officer & Gen. Mgr.)*
Dennis Teter *(Controller)*

No. of Mfg. Plants/Facilities: 8

Computer Systems/Hardware:
IBM Model 80

Outside Service Firm(s):

Lindburg & Vogel*(Auditors)*
Hutchinson, KS

Farmland Insurance*(Group Insurer)*
1963 Bell Ave.
Des Moines, IA 50315

Terry Berthoff*(Legal Firm)*
Hutchinson, KS

Citizens State Bank*(Major Banking Relationship)*
Moundridge, KS

MID-SOUTH FORD TRUCK SALES, INC.
673 E. Brooks Rd.
Memphis, TN 38116
Tel.: 901-332-8990
Fax: 901-332-5226
Approx.Sls.: $35,000,000
Emp.: 80
Retail & Leases Trucks
S.I.C.: 5511; 7513
Gerald Ruden *(Pres.)*
Ed Rainisewski *(V.P.)*

MID-SOUTH MILLING COMPANY, INC.
785 Crossover Ln., Ste. 116
Memphis, TN 38117
Tel.: 901-767-0071
Fax: 901-681-4337
Year Founded: 1961
Approx.Sls.: $75,000,000
Emp.: 200
Manufacture Animal Feed Ingredients
S.I.C.: 2048
John L. Petty *(Pres. & Chief Exec. Officer)*
James L. Petty *(V.P.)*

Outside Service Firm(s):

Coopers & Lybrand*(Auditors)*
1000 Morgan-Keegan Tower, 50 N. Front St.
Memphis, TN 38103
Tel.: 901-529-1100

MID SOUTH SALES
520 Walnut
Helena, AR 72342
Mailing Address:
P.O. Box 709
Helena, AR 72342
Tel.: 501-338-3464 **AR**
Fax: 501-338-8667
Year Founded: 1962
Approx.Sls.: $23,000,000
Emp.: 165
Fiscal Year-end: 11/30/88
Wholesale & Retail Oil Products, Convenience Stores
S.I.C.: 5172; 5411
William B. Benton *(Chm. Bd., Chief Exec. Officer & Chief Fin. Officer)*
Ernest Atkeison *(Dir.-Data Processing)*
Murray Benton *(Dir.-Personnel & Treas.)*

Computer Systems/Hardware:
Datapoint

Outside Service Firm(s):

Fred T. Neely*(Auditors)*
Greenwood, MS

Raff & Galloway*(Legal Firm)*
Helena, AR

Merchants & Farmers Bank*(Major Banking Relationship)*
West Helena, AR

Planters National Bank*(Major Banking Relationship)*
Hughes, AR

MID-STATES PETROLEUM INC.
2146 Livernois
Troy, MI 48099
Mailing Address:
P.O. Box 400
Troy, MI 48099
Tel.: 313-528-3577 **MI**
Fax: 313-689-7492
Approx.Sls.: $86,500,000
Emp.: 300
Wholesale & Retail Petroleum Products
S.I.C.: 5171; 5541; 5983
James M. Butler *(Pres.)*
Reginald H. Butler *(Chief Exec. Officer)*
Ken Frank *(Chief Fin. Officer)*
Harry P. Butler *(Exec. V.P.)*

Outside Service Firm(s):

Michigan National Bank*(Major Banking Relationship)*
Troy, MI

MID-WEST AUTOMATION SYSTEMS
1400 Busch Pkwy.
Buffalo Grove, IL 60089
Tel.: 708-541-3570 **IL**
Fax: 708-541-8562
Approx.Sls.: $17,000,000
Emp.: 160
Custom Designed Machinery For The Automotive & Electronic Industry
S.I.C.: 3559
Robert Eitzinger *(Pres.)*
Kenneth Vernon *(V.P.-Fin.)*
Gisela Eitzinger *(Treas. & Sec.)*
Al Pakosta *(Gen. Mgr.)*

Outside Service Firm(s):

Ronald L. Panter & Assoc.*(Legal Firm)*
Chicago, IL

The Northern Trust Co.*(Major Banking Relationship)*
50 S. LaSalle St.
Chicago, IL 60675
Tel.: 312-630-6000
Fax: 312-444-7028

MID-WEST PAPER PRODUCTS COMPANY
12350 E. Nine Mile Rd.
Warren, MI 48089
Tel.: 313-758-6700 **MI**
Fax: 313-758-5288
Year Founded: 1939
Approx.Sls.: $10,000,000

Emp.: 12
Fiscal Year-end: 6/30/90
Office Products & Furniture Distributor
S.I.C.: 5021; 5943; 5044
Floyd E. Allen *(Chm. Bd.)*
John N. Henderson, III *(Pres. & Chief Exec. Officer)*
Howard C. McFarland, III *(Chief Oper. Officer & Chief Fin. Officer)*
Daniel G. Danner *(Controller)*
Jim Collier *(Gen. Mgr.)*

Principal(s):
Floyd E. Allen
John N. Henderson, III
Howard C. McFarland, III

Computer Systems/Hardware:
Datapoint

Outside Service Firm(s):

National City Bank*(Major Banking Relationship)*
P.O. Box 92301,
Cleveland, OH 44101-0900
Tel.: 216-575-2529
Tel.: 800-622-6757
Fax: 216-575-9396

MIDCO INTERNATIONAL INC.
4140 W. Victoria
Chicago, IL 60646
Tel.: 312-604-8700
Fax: 312-604-4070
Approx.Sls.: $10,000,000
Emp.: 110
Heating & Commercial Restaurant Equip. Economite, Ember-Glo, Unipower, Incinomite
S.I.C.: 3433; 3589
Sonya Z. Beyer *(Chm., Pres. & Chief Exec. Officer)*
Robert Mechling *(V.P.-Sls.)*
Robert Stacho *(V.P.-Opers)*

MIDCOAST INDUSTRIAL SERVICES CORPORATION
1620 E Ave., N.E.
Cedar Rapids, IA 52402
Mailing Address:
P.O. Box 1211
Cedar Rapids, IA 52406
Tel.: 319-363-2073 **IA**
Fax: 319-363-8311
Year Founded: 1986
Assets: $5,930,213
Liabilities: $5,046,053
Net Worth: $884,160
Sales Range: $20-39 Million
Emp.: 10
Fiscal Year-end: 2/28/90
Holding Company; Commercial Real Estate Rental; Roofing Contractors; Roofing Material & Supplies, Roofing Consultants
S.I.C.: 2952; 6719; 8742; 1761
William W. Taylor *(Chm. Bd. & Pres.)*
Mary M.T. Suess *(V.P.)*
Jane Carlson *(Sec. & Treas.)*

Principal(s):
William W. Taylor
Mary M.T. Suess

No. of Mfg. Plants/Facilities: 1
No. of U.S. Offices: 1

Computer Systems/Hardware:
DEC-VAX 11750

Outside Service Firm(s):

Ernst & Young*(Auditors)*
Cedar Rapids, IA

Maryland Casualty Co.*(Commercial Insurance Carrier)*
Baltimore, MD

Frank B. Hall*(Group Insurer)*
Omaha, NE

Novak, Rosser & Benz*(Legal Firm)*
Cedar Rapids, IA

Firstar Bank Cedar Rapids, N.A.*(Major Banking Relationship)*
222 Second Ave. S.E.
Cedar Rapids, IA 52406
Tel.: 319-398-4224

Subsidiaries:

D. C. Taylor Co. **(1)**
1620 E Ave., N.E.
Cedar Rapids, IA 52402
Tel.: 319-363-2073 (100%)
Fax: 319-363-8311
Emp.: 150
Roofing Contractor
S.I.C.: 1761
William W. Taylor *(Chm. Bd., Chief Exec. Officer & Technical Dir.)*
Michael W. Murphy *(Pres.)*
Philip J. Suess *(V.P.-Field Opers.)*
Larry Stein *(V.P.-Sls.)*
Gregory J. Thirnbeck *(V.P.-Opers.)*
Jane R. Carlson *(Sec. & Treas.)*

Taylor Associates **(1)**
1620 E. Ave. N.E.
Cedar Rapids, IA 52402
Tel.: 319-363-2073 (100%)
Fax: 319-363-6419
Approx.Sls.: $1,500,000
Emp.: 35
Roof Consulting & Construction Management
S.I.C.: 1761; 8712
William W. Taylor *(Chm. Bd.)*
Kent D. Mattison *(Pres.)*
Jane Carlson *(Treas.)*
Christine Zaugg *(Sec.)*

Taylor Associates **(1)**
701 Center Point Rd., N.E.
Cedar Rapids, IA 52402
Tel.: 319-365-8083
Roof Consulting & Construction Management
S.I.C.: 1761; 8712
William W. Taylor *(Chm. Bd.)*

MIDCOAST MORTGAGE CORPORATION
275 Broad Hollow Road
Melville, NY 11747
Tel.: 516-293-6900 **NY**
Mortgage Banking
S.I.C.: 6162
William Hirschfeld *(Pres.)*

MIDDLESEX/PATRIOT GENERAL INSURANCE COMPANIES
Route 2
Concord, MA 01742
Tel.: 508-369-8600
Approx.Sls.: $141,000,000
Emp.: 215
Fiscal Year-end: 12/31/90
Insurance
S.I.C.: 6411
Larry Ballard *(Pres.)*
Beverly Nelson *(Dir.-Human Resources)*
John Noone *(Dir.-Agency Mktg.)*
Fred Orlosk *(Dir.-Commerical Line Underwriting)*

Subsidiaries:

Middlesex Insurance Co. **(1)**
Route 2
Concord, MA 01742
Tel.: 617-369-8600
S.I.C.: 6411

Patriot General Insurance Co. **(1)**
Route 2
Concord, MA 01742
Tel.: 508-369-8600
S.I.C.: 6411

MIDLAND MUTUAL LIFE INSURANCE CO.
250 E. Broad
Columbus, OH 43215
Tel.: 614-228-2001
Year Founded: 1905
Approx.Sls.: $210,000,000
Emp.: 300
Fiscal Year-end: 12/31/91
Individual Life Insurance and Annuities
S.I.C.: 6311
G.E. Mayo *(Chm. Bd.)*
Mary G. Pollman *(Dir.-Adv.)*

MIDLAND PAPER CO.
5860 N. Pulaski Rd.
Chicago, IL 60646
Tel.: 312-583-0717 **IL**
Fax: 312-583-6917
Approx.Sls.: $100,000,000
Emp.: 60
Wholesale Paper Distributor
S.I.C.: 5111
E. Stanton Hooker *(Pres. & Chief Exec. Officer)*
Francis W. Morley *(Chief Oper. Officer)*

Computer Systems/Hardware:
IBM

Outside Service Firm(s):

LaSalle National Bank*(Major Banking Relationship)*
135 S. LaSalle St., Rm.260
Chicago, IL 60603

MIDWAY FORD TRUCK CENTER INC.
7601 N.E. 38th St.
Kansas City, MO 64161
Tel.: 816-455-3000 **DE**
Fax: 816-454-3796
Year Founded: 1961
Approx.Sls.: $96,183,000
Emp.: 200
Wholesale & Retail Trucks & Truck Parts
S.I.C.: 5511; 5013; 5012
Donald C. Ahnger *(Chm. Bd.)*
Gary N. McClung *(Pres. & Gen. Mgr.)*
Michael W. Doran *(Treas. & Sec.)*

Computer Systems/Hardware:
Microdata

Outside Service Firm(s):

First National Bank of Kansas City*(Major Banking Relationship)*
10th & Baltimore
Kansas City, MO 64105
Tel.: 816-221-2800

MIDWAY PRODUCTS CORPORATION
523 Detroit Ave.
Monroe, MI 48161
Tel.: 313-241-7242
Fax: 313-241-7511
Approx.Sls.: $21,000,000
Emp.: 100
Automotive Stampings
S.I.C.: 3465
James E. Hoyt *(Pres.)*
George W. Hess *(V.P.-Opers.)*
Lloyd A. Miller *(V.P., Treas. & Sec.)*
Kevin Trares *(Controller)*
Cecil H. Lewis *(Dir.-Engrng.)*
Norbert Czernia *(Pur. Agent)*

Outside Service Firm(s):

Monroe Bank & Trust*(Major Banking Relationship)*
102 E. Front St.
Monroe, MI 48161
Tel.: 313-241-3431

MIDWESCO INC.
7720 Lehigh Ave.
Niles, IL 60648
Tel.: 708-966-2150
Fax: 708-966-8563
Approx.Sls.: $80,000,000
Emp.: 550
Mechanical Contracting; Heating & Air Conditioning Service; Boiler Conversions; Prefabricated Underground Pipe
S.I.C.: 1711; 3498; 3585; 3823; 7349; 7623
Henry Mautner *(Chm. Bd.)*
David Unger *(Pres.)*
Michael Bennett *(Chief Fin. Officer & V.P.-Fin.)*

Computer Systems/Hardware:
IBM

Outside Service Firm(s):

Ernst & Young*(Auditors)*
233 S. Wacker Dr.
Chicago, IL 60606
Tel.: 312-368-1800
Fax: 312-645-3095

Greenberg, Keele, Lunn & Aronberg*(Legal Firm)*
One IBM Plaza
Chicago, IL 60611
Tel.: 312-828-9600

Continental Bank N. A.*(Major Banking Relationship)*
231 S. LaSalle St.
Chicago, IL 60697
Tel.: 312-828-2345
Tel.: 800-426-5754
Telex: 312-828-1783

Divisions:

Midwesco Energy Systems Div. **(1)**
7720 Lehigh Ave.
Niles, IL 60648
Tel.: 708-966-2150
Turnkey Fuel Conversions, Air Waste Recovery Systems, Solid Waste Incinerators, Hazardous Waste Incinerators, Hazardous Waste Tank Farms, Turnkey Solid Fuel Boiler Plants Pollution Control Equip.
Bob Sharra *(Mgr.-Sls.)*

Midwesco Mechanical **(1)**
7720 Lehigh Ave.
Niles, IL 60648
Tel.: 708-966-2150
Mechanical Contractors
Robert Spreenberg *(V.P.)*
Ed Crylen *(Sls. Mgr.)*

Mid Res Service Div. **(1)**
7720 Lehigh Ave.
Niles, IL 60648
Tel.: 708-966-2150
Air Conditioning, Heating, Boiler Repairs, Plumbing
Dave Snuttjer *(Mgr.-Sls.)*
Caryl Schmidt *(Mgr.-Mktg.)*

Perma-Pipe Div. **(1)**
7720 Lehigh Ave.
Niles, IL 60648
Tel.: 708-966-2150
Pre-Fabricated Insulated Pipe
Ronald Sabala *(Mgr.-Sls.)*

Thermal-Care Div. **(1)**
7720 Lehigh Ave.
Niles, IL 60648
Tel.: 708-966-2150
Plastic Mold Chillers & Heaters
Don Gruenberg *(Pres.)*
Tom Benson *(Mgr.-Sls.)*

Subsidiary:

Midwesco Filter Resources **(1)**
400 Battaile Dr.
Winchester, VA 22601
Tel.: 703-667-8500
Fax: 703-667-9074
Approx.Sls.: $20,000,000
Emp.: 165
Protective Clothing, Filter Bags & Seamless Tube Filter Bags
S.I.C.: 2211
G. Ogilvie *(Pres.)*
H. Sturm *(V.P.-Mktg. Services)*
T. Headley *(V.P.-Sls.)*

MIDWEST AUTO PARTS DISTRIBUTORS, INC.
2565 Kasota Ave.
Saint Paul, MN 55108
Tel.: 612-644-6448
Fax: 612-644-7204
Wholesale Automobile Parts & Supplies
S.I.C.: 5013
Herb Lohse *(Pres.)*

Outside Service Firm(s):

McGladrey & Pullen*(Auditors)*
1800 Town Square, 445 Minnesota St.
St. Paul, MN 55101

MIDWEST BODY CORPORATION
2109 S. Central Ave.
Paris, IL 61944
Mailing Address:
P.O. Box 250,
Paris, IL 61944
Tel.: 217-465-6414
Fax: 217-463-1236
Year Founded: 1943
Sales Range: $10-19 Million
Emp.: 125
Fiscal Year-end: 12/31/90
Export
Farm & Commercial Truck Bodies & Steel Stampings
S.I.C.: 3469; 3713
Lanny A. Passaro *(Chm. Bd.)*
John J. Jeffers *(Pres.)*
R. Merrell *(V.P.-Mfg.)*
R.T. Thompson *(Controller)*
Fred Alwardt *(Mgr.-Sls.-Admin.)*
Robert Kruger *(Mgr. Sls.-Distribution)*
Principal(s):
Lanny A. Passaro
John J. Jeffers

No. of Mfg. Plants/Facilities: 1
No. of U.S. Offices: 1

Computer Systems/Hardware:
Wells American; IBM

Outside Service Firm(s):

Deloitte & Touche*(Auditors)*
Two Prudential Plaza, 180 N. Stetson
Chicago, IL 60601
Tel.: 312-946-2039

Massey, Anderson & Gibson*(Legal Firm)*
Paris, IL

American National Bank & Trust Company of Chicago*(Major Banking Relationship)*
33 N. LaSalle St.
Chicago, IL 60602
Tel.: 312-661-5000
Fax: 312-661-6417

Division:

Anthony Division **(1)**
2109 S. Central Ave.
Paris, IL 61944
Tel.: 217-465-6414
Manufacture Dump Trucks
S.I.C.: 3714
John Jeffers *(Pres.)*

MIDWEST COAST TRANSPORT L.P.
1600 E. Benson Rd.
Sioux Falls, SD 57117
Tel.: 605-339-8400
Fax: 605-339-8457
Approx.Sls.: $93,000,000
Emp.: 140
Transportation Of Perishable & General Commodities
S.I.C.: 4215
M.T. Smith *(Pres.)*
L.L. Engeltjes *(V.P.-Opers.)*
P. Nelson *(V.P.-Sls.)*
D.J. Odland *(V.P.-Safety & Fleet Devel.)*
Gregg Klatt *(Chief Fin. Officer)*

Outside Service Firm(s):

KPMG Peat Marwick*(Auditors)*
4200 Norwest Center, 90 S. 7th St.
Minneapolis, MN 55402
Tel.: 612-341-2222

Davenport, Evans, Hurwitz & Smith*(Legal Firm)*
Sioux Falls, SD

First National Bank In Sioux Falls*(Major Banking Relationship)*
Sioux Falls, SD

MIDWEST FASTENERS CORPORATION
9031 Shaver Rd.
Kalamazoo, MI 49002
Tel.: 616-327-6917
Fax: 616-327-9798
Approx.Sls.: $15,000,000
Emp.: 85
Hardware; Nuts, Bolts, Brads, Tacks
S.I.C.: 3452
Henry De Vries *(Pres.)*
Robert De Vries *(V.P.)*

Outside Service Firm(s):

NBD Portage Bank*(Major Banking Relationship)*
Portage, MI

MIDWEST INDUSTRIES, INC.
Hwy. 59 & 175
Ida Grove, IA 51445
Mailing Address:
P.O. Box 235,
Ida Grove, IA 51445
Tel.: 712-364-3365
Fax: 712-364-3361
Year Founded: 1954
Approx.Sls.: $30,000,000
Emp.: 250
Fiscal Year-end: 12/31/91
Export
Shore-Station Boat Hoist & Dock, Midwest Bolster Hoist, Harrow Handler, Husky Harrow, Buster Bar, Shore-Land'r Boat Trailers
Byron Godbersen *(Chief Exec. Officer)*
Andy Brosius *(Pres.)*
Bruce Godbersen *(Pres.-Byron Originals)*
Gerry Wiertsema *(Dir.-Engrng.)*
Urban Badenhop *(Mgr.-Farm Equip. Sls.)*
Van Corr *(Mgr.-Personnel)*
Dan Dose *(Mgr.-Data Processing)*
Ken Harriman *(Mgr.-Plant)*
Don Rusch *(Mgr.-Mktg.)*
Scott Saemich *(Mgr.-Adv.)*
Tony Schmall *(Mgr.-Pur.)*

Computer Systems/Hardware:
IBM System AS400

MIDWEST MECHANICAL CONTRACTORS INC.
2720 E. 88th Terrace
Kansas City, MO 64132
Tel.: 816-361-2500
Fax: 816-361-1107
Year Founded: 1932
Approx.Sls.: $155,000,000
Emp.: 500
International Mechanical/Industrial Contractor
S.I.C.: 1711
Michael W. Grossman *(Pres.)*
Marvin E. Andrews *(V.P.)*
William F. McDermott *(V.P.-Fin.)*
Don Sanders *(V.P.)*
Principal(s):
Michael W. Grossman
Don Sanders

Computer Systems/Hardware:
Qantel

Outside Service Firm(s):

Grant Thornton*(Auditors)*
1101 Walnut, Ste. 1600
Kansas City, MO 64106

MIDWEST PETROLEUM CO.
3940 S. 1st St.
Saint Louis, MO 63118
Tel.: 314-481-4300 **MO**
Fax: 314-481-4632
Year Founded: 1946
Approx.Sls.: $90,000,000
Emp.: 65
Wholesale & Retail Petroleum
S.I.C.: 5172; 5541
Louis M. Levin *(Pres. & Treas.)*
Don McNutt *(V.P.)*
Anne Levin *(Sec.)*

Outside Service Firm(s):

Rubin Brown Gornstein & Co.*(Auditors)*
230 S. Bemiston Ave.
St. Louis, MO 63105
Tel.: 314-727-8150

Royal Bank*(Major Banking Relationship)*
St. Louis, MO

MIDWEST TIRE & MUFFLER, INC.
P.O. Box 4510
Rapid City, SD 57701
Tel.: 605-348-2160
Fax: 605-348-2313
Approx.Sls.: $15,000,000
Emp.: 90
Tires, Wheels & Accessories
S.I.C.: 5014; 5013; 7533
Russell J. Haley *(Chm. Bd. & Pres.)*
Dean Kurtz *(Treas. & Sec.)*
H.W. Hinzman *(Controller)*

Outside Service Firm(s):

K.C. Peterson & Associates*(Auditors)*
Rapid City, SD

Sieler & Trimble*(Legal Firm)*
Rapid City, SD

Norwest Bank of Minneapolis N.A.*(Major Banking Relationship)*
P.O. Box 738, 161 N. Concord Exchange
So. St. Paul, MN 55075-0738
Tel.: 612-450-4064
Fax: 612-450-4078

MIDWEST VISION CENTERS
2672 Hwy. 23 N.E.
Sauk Rapids, MN 56379
Mailing Address:
P.O. Box 570,
St. Cloud, MN 56302
Tel.: 612-252-6006
Fax: 612-259-7270
Assets: $4,420,629
Liabilities: $3,770,479
Net Worth: $650,150
Approx.Sls.: $15,000,000
Emp.: 250
Fiscal Year-end: 12/31/90
Retail Sale of Prescription Eyewear, Contacts & Accessories
S.I.C.: 5995; 8042
Dr. Myrel Neumann *(Pres. & Chief Exec. Officer)*
Ken Hagemeier *(V.P.-Oper.)*
Patrick J. Miller *(V.P.-Fin.)*
Yvonne Cooney *(Dir.-Acctg.)*
Principal(s):
Dr. Myrel Neumann

No. of Mfg. Plants/Facilities: 1
No. of U.S. Offices: 50

Computer Systems/Hardware:
IBM System 34

Outside Service Firm(s):

Hartmann & Amundson*(Auditors)*
St. Cloud, MN

Hall, Byers, Hanson, Still & Weinberger*(Legal Firm)*
St. Cloud, MN

First American National Bank*(Major Banking Relationship)*
Saint Cloud, MN

Distributing System

MIGHTY DISTRIBUTING SYSTEM
50 Technology Park,/Atlanta
Norcross, GA 30092
Tel.: 404-448-3900
Fax: 404-446-8627
Approx.Sls.: $60,000,000
Emp.: 500
Franchise System of Distributing Automotive Parts to Professional Shops
S.I.C.: 5013
Jerry Beck *(Chm. Bd., Pres. & Chief Exec. Officer)*
Gary Vann *(V.P.-Sls. & Mktg.)*

MARILYN MIGLIN, INC.
112 E. Oak St.
Chicago, IL 60611
Tel.: 312-943-1120
Fax: 312-943-1184
Year Founded: 1963
Approx.Sls.: $15,000,000
Emp.: 50
Import
Wholesale and Retail Distributor of Cosmetics and Pheromone Fragrance
S.I.C.: 5122
Marilyn Miglin *(Pres.)*
Pam Lassers *(V.P.-Adv. & Public Rels.)*
Julie McLeod *(Dir.-Mktg.)*

MIKEN COMPANIES, INC.
(Formerly Miken Systems Inc.)
75 Boxwood Lane
Cheektowaga, NY 14227
Tel.: 716-668-6311 **NY**
Fax: 716-668-7630
Year Founded: 1972
Approx.Sls.: $21,500,000
Emp.: 150
Fiscal Year-end: 12/31/88
Lithographics Specializing in Book Covers, Stamps, Packaging
S.I.C.: 2752; 2789
Walter J. Jaworski *(Chm. Bd., Pres. Chief Exec. Officer & Chief Oper. Officer)*
Brian Carroll *(V.P.-Fin.)*
Pauline Jaworski *(V.P.-Personnel)*
Douglas Kirkpatrick *(Sec. & Gen. Counsel)*
John Mack *(Controller)*
Ralph Leskin *(Dir.-Pur.)*
Principal(s):
Walter J. Jaworski
Pauline Jaworski

No. of Mfg. Plants/Facilities: 2
No. of U.S. Offices: 2

Computer Systems/Hardware:
IBM

Outside Service Firm(s):

Brock, Schechter & Polakoff*(Auditors)*
Buffalo, NY

Naylan Financial Services*(Commercial Insurance Carrier)*
Buffalo, NY

Cohen Swados Wright Hanifin Bradfordt & Brett*(Legal Firm)*
Buffalo, NY

Marine Midland Bank*(Major Banking Relationship)*
P.O. Box 803, 1 Marine Midland Center, 23rd Floor
Buffalo, NY 14203
Tel.: 716-841-2582

MIL-MOR MEDIA, INC.
1407 Sherwood Ave.
Richmond, VA 23220
Tel.: 804-257-2875
Year Founded: 1975
Approx.Billings: $55,600,000
Emp.: 18
Media Planning & Buying for Consumer Package Goods & Ethical Products, Active in all Media
Richard Feldheim *(Pres.)*
Fran Slaughter *(V.P., Gen. Mgr.)*
Maria Brodecki *(Mgr.-Billing)*

MILADY BRASSIERE & CORSET CO., INC.
6 E. 32nd St.
New York, NY 10016
Tel.: 212-679-8060 NY
Fax: 212-889-7686
Year Founded: 1911
Sales Range: $20-39 Million
Emp.: 1,500
Import Export
Mfr. of Brassieres, Corsets & Swim Suits
S.I.C.: 2342; 2339
Irving H. Engel *(Pres.)*
Arthur Bernstein *(V.P.-Pur., Sportswear)*
Sandor J. Engel *(V.P.)*
Sheldon Bernstein *(Sec. & Treas.)*
Celia Albert *(Office Mgr.)*

Principal(s):
Arthur Bernstein
Sandor J. Engel
Sheldon Bernstein

No. of Mfg. Plants/Facilities: 8
No. of U.S. Offices: 6

Computer Systems/Hardware:
IBM System 38

Outside Service Firm(s):

H. J. Behrman Co.*(Auditors)*
New York, NY

National Westminster Bank plc*(Major Banking Relationship)*
Astor Plaza, 1515 Broadway
New York, NY 10036

Division:

Roxanne Swim Suits Co., Inc. **(1)**
1411 Broadway
New York, NY 10018
Tel.: 212-679-8060
Fax: 212-889-7686
Mfr. of Swimsuits
S.I.C.: 2339
Irving H. Engel *(Pres.)*
Arthur Bernstein *(V.P.)*
Sheldon Bernstein *(V.P.)*
Sandor J. Engel *(V.P.)*
Celia Albert *(Office Mgr.)*

Subsidiaries:

Harbour Casuals, Ltd. **(1)**
1411 Broadway
New York, NY 10018
Tel.: 212-679-8060 (100%)
Women's Intimate Apparel
S.I.C.: 2342

Qismet Ltd. **(1)**
6 E. 32nd St.
New York, NY 10016
Tel.: 212-679-8060 (100%)
Women's Intimate Apparel
S.I.C.: 2342

Quantum Sportswear, Ltd. **(1)**
1411 Broadway
New York, NY 10018
Tel.: 212-679-8060 (100%)
Women's Intimate Apparel
S.I.C.: 2342

MILES SAND & GRAVEL COMPANY
12th & M St., S.E.
Auburn, WA 98002
Mailing Address:
P.O. Box 130
Auburn, WA 98071
Tel.: 206-833-3700 WA
Fax: 206-833-3746
Year Founded: 1943
Emp.: 20
Ready Mixed Concrete; Sand & Gravel, Sand
S.I.C.: 3272; 5032
Frank Miles *(Pres.)*
Carl Schenk *(V.P.)*
Jerome Koch *(Treas. & Sec.)*

Outside Service Firm(s):

Bogle & Gates*(Legal Firm)*
Two Union Square, 601 Union St.
Seattle, WA 98101-2322
Tel.: 206-682-5151

MILEX OF AMERICA, INC.
4914 N. Lincoln
Chicago, IL 60625
Tel.: 312-334-3880
Tel.: 800-288-6030
Fax: 312-561-5026
Emp.: 15
Franchisor of Milex Car Care Centers
S.I.C.: 6794
Werner E. Ament *(Chm. Bd., Pres., Chief Exec. Officer & Sec.)*

Outside Service Firm(s):

Winkler & McDavid & Associates*(Auditors)*
Chicago, IL

Mayer, Brown & Platt*(Legal Firm)*
190 S. LaSalle St., Ste. 3900
Chicago, IL 60603
Tel.: 312-782-0600

THE MILFORD AGENCY
30 Rockefeller Plaza, Ste. 3021
New York, NY 10020
Tel.: 212-957-9090
Fax: 212-262-2656
Year Founded: 1976
Approx.Billings: $11,010,000
Howard Milstein *(Chm. & Pres.)*
Rick Silberman *(Exec. Dir.)*

MILK MARKETING INC.
8257 Dow Circle
Strongsville, OH 44136
Tel.: 216-826-4730
Fax: 216-826-1971
Year Founded: 1970
Approx.Sls.: $325,000,000
Emp.: 575
Fiscal Year-end: 6/30/92
Dairy Cooperative
S.I.C.: 5143
Herman Brubaker *(Pres.)*
Clarence Conrad *(V.P.)*
Rolland Higgins *(V.P.)*
J. Gordon Riehl *(Gen. Mgr.)*
Paul Ramsey *(Treas.)*
Galen Yoder *(Sec.)*
Rodney K. Carlson *(Dir.-Mktg.)*
Ann Marie Emerich *(Dir.-Adv.)*
John Fisher *(Dir.-Personnel)*
Merle E. Koppenhafer *(Dir.-Fin.)*
Cecil Parker *(Dir.-Data Processing)*

Computer Systems/Hardware:
Hewlett-Packard

MILK SPECIALTIES COMPANY
P.O. Box 278
Dundee, IL 60118
Tel.: 708-426-3411
Fax: 708-426-4121
Year Founded: 1944
Approx.Sls.: $85,000,000
Emp.: 260
Fiscal Year-end: 1/31/91
Export
Manufacture of Milk Products for Baby Animal Nutrition; Mink & Fox Food Products
S.I.C.: 2048
George Gill *(Chm. Bd. & Chief Exec. Officer)*
Erwin Clark *(Sr. V.P.)*
Terry Clark *(V.P.-Fin.)*
William Denison *(V.P.-Sls. & Mktg.)*
Dave Elesenbast *(Dir.-Pur.)*
F.D. Garret *(Dir.-Intl. Sls.)*
Susan Sijersen *(Dir.-Personnel)*

Computer Systems/Hardware:
IBM

Outside Service Firm(s):

Price Waterhouse*(Auditors)*
200 E. Randolph
Chicago, IL 60601
Tel.: 312-565-1500

Subsidiary:

Pet Ag Inc. **(1)**
30 W. 432 Route 20
Elgin, IL 60120
Tel.: 708-741-3131
Fax: 708-741-5135
Export
Produce Feed for Small Animals; Companion Animal Products
S.I.C.: 2048
Wally Quedmau *(Pres.)*

MILLER ADVERTISING AGENCY INC.
71 Fifth Ave.
New York, NY 10003
Tel.: 212-929-2200
Tel.: 800-229-6574
Fax: 212-727-4734
Year Founded: 1919
Approx.Billings: $63,000,000
Emp.: 125
Automotive, Real Estate, Recruitment & General Advertising
Leonard J. Miller *(Chm. Bd.)*
Robert Miller *(Pres.)*
David Green *(Sr. V.P.)*
Edward N. Hoffman *(Sr. V.P.)*
Howard Bauman *(V.P.)*
Daniel B. Miller *(V.P. & Auditor)*
Andrew Miller *(V.P. & Treas.)*
San Miller *(V.P. & Supvr.-Classified)*
James T. Curry *(Controller)*
Nicole Miller *(Sec.)*
M.S. Bowie *(Asst. Sec.)*

MILLER BROS. INDUSTRIES, INC.
3301 Castlewood
Richmond, VA 23234
Tel.: 804-231-0211 NY
Fax: 804-233-0972
Year Founded: 1944
Assets: $9,458,206
Liabilities: $2,683,690
Net Worth: $6,774,516
Approx.Sls.: $11,072,777
Emp.: 300
Mfr. Headwear
S.I.C.: 2353
Irving Joel *(Pres.)*
Andrew Joel *(V.P.)*
Jim Starnes *(V.P.-Sls. & Mktg.)*
Bill Throckmorton *(V.P.-Mngmt. Information Systems)*
Earl Griffin *(Treas.)*
Debbie Hall *(Sec.)*

Computer Systems/Hardware:
IBM System 34

Outside Service Firm(s):

Eldredge, Goggins & Weiss*(Legal Firm)*
1st Natl. Bank Bldg.
Dallas, TX 75226
Tel.: 214-747-9151

MILLER BUILDING CORP.
1410 Commonwealth Dr.
Wilmington, NC 28403
Mailing Address:
P.O. Box 2046
Wilmington, NC 28402
Tel.: 919-256-2613
Fax: 919-256-3822
Approx.Sls.: $54,000,000
Emp.: 300
General Contractor Industrial, Institutional & Commercial Construction
S.I.C.: 1541; 1542
Henry E. Miller, Sr. *(Chm. Bd.)*
Henry E. Miller, Jr. *(Pres.)*
J. C. Ballantine *(V.P., Sec. & Treas.)*
Larry P. Harkey *(V.P.)*
Richard J. Hurst *(V.P.)*

No. of U.S. Offices: 2

Outside Service Firm(s):

McGladrey & Pullen*(Auditors)*
Wilmington, NC

Marshall, Williams, Gorham & Brawley*(Legal Firm)*
Wilmington, NC

NationsBank Carolinas*(Major Banking Relationship)*
One NCNB Plaza T18-7
Charlotte, NC 28255

MILLER BUSINESS SYSTEMS, INC.
223 Ave. J
Arlington, TX 76006
Tel.: 817-640-1541
Fax: 817-640-1100
Earnings: $1,951,273
Approx.Sls.: $37,776,080
Emp.: 300
Fiscal Year-end: 6/30/91
Office Supplies & Furniture
S.I.C.: 5021; 5044; 5943
James B. Miller *(Chm. Bd. & Chief Exec. Officer)*
Michael J. Miller *(Pres.)*
Karen Kendrick *(V.P.-Fin.)*
Bud Mundt *(V.P.-Sls. & Mktg.)*
Stan Feldman *(V.P.-Opers.)*

Outside Service Firm(s):

KPMG Peat Marwick*(Auditors)*
1601 Elm St., Ste. 1600
Dallas, TX 75201
Tel.: 214-754-2000
Fax: 214-754-2297

Hill, Heard, O'Neal, Gilstrop & Goe*(Legal Firm)*
Dallas, TX

Texas Commerce Bank*(Major Banking Relationship)*
2200 Ross Ave.
Dallas, TX 75266

MILLER & CO.
500 Hooper Dr.
Selma, AL 36701
Mailing Address:
P.O. Box 779
Selma, AL 36701
Tel.: 205-874-8271

Miller & Co.—(Continued)

Fax: 205-875-9109
Sales Range: $10-19 Million
Emp.: 355
Hardwood Lumber & Logs, Oak Flooring
S.I.C.: 2426; 2435
Opha H. Miller *(Chm. Bd.)*
William H. Deramus *(Pres.)*
Zack Crittenden *(V.P.-Sls. & Gen. Mgr.)*
Cleve Hawkins *(Treas.)*
Robert Dease *(Dir.-Pur.)*
Principal(s):
Opha H. Miller
William H. Deramus

Computer Systems/Hardware:
Burroughs

Outside Service Firm(s):

Peoples Bank*(Major Banking Relationship)*
Birmingham, AL

MILLER COMPANY
99 Center St.
Meriden, CT 06450
Tel.: 203-235-4474
Fax: 203-634-6926
Year Founded: 1844
Sales Range: $10-19 Million
Emp.: 150
Strip & Coil Brass, Phosphor Bronze, Nickel Silver
S.I.C.: 3356
B.G. Tremaine, Jr. *(Chm. Bd.)*
B.G. Tremaine, III *(Pres.)*
Robert Flyntz *(V.P.-Admin.)*
R. Dlugos *(Pur. Agent)*
Principal(s):
B.G. Tremaine, Jr.

Computer Systems/Hardware:
Unisys

Outside Service Firm(s):

Coopers & Lybrand*(Auditors)*
280 Trumbull St.
Hartford, CT 06103

Robinson & Cole*(Legal Firm)*
Hartford, CT

MILLER CURTAIN CO., INC.
1734 Centennial
San Antonio, TX 78211
Mailing Address:
P.O. Box 3479
San Antonio, TX 78285
Tel.: 210-923-4587
Fax: 210-923-5619
Year Founded: 1947
Approx.Sls.: $45,000,000
Emp.: 850
Manufacture Drapes, Curtains & Bedspreads
S.I.C.: 2391; 2392
Gerd Miller *(Chm. Bd. & Pres.)*
Ronald Miller *(V.P.)*
Al Swerdlow *(Mgr.-Sls.)*

Outside Service Firm(s):

Padgett, Stratemann & Co.*(Auditors)*
San Antonio, TX

National Bank of Commerce*(Major Banking Relationship)*
San Antonio, TX

MILLER ELECTRIC COMPANY
2251 Rosselle St.
Jacksonville, FL 32204
Tel.: 904-388-8000 **FL**
Fax: 904-389-8653
Assets: $10,014,000
Liabilities: $3,512,000
Net Worth: $6,502,000
Approx.Sls.: $35,000,000
Emp.: 400
Fiscal Year-end: 9/30/92
Electrical Contractors
S.I.C.: 1731
Corporate Giving Program: 5% of Annual Net Profits to Charity
H.E. Autrey *(Pres.)*
Jane M. Wynn *(Exec. V.P., Sec. & Treas.)*
Edward E. Witt *(Sr. V.P.-Pur. & Sls.)*
Ronald A. Autrey *(V.P.-Estimating & Engrng.)*
Myron T. Gower *(V.P.-Engrng. Sls.)*
Hal Nelson *(V.P.)*
Susan L. Walden *(Asst. Sec. & Treas.)*
Susan A. Walden *(Mgr.-Fin. & Data Proecessing)*

Outside Service Firm(s):

John I. Bishop*(Auditors)*
Jacksonville, FL

Ulmer, Murchison, Ashby, Taylor & Corrigan*(Legal Firm)*
1600 Atlantic Bank Bldg.
Jacksonville, FL 32202
Tel.: 904-354-5652

Barnett Banks Trust Company, N.A.*(Major Banking Relationship)*
9000 Southside Blvd., P.O. Box 40200
Jacksonville, FL 32202-0200
Tel.: 904-464-2802

First Union National Bank*(Major Banking Relationship)*
P.O. Box 2565,
Jacksonville, FL 32203

MILLER ELECTRIC MFG. CO.
1635 W. Spencer
Appleton, WI 54914
Mailing Address:
P.O. Box 1079
Appleton, WI 54912
Tel.: 414-735-4248 **WI**
Fax: 414-735-4013
Year Founded: 1929
Approx.Sls.: $230,000,000
Emp.: 1,500
Fiscal Year-end: 9/30/92
Export
Mfr. Electric Arc Welders, Portable & Stationary Spot Welders
S.I.C.: 3548
K.L. Booher *(Pres.)*
R.M. Erbland *(Exec. V.P.-Mktg.)*
R.L. Geissbuhler *(Exec. V.P.-Domestic Sls.)*
J.B. Stearns *(Exec. V.P.-Intl. Sls.)*
R.R. Marquardt *(Chief Fin. Officer, Sec. & Treas.)*
L.W. Blank *(V.P.-Engrng. & Res.)*
B.D. Blazer *(V.P.-Mktg. Services)*
L.C. Lindgren *(V.P.-Employee Rels.)*
T.A. Martin *(V.P.-Matls.)*
W.B. Wieckert *(V.P. & Controller)*
W.C. Zinno *(V.P.-Mfg.)*
William E. Berglind *(Dir.-Adv.)*
W. Brooks *(Dir.-Mktg.)*
Wayne J. Dorsey *(Mgr.-Pur.)*
R. Gilson *(Dir.-Sls.)*
N. Ktiely *(Dir.-Intl.)*
M. Weller *(Mgr.-Personnel)*

Outside Service Firm(s):

Schenck & Associates*(Auditors)*
Appleton, WI

Foley & Lardner*(Legal Firm)*
777 E. Wisconsin Ave.
Milwaukee, WI 53202
Tel.: 414-271-2400

Bank One Milwaukee, N.A.*(Major Banking Relationship)*
111 E. Wisconsin Ave.
Milwaukee, WI
Tel.: 414-765-3000

Non-U.S. Holding:

The Miller Group (UK) Ltd. **(1)**
Unit 69 Hortonwood 32,
Hortonwood Telford, United Kingdom
Distributor
S.I.C.: 3548
Luigi Vacchini *(Mng. Dir.)*

MILLER FLUID POWER CORP.
800 N. York Rd.
Bensenville, IL 60106
Tel.: 708-766-3400
Fax: 708-766-3012
Approx.Sls.: $53,000,000
Emp.: 500
Fiscal Year-end: 12/31/90
Mfr. of Air & Hydraulic Components & Systems
S.I.C.: 3593; 3599
Go Sudiura *(Pres. & Owner)*
Frank Cushman *(V.P.-Opers.)*
James Taber *(V.P.-Sls.)*
Bernie Clark *(V.P.-Mktg.)*

H. C. MILLER COMPANY
8111 N. 87th St.
Milwaukee, WI 53224
Mailing Address:
P.O. Box 83347
Milwaukee, WI 53223
Tel.: 414-357-8111 **WI**
Fax: 414-357-7676
Year Founded: 1888
Approx.Sls.: $14,000,000
Emp.: 170
Import Export
Manufacture Loose Leaf Binders, Indexes; Commercial/Contract Office Supplies; Commercial Printing, Legal Forms
S.I.C.: 2782; 2759; 2752
Employee Matching Gifts Program: United Way
John G.H. Lotter *(Chm. Bd. & Chief Exec. Officer)*
Donald G. Schneeberger *(Pres. & Chief Oper. Officer)*
Margaret Johnson *(Controller)*
George Curtis *(Gen. Mgr.-Office Prods.)*
Ronald Demske *(Gen. Mgr., Green Bay Opers.)*
Ken Green *(Mgr.-Loose Leaf Bindery)*
Mark Nelson *(Mgr.-Mngmt. Information Systems)*
Lorrie Wallersheim *(Mgr.-Human Resources)*
Principal(s):
John G.H. Lotter
Donald G. Schneeberger

No. of Mfg. Plants/Facilities: 2
No. of U.S. Offices: 2

Computer Systems/Hardware:
Micro Data Reality

Outside Service Firm(s):

Arthur Andersen & Co.*(Auditors)*
777 E. Wisconsin Ave., P.O. Box 1215
Milwaukee, WI 53202
Tel.: 414-271-5100
Fax: 414-283-3200

Associated Kellogg Bank*(Major Banking Relationship)*
Milwaukee, WI

HOWARD MILLER CLOCK COMPANY
860 East Main Ave.
Zeeland, MI 49464
Tel.: 616-772-9131
Fax: 616-772-1670
Approx.Sls.: $50,000,000
Emp.: 500
Import Export
Mfr. Clocks
S.I.C.: 5094
Howard Miller *(Chm. Bd.)*
Jack H. Miller *(Pres.)*
Philip D. Miller *(Exec. V.P.)*
Robert LeHocky *(V.P.-Sls.)*
Dale E. Cramer *(Dir.-Personnel)*
Henry Dykstra *(Dir.-Procurement)*
Harold Elliott *(Dir.-Mfg.)*

MILLER & LONG CO. INC.
4824 Rugby Ave.
Bethesda, MD 20814
Tel.: 301-657-8000 **MD**
Fax: 301-657-1257
Year Founded: 1947
Approx.Sls.: $188,000,000
Emp.: 2,300
High-Rise Concrete Building Construction
S.I.C.: 1771
John F. Miller, III *(Chm. Bd. & Chief Exec. Officer)*
John M. McMahon *(Pres. & Chief Oper. Officer)*
Nicholas G. Paleologos *(V.P.)*
John W. Wharton *(V.P.)*
Herman L. Willis *(V.P.)*
Myles Gladstone *(Dir.-Personnel)*

Outside Service Firm(s):

Leonard Lipski*(Auditors)*
Gaithersburg, MD

Arent, Fox, Kintner, Plotkin & Kahn*(Legal Firm)*
1815 H St. N.W.
Washington, DC 20006
Tel.: 202-857-6000

NS & T Bank*(Major Banking Relationship)*
15th & New York Ave.
Washington, DC 20005
Tel.: 202-879-6000

Riggs National Bank of Washington, D.C.*(Major Banking Relationship)*
P.O. Box 96206, 1120 Vermont Ave. N.W.
Washington, DC 20090-6206
Tel.: 202-835-4082

MILLER MEESTER ADVERTISING INC.
17 N. Washington
Minneapolis, MN 55401
Tel.: 612-337-6600
Fax: 612-337-9100
Year Founded: 1975
Approx.Billings: $55,000,000
Emp.: 105
Food, Agriculture & Retail & Real Estate Advertising
S.I.C.: 7311
Robert V. Miller *(Chm.)*
Paul Durham *(Pres.)*
Steve Strande *(Chief Fin. Officer)*
Doug Engel *(Sr. V.P. & Exec. Dir.-Creative)*
Tom Gahm *(Sr. V.P.-Pub. Rels.)*
Diane North *(Sr. V.P.-Direct Mktg.)*

Outside Service Firm(s):

Oppenheimer, Wolff & Donnelly*(Legal Firm)*
332 Minnesota St.
St. Paul, MN 55101
Tel.: 612-227-7271

First National Bank*(Major Banking Relationship)*
River Falls, WI

MILLER OIL CO., INC.
1000 E. City Hall Ave.
Norfolk, VA 23504
Tel.: 804-623-6600 **VA**
Fax: 804-543-8462
Year Founded: 1977
Assets: $24,000,000
Liabilities: $18,000,000
Net Worth: $6,000,000
Approx.Sls.: $95,000,000
Emp.: 385
Fiscal Year-end: 9/30/91
Distribute Petroleum Products
S.I.C.: 5172
Augustus C. Miller *(Chm. Bd., Pres., Chief Exec. Officer)*
Mike J. Miller *(Chief Fin. Officer)*
Principal(s):
Augustus C. Miller

No. of Mfg. Plants/Facilities: 4
No. of U.S. Offices: 4

Computer Systems/Hardware:
Data General; NCR

Outside Service Firm(s):

Frederick B. Hill*(Auditors)*
Norfolk, VA

Adler & Rosen*(Legal Firm)*
Norfolk, VA

Crestar Bank*(Major Banking Relationship)*
P.O. Box 2642,
Norfolk, VA 23514
Tel.: 804-624-5507
Fax: 804-624-5538

Crestar Bank*(Pension Manager)*
P.O. Box 2642,
Norfolk, VA 23514
Tel.: 804-624-5507
Fax: 804-624-5538

MILLER PERSONNEL, INC.
720 Rte. 1 North
North Brunswick, NJ 08902
Mailing Address:
P.O. Box 7262
North Brunswick, NJ 08912
Tel.: 908-247-5600
Fax: 908-247-9022
Emp.: 300
Full Service Employment Agency
S.I.C.: 7361
Steven Miller *(Chm. Bd., Pres. & Chief Exec. Officer)*

Computer Systems/Hardware:
Data General

Outside Service Firm(s):

Connecticut General Life Insurance Co.*(Group Insurer)*
P.O. Box 2975,
Hartford, CT 06104
Tel.: 203-726-6000

MILLER PRODUCTS COMPANY, INC.
2220 91st St.
North Bergen, NJ 07047
Tel.: 201-662-2010
Fax: 201-662-0912
Approx.Sls.: $400,000,000
Emp.: 40
Manufacture Rubber & Synthetic Rubber Products; Molded Plastic Products; Gloves & Safety Equipment
S.I.C.: 3069; 3089
Stuart A. Miller *(Pres.)*
A.B. Yarsin *(Exec. V.P., Gen Mgr. & Human Resources Mgr.)*
Hector Ortiz *(V.P.-Sls.)*
Principal(s):
Stuart A. Miller

Computer Systems/Hardware:
IBM PC

Outside Service Firm(s):

Konigberg, Wolf & Co.*(Auditors)*
New York, NY

Affiliate:

Export Corporation **(1)**
2220 91st St.
North Bergen, NJ 07047
Tel.: 201-662-2010

MILLER-ST. NAZIANZ, INC.
511 E. Main St.
Saint Nazianz, WI 54232-0127
Mailing Address:
P.O. Box 127
St. Nazianz, WI 54232-0127
Tel.: 414-773-2121 **WI**
Fax: 414-773-2649
Year Founded: 1899
Approx.Sls.: $12,000,000
Emp.: 100
Import Export
Manufacturer & Wholesaler of Farm Equipment
S.I.C.: 3523; 5083
John C. Miller *(Pres.)*
Michael Malesevich *(Chief Fin. Officer)*
Dennis Weigard *(Mgr.-Mfg.)*
Greg Brace *(Pur. Agent)*
Principal(s):
John C. Miller

Computer Systems/Hardware:
IBM AS 400

Outside Service Firm(s):

Clifton, Gunderson & Co.*(Auditors)*
Milwaukee, WI

M & I Marshall & Ilsley Bank*(Major Banking Relationship)*
770 N. Water St.
Milwaukee, WI 53202
Tel.: 414-765-8700

MILLER & SMITH, INC.
1568 Spring Hill Rd.
McLean, VA 22102
Tel.: 703-821-2500
Fax: 703-821-2040
Emp.: 130
Operative Builder & Developer
S.I.C.: 1531; 6552
Gordon V. Smith *(Chm. Bd.)*
Alvin D. Hall *(Pres. & Chief Exec. Officer)*
Pat Powers *(Grp. Pres.-Maryland Homes Div.)*
Robert B. Young *(Grp. Pres.-Virginia Homes Div.)*
Richard J. North *(V.P., Sec. & Treas.)*
Spencer R. Stouffer *(V.P.-Sls. & Adv.)*

Outside Service Firm(s):

Ernst & Young*(Auditors)*
McLean, VA

Riggs National Bank of Washington, D.C.*(Major Banking Relationship)*
P.O. Box 96206, 1120 Vermont Ave. N.W.
Washington, DC 20090-6206
Tel.: 202-835-4082

MILLERS' MUTUAL INSURANCE ASSN. OF ILLINOIS
111 E. Fourth St.
Alton, IL 62001
Mailing Address:
P.O. Box 9006
Alton, IL 62002-9006
Tel.: 618-463-3636 **IL**
Fax: 618-463-3614
Year Founded: 1877
Assets: $145,855,000
Liabilities: $102,152,000
Net Worth: $43,703,000
Sales Range: $60-79 Million
Emp.: 475
Fiscal Year-end: 12/31/91
Export
Property & Casualty Insurance
S.I.C.: 6321; 6331
Corporate Giving Program: Requests must be in Writing & Reviewed by our Committee. Annual Program Allocation Approved by Policyholders at Annual Meeting
M.W. Welge *(Chm. Bd.)*
G.S. Milnor *(Pres. & Chief Exec. Officer)*
R.L. Mawhorter *(Sr. V.P.-Fin.)*
T.M. Moore *(Sr. V.P.-Insurance Oper.)*
D.A. Carter *(V.P.-Underwriting)*
R.D. Perry *(V.P.-Mktg.)*
J.H. Wohlfeil *(V.P.-Sls.)*
J.W. Carpenter *(V.P.-Mngmt. Information Systems)*
Marcella J. Eggemann *(V.P.-Human & Admin. Resources)*
J.E. Eccles *(Treas.)*
Sandra J. Leeson *(Sec.)*
Robert J. Holtzman *(Controller)*

Outside Service Firm(s):

Coopers & Lybrand*(Auditors)*
One Metropolitan Square
St. Louis, MO 63102
Tel.: 314-436-3200

Hoagland, Fitzgerald, Smith & Pranaitis*(Legal Firm)*
Alton, IL

Mercantile Bank of Illinois*(Major Banking Relationship)*
Alton, IL

Subsidiaries:

Classified Insurance Company, Inc. **(1)**
20800 Swenson Dr., Ste. 200
Waukesha, WI 53187-1407
Tel.: 414-796-1111
Auto Insurance
S.I.C.: 6331
George S. Milnor *(Pres.)*

Millers' General Insurance Company **(1)**
111 E. Fourth St.
Alton, IL 62002 (100%)
George I. Milnor *(Pres.)*

THE MILLGARD CORP.
12822 Stark Rd.
Livonia, MI 48150
Tel.: 313-425-8550 **MI**
Telex: 230-331
Fax: 313-425-0624
Sales Range: $20-39 Million
Emp.: 350
Fiscal Year-end: 7/31/92
Excavating & Foundation Work; Heavy FDN Contractor
S.I.C.: 1794; 1771
V. Dennis Millgard *(Pres. & Chief Exec. Officer)*
C. Richard Millgard *(Exec. V.P.)*
Michael Carroll *(V.P.-Fin. & Chief Fin. Officer)*
John J. O'Rourke *(V.P.)*
W.O. Koch *(Sec.)*
Christine Millgard *(Asst. Treas.)*

Outside Service Firm(s):

BDO Seidman*(Auditors)*
Detroit, MI

Bodman, Longley & Dahling*(Legal Firm)*
100 Renaissance Center
Detroit, MI 48243
Tel.: 313-259-7777

Manufacturers Bank*(Major Banking Relationship)*
P.O. Box 33-400,
Detroit, MI 48226
Tel.: 313-222-7572

MILLIKEN & CO., INC.
P.O. Box 1926
Spartanburg, SC 29304
Tel.: 803-573-2020
Fax: 803-573-2100
Year Founded: 1865
Approx.Sls.: $2,400,000,000
Emp.: 20,000
Import Export
Mfr. Cottons, Yarns & Synthetic Blend Fabrics, Carpets, Textiles, Industrial Mats, Shop Towels, Packaging Products & Chemicals
S.I.C.: 2231; 2221; 2273; 2823; 2824; 2299; 2843; 2392
Roger Milliken *(Chm. Bd. & Chief Exec. Officer)*
Minot Milliken *(Chief Fin. Officer)*
Tom Malone *(Pres.)*
Newt Hardie *(V.P.-Quality)*
Bill Petry *(V.P. & Legal Counsel)*
Larry Heagney *(Sec. & Treas.)*
Spence Wise *(Controller)*
John Gieser *(Dir.-Data Processing)*
Tommy Hodge *(Dir.-Personnel)*
Kurt Lambert *(Dir.-Mktg.-Textured Yarns)*
Hans Peyer *(Dir.-Mktg.-Greige Fine Goods)*
Kay Shannon *(Dir.-Mktg.)*
Rick Strasser *(Dir.-Telecommunications)*
Pat Bowie *(Gen. Mgr.-Callaway Carpets)*
D. Nash *(Bus. Mgr.-Uniforms Fabrics)*
Jack Burch *(Mgr.-Matl.)*
Jim Lewis *(Mgr.-Risk)*
Jim Rook *(Mgr.-Employee Benefits)*
Principal(s):
Milliken Family

No. of Mfg. Plants/Facilities: 65

Outside Service Firm(s):

Provident Life & Accident Insurance Co.*(Group Insurer)*
New York, NY

Citibank N.A.*(Major Banking Relationship)*
Corporate Trust Services, 399 Park Ave.
New York, NY 10043
Tel.: 212-559-1605

Aetna Life & Casualty*(Pension Manager)*
151 Farmington Avenue
Hartford, CT 06156
Tel.: 203-273-2128
Fax: 203-729-4295

Citibank N.A.*(Pension Manager)*
Corporate Trust Services, 399 Park Ave.
New York, NY 10043
Tel.: 212-559-1605

Divisions:

Milliken Fine Goods Div. **(1)**
P.O. Box 1926
Spartanburg, SC 29304
Tel.: 803-573-2020
Fax: 803-573-2100
S.I.C.: 2231
Bill Humphrey *(Pres.)*

Milliken Finished Apparel Div. **(1)**
P.O. Box 1926
Spartanburg, SC 29304
Tel.: 803-573-2020
Fax: 803-573-2100
S.I.C.: 2231
Tom Hannah *(Pres.)*

Milliken Industrial Div. **(1)**
P.O. Box 1926
Spartanburg, SC 29304
Tel.: 803-573-2020
Fax: 803-573-2100
S.I.C.: 2231
Ralph Gillespie *(Pres.)*

Milliken Interior Furnishings Div. **(1)**
P.O. Box 1926
Spartanburg, SC 29304
Tel.: 803-573-2020
Fax: 803-573-2100
Wayne Hunter *(Pres.)*

MILLMASTER ONYX GROUP, INC.
500 Post Rd. E.
Westport, CT 06880
Tel.: 203-454-1800
Fax: 203-227-0558
Year Founded: 1940
Approx.Sls.: $100,000,000
Emp.: 25
Organic & Inorganic Chemicals, Intermediates, Shellac, Specialty Chemicals, Surfactants, Textile Chemicals, Detergents, Printing Inks, Rigid Urethane Foam Roof Insulation Panels
S.I.C.: 2869; 2819; 2822; 2841; 2843; 2851; 2893
Employee Matching Gifts Progra
Ronald Baker *(Chm. Bd., Pres. & Chief Exec. Officer)*
William Barrie *(V.P.)*

Millmaster Onyx Group, Inc.—(Continued)

Dennis A. Sadlowski *(V.P., Sec. & Gen. Counsel)*
Rose Appelt *(Dir-Data Processing)*
Al Whitman *(Dir.-Trade Sls.)*
Joyce Barber *(Mgr.-Personnel)*

Computer Systems/Hardware:
Data General

Outside Service Firm(s):

Westminster National Bank*(Major Banking Relationship)*
New York, NY

Division:

Mantrose Haeuser Co. **(1)**
500 Post Road E.
Westport, CT 06880
Tel.: 203-454-1800
Fax: 203-227-0558
Approx.Sls.: $12,000,000
Emp.: 500
Importers of Gum Shellac, Bleachers of Shellac & Mfrs. of Shellac Varnishes & Sundry Paint Products
S.I.C.: 2851; 5198
Ronald Baker *(Chm. & Chief Exec. Officer)*
Paul R. Donovan, Jr. *(Asst. Gen. Mgr. & Dir.-Industry)*
Al Whitman *(Dir.-Trade Sls.)*

MILLS HALL WALBORN & ASSOCIATES
5915 Landerbrook Dr.
Mayfield Heights, OH 44124
Tel.: 216-646-9400
Fax: 216-646-9413
Year Founded: 1956
Approx.Billings: $18,000,000
Emp.: 37
Full Service Agency
Michael A. Mooney *(Pres.)*
Alfred J. Hall *(Exec. V.P.)*
Raymond Serraglio *(Sr. V.P.)*
Jerry Gilles *(Sr. V.P.)*
Steve Wheeler *(V.P.)*
Carol Kuk *(V.P.)*
Henry Dietz *(V.P., Chief Fin. Officer)*

OLAN MILLS, INC.
4325 Amnicola Hwy.
Chattanooga, TN 37406
Tel.: 615-622-5141 **DE**
Fax: 615-624-4815
Year Founded: 1932
Approx.Sls.: $200,000,000
Emp.: 6,300
Photographic Studios
S.I.C.: 7221
Olan Mills, III *(Chm. Bd. & Sec.)*
Olan Mills II *(Chm. Exec. Committee)*
Hampton Johnston *(Pres.)*
Brenda Grayson *(Gen. Mgr.)*

Outside Service Firm(s):

Central Bank & Trust Co.*(Major Banking Relationship)*
Lexington, KY

Divisions:

Olan Mills Inc. of Ohio **(1)**
329 Mt. Vernon Ave.
Springfield, OH 45503
Tel.: 513-323-5528
Photographic Studios
S.I.C.: 7221
Jean Glass *(Gen. Mgr.)*

Olan Mills Inc. of Texas **(1)**
701 W. Loop 340
Waco, TX 76702
Tel.: 817-776-7892
Approx.Sls.: $118,000,000
Emp.: 3,000
Photographic Studios
S.I.C.: 7221
Brenda Grayson *(Gen. Mgr.)*

W.G. MILLS, INC.
3301 Whitfield Ave.
Sarasota, FL 34243
Tel.: 813-758-6441 **FL**
Fax: 813-753-2235
Year Founded: 1972
Approx.Sls.: $50,000,000
Emp.: 80
General Contractor; Commercial, Institutional & Multi-Family
S.I.C.: 1522; 1541; 1542
Walter G. Mills *(Chm. Bd., Chief Exec. Officer & Treas.)*
Lemuel Sharp, III *(Pres.)*
Timothy D. Hensey *(V.P.)*
Steven E. Baker *(Sec.)*

Outside Service Firm(s):

Kerkering, Barberio & Co.*(Auditors)*
Sarasota, FL

Abel, Band, Brown, Russell, Collier, Petchford & Gordon*(Legal Firm)*
Sarasota, FL

Sun Bank, N.A.*(Major Banking Relationship)*
Sarasota, FL

MILLSTEIN INDUSTRIES
4th & Gaskill Ave.
Jeannette, PA 15644
Tel.: 412-523-5531
Fax: 412-523-5450
Emp.: 6
Real Estate Holding Company
S.I.C.: 6719
Jack H. Millstein, Sr. *(Chm. Bd.)*
Jack H. Millstein, Jr. *(Pres.)*

Outside Service Firm(s):

Gallatin Bank*(Major Banking Relationship)*
Greensbury, PA

Subsidiary:

National Plastics Corporation **(1)**
4th & Gaskill Aves.
Jeannette, PA 15644
Tel.: 412-523-5531
Approx.Sls.: $10,000,000
Emp.: 75
Manufacture Lighting Glassware & Electric Residential Lighting Fixtures
S.I.C.: 3229; 3645
Jack H. Millstein, Sr. *(Chm. Bd.)*
Jack H. Millstein, Jr. *(Pres.)*

MILLSTONE COFFEE, INC.
729 100th St., S.E.
Everett, WA 98208
Tel.: 206-347-3995 **WA**
Fax: 206-355-9310
Year Founded: 1981
Approx.Sls.: $33,000,000
Emp.: 150
Coffee Roasting
S.I.C.: 2095
Philip L. Johnson *(Pres.)*
Luther Johnson *(Sr. V.P. & Chief Oper. Officer)*
Don Emary *(V.P.-Sls.)*
Tim Kirstein *(V.P.-Fin.)*
Richard Robenseifner *(V.P.-Opers.)*

Outside Service Firm(s):

Langabeer, McKeman & Bauer*(Auditors)*
Everett, WA

THE MILNOT COMPANY
100 S. Fourth St.
Saint Louis, MO 63102
Tel.: 314-436-7667
Fax: 314-436-7679
Approx.Sls.: $45,000,000
Emp.: 126
Fiscal Year-end: 12/31/90
Mfr. of Canned Milk & Canned Meats; Chili Man Chili
S.I.C.: 2023; 2013
Michael E. Osborne *(Pres. & Chief Exec. Officer)*
Richard Cramer *(V.P.-Mktg. & Sls.)*
Ron Godier *(V.P.-Fin. & Admin.)*
Jeffrey King *(Mgr.-Mktg.)*

MILTON CAN CO., INC.
580 Division St.
Elizabeth, NJ 07201
Tel.: 908-289-8100
Fax: 908-289-2397
Approx.Sls.: $35,000,000
Emp.: 315
Manufacturer Metal, Plastic & Composite Cans & Pails
S.I.C.: 3411; 2655; 3089
James W. Milton *(Pres.)*
Alfred Benway *(V.P.-Admin.)*
Joan Bacon *(Dir.-Data Processing)*
Charles J. Carroll *(Pur. Agent)*

Computer Systems/Hardware:
IBM

Outside Service Firm(s):

KPMG Peat Marwick*(Auditors)*
345 Park Ave.
New York, NY 10154
Tel.: 212-758-9700
Fax: 212-872-3308

United Counties Trust Co.*(Major Banking Relationship)*
Elizabeth, NJ

MILTON INDUSTRIES, INC.
4500 W. Cortland St.
Chicago, IL 60639
Tel.: 312-235-9400 **IL**
Fax: 312-235-3221
Year Founded: 1984
Approx.Sls.: $23,000,000
Emp.: 180
Mfr. of Industrial & Hard Rubber Pressure Valves & Regulators; Mechanic's Hand Tools; Aircraft & Motor Vehicle Measurement Equipment; Battery Testers; Electrical Filters; Lubrication Equipment, Industrial
S.I.C.: 3491; 3069; 3423; 3829; 3825; 3569
Marc Goldish *(Pres.)*
John Santina *(Exec. V.P. & Chief Fin. Officer)*
Jerry Ginsberg *(V.P.-Pur.)*

Outside Service Firm(s):

Grant Thornton*(Auditors)*
700 One Prudential Plaza, 130 East Randolph St.
Chicago, IL 60601
Tel.: 312-856-0200
Fax: 312-565-4719

Harris Bank*(Major Banking Relationship)*
Chicago, IL

MILTON SHOE MANUFACTURING COMPANY, INC.
700 Hepburn St.
Milton, PA 17847
Tel.: 717-742-9621
Fax: 717-742-4340
Emp.: 650
Women's & Childrens Shoes
S.I.C.: 3144; 3149
Saul Putterman *(Pres. & Treas.)*
Lawrence Putterman *(Exec. V.P.)*
Julian Niernberg *(V.P.-Sls.)*
Klaus Schreiner *(V.P.-Mfg.)*
Florence G. Putterman *(Sec.)*
David Bamberger *(Controller)*

Outside Service Firm(s):

KPMG Peat Marwick*(Auditors)*
P.O. Box 1190, 225 Market St., Ste. 300
Harrisburg, PA 17108-1190
Tel.: 717-238-7131

Seligman & Seligman*(Legal Firm)*
405 Lexington Ave.
New York, NY 10017
Tel.: 212-661-4700

Fidelity Bank*(Major Banking Relationship)*
Harrisburg, PA

MILWAUKEE BUCKS, INC.
1001 N. 4th St.
Milwaukee, WI 53203
Tel.: 414-227-0500
Year Founded: 1968
Approx.Sls.: $25,000,000
Emp.: 45
Fiscal Year-end: 6/30/91
Professional NBA Basketball Entertainment
S.I.C.: 7941
Herb Kohl *(Pres.)*
John Steinmiller *(V.P.-Bus. Opers. & Mktg.)*

MINARIK ELECTRIC COMPANY
901 E. Thompson St.
Glendale, CA 91201
Tel.: 818-507-6500
Fax: 818-502-9002
Year Founded: 1952
Approx.Sls.: $25,000,000
Emp.: 200
Export
Wholesale Distributor & Manufacturer of Electric Motors; Switchgear & Switchboard Appartus; Time Switches
S.I.C.: 5063; 3613
William Minarik *(Chm. Bd.)*
Charles E. Carson *(Pres.)*

Outside Service Firm(s):

Bank of America*(Major Banking Relationship)*
701 S. Western Ave.
Los Angeles, CA 91201

MINCO PRODUCTS, INC.
7300 Commerce Lane
Minneapolis, MN 55432
Tel.: 612-571-3121
Fax: 612-571-0927
Approx.Sls.: $28,000,000
Emp.: 480
Flexible Interconnect Circuits, Thin, Flexible Heaters, Temperature Detectors, Instruments & Controls
S.I.C.: 3679; 3823
Karl Schurr *(Pres.)*
Larry Hanson *(Exec. V.P.-Mktg.)*

MINDGAMES, INC.
2720 W. 28th St.
Pine Bluff, AR 71613
Mailing Address:
P.O. Box 1429
Pine Bluff, AR 71613
Tel.: 501-536-3800
Fax: 501-535-2840
Approx.Sls.: $10,000,000
Emp.: 6
Mfr. Games
S.I.C.: 3944
Lawrence Blackwell *(Pres.)*
Becky McIntire *(Mgr.-Office)*

MINER ENTERPRISES INC.
1200 E. State St.
Geneva, IL 60134
Mailing Address:
Box 471
Geneva, IL 60134
Tel.: 708-232-3000 **DE**
Fax: 708-232-3123
Year Founded: 1894
Assets: $40,700,000
Liabilities: $23,600,000

Net Worth: $17,100,000
Approx.Sls.: $70,000,000
Emp.: 450
Fiscal Year-end: 3/31/92
Export
Transportation & Matl. Handling Equip.
S.I.C.: 3429; 3743; 3799
William E. Withall *(Chm. Bd. & Chief Exec. Officer)*
David W. Withall *(Pres.)*
Gary A. Withall *(Exec. V.P.)*
James M. Meyers *(V.P.-Admin.)*
Kris Jurasek *(V.P. & Treas.)*
Gregory Beling *(Controller)*

Computer Systems/Hardware:
IBM System AS/400

Outside Service Firm(s):

Coopers & Lybrand*(Auditors)*
203 N. LaSalle St.
Chicago, IL 60601
Tel.: 312-701-5500

Drendel, Schanlaber, Horwitz & Tatnall*(Legal Firm)*
Aurora, IL

Harris Trust & Savings Bank*(Major Banking Relationship)*
111 W. Monroe St.
Chicago, IL 60690
Tel.: 312-461-2265
Tel.: 800-858-0840

The Mingo Group, Inc.

THE MINGO GROUP, INC.
228 East 45th St.
New York, NY 10017
Tel.: 212-697-4515
Tel.: 800-777-2912
Fax: 212-661-7729
Year Founded: 1977
Approx.Billings: $60,000,000
Emp.: 60
General, African-American & Hispanic Markets
Samuel J. Chisholm *(Pres.)*
DeLisle Callender *(Sr. V.P., Chief Fin. Officer)*

MINI MART, INC.
907 N. Poplar, Ste. 260
Casper, WY 82601
Mailing Address:
P.O. Box 3259,
Casper, WY 82602
Tel.: 307-266-1230
Year Founded: 1968
Approx.Sls.: $120,000,000
Emp.: 850
Fiscal Year-end: 12/31/90
111 Convenience Stores in Six States
S.I.C.: 5411
Dan McMullin *(Pres.)*
Jeanne Aro *(V.P.-Fin & Admin.)*
Dick Lemm *(Dir.-Mktg. & Adv.)*
Principal(s):
Jeanne Aro

No. of Mfg. Plants/Facilities: 111
No. of U.S. Offices: 1

Computer Systems/Hardware:
IBM

ED MINIAT, INC.
945 W. 38th St.
Chicago, IL 60609
Tel.: 312-927-9200 **IL**
Fax: 312-927-8839
Year Founded: 1958
Approx.Sls.: $101,000,000
Fiscal Year-end: 12/31/91
Food Processing for Restaurants, Supermarket Chains Food Service Distributor
S.I.C.: 5147
Ronald Miniat *(Chm., Pres. & Chief Exec. Officer)*
Edmund Miniat *(Chief Fin. Officer & Treas.)*
Edmund Miniat, Jr. *(Exec. V.P.)*
David Miniat *(V.P.-Admin.)*
John Molton *(Controller)*
Patrick J. Shannon *(Gen. Counsel)*
Mike Broderick *(Dir.-Personnel)*
Verland Burkhart *(Dir.-Pur.)*
Bill Goldner *(Dir.-Research & Devel.)*
Albert Mosthof *(Dir.-Mktg.)*
Principal(s):
Ronald Miniat
Edmund Miniat
Edmund Miniat, Jr.

No. of Mfg. Plants/Facilities: 1

Computer Systems/Hardware:
Tandy 6000

Outside Service Firm(s):

Peter Shannon & Co.*(Auditors)*
Hinsdale, IL

American National Bank & Trust Company of Chicago*(Major Banking Relationship)*
33 N. LaSalle St.
Chicago, IL 60602
Tel.: 312-661-5000
Fax: 312-661-6417

Suburban Health Care Benefits*(Group Insurer)*
Bolingbrook, IL

Consolidated Pension Consulting, Inc.*(Pension Manager)*
Orland Park, IL

MINIATURE PRECISION COMPONENTS
Walworth Industrial Park
Walworth, WI 53184
Tel.: 414-275-5791 **WI**
Fax: 414-275-6346
Year Founded: 1973
Approx.Sls.: $35,000,000
Emp.: 750
Manufacture Miscellaneous Plastic Products, Measuring & Controlling Devices
S.I.C.: 3089; 3829
Jay Brost *(Pres. & Chief Exec. Officer)*
Laurence Austin *(V.P.-Fin., Sec. & Treas.)*
Steve Schalk *(V.P.-Engrng.)*
Cliff Shuld *(V.P.-Mfg.)*
Ron Hardwick *(Dir.-Pub. Rels. & Personnel)*
Roger Nehls *(Dir.-Mngmt. Information Systems)*

Computer Systems/Hardware:
IBM System 37 & PC

Outside Service Firm(s):

Wolf & Co.*(Auditors)*
Milwaukee, WI

Godfrey & Kahn*(Legal Firm)*
780 N. Water St.
Milwaukee, WI 53202
Tel.: 414-273-3500
Fax: 414-273-5198

M & I Marshall & Ilsley Bank*(Major Banking Relationship)*
770 N. Water St.
Milwaukee, WI 53202
Tel.: 414-765-8700

MINISTERS LIFE INSURANCE COMPANY
3100 W. Lake St.
Minneapolis, MN 55416
Mailing Address:
P.O. Box 910
Minnesota, MN 55440
Tel.: 612-927-7131
Tel.: 800-328-6124 **MN**
Fax: 612-925-3582
Year Founded: 1900
Assets: $246,609,366
Liabilities: $233,090,091
Net Worth: $13,519,275
Approx.Premiums: $65,251,216
Emp.: 81
Fiscal Year-end: 12/31/91
Life & Health Insurance for Religious Professionals
S.I.C.: 6311; 6321
Corporate Giving Program: Charitable *Gifts as Directed by President;* Employee Contributions on a One to One Basis; In Most Instances Gifts are Designated without Matching Requirements or Limitations
David E. Johnston *(Chm.)*
Jack B. McElhaney *(Pres. & Chief Exec. Officer)*
Arnold D. Henkel *(Sr. V.P. & Chief Mktg. Officer)*
Kevin J. Stangler *(Sr. V.P., Chief Oper. & Fin. Officer & Treas.)*
Mark Zingle *(Sr. V.P. & Chief Actuary)*
Frank Radermacher *(V.P. & Controller)*
Pamela S. Rose *(Asst. V.P. & Corp. Sec.)*
James M. Christenson *(Gen. Counsel)*
Michael R. Braun *(Dir.-Mngmt. Information Systems)*
Carolyn Lamuth *(Mgr.-Admin. Services, Pur. & Dir.-Telecommunications)*

Computer Systems/Hardware:
IBM 4381 Model Q13

Outside Service Firm(s):

Deloitte & Touche*(Auditors)*
900 Pillsbury Ctr.
Minneapolis, MN 55402
Tel.: 612-332-2301
Fax: 612-375-5418

Frank B. Hall*(Commercial Insurance Carrier)*
Minneapolis, MN

Oppenheimer, Wolff & Donnelly*(Legal Firm)*
IDS Ctr., 45 S. Seventh St.
Minneapolis, MN 55402
Tel.: 612-344-9300
Fax: 612-344-9376

Norwest Bank Minnesota, N.A.*(Major Banking Relationship)*
8th & Marquette
Minneapolis, MN 55479
Tel.: 612-372-8123

IAI-Venture Capital*(Pension Manager)*
Minneapolis, MN

MIMLIC Asset Management*(Pension Manager)*
Saint Paul, MN

WSA*(Pension Manager)*
Minneapolis, MN

MINN-DAK GROWERS, LTD.
Highway 81 N.
Grand Forks, ND 58203
Tel.: 701-746-7453 **MN**
Fax: 701-780-9050
Approx.Sls.: $25,000,000
Emp.: 44
Crop Preparation Services for Market
S.I.C.: 0723
H.A. Peterson *(Pres.)*
H.C. Peterson *(Gen. Mgr.)*

Outside Service Firm(s):

Brink, Sobolik, Severson & Vroom*(Legal Firm)*
Hallock, ND

First National Bank*(Major Banking Relationship)*
Grand Forks, ND

MINNESOTA BREWING COMPANY
882 W. 7th St.
Saint Paul, MN 55102
Tel.: 612-228-9173
Brewery; Grain Belt Beer, Landmark Beer
S.I.C.: 2082
Richard McMahon *(Pres.)*
Dennis Barrett *(Chief Fin. Officer)*
Karen Karels *(Opers. Mgr.)*
Sig G. Plagens *(Brewmaster & Plant Mgr.)*
Mike Dougherty *(Dir.-Mktg.)*
Pat Zettel *(Dir.-Sls.)*

MINNESOTA ELECTRIC SUPPLY COMPANY
1209 E. Hwy. 12
Willmar, MN 56201
Tel.: 612-235-2255
Fax: 612-235-5654
Approx.Sls.: $14,000,000
Emp.: 65
Distributor Of Electrical Supplies, Lighting & Lamps
S.I.C.: 5063
H. Willard Linder *(Pres. & Sec.)*
Steven W. Linder *(Exec. V.P.)*
Donald O. Linder *(Treas.)*
Dennis Anfinson *(Gen. Mgr.)*
Jeff Eklund *(Mgr.-Whlse.)*
Janet Haugon *(Mgr.-Data Processing)*
John Klaers *(Mgr.-Credit)*
David Stuhr *(Mgr.-Sls.)*

Outside Service Firm(s):

McMahon, Hartman & Amundson*(Auditors)*
Willmar, MN

Schmidt, Thompson, Thompson, Johnson & Moody*(Legal Firm)*
Willmar, MN

First American Bank, N.A.*(Major Banking Relationship)*
Willmar, MN

THE MINNESOTA MUTUAL LIFE INSURANCE COMPANY
400 N. Robert St.
Saint Paul, MN 55101
Tel.: 612-298-3500 **MN**
Fax: 612-223-4488
Year Founded: 1880
Assets: $6,177,286,122
Earnings: $31,593,416
Liabilities: $5,957,797,951
Net Worth: $219,488,171
Approx.Sls.: $1,600,000,000
Emp.: 1,764
Fiscal Year-end: 12/31/91
Life Insurance Company
S.I.C.: 6311
Corporate Giving Program: Must be an Organization Deductible According to IRS Code Section 170(c)
Employee Matching Gifts Program: Must be a Non-profit Organization, Minimum Amount Matched $35, Maximum Per Employee Annually $1,000
Coleman Bloomfield *(Chm. Bd. & Chief Exec. Officer)*
John A. Clymer *(Pres. & Chief Oper. Officer)*
Robert E. Hunstad *(Exec. V.P.)*
John Bruder *(Sr. V.P.-Fin. Services Div.)*
James E. Johnson *(Sr. V.P.-Group Div.)*

The Minnesota Mutual Life Insurance Company—(Continued)

Keith M. Campbell *(V.P.-Human Resources & Mngmt. Svcs.)*
Robert J. Hasling *(V.P., Gen. Counsel & Sec.)*
Joel W. Mahle *(V.P.-Information Services)*
Gregory S. Strong *(V.P.-Fin. Mngmt.)*
Terrence M. Sullivan *(V.P.-Ordinary Sls.)*
Randy Wallake *(V.P.-Pension Div.)*
Paul Gooding *(V.P.-Asset Mngmt. Div.)*
Mark Hier *(Dir.-Pub. Rels. & Adv.)*
Allen Peterson *(Dir.-Acctg. & Cash Mngmt.)*
Gary Christensen *(Mgr.-Employee Benefits.)*
Barbara Mueller *(Mgr.-Pur.)*
Margaret O'Donnell *(Mgr.-Training & Devel.)*
Jeanne Malone *(Mgr.-Telecommunications)*
William Smith *(Corp. Grants Contact)*
Marian McLain-Johnson *(Media Rels.)*

Computer Systems/Hardware:
IBM 3090 300E

Outside Service Firm(s):

KPMG Peat Marwick*(Auditors)*
1600 Meritor Tower, 444 Cedar St.
St. Paul, MN 55102

First Bank of St. Paul*(Major Banking Relationship)*
St. Paul, MN

Subsidiaries:

Adjustable Life Insurance Company **(1)**
400 N. Robert St.
Saint Paul, MN 55101
Tel.: 612-298-3500 (100%)
Life Insurance Company
S.I.C.: 6311
Coleman Bloomfield *(Pres.)*

MIMLIC Corp. **(1)**
400 N. Robert St.
Saint Paul, MN 55101
Tel.: 612-298-3826 (100%)
Holding Company
S.I.C.: 6719

Subsidiaries:

MIMLIC Asset Management Company **(2)**
400 N. Robert St.
Saint Paul, MN 55101
Tel.: 612-298-3826 (100%)
Emp.: 28
Investment Advisor
S.I.C.: 6282

MIMLIC Sales Corporation **(2)**
400 N. Robert St.
Saint Paul, MN 55101
Tel.: 612-228-4921 (100%)
Broker/Dealer
S.I.C.: 6311
Paul H. Gooding *(Pres.)*

Personal Finance Co. **(2)**
Box 708, First Natl. Plaza,
Chicago Heights, IL 60411
Tel.: 708-754-2700 (100%)
Emp.: 150
Personal Loans
S.I.C.: 6141
Dominic Sesto *(Exec. V.P.)*

Nesota Co. **(1)**
400 N. Robert St.
Saint Paul, MN 55101
Tel.: 612-298-3826 (100%)
Premium Financing
S.I.C.: 6141
Richard D. Lee *(Pres.)*

MINNESOTA TWINS BASEBALL CLUB
501 Chicago Ave. S.
Minneapolis, MN 55415
Tel.: 612-375-1366
Fax: 612-375-7473
Year Founded: 1901
Emp.: 40
Fiscal Year-end: 11/ 1/90
Professional Baseball Team
S.I.C.: 7941
Carl Pohlad *(Owner)*
Jerry Bell *(Pres.)*
Andy MacPhail *(Exec. V.P.)*
Bob Gebhard *(V.P.-Player Personnel)*
David D. Moore *(V.P.-Sls.)*
Matt Hoy *(Dir.-Opers.)*
Kevin Mather *(Dir.-Fin.)*

Computer Systems/Hardware:
IBM

Outside Service Firm(s):

Arthur Andersen & Co.*(Auditors)*
45 S. 7th St.
Minneapolis, MN 55402

Divisions:

Elizabethton Twins Baseball Club **(1)**
Holly Ln.
Elizabethton, TN 37643
Tel.: 615-543-3551

Fort Myers Miracles **(1)**
Lee County Stadium, 14100 Six Mile Cypress Pkwy.
Fort Myers, FL 33912
Tel.: 813-768-4210
Mike Veeck *(Mgr.)*

Fort Wayne Wizards **(1)**
927 S. Harrison
Fort Wayne, IN 46802
Tel.: 219-423-6400
Mike Tatoian *(Mgr.)*

Gulf Coast League Twins **(1)**
Lee County Stadium, 14200 Six Mile Cypress Pkwy.
Fort Myers, LA 33912
Tel.: 813-768-4280
Jim Rantz *(Mgr.)*

Kenosha Twins Baseball Club **(1)**
7619 Sheridan Rd.
Kenosha, WI 53141
Tel.: 414-657-7997
Bob Lee *(Gen. Mgr.)*

New Orleans Pelicans **(1)**
321 Veterans Blvd.
Metaire, LA 70005
Tel.: 504-837-0730
Tom Benson *(Mgr.)*
Bob Zander *(Mgr.)*

Orlando Sun Rays **(1)**
287 S. Tampa Ave.
Orlando, FL 32805
Tel.: 407-872-7593
Pat Williams *(Gen. Mgr.)*

Portland Beavers **(1)**
1844 S.W. Morrison Ave.
Portland, OR 97207
Tel.: 503-223-2838
Mark Helminiak *(Gen. Mgr.)*

Visalia Oaks Baseball Club **(1)**
440 N. Giddings
Visalia, CA 93279
Tel.: 209-625-0480
Bruce Bucz *(Gen. Mgr.)*

P.W. MINOR & SON, INC.
3 Treadeasy Ave.
Batavia, NY 14020
Tel.: 716-343-1500 **NY**
Year Founded: 1956
Approx.Sls.: $14,000,000
Emp.: 240
Export
Manufacturer of Women's & Men's Footwear, Except Athletic
S.I.C.: 3144; 3143
Henry H. Minor, Jr. *(Chm. Bd.)*
Henry H. Minor, III *(Pres.)*
Wolcott T. Hinchey *(V.P.-Fin.)*
Travis Minor *(V.P.-Mfg.)*
John T. Minor, Sr. *(V.P.)*
Laura Menor *(Mgr.-Adv.)*

Outside Service Firm(s):

Fleet Bank*(Major Banking Relationship)*
Deer Park, NY 14202

MINOR RUBBER CO., INC.
49 Ackerman St.
Bloomfield, NJ 07003
Tel.: 201-338-6800
Tel.: 800-433-6886
Fax: 201-893-1399
Year Founded: 1914
Approx.Sls.: $10,000,000
Emp.: 120
Export
Manufacturer of Molded, Extruded, Industrial Rubber & Synthethic Rubber Components & Assemblies
S.I.C.: 2822; 3069
C.A. Humphreys *(Chm. Bd.)*
R.W. Krumscheid Jr. *(Pres.)*
David Hymphreys *(Exec. V.P.)*
Russ Steinmann *(V.P.-Mfg.)*
Theresa Trumpore *(Treas.)*
Sandy Humphreys *(Sec.)*

Computer Systems/Hardware:
IBM 38

Divisions:

Minor Rubber Co. **(1)**
2425 McIver Ln., Ste. 180
Carrollton, TX 75006
Tel.: 214-484-6477
Tel.: 800-433-6886
Fax: 214-247-3703
Export
Mfr. of Molded, Extruded, Industrial Rubber & Synthetic Rubber Components & Assemblies
S.I.C.: 2822; 3069

MINOT BUILDERS SUPPLY ASSOCIATION
2626 Burdick Expwy., W.
Minot, ND 58701
Tel.: 701-852-1301
Fax: 701-852-8929
Year Founded: 1946
Approx.Sls.: $16,000,000
Emp.: 85
Wholesale Distribution of Rough, Dressed & Finished Lumber; Millwork
S.I.C.: 5031
Robert M. Pope *(Pres.)*
Dick Winje *(V.P.-Fin.)*
Joel Bosch *(Treas. & Sec.)*

Outside Service Firm(s):

Brady, Martz & Associates*(Auditors)*
Minot, ND

First Bank, N.A.*(Major Banking Relationship)*
Minot, ND

MINSTAR, INC.
(Wholly-Owned Sub. of I J Holdings Corp.)
100 S. Fifth St., Ste. 2400
Minneapolis, MN 55402
Mailing Address:
P. O. Box 635
Thief River Falls, MN 56701
Tel.: 612-339-7900 **DE**
Fax: 612-337-1930
Year Founded: 1962
Assets: $213,737,000
Earnings: ($46,010,000)
Liabilities: $287,310,000
Net Worth: $73,573,000
Approx.Rev.: $232,175,000
Emp.: 2,400
Fiscal Year-end: 12/31/91
Export
Manufacture Pleasure Boats
S.I.C.: 3731; 3732; 5551
Irwin L. Jacobs *(Chm. Bd. & Chief Exec. Officer)*
Robert J. Sutter *(Pres.)*
James B. Farrell *(V.P., Gen. Counsel & Sec.)*
Edward J. Laginess *(V.P.-Risk Mngmt.)*
Arlyn J. Lomen *(V.P., Treas. & Chief Fin. Officer)*
William A. Munsell *(V.P.)*
Lenny Tierney *(Corp. Travel Planner)*
Jim Weiss *(Controller)*
Lesly V. Larson *(Asst. Sec.)*

Outside Service Firm(s):

Arthur Andersen & Co.*(Auditors)*
45 S. 7th St.
Minneapolis, MN 55402

Weil, Gotshal & Manges*(Legal Firm)*
767 5th Ave.
New York, NY 10153
Tel.: 212-310-8000

Divisions:

Hatteras Yachts **(1)**
2100 Kivett Dr.
High Point, NC 27260
Tel.: 919-889-6621
Fax: 919-889-4257
Export
Hatteras Yachts
S.I.C.: 3732
D. Alton Herndon *(Pres.)*
Phil Fowler *(V.P.-Sls. & Mktg.)*
Timothy Strawn *(V.P. & Controller)*
Bryant Phillips *(Dir.-Mktg.)*

Larson Boats **(1)**
Paul Larson Memorial Dr.
Little Falls, MN 56345
Tel.: 612-632-5481
Fax: 612-632-5481 ext. 120
Fiberglass Boats
S.I.C.: 3732
Clint Moore *(Pres.)*
Thomas Boyer *(Sr. V.P.-Admin.)*

Minnetonka Boat Works **(1)**
P.O. Box 549
Wayzata, MN 55391
Tel.: 612-473-7305
Fax: 612-476-6711
Retail Boat Dealership
S.I.C.: 5551
Franklin Pillsbury *(Gen. Mgr.)*
Beth Whittaker *(Mgr.-Admin.)*

Subsidiaries:

Carver Boat Corp. **(1)**
790 Markham Dr.
Pulaski, WI 54162
Tel.: 414-822-3214
Fax: 414-822-8800
Approx.Sls.: $85,000,000
Emp.: 950
Fiscal Year-end: 12/31/90
Computer Systems/Hardware:
IBM System 38
Manufacture Pleasure Boats
S.I.C.: 3792; 3732; 5551
Edwin T. Veith *(Pres.)*
Larry H. Volz *(Chief Fin. Officer)*
Bob Van *(V.P.-Mktg.)*
Rick Kubiak *(Mgr.-Mktg. & Communications)*
Frank Kessler *(Pur. Agent)*

Subsidiary:

Marine Tech **(2)**
167 Greenfield Rd.
Lancaster, PA 17602
Tel.: 717-397-2471
Fax: 717-393-0689
Emp.: 150
Fiscal Year-end: 7/31/91
Inboard Cruisers & Motor Yachts
O.R. Smita *(Chief Exec. Officer)*

Cherco Compressors, Inc. **(1)**
21 FRJ Dr., P.O. Box 7516
Longview, TX 75607
Tel.: 903-753-4488
Designs & Fabricates Specialized Compression Systems for Natural Gas Handling & Seismic Applications
S.I.C.: 3563
B. H. Wilder *(Pres.)*
Robert Wilder *(Pres.)*

Crestliner, Inc. **(1)**
609 13th Ave. NE
Little Falls, MN 55345
Tel.: 612-632-6686 (100%)
Fax: 612-632-3888
Aluminum Boat Manufacture
S.I.C.: 3732
Al Kuebelbeck *(Pres.)*
Vern Nelson *(Mgr.-Natl. Sls.)*

Genmar Industries, Inc. **(1)**
100 S. Fifth St., Ste. 2400
Minneapolis, MN 55402
Tel.: 612-339-7600 (100%)
Fax: 612-337-1930
Approx.Sls.: $232,175,000
Emp.: 2,450
Fiscal Year-end: 12/31/91
Mfr. & Mkt. Pleasure Boats
S.I.C.: 3732; 3731; 5551
I.L. Jacobs *(Chm. Bd.)*
Robert J. Sutter *(Pres. & Chief Oper. Officer)*
A.J. Lomen *(V.P., Treas. & Chief Fin. Officer)*
James B. Farrell *(V.P., Gen. Counsel & Sec.)*
William A. Munsell *(V.P.)*
J. Robert Long *(V.P.)*
Larry H. Lovold *(V.P.)*
Edward Laginess *(V.P.-Employee Rels.)*
Bert Thompson *(Dir.-Sls. & Mktg.)*
Lesly V. Larson *(Asst. Sec.)*

Glastron Boats **(1)**
700 West River Rd.
Little Falls, MN 56345
Tel.: 612-632-8395 (100%)
Fax: 612-632-1438
Approx.Sls.: $20,000,000
Emp.: 250
Fiscal Year-end: 12/31/92
Export
Mfr. Fiberglass Boats
S.I.C.: 3732
Russell Kelly *(Pres.)*
Bruce Sargent *(V.P.-Sls. & Mktg.)*

Lund Boats **(1)**
W. Front St.
New York Mills, MN 56567
Tel.: 218-385-2235
Fax: 218-385-2227
Aluminum & Fiberglass Boats
S.I.C.: 3732
Larry Lovold *(Pres.)*
Gary Schultz *(Controller)*
Ken Zimmerman *(Dir.-Sls.)*
Lanny Orvala *(Dir.-Mktg.)*

Marine Tech **(1)**
167 Greenfield Rd.
Lancaster, PA 17602
Tel.: 717-397-2471
Fax: 717-393-0689
Approx.Sls.: $26,700,000
Emp.: 150
Fiscal Year-end: 7/31/91
Export
Inboard Cruisers & Motor Yachts
S.I.C.: 5551; 3732
Corporate Giving Program: United Way
Employee Matching Gift Program: United Way
O.R. Smita *(Chm. Bd. & Chief Exec. Officer)*

Mastercraft Corporation **(1)**
Rt. 3, Box 333
Winnsboro, IA 71295
Tel.: 318-435-9431 (100%)
Fax: 318-435-6918
Mfg. Fiberglass Bass Boats
S.I.C.: 3732
Samuel Davidson *(Pres.)*
Wilma Stevens *(V.P.-Sls.)*
Richard Ainsworth *(Controller)*

Wellcraft Marine **(1)**
1651 Whitfield Ave., P.O. Box 13011
Sarasota, FL 34234
Tel.: 813-753-7811
Fax: 813-755-1600
Mfr. of Fiberglass Pleasure Boats
S.I.C.: 3732
J. Robert Long *(Pres.)*
Bill Erickson *(Sr. V.P.-Sls. & Mktg.)*
Mac Spencer *(Sr. V.P.)*
Howard Bleser *(Controller)*

THE MINSTER MACHINE COMPANY
240 W. Fifth St.
Minster, OH 45865
Mailing Address:
P.O. Box 120,
Minster, OH 45865
Tel.: 419-628-2331
Telex: 242-427
Fax: 419-628-3517
Year Founded: 1901
Approx.Sls.: $90,000,000
Emp.: 750
Export
Manufacture Metal Forming Presses
S.I.C.: 3542
Harold Winch *(Chm. Bd. & Chief Exec. Officer)*
John J. Winch *(Pres.)*
Robert Sudhoff *(Chief Fin. Officer & Sec.)*
Stephen Kill *(V.P.-Human Resources)*
Harold Niekamp *(Mgr.-Data Processing)*

Computer Systems/Hardware:
IBM 4381

Outside Service Firm(s):

Ernst & Young*(Auditors)*
One Sea Gate
Toledo, OH 43604
Tel.: 419-244-8000

Bank One*(Major Banking Relationship)*
Kettering Tower
Dayton, OH 45401
Tel.: 513-449-8600

Society National Bank*(Pension Manager)*
900 Euclid Ave., P.O. Box 6477
Cleveland, OH 44101-6477
Tel.: 216-737-5000
Fax: 216-566-8947

Bank One*(Pension Manager)*
Kettering Tower
Dayton, OH 45401
Tel.: 513-449-8600

First Chicago Investment Advisors*(Pension Manager)*
Chicago, IL

First National Bank of Chicago*(Pension Manager)*
One First National Plaza
Chicago, IL 60670
Tel.: 312-732-9781
Tel.: 312-732-4050
Fax: 312-732-4840
Fax: 312-732-3055

Stein, Roe & Farnham*(Pension Manager)*
One S. Wacker Dr.
Chicago, IL 60606
Tel.: 312-368-7700

Subsidiary:

Minster Automation Inc. **(1)**
Industrial Park, Parker Dr.
Beaufort, SC 29903
Tel.: 803-846-2291 (100%)

MINTZ & HOKE INC.
40 Tower Lane
Avon, CT 06001
Tel.: 203-678-0473
Fax: 203-679-9850
Year Founded: 1971
Approx.Billings: $45,000,000
Emp.: 86
Consumer, Business-To-Business, Issues Awareness, Healthcare, Advertising & Public Relations
Joe Hoke *(Chm., Pres. & Chief Exec. Officer)*
John F. Mennis *(Chief Fin. Officer)*
James C. Steuer *(Exec. V.P., Dir.-Res., & Sec.)*
Karen Dinsmore *(V.P.-Boston Office)*
Diane Edwards *(V.P.& Assoc. Dir.-Pub. Rels.)*
Chris Knopf *(V.P. & Dir.-Opers. & Creative)*
Carol Mooney *(V.P.& Dir. Admin. & Human Resources)*
Michael Linsalato *(Controller)*
Michael Small *(Dir.-Automated Systems)*
Tom Bradley *(Assoc. Dir.-Pub. Rels.)*

MINUTEMAN PRESS INTERNATIONAL
1640 New Hwy.
Farmingdale, NY 11735
Tel.: 516-249-1370
Fax: 516-249-5618
Year Founded: 1973
Approx.Sls.: $18,000,000
Emp.: 120
Printing & Copying Franchisor
S.I.C.: 2759
Roy W. Titus *(Pres.)*
Stanley M. Katz *(Exec. V.P.)*
Jeffrey Haber *(V.P. & Gen. Mgr.)*
Stanley Swanson *(Sec. & Treas.)*

Outside Service Firm(s):

Chemical Bank*(Major Banking Relationship)*
Westbury, NY

MINYARD FOOD STORES
P.O. Box 518, 777 Freeport Pkwy.
Coppell, TX 75019
Tel.: 214-393-8700 **TX**
Fax: 214-462-9592
Year Founded: 1932
Assets: $148,000,000
Liabilities: $98,000,000
Net Worth: $50,000,000
Approx.Sls.: $650,000,000
Emp.: 5,900
Fiscal Year-end: 6/28/92
Import
Wholesale & Retail Groceries & Meat
S.I.C.: 5411; 5141
Corporate Giving Program: To Organizations in the Dallas Ft. Worth Area
Lisbeth Minyard *(Co-Chm. Bd. & Treas.)*
Gretchen Williams *(Co-Chm. Bd. & Sec.)*
Bob L. Minyard *(Chm. Exec. Committee)*
J.L. Williams *(Pres.)*
John P. Bennett *(Sr. V.P.-Fin.)*
Delbert Duncan *(Sr. V.P.-Admin.)*
Prudencio Pineda *(Sr. V.P.-Distr.)*
Charles Burns *(V.P.-Adv.)*
Jim Conine *(V.P.-Real Estate)*
Ron McDearmon *(V.P.-Retail Opers.)*
Arley Morrison *(V.P.-Meat Opers.)*
Joe Sealey *(V.P.-Warehouse Opers.)*
Joe Tarver *(V.P.-Pur.)*
David Westbrook *(V.P.-Produce Opers.)*
Loretta Denning *(Dir.-Pub. Rels.)*
Rick Frost *(Dir.-Data Processing)*
Mario J. LaForte *(Dir.-Fin.)*
Alan Vaughan *(Dir.-Human Resources)*

Principal(s):
Lisbeth Minyard
Gretchen Williams
Bob L. Minyard

Computer Systems/Hardware:
IBM

Outside Service Firm(s):

Arthur Andersen & Co.*(Auditors)*
901 Main St., Ste. 5600
Dallas, TX 75202
Tel.: 214-741-8300

CNA Insurance*(Commercial Insurance Carrier)*
Dallas, TX

CNA Insurance*(Group Insurer)*
Dallas, TX

Citicorp North America, Inc.*(Investment Banker)*
777 Long Ridge Rd.
Stamford, CT 06902
Tel.: 203-326-5023

Johnson & Swanson*(Legal Firm)*
100 Founders Sq., 900 Jackson St.
Dallas, TX 75202
Tel.: 214-977-9000

Cullen/Frost Bank of Dallas*(Major Banking Relationship)*
Dallas, TX

Subsidiaries:

Minyard Properties, Inc. **(1)**
777 Freeport Pkwy.
Coppell, TX 75019
Tel.: 214-393-8700
Emp.: 6
Management Services
S.I.C.: 8741; 6531
Jim Conine *(V.P.-Real Estate)*

MISCO INDUSTRIES
257 N. Broadway, Ste. 200
Wichita, KS 67202
Tel.: 316-265-6641 **KS**
Fax: 316-267-5534
Year Founded: 1910
Approx.Sls.: $15,000,000
Emp.: 20
Fiscal Year-end: 12/31/91
Holding Company Real Estate Investments
S.I.C.: 6719; 6531
S.O. Beren *(Chm. Bd., Pres. & Chief Exec. Officer)*
Peter Beren *(Exec. V.P.)*
V. Dale Shelley *(V.P. & Treas.)*
Richard W. Stavely *(V.P., Sec. & Gen. Counsel)*
Jeanneen Campbell *(Mgr.-Personnel)*

Computer Systems/Hardware:
Altos 986

Outside Service Firm(s):

KPMG Peat Marwick*(Auditors)*
Wichita, KS

Fourth National Bank Wichita*(Major Banking Relationship)*
Wichita, KS

Mission Bank*(Major Banking Relationship)*
Mission, KS

Blue Cross & Blue Shield of Kansas*(Group Insurer)*
1133 S.W. Topeka
Topeka, KS 66612

MISENER MARINE CONSTRUCTION
5440 W. Tyson Ave.
Tampa, FL 33611
Tel.: 813-839-8441
Fax: 813-839-7498
Year Founded: 1956
Assets: $25,000,000
Earnings: $4,000,000
Net Worth: $25,000,000
Approx.Sls.: $75,000,000
Emp.: 800
Heavy Marine Construction, Foundation Piling
S.I.C.: 1629; 1794; 1622
Theodore H. Knight *(Chm. Bd. & Pres.)*
Jack Crittenden *(Exec. V.P.)*
Robert D. Donaldson *(V.P., Chief Fin. Officer, Treas. & Controller)*
Richard Kermode *(Exec. V.P.-Admin. & Treas.)*
Bert Potts *(Dir.-Personnel)*
Deborah Powell *(Dir.-Data Processing)*

Misener Marine Construction—(Continued)

Computer Systems/Hardware:
Wang VS

Outside Service Firm(s):

Darby, Sheahen, Weissman & Morgenstern*(Auditors)*
Tampa, FL

United States Fidelity & Guaranty Co.*(Commercial Insurance Carrier)*
100 Light Street
Baltimore, MD 21202
Tel.: 301-547-3000

Florida Union National Bank*(Investment Banker)*
St. Petersburg, FL

First National Bank Tampa*(Major Banking Relationship)*
Tampa, FL

Florida Union National Bank*(Major Banking Relationship)*
St. Petersburg, FL

Subsidiaries:

Gulf Foundation Inc. (1)
5440 W. Tyson Ave.
Tampa, FL 33611
Tel.: 813-839-8441 (100%)

Misener Marine P.R. (1)
5440 W. Tyson Ave.
Tampa, FL 33611
Tel.: 813-839-8441 (100%)

MISS ELAINE INC.
1717 Olive St.
Saint Louis, MO 63103
Tel.: 314-421-3312
Fax: 314-421-6339
Year Founded: 1925
Approx.Sls.: $45,000,000
Emp.: 800
Manufacture Women's Lingerie & Sleepwear
S.I.C.: 2341
S.G. Seldin *(Chm. Bd.)*
Marc A. Seldin *(Pres.)*
H. Gerstein *(V.P.)*
S.I. Golman *(V.P.)*
Steve Marglous *(Controller)*
Adell Branz *(Dir.-Personnel)*

Outside Service Firm(s):

Rubin Brown Gornstein & Co.*(Auditors)*
230 S. Bemiston Ave.
St. Louis, MO 63105
Tel.: 314-727-8150

Mercantile Bank*(Major Banking Relationship)*
Saint Louis, MO

MISS ELLIETTE, INC.
4701 S. Santa Fe Ave
Los Angeles, CA 90058
Tel.: 213-585-2222
Tel.: 800-366-4773 CA
Fax: 213-587-8036
Year Founded: 1943
Approx.Sls.: $12,000,000
Emp.: 250
Fiscal Year-end: 12/13/89
Import
Manufacture Misses Dresses
S.I.C.: 2335
Kim Bryan *(V.P.)*
Larry Ramos *(Mgr.-Office)*
Elvira Kanim *(Sec. & Treas.)*

Outside Service Firm(s):

Leibowitz Wasser & Co.*(Auditors)*
Los Angeles, CA

First Business Bank*(Major Banking Relationship)*
Los Angeles, CA

MISSION INDUSTRIES
2936 De La Vina St.
Santa Barbara, CA 93105
Tel.: 805-682-8588 CA
Fax: 805-687-9505
Year Founded: 1930
Approx.Sls.: $200,000,000
Emp.: 4,000
Fiscal Year-end: 12/31/91
Import
Textile Linen & Industrial Supply Service; Industrial Launderers; Wholesale & Retail Industrial & Personal Service Paper
S.I.C.: 5113; 7213; 7218; 7299
Cass Landon *(Co-Pres. & Chief Exec. Officer)*
James Page *(Co-Pres. & Chief Oper. Officer)*
Homer Clements *(V.P.-Group)*
Sandra Helps *(V.P.-Fin.)*
Tom Hergenroeder *(V.P.-Opers.)*
Ralph Johnson *(V.P.-Admin.)*
Jack McCormack *(V.P.-Sls. & Mktg.)*
Steve Consorti *(Dir.-Sls.)*
Juan Fernandez *(Dir.-Mktg. Analysis)*
Jack Kotowski *(Dir.-Mktg.)*
Kristine Stall *(Dir.-Adv.)*
Raymond Fann *(Pur. Agent)*

Outside Service Firm(s):

Deloitte & Touche*(Auditors)*
Santa Barbara, CA

Henry Logan*(Legal Firm)*
Santa Barbara, CA

First Interstate Bank*(Major Banking Relationship)*
Santa Barbara, CA

MISSISSIPPI CHEMICAL CORPORATION
U.S. Hwy. 49 E.
Yazoo City, MS 39194
Mailing Address:
P.O. Box 388,
Yazoo City, MS 39194
Tel.: 601-746-4131 MS
Telex: 58-5449
Fax: 601-746-9158
Year Founded: 1949
Assets: $324,540,000
Earnings: ($7,383,000)
Liabilities: $185,777,000
Net Worth: $138,763,000
Approx.Sls.: $321,841,000
Emp.: 920
Fiscal Year-end: 6/30/92
Export
Mfr. & Distribution of Chemical Fertilizers & Newsprint Paper
S.I.C.: 2873; 2621; 5191; 5111
Coley L. Bailey *(Chm. Bd.)*
John S. Howie *(Vice Chm.)*
Tom C. Parry *(Pres. & Chief Exec. Officer)*
Charles O. Dunn *(Exec. V.P. & Chief Oper. Officer)*
Dave W. Arnold *(Sr. V.P.-Technical Grp.)*
William F. Hawkins *(Sr. V.P.-Fin. & Admin.)*
Gene A. Triggs *(V.P.-Govt. Affairs)*
Rosalyn B. Glascoe *(Sec.)*
Timothy A. Dawson *(Treas.)*
Robert E. Jones *(Gen. Counsel)*
Joe Ewing *(Dir.-Personnel & Services)*
Tim Sterling *(Dir.-Risk Mngmt. & Property Taxes)*
Ruben Smith *(Dir.-Data Processing)*
Wilson Harvey *(Mgr.-Pur.)*
Melinda Brewer Hood *(Mgr.-Corp. Communications)*
Robert Manning *(Mgr.-Cash Mngmt.)*

No. of Mfg. Plants/Facilities: 3
No. of U.S. Offices: 1

Computer Systems/Hardware:
IBM System 4381

Outside Service Firm(s):

Deloitte & Touche*(Auditors)*
Memphis, TN

Subsidiaries:

Mississippi Phosphates Corp. (1)
P.O. Box 848,
Pascagoula, MS 39568-0804
Import Export
Computer Systems/Hardware:
IBM
S.I.C.: 2873
Tom C. Parry *(Pres. & Chief Exec. Officer)*
Mack Barber *(V.P. & Gen. Mgr.)*

Newsprint South, Inc. (1)
P.O. Box 1499
Yazoo City, MS 39194
Tel.: 601-746-4222 (100%)
Fax: 601-746-9158
Approx.Sls.: $106,000,000
Emp.: 209
Fiscal Year-end: 6/30/91
Computer Systems/Hardware:
IBM
Newsprint Mill
S.I.C.: 2621
Leroy Percy *(Chm. Bd.)*
Charles O. Dunn *(Vice Chm. & Chief Exec. Officer)*
Frank C. Breese III *(Pres. & Chief Oper. Officer)*
Rod Brown *(Sr. V.P. & Gen. Mgr.)*
David W. Arnold *(V.P.-Engrng.)*
Timothy A. Dawson *(V.P.-Fin. & Treas.)*
Ethel Truly *(Gen. Counsel)*
Roslyn Glascoe *(Sec.)*
Melinda Brewer Hood *(Mgr.-Communications)*

Newsprint South Sales Corp. (1)
8111 LBJ Fwy., Ste. 1265
Dallas, TX 75251-1342
Tel.: 214-644-1100 (100%)
Fax: 214-644-6411
Emp.: 5
Computer Systems/Hardware:
IBM
Wholesale Newsprint Distribution
S.I.C.: 5111
J.W. Price *(Pres.)*
Robert Reynolds *(Exec. V.P.)*
W.F. Hawkins *(V.P.-Fin. & Treas.)*

MISSISSIPPI LIME CO.
7 Alby St.
Alton, IL 62002
Tel.: 618-465-7741
Fax: 618-465-7786
Emp.: 900
Limestone Mining & Lime Manufacturing
S.I.C.: 3274; 1411
Mrs. M. M. Jenks *(Chm. Bd. & Chief Exec. Officer)*
Charles Y. White *(Pres. & Chief Oper. Officer)*
John Green *(V.P.-Pur.)*
R.A. Zipprich *(V.P.-Plng. & Information Services)*
Michael V. Aimone *(Chief Fin. Officer & V.P.)*
James Pearce *(Mgr.-Admin. & Personnel)*

Computer Systems/Hardware:
IBM System 36

Outside Service Firm(s):

Ernst & Young*(Auditors)*
701 Market St.
St. Louis, MO 63101
Tel.: 314-259-1000

Blue Cross & Blue Shield of Illinois*(Group Insurer)*
100 Tower Drive
Burr Ridge, IL 60521
Tel.: 708-323-3666

New York Life*(Group Insurer)*
New York, NY

Boatmen's Trust Company*(Investment Banker)*
100 North Broadway
St. Louis, MO 63102
Tel.: 314-466-2469

Mercantile Commerce Trust*(Investment Banker)*
Saint Louis, MO

Mercantile Commerce Trust*(Major Banking Relationship)*
Saint Louis, MO

Mercantile Trust Co., N.A.*(Pension Manager)*
St. Louis, MO

Travelers Insurance Co.*(Pension Manager)*
1 Tower Square
Hartford, CT 06183
Tel.: 203-222-7821
Fax: 203-222-7813

MISSOURI LOTTERY
1823 Southridge Dr.
Jefferson City, MO 65109
Mailing Address:
P.O. Box 1603,
Jefferson City, MO 65102
Tel.: 314-751-4050
Fax: 314-751-5188
Year Founded: 1985
Approx.Sls.: $200,000,000
Emp.: 175
Fiscal Year-end: 6/30/91
State Lottery
S.I.C.: 7999
Michael Morris *(Dir.)*
Pam Koupal *(Dir.-Communications)*

MRS. ALISON'S COOKIE COMPANY
1780 Burns
Saint Louis, MO 63132
Tel.: 314-429-2111
Fax: 314-429-7906
Year Founded: 1939
Approx.Sls.: $30,000,000
Emp.: 250
Bakery Products; Mrs. Allison's Cookies, Dad's Cookies
S.I.C.: 2052
R.O. Merritt *(Pres. & Gen. Mgr.)*
J.C. Elliott *(Chief Exec. Officer)*
J. Allen *(V.P.-Opers.)*
Tom Harting *(V.P.-Sls.)*

Subsidiary:

Dad's Cookies (1)
2615 Hwy. 92 East
Plant City, FL 33566
Tel.: 813-754-5565
Fax: 813-752-5620
S.I.C.: 2052

MRS. BAIRD'S BAKERIES, INC.
7301 S. Frwy.
Fort Worth, TX 76134
Mailing Address:
P.O. Box 937
Fort Worth, TX 76101-0937
Tel.: 817-293-6230
Fax: 817-568-3690
Emp.: 450
Mrs. Baird's Bread, Cakes & Sweet Goods
S.I.C.: 2051; 5461
Clayton D. Baird *(Chm. Bd.)*
J. Allen Baird *(Pres. & Chief Exec. Officer)*
F. Carroll Baird *(Exec. V.P.)*
Steve Hileman *(Controller)*
Brad Lummus *(Sec.)*

Computer Systems/Hardware:
IBM System 38

Outside Service Firm(s):

Aetna Life & Casualty*(Group Insurer)*
151 Farmington Avenue
Hartford, CT 06156

Tel.: 203-273-2128
Fax: 203-729-4295

Team Bank*(Major Banking Relationship)*
P.O. Box 2604,
Fort Worth, TX 76113
Tel.: 817-884-4614

MRS. FIELDS' INC.
333 Main St.
Park City, UT 84060
Mailing Address:
P.O. Box 4000
Park City, UT 84060
Tel.: 801-649-1304 **CA**
Fax: 801-649-2753
Year Founded: 1977
Sales Range: $60-79 Million
Emp.: 2,000
Holding Company; Food Products
S.I.C.: 6719; 2052; 5461
Debra Fields *(Chm. Bd., Pres. & Chief Exec. Officer)*
Steven Hooker *(Sr. V.P.-Real Estate)*
Linda Ponder *(Project Coord.-Mktg.)*

Principal(s):

Computer Systems/Hardware:
IBM System 38

Outside Service Firm(s):

Price Waterhouse*(Auditors)*
Park City, UT

Divisions:

Fairfield Foods **(1)**
P.O. Box 4000, 12 Commerce Rd.
Fairfield, NJ 07006
Tel.: 201-227-5896 (100%)
Holding Co.
S.I.C.: 6719
Will Dunlavy *(Chief Oper. Officer)*

Mrs. Fields Cookies Inc. **(1)**
333 Main St.
Park City, UT 84060
Tel.: 801-649-1304
Fax: 801-649-1403
Approx.Sls.: $118,000,000
Emp.: 5,000
Fiscal Year-end: 12/31/90
Cookie Mfr. & Retailer
S.I.C.: 2052; 5461
Debra Fields *(Pres., Chief Exec. & Chief Oper. Officer)*
Michael Murphy *(Sr. V.P.-Real Estate)*
Randall K. Fields *(V.P.)*
Robert Burden *(V.P.-Oper. Support)*
Linda Ponder *(Project Coord.-Mktg.)*

Subsidiaries:

La Petite Boulangerie, Inc. **(1)**
P.O. Box 4000, 333 Main St.
Park City, UT 84060
Tel.: 801-649-1304
Fax: 801-649-7651
Emp.: 80
Fiscal Year-end: 1/ 3/91
Retail Specialty Bakeries, Company Owned & Franchised Stores
S.I.C.: 5461
Randall Fields *(Chm. Bd.)*
Debra Fields *(Pres. & Chief Exec. Officer)*

MRS. GOOCHS NATURAL FOOD MARKETS
15315 Magnolia Blvd., Ste. 320
Sherman Oaks, CA 91403
Tel.: 818-501-8484 **CA**
Fax: 818-990-7089
Year Founded: 1976
Approx.Sls.: $75,000,000
Emp.: 800
Retail Sales of Health Foods; Wholesale Distribution of Fresh Fruits & Vegetables
S.I.C.: 5499; 5148
John R. Moorman *(Chief Exec. Officer)*
Dan Volland *(Chief Oper. Officer)*
Mindy Pedlar *(Chief Fin. Officer)*
Sandra Gooch *(Dir.-Mktg. & Admin.)*

MRS. WINNER'S CHICKEN & BISCUIT RESTAURANTS
(Div. of Winners Corp.)
5995 Barfield Rd.
Atlanta, GA 30328
Tel.: 404-256-4900
Fax: 615-377-4429
Approx.Sls.: $120,000,000
Emp.: 3,000
Franchised Family Restaurants
S.I.C.: 5812
Russ Umphenour *(Chm., Pres. & Chief Exec. Officer)*
Doug Benham *(V.P.-Fin.)*

MR. CHRISTMAS INC.
41 Madison Ave.
New York, NY 10010
Tel.: 212-889-7220
Fax: 212-779-9035
Year Founded: 1933
Approx.Sls.: $85,000,000
Emp.: 250
Fiscal Year-end: 12/31/91
Import Export
Mfr. Artificial Christmas Trees; Light Sets; Wreaths & Electronic Musical Prods.
S.I.C.: 3999; 3699
Merril Hermanson *(Chm. Bd. & Chief Exec. Officer)*
Terry Hermanson *(Pres.)*
Fred Gabbe *(V.P.-Production)*
Michael Sheppard *(V.P. & Reg. Sls. Mgr.-West)*
Jeff Wilner *(V.P.)*
Charles Scott *(Chief Fin. Officer & Controller)*
Lydia Hermanson *(Sec.)*

Computer Systems/Hardware:
DEC; IBM PC

Outside Service Firm(s):

Empire Blue Cross & Blue Shield*(Group Insurer)*
New York, NY

First National Bank of Boston*(Major Banking Relationship)*
P.O. Box 644,
Boston, MA 02102-0644
Tel.: 617-575-2900
Fax: 617-575-2549

MR. GASKET COMPANY
8700 Brookpark Rd.
Cleveland, OH 44129
Tel.: 216-398-8300
Fax: 216-398-0007
Year Founded: 1965
Earnings: ($1,800,000)
Approx.Sls.: $100,000,000
Emp.: 600
Fiscal Year-end: 12/31/90
Import Export
Mfr. Automotive Accessories & Specialty Equipment; Engine Parts, Gaskets, Clutches, Suspension, Shifters, Ignition, Traction Bars, Bellhousings, Safety Equipment; Mini-Car Parts & Accessories
S.I.C.: 3714; 3053; 3694
Joseph F. Hrudka *(Chm., Pres. & Chief Exec. Officer)*
Ray Friant *(Chief Oper. Officer)*
Albert A. Garceau *(V.P., Chief Fin. Officer & Treas.)*
Tom Hrudka *(V.P.-Opers.)*
Mike Stasko *(Mgr.-Mktg.)*
Howard B. Gardner *(Sec.)*
Susan Akers *(Controller)*
Terry Hrudka *(Plant Mgr.)*

Divisions:

Cragar Industries **(1)**
19007 S. Reyes
Compton, CA 90221
Tel.: 310-639-6211
Fax: 310-639-8287
Approx.Sls.: $30,000,000
Emp.: 200
Fiscal Year-end: 12/31/90
Import Export
Computer Systems/Hardware:
IBM System 38
Mfr. Custom Wheels & Related After-Market Products
S.I.C.: 3465
Joe Hradko *(Chm. Bd. & Pres.)*
Gary Biggs *(Exec. V.P.-Mktg.)*
Glen Cox *(V.P.-Sls., Exhaust & Off-Road)*
Tom Fry *(V.P.-Sls., Wheel Access.)*
Michael Miller *(V.P.-Opers., Wheel & Exhaust Grp.)*
Tom Hrudko *(V.P.-Opers., Performance Grp.)*
Rick Rackeman *(V.P.-Sls., Wheel & Tire)*
Jim Trent *(V.P.-Mktg.-Performance Grp.)*
Albert Garcema *(Chief Fin. Officer & Treas.)*
Howard Gardner *(Sec.)*
Susan Akers *(Controller)*
Fran Bartsch *(Dir.-Sls., Tires)*
Patricia Fox *(Dir.-Pur.)*
Tom Griggs *(Dir.-Sls., Wheels)*
Terry Johnson *(Mgr.-Opers.)*
Cindy Tange *(Mgr.-Personnel)*

Subsidiary:

Hurst Performances, Inc. **(1)**
8700 Brook Park Rd.
Cleveland, OH 44129
Tel.: 216-398-8300
Fax: 216-398-0007
Emp.: 215
Import
Automatic & Manual Shifter Controls, Automotive Accessories; Competition/Plus, Airheart Disc Brakes; Hallcraft's Motorcycle Accessories
S.I.C.: 3999
Joseph Hrudka *(Chm. Bd. & Pres.)*
Craig Manchem *(Exec. V.P.-Sls. & Mktg.)*
Rich Smith *(V.P. & Dir.-Pur.)*
Jim Trent *(V.P.-Sls.)*
Mike Stasko *(Mgr.-Mktg.)*

MITCHEL & SCOT MACHINE CO., INC.
1841 Ludlow Ave.
Indianapolis, IN 46201
Tel.: 317-639-5331 **IN**
Fax: 317-684-8245
Year Founded: 1933
Approx.Sls.: $23,000,000
Emp.: 275
Fiscal Year-end: 12/31/90
Export
Mfr. of Screw Machine Products; Steel Service Center
S.I.C.: 3451; 5051
Thomas L. Mitchel *(Chm. Bd. & Pres.)*
David Mitchel *(V.P.-Mfg.)*
Stephen Mitchel *(V.P., Sec. & Treas.)*
Gary Williams *(Controller)*
John C. McKeown *(Dir.-Pur.)*
John Mikuta *(Dir.-Personnel)*
Bruce W. Cox *(Mgr.-Quality Control)*
Gary L. Cox *(Mgr.-Mktg. & Sls.)*
John Mitchel *(Mgr.-Network)*

Outside Service Firm(s):

Stilwell Hackemeyer & Life*(Legal Firm)*
Indianapolis, IN

Merchants National Bank & Trust Company of Indianapolis*(Major Banking Relationship)*
One Merchants Plaza, Ste. 901E
Indianapolis, IN 46255
Tel.: 317-267-7109

MITCHELL & ASSOC., INC.
7830 Old Georgetown Rd.
Bethesda, MD 20814
Tel.: 301-986-1772
Fax: 301-907-9255
Year Founded: 1981
Approx.Billings: $12,750,000
Emp.: 12
Ronald B. Mitchell *(Chm. Bd. & Pres.)*
Eve S. Wallace *(Exec. V.P.)*
Deborah S. McGregor *(V.P., Controller)*

MITCHELL COACH MANUFACTURING
4 1/2 Mile S. U.S. Hwy. 69
Pryor, OK 74361
Tel.: 918-825-7000
Fax: 718-825-2105
Year Founded: 1988
Approx.Sls.: $30,000,000
Emp.: 150
Manufacture Motor Homes
S.I.C.: 3792

MITCHELL CORPORATION OF OWOSSO
123 N. Chipman St.
Owosso, MI 48867
Tel.: 517-725-2171 **MI**
Fax: 517-725-2171, Ext. 237
Year Founded: 1937
Approx.Sls.: $80,000,000
Emp.: 1,200
Fiscal Year-end: 7/31/90
Mfr. of Automotive & Truck Interior Trims, Seat Frames & Foam Products
S.I.C.: 3714; 3465; 3069; 2273; 3544
William F. Mitchell *(Chm. Bd., Pres. & Chief Exec. Officer)*
Helen Malik *(Sec. & Treas.)*
Joseph Cebulski *(Gen. Mgr.-Mfg.)*
William Janego *(Dir.-Pur.)*
Martin Landino *(Dir.-Data Processing)*
Richard Snow *(Mgr.-Sls.)*

Principal(s):
William F. Mitchell

No. of Mfg. Plants/Facilities: 13
No. of U.S. Offices: 4
No. of Foreign Offices: 1

Computer Systems/Hardware:
IBM System 38

Outside Service Firm(s):

Coopers & Lybrand*(Auditors)*
400 Renaissance Center
Detroit, MI 48243
Tel.: 313-446-7100
Fax: 313-446-7117

Law, Weathers & Richardson*(Legal Firm)*
Grand Rapids, MI

Manufacturers National Bank N.A.*(Major Banking Relationship)*
38th Fl., 100 Renaissance Center
Detroit, MI 48243
Tel.: 313-222-4227

Old Kent Bank*(Major Banking Relationship)*
Detroit, MI

Divisions:

Benzonia Manufacturing **(1)**
2532 Benzie Hwy.
Benzonia, MI 49616
Tel.: 616-882-4453
Emp.: 250
Mfr. of Automobile Seat Covers, Door Panels, Carpets, Bucket Seats & Metal Seat Frames
S.I.C.: 3714
Larry Biedron *(Plant Mgr.)*

Mitchell Corporation, Clare Div. **(1)**
528 Holly St.
Clare, MI 48617
Tel.: 517-386-2325
Emp.: 350
Mfr. of Automobile Bucket Seats, Seat Covers, Door Panels, Metal Frames & Pocket Panels
S.I.C.: 3714
Donald Scollen *(Plant Mgr.)*

Mitchell Corporation, Elberta Manufacturing Div. **(1)**
100 Furnace St.
Elberta, MI 49628
Tel.: 616-352-9606
Emp.: 60

Mitchell Corporation of Owosso—(Continued)

Mfr. of Automobile Bucket Seats, Seat Covers, Door Panels, Metal Frames & Pocket Panels
S.I.C.: 3714
Brad Schnell *(Plant Mgr.)*

Mitchell Corporation, Hanchett Manufacturing Co. **(1)**
906 N. State
Big Rapids, MI 49307
Tel.: 616-796-7678
Mfr. of Grinding Machine & Sharpeners for Wood Industry
S.I.C.: 3544

JOHN PAUL MITCHELL SYSTEMS
P.O. Box 10597,
Beverly Hills, CA 90213-3597
Tel.: 805-298-0400 **CA**
Fax: 805-298-0390
Year Founded: 1980
Approx.Sls.: $145,000,000
Emp.: 45
Import Export
Wholesale Distribution of Hair Preparations
S.I.C.: 5122
John Paul DeJoris *(Chm. Bd. & Pres.)*
Debbie White *(Controller)*

MITEK, INC.
14515 N. Outer Forty Rd.
Chesterfield, MO 63017
Tel.: 314-434-1200
Tel.: 800-325-8075
Fax: 314-434-5334
Approx.Sls.: $150,000,000
Emp.: 1,300
Export
Steel Fasteners & Hydraulic & Pneumatic Presses
S.I.C.: 3542
Paul F. Cornelsen *(Chm. Bd. & Chief Exec. Officer)*
Eugene M. Toombs *(Pres.)*
Jack M. Casper *(Exec. V.P.)*
Barry J. Griffin *(V.P.)*
Art Sordo *(V.P.-Mfg.)*
Joseph C. Carr, Jr. *(Sec. & Gen. Counsel)*
William Watson *(Dir.-Human Resources)*
Jack Casper *(Mgr.-Exports)*

Plant:

Mitek Industries **(1)**
4203 Shoreline Dr.
Saint Louis, MO 63045
Tel.: 314-298-8088
Steel Fasteners & Hydraulic & Pneumatic Presses
S.I.C.: 3542
Arturo P. Sordo *(Mgr.-Opers.)*

MITRE CORPORATION
Burlington Rd.
Bedford, MA 01730
Tel.: 617-271-2000
Fax: 617-271-2271
Year Founded: 1958
Approx.Rev.: $500,000,000
Emp.: 6,000
Fiscal Year-end: 7/31/91
Systems Engineering; Research & Development; Non-Profit
S.I.C.: 8731
James R. Schlesinger *(Chm. Bd.)*
Dr. Barry M. Horowitz *(Pres. & Chief Exec. & Oper. Officer)*
Larry F. Myers *(Sr. V.P., Chief Fin. Officer, Sec. & Treas.)*
Bernard Cookson *(Controller)*

Computer Systems/Hardware:
IBM

Outside Service Firm(s):

Coopers & Lybrand*(Auditors)*
1 Post Office Square
Boston, MA 02110
Tel.: 617-574-5000
Fax: 617-345-0398

Ropes & Gray*(Legal Firm)*
One International Place
Boston, MA 02110
Tel.: 617-423-6100

First National Bank of Boston*(Major Banking Relationship)*
P.O. Box 644,
Boston, MA 02102-0644
Tel.: 617-575-2900
Fax: 617-575-2549

MOBILE TECHNOLOGY INC.
9841 Airport Blvd., 12th Fl.
Los Angeles, CA 90045
Tel.: 310-641-8614
Fax: 310-641-4512
Year Founded: 1983
Approx.Sls.: $100,000,000
Emp.: 650
Rental of Medical Equipment
S.I.C.: 7352
Fred Warren *(Chm. Bd.)*
Joe Cilurao *(Pres. & Chief Exec. Officer)*
Raymond Almieri *(V.P.-West Region)*
Cheryl Ford *(V.P.-Northeast Region)*
Jim Pike *(V.P. & Treas.)*
Larry D. Seston *(V.P.-South Region)*
Susan R. Silver *(V.P.-Business Devel.)*
Brian Woodbury *(V.P.-Midwest Region)*
Jeanne Y. McGill *(Mgr.-South Cental Region)*

Outside Service Firm(s):

Continental Bank N. A.*(Major Banking Relationship)*
231 S. LaSalle St.
Chicago, IL 60697
Tel.: 312-828-2345
Tel.: 800-426-5754
Telex: 312-828-1783

Subsidiary:

Mobile Technology Inc., North East Region **(1)**
30 Waterside Dr.
Farmington, CT 06032
Tel.: 203-677-8700
Provider of Mobile Shared MRI Scanner Services
S.I.C.: 8099
Cheryl Ford *(V.P.-Northeast Region)*

MODEL GLASS, INC.
4887 E. La Palma, Ste. 704
Anaheim, CA 92807
Tel.: 714-777-7714
Fax: 714-777-4402
Approx.Sls.: $20,000,000
Emp.: 145
Glass & Glazing Work; Glass Construction Materials
S.I.C.: 1793; 5039
Charles Boniols *(Chief Exec. Officer)*
Tom Metz *(Pres.)*
Bill Weidemann *(Exec. V.P.)*

Outside Service Firm(s):

First Business Bank*(Major Banking Relationship)*
Irvine, CA

HENRY MODELL & COMPANY, INC.
34-24 Vernon Blvd.
Long Island City, NY 11106
Tel.: 718-956-8600 **NY**
Fax: 718-278-1287
Year Founded: 1889
Approx.Sls.: $91,000,000
Emp.: 1,000
Fiscal Year-end: 1/31/90
Men's Clothing, Work Clothes, Footwear, Sports Equipment & Sundries
S.I.C.: 5611; 5661; 5941
William Modell *(Chm. Bd.)*
Michael S. Modell *(Pres.)*
Mitchell B. Modell *(Chief Oper. Officer)*
Lawrence Brustein *(Chief Fin. Officer, Sec. & Treas.)*
Aaron Fleishaker *(Gen. Counsel)*
Sam Golden *(Dir.-Mngmt. Information Systems)*

Outside Service Firm(s):

Richard Janover & Co.*(Auditors)*
New York, NY

Summit, Solomon & Feldesman*(Legal Firm)*
445 Park Ave.
New York, NY 10022
Tel.: 212-702-2200

Barclays Bank plc*(Major Banking Relationship)*
75 Wall St.
New York, NY 10265
Tel.: 212-412-4000

MODERN CONCRETE SEPTIC TANK COMPANY
Durham Rd.
Ottsville, PA 18942
Mailing Address:
P.O. Box 339
Ottsville, PA 18942
Tel.: 215-847-5112 **PA**
Fax: 215-847-8760
Year Founded: 1946
Approx.Sls.: $10,000,000
Emp.: 80
Fiscal Year-end: 4/30/92
Manufacture Concrete Septic Tanks, Wall Panels, Trash Receptacles, Planters, Headwalls, Seepage Tanks, Precast Steps, Sewer Manholes & Inlets; Wholesale Plumbing, Wastewater Treatment Plants
S.I.C.: 3272; 5074; 3589
Woodrow Wehrung *(Chm. Bd.)*
Vernon Wehrung *(Pres.)*
James P. Loew *(V.P.-Fin. & Controller & Treas.)*
S. Blanche Wehrung *(Sec.)*
Anne M. Slifer *(Dir.-Personnel & Mktg.)*
Jeff Weisberg *(Dir.-Pur.)*
Mike Seaman *(Mgr.-Plant)*

No. of Mfg. Plants/Facilities: 1

Outside Service Firm(s):

Niessen, Dunlap & Pritchard*(Auditors)*
Colmar, PA

Drake & Hileman*(Legal Firm)*
Doylestown, PA

Bucks County Bank & Trust Company*(Major Banking Relationship)*
Plumsteadville, PA

Subsidiary:

Wehrung Family Home Center **(1)**
Route 611
Ottsville, PA 18942
Tel.: 215-847-2066
Home Center Products
S.I.C.: 3272
Jim Loew *(Chief Fin. Officer)*
David Sliser *(Gen. Mgr.)*
Anne Slifer *(Dir.-Mktg.)*

MODERN DROP FORGE CO.
13810 S. Western Ave.
Blue Island, IL 60406
Tel.: 708-388-1806
Fax: 708-597-3633
Year Founded: 1914
Approx.Sls.: $50,000,000
Emp.: 500
Fiscal Year-end: 6/30/90
Manufacture Steel Drop Forgings
S.I.C.: 3462
Greg Heim *(Exec. V.P. & Chief Exec. Officer)*
Richard Heim *(Exec. V.P.)*
Patrick Thompson *(V.P.-Fin. & Chief Fin. Officer)*
Jack Hennessey *(V.P.-Human Resources)*
Thomas Bartley *(Controller)*
Delbert Bellah *(Dir.-Data Processing)*
Robert Bracey *(Dir.-Pur.)*

Computer Systems/Hardware:
IBM AS400

Outside Service Firm(s):

Wilkes Besterfield Co.*(Auditors)*
Olympia Fields, IL

John Hancock Mutual Life Insurance Co.*(Group Insurer)*
John Hancock Place, P.O. Box 111
Boston, MA 02117

The Northern Trust Co.*(Major Banking Relationship)*
50 S. LaSalle St.
Chicago, IL 60675
Tel.: 312-630-6000
Fax: 312-630-6516

Fiduciary Management, Inc.*(Pension Manager)*
Chicago, IL

John Hancock Mutual Life Insurance Co.*(Pension Manager)*
John Hancock Place, P.O. Box 111
Boston, MA 02117

Subsidiaries:

Mid-States Forging Die & Tool Co. **(1)**
P.O. Box5025
Rockford, IL 61125

Modern Forge/Tennessee **(1)**
Tri County Industrial Pk.
Piney Flats, TN 37686
Tel.: 615-282-0327

Tri-State Dies, Inc. **(1)**
913 W. 119th St.
Chicago, IL 60643
Tel.: 312-785-2842

MODERN GROUP LTD.
2501 Durham Rd.
Bristol, PA 19007
Mailing Address:
P.O. Box 710,
Bristol, PA 19007
Tel.: 215-943-9100 **PA**
Fax: 215-943-8901
Year Founded: 1979
Assets: $43,527,174
Earnings: $260,952
Liabilities: $26,542,828
Net Worth: $16,984,346
Approx.Sls.: $66,446,413
Emp.: 454
Fiscal Year-end: 10/25/91
Truck & Equipment Rental & Leasing; Parts & Service; Wholesale Material Handling
S.I.C.: 5084; 7359; 7513
Joseph McEwen *(Chm. Bd. & Chief Exec. Officer)*
John Smith *(Pres.)*
George S. Wilkinson *(Chief Fin. Officer & Exec. V.P.)*
Felicia Smith *(V.P.-Human Resources)*
Robert Holtz *(Treas.)*
John Lauf *(Controller)*
Anne L. McEwen *(Sec.)*
Mary Lou Schroeder *(Asst. Sec. & Asst. Treas.)*

Computer Systems/Hardware:
Prime 9750 & 4150

Outside Service Firm(s):

KPMG Peat Marwick*(Auditors)*
Lawrenceville, NJ

Stradley, Ronon, Stevens & Young*(Legal Firm)*
2600 One Commerce Square
Philadelphia, PA 19103
Tel.: 215-564-8000

Delaware Trust*(Major Banking Relationship)*
Wilmington, DE

Philadelphia National Bank*(Major Banking Relationship)*
P.O. Box 13834, Broad & Chestnut Streets
Philadelphia, PA 19101-7618
Tel.: 215-973-8327

Subsidiaries:

Material Handling Equipment Co. **(1)**
2501 Durham Rd.
Bristol, PA 19007
Tel.: 215-547-3700 (100%)
Fax: 215-943-5228
Emp.: 4
Sales and Distribution of Material Handling Equipment.
S.I.C.: 5084
John F. Smith *(Pres.)*
George S. Wilkerson *(V.P. & Treas.)*

Modern Equipment Rentals Inc. **(1)**
24 Brookside Dr.
Wilmington, DE 19804
Tel.: 302-658-5257 (100%)
Fax: 302-658-0135
Emp.: 56
Equipment Rentals
S.I.C.: 7359
Lawrence J. Norton *(Pres.)*
George S. Wilkinson *(V.P. & Treas.)*
Milt Hutchinson *(Dir.-Pur.)*
Clint Koch *(Dir.-Sls.)*

Modern Handling Equipment Co. **(1)**
2501 Durham Rd.
Bristol, PA 19007
Tel.: 215-943-9100 (100%)
Fax: 215-943-4978
Emp.: 175
Sales of Material Handling Equipment, Rentals, Parts and Service
S.I.C.: 5084; 7359
John F. Smith *(Pres.)*
George S. Wilkinson *(V.P. & Treas.)*
Daniel Luongo *(Dir.-Sls.)*

Modern Handling Equipment Co. of NY **(1)**
1176 Farmingdale Rd., Rte. 109
Lindenhurst, NY 11757
Tel.: 516-226-7900
Fax: 516-226-8491
Emp.: 15
Sales of Material Handling Equipment, Rentals, Parts and Service
S.I.C.: 5084; 7359
Carl P. Rathemacher *(V.P.)*
George S. Wilkinson *(V.P. & Treas.)*
Tom Sylvester *(Dir.-Sls.)*

Modern Handling Equipment of N.J., Inc. **(1)**
75 New St.
Edison, NJ 08837
Tel.: 908-738-9200 (100%)
Fax: 908-738-4077
Emp.: 90
Sales of Material Handling Equipment, Rentals, Parts and Service
S.I.C.: 5084; 7359
Carl P. Rathemacher *(Pres.)*
George S. Wilkinson *(V.P. & Treas.)*
Tom Sylvester *(Dir.-Sls.)*

Modern Hilift Equipment Co. **(1)**
1165 Matsonford Rd.
West Conshohocken, PA 19428
Tel.: 215-825-6010 (100%)
Fax: 215-825-1952
Emp.: 14
Sale, Lease & Service Cranes & Aerial Lifts
S.I.C.: 5084
Albert Funk *(Pres.)*
George S. Wilkenson *(V.P. & Treas.)*
Donald Sherow *(Dir.-Sls.)*

Moreco Inc. **(1)**
2501 Durham Rd.
Bristol, PA 19007
Tel.: 215-943-9100 (100%)
Fax: 215-943-8901
Real Estate
S.I.C.: 6531
Joseph McEwen *(Pres.)*
George S. Wilkinson *(V.P. & Treas.)*

Seely Equipment & Supply Co., Inc. **(1)**
1325 Hwy. 34
Wall, NJ 07719
Tel.: 908-938-2900
Fax: 908-938-5382
Emp.: 31
Distributor of Road Maintenance, Snow & Ice Equipment & Supplies; Signs; Safety Items
S.I.C.: 5084
Robert Held *(Pres.)*
George S. Wilkinson *(V.P. & Treas.)*

MODERN WELDING CO., INC.
2880 New Hartford Rd.
Owensboro, KY 42303
Mailing Address:
P.O. Box 1450
Owensboro, KY 42302
Tel.: 502-685-4400
Fax: 502-684-6972
Year Founded: 1932
Approx.Sls.: $80,000,000
Emp.: 775
Steel Storage Tanks, Code Tanks, Pressure Vessels
S.I.C.: 3443; 3441
John W. Jones *(Pres. & Chief Exec. Officer)*
James E. Jones *(Chief Fin. Officer, Sec. & Treas.)*
Ronald Ecleberry *(V.P.-Sls.)*

No. of Mfg. Plants/Facilities: 14

Outside Service Firm(s):

Arthur Andersen & Co.*(Auditors)*
2300 Meidinger Tower
Louisville, KY 40202
Tel.: 502-589-4160

Owensboro National Bank*(Major Banking Relationship)*
Owensboro, KY

MODERN WOODMEN OF AMERICA
1701 1st Ave.
Rock Island, IL 61201
Tel.: 309-786-6481
Fax: 309-786-7084
Year Founded: 1883
Approx.Rev.: $175,513,269
Emp.: 2,500
Fiscal Year-end: 12/31/90
Fraternal Life Insurance
W.B. Foster *(Pres.)*
James V. Standaert *(Natl. Sec.)*
Gary E. Stoefen *(Treas. & Investments Mgr.)*
Gloria Bergh *(Mgr.-Pub. Rels.)*

MODULITE CORPORATION
921 W. Artesia Blvd.
Compton, CA 90220
Tel.: 310-608-2200
Telex: 310-472-0884
Fax: 310-608-5818
Year Founded: 1979
Assets: $5,200,000
Earnings: $860,000
Net Worth: $5,200,000
Approx.Sls.: $10,000,000
Emp.: 140
Fiscal Year-end: 12/31/88
Manufacture Modular Lighting Systems
S.I.C.: 3645
Franz Kent Weber *(Chm. Bd., Pres. & Chief Exec. Officer)*
George Vargis *(V.P.-Admin. & Chief Fin. Officer)*
John Webber *(Treas.)*
Lynn B. Weber *(Sec.)*
Diane Palmer *(Dir.-Personnel)*
Leroy Baker *(Mgr.-Credit)*
Richard Castillo *(Mgr.-Opers.)*

Computer Systems/Hardware:
IBM PC

Outside Service Firm(s):

A. Dean Lynn*(Auditors)*
Tarzana, CA

AEGON USA, Inc.*(Group Insurer)*
1111 North Charles St.
Baltimore, MD 21201
Tel.: 410-576-4571
Telex: 464414
Fax: 410-347-8685

American Insurance*(Group Insurer)*
Sherman Oaks, CA

James Dumas*(Legal Firm)*
Santa Monica, CA

Subsidiary:

Universal Glass Corp. **(1)**
666 Union St.
Montebello, CA 90640
Tel.: 213-728-6700

MOGAS INDUSTRIES, INC.
P.O. Box 11529
Houston, TX 77293-1529
Tel.: 713-449-0291
Fax: 713-590-3412
Year Founded: 1973
Approx.Sls.: $10,000,000
Emp.: 50
Fiscal Year-end: 12/31/89
Manufacturer of Industrial Valves
S.I.C.: 3491
V. Louis Mogas *(Pres. & Chief Exec. Officer)*
Tommy Bright *(V.P.-Opers.)*
Sam Furman *(V.P.-Mfg.)*
Bob Kaufman *(V.P.-Sls. & Mktg.)*
Carol McArthur *(Controller)*

No. of Mfg. Plants/Facilities: 1
No. of U.S. Offices: 32
No. of Foreign Offices: 5

Computer Systems/Hardware:
Compaq

Outside Service Firm(s):

Green, Wheeler & Co.*(Auditors)*
Houston, TX

Utica National*(Commercial Insurance Carrier)*
Tulsa, OK

George Washington Life Insurance Co.*(Group Insurer)*
Jacksonville, FL

Texas Commerce Bank*(Major Banking Relationship)*
600 Travis Street, Suite 1150
Houston, TX 77002
Tel.: 713-236-4865

MOHAWK DISTILLED PRODUCTS
11900 Biscayne Blvd.
North Miami, FL 33181-2726
Tel.: 305-893-3394 **MI**
Fax: 305-891-6577
Year Founded: 1989
Approx.Sls.: $40,000,000
Emp.: 15
Blender & Distr. of Spirits
S.I.C.: 2084
Marshall L. Berkowitz *(Pres. & Chief Exec. Officer)*
Paul Berkowitz *(Sr. V.P.)*
Joseph Peiken *(V.P. & Chief Fin. Officer)*
Nancy D. Berkowitz *(V.P. & Dir.-Mktg.)*
Joseph Garuckas *(V.P. & Natl. Sls. Mgr.)*
Hubert Surville *(V.P.-Devel. & Export)*

MOHAWK PAPER MILLS, INC.
465 S. Saratoga St.
Cohoes, NY 12047
Mailing Address:
P.O. Box 497
Cohoes, NY 12047
Tel.: 518-237-1740
Tel.: 800-THE-MILL **NY**
Fax: 518-237-7394
Year Founded: 1931
Sales Range: $60-79 Million
Emp.: 330

Import Export
Mfr. of Coated Text, Cover & Uncoated Printing Papers
S.I.C.: 2621
Thomas D. O'Connor *(Chm., Pres. & Chief Exec. Officer)*
Phillip W. LaBatte *(Chief Fin. Officer)*
Dan Schimp *(Controller)*
Scott O. Petrequin *(Sr. V.P.)*
Keith Anderson *(V.P.-Admin.)*
William Monks *(V.P.-Mfg.)*
Clifford Bouchard *(Dir.-Personnel)*
David Fenton *(Dir.-Pur.)*
George Milner *(Dir.-Environmental Natural Resources)*
Thomas O'Connor, Jr. *(Dir.-Opers.)*
Laura Des Enfants *(Mgr.-Mktg.)*
Ted O'Connor *(Mgr.-Sls.)*
F. Joseph O'Connor *(Mgr.-Imports/ Exports)*
Laura Shore *(Mgr.-Communications & Promo. Services)*

No. of Mfg. Plants/Facilities: 2
No. of U.S. Offices: 1

Computer Systems/Hardware:
IBM

Outside Service Firm(s):

KPMG Peat Marwick*(Auditors)*
74 N. Pearl St.
Albany, NY 12207
Tel.: 518-455-8809

Norstar Bank, N.A.*(Major Banking Relationship)*
Albany, NY

MOHAWK PLASTICS, INC.
Northfield Rd.
Bernardston, MA 01337
Tel.: 413-648-9211
Fax: 413-648-5341
Approx.Sls.: $19,000,000
Emp.: 150
Manufacture Plastic Products
S.I.C.: 3081
Art Binner *(Acting Pres.)*
Evelyn Walsh *(Treas.)*

Outside Service Firm(s):

Roy B. Chapin & Associates*(Auditors)*
Bernardston, MA

Bank of New England*(Major Banking Relationship)*
Bernardston, MA

WALLACE MOIR CO.
9595 Wilshire Blvd., 10th Fl.
Beverly Hills, CA 90212
Tel.: 310-273-7300
Fax: 310-271-7661
Year Founded: 1972
Emp.: 100
Real Estate Investor, Developer; Pension Fund Manager
S.I.C.: 6552; 6411
Parker Jackson *(Pres.)*

Computer Systems/Hardware:
Data General

MOLDED FIBER GLASS COMPANIES
1601 W. 29th St.
Ashtabula, OH 44004
Mailing Address:
P.O. Box 675,
Ashtabula, OH 44004
Tel.: 216-997-5851 **OH**
Fax: 216-992-2695
Year Founded: 1948
Assets: $28,500,000
Liabilities: $12,500,000
Net Worth: $16,000,000
Approx.Sls.: $60,000,000
Emp.: 1,000
Fiscal Year-end: 8/31/91
Export
Mfr. of Fiberglass-Reinforced Plastic Products
S.I.C.: 3089
Richard S. Morrison *(Pres. & Chief Exec. Officer)*
Robert E. Mollman *(Chief Oper. Officer)*
Doy Gillespie *(Sr. V.P.)*
William Kane *(V.P., Sec., Treas. & Chief Fin. Officer)*
E.T. Warren *(Gen. Counsel)*
John Ehrlinger *(Dir.-Data Processing)*
Richard Fortune *(Dir.-Pur.)*
Andy Juhola *(Dir.-Personnel)*
Glen Warner *(Dir.-Adv.)*
Lawrence Narducci *(Mgr.-Mfg.)*

No. of Mfg. Plants/Facilities: 5
No. of U.S. Offices: 4

Computer Systems/Hardware:
ICL System 25

Outside Service Firm(s):

Deloitte & Touche*(Auditors)*
1717 East Ninth St.
Cleveland, OH 44114
Tel.: 216-589-1300

Liberty Mutual Insurance*(Commercial Insurance Carrier)*
Cincinnati, OH

Manning & Napier*(Investment Banker)*
Rochester, NY

Warren & Young*(Legal Firm)*
Ashtabula, OH

AmeriTrust Company*(Major Banking Relationship)*
Ashtabula, OH

Marine Bank*(Pension Manager)*
Erie, PA

Divisions:

Molded Fiber Glass Co. **(1)**
55 4th Ave.
Union City, PA 16438
Tel.: 814-438-3841
Tel.: 800-458-0863 (100%)
Fax: 814-438-2284
Approx.Sls.: $16,000,000
Emp.: 200
Computer Systems/Hardware:
ICL
Supplying Contractors with Fiberglass, Plastic, Standard & Special Forms & Custom Molding
S.I.C.: 3089
Gerald Bender *(Pres. & Gen. Mgr.)*
Phil Hancock *(Chief Oper. Officer)*
Jack Slocum *(Chief Fin. Officer)*
A.H. Fortune *(V.P.-Sls.)*
Louise M. Raffa *(V.P.-Corp. Communications & Adv.)*
Wesley Shamp *(Dir.-Sls.)*
Drew Mager *(Dir.-Mktg.)*

Molded Fiber Glass Co. **(1)**
4401 Benefit Ave.
Ashtabula, OH 44004
Tel.: 216-997-5851
Tel.: 800-456-5263 (100%)
Fax: 216-992-0542
Approx.Sls.: $31,000,000
Emp.: 425
Computer Systems/Hardware:
ICL
Mfr. of Fiberglass-Plastic Custom Molding
S.I.C.: 3089
Ron Orr *(Pres. & Gen. Mgr.)*
Larry Darducci *(Chief Oper. Officer)*
Dave Parker *(Chief Fin. Officer)*
Glen Warner *(Dir.-Sls.)*
Michelle Hoeferlia *(Dir.-Mktg.)*
Richard Fortune *(Dir.-Pur.)*

Subsidiaries:

Molded Fiber Glass Tray Co. **(1)**
E. Erie St.
Linesville, PA 16424
Tel.: 814-683-4500
Tel.: 800-458-0863 (100%)
Fax: 814-683-4504
Approx.Sls.: $13,300,000
Emp.: 150
Mfr. of Fiberglass Plastic Trays, Boxes & Custom Molding
S.I.C.: 3089

Molded Fiber Glass/West **(1)**
9400 Holly Rd.
Adelanto, CA 92301-0370
Tel.: 619-246-4042 (100%)
Fax: 619-246-5500
Approx.Sls.: $7,400,000
Emp.: 125
Supplying Contractors with Fiberglass, Plastic, Standard & Special Forms & Custom Molding
S.I.C.: 5033; 5162; 5031
Gary Trafican *(Gen. Mgr.)*

MOLESPHINI & TOBIN, INC.
301 East 45th St.
New York, NY 10017
Tel.: 212-972-6232
Fax: 212-661-3436
Year Founded: 1985
Approx.Billings: $23,500,000
Emp.: 6
Media Planning & Purchase, Strategic Marketingg & Planning
Arthur J. Molesphini *(Chm. & Media Dir.)*
John J. Tobin *(Pres.)*
Florence Horowitz *(Treas.)*

MOLIN AUTO PARTS INC.
3896 Union Rd.
Buffalo, NY 14225
Mailing Address:
P.O. Box 625
Buffalo, NY 14225
Tel.: 716-633-4455 **NY**
Fax: 716-633-5749
Year Founded: 1922
Assets: $8,200,000
Liabilities: $6,100,000
Net Worth: $2,100,000
Approx.Sls.: $20,000,000
Emp.: 160
Fiscal Year-end: 12/25/91
Wholesale & Retail Automotive Parts & Supplies
S.I.C.: 5013; 5531
Carl E. Molin, Jr. *(Chm. Bd.)*
Kim E. Molin *(Pres.)*
Carl E. Molin, III *(Treas.)*
Thomas H. Brown, Jr. *(Sec.)*
Neil Bedell *(Dir.-Pur.)*
John Edlund *(Dir.-Mktg.)*
Raymond Vigneron *(Dir.-Opers.)*
Anthony Vitrano *(Dir.-Data Processing)*

Outside Service Firm(s):

Urbach, Kahn, Werlin*(Auditors)*
Buffalo, NY

William R. Brennan*(Legal Firm)*
Buffalo, NY

Marine Midland Bank*(Major Banking Relationship)*
P.O. Box 803, 1 Marine Midland Center, 23rd Floor
Buffalo, NY 14203
Tel.: 716-841-2582

MOLINE CORPORATION
Dean St.
Saint Charles, IL 60174
Mailing Address:
P.O. Box 529
St. Charles, IL 60174
Tel.: 708-584-4600
Fax: 708-584-1999
Year Founded: 1869
Approx.Sls.: $12,000,000
Emp.: 200
Import Export
Iron Foundries, Job Castings & Power Transmission Prods.
S.I.C.: 3321; 3569; 3599
Dort Fauntleroy *(Pres.)*
Chuck Vaccarello *(Treas.)*
John Faber *(Dir.-Pur.)*
David Fauntleroy *(Mgr.-Sls.-Castings)*

Computer Systems/Hardware:
IBM 400

Outside Service Firm(s):

Altschuler, Melvoin & Glasser*(Auditors)*
30 S. Wecker Dr.
Chicago, IL 60606
Tel.: 312-207-2800

Michigan Avenue National Bank*(Major Banking Relationship)*
Chicago, IL

Adelman, Gettleman & Merens, Ltd.*(Legal Firm)*
Chicago, IL

MOLLENBERG-BETZ INC.
300 Scott St.
Buffalo, NY 14204
Tel.: 716-852-7138
Fax: 716-852-7180
Year Founded: 1910
Approx.Sls.: $20,390,000
Emp.: 110
Mechanical Contractor Specializing in Refrigeration Systems, Design & Installation, Process Piping, HVAC, Service Work, Boiler Plants, Heat Vent & Air Handling Installation; Distributor of Parts
S.I.C.: 1711; 5074; 5075; 5078; 5722
H. Van Mollenberg *(Chm. Bd., Pres. & Chief Exec. Officer)*
James S. Witter *(V.P.)*
Jim Camarre *(Controller & Dir.-Mngmt. Information Systems)*

Outside Service Firm(s):

KPMG Peat Marwick*(Auditors)*
700 Empire Tower
Buffalo, NY 14202-3786
Tel.: 716-854-1830
Fax: 716-856-8063

Phillips, Lytle, Hitchcock, Blaine & Huber*(Legal Firm)*
3400 Marine Midland Center
Buffalo, NY 14203
Tel.: 716-847-8400

Manufacturers & Traders Trust Company*(Major Banking Relationship)*
1 M & T Plaza
Buffalo, NY 14240
Tel.: 716-842-4200

MOLON MOTOR & COIL CORP.
3737 Industrial Ave.
Rolling Meadows, IL 60008
Tel.: 708-253-6000
Fax: 708-259-5491
Year Founded: 1955
Approx.Sls.: $20,000,000
Emp.: 340
Manufacture Subfractional Horsepower Motors
S.I.C.: 3621; 3564; 3566
Earl Moloney *(Chm. Bd. & Chief Exec. Officer)*
Bob Clancy *(Controller)*
S.H. Hollander *(Dir.-Admin.)*
Charles George *(Gen. Mgr.)*
Principal(s):
Earl Moloney

No. of Mfg. Plants/Facilities: 3

Computer Systems/Hardware:
Data General

Outside Service Firm(s):

First National Bank of Chicago*(Major Banking Relationship)*
One First National Plaza
Chicago, IL 60670
Tel.: 312-732-9781
Tel.: 312-732-4050
Fax: 312-732-4840
Fax: 312-732-3055

MOLTRUP STEEL PRODUCTS COMPANY
14th St. & 2nd Ave.
Beaver Falls, PA 15010
Mailing Address:
P.O. Box 331
Beaver Falls, PA 15010
Tel.: 412-846-3100
Fax: 412-846-3110
Sales Range: $10-19 Million
Emp.: 100
Cold Drawn Steel Bars, Steel Specialties
S.I.C.: 3316
Michael P. Pitterich *(Chm. Bd. & Pres.)*
George Ebel *(Chief Fin. Officer)*
John Modaffari *(Pur. Agent)*
Richard D. Reisinger *(Supvr.-Plant)*

Outside Service Firm(s):

Coopers & Lybrand*(Auditors)*
600 Grant St., 35th Fl.
Pittsburgh, PA 15219
Tel.: 412-355-8000
Fax: 412-355-8089

Mellon Bank, N.A.*(Major Banking Relationship)*
P.O. Box 444,
Pittsburgh, PA 15230
Tel.: 412-236-8000
Tel.: 1-800-451-7392
Fax: 412-236-8157

MONA INDUSTRIES, INC.
76 E. 24th St.
Paterson, NJ 07544-0425
Mailing Address:
P.O. Box 425,
Paterson, NJ 07544-0425
Tel.: 201-345-8220
Tel.: 800-553-6662
Telex: 130308
Fax: 201-345-3527
Year Founded: 1951
Approx.Sls.: $30,000,000
Emp.: 120
Fiscal Year-end: 7/31/91
Export
Mfr. of Surface Active Agents: Detergents, Synthetic or Inorganic
S.I.C.: 2843; 2841; 8711
J.W. Braitmayer *(Chm. Bd. & Chief Exec. Officer)*
J.J. McAndrews *(Pres. & Chief Oper. Officer)*
Joseph Lafferty *(Chief Info. Officer & Sr. V.P.-Data Processing)*
Paul Hiznay *(Sr. V.P.-Sls. & Mdsg.)*
Gehr W. Brown *(V.P.-Fin.)*
Dennis L. Fost *(V.P.-Mktg. & Comml. Devel.)*
Karl Heyman *(V.P.-Technology)*
Frank Kay *(V.P.-Opers.)*
Joseph Komor *(V.P.-Res. & Devel.)*
Joseph S. Schoen *(V.P.-Engrng.)*
Reed W. Easton *(Gen. Counsel)*
Wallace G. Clarke *(Dir.-Pur.)*
Frank Kay *(Mgr.-Opers.)*
George W. Lowry *(Mgr.-Regulatory Affairs)*
John Raggi *(Mgr.-Quality Control)*

Computer Systems/Hardware:
UNISYS

Outside Service Firm(s):

Arthur Andersen & Co.*(Auditors)*
Paterson, NJ

Chemical Bank*(Major Banking Relationship)*
Paterson, NJ

EDWARD V. MONAHAN INC.
21321 Kelly Rd.
Eastpointe, MI 48021
Tel.: 313-774-3800 **MI**
Fax: 313-774-2530
Year Founded: 1922
Approx.Sls.: $10,000,000
Emp.: 15
General Contractors Commercial Buildings.
S.I.C.: 1542; 8741
William D. Monahan *(Pres. & Chief Exec. Officer)*
Daniel J. Monahan *(V.P.)*
Edward J. Monahan *(V.P.)*
Michael J. Monahan *(V.P.)*
Michael P. Monahan *(Controller)*

Outside Service Firm(s):

Doeren & Mayhew*(Auditors)*
Troy, MI

National Bank of Detroit*(Major Banking Relationship)*
611 Woodward
Detroit, MI 48226
Tel.: 313-225-1000

MONARCH AVALON, INC.
4517 Harford
Baltimore, MD 21214
Tel.: 410-254-9200
Tel.: 800-999-3222 (Orders)
Fax: 410-254-0991
Year Founded: 1958
Approx.Sls.: $23,000,000
Emp.: 950
Fiscal Year-end: 4/30/91
Export
Publisher of Avalon Hill; Strategy Games, Leisure Time Games, Card Games, Financial Games, Sports Illustrated Games, Micro Computer Games & Victory Games
S.I.C.: 5092
A. Eric Dott *(Chm. Bd. & Chief Exec. Officer)*
Jackson Y. Dott *(Pres.)*
Thomas N. Shaw *(Exec. V.P. & Dir.-Adv. & Sls.)*
Donald J. Greenwood *(Sr. V.P. & Dir.-Res. & Devel.)*
Frank Fontenazza *(Chief Fin. Officer & Controller)*
Steven Szekely *(Sec. & Treas.)*
Phyllis Opolko *(Dir.-Mktg. & Pub. Rels.)*

Divisions:

The Avalon Hill Game Company **(1)**
4517 Harford
Baltimore, MD 21214
Tel.: 410-254-9200
Fax: 410-254-0991

Leisure Time Games **(1)**
4517 Harford
Baltimore, MD 21214
Tel.: 410-254-9200

Microcomputer Games **(1)**
4517 Harford Rd.
Baltimore, MD 21214
Tel.: 410-254-9200
Fax: 410-254-0991

Monarch Toy Co., Ltd. **(1)**
4517 Harford
Baltimore, MD 21214
Tel.: 410-254-9200
Fax: 410-254-0991

Strategy Games **(1)**
4517 Harford
Baltimore, MD 21214
Tel.: 410-254-9200

Victory Games, Inc. **(1)**
4517 Harford
Baltimore, MD 21214
Tel.: 410-254-9200
Fax: 410-254-0991

Subsidiary:

Avalon Hill/Sports Illustrated Games **(1)**
4517 Harford Rd.
Baltimore, MD 21214
Tel.: 410-254-9200

THE MONARCH COMPANY, INC.

THE MONARCH COMPANY, INC.
16 Perimeter Park Dr.,
Ste. 110
Atlanta, GA 30341

Tel.: 404-455-3908
Fax: 404-457-6797
Emp.: 45
Fiscal Year-end: 12/31/90
Mfr. & Distributor of Soft Drinks
S.I.C.: 2086; 5149
Frank A. Armstrong *(Chm. Bd.)*
Mark Armstrong *(Pres.)*
J. Alfred Pate III *(V.P.-Fin.)*
Ann Burton *(Controller)*

Outside Service Firm(s):

Alston & Bird*(Legal Firm)*
One Atlantic Center, 1201 West Peachtree St.
Atlanta, GA 30309-3424
Tel.: 404-881-7000

Subsidiaries:

Bubble-Up **(1)**
651 W. Washington St., Ste. 401
Chicago, IL 60661
Tel.: 312-559-9200
Telex: 206641UD
Fax: 312-559-1816
Mfr. Soft Drinks
S.I.C.: 2086
William Hill *(Exec. V.P.)*

Dad's Root Beer **(1)**
651 W. Washington Blvd., Ste. 401
Chicago, IL 60661
Tel.: 312-559-9200
Telex: 206641UD
Fax: 312-559-1816
Mfr. Soft Drinks
S.I.C.: 6794; 2086
Mark Armstrong *(Pres.)*
William C. Hill *(V.P.-Mktg.)*
Marie Centenail *(Controller)*

Non-U.S. Holding:

Suncrest Company of Canada **(1)**
170 Attwell Drive, Ste. 603
Rexdale, ON M9W 6A3, Canada
Tel.: 416-674-0136
Mfr. of Soft Drinks
S.I.C.: 2086; 5149
Joseph Stutz *(Pres.)*

MONARCH CONSTRUCTION COMPANY
1654 Sherman Ave.
Cincinnati, OH 45212
Tel.: 513-351-6900 **KY**
Fax: 513-351-0979
Year Founded: 1963
Approx.Sls.: $50,000,000
Emp.: 100
New Construction of Commercial, Office, Institutional & Industrial Buildings & Schools; Renovation & Repair of Commercial & Office Buildings;
S.I.C.: 1542; 1541

Ronald A. Koetters *(Chm. Bd. & Chief Exec. Officer)*
Michael Kocheck *(Pres.)*

MONARCH IMPORT CO., INC.
(Formerly Monarch Wine Co., Inc.)
845 3rd Ave.
New York, NY 10022
Tel.: 212-421-3900
Fax: 212-421-3913
Approx.Sls.: $20,000,000
Emp.: 35
Fiscal Year-end: 3/31/90
Importers & Distributors of Wine, Champagne, Vermouth
S.I.C.: 5182; 5181
Elis Goodman *(Chief Exec. Officer)*

Computer Systems/Hardware:
IBM

Outside Service Firm(s):

Anchin, Block & Anchin*(Auditors)*
1375 Broadway
New York, NY 10018

Chemical Bank*(Major Banking Relationship)*
450 West 33rd St.
New York, NY 10001
Tel.: 212-613-7197
Fax: 212-947-7628

MONARCH LUGGAGE CO. INC.
5 Delavan St.
Brooklyn, NY 11231
Tel.: 718-858-6900
Fax: 718-797-5626
Year Founded: 1946
Approx.Sls.: $15,000,000
Emp.: 300
Import Export
Mfr. Luggage; Monarch, Holiday
S.I.C.: 3161
R. Fried *(Pres.)*
D. Leibowitz *(V.P.)*
S. Schwartz *(V.P.)*
J. Steinhardt *(Comptroller)*
C. Barresi *(Dir.-Pur.)*
A. Hartenstein *(Dir.-Sls.)*
R. Schwartz *(Dir.-Mktg.)*
M. McCluskey *(Mgr.-Personnel)*

Computer Systems/Hardware:
IBM-RISC 6000

MONARK EGG CORPORATION
601 E. Third St.
Kansas City, MO 64106
Tel.: 816-421-1970
Fax: 816-842-6727
Approx.Sls.: $17,000,000
Emp.: 120
Fiscal Year-end: 12/31/90
Dried, Frozen & Liquid Egg Products
S.I.C.: 2015
Dean Hughson *(Pres.)*

MONEX INTERNATIONAL, LTD.
4910 Birch St.
Newport Beach, CA 92660
Tel.: 714-752-1400
Fax: 714-752-7214
Approx.Sls.: $8,000,000,000
Emp.: 300
Fiscal Year-end: 12/31/90
Trader of Precious Metals, Selective Foreign Currency, Dealer & Exchange Traded Options
S.I.C.: 5094; 6289
Louis E. Carabini *(Chm. Bd. & Pres.)*
George R. Hall *(V.P.-Mktg.)*
John S. Tate *(V.P.-Sls.)*
Gerald H. Hastings *(Dir.-Adv. & Sls. Promo.)*

MONEY POINT DIAMOND CO.
4300 Buell St.
Chesapeake, VA 23324
Mailing Address:
P.O. Box 7596
Chesapeake, VA 23324
Tel.: 804-543-2066
Fax: 804-543-6632
Sales Range: $20-39 Million
Emp.: 90
Export
Processing of Ferrous & Non-Ferrous Metals
S.I.C.: 3325
Fred Jacobson *(Pres.)*
George B. Ginsburg *(Sec. & Gen. Mgr.)*

Outside Service Firm(s):

Goodman & Company*(Auditors)*
Norfolk, VA

S. L. Nussbaum*(Commercial Insurance Carrier)*
Norfolk, VA

Signet Bank*(Major Banking Relationship)*
Norfolk, VA

Subsidiary:

Jacobson Metal Company **(1)**
P.O. Box 7596
Chesapeake, VA 23324
Tel.: 804-543-2066

MONICO ALLOYS, INC.
2301 E. 15th St.
Los Angeles, CA 90021-4848
Tel.: 213-629-4767
Fax: 213-627-2880
Year Founded: 1979
Approx.Sls.: $12,000,000
Emp.: 30
Fiscal Year-end: 7/31/91
Import Export
Wholesale High Temperature Metal Alloys
S.I.C.: 5051
Henri Kahn *(Pres.)*
Saul Zenk *(V.P. & Treas.)*
Nelly Kahn *(Sec.)*

Outside Service Firm(s):

Bernard Melamed Company*(Auditors)*
Los Angeles, CA

Bank of America NT&SA*(Major Banking Relationship)*
555 So. Flower St.
Los Angeles, CA 90071
Tel.: 213-683-3868

MONIER ROOF TILE, INC.
750 The City Dr. S., Ste. 200
Orange, CA 92668
Mailing Address:
P.O. Box 5567,
Orange, CA 92613
Tel.: 714-750-5366
Fax: 714-750-0751
Approx.Sls.: $50,000,000
Emp.: 28
Fiscal Year-end: 12/30/90
Mfr. Concrete Roof Tile
S.I.C.: 3272
Richard B. Lyons *(Pres.)*
John F. Thomas *(V.P.-Tech. & Prod.)*
James C. Albright *(V.P. & Controller)*
Anthony F. Gillett *(V.P.-Mktg.)*
Sal Mattera *(Gen. Mgr.)*
Guy E. Winters *(Gen. Mgr.)*
Jim Cowell *(Gen. Mgr.)*
Scott Weber *(Gen. Mgr.)*

MONITOR AEROSPACE CORPORATION
1000 New Horizons Blvd.
Amityville, NY 11701
Tel.: 516-957-2300
Fax: 516-957-2432
Year Founded: 1948
Approx.Sls.: $44,000,000
Emp.: 440
Manufacture Component Airplane Parts
S.I.C.: 3728
Guy Lepore *(Pres.)*
Douglas Monitto *(Exec. V.P.)*
Lawrence G. Goldberg *(V.P. & Treas.)*
Edwin Markowitz *(Sec.)*
Lawrence Teicher *(Controller)*

Outside Service Firm(s):

Holtz, Rubenstein & Co.*(Auditors)*
445 Broad Hollow Rd.
Melville, NY 11747-3696

Edward McCoyd*(Legal Firm)*
Garden City, NY

European American Bank*(Major Banking Relationship)*
East Farmingdale, NY

A.C. MONK CO., INC.
P.O. Box 166
Farmville, NC 27828
Tel.: 919-753-2121 NC
Fax: 919-753-8200
Approx.Sls.: $175,000,000
Emp.: 1,000
Fiscal Year-end: 4/30/89
Leaf Tobacco Processors, Dealers & Exporters
S.I.C.: 5154; 5159; 0132
William C. Monk *(Chm. Bd., Chief Exec. Officer & Treas.)*
Albert C. Monk, III *(Pres. & Chief Oper. Officer)*
John M. Hines *(Exec. V.P. & Sec.)*
T.S. Ryon *(Sr. V.P.)*
T.A. Lewis *(V.P. & Controller)*

Computer Systems/Hardware:
IBM

Outside Service Firm(s):

Price Waterhouse*(Auditors)*
Raleigh, NC

Blue Cross & Blue Shield of North Carolina*(Group Insurer)*
Durham, NC

State Mutual Life Assurance Co. of America*(Group Insurer)*
440 Lincoln St.
Worcester, MA 01605
Tel.: 508-852-1000

Wachovia Bank & Trust Co.*(Major Banking Relationship)*
P.O. Box 3001,
Winston-Salem, NC 27102
Tel.: 800-633-4236

Wachovia Bank & Trust Co.*(Pension Manager)*
P.O. Box 3001, 301 N. Church St.
Winston-Salem, NC 27101
Tel.: 919-770-5000

Subsidiaries:

Eastern Tobacco Co. **(1)**
P.O. Box 166
Farmville, NC 27828
Tel.: 919-753-2121 (100%)

Monk-Henderson Tobacco Co. **(1)**
P.O. Box 166
Farmville, NC 27828
Tel.: 919-753-2121 (100%)

Wendel Tobacco Co. **(1)**
P.O. Box 166
Farmville, NC 27828
Tel.: 919-753-2121 (100%)

MONROC, INC.
1730 Beck St.
Salt Lake City, UT 84110
Mailing Address:
P.O. Box 537,
Salt Lake City, UT 84110
Tel.: 801-359-3701 DE
Fax: 801-359-9882
Year Founded: 1986
Assets: $22,000,000
Earnings: $1,500,000
Liabilities: $17,000,000
Net Worth: $5,000,000
Approx.Sls.: $35,000,000
Emp.: 250
Fiscal Year-end: 12/31/89
Nonmetallic Minerals; Stone Prods.; Ready Mix Concrete; Asphalt; Construction Supplies
S.I.C.: 5052; 5032; 3281
Robert A. Parry *(Chm. Bd., Pres. & Chief Exec. Officer)*
L. William Rands *(Chief Fin. Officer, V.P. & Treas.)*
Michael Bunn *(Controller)*
Stanton E. Wilson *(Sec.)*
Frank Metcalf *(Dir.-Employee Benefits)*

Computer Systems/Hardware:
Tandem

Outside Service Firm(s):

Grant Thornton*(Auditors)*
Salt Lake City, UT

Alta Health Strategies*(Group Insurer)*
Salt Lake City, UT

Zions First National Bank*(Major Banking Relationship)*
One South Main St.
Salt Lake City, UT 84111
Tel.: 801-582-4812

The Principal Financial Group*(Pension Manager)*
Des Moines, IA

MONROE SYSTEMS FOR BUSINESS, INC.
1000 The American Rd.
Morris Plains, NJ 07950
Mailing Address:
P.O. Box CN 1941
Morristown, NJ 17962-1941
Tel.: 201-993-2000
Tel.: 800-666-7631
Fax: 201-993-2643
Year Founded: 1912
Emp.: 1,630
Fiscal Year-end: 8/30/91
Import Export
Mfr. of Electronic Programmable Printing & Display Calculators, Accounting Systems, Copiers, Shredders, Facsimile Machines
S.I.C.: 3578; 3579
Jeffry Picower *(Chm. Bd. & Chief Exec. Officer)*
David Bocksch *(Pres. & Chief Oper. Officer)*
Joseph V. Fusco *(V.P. & Chief Fin. Officer)*
Salvatore Cimbolo *(V.P.-Sls. & Mktg.)*
Richard B. Kelsky *(V.P. & Gen. Counsel)*
Bonnie Rhodes *(V.P.-Human Resources)*
Harry Short *(V.P.-Admin. & Plng.)*
Richard Lytton *(Asst. V.P.-Natl. & Govt. Acct. Sls.)*
John Miskew *(Asst. V.P.-Field Engrng.)*
Jeffrey Hecht *(Mgr.-Fin. Services)*
Stephen Hess *(Mgr.-European Opers.)*
Robert Lakeland *(Dir.-Admin.)*
Arnold B. McAllister *(Dir.-Mktg.)*

Outside Service Firm(s):

Mellon Bank, N.A.*(Major Banking Relationship)*
Mellon Independence Center, 7th & Market
Philadelphia, PA 19101-7899

MONROVIA NURSERY CO.
18331 E. Foothill Blvd.
Azusa, CA 91702
Mailing Address:
P.O. Box Q
Azusa, CA 91702
Tel.: 818-334-9321
Fax: 818-334-3126
Approx.Sls.: $25,000,000
Emp.: 800
Fiscal Year-end: 9/30/90
Wholesale Grower of Ornamental Nursery Stock
S.I.C.: 5193; 0181
Miles Rosedale *(Chm. Bd., Pres. & Chief Exec. Officer)*
Nils Bjerg *(Sec. & Chief Fin. Officer)*
Rodger Duer *(Dir.-Pub. Rels.)*
Mark Marko *(Mgr.-Adv.)*
Ron Cramer *(Pur. Agent)*

Subsidiary:

Monrovia Nursery Co.-Oregon **(1)**
12600 S.E. Alderman
Dayton, OR 97114
Tel.: 503-868-7941

MONSEY PRODUCTS COMPANY
Coldstream Rd.
Kimberton, PA 19442
Mailing Address:
P.O. Box 368
Kimberton, PA 19442
Tel.: 215-933-8888
Tel.: 800-523-0268 PA
Fax: 215-933-4598
Year Founded: 1939
Emp.: 350
Fiscal Year-end: 12/31/91
Import Export
Mfr. Protective Roof Coatings
S.I.C.: 2952
Joseph T. Mooney, Jr. *(Pres.)*
Edward P. Mooney *(V.P. & Chief Oper. Officer)*
Norman F. Nickerson *(V.P.-Sls.)*
John T. Mader *(Dir.-Mktg.)*
Brendan Walsh *(Treas. & Controller)*
J. Michael McFadden *(Sec. & Corp. Fin. Mgr.)*
Michael P. Manning *(Asst. to Pres.)*
Steven W. Landsfra *(Dir.-Pur.)*
William Buck *(Mgr.-Acctg.)*

No. of U.S. Offices: 6

Computer Systems/Hardware:
Unisys

Outside Service Firm(s):

Ernst & Young*(Auditors)*
1800 John F. Kennedy Blvd.
Philadelphia, PA 19103-7499
Tel.: 215-864-3300

Divisions:

Monsey Products Co. **(1)**
P.O. Box 3547
Rock Hill, SC 29731
Tel.: 803-366-8113
Fax: 803-366-5255
Export

Monsey Products Co. **(1)**
3802 Miller Park Dr.
Garland, TX 75042
Tel.: 214-272-5488
Fax: 214-276-7948

Monsey Products Co. **(1)**
4351 W. Morris St.
Indianapolis, IN 46241
Tel.: 317-248-1344
Fax: 317-243-6619

Monsey Products Co. **(1)**
SR 60 West
Bartow, FL 33830
Tel.: 813-533-0522
Fax: 813-533-4637

Monsey Products Co., Inc. **(1)**
P.O. Box 340
Waterford, NY 12188
Tel.: 518-235-7525
Fax: 518-235-7602

F.G. MONTABERT
175 Paterson Ave.
Midland Park, NJ 07432
Tel.: 201-444-1250
Fax: 201-444-4259
Sales Range: $10-19 Million
Emp.: 250
Woven Labels & Decorative Trim
S.I.C.: 2241
F. Condon *(Pres.)*
F. Gaffney *(Sr. V.P.-Admin.)*
John M. McGrath *(Sr. V.P.-Mktg. & Sls.)*
P. Hornik *(V.P.-Natl. Sls.)*
M. Martin *(V.P.-Natl. Acct. Sls.)*

B. L. MONTAGUE CO.
303 E. Liberty St.
Sumter, SC 29150
Mailing Address:
P.O. Box 250
Sumter, SC 29151
Tel.: 803-775-1102 SC
Fax: 803-773-8090
Year Founded: 1914
Approx.Sls.: $45,000,000
Emp.: 380
Manufacture Bulk Handling Conveyors; Industrial Supplies Sales & Distributors
S.I.C.: 3535; 5085
B.L. Montague II *(Chm. Bd. & Chief Exec. Officer)*
L.D. Montague, Jr. *(Pres.)*
Frank J. Warmoth *(Pres. & Chief Oper. Officer)*
T. Mitchell Watson *(Chief Fin. Officer & Treas.)*
Nancy M. Cromer *(V.P.-Admin. & Human Resources)*

No. of Mfg. Plants/Facilities: 1
No. of U.S. Offices: 10

Outside Service Firm(s):

Arthur Andersen & Co.*(Auditors)*
Columbia, SC

Citizens & Southern National Bank*(Major Banking Relationship)*
Columbia, SC

Nexen, Pruitt, Jacobs & Pollad*(Legal Firm)*
Columbia, SC

MONTANA LOTTERY
2525 N. Montana Ave.
Helena, MT 59601
Tel.: 406-444-5825
Fax: 406-444-5830
Year Founded: 1987
Approx.Sls.: $28,000,000
Emp.: 35
Fiscal Year-end: 6/30/92
State Lottery
S.I.C.: 7999
Sandra Guedes *(Dir.)*
John Onstad *(Dir.-Security)*
Jerry LaChere *(Dir.-Opers.)*
Janet Drexel-Bone *(Dir.-Mktg.)*

MONTE VISTA CO-OP ASSOCIATION, INC.
1901 E. Hwy. 160
Monte Vista, CO 81144
Tel.: 719-852-5181 CO

Fax: 719-852-3418
Year Founded: 1949
Approx.Sls.: $17,000,000
Emp.: 50
Wholesale Distribution of Fertilizer & Fertilizer Materials; Gasoline Filling Stations; Agricultural Machinery & Equipment
S.I.C.: 5191; 5541; 5083
Jon Brownell *(Pres.)*
Randy Brown *(V.P.)*
Everett Myers *(Sec.)*
Keith Jacobson *(Dir.-Fin.)*
Gerald Palmgren *(Gen. Mgr.)*

Outside Service Firm(s):

Gary A. Scofield*(Auditors)*
Littleton, CO

Bank of Monte Vista*(Major Banking Relationship)*
Monte Vista, CO

MONTEBELLO BRANDS INC.
1919 Willow Spring Rd.
Baltimore, MD 21222
Tel.: 410-282-8800
Fax: 410-282-8809
Year Founded: 1933
Approx.Sls.: $18,000,000
Emp.: 45
Fiscal Year-end: 4/30/90
Import Export
Liquor Manufacturer
S.I.C.: 5182; 2085; 5181
Alfred Bernstein *(Pres.)*
Leo Conte *(Exec. V.P.)*
Ellen S. Kier *(Dir.)*

Computer Systems/Hardware:
IBM System 36

Outside Service Firm(s):

London, Selenkow, Carton & Wolf*(Auditors)*
Baltimore, MD

Alexander & Alexander*(Commercial Insurance Carrier)*
P.O. Box 73223
Baltimore, MD 21273
Tel.: 310-547-2800

Maryland National Bank*(Major Banking Relationship)*
Baltimore, MD 21202

MONTEREY MECHANICAL COMPANY
8275 San Leandro St.
Oakland, CA 94621
Tel.: 415-632-3173
Fax: 415-632-0732
Year Founded: 1941
Approx.Sls.: $34,000,000
Emp.: 125
Fiscal Year-end: 7/31/91
Water Disposal Waste; Water Treatment Plant & Mechanical Contractor Boiler Work; Sheet Metal Fabrication
S.I.C.: 1629; 1711; 3444
Richard F. Hamilton *(Pres.)*
Milt Burleson *(Exec. V.P.)*
Robert A. Depolo *(Mgr.-Personnel, Treas. & Sec.)*
William P. Francis *(Mgr.-Opers.)*

Outside Service Firm(s):

KPMG Peat Marwick*(Auditors)*
Oakland, CA

First Interstate Bank*(Major Banking Relationship)*
Oakland, CA

Aiken, Kramer & Cummings*(Legal Firm)*
Oakland, CA

MONTEREY'S TEX MEX CAFE
4441 W. Airport Fwy.
Irving, TX 75062
Mailing Address:
P.O. Box 152077,
Irving, TX 75062
Tel.: 214-258-8508
Approx.Sls.: $17,000,000
Emp.: 1,100
Fiscal Year-end: 1/ 3/92
Mexican Restaurants
S.I.C.: 5812
Richard Frank *(Pres. & Chief Oper. Officer)*
Richard Huston *(Exec. V.P.-Mktg.)*
Curt Glowacki *(V.P. & Dir.-Opers.)*
Lois Perry *(Dir.-Adv.)*

BOB MONTGOMERY CHEVROLET/HONDA
5340 Dixie Hwy.
Louisville, KY 40216
Tel.: 502-448-2820
Fax: 502-448-2820, Ext. 212
Approx.Sls.: $27,000,000
Emp.: 95
New & Used Automobiles, Pickups & Vans
S.I.C.: 5511
Robert Montgomery *(Pres.)*
Joe Trent *(Controller)*
Rick Rickert *(Dir.-Personnel)*
Tom Hagan *(Mgr.-Acctng.)*
Steve Montgomery *(Gen. Mgr.)*

Outside Service Firm(s):

Citizens Fidelity Bank & Trust Co.*(Major Banking Relationship)*
Louisville, KY

MONTGOMERY ELEVATOR COMPANY
One Montgomery Court
Moline, IL 61265
Tel.: 309-757-1474 **DE**
Telex: 468436
Fax: 309-764-1469
Year Founded: 1892
Emp.: 3,000
Fiscal Year-end: 12/31/92
Manufacture Elevators, Escalators & Moving Ramps & Walks; Special Trade Contractors; Miscellaneous Repair Services
S.I.C.: 3534; 5084; 1796
B.J. Hank, Jr. *(Chm. Bd. & Chief Exec. Officer)*
Dan S. Blount *(Pres. & Chief Oper. Officer)*
Kathryn H. Collett *(Deputy Chm. & Sr. V.P.)*
Daniel J. Blount *(Sr. V.P.-Fin.)*
James G. Claassen *(Sr. V.P.-Mktg. & Sls.)*
A.M. Hallene, Jr. *(Sr. V.P.-Mfg.)*
Dennis Lauterbach *(Sr. V.P.-Branch Oper.)*
Arthur H. Marsh *(Sr. V.P.-Tech.)*
Michael Bauschka *(V.P. & Controller)*
John N. Hanshaw *(V.P.-Planning)*
Kevin Hogan *(V.P.-Corp. Pur.)*
E.J. Kiely II *(V.P.-Mktg.)*
Thomas Kinney *(V.P.-Information Processing)*
John F. White *(V.P.-Human Resources)*
James T. Widdop *(Treas.)*
Shirley J. Wilkins *(Sec.)*

No. of Mfg. Plants/Facilities: 7
No. of U.S. Offices: 200

Outside Service Firm(s):

Grant Thornton*(Auditors)*
700 One Prudential Plaza, 130 East Randolph St.
Chicago, IL 60601
Tel.: 312-856-0200
Fax: 312-565-4719

Liberty Life Assurance Company*(Group Insurer)*
Boston, MA

Goedert & Huntington*(Legal Firm)*
Oak Park, IL

First Midwest Bank/Western Illinois*(Major Banking Relationship)*
Moline, IL

Divisions:

Moline Accessories Company **(1)**
325 19th St.
Moline, IL 61265
Tel.: 309-762-6888
Fax: 309-762-7475
Manufactures Operator that Opens the Door
S.I.C.: 3534
John Mann Jr. *(Pres.)*

Montgomery Elevator Architectural Products Division **(1)**
Strother Field Industrial Park, P.O. Box 987
Arkansas City, KS 67005
Tel.: 316-442-2510
Manufacturers Passenger Elevators & Cabs
S.I.C.: 3534
Bill Lundell *(Div. Mgr.)*

Montgomery Elevator Controls Division **(1)**
U.S. Hgwy. 11
Commerce, TX 75428
Tel.: 903-886-2984
Manufacturers Controls for Escalators & Elevators
S.I.C.: 3534
Ansis Veiland *(Div. Mgr.)*

Montgomery Elevator Division **(1)**
2101 Couch Dr.
McKinney, TX 75069
Tel.: 214-542-0351
Manufactures Elevators
S.I.C.: 3534
Ansis Veiland *(Div. Mgr.)*

Montgomery Elevator Parts Distribution Center **(1)**
108 17th St.
Moline, IL 61265
Tel.: 309-764-5656
Warehouse
S.I.C.: 4225
Gary Wildermuth *(Div. Mgr.)*

Montgomery Escalator Division **(1)**
Rte. 6, East of Airport
Moline, IL 61265
Tel.: 309-949-2101
Manufacturers Escalators
S.I.C.: 3534
Kent Aufdengarten *(Div. Mgr.)*

Subsidiaries:

Clarion Enterprises, Inc. **(1)**
300 NW Bank Tower
Bettendorf, IA 52722
Tel.: 319-344-0535
Real Estate Development
S.I.C.: 6531

Moline Accessories Corporation **(1)**
430 W. Seventh St.
Kansas City, MO 64105 (100%)
Real Estate Holding Company
S.I.C.: 6519

Montgomery Elevator Export Corporation **(1)**
One Montgomery Court
Moline, IL 61265
Tel.: 309-764-6771
Foreign International Sales
S.I.C.: 5084

Sterling Machinery Co., Inc. **(1)**
104 Port Arthur
Mena, AR 71953
Tel.: 501-394-4248
Machining Center
S.I.C.: 3534

JAMES M. MONTGOMERY CONSULTING ENGINEERS
300 N. Lake St., Ste. 1200
Pasadena, CA 91101
Tel.: 818-796-9141 **CA**
Fax: 818-568-6619
Approx.Sls.: $155,000,000
Emp.: 1,200
Civil Engineering
S.I.C.: 8711
Richard S. Holmgren, Jr. *(Chm. Bd.)*
John E. Somerville *(Vice Chm.)*
Murly Tolaney *(Pres. & Chief Exec. Officer)*
James Lackman *(Sr. V.P. & Sec.)*
Robert B. Uhler *(Dir.-Mktg.)*

Outside Service Firm(s):

Price Waterhouse*(Auditors)*
555 California
San Francisco, CA 94104
Tel.: 415-393-8500

First Interstate Bank*(Major Banking Relationship)*
345 California St., 8th Flr.
San Francisco, CA 94104
Tel.: 415-773-7801

MONTGOMERY WARD & CO., INC.
Montgomery Ward Plaza, 619 W. Chicago Ave.
Chicago, IL 60671
Tel.: 312-467-2000 **IL**
Fax: 312-467-2043
Year Founded: 1872
Assets: $3,887,000,000
Earnings: $135,000,000
Liabilities: $3,248,000,000
Net Worth: $639,000,000
Approx.Sls.: $5,294,000,000
Emp.: 62,400
Fiscal Year-end: 12/28/91
Import
Retail Specialty Stores
S.I.C.: 5311
Employee Matching Gifts Program:
Montgomery Ward Foundation
Bernard F. Brennan *(Chm. Bd. & Chief Exec. Officer)*
Daniel H. Levy *(Vice Chm. & Chief Oper. Officer)*
Harold Kahn *(Pres.)*
Richard Bergel *(Pres.-Specialty Catalogs)*
William J. McCarthy *(Pres.-Stores & Mktg.)*
Donald L. Docken *(Exec. V.P.-Strategic Plng. & Devel.)*
Spencer H. Heine *(Exec. V.P.-Legal & Fin. Services)*
Robert A. Kasenter *(Exec. V.P.-Human Resources)*
Gene McCaffrey *(Exec. V.P.-Mktg.)*
Malvin Pavik *(Exec. V.P.-East Territory)*
Edwin G. Pohlmann *(Exec. V.P.-Stores & Fin.)*
Tom Cato *(Sr. V.P.-Logistics & Prod. Service)*
Bill Marginsm *(Sr. V.P.-West Territory)*
Bob Schoeberl *(Sr. V.P.-Electric Ave.)*
Larry Day *(V.P.-Auto Express)*
Carol Harms *(V.P. & Treas.)*
Charles H. Knittle *(V.P.-Govt. Affairs)*
Ann Raives *(V.P.-Customer Service & Corp. Communications)*
John Workman *(V.P.-Fin.)*
Jerry C. Jordan *(Controller-Store Opers.)*
Bill Motsinger *(Dir.-Mktg.)*
Raymond Stokes *(Mgr.-Pur.)*
Gena Schoen *(Librarian)*

No. of Mfg. Plants/Facilities: 323

Outside Service Firm(s):

Arthur Andersen & Co.*(Auditors)*
33 W. Monroe St.
Chicago, IL 60603-4067
Tel.: 312-580-0033
Fax: 312-507-6748

Montgomery Ward & Co., Inc.—(Continued)

Subsidiary:

The Signature Group **(1)**
200 N. Martingale
Schaumburg, IL 60173-2096
Tel.: 708-605-3000 (100%)
Approx.Sls.: $400,000,000
Emp.: 2,585
Insurance, Auto Club, Senior Citizen, Telemarketing, Direct Mail Services
S.I.C.: 6331; 6311; 8699; 7389; 7331
Spencer Heine *(Pres. & Chief Exec. Officer)*
Alan Portelli *(Sr. V.P.-Fin.)*

MONTGOMERY, ZUKERMAN, DAVIS, INC.
1800 N. Meridian St.
Indianapolis, IN 46202
Tel.: 317-924-6271
Fax: 317-925-3854
Year Founded: 1950
Approx.Billings: $32,000,000
Emp.: 63
Full Service Advertising, Retail & Consumer Marketing, Public Relations, Media Production, Audio & Video Production, Interactive Video
Employee Matching Gifts Progra
Robert L. Montgomery *(Chm. & Chief Exec. Officer)*
Allan B. Zukerman *(Pres. & Chief Oper. Officer)*
Harry L. Davis *(Exec. V.P.)*
Fred Bingle *(V.P., Dir. Mktg. Research)*
Dan Smith *(Comptroller)*

Computer Systems/Hardware:
Adware

MONUMENTAL MILLWORK, INC.
344 Manchester Rd.
Westminster, MD 21157
Mailing Address:
P.O. Box 526
Westminster, MD 21158
Tel.: 410-876-6262 **MD**
Fax: 410-848-6215
Approx.Sls.: $10,000,000
Emp.: 85
Wholesale Millwork
S.I.C.: 5031
N. Stanley Rosenzwog *(Chm. Bd.)*
John W. Tomlinson *(Pres.)*
Harvey Rosenzwog *(Exec. V.P.-Mktg.)*
William Burk *(V.P.-Sls.)*
Edith Rosenzwog *(Sec.)*
Stephen Malls *(Controller)*

Outside Service Firm(s):

Offit & Roth*(Auditors)*
Baltimore, MD

Offit & Batoff*(Legal Firm)*
Baltimore, MD

Sovran Bank*(Major Banking Relationship)*
Baltimore, MD

M. D. MOODY & SONS INC.
4652 Phillips Hwy.
Jacksonville, FL 32207
Tel.: 904-737-4401
Fax: 904-636-0532
Year Founded: 1914
Approx.Sls.: $25,000,000
Emp.: 110
Wholesale Construction Equipment
S.I.C.: 5082
Maxey D. Moody III *(Pres.)*
T.B. Moody *(V.P.)*
J.R. Tompkins *(Controller)*
Principal(s):
Maxey D. Moody III
T.B. Moody

Computer Systems/Hardware:
In-House System

Outside Service Firm(s):

Deloitte & Touche*(Auditors)*
Jacksonville, FL

First Union National Bank*(Major Banking Relationship)*
P.O. Box 2565,
Jacksonville, FL 32203

MOONEY AIRCRAFT CORPORATION
Louis Schreiner Airport, Box 72
Kerrville, TX 78029
Tel.: 210-896-6000
Fax: 210-896-7333
Year Founded: 1984
Approx.Sls.: $25,000,000
Emp.: 400
Export
Mfr. of 4-Place, Single Engine, Retractable Gear Aircraft & Parts
S.I.C.: 3721; 3728; 5088
Alexandre Couvelaire *(Pres. & Treas.)*
Jacques Esculier *(Chief Exec. Officer)*
Kyle M. Joster *(V.P.-Fin.)*
Keith Russey *(Dir.-Mfg.)*
Robert L. McDonnell *(Dir.-Engrng.)*

MOONEY CHEMICALS
2301 Scranton Rd.
Cleveland, OH 44113
Tel.: 216-781-8383
Fax: 216-781-5919
Year Founded: 1946
Emp.: 100
Petroleum Refining
S.I.C.: 2869; 2819; 2816
James P. Mooney *(Chm. Bd. & Chief Exec. Officer)*
Gene Bak *(Pres.)*
Michael Scott *(Gen. Counsel)*
John Holtzhauser *(Controller)*

Computer Systems/Hardware:
IBM 6251

Outside Service Firm(s):

KPMG Peat Marwick*(Auditors)*
1500 National City Center
Cleveland, OH 44114
Tel.: 216-696-9100

National City Bank*(Major Banking Relationship)*
P.O. Box 92301, Corp. Trust Dept.
Cleveland, OH 44101
Tel.: 216-575-2000

MOORE COMPANY
36 Beach St.
Westerly, RI 02891
Tel.: 401-596-2816
Fax: 401-596-6801
Emp.: 1,500
Fabric Finishing, Warp Knit; Manmade Fiber; Narrow Woven Fabrics; Pressure Sensitive Tape; Rubber; Thread; Mechanical Rubber Goods; Battery Separators, Wood
S.I.C.: 6719; 2258; 2241; 3069; 3061; 2499
Thomas F. Moore *(Chm. Bd.)*
George C. Moore *(Chief Oper. Officer)*
Dorothea Moore *(V.P.-Sls.)*
William R. Scott *(Treas.)*
Edward E. Davis *(Sec.)*
Peter F. Moore *(Deputy Sec.)*
Norman Dime *(Dir.-Adv.)*
Jim Dime *(Dir.-Pur.)*

Outside Service Firm(s):

Ernst & Young*(Auditors)*
One Old Stone Square
Providence, RI 02903
Tel.: 401-331-7000

Fleet National Bank*(Major Banking Relationship)*
Corporate Trust Department, 125 Dupont Dr.
Providence, RI 02907
Tel.: 401-278-5400

Subsidiary:

Moeller Marine Products **(1)**
850 Springfield Hwy.
Goodlettsville, TN 37072
Tel.: 615-815-5460
Fax: 601-332-9056
Emp.: 124
Export
Computer Systems/Hardware:
NCR
Oil Level Gauge Dipstick Assemblies, Snap-Tite, Twis-Tite, Turn-Tite, Urethane Products, Tubes, Guide Assemblies, Guide Assemblies (Tube), Oil Filter Caps
S.I.C.: 3466; 3429; 3069; 3499; 2822
Doug Estes *(Gen. Mgr.)*
Warren F. Fisher *(V.P.-Sls.)*
John Sevier *(Production Mgr.)*

E. R. MOORE CO.
1810 W. Grace St.
Chicago, IL 60613
Tel.: 312-549-4696
Fax: 312-549-6918
Approx.Sls.: $15,000,000
Emp.: 300
Mfr. Apparel for Schools, Colleges & Churches, Including Caps & Gowns, Choir Robes, Judicial & Pulpit Robes
S.I.C.: 2389
John P. Hines *(Pres.)*
William J. Donnelly *(V.P.)*
Alan I. Grove *(Pur. Agent)*

Computer Systems/Hardware:
Data General

MOORE, EPSTEIN, MOORE
3102 N. Habana Ave.
Tampa, FL 33607
Tel.: 813-877-8660
Year Founded: 1983
Approx.Billings: $11,000,000
Emp.: 15
Jim Epstein *(Pres.)*
Marianne Moore *(Exec. V.P. & Media Dir.)*
Ted Moore *(Exec. V.P. & New Bus. Contact)*

THE J.W. MOORE GROUP
7025 Albert Pick Rd.
Greensboro, NC 27409
Tel.: 919-665-1789
Year Founded: 1989
Approx.Billings: $10,150,000
Emp.: 10
Full Service Marketing Communications Programs
Jerry W. Moore *(Chm. Bd., Chief Exec. Officer & New Bus. Contact)*
Larry E. Clapp *(Pres. & Dir.-Creative)*
Catherine Schlecht *(Mgr.-Admin.)*

HAROLD MOORE & ASSOCIATES, INC.
1798 Wilson Pkwy.
Fayetteville, TN 37334
Mailing Address:
P.O. Box 756
Fayetteville, TN 37334
Tel.: 615-433-7702 **TN**
Fax: 615-433-3128
Year Founded: 1980
Assets: $2,815,024
Liabilities: $1,005,131
Net Worth: $1,809,893
Approx.Sls.: $16,000,000
Emp.: 40
General Contractor-Single & Multi-Family Housing Units
S.I.C.: 1521; 1522
Harold Moore *(Chm. Bd.)*
John W. Landers *(Pres.)*
Harold Cary *(V.P. & Treas.)*
Elizabeth Moore *(Sec.)*
Principal(s):
Harold Moore

Computer Systems/Hardware:
MAI Basic 4

Outside Service Firm(s):

Harshman, Lewis & Assoc., P.C.*(Auditors)*
Nashville, TN

Marsh & McLennan*(Group Insurer)*
Nashville, TN

Dominion Bank*(Major Banking Relationship)*
Fayetteville, TN

Moore-Hudson Oldsmobile GMC, Inc.
(Name Changed To Jim Hudson, Pontiac, Oldsmobile GMC)

REX MOORE ELECTRICAL CONTRACTORS & ENGINEERS
P.O. Box 915
West Sacramento, CA 95691
Tel.: 916-372-1300
Fax: 916-372-4013
Year Founded: 1922
Sales Range: $20-39 Million
Electrical Contractors & Engineers
S.I.C.: 5063
Rex Moore *(Chm. Bd.)*
Steven R. Moore *(Pres.)*
Rodney R. Weckworth *(Exec. V.P.)*
Barbara Larsen *(Controller)*
Karen Hussko *(Dir.-Personnel)*
Jim Lyons *(Dir.-Pur.)*
Principal(s):
Steven R. Moore
Rodney R. Weckworth

MOORE SPECIAL TOOL CO., INC.
800 Union Ave.
Bridgeport, CT 06607-0088
Mailing Address:
P. O. Box 4088
Bridgeport, CT 06607-0088
Tel.: 203-366-3224
Telex: 6711498
Fax: 203-367-0418
Year Founded: 1924
Approx.Sls.: $25,000,000
Emp.: 250
Fiscal Year-end: 12/31/92
Export
Jig Boring, Jig Grinding & Measuring Machines,Diamond Turning Machines & Accessories, Flexible Machining Systems
S.I.C.: 3541; 3544; 3545; 3549; 5064
Wayne R. Moore *(Chm. Bd., Pres. & Chief Exec. Officer)*
William G. Cogger *(Exec. V.P.)*
Glenn M. Collings *(V.P.-Fin. & Treas.)*
E. Ray McClure *(Dir.-Technical)*
Joseph H. Jakab *(Gen. Sls. Mgr.)*
Kathy Logan *(Adv. Asst.)*

Non-U.S. Holding:

Moore Special Tool AG **(1)**
Hohlstrasse 608 8048
Zurich, Switzerland
Tel.: 01/432 4034
Telex: 822 290
Emp.: 6
Precision Machine Tools and Metrology Equipment, European Headquarters
S.I.C.: 5084
Walter Zindel *(Sls. Application Engr.)*

MOORGATE ADVERTISING AGENCY
(A Div. of The Gillette Co.)
Prudential Tower Bldg.
Boston, MA 02199
Tel.: 617-421-8239
Year Founded: 1970

Approx.Billings: $60,000,000
Emp.: 18
Michael Nadelberg *(Pres.)*

MOORMAN MFG. COMPANY
1000 N. 30th St.
Quincy, IL 62305-3115
Mailing Address:
P.O. Box C1
Quincy, IL 62305-3115
Tel.: 217-222-7100
Fax: 217-222-4069
Year Founded: 1885
Approx.Sls.: $315,000,000
Emp.: 4,000
Fiscal Year-end: 3/31/91
Moorman's Feeds for Livestock & Poultry; Livestock Equipment; About 35 Outlying Locations
S.I.C.: 2048; 2834; 3523; 2075
Tom Shade *(Pres. & Chief Exec. Officer)*
Tom McKenna *(Chief Oper. Officer)*
Richard Jackson *(Treas. & Chief Fin. Officer)*
Terry Lunt *(Dir.-Human Resources)*
Larry Williams *(Dir.-Sls.)*
Lewin Davis *(Mgr.-Personnel & Corp. Rels.)*
John R. Nelson *(Mgr.-Data Processing)*
John R. Read *(Mgr.-Production Matls. Pur.)*
P.G. Wensing *(Mgr.-Credit)*
William Wolters *(Mgr.-Mktg. Opers.)*

Computer Systems/Hardware:
IBM 4341

Outside Service Firm(s):

Deloitte & Touche*(Auditors)*
Peoria, IL

Fireman's Fund Insurance Co.*(Commercial Insurance Carrier)*
San Francisco, CA

Travelers Insurance Co.*(Group Insurer)*
1 Tower Square
Hartford, CT 06183-2492
Tel.: 203-277-4542
Fax: 203-277-5038

Continental Bank N. A.*(Major Banking Relationship)*
231 S. LaSalle St.
Chicago, IL 60697
Tel.: 312-828-2345
Tel.: 800-426-5754
Telex: 312-828-1783

Continental Bank N. A.*(Pension Manager)*
231 S. LaSalle St.
Chicago, IL 60697
Tel.: 312-828-2345
Tel.: 800-426-5754
Telex: 312-828-1783

Divisions:

Moorman Mfg. Co. **(1)**
P.O. Box 309, 159 North Rd.
Alpha, IL 61413-0309
Tel.: 309-529-4121
S.I.C.: 2048
Ray Markword *(Mgr.)*

Moorman Mfg. Co. **(1)**
P.O. Box 498
Bluffton, IN 46714-0498
Tel.: 219-824-0079
S.I.C.: 2048
John Whicker *(Mgr.)*

Moorman Mfg. Co. **(1)**
P.O. Box 1029
Columbus, NE 68602-1028
Tel.: 402-564-3155
S.I.C.: 2048
Brian Sneeden *(Mgr.)*

Moorman Mfg. Co. **(1)**
P.O. Box 743, Moorman Rd.
Comanche, TX 76442-0743
Tel.: 915-356-2512
S.I.C.: 2048
Truman Hazelrigg *(Mgr.)*

Moorman Mfg. Co. **(1)**
P.O. Box 1137
Cordele, GA 31015
Tel.: 912-273-7400
S.I.C.: 2048
George Rischar *(Mgr.-Opers.)*

Moorman Mfg. Co. **(1)**
P.O. Box 1918
Hereford, TX 79045-1918
Tel.: 806-364-5211
S.I.C.: 2048
Andy Radford *(Mgr.)*

Moorman Mfg. Co. **(1)**
P.O. Box 210
Le Mars, IA 51031-0210
Tel.: 712-546-7029
S.I.C.: 2048
Chuck Bedford *(Mgr.)*

Subsidiaries:

Bell Grain & Milling, Inc. **(1)**
P.O. Box 758
Perris, CA 92370
Tel.: 909-657-5121
S.I.C.: 2048
Howard Waterhouse *(Gen. Mgr.)*

Moorman Mfg. Co. of California, Inc. **(1)**
250 E. Roth Rd.
Lathrop, CA 95330-9724
Tel.: 209-983-0123
S.I.C.: 2048
Don Smith *(Gen. Mgr.)*

Quincy Soybean Co. **(1)**
1900 Gardner Expressway
Quincy, IL 62301
Tel.: 217-224-1800
S.I.C.: 2048
Mike Foster *(Pres.)*

MORAN INDUSTRIES, INC.
(d/b/a Mr. Transmission & Multistate Transmission)
4444 W. 147th St.
Midlothian, IL 60445
Tel.: 708-389-5922
Telex: 800-377-9247
Fax: 708-389-9882
Year Founded: 1958
Approx.Sls.: $65,000,000
Emp.: 800
Fiscal Year-end: 6/30/92
Import Export
Franchisors of Multistate Transmissions,Transmission Repair & Service Centers
S.I.C.: 6794
Dennis Moran *(Chm. Bd. & Chief Exec. Officer)*
Richard Morton *(Exec. V.P.)*
Dan Lyons *(Controller, Mgr.-Personnel)*
Mel Patterson *(Dir.-Mktg.)*
Jose Rodriguez *(Dir.-Technology)*
Jack Yost *(Dir.-Opers.)*
Pam Burgher *(Mgr.-Pub. Rels.)*

Subsidiary:

U.S. Transparts **(1)**
4444 W. 147th St.
Midlothian, IL 60445
Tel.: 708-633-0200
Transmission Repair
S.I.C.: 7537
Dennis Moran *(Pres. & Chief Exec. Officer)*
Mel Patterson *(Dir.-Mktg., Pur. & Personnel)*

ART MORAN PONTIAC-GMC INC.
29300 Telegraph Rd.
Southfield, MI 48034
Tel.: 313-353-9000 **MI**
Fax: 313-353-7348
Year Founded: 1972
Approx.Sls.: $71,551,385
Emp.: 137
Fiscal Year-end: 7/31/90
Import Export
Automobile Dealership
S.I.C.: 5511
Arthur Moran *(Pres.)*
Bob Moran *(V.P.)*
Carol Charron *(Sec. & Treas.)*
Bill Curry *(Mgr.-Sls.)*

Outside Service Firm(s):

Manufacturers National Bank N.A.*(Major Banking Relationship)*
38th Fl., 100 Renaissance Center
Detroit, MI 48243
Tel.: 313-222-4227

Division:

Art Moran Auto Plaza, Inc. **(1)**
3720 N. Lake Blvd.
Lake Park, FL 33404
Tel.: 407-622-8220
Automobile Dealership
S.I.C.: 5511
William Reno *(Gen. Mgr.)*

MORAN TOWING & TRANSPORTATION CO. INC
Two Greenwich Plaza
Greenwich, CT 06830
Tel.: 203-625-7800 **NY**
Twx: 710-474-0051
Fax: 203-625-7857
Year Founded: 1926
Approx.Sls.: $45,000,000
Emp.: 400
Fiscal Year-end: 12/31/89
Tug & Barge Transportation; Ocean Towing
S.I.C.: 4492; 4499
Thomas E. Moran *(Chm. Bd.)*
Malcolm W. MacLeod *(Pres. & Chief Exec. Officer)*
Lee R. Christensen *(Chief Fin. Officer & V.P.)*
William A. Watt *(V.P.-Sls.)*
Joseph A. DeAngelo *(Treas.)*
Alan L. Marchisotto *(Sec. & Gen. Counsel)*
Jean Cuff *(Asst. Sec.)*
Fred Coseglia *(Dir.-Pur.)*
Principal(s):
Thomas E. Moran
Malcolm W. MacLeod
Lee R. Christensen
William A. Watt
Russell G. McVay
Edmond J. Moran, Jr.

Computer Systems/Hardware:
IBM System 36

Outside Service Firm(s):

Price Waterhouse*(Auditors)*
300 Atlantic St.
Stamford, CT 06904

Connecticut General Life Insurance Co.*(Group Insurer)*
P.O. Box 2975,
Hartford, CT 06104
Tel.: 203-726-6000

Estabrook Capital*(Investment Banker)*
New York, NY

Lazard Freres & Co.*(Investment Banker)*
One Rockefeller Plaza
New York, NY 10020
Tel.: 212-632-6287

Oppenheimer & Co., Inc.*(Investment Banker)*
New York, NY

White & Case*(Legal Firm)*
1155 Avenue of The Americas
New York, NY 10036

Chase Manhattan Bank, N.A.*(Major Banking Relationship)*
One Chase Manhattan Plaza
New York, NY 10081
Tel.: 212-552-2222
Tel.: 800-526-0801
Fax: 212-552-7175

Chemical Banking Corp.*(Major Banking Relationship)*
277 Park Ave.
New York, NY 10041
Tel.: 212-310-6407
Fax: 212-310-4526

Citibank N.A.*(Major Banking Relationship)*
Corporate Trust Services, 399 Park Ave.
New York, NY 10043
Tel.: 212-559-1605

Equitable Life*(Pension Manager)*
1221 Ave. of the Americas
New York, NY 10022
Tel.: 212-382-8038
Fax: 212-382-8089

Subsidiaries:

Moran Towing of Florida **(1)**
9485 Regency Blvd., Ste. 460
Jacksonville, FL 32225
Tel.: 904-721-7000

Moran Towing of Maine **(1)**
72 Commercial St., Ste. 04111
Portland, ME 04112
Tel.: 207-772-8319

Moran Towing of Maryland **(1)**
World Trade Center, 401 E. Pratt St., Ste. 800
Baltimore, MD 21202
Tel.: 410-962-6500

Moran Towing of Pennsylvania, Inc. **(1)**
1101 Market St., Ste. 2601
Philadelphia, PA 19107
Tel.: 215-925-3500

Moran Towing of Texas **(1)**
2300 Hwy. 365, Ste. 570
Nederland, TX 77627
Tel.: 409-727-7020

Moran Towing of Virginia **(1)**
Wheat Building, 109 Main St.
Norfolk, VA 23514
Tel.: 804-625-6001

MORGAN CONSTRUCTION COMPANY
15 Belmont St.
Worcester, MA 01605
Tel.: 508-755-6111
Fax: 508-755-6140
Year Founded: 1888
Assets: $58,000,000
Liabilities: $36,000,000
Net Worth: $22,000,000
Approx.Sls.: $110,000,000
Emp.: 550
Fiscal Year-end: 12/31/90
Manufacture Rolling Mill Machinery ; Furnace Control Equipment; Morgoil Bearings
S.I.C.: 3547; 3548; 3562
Paul S. Morgan *(Chm. Bd.)*
Phillip R. Morgan *(Pres. & Chief Exec. Officer)*
John W. Newton *(Chief Fin. Officer)*
John W. Bergan *(V.P. & Treas.)*
L. Scott Salter *(V.P.)*
William C. St. Martin *(Controller)*
Steven P. Scott *(Mgr.-Pur.)*
Russ Vanderbaan *(Mgr.-Human Resources)*
Gail Wilcox *(Clerk-Admin.)*

No. of Mfg. Plants/Facilities: 1
No. of Foreign Offices: 2

Computer Systems/Hardware:
Digital Vax 785; Vax 6440

Outside Service Firm(s):

Coopers & Lybrand*(Auditors)*
1 Post Office Square
Boston, MA 02110
Tel.: 617-574-5000
Fax: 617-345-0398

Morgan Construction Company—(Continued)

State Mutual Life Assurance Co. of America*(Group Insurer)*
440 Lincoln St.
Worcester, MA 01605
Tel.: 508-852-1000

State Street Bank & Trust Co.*(Investment Banker)*
P.O. Box 366,
Boston, MA 02101
Tel.: 617-426-5523

Citibank N.A.*(Major Banking Relationship)*
Corporate Trust Services, 399 Park Ave.
New York, NY 10043
Tel.: 212-559-1605

Mechanics Bank*(Major Banking Relationship)*
Worcester, MA

Connecticut General Life Insurance Co.*(Pension Manager)*
P.O. Box 2975,
Hartford, CT 06104
Tel.: 203-726-6000

Equitable Life*(Pension Manager)*
1221 Ave. of the Americas
New York, NY 10022
Tel.: 212-382-8038
Fax: 212-382-8089

Subsidiary:

Morgan Technical Services, Inc **(1)**
1 Station Square Ste. 230
Pittsburgh, PA 15219
Tel.: 617-755-6111 (100%)

MORGAN FOODS, INC.
90 W. Morgan St.
Austin, IN 47102
Tel.: 812-794-1170 **IN**
Fax: 812-794-1211
Year Founded: 1907
Approx.Sls.: $61,000,000
Emp.: 500
Fiscal Year-end: 6/30/92
Import Export
Vegetable & Soup Canning
S.I.C.: 2032; 2033
John S. Morgan *(Chm., Pres. & Chief Exec. Officer)*
Culver Field *(Sr. V.P.-Corp. Plng. & Devel.)*
James Barnhill *(V.P.-Engrng./Maint.)*
Phillip Bundy *(V.P.-Personnel & Labor Rels.)*
Donald M. Craig *(V.P.-Sls.)*
Michael L. Craig *(V.P.-Quality Assurance/Proc. Control)*
James Herald *(V.P.-Fin., Sec & Treas.)*
Lawrence Higdon *(V.P.-Pur.)*
Bert Turner *(V.P.-Mfg.)*
Roger Heaverin *(Dir.-Mngmt. Information Systems)*
Ronald Weir *(Dir.-Research & Devel.)*
Principal(s):
John S. Morgan

No. of Mfg. Plants/Facilities: 1
No. of U.S. Offices: 1

Computer Systems/Hardware:
Sperry Univac System 80

Outside Service Firm(s):

Ernst & Young*(Auditors)*
One Indiana Square, Ste. 3400
Indianapolis, IN 46204
Tel.: 317-236-1100

Aetna Life & Casualty*(Group Insurer)*
151 Farmington Avenue
Hartford, CT 06156
Tel.: 203-273-2128
Fax: 203-729-4295

Marsh & McLennan*(Group Insurer)*
135 N. Pennsylvania St., Ste. 1600
Indianapolis, IN 46204
Tel.: 317-261-9300
Fax: 317-261-9333

Ice, Miller, Donadio & Ryan*(Legal Firm)*
One American Square, Box 82001
Indianapolis, IN 46282
Tel.: 317-236-2219

Austin State*(Major Banking Relationship)*
Austin, IN

Citizens Fidelity Bank & Trust Co.*(Pension Manager)*
Louisville, KY

MORGAN INDUSTRIES INC.
One Presidential Blvd.
Bala-Cynwyd, PA 19004
Tel.: 215-668-2900
Fax: 215-664-4570
Sales Range: $80-99 Million
Emp.: 650
Owners & Franchisors of Auto Parts Patents; Equipment Leasing
S.I.C.: 5013; 6794; 7359
Robert Morgan *(Chm. Bd., Pres. & Chief Exec. Officer)*
William Shnycer *(Chief Oper. Officer & Exec. V.P.)*
Suzanne Morgan *(V.P. & Sec.)*

Outside Service Firm(s):

Deloitte & Touche*(Auditors)*
1700 Market St.
Philadelphia, PA 19103
Tel.: 215-246-2322
Fax: 215-569-2441

Blank, Rome, Comisky & McCauley*(Legal Firm)*
Four Penn Center Plaza
Philadelphia, PA 19103
Tel.: 215-209-3700

First Chicago Shareholder Services Trust Co.*(Major Banking Relationship)*
153 West 51st St.
New York, NY 10019
Tel.: 212-791-6422
Fax: 212-385-9798

MORGAN MANUFACTURING COMPANY, INC.
1900 S. Marshall St.
Paris, IL 61944
Mailing Address:
P.O. Boxes 877 & 878
Paris, IL 61944
Tel.: 217-465-8577
Fax: 217-463-2844
Year Founded: 1978
Approx.Sls.: $10,000,000
Emp.: 80
Fiscal Year-end: 12/31/91
Manufacture Pet Food, Livestock Feeds, Food & Industry. Grade Spray Chill & Flake Emulsifiers & Fats
S.I.C.: 2047; 2099
Robert Morgan *(Pres.)*
Norma Pruiett *(Mgr.-Admin.)*
Principal(s):
Robert Morgan

No. of Mfg. Plants/Facilities: 4
No. of U.S. Offices: 1

Outside Service Firm(s):

Larsson, Woodyard & Henson*(Auditors)*
Paris, IL

Diliavou, Overaker, Asher*(Legal Firm)*
Paris, IL

Edgar County Bank*(Major Banking Relationship)*
Paris, IL

Subsidiary:

Morgan Food Products **(1)**
1808 S. Main
Paris, IL 61944
Tel.: 217-465-8577
S.I.C.: 2047; 2099

Robert Morgan *(Chief Oper. Officer)*

MORGAN REALTY ASSOCIATES
P.O. Box 655
Englishtown, NJ 07726
Tel.: 908-780-0470 **NJ**
Fax: 908-780-0150
Sales Range: $20-39 Million
Emp.: 200
Real Estate Investment Firm
S.I.C.: 6531
Ronald Pearl *(Controller)*
Principal(s):
George W. Nirenberg
Alan Vituli
Peter J. Weidhorn

Computer Systems/Hardware:
Prime

Outside Service Firm(s):

The Trust Co. of New Jersey*(Major Banking Relationship)*
35 Journal Square
Jersey City, NJ 07306
Tel.: 201-420-2622

MORITZ CADILLAC-SAAB INC.
2001 N. Collins
Arlington, TX 76011
Tel.: 817-461-2222 **TX**
Fax: 817-275-3035
Year Founded: 1973
Approx.Sls.: $66,000,000
Emp.: 150
Retail New & Used Automobiles
S.I.C.: 5511
John D. Moritz *(Pres.)*
Kelly Bailey *(Sec.)*
Chuck Mamach *(Controller)*

MORLEY GROUP
2901 28th St.
Santa Monica, CA 90409
Tel.: 310-399-1600
Fax: 310-314-7347
Year Founded: 1947
Approx.Sls.: $135,000,000
Emp.: 600
Concrete Work; New Construction of Condominium Construction; Commercial & Office Building Construction
S.I.C.: 1771; 1522; 1542
Morley Benjamin *(Chm. Bd.)*
Mark Benjamin *(Pres. & Chief Exec. Officer)*
C. Terry Dooley *(Sr. V.P.)*
Tod Paris *(V.P.-Fin.)*

Subsidiary:

Morley Construction Co., Inc. **(1)**
2901 28th St.
Santa Monica, CA 90405
Tel.: 310-399-1600
Bert Lewitt *(Pres.)*

MORMAC MARINE TRANSPORT, INC.
3 Landmark Sq.
Stamford, CT 06901
Tel.: 203-977-8900 **DE**
Fax: 203-977-8989
Year Founded: 1987
Approx.Sls.: $26,000,000
Emp.: 120
Deep Sea Foreign Transportation Of Freight
S.I.C.: 4412
Wycliff F. Bennett *(Chief Fin. Officer)*
W. Robert Germain *(V.P.)*

Outside Service Firm(s):

KPMG Peat Marwick*(Auditors)*
Stamford Square, 3001 Summer St.
Stamford, CT 06905
Tel.: 203-356-9800

Chase Manhattan Bank, N.A.*(Major Banking Relationship)*
One Chase Manhattan Plaza
New York, NY 10081
Tel.: 212-552-2222
Tel.: 800-526-0801
Fax: 212-552-7175

MORNING GLORY FARMS REGION
(A Co. of Associated Milk Producers, Inc.)
116 N. Main St.
Shawano, WI 54166
Mailing Address:
P.O. Box 397,
Shawano, WI 54166
Tel.: 715-526-2131 **WI**
Fax: 715-526-6440
Year Founded: 1931
Approx.Sls.: $775,000,000
Emp.: 700
Fiscal Year-end: 12/31/90
Mfr. Dairy Prods.
S.I.C.: 2022; 2023; 2024; 2026; 5143
Philip L. Peterson *(Chm. Bd.)*
J.A. Kasten *(Reg. Mgr.)*
Wayne Bushweiler *(Controller)*
Ken McKenzie *(Communications Dir.)*
Jerry Kufahl *(Pur. Dir.)*
Tom Hudock *(Consumer Products Div. Mgr.)*
Mark Eggert *(Mktg. & Opers. Mgr.)*

Computer Systems/Hardware:
Hewlett-Packard 3000

Outside Service Firm(s):

Hill Christiansen*(Auditors)*
Marshfield, WI

Blue Cross & Blue Shield United of Wisconsin*(Group Insurer)*
Milwaukee, WI

Werner, Beyer & Lindgren*(Legal Firm)*
New London, WI

Citizens State Bank*(Major Banking Relationship)*
Shawano, WI

Valley National Bank*(Major Banking Relationship)*
Shawano, WI

M & I Marshall & Isley Bank*(Pension Manager)*
Milwaukee, WI

MOROCH & ASSOC., INC.
3625 N. Hall, Ste. 1200
Dallas, TX 75219
Tel.: 214-520-9700
Fax: 214-520-6464
Year Founded: 1981
Approx.Billings: $33,380,000
Emp.: 86
Retail & Consumer Accounts
Thomas F. Moroch *(Chm. Bd.)*
Bill Farmer *(Vice Chm. & Exec. Dir.-Creative)*
Pat Kempf *(Pres.)*
Mark Stepanek *(Chief Fin. Officer)*

Computer Systems/Hardware:
MacIntosh; Ad Aid Accounting System, Media Management Plus

Branches:

Moroch & Associates, Inc. **(1)**
4295 San Felipe, #200
Houston, TX 77027
Tel.: 713-623-2788
Fax: 713-580-5643
Don Rauch *(V.P., Gen. Mgr.)*

Moroch & Associates, Inc. **(1)**
85 NE Loop, #300
San Antonio, TX 78216
Tel.: 210-525-8923
Fax: 713-377-0939

David Perry *(Gen. Mgr., Acct. Supvr.)*

Moroch, Inc. **(1)**
7136 S. Yale, Ste. 300
Tulsa, OK 74136
Tel.: 918-663-1050
Tel.: 918-488-1905
Doris Coon *(Acct. Exec.)*

Moroch, Inc. **(1)**
6801 N. Broadway, Ste. 200
Oklahoma City, OK 73116
Tel.: 405-848-6800
Fax: 405-842-3607
Robert Boswell *(V.P., Gen. Mgr.)*

WILLIAM MORRIS AGENCY, INC.
151 El Camino
Beverly Hills, CA 90212
Tel.: 310-274-7451
Fax: 310-859-4462
Year Founded: 1898
Emp.: 500
Talent Agency
S.I.C.: 7389
Louis P. Weiss *(Chm. Bd. Emeritus)*
Norman Brokaw *(Chm. Bd. & Chief Exec. Officer)*
Jerry F. Katzman *(Pres.)*
Irving J. Weintraub *(Chief Fin. Officer & Sr. V.P.)*
Larry Averbach *(Exec. V.P.)*
Roger Davis *(Exec. V.P.)*
Anthony Fantozzi *(Exec. V.P.)*
Leonard Hirshan *(Exec. V.P.)*
Owen Laster *(Exec. V.P.)*
Walter Zifkin *(Exec. V.P., Chief Oper. Officer & Sec.)*

No. of U.S. Offices: 3

Computer Systems/Hardware:
IBM Systems 34 & 38

Outside Service Firm(s):

Wallin Simon & Black*(Auditors)*
New York, NY

Travelers Insurance Co.*(Commercial Insurance Carrier)*
One Tower Square
Hartford, CT 06183-6130
Tel.: 203-277-4542
Fax: 203-277-5038

Prudential Insurance Co. of America*(Group Insurer)*
751 Broad St.
Newark, NJ 07102-3777
Tel.: 201-802-6000

Bank of America NT&SA*(Major Banking Relationship)*
555 So. Flower St., 5th Fl.
Los Angeles, CA 90071
Tel.: 213-228-3526
Fax: 213-228-4062

Irving Trust Co.*(Major Banking Relationship)*
New York, NY

T.J. MORRIS COMPANY, INC.
Highway 301 S.
Statesboro, GA 30458
Tel.: 912-681-4580
Fax: 912-681-1817
Emp.: 220
Wholesale Groceries
S.I.C.: 5141
Thad J. Morris *(Chm. Bd.)*
W.I. Griffis *(Pres. & Chief Exec. Officer)*
Charles R. Fennell *(V.P.)*
Robert F. Morris, Jr. *(V.P.)*
Edwin E. Akins *(Treas., Sec. & Dir.-Personnel)*

Outside Service Firm(s):

Dabb Deal Hickman & Hill*(Auditors)*
Statesboro, GA

Franklin & Taulbee*(Legal Firm)*
Statesboro, GA

Wachovia Bank & Trust & Co.*(Major Banking Relationship)*
Statesboro, GA

Morris Corporation
(See listing under T.J. Morris Company, Inc.)

MORRIS COUPLING CO.
2240 W. 15th St.
Erie, PA 16505
Tel.: 814-459-1741
Tel.: 800-426-1579
Fax: 814-453-5155
Year Founded: 1941
Approx.Sls.: $10,000,000
Emp.: 90
Fiscal Year-end: 12/31/90

Export
Mfr. of Couplings, Repair Clamps & Tube Bends,Pipe Coils & Other Welded Pipe & Tube Fabrications
S.I.C.: 3317; 3494; 3429
Louis I. Pollock *(Chm. Bd. & Pres.)*
William T. Godfrey *(V.P.-Mfg. & Mktg.)*
Jon Whiteman *(V.P. & Chief Fin. Officer)*
B.R. Pollock *(Sec. & Treas.)*
Robert W. Myers *(Mgr.-Sls. & Mktg.)*
George Shabla *(Mfg. Supt.)*
Kathie McLaughlin *(Pur. Agent)*

No. of Mfg. Plants/Facilities: 2
No. of U.S. Offices: 2

Computer Systems/Hardware:
IBM AS/400

Subsidiary:

Tennessee Tubebending Inc. **(1)**
5320 S. National Dr.
Knoxville, TN 37914
Tel.: 615-546-6511
Tel.: 800-426-1579
Export
Richard Perrotta *(Plant Mgr.)*

MORRIS NEWSPAPER CORPORATION
27 Abercorn St.
Savannah, GA 31401
Tel.: 912-233-1281
Fax: 912-232-4639
Emp.: 1,000
Newspaper Publishers; Commercial Printing; Broadcasting
S.I.C.: 2711; 2759; 4832; 4833
Charles H. Morris *(Pres.)*
H. Edward Brooks, Jr. *(Chief Fin. Officer & V.P.)*
Alden M. Maier *(V.P. & Sec.)*
Miriam Potter *(V.P.)*

Outside Service Firm(s):

Ernst & Young*(Auditors)*
600 Peachtree St. N.E.
Atlanta, GA 30308
Tel.: 404-874-8300

Adams, Gardner & Ellis*(Legal Firm)*
Savannah, GA

NationsBank*(Major Banking Relationship)*
35 Broad St.
Atlanta, GA 30303
Tel.: 404-581-2121
Tel.: 800-848-8198

Subsidiary:

Sun-Litho **(1)**
7950 Haskell Ave.
Van Nuys, CA 91406
Tel.: 818-787-4100
Fax: 818-787-0164
Printing
S.I.C.: 2711; 2759
Robert Valenzuela *(Pres.)*

THE ROBERT E. MORRIS COMPANY
17 Talcott Notch Rd.
Farmington, CT 06032
Tel.: 203-678-0200 **CT**
Twx: 710-423-2034
Fax: 203-678-9365
Approx.Sls.: $75,000,000
Emp.: 200
Wholesale Distributor Metalworking Machinery & Tools
S.I.C.: 5084
Mike Wicken *(Chm. Bd.)*
Frank M. Clark *(Vice. Chm.)*
Michael A. Whitney *(Pres.)*
John Bowen *(V.P.-Fin. & Controller)*
Dorothy M. Morris *(Sec.)*
Glenn Eigabruadt *(Mgr.-Data Processing)*
Richard Trudell *(Mgr.-Sls.-Northern New England)*
Dave Young *(Mgr.-Sls.-Small Accts.)*

Outside Service Firm(s):

Arthur Andersen & Co.*(Auditors)*
One Financial Plaza
Hartford, CT 06103
Tel.: 203-280-0649
Fax: 203-280-0898

Reide & Riege*(Legal Firm)*
Hartford, CT

Connecticut Bank & Trust*(Major Banking Relationship)*
One Constitution Plaza,
Hartford, CT 06115

The Morrison Agency

THE MORRISON AGENCY
950 E. Paces Ferry Rd., Ste. 1575
Atlanta, GA 30326
Tel.: 404-233-3405
Year Founded: 1986
Approx.Billings: $12,000,000
Emp.: 25
Business-to-Business, Hospitlaity, Heathcare, Real Estate & Technology
Robert B. Morrison *(Pres. & New Bus. Contact)*
Kathryn D. Morrison *(V.P., Sec., Treas. & Pub. Rels. Dir.)*
Bonnie Worthy *(Pub. Rels. Acct. Supvr.)*

MORRISON, INC.
1834 Summer St.
Hammond, IN 46320
Tel.: 219-932-5036 **IN**
Year Founded: 1966
Approx.Sls.: $46,000,000
Emp.: 340
Heating, Ventilation & Air Conditioning Contractor
S.I.C.: 1711
J.M. Morrison *(Chm. Bd. & Pres.)*
H.B. Clark *(V.P.)*
William Short *(V.P.-Fin.)*
Joseph C. Shimala *(Sec.)*

Outside Service Firm(s):

INB National Bank*(Major Banking Relationship)*
One Indiana Sq.
Indianapolis, IN 46266
Tel.: 317-266-6000

MORRISON TEXTILE MACHINERY CO.
Hwy. #9
Fort Lawn, SC 29714
Mailing Address:
P.O. Drawer 1
Fort Lawn, SC 29714
Tel.: 803-872-4401
Fax: 803-872-4443
Sales Range: $10-19 Million
Emp.: 200
Manufacturer Textile Machinery
S.I.C.: 3552
John J. O'Neill *(Pres.)*
H.S. McManus *(V.P.-Mfg.)*
J.E. Talbert *(V.P.-Engrng.)*
E.R. Khoury *(Treas. & Controller)*
A.W. Caudill *(Dir.-Pur.)*
Lori Rollins *(Mgr.-Communications)*

Outside Service Firm(s):

KPMG Peat Marwick*(Auditors)*
Two First Union Center
Charlotte, NC
Tel.: 704-335-5300

General Administrators*(Group Insurer)*
Greenville, SC

Citizens & Southern National Bank*(Major Banking Relationship)*
Rock Hill, SC

MORSE DIESEL INTERNATIONAL
1515 Broadway
New York, NY 10036
Tel.: 212-730-4000 **NY**
Fax: 212-704-4143
Approx.Sls.: $600,000,000
Emp.: 500
Fiscal Year-end: 12/31/90
General Building Contractors; Construction Management
S.I.C.: 8741; 1542
Donald H. Piser *(Chm. Bd. & Chief Exec. Officer)*
John Cavanagh *(Exec. Dir.)*
Edward Collins *(Exec. V.P.)*
Mitchel Becker *(Sr. V.P. & Gen. Counsel)*
Norman G. Fornella *(Sr. V.P. & Chief Fin. Officer)*
Irwin Wecker *(Sr. V.P.-Human Resources)*
Ronni Meltzer *(V.P. & Controller)*

Outside Service Firm(s):

KPMG Peat Marwick*(Auditors)*
345 Park Ave.
New York, NY 10154
Tel.: 212-758-9700
Fax: 212-872-3308

AIG (American International Group)*(Commercial Insurance Carrier)*
70 Pine St.
New York, NY 10270
Tel.: 212-770-7000

Connecticut General Life Insurance Co.*(Group Insurer)*
P.O. Box 2975,
Hartford, CT 06104
Tel.: 203-726-6000

Savrin & Berson*(Legal Firm)*
New York, NY

Chase Manhattan Bank, N.A.*(Major Banking Relationship)*
One Chase Manhattan Plaza
New York, NY 10081
Tel.: 212-552-2222
Tel.: 800-526-0801
Fax: 212-552-7175

Harris Trust & Savings Bank*(Major Banking Relationship)*
P.O. Box 755, 111 W. Monroe
Chicago, IL 60603
Tel.: 312-461-2121

Morse Diesel International—(Continued)

Morgan Guaranty Trust Company of New York*(Major Banking Relationship)*
23 Wall St.
New York, NY 10015
Tel.: 212-483-2323

MORSE OPERATIONS INC.
1240 N. Federal Hwy.
Ft. Lauderdale, FL 33304
Tel.: 305-568-0770 **FL**
Fax: 305-568-5190
Assets: $448,947,729
Liabilities: $398,100,291
Net Worth: $50,847,438
Approx.Sls.: $1,459,897,273
Emp.: 541
Fiscal Year-end: 12/31/91
Retail New & Used Automobiles; Management Offices
S.I.C.: 5511; 8741
Edward J. Morse, Sr. *(Chm. Bd. & Pres.)*
Donald A. MacInnes *(Chief Fin. Officer & V.P.)*
Edward J. Morse, Jr. *(V.P.)*
Principal(s):
Edward J. Morse, Sr.
Edward J. Morse, Jr.

No. of U.S. Offices: 9

Computer Systems/Hardware:
Reynolds & Reynolds, UCS & ADP

Outside Service Firm(s):

Coopers & Lybrand*(Auditors)*
5959 Blue Lagoon Dr.
Miami, FL 33126
Tel.: 305-263-8200

PDP Group*(Commercial Insurance Carrier)*
Hunt Valley, MD 21031

Stracher & Harmon, P.A.*(Legal Firm)*
Plantation, FL

NCNB Bank Maryland*(Major Banking Relationship)*
Hunt Valley, MD

Subsidiaries:

Ed Morse Chevrolet Inc. **(1)**
1640 N.W. 40th Ave.
Fort Lauderdale, FL 33313
Tel.: 305-733-6000
New & Used Automobile Dealership
S.I.C.: 5511
Edward J. Morse, Jr. *(Pres.)*
Daniel Bischof *(Gen. Mgr.)*

Ed Morse Dodge, Inc. **(1)**
5401 W. Sample Rd.
Coconut Creek, FL 33083
Tel.: 305-974-1888
S.I.C.: 5511
Edward J. Morse, Sr. *(Pres.)*
Richard Danahy *(V.P.)*

MORSE SHOE, INC.
555 Turnpike St.
Canton, MA 02021
Tel.: 617-828-9300 **DE**
Telex: 92 4469
Fax: 617-784-7205
Approx.Sls.: $529,000,000
Emp.: 7,400
Fiscal Year-end: 12/28/91
Import
Retail, Manufacture & Distribute Shoes
S.I.C.: 5661; 3143; 3144; 5139
David Pulver *(Chm. Bd.)*
Malcolm Sherman *(Pres. & Chief Exec. Officer)*
Joseph Gajda *(Sr. V.P. & Gen. Mgr.)*
David Murphy *(Sr. V.P. & Gen. Mgr.-Fayva)*
Earl Spokane *(Sr. V.P. & Chief Fin. Officer)*
Lee J. Belitsky *(V.P., Treas. & Comptroller)*
Vincent Brown *(V.P.-Real Estate)*
Kenneth C. Cummins *(V.P., Sec. & Gen. Counsel)*
John M. Fiore *(V.P.-Mngmt. Information Systems)*
Steven F. Huggins *(V.P.-Business Plng.)*
Mark Rich *(V.P.-Personnel & Admin.)*
Laura Katz *(Dir.-Morse Shoe International)*
Jim Johnston *(Mgr.-Pur.)*

Outside Service Firm(s):

KPMG Peat Marwick*(Auditors)*
One Boston Place
Boston, MA 02108
Tel.: 617-723-7700

Bank of Boston*(Major Banking Relationship)*
55 Broadway, 1 Exchange Plaza
New York, NY 10006
Tel.: 800-442-2001

Divisions:

Fayva **(1)**
555 Turnpike St.
Canton, MA 02021
Tel.: 617-828-9300
Retail Shoes
S.I.C.: 5661
David J. Murphy, III *(Sr. V.P.)*
Steven F. Albert *(V.P.-Opers.)*
Vince Brown *(V.P.-Real Estate)*
Steve Huggins *(V.P.-Bus. Plng.)*
Glenn Stewart *(V.P.-Mktg.)*
Gary Davis *(Dir.-Dist. & Mds. Plng.)*
Rene Menard *(Assoc. Mgr.-Gen. Mds.)*

Morse Shoe Leased Div. **(1)**
555 Turnpike St.
Canton, MA 02021
Tel.: 617-828-9300
Retail Shoes in Leased Departments
S.I.C.: 5661
Joe Gadja *(Sr. V.P.-Leasing)*
James J. Hughes *(V.P.-Sls. & Mktg.)*
Merle Pyne *(V.P.-Field Opers.)*

Subsidiary:

Lowell Shoe, Inc. **(1)**
8 Hampshire Dr.
Hudson, NH 03501
Tel.: 603-880-8900 (100%)
Mfr. Women's Service & Casual Shoes
S.I.C.: 3144; 3149
Jordan Elliot *(Pres. & Chief Oper. Officer)*
John J. Nannicelli, Jr. *(Exec. V.P.-Fin. & Opers.)*

M. A. MORTENSON COMPANY
700 Meadow Ln. N.
Minneapolis, MN 55422
Mailing Address:
P.O. Box 710,
Minneapolis, MN 54400
Tel.: 612-522-2100
Fax: 612-520-3430
Year Founded: 1954
Approx.Sls.: $720,000,000
Emp.: 1,700
General Contractors
S.I.C.: 1541; 1542; 1629
M.A. Mortenson, Jr. *(Chm. Bd., Chief Exec. Officer & Pres.)*
Tom McCune *(Exec. V.P., Chief Exec. Officer-Building Div.)*
Ron Attig *(V.P.-Heavy Division)*
Paul Campbell *(V.P.-Northwest Region)*
Greg Clark *(V.P.-Estimating)*
Peter Conzemius *(V.P. & Chief Fin. Officer)*
Jeanne Forneris *(V.P. & Gen. Counsel)*
Tom Gunkel *(V.P.)*
Steve Halverson *(V.P.-Western Region)*
Robert Hardin *(V.P.)*
Ralph McCoy *(V.P.-Special Projects Group)*
Jon Morgan *(V.P.-Corp. Planning)*
Don Myers, Jr. *(V.P.-Admin.)*
Dean Nelson *(V.P.-Opers, Western Region)*
Dan Vertanan *(V.P.-Opers, Heavy Division)*
John Wood *(V.P.-Midwest Region)*
Fred Van Vurst *(V.P.-Fedral Contracting Group)*
Mark Westin *(V.P.)*
Earl Hacking *(Sec.)*
Owen Jensen *(Treas. & Controller)*
Principal(s):
Ron Attig

No. of U.S. Offices: 5

Computer Systems/Hardware:
IBM

Outside Service Firm(s):

Travelers Insurance Co.*(Group Insurer)*
Minneapolis, MN

MOSLER INC.
1561 Grand Blvd.
Hamilton, OH 45012
Tel.: 513-867-4000
Fax: 513-867-4062
Year Founded: 1867
Approx.Sls.: $220,000,000
Emp.: 2,200
Fiscal Year-end: 6/30/92
Import Export
Security Products-Fixtures for Financial Institutions, Electronic Security Services, Mfr. of Locks & Security Devices; Safes, Vaults, Safe Deposit Boxes, Burglar Alarms, Night Deposit Box Hardware
S.I.C.: 3499; 7382; 2542; 3669; 3429; 3599; 3663
A.M. Marzano *(Chm. Bd. & Chief Exec. Officer)*
Michael S. Battaglia *(Pres. & Chief Oper. Officer)*
Joseph F. Lingg *(Chief Fin. Officer & Controller)*
Arthur D. Lewis *(V.P.-Intl.)*
J. Pilcher *(V.P.-Mfg.)*
J. Tamashasky *(V.P.-Human Resources)*
D.F. Yorke *(V.P.-Electronic Systems Div.)*
Paul Jeanmougin *(Treas.)*
Sandra Sheffer *(Gen. Counsel)*
John Jacobs *(Dir.-Mngmt. Information Systems)*
Lisa B. Lawson *(Dir.-Mktg. Communications)*
Ruth Jacobs *(Mgr.-Pub. Rels.)*

Computer Systems/Hardware:
AS 400; 4331

Outside Service Firm(s):

Ernst & Young*(Auditors)*
1300 Chiquita Center, 250 E. Fifth St.
Cincinnati, OH 45202
Tel.: 513-621-6454

National City Bank*(Investment Banker)*
Cincinnati, OH

Divisions:

Mosler Counter Systems Div. **(1)**
200 Race St.
Buffalo, NY 14027
Tel.: 716-874-4200
Export
Mfr. of Metal Counter Tops & Fixtures for Financial Institutions
S.I.C.: 2542
J. Pilcher *(V.P.)*

Mosler Dropository Div. **(1)**
Dropositories, Dropository Envelopes & Dispensers
S.I.C.: 3499

Mosler Electronic Systems Div. **(1)**
415 Paterson-Hamburg Turnpike
Wayne, NJ 07470
Tel.: 201-595-4000
Mfrs. Electronic Surveillance Systems
S.I.C.: 3669; 7382
D.F. Yorke *(V.P. & Gen. Mgr.)*

Mosler, Inc. **(1)**
P.O. Box 2165
Orangeburg, SC 29116
Tel.: 803-534-3820
Mfr. of Safes, Vaults, & other Security Hardware
S.I.C.: 3499
Dennis Goldbach *(Gen. Mgr.)*
J. Pilcher *(V.P.)*

Non-U.S. Holding:

Mosler SA de C.D. **(1)**
Rio Lerma 69
Mexico, 5 D.F. Mexico
Tel.: 905-525-1935
Mfr. of Security Products for Financial Institutions
S.I.C.: 3499; 2542; 3429; 3669
Emilio Roaro *(Gen. Mgr.)*

MOSS AND COMPANY INC

MOSS AND COMPANY, INC.
49 W. 38th St.
New York, NY 10018
Tel.: 212-575-0808
Fax: 212-730-6020
Year Founded: 1950
Approx.Billings: $16,500,000
Murray Brauman *(Chm. Bd. & Chief Exec. Officer)*
Richard Yacenda *(Pres.)*
Bruce Thaler *(V.P., Direct Mktg. Services)*
Cheryl Sergiano *(Asst. Treas.)*

MOSS TELECOMMUNICATIONS SERVICES
561 Century Ave.
Grand Rapids, MI 49503
Tel.: 616-451-9933 **MI**
Fax: 616-451-8187
Year Founded: 1977
Assets: $1,198,000
Liabilities: $361,320
Net Worth: $836,680
Emp.: 52
Fiscal Year-end: 3/31/90
Installation Wiring Data Phone Systems
S.I.C.: 1731
Gerard J. Schaefer *(Pres.)*
Glen Hunter *(V.P.)*
Sandra Burton *(Mgr.-Fin.)*
Darlene Emery *(Mgr.-Pur.)*

No. of Mfg. Plants/Facilities: 2
No. of U.S. Offices: 2

Computer Systems/Hardware:
Novell Network On PC XT

Outside Service Firm(s):

Beene, Garter & Co.*(Auditors)*
Grand Rapids, MI

McShane & Bowie*(Legal Firm)*
Grand Rapids, MI

Old Kent Bank & Trust Co.*(Major Banking Relationship)*
One Vandenberg Center
Grand Rapids, MI 49503
Tel.: 616-774-5000

Union Central Life*(Pension Manager)*
Grand Rapids, MI

MOSSBERG INDUSTRIES, INC.
160 Bearhill Rd.
Cumberland, RI 02864
Tel.: 401-334-1800
Fax: 401-732-1562

Approx.Sls.: $15,000,000
Emp.: 150
Mfr. of Wood, Metal & Plastic Spools
S.I.C.: 3499; 3089
Malcolm G. Chase, III *(Chm. Bd.)*
Douglas G. McClurg *(Pres. & Chief Exec. Officer)*
Harold Wirts *(V.P.)*
Alfred Adessi *(Treas. & Sec.)*

Outside Service Firm(s):

Murphy & Company*(Auditors)*
Providence, RI

Hinkley, Allen, Snyder & Comen*(Legal Firm)*
1500 Fleet Ctr.
Providence, RI 02903
Tel.: 401-274-2000

Rhode Island Hospital Trust National Bank*(Major Banking Relationship)*
Warren, RI

Division:

Mossberg Industries, Hubbard Division **(1)**
2047 Second St.
Garrett, IN 46738
Tel.: 219-357-5141
S.I.C.: 3499; 3089
Harold Wirts *(Plant Mgr.)*

O. F. MOSSBERG & SONS, INC.
7 Grasso Ave.
North Haven, CT 06473
Tel.: 203-288-6491 **CT**
Fax: 203-288-2404
Year Founded: 1919
Approx.Sls.: $30,000,000
Emp.: 450
Fiscal Year-end: 9/30/90
Mfr. Shotguns
S.I.C.: 3484
Alan I. Mossberg *(Pres., Chief Exec. & Chief Oper. Officer & Treas.)*
Henry M. Beach *(Exec. V.P.-Mfg.)*
Richard Pelton *(Exec. V.P.)*
Iver Mossberg *(V.P.-Quality Control)*
William H. Schoner *(V.P.-Fin.)*
Warren Tomek *(V.P.-Mktg. & Law Enforcement Sls.)*
Nick A. Iacuone, Jr. *(Controller)*
Arthur S. Sachs *(Sec.)*
Joseph Witt *(Chief Information Officer)*
Tom Geirin *(Dir.-Data Processing)*
Dottie Ruotolo *(Mgr.-Personnel)*
Jack Guetens *(Pur. Agent)*
Georgia Nichols *(Legal Officer)*
Alice M. Zawadski *(Exec. Asst.)*
Principal(s):
Alan I. Mossberg

No. of Mfg. Plants/Facilities: 3
No. of U.S. Offices: 2

Computer Systems/Hardware:
IBM System 34

Outside Service Firm(s):

Ernst & Young*(Auditors)*
New Haven, CT

Travelers Insurance Co.*(Group Insurer)*
1 Tower Square
Hartford, CT 06183-2492
Tel.: 203-277-4542
Fax: 203-277-5038

MOTEK ENGINEERING & MANUFACTURING COMPANY
625 Second Ave., S.E.
Cambridge, MN 55008
Tel.: 612-689-1333 **MN**
Fax: 612-689-3126
Year Founded: 1967
Approx.Sls.: $15,000,000
Emp.: 160
Job Machine Shop
S.I.C.: 3599
Donald W. Ricke *(Chm. Bd. & Chief Exec. Officer)*
Robert Skawski *(Pres.)*
Gerald I. Pearson *(V.P.)*
Beatrice Ricke *(Sec. & Treas.)*
Steve Buckholz *(Dir.-Engrng.)*
K. Gordon *(Dir.-Pur.)*

Outside Service Firm(s):

Peoples State Bank*(Major Banking Relationship)*
Detroit, MI

MOTHER EARTH NEWS
24 E. 23rd St., 5th Fl.
New York, NY 10010
Tel.: 212-260-7210
Fax: 212-727-2326
Year Founded: 1991
Approx.Sls.: $15,000,000
Emp.: 20
Fiscal Year-end: 12/31/92
Import Export
Magazine Publishers & Book Plans & Product Sellers; Distr. of Four Handbooks Published by Simon & Schuster
S.I.C.: 2721; 2741
Bea Hanks *(Assoc. Publr.)*
John Colman *(Chief Exec. Officer)*
Vince McCann *(Chief Fin. Officer)*
Peter Millard *(V.P.-Adv.)*
Janice Motsinger *(Controller)*
Cathy Roach *(Gen. Mgr. Ancillary Products)*
Sheryl-Sue Sober *(Adv. Production Coord.)*

Division:

Mother's Bookshelf **(1)**
P. O. Box 10941
Des Moines, IA 50340
Tel.: 800-888-9098
Mail-order Books
S.I.C.: 5961
Cathy Roach *(Gen. Mgr.-Ancillary Products)*

Subsidiary:

Mothers Back Issues, Inc. **(1)**
P.O. Box 10941
Des Moines, IA 50340
Tel.: 800-888-9098
Mail-order Back Issues of Mother Earth News
S.I.C.: 5961
Cathy Roach *(Gen. Mgr.-Ancillary Products)*

MOTO, INC.
721 Main
Belleville, IL 62220
Tel.: 618-233-6754
Fax: 618-233-5724
Year Founded: 1974
Approx.Sls.: $46,000,000
Emp.: 400
Filling Stations; Grocery Stores; Bituminous Coal & Lignite Surface Mining
S.I.C.: 5541; 5411; 1221
James G. Forsyth, III *(Pres.)*
James M. Louery *(Treas. & Sec.)*

Outside Service Firm(s):

Magna Bank*(Major Banking Relationship)*
Belleville, IL

Subsidiary:

FKG Oil Company **(1)**
721 Main
Belleville, IL 62220
Tel.: 618-233-6754
Filling Stations
S.I.C.: 5541
David Howelman *(Pres.)*
Jeannie Eckenrod *(Treas. & Sec.)*
Robert Forsyth *(V.P.-Admin.)*

Motor Convoy Inc.
(Name Changed To Allied Systems, Ltd.)

MOTOR WHEEL CORPORATION
4000 Collins Rd.
Lansing, MI 48910
Tel.: 517-337-5700 **OH**
Fax: 517-337-5899
Year Founded: 1903
Approx.Sls.: $500,000,000
Emp.: 2,000
Fiscal Year-end: 12/31/90
Export
Manufacture Wheels, Hubs & Brake Parts for Cars, Trucks, Buses & Trailers
S.I.C.: 3714; 3429
Joseph C. Overbeck *(Chief Exec. Officer)*
G.D. Friedrichsen *(Exec. V.P., Gen. Mgr.-Comml. Hwy. & Military Prods.)*
J.R. Kinstler *(Exec. V.P.-Mfg.)*
A.N. McCotter *(Exec. V.P. & Gen. Mgr.-Automotive Prods. Div.)*
C.W. Brown *(V.P.-Pur.)*
T.R. Collins *(V.P.-Fin. & Treas.)*
L.R. Hoyt *(V.P.-Human Resources)*
D. Martin *(V.P., Sec. & Gen. Counsel)*
D.R. Lamison *(Asst. Treas.)*
D.F. Bush *(Dir.-Employee Benefits)*
R.A. Engle *(Dir.-Mktg., Comml. Hwy. & Military Prods.)*
D.E. Haviland *(Dir.-Mktg., Automotive Prods. Div.)*

Computer Systems/Hardware:
IBM System 38

Outside Service Firm(s):

Price Waterhouse*(Auditors)*
200 Renaissance Center, Ste. 3900
Detroit, MI 48243

Manufacturers National Bank N.A.*(Major Banking Relationship)*
38th Fl., 100 Renaissance Center
Detroit, MI 48243
Tel.: 313-222-4227

MOTORISTS MUTUAL INSURANCE CO.
471 E. Broad
Columbus, OH 43215
Tel.: 614-225-8211
Fax: 614-225-8407
Year Founded: 1928
Approx.Sls.: $260,000,000
Emp.: 857
Fiscal Year-end: 12/31/90
Property, Casualty & Life Insurance
S.I.C.: 6321; 6311; 6331
Robert E.H. Rabold *(Chm., Pres. & Chief Exec. Officer)*
John Cooper *(Sr. V.P.-Life Opers.)*
Richard Greathouse *(Sr. V.P. & Treas.)*
Garry Wharton *(Sr. V.P., Corp. Counsel & Sec.)*
Duane Swartz *(Sr. V.P.-Corp. Services)*
John J. Bishop *(V.P.-Mktg.)*
Thomas Ogg *(V.P.-Claims)*
Carl Meyer *(V.P.-Acctg.)*
Dorothy Heltzel *(V.P.-Res.)*
Daniel Crawford *(V.P.-Investment)*
Mike Wiseman *(V.P.-Actuarial)*
Jerry Merrell *(V.P.-Corp. Communications)*
John H. Huey *(V.P.-Information Systems)*
Mike Finch *(V.P.-Underwriting)*
Orville Lyons *(V.P.-Life Opers.)*
H. Steven Loy *(V.P.-Human Resources)*

THE MOTORLEASE CORP.
1506 New Britain Ave.
Farmington, CT 06032
Tel.: 203-677-9711
Fax: 203-674-8677
Approx.Sls.: $16,000,000
Emp.: 25
Passenger Automobile Leasing
S.I.C.: 7515
Jack Leary *(Pres.)*
Beth Foradari *(V.P. & Treas.)*
Robert Ferraresso *(V.P.-Opers.)*
Elizabeth Leary *(Sec.)*

Mount Vernon Realty, Inc.
(Acquired by Weichert Company, name changed to Weichert Realty, Inc.)

MOUNTAIN AIR DELIVERY
728 Spice Island Dr.
Sparks, NV 89431
Mailing Address:
P.O. Box 11246,
Reno, NV 89510
Tel.: 702-331-8010 **NV**
Telex: 361679
Fax: 702-331-6500
Year Founded: 1975
Sales Range: $10-19 Million
Emp.: 15
Import Export
Trucking; Customs Brokerage; Freight Forwarding
S.I.C.: 4213; 4212; 4731
Jeff Griffin *(Chm. Bd., Pres. & Chief Exec. Officer)*
Marna W. Griffin *(Sec.)*
Elizabeth Holt *(Mgr.)*
Eric Paulson *(Mgr.-Opers.)*
Russel Romine *(Mgr.-Mktg.)*
Barbara Stoddard *(Mgr.-Import)*
Terry D. Graff *(Legal Officer)*

No. of Mfg. Plants/Facilities: 1
No. of U.S. Offices: 1

Computer Systems/Hardware:
IBM; Apple; Tandy Radio Shack

Outside Service Firm(s):

Dean Albright & Associates*(Auditors)*
Reno, NV

Farmers Insurance*(Commercial Insurance Carrier)*
Reno, NV

Farmers Insurance*(Group Insurer)*
Reno, NV

Wool, Richardson & Graff*(Legal Firm)*
San Jose, CA

First Interstate Bank*(Major Banking Relationship)*
Reno, NV

Valley Bank of Nevada*(Major Banking Relationship)*
Reno, NV

MOUNTAIN STATES CONSTRUCTORS, INC.
West Frontage Rd. N.E.
Albuquerque, NM 87197
Tel.: 505-345-4401 **NM**
Fax: 505-345-4406
Year Founded: 1980
Approx.Sls.: $24,000,000
Emp.: 174
General Contractor, Highway & Street Construction; Earthmoving Contractor
S.I.C.: 1611; 1629
Steve Benoit *(Pres.)*
Melvin Morris *(Treas. & Sec.)*

Outside Service Firm(s):

Arthur Andersen & Co.*(Auditors)*
AmericaWest Financial Ctr., 6501 Americas Parkway N.E., Ste. 400
Albuquerque, NM 87110
Tel.: 505-889-4700

MOUNTAIN STATES PIPE & SUPPLY COMPANY
111 W. Las Vegas
Colorado Springs, CO 80903
Mailing Address:
P.O. Box 698,
Colorado Springs, CO 80903
Tel.: 719-634-5555 CO
Fax: 719-634-5551
Year Founded: 1986
Approx.Sls.: $10,000,000
Emp.: 33
Fiscal Year-end: 9/30/91
Wholesale Distribution of Plumbing & Hydronic Heating Supplies
S.I.C.: 5074
David Wilcox *(Pres.)*
Donald Cole *(V.P.-Sls.)*
Noel Frakes *(V.P.)*
Frank Milliron *(Dir.-Pur.)*
Jane T. Wilcox *(Treas. & Sec.)*
Gary R. Ferguson *(Controller)*

Principal(s):
David Wilcox
Maurice Baker
Ben Glidden

No. of U.S. Offices: 1

Computer Systems/Hardware:
Honeywell 1410

Outside Service Firm(s):

Mountain States Pipe & Supply Company*(Auditors)*
111 W. Las Vegas
Colorado Springs, CO 80903
Tel.: 719-634-5555
Fax: 719-634-5551

National Target Group Administrators*(Group Insurer)*
Pueblo, CO

Hendricks & Hendricks*(Legal Firm)*
Colorado Springs, CO

UMB Bank*(Major Banking Relationship)*
Nevada & Pikes Peak
Colorado Springs, CO

UMB Bank*(Pension Manager)*
Nevada & Pikes Peak
Colorado Springs, CO

ERIC MOWER AND ASSOCIATES, INC.
500 Plum St.
Syracuse, NY 13204
Tel.: 315-466-1000 NY
Fax: 315-466-2000

Approx.Billings: $82,015,895
Emp.: 170
Full-Service Advertising Agency
S.I.C.: 7311
Eric Mower *(Chm. & Chief Exec. Officer)*
Jay Quinn *(Pres. & Chief Oper. Officer)*
Ann G. Higbee *(Pres.-EMA Pub. Rels. Services)*
Francis T. Nichols *(Pres. & Gen. Mgr.-EMA Mngmt. Services Group, Inc.)*
Michael Cunningham *(Sr. V.P. & Exec. Dir.-Creative)*
Hal Goodman *(V.P.-Fin.)*
Trish Kyle *(Dir.-Human Resources)*

No. of U.S. Offices: 2

Branches:

Eric Mower and Associates/Buffalo, Inc. **(1)**
360 Delaware Ave.
Buffalo, NY 14202
Tel.: 716-842-2233
Fax: 716-842-6676
Advertising Agency
S.I.C.: 7311
Eric Mower *(Chm. & Chief Exec. Officer)*
Strattan S. White *(Sr. Partner)*
Doug Bean *(Partner)*
Judith Hojnacki *(Partner)*

Eric Mower and Associates/ Rochester, Inc. **(1)**
96 College Ave.
Rochester, NY 14607
Tel.: 716-473-0440
Fax: 716-473-8454
Advertising Agency
S.I.C.: 7311
John W. Huppertz, Ph.D. *(Pres. & Chief Oper. Officer)*
John Brown *(Sr. V.P. & Chief Creative Officer)*
Cynthia Hoenig *(V.P. & Dir.-Pub. Rels.)*
Susanne Perrone *(V.P. & Supvr.-Mngmt.)*

MOYER MITCHELL COMPANY, INC.
1014 Rural Ave.
Voorhees, NJ 08043
Tel.: 609-429-2696
Fax: 609-429-2878
Approx.Sls.: $20,000,000
Emp.: 22
Poultry Distribution
S.I.C.: 5144
Richard S. Mitchell, Jr. *(Pres.)*
Steve Moyer *(V.P.)*

Outside Service Firm(s):

Capehart & Scatchard*(Legal Firm)*
Mt. Laurel, NJ

Glendale National Bank*(Major Banking Relationship)*
Voorhees, NJ

MOYER PACKING COMPANY
249 Allentown Rd.
Souderton, PA 18964
Mailing Address:
P.O. Box 395,
Souderton, PA 18964-0395
Tel.: 215-723-5555 PA
Fax: 215-723-1018
Year Founded: 1925
Sales Range: $100-499 Million
Emp.: 1,200
Export
Meat Packing & Rendering
S.I.C.: 2011; 2077
Curtis F. Moyer *(Pres.)*
Dolores Howell *(Exec. V.P. & Sec.)*
John Hendricks *(V.P.-Rendering)*
William G. Morral *(V.P.-Fin. & Treas.)*
Michael Silverberg *(V.P.-Beef)*
Ella M. Roush *(Dir.-Pub. Rels.)*

MOYER PRODUCTS, INC.
1540 E. Shaw, Ste. 101
Fresno, CA 93710
Mailing Address:
P.O. Box 5434
Fresno, CA 93755
Tel.: 209-226-4664 CA
Fax: 209-227-2235
Year Founded: 1946
Approx.Sls.: $44,000,000
Emp.: 155
Fiscal Year-end: 11/30/89
Pesticides & Fertilizers; Growing Nurseries
S.I.C.: 2875; 2879; 0181
James H. Lindley *(Pres.)*
Donald D. Holbrook *(V.P.)*
Richard L. Maul *(V.P.)*
Lonnie L. Stivers *(Dir.-Pur.)*

No. of U.S. Offices: 10

Computer Systems/Hardware:
IBM

Outside Service Firm(s):

Deloitte & Touche*(Auditors)*
Suite 107, 1550 E. Shaw Ave.
Fresno, CA 93170
Tel.: 209-226-0560

Frank B. Hall*(Group Insurer)*
Suite 400, 5260 N. Palm Ave.
Fresno, CA 93704
Tel.: 209-449-1900

McCormick, Barstow, Sheppard, Wayte & Carruth*(Legal Firm)*
1331 Fulton Mall
Fresno, CA 93721
Tel.: 209-442-1150

Union Bank*(Major Banking Relationship)*
Suite 1000, 5250 N. Palm
Fresno, CA 93704

Lincoln National Life Insurance Co.*(Pension Manager)*
116 E. Berry
Ft. Wayne, IN 46802
Tel.: 219-423-6111

MOZEL DEVELOPMENT CORP.
6031 Leesburg Pike
Baileys Crossroads, VA 22041
Tel.: 703-578-4000
Approx.Sls.: $30,000,000
Emp.: 25
General Building Contractors
S.I.C.: 1522; 1542
Dr. Cyrus Katzen *(Pres. & Chief Exec. Officer)*
Harry Cohen *(Chief Fin. Officer, Treas. & Sec.)*

Computer Systems/Hardware:
Wang & IBM

MUELHENS, INC.
(Formerly Colonia Inc.)
15 Executive Blvd.
Orange, CT 06477
Tel.: 203-787-4711
Tel.: 800-243-5555
Fax: 203-865-8329
Approx.Sls.: $60,000,000
Emp.: 200
Import Export
Fragrances: Gucci Parfum I, Eau du Gucci, Gucci Pour Homme, 4711, Pavlova, Amun; Payot Creams & Makeup, Gucci No. 3
S.I.C.: 5122
Antoine Maintz *(Pres.)*
John McCoy *(Chief Fin. Officer)*
John Gordon *(V.P.-Pur.)*
Marcia Levis *(V.P.-Mktg./Sls.)*
Heidi Scholten *(Corp. Sec.)*
Ms. Pat Glennon *(Dir.-MIS)*
Leo Mahoney *(Dir.-Plant Opers.)*
Lois Kennedy *(Mgr.-Personnel)*
Amin Rizk *(Mgr.-Mktg.)*
Scott Sanserino *(Mgr.-Sls. Admin./ Opers.)*

MUELLER MACK
510 1st Ave. N., Ste. 200
Minneapolis, MN 55403
Tel.: 612-338-8089
Year Founded: 1989
Approx.Billings: $10,000,000
Emp.: 10
Food, Retail & Consumer Durables Advertising
Principal(s):
Bill Mueller
John Mack

R.A. MUELLER, INC.
11270 Cornell Park Dr.
Cincinnati, OH 45242
Tel.: 513-489-5200
Fax: 513-489-7554
Approx.Sls.: $10,000,000
Emp.: 45
Mfr. of Liquid Process Pumps; Fiberglass Pipe; Fluid Agitation; Ion Exchangers; Heat Exchangers
S.I.C.: 5084
Duane W. Larock *(Pres.)*
Kevin Delaney *(Mgr.-Sls.)*

MUELLER SPORTS MEDICINE, INC.
One Quench Dr.
Prairie du Sac, WI 53578
Tel.: 608-643-8530
Tel.: 800-356-9522
Fax: 608-643-2568
Approx.Sls.: $10,000,000
Emp.: 70
Fiscal Year-end: 11/30/90
Training Room Pharmaceuticals for Athletes
Curt Mueller *(Pres.)*
John Swafford *(Sr. V.P.)*
April Jacobs *(V.P.-Sls. & Mktg.)*
Brett Mueller *(V.P.-Sls. & Mktg.)*
O.P. Mueller *(Treas.)*
Rose Ballweg *(Sec.)*

MUENCH-KREUZER CANDLE COMPANY
617 E. Hiawatha Blvd.
Syracuse, NY 13208
Mailing Address:
P.O. Box 4969
Syracuse, NY 13221
Tel.: 315-471-4515
Tel.: 800-448-7884
Fax: 315-471-4581
Approx.Sls.: $12,000,000
Emp.: 175
Fiscal Year-end: 4/30/91
Emkay Decorative & Religious Candles
S.I.C.: 5199
M.A. Muench *(Pres.)*
Michael Swimm *(V.P.)*
Carol Egle *(V.P.-Sls.)*
Renee Roy *(V.P.-Sls.)*

C. A. MUER CORP.
1548 Porter St.
Detroit, MI 48216
Tel.: 313-965-5555
Fax: 313-965-5489
Year Founded: 1964
Approx.Sls.: $70,000,000
Emp.: 1,400
Fine Dining Restaurants Specializing in Fresh Seafood; Tavernhouse Restaurants Specializing in Seafood, Beef, Ribs & Pasta
S.I.C.: 5812
Charles A. Muer *(Pres.)*
Leo Beil *(V.P. & Treas.)*
Greg Ochoa *(Controller)*
Tony Adams *(Dir.-Pur.)*
Ruth Mayhall *(Dir.-Mktg.)*

Principal(s):
Charles A. Muer

No. of U.S. Offices: 1

Computer Systems/Hardware:
IBM System 38, PC & PC Compatibles; NCR Tower XP-Convergent Technologies Mini-Frame II

Outside Service Firm(s):

Arthur Andersen & Co.*(Auditors)*
400 Renaissance Center
Detroit, MI 48243
Tel.: 313-259-8100

Michigan National Bank*(Major Banking Relationship)*
Detroit, MI

MUHLHAUSER & YOUNG
544 Pacific Ave., Ste. 300
San Francisco, CA 94133
Tel.: 415-392-0542
Year Founded: 1976
Approx.Billings: $15,000,000
Emp.: 10
Apparel, Communications, Real Estate, Travel & Leisure
Barbara Muhlhauser *(Chm. Bd. & Creative Dir.)*
Jill Young *(Pres.)*
Bonnie Matza *(Exec V.P.)*
Jim Kelley *(Dir., Mktg, Hospitality/ Travel & Leisure)*
Suzanne Izzi *(Mktg. Asst., Media Contact)*
Al Ping *(Controller)*

MULACH STEEL CORPORATION
100 Hickory Grade Rd.
Bridgeville, PA 15017
Tel.: 412-257-1111
Fax: 412-221-1760
Assets: $11,000,000
Net Worth: $11,000,000
Approx.Sls.: $50,000,000
Emp.: 150
Mfr. Fabricated Structural Metal; Architectural & Ornamental Metal Work; General Contractor Nonresidential Buildings; Wholesale Metals
S.I.C.: 1542; 3441; 3446; 5051
Joseph F. Mulach, Jr. *(Chm. Bd.)*
Steven C. Thomas *(Vice Chm.)*
Albert Lepore *(Pres.)*
Raymond D. Horsman *(V.P. & Chief Fin. Officer)*

Outside Service Firm(s):

Deloitte & Touche*(Auditors)*
2400 One PPG Place
Pittsburgh, PA 15222
Tel.: 412-281-2232

Subsidiary:

Mulach Parking Structures Corp. **(1)**
100 Hickory Grade Rd.
Bridgeville, PA 15017
Tel.: 412-257-8100
Emp.: 40
Design & Construct Parking Structures
S.I.C.: 8712; 1542
Steven C. Thomas *(Vice Chm.)*
Raymond Horsman *(V.P.)*
Charles Churches *(V.P.-Opers.)*

MULBERRY METAL PRODUCTS, INC.
2199 Stanley Terrace
Union, NJ 07083
Mailing Address:
P.O. Box 443,
Union, NJ 07083
Tel.: 908-688-8850
Fax: 908-688-7294
Year Founded: 1921
Approx.Sls.: $10,000,000
Emp.: 140
Mfr. Metal Wall Plates, Wiring Devices, Outlet Boxes & Covers, Installation Accessories
S.I.C.: 3644
Richard Horn *(Pres. & Treas.)*
Richard E. Mueller *(Exec. V.P.-Sls.)*
Lony Mueller *(Sec.)*
Nancy Lemeiux *(Mgr.-Personnel)*
Bruce Burck *(Pur. Agent)*

MULHERN BELTING, INC.
148 Bauer Dr.
Oakland, NJ 07436
Tel.: 201-337-5700 **NJ**
Fax: 201-337-6540
Year Founded: 1932
Sales Range: $10-19 Million
Emp.: 75
Import Export
Mfr. of Industrial Conveyor Belting
S.I.C.: 3052
James A. Mulhern *(Chm. Bd.)*
Patrick M. Mulhern *(Pres.)*
Matthew T. Mulhern *(V.P.-Sls.)*

No. of Mfg. Plants/Facilities: 4
No. of U.S. Offices: 4

Computer Systems/Hardware:
Basic IV

Outside Service Firm(s):

Czonka & Youhas*(Auditors)*
Paramus, NJ

Citizens First National Bank*(Major Banking Relationship)*
Passaic, NJ

MULLE/BREEN ADVERTISING
10137 Riverside Dr.
Toluca Lake, CA 91602
Tel.: 818-761-0666
Year Founded: 1958
Approx.Billings: $10,000,000
Sherman G. Mulle *(Pres.)*
Charles I. Mulle *(V.P.)*
Paula Zoss *(Office Mgr.)*
Jane Rasak *(Asst. Dir., Pub. Rels.)*
Insang Kim *(Acctg. Supvr.)*

MULLEN ADVERTISING, INC.
36 Essex St.
Wenham, MA 01984
Tel.: 508-468-1155
Fax: 508-468-1133
Year Founded: 1970
Approx.Billings: $104,700,000
Emp.: 135
General Advertising, Public Relations, Design & Research
James X. Mullen *(Pres. & Chief Exec. Officer)*
Joseph M. Grimaldi *(Chief Oper. Officer)*
Carin Warner *(Exec. V.P.-Pub. Rels.)*
James E. Hartrich *(Sr. V.P. & Dir.-Res.)*
Jeanne Ridgway *(V.P.-Fin. & Treas.)*
Susan Schumacher *(V.P.-Pub. Rels.)*
Paul Slack *(V.P & Controller)*
Janet Swaysland *(V.P. & Assoc. Dir.-Pub. Rels.)*
Katie Greenler *(Telecommunications & Corp. Video Systems)*

Mulligan Sales
(See M M M Sales, Inc. Listing)

ED MULLINAX FORD, INC.
P.O. Box 280
Amherst, OH 44001
Tel.: 216-984-2431
Fax: 216-984-2431, Ext. 300
Approx.Sls.: $100,000,000
Emp.: 300
Retail New & Used Automobiles
S.I.C.: 5511
Charles E. Mullinax *(Pres.)*
Larry Mullinax *(Treas., Dir.-Pur., Data Processing, & Personnel)*
Joe Capps *(Comptroller)*

Outside Service Firm(s):

Hyman, Hyman & Noll Co.*(Legal Firm)*
Elyria, OH

The Central Trust Company, N.A.*(Major Banking Relationship)*
Amherst, OH

MULTI-AD SERVICES, INC.
1720 W. Detweiller Dr.
Peoria, IL 61615
Tel.: 309-692-1530
Fax: 309-692-6566
Emp.: 350
Fiscal Year-end: 12/31/90
Graphics Art Producers; Syndicated Newspaper Service, Retail Radio Ad Materials, Product Illustration Systems, Manufacturer Retail Advertising Materials & Programs, Co-op Information System, Color Food Service
S.I.C.: 2759
Larry Clore *(Pres.)*
Roy M. Endres *(Exec. V.P.)*
George Messer *(V.P.-Media Sls.)*
Steve Mylott *(V.P. Pre-Press)*
Bruce Taylor *(V.P.-Fin.)*
Larry Ziegler *(V.P.-Mfg. & Sls.)*
Jerry Ireland *(Plant Mgr.)*

Outside Service Firm(s):

Clifton Gunderson & Co.*(Auditors)*
Peoria, IL

Sutkowski & Washkuhn*(Legal Firm)*
Jefferson Bank Bldg., Ste. 505, 123 S.W. Adams St.
Peoria, IL 61602
Tel.: 309-673-4500

First America Bank*(Major Banking Relationship)*
Peoria, IL

Divisions:

Custom Ad-Planner **(1)**
1720 W. Detweiller Dr.
Peoria, IL 61615
Tel.: 309-692-1530

KRBS Radio **(1)**
1720 W. Detweiller Dr.
Peoria, IL 61615
Tel.: 309-692-1530

Kwikee Systems **(1)**
1720 W. Detweiller Dr.
Peoria, IL 61615
Tel.: 309-692-1530

Re Cas **(1)**
1720 W. Detweiller Dr.
Peoria, IL 61615
Tel.: 309-692-1530

MULTI-MEDIA MARKETING COMMUNICATIONS, INC. (M.M.M.C., INC.)
3030 Old Ranch Pkwy., Ste. 210
Seal Beach, CA 90740-2752
Tel.: 310-431-7885
Fax: 310-431-6285
Year Founded: 1982
Approx.Billings: $38,000,000
Emp.: 12
Packaged Goods & Consumer Adv.
Bruce C. Walter *(Chm. Bd., Pres. & Mktg. Dir.)*
Sherry L. Riach *(Admin. Asst.)*
Coleen D. Walter *(Treas.)*

Computer Systems/Hardware:
Macintosh SE/30

MULTI MEDIA SERVICES CORP.
801 N. Fairfax St., Ste. 312
Alexandria, VA 22314
Tel.: 703-739-2160
Fax: 703-739-0664
Year Founded: 1983
Approx.Billings: $10,000,000
Emp.: 6
Political Media Buying
Anthony M. Fabrizio *(Chm. Bd., Pres. & New Bus. Contact)*
Ronald W. Finkelstein *(Sec. & Treas.)*

MULTIMATIC CORPORATION
162 Veteran Drive
Northvale, NJ 07647
Tel.: 201-767-9660 **NJ**
Fax: 201-767-7037
Approx.Sls.: $11,000,000
Emp.: 70
Manufactures Commercial Dry Cleaning Machines
S.I.C.: 3582
Horst Hahn *(Chief Exec. Officer & Gen. Mgr.)*
Harold Yancek *(Controller)*

MULTIPLE ALLIED SERVICES, INC.
3157 Corporate Pl.
Hayward, CA 94545
Tel.: 510-887-2211
Fax: 510-887-3092
Year Founded: 1953
Approx.Sls.: $32,000,000
Emp.: 100
Fiscal Year-end: 9/30/92
Miracle Auto Painting & Body Repair Centers
S.I.C.: 7538; 7532
Lester R. Thayer *(Chm. Bd. & Pres.)*
Weyne Abbott *(Exec. V.P.)*
James L. Fowler *(V.P. & Sec.)*
Rolf Filosa *(Controller)*
James Jordan *(Dir.-Mktg. & Adv.)*
Robert Manchester *(Dir.-Pur.)*

MICHAEL J. MUNGO COMPANY, INC.
4400 St. Andrews Rd.
Columbia, SC 29210
Tel.: 803-772-9444
Fax: 803-731-6292
Approx.Sls.: $960,000,000
Emp.: 25
Residential Building Operator
S.I.C.: 6514
Michael J. Mungo *(Chm. Bd.)*
Stewart Mungo *(Pres.)*
Billy Mungo *(Exec. V.P.)*
Steven Mungo *(V.P.)*
Brian Graham *(Controller)*

Outside Service Firm(s):

Finch, Hamilton, Oxner & Co.*(Auditors)*
Columbia, SC

Gertz & Moore*(Legal Firm)*
Columbia, SC

South Carolina National Bank*(Major Banking Relationship)*
Columbia, SC

MUNIGLE CORPORATION
28 N. Main St.
West Hartford, CT 06107
Tel.: 203-561-5590
Fax: 203-561-4414
Approx.Sls.: $38,000,000
Emp.: 200
New Construction of Office & Industrial Buildings & Warehouses
S.I.C.: 1542; 1541; 6552
Charles L. Munigle *(Pres.)*
Jo Ann Munigle *(Sec.)*

MUNRO & COMPANY, INC.
120 Elmwood Rd.
Hot Springs, AR 71901
Mailing Address:
P.O. Box 1157
Hot Springs, AR 71902
Tel.: 501-262-6000 **AR**
Fax: 501-262-6084
Year Founded: 1972
Approx.Sls.: $100,000,000
Emp.: 2,500
Import Export
Manufacture Private Label & Military Shoes
S.I.C.: 3143; 3149; 3142
Donald Munro *(Chm. Bd., Chief Exec. Officer & Treas.)*
Michael Hennessy *(Pres.)*
Hayward D. Ervin *(V.P.)*
Stanley Grise, Jr. *(V.P.-Fin.)*

No. of Mfg. Plants/Facilities: 8

Munro & Company, Inc.—(Continued)

Computer Systems/Hardware:
IBM System AS/400

Outside Service Firm(s):

Bernard Johnson & Co.*(Auditors)*
Danvers, MA

Arkansas Blue Cross & Blue Shield, Inc.*(Group Insurer)*
Little Rock, AR

First National Bank of Boston*(Investment Banker)*
P.O. Box 644,
Boston, MA 02102-0644
Tel.: 617-575-2900
Fax: 617-575-2549

Arnold, Grobmyer & Haley*(Legal Firm)*
Little Rock, AR

First National Bank of Boston*(Major Banking Relationship)*
P.O. Box 644,
Boston, MA 02102-0644
Tel.: 617-575-2900
Fax: 617-575-2549

Stephens Inc.*(Pension Manager)*
Little Rock, AR

Subsidiary:

Lake Catherine **(1)**
190 Elmwood Rd.
Hot Springs, AR 71902
Tel.: 501-262-1440

MUNROE, INC.
1820 N. Franklin St.
Pittsburgh, PA 15233
Tel.: 412-231-0600
Fax: 412-231-0647
Approx.Sls.: $13,500,000
Emp.: 200
Mfr. & Wholesale Distributor of Boiler Components, Pressure Vessels, Heat Exchangers, Chemical Plant Construction Equipment; Replacement Parts & Repair Service; Resale Of Steel Mill Equipment; Water Cooled Duct & Boiler Repair
S.I.C.: 3433; 3443; 3569; 5074; 5084; 7692; 7699
Edward Young *(Chm. Bd.)*
Philip F. Muck *(Pres., Chief Exec. Officer & Treas.)*
S. Zemba *(Controller)*
E. Schoyer *(Gen. Counsel)*
C. Emerick *(Sec.)*
Donald W. Capone *(Mgr.-Sls.)*
J. Onuscheck *(Mgr.-Cabs, Pulpits & Equip.)*
R. Rigatti *(Mgr.-Construction)*
J. Walkolich *(Mgr.-Quality Control)*
D. Traviglini *(Pur. Agent)*
P. Isager *(Chief Engr.)*

Outside Service Firm(s):

Ernst & Young*(Auditors)*
2000 Pittsburgh Natl. Bldg.
Pittsburgh, PA 15222
Tel.: 412-644-7800
Fax: 412-644-7419

Buchanan, Ingersoll p.c.*(Legal Firm)*
600 Grant St., 57th Flr.
Pittsburgh, PA 15219
Tel.: 412-562-8800

Union National Bank*(Major Banking Relationship)*
Pittsburgh, PA

MUNSEN'S DISCOVERY ENTERPRISES
120 E. Ogden Ave.
Hinsdale, IL 60521
Tel.: 708-920-7960
Fax: 708-920-7982
Year Founded: 1974
Earnings: $274,871
Emp.: 75
Tour Operator Throughout the United States & Canada for Individuals 55 Years Old & Over
S.I.C.: 4725
Paul Munsen *(Pres. & Chief Exec. Officer)*
Debbie Vaice *(Office Mgr.)*
Ken Snyder *(Gen. Mgr.)*

Computer Systems/Hardware:
MAI Basic Four

Outside Service Firm(s):

Benjamin & Rees Ltd.*(Auditors)*
Chicago, IL

Lincoln National Life Insurance Co.*(Group Insurer)*
PO Box 208, 1300 S. Clinton
Fort Wayne, IN 46801
Tel.: 219-455-2926
Fax: 219-455-7619

North Shore National Bank*(Major Banking Relationship)*
Chicago, IL

Subsidiary:

Munsen's Discovery Travel **(1)**
120 E. Ogden Ave.
Hinsdale, IL 60521
Tel.: 708-920-7960

MURALO CO., INC.
148 E. Fifth St.
Bayonne, NJ 07002
Tel.: 201-437-0770
Fax: 201-437-2316
Sales Range: $20-39 Million
Emp.: 350
Paints & Brushes
S.I.C.: 2851; 3991
James Norton *(Pres.)*
Charles P. Lee *(Exec. V.P.)*
Michael Carey *(Mgr.-Sls.)*

Outside Service Firm(s):

United Jersey Bank*(Major Banking Relationship)*
Bayonne, NJ

MURDOCK, INC.
15800 S. Avalon
Compton, CA 90220
Mailing Address:
P.O. Box 4249
Compton, CA 90224-4249
Tel.: 310-770-0220 **CA**
Fax: 310-538-1673
Year Founded: 1953
Sales Range: $20-39 Million
Emp.: 400
Fiscal Year-end: 5/31/91
Import Export
Air Frame & Missile Tool, Components & Assemblies, Nuclear & Offshore Oil Components, Special Equipment, Metal Forming & Hot Presses & Machine for Composite Materials
S.I.C.: 3728; 3443; 3533; 3542; 3549; 3769
Harold G. Murdock, Jr. *(Pres.)*
H. Hollenbach *(V.P.-Mfg.)*
W.B. Parker *(V.P.-Quality Assur.)*
Allan Roberts *(V.P.-Fin. & Admin.)*
Joanne E. Murdock *(Corp. Sec.)*
Dennis Musial *(Controller)*
William Bottin *(Mgr.-Direct Mktg.)*
Gerry Thomas *(Mgr.-Pur.)*
Ron Williams *(Dir.-Human Resources)*
Karen Camarena *(Asst. Corp. Sec.)*

Outside Service Firm(s):

Frazer & Torbet*(Auditors)*
Los Angeles, CA

Josi & Dold*(Commercial Insurance Carrier)*
Long Beach, CA

Sanwa Bank*(Major Banking Relationship)*
601 S. Figueroa St.
Los Angeles, CA 90017
Tel.: 213-896-7817
Fax: 213-489-1977

Andy J. Davis*(Pension Manager)*
Paramount, CA

MURO PHARMACEUTICAL, INC.
890 East St.
Tewksbury, MA 01876
Tel.: 508-851-5981
Fax: 508-851-7346
Year Founded: 1978
Approx.Sls.: $30,000,000
Emp.: 177
Fiscal Year-end: 3/31/92
Mfr. of Pharmaceuticals, Asthma & Allergy Products
S.I.C.: 2834
Corporate Giving Program: Primarily to Non-Profit Organizations
George D. Behrakis *(Pres. & Treas.)*
Stephen Meli *(Chief Oper. Officer)*
Erene Koukias *(Chief Fin. Officer)*
Judith Musgrove *(Exec. Sec.)*
Richard Floor *(Sec.)*
Lisa A. Myers *(Controller)*
Joseph Celona *(Dir.-Regulatory)*
Eleanor Eckhoff *(Dir.-Meeting Plng.)*
Themmi Evangelatos *(Dir.-Mktg.)*
Marilyn Komulainen *(Dir.-Personnel)*
Richard L. Marden *(Dir.-Govt. Affairs)*
Barbara Morin *(Dir.-Quality Control)*
Kenneth Morse *(Dir.-Sls.)*
Steve Parisi *(Dir.-Data Processing)*
Brant T. Sayre *(Dir.-Opers.)*
Dr. Jonathan Shilstone *(Dir.-Res. & Devel.)*
David Batt *(Mgr.-Mfg.)*

Computer Systems/Hardware:
Wang VS

MURPHY COMPANY
P.O. Box 2810
Eugene, OR 97402
Tel.: 503-344-4747
Fax: 503-344-2434
Approx.Sls.: $75,000,000
Emp.: 450
Lumber & Wood Products
S.I.C.: 2499
Peter Murphy, Jr. *(Chm. Bd., Pres. & Chief Exec. Officer)*
Kevin Murphy *(V.P. & Treas.)*
John Murphy *(Sec.)*
Jess Hamby *(Controller)*

Computer Systems/Hardware:
IBM PC; Wang VS

Outside Service Firm(s):

Sanderson, Hull & Gunderson*(Auditors)*
Portland, OR

Houston General*(Group Insurer)*
Eugene, OR

Herb Lombard*(Legal Firm)*
Eugene, OR

Oregon Bank*(Major Banking Relationship)*
Portland, OR

Subsidiaries:

Murphy International **(1)**
P.O. Box 2810
Eugene, OR 97402
Tel.: 503-344-4747

Murphy Plywood **(1)**
P.O. Box 2810
Eugene, OR 97402
Tel.: 503-344-4747

Murphy Properties, Inc. **(1)**
P.O. Box 2810
Eugene, OR 97402
Tel.: 503-344-4747

Murphy Timber **(1)**
P.O. Box 2810
Eugene, OR 97402
Tel.: 503-344-4747

MURPHY FARMS INC.
Hwy. 117
Rose Hill, NC 28458
Mailing Address:
P.O. Box 759
Rose Hill, NC 28458
Tel.: 919-289-2111 **NC**
Fax: 919-289-2627
Year Founded: 1962
Approx.Sls.: $125,000,000
Emp.: 400
Fiscal Year-end: 10/31/90
Pork Producer
S.I.C.: 0213
Wendell H. Murphy *(Pres.)*
James E. Stocker *(Exec. V.P.)*
Randy Stoecker *(Grp. V.P.)*
Brewer M. Ezzell *(Treas.)*
William B. Saunders *(Sec.)*

MURRAY-CARVER
15 Witman St.
East Bridgewater, MA 02333
Mailing Address:
P.O. Box 814449
Dallas, TX 75234
Tel.: 508-378-3111
Fax: 508-378-7205
Approx.Sls.: $20,000,000
Emp.: 175
Mfrs. & Distributes Cotton Gins & Oil Seed Processing Machinery
S.I.C.: 3559
John E. Lee *(Pres. & Chief Exec. Officer)*
Louis Gejoff *(Chief Fin. Officer, Treas., Controller & Sec.)*
Deborah Cooper *(Dir.-Data Processing)*

ARTHUR MURRAY INTL., INC.
1077 Ponce De Leon Blvd.
Coral Gables, FL 33134
Tel.: 305-445-9645
Fax: 305-445-0451
Year Founded: 1912
Approx.Sls.: $50,000,000
Emp.: 30
Fiscal Year-end: 6/30/90
American, Latin, Social & Other Ballroom Dance Instruction Franchised Schools
S.I.C.: 7911
Philip S. Masters *(Chm. Bd.)*
George B. Theiss *(Pres. & Chief Operating Officer)*
Samuel A. Costello *(Chief Exec. Officer)*
John Kimmins *(Exec. V.P.)*
Luz Del Rio *(Chief Fin. Officer & Asst. Sec.)*
James A. Griffith *(Sec.)*

Subsidiary:

Arthur Murray Enterprises, Inc. **(1)**
1077 Ponce de Leon Blvd.
Coral Gables, FL 33134
Tel.: 305-445-9646
Fax: 305-445-0451
Franchisor; Dance Studios

JOHN F. MURRAY ADVERTISING AGENCY INC.

685 Third Ave.
New York, NY 10017
Tel.: 212-878-5200
Fax: 212-878-5062
Year Founded: 1912

Approx.Billings: $295,000,000
Emp.: 30
Richard Feldheim *(Pres.)*
William Levengood *(V.P., Dir. Computer Opers.)*
Ingrid Loeuis *(V.P., Treas.)*

MURRAY'S DISCOUNT AUTO STORES
21500 Trolley Industrial Dr.
Taylor, MI 48180
Tel.: 313-292-2800 **MI**
Fax: 313-292-5772
Approx.Sls.: $75,000,000
Emp.: 650
Retail Automotive Supplies
S.I.C.: 5531
Irving E. Pitt *(Pres.)*
Michael Klein *(Chief Fin. Officer)*
Murray C. Pitt *(V.P.)*
Jerry Rosenfield *(Gen. Mgr.)*
Grace Haver *(Mgr.-Data Processing)*

Principal(s):
Irving E. Pitt

Computer Systems/Hardware:
Wang

Outside Service Firm(s):

Rubinstein, Isaacs, Lax & Bordman*(Legal Firm)*
Southfield, MI

Manufacturers National Bank N.A.*(Major Banking Relationship)*
38th Fl., 100 Renaissance Center
Detroit, MI 48243
Tel.: 313-222-4227

MURRY'S, INC.
8300 Pennsylvania Ave.
Forestville, MD 20747
Tel.: 301-420-6400
Fax: 301-967-4816
Year Founded: 1948
Approx.Sls.: $200,000,000
Emp.: 1,500
Fiscal Year-end: 5/31/91
Retail Food Stores, Specializing in Meat. Frozen & Packaged Goods

S.I.C.: 5411; 5499
Murry Mendelson *(Chm. Bd.)*
Ira Mendelson *(Pres. & Chief Exec. Officer)*
Matthew Young *(Exec. V.P.)*
Jack Luber *(Sr. V.P.-Purch.)*
Stuart Mendelson *(Sr. V.P.-Food Service)*
Yaacov Nagler *(Sr. V.P.-Pur.)*
Alvan Siegel *(Sr. V.P.-Production)*
Robert Krissoff *(Sr. V.P.-Consumer Div.)*
Martin Rosenhaft *(V.P. & Controller)*
Herb Helman *(Treas.)*
Ida Mendelson *(Sec.)*
Louis Ford *(Dir.-Mngmt. Information Systems)*
Carol Levie *(Adv. Mgr.)*
Becky Taylor *(Admin. Asst.)*

MUSCUM BOUTIQUE INTERCONTINENTAL, LTD.
(Formerly Mari Hube Ltd.)
26 E. 64th St.
New York, NY 10021
Tel.: 212-759-0777 **DE**
Fax: 212-753-0179
Year Founded: 1992
Sales Range: $10-19 Million
Emp.: 4
Import Export
Publishing & Marketing Specialists: Licensing of Major Art Estates, Advertising, Museum Boutique Products, Publishing of Limited Edition Prints; Wholesalers of Museum Boutique Products to the Trade
S.I.C.: 2741; 7389
David Kass *(Pres.)*
Joseph Sprung *(Chief Fin. Officer)*
Marilyn Huberman Goldberg *(Sr. V.P.)*
Georgette Huberman *(V.P.)*
Lisa Cassese *(Jr. V.P.)*
Lisa Salvatore *(Jr. V.P.)*

Principal(s):
Marilyn Huberman Goldberg

No. of U.S. Offices: 1
No. of Foreign Offices: 1

Computer Systems/Hardware:
IBM

Outside Service Firm(s):

Abrams & Sprung*(Auditors)*
New York, NY

Greenbaum Stern & Friedman*(Group Insurer)*
Great Neck, NY

Cutner & Rathkopf*(Legal Firm)*
New York, NY

MUSE CORDERO CHEN, INC.
6100 Wilshire Blvd., Ste. 1600
Los Angeles, CA 90048
Tel.: 213-954-1655
Fax: 213-954-9171
Year Founded: 1986
Approx.Billings: $27,000,000
Emp.: 35
Multicultural Advertising
J. Melvin Muse *(Chm.)*
Mavis Cordero *(Mng. Partner)*
David Chen *(Mng. Partner)*
Bill Reeher *(Chief Fin. Officer)*
Berni Neal *(Mgr.-Mktg. Services)*
Michelle Sterling *(Mgr.-Opers.)*
John Agnew *(Mktg. Services Coord.)*
Chris Dwight *(Asst. Mgr.-Mktg. Services)*

Computer Systems/Hardware:
Macintosh

MUSIC SALES CORPORATION
225 Park Ave. S.
New York, NY 10003
Tel.: 212-254-2100
Tel.: 800-431-7187 **NY**
Fax: 212-255-2013
Year Founded: 1935
Sales Range: $20-39 Million
Emp.: 80
Fiscal Year-end: 6/30/91
Import Export
Music Publishing
S.I.C.: 2741
Barrie Edwards *(Pres.)*
John Castaldo *(Controller)*
Lisa Lewis *(Dir.-Sls, Mktg. & Adv.)*
Ron Sherman *(Mgr.-Export)*
Peter Pickow *(Chief Editor)*

Computer Systems/Hardware:
IBM

Outside Service Firm(s):

Empire Blue Cross & Blue Shield*(Group Insurer)*
New York, NY

Guardian Life Insurance Co.*(Group Insurer)*
New York, NY

Subsidiaries:

Associated Music Publishers **(1)**
24 E. 22nd St.
New York, NY 10010
Tel.: 212-254-2100
S.I.C.: 2741
Barrie Edwards *(Pres.)*

G. Schirmer, Inc. **(1)**
24 E. 22nd St.
New York, NY 10010
Tel.: 212-254-2100
S.I.C.: 2741
Barrie Edwards *(Pres.)*

Shawnee Press, Inc. **(1)**
1 Waring Dr.
Delaware Water Gap, PA 18327-1099
Tel.: 717-476-0550
Music Publishers
S.I.C.: 2741
Ruth Sibley *(V.P.)*

MUSKA ELECTRIC COMPANY
1985 Oakcrest Ave.
Saint Paul, MN 55113
Tel.: 612-636-5820
Fax: 612-636-0916
Approx.Sls.: $15,200,000
Emp.: 150
Electrical Contractor
S.I.C.: 1731
Mahlon Christensen *(Pres. & Chief Exec. Officer)*
Gary Nelson *(V.P.)*
Randy Luhrs *(Treas.)*

Outside Service Firm(s):

McGladrey & Pullen*(Auditors)*
1800 Town Square, 445 Minnesota St.
St. Paul, MN 55101

Liberty State Bank*(Major Banking Relationship)*
St. Paul, MN

MUSKIN LEISURE PRODUCTS, INC.
(Sub. of Zodiac North America)
401 E. Thomas St.
Wilkes-Barre, PA 18705-3897
Tel.: 717-825-4501
Fax: 717-823-1150
Year Founded: 1991
Approx.Sls.: $40,000,000
Emp.: 400
Import Export
Mfr. of Above Ground Swimming Pools & Pool Access., Vacuum Formed Wading Pools
S.I.C.: 3949; 3589; 3089
Jean-Marc Dailance *(Pres.)*
Joseph P. Serieno *(Exec. V.P. & Gen. Mgr.)*
Jean-Pierre Parent *(V.P.-Opers.)*
Richard Raffaelli *(V.P.-Sls. & Mktg.)*
Leonard Tomchak *(Controller)*

MUSTANG MANUFACTURING COMPANY, INC.
Country Rd. 45 N
Owatonna, MN 55060
Mailing Address:
P.O. Box 547
Owatonna, MN 55060
Tel.: 507-451-7112
Telex: 933001
Fax: 507-451-8209
Approx.Sls.: $30,000,000
Emp.: 160
Fiscal Year-end: 6/30/91
Mfr. of Mustang Loaders
S.I.C.: 3531; 3537
Donald A. Kalkman *(Pres.)*
Stan Smith *(V.P.-Mfg.)*
Mike Spear *(V.P.-Mktg. & Sls.)*
Robert Tighe *(Controller)*
Bruce Collins *(Mgr.-Admin.)*

MUSTANG TRACTOR & EQUIP. CO.
12800 NW Freeway
Houston, TX 77040
Mailing Address:
P.O. Box 1373
Houston, TX 77251
Tel.: 713-460-2000
Fax: 713-462-4032
Year Founded: 1952
Approx.Sls.: $120,000,000
Emp.: 630
Fiscal Year-end: 11/30/92
Construction Equipment Dealer
S.I.C.: 5082; 3519; 3537; 3523; 3531
Leonard Martin *(Chm. Bd.)*
F. Louis Tucker Jr. *(Pres.)*
Douglas R. Fisk *(Exec. V.P. & Chief Oper. Officer)*
Bradford Tucker *(Exec. V.P. & Gen. Counsel)*
Stephen R. Christo *(Treas.)*
Jeffrey C. Alt *(Mgr.-Mktg.)*

Computer Systems/Hardware:
IBM 4341

Outside Service Firm(s):

Ernst & Young*(Auditors)*
1 Houston Ctr., 1200 McKinney
Houston, TX 77002
Tel.: 713-750-1500

ALTA Health Strategies*(Group Insurer)*
Phoenix, AZ

Childs, Fortenbach, Beck & Guyton*(Legal Firm)*
402 Pierce
Houston, TX 77002
Tel.: 713-659-6681

First City National Bank*(Major Banking Relationship)*
Houston, TX

First City National Bank*(Pension Manager)*
Houston, TX

Divisions:

Mustang Industrial Equipment Co. **(1)**
7607 Wallisville Rd.
Houston, TX 77020
Tel.: 713-675-1552
Lift Truck Div.
S.I.C.: 3537

Mustang Power Systems **(1)**
12800 N. W. Freeway
Houston, TX 77040
Tel.: 713-460-2000
Import Export
New Engine Sales
S.I.C.: 5084
Terry Sears *(Gen. Mgr.)*

MUTUAL OF AMERICA
(Formerly Mutual of America Life Insurance Company)
666 Fifth Ave.
New York, NY 10103
Tel.: 212-399-1600
S.I.C.: 6311
William J. Flynn *(Pres.)*
Manfred Altstadt *(Chief Fin. Officer & Sr. V.P.)*
Thomas J. Moran *(Chief Exec. Officer)*
Joan M. Casson *(Exec. V.P. & Chief Investment Officer)*
Stephanie J. Kopp *(Exec. V.P. & Sec.)*
Paul R. Zwilling *(Exec. V.P. & Chief Actuary)*

Mutual of America—(Continued)

Liane Bronstein *(Sr. V.P.)*
Allen J. Bruckheimer *(Sr. V.P. & Asst. Treas.)*
J. Thomas Burkard *(Sr. V.P.-Special Markets)*
John Cerrato *(Sr. V.P.-Corp. Services)*
William C. Conway *(Sr. V.P.)*
Rita Conyers *(Sr. V.P.-Corp. Communications & Exec. Training)*
William A. DeMilt *(Sr. V.P. & Treas.)*
Warren A. Essner *(Sr. V.P. & Auditor)*
Roger C. Ferrara *(Sr. V.P.-Fin. Advisory Services)*
Fiske Field *(Sr. V.P.- National Accts.)*
Vivian P. Giacini *(Sr. V.P.-Human Resources)*
Thomas Gilliam *(Sr. V.P.- Technical Opers.)*
Raymond J. Hayes *(Sr. V.P.-Real Estate Mngmt.)*
Gregory A. Kleva, Jr. *(Sr. V.P. & Deputy Gen. Counsel)*
John E. Manley *(Sr. V.P.-Fin. Advisory Services)*
Robert W. Maull *(Sr. V.P. & Actuary)*
Dolores J. Morrisey *(Sr. V.P.)*
Lynn M. Nadler *(Sr. V.P.-Technical Services)*
Roger F. Napoleon *(Sr. V.P. & Assoc. Gen. Counsel)*
Richard J. O'Brien *(Sr. V.P.- Pub. Rels.)*
Raymond C. Peterson *(Sr. V.P.- Systems)*
William G. Shannon *(Sr. V.P.- Individual Fin. Plng.)*
Thomas J. Varage *(Sr. V.P. & Chief Investment Officer)*
William R. White *(Sr. V.P.-Corp. Communications)*
Donald E. Wissell *(Sr. V.P.-Admin. Services)*

Subsidiaries:

American Life Insurance Company of New York **(1)**
666 Fifth Ave.
New York, NY 10103
Tel.: (212) 399-5555
Theodore L. Herman *(Vice Chairman)*
Howard Lichtenstein *(Pres. & Chief Oper. Officer)*
John E. Thompson *(V.P.)*
Evelyn F. Barrington *(Second V.P. & Asst. to Vice Chairman)*
Ann Richmond *(Second V.P.)*

Mutual of America Financial Services Corp. **(1)**
666 Fifth Ave.
New York, NY 10103
Tel.: (212) 399-1730
Ronald S. Scowby *(Pres.)*

National Pension Life Insurance Company **(1)**
666 Fifth Ave.
New York, NY 10103
Tel.: (212) 399-1600

MUTUAL BENEFIT LIFE INSURANCE COMPANY

(Undergoing Reorganization)
520 Broad St.
Newark, NJ 07102-3184
Tel.: 201-481-8000 **NJ**
Fax: 201-268-4262
Year Founded: 1845
Assets: $11,600,000,000
Earnings: $42,600,000
Liabilities: $11,188,500,000
Net Worth: $411,500,000
Approx.Rev.: $3,883,964,093
Emp.: 1,000
Fiscal Year-end: 12/31/91
Life & Health Insurance; Financial Services
S.I.C.: 6411; 6311

Victor Palmieri *(Chief Exec. Officer)*
Ken Watson *(Sr. Exec. V.P.-Fin. & Plng.)*
No. of U.S. Offices: 85

Computer Systems/Hardware:
IBM Systems 3081 & 3090

Outside Service Firm(s):

Bankers Trust Co.*(Major Banking Relationship)*
P.O. Box 318, Church St. Station
New York, NY 10008
Tel.: 212-454-2212
Fax: 212-454-2783

Subsidiaries:

MBL Holding Corporation **(1)**
520 Broad St.
Newark, NJ 07102
Tel.: 201-481-8000 (100%)
Holding Co.
S.I.C.: 6719

Subsidiaries:

Muben Realty Co. **(2)**
520 Broad St.
Newark, NJ 07101
Tel.: 201-481-8000 (100%)
Emp.: 8
Real Estate & Development
S.I.C.: 6531

Mutual Benefit Financial Service Co. **(2)**
290 Westminster St.
Providence, RI 02903
Tel.: 401-451-8600 (100%)
Broker-Dealer Securities
S.I.C.: 6211
Betsy Hickey *(Pres.)*

MBL Life Assurance Corp. **(1)**
520 Broad St.
Newark, NJ 07102
Tel.: 201-481-8000
S.I.C.: 6411

MUTUAL DISTRIBUTORS LTD.

320 C Waiakamilo Rd.
Honolulu, HI 96817
Mailing Address:
P.O. Box 3290,
Honolulu, HI 96817
Tel.: 808-847-5941 **HI**
Fax: 808-847-2487
Year Founded: 1958
Approx.Sls.: $15,000,000
Emp.: 65
Wholesale Nondurable Goods; Electrical Appliances; Paints, Paint Supplies & Automotive Items; Hardware & Automotive Aftermarket; Hand & Power Tools, Plumbing, Large Home Appliances, Televisions, VCR's, Camcorders, Household Telephones, Answering Machines, Cellular Telephones
S.I.C.: 5064; 5198; 5199; 5072; 5013
Jack Leong *(Chm. Bd., Pres. & Chief Exec. Officer)*
Bob Hong *(V.P.-Admin.)*
James Leong *(V.P.-Sls., Mktg. & Adv.)*
Robert Leong *(V.P.)*
Edith Leong *(Treas. & Sec.)*

Outside Service Firm(s):

Leong & Fong*(Auditors)*
Honolulu, HI

First Hawaiian Bank*(Major Banking Relationship)*
165 South King St.
Honolulu, HI 96813
Tel.: 808-525-5876
Fax: 808-525-5791

First Interstate Bank*(Major Banking Relationship)*
Honolulu, HI

Hawaii National Bank*(Major Banking Relationship)*
Honolulu, HI

THE MUTUAL LIFE INSURANCE COMPANY OF NEW YORK (MONY)

1740 Broadway
New York, NY 10019
Tel.: 212-708-2000 **NY**
Fax: 212-708-2399
Year Founded: 1842
Assets: $19,015,233,000
Earnings: $4,695,000,000
Liabilities: $9,066,568,250
Net Worth: $9,948,664,750
Approx.Premiums: $3,138,799,000
Emp.: 4,496
Fiscal Year-end: 12/31/90
Life Insurance, Annuities; Accident & Health Insurance; Disability Income, Pensions & Investment Management Services
S.I.C.: 6411; 6311; 6289; 6552; 6719; 6371; 6321
Corporate Giving Program: Gives to Innovative 501C3 Organizations in the Communities Where It Maintains Offices. Each Principal Site has Specific Funding Priorities
Employee Matching Gifts Program: Company Matches Gifts up to $1000 in Contributions Made by Eligible Employees & Sales Representatives Throughout the U.S.
James B. Farley *(Chm. Bd.)*
Gordon E. Perry *(Vice Chm.)*
Floyd L. Smith *(Vice Chm.)*
Michael I. Roth *(Pres., Chief Oper. Officer & Chief Exec. Officer)*
Michael J. Drabb *(Exec. V.P.- Investment Mngmt.)*
Samuel J. Foti *(Exec. V.P.-Insurance Opers.)*
Weaver H. Gaines, Jr. *(Exec. V.P. & Gen. Counsel)*
Kenneth M. Levine *(Exec. V.P. & Chief Investment Officer)*
Thomas J. Conklin *(Sr. V.P. & Sec.)*
Richard Daddario *(Sr. V.P. & Chief Fin. Officer)*
Louis J. LaFontaine *(Sr. V.P.-Corp. Affairs)*
Richard E. Mulroy *(Sr. V.P. & Gen. Counsel)*
Tom A. Schlossberg *(Sr. V.P.- Pension Opers.)*
Theodore J. Shalack *(Sr. V.P.- Insurance Opers.)*
Kihong Sung *(Sr. V.P. & Chief Actuary)*

Computer Systems/Hardware:
IBM Systems 36 & 3777

Outside Service Firm(s):

Coopers & Lybrand*(Auditors)*
1301 Avenue of The Americas
New York, NY 10019
Tel.: 212-536-2000

Citibank N.A.*(Major Banking Relationship)*
Corporate Trust Services, 399 Park Ave.
New York, NY 10043
Tel.: 212-559-1605

First Chicago Shareholder Services Trust Co.*(Major Banking Relationship)*
153 West 51st St.
New York, NY 10019
Tel.: 212-791-6422
Fax: 212-385-9798

Subsidiaries:

Bell Investment Acquisition Corporation **(1)**
418 6th Ave., Ste. 240
Des Moines, IA 50309
Tel.: 515-280-4115
Thomas Steen *(Pres.)*

The Enterprise Group **(1)**
1200 Ashwood Pky., Ste. 290
Atlanta, GA 30338
Tel.: 404-396-8118
Victor Ugolyn *(Pres. & Chief Exec. Officer)*

MONY Advisers, Inc. **(1)**
1740 Broadway
New York, NY 10019
Tel.: 212-708-2960 (100%)
Approx.Rev.: $28,918
Investment Adviser
S.I.C.: 6282
John V. Rock *(Pres.)*

MONY Brokerage, Inc. **(1)**
P.O. Box 8009,
Harrisburg, PA 17105
Tel.: 717-541-8164
Tel.: 800-487-6244
Fax: 717-541-8370
Walter R. White *(Pres.)*
Paul Lightcap *(V.P.)*

MONY Credit Corporation **(1)**
West Bldg., 500 Frank W. Burr Blvd.
Teaneck, NJ 07666-6888
Tel.: 201-907-6599
Theodore J. Shalack *(Chief Exec. Officer)*

MONY CS, Inc. **(1)**
9810 FM 1960, Bypass Ste. 270
Humble, TX 77338
Tel.: 713-548-3580
Fax: 713-548-3582
J. Keith Baker *(Pres.)*

MONY Funding, Inc. **(1)**
1740 Broadway
New York, NY 10019
Tel.: 212-708-2634
Kenneth M. Levine *(Pres.)*

MONY Life Insurance Co. of America **(1)**
500 Frank W. Burr Blvd.
Teaneck, NJ 07666
Tel.: 201-907-6669 (100%)
Approx.Premiums: $18,632,915
Life Insurance, Annuities
S.I.C.: 6411
David S. Waldman *(Sec.)*

MONY Realty Partners, Inc. **(1)**
Frank W. Burr Blvd.
Teaneck, NJ 07666
Tel.: 201-907-6669
Charles A. Coolidge, III *(Pres.)*

MONY Securities Corp. **(1)**
MONY Glenpointe Centre West, 500 Frank W. Burr Blvd., MD 75-26
Teaneck, NJ 07666
Tel.: 201-907-5712
Lawrence F. Sherman *(Pres.)*

MONY Securities Corp. **(1)**
1740 Broadway
New York, NY 10019
Tel.: 212-708-2000 (100%)
Approx.Rev.: $599,792
Broker-Dealer
S.I.C.: 6211
Lawrence F. Sherman *(Pres.)*

MONY TAX Consulting Services, Inc. **(1)**
1740 Broadway
New York, NY 10019
Tel.: 212-708-2036
Richard C. Scott *(Pres.)*

Subsidiary:

1740 Ventures, Inc. **(2)**
1740 Broadway
New York, NY 10019
Tel.: 212-708-2000 (100%)
Approx.Rev.: $66,032
Real Estate Investment & Devel. Co.
S.I.C.: 6552
Norcross Teel *(Pres.)*

MUTUAL MANUFACTURING & SUPPLY CO.

3300 Spring Grove Ave.
Cincinnati, OH 45225
Tel.: 513-541-2330
Fax: 513-681-0900
Approx.Sls.: $36,000,000
Emp.: 205
Wholesale Plumbing, Heating & Industrial Supplies
S.I.C.: 5074; 5075

A.P. Barton, Jr. *(Chm. Bd., Pres. & Chief Exec. Officer)*
James Foley *(V.P.-Sls.)*
Carol Liebisch *(Dir.-Mngmt. Information Systems)*
John Robinson *(Mgr.-Opers.)*
James Sharpe *(Mgr.-Pur.)*

Computer Systems/Hardware:
IBM System 38

Outside Service Firm(s):

Ernst & Young*(Auditors)*
1300 Chiquita Center, 250 E. Fifth St.
Cincinnati, OH 45202
Tel.: 513-621-6454

The Central Trust Company, N.A.*(Major Banking Relationship)*
Cincinnati, OH
Tel.: 513-651-8896

MUTUAL OF OMAHA INSURANCE COMPANY
Mutual of Omaha Plaza
Omaha, NE 68175
Tel.: 402-342-7600 **NE**
Fax: 402-978-2775
Year Founded: 1909
Assets: $2,488,202,463
Earnings: $27,261,924
Liabilities: $1,742,996,386
Net Worth: $745,206,077
Approx.Sls.: $2,019,420,260
Emp.: 5,742
Fiscal Year-end: 12/31/91
Accident & Health Insurance
S.I.C.: 6321
Corporate Giving Program: The Recipient Organization Must Have Proper IRS Not-For-Profit Standing. The Companies Will Give Careful Consideration to Umbrella Fund-Raising Organizations Such as United Way. The Companies Will Generally Not Grant Requests for gifts if Services, Materials, or Use of Company Equipment or Systems Services, Materials or Use of Company Equipment or System
Employee Matching Gifts Program: Public & Private Schools are Eligible for the Program as Long as they Meet the Standards at the Time of the Companies' Donation. The Maximum Matching Gift is $1,000 in any Calandar Year.
Thomas J. Skutt *(Chm. Bd. & Chief Exec. Officer)*
John W. Weekly *(Pres. & Chief Oper. Officer)*
G. Ronald Ames *(Sr. Exec. V.P. & Dir.-Mktg. Opers.)*
Cecil D. Bykerk *(Sr. Exec. V.P. & Chief Actuary)*
Donald J. Goaley *(Sr. Exec. V.P.-Casualty & Canadian Opers.)*
Ernest B. Johnston *(Sr. Exec. V.P. & Dir.-Opers.)*
John L. Maginn *(Sr. Exec. V.P., Chief Investment Officer & Treas.)*
Richard J. Sampson *(Sr. Exec. V.P. & Dir.-Grp. Oper.)*
Thomas T. Sawicz *(Sr. Exec. V.P. & Dir.-Supplemental Distr.)*
John A. Sturgeon *(Sr. Exec. V.P. & Gen. Comptroller)*
Jerry E. Furlong *(Exec. V.P. & Asst. to Chm.)*
Lawrence F. Harr *(Exec. V.P. & Chief Counsel)*
Dwain R. Horn *(Exec. V.P. & Dir.-Grp. Pensions)*
M. Jane Huerter *(Exec. V.P. & Corp. Sec.)*
Michael J. Jareske *(Exec. V.P. & Dir.-Grp. Fin. Reporting & Admin. Services)*
Burton D. Jay *(Exec. V.P. & Actuary)*
Stephen E. Kohoskie *(Exec. V.P. & Dir.-Grp. Mktg.)*
David R. LaFayette *(Exec. V.P. & Chief Agent-Canada)*
William C. Mattox *(Exec. V.P.-Fed. Govt. Affairs)*
Thomas J. McCusker *(Exec. V.P. & Counsel to Chm. & Pres.)*
David R. Pepple *(Exec. V.P. & Dir.-Computer Data Services Opers.)*
Charles J. Stack *(Exec. V.P. & Dir.-Personnel Div.)*
E.L. Sulentic *(Exec. V.P. & Dir.-Admin. Opers.)*
Milton L. Brock, Jr. *(Sr. V.P. & Dir.-Agency Sls.)*
Terry A. Calek *(V.P. & Dir.-Pub. Affairs)*
Joseph E. Pittman *(Pub. Rels. Coord.)*
Amy Protexter *(Pub. Rels. Coord.)*

No. of Foreign Offices: 9

Computer Systems/Hardware:
IBM

Outside Service Firm(s):

Mutual of Omaha Insurance Company*(Group Insurer)*
Mutual of Omaha Plaza,
Omaha, NE 68175
Tel.: 800-228-7775

Subsidiaries:

Fund Management Co. **(1)**
10235 Regency Ct.
Omaha, NE 68114
Tel.: 402-397-8555

Omaha Property & Casualty Co. **(1)**
3102 Farnam St.
Omaha, NE 68131
Tel.: 402-342-3326
Fax: 402-978-2650
Approx.Sls.: $110,515,154
Emp.: 147
Property & Casualty Insurance
S.I.C.: 6331
Eric Lundby *(Pres.)*
Gordon E. Jensen *(V.P., Treas., Comptroller & Asst. Sec.)*
Edward L. Felchner *(V.P. & Dir.-Product Devel., Mktg. & Underwriting Opers.)*

United World Life Insurance Company **(1)**
Dodge at 33rd
Omaha, NE 68175
Tel.: 402-978-5127 (100%)
Approx.Sls.: $9,901,802
Insurance
S.I.C.: 6399
Thomas J. Skutt *(Chm. Bd.)*
Thomas T. Sawicz *(Pres.)*
Mark L. Prauner *(V.P.-Acct.)*
John E. Thomas *(V.P.-Mktg.)*

Affiliates:

Companion Life Insurance Co. **(1)**
401 Theodore Fremd Ave.
Rye, NY 10580-1493
Tel.: 914-921-0350 (100%)
Fax: 914-935-8475
Approx.Sls.: $39,492,448
Emp.: 66
Insurance
S.I.C.: 6311
Ernest B. Johnston *(Pres.)*
Daniel Varona *(Chief Admin. Officer, Sec. & Gen. Counsel)*

Health America/CapitalCare, Inc. **(1)**
220 S. 17th St.
Lincoln, NE 68508
Tel.: 402-473-7872
Approx.Sls.: $18,364,299
Emp.: 137
Health Insurance; HMO
S.I.C.: 6321
Dick L. Easley *(Chm. Bd. & Pres.)*
Kenneth W. Klaasmeyer *(V.P. & Chief Oper. Officer)*
Robert J. Kruml *(Chief Fin. Officer & Treas.)*

Kirkpatrick Pettis **(1)**
10250 Regency Cir., Ste. 200
Omaha, NE 68114
Tel.: 402-397-5777 (100%)
Fax: 402-393-7935
Approx.Sls.: $19,056,000
Emp.: 201
Investment Banking & Securities, Brokerage & Money Management
S.I.C.: 6799
L.C. Petersen *(Chm. Bd. & Chief Exec. Officer)*
Randall D. Greer *(Pres. & Chief Oper. Officer)*
Robert E. Brady *(Exec. V.P. & Dir.-Sls. & Mktg.)*
Rodney D. Cerny *(Exec. V.P. & Chief Investment Officer)*
Robert F. Kathol *(Exec. V.P. & Dir.-Investment Banking)*
Lamar S. Jones *(Sr. V.P., Chief Fin. Officer, Sec. & Dir.-Admin.)*

Mutual of Omaha **(1)**
Mutual of Omaha Plaza
Omaha, NE 68175
Tel.: 402-342-7600 (100%)
Fiscal Year-end: 12/31/91
Life Insurance
S.I.C.: 6311
Thomas J. Skutt *(Chm. Bd. & Chief Exec. Officer)*
John W. Weekly *(Pres. & Chief Oper. Officer)*
G. Ronald Ames *(Sr. Exec. V.P. & Dir.-Mktg. Opers.)*
Cecil D. Bykerk *(Sr. Exec. V.P. & Chief Actuary)*
Donald J. Goaley *(Sr. Exec. V.P.-Casualty & Canadian Opers.)*
Ernest B. Johnston *(Sr. Exec. V.P.-Opers.)*
John L. Maginn *(Sr. Exec. V.P., Chief Investment Officer & Treas.)*
Richard J. Sampson *(Sr. Exec. V.P. & Dir.-Grp. Opers.)*
Thomas T. Sawicz *(Sr. Exec. V.P. & Dir.-Supplemental Distr.)*
John A. Sturgeon *(Sr. Exec. V.P. & Gen. Comptroller)*
Lawrence F. Harr *(Exec. V.P. & Chief Counsel)*
Dwaine R. Horn *(Exec. V.P.& Dir.-Grp. Pensions)*
M. Jane Huerter *(Exec. V.P. & Corp. Sec.)*
Burton D. Jay *(Exec. V.P. & Chief Actuary)*
Stephen E. Kohoskie *(Exec. V.P. & Dir.-Grp. Mktg.)*
Thomas J. McCusker *(Exec. V.P. & Counsel to Chm. & Pres.)*
David R. Pepple *(Exec. V.P. & Dir.-Computer Data Services)*
E.L. Sulentic *(Exec. V.P. & Dir.-Admin.)*
Charles J. Stack *(Exec. V.P. & Dir.-Personnel)*
Jerry E. Furlong *(Exec. V.P. & Asst. to Chm.)*
David R. LaFayette *(Exec. V.P. & Chief Agent-Canada)*
William C. Mattox *(Exec. V.P.-Fed. Govt. Affairs)*
Milton L. Brock, Jr. *(Sr. V.P. & Dir.-Agency Sls.)*
Terry A. Calek *(V.P. & Dir.-Pub. Affairs)*
Ronald W. Leach *(V.P. & Deputy Dir.-Agency Sls. Div.)*
Douglas H. Parr *(V.P. & Dir.-Materials Procurement & Mngmt.)*
James R. Getscher *(V.P. & Mgr.-Admin. Services)*
Clifford E. Lord *(V.P. & Dir.-Quality Devel.)*

Mutual of Omaha Fund Management Co. **(1)**
10235 Regency Cir.
Omaha, NE 68114
Tel.: 402-397-8555
Tel.: 800-228-9596 (100%)
Fax: 402-397-3836
Approx.Sls.: $13,352,917
Emp.: 87
Mutual Funds
S.I.C.: 6722
Thomas J. Skutt *(Chm. Bd.)*
John M. Delich *(Chief Exec. Officer)*
J. Paul Erickson *(Pres. & Chief Oper. Officer)*
Michael P. Manning *(Sr. Exec. V.P. & Chief Investment Officer)*
Larry Pence *(V.P.-Sls.)*
Eugenia M. Simpson *(V.P., Dir.-Res. & Portfolio Mgr.)*

Omaha Property & Casualty **(1)**
3102 Farnam St.
Omaha, NE 68131
Tel.: 402-342-3326
Fax: 402-978-2650
Auto & Homeowners Insurance
S.I.C.: 6331
J. Eric Lundby *(Pres.)*
Gordon E. Jensen *(V.P.-Comptroller, Treas. & Asst. Sec.)*
Edward L. Felchner *(V.P. & Dir.-Prdouct Devel., Mktg. & Underwriting)*

Tele-Trip Co. **(1)**
Mutual Of Omaha Plaza
Omaha, NE 68175
Tel.: 402-345-2400 (100%)
Approx.Sls.: $13,410,171
Emp.: 188
Travel Insurance
S.I.C.: 6399
Thomas T. Sawicz *(Pres.)*
Jim White *(V.P., Treas. & Chief Fin. Officer)*
Holly Richmond *(V.P. & Dir.-Mktg.)*

Mutual Service Insurance
(Name Changed to MSI Insurance Companies)

MUTUAL TRADING CO., INC.
431 Crocker St.
Los Angeles, CA 90013
Tel.: 213-626-9458 **CA**
Fax: 213-626-5130
Year Founded: 1926
Assets: $10,473,151
Liabilities: $6,624,171
Net Worth: $3,848,980
Approx.Sls.: $35,000,000
Emp.: 120
Fiscal Year-end: 12/31/90
Wholesaler Japanese Foods
S.I.C.: 5149
Noritoshi Kanai *(Pres.)*
Seicho Fujikawa *(V.P.)*
Yasuo Katsumata *(V.P.)*
Mori Shigeru *(V.P.)*
Kotaro Hoshizaki *(Treas. & Sec.)*
Nakamura Tetsujiro *(Gen. Counsel)*
Katsumata Yasuo *(Dir.-Pur.)*
Principal(s):
Noritoshi Kanai

Outside Service Firm(s):

Kaz Yamamoto*(Auditors)*
Los Angeles, CA

Union Bank*(Major Banking Relationship)*
Trust Dept., 8155 Mercury Ct.
San Diego, CA 92112
Tel.: 619-230-4487

MUTUAL WELDING CO., LTD
739 Ahua
Honolulu, HI 96819
Tel.: 808-839-5111 **HI**
Fax: 808-833-9534
Year Founded: 1949
Approx.Sls.: $12,000,000
Emp.: 120
Structural Steel Fabrication & Erection, Miscellaneous Iron, Steel, Tanks, U.L.-A.P.I-A.S.M.E. Prefab Steel Buildings
S.I.C.: 3441; 3443; 3448
Thomas T.W. Chun *(Pres.)*
Rupert K. Chun *(Exec. V.P.)*
Tai Vee Chun *(V.P.-Prod.)*
Clyde H. Yagi *(Dir.-Data Processing, Sec. & Treas.)*
William Cooper *(Mgr.-Traffic & Pur. Agent)*
Principal(s):
Thomas T.W. Chun
Rupert K. Chun
Tai Vee Chun
Loretta M. Chun

No. of Mfg. Plants/Facilities: 1
No. of U.S. Offices: 1

Outside Service Firm(s):

Ishimoto Imamoto & Co.*(Auditors)*
Honolulu, HI

Liberty Bank & Trust*(Major Banking Relationship)*
Honolulu, HI

MY OWN MEALS, INC.
400 Lake Cook Rd.
Deerfield, IL 60015
Mailing Address:
P.O. Box 334,
Deerfield, IL 60015
Tel.: 708-948-1118 **DE**
Fax: 708-948-0468
Year Founded: 1986
Fiscal Year-end: 12/31/91
Export

My Own Meals, Inc.—(Continued)

Mfr. of Quality Shelf Stable Kosher Meals
S.I.C.: 2099
Mary Anne Jackson *(Chm., Pres. & Chief Oper. Officer)*
Elizabeth A. Doyle *(V.P.-Admin. & Production & Corp. Sec.)*
Alice Mikkelsen *(Dir.-Mktg. Services)*
Lynda Bigda *(Mgr.-Sls.)*
Chuck Courtney *(Govt. Affairs)*
Cathy Frangos *(Adv., Traffic & Media Planner)*

Computer Systems/Hardware:
IBM

Outside Service Firm(s):

Price Waterhouse*(Auditors)*
200 E. Randolph
Chicago, IL 60601
Tel.: 312-565-1500

Llama Co.*(Investment Banker)*
Fayetteville, AR

Butler, Rubin, Newcomer, Saltarelli & Boyd*(Legal Firm)*
3 First National Plaza, 70 W. Madison St., Ste. 1505
Chicago, IL 60602
Tel.: 312-444-9660

Subsidiary:

J & M Advertising **(1)**
400 Lake Cook Road
Deerfield, IL 60015
Tel.: 708-948-1290

MYERS & ASSOCIATES, INC.
3727 S.E. Ocean Blvd., Ste. 203
Stuart, FL 34996
Tel.: 407-287-1990
Fax: 407-287-1995
Year Founded: 1973
Approx.Billings: $12,100,000
Emp.: 8
Corporate, Business-to-Business, Direct Response, Financial, Public Relations
Kip Myers *(Pres. & Creative Dir.)*

THE MYERS GROUP (U.S) INC.
Myers Bldg., 72 Lake St.
Rouses Point, NY 12979-1091
Tel.: 518-297-2222 **NY**
Fax: 518-297-6650
Year Founded: 1860
Emp.: 602
Door-to-Door Transportation Package; Customs Clearance, Domestic Transportation, Air & Ocean Freight Forwarding, NVOCC, Warehousing & Distribution, EDI, Chartering & Insurance; Offices at All Major U.S. Ports of Entry Including Along the Canadian & Mexican Borders; Also Has a Worldwide Network of Affiliated Service Providers to Handle Import/Export Services for All Major Trade Lanes
S.I.C.: 4731; 4213; 4412; 4491; 4512; 4225; 4226
William R. Casey *(Chm. Bd. & Chief Exec. Officer)*
Kevin C. O'Shea *(Co-Pres.)*
Richard T. Casey *(Co-Pres.)*
Gregory L. MacConnell *(V.P.-Mktg. & Plng.)*
Roslyn Duley *(Controller)*

No. of U.S. Offices: 49

Subsidiaries:

F.W. Myers & Co. **(1)**
Myers Bldg., 72 Lake St.
Rouses Point, NY 12979
Tel.: 518-297-2222
Fax: 518-297-6650
Door-to-Door Transportation Package; Customs Clearance, Domestic Transportation, Air & Ocean Freight Forwardimg. NVOCC, Warehousing & Distribution, EDI, Chartering & Insurance, Offices at All Major U.S. Ports of Entry Including the Canadian & Mexican Borders; also Has a Worldwide Network of Affiliated Service Providers to Handle Import/Export Services for All Major Trade Lanes
S.I.C.: 4731; 4213; 4412; 4491; 4512; 4225; 4226
Richard T. Casey *(Pres.)*

Myers Group U.S., Inc. **(1)**
Myers Bldg., 72 Lake St.
Rouses Point, NY 12979
Tel.: 518-297-2222
Fax: 518-297-6650
Door-to-Door Transportation Package; Customs Clearance, Domestic Transportation, Air & Ocean Freight Forwarding, NVOCC, Warehousing & Distribution, EDI, Chartering & Insurance, Offices at All Major U.S. Ports of Entry Including the Canadian & Mexican Borders; Also Has a Worldwide Network of Affiliated Service Providers to Handle Import/Export Services for All Major Trade Lanes
S.I.C.: 4731; 4213; 4412; 4491; 4512; 4225; 4226
Kevin C. O'Shea *(Pres.)*

C. C. MYERS, INC.
3286 Fitzgerald Rd.
Rancho Cordova, CA 95742
Tel.: 916-635-9370 **CA**
Fax: 916-635-2734
Year Founded: 1977
Sales Range: $100-499 Million
Emp.: 400
Heavy Engineering & Bridge Contractor
S.I.C.: 1622
C.C. Myers *(Pres. & Chief Exec. Officer)*
Gary Janco *(Exec. V.P.)*
Carl Bauer *(Chief Oper. Officer)*
Linda J. Clifford *(Chief Fin. Officer, Treas. & Real Estate Dir.)*
Delores Lewis *(Sec.)*

Principal(s):
C.C. Myers

No. of U.S. Offices: 2

Computer Systems/Hardware:
IBM/PAC

Outside Service Firm(s):

S. J. Gallina & Co.*(Auditors)*
Sacramento, CA

Corroon & Black*(Group Insurer)*
San Francisco, CA

Wells Fargo Bank*(International Bank Affiliate)*
Sacramento, CA

McDonough, Holland & Allen*(Legal Firm)*
Sacramento, CA

Wells Fargo Bank*(Major Banking Relationship)*
Sacramento, CA

BEN MYERSON CANDY COMPANY, INC.
928 Towne Ave.
Los Angeles, CA 90021
Tel.: 213-623-6266 **CA**
Fax: 213-624-4948
Year Founded: 1951
Approx.Sls.: $100,000,000
Emp.: 360
Export
Wine; Neutral Spirits; Fruits; Candied, Crystallized or Glazed; Candy Bars, Including Chocolate Covered Bars
S.I.C.: 5182; 2064
Robert Myerson *(Chm. Bd.)*
James Parker Myerson *(Pres.)*
Evans Malanga *(V.P.)*
James Myerson *(Treas. & Sec.)*

Outside Service Firm(s):

Union Bank*(Major Banking Relationship)*
3810 Wilshire Blvd.
Los Angeles, CA 90010
Tel.: 213-480-6566

MYRICK CONSTRUCTION INC.
Shady Oak Dr.
Biscoe, NC 27209
Mailing Address:
P.O. Box 728
Biscoe, NC 27209
Tel.: 919-428-2106 **NC**
Fax: 919-428-9645
Year Founded: 1968
Approx.Sls.: $40,000,000
Emp.: 375
General Contractors Industrial & Commercial Buildings
S.I.C.: 1541; 1542
Bobby H. Myrick *(Pres. & Treas.)*
W. Parker Canady *(V.P.-Pur. & Engrng.)*
James Jackson *(V.P.-Opers.)*
B. Harold Myrick, Jr. *(V.P. & Sec.)*
Charles Myrick *(V.P.-Sls.)*
Norman Hartis *(Controller)*

Outside Service Firm(s):

J. B. Watson*(Auditors)*
Asheboro, NC

MYRON MANUFACTURING CORPORATION
205 Maywood Ave.
Maywood, NJ 07607
Tel.: 201-843-6464
Fax: 201-843-8390
Sales Range: $40-59 Million
Emp.: 600
Vinyl Covered Calendars & Advertising Specialties
S.I.C.: 2782
Myron Adler *(Chief Exec. Officer)*
Michael Adler *(Pres.)*
Roberta Glucksman *(V.P.-Mktg. Services)*
M. Adler Kravecas *(V.P.-Mktg.)*
Gwen Zaffe *(Treas.)*
Elaine Adler *(Sec.)*
Craig Van Tatenhove *(Dir.-Mfg.)*

Outside Service Firm(s):

National Westminster Bank plc*(Major Banking Relationship)*
One Exchange Place
Jersey City, NJ 07303
Tel.: 201-547-7000

N E D CORP.
18 Grafton St.
Worcester, MA 01604
Tel.: 508-798-8546
Fax: 508-799-2796
Emp.: 82
Diamond Cutting Tools For Turning, Boring & Burnishing
S.I.C.: 3545
Peter F. Wyatt *(Pres.)*
Paul A. La Forte *(V.P.)*
George A. White, Jr. *(Treas.)*

Outside Service Firm(s):

Fleet National Bank*(Major Banking Relationship)*
Worcester, MA

NBBJ
55 Nationwide Blvd.
Columbus, OH 43215
Tel.: 614-224-7145
Fax: 614-224-0218
Year Founded: 1943
Approx.Sls.: $56,062,000
Emp.: 500
Architectural Services, Interior Design, Management & Planning Services, Project & Cost Management, Graphic Design, Retail Planning, Land Planning & Landscape Architecture
S.I.C.: 8712; 8742; 7389
Friedrich K.M. Bohm *(Mng. Partner)*
Michael Ball *(Dir.-Mktg.)*

Principal(s):
Friedrich K.M. Bohm
William J. Bain, Jr.
Lawrence Helman
David C. Hoedemaker
James O. Jonassen
John R. Pangrazio
David R. Zimmerman

No. of U.S. Offices: 9

Outside Service Firm(s):

Deloitte & Touche*(Auditors)*
155 E. Broad St.
Columbus, OH 43215
Tel.: 614-221-1000
Fax: 614-229-4647

Bricker & Eckler*(Legal Firm)*
100 E. Broad St.
Columbus, OH 43215
Tel.: 614-227-2300

The Huntington National Bank*(Major Banking Relationship)*
41 S. High St.
Columbus, OH 43216

Subsidiaries:

NBBJ/LPA **(1)**
3780 Wilshire Blvd., Ste. 300
Los Angeles, CA 90010
Tel.: 213-738-7655
Architectural Services
S.I.C.: 8712

NBBJ-Rosenfield **(1)**
58 W. 40th St.
New York, NY 10018
Tel.: 212-391-9010
Architectural Services
S.I.C.: 8712

NBO STORES INC.
(Sub. of Dylex Holdings Inc.)
33-00 Broadway
Fair Lawn, NJ 07410
Tel.: 201-794-9400
Year Founded: 1984
Approx.Sls.: $102,000,000
Emp.: 1,000
Men's Clothing Stores
S.I.C.: 5611
Eugene Kosack *(Chief Exec. Officer)*
Barry Miller *(Chief Fin. Officer)*
Cynthia McNamara *(Controller)*
Alan Hecht *(Dir.-Mktg.)*

NFM CREATIVE COMMUNICATIONS
1340 Three Gateway Ctr.
Pittsburgh, PA 15222
Tel.: 412-394-6400
Fax: 412-394-6411
Year Founded: 1987
Approx.Billings: $13,150,000
Emp.: 12
Vendor & Sports Advertising
John P. Foley *(Pres.)*
Judith K. Foley *(Partner)*

NFO RESEARCH, INC.
2 Pickwick Plaza
Greenwich, CT 06830
Tel.: 203-629-8888
Year Founded: 1946
Approx.Sls.: $50,000,000
Emp.: 800
Fiscal Year-end: 12/31/91
Market Research Services
S.I.C.: 7389
Corporate Giving Program: United Way; Red Cross

William E. Lipner *(Pres. & Chief Exec. Officer)*
Alan L. Harvey *(Exec. V.P.-Fin.)*
Richard A. Spitzer *(Exec. V.P.-Opers.)*
Lawrence D. White *(Exec. V.P.-Mktg.)*
Robert F. Ampthor *(V.P.)*
David H. Anderson *(V.P.-Information Services)*
Candace S. Burch *(V.P.-Human Resources)*
Jennifer S. Clarke *(V.P.-Opers. Plng.)*
Diane M. Gerald *(V.P.)*
David J. Gorman *(V.P. & Controller)*
Jonathan K. Harding *(V.P.)*
Laurie L. Harris *(V.P.-Mktg.)*
Bruce E. Johnson *(V.P.-Res. Services)*
Diane F. Kosobud *(V.P.-Interviewing Services)*
Donald J. Morrison *(V.P.)*
Karen A. Stanley *(V.P.)*
Nancy J. Tope *(V.P.-Estimating & Project Control)*
Brent White *(V.P.)*
Eileen C. Wolford *(V.P.)*
Melanie Mumper *(Mgr.-Mktg. Services)*

Division:

National Yellow Pages Monitor (NYPM) **(1)**
785 Market St.
San Francisco, CA 94103
Tel.: 415-543-2200 (100%)
Audience Measurement for Yellow Pages
S.I.C.: 7389
Mary Ann Packo *(Pres.)*

NKH&W, Inc.

NKH&W, INC.
600 Broadway
Kansas City, MO 64015
Mailing Address:
P.O. Box 410977,
Kansas City, MO 64141
Tel.: 816-842-8881
Fax: 816-842-6340
Year Founded: 1981
Approx.Billings: $20,667,000
Emp.: 41
Business-to-Business Adv.
F. Peter Kovac *(Pres., Chief Exec. Officer)*
C.W. (Chuc) Barnes, III *(Chief Oper. Officer)*
Paul J. Welsh *(Exec. V.P.)*
J. David Tinnen *(V.P., Dir. Pub. Rels.)*
Reg Rowe *(Sr. Pub. Rels. Supvr.)*
Clarence N. Foxworthy *(Treas.)*

NMC OF NORTH AMERICA, INC.
501 NMC Drive
Zebulon, NC 27597
Tel.: 919-269-6500 **DE**
Fax: 919-269-7936
Year Founded: 1979
Emp.: 100
Fiscal Year-end: 12/31/90
Manufacture Packaging for Polyethelene Foam; Consumer Sports & Leisure Products
S.I.C.: 3086; 3089
Frederick Bowers *(Chm. Bd.)*
Marc Noel *(Pres. & Chief Exec. Officer)*
Edward Lauer *(V.P.)*
John B. Leeming *(V.P.)*

No. of Mfg. Plants/Facilities: 1
No. of U.S. Offices: 2

Computer Systems/Hardware:
NCR

Outside Service Firm(s):

Andy Bodane Accounting Firm*(Auditors)*
Rolly, NC

Subsidiary:

NCM Decoration, Inc. **(1)**
501 NCM Drive
Zebulon, NC 27597
Tel.: 914-269-7936

NPS CORPORATION
25 Chobot Lane
Elmwood Park, NJ 07407
Tel.: 201-794-9111 **NJ**
Fax: 201-794-9165
Year Founded: 1974
Sales Range: $100-499 Million
Emp.: 300
Plumbing, Heating & Air Conditioning Contractor; Manufacture Fabricated Pipe; Distribute Industial Supplies, Engineering Equipment; General Contractor Industiral & Commercial Buildings.
S.I.C.: 8711; 1711; 3498; 5085; 1542; 1541
Colin Halpern *(Chm. Bd. & Pres.)*

NRM CORPORATION
400 W. Railroad St.
Columbiana, OH 44408
Tel.: 216-253-2525
Approx.Sls.: $40,000,000
Emp.: 200
Fiscal Year-end: 12/31/90
Mfr. Machinery for Production of Steel Belting, Turnkey Extrusion Systems; Computer Process Control Systems; Retreading Equipment; Cold Feed Extruders
S.I.C.: 3559; 3541; 3542; 3823
John D. Vazzana *(Chm. Bd.)*
Richard K. Harr *(V.P.-Fin. & Treas.)*
Brian R. Fetzer *(V.P.-Procurement & Production)*

Subsidiary:

NRM-Steelastic **(1)**
1557 Industrial Pkwy.
Akron, OH 44310
Tel.: 216-633-0505
Tel.: 800-234-WE-SERVE
Fax: 216-633-0527
Emp.: 800
Fiscal Year-end: 3/31/91
Tire Tread Application Equipment; Orbitread Process/Flexcure; Systems for the Production of Steel Breaker Belts & Steel Body Ply Material; Rubber & Plastic Extruders; Process Control Systems; Tire Building Machinery; Hydraulic Tire Presses; Fabric Calendering Systems; Retreading Equipment; Recycling Machines for Rubber & Plastics
S.I.C.: 7534
John D. Vazzana *(Chm. Bd., Pres. & Chief Exec. Officer)*
James M. Myers *(Vice Chm.)*
Richard Harr *(Sr. V.P.-Fin.)*
John L. McCormick *(Sr. V.P.-Tire Equip. & Sls.)*
Edward M. Spear *(Sr. V.P.-Customer Support)*
David Caniglia *(Dir.-Adv.)*

NTC GROUP
Three Pickwick Plaza
Greenwich, CT 06830
Tel.: 203-862-2800 **DE**
Fax: 203-622-6538
Approx.Rev.: $570,000,000
Emp.: 8,000
Fiscal Year-end: 12/31/90
Financial-Leverage Buyouts, Holding Company for Textiles, Inorganic Chemicals & Transmissions
S.I.C.: 6282; 6289; 2281; 2211; 2221; 2819; 3462
Thomas C. Foley *(Chm. Bd. & Chief Exec. Officer)*
Kurt A. Herwald *(V.P.-Fin.)*
Randi Hanover *(Controller & Mgr.-Office)*

Outside Service Firm(s):

Arthur Andersen & Co.*(Auditors)*
133 Peachtree St., N.E.
Atlanta, GA 30303
Tel.: 404-658-1776

Subsidiaries:

The Bibb Company **(1)**
237 Coliseum Dr.
Macon, GA 31201
Tel.: 912-752-6700
Fax: 912-752-6734
Earnings: $6,366,000
Approx.Sls.: $226,819,000
Emp.: 4,500
Fiscal Year-end: 3/31/91
Computer Systems/Hardware:
IBM; Hewlett-Packard; Bell
Manufacture of Apparel Fabrics, Engineered Products for Industrial Use & Consumer Products
S.I.C.: 2281
Thomas H. Foley *(Chm. Bd.)*
Alan V. Davis *(Pres. & Chief Oper. Officer)*
Dennis L. Wolforth *(Sr. V.P. & Chief Fin. Officer)*
R. Steve Boyter *(Sr. V.P.-Mfg.)*
Lindsey L. Crosby *(Sr. V.P.)*
Donald G. Vereen *(V.P.-Fin. & Treas.)*
Lowell Belk *(V.P.-Admin. & Sec.)*
Frank Sheehan *(V.P.-Indus. Rels.)*
Tim Adams *(Gen. Counsel)*
Robert E. Bridgeman *(Asst. Sec.)*
Joe Wunsch *(Dir.-Pur.)*
Jim Hooper *(Dir.-Transportation)*

Divisions:

NTC Apparel Fabrics Division **(2)**
237 Coliseum Drive
Macon, GA 31208
Mfr. of Apparel Fabrics
S.I.C.: 2211; 2221; 2231
W.E. Hinshaw *(Pres.)*

NTC Consumer Products Div. **(2)**
237 Coliseum Drive
Macon, GA 31208
S.I.C.: 2281
Lindsey Crosby *(Pres.)*

NTC Engineered Products Div. **(2)**
237 Coliseum Drive
Macon, GA 31208
S.I.C.: 2281
R.E. Major *(Pres.)*

Plants:

The Bibb Company-Brucknell Plant **(3)**
Hwy. 501 North
Brucknell, VA 24528
Tel.: 804-376-2311
Mfr. of Terry Cloth & Institutional Towels
S.I.C.: 2281
Lindsey Crosby *(Pres.)*

The Bibb Company-Roanoke Rapids Plant **(3)**
Fifth & Jackson
Roanoke Rapids, NC 27870
Tel.: 919-537-4171
Mfr. of Terry Cloth & Institutional Towels
S.I.C.: 2281
Lindsey Crosby *(Pres.)*

The Bibb Company-White Horse Rd. Plant **(3)**
White Horse Rd.
Greenville, SC 29611
Tel.: 803-233-4952
Mfr. of Terry Cloth & Institutional Towels
S.I.C.: 2281
Lindsey Crosby *(Pres.)*

Bibb-Disc, Inc. **(1)**
237 Coliseum Dr.
Macon, GA 31201
Tel.: 912-743-3731 (100%)

NTH CONSULTANTS, LTD.
38955 Hills Tech Dr.
Farmington Hills, MI 48331
Tel.: 313-553-6300 **MI**
Fax: 313-489-0727
Year Founded: 1968
Assets: $8,200,000
Liabilities: $3,200,000
Net Worth: $5,000,000
Approx.Sls.: $15,000,000
Emp.: 175
Fiscal Year-end: 12/31/91
Engineering Consulting & Environmental Services
S.I.C.: 8711; 8999
Employee Matching Gifts Program: Minimum Donation of $25 & A Maximum Donation of $500, Match 1 to 1 to Eligible Institutions, Accredited Colleges, Universities & Junior Colleges
Jerome C. Neyer *(Chm. & Chief Exec. Officer)*
Benedict Tiseo *(Pres.)*
Robert L. Bailey *(Sr. V.P.)*
Kal R. Hindo *(Sr. V.P.-Corp. Devel.)*
Keith M. Swaffer *(V.P.)*
Rhonda Powell *(Controller)*
Kevin L. Martin *(Dir.-Mktg.)*
Stephanie Redman *(Dir.-Human Resources)*
Tom O'Brien *(Office Mgr.)*

No. of U.S. Offices: 3

Computer Systems/Hardware:
BST/DEC VAX

Outside Service Firm(s):

Chaness & Simon*(Auditors)*
Farmington Hills, MI 48018

Professional Underwriters, Inc.*(Commercial Insurance Carrier)*
31731 Northwestern Hwy., Ste. 152
Farmington Hills, MI 48018

Schier, Deneweth & Parfitt, P.C.*(Legal Firm)*
Troy, MI

NBD Bank, N.A.*(Major Banking Relationship)*
Novi, MI

Felker Benefits Services*(Pension Manager)*
440 No. 4th St.
St. Louis, MO 63102

Subsidiaries:

NTH Consultants, Ltd. **(1)**
860 Spring Lane
Exton, PA 19341
Tel.: 215-524-2300

NTH Consultants, Ltd. **(1)**
65 Cadillac Square, Ste. 2223
Detroit, MI 48226
Tel.: 313-965-0036

NTS CORPORATION
10172 Linn Station Rd.
Louisville, KY 40223
Tel.: 502-426-4800 **KY**
Fax: 502-426-4994
Assets: $160,000,000
Liabilities: $100,000,000
Net Worth: $60,000,000
Sales Range: $60-79 Million
Emp.: 350
Fiscal Year-end: 12/31/89
Real Estate Develoment & Management
S.I.C.: 6552; 6531
J.D. Nichols *(Chm. Bd. & Chief Exec. Officer)*
Richard L. Good *(Pres. & Chief Oper. Officer)*
John W. Hampton *(Sr. V.P. & Controller)*
James Mulrooney *(Sr. V.P.-Fin.)*
Stephen C. Wallace *(V.P.-Residential)*
Gregory A. Compton *(Gen. Counsel)*

N.W. TRANSPORT SERVICE, INC.
5601 Holly St.
Commerce City, CO 80022
Tel.: 303-289-3511
Fax: 303-289-4649
Year Founded: 1958
Approx.Sls.: $150,000,000

N.W. Transport Service, Inc.—(Continued)

Emp.: 1,700
Long Distance Trucking Company
S.I.C.: 4213
Jerry McMorris *(Pres. & Chief Exec. Officer)*
Wayne Follick *(Sr. V.P.)*
Monte Hutchinson *(Sr. V.P.-Opers.)*
Bill Ward *(Sr. V.P., Sec. & Treas.)*
Jeff McMorris *(V.P.-Industrial Devel.)*

Outside Service Firm(s):

Coopers & Lybrand*(Auditors)*
370 17th St., Ste. 3300
Denver, CO 80202
Tel.: 303-573-2800

Jones, Meiklejohn, Kehl & Lyons*(Legal Firm)*
Denver, CO

NWA, INC.
Minneapolis-St. Paul Intl. Airport
Saint Paul, MN 55111
Mailing Address:
5101 Northwest Dr.
St. Paul, MN 55111-3034
Tel.: 612-726-2111 **DE**
Fax: 612-726-6599
Year Founded: 1926
Earnings: $3,100,000
Approx.Rev.: $7,530,000,000
Emp.: 47,000
Fiscal Year-end: 12/31/91
Holding Company; Air Transportation
S.I.C.: 6719; 4512
Alfred Checchi *(Co-Chm. Bd.)*
Gary Wilson *(Co-Chm. Bd.)*
Frederick V. Malek *(Vice Chm.)*
John H. Dasburg *(Pres. & Chief Exec. Officer)*
Richard B. Hirst *(Exec. V.P. & Gen. Counsel)*
Joseph E. Francht *(Sr. V.P.-Fin. & Treas.)*
Christoper Clouser *(Sr. V.P.-Corp. Communications & Adv.)*
Ben Hirst *(Sr. V.P.-Gen. Counsel)*
Herbert Ihle *(Sr. V.P.-Fin. & Controller)*
Allen Johnson *(Sr. V.P.-Intl.)*
Mark Abels *(V.P.-Corp. Communications)*
Richard Anderson *(V.P.-Deputy Gen. Counsel)*
Dan Cohrs *(V.P.-Intl. Fin.)*
Philip Hahn *(V.P.-Revenue Mngmt.)*
Myles Itkin *(V.P.-Fin.)*
John Klinkenberg *(V.P.-Audit & Security)*
David Mishkin *(V.P.-Intl. & Regulatory Affairs)*
R. Terrence Rendleman *(V.P.-Tech. Opers.)*
Douglas Steenland *(V.P., Deputy Gen. Counsel & Sec.)*
Douglas B. Hultberg *(Asst. Treas.-Cash Mgmnt.)*
Harding E. Van Schaack *(Dir.-Comp. & Benefits)*
Wesley G. Carlson *(Dir.-Pensions)*

Outside Service Firm(s):

Ernst & Young*(Auditors)*
50 S. Main, Ste. 1400
Salt Lake City, UT 84144
Tel.: 801-538-2500

CIGNA*(Group Insurer)*
Hartford, CT
Tel.: 203-726-6000

Mutual Life*(Group Insurer)*
Boston, MA

Merrill Lynch*(Investment Banker)*
P.O. Box 20, World Trade Center
New York, NY 10281
Tel.: 212-449-4843

Salomon Brothers*(Investment Banker)*
7 World Trade Center
New York, NY 10048
Tel.: 212-783-7000

Dorsey & Whitney*(Legal Firm)*
2200 First Bank Place East
Minneapolis, MN 55402
Tel.: 612-340-2600
Fax: 612-340-2600

First Bank Minneapolis*(Major Banking Relationship)*
P.O. Box A700, 120 S. Sixth St.
Minneapolis, MN 55480
Tel.: 612-370-4141

Norwest Bank Minnesota, N.A.*(Major Banking Relationship)*
6th St. & Marquette Ave.
Minneapolis, MN 55479-0065
Tel.: 612-667-8101

Alliance Capital Management*(Pension Manager)*
Minneapolis, MN

Denver Investment Advisors Inc.*(Pension Manager)*
633 Seventeenth St.
Denver, CO 80217

Standish, Ayer & Wood*(Pension Manager)*
One Financial Center
Boston, MA 02111
Tel.: 617-350-6100

Subsidiaries:

MLT Vacations, Inc. **(1)**
5130 Highway 101
Minnetonka, MN 55345
Tel.: 612-474-2540 (100%)
Fax: 612-474-9730
Emp.: 192
Wholesaler of Vacation Travel Packages
S.I.C.: 4789
Edward A. Neer, Jr. *(Pres. & Chief Exec. Officer)*

Northwest Aerospace Training Corporation **(1)**
Minneapolis-St. Paul Intl. Airport
Saint Paul, MN 55111
Tel.: 612-726-6000 (100%)
Fax: 612-726-6132
Emp.: 150
Flight Training Unit
S.I.C.: 4581
Howard DeCastro *(Pres. & Chief Exec. Officer)*

Northwest Aircraft Inc. **(1)**
Minneapolis-St. Paul Intl. Airport
Saint Paul, MN 55111
Tel.: 612-726-2246 (100%)
Fax: 612-726-3947
Emp.: 3
Aircraft Lessor
S.I.C.: 4581
Lawrence Kahn *(Staff V.P.-Fleet Mngmt.)*

Northwest Airlines, Inc. **(1)**
5101 Northwest Dr.
Saint Paul, MN 55111-3034
Tel.: 612-726-2111 (100%)
Approx.Sls.: $7,530,000,000
Emp.: 47,000
Fiscal Year-end: 12/31/91
Air Transportation
S.I.C.: 4512
Employee Matching Gift Program: For *Colleges & Universities*
Alfred Checchi *(Co-Chm. Bd.)*
Gary Wilson *(Co-Chm. Bd.)*
Frederick V. Malek *(Vice Chm.)*
John Dasburg *(Pres. & Chief Exec. Officer)*
Richard B. Hirst *(Exec. V.P. & Gen. Counsel)*
Joseph Leonard *(Exec. V.P.-Customer Services)*
Michael E. Levine *(Exec. V.P.-Mktg.)*
William Slattery *(Exec. V.P.-Opers. & Chief Safety Officer)*
Christopher E. Clouser *(Sr. V.P.-Communications & Adv.)*
Robert L. Fornaro *(Sr. V.P.-Mkt. Plng.)*
Joseph E. Francht, Jr. *(Sr. V.P. & Treas.)*
Herbert D. Ihle *(Sr. V.P.-Fin. & Controller)*
Allen Johnson *(Sr. V.P.-Intl.)*
Barry A. Kotar *(Sr. V.P.-Quality, Human Resources & Info. Services)*
Terrence Rendleman *(Sr. V.P.-Technical Opers.)*
John Wilson *(Sr. V.P.-Corp. Plng.)*
Mary Barker *(Reg. V.P.-Ground Opers., Detroit Reg.)*
Robert Ronning *(Reg. V.P.-Ground Opers., Western Reg.)*
Ted Sartoian *(Reg. V.P.-Customer Service, Eastern Reg.)*
Jack Smith *(Reg. V.P.-Ground Opers., Southern Reg.)*
Mark E. Abels *(V.P.-Corp. Communications)*
Fay Beauchine *(V.P.-Reservation Sls. & Services)*
David Behrends *(V.P.-Cargo)*
Rick Blake *(V.P.-Product Devel.-Aircraft Projects)*
Malcolm Bromham *(V.P.-Atlantic Reg.)*
Dan Cohrs *(V.P.-Intl. Fin.)*
James Conte *(V.P.-Intl. Mktg.)*
Geoff Crowley *(V.P.-Affil. Airline Opers.)*
Thomas Devine *(V.P.-Maintenance & Engrng. ATL Base)*
Chris Doan *(V.P.-Maintenance Opers. MSP Base)*
Lew Elsworthy *(V.P.-Mktg. Sales & Information Systems)*
Terry Erskine *(V.P.-Labor Rels.)*
Michael Fahey *(V.P.-Labor Rels.)*
David A. Fielding *(V.P.-Customer Service)*
John Garel *(V.P.-Scheduling & Plng.)*
James Greenwald *(V.P.-Facilities)*
Harry L. Gregory *(V.P.-Matls. Mngmt)*
Myles R. Itkin *(V.P.-Fin.)*
Larry Kahn *(V.P.-Fleet Mngmt.)*
John S. Kern *(V.P.-Flight Opers.)*
John Klinkenberg *(V.P.-Audit & Security)*
Kenneth Levinson *(V.P.-Tax)*
Ruth McKee *(V.P.-Customer Service, Ground)*
Sally Macut *(V.P.-Opers. Control)*
Louis Mancini *(V.P.-Maintenance Process & Automation)*
David Mishkin *(V.P.-Intl. & Regulatory Affairs)*
Ken Neher *(V.P.-Mktg.)*
Mark Osterberg *(V.P. & Chief Acctg. Officer)*
Robert Page *(V.P.-Corp. Pur. & Services)*
Douglas Podolak *(V.P. & G.M.-Fuel Service)*
Cynthia Potter *(V.P.-Quality Mngmt. & Education)*
Ron Roberts *(V.P.-Powerplant & Shop Opers. MSP Base)*
Glen Rothe *(V.P.-Plng. Information Service)*
Douglas M. Steenland *(V.P., Deputy Gen. Counsel & Sec.)*
Dan Taylor *(V.P.-Line Opers.)*
John Temple *(V.P.-Sales)*
John Temple *(V.P.-Sales)*
Kathy Higgins Victor *(V.P.-Human Resources)*
Lloyd Warren *(V.P.-In-Flight Services)*
John Whisnant *(V.P.-Corp. Plng.)*
William Wren *(V.P.-Corp. Rels.)*
Frederick Dow *(Mng. Dir.-Worldwide Adv.)*

NWS, INC.
(d/b/a Union Liquors Co.)
3247 S. Kedzie Ave.
Chicago, IL 60623
Tel.: 312-254-9020
Tel.: 800-944-9450
Telex: 25-5131
Fax: 312-254-9033
Year Founded: 1933
Approx.Sls.: $91,000,000
Emp.: 295
Fiscal Year-end: 6/30/90
Import Export
Wholesale Liquors, Wines & Liqueurs
S.I.C.: 2085; 2084; 5182
Jim LaCrosse *(Chm. Bd.)*
Greg Mauloff *(Pres.)*
Joe Bridwell *(V.P.-Opers.)*
George Briskie *(V.P.-Mktg.)*
Louis Defalco *(V.P.-Brand Devel.)*
Milton C. Yong *(V.P.-Fin.)*
Dwight Deming *(Dir.-Data Processing)*

Principal(s):
Jim LaCrosse
Greg Mauloff

Computer Systems/Hardware:
Hewlett-Packard 3000-68

Outside Service Firm(s):

KPMG Peat Marwick*(Auditors)*
Peat Marwick Plaza, 303 E. Wacker Dr.
Chicago, IL 60601
Tel.: 312-938-1000

McDermott, Will & Emery*(Legal Firm)*
227 W. Monroe St.
Chicago, IL 60606-5096
Tel.: 312-372-2000

American National Bank & Trust Co.*(Major Banking Relationship)*
Chicago, IL

American National Bank & Trust Company of Chicago*(Major Banking Relationship)*
33 N. LaSalle St.
Chicago, IL 60602
Tel.: 312-661-5000
Fax: 312-661-6417

Subsidiary:

Consolidated Distilled Products **(1)**
3201 S. Kedzie Ave.
Chicago, IL 60623
Tel.: (312) 927-4161

NABHOLZ CONSTRUCTION CORP.
612 Garland
Conway, AR 72032
Tel.: 501-327-7781 **AR**
Fax: 501-327-8231
Year Founded: 1949
Approx.Sls.: $51,800,000
Emp.: 500
Fiscal Year-end: 3/31/90
General Building Contractors
S.I.C.: 1542; 1541
Robert D. Nabholz *(Chm. Bd.)*
Robert D. Nabholz, Jr. *(Chief Exec. Officer)*
Robert Tyler *(Pres. & Gen. Mgr.)*
M.H. Moix, Jr. *(Sr. V.P.)*
Bob Nutter *(Sr. V.P.)*
Lonnie Williams *(Sr. V.P.)*
Ron Montgomery *(V.P.)*
Norbert Moix *(Sec. & Treas.)*

Outside Service Firm(s):

Wright, Lindsey, & Jennings*(Legal Firm)*
2200 Worthen Bank Bldg.
Little Rock, AR 72201
Tel.: 501-371-0808
Fax: 501-375-1617

First National Bank of Conway*(Major Banking Relationship)*
Conway, AR

NA-CHURS PLANT FOOD COMPANY
421 Leader St.
Marion, OH 43302
Tel.: 614-382-5701
Year Founded: 1946
Approx.Sls.: $16,000,000
Emp.: 55
Fiscal Year-end: 9/30/92
Liquid Fertilizer
S.I.C.: 2875
John D. Kelly *(Pres. & Chief Exec. Officer)*
George Berg *(V.P.-Sls.)*
Orville E. Gaffney *(V.P.-Mkt. Expansion)*
Robert Hopp *(V.P.-Opers.)*
Tim Bailey *(Mgr.-Mkt. Devel.)*

NACOMA CONSOLIDATED, INC.
7516 U.S. 59 North
Nacogdoches, TX 75961
Tel.: 409-560-1432
Fax: 409-560-4707
Approx.Sls.: $10,000,000
Emp.: 80
Building & Installation Of Wooden Office Cabinets, Desks
S.I.C.: 2521; 1751
Jeff Fuller *(Pres.)*
Shawan Abernathy *(V.P. & Treas.)*
Paul Miller *(Sec.)*

Outside Service Firm(s):

Southside National Bank*(Major Banking Relationship)*
Nacogdoches, TX

NADEL PARTNERSHIP, INC.
1990 S. Bundy, Ste. 400
Los Angeles, CA 90025
Tel.: 310-826-2100 **CA**
Fax: 310-826-0182
Year Founded: 1973
Approx.Sls.: $19,000,000
Emp.: 140
Architectural Services
S.I.C.: 8712
Herbert Nadel *(Pres.)*
Rochelle Nadel *(V.P.)*

Outside Service Firm(s):

Roth, Bookstein & Zaslow*(Auditors)*
Los Angeles, CA

Security Pacific National Bank*(Major Banking Relationship)*
P.O. Box 60228, Terminal Annex,
Los Angeles, CA 90060
Tel.: 213-580-2829

Branches:

The Nadel Partnership, Inc. **(1)**
1760 Creekside Oaks Dr., Ste. 140
Sacramento, CA 95833
Tel.: 916-567-3000
Emp.: 25
S.I.C.: 8712

The Nadel Partnership, Inc. **(1)**
3090 Bristol St., Ste. 200
Costa Mesa, CA 92626
Tel.: 714-540-5000
Emp.: 15
S.I.C.: 8712

NADY SYSTEMS, INC.
6701 Bay St.
Emeryville, CA 94608
Tel.: 510-652-2411 **CA**
Fax: 510-652-5075
Year Founded: 1976
Assets: $3,500,000
Net Worth: $3,500,000
Approx.Sls.: $15,000,000
Emp.: 90
Fiscal Year-end: 12/31/91
Export
Mfr. Wireless Microphones & Communicators
S.I.C.: 3651
John Nady *(Pres. & Chief Exec. Officer)*
Charles Tsou *(Controller)*
Gene Campbell *(Gen. Mgr.)*
Jonathon Cohen *(Dir.-OEM & New Prod. Devel.)*
Tono Rondono *(Dir.-Adv.)*
Randy Stearns *(Dir.-Mngmt. Information Systems)*
Howard Zimmerman *(Dir.-Sls.)*
Principal(s):
John Nady

No. of Mfg. Plants/Facilities: 1
No. of U.S. Offices: 1
No. of Foreign Offices: 1

Computer Systems/Hardware:
IBM

Outside Service Firm(s):

Moss Adams*(Auditors)*
San Francisco, CA

Woodruff-Sawyer & Co.*(Commercial Insurance Carrier)*
San Francisco, CA

Massachusetts Indemnity & Life Insurance Co.*(Group Insurer)*
Santa Monica, CA

Wells Fargo Bank*(Major Banking Relationship)*
420 Montgomery St.
San Francisco, CA 94104

Shearson Lehman Brothers, Inc.*(Pension Manager)*
World Financial Center
New York, NY 10285
Tel.: 212-298-2000

FRANK C. NAHSER INC.
10 S. Riverside Plaza
Chicago, IL 60606
Tel.: 312-845-5000
Fax: 312-845-9075
Year Founded: 1939
Approx.Billings: $36,000,000
Emp.: 43
Consumer & Business-to-Business Advertising
F. Byron Nahser *(Pres. & Chief Exec. Officer)*
Donald F. Burke *(Chief Fin. Officer)*
Deb Kirby *(V.P., Prog. Devel.)*
Edward Bradley *(Gen. Counsel)*

NAMICO, INC.
4601 Flat Rock Rd.
Philadelphia, PA 19127
Mailing Address:
P.O. Box 4684,
Philadelphia, PA 19127
Tel.: 215-482-6600
Fax: 215-482-9182
Sales Range: $10-19 Million
Emp.: 70
Import Export
Industrial Soaps, Detergents, Cleaning Compounds & Rubber Processing Chemicals
S.I.C.: 2841
Robert McAlaine *(Chm. Bd. & Pres.)*
David Ward *(Exec. V.P.)*
Winfield W. Howe *(V.P.-Mfg.)*
Colby H. Snyder *(V.P.-Fin. & Sec.)*
George Sas *(Chief Chemist)*

Outside Service Firm(s):

Isdaner & Co.*(Auditors)*
Philadelphia, PA

Braemer, Ableson & Hitchner*(Legal Firm)*
18th Fl., 1515 Market St.
Philadelphia, PA 19102
Tel.: 215-665-8300

Meridian Bank*(Major Banking Relationship)*
One Meridian Plaza, 36th Fl.
Philadelphia, PA
Tel.: 215-854-3900

NANA REGIONAL CORPORATION, INC.
1001 E. Benson
Anchorage, AK 99508
Tel.: 907-265-4100 **AK**
Fax: 907-265-4123
Year Founded: 1972
Approx.Sls.: $24,000,000
Emp.: 300
Oil Field Services; Electric Power, Hotels
S.I.C.: 1389; 4911; 7011
Christina Westlake *(Chm. Bd.)*
Charley Curtis *(Pres.)*
John T. Shively *(Pres.-Nana Devel. Corp.)*
Maryanne Burke *(V.P.-Fin.)*
John A. Rense *(V.P.)*
Walter Sampson *(V.P.)*
Sarah Scanlan *(V.P.)*
Pete Schaeffer *(V.P.)*
Andrea Miller *(Controller)*

Outside Service Firm(s):

KPMG Peat Marwick*(Auditors)*
Anchorage, AK

Subsidiary:

Nana Development Corporation **(1)**
P.O. Box 49
Katzebue, AK 99752
Tel.: 907-442-3301
Fax: 907-442-2866
Hotel Management
S.I.C.: 7011; 8741
John T. Shivley *(Pres.)*
Maryanne Burke *(V.P.)*
Thomas M. Dow *(V.P.)*

THE NAPIER COMPANY
74 Cambridge St.
Meriden, CT 06450
Tel.: 203-237-5522
Tel.: 800-243-3106 **CT**
Fax: 203-237-6908
Year Founded: 1875
Approx.Sls.: $60,000,000
Emp.: 1,000
Fiscal Year-end: 12/31/91
Import Export
Mfr. of Fashion Jewelry
S.I.C.: 3911; 3961
Ronald J. Meoni *(Pres. & Chief Exec. Officer)*
John E. Benison *(Exec. V.P.-Sls. Mktg. & Prod. Devel.)*
Michael G. Consolini *(Exec. V.P.-Opers. & Sec.)*
Graham Brewster *(Sr. V.P.-Sls. & Mktg.)*
C. Martin Antisdale *(V.P.-Matls. & Systems)*
Karl S. Harkenreader *(V.P.-Fin.)*
John J. Keyes, Jr. *(V.P.-Sls.)*
Michael Ruggiero *(V.P.-Design)*
Jean Starr-McCarty *(V.P.-Human Resources)*
Herbert Ziemelis *(V.P.-Mfg.)*
James Vumbaco *(Treas.)*
Patricia Boyle *(Mgr.-Adv. & Sls. Promo.)*

No. of Mfg. Plants/Facilities: 2
No. of U.S. Offices: 8
No. of Foreign Offices: 2

Computer Systems/Hardware:
Burroughs Systems 1855, CP 9500 & A 3

Outside Service Firm(s):

Price Waterhouse*(Auditors)*
One Financial Plaza
Hartford, CT 06103
Tel.: 203-240-2000

Blue Cross & Blue Shield of Connecticut, Inc.*(Group Insurer)*
North Haven, CT

Shipman & Goodman*(Legal Firm)*
One American Row
Hartford, CT 06103

Chemical Banking Corp.*(Major Banking Relationship)*
277 Park Ave.
New York, NY 10041
Tel.: 212-310-6407
Fax: 212-310-4526

Fleet National Bank*(Major Banking Relationship)*
111 Westminster St.
Providence, RI 02903
Tel.: 401-278-6000

Rhode Island Hospital Trust National Bank*(Major Banking Relationship)*
Providence, RI

Chemical Banking Corp.*(Pension Manager)*
277 Park Ave.
New York, NY 10041
Tel.: 212-310-6407
Fax: 212-310-4526

Subsidiary:

Mildrum Manufacturing Co. **(1)**
Napier Park
Meriden, CT 06450
Tel.: 203-237-5522

Division:

RLJC, Inc. **(1)**
74 Cambridge St.
Meriden, CT 06450
Tel.: 800-245-5561
Mfg. and Distrubites Designer Jewelry
S.I.C.: 3911
Ronald J. Meoni *(Chm. Bd.)*

NARRAGANSETT CAPITAL INC.
50 Kennedy Plaza
Providence, RI 02903
Tel.: 401-751-1000 **RI**
Fax: 401-751-9340
Emp.: 22
Investment Banker; Television Broadcasting
S.I.C.: 6799; 4833
Gregory P. Barber *(Mng. Dir.)*
Jonathan M. Nelson *(Mng. Dir.)*
Roger A. Vandenberg *(Mng. Dir.)*
Raymond M. Mathieu *(Chief Fin. Officer & Treas.)*

Outside Service Firm(s):

Ernst & Young*(Auditors)*
One Old Stone Square
Providence, RI 02903
Tel.: 401-331-7000

Edwards & Angell*(Legal Firm)*
2700 Hospital Trust Twr.
Providence, RI 02903
Tel.: 401-274-9200

Fleet National Bank*(Major Banking Relationship)*
Corporate Trust Department, 125 Dupont Dr.
Providence, RI 02907
Tel.: 401-278-5400

Operations:

WPRI-TV **(1)**
25 Catamore Blvd.
East Providence, RI 02914
Tel.: 401-438-7200 (100%)
Television Broadcasting
S.I.C.: 4833
Robert Finke *(Gen. Mgr.)*
Robert McCaughey *(Gen. Sls. Mgr.)*

WTKR-TV **(1)**
720 Boush St.
Norfolk, VA 23510
Tel.: 804-446-1000 (100%)
Television Broadcasting
S.I.C.: 4833
Christopher Pike *(Gen. Mgr.)*

NARROW FABRIC INDUSTRIES, INC.
7th & Reading Aves.
West Reading, PA 19611
Mailing Address:
P.O. Box 6948,
Wymossing, PA 19610
Tel.: 215-376-2891
Twx: 5106510412
Year Founded: 1900
Approx.Sls.: $24,000,000
Emp.: 320
Fiscal Year-end: 9/30/90
Mfr. of Woven, Knitted & Braided Narrow Fabrics
S.I.C.: 2241
Stewart R. Tait *(Pres.)*
Charles Miller *(V.P.-Mfg.)*
Irwin Noll *(V.P.-Sls.)*
William P. Wisser *(V.P.-Fin.)*
Norman Kahl *(Dir.-Engrng.)*
Chris Pettis *(Dir.-Pur.)*
Michelle Hettinger *(Mgr.-Personnel)*
Neil Magerman *(Mgr.-Plant)*
Lori Walton *(Mgr.-Mdsg.)*
Mary Orlando *(Customer Service)*

THE NASH ENGINEERING COMPANY
310 Wilson Ave.
Norwalk, CT 06856
Tel.: 203-852-3900
Fax: 203-852-3988
Emp.: 700
Import Export
Manufacture Pumps & Compressors
S.I.C.: 3561; 3563
John W. Kubovic *(Pres. & Chief Exec. Officer)*
Jack Horan *(Pres. & Gen. Mgr.-Nash Canada)*

The Nash Engineering Company—(Continued)
Adam R. Taloni *(Pres.-Nash Europe)*
Dennis J. Hennessy *(Chief Fin. Officer, Treas. & V.P.-Fin.)*
Edward R. Tarczali *(V.P.-Human Resources)*
Robert Thompson *(V.P.-Mngmt. Information Systems)*
Phil Confaloni *(Mgr.-Data Processing)*
Arthur B. Ward *(Mgr.-Corp. Communications)*

Computer Systems/Hardware:
IBM 4381; Hewlett-Packard 3000

Outside Service Firm(s):

KPMG Peat Marwick*(Auditors)*
345 Park Ave.
New York, NY 10154
Tel.: 212-758-9700
Fax: 212-872-3308

Sherman & Sterling*(Legal Firm)*
New York, NY

Connecticut Bank & Trust*(Major Banking Relationship)*
Darien, CT

Non-U.S. Holdings:

Nash do Brasil Bombas Ltda. **(1)**
Ave. Mercedes Benz 700 13056
Campinas, S.P. Brazil
Tel.: 192 0475833 (100%)
Mfr. of Air Compressors
S.I.C.: 3563
Sidney Durval John *(Mgr.)*

Nash Engineering Co. (Great Britain) Ltd. **(1)**
Rd. 1, Industrial Estate,
Winsford, Cheshire CW7 3PL, United Kingdom
Tel.: 0606 594242
Telex: 668364 NASGGB G
Fax: 0606 551994
Vacuum System Engineers
S.I.C.: 8711; 3563
Bernard Harvey *(Mng. Dir.)*

The Nash Engineering Company of Canada, Ltd. **(1)**
1149 Northside Rd.
Burlington, ON L7P 3S9, Canada
Tel.: 416-335-0145
Emp.: 30
Mfr. Pumps & Pumping Equipment
S.I.C.: 3561
Jack Horan *(V.P.-Mfg.)*

NASHUA HOMES OF IDAHO INC.
5200 Federal Way
Boise, ID 83707
Mailing Address:
P.O. Box 8449,
Boise, ID 83707
Tel.: 208-345-0222
Fax: 208-345-1144
Approx.Sls.: $24,000,000
Emp.: 135
Mfr. Mobile Homes
S.I.C.: 2451
Ron Yanke *(Pres. & Owner)*
Milton Barningham *(V.P. & Gen. Mgr.)*

NASHVILLE MACHINE CO. INC.
530 Woodycrest Ave.
Nashville, TN 37210-4394
Mailing Address:
P.O. Box 101603
Nashville, TN 37224-1603
Tel.: 615-244-2030
Fax: 615-259-2936
Year Founded: 1887
Assets: $9,063,650
Liabilities: $3,720,713
Net Worth: $5,342,937
Approx.Sls.: $29,500,000
Emp.: 300
Fiscal Year-end: 9/30/90
Mechanical Construction; Sales & Service of Elevators; Machine Shop Sheet Metal Fabrication
S.I.C.: 1711; 5084; 3599; 3441; 1796
Robert L. Bibb, Jr. *(Chm. Bd.)*
Donald C. Orr *(Pres.)*
John Coben *(V.P.-Engrng.)*
David Crews *(V.P.)*
Donald B. Orr *(V.P.)*
Wallace R. Kinkade *(Sec. & Treas.)*
Robert Sharber *(Dir.-Pur.)*

Computer Systems/Hardware:
IBM System 34

Outside Service Firm(s):

Davidson & Kruse*(Auditors)*
Nashville, TN

Dearborn & Ewing*(Legal Firm)*
1 Commerce Pl., Ste. 1200
Nashville, TN 37219
Tel.: 615-259-3560

Manier, Herod, Hollabaugh & Smith*(Legal Firm)*
2200 One Nashville Pl., 150 4th Ave. N
Nashville, TN 37219

First American National Bank*(Major Banking Relationship)*
Nashville, TN

NASHVILLE STEEL CORP.
7211 Centennial Blvd.
Nashville, TN 37209
Mailing Address:
P.O. Box 90267
Nashville, TN 37209
Tel.: 615-350-7933 **TN**
Year Founded: 1960
Approx.Sls.: $35,000,000
Emp.: 150
Steel Service Warehouse
S.I.C.: 5051
Okey B. Johnson, Jr. *(Chm. Bd. & Pres.)*

Computer Systems/Hardware:
Data General

Outside Service Firm(s):

Commerce Union*(Major Banking Relationship)*
Nashville, TN

Subsidiary:

White Star Steel **(1)**
2200 Harbor Blvd.
Houston, TX 77020
Tel.: 713-675-6501
Fax: 713-678-8568
Steel Service Center
S.I.C.: 5051
O.B. Johnson, III *(Pres.)*

NASHVILLE WIRE PRODUCT CO.
199 Polk Ave.
Nashville, TN 37210
Mailing Address:
P.O. Box 491,
Nashville, TN 37202-0491
Tel.: 615-255-9874
Fax: 615-242-4225
Year Founded: 1933
Approx.Sls.: $38,000,000
Emp.: 550
Fiscal Year-end: 12/31/90
Manufacture & Market Wire Containers; Wire Pallets; Wire Baskets; Conveyor Guards; Point of Purchase Display Racks; Oven Racks; Refrigerator Racks; Fan Guards
S.I.C.: 3315; 3496
Clark Rollins *(Chm. Bd.)*
David Rollins *(Pres. & Chief Exec. Officer)*
Jeff McCann *(Chief Fin. Officer)*
R.C. Devor, Jr. *(Legal Officer)*
Michael Anglin *(Dir.-Mngmt. Information Systems)*
Bud Givan *(Dir.-Pur.)*
Ann Krafft *(Dir.-Human Resource)*

No. of Mfg. Plants/Facilities: 13

Computer Systems/Hardware:
IBM AS 400

Outside Service Firm(s):

Lattimore, Black, Morgan & Cain*(Auditors)*
Nashville, TN

First American National Bank*(Major Banking Relationship)*
First American Center
Nashville, TN 37237
Tel.: 615-748-2000

NASON AND CULLEN, INC.
Walnut Hill Plaza, 150 S. Warner Rd.
Wayne, PA 19087
Mailing Address:
P.O. Box 6730
Wayne, PA 19087
Tel.: 215-687-6100
Fax: 219-341-8697
Year Founded: 1926
Approx.Sls.: $95,000,000
Emp.: 205
Fiscal Year-end: 3/31/90
Construction Management; General Contractor
S.I.C.: 1541; 1542; 8741
Walton H. Nason, Jr. *(Chm. Bd.)*
J. Russell Cullen, Jr. *(Pres.)*
Loretta L. Simon *(Exec. V.P.)*
Robert L. Potter *(Sr. V.P.-Special Projects)*
Anthony J. DiLouis *(V.P.-Field Opers.)*
Albert P. Matulis *(V.P.-Estimating)*
David L. Oles *(V.P.-Project Mngmt.)*
Edward J. Tannebaum *(V.P.-Mktg.)*
Margaret A. Maltz *(Sec. & Controller)*
Marianne Beck *(Dir.-Contract Admin.)*
Michael Berardi *(Dir.-Delaware Div.)*
Theodore Daniels *(Dir.-New Construction)*
Henry W. Hudson, IV *(Dir.-Bus. Devel.)*

Principal(s):
Walton H. Nason, Jr.
J. Russell Cullen, Jr.

No. of U.S. Offices: 2

Computer Systems/Hardware:
HP 3000XE

Outside Service Firm(s):

Ernst & Young*(Auditors)*
1800 John F. Kennedy Blvd.
Philadelphia, PA 19103-7499
Tel.: 215-864-3300

Aetna Life & Casualty*(Commercial Insurance Carrier)*
Des Moines, IA

McCrea, Gallen, Missett & Associates*(Group Insurer)*
Wayne, PA

CoreStates Corporate Trust Services*(Investment Banker)*
P.O. Box 7907,
Philadelphia, PA 19101
Tel.: 215-629-8400

Jacoby, Donner & Jacoby*(Legal Firm)*
Wayne, PA

CoreStates Financial Corp.*(Major Banking Relationship)*
Philadelphia, PA

Principal Mutual Life Insurance Co.*(Pension Manager)*
711 High St.
Des Moines, IA 50309

NATHAN'S FAMOUS INC.
1400 Old Country Rd., Ste. 400
Westbury, NY 11590
Tel.: 516-338-8500
Fax: 516-338-7220
Year Founded: 1916
Assets: $22,451,000
Liabilities: $10,234,000
Net Worth: $12,217,000
Approx.Sls.: $70,000,000
Emp.: 500
Fiscal Year-end: 3/29/92
Fast Food Franchisor
S.I.C.: 5812
Wayne Norbitz *(Pres. & Chief Oper. Officer)*
William Handwerker *(Sr. V.P.)*
Raymond T. DioGuardi *(V.P.-Fin. & Chief Fin. Officer)*
Larry Feierstein *(V.P.-Mktg.)*
Donald Schedler *(V.P.-Architecture & Construction)*
Bob Varma *(V.P.-Opers.)*

Computer Systems/Hardware:
IBM System 36

Outside Service Firm(s):

Patrusky, Mintz & Semel*(Auditors)*
22 Cortlandt St.
New York, NY 10007
Tel.: 212-732-2600
Fax: 212-374-1967

JLS Group*(Commercial Insurance Carrier)*
228 E. 45th St.
New York, NY 10017
Tel.: 212-682-6700
Fax: 212-490-2475

Dreyer & Traub*(Legal Firm)*
101 Park Ave.
New York, NY 10016
Tel.: 212-661-8800

National Westminster Bank plc*(Major Banking Relationship)*
Astor Plaza, 1515 Broadway
New York, NY 10036

NATIONAL ACADEMY SCIENCES USA
2101 Constitution Ave., N.W.
Washington, DC 20418
Tel.: 202-334-2000 **DC**
Fax: 202-334-1597
Year Founded: 1863
Approx.Sls.: $178,000,000
Emp.: 1,120
Scientific Research Organization
S.I.C.: 8733
Frank Press *(Pres.)*
David Williams *(Chief Fin. Officer)*

Outside Service Firm(s):

Price Waterhouse*(Auditors)*
1801 K. Street, N.W.
Washington, DC 20006
Tel.: 202-296-0800

NATIONAL AMUSEMENTS, INC.
200 Elm St.
Dedham, MA 02026
Tel.: 617-461-1600
Operator of 750 Movie Theatres in the U.S. & England; Holding Company for Television & Motion Picture Companies, Cable Systems, Television & Radio Stations
S.I.C.: 7833; 7822; 6794; 7812; 4833; 4832; 4841; 6719
Sumner M. Redstone *(Chm. Bd.)*
Neil S. Braun *(Sr. V.P.-Corp. Dev. & Admin.)*
Edward D. Horowitz *(Sr. V.P.)*
Henry S. Schleiff *(Sr. V.P.)*
George S. Smith, Jr. *(Sr. V.P. & Chief Fin. Officer)*
Mark M. Weinstein *(Sr. V.P.-Gen. Counsel & Sec.)*
Thomas E. Dooley *(V.P.-Fin. & Treas.)*

Kevin C. Lavan *(V.P.-Controller & Chief Acctg. Officer)*
William A. Roskin *(V.P.-Human Resources & Admin.)*

Subsidiary:

Viacom Inc. **(1)**
1515 Broadway
New York, NY 10036
Tel.: 212-258-6000
Fax: 212-258-6354
Assets: $4,027,927,000
Earnings: ($49,656,000)
Liabilities: $3,661,764,000
Net Worth: $366,163,000
Approx.Rev.: $1,711,562,000
Emp.: 4,900
Fiscal Year-end: 12/31/91
Export
Holding Company
S.I.C.: 6719; 4899; 7822; 4832; 4833
Sumner M. Redstone *(Chm. Bd.)*
Frank J. Biondi, Jr. *(Pres. & Chief Exec. Officer)*
Winston H. (Tony) Cox *(Chm. & Chief Exec. Officer-Showtime Networks)*
Tom Freston *(Chm. & Chief Exec. Officer-MTV Networks)*
Neil S. Braun *(Sr. V.P. & Chm. & Chief Exec. Officer-Viacom Entertainment)*
Edward D. Horowitz *(Sr. V.P.-Tech. & Opers.)*
Scott Davis *(Exec. V.P.-Network Opers.)*
Gregory J. Ricca *(Exec. V.P.-Bus. Affairs & Networks Grps.)*
Lois Peel Eisenstein *(Sr. V.P.-Bus. Affairs & Gen. Counsel-MTV Networks)*
H. Gwen Marcus *(Sr. V.P. & Gen. Counsel-Showtime Networks)*
Raymond A. Boyce *(Sr. V.P.-Corp. Rels.)*
Thomas E. Dooley *(Sr. V.P.-Corp. Devel.)*
John W. Goddard *(Sr. V.P., Pres. & Chief Exec. Officer/Viacom Cable)*
Paul A. Heimbach *(Sr. V.P.-Engrng./Viacom Networks)*
Katherine A. Hogan *(Sr. V.P., Gen. Counsel/Entertainment)*
Ira A. Korff *(Sr. V.P.)*
William A. Roskin *(Sr. V.P.-Human Resources & Admin.)*
Edward N. Schor *(Sr. V.P.-Gen. Counsel/ Communications)*
George S. Smith, Jr. *(Sr. V.P. & Chief Fin. Officer)*
Mark M. Weinstein *(Sr. V.P. & Gen. Counsel)*
John V. Berna *(V.P.-Taxes)*
Hilary Condit *(V.P.-Corp. Rels.)*
Mark A. Harrad *(V.P.-Corp. Rels.)*
Richard Eigendorf *(V.P. & Asst. Treas.)*
Susan Gordon *(V.P.-Internal Audit)*
Gretchen Grant *(V.P.-Fin. Plng. & Analysis)*
Kevin C. Lavan *(V.P., Controller & Chief Acctg. Officer)*
Nancy Rosenfeld *(V.P., Deputy Gen. Counsel/Corporate)*
Patricia A. Ross *(V.P.-Personnel & Employee Rels.)*
Leslie Schine *(V.P.-Corp. Development)*
Kenneth Sullivan *(V.P.-Facilities Mngmt.)*
Hank Leingang *(V.P. & Chief Info. Officer)*

Subsidiaries:

Viacom Cable **(2)**
5924 Stoneridge Dr.
Pleasanton, CA 94566
Tel.: 510-463-0870
Cable Television Services
S.I.C.: 4841
John W. Goddard *(Pres. & Chief Exec. Officer)*
Garrett J. Girvan *(Exec. V.P. & Chief Oper Officer)*
John Kopchik *(Exec. V.P. & Chief Fin. Officer)*
Kurt E. Jorgensen *(Sr. V.P.-California/ Oregon)*
Eric Kronen *(Sr. V.P.-Puget Sound)*
Edward N. Schor *(Sr. V.P., Gen. Counsel/ Communications)*
Susan Dolce *(V.P. & Controller)*
Bruce Gillman *(V.P.-Human Resources)*
Stephanie Storms *(V.P.-Law & Govt. Rels.)*
Del Heller *(V.P.-Engrng.)*
Michael Johnson *(V.P.-MIS)*
Diane Schneiderjohn *(V.P.-Mktg.)*
Susan Evans *(Dir.-Public Rels.)*

Subsidiary:

KIKK AM/FM **(3)**
6306 Gulfton
Houston, TX 77081
Tel.: 713-772-4433 (100%)
Broadcasting
S.I.C.: 4832
Craig Magee *(G.M.)*

Subsidiary:

KIKK-FM Tower Corp. **(4)**
1515 Broadway
New York, NY 10036
FM Radio Broadcasting
S.I.C.: 4832

Viacom International Inc. **(2)**
1515 Broadway
New York, NY 10036
Tel.: 212-258-6000
Worldwide Syndication of TV Programs & Motion Pictures; Owns & Operates Cable TV Systems; Operates Pay & Advertiser-Supported Cable Services; Owns & Operates TV & Radio Stations; Advertising Services; Produced TV Programming, Develops International Business Opportunities in the Areas of Cable, Pay Television, Satellite Networking & Related Technologies; Video Entertainment & Information Services
S.I.C.: 4832; 4833; 4841; 6794; 7812; 7822
Sumner M. Redstone *(Chm. Bd.)*
Frank J. Biondi *(Pres. & Chief Exec. Officer)*
Scott Davis *(Exec. V.P.-Network Opers.)*
Gregory J. Ricca *(Exec. V.P.-Bus. Affairs)*
George S. Smith *(Sr. V.P. & Chief Fin. Officer)*
Mark M. Weinstein *(Sr. V.P. & Gen. Counsel)*

Divisions:

Viacom Broadcasting Inc. **(3)**
1515 Broadway
New York, NY 10036
Tel.: 212-258-6000
Radio & Television Broadcasting
S.I.C.: 4832
Edward D. Horowitz *(Chm. & Chief Exec. Officer)*
Kevin L. Reymond *(V.P. & Chief Fin. Officer)*
Francis P. Brady *(Sr. V.P. & Pres.-Television Div.)*
Thomas Dooley *(Sr. V.P.-Corp. Devel.)*
William R. Figenshu *(Sr. V.P. & Pres.-Radio Div.)*
William Roskin *(Sr. V.P.-Human Resources)*
Edward N. Schor *(Sr. V.P. & Gen. Counsel/ Communications)*
George Wolfson *(Sr. V.P.-Opers./Radio Div.)*
Betsy Vorce *(V.P.-Pub. Rels.)*

Viacom Entertainment **(3)**
1515 Broadway
New York, NY 10036
Tel.: 212-258-6000 (100%)
Communication Services; Film or Tape Distribution for TV & Production of Television Programming; Consists of Viacom Productions, Viacom Enterprises, Viacom Worldwide, MGS Services and Viacom Licensing & Merchandising Department
S.I.C.: 4899; 7822
Neil S. Braun *(Chm. & Chief Exec. Officer)*
Deborah Beece *(Pres.-Programming & Production)*
Gus Lucas *(Pres.-Viacom's West Coast Opers; Exec. V.P.-Entertainment Grp.)*
Michael Keslo *(Exec. V.P.-Opers.)*
Katherine A. Hogan *(Sr. V.P. & Gen. Counsel)*
Michael Klinghoffer *(Sr. V.P.-Television Programming & Production)*
Susan Kolar *(Sr. V.P. & Chief Fin. Officer)*
Cecelia Holloway *(V.P.-Human Resources & Admin.)*
Betsy Vorce *(Sr. V.P.-Pub. Rels.)*

Division:

Viacom Enterprises **(4)**
1515 Broadway
New York, NY 10036
Tel.: 212-258-6000
Develope & Distribute Television Programs & Motion Pictures
S.I.C.: 7822
Michael H. Gerber *(Pres.-First-Run, International Distr. & Acquisitions)*
Dennis G. Gillespie *(Pres.-Worldwide Mktg. & Domestic Sls.)*
Raul Lefcovich *(Pres.-International Sls.)*
Dennis Emerson *(Sr. V.P.-Sls.-West)*
Frank Flanagan *(Sr. V.P.-Sls.-East)*
Tony Guido *(Sr. V.P.-Business Affairs & Acquisitions)*
Elissa Leback *(Sr. V.P.-Mktg. Strategy)*
Peter A. Newman *(Sr. V.P.-Ancillary Rights & Special Projects)*
Eric Veale *(Sr. V.P.-Opers.)*
David Archer *(V.P.-Bus. Devel.-Viacom World Wide)*
Sean Deneny *(V.P. & Gen. Sls. Mgr.-First Run)*
Lynn Fero *(V.P.-Bus. Affairs Admin.)*
Julia Pistor *(V.P.-Program Production & Devel.)*
Judy Pless *(V.P.-Bus. Devel.-Viacom World Wide)*

Subsidiary:

Viacom Productions Inc. **(4)**
10 Universal City Plaza
Universal City, CA 91608
Tel.: 818-505-7500 (100%)
Television Production
S.I.C.: 7812
Gus Lucas *(Exec. V.P.-West Coast Opers.)*
Roger Kirman *(Sr. V.P.-Business Affairs)*
Gerard DiCanio *(Sr. V.P.-Fin.)*
Robert Greenfield *(Sr. V.P.-Bus. Admin.)*
Paul Mason *(Sr. V.P.-Productions)*
Steven Gordon *(Sr. V.P.-Devel./Drama)*

Subsidiary:

Viacom Networks Inc. **(3)**
1515 Broadway
New York, NY 10036
Tel.: 212-575-5175 (100%)
100% Interest in Showtime Networks Inc. and MTV Networks
S.I.C.: 4899
Gregory J. Ricca *(Exec. V.P.-Business Affairs)*

Subsidiaries:

MTV: Music Television **(4)**
1515 Broadway
New York, NY 10036
Tel.: 212-258-6000
Sara Levinson *(Exec. V.P.-Bus. Opers.)*
Judith McGrath *(Exec. V.P. & Dir.-Creative)*
John Cannelli *(Sr. V.P.-Music & Talent)*
Howard Handler *(Sr. V.P.-Mktg. & Promotions)*
Douglas Herzog *(Sr. V.P.-Programming)*
Carole Robinson *(Sr. V.P.-Press Rels.)*
Andy Schoun *(Sr. V.P.-Music Programming & Promotions)*
Van Toffler *(Sr. V.P.-Entertainment & Bus. Devel.)*

MTV Networks **(4)**
1515 Broadway
New York, NY 10036
Tel.: 212-258-8000
Fax: 212-258-6100
Emp.: 600
National Distributor of Cable TV Programming; Nickelodeon/Nick at Nite; MTV: Music Television; VH-1 & HA! The Comedy Network
S.I.C.: 4833
Thomas Freston *(Chm. & Chief Exec. Officer)*
Edward Bennett *(Pres.-The TV Comedy Network & VH-1)*
Scott Davis *(Exec. V.P.-Network Opers. & Gen. Mgr.-Nickelodeon Studios)*
Harvey Ganot *(Exec. V.P.-Adv. Sls.)*
Douglas Greenlaw *(Exec. V.P.-Adv. Sls.)*
Sara Levinson *(Exec. V.P.-New Bus. Devel.)*
Gregory Ricca *(Exec. V.P. & Gen. Counsel)*
Mark Rosenthal *(Exec. V.P.-Affil. Sls. & Mktg.)*
James M. Shaw *(Exec. V.P.)*
Nicole Browing *(Sr. V.P.-Affil. Sls.)*
Lois Eisenstein *(Sr. V.P.-Business Affairs & Gen. Counsel)*
Laurie Goldstein *(Sr. V.P.-Production Mngmt.)*
Paul A. Heimbach *(Sr. V.P.-Engrng./ Network Opers. Ctr.)*
Deborah Johns *(Sr. V.P.-Communications/ MTVN)*
Barry Kluger *(Sr. V.P.-Media & Network Talent Rels./VH-1)*
Rick Levy *(Sr. V.P.-Syndication Sls.)*
John Popkowski *(Sr. V.P.-Adv. Sls.)*
Dwight Tierney *(Sr. V.P.-Admin.)*
Susan White *(V.P.- Human Resources)*
Carole Robinson *(V.P.-Press Rels., MTV)*
Martin Von Ruden *(V.P.-Press Rels./ Nickelodeon & Nick at Nite)*
Christine Gorham *(Dir.-Press & Publicity/ MTV Europe)*

Non-U.S. Branches:

MTV Asia **(5)**
c/o Star TV, 12th Floor, Hutchison House
10 Harcourt Road,
Hong Kong, Hong Kong
Tel.: 011-85-2-532-1888

MTV Australia **(5)**
TCN Channel 9, 24 Artarmon Road
Willoughby, N.S.W. 2064, Australia
Tel.: 011-61-2-906-9999

MTV Brazil **(5)**
Avenida Prof. Alfonso Bovero #52 Sumere,
Sao Paolo, 01254, Brazil
Tel.: 011-55-11-262-7444

MTV Europe **(5)**
Centro House, 20-23 Mandela Street
Hamden Town,
London, NW1 0DU, United Kingdom
Tel.: 011-44-71-383-4250
William Roedy *(Mng. Dir.)*

MTV Japan **(5)**
6F Tango 33 Bldg. 3-25-11, Higashi,
Shibuya-ku,
Tokyo, 150, Japan
Tel.: 011-81-3-5466-1105

Nickelodeon/Nick At Nite **(4)**
1515 Broadway
New York, NY 10036
Tel.: 212-258-8000
Cable Television Services
S.I.C.: 4841
Dick Van Dyke *(Chm.-Nick at Nite)*
Geraldine Laybourne *(Pres.)*
Scott Davis *(Gen. Mgr.-Nickelodeon Studios)*
Linda Kahn *(Sr. V.P.-Intl. Program Sls.)*
Anne Sweeney *(Sr. V.P.-Program Enterprises)*
Richard Cronin *(Sr. V.P.-Mktg.)*
Herb Scannell *(Sr. V.P.-Programming)*
Scott Webb *(Sr. V.P. & Dir.-Creative)*
Sam Moser *(V.P.-Adv. Sls.)*
Heidi Diamond *(V.P.-Mktg.)*

VH-1/Video Hits One **(4)**
1515 Broadway
New York, NY 10036
Cable Television Services
S.I.C.: 4841
Edward A. Bennett *(Pres.)*
Juli Davidson *(Sr. V.P.-Programming)*
Barry Kluger *(Sr. V.P.-Media & Network Talent Rels.)*
Lesly Schaefer *(Sr. V.P.-Mktg. & Promotions)*

Subsidiaries:

Showtime Satellite Networks, Inc. **(5)**
1633 Broadway
New York, NY 10019
Tel.: 212-575-5175 (100%)
Cable Services
S.I.C.: 4899

Showtime/The Movie Channel Inc. (U.K.) **(5)**
1633 Broadway
New York, NY 10019
Tel.: 212-575-5175 (100%)
Pay-Per-View Cable Television
S.I.C.: 4899
Winston H. Cox *(Chief Exec. Officer)*

Viacom Satellite Networks Inc. **(5)**
1515 Broadway
New York, NY 10036
Tel.: 212-258-6000 (100%)
Cable Services
S.I.C.: 4899

Non-U.S. Holdings:

Viacom Canada Ltd. **(1)**
45 Charles St. E.
Toronto, ON M4Y 1S2, Canada
Tel.: 416-925-3161 (100%)
Inactive
S.I.C.: 4841
Alastair Banks *(Gen. Mgr.)*

Viacom Enterprises Canada Ltd. **(1)**
45 Charles St. E.
Toronto, ON M4Y 1S2, Canada
Tel.: 416-925-3161 (100%)
Communication Services
S.I.C.: 4833; 4841; 4832
Alastair Banks *(Gen. Mgr.)*

Viacom Intl. Ltd. **(1)**
40 Conduit St.
London, W1R 9FB, United Kingdom
Tel.: 44-71-434-4483 (100%)

National Amusements, Inc.—(Continued)

Communication Services
S.I.C.: 4833; 4841; 4832

Viacom Intl. Pty. Ltd. **(1)**
16th St., St. Martin's Tower, 31 Market St.
Sydney, N.S.W. 2000, Australia
Tel.: 61-2-261-5391 (100%)
Communication Services
S.I.C.: 4833; 4841; 4832
Peter Press *(Gen. Mgr.)*

Viacom Japan, Inc. **(1)**
4F, Mitsuwa Bldg. 7-2 Ginza 6-chome,
Chuo-Ku,
Tokyo, 104, Japan
Tel.: 81-3-3573-0551
Communication Services
S.I.C.: 4833; 4841; 4832
Hiro Kuno *(Pres.)*

Viacom S.A. **(1)**
Chamerstrasse 18 CH-6300
Zug, Switzerland
Tel.: 41-42-21-8122 (100%)
Communication Services
S.I.C.: 4833; 4841; 4832
Manfred Metzger *(Gen. Mgr.)*

Viacom Video-Audio Comunicacoes, Ltda. **(1)**
Alameda Jau', 1742-11 Andar Caixa Postal 51521, 01420
Sao Paulo, 01420, Brazil
Tel.: 55-11-853-4633 (100%)
Communication Services
S.I.C.: 4833; 4841; 4832
Ivan Aragon *(Gen. Mgr.)*

NATIONAL ATTORNEYS TITLE INSURANCE COMPANY
111 Church St.
White Plains, NY 10601
Tel.: 914-946-3400
Tel.: 800-221-1621
Fax: 914-946-0179
Year Founded: 1937
Emp.: 35
Title Insurance
S.I.C.: 6361

Computer Systems/Hardware:
Alpha Micro; Burroughs

Outside Service Firm(s):

Colley, Trumbower & Howell*(Auditors)*
Orlando, FL

Thacher, Proffitt & Wood*(Legal Firm)*
Two World Trade Center
New York, NY 10005
Tel.: 212-483-5836

Chemical Bank*(Major Banking Relationship)*
White Plains, NY

Division:

National Attorneys Title Insurance Company--National Div. **(1)**
32 Broadway
New York, NY 10004
S.I.C.: 6361

NATIONAL BAND & TAG CO.
721 York
Newport, KY 41071
Mailing Address:
P.O. Box 430
Newport, KY 41071-0430
Tel.: 606-261-2035
Fax: 606-261-TAGS (8247)
Year Founded: 1902
Emp.: 35
Fiscal Year-end: 6/30/90
Export
National Poultry & Turkey Leg Bands, Wing Bands, Cage & Nest Markers, Terminal Tags, Tool Checks, Dog License & Rabies Vaccination Tags, Swim Pool Tags, Advertising Specialty Tags
S.I.C.: 3999
Donald J. Haas *(Pres.)*
Joseph D. Haas *(V.P.)*
Fred Haas Jr. *(Sec. & Treas.)*
Eric Haas *(Mgr.-Adv.)*

NATIONAL BANNER COMPANY
11938 Harry Hines Blvd.
Dallas, TX 75229
Tel.: 214-241-2131
Tel.: 800-527-0860
Fax: 214-241-6282
Fax: 800-468-0700
Approx.Sls.: $10,000,000
Emp.: 200
Fiscal Year-end: 12/31/90
Mfr. of Banners, Pennants, Flags, & Decals
S.I.C.: 2399; 2752
Abraham Goldfarb *(Pres.)*
William Gallemore II *(Sr. V.P.-Opers.)*
Marc Goldfarb *(V.P. & Natl. Sls. Mgr.)*
Ken Looney *(Dir.-Sls.)*
Francois Louis *(Dir.-Mktg.)*
Judy Tapscott *(Asst. Sls. Dir.)*

NATIONAL BASKETBALL ASSOCIATION
Olympic Tower, 645 Fifth Ave.
New York, NY 10022
Tel.: 212-826-7000
Fax: 212-826-0579
Administrators for the 27 Teams of the National Basketball League
S.I.C.: 7941
David J. Stern *(Commissioner)*
Russell Granik *(Deputy Commissioner & Chief Oper. Officer)*
Gary B. Bettman *(Sr. V.P. & Gen. Counsel)*
Robert Criqui *(V.P.-Fin.)*

No. of U.S. Offices: 1

Computer Systems/Hardware:
Digital; DEC

Outside Service Firm(s):

Prudential Insurance Co. of America*(Group Insurer)*
751 Broad St.
Newark, NJ 07102-3777
Tel.: 201-802-6000

Proskauer, Rose, Goetz & Mendelsohn*(Legal Firm)*
1585 Broadway
New York, NY 10036
Tel.: 212-969-3000

NATIONAL BEDDING & FURNITURE INDUSTRIES
736 S. Dudley
Memphis, TN 38104
Tel.: 901-774-7013
Fax: 901-942-5132
Emp.: 550
Beddings; Wood Dinette Furniture
S.I.C.: 2511; 2515
J.H. Patton, III *(Chm. Bd. & Pres.)*
Maury Knowldon *(Exec. V.P.)*
Jerry Loftin *(V.P.-Treas. & Controller)*
Lawson Apperson *(Gen. Counsel)*

Outside Service Firm(s):

Rhea & Ivy*(Auditors)*
Memphis, TN

Boone, Wellford, Clark, Langschmidt & Apperson*(Legal Firm)*
One Commerce Sq.
Memphis, TN 38103
Tel.: 901-523-0311

Subsidiary:

Desoto Hardwood Flooring Company **(1)**
977 Sledge Ave.
Memphis, TN 38101
Tel.: 901-774-9672
Approx.Sls.: $16,000,000
Emp.: 240
Mfr. & Wholesale Hardwood Strip & Plank Flooring; Planing Mills, & Rough Lumber
S.I.C.: 2421; 2426; 5031
David Hilley *(Pres.)*
Lanny Trottman *(V.P.-Sls. & Mktg.)*

NATIONAL BRANDS, INC.
4633 W. Polk,
Phoenix, AZ 85043
Tel.: 602-269-3201 **AZ**
Fax: 602-272-3741
Year Founded: 1975
Wholesale Electrical Appliances, Parts & Equipment., Home Furnishings, Commercial Machines & Equipment.
S.I.C.: 5064; 5023; 5045; 5065
Terry Thomas *(Chm. Bd.)*
Richard Hollenbeck *(Pres.)*
Ken Grogan *(V.P. & Mgr.-Gen. Sls.)*
Ned Dryer *(Sec. & Treas.)*

Computer Systems/Hardware:
IBM System 38

Outside Service Firm(s):

Ernst & Young*(Auditors)*
1100 CitiBank Tower, One S. Church Ave.
Tucson, AZ 85701
Tel.: 602-622-5801

Valley National Bank*(Major Banking Relationship)*
241 North Central Ave., 11th Floor
Phoenix, AZ 85001

NATIONAL BULK CARRIERS, INC.
1345 Ave. of the Americas
New York, NY 10105
Tel.: 212-765-3000
Fax: 212-765-3000 x322
Emp.: 400
Management Services & Real Estate Development
S.I.C.: 6552
James R. Kertz *(Chm. Bd.)*
Edward A. McDermitt, Jr. *(Pres. & Chief Exec. Officer)*
Frank Hess *(Chief Fin. Officer)*
R. Sun *(Treas.)*
Jo Janice *(Controller)*

Outside Service Firm(s):

Arthur Andersen & Co.*(Auditors)*
1345 Ave. of the Americas
New York, NY 10105
Tel.: 212-708-4000

Blue Cross & Blue Shield of Massachusetts*(Group Insurer)*
100 Summer St.
Boston, MA 02110

United States Trust Company of New York*(Pension Manager)*
45 Wall Street
New York, NY 10005

NATIONAL CAR RENTAL SYSTEM, INC.
7700 France Ave., S.
Minneapolis, MN 55435
Tel.: 612-830-2121
Tel.: 800-227-7368
Fax: 612-830-2087
Year Founded: 1947
Approx.Sls.: $750,000,000
Emp.: 9,500
Fiscal Year-end: 12/31/90
Car Rental
S.I.C.: 7514; 7515
Thomas N. Murphy *(Chm. Bd.)*
Robert J. McKenna *(Pres. & Chief Oper. Officer)*
John L. Yurish *(Exec. V.P.)*
William B. Baker *(Corp. V.P.)*
Ronald Knez *(Corp. V.P.)*
Ronald Knez *(V.P.)*
Dan Knudsen *(V.P.-Mktg.)*
Michael J. Olsen *(V.P.-Communications)*
Jack Livingston *(Chief Information Officer)*
Michael Becker *(Treas.)*

Principal(s):
Fidelco Capital Corp.
Ard Shiel Inc.
General Motors Corp.

NATIONAL CLEANING CONTRACTORS, INC.
375 Hudson St.
New York, NY 10014-3658
Tel.: 212-229-4000 **DE**
Fax: 212-229-4141
Year Founded: 1886
Approx.Sls.: $400,000,000
Emp.: 15,000
Fiscal Year-end: 9/30/90
Janitorial, Cleaning & Maintenance Services
S.I.C.: 7349
Morton A. Sweig *(Chm. Bd. & Chief Exec. Officer)*
Robert J. Carroll *(Pres. & Chief Oper. Officer)*
John Agnello *(Exec. V.P.)*
Andy Perez *(Sr. V.P.-Pur.)*
Burton Waxler *(Sr. V.P. & Treas.)*
George Staniuk *(V.P.)*
James Greco *(Controller)*
Burt Haimes *(Gen. Counsel & Sec.)*
Harry Chrispen *(Dir.-Human Resources)*
Mitch Freman *(Dir.-Data Processing)*
Bruce Levy *(Dir.-Sls.)*
Ronald Miller *(Dir.-Leasing)*
Janet Schaefer *(Dir.-Employee Benefits)*
Maggie Schneider *(Dir.-Pub. Rels.)*

No. of U.S. Offices: 28

Computer Systems/Hardware:
IBM System 400

Outside Service Firm(s):

Coopers & Lybrand*(Auditors)*
1301 Avenue of The Americas
New York, NY 10019
Tel.: 212-536-2000

National Westminster Bank plc*(Major Banking Relationship)*
Astor Plaza, 1515 Broadway
New York, NY 10036

NATIONAL COMPUTER PRINT, INC.
5200 E. Lake Blvd.
Birmingham, AL 35217
Tel.: 205-849-5200 **AL**
Fax: 205-849-6926
Year Founded: 1974
Assets: $22,000,000
Liabilities: $14,255,000
Net Worth: $7,745,000
Approx.Sls.: $27,000,000
Emp.: 325
Fiscal Year-end: 2/28/90
Payment Systems for Financial Services
S.I.C.: 6159
Grady Burrow *(Pres. & Chief Exec. Officer)*
Sharon Burrow *(Sec.)*
Ray Burrow *(Sr. V.P.-Opers. & Fin.)*
Rodney Burrow *(V.P.-Security)*
Curtis Liles *(Gen. Counsel)*
Mark Frechette *(Pur. Agent)*

Principal(s):
Grady Burrow
Ray Burrow

No. of Mfg. Plants/Facilities: 1
No. of U.S. Offices: 1

Computer Systems/Hardware:
IBM

Outside Service Firm(s):

McGriff, Siebels & Williams, Inc.*(Commercial Insurance Carrier)*
2211 Seventh Av.
Birmingham, AL 35202-0265

McGriff, Siebels & Williams, Inc.*(Group Insurer)*
2211 Seventh Av.
Birmingham, AL 35202-0265

Maynard, Cooper, Frierson & Gale*(Legal Firm)*
Birmingham, AL

First Alabama Bank*(Pension Manager)*
Montgomery, AL

NATIONAL CONCRETE PRODUCTS COMPANY
939 S. Mill St.
Plymouth, MI 48170
Tel.: 313-453-8448
Emp.: 70
Sewer Pipe, Concrete or Lined with Concrete
S.I.C.: 3272
Jack E. Cook *(Pres.)*
James J. Manson *(V.P. & Sec.)*
Bob Terwin *(V.P. & Treas.)*

NATIONAL COOPERATIVE REFINERY ASSOCIATION
2000 S. Main St.
McPherson, KS 67460
Mailing Address:
P.O. Box 1404,
McPherson, KS 67460
Tel.: 316-241-2340 **KS**
Telex: 910-740-1318
Fax: 316-241-5531
Year Founded: 1943
Assets: $401,342,032
Earnings: $55,577,793
Liabilities: $159,860,466
Net Worth: $241,481,566
Approx.Rev.: $847,280,629
Emp.: 550
Fiscal Year-end: 6/30/91
Crude Oil Production & Refining
S.I.C.: 2911
Corporate Giving Program: Annual Contributions Authorized by Board of Directors
Noel K. Estenson *(Chm. Bd.)*
Larry E. Williams *(Pres. & Chief Exec. Officer)*
John G. Buehrle *(V.P.-Fin. & Chief Fin. Officer)*
Fred J. Pierce *(V.P.-Refining)*
Kenneth I. Roane *(V.P.-Supply & Transportation)*
Ron Schaumburg *(V.P.-Human Resources)*
Kerry L. Domke *(Controller)*
Darryl Leffler *(Treas. & Asst. Sec.)*
Kenneth W. Cummings *(Mgr.-Data Processing & Systems)*
Merlin D. Fields *(Mgr.-Bldg. & Grounds)*
Dennis McMurray *(Mgr.-Employee Relations)*
Michael O'Connor *(Mgr.-Economic & Plng.)*
Dean Whetstone *(Mgr.-Matls.)*
Charles W. Pauls *(Chief Mech. Engr.)*
Vicky Kline *(Personnel Asst.)*

Computer Systems/Hardware:
IBM 9370 & 4341

Outside Service Firm(s):

KPMG Peat Marwick*(Auditors)*
1000 Walnut St.
Kansas City, MO 64106

Klenda, Mitchell, Ausherman & Zuercher*(Legal Firm)*
Wichita, KS

Mellon Bank*(Major Banking Relationship)*
New York, NY

Subsidiary:

Clear Creek, Inc. **(1)**
2000 S. Main
McPherson, KS 67460
Tel.: 316-241-2340
Emp.: 60
Crude Oil Trucking & Pipeline
S.I.C.: 4612

NATIONAL CORSET SUPPLY HOUSE
3240 E. 26th St.
Los Angeles, CA 90023
Tel.: 213-261-0265 **CA**
Fax: 213-261-6693
Year Founded: 1948
Approx.Sls.: $17,000,000
Emp.: 180
Export
Wholesale Distributor & Manufacturer of Women's Chemises, Camisoles, Teddies & Corsets
S.I.C.: 2341; 5137
Roy Schlobohm *(Pres.)*
Herman Schlobohm *(V.P.)*
Jon Schlobohm *(Sec. & Treas.)*

Principal(s):
Roy Schlobohm
Jon Schlobohm

Outside Service Firm(s):

First Business Bank*(Major Banking Relationship)*
Los Angeles, CA

Division:

Finebrand Division **(1)**
3240 E. 26th St.
Los Angeles, CA 90023
Tel.: 213-261-0265
Corsets; Women's & Children's Accessories
S.I.C.: 2342
Roy Schlobohm *(Pres.)*

NATIONAL DISTRIBUTING CO., INC.
1 National Dr. S.W.
Atlanta, GA 30336
Tel.: 404-696-9440 **GA**
Fax: 404-691-0364
Approx.Sls.: $280,000,000
Emp.: 1,500
Wholesale Distribution of Wines, Spirits & Beer; Linen Supply
S.I.C.: 5182; 7213
Michael C. Carlos *(Chm. Bd. & Chief Exec. Officer)*
Jay M. Davis *(Pres. & Chief Oper. Officer)*
Andrew C. Carlos *(Exec. V.P. & Treas.)*
Dick May *(V.P. & Data Processing Dir.)*
Lee Howard *(V.P.-Mktg.)*
Robert Schussel *(Controller)*

Computer Systems/Hardware:
IBM System 34

Outside Service Firm(s):

Pilot Life*(Group Insurer)*
Greensboro, NC

Arnall, Golden & Gregory*(Legal Firm)*
55 Park Place
Atlanta, GA 30335
Tel.: 404-577-5100

Bank of America, N.T. & S.A.*(Major Banking Relationship)*
P.O. Box 37002,
San Francisco, CA 94137

First American Bank, N.A.*(Major Banking Relationship)*
Atlanta, GA

First National Bank of Atlanta*(Major Banking Relationship)*
2 Peachtree Street N.W.
Atlanta, GA 30383

Bank South, N.A.*(Pension Manager)*
P.O. Box 4387
Atlanta, GA 30302
Tel.: 404-529-4111

Wine & Liquor Group:

Subsidiaries:

National Distributing Co., Inc. **(1)**
4109 Savarese Circle N.
Tampa, FL 33614
Tel.: 813-885-3200
Wine & Liquor Distr.
S.I.C.: 5182
Gene Davis *(Exec. V.P. & Mng. Dir.)*

National Distributing Co., Inc. **(1)**
10700 E. 40th Ave.
Denver, CO 80239
Tel.: 303-292-9977
S.I.C.: 5182
Jim Calvert *(Exec. V.P. & Mng. Dir.)*

National Distributing Co., Inc. **(1)**
3316 Perkins Rd.
Augusta, GA 30906
Tel.: 706-790-4444
S.I.C.: 5182
Nick Petkas *(V.P. & Mng. Dir.)*

National Distributing Co., Inc. **(1)**
109 Booker Ave.
Albany, GA 31701
Tel.: 912-883-6151
S.I.C.: 5182
Warren Johnson *(V.P. & Mng. Dir.)*

National Distributing Co., Inc. **(1)**
513 14th St.
Columbus, GA 31904
Tel.: 706-322-6526
S.I.C.: 5182
Steve Marinos *(V.P. & Mng. Dir.)*

NDC Distributors, Inc. **(1)**
8000 Maie St.
Los Angeles, CA 90001
Tel.: 213-586-2000
Approx.Sls.: $100,000,000
Emp.: 385
S.I.C.: 5182
Jack T. Stout *(Pres.)*
Alfred A. Davis *(Chm.-Exec. Committee)*
Joe Hirsh *(Sr. V.P. & Dir.-Sls.)*
Wayne Millsap *(V.P. & Dir. Opers.)*
Juanne Pesick *(Gen. Office Mgr.)*

Branches:

NDC Distributors, Inc. **(2)**
530 E. Cerritos Ave.
Anaheim, CA 92805
Tel.: 714-772-5842
S.I.C.: 5182
Frank Fiorentino *(Branch Mgr.)*

National Distributing Co., Inc. **(2)**
1 National Dr. S.W.
Atlanta, GA 30336
Tel.: 404-696-9440
Wholesale Distr. of Beer
S.I.C.: 5182
Bob Ware *(V.P. & Mng. Dir.)*

National Distributing Co., Inc. **(2)**
Two Servitex Dr.
Macon, GA 31297
Tel.: 912-746-8166
S.I.C.: 5182
Gerald Neal *(V.P. & Mng. Dir.)*

Standard Distributing Co., Inc. **(1)**
1414 Mills B. Lane Blvd.
Savannah, GA 31405
Tel.: 912-233-2201
S.I.C.: 5182
Gordon Johnson *(V.P. & Mng. Dir.)*

Branches:

Standard Distributing Co. Inc. **(2)**
1725 T St.
Brunswick, GA 31520
Tel.: 912-265-0900
S.I.C.: 5182
Gordon Johnson *(V.P. & Mng. Dir.)*

Standard Distributing Co., Inc. **(2)**
1003 "M" St.
Waycross, GA 31501
Tel.: 912-283-7284
Wholesaler of Beer
S.I.C.: 5182
Don Wiggins *(Branch Mgr.)*

Standard Distributing Co., Inc. **(2)**
P.O. Box 1305
Vidalia, GA 30474
Tel.: 912-537-4114
Wholesale Beer Distr.
S.I.C.: 5182

National Distributing Co., Inc. **(2)**
9423 No. Main St.
Jacksonville, FL 32218
Tel.: 904-751-0090
Wholesale Distr. of Beer
S.I.C.: 5182
Gerard Fisher *(Sr. V.P. & Mng. Dir.)*

National Distributing Co., Inc. **(2)**
16601 N.W. 8th Ave.
Miami, FL 33169
Tel.: 305-621-1441
Wholesale Beer Distr.
S.I.C.: 5182
Michael Berns *(Sr. V.P. & Mng. Dir.)*

National Distributing Co., Inc. **(2)**
3785 Bryn Mawr St.
Orlando, FL 32808
Tel.: 407-298-2300
Wholesale Beer Distr.
S.I.C.: 5182
Donald M. Hanley *(V.P. & Mng. Dir.)*

National Distributing Co., Inc. **(2)**
4268 Westroads Dr.
West Palm Beach, FL 33407
Tel.: 407-842-4683
Wholesale Distr. of Beer
S.I.C.: 5182
Thomas Colombrito *(V.P. & Mng. Dir.)*

National Distributing Co., Inc. **(2)**
P.O. Box 17168, 3333 Palafox St.
Pensacola, FL 32522
Tel.: 904-432-4128
Wholesale Distr. of Beer
S.I.C.: 5182
John Carlos *(V.P. & Mng. Dir.)*

Linen Supply Group:

Servitex, Inc. **(1)**
717 Summit Ave.
Kinston, NC 28501
Tel.: 919-523-3191
Linen Supply Service
S.I.C.: 7213
Donald Joyner *(Plant Mgr.)*

Servitex, Inc. **(1)**
3301 Hillsborough St.
Raleigh, NC 27602
Tel.: 919-828-7491
Linen Supply Service
S.I.C.: 7213
Alan D. Wilson *(Exec. V.P. & Dir.-Opers.)*

Branches:

Servitex, Inc. **(2)**
One Servitex Dr.
Macon, GA 31297
Tel.: 912-742-1471
Linen Supply Service
S.I.C.: 7213
W. G. Randolph *(Plant Mgr.)*

Servitex, Inc. **(2)**
270 Piney Forest Rd.
Danville, VA 24541
Tel.: 804-793-5111
Linen Supply Service
S.I.C.: 7213
Phil Harris *(Plant Mgr.)*

Servitex, Inc. **(2)**
1720 Lawson
Durham, NC 27703
Tel.: 919-596-2186
Linen Supply Service
S.I.C.: 7213
Leo Watkins *(Plant Mgr.)*

National Distributing Co., Inc.—(Continued)

Servitex, Inc. **(2)**
123 W. Lewis St.
Greensboro, NC 27406
Tel.: 919-272-7182
Linen Supply Service
S.I.C.: 7213
Jimmy Burchfield *(Service Mgr.)*

Servitex, Inc. **(2)**
5616 Shell Rd.
Virginia Beach, VA 23455
Tel.: 804-460-1681
Linen Supply Service
S.I.C.: 7213
Homer Spears *(Plant Mgr.)*

Servitex, Inc. **(2)**
P.O. Box 628
Bedford, VA 24523
Tel.: 703-586-0704
Linen Supply Srvc.
S.I.C.: 7213

NATIONAL EMERGENCY SERVICES, INC.
P.O. Box 156, 39 Main St.
Tiburon, CA 94920
Tel.: 415-435-4591 IL
Fax: 415-435-2930
Year Founded: 1975
Approx.Sls.: $100,000,000
Emp.: 125
Physician Staffing for Emergency Rooms
S.I.C.: 7361
Dr. Allan Rappaport *(Chm. Bd., Pres. & Chief Exec. Officer)*
Mitchell G. Billing *(Chief Oper. Officer)*
Darrell Eckstein *(Chief Fin. Officer)*
Thomas M. Botts *(Exec. V.P.)*
Sanford E. Pomerantz *(Legal Counsel)*
Patrisha Rogers *(Mgr.-Office)*

Computer Systems/Hardware:
IBM Compatible Laser Digital System

Outside Service Firm(s):

Deloitte & Touche*(Auditors)*
50 Fremont St.
San Francisco, CA 94105-2230
Tel.: 415-393-4300
Fax: 415-227-0452

Sanford, Pomerantz*(Legal Firm)*
St. Louis, MO

NATIONAL ENGINEERING & CONTRACTING CO.
12608 Alameda Dr.
Strongsville, OH 44136
Tel.: 216-238-3331
Telex: 467982
Fax: 216-238-3335
Year Founded: 1933
Assets: $35,000,000
Liabilities: $21,300,000
Net Worth: $13,700,000
Approx.Sls.: $96,100,000
Emp.: 450
Fiscal Year-end: 12/31/91
General Contractors: Highways, Bridges, Sewage Treatment Plants
S.I.C.: 1622; 1623; 1629; 1791; 1794
Robert J. Ibos *(Chm. Bd., Pres. & Chief Exec. Officer)*
John DeLuca *(V.P. & Treas.)*
W.E. Jynod *(V.P. & Area Mgr.)*
John S. Shott *(V.P. & Sec.)*
Thomas Hesmond *(Dir.-Pur.)*
Duane Kryz *(Chief Fin. Officer)*
Fred Ode *(Mgr.-Data Processing)*
Tom Hurless *(Chief Engineer)*

Computer Systems/Hardware:
Wang

Outside Service Firm(s):

Tishler Beard Wallace*(Auditors)*
Cleveland, OH

Liberty Mutual*(Commercial Insurance Carrier)*
Cleveland, OH

Great-West Life Assurance Co.*(Group Insurer)*
Columbus, OH

Weston, Hurd, Fallon, Paisley & Howley*(Legal Firm)*
Cleveland, OH

National City Bank*(Major Banking Relationship)*
P.O. Box 92301, Corp. Trust Dept.
Cleveland, OH 44101
Tel.: 216-575-2000

Subsidiaries:

Lee Construction Co. **(1)**
P.O. Box 240927
Charlotte, NC 28231
Tel.: 704-588-5272
Emp.: 75
Heavy Construction
S.I.C.: 1622; 1623; 1629; 1794
Jimmie Neese *(Pres.)*

Transbulk, Inc. **(1)**
12608 Alameda Dr.
Strongsville, OH 44136
Tel.: 216-238-6566
Emp.: 3
Bulk Material Handling Equip. For Railroad Utilities & Ships
S.I.C.: 3625
Alan Rowen *(Pres.)*

Tri State Steel Construction **(1)**
12608 Alameda Dr.
Strongsville, OH 44136
Tel.: 216-238-3331
Emp.: 35
Structured Steel Erection
S.I.C.: 3448
Allan Shepard *(Pres.)*

THE NATIONAL ENQUIRER
600 S. East Coast Ave.
Lantana, FL 33464
Tel.: 407-586-1111
Fax: 407-540-1017
Approx.Sls.: $159,000,000
Emp.: 1,300
Weekly Newspaper
S.I.C.: 2711
Iain Calder *(Chm. Bd. & Pres.)*
Patrick M. Linskey *(Exec. V.P. & Dir.-Mktg.)*
Barbara H. Marks *(Sr. V.P. & Grp. Publr.)*
Ralph Gallagher *(V.P.-Agency & Client Rels.)*
Katherine Jose *(V.P. & Dir.-Adv.)*
Dan Schwartz *(Editor)*
Guy Galiardao *(Sec.)*
Richard Pickert *(Treas.)*

Subsidiary:

The National Enquirer **(1)**
Graybar Building, 420 Lexington Avenue, Ste. 440
New York, NY 10170
Tel.: 212-682-4022
Fax: 212-697-8793

NATIONAL FINANCIAL INSURANCE COMPANY
(Dallas Regional Office)
403 S. Akard
Dallas, TX 75202
Mailing Address:
P.O. Box 660254,
Dallas, TX 75266
Tel.: 214-670-9700
Approx.Rev.: $202,000,000
Emp.: 150
Fiscal Year-end: 12/31/90
Insurance Company; Life Insurance, Health Insurance & Annuities
S.I.C.: 6311; 6321
C.W. Boykin, Jr. *(Chief Oper. Officer)*
Ray L. Gonzalez *(V.P.-Insurance Services)*
Robert H. Choate *(V.P.-Claims)*
Donald M. Woodard *(V.P.-Fin. Services)*

NATIONAL FIRE PROTECTION ASSOCIATION
One Batterymarch Park
Quincy, MA 02269
Tel.: 617-770-3000
Fax: 617-770-0700
Year Founded: 1896
Approx.Sls.: $34,500,000
Emp.: 300
Fiscal Year-end: 12/31/92
Fire Prevention Books, Films & Magazines
S.I.C.: 8611; 7812
George D. Miller *(Pres. & Chief Exec. Officer)*
Anthony O'Neill *(V.P. & Chief Oper. Officer)*
Robert Coneys *(V.P.-Fin.)*
Richard Griessel *(V.P.-Mktg. & Sls.)*

NATIONAL FOOD STORES, INC. T/A KRAUSZER'S
(Formerly Dairy Stores, Inc.)
76 National Rd.
Edison, NJ 08818-3031
Mailing Address:
P.O. Box 3031,
Edison, NJ 08818
Tel.: 908-287-2800 NJ
Fax: 908-287-8064
Year Founded: 1909
Approx.Sls.: $100,000,000
Emp.: 18
Fiscal Year-end: 12/29/90
Retail Convenience Stores
S.I.C.: 2111; 5194; 2064; 5141; 5411
Harry Shah *(Pres.)*
Martin H. Kern *(Chief Exec. Officer)*
Don Obrzut *(V.P.-Mktg.)*
Harry Patel *(V.P.)*
Sohini Patel *(V.P.)*
Mark D. Kleczka *(Gen. Counsel)*

Computer Systems/Hardware:
IBM System 38

Outside Service Firm(s):

Deloitte & Touche*(Auditors)*
1700 Market St.
Philadelphia, PA 19103
Tel.: 215-246-2322
Fax: 215-569-2441

NATIONAL FOODS INC.
600 Food Center Dr.
Bronx, NY 10474
Tel.: 718-842-5000
Fax: 718-842-5664
Approx.Sls.: $140,000,000
Emp.: 900
Fiscal Year-end: 12/31/90
Export
Meat Products, Poultry Products, Pickled Products
S.I.C.: 2013; 2035; 2015
Isidore Pines *(Chm. Bd. & Chief Exec. Officer)*
Harvey Potkin *(Pres. & Chief Oper. Officer)*
Martin Silver *(Exec. V.P.)*
Alan Aronovitz *(Sr. V.P. & Chief Fin. Officer)*
Chuck Brown *(Sr. V.P.-Quality)*
David Palmer *(Sr. V.P.-Mktg. & Sls.)*
Jonathan Bernstein *(V.P., Treas. & Sec.)*
Vic Bevilaqua *(V.P.-Mktg.)*
Andrew Janover *(V.P.-Mfg. & Distr.)*
Robert Lichtman *(V.P.-Florida Opers.)*
Jerome M. Luks *(V.P. & Gen. Counsel)*
Ronald Potkin *(V.P.-Sls.)*
Ervin Schwarzmann *(V.P.-Pur.)*
Phil White *(V.P.-West Coast Opers.)*
Walt Dlugolecki *(Controller)*
Arnold Glick *(Dir.-Mngmt. Information Systems)*

Outside Service Firm(s):

Anchin, Block & Anchin*(Auditors)*
1375 Broadway
New York, NY 10018

Marine Midland Bank*(Major Banking Relationship)*
250 Park Ave.
New York, NY 10017
Tel.: 212-503-6642

Subsidiary:

Hebrew National Kosher Foods Div. **(1)**
602 W. Ray St.
Indianapolis, IN 46225
Tel.: 317-637-5093
Meat Products
S.I.C.: 2013
Charles Brown *(Sr. V.P.-Quality)*

NATIONAL FOOTBALL LEAGUE PROPERTIES, INC.
(Wholly-Owned by 28 National Football League Teams)
410 Park Ave.
New York, NY 10022
Tel.: 212-838-0660
Fax: 212-758-4239
Year Founded: 1963
Approx.Sls.: $2,000,000,000
Emp.: 100
Fiscal Year-end: 3/31/91
Import Export
Sales Promo., Licensing, Publishing; National Football League Team Names, Insignia, Designs & Publications
S.I.C.: 7941
Norman Braman *(Chm.-Exec. Committee)*
John J. Bello *(Pres.)*
John Flood *(Exec. V.P. & Legal Counsel)*
Alex MacFadyen *(V.P.-Fin.)*
Jim Schwebel *(V.P.-Mktg.)*
Frank Vuono *(V.P.-Retail Licensing)*
John Wiebusch *(V.P.-Creative Services)*
Ed Adams *(Dir.-Natl. Sls.)*
Jim Connelly *(Dir.-Intl. Licensing)*
Don Garber *(Dir.-New Business)*
Rusty Hawley *(Dir.-Communications)*
Tom Richardson *(Dir.-Publishing)*
Bill Barron *(Gen. Mgr.-Creative Services)*

Computer Systems/Hardware:
DEC VAX

NATIONAL FORGE COMPANY
One Front St.
Irvine, PA 16329
Tel.: 814-563-7522 DE
Telex: 091-4446
Fax: 814-563-9209
Year Founded: 1915
Assets: $91,000,000
Liabilities: $54,000,000
Net Worth: $37,000,000
Approx.Sls.: $78,000,000
Emp.: 889
Fiscal Year-end: 12/31/91
Export
Mfr. of Finish-Machined Steel Forgings; Hot & Cold Isostatic Presses
S.I.C.: 3312; 3462; 3544; 3399; 3479
Corporate Giving Program: Donations to Various Local Charities
Robert O. Wilder *(Chm. Bd., Pres. & Chief Exec. Officer)*
W.E. Erickson *(Exec. V.P.)*
John G. Koedel, Jr. *(V.P. & Chief Fin. Officer)*
Maurice Cashman *(Treas.)*
John H. Morse *(Sec.)*
Thomas Jackson *(Controller)*
R. D'Alessandro *(Dir.-Plng.)*
G.R. Charles *(Dir.-Mktg.)*
Joseph Gabriel *(Dir.-Mngmt. Information Systems)*

George O. Loomis *(Dir.-Operational Services)*
C.R. Olson *(Dir.-Opers.)*
Robert Kaemmerer *(Mgr.-Risk)*
Clarence Mason *(Mgr.-Purchase)*

No. of Mfg. Plants/Facilities: 6
No. of U.S. Offices: 5
No. of Foreign Offices: 2

Computer Systems/Hardware:
IBM System 400; IBM 4341

Outside Service Firm(s):

Price Waterhouse*(Auditors)*
600 Grant St., Ste. 4400
Pittsburgh, PA 15219
Tel.: 412-355-6000
Fax: 412-391-0609

Liberty Mutual*(Group Insurer)*
175 Berkeley St.
Boston, MA

Moses & Singer*(Legal Firm)*
1271 Ave. of the Americas
New York, NY 10020
Tel.: 212-246-3700

Chemical Bank*(Major Banking Relationship)*
450 West 33rd St.
New York, NY 10001
Tel.: 212-613-7197
Fax: 212-947-7628

Subsidiaries:

Industrial Materials Technology **(1)**
155 River St.,
Andover, MA 01810
Tel.: 508-470-1620 (100%)
Emp.: 50
Service Unit Providing Isostatic Pressing Service, Research, Developing & Consulting
S.I.C.: 8731; 8734
Dr. Robert Widmer *(Pres.)*
Arthur Brennan *(Controller)*

Plant:

Industrial Materials Technology **(2)**
6651 S.E. Crosswhite Way
Portland, OR 97206
Tel.: 503-777-8003
Isostatic Pressing Services, Consulting, Research & Development
S.I.C.: 8731; 8734

National Forge Engineered Systems Div. **(1)**
155 River Rd.
Andover, MA 01810
Tel.: 508-470-1620 (100%)
Fax: 508-475-2951
Manufacture & Design High Pressure Equipment
S.I.C.: 3823
Andrew Crum *(Gen. Mgr.)*
Arthur Brennan *(Controller)*

National Forge Export Corp. **(1)**
Front St.
Irvine, PA 16329
Tel.: 814-563-7522 (100%)
Sales of Steel Forgings; Hot & Cold Isostatic Presses
S.I.C.: 5051

IMT **(1)**
155 River Rd.
Andover, MA 01810
Tel.: 508-470-1620 (100%)
Fax: 508-475-2951
Emp.: 50
Hot & Cold Isostatic Pressing Services, Research, Development & Consulting
S.I.C.: 3462; 8731; 8734
Dr. Robert Widmer *(Chief Oper. Officer)*

Non-U.S. Holdings:

Mitchell Shackleton & Co. Ltd. **(1)**
Green Lane Patricroft
Manchester, M30 8AD, United Kingdom
Tel.: 61-789-2241 (100%)
Fax: 61-787-7672
Emp.: 100
Mfr. of Crankshafts
S.I.C.: 3462
Brian McGuinness *(Mng. Dir.)*
Brian McGuinness *(Chief Oper. Officer)*

National Forge Europe NV **(1)**
Industrie Park 7
Sint-Niklaas, Belgium
Tel.: 3 777 3511 (100%)
Emp.: 50
Manufacture & Designer of High Pressure Equipment; Isostatic Pressing Services
S.I.C.: 3823
Herman D.B. Raes *(V.P. & Gen. Mgr.)*

NATIONAL FROZEN FOODS CORP.
2371 Eastlake Ave. East
Seattle, WA 98102
Mailing Address:
P.O. Box 9366
Seattle, WA 98109
Tel.: 206-322-8900 **WA**
Fax: 206-322-4458
Year Founded: 1912
Approx.Sls.: $55,000,000
Emp.: 350
Export
Process Frozen Vegetables
S.I.C.: 2037
S.J. McCaffray *(Chm. Bd. & Pres.)*
Celeste Gazarek *(V.P.-Fin. & Treas.)*
R.H. Grader *(V.P.-Sls.)*
W.H. Rosenbach *(V.P.-Opers.)*
R.E. Ashmun *(Sec.)*
L.A. Cravens *(Controller)*
A.J. Alleman *(Mgr.-Sls. Service & Export)*
J.J. Bafus *(Mgr.-Corp. Quality Assurance)*
C.M. McCaffray *(Mgr.-Human Resources)*

Principal(s):
McCaffray Family

No. of Mfg. Plants/Facilities: 4

Outside Service Firm(s):

Coopers & Lybrand*(Auditors)*
1800 First Interstate Center, 999 Third Ave.
Seattle, WA 98104-4098
Tel.: 206-622-8700

Davis, Wright, Tremaine*(Legal Firm)*
2200 One Union Square
Seattle, WA 98101-1688
Tel.: 206-622-3150

Seafirst Bank*(Major Banking Relationship)*
Columbia-SeaFirst Center, 701 5th Ave., 11th Flr.
Seattle, WA 98124
Tel.: 206-358-3039
Fax: 206-358-3113

Divisions:

National Frozen Foods Corporation - Albany **(1)**
745 - 30th Ave. S.W.
Albany, OR 97321
Tel.: 503-928-3306
S.I.C.: 2037
Bill Kiewel *(Gen. Mgr.)*

National Frozen Foods Corporation - Burlington **(1)**
200 Washington Ave.
Burlington, WA 98233
Tel.: 206-755-0211
S.I.C.: 2037
Chip Wiles *(Gen. Mgr.)*

National Frozen Foods Corporation - Chehalis **(1)**
188 Sturdevant Rd.
Chehalis, WA 98532
Tel.: 206-748-4403
S.I.C.: 2037
Coe Johnson *(Gen. Mgr.)*

National Frozen Foods Corporation - Moses Lake **(1)**
Wheeler Rd.
Moses Lake, WA 98837
Tel.: 506-766-0793
S.I.C.: 2037
Tom Schultz *(Plant Mgr.)*

Subsidiary:

Cuizina Italia, Inc. **(1)**
18744 - 142nd N.E.
Woodinville, WA 98072
Tel.: 206-486-7000
S.I.C.: 2037
Ric Ferrera *(Pres.)*

NATIONAL FRUIT PRODUCT COMPANY
550 Fairmont Ave.
Winchester, VA 22601-3931
Mailing Address:
P.O. Box 2040
Winchester, VA 22604-1240
Tel.: 703-662-3401 **VA**
Fax: 703-665-4670
Fax: 703-665-4671
Year Founded: 1908
Sales Range: $100-499 Million
Emp.: 1,600
Fiscal Year-end: 6/31/92
Export
White House Apple Sauce, Apple Juice, Sliced Apples, Apple Cider Vinegar; White Distilled Vinegar, Wine Vinegar; Apple Butter
S.I.C.: 2099
Frank Armstrong III *(Chm. & Pres.)*
V.R. Strader, Jr. *(V.P. & Treas.)*
V.M. Miller *(V.P.-Mfg.)*
Daniel Troup *(V.P.-Mktg. & Sls.)*
L.M. Johns, Jr. *(Controller)*
Margaret H. Marlowe *(Sec.)*
Herbert Glass *(Mgr.-Human Resources)*
David Coco *(Chief Engineer)*

Outside Service Firm(s):

Grant Thornton*(Auditors)*
Washington, DC 20090

Hazel & Thomas, PC*(Legal Firm)*
Washington, DC
Tel.: 202-659-7000

Farmers & Merchants National Bank*(Major Banking Relationship)*
Winchester, VA

NATIONAL GEOGRAPHIC SOCIETY
17th & M Sts. N.W.
Washington, DC 20036
Tel.: 202-857-7000 **DC**
Fax: 202-828-5658
Year Founded: 1888
Publishers of Books & Magazines
S.I.C.: 2721; 2731
Gilbert M. Grosvenor *(Chm. Bd. & Pres.)*
Robert Sims *(Sr. V.P.)*
Michela English *(V.P.-Membership)*
Joan McCraw *(V.P.-Natl Adv.)*
Sarita L. Moffat *(Dir.-Magazine Opers.)*
Pandora Todd *(Dir.-Adv. Promo.)*
William Graves *(Editor)*

NATIONAL GRAPE CO-OP ASSOCIATION, INC.
Two S. Portage St.
Westfield, NY 14787
Tel.: 716-326-3131 **NY**
Fax: 716-326-5111
Year Founded: 1945
Assets: $197,921,000
Earnings: $54,810,000
Liabilities: $117,659,000
Net Worth: $80,262,000
Approx.Sls.: $419,254,000
Emp.: 1,297
Fiscal Year-end: 8/31/91
Cooperative Marketing of Grape Juice Products
S.I.C.: 2037; 2033
J. Roy Orton *(Pres.)*
Patrick J. O'Donnell *(Chief Oper. Officer, Treas. & Gen. Mgr.)*
Tim L. St. Hilaire *(V.P.)*
Douglas P. Moorhead *(V.P.)*
Daniel C. Schultz *(V.P.)*
James Weidman III *(V.P.-Corp. Communications)*

No. of Mfg. Plants/Facilities: 5
No. of U.S. Offices: 4

Computer Systems/Hardware:
IBM; National Advance System

Outside Service Firm(s):

KPMG Peat Marwick*(Auditors)*
700 Empire Tower
Buffalo, NY 14202-3786
Tel.: 716-854-1830
Fax: 716-856-8063

Aetna Life & Casualty*(Group Insurer)*
151 Farmington Avenue
Hartford, CT 06156
Tel.: 203-273-2128
Fax: 203-729-4295

Travelers Insurance Co.*(Group Insurer)*
1 Tower Square
Hartford, CT 06183-2492
Tel.: 203-277-4542
Fax: 203-277-5038

Goldman, Sachs & Co.*(Investment Banker)*
85 Broad St.
New York, NY 10004
Tel.: 212-902-1000
Fax: 212-902-4451

Bond, Schoeneck & King*(Legal Firm)*
One Lincoln Center
Syracuse, NY 13202
Tel.: 315-422-0121

Bankers Trust Co.*(Major Banking Relationship)*
Des Moines, IA

Citibank N.A.*(Major Banking Relationship)*
Corporate Trust Services, 399 Park Ave.
New York, NY 10043
Tel.: 212-559-1605

Bankers Trust Co.*(Pension Manager)*
One Bankers Trust Plaza
New York, NY 10006
Tel.: 212-250-6902

Subsidiary:

Welch's **(1)**
100 Main St.
Concord, MA 01742
Tel.: 508-371-1000 (100%)
Fax: 508-371-2832
Approx.Sls.: $464,000,000
Emp.: 1,300
Fiscal Year-end: 8/31/92
Export
Computer Systems/Hardware:
IBM
Mfr. & Marketing of Juices, Jellies & Concentrates
S.I.C.: 2033; 2037
J. Roy Orton *(Chm. Bd.)*
Everett N. Baldwin *(Pres. & Chief Exec. Officer)*
T.J. Wolfe *(Exec. V.P.)*
T. E. Callahan *(V.P.-Fin.)*
D.P. Dillon *(V.P.)*
T.E. Gettig *(V.P.-Human Resources)*
S.S. Hart *(V.P.-Mktg.)*
William C. Hewins *(V.P.-Intl. Oper.)*
G.H. Kilpatrick *(V.P.-Sls.)*
T.W. Lance *(V.P.-Opers.)*
James Weidman III *(V.P.-Corp. Communications)*
Albert B. Wright III *(V.P.-Corp. Plng.)*
D.E. Riederer *(Treas.)*
R.W. McMillen III *(Controller)*
V. Tseng *(Dir.-Legal)*

Division:

Welch's International Div. **(2)**
100 Main St.
Concord, MA 01742
Tel.: 508-371-1000
Fax: 508-371-2832
Sales & Marketing of Frozen Fruit Juices & Vegetables
S.I.C.: 5142

NATIONAL GROUP, INC.
2464 Amnicola Hwy.
Chattanooga, TN 37406
Mailing Address:
P.O. Box 1448,
Chattanooga, TN 37401
Tel.: 615-622-2254 **TN**
Fax: 615-622-7623
Year Founded: 1958
Approx.Sls.: $25,000,000
Emp.: 370
Screen Printing; Posters, Lithographed
S.I.C.: 2759; 2752
George Diamantis *(Pres.)*
Leland L. Gaddis *(Exec. V.P.-Admin.)*
James Huskey *(Exec. V.P.-Fin.)*
Carole J. Daniel *(V.P. & Asst. Treas.)*
Doris J. Thomas *(Sec.)*

Outside Service Firm(s):

Hazlett, Lewis & Bieter *(Auditors)*
Tivoli Cener, Ste. 300, 701 Broad St.
Chattanooga, TN 37402-1802
Tel.: 615-756-6133

Divisions:

National Posters, Inc. **(1)**
1001 Latta St.
Chattanooga, TN 37406
Tel.: 615-622-1106
Approx.Sls.: $16,000,000
Emp.: 135
Posters, Lithographed
S.I.C.: 2752
William H. Price *(Chm. Bd.)*
Philip H. Brown *(Pres.)*
L.L. Gaddis *(V.P. & Sec.)*
George Diamantis *(V.P.)*
Mack N. Jordan, Jr. *(V.P.)*
Linda N. Matthews *(V.P.)*
Leonard E. Scott *(V.P.)*
C.D. Spain *(V.P.)*
Carole Daniel *(Asst. Treas.)*

Spectra National **(1)**
1401 Godson Ave.
Chattanooga, TN 37406
Tel.: 615-622-2155

NATIONAL GYPSUM COMPANY
(Sub. of Aancor Holdings, Inc.)
2001 Rexford Rd.
Charlotte, NC 28211
Tel.: 704-365-7300 **DE**
Year Founded: 1925
Assets: $887,800,000
Earnings: ($95,800,000)
Liabilities: $1,469,600,000
Net Worth: $581,800,000
Approx.Sls.: $1,136,300,000
Emp.: 6,000
Fiscal Year-end: 12/31/91
Mfr. & Supplier of Gypsum Wallboard & Other Gypsum Products; Commercial & Industrial Design; Construction Services
S.I.C.: 1541; 3275; 8711; 1542; 5039
Peter C. Browning *(Chm. & Chief Exec. Officer)*
J. Michael Conaway *(Chief Fin. Officer & V.P.)*
Allan V. Cecil *(V.P.-Pub. Affairs)*
Cynthia Hartley *(V.P.-Human Resources)*
Edward A. Porter *(V.P.-Admin., Gen. Counsel & Corp. Sec.)*

Computer Systems/Hardware:
IBM 5150

Outside Service Firm(s):

Ernst & Young *(Auditors)*
2121 San Jacinto, Ste. 500
Dallas, TX 75201
Tel.: 214-969-8000

Divisions:

The Austin Company **(1)**
3650 Mayfield Rd.
Cleveland, OH 44121
Tel.: 216-382-6600
Fax: 216-291-6684
Approx.Sls.: $2,300,000
Emp.: 2,500
Fiscal Year-end: 12/31/91
Consulting, Design, Engineering & Construction of Governmental, Institutional, Commercial Buildings & Industrial Facilities
S.I.C.: 1541; 1542; 8711; 8712
Corporate Giving Program: Company Supports a Variety of Eleemosynary, Educational, Cultural and Civic Organizations and Institutions Through Direct Donations
Thomas J. Judge *(Pres. & Chief Exec. Officer)*
J. William Melsop *(Grp. V.P.-Domestic Oper. Units)*
Richard Moran *(Grp. V.P.-Intl. Oper. Units)*
James R. Anderson *(V.P.-Fin., Sec. & Treas.)*
William P. Buettner *(V.P. & Controller)*
James G. Peterson *(V.P.-Construction & Pur.)*
Theodore D. Puckorius *(V.P.-Govt. & Consulting Services)*
David A. Robichaux *(V.P.-Mktg. & Plng.)*
Gene Roe *(V.P.-Personnel)*
Stuart R. Wetterschneider *(V.P.-Design & Engrng.)*
Marvin M. Epstein *(Dir.-Pub. Rels. & Adv.)*
Dennis M. Raymond *(Dir.-Personnel)*
Joan L. Mascio *(Asst. Mgr.-Pub. Rels. & Adv.)*

Division:

Austin Consulting **(2)**
9801 W. Higgins Road
Rosemont, IL 60018
Tel.: 708-696-0500
Fax: 708-698-6359
Consultants: Productivity Improvement, Material Flow, Logistics, Equipment Condition Analysis, Inventory Systems Evaluation, Facility Modernization, System Configuration & Interface Definition, Detail Systems Design, Network Design, Concept Development, Total Systems Integration
S.I.C.: 8742; 7371; 7373; 7379
Theodore D. Puckorius *(Grp. V.P.)*
R.J. Tadlock *(Gen. Mgr.)*
T.J. Frey *(Dir.-Sls.)*

Gold Bond Building Products **(1)**
2001 Rexford Rd.
Charlotte, NC 28211
Tel.: 704-365-7300
Export
Mfr. & Supplier of Gypsum Wallboard, Predecorated Wallboard & Wallboard Systems
S.I.C.: 3275; 5039
Peter C. Browning *(Pres.)*
E.J. Fitzgerald *(V.P.-Mktg.)*
E.E. Stenstrom *(Dir.-Mktg. Communications)*

Plants:

Gold Bond Building Products **(2)**
Roll Rd.
Clarence Center, NY 14032
Tel.: 716-741-2811
Mfr. of Gypsum Wallboard & Wallboard Systems
S.I.C.: 3275

Gold Bond Building Products **(2)**
P.O. Box 566,
East Greenbush, NY 12061
Tel.: 518-449-7354
Mfr. of Gypsum Wallboard & Wallboard Systems
S.I.C.: 3275

Gold Bond Building Products **(2)**
1850 W. 8th
Long Beach, CA 90813
Tel.: 310-435-4465
Mfr. of Gypsum Products; Wallboard & Wallboard Systems
S.I.C.: 3275
R. Britt *(Plant Mgr.)*

Gold Bond Building Products **(2)**
P.O. Box 308,
Richmond, CA 94806
Tel.: 510-234-6740
Mfr. of Gypsum Board
S.I.C.: 3275
K.O. Reid *(Plant Mgr.)*

Gold Bond Gypsum Products **(2)**
P.O. Box 14,
National City, MI 48748
Tel.: 517-362-2696
Mfr. of Gypsum Products
S.I.C.: 3275
D.C. Lane *(Plant Mgr.)*

Gold Bond Building Products **(2)**
2301 S. Newkirk St.
Baltimore, MD 21224
Tel.: 410-732-9200
Mfr. of Gypsum Products
S.I.C.: 3275
J.A. Ciampaglio *(Plant Mgr.)*

Gold Bond Building Products **(2)**
1901 Henderson Dr.
Lorain, OH 44052
Tel.: 216-288-9101
Mfr. of Gypsum Products
S.I.C.: 3275
T.R. Fout *(Plant Mgr.)*

Gold Bond Building Products **(2)**
P.O. Box 7016,
Garden City, GA 31408
Tel.: 912-964-1561
Mfr. of Gypsum Products
S.I.C.: 3275
R.E. Rowan *(Plant Mgr.)*

Gold Bond Building Products **(2)**
P.O. Box 100,
Burlington, NJ 08016
Tel.: 609-499-3300
Mfr. of Gypsum Products
S.I.C.: 3275
G.T. Noakes *(Plant Mgr.)*

Gold Bond Building Products **(2)**
515 Sea Horse Dr.
Waukegan, IL 60085
Tel.: 708-623-8100
Mfr. of Gypsum Products
S.I.C.: 3275
L.P. Massey *(Plant Mgr.)*

Gold Bond Building Products **(2)**
1414 E. Hadley
Phoenix, AZ 85034
Tel.: 602-258-6106
Mfr. of Gypsum Products
S.I.C.: 3275
H.E. Skelly *(Plant Mgr.)*

Gold Bond Building Products **(2)**
1584 S. 22nd St., P.O. Box 977
Fort Dodge, IA 50501
Tel.: 515-576-4186
Mfr. of Gypsum Products
S.I.C.: 3275
John Wade *(Plant Mgr.)*

Gold Bond Building Products **(2)**
P.O. Box 250,
Shoals, IN 47581
Tel.: 812-247-2424
Mfr. of Gypsum Products
S.I.C.: 3275
W.M. Adamczyk *(Plant Mgr.)*

Gold Bond Building Products **(2)**
P.O. Box 270,
Portsmouth, NH 03801
Tel.: 603-436-4840
Mfr. of Gypsum Products
S.I.C.: 3275
R.L. Alessi *(Plant Mgr.)*

Gold Bond Building Products **(2)**
10 Louisiana St.
Westwego, LA 70094
Tel.: 504-341-8596
Mfr. of Wallboard & other Gypsum Products
S.I.C.: 3275
Tom Brooks *(Plant Mgr.)*

Gold Bond Building Products **(2)**
P.O. Drawer "B",
Rotan, TX 79546
Tel.: 915-735-2221
Mfr. of Wallboard & other Gypsum Products
S.I.C.: 3275
J.L. Presler *(Plant Mgr.)*

Gold Bond Building Products **(2)**
P.O. Box 19307,
Tampa, FL 33604
Tel.: 813-839-2111
Mfr. of Gypsum Products
S.I.C.: 3275
R.G. Moore *(Plant Mgr.)*

Gold Bond Building Products **(2)**
P.O. Drawer "B",
Medicine Lodge, KS 66860
Tel.: 316-886-5613
Mfr. of Wallboard & Other Gypsum Products
S.I.C.: 3275
J.N. Dooley *(Plant Mgr.)*

Gold Bond Building Products **(2)**
P.O. Box 1379,
Wilmington, NC 28402
Tel.: 919-799-3954
Mfr. of Wallboard & Other Gypsum Products
S.I.C.: 3275
W.L. Dungan *(Plant Mgr.)*

Gold Bond Building Products **(2)**
504 Walnut St.
Niles, OH 44446
Tel.: 216-652-2558
Mfr. of Metal Products
S.I.C.: 3469
D.M. Rotolo *(Plant Mgr.)*

Gold Bond Building Products **(2)**
Birmingham Hwy.
Anniston, AL 36201
Tel.: 205-831-6900
Mfr. of Paperboards
S.I.C.: 2679
H.B. McComb *(Plant Mgr.)*

Gold Bond Building Products **(2)**
P.O. Box 338,
Milton, PA 17847
Tel.: 717-538-2531
Mfr. of Paperboard Products
S.I.C.: 2679
L.R. Erhardt *(Plant Mgr.)*

Gold Bond Building Products **(2)**
P.O. Box 428,
Pryor, OK 74361
Tel.: 918-825-0142
Mfr. of Liner Paper
S.I.C.: 2679
T.L. May *(Plant Mgr.)*

Non-U.S. Holdings:

Austin-Australia **(1)**
3 Bowen Crescent
Melbourne, Victoria 3004, Australia
Tel.: 3 266-3255 (100%)
Design, Engineering & Construction of Industrial & Commercial Facilities
S.I.C.: 1541; 8711; 8712

Austin-Australia **(1)**
52-56 Atchinson St.
St. Leonards, N.S.W. 2065, Australia
Tel.: 439-4255 (100%)
Design, Engineering & Construction of Industrial & Commercial Facilities
S.I.C.: 1541; 8711; 8712

The Austin Co. **(1)**
1-9, Kanda Nishikicho., Chiyoda-ku
Tokyo, 101, Japan
Tel.: 03-3294-3236 (100%)
Design, Engineering & Construction of Industrial & Commercial Facilities
S.I.C.: 1541; 8711; 8712

The Austin Co. of Canada **(1)**
304 E. Mall, Ste. 701
Islington, ON M9B 6E2, Canada
Tel.: 416-239-4309 (100%)
Sales of Gypsum Products
S.I.C.: 5039
Peter C. Browning *(Chm. Bd.)*

The Austin Co. of U.K. Ltd. **(1)**
35 Ballards Lane
London, N3 IXW, United Kingdom
Tel.: 071-346-9351 (100%)
Design, Engineering & Construction of Industrial & Commercial Facilities
S.I.C.: 8711; 1541; 8712

The Austin Co. S.A. **(1)**
Magallanes 3, 10 piso 28015
Madrid, Spain
Tel.: 91-447-7300 (100%)
Design, Engineering & Construction of Industrial & Commercial Facilities
S.I.C.: 8711; 1541; 8712
Manuel S. Costales *(Mng. Dir.)*

Austin Italia S.p.A. **(1)**
Via Romagnoli 6 20146
Milan, Italy
Tel.: 2 422-82-46 (100%)
Design, Engineering & Construction of Industrial & Commercial Facilities
S.I.C.: 8711; 1541; 8712

Austin-Nederland B.V. **(1)**
Turfstekerstraat 63 1431 GD Aalsmeer, Amsterdam, Netherlands
Tel.: 2977 40201 (100%)
Design, Engineering & Construction of Industrial & Commercial Bldgs.
S.I.C.: 1541; 8711; 8712

NATIONAL HEALTH CARE AFFILIATES, INC.
651 Delaware Ave.
Buffalo, NY 14202
Tel.: 716-881-4425 **FL**
Fax: 716-881-5237
Year Founded: 1977
Assets: $59,875,000
Earnings: $803,000
Liabilities: $54,113,000
Net Worth: $5,762,000
Approx.Sls.: $48,790,000
Emp.: 1,900
Fiscal Year-end: 12/31/91
Owners & Managers of Nursing Homes & Retirement Centers
S.I.C.: 8051; 8099
Mark E. Hamister *(Chm. Bd., Pres. & Chief Exec. Officer)*
David Taber *(Chief Fin. Officer & V.P.-Fin.)*
George E. Hamister *(Sr. V.P.-Asset Mngmt.)*
Lisa Clark Driscoll *(V.P.)*
Darrel Hager *(V.P.-Southeast Region)*
Oliver C. Hamister *(V.P.-Admin., Treas. & Sec.)*
George E. Hart *(V.P. & Corp. Counsel)*
Jack A. Turesky *(V.P.-Northeast Region)*
Mark S. Tedesco *(Asst. V.P. & Controller)*
Robert J. Dorian *(Mgr.-Payroll)*
Nancy M. Harezga *(Mgr.-Payroll)*
Joan K. Meier *(Mgr.-Data Processing)*

Principal(s):
Mark E. Hamister
George E. Hamister
Oliver C. Hamister

No. of Mfg. Plants/Facilities: 15
No. of U.S. Offices: 3

Computer Systems/Hardware:
IBM System 36

Outside Service Firm(s):

Ernst & Young*(Auditors)*
1400 Key Tower - 50 Fountain Plaza
Buffalo, NY
Tel.: 716-843-5000
Fax: 716-847-6949

Continental Insurance*(Commercial Insurance Carrier)*
180 Maiden Lane
New York, NY

Blue Cross of Western New York, Inc.*(Group Insurer)*
P.O. Box 828, 275 Oak St.
Buffalo, NY 14240

Kidder, Peabody & Co.*(Investment Banker)*
Buffalo, NY

Hodgson, Russ, Andrews, Woods & Goodyear*(Legal Firm)*
1800 One M & T Plaza
Buffalo, NY 14203
Tel.: 716-856-4000

Chase Lincoln First Bank, N.A.*(Major Banking Relationship)*
295 Main St.
Buffalo, NY 14203
Tel.: 716-849-8531

Empire of America*(Major Banking Relationship)*
Buffalo, NY

Manufacturers & Traders Trust Company*(Major Banking Relationship)*
1 M & T Plaza
Buffalo, NY 14240
Tel.: 716-842-4200

NATIONAL HEALTH PRODUCTS
731 Kirkman Rd.
Orlando, FL 32811
Tel.: 407-297-7671
Tel.: 800-537-7671
Fax: 407-290-2788
Year Founded: 1975
Mfr. of Supplements For Body Builders
S.I.C.: 2833
Tom Ciola *(Pres.)*
Marsha Ciola *(Sec.)*

NATIONAL LABEL COMPANY
2025 Joshua Rd.
Lafayette Hill, PA 19444
Tel.: 215-825-3250
Fax: 215-834-8854
Year Founded: 1917
Sales Range: $10-19 Million
Emp.: 170
Paper Labels, Converted Paper & Paperboard Products
S.I.C.: 2851
James H. Shacklett, Jr. *(Chm. Bd.)*
James Shacklett III *(Chief Exec. Officer)*
Dean R. Shacklett *(Chief Oper. Officer)*
William T. Lambe *(Controller)*
Volker Hehlinger *(Dir.-Mfg.)*

Outside Service Firm(s):

Margolis & Co.*(Auditors)*
Bala Cynwyd, PA

Dilworth, Paxson, Kalish & Kauffman*(Legal Firm)*
Lafayette Hill, PA

Fidelity Bank*(Major Banking Relationship)*
Broad & Walnut St.
Philadelphia, PA 19109

THE NATIONAL LATEX PRODUCTS CO.
246 E. Fourth St.
Ashland, OH 44805
Tel.: 419-289-3300
Tel.: 800-437-5144(Cust. Serv.)
Fax: 419-289-7118
Year Founded: 1941
Approx.Sls.: $25,000,000
Emp.: 300
Mfr. of Rubber Toy Balloons & Plastic Playballs
S.I.C.: 3069; 3089
Harry R. Gill II *(Chm. Bd.)*
H. Ross Gill III *(Pres.)*
Rick C. Geething *(Exec. V.P.)*
Mick L. Briggs *(V.P.-Sls.)*
Ronald Kahn *(V.P.-Mktg.)*
Robert L. Frey *(Sec.)*
Dave Cheviron *(Mgr.-Adv.)*
Nancy Kolp *(Dir.-Pur.)*
R. Dean Strine *(Dir.-Personnel)*

NATIONAL LIBERTY
(Sub. of the Capitol Holding Corp.)
20 Moores Rd.
Frazer, PA 19355
Tel.: 215-648-5000
Approx.Sls.: $100,000,000
Emp.: 1500
Fiscal Year-end: 12/31/90
Marketer of Life & Health Financial Products
S.I.C.: 6311
Norman Phelps *(Pres. & Chief Exec. Officer)*
Pamela H. Godwin *(Sr. V.P.-Insurance Opers.)*
John Hoey *(Sr. V.P.-Mktg. & Adv.)*
Donald D. Kennedy, Jr. *(Sr. V.P. & Legal Counsel)*
Richard Smith *(Chief Fin. Officer)*

NATIONAL LIFE INSURANCE COMPANY
National Life Dr.
Montpelier, VT 05604
Tel.: 802-229-3333 **VT**
Fax: 802-229-9281
Year Founded: 1850
Assets: $4,700,000,028
Liabilities: $4,447,667,000
Net Worth: $252,333,028
Approx.Premiums: $520,851,000
Emp.: 940
Fiscal Year-end: 12/31/91
Life Insurance; Annuities; Accident & Sickness Insurance; Variable Annuities; Mutual Funds & Outside Investment Programs
S.I.C.: 6311; 6321; 6211
Corporate Giving Program: Limited to Vermont
Frederic H. Bertrand *(Chm. Bd. & Chief Exec. Officer)*
John H. Harding *(Pres. & Chief Oper. Officer)*
William L. Cassidy *(Sr. V.P.-Service)*
Thomas F. Commito *(Sr. V.P.-Mktg.)*
William W. Fenniman *(Sr. V.P. & Chief Mktg. Officer)*
Mark J. Levesque *(Sr. V.P.-Information Systems & Mngmt. Services)*
Thomas H. MacLeay *(Sr. V.P. & Chief Fin. Officer)*
Keniston P. Merrill *(Sr. V.P. & Chief Investment Officer)*
L. James L. Rivers *(Sr. V.P.-Plng.)*
John L. Stotler *(Sr. V.P. & Gen. Counsel)*
Theodore N. von Wallmenich *(Sr. V.P. & Chief Actuary)*
William L. Wagner, Jr. *(Sr. V.P.-New Bus.)*
Beverly Bagalio *(V.P.-Retirement Services)*
Bryan J. Cerutti *(V.P.-Information Systems Plng. & Service)*
Jon E. Desilets *(V.P.-Corp. Systems Devel.)*
Christopher Graham *(V.P.-Underwriting)*
Edward Lamorey *(V.P.-Data Center & Telecommunications Services)*
Richard H. Lashoones *(V.P.-Auditing)*
John L. Stotler *(V.P. & Gen. Counsel)*
John Trepanier *(V.P.-Agency Services)*
Brian Vachon *(V.P.-Communications)*
David O. Wesley *(V.P. & Chief Medical Dir.)*
Donn W. Blodgett *(2nd V.P.-Facilities Mngmt.)*
Susan Chiappetta *(2nd V.P.-Human Resources)*
Jerald A. Johnson *(2nd V.P.-Benefits)*
Margaret Arthur *(Sec.)*
Charles C. Kittredge *(Treas.)*
Jean K. Landolt *(Asst. Sec.)*
Lynn R. Averill *(Dir.-Conferences & Travel)*
Jane W. Robb *(Dir.-Corp. Rels.)*
Judith Hebert *(Mgr.-Mktg. Services)*
Reginald Morse *(Mgr.-Data Center Control)*
Charles Haynes *(Pur. Agent)*

No. of U.S. Offices: 68

Computer Systems/Hardware:
IBM Systems 3090-600E

Outside Service Firm(s):

Price Waterhouse*(Auditors)*
One Financial Plaza
Hartford, CT 06103
Tel.: 203-240-2000

National Life Insurance Company*(Group Insurer)*
Montpelier, VT

Subsidiaries:

Administrative Services, Inc. **(1)**
National Life Dr.
Montpelier, VT 05604
Tel.: 802-229-3333 (100%)
Fax: 802-229-9281
Admin. of Plans Sold by National Life Insurance Company, Vermont Life Insurance Company, Champlain Life Insurance Company & Equity Services, Inc.
S.I.C.: 6411; 8741
William L. Cassidy *(Pres. & Chief Oper. Officer)*
John H. Harding *(Chm. & Chief Exec. Officer)*

National Life Investment Management Co., Inc. **(1)**
National Life Dr.
Montpelier, VT 05604
Tel.: 802-229-3333
Insurance Holding Company
S.I.C.: 6282; 6719
Keniston P. Merrill *(Chm., Pres. & Chief Exec. Officer)*

Subsidiaries:

Equity Services, Inc. **(2)**
National Life Dr.
Montpelier, VT 05604
Tel.: 802-229-3900
Tel.: 800-233-4332 (100%)
Fax: 802-229-3596
Approx.Sls.: $171,000,000
Emp.: 55
Fiscal Year-end: 12/31/90
Broker in Mutual Fund Shares & other Securities
S.I.C.: 6211
Joseph M. Rob *(Chm. Bd., Pres. & Chief Exec. Officer)*
John M. Grab, Jr. *(Sr. V.P. & Chief Fin. Officer)*
Steven A. Englese *(V.P.-Due Dilligence)*
Marvin Aber *(V.P.)*
Brian K. Martin *(Treas.)*
D. Russell Morgan *(Gen. Counsel)*
John R. Feeney *(Mgr.-Proprietary Prod.)*
Budd A. Shedaker *(Dir.-Equity Communications)*
Pauline Stebar *(Dir.-Compliance)*
Douglas G. Newman *(Asst. V.P.-Equity Mktg.)*

Subsidiary:

Sentinel Administrative Service Corporation **(3)**
National Life Dr.
Montpelier, VT 05604
Tel.: 800-282-3863
Approx.Rev.: $2,100,000
Fiscal Year-end: 12/31/90
Shareholder Services & Fund Accounting to Sentinel Mutual Funds
S.I.C.: 6289
Nancy K. Port *(Pres. & Chief Oper. Officer)*
John M. Grab, Jr. *(Sr. V.P. & Chief Fin. Officer)*

Champlain Life Insurance Company **(2)**
National Life Dr.
Montpelier, VT 05604
Tel.: 802-229-3333
Fax: 802-229-9281
S.I.C.: 6311
John H. Harding *(Chief Oper. Officer)*

Redstone Properties, Inc. **(2)**
National Life Drive
Montpelier, VT 05604
Tel.: 802-229-3333

Sentinel Advisors, Inc. **(2)**
National Life Dr.
Montpelier, VT 05604
Tel.: 802-223-9300 (100%)
Investment Advisor to Sentinel Funds
S.I.C.: 6282
Keniston P. Merrill *(Chm., Pres. & Chief Exec. Officer)*

National Life Insurance Company—(Continued)

Vermont Life Insurance Company **(2)**
National Life Dr.
Montpelier, VT 05604
Tel.: 802-229-3333
S.I.C.: 6311
John H. Harding *(Pres. & Chief Oper. Officer)*

NATIONAL LIVE STOCK & MEAT BOARD
444 N. Michigan Ave.
Chicago, IL 60611
Tel.: 312-467-5520
Fax: 312-467-9729
Year Founded: 1922
Emp.: 96
Non-Profit Commodity Promotion & Consumer Education Research
S.I.C.: 8742; 8748
John L. Huston *(Pres.)*
Jeanne M. Sowa *(Exec. V.P.-Mktg.)*
Mark W. Thomas *(Exec. V.P.-Fin. & Opers.)*
Jay H. Wardell *(Exec. V.P.-Beef Industry Council)*
Mary M. Adolf *(V.P.-Adv. Promotions)*
Tim Downey *(V.P.-Pork Industry Grp.)*
David Hurt *(V.P.-Res.)*
H. Kenneth Johnson *(V.P.-Meat Science Div.)*
Gary Born *(Comptroller)*
Leslie Nelson *(Dir.-Human Resources)*
Donna Schmidt *(Dir.-Pub. Rels.)*
William D. Siarny *(Dir.-Library Services)*
Eric Hentges *(Dir.-Nutrition Res.)*

Computer Systems/Hardware:
MAI Basic 4

Outside Service Firm(s):

Hutton, Nelson & McDonald*(Auditors)*
Chicago, IL

Mayer, Brown & Platt*(Legal Firm)*
190 S. LaSalle St., Ste. 3900
Chicago, IL 60603
Tel.: 312-782-0600

Divisions:

Beef Industry Council **(1)**
444 N. Michigan Ave.
Chicago, IL 60611
Tel.: 312-467-5520
Fax: 312-467-9767
Emp.: 100
S.I.C.: 0751; 8741
Jay Wardell *(Exec. V.P.)*
Jeanne M. Sowa *(Exec. V.P.)*
Monica B. Eorgoff *(Dir.-Adv.)*

Lamb Committee **(1)**
444 N. Michigan Ave.
Chicago, IL 60611
Tel.: 312-467-5520
S.I.C.: 8741
H. Kenneth Johnson *(V.P.)*

Pork Industry Group **(1)**
444 N. Michigan Ave.
Chicago, IL 60611
Tel.: 312-467-5520
S.I.C.: 8741
Tim Downey *(V.P.)*

NATIONAL LUMBER CO.
24595 Groesbeck Hwy.
Warren, MI 48089
Mailing Address:
P.O. Box 1003
Warren, MI 48090
Tel.: 313-775-8200 **MI**
Fax: 313-775-4110
Approx.Sls.: $68,100,000
Emp.: 212
Wholesale & Retail Lumber, Manufacturer, Rough Lumber, Trusses, Apartment, & Building Operations
S.I.C.: 5211; 5031; 6512; 6513; 2439
Marvin Rosenthal *(Pres.)*
James Rosenthal *(V.P.)*
Allen Strickstein *(V.P.)*
Irvin Strickstein *(V.P. & Sec.)*
David Bittker *(Treas.)*
Ron Bittker *(Mgr.-Sls.)*

Outside Service Firm(s):

Kleiman, Carney & Greenbaum*(Auditors)*
Farmington Hills, MI

Comerica Bank*(Major Banking Relationship)*
Roseville, MI

NATIONAL MACHINERY ADV. SERVICES

161 Greenville St.
Tiffin, OH 44882
Tel.: 419-447-5211
Approx.Sls.: $55,000,000
Emp.: 800
Manufacturer of forging and forming machines
S.I.C.: 3542
Jim Wade *(Adv. Mgr.)*
Douglas Niemeyer *(Chief Fin. Officer, Sec. & Treas)*

NATIONAL MACHINERY COMPANY
161 Greenfield St.
Tiffin, OH 44883
Mailing Address:
P.O. Box 747
Tiffin, OH 44883
Tel.: 419-447-5211
Telex: 286450
Fax: 419-447-5299
Year Founded: 1874
Approx.Sls.: $100,000,000
Fiscal Year-end: 12/31/90
Import Export
Mfr. Forging & Forming Machines
S.I.C.: 3542
Paul N. Aley *(Pres. & Chief Exec. Officer)*
John Richards *(Sr. V.P.)*
Larry Baker *(V.P.-Human Rels.)*
John Bolte *(V.P.-Mfg.)*
Robert J. Foster *(V.P.-Fin.)*
Thomas Hay *(V.P.-Engrng.)*
Patrick Bowers *(Controller)*
Richard Hummerding *(Mgr.-Pur.)*
Larry Wilson *(Mgr.-Sls.)*

Computer Systems/Hardware:
IBM PC

Outside Service Firm(s):

Deloitte & Touche*(Auditors)*
Two Prudential Plaza, 180 N. Stetson
Chicago, IL 60601
Tel.: 312-946-2039

Continental Bank N. A.*(Major Banking Relationship)*
231 S. LaSalle St.
Chicago, IL 60697
Tel.: 312-828-2345
Tel.: 800-426-5754
Telex: 312-828-1783

The Huntington National Bank*(Major Banking Relationship)*
41 S. High St.
Columbus, OH 43216

National City Bank*(Major Banking Relationship)*
P.O. Box 92301, Corp. Trust Dept.
Cleveland, OH 44101
Tel.: 216-575-2000

National Bank of Detroit*(Major Banking Relationship)*
611 Woodward
Detroit, MI 48226
Tel.: 313-225-1000

NATIONAL MEDIA MAIL, INC.
1820 E. First St., Ste. 500
Santa Ana, CA 92705
Tel.: 714-836-9472
Tel.: 800-524-6245
Fax: 714-836-1293
Year Founded: 1985
Approx.Billings: $10,000,000
Emp.: 20
Pre-Print Media Buying Service: FSI's, Shared & Solo Mail Programs, Newspaper Inserts, Printing, Production & Freight
Barbara Gorla *(Pres.)*
Rita Campbell *(Gen. Mgr. & New Bus. Contact)*
Angela Garcia *(Acctg.)*

NATIONAL MEDIA SERVICES, INC.
600 Morgan Falls Rd., Ste. 125
Atlanta, GA 30350
Tel.: 404-551-5930
Fax: 404-551-5946
Year Founded: 1980
Approx.Billings: $13,000,000
Emp.: 16
National Yellow Pages Placement Services for Advertising Agencies & Direct Clients
Mark V. Church *(Pres.)*
Geri Haas *(Mgr.-Acctg.)*
Nan Hartup *(Mgr.-Client Services)*

NATIONAL MERCHANDISE CO., INC.
2321 Liberty St.
Jacksonville, FL 32206
Tel.: 904-757-2700 **FL**
Fax: 904-350-9544
Approx.Sls.: $175,000,000
Emp.: 400
Wholesaler of Drugs, Dry Goods & Domestic Items
S.I.C.: 5122; 5023; 5100
Leonard Setzer *(Pres. & Chief Exec. Officer)*
David Lehnartz *(V.P.-Sls.)*
Alan Bentley *(Sec. & Treas.)*
James Anderson *(Controller)*

Computer Systems/Hardware:
IBM 4341

Outside Service Firm(s):

Joseph Hartman & Associates*(Auditors)*
Jacksonville, FL

Selber & Selber*(Legal Firm)*
Jacksonville, FL

First Union National Bank*(Major Banking Relationship)*
P.O. Box 2565,
Jacksonville, FL 32203

NATIONAL MORTGAGE COMPANY
4041 Knight Arnold Rd.
Memphis, TN 38118
Tel.: 901-362-1171 **TN**
Fax: 901-367-4594
Year Founded: 1951
Emp.: 375
Mortgage Bankers & Correspondents; Insurance Agents, Brokers & Service
S.I.C.: 6162; 6411
Sam S. Margolin *(Pres. & Chief Exec. Officer)*
Frank Robinson *(Chief Fin. Officer & Treas.)*
Martin Graber *(Sr. V.P.)*
Sidney M. Katz *(Sr. V.P. & Gen. Counsel)*
David Katz *(V.P.-Secondary Mortgage)*
Stanley L. Wender *(Sec.)*

Outside Service Firm(s):

First National Bank*(Major Banking Relationship)*
New Orleans, LA

NATIONAL OUT-OF-HOME MEDIA/METRO 8
51 East 42nd St., Ste. 1208
New York, NY 10017
Tel.: 212-867-7557
Tel.: 800-438-7328
Fax: 212-867-7571
Year Founded: 1971
Approx.Billings: $18,000,000
Emp.: 16
Free Rates, Data Allotments, Competitive Data, Plng. Services & Out-of-Home Media
Robert Dragotta *(Chm. Bd. & Pres.)*
Richard Briggs *(Exec. V.P.)*
Allan Rothman *(Sr. V.P.)*
John Russick *(V.P., Chief Oper. Officer)*
Mary Robertson *(Admin.)*

Computer Systems/Hardware:
NEC

NATIONAL PROPERTY ANALYSTS, INC.
230 S. Broad St., Mezzanine
Philadelphia, PA 19102
Tel.: 215-790-4700
Fax: 215-790-4733
Year Founded: 1976
Approx.Sls.: $65,000,000
Emp.: 90
Real Estate Agents, Brokers & Managers
S.I.C.: 6531
Howard N. Brownstein *(Chm. Bd.)*
Edward B. Lipkin *(Pres.)*
George Alburger *(V.P.-Fin.)*
Howard Lezy *(V.P.)*
Al Lipkin *(V.P.)*
David Simon *(Controller)*
Principal(s):
Howard N. Brownstein
Edward B. Lipkin

Outside Service Firm(s):

KPMG Peat Marwick*(Auditors)*
1600 Market St.
Philadelphia, PA 19103
Tel.: 215-299-3100

Clair Insurance*(Group Insurer)*
Philadelphia, PA

Philadelphia National Bank*(Major Banking Relationship)*
P.O. Box 13834, Broad & Chestnut Streets
Philadelphia, PA 19101-7618
Tel.: 215-973-8327

NATIONAL R.V., INC.
3411 N. Perris Blvd.
Perris, CA 92370
Tel.: 909-943-6007 **CA**
Fax: 909-943-5204
Year Founded: 1963
Approx.Sls.: $43,000,000
Emp.: 250
Fiscal Year-end: 8/ 1/90
Manufacturer of Motor Homes
S.I.C.: 3792
Wayne Mertes *(Pres.)*
Kenneth Ashley *(Chief Fin. Officer, Sec. & Treas.)*
Morley Mendelson *(Gen. Counsel)*
Peter Thomas *(Dir.-Pur.)*
Lewis Howard *(Gen. Mgr.)*
Ronald Sutter *(Mgr.-Prod.)*

Mike Woods *(Mgr.-Natl. Sls.)*
Principal(s):
Wayne Mertes

No. of Mfg. Plants/Facilities: 1
No. of U.S. Offices: 1

Outside Service Firm(s):

Goode & Kiernan*(Auditors)*
Reseda, CA

Union Bank*(Major Banking Relationship)*
8155 Mercury Ct., P.O. Box 2529
San Diego, CA 92112

NATIONAL REPRODUCTIONS CORPORATION
29400 Stephenson Hwy.
Madison Heights, MI 48071
Tel.: 313-398-7900 **MI**
Fax: 313-398-7081
Year Founded: 1953
Approx.Sls.: $11,000,000
Emp.: 200
Lithographic Commercial Printing, Duplicating, Blueprinting, Computer Printing & Microfilming; Short-run Book Printing Facilities Management
S.I.C.: 2752
James P. Pamel *(Pres. & Treas.)*
John Markoul *(Sr. V.P.)*
Robert Berardino *(V.P.-Opers.)*
George Elian *(V.P.-Sls.)*
Peter J. Pamel *(V.P.-Opers.)*
James E. Stone *(V.P.-Mktg.)*
James Valentine *(V.P.-Opers.)*

Outside Service Firm(s):

Plante & Moran*(Auditors)*
Detroit, MI

Divisions:

Alberts Copying Div. **(1)**
115 W. Warren
Detroit, MI 48202
Tel.: 313-831-1170
Printing
S.I.C.: 2752

Book Publishing Div. **(1)**
12749 Richfield Ct.
Livonia, MI 48150
Tel.: 313-591-4130
Book Publishing
S.I.C.: 2731
Cathy Franczek *(Branch Mgr.)*

Computer Printing Div. **(1)**
433 E. Larned
Detroit, MI 48226
Tel.: 313-961-5252
Lazer Printing, Mailing & Complete Fulfillment Services
S.I.C.: 2752
Pricella Davis *(Mgr.)*

Shelly Data Systems **(1)**
48733 West Rd.
Wixom, MI 48393
Tel.: 313-380-8070
Microfilm & Computer Aided Retrival
S.I.C.: 7389
Alex Brunner *(Chief Oper. Officer)*

NATIONAL RESTAURANT SUPPLY COMPANY
320 W. San Antonio
El Paso, TX 79901
Tel.: 915-544-2121 **TX**
Fax: 915-544-2141
Sales Range: $10-19 Million
Emp.: 60
Wholesale Distributor of Restaurant Equipment & Supplies; Industrial & Personal Service Paper, Janitorial Supplies
S.I.C.: 5046; 5113; 5087
Bruce Gulbas *(Pres. & Chief Exec. Officer)*
Paul Gulbas *(V.P.)*
Jacqueline Gulbas *(Sec. & Treas.)*

Outside Service Firm(s):

Tune & Henderson*(Auditors)*
El Paso, TX

Texas Commerce Bank*(Major Banking Relationship)*
El Paso, TX

NATIONAL RETAIL HARDWARE ASSN.
(Retail Hardware Stores & Home Centers)
5822 W. 74th St.
Indianapolis, IN 46278
Tel.: 317-290-0338
Year Founded: 1901
Approx.Sls.: $15,000,000
Emp.: 80
Export
Various Retail Hardware Associations ThroughoutNorth America
Kenneth L. Army *(V.P.-Fin. & Opers.)*
John P. Hammond *(V.P. & Publisher)*
Stephen Johnson *(Dir.-Member Services)*
Richard Lindsai *(Dir.-Industry Affairs)*

NATIONAL RIVET & MANUFACTURING COMPANY
21 E. Jefferson St.
Waupun, WI 53963
Mailing Address:
P.O. Box 471,
Waupun, WI 53963
Tel.: 414-324-5511 **WI**
Fax: 414-324-3388
Year Founded: 1928
Emp.: 250
Fiscal Year-end: 12/31/88
Mfr. Rivets & Automatic Rivet Setting Machines
S.I.C.: 3452
J.G. Zeratsky *(Pres.)*
E.E. Fletcher *(V.P.-Sls.)*
J.J. Statz *(V.P. & Treas.)*
A.A. Zeratsky *(V.P.-Opers.)*
Drew Zeratsky *(Pur. Agent)*

Computer Systems/Hardware:
Alpha Micro

Outside Service Firm(s):

Wisconsin Physicians Service*(Group Insurer)*
Madison, WI

National Bank of Waupun*(Major Banking Relationship)*
Waupun, WI

Subsidiary:

The Shaler Company **(1)**
21 E. Jefferson St.
Waupun, WI 53963
Tel.: 414-324-2211
Emp.: 10
Automotive Oil & Gas Additives
S.I.C.: 5169
J.G. Zeratsky *(Pres.)*
J.J. Statz *(V.P. & Treas.)*
A.A. Zeratsky *(V.P.-Opers.)*
Edwin P. Wiley *(Sec.)*
William R. Cook *(Sls. Mgr.)*
J. Bur Zeratsky *(Mktg. Mgr.)*
Eugene Buchholz *(Pur. Agent)*

NATIONAL SAFETY ASSOCIATES
4260 E. Raines Rd.
Memphis, TN 38118
Tel.: 901-366-9288 **TN**
Fax: 901-795-2726
Year Founded: 1970
Assets: $126,000,000
Liabilities: $50,000,000
Net Worth: $76,000,000
Approx.Sls.: $250,000,000
Emp.: 450
Fiscal Year-end: 4/30/92
Export
Mfr. of Household Water Filters & Air Filters
S.I.C.: 3589
A. Jay Martin *(Pres.)*
George Pateet *(V.P.-Mfg.)*
Roger Pearsall *(V.P.-Mktg.)*
Marvin E. Orr *(V.P.)*
Fred G. Swindle *(V.P.)*
L. Frank Swords *(V.P., Treas. & Sec.)*
Richard Waak *(Gen. Counsel)*

Outside Service Firm(s):

Deloitte & Touche*(Auditors)*
Memphis, TN

National Bank of Commerce*(Major Banking Relationship)*
Memphis, TN

NATIONAL SEATING CO.
200 National Dr.
Vonore, TN 37885
Tel.: 615-884-6651
Fax: 615-884-6166
Approx.Sls.: $30,000,000
Emp.: 200
Mfrs. Bus & Truck Seating
S.I.C.: 2531
Donald R. Kegley *(Pres.)*
Raymond Miller *(Exec. V.P.)*
Mike Comroy *(V.P.-Fin.)*
Richard Krempasky *(Mgr.-Truck Prods.-Seat)*
Doug Studer *(Mgr.-Business Prods.-Seat)*

Outside Service Firm(s):

Arthur Andersen & Co.*(Auditors)*
Third Natl. Fin. Cntr., 424 Church St., Ste. 1100
Nashville, TN 37219

Bass, Berry & Sims*(Legal Firm)*
27th Fl., First American Ctr.
Nashville, TN 37238
Tel.: 615-244-5370

First American National Bank*(Major Banking Relationship)*
First American Center
Nashville, TN 37237
Tel.: 615-748-2000

NATIONAL SOLVENT CORPORATION
955 W. Smith Rd.
Medina, OH 44256
Tel.: 216-725-4991
Fax: 216-722-2281
Approx.Sls.: $10,000,000
Emp.: 31
Mfr. of Paint Removers, Solvents, Wood Preservatives, Stains & Fuel
S.I.C.: 2851; 2992
Vir K. Sondhi *(Chm. Bd. & Pres.)*
Ijaz H. Shah *(V.P.)*
Principal(s):
Vir K. Sondhi

Outside Service Firm(s):

Society National Bank*(Major Banking Relationship)*
900 Euclid Ave., P.O. Box 6477
Cleveland, OH 44101-6477
Tel.: 216-737-5000
Fax: 216-566-8947

NATIONAL SPINNING CO., INC.
183 Madison Ave.
New York, NY 10016
Tel.: 212-889-3800 **NY**
Fax: 212-951-3550
Year Founded: 1910
Approx.Sls.: $187,000,000
Emp.: 2,500
Manufacture Yarn
S.I.C.: 2281
Joseph Leff *(Chm. Bd.)*
Morgan Miller *(Vice Chm.)*
Henry Humphreys *(Pres.)*
Philip Wander *(Exec. V.P.)*
Thomas Markey *(V.P., Treas. & Sec.)*
D. Lembo *(Mgr.-Sls.)*
K. Norman *(Mgr.-Sls.)*
Principal(s):
Joseph Leff

Computer Systems/Hardware:
IBM

Outside Service Firm(s):

KPMG Peat Marwick*(Auditors)*
345 Park Ave.
New York, NY 10154
Tel.: 212-758-9700
Fax: 212-872-3308

Chemical Banking Corporation*(Major Banking Relationship)*
450 W. 33rd. St.
New York, NY 10001
Tel.: 212-613-7147

Plants:

National Spinning Co. **(1)**
P. O. Box 191
Washington, NC 27889
Tel.: 919-946-8111
S.I.C.: 2281
H. Wetmore *(Plant Mgr.-Dyeing)*

National Spinning Co. **(1)**
P.O. Box 547,
Whiteville, NC 28472
Tel.: 919-642-4181
S.I.C.: 2281
R. Deans *(Plant Mgr.)*

National Spinning Co. **(1)**
P. O. Box 545
Warsaw, NC 28398
Tel.: 919-293-7101
S.I.C.: 2281
B. Hutchins *(Plant Mgr.)*

National Spinning Co. **(1)**
P.O. Box 49,
Beulaville, NC 28518
Tel.: 919-298-3131
S.I.C.: 2281
E. Jeffords *(Plant Mgr.)*

National Yarn Crafts **(1)**
183 Madison Ave
New York, NY 10016
Tel.: 212-889-3800
S.I.C.: 2281
M. Miller *(Pres.)*
H.R. Miller *(Sr. V.P. & Gen. Mgr.)*

NATIONAL STEEL CORPORATION
4100 Edison Lakes Pky.
Mishawaka, IN 46545
Tel.: 219-273-7000
Fax: 412-394-4688
Approx.Sls.: $2,600,000,000
Emp.: 12,000
Fiscal Year-end: 12/31/90
Steel Mfr.
S.I.C.: 3312; 3316
Kokichi Hagiwara *(Chm. Bd. & Chief Exec. Officer)*
Ronald H. Doerr *(Pres. & Chief Oper. Officer)*
Rich Newsted *(V.P.-Fin. & Treas.)*
Richard P. Coffee *(V.P.-Human Resources)*
E. Krivoshia, Jr. *(V.P., Gen. Counsel & Sec.)*
Hugh Givens *(Controller & Asst. Sec.)*
Bob Toothman *(Dir.-Communications)*

Computer Systems/Hardware:
IBM 381K2

Outside Service Firm(s):

Ernst & Young*(Auditors)*
2000 Pittsburgh Natl. Bldg.
Pittsburgh, PA 15222
Tel.: 412-644-7800
Fax: 412-644-7419

Morgan Guaranty Trust Company of New York*(Major Banking Relationship)*
23 Wall St.
New York, NY 10015

National Steel Corporation—(Continued)

Tel.: 212-483-2323

Divisions:

National Steel, Granite City Div. (1)
20th & State Sts.
Granite City, IL 62040
Tel.: 618-451-3456
Steel Plant
S.I.C.: 3312
William D. Swanson *(V.P. & Gen. Mgr.)*

National Steel Great Lakes Div. (1)
1 Quality Dr.
Ecorse, MI 48229
Tel.: 313-297-2100
Steel Plant
S.I.C.: 3312
James Howell *(V.P. & Gen. Mgr.)*

National Steel Midwest Div. (1)
U.S. Hwy. 12
Portage, IN 46368
Tel.: 219-762-3131
Steel Plant
S.I.C.: 3312
Dr. D.A. Chatfield *(V.P. & Gen. Mgr.)*

Subsidiaries:

American Steel Corp. (1)
717 E. McNichols
Detroit, MI 48212
Tel.: 313-365-7000
Steel Processing Facility
S.I.C.: 3312

Mathies Coal Co. (1)
Dowling St.
Library, PA 15129
Tel.: 412-941-7071 (100%)
Coal Mine
S.I.C.: 1221

Mesaba-Cliffs Mining Co. (1)
Union Commerce Bldg., 14th Floor
Cleveland, OH 44115
Tel.: 216-241-2356 (100%)
Iron Ore Mines
S.I.C.: 1011

National Mines Corp. (1)
101 E. Vine St.
Lexington, KY 40507
Tel.: 606-233-4141 (100%)
Coal Mines & Properties In PA, KY & WV
S.I.C.: 1221
William E. Cotter, Jr. *(Pres.)*

NS Land Company (1)
20 Stanwix St.
Pittsburgh, PA 15222
Tel.: 412-394-4100 (100%)
S.I.C.: 6552

Affiliates:

Carryore, Limited (1)
c/o Hanna Co., 100 Erieview Plaza, 36th Floor
Cleveland, OH 44114
Tel.: 216-589-4000 (50%)
Iron Ore Transportation
S.I.C.: 5088

Presque Isle Corp. (1)
1815 Republic Bldg.
Cleveland, OH 44114
Tel.: 216-574-7992 (100%)
Limestone Quarry
S.I.C.: 1411

Joint Venture:

DNN Galvanizing Corporation (1)
300 Sprucewood Ave. P.O. Box 7069,
Windsor, ON N9Z 3X6, Canada
Tel.: 519-250-2146
Fax: 519-250-2199
Hot Dip Galvanized Flat Rolled Steels
S.I.C.: 3479
B.J. Cipriettl *(Pres.)*

Serevco & Company Ltd. (1)
Parc Industriel, P.O. Box 670,
Coteau du Lac, PQ J0P 1B0, Canada
Tel.: 514-763-0915
Fax: 514-763-0922
Hot Dip Galvanized Flat Rolled Steels
S.I.C.: 3479

T.J. Nadeau *(Pres.)*

NATIONAL STEEL & SHIPBUILDING COMPANY
Harbor Dr. at 28th
San Diego, CA 92113
Mailing Address:
P.O. Box 85278,
San Diego, CA 92186-5278
Tel.: 619-544-3400 **NV**
Telex: 695034
Fax: 619-544-3541
Approx.Sls.: $317,400,000
Emp.: 4,000
Shipbuilding & Repair, Construction of Offshore Modules
S.I.C.: 3731
R.H. Vortmann *(Pres. & Chief Exec. Officer)*
A.W. Lutter, Jr. *(Sr. V.P.-Mktg. & Bus. Affairs)*
D.A. Spanninga *(Sr. V.P.-Opers.)*
Spencer French *(V.P.-New Construction Production)*
F.N. Hallett *(V.P.-Fin.)*
S.D. Timmons *(V.P.-Bus. Affairs & Legal)*
James M. Temenek *(V.P.-Bus. Opers., Wash.)*
Eric Murray *(Controller)*

Outside Service Firm(s):

Coopers & Lybrand*(Auditors)*
402 W. Broadway, Ste. 400
San Diego, CA 92109
Tel.: 619-232-8000

Union Bank*(Major Banking Relationship)*
Trust Dept., 8155 Mercury Ct.
San Diego, CA 92112
Tel.: 619-230-4487

THE NATIONAL SUPER SERVICE CO.
3115 Frenchmens Rd.
Toledo, OH 43607
Tel.: 419-531-2121
Fax: 419-531-3761
Approx.Sls.: $20,000,000
Emp.: 120
Mfr. of Floor & Carpet Cleaning Equipment; Vacuum Cleaners
S.I.C.: 3589
John F. Bevington *(Pres. & Chief Exec. Officer)*
Mark Bevington *(V.P.-Sls. & Mktg.)*
David A. Hiatt *(Sec. & Treas.)*
Stepfen Senn *(Dir.-Pur.)*
Michael Savidge *(Dir.-Engrng.)*

NATIONAL SYSTEMS & RESEARCH CO.
5475 Mark Dabling
Colorado Springs, CO 80918
Tel.: 719-590-8880 **CO**
Fax: 719-590-8983
Year Founded: 1980
Approx.Sls.: $24,000,000
Emp.: 400
Developing or Modifying Computer Software
S.I.C.: 7373
Celestino E. Archuleta *(Pres.)*
Tommy W. Harman *(V.P.)*
Maria Archuleta *(Sec.)*

Outside Service Firm(s):

Ernst & Young*(Auditors)*
Colorado Springs, CO

United Bank*(Major Banking Relationship)*
Colorado Springs, CO

NATIONAL TOOL & MANUFACTURING COMPANY
100-124 N. 12th St.
Kenilworth, NJ 07033
Tel.: 908-276-1600
Fax: 908-276-8616

Approx.Sls.: $23,000,000
Emp.: 300
Standard Mold Sets & Components For Plastic Molds, Die Casting
S.I.C.: 3544; 3089; 3451
William Zeus, Jr. *(Pres. & Chief Exec. Officer)*
Bela B. Lukacs *(Exec. V.P. & Sec.)*
George Wahlgren *(Chief Engr. & Factory Mgr.)*
Burt Purcell *(Mgr.-Data Processing)*

Outside Service Firm(s):

Manheim, Kosson & Novick*(Auditors)*
Millburn, NJ

Lum, Hoens, Abeles, Conant & Danzis*(Legal Firm)*
Roseland, NJ

National State Bank*(Major Banking Relationship)*
Roseland, NJ

NATIONAL TRAVELERS LIFE CO.
820 Keo Way
Des Moines, IA 50309
Tel.: 515-283-0101
Year Founded: 1907
Approx.Sls.: $500,000,000
Emp.: 200
Fiscal Year-end: 12/31/90
Life & Health Insurance
S.I.C.: 6311; 6321
Maynard Axtell *(Pres.)*
Gerald Walsworth *(V.P.-Mktg.)*
Don J. Schmidt *(Dir.-Sls. Promotion)*

NATIONAL TRUCK LEASING SYSTEM
One S. 450 Summit Ave., Ste. 300
Oakbrook Terrace, IL 60181
Tel.: 708-953-8878
Tel.: 800-SAY-NTLS **IL**
Fax: 708-953-0040
Year Founded: 1944
Emp.: 10
Fiscal Year-end: 12/31/90
Full Service Truck, Tractor & Trailer Leasing
S.I.C.: 7513; 7519
Thomas Fleming *(Chm. Bd.)*
William Ilett *(Vice Chm.)*
William J. Ford *(Pres.)*
David Gerrard *(Chief Fin. Officer & Mktg. Dir.)*
Jon Fogelberg *(V.P. & Gen. Mgr.)*

Computer Systems/Hardware:
IBM PC

Outside Service Firm(s):

Selden Fox & Associates*(Auditors)*
Oak Brook, IL

Coghlan, Joyce & Kukankos*(Legal Firm)*
Chicago, IL

Merchandise National Bank*(Major Banking Relationship)*
Chicago, IL

NATIONAL UTILITY SERVICE, INC.
1 Maynard Dr.
Park Ridge, NJ 07656
Tel.: 201-391-4300 **NY**
Fax: 201-391-8158
Year Founded: 1990
Approx.Sls.: $45,000,000
Emp.: 1,000
Business Consultants
S.I.C.: 8748
Sarkis Soultanian *(Chm. & Pres.)*
Marvin Lauterbach *(Exec. V.P.)*
Brian Bell *(V.P.-Human Resources)*
Peter Bedrosian *(V.P.-Mktg.)*
Arnold Frankel *(V.P.)*
Stuart Gilbert *(V.P.)*

Craig Thalmann *(V.P.-Mktg. & Sls.)*
John J. Donnellan *(Sec. & Controller)*

NATIONAL VAN LINES, INC.
2800 W. Roosevelt Rd.
Broadview, IL 60153
Tel.: 708-450-2900
Approx.Sls.: $17,000,000
Emp.: 100
Household Goods Carrier
S.I.C.: 4214
Frank McKee, Sr. *(Pres.)*
Frank McKee, Jr. *(Exec. V.P.)*
Bob Buti *(V.P.-Fin.)*

NATIONAL WELDERS SUPPLY CO. INC.
810 Gesco St.
Charlotte, NC 28208
Mailing Address:
P.O. Box 31007
Charlotte, NC 28231
Tel.: 704-333-5475 **NC**
Fax: 704-342-0260
Year Founded: 1941
Sales Range: $40-59 Million
Emp.: 700
Fiscal Year-end: 9/25/91
Manufacture Industrial & Medical Gases, Cryogenics; Distribute Welding Supplies & Equipment
S.I.C.: 2813; 5084; 5099
Judith Carpenter *(Chm. Bd.)*
James A. Turner III *(Vice Chm.)*
James A. Turner, Jr. *(Chief Exec. Officer)*
Erroll Sult *(Pres.)*
Alan W. DeMart *(Sr. V.P.-Fin.)*
Tony Harrington *(Sr. V.P.-Opers.)*
Linerieux Turner *(V.P.)*
A.C. Pease *(V.P.-Mktg.)*
Tom Sheridan *(V.P.-Human Resources)*
Tony Martin *(Controller)*
Pat Surhan *(Sec.)*
Mike Mulinini *(Dir.-Plng. & Devel.)*
G. Lewis Barber *(Mgr.-Mktg.)*
Howard Hill *(Mgr.-Sls.)*
Tom Privott *(Pur. Agent)*

No. of Mfg. Plants/Facilities: 45

Outside Service Firm(s):

Arthur Andersen & Co.*(Auditors)*
2300 Charlotte Plaza
Charlotte, NC 28244
Tel.: 704-332-0092

Grier, Parker, Poe, Thompson, Bernstein, Gage & Preston*(Legal Firm)*
2600 Charlotte Plaza
Charlotte, NC 28244
Tel.: 704-372-9000

First Union National Bank*(Major Banking Relationship)*
P.O. Box 120
Charlotte, NC 28255
Tel.: 704-374-2698

NATION'S BUSINESS
(Published by the Chamber of Commerce of the U.S.)
1615 H St., N. W.
Washington, DC 20062
Tel.: 202-463-5636
Fax: 202-887-3437
Year Founded: 1912
Approx.Sls.: $20,000,000
Emp.: 60
Fiscal Year-end: 12/31/91
Monthly Business Magazine
S.I.C.: 5192
Dr. Richard Lesher *(Pres.)*
Dr. Carl Grant *(Sr. V.P.-Communications)*
Larry Kraus *(Sr. V.P. & Chief Fin. Officer)*

David Roe (V.P.-Publishing)
Bob Gray (Editor)
Mary McElveen (Asst. Editor)
Robert H. Gotshall (Dir.-Adv.)
Leonard Rippa (Mgr.-Bus.)
Nancy Swanson (Mgr.-Res.)

NATIONWIDE BEEF, INC.
219 N. Green St.
Chicago, IL 60607
Tel.: 312-829-4900 **DE**
Fax: 312-829-4788
Approx.Sls.: $34,000,000
Emp.: 250
Fresh Meats; Corned Beef from Purchased Meat
S.I.C.: 5147; 2013
Frank Swan *(Pres.)*
Erwin Rabin *(Sec. & Treas.)*

Outside Service Firm(s):

Miller, Cooper & Co.*(Auditors)*
Skokie, IL

Exchange National Bank*(Major Banking Relationship)*
Chicago, IL

NATIONWIDE HOMES, INC.
1100 Rives Rd.
Martinsville, VA 24115
Mailing Address:
P.O. Box 5511,
Martinsville, VA 24115
Tel.: 703-632-7100 **VA**
Fax: 703-632-1181
Year Founded: 1959
Approx.Sls.: $22,000,000
Emp.: 290
Fiscal Year-end: 12/31/92
Manufacture Modular Housing
S.I.C.: 2452
Employee Matching Gifts Progra
John A. McLendon *(Chm. Bd.)*
Frederic J. Betz *(Pres. & Chief Exec. Officer)*
Marvin L. Foster *(Sr. V.P. & Sec.)*
Ronald C. Evans *(V.P.-Sls.)*
Samuel C. Lawrence *(V.P.-Prod.)*
R. Noel Ward *(V.P.-Sls.)*
Michael Grisetti *(Controller)*

No. of Mfg. Plants/Facilities: 4
No. of U.S. Offices: 2

Computer Systems/Hardware:
IBM 36; AST-Premium 486

Outside Service Firm(s):

Arthur Andersen & Co.*(Auditors)*
One Southern Life Center
Greensboro, NC 27401
Fax: 919-378-1445

Chas. Lunsford & Associates*(Commercial Insurance Carrier)*
Roanoke, VA

Lincoln National Life Insurance Co.*(Group Insurer)*
PO Box 208, 1300 S. Clinton
Fort Wayne, IN 46801
Tel.: 219-455-2926
Fax: 219-455-7619

Hunton & Williams*(Legal Firm)*
951 E. Byrd St.
Richmond, VA 23219-4074
Tel.: 804-788-8200

Piedmont Trust Bank*(Major Banking Relationship)*
Martinsville, VA

NATIONWIDE MUTUAL INSURANCE COMPANY
One Nationwide Plaza
Columbus, OH 43216
Tel.: 614-249-7111 **OH**
Fax: 614-249-7705
Assets: $10,087,766,000
Liabilities: $6,986,688,000
Net Worth: $3,101,078,000
Approx.Rev.: $4,632,665,000
Emp.: 13,863
Fiscal Year-end: 12/31/91
Insurance Holding Company
S.I.C.: 6719; 6321; 6331
John E. Fisher *(Gen. Chm. & Chief Exec. Officer)*
D. Richard McFerson *(Pres. & Gen. Mgr.)*
Thomas E. Kryshak *(Exec. V.P.-Fin.)*
Gordon E. McCutchan *(Exec. V.P., Gen. Counsel & Sec.)*
William P. DeMeno *(Sr. V.P.-Bus Opers.)*
Herbert E. Cunningham *(V.P.-Human Resources)*
Patrick L. Doyle *(V.P.-Office of Gen. Chm.)*
Joseph Gasper *(V.P.-Agency Opers.)*
R. Steven Johnson *(V.P.-Adv. & Promo.)*
Robert A. Oakley *(V.P. & Controller)*
Stephen A. Rish *(V.P.-Pub. Rels.)*
Douglas C. Robinette *(V.P. & Treas.)*
Louis V. Fabro *(Dir.-Media Rels.)*
William C. Lamneck *(Dir.-Communications)*

Computer Systems/Hardware:
IBM

Outside Service Firm(s):

KPMG Peat Marwick*(Auditors)*
Two Nationwide Plaza
Columbus, OH 43215
Tel.: 614-249-2300

Nationwide Insurance*(Commercial Insurance Carrier)*
One Nationwide Plaza
Columbus, OH 43216
Tel.: 614-249-6488

Subsidiary:

Nationwide Corporation **(1)**
One Nationwide Plaza,
Columbus, OH 43215
Tel.: 614-249-7111 (100%)
Fax: 614-249-7705
Approx.Premiums: $805,250,000
Emp.: 18
Fiscal Year-end: 12/31/90
Computer Systems/Hardware:
IBM
Holding Co. with Major Investments in Life Insurance Companies & other Financial Products & Services
S.I.C.: 6719
John E. Fisher *(Gen. Chm.)*
W. Barton Montgomery *(Chm. Bd.)*
Peter F. Frenzer *(Pres.)*
Thomas E. Kryshak *(Exec. V.P.-Fin.)*
Gordon E. Mc Curthan *(Exec. V.P., Gen. Counsel Sec.)*
Harvey S. Galloway, Jr. *(Sr. V.P. & Chief Actuary)*
David A. Diamond *(Treas.)*
Louis V. Fabro *(Dir.-Media Rels.)*

Subsidiaries:

Gates, McDonald & Co. **(2)**
Three Nationwide Plaza,
Columbus, OH 43216
Tel.: 614-249-7211 (100%)
Fax: 614-249-7705
Approx.Rev.: $36,245,132
Emp.: 808
Unemployment & Workers' Compensation Programs
S.I.C.: 6411
Robert W. Witty *(Pres. & Chief Oper. Officer)*
Richard H. Hoyt *(V.P.-Sls. & Service)*
Dori D. Jennings *(Mgr.-Communications & Publications)*
John Morrow *(Pur. Supvr.)*

Insurance Intermediaries, Inc. **(2)**
5774 Shier-Rings Rd.
Dublin, OH 43017
Tel.: 614-766-0222
Insurance Serives
S.I.C.: 6411
R. Lee Ayotte *(Pres.)*

National Casualty Co. **(2)**
One City Centre, 515 N. Sixth St., Suite 1800
Saint Louis, MO 63101-1877
Tel.: 314-421-4626 (100%)
Fax: 314-421-6148
Approx.Rev.: $50,447,524
Emp.: 199
Individual, Group, Accident & Health Insurance; Casualty Reinsurance
S.I.C.: 6411
Sherrod E. Turner *(Pres.)*
John F. Delaloye *(V.P., Sec. & Treas.)*
Gary Johnston *(Adv. Mgr.)*
Manfred Nahser *(Pur. Agent)*

Subsidiary:

Hickey-Mitchell Company **(3)**
One City Centre, 515 N. Sixth St., Suite 1800
Saint Louis, MO 63101-1877
Tel.: 314-421-4626
Fax: 314-421-6148
Approx.Rev.: $14,509,336
Insurance Agency
S.I.C.: 6411
Sherrod E. Turner *(Pres.)*
John F. Delaloye *(V.P., Sec. & Treas.)*
John O'Brien *(V.P.-Mktg.)*
Gary Johnston *(Adv. Mgr.)*
Manfred Nasher *(Pur. Agent)*

Nationwide Financial Services, Inc. **(2)**
One Nationwide Plaza,
Columbus, OH 43216
Tel.: 614-249-7855 (100%)
Fax: 614-249-7705
Approx.Rev.: $13,080,474
Emp.: 50
Investment Mgr. & Principal Underwriter for Mutual Investment Foundation
S.I.C.: 6722
Marian A. Trimble *(Pres.)*
James Laird Jr. *(Treas.)*
William Wright *(Dir.-Distr.)*
Douglas Papp *(Mgr.-Publications)*

Nationwide Funding Inc. **(2)**
1275 Market St.
San Francisco, CA 94119
Tel.: 415-552-6200 (100%)
Approx.Rev.: $30,227
Emp.: 1
Insurance Premium Financing
S.I.C.: 6371
John U. Metzger *(Pres.)*

Nationwide Life Insurance Co. **(2)**
One Nationwide Plaza
Columbus, OH 43216
Tel.: 614-227-7111 (89%)
Approx.Rev.: $710,125,000
Emp.: 2,298
Individual & Group Life, Annuities & Accident & Health Coverages
S.I.C.: 6311
Peter Frenzer *(Pres.)*
Thomas Kryshak *(Exec. V.P.-Fin.)*
Richard Karas *(V.P.-Sls., Fin. Svcs.)*
Larry M. Robinson *(V.P.-Life Mktg.)*

Nationwide Health Care Corp. **(2)**
One Nationwide Plaza
Columbus, OH 43216
Tel.: 614-227-7111 (100%)
Fax: 614-249-7705
Approx.Rev.: $250,490
S.I.C.: 6321
Harvey S. Galloway, Jr. *(Pres.)*
Thomas Kryshak *(Exec. V.P.-Fin.)*
Ronald Hunt *(V.P. & Chief Oper. Officer)*
Larry M. Robinson *(V.P.-Mktg.)*

Pebsco Inc. **(2)**
One Nationwide Plaza
Columbus, OH 43216
Tel.: 614-227-7111 (100%)
Fax: 614-249-7705
Approx.Rev.: $24,814,298
Ins. Agents Brokers & Services
S.I.C.: 6411
Jay G. Wilkinson *(Pres.)*
Thomas E. Kryshak *(V.P.-Fin.)*
Michael Studebaker *(V.P.-Sls. Devel.)*
William Dearnbarger *(Mgr.-Fin.)*

West Coast Life Insurance Co. **(2)**
343 Sansome St.
San Francisco, CA 94104
Tel.: 415-433-6200
Tel.: 800-366-9378 (100%)
Fax: 415-433-1372
Approx.Rev.: $35,371,559
Emp.: 135
Indiv. & Group Life, Annuities, Accident & Health Insurance
S.I.C.: 6311
John U. Metzger *(Pres. & Chief Oper. Officer)*
Leigh Harrington *(Sr. V.P.-Actuary)*
Dale F. Moon *(Sr. V.P.-Insurance Opers.)*
Bernard Robins *(Sr. V.P.-Mktg.)*
Karl Snover *(Sr. V.P.-Fin.)*
Valentine Chmel *(V.P.-Communications)*
Mutsumi M. Hada *(Sec.)*
Mike Whelan *(Natl. Dir.-Agencies)*
Charles G. Barnett, M.D. *(Dir.-Mediacal)*

Affiliate:

Employers Insurance of Wausau a Mutual Co. **(1)**
2000 Westwood Dr.
Wausau, WI 54401
Tel.: 715-845-5211
Fax: 715-842-6947
Assets: $2,915,585,000
Liabilities: $2,486,785,000
Net Worth: $428,800,000
Sales Range: $1 Billion +
Emp.: 5,600
Computer Systems/Hardware:
IBM 3090, 200 & 3081
Property & Casualty Insurance
S.I.C.: 6331
John E. Fisher *(Gen. Chm.)*
Arden Shisler *(Chm. Bd.)*
Leon J. Weinberger *(Pres. & Chief Exec. Officer)*
Thomas E. Kryshak *(Exec. V.P.-Fin.)*
Gordon E. McCutchan *(Exec. V.P. & Gen. Counsel)*
Carl J. Santillo *(Exec. V.P.-Opers.)*
Bill D. Wymore *(Exec. V.P.-Admin. Services)*
Dwight Davis *(Sr. V.P.-Western Division)*
Scott Isaacson *(Sr. V.P.-Mktg.)*
David R. Jahn *(Sr. V.P.-South Central Division)*
J.M. Magalska *(Sr. V.P., Grp. & Retire Oper.)*
Richard J. Byron *(V.P., Assoc. Gen. Counsel & Sec.)*
Warren L. Fabel *(V.P.-Personnel)*
Mark E. Fiebrink *(V.P. & Actuary)*
W.H. Gustavson *(V.P. & Dir.-Med.)*
Floyd R. Luettgens *(V.P.-Audit)*
Virden H. Morrison *(V.P.-Office Services)*
Willard C. Sanford *(V.P. & Treas.)*
Bruce Thornton *(V.P. & Controller)*
Phil Wirtanen *(V.P. & Dir.-Sls.)*
Vicki Amundson *(Asst. Treas.)*
Brad Zweck *(Mgr.-Pub. Rels.)*

Non-U.S. Holding:

Nekura Versicherungs AG **(1)**
Oberstedter Strasse 14 D-6370
Oberursel, Hessen Germany
Tel.: 617 1690
Life Insurance, Accident & Health
S.I.C.: 6311; 6321
Uwe Jacobsen *(Pres.)*

Subsidiaries:

Auto Direkt Versicherungs AG **(2)**
Oberstedter Strasse 14 D-6370
Oberursel, Hessen Germany
Tel.: 617 1690
Accident & Health Insurance
S.I.C.: 6321

Columbus Versicherungs Vermittlungs **(2)**
Oberstedter Strasse 14 D-6370
Oberursel, Hessen Germany
Tel.: 617 1690
Insurance Agents
S.I.C.: 6411

NATIONWISE AUTOMOTIVE, INC.
3750 Courtright Ct.
Columbus, OH 43227
Tel.: 614-239-1111
Fax: 614-239-5160
Year Founded: 1963
Approx.Sls.: $300,000,000
Emp.: 3,000
Fiscal Year-end: 1/31/91
Retailer of Auto Parts
S.I.C.: 5531; 5015
Saul Levy *(Chm. Bd.)*
Barry Feinberg *(Pres.)*
Jim Schoenberger *(Sr. V.P.-Mktg.)*
Kent Stickley *(Sr. V.P.-Mdse.)*
Lee Tenenbaum *(Sr. V.P.-Legal/ Personnel)*

Nationwise Automotive, Inc.—(Continued)

Jim Ardery *(V.P.-Retail Div. Training)*
Keith Byrd *(V.P.-Mngmt. Information Systems)*
Hal Cook *(V.P.-Service Div.)*
Ron Schubert *(V.P. & Treas.)*
Mike Hall *(Dir.-Adv.)*

Principal(s):
Saul Levy
Barry Feinberg

No. of Mfg. Plants/Facilities: 170

Computer Systems/Hardware:
IBM

Outside Service Firm(s):

KPMG Peat Marwick*(Auditors)*
1000 Walnut St.
Kansas City, MO 64106

McDonough Caperton Insurance Group*(Group Insurer)*
Charleston, WV

NATURE'S RECIPE PET FOODS
341 Bonnie Circle
Corona, CA 91720
Tel.: 909-278-4280
Tel.: 800-843-4008
Year Founded: 1981
Approx.Sls.: $28,000,000
Mfr. of Pet Foods
S.I.C.: 2047
Jeffrey Bennett *(Pres. & Chief Exec. Officer)*
Frank Koch *(Exec. V.P.-Sls.)*
Bill Dibert *(V.P.-Opers.)*
Tracy Reppert *(Controller)*
Nancy Bennett *(Treas.)*
Skip McCabe *(Mgr.-Adv. & Mktg.)*

NAUGATUCK GLASS COMPANY
Church & Bridge Sts.
Naugatuck, CT 06770
Mailing Address:
P.O. Box 71
Naugatuck, CT 06770
Tel.: 203-729-5227 **CT**
Fax: 203-729-8781
Year Founded: 1978
Approx.Sls.: $15,000,000
Emp.: 224
Process Glass Parts To Customer Specifications
S.I.C.: 3231
Jeffrey T. Witherwax *(Pres. & Treas.)*
William T. Cremins *(Exec. V.P., Gen. Counsel & Sec.)*
Harold A. Racevicius *(V.P.-Opers.)*
Richard Samiglietti *(V.P.-Sls.)*

Outside Service Firm(s):

Charles Heaven & Co.*(Auditors)*
Waterbury, CT

Carmody & Torrance*(Legal Firm)*
Waterbury, CT

First National Bank of Boston*(Major Banking Relationship)*
P.O. Box 644,
Boston, MA 02102-0644
Tel.: 617-575-2900
Fax: 617-575-2549

NAUTILUS
709 Powerhouse Rd.
Independence, VA 24348
Mailing Address:
P.O. Box 708
Independence, VA 24348
Tel.: 703-773-2881
Tel.: 800-NAUTILUS
Fax: 703-773-3733
Year Founded: 1970
Emp.: 250
Fiscal Year-end: 6/30/92
Export
Mfr. of Conditioning & Rehabilitation Equipment, Fitness Systems; Diet & Nutrition Programs
S.I.C.: 3949
Dan D. Baldwin *(Pres. & Chief Exec. Officer)*
Tom Jones *(Exec. V.P.)*
John Donati *(V.P.)*
Ralph Pini *(V.P.-Fin.)*
Al Dickerson *(Controller)*
Ralph Griesser *(Natl. Sls. Mgr.)*

No. of Mfg. Plants/Facilities: 3
No. of U.S. Offices: 12
No. of Foreign Offices: 4

Computer Systems/Hardware:
IBM; DEC

Subsidiary:

Nautilus Virginia Inc. **(1)**
709 Powerhouse Rd., P.O. Box 160
Independence, VA 24348
Tel.: 703-773-2881
Fax: 703-773-3733
Emp.: 300
Bill Gates *(Mgr.)*

NAVAJO FOREST PRODUCTS INDUSTRIES
P.O. Box 1280
Navajo, NM 87328
Tel.: 505-777-2211
Fax: 505-777-2415
Year Founded: 1959
Assets: $26,000,000
Liabilities: $12,500,000
Net Worth: $13,500,000
Approx.Sls.: $17,000,000
Emp.: 285
Fiscal Year-end: 3/31/91
Lumber, Moulding, Particleboard
S.I.C.: 2426; 2431; 2491; 2493
Thomas J. Boyd *(Chm. Bd. & Pres.)*
Clarence W. Richen *(Vice Chm.)*
Frank Curley, Jr. *(Controller)*
Edward S. Richards *(Gen. Mgr.)*
Genevieve Chato *(Gen. Counsel)*
Normand Birtcher *(Mgr.-Opers.)*
Mitchell D. Boone *(Mgr.-Sls.)*
Cecil Hubbard *(Mgr.-Maintenance)*
Elvira J. Mitchell *(Mgr.-Personnel & Pub. Rels.)*
Larry Gash *(Pur. Agent)*

No. of Mfg. Plants/Facilities: 1
No. of U.S. Offices: 1

Computer Systems/Hardware:
Networking-Televideo

Outside Service Firm(s):

KPMG Peat Marwick*(Auditors)*
Two Park Square, 6565 Americas Pkwy., N.E., Ste. 700
Albuquerque, NM 87110
Tel.: 505-884-3939
Fax: 505-884-8348

Citibank N.A.*(Major Banking Relationship)*
Phoenix, AZ

Towers, Perrin, Forster & Crosby*(Pension Manager)*
1925 Century Park East
Los Angeles, CA 90069
Tel.: 310-556-0330
Fax: 310-551-5859

NAVCOM DEFENSE ELECTRONICS, INC.
4323 N. Arden Dr.
El Monte, CA 91731
Tel.: 818-579-8689
Fax: 818-442-4405
Year Founded: 1932
Approx.Sls.: $53,744,000
Emp.: 320
Fiscal Year-end: 12/31/90
Export
Mfr. Airborne Electronic Equip., Military Electronic Equipiment, Airborne Navigation Systems, TACAN, LF Navigation Systems, Test Equipment, Radar Altimeters, Surface TACAN Beacons, Automatic Test Equip.
S.I.C.: 3812
Clifford C. Christ *(Pres. & Gen. Mgr.)*
William W. Belcher *(V.P.-Opers.)*
Wayne Ketterling *(V.P.-Bus. Devel.)*
Frank Scalfaro *(Chief Fin. Officer)*
Vicki Halford *(Mktg. Admin.)*

NAYLOR PIPE COMPANY
1230 E. 92nd St.
Chicago, IL 60619
Tel.: 312-721-9400
Fax: 312-721-9494
Year Founded: 1925
Approx.Sls.: $12,000,000
Emp.: 200

Export
Mfr. of Steel Pipe
S.I.C.: 3312; 3317
William B. Skeates *(Pres.)*
Russell A. Blais *(V.P.-Mktg. & Sls.)*
Kevin E. Joyce *(V.P.-Sls.)*
Allan Proper *(V.P.-Engrng.)*
John J. Czulno *(Comptroller)*
Michael O'Rourke *(Dir.-Pur.)*

NEAL & STEPHENS ADVERTISING, INC.
417 E. Stroop Rd.
Kettering, OH 45429
Tel.: 513-299-4993
Fax: 513-299-9355
Year Founded: 1981
Approx.Billings: $10,000,000
Emp.: 20
Financial, Healthcare, Business-to-Business & Retail Advertising
John F. Neal *(Chm. Bd. & Creative Dir.)*
Phillip K. Stephens *(Pres., New Bus. Contact & Acct. Supvr.)*
Julie Ferneding *(V.P.)*

NEBRASKA DEPT. OF ECONOMIC DEVELOPMENT
P.O. Box 94666, 301 Centennial Mall South
Lincoln, NE 68509-4666
Tel.: 402-471-3111
Tel.: 800-426-6505
Fax: 402-471-3778
Year Founded: 1967
Approx.Sls.: $17,000,000
Emp.: 72
Fiscal Year-end: 6/30/92
Area & Tourism Development
S.I.C.: 9611
Steve Buttress *(Dir.)*
Peggy Briggs *(Dir.-Travel)*
Jenne Rodriguez *(Dir.-Community Devel. Div.)*
Jack Ruff *(Dir.-Business Div.)*
Mary Simmons *(Dir.-Bus. Recruitment)*
Donald G. Wright *(Dir.-Pub. Information)*
Stu Miller *(Deputy Dir.)*

Computer Systems/Hardware:
IBM PCs

NEBRASKA-IOWA SUPPLY COMPANY
1160 Lincoln
Blair, NE 68008
Tel.: 402-426-2171 **NE**
Fax: 402-426-2360
Approx.Sls.: $28,000,000
Emp.: 150
Fiscal Year-end: 12/31/90
Distributes Petroleum Products
S.I.C.: 5172
Thomas J. Lippincott *(Pres. & Treas.)*
Mark T. Lippincott *(V.P.)*
Glenn L. Valier *(Sec.)*

Outside Service Firm(s):

Masimore & Associates*(Auditors)*
Blair, NE

Baird, Holm, McEachen, Pedersen, Hammann & Strasheim*(Legal Firm)*
Woodmen Twr.
Omaha, NE 68102
Tel.: 402-344-0500

Washington County Bank*(Major Banking Relationship)*
Blair, NE 68008

NEBRASKA PUBLIC POWER DISTRICT
(Subdivision of the State of Nebraska)
1414 15th St.
Columbus, NE 68602-0499
Mailing Address:
P.O. Box 499,
Columbus, NE 68602-0499
Tel.: 402-564-8561 **NE**
Fax: 706-563-5551
Year Founded: 1940
Assets: $658,723,000
Earnings: $3,665,000
Liabilities: $438,205,000
Net Worth: $220,518,000
Approx.Rev.: $377,123,000
Emp.: 2,250
Fiscal Year-end: 12/31/91
Electric Utility Company Owned By Electricity Users
S.I.C.: 4911
Corporate Giving Program: United Fund-Employee Participation Only.
David Duren *(Chm. Bd.)*
Ronald W. Watkins *(Pres. & Chief Exec. Officer)*
Robert L. Gangel *(V.P.-Fin. & Admin.)*
William A. Merrill *(V.P.-Opers.)*
Hugh G. Parris *(V.P.-Production)*
Ron D. Asche *(Controller, Treas. & Div. Mgr.-Fin. & Acct.)*
Gene D. Watson *(Gen. Counsel)*
R. Annette Bailey *(Bd. Sec.)*
D.J. Valentine *(Div. Mgr.-External Affairs)*
Ronnie E. Hitch *(Div. Mgr.-Pur.)*
John R. McPhail *(Div. Mgr.-Human Resources)*
Larry Kuncl *(Div. Mgr.-Environment & Natural Resources)*
Dennis Grennan *(Div. Mgr.-Reg. Opers.)*
Bill D. Nickeson *(Div. Mgr.-Data Information Services)*
R.E. Breuer *(Div. Mgr.-Systems Plng. & Engrng.)*
C. Lloyd Castner *(Mgr.-Mktg.)*
Robert L. Walgren *(Mgr.-Employee Benefits)*
Elizabeth L. Boesch *(Mgr.-Communications & Community Rels.)*
William H. Irby *(Mgr.-Safety & Training)*
Ron Bogus *(Mgr.-Pub. Affairs)*
Nola Tooley *(Coord.-Travel)*

Computer Systems/Hardware:
IBM 3090-180'S, MVS/ESA V3

Outside Service Firm(s):

Coopers & Lybrand*(Auditors)*
1200 Landmark Center
Omaha, NE
Tel.: 402-344-4545

Diversified Services Inc.*(Group Insurer)*
Omaha, NE

Lazard Freres & Co.*(Investment Banker)*
One Rockefeller Plaza
New York, NY 10020
Tel.: 212-632-6287

Mudge, Rose, Guthrie, Alexander & Ferdon*(Legal Firm)*
180 Maiden Lane
New York, NY 10038
Tel.: 212-510-7000
Fax: 212-248-2655

American National Bank & Trust Company of Chicago*(Major Banking Relationship)*
33 N. LaSalle St.
Chicago, IL 60602
Tel.: 312-661-5000
Fax: 312-661-6417

Chase Manhattan Bank, N.A.*(Major Banking Relationship)*
One Chase Manhattan Plaza
New York, NY 10081
Tel.: 212-552-2222

First Tier Bank of Lincoln*(Pension Manager)*
Lincoln, NE

NEEB CORPORATION
136 W. Huron
Bad Axe, MI 48413
Tel.: 517-269-6481
Fax: 517-269-6482
Approx.Sls.: $125,000,000
Emp.: 50
Wholesaler Petroleum & Petroleum Products
S.I.C.: 5172
Philip Neeb *(Pres.)*
Carol Long *(Mgr.-Mngmt. Information Systems)*

Computer Systems/Hardware:
Accurate Data

Outside Service Firm(s):

Hyser, Hill & Booms*(Auditors)*
Bad Axe, MI

Hartford Life Insurance Co.*(Commercial Insurance Carrier)*
Hartford, CT 06104-2999

Blue Cross & Blue Shield of Michigan*(Group Insurer)*
Detroit, MI

NEENAH FOUNDRY COMPANY
2121 Brooks Ave.
Neenah, WI 54956
Mailing Address:
P.O. Box 729
Neenah, WI 54956
Tel.: 414-725-7000
Fax: 414-729-3682
Approx.Sls.: $95,000,000
Emp.: 1,000
Fiscal Year-end: 3/31/91
Construction & Industrial Castings
S.I.C.: 3321; 3543
E.W. Aylward *(Pres. & Gen. Mgr.)*
Bill Aylward, Jr. *(Exec. V.P. & Chief Oper. Officer)*
J.P. Keating, Jr. *(Sr. V.P.)*
A. Aylward *(V.P.-Sls. & Mktg.)*
T.R. Franklin *(V.P.-Fin. & Treas.)*
John Rader *(V.P.-Human Resources)*
W. Wilson *(V.P.-Mfg.)*
G. Lachey *(Controller & Asst. Treas.)*
Kit Sorenson *(Dir.-Corp. Services)*
R.A. Hagen *(Mgr.-Sls./Construction Div.)*
J.D. Waite *(Mgr.-Credit)*
Philip Zehner *(Mgr.-Gen. Acctg.)*
Richard Ziebell *(Mgr.-Sls./Indus. Div.)*
D.F. Schuh *(Mktg. Specialist)*

NEER MANUFACTURING COMPANY
265 S. Mill St.
Lexington, OH 44904
Tel.: 419-884-2274 **OH**
Fax: 419-884-2209
Emp.: 155
Electric Conduits & Fittings
S.I.C.: 3644
Robert M. Lape *(Pres. & Treas.)*
Gary Conlan *(Exec. V.P.)*
Tony Fasano *(V.P.-Mktg. & Sls.)*
Dianne Christie *(Mgr.-Pur.)*

Outside Service Firm(s):

Willis, Osmond & Beilstein*(Auditors)*
Mansfield, OH

Calhoun, Benzin, Kademenos & Hichel*(Legal Firm)*
Mansfield, OH

Bank One, Mansfield*(Major Banking Relationship)*
28 Park Avenue W.
Mansfield, OH 44902
Tel.: 419-525-5700

NEILL-LAVIELLE SUPPLY CO.
1711 S. Floyd St.
Louisville, KY 40217
Tel.: 502-637-5401
Fax: 502-637-5450
Year Founded: 1881
Approx.Sls.: $25,000,000
Emp.: 150
Distribute Mill Supplies, Machine Tools, Ball & Roller Bearings, Steel Fabrications
S.I.C.: 5085; 5051
Robert G. Pfeiffer *(Chm. Bd. & Chief Exec. Officer)*
Richard N. Pfeiffer *(Pres.)*
Kent Crosthwait *(V.P.-Sls. & Pur.)*
Janie Becker *(Dir.-Pur.)*

No. of U.S. Offices: 3

Outside Service Firm(s):

Jones, Nale & Mattingly*(Auditors)*
Louisville, KY

Boehl, Stopher, Graves & Deindoerfer*(Legal Firm)*
Louisville, KY

Liberty National Bank & Trust Co.*(Major Banking Relationship)*
416 W. Jefferson St.
Louisville, KY 40202
Tel.: 502-566-2000

NELLA OIL COMPANY
2349 Rickenbacker Way
Auburn, CA 95603
Tel.: 916-885-0401
Fax: 916-885-5851
Year Founded: 1967
Approx.Sls.: $38,000,000
Emp.: 160
Brand X Retail Gasoline Service Stations
S.I.C.: 5541
T.A. Dwelle *(Pres.)*

Outside Service Firm(s):

Hume & Bobst*(Auditors)*
Auburn, CA

Bank of America NT&SA*(Major Banking Relationship)*
Auburn, CA

NELSEN STEEL & WIRE CO.
9400 W. Belmont Ave.
Franklin Park, IL 60131
Tel.: 708-671-9700
Tel.: 800-247-9700 **IL**
Fax: 708-671-9700
Year Founded: 1939
Approx.Sls.: $100,000,000
Emp.: 180
Import Export
Mfr. Cold-Drawn Steel Bars & Wire
S.I.C.: 3316; 3315; 3496
Clifford D. Nelsen *(Chm. Bd. & Pres.)*
C. Davis Nelsen, II *(Exec. V.P.)*
Leif A. Nelsen *(Treas.)*
Principal(s):
Clifford D. Nelsen
C. Davis Nelsen, II
Leif A. Nelsen

No. of Mfg. Plants/Facilities: 3
No. of U.S. Offices: 6

Computer Systems/Hardware:
SYS 10; ST-1; MACH 3

Outside Service Firm(s):

Grant Thornton*(Auditors)*
700 One Prudential Plaza, 130 East Randolph St.
Chicago, IL 60601
Tel.: 312-856-0200
Fax: 312-565-4719

Wausau Insurance*(Group Insurer)*
2000 Westwood Dr.
Wausau, WI 54401-7881
Tel.: 715-842-6902
Fax: 715-847-8534

American National Bank*(Major Banking Relationship)*
33 North LaSalle St.
Chicago, IL 60690
Tel.: 312-661-6967

Affiliate:

Union Drawn Steel Co., Ltd. **(1)**
1350 Burlington St. East P.O. Box 98,
Hamilton, ON L8N 3AZ, Canada
Tel.: 416-547-4480
Mfr. of Cold-Drawn Steel Bars & Wire
S.I.C.: 3316; 3315
James J. Yelland *(Pres.)*

NELSON BROTHERS FURNITURE CO.
2750 W. Grand Ave.
Chicago, IL 60612
Tel.: 312-489-3333
Fax: 312-489-1743
Approx.Sls.: $30,000,000
Emp.: 265
Retail Furniture, Appliances, Rugs & Carpets
S.I.C.: 5712; 5713; 5722
James F. Blinder *(Pres. & Treas.)*
Mike Steinberg *(Chief Fin. Officer)*
Max Gomberg *(V.P.)*
Alice D. Blinder *(Sec.)*
John Melus *(Pur. Agent)*
Principal(s):
James F. Blinder

Computer Systems/Hardware:
MAI Basic 4; NCR

Outside Service Firm(s):

Sidney L. Gimbel Co.*(Auditors)*
Chicago, IL

Sidley & Austin*(Legal Firm)*
One First National Plaza, 42nd Fl.
Chicago, IL 60603
Tel.: 312-853-7000
Fax: 312-853-7036

American National Bank & Trust Co.*(Major Banking Relationship)*
Chicago, IL

NELSON COMMUNICATIONS, INC.
41 Madison Ave., 27th Fl.
New York, NY 10010
Tel.: 212-779-1547
Fax: 212-213-4694
Year Founded: 1987
Approx.Billings: $242,347,000
Emp.: 421
Healthcare Marketing Services
Wayne K. Nelson *(Chm. & Chief Exec. Officer)*
Thomas C. Mackay *(Chief Fin. Officer)*
Blanca M. Stephens *(Sr. V.P.-Human Resources & Opers.)*
James Zambito *(Sr. V.P.-Fin.)*
Matthew J. Hayden *(V.P.-Fin.)*

L. R. NELSON CORPORATION
7719 N. Pioneer Lane
Peoria, IL 61615
Tel.: 309-692-2200
Fax: 309-692-5847
Year Founded: 1911
Emp.: 400
Fiscal Year-end: 7/31/90
Import Export
Manufacture Above-Ground & Underground Lawn Sprinklers & Accessories, Valves & Electronic Controllers
S.I.C.: 3432
David P. Ransburg *(Chm. Bd.)*
Nick Owens *(Pres.)*
Ray Busam *(Controller)*
Gary Bartholomew *(Mgr.-Pur.)*
Ken Bruninga *(Mgr.-Engrng.)*
Dave Eglinton *(Mgr.-Sls. & Mktg.)*
Cindy McCollum *(Mgr.-Adv.)*
Lois Stumetz *(Admin. Asst.)*

Computer Systems/Hardware:
IBM 36; ARS 400 D

Outside Service Firm(s):

Travelers Insurance Co.*(Group Insurer)*
1 Tower Square
Hartford, CT 06183-2492
Tel.: 203-277-4542
Fax: 203-277-5038

NELSON PHOTO SUPPLIES
722 33rd St.
San Diego, CA 92102
Mailing Address:
P.O. Box 85127
San Diego, CA 92186-5127
Tel.: 619-231-1700 **CA**
Fax: 619-696-9939
Year Founded: 1950
Approx.Sls.: $33,000,000
Emp.: 87
Wholesale Distribution of Photographic Cameras, Projectors, Equipment & Supplies
S.I.C.: 5043; 5946
Gary R. Nelson *(Chm. Bd. & Chief Exec. Officer)*
John T. Nelson, Sr. *(Pres.)*
John Lake *(V.P.)*
Carl Nelson *(V.P.-Sls.)*
Norris Padfield *(V.P.-Retail)*
Virginia Dickerson *(Sec.)*

Outside Service Firm(s):

Davies & Firman*(Auditors)*
San Diego, CA

Harmsen, Carpenter, Sidell & Olson*(Legal Firm)*
San Diego, CA
Tel.: 619-232-1800

San Diego Trust & Savings*(Major Banking Relationship)*
San Diego, CA

NELSON & SCHMIDT, INC.
111 E. Wisconsin Ave., Ste. 1000
Milwaukee, WI 53202
Tel.: 414-224-0210
Fax: 414-224-9463
Year Founded: 1971
Approx.Billings: $16,700,000
Emp.: 26
Fiscal Year-end: 9/30/91
Advertising Agency
S.I.C.: 7311
Dan Nelson *(Chm. & Chief Exec. Officer)*
Charles Frey *(V.P.-Pub. Rels.)*
David McGinn *(V.P.-Fin.)*
Werner Randelzhoffer *(V.P.)*
Tom Ristow *(V.P.- Acct. Services)*
Kathleen Peterson *(Mgr.-Traffic)*

Division:

Technical Publishing **(1)**
111 E. Wisconsin Ave.
Milwaukee, WI 53202
Tel.: 414-224-0210
Emp.: 2
Database Publishing; Engineering Manuals
S.I.C.: 7375; 2721
Dan Nelson *(Pres.)*

Nelson & Schmidt, Inc.—(Continued)

Hans Ziegler *(Dir.)*

NELSON & SMALL INC.
212 Canco Rd.
Portland, ME 04103
Mailing Address:
P.O. Box 1420
Portland, ME 04104
Tel.: 207-775-5661
Fax: 207-775-4303
Approx.Sls.: $74,000,000
Emp.: 170
Wholesale Electrical Appliances & Electronics, Snowmobiles, Kitchen Cabinets, Carpets & Flooring & Sporting & Recreational Goods
S.I.C.: 5064; 5023; 5091
Harold P. Nelson *(Chm. Bd.)*
Kenneth M. Nelson *(Pres.)*
Peter La Rose *(Sr. V.P.-Electronics)*
Donald M. Brown *(V.P.-Flooring)*
Bernard M. Resnick *(V.P.-Manchester Branch)*
David L. Small *(Treas.)*
Cathy Hanscom *(Dir.-Personnel)*

Outside Service Firm(s):

KPMG Peat Marwick*(Auditors)*
100 Middle St. Plaza
Portland, ME

JEFFREY NEMETZ & ASSOCIATES, INC.
750 N. Orleans, Ste. 401
Chicago, IL 60610
Tel.: 312-664-8112
Fax: 312-664-0943
Year Founded: 1978
Approx.Billings: $10,000,000
Emp.: 18
Jeffrey A. Nemetz *(Pres.)*
Harriet Karzen *(V.P., Strategic Counsel)*
Lee Uerkwitz *(V.P., Bus. Affairs)*

NEMSCHOFF CHAIRS, INC.
2218 W. Water
Sheboygan, WI 53081
Mailing Address:
P.O. Box 129
Sheboygan, WI 53082-0129
Tel.: 414-457-7726
Fax: 414-457-7537
Year Founded: 1950
Emp.: 400
Export
Furniture & Institutional Furnishings
S.I.C.: 2531
Leonard Nemschoff *(Chm. Bd. & Sec.)*
Mark Nemschoff *(Pres., Chief Exec. Officer & Treas.)*
Steve Oppeneer *(V.P.-Mfg.)*
Dave Seifert *(V.P.-Fin.)*
Tom Rice *(Dir.-Personnel)*
David N. Stinson *(Dir.-Govt. Sls.)*
John Rademacher *(Mgr.-Mktg.)*
Dave Goodlund *(Mgr.-Sls.)*

Computer Systems/Hardware:
Prime 2655

Outside Service Firm(s):

Arthur Andersen & Co.*(Auditors)*
777 E. Wisconsin Ave., P.O. Box 1215
Milwaukee, WI 53202
Tel.: 414-271-5100
Fax: 414-283-3200

Reinhart, Boerner, Van Deuren, Norris & Rieselbach, S.C.*(Legal Firm)*
1000 N. Water St., Ste. 2100
Milwaukee, WI 53202
Tel.: 414-298-1000

American National Bank & Trust Company of Chicago*(Major Banking Relationship)*
33 N. LaSalle St.
Chicago, IL 60602
Tel.: 312-661-5000
Fax: 312-661-6417

THE NERLAND AGENCY, INC.
808 "E" St.
Anchorage, AK 99501
Tel.: 907-274-9553
Fax: 907-274-9990
Year Founded: 1975
Approx.Billings: $10,200,000
Emp.: 20
Rick Nerland *(Chm. Bd., Pres. & New Bus. Contact)*
Betty L. Fauber *(Mgr.-Office)*
Lisa King *(Mgr.-Fin.)*
Rick Barrier *(Sec.)*

NESCO, INC.
6140 Parkland Blvd.
Mayfield Heights, OH 44124
Tel.: 216-461-6000 DE
Fax: 216-449-3111
Approx.Sls.: $200,000,000
Emp.: 5,000
Holding Company of Engineering & Manufacturing Firms
S.I.C.: 6719; 8711; 3569; 3599
Robert J. Tomsich *(Chm.)*
Ralph Nehrig *(Sr. V.P.)*
Joseph Mandia *(Group V.P.-Opers.)*
Frank Rzicznek *(V.P.-Fin. & Chief Fin. Officer)*
John Biacofsky *(Auditor)*
Peter A. Vinocur *(Legal Counsel)*

Computer Systems/Hardware:
IBM PC

Outside Service Firm(s):

Ernst & Young*(Auditors)*
1300 Huntington Bldg.
Cleveland, OH 44115
Tel.: 216-861-5000

Baker & Hostetler*(Legal Firm)*
3200 National City Center
Cleveland, OH 44114
Tel.: 216-621-0200
Fax: 216-696-0740

Society National Bank*(Major Banking Relationship)*
Cleveland, OH

Subsidiary:

Continental Conveyor & Equipment Company **(1)**
4th Ave. S., Industrial Pk. Rd.
Winfield, AL 35594
Tel.: 205-487-6492 (100%)
Telex: 59769
Fax: 205-487-4233
Approx.Sls.: $60,000,000
Emp.: 450
Fiscal Year-end: 12/31/90
Import Export
Mfr. Materials Handling Equipment, Conveyors & Components, Mobile Home Undercarriages, Natural & Synthetic Fiber Processing Equipment.
S.I.C.: 3535; 3569
C. Edward Bryant, Jr. *(Pres.)*
James A. Key *(V.P.-Adv., Pub. Rels. & Sls. Promo.)*
Ray McGaha *(V.P.-Sls. & Engrng.)*
James Simpson *(V.P.-Matls.)*
Clinton Butler *(Dir.-Personnel & Recruitment)*
Jack Russell *(Mgr.-Export)*

NESLAB INSTRUMENTS, INC.
25 Nimble Hill Rd.
Newington, NH 03801
Mailing Address:
P.O. Box 1178
Portsmouth, NH 03802-1178
Tel.: 603-436-9444
Tel.: 800-258-0830
Fax: 603-436-8411
Year Founded: 1963
Sales Range: $10-19 Million
Emp.: 250
Fiscal Year-end: 7/30/92
Export
Liquid Temperature Control Systems; Laboratory Equipment
S.I.C.: 3821; 3822
Andrew Bebbington *(Chief Exec. Officer)*
Van Ballantyre *(V.P.-Finance)*
Gerald Becker *(V.P.-Engrng.)*
Timothy LeFebvre *(V.P.-Domestic Sls. & Mktg.)*
Mark Zarembo *(V.P.-Intl. Sls. & Mktg.)*
David Laub *(Mgr.-Pur.)*
Deborah Ludington *(Mgr.-Adv.)*
Bruce Manchester *(Mgr.-Intl. Sls.)*
Lisa Trial *(Mgr.-Personnel)*
Jayne Walker *(Adv. Coord.)*

No. of Mfg. Plants/Facilities: 1
No. of U.S. Offices: 7
No. of Foreign Offices: 3

Outside Service Firm(s):

Grant Thornton*(Auditors)*
53 State St.
Boston, MA 02109
Tel.: 617-723-7900

G.L. NESS AGENCY, INC.
3100 13th Ave. South, Ste. 302
Fargo, ND 58103
Tel.: 701-280-1768
Year Founded: 1978
Approx.Billings: $14,400,000
Emp.: 23
Corporate/Brand Image, Graphic Design, Broadcast Production, Media Planning & Buying, Public Relations, Multi-Unit Retail, Dairy, Medical, Travel & Tourism, Agricultural, Floral Industry, Aeronautics, Beverages
Greg Ness *(Pres.)*
Michael Philpot *(Controller)*

Computer Systems/Hardware:
IBM, Macintosh

NETWORK REAL ESTATE OF CALIFORNIA, INC.
2425 Porter St., Ste. 16
Soquel, CA 95073
Tel.: 408-462-6200 CO
Year Founded: 1986
Assets: $8,324,000
Earnings: ($391,000)
Liabilities: $5,011,000
Net Worth: $3,313,000
Approx.Rev.: $10,133,000
Fiscal Year-end: 6/30/91
Real Estate Brokerage
S.I.C.: 6531
Leon J. Danna *(Chm. Bd. & Chief Exec. Officer)*
David R. Barton *(Vice Chm.)*
Edward R. Gresham *(Pres. & Chief Oper. Officer)*
James D. Tucker *(Sec./Treas.)*

Outside Service Firm(s):

Comiskey & Holscher*(Auditors)*
Pavilion Towers, Ste. 1125, 2851 S. Parker Rd.
Aurora, CO 80014
Tel.: 303-695-6306

Subsidiaries:

Network Capital Group **(1)**
1999 S. Bascom, Ste. 400
Campbell, CA 95008
Tel.: 408-559-8030 (100%)
Mortgage Banking Co.
S.I.C.: 6162
Leo G. Raiche *(Chm. Bd.)*
Donald L. Ryals *(Pres. & Chief Oper. Officer)*

Network Real Estate, Inc. **(1)**
2425 Porter St., Ste. 16
Soquel, CA 95073
Tel.: 408-462-6200 (100%)
Real Estate Brokerage
S.I.C.: 6531
Leon J. Danna *(Chm. Bd. & Chief Exec. Officer)*
Edward R. Gresham *(Pres. & Chief Oper. Officer)*
James D. Tucker *(Sec./Treas.)*

Subsidiaries:

Network Home Services, Inc. **(2)**
2425 Porter St., Ste 16
Soquel, CA 95073
Tel.: 408-462-6200 (100%)
Real Estate & Financial Services, Mortgages, Insurance, Leasing
S.I.C.: 6162; 6411; 6159
Leon J. Danna *(Chm. Bd. & Chief Exec. Officer)*
Edward R. Gresham *(Pres. & Chief Oper. Officer)*

Network Real Estate of Central California, Inc. **(2)**
2425 Porter St., Ste. 16
Soquel, CA 95073
Tel.: 408-462-6200 (100%)
Real Estate Brokerage
S.I.C.: 6531
William Papola, Jr. *(Pres.)*

Network Real Estate of Los Angeles, Inc. **(2)**
2425 Porter St., Ste. 16
Soquel, CA 95073
Tel.: 408-462-6200 (100%)
Real Estate Brokerage
S.I.C.: 6531

Network Real Estate of Northern California, Inc. **(2)**
2425 Porter St., Ste. 16
Soquel, CA 95073
Tel.: 408-462-6200 (100%)
Real Estate Brokerage
S.I.C.: 6531

Network Real Estate of Southern California, Inc. **(2)**
2425 Porter St., Ste. 16
Soquel, CA 95073
Tel.: 408-462-6200 (100%)
Real Estate Brokerage
S.I.C.: 6531
William Papola, Jr. *(Pres.)*

NETWORK SERVICES COMPANY OF CHICAGO
1550 Bishop Court
Mount Prospect, IL 60056
Tel.: 708-803-4888
Fax: 708-803-0482
Approx.Sls.: $1,000,000,000
Emp.: 2,000
Wholesale Supplier of Branded Paper & Plastic Prods. & Cleaning Materials
S.I.C.: 5113
Walt Dethlefsen *(Acting Pres. & V.P.-Adv. & Mktg.)*
Ronald Lee *(V.P. & Dir.-Data Processing)*
Bill Miller *(V.P. & Controller)*
Mark Payette *(V.P.-Sls.)*

NETZSCH, INC.
119 Pickering Way
Exton, PA 19341
Tel.: 215-363-8010
Fax: 215-363-0971
Year Founded: 1969
Approx.Sls.: $20,000,000
Emp.: 123
Import Export
Mfr. of Special Industrial Machinery, Pumps, Grinding & Filtering Equipment
S.I.C.: 3559; 3561; 3569
Thomas Netzsch *(Chm. Bd.)*
Hanno W. Spranger *(Pres. & Chief Exec. Officer)*
Rick E. Strait *(Exec. V.P.)*
David Brennan *(Chief Information Officer-Mngmt. Information Systems)*
Joe Graham *(Controller)*
Wolfgang Netzsch *(Sec. & Treas.)*
Michael Ryan *(Gen. Counsel)*
Bob Hoffman *(Dir.-Pur.)*
Boyd Peart *(Dir.-Engrng.)*
Bob Karr *(Mgr.-Mfg.)*

NEW BALANCE ATHLETIC SHOE, INC.
38 Everett St.
Boston, MA 02134
Tel.: 617-783-4000
Fax: 617-787-9355
Emp.: 500
Fiscal Year-end: 12/31/91
Mfr. of Racing, Running, Tennis, Hiking, Soccer, Walking, Squash, Basketball, Aerobic Fitness Shoes, Running Clothing, Active Wear, Bags, T-Shirts & Cycling Apparel
S.I.C.: 3149; 2329
John Lawsen *(Pres.)*
Ed Juengst *(Exec. V.P.-Mngmt. Information Systems & Distr.)*
Anne Davis *(V.P.-Admin.)*
John Gardner *(V.P.-Fin.)*
Paul Heffernan *(V.P.-Mktg.)*
Martin Walter *(V.P.-Intl.)*
J. Wilson *(V.P.-Mfg.)*
David G. Shelbourne *(Dir.-Intl.)*

Computer Systems/Hardware:
IBM 4341; Prime 750

Outside Service Firm(s):

Metropolitan Life Insurance Co.*(Group Insurer)*
One Madison Avenue
New York, NY 10010-3690

Non-U.S. Holding:

New Balance Canada Inc. **(1)**
5 Manitou Dr., Unit 15-A
Kitchener, ON N2C 2J6, Canada
Tel.: 519-895-1320 (100%)
Telex: 06-955178
Fax: 519-895-1321
Mktg. of Athletic Shoes
S.I.C.: 5139
Gail Maxwell *(Office Mgr.)*

NEW BEDFORD PANORAMEX CORPORATION
1037 W. 9th St.
Upland, CA 91786
Tel.: 909-982-9806 **CA**
Fax: 909-985-6217
Year Founded: 1966
Approx.Sls.: $20,000,000
Emp.: 220
Mfr. of Airborne Radio, Marine Radio & Space Satellite Communications Equipment
S.I.C.: 3663
Robert Ozuna *(Pres.)*
Rosemary Ozuna *(Treas. & Sec.)*

Outside Service Firm(s):

Sanwa Bank*(Major Banking Relationship)*
Santa Fe Springs, CA

NEW COOPERATIVE INC.
2626 1st Ave., S.
Fort Dodge, IA 50501
Mailing Address:
P.O. Box 818,
Fort Dodge, IA 50501
Tel.: 515-955-2040
Fax: 515-955-5565
Year Founded: 1972
Assets: $35,745,000
Earnings: $2,207,619
Liabilities: $18,325,000
Net Worth: $17,420,000
Approx.Sls.: $101,307,532
Emp.: 100
Fiscal Year-end: 6/30/91
Agri-Production, Crops & Services; Food & Kindred Products; Wholesale Trade Nondurable Goods
S.I.C.: 5153; 5191
Paul Pingel *(Chm. Bd. & Pres.)*
Robert Wallentine *(Chief Exec. Officer & Gen. Mgr.)*
Gene Black *(V.P.)*
John R. Bonnstetter *(Dir.-Fin.)*
Vernon Niemeyer *(Sec.)*

Computer Systems/Hardware:
IBM AS/400

Outside Service Firm(s):

Gardiner & Co.*(Auditors)*
Urbandale, IA

Associated Benefits Corp.*(Group Insurer)*
2929 Westown Pkwy.
Des Moines, IA 50265

Johnson Law Firm*(Legal Firm)*
Fort Dodge, IA

Associated Benefits Corp.*(Pension Manager)*
2929 Westown Pkwy.
Des Moines, IA 50265

NE The New England
Your Financial Partner

THE NEW ENGLAND
501 Boylston St.
Boston, MA 02117
Tel.: 617-578-2000 **MA**
Fax: 617-247-6841
Year Founded: 1835
Assets: $17,130,600,000
Earnings: $48,000,000
Liabilities: $16,450,400,000
Net Worth: $680,200,000
Approx.Sls.: $2,252,100,000
Emp.: 2,800
Fiscal Year-end: 12/31/91
Life & Health Insurance, Annuities, Investment Management, Mutual Funds
S.I.C.: 6311; 6411; 6321; 6211
Corporate Giving Program: Grants are Restricted to the Greater Boston Area with a Special Focus on Elderly, Low Income & Minorities. The Company Supports Charitable, Educational, Cultural, Social Service, Civic & other Organizations Which Improve the Quality of Life in our Community
Employee Matching Gifts Program: Employees Contributions to Accredited Institutions of Higher Learning Will be Matched by Contributions From The Company; Yearly Maximum $1,000 per Employee
Edward E. Phillips *(Chm. Bd.)*
Robert A. Shafto *(Pres. & Chief Exec. Officer)*
Ralph F. Verni *(Pres. & Chief Exec. Officer, New England Investment Companies)*
Michael I. Brown *(Exec. V.P.-Corporate Mngmt. Serv. Admin.)*
Edward C. Hall *(Exec. V.P.-Client Services)*
Kernan F. King *(Exec. V.P.-Admin. & Gen. Counsel)*
Robert E. Schneider *(Exec. V.P. & Chief Fin. Officer)*
Daniel J. Toran *(Exec. V.P.-Agency Opers. Admin.)*
James W. Zilinski *(Exec. V.P. & Chief Mktg. Officer)*
Chester R. Frost *(Sr. V.P.-Fin. Admin.)*
Daniel J. Kelliher, Jr. *(Sr. V.P. & Assoc. Gen. Counsel-Investments)*
F. Daniel Logan, Jr. *(Sr. V.P.-Mktg. Services Grp.)*
Gordon D. MacKay *(Sr. V.P.-Pub. Affairs/Pub. Rels.)*
Francis J. Malone *(Sr. V.P.-Mktg. Services)*
Gerard P. Maus *(Sr. V.P.-Investment Fin. Services)*
John G. Small *(Sr. V.P.-New Bus. Service Admin.)*
Edward N. Wadsworth *(Sr. V.P. & Assoc. Gen. Counsel)*
H. James Wilson *(Sr. V.P. & Assoc. Gen. Counsel-Insurance)*
Gail E. Weber *(Sr. V.P.-Human Resources & Corp. Serv.)*
Frederick K. Zimmermann *(Sr. V.P.-Investment Admin.)*
John W. Wright *(Grp. V.P.-Employee Benefits Sls. & Mktg.)*
William W. Batchelor *(V.P.-Field Comm., Meetings & Travel)*
William A. Benson *(V.P. & Chief Training & Devel. Officer)*
F. Brooks Cowgill *(V.P. & Treas.)*
James A. Gallaher *(V.P.-Pub. Affairs/ Pub. Rels. & Sec.)*
Peter N. Harrington *(V.P.-Public Rels.)*
Thomas W. Holland, Jr. *(V.P.-Pension Plan & Prod. Services)*
Frederick W. Knier *(V.P.-Computer Services, Telecommunications & Office Services)*
James A. Medeiros *(V.P.-Quality Commitment)*
Roger J. Montalto *(V.P.-Facilities Mngmt.)*
Alvaro M. Sousa *(V.P.-State Govt. Rels.)*
Robert D. Zuar *(V.P. & Controller)*
Stephen A. Conopka *(2nd V.P.-Information Mngmt. Services)*
Richard L. Gersh *(2nd V.P.-Treasury Opers.)*
Kathryn F. Plazak *(2nd V.P.-Community Rels.)*
Adrienne Korman *(Dir.-Corp. Library Services)*
Nancy Michalowski *(Dir.-Adv.)*
Kernan F. King *(Gen. Counsel)*
Gail E. Weber *(Human Resources)*

Computer Systems/Hardware:
IBM System 3090

Outside Service Firm(s):

Coopers & Lybrand*(Auditors)*
1 Post Office Square
Boston, MA 02110
Tel.: 617-574-5000
Fax: 617-345-0398

New England Mutual Life Insurance Co.*(Group Insurer)*
Boston, MA

Subsidiaries:

The New England Companies, Inc. **(1)**
501 Boylston St.
Boston, MA 02117
Tel.: 617-578-2000 (100%)
S.I.C.: 6719
Robert A. Shafto *(Pres. & Chief Exec. Officer)*

Subsidiaries:

TNE Funding Corporation **(2)**
501 Boylston St.
Boston, MA 02117
Tel.: 617-578-2000 (100%)
Issue & Sell Bonds, Notes, Stocks & Other Obligations
S.I.C.: 6211
F. Brooks Cowgill *(Pres.)*

New England Life Mortgage Funding Corp. **(2)**
501 Boylston St.
Boston, MA 02117
Tel.: 617-578-2000 (100%)
Issuer of Mortgage-Backed Bonds
S.I.C.: 6162
F. Brooks Cowgill *(Pres.)*

New England Investment Companies, Inc. **(2)**
501 Boylston St.
Boston, MA 02117
Tel.: 617-578-3500 (100%)
Fax: 617-578-2399
Emp.: 72
Holding Company
S.I.C.: 6719
Ralph F. Verni *(Pres. & Chief Exec. Officer)*
Gerald P. Maus *(Exec. V.P.)*

Subsidiaries:

Back Bay Advisors, Inc. **(3)**
399 Boylston St.
Boston, MA 02116
Tel.: 617-578-1500 (100%)
Emp.: 22
Investment Advisors
S.I.C.: 6282
Charles T. Wallis *(Pres. & Chief Exec. Officer)*
Michael Martino *(Exec. V.P. & Chief Investment Officer)*

Boylston Capital Advisors **(3)**
501 Boylston St.
Boston, MA 02117
Tel.: 617-578-2809 (100%)
Emp.: 60
Investment Advisors
S.I.C.: 6282
Fredrick K. Zimmermann *(Pres. & Chief Exec. Officer)*

Subsidiary:

New England Portfolio Advisors, Inc. **(4)**
501 Boylston Street
Boston, MA 02117
Tel.: 617-578-2000 (100%)
Investment Advisory Services for Pension Funds
S.I.C.: 6282; 6371
John F. Guthrie, Jr. *(Pres.)*

Copley Real Estate Advisors, Inc. **(3)**
399 Boylston St.
Boston, MA 02116
Tel.: 617-578-1200 (80%)
Approx.Sls.: $50,000,000
Emp.: 159
Real Estate Advisory & Management Services
S.I.C.: 6531
Joseph W. O'Connor *(Pres. & Chief Exec. Officer)*
Daniel J. Coughlin *(Mng. Dir.-Asset & Portfolio Mngmt.)*
John C. Phillips, Jr. *(Mng. Dir.-Client Rels.)*

Loomis, Sayles & Co. **(3)**
One Financial Center
Boston, MA 02111
Tel.: 617-482-2450 (95%)
Fax: 617-482-1985
Emp.: 240
Investment Counseling
S.I.C.: 6282
Donald R. Shepherd *(Chm. Bd. & Chief Exec. Officer)*
Ralph F. Verni *(Pres.-Institutional Investment Group TNE)*

Marlborough Capital Advisors, Inc. **(3)**
399 Boylston St.
Boston, MA 02116
Tel.: 617-578-1722 (100%)
Emp.: 6
Investment Advisors
S.I.C.: 6282
Margaret L. Lanoix *(Pres.)*

New England Securities Corp. **(3)**
399 Boylston St.
Boston, MA 02116
Tel.: 617-267-6600 (100%)
Emp.: 165
Broker-Dealer
S.I.C.: 6211
Henry L.P. Schmelzer *(Pres.)*

New England Investment Marketing, Inc. **(3)**
339 Boylston St.
Boston, MA 02116
Tel.: 617-578-1300 (100%)
Emp.: 10
Insurance Company Services
S.I.C.: 6411
Ralph F. Verni *(Pres. & Chief Exec. Officer)*
Antwine Jefferson, III *(Exec. V.P.)*
Elliott M. Gartner *(Exec. V.P.)*

TNE Investment Services Corp. **(3)**
399 Boylston St.
Boston, MA 02116
Tel.: 617-578-1388 (100%)
Emp.: 12
Security Broker/Dealers
S.I.C.: 6211
Henry L.P. Schmelzer *(Pres.)*

Westpeak Investment Advisors, Inc. **(3)**
1050 Walnut St., Ste. 300
Boulder, CO 80302
Tel.: 303-786-7700 (100%)
Emp.: 5
Investment Advice
S.I.C.: 6282

The New England—(Continued)

Gerald H. Scriver *(Pres. & Chief Exec. Officer)*

New England Pension & Annuity Co. **(1)**
501 Boylston St.
Boston, MA 02117
Tel.: 617-578-2000 (100%)
Life, Accident & Health Insurance
S.I.C.: 6311
Ralph F. Verni *(Pres. & Chief Exec. Officer)*

New England Variable Life Insurance Co **(1)**
501 Boylston St.
Boston, MA 02117
Tel.: 617-578-2000 (100%)
Life, Annuities & Variable Life
S.I.C.: 6311
Robert A. Shafto *(Pres.)*

Non-U.S. Holdings:

Draycott Partners, Ltd. **(1)**
12-14 Masons Ave.
London, EC2V 5BT, United Kingdom (100%)
Emp.: 8
Investment Advisors; Subsidiary of New England Investment Companies, Inc.
S.I.C.: 6282
Nicholas D.P. Carn *(Pres. & Chief Exec. Officer)*

Newbury Insurance Co. **(1)**
Hamilton, Bermuda
Captive Insurance Company; Subsidiary of New England Companies, Inc.
S.I.C.: 6411
Chester R. Frost *(Pres.)*

NEW ENGLAND COFFEE COMPANY
100 Charles St.
Malden, MA 02148
Tel.: 617-324-8094 **MA**
Fax: 617-397-7580
Year Founded: 1916
Assets: $10,211,403
Liabilities: $6,836,398
Net Worth: $3,375,005
Approx.Sls.: $36,954,000
Emp.: 125
Fiscal Year-end: 12/31/91
Wholesale Coffee, Tea & Hot Chocolate
S.I.C.: 5149
Stephen Kaloyanides *(Pres.)*
James P. Feeney *(Chief Fin. Officer & V.P.)*
Bob Ristaino *(V.P.-Sls., Mktg. & Service)*
Steven Dostov *(Treas.)*
Jim Kaloyanides *(Dir.-Mktg.)*
Steve Kaloyanides, Jr. *(Dir.-Pur.)*
Principal(s):
Stephen Kaloyanides
Steven Dostov
Basil Kaloyanides

No. of Mfg. Plants/Facilities: 1
No. of U.S. Offices: 3

Computer Systems/Hardware:
IBM AS-400

Outside Service Firm(s):

KPMG Peat Marwick*(Auditors)*
One Boston Place
Boston, MA 02108
Tel.: 617-723-7700

Commercial Union Insurance Co.*(Commercial Insurance Carrier)*
Foxboro, MA

Prucare Insurance*(Group Insurer)*
Boston, MA

Shearson Lehman Brothers, Inc.*(Investment Banker)*
Boston, MA

Kaye, Fialkow, Richmond & Rothstein*(Legal Firm)*
Boston, MA

Bay Bank Boston, N.A.*(Major Banking Relationship)*
Boston, MA

Shearson Lehman Brothers, Inc.*(Pension Manager)*
Boston, MA

NEW ENGLAND CORPORATION
P.O. Box 5427
Hamden, CT 06518
Tel.: 203-562-9981
Fax: 203-782-2785
Approx.Sls.: $13,000,000
Emp.: 115
Distributes Pre-cut Logs
S.I.C.: 5099
Len Suzio *(Pres. & Chief Exec. Officer)*
Joseph DiChello *(Controller)*

No. of Mfg. Plants/Facilities: 3
No. of U.S. Offices: 5

Outside Service Firm(s):

Vechitto, Macca & Co.*(Auditors)*
Rocky Hill, CT

Sklarz & Early*(Legal Firm)*
New Haven, CT

American National Bank*(Major Banking Relationship)*
Hamden, CT

Subsidiary:

New England Log Homes, Inc. **(1)**
2301 State St.
Hamden, CT 06518
Tel.: 203-562-9981
Fax: 203-782-2785
Approx.Sls.: $14,000,000
Emp.: 100
Manufacture Log Home Packages
S.I.C.: 2452
Len Suzio *(Pres.)*
Peter Hart *(V.P.-Mktg.)*
Joseph DiChello *(Treas.)*

NEW ENGLAND DAIRIES, INC.
255 Homestead Ave.
Hartford, CT 06112
Tel.: 203-241-2700 **CT**
Fax: 203-241-0326
Year Founded: 1983
Approx.Sls.: $50,000,000
Emp.: 250
Mfr. of Fluid Milk & Dairy Products
S.I.C.: 2021; 2022; 2026
James Conley *(Chm. Bd.)*
Frank A. Starvel *(Pres. & Chief Exec. Officer)*
Ken Reynolds *(V.P.-Sls.)*
Mike Rizzo *(V.P.-Fin.)*
Ralph Birkanshaw *(Sec.)*

Outside Service Firm(s):

Shawmut Bank*(Major Banking Relationship)*
One Federal St.
Boston, MA 02211
Tel.: 617-292-2969
Fax: 617-292-4417

NEW ENGLAND FROZEN FOODS
1 Harvest Lane
Southborough, MA 01772
Mailing Address:
P.O. Box 1409,
Southboro, MA 01772
Tel.: 508-481-0300 **MA**
Fax: 508-481-6456
Year Founded: 1932
Assets: $24,245,000
Liabilities: $15,554,000
Net Worth: $8,691,000
Sales Range: $100-499 Million
Emp.: 175
Fiscal Year-end: 12/31/91
Distributor of Frozen Foods & Ice Cream
S.I.C.: 2024; 4212; 4222; 5143
Robert G. White *(Chm. Bd., Pres. & Chief Exec. Officer)*
Walter M. Stella *(Exec. V.P. & Chief Oper. Officer)*
William Cicchese *(Sr. V.P.-Sls. & Pur.)*
Robert Frotten *(V.P.-Fin. & Admin.)*
Donald Ziniti *(V.P.-Opers.)*
Robert Dwyer *(Sec.)*
Jeffrey Stone *(Mgr.-Data Processing)*

Computer Systems/Hardware:
Bull Worldwide

Outside Service Firm(s):

Deloitte & Touche*(Auditors)*
125 Summer St.
Boston, MA 02110
Tel.: 617-261-8000
Fax: 617-261-8111

Blue Cross & Blue Shield Association*(Group Insurer)*
New York, NY

Hale and Dorr*(Legal Firm)*
60 State St.
Boston, MA 02109-6098
Tel.: 617-526-6000

South Shore Bank*(Major Banking Relationship)*
Quincy, MA

Massachusetts Mutual Life Insurance Co.*(Pension Manager)*
1295 State Street
Springfield, MA 01111
Tel.: 413-788-8411

NEW ENGLAND MACHINERY, INC.
6204 29th St. E.
Bradenton, FL 34203
Tel.: 813-755-5550
Telex: 6813344 NEM INC
Fax: 813-751-6281
Approx.Sls.: $10,000,000
Emp.: 75
Fiscal Year-end: 8/31/91
Export
Mfr. of Packaging Machinery & Equipment
S.I.C.: 3565
Geza E. Bankuty *(Chm. Bd., Pres. & Chief Exec. Officer)*
John Nieves *(Sr. V.P.-Mktg. & Sls.)*
Andrew J. May *(Dir.-Mktg)*

Computer Systems/Hardware:
MacIntosh

NEW ENGLAND NEWSPAPER SUPPLY COMPANY, INC.
49 Railroad Ave.
Millbury, MA 01527
Tel.: 508-865-5205
Fax: 508-865-1854
Approx.Sls.: $31,000,000
Emp.: 160
Printing Trades Machinery, Equipment & Supplies
S.I.C.: 5084
Alfred T. Beaton *(Chm. Bd.)*
Bradford Beaton *(Pres. & Chief Exec. Officer)*
Larry E. Erwin *(Exec. V.P.)*
William Graves *(V.P.)*
Wayne Parker *(V.P.)*
Maurice Croteau *(Controller)*

Outside Service Firm(s):

Singer & Lusardi*(Auditors)*
Worcester, MA

Shawmut Bank*(Major Banking Relationship)*
Worcester, MA

NEW ENGLAND STONE INDUSTRIES, INC.
15 Branch Pike
Esmond, RI 02917-1223
Tel.: 401-232-2040 **RI**
Fax: 401-232-2087
Year Founded: 1966
Approx.Sls.: $15,000,000
Emp.: 100
Fiscal Year-end: 10/31/91
Export
Granite Quarried, Cut & Fabricated To Specifications
S.I.C.: 1411; 1743; 3281
Antonio C. Ramos *(Pres. & Treas.)*
Ana Marie Ajami *(Chief Fin. Officer)*
Joseph D'Orsi *(Gen. Mgr.)*

No. of Mfg. Plants/Facilities: 2

Computer Systems/Hardware:
Compaq; Unix

Outside Service Firm(s):

Priest, Kortick & Gesmondi*(Auditors)*
Providence, RI

Fleet National Bank*(Major Banking Relationship)*
125 Dupont Dr.
Providence, RI 02907-3178
Tel.: 401-278-5335

Subsidiary:

Georgia Stone Industries, Inc. **(1)**
Hwy. 72 W.
Elberton, GA 30635
Tel.: 404-283-2254
Fax: 404-283-7632
Emp.: 50
Granite Quarrying
S.I.C.: 1411; 3281
Antonio C. Ramos *(Pres.)*

NEW FORTIS CORP.
151 Jefferson Church Rd.
King, NC 27021
Mailing Address:
P.O. Box 485
King, NC 27021
Tel.: 919-983-4321 **NC**
Fax: 919-983-6608
Year Founded: 1985
Approx.Sls.: $40,000,000
Emp.: 88
Fiscal Year-end: 4/30/92
Builders of Single & Multi-Family Homes
S.I.C.: 1531
Marvin D. Gentry *(Chm. Bd. & Pres.)*
John A. Bush *(Sr. V.P.-Fin.)*
Samuel D. Burns *(V.P.-Mktg.)*
John E. Davis *(V.P.-Construction)*
R. Randolph Reid *(V.P.-Sls.)*

Outside Service Firm(s):

Kenneth Leventhal & Co.*(Auditors)*
805 Third Ave.
New York, NY 10022

Blue Cross & Blue Shield of North Carolina*(Group Insurer)*
Durham, NC

Petree Stockton & Robinson*(Legal Firm)*
1001 W. Fourth St.
Winston-Salem, NC 27101
Tel.: 919-725-2351

Old North State Bank*(Major Banking Relationship)*
King, NC

NEW HAMPSHIRE OAK
Liberty Lane
Hampton, NH 03842
Tel.: 603-926-5911
Fax: 603-929-2404
Approx.Sls.: $605,327,000
Emp.: 3,700
Fiscal Year-end: 12/31/90

Production of a Variety of Industrial Chemicals & the Manufacture of Various Products for the Automotive & other Industries
S.I.C.: 2842; 2893
Michael D. Dingman *(Chm., Chief Fin. Officer & Mng. Dir.)*
Paul M. Montrone *(Pres. & Mng. Dir.)*
Edward F. Kavanaugh *(V.P., Treas., Controller & Mng. Dir.)*
Edwin H. Danenhauer *(Sec.)*

Outside Service Firm(s):

Arthur Andersen & Co.*(Auditors)*
1345 Ave. of the Americas
New York, NY 10105
Tel.: 212-708-4000

Deluvaine & Plimpton*(Legal Firm)*
New York, NY

Mellon Bank, N.A.*(Major Banking Relationship)*
New York, NY

Subsidiaries:

Balcrank Products **(1)**
1 Balcrank Way
Weaverville, NC 38787
Tel.: 704-645-4261
Mfrs. & Sells Products for the Automotive Service Market
S.I.C.: 7539; 3549
John R. Fahey *(Chief Exec. Officer)*
C. Roy Mendenhall *(Pres.)*

General Chemical Corporation **(1)**
90 E. Halsey Rd.
Parsippany, NJ 07054
Tel.: 201-515-0900
Approx.Sls.: $435,000,000
Production of Industrial & Specialty Chemicals; Sulfuric Acid, Soda Ash, Aluminum Sulfate, Fertilizers, Metals, Integrated Circuits & Photographic Supplies
S.I.C.: 3861; 2869; 2873; 2812
Richard Russell *(Pres.)*
David A. Brooks *(V.P.-Sls. & Mktg.)*
Thomas J. Germine *(V.P. & Gen. Counsel)*
Ralph M. Passino *(V.P.-Fin.)*
Christopher J. Reinhard *(V.P. & Sec.)*

Prestolite Wire Corporation **(1)**
32871 Middlebelt Rd.
Farmington Hills, MI 48334
Tel.: 313-626-1336 (100%)
Supplies Automotive Wire Products, Ignition Wire, Battery Cable Assemblies & Harnesses & Primary Wire & Non-automotive or Specialty Wire Products, Including Wire & Cable, to the Automotive Industry & other Industries, Primarily in North America & Europe
S.I.C.: 3357

Printing Developments, Inc. **(1)**
2010 Indiana St.
Racine, WI 53405
Tel.: 414-554-1030
Mfr. of Lithographic Plates, Plate & Pressroom Chemicals & Automatic Plate Processors
S.I.C.: 2796

Toledo Stamping & Manufacturing Co. **(1)**
P.O. Box 596
Toledo, OH 43693
Tel.: 419-382-3407 (100%)
Designs & Manufactures Medium & Heavy Specialty Stampings For The Automotive & Off-Highway Equipment Markets
S.I.C.: 3469

NEW HAMPSHIRE SWEEPSTAKES COMMISSION
75 Fort Eddy Rd.
Concord, NH 03301
Mailing Address:
P.O. Box 1217
Concord, NH 03302-1217
Tel.: 603-271-3391
Fax: 603-271-1160
Year Founded: 1963
Approx.Sls.: $100,000,000
Emp.: 52
Fiscal Year-end: 6/30/91
Lottery, Bingo, Charity Tickets
S.I.C.: 7999
James E. Wimsatt *(Exec. Dir.)*
Howard W. Keegan *(Commission Chm.)*

Computer Systems/Hardware:
Ibex 386/25

NEW HAMPTON, INC.
235 E. 45th St.
New York, NY 10017
Tel.: 212-986-2585 **DE**
Fax: 212-916-8375
Year Founded: 1987
Assets: $152,000,000
Liabilities: $119,000,000
Net Worth: $33,000,000
Approx.Sls.: $270,000,000
Emp.: 1,100
Fiscal Year-end: 12/31/91
Import
Catalog & Mail-Order Houses
S.I.C.: 5961
Raymond B. Rudy *(Chm. Bd.)*
George Ittner *(Pres. & Chief Oper. Officer)*
James Brewster *(V.P. & Chief Fin. Officer)*
Stephen Enroth *(V.P.)*
Robert Kramer *(V.P.-Information Services)*
James Lant *(V.P.)*
Michael Lutz *(V.P.-Opers.)*
Stewart Tarkington *(V.P.-Mktg.)*
Marianne Taylor *(V.P.-Human Resources)*
Constance Waters *(V.P.)*

Outside Service Firm(s):

KPMG Peat Marwick*(Auditors)*
345 Park Ave.
New York, NY 10154
Tel.: 212-758-9700
Fax: 212-872-3308

Crestar Bank*(Major Banking Relationship)*
P.O. Box 26665,
Richmond, VA 23261
Tel.: 804-782-5995

NEW HAVEN MFG. CORP.
446 Blake St.
New Haven, CT 06515
Tel.: 203-387-2572
Year Founded: 1989
Approx.Sls.: $18,000,000
Emp.: 275
Fiscal Year-end: 5/31/90
Time Recording Equipment & Hydraulic & Pneumatic Valves, Electronic Hardware
S.I.C.: 3579; 3492
W. Ryan *(Pres.)*
A. Karpuk *(Treas.)*
J. Marshall *(Sec.)*

NEW HAVEN SAVINGS BANK
195 Church St.
New Haven, CT 06510
Tel.: 203-787-1111
Fax: 203-789-2650
Year Founded: 1838
Approx.Rev.: $1,800,000,000
Emp.: 510
Bank & Lending Instituitions
S.I.C.: 6036
Charles Terrell *(Pres., Treas. & Chief Exec. Officer)*
David Rice *(V.P.-Mktg. & Corp. Sec.)*

NEW HERMES INCORPORATED
535 Connecticut Ave.
Norwalk, CT 06854
Mailing Address:
P.O. Box 6059,
Norwalk, CT 06851
Tel.: 203-852-7000
Tel.: 800-8-HERMES
Approx.Sls.: $45,000,000
Emp.: 300
Fiscal Year-end: 12/31/90
Engraving Machines: Computerized & Engravograph Adjustable Pantograph Engraving Machines; Accessories for Engraving & Profiling of Plastics & Metals; Engravable Plastic & Metal
S.I.C.: 3555
Jon C. Estes *(Pres.)*
James Bernstein *(V.P.-Sls.)*
Kenneth Chin *(V.P. & Controller)*
Deborah Gunzelman *(Dir.-Matls. Mgmnt.)*
Gail Liddell *(Mgr.-Communications)*

Divisions:

New Hermes Inc-Midwest **(1)**
3642 W. 128th Pl.
Alsip, IL 60658
Tel.: 312-371-3744
Fax: 312-371-2380
Pieter Kes *(Mgr.)*

New Hermes Inc. Northeast **(1)**
20 Cooper Sq.
New York, NY 10003
Tel.: 212-777-3080
Fax: 212-460-8508
Dolores Altonaga *(Mgr.)*

New Hermes Inc-South **(1)**
5680 NW 161st St.
Hialeah, FL 33014

New Hermes Inc.-Southeast **(1)**
2620 Park Central Blvd.
Decatur, GA 30035
Tel.: 404-981-2563
Fax: 404-981-7407
Ernie Cole *(Mgr.)*

New Hermes Inc-Southwest **(1)**
12243 E. Northwest Hwy.
Dallas, TX 75228
Tel.: 214-328-9835
Fax: 214-328-6681
Howard Kletter *(Mgr.)*

New Hermes Inc.-West Coast **(1)**
11711 Monarch St.
Garden Grove, CA 92641
Tel.: 714-898-9265
Fax: 714-897-6633
Linda Stevens *(Mgr.)*

Non-U.S. Holding:

New Hermes, Ltd. **(1)**
1561 Courtneypark Dr. East
Mississauga, ON L5T 1V9, Canada
Tel.: 416-670-2224
Tel.: 800-387-3130 (100%)
Fax: 416-670-9491

NEW JERSEY PRESS, INC.
3601 Highway 66
Neptune, NJ 07754
Mailing Address:
P.O. Box 1550,
Neptune, NJ 07754
Tel.: 908-922-6000
Fax: 908-922-6326
Year Founded: 1879
Approx.Sls.: $95,000,000
Emp.: 1,500
Newspaper Publisher; Direct Mail; Travel Agency, Radio & TV
S.I.C.: 2711; 7331; 4724
Jules Plangere, Jr. *(Chm. Bd.)*
E. Donald Lass *(Pres., Editor & Chief Exec. Officer)*
Jules Plangere, III *(Exec. V.P.)*
Alfred Colantoni *(V.P.-Corp. Services)*
Anthony Ordino *(V.P.-Opers.)*
Charles W. Ritscher *(V.P.-Mktg., Sls. & Sec.)*
Richard Morena *(Controller)*
Richard Orloff *(Dir.-Mktg.)*
Stephen Rice *(Dir.-Human Resources)*
Bob Hoffman *(Mgr.-Mktg.)*
Timothy P. Zeiss *(Mgr.-Pub. Rels.)*

Outside Service Firm(s):

Price Waterhouse*(Auditors)*
Princeton, NJ

McCarter & English*(Legal Firm)*
Four Gateway Center, 100 Mulberry St.
Newark, NJ 07102-4096
Tel.: 201-622-4444

Subsidiaries:

Press Broadcasting Co. **(1)**
600 Essex Rd.
Neptune, NJ 07754
Tel.: 908-922-4700
Tel.: 800-678-9599
Fax: 908-922-3085
Emp.: 80
Fiscal Year-end: 12/31/90
Television & Radio Stations; WKCF-TV Television Station, Orlando, Daytona Beach, Melbourne Florida; NJ101.5 FM & WBUD (AM) Radio Stations, Trenton, New Jersey
S.I.C.: 4832
Robert McAllan *(Pres.)*
Alfred D. Colantoni *(V.P. & Chief Fin. Officer)*
E. Donald Lass *(V.P.)*
Jules L. Plangere, III *(V.P.)*
Jules L. Plangere, Jr. *(V.P.)*
Perry M. Simon *(Asst. to Pres.)*
Charles W. Ritscher *(Sec.)*
Janice Gundacker *(Mgr.-Mktg.)*

Asbury Park Press, Inc. **(1)**
3601 Highway 66
Neptune, NJ 07754
Tel.: 908-922-6000
Newspaper Publisher; Direct Mail; Travel Agency; Radio & TV
S.I.C.: 2711; 7331; 4724
Jules L. Plangere, Jr. *(Chm. Bd.)*

Subsidiary:

Addresses Unlimited **(2)**
3601 Highway 66
Neptune, NJ 07754
Tel.: 908-922-6000
Direct Mail Advertising Services
S.I.C.: 5961
S. Serlazzo *(Gen. Mgr.)*

NEW JERSEY STATE LOTTERY
One Lawrence Park Complex,
Brunswick Ave. Circle
Trenton, NJ 08648
Mailing Address:
CN 041
Trenton, NJ 08625-0041
Tel.: 609-599-5800
Approx.Sls.: $1,174,330,047
Emp.: 214
Fiscal Year-end: 6/30/91
Lottery Commission-Sale & Distribution of Lottery Tickets
S.I.C.: 7999
Phillip Gelber *(Commission Chm.)*
Stephen Crane *(Treas. & Commissioner)*
Frank Telly *(Acting Exec. Dir.)*
Russell R. Hart *(Deputy Dir.)*
Lauren Lichtenderger *(Acting Sls. Field Mgr.)*
Larry Brothy *(Deputy Dir.-EDP Audit)*
Joseph DeCicco *(Mgr.-Opers.)*
John J. Majarwitz *(Deputy Dir.-Security, Auditing & Licensing)*
John J. Gallagher *(Controller)*

NJ TRANSIT
One El Plaza E.
Newark, NJ 07105
Tel.: 201-491-7000
Fax: 201-491-8218
Approx.Sls.: $324,000,000
Emp.: 9,701
Fiscal Year-end: 6/30/91
Bus/Rail Mass Transportation
S.I.C.: 4111
Shirley A. DeLibero *(Exec. Dir.)*
George Warrington *(Chief Oper. Officer)*
William Hempel *(Reorganization Project Mgr.)*
Joseph Crawford *(V.P. & Gen. Mgr.-Retail Opers.)*
Bill McManimon *(Chief Fin. Officer/ Comptroller)*
Fran Hooper *(Chief-Admin. Staff)*

NJ Transit—(Continued)

Janet Recca *(Dir.-Mktg.)*
Frank Hopper *(Asst. Dir.-Procurement)*

Division:

NJ Transit Corporation **(1)**
Market St. & McCarter Hwy.
Newark, NJ 07101
Tel.: 201-643-7400
S.I.C.: 4111

Subsidiaries:

NJ Transit Bus Operations **(1)**
180 Boyden Ave.
Maplewood, NJ 07040
Tel.: 201-378-6369
S.I.C.: 4111

NJ Transit Rail Operations **(1)**
1160 Raymond Blvd.
Newark, NJ 07101
Tel.: 201-468-8000
S.I.C.: 4111
George Warrington *(V.P. & Gen. Mgr.)*

NEW MECH COMPANIES, INC.
1633 Eustis St.
Saint Paul, MN 55108
Tel.: 612-645-0451
Fax: 612-642-5591
Approx.Sls.: $36,000,000
Emp.: 325
Mechanical Contractors
S.I.C.: 1711
Richard A. Newman *(Chm. Bd.)*
Ronald A. Pearson *(Pres.)*
Larry C. Jordon *(V.P.)*
John A. Pepera *(V.P.)*
Gerald J. Poser *(V.P.)*
Wayne K. Henquinet *(Sec. & Treas.)*

Outside Service Firm(s):

Wilkerson, Guthmann & Johnson*(Auditors)*
Minneapolis, MN

Grossman, Karlins, Siegel, Brill, Gruetner & Duffy*(Legal Firm)*
Minneapolis, MN

North Star State Bank of Roseville*(Major Banking Relationship)*
St. Paul, MN

NEW STANDARD CORPORATION
Pinkerton Rd.
Mount Joy, PA 17552
Mailing Address:
P.O. Box 420
Mount Joy, PA 17552
Tel.: 717-653-1811 **PA**
Fax: 717-653-4678
Year Founded: 1940
Approx.Sls.: $25,000,000
Emp.: 265
Fiscal Year-end: 12/31/90
Manufacture Metal Stampings, Assemblies & Automotive Stampings
S.I.C.: 3465; 3469
Morton F. Zifferer, Jr. *(Pres. & Chief Exec. Officer)*
William Neff *(Sec.)*
Thomas P. McEvoy *(Treas. & Controller)*
Kevin Brewer *(Dir.-Engrng.)*
Barry Enos *(Mgr.-Sls.)*
Victor Hetrick *(Mgr.-Personnel)*
Richard Kern *(Mgr.-Opers.)*
Charles Keznor *(Mgr.-Quality Assurance)*
Robert Traup *(Mgr.-Materials)*
Principal(s):
Morton F. Zifferer, Jr.

No. of Mfg. Plants/Facilities: 2
No. of U.S. Offices: 1

Computer Systems/Hardware:
Mai Basic Four

Outside Service Firm(s):

Arthur Andersen & Co.*(Auditors)*
101 Eisenhower Pkwy.
Roseland, NJ 07068
Tel.: 201-403-6100

Stock & Leader*(Legal Firm)*
York, PA

Hamilton Bank*(Major Banking Relationship)*
York, PA

NEW TEXAS TUMBLEWEED
10304 Interstate 10 E., Ste. 350
Houston, TX 77029
Tel.: 713-675-4900 **TX**
Fax: 713-673-7339
Year Founded: 1977
Approx.Sls.: $18,000,000
Emp.: 300
Fiscal Year-end: 8/31/88
Chain of Steak & Seafood Houses
S.I.C.: 5812
Duncan McCoy *(Pres. & Chief Exec. Officer)*
Principal(s):
Duncan McCoy

Computer Systems/Hardware:
IBM 9000

Outside Service Firm(s):

U.S. Health*(Group Insurer)*
Ft. Worth, TX

William King*(Legal Firm)*
Houston, TX

Capital Bank*(Major Banking Relationship)*
Houston, TX

IDS Advisory Group*(Pension Manager)*
Minneapolis, MN

Subsidiary:

Daddy Did It **(1)**
10304 Interstate 10 E, Ste. 350
Houston, TX 77029
Tel.: 713-672-6909 (100%)

NEW YORK CARPET WORLD INC.
23840 W. Eight Mile Rd.
Southfield, MI 48034
Tel.: 313-353-0160 **MI**
Fax: 313-353-6621
Approx.Sls.: $356,300,000
Emp.: 2,250
Retail & Wholesale Carpeting, Linoleum & Rugs
S.I.C.: 5713; 5023
Irving Nusbaum *(Pres. & Chief Exec. Officer)*
Earle Stackpole *(Sr. V.P.)*
James Telfer *(V.P.)*
Marvin Berlin *(Sec. & Treas.)*

Outside Service Firm(s):

Broder, Feinberg & Sukenic*(Auditors)*
Southfield, MI

NEW YORK CITY DEPT. OF GENERAL SERVICES
(Div. of Real Property)
2 Lafayette St., Rm. 2200
New York, NY 10007
Tel.: 212-566-7530
Fax: 212-566-5786
Approx.Sls.: $43,000,000
Emp.: 300
Management & Disposition of City-Owned Industrial & Commercial Estate
S.I.C.: 8748
Nancy Rosen *(Dir.-Opers.)*

NEW YORK CITY OFF TRACK BETTING CORP.
1501 Broadway
New York, NY 10036
Tel.: 212-704-5201
Fax: 212-704-5295
Approx.Sls.: $1,200,000,000
Emp.: 2,600
Legalized Pari-Mutuel Wagering On Horse Racing
S.I.C.: 6159
Edward Lewis *(Chm. Bd.)*
Lewis J. Rappoport *(Vice Chm.)*
David L. Vaughn *(Chief Exec. Officer)*
Hazel N. Dukes *(Pres.)*
Richard R. Dangler *(Sr. V.P.-Admin.)*
Nick Cirillo *(V.P.-Racing Opers.)*
Lorraine D. Melton *(V.P.-Mktg. & Special Events)*
Robert Palumbo *(V.P.-Personnel)*
Joseph Magnani *(Controller)*
Harry Scott *(Gen. Counsel)*
Margaret Longley *(Dir.-Pub. Affairs)*
Donna Watson *(Dir.-Promo. & Special Services)*

NEW YORK LIFE INSURANCE COMPANY
51 Madison Ave.
New York, NY 10010
Tel.: 212-576-7000 **NY**
Fax: 212-576-6794
Year Founded: 1845
Assets: $54,066,000,000
Liabilities: $51,446,000,000
Net Worth: $2,620,000,000
Approx.Sls.: $5,300,000,000
Emp.: 8,200
Fiscal Year-end: 12/31/91
Life, Group & Health Insurance; Financial Services
S.I.C.: 6411; 6311; 6159; 6321; 6324; 6371; 6726; 6722
Harry G. Hohn *(Chm. Bd. & Chief Exec. Officer)*
William F. Yelverton *(Chm. & Chief Exec. Officer-New York Worldwide Holding, Inc.)*
George A.W. Bundschuh *(Pres.)*
Lee M. Gammill, Jr. *(Exec. V.P.-Individual Opers.)*
Alice T. Kane *(Exec. V.P., Gen. Counsel & Sec.)*
Thomas P. O'Connor *(Exec. V.P.-Pensions, Mutual Funds, Partnership Investments)*
Walter Shur *(Exec. V.P.)*
Seymour Sternberg *(Exec. V.P.-Grp. Dept.)*
Patrick Boyle *(Sr. V.P.-Pension)*
Walter M. Brady *(Sr. V.P.-Agency)*
C. Andrew Brauer *(Sr. V.P.-Merger & Acquisition)*
Herbert L. Cheskis *(Sr. V.P.-Northeastern Agencies)*
John B. Foy *(Sr. V.P.-Information Systems & Services)*
Sam Goldfinger *(Sr. V.P.-Individual Life)*
Richard A. Hansen *(Sr. V.P.-Mutual Funds Investments)*
Jean E. Hoysradt *(Sr. V.P.-Investment)*
L. Michael Keone *(Sr. V.P.-Pacific Agencies)*
Michael J. McLaughlin *(Sr. V.P. & Deputy Gen. Counsel)*
Frank J. Ollari *(Sr. V.P.-Mortgage Finance)*
Richard O. Painter *(Sr. V.P.-Southeastern Agencies)*
Lyle R. Paul *(Sr. V.P.-Agency)*
Michael W. Reeves *(Sr. V.P.-Western Agencies)*
Robert D. Rock *(Sr. V.P.-Individual Annuity)*
Lester L. Schoenberg *(Sr. V.P.-Individual Policy Services)*
Frederick Sievert *(Sr. V.P. & Chief Fin. Officer)*
Paul T. Smith *(Sr. V.P.-Investments)*
Stephen N. Steinig *(Sr. V.P. & Controller & Chief Actuary)*
George J. Trapp *(Sr. V.P.-Human Resources)*
F. Barrie Usher *(Sr. V.P.-Canada)*
Richard A. Wecker *(Sr. V.P.-Mktg.)*
Edward G. Wendt, Jr. *(Sr. V.P.-Grp. Dept. Ins.)*
Robin B. Welch *(Sr. V.P.-Grp. Ins. Dept.)*
John W. Zorio *(Sr. V.P.-No. Central Agencies)*
Jessie M. Colgate *(V.P.-Govt. Affairs)*
Bruce J. Davey *(V.P. & Treas.)*
Wynne M. Gannon *(V.P.-Corp. Quality)*
Julia A. Romano *(V.P.-Information Systems & Services)*
Linda B. Staniar *(V.P.-Pub. Rels., Adv. & Video Systems)*
Charles A. Stringfellow *(V.P.-Employees' Health)*
Thomas J. Warga *(V.P. & Gen. Auditor)*

No. of Mfg. Plants/Facilities: 1
No. of U.S. Offices: 316
No. of Foreign Offices: 16

Computer Systems/Hardware:
IBM System 3090

Outside Service Firm(s):

Price Waterhouse*(Auditors)*
153 E. 53rd St., 44th Fl.
New York, NY 10022
Tel.: 212-371-2000

New York Life*(Group Insurer)*
51 Madison Ave.
New York, NY 10010
Tel.: 212-576-6367
Fax: 212-576-6630

MacKay-Shields Financial Corp.*(Pension Manager)*
9 W. Fifth Av.
New York, NY 10019
Tel.: 212-230-3844
Fax: 212-935-1083

Subsidiaries:

New York Life Insurance and Annuity Corporation **(1)**
51 Madison Ave.
New York, NY 10010
Tel.: 212-576-7000 (100%)
S.I.C.: 6311; 6321
Lee Gammill *(Pres.)*

New York Life & Health Insurance Company **(1)**
300 Delaware Ave.
Wilmington, DE 19801
Tel.: 302-656-9491 (100%)
Group Life & Health Insurance
S.I.C.: 6311; 6321
Seymour Sternberg *(Pres.)*

NYLIFE Inc. **(1)**
372 Park Ave., So.
New York, NY 10010
Tel.: 212-576-7000 (100%)
Insurance Holding Company
S.I.C.: 6719
Richard M. Kernan *(Chm.)*
Seymour Sternberg *(Pres.)*

Subsidiaries:

CoMed Management Inc. **(2)**
525 Metro Place North
Dublin, OH 43017
Tel.: 614-766-0061
Fax: 614-889-2148
Healthcare Management Services & Health Benefit Plan Design Consulting
S.I.C.: 8742
Edward G. Wendt, Jr. *(Chm. Bd.)*
Janice Spillane *(Pres.)*

Greystone Realty Corporation **(2)**
2 Pickwick Plaza, 3rd Floor
Greenwich, CT 06830
Tel.: 203-629-1166
Fax: 203-629-9859
Real Estate Investment Advisors
S.I.C.: 6282
Thomas P. O'Connor *(Chm. Bd.)*
Donald E. Conover *(Pres. & Chief Exec. Officer)*

Hillhouse Associates Insurance, Inc. **(2)**
8834 Capital of Texas Hwy. N., Ste. 300
Austin, TX 78720
Tel.: 512-343-5555
Fax: 512-343-5566
Group Insurance
S.I.C.: 6324
Ronald Hillhouse *(Pres. & Chief Exec. Officer)*

Monitor Capital Advisors Inc. **(2)**
51 Madison Ave.
New York, NY 10010
Tel.: 212-576-7000
Pension Fund Investment Advisors
S.I.C.: 6282
Thomas P. O'Connor *(Pres.)*

New York Life Acceptance Corp. **(2)**
51 Madison Ave.
New York, NY 10010
Tel.: 212-576-7000
Life Insurance
S.I.C.: 6311
Richard A. Wecker *(Pres.)*

New York Life Foundation **(2)**
51 Madison Ave.
New York, NY 10010
Tel.: 212-576-7000
Health & Life Insurance
S.I.C.: 6311; 6321
Harry Hohn *(Chm. Bd.)*
Carol Reuter *(Pres.)*

New York Life International Investment **(2)**
51 Madison Ave.
New York, NY 10010
Tel.: 212-576-7000
Holding Company For Worldwide Investments
S.I.C.: 6719
Richard M. Kernan, Jr. *(Chm. Bd. & Chief Exec. Officer)*

New York Life Worldwide Holding, Inc. **(2)**
51 Madison Ave.
New York, NY 10010
Tel.: 212-576-7000
Holds Title to Life Insurance Companies Outside U.S.
S.I.C.: 6719
William F. Yelverton *(Chm. & Chief Exec. Officer)*
Ralph Casale *(Exec. V.P. & Chief Mktg. Officer)*
James Kelly *(V.P.)*

NYLIFE Advisers, Inc. **(2)**
51 Madison Ave.
New York, NY 10010
Tel.: 212-576-7000
Financial Planning Services
S.I.C.: 6282
Lester L. Schoenberg *(Pres.)*

NYLIFE Depositary Corporation **(2)**
51 Madison Ave.
New York, NY 10010
Tel.: 212-576-7000
Limited Programs for Public Mortgage-Backed Securities & Real Estate Programs
S.I.C.: 6798
Michael J. Nocera *(Pres.)*

NYLIFE Equity Inc. **(2)**
51 Madison Ave.
New York, NY 10010
Tel.: 212-576-7000 (100%)
Oil & Gas Limited Partnerships
S.I.C.: 6799
Michael J. Nocera *(Pres.)*

NYLIFE Funding Inc. **(2)**
Ste. 780, 1100 N. Market St.
Wilmington, DE 19801-1281
Tel.: 302-428-3942
Insurance Mortgage Related Securities
S.I.C.: 6211
Frank J. Ollari *(Pres.)*

NYLIFE Leasing Inc. **(2)**
51 Madison Ave.
New York, NY 10010
Tel.: 212-576-7000
Consults On & Sponsors Public/Private Equipment Leasing Programs
S.I.C.: 8742
Michael J. Nocera *(Pres.)*

NYLIFE Mortgage Inc. **(2)**
12201 Merit Dr., Ste. 1000
Dallas, TX 75251
Tel.: 214-387-2929 (100%)
Insurance Collateralized Mortgage Obligations
S.I.C.: 6211
Richard M. Kernan, Jr. *(Pres.)*

NYLIFE Realty Inc. **(2)**
51 Madison Ave.
New York, NY 10010
Tel.: 212-576-7000 (100%)
Real Estate Limited Partnerships
S.I.C.: 6799
Michael J. Nocera *(Pres.)*

NYLIFE Securities Inc. **(2)**
51 Madison Ave.
New York, NY 10010
Tel.: 212-576-7000 (100%)
S.I.C.: 6211
Richard A. Topp *(Pres. & Chief Exec. Officer)*

MacKay-Shields Financial Corp. **(2)**
9 West 57th St.
New York, NY 10019
Tel.: 212-758-5400 (100%)
Fax: 212-935-1083
Financial Services
S.I.C.: 6159
Ravi Akhoury *(Chm. & Chief Exec. Officer)*
John R. O'Brien *(Vice Chm.)*

Sanus Corp. Health Systems **(2)**
One Parker Plaza, 400 Kelby St.
Fort Lee, NJ 07024
Tel.: 201-947-6000
Health Maintenance Organization; Health Srvc. Consulting
S.I.C.: 6324; 8742
Howard L. Waltman *(Chm. Bd. & Chief Exec. Officer)*
Joseph T. Lynaugh *(Pres.)*

NYLIFE Insurance Company of Arizona **(1)**
6263 Scottsdale Rd., Ste. 300
Scottsdale, AZ 85250
Tel.: 602-443-6800
Life & Health Insurance
S.I.C.: 6311; 6321
Lester L. Schoenberg *(Chm. Bd. & Pres.)*

Non-U.S. Holdings:

New York Life Insurance Co. of Canada **(1)**
121 Bloor Street East Ste. 1600,
Toronto, ON M4W 3N2, Canada
Tel.: 416-960-4500
Insurance Co.
S.I.C.: 6311; 6411
F. Barrie Usher *(Pres.)*

New York Life Insurance Worldwide Ltd. **(1)**
Cedar House, 41 Cedar Ave.
Hamilton, 21, Bermuda
Life Insurance Company
S.I.C.: 6311
William F. Yelverton *(Pres.)*

Windsor Group Limited **(1)**
Windsor House, Telford Centre
Telford, TF3 4NB, United Kingdom
Tel.: 011-44-952-29-2929
Life Insurance
S.I.C.: 6311
William F. Yelverton *(Chm. Bd.)*

NEW YORK RACING ASSOCIATION
P.O. Box 90
Jamaica, NY 11417
Tel.: 718-641-4700
Fax: 718-843-7673
Approx.Sls.: $250,000,000
Emp.: 5,000
Aqueduct, Belmont Park, & Saratoga Racetracks
S.I.C.: 7948
Allan R. Dragone *(Chm. Bd.)*
Gerard J. McKeon *(Pres.)*
Richard Barone *(V.P.-Mktg. & Pub. Rels.)*
Fred Lief *(Dir.-Promo.)*
Sal Cartagine *(Human Resources Exec. Dir.)*
Elaine Poreda *(Pur. Agent)*

THE NEW YORKER MAGAZINE
20 W. 43rd St.
New York, NY 10036
Tel.: 212-840-3800
Fax: 212-944-6367
Approx.Sls.: $74,732,495
Emp.: 350
Fiscal Year-end: 12/31/90
Periodical
S.I.C.: 2721
Steven T. Florio *(Pres. & Chief Exec. Officer)*
Tina Brown *(Editor)*
Ginger Jesperson *(V.P.-Bus. Mngmt.)*
Pam Older *(V.P.-Production)*
Rhonda Sherman *(V.P.-Advertising Promo. & New Business)*
Lynn Guthrie Heiler *(Assoc. Publisher)*

Subsidiary:

Boulder Enterprise, Inc. **(1)**
3550 Frontier Ave.
Boulder, CO 80301
Tel.: 303-449-8011
S.I.C.: 2721
James E. Noel *(Pres.)*

NEW ZEALAND LAMB CO., INC.
555 Paxter Rd.
Elmsford, NY 10523
Tel.: 914-347-5488
Fax: 914-347-3637
Approx.Sls.: $34,000,000
Emp.: 75
Fiscal Year-end: 12/31/90
Importer & Wholesaler of Lamb
S.I.C.: 5147
Richard Lawrence *(V.P.)*

NEWAGE INDUSTRIES INC.
2300 Maryland Rd.
Willow Grove, PA 19090-1799
Tel.: 215-657-3151 **NY**
Telex: 263780
Fax: 215-657-6594
Year Founded: 1951
Approx.Sls.: $12,500,000
Emp.: 55
Fiscal Year-end: 12/31/90
Import Export
Holding Company: Plastics Testing Instruments
S.I.C.: 6719
Raymond E. Baker *(Chm. Bd.)*
Ken Baker *(Chief Exec. Officer & Gen. Mgr.-Plastics Div.)*
Gordon Baker *(Pres. & Gen. Mgr.-Instrument Div.)*
Stephen Midgette *(Controller)*
Constance Schmitt *(Mgr.-Quality Control)*
Catherine A. Wallace *(Mgr.-Pur.)*
Donald G. Warner *(Mgr.-Mktg.)*
David Greer *(Dir.-Management Information Systems)*
Stephen Kuhns *(Dir.-Sls.)*

Principal(s):
Raymond E. Baker

No. of Mfg. Plants/Facilities: 1
No. of U.S. Offices: 1

Computer Systems/Hardware:
C. Itoh Minicomputer; Pick Operating Systems; Prelude, Inc.-Program

Outside Service Firm(s):

Samuel N. Ramsey*(Auditors)*
Willow Grove, PA

Timoney, Knox, Hasson, Weand*(Legal Firm)*
Ambler, PA

Philadelphia National Bank*(Major Banking Relationship)*
P.O. Box 13834, Broad & Chestnut Streets
Philadelphia, PA 19101-7618
Tel.: 215-973-8327

Divisions:

Newage Industries Inc., Plastics Division **(1)**
2300 Maryland Rd.
Willow Grove, PA 19090-1799
Tel.: 215-657-3151
Telex: 263780
Fax: 215-657-6594
Approx.Sls.: $8,500,000
Emp.: 35
Fiscal Year-end: 12/31/90
Import Export
Computer Systems/Hardware:
C. Itoh-Pick Operating System
Mfr. of Industrial Plastic Products
S.I.C.: 3089
Raymond E. Baker *(Pres.)*
Kenneth D. Baker *(Chief Exec. Officer & Gen. Mgr.-Plastics Div.)*
Bernard Vieille *(Controller)*
Stephen Kuhns *(Dir.-Sls.)*
Thomas DeBow *(Mgr.-Fabrication)*
Jerry Schmitt *(Mgr.-Mfg. & Quality Assurance)*
Catherine A. Wallace *(Mgr.-Pur. & Dir.-Import)*
Donald G. Warner *(Mgr.-Mktg.)*

Newage Industries Inc., Testing Instruments Division **(1)**
2300 Maryland Rd.
Willow Grove, PA 19090
Tel.: 215-657-6040
Telex: 273-780
Fax: 215-657-1697
Approx.Sls.: $3,500,000
Emp.: 15
Fiscal Year-end: 12/31/90
Import Export
Mfr. of Metal Hardness Testers
S.I.C.: 3829
R.E. Baker *(Chm. Bd.)*
Gordon Baker *(Pres.)*
Ken Baker *(Chief Oper. Officer)*
Steve Midgette *(Controller)*
Kathi Lohr *(Dir.-Pur.)*
G. Mazzoleni *(Dir.-Engrng.)*
Carmen Phillips *(Mgr.-Admin.)*
Richard Walsh *(Mgr.-Natl. Sls.)*
Janet Wordel *(Admin. Asst.)*

GUST K. NEWBERG CONSTRUCTION CO.
2040 N. Ashland Ave.
Chicago, IL 60614
Tel.: 312-489-1400 **IL**
Fax: 312-489-1408
Approx.Sls.: $167,000,000
Emp.: 2,000
General Contractors; Industrial & Commercial Buildings
S.I.C.: 1541; 1542
Francis W. Durocher *(Chm. Bd., Pres. & Treas.)*
Kevin J. Woods *(Exec. V.P.)*
Jack S. Dibie *(V.P.-Estimating)*
Dale H. Gold *(V.P.-West Coast Opers.)*
James R. Hansen *(V.P.-Contract Admin.)*
Joseph M. Orr *(V.P.-Florida Div.)*
Donald L. Stegemoller, Sr. *(V.P.-Power Construction)*
Peter C. Luedeking *(Sec.)*

Outside Service Firm(s):

Alexander X. Kuhn & Co.*(Auditors)*
Chicago, IL

Carey, Filter, White & Boland*(Legal Firm)*
Chicago, IL

First National Bank of Chicago*(Major Banking Relationship)*
One First National Plaza
Chicago, IL 60670
Tel.: 312-732-9781
Tel.: 312-732-4050
Fax: 312-732-4840
Fax: 312-732-3055

NEWBURY INDUSTRIES, INC.
10975 Kinsman Rd.
Newbury, OH 44065
Tel.: 216-564-2285
Fax: 216-564-7152
Approx.Sls.: $18,000,000
Emp.: 165
Mfr. of Plastic Injection Molding Machines
S.I.C.: 3559
Glenn H. Frohring *(Pres.)*
George W. Dallas *(Sls. Mgr.)*
Barbara Gorka *(Pur. Mgr.)*

D. W. NEWCOMER'S SONS, INC.
1331 Brush Creek Blvd.
Kansas City, MO 64110
Mailing Address:
P.O. Box 27056,
Kansas City, MO 64110
Tel.: 816-561-0024 **MO**
Fax: 816-931-7246
Year Founded: 1893
Sales Range: $20-39 Million
Emp.: 250
Fiscal Year-end: 12/31/89
Funeral Home & Cemeteries
S.I.C.: 6553; 7261
David W. Newcomer IV *(Pres. & Partner)*
Frank Newcomer III *(Partner)*
F. Peter Newcomer *(Partner)*
E. Thomas Turner, Jr. *(V.P.-Fin.)*
Robert T. Kelly *(V.P.-Admin.)*
Daniel Hocklander *(Dir.-Pub. Rels.)*

Principal(s):
David W. Newcomer IV
Frank Newcomer III
F. Peter Newcomer

Computer Systems/Hardware:
IBM System AS/400

Outside Service Firm(s):

Northwestern National Life*(Group Insurer)*
Kansas City, MO

Wassberg & Gallagher*(Legal Firm)*
Kansas City, MO

Subsidiary:

Funeral Security Plans, Inc. **(1)**
1331 Brush Creek Blvd.
Kansas City, MO 64110
Tel.: 816-561-0024
S.I.C.: 7261
David W. Newcomer *(Pres.)*
Gary Davis *(V.P.-Sls.)*
E. Thomas Turner, Jr. *(Treas.)*

HENRY NEWGARD & COMPANY
77 W. Seegers Rd.
Arlington Heights, IL 60005
Tel.: 708-640-8900 **IL**
Fax: 708-640-1719
Year Founded: 1882
Approx.Sls.: $28,000,000
Emp.: 340
Fiscal Year-end: 9/30/92
General Electrical Contractor
S.I.C.: 1731
J. Richard Newgard *(Pres. & Chief Exec. Officer)*
Robert N. Sieb *(Exec. V.P. & Chief Oper. Officer)*
James H. Newgard *(Sec. & Treas.)*

Principal(s):
J. Richard Newgard
James H. Newgard

No. of Foreign Offices: 1

Computer Systems/Hardware:
ARIX

Outside Service Firm(s):

McGreal, Johnson & McGreal*(Auditors)*
Chicago, IL

Phelan & Doyle*(Legal Firm)*
Chicago, IL

NEWLY WEDS FOODS INC.
4140 W. Fullerton Ave.
Chicago, IL 60639
Tel.: 312-489-7000
Fax: 312-489-2799
Year Founded: 1932
Approx.Sls.: $100,000,000
Emp.: 600
Fiscal Year-end: 12/31/91
Import Export
Mfr. of Breads & Batters, English Muffins, Foodservice Mixes; Exports Batters, Seasoning Blends, Spices, Marinades, Ice Cream Cake, Roll Cake
S.I.C.: 2024; 2099; 2051
Charles T. Angell *(Pres.)*
Jim Angell *(V.P.-Mngmt. Information Services)*
Frank Davis *(V.P.-Opers.)*
Don K. Harr *(V.P.-Spicecraft Div.)*
Bruce A. Leshiniski *(V.P.-Sls. & Mktg.)*
Leslie Minkus *(V.P. & Chief Fin. Officer)*
Richard J. Neidhardt *(V.P.-Pur.)*
Bruce Nevers *(V.P.-Human Resources)*
Hosen Oshita *(V.P., Sec. & Treas.)*
John J. Seely *(V.P. & Gen. Counsel)*
Chris Swain *(V.P.-Engrng.)*
William G. Readdy *(Dir.-Mktg.)*

No. of Mfg. Plants/Facilities: 3
No. of Foreign Offices: 6

Outside Service Firm(s):

Ernst & Young*(Auditors)*
233 S. Wacker Dr.
Chicago, IL 60606
Tel.: 312-368-1800
Fax: 312-645-3095

Schuyler, Roche & Zwirner*(Legal Firm)*
130 E. Randolph Dr.
Chicago, IL

Mellon Bank, N.A.*(Major Banking Relationship)*
Four Station Sq., Third Fl.
Pittsburgh, PA 15219
Tel.: 412-326-8000

Divisions:

Newly Weds Foods, Inc. **(1)**
70-80 Grove St.
Watertown, MA 02172
Tel.: 617-926-7600
Processes Batter Mixes & Bread Crumbs
S.I.C.: 2041; 2099
John Lincoln *(Gen. Mgr.)*

Newly Weds Foods, Inc. **(1)**
1111 Angell Dr.
Springdale, AR 72764
Tel.: 501-756-7300
Mfr. of Food Coatings
S.I.C.: 2099
John Kandl *(Gen. Mgr.)*

Newly Weds Foods, Inc. **(1)**
Gerald, MO
Tel.: 314-764-3397
Processes Seasoning Blends; Cleans, Grinds Spices
S.I.C.: 2099
Fred Edwards *(Mgr.-Plant)*
Rich Greenwood *(Quality Analyst)*

Non-U.S. Holdings:

M. Alkalay Agencies, Ltd. **(1)**
Industrial Area, P.O. Box 352,
Yavne, 70650, Israel
Tel.: 8 435572
Fax: 8 430418
Mfr. of Batters, Breading, etc.
S.I.C.: 2045; 2099; 2035

CIQYA/Bravo Foods de Mexico **(1)**
Prol. Morelos 2277 C.P. 64820 Col. Buenos Aires,
Monterrey, Nuevo Leon Mexico
Tel.: 83 597919
Fax: 83 591929
Marketing & Sales Office
S.I.C.: 5141

New Food Ingredients, Ltd. **(1)**
Owl Lane
Ossett, West Yorkshire WF5 9AX, United Kingdom
Tel.: 924 281040
Fax: 924 281041
Marketing & Sales Office
S.I.C.: 5149

Newly Weds Foods Asia/Pacific **(1)**
32 Davis Rd.
Wetherill Park, N.S.W. 2164, Australia
Tel.: 2 604 5966
Fax: 2 609 4728
Manufacturing of Custom Blended Spices, Seasonings & Batters
S.I.C.: 2035; 2099; 2045

Newly Weds Foods Thailand **(1)**
Industrial Estate, 139/11 Moo 17, Bang Plee Bagna Trao Road, Banghplee, Samutprakan, 10540, Thailand
Tel.: 2 3151502
Fax: 2 3151503
Mfr. of Batter Mixes, Breadings
S.I.C.: 2045; 2041

Nippon Flour Mills Co., Ltd. **(1)**
2715 Sendagaya Shibuya-ku 4-chome, Tokyo, 151, Japan
Tel.: 03 33502411
Fax: 03 33565175
Manufacturers of Batter Mixes
S.I.C.: 2045

RHM Ingredients, Ltd. **(1)**
Owl Lane
Ossett, West Yorkshire W5F 9AX, United Kingdom
Tel.: 924 280444
Fax: 924 281042
Mfr. of Food Ingredients
S.I.C.: 2099; 2045; 2035

UFL Foods, Inc. **(1)**
6320 Northwest Dr.
Mississauga, ON L4V 1J7, Canada
Tel.: 416-671-0808
Fax: 416-671-0809
Sales & Marketing Office for Custom Blend Spices, Seasonings & Batters
S.I.C.: 5149

NEWMAN, SAYLOR & GREGORY
2817 Millwood Ave.
Columbia, SC 29205
Tel.: 803-254-8158
Fax: 803-253-2016
Year Founded: 1970
Approx.Billings: $17,550,000
Emp.: 40
Business-to-Business, Direct Marketing, Planning & Retail
Van Newman *(Chm. Bd. & Treas.)*
Ralph Gregory *(Pres.)*
Lee Bussell *(Sr. V.P., Acct. Services)*
Howard Hellams *(Sr. V.P., Creative Services)*
Nickie Dickson *(Sr. V.P., Admin. & Fin.)*
David Anderson *(Sr. V.P., Mktg. Services)*

NEWMAN'S OWN, INC.
246 Post Road E.
Westport, CT 06880
Tel.: 203-222-0136
Year Founded: 1982
Approx.Sls.: $50,000,000
Fiscal Year-end: 12/31/90
Mfr. & Distribute Spaghetti Sauce, Popcorn, Salad Dressing & Lemonade
S.I.C.: 2033; 2099; 2035; 2086
Paul Newman *(Pres.)*
A.E. Hotchner *(Exec. V.P.)*
Ursula Hotchner *(Sr. V.P.)*

NEWMARK, POSNER & MITCHELL, INC.
300 East 42nd St.
New York, NY 10017
Tel.: 212-867-3900
Tel.: 800-486-1250
Fax: 212-818-0083
Year Founded: 1959
Approx.Billings: $25,280,000
Emp.: 55
Healthcare, Financial, Real Estate, Human Resources Recruitment, School & Business-to-Business Communications
Sidney Posner *(Chm. Bd., Chief Exec. Officer, Treas.)*
Peter S. Posner *(Pres., Chief Oper. Officer, New Bus. Contact)*
Robert K. Posner *(Exec. V.P.)*
Roy Schwartz *(Sr. V.P.)*
Richard Pines *(V.P.)*
Ron Shafran *(V.P.)*
Charles J. Barber *(Admin./Opers.)*
Nancy Reiher *(Chief Fin. Officer, Controller)*
Miriam Posner *(Corp. Sec.)*

NEWPORT/CAPE DORY YACHTS, INC.
(Formerly Cape Dory Yachts, Inc.)
308 Line Rd.
Manorville, NY 11949
Tel.: 516-727-1313
Fax: 401-253-0087
Year Founded: 1964
Approx.Sls.: $10,000,000
Emp.: 200
Boat Building & Repairing
S.I.C.: 3732
Russell Handler *(Pres.)*
Dana Marnane *(Sec.)*

NEWS-PRESS & GAZETTE COMPANY
P.O. Box 29,
St. Joseph, MA 64502
Mailing Address:
P.O. Box 29
St. Joseph, MO 64502
Approx.Sls.: $30,000,000
Emp.: 400
Newspaper Publishing, Cable Television, Television Broadcasting
S.I.C.: 2711; 4899; 4833
Henry H. Bradley *(Chm., Treas. & Publisher)*
David R. Bradley Jr. *(Pres. & Editor)*
Lyle Leimkuhler *(V.P.-Fin. & Sec.)*
Douglas B. Fuller *(V.P.-Cablevision)*
Carroll C. Hicks *(Asst. Treas.)*
Robert M. Lindsay *(Mgr.-Production & Circulation)*
Richard A. Heath *(Mgr.-Adv.)*

Subsidiaries:

Broadcasters of Mississippi, Inc. **(1)**
1820 TV Road, P.O. Box 8887
Jackson, MS 39204
Tel.: 601-372-6311 (100%)
Television Broadcasting
S.I.C.: 4833
John A. MacGregor *(Pres.)*

Stations:

WHLT **(2)**
990 Hardy St., Box 232
Hattiesburg, MS 39403
Tel.: 601-545-2077
Television Broadcasting
S.I.C.: 4833
Randy Cleland *(Gen. Mgr.)*

WJTV **(2)**
1820 TV Road, Box 8887
Jackson, MS
Tel.: 601-372-6311
Television Broadcasting
S.I.C.: 4833
William M. Dilday, Jr. *(V.P. & Gen. Mgr.)*

SDTV, Inc. **(1)**
300 No. Dakota Ave.
Sioux Falls, SD 57102
Tel.: 605-336-1300 (100%)
Television Broadcasting
S.I.C.: 4833
David R. Bradley, Jr. *(Pres.)*

Station:

KSFY-TV **(2)**
300 No. Dakota Ave.
Sioux Falls, SD 57102
Tel.: 605-336-1300
Television Broadcasting
S.I.C.: 4833
Mike Smith *(Gen. Mgr.)*
R. Gary Pierone *(Gen. Sls. Mgr.)*

NPG of Arizona, Inc. **(1)**
115 W. Drachman
Tucson, AZ 85705
Tel.: 602-624-2511
S.I.C.: 4833
Marge Wilson *(Mgr.)*

Station:

KOLD-TV **(2)**
115 W. Drachman
Tucson, AZ 85705
Tel.: 602-624-2511
Television Station
S.I.C.: 4833
Marge Wilson *(Mgr.)*

NEWSPAPER ADVERTISING SPECIALISTS, INC. (N.A.S.)
333 N. Michigan Ave.
Chicago, IL 60601
Tel.: 312-853-1195
Year Founded: 1981
Approx.Billings: $12,000,000
Emp.: 11
National, Regional, Local Newsp. Research, Planning, Estimating & Scheduling
C. Randall Choate *(Pres.)*
Judith F. Sandlin *(Exec. V.P.)*

O. A. NEWTON & SON CO.
P.O. Box 397,
Bridgeville, DE 19933
Tel.: 302-337-8211
Fax: 302-337-3780
Year Founded: 1916
Approx.Sls.: $14,000,000
Emp.: 85
Fiscal Year-end: 10/31/92
Export
Mfr. of Industrial & Farm Machinery; Feed Milling & Grain Handling Equipment; Modular Homes; Plastics Material Handling Systems
S.I.C.: 3523; 3452; 3537; 3559
Robert F. Rider *(Chm., Chief Exec. Officer & Treas.)*
William S. Farlow *(Pres.)*
John Herrmann *(V.P.-Sls. & Mktg.)*
Robert F. Rider, Jr. *(Asst. V.P.-Parts & Service Div.)*
Robert E. Walls *(Asst. V.P.-Agri. Div.)*
Grace Adams *(Sec.)*

Computer Systems/Hardware:
IBM

NEWTRON GROUP INC.
8183 W. El Cajon Dr.
Baton Rouge, LA 70815
Tel.: 504-927-8921
Year Founded: 1973
Approx.Sls.: $80,000,000
Emp.: 1,200
Fiscal Year-end: 12/31/90
Electrical & Industrial Contractors; Installation & Repair Instrumentation
S.I.C.: 1731; 7699
Newton B. Thomas *(Chm. Bd. & Pres.)*
Alberto J. De Jongh *(V.P. & Sec.)*

Outside Service Firm(s):

Hannis T. Bourgois*(Auditors)*
Baton Rouge, LA

Taylor, Porter, Brooks & Phillips*(Legal Firm)*
Baton Rouge, LA

Premier Bank*(Major Banking Relationship)*
P.O. Box 1511
Baton Rouge, LA 70821

NEXT, INC.
900 Chesapeake Dr.
Redwood City, CA 94063
Tel.: 415-424-8500
Tel.: 415-366-0900
Fax: 415-780-3714
Year Founded: 1988
Approx.Sls.: $127,000,000
Custom Computer Software Developers
S.I.C.: 7371; 7372; 7373
Steven P. Jobs *(Chm. & Chief Exec. Officer)*
Peter van Cuylenberg *(Pres. & Chief Oper. Officer)*
Mike Slade *(V.P.-Mktg.)*
Marcel Gani *(Chief Fin. Officer)*

NEXUS PLASTICS, INC.
One Loretto Ave.
Hawthorne, NJ 07506
Tel.: 201-427-3311
Tel.: 800-486-3987
Fax: 201-427-4847
Year Founded: 1982
Approx.Sls.: $14,500,000
Emp.: 100
Fiscal Year-end: 8/31/91
Export
Mfr. of Polyethylene Bags, Tubing & Sheeting
S.I.C.: 3081
J. Ronald Esak *(Pres. & Chief Exec. Officer)*
Marwan Sholakh *(V.P. & Chief Oper. Officer)*
Mary Lynn Esak *(Controller)*
Doug Boyd *(Mgr.-Sls.)*
Wayne Dzierzanowski *(Mgr.-Quality Control)*
Fred Qualigari *(Mgr.-Production)*
Kariman Sholakh *(Mgr.-Human Resources)*
Ken Tashjy *(Mgr.-Mktg.)*

Computer Systems/Hardware:
UNIX/FILE Pro

Divisions:

C-J Extruders Inc. **(1)**
One Loretto Ave.
Hawthorne, NJ 07506
Tel.: 201-427-3311
Mfrs. Plastics
S.I.C.: 3081
J. Ronald Esak *(Prex. & Chief Exec. Officer)*

THE J. M. NEY COMPANY
Ney Industrial Park
Bloomfield, CT 06002
Tel.: 203-242-2281 **CT**
Telex: 6288 7937
Fax: 203-242-5688
Year Founded: 1812
Approx.Sls.: $45,000,000
Emp.: 350
Fiscal Year-end: 12/25/90
Manufactures Precious Metals for Dental & Electronic Uses
S.I.C.: 3843; 3339
Frank S. Wilson *(Chm. Bd.)*
Robert H. Saunders, Jr. *(Pres. & Chief Exec. Officer)*
Lois C. Dowd *(V.P.-Human Resources)*
H. George Wolfe *(V.P.-Dental Div.)*
Pauline V. Dougan *(Sec.)*
Jack Volinski *(Controller)*
Melvyn A. Barham *(Dir.-West Coast Opers.)*
Michael W. Conroy *(Dir.-Mktg.)*
Richard Daly *(Dir.-Information Services)*
Thomas W. Lindenmuth *(Dir.-East Coast Opers.)*
Dr. Edward F. Smith *(Dir.-Res. & Devel. Div.)*
Joyce E. Thompson *(Dir.-Pur.)*

No. of Mfg. Plants/Facilities: 3
No. of Foreign Offices: 1

Computer Systems/Hardware:
IBM 4341; IBM 36

Outside Service Firm(s):

Coopers & Lybrand*(Auditors)*
280 Trumbull St.
Hartford, CT 06103

Connecticut General Life Insurance Co.*(Group Insurer)*
P.O. Box 2975,
Hartford, CT 06104
Tel.: 203-726-6000

Robinson & Cole*(Legal Firm)*
Hartford, CT

Connecticut National Bank*(Major Banking Relationship)*
777 Main St.
Hartford, CT 06115
Tel.: 203-728-2000

Aetna Life & Casualty*(Pension Manager)*
151 Farmington Avenue
Hartford, CT 06156
Tel.: 203-273-2128
Fax: 203-729-4295

Connecticut National Bank*(Pension Manager)*
777 Main St.
Hartford, CT 06115
Tel.: 203-728-2000

Divisions:

Barkmeyer Div. **(1)**
P.O. Drawer C
Yucaipa, CA 92399
Tel.: 909-795-2461
S.I.C.: 3843
Mel A. Barham *(West Coast Oper. Mgr.)*

Dental Div. **(1)**
Ney Industrial Park
Bloomfield, CT 06002
Tel.: 203-242-2281
Fax: 203-242-5688
S.I.C.: 3843
H. George Wolfe *(Div. Dir.)*

Electronics Div. **(1)**
Ney Industrial Park
Bloomfield, CT 06002
Tel.: 203-242-2281
Fax: 203-242-5688
S.I.C.: 3843
John J. Patsky *(Opers. Mgr.)*
T. Lindenmouth *(Dir.-East Coast Opers.)*

Precision Machine Div. **(1)**
Redmond, WA 98052
Tel.: 206-885-1921
S.I.C.: 3843
Mel A. Barham *(West Coast Opers. Mgr.)*

Refining Div. **(1)**
Ney Industrial Park
Bloomfield, CT 06002
Tel.: 203-242-2281
S.I.C.: 3339

AL NEYER, INC.
3800 Red Bank Rd.
Cincinnati, OH 45227
Tel.: 513-271-6400 **OH**
Fax: 513-271-1350
Year Founded: 1894
Approx.Sls.: $25,000,000
Emp.: 80
Import Export
New Construction of Commercial, Office & Institutional Buildings; Subdividers & Developers
S.I.C.: 1542; 1541; 6552
Corporate Giving Program: Supports Organizations Sponsored by Employees & Approved by Board
Employee Matching Gifts Program: To Educational Foundations
Donald L. Neyer *(Chm. Bd. & Pres.)*
Thomas Neyer *(Exec. V.P. & Treas.)*
Dan Neyer *(V.P. & Asst. Treas.)*
David F. Neyer *(V.P.-Opers.)*
Thomas L. Neyer Jr. *(V.P.-Mktg.)*
John Neyer *(V.P.)*
Jennifer Berg *(Controller)*
William Neyer *(Sec.)*

Outside Service Firm(s):

Provident Bank*(Major Banking Relationship)*
One E. Fourth St.
Cincinnati, OH 45202
Tel.: 513-579-2731

NIAGARA BLOWER COMPANY
673 Ontario
Buffalo, NY 14207
Tel.: 716-875-2000
Tel.: 800-426-5169
Fax: 716-875-1077
Approx.Sls.: $12,000,000
Emp.: 99
Fiscal Year-end: 11/30/91
Import Export
Process Equipment for Industry & Heat Transfer Equipment, Custom HVAC Central Station Air Handling Units
S.I.C.: 3443
George C. Morris *(Pres.)*
Ronald W. Pokorski *(V.P.-Sls.)*
Charles L. Gornick *(V.P.-Resorcon)*
Craig D. Boyce *(Controller)*

Computer Systems/Hardware:
IBM CAD

NIAGARA CUTTER, INC.
Niagara Cutter Plaza, 889 Erie Ave.
North Tonawanda, NY 14120
Tel.: 716-693-8400
Fax: 716-693-2236
Sales Range: $10-19 Million
Emp.: 90
Manufacture Metal Cutting Tools
S.I.C.: 3541
Roger D. Bollier *(Pres.)*
Bill Szabo *(Controller)*
Terry Covert *(Mgr.-Data Processing)*
Bill Reece *(Mgr.-Pur.)*
Principal(s):
Roger D. Bollier

No. of Mfg. Plants/Facilities: 2

Computer Systems/Hardware:
IBM System 36

Outside Service Firm(s):

J. D. Elliott & Co.*(Auditors)*
Buffalo, NY

The Bank of New York*(Major Banking Relationship)*
One Wall Street
New York, NY 10286
Tel.: 212-635-6805
Fax: 212-635-3201

NIAGARA ENVELOPE COMPANY, INC.
(Formerly Niagara Envelope Group, Inc.)
693 Seneca St., 5th Fl.
Buffalo, NY 14210
Tel.: 716-854-8204
Fax: 716-852-8680
Year Founded: 1863
Sales Range: $40-59 Million
Emp.: 550

Niagara Envelope Company, Inc.—(Continued)

Import Export
Manufacture Envelopes
S.I.C.: 2677; 5112
Frederick G. Pierce II *(Chm. Bd., Pres. & Chief Exec. Officer)*
David Hecht *(V.P.)*
Robert Woollacott *(V.P.-Mktg.)*
Jeffery Lennox *(Controller)*
Patricia Larkin *(Sec.)*
Cheryl Byrne *(Dir.-Personnel)*
Cynthia J. Herrigan *(Mgr.-Sls. Promo. & Adv.)*
Principal(s):
Frederick G. Pierce II
David Hecht
Jeffery Lennox

No. of Mfg. Plants/Facilities: 6

Computer Systems/Hardware:
Data General System 12

Outside Service Firm(s):

Lucker, Kennedy & Felmeden*(Auditors)*
Buffalo, NY

Phillips, Lytle, Hitchcock, Blaine & Huber*(Legal Firm)*
3400 Marine Midland Center
Buffalo, NY 14203
Tel.: 716-847-8400

Marine Midland Bank*(Major Banking Relationship)*
250 Park Ave.
New York, NY 10017
Tel.: 212-503-6642

Divisions:

Niagara Envelope Co., Inc. **(1)**
701 Seneca St.
Buffalo, NY 14210
Tel.: 716-854-8251
Fax: 716-856-6388
Envelope Converter
S.I.C.: 2677
Gary Marella *(V.P. & Gen. Mgr.)*

Niagara Envelope Co. of Colorado **(1)**
14101 E. 33rd. Place
Aurora, CO 80011
Tel.: 303-373-1780
Tel.: 800-333-1780
Fax: 303-371-7765
Envelope Converter
S.I.C.: 2677
Kurt Braun *(Opers. Mgr.)*

Niagara Envelope Co. of Florida **(1)**
5560 Shawland Rd.
Jacksonville, FL 32205
Tel.: 904-783-0601
Tel.: 800-477-3577
Fax: 904-783-6456
Envelope Converter
S.I.C.: 2677
Adrian S. Jewett *(Opers. Mgr.)*

Niagara Envelope Co. of Illinois **(1)**
2001 W. Arthur St.
Elk Grove Village, IL 60007
Tel.: 708-364-5588
Tel.: 800-395-5580
Fax: 708-364-6894
Envelope Converter
S.I.C.: 2677
T.J. McNeill *(V.P. & Gen. Mgr.)*

Niagara Envelope Co. of Texas **(1)**
10231 Plano Rd.
Dallas, TX 75238
Tel.: 214-348-5511
Tel.: 800-825-9998
Fax: 214-343-8100
Envelope Converter
S.I.C.: 2677
Frank J. Artinger, Jr. *(V.P. & Gen. Mgr.)*

NIAGARA FRONTIER TRANSPORATION METRO SYSTEM, INC.
181 Ellicott St.
Buffalo, NY 14203
Mailing Address:
P. O. Box 5008
Buffalo, NY 14205
Tel.: 716-855-7226
Fax: 716-855-7657
Approx.Sls.: $32,000,000
Emp.: 1,100
Fiscal Year-end: 12/31/90
Transportation
S.I.C.: 4111
Anthony Schill *(Exec. V.P.)*
Terry Kelly *(Admin. Supvr.)*
John Gross *(Mgr.-Matls. & Procurement)*
Darryl Rasuli *(Mgr.-Pub. Rels.)*

NIAGARA THERAPY MFG. CORP.
1100 Hwy. 27 S.
Stanley, NC 28164
Mailing Address:
P.O. Box 1100
Stanley, NC 28164
Tel.: 704-263-1451
Fax: 704-263-4345
Approx.Sls.: $30,000,000
Emp.: 150
Manufacture Electrical Massage Equipment
S.I.C.: 3999
Robert Egan *(Pres.)*
Mark Nye *(Chief Exec. Officer & V.P.)*
Daryle Hall *(V.P.-Fin.)*
John J. Luptak *(V.P.-Mktg. & Sec.)*

Outside Service Firm(s):

Millard & Company*(Auditors)*
Ft. Lauderdale, FL

Diamond & Golomb*(Legal Firm)*
999 Park Ave.
New York, NY 10016
Tel.: 212-687-7550

First Union National Bank*(Major Banking Relationship)*
CMG-5, Two First Union Center
Charlotte, NC 28288-1154
Tel.: 704-374-2698
Fax: 704-374-6987

NIAGARA TRANSFORMER CORP.
1747 Dale Rd.
Buffalo, NY 14225
Mailing Address:
P.O. Box 233
Buffalo, NY 14225
Tel.: 716-896-6500
Fax: 716-896-8871
Approx.Sls.: $10,000,000
Emp.: 100
Fiscal Year-end: 1/ 1/91
Power, Lighting & Distribution Transformer
Fred W. Darby *(Pres.)*
Francis J. Winnert *(V.P.-Fin.)*
Gerald H. Asmus *(V.P.-Sls.)*

NIBBLE WITH GIBBLE'S, INC.
6647 Molly Pitcher Hwy. S.
Chambersburg, PA 17201
Tel.: 717-375-2243
Tel.: 800-843-2447
Fax: 717-375-2762
Year Founded: 1959
Approx.Sls.: $21,000,000
Emp.: 220
Fiscal Year-end: 6/30/91
Mfr. Potato Chips & Snacks
S.I.C.: 2096
Robert W. Luttman *(Pres.)*
David L. Rank *(V.P.-Fin. & Treas.)*
Hershey Bowers, Jr. *(Sec.)*
Darrell K. Miller *(Mgr.-Quality Control)*
W. Keith Starliper *(Mgr.-Opers.)*

Computer Systems/Hardware:
IBM System 38

Outside Service Firm(s):

Ciardi, Fishbane & Didonato*(Legal Firm)*
Philadelphia, PA

NIBCO, INC.
500 Simpson Ave.
Elkhart, IN 46516
Mailing Address:
P.O. Box 1167
Elkhart, IN 46515
Tel.: 219-295-3000 **IN**
Fax: 219-295-3307
Year Founded: 1904
Earnings: $8,500,000
Approx.Sls.: $288,000,000
Emp.: 2,700
Fiscal Year-end: 12/31/91
Import Export
Manufacture of Pipe Fittings, Valves & Plumbing Faucets
S.I.C.: 3432; 3089; 3494
Lee Martin *(Chm. Bd.)*
Rex Martin *(Pres. & Chief Exec. Officer)*
Larry Birch *(V.P.-Residential Mktg.)*
Robert L. Krok *(V.P.-Comml. & Indus. Div.)*
Dennis J. Parker *(V.P.-Fin., Chief Fin. Officer & Treas.)*
James I. Pullen *(V.P.-Admin.)*
Thomas M. Smith *(V.P.-Valve Mfg.)*
James N. Davis *(Controller)*
Thomas Eisele *(Sec. & Legal Counsel)*
William Frymoyer *(Dir.-Personnel)*
David Grumm *(Dir.-ICS)*
Kevin Caldwell *(Mgr.-Quality Control)*
Garry Fileccia *(Mgr.-Adv.)*
Bill Good *(Mgr.-Engrng.)*
Joe Hlade *(Mgr.-Natural Resources)*
Deb Huss *(Mgr.-Cash)*
Jeff Robertson *(Mgr.-International)*
Lynn Sayre *(Mgr.-Research & Devel.)*
Principal(s):
Martin Family

Computer Systems/Hardware:
IBM 4381; H.P.

Outside Service Firm(s):

Coopers & Lybrand*(Auditors)*
211 W. Washington, Ste. 2200
South Bend, IN 46601
Tel.: 219-234-4021

Prudential Insurance Co. of America*(Group Insurer)*
751 Broad St.
Newark, NJ 07102-3777
Tel.: 201-802-6000

Barnes & Thornburg*(Legal Firm)*
100 N. Michigan., Ste. 600
South Bend, IN 46601
Tel.: 219-233-1171

Bank One, Indianapolis, N.A.*(Major Banking Relationship)*
111 Monument Circle, Ste. 1611
Indianapolis, IN 46204-1611
Tel.: 317-321-8110

Continental Bank N. A.*(Major Banking Relationship)*
231 S. LaSalle St.
Chicago, IL 60697
Tel.: 312-828-2345
Tel.: 800-426-5754
Telex: 312-828-1783

Irving Trust Co.*(Major Banking Relationship)*
New York, NY

National Bank of Detroit*(Major Banking Relationship)*
611 Woodward
Detroit, MI 48226
Tel.: 313-225-1000

Townley Capital Management*(Pension Manager)*
New York, NY

Warehouses:

NIBCO SWM Marketing Corp. **(1)**
Carrollton, TX 75006
Tel.: 214-241-3900 (100%)
Fax: 214-241-0089
Approx.Sls.: $12,000,000
Emp.: 21
Distributor of Nibco Products
S.I.C.: 5074

NIBCO Piping Products East **(1)**
P.O. Box 1387, 1510 Gehman Rd.
Kulpsville, PA 19443
Tel.: 800-836-4260
Fax: 215-256-4020
S.I.C.: 5074

QPP Quality Piping Products **(1)**
10516 Commerce Way
Fontana, CA 92335
Tel.: 909-822-5044
Fax: 800-447-7865
S.I.C.: 5074

Non-U.S. Holding:

Nibchem Inc. **(1)**
50 Dynamic Dr. Unit 1
Scarborough, ON M1V 2W2, Canada
Tel.: 416-291-8167 (100%)
Fax: 416-291-5151
Approx.Sls.: $4,000,000
Emp.: 10
Wholesale Industrial & Plumbing Supplies
S.I.C.: 5074
Frank LeMay *(Pres.)*

NICKERSON LUMBER COMPANY
15 Main St.
Orleans, MA 02653
Mailing Address:
P.O. Box 99
Orleans, MA 02563
Tel.: 508-255-0200
Fax: 508-255-0599
Sales Range: $20-39 Million
Emp.: 250
Sawmill Products; Millwork; Structural Lumber; Prefabricated Homes
S.I.C.: 5211; 2421; 2439; 2452
Joshua A. Nickerson, Jr. *(Chm. Bd. & Pres.)*
Douglas Bohannon *(V.P. & Gen. Mgr.)*
William Durgin *(V.P. & Treas.)*
Kenneth Krammer *(V.P.-Personnel)*
Louise Nickerson *(Sec.)*

Outside Service Firm(s):

Price Waterhouse*(Auditors)*
160 Federal St.
Boston, MA 02110
Tel.: 617-439-3308
Fax: 617-439-3308

Hill & Barlow*(Legal Firm)*
One International Place
Boston, MA 02110
Tel.: 617-439-3555

Cape Bank & Trust Co.*(Major Banking Relationship)*
Orleans, MA

ALFRED NICKLES BAKERY, INC.
26 Main St.
Navarre, OH 44662
Tel.: 216-879-5635
Fax: 216-879-5896
Year Founded: 1909
Approx.Sls.: $100,000,000
Emp.: 1,900
Baker of Bread, Buns, Sweet Rolls, Doughnuts, Cake
S.I.C.: 2051
Ernest A. Nickles *(Chm. & Chief Exec. Officer)*
David E. Gardner *(Pres. & Sec.)*
James L. Gerber *(Sr. V.P.-Mktg.)*

T. Robert Wolfe *(V.P.-Production)*
M.J. Arciello *(V.P.-Fin.)*
Walter Hern *(V.P.-Sls.)*
David A. Gardner *(V.P.-Plant Mngmt.)*

Divisions:

Nickles Bakery Inc., Elkhart **(1)**
600 Harrison St.
Elkhart, IN 46516
Tel.: 219-293-0608
Approx.Sls.: $13,200,000
Emp.: 165
Mfr. Bread, Cake & Related Products
S.I.C.: 2051
W. Carter *(Gen. Mgr.)*

Nickles Bakery Inc., Lima **(1)**
775 W. North St.
Lima, OH 45801
Tel.: 419-224-7080
Approx.Sls.: $8,000,000
Emp.: 100
Mfr. Bread, Cake & Related Products
S.I.C.: 2051
Ernest Nickles *(Chm. & Chief Exec. Officer)*

Subsidiary:

Nickles Bakery, Inc. **(1)**
1000 Broadway
Martins Ferry, OH 43935
Tel.: 614-633-1711
Approx.Sls.: $30,000,000
Emp.: 300
Wholesale Bread, Buns
S.I.C.: 5141
Ernest A. Nickles *(Chm. & Chief Exec. Officer)*
David A. Gardner *(Pres. & Sec.)*
M.J. Arciello *(V.P.-Fin. & Treas.)*
James L. Gerber *(V.P.-Mktg. & Distr.)*
Walter Hern *(V.P.)*
Jim Kettlewell *(V.P.-Pur.)*
T.R. Wolfe *(V.P.-Production)*
William Icenhower *(Mgr.-Area)*
Gerald Spieth *(Mgr.-Plant)*

THE NIELSEN COMPANY
(Formerly Nielsen Lithographing Company)
3731 Eastern Hills Lane
Cincinnati, OH 45209
Tel.: 513-321-5200
Fax: 513-321-5315
Approx.Sls.: $17,000,000
Emp.: 160
Commercial Lithographing
S.I.C.: 2752
Eric C. Nielsen *(Chm. Bd.)*
S. Christian Nielsen, III *(Pres.)*
Steve Jones *(V.P.-Opers.)*
Allan J. Fritsch *(Treas.)*
Gene Rich *(Mgr.-Sls.)*

Outside Service Firm(s):

Grant Thornton*(Auditors)*
1600 Atrium One
Cincinnati, OH 45202
Tel.: 513-762-5000

Taft, Stettinius & Hollister*(Legal Firm)*
First Natl. Bank Center
Cincinnati, OH 45202
Tel.: 513-381-2838

Star Bank*(Major Banking Relationship)*
425 Walnut Street
Cincinnati, OH 45202
Tel.: 513-632-4000

Divisions:

Ohio Valley Litho Div. **(1)**
7405 Industrial Drive Rd.
Florence, KY 41042
Tel.: 606-525-7405
Lithographers, Commercial Printing
S.I.C.: 2752
Ronald Kurg *(V.P.)*

Queensgate Press **(1)**
3956 Virginia Ave.
Cincinnati, OH 45227
Tel.: 513-271-1200
Commercial Lithographing
S.I.C.: 2752
Richard Arnold *(Pres.)*

NIELSEN CONSTRUCTION COMPANY
3127 Jefferson St.
San Diego, CA 92110
Mailing Address:
P.O. Box 80367
San Diego, CA 92138
Tel.: 619-291-6330
Fax: 619-293-7620
Year Founded: 1945
Assets: $39,000,000
Liabilities: $30,500,000
Net Worth: $8,500,000
Approx.Sls.: $180,000,000
Emp.: 450
Fiscal Year-end: 9/30/91
General Building Contractor
S.I.C.: 1541; 1542
L. Richard Myers *(Chm. Bd.)*
Stephen C. Marble *(Pres. & Chief Exec. Officer)*
Jeffrey E. Platt *(Sr. V.P.-Fin.)*
Thomas E. Tourtellott *(Sr. V.P.-Mktg. & Admin.)*
Timothy Kelly *(V.P.-Estimating)*
Dennis Walters *(V.P.-Field Opers.)*
Barbara J. Roth *(Controller)*

No. of U.S. Offices: 3

Outside Service Firm(s):

Larson, Ludwig, Stokes, Pecoraro, Combs & Bohne*(Auditors)*
San Diego, CA

Hillyer & Irwin*(Legal Firm)*
San Diego, CA

Union Bank*(Major Banking Relationship)*
8155 Mercury Ct., P.O. Box 2529
San Diego, CA 92112

NIGHTINGALE-CONANT CORP.
7300 N. Lehigh Ave.
Niles, IL 60714
Tel.: 708-588-6217
Tel.: 800-323-5552
Fax: 708-647-7145
Approx.Sls.: $60,000,000
Emp.: 250
Fiscal Year-end: 2/28/91
Audio & Video Training & Self-Development Programs, Lead the Field, Keep It Simple, Salesman, The Psychology of Winning, The Strangest Secret, The Boss, Megatrends, How to Be a No-Limit Person, The Iacocca Tapes
S.I.C.: 3652; 5735
Victor Conant *(Pres. & Chief Exec. Officer)*
Kevin McEneely *(Exec. V.P.)*

Outside Service Firm(s):

NBD Bank, N.A.*(Major Banking Relationship)*
Evanston, IL

Divisions:

Broadcast Div. **(1)**
7300 N. Lehigh Ave.
Chicago, IL 60648
Tel.: 312-588-6217
Barbara Andreski *(Gen. Mgr.)*

Nightingale-Conant Div. **(1)**
7300 N. Lehigh Ave.
Chicago, IL 60648
Tel.: 312-588-6217
Nick Carter *(V.P. & Natl. Sls. Dir.)*
Vic Conant *(V.P. & Dir.-Opers.)*
David Nightingale *(V.P.-Mail Order Syndication & Prod. Devel.)*
Don Reaser *(V.P.-Adv. & Devel.)*
Toni Boyle *(Exec. Producer)*

Nightingale-Conant Recording & Tape Duplicating Div. **(1)**
Howard Commons, 6245 W. Howard St.
Niles, IL 60648
Tel.: 312-647-0300
Jim Reising *(V.P.)*

Nightingale-Conant Retail Div. **(1)**
7300 N. Lehigh Ave.
Chicago, IL 60648
Tel.: 312-588-6217
Fred Walski *(V.P.)*

Nightingale-Conant Specialty Mail Services Div. **(1)**
7300 N. Lehigh Ave.
Chicago, IL 60648
Tel.: 312-588-6217
Dorothy Peara *(V.P. & Pur. Agent)*

THE NIKKEL CORPORATION
3091 Fair Oaks Blvd.
Sacramento, CA 95824
Tel.: 916-488-6170
Approx.Sls.: $15,000,000
Emp.: 70
Mfr. of Wood Mouldings & Lumber
S.I.C.: 2431; 5031
Robert F. Nikkel *(Pres. & Chief Fin. Officer)*
Margarita Nikkel *(Sec. & Treas.)*

NIMNICHT CHEVROLET COMPANY
1550 Cassat Ave.
Jacksonville, FL 32210
Tel.: 904-387-4041
Fax: 904-388-8016
Year Founded: 1941
Sales Range: $40-59 Million
Emp.: 157
New & Used Automobiles & Trucks
S.I.C.: 5511
Billie N. Nimnicht, Jr. *(Pres.)*
Edward A. Nimnicht, II *(V.P. & Gen. Mgr.)*
Ann Nimnicht *(Controller, Treas. & Sec.)*
Nancy Bane *(Dir.-Personnel & Bus. Mgr.)*
W.J. McMenany *(Gen. Sls. Mgr.)*
Lucy Merrell *(Pur. Agent & Credit Mgr.)*
Brent Penn *(Mgr.-Sls., New Cars)*

Outside Service Firm(s):

Masters, Smith & Wisby*(Auditors)*
Jacksonville, FL

Mahoney, Hadlow, Adams, Milan, Surface & Grimsley*(Legal Firm)*
800 Barnett Bank Bldg., 100 Laura St., P.O. Box 4099
Jacksonville, FL 32201-4099
Tel.: 904-354-1100

Florida Union National Bank*(Major Banking Relationship)*
Jacksonville, FL

NINE WEST GROUP, INC.
(Formerly Fisher Camuto Retail Corporation)
9 W Broad St.
Stamford, CT 06902
Tel.: 203-324-7567
Fax: 203-324-9045
Emp.: 1,500
Retail Women's Shoes
S.I.C.: 5661
Jerome Fisher *(Chm. Bd.)*
Vincent Camuto *(Co-Chm. Bd.)*
Wayne Weaver *(Pres. & Chief Exec. Officer)*
Barbara Polman *(Dir.-Personnel)*

NITRAM ENERGY INC.
227 Thorn Ave.
Orchard Park, NY 14127
Tel.: 716-662-6540
Fax: 716-662-6548
Approx.Sls.: $22,000,000
Emp.: 250
Fiscal Year-end: 12/31/90
Mfr. Heat Exchangers
S.I.C.: 3443
W.G. Martin *(Pres.)*
Art Cagney *(V.P.-Sls.)*

Subsidiary:

Burgess Manning, Inc. **(1)**
227 Thorn Ave.
Orchard Park, NY 14127
Tel.: 716-662-6540
Fax: 716-662-6548
Approx.Sls.: $21,000,000
Emp.: 295
Fiscal Year-end: 12/31/90
Liquid/Gas/Air Separation, Filteration, Cleaning, Pulsation, & Noise Pollution Control Standard & Special Engineered Equip. & Products
S.I.C.: 3799; 3599
W.G. Martin *(Pres.)*
Art Cagney *(V.P.)*

NIXDORFF KREIN INDUSTRIES INC.
760 Office Pkwy., Ste. 48
Saint Louis, MO 63141
Mailing Address:
P.O. Box 419050,
St. Louis, MO 63141-9050
Tel.: 314-872-8500 **DE**
Fax: 314-872-8517
Year Founded: 1854
Sales Range: $10-19 Million
Emp.: 70
Fiscal Year-end: 6/30/90
Import Export
Mfr. Sporting Goods
S.I.C.: 3949
Millard S. Cohen *(Pres.)*
C.B. Baron *(Sec.)*

No. of Mfg. Plants/Facilities: 3
No. of U.S. Offices: 4

Computer Systems/Hardware:
IBM

Outside Service Firm(s):

KPMG Peat Marwick*(Auditors)*
1010 Market St.
Saint Louis, MO 63101
Tel.: 314-444-1400

Thompson & Mitchell*(Legal Firm)*
One Mercantile Center
St. Louis, MO 63101
Tel.: 314-231-7676

Comerica Bank*(Major Banking Relationship)*
211 W. Fort St.
Detroit, MI 48226
Tel.: 313-222-3300

Subsidiary:

Gared Sports Inc. **(1)**
1107 Mullanphy
Saint Louis, MO 63106
Tel.: 314-421-0044
Sporting Goods
S.I.C.: 3949
C.J. Engle *(Pres.)*

NOB HILL GENERAL STORE, INC.
200 E. 10th St.
Gilroy, CA 95020
Tel.: 408-842-6441
Fax: 408-842-3546
Year Founded: 1961
Approx.Sls.: $400,000,000
Emp.: 2,600
Fiscal Year-end: 2/28/92
Supermarket Chain/Retail Grocer
S.I.C.: 5411
Michael Bonfante *(Pres. & Chief Exec. Officer)*
Greg Barr *(Exec. V.P. & Chief Oper. Officer)*
James Oteri *(Sr. V.P.)*
Norman Kato *(Sr. V.P.-Opers.)*
Lynda Trelut *(V.P.-Adv. & Pub. Rels.)*
Rick Rae *(V.P.-Corp. Fin.)*
Terry Hall *(V.P.-Distr.)*
James Trelut *(V.P.-Human Resources)*
Alan Oteri *(V.P.-Mdsg.)*
Javier Mercado *(V.P.-Produce)*

Nob Hill General Store, Inc.—(Continued)

Computer Systems/Hardware:
IBM

Outside Service Firm(s):

Bank of the West*(Major Banking Relationship)*
Gilroy, CA

NOBART, INC.
1133 S. Wabash Ave.
Chicago, IL 60605
Tel.: 312-427-9800
Fax: 312-427-4603
Year Founded: 1948
Sales Range: $20-39 Million
Emp.: 325
Export
Catalog Design & Production Company for Major Manufacturers, Service Companies, Retail & Direct Marketing Firms
S.I.C.: 7336
Noby Yamakoshi *(Chm. Bd. & Chief Exec. Officer)*
Warren Yamakoshi *(Pres.)*

No. of Mfg. Plants/Facilities: 5
No. of U.S. Offices: 5
No. of Foreign Offices: 1

Outside Service Firm(s):

Arthur Andersen & Co.*(Auditors)*
33 W. Monroe St.
Chicago, IL 60603-4067
Tel.: 312-580-0033
Fax: 312-507-6748

Dai-Ichi Kangyo, Ltd.*(Major Banking Relationship)*
Chicago, IL

NOBLE & ASSOCIATES
1949 E. Sunshine
Springfield, MO 65804
Mailing Address:
P.O. Box 9011,
Springfield, MO 65808
Tel.: 417-882-5050
Fax: 417-882-3309
Year Founded: 1969
Approx.Billings: $85,000,000
Emp.: 175
Advertising, Promotion, Marketing, Public Relations & Product Development for Food & Food Related Products
Robert B. Noble *(Chm. & Chief Exec. Officer)*
David Allemeier *(Pres., Chief Creative Officer)*
J. Michael Cooper *(Chief Fin. Officer)*
John Morrison *(Chief Mktg. Officer)*

NOBLES INDUSTRIES, INC.
645 E. 7th St.
Saint Paul, MN 55106
Tel.: 612-771-5581
Fax: 612-771-7855
Approx.Sls.: $12,000,000
Emp.: 150
Fiscal Year-end: 12/31/90
Mfr. Floor Maintenance Equipment
S.I.C.: 3728; 3589; 3821
V.D. Riediger *(Pres.)*
Jerry Falksen *(V.P. & Treas.)*

NODAK ELECTRIC CO-OP
(Formerly Nodak Rural Electric Co-op)
1405 First Ave., N.
Grand Forks, ND 58201
Mailing Address:
P.O. Box 1478,
Grand Forks, ND 58206-1478
Tel.: 701-746-4461
Fax: 701-746-7431
Approx.Sls.: $21,500,000
Emp.: 70
Electric Utility
S.I.C.: 4911
Lee Kaldor *(Pres.)*
George Berg *(Gen. Mgr.)*
C.T. Marhula *(Mgr.-Bus.)*
John Rodgers *(Mgr.-Engrng.)*
Dale West *(Mgr.-Member Services)*

Outside Service Firm(s):

Brady, Martz & Associates*(Auditors)*
Grand Forks, ND

W.R. Coulet, Jr.*(Legal Firm)*
Grafton, ND

First National Bank*(Major Banking Relationship)*
Grand Forks, ND

NODAK MUTUAL INSURANCE COMPANY
1101 First Ave., N.
Fargo, ND 58102
Mailing Address:
P.O. Box 2502
Fargo, ND 58108
Tel.: 701-298-4200
Fax: 701-234-0811
Assets: $45,739,187
Liabilities: $24,202,848
Net Worth: $21,536,339
Approx.Sls.: $41,929,497
Emp.: 100
Non Profit Organization
S.I.C.: 8699
Corporate Giving Program: Supports United Way
Howard G. Schmid *(Pres.)*
Kevin D. Pifer *(Exec. V.P. & Chief Exec. Officer)*
Joseph T. Steier *(V.P.)*
David L. Johnson *(V.P.-Opers. & Corp. Communications)*
Allen F. Fabricius *(V.P.-Mktg.)*
J. Robert Belsly *(Treas.)*
David Klatt *(Controller)*
Darwin T. Wittmier *(Dir.-Human Resources)*
Larry Marxen *(Mgr.-Mngmt. Information Services)*
Principal(s):

No. of U.S. Offices: 5

Outside Service Firm(s):

Meriwether, Wilson & Co.*(Auditors)*
1200 35th St., Ste. 400
Des Moines, IA 50265

First Interstate Bank*(Major Banking Relationship)*
Fargo, ND

Nilles, Hansen & Davies Ltd.*(Legal Firm)*
1800 Radison Tower, 201 North 5th St.,
P.O. Box 2626
Fargo, ND 58102
Tel.: 701-237-5544

Division:

Nodak Mutual Insurance Co. **(1)**
1101 First Ave., N.
Fargo, ND 58102
Tel.: 701-298-4200
Approx.Sls.: $22,000,000
Emp.: 80
Property & Casualty Insurance
S.I.C.: 6331
Howard Schmid *(Pres.)*
Kevin Pifer *(Exec. V.P.)*
David Johnston *(V.P.-Opers.)*
Ed Gross *(V.P.-Claims)*
Allen Fabricuis *(V.P.-Mktg.)*
J. Robert Belsly *(Treas.)*
Darwin Wittmier *(Dir.-Personnel)*

NOEL CANNING CORPORATION
1001 S. 1st St.
Yakima, WA 98907
Tel.: 509-248-4545
Fax: 509-575-1729
Year Founded: 1940
Approx.Sls.: $100,000,000
Emp.: 600
Can Soft Drinks
S.I.C.: 2086
Rodger Noel *(Pres.)*
Carolyn Noel *(1st V.P.)*
Larry Estes *(Chief Fin. Officer)*
Jerry Aucutt *(Dir.-Sls.)*
Principal(s):
Noel Family

Outside Service Firm(s):

Boyd Olofoson & Company*(Auditors)*
Yakima, WA

NOEL-JOANNA, INC.
22942 Arroyo Vista
Rancho Santa Margarita, CA 92688
Tel.: 714-858-9717
Tel.: 800-854-8760
Telex: 362 882
Fax: 714-858-9686
Year Founded: 1975
Approx.Sls.: $15,000,000
Emp.: 78
Fiscal Year-end: 12/31/90
Import Export
Mfr. of Infant Bedding & Accessories
S.I.C.: 2211; 2515; 2392
Shirley Pepys *(Chm., Pres. & Chief Exec. Officer)*
Perry Schneider *(Exec. V.P.)*
Donna McGovern *(Controller)*
Renee Pepys *(Dir.-Sls. & Mktg.)*
Bob Blume *(Mgr.-Mfg.)*
Louisa McInnis *(Mgr.-Sls.)*
Lynne Powers *(Sls. & Mktg. Coord.)*
Principal(s):
Shirley Pepys

No. of Mfg. Plants/Facilities: 1
No. of U.S. Offices: 1

Outside Service Firm(s):

Arthur Andersen & Co.*(Auditors)*
18500 Von Karman Ave., Ste. 1100
Irvine, CA 92715
Tel.: 714-757-3100

Fireman's Fund Insurance Co.*(Group Insurer)*
New York, NY

Pilot Life*(Group Insurer)*
Greensboro, NC

Security Pacific National Bank*(Major Banking Relationship)*
Irvine, CA

NOMA-INTERNATIONAL, INC.
7400 W. Industrial Dr.
Forest Park, IL 60130
Tel.: 708-771-9400
Tel.: 800-872-8072
Fax: 708-771-8856
Approx.Sls.: $90,000,000
Emp.: 150
Import
Manufacturer of Christmas Tree Light Sets, Patio & Halloween Lights, Low Voltage Lighting
S.I.C.: 3699
Richard Krelstein *(Pres.)*
Tad Cook *(V.P.-Sls.)*
Mike Sular *(V.P.-Admin.)*
Alex Campbell *(Dir.-Mktg.)*
Raymond Waligurski *(Controller)*
Dan Daun *(Dir.-Mktg.)*

Computer Systems/Hardware:
WANG

NOOTER CORPORATION
1400 S. Third St.
Saint Louis, MO 63104
Mailing Address:
P.O. Box 451
St. Louis, MO 63166
Tel.: 314-621-6000
Telex: 044-849
Fax: 314-421-7580
Year Founded: 1896
Assets: $115,000,000
Liabilities: $60,000,000
Net Worth: $55,000,000
Approx.Sls.: $257,000,000
Emp.: 1,500
Fiscal Year-end: 11/30/91
Import Export
Steel & Alloy Plate Fabricators & Erectors
S.I.C.: 3443
George Hays *(Chm. Bd.)*
Gene R. Smith *(Pres.)*
G.P. Bouckaert *(Exec. V.P.)*
Raymond B. Rohrbacker *(V.P., Sec. & Treas.)*
R.H. Arb *(Dir.-Personnel)*
D.R. Herr *(Dir.-Pur.)*
W.L. Kirchner *(Dir.-Mktg.)*
John Meyer *(Dir.-Research & Devel.)*
W.H. Schawacker *(Dir.-Adv.)*

No. of Mfg. Plants/Facilities: 2
No. of U.S. Offices: 3
No. of Foreign Offices: 5

Computer Systems/Hardware:
Hewlett Packard

Outside Service Firm(s):

Deloitte & Touche*(Auditors)*
One City Centre
St. Louis, MO 63101
Tel.: 314-342-4900
Fax: 314-342-1100

Lewis & Rice*(Legal Firm)*
611 Olive St., Suite 1400
St. Louis, MO 63101
Tel.: 314-231-5833

Boatmen's National Bank of St. Louis*(Major Banking Relationship)*
One Boatmen's Plaza, 800 Market St.
St. Louis, MO 63101
Tel.: 314-466-6000

Divisions:

Missouri Boiler & Tank Co. **(1)**
2300 Papin St.
Saint Louis, MO 63103
Tel.: 314-231-5800
Rick Uebel *(Gen. Mgr.)*

Nooter/Eriksen Cogeneration Systems, Inc. **(1)**
3630 S. Geyer Rd.,Ste. 310
Saint Louis, MO 63127
Tel.: 314-957-7800
Fax: 314-966-6989
Vern Eriksen *(Pres.)*

Subsidiaries:

McGrath & Associates **(1)**
1920 S. Kings Hwy.
Saint Louis, MO 63110
Tel.: 314-772-7600
J. B. McGrath *(Chief Oper. Officer)*

Nooter Construction Co. **(1)**
1400 So. Third St.
Saint Louis, MO 63104
Tel.: 314-421-7600
Kenneth Kolkmeier *(Pres.)*

St. Louis Metallizing Co. **(1)**
4123 Sarpy Ave.
Saint Louis, MO 63110
Tel.: 314-531-5253
Frank A. Martin *(Chm. Bd.)*

Wyatt Field Service Co. **(1)**
P.O. Box 3052
Houston, TX 77253
Tel.: 713-956-2020
Frank Rister *(Pres.)*

NOR-CAL BEVERAGE CO., INC.
2286 Stone Blvd.
West Sacramento, CA 95691
Tel.: 916-372-0600

Fax: 916-372-3451
Year Founded: 1936
Approx.Sls.: $45,000,000
Emp.: 304
Bottler/Wholesaler of Soft Drinks
S.I.C.: 2086; 2082
Roy G. Deary, Jr. *(Pres.)*
Donald R. Deary *(V.P.-Mfg.)*
Peter D. Ruhkala *(Treas.)*
Duane Reeder *(Dir.-Pur.)*
Andy Mendoza *(Mgr.-Sls.)*

Computer Systems/Hardware:
IBM AS400

NORANDEX INC.
8450 S. Bedford Rd.
Macedonia, OH 44056
Tel.: 216-468-2200
Approx.Sls.: $250,000,000
Emp.: 1,000
Mfr. & Distribute of Aluminum, Steel & Vinyl Bldg. Materials
S.I.C.: 5031; 2431
R. W. Johnston *(Pres.)*
J. Blanchard *(V.P.-Sls.)*
R. Valle *(V.P.-Mktg.)*
B. Virostek *(V.P.-Admin.)*
Van L. Garber *(Dir.-Mktg. Services)*

NORBEST, INC.
6875 S. 900 E.
Midvale, UT 84047
Mailing Address:
P.O. Box 1000
Midvale, UT 84047-1000
Tel.: 801-566-5656 UT
Fax: 801-255-2309
Year Founded: 1930
Sales Range: $100-499 Million
Emp.: 36
Export
Market Wholesale Turkeys
S.I.C.: 5144
Joseph Nielsen *(Chm. Bd.)*
Steven Jensen *(Pres. & Chief Exec. Officer)*
John B. Hall *(Sr. V.P. & Sec.)*
Ronald L. Attebury *(Chief Fin. Officer & Treas.)*
Allen Pulfipher *(Controller)*
Steven Johnson *(Gen. Counsel & Dir.-Legal Services)*
Tom Becker *(Mgr.-Data Processing)*
Jim Draper *(Mgr.-Product Devel.)*
Carmi McDougal *(Mgr.-Office)*
Sherry Talbot *(Mgr.-Personnel)*

Computer Systems/Hardware:
DEC Micro VAX 2/MV 4000

Outside Service Firm(s):

Jones, Waldo, Holbrook & McDonough*(Legal Firm)*
1500 First Interstate Plaza, 170 South Main St.
Salt Lake City, UT 84101
Tel.: 801-521-3200

First Security Bank of Utah*(Major Banking Relationship)*
Salt Lake City, UT

National Bank for Cooperatives*(Major Banking Relationship)*
5500 S. Quebec St.
Englewood, CO 80111
Tel.: 303-740-4000
Fax: 303-740-4002

Affiliates:

Moroni Feed Co. **(1)**
P.O. Box 368
Moroni, UT 84646
Tel.: 801-436-8221
S.I.C.: 2048

Nebraska Turkey Growers **(1)**
Railroad & Lawn Ave.
Gibbon, NE 68840
Tel.: 308-468-5711
S.I.C.: 5144; 0253

Oregon Turkey Growers **(1)**
740 NW Bassett
Salem, OR 97304
Tel.: 503-364-3323
S.I.C.: 5144; 0253

Utah Turkey Growers **(1)**
Salina, UT 84654
Tel.: 801-529-7441

West Central Turkeys **(1)**
P.O.B. Turkey
Pelican Rapids, MN 56572
Tel.: 218-863-3131
S.I.C.: 5144; 0253

NORCOSTCO, INC.
3203 N. Hwy. 100
Minneapolis, MN 55422
Tel.: 612-533-2791
Fax: 612-533-3718
Approx.Sls.: $10,000,000
Emp.: 180
Retail & Rental of Formal Wear; Mens, Boy & Womens Clothing & Theatrical Supplies, Costumes
S.I.C.: 5699; 7299
James T. Scott *(Chm. Bd., Chief Exec. Officer & Treas.)*
Roger E. Deters *(Pres.)*
Wayne Murphy *(Sec.)*

Outside Service Firm(s):

Norwest Bank Minnesota, N.A.*(Major Banking Relationship)*
P.O. Box 738, 161 North Concord Exchange
St. Paul, MN 55075
Tel.: 612-450-4046

NORCRAFT COMPANIES, INC.
30 E. Plato Blvd.
Saint Paul, MN 55107
Tel.: 612-297-0661
Tel.: 612-221-0337 MN
Fax: 612-221-9734
Year Founded: 1974
Approx.Sls.: $50,000,000
Emp.: 450
Fiscal Year-end: 4/30/92
Mfr. of Kitchen Cabinets
S.I.C.: 2434
Harold B. Dokmo, Jr. *(Chm. Bd., Pres., Treas. & Sec.)*
Thomas Botten *(V.P.-Fin.)*
Terry Dickey *(V.P.-Mfg.)*
Dave Van Horne *(V.P.-Sls.)*
Principal(s):
Harold B. Dokmo, Jr.
Leonard Gasparre'
Gary Holmes

No. of Mfg. Plants/Facilities: 3

Outside Service Firm(s):

Hoffman & Brobst*(Auditors)*
Marshall, MN

Robins, Kaplan, Miller & Ciresi*(Legal Firm)*
Minneapolis, MN

First American Bank Metro*(Major Banking Relationship)*
South Saint Paul, MN

Plant:

Norcraft Companies **(1)**
900 S. Meridian Ave.
Newton, KS 67114
Emp.: 320
Manufacturing Plant
S.I.C.: 2434

NORCROSS INDUSTRIES, INC.
11405 Park Rd.
Louisville, KY 40223
Tel.: 502-244-1153
Fax: 502-244-8253
Emp.: 29
Holding Company
S.I.C.: 6719; 3021
Michael Cappy *(Chm. Bd. & Pres.)*

Outside Service Firm(s):

KPMG Peat Marwick*(Auditors)*
444 S. Fifth St.
Louisville, KY 40202
Tel.: 502-587-0535
Fax: 502-587-1549

Midlantic National Bank*(Major Banking Relationship)*
Paterson, NJ

Subsidiary:

Kaysam Corporation Of America **(1)**
27 Kentucky Ave.
Paterson, NJ 07053
Tel.: 201-684-5700
Vinyl Footwear, Vinyl Compounds
S.I.C.: 3021
Steven L. Fell *(Gen. Mgr.)*
Edward Shain *(Dir.-Sls.)*
Lita Spinella *(Dir.-Sls.)*

NORDEN FRUIT COMPANY, INC.
1601 E. Olympic Blvd.
Los Angeles, CA 90021
Tel.: 213-629-2100 CA
Fax: 213-623-0803
Year Founded: 1963
Approx.Sls.: $124,000,000
Emp.: 175
Wholesale Distribution of Fresh Fruits
S.I.C.: 5148
Norman Gilfenbain *(Pres.)*
Danny Gill *(V.P. & Sec.)*

NORDIC GROUP OF COMPANIES, LTD.
522 South Boulevard
Baraboo, WI 53913
Tel.: 608-356-5551
Telex: 910-280-2644
Fax: 608-356-5773
Year Founded: 1947
Approx.Sls.: $125,000,000
Emp.: 1,400
Fiscal Year-end: 6/30/92
Export
Holding Company
S.I.C.: 6719; 3949; 3544; 7373; 3799; 3944; 3089
Corporate Giving Program: Corporate *Angel Network (CAN) Makes the* Corporate Business Jet Available to Cancer Patients for Transport to Treatment Centers.
W.R. Sauey *(Chm. Bd., Pres. & Treas.)*
Richard Koenings *(V.P. & Sec.)*
Principal(s):
W.R. Sauey

No. of Mfg. Plants/Facilities: 8
No. of U.S. Offices: 8

Computer Systems/Hardware:
Artecon

Outside Service Firm(s):

Arthur Andersen & Co.*(Auditors)*
777 E. Wisconsin Ave., P.O. Box 1215
Milwaukee, WI 53202
Tel.: 414-271-5100
Fax: 414-283-3200

Liberty Mutual*(Group Insurer)*
Milwaukee, WI

Michael, Best & Friedrich*(Legal Firm)*
100 East Wisconsin Avenue
Milwaukee, WI 53202
Tel.: 414-271-6560

First Wisconsin National Bank*(Major Banking Relationship)*
777 E. Wisconsin Ave.
Milwaukee, WI 53202
Tel.: 414-765-4321
Fax: 414-355-6903

Subsidiaries:

Artecon, Inc. **(1)**
2440 Impala Dr., Dept. 5500
Carlsbad, CA 92008
Tel.: 619-931-5500
Fax: 619-931-5527
Emp.: 48
Import Export
Computer Systems/Hardware:
Sun Microsystems
Manufacture Hardware & Software to Fit System Needs. Produce Line of Aftermarket Products
S.I.C.: 7373
James L. Lambert *(Pres. & Chief Exec. Officer)*
Dana W. Kammersgard *(V.P.-Sls. & Mktg.)*
Tesfaye Hailemichael *(Controller)*

Columbia ParCar Corp. **(1)**
P.O. Box One, One Golf Car Rd.
Deerfield, WI 53531
Tel.: 608-764-5474
Fax: 608-764-8246
Approx.Sls.: $12,000,000
Emp.: 85
Manufacture Golf Cars, Passenger, Commercial & Utility Vehicles
S.I.C.: 3799

Flambeau Corporation **(1)**
801 Lynn Ave.
Baraboo, WI 53913
Tel.: 608-356-5551
Approx.Sls.: $88,000,000
Emp.: 1,300
Fiscal Year-end: 6/29/92
Export
Computer Systems/Hardware:
Burroughs System 1955
Manufacture Plastic Products for Industrial, Commercial & Consumer Use; Plastic Boxes & Storage Units; Sporting Goods Products; Mold & Tool Fabrication; Prototype Services & Cad Cam Capabilities
S.I.C.: 3949; 3089; 3944; 3544; 3952; 3799
W.R. Sauey *(Chm. Bd.)*
Craig L. Sauey *(Pres. & Chief Exec. Officer)*
Dave Harris *(V.P.-Engrng. & Tech. Services)*
Harold R. Siekert *(V.P.-Fin.)*
Bill Flint Jr. *(V.P.-Mktg.)*
Chuck Frank *(V.P.-Mfg.)*
Robert Storandt *(Dir.-Data Processing)*

Subsidiaries:

Flambeau Micro Co. **(2)**
3696 Burke Rd.
Madison, WI 53704
Tel.: 608-241-1975 (100%)
Emp.: 75
Manufacture Precision Engineered Plastics & Related Medical Products
S.I.C.: 3089

Flambeau Plastics Co. **(2)**
801 Lynn Ave.
Baraboo, WI 53913
Tel.: 608-356-5551 (100%)
Emp.: 400
Manufacture Engineered Plastic Products for Original Equipment
S.I.C.: 3089
Chuck Frank *(V.P. & Gen. Mgr.)*
Dick Falk *(Mgr.-Matls.)*
Joe Chenoweth *(Mgr.-Personnel)*
Bob Neidigh *(Mgr.-Plant)*

Flambeau Southeast Co. **(2)**
1533 S. Broad St.
Monroe, GA 30655
Tel.: 706-267-7543 (100%)
Fax: 706-267-3763
Approx.Sls.: $7,000,000
Emp.: 95
Manufacture Engineered Plastic Products & Fluid Systems (Cap, Tanks, Fittings)
S.I.C.: 3088; 3089

Flambeau Products Corp. **(1)**
15981 Valpast Rd.
Middlefield, OH 44062
Tel.: 216-632-1631 (100%)
Emp.: 200
Mfr. Sporting Goods, Recreational & Floral Prods., Hardware Prods., Commercial Plastic Boxes, Art Bin Boxes & Accessories, Engineered Plastic Prods. & Housewares
S.I.C.: 3949; 3089
Marc Mason *(Co-Pres. & Chief Oper. Officer-Production Sector)*
Jason Savey *(Co-Pres.-Mktg. & Fin. Sector)*
Stan Parker *(Chief Fin. Officer)*
Marsha Bryant *(Mktg. Services Coord.)*
Steve Drotos *(Pur. Dir.)*

Nordic Group of Companies, Ltd.—(Continued)

Subsidiaries:

Duncan Toys Company **(2)**
15981 Valplast Rd.
Middlefield, OH 44062
Tel.: 216-632-1631 (100%)
Approx.Sls.: $5,000,000
Emp.: 10
Manufacture Duncan YoYo's & Wheeled Action Toys
S.I.C.: 3944
Jerry Kaplan *(Natl. Sls. Mgr.)*

Flambeau Products-Columbus **(2)**
4325 Middle Rd.
Columbus, IN 47202
Tel.: 812-372-4899
Hardware Boxes & Cabinets & Toolboxes
S.I.C.: 3083; 3089
Steve Keefe *(Mgr.-Natl. Sls.)*

Seats Incorporated **(1)**
1515 Industrial St.
Reedsburg, WI 53959
Tel.: 608-524-4316
Fax: 608-524-6004
Approx.Sls.: $17,000,000
Emp.: 225
Fiscal Year-end: 5/31/92
Export
Mfr. of Industrial, Recreational & Transportational Seating
S.I.C.: 2531
Eric W. Sauey *(Pres.)*
Gerald L. Ward *(V.P.-Admin.)*
James Kreger *(V.P.-Sls.)*
James Hofrichter *(Dir.-Design Engrng.)*

NOREL PAPER CORPORATION
223 Gates Rd.
Little Ferry, NJ 07643
Tel.: 201-440-4400
Fax: 201-440-5901
Year Founded: 1955
Approx.Sls.: $40,000,000
Emp.: 150
Mfr. of Styrofoam & Paper Packaging Materials
S.I.C.: 3089; 2671
Richard Horstein *(Pres.)*
Saul Srour *(V.P.-Fin.)*
Jack Traverso *(V.P- Fin.)*

NORFOLK SHIPBUILDING & DRYDOCK CORPORATION
P.O. Box 2100
Norfolk, VA 23501-2100
Mailing Address:
750 Berkley Ave.
Norfolk, VA 23523
Tel.: 804-494-4000
Tel.: 800-368-3637 **VA**
Telex: 823613
Fax: 804-494-4307
Year Founded: 1915
Approx.Sls.: $220,000,000
Emp.: 3,000
Fiscal Year-end: 12/31/90
Ship Building, Conversion & Repair
S.I.C.: 3731
Corporate Giving Program: Charity Trust-Types And Amounts Of Contributions Are Subject To Board Of Directors Approval.
John L. Roper III *(Pres. & Chief Exec. Officer)*
Richard H. Winslow *(Chief Fin. Officer, V.P.-Fin., Controller & Treas.)*
John L. Roper, IV *(Exec. V.P.-Opers. & Sec.)*
C.E. Agnese *(V.P.-Estimating & Contract Admin.)*
George H. Curtis, III *(V.P.-Engineering & Facilities)*
F.A. Ganter *(V.P.-Mktg.)*
John W. Humphreys *(V.P.-Admin.)*
B.L. Moyer *(Dir.-Pur.)*
James R. Wermeister *(Dir.-Indus. Rels.)*
Mary Sharp *(Mgr.-Employment & Corp. Training)*

No. of Mfg. Plants/Facilities: 2
No. of U.S. Offices: 2

Computer Systems/Hardware:
Hewlett Packard

Outside Service Firm(s):

KPMG Peat Marwick*(Auditors)*
2100 Dominion Tower, 999 Waterside Dr.
Norfolk, VA 23510
Tel.: 804-622-6533

Blue Cross & Blue Shield of Virginia*(Group Insurer)*
2015 Staples Mill Rd.
Richmond, VA 23230
Tel.: 804-359-7000
Fax: 804-354-7397

Virginia Investment Counselors*(Investment Banker)*
Norfolk, VA

Vandeventer, Black, Meredith & Martin*(Legal Firm)*
Norfolk, VA

Sovran Bank*(Major Banking Relationship)*
One Commercial Place
Norfolk, VA
Tel.: 804-441-4849
Fax: 804-624-2965

Equitable Life*(Pension Manager)*
1221 Ave. of the Americas
New York, NY 10022
Tel.: 212-382-8038
Fax: 212-382-8089

Subsidiaries:

Diesel Marine Norshipco **(1)**
P.O. Box 2100
Norfolk, VA 23501
Tel.: 804-494-2963
S.I.C.: 3731

Norshipco Industrial Enterprises **(1)**
P.O. Box 2100
Norfolk, VA 23501
Tel.: 804-494-4000

NORFOODS, INC.
7101 College Ave, Ste. 8000
Overland Park, KS 66210
Tel.: 913-661-6100 **DE**
Fax: 913-661-6159
Year Founded: 1985
Emp.: 500
Export
Holding Company; Grains; Soybeans; Wheat; Green Or Roasted Coffee; Powdered Cocoa; Candy & Other Confectionery Products; Brokerage Services
S.I.C.: 5153; 5149; 2066; 2064; 7389; 6719; 2393; 2099
Raymond Cretegny *(Pres.)*
Paul Meschler *(Exec. V.P. & Treas.)*
Walter Muff *(Sec.)*
Berman Blackwell *(Mgr.-Personnel)*

Outside Service Firm(s):

Chase Manhattan Bank, N.A.*(Major Banking Relationship)*
One Chase Manhattan Plaza
New York, NY 10081
Tel.: 212-552-2222
Tel.: 800-526-0801
Fax: 212-552-7175

Subsidiaries:

Cofinco, Inc. **(1)**
99 Park Ave., 11th Fl.
New York, NY 10016
Tel.: 212-309-1500
Coffee Importer
S.I.C.: 5149
B. Bialt *(Gen. Mgr. & Treas.)*

Drumheller Bag & Supply **(1)**
1105 E. Hill Ave.
Valdosta, GA 31603
Tel.: 912-247-0670
Mfr. of Multiwall Paper & Textile Bags
S.I.C.: 2393
George Smith *(Pres.)*
A. Lloyd *(Controller)*

Finora Company, Inc. **(1)**
99 Park Ave., 11th Fl.
New York, NY 10016
Tel.: 212-309-1500
Approx.Sls.: $46,000,000
Brokers' Services
S.I.C.: 7389
H. Peter Steffler *(Pres.)*
Stewart Cofsky *(V.P. & Controller)*
Randolph Rades *(V.P. & Sec.)*
Richard Demaurex *(V.P.)*

Garnac Grain Co., Inc. **(1)**
8000 W. 110th St., Ste. 300
Overland Park, KS 66210-2315
Tel.: 913-661-6100
Approx.Sls.: $150,000,000
Emp.: 225
Grain Elevators; Grains, Soybeans; Wheat; Canal Barge Operations
S.I.C.: 5153; 4449
Frank Bisang *(Pres. & Chief Exec. Officer)*
Bill Boslievac *(Treas.)*
Walter Muff *(Sec.)*

Shade Foods, Inc. **(1)**
33063 Western Ave.
Union City, CA 94587
Tel.: 415-489-2800
Approx.Sls.: $56,000,000
Emp.: 250
Mfr. of Chocolate & Cocoa Products; Candy & Other Confectionery Products
S.I.C.: 2066; 2064
Jerome Clark *(Pres.)*
Addison Bergfalk *(Exec. V.P.)*
Todd Andrews *(V.P.-Eastern Sls.)*
Thomas Seymour *(V.P.-Western Sls.)*
William G. Frimel *(V.P.)*
Claude Bielman *(V.P.)*

Shade Pasta, Inc. **(1)**
805 S. Union
Fremont, NE 68025
Tel.: 402-727-8412
Mfr. of Pasta
S.I.C.: 2099
Maurice Shanley *(V.P. & Gen. Mgr.)*

NORMAN BROTHERS NISSAN INC.
1983 N. Semoran Blvd.
Orlando, FL 32807
Tel.: 407-657-9500 **FL**
Fax: 407-678-7498
Year Founded: 1976
Assets: $1,154,208
Liabilities: $422,243
Net Worth: $731,965
Approx.Sls.: $37,000,000
Emp.: 131
Import
Automobile Dealership
S.I.C.: 5511
Jack Norman, Sr. *(Chm. Bd.)*
George J. Norman *(Pres.)*
Forrest A. Norman *(V.P.)*
James G. Norman *(Sec. & Treas.)*
Amy Du Bois *(Dir.-Admin. & Opers. & Comptroller)*
Nancy Graham *(Dir.-Adv.)*
Paul Norman *(Mgr. Sls.-New & Used Cars)*
Ray Eaglefield *(Mgr.-Service)*
Marvin Roads *(Gen. Counsel)*
Neil Norman *(Service Coord.)*

Computer Systems/Hardware:
Reynolds & Reynolds

Outside Service Firm(s):

Kane & Associates*(Auditors)*
Winter Park, FL

First Southern Insurance Co.*(Commercial Insurance Carrier)*
Tampa, FL

Barnett Banks Trust Company, N.A.*(Major Banking Relationship)*
Orlando, FL

NORMARK CORPORATION
1710 E. 78th St.
Minneapolis, MN 55423
Tel.: 612-869-3292
Fax: 612-869-0653
Approx.Sls.: $20,000,000
Emp.: 30
Fiscal Year-end: 7/31/92
Import
Fishing Lures, Fillet Knifes & Boards, Whetstones
S.I.C.: 3949
R.W. Weber *(Chief Exec. Officer)*
Donald Addy *(Pres.)*
Robert Miller *(Controller)*
Jerry Calengor *(Dir.-Mktg.)*
Warren Reader *(Mgr.-Natl. Sls.)*

Computer Systems/Hardware:
Wang

Division:

Sporting Goods Div. **(1)**
1710 E. 78th St.
Minneapolis, MN 55423
Tel.: 612-869-3292
S.I.C.: 3949

Subsidiaries:

Blue Fox Tackle Co. **(1)**
645 N. Emerson
Cambridge, MN 55008
Tel.: 612-689-3402
Import
S.I.C.: 3949
Marc Jensen *(Gen. Mgr.)*

Vibrax/MCA Inc. **(1)**
645 N. Emerson
Cambridge, MN 55008
Tel.: 612-689-3402
S.I.C.: 3949

NORPAC FOODS, INC. COOPERATIVE
(Formerly Stayton Canning Co. Cooperative)
930 W. Washington St.
Stayton, OR 97383
Mailing Address:
P.O. Box 458,
Stayton, OR 97383-0458
Tel.: 503-769-2101
Fax: 503-769-5411
Year Founded: 1923
Assets: $159,994,505
Earnings: ($3,330,672)
Liabilities: $122,257,109
Net Worth: $37,737,396
Approx.Sls.: $220,649,488
Emp.: 325
Fiscal Year-end: 3/31/92
Import Export
Processor of Frozen & Canned Fruits & Vegetables
S.I.C.: 2037; 2033
Don Nielson *(Chm. Bd.)*
Arthur Christionson *(Pres. & Gen. Mgr.)*
Richard C. Hull *(Controller)*
David M. Karr *(Sec. & Treas.)*
Alan Dozler *(Dir.-Purch.)*
James F. Enger *(Dir.-Personnel)*
Renee Luke *(Dir.-Cash Mngmt.)*
James Stromvig *(Mgr.-Info. Systems)*

Computer Systems/Hardware:
Unysis

NORRELL CORPORATION
Bldg. #14, 3535 Piedmont Rd. N.E.
Atlanta, GA 30305
Tel.: 404-240-3000
Fax: 404-240-3312
Year Founded: 1961
Assets: $132,692,000
Earnings: $8,918,000
Liabilities: $91,303,000
Net Worth: $41,389,000
Approx.Sls.: $493,507,000
Emp.: 350
Fiscal Year-end: 11/30/91
Temp. Personnel Services
S.I.C.: 7363; 7371
Corporate Giving Program: United Way of Metro Atlanta, GA

Guy W. Millner *(Chm. & Chief Exec. Officer)*
C. Douglas Miller *(Pres.-NorrellTemporary Services)*
Larry J. Bryan *(Exec. V.P. & Chief Fin. Officer)*
Linda Arnold *(V.P.-Human Resources)*
Mark Hain *(V.P. & Gen. Counsel)*
Madison F. Cole, Jr. *(Treas.)*
Fred Herbert *(Asst. Treas.)*
Edward Nubel *(Dir.-Mktg.)*

Outside Service Firm(s):

Arthur Andersen & Co.*(Auditors)*
Avenue des Arts 56 1040
Brussels, Belgium

Arthur Andersen & Co.*(Auditors)*
133 Peachtree St., N.E.
Atlanta, GA 30303
Tel.: 404-658-1776

Powell, Goldstein, Frazer & Murphy*(Legal Firm)*
191 Peachtree St. NE, 16th Fl.
Atlanta, GA 30303
Tel.: 404-572-6700
Fax: 404-572-5958

Trust Company Bank*(Major Banking Relationship)*
Stock Trans. Dept. P.O.B. 4625, Trust Company of Georgia Bldg.
Atlanta, GA 30302
Tel.: 404-588-7831

Subsidiary:

Norrell Health Care Inc. **(1)**
3535 Piedmont Rd., N.E.
Atlanta, GA 30305
Tel.: 404-240-3000
Home Health Care & Medical Temporary Personnel Supply Services
S.I.C.: 8082; 7363
Guy W. Millner *(Pres.)*

NORTH AMERICAN COMPANY
P.O. Box 14758
Fort Lauderdale, FL 33302
Tel.: 305-463-0681
Fax: 305-527-0904
Approx.Sls.: $35,000,000
Emp.: 200
Venture Capital Investments; Real Estate Development
S.I.C.: 6799; 6552
Charles L. Palmer *(Chm. Bd. & Chief Exec. Officer)*
Allan C. Hanselman *(V.P. & Comptroller)*
G. H. Gore *(Sec. & Gen. Counsel)*

Outside Service Firm(s):

Arthur Andersen & Co.*(Auditors)*
2100 One Biscayne Tower
Miami, FL 33131
Tel.: 305-374-3700

Saunders, Curtis, Ginestra & Gore*(Legal Firm)*
Fort Lauderdale, FL

Citizens & Southern National Bank*(Major Banking Relationship)*
Fort Lauderdale, FL

NORTH AMERICAN ENCLOSURES, INC.
85 Jetson Lane
Central Islip, NY 11722
Mailing Address:
P.O. Box 177
Central Islip, NY 11722
Tel.: 516-234-9500
Tel.: 800-645-9209 NY
Fax: 516-234-9504
Year Founded: 1963
Approx.Sls.: $18,000,000
Emp.: 225
Fiscal Year-end: 4/30/91
Export
Wood, Metal & Plastic Picture Frames
S.I.C.: 2499
Richard Schwartz *(Pres.)*
NormanGrafstein *(V.P.)*
Marie Neubert *(Sec.)*

No. of Mfg. Plants/Facilities: 2
No. of U.S. Offices: 2

Outside Service Firm(s):

Schultz & Sage*(Auditors)*
Great Neck, NY

Albin & Richman*(Legal Firm)*
Garden City, NY

National Westminster Bank Plc*(Major Banking Relationship)*
Central Islip, NY

Subsidiary:

North American Enclosures, Inc. **(1)**
501 Airpark Drive
Fullerton, CA 92633
Tel.: 714-447-8700
Tel.: 800-852-5356

THE NORTH AMERICAN MANUFACTURING CO.
4455 E. 71st St.
Cleveland, OH 44105
Tel.: 216-271-6000
Fax: 216-641-7852
Approx.Sls.: $40,000,000
Emp.: 500
Manufacture Industrial Furnace Components & Edge Guide Materials; Electrical & General Engineering
S.I.C.: 3433; 3494; 3564; 8711
Robert J. Neville *(Chm. Bd., Pres. & Chief Exec. Officer)*
James D. Neville *(Exec. V.P., Chief Fin. Officer, Treas. & Sec.)*
John J. Skoczen *(V.P. & Gen. Mgr.-Empl. Ben.)*

Computer Systems/Hardware:
Hewlett-Packard

Outside Service Firm(s):

Ernst & Young*(Auditors)*
1300 Huntington Bldg.
Cleveland, OH 44115
Tel.: 216-861-5000

Eugene Schwartz*(Legal Firm)*
Cleveland, OH

National City Bank*(Major Banking Relationship)*
P.O. Box 92301, Corp. Trust Dept.
Cleveland, OH 44101
Tel.: 216-575-2000

Society National Bank*(Major Banking Relationship)*
800 Superior Ave.
Cleveland, OH 44114
Tel.: 216-689-5931
Fax: 216-689-3814

Prudential Insurance Co. of America*(Pension Manager)*
751 Broad St.
Newark, NJ 07102-3777
Tel.: 201-802-6000

NORTH AMERICAN PRODUCTS CORP.
1180 Wernsing Rd.
Jasper, IN 47546
Mailing Address:
P.O. Box 647,
Jasper, IN 47547
Tel.: 812-482-2000
Tel.: 800-634-TOOL
Fax: 800-457-7458
Year Founded: 1941
Approx.Sls.: $27,000,000
Emp.: 450
Fiscal Year-end: 12/31/91
Export
Carbide Cutting Tools for Woodworking, Metals
S.I.C.: 3545
Steven A. Segal *(Chm. Bd.)*
John Segal *(Pres.)*
Thomas Kennedy *(V.P.-Central Sls.)*
Michael E. Sutton *(V.P.-Mfg.)*
Jeffery Jahn *(Mgr.-Quality)*
Paula Maxey *(Mgr.-Personnel)*
Ralph Werner *(Mgr.-Pur.)*

Subsidiaries:

Precision Disc Corp. **(1)**
5055 S. National Dr.
Knoxville, TN 37914
Tel.: 615-525-1111
Fax: 615-524-2270
Anthony Holzer *(V.P. & Gen. Mgr.)*

S & J Industries **(1)**
2130 Barrett Park Dr., Ste. 103
Kennesaw, GA 30144
Tel.: 404-424-1844
Fax: 404-424-2041
S.I.C.: 3545
Stephen Hansen *(V.P. & Gen. Mgr.)*

NORTH AMERICAN PUBLISHING COMPANY
401 N. Broad St.
Philadelphia, PA 19108
Tel.: 215-238-5300
Fax: 215-238-5457
Year Founded: 1944
Approx.Sls.: $30,000,000
Emp.: 320
Publisher of Business, Professional & Consumer Magazines; Business Forms & Systems, Printing Impressions, Magazine & Bookseller, American School & University, In Plant Reproductions & Electronic Publishing, Custom House Guide, Package Printing & Converting, Target Marketing, Official Export Guide, Global Trade, Dealerscope Merchandising, Print Cards, The Designer, Publishing Technology, Forms Professi
S.I.C.: 2731; 2711; 2721
I.J. Borowsky *(Chm. Bd.)*
Ned S. Borowsky *(Pres. & Chief Oper. Officer)*
Bob Gibbons *(V.P.-Mfg.)*
Maxine Jaffe *(V.P.-Editorial)*
Marshall Siegel *(V.P.-Sls.)*
Ernie Kollias *(Controller)*

Outside Service Firm(s):

Fax, Rothchild, O'Brian & Frankel*(Legal Firm)*
Philadelphia, PA

Meridian Bank*(Major Banking Relationship)*
One Meridian Plaza, 36th Fl.
Philadelphia, PA
Tel.: 215-854-3900

NORTH AMERICAN REFRACTORIES COMPANY
1228 Euclid
Cleveland, OH 44115
Tel.: 216-621-5200
Fax: 216-621-8143
Approx.Sls.: $200,000,000
Emp.: 1,500
Fire, Basic & Silica Brick; High Temp Cements, Plastics, Castables & Mortars
S.I.C.: 3255; 3297
Edmund S. Wright *(Pres. & Chief Exec. Officer)*
N.G. Taylor *(Sr. V.P.-Industrial Sls. & Mktg.)*
R.B. Nightingale *(V.P.-Fin.)*
A.F. Rosa *(V.P.-Human Resources)*
J.S. Ehrle *(Gen. Counsel & Sec.)*
N.E. Bruncak *(Dir.-Transportation)*
W.A. Fluka *(Dir.-Information Services)*

Outside Service Firm(s):

Price Waterhouse*(Auditors)*
BP America Bldg., 200 Public Square, 27th Floor
Cleveland, OH 44114-2301
Tel.: 216-781-3700

Jones, Day, Reavis & Pogue*(Legal Firm)*
901 Lakeside Ave.
Cleveland, OH 44114
Tel.: 216-586-3939
Fax: 216-579-0212

National City Bank*(Major Banking Relationship)*
P.O. Box 92301, Corp. Trust Dept.
Cleveland, OH 44101
Tel.: 216-575-2000

NORTH AMERICAN ROOFING COMPANY, INC.
9700 N. Michigan Rd.
Carmel, IN 46032
Tel.: 317-875-5434
Tel.: 800-551-5602
Fax: 317-872-8253
Approx.Sls.: $30,000,000
Emp.: 300
Roofing Contractor
S.I.C.: 1761
C. Michael Verble *(Pres. & Chief Exec. Officer)*
Charles Hill *(V.P. & Gen. Mgr.)*

Outside Service Firm(s):

Burke, Gross, Bell & Coulter*(Auditors)*
Indianapolis, IN

Merchants National Bank & Trust Company of Indianapolis*(Major Banking Relationship)*
One Merchants Plaza, Ste. 901E
Indianapolis, IN 46255
Tel.: 317-267-7109

NORTH AMERICAN ROYALTIES, INC.
200 E. Eighth St.
Chattanooga, TN 37402
Tel.: 615-265-3181 DE
Fax: 615-756-6516
Year Founded: 1866
Assets: $108,000,000
Liabilities: $82,000,000
Net Worth: $26,000,000
Approx.Sls.: $132,000,000
Emp.: 1,100
Fiscal Year-end: 4/30/92
Mfr. of Gray & Ductile Iron Castings; Exploration & Development of Oil & Gas Properties
S.I.C.: 1311; 3321
Corporate Giving Program:
Scholarships are Funded through Grants to Colleges for Dependents of Employees, also Funds to Local Charities
Gordon P. Street, Jr. *(Chm. Bd., Pres. & Chief Exec. & Chief Oper. Officer)*
Jack W. Money *(V.P.-Fin. & Treas.)*
Harry F. Faulkner III *(V.P.-Admin. & Sec.)*
Gordon L. Smith, Jr. *(V.P.-Plng.)*
David R. Williams *(Controller)*
Gary C. McGee *(Dir.-Personnel)*
S.E. Blair *(Mgr.-Pur.-Wheland Foundry Div.)*
Jack K. Matens *(Mgr.-Employee Devel.)*
Benny R. Cogdill *(Mgr.-Information Services)*
G.L. Smith III *(Mgr.-Engrng.-Oil & Gas Div.)*

No. of Mfg. Plants/Facilities: 3
No. of U.S. Offices: 4

Computer Systems/Hardware:
Burroughs System B2930 & DEC

Outside Service Firm(s):

Arthur Andersen & Co.*(Auditors)*
133 Peachtree St., N.E.
Atlanta, GA 30303
Tel.: 404-658-1776

North American Royalties, Inc.—(Continued)

Provident Life & Accident Insurance Co.*(Group Insurer)*
P.O. Box 12015
Chattanooga, TN 37401
Tel.: 615-755-7088

Blue Cross & Blue Shield of Tennessee*(Group Insurer)*
Chattanooga, TN

Witt, Gaither & Whitaker*(Legal Firm)*
1100 American Natl. Bank Bldg.
Chattanooga, TN 37402
Tel.: 615-265-8881

First Tennessee Bank, N.A.*(Major Banking Relationship)*
701 Market St.
Chattanooga, TN 37402

Texas Commerce Bank*(Major Banking Relationship)*
600 Travis Street, Suite 1150
Houston, TX 77002
Tel.: 713-236-4865

Morgan Guaranty Trust Company of New York*(Pension Manager)*
23 Wall St.
New York, NY 10015
Tel.: 212-483-2323

Divisions:

The Oil & Gas Div. **(1)**
200 E. Eighth St.
Chattanooga, TN 37402
Tel.: 615-265-3181
Approx.Sls.: $14,000,000
Emp.: 1200
Exploration & Development of Oil & Gas Properties
S.I.C.: 1311
Gordon P. Street, Jr. *(Chief Oper. Officer)*
Gordon L. Smith III *(Div. Engr.)*

The Wheland Foundry Div. **(1)**
2800 Broad St.
Chattanooga, TN 37402
Tel.: 615-265-3181
Fax: 615-756-3179
Approx.Sls.: $126,000,000
Emp.: 1,160
Computer Systems/Hardware:
Burroughs
Manufacture Grey Iron Castings
S.I.C.: 3321
Ron Reese *(V.P.)*
Gary C. McGee *(Dir.-Personnel)*
Tim Roberts *(Gen. Mgr.)*
S.E. Blair *(Mgr.-Pur.)*

NORTH AMERICAN SALT COMPANY
8300 College Blvd.
Overland Park, KS 66210
Tel.: 913-344-9100 **DE**
Fax: 913-338-7935
Approx.Sls.: $200,000,000
Emp.: 1,100
Fiscal Year-end: 3/31/91
Export
Processors of Agricultural, Industrial, Chemical & Water Softener Salts; Food Processing Salts
S.I.C.: 2899; 1389; 5169
D. George Harris *(Chm. Bd.)*
Anthony Petrocelli *(Vice Chm.)*
Peter McConnell *(Pres.)*
Michael Boyce *(Chief Oper. Officer)*
Richard Nick *(Chief Fin. Officer)*
Gerry Murphy *(V.P.-Fin.)*
Charles R. Sheppard *(V.P.-Mfg.)*
W. Sichko *(V.P.-Human Resources)*
Timothy J. Sullivan *(V.P.-Sls. & Mktg.)*
Susan Day *(Treas.)*
T. Hushion *(Dir.-Mngmt. Information Systems)*
Mike Runyon *(Dir.-Pur.)*

No. of Mfg. Plants/Facilities: 12
No. of U.S. Offices: 2

Computer Systems/Hardware:
Hewlett Packard

Outside Service Firm(s):

Coopers & Lybrand*(Auditors)*
Kansas City, MO

Blackwell, Sanders, Matheny, Weary & Lombardi*(Legal Firm)*
Overland Park, KS

United Missouri Bank*(Major Banking Relationship)*
Kansas City, MO

Non-U.S. Holdings:

Sifto Canada, Inc. **(1)**
1136 Matheson Blvd.
Mississauga, ON L4W 2V4, Canada
Tel.: 416-624-5700
Manufacture Salt
S.I.C.: 2899
Peter McConnell *(Mgr.)*

Siftco Canada, Inc. **(1)**
5430 Timberlan Blvd.
Mississauga, ON L4W 2T7, Canada
Tel.: 416-629-7082 (100%)
Fax: 416-629-8911
Approx.Sls.: $125,000,000
Emp.: 660
Processors of Agricultural, Industrial, Chemical & Water Softener Salts; Food Processing Salts
S.I.C.: 2899
Peter McConnell *(Pres.)*
Gerry Murphy *(V.P.-Fin.)*
David Ibbott *(V.P.-Mktg.-Highway & Chemical)*
Steven Baimel *(V.P.-Mktg.-Gen. Trade)*
Keith Davey *(Dir.-Business Devel.)*

NORTH AMERICAN WATCH CORPORATION
125 Chubb Ave.
Lyndhurst, NJ 07071
Tel.: 201-460-4800 **NY**
Telex: 421872 PIAG UI
Fax: 212-460-3876
Year Founded: 1967
Assets: $161,105,000
Earnings: ($986,000)
Liabilities: $114,292,000
Net Worth: $46,813,000
Approx.Sls.: $152,722,000
Emp.: 614
Fiscal Year-end: 1/31/91
Import Export
Mfr., Import & Distribution of Piaget, Corum, Concord & Movado Watches, MMDI Jewelry, Luggage, Small Accessories, Leather Goods, Desk Accessories & Sunglasses
S.I.C.: 5094; 3873; 3851
Gedalio Grinberg *(Chm. Bd. & Chief Exec. Officer)*
Efraim Grinberg *(Pres. & Chief Oper. Officer)*
William Diamond *(Exec. V.P. & Chief Fin. Officer)*
John Pistner *(Sr. V.P.-Sales)*
Robert Vuillet *(Sr. V.P.-Natl. Sls.)*
Harvey Driansky *(V.P.-Opers.)*
Mario Larosa *(V.P.-Corp. M.I.S.)*
Damon Lupu *(V.P.-Human Resources)*
Harry Viola *(V.P.-Adv.)*
Marquerite Nougus-Sans *(Corp. Sec., Asst. Gen. Counsel)*
Howard Regenbogen *(Treas.)*
Sol E. Flick *(Gen. Counsel)*
Paul Messina *(Controller)*

Outside Service Firm(s):

Price Waterhouse*(Auditors)*
153 E. 53rd St., 44th Fl.
New York, NY 10022
Tel.: 212-371-2000

Seyfarth, Shaw, Fairweather & Geraldson*(Legal Firm)*
520 Madison Ave.
New York, NY 10022
Tel.: 212-715-9000

Subsidiaries:

Concord Watch Co. **(1)**
650 Fifth Ave.
New York, NY 10019
Tel.: 212-676-5753 (100%)
Exclusive Importer and Distributor of Swiss Mfr. Watches
S.I.C.: 5094
James P. Reilly *(Chief Oper. Officer)*

Corum Watch Corporation **(1)**
650 Fifth Ave.
New York, NY 10019
Tel.: 212-397-7800 (100%)
Exclusive Importer and Distr. of Corum Products
S.I.C.: 5094
James P. Reilly *(Chief Oper. Officer)*

Movado Museum Designs International Ltd. **(1)**
650 Fifth Ave.
New York, NY 10019
Tel.: 212-397-7800 (100%)
Exclusive Worldwide Licensor and/or Manufacturer Of All Movado Products Other Than Watches
Stanley Schwartz *(Chief Oper. Officer)*

Movado Watch Co. **(1)**
125 Chubb Ave.
Lyndhurst, NJ 07071
Tel.: 201-460-4800 (100%)
Emp.: 50
Mfr. Watches
S.I.C.: 3873
Efraim Grinberg *(Pres.)*
Harry Viola *(V.P.-Adv.)*
William Diamond *(Chief Fin. Officer)*
Paul Messing *(Controller)*

Piaget Watch Corporation **(1)**
650 Fifth Ave.
New York, NY 10019
Tel.: 212-397-7800 (100%)
Exclusive Importer and Distr. of Piaget Products
S.I.C.: 5094
James P. Reilly *(Chief Oper. Officer)*

Non-U.S. Holdings:

Concord Watch Company, S.A. **(1)**
63 Rue Central CH2501
Bienne, Switzerland (100%)
Mfr. Concord Watches
S.I.C.: 3873

Montres Movado, S.A. **(1)**
63 Rue Central CH2501
Bienne, Switzerland (100%)

Movado Watch Company, S.A. **(1)**
Bettlach Strasse 8 CH2540
Grenchen, Switzerland (100%)
Mfr. Movado Watches
S.I.C.: 3873

North American Watch of Canada, Ltd. **(1)**
2001 Sheppard Ave., West
Willowdale, Ontario MZJ4Z7, Canada
Tel.: 416-497-1606 (100%)
Retail & Wholesale Watches
S.I.C.: 5094; 5944

N.A. Trading Ltd. **(1)**
Bettlach Strasse 8 CH2540
Grenchen, Switzerland (100%)
Retail & Wholesale Watches
S.I.C.: 5094; 5944

NORTH & JUDD
699 Middle St.
Middletown, CT 06457
Tel.: 203-632-2600
Fax: 203-632-1436
Approx.Sls.: $25,000,000
Emp.: 250
Fiscal Year-end: 7/31/90
General Hardware, Riding & Saddlery Hardware, Metal Closures & Trimmings for Clothing & Shoes, Hook-Flex Waistband Closures, T-Nuts, Industrial & Safety Hardware, Marine Hardware, Lights, Marine Sanitation Systems, Wilcox-Crittenden, Con-Torq
S.I.C.: 3429; 3965
A. Garcia *(Pres.)*
D. Allen *(V.P.-Sls.)*
J. Morris *(V.P.-Hardware)*
Jack Butler *(Mgr.-Quality Control)*
Shirley Muter *(Asst. Mgr.-Sls.)*

NORTH ATLANTIC INDUSTRIES, INC.
60 Plant Ave.
Hauppauge, NY 11788-3890
Tel.: 516-582-6500
Fax: 516-582-8079
Year Founded: 1954
Assets: $33,817,000
Earnings: $3,900,000
Liabilities: $14,920,000
Net Worth: $18,897,000
Approx.Sls.: $59,412,000
Emp.: 331
Fiscal Year-end: 12/31/91
Designs, Manufactures & Markets Computers, Computer Systems, Computer Peripherals & Electronic Signal Measuring Equipment
S.I.C.: 3572; 3812; 3577
Robert A. Carlson *(Chm. Bd. & Pres.)*
William Bouverie *(V.P.-Engrng.)*
Edwardo Delgado *(V.P.-Sls., Military Prods. U.S.)*
Richard A. Schneider *(V.P.-Fin., Sec. & Treas.)*
Frank Tortorelli *(V.P.-Mktg., Military Prods.)*
John Barry *(Dir.-Data Processing)*
Fred Delp *(Dir.-Int'l Sls.)*
Timothy Hensch *(Dir.-Mfg.)*
Joseph LaBarca *(Dir.-Quality Control)*
Maureen Nurray *(Dir.-Pub. Rels.)*
Len Stanton *(Dir.-Human Resources)*
Paul Witkowski *(Dir.-Pur.)*

Divisions:

North Atlantic Industries Systems Division **(1)**
7125 Riverwood Dr.
Columbia, MD 21046
Tel.: 410-312-5800 (100%)
Fax: 410-312-5850
Approx.Sls.: $14,000,000
Emp.: 45
Computer Systems/Hardware:
Tempest Computer Systems Integrator
S.I.C.: 3577
Kenneth Weiss *(Pres.)*
Mark Figley *(Controller)*
Steven Rice *(Dir.-Sls.)*
Keith Wood *(Dir.-Mktg.)*

Wilcom Products, Inc. **(1)**
Rt. 3 Daniel Webster Hwy.
Laconia, NH 03248
Tel.: 603-524-2622
Approx.Sls.: $7,000,000
Emp.: 100
Mfr. of Telecommunication Test Equipment
S.I.C.: 3825
Mark Farrant *(Gen. Mgr.)*

NORTH CAROLINA EQUIPMENT CO.
3101 Hillsboro St.
Raleigh, NC 27602
Mailing Address:
P.O. Box 431
Raleigh, NC 27602
Tel.: 919-833-4811
Fax: 919-828-6619
Approx.Sls.: $45,000,000
Emp.: 300
Fiscal Year-end: 2/28/90

Wholesale Construction & Industrial Machinery & Supplies
S.I.C.: 5082; 5084
Van C. Calton *(Chm. Bd.)*
Kenneth J. Calton *(Pres.)*
Charles Attardi, Jr. *(Sec. & Treas.)*

No. of Mfg. Plants/Facilities: 13

Outside Service Firm(s):

Poyner & Spruill*(Legal Firm)*
Raleigh, NC

Wachovia Bank of North Carolina, N.A.*(Major Banking Relationship)*
P.O. Box 27886, 227 Fayetteville St.
Raleigh, NC 27611
Tel.: 919-755-7730

NORTH CAROLINA MUTUAL LIFE INSURANCE CO.
411 W. Chapel Hill St.
Durham, NC 27701
Tel.: 919-682-9201
Fax: 919-683-1794
Year Founded: 1898
Approx.Sls.: $68,000,000
Emp.: 1,200
Fiscal Year-end: 12/31/90
Life Insurance
S.I.C.: 6311
W.J. Kennedy III *(Chm. Bd.)*
Bert Collins *(Pres. & Chief Exec. Officer)*
James Parrish *(Exec. V.P.)*
Charles Blackmon *(Sr. V.P.)*
Edward Bowser *(V.P.-Data Processing)*
Willie Closs *(V.P. & Controller)*
Albert Willis *(Gen. Counsel)*
Theresa Lyons *(Sec.)*
Keith Corbett *(Treas.)*
Daryl Banks *(Dir.-Mktg.)*
Lillian Bowser *(Dir.-Pur.)*
D. Robert Drake *(Dir.-Plng. & Devel.)*
Carlton Spaulding *(Dir.-Sls.)*
Roger Gregory *(Mgr.-Personnel)*

NORTH CAROLINA MUTUAL WHOLESALE DRUG CO.
816 Ellis Rd.
Durham, NC 27703
Mailing Address:
P.O. Box 411
Durham, NC 27702
Tel.: 919-596-2151 **NC**
Fax: 919-596-1453
Approx.Sls.: $85,000,000
Emp.: 118
Fiscal Year-end: 3/31/91
Wholesaler of Drugs, Health & Beauty Aids, Sundries
S.I.C.: 5122; 5100
Robert Bowers *(Pres.)*
Donald V. Peterson *(Chief Exec. Officer)*
Eugene W. Hackney *(Sec.)*
Mike Bromme *(Comptroller)*
D.E. Tilley *(Dir.-Opers.)*
W.V. O'Quinn *(Mgr.-Sls.)*

Outside Service Firm(s):

Thomas, Knight, Trent, King & Co.*(Auditors)*
Durham, NC

Stubbs, Cole, Breedlove, Prentis & Poe*(Legal Firm)*
Durham, NC

First Union National Bank*(Major Banking Relationship)*
Durham, NC

NORTH CENTRAL LIFE INSURANCE COMPANIES
445 Minnesota St.
Saint Paul, MN 55101
Mailing Address:
P.O. Box 64139
St. Paul, MN 55164
Tel.: 612-227-8000
Tel.: 800-888-8625 **MN**
Fax: 612-292-1830
Year Founded: 1951
Assets: $164,024,000
Liabilities: $152,159,000
Net Worth: $11,865,000
Approx.Income: $54,005,000
Emp.: 165
Fiscal Year-end: 12/31/88
Insurance & Investment Holding Company
S.I.C.: 6719; 6311; 6321; 6799
Bruce Sanborn *(Chm. Bd., Pres. & Chief Exec. Officer)*
John Drake *(Chief Fin. Officer)*
Frank McCarthy *(Gen. Counsel)*
Karin Fischer *(Dir.-Pur.)*
Dave Lawson *(Dir.-Data Processing)*
Mike McLaughlin *(Dir.-Adv. & Pub. Rels.)*
April Sweigart *(Dir.-Personnel)*

Principal(s):
Sanborn Family

No. of U.S. Offices: 1

Outside Service Firm(s):

Deloitte & Touche*(Auditors)*
900 Pillsbury Ctr.
Minneapolis, MN 55402
Tel.: 612-332-2301
Fax: 612-375-5418

Norwest Bank Minnesota, N.A.*(Major Banking Relationship)*
6th St. & Marquette Ave.
Minneapolis, MN 55479-0065
Tel.: 612-667-8101

Subsidiary:

Financial Life Companies, Inc. **(1)**
445 Minnesota St.
St. Paul, MN 55101
Tel.: 612-227-8000
Fax: 612-292-1830
Emp.: 147
Life Insurance, Computer Programming Services, Advertising Agency
S.I.C.: 6311; 7311; 7372
Bruce C. Sanborn *(Chm. Bd., Pres. & Chief Exec. Officer)*
David Sanborn *(Sec. & Treas.)*

NORTH COAST ELECTRIC COMPANY
110 110th Ave., N.E., Ste. 616
Bellevue, WA 98004
Mailing Address:
P.O. Box 97010,
Bellevue, WA 98009
Tel.: 206-454-1747
Fax: 206-454-7497
Year Founded: 1913
Sales Range: $100-499 Million
Emp.: 400
Fiscal Year-end: 12/31/89
Electrical Distributor
Robert L. Lemman *(Chm. Bd.)*
Peter R. Lemman *(Pres.)*
Paul E. Perko *(Chief Exec. Officer)*
Ronald G. Stewart *(Chief Fin. Officer)*
Richard Bumpus *(V.P.-Mktg. & Training)*
Dean M. Lemman *(V.P.)*
Patrick Moore *(V.P.-Corp. Credit)*

No. of U.S. Offices: 22

Computer Systems/Hardware:
Data General

NORTH DAKOTA MILL & ELEVATOR ASSOCIATION
1823 Mill Road
Grand Forks, ND 58201
Mailing Address:
P.O. Box 1078
Grand Forks, ND 58206-1078
Tel.: 701-795-7000 **ND**
Fax: 701-772-9387
Year Founded: 1922
Approx.Sls.: $50,000,000
Emp.: 120
Fiscal Year-end: 6/30/90
Spring Wheat Flour, Semolina
S.I.C.: 2041; 5149
Roger Dunning *(Pres. & Gen. Mgr.)*
Mark Bandy *(Mgr.-Quality Assurance)*
Steve Gorman *(Mgr.-Sls.)*
Corky Haugen *(Mgr.-Admin. & Fin.)*
Chris LeMoine *(Mgr.-Production)*

Outside Service Firm(s):

Bank of North Dakota*(Major Banking Relationship)*
Bismark, ND

NORTH ELECTRIC SUPPLY, INC.
1290 N. Opdyke Rd.
Auburn Hills, MI 48326
Tel.: 313-373-1070 **MI**
Fax: 313-373-0180
Year Founded: 1972
Sales Range: $10-19 Million
Emp.: 20
Distributor Of Electrical Construction Materials
S.I.C.: 5063
Harry Scarfe, Jr. *(Pres.)*
Robert J. Sleva *(V.P.)*
Raymond Wickersham *(V.P.)*
Frank Nutt *(Treas.)*
Phillip Kurkowski *(Sec.)*

Outside Service Firm(s):

Miller, Canfield, Paddock & Stone*(Legal Firm)*
Birmingham, MI

NORTH PACIFIC LUMBER COMPANY
1505 SE Gideon St.
Portland, OR 97208
Mailing Address:
P.O. Box 3915,
Portland, OR 97208
Tel.: 503-231-1166
Twx: 360564
Fax: 503-238-2650
Year Founded: 1948
Approx.Sls.: $500,000,000
Emp.: 370
Fiscal Year-end: 12/31/91
Import Export
Wholesale Forest & Agricultural Products; General Commodities; Steel, Waste Paper
S.I.C.: 5031; 5191; 5093
Thomas J. Tomjack *(Chm Bd. & Pres.)*
George R. Thurston *(Exec. V.P.-Fin., Intl.)*
Donald R. Lester *(Sr. V.P.-Panel Prods.)*
Bradley A. Manelin *(Sr. V.P.-Sls.)*
Kenneth N. McCoun, Jr. *(Sr. V.P.-Sls.)*
Dwight D. Foy *(V.P.-Mktg. & Transportation)*
Richard D. Hutson *(V.P. & Asst. Treas.)*
Irwin W. Rogers *(V.P., Controller & Sec.)*
M. Tamura *(V.P.-Mngmt. Information Services)*

Outside Service Firm(s):

KPMG Peat Marwick*(Auditors)*
1211 S.W. Fifth Ave.
Portland, OR 97204

Dunn, Carney, Allen, Higgins & Tongue*(Legal Firm)*
Portland, OR

First Interstate Bank*(Major Banking Relationship)*
P.O. Box 3131,
Portland, OR 97208
Tel.: 503-220-4855
Fax: 503-225-7153

NORTH PARK LINCOLN MERCURY INC.
9207 San Pedro
San Antonio, TX 78216
Tel.: 210-341-8841 **TX**
Fax: 210-341-5178
Assets: $15,996,062
Liabilities: $10,711,773
Net Worth: $5,284,289
Approx.Sls.: $90,000,000
Emp.: 164
Fiscal Year-end: 12/13/91
New & Used Automobile Dealership
S.I.C.: 5511
Clarence J. Kahlig *(Pres.)*
Sandra Kahlig *(Treas. & Sec.)*
David Hoyer *(Controller)*
Jim Tatum *(Dir.-Sls.)*
Billy Vaughn *(Gen. Mgr.)*
Principal(s):
Clarence J. Kahlig

Computer Systems/Hardware:
Oakleaf

Outside Service Firm(s):

John Deere Insurance*(Commercial Insurance Carrier)*
Moline, IL

Humana Health Care Plan*(Group Insurance Broker/Consult)*
San Antonio, TX

Foster, Lewis, et al*(Legal Firm)*
San Antonio, TX

National Bank of Commerce*(Major Banking Relationship)*
San Antonio, TX

Austin Group*(Pension Manager)*
Austin, TX

NORTH SHORE MOVERS
600 Waukegan Rd.,
Northbrook, IL 60062
Mailing Address:
P.O. Box 189,
Northbrook, IL 60062
Tel.: 708-498-6560 **IL**
Fax: 708-498-6935
Year Founded: 1968
Emp.: 75
Export
Local & Long Distance Moving & Storage; Corporate & Office Relocation
S.I.C.: 4213; 4214; 4212
Frank Larkin *(Chm. Bd. & Investor Rels. Dir.)*
William L. Owens *(Pres.-Corp. Relocation)*
James A. Larkin *(Sr. Exec. V.P.-Sales)*
Barry Litberg *(Gen. Mgr.)*
Linda Larkin *(Treas.)*
Laura Klaus-Owens *(Controller)*
Jerry Rason *(Gen. Counsel)*
Dorothy Steubben *(Corp. Sec.)*
Mike Klaus *(Dir.-Direct Mktg.)*
Steve Klaus *(Dir.-Admin. & Opers.)*
Mike Klein *(Dir.-Fin.)*

No. of U.S. Offices: 1

Computer Systems/Hardware:
IBM PC

Outside Service Firm(s):

Vincent Brandband*(Group Insurer)*
Park Ridge, IL

NORTHEAST TEXAS FARMERS CO-OP
428 N. Jackson
Sulphur Springs, TX 75482
Tel.: 903-885-3143
Fax: 903-885-4359
Approx.Sls.: $22,000,000
Emp.: 78
Retail Feed & Farm Supplies; Wholesale Grain
S.I.C.: 5153; 5191
Richard C. Thomas *(Chief Exec. Officer)*
Jerry Gibby *(Pres.)*
Lanny R. Dodd *(Controller)*

Outside Service Firm(s):

Scott, Singleton & Fincher*(Auditors)*
Greenville, TX

Sulphur Springs State Bank*(Major Banking Relationship)*
Sulphur Springs, TX

NORTHEASTERN GRAPHIC SUPPLY, INC.
14 Industrial Way
Portland, ME 04102
Mailing Address:
P.O. Box 1418
Portland, ME 04104
Tel.: 207-797-9982
Fax: 207-797-9538
Sales Range: $10-19 Million
Emp.: 20
Graphic Art Supplies
S.I.C.: 3952
Hyman Kroot *(Chm. Bd.)*
Brian Kroot *(Pres.)*

Outside Service Firm(s):

Ralph Morton & Nicholas*(Auditors)*
South Portland, ME

Greenberg & Greenberg*(Legal Firm)*
Portland, ME

Key Bank Of Southern Maine*(Major Banking Relationship)*
South Portland, ME

NORTHERN DRUG COMPANY
4444 Haines Rd.
Duluth, MN 55811
Mailing Address:
P.O. Box 16657
Duluth, MN 55816
Tel.: 218-722-4791
Fax: 218-722-0116
Approx.Sls.: $48,000,000
Emp.: 49
Wholesaler of Drugs & Sundries
S.I.C.: 5122; 5100
Erwin L. Goldfine *(Chm. Bd.)*
Steven B. Goldfine *(Pres.)*
G. Jay Coughlin *(Exec. V.P.-Sls.)*
Manley Goldfine *(Treas.)*
John J. Goldfine *(Sec.)*

Computer Systems/Hardware:
IBM

Outside Service Firm(s):

Esterbrooks, Lomen, Scott, Signorelli Ltd.*(Auditors)*
Duluth, MN

Norwest Business Credit, Inc.*(Major Banking Relationship)*
Minneapolis, MN

NORTHERN MICHIGAN VENEERS, INC.
Gladstone Industrial Park
Gladstone, MI 49837
Mailing Address:
P.O. Box 352,
Gladstone, MI 49837
Tel.: 906-428-3113 **MI**
Fax: 906-428-3310
Year Founded: 1966
Approx.Sls.: $17,000,000
Emp.: 80
Fiscal Year-end: 12/31/90
Export
Veneer Stock, Hardwood
S.I.C.: 2435
John Besse *(Pres.)*
Melissa Besse *(Treas.)*
Grey Besse *(Sec.)*
Ray Oelmont *(Controller)*
Al Hurtibuse *(Mgr.-Sls.)*

NORTHERN WIRE & CABLE, INC.
1902 Northwood
Troy, MI 48084
Mailing Address:
P.O. Box 1026
Troy, MI 48099
Tel.: 313-244-8100
Tel.: 800-521-2756 **MI**
Fax: 313-244-9840
Year Founded: 1976
Assets: $11,087,956
Liabilities: $9,887,956
Net Worth: $1,200,000
Approx.Sls.: $40,602,305
Emp.: 189
Fiscal Year-end: 12/31/91
Import Export
Distribute Electrical & Electronic Wire & Cable, Connectors & Accessories
S.I.C.: 5063; 3678
Robert Brzustewicz *(Chief Exec. Officer & Sec.)*
Glen M. Nast *(Pres. & Treas.)*
Wayne Biederman *(Exec. V.P.)*
Michael Arnett *(V.P.-Fin.)*
Brian Cronin *(V.P.-Western Reg.)*
George Dann *(V.P.-Sls.)*
Frances Hudgins *(V.P.-Admin.)*
Paul Waleke *(V.P.-Pur.)*
Lisa Hendry *(Dir.-Personnel)*
Paul Adams *(Mgr.-Information Systems)*
Rodney A. Hoover *(Mgr.-Adv.)*
Toni Lotz *(Admin. Asst.)*
Claudia Oliver *(Insurance Specialist)*
Principal(s):
Glen M. Nast
Wayne Biederman
Robert Brzustewicz

No. of U.S. Offices: 5

Computer Systems/Hardware:
IBM

Outside Service Firm(s):

Mallin, Kushner, Chupack & Kippelman*(Auditors)*
Southfield, MI

Midwest Benefits*(Group Insurer)*
Suite 3000, 2205 W. 12 Mile Rd.
Southfield, MI 48034-8339
Tel.: 313-351-0200

Michigan National Bank*(Investment Banker)*
Troy, MI

Lipson, Neilson, Jacobs & Cole, P.C.*(Legal Firm)*
Troy, MI

Barnett Banks Trust Company, N.A.*(Major Banking Relationship)*
Atlanta, GA

Michigan National Bank*(Major Banking Relationship)*
Detroit, MI

Valley Bank of Nevada*(Major Banking Relationship)*
300 S. Fourth St.
Las Vegas, NV 89101

Great Lakes Benefit*(Pension Manager)*
Birmingham, MI

Prudential-Bache*(Pension Manager)*
9 West 57th St.
New York, NY 10019
Tel.: 212-415-5800
Fax: 212-415-5885

NORTHLAND ALUMINUM PRODUCTS, INC.
Hwy. 7 at 100
Minneapolis, MN 55416
Tel.: 612-920-2888
Fax: 612-920-3762
Year Founded: 1946
Approx.Sls.: $65,000,000
Emp.: 550
Manufacture Aluminum, Clay Cookware, Small Electrical Appliances, Barbecue Grills; Industrial Diecastings; Commercial Coatings; Commercial Magnetic Recording Heads
S.I.C.: 3469; 3269; 3341; 3365; 3479; 3589; 3679; 3089
H. David Dalquist, Sr. *(Chm. Bd. & Chief Exec. Officer)*
H. David Dalquist, III *(Pres.)*
Robert Franklin *(Controller)*
Dennis Siddall *(Pur. Agent)*

Computer Systems/Hardware:
IBM PC

Outside Service Firm(s):

McGladrey & Pullen*(Auditors)*
Minneapolis, MN

Hessian, McKasy & Soderberg*(Legal Firm)*
Minneapolis, MN

First Bank Minneapolis*(Major Banking Relationship)*
Minneapolis, MN

NORTHLAND CONTAINER CORP.
9070 General Dr.
Plymouth, MI 48170
Tel.: 313-459-2000
Tel.: 800-331-2089 **TX**
Fax: 313-459-3833
Year Founded: 1971
Approx.Sls.: $15,000,000
Emp.: 48
Fiscal Year-end: 12/31/90
Import
Warehousing & Distribution of Packaging Products
S.I.C.: 4226; 5199
Harold Bergquist *(Chm. & Chief Exec. Officer)*
David Bergquist *(Pres.)*
Irvin Levy *(V.P.)*
Raymond Stachura *(V.P.-Fin. & Sec.)*
John Holden *(Mgr.-Pur. & Adv.)*
Charisse Miller *(Mgr.-Data Processing)*

Outside Service Firm(s):

Ernst & Young*(Auditors)*
One Detroit Center, 500 Woodward, Ste. 1700
Detroit, MI 48243
Tel.: 313-259-9600

Draugelis, Ashton, Scully, Haynes, MacLean & Pollard*(Legal Firm)*
Detroit, MI

Comerica Bank*(Major Banking Relationship)*
211 W. Fort St.
Detroit, MI 48226
Tel.: 313-222-3300

NORTHLAND ELECTRIC SUPPLY COMPANY
521 S. 10th St.
Minneapolis, MN 55440
Tel.: 612-341-6100
Fax: 612-341-6179
Approx.Sls.: $38,000,000
Emp.: 140
Wholesale Distributor of Electrical Plumbing Supplies
S.I.C.: 5063; 5074
J.M. Vilett, Jr. *(Pres.)*
Marvin Spartz *(Treas.)*
Fred Eiseman *(Gen. Mgr.)*

Outside Service Firm(s):

Robert F. Stringer Co., Ltd.*(Auditors)*
Minneapolis, MN

Lang, Pauly & Gregerson*(Legal Firm)*
4400 IDS Center
Minneapolis, MN 55402
Tel.: 612-338-0755
Fax: 612-349-6718

Marquette Bank*(Major Banking Relationship)*
777 Marquette Ave.
Minneapolis, MN 55402
Tel.: 612-370-2182

NORTHLICH STOLLEY LAWARRE
200 W. Fourth St.
Cincinnati, OH 45202
Tel.: 513-421-8840
Fax: 513-287-1855
Year Founded: 1949
Approx.Billings: $45,000,000
Emp.: 75
William M. LaWarre *(Pres.)*
Mark A. Serrianne *(Exec. V.P.)*
Bruce W. Mackey *(Sr. V.P., Dir. Plng. & Mktg. Services)*
Barbara Heldman *(Sec., Treas.)*

Computer Systems/Hardware:
IBM Compatibles, McIntosh/Apple

NORTHVILLE INDUSTRIES CORP.
P.O. Box 2937, 25 Melville Pk. Rd.
Melville, NY 11747
Tel.: 516-293-4700
Fax: 516-293-4780
Approx.Sls.: $304,000,000
Emp.: 320
Wholesale & Retail Gasoline
S.I.C.: 5541; 5172
Jay Bernstein *(Chm. Bd.)*
Gene M. Bernstein *(Pres.)*
Peter Ripp *(Sr. V.P. & Chief Fin. Officer)*
Steve Lessman *(Controller)*

Outside Service Firm(s):

Empire Blue Cross & Blue Shield*(Group Insurer)*
New York, NY

NORTHWAY MOTORCAR CORPORATION
727 New Loudon Rd.
Latham, NY 12110
Tel.: 518-783-1951
Fax: 518-783-1737
Year Founded: 1967
Approx.Sls.: $30,000,000
Emp.: 64
Retail New & Used Automobiles
S.I.C.: 5511
Kevin Langan *(Pres.)*
Conrad Kupillas *(V.P.)*

NORTHWEST PAPER CONVERTING COMPANY
6416 N.W. Whitney Rd.
Vancouver, WA 98665
Tel.: 206-695-7771 **WA**
Fax: 206-694-0943
Year Founded: 1976
Assets: $4,000,000
Liabilities: $3,100,000
Net Worth: $900,000
Approx.Sls.: $13,000,000
Emp.: 96
Import Export

Holding Company
S.I.C.: 6719
John T. Fike *(Pres. & Chief Exec. Officer)*
V. Harley Morgan *(Exec. V.P. & Sec.)*
Richard Raivio *(Controller)*
Carol Brain *(Dir.-Employee Benefits)*
Robert M. Fike *(Dir.-Mktg.)*
Robert Kenney *(Dir.-Mfg.)*

Principal(s):
John T. Fike
V. Harley Morgan

No. of Mfg. Plants/Facilities: 1
No. of U.S. Offices: 1

Computer Systems/Hardware:
386 PC

Outside Service Firm(s):

Fitzpatrick & Countryman*(Auditors)*
McMinnville, OR

Ragen, Tremaine, Kreiger, Schneer & Neill*(Legal Firm)*
Portland, OR

Northwest National Bank*(Major Banking Relationship)*
Vancouver, WA

Subsidiary:

Pac Paper, Inc. **(1)**
6416 N.W. Whitney Rd.
Vancouver, WA 98665
Tel.: 206-695-7771
Approx.Sls.: $14,000,000
Emp.: 91
Paper Converting
S.I.C.: 5113
John T. Fike *(Chm. Bd., Pres. & Chief Exec. Officer)*
Robert M. Fike *(Chief Oper. Officer)*
J. Harley Morgan *(V.P.-Sls.)*
Richard Ravio *(Chief Fin. Officer)*
Robert Kenney *(Gen. Mgr.)*

NORTHWEST PIPE FITTINGS, INC.
33 S. 8th St. W.
Billings, MT 59103
Tel.: 406-252-0142 **DE**
Fax: 406-248-8072
Approx.Sls.: $16,000,000
Emp.: 75
Plumbing & Hydronic Heating Supplies; Valves & Fittings; Pipe & Tubing; Steel Copper Sheets, Plates, Bars, Rods & Pipes; Drilling Equipment
S.I.C.: 5074; 5085; 5051; 5084
Robert W. Kuhns, Jr. *(Chm. Bd.)*
Jerry Evenson *(Pres.)*
Dick L. Dede *(V.P.)*
Hank Mellgren *(Treas.)*
W. Robert Barbour *(Sec.)*
Dean Lehman *(Pur. Agent)*

Outside Service Firm(s):

Anderson, Cebull & Gerbuse*(Legal Firm)*
Billings, MT

First Bank Billings*(Major Banking Relationship)*
Billings, MT

NORTHWEST TOBACCO & CANDY CO.
612 W. Center
Fayetteville, AR 72701
Mailing Address:
P.O. Box 4215
Fayetteville, AR 72702
Tel.: 501-442-8121 **AR**
Year Founded: 1960
Approx.Sls.: $12,000,000
Emp.: 21
Wholesale Distribution of Tobacco, Tobacco Products & Candy
S.I.C.: 5194; 5145
Grace M. Tancred *(Pres.)*
Faye M. Williams *(Treas. & Sec.)*
Tony Harp *(Gen. Mgr.)*

Outside Service Firm(s):

Ted Fisher*(Auditors)*
Fayetteville, AR

First National Bank*(Major Banking Relationship)*
Fayetteville, AR

NORTHWESTERN ENGINEERING CO.
P.O. Box 2320
Rapid City, SD 57709
Tel.: 605-394-3310
Fax: 605-341-3446
Approx.Sls.: $22,000,000
Emp.: 250
Holding Company; Real Estate Management, Highway & Street Construction, Quarrying; Ready-Mix Concrete
S.I.C.: 6719; 6552; 8741; 6531; 1611; 3241
Stanford M. Adelstein *(Pres.)*
Patrick Tlustos *(V.P.)*
Robert M. Adelstein *(Sec.)*

Outside Service Firm(s):

McGladrey & Pullen*(Auditors)*
1700 Lincoln St.
Denver, CO 80203
Tel.: 303-861-4545

Banks, Johnson, Johnson, Colbath & Huffman, P.C.*(Legal Firm)*
Rapid City, SD

Norwest Bank Minnesota, N.A.*(Major Banking Relationship)*
Rapid City, SD

Subsidiary:

Hills Materials Co. **(1)**
P.O. Box 2320
Rapid City, SD 57709
Tel.: 605-342-3875
Approx.Sls.: $18,000,000
Emp.: 200
Highway & Street Construction, Building Quarries & Ready-mix Concrete
S.I.C.: 1611; 3241; 5032
Stanford M. Adelstein *(Chm. Bd. & Treas.)*
Pat Tlustos *(Pres.)*

NORTHWESTERN GOLF COMPANY
4701 N. Ravenswood Ave.
Chicago, IL 60640
Tel.: 312-275-0500 **IL**
Fax: 312-275-0949
Sales Range: $20-39 Million
Emp.: 280
Golf Clubs & Equipment
S.I.C.: 3949
Nat C. Rosasco *(Chm. Bd.)*
Nat G. Rosasco *(Pres.)*
Paul Runkel *(V.P.-Fin.)*
H. Charles Stickelmater *(V.P.-Mktg.)*
Robert Evert *(V.P. & Gen. Mgr.)*

Outside Service Firm(s):

Rome & Associates*(Auditors)*
Chicago, IL

Division:

Pro-Select **(1)**
2151 Cermak Rd.
Broadview, IL 60153
Tel.: 708-343-0430
Golf Clubs & Equipment
S.I.C.: 3949
Nat C. Rosasco *(Chm. Bd.)*

NORTHWESTERN INDUSTRIAL PIPING
7475 Oak Park Ave.
Niles, IL 60714
Tel.: 312-775-1455 **DE**
Fax: 312-775-5455
Year Founded: 1958
Approx.Sls.: $20,000,000
Emp.: 100
Warm Air Heating & Air Conditioning Contractors
S.I.C.: 1711
Joseph S. Kearney, Jr. *(Pres.)*
George Kearney *(Exec. V.P. & Treas.)*
Marshall I. McMahon, Jr. *(Sec.)*

Outside Service Firm(s):

Bansley & Keiner*(Auditors)*
Chicago, IL

NORTHWESTERN MEATS INC.
2100 N.W. 23rd St.
Miami, FL 33142
Tel.: 305-633-8112 **FL**
Fax: 305-633-6907
Approx.Sls.: $119,000,000
Emp.: 76
Wholesale & Export Meat, Poultry & Seafood
S.I.C.: 5144; 5146; 5147
Elpidio Nunez *(Pres. & Chief Exec. Officer)*
Ramon N. Gonzalez *(V.P.-Opers.)*
Alvin Y. Nance *(V.P.-Sls.)*
Elpidio P. Nunez, Jr. *(V.P.-Fin.)*
Olga M. Nunez *(Sec.)*

Outside Service Firm(s):

Kaufman & Rossin*(Auditors)*
Miami, FL

Paul, Landy, Bailey*(Legal Firm)*
Miami, FL

First Union National Bank*(Major Banking Relationship)*
1 S.E. Financial Ctr.
Miami, FL 33131
Tel.: 305-666-5656

NORTHWESTERN MUTUAL LIFE INSURANCE CO.
720 E. Wisconsin Ave.
Milwaukee, WI 53202
Tel.: 414-271-1444 **WI**
Fax: 414-299-2463
Assets: $35,744,000,000
Liabilities: $33,033,000,000
Net Worth: $2,711,000,000
Approx.Premiums: $4,658,000,000
Emp.: 3,000
Fiscal Year-end: 12/31/92
Life Disability Income Insurance & Annuities
S.I.C.: 6311
Donald J. Schuenke *(Chm. Bd. & Chief Exec. Officer)*
James D. Ericson *(Pres. & Chief Oper. Officer)*
Robert E. Carlson *(Exec. V.P.-Agencies & Mktg.)*
Peter W. Bruce *(Sr. V.P.-Insurance Opers.)*
James W. Ehrenstrom *(Sr. V.P.-Human Resources & Admin.)*
Mason G. Ross *(Sr. V.P.-Real Estate)*
Frederic H. Sweet *(Sr. V.P.-Govt. Rels.)*
Dennis Tamcsin *(Sr. V.P.-Agencies)*
Walter J. Wojcik *(Sr. V.P.-Plng. & Fin.)*
Edward J. Zore *(Sr. V.P.-Chief Fin. Officer & Investments)*
Deborah A. Beck *(V.P.-New Bus.)*
John M. Bremer *(V.P., Gen. Counsel & Sec.)*
Robert O. Carboni *(V.P.-Corp. Offices)*
Mark G. Doll *(V.P. & Treas.)*
Thomas Dyer *(V.P.-Policyowner Services)*
Edward A. Flitz *(V.P.-Information Systems)*
Madonna M. Hostetter *(V.P.-Underwriting Standards & Services)*
William C. Koenig *(V.P. & Chief Actuary)*
Gary E. Long *(V.P. & Controller)*
Donald L. Mellish *(V.P.-Field Fin. Services)*
Barbara F. Piehler *(V.P.-Corp. Services)*
James F. Reiskytl *(V.P.-Tax & Fin. Plng.)*
Virgil L. Renne *(V.P.-Employer Prod. Mktg.)*
Leonard F. Stecklein *(V.P.-Individual Prod. Mktg.)*
Casey J. Sylla *(V.P.-Securities)*
Martha M. Valerio *(V.P.-Policy Benefits)*
W. Ward White *(V.P.-Communications)*
William L. Hegge *(Mgr.-Telecommunications)*
David L. Wild *(Mgr.-Pur.)*

Computer Systems/Hardware:
Amdahl 5870; IBM 3081 XK; Amdahl V8

Outside Service Firm(s):

Price Waterhouse*(Auditors)*
1500 Bank One Plaza, 100 E. Wisconsin Ave.
Milwaukee, WI 53202

Northwestern Mutual*(Group Insurer)*
Milwaukee, WI

Subsidiary:

MGIC Investment Corporation **(1)**
P.O. Box 488,
Milwaukee, WI 53201
Tel.: 414-347-6480 (95%)
Approx.Income: $75,006,000
Fiscal Year-end: 12/31/91
Financial Services
S.I.C.: 6159

NORTHWESTERN STEEL & WIRE CO.
121 Wallace St.
Sterling, IL 61081
Tel.: 815-625-2500 **IL**
Fax: 815-625-2500
Year Founded: 1879
Assets: $342,899,000
Earnings: ($19,547,000)
Liabilities: $313,591,000
Net Worth: $29,308,000
Approx.Rev.: $477,429,000
Emp.: 2,700
Fiscal Year-end: 7/31/92
Export
Steel Producers
S.I.C.: 3312; 3315
Michael J. Rosenthal *(Chm. Bd.)*
Robert N. Gurnitz *(Pres. & Chief Exec. Officer)*
Charles H. Biermann *(Sr. V.P.-Sls.)*
Edward G. Maris *(Sr. V.P. & Chief Fin. Officer)*
K.J. Burnett *(V.P.-Steel Opers.-Sterling)*
Robert W. Martin *(V.P.-Pur.)*
John C. Meyer *(V.P.-Human Resources)*
M.J. Mullen *(V.P. & Gen. Mgr.-Houston Opers.)*
D.C. Oberbillig *(V.P.-Wire Prod. Sls.)*
Gerald T. Shinville *(V.P.-Quality Assurance & Tech.)*
Frank L. Rausa *(Mgr.-Training & Devel.)*
Thomas M. Vercillo *(Mgr.-Corp. Acctg.)*

NORTON ASSOCIATES, INC.
203 N. Wabash Ave., Ste. 1220
Chicago, IL 60601
Tel.: 312-899-1960
Fax: 312-899-1122
Year Founded: 1974
Approx.Billings: $18,000,000
Emp.: 25
Foodservice Advertising
Timothy C. Norton *(Chm. Bd.)*

W.W. NORTON & COMPANY, INC.
500 Fifth Ave.
New York, NY 10110
Tel.: 212-354-5500

W.W. Norton & Company, Inc.—(Continued)

Fax: 212-869-0856
Emp.: 320
Publisher of Books
S.I.C.: 2731
Donald S. Lamm *(Chm. Bd. & Pres.)*
Eric P. Swenson *(Vice Chm.)*
Edwin Barber *(V.P., Editor & Dir.-Trade Books)*
Iva K. Ashner *(V.P. & Mgr.-Adv.)*
Genevieve Luciano *(V.P. & Dir.-Subsidiary Rights)*
William F. Rusin *(V.P.-Sls.- Trade Dept.)*
Warren Tiley *(V.P. & G.M.)*
Victor Schmalzer *(Treas.)*
Jack Rizzitello *(Co. Sec.)*
Julia Reidhead *(Adv.-College Dept.)*
Pearl Axson *(Personnel Dir.)*
Lisa Gaeth *(Personnel Mgr.)*

Subsidiaries:

Liveright Publishing Corp. **(1)**
500 Fifth Ave.
New York, NY 10110
Tel.: 212-354-5500
Fax: 212-869-0856
Publishing
S.I.C.: 2621

National Book Company Inc. **(1)**
Keystone Industrial Park
Scranton, PA 18512
Tel.: 717-346-2020
Fax: 717-346-1442
Book Distr.
S.I.C.: 5192
Michael Charnogursky *(Exec. V.P.)*

J. R. NORTON COMPANY
3200 E. Camelback Rd., Ste. 389
Phoenix, AZ 85018
Tel.: 602-954-8812 **AZ**
Fax: 602-954-8908
Year Founded: 1955
Sales Range: $40-59 Million
Emp.: 1,800
Fiscal Year-end: 9/30/88
General Crop Farm
S.I.C.: 0191
John R. Norton, III *(Chm. Bd. & Chief Exec. officer)*
Owen L. Cotton *(V.P.-Fin. & Treas.)*
Robert A. Micalizio *(V.P.)*
John Phelps Norton *(V.P.-Prod.)*
Roger L. Stevenson *(V.P.-Devel.)*

Computer Systems/Hardware:
IBM System 38

Outside Service Firm(s):

Ernst & Young*(Auditors)*
40 North Central, Ste. 900
Phoenix, AZ 85004
Tel.: 602-258-3366

Beus, Gilbert & Morrill*(Legal Firm)*
Phoenix, AZ

Jennings, Strouss & Salmon*(Legal Firm)*
2 N. Central, Ste. 1600
Phoenix, AZ 85004
Tel.: 602-942-8659

Valley National Bank*(Major Banking Relationship)*
241 North Central Ave., 11th Floor
Phoenix, AZ 85001

NORTOWN OLDSMOBILE INC.
7601 N. Skokie Blvd.
Skokie, IL 60077
Tel.: 708-982-9500
Fax: 708-982-9500, Ext. 203
Year Founded: 1974
Approx.Sls.: $19,000,000
Emp.: 55
Oldsmobile Dealership
S.I.C.: 5511
Julius Alvarez *(Pres.)*

Outside Service Firm(s):

Shapiro Olefsky & Co.*(Auditors)*
Dundee, IL

Rosenthal Schanfield*(Legal Firm)*
Chicago, IL

First Chicago Bank*(Major Banking Relationship)*
One First National Plaza
Chicago, IL 60670

NORWALK CO., INC.
20 N. Water St.
South Norwalk, CT 06854
Mailing Address:
P.O. Box 548,
South Norwalk, CT 06856
Tel.: 203-838-4766
Tel.: 800-556-5001
Telex: 4759017
Fax: 203-838-6140
Year Founded: 1864
Approx.Sls.: $15,000,000
Emp.: 100
Fiscal Year-end: 7/31/91
Export
High & Low Pressure Air & Gas Compressors
S.I.C.: 3563
Arthur McCauley *(Chm. & Pres.)*
George Ward *(V.P.-Mktg.)*
Vona Limone *(Admin. Asst.)*
Denice Hall *(Mgr.-Data Processing)*

Computer Systems/Hardware:
IBM

NORWALK FURNITURE CORPORATION
100 Furniture Pkwy.
Norwalk, OH 44857
Tel.: 419-668-4461
Fax: 419-668-6223
Year Founded: 1902
Approx.Sls.: $60,000,000
Emp.: 900
Upholstered Livingroom Furniture & Tables
S.I.C.: 2512; 2426; 2511
Edward Gerken *(Chm. Bd. & Pres.)*
Jack Arthur *(V.P.)*
John V. Arthur *(V.P.)*
John Francisco *(V.P.-Mfg.)*

Outside Service Firm(s):

Deloitte & Touche*(Auditors)*
One Cascade Plaza, Ste. 1600
Akron, OH 44303-1187
Tel.: 216-253-2022

National City Bank*(Major Banking Relationship)*
Norwalk, OH

Subsidiary:

Hickory Hill Furniture Corporation **(1)**
501 Hoyle St.
Valdese, NC 28690
Tel.: 704-874-2124
Sales Range: $60-79 Million
Emp.: 1,550
Mfr. Upholstered Living Room Furniture
S.I.C.: 2512
A. Wayne Annas *(V.P.-Mfg.)*
Carlton Caruso *(Dir.-Pur.)*
William E. Adkins *(Gen. Mgr.)*

NORWALK POWDERED METALS, INC.
Muller Park
Norwalk, CT 06852
Mailing Address:
P.O. Box 271
Norwalk, CT 06852
Tel.: 203-847-4537
Fax: 203-849-1876
Year Founded: 1958
Approx.Sls.: $10,000,000
Emp.: 100
Fiscal Year-end: 12/31/90
Export
Powdered Metal Gears, Bushings, Structural Parts, Etc.
S.I.C.: 3499
Thomas A. Blumenthal *(Chm. Bd, Pres. & Chief Exec. Officer)*
Henry Adams *(V.P.-Sls., Mktg., Adv. & Tech. Services)*
Richard Webb *(V.P.-Opers.)*
Nick Mozzillo *(Controller)*
Fred Baechtold *(Dir.-Res. & Devel.)*
Lucile DiMiglio *(Dir.-Personnel & Pur.)*
Robert Lampe *(Dir.-Quality Control)*
L.D. Meglio *(Dir.-Pur. & Office Mgr.)*
Brenda Donnelly *(Mgr.-Info. Services)*
F. Farahani *(Mgr.-Production)*
F. Baechtold *(Chief Engr.)*

Computer Systems/Hardware:
PC, Several Brands

NORWECO, INC.
(d/b/a Oxarc)
E. 4003 Broadway Ave.
Spokane, WA 99220
Tel.: 509-535-7794
Emp.: 65
Welding Supplies & Gases
S.I.C.: 5084; 5169; 7692
Jerry T. Walmsley *(Chief Exec. Officer)*
Gregory H. Walmsley *(Pres.)*
Jana Nelson *(V.P.-Admin.)*
Jane Virgine *(Pur. Agent)*

Outside Service Firm(s):

LeMasters & Daniels*(Auditors)*
Spokane, WA

Lukins & Annis*(Legal Firm)*
Spokane, WA

Security Pacific National Bank*(Major Banking Relationship)*
Spokane, WA

NORWEGIAN CRUISE LINE
95 Merrick Way
Coral Gables, FL 33134
Tel.: 305-447-9660
Tel.: 800-327-7030
Telex: 305-448-6406
Approx.Sls.: $735,000,000
Emp.: 5,597
Fiscal Year-end: 12/31/91
Bahamas, Caribbean, Bermuda, California & Mexico Cruises
S.I.C.: 4481
Trygve Hegnar *(Chm. Bd. & Chief Exec. Officer)*
Hans Golteus *(Pres. & Chief Oper. Officer)*
Doug Falk *(Exec. V.P.-Sls. & Mktg.)*
Robert Walters *(Exec. V.P. & Chief Fin. Officer)*
Joan Di Pietro *(V.P.-Mktg.)*
Fran Sevcik *(Dir.-Pub. Rels.)*
Jeff Stutin *(Dir.-Mktg. Services)*
Jill Miller *(Mgr.-Mktg. & Promo.)*

Division:

Royal Viking Line **(1)**
Two Alhambra Plaza
Coral Gables, FL 33134
Tel.: 305-447-9660
Tel.: 800-422-8000
Cruise Line
Spencer Frazier *(V.P.)*

NORWESCO, INC.
1650 W. 82nd. St., Ste. 1000
Minneapolis, MN 55431
Tel.: 612-885-5900
Tel.: 612-446-1945 **MN**
Fax: 612-885-5940
Year Founded: 1939
Approx.Sls.: $40,000,000
Emp.: 270
Fiscal Year-end: 12/31/90
Import Export
Plastic Molding
S.I.C.: 6719; 3089
Edward T. Michalek *(Chm. Bd. & Chief Exec. Officer)*
Thomas J. Smith *(Pres.)*
Dale H. Sandberg *(V.P. & Chief Fin. Officer)*

Computer Systems/Hardware:
IBM AS 400

Divisions:

Norwesco Components Div. **(1)**
Box 3876,
Gastonia, NC 28052
Tel.: 704-866-9161
Approx.Sls.: $9,000,000
Emp.: 95
Plastic Molding
S.I.C.: 3089
G.W. Munn *(V.P. & Gen. Mgr.)*
Bill Blalock *(Dir.-Pur.)*
Gayle Crowson *(Dir.-Data Processing)*

Norwesco Contract Manufacturing Div. **(1)**
311 B Avenue
Grundy Center, IA 50638
Tel.: 319-824-5201
Approx.Sls.: $9,000,000
Emp.: 95
Plastic Molding
S.I.C.: 3089
J.L. Bakker *(V.P. & Gen. Mgr.)*

Norwesco Fluid Systems Div. **(1)**
4365 Steiner St.
Saint Bonifacius, MN 55375
Tel.: 612-446-1945
Approx.Sls.: $18,000,000
Emp.: 64
Rotational Molding
S.I.C.: 3089
T.J. Smith *(V.P. & Gen. Mgr.)*
Jim Baker *(Dir.-Data Processing)*

NORWOOD SHOE CORPORATION
One Penaljo Dr.
De Soto, MO 63020
Tel.: 314-586-0770
Approx.Sls.: $10,000,000
Emp.: 80
Mfrs. & Distr. Women's Shoes
S.I.C.: 3144
James Norwood *(Pres.)*

THE NOTEWORTHY COMPANY
100 Church St.
Amsterdam, NY 12010
Tel.: 518-842-2660 **NY**
Fax: 800-866-8317
Year Founded: 1954
Approx.Sls.: $13,000,000
Emp.: 205
Plastic & Paper Litterbags, Take-Home Bags, Photo Finishing Bags, Coloring Books, Book Jackets & Envelopes
S.I.C.: 2673; 2674; 2677; 2679
Carol Constantino *(Pres.)*
John Colangelo *(V.P.-Fin.)*
Thomas J. Cummings *(V.P.-Opers. & Chief Engr.)*
Dianne Santos *(Corp. Sec.)*
Steve Smeltzer *(Dir.-Corp. Plng.)*
Barry C. Connor *(Mgr.-Natl. Sls.)*

No. of Mfg. Plants/Facilities: 2

Computer Systems/Hardware:
IBM-36

Outside Service Firm(s):

Stanley J. Wawrejko & Co.*(Auditors)*
Albany, NY

DiFabio, Tommaney & Legnard*(Legal Firm)*
Albany, NY

First American Bank, N.A.*(Major Banking Relationship)*
New York, NY

NOVA POWER, INC.
1231 E. Dyer Rd., Ste. 110
Santa Ana, CA 92705
Tel.: 714-641-4727 CA
Fax: 714-966-2889
Year Founded: 1978
Approx.Sls.: $16,000,000
Emp.: 130
Export
Engineering Consulting & Electrical Contractor
S.I.C.: 1731
Gabriel Chavez *(Pres. & Gen. Mgr.)*
Thomas D. Teichman *(V.P. & Treas.)*
Thomas R. Linn *(Controller)*
Marian E. Schomer *(Sec.)*

Outside Service Firm(s):

Wells Fargo Bank*(Major Banking Relationship)*
Santa Ana, CA

NOVAMETRIX MEDICAL SYSTEMS INC.
1 Barnes Industrial Park Rd.
Wallingford, CT 06492
Mailing Address:
P.O. Box 690,
Wellingford, CT 06492
Tel.: 203-265-7701 DE
Telex: 956-054
Fax: 203-284-0753
Assets: $25,885,000
Earnings: ($2,423,000)
Liabilities: $21,147,000
Net Worth: $4,738,000
Approx.Rev.: $17,692,000
Emp.: 150
Fiscal Year-end: 4/28/91
Mfr., Development & Marketing of Medical Electronic Instruments & Disposable Products
S.I.C.: 3841; 5049
William J. Lacourciere *(Chief Exec. Officer, Chm. Bd., Pres.)*
John A. Ramadei *(V.P.-Fin. & Treas.)*
Morton F. Reich *(V.P.)*
Thomas M. Haythe *(Sec. & Gen. Counsel)*

Subsidiary:

Cascadia Technology Corporation **(1)**
2877 1052 Ave. N.E.
Redman, WA 95052
Tel.: 206-882-3500
Lesly Mace *(V.P.-Engrng.)*

NOVAR ELECTRONICS
24 Brown St.
Barberton, OH 44203
Tel.: 216-745-0074
Fax: 216-745-7401
Assets: $16,800,000
Earnings: ($122,084)
Net Worth: $16,800,000
Approx.Sls.: $11,875,258
Emp.: 320
Fiscal Year-end: 12/31/89
Mfr. of Burglary Deterrents & Involved with Energy Management & Building Management Computer Systems
S.I.C.: 3669
James H. Ott *(Chm.)*
Andrew Federico *(Pres. & Chief Exec. Officer)*
Patrick L. O'Neill *(Treas.)*

Subsidiaries:

Leasing Services Corp. **(1)**
24 Brown St.
Barberton, OH 44203
Tel.: 216-745-0074
Leasing of Burglary Deterrent Systems
S.I.C.: 7382

Novar Controls Corp. **(1)**
24 Brown St.
Barberton, OH 44203
Tel.: 216-745-0074
Manufacturer of Controls for Energy Management Systems
S.I.C.: 3823

Novar Corp. **(1)**
24 Brown St.
Barberton, OH 44203
Tel.: 216-745-0074
Sales & Marketing of Systems
S.I.C.: 5084; 7382

NOVILLE ESSENTIAL OIL CO., INC.
1312 Fifth St.
North Bergen, NJ 07047
Tel.: 201-867-9080 DE
Fax: 201-867-1914
Year Founded: 1939
Approx.Sls.: $15,000,000
Emp.: 120
Fragrances & Flavors
S.I.C.: 2844; 2869; 2899
W.B. Widlund *(Chm. Bd.)*
D.J. Carey *(Pres.)*
A. Galante *(Sr. V.P. & Treas.)*
John E. Porter *(V.P.-Research & Devel.)*
William J. Wichmann *(V.P.-Opers.)*
E. Widlund *(V.P.-Mktg.)*

Outside Service Firm(s):

Paddell & Nadell*(Auditors)*
New York, NY

National Community Bank*(Major Banking Relationship)*
North Bergen, NJ

NU SKIN INTERNATIONAL
145 E. Center St.
Provo, UT 84606
Mailing Address:
75 W. Center St.
Provo, UT 84606
Tel.: 801-345-1000
Fax: 801-377-2850
Year Founded: 1984
Approx.Sls.: $363,000,000
Emp.: 1,200
Distribute of Cosmetics, Vitamins, Hair Care Products, Personal Care & OTC Products
S.I.C.: 5122
Blake M. Roney *(Pres.)*
Kirk Roney *(V.P.-Devel.)*
Sandy Tillotson *(V.P.-Mktg.)*

NUARC COMPANY, INC.
6200 W. Howard St.
Niles, IL 60714
Tel.: 708-967-4400 IL
Fax: 708-967-9664
Year Founded: 1946
Sales Range: $20-39 Million
Emp.: 145
Fiscal Year-end: 6/30/91
Export
Graphic Arts Equipment
S.I.C.: 3861
Henry Weisman *(Pres. & Treas.)*
Donald V. Cims *(Exec. V.P.)*
Joseph M. Dixler *(Exec. V.P.)*
Barbara Morgenstern *(Exec. V.P.)*
Julian Koren *(V.P.-Technical Services)*
Charles Leonhart *(V.P.-Engrng.)*
Robert Epifano *(Sec. & Asst. Treas.)*
Eli Jacobs *(Dir.-Pur.)*
Donald Jancula *(Dir.-Information Systems)*
Conrad Aaknes *(Plant Mgr.)*
Fred Posner *(Supvr.-Acctg.)*
William Urian *(Adv. Coord.)*

No. of U.S. Offices: 16

Computer Systems/Hardware:
IBM System 38

Outside Service Firm(s):

Blue Cross & Blue Shield of Illinois*(Group Insurer)*
100 Tower Drive
Burr Ridge, IL 60521
Tel.: 708-323-3666

Divisions:

Nuarc Eastern Div. **(1)**
175 Varick St.
New York, NY 10014
Tel.: 212-255-7330
Joe Fontanella *(V.P.)*

Nuarc Mid-Atlantic Div. **(1)**
14254 Cherry Lane
Laurel, MD 20707
Tel.: 301-470-3851
Bob McMillan *(Gen. Mgr.)*

Nuarc Northeastern Div. **(1)**
180 Second St.
Chelsea, MA 02150
Tel.: 617-889-8000
Ernest M. Fobert *(Mgr.-New England Branch)*

Nuarc Northwestern Div. **(1)**
1800 Westlake Ave. North #206
Seattle, WA 98109
Tel.: 206-283-9550

Nuarc Southeastern Div. **(1)**
555 Armour Circle N.E.
Atlanta, GA 30324
Tel.: 404-892-4800
Edwin Moehring *(Gen. Mgr.)*

Nuarc Southern Div. **(1)**
3912 N. 29th Ave.
Hollywood, FL 33020
Tel.: 305-921-5111
Ron Hopkins *(Gen. Mgr.)*

Nuarc Southwestern Div. **(1)**
1931 Market Center Blvd., Ste. 109
Dallas, TX 75207
Tel.: 214-748-0841
James Dowlen *(Gen. Mgr.)*

Nuarc Western Div. **(1)**
12130 Mora Dr., Unit # 1
Santa Fe Springs, CA 90670
Tel.: 310-944-0045
Dennis Dobranski *(Gen. Mgr.)*

Groups:

Central, East Central, West Central Divs. **(1)**
6200 W. Howard St.
Niles, IL 60648
Tel.: 708-967-4400
Red Koren *(V.P.-Tech. Services)*
R. Adrian *(Gen. Mgr.)*

NuArc Co. **(1)**
909 Oakland Park
Cleveland, OH 43224
Tel.: 614-268-9907
Jim Stephenson *(Mgr.-Sls. & Service)*

NuArc Co. **(1)**
9810 Ashton Rd.
Philadelphia, PA 19114
Tel.: 215-969-6300
Chuck Frey *(Gen. Mgr.)*

NuArc Co. **(1)**
130 Produce Ave., Ste. E
South San Francisco, CA 94080
Tel.: 415-952-6777
Art Lopez *(Mgr.-Sls. & Service)*

NuArc Co. **(1)**
5855 Sovereign Dr., Ste. 135
Houston, TX 70036
Tel.: 713-995-9045
David Kageler *(Mgr.-Sls. & Service)*

NuArc Co. **(1)**
301 W. Armour Blvd.
Kansas City, MO 64111
Tel.: 816-283-9046
Jim Tharp *(Mgr.-Sls. & Service)*

NuArc Co. **(1)**
13540 N. Florida Ave., Ste. 103
Tampa, FL 33613
Tel.: 813-961-7702
Erik Sperry *(Mgr.-Sls. & Service)*

NuArc Co. **(1)**
501 Archdale Dr., Ste. 209
Charlotte, NC 28210
Tel.: 704-527-9143
Phillip Seaman *(Mgr.-Sls. & Service)*

NuArc Co. **(1)**
478 Thurston Rd., Suite S-22
Rochester, NY 14619
Tel.: 716-235-2840

NUHAHN, INC.
614 W. 184th St.
Gardena, CA 90248
Tel.: 310-515-2862
Fax: 310-323-7725
Year Founded: 1981
Approx.Sls.: $50,000,000
Emp.: 30
New Construction of Commercial & Office Buildings; Renovation & Repair; Shopping Center Construction
S.I.C.: 1542; 1541
John Yarnall *(Pres.)*
William Roberts *(V.P.)*

Outside Service Firm(s):

Deloitte & Touche*(Auditors)*
Gardena, CA

First Interstate Bank*(Major Banking Relationship)*
Lomita, CA

NULAID FOODS
200 W. 5th St.
Ripon, CA 95366
Tel.: 209-599-2121
Fax: 209-599-4822
Year Founded: 1963
Approx.Sls.: $60,000,000
Emp.: 130
Wholesale Distributor of Shell Eggs, Fresh, Frozen & Dried Egg Products; Poultry Feed; Dry Dog & Cat Feed
S.I.C.: 5144; 2048; 2047
Jeff Ovadia *(Pres.)*
Stan Andre *(Sr. V.P.-Mktg.)*
Teresa Butts *(V.P. & Sec.)*

Outside Service Firm(s):

Wells Fargo Bank*(Major Banking Relationship)*
Modesto, CA

#1 COCHRAN, INC.
4200 William Penn Hwy.
Monroeville, PA 15146
Tel.: 412-373-3333 PA
Fax: 412-373-4288
Year Founded: 1965
Emp.: 400
Retail Motor Vehicles
S.I.C.: 5511
R.W. Cochran *(Pres. & Chief Exec. Officer)*
R.E. Cochran *(V.P. & Chief Oper. Officer)*
Carol Cochran Tsudis *(Corp. Sec. & Treas.)*

Outside Service Firm(s):

Schneider, Downs & Company*(Auditors)*
Pittsburgh, PA

Mollica, Murray & Hogue*(Legal Firm)*
Pittsburgh, PA

Pittsburgh National Bank*(Major Banking Relationship)*
5th Ave. & Wood St.
Pittsburgh, PA 15222
Tel.: 412-355-3000

NUTECH, INC.
145 Martinvale Ln.
San Jose, CA 95119
Tel.: 408-629-9800 **CA**
Fax: 408-281-6186
Year Founded: 1974
Assets: $20,000,000
Liabilities: $4,000,000
Net Worth: $16,000,000
Approx.Sls.: $30,000,000
Emp.: 330
Fiscal Year-end: 12/31/88
Engineering Consulting Services For Power Industry, Ranging From Production Engineering To Hi-Technology Specialty Applications
S.I.C.: 8711
Michael Scholtens *(Chm., & Chief Exec. Officer)*
T.N. Vogel *(Pres.)*
W. L. Potts, Jr. *(Chief Fin. Officer, Treas. & Controller)*
T. J. Van Bogart *(Controller & Asst. Sec.)*
K. A. Hoedeman *(Dir.-Purchasing)*
M. C. Metts *(Dir.-Telecommunications)*

No. of U.S. Offices: 5
No. of Foreign Offices: 4

Computer Systems/Hardware:
Apple; Hewlett-Packard; IBM PC/ Compatible, Sun Microsystem

Outside Service Firm(s):

Ernst & Young*(Auditors)*
55 Almaden Blvd.
San Jose, CA 95115
Tel.: 408-947-5476
Fax: 408-294-2744

Northwestern National Life*(Group Insurer)*
20 Washington Ave. S.
Minneapolis, MN 55401

Thelen, Marrin, Johnson & Bridges*(Legal Firm)*
Two Embarcadero Center
San Francisco, CA 94111
Tel.: 415-392-6320

Bank of America NT&SA*(Major Banking Relationship)*
San Jose, CA

Subsidiaries:

NUTECH Engineers, Inc. **(1)**
145 Martinvale Ln.
San Jose, CA 95119
Tel.: 408-629-9800 (100%)
Emp.: 200
Engineering Consulting Firm Offering Technical & Management Support To Domestic Power Industries
S.I.C.: 8711
T.N. Vogel *(Pres.)*

NUTECH International, Inc **(1)**
145 Martinvale Lane
San Jose, CA 95119
Tel.: 408-629-9800 (100%)
Emp.: 40
Engineering Firm Offering Technical & Managment Support to International Power Industries
S.I.C.: 8711
T.N. Vogel *(Pres.)*

Pacific Nuclear Systems, Inc. **(1)**
1010 S. 336th St., Ste. 220
Federal Way, WA 98003
Tel.: 206-874-2235
Earnings: $1,561,000
Approx.Rev.: $66,423,000
Fiscal Year-end: 12/31/91

NUTRI/SYSTEM INC.
380 Sentry Pkwy.
Blue Bell, PA 19422-2332
Tel.: 215-940-3000 **PA**
Fax: 215-940-3023
Assets: $179,739,000
Earnings: $113,063,000
Liabilities: $163,526,000
Net Worth: $16,213,000
Approx.Sls.: $665,198,000
Emp.: 5,000
Fiscal Year-end: 7/31/91
Weight Loss Centers & Franchising
S.I.C.: 7991; 7299
A. Donald McCulloch, Jr. *(Chm. Bd. & Chief Exec. Officer)*
Albert J. DeMarco *(Pres. & Chief Oper. Officer)*
Richard J. Gyde *(Exec. V.P.-Mktg.)*
Joseph T. Dono *(Sr. V.P.-Mktg. & Adv.)*
William R. Lewis *(Sr. V.P.-Fin.)*
John E. Sylvester *(Sr. V.P.-Opers.)*
Edward Walsh *(Sr. V.P.-Human Resources)*
W. John Coats *(V.P.-Fin.)*
Jeffrey Landau *(V.P.-Mngmt. Information Systems)*
James Kemper Millard *(V.P.-Communications)*
Reef C. Ivey III *(Gen. Counsel)*
Thomas Stone *(Treas.)*
Delphine Carroll *(Dir.-Pub. Rels.)*
Marianne Pishock *(Dir.-Corp. Admin.)*
Elaine Schleigh *(Dir.-Meetings Plng.)*
Lynn Bellucci *(Mgr.)*

No. of Mfg. Plants/Facilities: 795
No. of Foreign Offices: 1

Outside Service Firm(s):

Arthur Andersen & Co.*(Auditors)*
1601 Market St.
Philadelphia, PA 19103
Tel.: 215-241-7300

Dilworth, Paxson, Kalish & Kauffman*(Legal Firm)*
2600 Fidelity Bldg., 123 S. Broad St.
Philadelphia, PA 19109
Tel.: 215-875-7000

NUTRITION WORLD
(Sub. of Health Foods Inc.)
155 W. Old Higgins Rd.
Des Plaines, IL 60018
Tel.: 708-298-8220
Approx.Sls.: $10,000,000
Emp.: 200
Fiscal Year-end: 12/31/90
Natural Foods, Vitamins & Health Food Stores
S.I.C.: 5499
Jim Zedella *(Pres.)*
Bill S. Zramek *(Gen. Mgr.-Retail Opers.)*

NUTTALL EQUIPMENT CO. INC.
128 E. Main St.
Sherman, NY 14781
Mailing Address:
P.O. Box 990,
Sherman, NY 14781
Tel.: 716-761-6111 **NY**
Fax: 716-761-6110
Approx.Sls.: $12,000,000
Emp.: 65
Wholesale Trucks & Construction Equipment; Fire Truck Repair
S.I.C.: 5012; 5082; 7538
Grant Lesswing *(Chm. Bd. & Chief Exec. Officer)*

No. of U.S. Offices: 2

Outside Service Firm(s):

Lumsden McCormick & Co.*(Auditors)*
Buffalo, NY

Boniello, Anton, Conti, Boniello*(Legal Firm)*
Niagara Falls, NY

Norstar Bank, N.A.*(Major Banking Relationship)*
Jamestown, NY

NUTTALL GEAR CORPORATION
2221 Niagara Falls Blvd.
Niagara Falls, NY 14302
Mailing Address:
P.O. Box 1032
Niagara Falls, NY 14302
Tel.: 716-731-5180 **DE**
Telex: 466950
Fax: 716-731-9329
Year Founded: 1982
Approx.Sls.: $10,781,974
Emp.: 125
Fiscal Year-end: 9/30/91
Export
Mfr. Enclosed Gear Drives
S.I.C.: 3566
Christopher C. Collins *(Chm. Bd., Pres. & Chief Exec. Officer)*
A. Carl Becker *(V.P.-Pur. & Engrng.)*
W. Charles Kolkebeck *(V.P.-Mktg. & Sls.)*
Richard Danni *(Mgr.-Opers.)*
Michael Graves *(Mgr.-Pur.)*
Jeffrey Somerville *(Mgr.-Quality Assurance)*
Principal(s):
Christopher C. Collins
A. Carl Becker
W. Charles Kolkebeck

No. of Mfg. Plants/Facilities: 1

Computer Systems/Hardware:
Altos Computer Systems

Outside Service Firm(s):

Deloitte & Touche*(Auditors)*
50 Fountain Plaza
Buffalo, NY 14202
Tel.: 716-843-7200

Alexander & Alexander*(Commercial Insurance Carrier)*
Buffalo, NY

Hiscock & Barclay*(Legal Firm)*
Buffalo, NY

Marine Midland Bank, N.A.*(Major Banking Relationship)*
Niagara Falls, NY

NYLON CORPORATION OF AMERICA
333 Sundial Ave.
Manchester, NH 03103
Tel.: 603-669-5015
Fax: 603-627-5154
Year Founded: 1983
Sales Range: $10-19 Million
Emp.: 80
Nylon Resins
S.I.C.: 2821
Steven Hudson *(Pres.)*
William Baker *(V.P.-Mfg.)*
Carlo Pacchini *(V.P.-Human Resources)*
John Kittle *(Controller)*
John Pollono *(Chief Engr.)*

Outside Service Firm(s):

Deloitte & Touche*(Auditors)*
Manchester, NH

Wiggin & Nourie*(Legal Firm)*
Manchester, NH

Bank of New England*(Major Banking Relationship)*
Randolph, MA

OCTUS
9940 Barnes Canyon Rd.
San Diego, CA 92121
Tel.: 619-452-9400 **CA**
Fax: 619-452-2427
Year Founded: 1983
Assets: $22,000,000
Liabilities: $9,000,000
Net Worth: $13,000,000
Sales Range: $20-39 Million
Emp.: 131
Manufacture Laser Printers, Raster Image Controllers & Interface Products
S.I.C.: 3571
John Belden *(Pres. & Chief Exec. Officer)*
Gene Candalore *(Exec. V.P.-Opers.)*
Jill Beckman-Donley *(Dir.-Human Resources)*
Brian Herman *(Dir.-Data Processing)*
Steve Nelson *(Dir.-Materials)*
Steve Rogers *(Dir.-Mktg.)*
Robert Kuncilo *(Mgr.-Mktg./ Communications)*
Principal(s):
John Belden

No. of Mfg. Plants/Facilities: 1
No. of U.S. Offices: 11
No. of Foreign Offices: 2

Computer Systems/Hardware:
LaserPro

Outside Service Firm(s):

Price Waterhouse*(Auditors)*
750 B St.
San Diego, CA 92101
Tel.: 619-231-9830

Prudential Insurance Co. of America*(Group Insurer)*
San Diego, CA

Thomas Green*(Investment Banker)*
San Diego, CA

Latham & Watkins*(Legal Firm)*
633 West Fifth St.
Los Angeles, CA 90071
Tel.: 213-485-1234
Fax: 213-643-9086

Imperial Bank*(Major Banking Relationship)*
San Diego, CA

The Prudential Asset Management Company*(Pension Manager)*
751 Broad St., 19th Fl.
Newark, NJ 07102-3777
Tel.: 201-802-8400
Fax: 201-802-8456

ODI
(Formerly Organizational Dynamics, Inc.)
25 Mall Rd.
Burlington, MA 01803
Tel.: 617-272-8040 **MA**
Telex: 7103321067
Fax: 617-273-2558
Year Founded: 1970
Assets: $7,000,000
Earnings: $1,700,000
Liabilities: $4,000,000
Net Worth: $3,000,000
Approx.Sls.: $17,000,000
Emp.: 160
Fiscal Year-end: 6/30/89
Design & Implementation of Management Development, Quality Improvement & Performance Management Training Systems
S.I.C.: 8742
Dr. George H. Labovitz *(Chm. Bd., Pres. & Chief Exec. Officer)*
Richard L. Murphy *(Pres.-ODI Intl.)*
Paul Hesselschwerdt *(Chief Fin. Officer & V.P.)*
Steven J. Aronson *(Sr. V.P.)*
Victor Rosansky *(Sr. V.P.-Training & Devel.)*
Donald Weintraub *(Sr. V.P.-Bus. Devel.)*
Thomas J. Varian *(V.P.-Mktg. Communications)*
Principal(s):
Dr. George H. Labovitz

No. of U.S. Offices: 12
No. of Foreign Offices: 4

Computer Systems/Hardware:
IBM PC

Outside Service Firm(s):

Alan Edelstein*(Auditors)*
Boston, MA

Chubb Group*(Commercial Insurance Carrier)*
P.O. Box 1615,
Warren, NJ 07061
Tel.: 201-580-2000

Blue Cross of Massachusetts, Inc.*(Group Insurer)*
Boston, MA

Kassler & Feuer*(Legal Firm)*
Boston, MA

U.S. Trust Co.*(Major Banking Relationship)*
40 Court St.
Boston, MA 02108
Tel.: 617-726-7371
Fax: 617-726-7380

U.S. Trust Co.*(Pension Manager)*
40 Court St.
Boston, MA 02108
Tel.: 617-726-7371
Fax: 617-726-7380

Subsidiary:

ODI **(1)**
25 Mall Rd.n Woods Dr.
Burlington, MA 01803
Tel.: 617-272-8040
Management Training & Consulting
S.I.C.: 8742

ODL INCORPORATED
215 E. Roosevelt Rd.
Zeeland, MI 49464
Tel.: 616-772-9111
Tel.: 800-288-1800
Fax: 616-772-9110
Year Founded: 1948
Approx.Sls.: $45,000,000
Emp.: 325
Fiscal Year-end: 12/31/91
Import Export
Mfr. Building Products
S.I.C.: 2431
Lawrence Mulder *(Chm. Bd.)*
Thomas Jurgens *(Pres. & Chief Exec. Officer)*
David Killoran *(V.P. & Gen. Mgr.-Retail)*
Paul Meeuwsen *(V.P. & Gen. Mgr.-Distr.)*
G. Ronald Wright *(V.P.-Fin.)*
Craig Weaver *(Product Mgr., Retail)*

Computer Systems/Hardware:
MAI Basic 4

O/E AUTOMATION, INC.
3290 W. Big Beaver, Ste. 132
Troy, MI 48084
Tel.: 313-643-2035
Fax: 313-643-0728
Approx.Sls.: $70,000,000
Emp.: 600
Leasing Computer Equipment
S.I.C.: 6159; 7379
Thomas Doonan *(Chm. Bd.)*
Richard K. Austin *(Pres.)*
Robert Smith *(Sec.)*

Outside Service Firm(s):

Arthur Andersen & Co.*(Auditors)*
400 Renaissance Center
Detroit, MI 48243
Tel.: 313-259-8100

National Westminster Bank plc*(Major Banking Relationship)*
175 Water St.
New York, NY 10038-4924
Tel.: 212-602-3364

OEI Business Forms
(Name Changed To Office Electronics, Inc.)

OMCO MOULD, INC.
One OMCO Square
Winchester, IN 47394
Mailing Address:
P.O. Box 5,
Muncie, IN 47305
Tel.: 317-584-4000 **IN**
Fax: 317-584-4982
Assets: $13,425,162
Earnings: ($1,714,863)
Liabilities: $7,832,676
Net Worth: $5,592,486
Approx.Sls.: $43,327,785
Emp.: 471
Fiscal Year-end: 12/31/89
Export
Moulds for Glass Container Indus.; Gray & Ductile Iron Castings for Several Industries
S.I.C.: 3321; 3544; 3599
C. Donald Cunningham *(Pres.)*
George C. Bowyer *(V.P.)*
Billie Hart *(Admin.-Personnel)*

Outside Service Firm(s):

Arthur Andersen & Co.*(Auditors)*
111 Monument Circle, Ste. 4300
Indianapolis, IN 46204-5143
Tel.: 317-634-3210
Fax: 317-632-3973

Barnes & Thornburg*(Legal Firm)*
11 S. Meridian St.
Indianapolis, IN 46204
Tel.: 317-638-1313

Subsidiaries:

OMCO Cast Metals, Inc. **(1)**
900 N. Main St.
Winchester, IN 47394
Tel.: 317-584-4000
Emp.: 119
Gray & Ductile Iron Castings
S.I.C.: 3321; 3369

OMCO Machining Concepts, Inc. **(1)**
828 N. Main St.
Winchester, IN 47394
Tel.: 317-584-4006
S.I.C.: 3599

OPT INDUSTRIES, INC.
300 Red School Lane
Phillipsburg, NJ 08865
Tel.: 908-454-2600
Fax: 908-454-3742
Year Founded: 1972
Approx.Sls.: $15,000,000
Emp.: 275
Fiscal Year-end: 10/31/91
Mfrs. of Power Supplies, Data Networking Prods. & Magnetic Components
Jerome Potash *(Pres.)*
William Chakeres *(Sr. V.P.)*
Jack Smith *(V.P.-Corp. Accts.)*
Paul Folla *(V.P.-Data Prods. Div.)*

OSC CORPORATION D/B/A OLYMPIC SALES CO.
134 W. 131st St.
Los Angeles, CA 90061
Tel.: 310-719-9500
Fax: 310-719-9518
Approx.Sls.: $15,000,000
Emp.: 20
Fiscal Year-end: 12/31/90
Sales of Electronic Equipment; Computers, Calculators, Etc.
S.I.C.: 5734
Francis Ravel *(Pres.)*
Liliane Ravel *(V.P.)*

OAK RUBBER COMPANY
219 S. Sycamore St.
Ravenna, OH 44266-1203
Tel.: 216-296-3416
Fax: 216-296-6117
Approx.Sls.: $25,000,000
Emp.: 350
Design & Manufacture of Polyvinylchloride & Latex Rubber Products
S.I.C.: 3069
W.R. Collette *(Chm. Bd.)*
Murray P. Collette *(Pres. & Chief Exec. Officer)*
C.P. Tushar *(Treas. & Controller)*
Jerry Beach *(Dir.-Human Resources)*
Angela Burnes *(Pur. Agent)*

Subsidiary:

Oak Technical, Inc. **(1)**
219 S. Sycamore St.
Ravenna, OH 44266
Tel.: 216-296-3416
S.I.C.: 3069

OAKHURST DAIRY
364 Forest Ave.
Portland, ME 04101
Tel.: 207-772-7468
Year Founded: 1921
Approx.Sls.: $40,000,000
Emp.: 155
Milk Processing
S.I.C.: 2026
Donald H. Bennett *(Chm. Bd.)*
Stanley T. Bennett *(Pres.)*
William P. Bennett *(V.P.)*
John F. Barry *(Treas.)*

OAKLAND TOOL & MANUFACTURING COMPANY
34700 Commerce
Fraser, MI 48026
Tel.: 313-294-0100 **MI**
Fax: 313-294-6139
Year Founded: 1963
Approx.Sls.: $13,000,000
Emp.: 79
Fiscal Year-end: 10/31/91
Automobile Auto Parts, Stamped Metal
S.I.C.: 3465
Thelma Krause *(Pres.)*
Joanna Saunders *(V.P. & Treas.)*
Karen Malburg *(Controller)*
Royal Clippert *(Dir.-Engrng.)*
Dave Motyka *(Dir.-Pur.)*
Al Young *(Dir.-Sls.)*

Outside Service Firm(s):

Comerica Bank*(Major Banking Relationship)*
211 W. Fort St.
Detroit, MI 48226
Tel.: 313-222-3300

BRUCE OAKLEY, INC.
3700 Lincoln
North Little Rock, AR 72114
Tel.: 501-945-0875 **AR**
Fax: 501-945-6970
Year Founded: 1972
Approx.Sls.: $42,000,000
Emp.: 42
Wholesale Grain & Fertilizer; Retail Nursery, Garden Supplies
S.I.C.: 5153; 5191; 5261
Bruce Oakley *(Pres.)*
Mike Fisher *(Gen. Mgr.)*

Outside Service Firm(s):

Richard L. Bell*(Auditors)*
Little Rock, AR

First Commercial Bank*(Major Banking Relationship)*
P.O. Box 1331,
Little Rock, AR 72201

BENJAMIN OBDYKE, INC.
Jacksonville Rd.
Warminster, PA 18974
Tel.: 215-672-7200
Fax: 215-672-3731
Approx.Sls.: $22,000,000
Emp.: 75
Residential Building Products
S.I.C.: 3444
Richard J. Campbell *(Pres.)*
David Campbell *(Chief Oper. Officer)*
Mike Coulton *(Gen. Mgr.)*

Outside Service Firm(s):

Coopers & Lybrand*(Auditors)*
2400 Eleven Penn Center
Philadelphia, PA 19103-2962
Tel.: 215-963-8000

Kevlin & Irwin*(Legal Firm)*
Philadelphia, PA

Philadelphia National Bank*(Major Banking Relationship)*
5th & Market Sts.
Philadelphia, PA 19101
Tel.: 215-629-3100
Fax: 215-834-2069

OBERDORFER INDUSTRIES, INC.
P.O. Box 4811
Syracuse, NY 13221
Tel.: 315-437-7588
Fax: 315-434-9826
Year Founded: 1878
Approx.Sls.: $25,000,000
Emp.: 200
Export
Manufacture Aluminum Sand Castings, Permanent Mold Castings
S.I.C.: 3365
Kenneth L. Evans *(Pres. & Chief Exec. Officer)*
Paul Whittaker *(Exec. V.P.)*
K. Lynch *(Mgr.-Personnel)*

Computer Systems/Hardware:
IBM System 34

OBERG INDUSTRIES CO.
Silverville Rd.
Freeport, PA 16229
Tel.: 412-295-2121
Fax: 412-295-2588
Year Founded: 1948
Approx.Sls.: $35,000,000
Emp.: 360
Manufacture Carbide Stamping Dies, Ultra-Precision Components, Stampings
S.I.C.: 3544; 3469
Donald E. Oberg, II. *(Chm. Bd.)*
Donald E. Oberg *(Emeritus)*
David O. Shondeck *(Pres.)*
Les Freehling *(Sec.)*
Tom Polczynski *(Pur. Agent)*

Computer Systems/Hardware:
Hewlett-Packard

Outside Service Firm(s):

Ernst & Young*(Auditors)*
2000 Pittsburgh Natl. Bldg.
Pittsburgh, PA 15222
Tel.: 412-644-7800
Fax: 412-644-7419

Buchanan, Ingersoll p.c.*(Legal Firm)*
600 Grant St., 57th Flr.
Pittsburgh, PA 15219
Tel.: 412-562-8800

Citizens National Bank of Evans City*(Major Banking Relationship)*
Evans City, PA

Divisions:

Independent Tool & Die **(1)**
Silverville Rd.
Freeport, PA 16229
Tel.: 412-295-2588
S.I.C.: 3544

Oberg Arizona **(1)**
Chandler, AZ
Tel.: 602-961-0622

Oberg Industries Co.—(Continued)

Oberg Carbide Punch & Die **(1)**
Silverville Rd.
Freeport, PA 16229
Tel.: 412-295-2558
S.I.C.: 3544

Oberg Mfg. Co. **(1)**
Silverville Rd.
Freeport, PA 16229
Tel.: 412-295-2121
S.I.C.: 3469; 3544

OBERWEIS DAIRY, INC.
945 N. Lake St.
Aurora, IL 60506
Tel.: 708-897-0512
Fax: 708-897-0562
Approx.Sls.: $12,000,000
Emp.: 100
Mfr. Ice Cream; Wholesale Dairy Prods.; Retail Milk, Ice Cream & Other Dairy Prods.
S.I.C.: 2024; 5143; 5451
Elaine Oberweis *(Pres.)*
Jim Oberweis *(V.P.)*
Marie Oberweis *(Sec.)*
Carole Arliskis *(Dir.-Mktg. & Gen. Mgr.)*

Principal(s):
Elaine Oberweis
Marie Oberweis

Computer Systems/Hardware:
IBM

Outside Service Firm(s):

Sikich, Gardner & Co.*(Auditors)*
Aurora, IL

Drendel, Schanlaber, Horwitz, Tatnall & McCracken*(Legal Firm)*
Chicago, IL

Suburban National Bank*(Major Banking Relationship)*
Aurora, IL
Tel.: 312-844-5000

Division:

Roney Div. of Oberweis Dairy, Inc. **(1)**
735 Prairie St.
Aurora, IL 60506
Tel.: 708-859-2800
Emp.: 80
Manufacturer of Ice Cream Specialties
S.I.C.: 2024; 2023; 2052
Dennis Roney *(Pres.)*
Marshall Cunz *(Mgr.-Opers.)*
Dave Lucas *(Mgr.-Sls.)*

THE O'BRIEN CORPORATION
450 E. Grand Ave.
South San Francisco, CA 94080
Tel.: 415-761-2300 **IN**
Fax: 415-873-2628
Year Founded: 1875
Assets: $66,475,000
Liabilities: $28,914,000
Net Worth: $37,561,000
Approx.Sls.: $130,000,000
Emp.: 750
Fiscal Year-end: 12/31/91
Export
Mfr. Paints, Enamels, Varnishes, Lacquers, Stains, Resins, Powder Coatings, Industrial Metal Finishes
S.I.C.: 2851; 2821
Jerome J. Crowley, Jr. *(Pres.)*
Thomas H. Cahir *(V.P.-Pur.)*
Edward P. Daly *(V.P.-Opers.)*
Eric Swanson *(V.P.-Sls.)*
John E. Trewin *(V.P. & Treas.)*
Mark R. Allen *(Sec.)*
Karl Seiter *(Dir.-Natl. Mktg. Communications)*
Charles Hogue *(Mgr.-Mktg.)*

Outside Service Firm(s):

Price Waterhouse*(Auditors)*
202 S. Michigan
South Bend, IN 46624

Crowley, Barrett & Karaba*(Legal Firm)*
111 W. Monroe St.
Chicago, IL 60603
Tel.: 312-726-2468

Wells Fargo Bank*(Major Banking Relationship)*
420 Montgomery St.
San Francisco, CA 94104

Subsidiaries:

Fuller O'Brien Paints **(1)**
450 E. Grand Ave.
South San Francisco, CA 94080
Tel.: 415-761-2300
Approx.Sls.: $150,000,000
Emp.: 900
Mfr. & Wholesaler-Retailer of Paints, Coatings & Related Prods.; Fuller-O'Brien Paints
S.I.C.: 2851; 5198
J.J. Crowley, Jr. *(Pres. & Chief Exec. Officer)*
Roger Adams *(Pres.-Trade Sls.)*
Mark R. Allen *(V.P. & Sec.)*
E.P. Daly *(V.P.-Trade Sls. Opers.)*
Frank Karaba *(Gen. Counsel)*
Greg Hatch *(Dir. Mktg.-Trade Sls.)*

Nason Automotive **(1)**
450 Grand Avenue
South San Francisco, CA 94080
Tel.: 415-761-2300
Jon Owen *(V.P.)*

O'Brien Powder Products, Inc. **(1)**
9800 Genard Rd.
Houston, TX
Emp.: 180
Mfg. & Sales of Powder Coating
S.I.C.: 2851
John Bruenik *(Pres.)*
Douglas Bach *(V.P.-Mktg.)*
John Bethea *(V.P.-Sls.)*
Lyle Schott *(V.P.-Opers.)*
John Biesmann *(Controller)*

O'Brien Powder Products, Inc. **(1)**
9800 Genard
Houston, TX 77041
Tel.: 713-641-0661
Tel.: 800-247-3886
Approx.Sls.: $33,000,000
Emp.: 175
Fiscal Year-end: 12/31/90
Export
Mfr. of Thermoset Powder Coatings in Epoxy; Hybrid; TGIC-Polyester & Urethane Chemistries
S.I.C.: 2851
John R. Brvenik *(Pres.)*
W. Douglas Bach *(V.P.-Mktg. & Bus. Devel.)*
Lyle W. Schott *(V.P. & Opers. Mgr.)*
Mark R. Allen *(Sec.)*
Noel H. Isham *(Mgr.-Nat'l Sls.-Deco Products)*
John Biesmann *(Controller)*

O'BRIEN ENERGY SYSTEMS INC.
225 S. Eighth St.
Philadelphia, PA 19106
Tel.: 215-627-5500
Approx.Sls.: $22,000,000
Emp.: 212
Cogeneration & Alternative Fuel Projects
S.I.C.: 5084; 4911
F.L. O'Brien, III *(Chm., Pres. & Chief Exec. Officer)*
Sanders D. Newman *(Sr. V.P., Sec. & Gen. Counsel)*
J.D. Cooperman *(V.P.-Fin.)*
Bruce Levy *(V.P.-Mktg.)*

Non-U.S. Holdings:

Kartret Switchgear Ltd. **(1)**
Switchgear House, Mill Lane
Croydon, Surrey CR0 4AA, United Kingdom
Tel.: 081-681 0751
Telex: 946794 KSPLTD G
Fax: 081-680 1520
Mfr. Electrical Switchgear
S.I.C.: 3613
Norman O'Hara *(Mng. Dir.)*

Puma Manufacturing Ltd. **(1)**
37 Sandwich Rd.
Ash, Kent CT3 2AJ, United Kingdom
Tel.: 0304 812818
Telex: 96366 PUMAUK G
Fax: 0304 813331
Mfr. Diesel Electric Generating Sets
S.I.C.: 3621
Brian Tatton *(Mng. Dir.)*

O'BRIEN MACHINERY COMPANY
100 Green St.
Downingtown, PA 19335
Tel.: 215-873-1700
Tel.: 800-879-0879
Telex: 875319
Fax: 215-873-7711
Year Founded: 1915
Approx.Sls.: $40,000,000
Emp.: 50
Export
Generator Sets & Related Equip.
S.I.C.: 3621
Clarence J. O'Brien II *(Chm.)*
Wm. Glockner *(Pres.)*
Dave Reilly *(V.P.-Sls. & Mktg.)*

ROY O'BRIEN INC.
22201 E. Nine Mile Rd.
St. Clair Shores, MI 48080
Mailing Address:
P.O. Box 98,
St. Claire Shores, MI 48080
Tel.: 313-776-7600 **MI**
Fax: 313-776-2360
Year Founded: 1946
Assets: $9,285,000
Liabilities: $5,838,000
Net Worth: $3,447,000
Approx.Sls.: $35,000,000
Emp.: 110
Fiscal Year-end: 12/31/91
Ford Automobile & Truck Dealership
S.I.C.: 5511
Roy E. O'Brien, Jr. *(Pres.)*
Raymond R. Northrup *(V.P.)*
Harold L. Matyn *(Treas.)*
James D. Tracy *(Sec.)*

Outside Service Firm(s):

Dykema, Gossett*(Legal Firm)*
400 Renaissance Ctr., 35th Fl.
Detroit, MI 48243
Tel.: 313-568-6800

Comerica Bank*(Major Banking Relationship)*
211 W. Fort St.
Detroit, MI 48226
Tel.: 313-222-3300

O'BRYAN BROTHERS INC.
4220 W. Belmont Ave.
Chicago, IL 60641
Tel.: 312-283-3000 **IL**
Fax: 312-283-5878
Year Founded: 1930
Approx.Sls.: $40,000,000
Emp.: 725
Lingerie Manufacturer
S.I.C.: 2341
Michael L. O'Bryan *(Pres.)*
James Mattingly *(V.P.-Sls.)*
Stephen F. O'Bryan *(V.P.)*

Principal(s):
Michael L. O'Bryan
Stephen F. O'Bryan

Computer Systems/Hardware:
IBM 4361

Outside Service Firm(s):

Ernst & Young*(Auditors)*
233 S. Wacker Dr.
Chicago, IL 60606
Tel.: 312-368-1800
Fax: 312-645-3095

McDermott, Will & Emery*(Legal Firm)*
227 W. Monroe St.
Chicago, IL 60606-5096
Tel.: 312-372-2000

American National Bank & Trust Co.*(Major Banking Relationship)*
Chicago, IL

OCEAN CHEVROLET, INC.
(Formerly Autoland Chevrolet, Inc.)
Rte. 37 & Peter Ave.
Toms River, NJ 08753
Tel.: 908-244-8400 **NJ**
Fax: 908-349-6018
Year Founded: 1981
Approx.Sls.: $50,000,000
Emp.: 106
Automobile Dealer; New & Used Car Franchise, Sales & Service
S.I.C.: 5511; 6794; 7538
Donald Toresco *(Pres.)*
Mike Margolies *(Controller)*
Andrea Karsian *(Sec.)*

Computer Systems/Hardware:
ADP

Outside Service Firm(s):

Mironov, Goldman & Wortzel*(Auditors)*
East Brunswick, NJ

Martin G. Margolis*(Legal Firm)*
Toms River, NJ

First National Bank of Toms River*(Major Banking Relationship)*
Toms River, NJ

OCEAN PROPERTIES, LTD.
1755 N. Congress Ave.
Boynton Beach, FL 33426
Tel.: 407-364-8800
Fax: 407-737-7580
Year Founded: 1975
Approx.Sls.: $58,000,000
Emp.: 1,230
Hotel Managment; Commercial Land Development
S.I.C.: 7011; 6552
Michael Walsh *(Pres.)*
Steven Updike *(V.P.-Food & Beverage Opers.)*
William Walsh *(V.P.)*
Orman G. Twitchell *(Sec.)*
Mark Walsh *(Treas.)*

OCEAN SPRAY CRANBERRIES, INC.
One Ocean Spray Dr.
Lakeville, MA 02349
Tel.: 508-946-1000 **DE**
Telex: 710391598
Fax: 508-946-7704
Year Founded: 1930
Assets: $548,009,000
Earnings: $210,415,000
Liabilities: $336,894,000
Net Worth: $211,115,000
Approx.Sls.: $974,288,000
Emp.: 2,000
Fiscal Year-end: 8/31/91
Import Export
Co-op Manufacture & Market Cranberry & Grapefruit Products
S.I.C.: 2033; 2037
Corporate Giving Program:
Cooperative $ Program Matches .50 For Every 1.00 Invested
Robert St. Jacques *(Chm. Bd.)*
John S. Llewellyn, Jr. *(Pres. & Chief Exec. Officer)*
Alexander W. Turnbull *(Sr. V.P. & Chief Fin. Officer)*
Thomas Wagner *(Sr. V.P.-Mfg.)*
Patrick M. McCarthy *(Grp. V.P.-Sls. & Mktg.)*
Kenneth J. Beeby *(V.P., Sec. & Gen. Counsel)*
Thomas Bullock *(V.P.-Retail Sls.)*

S. Woodworth Chittick *(V.P.-Plng. & Bus. Devel.)*
Lawrence Kuzminski *(V.P.-Tech. Res. & Devel.)*
James Lange *(V.P.-Mfg.)*
John S. Ropes *(V.P.-Grower Rels.)*
Michael J. Shea *(V.P.-Logistics)*
Charles R. Dulany *(Treas.)*
Nancy McDermott *(Controller)*
Richard Brooks *(Dir.-Human Resources)*
Stephen Dinsmore *(Dir.-Mktg. Services)*
John Emerson *(Dir.-Trade Mktg.)*
Mary Furlong *(Dir.-Quality Control)*
Kevin Kavanaugh *(Dir.-Food Services & Ingredients)*
Thomas Modestino *(Dir.-Mngmt. Information Systems)*
James McDonough *(Dir.-Pur.)*
Mary Ann Rood *(Dir.-Communications)*
John Lawlor *(Mgr.-Pub. Rels.)*
John Ferullo *(Mgr.-Compensation & Benefits)*
Christopher Perry *(Asst. Treasurer)*
Principal(s):
Robert St. Jacques
John S. Llewellyn, Jr.

No. of Mfg. Plants/Facilities: 6
No. of U.S. Offices: 4
No. of Foreign Offices: 1

Computer Systems/Hardware:
IBM 3083

Outside Service Firm(s):

Deloitte & Touche*(Auditors)*
125 Summer St.
Boston, MA 02110
Tel.: 617-261-8000
Fax: 617-261-8111

Employee's Insurance of Wausau*(Group Insurer)*
Wausau, WI

Kemper Insurance*(Group Insurer)*
Long Grove, IL 60049-0001

Goldman, Sachs & Co.*(Investment Banker)*
85 Broad St.
New York, NY 10004
Tel.: 212-902-1000
Fax: 212-902-4451

Springfield Bank for Co-operatives*(Major Banking Relationship)*
Springfield, MA

Subsidiary:

Milne Fruit Products **(1)**
804 Bennett Ave.
Prosser, WA 99350
Tel.: 509-786-2611
Fax: 509-786-1724
Fruit Processor/Concentrator
S.I.C.: 2037; 2087
Bob White *(Gen. Mgr.)*
John Schroeder *(Mgr.-Sls.)*

OCHOCO LUMBER COMPANY
416 Combs Flat Rd.
Prineville, OR 97754
Mailing Address:
P.O. Box 668
Prineville, OR 97754
Tel.: 503-447-6296
Fax: 503-447-3432
Year Founded: 1980
Approx.Sls.: $57,000,000
Emp.: 320
Manufacturer of Pine Fir & Other Types of Lumber
S.I.C.: 2421
S.J. Sheik, Jr. *(Pres.)*
Bruce Daucsavage *(V.P.)*

Outside Service Firm(s):

Arthur Andersen & Co.*(Auditors)*
111 S.W. Columbia, Ste. 1400
Portland, OR 97201
Tel.: 503-226-1331

First Interstate Bank*(Major Banking Relationship)*
P.O. Box 3131,
Portland, OR 97208
Tel.: 503-220-4855
Fax: 503-225-7153

O'CONNOR MACCIOLI, INC.
2828 Routh St., Ste. 590
Dallas, TX 75201
Tel.: 214-871-2225
Fax: 214-871-2536
Year Founded: 1983
Approx.Billings: $10,000,000
Emp.: 15
Retail Adv.
Ellen Cook O'Connor *(Pres.)*

OCTAGON PROCESS INC.
725 River Rd.
Edgewater, NJ 07020
Tel.: 201-945-9400 **NJ**
Fax: 201-945-1203
Year Founded: 1940
Sales Range: $20-39 Million
Emp.: 60
Fiscal Year-end: 12/31/90
Import Export
Metal Treating Chemical Compounds, Rust Proofing Phosphate Coatings & Oils, Cold Degreasing Solvents, Industrial Chemicals & Solvents, Lubricating Oils & Hydraulic Fluids, Metal Cleaning Equipment, Cleansing & Polishing Preparations, Insecticides, Commercial Aerospace Chemical Products, Aviation De-Icing & Anti-Icing Fluids, Runway De-Icing Fluids
S.I.C.: 2992; 2842; 2879; 2899
Corporate Giving Program: Supports Local Community Organizations Only
Harold Rosenberg *(Chm. Bd.)*
Louis L. Teller *(Vice Chm. & Chief Exec. Officer)*
James R. Braby *(Pres. & Chief Oper. Officer)*
Joan A. Benvenuti *(V.P.-Admin. & Sec.)*
Jane K. Hinkle *(V.P.-Sls. & Mktg.)*
Douglas P. Jackson *(V.P.-Res. & Devel.)*
Frank J. Piazza *(V.P.-Mfg.)*
Joseph J. Burgard *(Dir.-Enviornmental Compliance & Safety Admin.)*
Iris Charms *(Dir.-Product Pricing & Supply)*
Cathy Murphy *(Dir.-MIS)*
Marian Terminato *(Dir.-Acctg. & Treas.)*
Scott Braby *(Administrator-Saftey & Training)*
Antionette Maro-Koehler *(Administrator-Sls. & Mktg.)*
John Wakelin *(Mgr.-Tech. Services)*
Tom Wilson *(Mgr.-Warehouse & Traffic)*
Susan James *(Govt. Affairs Sls. Coordinator)*
Frank Kelley *(Plant Engr.)*
Principal(s):
Harold Rosenberg

No. of Mfg. Plants/Facilities: 1
No. of U.S. Offices: 2

Outside Service Firm(s):

Diamond, Kerbis & Weinstein, P.C.*(Auditors)*
New York, NY

Hobbs Group*(Commercial Insurance Carrier)*
Hackensack, NJ

Home Life Insurance Co.*(Group Insurer)*
Hackensack, NJ

Cole, Schotz, Bernstein, Meisel & Forman*(Legal Firm)*
Hackensack, NJ

National Community Bank*(Major Banking Relationship)*
Edgewater, NJ

Laiken Associates*(Pension Manager)*
605 Third Avenue
New York, NY 10158

OCTOBER FILMS, INC.
45 Rockefeller Plaza, Ste. 3014
New York, NY 10111
Tel.: 212-332-2480
Fax: 212-332-2499
Approx.Sls.: $13,000,000
Emp.: 24
Film Production & Distribution
S.I.C.: 7829
Jeff Lipsky *(Chm. Bd.)*
Amir J. Malin *(Co-Pres. & Chief Exec. Officer)*
Bingham Ray *(Co-Chief Exec. Officer)*
John Schmidt *(Co-Chief Exec. Officer)*

THE ODOM CORPORATION
26 S. Hanford
Seattle, WA 98134
Tel.: 206-623-3256 **DE**
Fax: 206-622-5112
Year Founded: 1947
Approx.Sls.: $110,000,000
Emp.: 310
Holding Company; Groceries & Related Items
S.I.C.: 6719; 5149
John P. Odom *(Co-Chm. Bd. & Chief Exec. Officer)*
William Odom *(Co-Chm. Bd.)*
Gordon Swenson *(V.P.-Fin., Treas. & Sec.)*
Jerry Dunn *(Gen. Mgr.)*

Outside Service Firm(s):

Laycock & Grundhauser*(Auditors)*
Seattle, WA

Aiken, St. Louis & Siljeg*(Legal Firm)*
Seattle, WA

Seafirst Bank*(Major Banking Relationship)*
Columbia-SeaFirst Center, 701 5th Ave., 11th Flr.
Seattle, WA 98124
Tel.: 206-358-3039
Fax: 206-358-3113

ODYSSEY PARTNERS
31 W. 52nd St., 17th Fl.
New York, NY 10019
Tel.: 212-708-0600
Telephone & Telegraph Apparatus; Children's Games/Toys
S.I.C.: 3661; 3944; 6799
Lawrence Levitt *(Chief Fin. Officer)*

Subsidiary:

Pollenex Corporation **(1)**
165 N. Canal
Chicago, IL 60606
Tel.: 312-454-5400
Tel.: 800-767-6020
Telex: 910-2212197 POLLENEX CGO
Fax: 312-454-7941
Approx.Sls.: $50,000,000
Emp.: 100
Fiscal Year-end: 5/31/92
Import Export
Computer Systems/Hardware:
IBM System AS/400
Mfr. of Air & Water Purifiers, Massagers, Massaging Showerheads, Whirlpool Baths, Footbaths, Humidifiers, Heating Pads, Fitness Equipment, Specialty Radios
S.I.C.: 3634; 3842; 3800
Elliott Millenson *(Pres.)*
Gary Bjarnson *(V.P.-Fin.)*
Alan Murry *(V.P.-Sls.)*
Joe Ford *(V.P.-Pur.)*
Don Hallagan *(Controller)*
Mary Morgan *(Dir.-Mktg.)*
Sid Kaplan *(Dir.-Adv.)*
Dale Brandt *(Dir.-Mngmt. Information Systems)*
Joyce Becella *(Mgr.-Human Resources)*
Phil Gyori *(Mgr.-Mktg.)*

Office Automation Systems, Inc.
(Name Changed To OCTus)

OFFICE CONNECTION, INC.
(Formerly Stoddard Office Supply, Inc.)
5301 N.W. 9 Ave.
Fort Lauderdale, FL 33310-9157
Tel.: 305-751-1856
Fax: 305-751-0986
Year Founded: 1957
Approx.Sls.: $10,000,000
Emp.: 70
Fiscal Year-end: 12/31/92
Retail Office Forms; Wholesale Commercial Machines & Equipment
S.I.C.: 5112; 5044; 2761
Arnold Malm *(Pres.)*
Richard Stoddard *(V.P.)*
Don Mahaffey *(V.P.)*
Steve Nipe *(V.P.)*
Vic Spellberg *(Sec.)*
Richard Thompson *(Treas.)*

OFFICE ELECTRONICS, INC.
865 W. Irving Park Rd.
Itasca, IL 60143
Tel.: 708-773-2270 **IL**
Fax: 708-773-3915
Year Founded: 1956
Assets: $36,056,000
Liabilities: $23,153,000
Net Worth: $12,903,000
Approx.Sls.: $111,300,000
Emp.: 575
Fiscal Year-end: 12/31/91
Import Export
Offset Printing; Business Forms, Tab Cards, Labels
S.I.C.: 2754; 2759; 2752; 2761
Corporate Giving Program: Contact Co. Directly for Details
Robert A. Houston *(Chm. Bd.)*
Mikel S. Briggs *(Pres.)*
Peter J. Raymond *(V.P.-Eastern Zone)*
Edward Richert *(V.P.-Fin. & Admin., & Treas.)*
John K. Stephens *(V.P.-Western Zone)*
William L. Troth *(V.P.-Mfg.)*
Charles Veit *(V.P.-Mktg.)*
John Kloempken *(Corp. Sec.)*
James F. Broz *(Controller & Asst. Treas.)*
Amy Schuett *(Dir.-Human Resources)*

No. of U.S. Offices: 16

Computer Systems/Hardware:
IBM AS/400

Outside Service Firm(s):

American National Bank & Trust Company of Chicago*(Major Banking Relationship)*
33 N. LaSalle St.
Chicago, IL 60602
Tel.: 312-661-5000
Fax: 312-661-6417

OFFICE EQUIPMENT COMPANY OF CHICAGO
223 W. Lake St.
Chicago, IL 60606
Tel.: 312-236-6016 **IL**
Fax: 312-236-6494
Approx.Sls.: $48,000,000
Emp.: 170
Wholesale Distributor of Office Furniture
S.I.C.: 5021
Raymond R. Rha *(Pres.)*
R.R. Riha, Jr. *(V.P.)*
Fred Trumm *(V.P.)*
Frances Riha *(Sec. & Treas.)*

Office Equipment Company Of Chicago—(Continued)

Outside Service Firm(s):

LaSalle National Bank*(Major Banking Relationship)*
120 S. LaSalle St.
Chicago, IL 60603
Tel.: 312-781-8000

C.M. OFFRAY & SON INC.
P.O. Box 601, Rte. 24
Chester, NJ 07930
Tel.: 908-879-4700
Telex: 837724
Fax: 908 879 8585
Approx.Sls.: $15,000,000
Ribbons, Bindings, Webbings & Tapes
S.I.C.: 3269
Claude Offray, Jr. *(Pres. & Chief Exec. Officer)*

Subsidiaries:

Lion Ribbon Company **(1)**
100 Metro Way
Secaucus, NJ 07094
Tel.: 201-348-4500
Creates Decorative Ribbon for the Florist Industry
S.I.C.: 3269
James McDermott *(Chief Oper. Officer)*

Maryland Ribbon Company **(1)**
857 Willow Circle
Hagerstown, MD 21740
Tel.: 301-739-6314
Woven & Craft Ribbons
S.I.C.: 3269
Philip Portner *(Gen. Mgr.)*

OGLETHORPE POWER CORP.
2100 E. Exchange Pl.
Tucker, GA 30085
Mailing Address:
P.O. Box 1349
Tucker, GA 30085
Tel.: 404-270-7600 **GA**
Fax: 404-270-7872
Year Founded: 1974
Approx.Sls.: $1,000,000,000
Emp.: 550
Fiscal Year-end: 12/30/91
Electric Utility Cooperative
S.I.C.: 4911
J. Calvin Earwood *(Chm. Bd.)*
Sammy Jenkins *(Vice Chm.)*
Tom D. Kilgore *(Pres. & Chief Exec. Officer)*
Charles T. Autry *(Sr. V.P.-Governmental Affairs & Gen. Counsel)*
George Heckman *(Sr. V.P.-Capital Projects)*
Gene Heckl *(Sr. V.P.-Fin. Acctng.)*
G. Stanley Hill *(Sr. V.P.-Mktg. & Customer Service)*
Jerry Pate *(V.P.-External Affairs)*
John S. Dean *(Sec. & Treas.)*

Outside Service Firm(s):

Arthur Andersen & Co.*(Auditors)*
133 Peachtree St., N.E.
Atlanta, GA 30303
Tel.: 404-658-1776

Smith Barney, Harris Upham & Company, Inc.*(Investment Banker)*
1345 Avenue of the Americas
New York, NY
Tel.: 212-698-6559
Fax: 212-698-5735

Paul, Hastings, Janofsky & Walker*(Legal Firm)*
Atlanta, GA

Trust Company Bank*(Major Banking Relationship)*
Stock Trans. Dept. P.O.B. 4625, Trust Company of Georgia Bldg.
Atlanta, GA 30302
Tel.: 404-588-7831

OH BOY CORPORATION
1516 First St.
San Fernando, CA 91340
Tel.: 818-361-1128
Fax: 818-361-7651
Approx.Sls.: $14,000,000
Emp.: 195
Fiscal Year-end: 12/31/90
Oh Boy Sandwiches, Italian Brand Fruit Ices, Pizzas, Stuffed Frozen Potatoes, Garlic Bread & Italian Specialties
S.I.C.: 2099; 2038; 2037
Pietro Vitale *(Pres.)*
Lou De Vita *(Exec. V.P.)*

O'HALLORAN ADVERTISING, INC.
116 Danbury Rd.
Wilton, CT 06897
Tel.: 203-762-0054
Year Founded: 1971
Approx.Billings: $10,000,000
National Yellow Pages
James J. O'Halloran *(Pres.)*
Lynn O'Halloran *(V.P., Treas.)*
Mark O'Halloran *(V.P., Client Services & Sls.)*
Gordon Hewetson *(Opers. Supvr.)*
Chantal Donaghy *(Admin. Supvr.)*

OHAUS CORPORATION
29 Hanover Rd.
Florham Park, NJ 07932
Tel.: 201-377-9000
Tel.: 800-672-7722
Telex: 6853191 Ohaus UW
Fax: 201-593-0359
Year Founded: 1907
Emp.: 350
Export
Mfr. Mechanical & Electronic Balances
S.I.C.: 3596; 3821
James Ohaus *(Pres.)*
Steve Drozdow *(V.P.-Sls. & Mktg.)*
John Powers *(V.P.-Fin. & Opers.)*
Richard G. Stebbins *(Controller)*
Paul Fein *(Dir.-Human Resources)*
Mike Zakrzewski *(Natl. Sls. Mgr.)*
Paula Mylenki *(Supvr.-Mktg. Communications)*

Computer Systems/Hardware:
IBM System 38

Outside Service Firm(s):

Price Waterhouse*(Auditors)*
4 Headquarters Plaza North, 9th Fl.
Morristown, NJ 07962
Tel.: 201-540-8980

Pitney, Hardin, Kipp & Szuch*(Legal Firm)*
163 Madison Ave.
Morristown, NJ 07960
Tel.: 201-267-3333

First Fidelity Bank, N.A.*(Major Banking Relationship)*
Florham Park, NJ

OHIO GAS COMPANY
200 W. High
Bryan, OH 43506
Tel.: 419-636-1117
Tel.: 800-331-7396
Year Founded: 1914
Approx.Sls.: $32,800,000
Emp.: 103
Fiscal Year-end: 12/31/91
Natural Gas Utility
S.I.C.: 4924
J.L. Tuttle *(Pres. & Chief Exec. Officer)*
Richard P. Hallett *(V.P.)*
J.C. Webster *(V.P. & Chief Engineer)*
G.A. Richards *(Treas.)*
Kim A. Watkins *(Controller)*
Myrna L. Tuttle *(Sec.)*
Todd Campbell *(Pur. Agent)*

Computer Systems/Hardware:
NCR

OHIO LOTTERY COMMISSION
615 W. Superior
Cleveland, OH 44113
Tel.: 216-787-3200
Fax: 216-787-3718
Year Founded: 1974
Approx.Sls.: $1,600,000,000
Emp.: 300
Fiscal Year-end: 6/30/91
Lottery Games of Chance, Computerized & Instant Scratch-Offs
S.I.C.: 7999
Irene Kay *(Commission Chm.)*
Virgal E. Crown *(Exec. Dir.)*
Michael M. Migieliez *(Asst. Exec. Dir.)*
John P. Forristal *(Deputy Dir.-Admin.)*
Sandy Lesko Mounts *(Deputy Dir.-Pub. Rels.)*
Cynthia Rowser *(Deputy Dir.-Sls.)*
Dennis Smolinski *(Deputy Dir.-Opers.)*
Cathlean G. Weiss *(Chief Legal Counsel)*
Stephen E. DeJohn *(Legal Counsel)*

OHIO MACHINERY CO.
3993 E. Royalton Rd.
Cleveland, OH 44147
Tel.: 216-526-6200 **OH**
Fax: 216-526-9513
Year Founded: 1946
Approx.Sls.: $90,000,000
Emp.: 340
Fiscal Year-end: 12/31/90
Caterpillar Tractor Distributor
S.I.C.: 5082; 7538
Thomas H. Taylor, Jr. *(Pres. & Chief Exec. Officer)*
Robert E. Hammel *(Chief Fin. Officer, Treas. & Sec.)*
Carl W. Bowen *(Controller)*
Paul Liesem *(V.P.-Sls.)*
Kelly Love *(V.P.-Mktg.)*
Richard Johnston *(Dir.-Data Processing)*

No. of U.S. Offices: 6

Computer Systems/Hardware:
Sperry Univac 1171

Outside Service Firm(s):

Ernst & Young*(Auditors)*
1300 Huntington Bldg.
Cleveland, OH 44115
Tel.: 216-861-5000

Caterpiller Insurance Co.*(Commercial Insurance Carrier)*
St. Paul, MN

John Hancock Mutual Life Insurance Co.*(Group Insurer)*
John Hancock Place, P.O. Box 111
Boston, MA 02117

Zellmer & Gruber*(Legal Firm)*
Cleveland, OH

National City Bank*(Major Banking Relationship)*
P.O. Box 92301, Corp. Trust Dept.
Cleveland, OH 44101
Tel.: 216-575-2000

Society National Bank*(Pension Manager)*
127 Public Square
Cleveland, OH 44114
Tel.: 216-689-3000

OHIO RIVER ASSOCIATES, INC.
State Rt. 7, 2 Miles N.
Hannibal, OH 43931
Tel.: 614-483-1381
Fax: 614-483-2622
Holding Company
S.I.C.: 6719
R.E. Boyle *(Chm. Bd. & Chief Exec. Officer)*
Alex Nagem *(Controller)*
Debra Boger *(Sec.)*

Outside Service Firm(s):

Price Waterhouse*(Auditors)*
600 Grant St., Ste. 4400
Pittsburgh, PA 15219
Tel.: 412-355-6000
Fax: 412-391-0609

Eckert, Seamans, Cherin & Mellott*(Legal Firm)*
600 Grant St., 42nd Fl.
Pittsburgh, PA 15219
Tel.: 412-566-6000

Mellon Bank, N.A.*(Major Banking Relationship)*
Portland, OR

Subsidiary:

Ormet Corporation **(1)**
State Rt. 7, 2 Miles N
Hannibal, OH 43931
Tel.: 614-483-1381
Emp.: 1,700
Manufacture Primary Aluminum
S.I.C.: 3334
R.E. Boyle *(Chm. Bd., Pres. & Chief Exec. Officer)*
T.G. Temple *(V.P.-Aluminum Opers.)*
Debra J. Boger *(Sec.)*

OHIO TRANSMISSION CORPORATION
666 Parsons Ave.
Columbus, OH 43206
Tel.: 614-444-2172 **OH**
Fax: 614-444-1235
Approx.Sls.: $35,000,000
Emp.: 175
Industrial Machinery & Equipment; Materials Handling Machinery, Compressors Except Air Conditioning; Pumps & Pumping Equipment
S.I.C.: 5084
David D. Derrow *(Chm. Bd.)*
George Babyak *(Pres.)*
Alida L. Breen *(V.P.-Fin.)*

Outside Service Firm(s):

KPMG Peat Marwick*(Auditors)*
Two Nationwide Plaza
Columbus, OH 43215
Tel.: 614-249-2300

Riley, Ucker & Lavinsky*(Legal Firm)*
Colubmus, OH

BancOhio National Bank*(Major Banking Relationship)*
Columbus, OH

OHIO VALLEY ELECTRIC CORPORATION
U.S. Rte. 23
Piketon, OH 45661
Mailing Address:
P.O. Box 468
Piketon, OH 45661
Tel.: 614-289-2376 **OH**
Fax: 614-289-2376, Ext. 253
Year Founded: 1952
Assets: $140,762,321
Liabilities: $130,730,483
Net Worth: $10,031,838
Emp.: 789
Fiscal Year-end: 12/31/90
Electrical Company
S.I.C.: 4911
R.E. Disbrow *(Pres.)*
David L. Hart *(V.P. & Asst to Pres.)*
David E. Jones *(V.P.-Opers.)*
G. Maloney *(V.P.)*
John D. Brodt *(Treas. & Sec.)*

Outside Service Firm(s):

Arthur Andersen & Co.*(Auditors)*
Columbus, OH

Wyatt Co.*(Group Insurer)*
1700 One Penn Center, 1617 Kennedy Blvd.
Philadelphia, PA 19103
Tel.: 215-569-4393

Simpson, Thacher & Bartlett*(Legal Firm)*
Columbus, OH

Subsidiary:

Indiana Kentucky Electric Corporation **(1)**
P.O. Box 468
Piketon, OH 45661
Tel.: 614-289-2376
Electric Utility
S.I.C.: 4911

OHMITE MANUFACTURING COMPANY
3601 Howard St.
Skokie, IL 60076
Tel.: 708-675-2600
Fax: 708-675-1505
Year Founded: 1927
Assets: $12,300,000
Liabilities: $9,300,000
Net Worth: $3,000,000
Approx.Sls.: $25,000,000
Emp.: 300
Fiscal Year-end: 12/31/90
Import Export
Produces Resistors & Rheostats
S.I.C.: 3676; 3679
Max D. Sanders *(Chm. Bd. & Pres.)*
Bill Acuff *(Dir.-Mfg.)*
Howard Bloom *(Dir.-Fin.)*
Elizabeth Maciejewski *(Dir.-Personnel)*
Alex Weissner *(Pur. Agent)*
Principal(s):
Max D. Sanders

No. of Mfg. Plants/Facilities: 3
No. of U.S. Offices: 2

Outside Service Firm(s):

KPMG Peat Marwick*(Auditors)*
Peat Marwick Plaza, 303 E. Wacker Dr.
Chicago, IL 60601
Tel.: 312-938-1000

Gardner Denver*(Legal Firm)*
Chicago, IL

Cole Taylor Bank*(Major Banking Relationship)*
Skokie, IL

OIL & GAS SUPPLY COMPANY
8601 Boone Rd.
Houston, TX 77099
Tel.: 713-498-6331
Fax: 713-498-4464
Approx.Sls.: $15,000,000
Emp.: 50
Manufacture Air & Gas Compressors
S.I.C.: 3563
William F. Joplin *(Pres.)*
John F. Joplin *(V.P.)*
Jean Joplin *(Treas. & Sec.)*
Steve Beverding *(Controller)*
Bob Linsemeyer *(Mgr.-Sls.)*
Will Richmond *(Gen. Mgr.)*
Don Watters *(Pur. Agent)*

Outside Service Firm(s):

Ernst & Young*(Auditors)*
1 Houston Ctr., 1200 McKinney
Houston, TX 77002
Tel.: 713-750-1500

Bracewell & Patterson*(Legal Firm)*
2900 South Tower, Pennzoil Place
Houston, TX 77002
Tel.: 713-223-2900

Cullen Center Bank & Trust*(Major Banking Relationship)*
Houston, TX

O'KEEFFE'S, INC.
75 Williams Ave.
San Francisco, CA 94124
Tel.: 415-822-4222
Tel.: 800-227-3305 CA
Fax: 415-822-5222
Approx.Sls.: $15,000,000
Emp.: 100
Import Export
Custom & Standard Glass & Plastic Skylights, Smoke Vents, Glass Fire Doors & Walls, Aluminum Ladders; Architectural Metal & Sheet Work
S.I.C.: 3211; 3083; 3442; 3449; 5039
William F. O'Keeffe *(Pres.)*
A. Garrett *(V.P.)*
Nick Luria *(Gen. Mgr.)*
Stacey Westhoff *(Dir.-Mktg. & Adv.)*
Mike Vizcarra *(Mgr.-Standard Sls.)*
Jim Watkins *(Mgr.-Custom Sls.)*

Outside Service Firm(s):

Moss Adams*(Auditors)*
San Francisco, CA

First Interstate Bank*(Major Banking Relationship)*
345 California St., 8th Flr.
San Francisco, CA 94104
Tel.: 415-773-7801

Subsidiary:

Safety And Fire Technology, Inc. **(1)**
1240 Fitzgerald St.
San Francisco, CA 94124
Tel.: 415-822-4234
Tel.: 800-822-5222
Distributor of Fire & Safety Rated Glass
William O'Keeffe *(Pres.)*
Kirk Ratzel *(V.P.)*

THE OKONITE COMPANY
102 Hilltop Rd.
Ramsey, NJ 07446
Mailing Address:
P.O. Box 340,
Ramsey, NJ 07446
Tel.: 201-825-0300 NJ
Fax: 201-825-7633
Year Founded: 1878
Assets: $148,000,000
Liabilities: $79,000,000
Net Worth: $69,000,000
Approx.Sls.: $298,000,000
Emp.: 1,400
Fiscal Year-end: 12/31/90
Export
Manufacture Wire & Cable
S.I.C.: 3357
Victor A. Viggiano *(Chm. Bd.)*
Alfred C. Coppola *(Pres. & Chief Oper. Officer)*
William Blowers *(V.P.-Mngmt. Information Systems)*
Robert T. Brennan *(V.P.-Fin.)*
Jack S. Lasky *(V.P.-Research & Engrng.)*
Donald Nelson *(V.P.-Mfg.)*
Frank R. Postma *(V.P.-Mktg.)*
Robert A. Sauerwein *(V.P. & Controller)*
Thomas M. Scanlon *(V.P.-Employee Rels.)*
Donald F. Schwamb, Jr. *(V.P.-Sls.)*
David J. Sokira *(V.P. & Treas.)*
Richard Brill *(Dir.-Pur.)*

No. of Mfg. Plants/Facilities: 5
No. of U.S. Offices: 27

Computer Systems/Hardware:
IBM 4300

Outside Service Firm(s):

Coopers & Lybrand*(Auditors)*
Morris County Financial Center, One Sylvan Way
Parsippany, NJ 07054

Travelers Insurance Co.*(Group Insurer)*
1 Tower Square
Hartford, CT 06183-2492
Tel.: 203-277-4542
Fax: 203-277-5038

Lowenstein, Sandler, Kohl, Fisher & Boylan*(Legal Firm)*
65 Livingston Ave.
Roseland, NJ 07068
Tel.: 908-992-8700

Midlantic National Bank*(Major Banking Relationship)*
West Paterson, NJ

National Westminster Bank plc*(Major Banking Relationship)*
Teaneck, NJ

The Northern Trust Co.*(Pension Manager)*
50 S. LaSalle St.
Chicago, IL 60675
Tel.: 312-630-6000
Fax: 312-630-6516

OLD AMERICAN POTTERY COMPANY
811 N. Collins Fwy. 75 N.
Howe, TX 75459
Tel.: 903-532-5547 TX
Fax: 903-532-6762
Year Founded: 1988
Approx.Sls.: $50,000,000
Emp.: 650
Retail Sales of Artifical Flowers; Ready Made Picture Frames; Wicker, Rattan Or Reed Home Furnishings
S.I.C.: 5999; 5719
Wayne Brush *(Pres.)*
Bob Mickey *(Chief Fin. Officer)*
Johnny Hightower *(V.P.-Adv.)*
Max Johnson *(V.P.)*

Outside Service Firm(s):

Groos Bank*(Major Banking Relationship)*
San Antonio, TX

OLD DUTCH FOODS, INC.
2375 Terminal Rd.
Saint Paul, MN 55113
Tel.: 612-633-8810
Fax: 612-633-8894
Approx.Sls.: $48,000,000
Emp.: 400
Fiscal Year-end: 12/31/90
Produces Old Dutch Potato Chips, Corn Chips, Cheese Corn, Carmel Corn, Popcorn, Pretzels, Nuts & Other Items
S.I.C.: 2096; 2064; 2099
Vernon O. Aanenson *(Pres. & Treas.)*
Lewis J. Buckingham, Jr. *(Gen. Sls. Mgr.)*

OLD HOME FOODS, INC.
370 University Ave.
Saint Paul, MN 55103
Tel.: 612-228-9035 MN
Fax: 612-228-1820
Sales Range: $10-19 Million
Emp.: 100
Manufacture Dairy Products
S.I.C.: 2026; 2021; 2023
George V. Hanson *(Chm. Bd., Pres. & Chief Exec. Officer)*
Larry B. Oppegaard *(Chief Fin. Officer & Exec. V.P.)*
Chuck Bailey *(V.P.)*
Joel P. Bachul *(V.P.)*
June C. Harris *(V.P. & Sec.)*
John Bonifaci *(Treas. & Controller)*
Ardell Baldwin *(Dir.-Mfg.)*
Mike Punton *(Dir.-Mktg. & Adv.)*
Nancy Rose *(Dir.-Quality Control)*
Bob Long *(Mgr.-Sls.)*
Principal(s):
George V. Hanson
June C. Harris
Richard G. Hanson

No. of Mfg. Plants/Facilities: 1
No. of U.S. Offices: 1

Outside Service Firm(s):

McGladrey & Pullen*(Auditors)*
1800 Town Square, 445 Minnesota St.
St. Paul, MN 55101

Felhaber, Larson, Fenlon & Vogt*(Legal Firm)*
222 S. Ninth St., Ste. 1935
Minneapolis, MN 55402
Tel.: 612-339-6321
Fax: 612-339-4714

First Bank of St. Paul*(Major Banking Relationship)*
St. Paul, MN

OLD QUAKER PAINT CO.
2209 S. Main St.
Santa Ana, CA 92707
Tel.: 714-540-2155
Fax: 714-556-6626
Year Founded: 1939
Approx.Sls.: $30,000,000
Emp.: 182
Manufacture & Retail Paints, Lacquers, Enamels & Allied Products
S.I.C.: 2851; 5231
Ronald S. Goodman *(Pres.)*
Michael B. Goodman *(V.P.)*
Ted Bachrach *(Dir.-Prod. & Pur.-Raw Materials)*
Richard Rante *(Dir.-Fin.)*

Outside Service Firm(s):

Friedman, Rosenthal & Co.*(Auditors)*
Los Angeles, CA

Janoff, Karpel & Company*(Legal Firm)*
Carson City, CA

Bank of America NT&SA*(Major Banking Relationship)*
Carson City, CA

OLD STONE OF CALIFORNIA, INC.
9449 Balboa Ave., Ste.300
San Diego, CA 92133
Tel.: 619-492-9000
Makes Commercial & Residential Construction Loans
S.I.C.: 6159
Berit N. Durler *(Pres. & Chief Exec. Officer)*

Subsidiary:

Old Stone Bank of California **(1)**
24970 Hesperian Blvd.
Hayward, CA 94545
Tel.: 510-887-6000
Approx.Assets: $269,000,000
Banking
S.I.C.: 6011
Loretta M. Pain *(Pres. & Chief Exec. Officer)*

OLD WORLD INDUSTRIES, INC.
(Formerly Old World Trading Company, Inc.)
4065 Commercial Ave.
Northbrook, IL 60062
Tel.: 708-559-2000 IL
Fax: 708-559-1329
Year Founded: 1968
Emp.: 200
Import Export
Mfr. Automotive & Industrial Chemicals, Including Windshield Wiper Fluid & Antifreeze
S.I.C.: 2819; 2899
Tom Hurvis *(Chm. Bd.)*
Steven Warrenfeltz *(Pres. & Chief Exec. Officer)*
Riaz Waraich *(Mng. Dir.)*
Mark Allbers *(V.P. & Controller)*

No. of Mfg. Plants/Facilities: 2
No. of U.S. Offices: 16
No. of Foreign Offices: 2

Computer Systems/Hardware:
AS400 HFA

Outside Service Firm(s):

Duggan & Clesceri*(Auditors)*
Chicago, IL

Old World Industries, Inc.—(Continued)

Boulevard Bank*(Major Banking Relationship)*
410 N. Michigan Ave.
Chicago, IL 60611
Tel.: 312-836-6500

Subsidiary:

Old World Automotive Products **(1)**
4065 Commercial Ave.
Northbrook, IL 60062
Tel.: 708-559-2000
Fax: 708-559-1329
Computer Systems/Hardware:
AS400/HFA
Mfr. Antifreeze
S.I.C.: 2899
Steven Warrenfeltz *(Chief Exec. Officer)*
Michael Barcam *(Pres.)*
Rick Jago *(Mktg. Dir.)*
Tim Burns *(Sls. Dir.)*

Splitfire, Inc. **(1)**
4065 Commercial Ave.
Northbrook, IL 60062
Tel.: 708-559-2000
Fax: 708-559-1329
Computer Systems/Hardware:
AS400/HFA
Mfr. of Splitfire Spark Plugs
S.I.C.: 3624
Michael Baucum *(Pres.)*
Rick Jago *(Mktg. Dir.)*
Mike Wilson *(Sls. Mgr.)*

THE OLDENBURG GROUP COMPANIES

8600 W. Bradley
Milwaukee, WI 53224
Tel.: 414-357-8600
Fax: 414-357-8613
Holding Company
S.I.C.: 6719
Wayne C. Oldenburg *(Pres. & Chief Exec. Officer)*
David Drury *(Chief Fin. Officer & Exec. V.P.)*

Outside Service Firm(s):

Price Waterhouse*(Auditors)*
1500 Bank One Plaza, 100 E. Wisconsin Ave.
Milwaukee, WI 53202

Foley & Lardner*(Legal Firm)*
777 E. Wisconsin Ave.
Milwaukee, WI 53202
Tel.: 414-271-2400

First Wisconsin National Bank*(Major Banking Relationship)*
777 E. Wisconsin Ave.
Milwaukee, WI 53202
Tel.: 414-765-4321
Fax: 414-355-6903

Subsidiary:

Lake Shore, Inc. **(1)**
900 W. Breitung Ave.
Kingsford, MI 49801
Tel.: 906-774-1500
Fax: 906-744-1500, Ext. 501
Sales Range: $80-99 Million
Emp.: 560
Wayne C. Oldenburg *(Pres. & Chief Exec. Officer)*
E. Coughlin *(Exec. V.P.)*
R. Lehmann *(V.P.-Mining)*
Stephen Burkhammer *(V.P.-Mfg.)*
Lon Prekop *(Controller)*

L. L. OLDS SEED COMPANY

2901 Packers Ave.
Madison, WI 53704
Mailing Address:
P.O. Box 7790
Madison, WI 53707-7790
Tel.: 608-249-9291
Fax: 608-249-0695
Year Founded: 1888
Approx.Sls.: $11,000,000
Emp.: 75
Fiscal Year-end: 10/31/91
Old Gold Brand & Agripro Brand Forage Seeds, Olds Brand Seed Corn
S.I.C.: 0181; 0115
Raymond Reisdorf *(Pres.)*
Carolyn Becker *(Chief Fin. Officer)*
Robert O'Donnell *(Dir.-Sls.)*
Chris Wendrof *(Pur. Agent)*

VIC OLESEN & PARTNERS, INC.

1631 Pontius Ave.
Los Angeles, CA 90025
Tel.: 310-479-8999 **CA**
Fax: 310-479-8006
Year Founded: 1984
Approx.Billings: $18,000,000
Emp.: 10
Advertising Agency
S.I.C.: 7311
Victor L. Olesen *(Pres.)*
Bill Donaldson *(Partner)*
Principal(s):
Victor L. Olesen
Irwin S. Davis
Eric Davison
Bill Donaldson

No. of U.S. Offices: 2

Outside Service Firm(s):

Arthur Andersen & Co.*(Auditors)*
633 W. Fifth St.
Los Angeles, CA 90071
Tel.: 213-614-6500

Aetna Life & Casualty*(Group Insurer)*
151 Farmington Avenue
Hartford, CT 06156
Tel.: 203-273-2128
Fax: 203-729-4295

Branch:

Vic Olesen & Partners, Inc. **(1)**
2350 Franklin, Ste. 230
Bloomfield Hills, MI 48302
Tel.: 313-333-7530
Fax: 313-335-5997
S.I.C.: 7311
Mike Breazeale *(Gen. Mgr.)*

B. OLINDE & SONS COMPANY, INC.

9536 Airline Hwy.
Baton Rouge, LA 70815
Tel.: 504-926-3380
Fax: 504-924-2063
Year Founded: 1900
Approx.Sls.: $26,000,000
Emp.: 100
Wholesale Beer; Retail Furniture; Financial Agency; Wholesale & Retail Miscellaneous Commodities
S.I.C.: 5181; 5199; 5712; 5999
J. Beauregard Olinde *(Pres.)*
Humphrey T. Olinde, Jr. *(Treas. & Sec.)*

Outside Service Firm(s):

H. J. Lowe & Associates*(Auditors)*
Baton Rouge, LA

Kantrow, Spaht, Weaver & Blitzer*(Legal Firm)*
P.O. Box 2997
Baton Rouge, LA 70821
Tel.: 504-383-4703

Baton Rouge Bank & Trust Company*(Major Banking Relationship)*
Baton Rouge, LA

OLIVER OIL COMPANY, INC.

875 S. Main St.
Chambersburg, PA 17201
Tel.: 717-264-5165 **PA**
Year Founded: 1966
Approx.Sls.: $24,000,000
Emp.: 110
Fuel Oil Dealers; Filling Stations; Petroleum Bulk Stations
S.I.C.: 5983; 5541; 5171
Richard Mackey, Jr. *(Pres.)*
Richard Mackey, Sr. *(V.P.)*
Carlton Speer *(V.P. & Sec.)*
Randall Zook *(Treas.)*

Outside Service Firm(s):

Miller & Company*(Auditors)*
York, PA

Valley Bank & Trust Co.*(Major Banking Relationship)*
Chambersburg, PA

OLIVER PRODUCTS COMPANY

445 6th St., N.W.
Grand Rapids, MI 49504
Tel.: 616-456-7711 **MI**
Fax: 616-456-7791
Year Founded: 1981
Approx.Sls.: $18,000,000
Emp.: 180
Mfr. of Bakery Machinery; Commercial Lithographic Label Printing
S.I.C.: 2752
Victor P. Tuthill *(Chm. Bd.)*
Robert L. Porter *(Pres. & Chief Oper. Officer)*
Joseph Schmieder *(V.P.-Sls. & Mktg.)*
Albert R. Gauthier *(Controller & Treas.)*
Susan Hammer *(Sec.)*

Outside Service Firm(s):

Old Kent Bank & Trust Co.*(Major Banking Relationship)*
One Vandenberg Center
Grand Rapids, MI 49503
Tel.: 616-774-5000

JOHN M. OLSON COMPANY

26210 Harper
Saint Clair Shores, MI 48081
Tel.: 313-771-9330
Fax: 313-771-2440
Approx.Sls.: $19,000,000
Emp.: 28
Commercial & Industrial Contractor
S.I.C.: 1541; 1542
John M. Olson *(Pres.)*

Outside Service Firm(s):

Danville & Deering*(Auditors)*
Detroit, MI

First America Bank*(Major Banking Relationship)*
Detroit, MI

OLSON RUG COMPANY

832 S. Central Ave.
Chicago, IL 60644
Tel.: 312-921-1300 **DE**
Year Founded: 1874
Approx.Sls.: $25,000,000
Emp.: 95
Fiscal Year-end: 12/31/90
Carpet Retailer
S.I.C.: 5713
Richard Walters *(Pres.)*
John Kosik *(Controller)*
Beverly Brennan *(Dir.-Adv. & Mktg.)*

No. of Mfg. Plants/Facilities: 14

Computer Systems/Hardware:
Motorola Phase 4

Outside Service Firm(s):

Goldstein, Berger & Co.*(Auditors)*
Chicago, IL

Pfeiffer & Associates*(Legal Firm)*
Chicago, IL

Oak Park Trust & Savings Bank*(Major Banking Relationship)*
Oak Park, IL

OLSON-TRAVELWORLD LTD.

1334 Parkview Ave., Ste. 210
Manhattan Beach, CA 90266
Tel.: 310-546-8400
Fax: 310-546-8450
Approx.Sls.: $20,000,000
Emp.: 40
Foreign & Superior Domestic Travel Tours; Deluxe & First Class to Europe, To Orient & China, Africa, India, South Pacific, South America; Independent Vacations
S.I.C.: 4724
David Elmore *(Chm. Bd. & Pres.)*
Dawn Suart *(Chief Exec. Officer)*
Joanne Sterbenz *(Chief Fin. Officer & Treas.)*

Computer Systems/Hardware:
Prime

Outside Service Firm(s):

Grant Thornton*(Auditors)*
700 One Prudential Plaza, 130 East Randolph St.
Chicago, IL 60601
Tel.: 312-856-0200
Fax: 312-565-4719

Metropolitan Life Insurance Co.*(Group Insurer)*
One Madison Avenue
New York, NY 10010-3690

First Interstate Bank*(Major Banking Relationship)*
Glendale, CA

OLSONITE CORPORATION

8801 Conant Ave.
Detroit, MI 48211-1403
Tel.: 313-875-5831
Fax: 313-874-2846
Year Founded: 1905
Approx.Sls.: $35,000,000
Emp.: 500
Manufacturer Plastic Seats
S.I.C.: 3089; 3325; 3714
Oscar L. Olson *(Chm. Bd. & Chief Exec. Officer)*
Thomas A. Caponi *(Pres.)*
Marjory Williams *(Pur. Agent)*

Outside Service Firm(s):

Coopers & Lybrand*(Auditors)*
400 Renaissance Center
Detroit, MI 48243
Tel.: 313-446-7100
Fax: 313-446-7117

Peoples State Bank*(Major Banking Relationship)*
Detroit, MI

OLTMANS CONSTRUCTION COMPANY

10005 Mission Mill Rd.
Whittier, CA 90608
Tel.: 310-948-4242
Fax: 310-695-2939
Year Founded: 1928
Approx.Sls.: $150,000,000
Emp.: 350
Construction Contractors
S.I.C.: 1542
Robert M. Holmes *(Chm. Bd. & Chief Exec. Officer)*
Joseph O. Oltmans, II *(Pres.)*
Basil Johnson *(V.P.)*
Robert C. Roy *(V.P.)*
John E. Rowe *(Treas. & Sec.)*

Outside Service Firm(s):

KPMG Peat Marwick*(Auditors)*
725 S. Figueroa St.
Los Angeles, CA 90017
Tel.: 213-972-4000

Acret & Perrochet*(Legal Firm)*
Los Angeles, CA

Security Pacific Corporation*(Major Banking Relationship)*
Security Pacific Plaza
Los Angeles, CA 90071
Tel.: 213-345-6211
Fax: 213-625-0809

OLYMPIC STEEL INC.
5080 Richmond Rd.
Bedford Heights, OH 44146
Tel.: 216-292-3800
Tel.: 800-321-6290 **OH**
Fax: 216-292-3974
Year Founded: 1954
Assets: $120,431,000
Earnings: $7,916,000
Liabilities: $101,010,000
Net Worth: $19,421,000
Approx.Sls.: $260,000,000
Emp.: 380
Fiscal Year-end: 12/31/90

Import Export
Carbon & Stainless Steel, Aluminum & Alloy Service Center
S.I.C.: 5051
Sol Siegal *(Chm. Bd.)*
Harvey Adelstein *(Vice Chm.)*
Michael D. Siegal *(Pres. & Chief Exec. & Chief Oper. Officer)*
Bruce S. Adelstein *(Exec. V.P. & Sec.)*
R. Louis Schneeberger *(V.P. & Chief Fin. Officer)*
David Wolfort *(V.P.)*
Ronald Stalle *(Dir.-Mngmt. Information Systems)*
Toni White *(Dir.-Human Resources)*
Jose Jandenes *(Gen. Mgr.-Import & Export)*
Kim Buhrow *(Mgr.-Personnel)*
Darrel Johnson *(Mgr.-Pur.)*
Dan Radish *(Mgr.-Fin. Reporting)*
Debbie Jadrych *(Analyst-Mngmt. Information Systems)*

Principal(s):
Bruce S. Adelstein
R. Louis Schneeberger
Michael D. Siegal
David Wolfort

No. of Mfg. Plants/Facilities: 6
No. of U.S. Offices: 8

Computer Systems/Hardware:
Digital Equipment

Outside Service Firm(s):

Arthur Andersen & Co.*(Auditors)*
1717 E. 9th St.
Cleveland, OH 44114
Tel.: 216-781-2140
Fax: 216-781-3683

McDonough Caperton Insurance Group*(Commercial Insurance Carrier)*
Cleveland, OH

Cigna*(Group Insurer)*
525 W. Monroe St., Ste. 1900
Chicago, IL 60606
Tel.: 312-648-3742

Kahn, Kleinman, Yanowitz & Arnson*(Legal Firm)*
1301 East Ninth St., Ste. 2600
Cleveland, OH 44114
Tel.: 216-696-3311
Fax: 216-696-1009

National City Bank*(Major Banking Relationship)*
P.O. Box 92301, Corp. Trust Dept.
Cleveland, OH 44101
Tel.: 216-575-2000

Division:

Eastern Steel & Metal Company **(1)**
1 Eastern Steel Rd.
Milford, CT 06460
Tel.: 203-878-9381
Fax: 203-877-9819
Approx.Sls.: $85,000,000
Emp.: 100
Cold & Hot Rolled Sheet & Strip, Galvanized & Electro Zinc Coated & In Coils, Sheets, Blanks, Warehouse Distribution & Processor
S.I.C.: 5051; 5033; 5039
Ron Trone *(Gen. Mgr.)*

OMAHA CREATIVE GROUP

P.O. Box 3300, 10909 John Galt Blvd.
Omaha, NE 68103
Tel.: 402-597-3000
Tel.: 800-228-2778
Fax: 402-597-8120
Year Founded: 1980
Approx.Billings: $12,000,000
Emp.: 10
Direct Marketing of Steaks & Gourmet Foods
Frederick J. Simon *(Chm. Bd. & Pres.)*
Curtis Todd *(V.P., Controller)*
Vickie Hagen *(Gen. Mgr.)*
Stephen H. Simon *(Sec.)*
Alan D. Simon *(Treas.)*
Marilyn Pred *(Dir., Pub. Rels.)*
Laura Ramirez *(Telecommunications)*

OMAHA PUBLIC POWER DISTRICT
Energy Plaza, 444 S. 16th St. Mall
Omaha, NE 68102-2247
Tel.: 402-636-2000 **NE**
Telex: 402-636-3229
Fax: 402-636-3229
Year Founded: 1946
Assets: $1,833,577,000
Earnings: $35,339,000
Liabilities: $1,197,882,000
Net Worth: $635,695,000
Approx.Sls.: $382,000,000
Emp.: 2,450
Fiscal Year-end: 12/31/91
Electric Utility Company Providing Services for Southeast Nebraska
S.I.C.: 4911
Frank J. Wear *(Chm. Bd.)*
Fred M. Petersen *(Pres., Chief Exec. Officer & Chief Oper. Officer)*
Eldon C. Pape *(Chief Fin. Officer, Chief Plng. Officer & Exec. V.P.)*
Ken Fielding *(Chief Information Officer)*
William Dermyer *(V.P.)*
William C. Jones *(V.P.)*
Dayton D. Wittke *(V.P.)*
John Green *(Treas.)*
Michael O'Hara *(Sec.)*
John Leifert *(Mgr.-Pension Admin. & Investor Rels.)*

No. of Mfg. Plants/Facilities: 3
No. of U.S. Offices: 14

Computer Systems/Hardware:
IBM

Outside Service Firm(s):

Deloitte & Touche*(Auditors)*
2000 First National Center
Omaha, NE 68102
Tel.: 402-346-7788

Fraser, Stryker, Veach, Vaughn, Meusey, Olson, Boyer*(Legal Firm)*
409 S. 17th
Omaha, NE

FirsTier Bank*(Major Banking Relationship)*
Omaha, NE

First National Bank of Omaha*(Major Banking Relationship)*
One First National Center
Omaha, NE 68102

Norwest Bank Minnesota, N.A.*(Major Banking Relationship)*
Omaha, NE

Denver Investment Advisors Inc.*(Pension Manager)*
633 Seventeenth St.
Denver, CO 80217

FirsTier Bank*(Pension Manager)*
Omaha, NE

First National Bank of Omaha*(Pension Manager)*
One First National Center
Omaha, NE 68102

Kirkpatrick Pettis Management*(Pension Manager)*
Omaha, NE

Merrill Lynch Asset Management*(Pension Manager)*
Omaha, NE

Norwest Capital Management & Trust*(Pension Manager)*
Omaha, NE

Sanford C. Bernstein & Co., Inc.*(Pension Manager)*
767 Fifth Ave.
New York, NY 10153
Tel.: 212-756-4383
Fax: 212-756-4405

Smith Barney Capital Management*(Pension Manager)*
1345 Ave. of the Americas
New York, NY 10105

OMAHA STEAKS INTERNATIONAL
10909 John Galt Blvd.
Omaha, NE 68103
Mailing Address:
P.O. Box 3300
Omaha, NE 68103
Tel.: 402-331-1010
Tel.: 800-228-2778
Fax: 402-597-8120
Year Founded: 1917
Approx.Sls.: $114,000,000
Emp.: 600
Fiscal Year-end: 12/31/91

Export
Mail Order Meats & Meats for Restaurants & Institutions
S.I.C.: 5961; 5147
Corporate Giving Program: United Way, Combined Health Agencies, United Arts Omaha
Alan D. Simon *(Chm. Bd. & Pres.)*
Frederick J. Simon *(Exec. V.P.)*
Richard Bezousek *(V.P.-Production & Chief Oper. Officer)*
JoAnn Kozeny *(V.P.-Human Resources)*
Bruce Simon *(V.P.-Pur.)*
Stephen H. Simon *(V.P. & Gen. Mgr.-Food Service Div.)*
Curt Todd *(Chief Fin. Officer)*
Dave Hershiser *(Controller)*
Todd Simon *(Gen. Mgr.-Omaha Steakshops)*
Jeff Carter *(Dir.-Mngmt. Info. Systems)*
Marilyn Pred *(Dir.-Pub. Rels.)*
Laura Ramirez *(Dir.-Telecommunications)*

Computer Systems/Hardware:
AS400s

Outside Service Firm(s):

Coopers & Lybrand*(Auditors)*
1200 Landmark Center
Omaha, NE
Tel.: 402-344-4545

Norwest Bank Minnesota, N.A.*(Major Banking Relationship)*
Omaha, NE

Divisions:

Gourmet Foods Div. **(1)**
10909 John Galt Blvd.
Omaha, NE 68103
Tel.: 402-597-3000
Tel.: 800-228-2778
Fax: 402-597-8120
Direct Marketing Of Steaks And Other Frozen Gourmet Foods
S.I.C.: 5147
Frederick J. Simon *(Pres.)*
Vickie Hagen *(V.P. & G.M.)*
Ron Bruggeman *(Dir.-Sls.)*
Ron Eike *(Dir.-Opers.)*
Gary Pelphrey *(Dir.-Mktg.)*

Omaha Steaks Food Service **(1)**
10909 John Galt Blvd.
Omaha, NE 68103
Tel.: 402-597-8135
Fax: 402-597-8222
Export
Purveyors Of Frozen, Portion Control Steaks To Restaurants, Hotels & Other Institutions
S.I.C.: 5147
Alan Simon *(Pres.)*
Stephen H. Simon *(V.P. & Gen. Mgr.)*

O'MALIA FOOD MARKETS INC.
1555 Westfield Rd.
Noblesville, IN 46060
Tel.: 317-773-8074 **IN**
Fax: 317-776-4129
Year Founded: 1966
Approx.Sls.: $73,000,000
Emp.: 950
Grocery Stores
S.I.C.: 5411
Corporate Giving Program: Charitible Groups Must Register and be Approved; We Contribute 1 Percent of Amount of Stamped Receipts Turned in to us by the Group; The Program is Called "Joe Cares"
George Joe O'Malia *(Chm. Bd.)*
Daniel J. O'Malia *(Pres. & Chief Exec. Officer)*
David T. O'Malia *(Exec. V.P. & Gen. Counsel)*
Dennis S. O'Malia *(V.P.)*
Kent Francis *(Chief Fin. Officer & Treas.)*
Sharon Pettygrove *(Asst. Treas.)*
Barbara Ash *(Mgr.-Human Resources)*
Tom Mathey *(Mgr.-Mdse. & Purch.)*
Daniel O'Malia *(Mgr.-Adv.)*

Principal(s):
George Joe O'Malia

Outside Service Firm(s):

Blue & Co.*(Auditors)*
Indianapolis, IN

Stark, Doninger, Mernitz & Smith*(Legal Firm)*
Indianapolis, IN

Merchants National Bank & Trust Company of Indianapolis*(Major Banking Relationship)*
One Merchants Plaza, Ste. 901E
Indianapolis, IN 46255
Tel.: 317-267-7109

OMAN CONSTRUCTION CO. INC.
200 42nd Ave. N.
Nashville, TN 37209
Mailing Address:
P.O. Box 146
Nashville, TN 37202
Tel.: 615-385-2500 **TN**
Fax: 615-385-2507
Year Founded: 1950
Approx.Sls.: $44,000,000
Emp.: 500
Highway & Bridge Construction
S.I.C.: 1541; 1611; 1622; 1623; 1629
Jack A. Oman *(Chm. Bd. & Pres.)*
Joseph Kanady, Jr. *(Sr. V.P.-Construction)*
William A. Brown *(V.P.)*

Oman Construction Co. Inc.—(Continued)

John A. Oman, Jr. *(V.P.)*
Jimmy Dale *(Treas. & Mgr.-Acct.)*
B.D. Horn *(Sec.)*

Computer Systems/Hardware:
IBM

Outside Service Firm(s):

Lattimore, Black, Morgan & Cain*(Auditors)*
Brentwood, TN

Chambers & Kinnard*(Legal Firm)*
Nashville, TN

First American National Bank*(Major Banking Relationship)*
Nashville, TN

OMEGA PERFORMANCE GROUP
71 Stevenson St., Ste. 1450
San Francisco, CA 94105
Tel.: 415-543-1836
Fax: 415-495-0240
Year Founded: 1976
Approx.Sls.: $10,000,000
Emp.: 70
Consulting & Training of Bank Management
S.I.C.: 8742
David Bennett *(Chm. Bd.)*
Carter Brown *(Pres. & Chief Exec. Officer)*
Stephen A. Royal *(Chief Fin. Officer)*
Morgan Reis *(Chief Admin. Officer)*

Computer Systems/Hardware:
Stride; MacIntosh; IBM PC

Outside Service Firm(s):

Deloitte & Touche*(Auditors)*
50 Fremont St.
San Francisco, CA 94105-2230
Tel.: 415-393-4300
Fax: 415-227-0452

OMEGA WORLD TRAVEL, INC.
5203 Leesburg Pike
Falls Church, VA 22041
Tel.: 703-931-8585
Fax: 703-820-0983
Year Founded: 1972
Assets: $10,863,700
Liabilities: $8,527,354
Net Worth: $2,336,346
Approx.Sls.: $295,000,000
Emp.: 750
Fiscal Year-end: 12/31/91
Travel Agency
S.I.C.: 4724
Gloria Bohan *(Pres. & Chief Oper. Officer)*
Gil F. Stromvall *(Chief Fin. Officer)*
Daniel P. Bohan *(Exec. V.P., Treas. & Sec.)*
Leona Strampel *(Dir.-Personnel)*

Principal(s):
Gloria Bohan
Daniel P. Bohan

No. of U.S. Offices: 190

Outside Service Firm(s):

Grant Thornton*(Auditors)*
Washington, DC 20090

Aetna Casualty & Surety*(Commercial Insurance Carrier)*
P.O. Box 10127,
Fairfax, VA

MDIPA*(Group Insurer)*
4 Taft Ct.
Rockville, MD

Pestronk & Associates*(Legal Firm)*
1350 I St., S.W.
Washington, DC

NationsBank*(Major Banking Relationship)*
8300 Greensboro Dr., Ste. 1070
McLean, VA

OMNI FLIGHT HELICOPTERS, INC.
Rte. 4031, Hwy. 515
Janesville, WI 53546
Tel.: 608-756-3631
Fax: 608-755-4714
Year Founded: 1962
Sales Range: $40-59 Million
Emp.: 450
Air Transportation
S.I.C.: 4522
Mark Wittman *(Exec. V.P.)*

Outside Service Firm(s):

Continental Bank N. A.*(Major Banking Relationship)*
231 S. LaSalle St.
Chicago, IL 60697
Tel.: 312-828-2345
Tel.: 800-426-5754
Telex: 312-828-1783

OMNI HOTELS
500 Lafayette Rd.
Hampton, NH 03842
Tel.: 603-926-8911
Tel.: 800-THE-OMNI
Fax: 603-926-9122
Year Founded: 1958
Approx.Sls.: $400,000,000
Emp.: 9,700
Fiscal Year-end: 12/31/90
Ownership & Management of Hotels, Restaurants & Lounges
S.I.C.: 7011
Jon Canas *(Vice Chm.)*
William J. Sheehan *(Pres. & Chief Exec. Officer)*
Charles H. Adams *(Sr. V.P. & Chief Fin. Officer)*
John M. Bolis *(Sr. V.P. & Gen. Counsel)*
Paul Hanley *(Sr. V.P.-Rooms Mngmt. & Mktg.)*
Peter Hothorn *(Sr. V.P.-Food & Beverage)*
David M. June *(Sr. V.P. & Controller)*
Stephen H. Lewy *(Sr. V.P. & Treas.)*
Robert McIntosh *(Sr. V.P. & Dir.-Service Mngmt.)*
Paul Sacco *(Sr. V.P.-Hotel Sls. & Mktg.)*
James E. Fitzgerald III *(V.P.-Asset Mngmt.)*
John L. Hopkins *(V.P.-Asset Mngmt.)*
Sheila Schofield *(Dir.-Adv. & Pub. Rels.)*

OMNI LENS CORPORATION
One Arlington Rd.
Forty Fort, PA 18704
Tel.: 717-287-4955
Year Founded: 1952
Sales Range: $10-19 Million
Emp.: 27
Import Export
Mfr. of Contact Lens
S.I.C.: 3851
Joseph H. Smith *(Pres.)*
Jason Smith *(V.P.)*
Libby Leibman *(Sec.)*
Richard Kramer *(Controller)*

Computer Systems/Hardware:
IBM PC

Outside Service Firm(s):

Earl Herbert*(Auditors)*
Kingston, PA

First State Bank of Wyoming*(Major Banking Relationship)*
Wyoming, PA

Kluger*(Legal Firm)*
Wilkes-Barre, PA

OMNI SOURCE CORPORATION
1610 N. Calhoun St.
Fort Wayne, IN 46808
Tel.: 219-422-5541 **IN**
Fax: 219-422-9154
Year Founded: 1946
Approx.Sls.: $350,000,000
Emp.: 400
Wholesale Metal Scrap; Processing & Recycling Scrap Materials
S.I.C.: 5093; 4953
Leonard Rifkin *(Chm. Bd. & Pres.)*
Barry Dorman *(Vice Chm., Sr. V.P. & Sec.)*
Daniel M. Rifkin *(Exec. V.P.)*
Richard S. Rifkin *(V.P.)*
Charles Quinby *(Controller)*

Principal(s):
Family-Owned

Outside Service Firm(s):

Ernst & Young*(Auditors)*
2300 Fort Wayne Natl. Bank Bldg.
Fort Wayne, IN 46802

Barrett & McNaghy*(Legal Firm)*
Ft. Wayne, IL

Summit Bank*(Major Banking Relationship)*
P.O. Box 2345,
Fort Wayne, IN 46801-2345
Tel.: 219-427-8333

OMNICARE HEALTH PLAN
1155 Brewery Park Blvd., Ste. 250
Detroit, MI 48207-2602
Tel.: 313-259-4000
Fax: 313-393-7944
Year Founded: 1971
Approx.Sls.: $53,000,000
Emp.: 194
Fiscal Year-end: 12/31/92
Health Maintenance Organization
S.I.C.: 8099
Dr. Julius V. Combs *(Chm. Bd.)*
Ronald R. Dobbins *(Pres.)*
Bobby Jones *(Sr. V.P.)*
Harold Roberts *(Sr. V.P.-Mktg.)*
Jagu Vanaharam *(Sr. V.P.-Finance, Accounting & Treas.)*
Denice Davis *(V.P.-Plng. & Devel.)*
Dr. Hills Howard *(Dir.-Medical/ OmniCare Health Plan)*
James Jackson, Jr. *(Dir.-Human Resources)*
Dr. William Sharp *(Medical Dir.-TPA/ PPO)*

Divisions:

U. A. Health Care Corporation **(1)**
Bank One Bldg., 1255 Euclid Ave., Ste. 500
Cleveland, OH 44115-1807
Tel.: 216-687-0015
Fax: 216-0687-9484

United American Healthcare Corp. **(1)**
1155 Brewery Park Blvd., Ste. 200
Detroit, MI 48207-2602
Tel.: 313-393-0200
Fax: 313-393-7944
Earnings: $4,349,000
Approx.Rev.: $36,031,000
Fiscal Year-end: 6/30/91
A Management Company for HMO, PPO for Profit
S.I.C.: 8099
Dr. Julius Combs *(Chm. Bd. & Chief Exec. Officer)*
Ronald Dobbins *(Pres. & Chief Oper. Officer)*
Bobby L. Jones *(Sr. V.P.)*
Jagu Vanaharam *(V.P.-Fin., Accounting & Treas.)*
Denice Davis *(V.P.-Plng. & Devel.)*
Harold Roberts *(Sr. V.P.-Mktg. & Sls.)*
Wilton Savage *(V.P.-U. A. Health Care Corp.)*
James Jackson Jr. *(Dir.-Human Resources & Admin.)*

OMNIFLIGHT, INC.
4650 Airport Pkwy.
Dallas, TX 75248
Tel.: 214-233-6464
Fax: 214-490-1486
Year Founded: 1957
Approx.Sls.: $50,000,000
Emp.: 400
Fiscal Year-end: 3/31/92
Aircraft Operators; Helicopter Flight & Maintenance Services
S.I.C.: 4522
JoAnn Parker *(Chm. Bd. & Chief Exec. Officer)*
Robert Buffum *(Pres. & Chief Oper. Officer)*
Roland Wisner *(Chief Fin. Officer)*
Hans Hilkhuysen *(V.P.-Technical)*
Gaylan A. Crowell *(Dir.-Mktg.)*
Rod Means *(Dir.-Pur.)*
Gary Cochran *(Mgr.-Safety)*
Mike Aslaksen *(Gen. Mgr.-Aviation Services Div.)*
John Cox *(Gen. Mgr.-Technical Services Div., Addison, TX)*
John Nielson *(Gen. Mgr.-Air Medical Services Div.)*
Mark Wittman *(Gen. Mgr.-Technical Services Div., Janesville, WI)*

Computer Systems/Hardware:
IBM AS400

Outside Service Firm(s):

Arthur Andersen & Co.*(Auditors)*
Columbia, SC

Ober, Kaler, Grimes & Schreiber*(Legal Firm)*
Baltimore, MD

NationsBank Carolinas*(Major Banking Relationship)*
Hickory, NC

Subsidiary:

Omniflight Helicopters, Inc. **(1)**
4650 Airport Pkwy.
Dallas, TX 75248
Tel.: 214-233-6464
Provides Helicopter Services
S.I.C.: 4522

OMON, NEW YORK LTD.
23 Watts St.
New York, NY 10013
Tel.: 212-925-5533
Fax: 212-941-6790
Year Founded: 1989
Approx.Billings: $25,000,000
Emp.: 19
Print, Out-of-Home & Broadcast Advertising
Joanne M. Davis *(Pres.)*
Marisa Parilla *(Office Mgr.)*

ON-COR FROZEN FOODS INC.
1227 W. Fulton
Chicago, IL 60607
Tel.: 312-738-1040
Fax: 312-738-0214
Year Founded: 1946
Frozen Entrees
S.I.C.: 2038
Sol Friend *(Pres.)*
Howard Friend *(Exec. V.P.-Sls. & Mktg.)*
Joel Bauer *(Controller)*
Howard Leafstone *(Mgr.-Natl. Sls.)*

Subsidiary:

Redi-Serve Foods **(1)**
P. O. Box 82
Ft. Atkinson, WI 53538
Tel.: 414-563-6391
S.I.C.: 2038
Gary Schimek *(Sr. V.P.-Gen. Mgr.)*

ONE HOUR MARTINIZING DRY CLEANING FRANCHISE (SYSTEM)
(Formerly Martin Franchises Inc.)
2005 Ross Ave.
Cincinnati, OH 45212
Tel.: 513-351-6211
Tel.: 800-827-0207
Fax: 513-731-5513
Year Founded: 1949
Approx.Sls.: $150,000,000
Emp.: 16
Fiscal Year-end: 12/31/92

Import Export
Franchised One Hour Martinizing Dry Cleaning Stores, Dry Cleaning Equipment
S.I.C.: 7389
George L. Strike *(Chm. Bd.)*
John L. Strike *(Vice Chm.)*
Anthony Strike *(Pres.)*
Larry Bosley *(V.P.-Admin. & Chief Fin. Officer)*
Theodore Hyde *(V.P.-Human Resources)*
Jerry Laesser *(V.P.-Mktg. & Franchise Devel. & Chief Oper. Officer)*
Leslie Alexander *(Dir.-Training)*
Michael Gates *(Dir.-Company Opers. & Reg. Mgr.)*
Michael Lyon *(Sr. Mgr.-Technical Services)*
Margaret Muething *(Mgr.-Adv.)*

ONE STOP SUPPLY
P.O. Box 689,
Tyler, TX 75710
Tel.: 903-592-0268
Fax: 903-597-1724
Year Founded: 1976
Approx.Sls.: $10,000,000
Emp.: 10
Wholesale Distributor of Waterbeds & Furniture
S.I.C.: 5021
Steve Arnold *(Pres. & Chief Exec. Officer)*

Principal(s):
Steve Arnold

No. of Mfg. Plants/Facilities: 3

Outside Service Firm(s):

First Business Bank*(Major Banking Relationship)*
Tyler, TX

O'Neal &Prelle
Advertising/Marketing/Public Relations

O'NEAL & PRELLE
95 Elm St., P.O. Box 1139
Hartford, CT 06143-1139
Tel.: 203-527-3233
Fax: 203-524-9234
Year Founded: 1934
Approx.Billings: $24,500,000
Emp.: 35
William J. O'Neal *(Chm.)*
William W. Ervin *(Pres. & Chief Exec. Officer)*
Michael Kintner *(V.P.-Pub. Rels.)*
Elizabeth Namnoum *(V.P.-Finance)*
Thomas P. Fontaine *(Sec.)*
Nancy Smith *(Dir.-Mktg. Services)*

Computer Systems/Hardware:
TSI, MMPlus, MacDesign

O'NEAL STEEL INC.
744 N. 41 St.
Birmingham, AL 35222
Mailing Address:
P.O. Box 2623
Birmingham, AL 35202
Tel.: 205-599-8000 **AL**
Fax: 205-599-8037
Year Founded: 1922
Sales Range: $100-499 Million
Emp.: 1,630
Fiscal Year-end: 6/30/91
Metal Service Center
S.I.C.: 5051
Emmet O'Neal *(Chm. Bd. & Chief Exec. Officer)*
Emmet O'Neal, III *(Vice Chm. & Chief Oper. Officer)*
Max DeJonge *(Pres.)*
Donald Freriks *(V.P.-Fin.)*
Don Donaldson *(V.P.-Admin.)*
Gayle Morgan *(Controller)*
G.P. Thornton *(Treas.)*
Elizabeth O'Neal Shannon *(Sec.)*
Glenn Davis *(Dir.-Pur.)*
Vicky Stewart *(Dir.-Data Processing)*
Doris Parks *(Mgr.-Risk)*

No. of Mfg. Plants/Facilities: 23

Computer Systems/Hardware:
IBM 9121

Outside Service Firm(s):

Deloitte & Touche*(Auditors)*
417 No. 20th St., Ste. 1000
Birmingham, AL 35203-3289
Tel.: 205-322-0534

Arkwright Mutual Insurance*(Commercial Insurance Carrier)*
Charlotte, NC

Provident Life & Accident Insurance Co.*(Group Insurer)*
Newark, NJ

Weiss, Peck & Greer*(Investment Banker)*
One New York Plaza
New York, NY 10004
Tel.: 212-908-9500
Fax: 212-908-9652

Cabaniss, Johnston, Gardner, Dumas & O'Neal*(Legal Firm)*
Birmingham, AL

NationsBank*(Major Banking Relationship)*
35 Broad St.
Atlanta, GA 30303
Tel.: 404-581-2121
Tel.: 800-848-8198

SouthTrust Bank*(Major Banking Relationship)*
Birmingham, AL
Tel.: 205-254-5068

Weiss, Peck & Greer*(Pension Manager)*
One New York Plaza
New York, NY 10004
Tel.: 212-908-9500
Fax: 212-908-9652

O'NEIL GRIFFIN & ASSOCIATES, INC.
324 Commercial St.
Manchester, NH 03101
Tel.: 603-625-5713
Year Founded: 1974
Approx.Billings: $18,800,000
Emp.: 30
Consumer Service/Public Sector Accounts
Gary M. O'Neil *(Pres. & Chief Exec. Officer)*
Patrick W. Griffin *(Exec. V.P.)*
Jane P. Tyson *(Sr. V.P., Chief Fin. Officer)*
Mark M. Bodi *(V.P., Pub. Rels.)*
Rose White *(Travel Planner)*

O'NEIL INDUSTRIES INC.
2751 N. Clybourn Ave.
Chicago, IL 60614
Tel.: 312-327-1611 **IL**
Fax: 312-327-4784
Assets: $58,729,375
Liabilities: $46,722,033
Net Worth: $12,007,342
Approx.Sls.: $219,000,000
Emp.: 450
Fiscal Year-end: 12/31/89
General Contracting & Construction Management; Office Buildings, Hospitals, Hotels, Manufacturing Facilities, Schools, Apartments
S.I.C.: 1541; 1522; 1542
J.R. Rotunno *(Chm. Bd.)*
W.E. O'Neil *(Pres.)*
A.F. O'Neil *(Sr. V.P.)*
R.R. Dukes *(Chief Fin. Officer)*
P.A. O'Neil *(Treas. & Sec.)*
K. Kopach *(Dir.-Mngmt. Info. Systems)*

Principal(s):
J.R. Rotunno
W.E. O'Neil

No. of U.S. Offices: 5

Computer Systems/Hardware:
Hewlett-Packard System 42

Outside Service Firm(s):

Arthur Andersen & Co.*(Auditors)*
33 W. Monroe St.
Chicago, IL 60603-4067
Tel.: 312-580-0033
Fax: 312-507-6748

Maryland National Bank*(Commercial Insurance Carrier)*
Chicago, IL

Massachusetts Mutual Life Insurance Co.*(Group Insurer)*
1295 State St.
Springfield, MA 01111
Tel.: 413-788-8411
Fax: 413-730-6144

Vedder, Price, Kaufman & Kammholz*(Legal Firm)*
115 S. La Salle
Chicago, IL 60603
Tel.: 312-781-2200

American National Bank & Trust Co.*(Major Banking Relationship)*
Chicago, IL

Chicago Title & Trust Co.*(Pension Manager)*
111 W. Washington St.
Chicago, IL 60602
Tel.: 312-630-2000
Fax: 312-368-4736

Subsidiary:

W. E. O'Neil Construction Company **(1)**
2751 N. Clybourn Ave.
Chicago, IL 60614
Tel.: 312-327-1611
Fax: 312-327-4684
Construction Company
S.I.C.: 1522
W.E. O'Neil *(Chm. Bd.)*
M.J. Faron *(Chief Oper. Officer)*
P.A. O'Neil *(Dir.-Mktg.)*

WILLIAM O'NEIL & CO., INC.
12655 Beatrice St.
Los Angeles, CA 90066
Tel.: 310-448-6800
Fax: 213-447-3369
Approx.Sls.: $47,000,000
Emp.: 300
Security Brokers, Financial Newspaper Publisher, Data Service & Technical Printing
S.I.C.: 6211; 7374
William J. O'Neil *(Pres.)*
Don Drake *(Chief Fin. Officer)*
Peter Marin *(V.P.-Sls.)*

Outside Service Firm(s):

Arthur Andersen & Co.*(Auditors)*
633 W. Fifth St.
Los Angeles, CA 90071
Tel.: 213-614-6500

Security Pacific National Bank*(Major Banking Relationship)*
333 S. Beaudry Ave., 24th Fl.
Los Angeles, CA 90017
Tel.: 213-345-2829

Subsidiary:

O'Neil Data Systems, Inc. **(1)**
2005 Armacost Ave.
Los Angeles, CA 90025
Tel.: 310-820-8343
Approx.Sls.: $12,000,000
Emp.: 150
Data Processing & Technical Printing
S.I.C.: 7374; 2741; 2754; 2791
William J. O'Neil *(Chm. Bd., Pres. & Treas.)*
Hamid Fereydouni *(V.P.)*
Sam Dickey *(Sec. & Treas.)*

OOMPHIES, INC.
5 Franklin St.
Lawrence, MA 01840
Tel.: 508-682-5268 **NH**
Fax: 508-685-7868
Approx.Sls.: $10,000,000
Emp.: 150
Mfr. Women's Shoes
S.I.C.: 3144
James G. Di Zazzo *(Chm. Bd. & Pres.)*

Principal(s):
James G. Di Zazzo

No. of Mfg. Plants/Facilities: 1
No. of U.S. Offices: 2

Computer Systems/Hardware:
IBM System 34

Outside Service Firm(s):

Henry & Co.*(Auditors)*
North Andover, MA

Palmer & Dodge*(Legal Firm)*
One Beacon St.
Boston, MA 02108

ComFed Savings Bank*(Major Banking Relationship)*
Chelmsford, MA

OPTIC GRAPHICS, INC.
101 Dover Rd.
Glen Burnie, MD 21060
Tel.: 410-768-3000
Fax: 410-760-4082
Year Founded: 1900
Approx.Sls.: $29,000,000
Emp.: 375
Mfr. of Looseleaf Products & Software Packaging & Offset Printing
S.I.C.: 2782; 2752
David Kinlein *(Pres.)*
John Strauss *(V.P.)*

Outside Service Firm(s):

Bauerman & Druzala*(Auditors)*
Townson, MD

Wright & Parks*(Legal Firm)*
Baltimore, MD

Philadelphia National Bank*(Major Banking Relationship)*
5th & Market Sts.
Philadelphia, PA 19101
Tel.: 215-629-3100
Fax: 215-834-2069

OPTICAL CORP. OF AMERICA
640 Fourth Ave.
Louisville, KY 40202
Mailing Address:
P.O. Box 1063
Louisville, KY 40201
Tel.: 502-583-5606 **KY**

Optical Corp. of America—(Continued)

Fax: 502-625-0392
Year Founded: 1897
Sales Range: $10-19 Million
Emp.: 10
Import
Optical Retailer
S.I.C.: 5995
Frank Sanning *(Pres.)*
Norman Walker *(V.P.-Mktg.)*
Paul Clemens *(Dir.-Fin. & Admin.)*
Jake Krill *(Dir.-Production)*
Granville Smith *(Dir.-Retail Optical)*

No. of Mfg. Plants/Facilities: 1
No. of U.S. Offices: 45

Computer Systems/Hardware:
Digital

Outside Service Firm(s):

Alexander & Alexander*(Commercial Insurance Carrier)*
220 W. Main St., Ste. 1800
Louisville, KY 40202-1395
Tel.: 502-561-1500
Fax: 502-561-1535

Liberty National Bank & Trust Co.*(Investment Banker)*
416 W. Jefferson St.
Louisville, KY 40202
Tel.: 502-566-2000

Liberty National Bank & Trust Co.*(Major Banking Relationship)*
Louisville, KY

Divisions:

Kentucky Optical **(1)**
640 Fourth Ave.
Louisville, KY 40201
Tel.: 502-584-0253
Emp.: 30
Wholesale Optical Lab

Lugene Opticians **(1)**
640 Fourth Ave.
Louisville, KY 40201
Tel.: 502-583-5606
Emp.: 60
Optical Retailers

Southern Optical **(1)**
640 Fourth Ave.
Louisville, KY 40201
Tel.: 502-583-0687
Emp.: 50
Optical Retailer

OPTIWORLD
1820 The Exchange, Ste. 450
Atlanta, GA 30339
Tel.: 404-916-2020
Fax: 404-916-2030
Emp.: 1,100
Optical Centers
S.I.C.: 5995
Donald Chapman *(Chm. Bd. & Chief Exec. Officer)*
Carl Hopper *(Exec. V.P.)*
Marlin Alsup *(Sr. V.P.-Fin.)*
Lisa Evans *(V.P.-Opers.)*
Trish Matthews *(Dir.-Mktg.)*

Outside Service Firm(s):

First Atlanta Bank*(Major Banking Relationship)*
Atlanta, GA

OPTYL EYEWEAR FASHION INTERNATIONAL CORP.
35 Maple St.
Norwood, NJ 07648
Tel.: 201-767-3820
Fax: 201-767-8984
Approx.Sls.: $50,000,000
Emp.: 210
Fiscal Year-end: 12/31/89
Manufacturer & Distributor of Designer Eyewear
S.I.C.: 3851

Tony Sperduto *(Sr. V.P.-Fin. & Admin.)*
Tom Maskery *(Dir.-Mktg.)*
Rick Grossman *(Dir.-Sls.)*

OPUS CORP.
(Affiliate of OPUS U.S. Corporation)
800 OPUS Center, 9900 Bren Road E.
Minnetonka, MN 55343
Mailing Address:
P.O. Box 150
Minnetonka, MN 55440
Tel.: 612-936-4444 **MN**
Fax: 612-936-4529
Year Founded: 1953
Approx.Sls.: $200,000,000
Emp.: 500
Architecture & Engineerring Services, Commercial & Industrial Construction, Real Estate Management & Development
S.I.C.: 8711; 8712; 1542; 1541; 6552
Gerald Rauenhorst *(Chm. Bd. & Chief Exec. Officer)*
Gene Haugland *(Vice Chm.)*
Mark Rauenhorst *(Pres. & Chief Oper. Officer)*
Robert J. Korkowski *(Sr. V.P.-Fin. & Admin.)*
James L. Tucker *(Sr. V.P., Sec. & Gen. Counsel)*
Vicki Strahan *(Mgr.-Mktg. Services)*
Dyann Myers *(Mktg.-Coord.)*

No. of U.S. Offices: 6

Outside Service Firm(s):

KPMG Peat Marwick*(Auditors)*
4200 Norwest Center, 90 S. 7th St.
Minneapolis, MN 55402
Tel.: 612-341-2222

OPUS SOUTH CORPORATION
SUITE 444, 4200 W. Cypress
Tampa, FL 33607
Tel.: 813-877-4444
Fax: 813-877-1222
Year Founded: 1906
Approx.Sls.: $50,000,000
Emp.: 150
Fiscal Year-end: 3/31/92
General Building Contractors, Developers & Architects
S.I.C.: 1542; 1541; 8712
George X. Connor *(Chm. Bd.)*
Rauenhorst, Neil *(Pres.)*
Barry Greenfield *(Treas.)*
Joe Dusek *(Gen.-Mgr.)*
Betsy Luker *(Dir.-Data Processing)*
Jim Lee *(Mgr.)*
Jerry Shaw *(Mgr.)*

No. of U.S. Offices: 3

Computer Systems/Hardware:
IBM System 36; IBM XT's

Outside Service Firm(s):

KPMG Peat Marwick*(Auditors)*
201 N. Franklin St., Ste. 3000
Tampa, FL 33602
Tel.: 813-223-1466
Fax: 813-229-3976

St. Paul Insurance Companies*(Commercial Insurance Carrier)*
St.Paul, MN

Hill, Ward & Henderson*(Legal Firm)*
Tampa, FL

Barnett Banks Trust Company, N.A.*(Major Banking Relationship)*
Pensacola, FL

Subsidiary:

Normandale Properties **(1)**
4350 W. Cypress, Ste. 701
Tampa, FL 33622
Tel.: 813-873-3675
Emp.: 15
Property Management
S.I.C.: 6531

Orange County Auto Auction Inc.
(Name Changed To Greater Orlando Auto Auction)

ORANGE GROVE CO-OPERATIVE
P.O. Box 310
Orange Grove, TX 78372
Tel.: 512-384-2766
Sales Range: $100-499 Million
Farmers' Co-operative; Grain Elevator, Milo, Corn & Wheat Sales
S.I.C.: 4221; 5153
James Gwosdz *(Chm. Bd. & Pres.)*
Willie S. Schmidt, Jr. *(Gen. Mgr.)*

Computer Systems/Hardware:
IBM System 36

Outside Service Firm(s):

Rob Hamilton*(Auditors)*
Corpus Christi, TX

Producers Exchange*(Group Insurer)*
Dallas, TX 75235

ORANGE MOTOR COMPANY INC.
799 Central Ave.
Albany, NY 12206
Tel.: 518-489-5414 **NY**
Fax: 518-489-8548
Year Founded: 1916
Approx.Sls.: $40,000,000
Emp.: 117
Retail New & Used Automobiles
S.I.C.: 5511
Carl E. Touhey *(Pres. & Treas.)*
Jim Howlan *(V.P.)*
Carl Keegan *(V.P.)*
Charles L. Touhey *(V.P. & Sec.)*

Outside Service Firm(s):

Stulmaker Roach & Co.*(Auditors)*
Albany, NY

Louis Dempf*(Legal Firm)*
Albany, NY

Key Bank*(Major Banking Relationship)*
Albany, NY

ORBEL CORPORATION
150 Anderson St.
Phillipsburg, NJ 08865
Tel.: 908-859-1000
Fax: 908-859-3594
Emp.: 24
Mfr. of Electroplated Wire & Strip
S.I.C.: 3496; 3316; 3357
Kenneth Marino *(Pres.)*
A.S. Marino *(V.P.)*
D.T. Kinghorn *(Mgr.-Plant)*

Outside Service Firm(s):

Phillipsburg National Bank & Trust Co.*(Major Banking Relationship)*
Phillipsburg, NJ

ORBIT VALVE INTERNATIONAL, INC.
7200 Interstate 30
Little Rock, AR 72209
Tel.: 501-568-6000 **AR**
Fax: 501-562-8564
Year Founded: 1979
Approx.Sls.: $46,000,000
Emp.: 550
Mfr. of Valves & Pipe Fittings
S.I.C.: 3494
Ed D. Ligon *(Chm. Bd. & Pres.)*
W. Ray Gabbard *(Treas.)*
Anne Moore *(Sec.)*

Outside Service Firm(s):

Frost & Co.*(Auditors)*
Little Rock, AR

Friday, Eldridge & Clark*(Legal Firm)*
2000 First Commercial Bldg.
Little Rock, AR 72201
Tel.: 501-376-2011

First Tennessee Bank, N.A.*(Major Banking Relationship)*
P.O. Box 84
Memphis, TN 38101-0034
Tel.: 901-523-4541

Subsidiary:

Orbit Valve Co. **(1)**
7200 Interstate 30
Little Rock, AR 72209
Tel.: 501-568-6000
Mfr. of Valves & Pipe Fittings
S.I.C.: 3494
Ed D. Ligon *(Pres.)*
John Stone *(V.P.-Fin.)*
Ray Gorcyca *(V.P.-Mfg.)*
Howard Fikes *(Dir.-Personnel)*
Paul Benson *(Mgr.-Pur.)*

ORBITAIR INTERNATIONAL LTD.
(d/b/a Russian Travel Bureau Inc.)
225 E. 44th St.
New York, NY 10017-4302
Tel.: 212-986-1500
Fax: 212-490-1650
Year Founded: 1959
Approx.Sls.: $10,000,000
Emp.: 16
Fiscal Year-end: 11/30/90
Tourist Promotion
S.I.C.: 7389
E.W. Lawrence III *(Chm. Bd. & Chief Exec. Officer)*
Caroline Cavalli *(Pres. & Sec.)*
Libby Gardner *(V.P.)*
Chris Mangan *(V.P. & Treas.)*

Subsidiaries:

China Travel Bureau Ltd. **(1)**
Orbitair International Bldg., 225 E. 44th St.
New York, NY 10017
Tel.: 212-986-1500
Wholesales; Tour Operator
S.I.C.: 7389

Russian Travel Bureau, Inc. **(1)**
Orbitair International Bldg., 225 E. 44th St.
New York, NY 10017
Tel.: 212-986-1500
Wholesales; Tour Operator
S.I.C.: 7389

ORCAD L.P.
3175 N.W. Aloclek Dr.
Hillsboro, OR 97124
Tel.: 503-690-9881
Electronic Design Automation Software
S.I.C.: 7372
John Durbetaki *(Owner)*

ORCHARD SUPPLY HARDWARE
6450 Via Del Oro
San Jose, CA 95119
Tel.: 408-281-3500
Fax: 408-629-7174
Retail Hardware & Home Improvement Stores; 23 Locations In Northern California
S.I.C.: 5211; 5231; 5251
Maynard Jenkins *(Pres. & Chief Exec. Officer)*
Steve Hilberg *(Chief Fin. Officer)*

No. of U.S. Offices: 34

ORCO BLOCK COMPANY
8042 Katella Ave.
Stanton, CA 90680
Tel.: 714-527-2239

Fax: 714-895-4021
Approx.Sls.: $10,000,000
Emp.: 198
Concrete Blocks & Bricks
S.I.C.: 3271
Peter G. Muth *(Chm. Bd.)*
Richard Muth *(Pres.)*
Mary M. Muth *(Sec.)*

ORDERS DISTRIBUTING CO.
501 Congaree Rd.
Greenville, SC 29607
Mailing Address:
P.O.Box 17189,
Greenville, SC 29606
Tel.: 803-288-4220 **SC**
Fax: 803-458-7348
Year Founded: 1955
Approx.Sls.: $37,000,000
Emp.: 180
Fiscal Year-end: 12/31/90
Wholesale Home Furnishings
S.I.C.: 5023
William H. Orders *(Chm. Bd., Chief Exec. Officer & Treas)*
C. Michael Smith *(Pres., Chief Oper. Officer & Sec.)*
Jim Kelley *(Sr. V.P.)*
Tim Cook *(V.P.-Sls.)*
Wiley Johnson *(V.P.-Personnel)*
Jim Mitcheltree *(V.P.)*
Maury Pulliam *(V.P.)*
Bill Thomas *(V.P.)*
David H. Williams *(V.P.-Fin.)*
C.R. Atkins *(Dir.-Data Processing)*

No. of U.S. Offices: 9

Computer Systems/Hardware:
IBM-System 36

Outside Service Firm(s):

Ernst & Young*(Auditors)*
C & S Bank Tower, Two Shelter Centre, Ste. 800
Greenville, SC 29603

Love, Thornton, Arnold & Thomason*(Legal Firm)*
Greenville, SC

First Citizens Bank*(Major Banking Relationship)*
Greenville, SC

OREGON FREEZE DRY, INC.
525 25th Ave., S.W.
Albany, OR 97321
Mailing Address:
P.O. Box 1048
Albany, OR 97321
Tel.: 503-926-6001
Tel.: 800-547-4060
Fax: 503-967-6527
Year Founded: 1963
Assets: $27,000,000
Liabilities: $8,000,000
Net Worth: $19,000,000
Sales Range: $80-99 Million
Emp.: 425
Fiscal Year-end: 12/31/90
Export
Mfr. Freeze Dried Foods and Ingredients
S.I.C.: 2099
Corporate Giving Program:
Contributions to Local Charitable, Educational, Cultural and Civic Organizations
Herbert Aschkenasy *(Pres.)*
Phillip Unverzagt *(Chief Fin. Officer & V.P.)*
William Impey *(V.P.-Mktg. & Prod. Devel.)*
Larry Kleven *(V.P.-Mfg.)*
James Baglien *(Mgr.-Mkt. Devel.)*
Jack Glaser *(Mgr.-Food Ingredients/ Industrial Sls.)*
Mickey E. Lancer *(Mgr.-Customer & Mktg. Services)*
Larry Von Deylen *(Mgr.-Mfg.)*

Computer Systems/Hardware:
IBM System 36

Outside Service Firm(s):

Price Waterhouse*(Auditors)*
1221 S.W. Morrison, Suite 1800
Portland, OR 97204
Tel.: 503-224-9040

Lindsay, Hart, Neil & Weigler*(Legal Firm)*
Portland, OR

First Interstate Bank*(Major Banking Relationship)*
P.O. Box 3131,
Portland, OR 97208
Tel.: 503-220-4855
Fax: 503-225-7153

OREGON STATE LOTTERY
2767 22nd St. SE
Salem, OR 97302
Mailing Address:
P.O. 12649
Salem, OR 97309
Tel.: 503-378-3545
Fax: 503-373-0248
Year Founded: 1985
Approx.Sls.: $150,000,000
Emp.: 300
Fiscal Year-end: 6/30/92
State Lottery
S.I.C.: 7999
Steve Caputo *(Deputy Dir.)*
John McCafferty *(Deputy Dir., Security)*
Jim Davey *(Dir.)*
Carl Bewley *(Mgr.-Fiscal)*
Greg Henkel *(Mgr.-Sls.)*
Marlene Meissner *(Mgr.-Pub. Rels.)*
Carole Walsh *(Mgr.-Adv.)*

O'REILLY AUTO INC.
233 S. Patterson
Springfield, MO 65802
Tel.: 417-862-2333 **MO**
Fax: 417-869-8903
Year Founded: 1957
Assets: $43,457,396
Liabilities: $14,130,000
Net Worth: $29,327,396
Approx.Sls.: $100,000,000
Emp.: 935
Fiscal Year-end: 12/31/91
Import
Wholesale Distributor of Automotive Supplies & Parts; Commercial & Industrial Building Operation
S.I.C.: 5013; 6512
C.H. O'Reilly *(Chm. Bd.)*
Charlie O'Reilly *(Pres.)*
David O'Reilly *(Pres.-Ozark Automotive Dist.)*
Larry O'Reilly *(Pres.-Corp. Sls.)*
Rosalie Wooten *(Exec. V.P.)*
Ted Wise *(V.P.)*

Outside Service Firm(s):

Green & Curtis*(Legal Firm)*
Springfield, MO

Boatmen's National Bank*(Major Banking Relationship)*
Springfield, MO

ORGANICALLY GROWN CORPORATION
12840 Sunset Blvd.
Los Angeles, CA 90049
Tel.: 310-393-3039
Fax: 310-393-7303
Approx.Sls.: $40,000,000
Emp.: 150
Manufacturer of Women's Clothing
S.I.C.: 5137
Stephen Abrams *(Pres.)*
Anoush Akaraguian *(V.P. & Treas.)*

Organizational Dynamics, Inc.
(See Organically Grown Corporation)

ORIEL CORPORATION
250 Long Beach Blvd.
Stratford, CT 06497
Tel.: 203-377-8282 **CT**
Telex: 4750361
Fax: 203-378-2457
Approx.Rev.: $17,000,000
Emp.: 130
Mfr. of Optical Systems & Components
S.I.C.: 3827; 3674; 3826
Francis X. Boes *(Pres. & Chief Exec. Officer)*
Allen J. Smith *(Exec. V.P.)*
Robert St. John *(V.P.-Fin.)*
Eugene Arthurs *(V.P.-Engrng.)*
William Malin *(V.P.-Mfg.)*

ORIX REAL ESTATE EQUITIES, INC.
100 N. Riverside Plaza
Chicago, IL 60606
Tel.: 312-669-6400 **DE**
Fax: 312-368-5330
Year Founded: 1930
Sales Range: $10-19 Million
Import Export
Real Estate Investment & Management
S.I.C.: 6531; 6552
Stephen Sinclair *(Pres. & Chief Exec. Officer)*
J.W. Kullman *(Exec. V.P. & Chief Oper. Officer)*
Jeff Plack *(Treas., Controller & Corp. Sec.)*
Yoshi Nakamura *(Sr. V.P.)*
Barbara Stanko *(Dir.-Personnel)*

No. of Mfg. Plants/Facilities: 2
No. of U.S. Offices: 2

Outside Service Firm(s):

Arthur Andersen & Co.*(Auditors)*
33 W. Monroe St.
Chicago, IL 60603-4067
Tel.: 312-580-0033
Fax: 312-507-6748

Great American Insurance Co.*(Commercial Insurance Carrier)*
Cincinnati, OH

William Blair & Co.*(Investment Banker)*
135 S. LaSalle St.
Chicago, IL 60603
Tel.: 312-236-1600

Sidley & Austin*(Legal Firm)*
One First National Plaza, 42nd Fl.
Chicago, IL 60603
Tel.: 312-853-7000
Fax: 312-853-7036

First National Bank of Chicago*(Major Banking Relationship)*
One First National Plaza
Chicago, IL 60670
Tel.: 312-732-9781
Tel.: 312-732-4050
Fax: 312-732-4840
Fax: 312-732-3055

Harris Trust & Savings Bank*(Major Banking Relationship)*
111 W. Monroe St.
Chicago, IL 60690
Tel.: 312-461-2265
Tel.: 800-858-0840

LaSalle National Bank*(Pension Manager)*
135 S. LaSalle St.
Chicago, IL 60690
Tel.: 312-443-2000

Subsidiaries:

Lake Michigan Construction, Inc. **(1)**
100 N. Riverside Plaza
Chicago, IL 60606
Tel.: 312-669-6400
Emp.: 46
Real Estate
S.I.C.: 6531; 6552

Lake Michigan Construction II, Inc. **(1)**
100 N. Riverside Plaza
Chicago, IL 60606
Tel.: 312-669-6400

Lake Michigan Construction III, Inc. **(1)**
100 N. Riverside Plaza
Chicago, IL 60606
Tel.: 312-669-6400

Lake Michigan Properties, Inc. **(1)**
100 N. Riverside Plaza
Chicago, IL 60606
Tel.: 312-669-6400

Lake Michigan Properties II, Inc. **(1)**
100 N. Riverside Plaza
Chicago, IL 60606
Tel.: 312-669-6400

Lake Michigan Properties III, Inc. **(1)**
100 N. Riverside Plaza
Chicago, IL 60606
Tel.: 312-669-6400

Lake Michigan Properties IV, Inc. **(1)**
100 N. Riverside Plaza
Chicago, IL 60606
Tel.: 312-669-6400

Renaissance Center Management Co. **(1)**
100 N. Riverside Plaza
Chicago, IL 60606
Tel.: 312-669-6400

Arthur Rubloff & Co. of Florida **(1)**
100 N. Riverside Plaza
Chicago, IL 60606
Real Estate Developer, Management & Brokerage
S.I.C.: 6531; 6552

Rubloff Capital Inc. **(1)**
100 N. Riverside Plaza
Chicago, IL 60606

Rubloff Capital Investments Inc. **(1)**
100 N. Riverside Plaza
Chicago, IL 60606
Tel.: 312-669-6400

Rubloff-Colonial Oaks, Inc. **(1)**
100 N. Riverside Plaza
Chicago, IL 60606
Tel.: 312-669-6400

Rubloff Corporate Services, Inc. **(1)**
100 N. Riverside Plaza
Chicago, IL 60606
Tel.: 312-669-6400

ORLEANS INTERNATIONAL, INC.
6441 Inkster, Suite 140
Bloomfield Hills, MI 48301
Tel.: 313-855-5556
Fax: 313-855-5668
Approx.Sls.: $170,000,000
Emp.: 15
Wholesale Distrbutor & Importer Poultry, Pork & Beef Products
S.I.C.: 5144; 5147
Earl Tushman *(Pres.)*
J. Lawrence Tushman *(Chief Exec. Officer & Sec.)*
Jerry Linderman *(Controller)*
Fred Babbin *(Gen. Counsel)*

Outside Service Firm(s):

BDO Seidman*(Auditors)*
Detroit, MI

Manufacturers National Bank N.A.*(Major Banking Relationship)*
38th Fl., 100 Renaissance Center
Detroit, MI 48243
Tel.: 313-222-4227

ORLEANS MATERIALS & EQUIPMENT CO., INC.
5501 France Rd.
New Orleans, LA 70216
Mailing Address:
P.O. BOx 26307
New Orleans, LA 70186
Tel.: 504-288-6361
Fax: 504-282-6633
Approx.Sls.: $20,000,000
Emp.: 150
Fabricated Structural Steel, Reinforcing Steel Service Center
S.I.C.: 5051; 3441
John J. Housey, Jr. *(Pres.)*
Daniel H. Housey *(V.P. & Dir.-Pur.)*
Frank Mikovich *(Sec. & Treas.)*

Outside Service Firm(s):

Pepperman, Emboulas, Schwartz & Todaro*(Auditors)*
New Orleans, LA

Whitney National Bank of New Orleans*(Major Banking Relationship)*
P.O. Box 61260
New Orleans, LA 70161
Tel.: 504-586-7422

THE ORMOND SHOPS, INC.
7300 West Side Ave.
North Bergen, NJ 07047
Tel.: 201-861-5800
Fax: 201-348-2127
Year Founded: 1950
Emp.: 1,800
Retail Women's Apparel & Accessories
S.I.C.: 5632
Lawrence B. Goodman *(Chm. Bd. & Treas.)*
Neil Flechner *(V.P.-Fin. & Sec.)*
Richard F. Goodman *(V.P.-Real Estate)*
Glen Lyon *(V.P. & Gen. Mgr.-Mdse.)*
Robert Di Carlo *(Controller)*

Outside Service Firm(s):

Ernst & Young*(Auditors)*
787 Seventh Ave.
New York, NY 10019
Tel.: 212-773-1243

Moore, Berson, Lifflander & Mewhinney*(Legal Firm)*
595 Madison Ave.
New York, NY 10022
Tel.: 212-838-0600

Chemical Bank*(Major Banking Relationship)*
450 West 33rd St.
New York, NY 10001
Tel.: 212-613-7197
Fax: 212-947-7628

OROAMERICA, INC.
443 N. Varney St.
Burbank, CA 91502
Tel.: 818-848-5555 **CA**
Fax: 818-841-4342
Year Founded: 1977
Approx.Sls.: $190,000,000
Emp.: 300
Mfr. of Precious Metal Jewlery
S.I.C.: 3911
Guy Benhamou *(Pres.)*
Shiu Shao *(Chief Fin. Officer & Sr. V.P.)*
Andrew Concool *(V.P.)*
Betty Sou *(Controller)*

Outside Service Firm(s):

Price Waterhouse*(Auditors)*
400 S. Hope St.
Los Angeles, CA 90071-2889
Tel.: 213-236-3000

BankAmerica Corp.*(Major Banking Relationship)*
Anaheim, CA

THE ORR FELT COMPANY
750 S. Main St.
Piqua, OH 45356
Mailing Address:
P.O.Box 908,
Piqua, OH 45356
Tel.: 513-773-0551
Fax: 513-778-9670
Year Founded: 1963
Approx.Sls.: $25,000,000
Emp.: 225
Fiscal Year-end: 12/31/90
Import Export
Papermakers Felts
S.I.C.: 2299
Donna H. Nicholas *(Chm. Bd.)*
Tom Cheney *(Pres.)*
Carl M. Thomas *(Chief Exec. Officer)*
Pieter Diehl *(V.P.-Tech. Design & Service)*
James Rigola *(V.P.-Sls.)*
Richard V. Wendeln *(Controller)*
J. Richard Gaier *(Sec.)*

Computer Systems/Hardware:
Qantel; Signature

ORR SAFETY EQUIPMENT COMPANY
2360 Millers Lane
Louisville, KY 40216
Tel.: 502-774-5791
Fax: 502-776-8030
Approx.Sls.: $18,000,000
Emp.: 145
Wholesale Industry Safety Equipment
S.I.C.: 5099; 5169
Clark Orr, Jr. *(Pres. & Chief Exec. Officer)*
Richard Harper *(V.P.)*
Larry Clements *(Dir.-Human Resources)*

ORTEL CORPORATION
2015 W. Chestnut
Alhambra, CA 91803
Tel.: 818-281-3636 **CA**
Fax: 818-281-8231
Year Founded: 1980
Assets: $20,000,000
Liabilities: $2,000,000
Net Worth: $18,000,000
Sales Range: $10-19 Million
Emp.: 125
Fiscal Year-end: 4/30/91
Import Export
Mfr. of Components & Systems for High Performance Fiber Optic Applications Such as Communications, CATV, Cellular & Microwave
S.I.C.: 3663
Wim H.J. Selders *(Pres. & Chief Exec. Officer)*
Stephan Workman *(Chief Fin. Officer & V.P.-Fin.)*
Dr. Nadav Bar-Chaim *(V.P.-Device Structures)*
Claude L. Mathews *(V.P.-Mfg.)*
Robert J. Mielke *(V.P.-Quality Assurance)*
Dr. Israel Ury *(V.P. & Chief Tech. Officer)*
Kimberly Congdon *(Dir.-Human Resources)*
Jack May *(Dir.-Pur.)*

No. of Mfg. Plants/Facilities: 1
No. of U.S. Offices: 1

Outside Service Firm(s):

KPMG Peat Marwick*(Auditors)*
Woodland Hills, CA

Latham & Watkins*(Legal Firm)*
633 West Fifth St.
Los Angeles, CA 90071
Tel.: 213-485-1234
Fax: 213-643-9086

First Interstate Bank*(Major Banking Relationship)*
Alhambra, CA

ORTHO-KINETICS, INC.
W220 N507 Springdale Rd.
Waukesha, WI 53186
Mailing Address:
P.O. Box 1647
Waukesha, WI 53187
Tel.: 414-542-6060
Year Founded: 1963
Approx.Sls.: $23,000,000
Emp.: 250
Fiscal Year-end: 3/31/91
Mfr. of Rehabilitation, Mobility & Medical Equipment for Adults & Children
S.I.C.: 3829; 3842; 3800
Edward J. Gaffney *(Pres. & Treas.)*
Ken Kanack *(Chief Oper. Officer)*
Jim Lotz *(Chief Fin. Officer)*
Robert Cowan *(Mgr.-Production)*
Mary Kallenbach *(Mgr.-Mktg.)*

ORTRONICS, INC.
595 Greenhaven Shores
Pawcatuck, CT 06379
Tel.: 203-599-1760
Fax: 203-599-1774
Approx.Sls.: $14,000,000
Emp.: 200
Manufacture Insulating Connectorized Cable, Electronic Circuits & Coils; Wholesale Non-insulated Wire Cable
S.I.C.: 3357; 3677; 3679; 5051
Stephen Orlando *(Pres.)*
Maurice V. Orlando *(Chief Exec. Officer)*
Ida L. Orlando *(Treas. & Sec.)*
Walter Schwer *(Dir.-Engrng.)*

Outside Service Firm(s):

Benevides, Wiseman & Cooper, LTD*(Auditors)*
Westerly, RI

Connecticut National Bank*(Major Banking Relationship)*
777 Main St.
Hartford, CT 06115
Tel.: 203-728-2000

THE ORVIS COMPANY, INC.
U.S. Rte. #7
Manchester, VT 05254
Tel.: 802-362-3622
Fax: 802-362-3525
Year Founded: 1856
Assets: $33,000,000
Liabilities: $18,000,000
Net Worth: $15,000,000
Approx.Sls.: $86,000,000
Emp.: 550
Fiscal Year-end: 9/30/91

Import Export
Retail Mail Order & Manufacture Fishing Rods
S.I.C.: 3949; 5961
Leigh H. Perkins, Jr. *(Pres.)*
Leigh H. Perkins *(Chief Exec. Officer)*
Thomas S. Vaccaro *(V.P.-Fin. & Sec.)*
John Moticha *(V.P.-Opers.)*
Joseph Cassidy *(V.P.-Mktg.)*
Roxanna Kayton *(Controller)*

Outside Service Firm(s):

Grant Thornton*(Auditors)*
Cleveland, OH

Baker & Hostetler*(Legal Firm)*
3200 National City Center
Cleveland, OH 44114
Tel.: 216-621-0200
Fax: 216-696-0740

Fleet Bank of Massachusetts*(Major Banking Relationship)*
10 Post Office Sq.,6th Fl.
Boston, MA 02109
Tel.: 617-742-4000

OSBORN & BARR COMMUNICATIONS
(Formerly BTB Communications)
7800 Forsyth Blvd., 7th Fl.
Clayton, MO 63105
Tel.: 314-726-5511
Tel.: 800-666-1765
Fax: 314-726-6350
Year Founded: 1988
Approx.Billings: $17,850,000
Emp.: 25
Agriculture, Business-to-Business, Educational, Training Programs
Joseph Osborn *(Pres. & Creative Dir.)*
Stephen Barr *(Chief Exec. Officer)*
Robert Bryan *(Controller)*
Billie Jo Keller *(Office Services)*

Computer Systems/Hardware:
Admark, Data General, MacIntosh, IBM PC

OSCO INDUSTRIES INC.
Eleventh & Chillicothe
Portsmouth, OH 45662
Mailing Address:
P.O. Box 1388,
Portsmouth, OH 45662
Tel.: 614-354-3183 **OH**
Fax: 614-353-1504
Year Founded: 1872
Assets: $17,970,000
Liabilities: $5,764,000
Net Worth: $12,206,000
Approx.Sls.: $26,000,000
Emp.: 350
Fiscal Year-end: 12/31/90
Import Export
Commercial Gray Iron Castings
S.I.C.: 3321
Keith Spires *(Pres. & Chief Exec. Officer)*
Charles R. Vetter *(V.P.-Fin. & Sec.)*
William J. Burke *(V.P.-Sls.)*
John M. Burke *(V.P.-Pur.)*
Jeffrey A. Burke *(V.P.)*
Philip L. Vetter *(Treas.)*
Richard Roberts *(Dir.-Personnel)*

No. of Mfg. Plants/Facilities: 2

Computer Systems/Hardware:
IBM 38

Outside Service Firm(s):

KPMG Peat Marwick*(Auditors)*
Two Nationwide Plaza
Columbus, OH 43215
Tel.: 614-249-2300

Ohio Company*(Investment Banker)*
Portsmouth, OH

McCurdy, Johnson, Ruggiero, McKenzie & Bender*(Legal Firm)*
Portsmouth, OH

Bank One*(Major Banking Relationship)*
Portsmouth, OH

Bank One*(Major Banking Relationship)*
Kettering Tower
Dayton, OH 45401
Tel.: 513-449-8600

Subsidiary:

Mid State Products Co. **(1)**
P.O. Box 1388
Portsmouth, OH 45662
Tel.: 614-354-3183
Emp.: 4
Real Estate Holding Co.
S.I.C.: 6719; 6531

OSMOSE WOOD PRESERVING CO.
980 Ellicott St.
Buffalo, NY 14209
Tel.: 716-882-5905 **NY**

Fax: 716-882-5139
Approx.Sls.: $79,000,000
Emp.: 350
Mfr. & Contract Application of Wood Preservatives
S.I.C.: 2491
John L. Surdam *(Chm. Bd.)*
Robert E. Webber *(Pres.)*
Ronald J. Orlowski *(Chief Fin. Officer & V.P.-Admin.)*
Paul A. Goydan *(V.P.-Wood Preserving Div.)*
James R. Spengler *(V.P.-Utilities Div.)*
C. Frank Robertson *(Mgr.-Natl. Mktg.)*
John D. Horton *(Mgr.-Tech. Services)*
Al Hebner *(Dir.-Adv. & Natl. Sls.)*

Outside Service Firm(s):

J. D. Elliott & Co.*(Auditors)*
Buffalo, NY

Manufacturers & Traders Trust Company*(Major Banking Relationship)*
1 M & T Plaza
Buffalo, NY 14240
Tel.: 716-842-4200

Manufacturers & Traders Trust Company*(Investment Banker)*
1 M & T Plaza
Buffalo, NY 14240
Tel.: 716-842-4200

OSTARR CORPORATION
5240 So. Archer Ave.
Chicago, IL 60632
Tel.: 312-581-5800
Fax: 312-581-9549
Year Founded: 1976
Assets: $880,000
Liabilities: $285,000
Net Worth: $595,000
Emp.: 15
Fiscal Year-end: 9/30/89
Manfacture & Distribution of Ostarr Concrete Repair Products; Concrete Repair Centers
S.I.C.: 3599; 3699
James R. Post *(Pres., Chief Exec. Officer, Chief Fin. Officer)*
Cindy Schebo *(Treas., Sec. & Dir.-Personnel)*

No. of Mfg. Plants/Facilities: 1
No. of U.S. Offices: 3

Computer Systems/Hardware:
Apple Macintosh SE II

Outside Service Firm(s):

Van Eck & Dykstra*(Auditors)*
Countryside, IL

American States Insurance Co.*(Commercial Insurance Carrier)*
500 N. Meridian St.
Indianapolis, IN 46204-1275
Tel.: 317-262-6262
Fax: 317-262-6290

American Family Insurance Group*(Group Insurer)*
Madison, WI

Edward Mossner*(Legal Firm)*
La Grange, IL

Harris Bank Naperville*(Major Banking Relationship)*
503 N. Washington St.
Naperville, IL 60540
Tel.: 708-420-3500

THE OSTERNECK CO. INC.
Hwy. 72 E.
Lumberton, NC 28358
Mailing Address:
P.O. Box 859
Lumberton, NC 28359
Tel.: 919-738-2416
Tel.: 800-682-2416 **NC**
Fax: 919-739-2881
Year Founded: 1971
Assets: $4,702,475
Liabilities: $2,660,715
Net Worth: $2,041,760
Approx.Sls.: $12,000,000
Emp.: 256
Import Export
Manufacture & Processor of Woven Polypropylene Slit Yarn, Bale Wraps & Tubular Material, Burlap & Nylon
S.I.C.: 2281; 2295
Guy-Kenneth Osterneck *(Chm. Bd., Pres. & Treas.)*
Ben F. Morris *(V.P.-Admin. & Sec.)*
Myles Osterneck *(V.P.-Sls.)*
Kenneth Davis *(Comptroller)*

Principal(s):
Guy-Kenneth Osterneck
Myles Osterneck

No. of Mfg. Plants/Facilities: 1
No. of U.S. Offices: 1

Computer Systems/Hardware:
Micro Systems; Lotus

Outside Service Firm(s):

Kenneth C. Davis*(Auditors)*
Red Springs, NC

Dunbar Insurance*(Commercial Insurance Carrier)*
Raleigh, NC

Lincoln National Life Insurance Co.*(Group Insurer)*
PO Box 208, 1300 S. Clinton
Fort Wayne, IN 46801
Tel.: 219-455-2926
Fax: 219-455-7619

McLean, Stacy, Henry & McLean*(Legal Firm)*
P.O. Drawer 1087
Lumberton, NC 28359
Tel.: 919-738-5257

Southern National Bank of North Carolina*(Major Banking Relationship)*
Securities Transfer Services, 500 N. Chestnut St.
Lumberton, NC 28358

OSTROW TEXTILE CO., INC.
923 Standard & High Sts.
Rock Hill, SC 29730
Tel.: 803-324-4284 **SC**
Fax: 803-324-7942
Approx.Sls.: $40,000,000
Emp.: 500
Wholesale & Retail Linens & Home Furnishings
S.I.C.: 5023; 5719
Joel J. Ostrow *(Pres.)*
Al Levenson *(Sr. V.P.)*
John Hecimovich *(V.P.-Fin.)*
Lane Ostrow *(V.P.-Retail Sls.)*
Steve Pinner *(Dir.-Warehouse Distribution)*
Bill Wallace *(Dir.-Adv.)*
Gary Strunck *(Mgr.-Wholesale Opers.)*
Pete Vulin *(Mgr.-Inventory Control)*

Outside Service Firm(s):

Pollack, Sage & Co.*(Auditors)*
Great Neck, NY

Holland & Knight*(Legal Firm)*
P.O. Box 1288
Tampa, FL 33601
Tel.: 813-223-1621

South Carolina National Bank*(Major Banking Relationship)*
Columbia, SC

OTT COMMUNICATIONS, INC.
ADVERTISING / DESIGN GROUP

OTT COMMUNICATIONS, INC.
3321 Ruckreigel Pkwy.
Louisville, KY 40299
Tel.: 502-267-6999
Fax: 502-267-5445
Year Founded: 1970
Approx.Billings: $18,000,000
Emp.: 41
Food Marketing
Jerry E. Ott *(Chm. Bd.)*
Larry Pizer *(Pres. & New Bus. Contact)*
Christopher J. Ott *(Exec. V.P.)*
Woody Downer *(V.P., Gen. Mgr. & Creative Services)*
Paula Matthews *(V.P., Food Mktg.)*
Susan Ott *(Sec.)*

OTT FOOD PRODUCTS
705 W. Fairview
Carthage, MO 64836
Mailing Address:
P.O. Box 816,
Carthage, MO 64836
Tel.: 417-358-2585 **MO**
Year Founded: 1954
Emp.: 13
Mfr., Wholesaler & Retailer Salad Dressings & Barbecue Sauces
S.I.C.: 2035; 2079; 5149; 5499
Wayne Marti *(Pres.)*
Jack Crede *(V.P.)*
Roy Moore *(Treas.)*

Computer Systems/Hardware:
IBM 60

Outside Service Firm(s):

General American Life Insurance Co.*(Group Insurer)*
700 Market
Saint Louis, MO 63101
Tel.: 314-525-5458
Fax: 314-525-3677

Day McGuire*(Legal Firm)*
Carthage, MO

Southwest Missouri Bank*(Major Banking Relationship)*
Carthage, MO

OTTENHEIMER & COMPANY, INC.
2275 Half-Day Rd.
Bannockburn, IL 60015
Tel.: 708-940-8000
Tel.: 800-222-3834
Tel.: 800-937-7177 **IL**
Fax: 708-940-9118
Year Founded: 1896
Sales Range: $20-39 Million
Emp.: 560
Fiscal Year-end: 6/30/90
Mfr. of Healthcare Uniforms & Career Identity Uniforms
S.I.C.: 2326; 2339
K.A. Merlav *(Chm. Bd., Pres. & Chief Exec. Officer)*
Bob Jones *(Sr. V.P.-Fin. & Admin.)*
C.S. Fields *(Chief Fin. Officer)*
R. Foggl *(V.P.-Sls.)*
A. Gstroff *(V.P.-Opers.)*
Sandra Hamden *(Dir.-Adv.)*

Outside Service Firm(s):

Altschuler, Melvoin & Glasser*(Legal Firm)*
30 S. Wecker Dr.
Chicago, IL 60606
Tel.: 312-207-2800

D'Ancona & Pflaum*(Legal Firm)*
30 No. LaSalle St.
Chicago, IL 60602
Tel.: 312-580-2000

Harris Trust & Savings Bank*(Major Banking Relationship)*
111 W. Monroe St.
Chicago, IL 60690
Tel.: 312-461-2265
Tel.: 800-858-0840

OUACHITA COCA-COLA BOTTLING COMPANY
P.O. Box 1571
Monroe, LA 71210
Tel.: 318-388-4900
Fax: 318-387-7985
Soft Drink Bottler
S.I.C.: 2086
Hank Biedenharn *(Pres.)*
Harlin Sager *(V.P.-Personnel)*

Subsidiary:

Coca-Cola/Dr. Pepper Bottling Co. Of South Arkansas **(1)**
205 E. Second Ave.
Pine Bluff, AR 71601
Tel.: 501-534-0621
Fax: 501-534-0621
Soft Drink Bottler
S.I.C.: 2086
Ralph Hatch *(Gen. Mgr.)*

OUIMET INDUSTRIES
22D Patterson Brook Rd.
West Wareham, MA 02576
Mailing Address:
P.O. Box 520
West Wareham, MA 02576
Tel.: 508-295-8886 **DE**
Fax: 508-295-8776
Year Founded: 1940
Approx.Sls.: $25,000,000
Emp.: 300
Fiscal Year-end: 9/30/91
Import Export
Holding Company; Mfr. Rubber, Plastics, Leather & Textiles, Hook & Loop Fasteners
S.I.C.: 6719; 2299; 3069; 3089; 3111; 3131
Emil R. Ouimet *(Chm. Bd. & Treas.)*
Principal(s):
Emil R. Ouimet

No. of Mfg. Plants/Facilities: 3
No. of U.S. Offices: 3

Computer Systems/Hardware:
Burroughs

Outside Service Firm(s):

Ernst & Young*(Auditors)*
200 One Commerce Place
Nashville, TN 37239

Third National Bank*(Major Banking Relationship)*
201 4th Ave. No., Uptown Sta., Box 2844
Nashville, TN 37167
Tel.: 615-748-4742

Subsidiaries:

Ouimet Corp. **(1)**
2967 Sidco Dr.
Nashville, TN 37204
Tel.: 508-295-8886
Fax: 508-295-8776
Mfr. Rubber, Plastics, Leather & Textiles, Hook & Loop Fasteners
S.I.C.: 2299; 3069; 3089; 3111; 3131
Emil R. Ouimet *(Chm. Bd. & Treas.)*
Richard J. Ouimet *(Pres.)*
Richard Best *(Plant Mgr.)*

Ouimet Stay & Leather Co. **(1)**
650 Armory Dr.
Nashville, TN 37204
Tel.: 615-242-5478
Shoe & Auto Trimmings, Plastic Extrusions & Textile Fasteners
S.I.C.: 5199; 2396; 3089; 3199
Richard J. Ouimet *(Pres.)*
Emil R. Ouimet *(Treas.)*

Ouimet Industries—(Continued)

Richard Best *(V.P.-Opers.)*

OUR OWN HARDWARE COMPANY
2300 W. Hwy. 13
Burnsville, MN 55337
Mailing Address:
P.O. Box 720
Minneapolis, MN 55440
Tel.: 612-890-2700
Fax: 612-890-4233
Year Founded: 1913
Approx.Sls.: $160,000,000
Emp.: 380
Import
Wholesale Distribute of General Hardware, Sporting Goods, Electrical Appliances, Paints, Major Appliances, Housewares & Lumber
S.I.C.: 5072; 5031; 5091; 5064; 5198; 5251
James Mahowald *(Chm. Bd.)*
J. Weyrens *(Pres. & Chief Exec. Officer)*
H.D. Thompson *(Chief Fin. Officer, V.P., Treas. & Sec.)*
S. Saefke *(V.P.-Mdse. & Adv.)*
D. Schneider *(V.P.-Sls.)*
Darwin Wilde *(V.P.-Personnel)*

Computer Systems/Hardware:
IBM 4341

Outside Service Firm(s):

Coopers & Lybrand*(Auditors)*
1000 TCF Bldg.
Minneapolis, MN 55402
Tel.: 612-293-2929
Fax: 612-370-9395

American Hardware Mutual*(Commercial Insurance Carrier)*
Minneapolis, MN

National Cooperative Bank*(Major Banking Relationship)*
Minneapolis, MN

Norwest Bank Minnesota, N.A.*(Major Banking Relationship)*
6th St. & Marquette Av.
Minneapolis, MN 55479
Tel.: 612-667-1234

Subsidiary:

Jeffersonville Distribution Center **(1)**
3230 Industrial Pkwy.
Jeffersonville, IN 47130
Tel.: 812-283-6661
Fax: 812-283-4105
Approx.Sls.: $30,000,000
Emp.: 130
Wholesale Hardware Distributor Serving Franchised S & T & Blue Grass Stores
S.I.C.: 5072
Charles E. Redmon *(Chm. Bd.)*
James Koetter *(V.P.-Sls.)*
Yandell Martin *(Dir.-Data Processing)*
Richard Jecker *(Mgr.-Opers.)*
James Lehrer *(Mgr.-Mktg.)*
Marvin Wiley *(Mgr.-Sls., Field)*

OUR SUNDAY VISITOR, INC.
100 Noll Plaza
Huntington, IN 46750
Tel.: 219-356-8400
Fax: 219-356-8472
Year Founded: 1912
Approx.Sls.: $10,000,000
Emp.: 48
Fiscal Year-end: 6/30/91
Publisher of Religious Books & Materials
S.I.C.: 2731
Employee Matching Gifts Program:
Dollar For Dollar To United Way
Robert Lockwood *(Pres.& Chief Exec. Officer)*
Alan Buck *(Dir.-Data Processing)*
Thomas Smith *(Bus. Mgr.)*

Computer Systems/Hardware:
IBM 4300 & PC

Outside Service Firm(s):

Coopers & Lybrand*(Auditors)*
490 Lincoln Bank Tower
Fort Wayne, IN 46802
Tel.: 219-423-1531
Fax: 219-426-7870

Subsidiary:

Noll Printing Corporation **(1)**
100 Noll Plaza
Huntington, IN 46750
Tel.: 219-356-8400
Approx.Sls.: $42,200,000
Emp.: 425
Offset Printing; Magazines, Inserts, Flyers, Catalogs
S.I.C.: 2759
James Denman *(Chief Exec. Officer)*

OURSO INVESTMENT CORPORATION
110 Railroad Ave.
Donaldsonville, LA 70346
Mailing Address:
P.O. Box 609,
Donaldsonville, LA 70346
Tel.: 504-473-8654 LA
Fax: 543-473-8010
Year Founded: 1970
Assets: $23,619,527
Liabilities: $9,179,581
Net Worth: $14,439,946
Approx.Sls.: $67,053,140
Emp.: 3
Fiscal Year-end: 12/31/91
Holding Co.; Life & Fire Insurance Co., Cemetery Sales, Funeral Homes & Flower Shops
S.I.C.: 6719; 6311; 6553; 7261
E.J. Ourso *(Chm., Pres. & Chief Exec. Officer)*
Jesse P. Arboneaux *(V.P., Chief Fin. Officer, Treas. & Sec.)*
John H. Fritz *(Exec. V.P.-Fin.)*
Principal(s):
E.J. Ourso

No. of U.S. Offices: 1

Outside Service Firm(s):

Ernst & Young*(Auditors)*
4200 One Shell Square, 701 Poydras St.
New Orleans, LA 70139
Tel.: 504-581-4200

Malcolm M. Dienes & Company*(Auditors)*
New Orleans, LA

Talbot Sotile & Carmouch*(Legal Firm)*
Donaldsonville, LA

Premier Bank*(Major Banking Relationship)*
P.O. Box 1511
Baton Rouge, LA 70821

Subsidiaries:

Bultman Funeral Home **(1)**
3338 St. Charles Ave.
New Orleans, LA 70115
Tel.: 504-895-7766
Funeral Home
S.I.C.: 7261
Stephen L. Santheimer *(Chm. Bd.)*
Jesse P. Abroneaux *(Chief Fin. Officer)*

Security Industrial Insurance Co., Inc. **(1)**
P.O. Box 609
Donaldsonville, LA 70346
Tel.: 504-473-8654 (100%)
Fax: 504-473-8010
Assets: $156,341,776
Earnings: $1,333,271
Liabilities: $141,411,653
Net Worth: $14,930,123
Emp.: 700
Fiscal Year-end: 12/31/91
Life & Fire Insurance Co., Cemetery Sales & Funeral Homes
S.I.C.: 6311; 6331; 6553; 7261
Eucharist J. Ourso *(Chief Exec. Officer)*
Dennis P. Caballero *(Pres.)*
Sidney L. Harp, II *(Exec. V.P. & Agency Dir.)*
James V. Morris *(Sr. V.P.)*
Jesse P. Arboneaux *(V.P., Treas. & Sec.)*

BUTCH OUSTALET FORD SAAB, INC.
9274 Hwy. 49
Gulfport, MS 39503
Tel.: 601-863-5525
Fax: 601-863-9612
Approx.Sls.: $18,000,000
Emp.: 60
New & Used Automobiles & Pickups
S.I.C.: 5511
A.J.M. Butch Oustalet *(Pres.)*
Larry Clark *(V.P.)*
Gene Fortenbery *(V.P.)*

Outside Service Firm(s):

Hancock Bank*(Major Banking Relationship)*
Gulfport, MS

OHMS

OUT OF HOME MEDIA SERVICES, INC.
42 W. 38th St.
New York, NY 10018
Tel.: 212-391-2121
Fax: 212-827-0283
Year Founded: 1916
Approx.Billings: $35,000,000
Emp.: 15
Out of Home Media Planning & Placement
Henry E. Prasse *(Chm. Bd. & Pres.)*
Len Tudisco *(Exec. V.P.)*
Gordon Bring *(V.P., Mktg. Dir. & New Bus. Contact)*
Louis Basso *(Personnel Mgr.)*
David Wells *(Dir., Information Services)*
Salvatore Palilla *(Controller)*
Jean Seepaul *(Acctg. Mgr.)*

Computer Systems/Hardware:
IBM AS/400, PC Local Area Network

OUTDOOR VENTURE CORP.
Hwy. 92
Stearns, KY 42647
Mailing Address:
P.O. Box 337
Stearns, KY 42647
Tel.: 606-376-5021
Fax: 606-376-3341
Year Founded: 1978
Approx.Sls.: $14,000,000
Emp.: 210
Military Tents & Canvas Products
S.I.C.: 2394; 2399
Garry Lockhart *(Pres.)*
Carmen Perry *(Sec., Treas. & Controller)*

Outside Service Firm(s):

Dulworth & Breeding*(Auditors)*
Lexington, KY

Baker, Worthington, Crossley, Stansberry & Woolf*(Legal Firm)*
Knoxville, TN

Bank of McCreary County*(Major Banking Relationship)*
Stearns, KY

OVATION MARKETING, INC.
201 Main St., 6th Fl.
La Crosse, WI 54601
Tel.: 608-785-2460
Fax: 608-785-2496
Year Founded: 1978
Approx.Billings: $15,000,000
Emp.: 36
Direct Marketing
Ralph S. Heath, III *(Pres.)*
Nancy Halverson *(Treas.)*
Lee Mullally *(Pub. Rels. Dir.)*
Kathy Sierp *(Personnel Dir.)*
Deb Culbert *(Production Mgr.)*

OVERHEAD CONVEYOR CO.
1330 Hilton Rd.
Ferndale, MI 48220
Tel.: 313-547-3800 MI
Fax: 313-547-8344
Year Founded: 1945
Assets: $4,821,339
Liabilities: $1,844,266
Net Worth: $2,977,073
Approx.Sls.: $12,000,000
Emp.: 50
Fiscal Year-end: 12/31/90
Export
Manufacture of Conveyors, Structural & Miscellaneous Iron Fabrication
S.I.C.: 3535; 1791
Milford E. Woodbeck *(Chm. Bd.)*
Milford E. Woodbeck, Jr. *(Pres.)*
Thomas M. Woodbeck *(Exec. V.P.)*
Charles E. Whiting *(V.P.)*
Thomas F. Fay *(Treas. & Sec.)*
Principal(s):
Milford E. Woodbeck
Milford E. Woodbeck, Jr.

No. of Mfg. Plants/Facilities: 3
No. of U.S. Offices: 2

Computer Systems/Hardware:
IBM

Outside Service Firm(s):

Joseph, Dise, Grady*(Auditors)*
Troy, MI

Travelers Insurance Co.*(Commercial Insurance Carrier)*
Detroit, MI

Travelers Insurance Co.*(Group Insurer)*
Detroit, MI

N.B.D. Bank, N.A.*(Major Banking Relationship)*
611 Woodward Ave.
Detroit, MI 48226
Tel.: 313-225-1122
Fax: 313-225-3420

Overhill Farms
(See IBM Foods Listing)

OVERLAND TRANSPORTATION SYSTEM, INC.
6500 E. 30th St.
Indianapolis, IN 46219
Mailing Address:
P.O. Box 7004
Indianapolis, IN 46207
Tel.: 317-543-1234
Tel.: 800-366-0150 IN
Fax: 317-543-1230
Year Founded: 1971
Assets: $14,500,009
Liabilities: $7,880,667
Net Worth: $6,619,342
Approx.Sls.: $49,572,200
Emp.: 150
Import Export
Common & Contract Carrier
S.I.C.: 4212; 4213
Carl Cook *(Chm. Bd. & Pres.)*
C. Larry Cook *(Vice Chm.)*
Stephen A. Cook *(V.P. & Chief Oper. Officer)*
Daniel L. Cook *(V.P. & Chief Fin. Officer)*
John G. Hoefle *(V.P. & Chief Information Officer)*
Michael Mills *(V.P. & Controller)*
Mark E. Kern *(V.P.-Pur.)*
Larry D. Parrish *(V.P.-Quality Control)*
William Evans *(Gen. Sls. Mgr.)*

Ann Stegeman *(Mgr.-Personnel Training & Devel.)*
Jennifer Brake *(Dir.-Data Processing)*
Doug Compton *(Asst. to V.P. of Pur.)*
Velma Kaufman *(Corp. Travel Planner)*
Principal(s):
Carl Cook
C. Larry Cook
Stephen A. Cook
Daniel L. Cook

No. of Mfg. Plants/Facilities: 20
No. of U.S. Offices: 20

Computer Systems/Hardware:
IBM

Outside Service Firm(s):

Katz, Sapper & Miller*(Auditors)*
Indianapolis, IN

Baldwin & Lyons*(Commercial Insurance Carrier)*
Indianapolis, IN

Prucare*(Group Insurer)*
Indianapolis, IN

City Securities Corp.*(Investment Banker)*
Indianapolis, IN

Baker & Daniels*(Legal Firm)*
810 Fletcher Bldg., 108 N. Pennsylvania
Indianapolis, IN 46204
Tel.: 317-237-4535

Scopelitis & Garvin*(Legal Firm)*
Inidanapolis, IN

Bank One, Indianapolis, N.A.*(Major Banking Relationship)*
111 Monument Circle, Ste. 1611
Indianapolis, IN 46204-1611
Tel.: 317-321-8110

Jefferson National Life Insurance*(Pension Manager)*
Indianapolis, IN

Subsidiaries:

Frontier Transport Corporation **(1)**
1560 E. Raymond St.
Indianapolis, IN 46203
Tel.: 317-636-1641
Tel.: 800-326-4644
Fax: 317-636-4690
Emp.: 190
Common Carrier
S.I.C.: 4213
Steve Harris *(Pres.)*
Jeffery Davis *(V.P.)*
Thom Schmidt *(Dir.-Sls.)*

Pioneer Express Inc. **(1)**
1560 West Raymond St.
Indianapolis, IN 46206
Tel.: 317-636-1641
Tel.: 800-733-6613
Fax: 317-634-0321
Emp.: 30
Contract & Common Carrier
S.I.C.: 4213
Tony Witt *(V.P.)*
Randy Mitchell *(Dir.-Sls.)*

OVERLY MANUFACTURING CO.
574 W. Otterman
Greensburg, PA 15601
Mailing Address:
P. O. Box 70
Greensburg, PA 15601
Tel.: 412-834-7300
Fax: 412-830-2871
Year Founded: 1888
Approx.Sls.: $12,000,000
Emp.: 150
Export
Metal Doors, Frames, Nuclear Products, Roofs, Church Steeples, Aluminum Swimming Pools
S.I.C.: 3442; 3444
Terry Reese *(Chm. Bd.)*
John Harts *(Pres.)*
D.C. Smeltzer *(V.P.-Res. & Devel.)*
K. Lars Held *(Treas. & Sec.)*
John T. Brooks *(Mgr.-Sls. & Mktg.)*

Computer Systems/Hardware:
Prime/PC Network

Division:

Overly Manufacturing **(1)**
1501 S. Mission Rd.
Fallbrook, CA 92028
Tel.: 619-723-1105
Fax: 619-728-7512
S.I.C.: 3442

OVERSEAS MILITARY SALES CORPORATION
100 Crossways Park W.
Woodbury, NY 11797
Tel.: 516-921-2800 **NY**
Fax: 516-496-1835
Approx.Sls.: $275,000,000
Emp.: 16
Retail Sales of New & Used Automobiles
S.I.C.: 5511
Allen A. Goldring *(Pres.)*
Leo Breittholz *(V.P.)*
Muriel Logan *(Asst. to Pres.)*

Outside Service Firm(s):

Citibank N.A.*(Major Banking Relationship)*
Jericho, NY

OVERSEAS PARTNERS, INC.
375 Park Ave.
New York, NY 10152
Tel.: 212-308-0680
Fax: 212-421-5704
Holding Company
S.I.C.: 6719; 3325; 3471; 3544
Emanuele Costa *(Pres.)*
Donald W. Dick *(Treas.)*

Outside Service Firm(s):

Ernst & Young*(Auditors)*
787 Seventh Ave.
New York, NY 10019
Tel.: 212-773-1243

Citibank N.A.*(Major Banking Relationship)*
Corporate Trust Services, 399 Park Ave.
New York, NY 10043
Tel.: 212-559-1605

OVERSEAS SERVICE CORPORATION
1100 Northpoint Parkway
West Palm Beach, FL 33407
Tel.: 407-683-4090
Fax: 407-683-4031
Emp.: 175
Manufacturers Representative
S.I.C.: 8742
Frank J. Hogan *(Pres. & Chief Exec. Officer)*
Richard Cullen *(Chief Fin. Officer)*
William Vickers *(V.P.-Mktg.)*

Divisions:

Commissary Div. **(1)**
1100 Northpoint Parkway
West Palm Beach, FL 33407
Tel.: 407-683-4090
Mfr. Rep For The Military Commissaries
S.I.C.: 8742
R.S. Van Emburg *(Gen. Mgr.)*

Exchange Div. **(1)**
12700 Park Center Dr., Ste. 1409
Dallas, TX 75251
Tel.: 214-991-9390
Mfrs. Rep, Exchanges Only
S.I.C.: 8742
R.E. Denson *(Gen. Mgr.)*

OVERSTREET PAVING COMPANY
1390 Donegan Rd.
Largo, FL 34641
Tel.: 813-585-4786 **FL**
Fax: 813-585-3139
Year Founded: 1969
Approx.Sls.: $21,000,000
Emp.: 150
Surfacing & Paving; Underground Utilities Contractor
S.I.C.: 1611; 1623
Thomas E. Overstreet *(Pres.)*
Dorothy M. Overstreet *(Sr. V.P. & Sec.)*
Thomas E. Overstreet, Jr. *(V.P.)*
Monica Kramen *(V.P.)*

Outside Service Firm(s):

Morrison & Delarbre*(Auditors)*
Tampa, FL

NCNB National Bank of Florida*(Major Banking Relationship)*
Tampa, FL

OVERTON MOORE & ASSOCIATES
1125 W. 190th St., Ste. 200
Gardena, CA 90248
Tel.: 310-323-9100 **CA**
Fax: 310-608-7997
Year Founded: 1973
Approx.Sls.: $25,000,000
Emp.: 60
Real Estate Developers
S.I.C.: 1531
Stanley A. Moore *(Pres.)*
Doug Carlton *(V.P.)*
Don Koch *(V.P.)*
Kathy Rodgers *(V.P.)*

OWATONNA CANNING COMPANY
900 N. Cedar Ave.
Owatonna, MN 55060
Mailing Address:
P. O. Box 447
Owatonna, MN 55060
Tel.: 507-451-7670 **MN**
Telex: 62921160
Fax: 507-451-5607
Year Founded: 1921
Approx.Sls.: $56,000,000
Emp.: 400
Fiscal Year-end: 2/29/92
Export
Canned Asparagus, Peas, Corn, Pumpkin, Wax Beans & Green Beans & Prepared Salads
S.I.C.: 2033
Stephens J. Lange *(Chm. Bd.)*
Chadwick S. Lange *(Pres.)*
Jerome F. Erck *(V.P.)*
Dean Christianson *(Controller)*
Karen E. Lange *(Sec.)*
Elvin Halverson *(Mgr.-Human Resources)*
David E. Hanna *(Mgr.-Sls. & Mktg.)*
Principal(s):
Stephens J. Lange
Chadwick S. Lange

No. of Mfg. Plants/Facilities: 5

Outside Service Firm(s):

Hutton, Nelson & McDonald*(Auditors)*
Chicago, IL

Dorsey & Whitney*(Legal Firm)*
2200 First Bank Place East
Minneapolis, MN 55402
Tel.: 612-340-2600
Fax: 612-340-2600

Norwest Bank Minnesota, N.A.*(Major Banking Relationship)*
Owatonna, MN

Subsidiary:

Princeville Canning Co. **(1)**
Princeville, IL 61559
Tel.: 309-385-4301
Canned Salads, Asparagus & Pumpkin
S.I.C.: 2033
David Stoner *(Gen. Mgr.)*

OWEN-AMES-KIMBALL CO.
300 Ionia Ave. N.W.
Grand Rapids, MI 49503
Tel.: 616-456-1521 **MI**
Fax: 616-458-0770
Year Founded: 1891
Assets: $15,200,000
Liabilities: $11,100,000
Net Worth: $4,100,000
Approx.Sls.: $50,000,000
Emp.: 125
Fiscal Year-end: 12/31/91
Non-Residential Bldg. Contractors
S.I.C.: 1541; 1542
Thomas Healy *(Pres.)*
John S. Keelean *(V.P.)*
Ronnell P. Denhof *(Sec.)*
David H. Gibbs *(Treas.)*

Outside Service Firm(s):

Ernst & Young*(Auditors)*
171 Monroe Ave. NW
Grand Rapids, MI 49503
Tel.: 616-774-0710
Fax: 616-774-0190

Warner, Norcross & Judd*(Legal Firm)*
One Vandenberg Center
Grand Rapids, MI 49502
Tel.: 616-459-6121

Old Kent Bank*(Major Banking Relationship)*
Grand Rapids, MI

Subsidiaries:

Muskegon Construction Company **(1)**
425 Catawba Ave.
Muskegon, MI 49443
Tel.: 616-726-3177
Fax: 616-728-3547
General Contractors
S.I.C.: 1541; 1542
Gary Post *(Pres. & Chief Oper. Officer)*

Owen-Ames-Kimball Co. **(1)**
11941 Fairway Lakes Dr
Fort Myers, FL 33913-8338
Tel.: 813-561-4141
Fax: 813-561-1996
General Contractors
S.I.C.: 1541; 1542
Steven C. Shimp *(Chief Oper. Officer)*

Owen-Ames-Kimball Engineering, Inc. **(1)**
300 Ionia Ave. N.W.
Grand Rapids, MI 49503
Tel.: 616-456-1521
Fax: 616-458-0770
General Contractors
S.I.C.: 1541; 1542
John S. Keelean *(Chief Oper. Officer)*

OWEN HEALTH CARE
9800 Centre Pkwy.
Houston, TX 77036
Mailing Address:
P.O. Box 742587,
Houston, TX 77274-2587
Tel.: 713-777-8173
Fax: 713-777-5417
Sales Range: $100-499 Million
Emp.: 1,600
Fiscal Year-end: 5/31/91
Hospital Pharmacy Management
S.I.C.: 8099
Dian G. Owen *(Chm. Bd.)*
Carl E. Isgren *(Pres.)*
Harlan C. Stai *(Exec. V.P.)*
Donald M. Jones *(Sr. V.P.)*
M. Andy Marlatt *(Sr. V.P.)*
Robert J. Rasmussen *(Sr. V.P.-Sls.)*
Dennis S. Stepanik *(Sr. V.P.)*
Edward D. Zost *(Sr. V.P.)*
Robert M. Rutledge *(V.P.)*
Principal(s):
Dian G. Owen

Outside Service Firm(s):

Price Waterhouse*(Auditors)*
1201 Louisiana, Ste. 2900
Houston, TX 77002
Tel.: 713-654-4100

Owen Health Care—(Continued)

Wood, Lucksinger & Epstein*(Legal Firm)*
Houston, TX

First National Bank of Abilene*(Major Banking Relationship)*
Abilene, TX

OWEN INDUSTRIES, INC.
5th & Ave. H
Carter Lake, IA 51510
Mailing Address:
P.O. Box 1085,
Omaha, NE 68101
Tel.: 712-347-5500 **NE**
Year Founded: 1979
Approx.Sls.: $75,000,000
Emp.: 400
Import
Mfr. Fabricated Structural Metal; Metal Service Center
S.I.C.: 3441; 5051
Robert E. Owen *(Chm. Bd. & Pres.)*
John Dobson *(Sr. V.P.)*
Sid Blaauw *(V.P.)*
Richard Carlin *(V.P.)*
Roger Goodwin *(V.P.)*
Carl Harrison *(V.P.)*
John T. Hurley *(V.P.)*
Robert Jacobsen *(V.P.)*
William R. Nessen *(V.P.)*
Dolores Owen *(Sec. & Treas.)*

Outside Service Firm(s):

First National Bank*(Major Banking Relationship)*
Omaha, NE

Divisions:

Lincoln Steel **(1)**
P.O. Box 81668,
Lincoln, NE 68501
Approx.Sls.: $6,000,000
Emp.: 50
Fiscal Year-end: 12/31/91
Steel Distributors & Fabricators
S.I.C.: 3499
Robert E. Owen *(Pres.)*
William R. Nessen *(V.P. & Gen. Mgr.)*
Carl W. Harrison *(Sec. & Treas.)*
Michael Herzog *(Office Mgr.)*

Paxton & Vierling **(1)**
P.O. Box 1085
Omaha, NE 68101
Tel.: 712-347-5500
Machine Shops; Steel Service Center; Structural Steel
S.I.C.: 5051; 3441; 3449; 3599
Sid Blaauw *(V.P. & Gen. Mgr.)*

OWEN PACIFIC
1236 S. Compton Ave.
Los Angeles, CA 90021
Mailing Address:
P.O. Box 21097
Los Angeles, CA 90021
Tel.: 213-747-7125 **CA**
Fax: 213-746-2714
Year Founded: 1916
Approx.Sls.: $15,000,000
Emp.: 200
Fiscal Year-end: 4/30/88
Commercial & Industrial Roofing
S.I.C.: 1761
John R. McClain *(Pres.)*
Mark R. McClain *(V.P.)*
David Sirignano *(Treas.)*
Stuart Hsieh *(Sec.)*

No. of Mfg. Plants/Facilities: 3
No. of U.S. Offices: 3

Computer Systems/Hardware:
Basic Four 9000

Outside Service Firm(s):

Grant & Popovich*(Legal Firm)*
Los Angeles, CA

First Business Bank*(Major Banking Relationship)*
Los Angeles, CA

OWEN STEEL CO., INC.
801 Blossom St.
Columbia, SC 29202
Mailing Address:
P.O. Box 18
Columbia, SC 29202
Tel.: 803-251-7680 **SC**
Fax: 803-251-7665
Year Founded: 1936
Sales Range: $100-499 Million
Emp.: 1,650
Manufacture Fabricated Structural & Reinforcing Steel
S.I.C.: 3441; 3449
Dorothy G. Owen *(Chm. Bd.)*
Ralph H. Moore, Jr. *(Vice Chm.)*
Lawrence P. Flood *(Pres. & Chief Exec. Officer)*
Guy W. Hendley *(Exec. V.P.-Corp. Fin. & Treas.)*
James McGready *(V.P.-Sls.)*
Bill Saunders *(V.P.-Sls.)*
Michael J. Senneway *(V.P. & Gen. Mgr.)*
Elizabeth G. Owen *(Sec.)*
Charles W. Harris *(Dir.-Safety)*
Frank Parks *(Dir.-Personnel)*
Donald M. Parris *(Mgr.-Data Processing)*

Outside Service Firm(s):

Derrick, Stubbs & Stith*(Auditors)*
Columbia, SC

South Carolina National Bank*(Major Banking Relationship)*
Columbia, SC

OWENS POLLICK & ASSOCIATES, PHOENIX, INC.
2800 N. Central Ave., Ste. 1500
Phoenix, AZ 85004
Tel.: 602-230-7557
Fax: 602-230-8396
Year Founded: 1991
Approx.Billings: $18,000,000
Emp.: 20
Bill M. Owens *(Chm. Bd. & Chief Exec. Officer)*
Terry Kramer *(Office Mgr. & Telecommunications)*

R.S. OWENS
5535 N. Lynch Ave.
Chicago, IL 60630
Tel.: 312-282-6000
Tel.: 800-282-6200 **IL**
Fax: 312-545-4501
Year Founded: 1938
Approx.Sls.: $15,000,000
Emp.: 300
Import Export
Trophies, Plaques, Custom Recognition & Incentive Awards
S.I.C.: 3499; 3914
Owen R. Siegel *(Chm. Bd. & Chief Exec. Officer)*
Scott Siegel *(Pres.)*
S.L. Siegel *(Treas. & Sec.)*
Bert Marcelo *(Controller)*
Kathy Wemlinger *(Dir.-Human Resources)*
Don Esposito *(Mgr.-Inventory Controll)*
Dick Gertz *(Mgr.-Pur.)*
Tom Lueken *(Mgr.-Sls. & Mktg., Retail Div.)*
Frank Poradek *(Mgr.-Mfg. & Plant Mgr.)*
Principal(s):
Owen R. Siegel

No. of Mfg. Plants/Facilities: 1

Outside Service Firm(s):

Miller, Cooper & Co.*(Auditors)*
Northbrook, IL

Levin & Rosen*(Legal Firm)*
Chicago, IL

LaSalle National Bank*(Major Banking Relationship)*
135 S. LaSalle St.
Chicago, IL 60603
Tel.: 312-443-2440
Fax: 312-443-2819

OWENSBORO GRAIN CO., INC.
719 E. 2nd St.
Owensboro, KY 42301
Tel.: 502-686-6509
Fax: 502-684-1166
Sales Range: $100-499 Million
Emp.: 125
Soybean Processor; Grain Merchandiser
S.I.C.: 2075; 5153; 5191
Patrick E. Wright *(Pres.)*
Jeffrey L. Erb *(Chief Fin. Officer)*
Henry E. O'Bryan *(Exec. V.P.)*
Julian G. Hayden, Jr. *(V.P.-Mktg.)*
John M. Wright *(V.P.-Opers.)*
Patrick Conder *(Treas.)*
Ronald Prater *(Sec.)*

Computer Systems/Hardware:
IBM System 36

Outside Service Firm(s):

Arthur Andersen & Co.*(Auditors)*
2300 Meidinger Tower
Louisville, KY 40202
Tel.: 502-589-4160

Liberty Life Assurance Company*(Group Insurer)*
Greenville, SC

Holbrook, Wible, Sullivan & Helmers*(Legal Firm)*
Owensboro, KY

Owensboro National Bank*(Major Banking Relationship)*
Owensboro, KY

First National Bank of Louisville*(Pension Manager)*
P.O. Box 36000,
Louisville, KY 40233

OWSLEY & SONS, INC.
Gold Hill Rd. at I-77 S.
Fort Mill, SC 29716-1449
Mailing Address:
P.O. Box 1449,
Fort Mill, SC 29715
Tel.: 803-548-3636
Fax: 803-548-7115
Approx.Sls.: $30,000,000
Emp.: 90
Export
Wholesale Rental & Sales of Construction & Industrial Equipment
S.I.C.: 5082
T. Reed Owsley *(Pres.)*
R.M. Owsley *(Exec. V.P.)*
John Wall *(V.P.-Sls.)*
Principal(s):
T. Reed Owsley

Outside Service Firm(s):

Ernst & Young*(Auditors)*
1100 Independence Center
Charlotte, NC 28246
Tel.: 704-372-6300

Henderson Henderson & Shuford*(Legal Firm)*
Charlotte, NC

First Citizens Bank & Trust Co.*(Major Banking Relationship)*
Charlotte, NC

OXBOW CORPORATION
1601 Forum Pl.
West Palm Beach, FL 33401
Tel.: 407-697-4300
Fax: 407-697-1876
Approx.Sls.: $1,250,000,000
Emp.: 80
Investment Company; Oil Trading; Energy Production
S.I.C.: 6799; 6211; 1311
William I. Koch *(Pres.)*
John M. Klarfeld *(Press Officer)*

OXFORD FIRST CORPORATION
7300 Old York Rd.
Philadelphia, PA 19126-1884
Tel.: 215-782-7000 **PA**
Fax: 215-782-7305
Year Founded: 1948
Assets: $550,000,000
Earnings: $6,502,000
Liabilities: $485,000,000
Net Worth: $65,000,000
Approx.Rev.: $70,000,000
Emp.: 340
Fiscal Year-end: 12/31/91
Financial Holding Co.
S.I.C.: 6153; 6552; 6719; 7371; 6159; 6162
Aaron A. Gold *(Chm. Bd. & Chief Exec. Officer)*
Bert Blicher *(Pres. & Chief Oper. Officer)*
Gerard J. Leimkuhler, Jr. *(Exec. V.P., Sec. & Chief Admin. Officer)*
Donald M. Rosenberg *(Exec. V.P., Treas. & Chief Fin. Officer)*
Joshua S. Gold *(Sr. V.P.-Port Folio Acquisition)*
Frank J. Nicastro *(Sr. V.P. & Gen. Counsel)*
Kurt V. Christensen *(V.P.)*
Kenneth R. Gingrich, Jr. *(V.P. & Controller)*
Marie Wilkens *(V.P.-Personnel)*

No. of U.S. Offices: 2

Computer Systems/Hardware:
IBM ES 9000

Outside Service Firm(s):

Coopers & Lybrand*(Auditors)*
2400 Eleven Penn Center
Philadelphia, PA 19103-2962
Tel.: 215-963-8000

Bankers Trust Co.*(Investment Banker)*
P.O. Box 9050, Church St. Station
New York, NY 10008
Tel.: 212-250-6037

Blank, Rome, Comisky & McCauley*(Legal Firm)*
Four Penn Center Plaza
Philadelphia, PA 19103
Tel.: 215-209-3700

Philadelphia National Bank*(Major Banking Relationship)*
P.O. Box 13834, Broad & Chestnut Streets
Philadelphia, PA 19101-7618
Tel.: 215-973-8327

Stratton Management Co.*(Pension Manager)*
Blue Bell, PA

Subsidiaries:

Computer Information Services, Inc. **(1)**
7300 Old York Rd.
Philadelphia, PA 19126
Tel.: 215-782-7000 (100%)
Fax: 215-782-7019
Approx.Sls.: $1,000,000
Emp.: 10
Computer Service Bureau
S.I.C.: 7372
Aaron A. Gold *(Chm.)*
Bert Blicher *(Pres.)*
Gerard J. Leimkuhler, Jr. *(Exec. V.P.)*
Donald M. Rosenberg *(Exec. V.P. & Chief Fin. Officer)*
Joseph DeAngelo *(V.P. & Dir.-Data Processing)*

Oxford Communities, Inc. **(1)**
7300 Old York Blvd.
Philadelphia, PA 19126
Tel.: 215-782-7000 (100%)
Fax: 215-782-7019
Approx.Sls.: $4,000,000
Emp.: 4
Real Estate Development
S.I.C.: 6552
Aaron A. Gold *(Chm.)*
Bert Blicher *(Pres.)*
Donald M. Rosenberg *(Exec. V.P. & Chief Fin. Officer)*
Joshua Gold *(Sr. V.P. & Dir.-Real Estate)*

Oxford Finance Companies, Inc. **(1)**
7300 Old York Rd.
Philadelphia, PA 19126
Tel.: 215-782-7019 (100%)
Fax: 215-782-7019
Approx.Sls.: $70,000,000
Emp.: 200
Purchase & Liquidation of Accounts Receivable
S.I.C.: 6162; 6159; 6153
Aaron A. Gold *(Chm. Bd. & Chief Exec. Officer)*
Bert Blicher *(Pres. & Chief Oper. Officer)*
Donald M. Rosenberg *(Exec. V.P., Treas. & Chief Fin. Officer)*
Gerard J. Leimkuhler, Jr. *(Exec. V.P., Sec. & Chief Admin. Officer)*
Kenneth R. Gingrich, Jr. *(V.P. & Controller)*
Kurt V. Christensen *(V.P. & Dir.-Fin. Services)*
Joseph DeAngelo *(V.P. & Dir.-Data Processing)*

OXFORD REALTY SERVICES CORP.
7316 Wisconsin Ave.
Bethesda, MD 20814
Tel.: 301-654-3100 **IN**
Fax: 301-951-3495
Year Founded: 1949
Sales Range: $100-499 Million
Emp.: 1,955
Fiscal Year-end: 3/31/91
Manage & Finance Multi-Family Housing & Senior Living
S.I.C.: 6719; 1522; 1531; 6513; 6531; 6552
Leo E. Zickler *(Pres. & Chief Exec. Officer)*
Donald Boardman *(Exec. V.P.)*
Wesley D. Minami *(Sr. V.P. & Chief Fin. Officer)*
Robert B. Downing *(Sr. V.P.)*
Karl Mayer *(Sr. V.P.)*
Mark E. Schifrin *(Sr. V.P.)*
Richard R. Singleton *(Sr. V.P.)*
Timothy Danello *(V.P., Gen. Counsel & Asst. Sec.)*
Laura M. Grabow *(V.P. & Sec.)*
Ken Willard *(V.P. & Treas.)*

Principal(s):
Leo E. Zickler

No. of U.S. Offices: 7

Computer Systems/Hardware:
WANG

Outside Service Firm(s):

Arthur Andersen & Co.*(Auditors)*
1666 K Street, N.W.
Washington, DC 20006

Jones, Day, Reavis & Pogue*(Legal Firm)*
Dallas, TX

OZARK MOTOR LINES
3934 Homewood Rd.
Memphis, TN 38181
Mailing Address:
P.O. Box 181077
Memphis, TN 38181
Tel.: 901-795-9711 **TN**
Fax: 901-360-1250
Year Founded: 1967
Trucking, Except Local
S.I.C.: 4213
Steve F. Higginbotham *(Pres.)*
Tommy Higginbotham *(V.P.)*
Dorothy Higginbotham *(Sec.)*

Outside Service Firm(s):

Boatmen's Bank of Tennessee*(Major Banking Relationship)*
200 Madison
Memphis, TN
Tel.: 901-529-5900

P M COMPANY
(Formerly Paper Manufacturers Co.)
9800 Bustleton Ave.
Philadelphia, PA 19115
Tel.: 215-673-4500
Tel.: 800-999-PMCO
Twx: 710-670-0595
Fax: 215-676-1311
Year Founded: 1905
Approx.Sls.: $100,000,000
Emp.: 650
Fiscal Year-end: 9/30/91
Import Export
Convertor of Rolled Paper Products & Other Office Consumables; Felxible Medical Packaging Materials
S.I.C.: 2672; 2678
Corporate Giving Program:
Contributes to United Way
Donald F. O'Neill *(Pres. & Chief Exec. Officer)*
Jerry Morris *(Sr. V.P.-Sls.)*
Robert Burgess *(Grp. Pres.-Health Care)*
James O'Brien *(V.P.-Sls. & Mktg.)*
Douglas Tryon *(V.P.-Human Resources)*
Jack Omlor *(Chief Fin. Officer & Treas.)*
Wayne Romanczuk *(Sec. & Controller)*
Jeffrey Brown *(Dir.-Sls. & Mktg.)*
Richard Craig *(Dir.-Quality Control)*
Richard Stover *(Dir.-Mngmt. Information Systems)*
Dan Craft *(Mgr.-Tech.)*
Greg Olson *(Mgr.-Personnel)*

No. of Mfg. Plants/Facilities: 4
No. of U.S. Offices: 6
No. of Foreign Offices: 2

Computer Systems/Hardware:
IBM System 36

Outside Service Firm(s):

KPMG Peat Marwick*(Auditors)*
1600 Market St.
Philadelphia, PA 19103
Tel.: 215-299-3100

Arkwright Mutual Insurance*(Commercial Insurance Carrier)*
225 Wyman St.
Waltham, MA 02254-9198
Tel.: 617-890-9300
Fax: 617-890-0075

Liberty Mutual*(Commercial Insurance Carrier)*
Boston, MA

Connecticut General Life Insurance Co.*(Group Insurer)*
P.O. Box 2975,
Hartford, CT 06104
Tel.: 203-726-6000

Ballard, Spahr, Andrews & Ingersoll*(Legal Firm)*
1735 Market St., 51st Fl.
Philadelphia, PA 19103-7599
Tel.: 215-665-8500

Meridian Bank*(Major Banking Relationship)*
Reading, PA

Philadelphia National Bank*(Major Banking Relationship)*
P.O. Box 13834, Broad & Chestnut Streets
Philadelphia, PA 19101-7618
Tel.: 215-973-8327

Divisions:

P.M. Health Care Div. **(1)**
9800 Bustleton Ave.
Philadelphia, PA 19115
Tel.: 215-673-4500
Tel.: 800-999-PMCO
Anthony Cook *(Pres.)*
Jim O'Brien *(V.P.-Sls. & Mktg.)*
Barbara Bullard *(Mgr.-Adv.)*

P.M. Paper Products Div. **(1)**
8525 E. 33rd St.
Indianapolis, IN 46226
Tel.: 317-899-5100
William Fecht *(Pres.)*

P/A INDUSTRIES, INC.
522 Cottage Grove Rd.
Bloomfield, CT 06002
Tel.: 203-243-8306
Fax: 203-242-4870
Year Founded: 1954
Approx.Sls.: $10,000,000
Emp.: 100
Fiscal Year-end: 12/31/90
Import Export
Mfr. of Machine Tools For The Metal Stamping & Fabricating Industry & Converting Equip. For The WEB Processing & Converting Accessor Manufacturer
S.I.C.: 3545
Jerome Finn *(Pres.)*
E. Tremblay *(V.P. & Chief Oper. Officer)*
William J. Pitney *(V.P. & Chief Fin. Officer)*
Steve Miller *(Gen. Counsel)*
Tom Owens *(Controller)*
Tom Carrigan *(Dir.-Sls.)*
Norm Lubeach *(Mgr.-Personnel)*
M.A. Sirois *(Mgr.-Data Processing)*
B. Cooper *(Mgr.-Corp. Travel Planner)*

Computer Systems/Hardware:
IBM

Divisions:

Metal Stamping Equip. Div. **(1)**
522 Cottage Grove Rd.
Bloomfield, CT 06002
Tel.: 203-243-8306
Tel.: 800-243-8306
Fax: 203-242-4870
Import Export
Metal Forming Equipment
S.I.C.: 3545
J. Finn *(Pres.)*

Web Processing Equip. Div. **(1)**
522 Cottage Grove Rd.
Bloomfield, CT 06002
Tel.: 203-243-8306
Tel.: 800-243-8306
Fax: 203-242-4870
Computer Systems/Hardware:
IBM
S.I.C.: 3545
William Pitney *(Treas.)*

PBM OFFICE PRODUCTS
7820 E. Pleasant Valley Rd.
Cleveland, OH 44131
Tel.: 216-447-1200 **OH**
Fax: 216-447-9214
Year Founded: 1974
Approx.Sls.: $15,000,000
Emp.: 105
Commercial Distributor of Office Products
S.I.C.: 5044; 5112
Alex S. Toth *(Chm. Bd., Pres. & Chief Exec. Officer)*
Frank Buchwald *(V.P.-Opers.)*
Mark Honeycutt *(V.P.-Admin. & Chief Fin. Officer)*

Principal(s):
Alex S. Toth

No. of Mfg. Plants/Facilities: 3
No. of U.S. Offices: 3

Computer Systems/Hardware:
Hewlitt Packard 9000

Outside Service Firm(s):

Ernst & Young*(Auditors)*
1300 Huntington Bldg.
Cleveland, OH 44115
Tel.: 216-861-5000
Fax: 303-291-6234

Republic Hogg Robinson*(Commercial Insurance Carrier)*
Cleveland, OH

Arter & Hadden*(Legal Firm)*
1144 Union Commerce Bldg.,
Cleveland, OH 44115
Tel.: 216-696-1144

Society National Bank*(Major Banking Relationship)*
900 Euclid Ave., P.O. Box 6477
Cleveland, OH 44101-6477
Tel.: 216-737-5000
Fax: 216-566-8947

Subsidiary:

PBM Publishing **(1)**
7820 E. Pleasant Valley Rd.
Independence, OH 44131
Tel.: 216-447-1200
Book Publishing
S.I.C.: 2731
Al Toth *(Pres.)*

PBS BUILDING SYSTEMS OF AMERICA
155 N. Riverview Dr.
Anaheim, CA 92808
Tel.: 714-998-4777
Fax: 714-283-1504
Year Founded: 1980
Approx.Sls.: $29,000,000
Emp.: 201
Mfr. of Prefabricated Wood Buildings
S.I.C.: 2452
Lance L. Knox *(Chm. Bd.)*
John B. Harty *(Pres. & Chief Exec. Officer)*
James W. Gasper *(Sr. V.P. & Gen. Mgr.)*
Kathryn M. Gray *(V.P.)*
John J. Horn *(V.P.-Engrng.)*
Steven J. Mozer *(V.P. & Gen. Mgr.)*
Brian B. Ruttencutter *(V.P.-Fin. & Admin.)*
Steven J. Treicher *(V.P.-Sls.)*
Conrad A. Plimpton *(Sec.)*

PC DISTRIBUTING INC.
2080 Carboy Rd.
Mount Prospect, IL 60056
Tel.: 708-228-0700 **IL**
Fax: 708-228-5560
Year Founded: 1982
Assets: $15,312,236
Liabilities: $13,947,325
Net Worth: $1,364,911
Approx.Sls.: $60,000,000
Emp.: 125
Fiscal Year-end: 7/31/91
Wholesale Distribution of Micro Computer Hardware and Peripherals
S.I.C.: 5045
Glen Peterson *(Chm. Bd.)*
Joe Muldoon *(Pres.)*
Martin Glotzon *(Treas. & Sec.)*
Kim Kehoe *(Dir.-Sls.)*
Cleo Mancini *(Dir.-Adv.)*
Mark Sanderson *(Dir.-Personnel)*
Jeff Sirt *(Dir.-Pur.)*

No. of Mfg. Plants/Facilities: 1
No. of U.S. Offices: 6

Computer Systems/Hardware:
Fujitsu

Outside Service Firm(s):

Arthur Andersen & Co.*(Auditors)*
33 W. Monroe St.
Chicago, IL 60603-4067
Tel.: 312-580-0033
Fax: 312-507-6748

Griffin & Fadden Ltd.*(Legal Firm)*
Chicago, IL

PC Distributing Inc.—(Continued)

LaSalle National Bank*(Major Banking Relationship)*
120 S. LaSalle St.
Chicago, IL 60603
Tel.: 312-781-8000

PCI
12416 Hymeadow Dr.
Austin, TX 78750
Tel.: 512-250-9023
Tel.: 1-800-678-9724 TX
Fax: 512-331-3900
Year Founded: 1979
Assets: $3,977,659
Liabilities: $517,233
Net Worth: $3,460,426
Sales Range: $10-19 Million
Emp.: 52
Fiscal Year-end: 9/30/91
Export
Computer Trade Publications
S.I.C.: 2721
Gary Pittman *(Chm. Bd., Pres., Chief Exec., Chief Oper. & Chief Fin. Officer)*
Bill Lifland *(V.P.-Circulation & Data Processing)*
Clayton P. Peters *(V.P.-Meetings & Planning)*
Tom Clark *(V.P.)*
Jim Boone *(Treas.)*
Dean Buchanan *(Mgr.-Fin. & Admin.)*
Tracey Yelverton *(Mgr.-Human Resources)*

No. of U.S. Offices: 2
No. of Foreign Offices: 1

Computer Systems/Hardware:
Convergent; NCR; IBM; Texas Instruments; Apple; Hewlett-Packard; Macintosh

Outside Service Firm(s):

Tommy Bargsley, CPA*(Auditors)*
Austin, TX

Mass Mutual*(Group Insurer)*
Austin, TX

Bankston, Wright & Greenhill*(Legal Firm)*
Austin, TX

Hill Country Bank*(Major Banking Relationship)*
Austin, TX

Rauscher Pierce Refsnes, Inc.*(Pension Manager)*
InterFirst Tower, Sixth & Congress
Austin, TX 78701
Tel.: 512-476-7131

Subsidiaries:

PD News **(1)**
12416 Hymeadow Dr.
Austin, TX 78750
Tel.: 512-250-8388

Software Video Production **(1)**
12416 Hymeadow Dr.
Austin, TX 78750
Tel.: 512-250-9563
Emp.: 50
Publ. of Computer Journals
S.I.C.: 2721
Gary Pittman *(Chief Oper. Officer)*
Dusty Miller *(Publr.)*

P.D. FASHIONS
(Formerly Dubrowsky & Perlbinder, Inc.)
512 Seventh Ave.
New York, NY 10018
Tel.: 212-221-1450
Fax: 212-819-1268
Approx.Sls.: $12,000,000
Emp.: 50
Mfr. of Women's Fun Fur Coats, Leather Long Coats & Short Jackets; With Fur & Without
S.I.C.: 2337
Arnold Perlbinder *(Pres.)*
Paul Dubrowsky *(V.P.)*
Seymour Goldstein *(Mgr.-Sls.)*

Outside Service Firm(s):

Chemical Banking Corp.*(Major Banking Relationship)*
277 Park Ave.
New York, NY 10041
Tel.: 212-310-6407
Fax: 212-310-4526

PE SYSTEMS
1851 Alexander Bell Drive, Ste. 105
Reston, VA 22091
Tel.: 703-391-9811
Fax: 703-391-9435
Approx.Sls.: $10,000,000
Emp.: 120
Analysis of Military Based Systems; Communications Security; Manufacturer of Security Devices
S.I.C.: 8999; 7382
David Pronko *(Chm. Bd., Pres. & Chief Exec. Officer)*
Elizabeth A. Pronko *(Chief Fin. Officer, V.P. & Controller)*
Gail De Segurintz *(Dir.-Personnel)*

Computer Systems/Hardware:
IBM PC

Outside Service Firm(s):

Price Waterhouse*(Auditors)*
1801 K. Street, N.W.
Washington, DC 20006
Tel.: 202-296-0800

Lincoln National Life Insurance Co.*(Group Insurer)*
PO Box 208, 1300 S. Clinton
Fort Wayne, IN 46801
Tel.: 219-455-2926
Fax: 219-455-7619

Bank of Virginia*(Major Banking Relationship)*
Springfield, VA

McLean Financial*(Pension Manager)*
McLean, VA

PHB PARKER DIE CASTINGS
7900 W. Ridge Rd.
Fairview, PA 16415
Tel.: 814-474-5511
Year Founded: 1906
Approx.Sls.: $52,000,000
Emp.: 500
Export
Precision Aluminum & Zinc Die Castings
S.I.C.: 3363; 3364
William M. Hilbert *(Pres. & Chief Oper. Officer)*
Edward V. Bolt *(Exec. V.P.)*
James O. Benson *(V.P. & Treas.)*
A.J. Kalil *(V.P.-Sls. & Mktg.)*
J.D. McDonald Jr. *(Sec.)*

Computer Systems/Hardware:
IBM AS/400 & IBM 4341

Division:

PHB Parker Die Castings **(1)**
P.O. Drawer D
Beaufort, SC 29903
Tel.: 803-846-2201
Approx.Sls.: $53,000,000
Emp.: 125
S.I.C.: 3363; 3364
William M. Hilbert Sr. *(Chief Exec. Officer)*
Bill O'Neal *(Sls. Mgr.)*
Don Bennett *(Gen. Mgr.)*

PMC PARTNERSHIP, LTD.
90 Post Rd., West
Westport, CT 06880
Tel.: 203-227-8478
Year Founded: 1973
Approx.Billings: $14,000,000
Emp.: 12
Full Service Sales Promotion Agency
Joseph R. Geer *(Pres., Chief Exec. Officer)*
C. Samuel Stryker, Jr. *(Chief Oper. Officer, Exec. V.P., New Bus. Contact)*
Nicholas A. Noell *(Sr. V.P. & Treas.)*
Elsebeth Sexton Stryker *(Sr. V.P. & Sec.)*

PMC, INC.
12243 Branford St.
Sun Valley, CA 91353
Tel.: 818-896-1101 DE
Fax: 818-897-0180
Year Founded: 1964
Assets: $345,000,000
Net Worth: $345,000,000
Approx.Sls.: $1,000,000,000
Emp.: 4,500
Fiscal Year-end: 12/31/89
Import Export
Manufacture of Miscellaneous Plastic Products, Chemicals & Equipment
S.I.C.: 2819; 2821; 2865
Philip E. Kamins *(Pres.)*
T.C. Cheong *(Chief Fin. Officer)*
Lori M. Johnson *(V.P.)*

Outside Service Firm(s):

Coopers & Lybrand*(Auditors)*
350 S. Grand Ave.
Los Angeles, CA 90071
Tel.: 213-481-1000
Fax: 213-482-6440

PMC INDUSTRIES INC.
29100 Lakeland Blvd.
Wickliffe, OH 44092
Tel.: 216-943-3300
Fax: 216-944-1974
Approx.Sls.: $33,000,000
Emp.: 200
Fiscal Year-end: 12/31/90
Mfr. Machinery, Cutting Tools, Gages, Couplings
S.I.C.: 3541; 3398; 3498; 3544; 3545; 3599
Jack F. Roche *(Chm. Bd., Pres. & Chief Exec. Officer)*
Richard J. Jeschelnig *(V.P.-Sls. & Engrng.)*
Edward K. Novak *(V.P.-Mfg.)*
Michael A. Brackman *(Controller)*
J. Popovic *(Mgr.-Sls.)*
R. Terrill *(Mgr.-Intl. Sls.)*
Dennis A. Yeager *(Mgr.-Pur.)*

Outside Service Firm(s):

Ernst & Young*(Auditors)*
1300 Huntington Bldg.
Cleveland, OH 44115
Tel.: 216-861-5000

PPA INDUSTRIES, INC.
8222 Douglas Ave., Ste. 660
Dallas, TX 75225
Tel.: 214-373-1844
Fax: 214-373-1825
Approx.Sls.: $40,000,000
Emp.: 500
Fiscal Year-end: 12/31/90
Holding Co.; Mfr. of Chain Link Fence, Communication Crystals & Metal Enclosures for Electronics Industry; Aluminum & Die Cast Products
S.I.C.: 1799; 3469; 3496; 3677; 5039; 5065; 6719; 3679
David E. Crandall *(Chm. Bd. & Chief Exec. Officer)*
Arthur J. Harding Jr. *(Pres. & Chief Oper. Officer)*
Stanley F. Kwasnicki *(V.P.)*
Tony H. Wilson *(V.P.-Fin. & Sec.)*

Computer Systems/Hardware:
IBM PC

Outside Service Firm(s):

Coopers & Lybrand*(Auditors)*
1999 Bryan St., Ste. 3000
Dallas, TX 75201
Tel.: 214-754-5000

MBank Dallas*(Major Banking Relationship)*
1900 Pacific
Dallas, TX 75265

Divisions:

Anchor Fence Company **(1)**
8451 Rovana Cir., Ste. 1
Sacramento, CA 95828
Tel.: 916-387-6412
Mfr. of Fences
S.I.C.: 1799; 3469; 3496
George Kruse *(Branch Mgr.)*

Anchor Post Products-Washington Div. **(1)**
13202 NE 177th Pl.
Woodinville, WA 98072
Tel.: 206-364-0121

Premier Metal Products Company **(1)**
381 Canal Place
Bronx, NY 10451
Tel.: 718-993-9200
Fax: 718-993-9211
Approx.Sls.: $7,000,000
Emp.: 70
Mfg. Electronic Cabinets, Cases & Access.; Trimline Enclosures
S.I.C.: 3651
Stanley Kwasnicki *(Pres.)*
Anthony Bozza *(Sls. Mgr.)*
Lafayette Adams *(Pur. Agent)*

PQ CORPORATION
500 E. Swedesford Rd.
Valley Forge, PA 19482
Mailing Address:
P.O. Box 840,
Valley Forge, PA 19482
Tel.: 215-293-7200 PA
Fax: 215-688-3835
Year Founded: 1831
Approx.Sls.: $265,000,000
Fiscal Year-end: 12/31/91
Export
Sodium & Potassium Silicates, Colloidal Silicas, Silica Gels (Hydrated & Anhydrous), Magnesium Silicate, Antimony Pentoxide, Epsom Salt, Glass Beads & Hollow Microspheres, Zeolites & Zeolite Catalysts, Silica Catalysts & Catalyst Supports
S.I.C.: 2819; 3231
Corporate Giving Program: Education Health, Human Services & Cultural Programs
Employee Matching Gifts Program: Education Health, Human Services & Cultural Programs
G.P. Keeley *(Chm. Bd.)*
R.W. Kelso *(Pres. & Chief Exec. Officer)*
S.W. Silverman *(Exec. V.P. & Chief Oper. Officer)*
D.J. Shimer *(Exec. V.P. & Chief Fin. Officer)*
J.R. Carroll *(V.P.-Technology)*
W.C. Combs *(V.P. & Pres.-Potters Industries, Inc.)*
J.I. Grams *(V.P. & Gen. Mgr.-Industrial Chems. Div.)*
M.R. Imbriani *(V.P. & Mng. Dir.-Akzo-PQ Silica)*
E.G. Posner *(V.P., Sec. & Gen. Counsel)*
H.S. Sherry *(V.P. & Gen. Mgr.-Zeolites & Catalysts Div.)*
H.F. Whalen *(V.P. & Dir.-Corp. Devel.)*
J.L. DeRito *(Controller)*
E.T. Kautz *(Mgr.-Employee Rels.)*
J.M. Reed *(Mgr.-Corp. Communications)*

E.F. Blessing *(Mgr.-Pur.)*

No. of Mfg. Plants/Facilities: 58
No. of U.S. Offices: 6

Computer Systems/Hardware:
IBM 4361 Model LK5

Outside Service Firm(s):

Coopers & Lybrand*(Auditors)*
2400 Eleven Penn Center
Philadelphia, PA 19103

Montgomery, McCracken, Walker & Rhoads*(Legal Firm)*
3 Parkway
Philadelphia, PA 19103
Tel.: 215-563-0650

Philadelphia National Bank*(Major Banking Relationship)*
P.O. Box 13834, Broad & Chestnut Streets
Philadelphia, PA 19101-7618
Tel.: 215-973-8327

Provident National Bank*(Major Banking Relationship)*
P.O. Box 7648
Philadelphia, PA 19101
Tel.: 215-585-5000

Divisions:

Industrial Chemicals Div. **(1)**
P.O. Box 840,
Valley Forge, PA 19482
Tel.: 215-293-7200
Sodium Silicate, Liquid & Solid, Magnesium Sulfate
S.I.C.: 2819
J.I. Grams *(V.P. & Gen. Mgr.)*
D.N. Fleming *(Mgr.-Natl. Sls.)*
D.T. Hermann *(Mgr.-Mktg.)*

Specialty Chemicals Div. **(1)**
P.O. Box 840,
Valley Forge, PA 19482
Tel.: 215-293-7200
Industrial Inorganic Chemicals, Silica Gels, Hollow Microspheres, Silica Sols
S.I.C.: 2819
J.R. McLaughlin *(V.P. & Gen. Mgr.)*
V.J. Cassella *(Mgr.-Sls.)*

Subsidiaries:

Nyacol Products, Inc. **(1)**
Megunco Rd., P.O. Box 349
Ashland, MA 01721
Tel.: 508-881-2220
Export
Inorganic Colloids, Antimony Pentoxides, Silica Sols
S.I.C.: 2819
J.T. Robinson *(Pres.)*

Potters Industries, Inc. **(1)**
Waterview Corporate Centre, 20 Waterview Blvd.
Parsippany, NJ 07054
Tel.: 201-288-4700
Telex: 219054 POTTR VR
Fax: 201-335-9350
Emp.: 650
Glass Spheres for Road Marking, Shot Peening & Reinforcement & Filler Material
S.I.C.: 3231
W.C. Combs *(Pres. & Chief Exec. Officer)*
W. Grainger *(V.P.-Mfg. & Engrng.)*
D.T. Kelly *(V.P.-Fin. & Admin.)*
C.A. Schneider *(V.P.-Domestic)*
B.J. Sutker *(V.P.-Technology)*
James W. Brinkerhoff *(Dir.-Human Resources)*
R. Brown *(Indus. Mgr.-Polymer Additives)*
D. Mastro *(Indus. Mgr.-Hwy. Prods.)*
R.C. McClure *(Mgr.-Sls. & Mktg., Hwy. Prods.)*
R. Mulhall *(Indus. Mgr.-Conductive Prods.)*

Spherical Products Corp. **(1)**
601 Cumberland
Chattanooga, TN 37409
Tel.: 615-629-7160
Export
Hollow Microspheres
S.I.C.: 2819
R.A. Ruhno *(Pres.)*

Non-U.S. Holdings:

National Silicates Ltd. **(1)**
429 Kipling Ave. Station N,
Toronto, ON M8V 3S7, Canada
Tel.: 416-255-0170
Soluble Silicates
S.I.C.: 2819
M.F. Irwin *(Pres.)*

PQ Australia Pty., Ltd. **(1)**
Lot 2, Ruhr Ct.,
Dandenong, Victoria 3175, Australia
Tel.: 61-3-7914066
Hollow Microspheres, Sodium Silicate
S.I.C.: 2819
Alfred G. Baker *(Pres.)*

PQ Zeolites B.V. **(1)**
Stationsweg 26 2312 AV
Leiden, Netherlands
Tel.: 71-125333
Zeolites & Zeolite Catalysts
S.I.C.: 2819

P. S. INTERNATIONAL INC.
8910 Purdue Rd., Ste. 260
Indianapolis, IN 46268
Tel.: 317-875-7777
Fax: 317-875-4064
Year Founded: 1985
Approx.Sls.: $81,657,000
Emp.: 16
International Trading of Commodities, Processed Foods, Building Materials, Secondary Textiles
S.I.C.: 6221; 5141; 5039; 5031; 5131
Catherine M. Fields *(Pres. & Chief Exec. Officer)*
Frank C. Kinzer *(V.P.)*
Melvin C. Fields *(Dir.)*

PSI GROUP OF COMPANIES
1790 Kirby Pkwy., Ste. 300
Memphis, TN 38138
Tel.: 901-756-8250 **TN**
Telex: 910-240-6506
Fax: 901-756-8253
Year Founded: 1974
Sales Range: $20-39 Million
Emp.: 175
Fiscal Year-end: 8/31/88
Process Design; Engineering & Construction Management Specializing in the Food Processing Industry
S.I.C.: 8711; 1799; 8741
Tiny Jenkins *(Chm. Bd. & Chief Exec. Officer)*
Beverly Vaughan *(Pres.)*
Mike Flippin *(Chief Fin. Officer)*
Dennis Nerby *(Exec. V.P.)*
Leo McKittrick *(V.P.)*
Edward Turk *(V.P.)*
Richard Veazie *(V.P.)*
Sharon Bell *(Dir.-Pur.)*
Dennis Jones *(Dir.-Data Processing)*
Principal(s):
Beverly Vaughan
Dennis Nerby
Leo McKittrick
Edward Turk
Richard Veazie

No. of Mfg. Plants/Facilities: 3
No. of U.S. Offices: 3

Computer Systems/Hardware:
IBM PC; Prime; Cal-Comp; Compaq

Outside Service Firm(s):

Coopers & Lybrand*(Auditors)*
1000 Morgan-Keegan Tower, 50 N. Front St.
Memphis, TN 38103
Tel.: 901-529-1100

DPIC*(Commercial Insurance Carrier)*
Memphis, TN

Hartford Life Insurance Co.*(Commercial Insurance Carrier)*
Hartford, CT 06104-2999

Hartford Life Insurance Co.*(Group Insurer)*
Hartford, CT 06104-2999

Wildman, Harrold, Allen & Dixon*(Legal Firm)*
Memphis, TN

Sovran Bank*(Major Banking Relationship)*
Memphis, TN

Central Trust Company, N.A.*(Pension Manager)*
Memphis, TN

Subsidiaries:

PSI Fabricators, Inc. **(1)**
1790 Kirby Pkwy., Ste. 300
Memphis, TN 38138
Tel.: 901-756-8250 (100%)
Emp.: 44
General Contractor & Fabricator Specializing in Food Processing, Specialty Chemical & Material Handling Projects
S.I.C.: 8711; 1799
Jim Woodard *(Chief Oper. Officer)*

Process Systems, Inc. Construction Co. **(1)**
1790 Kirby Pkwy. Ste. 300
Memphis, TN 38138
Tel.: 901-756-8250 (100%)
Emp.: 200
Specialty Food Processing Projects
S.I.C.: 8711; 1799
Jim Woodward *(Chief Oper. Officer)*

PST VANS, INC.
1901 W. 2100 St. S.
Salt Lake City, UT 84119
Tel.: 801-972-6690
Fax: 801-975-2515
Year Founded: 1984
Approx.Sls.: $110,000,000
Emp.: 890
Truck Leasing & Rental Without Drivers; Contract Haulers; Household Goods Transport; Refrigerated Products Transport
S.I.C.: 7513; 4213
Kenneth R. Norton *(Chm. Bd. & Chief Exec. Officer)*
Robert D. Hill *(Pres.)*
Jerry Carter *(V.P.-Sls.-North Eastern Region)*
Robert Trapp *(V.P.-Sls.-North Eastern Region)*
Michael Smith *(V.P.-Sls.-Western Region)*
Mark Pfuehler *(V.P.-Sls.-Central North Region)*
Joseph Schumacher *(V.P.-Sls.-Central South Region)*
Jeffrey L. Theurer *(Sec.)*
Steven R. Orme *(Controller)*
Brent Martin *(Dir.-Human Resources)*
Jody Bramble *(Supvr.-Pur.)*

Outside Service Firm(s):

Arthur Andersen & Co.*(Auditors)*
36 South State St., Ste. 1600
Salt Lake City, UT 84111
Tel.: 801-533-0820
Fax: 801-534-0550

PTA CORPORATION
178 Christian St.
Oxford, CT 06483
Tel.: 203-888-0585
Year Founded: 1953
Approx.Sls.: $14,000,000
Emp.: 180
Mfr. of Industrial Molds & Plastic Products
S.I.C.: 3544; 3089
Peter W. Cherry *(Chm. Bd.)*
Raynor M. Seeley, Sr. *(Pres.)*
Raynor M. Seeley, Jr. *(V.P., Chief Fin. Officer & Sec.)*
Shaun Dwyer *(Controller)*
Marc Dubreuil *(Dir.-Mktg.)*

PTC AEROSPACE, INC.
P.O. Box 140,
Litchfield, CT 06759
Year Founded: 1938
Approx.Sls.: $70,000,000
Emp.: 500
Fiscal Year-end: 2/28/93
Import Export
Commercial & Commuter Aircraft Passenger Seats
S.I.C.: 3728
D.H. Woodford *(Pres.)*
E.J. Brennan *(V.P.-Engrng.)*
A. Cutrali *(V.P.-Fin.)*
T. Sayers *(V.P.-Mfg. Opers.)*
W. Dausey *(V.P.-Sls. & Mktg.)*
P. Courtney *(Pur. Mgr.)*

Computer Systems/Hardware:
IBM AS System 400

Divisions:

PTC Aerospace **(1)**
11752 Markon Dr.
Garden Grove, CA 92641
Tel.: 714-891-3681
D.D. Rutter *(V.P. & G.M.)*
William Beasley *(Controller)*
John Wiggans *(Dir.-Sls.)*

PTC Aerospace **(1)**
The Plaza Bldg., 10900 N. E. 8th St., Ste.1023
Renton, WA 98055
Tel.: 206-455-2685
H. Durussell *(Northwest Field Service Mgr.)*

PTS ELECTRONICS CORPORATION
5233 S. Hwy. 37
Bloomington, IN 47401
Mailing Address:
P.O. Box 272
Bloomington, IN 47401
Tel.: 812-824-9331
Fax: 812-824-2848
Year Founded: 1967
Approx.Sls.: $12,000,000
Emp.: 150
Import Export
Repair Service for TV Tuners & Modules, MATV/CATV Amplifiers & Converters, VCR Boards & Microwave Panels; Distr. MATV Equip.; Complete Circuit Board Assembly, Finished Product Assembly
S.I.C.: 7622
Jack Craig *(Chief Exec. Officer)*
J.A. Hamilton *(Pres.)*
Joe King *(V.P.-Mktg.)*

PVS CHEMICALS, INC.
10900 Harper Ave.
Detroit, MI 48213
Tel.: 313-921-1200 **MI**
Fax: 313-921-1378
Year Founded: 1945
Assets: $65,000,000
Liabilities: $42,000,000
Net Worth: $23,000,000
Approx.Sls.: $100,000,000
Emp.: 310
Fiscal Year-end: 12/31/91
Export
Production Of Sulfuric Acid, Sulfan, Oleum; Distr. Of Sulfuric, Muriatic, Nitric, Phosphoric, Hydrofluosilicic, Hydrofluoric Liquid Caustic
S.I.C.: 2819; 5169
Donald Harrison *(Chm. Bd. & Gen. Counsel)*
James B. Nicholson *(Pres. & Chief Exec. Officer)*
Donald S. Sosnoski *(Chief Fin. Officer, V.P. & Treas.)*
Robert G. Olson *(Grp. V.P.)*
Allan A. Schlumberger *(Grp. V.P.)*
Jon Taub *(Sec.)*
Marc Robinson *(Controller)*
Judy Smith *(Asst. Treas. & Coord.-Employee Benefits)*

PVS Chemicals, Inc.—(Continued)

Beth Bania *(Dir.-Quality Control)*
Ray Hale *(Dir.-Data Processing)*
Don King *(Dir.-Mktg.)*
Mary Shank *(Dir.-Environment/ Natural Resources)*
Principal(s):
James B. Nicholson

No. of Foreign Offices: 1

Computer Systems/Hardware:
IBM System 36's

Outside Service Firm(s):

Arthur Andersen & Co.*(Auditors)*
400 Renaissance Center
Detroit, MI 48243
Tel.: 313-259-8100

Amerisure Companies*(Commercial Insurance Carrier)*
Farmington Hills, MI

Connecticut General Life Insurance Co.*(Group Insurer)*
Southfield, MI

William Blair & Co.*(Investment Banker)*
135 S. LaSalle St.
Chicago, IL 60603
Tel.: 312-236-1600

Cross Wrock*(Legal Firm)*
Detroit, MI

The Bank of New York*(Major Banking Relationship)*
One Wall Street
New York, NY 10286
Tel.: 212-635-6805
Fax: 212-635-3201

Connecticut General Life Insurance Co.*(Pension Manager)*
Southfield, MI

Subsidiaries:

Dynecol, Inc. (1)
6520 Georgia
Detroit, MI 48211
Tel.: 313-571-7141
Emp.: 37
Processor of Waste Chemicals
S.I.C.: 5169
Frank J. Biermann *(Pres.)*

PVS Chemicals, Inc. (1)
55 Lee St.
Buffalo, NY 14210
Tel.: 716-825-5762
Emp.: 52
Mfg. of Chemicals
S.I.C.: 2819
William Decker *(Pres.)*

PVS Chemicals, Inc. (1)
3149 Copley Rd.
Copley, OH 44321
Tel.: 216-666-0888
Emp.: 16
Distributor of Chemicals
S.I.C.: 5169
Dean Larson *(Pres.)*

PVS Chemicals, Inc. (1)
12260 S. Carondolet
Chicago, IL 60633
Tel.: 312-933-8800
Emp.: 61
Mfg. of Chemicals
S.I.C.: 2819
Jerrold Panock *(Pres.)*

PVS Chemicals, Inc. (1)
503 E. Grove
Terrell, TX 75160
Tel.: 214-563-3301
Emp.: 10
Mfg. of Chemicals
S.I.C.: 2819
Michael G. McGuirk *(Pres.)*

PVS-Nolwood Chemicals, Inc. (1)
10900 Harper Ave.
Detroit, MI 48213
Tel.: 313-925-0300
Emp.: 62
Distributor of Chemicals
S.I.C.: 5169
Richard Peacock *(Pres.)*

PVS Technologies, Inc. (1)
10900 Harper Ave.
Detroit, MI 48213
Tel.: 313-571-1100
Emp.: 50
Mfg. of Chemicals
S.I.C.: 2819
Michael G. McGuirk *(Pres.)*

Non-U.S. Holding:

Fanchem, Ltd. (1)
1141 S. Service Road, West, Unit A
Oakville, Ontario L6L 6K4, Canada
Tel.: 416-825-9810
Emp.: 5
Distributor of Chemicals
S.I.C.: 5169
Frank J. Biermann *(Pres.)*

PACE COLLECTION, INC.
11-11 34th Ave.
Long Island City, NY 11106
Tel.: 718-721-8201
Fax: 718-274-5530
Emp.: 70
Mfr. of Residential & Office Furniture, Cabinets, Desks, Wall Systems & Seating Tables
S.I.C.: 2517; 2511; 2521
Leon Rosen *(Pres.)*
Arthur Rosen *(Exec. V.P.)*
James Rosen *(V.P.)*

Outside Service Firm(s):

Berenson, Berenson, Adler & Co.*(Auditors)*
New York, NY

Danziger, Bangser, Klipstein, Goldsmith, Greenwald & Weiss*(Legal Firm)*
New York, NY

Manufacturers & Traders Trust Company*(Major Banking Relationship)*
654 Madison Ave.
New York, NY 10021
Tel.: 212-303-0400

PACE FOODS, INC.
3750 N. Pan Am Expwy.
San Antonio, TX 78219
Mailing Address:
P.O. Box 12636
San Antonio, TX 78212
Tel.: 210-224-2211
Fax: 210-222-8818
Approx.Sls.: $35,000,000
Emp.: 400
Fiscal Year-end: 12/31/90
Manufacturer of Sauces & Salad Dressings
S.I.C.: 2035
Christopher Goldsbury *(Pres.)*
Rod Sands *(Exec. V.P.)*

PACE INDUSTRIES, INC.
One McIlroy Plaza
Fayetteville, AR 72701
Mailing Address:
P.O. Box 309
Fayetteville, AR 72702
Tel.: 501-443-1455 **AR**
Fax: 501-443-7058
Year Founded: 1975
Approx.Sls.: $90,000,000
Emp.: 450
Manufacturing Die-Castings of Aluminum
S.I.C.: 3363
James F. Keenan *(Chm. Bd. & Chief Exec. Officer)*
Bob L. Gaddy *(Pres.)*
Terry C. Bellora *(V.P.-Fin. & Treas.)*
Richard Ardemagni *(V.P.-Admin.)*
Jim D. Alford *(V.P.)*
Scott Bull *(V.P.)*
Howard N. Higgins *(Controller)*
Carolyn B. Madison *(Sec.)*
Steve Flynn *(Mgr.-Personnel)*
J.W. Moore *(Mgr.-Pur.)*

Outside Service Firm(s):

Frost & Co.*(Auditors)*
Little Rock, AR

Plant:

Pace Industries, Inc. (1)
P.O. Box 1198
Harrison, AR 72601
Tel.: 501-741-8255
Dale Randall *(Mgr.)*

PACE INTERNATIONAL CORPORATION
500 7th Ave., S.
Kirkland, WA 98033
Tel.: 206-827-8711 **WA**
Fax: 206-822-8261
Sales Range: $20-39 Million
Emp.: 175
Export
Mfr. of Window Cleaning Preparations; Agricultural & Household Pesticides; Fungicides, Herbicides; Plant Foods; Water Treating Compounds; Emulsifiers; Specialty Chemicals; Fruit & Vegetable Waxes & DPA
S.I.C.: 2842; 2879; 2873; 2899; 2843; 2992
Herman Sarckowsky *(Chm. Bd.)*
Brooke Van Wyk *(Pres. & Chief Exec. Officer)*
Sheryl Hildebrand *(Chief Fin. Officer, Dir.-Human Resources & Employee Benefits)*
Gary Gelly *(Chief Information Officer & Dir.-Data Processing)*
Dan Baker *(Exec. V.P. & Dir.-Quality Control & Res. & Devel.)*
Glen Gay *(V.P.-Sls., Mktg. & Export)*
Nancy Templeton *(Corp. Sec.)*
Vicki Dee *(Dir.-Govt. Affairs)*
Tammy Elliott *(Dir.-Adv.)*
Will Ferguson *(Dir.-Admin., Opers., Pur. & Import)*
Frank Kemery *(Dir.-Mktg.)*
David Searles *(Dir.-Mfg.)*
George Lobisser *(Dir.)*
Principal(s):
Herman Sarckowsky
Brooke Van Wyk
George Lobisser

No. of Mfg. Plants/Facilities: 4
No. of U.S. Offices: 1

Computer Systems/Hardware:
IBM 6000 & Datalogics

Outside Service Firm(s):

Deloitte & Touche*(Auditors)*
700 Fifth Ave., Suite 4500
Seattle, WA 98104-5044
Tel.: 206-292-1800

George Lobisser*(Legal Firm)*
Seattle, WA

Seattle First National Bank*(Major Banking Relationship)*
Seattle, WA

Division:

InVireChem (1)
1500 7th Ave. S.
Kirkland, WA 98033
Tel.: 706-827-8711
Enviro-friendly Paint Booth Defloculents
S.I.C.: 2899
Brooke Van Wyk *(Pres. & Chief Exec. Officer)*

PACE OIL CO., INC.
150 Stratford Court SW
Winston-Salem, NC 27103
Mailing Address:
P.O. Box 15047
Winston-Salem, NC 27113
Tel.: 919-723-9982 **NC**
Year Founded: 1959
Approx.Sls.: $35,000,000
Emp.: 30
Wholesale Trade-Petroleum Products
S.I.C.: 5172
F. Roger Page *(Chm. Bd., Pres., Chief Exec. & Fin. Officer)*
Doris B. Page *(Treas. & Sec.)*
Paul Jones *(Controller)*
Principal(s):
F. Roger Page
Doris B. Page

Outside Service Firm(s):

Deloitte & Touche*(Auditors)*
Greensboro, NC

Blue Cross & Blue Shield of North Carolina*(Group Insurer)*
Durham, NC

NationsBank Carolinas*(Investment Banker)*
Winston-Salem, NC

Lanier & Fountain*(Legal Firm)*
Winston-Salem, NC

Branch Banking & Trust Co.*(Major Banking Relationship)*
Winston-Salem, NC

Carolina Bank*(Major Banking Relationship)*
Sanford, NC

First Union National Bank*(Major Banking Relationship)*
Winston-Salem, NC

NationsBank*(Major Banking Relationship)*
35 Broad St.
Atlanta, GA 30303
Tel.: 404-581-2121
Tel.: 800-848-8198

NationsBank Carolinas*(Major Banking Relationship)*
One NCNB Plaza T18-7
Charlotte, NC 28255

PACE PRESS, INC.
636 11th Ave.
New York, NY 10036
Tel.: 212-246-8100 **NY**
Fax: 212-256-3091
Year Founded: 1969
Approx.Sls.: $22,000,000
Emp.: 100
Lithographic Printing
S.I.C.: 2752
Julius Briskie *(Pres.)*
Jack Mangi *(V.P.-Sls.)*
David Savitt *(V.P. & Treas.)*
Seymour Strau *(V.P.)*
Charles Licata *(Mgr.-Production)*

Outside Service Firm(s):

Irving Handel & Co.*(Auditors)*
New York, NY

Julian Shestack*(Legal Firm)*
New York, NY

Manufacturers Hanover Trust Co.*(Major Banking Relationship)*
450 W. 33rd St.-Bay 13
New York, NY 10001
Tel.: 212-613-7198

PACE RESOURCES, INC.
40 S. Richland Ave.
York, PA 17405
Tel.: 717-854-5564 **PA**
Fax: 717-845-5716
Year Founded: 1946

Approx.Sls.: $32,000,000
Emp.: 580
Fiscal Year-end: 10/31/92
Consulting Engineers; Architects
Printers; Computer Service Bureau
S.I.C.: 2752; 7372
Russell E. Horn, Sr. *(Chm. Bd.)*
Russell E. Horn, Jr. *(Co-Pres.)*
John B. Jung *(Co-Pres.)*
Samuel Wornom *(V.P. & Chief Fin. Officer)*

Outside Service Firm(s):

Coopers & Lybrand*(Auditors)*
5 North Fifth Street
Harrisburg, PA 17101

Blakey, Yost, Bupp & Schaumann*(Legal Firm)*
York, PA

Subsidiary:

Print-O-Stat, Inc. **(1)**
1011 W. Market St.
York, PA 17405
Tel.: 717-854-7821
Approx.Sls.: $10,000,000
Emp.: 115
Offset Printing; Retail Engineering Supplies; Office Furnishings
S.I.C.: 2752; 5021
Russell E. Horn, Jr. *(Pres.)*
Ralph E. Horn *(V.P.)*
Albert Wankmiller *(V.P.-Sls. & Mktg.)*

PACESETTER CORPORATION
4343 S. 96th St.
Omaha, NE 68127
Tel.: 402-331-9400 **NE**
Fax: 402-331-0747
Year Founded: 1962
Approx.Sls.: $95,000,000
Emp.: 1,800
Fiscal Year-end: 12/31/90
Mfr. Home Improvement Products, Aluminum Storm Windows & Doors, Sliding Glass Doors, Fiberglass Awnings & Patio Covers, Aluminum Siding
S.I.C.: 3442; 3089; 5031; 5039
Phillip G. Schrager *(Chm. Bd. & Chief Exec. Officer)*
Harley Schrager *(Pres. & Chief Oper. Officer)*
Bill Blaha *(Pres.-Sls.)*
Patrick Hoy *(Chief Fin. Officer & V.P.)*
Dale Anthony *(V.P.-Mfg.)*
Robert Campney *(V.P. & Treas.)*
Wayne Corey *(V.P. & Controller)*
Ivan Gerard *(V.P.-Human Resources)*
Robert Schmidt *(V.P.-Data Processing)*
James Miller *(Gen. Counsel)*
Stanley Edelstein *(Sec.)*
Tim Curtis *(Asst. V.P.-Telecommunications)*
Rick Holstein *(Asst. V.P.-Personnel)*
Steve Jensen *(Asst. V.P.-Mktg.)*
Dana Hamik *(Dir.-Leasing)*
Earl Richter *(Dir.-Purchasing)*
Matthew Lamb *(Engineer)*

No. of Mfg. Plants/Facilities: 1
No. of U.S. Offices: 73

Computer Systems/Hardware:
IBM 4381

Outside Service Firm(s):

Coopers & Lybrand*(Auditors)*
1200 Landmark Center
Omaha, NE
Tel.: 402-344-4545

Mutual of Omaha Insurance Company*(Group Insurer)*
Mutual of Omaha Plaza,
Omaha, NE 68175
Tel.: 800-228-7775

McGrath, North, Mullin & Kratz*(Legal Firm)*
One Central Park Plaza, Ste. 1100
Omaha, NE 68102
Tel.: 402-341-3070

Continental Bank N. A.*(Major Banking Relationship)*
231 S. LaSalle St.
Chicago, IL 60697
Tel.: 312-828-2345
Tel.: 800-426-5754
Telex: 312-828-1783

First National Bank of Omaha*(Major Banking Relationship)*
One First National Center
Omaha, NE 68102

Omaha National Bank*(Major Banking Relationship)*
Omaha, NE

PACESETTER STEEL SERVICE, INC.
1100 Shallowford Rd.
Marietta, GA 30066
Mailing Address:
P.O. Box 1729,
Woodstock, GA 30188
Tel.: 404-926-8900 **GA**
Fax: 404-928-5753
Year Founded: 1977
Approx.Sls.: $118,000,000
Emp.: 148
Steel Service Center
S.I.C.: 5051
Steven Leebow *(Chm. Bd., Pres. & Chief Exec. Officer)*
Jonathan Rapaport *(Chief Fin. Officer, V.P. & Treas.)*
Margie O'Bryne *(V.P.-Credit)*
Lonnie J. Taylor *(V.P.-Opers.)*
Principal(s):
Steven Leebow

No. of Mfg. Plants/Facilities: 4
No. of U.S. Offices: 4

Computer Systems/Hardware:
MAI Basic Four

Outside Service Firm(s):

Babush, Neiman, Kornman & Johnson*(Auditors)*
Atlanta, GA

Alexander & Alexander*(Commercial Insurance Carrier)*
Two Piedmont Center, 3565 Piedmont Rd. N.E.
Atlanta, GA 30363

Great-West Life Assurance Co.*(Group Insurer)*
8505 East Orchard Rd.
Englewood, CO 8011
Tel.: 800-537-2033

Altman, Kritzer & Levick*(Legal Firm)*
6400 Powers Ferry Rd.
Atlanta, GA 30339

Bank South, N.A.*(Major Banking Relationship)*
P.O. Box 4387
Atlanta, GA 30302
Tel.: 404-529-4111

Manufacturers Hanover Trust Co.*(Major Banking Relationship)*
270 Park Ave.
New York, NY 10017
Tel.: 212-286-3229

PACHMAYR GUN WORKS INC.
1875 S. Mountain
Monrovia, CA 91016
Mailing Address:
P.O. Box 667
Monrovia, CA 91017-0667
Tel.: 818-357-7771
Tel.: 800-423-9704
Telex: 181240 PGUN LSA
Fax: 818-358-7251
Year Founded: 1929
Approx.Sls.: $10,500,000
Emp.: 90
Fiscal Year-end: 12/31/91
Import Export
White Line, Lo-Swing, Presentation, Signature & Pachmayr Gun Equip.
S.I.C.: 3484
W.G. Baker, Jr. *(Chm. Bd. & Chief Exec. Officer)*
Laura Watson *(Chief Fin. Officer & Controller)*
Bruce Baker *(Pres.)*
Ron Plue *(V.P.)*
Alicia Sugarman *(Sec.)*
Carl Cupp *(Engineer)*
Bob Blair *(Mgr.-Natl. Sls.)*
Scott Young *(Mgr.-MIS)*

Computer Systems/Hardware:
Varnet Software With Bridgeware
MPS Software Data General

PACIFIC CAPITAL BANCORP
1001 S. Main St.
Salinas, CA 93901
Mailing Address:
P.O. Box 1786,
Salinas, CA 93902-1786
Tel.: 408-757-4900 **CA**
Fax: 408-757-5061
Year Founded: 1983
Assets: $291,000,000
Liabilities: $261,000,000
Net Worth: $30,000,000
Fiscal Year-end: 12/31/91
Bank Holding Company
S.I.C.: 6712; 6022
William H. Pope *(Chm. Bd.)*
Stanley R. Haynes *(Pres.)*
D. Vernon Horton *(Chief Exec. Officer)*
Dennis A. DeCius *(Chief Fin. Officer, Exec. V.P. & Asst. Sec.)*
June C. Duran-Stock *(Sec.)*

Outside Service Firm(s):

KPMG Peat Marwick*(Auditors)*
50 W. San Fernando
San Jose, CA 95113-2413
Tel.: 408-279-2000

Lillick & Charles*(Legal Firm)*
Two Embarcadero Center
San Francisco, CA 94111
Tel.: 415-984-8200
Fax: 415-421-4799

First Interstate Bank*(Major Banking Relationship)*
P.O.Box 54168, Terminal Annex
Los Angeles, CA 90054-0168
Tel.: 800-522-6645

Subsidiary:

First National Bank of Central California **(1)**
P.O. Box 1786,
Salinas, CA 93902-1786
Tel.: 408-757-4900
Emp.: 166
Commercial Bank
S.I.C.: 6022
Dennis A. DeCius *(Chief Fin. Officer & Sr. V.P.)*

PACIFIC COAST BUILDING PRODUCTS INC.
3001 I St.
Sacramento, CA 95816
Mailing Address:
P.O. Box 160488,
Sacramento, CA 95816
Tel.: 916-444-9304
Fax: 916-325-3697
Year Founded: 1953
Approx.Sls.: $333,000,000
Emp.: 2,200
Roofing & Drywall Insulation Contractors, Wholesale & Retail Building Materials & Veneer, Manufacture Clay, Pipe, Floor & Roof Tile & Local Trucking
S.I.C.: 1761; 3259; 4213; 5039; 5211
F.E. Anderson *(Chm. Bd.)*
D.J. Lucchetti *(Pres.)*
Nick Kalanges *(Chief Fin. Officer)*
James B. Thompson *(Sec.)*

Outside Service Firm(s):

Price Waterhouse*(Auditors)*
455 Capitol Mall
Sacramento, CA 95814
Tel.: 916-441-2370

Skirving, Thompson & Fenneli*(Legal Firm)*
Sacramento, CA

First Interstate Bank*(Major Banking Relationship)*
345 California St., 8th Flr.
San Francisco, CA 94104
Tel.: 415-773-7801

Subsidiary:

Interstate Brick Company **(1)**
9780 So. 5200 West
West Jordan, UT 84084
Tel.: 801-565-5200 (100%)
Fax: 802-561-1471
Approx.Rev.: $14,300,000
Emp.: 170
Manufacturer & Sale of Bricks
S.I.C.: 3251; 5032
Jerry Waitrovich *(Div. Mgr.)*

PACIFIC COAST PRODUCERS
P.O. Box 1600
Lodi, CA 95241-1600
Tel.: 209-367-8800 **CA**
Fax: 209-367-1084
Year Founded: 1971
Assets: $100,778,000
Earnings: $2,575,000
Liabilities: $53,174,000
Net Worth: $47,604,000
Approx.Sls.: $172,232,000
Emp.: 5,000
Fiscal Year-end: 5/31/91
Export
Mfr. Canned Fruits & Vegetables
S.I.C.: 2033
Robert P. Moser *(Chm. Bd.)*
Tony Turkovich *(Vice Chm.)*
Larry D. Clay *(Pres. & Chief Exec. Officer)*
Robert Graf *(Exec. V.P.)*
James Scarpace *(V.P.-Opers.)*
Mark M. Wahlman *(V.P.-Fin.)*
Cynthia Irwin *(Corp. Sec.)*
Stewart Easton *(Controller)*
James Schweickardt *(Dir.-Human Resources)*
Peter C. Wtulich *(Dir.-Mngmt. Information Systems)*

No. of Mfg. Plants/Facilities: 3
No. of U.S. Offices: 1

Computer Systems/Hardware:
IBM System AS/400

Outside Service Firm(s):

KPMG Peat Marwick*(Auditors)*
50 W. San Fernando
San Jose, CA 95113-2413
Tel.: 408-279-2000

Jardine Insurance Brokers of Stockton, Inc.*(Commercial Insurance Carrier)*
Stockton, CA

Lincoln National Life Insurance Co.*(Group Insurer)*
PO Box 208, 1300 S. Clinton
Fort Wayne, IN 46801
Tel.: 219-455-2926
Fax: 219-455-7619

Boutin, Lassner, Gibson & Delehant*(Legal Firm)*
Sacramento, CA

Bank of America NT&SA*(Major Banking Relationship)*
Sacramento, CA

Sanwa Bank*(Major Banking Relationship)*
Sacramento, CA

Pacific Coast Producers—(Continued)

Subsidiary:

California Custom Foods **(1)**
P.O. Box 2695
Lodi, CA 95241
Tel.: 209-367-8800
Emp.: 5
Food Processing
S.I.C.: 2033
Robert Brewer *(Pres.)*
William J. Benapfl *(Controller)*
William Fletcher *(Dir.-Mktg.)*

PACIFIC ENTERPRISES OIL COMPANY (USA)
1700 Pacific Ave., Ste. 1200
Dallas, TX 75201-4697
Tel.: 214-953-0088 **LA**
Fax: 214-953-5299
Year Founded: 1970
Approx.Sls.: $270,000,000
Emp.: 550
Fiscal Year-end: 12/31/90
Oil & Gas Exploration & Production
S.I.C.: 1382
H. E. Lepape *(Chm. Bd. & Chief Exec. Officer)*
R. E. Rinard *(Pres. & Chief Oper. Officer)*
Jere Hayes *(V.P., Gen. Counsel & Sec.)*
Daniel Thorne *(V.P.-Fin. & Treas.)*
R. S. Dinkins *(V.P.-Human Resources)*
W. M. Sweat *(V.P.-Oper.)*
J. L. Pritchett III *(V.P.-Exploration)*
R. K. Samuel *(Controller)*
R. B. Dunie *(Mgr.-Fin. Plng.)*
S. Kuykendall *(Mgr.-Pur.)*
G. C. Spence *(Dir.-Mktg.)*
Bob Raed *(Dir.-Information Systems)*

Outside Service Firm(s):

Deloitte & Touche*(Auditors)*
Ste. 200, Two Windsor Dr., 7540 Windsor Dr.
Allentown, PA 18195
Tel.: 215-366-5100

Locke, Purnell, Rain, Harrell*(Legal Firm)*
First Republic Bank Center, 3600 Tower II
Dallas, TX 75201-3989
Tel.: 214-754-7400

PACIFIC ENVELOPE COMPANY
1600 E. Winston Rd.
Anaheim, CA 92805
Mailing Address:
P.O. Box 68,
Anaheim, CA 92805
Tel.: 714-758-0775 **CA**
Fax: 714-991-4729
Year Founded: 1959
Assets: $27,916,400
Earnings: $1,761,430
Liabilities: $12,814,991
Net Worth: $15,101,409
Approx.Sls.: $41,657,200
Emp.: 382
Fiscal Year-end: 6/30/90
Mfr. & Print Envelopes
S.I.C.: 2677
Robert L. Cashman *(Chm. Bd., Pres. & Chief Exec. Officer)*
John Vilagi *(Controller & Chief Fin. Officer)*
G. E. Cashman *(V.P.)*
Georgia Cashman *(Treas.)*
Bret Brandt *(Dir.-Pur.)*
Principal(s):
Robert L. Cashman
G. E. Cashman

No. of Mfg. Plants/Facilities: 5
No. of U.S. Offices: 5

Computer Systems/Hardware:
IBM System 36; IBM PC

Outside Service Firm(s):

Price Waterhouse*(Auditors)*
660 Newport Center Dr., Ste. 600
Newport Beach, CA 92660
Tel.: 714-640-9200

Singer, Lewak, Greenbaum & Goldstein*(Auditors)*
Annaheim, CA

Nationwide Insurance*(Commercial Insurance Carrier)*
One Nationwide Plaza
Columbus, OH 43216
Tel.: 614-249-6488

Nationwide Insurance*(Group Insurer)*
One Nationwide Plaza
Columbus, OH 43216
Tel.: 614-249-6488

Saxon, Alt, Dean Mason, Brewer & Kincannon*(Legal Firm)*
333 City Blvd. West, Ste. 1600
Orange, CA 92666

City National Bank*(Major Banking Relationship)*
LaMirada, CA

Subsidiaries:

Hallmark Litho Co. **(1)**
1230 S. Sherman St.
Anaheim, CA 92805
Tel.: 714-758-0440
Emp.: 37
Commercial Printer
S.I.C.: 2759
Georgia E. Cashman *(Chief Oper. Officer)*

Premier Publishing Co. **(1)**
1600 E. Winston Rd.
Anaheim, CA 92805
Tel.: 714-758-0775
Emp.: 4
Book Publisher
S.I.C.: 2731
Robert L. Cashman *(Pres.)*

PACIFIC FOODS, INC.
(Formerly Crescent Foods, Inc.)
21612 88th Ave. S.
Kent, WA 98031
Tel.: 206-395-9400
Tel.: 800-347-9444
Fax: 206-395-3330
Year Founded: 1883
Approx.Sls.: $20,000,000
Emp.: 80
Fiscal Year-end: 3/31/91
Import Export
Marketing of Mapleine, Raw & Salted Nuts, Spices, Extracts & Seasoning Mixes
S.I.C.: 5441; 5149
Charles Eggert *(Chm. Bd.)*
Michael A. Prosser *(Pres.)*
Carolyn Rayback *(Controller)*
Susan Black *(Dir.-Technical Services)*
Dave Dowling *(Mgr.-Sls.)*
Chuck Gray *(Mgr.-Opers.)*
John Loughridge *(Mgr.-Mktg. & Intl. Mngmnt. Information Systems)*

Computer Systems/Hardware:
Hewlett-Packard; IBM Compatible PC

PACIFIC HAWAIIAN LTD.
(d/b/a Food Fair Supermarkets)
1990 Kinoole St.
Hilo, HI 96720
Tel.: 808-959-9126 **HI**
Fax: 808-959-6587
Year Founded: 1950
Approx.Sls.: $17,000,000
Emp.: 164
Fiscal Year-end: 9/30/91
Import
Independent Supermarkets
S.I.C.: 5411
Eijiro Kaneshiro *(Chm. Bd.)*
Glenn Kaneshiro *(Pres.)*
Seiko Kaneshiro *(V.P.)*
Lynnette Kaneshiro *(Sec.)*
Frank Clay *(Treas. & Controller)*
Wayne Hashimoto *(Dir.-Pur.)*
Charlie Umanoro *(Dir.-Adv.)*

Computer Systems/Hardware:
IBM System 34

Outside Service Firm(s):

Namahira & Yokoyama*(Auditors)*
Hilo, HI

Cook Choi & Quitiquit*(Legal Firm)*
Honolulu, HI

First Hawaiian Bank*(Major Banking Relationship)*
165 South King St.
Honolulu, HI 96813
Tel.: 808-525-5876
Fax: 808-525-5791

Bishop Trust Co., Ltd.*(Pension Manager)*
P.O. Box 2390
Honolulu, HI 96804
Tel.: 808-523-2111

PACIFIC HIDE & FUR DEPOT
P.O. Box 1549
Great Falls, MT 59403
Tel.: 406-727-6222
Fax: 406-453-4269
Emp.: 400
Fiscal Year-end: 8/31/91
Steel & Hardware Sales; Buys & Recycles Hides, Furs, Scrap Iron & Metals
S.I.C.: 5051; 5072; 5632
N.E. Vosburg *(Pres. & Chief Exec. Officer)*
Leroy Stevens *(Exec. V.P.)*
Dave Richards *(Treas. & Controller)*
Robert Short *(Mgr.-Personnel)*

Computer Systems/Hardware:
IBM System 36

Outside Service Firm(s):

Junkemeyer & Clark*(Auditors)*
Great Falls, MT

Dorsey & Whitney*(Legal Firm)*
2200 First Bank Place East
Minneapolis, MN 55402

Norwest Bank Minnesota, N.A.*(Major Banking Relationship)*
Great Falls, MT

PACIFIC HOLDING CORPORATION
Murdock Plaza, 10900 Wilshire Blvd.
Los Angeles, CA 90024
Tel.: 310-208-6055 **DE**
Fax: 213-824-2159
Approx.Sls.: $998,907,000
Emp.: 20,595
Holding Company; Natural Resources; Ceramic Tile; Land Development
S.I.C.: 3255; 6531; 3253; 3297; 6552; 6719
David H. Murdock *(Pres. & Chief Exec. Officer)*
Allen Sellers *(Exec. V.P.)*
Principal(s):
David H. Murdock

Outside Service Firm(s):

Arthur Andersen & Co.*(Auditors)*
633 W. Fifth St.
Los Angeles, CA 90071
Tel.: 213-614-6500

O'Melveny & Myers*(Legal Firm)*
611 W. Sixth St.
Los Angeles, CA 90017
Tel.: 213-620-1120

Continental Bank N. A.*(Major Banking Relationship)*
231 S. LaSalle St.
Chicago, IL 60697
Tel.: 312-828-2345
Tel.: 800-426-5754
Telex: 312-828-1783

Subsidiary:

PHC Holdings, Inc. **(1)**
10900 Wilshire Blvd., Ste. 1600
Los Angeles, CA 90024
Tel.: 310-208-6055 (100%)
Holding Co.
S.I.C.: 6719
David H. Murdock *(Chm. Bd. & Pres.)*

Subsidiaries:

Huntington Tile, Inc. **(2)**
1315 E. Third St.
Pomona, CA 91766
Tel.: 909-623-6481 (100%)
Ceramic Tile
S.I.C.: 3253
Donald A. Quick *(Pres.)*

Pacific Clay Products **(2)**
P.O. Box 1149,
Corona, CA 91720
Tel.: 909-735-6020 (100%)
Clay Building Products-Pipe
S.I.C.: 3255
Walter M. Colley *(Pres.)*

Affiliate:

Dole Food Company, Inc. **(1)**
31355 Oak Crest Dr.
Westlake Village, CA 91361
Tel.: 818-879-6600
Telex: 340295
Fax: 818-879-6622
Assets: $2,423,270,000
Earnings: $133,726,000
Liabilities: $616,077,000
Net Worth: $1,807,193,000
Approx.Rev.: $3,215,999,000
Emp.: 51,000
Fiscal Year-end: 12/28/91
Food Processing, Merchandising, Manufacturing, Real Estate, Produce & Market Fresh Fruits, Vegetable Juices & Nuts
S.I.C.: 0179; 0161; 5148; 6552; 2033; 6512; 0182; 2086; 6519; 7359; 2037; 2024
David H. Murdock *(Chm. Bd. & Chief Exec. Officer)*
David A. DeLorenzo *(Pres., Dole Food Co. & Exec. V.P., Dole Food Co., Inc.)*
Alan B. Sellers *(Exec. V.P.-Admin. & Legal, Corp. Sec.)*
Gerald W. LaFleur *(Exec. V.P.)*
David Cooper *(V.P. & Treas.)*
William Hain Jr. *(V.P.-Fin.)*
Carol J. Klein *(V.P.-Corp. Affairs)*
Linda S. Graebner *(V.P.-Mktg. Communications)*
George R. Horne *(V.P.-Human Resources)*
Patricia A. McKay *(V.P. & Controller)*
James Marc Albright *(Asst. Treas.)*
Claire Creighton *(Dir.-Employee Benefits)*

PACIFIC LUMBER & SHIPPING CO.
3131 Rainier Bank Tower
Seattle, WA 98101
Mailing Address:
P.O. Box 21785
Seattle, WA 98111
Tel.: 206-682-7262
Fax: 206-683-8152
Year Founded: 1932
Approx.Sls.: $244,000,000
Emp.: 500
Lumber & Wood Products
S.I.C.: 5099; 5031; 2421; 2436; 2493
Charles L. Spence *(Chm. Bd.)*
Robert L. Spence *(Pres. & Chief Exec. Officer)*
Jay Williams *(Chief Fin. Officer & Treas.)*

Computer Systems/Hardware:
IBM PC

Outside Service Firm(s):

Deloitte & Touche*(Auditors)*
700 Fifth Ave., Suite 4500
Seattle, WA 98104-5044
Tel.: 206-292-1800

Lincoln National Life Insurance Co.*(Group Insurer)*
PO Box 208, 1300 S. Clinton
Fort Wayne, IN 46801
Tel.: 219-455-2926
Fax: 219-455-7619

First Interstate Bank of Washington, N.A.*(Major Banking Relationship)*
P.O. Box 21927, 999 Third Ave.
Seattle, WA 98111
Tel.: 206-292-3522
Tel.: 800-522-6645

The Principal Financial Group*(Pension Manager)*
711 High St.
Des Moines, IA 50309
Tel.: 515-247-4593
Tel.: 800-543-4015

PACIFIC METAL COMPANY
3400 SW Bond Ave.
Portland, OR 97201
Tel.: 503-227-0691 **OR**
Fax: 503-227-2118
Approx.Sls.: $53,000,000
Emp.: 144
Aluminum Bars, Rods, Ingots, Sheets, Pipes, Plates; Steel; Nonferrous Products
S.I.C.: 5051
Donald E. Peck *(Pres.)*
Eugene C. Comfort *(V.P. & Treas.)*
Sandy Noster *(V.P.-Sls.)*
Robert S. Perry *(V.P.-Opers.)*

Outside Service Firm(s):

Perkins & Co.*(Auditors)*
Portland, OR

Hanna, Spencer, Kerns & Strader*(Legal Firm)*
Portland, OR

United States National Bank of Oregon*(Major Banking Relationship)*
P.O. Box 3850,
Portland, OR 97208
Tel.: 503-275-6111

PACIFIC MUTUAL LIFE INSURANCE COMPANY
700 Newport Ctr. Dr.
Newport Beach, CA 92660
Mailing Address:
P.O. Box 9000
Newport Beach, CA 92658-9030
Tel.: 714-640-3011
Tel.: 800-800-7646 **CA**
Fax: 714-640-7614
Year Founded: 1868
Assets: $10,650,016,000
Liabilities: $10,303,635,000
Net Worth: $346,381,000
Approx.Sls.: $2,572,143,000
Emp.: 2,412
Fiscal Year-end: 12/31/91
Life & Health Insurance; Equity Sales; Investment Management
S.I.C.: 6311; 6321; 6371; 6799
Corporate Giving Program: Pacific Mutual Foundation
Employee Matching Gifts Program: Pacific Mutual Foundation
Thomas C. Sutton *(Chm. Bd. & Chief Exec. Officer)*
William D. Cvengros *(Vice Chm. & Chief Investment Officer)*
Arthur M. Kesselhaut *(Exec. V.P.-Individual Insurance)*
Glenn S. Schafer *(Exec. V.P. & Chief Fin. Officer)*
Daryle G. Johnson *(Sr. V.P.-Pension Investments)*
Stephen T. O'Hare *(Sr. V.P.-Corp. Services)*
David R. Carmichael *(Sr. V.P. & Gen. Counsel)*
Khahn T. Tran *(V.P. & Treas.)*
Robert G. Haskell *(V.P.-Pub. Affairs)*
Anthony J. Bonno *(V.P.-Corp. Services)*
Edgar R. Lehman *(V.P.-Human Resources)*
Audrey L. Milfs *(V.P. & Sec.)*
Edward R. Byrd *(V.P. & Controller)*
Andrew Morrison *(Asst. V.P.-Pub. Affairs)*
Milda C. Goodman *(Mgr.-Adv.)*

No. of U.S. Offices: 75

Computer Systems/Hardware:
IBM Systems 3081 & 4341; Hewlett-Packard 3000; Wang VS100

Outside Service Firm(s):

Deloitte & Touche*(Auditors)*
695 Town Center Dr.
Costa Mesa, CA 92626
Tel.: 714-436-7100

Pacific Mutual*(Group Insurer)*
700 Newport Center Dr.
Newport Beach, CA 92660
Tel.: 714-640-3011
Fax: 714-759-3372

First Interstate Bank*(Major Banking Relationship)*
Pomona, CA

Security Pacific Corporation*(Major Banking Relationship)*
Security Pacific Plaza
Los Angeles, CA 90071
Tel.: 213-345-6211
Fax: 213-625-0809

Subsidiaries:

Cadence Capital Management **(1)**
10 Liberty Sq., 4th Fl.
Boston, MA 02109
Tel.: 617-451-0250
Investment & Equity Management
S.I.C.: 6799
Mark W. England-Markun *(Chief Exec. Officer & Mgr. Dir.)*
David B. Breed *(Mng. Dir.)*
John A. McQuilkin *(Mng. Dir.)*

Employee Benefits America **(1)**
17360 Brookhurst
Fountain Valley, CA 92708
Tel.: 800-733-7020
National Administration of Insurance Claims
S.I.C.: 6411
Lawrence Halpin *(Pres. & Chief Oper. Officer)*

Mutual Service Corporation **(1)**
701 N. Federal Hwy.
North Palm Beach, FL 33408
Tel.: 407-863-7990
Broker/Dealer; Investments & Insurance Products
S.I.C.: 6411
John Dixon *(Pres.)*

NJF Investment Group, Inc. **(1)**
2121 San Jacinto, Ste. 1440
Dallas, TX 75201
Tel.: 214-754-1780
Investments-Equity Mgr.
S.I.C.: 6799
Ben Fischer *(Mng. Dir.)*
John Johnson *(Mng. Dir.)*
Chris Najork *(Mng. Dir.)*

PM Group Life Insurance Company **(1)**
17360 Brookhurst St.
Fountain Valley, CA 92708
Tel.: 714-760-4310
Life Insurance
S.I.C.: 6311
William Ferris *(Pres. & Chief Exec. Officer)*
Michael Berumen *(Sr. V.P.)*

PMRealty Advisors, Inc. **(1)**
800 Newport Center Dr., Ste 300
Newport Beach, CA 92660
Tel.: 714-721-5005
Investment Counseling; Real Estate Management
S.I.C.: 6282; 6531
Glenn L. Hammer, Jr. *(Mng. Dir.)*
James G. McWalters *(Mng. Dir.)*
Michael R. Neill *(Mng. Dir.)*
Larry K. Sullivan *(Mng. Dir.)*

Pacific Equities Network **(1)**
700 Newport Center Dr.
Newport Beach, CA 92660
Tel.: 714-640-3881 (100%)
Holding Company for Mutual Service Corp. & United Planners' Group, Inc.
S.I.C.: 6211
Richard Meehan *(V.P.-Mktg. & Sls.)*

Pacific Financial Asset Management Corporation **(1)**
700 Newport Center Dr.
Newport Beach, CA 92660
Tel.: 714-640-3030
Investment Management Co. with Subsidiary Firms
S.I.C.: 6719
Steven T. Bailey *(Mng. Dir.)*

Pacific Investment Management Co. **(1)**
840 Newport Center Dr., Ste. 360
Newport Beach, CA 92660
Tel.: 714-640-3031 (100%)
Approx.Sls.: $3,022,000,000
Investment Advisor
S.I.C.: 6282
William F. Podlich *(Chief Exec. Officer & Mng. Dir.)*
Chris P. Dialynas *(Mng. Dir.)*
William H. Gross *(Mng. Dir.)*
Dean S. Meiling *(Mng. Dir.)*
James F. Muzzy *(Mng. Dir.)*

Parametric Portfolio Associates, Inc. **(1)**
7310 Columbia Center, 701 5th Ave.
Seattle, WA 98104
Tel.: 206-386-5575
Investment & Global Equity Management
S.I.C.: 6211; 6282
Mark W. England-Markun *(Chief Exec. Officer & Mng. Dir.)*
William E. Cornelius *(Mng. Dir.)*

United Planners' Group, Inc. **(1)**
7333 E. Doubletree Rd., Ste. 120
Scottsdale, AZ 85258
Tel.: 602-991-0225
Broker/Dealer-Limited Partnership
S.I.C.: 6282
Edward B. Burr *(Pres. & Chief Exec. Officer)*

PACIFIC NORTHERN OIL CORP.
100 W. Harrison, North Tower Ste. 200
Seattle, WA 98119
Tel.: 206-282-4421 **WA**
Fax: 206-282-6574
Approx.Sls.: $200,000,000
Emp.: 180
Wholesale Oil for Ocean Going Vessels; Petroleum Bulk Stations & Terminals
S.I.C.: 5172; 5171
David Arnold *(Pres. & Chief Exec. Officer)*
J. Douglas Lennon *(V.P.)*
David Waldschmidt *(Sec.)*
Loran Pace *(Treas.)*

Outside Service Firm(s):

Coopers & Lybrand*(Auditors)*
1800 First Interstate Center, 999 Third Ave.
Seattle, WA 98104-4098
Tel.: 206-622-8700

NMB Bank*(Major Banking Relationship)*
Los Angeles, CA

PACIFIC SCENE INC.
3900 Harney St.
San Diego, CA 92110
Tel.: 619-299-5100 **CA**
Fax: 619-294-8361
Approx.Sls.: $350,000,000
Emp.: 330
General Contractor; Residential, Commercial & Industrial Buildings
S.I.C.: 1521; 1522; 1541
Tawfig N. Khoury *(Chm. Bd. & Chief Exec. Officer)*
Richel G. Khoury *(Vice Chm., Sec. & Treas.)*
Russell R. Richard *(Pres. & Chief Oper. Officer)*
A.J. Moxhan *(Sr. V.P.)*
Ed Peterson *(Sr. V.P. & Chief Fin. Officer)*
Jon B. Werner *(Sr. V.P.)*

Outside Service Firm(s):

Ernst & Young*(Auditors)*
501 W. Broadway, Ste. 1200
San Diego, CA 92101

Bank of America NT&SA*(Major Banking Relationship)*
San Diego, CA

PACIFIC SOUND RESOURCES
2801 S.W. Florida St.
Seattle, WA 98126
Tel.: 206-932-0445 **WA**
Fax: 206-932-0237
Year Founded: 1966
Approx.Sls.: $12,000,000
Emp.: 70
Fiscal Year-end: 12/31/90
Export
Forest Products Treated with Preservatives, Piling, Lumber, Ties, Poles & Plywood
S.I.C.: 2491
Ted DePriest *(Pres. & Chief Oper. Officer)*
Bruce Lines *(V.P.-Sls.)*
Charles Mullen *(Sec.)*

No. of Mfg. Plants/Facilities: 2
No. of U.S. Offices: 1

Computer Systems/Hardware:
NCR

Outside Service Firm(s):

Deloitte & Touche*(Auditors)*
700 Fifth Ave., Suite 4500
Seattle, WA 98104-5044
Tel.: 206-292-1800

Graham & Dunn*(Legal Firm)*
1301 5th Ave., 34th Floor
Seattle, WA 98101
Tel.: 206-624-8300

PACIFIC STATES CASUALTY CO.
4021 Rosewood, Ste. 300
Los Angeles, CA 90004
Tel.: 213-666-8694 **CA**
Fax: 213-666-0743
Year Founded: 1983
Assets: $97,513,000
Liabilities: $78,494,000
Net Worth: $19,019,000
Approx.Sls.: $53,494,000
Emp.: 180
Fiscal Year-end: 12/31/90
Property Damage Insurance
S.I.C.: 6331
Rudolph Lowy *(Chm. Bd., Pres. & Chief Exec. Officer)*
Steve Porress *(Chief Oper. Officer & Mng. Dir.)*
Steve Mayberry *(Chief Fin. Officer)*
Martin G. Boost *(Exec. V.P.)*
R. Hollingshead *(V.P.-Claims)*
Sandy Weaver *(Treas.)*
Chris Bryson *(Gen. Counsel)*
E. Lowy *(Sec.)*

No. of U.S. Offices: 4

Computer Systems/Hardware:
IBM

Outside Service Firm(s):

Chubb Group*(Commercial Insurance Carrier)*
Los Angeles, CA

Union Bank*(Major Banking Relationship)*
Beverly Hills, CA

PACIFIC STEEL CASTING CO.
1333 2nd St.
Berkeley, CA 94710
Tel.: 510-525-9200
Fax: 510-524-4673
Emp.: 250
Manufacture Steel Castings
S.I.C.: 3325

Pacific Steel Casting Co.—(Continued)

Robert J. Delsol *(Pres.)*
Calvin Wong *(Chief Fin. Officer & V.P.)*
N.V. Davi *(Sr. V.P.-Opers.)*
Richard D. Genger *(V.P.)*
Ralph E. Hoover *(Comptroller)*

Computer Systems/Hardware:
Hewlett Packard

Outside Service Firm(s):

Coopers & Lybrand*(Auditors)*
1333 Broadway
Oakland, CA 94612
Tel.: 415-834-5400

Wells Fargo Bank*(Major Banking Relationship)*
420 Montgomery St.
San Francisco, CA 94104

PACIFIC WOOD TREATING COPORATION
(d/b/a Niedermeyer-Martin Co.)
111 W. Division, P.O. Box 518
Ridgefield, WA 98642
Tel.: 206-887-3562
Tel.: 800-547-6952 **WA**
Fax: 503-287-7225
Approx.Sls.: $17,000,000
Emp.: 125
Fiscal Year-end: 3/31/92
Import Export
Poles; Posts; Pillings; Softwoods; Hardwoods; Treated & Untreated Wood
S.I.C.: 2491
Edward C. Niedermeyer *(Pres.)*
Matt S. Masco *(Exec. V.P., Treas. & Sec.)*
Chad Niedermeyer *(V.P.)*
Dave Howland *(Dir.-Quality Control)*
Bev Dianich *(Mgr.-Sls. & Mktg.)*
Terry Niedermeyer *(Mgr.-Exports)*
Jo Waggoner *(Mgr.-Personnel)*
Geoffrey Watkins *(Mgr.-Data Processing)*
David Xochihua *(Mgr.-Imports)*

No. of Mfg. Plants/Facilities: 1
No. of U.S. Offices: 2

Computer Systems/Hardware:
IBM Systems 400

Outside Service Firm(s):

Schwab, Hilton & Howard*(Legal Firm)*
Portland, OR

First Interstate Bank*(Major Banking Relationship)*
P.O. Box 3131,
Portland, OR 97208
Tel.: 503-220-4855
Fax: 503-225-7153

PACIFICA REAL ESTATE GROUP
200 E. Carrillo St., Ste. 200
Santa Barbara, CA 93101
Tel.: 805-963-1631
Sales Range: $10-19 Million
Holding Company
S.I.C.: 6719; 6531
Dale Marquis *(Pres.)*

Subsidiaries:

Beaver Free Corp. **(1)**
200 E. Carrillo St., Ste. 200
Santa Barbara, CA 93101
Tel.: 805-963-1631
Real Estate & Commercial Brokerage
S.I.C.: 6531

Invest West Financial Corporation **(1)**
Ste. 302, 200 E. Carrillo St.
Santa Barbara, CA 93101
Tel.: 805-965-3025
Fax: 805-966-5670
Sales Range: $10-19 Million
Commercial Real Estate Investment & Development
S.I.C.: 6531
Dale M. Marquis *(Pres.)*
Thomas J. Gamble *(V.P.)*
Arlene M. Kostock *(V.P.)*

PACIFICA SERVICES, INC.
106 S. Mentor Ave., Ste. 200
Pasadena, CA 91106
Tel.: 818-405-0131 **CA**
Fax: 818-405-0059
Year Founded: 1979
Approx.Sls.: $60,000,000
Emp.: 600
Civil Engineering; Electronic Equipment Repair; Business Consultant
S.I.C.: 8711; 7629; 8742
Ernest M. Camacho *(Pres.)*
Stephen Caropino *(Exec. V.P.)*
Dave McClelland *(Sr. V.P.)*
Nelson Darquea *(V.P. & Controller)*

Outside Service Firm(s):

Bank of America NT&SA*(Major Banking Relationship)*
555 So. Flower St.
Los Angeles, CA 90071
Tel.: 213-683-3868

PACKAGE SERVICE COMPANY, INC.
10525 N.W. Ambassador, Ste. 208
Kansas City, MO 64153
Tel.: 816-891-8300 **MO**
Fax: 816-891-9032
Year Founded: 1963
Approx.Sls.: $35,000,000
Emp.: 235
Mfr. of Adhesive Papers, Labels or Tapes From Purchased Materials; Paper Products; Plastic Bands & Christmas Tree Ornaments Except Electrical & Glass
S.I.C.: 2672; 2679; 3089; 3999
G. Wesley Nedblake *(Pres.)*
Charles Adams *(Chief Exec. Officer)*
Karl Kimes *(V.P.)*
Jeff Nedblake *(V.P. & Treas.)*
Bill Toyne *(V.P.-Fin.)*
Steve McGinnis *(Asst. Controller)*

Outside Service Firm(s):

KPMG Peat Marwick*(Auditors)*
1000 Walnut St.
Kansas City, MO 64106

PACKAGING PRODUCTS & DESIGN
2120 S. Susan St.
Santa Ana, CA 92704-4494
Tel.: 714-546-9790 **CA**
Approx.Sls.: $11,000,000
Emp.: 65
Fiscal Year-end: 12/31/90
Export
Mfr. Plastic Bags & Polyethylene Film
S.I.C.: 2673; 3089
Lee Marteney *(Pres.)*
Virginia Marteney *(Sr. V.P.)*
R. Hare *(V.P.-Sls.)*
Joe Tiscareno *(Mgr.-Plant)*

No. of Mfg. Plants/Facilities: 1

Outside Service Firm(s):

Arthur Andersen & Co.*(Auditors)*
18500 Von Karman Ave. #1100
Irvine, CA
Tel.: 714-757-3100

PACO RABANNE PARFUMS
(Affil. of Puig of Barcelona, Spain)
70 E. 55th St.
New York, NY 10022
Tel.: 212-980-9620
Approx.Sls.: $25,000,000
Emp.: 110
Distr. of Paco Rabanne & Quorum-Puiq Cologne for Men; Calandre & Metal Cologne For Women; Men's Skin Care Prods.
S.I.C.: 5122
Dr. Fernando Aleu *(Pres.)*
John Lamie *(Sr. V.P.-Sls.)*
Robert McCormick *(V.P.-Opers. & Controller)*
Pat Snow *(V.P.-Sls.)*
Craig Morton *(Dir.-Mktg. & Adv.)*

PACOR, INC.
1900 N. Sixth St.
Philadelphia, PA 19122
Mailing Address:
P.O. Box 29278,
Philadelphia, PA 19128
Tel.: 215-978-7100
Fax: 215-978-7107
Approx.Sls.: $15,000,000
Emp.: 275
Thermal Insulation
S.I.C.: 3296
James E. Sullivan *(Chm. Bd.)*
Paul Fraatz, Jr. *(Pres. & Treas.)*
James D. Brown *(Exec. V.P. & Sec.)*

Outside Service Firm(s):

Jacoby, Donner & Jacoby*(Legal Firm)*
Philadelphia, PA

Philadelphia National Bank*(Major Banking Relationship)*
5th & Market Sts.
Philadelphia, PA 19101
Tel.: 215-629-3100
Fax: 215-834-2069

PADDOCK POOL CONSTRUCTION CO.
6525 E. Thomas Rd.
Scottsdale, AZ 85251
Tel.: 602-947-7261
Fax: 602-945-4925
Approx.Sls.: $21,000,000
Emp.: 220
Fiscal Year-end: 6/30/91
Special Trade Contractors; Retail of Misc. Merchandise; Business Services
S.I.C.: 1799; 5999
George Ghiz *(Chm. Bd.)*
Lewis Ghiz *(Pres.)*
Norman Bennett *(V.P.)*
Sally Ghiz *(Sec.)*
Gary Litton *(Dir.-Adv.)*

PADDOCK PUBLICATIONS, INC.
217 W. Campbell St.
Arlington Heights, IL 60005
Mailing Address:
P.O. Box 280
Arlington Heights, IL 60006
Tel.: 708-870-3600 **DE**
Fax: 708-398-0172
Year Founded: 1872
Approx.Sls.: $60,000,000
Emp.: 520
Fiscal Year-end: 3/31/92
Newspaper Publishing
S.I.C.: 2711
S. R. Paddock, Jr. *(Chm., Chief Exec. Officer & Publr.)*
R. Y. Paddock *(Vice Chm.)*
Daniel E. Baumann *(Pres. & Chief Oper. Officer)*
Robert F. Donahue *(V.P. & Treas.)*
Margie S. Flanders *(V.P. & Asst. Treas.)*
Judi Orgell *(V.P.-Human Resources)*
Douglas K. Ray *(V.P. & Editor)*
William F. Schoepke *(V.P.-Production)*
James F. Walsh *(V.P.-Adv.)*
Principal(s):
S. R. Paddock, Jr.
R. Y. Paddock
Margie S. Flanders

No. of Mfg. Plants/Facilities: 1
No. of U.S. Offices: 1

Computer Systems/Hardware:
Digital Equipment VAX

Outside Service Firm(s):

Arthur Andersen & Co.*(Auditors)*
33 W. Monroe St.
Chicago, IL 60603-4067
Tel.: 312-580-0033
Fax: 312-507-6748

Marsh & McLennan*(Commercial Insurance Carrier)*
222 S. Riverside Plaza
Chicago, IL 60606
Tel.: 312-648-6652

Prudential Insurance Co. of America*(Group Insurance Broker/Consult)*
130 E. Randolph Dr.
Chicago, IL 60601
Tel.: 312-861-4500

Lord, Bissell & Brook*(Legal Firm)*
115 S. La Salle St.
Chicago, IL 60603
Tel.: 312-443-0700
Fax: 312-443-0336

American National Bank & Trust Company of Chicago*(Major Banking Relationship)*
33 N. LaSalle St.
Chicago, IL 60602
Tel.: 312-661-5000
Fax: 312-661-6417

PADILLA SPEER BEARDSLEY INC.
224 Franklin Ave., W.
Minneapolis, MN 55404
Tel.: 612-871-8877 **MN**
Fax: 612-871-7792
Year Founded: 1961
Emp.: 53
Fiscal Year-end: 6/30/92
Financial Relations & Corporate Public Relations Counseling; Publicity Programs & Strategic Communication Services
S.I.C.: 8743
Corporate Giving Program: Company gives up to 5% of pretax income
Employee Matching Gifts Program: Gives matching gifts for education; post secondary schools
John R. Beardsley *(Chm. Bd. & Chief Exec. Officer)*
Jerry L. Erickson *(Chief Fin. Officer)*
Barbara Kuklock *(V.P.-Admin.)*

No. of U.S. Offices: 3

Computer Systems/Hardware:
AT&T/Contel

Outside Service Firm(s):

Price Waterhouse*(Auditors)*
3100 Multifoods Tower, 33 S. Sixth St.
Minneapolis, MN 55402

Royal Insurance Co.*(Commercial Insurance Carrier)*
Charlotte, NC

Blue Cross & Blue Shield Association*(Group Insurer)*
Minneapolis, MN

Robins, Kaplan, Miller & Ciresi*(Legal Firm)*
1800 International Center, 900 Second Ave. So.
Minneapolis, MN 55402

LOUIS PADNOS IRON & METAL CO.
120 S. River Ave.
Holland, MI 49423
Mailing Address:
P.O. Box 1979
Holland, MI 49422
Tel.: 616-396-6521

Fax: 616-396-7789
Year Founded: 1947
Approx.Sls.: $40,000,000
Emp.: 220
Process Secondary Metals & Fibres, Merchandise Mill Supplies, Machinery & Equipment
S.I.C.: 3339; 5084; 5093
Jeffrey S. Padnos *(Pres. & Chief Oper. Officer)*
Mitchell W. Padnos *(V.P.-Sls. & Mktg.)*
Barbara Padnos *(Sec.)*
James Den Braker *(Controller)*
Karen Gardner *(Dir.-Human Resources)*
Robert Eller *(Mgr.-Data Processing)*
Bruce Karger *(Pur. Agent)*

Outside Service Firm(s):

BDO Seidman*(Auditors)*
700 Commercial Bldg.
Kalamazoo, MI 49007-4758

Warner, Norcross & Judd*(Legal Firm)*
Grand Rapids, MI

First Michigan Bank*(Major Banking Relationship)*
Holland, MI

Division:

Padnos-Summit **(1)**
P.O. Box 13070
Lansing, MI 48901
Tel.: 517-372-6600
Fax: 210-372-0356
Processed Ferrous & Non-ferrous Scrap For Remelting Purposes; Primary Metals Distribution
S.I.C.: 3399; 5093
Bill Clay *(V.P.-Opers.)*

PAGANO, SCHENCK & KAY, INC.
1 Old Stone Square
Providence, RI 02903
Tel.: 401-456-0650
Fax: 401-861-8170
Year Founded: 1986
Approx.Billings: $20,000,000
Emp.: 33
Consumer & Business-to-Business Adv.
Robert P. Pagano *(Pres. & New Bus. Contact)*
John Malley *(Dir.-Finance & Admin.)*

Computer Systems/Hardware:
Unisys

PAGE BOY COMPANY, INC.
8918 Governors Row
Dallas, TX 75247
Tel.: 214-951-0055
Approx.Sls.: $10,000,000
Emp.: 200
Maternity Wear
S.I.C.: 2339
Elsie Frankfurt Pollock *(Pres.)*
Edna Ravkind *(V.P.)*
Robert Pollock *(Chief Oper. Officer)*

PAINE FURNITURE CO.
160 Lenox St.
Norwood, MA 02062
Tel.: 617-551-0770
Fax: 617-551-0914
Year Founded: 1835
Approx.Sls.: $15,000,000
Emp.: 60
Fiscal Year-end: 4/30/91
Retail Home Furnishings
S.I.C.: 5932
William L. Shearer III *(Chm. Bd. & Treas.)*
Jonathan Shearer *(Pres.)*
Thomas Calt *(V.P.)*
John Maguire *(V.P.)*
William McBirney *(V.P.)*
Barbara Ready *(V.P.-Sls. & Adv.)*
Catherine Morgan *(Controller)*

PAISANO PUBLICATIONS, INC.
28210 Dorothy Dr.
Agoura, CA 91301
Tel.: 818-889-8740 **CA**
Fax: 818-889-4726
Year Founded: 1970
Approx.Sls.: $30,000,000
Emp.: 120
Fiscal Year-end: 12/31/91
Export
Magazine Publishing Only, Not Printed On Site
S.I.C.: 2721
Joseph Teresi *(Pres.)*
Brian Wood *(Chief Oper. Officer & V.P.)*
Ellen Meagher *(Chief Fin. Officer & Treas.)*
Keith Ball *(V.P. & Dir.-Editorial)*
Alan P. Ribakoff *(V.P.)*
Brian Van Mols *(V.P.-New Business Devel.)*
Lizette Hotinger *(Dir.-Adv.)*
Tom Mulholland *(Dir.-Opers.)*
Bevi Whitehouse *(Dir.-Sls.)*

Principal(s):
Joseph Teresi

Outside Service Firm(s):

Union Bank*(Major Banking Relationship)*
Woodland Hills, CA

PAKULA & COMPANY
(Filed Chapter 11 Bankruptcy on July 2, 1992)
350 N. Orleans, Ste. 1001
Chicago, IL 60654-1588
Tel.: 312-644-2300
Fax: 312-836-5101
Year Founded: 1932
Approx.Sls.: $30,000,000
Emp.: 400
Fiscal Year-end: 3/31/91
Mfr. & Distribute Fashion Jewelry
S.I.C.: 3961; 5094
Milton S. Axelrad *(Chm. Bd.)*
James A. Axelrad *(Pres. & Chief Exec. Officer)*
Dick Franzen *(V.P.-Opers., Chicago)*
Marilyn Axelrad *(Sec.)*
John Weglarz *(Controller)*
Terri Flood *(Mgr.-Acct.)*
Ray Harnarine *(Mgr.-Data Processing)*

Principal(s):
Milton S. Axelrad
James A. Axelrad

No. of Mfg. Plants/Facilities: 1
No. of U.S. Offices: 7

Computer Systems/Hardware:
IBM System 38

Outside Service Firm(s):

Beiderman, Stetter, Silverman & Co.*(Auditors)*
Northfield, IL

Slater & Lieberman*(Legal Firm)*
Chicago, IL

Continental Bank N. A.*(Major Banking Relationship)*
231 S. LaSalle St.
Chicago, IL 60697
Tel.: 312-828-2345
Tel.: 800-426-5754
Telex: 312-828-1783

Division:

Cranston Manufacturing Facility **(1)**
One Pakula Park
Cranston, RI 02910
Tel.: 401-941-9000
Fax: 401-941-1720
S.I.C.: 3961

PALA GROUP, INC.
(Formerly Riana Enterprises Inc.)
16347 Old Hammond Hwy.
Baton Rouge, LA 70816
Mailing Address:
P.O. Box 15949
Baton Rouge, LA 70895
Tel.: 504-272-5194 **LA**
Fax: 504-272-5239
Year Founded: 1986
Approx.Sls.: $34,000,000
Emp.: 500
Industrial Contractor
S.I.C.: 1541
Ana M. Tarajano *(Pres.)*
Jorge L. Tarajano *(V.P.)*
John R. Hanson *(Treas.)*
Jose Tarajano *(Gen. Counsel & Mgr.-Personnel)*
Frank Olinde *(Dir.-Pur.)*

Subsidiary:

Pala Interstate **(1)**
16347 Old Hammond Hwy.
Baton Rouge, LA 70816
Tel.: 504-272-5194
Fax: 504-272-5194
Emp.: 400
Industrial Maintenance & Construction
S.I.C.: 1541

PALLAS ADVERTISING, INC.
1160 Battery St., Ste. 200
San Francisco, CA 94111
Tel.: 415-421-1414
Fax: 415-421-2950
Year Founded: 1985
Approx.Billings: $20,000,000
Emp.: 17
Robert M. Pallas *(Pres.)*
Joe Jackson *(Mktg. Dir.)*

PALM BEACH BEAUTY PRODUCTS CO.
950 Xenia Ave., S.
Minneapolis, MN 55416
Tel.: 612-546-0322
Tel.: 800-326-7256 **MN**
Fax: 612-546-0322, Ext. 112
Year Founded: 1941
Approx.Sls.: $10,500,000
Emp.: 102
Fiscal Year-end: 6/30/92
Export
Mfr. of Cosmetics, Hair Care Products & Medical Products
S.I.C.: 2834; 2844
Ben B. Kaitz *(Pres.)*
Richard A. Kaitz *(Exec. V.P.)*
Rich Halliday *(V.P.-Mktg.)*
David P. Bellizi *(V.P.-Sls.)*
Miriam Collins Kaitz *(Sec. & Treas.)*
David Darsow *(Controller)*
Bob Cordell *(Gen. Mgr.)*
Bruce Vetsch *(Dir.-Pur.)*
Michelle Reed *(Data Processing Dir.)*

Principal(s):
Ben B. Kaitz
Richard A. Kaitz
Miriam Collins Kaitz

No. of Mfg. Plants/Facilities: 1
No. of U.S. Offices: 1

Computer Systems/Hardware:
Micro Data/Reality

Outside Service Firm(s):

Chubb Group*(Commercial Insurance Carrier)*
Minneapolis, MN

P-H-P/Mutual Benefit Life*(Group Insurer)*
Minneapolis, MN

Lindquist & Vennum*(Legal Firm)*
4200 IDS Center, 80 South 8th St.
Minneapolis, MN 55402
Tel.: 612-371-3211

Norwest Bank Minnesota, N.A.*(Major Banking Relationship)*
Golden Vallley, MN

PALM HARBOR HOMES, INC.
15301 Dallas Parkway, Ste. 800
Dallas, TX 75248
Tel.: 214-991-2422
Fax: 214-991-5949
Emp.: 1,500
Mobile Homes Except Recreational
S.I.C.: 2451
Lee Posey *(Pres. & Chief Exec. Officer)*
James Nicholson *(V.P.-Fin.)*

Outside Service Firm(s):

North Park National Bank*(Major Banking Relationship)*
Dallas, TX

Subsidiaries:

Palm Harbor Homes, d/b/a V.P. Homes, Inc. **(1)**
Rte. 22 E.
Sabina, OH 45169
Tel.: 513-584-2401
Mobile Homes
S.I.C.: 2451
Allen Reitmeier *(Mgr.)*

Palm Harbor Homes, d/b/a V.P. Homes, Inc. **(1)**
Hwy. 421 N.
Silver City, NC 27344
Tel.: 919-663-2182
Mobile Homes
S.I.C.: 2451

PALM IRON & BRIDGE WORKS, INC.
8845 Elder Creek Rd.
Sacramento, CA 95828
Tel.: 916-386-1010
Fax: 916-381-7787
Year Founded: 1886
Approx.Sls.: $30,000,000
Emp.: 200
Fabricated Steel
S.I.C.: 1791
Steve Schwartz *(Pres.)*
Alan Messick *(Sec. & Treas.)*
Jan Steinberg *(Controller)*
Gary Rogers *(Pur. Agent)*

Outside Service Firm(s):

Swanson & Kinney*(Auditors)*
Sacramento, CA

Diepenbrock, Wulff, Plant & Hannegan*(Legal Firm)*
Sacramento, CA

Wells Fargo Bank*(Major Banking Relationship)*
420 Montgomery St.
San Francisco, CA 94104

R.M. PALMER COMPANY
77 Second Ave.
West Reading, PA 19611
Tel.: 215-372-8971
Approx.Sls.: $35,000,000
Emp.: 500
Mfr. of Seasonal Chocolates
S.I.C.: 2064
Richard M. Palmer, Jr. *(Chm. Bd. & Pres.)*
Roderick Eaken *(Exec. V.P.)*
William Newton *(V.P.-Mfg.)*
James E. Tucker *(V.P.-Sls. & Mktg.)*
William J. Lucas *(Treas.)*
Ronald Leeper *(Sec.)*

PALMER ELECTRIC CO.
875 Jackson Ave.
Winter Park, FL 32789
Tel.: 407-646-8700
Fax: 407-644-8843

Palmer Electric Co.—(Continued)

Approx.Sls.: $19,500,000
Emp.: 325
Fiscal Year-end: 9/30/90
Electrical Contractor Commercial & Residential Lighting; Wholesale & Retail Household Appliances
S.I.C.: 1731; 5063; 5064; 5722
Charles H. Tindal *(Chm. Bd., Pres. & Chief Exec. Officer)*
Thomas G. Beard *(V.P.-Admin., Treas., Controller & Sec.)*
Henry C. Eure *(V.P.-Lighting & Signs)*
Principal(s):
Employee Owned

Outside Service Firm(s):

Cuthill & Eddy*(Auditors)*
Winter Park, FL

Maguire, Voorhis & Wells*(Legal Firm)*
Two S. Orange Plz.
Orlando, FL 32801
Tel.: 407-843-4421

Sun Bank, N.A.*(Major Banking Relationship)*
200 S. Orange Ave., 8th Fl. SOAB
Orlando, FL
Tel.: 407-237-4141

R.J. Palmer Inc
MEDIA SERVICES AND PROGRAM SYNDICATION

R.J. PALMER, INC.
1350 Ave. of the Americas
New York, NY 10019
Tel.: 212-541-6770
Fax: 212-541-6769
Year Founded: 1981
Approx.Billings: $60,000,000
Emp.: 13
Network and Cable TV
Robert J. Palmer *(Pres.)*
Peter T. Knobloch *(Exec. V.P.)*
Laurence E. Reynolds *(V.P., Mktg.)*
Olga Mendez *(Comptroller)*

PALMER INTERNATIONAL, INC.
Rte. 73
Worcester, PA 19490
Tel.: 215-584-4241
Fax: 215-584-4817
Sales Range: $10-19 Million
Emp.: 65
Mfr. of Synthetic Resins, Epoxy & Urea Adhesives
S.I.C.: 2822; 2821; 2891
Stephen T. Palmer, Jr. *(Chm. Bd. & Chief Exec. Officer)*
Wayne L. Palmer *(Pres.)*
Bruce Palmer *(Exec. V.P.-Opers.)*
Roberta Palmer *(Sec.)*

Outside Service Firm(s):

Deloitte & Touche*(Auditors)*
1700 Market St.
Philadelphia, PA 19103
Tel.: 215-246-2322
Fax: 215-569-2441

Mellon Bank, N.A.*(Major Banking Relationship)*
Mellon Independence Center, 7th & Market
Philadelphia, PA 19101-7899

PALMER MANUFACTURING COMPANY
243 Medford St.
Malden, MA 02148
Tel.: 617-321-0480
Fax: 617-321-2226
Approx.Sls.: $15,000,000
Emp.: 130
Manufacture Aircraft Engine Components
S.I.C.: 3724
Frank Mode, Jr. *(Pres.)*
Raymond Gosselin *(V.P.-Sls.)*
Donald A. Fiore *(Treas. & Mgr.-Personnel)*
Sonny Panbianco *(Pur. Agent)*

Outside Service Firm(s):

Giantz & Saperstein*(Auditors)*
Boston, MA

George M. Beisky*(Legal Firm)*
Boston, MA

Bay Bank*(Major Banking Relationship)*
Burlington, MA

PALMER MOVING & STORAGE CO.
31751 Enterprise Dr.
Livonia, MI 48150
Mailing Address:
P.O. Box 2496,
Livonia, MI 48151
Tel.: 313-458-8000 **MI**
Fax: 313-422-5311
Year Founded: 1910
Approx.Sls.: $12,600,000
Emp.: 193
Local Moving & Storage; Long Distance Moving
S.I.C.: 4214; 4213
Richard F. Palmer *(Chm. Bd.)*
Jeffrey W. Palmer *(Pres.)*
Joan R. Palmer *(V.P.)*

PALMETTO SPINNING CORP.
1100 Church St.
Laurens, SC 29360
Tel.: 803-984-3556
Fax: 803-984-6232
Year Founded: 1946
Approx.Sls.: $20,000,000
Emp.: 200
Mfr. Carpet Yarns
S.I.C.: 2281; 2282
W.F. Davis, Jr. *(Pres., Chief Exec. Officer & Treas.)*
Mary Davis *(V.P. & Corp. Sec.)*
Eugene Tollison *(Mgr.-Personnel)*

Outside Service Firm(s):

Ernst & Young*(Auditors)*
C & S Bank Tower, Two Shelter Centre, Ste. 800
Greenville, SC 29603

Wyche, Burgess, Freeman & Parham, P.A.*(Legal Firm)*
44 E. Camperdown Way
Greenville, SC 29602
Tel.: 803-242-3131

Palmetto Bank*(Major Banking Relationship)*
Laurens, SC

PALMETTO WHOLESALE CO., INC.
850 Rosewood Dr.
Columbia, SC 29201
Mailing Address:
P.O. Box 998,
Columbia, SC 29202
Tel.: 803-799-1662 **SC**
Fax: 803-779-0564
Year Founded: 1946
Approx.Sls.: $17,266,000
Emp.: 105
Fiscal Year-end: 12/31/91
Import
Wholesale Hardware & Building Materials
S.I.C.: 5072; 5039
John H. Saunders, Sr. *(Chm. Bd. & Chief Exec. Officer)*
Harry L. Bauknight *(Pres. & Chief Oper. Officer)*
Linda P. Kaneft *(Exec. V.P.)*
Ted Cooper *(V.P.-Door & Hardware Div.)*
Mark Christopher *(Controller)*
Joseph Shealy *(Dir.-Pur.)*
Michael P. Owen *(Dir.-Adv. & Stores Programs)*
Ray Justice *(Gen. Mgr.-Dealer Div.)*
Steve McKelvey *(Mgr.-Sls.)*

No. of Mfg. Plants/Facilities: 1
No. of U.S. Offices: 1

Computer Systems/Hardware:
Wang VS-5000

Outside Service Firm(s):

C. C. McGregor & Co.*(Auditors)*
Columbia, SC

Self-Insured*(Group Insurer)*

The McNair Firm*(Legal Firm)*
Columbia, SC

South Carolina National Bank*(Major Banking Relationship)*
Columbia, SC

R. B. PAMPLIN CORP.
900 S.W. 5th Ave., Ste. 1800
Portland, OR 97204
Tel.: 503-248-1133 **DE**
Fax: 503-248-1175
Year Founded: 1957
Approx.Sls.: $572,000,000
Emp.: 5,500
Fiscal Year-end: 5/31/92
Holding Co.; Sand, Gravel, Concrete & Asphalt Materials; Textile Manufacturing
S.I.C.: 5039; 2297; 6719; 2911; 2951
Robert B. Pamplin, Sr. *(Chm. Bd. & Chief Exec. Officer)*
Dr. Robert B. Pamplin, Jr. *(Pres., Chief Oper. Officer & Sec.)*
David Meek *(Treas.)*

Computer Systems/Hardware:
IBM System 38

Outside Service Firm(s):

Deloitte & Touche*(Auditors)*
1200 NCNB Plaza, 7 N. Laurens St.
Greenville, SC 29601
Tel.: 803-242-3640

Travelers Insurance Co.*(Commercial Insurance Carrier)*
One Tower Square
Hartford, CT 06183-6130
Tel.: 203-277-4542
Fax: 203-277-5038

Blue Cross & Blue Shield of South Carolina*(Group Insurer)*
1517 Laurel St.
Columbia, SC 29201

Haynsworth, Marion, McKay & Guerard*(Legal Firm)*
75 Beattie Place, 2 Shelter Centre 11th Fl
Greenville, SC 29601
Tel.: 803-240-3300

Wachovia Bank & Trust Co.*(Major Banking Relationship)*
Charlotte, NC

Subsidiaries:

Mount Vernon Mills, Inc. **(1)**
One Shelter Pl., Ste. 700
Greenville, SC 29601
Tel.: 803-233-4151
Fax: 803-370-2315
Approx.Sls.: $450,000,000
Emp.: 5,000
Import Export
Mfr. of Textiles & Home Furnishings
S.I.C.: 2211; 2241; 2269; 2341; 2392; 4213; 5131
R.B. Pamplin, Sr. *(Chm. Bd.)*
Dr. R.B. Pamplin, Jr. *(Vice Chm.)*
J.L. Jennings, Jr. *(Pres.)*
Roger W. Chastain *(Exec. V.P. & Pres.-Riegel Textile Div.)*
Ligon King *(Exec. V.P. & Pres.-Mt. Vernon Grp.)*
C. Ray Mabry *(V.P. & Pres.-Mt. Vernon Textile Grp.)*
David C. Meek *(V.P. & Treas.)*
Jim Knight *(Controller)*
E.G. Cochrane II *(Sec. & Gen. Counsel)*
H.B. Leonard *(Credit Mgr.)*

Divisions:

Mount Vernon Mills, Inc., Consumer Products Div. (McCormick) **(2)**
Augusta Hwy.
McCormick, SC 29835
Tel.: 803-465-2632
Emp.: 255
Infant's Wear
S.I.C.: 2341
J.M. Spinner *(Pres.)*
M. Wideman *(Plant Mgr.)*

Mount Vernon Mills, Inc., Clarkton, NC **(2)**
Clarkton, NC 28433
Tel.: 919-647-4011
Yarn Spinning Mill
S.I.C.: 2281

Mount Vernon Mills, Inc. **(2)**
689 S. Elm St.
Commerce, GA 30529
Tel.: 706-335-3171
Fax: 706-335-6381
Emp.: 300
Mfr. of Greige Goods for Home Furnishings & Apparel
S.I.C.: 2211
John Klugh *(Gen. Mgr.)*

Mount Vernon Mills, Inc., LaFrance Industries **(2)**
P.O. Box 500
La France, SC 29656
Tel.: 803-646-3213
Emp.: 850
Mfr. of Upholstery Fabrics for Furniture
S.I.C.: 2221
R.E. King *(Pres.)*

Mount Vernon Mills, Inc., Mount Vernon Forming Fabrics **(2)**
P.O. Box 607
Weaverville, NC 28787
Tel.: 704-645-4251
Mfr. of Monofilament for Industrial Paper Making Machines
S.I.C.: 2282

Mount Vernon Mills, Inc., Riegel Consumer Products Div. **(2)**
P.O. Box E
Johnston, SC 29832
Tel.: 803-275-2541
Emp.: 423
Infant's & Domestic Products
S.I.C.: 2392; 2211
J.M. Spinner *(Pres.)*
T.L. Whitlock *(Plant Mgr.)*

Mount Vernon Mills, Inc., Tallassee, AL **(2)**
Tallassee, AL 36078
Tel.: 205-283-6501
S.I.C.: 2221

Mount Vernon Mills, Inc., Riegel Textile Div. **(2)**
P.O. Box 3478
Greenville, SC 29602
Tel.: 803-233-4151
Mill & Finishing Plant
S.I.C.: 2211; 2269
Roger Chastain *(Pres.)*

Divisions:

Mount Vernon Mills, Inc., Riegel Textile Div. (Alto) **(3)**
P.O. Box 649
Alto, GA 30510
Tel.: 706-778-2141
Emp.: 622
Manufacture of Textile
S.I.C.: 2241
L.E. Porter *(Chief Exec. Officer)*

Mount Vernon Mills, Inc., Riegel Textile Div. (Trion) **(3)**
P.O. Box 7
Trion, GA 30753
Tel.: 706-734-2311
Emp.: 3,000
Manufacturer of Textiles
S.I.C.: 2211; 2281
H.L. Peek *(V.P.)*

Mount Vernon Mills, Inc., Williamston (2)
P.O. Box 339
Williamston, SC 29697
Tel.: 803-845-5447
S.I.C.: 2211
Jerald Miles *(Gen. Mgr.)*

Mount Vernon Mills, Inc., Woodruff (2)
P.O. Box 459
Woodruff, SC 29388
Tel.: 803-476-8174
Yarn Spinning Mill & Finishing Plant
S.I.C.: 2269; 2281
J.T. Moore *(Gen. Mgr.)*

Subsidiaries:

Mount Vernon Dryer Fabrics **(2)**
P.O. Box 5837
Greenville, SC 29606
Tel.: 803-967-7641
Emp.: 100
Textile Goods
S.I.C.: 2299
R.L. King, Jr. *(Pres.)*

Mount Vernon Mills, Smith & Waters, Inc. **(2)**
Nation Rd.
Ware Shoals, SC 29692
Tel.: 803-456-7421 (100%)
Emp.: 29
Trucking
S.I.C.: 4213
P.H. Balentine *(Pres.)*

Ross Island Sand & Gravel Co., Inc. **(1)**
4315 S.E. McLoughlin Blvd.
Portland, OR 97202
Tel.: 503-239-5504 (100%)
Approx.Sls.: $30,500,000
Emp.: 250
Mining of Sand & Gravel; Manufacturer of Concrete, Asphalt & Dry Mix Products
S.I.C.: 1442; 3271; 3272; 3273; 2951; 2952
Dr. R.B. Pamplin, Jr. *(Pres. & Sec.)*
Charles Steinwandel *(Exec. V.P.)*

Subsidiary:

K.F. Jacobson Co. **(2)**
4315 S.E. McLoughlin Blvd.
Portland, OR 97202
Tel.: 503-239-5532 (100%)
Sand & Gravel Mining; Mfr. of Concrete, Asphalt & Dry Mix Products
S.I.C.: 1442; 3271; 3272; 3273; 2951; 2952
Dr. R.B. Pamplin, Jr. *(Pres. & Sec.)*
Charles Steinwandel *(Exec. V.P.)*

PAN-AMERICAN LIFE INSURANCE COMPANY
601 Poydras St.
New Orleans, LA 70130
Mailing Address:
P.O. Box 60219
New Orleans, LA 70160
Tel.: 504-566-1300
Fax: 504-566-3459
Year Founded: 1911
Assets: $2,056,034,344
Liabilities: $1,932,078,079
Net Worth: $123,956,265
Approx.Sls.: $729,000,000
Emp.: 600
Fiscal Year-end: 12/31/91
Life & Health Insurance; Hospital & Medical Service Plans; Pension Plans & Administration
S.I.C.: 6311; 6321
Employee Matching Gifts Program: Matching Gifts to University Alma Maters of Employees
G. Frank Purvis; Jr. *(Chm. Bd.)*
Carl Giffir *(Pres.-Natl. Insurance Services)*
John K. Roberts, Jr. *(Pres. & Chief Exec. Officer)*
M. Steven Bumpas *(Sr. V.P.-Employee Benefits Opers.)*
James M. Cash, Jr. *(Sr. V.P.-Corp. Services)*
Robert S. Foster *(Sr. V.P.-Intl. Opers.)*
Michael Gereaue *(Sr. V.P.-Pensions)*
Sidney Albert Leblanc *(Sr. V.P.-Fin. Plng. & Control)*
Warren S. Newton, Jr. *(Sr. V.P.-U.S. Opers.)*
Theodore Tumminello *(Sr. V.P., Gen. Counsel & Sec.)*
Robert E. Van Arsdall *(Sr. V.P.-Investments)*
William Guion *(2nd V.P.-Communications)*

Outside Service Firm(s):

KPMG Peat Marwick*(Auditors)*
One Shell Center, Ste. 3500
New Orleans, LA 70139

First National Bank Of Commerce*(Major Banking Relationship)*
New Orleans, LA

PAN AMERICAN TRADE DEVELOPMENT CORP.
(Filed Ch. 11 Bankruptcy 8/91)
310 Madison Ave.
New York, NY 10017
Tel.: 212-599-3500 **NY**
Fax: 212-599-3509
Approx.Sls.: $300,000,000
Emp.: 450
Wholesale Steel & Forest Products, Chemicals, Rubber and Foods; Importing; International & Domestic Financing
S.I.C.: 5051; 5031; 5084; 5191; 5169; 5199
Peter L. Slotta *(Pres. & Treas.)*
Archie Abrams *(Sr. V.P.)*
Albert Baldassarri *(Sr. V.P.)*
Peter R. Klaus *(Sr. V.P.)*
Peter Liebgold *(Sr. V.P.)*
Albert Rode *(Sr. V.P.)*
Katherine M. Farrell *(Sec.)*

Outside Service Firm(s):

Spicer & Oppenheim*(Auditors)*
7 World Trade Center,
New York, NY 10048
Tel.: 212-422-1000

Chase Manhattan Bank, N.A.*(Major Banking Relationship)*
One Chase Manhattan Plaza
New York, NY 10081
Tel.: 212-552-2222
Tel.: 800-526-0801
Fax: 212-552-7175

PANARCO, INC.
480 Morris Ave.
Summit, NJ 07901
Tel.: 908-273-5398
Fax: 908-273-5896
Approx.Sls.: $15,000,000
Emp.: 95
Machine Engraved Printing Rollers, Embossing Rollers, Embossing Machines, Plate Cylinders For Printing & Converting
S.I.C.: 3555; 3579
Peter Callaghan *(Chm. Bd.)*
Maurice Buckley *(Pres. & Chief Exec. Officer)*

Outside Service Firm(s):

Crowe, Chizek & Co.*(Auditors)*
P.O. Box 3687,
Oak Brook, IL 60822
Tel.: 708-954-7408
Fax: 708-799-1299

I. Leo Motiuk*(Legal Firm)*
Flemington, NJ

National State Bank*(Major Banking Relationship)*
Roselle, NJ

PANCOM INTERNATIONAL CORP.
2015 W. Main St.
Stamford, CT 06902
Tel.: 203-357-7204
Fax: 203-964-0068
Approx.Billings: $31,000,000
Joseph F. Bartolone, Sr. *(Chm. & Chief Exec. Officer)*
Gary W. Kullberg *(Pres. & Chief Oper. Officer)*
Lynn D'Anna *(Exec. V.P.)*
Joseph F. Bartolone, Jr. *(Exec. V.P.)*

Operating Group
Joseph F. Bartolone, Sr. *(Chm. & Creative Services)*
Lynn D'Anna *(Exec. V.P., Dir. Mktg. Services)*
Martin Fiderer *(Sr. V.P., Acct. Services)*
Richard Kosmicki *(Sr. V.P., Dir. Pub. Rel.)*
George Nigro *(Sr. V.P., Intl.)*
Mike Keysivk *(Controller)*
Ruth Sitler *(Admin.)*

PANDUIT COMPANY
17301 Ridgeland Ave.
Tinley Park, IL 60477
Tel.: 708-532-1800
Fax: 708-532-1811
Approx.Sls.: $200,000,000
Emp.: 2,000
Mfr. Electrical Wire & Electronics Accessories
S.I.C.: 3643; 3644
Max Henderson *(Pres.)*
Dennis Colleran *(V.P.-Fin.)*
Bob Kenney *(Mgr.-Mktg.)*

Computer Systems/Hardware:
IBM

Outside Service Firm(s):

Blue Cross & Blue Shield of Illinois*(Group Insurer)*
100 Tower Drive
Burr Ridge, IL 60521
Tel.: 708-323-3666

Non-U.S. Holdings:

Advance Power Co. Ltd. **(1)**
150/49-51 Larn luang Road
Pomprab, Bangkok 10100, Thailand
Tel.: 2800150
Telex: 84829 CKSUE TH
Fax: 6622803684
S.I.C.: 3643; 3644; 5063

Allhabo Aktiebolag **(1)**
Alstromergatan 20 P.O. Box 49044, 10028
Stockholm, 49, Sweden
Tel.: 540700
Telex: 19015 ALLHABO S
Fax: 522600
S.I.C.: 3643; 3644; 5063

Burc Electronics & Machinery Corp. **(1)**
Refik Saydam cad. 89, Arsian Han Kat: 2
Sishane Istanbul, Turkey
Tel.: 1495788
Telex: 25883 BUEM TR
Fax: 1446182
S.I.C.: 3643; 3644; 5063

Commercial Espanola de Componentes S.A. **(1)**
Ofelia Nieto 43 28039
Madrid, Spain
Tel.: 4593441
Telex: 47010 ECCE E
S.I.C.: 3643; 3644; 5063

Cone, Lda. **(1)**
Urb. Colina do Sol, Lote 18-Alfornel 2700
Amadora, Portugal
Tel.: 990239
Telex: 18594 CONE P
S.I.C.: 3643; 3644; 5063

Dahms Electronik GmbH **(1)**
Wienerstr. 287 8051
Graz, Austria
Tel.: 64030-33
Telex: 311099-DAHMS A
S.I.C.: 3643; 3644; 5063

Electronica Del Pacifico **(1)**
Julio Prado 2118
Santiago, 9, Chile
Tel.: 2250356
Telex: 241055 ELFIN CL
S.I.C.: 3643; 3644; 5063

Electronik (Pty) Ltd. **(1)**
Fleetway House, Martin Hammerschlag Way P.O. Box 1020,
Cape Town, 8000, South Africa
Tel.: 457657
Telex: 52730 ELINK SA
S.I.C.: 3643; 3644; 5063

Oy Etra Ab **(1)**
Lampputie 2 00740
Helsinki, 74, Finland
Tel.: 366366
Telex: 124818 ETRA SF
S.I.C.: 3643; 3644; 5063

Hans Folsgaard, Agentur A/S **(1)**
Ejby Industrivej 2 2600
Glostrup, Denmark
Tel.: 963388
Telex: 33505 ELSHOP DK
Fax: 968855
S.I.C.: 3643; 3644; 5063

Interelectronic Oertli AG **(1)**
Kirchenweg 5 8032
Zurich, Switzerland
Tel.: 2512929
Telex: 816358 FBX CH
Fax: 2512379
S.I.C.: 3643; 3644; 5063

Iselco SF **(1)**
Skeifan 11/D, Reykjavik Ind. Centre P.O. Box 8060, 128, 105
Reykjavik, Iceland
Tel.: 686-466
Telex: 2203 ISELCO SF
S.I.C.: 3643; 3644; 5063

Klockner-Moeller Norsk A/S **(1)**
Hvamveien 4 Postboks 98, 2013
Skjetten, Norway
Tel.: 8420100
Telex: 76936 KLOMO N
Fax: 840125
S.I.C.: 3643; 3644; 5063

Mulder Hardenberg B.V. **(1)**
Westerhoutpark 1a,2012 JL P.O. Box 3059, 2001 DB
Haarlem, Netherlands
Tel.: 319184
Telex: 41431 HARMU NL
Fax: 325932
S.I.C.: 3643; 3644; 5063

Panduit S.N.C. **(1)**
Z.A. des Marais, 1 Ave. Louison Bobet 94124,
Fontenay-sous-Bois, Cedex France
Tel.: 48777633
Telex: 670156 PANFRAN
Fax: 48775617
S.I.C.: 3643; 3644; 5063

Panduit Aust. Pty. Ltd. **(1)**
No. 7 Conifer Crescent, Redwood Gardens Estate
Dingley, Victoria 3172, Australia
Tel.: 551-8844
Telex: 36857 PANAUS AA
Fax: 551-8080
S.I.C.: 3643; 3644; 5063

Panduit Canada Ltd. **(1)**
140 Amber St.
Markham, ON L3R 3J8, Canada
Tel.: 416-475-6922
Telex: 986810 PANDUIT MKHM
Fax: 476-6998
S.I.C.: 3643; 3644; 5063

Panduit Corp. **(1)**
Erlachplatz 2-4 A-1100,
Vienna, Austria
Tel.: 222-76-9639
Telex: 136538 PINC A
Fax: 6049734
S.I.C.: 3643; 3644; 5063

Panduit Company—(Continued)

Panduit Corp. **(1)**
Avenue de la Liberte, 80 1080
Brussels, Belgium
Tel.: 02-428-2944
Telex: 62810 PANDUIT B
Fax: 02-424-2319
S.I.C.: 3643; 3644; 5063

Panduit Corp. Japan Branch **(1)**
31-5, Omori Kita 6-chome Ota-ku,
Tokyo, 143, Japan
Tel.: 7677011
Telex: 2424527 PJLTYO J
Fax: 7677033
S.I.C.: 3643; 3644; 5063

Panduit GMbH **(1)**
Rudolf-Diesel-Strasse 18 P.O. Box 206, D-8012
Ottobrunn, Germany
Tel.: 6091040
Telex: 529260 PINCO D
Fax: 6094728
S.I.C.: 3643; 3644; 5063

Panduit Limited **(1)**
61-65 Revenge Road
Chatham, Kent ME5 8YT, United Kingdom
Tel.: 660811
Telex: 965393 PANDUK G
Fax: 685326
S.I.C.: 3643; 3644; 5063

Panduit Nederland **(1)**
P.O. Box 257, 4240 AG
Rosmalen, Holland Netherlands
Tel.: 31-4192-19000
Telex: 50435
Fax: 31-4192-19090
S.I.C.: 3643; 3644; 5063

Panduit Philippines **(1)**
Rm. 301, Ambrosio Bldg., Sen. Gil J. Puyat Ave. Corner Bautista St.,
Makati, Metro Manila Philippines
Tel.: 632-856481
Telex: 63199 ETPIMO PN
Fax: 632-8179742
S.I.C.: 3643; 3644; 5063

Panduit S.A.S. **(1)**
Via Como 10 1 20020
Lainate, Milan Italy
Tel.: 93570324
Telex: 332550
Fax: 93670333
S.I.C.: 3643; 3644; 5063

Panduit Singapore Pte. Ltd. **(1)**
5 Gul Lane
Singapore, Singapore
Tel.: 8613122
Telex: 35826 PANSPL
Fax: 8613161
S.I.C.: 3643; 3644; 5063

Panduit Trading Pte. Ltd. **(1)**
Unit 15, Block A, S/F, Tonic Industrial Centre 26 Kai Cheung Rd.,
Kowloon Bay, Kowloon Hong Kong
Tel.: 7967803
Cable: PANDUIT HK
Fax: 7967795
S.I.C.: 3643; 3644; 5063

Panduit Trading Pte. Ltd. **(1)**
Rm. 1015 Jungwoo Bldg., 13-25 Yoldo Dong Yungdongpo-ku,
Seoul, Korea
Tel.: 2-7849497
Fax: 2-7851357
S.I.C.: 3643; 3644; 5063

Panduit Trading Pte. Ltd. **(1)**
Rm. 807, 246 Chang An, East Road, Sector 2
Taipei, Taiwan
Tel.: 7812604
Fax: 7310324
S.I.C.: 3643; 3644; 5063

Patron Comercio E Representacoes Ltda. **(1)**
Rua Julio Ribeiro, 78 RJ CEP 21041,
Bonsucesso, Rio De Janiero Brazil
Tel.: 260-1377
S.I.C.: 3643; 3644

Srivathsa Electrical Corp. **(1)**
157, Angappa Street
Madras, 600001, India
Tel.: 510462
Telex: 417482 IOSA IN
S.I.C.: 3643; 3644; 5063

C.V. Sumber Sakti **(1)**
7 Jalan Dr Susilo
Bandung, 40171, Indonesia
Tel.: 434386-7
Telex: 28544 SUMTI IA
Fax: 435177
S.I.C.: 3643; 3644; 5063

Alexander Schneider Ltd. **(1)**
44 Petach Tikva Rd.
Tel Aviv, 81180, Israel
Tel.: 372089
Telex: 33613 Dygal IL
Fax: 370337
S.I.C.: 3643; 3644; 5063

Tecna Ltda. **(1)**
Carrara 32 No. 22-B-60/66
Bogota, D.E. Colombia
Tel.: 2681311
Telex: 44358 TECNA CO
Fax: 2692163
S.I.C.: 3643; 3644; 5063

S.K. Tsoumanis Representations **(1)**
29 Iroon Skopeftiriou and, Solomonidou Corner P.O. Box 74214,
Kessariani, Athens 16000, Greece
Tel.: 7291414
Telex: 214065 CONT GR
S.I.C.: 3643; 3644; 5063

Tylus SDN BHD **(1)**
3L. Ground Floor Block C, Jalan, Jubilee
55200 Off Jalan Loke Yew,
Kuala Lumpur, Malaysia
Tel.: 2222228
Fax: 03-2439637
S.I.C.: 3643; 3644; 5063

PANEL PRINTS, INC.
1001 Moosic Rd.
Old Forge, PA 18518
Tel.: 717-457-8334
Fax: 717-457-6440
Year Founded: 1974
Approx.Sls.: $38,000,000
Emp.: 475
Import
Lithographic Printing
S.I.C.: 2752
Karl Schaettle *(Pres.)*
Joseph S. Lieber *(V.P.-Fin.)*
Rick O'Hop *(Controller)*
William Titus *(Sec. & Pur. Agent)*
Dave Graber *(Mgr.-Production)*

Outside Service Firm(s):

Ernst & Young*(Auditors)*
1100 Independence Center
Charlotte, NC 28246
Tel.: 704-372-6300

Ginader, Jones & Company*(Auditors)*
Scanton, PA

First Eastern Bank N.A.*(Major Banking Relationship)*
Scranton, PA

PANEL PROCESSING, INC.
120 N. Industrial Hwy.
Alpena, MI 49707
Mailing Address:
P.O. Box 457
Alpena, MI 49707
Tel.: 517-356-9007
Fax: 517-356-9000
Year Founded: 1971
Approx.Sls.: $25,000,000
Emp.: 175
Mfr. of Painted & Fabricated Hardboard, Patricle Board & Fiberboard
S.I.C.: 2493
Robert M. Granum *(Chm. Bd. & Chief Exec. Officer)*
Robert W. Karsten *(Vice Chm. & Treas.)*
Phillip Hitchock *(Pres.)*
Carl F. Reitz *(Sec.)*

Outside Service Firm(s):

BDO Seidman*(Auditors)*
Flint, MI

Braun, Kendrick, Finkbeiner, Schafer & Murphy*(Legal Firm)*
Saginaw, MI

Second National Bank of Saginaw*(Major Banking Relationship)*
Saginaw, MI

CHARLES PANKOW BUILDERS, LTD.
2476 N. Lave Ave.
Altadena, CA 91001
Tel.: 213-684-2320
Fax: 818-794-1539
Year Founded: 1963
Approx.Sls.: $457,000,000
Emp.: 132
New Construction Of Commercial & Office Buildings & Multi-Family Dwellings, Retail & Pkg. Structures
S.I.C.: 1542; 1522
Charles J. Pankow, Jr. *(Pres. & Chief Exec. Officer)*
Tim Murphy *(Chief Fin. Officer)*
Gaylin Roeters *(Mgr.-Data Processing)*

Outside Service Firm(s):

Bank of America NT&SA*(Major Banking Relationship)*
555 S. Flower St.
Los Angeles, CA 90071
Tel.: 213-228-3868

PANNIER CORPORATION
207 Sandusky St.
Pittsburgh, PA 15212
Tel.: 412-323-4900
Fax: 412-323-4962
Approx.Sls.: $16,000,000
Emp.: 225
Export
Marking & Identification Systems; Fiberglass Imbedded Signs
S.I.C.: 3953; 3993; 3999
A.J. Carvelli *(Vice Chm. & Chief Exec. Officer)*
David E. Gibbs, Jr. *(Exec. V.P.-Fin.)*
Allan Schilling *(Exec. V.P.-Sls. & Mktg.)*
John E. Visconti *(Exec. V.P.-Mfg.)*
Frederick Armstrong *(V.P.-Sls. & Mktg.)*
Gary Datt *(Controller)*
William A. Matthews, Jr. *(Mgr.-Pur.)*

No. of Mfg. Plants/Facilities: 4
No. of U.S. Offices: 3

Outside Service Firm(s):

KPMG Peat Marwick*(Auditors)*
1 Mellon Bank Ctr.
Pittsburgh, PA 15219
Tel.: 412-391-9710

Brandt, Milnes, Rea & Wise*(Legal Firm)*
Pittsburgh, PA

Union National Bank*(Major Banking Relationship)*
Pittsburgh, PA

PANORAMA PRESS, INC.
1 Entin Rd.
Clifton, NJ 07014
Tel.: 201-779-8900
Fax: 201-779-3738
Year Founded: 1957
Assets: $4,301,506
Liabilities: $2,568,351
Net Worth: $1,733,155
Approx.Sls.: $15,966,156
Emp.: 135
Fiscal Year-end: 6/30/92
Offset & Letterpress Printing
S.I.C.: 2752
Stanley Roth *(Chm. Bd. & Pres.)*
Vito Seminara *(Sr. V.P.)*
L.W. Buchbinder *(V.P. & Treas.)*
Tony Sarubbi *(V.P.-Mfg.)*
David Herstine *(Controller)*
John Zalarick *(Mgr.-Mktg.)*
Gloria Poranski *(Mgr.-Employee Benefits)*
Alan Roth *(Sec.)*

No. of Mfg. Plants/Facilities: 1

Outside Service Firm(s):

J. H. Cohn & Co.*(Auditors)*
New York, NY

CPI Insurance Group*(Commercial Insurance Carrier)*
1201 Mt. Kemble Ave.
Morristown, NJ 07960
Tel.: 201-425-6000

Chubb Life America*(Group Insurance Broker/Consult)*
8 Sylvan Way
Parsippany, NJ

Wolff, Sampson*(Legal Firm)*
5 Becker Farm Rd.
Roseland, NJ

National Community Bank*(Major Banking Relationship)*
Patterson, NJ

THE PANTRY, INC.
1801 Douglas Dr.
Sanford, NC 27331
Mailing Address:
P.O. Box 1410
Sanford, NC 27331
Tel.: 919-774-6700 **NC**
Fax: 919-775-5464
Year Founded: 1967
Approx.Sls.: $375,000,000
Emp.: 2,600
Import Export
Convenience Stores
S.I.C.: 5399; 5411
Truby G. Proctor, Jr. *(Chm. Bd. & Chief Exec. Officer)*
Eugene B. Horne, Jr. *(Pres. & Chief Oper. Officer)*
Bobby L. Jones *(V.P.-Mngmt. Information Systems)*
Mark C. King *(V.P.-Fin. & Treas.)*
Terry Lehman *(V.P.-Opers.)*
James A. Rader *(V.P.-Mktg.)*
Faye Simerson *(Dir.-Personnel)*

Computer Systems/Hardware:
IBM System 38

Outside Service Firm(s):

Price Waterhouse*(Auditors)*
Raleigh, NC

Harrington & Gilleland*(Legal Firm)*
Sanford, NC

Moore & Van Allen*(Legal Firm)*
Durham, NC

First Union National Bank*(Major Banking Relationship)*
Raleigh, NC

PAOLI, INC.
524 N.E. Third St.
Paoli, IN 47454
Mailing Address:
P.O. Box 30
Paoli, IN 47454
Tel.: 812-723-2791
Tel.: 800-457-7415 **IN**
Fax: 812-723-3880
Year Founded: 1926
Approx.Sls.: $24,000,000
Emp.: 400
Fiscal Year-end: 12/31/90

Import Export
Manufacture Chairs & Desks
S.I.C.: 2521; 2511
Thomas A. Tolone *(Pres. & Chief Oper. Officer)*
Michael Heazlitt *(V.P.-Sls. & Mktg.)*
Michael McCraken *(V.P.-Opers.)*
Larry G. Apple *(Dir.-Personnel)*
Lindy Hopkins *(Mgr.-Plant)*
Joe Hutslar *(Pur. Agent-Supplies)*
Don Laird *(Plant Supvr.)*
Principal(s):
Thomas A. Tolone

No. of Mfg. Plants/Facilities: 3
No. of U.S. Offices: 3

Computer Systems/Hardware:
Wang 2200

Outside Service Firm(s):

Ernst & Young*(Auditors)*
1000 Brown & Williamson Tower
Louisville, KY 40202
Tel.: 502-585-1400

PAOLIN & SWEENEY
375 N. Kings Hwy.
Cherry Hill, NJ 08034
Tel.: 609-667-7700
Fax: 609-667-7178
Year Founded: 1969
Approx.Billings: $17,000,000
Emp.: 24
New Home Mktg., Business-to-Business, Retail & Consumer Adv.
John Paolin *(Pres.)*
Dolores Paolin *(Chief Fin. Officer)*
Tim Kelly *(V.P.-Pub. Rels.)*

PAPER CALMENSON & CO.
P.O. Box 64432
Saint Paul, MN 55164
Tel.: 612-631-1111 **MN**
Fax: 612-631-9076
Telecopier: 612-631-1939
Year Founded: 1891
Approx.Sls.: $35,000,000
Emp.: 300
Fiscal Year-end: 12/31/90
Import Export
Steel Parts & Sub-Assembly Fabricator; Manufacturer of Grader, Dozer, Scraper, Loader & Snow Plow Blades
S.I.C.: 3531; 3443
Willis M. Forman *(Pres., Chief Exec. Officer & Treas.)*
J. James Collova *(Chief Fin. Officer & Sec.)*
Roger A. Salway *(Chief Oper. Officer & Exec. V.P.)*
Penny Helberg *(V.P.-Human Resources)*
Frank Zimmy *(V.P.-Admin.)*
Warner Nibbe *(Dir.-Sls. & Mktg.)*
Bert Riveis *(Dir.-Opers.)*
Jack Arvig *(Facility Mgr.-Pacal Business Center)*

No. of Mfg. Plants/Facilities: 4
No. of U.S. Offices: 1

Computer Systems/Hardware:
Unisys

Outside Service Firm(s):

Ernst & Young*(Auditors)*
St. Paul, MN

Liberty Mutual*(Commercial Insurance Carrier)*
Boston, MA

Prudential Insurance Co. of America*(Group Insurer)*
Minneapolis, MN

Doherty, Rumble & Butler*(Legal Firm)*
2800 Minnesota World Trade Center
St. Paul, MN 55101-4999
Tel.: 612-291-9333

American National Bank & Trust of St. Paul*(Major Banking Relationship)*
Fifth & Minnesota Streets
St. Paul, MN 55101
Tel.: 612-298-6000

American National Bank & Trust of St. Paul*(Pension Manager)*
Fifth & Minnesota Streets
St. Paul, MN 55101
Tel.: 612-298-6000

PAPER ENTERPRISES, INC.
850 E. 140th St.
Bronx, NY 10454
Tel.: 718-402-1200 **NY**
Fax: 718-292-1240
Year Founded: 1961
Sales Range: $20-39 Million
Emp.: 60
Export
Wholesale Paper Cups, Bags & Dishes, Janitorial Supplies, Restaurant Equipment
S.I.C.: 5113; 5087
Herbert L. Sedler *(Pres.)*
Jordan B. Sedler *(V.P., Sec. & Treas.)*
James Tilzer *(V.P.-Sls.)*
James E. Sheridian *(Controller)*
Howard Cohen *(Dir.-MIS)*
George Febbraio *(Dir.-Pur.)*
Ron Miranda *(Dir.-Sls.)*
Tom Paolino *(Mgr.-Opers.)*
Principal(s):
Herbert L. Sedler
Jordan B. Sedler

Outside Service Firm(s):

Shapiro & Liebreman*(Auditors)*
Englewood, NJ

Rand, Smith & Rosensweig*(Legal Firm)*
New York, NY

Chemical Bank*(Major Banking Relationship)*
Bronx, NY

PAR ENTERPRISES, INC.
1535 Market St.
Wheeling, WV 26003
Tel.: 304-233-2222 **WV**
Fax: 304-232-2222
Approx.Sls.: $11,000,000
Emp.: 42
New & Used Automobiles
S.I.C.: 5511
Kenneth Straub *(Pres.)*
Martha Fato *(Sec. & Treas.)*

Outside Service Firm(s):

Pittsburgh National Bank*(Major Banking Relationship)*
5th Ave. & Wood St.
Pittsburgh, PA 15222
Tel.: 412-355-3000

Security National Bank*(Major Banking Relationship)*
Charleston, WV

PAR INDUSTRIES, INC.
305 Lake Rd.
Medina, OH 44258
Tel.: 216-725-7771
Fax: 216-728-1722
Approx.Sls.: $20,000,000
Emp.: 125
Fiscal Year-end: 12/31/90
Manufacture Metal Stampings & Plastic Injection Molding
S.I.C.: 3469; 3089
William Bobinchuck *(Chm. Bd.)*
Michael Bobinchuck *(Pres.)*
Mark Bobinchuck *(V.P.-Mktg.)*
Richard Taverna *(V.P.)*
Steve Wasylko *(V.P.-Mfg.)*
Charles Heath *(Mgr.-Personnel)*

Outside Service Firm(s):

Lewandowski & Company*(Auditors)*
Medina, OH

Calfee, Halter & Griswold*(Legal Firm)*
800 Superior Ave., Ste. 1800
Cleveland, OH 44115-2688
Tel.: 216-622-8200
Fax: 216-241-0816

Society National Bank*(Major Banking Relationship)*
Akron, OH

Subsidiary:

Flexible Flyer Inc. **(1)**
100 Tubb Ave.
West Point, MS 39773
Tel.: 601-494-4732
Fax: 601-494-8456
Approx.Sls.: $60,000,000
Emp.: 500
Mfr. of Toys
S.I.C.: 3944; 2514
William R. Bobinchuck *(Chm. Bd.)*
Michael J. Bobinchuck *(Vice Chm.)*
James Branson *(Pres.)*
G. Trull *(Exec. V.P.)*
Charles Seawright *(Exec. V.P.)*
Daniel Roberts *(V.P.-Mktg.)*
Bob Thacker *(V.P.-Engrng.)*
Bob Oswalt *(Procurement Mgr.)*
Cathy Brown *(Customer Service)*
Scott Saxman *(Mktg. Mgr.)*
Glenn Montgomery *(Natl. Sls. Mgr.)*

PARADATA COMPUTER NETWORKS, INC.
37695 Interchange Dr.
Farmington Hills, MI 48335
Tel.: 313-478-8400 **MI**
Fax: 313-478-6806
Year Founded: 1979
Sales Range: $10-19 Million
Emp.: 75
Fiscal Year-end: 5/31/90
Development And Sales Of Computer Hardware And Software Products
S.I.C.: 7371
Kenneth H. Schumacher *(Chm. Bd. & Pres.)*
Ann Murphy *(Controller)*
Rick Kubacka *(Dir.-Pur.)*
Principal(s):
Kenneth H. Schumacher

No. of Mfg. Plants/Facilities: 1
No. of U.S. Offices: 9

Computer Systems/Hardware:
AT&T

Outside Service Firm(s):

Arthur Andersen & Co.*(Auditors)*
Ann Arbor, MI

Wausau Insurance*(Commercial Insurance Carrier)*
Detroit, MI

Wausau Insurance*(Group Insurer)*
Detroit, MI

Schlussel-Lifton-Simon*(Legal Firm)*
Southfield, MI

N.B.D. Bank, N.A.*(Major Banking Relationship)*
611 Woodward Ave.
Detroit, MI 48226
Tel.: 313-225-1122
Fax: 313-225-3420

N.B.D. Bank, N.A.*(Pension Manager)*
611 Woodward Ave.
Detroit, MI 48226
Tel.: 313-225-1122
Fax: 313-225-3420

PARADE PUBLICATIONS INC.
750 Third Ave.
New York, NY 10017
Tel.: 212-573-7000
Approx.Sls.: $380,000,000
Emp.: 200
Publishers of Parade Magazine
S.I.C.: 2721
Carlo Vittorini *(Chm., Publisher & Chief Exec. Officer)*
Frank N. McNulty *(Pres. & Chief Oper. Officer)*
Walter Anderson *(Sr. V.P. & Editor)*
Milton Lieberman *(Sr. V.P.-Mktg.)*
Robert L. Forbes *(V.P.-West Coast Mgr.)*
John Garvey *(V.P.-Mfg.)*
Frederick H. Johnson *(V.P.-Dir. of Newspaper Rels.)*
Carl M. Krampert *(V.P.-Detroit Sls. Mgr.)*
John A. Meyer *(V.P.-Midwest Mgr.-Newspaper Rels.)*
Michael McDevitt *(V.P.-Western Mgr.-Newspaper Rels.)*
Marcel Schloss *(V.P.-Fin.)*
Theresa B. Sullivan *(V.P. & Dir.-Direct Response Adv.)*
James M. Urice *(V.P. & Midwest Sls. Mgr.)*
Kenneth W. Wallace *(V.P.-Adv. Sls.)*
Mary Jennings *(Dir.-Promo.)*
Ralph G. Papaccioli *(NY Sls. Mgr.)*
Clare E. Davis *(NY Sls. Mgr.)*
Kerry A. Clawson *(NY Sls. Mgr.)*
Michael Perry *(Northeastern Mgr.-Newspaper Rel.)*
William Shiver *(Southwestern Mgr.-Newspaper Rel.)*
Patricia Dent Kemp *(San Francisco Sls. Mgr.)*
Jodi Vevoda *(Los Angeles Sls. Mgr.)*

Subsidiary:

Parade Publications, Inc. **(1)**
830 Henderson Blvd.
Folcroft, PA 19032
Tel.: 215-532-6400
S.I.C.: 2721
John Plachter *(Mgr.)*

PARADIGM COMMUNICATIONS
5301 W. Cypress St., Ste. 314
Tampa, FL 33607
Tel.: 813-287-0028
Tel.: 800-749-0220
Fax: 813-286-0100
Year Founded: 1989
Approx.Billings: $45,000,000
Emp.: 83
Telecommunications, Travel, Retail, Healthcare & Automotive Adv.
Vincent J. Fabrizzi *(Pres., New Bus. Contact & Merger/Acquisitions Contact)*
Daniel R. Furlong *(Exec. V.P., Treas.)*
John D. Holmes *(Exec. V.P., Mktg. Dir. & Sec.)*
Julia Finkbiener *(Dir.-Telemarketing)*
Diane Gerber *(Dir.-MIS)*
Gay McGowan *(Dir.-Acct. & Fin.)*
David Spector *(Dir.-Pub. Rels.)*
Mary Hanyok *(Pur.)*

PARADISE FRUIT COMPANY, INC.
1200 W. Haines St.
Plant City, FL 33566
Tel.: 813-752-1155
Fax: 813-754-3168
Approx.Sls.: $21,100,000
Emp.: 150
Fiscal Year-end: 12/31/90
Acquisition, Mfg. & Sale of Fruit Prods.
S.I.C.: 2099
Frank A. Weaner *(Chm. Bd.)*
Melvin S. Gordon *(Pres.)*
Eugene L. Weiner *(Exec. V.P., Sec. & Treas.)*
Tracy W. Schulis *(V.P.)*

PARAGON GROUP, INC.
7557 Rambler Rd., Ste. 1200
Dallas, TX 75231
Tel.: 214-891-2000
Fax: 214-696-6318
Year Founded: 1979
Approx.Sls.: $493,000,000

Paragon Group, Inc.—(Continued)

Emp.: 1,300
Real Estate Development, Construction Management
S.I.C.: 6552; 8741
William R. Cooper *(Chm. Bd. & Pres.)*
Thomas D. Ferguson *(V.P.)*
Jerry Bonner *(Treas.)*
Principal(s):
Jeffrey B. Allen
James T. Cobb
Lewis A. Levey
Steven A. Means
Don Shine

Outside Service Firm(s):

Stutzman & Bromberg*(Legal Firm)*
Dallas, TX

PARAGON PAINT & VARNISH CORP.
5-49 46th Ave.
Long Island City, NY 11101
Tel.: 718-729-7420
Tel.: 800-221-9132 **NY**
Fax: 718-729-1717
Year Founded: 1924
Sales Range: $10-19 Million
Emp.: 100
Fiscal Year-end: 12/31/90
Export
Mfr. Paints & Varnishes
S.I.C.: 2851
Selma Rattner *(Pres.)*

Computer Systems/Hardware:
Hewlett Packard

Outside Service Firm(s):

U.S. HealthCare*(Group Insurer)*
New York, NY

Chemical Bank*(Major Banking Relationship)*
Long Island City, NY

Paragon Restaurant Group, Inc.
(Name Changed to Green Leaf Ventures, Inc.)

PARAMOUNT FITNESS EQUIPMENT CORP.
6450 E. Bandini Blvd.
Los Angeles, CA 90040-3185
Tel.: 213-721-2121
Fax: 213-721-8841
Sales Range: $10-19 Million
Emp.: 130
Export
Mfr. of Sports Trainer Line, Performance Line, Performance Free Weight Line, Fitness Equipment, Paramount FTX, Fitness Trainer Cycle, Paramount Fitness Center, ProTrainer 1000 & 2000
S.I.C.: 3949
W. Hubner *(Chm. Bd.)*
James Trisler *(Pres.)*
Steve Rhodes *(V.P.-Mktg. & Sls.)*
Harvey Voris *(V.P.-Engr.)*
Jeffrey Kolsin *(Controller)*
Cherie Duran *(Mgr.-Adv.)*
Johnson Yu *(Mgr.-Pur.)*

PARAMOUNT FOODS INC.
2800 Fern Valley Rd.
Louisville, KY 40213
Mailing Address:
P.O. Box 32150
Louisville, KY 40232-2150
Tel.: 502-969-9363
Fax: 502-969-6394
Year Founded: 1886
Emp.: 300
Fiscal Year-end: 4/30/91
Pickles, Dressings & Canned Meats
S.I.C.: 5149
Frank W. Fleischaker *(Chm. Bd.)*
F. Miller Owings *(Pres.)*
Ronald I. Sternberg *(Exec. V.P. & Treas.)*
Robert M. Hirsch *(V.P.)*
Joe Thomas *(Treas.)*
Doug Adams *(Controller)*
Charlotte Fowler *(Sec.)*
Ronald Fox *(Plant Mgr.)*
Jerry Taylor *(Pur. Agent)*

Outside Service Firm(s):

Ernst & Young*(Auditors)*
1000 Brown & Williamson Tower
Louisville, KY 40202
Tel.: 502-585-1400

Liberty National Bank & Trust Co.*(Major Banking Relationship)*
Louisville, KY

PARAMOUNT PACKAGING CORP.
202 Oak Ave.
Chalfont, PA 18914
Mailing Address:
P.O. Box 902,
Chalfont, PA 18914
Tel.: 215-822-2911 **DE**
Fax: 215-997-4528
Earnings: $1,109,000
Approx.Sls.: $55,937,000
Emp.: 530
Fiscal Year-end: 12/31/88
Mfr. Flexible Packaging
S.I.C.: 2673; 2679; 2671; 2672; 3089
Harold Isen *(Chm. Bd. & Chief Exec. Officer)*
Irvin Isen *(Pres. & Chief Oper. Officer)*
Frank W. Gallagher *(Chief Fin. Officer & Treas.)*
John Carr *(V.P.)*
Robert Isen *(V.P. & Sec.)*
Joseph Moi *(V.P.)*
Steve Ayers *(Dir.-Mngmt. Information Systems)*
Russell R. Mantione *(Controller)*

Outside Service Firm(s):

Ernst & Young*(Auditors)*
1800 John F. Kennedy Blvd.
Philadelphia, PA 19103-7499
Tel.: 215-864-3300

Blue Cross & Blue Shield of Florida, Inc.*(Group Insurer)*
532 Riverside
Jacksonville, FL 32231
Tel.: 904-363-5572
Fax: 904-363-5180

Dilworth, Paxson, Kalish & Kauffman*(Legal Firm)*
2600 Fidelity Bldg., 123 S. Broad St.
Philadelphia, PA 19109
Tel.: 215-875-7000

CoreStates First Pennsylvania Bank, N.A.*(Major Banking Relationship)*
Philadelphia, PA

Subsidiary:

Paramount Packaging Corp. **(1)**
106 Samsonite Blvd.
Murfreesboro, TN 37130
Tel.: 615-896-3970 (100%)
Emp.: 300
Mfr. Flexible Packaging
S.I.C.: 2671; 2672; 2673; 2679

PARAMOUNT PETROLEUM CORP.
14700 Downey Ave.
Paramount, CA 90723
Tel.: 310-531-2060 **DE**
Fax: 310-633-8211
Year Founded: 1988
Approx.Sls.: $350,000,000
Emp.: 200
Petroleum Refining
S.I.C.: 2911
J.T. Campbell *(Chm. Bd.)*
James H. McDonald *(Chief Exec. Officer)*
Glenn C. Lingle *(Pres.)*

Outside Service Firm(s):

NMB Bank*(Major Banking Relationship)*
Los Angeles, CA

PARIS PRESENTS
3800 Swanson Ct.
Gurnee, IL 60031
Tel.: 708-263-5500
Fax: 708-263-6002
Approx.Sls.: $24,000,000
Emp.: 65
Import
Imports & Wholesale Cosmetic Accessories; Bath & Beauty Related Items
S.I.C.: 5122
Lawrence Zall *(Pres.)*
Jeff Nitzkin *(V.P.-Sls.)*
Michael P. Wolf *(V.P.-Fin.)*
Betty Zall *(Treas. & Sec.)*

Outside Service Firm(s):

Altschuler, Melvoin & Glasser*(Auditors)*
30 S. Wecker Dr.
Chicago, IL 60606
Tel.: 312-207-2800

Lake Shore National Bank*(Major Banking Relationship)*
605 N. Michigan Ave.
Chicago, IL 60611
Tel.: 312-787-1900

PARISI, INC.
3031 Red Lion Rd.
Philadelphia, PA 19114
Tel.: 215-632-4495 **PA**
Fax: 215-632-1660
Year Founded: 1962
Approx.Sls.: $12,000,000
Emp.: 75
Fiscal Year-end: 6/30/90
Export
Restaurant Fast Food; Bank Furniture
S.I.C.: 2541; 2599
Joseph Parisi, Jr. *(Pres.)*
Jack Childs *(V.P.-Sls.)*
Gary Graf *(V.P. & Treas.)*
Frank McGothigan *(V.P.-Opers.)*
Eleanor Parisi *(V.P.)*
Alice Parisi *(Sec.)*
George Gibbs *(Mgr.-Engrng.)*
Thomas McKenna *(Mgr.-Pur.)*
Rodney P. Schmehl *(Mgr.-Plant)*

No. of Mfg. Plants/Facilities: 1
No. of U.S. Offices: 1

Outside Service Firm(s):

William J. Priest*(Auditors)*
Jenkintown, PA

Klehn Harrison*(Legal Firm)*
Philadelphia, PA

Philadelphia National Bank*(Major Banking Relationship)*
P.O. Box 13834, Broad & Chestnut Streets
Philadelphia, PA 19101-7618
Tel.: 215-973-8327

PARISIAN, INC.
750 Lakeshore Pkwy.
Birmingham, AL 35211
Tel.: 205-940-4000
Fax: 205-940-4987
Assets: $163,349,463
Liabilities: $83,297,121
Net Worth: $80,052,342
Approx.Sls.: $250,000,000
Emp.: 4,500
Fiscal Year-end: 1/ 3/91
Operates Chain of 18 Specialty Department Stores
S.I.C.: 5311
Emil C. Hess *(Chm. Bd.)*
Donald E. Hess *(Pres. & Chief Exec. Officer)*
Harold L. Abroms *(Chief Oper. Officer, Exec. V.P., Treas. & Sec.)*
D. Warren Bailey *(Chief Fin. Officer & Sr. V.P.-Fin.)*
Tom R. Amerman *(Sr. V.P.-Personnel & Loss Prevention)*
Gene Higuera *(V.P.-Credit)*
John W. Parrott *(V.P.-Opers.)*
Kenneth R. Scarborough *(V.P.-Information Systems)*
Gary A. Smith *(V.P.-Distr. & Controller)*
Patty Bystrom *(Dir.-Sls. Promo.)*

Outside Service Firm(s):

Coopers & Lybrand*(Auditors)*
1901 6th Ave. North, Ste. 1600
Birmingham, AL 35203-2602

Berkowicz, Lefkowicz, Isom & Kurshner*(Legal Firm)*
Birmingham, AL
Tel.: 205-328-0480

AmSouth Bank N.A.*(Major Banking Relationship)*
P.O. Box 11426
Birmingham, AL 35202
Tel.: 205-326-5321

THE PARK CIRCLE MOTOR CO.
1829 Reisterstown Rd.
Baltimore, MD 21208
Tel.: 301-484-0600
Fax: 301-484-2929
Year Founded: 1921
Approx.Sls.: $70,000,000
Emp.: 284
Automobile & Truck Sales & Service
S.I.C.: 5511; 7538
Leslie Legum *(Chm. Bd.)*
Jeffrey A. Legum *(Pres.)*
Thomas J. Karwacki *(Sec. & Treas.)*

Outside Service Firm(s):

Deloitte & Touche*(Auditors)*
1100 Mercantile Bank Bldg., 2 Hopkins Plaza
Baltimore, MD 21201
Tel.: 410-576-6700

Weinberg & Green*(Legal Firm)*
100 S. Charles St.
Baltimore, MD 21202
Tel.: 410-332-8795

Maryland National Bank*(Major Banking Relationship)*
2 N. Charles St.
Baltimore, MD 21201

PARK CONSTRUCTION COMPANY
7900 Beech St., N.E.
Minneapolis, MN 55432
Tel.: 612-786-9800
Fax: 612-786-2952
Approx.Sls.: $35,000,000
Emp.: 200
Highway Grading & Bridge Tunnel, Elevated Highway Construction
S.I.C.: 1611; 1622
Richard N. Carlson *(Chm. Bd.)*
Duane Prairie *(Pres. & Chief Exec. Officer)*
Tom Evered *(V.P.)*

Robert Swanson *(Treas.)*
Bruce Carlson *(Sec.)*

Outside Service Firm(s):

Charles Bailly & Co.*(Auditors)*
406 Main Ave., Ste. 3000
Fargo, ND 58126-0001
Tel.: 701-239-8500

First Bank, N.A.*(Major Banking Relationship)*
First Bank Place
Minneapolis, MN 55480

PARK CORPORATION
511 Lake Zurich Rd.
Barrington, IL 60010
Tel.: 708-381-8550
Tel.: 800-323-4976 **IL**
Fax: 708-381-8599
Year Founded: 1988
Approx.Sls.: $140,000,000
Emp.: 285
Fiscal Year-end: 1/31/92

Export
Coffee Roasting, Except By Wholesale Grocers; Powders, Drinks; Cake Mixes, Prepared From Purchased Flour; Detergents
S.I.C.: 2095; 2045; 2841
Thomas D. Stocks III *(Chm. Bd. & Chief Exec. Officer)*
Stanley A. Wilson *(Exec. V.P.-Fin. & Mfg.)*
Jeffrey Cartwright *(V.P-Opers.)*
Robert J. Gats *(V.P.-Mktg.)*
David Riesmeyer *(V.P.-Corp. Devel.)*
Keith Sheller *(V.P.-Sls.)*
John Nyquist *(Dir.-Tech Services)*
Tina Rubczyk *(Coord.-Admin. & Meetings Planning)*

Outside Service Firm(s):

Ernst & Young*(Auditors)*
233 S. Wacker Dr.
Chicago, IL 60606
Tel.: 312-368-1800
Fax: 312-645-3095

The Northern Trust Co.*(Major Banking Relationship)*
50 S. LaSalle St.
Chicago, IL 60675
Tel.: 312-630-6000
Fax: 312-444-7028

GEORGE W. PARK SEED CO., INC.
Hwy. 254 North
Greenwood, SC 29647
Mailing Address:
P.O. Box 31,
Greenwood, SC 29648
Tel.: 803-223-8555
Fax: 803-941-4239
Sales Range: $20-39 Million
Emp.: 400
Retail & Mail Order Seeds, Bulbs, Plants & Accessories
S.I.C.: 5961; 5261
J. Leonard Park *(Chm. Bd., Pres., Chief Exec. Officer & Treas.)*
Klaus Neubner *(Vice Chm. & Exec. V.P.)*
Karen P. Jennings *(Sr. V.P.-Mktg.)*
Leonard Richey *(Sr. V.P.)*
Wayne Lester *(V.P. & Corp. Controller)*
A. Russell Myrick *(Asst. V.P.-Data Processing)*

Computer Systems/Hardware:
Digital

Outside Service Firm(s):

Elliott, Davis & Co.*(Auditors)*
Greenwood, SC

Burns, McDonald, Bradford, Erwin, Patrick & Dean*(Legal Firm)*
Greenwood, SC

The County Bank*(Major Banking Relationship)*
Greenwood, SC

PARK MOTOR SALES COMPANY
18100 Woodward Ave.
Detroit, MI 48203
Tel.: 313-869-5000
Fax: 313-869-2109
Approx.Sls.: $25,000,000
Emp.: 62
Automobile Dealership
S.I.C.: 5511
Paul J. Kuhn *(Pres.)*
Paul J. Kuhn, II *(V.P.)*
Harold Kuhn *(V.P. & Sls. Mgr.)*
Daniel Abair *(Sec. & Treas.)*

PARK PLACE MOTORCARS
4023 Oak Lawn
Dallas, TX 75219
Tel.: 214-526-8701 **NV**
Fax: 214-443-8205
Year Founded: 1987
Approx.Sls.: $72,000,000
Emp.: 105
Retail New & Used Automobiles
S.I.C.: 5511
Kenneth L. Schnitzer, Jr. *(Pres.)*
Byron K. Dobbs *(Chief Fin. Officer)*
R. Jack Hayter *(V.P. & Gen. Mgr.)*

Principal(s):
Kenneth L. Schnitzer, Jr.

No. of U.S. Offices: 1

Computer Systems/Hardware:
Micro Data

Outside Service Firm(s):

Grant Thornton*(Auditors)*
1445 Ross Ave.
Dallas, TX 75202
Tel.: 214-855-7300

Business Men's Assurance*(Group Insurer)*
P.O. Box 419269
Kansas City, MO 64141

First City National Bank*(Major Banking Relationship)*
Dallas, TX

PARK RIDGE CORPORATION
225 Brae Blvd.
Park Ridge, NJ 07656
Tel.: 201-307-2000
Fax: 201-307-2644
Year Founded: 1987
Approx.Rev.: $2,626,225,000
Emp.: 18,100
Fiscal Year-end: 12/31/91
Management Company
S.I.C.: 8741; 6719
Frank A. Olson *(Chm. Bd. & Pres.)*
Albert L. Dowden *(Exec. V.P.)*
Malcolm Macdonald *(Exec. V.P. & Treas.)*
David McCammon *(Exec. V.P.)*
Joseph L. Nicolato *(Exec. V.P.)*
Peter J. Pestillo *(Exec. V.P.)*
Jurgen Reimnitz *(Exec. V.P.)*
William Sider *(Exec. V.P.-Fin.)*
Elizabeth S. Acton *(V.P. & Asst. Treas.)*
Leo Massad Jr. *(V.P. & Controller)*
Robert Rillings *(V.P. & Asst. Treas.)*
John Rintamaki *(V.P. & Sec.)*
Louis J. Ghilardi *(Asst. Sec.)*
Burton B. Smoliar *(Asst. Sec.)*
Peter H. Viall *(Asst. Treas.)*

Outside Service Firm(s):

Arthur Andersen & Co.*(Auditors)*
One Intl. Place, 100 Oliver St.
Boston, MA 02110
Tel.: 617-330-4000
Fax: 617-439-9731

Subsidiary:

The Hertz Corporation **(1)**
225 Brae Blvd.
Park Ridge, NJ 07656
Tel.: 201-307-2000 (100%)
Fax: 201-307-2644
Earnings: $48,400,000
Approx.Rev.: $2,626,225,000
Emp.: 18,100
Fiscal Year-end: 12/31/91
Renting & Leasing of Automobiles, Trucks & Equipment
S.I.C.: 7513; 7514
Frank A. Olson *(Chm. Bd., Chief Exec. & Oper. Officer)*
Craig R. Koch *(Exec. V.P.)*
Antoine Cau *(Exec V.P.-Intl. Opers.)*
Daniel I. Kaplan *(Exec. V.P.-HERC)*
Brian J. Kennedy *(Exec. V.P.-Sls. & Mktg.)*
William Sider *(Exec. V.P. & Chief Fin. Officer)*
Robert J. Bailey *(Sr. V.P.-Quality Assurance & Admin.)*
Paul M. Tschirhart *(Sr. V.P., Gen. Counsel & Sec.)*
John Blake *(Sr. V.P.-Properties & Facilities)*
Donald F. Steele *(Sr. V.P.-Employee Rels.)*
Joseph M. Russo *(V.P.-Pub. Affairs)*
Leo A. Massad, Jr. *(Controller)*
Robert H. Rillings *(Treas.)*

Subsidiary:

Hertz Equipment Rental Corp. **(2)**
225 Brae Blvd.
Park Ridge, NJ 07656
Tel.: 201-307-2000
Approx.Sls.: $233,000,000
Emp.: 1,300
Equipment & Truck for Construction & Industry
S.I.C.: 7353; 7359
Daniel I. Kaplan *(Pres.)*
William Sider *(V.P.)*
Joseph Gagliardi *(V.P.-Adv.)*
Paul M. Tschirhart *(V.P. & Sec.)*

PARKDALE MILLS
1630 W. Garrison Blvd.
Gastonia, NC 28053
Mailing Address:
P.O. Box 1787
Gastonia, NC 28053
Tel.: 704-864-8761
Tel.: 800-331-1843
Fax: 704-864-0358
Year Founded: 1918
Approx.Sls.: $410,000,000
Emp.: 2,800
Fiscal Year-end: 9/30/91

Export
Mfr. of Cotton & Cotton/Synthetic Yarns For Apparel & Industrial Applications
S.I.C.: 2281
W. Duke Kimbrell *(Chm. Bd. & Chief Exec. Officer)*
Anderson Warlick *(Pres. & Chief Oper. Officer)*
Max Huntley *(V.P.-Mfg.)*
Arthur R. Newcombe *(V.P.-Sls. & Mktg.)*
Dan Wilson *(Treas. & Dir.-Data Processing)*
Harold Davis *(Dir.-Personnel)*
Joe Ferguson *(Dir.-Engrng.)*
Larry Phillips *(Dir.-Pur.)*

No. of Mfg. Plants/Facilities: 17
No. of U.S. Offices: 1

Computer Systems/Hardware:
IBM

Outside Service Firm(s):

Arthur Andersen & Co.*(Auditors)*
2300 Charlotte Plaza
Charlotte, NC 28244
Tel.: 704-332-0092

Womble, Carlyle, Sandridge & Rice*(Legal Firm)*
Wachovia Bldg.
Winston Salem, NC 27102
Tel.: 919-721-3600

First Union National Bank*(Major Banking Relationship)*
CMG-5, Two First Union Center
Charlotte, NC 28288-1154
Tel.: 704-374-2698
Fax: 704-374-6987

First Wachovia Bank & Trust Co.*(Major Banking Relationship)*
301 N. Main St.
Winston-Salem, NC

Division:

Delmont Div. **(1)**
100 E. Woodrow Ave.
Belmont, NC 28012
Tel.: 704-825-4961
Mfr. Yarn
S.I.C.: 2281
Lee Thomas *(V.P.)*

PARKER FERTILIZER CO., INC.
201 W. Fourth St.
Sylacauga, AL 35150
Mailing Address:
P.O. Box 540,
Sylacauga, AL 35150
Tel.: 205-245-5282
Fax: 205-249-6859
Year Founded: 1904
Approx.Sls.: $20,000,000
Emp.: 100
Mfr. of Fertilizers
S.I.C.: 2875
J.T. Pursell *(Pres.)*
Duane Kennedy *(Dir.-Consumer Sls.)*

PARKER STEEL COMPANY
4239-41 Monroe St.
Toledo, OH 43606
Tel.: 419-473-2481 **OH**
Fax: 419-471-2655
Approx.Sls.: $13,000,000
Emp.: 21

Import Export
Metal Bars & Plates; Wire; Cold Finishing Of Steel Shapes; Cold Finished Bars, Hot Rolled Bars, Stainless Steel Bars
S.I.C.: 5051
Paul D. Goldner *(Pres.)*

Outside Service Firm(s):

Nachtrab, Cousino & O'Neil*(Auditors)*
Toledo, OH

PARKLANE HOSIERY CO., INC.
621 State Route 46
Hasbrouck Heights, NJ 07604
Tel.: 201-288-8822
Tel.: 800-PARKLAN **NY**
Fax: 201-288-7505
Year Founded: 1946
Approx.Sls.: $110,000,000
Emp.: 3,000
Fiscal Year-end: 12/31/90

Import
Retail Hosiery & Dance Wear Products
S.I.C.: 5632
Charlotte G. Fischer *(Pres. & Chief Exec. Officer)*
John Leberfinger *(V.P.-Human Resources)*
William Soncini *(V.P.-Store Opers.)*
Michael Knatz *(Chief Fin. Officer)*
John Stanish *(Mgr.-Adv.)*

Computer Systems/Hardware:
IBM System 5265; IBM System 38 Model 20; IBM Series 1

Outside Service Firm(s):

Coopers & Lybrand*(Auditors)*
1301 Avenue of The Americas
New York, NY 10019
Tel.: 212-536-2000

Lowen & Abbott*(Legal Firm)*
New York, NY

PARKS CORPORATION
1083 County St.
Somerset, MA 02726
Tel.: 508-679-5938 **MA**
Fax: 508-674-8404
Year Founded: 1962
Approx.Sls.: $35,000,000
Emp.: 100
Mfr. of Shellac, Lacquer, Thinner, Solvents, Wood Stains & Enamels
S.I.C.: 2851; 2869
F. Lee Davidson *(Pres. & Chief Exec. Officer)*
Dennis Dussault *(Controller)*

Outside Service Firm(s):

Bank of New England*(Major Banking Relationship)*
One Washington Mall
Boston, MA 02108
Tel.: 617-742-4000

PARKS PRODUCTS, INC.
3611 Cahuenga
Hollywood, CA 90068
Tel.: 213-876-5454 **CA**
Fax: 213-876-5634
Year Founded: 1957
Import Export
Mfr. Shavers & Shaving Accessories
S.I.C.: 2844; 3421; 3991
Robert M. Parks *(Chm. Bd. & Pres.)*
A.L. Parks *(Sec. & Treas.)*
John Roberts *(Mgr.-Adv. & Customer Service)*

Outside Service Firm(s):

Bank of America NT&SA*(Major Banking Relationship)*
Universal City, CA

PARKS SAUSAGE COMPANY
3330 Henry G. Parks Jr. Circle
Baltimore, MD 21215
Mailing Address:
P.O. Box 854
Baltimore, MD 21203
Tel.: 410-664-5050 **MD**
Fax: 410-664-5093
Year Founded: 1951
Approx.Sls.: $29,000,000
Emp.: 240
Mfr. of Breakfast Meat Products & Pizza Toppings
S.I.C.: 2011; 2013
Corporate Giving Program: United Way Campaign
Employee Matching Gifts Program: United Way Campaign
Raymond V. Haysbert, Sr. *(Chm. Bd., Pres. & Chief Exec. Officer)*
Reginald G. Haysbert *(Sr. V.P.)*
William Gordon *(Controller)*
Don Alden *(Dir.-Tech. Services)*
E. Ken Brown *(Dir.-Mktg.)*
Mark S. Shevbrooks *(Mgr.-Plant)*
John Snyder *(Mgr.-Information Systems)*
Darnelle Street *(Mgr.-Human Resources)*
Sam Sydnor *(Mgr.-Gen. Sls.)*

Computer Systems/Hardware:
IBM

Outside Service Firm(s):

Arthur Andersen & Co.*(Auditors)*
120 E. Baltimore St.
Baltimore, MD 21202
Tel.: 301-727-5800

PARLIAMENT CO.
30200 Telegraph Rd., Ste. 251
Bingham Farms, MI 48025
Tel.: 313-645-6680 **MI**
Fax: 313-645-0225
Year Founded: 1959
Approx.Sls.: $40,000,000
Emp.: 30
Fiscal Year-end: 5/31/89
Construction Management; General Contractor Commercial Construction
S.I.C.: 8741; 1542
Jack D. Hamburger *(Chm. Bd.)*
John A. Hamburger *(V.P.)*

THE PARMAN CORPORATION
(d/b/a Parman Oil Co.)
7101 Cockrill Bend Blvd.
Nashville, TN 37209
Tel.: 615-350-7920
Fax: 615-350-8561
Year Founded: 1958
Approx.Sls.: $55,000,000
Emp.: 150
Wholesale Petroleum Products; Convenience Stores
S.I.C.: 5171; 5541
John B. Jewell *(Pres.)*
Barry Shipp *(Pres.-Oils & Lubes)*
Norma Bass *(Treas. & Sec.)*
Wayne Franklin *(Dir.-Mktg.)*
Don Grubbs *(Pur. Mgr.-Petroleum)*

Computer Systems/Hardware:
Wang

Outside Service Firm(s):

Edward Skulley & Associates*(Auditors)*
Nashville, TN

Blue Cross & Blue Shield of Indiana*(Group Insurer)*
P.O. Box 7700,
Indianapolis, IN 46277-3772

Bass, Berry & Sims*(Legal Firm)*
27th Fl., First American Ctr.
Nashville, TN 37238
Tel.: 615-244-5370

Subsidiaries:

Parman Oil Co. **(1)**
5901 Cockrill Industrial Dr.
Nashville, TN 37209
Tel.: 615-385-9106
Wholesale Petroleum Products
S.I.C.: 5171; 5541
John B. Jewell *(Pres.)*

Parmart Stores **(1)**
5901 Cockrill Industrial Dr.
Nashville, TN 37209
Tel.: 615-383-9106
Convenience Stores
S.I.C.: 5421; 5411
J. R. Lanier *(Gen. Mgr.)*

PARRISH TIRE COMPANY, INC.
8800 N. Point Blvd.
Winston-Salem, NC 27106
Tel.: 919-759-0202
Fax: 919-759-2963
Approx.Sls.: $50,000,000
Emp.: 230
Wholesale Tires
S.I.C.: 5014; 5531; 7534
William L. Jackson *(Chm. Bd. & Pres.)*
Michael Everhart *(Treas.)*
Shirley Long *(Sec.)*

Outside Service Firm(s):

Butler & Burke*(Auditors)*
Winston-Salem, SC

Southern National Bank*(Major Banking Relationship)*
Winston-Salem, NC

PARSONS BRINCKERHOFF INC.
1 Penn Plaza, 5th Fl.
New York, NY 10119
Tel.: 212-465-5000
Telex: RCA 232 117
Fax: 212-465-5096
Year Founded: 1885
Sales Range: $100-499 Million
Emp.: 3,024
Fiscal Year-end: 10/19/91
Holding Company; Engineering Consultants
S.I.C.: 6719; 8711
Henry L. Michel *(Chm. Bd.)*
J.L. Lammie *(Pres. & Chief Exec. Officer)*
Allan J. Stevenson *(Sr. V.P., Chief Fin. Officer & Controller)*
Kevin J. Curran *(Sec. & Gen. Counsel)*
John J. Cosgrove *(Dir.-Pur.-PBQD, Inc.)*
Robert Prieto *(Dir.-Corp. Devel.)*
John Ryan *(Dir.-Human Resources-PBQD, Inc.)*
Richard A. Schrader *(Dir.-Fin. & Admin.)*
Robert P. Dallesandro *(Mgr.-Data Processing-PBQD, Inc.)*

Computer Systems/Hardware:
IBM 4361 & 4365; DEC VAX 6310

Outside Service Firm(s):

KPMG Peat Marwick*(Auditors)*
345 Park Ave.
New York, NY 10154
Tel.: 212-758-9700
Fax: 212-872-3308

Continental Insurance*(Commercial Insurance Carrier)*
180 Maiden Lane
New York, NY

Equitable Real Estate Investment Managment Inc.*(Group Insurer)*
3414 Peachtree Rd. N.E.
Atlanta, GA 30326-1162

Reid & Priest*(Legal Firm)*
40 W. 57th St.
New York, NY 10019
Tel.: 212-603-2000

National Westminster Bank plc*(Major Banking Relationship)*
Astor Plaza, 1515 Broadway
New York, NY 10036

T. Rowe Price Associates*(Pension Manager)*
100 E. Pratt St.
Baltimore, MD 21202
Tel.: 410-547-2000
Fax: 410-659-0965

Subsidiaries:

Parsons Brinckerhoff Construction Services, Inc. **(1)**
475 Spring Park Place, Ste. 500
Herndon, VA 22070
Tel.: 703-834-1717
S.I.C.: 8711
Christopher Reseigh *(Pres.)*

Parsons Brinckerhoff Development Corp. **(1)**
One Penn Plaza, 5th Fl.
New York, NY 10119
Tel.: 212-465-5000
Richard A. Schrader *(Pres.)*

Parsons Brinckerhoff International, Inc. **(1)**
One Penn Plaza, 5th Fl.
New York, NY 10119
Tel.: 212-465-5000
S.I.C.: 8711
Woodrow W. Hitchcock *(Chief Oper. Officer)*

Parsons Brinckerhoff Facilities Services, Inc. **(1)**
475 Spring Park Place, Ste. 500
Herndon, VA 22070
Tel.: 703-834-1717
S.I.C.: 7349
Richard C. Noakes *(Chief Oper. Officer)*

Parsons Brinckerhoff Quade & Douglas, Inc. **(1)**
One Penn Plaza
New York, NY 10119
Tel.: 212-465-5000
Engrng. Consultants
S.I.C.: 8711
Paul H. Gilbert *(Chm. Bd.)*
James L. Lammie *(Pres.)*
Paul D. Shein *(Controller)*
Kevin J. Curran *(Sec.)*

PARSONS & WHITTEMORE ENTERPRISES
4 International Dr.
Rye Brook, NY 10573
Tel.: 914-937-9009
Holding Company for Wood Industries
S.I.C.: 6719; 2611
George Landegger *(Chm. Bd.)*
Carl C. Landegger *(Vice Chm.)*
Arthur L. Schwartz *(Pres.)*
Robert H. Masson *(V.P.-Fin.)*
Frank Grasso *(Treas.)*
Stephen J. Sweeney *(Controller)*

Outside Service Firm(s):

Ernst & Young*(Auditors)*
787 Seventh Ave.
New York, NY 10019
Tel.: 212-773-1243

Non-U.S. Holdings:

St. Anne Chemical Co., Ltd. **(1)**
P.O. Box 1000
Nackawic, NB E0H 1P0, Canada
Tel.: 506-575-2206
Chemicals
S.I.C.: 2819

St. Anne Industries Ltd. **(1)**
Main Rd.
Nackawic, New Brunswick EOH 1PO, Canada
Tel.: 506-575-2221
S.I.C.: 5099

St. Anne - Nackawic Pulp Co., Ltd. **(1)**
P.O. Box 1000
Nackawic, NB E0H 1P0, Canada
Tel.: 506-575-2221
PulpMill
S.I.C.: 2611

St. Anne Pulp Sales Co. Ltd. **(1)**
250 Bloor Street EAst, Suite 1420
Toronto, ON M4W 1E6, Canada
Tel.: 416-968-2900
Pulp Sales
S.I.C.: 5099

Southampton Sawmills, Ltd. **(1)**
P.O. Box 1000
Nackawic, NB E0H 1P0, Canada
Tel.: 506-575-2388
Sawmill
S.I.C.: 2421

PARTNERS MEANY, INC.
382 Broadway
Albany, NY 12207
Tel.: 518-465-4573
Fax: 518-465-4937
Year Founded: 1959
Approx.Billings: $13,000,000
Emp.: 19
Full Service, Events Mktg., Food, Beverage & Alcohol, Financial Services/Banks, Sporting Goods, Sales Promotion, Marketing & Public Relations
Richard N. Beckman *(Chm.)*
Kevin C. Meany *(Pres., Chief Exec. & New Bus. & Merger/Aquisition Contact)*
William T. Scully *(Chief Fin. Officer)*
Carolyn Hapeman *(Pub. Rels.)*
Michael Citrin *(Mktg., Res. & Devel. Dir.)*

Computer Systems/Hardware:
IBM, Macintosh

PARTNERS & SHEVACK, INC.
1350 Ave. of the Americas
New York, NY 10019-4701
Tel.: 212-245-7300
Fax: 212-245-8478
Approx.Billings: $149,000,000
Henry Kornhauser *(Chm.)*
Brett Shevack *(Pres. & Chief Exec. Officer)*
Neil Miller *(Exec. V.P., Chief Fin. Officer)*
Lynne Seid *(Exec. V.P., Dir. Mktg. Services)*
Barry Martin *(Sr. V.P., Dir. Strategic Plng.)*

PASCHEN CONTRACTORS, INC.
2739 N. Elston Ave.
Chicago, IL 60647
Tel.: 312-278-4700
Fax: 312-278-4438
Year Founded: 1932
Approx.Sls.: $75,000,000
Emp.: 1,000
Fiscal Year-end: 12/31/88
General Building Contractors; Heavy Construction Contractors
S.I.C.: 1542; 1796
Robert L. O'Neil, II *(Pres.)*

Computer Systems/Hardware:
IBM System 36

Outside Service Firm(s):

KPMG Peat Marwick*(Auditors)*
Peat Marwick Plaza, 303 E. Wacker Dr.
Chicago, IL 60601
Tel.: 312-938-1000

Prudential Insurance Co. of America*(Group Insurer)*
751 Broad St.
Newark, NJ 07102-3777
Tel.: 201-802-6000

Sonnenschein, Nath & Rosenthal*(Legal Firm)*
800 Sears Tower
Chicago, IL 60606
Tel.: 312-876-8035

Continental Bank N. A.*(Major Banking Relationship)*
231 S. LaSalle St.
Chicago, IL 60697
Tel.: 312-828-2345
Tel.: 800-426-5754
Telex: 312-828-1783

First National Bank of Chicago*(Major Banking Relationship)*
One First National Plaza
Chicago, IL 60670
Tel.: 312-732-9781
Tel.: 312-732-4050
Fax: 312-732-4840
Fax: 312-732-3055

Subsidiaries:

PCI Investments Inc. **(1)**
2739 N. Elston Ave.
Chicago, IL 60647
Tel.: 312-278-4700

PASCOE BUILDING SYSTEMS, INC.
P.O. Box 7186,
Columbus, GA 31908
Mailing Address:
P.O. Box 7186,
Columbus, GA 31908
Year Founded: 1947
Approx.Sls.: $20,000,000
Emp.: 140
Fiscal Year-end: 2/28/89
Pre-Engineered Metal Bldgs.
S.I.C.: 3449; 1791; 3448
John Grot *(Chm. Bd. & Pres.)*
Richard McGauran *(Exec. V.P.-Opers.)*
Leonard Grabia *(V.P.-Sls.)*
Charles Nangia *(V.P.-Engrng. Services)*
Larry Reagan *(Treas.)*
Rod Harrelson *(Dir.-Pur.)*
Cindy Grot *(Coord.-Mktg.)*

Outside Service Firm(s):

Warren Averett*(Auditors)*
Birmingham, AL

Warren Averett*(Auditors)*
Birmingham, AL

Barnett Bank*(Major Banking Relationship)*
Columbus, GA

Barnett Bank*(Major Banking Relationship)*
Columbus, GA

Columbus Bank & Trust Company*(Major Banking Relationship)*
Trust Dept., P.O. Box 120
Columbus, GA 31902
Tel.: 706-649-2311

PASOTEX CORPORATION
310 N. Mesa, Ste. 614
El Paso, TX 79901
Tel.: 915-544-6000
Fax: 914-544-0624
Stephen Curl *(Pres.)*

Subsidiary:

Pipeco, Inc. **(1)**
8223 Willow Place South
Houston, TX 77070
Tel.: 713-955-3500
Mfr. of Pipes & Pipe Fittings
S.I.C.: 3498

Division:

Tubular Services, Inc. **(2)**
1010 McCarty
Houston, TX 77029
Tel.: 713-675-6212
Mfr. of Pipes & Tubular Goods
S.I.C.: 3498
Russell Rhodes *(V.P.)*

PATCH COMMUNICATIONS
5211 S. Washington Ave.
Titusville, FL 32780
Tel.: 407-268-5010
Fax: 407-267-7216
Emp.: 100
Publishes Shutter-Bug Magazine
S.I.C.: 2741
Glenn E. Patch *(Chm. Bd.)*
Donald Welk *(Pres.)*
Bonnie Paulk *(Mng. Editor)*

Outside Service Firm(s):

Florida Union National Bank*(Major Banking Relationship)*
Titusville, FL

PATERNO IMPORTS
CHICAGO, ILLINOIS

PATERNO IMPORTS LIMITED
2701 S. Western Ave.
Chicago, IL 60608
Tel.: 312-247-7070
Fax: 312-247-0072
Year Founded: 1977
Emp.: 126
Import
Importers & Distributors of Wines, Beers & Spirits
S.I.C.: 5182; 5181
Anthony Terlato *(Pres. & Chief Exec. Officer)*
Leslie Lentino *(Exec. V.P. & Sec.)*
John Scribner *(V.P. & Chief Fin. Officer)*
William A. Terlato *(V.P. & Chief Oper. Officer)*
John Terlato *(V.P. & Asst. Legal Counsel)*
Greg Christoff *(Dir.-Mktg.)*
Mark Gould *(Dir.-Pub. Rels.)*
Associated Company:

Pacific Wine Co. **(1)** (100%)
2701 S. Western Ave.
Chicago, IL 60608
Tel.: 312-247-8000
Fax: 312-247-0072
Emp.: 75
Wine Distributor
S.I.C.: 5182
Anthony Terlato *(Pres.)*
Leslie Lentino *(Exec. V.P. & Sec.)*
William A. Terlato *(V.P. & Chief Oper. Officer)*
John Scribner *(V.P. & Chief Fin. Officer)*
John Terlato *(V.P. & Asst. Legal Counsel)*
Greg Christoff *(Dir.-Mktg.)*
Mark Gould *(Dir.-Pub. Rels.)*

SID PATERSON ASSOC., INC.
22 East 29th St.
New York, NY 10016
Tel.: 212-725-9600
Fax: 212-779-7291
Year Founded: 1963
Approx.Billings: $18,000,000
Emp.: 25
Sid Paterson *(Pres. & Acct. Exec.)*

PATIENT CARE, INC.
59 Main St.
West Orange, NJ 07052
Tel.: 201-325-8038
Fax: 201-325-8823
Year Founded: 1975
Approx.Sls.: $31,000,000
Emp.: 1,200
Home Health Agency; Infusion Therapy Services
S.I.C.: 8082
Lawrence I. Sosnow *(Pres.)*
Elaine Boardman *(Sr. V.P.)*
Louis Tamburro *(V.P.-Fin. & Admin.)*
Sally Yingling *(V.P.-Opers. & Mktg.)*
Elizabeth Swanson *(Sec.)*

THE PATRICIAN GROUP
502 Park Ave.
New York, NY 10022
Tel.: 212-371-6262
Fax: 212-223-3871
Real Estate Investment Firm
S.I.C.: 6798; 6552
Ted Shapiro *(Chm. Bd.)*
Edward Fingerman *(Pres.)*
Robert Grossman *(Exec. V.P.)*
Robert Testa *(V.P.)*

PATSON'S PRESS
508 Tasman Dr.
Sunnyvale, CA 94089
Tel.: 408-744-0911
Fax: 408-747-0512
Year Founded: 1958
Emp.: 45
Commercial Printing
S.I.C.: 2759; 2752
Patricia Dellamano *(Pres. & Chief Exec. & Chief Fin. Officer)*
Joseph Dellamano *(Mgr.-Production)*
Mark Dellamano *(Mgr.-Sls. & Data Processing)*

Computer Systems/Hardware:
NCR PC

Outside Service Firm(s):

Frank Scarpace*(Auditors)*
Oakland, CA

Nationwide Insurance*(Group Insurer)*
One Nationwide Plaza
Columbus, OH 43216
Tel.: 614-249-6488

PATSY'S, INC.
24 Hall St.
Concord, NH 03301
Mailing Address:
P.O. Box 513,
Concord, NH 03302-0513
Tel.: 603-224-5366
Fax: 603-226-2001
Year Founded: 1929
Approx.Sls.: $10,000,000
Emp.: 100
Retail Truck & Car Sales, Service & Parts
S.I.C.: 5511; 5531; 7538
Joseph R. Alosa *(Pres. & Treas.)*
Anthony M. Waterman *(V.P.)*
Arthur Perkins *(Sec.)*

Outside Service Firm(s):

Anderson & Cloues*(Auditors)*
Concord, NH

Perkins, Phillips & Waters*(Legal Firm)*
Concord, NH

New Hampshire Savings Bank*(Major Banking Relationship)*
Concord, NH

PATTERSON DENTAL COMPANY
1100 E. 80th St.
Minneapolis, MN 55420
Tel.: 612-854-2881
Tel.: 800-328-5536 **DE**
Fax: 612-854-8381
Year Founded: 1877
Assets: $65,000,000
Liabilities: $49,000,000
Net Worth: $16,000,000
Approx.Sls.: $240,000,000
Emp.: 1,340
Fiscal Year-end: 4/27/91
Export
Distributor of Dental Equipment & Supplies
S.I.C.: 5047; 3843
Peter L. Frechette *(Pres. & Chief Exec. Officer)*
Guy F. Bradley II *(V.P.-Mktg.)*
John Dodd *(V.P.-Mngmt. Information Systems)*
Ronald E. Ezerski *(V.P.-Fin. & Treas.)*
James W. Wiltz *(V.P.)*
Thomas E. Alderman *(Controller)*
Matthew Levitt *(Gen. Counsel)*

No. of U.S. Offices: 77

Computer Systems/Hardware:
Tandem, Alpha Micro, IBM

Outside Service Firm(s):

Ernst & Young*(Auditors)*
1400 Pillsbury Center
Minneapolis, MN 55402
Tel.: 612-343-1000

First Bank, N.A.*(Major Banking Relationship)*
Minneapolis, MN

Subsidiary:

Direct Dental Supply Co. **(1)**
879 Deming Way
Sparks, NV 89431
Tel.: 702-331-4300
Tel.: 800-648-5628
Emp.: 8
Mail Order Distributor of Dental Supplies
S.I.C.: 5961; 5047
Peter L. Frechette *(Pres.)*
Ronald E. Ezerski *(Chief Fin. Officer)*
Dee Stagner *(Mgr.)*

PATTERSON FROZEN FOODS, INC.
100 W. Las Palmas
Patterson, CA 95363
Mailing Address:
P.O. Box 114
Patterson, CA 95363
Tel.: 209-892-2611 CA
Fax: 209-892-5209
Year Founded: 1946
Approx.Sls.: $60,000,000
Emp.: 800
Frozen Vegetables & Fruits
S.I.C.: 2037
John Ielmini *(Pres.)*
Angelo Ielmini *(Exec. V.P.)*
Bud Ingebretsen *(V.P.-Opers.)*
Neil Morosa *(V.P.-Fin.)*
Bill Rembold *(V.P.-Sls.)*
Sam Hibma *(Controller)*
Steve Martin *(Mgr.-Quality Control)*
Doug Price *(Mgr.-Res. & Devel.)*

Principal(s):
John Ielmini
Angelo Ielmini

Outside Service Firm(s):

Atherton, Ludlow & Schonhoff*(Auditors)*
Modesto, CA

Orrick, Herrington & Sutcliffe*(Legal Firm)*
Old Federal Reserve Bank Bldg., 400 Sansome St.
San Francisco, CA 95814
Tel.: 415-392-1122

Wells Fargo Bank*(Major Banking Relationship)*
420 Montgomery St.
San Francisco, CA 94104

PATTERSON LABORATORIES, INC.
11930 Pleasant Ave.
Detroit, MI 48217
Tel.: 313-843-4500
Fax: 313-843-9416
Year Founded: 1935
Approx.Sls.: $10,000,000
Emp.: 30
Fiscal Year-end: 9/30/90
Ful-Vue Windshield Washer Solvent & De-Icer Solution; Blue Ribbon Ammonia, Rinse (Fabric Softener), Bleach, & Glass Polish & Blue Ribbon Liquid Starch, Blue Ribbon All Fabric Bleach & Blue Ribbon Dish Detergents
S.I.C.: 2842; 2843
J.S. Moon *(Pres.)*
R. Hodgkinson *(V.P.-Admin.)*
R. Dilcher *(Mgr.-Sls.)*

THE PATY COMPANY
220 Piney Flats Rd.
Piney Flats, TN 37686
Mailing Address:
P.O. Box 250
Piney Flats, TN 37686
Tel.: 615-538-8101
Fax: 615-538-8101, Ext. 226
Approx.Sls.: $65,000,000
Emp.: 550
Retail Building Supplies
S.I.C.: 5211
John C. Paty, Jr. *(Chm. Bd.)*
John E. Seward, Jr. *(Pres. & Chief Exec. Officer)*
Bill T. McClellan *(Sr. V.P.)*
John E. Seward, Sr. *(Sr. V.P.)*
John Kiss *(V.P.-Mktg.)*
JoAnne Paty *(V.P.-Human Resources)*
Robert Salyer *(V.P. & Treas.)*
Elizabeth P. Snead *(Sec.)*
Lester Bennett *(Mgr.-Production)*
Rita Catron *(Mgr.-Data Processing)*
Mike Farmer *(Mgr.-Contract Sls.)*
Eugene Garity *(Mgr.-Inventory)*
Dean Privette *(Mgr.-Adv.)*

Principal(s):
John C. Paty, Jr.

No. of Mfg. Plants/Facilities: 1

Computer Systems/Hardware:
IBM AS-400

Outside Service Firm(s):

Price Waterhouse*(Auditors)*
1800 One Triad Plaza
Winston-Salem, NC 27101
Tel.: 919-725-0691
Fax: 919-725-5022

Third National Bank*(Major Banking Relationship)*
201 Fourth Ave. N.
Nashville, TN 37219
Tel.: 615-748-4742

PAVEY ENVELOPE & TAG CORP.
25 Linden Ave. E.
Jersey City, NJ 07305
Tel.: 201-434-2100 NJ
Fax: 201-434-8431
Year Founded: 1907
Approx.Sls.: $15,500,000
Emp.: 170
Mfr. & Printer of Envelopes
S.I.C.: 2677
Gerald F. Mahoney *(Pres.)*
Albert Logan *(V.P. & Gen. Mgr.)*
Sanford Rothbard *(V.P.-Fin.)*
William Light *(V.P.-Opers.)*

Outside Service Firm(s):

J. H. Cohn & Co.*(Auditors)*
75 Eisenhower Pkwy.
Roseland, NJ 07068-1697
Tel.: 201-228-3500

Midlantic National Bank*(Major Banking Relationship)*
Metro Park Plaza,
Edison, NJ 08818
Tel.: 908-321-8000

Affiliate:

Standard Tag Mfg. Co. **(1)**
25 Linden Ave. E.
Jersey City, NJ 07305
Tel.: 201-333-8800
Fax: 201-434-0527
Gerald F. Mahoney *(Pres.)*
Robert Socozzo *(Dir.-Mktg.)*

PAVION LTD.
60 Cedar Hill Avenue
Nyack on Hudson, NY 10960
Mailing Address:
P.O. Box 996,
Nyack on Hudson, NY 10960
Tel.: 914-353-3000
Fax: 914-353-1625
Year Founded: 1979
Approx.Sls.: $40,000,000
Emp.: 350
Fiscal Year-end: 12/31/91
Manufactures & Distributes a Branded Line of Budget Priced Cosmetics
S.I.C.: 5122
Stanley Acker *(Chm., Pres. & Chief Exec. Officer)*
Stephen A. Heit *(Chief Fin. Officer & Treas.)*
Karen Acker *(V.P.-International & Sec.)*
Mark Acker *(V.P.-Operations)*
Denis Corrigan *(Controller)*
Fran Garner *(Dir.-Human Resources)*
Eric Ludlow *(Dir.-Pur.)*

PAWLING CORPORATION
157 Charles Colman Blvd.
Pawling, NY 12564
Tel.: 914-855-1000
Fax: 914-855-3150
Year Founded: 1945
Approx.Sls.: $50,000,000
Emp.: 340
Fiscal Year-end: 7/31/91
Import Export
Mfr. Rubber & Plastic Extrusions, Link Mats & Matting, Molded Rubber Prods., Pneumatic Seals, Protective Door, Wall & Corner Guards, Custom Mixed Rubber Compounds, Handrails
S.I.C.: 3089; 3446; 3069; 3061; 3053; 3084
Howard W. Smith *(Chm. Bd.)*
Roger W. Smith *(Pres.)*
Robert B. Busby *(Exec. V.P. & Dir.-Sls.)*
Maurice V. Smith *(V.P.-Custom Mixing Div.)*
Steve J. Smith *(V.P.-Mktg.)*
Ralph J. Skokan *(Treas.)*
Valerie S. Busby *(Sec.)*
Barbara LaForce *(Mktg. Coord.)*
Richard Meyer *(Chief Engineer)*
Mary Tripp *(Mgr.-Export & Import)*

Outside Service Firm(s):

KPMG Peat Marwick*(Auditors)*
Stamford Square, 3001 Summer St.
Stamford, CT 06905
Tel.: 203-356-9800

Marine Midland Bank*(Major Banking Relationship)*
White Plains, NY

Subsidiary:

Presray Corp. **(1)**
159 Charles Colman Blvd.
Pawling, NY 12564
Tel.: 914-855-1000
Theodore C. Hollander, Jr *(Pres.)*

PAWNEE INDUSTRIES, INC.
2024 No. Woodlawn St.
Wichita, KS 67208
Mailing Address:
P.O. Box 21110
Wichita, KS 67208
Tel.: 316-652-9500 DE
Fax: 316-652-9600
Year Founded: 1964
Approx.Sls.: $130,000,000
Emp.: 600
Custom Extruded Thermoplastic Sheet Material For Industrial Application
S.I.C.: 3085
David Prochey *(Chm. Bd. & Pres.)*
Will Maxwell *(Dir.-Personnel)*

No. of Mfg. Plants/Facilities: 7
No. of U.S. Offices: 8

Computer Systems/Hardware:
IBM

Outside Service Firm(s):

Ernst & Young*(Auditors)*
Wichita, KS

Heller Financial Services*(Investment Banker)*
Glendale, CA

Baker, Hoster, McSpadden, Clark, Rasure & Slicker*(Legal Firm)*
Wichita, KS

First National Bank of Wichita*(Major Banking Relationship)*
Box One
Wichita, KS 67201
Tel.: 316-268-1201

Subsidiaries:

Pawnee Extrusions **(1)**
2401 Dillard
Grand Prairie, TX 75051
Tel.: 214-647-1212
Fax: 214-660-4306
Manufacture Sheet Plastic
S.I.C.: 3081
Anthony S. Vaudo *(Pres.)*
George Howell *(V.P.-Tech.)*
James R. Gilmore *(V.P.-Fin.)*
William Phillips *(V.P.-Sls.)*

Pawnee Specialty Products **(1)**
2024 No. Woodlawn
Wichita, KS 67208
Tel.: 316-652-9500
Mfr., Rotationally Molded Products, Color Concentrates & Composite Fabrication
S.I.C.: 2816; 3089
William Leahy *(Pres.)*

PAWTUCKET FASTENERS INC.
327 Pine St.
Pawtucket, RI 02862
Mailing Address:
P.O. Box 879
Pawtucket, RI 02862
Tel.: 401-725-3880
Fax: 401-725-0817
Approx.Sls.: $10,000,000
Emp.: 100
Fiscal Year-end: 6/30/90
High Carbon Steel, Stainless Steel & Special Alloy Bolts, Studs & Other Threaded Fastening Devices
S.I.C.: 3452
D.M. Hirsch *(Pres.)*
Joel Roseman *(V.P.-Sls.)*
Judy Croone *(Sec.)*

THE PAXALL GROUP, INC.
7515 N. Linder Ave.
Skokie, IL 60077
Tel.: 708-677-7800 DE
Fax: 708-677-7139
Approx.Sls.: $25,000,000
Emp.: 160
Fiscal Year-end: 12/31/90
Mfr. Packaging Machinery
S.I.C.: 3565
Earl Ritchie *(Pres.)*
David A. Chenoweth *(V.P.-Sls. & Mktg.)*
T. Russell Davis *(V.P.-Engrng. (Hayward))*

Divisions:

Paxall Circle Machinery **(1)**
7515 N. Linder Ave.
Skokie, IL 60077
Tel.: 708-677-7800
Fax: 201-427-1140
Import Export
S.I.C.: 3565

Paxall Clybourn Machinery **(1)**
7515 N. Linder Ave.
Skokie, IL 60077
Tel.: 708-677-7800
Fax: 708-677-7139
Import Export
Carton-Filling & Packaging Machines
S.I.C.: 3565

Paxall Pak-Master Machinery **(1)**
31800 Hayman St.
Hayward, CA 94544
Tel.: 510-489-3900
Fax: 510-489-7621
Mfr. Wraparound Casepackers & Palletizers
S.I.C.: 3565

Paxall Parsons Machinery **(1)**
31800 Hayman St.
Hayward, CA 94544
Tel.: 510-489-3900
Fax: 510-489-7621
Packaging Systems, Batchers, Fillers, Weighers, Scales
S.I.C.: 3565

PAY LESS SUPER MARKETS, INC.
First Savings Tower, 33 W. 10th St.
Anderson, IN 46015
Mailing Address:
P.O. Box 639
Anderson, IN 46015
Tel.: 317-649-3526
Fax: 317-640-2496
Year Founded: 1954
Approx.Sls.: $156,000,000

Emp.: 1,400
Grocery Stores
S.I.C.: 5411
Glenn Falls *(Chm. Bd.)*
Larry D. Contos *(Pres.)*
Robert Albregts *(V.P.-Human Resources)*
Bill Fleming *(V.P.-Sls. & Mdsg.)*
Judy C. Miller *(V.P.-Adv.)*
Everett Muterspaugh *(V.P.-Opers.)*
Paul Nicholson *(V.P.-Fin. & Treas.)*
Richard F. Davisson *(Sec. & Gen. Counsel)*
Richard Scott *(Dir.-Mngmt. Information Systems)*
Dixie Contos Wilson *(Dir.-Pub. Rels.)*
Principal(s):
Larry D. Contos

Outside Service Firm(s):

Arthur Andersen & Co.*(Auditors)*
111 Monument Circle, Ste. 4300
Indianapolis, IN 46204-5143
Tel.: 317-634-3210
Fax: 317-632-3973

Davisson & Davisson*(Legal Firm)*
Anderson, IN

Anderson Banking Co.*(Major Banking Relationship)*
Anderson, IN

PAYLESS CAR RENTAL SYSTEM, INC.
2350 34th Street North
Saint Petersburg, FL 33713
Tel.: 813-321-6352
Telex: 403066
Fax: 813-323-3529
Year Founded: 1971
Assets: $2,286,457
Liabilities: $991,398
Net Worth: $1,295,059
Sales Range: $60-79 Million
Emp.: 55
Franchisor; Car Rentals
S.I.C.: 6794
Fred Lin *(Chm. Bd.)*
Jay Vahl *(Pres.)*
Joe Dinicoli *(Sr. V.P.)*
Linster E. Brinkley *(Gen. Counsel)*

No. of U.S. Offices: 100
No. of Foreign Offices: 8

Computer Systems/Hardware:
Dec. Vax 8200; Dec. PDP 11/84

Outside Service Firm(s):

Coopers & Lybrand*(Auditors)*
101 E. Kennedy Blvd., Ste. 1500
Tampa, FL 33602
Tel.: 813-229-0221

Life General Security*(Group Insurer)*
New York, NY

Security Mutual Insurance Company of New York*(Group Insurer)*
New York, NY

J. Patrick McElroy*(Legal Firm)*
Clearwater, FL

Citizens & Southern National Bank*(Major Banking Relationship)*
St. Petersburg, FL

PAYLESS CASHWAYS, INC.
2300 Main St.
Kansas City, MO 64108
Mailing Address:
P.O. Box 419466,
Kansas City, MO 64141-0466
Tel.: 816-234-6000 **IA**
Fax: 816-234-6040
Year Founded: 1930
Sales Range: $1 Billion +
Emp.: 350
Operate Approximately 197 Lumber & Building Materials Retail Outlets
S.I.C.: 5211
Corporate Giving Program: Human & Neighborhood Services; Education (Programs Supportive of At-Risk Youths); Civic Efforts; The Arts.
David Stanley *(Chm. Bd. & Chief Exec. Officer)*
Larry P. Kunz *(Pres. & Chief Oper. Officer)*
Linda French *(Sr. V.P., Gen. Counsel & Sec.)*
Stephen Lightstone *(Sr. V.P.-Fin. & Chief Fin. Officer)*
John Fischer *(V.P.-Western Region)*
David Krumbholz *(V.P.-Midwestern Region)*
Dick Luse *(V.P. & Controller)*
Kris Maynard *(V.P.-Eastern Region)*
Roger Weverka *(V.P.-Southern Region)*
John White *(V.P.-Distr. & Trans.)*
Ritchy Brown *(Dir. Facility Devel.)*
Karen Garrison *(Dir.-Communications)*
Jim Neustadt *(Dir.-Adv.)*
Paul Van Dyne *(Dir.-Compensation & Benefits)*
Greg Drown *(Mgr.-Treasury Opers.)*
Jim O'Keefe *(Mgr.-Real Estate)*
Brenda Nolte *(Pub. Affairs Officer)*

Outside Service Firm(s):

KPMG Peat Marwick*(Auditors)*
1000 Walnut St.
Kansas City, MO 64106

Blackwell, Sanders, Matheny, Weary & Lombardi*(Legal Firm)*
2300 Main Street
Kansas City, MO 64108
Tel.: 816-474-5700

NationsBank Texas*(Major Banking Relationship)*
NCNB Plaza, 16th Fl., P.O. Box 830501
Dallas, TX 75283-1402
Tel.: 214-508-1729

Subsidiaries:

Knox Lumber Co. **(1)**
573 N. Prior
Saint Paul, MN 55114
Tel.: 612-646-4893 (100%)
Emp.: 1,045
Retail Sales of Lumber & Bldg. Materials
S.I.C.: 5211
Mike Carver *(Pres.)*

Somerville Lumber & Supply Co. **(1)**
779 McGrath Hwy.
Somerville, MA 02145
Tel.: 617-623-2800 (100%)
Emp.: 1,243
Building Materials Retailer
S.I.C.: 5211
Harold Cohen *(Pres.)*

PAYSON CASTERS, INC.
2323 Delaney Rd.
Gurnee, IL 60031
Tel.: 708-336-6200
Fax: 708-336-6542
Year Founded: 1873
Approx.Sls.: $16,000,000
Emp.: 155
Fiscal Year-end: 9/30/91
Casters & Wheels
S.I.C.: 3429
Harold Sullivan, III *(Pres.)*
J. Katherine Kuroski *(V.P.-Acctg.)*
Cynthia Martinaitis *(Mgr.-Adv.)*

Outside Service Firm(s):

Hendricks & Associates*(Legal Firm)*
Oak Brook, IL

Subsidiaries:

Payson Bronco, Inc. **(1)**
6900 Cherry Ave.
Long Beach, CA 90805
Tel.: 310-602-2400
Casters & Wheels
S.I.C.: 3429
Ken Conway *(Gen. Mgr.)*

Payson Georgia, Inc. **(1)**
3480 Oakcliff Rd.
Andoraville, GA 30340
Tel.: 404-457-2969
Casters & Wheels
S.I.C.: 3429
Floyd Kingston *(Pres.)*

Payson Texas, Inc. **(1)**
2688 Freewood Dr.
Dallas, TX 75220
Tel.: 214-352-1765
Casters & Wheels
S.I.C.: 3429
Evelyn Shaw *(Gen. Mgr.)*

PEABODY OFFICE FURNITURE CORPORATION
234 Congress St.
Boston, MA 02110
Tel.: 617-542-1902
Fax: 617-542-1609
Year Founded: 1899
Approx.Sls.: $30,000,000
Emp.: 90
Fiscal Year-end: 12/31/90
Wholesale Office Furniture
S.I.C.: 5021
Lester C. Peabody *(Chm. Bd.)*
John B. Halloran *(Pres.)*
Jonathan C. Peabody *(V.P. & Treas.)*
Principal(s):
Lester C. Peabody
Jonathan C. Peabody

PEAKE PRINTERS, INC.
2500 Schuster Dr.
Cheverly, MD 20781
Tel.: 301-341-4600
Fax: 301-341-1162
Approx.Sls.: $24,000,000
Emp.: 175
Complete Commercial Printing
S.I.C.: 2752
Jay Rupard *(Pres.)*
Charles Slaugh *(V.P.-Fin.)*
Ed Webb *(V.P.-Sls.)*
Principal(s):
Virginia Rupard

Outside Service Firm(s):

First American Bank Of Maryland*(Major Banking Relationship)*
Baltimore, MD

PEARCE INDUSTRIES INC.
12320 S. Main St.
Houston, TX 77035
Mailing Address:
P.O. Box 35068,
Houston, TX 77235
Tel.: 713-723-1050
Fax: 713-551-0454
Year Founded: 1924
Emp.: 485
Wholesale Distribution of Gas & Diesel Engines & Construction Machinery; Manufacture & Sales of Oil Field Equipment
S.I.C.: 5084; 5082; 5013; 3586
Louis M. Pearce, Jr. *(Chm. Bd.)*
Gary M. Pearce *(Vice Chm. & Pres.)*
Richard E. Bean *(Chief Fin. Officer & Exec. V.P.-Fin.)*
Louis Pearce, III *(V.P. & Sec.)*
Stephen R. Pearce *(V.P. & Treas.)*
Al Bentley *(Controller)*
John Gutta *(Dir.-Indus. Rels.)*
John MacNamara *(Dir.-Information Systems)*

Computer Systems/Hardware:
Sperry Univac

Outside Service Firm(s):

American General Life Insurance Co.*(Group Insurer)*
2727 Allen Pkwy.
Houston, TX 77019
Tel.: 713-522-1111

Fulbright & Jaworski*(Legal Firm)*
1301 McKinney St.
Houston, TX 77010
Tel.: 713-651-5151

First City National Bank*(Major Banking Relationship)*
Houston, TX

Texas Commerce Bank*(Major Banking Relationship)*
717 Travis St.
Houston, TX 77002
Tel.: 713-236-4636
Fax: 713-236-5476

Subsidiaries:

Paloma Production Co. Inc. **(1)**
12320 S. Main St.
Houston, TX 77235
Tel.: 713-723-1050

Pearce Equipment Leasing **(1)**
12320 S. Main St.
Houston, TX 77235
Tel.: 713-723-1050

Pearce International Inc. **(1)**
12320 S. Main St.
Houston, TX 77235
Tel.: 713-723-1050

Texas Iron Works Inc. **(1)**
12320 S. Main St.
Houston, TX 77235
Tel.: 713-723-1050

Waukesha-Pearce Industries **(1)**
12320 S. Main St.
Houston, TX 77235
Tel.: 713-723-1050

PEARL-PRESSMAN-LIBERTY COMMUNICATIONS GROUP
(Formerly Pearl-Pressman-Liberty, Inc.)
5th & Poplar Sts.
Philadelphia, PA 19123
Tel.: 215-925-4900
Fax: 215-925-2302
Approx.Sls.: $15,500,000
Emp.: 150
Color Lithography; Computerized Typesetting
S.I.C.: 2752; 2791
Harold B. Pressman *(Chm. Bd.)*
Morris Rosen *(Pres.)*
William Conners *(Exec. V.P.)*
Marvin Bergman *(V.P.)*
Gary Fay *(V.P.-Sls.)*
David Van Dusen *(V.P.)*
Manny Pearl *(Sec. & Treas.)*
Thomas Derham *(Mgr.-Data Processing)*
Louis Levicoff *(Pur. Agent)*
Eugene Peters *(Chief Engr.)*

Outside Service Firm(s):

Rudolph, Palitz & Co.*(Auditors)*
Philadelphia, PA

Wolf, Block, Schorr & Solis-Cohen*(Legal Firm)*
Packard Bldg.
Philadelphia, PA 19102
Tel.: 215-977-2000

Continental Bank, N.A.*(Major Banking Relationship)*
1500 Market St.
Philadelphia, PA 19102
Tel.: 215-564-7475

PEARLSTINE DISTRIBUTORS INC.
4550 Gaynor Ave.
Charleston, SC 29411
Mailing Address:
P.O. Box 10247,
Charleston, SC 29411
Tel.: 803-554-1022 **SC**
Fax: 803-745-1808
Approx.Sls.: $56,000,000

Pearlstine Distributors Inc.—(Continued)

Emp.: 265
Wholesale Beer & Wine
S.I.C.: 5181; 5182
Edwin Pearlstine, Jr. *(Pres.)*
Arthur Brabham *(V.P.-Sls.)*
Charles B. Marquardt, Jr. *(V.P. & Controller)*
Walker Spann *(V.P.-Opers.)*
John D. Sullivan *(V.P.)*
Karla Taylor *(V.P.-Mktg. & Adv.)*

Outside Service Firm(s):

Thiem, Jackson & Pace*(Auditors)*
Charleston, SC

David Jennings*(Legal Firm)*
Charleston, SC

Citizens & Southern National Bank*(Major Banking Relationship)*
Charleston, SC

PEASE INDUSTRIES, INC.
7100 Dixie Hwy.
Fairfield, OH 45014
Mailing Address:
P.O. Box 14-8001,
Fairfield, OH 45014-8001
Tel.: 513-870-3600
Tel.: 800-875-3691 **OH**
Telex: 332019
Fax: 513-870-3602
Fax: 513-870-3670
Year Founded: 1893
Assets: $15,000,000
Liabilities: $11,300,000
Net Worth: $3,700,000
Approx.Sls.: $50,000,000
Emp.: 300
Fiscal Year-end: 12/31/90
Import
Mfr. & Distribution of Residential Steel, Fiberglass and Wood Door Entry Systems
S.I.C.: 3442; 2431
David H. Pease, Jr. *(Chm. Bd. & Chief Exec. Officer)*
Leonard W. Cavens *(Pres.)*
David A. Aluise *(V.P.-Logistics)*
Neil W. Jackman *(V.P.-Sls. & Human Resources)*
David H. Pease III *(V.P.-Engrng. & Mfg.)*
Alan Buckley *(Chief Fin. Officer, Sec., Treas. & Legal Officer)*
Harriet O'Hara *(Controller)*
Sue Calardo *(Mgr.-Adv.)*

No. of Mfg. Plants/Facilities: 4
No. of U.S. Offices: 1

Computer Systems/Hardware:
IBM System 38

Outside Service Firm(s):

Ernst & Young*(Auditors)*
1300 Chiquita Center, 250 E. Fifth St.
Cincinnati, OH 45202
Tel.: 513-621-6454

Kemper Insurance*(Commercial Insurance Carrier)*
Cincinnati, OH

Clark & Eyrich*(Legal Firm)*
Hamilton, OH

The Central Trust Company, N.A.*(Major Banking Relationship)*
201 E. Fifth
Cincinnati, OH 45202
Tel.: 513-651-8255

PEAVEY ELECTRONIC CORP.
711 A St.
Meridian, MS 39301
Mailing Address:
P.O. Box 2898,
Meridian, MS 39302
Tel.: 601-483-5365 **DE**
Fax: 601-484-4278
Year Founded: 1965
Emp.: 1,900
Manufactures Portable Sound Equipment, Electric Musical Instruments, Amplifiers, Microphones, Public Address Systems, Commercial Sound Equipment & Components
S.I.C.: 3651
Melia Peavey *(Pres.)*
Hartley D. Peavey *(Chief Exec. Officer)*
Jack Wilson *(V.P.)*

No. of Mfg. Plants/Facilities: 18
No. of U.S. Offices: 2
No. of Foreign Offices: 3

Computer Systems/Hardware:
IBM System 3090

Outside Service Firm(s):

Sandusky, Bailey & Fortenberry*(Legal Firm)*
Meridian, MS

Subsidiary:

AMR (Audio Media Research) **(1)**
711 A St.
Meridian, MS 39301
Tel.: 601-483-5365

PECK IRON & METAL COMPANY, INC.
3500 Elm Ave.
Portsmouth, VA 23704
Tel.: 804-399-4075 **VA**
Fax: 804-399-3949
Year Founded: 1945
Approx.Sls.: $24,000,000
Emp.: 150
Wholesale Distribution of Ferrous & Nonferrous Metal Scrap & Waste
S.I.C.: 5093
Julius S. Peck *(Pres.)*
Barry D. Peck *(V.P.)*
Aaron M. Peck *(Treas. & Sec.)*

Outside Service Firm(s):

Sherman, Spero & Safarino Ltd.*(Auditors)*
Virgina Beach, VA

Crestar Bank*(Major Banking Relationship)*
P.O. Box 26665,
Richmond, VA 23261
Tel.: 804-782-5995

PECK JONES CONSTRUCTION
(Formerly Peck Jones, Inc.)
10866 Wilshire Blvd., 7th Fl.
Los Angeles, CA 90024
Tel.: 213-470-1885 **CA**
Fax: 213-470-3175
Year Founded: 1915
Approx.Sls.: $300,000,000
Emp.: 250
Fiscal Year-end: 12/31/91
General Building Contractors; Heavy Construction Contractors
S.I.C.: 1541; 1542; 1629
J. Gregory Jones *(Pres. & Chief Fin. Officer)*
Jerve M. Jones *(Chief Exec. Officer)*
Dan Penn *(Controller)*
J. Kevin Jones *(Exec. V.P.-Mktg.)*
George W. Fenimore *(Sr. V.P.-Pub. Affairs)*
Susan Ichikawa *(Corp. Sec.)*
Joseph D. Irish *(Mgr.-Opers.)*
Principal(s):
J. Gregory Jones
Jerve M. Jones
J. Kevin Jones

Computer Systems/Hardware:
Digital

Outside Service Firm(s):

Arthur Andersen & Co.*(Auditors)*
633 W. Fifth St.
Los Angeles, CA 90071
Tel.: 213-614-6500

Pacific Mutual*(Group Insurer)*
700 Newport Center Dr.
Newport Beach, CA 92660
Tel.: 714-640-3011
Fax: 714-759-3372

Monteleone & McCrory*(Legal Firm)*
5900 Wilshire Blvd. Los Angeles
Los Angeles, CA 90010
Tel.: 213-937-1533

First Interstate Bank of California, N.A.*(Major Banking Relationship)*
P.O. Box 3667,
Los Angeles, CA 90051
Tel.: 213-614-4000

Pacific Mutual*(Pension Manager)*
700 Newport Center Dr.
Newport Beach, CA 92660
Tel.: 714-640-3011
Fax: 714-759-3372

Peck Lynn Group Ltd.
(Name Changed To H.P.H. Industries Ltd.)

PECK ROAD FORD TRUCK SALES
2450 Kella Ave.
Whittier, CA 90601
Tel.: 310-692-7267 **DE**
Fax: 310-692-8390
Year Founded: 1970
Approx.Sls.: $60,000,000
Emp.: 82
Export
Wholesale Distributor of Commercial Trucks
S.I.C.: 5012
Arthur W. Fraser *(Pres.)*
Betty Ann Fraser *(V.P.)*
Sam Treynor *(Sec., Treas. & Controller)*
Randy Carter *(Gen. Mgr.-Sls.)*

PECK SIMS MUELLER, INC.
1170 Waimanu St.
Honolulu, HI 96814
Tel.: 808-526-1134
Fax: 808-533-1750
Year Founded: 1972
Approx.Billings: $25,000,000
Emp.: 47
R. Sanderson Sims *(Pres.)*
Donald R. Mueller *(Exec. V.P.)*
Martha Ball *(Controller)*

PECK SPRING COMPANY
89 Whiting St.
Plainville, CT 06062
Tel.: 203-747-5715 **CT**
Fax: 203-747-5008
Year Founded: 1979
Approx.Sls.: $10,000,000
Emp.: 135
Mfr. of Unassembled Furniture Springs; Screw Machine Products
S.I.C.: 3495; 3451
James M. Batt *(Pres. & Chief Exec. Officer)*
Leonard Bachand *(V.P.)*
Roger Fekete *(V.P. & Sec.)*
Donald Fournier *(Pur. Agent)*

Outside Service Firm(s):

Harper & Whitfield*(Auditors)*
Farmington, CT

PECKHAM INDUSTRIES, INC.
20 Haarlem Ave.
White Plains, NY 10603
Tel.: 914-949-2000
Fax: 914-949-2075
Approx.Sls.: $50,000,000
Emp.: 150
Road Contractors, Road Building Supplies, Crushed Stone, Liquid Asphalt & Crushed Limestone
S.I.C.: 1611; 2911; 2951; 3281
Janet G. Peckham *(Chm. Bd.)*
James V. DeForest *(Pres.)*
John R. Peckham *(Exec. V.P.)*
Joseph V. Kuch *(V.P.)*
Frank J. Franco *(Treas. & Sec.)*

Outside Service Firm(s):

BDO Seidman*(Auditors)*
White Plains, NY

Chemical Bank*(Major Banking Relationship)*
White Plains, NY

PECO INC.
4707 S.E. 17th Ave.
Portland, OR 97202-0189
Mailing Address:
P. O. Box 82189
Portland, OR 97282
Tel.: 503-233-6401
Fax: 503-233-6407
Approx.Sls.: $25,000,000
Emp.: 250
Fiscal Year-end: 6/30/92
Import Export
Speeometer Seals, Material Handling Prods., Zinc & Aluminum Die Castings, Injection Moldings, Screw Machine Prods., Memory Disc Packs, Temperature Controls, Electrical, Electronic & Mechanical Assembly Machining
S.I.C.: 3363; 3364; 5084
E.D. Schamp *(Pres.)*
J.M. Stocks *(V.P.-Mfg.)*
H.J. Taylor *(V.P.-Sls.)*
Brian Leckband *(Controller)*
Lynn Sanders *(Dir.-Personnel)*
Steve Sather *(Mgr.-Pur.)*

Divisions:

Cartall Div. **(1)**
4720 S.E. 17th Ave.
Portland, OR 97202
Tel.: 503-233-6401
H.J. Taylor *(V.P.)*

Peco Mfg. Co. **(1)**
4720 S.E. 17th Ave.
Portland, OR 97202
Tel.: 503-233-6401
E.D. Schamp *(Pres.)*

Sunne Controls Div. **(1)**
4720 S.E. 17th Ave.
Portland, OR 97202
Tel.: 503-233-6401

PEDONE & PARTNERS
100 Fifth Ave.
New York, NY 10011

Tel.: 212-627-3300
Fax: 212-672-3966
Year Founded: 1987
Approx.Billings: $45,000,000
Emp.: 37
Michael F. Pedone *(Pres. & Chief Exec. Officer)*
James F. Coakley *(V.P., Bus. Devel.)*
John P. Green *(Dir., Res. & Strategic Plng.)*
Peter Daly *(Comptroller)*

PEDUS SERVICES, INC.
3500 W. First St.
Los Angeles, CA 90004
Tel.: 213-386-8480
Fax: 213-739-0064
Year Founded: 1979
Approx.Sls.: $81,000,000
Emp.: 7,000
Building, Security & Food Services
S.I.C.: 7382; 5812
Tony Caminitti *(Pres.)*
Andre Nicassio *(V.P.)*
Robert Fenn *(Dir.-Personnel)*

No. of U.S. Offices: 3

Computer Systems/Hardware:
IBM PC-XT

Outside Service Firm(s):

Buchalter, Nemer, Fields & Younger*(Legal Firm)*
601 S. Figueroa St., Ste. 2500
Los Angeles, CA 90017-5704
Tel.: 213-891-0700

Wells Fargo Bank*(Major Banking Relationship)*
420 Montgomery St.
San Francisco, CA 94104

Subsidiaries:

Pedus Building Services **(1)**
3500 W. First St.
Los Angeles, CA 90004
Tel.: 213-484-9600 (100%)
S.I.C.: 7382
Tony Caminetti *(Pres.)*

Pedus Food Services **(1)**
3500 W. First St.
Los Angeles, CA 90004
Tel.: 213-484-9600
S.I.C.: 5812
Tony Caminetti *(Pres.)*

Pedus Office Services **(1)**
3500 W. First St.
Los Angeles, CA 90004
Tel.: 213-484-9600
S.I.C.: 8741
Tony Caminetti *(Pres.)*

Pedus Security Services **(1)**
3500 W. First St.
Los Angeles, CA 90004
Tel.: 213-484-9600 (100%)
S.I.C.: 7382
Tony Caminetti *(Pres.)*

PEEBLES, INC.
One Peebles St.
South Hill, VA 23970
Tel.: 804-447-7671
Fax: 804-447-2387
Operators of 49 Department Stores
S.I.C.: 5311
Michael F. Moorman *(Pres.)*
Steve Hannah *(V.P.-Mktg.)*
Randi Lail *(V.P.-Fin.)*
Stanley Spencer *(V.P.-Mngmt. Information Systems)*
Dan Terrell *(Controller)*
Rebecca Avans *(Dir.-Pur.)*

Outside Service Firm(s):

Ernst & Young*(Auditors)*
One James Center, 901 E. Cary St.,Ste. 1000
Richmond, VA 23219
Tel.: 804-780-0010

McQuire, Woods, Battle & Booth*(Legal Firm)*
8th & Main Sts.
Richmond, VA 23219
Tel.: 804-644-4131

Central Fidelity Bank*(Major Banking Relationship)*
Richmond, VA

PEELERS RUG COMPANY, INC.
1224 Champion Ferry Rd.
Gaffney, SC 29341
Tel.: 803-489-3010 **SC**
Fax: 803-489-4131
Year Founded: 1962
Approx.Sls.: $11,000,000
Emp.: 400
Mfr. of Tufted & Machine Woven Rugs; Screen Printing of Cotton Broadwoven Fabrics
S.I.C.: 2273; 2261
Bobby J. Peeler *(Pres.)*
Nancy Carole Peeler *(Treas. & Sec.)*

PEERLESS CHAIN CO.
1416 E. Sanborn St.
Winona, MN 55987
Tel.: 507-457-9100
Year Founded: 1917
Approx.Rev.: $37,000,000
Emp.: 345
Fiscal Year-end: 3/31/91
Chain & Wire Forms
S.I.C.: 3496
H. Andrew Thornburg *(Chm. Bd.)*
V. Lynn Graybill *(Pres.)*
Sheila Lind *(Sec.)*
Robert Deter *(Controller)*
Curt Mihm *(Mgr.-Human Resources)*
Gary Stenzel *(Mgr.-Pur.)*

PEERLESS CONFECTION COMPANY
1250 W. Schubert Ave.
Chicago, IL 60614
Tel.: 312-281-6100
Fax: 312-281-5812
Emp.: 120
Manufacture Hard Candy
S.I.C.: 2064
Robert F. Picken *(Chm. Bd. & Pres.)*
James E. Wilson *(V.P. & Treas.)*
F. Roger Curtis *(V.P.-Sls.)*
R.C. Lyman *(V.P.-Mngmt. Information Systems)*
John A. Kelly, Jr. *(Sec.)*
Stanley Mazurek *(Pur. Agent)*
Carl Holmberg *(Chief Engr.)*

Outside Service Firm(s):

Swanson, Ogilvie & McKenzie*(Auditors)*
Chicago, IL

Kelly, Olson, Rogan & Siepker*(Legal Firm)*
Chicago, IL

American National Bank*(Major Banking Relationship)*
33 North LaSalle St.
Chicago, IL 60690
Tel.: 312-661-6967

PEERLESS IMPORTERS, INC.
16 Bridgewater St.
Brooklyn, NY 11222
Tel.: 718-383-5500
Fax: 718-383-5500
Emp.: 900
Importer of Alcohol
S.I.C.: 5182
John Magliocco *(Chm. Bd. & Chief Exec. Officer)*
Terry Arlotta *(Chief Fin. Officer)*
Antonio Magliocco, Jr. *(Pres.)*
Joseph Magliocco *(V.P.)*
T. Bruno *(Gen. Mgr.-Sls.)*
E. Einseidler *(Gen. Mgr.-Sls.)*
Bob Lento *(Gen. Mgr.)*
Allen Paul *(Gen. Mgr.-Sls.)*
C. Silverstein *(Gen. Mgr.-Sls.)*
J. Deptulski *(Mgr.-Sls.)*
F. Ferrara *(Mgr.-Sls.)*
E. Sullivan *(Mgr.-Sls.)*
Mel Telsey *(Dir.-Sls. & Mktg.)*

Computer Systems/Hardware:
IBM

Outside Service Firm(s):

KPMG Peat Marwick*(Auditors)*
345 Park Ave.
New York, NY 10154
Tel.: 212-758-9700
Fax: 212-872-3308

Empire Blue Cross & Blue Shield*(Group Insurer)*
New York, NY

Chase Manhattan Bank, N.A.*(Major Banking Relationship)*
One Chase Manhattan Plaza
New York, NY 10081
Tel.: 212-552-2222
Tel.: 800-526-0801
Fax: 212-552-7175

Division:

Chatham Importers **(1)**
666 3rd Ave., 10th Fl.
New York, NY 10017
Tel.: 212-983-8427
S.I.C.: 5182

PEERLESS LIGHTING CORP.
2246 Fifth St.
Berkeley, CA 94710
Mailing Address:
P.O. Box 2556
Berkeley, CA 94702
Tel.: 510-845-2760
Fax: 510-845-2776
Year Founded: 1932
Approx.Sls.: $13,000,000
Emp.: 140

Import Export
Mfr. of Architectural Lighting Systems
S.I.C.: 3648
Douglas J. Herst *(Chm. Bd. & Pres.)*
Dick Kraber *(Chief Oper. Officer)*
Guy Esberg *(V.P.-Mktg.)*
Peter Ngai *(V.P.)*
Gary Owens *(Sec.)*
Donald L. Beeson *(Gen. Counsel)*
Joanne Schweibinz *(Mgr.-Mfg.)*

PEERLESS POTTERY, INC.
No. Lincoln Ave.
Rockport, IN 47635
Mailing Address:
P.O. Box 145
Rockport, IN 47635-0145
Tel.: 812-649-6430
Tel.: 800-457-5785
Fax: 812-649-6429
Year Founded: 1902
Approx.Sls.: $16,000,000
Emp.: 245

Export
Mfr. Vitreous China Plumbing Fixtures
S.I.C.: 3261
Charles S. Weaver *(Pres.)*
Thomas M. Broyles *(V.P.-Fin. & Corp. Sec.)*
Charles A. Porter *(V.P.-Sls. & Mktg.)*
R.W. Sears *(Pur. Agent)*

Outside Service Firm(s):

Umbach & Vowells*(Auditors)*
Evansville, IN

Johnson, Carroll & Griffith*(Legal Firm)*
Evansville, IN

One National Bank*(Major Banking Relationship)*
Evansville, IN

PEERLESS UMBRELLA CO., INC.
600 7th St.
Harrison, NJ 07029
Tel.: 201-485-4900
Fax: 201-485-5372
Year Founded: 1929
Emp.: 32
Manufacture Umbrellas
S.I.C.: 3999
Edwin Moscowitz *(Pres.)*
Gene Moscowitz *(V.P.)*

Computer Systems/Hardware:
IBM PC

Outside Service Firm(s):

Shubert, Silver & Rosen*(Auditors)*
New York, NY

Blue Cross of New Jersey*(Group Insurer)*
Newark, NJ

PEET PACKING CO. INC.
P.O. Box 187
Chesaning, MI 48616
Tel.: 517-845-3021
Fax: 517-845-7898
Year Founded: 1886
Approx.Sls.: $46,000,000
Emp.: 325
Food Processing, Packing & Distributing
S.I.C.: 2011

Computer Systems/Hardware:
IBM System 34

Outside Service Firm(s):

Pennsylvania General Insurance Co.*(Group Insurer)*
Philadelphia, PA

Old Kent Bank*(Major Banking Relationship)*
Detroit, MI

PEGASUS INTERNATIONAL CORPORATION
Straube Center, 114 W. Franklin Ave.
Pennington, NJ 08534
Tel.: 609-737-3538 **NJ**
Fax: 609-737-6829
Year Founded: 1951
Approx.Sls.: $21,000,000
Emp.: 25

Export
Steel Sheet, Strip, Bars, Pipe, Tubes; Brass & Bronze, Wire and Other Speciality Metals, Including Titanium, Pure Nickel & Nickel Alloys, Stainless Steels, Resistance Alloys, Be Cu, Etc.; Aerosol Valves & Components As Well As Branded or Private Label Aerosols (Not Personal Care) for the Industrial, Automotive, Hardware, DIY & Graphic Arts Markets; Car Wax; Computer & Electronic Equipment
S.I.C.: 3316; 3317; 3577; 3679; 5045; 5051; 5065; 7372; 8741; 8748
Win Straube *(Chm. Bd.)*
Dietrich von Riesen *(Vice Chm. & Chief Exec. Officer)*
J.D. Foote *(Pres.)*
Mary B. Deubler *(V.P. & Gen. Mgr.)*
Joan C. Borocz *(Mgr.-Export)*

No. of U.S. Offices: 1
No. of Foreign Offices: 3

Computer Systems/Hardware:
Apple, Macintosh

PEIRCE-PHELPS, INC.
2000 N. 59th St.
Philadelphia, PA 19131
Tel.: 215-879-7000 **DE**
Fax: 215-878-5252
Year Founded: 1926
Assets: $64,250,000
Liabilities: $38,250,000
Net Worth: $26,000,000
Approx.Sls.: $175,000,000
Emp.: 400
Fiscal Year-end: 12/31/91
Distribution of Consumer Electronics & Home Appliance Products; Communications & Telecon Fencing Systems
S.I.C.: 5064; 5074; 5075; 5065; 5045; 1731
R. Richard Dyer *(Chm. Bd.)*
Brian Peirce *(Pres. & Chief Exec. Officer)*
James M. Tholey *(Chief Oper. Officer, Chief Fin. Officer, & Treas.)*
Robert P. Subranni *(Controller)*
Ann P. Morris *(Sec.)*
Daniel Fogerty *(Dir.-Personnel & Employee Benefits)*
R. Shulman *(Dir.-Data Processing)*
Michael Wetmore *(Dir.-Mngmt. Information Systems)*
Principal(s):

Peirce-Phelps, Inc.—(Continued)

Brian Peirce
Ann P. Morris

No. of Mfg. Plants/Facilities: 2
No. of U.S. Offices: 9

Computer Systems/Hardware:
IBM 4381-22

Outside Service Firm(s):

Deloitte & Touche*(Auditors)*
1700 Market St.
Philadelphia, PA 19103
Tel.: 215-246-2322
Fax: 215-569-2441

Transamerica*(Commercial Insurance Carrier)*
Boston, MA

Canada Life Assurance*(Group Insurer)*
330 University Ave.
Toronto, ON Toronto, Canada

Pennsylvania Blue Shield*(Group Insurer)*
Camp Hill, PA

Dechert, Price & Rhoads*(Legal Firm)*
4000 Bell Atlantic Tower, 1717 Arch St.
Philadelphia, PA 19103
Tel.: 215-994-4000
Tel.: 2000

CoreStates Corporate Trust Services*(Major Banking Relationship)*
P.O. Box 7907,
Philadelphia, PA 19101
Tel.: 215-629-8400

CoreStates First Pennsylvania Bank, N.A.*(Major Banking Relationship)*
Center Sq. West Tower, 15th & Market Streets
Philadelphia, PA 19101

Meridian Bank*(Major Banking Relationship)*
Reading, PA

PNC Financial*(Major Banking Relationship)*
Philadelphia, PA

Vanguard Group*(Pension Manager)*
Vanguard Financial Ctr., P.O. Box 876
Valley Forge, PA 19482
Tel.: 215-648-6000
Fax: 215-648-6321

DAVID L. PEISTER CO., INC.
29 W. 38th St.
New York, NY 10018
Tel.: 212-764-6444
Fax: 212-730-6094
Sales Range: $10-19 Million
Emp.: 45
Dry Heat Transfers, Laces, Embroderies
S.I.C.: 2752; 2241; 2395
Alan Peister *(Pres.)*
Milton Peister *(Exec. V.P.)*

Outside Service Firm(s):

Friedman, Alpren & Green*(Auditors)*
New York, NY

National Westminster Bank plc*(Major Banking Relationship)*
Astor Plaza, 1515 Broadway
New York, NY 10036

PELICAN PRODUCTS
2255 Jefferson St.
Torrance, CA 90501
Tel.: 213-328-9910 **CA**
Fax: 213-533-8160
Year Founded: 1976
Sales Range: $10-19 Million
Emp.: 125
Fiscal Year-end: 10/31/88
Mfr. Sports & Marine Accessories
S.I.C.: 5091
David H. Parker *(Chm. Bd., Pres. & Chief Exec. Officer)*
Gerald F. Linehan *(Exec. V.P., Chief Fin. Officer)*
Arlene F. Parker *(Treas.)*

Outside Service Firm(s):

Republic Bank Inc.*(Major Banking Relationship)*
Torrance, CA

PELLA CORPORATION
(Formerly Pella/Rolscreen Company)
102 Main St.
Pella, IA 50219
Tel.: 515-628-1000
Telex: 47-8459
Fax: 515-628-6070
Year Founded: 1925
Approx.Sls.: $300,000,000
Emp.: 3,000
Import Export
Manufacture Wood Windows, Entry, Sliding & Folding Doors
S.I.C.: 2431; 3211; 3231
Joan Farver *(Co.-Chm. Bd.)*
Peter Kuiper *(Co.-Chm Bd.)*
J. Wayne Bevis *(Pres. & Chief Exec. Officer)*
Gary Christensen *(Sr. V.P.-Mktg. & Sls.)*
Hilliard Keeney *(Sr. V.P.-Opers.)*
Steve Bragg *(V.P.-Human Resources)*
Gene DeBoef *(V.P.-Engrng.)*
Mel Haught *(V.P.-Mfg.)*
Randy Iles *(V.P.-Mktg.)*
Herbert Gene Lienenbrugger *(V.P.-Fin.)*
William J. Anderson *(Sec. & Treas.)*

Computer Systems/Hardware:
Pella Designer

Outside Service Firm(s):

Arthur Andersen & Co.*(Auditors)*
33 W. Monroe St.
Chicago, IL 60603-4067
Tel.: 312-580-0033
Fax: 312-507-6748

Grefe & Sidney*(Legal Firm)*
Des Moines, IA

First Interstate Bank*(Major Banking Relationship)*
Locust at Sixth
Des Moines, IA 50304
Tel.: 515-245-7047
Fax: 515-245-7225

PELOUZE SCALE CO.
2120 Greenwood
Evanston, IL 60201
Tel.: 708-328-8330
Tel.: 800-654-8330
Tel.: 800-654-7330
Fax: 800-654-7330
Year Founded: 1894
Approx.Sls.: $15,000,000
Emp.: 50
Fiscal Year-end: 10/30/91
Import Export
Scales: Postal, Dairy, Dietetic, Photographic & Restaurant Portioning, Digital Computing Postal Scales
S.I.C.: 3596
Richard Hutner *(Pres.)*
Paul D. Nizzere *(V.P.-Sls. & Mktg.)*

PEMCO DIE CASTING CORPORATION
9864 Church St.
Bridgman, MI 49106
Tel.: 616-465-6000
Fax: 616-465-3721
Approx.Sls.: $20,000,000
Emp.: 158
Aluminum Die-Castings, Zinc & Zinc-Base Alloy; Special Dies, Tools, Jigs & Fixtures
S.I.C.: 3363; 3369; 3544
Terrence J. Allen *(Chm. Bd. & Pres.)*
William Baker *(V.P.)*
Thomas Diener *(V.P.)*
Harrison Lyons *(V.P.)*
Elizabeth Allen *(Sec.)*
Robert Jorgensen *(Pur. Agent)*

Outside Service Firm(s):

Vedder, Price, Kaufman & Kammholz*(Legal Firm)*
115 S. La Salle
Chicago, IL 60603
Tel.: 312-781-2200

National Bank of Detroit*(Major Banking Relationship)*
Benton Harbor, MI

PEMKO MANUFACTURING COMPANY
4226 Transport St.
Ventura, CA 93006
Tel.: 805-642-2600
Fax: 805-642-4109
Approx.Sls.: $20,000,000
Emp.: 160
Weatherstrip, Thresholds, Sills & Glazing Bead
S.I.C.: 3442
Paul F. Kops, Jr. *(Pres.)*
Vic Carpenter *(V.P.-Opers.-Memphis Branch)*
James C. Nonn *(Sec. & Treas.)*
Charles T. Kops *(Mgr.-Natl. Sls.)*
Mark Page *(Mgr.-Commercial Sls. Division)*

Outside Service Firm(s):

Joseph Lopez Accountancy Corp.*(Auditors)*
Walnut Creek, CA

Subsidiary:

Pemko Manufacturing **(1)**
5535 Distribution Dr.
Memphis, TN 38114
Tel.: 901-365-2160
Fax: 901-365-1354
Weatherstrip, Thresholds & Glazing Bead
S.I.C.: 3442
Vic Carpenter *(V.P.-Opers.)*
Steve Miller *(Asst. Mgr.-Opers.)*

PEN HOLDINGS, INC.
105 West Park Drive
Brentwood, TN 37027
Mailing Address:
P.O. Box 2248,
Brentwood, TN 37027-2248
Tel.: 615-370-9700 **DE**
Year Founded: 1988
Holding Company
S.I.C.: 6719; 3951
S. Dennis Thomas *(Vice Chm.)*
Charles Lieppe *(Pres. & Chief Exec. Officer)*
John A. Rynn *(V.P. & Treas.)*

Subsidiaries:

Berol Corporation **(1)**
105 West Park Drive
Brentwood, TN 370267
Tel.: 615-370-9700
Approx.Sls.: $235,000,000
Emp.: 2,700
Computer Systems/Hardware:
IBM Data General
Manufacture of Writing Instruments: Pen, Pencils, Markers; Artist Products; Drafting Products
S.I.C.: 3951; 3952; 3953
S. Denis Thomas *(Pres. & Chief Exec. Officer)*
Robert J. Spies *(Sr. V.P. & Chief Fin. Officer)*
Howard James *(V.P.-Mktg.)*
Ronald J. Bonelli *(V.P. & Corp. Controller)*
Keith A. McLusky *(V.P.-Intl. Opers.)*
John A. Rynn *(V.P. & Treas.)*
Anthony T. DelNegro *(V.P.-Human Resources)*
John E. Hassenfeld *(V.P.)*
Henry F. Skelsey *(V.P.)*
Robert D. Stillman *(V.P.)*
Christine J. Smith *(V.P. & Sec.)*

Empire Berol U.S.A. **(1)**
105 Westpark Dr.
Brentwood, TN 37027
Tel.: 615-371-1199
Fax: 615-684-9394
Sales Range: $20-39 Million
Emp.: 750
Fiscal Year-end: 12/31/91
Import Export
Computer Systems/Hardware:
IBM System 38 & AS/400
Manufactures, Imports & Sells a Broad Line of Pencils, Pens, School Supplies & Related Items; Under License for NFL, Disney, Snoopy, Garfield
S.I.C.: 3951; 3952
Patrick Fox *(V.P.-Fin.)*
David Clark *(V.P.-Mktg.)*
Emil Mongeon *(V.P.-Mass Market Sls.)*
Roger Thomas *(V.P.-Mfg.)*
Gary Hall *(V.P.-Human Resources)*
Bill Broslat *(Mgr.-Pkgng. Devel.)*
Fred Smith *(Opers. Mgr.-Materials & Logistics)*

Subsidiaries:

Blue Ribbon Pen & Pencil Co. **(2)**
Bourbon & Chambers St.
Georgetown, KY 40324
Tel.: 502-863-0954 (100%)
Mfr., Import & Sale of a Broad Line of Pencils, Pens, School Supplies & Related Items
S.I.C.: 3951; 3952
Sam Schapiro *(Pres.)*

Mallard Pen & Pencil Co. **(2)**
Bourbon & Chambers St.
Georgetown, KY 40324
Tel.: 502-863-0954 (100%)
Mfr., Import & Sale of a Broad Line of Pencils, Pens, School Supplies & Related Items
S.I.C.: 3951; 3952
Ian Ward *(Pres.)*

PEN-TAB INDUSTRIES, INC.
63-15 Traffic St.
Glendale, NY 11385
Tel.: 718-386-9000
Tel.: 800-221-0455
Fax: 718-821-9285
Approx.Sls.: $100,000,000
Emp.: 550
Export
Mfr. of Paper School Supplies & Stationery Products
S.I.C.: 2678; 2679
Alan Hodes *(Chm. Bd. & Pres.)*
William Leary *(Chief Exec. Officer & V.P.)*
James Diorio *(V.P.)*
Wayne Finholt *(V.P.)*
William C. McIlvain, Jr. *(Dir.-Opers.)*
Jim Arrollado *(Natl. Sls. Mgr.)*
Joseph Naugle *(Mgr.-Communication Products)*

Principal(s):
Alan Hodes

No. of Mfg. Plants/Facilities: 3
No. of U.S. Offices: 3

Outside Service Firm(s):

Ernst & Young*(Auditors)*
787 Seventh Ave.
New York, NY 10019
Tel.: 212-773-1243

Kemper Insurance*(Group Insurer)*
Long Grove, IL 60049-0001

Herzfeld & Rubin*(Legal Firm)*
40 Wall St.
New York, NY 10005
Tel.: 212-344-0680

Continental Bank N. A.*(Major Banking Relationship)*
231 S. LaSalle St.
Chicago, IL 60697
Tel.: 312-828-2345
Tel.: 800-426-5754
Telex: 312-828-1783

Division:

Vinylweld Division **(1)**
2011 W. Hastings
Chicago, IL 60608
Tel.: 312-243-0606
Tel.: 800-444-4020
Tape Cassette Holders
S.I.C.: 5099
Michael Greenberg *(Exec. V.P.)*
Tom Topmiller *(Controller)*

Subsidiary:

Pen-Tab Industries Of California, Inc. **(1)**
911 Bixby Dr.
City of Industry, CA 91747
Tel.: 818-961-7231
Tel.: 800-777-6276
Mfr. of Paper School Supplies & Stationery Products
S.I.C.: 2678; 2679

PENCO PRODUCTS
Brower Ave.
Oaks, PA 19456
Tel.: 215-666-0500
Fax: 215-666-7561
Approx.Sls.: $40,000,000
Emp.: 350
Fabricated Metal Products, Including Steel Lockers, Shelving, Shop Equipment, Cabinets, Storage Racks
S.I.C.: 2542
Arthur M. Muti *(Pres.)*
Howard Easton *(Dir.-Personnel)*
William H. Epp *(Mgr.-Mktg. & Sls.)*
Philip Krugler *(Mgr.-Mktg. Services)*
Allan J. Goss *(Pur. Agent)*

PENDA CORPORATION
N7660 Industrial Rd.
Portage, WI 53901
Mailing Address:
P.O. Box 449
Portage, WI 53901
Tel.: 608-742-5301
Fax: 608-742-9153
Year Founded: 1975
Sales Range: $80-99 Million
Emp.: 700
Export
Plastics Processor
S.I.C.: 3089; 5162
Dennis Markos *(Chief Exec. Officer)*
William Dresen *(Pres.)*
C. Martin Gavinski *(Chief Fin. Officer)*
Harlon Breezer *(V.P.- Custom Sls.)*
Jon Kuse *(V.P.-Matls. Mngmt.)*
George Thornton *(V.P.-Oper.)*
Peter Welsh *(V.P.-Corp. Devel.)*
Tom Tessman *(Controllor)*
Dan Brown *(Gen. Mgr.-Proprietary Prod.)*
Pam Barreau *(Mgr.-Data Proc.)*
Tom Drury *(Dir.-Human Resources)*
Principal(s):
Dennis Markos
William Dresen
C. Martin Gavinski

No. of Mfg. Plants/Facilities: 2
No. of U.S. Offices: 1

PENDLETON WOOLEN MILLS, INC.
220 N.W. Broadway
Portland, OR 97209
Mailing Address:
P.O. Box 3030
Portland, OR 97208
Tel.: 503-226-4801
Fax: 503-273-2599
Year Founded: 1909
Sales Range: $100-499 Million
Emp.: 2,500
Textile Mill Products; Apparel & Other Textile Products; Apparel & Accessory Stores
S.I.C.: 2231; 2329; 2339; 5699
B.H. Bishop *(Chm. Bd. & Co-Chief Exec. Officer)*
C.M. Bishop, Jr. *(Pres. & Co-Chief Exec. Officer)*
R.E. Poth *(Corp. V.P.)*
Robert Mathis *(Controller)*
D.A. Anderson *(Dir.-Mngmt. Information Systems)*
C.M. Bishop III *(Mgr.-Women's Mdse.)*
Gary Benson *(Mgr.-Personnel)*
Patti McGrath *(Mgr.-Adv.-Men's Wear)*
P.L. McKevitt *(Mgr.-Adv.-Women's Wear)*
W.A. Shoen *(Mgr.-Sls.-Men's Wear)*
Jon Stein *(Mgr. Sls.-Women's Wear)*
Principal(s):
B.H. Bishop
C.M. Bishop, Jr.

Computer Systems/Hardware:
IBM System 4381

Outside Service Firm(s):

Price Waterhouse*(Auditors)*
1221 S.W. Morrison, Suite 1800
Portland, OR 97204
Tel.: 503-224-9040

U.S. National Bank*(Major Banking Relationship)*
309 S.W. Sixth Ave.
Portland, OR 97208
Tel.: 503-275-4942

Columbia Mngmt. Co.*(Pension Manager)*
1300 S.W. Sixth Ave.
Portland, OR 97207
Tel.: 503-222-3600

PENGUIN INDUSTRIES, INC.
Airport Industrial Mall
Coatesville, PA 19320
Tel.: 215-384-6000
Fax: 215-857-5980
Approx.Sls.: $20,000,000
Emp.: 180
Fiscal Year-end: 12/31/90
Hoppe's Gun Care Prods., Shooting Access., Decorative Hangers, Protecto Gun Cases
S.I.C.: 3949
Robert D. McNeil *(Pres.)*

Division:

Protecto Plastics, Inc. **(1)**
201 Alpha Rd.
Wind Gap, PA 18091
Tel.: 215-863-6008
S.I.C.: 3949

PENHALL INTERNATIONAL
1801 Penhall Way
Anaheim, CA 92803
Tel.: 714-778-6677
Fax: 714-778-8437
Year Founded: 1958
Assets: $22,000,000
Liabilities: $6,000,000
Net Worth: $16,000,000
Approx.Sls.: $65,000,000
Emp.: 450
Fiscal Year-end: 6/30/91
Holding Company; Concrete Cutting, Sawing, Breaking & Removal
S.I.C.: 6719; 1795
Roger Stull *(Chm. Bd. & Pres.)*
Charles Steichem *(V.P. & Chief Fin. Officer)*

No. of U.S. Offices: 11

Outside Service Firm(s):

Moss Adams & Co.*(Auditors)*
Costa Mesa, CA

Bank of America NT&SA*(Major Banking Relationship)*
Anaheim, CA

Subsidiaries:

Penhall Co., Inc. **(1)**
P.O. Box 4609
Anaheim, CA 92803
Tel.: 714-778-6677
S.I.C.: 1795
John Sawyer *(Pres.)*

Phoenix Concrete Cutting **(1)**
3639 E. Superior Ave.
Phoenix, AZ 85040
Tel.: 602-967-5029
S.I.C.: 1795
George Bush *(Pres.)*

PENN COLOUR GRAPHICS, INC.
99 Buck Rd.
Huntingdon Valley, PA 19006 **PA**
Tel.: 215-364-4000
Fax: 215-364-2596
Approx.Sls.: $12,000,000
Emp.: 150
Photo Engraving
S.I.C.: 2796
John E. Carickhoff, Jr. *(Chm. Bd.)*
James M. Brennan *(Pres.)*
Theodore A. Oliveri *(Sec. & Treas.)*

Outside Service Firm(s):

Stockton, Bates & Co.*(Auditors)*
Philadelphia, PA

German, Gallagher & Murtaugh*(Legal Firm)*
Philadelphia, PA

Provident National Bank*(Major Banking Relationship)*
Broad & Chestnut Sts.
Philadelphia, PA 19101
Tel.: 215-585-5000

PENN-DANIELS, INC.
505 N. 24th St.
Quincy, IL 62301
Tel.: 217-224-2474 **DE**
Fax: 217-224-6621
Year Founded: 1962
Sales Range: $100-499 Million
Emp.: 1,950
Fiscal Year-end: 1/31/92
Retail General Merchandise
S.I.C.: 5399
William D. Daniels *(Chm. Bd. & Chief Exec. Officer)*
David P. Daniels *(Pres. & Chief Oper. Officer)*
Rob Armitage *(V.P.-Human Resources)*
Ken Ehli *(V.P.-Opers.)*
Richard A. Mettemeyer *(V.P.-Fin.)*
Joe De Angelo *(Dir.-Adv.)*
Ken Forman *(Dir.-Mngmt. Information Systems)*
David T. Steele *(Dir.-Real Estate & Construction)*
Denise Swink *(Dir.-Employee Benefits)*
Bill Wagner *(Dir.-Sls. Promo.)*
Principal(s):
William D. Daniels
David P. Daniels
Jane Daniels

No. of Mfg. Plants/Facilities: 17

Computer Systems/Hardware:
IBM AS400

Outside Service Firm(s):

Arthur Andersen & Co.*(Auditors)*
1010 Market St.
St. Louis, MO 63101

C.J. Thomas Company*(Commercial Insurance Carrier)*
St. Louis, MO

Lewis, Rice & Fingersh*(Legal Firm)*
611 Olive St.
St. Louis, MO 63101

Boatmen's Bank of Quincy*(Major Banking Relationship)*
Sixth & Hampshire
Quincy, IL 62301
Tel.: 217-228-6200

PENN EMBLEM CO.
10909 Dutton Rd.
Philadelphia, PA 19154
Tel.: 215-632-7800
Fax: 215-632-6166
Approx.Sls.: $20,000,000
Emp.: 500
Fiscal Year-end: 12/31/91
Designer & Manufacturer of Embroidered Emblems, Penn Text Printed Industrial Emblems, Penn Seal Identification Tapes for Industrial Launderies, Linen Supply Rental & Hospitals
S.I.C.: 2395; 2399
Robert Blumenthal *(Pres. & Chief Exec. Officer)*
Aaron Bitman *(Sr. V.P.)*
Frank Colgan *(V.P.-Admin. & Chief Fin. Officer)*

Divisions:

Penn Emblem Co. **(1)**
2428 E. 56th St.
Los Angeles, CA 90058
S.I.C.: 2395

Penn Emblem Co. **(1)**
P.O. Box 1157
Saint Charles, MO 63302
Tel.: 314-441-9940
S.I.C.: 2395

Outside Service Firm(s):

KPMG Peat Marwick*(Auditors)*
Wayne, PA

Kleinbard, Bell & Brecker*(Legal Firm)*
30 S. 17th St.
Philadelphia, PA 19103
Tel.: 215-568-2000

Philadelphia National Bank*(Major Banking Relationship)*
P.O. Box 13834, Broad & Chestnut Streets
Philadelphia, PA 19101-7618
Tel.: 215-973-8327

H.O. PENN MACHINERY CO. INC.
100 Business Park Dr.
Armonk, NY 10504
Tel.: 914-273-9800
Fax: 914-273-4147
Year Founded: 1923
Approx.Sls.: $130,000,000
Emp.: 380
Fiscal Year-end: 12/31/91
Mfr. Earth Moving & Material Handling Equipment: Diesel Engines, Tractors & Fork Lift Trucks
S.I.C.: 5082; 5084
Corporate Giving Program: United Way
C.E. Thomas Cleveland *(Pres.)*
Alfred Hahnfeldt *(V.P. & Treas.)*
Sylvia Stone *(Controller)*
Janice Gilligan *(Dir.-Personnel)*
Justi Rynders *(Dir.-Cash Mngmt.)*
Sally O'Hara *(Mgr.-Data Processing)*

Computer Systems/Hardware:
Vax System

Outside Service Firm(s):

David Tarlow*(Auditors)*
New York, NY

Empire Blue Cross & Blue Shield*(Group Insurer)*
New York, NY

H.O. Penn Machinery Co. Inc.—(Continued)

Citibank N.A.*(Major Banking Relationship)*
Corporate Trust Services, 399 Park Ave.
New York, NY 10043
Tel.: 212-559-1605

CIGNA*(Pension Manager)*
Hartford, CT
Tel.: 203-726-6000

THE PENN MUTUAL LIFE INSURANCE COMPANY
Independence Square, 530 Walnut St.
Philadelphia, PA 19172
Tel.: 215-956-8000 **PA**
Fax: 215-625-5661
Approx.Sls.: $834,000,000
Emp.: 3,000
Fiscal Year-end: 12/31/90
Life, Disability, Annuities, Pensions & Profit Sharing Insurance
S.I.C.: 6311
John E. Tait *(Chm. Bd., Pres. & Chief Exec. Officer)*
Thomas E. Stiles *(Exec. V.P. & Chief Fin. Officer)*
Donna D. Holton *(Sr. V.P.)*
Joseph J. Horvath *(Sr. V.P., Gen. Counsel & Sec.)*
Gerald J. Oyen *(V.P.-Acquisitions & Sr. Actuary)*

Computer Systems/Hardware:
IBM Systems 3081K & 4381; Amdahl System 470/B8

Outside Service Firm(s):

Coopers & Lybrand*(Auditors)*
2400 Eleven Penn Center
Philadelphia, PA 19103-2962
Tel.: 215-963-8000

Marsh & McLennan*(Commercial Insurance Carrier)*
3 Parkway
Philadelphia, PA 19102
Tel.: 215-963-2800

Dechert, Price & Rhoads*(Legal Firm)*
4000 Bell Atlantic Tower, 1717 Arch St.
Philadelphia, PA 19103
Tel.: 215-994-4000
Tel.: 2000

Subsidiaries:

Independence Square Properties **(1)**
Independence Square
Philadelphia, PA 19172
Tel.: 215-625-5000 (100%)
Insurance Buildings
S.I.C.: 6512

Janney Montgomery Scott Inc. **(1)**
1801 Market St.
Philadelphia, PA 19103
Tel.: 215-665-6000 (100%)
Investments
S.I.C.: 6211
Norman T. Wilde, Jr. *(Pres.)*
William L. Rulon-Miller *(First V.P.)*

Penn Insurance & Annuity Co. **(1)**
Independence Square
Philadelphia, PA 19172
Tel.: 215-625-6400 (100%)
Life Insurance
S.I.C.: 6311

Penn Mutual Equity Services Inc. **(1)**
1801 Market St.
Philadelphia, PA 19103
Tel.: 215-557-7700 (100%)
Insurance
S.I.C.: 6411
Vincent T. Cloud *(Pres. & Chief Exec. Officer)*

PENNEX PRODUCTS CO., INC.
One Pennex Dr.
Verona, PA 15147-3998
Tel.: 412-828-2900
Tel.: 800-245-6110 **PA**
Fax: 412-826-4720
Year Founded: 1934
Approx.Sls.: $90,000,000
Emp.: 265
Export
Mfr. of OTC Pharmaceuticals & Health & Beauty Aids
S.I.C.: 2834; 2844
William P. Lyons *(Chm. Bd.)*
Jack Van Hulst *(Pres. & Chief Exec. Officer)*
E.T. Betush, Jr. *(V.P.-Sls. & Mktg.)*
Dan M. Bryson *(V.P.-Fin.)*
A. Gallagher *(V.P.-Human Resources)*
Robert Pilson *(V.P.-Compliance)*
Hank Rosen *(V.P.-Opers.)*
Richard DeCecco *(Controller)*
Charlotte Brooks *(Dir.-Mngmt. Information Systems)*
Gregory Meinert *(Mgr.-Production/ Facilities)*
Principal(s):
William P. Lyons
Jack Van Hulst

No. of Mfg. Plants/Facilities: 2

Computer Systems/Hardware:
IBM PC's

PENNINSULAR MEAT COMPANY, INC.
4401 N. Westshore Blvd.
Tampa, FL 33614
Tel.: 813-879-2551
Fax: 813-879-3720
Year Founded: 1955
Approx.Sls.: $34,000,000
Emp.: 8
Wholesale Fresh & Frozen Meat
S.I.C.: 5147
Bernell Dale Gardner *(Chm. Bd.)*
Jean Gardner *(Pres.)*
Jacquelyn G. Marcus *(V.P.)*

Outside Service Firm(s):

CNS Bank*(Major Banking Relationship)*
Tampa, FL

PENNOCK
3027 Stokely Av.
Philadelphia, PA 19129
Tel.: 215-844-6600
Fax: 215-959-6498
Approx.Sls.: $200,000,000
Emp.: 600
Wholesale Trade-Nondurable Goods
S.I.C.: 5199
John A. Bauer, Jr. *(Chm. Bd.)*
Wayne Collins *(Pres. & Chief Exec. Officer)*
Harold Hartsig *(V.P. & Treas.)*
Domenick R. Sciole *(Controller)*
Jim Falvey *(Sec.)*
Tom Logue *(Mgr.)*

PENNSYLVANIA CRUSHER CORP.
600 Abbott Dr.
Broomall, PA 19008
Mailing Address:
P.O. Box 100
Broomall, PA 19008
Tel.: 215-544-7200 **PA**
Fax: 215-543-0190
Year Founded: 1905
Approx.Sls.: $17,000,000
Emp.: 95
Import Export
Design, Manufacturer, & Sale of Crushers, Parts & Service to Utility, Steel, Cement, Quarrying, Glass & General Materials Reduction Markets
S.I.C.: 3532; 3559
John D. Whalen *(Pres. & Chief Exec. Officer)*
Donald J. Carrozzino *(V.P.-Fin. & Treas.)*
Lee F. Doyer *(V.P.-Mktg.)*
Nancy S. Hansen *(V.P.-Admin. & Sec.)*
Bernard H. Schonbach *(V.P.-Engrng.)*
Frank Wallitsch *(V.P.-Mfg.)*
Herman L. Powers *(Mgr.-Pur.)*

No. of Mfg. Plants/Facilities: 1
No. of U.S. Offices: 1

Computer Systems/Hardware:
IBM System 38

Outside Service Firm(s):

Arthur Andersen & Co.*(Auditors)*
1601 Market St.
Philadelphia, PA 19103
Tel.: 215-241-7300

Sedgwick James*(Group Insurer)*
Public Ledger Bldg., 6 & Chestnut Sts.
Philadelphia, PA 19106

CoreStates First Pennsylvania Bank, N.A.*(Investment Banker)*
Center Sq. West Tower, 15th & Market Streets
Philadelphia, PA 19101

Pepper, Hamilton & Scheetz*(Legal Firm)*
123 S. Broad
Philadelphia, PA 19109
Tel.: 215-893-3000

CoreStates First Pennsylvania Bank, N.A.*(Major Banking Relationship)*
Center Sq. West Tower, 15th & Market Streets
Philadelphia, PA 19101

PENNSYLVANIA PETROLEUM PRODUCT COMPANY
1330 Industrial Hwy.
Southhampton, PA 18966
Tel.: 215-322-8510
Fax: 215-322-9484
Sales Range: $10-19 Million
Emp.: 49
Mfr. of Lubricating Oils & Additives
S.I.C.: 2992
Marc H. Steinberg *(Pres.)*
D.D. Barney *(Controller)*
J. Earl Epstein *(Sec.)*
J. Murland *(Pur. Agent)*

Outside Service Firm(s):

Morris J. Cohen & Co.*(Auditors)*
Philadelphia, PA

Epstein, Shapiro & Epstein*(Legal Firm)*
Philadelphia, PA

Meridian Bank*(Major Banking Relationship)*
One Meridian Plaza, 36th Fl.
Philadelphia, PA
Tel.: 215-854-3900

PENNSYLVANIA STATE LOTTERY
2850 Turnpike Industrial Dr., Bldg. #5
Middletown, PA 17057
Tel.: 717-787-2718
Tel.: 800-545-9467
Fax: 717-986-4767
Year Founded: 1973
Approx.Sls.: $1,567,000,000
Emp.: 187
Fiscal Year-end: 6/30/91
Lottery Sales (Tickets & Games)
S.I.C.: 7999
Conrad Stauffer *(Exec. Dir.)*
Ronald Fertal *(Security Dir.)*
Edward Bell *(Mktg. Dir.)*
Mark Schreiber *(Pub. Rels. Dir.)*
Judy Tyler *(Instant Game Controller)*
Michael Keyser *(On-Line Game Controller)*
Kim Troutman *(Pur. Agent)*

PENNY/OHLMANN/NEIMAN, INC.
1605 N. Main St.
Dayton, OH 45405
Tel.: 513-278-0681 **OH**
Fax: 513-277-1723
Year Founded: 1949
Approx.Billings: $20,054,000
Emp.: 35
Advertising Agency
S.I.C.: 7311
Robert L. Penny *(Chm. Bd.)*
Walter Ohlmann *(Pres. & Chief Exec. Officer)*
Rick Hamer *(Sr. V.P.- Fin.)*
Bruce Geiger *(V.P.)*
Dennis Nickell *(Dir.- Pub. Rels.)*

Computer Systems/Hardware:
NCR Tower, IBM

Outside Service Firm(s):

Roth & Co.*(Auditors)*
Dayton, OH

Altick & Corwin*(Legal Firm)*
Dayton, OH

First National Bank of Dayton*(Major Banking Relationship)*
1 First National Plaza
Dayton, OH 45402
Tel.: 513-226-2000

Subsidiaries:

P/O/N Product Corp. **(1)**
1605 N. Main
Dayton, OH 45405
Tel.: 513-278-0681
S.I.C.: 2741

P/O/N Service Corp. **(1)**
1605 N. Main St.
Dayton, OH 45405
Tel.: 513-278-0681
S.I.C.: 7311

PENNY PLATE, INC.
603 Kressan Rd.
Cherry Hill, NJ 08034
Mailing Address:
P.O. Box 3003
Cherry Hill, NJ 08034
Tel.: 609-429-7583
Fax: 609-429-7166
Approx.Sls.: $10,000,000
Emp.: 150
Mfr. of Aluminum Containers
S.I.C.: 3497
Helen Buff *(Pres.)*
George Buff, III *(Exec. V.P.)*
John Charles Buff *(V.P.)*
John J. Dillenschneider *(Treas.)*

Outside Service Firm(s):

Philadelphia National Bank*(Major Banking Relationship)*
5th & Market Sts.
Philadelphia, PA 19101
Tel.: 215-629-3100
Fax: 215-834-2069

PENNY & SPEIER INC.
1800 W. Loop South, Ste. 400
Houston, TX 77027
Tel.: 713-965-0331
Fax: 713-961-4128
Year Founded: 1953
Approx.Billings: $18,000,000
Emp.: 24
Dick Penny *(Chm. & Chief Exec. Officer)*
Stephen Speier *(Pres. & Chief Oper. Officer)*
Charles Lutz *(Sr. V.P., Chief Mktg. Officer)*
Shirley Nicola *(Sec., Treas. & Office Mgr.)*

PENOBSCOT FROZEN FOODS, INC.
One Pierce St.
Belfast, ME 04915
Tel.: 207-338-4360
Fax: 207-338-5742
Approx.Sls.: $10,000,000
Emp.: 200
Frozen Potato Skins, Baked Stuffed Potatos & Jo-Jo Potatoes
S.I.C.: 2037; 2038
Frederick D. Starrett, III *(Pres., Treas., Sls. & Mktg.)*
Robert Stansfield *(Mgr.-Materials)*
Ada L. Gordon *(Sec.)*
Dwight Patten *(Mgr.-Prod. & Chief Engr.)*

Outside Service Firm(s):

Haverlock, Estey & Curran*(Auditors)*
Bangor, ME

Eaton, Glass, Marsano & Woodward*(Legal Firm)*
Belfast, ME

Key Bank*(Major Banking Relationship)*
Augusta, ME

PENROD DRILLING CORPORATION
2100 Thanksgiving Tower,
1601 Elm Street
Dallas, TX 75201
Tel.: 214-880-1700
Fax: 214-880-1787
Year Founded: 1935
Emp.: 1,700
Oil & Gas Drilling Contractors
S.I.C.: 1381
Marshall Ballard *(Pres.)*
Gary James *(V.P.-Operations)*
J.M. Rowley *(V.P.-Contracts & Mktg.)*
Robert Isaac *(Sec. & Gen. Counsel)*
Richard Brown *(Mgr.-Safety & Environmental Compliance)*
Donald Gaddy *(Mgr.-Engineering)*
Shane Lein *(Mgr.-Pur. & Materials)*
Louis Mullenix *(Mgr.-Personnel)*
John Nilson *(Mgr.-Mktg.)*
Michael Wiley *(Mgr.-Admin.)*
Malinda Wineinger *(Mgr.-Cash)*
Buck Woods *(Mgr.-Mngmt. Information Systems)*

Computer Systems/Hardware:
IBM System 3683

Outside Service Firm(s):

KPMG Peat Marwick*(Auditors)*
1601 Elm St., Ste. 1600
Dallas, TX 75201
Tel.: 214-754-2000
Fax: 214-754-2297

Consolidated Medical Life Trust*(Group Insurer)*
Dallas, TX

Shank, Irwin & Conant*(Legal Firm)*
Dallas, TX

Chemical Bank*(Major Banking Relationship)*
450 West 33rd St.
New York, NY 10001
Tel.: 212-613-7197
Fax: 212-947-7628

First City National Bank*(Major Banking Relationship)*
Dallas, TX

Subsidiary:

Penrod International Drilling Company **(1)**
Denhelder, Netherlands
Tel.: 31 2550 33144 (100%)
Telex: 844-41379
Fax: 312230-37946
International Drilling Services
S.I.C.: 1381
Robert Bujol *(Dist. Mgr.)*

Non-U.S. Holdings:

Penrod Drilling Corporation (UK) **(1)**
Main Cross Road
Great Yarmouth, Norfolk NR30 3PD, United Kingdom
Tel.: 493-853346
Telex: 851 975468
Fax: 493 853086
Emp.: 192
International Drilling Services
S.I.C.: 1381
Raymond Huffman *(Mgr.-North Sea)*

Penrod International Drilling Company **(1)**
P.O. Box 1055, 8 Dagli St., 2nd Fl.,
Kavala, Greece
Tel.: 51 836 839 (100%)
Telex: 863 452173
International Drilling Services
S.I.C.: 1381
Manos Kouteranis *(Mgr.)*

PENSKE CORPORATION
13400 Outer Dr. W.
Detroit, MI 48239
Tel.: 313-592-7410 **PA**
Fax: 313-592-5256
Approx.Sls.: $2,800,000,000
Emp.: 10,000
Fiscal Year-end: 12/31/91
Diesel Manufacturing; Truck Leasing; Auto Dealerships
S.I.C.: 3519; 5511; 7513
Roger S. Penske *(Pres.)*
Walter P. Czarnecki *(Exec. V.P.)*
Norman H. Ahn *(V.P.)*
Lawrence Bluth *(V.P.- Sec. & Gen. Counsel)*
Robert Carter *(V.P.-Personnel)*
Solomon Cohen *(V.P.)*
Ursel T. Dougherty *(V.P.-Bus. Devel.)*
Dan R. Luginbuhl *(V.P.- Communications)*
John C. McGinley *(V.P.-Corp. Security)*
Richard J. Peters *(V.P. & Treas.)*
James H. Harris *(Controller)*

Computer Systems/Hardware:
IBM

Outside Service Firm(s):

Deloitte & Touche*(Auditors)*
1700 Market St.
Philadelphia, PA 19103
Tel.: 215-246-2322
Fax: 215-569-2441

Drinker, Biddle & Reath*(Legal Firm)*
1000 Westlakes Dr., Ste. 300
Berwyn, PA 19312
Tel.: 215-993-2200
Fax: 215-993-8585

Subsidiaries:

Detroit Diesel Corp. **(1)**
13400 W. Outer Dr.
Detroit, MI 48239
Tel.: 313-592-5000 (100%)
Emp.: 3,200
Export
Diesel Engines
S.I.C.: 3519
Roger S. Penske *(Chm. & Chief Exec. Officer)*
Ludvik F. Koci *(Pres. & Chief Oper. Officer)*
Robert R. Allran *(Sr. V.P.-Opers.)*
Lee Grubb *(Sr. V.P.-Fin.)*
David Merrion *(Sr. V.P.-Engrng.)*
Paul Walters *(Sr. V.P.-Admin.)*
Charles Yount *(Mgr.-Adv. & Promo.)*

Penske Transportation Inc. **(1)**
Rte. 10, Green Hills
Reading, PA 19603
Tel.: 215-775-6000
S.I.C.: 7513
Roger Penske *(Pres.)*

Subsidiary:

Penske Truck Leasing Corp. **(2)**
P.O. Box 563, Rte. 10
Reading, PA 19603
Tel.: 215-775-6000
Truck Leasing
S.I.C.: 7513; 4213
Roger Penske *(Chm. Bd.)*
Brian Hard *(Pres.)*
Sue Surrey *(V.P.-Admin.)*

Penske Truck Leasing **(1)**
14528 South Outer 40
Chesterfield, MO 63017
Tel.: 314-576-4848 (100%)
Approx.Sls.: $207,762,000
Emp.: 1,770
Full Service Maintenance Leasing of Trucks & Truck Tractors
S.I.C.: 7513
Ormond B. Kinney *(Pres. & Chief Exec. Officer)*
John Campbell *(Sr. V.P.)*
Edward V. Burns *(V.P.-Human Resources)*
Lin Dawson *(V.P.)*
Larry R. Dusenberry *(V.P.-Info. Systems)*
Ralph M. Lepak *(V.P.)*
Ronald L. Meinhardt *(V.P. & Chief Fin. Officer)*
George C. Neely *(V.P.)*
Paul E. Prang *(V.P.)*
Roger A. Rash *(V.P.-Maintenance)*
George Seely *(V.P.)*
Charles L. Tyrrell *(V.P.-Special Services)*
Alexander M. Urbani *(V.P.-Sls. & Mktg.)*
Thomas D. Vaughn *(V.P. & Gen. Counsel)*

Penske Truck Leasing **(1)**
1500 So. Greenwood Ave.
Montebello, CA 90640
Tel.: 213-724-4494
Truck & Trailer Leasing
S.I.C.: 7513
O. B. Kinney *(Pres.)*

Penske Truck Leasing **(1)**
6100 W. 65th St.
Little Rock, AR 72209
Tel.: 501-562-3744
Truck & Trailer Leasing
S.I.C.: 7513
O. B. Kinney *(Pres.)*

PENTAX PRECISION INSTRUMENTS CORP.
30 Ramland Rd.
Orangeburg, NY 10962-2699
Tel.: 914-365-0700
Telex: 910-240-6953
Fax: 914-365-0822
Emp.: 130
Fiscal Year-end: 3/31/92
Mfr. Endoscopes
S.I.C.: 3841
Ko Shirahata *(Pres.)*
Paul McGrath *(V.P.-Fin. & Admin.)*
Marc Pierce *(V.P.-Sls. & Mktg.)*
Kenji Takashima *(V.P., Sec., & Treas.)*
Susan K. Maxwell *(Dir.-Mktg.)*
Bette Francis *(Mgr.-Opers.)*
Keith Nelson *(Mgr.-Products)*

Computer Systems/Hardware:
DEC MicroVAX

Outside Service Firm(s):

Empire Blue Cross & Blue Shield*(Group Insurer)*
New York, NY

PEOPLES ELECTRIC COMPANY, INC.
277 E. Fillmore Ave.
Saint Paul, MN 55107
Tel.: 612-227-7711 **MN**
Fax: 612-227-9684
Year Founded: 1921
Approx.Sls.: $21,000,000
Emp.: 160
Import Export
Electrical Contractor
S.I.C.: 1731
Neal R. Lindberg *(Pres.)*
Phillip J. Scheidnes *(V.P.)*
Dennis Sorheim *(Sec. & Treas.)*

Outside Service Firm(s):

Steven DeWald*(Auditors)*
Maplewood, MN

Briggs & Morgan*(Legal Firm)*
Minneapolis, MN

First Bank Minneapolis*(Major Banking Relationship)*
120 S. Sixth St.
Minneapolis, MN 55480
Tel.: 612-370-4141

HARRY PEPPER & ASSOCIATES
119 W. 8th St.
Jacksonville, FL 32206
Tel.: 904-356-3954 **FL**
Fax: 904-355-0804
Year Founded: 1945
Approx.Sls.: $21,000,000
Emp.: 100
New Construction of Industrial Buildings
S.I.C.: 1541; 1629
Harry C. Pepper, Jr. *(Chm. Bd.)*
David Pepper *(Pres.)*
H. Cuy Broome, Jr. *(Exec. V.P.)*
Martha Pepper *(Sec.)*

Outside Service Firm(s):

Phillip Weinstein*(Legal Firm)*
Miami, FL

First Union National Bank*(Major Banking Relationship)*
P.O. Box 2565,
Jacksonville, FL 32203

THE PEPPER COMPANIES, INC.
643 N. Orleans St.
Chicago, IL 60610
Tel.: 312-266-4703 **DE**
Fax: 312-266-6010
Year Founded: 1927
Assets: $141,000,000
Earnings: $5,200,000
Liabilities: $91,000,000
Net Worth: $50,000,000
Approx.Sls.: $310,000,000
Emp.: 800
Fiscal Year-end: 9/30/92
General Contractor & Construction Manager
S.I.C.: 1541; 1542
J. Stanley Pepper *(Pres.)*
Richard S. Pepper *(Chief Exec. Officer)*
Thomas M. O'Leary *(Chief Fin. Officer & Gen Counsel)*
Bharat Gandhi *(Sr. V.P.)*
John H. Beasley *(V.P.-Personnel)*
Gordon B. Marshall *(V.P.-Fin. & Treas.)*
Joel Thomason *(Controller)*
J. David Pepper *(Sec.)*
Principal(s):
Richard S. Pepper

No. of U.S. Offices: 4

Computer Systems/Hardware:
IBM System 38, PE/2

Outside Service Firm(s):

Deloitte & Touche*(Auditors)*
Two Prudential Plaza, 180 N. Stetson
Chicago, IL 60601
Tel.: 312-946-2039

Artex Insurance Agency, Inc.*(Commercial Insurance Carrier)*
12222 Merit Drive, Suite 1660
Dallas, TX 75251

St. Paul/Seaboard Surety*(Group Insurer)*
Chicago, IL

First National Bank of Chicago*(Major Banking Relationship)*
One First National Plaza
Chicago, IL 60670
Tel.: 312-732-9781
Tel.: 312-732-4050
Fax: 312-732-4840
Fax: 312-732-3055

The Pepper Companies, Inc.—(Continued)

Harris Trust & Savings Bank*(Major Banking Relationship)*
111 W. Monroe St.
Chicago, IL 60690
Tel.: 312-461-2265
Tel.: 800-858-0840

Subsidiaries:

Pepper Construction Co. **(1)**
643 N. Orleans St.
Chicago, IL 60610
Tel.: 312-266-4700
Emp.: 800
General Contracting & Construction Management
S.I.C.: 1541; 1542
J. Stanley Pepper *(Pres.)*
Bharat Gandhi *(Chief Oper. Officer)*
John H. Beasley *(Sr. V.P.-Personnel)*
Richard H. Tilghman *(Sr V.P.-Mktg.)*

Pepper-Lawson **(1)**
4555 Katy Hocley Cut-off Rd.
Katy, TX 77449
Tel.: 713-371-3100
Fax: 713-371-2029
Emp.: 26
General Contractor & Construction Manager
S.I.C.: 1541; 1542
Paul Lawson *(Pres.)*
Bruce L. Ford *(Controller)*
Buddy Goodson *(Dir.-Mktg.)*

Pepper West, Inc. **(1)**
17941 Fitch
Irvine, CA 92714
Tel.: 714-261-7080
Fax: 714-261-7098
Emp.: 20
General Contracting & Construction Management
S.I.C.: 1541; 1542
Bharat Gandhi *(Pres.)*
Gary Gustafson *(Exec. V.P.)*
Mark Thurman *(Dir.-Mktg.)*

PEPPER, HAMILTON & SCHEETZ

3000 Two Logan Sq.,
Eighteenth & Arch Sts.
Philadelphia, PA 19103
Tel.: 215-981-4000
Fax: 215-981-4750
Year Founded: 1890
Approx.Billings: $90,000,000
Emp.: 760
Fiscal Year-end: 12/31/92
Law Firm
S.I.C.: 8111
William R. Klaus *(Co-Chm.)*
Edward W. Madiera, Jr. *(Co-Chm.)*
Jon A. Baughman *(Chm. of Exec. Committee)*
Barbara Mather *(Exec. Partner)*
Karen M. Knab *(Chief Admin. Officer)*
Monica L. Hill *(Dir.-Human Resources)*
Josette Marsh *(Dir.-Opers.)*
Thomas Petrillo *(Dir.-Applications)*
Robyn Beyer *(Librarian)*

No. of U.S. Offices: 8
No. of Foreign Offices: 3

Computer Systems/Hardware:
IBM AS-400; DEC (Various)

Branches:

Pepper, Hamilton & Scheetz **(1)**
1300 Nineteenth St., N.W.
Washington, DC 20036
Tel.: 202-828-1200
Fax: 202-828-1665

Pepper, Hamilton & Scheetz **(1)**
10 E. 53rd St., 32nd Fl.
New York, NY 10022
Tel.: 212-371-3670
Fax: 212-935-2690
Law Firm Branch
S.I.C.: 8111

Pepper, Hamilton & Scheetz **(1)**
200 One Keystone Plaza
Harrisburg, PA 17108
Tel.: 717-255-1155
Fax: 717-238-0575
Law Firm Branch
S.I.C.: 8111

Pepper, Hamilton & Scheetz **(1)**
1201 Markey St., Ste. 1401
Wilmington, DE 19801
Tel.: 302-571-6555
Fax: 302-656-8865
Law Firm Branch
S.I.C.: 8111

Pepper, Hamilton & Scheetz **(1)**
100 Renaissance Center, 36th Fl.
Detroit, MI 48243
Tel.: 313-259-7110
Fax: 313-259-7926
Law Firm Branch
S.I.C.: 8111

Pepper, Hamilton & Scheetz **(1)**
1235 Westlake Dr., Ste. 400
Berwyn, PA 19312
Tel.: 215-251-0777
Fax: 215-640-7835
Law Firm Branch
S.I.C.: 8111

Pepper, Hamilton & Scheetz **(1)**
Sentry Office Plaza, 216 Haddon Ave., Ste. 321
Westmont, NJ 08108
Tel.: 609-869-9555
Fax: 609-869-9595
Law Firm Branch
S.I.C.: 8111

Pepper, Hamilton & Scheetz **(1)**
City Tower, 40 Basinghall St.
London, EC2V 5DE, United Kingdom
Tel.: 071-628-1122
Fax: 071-628-6010
Law Firm Branch
S.I.C.: 8111

Pepper, Hamilton & Scheetz **(1)**
19-27 Grokholsky Per.
Moscow, Russia 129010
Tel.: 011-7095-280-4493
Law Firm Branch
S.I.C.: 8111

Pepper, Hamilton & Scheetz **(1)**
International Law Center, 2 Captain Shefaer St.
Vladivostok, Russian Federation
Tel.: 011-7423-211-1166
Law Firm Branch
S.I.C.: 8111

PEPSI-COLA ALBANY BOTTLING CO., INC.

One Pepsi-Cola Dr.
Latham, NY 12110
Tel.: 518-783-8811
Fax: 518-783-3303
Sales Range: $40-59 Million
Emp.: 200
Distributor & Bottlers of Carbonated Soft Drinks
S.I.C.: 2086
John R. Strachen *(Chm. Bd.)*
David A. Weir *(Pres.)*
Carlton Endemann, Jr. *(Sr. V.P.)*
Steve Fahey *(V.P.)*
Tom Herlihy *(Controller)*
Tony Lupino *(Chief Fin. Officer)*
Roy Roberts *(Gen. Mgr.)*
Jim DeStefano *(Mgr.-Plant)*

Outside Service Firm(s):

Evans & Bennett*(Auditors)*
Syracuse, NY

Chemical Bank*(Major Banking Relationship)*
Syracuse, NY

PEPSI-COLA BOTTLING CO.

3801 Brighton Blvd.
Denver, CO 80216
Tel.: 303-292-9220
Fax: 303-295-2741
Emp.: 550
Bottlers & Distributors of Soft Drinks
S.I.C.: 2086; 5149
Eric Reinhard *(Pres.)*

Computer Systems/Hardware:
Burroughs

Outside Service Firm(s):

Ernst & Young*(Auditors)*
4300 Republic Plaza
Denver, CO 80202
Tel.: 303-628-4406

Fairfield & Woods*(Legal Firm)*
Denver, CO

PEPSI-COLA BOTTLING COMPANY OF CHARLOTTE INC.

2820 South Blvd.
Charlotte, NC 28209
Mailing Address:
P.O. Box 241167
Charlotte, NC 28224
Tel.: 704-523-6761 **NC**
Fax: 704-523-7535
Year Founded: 1905
Approx.Sls.: $50,000,000
Emp.: 275
Import Export
Mfr. & Distribution of Soft Drinks
S.I.C.: 2086
Dale F. Halton *(Chm. Bd., Pres. & Chief Exec. Officer)*
Darrell M. Holland *(Exec. V.P.)*
Marilyn Gallagher *(V.P.-Human Resources)*
Stuart Menzel *(V.P.-Opers.)*
Charles F. Sullivan *(V.P.-Sls.)*
Barbara E. Burleson *(Sec.)*
Debbie Ollo *(Dir.-Data Processing)*

No. of Mfg. Plants/Facilities: 3

Outside Service Firm(s):

Scharf & Pera*(Auditors)*
Charlotte, NC

First Citizens Bank & Trust Co.*(Major Banking Relationship)*
Charlotte, NC

Royal Insurance Co.*(Major Banking Relationship)*
Charlotte, NC

First Citizens Bank & Trust Co.*(Investment Banker)*
Charlotte, NC

Provident Life & Accident Insurance Co.*(Group Insurer)*
Charlotte, NC

James, McElroy & Deihl*(Legal Firm)*
Charlotte, NC

PERDUE FARMS INC.

Old Ocean City Rd.
Salisbury, MD 21802
Mailing Address:
P.O. Box 1537
Salisbury, MD 21802-1537
Tel.: 410-543-3000
Fax: 410-543-3292
Year Founded: 1920
Approx.Sls.: $1,200,000,000
Emp.: 12,000
Fiscal Year-end: 4/ 1/92
Dressed Poultry, Soybean Products, Hatching Eggs, Grain, Poultry By-Products, Turkey & Chicken
S.I.C.: 2015; 0251; 0254
James A. Perdue *(Chm. Bd.)*
Pelham B. Lawrence *(Pres.)*
Dick Willey *(Pres.-Grain & Oil Seed)*
Roger Covey *(V.P.-Sls.)*
Thomas R. Moyers *(V.P.-Human Resources)*
George C. Reiswig *(V.P.-Fin. & Chief Fin. Officer)*
Thomas E. Mahn *(Treas.)*
Elaine Barnes *(Sec.)*
Robert Cook *(Dir.-Mngmt. Information Systems)*
Steve Evans *(Dir.-Mktg.)*
Connie Littleton *(Dir.-Mktg. Services)*
Frank MacKinnis *(Dir.-Pur.)*
Lois Lake *(Mgr.-Telecommunications)*
Kathy Sabo *(Mgr.-Media & Res. Data)*
Christine Whaley *(Mgr.-Pub. Rels. Promo.)*

Computer Systems/Hardware:
IBM System 4381

Outside Service Firm(s):

Price Waterhouse*(Auditors)*
7 St. Paul St.
Baltimore, MD 21202

Metropolitan Life Insurance Co.*(Group Insurer)*
One Madison Ave.
New York, NY 10010-3690
Tel.: 215-578-9292

Goldman, Sachs & Co.*(Investment Banker)*
85 Broad St.
New York, NY 10004
Tel.: 212-902-1000
Fax: 212-902-4451

Citibank N.A.*(Major Banking Relationship)*
Corporate Trust Services, 399 Park Ave.
New York, NY 10043
Tel.: 212-559-1605

First Chicago Shareholder Services Trust Co.*(Major Banking Relationship)*
153 West 51st St.
New York, NY 10019
Tel.: 212-791-6422
Fax: 212-385-9798

NationsBank Carolinas*(Major Banking Relationship)*
One NCNB Plaza T18-7
Charlotte, NC 28255

Subsidiaries:

FoodCraft Equipment Co., Inc. **(1)**
53 Industrial Circle
Lancaster, PA 17601-1537
Tel.: 717-656-0401
Fax: 717-656-0549
Emp.: 55
Export
Product Development
S.I.C.: 3523; 8734
Eugene Martin *(Pres.)*
Michael Lease *(V.P.-Research & Devel.)*
Skip Daiger *(Dir.-Adv. & Mktg.)*
Michael Curtis *(Personnel Mgr.)*

Perdue Foods Incorporated **(1)**
P.O. Box 1537
Salisbury, MD 21801
Tel.: 410-543-3000
S.I.C.: 2015; 0251

Perdue Incorporated **(1)**
P.O. Box 1537
Salisbury, MD 21801
Tel.: 410-543-3000
S.I.C.: 2015; 0251

Perdue Transportation Inc. **(1)**
P.O. Box 1537
Salisbury, MD 21802-1537
Tel.: 410-543-3000
S.I.C.: 4731

Shenandoah Products **(1)**
P.O. Box 1537
Salisbury, MD 21801
Tel.: 410-543-3000
S.I.C.: 2015; 0251

Shenandoah Valley Farms **(1)**
P.O. Box 1537
Salisbury, MD 21801
Tel.: 410-543-3000
S.I.C.: 2015; 0251

PEREZ TRADING CO. INC.
3490 N.W. 125th St.
Miami, FL 33167
Tel.: 305-769-0761 **NY**
Fax: 305-681-7963
Year Founded: 1946
Approx.Sls.: $80,000,000
Emp.: 130

Import Export
Wholesale & Export Printing Paper, Paper & Paperboard Equipment & Supplies
S.I.C.: 5113; 5199; 5084
John Perez *(Pres. & Chief Exec. Officer)*
Carl A. Perez *(V.P. & Sec. Of Bd.)*
Eduardo Lopez *(Dir.-Personnel)*

Outside Service Firm(s):

BDO Seidman*(Auditors)*
Miami, FL

Mishan, Sloto & Hoffman*(Legal Firm)*
Miami, FL

PERFECT FIT INDUSTRIES, INC.
201 Cuthbertson St.
Monroe, NC 28110
Mailing Address:
P.O. Box 709
Monroe, NC 28110
Tel.: 704-289-1531 **DE**
Fax: 704-283-8856
Year Founded: 1934
Approx.Sls.: $80,000,000
Emp.: 1,000
Fiscal Year-end: 12/31/91
Mfr. & Distribute Bedspreads, Comforters, Mattress Pads, Draperies & Bed Pillows
S.I.C.: 2392; 2391; 5023
M.L. Fontenot *(Chm. Bd. & Pres.)*
L.D. Sears *(Chief Fin. Officer & V.P.)*

No. of Mfg. Plants/Facilities: 7

Outside Service Firm(s):

Deloitte & Touche*(Auditors)*
2000 First Citizens Bank Plaza, 128 S. Tryon St.
Charlotte, NC 28202-5001
Tel.: 704-372-3560

Kennedy, Covington, Lobdell & Hickman*(Legal Firm)*
3300 NCNB Plaza
Charlotte, NC 28282
Tel.: 704-377-6000

NationsBank Carolinas*(Major Banking Relationship)*
One NCNB Plaza T18-7
Charlotte, NC 28255

PERFECT PEARL COMPANY, INC.
104 W. 29th St., 3rd Fl.
New York, NY 10001
Tel.: 212-736-2421 **NY**
Fax: 212-239-8036
Year Founded: 1955
Approx.Sls.: $12,000,000
Emp.: 30
Mfr. of Costume Jewelry, Precious Metal & Semiprecious Stones
S.I.C.: 3961
Joseph Spitzer *(Pres.)*
Albert Spitzer *(V.P. & Treas.)*

Outside Service Firm(s):

Fleet National Bank*(Major Banking Relationship)*
111 Westminster St.
Providence, RI 02903
Tel.: 401-278-6000

PERFECTION AUTOMOTIVE PRODUCTS CORPORATION
12445 Levan Rd.
Livonia, MI 48150
Tel.: 313-591-0111 **MI**
Fax: 313-591-3780
Year Founded: 1952
Approx.Sls.: $10,000,000
Emp.: 30
Mfr. of Automobile Parts & Accessories
S.I.C.: 3714
Jerome M. Ash *(Pres.)*
Norman Ash *(Exec. V.P.)*
Jay Melody *(V.P.-Mktg. & Adv.)*
Jared Kokubo *(Mgr.-Data Processing)*
Henry Kolo *(Pur. Agent)*

Outside Service Firm(s):

Kirschner, Hutton & Shevin, PC*(Auditors)*
Southfield, MI

Maddin, Hauser, Wartell, Roth, Heller & Pesses*(Legal Firm)*
Southfield, MI

PERFECTION BAKERIES INC.
350 Pearl St.
Fort Wayne, IN 46802
Tel.: 219-424-8245 **IN**
Fax: 219-424-5047
Year Founded: 1901
Approx.Sls.: $10,000,000
Emp.: 200
Fiscal Year-end: 9/30/90
Wholesale Bread & Buns
S.I.C.: 2053; 5149
John F. Popp *(Chm. Bd. & Pres.)*
Jay Miller *(V.P.-Fin., Treas. & Sec.)*
Bohn Popp *(Dir.-Mktg.)*
John Gluhofky *(Plant Mgr.)*
Joe Steele *(Chief Engineer)*

Computer Systems/Hardware:
Service Bureau

Outside Service Firm(s):

Coopers & Lybrand*(Auditors)*
490 Lincoln Bank Tower
Fort Wayne, IN 46802
Tel.: 219-423-1531
Fax: 219-426-7870

Nyhart Co.*(Group Insurer)*
Indianapolis, IN
Tel.: 1-800-428-7106

Barrett & McNagny*(Legal Firm)*
Lincoln Bank Tower, 3rd Fl.
Ft. Wayne, IN 46802
Tel.: 219-423-9551

Lincoln National Life Insurance Co.*(Major Banking Relationship)*
Fort Wayne, IN

Manufacturers National Bank N.A.*(Pension Manager)*
38th Fl., 100 Renaissance Center
Detroit, MI 48243
Tel.: 313-222-4227

Subsidiaries:

Gase Bakery Co. **(1)**
404 W. Genessee
Saginaw, MI 48602
Tel.: 517-752-6138
Bakery Goods
S.I.C.: 2051

Schafer Bakeries, Inc. **(1)**
2701 S. Logan Central Garage
Lansing, MI 48910
Tel.: 517-372-3920
Bakery Goods
S.I.C.: 2051
William Pasche *(V.P.-Sls.)*

Way Bakeries, Inc. **(1)**
2100 Enterprise Dr.
Jackson, MI 49203
Tel.: 517-750-1818
Bakery Goods
S.I.C.: 2051
John F. Popp *(Pres.)*
Jay Miller *(V.P.-Fin.)*
Mark Porter *(Plant Mgr.)*

PERFECTION-SCHWANK INC.
Hwy. 56, P.O. Box 749
Waynesboro, GA 30830-0749
Tel.: 706-554-2101
Tel.: 800-241-9727
Fax: 706-554-3933
Year Founded: 1882
Approx.Sls.: $20,000,000
Emp.: 170
Fiscal Year-end: 12/31/90
Manufacture Gas & Oil Room Heaters, Wall Furnaces & Gas Infra-Red Heaters
S.I.C.: 3433
Bernd H. Schwank *(Chm. Bd.)*
C.N. High *(Pres.)*
J.E. Smith *(V.P.-Mktg. & Sls.)*
E.R. Daughtry *(Controller)*
M.S. Osteen *(Dir.-Pur.)*

No. of Mfg. Plants/Facilities: 1

Computer Systems/Hardware:
IBM Mapics I & II

Outside Service Firm(s):

Blue Cross & Blue Shield of Georgia, Inc.*(Group Insurer)*
Atlanta, GA

PERFORMANCE CONTRACTING GROUP
5435 Seventy Seven Center Dr., Ste. 10
Charlotte, NC 28217
Tel.: 704-529-8000 **DE**
Fax: 704-528-8037
Approx.Sls.: $150,000,000
Emp.: 1,450
Building Insulation; Acoustical & Ceiling Work; Thermal Insulation
S.I.C.: 1742; 5033
Kenneth Spraetz *(Pres.)*
Robert Brand *(Treas. & Sec.)*

Outside Service Firm(s):

KPMG Peat Marwick*(Auditors)*
Two First Union Center
Charlotte, NC
Tel.: 704-335-5300

First Union National Bank*(Major Banking Relationship)*
CMG-5, Two First Union Center
Charlotte, NC 28288-1154
Tel.: 704-374-2698
Fax: 704-374-6987

Subsidiary:

Performance Contracting, Inc. **(1)**
5435 Seventy Seven Center Dr., Ste. 10
Charlotte, NC 28217
Tel.: 704-529-8000
Building Insulation; Acoustical & Ceiling Work; Thermal Insulation
S.I.C.: 1742; 5033
Kenneth Spaetz *(Pres.)*
Tom Carlisle *(V.P.)*
Craig Fallon *(V.P.)*
Michael Matthews *(V.P.)*
Robert Brand *(Treas. & Sec.)*

PERFORMANCE CONTRACTORS INC.
9865 Pecue Lane
Baton Rouge, LA 70810
Mailing Address:
P.O. Box 83630
Baton Rouge, LA 70884
Tel.: 504-751-4156 **LA**
Fax: 504-751-8409
Year Founded: 1979
Approx.Sls.: $36,000,000
Emp.: 700
Fiscal Year-end: 12/31/91
General Industrial Construction & Maintenance Contractor
S.I.C.: 1541
Art E. Favre *(Pres.)*
Mitch A. Rayner *(V.P., Chief Oper. Officer & Sec.)*
George Thompson *(Controller)*
Rick Bourgeois *(Mgr.-Pur.)*
Ron McMorris *(Mgr.-Quality Control)*

Principal(s):
Art E. Favre
Mitch A. Rayner

No. of Mfg. Plants/Facilities: 1
No. of U.S. Offices: 1

Computer Systems/Hardware:
IBM System 36; IBM RISC 6000

Outside Service Firm(s):

Dan Pritchard*(Auditors)*
Baton Rouge, LA

Financial Service Corporation*(Investment Banker)*
Baton Rouge, LA

Eldred, Claver & Davis*(Legal Firm)*
Baton Rouge, LA

Southern Pension Consultants Inc*(Pension Manager)*
Baton Rouge, LA

PERFORMANCE FOOD GROUP, INC.
(Formerly Pocahontas Food Group, Inc.)
25 Century Blvd., Ste. 509
Nashville, TN 37214
Mailing Address:
P.O. Box 9729
Richmond, VA 23228
Tel.: 615-391-0112 **VA**
Fax: 615-391-3547
Year Founded: 1987
Assets: $40,500,000
Earnings: $2,500,000
Liabilities: $31,000,000
Net Worth: $9,500,000
Approx.Sls.: $270,000,000
Emp.: 1,000
Fiscal Year-end: 12/31/91

Import
Food Service Distributor; Refrigerated Warehousing
S.I.C.: 5141; 5149; 4222; 4213
Kenneth O. Lester *(Chm. Bd.)*
Jerry Caro *(Vice Chm.)*
Robert C. Sledd *(Pres. & Chief Exec. Officer)*
Roger L. Boeve *(Chief Fin. Officer & Exec. V.P.)*
David W. Sober *(V.P.-Human Res.)*
Brenda McPeak *(Meetings Plng.)*

Computer Systems/Hardware:
IBM

Outside Service Firm(s):

KPMG Peat Marwick*(Auditors)*
1900 Nashville Center, 511 Union St.
Nashville, TN 37219

Third National Bank*(Major Banking Relationship)*
201 4th Ave. No., Uptown Sta., Box 2844
Nashville, TN 37167
Tel.: 615-748-4742

Subsidiaries:

B & R Foods **(1)**
3150 N. Gallagher Rd.
Dover, FL 33527
Tel.: 813-659-0811
S.I.C.: 5141
David Johnson *(Gen. Mgr.)*

Caro Produce & Institutional Foods **(1)**
2324 Bayou Blue Rd.
Houma, LA 70364
Tel.: 504-872-1483
S.I.C.: 5149

Performance Food Group, Inc.—(Continued)

Hale Brothers, Inc. **(1)**
530 E. Main
Morristown, TN 37816
Tel.: 615-586-6231
Food Distribution
S.I.C.: 5149
W.T. Hale *(Pres.)*

Kenneth O. Lester, Inc. **(1)**
825 Maddox Simpson Pkwy
Lebanon, TN 37087
Tel.: 615-443-0077
S.I.C.: 5141

Pocahontas Foods, USA **(1)**
7420 Ranco Rd.
Richmond, VA 23228
Tel.: 804-262-8614
Food Brokers
S.I.C.: 5141; 5149
C. Michael Gray *(Pres.)*

Performance Toyota of Louisiana, Inc.
(Name Changed to Colman Toyota)

PERGAMENT HOME CENTERS, INC.
101 Marcus Dr.
Melville, NY 11747
Tel.: 516-694-9300
Fax: 516-694-3922
Approx.Sls.: $290,000,000
Emp.: 2,500
Retail General Merchandise Store
S.I.C.: 5399; 5198
Donald Tattenbaum *(Pres.)*
Robert Silver *(Sr. V.P.-Human Resources)*

Periphonics CORPORATION

PERIPHONICS CORP.
4000 Veterans Memorial Hwy.
Bohemia, NY 11716
Tel.: 516-467-0500 **DE**
Fax: 516-737-8520
Year Founded: 1970
Sales Range: $20-39 Million
Emp.: 280
Export
Mfr. Voice Response & Audiotex Systems
S.I.C.: 7378; 3577
Peter J. Cohen *(Pres. & Chief Exec. Officer)*
Richard A. Daniels *(Sr. V.P.-Sls.)*
George Cole *(V.P.-Mktg.)*
Richard Giannotti *(V.P.-Tech. Services)*
Terry Meehan *(V.P. & Dir.-Software Devel.)*
Kevin O'Brien *(V.P.-Fin.)*
Jay Patel *(V.P.-Res. & Devel.)*
Janet Anderson *(Dir.-Employee Rels.)*
J. Demas *(Dir.-Pur.)*
Robert Tolsch *(Dir.-Mfg.)*
Karen L. Ferraro *(Mgr.-Mktg.)*
Principal(s):
Peter J. Cohen
George Cole
Richard A. Daniels
Richard Giannotti
Terry Meehan
Kevin O'Brien
Jay Patel

No. of Mfg. Plants/Facilities: 1
No. of U.S. Offices: 18
No. of Foreign Offices: 5

Computer Systems/Hardware:
Periphonics Proprietary Software & Hardware

Outside Service Firm(s):

Deloitte & Touche*(Auditors)*
Two Jericho Plaza
Jericho, NY 11753-1683

Industrial Risk Insurers*(Commercial Insurance Carrier)*
Hartford, CT

Norman Abrams*(Legal Firm)*
Huntington, NY

Marine Midland Bank*(Major Banking Relationship)*
Melville, NY

Non-U.S. Holdings:

Periphonics S.A. de C.V. **(1)**
San Francisco No.1626-301 03100 Col. del Valle,
Mexico, D.F. Mexico
Tel.: 525-682-9910
Fax: 525-682-9910

Periphonics Voice Processing Systems Ltd. **(1)**
Albany Court, Albany Park
Camberley, Surrey GU15 2XA, United Kingdom
Tel.: 0276 692 020 (100%)
Fax: 0276 692083
Computer Systems/Hardware:
VPS Series
Mktg. & Sales of Voice-Response Systems
S.I.C.: 5045
Jan Waterhouse *(Dir.-Mktg.)*
Joe McHugh *(Mgr.)*
Manoo Parmar *(Mgr.-Sls.)*

PERKASIE INDUSTRIES CORPORATION
50 E. Spruce St.
Perkasie, PA 18944
Tel.: 215-257-6581
Fax: 215-453-1703
Approx.Sls.: $14,000,000
Emp.: 158
Mfr. Lighting Fixtures, Interior Storm Windows & Wiring Devices
S.I.C.: 3442; 3643; 3646
Hubert Hassinger *(Pres.)*
Douglas Hassinger *(Treas. & Sec.)*
Shirley Heaverly *(Mgr.-Data Processing)*
Bill Kennedy *(Mgr.-Personnel)*
Terry Weirback *(Mgr.-Sls. & Mktg.)*

Outside Service Firm(s):

Landsburg, Pitt, Grenwalt & Felx*(Auditors)*
Philadelphia, PA

Rubin, Quinn, Moss*(Legal Firm)*
Philadelphia, PA

Union Bank*(Major Banking Relationship)*
Souderton, PA

PERLMUTER PRINTING COMPANY
4437 E. 49th St.
Cleveland, OH 44125
Tel.: 216-271-5300 **OH**
Fax: 216-271-7650
Year Founded: 1917
Assets: $28,002,855
Liabilities: $22,638,214
Net Worth: $5,364,641
Approx.Sls.: $40,000,000
Emp.: 300
Fiscal Year-end: 10/31/91
Commercial Lithographic & Letterpress Printing
S.I.C.: 2752
Employee Matching Gifts Program: Matches 10% of employee's comtribution
Ernest A. Perlmuter *(Chm. Bd.)*
Richard M. Perlmuter *(Pres. & Chief Exec. Officer)*
Kenneth C. Allen, Jr. *(Exec. V.P.)*
Michael Perlmuter *(Sr. V.P. & Gen. Counsel)*
Robert F. Angart *(Chief Oper. Officer, Chief Fin. Officer, V.P.-Fin.)*
Dick Hill *(V.P.-Mfg.)*
Ed Lipp *(V.P.-Sls. Projects)*
Bruce Perlmuter *(Sec., Treas. & V.P.-Opers.)*
Laurie Mueller *(Dir.-Government Affairs)*
Lynn Wightman *(Dir.-Pur.)*

Computer Systems/Hardware:
Data General, Nixdorf

Outside Service Firm(s):

Krasney, Polk, Friedman & Fish*(Auditors)*
Cleveland, OH

Society Bank*(Investment Banker)*
Cleveland, OH

Kahn, Kleinman, Yanowitz & Arnson*(Legal Firm)*
1301 East Ninth St., Ste. 2600
Cleveland, OH 44114
Tel.: 216-696-3311
Fax: 216-696-1009

AmeriTrust Company, N.A.*(Major Banking Relationship)*
P.O. Box 5937, 900 Euclid Ave.
Cleveland, OH 44101-0937

Bank One*(Major Banking Relationship)*
Cleveland, OH

PERPETUAL CORPORATION
800 17th St. NW, Ste. 301
Washington, DC 20006
Tel.: 202-789-2130 **DE**
Telex: 904011
Fax: 202-822-6749
Year Founded: 1958
Emp.: 12
Fiscal Year-end: 9/30/91
TV Broadcasting
S.I.C.: 4833; 6719
Joe L. Allbritton *(Chm. Bd. & Chief Exec. Officer)*
Lawrence I. Hebert *(Pres. & Chief Oper. Officer)*
Virginia L. White *(Treas. & Sec.)*

No. of U.S. Offices: 1

Computer Systems/Hardware:
IBM PC

Outside Service Firm(s):

Ernst & Young*(Auditors)*
1225 Connecticut Ave., NW
Washington, DC 20036

Fulbright & Jaworski*(Legal Firm)*
1301 McKinney St.
Houston, TX 77010
Tel.: 713-651-5151

Subsidiaries:

Allbritton Communications Company **(1)**
800 17th St., N.W., Ste. 301
Washington, DC 20006
Tel.: 202-789-2130 (100%)
Fax: 202-822-6749
Televison Broadcasting
S.I.C.: 4833
Joe L. Allbritton *(Chm. Bd. & Chief Exec. Officer)*
Lawrence I. Hebert *(Pres. & Chief Oper. Officer)*
Marvin A. Shirley *(Exec. V.P.)*
Jerald N. Fritz *(V.P. & Gen. Counsel)*
Michael H. Moore *(V.P.)*
Virginia L. White *(Sec. & Treas.)*

Division:

WJLA-TV **(2)**
3307 Tilden Street, N.W.
Washington, DC 20008
Tel.: 202-364-7777 (100%)
Fax: 202-364-1943
Emp.: 185
T.V. Broadcasting
S.I.C.: 4833
John D. Sawhill *(Pres. & Station Mgr.)*
Virgina L. White *(Sec. & Treas.)*

Subsidiaries:

Allbritton News Bureau, Inc. **(2)**
800 17th St. N.W., Ste. 301
Washington, DC 20006
Tel.: 202-789-2130 (100%)
Fax: 202-822-6749
Equipment Rental
S.I.C.: 7359
Joe L. Allbritton *(Chm. Bd.)*
Lawrence I. Hebert *(Pres.)*
Virginia L. White *(Sec. & Treas.)*

Allbritton Television Productions, Inc. **(2)**
Ste. 301, 800 17th St., N.W.
Washington, DC 20006
Tel.: 202-789-2130 (100%)
Fax: 202-822-6749
Television Program Production
S.I.C.: 7922
Lawrence I. Hebert *(Pres.)*
Virginia L. White *(Sec. & Treas.)*

KATV Television, Inc. **(2)**
P.O. Box 77,
Little Rock, AR 72203
Tel.: 501-372-7777 (100%)
Fax: 501-374-7909
Emp.: 99
TV Broadcasting
S.I.C.: 4833
L. Dale Nicholson *(Pres. & Chief Oper. Officer)*
Virginia L. White *(Sec. & Treas.)*

KTUL Television, Inc. **(2)**
P.O. Box 8,
Tulsa, OK 74101
Tel.: 918-446-3351 (100%)
Fax: 918-445-9316
Emp.: 100
TV Broadcasting
S.I.C.: 4833
Dan C. Bates *(Pres. & Chief Oper. Officer)*
Bernhard L. Gaarsoe *(V.P.)*
Virginia L. White *(Sec. & Treas.)*

The News Printing Company **(2)**
c/o Allbritton Communications, 800 17th St., N.W., Suite 301
Washington, DC 20006
Tel.: 202-789-2130 (100%)
Newspaper Publisher
S.I.C.: 2711
Michael H. Moore *(Pres. & Chief Oper. Officer)*

Trenton Times Corp. **(2)**
Ste. 301, 800 17th St., N.W.
Washington, DC 20006
Tel.: 202-789-2130 (100%)
Newspaper Publisher
S.I.C.: 2711
Michael H. Moore *(Pres. & Chief Oper. Officer)*

Allnewsco, Inc. **(1)**
7600D Boston Blvd.
Springfield, VA 22153
Tel.: 703-912-5300 (100%)
Fax: 703-866-6009
Cable Programming
S.I.C.: 4899
John D. Hillis *(Pres.)*

PERRY BROTHERS, INC.
107 W. Lufkin Ave.
Lufkin, TX 75901
Tel.: 409-634-6686 **TX**
Fax: 409-634-7648
Year Founded: 1924
Approx.Sls.: $47,000,000
Emp.: 1,200
Variety Stores
S.I.C.: 5331
Ray Baldwin *(Chm. Bd. & Chief Oper. Officer)*
Billy B. Jackson *(Vice Chm.)*
Jack Simpson *(Pres.)*
Jim Stephens *(V.P.)*
Billy Woodruff *(V.P.-Opers.)*
Clifford Schmidt *(Sec.)*

Outside Service Firm(s):

Axley & Rode*(Auditors)*
Lufkin, TX

First Bank, N.A.*(Major Banking Relationship)*
Lufkin, TX

PERRY & DERRICK CO.
2510 Highland Ave., Ste. 510
Cincinnati, OH 45212
Mailing Address:
P.O. Box 125215,
Cincinnati, OH 45212
Tel.: 513-351-5800
Tel.: 800-227-2468 **KY**
Fax: 513-351-3299
Year Founded: 1913
Approx.Sls.: $16,000,000
Emp.: 130
Fiscal Year-end: 11/30/91
Export
Mfr. Paint
S.I.C.: 2851
William J. Bradley *(Pres. & Chief Exec. Officer)*
Mark E. Derrick *(V.P.-Admin.)*
Everett Joles *(V.P.-Sls. & Mktg.)*
Dennis J. Dreyer *(Sec.)*
Ken Wagner *(Treas.)*
Vada Hammann *(Dir.-Pur.)*
Hugh Lowrey *(Dir.-Tech.)*
Dan McKeown *(Dir.-Data Processing)*
Greg Schott *(Mgr.-Production)*
Ken Stacy *(Mgr.-Quality Control)*
John J. Jones *(Plant Supt.)*

No. of Mfg. Plants/Facilities: 1

Computer Systems/Hardware:
MAI Basic 4

Outside Service Firm(s):

Clark, Schaeffer & Hackett*(Auditors)*
Cincinnati, OH

Santen & Hughes*(Legal Firm)*
Cincinnati, OH

The Central Trust Company, N.A.*(Major Banking Relationship)*
201 E. Fifth
Cincinnati, OH 45202
Tel.: 513-651-8255

Subsidiary:

Foy-Johnston, Inc. **(1)**
P.O. Box 125215
Cincinnati, OH 45212
Tel.: 513-351-5800
Approx.Sls.: $7,500,000
Emp.: 100
Mfr. of Paint
S.I.C.: 2851
Everett Joles *(V.P.-Sls. & Gen. Mgr.)*

PERRY EQUIPMENT CORPORATION
Wolters Industrial Park, P.O. Box 640
Mineral Wells, TX 76067
Tel.: 817-325-2575 **TX**
Twx: 758343
Fax: 817-325-4622
Year Founded: 1936
Approx.Sls.: $39,000,000
Emp.: 435
Fiscal Year-end: 5/31/90
Export
Mfr. Pipeline Launchers; Receivers Oil, Gas, Air & Water Filters; Replacement Elements & Flow Measurement Equipment
S.I.C.: 3443; 3599
M. Dunman Perry, Jr. *(Chm. Bd. & Chief Exec. Officer)*
J. Wayne Crandell *(Pres.)*
F. Baker *(V.P.-Opers.)*
M.C. Durkee *(V.P.-Fin.)*
Doyle Gould *(V.P.-Mktg.)*
D. Harcourt *(V.P.-Human Resources)*
D. Houston *(V.P.-Engrng.)*
R. Lauterbach *(V.P.-Intl. Sls.)*
D. Perry *(Sec.)*
John Allen *(Controller)*
M. Stuart *(Dir.-Mngmt. Information Systems)*
Principal(s):
M. Dunman Perry, Jr.
D. Perry

Outside Service Firm(s):

Grant Thornton*(Auditors)*
1445 Ross Ave.
Dallas, TX 75202
Tel.: 214-855-7300

L.J. Varnell, Jr.*(Legal Firm)*
Minerla Wells, TX

Overton Park National Bank*(Major Banking Relationship)*
Fort Worth, TX

Subsidiaries:

Flo-Line Filters, Inc. **(1)**
1501 S. Johnson
Amarillo, TX 79105
Tel.: 806-373-3224
S.I.C.: 3599
J. Wayne Crandell *(Pres. & Chief Oper. Officer)*
M.C. Durke *(V.P.)*
J. Menke *(V.P. & Gen. Mgr.)*

United Filters, Inc. **(1)**
1501 S. Johnson
Amarillo, TX 79105
Tel.: 806-373-8386
S.I.C.: 3599
J. Wayne Crandell *(Pres. & Chief Oper. Officer)*
M.C. Durke *(V.P.)*
J. Menke *(V.P. & Gen. Mgr.)*

PERRY GROUP, INC.
25 Mt. Laurel Rd.
Hainesport, NJ 08036
Tel.: 609-267-1600
Approx.Sls.: $22,000,000
Emp.: 110
Mfr. Metalworking Machinery; Process Vessels
S.I.C.: 5084; 3443
Perez Epstein *(Chm. Bd.)*
Jerome P. Epstein *(Pres.)*
Stanley Brooks *(V.P.-Sls.)*
Greg Epstein *(V.P.)*
Leonard Jacobs *(V.P. & Sec.)*
Mary K. Epstein *(Asst. Treas.)*

Subsidiary:

Perry Products Corp. **(1)**
Mt. Laurel Rd.
Hainesport, NJ 08036
Tel.: 609-267-1603
Fax: 609-267-4499
Approx.Sls.: $3,000,000
Emp.: 15
Fiscal Year-end: 12/31/90
Heat Exchangers Mfrs.
S.I.C.: 3443
P. Epstein *(Chm. Bd.)*
Jerome P. Epstein *(Pres.)*
J. Coia *(Mgr.-Sls.)*
A. McGill *(Mgr.-Mfg.)*
Suren Shah *(Mgr.-Engrng.)*

PERRY'S ICE CREAM CO., INC.
1 Ice Cream Plaza
Akron, NY 14001
Mailing Address:
P.O. Box 328,
Akron, NY 14001
Tel.: 716-542-5492
Tel.: 800-533-2300 **NY**
Fax: 716-542-2544
Year Founded: 1918
Assets: $16,600,000
Liabilities: $11,600,000
Net Worth: $5,000,000
Approx.Sls.: $42,000,000
Emp.: 250
Fiscal Year-end: 12/31/90
Import Export
Ice Cream Mfr.
S.I.C.: 2024
Dale Perry *(Co-Chm. Bd.)*
Thomas Perry *(Co-Chm. Bd.)*
Mike Bieger *(Pres.)*
Dave Hodgson *(Controller)*
Doug Farrell *(V.P.-Opers.)*
Mark Weigel *(V.P.-Sls.)*
Nancy Lynch *(Dir.-Human Resources)*
Leigh Menzel *(Dir.-Pur.)*
William Storr *(Dir.-Mgmt. Info. Systems)*
Robert Denning *(Mgr.-Credit & Lease)*
Sharon Doll *(Mgr.-Meetings Planning)*
Principal(s):
Dale Perry

No. of Mfg. Plants/Facilities: 1
No. of U.S. Offices: 1

Computer Systems/Hardware:
DEC

Outside Service Firm(s):

BDO Seidman*(Auditors)*
Buffalo, NY

Independent Health Association*(Group Insurer)*
777 International Dr.
Buffalo, NY
Tel.: 716-631-5392

Liberty Mutual*(Group Insurer)*
175 Berkeley St.
Boston, MA

Allbright, Mcquire, Heffern, Shonn*(Legal Firm)*
Akron, NY

PERRYTON EQUITY
202 S. Amherst
Perryton, TX 79070
Tel.: 806-435-4016
Fax: 806-435-7194
Approx.Sls.: $79,000,000
Emp.: 175
Fiscal Year-end: 12/31/88
Grain Co-op
S.I.C.: 5153
Doug Mitchell *(Chm. Bd. & Pres.)*
Don Dunler *(Treas. & Gen. Mgr.)*
Edgar Womble *(Controller)*
Aldena Endicott *(Mgr.-Data Processing)*

Computer Systems/Hardware:
Burroughs 1955

Outside Service Firm(s):

Balbaugh & Campbell*(Auditors)*
Enid, OK

Producers Exchange*(Commercial Insurance Carrier)*
Dallas, TX 75235

Lemmon, Close & Shearer*(Legal Firm)*
Perryton, TX

First National Bank Perryton*(Major Banking Relationship)*
Perryton, TX

PERSIS CORPORATION
605 Kapiolani Blvd.
Honolulu, HI 96813
Tel.: 808-525-8087
Emp.: 650
Newspaper & Magazine Publishing
S.I.C.: 2711; 2721
Thurston Twigg-Smith *(Chm., Pres. & Chief Exec. Officer)*
David Twigg-Smith *(Vice Chm. & Sec.)*
Philip T. Gialanella *(Exec. V.P. & Chief Oper. Officer)*
Paul DeVille *(V.P. & Chief Fin. Officer)*
Ken Uemura *(Treas.)*

Subsidiaries:

ASA Properties Hawaii Inc. **(1)**
605 Kapiolani Blvd.
Honolulu, HI 96813
Tel.: 808-525-8087
S.I.C.: 6552
Paul DeVille *(Pres.)*

Honolulu Advertiser, Inc. **(1)**
605 KapiolaniBlvd.
Honolulu, HI 808-525-8000
Newspaper Publishing
S.I.C.: 2711
Thurston Twigg-Smith *(Pres.)*

Knoxville Journal Corporation **(1)**
307 Harper St.
Maryville, TN 37801
Tel.: 615-981-1137
Newspaper Publishing, Sunday Feature Only
S.I.C.: 2711
Larry Walcott *(Pres.)*

Maryville-Alcoa Newspapers, Inc. **(1)**
307 Harper St.
Maryville, TN 37801
Tel.: 615-981-1137
Newspaper Publishing
S.I.C.: 2711
Larry Walcott *(Publr.)*

Northwest Media, Inc. **(1)**
1705 132nd Ave. N.E.
Bellevue, WA 98005
Tel.: 206-455-2222
Newspaper Publishing
S.I.C.: 2711
Thurston Twigg-Smith *(Chief Exec. Officer)*

PET LIFE FOODS, INC.
7628 Plaza Ct.
Willowbrook, IL 60521
Tel.: 708-789-5757
Tel.: 800-323-2267
Fax: 708-789-5762
Year Founded: 1934
Approx.Sls.: $30,000,000
Emp.: 250
Fiscal Year-end: 9/30/91
Import Export
Mfr. Private Label Dog & Cat Foods, Hi Life Dog & Cat Foods, Pet Life Dog & Cat Foods, Say Cheese, Doggie Donuts, People Crackers, Lolli-Pups, Dog Life & Cat Life Pet Foods
S.I.C.: 2047
John Donahue *(Chm. Bd.)*
Frank B. Sloup *(Pres.)*
Robert Gallian *(Exec. V.P.)*

PETCARE PLUS, INC.
2300 Windson Ct.
Addison, IL 60101
Tel.: 708-932-4440 **DE**
Fax: 708-932-7093
Year Founded: 1989
Approx.Sls.: $25,000,000
Emp.: 300
Fiscal Year-end: 1/31/92
Complete Line of Pet Supplies & Food
S.I.C.: 5999
Steve Jeske *(Chief Fin. Officer)*
Ray Guyer *(Pres. & Merger & Acquisition Contact)*
Mike Riggon *(Exec. V.P.-Mktg. & Mdse.)*
Wayne Fricano *(V.P.-Distr.)*
Terry McKee *(V.P.-Real Estate)*
Karen Morrison *(V.P.-Store Opers.)*
Chris Urgo *(Controller)*

No. of Mfg. Plants/Facilities: 21

Computer Systems/Hardware:
IBM AS400

Outside Service Firm(s):

Coopers & Lybrand*(Auditors)*
203 N. LaSalle St
Chicago, IL 60601
Tel.: 312-701-5500

PetCare Plus, Inc.—(Continued)

Spencer, Fane, Britt & Browne*(Legal Firm)*
106 W. 14th St.
Kansas City, MO 64105
Tel.: 816-474-8100

PETER LUMBER COMPANY
Washington & Lyons Court
Pleasantville, NJ 08232
Tel.: 609-641-9000
Fax: 609-641-8292
Approx.Sls.: $28,000,000
Emp.: 100
Retail Lumber
S.I.C.: 5211
Lee D. Bergen *(Chm. Bd. & Sec.)*
Hugh M. Peter, Jr. *(Pres.)*
Hugh M. Peter, Sr. *(Exec. V.P.)*
Peter Holter *(V.P. & Treas.)*

Outside Service Firm(s):

KPMG Peat Marwick*(Auditors)*
Trenton, NJ

Saul, Ewing, Remick & Saul*(Legal Firm)*
1500 Market St.
Philadelphia, PA 19102
Tel.: 215-972-7777

CoreStates First Pennsylvania Bank, N.A.*(Major Banking Relationship)*
16th & Market Sts.
Philadelphia, PA 19101
Tel.: 215-786-8030

PETER PAN BUS LINES, INC.
1776 Main St.
Springfield, MA 01102
Mailing Address:
P.O. Box 1776
Springfield, MA 01102-1776
Tel.: 413-781-2900 **MA**
Fax: 413-731-9721
Year Founded: 1933
Assets: $23,400,000
Liabilities: $8,700,000
Net Worth: $14,700,000
Approx.Sls.: $28,500,000
Emp.: 500
Fiscal Year-end: 12/31/90
Intercity Bus Line & Charter Bus Service
S.I.C.: 4142; 4131; 5013
Peter L. Picknelly *(Chm. Emeritus)*
Peter A. Picknelly, Jr. *(Pres. & Chief Exec. Officer)*
Brian R. Stefano *(Chief Fin. Officer & Controller)*
Robert Schwarz *(Exec. V.P.)*
Robert Dostal *(Sr. V.P.-Mktg. & Adv.)*
Carmen Picknelly *(Sr. V.P.)*
Paul Picknelly *(Sr. V.P.)*
Philip J. Shine *(Sec.)*
Paul Lemieux *(Dir.-Personnel)*
Michael Paton *(Dir.-Mktg.)*
Susan Brown *(Mktg. Coord.)*
Principal(s):
Peter A. Picknelly, Jr.
Peter L. Picknelly

No. of U.S. Offices: 3

Computer Systems/Hardware:
IBM System 36

Outside Service Firm(s):

Meyers Brothers & Adeletti, P.C.*(Auditors)*
Longmeadow, MA

Insurance Company of North America*(Commercial Insurance Carrier)*
Hartford, CT

Connecticut General Life Insurance Co.*(Group Insurer)*
P.O. Box 2975,
Hartford, CT 06104
Tel.: 203-726-6000

Philip J. Shine, Esq.*(Legal Firm)*
Springfield, MA

Santaniello, Posnik, Basile & Gelinas, P.C.*(Legal Firm)*
Springfield, MA

BayBank Valley Trust Company*(Major Banking Relationship)*
Springfield, MA

Pension Associates, Inc.*(Pension Manager)*
Springfield, MA

J. M. PETERS CO.
3501 Jamboree, Ste. 200
Newport Beach, CA 92660
Tel.: 714-854-2500
Earnings: ($107,981,000)
Approx.Rev.: $215,535,000
Fiscal Year-end: 2/28/91
Real Estate Development
S.I.C.: 6552
James M. Peters *(Pres.)*

PETERSEN ALUMINUM CORPORATION
955 Estes Ave.
Elk Grove Village, IL 60007
Tel.: 708-228-7150
Tel.: 800-323-1960 **IL**
Fax: 708-722-7150
Year Founded: 1965
Approx.Sls.: $34,000,000
Emp.: 100
Fiscal Year-end: 6/30/92
Import Export
Warehousing, Fabrication of Aluminum & Architectural Metals, Roll Formed Building Panels & Architectural Signage
S.I.C.: 4225; 3441
Maurice R. Petersen *(Chief Exec. Officer)*
Mike Petersen *(Pres.)*
Thomas Creigh *(V.P.)*
John Palesny *(V.P.)*
Jon Snyder *(V.P.)*
Ann R. Petersen *(Sec.)*

No. of Mfg. Plants/Facilities: 4
No. of U.S. Offices: 4

Computer Systems/Hardware:
IBM System/36, PCs, etc.

Outside Service Firm(s):

McCullough, Rossi & Co.*(Auditors)*
Hoffman Estates, IL

NBD Of Highland Park*(Major Banking Relationship)*
Elk Grove Village, IL

Subsidiary:

Charleston Industries **(1)**
One Industrial Park
Charleston, MS
Tel.: 800-647-2384
Sign Company
S.I.C.: 7389

PETERSEN GRAPHICS GROUP
2920 W. Sample
South Bend, IN 46619
Tel.: 219-233-6171
Fax: 219-288-4521
Year Founded: 1919
Approx.Sls.: $16,000,000
Emp.: 134
Commercial & Advertising Lithography
S.I.C.: 2752
Eric Petersen *(Chm. Bd. & Treas.)*
Marc Petersen *(Pres. & Sec.)*

Outside Service Firm(s):

John Z. Olcott & Co.*(Auditors)*
South Bend, IN

Rallo & Tepper*(Legal Firm)*
Chicago, IL

TrustCorp Bank*(Major Banking Relationship)*
South Bend, IN

PETERSEN PUBLISHING COMPANY
8490 Sunset Blvd.
Los Angeles, CA 90069
Tel.: 310-854-2222
Fax: 310-854-6825
Year Founded: 1948
Approx.Sls.: $200,000,000
Emp.: 800
Fiscal Year-end: 11/30/90
Consumer Magazines; 16 Monthlies, 7 Bimonthlies, Enthusiast Specialty Publications & Variety of One-Shots
S.I.C.: 2721
R.E. Petersen *(Chm. Bd.)*
F.R. Waingrow *(Pres.)*
Peter Clancey *(Sr. V.P. & Natl. Adv. Dir.)*
Robert MacLeod *(Sr. V.P. & Publr.-Teen)*
John Dianna *(V.P. & Grp. Publr.-Auto Performance Grp.)*
Nigel Heaton *(V.P.-Circulation & Mktg. Devel.)*
Lee Kelley *(V.P. & Grp. Publr.-Auto & Sport)*
James J. Krenek *(V.P.-Mfg.)*
Thomas Siatos *(V.P. & Grp. Publr.-Outdoor Div.)*
Philip E. Trimbach *(V.P.-Fin. & Admin.)*
Paul Tzimoulis *(V.P. & Grp. Publr.-Marine & Photography Div.)*
Richard Johnson *(Controller)*
James G. Adolph *(Publr.-Car Craft)*
Charles Alexander *(Dir.-Eastern Adv.)*
Vern Ball *(Dir.-Fulfillment Services)*
Carol Johnson *(Dir.-Adv. Opers.)*
James G. Kilbourne *(Dir.-Single Copy Sls.)*
Henson Lacon *(Dir.-Subscription Sls.)*
Leo D. LaRew *(Dir.-Human Resources)*
Don McGlathery *(Dir.-Adv. Research)*
Ralph Panico *(Dir.-Western Adv.)*
Duane Placko *(Dir.-Midwest Adv.)*
T.J. Prohaska *(Dir.-Real Estate)*
Bob Weggeland *(Dir.-Direct Mktg. Div.)*
Melissa Donnelly *(Mgr.-Adv. Admin.)*
Elizabeth Schroeder *(Mgr.-Promotion)*

Outside Service Firm(s):

Arthur Andersen & Co.*(Auditors)*
633 W. Fifth St.
Los Angeles, CA 90071
Tel.: 213-614-6500

Robert Gottlieb*(Legal Firm)*
Los Angeles, CA

First Interstate Bank of California*(Major Banking Relationship)*
707 Wilshire Blvd., 11th Fl.
Los Angeles, CA 90017
Tel.: 213-614-0111
Tel.: 800-522-6645

PETERSON AMERICAN CORP.
21200 Telegraph Rd.
Southfield, MI 48034
Tel.: 313-353-6400
Fax: 313-357-3176
Approx.Sls.: $75,000,000
Emp.: 650
Fiscal Year-end: 12/31/91
Export
Mfr. Springs, Fasteners, Hose Clamps, Metal Stampings
S.I.C.: 3495; 3496; 3493; 3429; 3469
Alfred H. Peterson III *(Chm. Bd.)*
Eric Peterson *(Pres.)*
Lawrence Luchi *(V.P.-Fin.)*
Gary Strunk *(V.P.-Sls.)*
G. Connor *(Dir.-Pur.)*
Michael S. Proffitt *(Dir.-Personnel)*
Gail A. Lauzzana *(Mgr.-Corp. Communications)*

No. of Mfg. Plants/Facilities: 20
No. of U.S. Offices: 14
No. of Foreign Offices: 7

Outside Service Firm(s):

Ernst & Young*(Auditors)*
One Detroit Center, 500 Woodward, Ste. 1700
Detroit, MI 48243
Tel.: 313-259-9600

Cross Wrock*(Legal Firm)*
Detroit, MI

N.B.D. Bank, N.A.*(Major Banking Relationship)*
611 Woodward Ave.
Detroit, MI 48226
Tel.: 313-225-1122
Fax: 313-225-3420

PETERSON BUILDERS, INC.
101 Pennsylvania St.
Sturgeon Bay, WI 54235
Mailing Address:
P.O. Box 650,
Sturgeon Bay, WI 54235
Tel.: 414-743-5577 **WI**
Telex: 26-3423
Fax: 414-743-6089
Year Founded: 1933
Sales Range: $60-79 Million
Emp.: 900
Fiscal Year-end: 8/31/92
Export
Shipbuilding, Boatbuilding & Repairs
S.I.C.: 3731; 3732
Ellsworth L. Peterson *(Pres. & Gen. Mgr.)*
Larry Maples *(V.P.-Fin. & Chief Fin. Officer)*
Dick Russell *(V.P.-Mfg.)*
Lloyd Shaffer *(V.P.-Contracts)*
Chuck St. Pierre *(V.P.-Human Resources)*
Fred J. Peterson II *(Sec.)*
Marsha L. Kerley *(Treas. & Asst. Sec.)*

No. of U.S. Offices: 1

Computer Systems/Hardware:
AS-400

Outside Service Firm(s):

Bank of Sturgeon Bay*(Major Banking Relationship)*
Sturgeon Bay, WI

PETERSON INDUSTRIES INC.
250 S. Main St.
Decatur, AR 72722
Tel.: 501-752-3211
Fax: 501-752-3250
Year Founded: 1939
Approx.Sls.: $80,000,000
Emp.: 1,200
Breeding Stock, Dressed Poultry
S.I.C.: 0212; 0251; 0253; 0259
Lloyd E. Peterson *(Chm. Bd.)*
L. Victor Evans *(Pres.)*
Dan Henderson *(Exec. V.P.-Fin.)*
E.J. Wilmoth *(Exec. V.P.)*
Gene Wilmoth *(Exec. V.P.)*
Bill Baisley *(V.P.-Mktg.)*
Lorrayne L. Peterson *(Sec.)*
Ray Wear *(Comptroller)*
Kerry Kenyon *(Pur. Agent)*
Curtis Vaugh *(Dir.-Personnel)*
Donna Amos *(Mgr.-Data Processing)*
Don Ellen *(Mgr.-Sls.)*

Outside Service Firm(s):

Frost & Co.*(Auditors)*
Little Rock, AR

Mitchell, Williams, Selig, Jackson & Tucker*(Legal Firm)*
Decatur, AR

Decatur State Bank*(Major Banking Relationship)*
Decatur, AR

PETERSON MOTOR COMPANY
9101 W. Fairview
Boise, ID 83704
Tel.: 208-378-9000 **ID**
Fax: 208-378-9090
Year Founded: 1958
Approx.Sls.: $18,000,000
Emp.: 80
Retail Sales of New & Used Automobiles
S.I.C.: 5511
Marvin Peterson *(Pres.)*
Mark Peterson *(V.P.)*
Jean Peterson *(Treas. & Sec.)*

Outside Service Firm(s):

First Security Bank, N.A.*(Major Banking Relationship)*
P.O. Box 2618,
Boise, ID 83701
Tel.: 208-338-2032

PETERSON TRACTOR COMPANY
955 Marina Blvd.
San Leandro, CA 94577
Tel.: 510-357-6200
Fax: 510-352-5952
Approx.Sls.: $100,000,000
Emp.: 500
Agriculture Implements, Construction Earth Moving, Mining & Industrial Machinery
S.I.C.: 5083; 5082; 5084
W.E. Doyle, Jr. *(Pres.)*
Ernie Fiero *(V.P.-Product Support)*
Jerry Lopus *(V.P.-Sls.)*
Walter Perry *(V.P.-Fin.)*
Jack Gallagher *(Treas.)*
Duane Doyle *(Gen. Mgr.)*
Jerry Evans *(Pur. Agent)*

Outside Service Firm(s):

Deloitte & Touche*(Auditors)*
50 Fremont St.
San Francisco, CA 94105-2230
Tel.: 415-393-4300
Fax: 415-227-0452

Fitzgerald, Abbot & Beardsley*(Legal Firm)*
Oakland, CA

PETRICCA INDUSTRIES, INC.
444 Merrill Rd.
Pittsfield, MA 01202
Mailing Address:
P.O. Box 1145
Pittsfield, MA 01202
Tel.: 413-442-6926
Fax: 413-499-9930
Approx.Sls.: $38,000,000
Emp.: 200
Heavy & Highway Construction, Supply Ready-mixed Concrete, Sand & Stone; Prestressed Concrete Forms; Landscaping Services
S.I.C.: 1611; 0781; 5032
Robert W. Petricca *(Pres.)*
Perric C. Petricca *(Exec. V.P.)*
Thomas Grof *(V.P.-Fin.)*
Virginia R. Petricca *(Treas.)*
Barbara Krupka *(Dir.-Personnel)*
Frank Zovistroski *(Mgr.-Data Processing)*
Donald K. Laws *(Chief Accountant)*
Holly Wroldson *(Pur. Agent)*

Outside Service Firm(s):

Coopers & Lybrand*(Auditors)*
2300 Bay Bank Tower, 1500 Main St.
Springfield, MA 01101
Tel.: 413-781-7200

Cain, Hibbard, Myers & Cook*(Legal Firm)*
Pittsfield, MA

First Agricultural Bank*(Major Banking Relationship)*
Pittsfield, MA

PETRO CHEM DEVELOPMENT COMPANY
122 E. 42nd St.
New York, NY 10017
Tel.: 212-697-7442
Fax: 212-557-6457
Emp.: 50
Fiscal Year-end: 12/31/91

Export
Refinery Heaters & Waste Heat Boilers For Oil & Petrochemical Industry; General Application Process Heaters For Oil & Chemical Plants; Industrial Dryers; Magnet Wire Equipment; Parts Washers & Paint Finishing Systems
S.I.C.: 1629
Anthony T. Limpe *(Chm. Bd.)*
William Bredin *(Dir.-Fin.)*
Andrew Alexander *(V.P.-Engrng.)*
Emily T. Limpe *(Exec. V.P.)*
D.J. Stoepker *(Mgr.-Opers.)*
Donald J. McCarthy *(Dir.-Pur.)*
Kenneth Catala *(Dir.-Quality Control)*

No. of Mfg. Plants/Facilities: 1
No. of U.S. Offices: 3

Outside Service Firm(s):

Ernst & Young*(Auditors)*
1300 Huntington Bldg.
Cleveland, OH 44115
Tel.: 216-861-5000
Fax: 303-291-6234

Orloff, Lowenbach, Stifelman & Siegel*(Legal Firm)*
Milburn, NJ

Citibank N.A.*(Major Banking Relationship)*
Corporate Trust Services, 399 Park Ave.
New York, NY 10043
Tel.: 212-559-1605

Subsidiary:

American Econo-Therm **(1)**
8282 South Memorial
Tulsa, OK 74133
Tel.: 918-254-8000
J.E. Gates *(V.P. & Gen. Mgr.)*
Lee Massey *(Dir.-Mktg.)*
Art Christian *(Mgr.-Pur.)*

PETRO-HUNT CORPORATION
3900 Thanksgiving Tower
Dallas, TX 75201
Tel.: 214-880-8400
Fax: 214-880-7101
Year Founded: 1983
Approx.Sls.: $25,000,000
Emp.: 150
Fiscal Year-end: 4/30/90
Oil & Gas Exploration & Extraction; Real Estate
S.I.C.: 1381; 1382
Bruce W. Hunt *(Pres. & Chief Exec. Officer)*
Tom Nelson *(V.P.-Fin.)*
Charles Rigdon *(V.P.-Opers.)*
Charlotte Bowland *(Treas.)*
Walter Roach *(Gen. Counsel)*
Randy Burrows *(Dir.-Data Processing)*
Bill Heidelberg *(Dir.-Personnel & Employee Benefits)*
Ron Stephens *(Dir.-Pur.)*

Computer Systems/Hardware:
IBM 3083

Outside Service Firm(s):

KPMG Peat Marwick*(Auditors)*
1601 Elm St., Ste. 1600
Dallas, TX 75201
Tel.: 214-754-2000
Fax: 214-754-2297

Bank One*(Major Banking Relationship)*
P.O. Box 655415,
Dallas, TX 75265-5415
Tel.: 214-290-2000

First City, Texas-Dallas*(Major Banking Relationship)*
P.O. Box 661700,
Dallas, TX 75266
Tel.: 214-939-8441

PETROLEUM INC.
301 N. Main , Ste. 900
Wichita, KS 67202
Tel.: 316-291-8200
Fax: 316-291-8201
Telecopier: 316-291-8211
Year Founded: 1948
Approx.Sls.: $100,000,000
Emp.: 70
Fiscal Year-end: 3/31/90
Oil & Gas Exploration
S.I.C.: 1382
John Garvey *(Chm. Bd. & Chief Exec. Officer)*
James A. Williams *(Pres. & Chief Oper. Officer)*
Thomas Beard *(Sr. V.P., Chief Fin. Officer, Treas. & Controller)*
Charlotte Weidman *(Sr. V.P. & Sec.)*
Richard D. Randall *(V.P. & Gen. Counsel)*
John C. Miles *(Controller & Asst. Treas.)*
Ben Whiteside *(Mgr.-Data Processing)*

Computer Systems/Hardware:
IBM System 38 Model 8

Outside Service Firm(s):

Price Waterhouse*(Auditors)*
1055 Broadway
Kansas City, MO 64105
Tel.: 816-474-6590

Andrews Davis Legg Bixler Milsten & Price*(Legal Firm)*
500 W. Main
Oklahoma City, OK 73102
Tel.: 405-272-9241

First National Bank Oklahoma City*(Major Banking Relationship)*
Oklahoma City, OK

Fourth National Bank Wichita*(Major Banking Relationship)*
Wichita, KS

PETROLEUM MARKETERS, INC.
5221 Valley Park Drive, Ste. 3
Roanoke, VA 24019
Mailing Address:
P.O. Box 12203,
Roanoke, VA 24023
Tel.: 703-362-4900
Fax: 703-366-2820
Assets: $21,699,898
Liabilities: $16,235,439
Net Worth: $5,464,459
Approx.Sls.: $150,000,000
Emp.: 368
Fiscal Year-end: 6/30/91
Retail Petroleum & Petroleum Products; Operator of Convenience Stores
S.I.C.: 5983; 5171; 5399
Terry M. Phelps *(Chm. Bd., Pres. & Chief Exec. Officer)*
Scott F. Blankinship *(Exec. V.P. & Sec.)*
Tina Sullivan *(Dir.-Personnel)*
Jack J. Jackson *(Mgr.-Credit)*
Principal(s):
Terry M. Phelps

No. of U.S. Offices: 8

Computer Systems/Hardware:
Sperry 1100/71; IBM PC

Outside Service Firm(s):

Dalton, Pennell & Co.*(Auditors)*
Richmond, VA

Maguire, Woods & Battle*(Legal Firm)*
Richmond, VA

Sovran Bank*(Major Banking Relationship)*
Roanoke, VA

Jefferson National Bank*(Pension Manager)*
Richmond, VA

Subsidiaries:

PM Properties Inc. **(1)**
5221 Valley Park Rd., Ste. 3
Roanoke, VA 24019
Tel.: 804-288-4124 (100%)
Emp.: 77
Retail & Wholesale Petroleum Prods.
S.I.C.: 5171; 5983
Scott F. Blankinship *(Pres.)*

PM Terminals, Inc. **(1)**
5221 Valley Park Dr., Ste. 3
Roanoke, VA 24019
Tel.: 804-232-6640 (100%)
Emp.: 4
Petroleum Products Terminalling
S.I.C.: 1321
John W. Smith *(Pres.)*

PM Transport, Inc. **(1)**
5221 Valley Park Dr., Ste. 3
Roanoke, VA 24019
Tel.: 804-528-3292 (100%)
Emp.: 18
Common Carrier
S.I.C.: 4213
John W. Smith *(Pres.)*

Stop In Food Stores **(1)**
5221 Valley Park Rd., Ste. 3
Roanoke, VA 24019
Tel.: 804-288-4577 (100%)
Emp.: 214
Retail Gasoline & Convenience Stores
S.I.C.: 5411
Ronald R. Hare *(Pres.)*

PETROLEUM PRODUCTS CORP.
900 Eisenhower Blvd.
Middletown, PA 17057
Mailing Address:
P.O. Box 2621
Harrisburg, PA 17105
Tel.: 717-939-0466 **PA**
Fax: 717-939-0294
Year Founded: 1960
Approx.Sls.: $250,000,000
Emp.: 20
Fiscal Year-end: 1/31/90
Wholesale Oil, Gasoline & Kerosene
S.I.C.: 5171
John A. Arnold *(Chm. Bd.)*
Paul E. Ermlich *(Vice Chm.)*
John M. Arnold *(Pres.)*
Barbara M. Arnold *(Treas.)*
Dennis M. Shaw *(Controller)*
Robert G. Bost *(Sec.)*

Computer Systems/Hardware:
STS Systems

Outside Service Firm(s):

Dauphin Deposit Bank & Trust Co.*(Major Banking Relationship)*
213 Market St.
Harrisburg, PA 17101

PETROLEUM TRADERS CORPORATION
1122 Thomas Rd.
Fort Wayne, IN 46804
Tel.: 219-432-6622 **IN**
Fax: 219-432-6564
Year Founded: 1979
Approx.Sls.: $135,000,000
Emp.: 62
Fiscal Year-end: 6/30/91

Petroleum Traders Corporation—(Continued)

Petroleum Product Wholesale- Owns No Bulk Stations or Terminals. Does Sell to Both.
S.I.C.: 5172
Michael B. Himes *(Chm. Bd., Pres. & Chief Exec. Officer)*
Vicki Himes *(Office Mgr.)*

Outside Service Firm(s):

Baden, Conrad, Gage & Schroeder*(Auditors)*
Ft. Wayne, IN

Lincoln National Life Insurance Co.*(Major Banking Relationship)*
Fort Wayne, IN

PETTY COMPANY, INC.
P.O. Box 250,
Effingham, IL 62401
Year Founded: 1956
Approx.Sls.: $70,000,000
Emp.: 500
Fiscal Year-end: 12/31/90
Lithographic Commercial Printing
S.I.C.: 2752
Jack W. Graham *(Chm. Bd., Sec. & Treas.)*
George Whaling *(Pres. & Chief Exec. Officer)*
Robert Kronenberger *(Chief Fin. Officer, Sr. V.P. & Treas.)*
David O. Field *(Exec. V.P.)*
Jerry Frailey *(Exec. V.P.)*
Dale Donsbach *(Sr. V.P.)*
Rick Havel *(Sr. V.P.)*
Micheal Patterson *(Sr. V.P.)*
Robert H. Pillers *(Sr. V.P.)*
William A. Waller *(Sr. V.P., Gen. Counsel & Sec.)*

No. of Mfg. Plants/Facilities: 2
No. of U.S. Offices: 5

Outside Service Firm(s):

KPMG Peat Marwick*(Auditors)*
Decatur, IL

Boatmen's National Bank of St. Louis*(Major Banking Relationship)*
One Boatmen's Plaza, 800 Market St.
St. Louis, MO 63101
Tel.: 314-466-6000

National Westminster Bank plc*(Major Banking Relationship)*
Astor Plaza, 1515 Broadway
New York, NY 10036

PFAUDLER-U.S., INC.
1000 West Ave.
Rochester, NY 14611
Mailing Address:
P.O. Box 1600,
Rochester, NY 14692
Tel.: 716-235-1000
Year Founded: 1884
Approx.Sls.: $55,000,000
Emp.: 450
Import Export
Corrosion Resistant Equipment & Systems for the Chemical Processing & Pharmaceutical Industries
S.I.C.: 3599
Robert Campbell *(Pres. & Chief Exec. Officer)*
William Hall *(Pres.-Eagle Industries Inc.)*
Rick Kinsley *(V.P.-Sls. & Mktg.)*
Joe Whalen *(V.P.-Mngmt. Information Systems)*
Brian Marks *(V.P.-Engrng.)*
Jim Malvaso *(V.P.-Mfg.)*
Steven Ley *(V.P.-Fin.)*
Joseph R. Mannara *(Dir.-Mktg. Communication)*
Paul Knight *(Dir.-Pur.)*
Don Doell *(Mgr.-Natl. Sls.)*

Bette Quinn *(Mgr.-Human Resources)*
Sid Smith *(Mgr.-Quality Control)*

Subsidiary:

Edlon Products, Inc. **(1)**
117 State Rd.
Avondale, PA 19311-0667
Tel.: 215-268-8898
Mfr. of Corrosion Resistance Teflon
S.I.C.: 3599
William Flannery *(Pres.)*
Brian Blauvelt *(Natl. Sls. Mgr.)*

PHAR-MOR, INC.
(Filed Ch. 11 Bankruptcy, Aug. 17, 1992)
20 Federal Plaza W.
Youngstown, OH 44503
Tel.: 216-746-6641
Fax: 216-740-2915
Year Founded: 1982
Approx.Sls.: $2,400,000,000
Emp.: 22,000
Fiscal Year-end: 6/30/91
Retail Drug Stores
S.I.C.: 5912
David Shapira *(Chm. Bd.)*
Antonio C. Alvarez *(Pres. & Chief Oper. Officer)*
Joe Pingue *(Sr. V.P.-Mktg.)*
James Teichman *(Sr. V.P.)*
Andrew Bremmer *(V.P.-Adv.)*

PHARMACAPS INC.
P.O. Box 547, 1111 Jefferson Ave.
Elizabeth, NJ 07201
Tel.: 908-354-6900
Approx.Sls.: $25,000,000
Emp.: 200
Mfg. of Pharmaceuticals, Vitamins, Dietary Products & Veterinary Products
S.I.C.: 2834; 2099
Stephen E. Fischer *(Pres.)*
Ira R. Berry *(Exec. V.P.)*
Wayne Phillips *(V.P.-Sls. & Mktg.)*
Theresa Telly *(Dir.-Personnel & Admin.)*

PHARMAVITE CORP.
15451 San Fernando Mission Blvd.
Mission Hills, CA 91345
Tel.: 818-837-3633
Fax: 818-637-6108
Approx.Sls.: $123,500,000
Emp.: 640
Fiscal Year-end: 2/28/92
Import Export
Mfr. Vitamins, Food Supplements, & Skin Care Prods.
S.I.C.: 5122; 2834
Kenneth M. Rosenberg *(Chm. & Chief Exec. Officer)*
Henry Burdick *(Pres.)*
Dick Mora *(Chief Oper. Officer)*
Claudette St. Onge *(Exec. V.P.-Sls. & Mktg.)*
Gerry Holly *(Sr. V.P.-Opers.)*
Jerry Caldera *(V.P.-Sls.)*
John Vickers *(V.P.-Fin.)*
Frank Sajovic *(Dir.-Mktg.)*

Computer Systems/Hardware:
AS400

Division:

International Tableting **(1)**
15451 San Fernando Mission Blvd.
Mission Hills, CA 91345
Tel.: 213-875-0948

Subsidiary:

Nature Made Nutritional Products Inc. **(1)**
15451 San Fernando Mission Blvd.
Mission Hills, CA 91345
Tel.: 213-875-0948

THE PHELPS GROUP
11999 San Vicente Blvd., Ste. 401
Los Angeles, CA 90049
Tel.: 310-471-6170
Fax: 310-471-2830
Year Founded: 1981
Approx.Billings: $16,000,000
Emp.: 28
Joe Phelps *(Pres.)*
Glenn Schieke *(V.P., Opers.)*
Judy Lynes *(V.P., Dir. Pub. Rels.)*

PHELPS TOINTON INC.
822 7th St., Ste. 700
Greeley, CO 80631
Mailing Address:
P.O. Box 1518
Greeley, CO 80632
Tel.: 303-353-7000 **DE**
Fax: 303-353-2434
Year Founded: 1897
Approx.Sls.: $70,000,000
Emp.: 500
Fiscal Year-end: 12/31/90
Export
Mfr. & Export Dentention Equipment, Jail Locks, Detention Windows
S.I.C.: 3312; 3429; 3442; 3449; 3272
Robert G. Tointon *(Pres.)*
Larry LaFollette *(Pres.-Rocky Mountain Prestress)*
Steve Allison *(V.P.)*
Joe Phelps *(V.P.)*
Martin G. Ariano *(Controller)*

Principal(s):
Robert G. Tointon
Joe Phelps

No. of Mfg. Plants/Facilities: 5

Outside Service Firm(s):

Price Waterhouse*(Auditors)*
950 17th St., Ste. 2600
Denver, CO 80202
Tel.: 303-893-8100

Division:

Southern Steel Company **(1)**
P.O. Box 2021
San Antonio, TX 78297
Tel.: 210-533-1231
Fax: 210-533-2211
Steel Company
S.I.C.: 3312
Michael Holland *(Pres.)*

THE PHILADELPHIA BOURSE, INC.
9602 A George Palmer Hwy.
Lanham, MD 20706
Mailing Address:
4601 Forbes Blvd.
Lanham, MD 20706
Tel.: 301-731-0811 **DC**
Fax: 301-731-6181
Year Founded: 1979
Holding Company
S.I.C.: 6719
McBee Butcher *(Chm.)*
John Hozik *(Pres. & Chief Exec. Officer)*
Howard Butcher IV *(V.P.)*
Johnathan Butcher *(V.P.)*

Divisions:

E. C. Ernst **(1)**
P.O. Box 4040
Capitol Heights, MD 20791
Tel.: 410-350-7770
Approx.Sls.: $10,000,000
Emp.: 200
Electrical Contracting
S.I.C.: 1731
R. C. Worch *(Pres.)*
John Hozik *(Chief Exec. Officer)*

Mitchell Business Equipment **(1)**
4855 Walden Lane
Lanham, MD 20706
Tel.: 301-306-1860
Fax: 301-306-9687
Retail Sales & Service Business Equipment
S.I.C.: 5044
Thomas Noble *(Gen. Mgr.)*

Sensenich Propeller Co. **(1)**
P.O. Box 5100, East Airport Rd.
Lancaster, PA 17601
Tel.: 717-560-3711
Fax: 717-560-3725
Manufacturing and Sales & Service Airplane Propellers
S.I.C.: 3724; 5088
Joseph Maus *(Pres.)*

PHILADELPHIA COCA-COLA BOTTLING CO.
725 Erie Ave. & 9th St.
Philadelphia, PA 19134
Tel.: 215-427-4500
Fax: 215-423-5557
Approx.Sls.: $256,000,000
Emp.: 850
Mfr. of Soft Drinks, Coca-Cola & Allied Products
S.I.C.: 2086
J. Bruce Llewellyn *(Chm. Bd.)*
Ronald D. Wilson *(Pres.)*
Lynn King *(V.P.-Fin.)*
John P. Kolb *(V.P.-Human Resources)*
Asa G. Murray *(V.P.-Sls. & Mktg.)*
Burton Rubin *(Treas.)*
Hubert Tipkin *(Controller)*

Outside Service Firm(s):

Ernst & Young*(Auditors)*
1800 John F. Kennedy Blvd.
Philadelphia, PA 19103-7499
Tel.: 215-864-3300

Philadelphia National Bank*(Major Banking Relationship)*
5th & Market Sts.
Philadelphia, PA 19101
Tel.: 215-629-3100
Fax: 215-834-2069

Trust Company Bank*(Major Banking Relationship)*
Trust Co. Tower
Atlanta, GA 30303
Tel.: 404-588-7963

PHILADELPHIA GEAR CORP.
181 S. Gulph Rd.
King of Prussia, PA 19406
Tel.: 215-265-3000
Fax: 215-337-5637
Year Founded: 1892
Approx.Sls.: $55,000,000
Emp.: 400
Fiscal Year-end: 12/31/90
Import Export
Mfr. Power Transmissions
S.I.C.: 3566
Thomas R. Kling *(Pres.)*
Joseph Gratzinger *(V.P.-Quality Assurance)*
Robert Murphy *(V.P.-Sls.)*
Jon Jensen *(Controller & Treas.)*
Rick Carson *(Dir.-Mngmt. Information Systems)*
Bruce Hamilton *(Dir.-Human Resources)*
William Liggett *(Dir.-Pur.)*
Joseph Pooler *(Dir.-Real Estate)*
Charles M. Slinghoff, Jr. *(Dir.)*
George W. Boisbrun *(Gen. Sls. Mgr.)*

Computer Systems/Hardware:
UMSYS 6000 Series

Outside Service Firm(s):

KPMG Peat Marwick*(Auditors)*
1600 Market St.
Philadelphia, PA 19103
Tel.: 215-299-3100

Morgan, Lewis & Bockius*(Legal Firm)*
2000 One Logan Square
Philadelphia, PA 19103-6993
Tel.: 215-963-5000
Fax: 215-963-5299

Mellon Bank, N.A.*(Major Banking Relationship)*
P.O. Box 444,
Pittsburgh, PA 15230
Tel.: 412-236-8000
Tel.: 1-800-451-7392
Fax: 412-236-8157

Philadelphia National Bank*(Major Banking Relationship)*
P.O. Box 13834, Broad & Chestnut Streets
Philadelphia, PA 19101-7618
Tel.: 215-973-8327

Dearden, McGuire & Weaver*(Pension Manager)*
Philadelphia, PA

PHILADELPHIA RESERVE SUPPLY COMPANY
400 Mack Dr.
Croydon, PA 19021
Tel.: 215-785-3141
Tel.: 800-347-7726 **PA**
Fax: 215-785-5806
Year Founded: 1930
Approx.Sls.: $65,710,000
Emp.: 35
Fiscal Year-end: 11/30/92
Lumber & Building Materials-Wholesale
S.I.C.: 5031; 5039
Harry T. Rosenheim, III *(Pres.)*
Frank Dalinsky *(Chief Exec. Officer & Exec. V.P.)*
Sandra Spadaccino *(V.P.-Sls. & Pur.)*
Howard J. Opdyke *(Treas.)*
Charles Gormley *(Controller)*
Peter Shearer *(Sec.)*
Janet Dinofa *(Dir.-Data Processing)*

No. of Mfg. Plants/Facilities: 1

Computer Systems/Hardware:
MCS/Digital

Outside Service Firm(s):

Seligman, Cupersmith, Wilensky & Co.*(Auditors)*
Philadelphia, PA

Dechert, Price & Rhoads*(Legal Firm)*
4000 Bell Atlantic Tower, 1717 Arch St.
Philadelphia, PA 19103
Tel.: 215-994-4000
Tel.: 2000

Philadelphia National Bank*(Major Banking Relationship)*
P.O. Box 13834, Broad & Chestnut Streets
Philadelphia, PA 19101-7618
Tel.: 215-973-8327

PHILADELPHIA SIGN COMPANY
707 W. Spring Garden St.
Palmyra, NJ 08065
Tel.: 609-829-1460
Fax: 609-829-8549
Approx.Sls.: $10,000,000
Emp.: 120
Electric Signs, Lighting Fixtures, Steel Fabrication, Plastic Forming & Fabrication, Controlled Environments, Prefabricated Buildings
S.I.C.: 3993; 2541; 2452; 3089; 3645
William Trucksess *(Pres.)*
John M. Lopez *(Sr. V.P.)*
Wright Rundle *(Mgr.-Sls.)*
Frank M. Lario, Jr. *(Gen. Counsel)*
Martin Marotta *(Pur. Agent)*

Outside Service Firm(s):

Gordon Meyers*(Auditors)*
Camden, NJ

Mellon Bank, N.A.*(Major Banking Relationship)*
Camden, NJ

PHILIPP BROTHERS CHEMICALS, INC.
One Parker Plaza
Fort Lee, NJ 07024
Tel.: 201-944-6020 **NY**
Fax: 201-944-7916
Year Founded: 1947
Assets: $120,000,000
Liabilities: $86,000,000
Net Worth: $34,000,000
Approx.Sls.: $175,000,000
Emp.: 700
Fiscal Year-end: 6/30/92
Import Export
Industrial & Agricultural Chemicals
S.I.C.: 2869; 2879
C.H. Bendheim *(Chm. Bd.)*
J.C. Bendhelm *(Pres.)*
Marvin Sussman *(Exec. V.P.-Pur.)*
Joseph Katzenstein *(Treas.)*
Nathan Bistricer *(Sec.)*

Outside Service Firm(s):

Edward Isaacs & Co.*(Auditors)*
380 Madison Ave.
New York, NY 10017

Weitzner, Levine & Hamburg*(Legal Firm)*
New York, NY

Citibank N.A.*(Major Banking Relationship)*
Corporate Trust Services, 399 Park Ave.
New York, NY 10043
Tel.: 212-559-1605

Non-U.S. Holding:

Ferro Metal & Chemical Corporation Ltd. **(1)**
179, Kings Rd.
Reading, RG1 4EX, United Kingdom
Tel.: 0734 591961
Telex: 847295 FERRO G
Fax: 0734 509216
Approx.Sls.: $15,000,000
Emp.: 45
Chemicals & Pharmaceutical Chemicals
S.I.C.: 5122; 5169
Joseph J. Norman *(Mng. Dir.)*

THE PHILLIES-A LIMITED PARTNERSHIP
Veterans Stadium, Broad St. & Pattison Ave.
Philadelphia, PA 19148
Mailing Address:
P.O. Box 7575
Philadelphia, PA 19101
Tel.: 215-463-6000
Fax: 215-389-3050
Sales Range: $40-59 Million
Emp.: 120
Import
Professional Baseball Team
S.I.C.: 7941
Bill Giles *(Pres.)*
David Montgomery *(Exec. V.P.)*
G.S. Clothier *(Sr. V.P.-Fin.)*
Larry Shenk *(V.P.-Pub. Rels.)*
Lee Thomas *(V.P. & Gen. Mgr.)*
Louis Perez *(Controller)*
Richard Deats *(Dir.-Sls.-Ticket Opers.)*
Mike DiMuzio *(Dir.-Stadium Opers.)*
Thomas T. Hudson *(Dir.-Plng./Devel.-Super Box)*
Dennis Mannion *(Dir.-Mktg.)*
Brian Lamoreaux *(Mgr.-Info. Systems)*
Jo-Anne Levy *(Mgr.-Adv. & Brdcst.)*
Dave Buck *(Mktg. Rep.)*
Ed Wade *(Player Personnel Admin.)*

No. of U.S. Offices: 2

Computer Systems/Hardware:
Data General MV 10,000

Outside Service Firm(s):

KPMG Peat Marwick*(Auditors)*
1600 Market St.
Philadelphia, PA 19103
Tel.: 215-299-3100

Sedgwick James*(Group Insurer)*
Philadelphia, PA

Kidder, Peabody & Co.*(Investment Banker)*
Philadelphia, PA

Ballard, Spahr, Andrews & Ingersoll*(Legal Firm)*
1735 Market St., 51st Fl.
Philadelphia, PA 19103-7599
Tel.: 215-665-8500

Mellon Bank, N.A.*(Major Banking Relationship)*
P.O. Box 444,
Pittsburgh, PA 15230
Tel.: 412-236-8000
Tel.: 1-800-451-7392
Fax: 412-236-8157

Subsidiary:

Clearwater Phillies **(1)**
800 Phillies Dr.
Clearwater, FL 33515
Tel.: 813-441-8638
Emp.: 6
Baseball Team
S.I.C.: 7941
John Timberlake *(Gen. Mgr.)*

THE PHILLIPS AGENCY
800 Business Center Dr., Ste. 100
Horsham, PA 19044
Tel.: 215-443-8080
Year Founded: 1988
Approx.Billings: $12,000,000
Emp.: 32
Business-to-Business, Healthcare, Technology
Kathleen Phillips *(Pres.)*
Leslie Adams *(V.P., Sls. & New Business Contact)*
Doris Kobulsky *(V.P., Opers. & Sec.)*
Joesph Kobulsky *(Treas.)*
Claude Carter *(Res. Dir.)*
Ellen Wilson *(Librarian)*

PHILLIPS FINE ART AUCTIONEERS
406 E. 79th St.
New York, NY 10021
Tel.: 212-570-4830
Fax: 212-570-2207
Year Founded: 1796
Approx.Sls.: $10,000,000
Emp.: 6
Fiscal Year-end: 3/31/91
Import Export
Fine Art Auctioneers & Appraisers
S.I.C.: 7999
Christopher J. Weston *(Chm. Bd.)*
Roger H. Hollest *(Exec. V.P.)*
Claudia Florian *(Branch Mgr. & Jewelery Dept. Head)*
Alexandra Peters *(Pub. Rels. & Adv.)*
Nicole Migeon *(Paintings & Prints Dept.)*
Benita Norrmen-Smith *(Auction Admin.)*
Christina Pstrag *(Admin. & Customer Service)*
Joe Winslow *(Shipping Dept.)*

PHILLIPS, MILLER, SPEYER & FROST, INC.
121 W. Oak St.
Amityville, NY 11701
Tel.: 516-691-1911
Fax: 516-691-1980
Year Founded: 1971
Approx.Billings: $12,760,101
Emp.: 23
Consumer & Trade Advertising
Harvey Miller *(Pres.)*
Guy Speyer *(V.P., Sec.)*
Paul Frost *(V.P.)*

Computer Systems/Hardware:
Data General, Macintosh

PHILLIPS PLASTICS CORPORATION
P.O. Box 29, Seven Long Lake Dr.
Phillips, WI 54555
Tel.: 715-339-3005 **WI**
Fax: 715-339-3092
Year Founded: 1964
Assets: $68,000,000
Liabilities: $35,000,000
Net Worth: $33,000,000
Approx.Sls.: $100,000,000
Emp.: 1,400
Fiscal Year-end: 6/30/92
Export
Decorative Custom Injection Molded Plastic Products
S.I.C.: 3089
Corporate Giving Program: Ann-Marie Foundation-Corporate Foundation contributes to local causes
Robert Cervenka *(Chief Exec. Officer)*
Larry Smith *(Pres.)*
David L. Eggebrecht *(Chief Fin. Officer & Treas.)*
James A. Solinsky *(V.P.-Fin. & Sec.)*
Dennis P. McArrhey *(Controller)*
Principal(s):
Robert Cervenka

No. of Mfg. Plants/Facilities: 15
No. of U.S. Offices: 2
No. of Foreign Offices: 1

Outside Service Firm(s):

DiRenzo, Simonis & Miller*(Auditors)*
Appleton, WI

Willet & Klein*(Legal Firm)*
Phillips, WI

Bank One Milwaukee, N.A.*(Major Banking Relationship)*
111 E. Wisconsin Ave.
Milwaukee, WI
Tel.: 414-765-3000

Frank Russell Company*(Pension Manager)*
Phillips, WI

Subsidiaries:

Browne Medical Systems, Inc. **(1)**
8990 Springbrook Dr., Ste. 120
Minneapolis, MN 55433
Tel.: 612-784-6644
Fax: 612-785-5828
Royce D. Pipes *(Pres.)*

Flexmedics Corporation **(1)**
620 Ford Center, 420 N. 5th St.
Minneapolis, MN 55401-1332
Tel.: 612-338-8265
Fax: 612-338-4564
Jim Stice *(Pres.)*

Micropure Medical, Inc. **(1)**
177 Neal Ave.N.
Stillwater, MN 55082
Tel.: 612-436-1919
Fax: 612-436-1013
Tom Brust *(Pres.)*

Microvena Corporation **(1)**
3600 Labore Rd., Ste. 1
Vadnais Heights, MN 55110
Tel.: 612-484-1235
Fax: 612-484-1361
Rudy A. Mazzocchi *(Pres.)*

Para Natal Care Services, Inc. **(1)**
1401 West 76th St., Ste. 245
Minneapolis, MN 55423
Tel.: 612-869-4434
Fax: 612-869-4414
Karen Warrings *(Chief Exec. Officer)*

Sharpe Endosurgical Corporation **(1)**
8990 Springbrook Dr., Ste. 202
Minneapolis, MN 55433
Tel.: 612-784-0460
Fax: 612-784-0031
Tim Miller *(Pres.)*

Phillips Plastics Corporation—(Continued)

Stratis Corporation **(1)**
159 Old Orchard Ln.
Neenah, WI 54956
Tel.: 414-725-5353
Fax: 414-725-5403
Andy Elder *(Pres.)*

PHILLIPS PUBLISHING INC.
7811 Montrose Rd.
Potomac, MD 20854
Tel.: 301-340-2100 **MD**
Fax: 301-424-7034
Year Founded: 1974
Approx.Sls.: $62,400,000
Emp.: 225
Fiscal Year-end: 6/30/91
Publishers of Magazines & Newsletters in the Areas of Investments, Communications, Computers & Finance; Publishes Telecommunications Directories
S.I.C.: 2721; 2741
Thomas L. Phillips *(Chm. Bd., Pres. & Chief Exec. Officer)*
Robert S. King *(Exec. V.P. & Gen. Mgr.)*
Thomas C. Thompson *(Exec. V.P. & Gen. Mgr.)*
James T. deGraffenreid *(Sr. V.P.)*
Stephen D. Peck *(Sr. V.P., Chief Fin. Officer & Treas.)*

Computer Systems/Hardware:
Radio Shack TRS 80; Apple 2E

Outside Service Firm(s):

Ritter & Assocs.*(Auditors)*
Vienna, VA

Guardian Life Insurance Co.*(Group Insurer)*
New York, NY

Shulman, Rogers, Gandal, Pordy & Ecker*(Legal Firm)*
Silver Spring, MD

First American Bank, N.A.*(Major Banking Relationship)*
Washington, DC

PHOENIX AMERICAN INCORPORATED
2401 Kerner Blvd.
San Rafael, CA 94901
Tel.: 415-485-4500 **CA**
Fax: 415-453-8203
Year Founded: 1981
Assets: $50,342,374
Earnings: $208,799,000
Liabilities: $37,786,990
Net Worth: $12,555,384
Approx.Rev.: $28,210,081
Emp.: 248
Fiscal Year-end: 6/30/91
Investors in Computer Data Processing & other High Technology Equipment
S.I.C.: 6799
Gus Constantin *(Chm. Bd., Pres. & Chief Exec. Officer)*
Paritosh K. Choksi *(Sr. V.P., Chief Fin. Officer & Treas.)*
Gary W. Martinez *(Sr. V.P.)*
Bryant J. Tong *(Sr. V.P.)*
Susan D. Ackerman *(V.P. & Sec.)*
Ronald Demer *(V.P.)*
Kirby Fiegel *(V.P.-Equip. Mktg.)*
Francis A. Juliano *(V.P.-Technical Opers.)*
Thomas A. Hurt *(V.P.)*
Norman H. Nelson *(V.P.)*
Cynthia E. Parks *(V.P. & Gen. Counsel)*
David W. Brunton *(Controller)*

Outside Service Firm(s):

Arthur Andersen & Co.*(Auditors)*
Spear Street Tower, One Market Plaza, Ste. 3500
San Francisco, CA 94105
Tel.: 415-546-8200

Provident Life & Accident Insurance Co.*(Group Insurer)*
P.O. Box 12015
Chattanooga, TN 37401
Tel.: 615-755-7088

Kindel & Anderson*(Legal Firm)*
555 S. Flower, Ste. 2600
Los Angeles, CA 90071
Tel.: 213-680-2222

Subsidiaries:

Phoenix American Alarm Affiliates, Inc. **(1)**
2401 Kerner Blvd.
San Rafael, CA 94901-5527
Tel.: 415-485-4500 (83%)
Leasing Investment Firm
S.I.C.: 6211

Phoenix Cable Incorporated **(1)**
2401 Kerner Blvd.
San Rafael, CA 94901
Tel.: 415-485-4500 (85%)
Owns & Operates Cable Systems in Several States
S.I.C.: 4841

Phoenix Fiber Link Inc. **(1)**
2401 Kerner Blvd.
San Rafael, CA 94901
Tel.: 415-485-4500
Leasing
S.I.C.: 7359

Phoenix Growth Capital Corp. **(1)**
2401 Kerner Blvd.
San Rafael, CA 94901
Tel.: 415-485-4500 (89%)
Venture Capital
S.I.C.: 6799

Phoenix Leasing Incorporated **(1)**
2401 Kerner Blvd.
San Rafael, CA 94901
Tel.: 415-485-4500 (100%)
Organizes & Manages Income-Oriented Limited Partnerships for Investment in High Technology Equipment Leasing
S.I.C.: 6799

Phoenix Securities, Inc. **(1)**
2401 Kerner Blvd.
San Rafael, CA 94901
Tel.: 415-485-4500 (100%)
Markets Partnership Interests
S.I.C.: 6211

Phoenix Systems Exchange, Inc. **(1)**
2401 Kerner Blvd.
San Rafael, CA 94901
Tel.: 415-485-4500 (88%)
Leasing of High Technology Equipment
S.I.C.: 7359

PHOENIX ENTERPRISES INC.
3100 W. End Ave., Ste. 910
Nashville, TN 37203
Tel.: 615-292-7328
Fax: 615-383-3990
Year Founded: 1980
Approx.Sls.: $50,000,000
Emp.: 750
Investment Firm; Manufacturing & Merchandising of Office Furniture
S.I.C.: 6211; 6719; 8742; 2522; 5021
J. Handley Sayers *(Pres.)*
Janice Sensing *(Sec. & Treas.)*

Computer Systems/Hardware:
IBM PC-AT

PHOENIX FUEL COMPANY, INC.
2343 N. 27th Ave.
Phoenix, AZ 85005
Tel.: 602-278-6271 **AZ**
Fax: 602-278-7196
Year Founded: 1927
Sales Range: $60-79 Million
Emp.: 70
Whlsle. Petroleum Bulk Stations
S.I.C.: 5171
Joseph W. Wilhoit *(Pres.)*
T.A. Wilhoit *(Sec.)*
Gary Dalke *(Controller)*
Principal(s):
Joseph W. Wilhoit
T.A. Wilhoit

Computer Systems/Hardware:
IBM

Outside Service Firm(s):

Arthur Andersen & Co.*(Auditors)*
Phoenix, AZ

Western Petroleum Marketers Association*(Group Insurer)*
Salt Lake City, UT

Lewis & Roca*(Legal Firm)*
Phoenix, AZ

First Interstate Bank*(Major Banking Relationship)*
P.O. Box 53441,
Phoenix, AZ 85072-3441
Tel.: 602-229-4049

PHOENIX HOME LIFE MUTUAL INSURANCE COMPANY
(Formerly Phoenix Mutual Life Insurance Company)
One American Row
Hartford, CT 06115
Tel.: 203-275-5000 **CT**
Fax: 203-275-5855
Year Founded: 1851
Assets: $6,629,510,085
Liabilities: $6,303,446,798
Net Worth: $326,063,287
Approx.Premiums: $1,153,285,000
Emp.: 3,700
Fiscal Year-end: 12/31/91
Import Export
Life Insurance
S.I.C.: 6311
Employee Matching Gifts Program: Colleges, Universities and Private Secondary Schools, also United Negro College & American College Funds; $1,000 Maximum Match, $25 Minimum Match per Person/per year
John Gummere *(Chm. Bd. & Chief Exec. Officer)*
William B. Wallace *(Vice Chm. & Chief Oper. Officer)*
Robert W. Fiondella *(Pres. & Principal)*
John F. Fabian *(Exec. V.P.-Investments)*
Philip R. McLoughlin *(Exec. V.P. & Investments)*
Charles J. Paydos *(Exec. V.P.)*
Kelly Carlson *(Sr. V.P.-Career Organizations)*
Martin J. Gavin *(Sr. V.P.-Investment Products)*
Randall C. Giangiullo *(Sr. V.P.-Grp. Sls.)*
Joan E. Herman *(Sr. V.P.-Group Ins.)*
Lee Lapioli *(Sr. V.P.-Data Processing)*
Gary J. Laughinghouse *(Sr. V.P. & Gen. Mgr.)*
Robert G. Lautensack, Jr. *(Sr. V.P.)*
Frederick W. Sawyer, III *(Sr. V.P.-Individual Ins. & Information Systems)*
David W. Searfoss *(Sr. V.P., Chief Fin. Officer & Treas.)*
Richard C. Shaw *(Sr. V.P.)*
John W. Schoeninger, Jr. *(Sr. V.P.-Individual Mktg.)*
Terence N. Towry *(Sr. V.P.)*
Dona D. Young *(Sr. V.P. & Gen. Counsel)*
Carl T. Chadburn *(V.P.-Human Resources)*
James F. Gleason *(V.P.-Corp. Services)*
Maura L. Melley *(V.P.-Govt. Affairs)*
Scott C. Noble *(V.P.-Real Estate Investments)*
Ann Cowen *(2nd V.P.-Human Resources)*
JoAnne Leventhal *(Asst. V.P.-Public Affairs)*
Keith D. Robbins *(Corp. Sec.)*
Marcia Brooks *(Mgr.-Meetings Plng.)*
Jeanne Manning *(Mgr.-Adv.)*
E.C. Hollingsworth *(Pub. Affairs Asst.)*
Elaine Loehr *(Librarian)*

Computer Systems/Hardware:
IBM Systems 1333 & 3090

Outside Service Firm(s):

Price Waterhouse*(Auditors)*
One Financial Plaza
Hartford, CT 06103
Tel.: 203-240-2000

Sullivan & Worcester*(Legal Firm)*
One Post Office Square
Boston, MA 02109
Tel.: 617-338-2800

Subsidiaries:

American Brokerage Corporation **(1)**
One American Row
Hartford, CT 06115
Tel.: 203-275-5000 (100%)
Fax: 203-275-5296
Approx.Sls.: $10,265,000
Emp.: 150
Property Casualty Insurance Agency Mngmt.
S.I.C.: 6411
Martin Vaughn *(Pres.)*

PM Holdings, Inc. **(1)**
One American Row
Hartford, CT 06115
Tel.: 203-275-5000 (100%)
Holding Co.
S.I.C.: 6719
John Gummere *(Chief Oper. Officer)*

Phoenix American Life Ins. Co. **(1)**
One American Row
Hartford, CT 06115
Tel.: 203-275-5000 (100%)
Approx.Premiums: $20,189,649
Stock Life Ins. Company.
S.I.C.: 6311
John Gummere *(Pres.)*

Phoenix Equity Planning Corp. **(1)**
100 Bright Meadow Blvd.
Enfield, CT 06082
Tel.: 203-353-1000 (100%)
Approx.Sls.: $5,500,000
Emp.: 52
Funds Mngmt.
S.I.C.: 6211; 6722

Subsidiary:

Phoenix Investment Counsel Inc. **(2)**
One American Row
Hartford, CT 06115
Tel.: 203-275-5000 (100%)
Approx.Sls.: $2,909,566
Funds Management
S.I.C.: 6289

Phoenix Founders, Inc **(1)**
One American Row
Hartford, CT 06115
Tel.: 203-275-5000 (100%)
Approx.Sls.: $100,000,000
Real Estate Investment
S.I.C.: 6726

PHOENIX INTERNATIONAL, INC.
450 Broad St.
Beverly, NJ 08010
Mailing Address:
P.O. Box 397,
Beverly, NJ 08010
Tel.: 609-387-8200 **DE**
Fax: 609-387-8421
Year Founded: 1987
Approx.Sls.: $18,500,000
Emp.: 300
Fiscal Year-end: 9/30/91
Export
Mfr. Aerospace Components, Dental Implants and Specialized Coatings
S.I.C.: 3724; 3463; 3843
James M. Matarese *(Chm., Pres. & Chief Exec. Officer)*
Betty H. Matarese *(Sr. V.P. & Sec.)*
Max F. Clark *(Gen. Mgr.-Quality Assurance, Tech./Engrng./Tech. Svcs.)*
Edward C. Swedin *(Mgr.-Plant)*
Jill L. Atzert *(Admin.)*

Outside Service Firm(s):

Coopers & Lybrand*(Auditors)*
350 S. Grand Ave.
Los Angeles, CA 90071
Tel.: 213-481-1000
Fax: 213-482-6440

Buchalter, Nemer, Fields & Younger*(Legal Firm)*
601 S. Figueroa St., Ste. 2500
Los Angeles, CA 90017-5704
Tel.: 213-891-0700

Wells Fargo Bank*(Major Banking Relationship)*
420 Montgomery St.
San Francisco, CA 94104

Subsidiaries:

Macrodyne Engineering Services **(1)**
Columbus Rd., P.O. Box 188
Burlington, NJ 08016
Tel.: 609-386-2900
S.I.C.: 8711
George F. Vogt *(Pres. & Gen. Mgr.)*

Precision Metal Prods., Inc. **(1)**
850 W. Bradley Ave.
El Cajon, CA 92022
Tel.: 619-448-2711 (100%)
Fax: 619-448-2005
Approx.Sls.: $6,300,000
Emp.: 100
High Energy Rate Precision Forging
S.I.C.: 3463
James M. Matarese *(Chm. Bd.)*
C. Thomas Cash *(Pres. & Chief Exec. Officer)*
Brent Conyers *(V.P. & Controller)*

Tactair Advanced Technology, Inc. **(1)**
Columbus Road, Box 188
Burlington, NJ 08016
Tel.: 609-386-5840
Engineering Services
S.I.C.: 8711
Joseph Weaver *(Pres. & Gen. Mgr.)*

Tactair Fluid Controls Corp. **(1)**
450 Broad St., P.O. Box 158
Beverly, NJ 08010
Tel.: 609-387-0010 (100%)
Approx.Sls.: $4,000,000
Emp.: 65
Pneumatic Valves & Hydraulic Controls
S.I.C.: 3494
Michael Sagolla *(Gen. Mgr.)*
Robert Tryon *(Pres.)*
James Van Dine *(Mgr.-Sls.)*

PHOENIX STEEL, INC.
2800 Melby St.
Eau Claire, WI 54703
Tel.: 715-835-6143
Fax: 715-835-0183
Year Founded: 1861
Approx.Sls.: $52,000,000
Emp.: 320
Steel Fabrication; Wholesale Steel
S.I.C.: 3441; 5051
Milton A. Lunda *(Pres.)*
Karl Murch *(Chief Fin. Officer)*
Paul Gehl *(V.P.)*
Larry Lunda *(V.P.)*
Robert Ridley *(Gen Mgr.)*

Outside Service Firm(s):

Wipfli, Ullrich, Bertleson*(Auditors)*
Eau Claire, WI

Carroll Parroni Posplewaite Anderson & Graham*(Legal Firm)*
Eau Claire, WI

First Wisconsin National Bank*(Major Banking Relationship)*
777 E. Wisconsin Ave.
Milwaukee, WI 53202
Tel.: 414-765-4321
Fax: 414-355-6903

PHOENIX VENTURES
(Formerly Phoenix Distributors, Inc.)
1890 S. Chris Lane
Anaheim, CA 92805
Tel.: 800-325-0946
Emp.: 400
Wholesale Industrial Gas & Welding Supplies
S.I.C.: 5085; 5172

Outside Service Firm(s):

Edwards & Angell*(Legal Firm)*
Boston, MA

First National Bank of Boston*(Major Banking Relationship)*
Mail Stop 44-02-09, P.O. Box 644
Boston, MA 02102-0644
Tel.: 617-575-2555

PHONEMATE, INC.
(Sub. of Asahi Overseas Corporation)
20665 Manhattan Pl.
Torrance, CA 90501
Mailing Address:
P.O. Box 2914
Torrance, CA 90509-2914
Tel.: 310-618-9910 **CA**
Telex: 215206 PHNMTUR
Fax: 310-533-0180
Year Founded: 1968
Assets: $68,607,000
Earnings: $2,537,000
Liabilities: $63,090,000
Net Worth: $5,517,000
Approx.Sls.: $133,039,000
Emp.: 289
Fiscal Year-end: 12/31/90
Import
Designs, Engineers & Markets Proprietary Telecommunications Products for Home, Professional Office & Small Business Use
S.I.C.: 3661; 3579
Shun Yamaura *(Pres. & Chief Exec. Officer)*
Tak Suzuki *(Exec. V.P. & Chief Fin. Officer)*
Larry Kloman *(V.P.-Mktg. & Sls.)*
Stephen B. Knuth *(V.P.-Opers. & Engrng.)*
Jay R. Spowart *(V.P.-Fin. & Corp. Sec.)*
Carol Jaramillo *(Dir.-Personnel)*
Jim Oblak *(Dir.-Mktg.)*
Mike Page *(Dir.-Data Processing)*
Dave Reed *(Dir.-Pur.)*
Pilar Rendon *(Dir.-Cash Mngmt.)*
Mark Karnowski *(Mgr.-Engr.)*

Computer Systems/Hardware:
IBM System 38 Model 600

PHONETICS, INC.
901 Tryens Rd.
Aston, PA 19014
Tel.: 215-558-2700 **PA**
Fax: 215-558-0222
Year Founded: 1985
Emp.: 22
Fiscal Year-end: 4/30/91
Export
Mfr. of Sensaphone & Environmental Monitors
S.I.C.: 3825
Kenneth E. Blanchard *(Chm. Bd., Pres. & Chief Oper. Officer)*
Robert J. Douglass *(V.P.-Tech. Opers.)*
Mary Ellen Gomeau *(V.P.-Sls. & Mktg.)*
Barbara T. Cella *(Controller)*
John H. Toal *(Gen. Counsel)*
Deborah R. Hargy *(Dir.-Pur.)*
Colleen McGill *(Dir.-Admin.)*

Outside Service Firm(s):

Coopers & Lybrand*(Auditors)*
2400 Eleven Penn Center
Philadelphia, PA 19103-2962
Tel.: 215-963-8000

Pray, Walker, Jackman, Williamson & Marlar*(Legal Firm)*
Ninth Floor-Okeok Plaza
Tulsa, OK 74153
Tel.: 918-584-4136
Fax: 918-584-1446

PHOTOGENIC MACHINE COMPANY, INC.
525 McClurg Rd.
Youngstown, OH 44512
Mailing Address:
P.O. Box 3365,
Youngstown, OH 44513
Tel.: 216-758-6658
Tel.: 800-682-7668
Fax: 216-758-3667
Year Founded: 1921
Emp.: 70
Mfr. Photographic Lighting Equipmrnt
S.I.C.: 3641; 3861
Anne Kubiac *(Pres.)*
Michael Markl *(Dir.-Pur.)*
Thomas Kubiac *(Gen. Mgr.)*
John Shirilla *(Mgr.-Gen. Sls.)*

Outside Service Firm(s):

Hill, Barth & King*(Auditors)*
Sharon, PA

Harold Stein*(Legal Firm)*
Youngstown, OH

Dollar Bank*(Major Banking Relationship)*
Youngstown, OH

PHOTOTYPE COLOR GRAPHICS, INC.
7890 Airport Hwy.
Pennsauken, NJ 08109
Tel.: 609-663-4100
Tel.: 800-523-4784
Fax: 609-663-6631
Year Founded: 1903
Sales Range: $10-19 Million
Emp.: 130
Fiscal Year-end: 12/31/90
Offset & Gravure Film Preparation & Printing House
S.I.C.: 2752; 2754
Joel Rubin *(Chm. Bd., Pres. & Chief Exec. Officer)*
Alan Stack *(Chief Fin. Officer)*
Hal Wilkinson *(Chief Information Officer)*
William Rubin *(V.P. & Mgr.-Human Resources)*
Dennis Stewart *(Chief Engr.)*
Chip Ridewood *(Pur. Agent)*
Principal(s):
Joel Rubin

Outside Service Firm(s):

H.R. Margolis & Co.*(Auditors)*
Bala Cynwyd, PA

Provident National Bank*(Major Banking Relationship)*
17th & Chestnut Sts.
Philadelphia, PA 19101
Tel.: 215-585-5625

PIASA MOTOR FUELS INC.
Piasa Lane & Hwy. 3
Hartford, IL 62048
Mailing Address:
P.O. Box 484
Alton, IL 62002
Tel.: 618-254-7341 **MO**
Fax: 618-254-8281
Year Founded: 1932
Approx.Sls.: $90,000,000
Emp.: 150
Wholesale & Retail Petroleum Products
S.I.C.: 5171; 5541
Bill Schrimpf *(Pres.)*
Donald F. Schrimpf *(V.P.)*
Mark Schrimpf *(V.P.-Opers.)*
S. Wiley Davis *(Sec.)*

Outside Service Firm(s):

Grace & Co.*(Auditors)*
St. Louis, MO

United Missouri Bank*(Major Banking Relationship)*
Saint Louis, MO

Subsidiaries:

Hartford-Wood River Terminal **(1)**
Piasa Lane & Hwy. 3
Hartford, IL 62048
Tel.: 618-254-7341
Approx.Sls.: $84,000,000
Emp.: 10
Wholesale Bulk Petroleum Products
S.I.C.: 5171
Robert Schrimpf *(Pres.)*
R. William Schrimpf *(Asst. Sec.)*

Piasa Oil Transport Inc. **(1)**
Piasa Lane at Hwy. 3
Hartford, IL 62048
Tel.: 618-254-7341
Bill Schrimpf *(Pres.)*

PIC N'PAY SUPERMARKETS, INC.
130 S.W. 1st Ave.
Dania, FL 33004
Tel.: 305-922-2274 **FL**
Approx.Sls.: $20,000,000
Emp.: 200
Operators of 6 Retail Grocery Stores; 5 Pic N'pay, 1 Payless
S.I.C.: 5411
Joseph Salamon *(Pres.)*
Robert Salamon *(V.P., Sec. & Treas.)*
Aaron Salamon *(V.P.-Pur. & Personnel Dir.)*
Diane Salamon *(Legal Counsel)*

Outside Service Firm(s):

Capital Bank*(Major Banking Relationship)*
Miami, FL

PICKERING INDUSTRIES INC.
2102 D St. E.
Tacoma, WA 98421
Tel.: 206-572-9212 **WA**
Fax: 206-272-2911
Year Founded: 1967
Assets: $6,982,943
Liabilities: $4,365,948
Net Worth: $2,616,995
Approx.Sls.: $16,000,000
Emp.: 60
Fiscal Year-end: 10/31/91
Import
Manufacture Low & High Pressure Decorative Laminates Using Particle Board & Plywood Substrates; Wholesale Plywood Products and Allied Products for the Fixture & Cabinet Industries; Marina Operator
S.I.C.: 2435; 5031
Corporate Giving Program: United Way, Washington State University, Festival of Trees, Save the Children, & Tacoma Rotary
Employee Matching Gifts Program: After 6 Months of Employment Gifts up to 6% of Annual Salary will be Matched up to 50% by Company
Gordon G. Pickering *(Chm. Bd., Pres. & Gen. Counsel)*
Allen Pickering *(Chief Exec. Officer, Treas. & Sec.)*
Lawrence Huffines *(V.P.-Mktg. & Sls.)*
Deborah Sanderson *(Controller)*
Allen Pukering *(Sec.)*
Robert Hutchins *(Gen. Counsel)*
Robert Goin *(Dir.-Pur.)*
Gordon Pukering *(Dir.-Mktg.)*

Pickering Industries Inc.—(Continued)

Principal(s):
Gordon G. Pickering
Virginia Pickering

No. of Mfg. Plants/Facilities: 1
No. of U.S. Offices: 1

Computer Systems/Hardware:
Cado/Cado

Outside Service Firm(s):

Moss Adams*(Auditors)*
Tacoma, WA

Bradrud-Middleton*(Commercial Insurance Carrier)*
Tacoma, WA

Puget Sound National Bank*(International Bank Affiliate)*
P.O. Box 11500
Tacoma, WA 98411
Tel.: 206-383-2871

Schwartz-Shela*(Group Insurer)*
Tacoma, WA

Robert Hutchins*(Legal Firm)*
Tocoma, WA

Spectrum Pension Consultants*(Pension Manager)*
Tacoma, WA

Subsidiary:

Pick's Cove Marina **(1)**
1930 East "D" St.
Tacoma, WA 98466
Tel.: 206-572-3625
Emp.: 60
Marina, Boat Shop & Rental
S.I.C.: 4493; 7999
Debbie Sanderman *(Comptroller)*

Affiliate:

JAG Northwest Inc. **(1)**
1616 E. St. Paul Ave.
Tacoma, WA 98421
Tel.: 206-272-1416
Machine Center; Processes Decorative Panels to Specifications
S.I.C.: 3569
Jeff Pickering *(Pres.)*

PICOU BROTHERS CONSTRUCTION COMPANY
12608 Airline Hwy.
Gonzales, LA 70737
Mailing Address:
P.O. Box 519,
Gonzales, LA 70737
Tel.: 504-644-6577 **LA**
Fax: 504-644-6570
Year Founded: 1973
Assets: $2,985,000
Liabilities: $1,764,000
Net Worth: $1,221,000
Approx.Sls.: $13,000,000
Emp.: 85
Fiscal Year-end: 12/31/88
Commercial Building Contractor
S.I.C.: 1542
Donald Picou *(Pres.)*
Richard Picou *(V.P., Sec. & Treas.)*
Principal(s):
Donald Picou
Richard Picou

No. of Mfg. Plants/Facilities: 1
No. of U.S. Offices: 1

Computer Systems/Hardware:
BIDTEK

Outside Service Firm(s):

Hannis T. Bourgois*(Auditors)*
Baton Rouge, LA

Hoffman, Sutterfield, Ensenat & Bankston*(Legal Firm)*
Baton Rouge, LA

Bank Of Gonzales*(Major Banking Relationship)*
Gonzales, LA

Subsidiary:

Picou Brothers Tractor & Rental Company of Gonzales **(1)**
12608 Airline Hwy.
Gonzales, LA 70737
Tel.: 504-644-6577
Tractor & Rental Company
S.I.C.: 3711

PIEDMONT MECHANICAL, INC.
(Formerly Piedmont Mechanical of Spartanburg, Inc.)
116 John Dodd Rd.
Spartanburg, SC 29303
Mailing Address:
P.O. Box 4925
Spartanburg, SC 29305
Tel.: 803-578-9114 **SC**
Fax: 803-578-5314
Year Founded: 1977
Assets: $4,081,721
Liabilities: $2,892,945
Net Worth: $1,188,776
Approx.Sls.: $15,031,000
Emp.: 211
Fiscal Year-end: 12/31/91
Mechanical Contractor; Machinery Installation & Fabrication; Process Piping & HVAC Fabrication & Installation
S.I.C.: 1711; 1796; 3498
Charles E. Blackwell *(Chm. Bd.)*
Winston H. Anderson *(Chief Oper. Officer)*
Robert B. Dannelly, Sr. *(Chief Fin. Officer & V.P.-Fin.)*
David E. Autrey *(Pres.)*
Thomas R. Holt *(V.P.)*
Paul Norris *(V.P.-Georgia Engrng.)*
Albert E. Smith *(V.P.-Georgia Opers.)*
Bruce Dannelly *(Controller)*
Julian Scruggs *(Dir.-Human Resources)*
James McMahan *(Shop Mgr.)*
Pam Rollins *(Office Mgr.)*
Principal(s):
Charles E. Blackwell

No. of Mfg. Plants/Facilities: 2
No. of U.S. Offices: 2

Computer Systems/Hardware:
Basic 4

Outside Service Firm(s):

Liberty Mutual*(Group Insurer)*
175 Berkeley St.
Boston, MA

Smith, Mullis, Helms*(Legal Firm)*
Charlotte, NC

Carolina Southern Bank*(Major Banking Relationship)*
Spartanburg, SC

NationsBank Carolinas*(Major Banking Relationship)*
Spartanburg, SC

Subsidiary:

Piedmont Mechanical, Inc. **(1)**
103 Cooley Industrial Way, P.O. Box 308
La Grange, GA 30241
Tel.: 706-882-4277
Fax: 706-884-2370
Emp.: 80
Mechanical Contractor
S.I.C.: 1711
A. E. Smith *(Chief Oper. Officer & V.P.)*

PIERCE MANUFACTURING, INC.
2600 American Dr.
Appleton, WI 54915
Tel.: 414-832-3000
Fax: 414-832-3092
Year Founded: 1913
Approx.Sls.: $80,000,000
Emp.: 1,100
Manufacture Motor Vehicle Passenger Car, Truck & Bus Bodies
S.I.C.: 3711; 3713
Michael R. Reese *(Chm Bd., Pres. & Chief Exec. Officer)*
David Ogilive *(V.P.)*
William Peters *(Controller)*

Outside Service Firm(s):

Arthur Andersen & Co.*(Auditors)*
777 E. Wisconsin Ave., P.O. Box 1215
Milwaukee, WI 53202
Tel.: 414-271-5100
Fax: 414-283-3200

Valley National Bank*(Major Banking Relationship)*
Appleton, WI

PIERCING PAGODA, INC.
3910 Adler Pl.
Bethlehem, PA 18016
Mailing Address:
P.O. Box 25007
Lehigh Valley, PA 18002-5007
Tel.: 215-691-0437
Fax: 215-694-9077
Approx.Sls.: $50,000,000
Emp.: 1,275
Fiscal Year-end: 3/31/91
Import
14k Gold & Sterling Silver Jewelry
S.I.C.: 5944
Employee Matching Gifts Program:
United Way-Equal Match
Richard H. Penske *(Chm. Bd., Pres. & Treas.)*
Sharon Jones Zondag *(Sr. V.P.-Field Opers.)*
Branden Lehman *(Controller)*
Kathy Biolsi *(Pur. Agent)*

Outside Service Firm(s):

KPMG Peat Marwick*(Auditors)*
4905 Tildgman St.
Allentown, PA 18104
Tel.: 215-391-6380

Haber & Corriere, P.C.*(Legal Firm)*
Bethlehem, PA

First Valley Bank*(Major Banking Relationship)*
Bethlehem, PA

JOS. J. PIETRAFESA CO., INC.
7400 Morgan Rd.
Liverpool, NY 13090
Tel.: 315-451-9120
Fax: 315-451-4073
Emp.: 500
Men's & Women's Tailored Clothing
S.I.C.: 2311; 2339
Richard C. Pietrafesa, Jr. *(Pres.)*
Donald Kagan *(Chief Fin. Officer)*
Joseph J. Pietrafesa, II *(Dir.-Mfg.)*

Outside Service Firm(s):

Firley, Morgan, Freer & Eassa*(Auditors)*
Syracuse, NY

MacKenzie, Smith, Lewis, Michell & Hughes*(Legal Firm)*
Syracuse, NY

Chase Lincoln First Bank, N.A.*(Major Banking Relationship)*
Syracuse, NY

PIKNIK PRODUCTS COMPANY, INC.
3806 Day St.
Montgomery, AL 36108
Tel.: 205-265-1567 **FL**
Fax: 205-265-9490
Year Founded: 1951
Approx.Sls.: $18,000,000
Emp.: 100
Mfr. of Mayonnaise, Prepared Wet Mustard, Salad Dressings, Soy Sauce
S.I.C.: 2035
Loeb Herman, Jr. *(Chm. Bd.)*
H. Richard Loeb *(Pres.)*
Charles R. Caraway *(V.P.)*
Leon Wium *(V.P.)*
Carol Loeb *(Treas. & Sec.)*

Outside Service Firm(s):

Blankenship, Lamar, Gilliland*(Auditors)*
Montgomery, AL

SouthTrust Bank, Montgomery*(Major Banking Relationship)*
2520 Eastern Bypass
Montgomery, AL 36117
Tel.: 205-279-6000
Fax: 205-270-2279

PILLOWTEX CORPORATION
4111 Mint Way
Dallas, TX 75237
Tel.: 214-333-3225
Fax: 214-330-6016
Approx.Sls.: $145,000,000
Emp.: 1,500
Mfr. of Pillows, Mattress Pads, Comforters
S.I.C.: 2392
John H. Silverthorne *(Chm. Bd.)*
Charles M. Hansen *(Pres. & Chief Exec. Officer)*
Scott Schmizo *(Exec. V.P.-Sls.)*
Richard Canter *(Sr. V.P.-Sls.)*
Russ Holbrook *(Sr. V.P.-Sls.)*
Dale Williams *(Sr. V.P.-Mktg.)*
Carl Choate *(V.P.-Corp. Services)*
Jeff Cordus *(V.P.-Plng. & Admin.)*
Michael G. Eipper *(V.P.-Sls.)*
John Peterson *(V.P.-Intl.)*
Rudy Fautaz *(Dir.-Human Resources)*

Computer Systems/Hardware:
Data General

Outside Service Firm(s):

KPMG Peat Marwick*(Auditors)*
1601 Elm St., Ste. 1600
Dallas, TX 75201
Tel.: 214-754-2000
Fax: 214-754-2297

NationsBank Texas*(Major Banking Relationship)*
901 Main St., 16th Fl.
Dallas, TX 75202
Tel.: 214-922-5000

PILOT AIR FREIGHT CORP.
314 N. Middletown Rd.
Lima, PA 19037
Tel.: 215-565-8100
Fax: 215-565-4267
Approx.Sls.: $75,000,000
Emp.: 125
Air Freight Forwarder
S.I.C.: 4513
Thomas P. Edwards *(Chm. Bd.)*
John J. Edwards *(Pres. & Chief Exec. Officer)*
Fred Molden *(Chief Fin. Officer)*
Richard Morris *(V.P.-Mktg.)*
William F. Edwards *(Sec. & Treas.)*
Neil McFadden *(Dir.-Mngmt. Information Systems)*

PINCUS BROS., INC.
Independence Mall East
Philadelphia, PA 19106
Tel.: 215-922-4900
Fax: 215-922-1140
Year Founded: 1911
Sales Range: $60-79 Million
Emp.: 1,000
Fiscal Year-end: 12/31/90
Import Export
Mfr. Men's Suits & Sportcoats, Women's Tailored Suits
S.I.C.: 2311; 2325; 2337
David Pincus *(Chm. Bd. & Chief Exec. Officer)*

Alvin Kohn *(Pres.)*
Bruce Fishberg *(Exec. V.P.)*
Naresh Jain *(Sr. V.P.)*
Principal(s):
David Pincus

No. of Mfg. Plants/Facilities: 4

Outside Service Firm(s):

Halbert, Katz & Company*(Auditors)*
Philadelphia, PA

Wolf, Block, Schorr & Solis-Cohen*(Legal Firm)*
Packard Bldg., 12th Fl., 15th & Chestnut Sts.
Philadelphia, PA 19102
Tel.: 215-569-4000

Philadelphia National Bank*(Major Banking Relationship)*
P.O. Box 13834, Broad & Chestnut Streets
Philadelphia, PA 19101-7618
Tel.: 215-973-8327

PINE STATE CREAMERY CO.
500 Glenwood Ave.
Raleigh, NC 27628
Mailing Address:
P.O. Box 6508
Raleigh, NC 27628
Tel.: 919-828-7401
Fax: 919-664-8362
Year Founded: 1919
Approx.Sls.: $48,000,000
Emp.: 400
Fiscal Year-end: 12/31/90
Processor & Distributor of Dairy Products
S.I.C.: 5143
Benjamin W. Kilgore, III *(Pres. & Chief Oper. Officer)*
William R. Lampley *(V.P.-Fin.)*
Benjamin Gibbs *(Treas.)*
Judy Glover *(Dir.-Personnel)*
Principal(s):
Benjamin W. Kilgore, III
Benjamin Gibbs

Computer Systems/Hardware:
Texas Instruments

Outside Service Firm(s):

KPMG Peat Marwick*(Auditors)*
3100 Smoketree Court
Raleigh, NC 27629
Tel.: 919-872-3600
Fax: 919-790-9731

Smith, Anderson, Blount, Mitchell*(Legal Firm)*
P.O. Box 12807
Raleigh, NC 27605

United Carolina Bank*(Major Banking Relationship)*
Raleigh, NC

PINE STATE TOBACCO & CANDY COMPANY
8 Ellis Ave.
Augusta, ME 04330
Tel.: 207-622-3741
Fax: 207-626-0150
Year Founded: 1940
Approx.Sls.: $80,000,000
Emp.: 250
Wholesale Tobacco, Confectionery, Beer, Wine & Operates Vending Machines
S.I.C.: 5145; 5182; 5194
Charles F. Canning, Jr. *(Pres.)*
John N. Canning *(V.P.-Sls. & Mktg.)*
Paul Cottrell, Jr. *(Controller)*
Terry Goddard *(Dir.-Data Processing & Opers. Coordinator)*
Sue Reed *(Dir.-Personnel)*
Paul Auger *(Mgr.-Opers.)*
Ron Bechard *(Mgr.-Beverage Opers.)*

Outside Service Firm(s):

Schatz & Fletcher*(Auditors)*
Augusta, ME

Lipman & Parks*(Legal Firm)*
Augusta, ME

Fleet National Bank*(Major Banking Relationship)*
125 Dupont Dr.
Providence, RI 02907-3178
Tel.: 401-278-5335

Subsidiaries:

Pine State Beverage **(1)**
8 Ellis Ave.
Augusta, ME 04330
Tel.: 207-622-3741
Malt Beverage & Wine
S.I.C.: 2084

Pine State Vending **(1)**
8 Ellis Ave.
Augusta, ME 04330
Tel.: 207-622-3741
Operates Vending Machines
S.I.C.: 5962

Pinkerton & Laws Co.
(See Pine State Tobacco & Candy Company)

PINNE/HERBERS ADVERTISING INC.
200 Vallejo St.
San Francisco, CA 94111
Tel.: 415-956-4210
Fax: 415-956-4285
Year Founded: 1975
Approx.Billings: $20,000,000
Emp.: 28
Robert A. Pinne *(Chm. Bd. & Chief Exec. Officer)*
Donald Herbers *(Pres. & Chief Oper. Officer)*
Claudia Ceneceros *(Pub. Rels. Dir.)*
Linda Utterberg *(Office Mgr.)*
Anthony Laruso *(Data Processing & Corp. Travel Planner)*

PIONEER ALUMINUM, INC.
3800 E. 26th St.
Los Angeles, CA 90023
Tel.: 213-268-7211
Tel.: 800-344-4972
Fax: 213-266-3761
Year Founded: 1950
Approx.Sls.: $65,000,000
Emp.: 134
Export
Aluminum Bars, Rods, Ingots, Sheets, Pipes & Plates
S.I.C.: 5051
John P. Cassel *(Pres.)*
Jerry Jacobs *(V.P.-Fin., Treas. & Sec.)*
Bob Landry *(V.P.-Sls. & Marketing)*

Outside Service Firm(s):

Deloitte & Touche*(Auditors)*
1000 Wilshire Blvd.
Los Angeles, CA 90017-2472
Tel.: 213-688-0800
Fax: 213-688-0100

Barclays Bank plc*(Major Banking Relationship)*
Los Angeles, CA

PIONEER COMMUNICATIONS OF AMERICA
600 E. Crescent Ave.
Upper Saddle River, NJ 07458
Tel.: 201-327-6400
Fax: 201-327-9379
Year Founded: 1973
Approx.Sls.: $100,000,000
Emp.: 125
Mfr. of Videodisc Players, Computer Storage Drives, Cable Television Systems
S.I.C.: 5065
K. Peter Imamura *(Pres.)*
Jerry Landskron *(Sr. V.P.-Admin.)*
Hank Evans *(V.P.-Mktg.)*
Thomas McPherson *(V.P.)*
Mike Koshiba *(Treas.)*
Robert Bennett *(Dir.-Pur.)*
Yuta Ito *(Dir.-Plng. & Devel.)*
Patricia Linton *(Personnel Mgr.)*

PIONEER/ECLIPSE CORP.
(Sub. of Amano Corp., Yokohama, Japan.)
Eclipse Rd. & Hwy. 18N
Sparta, NC 28675
Mailing Address:
P.O. Box 909
Sparta, NC 28675
Tel.: 919-372-8080
Tel.: 800-334-2246 **NC**
Fax: 919-372-2895
Year Founded: 1978
Sales Range: $20-39 Million
Emp.: 130
Fiscal Year-end: 3/31/92
Import Export
Mfr. Floor Cleaning Chemicals & Equipment For The Industrial & Institutional Markets; Develops High Speed High Tech Floor Maintenance Systems
S.I.C.: 2842; 3589
Minoru Iwasaki *(Chm. Bd.)*
William H. Wilson *(Pres. & Chief Exec. Officer)*
E.F. Reeves, IV *(Sr. V.P. & Gen. Mgr.)*
Robert Balsdon *(V.P.-Sls. & Mktg.)*
Byron Snyder *(V.P.-Intl. Sls.)*
Yoshio Misumi *(Treas.)*
G.A. Avram *(Gen. Counsel)*
Ralph M. Cooke *(Dir.-Human Resources)*
Mike Hanks *(Dir.-Machine Production)*
Warren Weaver *(Dir.-Chemical Production)*
David Wooten *(Dir.-Pur.)*
Nikki Larrowe *(Corp. Accountant)*
John Metzger *(Govt. Mkt. Mgr.)*
Principal(s):
William H. Wilson

No. of Mfg. Plants/Facilities: 1
No. of U.S. Offices: 15
No. of Foreign Offices: 1

Computer Systems/Hardware:
Hewlett-Packard 3000

Outside Service Firm(s):

Benson, Belvins, Drum & Thomas*(Auditors)*
N. Wilkesboro, NC

State Mutual Life Assurance Co. of America*(Group Insurer)*
3101 N. Elm St., Ste. 320
Greensboro, NC 27408
Tel.: 919-282-6660

Finger Parker Avram*(Legal Firm)*
P.O. Box 11633,
Winston-Salem, NC

First Citizens Bank*(Major Banking Relationship)*
Sparta, NC

Miller & Seaford*(Pension Manager)*
Elkin, NC

Subsidiary:

Topaka Scientific Safety Co. **(1)**
P.O. Box 486
Glade Valley, NC 28627
Tel.: 919-372-5656
Emp.: 3
Mfr. & Distr. Floor Slip Testers
S.I.C.: 2842

PIONEER ENGINEERING & MANUFACTURING CO.
2500 E. Nine Mile Rd.
Warren, MI 48091
Mailing Address:
P.O. Box 718
Warren, MI 48091
Tel.: 313-755-4400 **MI**
Fax: 313-754-9047
Year Founded: 1931
Approx.Sls.: $60,000,000
Emp.: 1,000
Fiscal Year-end: 12/31/90
Contract Engineering Services, Prototype Research & Development, Graphic Services
S.I.C.: 8711; 8731; 7389; 7363
David G. Fisher *(Pres. & Chief Exec. Officer)*
Lou Infante *(V.P.-Plng. & Devel.)*
Jackie Kurtz *(V.P.-Mktg. & Admin.)*
Bill Woehlke *(Asst. Treas. & Controller)*
Norm Ludtke *(Dir.-Res. & Devel.)*
Mary Aiello *(Mgr.-Data Processing)*
Debbi Celli *(Supvr.-Employee Benefits)*
Robin Craig *(Human Resources Admin.)*
Nancy Drobny *(Mktg. Assoc.)*
Principal(s):
D.T. Chase

No. of Mfg. Plants/Facilities: 9
No. of U.S. Offices: 9

Computer Systems/Hardware:
IBM System 36; Prime/Lundy; CADxx; CACMA

Outside Service Firm(s):

Arthur Andersen & Co.*(Auditors)*
400 Renaissance Center
Detroit, MI 48243
Tel.: 313-259-8100

Schmier, Fealk & Ellis*(Legal Firm)*
29200 Northwestern Highway
Southfield, MI 48034
Tel.: 313-355-2100

Manufacturers National Bank N.A.*(Major Banking Relationship)*
38th Fl., 100 Renaissance Center
Detroit, MI 48243
Tel.: 313-222-4227

Divisions:

Pioneer Industrial Engineering Div. **(1)**
32201 N. Avis
Madison Heights, MI 48071
Tel.: 313-589-3411
Approx.Sls.: $6,000,000
Emp.: 200
Indus. Design Srvs.
S.I.C.: 8711
David G. Fisher *(Chief Exec. Officer)*
D. P. Marneef *(V.P.)*

Pioneer Manufacturing Engineering Div. **(1)**
2500 E. Nine Mile Rd.
Warren, MI 48091
Ken Sommer *(V.P.)*

Pioneer Research & Development Div. **(1)**
2500 E. Nine Mile Rd.
Warren, MI 48091
Tel.: 313-755-4400
Approx.Sls.: $1,000,000
Emp.: 50
Test & Devel.
S.I.C.: 8731
N.F. Ludtke *(Dir.-Advanced Engrng. & Res.)*

PIONEER INDUSTRIAL PRODUCTS CO.
512 E. Tiffin St.
Willard, OH 44890
Tel.: 419-933-2211
Year Founded: 1918

Pioneer Industrial Products Co.—(Continued)

Approx.Sls.: $17,000,000
Emp.: 300
Export
Mfr. of Industrial & Consumer Latex Gloves
S.I.C.: 3069
J. Murawski *(Exec. V.P.)*
P. Sodeika *(V.P.-Fin.)*
Stan Hare *(Dir.-Indus. Sls.)*
Tom Jordan *(Mgr.-Info. Systems)*
Edward O'Connell *(Mgr.-Mktg.)*

PIONEER MUTUAL LIFE INSURANCE COMPANY
203 10th St., N.
Fargo, ND 58102
Tel.: 701-293-3300
Fax: 701-277-2445
Approx.Sls.: $30,000,000
Emp.: 108
Life Insurance & Annuity
S.I.C.: 6311
James M. Swedback *(Pres.)*
Mary Jean Olson *(V.P. & Sec.)*
Douglas C. Oksendahl *(V.P.-Fin.)*
Avery D. Baker *(V.P. & Comptroller)*
Duane Engebretson *(V.P.-Mktg.)*
Theodore Appel *(V.P.-Underwriting & Claims)*

Outside Service Firm(s):

KPMG Peat Marwick*(Auditors)*
4200 Norwest Center, 90 S. 7th St.
Minneapolis, MN 55402
Tel.: 612-341-2222

Norwest Bank Minnesota, N.A.*(Major Banking Relationship)*
Fargo, ND

PIONEER OIL COMPANY INC.
3420 E. Vickery
Fort Worth, TX 76105
Mailing Address:
P.O. Box 1838
Fort Worth, TX 76101
Tel.: 817-531-3776 **TX**
Fax: 817-531-2271
Approx.Sls.: $50,000,000
Emp.: 30
Fiscal Year-end: 6/30/90
Retail & Wholesale Petroleum Products
S.I.C.: 5541; 5172
R. Leon McDaniel *(Pres. & Chief Oper. Officer)*
Earl E. Frazier *(V.P.)*
Sam H. Gann *(Sec., Treas. & Dir.-Opers.)*

Computer Systems/Hardware:
Hewlett-Packard 3000

Outside Service Firm(s):

KPMG Peat Marwick*(Auditors)*
301 Commerce, Ste. 2500
Ft. Worth, TX 76102
Tel.: 817-335-2655

Morris & Hendelman*(Legal Firm)*
Fort Worth, TX

Overton Park National Bank*(Major Banking Relationship)*
Fort Worth, TX

PIONEER PAPER CORPORATION
50 Triangle Blvd.
Carlstadt, NJ 07072
Tel.: 201-935-0123
Fax: 201-935-3044
Approx.Sls.: $10,000,000
Emp.: 150
Blister Packaging, Paperboard Spools, Lithographic Printing
S.I.C.: 3089; 2655; 2752
Myron Gross *(Pres.)*
Lewis Gross *(Exec. V.P.)*
Steve Boross *(Comptroller)*

Outside Service Firm(s):

Bachmann, Schwartz & Abramson*(Auditors)*
New York, NY

PIONEER PLASTICS HOLDING, INC.
One Pionite Rd.
Auburn, ME 04210
Tel.: 207-784-9111 **DE**
Fax: 207-784-0392
Year Founded: 1989
Approx.Sls.: $77,000,000
Emp.: 1,000
Laminated Plastics Plate & Sheet; Particleboard
S.I.C.: 3083; 5031
Richard Schneider *(Pres.)*
Patrick Peyton *(V.P.-Fin.)*

Subsidiary:

Pioneer Plastics Corp. **(1)**
One Pionite Rd.
Auburn, ME 04210
Tel.: 207-784-9111
Approx.Sls.: $145,000,000
Emp.: 1,000
Laminated Plastics Plate & Sheet; Particleboard
S.I.C.: 3083; 5031
Richard Schneider *(Pres.)*
Douglas G. McDonald *(V.P.-Fin.)*
Clifford T. Marr *(V.P.-Mktg. & Sls.)*
Dale Larose *(V.P.-Mfg.)*

PIONEER SUPERMARKETS
(d/b/a Pioneer Foods, Inc.)
1625 Sunset Blvd.
Los Angeles, CA 90026
Tel.: 213-250-3783
Emp.: 178
Retail Groceries & Liquor
S.I.C.: 5411; 5921
Leonard R. Leum *(Pres.)*
Mike Leum *(V.P.)*
Tom Gardiner *(Controller)*

Outside Service Firm(s):

J.A. Rodgers & Co.*(Auditors)*
Los Angeles, CA

PIPE FABRICATING & SUPPLY COMPANY
9703 S. Norwalk Blvd.
Santa Fe Springs, CA 90670
Tel.: 310-692-7226
Fax: 310-699-8472
Sales Range: $10-19 Million
Emp.: 100
Engineering, Bending, Fabricating, Heat Treating, Sand, Shot & Grit Blasting, Painting Of High & Low Pressure Piping Systems
S.I.C.: 3498; 3356; 3398; 3443
J.M. Eagle *(Chm. Bd. & Chief Exec. Officer)*
A.R. Simmons *(Pres.)*
J. Eagle *(V.P.)*
M.J. Eagle *(Sec. & Treas.)*

Outside Service Firm(s):

Price Waterhouse*(Auditors)*
660 Newport Center Dr., Ste. 600
Newport Beach, CA 92660
Tel.: 714-640-9200

First Interstate Bank*(Major Banking Relationship)*
5000 Birch St.
Newport Beach, CA 92660

PIPER AIRCRAFT CORPORATION
2926 Piper Dr.
Vero Beach, FL 32960
Mailing Address:
P.O. Box 1328,
Vero Beach, FL 32961
Tel.: 407-567-4361 **PA**
Fax: 407-770-2237
Year Founded: 1937
Approx.Sls.: $125,000,000
Emp.: 260
Fiscal Year-end: 6/30/92
Mfr. of Personal, Training, Utility & Business Aircraft
S.I.C.: 3721; 3724; 3728
A. Stone Douglass *(Chm. Bd. & Owner)*
Charles M. Suma *(Pres. & Chief Oper. Officer)*
J. Earle Boyter *(V.P.-Mktg. & Sls.)*
Robert Mikolajczak *(Chief Fin. Officer)*
John Hopper *(Controller)*
E. Glenn Parr *(Gen. Counsel)*
Patrick Shepherd *(Dir.-Personnel & Employee Benefits)*
Bradley Smith *(Dir.-Fin.)*
Lee Walther *(Dir.-Mktg. & Sls.)*
John Mattingly *(Mgr.-Pur.)*
James Skinner *(Mgr.-MIS)*
Werner Hartlieb *(Mgr.-Quality Assurance)*
James Skinner *(Mgr.-Mngmt. Information Systems)*
George Watson *(Mgr.-Mfg.)*
Cindy Bedsole *(Corp. Travel Planner & Exec. Asst.)*
Principal(s):
A. Stone Douglass

No. of Mfg. Plants/Facilities: 1
No. of U.S. Offices: 1

Computer Systems/Hardware:
IBM 3178

PIPER INDUSTRIES, INC.
12001 Corporate Dr.
Dallas, TX 75228
Tel.: 214-686-4366 **TX**
Fax: 214-686-4336
Assets: $12,000,000
Liabilities: $2,200,000
Net Worth: $9,800,000
Sales Range: $10-19 Million
Emp.: 50
Fiscal Year-end: 8/31/90
Own & Lease Real Property; Investments
Paul P. Piper, Jr. *(Chm. & Chief Exec. Officer)*
David E. Chisum *(Chief Fin. Officer & Sec.)*
Edward Stahl *(Pres.)*

No. of Mfg. Plants/Facilities: 1
No. of U.S. Offices: 2

Computer Systems/Hardware:
AT&T

Outside Service Firm(s):

AIG (American International Group)*(Commercial Insurance Carrier)*
Boston, MA

Blue Cross & Blue Shield of Texas, Inc.*(Group Insurer)*
Dallas, TX

Decker, Hardt, Kopf, Harr, Munsch & Dinan*(Legal Firm)*
Dallas, TX

Texas Commerce Bank*(Major Banking Relationship)*
2200 Ross Ave.
Dallas, TX 75266

MALCOLM PIRNIE, INC.
2 Corporate Park Dr.
White Plains, NY 10602
Mailing Address:
P.O. Box 751,
White Plains, NY 10602
Tel.: 914-694-2100 **NY**
Telex: 137364
Fax: 914-694-9286
Year Founded: 1910
Approx.Sls.: $112,000,000
Emp.: 1000
Fiscal Year-end: 12/31/91
Environmental Engineers, Scientists & Planners
S.I.C.: 8711; 8731
John H. Foster *(Chm. Bd.)*
Dr. Paul L. Busch *(Pres. & Chief Exec. Officer)*
Kenneth W. Henderson *(V.P. & Sec.)*
Thomas J. Hickey *(V.P. & Gen. Counsel)*
Daniel R. Shevchik *(V.P. & Treas.)*
Michael T. Sobozak *(V.P.-Mktg.)*
David H. Harris *(Dir.-Data Processing)*
John T. O'Neal *(Dir.-Personnel)*
Thomas J. Furlong *(Mgr.-Fin. Plng. & Taxes)*

No. of U.S. Offices: 21

Computer Systems/Hardware:
Prime

Outside Service Firm(s):

Arthur Andersen & Co.*(Auditors)*
400 Atlantic St.
Stamford, CT 06901
Tel.: 203-327-6100

Atlantic Mutual Insurance*(Commercial Insurance Carrier)*
New York, NY

Chemical Bank*(International Bank Affiliate)*
450 West 33rd St.
New York, NY 10001
Tel.: 212-613-7197
Fax: 212-947-7628

Metropolitan Life Insurance Co.*(Group Insurer)*
One Madison Avenue
New York, NY 10010-3690

Chemical Bank*(Investment Banker)*
450 West 33rd St.
New York, NY 10001
Tel.: 212-613-7197
Fax: 212-947-7628

Chemical Bank*(Major Banking Relationship)*
450 West 33rd St.
New York, NY 10001
Tel.: 212-613-7197
Fax: 212-947-7628

MONY*(Pension Manager)*
New York, NY

PISTOL PETE'S PIZZA
2810 W. Camelback Rd.
Phoenix, AZ 85017
Tel.: 602-246-7125
Fax: 602-433-2482
Approx.Sls.: $60,000,000
Emp.: 65
Family Style Restaurants
S.I.C.: 5812
Steve Haberkorn *(Pres. & Mgr.-Adv.)*

HAROLD M. PITMAN CO., INC.
721 Union Blvd.
Totowa, NJ 07512
Tel.: 201-812-0400
Fax: 201-812-1815
Approx.Sls.: $150,000,000
Emp.: 350
Graphic Art Distributors
S.I.C.: 7336
John W. Dreyer *(Chm. Bd., Pres. & Chief Exec. Officer)*
Gerald R. Knueven *(Chief Fin. Officer, Treas. & Controller)*
Monte Phelps *(V.P.-Sls.)*
Robert Pitman Schmidt *(Dir.-Mktg.)*
William J. Ford *(Mgr.-Natl. Sls.)*
Francis X. McCarthy *(Mgr.-Data Processing)*

Computer Systems/Hardware:
Burroughs B 1955

Outside Service Firm(s):

KPMG Peat Marwick*(Auditors)*
Peat Marwick Plaza, 303 E. Wacker Dr.
Chicago, IL 60601
Tel.: 312-938-1000

The Atlantic Companies*(Commercial Insurance Carrier)*
New York, NY

Metropolitan Life Insurance Co.*(Group Insurer)*
Tampa, FL

Continental Bank N. A.*(Major Banking Relationship)*
231 S. LaSalle St.
Chicago, IL 60697
Tel.: 312-828-2345
Tel.: 800-426-5754
Telex: 312-828-1783

PITTSBURGH BREWING COMPANY
3340 Liberty Ave.
Pittsburgh, PA 15201
Tel.: 412-682-7400 **PA**
Fax: 412-682-2379
Approx.Sls.: $55,000,000
Emp.: 285
Export
Brewery
S.I.C.: 2082
Michael Carlow *(Chm. Bd.)*
Jack Isherwood *(Pres.)*
Michael Graham *(Sr. V.P.-Sls. & Mktg.)*
William Morrison *(V.P.-Fin. & Admin.)*

PITTSBURGH PIRATES PROFESSIONAL BASEBALL CLUB
(Sub. of Pittsburgh Athletic Company, Inc.)
600 Stadium Circle
Pittsburgh, PA 15212
Mailing Address:
P.O. Box 7000
Pittsburgh, PA 15212
Tel.: 412-323-5000
Fax: 412-323-5024
Year Founded: 1891
Approx.Sls.: $20,000,000
Emp.: 100
Fiscal Year-end: 10/31/89
Professional Baseball Team
S.I.C.: 7941
Douglas Danforth *(Chm. Bd.)*
Mark Sauer *(Pres. & Chief Exec. Officer)*
Bob Derda *(V.P.-Ticket Opers.)*
Steve Greenberg *(V.P.-Mktg.)*
Jim Lachima *(Dir.-Media Rels.)*

PITTSBURGH TUBE CO.
2060 Pennsylvania Ave.
Monaca, PA 15061
Tel.: 412-774-6830
Fax: 412-773-7160
Approx.Sls.: $90,000,000
Emp.: 550
Fiscal Year-end: 9/30/92
Cold Drawn Buttweld & Electric Weld Mechanical Steel Tubing
S.I.C.: 3317
Arnold Cogswell *(Chm. Bd.)*
Richard C. Huemme *(Pres. & Chief Exec. Officer)*
Warren MacKenzie *(V.P.-Sls. & Mktg.)*
John R. Meneely, Jr. *(V.P.-Fin.)*
Les Whitver *(V.P.-Opers.)*
Richard L. Budd *(Chief Engr.)*
Jeffrey T. Wehman *(Pur. Agent)*

No. of U.S. Offices: 7

Outside Service Firm(s):

Price Waterhouse*(Auditors)*
600 Grant St., Ste. 4400
Pittsburgh, PA 15219
Tel.: 412-355-6000
Fax: 412-391-0609

Reed, Smith, Shaw & McClay*(Legal Firm)*
Mellon Square, P.O. Box 2009
Pittsburgh, PA 15230
Tel.: 412-288-3131
Fax: 412-288-3063

Divisions:

Pittsburgh Tube Co. Fairbury Div. **(1)**
U.S. Rte. 24, E.
Fairbury, IL 61739
Tel.: 815-692-2311
Fax: 815-692-3513
Approx.Sls.: $20,000,000
Emp.: 150
Fiscal Year-end: 9/30/91
Manufacture Electric Welded Steel Tubing & Cold Drawn Tube
S.I.C.: 3317
Richard Samsa *(Gen. Mgr.)*

Pittsburgh Tube Darlington Div. **(1)**
Darlington, PA 16115
Tel.: 412-827-8101
H.E. Thompson *(Plant Mgr.)*

Pittsburgh Tube Jane Lew Div. **(1)**
Jane Lew, WV 26378
Tel.: 304-884-7801
R.F. Samsa *(Plant Mgr)*

Pittsburgh Tube Monaca Div. **(1)**
Monaca, PA 15061
Tel.: 412-774-6830
W.C. Downs *(Mfg. Mgr.)*

TEC Fab Div. **(1)**
1805 Sheridan St.
Richmond, IN 47374
Tel.: 317-962-4295
David Straw *(Gen. Mgr.)*

PIZZA HAVEN INC.
12860 Interurban Ave. S.
Seattle, WA 98168
Tel.: 206-241-2990
Fax: 206-246-0298
Year Founded: 1958
Emp.: 250
Fiscal Year-end: 1/31/91
Chain of Pizza Restaurants
S.I.C.: 5812
Ronald H. Bean *(Pres.)*
Terry Younggren *(Controller)*
Stan Pate *(Dir.-Opers.)*
Jim Scribner *(Pur. Agent)*

Computer Systems/Hardware:
MAI Basic Four

Outside Service Firm(s):

Deloitte & Touche*(Auditors)*
700 Fifth Ave., Suite 4500
Seattle, WA 98104-5044
Tel.: 206-292-1800

Perkins, Coie*(Legal Firm)*
1900 Washington Bldg.
Seattle, WA 98101
Tel.: 206-454-6363

PIZZAGALLI CONSTRUCTION CO.
55 Joy Drive
South Burlington, VT 05403
Mailing Address:
P.O. Box 2009
South Burlington, VT 05403
Tel.: 802-658-4100 **VT**
Fax: 802-865-4469
Year Founded: 1958
Approx.Sls.: $145,000,000
Emp.: 1,000
Heavy Construction & General Building Contractor; Power & Industrial Process Contracting
S.I.C.: 1629; 1542; 1541
Thomas E. Chase *(Pres.)*
Peter M. Bernhardt *(V.P.)*
Ronald I. Bouchard *(V.P.)*
Angelo P. Pizzagalli *(V.P.)*
James Pizzagalli *(V.P.)*
Remo Pizzagalli *(V.P.)*
Gary B. Warner *(V.P.)*

John C. Stewart *(Treas.)*

Outside Service Firm(s):

Deloitte & Touche*(Auditors)*
125 Summer St.
Boston, MA 02110
Tel.: 617-261-8000
Fax: 617-261-8111

Morgan Guaranty Trust Company of New York*(Major Banking Relationship)*
23 Wall St.
New York, NY 10015
Tel.: 212-483-2323

PLACID OIL COMPANY
3800 Thanksgiving Tower
Dallas, TX 75201
Tel.: 214-880-1000
Fax: 214-880-1185
Approx.Sls.: $400,000,000
Emp.: 110
Crude Oil & Natural Gas Production
S.I.C.: 1311
Jerry Wright *(Pres. & Chief Exec. Officer)*
Phil Clarke *(V.P.-Opers.)*
Jeff Jones *(Controller)*
Bob Adkins *(Mgr.-Employee Rels.)*

Outside Service Firm(s):

First City Bank, Texas-Dallas*(Major Banking Relationship)*
1401 Elm
Dallas, TX 75283
Tel.: 214-939-8000

Subsidiary:

Placid Refining Company **(1)**
3800 Thanksgiving Tower
Dallas, TX 75201
Tel.: 214-880-1000
Approx.Sls.: $200,000,000
Emp.: 150
Oil Refinery
S.I.C.: 2911
Jerry Wright *(Pres.)*

PLAID PANTRIES, INC.
10025 S.W. Allen Blvd.
Beaverton, OR 97005
Tel.: 503-646-4246
Fax: 503-646-3071
Approx.Sls.: $65,000,000
Emp.: 900
Convenience Store Chain
S.I.C.: 5411
Chris Girard *(Pres. & Chief Exec. Officer)*
Chuck Bode *(V.P.)*
Thomas Florey *(V.P.-Fin.)*
Mark Stine *(V.P.)*

Outside Service Firm(s):

First Independent Bank*(Major Banking Relationship)*
Vancouver, WA

PLAINS CO-OP OIL MILL
2901 Ave. A
Lubbock, TX 79404
Mailing Address:
P.O. Box 1889
Lubbock, TX 79408
Tel.: 806-747-3434
Fax: 806-744-3221
Earnings: $3,000,000
Approx.Sls.: $64,000,000
Emp.: 270
Cotton Seed Processor
S.I.C.: 2074
Keith Streety *(Chm. Bd.)*
Wayne Martin *(Pres. & Chief Exec. Officer)*
Jack Sebastian *(Chief Fin. Officer & Treas.)*
Gail Kring *(Sr. V.P.)*
Gary Cobb *(V.P.-Mktg.)*
J.R. Blumrosen *(Gen. Counsel)*
Jeffrey Tucker *(Mgr.-Mngmt. Information Systems)*

Computer Systems/Hardware:
MAI Basic 4

Outside Service Firm(s):

Coopers & Lybrand*(Auditors)*
1999 Bryan St., Ste. 3000
Dallas, TX 75201
Tel.: 214-754-5000

Protection Mutual*(Commercial Insurance Carrier)*
Boston, MA

Nationwide Insurance*(Group Insurer)*
One Nationwide Plaza
Columbus, OH 43216
Tel.: 614-249-6488

NationsBank Texas*(Major Banking Relationship)*
Lubbock, TX

Texas Bank for Co-ops*(Major Banking Relationship)*
Austin, TX

PLAINS COTTON CO-OP ASSOCIATION
3301 E. 50th St.
Lubbock, TX 79404
Mailing Address:
P.O. Box 2827
Lubbock, TX 79408
Tel.: 806-763-8011 **TX**
Fax: 806-762-7335
Year Founded: 1953
Assets: $178,841,005
Liabilities: $98,475,982
Net Worth: $80,365,023
Approx.Sls.: $718,678,404
Emp.: 800
Fiscal Year-end: 6/30/91
Import Export
Marketing & Merchandising Raw Cotton to Domestic & Foreign Mills; Manufacture Denims
S.I.C.: 5159; 4221; 2211
Jackie Mull *(Chm. Bd.)*
Van May *(Pres. & Chief Exec. Officer)*
Darryl Lindsey *(V.P.-Opers.)*
Billy Morton *(V.P.-Fin.)*
Suz-Ann Glover *(Controller)*
Lee Phenix *(Dir.-Personnel)*
J.R. Blomrosen *(Gen. Counsel)*

Outside Service Firm(s):

Coopers & Lybrand*(Auditors)*
Lubbock, TX

Transamerica Occidental Insurance Co.*(Group Insurer)*
P.O. Box 30253,
Los Angeles, CA 90099

CoBank-National Bank for Cooperatives*(Major Banking Relationship)*
P.O. Box 5110,
Denver, CO 80217
Tel.: 303-740-4000
Fax: 509-838-9223

Cullen/Frost Bank of Dallas*(Pension Manager)*
Dallas, TX

PLAINS ELECTRIC GENERATION TRANSMISSION CO-OP, INC.
2401 Aztec, N.E.
Albuquerque, NM 87107
Tel.: 505-884-1881 **NM**
Fax: 505-889-7636
Year Founded: 1952
Approx.Sls.: $125,000,000
Emp.: 300
Generation, Electric Power; Transmission Electric Power
S.I.C.: 4911
Kenneth Coker *(Pres. of Bd. Dir.)*
Russell Baker *(Vice Chm. Bd.)*
Stanley K. Bazant *(Exec. V.P., Chief Exec. Officer & Gen. Mgr.)*

Plains Electric Generation Transmission Co-Op, Inc.—(Continued)

Outside Service Firm(s):

KPMG Peat Marwick*(Auditors)*
Two Park Square, 6565 Americas Pkwy., N.E., Ste. 700
Albuquerque, NM 87110
Tel.: 505-884-3939
Fax: 505-884-8348

Sun West Bank of Albuquerque*(Major Banking Relationship)*
P.O. Box 25500
Albuquerque, NM 87125-0500
Tel.: 505-765-2698
Fax: 505-842-6661

PLAINVILLE STOCK COMPANY, INC.
104 South St.
Plainville, MA 02762
Mailing Address:
P.O. Box 1628,
Plainville, MA 02762
Tel.: 508-699-4434
Fax: 508-695-0836
Approx.Sls.: $17,000,000
Emp.: 115
Manufacture Precious Jewelry
S.I.C.: 3911
Stephen Weisman *(Pres.)*
William Weisman *(V.P.)*
Robert Weisman *(Treas.)*
Larry Weisman *(Expediter)*

Outside Service Firm(s):

Priest, Kortick & Gesmondi*(Auditors)*
Providence, RI

Abraham Belilove*(Legal Firm)*
Providence, RI

Rhode Island Hospital Trust National Bank*(Major Banking Relationship)*
Providence, RI

PLAN INTERNATIONAL U.S.A.
155 Plan Way, Dept. MO24
Warwick, RI 02886
Tel.: 401-738-5600
Tel.: 800-556-7918
Fax: 401-738-5608
Year Founded: 1937
Approx.Rev.: $30,466,534
Emp.: 80
Fiscal Year-end: 6/30/91
Childreach Sponsorship Provides Grassroots Assistance in Health, Education, Family Livelihood & Community Development to help Sponsored Children & Their Families Towards Long-Term Goal of Self-Sufficiency
S.I.C.: 8361
Robert H. Zirkle *(Chm. Bd.)*
Kenneth H. Phillips *(Pres.)*
Donna-Jean Rainville *(V.P. Admin. & Fin.)*
Michael A. Walsh *(V.P.-Mktg.)*
Stacey Pulner *(Dir.-Adv.)*
Julie Gross *(Dir.-Pub. Rels.)*

Computer Systems/Hardware:
IBM System 38

PLANES MOVING AND STORAGE, INC.
10115 Transportation Way
Cincinnati, OH 45246
Tel.: 513-874-9330
Fax: 513-874-8215
Year Founded: 1921
Approx.Sls.: $21,000,000
Emp.: 220
Moving And Storage
S.I.C.: 4214
John Planes *(Pres.)*
Marianne Posey *(Chief Fin. Officer)*
Carl DeBlasio *(Exec. V.P.)*
Linda DeBlasio *(Sec.)*
Principal(s):
John Planes
Carl DeBlasio

Outside Service Firm(s):

Kamphaus, Henning Hoad & Sicking*(Auditors)*
Cincinnati, OH

IMPO Glaztile*(Major Banking Relationship)*
7600 County Line Rd., Unit 1
Burr Ridge, IL 60521
Tel.: 708-655-4676
Fax: 708-655-4696

PLANNING SYSTEMS INC.
7923 Jones Branch Dr.
McLean, VA 22102-3304
Tel.: 703-734-3400 **MD**
Fax: 703-734-3456
Year Founded: 1972
Assets: $10,182,000
Earnings: ($1,200,000)
Liabilities: $5,060,000
Net Worth: $5,122,000
Approx.Sls.: $27,500,000
Emp.: 290
Fiscal Year-end: 7/31/92
Research & Analysis of Naval Warfare Systems
S.I.C.: 8731
Louis M. Brown, Jr. *(Chm. Bd.)*
Gilbert Jacobs *(Pres. & Chief Exec. Officer)*
Robert Falconi *(Chief Fin. Officer, Treas. & Sec.)*
Chris McCarrick *(Chief Information Offficer)*
Dr. Sherry Potts *(V.P.-Bus. Devel & Admin.)*
Robert Murphy *(Chief Accountant)*
Dr. Alan Friedman *(Dir.-Tech.)*
Doreen Harrigan *(Dir.-Meetings Plng.)*
Marilyn Holcomb *(Dir.-Human Resources)*
Candace Byers *(Mgr.-Pur.)*
Debora Stonell *(Admin.- Facilities)*

No. of U.S. Offices: 9

Outside Service Firm(s):

Grant Thornton*(Auditors)*
McLean, VA
Tel.: 703-749-2900

EmTrust*(Group Insurer)*
Alexandria, VA
Tel.: 703-960-2200

The Insurance Exchange*(Group Insurer)*
Rockville, MD
Tel.: 301-279-5500

Reliance Standard*(Group Insurer)*
Philadelphia, PA

Semmes, Bowen, Semmes*(Legal Firm)*
10 Light Equitable Bldg.
Baltimore, MD 21204
Tel.: 410-296-4400

Signet Bank*(Major Banking Relationship)*
Vienna, VA

PLANO MOLDING CO.
431 E. South St.
Plano, IL 60545
Tel.: 708-552-3111
Fax: 708-552-8989
Year Founded: 1932
Sales Range: $20-39 Million
Emp.: 500
Manufacture Plastic Tackle Boxes, Utility Boxes, Tool Boxes, Paramedic Boxes & Cosmetic Organizers
S.I.C.: 3089
Peter H. Henning *(Pres. & Chief Exec. Officer)*
H.R. Behrens *(Exec. V.P.)*
John Kippen *(V.P.-Sls.)*
Mitch Spratford *(V.P.-Mktg.)*
James E. Porter *(Pur. Agent)*

Computer Systems/Hardware:
IBM AS/400

Outside Service Firm(s):

Hillsman, Lynch & Co.*(Auditors)*
Chicago, IL

Alschuler, Putman, McWethy, Funkey & Lewis*(Legal Firm)*
Chicago, IL

Sandwich State Bank*(Major Banking Relationship)*
Sandwich, IL

PLANT MAINTENANCE SERVICE CORPORATION
3000 Fite Rd.
Memphis, TN 38128
Mailing Address:
P.O. Box 280883,
Memphis, TN 38168-0883
Tel.: 901-353-9880 **TN**
Fax: 901-353-0882
Year Founded: 1967
Approx.Sls.: $24,000,000
Emp.: 260
Fabricated Plate Work; Boiler Repair Shop
S.I.C.: 3443; 7699
Robert L. Baker *(Pres.)*
Harold Perry *(V.P. & Treas.)*
Enoch Radford *(V.P. & Sec.)*
Richard Edwards *(Pur. Agent)*

Outside Service Firm(s):

National Bank of Commerce*(Major Banking Relationship)*
Memphis, TN

PLANTATION FOODS INC.
2510 E. Lake Shore Dr.
Waco, TX 76705
Tel.: 817-799-6211
Fax: 817-799-6499
Year Founded: 1979
Approx.Sls.: $71,000,000
Emp.: 1,600
Producer & Marketers of Turkey Products
S.I.C.: 5144
Roane Lacy *(Chm. Bd.)*
Dick Taylor *(Pres.)*
Roane Lacy, Jr. *(Chief Exec. Officer)*
Peter Palesota *(Controller, Treas. & Sec.)*
William Lunz *(Dir.-Adv. & Mktg.)*

Principal(s):
Roane Lacy
Roane Lacy, Jr.

PLASCAL CORPORATION
361 Eastern Pkwy.
Farmingdale, NY 11735
Tel.: 516-249-2200 **NY**
Fax: 516-249-2256
Approx.Sls.: $12,000,000
Emp.: 25
Mfr. of Plastics Materials & Resins
S.I.C.: 2821
Gerald Zimand *(Pres.)*
Henry Chozick *(V.P.-Sls.)*
Martin Klein *(Sec. & Treas.)*
Fred Hurd *(Dir.-Mfg.)*
John Urizzo *(Mgr.-Product)*
Gus Collin *(Chief Engr.)*

Outside Service Firm(s):

Goldfinger, Fuchs & Lasser*(Auditors)*
New York, NY

Chemical Banking Corp.*(Major Banking Relationship)*
277 Park Ave.
New York, NY 10041
Tel.: 212-310-6407
Fax: 212-310-4526

PLASKOLITE INC.
1770 Joyce Ave.
Columbus, OH 43219
Mailing Address:
P O. Box 1497
Columbus, OH 43216
Tel.: 614-294-3281
Fax: 614-297-7287
Year Founded: 1950
Approx.Sls.: $60,000,000
Emp.: 350
Export
Home Improvement Prods.: Acrylic Glazing, Rust-Proof Shower Stalls, Bathtub Wall Kits, Interior Insulating Windows With a Magnetic System, Styrene Glazing, Lens For Flourescent Lighting Fixtures, Skylight Glazing, Pellets For Injection Molders; Points Of Sale Mdsg. Displays & Acrylic Table Tops
S.I.C.: 3088; 3089; 3648
Donald G. Dunn *(Chm. Bd.)*
James Dunn *(Pres.)*
Mitchell P. Grindley *(V.P.-Mktg.)*
Mark Grindley *(V.P.-Opers.)*
David Chan *(V.P.-Tech.)*
Doug Nielson *(Treas.)*

PLASMA TECHNOLOGY, INC.
1754 Crenshaw Blvd.
Torrance, CA 90501
Tel.: 310-320-3373
Fax: 310-533-1677
Approx.Sls.: $10,000,000
Emp.: 135
Metal Plasma Coating
S.I.C.: 3479
Gene Fosket *(Pres.)*
Robert D. Dowell *(V.P.)*
John Nikitich *(V.P.)*
Robert Wolfgram *(V.P.)*

Outside Service Firm(s):

Rutton & Tucker*(Legal Firm)*
Santa Ana, CA

First Business Bank*(Major Banking Relationship)*
Torrance, CA

PLASTECH CORPORATION
20 N. Lake St.
Forest Lake, MN 55025
Tel.: 612-464-8700 **MN**
Fax: 612-464-1814
Sales Range: $40-59 Million
Emp.: 600
Fiscal Year-end: 12/31/91
Plastic Injection Molding
S.I.C.: 3089
Dennis Frandsen *(Chm. Bd. & Owner)*
Tom Pesek *(Chief Fin. Officer)*
Robert Bullard *(V.P.-Admin.)*
Marcia Wegleitner *(Controller)*
Alan Stender *(Mgr.-Data Processing)*
Principal(s):
Dennis Frandsen

Outside Service Firm(s):

Boulay, Heutmaker, Zibell & Co.*(Auditors)*
Minneapolis, MN

Lindquist & Vennum*(Legal Firm)*
4200 IDS Center, 80 South 8th St.
Minneapolis, MN 55402
Tel.: 612-371-3211

PLASTEK GROUP
2425 W. 23rd. St.
Erie, PA 16506
Tel.: 814-838-9667
Fax: 814-833-4486
Year Founded: 1956
Sales Range: $40-59 Million
Emp.: 580
Export

Custom Injection Molding
S.I.C.: 3089
Joseph J. Prischak *(Chm. Bd.)*
Andrew M. Prischak *(Pres.)*
Nar Handa *(Sr. V.P.)*
Dennis J. Prischak *(V.P.-Engrng.)*
Isabel J. Prischak *(Treas.)*
James J. Sitter *(Sec. & Controller)*
Ron Checcio *(Gen. Mgr.-MA Fix)*
Al Costa *(Gen. Mgr.-Empire Cosmetics)*
Nar Handa *(Gen. Mgr.-Ultra-Pak)*
William Koehle *(Mgr.-Pur.)*
Genivieve Putnam *(Mgr.-Human Res.)*
Norbert J. Wroblewski *(Mgr.-Sls.)*

Outside Service Firm(s):

Ronald Midcap*(Auditors)*
Akron, OH

Penn Bank of Erie*(Major Banking Relationship)*
Erie, PA

Subsidiaries:

Applicator Co. **(1)**
2431 W. Grandview Blvd.
Erie, PA 16506
Tel.: 814-838-1119
Applicators, Daubers, etc.
S.I.C.: 2499; 3842
Eric Robbins *(Chief Oper. Officer)*

Color Cosmetics **(1)**
2310 Pittsburgh Ave.
Erie, PA 16506
Tel.: 814-454-0550
Packaging of Cosmetics
S.I.C.: 5122
Al Costa *(Gen. Mgr.)*

M & E Manufacturing Co. **(1)**
19 Durkee St.
Laconia, NH 03246
Tel.: 603-528-1217
Mfr. of Cosmetic Brushes
S.I.C.: 2844; 3991
G. Edmund Heim *(Gen. Mgr.)*

Penn Erie Div. **(1)**
2315 W. 23rd. St.
Erie, PA 16506
Tel.: 814-453-5081
Plastic Injection Molding
S.I.C.: 3089
Chip Hillen *(Gen. Mgr.)*

Plastek Industries, Inc. **(1)**
3001 W. 15th St.
Erie, PA 16505
Tel.: 814-838-9667
Engineered Plastics; Custom Injection Molding
S.I.C.: 3087
Walter Masnyk *(Gen. Mgr.)*

Plastek Tool, Inc. **(1)**
3001 W. 15th St.
Erie, PA 16505
Tel.: 814-838-9667
Plastic Injection Molding
S.I.C.: 3089
Steve Andersen *(Gen. Mgr.)*

Spectrum Molding **(1)**
2425 W. 23rd St.
Erie, PA 16506
Tel.: 814-838-9667
Injection Molding of Plastics
S.I.C.: 3089
Andy Prischak *(Gen. Mgr.)*

Triangle Tool Co. **(1)**
3230 W. 22nd St.
Erie, PA 16506
Tel.: 814-833-7727
Plastic Injection Molding; Tool & Die
S.I.C.: 3089; 3544
Ed Butlin *(Gen. Mgr.)*

PLASTI-KOTE COMPANY INC.
1000 Lake Rd.
Medina, OH 44256
Mailing Address:
P.O. Box 708
Medina, OH 44258
Tel.: 216-725-4511
Tel.: 800-431-5928 OH
Fax: 216-723-3674
Year Founded: 1923
Approx.Sls.: $50,000,000
Emp.: 250
Fiscal Year-end: 3/31/91
Manufacture Aerosol Paint & Enamel Products; Brushes
S.I.C.: 2851; 3991
P.W. McKenna *(Chm. Bd., Pres. & Chief Oper. Officer)*
Scott Williamson *(Chief Fin. Officer & Gen. Counsel)*
Bob Radigan *(Sr. Exec. V.P.)*
Christine McKenna *(Exec. V.P.-Mktg.)*
Todd P. Ruppelli *(Exec. V.P.-Sls.)*
James F. Rapp *(V.P.-Intl. Sls.)*
Kenneth J. Kerata *(Dir.-Data Processing & Telecommunications)*
Pat Maloy *(Dir.-Personnel)*
Dick Kyle *(Pur. Agent)*
Principal(s):
P.W. McKenna

No. of Mfg. Plants/Facilities: 1
No. of U.S. Offices: 4
No. of Foreign Offices: 1

Computer Systems/Hardware:
IBM System 38

Outside Service Firm(s):

Ernst & Young*(Auditors)*
1300 Huntington Bldg.
Cleveland, OH 44115
Tel.: 216-861-5000

Marsh & McLennan*(Commercial Insurance Carrier)*
1 Cleveland Center, Ste. 2500, 1375 E. 9th St.
Cleveland, OH 44114
Tel.: 216-241-0908

John Hancock Mutual Life Insurance Co.*(Group Insurer)*
One Financial Center, 44th Floor
Boston, MA 02111
Tel.: 617-348-3707
Fax: 617-350-0305

Fleet National Bank*(Investment Banker)*
125 Dupont Dr.
Providence, RI 02907-3178
Tel.: 401-278-5335

Calfee, Halter & Griswold*(Legal Firm)*
800 Superior Ave., Ste. 1800
Cleveland, OH 44115-2688
Tel.: 216-622-8200
Fax: 216-241-0816

Fleet National Bank*(Major Banking Relationship)*
125 Dupont Dr.
Providence, RI 02907-3178
Tel.: 401-278-5335

Subsidiaries:

Plasti-Kote Co., Pactra Hobby **(1)**
27201 Tourney Rd., Ste. 200
Valencia, CA 91355
Tel.: 805-255-7661
Fax: 818-997-1173
Emp.: 5
Fiscal Year-end: 12/31/89
Manufacture Paints
S.I.C.: 2851
Robert Radigan *(Pres.)*
Mike McKenna *(V.P.-Opers.)*
Gil Mercier *(Gen. Sls. Mgr.)*

Tempo Products Company **(1)**
6200 Cochran Rd.
Cleveland, OH 44139
Tel.: 216-248-1450
Emp.: 50
Fiscal Year-end: 3/31/91
Manufacture Paints
S.I.C.: 2851
Michael McKenna *(Pres.)*

PLASTIC ENGINEERING COMPONENTS INC.
2665 So. Moorland Ave., Ste. 210
New Berlin, WI 53151
Tel.: 414-782-2610
Tel.: 800-726-2060 DE
Fax: 414-782-5143
Year Founded: 1989
Approx.Sls.: $80,000,000
Emp.: 850
Fiscal Year-end: 6/30/92
Export
Machine Tool Manufacturing; Plastics Molding & Processing; Machine Process Controls
S.I.C.: 3541; 3089; 3829
Corporate Giving Program: United Way
Edward Mentzer *(Pres. & Chief Exec. Officer)*
Ronald L. DeCamp *(Chief Oper. Officer)*
Richard M. Koputich *(Chief Fin. Officer)*
Michael C. Sipek *(Grp. V.P.)*
Eric J. Lorenz *(Controller)*

Computer Systems/Hardware:
DEC; IBM

Operations:

Golden Triangle Plastics, Inc. **(1)**
1325 Perdale Rd.
El Paso, TX 79936
Tel.: 915-594-1095
Fax: 915-594-0016
Emp.: 200
Computer Systems/Hardware:
DEC
Custom Injection Molds
S.I.C.: 3089
Robert Kroll *(Gen. Mgr.)*

Los Angeles Die Mold **(1)**
1942 N. Rosemead Blvd.
South El Monte, CA 91733
Tel.: 213-283-5184
Fax: 818-443-0547
Emp.: 175
Louis Korbe *(Gen. Mgr.)*

Janlin Plastic Inc. **(1)**
1204 E. Lincoln St.
Mount Horeb, WI 53572
Tel.: 608-437-3021 (100%)
Emp.: 150
Computer Systems/Hardware:
DEC
Mfrs. Plastic Parts
S.I.C.: 3089
Michael Longworth *(Gen. Mgr.)*

Moark Mold, Inc. **(1)**
"PP" Highway & Miller Road
Poplar Bluff, MO 63901
Tel.: 314-785-0871 (100%)
Emp.: 175
Computer Systems/Hardware:
DEC
Injection Mold Builders & Plastic Parts Mfr.
S.I.C.: 3544; 3089
Harry Scharboneau *(Gen. Mgr.)*

Mol-Bee, Inc. **(1)**
1811 Vanderbilt Ave.
Kalamazoo, MI 49002
Tel.: 616-327-3023 (100%)
Mfrs. Steel Molds that Produce Plastic Parts
S.I.C.: 3544
John Linder *(Gen. Mgr.)*

Pan-O-Grav, Inc. **(1)**
1807 Vanderbilt Road
Kalamazoo, MI 49002
Tel.: 616-327-4486 (100%)
Plastic Injection Molding
S.I.C.: 3089
John Linder *(Div. Mgr.)*

Plastic Engineering, Inc. **(1)**
1825 Vanderbilt Road
Kalamazoo, MI 49002
Tel.: 616-327-6788 (100%)
Mfrs. Plastics
S.I.C.: 3089
James LaCroix *(Gen. Mgr.)*

PLASTIC MOLDINGS CORP.
2181 Grand Ave.
Cincinnati, OH 45214
Tel.: 513-921-5040
Fax: 513-921-5883
Approx.Sls.: $16,000,000
Emp.: 350
Custom Plastic Molding
S.I.C.: 3089
Thomas R. Gerdes *(Pres.)*
Robert Brohas *(V.P.-Engrng.)*
Dennis Blazer *(Treas.)*

Computer Systems/Hardware:
IBM

Outside Service Firm(s):

Ruby & Kingston*(Auditors)*
Cincinnati, OH

Schwartz, Manes & Ruby*(Legal Firm)*
Cincinnati, OH

Star Bank*(Major Banking Relationship)*
425 Walnut Street
Cincinnati, OH 45202
Tel.: 513-632-4000

PLASTIC PACKAGING, INC.
1246 Main Ave. S.E.
Hickory, NC 28601
Tel.: 704-328-2466
Year Founded: 1958
Approx.Sls.: $20,000,000
Emp.: 200
Mfr. of Plastic Packaging Materials
S.I.C.: 3089
Thomas C. Ballenger *(Chm. Bd.)*
Weldon S. Fanjoy *(Pres.)*
Jake Schoonderwoerd *(V.P.-Mfg.)*
James Teubner *(V.P.-Fin.)*
William Lipscomb *(V.P.-Sls. & Mktg.)*

PLASTIC REEL CORP. OF AMERICA
Brisbin Ave.
Lyndhurst, NJ 07071
Tel.: 201-933-5100
Fax: 201-933-9468
Approx.Sls.: $10,000,000
Emp.: 150
Mfg. Plio-Magic Plastic Film Shipping Cases, Reels & Accessories; Videotape & Magnetic Tape Reels; Micro Film Reels, Cores, Rollers, Bearings, Bushings; Moduline Storage Systems; Editing Equip. & Supplies; Videotape Boxes for Storage Cases, Computer Shipping & Carrying Cases, Plastic Video Cassette Storage Boxes for 1/2" & U-Matic Cassettes
S.I.C.: 3861
Ben Zuk *(Chm. Bd. & Pres.)*
Pat Baccarella *(V.P.)*

Division:

PRC of America Supply Corp. **(1)**
Brisbin Ave.
Lyndhurst, NJ 07071
Tel.: 201-933-5100
S.I.C.: 3861
Pat Baccarella *(Pres.)*

Subsidiary:

PRC of America Corp. **(1)**
Brisbin Ave.
Lyndhurst, NJ 07071
Tel.: 201-933-5100
S.I.C.: 3861
Ben Zuk *(Pres.)*

PLASTIC SUPPLIERS, INC.
2887 Johnstown Rd.
Columbus, OH 43219
Mailing Address:
P.O. Box 360478,
Columbus, OH 43236-0478
Tel.: 614-471-9100 NJ

Plastic Suppliers, Inc.—(Continued)

Fax: 614-471-9033
Year Founded: 1950
Approx.Sls.: $85,000,000
Emp.: 250
Fiscal Year-end: 11/ 2/91

Export
Manufacture Biaxially Oriented Polystyrene Distribution & Converter of Plastic Film & Sheet
S.I.C.: 3081; 3083; 3089
Peter Driscoll *(Chm. Bd.)*
Howard Callaghan *(Pres.)*
Theodore Riegert *(V.P.-Opers.)*
Marvin Goodman *(V.P.-Sls. & Mktg.)*
James P. Ansted *(Chief Fin. Officer, Treas., Sec.)*
Robert Stephens *(Mgr.-Pur.)*
Robert Weber *(Natl. Sls. Mgr.)*

No. of Mfg. Plants/Facilities: 8
No. of U.S. Offices: 6
No. of Foreign Offices: 2

Plants:

Plastic Suppliers Inc. **(1)**
12916 S. Broadway
Los Angeles, CA 90061
Tel.: 800-722-5577
Manufacture Plastic Film
S.I.C.: 3081
Ronald Cox *(Mgr.)*

Plastic Suppliers Inc. **(1)**
3330 Holman Ave.
Chicago Heights, IL 60411
Tel.: 800-722-5577
Converter & Manufacture Plastic Film
S.I.C.: 3081
Walter Smith *(Mgr.)*

Plastic Suppliers Inc. **(1)**
815 Mercury Street
Duncanville, TX 75137
Tel.: 800-722-5577
Manufacture Plastic Film
S.I.C.: 3081
Bill Adams *(Mgr.)*

Plastic Suppliers, Inc. **(1)**
1174 Hayes Industrial Dr.
Marietta, GA 30062
Tel.: 404-424-0702
Tel.: 800-722-5577
Manufacture Plastic Film
S.I.C.: 3081
John Hess *(Mgr.)*
Dennis Cheny *(Plant Mgr.)*

Plastic Suppliers, Inc. **(1)**
207 Lakeview Ave.
Blackwood, NJ 08012
Tel.: 609-228-5600
Fax: 609-228-5604
Mfr. of Plastic Film
S.I.C.: 3081

Plastic Suppliers, Inc **(1)**
2400 Marilyn Lane
Columbus, OH 43219
Tel.: 614-475-8010
Mfr. of Plastic Film
S.I.C.: 3081
Jim Allen *(Plant Mgr.)*

PLASTICS MANUFACTURING COMPANY
2700 S. Westmoreland
Dallas, TX 75233
Tel.: 214-330-8671
Fax: 214-337-7428
Approx.Sls.: $39,000,000
Emp.: 450
Mfr. of Molded Table & Housewares Products
S.I.C.: 3089
James H. Miller *(Pres. & Chief Exec. Officer)*
Robert Logan *(Exec. V.P.)*
Jim Forrester *(V.P.)*
Wayne Sullivan *(V.P.)*
Deryl E. Cochran *(Sec. & Treas.)*

Outside Service Firm(s):

KPMG Peat Marwick*(Auditors)*
1601 Elm St., Ste. 1600
Dallas, TX 75201
Tel.: 214-754-2000
Fax: 214-754-2297

PLASTIGAGE CORPORATION
2917 Wildwood Ave.
Jackson, MI 49202
Mailing Address:
P.O. Box 1167,
Jackson, MI 49204
Tel.: 517-788-8000 **MI**
Fax: 517-788-8215
Assets: $3,263,000
Liabilities: $1,410,000
Net Worth: $1,853,000
Approx.Sls.: $10,000,000
Emp.: 105
Manufacture & Wholesale Plastics Parts & Products
S.I.C.: 3087; 5162
Fred B. Hetherwick *(Chm. Bd., Pres. & Chief Exec. Officer)*
Albert Medler *(Vice Chm.)*
Carolyn Osborne *(Sec. & Dir.-Personnel)*
Tom Nelson *(Dir.-Pur.)*

Computer Systems/Hardware:
Zilog & Cado

Outside Service Firm(s):

Ernst & Young*(Auditors)*
188 E. Capital St., Ste. 400
Jackson, MI 39201-2157
Tel.: 601-948-6600

Ammon, Sullivan, Weeden, Thompson*(Legal Firm)*
Jackson, MI

Division:

Gordon Plastics Div. **(1)**
P.O. Box 1107,
Jackson, MI 49204
Tel.: 517-788-8000
Manufacture Thermal Plastics
S.I.C.: 3089
Fred Hetherwick *(Pres. & Chief Exec. Officer)*

PLASTIPAK PACKAGING INC.
9135 General Ct.
Plymouth, MI 48170
Tel.: 313-455-3600
Fax: 313-455-0556
Approx.Sls.: $96,000,000
Emp.: 1,100
Manufacture Miscellaneous Plastic Products
S.I.C.: 3089
William P. Young *(Chm. Bd.)*
William C. Young *(Pres.)*
Joseph Bongiomo *(V.P.-Admin.)*
William Slat *(V.P.-Opers. & Mfg. Dir.)*
Mary E. Young *(Treas.)*
John D. Schaefer *(Sec.)*
Gina Ferretti *(Dir.-Human Resources)*

PLASTOID CORPORATION
45 Gingerbread Castle Rd.
Hamburg, NJ 07419
Tel.: 201-827-7141
Approx.Sls.: $10,000,000
Emp.: 250
Coaxial Cable & Insulated Wire
S.I.C.: 3357
Jacqueline Traeger-Rado *(Pres.)*
J. Leon Brodsky *(V.P.-Engrng.)*
Dean Haggerty *(Mgr.-Pur.)*
Ferne Traeger *(Asst. Sec.)*

PLASTOMER CORP.
37819 Schoolcraft
Livonia, MI 48150
Tel.: 313-464-0700
Fax: 313-464-4792
Approx.Sls.: $33,000,000
Emp.: 400
Manufacture Gaskets, Packing & Sealing Devices; Polyurethane Foam; Laminations
S.I.C.: 3053; 3086; 3081; 3083
Walter P. Baughman *(Chm. Bd.)*
George K. Baughman *(Pres. & Treas.)*
David O. Baughman *(V.P.-Mktg.)*
Walter P. Baughman III *(V.P.-Mfg.)*

PLATT SACO LOWELL CORPORATION
P.O. Drawer 2327
Greenville, SC 29602
Tel.: 803-859-3211
Fax: 803-859-2908
Approx.Sls.: $50,000,000
Emp.: 750
Fiscal Year-end: 12/31/91
Mfrs. Yarn Preparatory Machinery Through Twisting, Indus. Robots
S.I.C.: 3599
T. Michael Papleacos *(Sr. Exec. V.P.)*
E.T. Cansler *(V.P.-Domestic Sls.)*
Doug Fraser *(Dir.-Fin.)*
Brent O'Shields *(Dir.-Employee Rels.)*
Mario Dihigo *(Mgr.-Mfg.)*

PLAYTEX APPAREL INC.
700 Fairfield Ave.
Stamford, CT 06904
Mailing Address:
P.O. Box 10064
Stamford, CT 06904
Tel.: 203-356-8000 **DE**
Fax: 203-356-8448
Year Founded: 1932
Approx.Sls.: $384,492,000
Emp.: 6,500
Fiscal Year-end: 12/31/89
Holding Company
S.I.C.: 6719; 2342
Donald J. Franceschini *(Pres.)*

Outside Service Firm(s):

KPMG Peat Marwick*(Auditors)*
Stamford Square, 3001 Summer St.
Stamford, CT 06905
Tel.: 203-356-9800

Metropolitan Life Insurance Co.*(Group Insurer)*
One Madison Avenue
New York, NY 10010-3690

E.F. Hutton*(Investment Banker)*
Jacksonville, FL

Latham & Watkins*(Legal Firm)*
885 Third Ave.
New York, NY 10022
Tel.: 212-906-1200

Chemical Banking Corporation*(Major Banking Relationship)*
450 W. 33rd. St.
New York, NY 10001
Tel.: 212-613-7147

Non-U.S. Holdings:

Gelmart Industries Philippines, Inc. **(1)**
PX Division, Km. 15, South Super Hwy.
CCPO Box 373, Makati,
Metro Manila, Rizal Philippines
Tel.: 828-75-81, 82
Telex: 762064115 GIPPX PN
Fax: 8179742, 8150756
Mfr. of Undergarments
S.I.C.: 2342

Intex **(1)**
AM Wartberg, Playtex Park Postfach, D-6508
Alzey, Germany
Tel.: 6731 49 40
Telex: 841-42429
Fax: 6731 1700
Mfr. of Undergarments
S.I.C.: 2342

Playtex Apparel Canada, Ltd. **(1)**
6363 Northam Dr. Airport Industrial Park,
Malton, ON L4V 1N5, Canada
Tel.: 416-677-6211 (100%)
Telex: 06968618 PLAYTEX TOR
Fax: 416-677-7965
Import
Computer Systems/Hardware:
IBM
Mfr. of Intimate Apparel
S.I.C.: 2342
M. Recone *(V.P. & Gen. Mgr.-Family Products Div.)*
P. Mischinski *(V.P. & Gen. Mgr.-Intl. Apparel Div.)*
R. Jessop *(Natl. Sls. Mgr.-Family Products Div.)*

Division:

Playtex Apparel Canada, Ltd., Renfrew **(2)**
550 Hall St.
Renfrew, ON K7V 2S9, Canada
Tel.: 613-432-3677
Fax: 613-432-9919
Mfr. of Intimate Apparel
S.I.C.: 2342

Playtex Espana S.A. **(1)**
Carretera de Sabadell S/N 08211
Castellar del Valles, Spain
Tel.: 3-7145600
Telex: 83151884 51884 PLYC E
Fax: 3 7148366

Playtex Espana S.A. **(1)**
Paseo de la Castellana 93 28046
Madrid, Spain
Tel.: 1-597-1517 (100%)
Fax: 1-55 54122
Mktg. & Sls. of Intimate Apparel
S.I.C.: 5137

Playtex France **(1)**
6 Rue de Penthievre 75008
Paris, France
Tel.: 14 266.90.91 (100%)
Telex: 842-660174
Fax: 14 266-6691
Fax: 14 266-6915
Marketing & Sales of Intimate Apparel
S.I.C.: 5137

Plant:

Playtex France **(2)**
B.P. 55, Zone Industrielle 38110
La Tour-du-Pin, France
Tel.: 74 97.10.96
Fax: 74 97.06.62
Mfr. of Intimate Apparel
S.I.C.: 2342

Playtex, Italia S.p.A. **(1)**
Piazza L. Sturzo, 31 00144
Rome, Italy
Tel.: 6-591-2751 (100%)
Telex: 612165
Fax: 6-592-4077
Marketing & Sales of Intimate Apparel
S.I.C.: 5137

Plant:

Playtex Italia S.p.A. **(2)**
Via Laurentian, Km. 27,200 00040
Pomezia, Italy
Tel.: 6-919 5041/5
Telex: 611040 PLAYTEX I
Fax: 6-919-6037
Mfr. of Intimate Apparel
S.I.C.: 2342

Playtex, Ltd. **(1)**
6363 Northam Dr. Airport IndustrialPark,
Malton, ON L4V 1N5, Canada
Tel.: 416-677-6211 (100%)
Telex: 06968618 PLAYTEX TOR
Fax: 416-677-7965
Mfr. of Intimate Apparel
S.I.C.: 2342

Division:

Playtex, Ltd., Arnprior **(2)**
Playtex Park P.O. Box 760,
Arnprior, ON K7S 1Z4, Canada
Tel.: 613-623-6531
Fax: 613-623-6820
Mfr. of Intimate Apparel
S.I.C.: 2342

Playtex Limited (1)
36 Chertsey Road
Woking, Surrey GU21 5BB, United Kingdom
Tel.: 4837 21121 (100%)
Telex: 851-859530 PLAYTEX LONDON
Fax: 4837-55272

Playtex Limited (1)
Playtex Park Port Glasgow,
Renfrewshire, United Kingdom
Tel.: 475-41631
Telex: 85177372 PLAYTEX G
Fax: 475-43119

Playtex Mexicana S.A. de C.V. (1)
Avenida Constitutyentes 908-C Col. Lomas Altas,
Mexico, D.F. 10, Mexico
Tel.: 905-570-4109 (100%)
Fax: 905-359-3496
Mktg. of Intimate Apparel
S.I.C.: 5137

Plant:

Playtex Mexicana S.A. de C.V. (2)
Calle 3 No. 28 1A. Seccion Alce Blanco,
Naucalpan de Juarez, Mexico
Tel.: 905-358-1000
Telex: 383-1774244 PLAYTEX MEX
Fax: 905-359-3496
Mfr. of Intimate Apparel
S.I.C.: 2342

Playtex (Pty.) Ltd. (1)
104 Briens Road
Northmead, N.S.W. 2152, Australia
Tel.: 2-630-770 (100%)
Fax: 2-683-2197

PLAYTEX FP GROUP INCORPORATED
700 Fairfield Ave.
Stamford, CT 06904
Mailing Address:
P.O. Box 10064,
Stamford, CT 06904
Tel.: 203-356-8000 **DE**
Year Founded: 1932
Assets: $694,381,000
Earnings: ($6,921,000)
Liabilities: $197,047,000
Net Worth: $497,334,000
Approx.Sls.: $405,477,000
Emp.: 1,600
Fiscal Year-end: 12/31/90
Holding Company; Manufacturer of Baby Feeding Systems, Gloves, Sanitary Products, Toothbrushes & Haircare Products
S.I.C.: 3069; 3991; 6719
Joel E. Smilow *(Chm. Bd. & Chief Exec. Officer)*
Hercules P. Sotos *(Vice Chm.)*
Calvin Gauss *(Pres.)*
William A. Heimerdinger *(Sr. V.P.-Opers. & Human Resources)*
Joel C. Coleman *(V.P., Gen. Counsel & Sec.)*

No. of Mfg. Plants/Facilities: 9
No. of U.S. Offices: 7
No. of Foreign Offices: 2

Outside Service Firm(s):

KPMG Peat Marwick*(Auditors)*
Stamford Square, 3001 Summer St.
Stamford, CT 06905
Tel.: 203-356-9800

Equitable Life*(Group Insurer)*
Charlotte, NC

Bankers Trust Co.*(Major Banking Relationship)*
P.O. Box 9050, Church St. Station
New York, NY 10008
Tel.: 212-250-6037

Latham & Watkins*(Legal Firm)*
885 Third Ave.
New York, NY 10022
Tel.: 212-906-1200

Subsidiaries:

Playtex Family Products Corp. (1)
700 Fairfield Ave.
Stamford, CT 06904
Tel.: 203-356-8000 (100%)
Assets: $700,877,000
Earnings: $3,363,000
Liabilities: $1,180,322,000
Net Worth: $479,445,000
Approx.Rev.: $382,862,000
Rubber Gloves, Sanitary Prods., Disposable Nursers, Baby Feeding Systems, Toothbrushes
S.I.C.: 3069; 3991; 2676
Joel E. Smilow *(Chm. & Chief Exec. Officer)*
Hercules P. Sotos *(Vice Chm.)*
Calvin J. Gauss *(Pres.)*
Irwin S. Butensky *(V.P.-Family Prods. Research & Devel.)*
William A. Heimerdinger *(V.P.-Opers. & Human Resources)*
Joel C. Coleman *(Gen. Counsel)*
Carlos L. Garcia *(Dir.-Corp. Fin.)*
Dan Riley *(Dir.-Res.)*

Subsidiaries:

Playtex Beauty Care, Inc. (2)
700 Fairfield Ave.
Stamford, CT 06904
Tel.: 203-356-8000 (100%)
Approx.Sls.: $75,000,000
Emp.: 200
Fiscal Year-end: 12/31/91
Manufacture Professional Hair Preparations
S.I.C.: 2844; 5122
Joel E. Smilow *(Chm. & Chief Exec. Officer)*
Calvin J. Gauss *(Pres.)*
Hercules P. Sotos *(Vice Chm.)*
Jim Cook *(Sr. V.P.-Opers. & Human Resources)*
I. Butensky *(Sr. V.P.-Res. & Devel.)*
Max Recone *(V.P.-Sls.)*

Playtex Investment Corp. (2)
700 Fairfield Ave.
Stamford, CT 06904
Tel.: 203-356-8000 (100%)
Holding Co.
S.I.C.: 6719

Playtex Marketing Corporation (2)
700 Fairfield Ave.
Stamford, CT 06904
Tel.: 203-356-8000 (100%)
Mktg. of Playtex Products
S.I.C.: 5137; 5122

PLIBRICO CO.
1800 N. Kingsbury St.
Chicago, IL 60614
Tel.: 312-549-7014
Fax: 312-549-0424
Year Founded: 1914
Approx.Sls.: $30,000,000
Emp.: 200
Fiscal Year-end: 12/31/90
Refractories, Boiler Setting & Furnace Construction
S.I.C.: 3255; 3297
Robert E. Fisher *(Pres.)*
Don Martosko *(Chief Oper. Officer)*
Robert G. Schultz *(V.P.-Mktg.)*
Joseph Milas *(Treas.)*
Daniel Wilke *(Mgr.-Benefits)*
Tom Wilke *(Mgr.-Data Processing)*
Jeri Rogus *(Pur. Agent)*

Computer Systems/Hardware:
IBM System 36

Outside Service Firm(s):

Hutton, Nelson & McDonald*(Auditors)*
Oak Brook, IL

First National Bank of Chicago*(Major Banking Relationship)*
One First National Plaza
Chicago, IL 60670
Tel.: 312-732-9781
Tel.: 312-732-4050
Fax: 312-732-4840
Fax: 312-732-3055

Subsidiaries:

Fireline Co. (1)
1800 N. Kingsbury St.
Chicago, IL 60614
Tel.: 312-549-7014
Fax: 312-549-0424
S.I.C.: 3255

Plibrico Sales & Service, Inc. (1)
1800 N. Kingsbury
Chicago, IL 60614
Tel.: 312-549-7014
Fax: 312-549-0424
Special Trade Contractor
S.I.C.: 1799
Robert E. Fisher *(Pres.)*

PLOOF TRUCK LINES, INC.
1414 Lindrose St.
Jacksonville, FL 32206
Tel.: 904-353-8641
Fax: 904-353-4326
Approx.Sls.: $36,000,000
Emp.: 600
Heavy Hauling
S.I.C.: 4213
William B. Copeland *(Chm. Bd.)*
Daniel M. Copeland *(Pres.)*
Robert W. Hooper *(Sr. V.P.-Sls.)*
Floyd Lee *(Sec.)*

Outside Service Firm(s):

KPMG Peat Marwick*(Auditors)*
Jacksonville, FL

Martin Sack, Jr.*(Legal Firm)*
Jacksonville, FL

Barnett Banks Trust Company, N.A.*(Major Banking Relationship)*
9000 Southside Blvd., P.O. Box 40200
Jacksonville, FL 32202-0200
Tel.: 904-464-2802

PLUNKETT-WEBSTER, INC.
2 Clinton Pl.
New Rochelle, NY 10802-0251
Tel.: 914-636-8770
Fax: 914-636-4477
Sales Range: $80-99 Million
Emp.: 220
Import Export
Lumber & Building Materials
S.I.C.: 2421
Robert G. Plunkett *(Pres.)*
H.H. Beecher *(V.P.)*
Jim A. Daniels *(V.P.)*
R.M. Tiffany *(V.P. & Sec.)*
W.E. Tufts *(V.P.)*

Outside Service Firm(s):

Edward Isaacs & Co.*(Auditors)*
New York, NY

PLYMOUTH CREAMERIES, INC.
Schwartz St. & Factory Rd.
Plymouth, WI 53073
Mailing Address:
P.O. Box 201,
Plymouth, WI 53073
Tel.: 414-893-0505
Approx.Sls.: $18,000,000
Emp.: 7
Wholesale Cream & Butter; Refrigerated Warehousing
S.I.C.: 4222; 5143
Howard E. Stoll *(Chm. Bd.)*
Ronald Nicolaus *(Pres.)*
Penny Nicolaus *(Sec. & Treas.)*

Outside Service Firm(s):

Vander, Jagt, Buss & Associates*(Auditors)*
Sheboygan, WI

First Wisconsin National Bank*(Major Banking Relationship)*
Sheboygan, WI

PLYMOUTH LAMSTON STORES, CORP.
45 Mayhill St.
Saddle Brook, NJ 07662
Tel.: 201-368-6900
Fax: 201-368-5858
Year Founded: 1987
Approx.Sls.: $200,000,000
Emp.: 3,300
Department & Accessories Stores
S.I.C.: 5311
Ronald DeFusco *(Pres.)*
Dennis Shae *(Chief Fin. Officer)*
Peter Devos *(Dir.-Visual Presentation)*

Outside Service Firm(s):

Grant Thornton*(Auditors)*
605 Third Ave.
New York, NY 10158
Tel.: 212-599-0100
Fax: 212-370-4520

Chemical Banking Corp.*(Major Banking Relationship)*
277 Park Ave.
New York, NY 10041
Tel.: 212-310-6407
Fax: 212-310-4526

Subsidiaries:

Lamston (1)
45 Mayhill St.
Saddle Brook, NJ 07662
Tel.: 201-368-6900
Neil Roth *(V.P. & Gen. Mdse. Mgr.)*
Barry Swartz *(V.P.-Store Opers.)*

Plymouth (1)
45 Mayhill St.
Saddle Brook, NJ 07662
Tel.: 201-368-6900

PLYMOUTH LOCOMOTIVE INTERNATIONAL, INC.
Bell & High Sts.
Plymouth, OH 44865
Tel.: 419-687-4641
Fax: 419-687-8112
Year Founded: 1987
Approx.Sls.: $15,000,000
Emp.: 140
Mfr. Industrial & Mining Locomotives; Extrucing & Processing Machinery; Heavy Duty Industrial Life Trucks; Narrow Aisle Electric Lift Trucks; 2, 000 Pound Articulated Loaders
S.I.C.: 3537; 3559; 3743
Ervin W. Howard *(Pres.)*
Donald Barnthoose *(Mgr.-Mktg.)*
Carl Ganzhorn *(Mgr.-Sls.)*
Larry Akers *(Buyer)*

Division:

Autolift Industrial Lift Trucks (1)
607 Bell St.
Plymouth, OH 44865
Tel.: 419-687-4641
S.I.C.: 3537

PLYMOUTH TUBE COMPANY
29 W. 150 Warrenville Rd.
Warrenville, IL 60555
Mailing Address:
Box 45,
Warrenville, IL 60555
Tel.: 708-393-4424 **MI**
Twx: 910-252-2160
Fax: 708-393-4427
Year Founded: 1924
Approx.Sls.: $105,000,000
Emp.: 850
Fiscal Year-end: 12/31/91
Import Export
Manufacturer & Distributor of Steel Pipes & Tubes
S.I.C.: 3317; 5051
Donald C. Van Pelt *(Chm. Bd., Pres. & Chief Exec. Officer)*
Gary Lloyd *(Exec. V.P.)*
Donald C. Van Pelt, Jr. *(Exec. V.P.)*
John W. Fikejs *(Treas. & Sec.)*

Plymouth Tube Company—(Continued)

Hugh Hawk *(Mgr.-New Business Devel.)*
Sharee L. Long *(Mgr.-Acctg.)*

No. of Mfg. Plants/Facilities: 10
No. of U.S. Offices: 10
No. of Foreign Offices: 1

Computer Systems/Hardware:
Sequent S16; UNIX

Outside Service Firm(s):

KPMG Peat Marwick*(Auditors)*
Peat Marwick Plaza, 303 E. Wacker Dr.
Chicago, IL 60601
Tel.: 312-938-1000

Liberty Mutual*(Commercial Insurance Carrier)*
Boston, MA

Winston & Strawn*(Legal Firm)*
One 1st Natl. Plaza, No. 5000
Chicago, IL 60603
Tel.: 312-558-5600

American National Bank & Trust Company of Chicago*(Major Banking Relationship)*
33 N. LaSalle St.
Chicago, IL 60602
Tel.: 312-661-5000
Fax: 312-661-6417

Securities Counselors of Iowa*(Pension Manager)*
Des Moines, IA

Non-U.S. Holdings:

Tubetec **(1)**
Calle Mayas, No. 12, Sta. Cruz Acatlan
Naucalpan De Juarez,
Mexico, D.F. Mexico
Tel.: 5-577-3040 (79%)
Manufacturer & Distributor of Steel Pipes & Tubes
S.I.C.: 3317; 5051
Carlos Lara *(Chief Oper. Officer)*

Universal Steel Tube Co. Limited **(1)**
Bertha Road Greet
Birmingham, B112 NN, United Kingdom
Tel.: 021-771-4256 (100%)
Telex: 336518 TUBUNIG
Fax: 021-766-6160
Approx.Sls.: $10,000,000
Emp.: 120
Mfr. of Cold Drawn & Hot Finished Seamless Steel Tube
S.I.C.: 3317
Peter J. Korbar *(Chief Oper. Officer)*
Margaret Barton *(Chief Fin. Officer)*

PLYWOOD PANELS, INC.
100 Napoleon Ave.
New Orleans, LA 70115
Mailing Address:
P.O. Box 15435
New Orleans, LA 70175
Tel.: 504-899-5691
Fax: 504-899-0118
Year Founded: 1966
Approx.Sls.: $205,000,000
Emp.: 1,000
Fiscal Year-end: 12/31/91
Wall Paneling, Unfinished Fancy Plywood, Veneer, Imported Lumber
S.I.C.: 2431; 2435; 5031
Thomas B. Roller *(Pres. & Chief Exec. Officer)*
Robert S. Taylor *(Chief Fin. Officer)*
Victor Johnson *(Sr. V.P.)*
Michael Swanson *(Sr. V.P.)*
Charles Rowe *(Controller)*
Donald Oaigle *(Dir.-Mngmt. Information Systems)*
Tom Stanchec *(Mgr.-Credit)*

No. of Mfg. Plants/Facilities: 4
No. of U.S. Offices: 7

Outside Service Firm(s):

Elmore R. Verlander & Company*(Auditors)*
New Orleans, LA

Jones, Walker, Waechter, Poitevent, Carrere & Denegre*(Legal Firm)*
Place St. Charles, 201 St. Charles Ave.
New Orleans, LA 70112
Tel.: 504-582-8000

Citizens & Southern National Bank*(Major Banking Relationship)*
New Orleans, LA

PLYWOOD PLASTICS INC.
111 Tonawanda St.
Buffalo, NY 14207
Tel.: 716-875-0800 **NY**
Fax: 716-875-8978
Year Founded: 1959
Approx.Sls.: $10,000,000
Emp.: 42
Export
Wholesale Distributor of Building Materials
S.I.C.: 5039; 5031
G. Fred Koch *(Pres. & Treas.)*
Frank Simpson *(Chief Fin. Officer & Controller)*
Peter Koch *(Exec. V.P.)*
Douglas Parker *(V.P.)*
John A. Wall *(V.P.)*
Elizabeth Koch *(Treas.)*

No. of Mfg. Plants/Facilities: 2
No. of U.S. Offices: 2

Outside Service Firm(s):

Freed, Maxick, Sachs & Murphy*(Auditors)*
Buffalo, NY
Tel.: 716-847-2651

Subsidiary:

Plywood Plastics, Inc. **(1)**
299 Burrows St.
Rochester, NY 14606
Tel.: 716-458-3636
Emp.: 18
Wholesale Distributor of Building Materials
S.I.C.: 5063
D. Parba *(Mgr.)*

PNEUMAFIL CORP.
4500 Chesapeake Dr.
Charlotte, NC 28216
Mailing Address:
P.O. Box 16348
Charlotte, NC 28297-6348
Tel.: 704-399-7441 **DE**
Fax: 704-391-7841
Year Founded: 1946
Approx.Sls.: $55,000,000
Emp.: 600
Manufacture Industrial Air Ventilation & Filtration Systems; Metal Cabinets for Military Electronics; Special Pump Systems; Chemical Process Equipment
S.I.C.: 3564; 3499; 3552; 3559; 3561; 3585
Robert P. Barbee *(Chm. Bd. & Chief Exec. Officer)*
Andreas H. Bechtler *(Vice Chm.)*
Harry S. Barr *(V.P.-Prod. Devel.)*
Paul Brusher *(V.P.-Human Resources)*
Harry S. Trimakas *(V.P.-Fin. & Treas.)*
Tom Mullen *(Dir.-Data Processing)*
Bill Helnes *(Mgr.-Pur.)*

Principal(s):
Andreas H. Bechtler

Outside Service Firm(s):

Ernst & Young*(Auditors)*
1100 Independence Center
Charlotte, NC 28246
Tel.: 704-372-6300

Fleming, Robinson, Bradshaw & Hinson, P.A.*(Legal Firm)*
First Union Plz.
Charlotte, NC 28801
Tel.: 704-377-2536

NationsBank Carolinas*(Major Banking Relationship)*
One NCNB Plaza T18-7
Charlotte, NC 28255

POINT COMMUNICATIONS, INC.
14001 Dallas Pkwy., Ste. 450
Dallas, TX 75240
Tel.: 214-851-1100
Fax: 214-851-1160
Year Founded: 1970
Approx.Billings: $20,000,000
Emp.: 32
Bill R. Neale *(Chm.)*
Willard Moon *(Pres. & Dir. Acct. Mngmt.)*
Sam J. Johnson *(Chief Exec. Officer)*
Duvan Polk *(V.P.)*
Debbie Johnson *(Controller)*

POLAR CORPORATION
40 Walcott St.
Worcester, MA 01603
Mailing Address:
P.O. Box 15011,
Worcester, MA 01615
Tel.: 508-753-4300
Tel.: 800-225-7410 **MA**
Fax: 508-793-0813
Year Founded: 1916
Approx.Sls.: $45,000,000
Emp.: 225
Fiscal Year-end: 12/31/90
Export
Mfr. of Carbonated Beverages including Seltzers & Bottled Water
S.I.C.: 2086
Corporate Giving Program: Local Institutions & Charities
Ralph D. Crowley *(Chm. Bd.)*
Ralph D. Crowley, Jr. *(Pres.)*
Scott Kumf *(Chief Fin. Officer)*
Christopher Crowley *(V.P.)*
Paul A. Salois *(V.P.-Mktg.)*
Denis M. Crowley *(Treas.)*
Davis Harmon *(Controller)*
Brian La Forte *(Sec.)*
Kathleen Crowley *(Dir.-Pub. Rels.)*
Gordon O. Davis *(Mgr.-Mktg.)*

Outside Service Firm(s):

Arthur Andersen & Co.*(Auditors)*
120 E. Baltimore St.
Baltimore, MD 21202
Tel.: 301-727-5800

Mirick, O'Connell, DeMalle & Lougee*(Legal Firm)*
Worcester, MA

Fleet National Bank*(Major Banking Relationship)*
111 Westminster St.
Providence, RI 02903
Tel.: 401-278-6000

POLAR WARE COMPANY
2806 N. 15th St.
Sheboygan, WI 53083
Mailing Address:
P.O. Box 211
Sheboygan, WI 53082
Tel.: 414-458-3561
Tel.: 800-237-3655
Fax: 414-458-2205
Year Founded: 1907
Approx.Sls.: $20,000,000
Emp.: 130
Fiscal Year-end: 12/31/91
Import Export
Polar Stainless Steel Deep Draw Hospital & Restaurant Utensils, Stainless Steel Sinks, Deep Drawn Stainless Steel Components
S.I.C.: 3431
Walter Vollrath III *(Pres. & Chief Exec. Officer)*
Tim Baiden *(V.P.-Mktg. & Sls.)*
Wes Peltier *(V.P.-Fin. & Treas.)*
Lee Wolf *(V.P.-Mfg.)*
Elizabeth Dubman *(Mgr.-Market Devel.)*
Dick Radloff *(Mgr.-Natl. Sls.-Contract Div.)*
Jim Stephani *(Mgr.-Natl. Sls.-Institution Div.)*

Outside Service Firm(s):

Schenck & Associates*(Auditors)*
Sheboygan, WI

First Wisconsin National Bank*(Major Banking Relationship)*
Sheboygan, WI

POLARIS POOL SYSTEMS, INC.
1709 LaCosta Meadows Dr.
San Marcos, CA 92069-5194
Mailing Address:
P.O. Box 1149
San Marcos, CA 92079-1149
Tel.: 619-471-0129
Tel.: 800-VAC-SWEEP **CA**
Fax: 619-471-1048
Year Founded: 1971
Approx.Sls.: $30,000,000
Emp.: 95
Export
Manufacture Automated Swimming Pool Cleaners, Spa Products
S.I.C.: 3589
Lyndol Cook *(Pres. & Chief Exec. Officer)*
Gregory Howard *(V.P.-Opers.)*
Greg Ritter *(V.P.-Prods. & Services)*
Robert Stuart *(V.P.-Sls.)*
Doug Bell *(Controller)*

Computer Systems/Hardware:
DEC PDP 11/73

Outside Service Firm(s):

Weber, Lipshie & Co.*(Auditors)*
Los Angeles, CA

MNC Commercial Corporation*(Major Banking Relationship)*
Towson, MD

Sheppard, Mullin, Richter & Hampton*(Legal Firm)*
San Diego, CA

Wells Fargo Bank*(Pension Manager)*
420 Montgomery St.
San Francisco, CA 94104

POLAROME MFG. CO. INC.
200 Theodore Conrad Dr.
Jersey City, NJ 07305
Tel.: 201-309-4500
Telex: ITT: 421-135
Fax: 201-433-0638
Year Founded: 1950
Approx.Sls.: $114,000,000
Emp.: 85
Fiscal Year-end: 8/31/90
Manufacture & Distribution of Essential Oils & Chemicals for Flavor & Fragrance Industries
S.I.C.: 2844; 2899; 5122
Ralph Barash *(Pres. & Chief Exec. Officer)*
Bernard Turret *(Controller & Chief Fin. Officer)*

POLERA BUILDING CORP.
180 Brook St.
Scarsdale, NY 10583
Tel.: 914-723-3767
Fax: 914-723-1503

Approx.Sls.: $20,000,000
Emp.: 30
General Building Contractors; Construction Managers
S.I.C.: 1542
Vito Polera *(Chm. Bd.)*
Anthony Polera *(Chief Exec., Chief Oper. & Info. Officer)*
Catherine Polera *(Pres., Chief Fin. Officer, Sec. & Treas.)*
Anthony Abatino *(Controller)*

Outside Service Firm(s):

Bertrand Kweskin*(Auditors)*
New York, NY

Chubb Group*(Commercial Insurance Carrier)*
P.O. Box 1615,
Warren, NJ 07061
Tel.: 201-580-2000

Empire Blue Cross & Blue Shield*(Group Insurer)*
New York, NY

United States Life Insurance Co.*(Group Insurer)*
New York, NY

National Westminster Bank plc*(Major Banking Relationship)*
Astor Plaza, 1515 Broadway
New York, NY 10036

Scarsdale National Bank*(Major Banking Relationship)*
Scarsdale, NY

Subsidiary:

Valley Cottage Machine Corp. **(1)**
180 Brook St.
Scarsdale, NY 10583
Tel.: 914-723-3853
Fax: 914-723-1503

THE POLIZOS AGENCY
220 W. Freemason St.
Norfolk, VA 23510
Tel.: 804-622-7033
Fax: 804-622-1308
Year Founded: 1964
Approx.Billings: $11,000,000
Emp.: 20
Retail, Tourism, Travel & Economic Development
Arthur G. Polizos *(Chm.)*
Chuck Applebach *(Pres. & Chief Oper. Officer)*
Cindy Lewark *(Asst. V.P., Systems Opers. Mgr.)*
Martha Burns *(Treas.)*
Catherine Polizos *(Sec.)*

R. L. POLK & CO.
1155 Brewery Park Blvd.
Detroit, MI 48207-2697
Tel.: 313-393-0880 **DE**
Fax: 313-393-2860
Year Founded: 1870
Assets: $250,000,000
Liabilities: $116,000,000
Net Worth: $134,000,000
Approx.Sls.: $293,000,000
Emp.: 7,000
Fiscal Year-end: 12/31/92
Publishers of City Directories & Bank Directories; Motor Vehicle Registration Statistics; Direct Mail Advertising; Lists & Warehouse Facilities; Manufacture & Distribute Calendars & Other Advertising Specialties
S.I.C.: 2741; 7331; 7389
John M. O'Hara *(Chm. Bd. & Chief Exec. Officer)*
Larry C. Helber *(Chief Fin. Officer)*
Stephen R. Polk *(Pres. & Chief Oper. Officer)*
Joseph C. Cirrincione *(Pres.-Motor Statistical)*
Loren G. Prange *(Pres.-City Directory Div.)*
W.T. Stumb *(Pres.-Bank Services Div.)*
Allen T. Francis *(Sr. V.P. & Mgr.-Data Processing & Production Methods)*
Robert Piehler *(Sr. V.P.-Corp. Communications & Planning)*
Timothy L. Williams *(Sr. V.P.-Human Resources)*
Charlotte Cupol *(V.P. & Mgr.-Compensation & Benefits)*
John. P. McGough *(V.P.-Taxes)*
D.E. McKenzie *(V.P. & Dir.-Pur.)*
Leo A. Marx, Jr. *(Sec. & Gen. Counsel)*
Gary O. Puvalowski *(Treas.)*
Suzanne F. Orlicki *(Dir.-Corp. Communications)*

Outside Service Firm(s):

Deloitte & Touche*(Auditors)*
200 Renaissance Center, 16th Fl.
Detroit, MI 48243
Tel.: 313-396-3000
Fax: 313-259-8087

Blue Cross & Blue Shield of Michigan*(Group Insurer)*
Detroit, MI

N.B.D. Bank, N.A.*(Major Banking Relationship)*
611 Woodward Ave.
Detroit, MI 48226
Tel.: 313-225-1122
Fax: 313-225-3420

National Bank of Detroit*(Pension Manager)*
611 Woodward Ave.
Detroit, MI 48226

The Principal Financial Group*(Pension Manager)*
711 High St.
Des Moines, IA 50309
Tel.: 515-247-4593
Tel.: 800-543-4015

Divisions:

Automotive Marketing Group **(1)**
1155 Brewery Park Blvd.
Detroit, MI 48207-2697
Tel.: 313-393-0880
Automotive Mail Advertising & Statistics
S.I.C.: 7389
J.C. Cirrincione *(Pres.)*

Direct Marketing Group **(1)**
6400 Monroe Blvd.
Taylor, MI 48180-1884
Tel.: 313-292-3200
Mail Advertising & Marketing
S.I.C.: 7331
Sidney Simon *(Pres.)*

Polk Bank Services Div. **(1)**
2001 Elm Hill Pike
Nashville, TN 37230-5100
Tel.: 615-889-3350
Publishes Bank Directories
S.I.C.: 2741
Hugh R. Boyd *(Pres.)*

Polk City Directory Div. **(1)**
1155 Brewery Park Blvd.
Detroit, MI 48207-2697
Tel.: 313-393-0880
Publishes City Directories
S.I.C.: 2741
Loren G. Prange *(Pres.)*

Polk Motor Vehicle Registrations Div. **(1)**
1155 Brewery Park Blvd.
Detroit, MI 48207-2697
Tel.: 313-393-0880
Motor Vehicle Registration Data
S.I.C.: 7389
Larry G. Majerus *(Sr. V.P. & Gen. Mgr.)*

POLKA DOT DAIRY
110 E. 17th St.
Hastings, MN 55033
Tel.: 612-437-9023
Fax: 612-438-2638
Year Founded: 1957
Approx.Sls.: $125,000,000
Emp.: 1,600
Wholesale Dairy Products
S.I.C.: 5143
Wallace Pettit *(Pres.)*
Bill Ludwig *(Dir.-Sls. & Mktg.)*

Computer Systems/Hardware:
MAI Basic 4

Outside Service Firm(s):

Wilkerson, Guthmann & Johnson*(Auditors)*
Hastings, MN

Norwest Bank Minnesota, N.A.*(Major Banking Relationship)*
6th St. & Marquette Av.
Minneapolis, MN 55479
Tel.: 612-667-1234

Subsidiary:

Thom Thumb Food Market Inc. **(1)**
110 E. 17th St.
Hastings, MN 55033
Tel.: 612-437-9023
Retail Groceries & Gasoline
S.I.C.: 5411; 5541
Wallace Pettit *(Pres.)*
Derrell Deming *(Dir.-Sls. & Mktg.)*
Dennis Tennessen *(Dir.-Personnel)*

POLLACK CORPORATION
600 Roundwood Dr.
Scarborough, ME 04074
Tel.: 207-883-8455
Fax: 207-883-1012
Year Founded: 1954
Approx.Sls.: $12,500,000
Emp.: 130
Fiscal Year-end: 9/30/92
Retail Jewelry; G.M. Pollack & Sons Jewelry Stores
S.I.C.: 5632; 5944
Gerald M. Pollack *(Pres.)*
Stanley C. Pollack *(Treas.)*
Nick Kleftkis *(Gen. Mgr.)*
Russ Leonard *(Mgr.-Adv.)*
Peter Warren *(Mgr.-Adv. & Prods.)*
Roger D. LeBlanc *(Controller)*

POLLAK LEVITT CHAIET ADVERTISING INC

POLLAK LEVITT CHAIET, ADVERTISING
One Piedmont Ctr., Ste. 505
Atlanta, GA 30305
Tel.: 404-261-1566
Fax: 404-261-2029
Year Founded: 1988
Approx.Billings: $12,500,000
Emp.: 22
James S. Pollak *(Chm. & Chief Exec. Officer)*
Alan H. Chaiet *(Vice Chm. & Dir. Media Services)*
Bruce Levitt *(Pres. & Chief Creative Officer)*
Phil Cuttino *(Exec. V.P., Creative Dir., Bus. Devel.)*
Barbara McMaken *(Mgr., Bus. Devel.)*

Computer Systems/Hardware:
MacIntosh

POLLENEX CORPORATION
(Formerly Associated Mills)
165 N. Canal St., Ste. 1460
Chicago, IL 60606
Tel.: 312-454-5400
Tel.: 800-767-6020
Telex: 910-2212197 POLLENEX CGO
Fax: 312-454-7941
Approx.Sls.: $50,000,000
Emp.: 350
Fiscal Year-end: 5/31/92
Import Export
Mfg. of Massagers, Shower Heads, Smokeless Ashtrays, Humidifiers, Air & Water Purifiers, Footbaths, Heating Pads, Fitness Equipment, Specialty Radios & Whirlpool Baths
S.I.C.: 3634; 5064; 3842
Elliott Millenson *(Pres. & Chief Exec. Officer)*
Gary Bjarnson *(V.P. & Chief Fin. Officer)*
Ed Brogan *(V.P.-Sls.)*
Jerome Drapekin *(V.P.-Mfg.)*
Robert Patterson *(V.P.-Intl.)*
Ira Pruzan *(V.P.-Mktg.)*
Judith Stern *(Sec.)*
Dale Brandt *(Dir.-Mngmt. Information Systems)*
Joyce Becella *(Mgr.-Human Resources)*

No. of Mfg. Plants/Facilities: 2
No. of U.S. Offices: 2
No. of Foreign Offices: 1

Computer Systems/Hardware:
IBM System AS/400

Outside Service Firm(s):

Arthur Andersen & Co.*(Auditors)*
33 W. Monroe St.
Chicago, IL 60603-4067
Tel.: 312-580-0033
Fax: 312-507-6748

Sidley & Austin*(Legal Firm)*
One First National Plaza, 42nd Fl.
Chicago, IL 60603
Tel.: 312-853-7000
Fax: 312-853-7036

THE POLLOCK CORP.
Industrial Hwy. & Kind Rd.
Pottstown, PA 19464
Mailing Address:
P.O. Box 759
Pottstown, PA 19464
Tel.: 215-323-5500
Fax: 215-323-5506
Year Founded: 1888
Approx.Sls.: $30,000,000
Emp.: 125
Fiscal Year-end: 1/31/90
Recycling & Sale of Scrap Metal; Steel Fabrication; Demolition Services
S.I.C.: 5093; 1795; 7389
Donald Orr *(Pres.)*
D.J. Owens *(Controller)*

Computer Systems/Hardware:
MAI Basic 4

Outside Service Firm(s):

Rudolph Palitz*(Auditors)*
Pottstown, PA

Fox, Rothschild, O'Brien & Frankel*(Legal Firm)*
2000 Market St., 10th Flr.
Philadelphia, PA 19103
Tel.: 215-299-2012

POLO/RALPH LAUREN CORPORATION
650 Madison Ave.
New York, NY 10019
Tel.: 212-318-7000
Fax: 212-888-5780
Approx.Sls.: $180,000,000
Manufacture Men's, Women's & Children's Clothing & Accessories, Fragrances, Home Furnishings, Luggage, Furs; Retail Sales; Licensing of Designer's Name
S.I.C.: 2311; 2329; 2844; 3161; 5136; 5611; 5632; 6794
Ralph Lauren *(Chm. Bd.)*
Peter Strom *(Vice Chm.)*
Michael Newman *(Pres. & Chief Exec. Officer)*
Buffy Birrittella *(Sr. V.P.-Adv. & Women's Design)*

Polo/Ralph Lauren Corporation—(Continued)

Lance Isham *(Sr. V.P.-Sls.)*
Jerry Lauren *(Sr. V.P.-Mens Design)*
Nancy Vignola *(Sr. V.P.-Home Collection Design)*
Victor Cohen *(V.P. & Gen. Counsel)*
Mary Randolph Carter *(V.P.-Adv.)*
Stan Lee Brown *(V.P.-Design Support)*
Mary Asphar *(Adv.)*
Principal(s):
Ralph Lauren
Peter Strom

Computer Systems/Hardware:
DEC

Outside Service Firm(s):

Mahoney Cohen & Co., P.C.*(Auditors)*
New York, NY

Skadden, Arps, Slate, Meagher & Flom*(Legal Firm)*
919 3rd Ave.
New York, NY 10022
Tel.: 212-371-6000
Fax: 212-735-2000

Chemical Bank*(Major Banking Relationship)*
450 West 33rd St.
New York, NY 10001
Tel.: 212-613-7197
Fax: 212-947-7628

Subsidiary:

Polo/Ralph Lauren Factory Store **(1)**
590 Commerce Blvd.
Carlstadt, NJ 07072
Tel.: 201-438-5900
Factory Stores In AL, CA, CO, IN, KY, ME, MA, MI, MO, MT, NH, NY, NC, PA, PR, SD, TN, VT, WV, WI & WY
S.I.C.: 5311
Larry Gore *(Pres.)*

POLY PAK AMERICA, INC.
2939 E. Washington Blvd.
Los Angeles, CA 90023
Tel.: 213-264-2400
Fax: 213-264-2407
Approx.Sls.: $15,000,000
Emp.: 125
Fiscal Year-end: 5/31/92
Mfr. of Plastic Mailers, Bags & Packaging
S.I.C.: 2673; 3081
Richard Gurewitz *(Chm. Bd. & Chief. Exec. Officer)*
Tom Hawley *(Controller)*
Lorrie Gurewitz *(Sec. & Treas.)*
Sheldon Kritzer *(Dir.-Sls.)*
Gallo Schreiber *(Dir.-Mfg.)*
Cheryl Schneider *(Dir.-Personnel)*
Jezabel Weeks *(Mgr.-Res. & Devel.)*

Outside Service Firm(s):

Security Pacific Bank & Trust Company*(Major Banking Relationship)*
333 S. Hope St.
Los Angeles, CA 90071
Tel.: 213-613-6211

POLY-SEAL CORPORATION
1810 Portal St.
Baltimore, MD 21224
Tel.: 410-633-1990 DE
Fax: 301-391-9581
Year Founded: 1934
Approx.Sls.: $80,000,000
Emp.: 800
Export
Plastic Closures, Fitments, Applicators & Droppers
S.I.C.: 3089
Corporate Giving Program: Johns Hopkins Children Center- 1992 $100,000; & Other Local Charities
R.N. Gillman *(Pres. & Chief Exec. Officer)*
Harry Baughan *(V.P.-Mfg.)*
Kenneth M. Gillamn *(V.P.-Sls.)*
Randall F. House *(V.P.-Mktg.)*
James Palinkas *(V.P.-Fin.)*
William Pate *(V.P.-Systems)*
William Baschke *(Dir.-Human Resources)*
Ata Mostoufi *(Dir.-Quality Control)*
Paul Hasskamp *(Mgr.-Pur.)*

No. of Mfg. Plants/Facilities: 2
No. of U.S. Offices: 4

Outside Service Firm(s):

Ellin & Tucker*(Auditors)*
Baltimore, MD

First National Bank of Maryland*(Major Banking Relationship)*
25 S. Charles St.
Baltimore, MD 21201
Tel.: 410-244-4025

Subsidiaries:

American National Can Co. **(1)**
Bedford Park, IL
Plastic Molding
S.I.C.: 3089

Moldcraft Plastics Inc. **(1)**
4211 Shannon Dr.
Baltimore, MD 21213
Tel.: 301-325-4090
Emp.: 202
Plastic Closures
S.I.C.: 3089
James Palinkas *(V.P.-Fin.)*
Kenneth Gillman *(V.P.-Sls.)*
Randall F. House *(V.P.-Mktg.)*
Jorg Freyer *(Gen. Mgr.)*

POLYCOAT SYSTEMS, INC.
5 Depot St.
Hudson Falls, NY 12839
Tel.: 518-747-0654
Fax: 518-747-5894
Year Founded: 1978
Approx.Sls.: $27,400,000
Emp.: 32
Insulation Roofing & Coating Materials
S.I.C.: 2952
George Carruthers *(Pres., Chief Exec. & Chief Fin. Officer, Controller)*

No. of Mfg. Plants/Facilities: 3
No. of U.S. Offices: 6

Computer Systems/Hardware:
Digital VAX; IBM PC

POLYMER DEVELOPMENT LABORATORIES, INC.
212 W. Taft Ave.
Orange, CA 92665
Tel.: 714-921-2300
Fax: 714-921-9643
Year Founded: 1974
Emp.: 30
Manufacture Polyurethane Liquid Systems, Foams & Coatings
S.I.C.: 3086; 2821
Louis Zenegy *(Chm. Bd., Pres. & Chief Exec. Officer)*
Rick Lenarth *(V.P.-Sls.)*
Michael P. McMahon *(Sec.)*

Computer Systems/Hardware:
IBM Compatible

Outside Service Firm(s):

Blue Shield of California*(Group Insurer)*
San Francisco, CA

POLYMER PLASTICS CORPORATION
65 Davids Dr.
Hauppauge, NY 11788
Tel.: 516-231-1300
Tel.: 800-777-6596
Fax: 516-231-1329
Year Founded: 1955
Approx.Sls.: $10,000,000
Emp.: 40
Fiscal Year-end: 12/31/92
Import Export
Mfr. Waterproofing Coatings, Adhesives & Sealants; Waterproofing, Roofing, Floors, Wall Systems
S.I.C.: 2899; 2891; 2542; 2851; 3089
Arthur Noskin *(Pres.)*
Steven Noskin *(Exec. V.P.)*

Computer Systems/Hardware:
Tandy

POLYVINYL FILMS, INC.
Depot St.
Sutton, MA 01590
Mailing Address:
P.O. Box 218
Sutton, MA 01590
Tel.: 508-865-3558 MA
Fax: 508-865-1562
Year Founded: 1965
Approx.Sls.: $10,000,000
Emp.: 115
Manufacture Polyvinylchloride Film
S.I.C.: 3081
John W. Baldwin *(Pres.)*
John J. Connor II *(V.P.)*
John J. Connor *(Treas.)*

Outside Service Firm(s):

O'Connor Maloney & Company*(Auditors)*
Worcester, MA

Mechanics Bank*(Major Banking Relationship)*
Worcester, MA

A. POMERANTZ & CO.
1525 Chestnut St.
Philadelphia, PA 19102
Tel.: 215-864-3000
Fax: 215-864-3202
Approx.Sls.: $63,000,000
Emp.: 325
Fiscal Year-end: 4/30/90
Wholesale Office Products & Furniture
S.I.C.: 5021; 5046
David Aubuchon *(Chief Fin. Officer)*
Samuel Weinberg *(Exec. V.P.)*
Charles Pagesy *(V.P.-Opers.)*
Gail M. Rubino *(Pres. & Chief Exec. Officer)*
Tom Byrne *(V.P.-Sls.)*
Allan Struzinski *(Chief Fin. Officer)*

Outside Service Firm(s):

Fox, Rothschild, O'Brien & Frankel*(Legal Firm)*
2000 Market St., 10th Flr.
Philadelphia, PA 19103
Tel.: 215-299-2012

POMPEIAN, INC.
4201 Pulaski Hwy.
Baltimore, MD 21224
Tel.: 410-276-6900
Fax: 410-276-3764
Approx.Sls.: $20,000,000
Emp.: 50
Fiscal Year-end: 9/30/90
Pompeian, Romanza & Laco Pure Olive Oil; Olives; Avallo-Blended Oils
S.I.C.: 2079
Roy Quinn *(Pres. & Controller)*
Jaan Slug *(V.P.-Opers.)*

PONY SPORTS & LEISURE INC.
15 Independent Blvd.
Warren, NJ 07059
Tel.: 908-580-0700
Tel.: 800-654-7669 DE
Fax: 908-580-1372
Year Founded: 1975
Approx.Sls.: $125,000,000
Emp.: 200
Fiscal Year-end: 12/31/90
Manufacture Athletic Shoes & Apparel
S.I.C.: 3021; 3161; 3949
C. William Lolas *(Chief Oper. Officer)*
Gary Simon *(V.P. & Gen. Counsel)*
George Case *(Mgr.-Natl. Sls.)*

Computer Systems/Hardware:
IBM System 38 & PC

Outside Service Firm(s):

KPMG Peat Marwick*(Auditors)*
Secaucus, NJ

Aetna Life & Casualty*(Group Insurer)*
151 Farmington Avenue
Hartford, CT 06156
Tel.: 203-273-2128
Fax: 203-729-4295

POOL COMMUNICATIONS
11828 LaGrange Ave.
Los Angeles, CA 90025
Tel.: 310-479-4166
Fax: 310-473-6476
Year Founded: 1979
Approx.Billings: $15,000,000
Emp.: 16
Travel, Franchises, Retail & Real Estate
S.I.C.: 7311
Harvey Pool *(Pres.)*
Renee Petruschin *(Comptroller)*

No. of U.S. Offices: 3

Computer Systems/Hardware:
Apple Mcintosh

Outside Service Firm(s):

Blum, Propper, & Hardacre*(Legal Firm)*
Los Angeles, CA

First Charter Bank*(Major Banking Relationship)*
Los Angeles, CA

Subsidiary:

Pool Communications - Chicago **(1)**
320 N. Michigan Ave.
Chicago, IL 60610
Tel.: 312-541-8610
Fax: 312-541-0187
Travel, Franchises, Retail & Real Estate
S.I.C.: 7311
Dennis Brown *(Gen. Mgr.)*

POPOFSKY ADVERTISING, INC.
60 Madison Ave.
New York, 350 Fifth Ave., NY 10010-1600
Tel.: 212-532-9700
Year Founded: 1971
Approx.Billings: $16,000,000
Emp.: 11
Healthcare/Consumer Packaged Goods
David Popofsky *(Chm. Bd., Pres. & Creative)*
Scott Popofsky *(V.P., Production Supvr. & Acct. Supvr.)*
Rosalie Stillo *(Office Mgr.)*

POPPE TYSON
40 W. 23rd St.
New York, NY 10010
Tel.: 212-727-5600
Fax: 212-727-5662
Year Founded: 1917
Approx.Billings: $55,000,000
Emp.: 80
Consumer & Business-to-Business Advertising
S.I.C.: 7311
Fergus F. O'Daly *(Chm. & Chief Exec. Officer)*
Dick Solay *(Sr. V.P., Grp. Supvr.)*
Thomas E. Wharton, Jr. *(V.P., Fin. & Admin.)*
Cheryl Benton *(V.P., Grp. Supvr.)*
Richard Sacks *(Pub. Rels. Dir.)*

PORCARO BLANKENSHIP ADVERTISING
433 West 9th Ave.
Anchorage, AK 99501
Tel.: 907-276-4262
Year Founded: 1982
Approx.Billings: $10,000,000
Emp.: 15
Michael F. Porcaro *(Chm. Bd. & New Bus. Contact)*
Michael W. Blankenship *(Pres. & Creative Dir.)*

PORCELAIN METALS CORP.
1400 S. 13th St.
Louisville, KY 40210
Mailing Address:
P.O. Box 3646,
Louisville, KY 40201-3646
Tel.: 502-635-7421
Fax: 502-635-1200
Year Founded: 1927
Approx.Sls.: $15,000,000
Emp.: 120
Fiscal Year-end: 12/31/90
Export
Mfr. of Major Appliance Parts; Electrostatic Powder Painting, Porcelain Enameling & Fabrication
S.I.C.: 3264; 3269; 3469
John H. McBride *(Pres. & Chief Exec. Officer)*
Allan Lerch *(Chief Oper. Officer & V.P.)*
Larry Weimer *(Controller)*
John Waugh *(Dir.-Sls. & Mktg.)*
Richard Palmer *(Mgr.-Pur.)*

Outside Service Firm(s):

Ernst & Young*(Auditors)*
1000 Brown & Williamson Tower
Louisville, KY 40202
Tel.: 502-585-1400

First National Bank of Louisville*(Major Banking Relationship)*
P.O. Box 36000,
Louisville, KY 40233

PORT OF GALVESTON
(Owned by the City of Galveston, TX)
123 Rosenberg, 8th Fl.
Galveston, TX 77550
Mailing Address:
P.O. Box 328
Galveston, TX 77553
Tel.: 409-765-9321
Telex: 765436 PRT GALV
Fax: 409-766-6107
Year Founded: 1825
Approx.Sls.: $12,000,000
Emp.: 63
Fiscal Year-end: 12/00/92
Port of Galveston
S.I.C.: 4491
John Unbehagen *(Chm. Bd.)*
B.B. Nelson *(Vice Chm.)*
Doug J. Marchand *(Gen. Mgr. & Port Dir.)*
C.E. Poe *(Deputy Port Dir.-Facilities Mngmt.)*
Ben Powell *(Gen. Counsel)*
D. Jack Collier *(Dir.-Port Devel.)*
Bernard C. Curran *(Dir.-Admin.)*
Robert Schultz *(Dir.-Opers.)*
Diane P. Falcioni *(Mgr.-Cruise Promo.)*
Joe Romano *(Mgr.-Office)*
Pat Rosenfield *(Mgr.-Acctg.)*
Judy Slocum *(Mgr.-Pub. Rels.)*
Ron R. Surovik *(Mgr.-Port Properties)*
Oscar Molina *(Harbor Master)*
H.L. Smith *(Rep.-Mktg. Services)*
S. Robison *(Pur. Agent)*

PORT OF HOUSTON AUTHORITY
111 East Lood North
Houston, TX 77029
Mailing Address:
P.O. Box 2562
Houston, TX 77252
Tel.: 713-670-2400
Fax: 713-670-2564
Year Founded: 1914
Approx.Sls.: $50,000,000
Emp.: 600
Fiscal Year-end: 1/30/91
World Trade Port Operations
S.I.C.: 9621
Ned Holmes *(Chm. Bd.)*
Tom Kornegay *(Acting Exec. Dir.)*
Bill Brady *(Controller)*
Dom Allee *(Dir.-Trade Devel.)*
James Baker *(Dir.-Port Opers.)*
Jeffield Jefferson *(Mgr.-Communcations)*
Len Waska *(Mgr.-Pur.)*

PORT OF OAKLAND
530 Water St.
Oakland, CA 94607
Tel.: 510-272-1100
Tel.: 800-227-2726
Approx.Sls.: $100,000,000
Emp.: 600
Airport, Marine Terminals, Jack London Square Restaurant & Shopping Complex, Embarcadero Cove Restaurant, Office & Marina Complex, Airport Business Park
S.I.C.: 4581
Employee Matching Gifts Progra
Mel Wax *(Dir.-Pub. Affairs)*
Robert Middleton *(Sr. Pub. Affairs Rep.)*

Porteous Mitchel & Braun Company
(Acquired by The Dunlap Companies)

ARTHUR PORTER CONSTRUCTION
11201 N. 23rd Ave., Suite 200
Phoenix, AZ 85029
Tel.: 602-943-2222
Fax: 602-943-2505
Year Founded: 1944
Sales Range: $20-39 Million
Emp.: 14
General Contracting & Construction Management
S.I.C.: 1521; 1531
Arthur Porter *(Pres.)*
W. Lawrence Hart *(V.P.)*
Principal(s):
Arthur Porter

Computer Systems/Hardware:
IBM

Outside Service Firm(s):

Ernst & Young*(Auditors)*
40 North Central, Ste. 900
Phoenix, AZ 85004
Tel.: 602-258-3366

Physicians Mutual*(Group Insurer)*
Phoenix, AZ

Ridenour, Swenson, Cleere & Evans*(Legal Firm)*
Phoenix, AZ

First Interstate Bank*(Major Banking Relationship)*
P.O. Box 53441,
Phoenix, AZ 85072-3441
Tel.: 602-229-4049

PORTLAND FOOD PRODUCTS COMPANY
5320 S.W. Macadam Ave.
Portland, OR 97201
Tel.: 503-228-8188
Fax: 503-228-8190
Approx.Sls.: $110,000,000
Emp.: 700
Fiscal Year-end: 3/31/91
Specialty/Gourmet Foods Manufacturing & Wholesale Distributing; Maraschino Cherries Packaged in Cans & Jars; Food Preparations; Candied, Crystallized or Glazed Fruits; Shampoos, Facial Washes & Hand Creams
S.I.C.: 2033; 2099; 2064; 2844
James G. Reynolds *(Chm. Bd. & Pres.)*
Robert I. Unger *(Exec. V.P.)*
Richard Bertellotti *(V.P.)*
Jeffrey Grimm *(V.P.-Fin. & Treas.)*
Ronald L. Greenman *(Sec.)*

Outside Service Firm(s):

Tonkon, Torp, Galen, Marmaduke & Booth*(Legal Firm)*
1600 Pioneer Tower, 888 S.W. Fifth Ave.
Portland, OR 97204
Tel.: 503-221-1440

First Interstate Bank*(Major Banking Relationship)*
P.O. Box 3131,
Portland, OR 97208
Tel.: 503-220-4855
Fax: 503-225-7153

Subsidiary:

American Specialty Foods **(1)**
5990 W. Touhy Ave.
Niles, IL 60648
Tel.: 708-647-0787
Telex: 325248
Fax: 312-772-2951
Assets: $16,227,472
Earnings: $2,625,623
Liabilities: $10,296,554
Net Worth: $5,930,918
Approx.Sls.: $35,606,655
Emp.: 150
Fiscal Year-end: 6/30/90
Imports, Packages & Distributes a Full Line of Gourmet Specialty Foods & Gift Packages
S.I.C.: 5149; 5141
Steve Reich *(Pres.)*
Stewart H. Reich *(V.P.-Sls.)*

Distribution Centers:

American Specialty Distributing **(2)**
2501 N. Elston Ave.
Chicago, IL 60647
Tel.: 312-772-8310
Approx.Sls.: $34,642,000
Emp.: 150
S.I.C.: 5141

American Specialty Distributing **(2)**
3231 W. 37th Place
Chicago, IL 60632
Tel.: 312-376-6663
S.I.C.: 5141

Portland Glass/Proglass
(See American Management Group Listing)

POSITRONIC INDUSTRIES, INC.
(Formerly Positronic Industry, Inc.)
423 N. Campbell
Springfield, MO 65806
Mailing Address:
P.O. Box 8247
Springfield, MO 65801
Tel.: 417-866-2322 **MO**
Fax: 417-866-4115
Year Founded: 1966
Approx.Sls.: $16,000,000
Emp.: 380
Export
Mfr. of Electronic Connectors
S.I.C.: 3678
Jack T. Gentry *(Chm. Bd. & Pres.)*
Mary Allen *(V.P.-Pur.)*
Wayne Gilbert *(V.P.-Admin.)*
Turner White *(Treas. & Sec.)*

Outside Service Firm(s):

Baird, Kurtz & Dobson*(Auditors)*
Springfield, MO

Commerce Bank*(Major Banking Relationship)*
Springfield, MO

POST BUCKLEY SCHUH & JERNIGAN
8600 NW 36th St.
Miami, FL 33166
Tel.: 305-592-7275
Tel.: 800-597-7275 **FL**
Fax: 305-599-3808
Year Founded: 1960
Assets: $27,360,000
Liabilities: $16,085,000
Net Worth: $11,275,000
Approx.Sls.: $83,600,000
Emp.: 1,000
Fiscal Year-end: 9/30/92
Engineering & Architectural Services
S.I.C.: 8712
William Randolph *(Chm. Bd. & Chief Exec. Officer)*
H. Michael Dye *(Pres. & Chief Oper. Officer)*
John Shearer *(Exec. V.P.-Environment & Natural Resources)*
David Twiddy *(Exec. V.P.)*
Kevin Cooley *(Sr. V.P.-Personnel Training & Devel.)*
James Killough *(Sr. V.P.)*
Phillip Searcy *(Sr. Exec. V.P.-Tech. & Engrng.)*
Richard Wickett *(Sr. V.P.-Investor Rels.)*
John B. Zumwalt, III *(Sr. V.P.-Plng. & Devel.)*
Walter Burkett *(V.P.-Mktg.)*
Richard Grubel *(V.P.-Leasing)*
Murray Pardue *(V.P.-Mktg.)*
Judith Squillante *(V.P.-Pur. & Employee Benefits)*
Steve Tracy *(Assoc. V.P.-Mktg. & Sls. Promo.)*
Scott Deloach *(Controller)*
Beth Ann Rufo *(Sec. & Meetings Plng.)*
Cathy Lerman *(Gen. Counsel)*
Dedra Blackwelder *(Dir.-Data Processing)*
Adrianna Holt *(Dir.-Telecommunications)*
Guada Lueck *(Mgr.-Adv. & Pub. Rels.)*

No. of U.S. Offices: 32
No. of Foreign Offices: 1

Outside Service Firm(s):

Coopers & Lybrand*(Auditors)*
5959 Blue Lagoon Dr.
Miami, FL 33126
Tel.: 305-263-8200

Baker McKenzie*(Legal Firm)*
Miami, FL

Post Buckley Schuh & Jernigan—(Continued)

NationsBank Florida*(Major Banking Relationship)*
P.O. Box 02-5337 DT MIA 4-3, 150 SE 3rd Ave.
Miami, FL 33102-5337

Sun Trust*(Pension Manager)*
Orlando, FL

Subsidiary:

HOH Associates **(1)**
1505 Prince St.
Alexandria, VA 22314
Tel.: 703-549-2614
Emp.: 40
Planning & Landscape Architects
S.I.C.: 0781
Jay Parker *(Pres.)*
Jim Warren *(Controller)*

POTAMKIN MANHATTAN
787 11th Ave. at 54th St.
New York, NY 10019
Tel.: 212-603-7200
Fax: 212-603-7034
Approx.Sls.: $856,000,000
Emp.: 3,000
Auto Dealerships
S.I.C.: 5511
Victor Potamkin *(Pres. & Chief Exec. Officer)*
Allen Potamkin *(Treas.)*
Robert Potamkin *(Sec.)*

POTAMKIN TOYOTA, INC.
19200 N.W. Second Ave.
Miami, FL 33169
Tel.: 305-652-6500
Year Founded: 1986
Approx.Sls.: $30,000,000
Emp.: 125
Retail New & Used Automobiles
S.I.C.: 5511
Alan Potamkin *(Pres.)*
Andy Adler *(V.P.)*
Dave Yusko *(Sec.)*
Glen Grosso *(Adv. Mgr.)*

POTATO SALES COMPANY, INC.
1601 E. Olympic Blvd., Ste. 311
Los Angeles, CA 90021
Tel.: 213-627-4261 **CA**
Fax: 213-895-6671
Year Founded: 1960
Approx.Sls.: $52,000,000
Emp.: 85
Wholesale Distributor of Fresh Fruits & Vegetables
S.I.C.: 5148
Jack Berlin *(Pres.)*
Don Beck *(V.P.)*
Leane Berlin *(V.P.)*
Alan Berlin *(Treas. & Sec.)*

Outside Service Firm(s):

Security Pacific National Bank*(Major Banking Relationship)*
P.O. Box 60228, Terminal Annex,
Los Angeles, CA 90060
Tel.: 213-580-2829

POTTER HAZLEHURST INCORPORATED
800 Quaker Lane
East Greenwich, RI 02818
Tel.: 401-885-4300 **RI**
Fax: 401-885-7299
Year Founded: 1960
Approx.Billings: $17,470,000
Emp.: 42
Fiscal Year-end: 12/31/90
Advertising Agency
S.I.C.: 7311
Thomas E. Hazlehurst *(Chm. Bd.)*
Herbert C. Sawyer *(Pres. & Treas.)*
Michael F. Moore *(Exec. V.P.)*
Barbara Wellnitz *(Pres.-PHI Public Relations)*

Principal(s):
Thomas E. Hazlehurst

No. of Mfg. Plants/Facilities: 1

Computer Systems/Hardware:
IBM Sys. 36-Finance/Opers. & Apple Mac-Creative

LUKE POTTER DODGE INC.
1050 N. Orlando Ave.
Winter Park, FL 32789
Tel.: 407-644-1919 **FL**
Fax: 407-628-9909
Year Founded: 1963
Assets: $58,100,000
Liabilities: $55,500,000
Net Worth: $2,600,000
Approx.Sls.: $177,000,000
Emp.: 84
Fiscal Year-end: 12/31/88
Automobile Dealership
S.I.C.: 5511
Luther D. Potter *(Pres.)*
Michael L. Potter *(V.P. & Gen. Sls. Mgr.)*
Jim Potter *(V.P.)*
Brett Hall *(Mgr.-New Cars)*
Murray Pendleton *(Mgr.-Service)*

Outside Service Firm(s):

Neff & Company*(Auditors)*
7001 Prospect Place N.E.
Alburquerque, NM

Marchman & Assoc.*(Legal Firm)*
Winter Park, FL

Barnett Banks Trust Company, N.A.*(Major Banking Relationship)*
Orlando, FL

Subsidiary:

Winter Park Leasing, Inc. **(1)**
1050 N. Orlando Ave.
Winter Park, FL 32789
Tel.: 407-644-1919
Emp.: 10
Fleet Leasing
S.I.C.: 7515
Luther D. Potter *(Pres.)*
Eugene K. Hall *(V.P.)*
John H. Outlan *(Sec. & Treas.)*

POTTER-SHACKELFORD CONSTRUCTION CO.
80 Villa Rd.
Greenville, SC 29615
Tel.: 803-242-9720
Fax: 803-242-9726
Approx.Sls.: $24,000,000
Emp.: 150
Building Construction
S.I.C.: 1541
Louis A. Seaborn *(Pres.)*
Arthur H. Baiden III *(Sr. V.P.)*
Clyde A. Glenn *(Sr. V.P.)*

Outside Service Firm(s):

Elliott, Davis & Co.*(Auditors)*
Greenville, SC

Haynsworth, Marion, McKay & Guerard*(Legal Firm)*
75 Beattie Place, 2 Shelter Centre 11th Fl
Greenville, SC 29601
Tel.: 803-240-3300

NationsBank Carolinas*(Major Banking Relationship)*
Spartanburg, SC

L. POWELL CO., INC.
8631 Hayden Pl.
Culver City, CA 90232
Mailing Address:
P.O. 1408
Culver City, CA 90232-1408
Tel.: 310-204-2224 **CA**
Fax: 213-837-6223
Year Founded: 1968
Approx.Sls.: $100,000,000
Emp.: 55
Import
Wholesale Distributor of Household Furniture
S.I.C.: 5021
Lawrence M. Powell *(Chm. Bd.)*
Richard M. Powell *(Pres. & Chief Exec. Officer)*
Joyce Powell *(V.P. & Sec.)*
Larry Woods *(V.P.)*
Robert Resnik *(Dir.-Mktg.)*

Outside Service Firm(s):

Kaufman & Enzer*(Auditors)*
Beverly Hills, CA

City National Bank*(Major Banking Relationship)*
120 S. Spalding Dr.
Beverly Hills, CA 90213
Tel.: 310-550-5821

POWELL ELECTRONICS INC.
S. Island Rd. & Enterprise Ave.
Philadelphia, PA 19153
Mailing Address:
P.O. Box 8765,
Philadelphia, PA 19101
Tel.: 215-365-1900 **PA**
Fax: 215-365-7245
Year Founded: 1946
Approx.Sls.: $60,000,000
Emp.: 351
Fiscal Year-end: 12/31/90
Import Export
Wholesale Distributor of Electrical/Electronic Components
S.I.C.: 5065; 5063
Harold H. Powell *(Chm. Bd.)*
Arthur Nannos *(Vice Chm.)*
Millard D. Brown *(Pres. & Chief Exec. Officer)*
Robert Carroll *(Sr. V.P.-East)*
Joseph Harris *(Sr. V.P. & Treas.)*
Ernest Schilling *(Sr. V.P.-Midwest & West)*
Richard Campbell *(V.P.-West)*
Bruce Cobb *(V.P.-Mktg.)*
David Golden *(V.P.-Fin.)*
Maurice Ayars *(Dir.-Warehouse)*
Robert R. Bastian *(Dir.-Mktg.)*
Vincent Calderaro *(Dir.-Opers.)*
John Lincavage *(Dir.-Mngmt. Information Systems)*
Maryann Todd *(Dir.-Human Resources)*
Larry Gallone *(Mgr.-Mktg. Communications)*

Principal(s):
Harold H. Powell

No. of U.S. Offices: 10

Computer Systems/Hardware:
IBM 4381

Outside Service Firm(s):

James Kelly & Assoc.*(Auditors)*
Ardmore, PA

Chase & Heckman*(Commercial Insurance Carrier)*
Philadelphia, PA

Connecticut Mutual*(Group Insurer)*
Hartford, CT

Krekstein, Wolfson & Krekstein*(Legal Firm)*
Philadelphia, PA

Central Penn National Bank*(Major Banking Relationship)*
Philadelphia, PA

Mellon Bank, N.A.*(Major Banking Relationship)*
P.O. Box 444,
Pittsburgh, PA 15230
Tel.: 412-236-8000
Tel.: 1-800-451-7392
Fax: 412-236-8157

ROBERT C. POWELL DEVELOPMENTS, INCORPORATED
3610 American River Dr., #150
Sacramento, CA 95864
Tel.: 916-485-9121 **CA**
Fax: 916-485-8179
Year Founded: 1961
Assets: $11,300,000
Liabilities: $2,400,000
Net Worth: $8,900,000
Approx.Sls.: $39,600,000
Emp.: 60
Fiscal Year-end: 4/30/91
Builder of Single-Family Homes
S.I.C.: 1531
Robert C. Powell *(Chm. Bd. & Pres.)*
Deborah D. Powell *(Chief Fin. Officer & Sec.)*
Robert J. Cassano *(V.P.)*
James M. Gross *(V.P.)*

Outside Service Firm(s):

S. J. Gallina & Co.*(Auditors)*
Sacramento, CA

John O. Bronson Co.*(Commercial Insurance Carrier)*
Sacramento, CA

Foundation Health*(Group Insurer)*
Sacramento, CA

McDonough, Holland & Allen*(Legal Firm)*
Sacramento, CA

Wells Fargo Bank*(Major Banking Relationship)*
420 Montgomery St.
San Francisco, CA 94104

THE WM. POWELL COMPANY
2503 Spring Grove Ave.
Cincinnati, OH 45214
Mailing Address:
P.O. Box 145434
Cincinnati, OH 45214
Tel.: 513-852-2000 **OH**
Fax: 513-852-2997
Year Founded: 1846
Approx.Sls.: $50,000,000
Emp.: 500
Fiscal Year-end: 12/31/90
Import Export
Fabricated Metal Products; Machinery; Manufacture Industrial Valves, All Pressures, & Metal Clasps
S.I.C.: 3494
V. Anderson Coombe *(Chm. Bd., Chief Exec. Officer, & Treas.)*
D.R. Cowart *(Pres.)*
John L. Schaefer *(V.P.-Fin., Chief Fin. Officer & Sec.)*
Dennis Willhoite *(V.P.-Pur.)*
Thomas Curran *(V.P.-Customer Service)*
Jim Strotman *(Controller)*
James Hengehold *(Chief Engrng.)*
William Teasley *(Dir.-Personnel)*
Don Ruter *(Mgr.-Adv.)*
Frank Glass *(Mgr.-Data Processing)*
Chris Mechler *(Mgr.-Quotations)*
Harry Herdeman *(Mgr.-Employee Rels.)*

Computer Systems/Hardware:
Burroughs

Outside Service Firm(s):

KPMG Peat Marwick*(Auditors)*
1600 Central Trust Ctr., 201 East Fifth St.
Cincinnati, OH 45202
Tel.: 513-421-6430

HMO*(Group Insurer)*
Cincinnati, OH

Taft, Stettinius & Hollister*(Legal Firm)*
First Natl. Bank Center
Cincinnati, OH 45202
Tel.: 513-381-2838

Star Bank*(Major Banking Relationship)*
425 Walnut Street
Cincinnati, OH 45202
Tel.: 513-632-4000

Star Bank*(Pension Manager)*
425 Walnut Street
Cincinnati, OH 45202
Tel.: 513-632-4000

Union Central Life*(Pension Manager)*
Cincinnati, OH

Subsidiaries:

The Starflo Corporation **(1)**
Hwy 301 N., Crosscreek Rd.
Orangeburg, SC 29115
Tel.: 803-536-9660
Fax: 803-534-8813
Import Export
Mfr. of Industrial Valves
S.I.C.: 3494
V.A. Coombe *(Chm. Bd.)*
D.R. Cowart *(Pres.)*
J.L. Schaefer *(V.P.-Fin.)*
Dennis Wilhoite *(V.P.-Pur.)*
Frank Parker *(Mgr.-Plant)*

The Starflo Corporation **(1)**
Rte. 5, Box 472
Marining, SC 29102
Tel.: 803-473-4046
Frank Parker *(Mgr.-Plant)*

J.D. POWER AND ASSOCIATES
30401 Agoura Rd.
Agoura Hills, CA 91301
Tel.: 818-889-6330 **CA**
Fax: 818-889-3719
Year Founded: 1968
Approx.Sls.: $20,000,000
Emp.: 180
Marketing Information Services, Publish The Power Report, The California Report & Magazine
S.I.C.: 8742
James D. Power, III *(Pres.)*
J. Ferron *(Sr. Partner)*
John H. Hammond, Jr. *(Sr. Partner)*
Adrian Heryford *(Partner & Chief Admin. Officer)*
Stephen Goodall *(Partner & Mgr.-Detroit Office)*
Tom Healey *(Partner & Dir.-Media & Adv.)*
Linda Hirneise *(Partner & Intl. Acct. Dir.)*
Don Keithley *(Partner & Dealer Rels.)*
Mark Rees *(Partner & Dir.-Res.)*
Marjorie Samuelson *(Partner & Chief Fin. Officer)*
Leonard Sherman *(Partner/Dir.-Tactical Consulting Practice)*

Outside Service Firm(s):

McGladrey & Pullen*(Auditors)*
222 S. Harbor Blvd. #800
Anaheim, CA 92815

Bank of America NT&SA*(Major Banking Relationship)*
Westlake Village, CA

Joint Venture:

R&D/J.D. Power **(1)**
3rd Fl., Nitta Building, 2-8 Tsukiji 2-Chome; Chou-Ku, 104
Tokyo, Japan
Tel.: 011-81-3-3545-1485
Marketing Information Services
S.I.C.: 8742
J.D. Power, III *(Chm. Bd.)*

POWER CONTRACTING & ENGINEERING CORP.
1895 Rohlwing Rd.
Rolling Meadows, IL 60008
Tel.: 708-259-1100 **DE**
Fax: 708-259-3026
Year Founded: 1926
Assets: $38,864,826
Liabilities: $27,233,575
Net Worth: $11,631,251
Approx.Sls.: $156,649,400
Emp.: 100
Fiscal Year-end: 12/31/91
Export
General Contractor
S.I.C.: 1541; 1542
Alvin L. Gorman *(Chm Bd.)*
Tom Settles *(Pres.*
Jeff Karp *(Exec. V.P.)*
Pete Hultman *(V.P.)*
Wynn Hultman *(V.P.)*
Dave Murphy *(V.P.)*
Marty Friedman *(Chief Fin. Officer, Treas, & Controller)*
Kay Petermeyer *(Sec.)*
Joe Beuttas *(Dir.-Business Devel.)*
Gerald W. Duray *(Dir.-Sls. & Mktg.)*
Kim Kloss *(Dir.-Data Processing)*

Computer Systems/Hardware:
IBM System 36

Outside Service Firm(s):

Michael Silver & Company*(Auditors)*
Skokie, IL

POWER CONVERSION, INC.
280 Midland Ave.
Saddle Brook, NJ 07662
Tel.: 201-796-4800
Tel.: 800-452-1211
Year Founded: 1970
Approx.Sls.: $20,000,000
Emp.: 690
Export
Mfr. of Lithium Cells & Batteries
S.I.C.: 3692; 2819
Joan Richardson *(Chm. Bd.)*
Bill Vlasich *(Pres.)*
Jerry Hoffman *(V.P.-Fin.)*
James Sullivan *(V.P.-Mktg.)*
Mike Freedmon *(Controller)*
Sandra Grayson *(Dir.-Pur.)*
Wayne Andruk *(Dir.-Engrng.)*
Marie Easton *(Mgr.-Mfg.)*
Carol Brown *(Mgr.-Quaity Control)*
George Thompson *(Mgr.-Human Resources)*

POWER ENGINEERING CO. INC.
4205 Salzado St.ve.
Coral Gables, FL 33146
Tel.: 305-567-2630 **FL**
Fax: 305-567-9317
Approx.Sls.: $95,000,000
Emp.: 250
Wholesale Electrical Apparatus & Equipment; Management & Engineering Services; Electric Utility; Automobile Dealer
S.I.C.: 4911; 5063; 5511; 8711; 8741
John N. Scopetta *(Chm. Bd., Pres. & Chief Exec. Officer)*
George Scopetta *(V.P.)*
John R. Scopetta *(V.P.)*
Ulijes E. Rodriguez *(Treas. & Sec.)*

Outside Service Firm(s):

KPMG Peat Marwick*(Auditors)*
One Biscayne Tower, 2 South Biscayne Blvd., Ste.2900
Miami, FL 33131

Flagship National Bank of Miami*(Major Banking Relationship)*
3737 Northwest 87th Ave.
Miami, FL 33166
Tel.: 305-579-7136

POWER KING PRODUCTS CO.
1100 Green Valley Rd.
Beaver Dam, WI 53916
Tel.: 414-881-3383
Fax: 414-881-7556
Year Founded: 1946
Approx.Sls.: $10,000,000
Emp.: 40
Fiscal Year-end: 8/31/91
Mfr. of Compact/Utility & Garden Tractors, 12 HP/20 HP Engines, Gear & Hydrostatic
S.I.C.: 3524; 3523
David Cargen *(Pres. & Chief Exec. Officer)*

Power Lawn Mower Parts, Inc.
(See Listing Under Foley-Belsaw Company; Name Changed To Foley-PLP Company)

POWER-ONE, INC.
740 Calle Plano
Camarillo, CA 93012
Tel.: 805-987-8741
Tel.: 800-678-9445
Approx.Sls.: $49,000,000
Emp.: 300
Export
Mfr. of DC Power Supplies-Liner & Switcher
S.I.C.: 3679
Steve Goldman *(Pres. & Chief Exec. Officer)*
Dennis Roark *(Exec. V.P.-Engrng.)*
Mark Weiss *(V.P.-Opers.)*
Julius Hirsch *(V.P.-Sls.)*
Sharyl Owen *(Sec., Treas. & Chief Fin. Officer)*
Donna Koep *(Dir.-Human Resources)*
Dennis Brondi *(Dir.-Mktg.)*
Ed Schnopp *(Dir.-Finance)*

POWER PROCESS PIPING, INC.
45780 Port St.
Plymouth, MI 48170
Mailing Address:
P.O. Box 8100 C
Plymouth, MI 48170
Tel.: 313-451-0130 **MI**
Fax: 313-451-0763
Year Founded: 1974
Assets: $9,212,676
Liabilities: $3,056,113
Net Worth: $6,156,563
Approx.Sls.: $38,172,731
Emp.: 225
Fiscal Year-end: 12/31/91
Mechanical Contractor, Installation of Piping & Related Equipment
S.I.C.: 1711; 1796; 1799
David J. Williams *(Chm. Bd., Pres. & Chief Exec. Officer)*
William Kurtzhals *(V.P.-Personnel)*
Royce Dickinson *(Sec., Treas. & Controller)*

Outside Service Firm(s):

Williams & Herbert*(Auditors)*
Trenton, MI

Charter National Bank*(Major Banking Relationship)*
Taylor, MI

POWER & TELEPHONE SUPPLY COMPANY
2701 Union Extended, Ste. 300
Memphis, TN 38112-4417
Tel.: 901-324-6116
Tel.: 800-238-7514 **TN**
Fax: 901-320-3083
Year Founded: 1963
Approx.Sls.: $30,000,000
Emp.: 250
Fiscal Year-end: 4/30/91
Export
Wholesale Telephones & Data Communications Equipment
S.I.C.: 5065
Corporate Giving Program: Funds Matched on Voluntary Contributions by Employees
Employee Matching Gifts Program: Minimal Individual Gift of $50 to a Registered Charity
J. Miller Pentecost *(Chm. Bd.)*
Jim Pentecost *(Pres.)*
Laburn R. Dye *(V.P.-Communications)*
Overton Lea, Sr. *(V.P.-Power)*
Boyd A. Pollard *(Sec. & Treas.)*
Daniel G. Melore *(Comptroller)*
Mary Bowen *(Dir.-Mktg. & Intl. Sls.)*
Tom Doddridge *(Mgr.-Sls.)*
Dale Stevenson *(Dir.-Data Processing)*
C. Dave Boykin *(Pur. Agent)*
Patty Cartner *(Employee Benefits Admin.)*
Inga Citrone *(Corp. Travel Planner)*

No. of U.S. Offices: 12

Outside Service Firm(s):

Bean & Ison*(Auditors)*
Memphis, TN

Armstrong, Allen, Prewitt, Gentry, Johnson & Holmes*(Legal Firm)*
1900 One Commerce Sq.
Memphis, TN 38103
Tel.: 901-523-8211

First Tennessee Bank, N.A.*(Major Banking Relationship)*
P.O. Box 101
Memphis, TN 38101
Tel.: 901-523-4555

POWERINE OIL COMPANY HOLDINGS
12354 E. Lakeland Rd.
Santa Fe Springs, CA 90670
Tel.: 310-944-6111 **CA**
Fax: 310-944-8522
Year Founded: 1936
Emp.: 380
Fiscal Year-end: 1/ 1/91
Import
Holding Company; Jet Diesel & Gasoline
S.I.C.: 2911; 6719
Albert L. Gualtieri *(Pres.)*
Henry Del Castillo *(Chief Fin. Officer)*
Michael Egner *(Controller)*

Outside Service Firm(s):

Bank of America*(Major Banking Relationship)*
701 S. Western Ave.
Los Angeles, CA 91201

Subsidiary:

Powerine Oil Company **(1)**
12354 E. Lakeland Rd.
Santa Fe Springs, CA 90670
Tel.: 310-944-6111
Emp.: 380
GasolineProduction
S.I.C.: 2911
Albert L. Gualtieri *(Pres.)*
Marshall Stein *(V.P.-Mktg.)*
Gary L. Petersen *(V.P.-Mfg.)*
Henry Del Castillo *(V.P.-Fin.)*
Ernest Houtz *(Gen. Mgr.-Crude Oil Supply)*

POWERS CONSTRUCTION CO., INC.
3091 S. Cashua Dr.
Florence, SC 29501
Tel.: 803-669-5213 **SC**
Fax: 803-664-0261
Approx.Sls.: $16,000,000
Emp.: 125
Commercial & Industrial Contractor
S.I.C.: 1542; 1541
W.O. Powers *(Chm. Bd.)*
John T. Rabun, Jr. *(Pres.)*
Asa Godbold *(V.P.)*
Ann Powers *(Sec.)*

Outside Service Firm(s):

Jordan Warren & Co.*(Auditors)*
Florence, SC

ARTHUR A. POZZI CO., INC.
5550 Southwest MacAdam Ave., Ste. 230
Portland, OR 97201
Mailing Address:
P.O. Box 416,
Portland, OR 97207
Tel.: 503-228-8160
Fax: 503-226-0284
Year Founded: 1963
Approx.Sls.: $56,000,000
Emp.: 10
Import Export
Wholesale Lumber
S.I.C.: 5031
Arthur A. Pozzi *(Chm. Bd.)*
Bob Borghorst *(Pres.)*
Lawrence Allison *(V.P.)*
Tonne Bailey *(Controller)*

Computer Systems/Hardware:
DEC

Outside Service Firm(s):

Hainley & Lavey*(Auditors)*
Portland, OR

Industrial Indemnity*(Commercial Insurance Carrier)*
San Francisco, CA

United States National Bank of Oregon*(Investment Banker)*
P.O. Box 3850,
Portland, OR 97208
Tel.: 503-275-6111

United States National Bank of Oregon*(Major Banking Relationship)*
P.O. Box 3850,
Portland, OR 97208
Tel.: 503-275-6111

PRAIRIE FARMS DAIRY, INC.
1100 N. Broadway
Carlinville, IL 62626
Mailing Address:
P.O. Box 560
Carlinville, IL 62626
Tel.: 217-854-2547 **IL**
Fax: 217-854-6426
Year Founded: 1938
Assets: $125,000,000
Earnings: $4,400,000
Liabilities: $46,000,000
Net Worth: $79,000,000
Approx.Sls.: $283,000,000
Emp.: 950
Fiscal Year-end: 9/30/91
Food Products: Milk & Butter
S.I.C.: 2021; 2026; 5143
Melvin Schweizer *(Chm. Bd. & Pres.)*
Leonard Southwell *(Chief Exec. Officer)*
Paul Benne *(V.P.-Corp. Fin.)*
Roger Capps *(V.P.-Production)*
Ron Dierolf *(V.P.-Engrng.)*
Don Kullmann *(V.P.-Mktg.)*
Jerry Lane *(V.P.-Internal Auditing)*
Ron McMillan *(V.P.-Data Processing)*
James Anderson *(Legal Officer)*
Tom Beichler *(Supvr.-Payroll)*
Principal(s):
Cooperative

Computer Systems/Hardware:
IBM System 38

Outside Service Firm(s):

Coopers & Lybrand*(Auditors)*
One Metropolitan Square
St. Louis, MO 63102
Tel.: 314-436-3200

Country Companies*(Group Insurer)*
Bloomington, IL

Paul Benne*(Investment Banker)*
Carlinville, IL 62626

Illinois Agricultural Association Trust Co.*(Legal Firm)*
Bloomington, IL

Boatmen's Trust Company*(Major Banking Relationship)*
100 North Broadway
St. Louis, MO 63102
Tel.: 314-466-2469

Carlinville National Bank*(Major Banking Relationship)*
Carlinville, IL

Co-Bank St. Louis Region*(Major Banking Relationship)*
1415 Olive St.
St. Louis, MO 63166

Illinois Agricultural Association Trust Co.*(Pension Manager)*
Bloomington, IL

Subsidiaries:

Hiland Dairy Company **(1)**
1133 E. Kearney
Springfield, MO 65803
Tel.: 417-862-9311
Fax: 417-837-1106
Approx.Sls.: $158,000,000
Emp.: 380
Dairy Products Except Dried or Canned
S.I.C.: 5143
Lynn Oller *(Gen. Mgr.)*

Ice Cream Specialties, Inc. **(1)**
1100 N. Broadway
Carlinville, IL 62626
Tel.: 217-854-2547
Emp.: 90
Produce Ice Cream Novelties
S.I.C.: 2657
Roger Capps *(Chief Oper. Officer)*

P.F.D. Supply Corp. **(1)**
1100 N. Broadway
Carlinville, IL 62626
Tel.: 217-854-2547
Emp.: 100
Service To Fast Food Outlets
S.I.C.: 5812
Jim McCulloch *(Chief Oper. Officer)*

Pevely Dairy Company **(1)**
1001 S. Grand Blvd.
Saint Louis, MO 63104
Tel.: 314-771-4400
Fax: 314-771-2791
Assets: $12,000,000
Liabilities: $8,000,000
Net Worth: $4,000,000
Approx.Sls.: $60,000,000
Emp.: 200
Computer Systems/Hardware:
IBM System 36
Producer Milk, Cottage Cheese, Ice Cream, etc.
S.I.C.: 2026; 5143
Richard D. Kerckhoff, Jr. *(Gen. Mgr.)*
Kim Wagner *(Mgr.-Mktg.)*

Steffen Dairy Foods Co., Inc. **(1)**
700 E. Central
Wichita, KS 67201
Tel.: 316-267-4221
Fax: 316-267-4947
Approx.Sls.: $50,000,000
Emp.: 250
Fiscal Year-end: 12/31/90
Dairy Processing, Distribution
S.I.C.: 3556; 2023
Charles Burgess *(V.P. & Gen. Mgr.)*
Kevin B. McEwen *(Sls. Coord.)*
Sandy Kilderbran *(Pur. Agent)*
Greg Thomas *(Plant Mgr.)*

H. C. PRANGE COMPANY
301 N. Washington St.
Green Bay, WI 54301
Tel.: 414-435-6611 **WI**
Fax: 414-436-5006
Year Founded: 1887
Assets: $200,000,000
Liabilities: $137,400,000
Net Worth: $62,600,000
Approx.Sls.: $420,000,000
Emp.: 9,000
Fiscal Year-end: 1/28/91
Operates Department, Discount & Specialty Stores
S.I.C.: 5311; 5632; 5719
Henry C. Prange *(Chm. Bd.)*
Gerald K. Donnelly *(Chief Exec. Officer)*
Milton E. Hartley *(Sr. V.P.)*
Howard Nielsen *(Sr. V.P.-Mngmt. Informations Systems)*
Robert J. Pfeil *(Sr. V.P., Chief Fin. Officer & Treas.)*
Larry Sommer *(Sr. V.P. & Pres.-Prange Way)*
Jennifer Blackstone *(V.P.-Admin.)*
Kathleen E. Mauer *(V.P. & Controller)*
Richard Unger *(V.P.-Mktg. & Sls.)*
Sue Toepel *(Dir.-Adv.)*
Perry Ziegler *(Dir.-Telecommunications)*

Computer Systems/Hardware:
IBM 4381

Outside Service Firm(s):

Deloitte & Touche*(Auditors)*
250 E. Wisconsin Ave.
Milwaukee, WI 53202-4283
Tel.: 414-271-3000

Industrial Risk Insurers*(Commercial Insurance Carrier)*
Hartford, CT

Liberty Mutual*(Commercial Insurance Carrier)*
Boston, MA

Foley & Lardner*(Legal Firm)*
777 E. Wisconsin Ave.
Milwaukee, WI 53202
Tel.: 414-271-2400

Rohde, Neuses & Dales*(Legal Firm)*
Sheboygan, WI

Bank One Milwaukee, N.A.*(Major Banking Relationship)*
111 E. Wisconsin Ave.
Milwaukee, WI
Tel.: 414-765-3000

First Interstate Bank*(Major Banking Relationship)*
Milwaukee, WI

M & I Marshall & Ilsley Bank*(Major Banking Relationship)*
770 N. Water St.
Milwaukee, WI 53202
Tel.: 414-765-8700

Strong/Corneliuson Capital Management Inc.*(Pension Manager)*
Milwaukee, WI

Subsidiaries:

Christmas & Things **(1)**
Edison Mall, 4125 Cleveland
Fort Myers, FL 33901
Tel.: 813-939-4699
Joan England *(Mgr.)*

Christmas & Things, Inc. **(1)**
Coastland Ctr., 1832 N. Tamiami Trail
Naples, FL 33940
Tel.: 813-262-1971
Retail Gift Stores
S.I.C.: 5947
Joan England *(Mgr.)*

Prange Way **(1)**
301 N. Washington St.
Green Bay, WI 54301
Tel.: 414-435-6611
Larry Sommer *(Pres.)*

Prange Specialty Stores Group, Inc. **(1)**
2800 So. Ashland Ave.
Green Bay, WI 54302
Tel.: 414-496-3300
Fax: 414-496-3300
Emp.: 1,500
220 Women's Specialty Stores
S.I.C.: 5621
William Prange *(Chm.)*

Thimbles Specialty Stores, Inc. **(1)**
2800 So. Ashland Ave.
Green Bay, WI 54302
Tel.: 414-496-3300
Retail Women's Wear
S.I.C.: 5621

PRATT-READ CORPORATION
1155 Railroad Av.
Bridgeport, CT 06605
Tel.: 203-366-4911 **CT**
Fax: 203-366-4911
Year Founded: 1798
Approx.Sls.: $12,000,000
Emp.: 150
Fiscal Year-end: 6/30/91
Manufacture Tools, Hardware & Wood Products
S.I.C.: 2421; 3423; 2499; 2426
Harwood B. Comstock *(Chm. Bd.)*
Steven Payer *(Pres.)*
Gerald LeVasseur *(Chief Fin. Officer)*

Outside Service Firm(s):

Arthur Andersen & Co.*(Auditors)*
One Financial Plaza
Hartford, CT 06103
Tel.: 203-280-0649
Fax: 203-280-0898

Jones, Day, Reavis & Pogue*(Legal Firm)*
901 Lakeside Ave.
Cleveland, OH 44114
Tel.: 216-586-3939
Fax: 216-579-0212

Connecticut National Bank*(Major Banking Relationship)*
E. Hartford, CT

Division:

The Cornwall & Patterson Co. **(1)**
1155 Railroad Ave.
Bridgeport, CT 06605
Tel.: 203-366-4911
Tools
S.I.C.: 3931; 3423
Harwood B. Comstock *(Pres.)*

PRAXIS INTERNATIONAL INC.
4 Cambridge Center
Cambridge, MA 02142-1489
Tel.: 617-492-8860
Fax: 617-497-1072
Year Founded: 1992
Approx.Rev.: $32,000,000
Emp.: 250
Fiscal Year-end: 6/30/90
Computer Software, Consulting, Application Development, Implementation & Integration for Networked Information Systems, Services for Direct Response Marketing
S.I.C.: 7371; 7372; 7373; 7375; 7379
Richard Stewart *(Chm., Pres. & Chief Exec. Officer)*
Francie Anhut *(Exec. V.P.)*
David Ehlke *(Exec. V.P.)*
John G. Dove *(V.P.-Quality & Prod. Engrng.)*
William Reed *(V.P. & Chief Fin. Officer)*
Richard Winter *(V.P.-Technical Mktg.)*
Victoria Winston *(Dir.-Mktg. Communications)*

Subsidiaries:

Computer Corporation of America **(1)**
Four Cambridge Center
Cambridge, MA 02142-1489
Tel.: 617-661-7970
Fax: 617-497-1072
Specializes in High Performance Information Management Software
S.I.C.: 7371
William D. Reed *(Pres. & Chief Oper. Officer)*

MarketPulse **(1)**
Four Cambridge Center
Cambridge, MA 02142-1489
Tel.: 617-661-9790
Fax: 617-497-1072
Application-Oriented Company that Provides Products and Services for Direct Response Marketing
S.I.C.: 7371

Francie Anhut *(Pres. & Chief Oper. Officer)*

Segue Partners **(1)**
Four Cambridge Center
Cambridge, MA 02142-1489
Tel.: 617-661-9790
Fax: 617-497-1072
Provides Specialized Know-How to Enable Organizations to Make the Transition to Networked Computing Environments; Offices in Chicago, St. Louis, Denver, Dallas, San Francisco, Washington D.C., Toronto & Maidenhead, England
S.I.C.: 7371; 7379
J. David Ehlke *(Pres. & Chief Oper. Officer)*

Non-U.S. Holdings:

Segway Partners **(1)**
Maidenhead, United Kingdom
Computer Services; International Headquarters for 20 Countries
S.I.C.: 7371; 7379

Segway Partners **(1)**
Toronto, ON Canada
Computer Services
S.I.C.: 7371; 7379

PRECISION CARBIDE TOOL COMPANY, INC.
7450 N. Natchez Ave.
Niles, IL 60714
Tel.: 708-647-6870
Fax: 708-647-1851
Approx.Sls.: $12,000,000
Emp.: 125
Export
Solid Carbide Rotary Cutting Tools
S.I.C.: 3425
Eugene Terry *(Chm. Bd. & Sec.)*
Douglas Johnson *(Pres.)*
Nicole Terry *(Treas.)*
Joseph Bracken *(Controller)*
James Ahern *(Mgr.-Natl. Sls.)*
Connie Berger *(Mgr.-Data Processing)*
Ruth Farrell *(Mgr.-Human Resources)*
Jack Hedquist *(Mgr.-Quality Control)*
Boru Rusic *(Supervisor-Plant)*

No. of Mfg. Plants/Facilities: 1

Outside Service Firm(s):

Blackman Kallick Bartelstein*(Auditors)*
300 Riverside Plaza
Chicago, IL 60606
Tel.: 312-207-1040

LaSalle National Bank*(Major Banking Relationship)*
135 S. LaSalle St.
Chicago, IL 60603
Tel.: 312-443-2440
Fax: 312-443-2819

PRECISION ECHO, INC.
3105 Patrick Henry Dr.
Santa Clara, CA 95054
Tel.: 408-988-0516
Fax: 408-727-7491
Year Founded: 1967
Approx.Sls.: $20,000,000
Emp.: 125
Fiscal Year-end: 3/31/91
Rotary, Disc Cassette, Longitudinal Data Storage Recorders
S.I.C.: 3651; 3652
Werner Christmann *(V.P.-Opers.)*
John A. Martin *(V.P.-Engrng.)*
R. Roger Watson *(V.P.-Advanced Prod. Devel.)*
Bob Carter *(Dir.-Bus. Devel.)*
Steve Conlisk *(Controller)*

PRECISION INDUSTRIES
(Formerly Precision Bearing Company)
4611 S. 96th St.
Omaha, NE 68127
Tel.: 402-593-7000
Fax: 402-593-7054
Approx.Sls.: $40,000,000
Emp.: 280
Bearings; Valves & Fittings; Hose, Belting & Packing; Material Handling Machinery
S.I.C.: 5084; 5085
Sebastian A. Circo *(Chm. Bd.)*
Dennis P. Circo *(Pres. & Chief Exec. Officer)*
Olive Circo *(V.P.)*

Outside Service Firm(s):

Norwest Bank Minnesota, N.A.*(Major Banking Relationship)*
Omaha, NE

PRECISION PARTS CORP.
4188 E. Andrew Johnson Hwy.
Morristown, TN 37814
Mailing Address:
P.O. Box 2159
Morristown, TN 37816-2159
Tel.: 615-587-9390 **TN**
Fax: 615-581-7749
Year Founded: 1942
Sales Range: $10-19 Million
Emp.: 40
Export
Manufacture Gas Boilers, Electric & Gas Hot Water Heaters
S.I.C.: 3639; 3433; 3443
Steve Richey *(Pres.)*
Curt Diedrick *(V.P.-Opers.)*
Jim Mathis *(V.P.-Mktg., Sec. & Treas.)*
Doc Husk *(Dir.-Pur.)*
Frank Broadhurst *(Mgr.-Sls.)*
Principal(s):
Steve Richey
Jim Mathis

No. of Mfg. Plants/Facilities: 1
No. of U.S. Offices: 1

Computer Systems/Hardware:
Tandy 3000, Epson IE, Epson 3865X

Outside Service Firm(s):

Russell, Purkey, Carter & Compton*(Auditors)*
Morristown, TN

First Tennessee Bank, N.A.*(Major Banking Relationship)*
Morristown, TN

PRECISION PLASTICS INC.
722 Sw
Columbia City, IN 46725
Mailing Address:
P.O. Box 329
Columbia City, IN 46725
Tel.: 219-244-6114
Fax: 219-244-5995
Plastic Injection Molders
S.I.C.: 3089
Frank Lessen *(Pres.)*

Division:

Precision Plastics **(1)**
1001 E. College St.
Crawfordsville, IN 47933
Tel.: 317-362-0400
Fax: 317-364-6908
Plastic Parts, Toilet Seats, Furniture Parts, Radio Containers, Showers, Computer Housings
S.I.C.: 2499; 2519; 2653; 3089
Frank Ressen *(Pres.)*
Paul Frankwich *(Plant Mgr.)*

PRECISION ROLL GRINDERS, INC.
R.D. 6
Allentown, PA 18105
Tel.: 215-395-6966
Fax: 215-481-9130
Approx.Sls.: $10,000,000
Emp.: 90
Export
Roll Grinding & Polishing
S.I.C.: 3599; 3471
Adam T. Schildge *(Chm. Bd.)*
Gerhard Sybrius *(Pres.)*
George Maniatty *(Exec. V.P.)*
George Schildge *(Treas.)*
Ronald Schildge *(Sec.)*
Terry R. Frick *(Mgr.-Sls.)*
Joseph Lampi *(Plant Mgr.)*

PRECISION TUNE, INC.
784 Miller Dr. S.E.
Leesburg, VA 22075
Tel.: 703-777-9095
Tel.: 800-231-0588 **VA**
Fax: 703-779-0136
Year Founded: 1975
Approx.Sls.: $24,000,000
Emp.: 60
Fiscal Year-end: 4/30/92
Export
Franchisor of Automotive Tune-Up Shops
S.I.C.: 6794; 7549
Joseph A. Grimaud, Jr. *(Pres. & Chief Exec. Officer)*
Robert N. Burguieres *(V.P.-Fin. & Treas.)*
William Carroll *(V.P.-Franchise Devel.)*
Dave Diranna *(V.P.-Franchise Services)*
David Groce *(V.P., Sec. & Gen. Counsel)*
Glynn Massingill *(V.P.-PAC Mfg. & Distr.)*
Carol Cothern *(Controller)*
Diana Kash *(Exec. Admin. Asst.)*
Diane Treanor *(Internal Auditor)*
Joel Burrows *(Dir.-Tech. Engrng.)*
Phil Trigg *(Dir.-Franchise Sls.)*
Scott Rolf *(Mgr.-Adv.)*
Principal(s):
Joseph A. Grimaud, Jr.

No. of Mfg. Plants/Facilities: 545
No. of U.S. Offices: 4

Computer Systems/Hardware:
NCR Tower

Outside Service Firm(s):

Ernst & Young*(Auditors)*
1225 Connecticut Ave., NW
Washington, DC 20036

Morgan, Lewis & Bockius*(Legal Firm)*
1800 M St. N.W.
Washington, DC 20036
Tel.: 202-467-7000

First Virginia Bank*(Major Banking Relationship)*
Leesburg, VA 22075

Subsidiary:

PAC Manufacturing & Distributing Co. **(1)**
1575 Lenoir Dr.
Winchester, VA 22601
Tel.: 800-727-8863
Emp.: 60
Retail/Franchise Auto Tune-Up Centers
S.I.C.: 7549
Glyn Massingill *(V.P. & Gen. Mgr.)*
John Wiegand *(Dir.-Sls.)*

PRECISION TWIST DRILL CO.
One Precision Plaza
Crystal Lake, IL 60039-9000
Mailing Address:
P.O. Box 9000,
Crystal Lake, IL 60039-9000
Tel.: 815-459-2040
Fax: 815-459-2804
Year Founded: 1952
Approx.Sls.: $100,000,000
Emp.: 1,700
Fiscal Year-end: 3/31/91
Export
Manufacture Standard & Special Twist Drills, Carbide-tipped & Solid Carbide Rotary Cutting Tools
S.I.C.: 3545; 3423
James H. Beck *(Chm. Bd. & Chief Exec. Officer)*
Arthur R. Beck *(Pres. & Chief Oper. Officer)*
Norman Margolin *(Chief Fin. Officer & Exec. V.P.-Fin.)*
Bud Matz *(Sr. V.P.-Opers.)*
John E. DeMond *(V.P.-Mktg. & Sls.)*
Dick Gulbrandsen *(V.P.-Engrng.)*
Joy Young *(Treas.)*
Eldon Conley *(Dir.-Production & Inventory Control)*
Susan M. Maxey *(Dir.-Mktg. Services)*
Dan McMullen *(Dir.-Human Resources)*
Kitch Ziebel *(Dir.-Pur.)*
Fred Guttas *(Natl. Sls. Mgr.)*
Ed Malinowski *(Mgr.-Credit)*
Steve Meyer *(Mgr.-Data Processing)*
Karen Miller *(Asst. to Chm.)*
Principal(s):
Arthur R. Beck

No. of Mfg. Plants/Facilities: 3
No. of U.S. Offices: 2

Computer Systems/Hardware:
IBM System 38

Outside Service Firm(s):

Friedman, Eisenstein, Raemer & Schwartz*(Auditors)*
Chicago, IL

Shefsky & Froehlich*(Legal Firm)*
Chicago, IL

American National Bank & Trust Company of Chicago*(Major Banking Relationship)*
33 N. LaSalle St.
Chicago, IL 60602
Tel.: 312-661-5000
Fax: 312-661-6417

Divisions:

Mohawk Tools **(1)**
P.O. Box 9000, One Precision Plaza
Crystal Lake, IL 60039-9000
Tel.: 815-459-2040
Fax: 815-459-0195
Export
Computer Systems/Hardware:
IBM PC
Manufactures Tools
S.I.C.: 3545
James H. Beck *(Chm. Bd. & Chief Exec. Officer)*
Arthur R. Beck *(Pres. & Chief Oper. Officer)*
Norman Margolin *(Exec. V.P. & Chief Fin. Officer)*
John E. Demond *(V.P.-Mktg. & Sls.)*
Susan Maxey *(Corp. Dir.-Mktg. Services)*
Kitch Ziebel *(Dir.-Pur.)*

TSC Carbide Co. **(1)**
P.O. Box 9000, One Precision Plaza
Crystal Lake, IL 60014
Tel.: 815-459-2040
Fax: 815-459-0430
Import Export
Manufactures Tools
S.I.C.: 3545
Art Beck *(Pres.)*
John Demond *(V.P.-Sls. & Mktg.)*
Susan Maxey *(Corp. Dir.-Mktg. Services)*

Triumph Twist Drill Co. **(1)**
One Precision Plaza, Box 9000
Crystal Lake, IL 60039-9000
Tel.: 815-459-6250
Fax: 815-459-2804
Import Export
Manufactures Tools
S.I.C.: 3423
Art Beck *(Pres. & Chief Oper. Officer)*
Norm Margolin *(Chief Fin. Officer)*
Susan Maxey *(Corp. Dir., Mktg. Services)*
Kitch Ziebel *(Pur. Dir.)*
Randy Beck *(Natl. Sls. Mgr.)*

PRECISION VALVE CORPORATION
700 Nepperham Ave.
Yonkers, NY 10703
Mailing Address:
P.O. Box 309
Yonkers, NY 10702
Tel.: 914-969-6500 **NY**
Fax: 914-969-0618
Year Founded: 1949

Precision Valve Corporation—(Continued)

Approx.Sls.: $200,000,000
Emp.: 2,000
Mfr. of Metal Aerosol Valves
S.I.C.: 3499
Robert H. Abplanalp *(Chm. Bd., Pres. & Chief Exec. Officer)*
Frederick K. Langford *(Sr. V.P.-Intl. Aerosol)*
Walter Camas *(V.P.-Mktg.)*
William A. Gregg *(V.P.-Res.)*
Robert H. Hawkey *(V.P.-Fin. & Admin.)*
Kenneth Radcliffe *(V.P.-Aerosol Mfg.)*
William E. Griffin *(Sec.)*
Albert Mariani, Jr. *(Controller)*
Chris Bayer *(Dir.-Mfg.)*
Edward Gunther *(Mgr.-Pur.)*

Outside Service Firm(s):

KPMG Peat Marwick*(Auditors)*
Stamford Square, 3001 Summer St.
Stamford, CT 06905
Tel.: 203-356-9800

Griffin, Letsen, Coogan & Veneruso, P.C.*(Legal Firm)*
Yonkers, NY

Hudson Valley National Bank*(Major Banking Relationship)*
Yonkers, NY

Divisions:

Aeroclo Metal Products **(1)**
700 Nepperham Ave.
Yonkers, NY 10703
Tel.: 914-969-6500
Fax: 914-969-0618
Mfr. of Cups For Metal Aerosol Valves
S.I.C.: 3499
John Lazzari *(Mgr.-Sls.)*

Tiros Plastics Div. **(1)**
700 Nepperham Ave.
Yonkers, NY 10703
Tel.: 914-969-6500
Fax: 914-969-0618
Plastic Extrusions
S.I.C.: 3089
John Lazzari *(Mgr.-Sls.)*

PRECISIONAIRE, INC.
2399 26th Ave. N.
Saint Petersburg, FL 33713
Tel.: 813-822-4411
Fax: 813-823-5510
Emp.: 550
Manufacture Air Conditioner & Heater Spun Glass Filters
S.I.C.: 3564
Emily C. Beck *(Chm. Bd.)*
Gus Hernandez *(Pres.)*
Robert V. Beck *(V.P.-Sls. & Mktg.)*
William C. Beck *(V.P.-Pur.)*
Steve Lackley *(V.P.-Sls.)*

Outside Service Firm(s):

Hanson & Tottle*(Auditors)*
St. Petersburg, FL

Trenam, Simmons, Kemker, Scharf, Barkin, Frye & O'Neil*(Legal Firm)*
P.O. Box 1102
Tampa, FL 33601
Tel.: 813-689-8161

Sun Bank, N.A.*(Major Banking Relationship)*
St. Petersburg, FL

PREFERRED RISK MUTUAL INSURANCE
1111 Ashworth Rd.
West Des Moines, IA 50265
Tel.: 515-225-5000 **CO**
Fax: 515-225-5088
Assets: $331,375,421
Liabilities: $218,444,493
Net Worth: $112,930,928
Sales Range: $100-499 Million
Emp.: 850
Fiscal Year-end: 12/31/91
Insurance Holding Company: Life, Health, Property & Casualty Coverage for Nondrinkers
S.I.C.: 6311; 6321; 6719; 6331
Employee Matching Gifts Program: Colleges & Universities Match $25 to $100 Gifts
Bernard Mercer *(Chm. Bd.)*
Robert Plunk *(Pres. & Chief Exec. Officer)*
Jack Kelly *(Sr. V.P.-Comml. Mktg.)*
Judy Brannon *(V.P.-Personal Lines)*
Michael Crain *(V.P.-Sls.)*
Greg Ellison *(V.P.-Comml. Lines)*
Thomas Farr *(V.P.-Claims & Gen. Counsel)*
Vern Shelton *(V.P. & Chief Information Officer)*
Ron Wilson *(V.P.-Indus. Agencies)*
David Withers *(V.P.-Actuary)*
Syd Vanderlinden *(V.P.-Field Quality)*
Philip Vanderah *(Treas. & Sec.)*
Conrey Combs *(Dir.-Human Resources)*
Deborah Marguardt *(Dir.-Personnel Training & Devel.)*
Lynsey Oster *(Dir.-Emp. Benefits)*
Max Vail *(Dir.-Admin.)*

Computer Systems/Hardware:
IBM System 3033

Outside Service Firm(s):

KPMG Peat Marwick*(Auditors)*
2500 Ruan Center
Des Moines, IA 50309
Tel.: 515-288-7465

Norwest Bank of Minneapolis N.A.*(Major Banking Relationship)*
P.O. Box 738, 161 N. Concord Exchange
So. St. Paul, MN 55075-0738
Tel.: 612-450-4064
Fax: 612-450-4078

West Des Moines State Bank*(Major Banking Relationship)*
West Des Moines, IA

Subsidiaries:

Midwest Mutual Insurance Co. **(1)**
1111 Ashworth Rd.
West Des Moines, IA 50265
Tel.: 515-223-2000 (100%)
Assets: $59,798,873
Earnings: $2,966,608
Liabilities: $35,009,309
Net Worth: $24,789,564
Approx.Premiums: $35,652,156
Emp.: 85
Fiscal Year-end: 12/31/91
Motorcycle, Recreational Vehicle, Non-Standard Auto, Mobile Home
S.I.C.: 6331
Chad Hensley *(Chm. Bd.)*
Robert D. Meyer *(Pres. & Chief Exec. Officer)*
Glenn Ballew *(V.P.-Underwriting & Sec.)*
Jim Johnson *(V.P.-Sls. & Mktg.)*
Dennis Carney *(Treas.)*

Preferred Risk Life Insurance Co. **(1)**
1111 Ashworth Rd.
West Des Moines, IA 50265
Tel.: 515-225-5000 (100%)
Assets: $195,382,136
Earnings: $5,677,992
Liabilities: $152,744,345
Net Worth: $42,637,791
Approx.Rev.: $30,867,142
Emp.: 45
Fiscal Year-end: 12/31/91
Health & Life Insurance
S.I.C.: 6311; 6321
Bernard Mercer *(Chm. Bd.)*
Michael Weiler *(Pres. & Chief Exec. Officer)*
Norm Larsen *(V.P.-Investments)*
William S. Gates *(Treas. & Sec.)*
Albert L. Clemens, M.D. *(Medical Dir.)*
Bruce Huisman *(Acct. Mgr.)*

PREFORMED LINE PRODUCTS
660 Beta Dr.
Cleveland, OH 44143
Mailing Address:
P.O. Box 91129,
Cleveland, OH 44101
Tel.: 216-461-5200
Telex: 980407
Fax: 216-442-8816
Year Founded: 1947
Earnings: $5,070,000
Approx.Sls.: $115,000,000
Emp.: 1,100
Manufacture Products for Construction of Electric Power Lines & Telecommunications Systems
S.I.C.: 3643; 3644; 3661; 3669
Jon R. Ruhlman *(Pres. & Chief Exec. Officer)*
Carl Gregory *(Chief Fin. Officer, V.P.-Fin. & Treas.)*
David P. Arnold *(V.P.-Sls.)*
Bill Hoppe *(V.P.-Mfg.)*
Gordon Meldrum *(V.P.-Intl. Opers.)*
E.J. Pleszko *(V.P.-Mktg.)*
Robert G. Ruhlman *(V.P.-Corp. Plng.)*
Ralph Siter *(V.P.-Research & Engrng.)*
Robert Weber *(V.P.-Employee Rels.)*
J. Richard Hamilton *(Sec.)*
Joseph Kreger *(Asst. Treas.)*
Richard L. Pardee *(Dir.-Mktg.)*

No. of Mfg. Plants/Facilities: 17

Computer Systems/Hardware:
IBM 4361; IBM PC-XT

Outside Service Firm(s):

Ernst & Young*(Auditors)*
1300 Huntington Bldg.
Cleveland, OH 44115
Tel.: 216-861-5000

John Hancock Mutual Life Insurance Co.*(Group Insurer)*
John Hancock Place, P.O. Box 111
Boston, MA 02117

Baker & Hostetler*(Legal Firm)*
3200 National City Center
Cleveland, OH 44114
Tel.: 216-621-0200
Fax: 216-696-0740

National City Bank*(Major Banking Relationship)*
P.O. Box 92301, Corp. Trust Dept.
Cleveland, OH 44101
Tel.: 216-575-2000

Non-U.S. Holdings:

Fanner-PLP **(1)**
150 Briens Rd.
Northmead, N.S.W. 2152, Australia
Tel.: 263 06388
Emp.: 100
Mfrs. Lighting Fixtures
S.I.C.: 3646; 3645
Richard Oakden *(Mng. Dir.)*

Foundation Instruments Inc. **(1)**
24 Colonnade Rd.
Ottawa, ON K2E 7J6, Canada
Tel.: 613-226-4000
Emp.: 60
Mfrs. Radio & Television Parts & Equipment
S.I.C.: 3663
Russell Smith *(Mgr.)*

PLP Produtos Para Linhas Proformados Ltda. **(1)**
R. Santa Elvira 465
Sao Paulo, SP-03086 Brazil
Tel.: 1129 58511
Emp.: 215
Mfrs. Electrical Equipment, Wiring & Supplies
S.I.C.: 3643; 3699
Aristheu Amaral Rosa *(Dir.)*

Preformados De Mexico SA **(1)**
Poniente 140, 526 Fracc Ind. Vallejo
Mexico, D.F. 02300, Mexico
Tel.: 587 4308
Mfrs. Wire
S.I.C.: 3357
J. Monetti Calanche *(Gen. Mgr.)*

Preformed Line Products Canada **(1)**
36 Raglan Pl.
Cambridge, ON N1R 7J2, Canada
Tel.: 519-740-6666
Emp.: 25
Mfr. Pole Line Hardware
S.I.C.: 3644; 3496
Gordon Meldrum *(Mng. Dir.)*

Preformed Line Products(Great Britain) Ltd. **(1)**
East Portway Industrial Estate
Andover, Hants SP10 3LH, United Kingdom
Tel.: 0264 366234
Telex: 47310 PLP G
Fax: 0264 356714
Mfrs. Overhead Transmission Fittings
S.I.C.: 3643
David Hearnshaw *(Mng. Dir.)*

PREMARC CORPORATION
7505 Hwy. M-71
Durand, MI 48429
Tel.: 517-288-2661
Holding Company for Manufacturers of Concrete Pipe
S.I.C.: 3272; 6719
Daniel C. Marsh *(Pres.)*
Thomas Haggar *(Exec. V.P.)*
David Marsh *(V.P.)*
Jack R. Marsh *(V.P.)*

Subsidiaries:

Cadillac Pipe **(1)**
5305 Hwy. M-115
Cadillac, MI 49601
Tel.: 616-775-3761
Mfr. Concrete Products
S.I.C.: 3272
Paul MArsh *(Gen. Mgr.)*

Lamar Corp. **(1)**
2696 Chicago Dr., S.W.
Grand Rapids, MI 45909
Tel.: 616-534-9645 (100%)
Mfr. of Pre-Cast Concrete Wastewater Pipelines
S.I.C.: 3272
Daniel C. Marsh *(Pres.)*

Marsh Products Co. **(1)**
7505 E. M-71
Durand, MI 48429
Tel.: 517-288-2661 (100%)
Mfr. of Concrete Products
S.I.C.: 3272
Daniel C. Marsh *(Pres.)*

Precision Pipe & Supply Co. **(1)**
4950 White Lake Rd.
Clarkston, MI 48346
Tel.: 313-625-8080 (100%)
Mfr. of Concrete Pipe
S.I.C.: 3272
Daniel C. Marsh *(Pres.)*

PREMIER COATINGS, INC.
2250 Arthur Ave.
Elk Grove Village, IL 60007
Tel.: 708-439-4200
Fax: 708-439-4211
Year Founded: 1946
Approx.Sls.: $18,500,000
Emp.: 80
A Full Line of Latex & Oil Exterior Stains & Varnish
S.I.C.: 2851; 5198
Edward R. Andrus *(Pres. & Chief Exec. Officer)*
Victor G. Meier *(Exec. V.P.-Sls.)*
Paul Petraitis *(V.P.-Sls. & Mktg.)*
Michael Miskewitch *(V.P.-Mfg.)*
Carl Helzing *(Sec. & Treas.)*

Computer Systems/Hardware:
IBM 3800

Division:

Maxum Exterior Coatings **(1)**
2250 Arthur Ave.
Elk Grove Village, IL 60007
Tel.: 708-439-4200
Fax: 708-439-4211

PREMIER DENTAL PRODUCTS COMPANY
1710 Romano Dr.
Norristown, PA 19404
Tel.: 215-277-3800
Fax: 215-277-4270
Approx.Sls.: $19,000,000
Emp.: 160

Wholesale Distributor of Dental Supplies & Instruments
S.I.C.: 5047
Morton Charlestein *(Chm. Bd.)*
Jerrold A. Frezel *(Pres.)*
Gary Charlestein *(Chief Exec. Officer & Treas.)*
William J. Frezel *(Exec. V.P. & Sec.)*
Joseph V. Hosack *(Controller)*

Outside Service Firm(s):

Simonson, Lipschutz & Fogel*(Auditors)*
Philadelphia, PA

Blank, Rome, Comisky & McCauley*(Legal Firm)*
Four Penn Center Plaza
Philadelphia, PA 19103
Tel.: 215-209-3700

Provident National Bank*(Major Banking Relationship)*
P.O. Box 7648
Philadelphia, PA 19101
Tel.: 215-585-5000

PREMIER INDUSTRIES, INC.
1019 Pacific Ave., Ste. 1501
Tacoma, WA 98402
Tel.: 206-572-5111
Fax: 206-383-7100
Sales Range: $500-999 Million
Emp.: 300
Holding Company; Chemical Manufacturers
S.I.C.: 2819; 6719
Michael Wall *(Pres.)*
James R. Johnson *(Chief Fin. Officer)*
Sam Felker *(Dir.-Mngmt. Information Systems)*

Computer Systems/Hardware:
IBM

Outside Service Firm(s):

Commerce Bank of Kansas City*(Major Banking Relationship)*
10th & Walnut
Kansas City, MO 64141
Tel.: 816-234-2000
Fax: 816-234-2548

Plants:

Manley Bros. **(1)**
P.O. Box C
Troy Grove, IL 61372
Tel.: 815-539-7486
Mfr. of Chemicals
S.I.C.: 2819
Derrol Lee *(Plant Mgr.)*

Manley Bros. **(1)**
Livingston Rd., P.O. Box 456
Bridgman, MI 49106
Tel.: 616-465-5833
Mfr. of Chemicals
S.I.C.: 2819
Wayne Williams *(Plant Mgr.)*

PREMIER MILL CORP.
30 West 21st St.
New York, NY 10010
Tel.: 212-727-3400
Telex: 423628 Premill
Fax: 212-727-9841
Year Founded: 1923
Approx.Sls.: $10,000,000
Emp.: 60
Fiscal Year-end: 6/30/91
Export
Mfr. Grinding & Mixing Systems & Dispersion Equip.
S.I.C.: 3559
Myron Segal *(Chm. Bd., Pres. & Chief Exec. Officer)*
Mark Fuhrer *(Exec. V.P.-Admin.)*
Chris Zoga *(Exec. V.P.-Mfg.)*
Amy Segal *(Coord.-Sls. & Mktg.)*

No. of Mfg. Plants/Facilities: 1
No. of U.S. Offices: 20

Computer Systems/Hardware:
IBM/Novell Network

Outside Service Firm(s):

Reitman & Reitman*(Auditors)*
New York, NY

Empire Blue Cross & Blue Shield*(Group Insurer)*
New York, NY

Meridian Bank*(Major Banking Relationship)*
Reading, PA

Plant:

Premier Mill Corp. **(1)**
Exeter Industrial Park, One Birchmont Dr.
Reading, PA 19606
Tel.: 215-779-9500
S.I.C.: 3559

PREMIER REFRACTORIES & CHEMICALS INC.
901 E. Eighth Ave.
King of Prussia, PA 19406
Tel.: 215-337-1100
Refractory Cement & Plastics
S.I.C.: 3297
Charles Gehret *(Pres.)*

Non-U.S. Holding:

Premier Refractories (Canada) Ltd. **(1)**
Prince Charles Dr.
Welland, ON L3B 5P4, Canada
Tel.: 416-732-4441 (100%)
Non-Clay Refractories
S.I.C.: 3297
William Lutes *(Pres.)*

PRENTISS INCORPORATED
21 Vernon St.
Floral Park, NY 11001
Mailing Address:
CB 2000,
Floral Park, NY 11002-2000
Tel.: 516-326-1919
Telex: 836254
Fax: 516-326-2312
Year Founded: 1919
Approx.Sls.: $16,000,000
Emp.: 42
Fiscal Year-end: 9/30/92
Import Export
Pesticide Formulator
S.I.C.: 2879
Malcolm Miller *(Chm. & Chief Exec. Officer)*
Richard A. Miller *(Pres.)*
Jeffrey S. Miller *(V.P.-Opers., Chief Oper. Officer)*
Larry Eichler *(V.P.-Sls. & Mktg.)*
Robert N. Miller *(V.P.-Fin. & Treas.)*
Nina J. Miller *(Sec.)*

Computer Systems/Hardware:
IBM 5363

PREPCO
6190 E. Slauson Av.
Los Angeles, CA 90040
Tel.: 213-726-2676
Fax: 213-726-0438
Year Founded: 1945
Sales Range: $20-39 Million
Emp.: 250
Fiscal Year-end: 12/31/90
Import Export
Specialty Baked Goods, Croutons, Stuffing, Breading, Bread Crumbs, Blended Seasonings, Snack Foods & Bottled Juices
S.I.C.: 5141; 2096; 2099; 2033; 5812
Mark Sedlacek *(Pres.)*
Thomas W. Lehmer *(Chief Exec. Officer)*
David Andrews *(Chief Fin. Officer)*
Colleen Cleveland *(V.P.-Mktg.)*
Principal(s):
Thomas W. Lehmer

No. of Mfg. Plants/Facilities: 3
No. of U.S. Offices: 3

Computer Systems/Hardware:
IBM System 36

Outside Service Firm(s):

McGladrey & Pullen*(Auditors)*
Los Angeles, CA

Bank of America NT&SA*(Major Banking Relationship)*
555 So. Flower St., 5th Fl.
Los Angeles, CA 90071
Tel.: 213-228-3526
Fax: 213-228-4062

GEORGE W. PRESCOTT PUBLISHING CO.
400 Crown Colony Dr.
Quincy, MA 02169
Tel.: 617-786-7000
Fax: 617-786-7120
Sales Range: $20-39 Million
Emp.: 400
Newspaper Publishing: The Patriot Ledger
S.I.C.: 2711
K. Prescott Low *(Chm. Bd., Pres. & Publr.)*
Frank Grueter *(Chief Fin. Officer & V.P.)*
Patrick J. DeGisa *(V.P. & Gen Mgr.)*
William B. Ketter *(V.P. & Editor)*
Scott Low *(Publr.)*

PRESERVATIVE PAINT COMPANY
5400 Airport Way
Seattle, WA 98108
Tel.: 206-763-0300
Fax: 206-767-2251
Year Founded: 1908
Approx.Sls.: $18,000,000
Emp.: 130
Paints, Varnishes & Lacquers
S.I.C.: 2851; 5198; 5231
Richard E. Wittig *(Pres.)*
Phillip Konopka *(V.P.-Fin.)*
Kenneth Skalsky *(V.P.-Sls.)*
Jim Todd *(V.P.-Mfg. & Sec.)*

Outside Service Firm(s):

Beresford, Booth, Baronsky & Trompeter*(Legal Firm)*
Seattle, WA

Key Bank of Puget Sound*(Major Banking Relationship)*
Seattle, WA

THE PRESMET CORP.
112 Harding St.
Worcester, MA 01604
Tel.: 508-792-6400
Fax: 508-792-6427
Year Founded: 1943
Approx.Sls.: $17,000,000
Emp.: 275
Fiscal Year-end: 9/30/90
Export
Manufactures Powder Metallurgy, Structurals & Bearings including Secondary Machining
S.I.C.: 3499
Stephen H. Climch *(Pres.)*
R.J. Stansoucy *(Exec. V.P.)*
Thaddeus Bauer *(Dir.-Sls. & Mktg.)*
R. Bellenoit *(Mgr.-Admin.)*
James Gusha *(Mgr.-Personnel)*

Subsidiary:

Massachusetts Steel Treating **(1)**
112 Harding St.
Worcester, MA 01604
Tel.: 508-753-6400
D. Weldon *(Mgr.)*

PRESS ENTERPRISE COMPANY
3512 14th St.
Riverside, CA 92501
Mailing Address:
P.O. Box 792
Riverside, CA 92501
Tel.: 909-684-1200 **CA**
Fax: 909-782-7630
Year Founded: 1878
Approx.Sls.: $70,000,000
Emp.: 1,400
Fiscal Year-end: 12/31/91
Daily Newspaper Publishing
S.I.C.: 2711
Howard H. Hays, Jr. *(Chm. Bd.)*
Marcia McQuern *(Pres. & Exec. Editor)*
Dr. Daniel M. Hays *(V.P.)*
Helen C. Hays *(Treas. & Sec.)*
Paul Ringdahl *(Controller)*
Dave Cornwall *(Dir.-Adv.)*
Nick Vance *(Dir.-Personnel)*
Jon Hays *(Gen. Mgr.)*
Howard Owens *(Mgr.-Prod.)*
Jim Zikratch *(Mgr.-Data Processing)*
William D. Rich *(Publr.)*
Klaus Rombach *(Pur. Agent)*

Outside Service Firm(s):

Best, Best & Krieger*(Legal Firm)*
P.O. Box 1028
Riverside, CA 92502
Tel.: 909-686-1450

Bank of America*(Major Banking Relationship)*
Riverside, CA

PRESSED STEEL TANK CO., INC.
1445 S. 66th St.
West Allis, WI 53214
Mailing Address:
P.O. Box 2180
Milwaukee, WI 53201-2180
Tel.: 414-476-0500
Fax: 414-476-7191
Year Founded: 1902
Approx.Sls.: $20,000,000
Emp.: 200
Fiscal Year-end: 12/31/91
Import Export
Mfr. Compressed Gas Cylinders, Pressure Vessels & Deep Drawn Shapes and Shells
S.I.C.: 3443
G.G. Finch *(Pres.)*
Conrad C. Cramer *(V.P.-Sls. & Mktg.)*

Computer Systems/Hardware:
Unisys

PRESSMAN TOY CORP.
200 Fifth Ave., Suite 1052
New York, NY 10010
Mailing Address:
745 Joyce Kilmer Ave.
New Brunswick, NJ 08901
Tel.: 212-675-7910 **NY**
Fax: 212-645-8512
Year Founded: 1947
Approx.Sls.: $40,000,000
Emp.: 325
Fiscal Year-end: 12/31/90
Import
Toys & Games
S.I.C.: 3944
Lynn Pressman *(Chm. Bd.)*
James R. Pressman *(Pres. & Chief Oper. Officer)*
Ralph Lancellotti *(Exec. V.P.-Sls.)*
Susan Adamo *(V.P.-Res. & Devel.)*
Ron Gurin *(V.P.-Pur. & Prod. Devel.)*
Murray Hellman *(V.P., Treas. & Sec.)*
Ronald Leona *(V.P.-Mktg.)*
Barry Schneider *(V.P.-Mfg.)*
Henry Schroeder *(Mgr.-Credit)*

No. of Mfg. Plants/Facilities: 1
No. of U.S. Offices: 2

Pressman Toy Corp.—(Continued)

Computer Systems/Hardware:
IBM 36

Outside Service Firm(s):

I. Weisman Associates*(Auditors)*
Mount Arlington, NJ

Moore, Wohl & Newman*(Legal Firm)*
New Brunswick, NJ

Midlantic National Bank*(Major Banking Relationship)*
Metro Park Plaza, P.O. Box 600
Edison, NJ 08818
Tel.: 908-321-8400

United Jersey Bank/Central N.A.*(Major Banking Relationship)*
Somerset, NJ

PRESSURE SYSTEMS
34 Research Dr.
Hampton, VA 23666
Mailing Address:
P.O. Box 7386
Hampton, VA 23666
Tel.: 804-865-1243 **VA**
Telex: 901-406
Fax: 804-766-2644
Year Founded: 1977
Sales Range: $10-19 Million
Emp.: 79
Manufacture Electronic Pressure Transducers & Measurement Systems
S.I.C.: 3829; 3825
Douglas B. Juanarena *(Pres. & Chief Exec. Officer)*
Mark Miller *(V.P.-Opers.)*
Sue Juanarena *(Treas.)*
Robert Savage *(Controller)*
LaSandra Owens *(Dir.-Personnel)*
Stephen Yakshe *(Mgr.-Sls.)*
Richard S. Gordon *(Legal Officer)*
Principal(s):
Douglas B. Juanarena

No. of Mfg. Plants/Facilities: 1
No. of U.S. Offices: 2

Computer Systems/Hardware:
IBM; Tandy; Hewlett-Packard

Outside Service Firm(s):

Goodman & Co.*(Auditors)*
Newport News, VA

New England Mutual Life Insurance Co.*(Commercial Insurance Carrier)*
Norfolk, VA

New England Mutual Life Insurance Co.*(Group Insurer)*
Norfolk, VA

Central Fidelity Bank*(Major Banking Relationship)*
Newport News, VA

PRESTIGE STAMPING, INC.
23513 Groesbeck Hwy.
Warren, MI 48089
Mailing Address:
P.O. Box 1086
Warren, MI 48089
Tel.: 313-773-2700 **MI**
Fax: 313-773-2298
Year Founded: 1967
Approx.Sls.: $15,000,000
Emp.: 86
Import Export
Metal Washers, Fasteners, Metal Stampings & Assemblies
S.I.C.: 3465; 3452
Robert A. Rink *(Pres. & Chief Exec. Officer)*
Robert J. Rink *(Chief Oper. Officer)*
James A. Rink *(V.P.-Sls. & Engrng.)*
Chris Rink *(V.P. & Gen. Mgr.)*
Jeff Rink *(V.P. & Mgr.-Sls.)*
M. Solonica *(Mgr.-Personnel)*
Alison Elmes *(Supvr.-Data Processing)*
William Fleming *(Buyer)*

No. of Mfg. Plants/Facilities: 1

Outside Service Firm(s):

James R. Graves*(Auditors)*
Grosse Pointe, MI

National Bank of Detroit*(Major Banking Relationship)*
Ann Arbor, MI

PRESTO FOOD PRODUCTS, INC.
18275 Arenth Ave.
City of Industry, CA 91748
Mailing Address:
P.O. Box 584
City of Industry, CA 91747
Tel.: 818-810-1775
Fax: 818-912-6473
Year Founded: 1937
Emp.: 500
Fiscal Year-end: 12/31/90
Export
Non-Dairy Creamers, Toppings & Sour Dressings, Salad Dressings & Frozen Bakery Products, Non-Dairy Frozen Dessert, Cultured Dressings, Aerosol Toppings, Non-Dairy Whipped Toppings
S.I.C.: 2033; 2099
Bruce Coffey *(Chm. & Chief Exec. Officer)*
Glynn Morris *(Pres. & Chief Oper. Officer)*
Richard Clark *(V.P.-Opers.)*
E.A. Gibbons *(V.P.-Mktg. & Food Service Sls.)*
Richard Van Wagenan *(V.P.-Fin. & Admin.)*
Donald G. Calzia *(Mgr.-Pur.)*

Subsidiary:

Jon Donaire Pastries, Inc. **(1)**
942 Sorensen Ave.
Santa Fe Springs, CA 90670
Tel.: 310-946-6344
Cheesecakes & Specialty Cakes
S.I.C.: 2051
Michael DelDuca *(Pres.)*
Ken Plank *(Plant Mgr.)*

PRESTO FOOD STORES, INC.
607 S. Alexander St.
Plant City, FL 33566
Tel.: 813-754-3511 **FL**
Fax: 813-752-5494
Year Founded: 1976
Assets: $17,839,500
Liabilities: $713,400,686,603
Net Worth: $713,382,847,103
Approx.Sls.: $36,141,500
Emp.: 325
Fiscal Year-end: 12/31/91
Presto & Gator Retail Grocery Stores; Wholesale & Retail Gasoline
S.I.C.: 5172; 5411; 5541
Employee Matching Gifts Program:
United Fund, Local Areas
Hugh C. Robinson III *(Pres.)*
Carol Robinson *(Exec. V.P.)*
John A. Brady *(V.P.-Security)*
Robert Stillings *(V.P.-Opers., Sls., Mktg. & Personnel Dir.)*
O. Keith Avery *(Sec. & Treas.)*

Outside Service Firm(s):

Bella Hermida Gillman & Co.*(Auditors)*
Plant City, FL

Trinkle Redman Moody*(Legal Firm)*
Plant City, FL

Hillsboro Sun Bank*(Major Banking Relationship)*
Plant City, FL

PRESTO LOCK, INC.
100 Outwater Lane
Garfield, NJ 07026
Tel.: 201-340-1000
Fax: 201-340-2705
Emp.: 350
Hardware For Luggage & Boxes; Personal Security Devices
S.I.C.: 3429
Eberhard Franzen *(Pres.)*
Joseph Held *(V.P.-Mfg.)*
Carl A. Mann *(V.P.-Sls.)*
John Fox *(Sec. & Treas.)*
Gus Schaller *(Chief Engr.)*
George King *(Pur. Agent)*

Outside Service Firm(s):

KPMG Peat Marwick*(Auditors)*
345 Park Ave.
New York, NY 10154
Tel.: 212-758-9700
Fax: 212-872-3308

Shapiro & Shapiro*(Legal Firm)*
Arlington, VA

Midlantic National Bank*(Major Banking Relationship)*
West Paterson, NJ

PRESTON ENERGY INC.
202 E. High St.
Kingwood, WV 26537
Tel.: 304-329-1778 **WV**
Fax: 304-329-3345
Year Founded: 1973
Assets: $25,000,000
Liabilities: $20,000,000
Net Worth: $5,000,000
Approx.Sls.: $30,000,000
Emp.: 50
Coal Mining
S.I.C.: 1222
John Hardesty *(Pres.)*
Larry L. Myers *(V.P.)*

Outside Service Firm(s):

Kenneth Maloney*(Auditors)*
Kingwood, WV

Dailey & Miller*(Legal Firm)*
Kingwood, WV

Albright National Bank*(Major Banking Relationship)*
Kingwood, WV

PRICE BROTHERS CO.
367 W. 2nd St.
Dayton, OH 45402
Mailing Address:
P.O. Box 825
Dayton, OH 45401
Tel.: 513-226-8700 **MI**
Telex: 155197
Fax: 513-226-8763
Year Founded: 1911
Approx.Sls.: $170,000,000
Emp.: 1,500
Manufacture Composite Construction Materials
S.I.C.: 3272; 3315; 3496
Gayle B. Price, Jr. *(Chm. Bd. & Chief Exec. Officer)*
Emerson W. Heisler *(Pres. & Chief Oper. Officer)*
Donald N. Lorenz *(Chief Fin. Officer & V.P.-Fin.)*
Bradley W. Evers *(V.P., Sec. & Gen. Counsel)*
Steven M. Paul *(Treas.)*
Ira H. Stanley *(Asst. Treas.)*
Wilson C. Miller *(Opers. Controller)*
Douglas Robbins *(Mgr.-Mngmt. Information Systems)*
John B. Tonkin *(Mgr.-Corp Services)*

Computer Systems/Hardware:
NCR

Outside Service Firm(s):

Deloitte & Touche*(Auditors)*
1700 Courthouse Plaza NE
Dayton, OH 45401
Tel.: 513-223-8821

Bank One*(Major Banking Relationship)*
Kettering Tower
Dayton, OH 45401
Tel.: 513-449-8600

NationsBank Carolinas*(Major Banking Relationship)*
One NCNB Plaza,
Charlotte, NC 28255
Tel.: 704-374-5000

N.B.D. Bank, N.A.*(Major Banking Relationship)*
611 Woodward Ave.
Detroit, MI 48226
Tel.: 313-225-1122
Fax: 313-225-3420

Bank One*(Pension Manager)*
Kettering Tower
Dayton, OH 45401
Tel.: 513-449-8600

NationsBank Carolinas*(Pension Manager)*
One NCNB Plaza,
Charlotte, NC 28255
Tel.: 704-374-5000

N.B.D. Bank, N.A.*(Pension Manager)*
611 Woodward Ave.
Detroit, MI 48226
Tel.: 313-225-1122
Fax: 313-225-3420

Scudder, Stevens & Clark*(Pension Manager)*
Cincinnati Commerce Center, 600 Vine St., Ste. 2000
Cincinnati, OH 45202-2884
Tel.: 513-621-2733
Fax: 513-621-5081

Subsidiaries:

McClean-Anderson **(1)**
10600 W. Glenbrook Ct.
Milwaukee, WI 53212
Tel.: 414-355-9720
Manufacture Industrial Equipment
S.I.C.: 3559
Raymond C. Hayes *(Opers. Mgr.)*

Price Brothers Composite Pipe, Inc. **(1)**
Hwy. 16
Green Cove Springs, FL 32043
Tel.: 904-284-3003
Manufacture Fiberglass Reinforced Plastic Products
S.I.C.: 3089
Charles Hammond *(V.P. & Gen. Mgr.)*

Price Chopper Foods
(See Town & Country Supermarket d/b/a Price Chopper Foods Listing)

PRICE/MCNABB, INC.
One N. Pack Square
Asheville, NC 28801
Tel.: 704-255-2700
Fax: 704-255-2666
Year Founded: 1967
Approx.Billings: $40,000,000
Emp.: 74
Charles R. Price, Jr. *(Chm.)*
Thomas E. Eppes *(Pres.)*
Laura Mercer *(Sr. V.P., Dir. Pub. Rels.)*
Charlie Elberson *(Sr. V.P.)*
Peter Lloyd *(Sr. V.P.)*
Joe Urey *(Sr. V.P.)*
Phil Yaeger *(Sr. V.P.)*
Lynn Fidler *(V.P., Controller)*

PRICE WATERHOUSE - U.S.
1251 Ave. of the Americas
New York, NY 10020
Tel.: 212-819-5000

Fax: 212-790-6620
Year Founded: 1849
Approx.Rev.: $1,300,000,000
Emp.: 350
Fiscal Year-end: 6/30/91
Accounting & Auditing; Tax & Management Consulting; Tax Planning & Preparation; Executive Financial Planning
S.I.C.: 8721; 7389
Employee Matching Gifts Program: Price Waterhouse Foundation Matches Gifts of $25 to $1000 per Staff Member Per Fiscal Year to Qualified Four-Year Degree Granting Universities in the U.S.
Shaun F. O'Malley *(Co-Chm. & Sr. Partner)*
James E. Daley *(Co-Chm.)*
Dominic A. Tarantino *(Co-Chm.)*
James M. Coriston *(Natl. Vice Chm.-Mktg.)*
Thomas H. Chamberlain *(Chief Fin. Officer)*
Eldon Olson *(Gen. Counsel)*
John Kavalkovich *(Natl. Dir.-World Communications)*
Richard P. Kearns *(Natl. Dir.-Human Resources)*
Sheldon J. Laube *(Natl. Dir.-Information & Tech.)*
Principal(s):
James E. Daley
Dominic A. Tarantino

No. of U.S. Offices: 115

Computer Systems/Hardware:
IBM MVS/SP; DEC VMS

PRICE WEBER MARKETING COMMUNICATIONS, INC.
2101 Production Dr.
Louisville, KY 40299
Tel.: 502-499-9220
Year Founded: 1968
Approx.Billings: $12,000,000
Emp.: 60
Promotional Marketing & Advertising
Shanna J. Columbus *(Chm. Bd., Pres. & New Bus. Contact)*
Robert S. Hudson *(Exec. V.P., Fin. & Treas.)*
Ruth F. Voll *(Sec.)*

Computer Systems/Hardware:
MAC, UNIX, DOS

PRIDE PRODUCTS, INC.
5 Slater Dr.
Elizabeth, NJ 07206
Tel.: 908-353-6800
Fax: 908-353-6974
Year Founded: 1982
Approx.Sls.: $13,000,000
Emp.: 125
Mfr. of Household Appliances; Toys
S.I.C.: 3631; 3632; 3633; 3634; 3635; 3639; 3942; 3069; 3944
William Yuan *(Chm. Bd.)*
John Hofmann *(V.P.-Sls. & Mktg.)*
Connie Lue *(Controller)*
Rickie Tee *(Plant Mgr.)*

Subsidiaries:

Frigid Products, Inc. **(1)**
5 Slater Dr.
Elizabeth, NJ 07206
Tel.: 908-353-6800
Fax: 908-353-6974
Approx.Sls.: $8,000,000
Emp.: 200
Mfr. of Industrial Fans, Blowers, Air Circulators, Household Fans, Elec. Heaters, Humidifiers
S.I.C.: 3564; 3634
John Hofmann *(Pres.)*
George Turin *(Dir.-Indus. Sls.)*

The Toy Factory **(1)**
5 Slater Dr.
Elizabeth, NJ 07206
Tel.: 908-654-6800
Fax: 908-353-6974
Mfr. Toys
S.I.C.: 3942; 3069; 3944
Tim Ames *(Pres.)*
Theresa Fields *(Pur. Mgr.)*

PRIDGEON & CLAY, INC.
50 Cottage Grove SW
Grand Rapids, MI 49507
Tel.: 616-241-5675
Fax: 616-241-1799
Year Founded: 1948
Assets: $24,500,000
Earnings: $1,900,000
Liabilities: $12,000,000
Net Worth: $12,500,000
Approx.Sls.: $53,000,000
Emp.: 300
Fiscal Year-end: 12/31/91
Export
Mfr. Automotive & Metal Stampings, Special Dyes, Tools, Dye Sets, Jigs, Fixtures & Indus. Molds
S.I.C.: 3465; 3469; 3544
Robert Earl Clay *(Chm. Bd. & Chief Exec. Officer)*
Robert Edwin Clay *(Pres. & Chief Oper. Officer)*
D. Bruce Penno *(Chief Fin. Officer & Treas.)*
Donald C. Clay *(V.P.-Data Processing)*
John McNeil *(Sec.)*
Ann Dumond *(Dir.-Telecommunications)*
William Landon *(Dir.-Personnel)*
Frederick Long *(Dir.-Pur.)*
Fern Pasholk *(Meetings Planner)*

PRIMARY INDUSTRIES CORPORATION
(Sub. of Primary Industries (U.K.) Ltd.)
666 Fifth Ave.
New York, NY 10103
Tel.: 212-581-9200
Fax: 212-582-4350
Year Founded: 1960
Approx.Sls.: $500,000,000
Emp.: 250
Steel & Coal Trading & Distribution
S.I.C.: 5051; 5052; 6221; 3444
Marc Ginzberg *(Chm. Bd., Pres. & Chief Exec. Officer)*
Gavin J. Parfit *(Chief Fin. Officer)*
Sam Schussler *(Treas.)*
Murray Relis *(Controller)*
Vicki Golodetz *(Dir.-Personnel)*

No. of Foreign Offices: 9

Computer Systems/Hardware:
IBM

Outside Service Firm(s):

David Lieb & Co.*(Auditors)*
New York, NY

First Chicago Shareholder Services Trust Co.*(Major Banking Relationship)*
153 West 51st St.
New York, NY 10019
Tel.: 212-791-6422
Fax: 212-385-9798

Bankers Trust Co.*(Investment Banker)*
P.O. Box 318, Church St. Station
New York, NY 10008
Tel.: 212-454-2212
Fax: 212-454-2783

Roe & Kramer*(Legal Firm)*
New York, NY

Subsidiaries:

Gary Metals Co., Inc. **(1)**
2400 E. Dominguez Blvd.
Long Beach, CA 90810
Tel.: 213-775-7501
Wholesale Steel & Steel Fabrication
S.I.C.: 5051; 3312; 3499
Robert A. Krauss *(V.P.)*

Primary Coal Inc. **(1)**
666 Fifth Ave.
New York, NY 10103
Tel.: 212-581-2400
Coal Trading & Distribution
S.I.C.: 6221; 5052
Lawrence Perlstein *(Pres.)*

Primary Steel Inc. **(1)**
200 McDermott Rd.
North Haven, CT 06473
Tel.: 203-865-2606
Steel Fabrication & Distribution
S.I.C.: 3312; 5051
Charles Pompea *(Pres.)*

PRIME HOSPITALITY CORP.
(Formerly Prime Motor Inns, Inc.)
P.O. Box 2700,
Fairfield, NJ 07007-2700
Emp.: 2,500
Operation of Hotels, Restaurants, Cocktail Lounges
S.I.C.: 7011; 5812; 5813
David A. Simon *(Pres. & Chief Exec. Officer)*
Michael J. Clarke *(Chief Fin. Officer, Exec. V.P.)*
Melvin S. Taub *(Sr. Exec. V.P. & Gen. Counsel)*
David L. Barsky *(Exec. V.P.)*
Herbert Kay *(Sr. V.P.)*
Gerald Bohm *(V.P., Corp. Counsel & Sec.)*
Joel Simon *(V.P.)*
Jon Gurkoff *(V.P.)*
Robert S. Bingham *(V.P.)*
Donald Stevens *(Data Processing Dir.)*
Janice Torchinsky *(Dir.-Employee Benefits)*
Ronnie Wyble *(Adv. Consultant)*

Subsidiaries:

Equity Construction Co., Inc. **(1)**
1030 Clifton Ave.
Clifton, NJ 07013
Tel.: 201-779-4100 (100%)
S.I.C.: 1623

Prime Construction Co. **(1)**
P.O. Box 2700, 700 Rte. 46 E.
Fairfield, NJ 07007
Tel.: 201-882-1010 (100%)
S.I.C.: 1623

Prime-Florida, Inc. **(1)**
P.O. Box 2700, 700 Rte. 46 E.
Fairfield, NJ 07007 (80%)
S.I.C.: 1623

Prime Management Co., Inc. **(1)**
P.O. Box 2700, 700 Rte. 46 E.
Fairfield, NJ 07007
Tel.: 201-882-1010 (100%)
S.I.C.: 1623

Prime Hospitality Corp Limited Partnership **(1)**
700 Route 48 East
Fairfield, NJ 07006
Tel.: 201-882-1010
Earnings: $4,200,000
Approx.Rev.: $18,000,000
Fiscal Year-end: 12/31/90
Operation of 16 Holiday Inns in Maryland, Pennsylvania & Connecticut
S.I.C.: 7011; 5812

PRIME TANNING CO., INC.
Sullivan St.
Berwick, ME 03901
Mailing Address:
P.O. Box 713
Berwick, ME 03901
Tel.: 207-698-1100
Fax: 207-698-7768
Approx.Sls.: $75,000,000
Emp.: 650
Export
Leather Tanning
S.I.C.: 3111
Leonard D. Kaplan *(Chm. & Treas.)*
Kenneth Purdy *(Pres.)*
Steven A. Goldberg *(Chief Fin. Officer, V.P.-Fin. & Admin.)*
Samuel Rubin *(Exec. V.P.)*
Ralph J. Amabile, Jr. *(V.P.-Sls., Asian)*
Dan Fitzgerald *(V.P.-Quality Controll)*
Michael Kaplan *(V.P.-Upholstery)*
Steven Kaplan *(V.P.-Sls., Domestic)*
Eliseo Pombo *(V.P.-Mfg.)*
Jeff Chappell *(Controller)*
Lawrence M. Levinson *(Sec.)*
Bob Brewster *(Dir.-Pur.)*
Rich Euler *(Dir.-Human Resources)*

No. of Mfg. Plants/Facilities: 2
No. of U.S. Offices: 2

Outside Service Firm(s):

Schneider & Schneider*(Auditors)*
Boston, MA

Burns & Levinson*(Legal Firm)*
50 Milk St.
Boston, MA 02109
Tel.: 617-451-3300

First National Bank of Boston*(Major Banking Relationship)*
P.O. Box 644,
Boston, MA 02102-0644
Tel.: 617-575-2900
Fax: 617-575-2549

PRIME TECHNOLOGY, INC.
4936 Kendrick St., SE
Grand Rapids, MI 49512
Tel.: 616-942-2104
Tel.: 800-882-8196 **MI**
Fax: 616-942-2108
Year Founded: 1982
Assets: $2,462,934
Liabilities: $1,734,609
Net Worth: $728,325
Approx.Sls.: $35,000,000
Emp.: 29
Fiscal Year-end: 1/31/91
Import Export
Distributors Of High-Technology Machine Tools
S.I.C.: 5084
Phil Pachulski *(Chm. Bd. & Pres.)*
Sheila Pachulski *(V.P.-Support Services)*
Lynn Calhoun *(Chief Fin. Officer & Controller)*
Cliff Maine *(Corp. Counsel)*
Mark Koetje *(Gen. Sls. Mgr.)*
Brad Stevens *(Dir.-Purch.)*
Principal(s):
Phil Pachulski

No. of Mfg. Plants/Facilities: 3
No. of U.S. Offices: 3
No. of Foreign Offices: 1

Computer Systems/Hardware:
Compaq PC-Based

Outside Service Firm(s):

Deloitte & Touche*(Auditors)*
Greensboro, NC

Tolley, Fisher & VerWys*(Legal Firm)*
Grand Rapids, MI

Subsidiaries:

Abrasives, Inc. **(1)**
4936 Kendrick St.
Grand Rapids, MI 49512
Tel.: 616-942-8995
Emp.: 1
Distributor of Abrasives
S.I.C.: 5085
Howard Frischman *(Opers. Mgr.)*

Prime Technology, Inc. **(1)**
56 So. Park Blvd.
Greenwood, IN 46142
Tel.: 317-889-2222
Fax: 317-889-2226
Machine Tool Distributor
S.I.C.: 5084
Ron Blake *(Regional Sls. Mgr.)*

Prime Technology, Inc.—(Continued)

Prime Technology Inc. (1)
21665 Melrose Ave., Bldg. 7
Southfield, MI 48075
Tel.: 313-352-4950
Fax: 313-352-4953
Emp.: 5
Mark Koejte *(Gen. Mgr.-Sls.)*

PRIMUS INC.
3110 Kettering Blvd.
Dayton, OH 45439
Tel.: 513-294-6878 **DE**
Fax: 513-293-9591
Year Founded: 1956
Assets: $112,565,768
Liabilities: $92,296,683
Net Worth: $20,269,085
Approx.Sls.: $368,438,000
Emp.: 1,600
Fiscal Year-end: 2/ 1/92
Import
Wholesale Plumbing & Heating Supplies & Equipment; Electrical, Air Conditioning, Refrigeration, Fasteners; Management Consulting
S.I.C.: 8742; 5074
Richard F. Schiewetz *(Pres.)*
Gerald Padilla *(V.P.)*
Richard Schwartz *(V.P.)*
Jack W. Johnston *(Treas.)*
Jim Marshall *(Sec.)*

No. of U.S. Offices: 200

Computer Systems/Hardware:
IBM

Outside Service Firm(s):

Dapsco Inc.*(Auditors)*
Dayton, OH

Bank One*(Major Banking Relationship)*
Kettering Tower
Dayton, OH 45401
Tel.: 513-449-8600

PRINCE CORPORATION
One Prince Center
Holland, MI 49423
Tel.: 616-392-5151
Fax: 616-394-8099
Approx.Sls.: $100,000,000
Emp.: 1,300
Visers For Automotives
S.I.C.: 3465
Edgar Prince *(Chm. Bd.)*
John Spoehof *(Pres.)*
Walter Jones *(V.P.-Fin.)*
Fred Sotok *(V.P.-Mfg.)*
Roger Baas *(Mgr.-Sls.)*

PRINCE GARDNER INCORPORATED
6245 Lemay Ferry Rd.
Saint Louis, MO 63129
Tel.: 314-487-3100
Fax: 314-487-7709
Approx.Sls.: $45,000,000
Emp.: 1,500
Fiscal Year-end: 12/31/90
Men's & Ladies' Personal Leather Goods
S.I.C.: 3171; 3172
Thomas Fey *(Pres.)*
R.L. Ryman *(Sr. V.P.-Sls. & Mktg.)*
Joe Burris, Jr. *(V.P.-Fin.)*
Larry Carney *(V.P.-Sls. & Mktg.-Royalle Div.)*

PRINCE MANUFACTURING, INC.
3 Princess Rd.
Lawrenceville, NJ 08648-2398
Mailing Address:
P.O. Box 2031
Princeton, NJ 08540
Tel.: 609-896-2500
Tel.: 800-283-6647 **NJ**
Fax: 609-895-7092
Year Founded: 1970
Approx.Sls.: $190,000,000
Emp.: 525
Fiscal Year-end: 9/30/91
Manufacture Tennis Equipment; Prince Ball Machines, Racquets, Shoes & Apparel
S.I.C.: 3949
John Sultivan *(Chm. Bd.)*
Arthur M. Bylin *(Pres.)*
George Meaney *(V.P.-Fin. & Sec.)*
David A. Haggerty *(V.P.-Mktg.)*
Jeff Rothstein *(V.P.-Intl. Sls.)*
Clifford R. Martin *(Treas.)*
Paul Kimaid *(Controller)*
Richard M. Miller *(Gen. Counsel)*
Mike Grafeld *(Dir.-Opers.)*
John McBride *(Dir.-Pur.)*

Computer Systems/Hardware:
Hewlett-Packard

Outside Service Firm(s):

Ernst & Young*(Auditors)*
202 Carnegie Center
Princeton, NJ 08640
Tel.: 609-243-0303
Fax: 609-243-9322

Subsidiaries:

American Ball Manufacturing (1)
1225 Tappan Circle
Carrollton, TX 75006
Tel.: 214-242-0300
Approx.Sls.: $1,000,000
Emp.: 24
Mfr. of Golf Balls, Baseballs, Footballs & Basketballs
S.I.C.: 3949
William V. Brown *(Pres.)*
Gary T. Mackey *(Sr. V.P.-Mfg.)*
Steve Spradlin *(Controller)*
Eddie French *(Natl. Sls. & Mktg. Mgr.)*

Ektelon Corp. (1)
8929 Aero Dr.
San Diego, CA 92123
Tel.: 619-560-0066
Fax: 619-492-9753
Approx.Sls.: $25,000,000
Emp.: 155
Fiscal Year-end: 9/30/90
Manufacturer of Racquetball Equipment & Related Accessories
S.I.C.: 3949
Norm Peck *(Pres.)*
Gil Vieira *(V.P.-Sls.)*
Brian Shaputis *(Controller)*
Lenita Colburn *(Mktg. Services Dir.)*
Tom Odisho *(Mgr.-Adv.)*
Frank Wolski *(Matls. Mgr.)*

Grafalloy Inc. (1)
1020 N. Marshall Ave.
El Cajon, CA
Tel.: 619-562-1020
Sporting Equipment
S.I.C.: 3949

Langert Golf Co., Inc. (1)
2774 Loker Ave. W.
Carlsbad, CA 92008
Sporting Equipment
S.I.C.: 3949
Peter C. Brooks *(Chief Exec. Officer)*

PRINCETON PARTNERS, INC.
2 Research Way, Princeton Forrestal Center
Princeton, NJ 08540
Tel.: 609-452-8500
Fax: 609-452-7212
Year Founded: 1965
Approx.Billings: $10,500,000
Emp.: 17
Consumer, Financial & Healthcare
Catherine A. Mathis *(Pres.)*
Thomas Sullivan *(Exec. V.P.)*

PRINCEVILLE CORPORATION
Princeville Center, 5-4280 Kuhio Hwy.
Princeville, HI 96722
Mailing Address:
P.O. Box 3040, Princeville Contract Station
Princeville, HI 96722
Tel.: 808-826-3040 **CO**
Fax: 808-826-9592
Year Founded: 1979
Assets: $77,102,383
Liabilities: $37,456,248
Net Worth: $39,646,135
Approx.Sls.: $17,389,708
Emp.: 175
Fiscal Year-end: 11/30/88
Resort Operations; Real Estate Development & Sales
S.I.C.: 6531; 7011; 1522; 4581
Christopher C. Skase *(Chm. Bd.)*
John E. Tabart *(Pres. & Chief Exec. Officer)*
Alan B. Davis *(Chief Oper. Officer)*
Walter W. Challenger *(V.P.-Fin. & Sec.)*
Thomas W. Giles *(V.P.-Real Estate Opers.)*
John R. Held *(Treas.)*

Outside Service Firm(s):

Coopers & Lybrand*(Auditors)*
Pacific Tower, 1001 Bishop St., Ste. 2500
Honolulu, HI 96813-3668
Tel.: 808-531-3400

Cades, Schutte, Fleming & Wright*(Legal Firm)*
P.O. Box 939, 1000 Bishop St.
Honolulu, HI 96813
Tel.: 808-521-9200

Subsidiaries:

Princeville Hotel Corporation (1)
Princeville Center, 5-4280 Kuhio Hwy.
Princeville, HI 96722
Tel.: 808-826-3040 (100%)
Fax: 808-826-9592
Hotel Mngmt.
S.I.C.: 1522; 7011
Alan B. Davis *(Chief Oper. Officer)*

Princeville Management Corporation (1)
Princeville Center, 5-4280 Kuhio Hwy.
Princeville, HI 96722
Tel.: 808-826-3040 (100%)
Fax: 808-826-9592
Emp.: 15
Condo Mngmt.
S.I.C.: 6531
Alan B. Davis *(Chief Oper. Officer)*

Princeville Realty Corporation (1)
Princeville Center, 5-4280 Kuhio Hwy.
Princeville, HI 96722
Tel.: 808-826-3040 (100%)
Fax: 808-826-9592
Real Estate Brokerage
S.I.C.: 6531
Alan B. Davis *(Chief Oper. Officer)*

Princeville Utilities Company, Inc. (1)
Princeville Center, 5-4280 Kuhio Hwy.
Princeville, HI 96722
Tel.: 808-826-3040 (100%)
Fax: 808-826-9592
Emp.: 5
Public Utility
S.I.C.: 4941
Alan B. David *(Chief Oper. Officer)*

Princeville Water Systems, Inc. (1)
Princeville Center, 5-4280 Kuhio Hwy.
Princeville, HI 96722
Tel.: 808-826-3040 (100%)
Fax: 808-826-9592
Public Utility
S.I.C.: 4941
Alan B. David *(Chief Oper. Officer)*

THE PRINCIPAL FINANCIAL GROUP
711 High St.
Des Moines, IA 50392-0150
Tel.: 515-247-5111 **IA**
Fax: 515-247-5930
Year Founded: 1879
Assets: $31,499,400,000
Earnings: $330,000,000
Liabilities: $30,175,800,000
Net Worth: $1,323,600,000
Approx.Sls.: $7,333,300,000
Emp.: 12,153
Fiscal Year-end: 12/31/91
Mutual Life Insurance Company
S.I.C.: 6311; 6799; 7389; 6331; 6324
Corporate Giving Program: Support Arts & Culture, Civic & Community, Education, Health & Human Services & United Way; Applications Accepted Throughout Year; Submit Written Proposal Outlining Purpose, Anticipated Budget, Proof of Tax Exemption, Audited Financial Statements
Employee Matching Gifts Program: Matching Grants to Higher Education for Employees & Qualified Agents, Brokers & their Spouses; Matching Grants to United Way for Qualified Agents & Brokers Only
G. David Hurd *(Chm. Bd., Pres. & Chief Exec. Officer)*
R.W. Ehrle *(Exec. V.P.)*
T.M. Hutchison *(Exec. V.P.)*
Ray Crabtree *(Sr. V.P.)*
Dave Kauf *(Sr. V.P.-Corp. & Fin. Service Devel.))*
C.E. Rohm *(Sr. V.P.-Individual Ins. Opers.)*
Don G. Keown *(V.P.-Human Resources)*
William Knowles *(V.P.-Commercial Real Estate)*
John S. Martin *(V.P.)*
Gregg Narber *(V.P. & Gen. Counsel)*
Walter J. Walsh *(V.P.-Corp. Rels.)*
Joyce Hoffman *(Sec.)*
Jerry G. Wisgerhof *(Treas.)*
Robert Delaney *(Dir.-Data Processing)*
Caesar Smith *(Dir.-Training & EEO Programs)*
Mark Tezak *(Asst. Dir.-Travel & Meeting Services)*
Debra J. Jensen *(Mgr.-Community Rels.)*
Mary O'Keefe *(Mgr.-Media Rels.)*
Janice Prosperi *(Mgr.-Adv.)*

Computer Systems/Hardware:
IBM Systems 3090-200, 3084 & 4381

Outside Service Firm(s):

Ernst & Young*(Auditors)*
317 6th Ave., Ste. 1100
Des Moines, IA 50309
Tel.: 515-243-2727

Principal Mutual Life Insurance Co.*(Group Insurer)*
Des Moines, IA

Norwest Bank Minnesota, N.A.*(Major Banking Relationship)*
Des Moines, IA

Subsidiaries:

Delaware Charter Guarantee & Trust Co. (1)
1013 Center Rd.
Wilmington, DE 19805
Tel.: 302-995-2131
Pension Management
S.I.C.: 7389
D.R. Butler *(Chm.)*
S.B. Tily III *(Pres.)*

HMO Iowa, Inc. (1)
1002 1st Interstate Bank Bldg., Locust at Sixth
Des Moines, IA 50309
Tel.: 515-244-6300
Health Maintenance Organization
S.I.C.: 6324
R.H. Neil *(Chm. Bd.)*
Janice Prosperi *(Mgr.-Adv.)*

Health Care Preferred (1)
1002 1st Interstate Bldg., Locust at 6th
Des Moines, IA 50309
Tel.: 515-244-6300

Health Maintenance Organization
S.I.C.: 6324
R.H. Neil *(Chm.)*

Invista Capital Management Corp. **(1)**
Hub Tower, 699 Walnut St.
Des Moines, IA 50309
Tel.: 515-247-5111 (100%)
Investment Advisors
S.I.C.: 6799
R.W. Ehrle *(Chm.)*
Janice Prosperi *(Mgr.-Adv.)*

Patrician Associates, Inc. **(1)**
711 High St.
Des Moines, IA 50309
Tel.: 515-247-5111 (100%)
Investment Company
S.I.C.: 6799
R.W. Ehrle *(Chm.)*

Petula Associates, Ltd. **(1)**
711 High St.
Des Moines, IA 50309
Tel.: 515-247-5111 (100%)
Investment Company
S.I.C.: 6799
R.W. Ehrle *(Chm.)*

Principal Casualty Insurance Company **(1)**
711 High St.
Des Moines, IA 50309
Tel.: 515-247-5111 (100%)
Insurance
S.I.C.: 6331
R. Crabtree *(Chm.)*

Principal Development Associates, Inc. **(1)**
711 High St.
Des Moines, IA 50309
Tel.: 515-247-5111 (100%)
Investment Company
S.I.C.: 6799
R.W. Ehrle *(Chm.)*

The Principal/EGT Financial Corporation **(1)**
2001 Bryan Tower, Ste. 2300
Dallas, TX 75201
S.I.C.: 6159
T.F. O'Toole *(Chm.)*

Principal Health Care, Inc. **(1)**
1801 Rockville Pike, Ste. 601
Rockville, MD 20852
Tel.: 301-881-1033
Health Care Marketing Organization
S.I.C.: 7389
K. Linde *(Pres. & Chief Exec. Officer)*
Janice Prosperi *(Mgr.-Adv.)*

Principal Marketing Services, Inc. **(1)**
711 High St.
Des Moines, IA 50309
Tel.: 515-247-5111 (100%)
Insurance Agencies
S.I.C.: 6411
C.E. Rohm *(Chm.)*

Principal Life Insurance Company **(1)**
711 High St.
Des Moines, IA 50309
Tel.: 515-247-5111 (100%)
Insurance
S.I.C.: 6311
C.E. Rohm *(Chm.)*

Principal Management Inc. **(1)**
711 High St.
Des Moines, IA 50309
Tel.: 515-247-5111 (100%)
Management Company
S.I.C.: 7389
Dave Kauf *(Chm.)*
Janice Prosperi *(Mgr.-Adv.)*

Principal Mutual Life Insurance Co. **(1)**
711 High St.
Des Moines, IA 50309-0001
Tel.: 515-247-5111
Fax: 515-247-5390
S.I.C.: 6311
G. David Hurd *(Chm., Pres. & Chief Exec. Officer)*
Janice Prosperi *(Mgr.-Adv.)*

Principal National Life Insurance Company **(1)**
711 High St.
Des Moines, IA 50309
Tel.: 515-247-5111 (100%)
Insurance
S.I.C.: 6311
C.E. Rohm *(Chm.)*

Principal Residential Advisors **(1)**
379 Thornall St.
Edison, NJ 08837
Tel.: 908-548-0101
Fax: 908-548-0286
Mortgage Broker
S.I.C.: 6162

Princor Financial Services Corporation **(1)**
711 High St.
Des Moines, IA 50309
Tel.: 515-247-5111 (100%)
Equity Services
S.I.C.: 7389
Dave Kauf *(Chm.)*
Janice Prosperi *(Mgr.-Adv.)*

PRINT NORTHWEST
4918 20th St.E.
Fife, WA 98424
Mailing Address:
P.O. Box 1418
Tacoma, WA 98401
Tel.: 206-922-9393
Tel.: 800-451-5742
Fax: 206-922-3383
Approx.Sls.: $14,000,000
Emp.: 125
Commercial Printing, Lithographic
S.I.C.: 2752
Brian Dammeier *(Pres.)*
Thomas Foley *(Chief Fin. Officer & V.P.)*
Janet A. Dammeier *(V.P.)*
Kurt B. Dammeier *(V.P.-Sls. & Mktg.)*
Les Gallamore *(V.P.)*

Outside Service Firm(s):

Knight, Vale & Gregory*(Auditors)*
Tacoma, WA

PRINT-O-TAPE
755 Tower Rd.
Mundelein, IL 60060
Mailing Address:
P.O. Box 308
Libertyville, IL 60048
Tel.: 708-362-1476 **IL**
Fax: 708-949-7449
Approx.Sls.: $10,000,000
Emp.: 72
Pressure Sensitive Tapes Made From Purchased Materials; Unprinted Gummed Labels Made From Purchased Materials
S.I.C.: 2672
Carl J. Walliser *(Pres.)*
Charles Stickels *(V.P.-Mfg.)*
Andrew Walliser *(V.P.)*

Outside Service Firm(s):

Edward Jacks & Co.*(Auditors)*
Bannockburn, IL

First of America Bank*(Major Banking Relationship)*
Libertyville, IL

PRINTCO, INC.
1321 Van Deinse
Greenville, MI 48838
Tel.: 616-754-3672
Fax: 616-754-7741
Emp.: 250
Commercial Printing, Lithographic
S.I.C.: 2752
John Stafford *(Chm. Bd.)*
James Pentecost *(Pres.)*
Jon Anderson *(V.P.-Mfg.)*
Richard Ellafrits *(V.P.-Fin.)*
Michael Traidman *(V.P.-Sls. & Mktg.)*

Outside Service Firm(s):

Arthur Andersen & Co.*(Auditors)*
Grand Rapids, MI

David Hecht*(Legal Firm)*
Grand Rapids, MI

Michigan National Bank*(Major Banking Relationship)*
77 Monroe Center
Grand Rapids, MI 49501
Tel.: 616-451-7600

PRINTED CIRCUIT CORPORATION
10 Micro Dr.
Woburn, MA 01801
Tel.: 617-935-9570 **MA**
Fax: 617-933-5124
Year Founded: 1961
Sales Range: $20-39 Million
Emp.: 210
Fiscal Year-end: 10/31/91
Printed Circuit Boards
S.I.C.: 3672
Peter Sarmanian *(Chm. Bd. & Chief Exec. Officer)*
Stephen Stepanian *(Pres. & Chief Oper. Officer)*
Robert Garabedian *(V.P.-Engrng.)*
Charles Krikorian *(Natl. Sls. Mgr.)*
Donald Tavano *(Mgr.-Personnel)*
Joe Corroon *(Pur. Agent)*

No. of Mfg. Plants/Facilities: 1

Outside Service Firm(s):

Bingham, Dana & Gould*(Legal Firm)*
150 Federal St.
Boston, MA 02110
Tel.: 617-951-8000
Fax: 617-951-8736

PRINTING HOUSE, INC.
P.O. Box 310
Quincy, FL 32353
Tel.: 904-875-1500
Tel.: 800-277-7687 **FL**
Fax: 904-875-1515
Year Founded: 1972
Approx.Sls.: $28,000,000
Emp.: 392
Fiscal Year-end: 12/31/91
Commercial Printing, Magazines
S.I.C.: 2752; 2741
Delbert M. Archibald *(Chm. Bd.)*
Robert Prince *(Pres.)*
Leon H. Cassels *(Chief Fin. Officer & V.P.-Fin.)*
Ronald K. Sauls *(Exec. V.P.)*
Allen Harrod *(V.P.-Mfg.)*
W. Needham *(V.P.-Corp. Services)*
Kathy R. Archibald *(Sec. & Treas.)*
Don Odham *(Dir.-Commercial Sls.)*
Harry Jones *(Mgr.-Pur.)*

No. of U.S. Offices: 2

Computer Systems/Hardware:
IBM; MAC

Outside Service Firm(s):

Williams, Cox Weidner & Cox*(Auditors)*
Tallahassee, FL

Roberts, Boggett, LaFace & Richard*(Legal Firm)*
Tallahassee, FL

Greenberg, Traurig, Hoffman, Lipoff, Rosen & Quentel, P.A.*(Legal Firm)*
1221 Brickell Ave.
Miami, FL 33131
Tel.: 305-579-0500

NationsBank Florida*(Major Banking Relationship)*
Tallahassee, FL

Pro Clinica

PRO CLINICA INC.
51 E. 42nd St.
New York, NY 10017
Tel.: 212-856-6440
Fax: 212-856-6453
Year Founded: 1976
Approx.Billings: $24,200,000
Emp.: 26
Medical & Pharmaceutical Adv.
Mel Snyder *(Pres.)*
Robin L. Hulton *(Exec. V.P., Gen. Mgr.)*
Leon Soriano *(V.P., Intl.)*
Laurie Edelman *(Controller)*

THE PRO CORPORATION
296 Nonotuck St.
Florence, MA 01060
Tel.: 413-584-1780 **DE**
Fax: 413-586-5762
Year Founded: 1845
Approx.Sls.: $18,000,000
Emp.: 225
Fiscal Year-end: 12/31/90
Export
Custom Injection Molding
S.I.C.: 3089
Terry Minnick *(Chm. Bd., Pres. & Chief Exec. Officer)*
Edward R. Cilento *(V.P.-Opers.)*
Walter Erwin *(V.P.-Fin. & Admin.)*
Daniel W. Kerkhoff *(V.P.-Mktg. & Sls.)*
Wayne Tangel *(Dir.-Quality Assurance)*
John Lankargo *(Mgr.-Pur.)*
Betty Trumble *(Mgr.-Personnel)*
Dorrie Ignatovich *(Mktg. Coord.)*

Principal(s):
Terry Minnick

No. of Mfg. Plants/Facilities: 1
No. of U.S. Offices: 1

Computer Systems/Hardware:
Hewlett-Packard

Outside Service Firm(s):

Grant Thornton*(Auditors)*
53 State St.
Boston, MA 02109
Tel.: 617-723-7900

A.W. Borawski Insurance*(Commercial Insurance Carrier)*
Northampton, MA 01060

Blue Cross of Massachusetts, Inc.*(Group Insurer)*
Boston, MA

Hutchins & Wheeler*(Legal Firm)*
100 Federal Street
Boston, MA 02110
Tel.: 617-951-6600
Fax: 617-951-1295

U.S. Trust Co.*(Major Banking Relationship)*
30 Court St.
Boston, MA 02108

PRO HARDWARE, INC.
Intl. Mktg. Hdqtrs.-Suite 360,
9137 E. Mineral Cir.-Box 6585
Englewood, CO 80155-6585
Tel.: 303-792-3000
Fax: 303-792-5589
Year Founded: 1956
Sales Range: $1 Billion +
Emp.: 35
Fiscal Year-end: 12/31/91
Hardware Distributor
S.I.C.: 5072

Pro Hardware, Inc.—(Continued)

Corporate Giving Program: Committee Reviews All Requests for any type of Donations-(Very Limited Budget)
Gary D. Cosgrave *(Chm. & Chief Exec. Officer)*
Hazel Cosgrove *(Vice Chm., Treas., & Corp. Sec.)*
Richard Paige *(Sr. V.P. & Chief Oper. Officer)*
Maria Forster *(Chief Fin. Officer & V.P.)*
William O. Kugler *(V.P.-Personnel & Wholesale Programs)*
John M. McGraw *(V.P.-Pro Stores Program)*
Karen Fox *(Dir.-Adv.)*
John Haste *(Dir.-Field Mktg.)*
Lisa Chesen *(Controller)*
Monte Buckley *(Mgr.-MIS)*
Karen Fox *(Mgr.-Adv.)*

Principal(s):
Gary D. Cosgrave
Hazel Cosgrove

Computer Systems/Hardware:
IBM PC Compatible

Outside Service Firm(s):

Parker, Chapin, Flattau & Klimpl*(Legal Firm)*
1211 Avenue of the Americas
New York, NY 10036
Tel.: 212-840-6200

PRO-LINE CORPORATION
2121 Panoramic Circle
Dallas, TX 75212
Tel.: 214-631-4247
Fax: 214-634-8155
Approx.Sls.: $26,000,000
Emp.: 320
Mfr. of Ethnic Hair Products
S.I.C.: 3999
Comer J. Cottrell *(Chm. Bd. & Pres.)*
Alfred Baker *(V.P.-Fin.)*
Renee C. Brown *(V.P.-Mktg. & Sls.)*
Eric Brown *(V.P.-Systems & Plng.)*
Doug Mark *(V.P.-Matl. Opers.)*
Felicia McAfee *(Dir.-Sls.)*
Til Pettis *(Dir.-Human Resources)*

Outside Service Firm(s):

Mahomes & Associates*(Legal Firm)*
Dallas, TX

Continental Bank, N.A.*(Major Banking Relationship)*
Dallas, TX

PRO-LOG CORPORATION
2555 Garden Rd.
Monterey, CA 93940
Tel.: 408-372-4593
Fax: 408-646-3568
Year Founded: 1972
Approx.Sls.: $15,000,000
Emp.: 100
Export
Manufacture Industrial Computer Systems
S.I.C.: 3571; 3577
Leland E. Dake *(Chm. Bd.)*
Richard P. McClellan *(Pres. & Chief Exec. Officer)*
Arthur W. Pasquinelli *(Chief Fin. Officer)*
Paul Virgo *(Dir.-Mktg. & Adv.)*

No. of Mfg. Plants/Facilities: 1
No. of U.S. Offices: 5

Computer Systems/Hardware:
Hewlett Packard 3000; IBM PC

Outside Service Firm(s):

Coopers & Lybrand*(Auditors)*
10 Almaden Blvd., Ste. 1600
San Jose, CA 95113
Tel.: 408-295-1020
Fax: 408-292-1382

Chubb Group*(Commercial Insurance Carrier)*
Minneapolis, MN

Wilson, Sonsini, Goodrich & Rosati*(Legal Firm)*
2 Palo Alto Square, Ste. 900
Palo Alto, CA 94306
Tel.: 415-493-9300
Fax: 415-493-6811

Silicon Valley Bank*(Major Banking Relationship)*
3000 Lakeside Dr.
Santa Clara, CA 95054

PRO MEDIA, INC.
160 Gould St.
Needham, MA 02194
Tel.: 617-455-8910
Fax: 617-455-8613
Year Founded: 1980
Approx.Billings: $40,000,000
Emp.: 22
Consumer & Political Media Management, Strategic Mktg., Media Planning & Buying
Nancy Ryan Greenberg *(Pres.)*
Rosemary Bell *(Sr. V.P.)*
Susan Ryan *(V.P., Dir. Political Div.)*
Les Greenberg *(V.P., Fin.)*
Tony Busa *(V.P.)*
Carol Cleveland *(V.P.)*
Joy Mildner *(Exec. Asst.)*

THE PRO-QUIP CORPORATION
8522 E. 61st St.
Tulsa, OK 74133
Tel.: 918-250-8522 **OK**
Fax: 918-250-6915
Year Founded: 1969
Emp.: 200
Fiscal Year-end: 6/30/90
Engineering, Design, Fabrication and Field Construction of Machinery For Process Industries
S.I.C.: 1629
J.D. Brandon *(Chm. Bd. & Pres.)*
J.E. Boles *(V.P.)*
D.M. Chernovetz *(V.P.)*
C.A. Daw *(V.P.)*
A.L. Hensley *(V.P.)*
R.S. Palmer *(V.P.)*
L.E. Reiners *(V.P.)*

No. of Mfg. Plants/Facilities: 1
No. of U.S. Offices: 1

Computer Systems/Hardware:
Prime

Outside Service Firm(s):

Arthur Andersen & Co.*(Auditors)*
901 Main St., Ste. 5600
Dallas, TX 75202
Tel.: 214-741-8300

Jackson & Walker*(Legal Firm)*
Tulsa, OK

PROCESSED PLASTIC COMPANY
1001 Aucutt Rd.
Montgomery, IL 60538
Tel.: 708-892-7981 **DE**
Fax: 708-892-6056
Year Founded: 1948
Approx.Sls.: $43,000,000
Emp.: 400
Fiscal Year-end: 12/31/90
Import Export
Toys
S.I.C.: 3944
Robert S. Bergman *(Pres. & Treas.)*
David R. Bergman *(Exec. V.P. & Sec.)*
Ronald F. Surma *(Chief Fin. Officer & Controller)*
David C. Bergman *(V.P.-Prod. Devel.)*
Jeffrey W. Soulsby *(V.P.-Sls.)*
Ritch Wingo *(Mgr.-Data Processing)*
Eugene Balis *(Pur. Agent)*

Principal(s):
Robert S. Bergman
David R. Bergman
The Bergman Family

No. of Mfg. Plants/Facilities: 2
No. of U.S. Offices: 2

Computer Systems/Hardware:
IBM AS/400

Outside Service Firm(s):

Blackman Kallick Bartelstein*(Auditors)*
300 Riverside Plaza
Chicago, IL 60606
Tel.: 312-207-1040

Drendel, Schanlaber, Horwitz, Tatnall & McCracken*(Legal Firm)*
Chicago, IL

Harris Bank*(Major Banking Relationship)*
Chicago, IL

PROCTOR & GARDNER ADVERTISING, INC.
111 E. Wacker Dr., Ste. 321
Chicago, IL 60601
Tel.: 312-565-5400 **IL**
Fax: 312-565-5450
Year Founded: 1970
Approx.Billings: $12,500,000
Emp.: 20
Advertising Agency
S.I.C.: 7311
Barbara G. Proctor *(Pres. & Chief Exec. Officer)*
George Miller *(Exec. V.P. & Supvr.-Mngmt.)*
David S. Mann *(Sec.)*
Rachelle Zupnik *(Controller)*

Computer Systems/Hardware:
IBM PC

Outside Service Firm(s):

McBride, Baker & Coles*(Legal Firm)*
500 W. Madison St., 40th Fl.
Chicago, IL 60606
Tel.: 312-715-5700

South Shore Bank*(Major Banking Relationship)*
Chicago, IL

PRODUCERS CO-OP ASSOCIATION, INC.
300 Buffalo St.
Girard, KS 66743
Mailing Address:
P.O. Box 323
Girard, KS 66743
Tel.: 316-724-8241 **KS**
Fax: 316-724-8243
Year Founded: 1948
Assets: $5,785,923
Earnings: $157,665
Liabilities: $356,000
Net Worth: $5,429,923
Approx.Sls.: $16,800,000
Emp.: 46
Fiscal Year-end: 5/31/91
Agricultural Products Wholesale
S.I.C.: 5153; 5191; 2048; 0723; 4221
Steve Murphy *(Chm. Bd.)*
Kenneth M. Taylor *(Pres.)*
Donald Ralph *(Sec.)*
Wayne Wigger *(Gen. Mgr.)*

No. of Mfg. Plants/Facilities: 2
No. of U.S. Offices: 1

Computer Systems/Hardware:
IBM

Outside Service Firm(s):

Lindburg & Vogel*(Auditors)*
Hutchinson, KS

Farmland Mutual Insurance Co.*(Commercial Insurance Carrier)*
Kansas City, MO

Blue Cross & Blue Shield of Kansas*(Group Insurer)*
1133 S.W. Topeka
Topeka, KS 66612

Girard National Bank*(Major Banking Relationship)*
Girard, KS

National Bank for Cooperatives*(Major Banking Relationship)*
Wichita, KS

PRODUCERS LIVESTOCK
170 W. Cudahy Ln.
North Salt Lake, UT 84054
Mailing Address:
P.O. Box 540477
North Salt Lake City, UT 84054
Tel.: 801-292-2424
Fax: 801-292-2426
Year Founded: 1935
Earnings: $342,540
Approx.Sls.: $298,400,000
Emp.: 400
Livestock Marketing
S.I.C.: 5154
Mike Urrutia *(Chm. Bd. & Pres.)*
Clair Okeleberry *(Chief Exec. Officer, Treas. & Gen. Mgr.)*
John Butler *(Controller)*

Computer Systems/Hardware:
IBM System 34

Outside Service Firm(s):

Sunniville, Griffin & Smith*(Auditors)*
Salt Lake City, UT

First Security Bank of Utah*(Major Banking Relationship)*
Salt Lake City, UT

Mutual Benefit Life Insurance*(Pension Manager)*
520 Broad St.
Newark, NJ 07102-3184
Tel.: 201-481-8000

PRODUCERS RICE MILL INC.
518 E. Harrison St.
Stuttgart, AR 72160
Mailing Address:
P.O. Box 461
Stuttgart, AR 72160
Tel.: 501-673-4444 **AR**
Telex: 536-455 Producers, STGT
Fax: 501-673-8131
Year Founded: 1943
Assets: $68,000,000
Liabilities: $38,000,000
Net Worth: $30,000,000
Approx.Sls.: $150,000,000
Emp.: 425
Fiscal Year-end: 7/31/92
Export
Farmers' Cooperative; Rice Drying, Milling & Processing
S.I.C.: 0112; 0723; 5149; 2044; 5153
Gary Sebree *(Chm. Bd.)*
Jerry Hoskyn *(Vice Chm.)*
Keith Glover *(Pres. & Gen. Mgr.)*
Kent Lockwood *(Chief Fin. Officer & V.P.-Fin.)*
Marvin Baden *(V.P.-Mktg. & Sls., Sec. & Treas.)*
John Grabbe *(V.P.-Opers.)*
Gary Reifeiss *(V.P.-Mktg. & Consumer Prods.)*
Don King *(Dir.-Human Resources)*

No. of Mfg. Plants/Facilities: 12
No. of U.S. Offices: 1

Computer Systems/Hardware:
IBM System AS-400

Outside Service Firm(s):

Erwin & Company*(Auditors)*
Little Rock, AR

Ranger Insurance Co.*(Commercial Insurance Carrier)*
Houston, TX

Co-Bank*(Investment Banker)*
Atlanta, GA

Malcolm Smith*(Legal Firm)*
Stuttgart, AR

Citibank N.A.*(Major Banking Relationship)*
Corporate Trust Services, 399 Park Ave.
New York, NY 10043
Tel.: 212-559-1605

Co-Bank*(Major Banking Relationship)*
Atlanta, GA

First Tennessee Bank, N.A.*(Major Banking Relationship)*
Memphis, TN

Liberty Life Assurance Company*(Pension Manager)*
Boston, MA

PRODUCTION MACHINERY CORPORATION
8500 Station St.
Mentor, OH 44060
Mailing Address:
P.O. Box 898,
Mentor, OH 44061-0898
Tel.: 216-255-3437 **OH**
Telex: 6873051
Fax: 216-255-3430
Year Founded: 1955
Approx.Sls.: $56,000,000
Emp.: 81
Fiscal Year-end: 9/30/91
Export
Manufacture Coil Processing Lines for Steel Mills, Metal Strip Processors
S.I.C.: 3549; 3547; 3535; 3541
Donald W. Games *(Chm. Bd.)*
Sam Friedlander *(Pres. & Chief Exec. Officer)*
John R. Deering *(Exec. V.P.-Fin., Chief Oper. Officer & Legal Officer)*
Bruce W. Eckstein *(V.P.-Sls.)*
Terry Robinson *(V.P.-Engrng.)*
Mario Mulig *(V.P.-Acctg. & Controller)*
William A. Tango *(Dir.-Pur.)*
Carol Dodson *(Personnel Admin.)*
David W. Hill *(Mgr.-Sls.)*

No. of U.S. Offices: 1
No. of Foreign Offices: 1

Computer Systems/Hardware:
Radio Shack

Outside Service Firm(s):

S. R. Snodgrass & Co.*(Auditors)*
Beaver Falls, PA

Pittsburgh National Bank*(International Bank Affiliate)*
5th Ave. & Wood St.
Pittsburgh, PA 15222
Tel.: 412-355-3000

Medical Life Insurance Co.*(Group Insurer)*
Cleveland, OH

Bank One*(Investment Banker)*
Painesville, OH

Pittsburgh National Bank*(Investment Banker)*
5th Ave. & Wood St.
Pittsburgh, PA 15222
Tel.: 412-355-3000

Hahn, Loeser & Parks*(Legal Firm)*
Natl. City E. 6 Bldg.
Cleveland, OH 44114
Tel.: 216-621-0150

Bank One*(Major Banking Relationship)*
Painesville, OH

The Principal Financial Group*(Pension Manager)*
711 High St.
Des Moines, IA 50309
Tel.: 800-543-4015

Subsidiary:

Mentor AGVS, Inc. **(1)**
8500 Station St.
Mentor, OH 44060
Tel.: 216-255-4051
Automatic Guided Vehicle Systems
S. Friedlander *(Pres.)*
J. Deering *(Exec. V.P.)*
M. Urban *(Gen. Mgr.)*

PRODUCTION MANAGEMENT COMPANIES, INC.
2439 Manhattan Blvd., Ste. 400
Harvey, LA 70058
Mailing Address:
P.O. Box 44
Harvey, LA 70059
Tel.: 504-366-3594
Fax: 504-366-4909
Year Founded: 1971
Assets: $12,300,000
Net Worth: $12,300,000
Approx.Sls.: $48,000,000
Emp.: 700
Oil & Gas Property Management; Fabrication & Construction of Production Facilities
S.I.C.: 1389; 4925; 3499; 3822; 3731; 8711; 1382
Michael C. Sport *(Chm. Bd., Pres. & Chief Exec. Officer)*
John D. Demarest *(Chief Fin. Officer, V.P. & Treas.)*
Stan Ellington *(V.P.-Corp. Devel.)*
Eldon Falgout *(Controller)*
Ralph Capdeville *(Dir.-Personnel)*
Carol Johnson *(Dir.-Data Processing)*
Michael Seymour *(Dir.-Mktg.)*
Marie Keeton *(Mgr.-Admin.)*
Principal(s):
Michael C. Sport

No. of Mfg. Plants/Facilities: 4
No. of U.S. Offices: 3

Computer Systems/Hardware:
IBM AS/400

Outside Service Firm(s):

Arthur Andersen & Co.*(Auditors)*
201 St. Charles Ave., Ste. 4500
New Orleans, LA 70170

Metropolitan Life Insurance Co.*(Group Insurer)*
Chattanooga, TN

Lemle, Kelleher, Kohlmayer & Matthews*(Legal Firm)*
New Orleans, LA

Hibernia National Bank*(Major Banking Relationship)*
New Orleans, LA

Subsidiaries:

Production Management Control Systems, Inc. **(1)**
1865 Industrial Hwy.
Harvey, LA 70058
Tel.: 504-340-3100
E. Patrick Ward *(Chief Oper. Officer)*

Production Management Corporation **(1)**
1980 Post Oak Blvd.
Houston, TX 77056
Tel.: 713-629-1820
Oscar L. Atkins *(Chief Oper. Officer)*

Production Management Industries, Inc. **(1)**
2804 Peters Rd.
Harvey, LA 70058
Tel.: 504-363-5900
Brian A. LaCour *(Chief Oper. Officer)*

Production Management Structural Systems, Inc. **(1)**
15160 Intracoastal Dr.
New Orleans, LA 70189
Tel.: 504-254-2135
Frank L. Anastasio, Jr. *(Chief Oper. Officer)*

PRODUCTION TOOL SUPPLY CO.
8655 E. 8 Mile Rd.
Warren, MI 48089
Tel.: 313-755-7770
Tel.: 800-366-2600 **MI**
Fax: 313-755-2156
Year Founded: 1951
Approx.Sls.: $100,000,000
Emp.: 247
Import Export
Wholesale Industrial Supplies & Tool Steels
S.I.C.: 5085
D. Dan Kahn *(Chm. Bd. & Chief Exec. Officer)*
Mark Kahn *(Pres.)*
Lawrence A. Wolfe *(Exec. V.P. & Sec.)*
Lester Yollich *(Exec. V.P.)*
Michael D. Brenner *(Controller)*
Roseanne Bochatyn *(Dir.-Inside Sls.)*
Robert Johnson *(Dor.-Mktg.)*
Bill Reno *(Dir.-Mngmt. Information Systems)*
John K. Stier *(Dir.-Pur.)*

No. of U.S. Offices: 18

Outside Service Firm(s):

Sidney Noveck & Co.*(Auditors)*
Southfield, MI

Hertzberg & Noveck*(Legal Firm)*
Birmingham, MI

Manufacturers National Bank N.A.*(Major Banking Relationship)*
38th Fl., 100 Renaissance Center
Detroit, MI 48243
Tel.: 313-222-4227

Affiliate:

Rex Supply Company **(1)**
3715 Harrisburg
Houston, TX 77001
Tel.: 713-222-2251
Industrial Sales
S.I.C.: 5085
Joe Madden *(Chief Oper. Officer)*

THE PRODUCTO MACHINE CO.
990 Housatonic Ave.
Bridgeport, CT 06606
Mailing Address:
P.O. Box 780,
Bridgeport, CT 06601-0780
Tel.: 203-367-8675
Tel.: 800-243-9898 **CT**
Fax: 203-368-2597
Year Founded: 1938
Approx.Sls.: $25,000,000
Emp.: 270
Fiscal Year-end: 3/31/92
Import Export
Mfr. of Machine Tools & Tooling Components
S.I.C.: 3544
Philip R. Marsilius *(Chm. Bd.)*
N.M. Marsilius III *(Pres. & Treas.)*
Kenneth Samonek *(Chief Fin. Officer)*
Richard A. Marsilius *(Exec. V.P. & Sec.)*
Jon A. Kochnavy *(V.P.-Opers.)*
Kevin Uhlig *(V.P.-Machine Tool Sls.)*
D.J. Williams, Jr. *(V.P.-Mktg. & Sls.)*
Maynard L. Cotler *(Mgr.-Mfg./Jamestown)*

Computer Systems/Hardware:
Hewlett Packard System 48

Outside Service Firm(s):

Milton H. Friedberg, Smith & Co.*(Auditors)*
855 Main St., 4th Fl.
Bridgeport, CT 06604
Tel.: 203-366-5876

Marsh, Day & Calhoun*(Legal Firm)*
955 Main St.
Bridgeport, CT 06604
Tel.: 203-368-4221

Connecticut National Bank*(Major Banking Relationship)*
Bridgeport, CT

Divisions:

Pierce-All Div. **(1)**
Turner Rd.
Jamestown, NY 14701
Tel.: 716-484-7131
Tel.: 800-828-2216
Fax: 800-828-2216
Emp.: 102
Export
Computer Systems/Hardware:
Hewlett Packard System 48
Mfr. of Unitized Tooling, Punches & Dies
S.I.C.: 3544
George A. Campbell *(V.P. & Chief Oper. Officer)*

Producto Machine Co. Ring Division **(1)**
Turner Rd.
Jamestown, NY 14701
Tel.: 716-484-7131
Tel.: 800-828-2216
Fax: 716-484-2235
Approx.Sls.: $8,500,000
Emp.: 110
Fiscal Year-end: 3/31/91
Export
Computer Systems/Hardware:
Hewlett Packard & ASK Software
Mfr. of Perforating Punches & Dies
S.I.C.: 3544
M.L. Cotter *(Gen. Mgr.)*
D.J. Williams, Jr. *(V.P.-Mktg.)*

Manufacturing Plants:

The Producto Machine Co. **(1)**
2950 Hart Dr., P.O. Box 366
Franklin Park, IL 60131
Tel.: 708-455-2241
Tel.: 312-889-5442
Fax: 708-455-8270
Mfr. of Die Sets
S.I.C.: 3544
Gerald Clark *(Plant Mgr.)*

The Producto Machine Co. **(1)**
15958 S. Downey Ave.
Paramount, CA 90723
Tel.: 310-774-2508
Fax: 310-634-4019
Mfr. of Die Sets
S.I.C.: 3544
James Kosinski *(Plant Mgr.)*

The Producto Machine Co. **(1)**
10200 Capital Ave.
Oak Park, MI 48237
Tel.: 313-546-7600
Tel.: 313-546-7823
Fax: 313-546-3281
Computer Systems/Hardware:
Hewlett Packard System 48
Mfr. of Die Sets
S.I.C.: 3544
William McCallion *(V.P. & G.M.)*

Non-U.S. Holding:

Producto Diemakers Supplies Ltd. **(1)**
620 Supertest Rd.
Downsview, ON M3J 2M8, Canada
Tel.: 416-661-0555
Mfr. of Machine Tools
S.I.C.: 3544
Robert J. Partington *(Mgr.)*

PROFESSIONAL APARTMENT MANAGEMENT, INC.
2020 W. Kettleman Ln.
Lodi, CA 95241
Mailing Address:
P.O. Box 1570,
Lodi, CA 95241
Tel.: 209-334-6565 **CA**

Professional Apartment Management, Inc.—(Continued)

Fax: 209-334-3712
Year Founded: 1969
Emp.: 175
Fiscal Year-end: 7/31/90
Real Estate Developer & Syndicator
S.I.C.: 6531; 6552
Joseph Michael *(Chm.)*
David Michael *(Pres.)*
Roger Barger *(Controller)*
Greg Frye *(Dir.-Pur.)*

No. of U.S. Offices: 3

Computer Systems/Hardware:
Burroughs

Outside Service Firm(s):

Coopers & Lybrand*(Auditors)*
Sacramento, CA

State Farm Insurance*(Commercial Insurance Carrier)*
Sacramento, CA

State Farm Insurance*(Group Insurer)*
Sacramento, CA

Union Bank*(Major Banking Relationship)*
Stockton, CA

PROFESSIONAL BOOK DISTRIBUTORS, INC.
1650 Bluegrass Lakes Pky.
Alpharetta, GA 30201
Tel.: 404-442-8633 **GA**
Fax: 404-442-9742
Year Founded: 1976
Assets: $6,200,000
Liabilities: $5,200,000
Net Worth: $1,000,000
Approx.Sls.: $14,000,000
Emp.: 75
Fiscal Year-end: 12/31/90
Import Export
Book Order Fulfillment
S.I.C.: 5961
James E. Dockter *(Pres.)*
Rebecca L. Dockter *(Treas. & Sec.)*
Principal(s):
James E. Dockter

No. of U.S. Offices: 1

Computer Systems/Hardware:
Wang VS 5000

Outside Service Firm(s):

Chubb Life Insurance Co. of America*(Commercial Insurance Carrier)*
Concord, NH

Benefit Trust*(Group Insurer)*
Jacksonville, FL

Glass, McCullough, Sherrill & Harrold*(Legal Firm)*
1409 Peachtree Street
Atlanta, GA 30309

First Union National Bank*(Major Banking Relationship)*
Atlanta, GA

Paine Webber*(Pension Manager)*
Columbus, OH

William Roebuck*(Pension Manager)*
Columbus, OH

Subsidiary:

Fulfillment Unlimited **(1)**
1650 Bluegrass Lakes Pky.
Alpharetta, GA 30201
Tel.: 404-442-8633
Emp.: 25
S.I.C.: 5961

PROFESSIONAL HEALTHCARE SYSTEMS, INC.
12960 Coral Tree Place
Los Angeles, CA 90066
Tel.: 310-578-7000
Fax: 310-301-7105
Approx.Sls.: $42,000,000
Emp.: 353
Computerized Hospital Financial Management Systems
S.I.C.: 7372; 7373; 7375
Walt Kaczor *(Sr. V.P. & Chief Fin. Officer)*
Kathleen Stevens *(V.P.-Client Services)*

Computer Systems/Hardware:
Data General

PROFESSIONAL TRAVEL, INC.
302 S. Thornton Ave.
Dalton, GA 30722
Mailing Address:
P.O. Box 1623,
Dalton, GA 30722
Tel.: 706-278-1010 **GA**
Fax: 706-226-5310
Year Founded: 1976
Earnings: $175,708
Approx.Sls.: $10,000,000
Emp.: 27
Retail Travel Agent
S.I.C.: 4724
Frank P. Stevens *(Chm. Bd., Pres., Treas., Chief Exec. Officer & Chief Fin. Officer)*
Mary Boldon *(Dir.-Data Processing)*
Ann Smith *(Dir.-Mktg.)*
Sherry Cochran *(Gen. Mgr.)*
Jessie Davis *(Asst. Gen. Mgr.)*
Principal(s):
Frank P. Stevens

No. of U.S. Offices: 2

Computer Systems/Hardware:
IBM XT

Outside Service Firm(s):

Gross, Collins, & Cress*(Auditors)*
Atlanta, GA

State Farm Insurance*(Commercial Insurance Carrier)*
Dalton, GA

Home Life Insurance Co.*(Group Insurer)*
P.O. Box 1326,
Newark, NJ

Citizens & Southern National Bank*(International Bank Affiliate)*
Dalton, GA

Joe Tuggle Legal Firm*(Legal Firm)*
Dalton, GA

The First National Bank of Dalton*(Major Banking Relationship)*
Dalton, GA

First Union National Bank*(Major Banking Relationship)*
Dalton, GA

Branch:

Professional Travel Inc. **(1)**
1015 B South Wall St.
Calhoun, GA 30701
Tel.: 706-629-1202
Tel.: 800-752-0845
Emp.: 4
Travel Agency
S.I.C.: 4724
Diane Randolph *(Office Mgr.)*

PROGRESS CASTING GROUP, INC.
2600 N. Niagara Ln.
Plymouth, MN 55447
Tel.: 612-557-1000
Fax: 612-557-0320
Approx.Sls.: $25,000,000
Emp.: 250
Manufacture Non-Ferrous Castings
S.I.C.: 3575
Kerry Krafthefer *(Pres.)*
David Leitten *(Exec. V.P.)*
Gary Fuerstenberg *(V.P.-Mktg.)*
Kenneth Nickell *(V.P.-Admin.)*
Gary Johnson *(Gen. Mgr.)*

Outside Service Firm(s):

Coopers & Lybrand*(Auditors)*
1000 TCF Bldg.
Minneapolis, MN 55402
Tel.: 612-293-2929
Fax: 612-370-9395

First Bank Systems*(Major Banking Relationship)*
120 So. Sixth St.
Minneapolis, MN 55402

PROGRESS PAINT MFG. CO.
826 W. Main St.
Louisville, KY 40202
Mailing Address:
P.O. Box 33188,
Louisville, KY 40232
Tel.: 502-587-8685
Fax: 502-583-1847
Year Founded: 1912
Approx.Sls.: $12,000,000
Emp.: 95
Fiscal Year-end: 11/30/92
Export
Mfr. & Wholesale Distributor of Paint & Paint Sundry
S.I.C.: 2851; 5198
Fairleigh Lussky *(Pres.)*
William Lussky *(V.P.-Sls.)*
Nick Lanning *(Dir.-Res. & Devel.)*
Keith Scully *(Dir.-Opers.)*
Noel Booker *(Mgr.-Trade Sls.)*
Ken Lawrence *(Mgr.-Indus. Sls.)*

Computer Systems/Hardware:
IBM System 36

Outside Service Firm(s):

Carpenter & Mounljoy*(Auditors)*
Louisville, KY

First National Bank*(Major Banking Relationship)*
Louisville, KY

PROGRESS PRINTING COMPANY
3523 Waterlick Rd.
Lynchburg, VA 24502
Tel.: 804-239-9213
Fax: 804-237-1618
Emp.: 265
Commercial Offset Printing
S.I.C.: 2752
T.D. Thornton II *(Pres. & Treas.)*
Daniel P. Thornton *(Sr. V.P.-Sls. & Mktg.)*
Michael A. Thornton *(V.P.-Prod.)*
P. Cornell Murphy *(Controller)*
Phillip Pryor *(Dir.-Pur.)*
J. Wayne Scroggs *(Plant Mgr.)*

Outside Service Firm(s):

Brockman Drinkard Pennington*(Auditors)*
Lynchburg, VA

Crestar Bank*(Major Banking Relationship)*
Lynchburg, VA

PROGRESS WEST
10180 L Street
Omaha, NE 68127
Tel.: 402-592-1800
Fax: 402-592-9617
Sales Range: $40-59 Million
Emp.: 15
Real Estate Investors, Brokers & Developers
S.I.C.: 6798; 6531; 6552
Monte Matz *(Pres.)*
Erick Wagner *(Exec. V.P.)*
Kenneth Amick *(V.P.)*
Lisa Showers *(Dir.-Opers.)*

Computer Systems/Hardware:
IBM

PROGRESSIVE DRIVER SERVICES, INC.
2000 Corporate Square Blvd.
Jacksonville, FL 32216
Mailing Address:
P.O. Box 17775,
Jacksonville, FL 32245
Tel.: 904-724-2864 **FL**
Fax: 904-724-2936
Year Founded: 1969
Assets: $1,810,343
Liabilities: $895,955
Net Worth: $914,388
Approx.Sls.: $20,000,000
Emp.: 600
Contract Driver Leasing
S.I.C.: 7361
Lowell D. Harmon *(Chm. Bd. & Pres.)*
Linda L. Harmon *(Chief Fin. Officer & Treas.)*
Robert R. Lee *(Exec. V.P.)*
Principal(s):
Lowell D. Harmon
Robert R. Lee

No. of U.S. Offices: 3

Computer Systems/Hardware:
Wang

Outside Service Firm(s):

Price Waterhouse*(Auditors)*
2500 Independent Square
Jacksonville, FL 32202

Insurex Agency, Inc.*(Group Insurer)*
Memphis, TN

Zisser, Robison*(Legal Firm)*
Jacksonville, FL

Ponte Vedre National Bank*(Major Banking Relationship)*
Jacksonville, FL

PROGRESSIVE TOOL & INDUSTRIES CO.
21000 Telegraph Rd.
Southfield, MI 48034
Tel.: 313-353-8888 **MI**
Fax: 313-353-5317
Approx.Sls.: $120,000,000
Emp.: 1,200
Manufacture Specialty Dies, Jigs & Tools
S.I.C.: 3544; 3542
Anthony Wisne *(Chm. Bd.)*
Lawrence A. Wisne *(Pres. & Chief Exec. Officer)*
Bob Stoutenberg *(V.P.-Mfg.)*
Alan Wisne *(V.P.)*
Joseph Wisne *(V.P.)*
Victor A. Winiarski *(Treas. & Sec.)*
Fred Beagle *(Dir.-Personnel)*

Outside Service Firm(s):

Coopers & Lybrand*(Auditors)*
400 Renaissance Center
Detroit, MI 48243
Tel.: 313-446-7100
Fax: 313-446-7117

National Bank of Detroit*(Major Banking Relationship)*
611 Woodward
Detroit, MI 48226
Tel.: 313-225-1000

PROPERTY MANAGEMENT SERVICES, INC.
205 E. 11th St., Ste. 100
Vancouver, WA 98660
Mailing Address:
P.O. Box 7,
Vancouver, WA 98666
Tel.: 206-696-9000
Fax: 206-696-9609
Sales Range: $500-999 Million
Emp.: 750
Property Management: Commercial & Multi-Family Residential Housing
S.I.C.: 6531
Al Naimo *(Pres.)*

Computer Systems/Hardware:
AT&T PC

Outside Service Firm(s):

Deloitte & Touche*(Auditors)*
700 Fifth Ave., Suite 4500
Seattle, WA 98104-5044
Tel.: 206-292-1800

Blue Cross of Washington & Alaska*(Group Insurer)*
Seattle, WA

Kaiser Insurance*(Group Insurer)*
Portland, OR

PTIC*(Group Insurer)*
Vancouver, WA

Samuels, Yoelin, Weiner, Kantor & Seymour*(Legal Firm)*
Portland, OR

Northwest National Bank*(Major Banking Relationship)*
Vancouver, WA

U.S. National Bank*(Major Banking Relationship)*
309 S.W. Sixth Ave.
Portland, OR 97208
Tel.: 503-275-4942

PROPPER MANUFACTURING CO., INC.
36-04 Skillman Ave.
Long Island City, NY 11101
Tel.: 718-392-6650
Fax: 718-482-8909
Year Founded: 1935
Approx.Sls.: $20,000,000
Emp.: 150
Fiscal Year-end: 7/31/90
Import
Mfr. & Importer of Surgical, Hospital & Laboratory Supplies
S.I.C.: 3841; 3842; 5047; 3800
Seymour Schuman *(Chm. Bd. & Sec.)*
Jane Schuman *(Vice Chm.)*
Kenneth Summer *(Pres.)*
Irving Speelman *(Exec. V.P.)*
Thomas A. Augurt *(V.P.-Product Plng.)*
John E. McGinley *(V.P.-Mktg.)*
Louis Rossman *(V.P.-Fin.)*

Outside Service Firm(s):

Douglas Greenberg*(Auditors)*
New York, NY

Chemical Banking Corp.*(Major Banking Relationship)*
277 Park Ave.
New York, NY 10041
Tel.: 212-310-6407
Fax: 212-310-4526

PROSPECT FOUNDRY, INC.
1225 Winter St., N.E.
Minneapolis, MN 55413
Tel.: 612-331-9282
Fax: 612-331-4122
Emp.: 275
Manufacture Castings
S.I.C.: 3321
Richard Sitarz *(Pres.)*
David B. Henderson *(Sec.)*
Joe Dougherty *(Controller)*

Outside Service Firm(s):

Grant Thornton*(Auditors)*
500 Pillsbury Center
Minneapolis, MN 55402-1459

Oppenheimer, Wolff & Donnelly*(Legal Firm)*
IDS Ctr., 45 S. Seventh St.
Minneapolis, MN 55402
Tel.: 612-344-9300
Fax: 612-344-9376

Norwest Bank Minnesota, N.A.*(Major Banking Relationship)*
6th St. & Marquette Av.
Minneapolis, MN 55479
Tel.: 612-667-1234

PROSPECT MOTORS, INC.
645 Hwy. 49-88
Jackson, CA 95642
Mailing Address:
P.O. Box 1025
Jackson, CA 95642
Tel.: 209-223-1740
Tel.: 800-538-3738 **CA**
Fax: 209-223-0395
Year Founded: 1970
Assets: $67,539,001
Liabilities: $66,546,535
Net Worth: $992,466
Approx.Sls.: $250,000,000
Emp.: 55
Fiscal Year-end: 5/30/91
New & Used Automobiles, Automobile Repair Shop, Passenger Car Leasing
S.I.C.: 5511; 7515
William Halvorson *(Pres.)*
Frank E. Halvorson *(V.P.)*
W.B. Smallfield *(V.P.)*
Lorraine Halvorson *(Sec. & Treas.)*
Principal(s):
William Halvorson
Frank E. Halvorson

Outside Service Firm(s):

Engilis, Payne & Kmetz*(Auditors)*
1400 Ethan Way #1
Sacramento, CA 95825

Delta Benefit Plans*(Group Insurer)*
P.O. Box 1147,
Stockton, CA

Freeman & Brown*(Legal Firm)*
1818 Grand Canal Blvd.
Stockton, CA 95207

Bank Of Amador*(Major Banking Relationship)*
Jackson, CA

Daugherty Insurance*(Major Banking Relationship)*
P.O. Box 7369,
Stockton, CA 95267

Edward D. Jones & Co.*(Pension Manager)*
P.O. Box 1267,
Jackson, CA 95642

Subsidiary:

Amador Motors **(1)**
P.O. Box 278,
Sutter Creek, CA 95685
Tel.: 209-267-5277
Emp.: 20
Automobile Dealer
S.I.C.: 5511

PROSTROLLO MOTOR COMPANY
1001 S. Washington St.
Madison, SD 57042
Tel.: 605-256-9111
Fax: 605-256-6824
New & Used Automobiles
S.I.C.: 5511
Jerry L. Prostrollo *(Pres.)*

Outside Service Firm(s):

Norwest Bank Minnesota, N.A.*(Major Banking Relationship)*
Madison, SD

Division:

Prostrollo Motor Sales, Inc. **(1)**
500 4th St., N.E.
Huron, SD 57350
Tel.: 605-352-6411
Approx.Sls.: $13,000,000
Emp.: 38
New & Used Automobiles
S.I.C.: 5511
Pat Prostrollo *(Pres.)*
John Deniger *(Gen. Mgr.)*

THE PROTECTOR CORPORATION
240 E. Lake St., Ste. 306
Addison, IL 60101
Tel.: 708-279-3010
Fax: 708-279-3207
Year Founded: 1980
Approx.Sls.: $37,000,000
Emp.: 20
Supplier to the Automotive Aftermarket
S.I.C.: 5013; 5169; 2899
Larry Bettendorf *(Pres.)*
Elaine Russo *(Controller)*
Pat Lavelle *(Mgr.-Natl. Sls.)*
Linda Richer *(Mgr.-Customer Service)*

Computer Systems/Hardware:
IBM System 36

Outside Service Firm(s):

KPMG Peat Marwick*(Auditors)*
345 Park Ave.
New York, NY 10154
Tel.: 212-758-9700
Fax: 212-872-3308

Aetna Life & Casualty*(Commercial Insurance Carrier)*
100 N. Riverside Plaza
Chicago, IL 60606

Syncor Administrative Services*(Group Insurer)*
Northbrook, IL

American National Bank & Trust Company of Chicago*(Major Banking Relationship)*
33 N. LaSalle St.
Chicago, IL 60602
Tel.: 312-661-5000
Fax: 312-661-6417

PROTIMEX CORPORATION
11846 Venture Blvd., Ste. 301
Studio City, CA 91604
Tel.: 818-509-9700 **CA**
Fax: 818-509-9572
Year Founded: 1975
Approx.Sls.: $192,000,000
Emp.: 98
Wholesale Distributor of Fresh Meats & Unpackaged Frozen, Live Or Dressed Poultry
S.I.C.: 5147; 5144
Frederick Goldberger *(Pres.)*
Joseph Jordan *(V.P.-Fin.)*
Harvey Lecker *(V.P.-Sls.)*

Outside Service Firm(s):

Bay Sherman & Co.*(Auditors)*
Studio City, CA

PROTO SYSTEMS OF ATLANTA
625 Simms Industrial Blvd.
Alpharetta, GA 30201
Tel.: 404-475-1330
Fax: 404-442-9751
Year Founded: 1979
Sales Range: $10-19 Million
Emp.: 200
Mfr. Printed Circuit Boards
S.I.C.: 3672
Gary W. Smith *(Chm. Bd., Pres. & Chief Exec. Officer)*
Arthur J. Allen *(V.P.-Fin.)*
Beverly B. Butner *(V.P.-Admin. & Sec.)*
Travis L. Langley *(V.P.-Mfg.)*
Bruce J. Smith *(V.P.-Mktg.)*
Karen Craft *(Dir.-Human Resources)*
Keith A. Koehle *(Mgr.-Natl. Sls.)*
Gisa Hacker *(Corp. Travel Planner)*
Nancie McLeod *(Pur. Agent)*
Principal(s):
Gary W. Smith

No. of Mfg. Plants/Facilities: 2
No. of U.S. Offices: 1

Computer Systems/Hardware:
IBM 3600

Outside Service Firm(s):

Arthur Andersen & Co.*(Auditors)*
133 Peachtree St., N.E.
Atlanta, GA 30303
Tel.: 404-658-1776

Mutual of Omaha Insurance Company*(Group Insurer)*
Mutual of Omaha Plaza,
Omaha, NE 68175
Tel.: 800-228-7775

St. Paul Insurance of Illinois*(Group Insurer)*
Chicago, IL

C&S National Bank*(Major Banking Relationship)*
Atlanta, GA

PROVIDENCE JOURNAL COMPANY
75 Fountain St.
Providence, RI 02902
Tel.: 401-277-7000 **RI**
Fax: 401-277-7802
Year Founded: 1829
Assets: $654,000,000
Liabilities: $254,000,000
Net Worth: $400,000,000
Approx.Sls.: $262,000,000
Emp.: 1,800
Fiscal Year-end: 12/31/91
Import Export
Newspaper Publishing, TV Broadcasting, Cable TV
S.I.C.: 2711; 4833; 3663
Stephen Hamblett *(Chm. Bd., Chief Exec. Officer & Publr.)*
Trygve Myhren *(Pres. & Chief Oper. Officer)*
John A. Bowers *(V.P.-Human Resources)*
Thomas Gregory *(V.P. & Corp. Comptroller)*
James F. Stack *(V.P. & Chief Fin. Officer)*
Joel Stark *(V.P.-Mktg. & Sls.)*
Howard G. Sutton *(V.P.-Admin.)*
James V. Wyman *(V.P. & Exec. Dir.)*
Harry Dyson *(Treas. & Sec.)*
Donald Almeida *(Dir.-Systems)*
Don Ross *(Mgr.-Adv.)*

Computer Systems/Hardware:
IBM 4381

Outside Service Firm(s):

Coopers & Lybrand*(Auditors)*
1 Post Office Square
Boston, MA 02110
Tel.: 617-574-5000
Fax: 617-345-0398

Blue Cross & Blue Shield of Rhode Island*(Group Insurer)*
Providence, RI

Ocean State*(Group Insurer)*
Providence, RI

Prudential Group Dental Claims*(Group Insurer)*
Lawrence, MA

Providence Journal Company—(Continued)

Rhode Island Group Health Associates*(Group Insurer)*
Providence, RI

Edwards & Angell*(Legal Firm)*
2700 Hospital Trust Twr.
Providence, RI 02903
Tel.: 401-274-9200

Rhode Island Hospital Trust National Bank*(Major Banking Relationship)*
Providence, RI

Subsidiaries:

Colony Communications Inc. **(1)**
75 Fountain St.
Providence, RI 02902
Tel.: 401-277-7000 (100%)

Providence Journal Broadcasting Corp. **(1)**
75 Fountain St.
Providence, RI 02902
Tel.: 401-277-7000 (100%)

Providence Journal Telecommunications, Inc. **(1)**
75 Fountain St.
Providence, RI 02902
Tel.: 401-277-7000 (100%)

PROVIDENT MUTUAL

PROVIDENT MUTUAL LIFE INSURANCE CO.
1600 Market St.
Philadelphia, PA 19103
Mailing Address:
P.O. Box 7378,
Philadelphia, PA 19101
Tel.: 215-636-5000 PA
Fax: 215-636-8166
Year Founded: 1865
Assets: $3,953,638,000
Earnings: $20,426,000
Net Worth: $3,953,638,000
Approx.Premiums: $644,980,000
Emp.: 1,308
Fiscal Year-end: 12/31/91
Life Insurance; Security Brokers & Dealers, Investment Advice & Mutual Fund Srvcs.
S.I.C.: 6311; 6211; 6282
L.J. Rowell, Jr. *(Chm. Bd., Pres. & Chief Exec. Officer)*
Gerald B. Beam *(Exec. V.P.-Corp.)*
John R. McClelland *(Exec. V.P. & Chief Fin. Officer)*
Stanley R. Reber *(Exec. V.P. & Chief Investment Officer)*
Lawrence R. Brown, Jr. *(Sr. V.P. & Corp. Counsel)*
Guy H. Edwards *(V.P.-Information Services)*
Mary Lynn Finelli *(V.P & Controller)*
Richard N. Herb *(V.P.-Pension)*
George Lambert *(V.P. & Gen. Counsel)*
Charlene Parsons *(V.P.-Human Resources)*
Craig Snyder *(V.P.-Mortgage Loans & Real Estate)*
Rosanne Gatta *(Asst. V.P. & Treas.)*
Wistar Kane *(Asst. V.P.-Fin. Reporting)*
Joseph Kenney *(Sec.)*
Keith Bratz *(Dir.-Communications)*
Judy Peck *(Dir.-Meetings Plng.)*
Michael Cohen *(Plng. Officer)*
Lori Pickford *(Pub. Rels.)*

No. of U.S. Offices: 58

Computer Systems/Hardware:
IBM

Outside Service Firm(s):

Coopers & Lybrand*(Auditors)*
2400 Eleven Penn Center
Philadelphia, PA 19103-2962
Tel.: 215-963-8000

Duane Morris & Heckscher*(Legal Firm)*
Philadelphia, PA

Subsidiaries:

Continental American Life Insurance Co. **(1)**
300 Continental Dr.
Newark, DE 19713
Tel.: 302-454-5000 (100%)
Fax: 302-731-1101
Approx.Premiums: $120,650,000
Emp.: 229
Fiscal Year-end: 12/30/90
Direct Response Marketing-Life Insurance
S.I.C.: 6311
William G. Copeland *(Chm. Bd.)*
John T. Unipan *(Pres. & Chief Exec. Officer)*

PML Securities Co. **(1)**
Christiana Executive Campus, 220 Continental Dr.
Wilmington, DE 19713
Tel.: 302-453-3800
Tel.: 800-828-9765 (100%)
Fax: 302-453-0703
Approx.Sls.: $4,000,000
Emp.: 11
Fiscal Year-end: 12/30/90
Securities Broker & Dealer
S.I.C.: 6211
Anthony Nappi *(Pres.)*

Provident Mutual Life & Annutiy Company of America **(1)**
1600 Market St.
Philadelphia, PA 19103
Tel.: 215-636-5000 (100%)
Fax: 215-636-8166
Approx.Sls.: $21,157,000
Emp.: 25
Life Insurance & Annuities
S.I.C.: 6311
Alfred F. Wilmouth *(Pres.)*

Sigma Group **(1)**
Christiana Executive Campus, 220 Continental Dr.
Wilmington, DE 19713
Tel.: 302-456-1010 (100%)
Fax: 302-731-5157
Approx.Rev.: $6,500,000
Emp.: 70
Investment Advisory & Mutual Fund Services
S.I.C.: 6211; 6282
Anthony Nappi *(Pres. & Chief Oper. Officer)*

PROVIMI VEAL CORPORATION
20800 Swenson Dr., Ste. 440
Waukesha, WI 53186
Tel.: 414-784-8520
Fax: 414-784-2245
Year Founded: 1961
Approx.Sls.: $75,000,000
Emp.: 180
Export
Slaughtering of Veal & Lamb
S.I.C.: 2011
Aat Groenevelt *(Chm. Bd. & Pres.)*

No. of Mfg. Plants/Facilities: 1
No. of U.S. Offices: 1

Outside Service Firm(s):

First Chicago Trust Co. of New York*(Major Banking Relationship)*
One First Natl. Plaza, Ste. 123
Chicago, IL 60670
Tel.: 312-407-4660

PROXIMA CORPORATION
6610 Nancy Ridge Dr.
San Diego, CA 92121
Tel.: 619-457-5500
Tel.: 800-447-7694 CA
Fax: 619-457-9647
Year Founded: 1982
Approx.Sls.: $32,000,000
Emp.: 300
Fiscal Year-end: 3/31/91
Export
Mfr. of Electronic Computing Equipment
S.I.C.: 3571; 3577
Ken Olson *(Chm. & Chief Exec. Officer)*
Paul Eichen *(Pres.)*
Fred Parker *(V.P.-Opers.)*
John Thomas *(V.P. & Bus. Unit Mgr.)*
Mary Zoeller *(V.P. & Bus. Unit Mgr., PDP)*
Dick Frost *(Dir.-Sls., Power)*
Jack Gausnell *(Dir.-Sls., PDP)*

Outside Service Firm(s):

Deloitte & Touche*(Auditors)*
701 "B" St., Ste. 1900
San Diego, CA 92101-8198

Imperial Bank*(Major Banking Relationship)*
San Diego, CA

Prudential Feldco Inc.
(Name Changed To Pen-Tab Industries, Inc.)

THE PRUDENTIAL INSURANCE COMPANY OF AMERICA
Prudential Plaza
Newark, NJ 07102
Mailing Address:
751 Broad St.
Newark, NJ 07102-3777
Tel.: 201-802-6000 NJ
Year Founded: 1875
Approx.Rev.: $50,958,000,000
Emp.: 105,000
Fiscal Year-end: 12/31/91
Life & Health Insurance, Annuities
S.I.C.: 6311; 6321; 6399; 6719; 8071; 8361; 6211; 6411; 6331
Corporate Giving Program: The Prudential Foundation Provides Grants to Qualified Organizations in Each of the 6 Major Funding Areas; Health & Human Services, Education, Urban & Community Devel., Business & Civic Affairs, Culture & Arts, & Lives & Living Conditions of Children
Employee Matching Gifts Program: The Foundation will Match Gifts to Private Colleges & Universities at a Ratio of 1&1/2 to 1, Gifts to all Other Eligible Institutions will be Matched Dollar for Dollar to a Maximum of $5,000
Robert C. Winters *(Chm. Bd. & Chief Exec. Officer)*
Eugene B. Heimberg *(Chm.-The Prudential Realty Grp.)*
Garnett L. Keith, Jr. *(Vice Chm.)*
Stephen R. Braswell *(Pres.-Prudential Property & Casualty Insurance Co.)*
S. Ross Johnson *(Pres.-Canadian Opers.)*
Hardwick Simmons *(Pres. & Chief Exec. Officer-Prudential Securities)*
Robert P. Hill *(Exec. V.P.-Individual Insurance)*
William P. Link *(Exec. V.P.)*
Robert E. Riley *(Exec. V.P.-Prudential Investment Corp. & Chm.-Prud. Realty Grp.)*
James W. Stevens *(Exec. V.P.)*
Edward D. Zinbarg *(Exec. V.P.)*
Robert M. Chmely *(Sr. V.P. & Actuary)*
Allen M. Haight *(Sr. V.P.-Grp. Dept.)*
James R. Gillen *(Sr. V.P. & Gen. Counsel)*
Eugene M. O'Hara *(Sr. V.P., Comptroller & Chief Fin. Officer)*
Samuel H. Havens *(Sr. V.P.-Grp. Dept.)*
William G. Hunt, Jr. *(Sr. V.P.-Ordinary Agencies Dept.)*
Malcolm D. MacKinnon *(Sr. V.P.-IIS & A)*
Kenneth E. MacWilliams *(Sr. V.P.-Gateway Investors)*
Donald C. Mann *(Sr. V.P.-Human Resources)*
I. Edward Price *(Sr. V.P.-Individual Ins. Systems & Admin.)*
Donald G. Southwell *(Sr. V.P.-District Agencies)*
Morton E. Spitzer *(Sr. V.P.-District Agencies)*
William H. Tremayne *(Sr. V.P.-Pub. Affairs)*
Ira J. Kleinman *(Sr. V.P.)*
Gerald Loev *(Sr. V.P.)*
Dorothy K. Light *(V.P. & Sec.)*
Martin Pfinsgraff *(V.P. & Treas.)*
Nicholas M. Graves *(Sr. Mng. Dir.-Corp. Fin. Grp.)*

Computer Systems/Hardware:
IBM Systems 3084-Q & 3090

Outside Service Firm(s):

Deloitte & Touche*(Auditors)*
Newark, NJ

Prudential Insurance Co. of America*(Group Insurer)*
Prudential Tower Suite 450, 800 Boylston St.
Boston, MA 02119

Bank of New England*(Major Banking Relationship)*
28 State Street
Boston, MA 02109
Tel.: 617-742-4000

Subsidiaries:

PRUCO Life Insurance Company **(1)**
213 Washington St.
Newark, NJ 07102
Tel.: 201-802-3707 (100%)
Coordinates Development & Operational Activities for Variable Life & Other Non-Participating, Insurance & Annuity Products
S.I.C.: 6311
William J. Kelly *(Pres.)*

Subsidiary:

Pruco Life Insurance Company of New Jersey **(2)**
213 Washington St.
Newark, NJ 07102
Tel.: 201-877-3707 (100%)
Individual Deferred Annuity & Group Issues Health Insurance
S.I.C.: 6311; 6321
Donald G. Southwell *(Pres.)*

PRUCO, Inc. **(1)**
751 Broad St.
Newark, NJ 07102 (100%)
Holding Company
S.I.C.: 6719
Robert C. Winters *(Pres.)*

Subsidiaries:

Chatham Eight Corporation **(2)**
Prudential Plaza
Newark, NJ 07102
Allen J. Green *(Pres.)*

Newark Rehabilitation, Inc. **(2)**
Prudential Plaza
Newark, NJ 07102 (100%)
Housing Rehabilitation Projects in Newark
S.I.C.: 8361; 1521; 1522
Claude J. Zinngrabe, Jr. *(Chm. Bd.)*

PIC Realty Corp. **(2)**
P.O. Box 1539,
Newark, NJ 07102 (100%)
Owns, Develops & Operates Real Estate
S.I.C.: 6531
Robert E. Riley *(Pres.)*

Pruco Securities Corp. **(2)**
Prudential Plaza,
Newark, NJ 07102
Tel.: 201-877-5730 (100%)
Registered Securities Broker-Dealer
S.I.C.: 6211
John T. Dillon *(Pres. & Chief Oper. Officer)*

Pruco Services, Inc. **(2)**
Prudential Plaza,
Newark, NJ 07102
Tel.: 201-877-6523 (100%)

Clinical Laboratory
S.I.C.: 8071
Robert P. Hill *(Chm. Bd. & Pres.)*

Prudential Agricultural Credit, Inc. **(2)**
Prudential Plaza,
Newark, NJ 07102
Tel.: 201-877-7042 (100%)
S.I.C.: 6159
Leslie G. Horsager *(Pres.)*

Prudential Funding Corp. **(2)**
2 Gateway Center 4, 100 Mulberry St.
Newark, NJ 07102
Tel.: 201-802-7679 (100%)
Provides Financial Services for Prudential & Its Subsidiaries
S.I.C.: 8741
John P. Murray *(Pres. & Chief Exec. Officer)*

Prudential Property & Casualty Insurance Company **(2)**
23 Main St.
Holmdel, NJ 07733
Tel.: 908-946-5000 (100%)
Provides Homeowners, Automobile & Personal Catastrophe Coverage
S.I.C.: 6331
Stephen R. Braswell *(Pres.)*

Subsidiaries:

Prudential Commercial Insurance Co. **(3)**
23 Main St.
Holmdel, NJ 07733
Tel.: 908-946-5000 (100%)
Offers Property & Casualty Insurance Not Written by Prudential Property & Casualty Insurance Co.
S.I.C.: 6399
Walter Barnes, Jr. *(Pres.)*

Prudential General Insurance Co. **(3)**
23 Main St.
Holmdel, NJ 07733
Tel.: 908-946-5000 (100%)
S.I.C.: 6411
Walter Barnes, Jr. *(Pres.)*

Prudential Reinsurance Co. **(2)**
100 Mulberry St.
Newark, NJ 07102
Tel.: 201-802-8000 (100%)
Commercial Property & Casualty Reinsurance through Brokers & Insurance Company Clients Worldwide
S.I.C.: 6411
James E. Dwane *(Pres.)*

Subsidiaries:

Dryden & Co., Inc. **(3)**
100 Mulberry St.
Newark, NJ 07102
Tel.: 201-877-8500 (100%)
Underwriting Manager & Surplus Line Broker for Gibraltar Casualty Co.
S.I.C.: 6411
LeRoy J. Simon *(Pres.)*

Gibraltar Casualty Co. **(3)**
100 Mulberry St.
Newark, NJ 07102
Tel.: 201-877-8000 (100%)
Writes Unusual & Non Standard Property & Casualty Risks on a Surplus Line Basis
S.I.C.: 6321
LeRoy J. Simon *(Pres.)*

Prudential Reinsurance **(3)**
4600 Post Oak Pl., Ste. 260
Houston, TX 77027
Tel.: 713-877-8814
Insure Insurance Companies
S.I.C.: 6351
James M. Heath *(Pres.)*

Prudential Capital & Investment Services, Inc. **(1)**
1 Seaport Plaza
New York, NY 10292
Tel.: 212-214-1315 (100%)
Holding Company; Subsidiaries Involved in Securities Brokerage, Commodities Brokerage, Investment Banking & Other Related Financial Services through its Primary Operating Subsidiary: Prudential-Bache Securities Inc.
S.I.C.: 6719
George L. Ball *(Chm. & Chief Exec. Officer)*

Subsidiaries:

PruCapital, Inc. **(2)**
100 Mulberry St.
Newark, NJ 07102
Tel.: 201-802-7151
Coordinated Fixed & Floating Rate Revolving Lines of Credit & Term Loans, Together With Lease Programs, Supply Programs & Equity Investments for Itself & Its Subsidiaries
S.I.C.: 6159
Kenneth E. MacWilliams *(Chm.)*

Subsidiaries:

PruCapital Management, Inc. **(3)**
100 Mulberry St.
Newark, NJ 07102
Tel.: 201-877-7151 (100%)
Provides Marketing & Administration Services for PruCapital, Inc. & Its Subsidiaries
S.I.C.: 8741
Rodney W. Reynolds *(Chm.)*

Prudential Interfunding Corp. **(3)**
100 Mulberry St.
Newark, NJ 07102
Tel.: 201-877-7151 (100%)
Provides Financial Services
S.I.C.: 6411
Rodney W. Reynolds *(Chm.)*

PruLease, Inc. **(3)**
100 Mulberry St.
Newark, NJ 07102
Tel.: 201-877-7151 (100%)
Provides Financing Services
S.I.C.: 6411
Rodney W. Reynolds *(Chm.)*

Subsidiary:

PruCapital Securities Co., Inc. **(4)**
100 Mulberry St.
Newark, NJ 07102
Tel.: 201-877-6000
S.I.C.: 6211
Rodney W. Reynolds *(Chm.)*

PruSupply, Inc. **(3)**
100 Mulberry St.
Newark, NJ 07102
Tel.: 201-877-7151 (100%)
Leasing of Fuel & Material Supplies
S.I.C.: 7389
Rodney W. Reynolds *(Chm.)*

Prudential Securities Group Inc. **(2)**
One Seaport Plaza
New York, NY 10292
Tel.: 212-214-3270 (100%)
Emp.: 17,000
Holding Company Controlling Securities & Commodities Brokerage Subsidiaries
S.I.C.: 6719
Robert Beck *(Chief Exec. Officer)*

Subsidiary:

Prudential Securities Inc. **(3)**
199 Gold St.
New York, NY 10292
Tel.: 212-214-1000
Emp.: 17,000
Investment Banking & Brokerage Firm
S.I.C.: 6211
Hardwick Simmons *(Pres. & Chief Exec. Officer)*
Howard A. Knight *(Pres.-Strategy & Investment Bnkg.)*
George Murray *(Pres.-Retail Brokerage)*
Loren Schechter *(Exec. V.P. & Gen. Counsel)*
Ronna G. Lichtenberg *(Sr. V.P. & Dir.-Mktg.)*
Barbara Glasser *(1st V.P. & Dir.-Adv.)*
David deMerlier *(Asst. V.P. & Adv. Mgr.)*

Prudential Support Operations, Inc. **(2)**
Prudential Plaza
Newark, NJ 07101
Tel.: 201-877-6600 (100%)
Provides Management Services to Pru Capital, Inc., Prudential-Bache Securities, Inc. & Their Subsidiaries
S.I.C.: 8741
George L. Ball *(Pres. & Chief Exec. Officer)*

Prudential Eastern Home Office **(1)**
P.O. Box 388,
Ft. Washington, PA 19034
Tel.: 215-784-2345
A Trust Company Providing Investment Services to Eligible Employee Benefit Trusts, Endowment Funds & Foundations
S.I.C.: 6311; 6371

The Prudential Investment Corp. **(1)**
Prudential Plaza
Newark, NJ 07102
Tel.: 201-802-6000 (100%)
Provides Investment Services to The Prudential's General & Separate Accounts & Other Entities
S.I.C.: 6211
Garnett L. Keith, Jr. *(Chief Exec. Officer)*

Subsidiaries:

The Prudential Asset Management Co., Inc. **(2)**
71 Hanover Road
Florham Park, NJ 07932
Tel.: 201-966-3215 (100%)
Emp.: 150
Sells Prudential's Investment Activities to Pension Funds & Foundations; Administers Pension Plans for Corporate Clients
S.I.C.: 6159; 6371; 6411
Scott Pierce *(Chm. & Chief Exec. Officer)*
Harold Hopkins *(V.P.-Defined Contribution Programs)*
Steven Benson *(V.P.-Sls. & Mktg.)*

Subsidiary:

Mercator Asset Management Co., Inc. **(3)**
Paragon Center, 2400 E. Commercial Blvd., Ste. 810
Fort Lauderdale, FL 33308
Tel.: 305-771-9660
Asset Management Co.
S.I.C.: 8741
John G. Thompson *(Chm. & Pres.)*

Prudential-LMI Commercial Insurance Company **(1)**
900 Springmill Rd.
Mansfield, OH 44906
Tel.: 419-525-9000
Fax: 419-522-5014
Assets: $189,148,000,000
Earnings: $2,280,000,000
Liabilities: $182,621,000,000
Net Worth: $6,527,000,000
Approx.Rev.: $29,716,000,000
Emp.: 400
Fiscal Year-end: 12/31/91
Property & Casualty Insurance Company; Commercial Package Policies
S.I.C.: 6331
Richard G. Cober *(Pres.)*
William J. Breslin *(Sr. V.P.)*
M. Kenneth McGreevy *(Sr. V.P.)*
Kenneth Frayer *(V.P.-Info. Systems)*

The Prudential Realty Group **(1)**
751 Broad St.
Newark, NJ 07102-3777
Tel.: 201-802-9399 (100%)
Real Estate Manager, Developer, Mortgage Lender
S.I.C.: 6531; 6552; 6512; 6162
Eugene Heimberg *(Chm.)*

Divisions:

Prudential Development & Retail Div. **(2)**
751 Broad St.
Newark, NJ 07102-3777
Tel.: 201-802-9399
Real Estate Management & Investment
S.I.C.: 6531
Brian J. Strum *(Pres.)*

Prudential Equity Investment Div. **(2)**
751 Broad St.
Newark, NJ 07102-3777
Tel.: 201-802-9399
Issues Zero Coupon Bonds Secured by Residential Mortgages.
S.I.C.: 6211
Ron Rayevich *(Pres.)*

Prudential Institutional Investment Management Div. **(2)**
751 Broad St.
Newark, NJ 07102-3777
Tel.: 201-802-9399
Real Estate Investment
S.I.C.: 6733
Richard Stearns *(Pres.)*

Prudential Mortgage Capital **(2)**
751 Broad St.
Newark, NJ 07102-3777
Tel.: 201-802-9399
Origination & Servicing of Residential & Commercial Mortgages & Packaging of Mortgage-Backed Securities
S.I.C.: 6162
Frank MacDougal *(Pres.)*

Non-U.S. Holdings:

Harrod Devitt Sociedad Anonima **(1)**
Avad. Diagonal,601,5.A 08028
Barcelona, Spain
Provides Administrative Services Required by PAMCO Espana, Sociedad Anonima de Seguros
S.I.C.: 8748
Jorge Mensa *(Dir.)*

Industrial Trust Company **(1)**
200 Consilium Place
Scarborough, ON M1H 3E6, Canada
Tel.: 416-296-0777
Trust & Loan Co.
S.I.C.: 6091; 6159

PAMCO Espana Sociedad Anonima de Seguros **(1)**
Diagonal, 601, 5-D
Barcelona, 08028, Spain
Tel.: 34-3-230-0900
Group Pension Contracts
Higinio Bartolome *(Pres.)*

PIC Realty Canada Ltd. **(1)**
200 Consilium Place
Scarborough, ON M1H 3E6, Canada
Tel.: 416-296-0777 (100%)
Fax: 416-296-3180
Real Estate Development
S.I.C.: 6552
John S. Batters *(Pres.)*

Prudential of America General Insurance Co. (Canada) **(1)**
200 Consilium Place
Scarborough, ON M1H 3E6, Canada
Tel.: 416-296-0777
Property & Casualty Insurances
S.I.C.: 6331
Ron Meredith-Jones *(Pres.)*

Prudential Asia Investments Limited **(1)**
Alexandra House, 32nd Fl., 16-20 Chater Rd.
Hong Kong, Hong Kong
Tel.: 852-5-844-1008
Holding Co.
S.I.C.: 6719
Victor K. Fung *(Pres.)*

Subsidiary:

Prudential Asia Capital Limited **(2)**
Alexandra House, 16-20 Chater Rd.
Hong Kong, Hong Kong
Provides Corp. Financial Services in the Far East
S.I.C.: 6082

Prudential Fund Management Canada Ltd. **(1)**
200 Consilium Place
Scarborough, ON M1H 3E6, Canada
Tel.: 416-296-0777 (100%)
Mutual Fund Management
S.I.C.: 6722
Ronald D. Barbaro *(Pres.)*

The Prudential Life Insurance Company, Ltd. **(1)**
Sogo Hanzomon Bldg., 1-7 Kojimachi Chiyoda-kee,
Tokyo, 102, Japan
Sells Traditional & Variable Life Insurance Products within Japan
S.I.C.: 6311
Kiyofumi Sakaguchi *(Pres.)*

Prudential Overseas Funding Corp. N.V. **(1)**
Labadera Plaza, Santa Rosaweg 129 E
Curacao, Netherlands Antilles (100%)
Provides Financial Services
S.I.C.: 8742

The Prudential Insurance Company of America—(Continued)

Martha Clark Briley *(Dir.)*

PruServicos Participacoes, S.A., c/o Prudential Atlantic Companhia Brasileira de Seguros **(1)**
Rua BoaVista 254,9, Andar,
Sao Paulo, 01014, Brazil
Tel.: 55-11-258-7455 (99.9%)
Holding Co.
S.I.C.: 6719
J.M. Pinheiro *(Pres.)*

Le Rocher, Compagnie de Reassurance, S.A. **(1)**
35 Square de Meeus BTE-1 1040
Brussels, Belgium
Tel.: (011-32-2) 513-9140 (99.9%)
Sub. of Prudential Reinsurance Co.;
Property & Casualty Reinsurance
S.I.C.: 6331
Claude E. Nyssen *(Mng. Dir.)*

Le Rocher UK, Ltd. **(1)**
37-39 Lime Street
London, EC3 M7AY, United Kingdom
Tel.: 071-621-1860
Property & Casualty Reinsurance
S.I.C.: 6331
Claude E. Nyssen *(Mng. Dir.)*

PRUDENTIAL METAL SUPPLY CORP.
171 Milton St.
East Dedham, MA 02026
Mailing Address:
P.O. Box 4159,
East Dedham, MA 02026
Tel.: 617-329-3232 MA
Fax: 617-326-0752
Year Founded: 1959
Approx.Sls.: $65,000,000
Emp.: 110
Import
Wholesale Building Materials
S.I.C.: 5039
Robert A. Kolikof *(Pres., Chief Exec. Officer & Chief Oper. Officer)*
Peter Daniels *(Pres.-Southern Div.)*
Richard H. Rossman *(Pres.-Northern Div.)*
Irving Helman *(Sec.)*
Martha Fisher *(Controller & Asst. Treas.)*

No. of U.S. Offices: 7

Computer Systems/Hardware:
DEC

Outside Service Firm(s):

Tobin & Waldstein*(Auditors)*
Newton, MA

Lumber Mutual*(Commercial Insurance Carrier)*
Framingham, MA

Guardian Life Insurance Co.*(Group Insurer)*
Boston, MA

Nutter, McClennen & Fish*(Legal Firm)*
One International Place
Boston, MA 02210-2699
Tel.: 617-439-2000

Bay Bank Boston, N.A.*(Major Banking Relationship)*
Boston, MA

First National Bank of Boston*(Major Banking Relationship)*
150 Royall St.
Canton, MA 02021
Tel.: 617-575-2900
Tel.: 800-442-2001

Westfield Management*(Pension Manager)*
Boston, MA

PSOMAS & ASSOCIATES
3420 Ocean Park Blvd.
Santa Monica, CA 90405
Tel.: 310-450-1217 CA
Fax: 310-452-7411
Year Founded: 1946
Approx.Sls.: $35,000,000
Emp.: 350
Surveying; Engineering Services & Planners
S.I.C.: 8713; 8711
George Psomas *(Chm. Bd.)*
Tim Psomas *(Pres.)*
George Colvan *(V.P.)*
Ronald Vinje *(Treas. & Sec.)*

Outside Service Firm(s):

Sanwa Bank*(Major Banking Relationship)*
601 S. Figueroa St.
Los Angeles, CA 90017
Tel.: 213-896-7817
Fax: 213-489-1977

PUBLIC MEDIA CENTER
466 Green St.
San Francisco, CA 94133
Tel.: 415-434-1403
Fax: 415-986-6779
Approx.Billings: $30,250,000
Advocacy, Unions, Government, Public Interest & Public Service
Herbert Chao Gunther *(Pres.)*
Dan Scharlin *(V.P., Fin.)*
Carolanne Allen *(Direct Mail Supvr.)*

PUBLIC STORAGE, INC.
600 N. Brant Blvd., Ste. 300
Glendale, CA 91203
Tel.: 818-244-8080
Fax: 818-244-9530
Approx.Rev.: $162,000,000
Emp.: 4,000
Fiscal Year-end: 12/31/90
Holding Company; Mini Warehouse Construction
S.I.C.: 4225; 1541; 6719
Kenneth G. Volk, Jr. *(Chm. Bd.)*
B. Wayne Hughes *(Pres. & Chief Exec. Officer)*
Robert K. Cole *(Pres.-Real Estate Fin. Grp.)*
Hugh W. Horne *(Pres.-Real Estate Devel. Grp.)*
Harvey Lenkin *(Pres.-Capital Markets Grp.)*
Marvin Lotz *(Pres.-Pub. Storage Mngmt., Inc. & Real Estate Aquisition Grp.)*
Mary Jayne Overman *(Pres.-Pub. Storage Commercial Properties Grp., Inc.)*
Ronald Havner *(Chief Fin. Officer)*
Ron Havner *(V.P. & Controller)*
Paul A Lund *(V.P.-Investor Services)*
Peggy A. McShane *(V.P.-Admin.)*
Peter J. Nelson *(V.P.-Corp. Information)*

Outside Service Firm(s):

Ernst & Young*(Auditors)*
515 S. Flower St.
Los Angeles, CA 90071
Tel.: 213-621-1666

Sachs & Phelps*(Legal Firm)*
Los Angeles, CA

Wells Fargo Bank*(Major Banking Relationship)*
9000 Flair
El Monte, CA

Subsidiaries:

Public Storage Commercial Properties Group, Inc. **(1)**
600 N. Brant Blvd., Ste. 300
Glendale, CA 91203
Tel.: 818-244-8080

Public Storage Management **(1)**
600 N. Brant Blvd., Ste. 300
Glendale, CA 91203
Tel.: 818-244-8080
Marvin Lotz *(Pres.)*

Public Storage Properties **(1)**
600 N. Brant Blvd., Ste. 300
Glendale, CA 91203
Tel.: 818-244-8080
Mary Jayne Overman *(Pres.)*

Western Storage Insurance Co. **(1)**
2929 N. 44th St., Suite 120
Phoenix, AZ 85018

Non-U.S. Holding:

Canadian Mini-Warehouse Properties, Ltd. **(1)**
1550 Meyerside Dr., Unit 7
Mississauga, ON L5T 1V4, Canada
Tel.: 416-564-2020 (100%)
Construction & Mngmt. of Mini-Warehouses
S.I.C.: 1541; 4225

PUBLISHERS CLEARING HOUSE
382 Channel Dr.
Port Washington, NY 11050
Tel.: 516-883-5432
Fax: 516-767-7219
Year Founded: 1953
Sales Range: $100-499 Million
Emp.: 700
Fiscal Year-end: 12/31/90
Direct Mail Marketing & Telemarketing of Magazine Subscriptions & Products
S.I.C.: 5961; 7389
Robin Smith *(Pres. & Chief Exec. Officer)*
Ralph Sabatini *(Chief Fin. Officer & V.P.)*
Bruce Pantano *(Exec. V.P.)*
Thomas P. Owens *(Sr. V.P.-Creative)*
Tom Lagan *(V.P.-Opers.)*
William Johnson *(Asst. V.P.)*
Nick Petrillo *(Asst. V.P.-Info. Services)*
Daniel P. Doyle *(Treas.)*
Ted Kasnicki *(Controller)*
Patricia A. Zerah *(Asst. Controller)*
David C. Sayer *(Exec. Dir.-Adv. & Pub. Rels.)*
Todd Sloane *(Assoc. Dir.-Adv.)*
Ellen Gorecici *(Mgr.-Risk Mgmt.)*

Computer Systems/Hardware:
REI System

Outside Service Firm(s):

Pannell, Kerr, Forster*(Auditors)*
420 Lexington Ave.
New York, NY 10170
Tel.: 212-867-8000

Morgan, Lewis & Bockius*(Legal Firm)*
101 Park Ave.
New York, NY 10178
Tel.: 212-309-6000

The Bank of New York*(Major Banking Relationship)*
Garden City, NY

European American Bank*(Major Banking Relationship)*
New York, NY

Morgan Stanley & Co.*(Pension Manager)*
1251 Avenue of the Americas
New York, NY 10020

Subsidiary:

The Power Line **(1)**
382 Channel Dr.
Port Washington, NY 11050
Tel.: 516-883-4300
Telemarketing
S.I.C.: 7389

PUBLIX GROUP
(Formerly Publix Shirt Corp.)
350 Fifth Ave.
New York, NY 10118
Tel.: 212-695-4700
Fax: 212-736-9522
Mfr. Mens Shirts & Sportswear; Career Club Men's Shirts, Bruxton Boy's Shirts
S.I.C.: 2321
David Zelmo *(Pres.)*
Wayne S. Miller *(Chief Fin. Officer)*
Herbert Holzer *(Exec. V.P.)*
Stanley Wagner *(Treas.)*
Irwin Goldman *(Pur. Agent)*

Outside Service Firm(s):

Richard A. Eisner & Co.*(Auditors)*
575 Madison Ave.
New York, NY 10022
Tel.: 212-355-1700

Bank of New York*(Major Banking Relationship)*
90 Washington St.
New York, NY 10015

Division:

Career Club Shirt Co. **(1)**
350 Fifth Ave.
New York, NY 10118
Tel.: 212-695-4700
Shirts, Sportswear, Knitwear
S.I.C.: 2321; 2326
Donald Sutherland *(Chm. Bd.)*
Ed Gilgallon *(Pres.)*
Wayne Miller *(Chief Fin. Officer)*
Margie Orlich *(Personnel Mgr.)*
Irwin Moss *(Export Mgr.)*
Irwin Goldman *(Pur. Agent)*

PUBLIX SUPERMARKETS INC.
1936 George Jenkins Blvd.
Lakeland, FL 33802
Mailing Address:
P.O. Box 407,
Lakeland, FL 33802
Tel.: 813-688-1188 FL
Fax: 813-680-5257
Year Founded: 1930
Assets: $1,475,000,000
Earnings: $149,000,000
Liabilities: $515,000,000
Net Worth: $960,000,000
Approx.Sls.: $5,758,000,000
Emp.: 65,000
Fiscal Year-end: 12/29/90
Retail Grocery
S.I.C.: 5411; 5421; 5461; 5912; 5921
George W. Jenkins *(Founder & Chm. Emeritus)*
Howard Jenkins *(Chm. Bd. & Chief Exec. Officer)*
Charles H. Jenkins, Jr. *(Chm.-Exec. Committee)*
Mark C. Hollis *(Pres. & Chief Oper. Officer)*
Hoyt Barnett *(Exec. V.P.-Admin.)*
Edward H. Ruth *(V.P.-Human Resources)*
Bill Curry *(V.P.-Real Estate)*
Dan Risener *(V.P.-Mngmt. Information Systems)*
Edward Shivers *(V.P.-Insurance & Safety)*
Mark Irby *(V.P.-Mktg. & Adv.)*
Ernestine Tye *(V.P.-Admin.)*
William H. Vass *(V.P.-Fin. & Treas.)*
David Phillips *(Controller)*
S. Keith Billups *(Sec.)*
Bob McDermott *(Dir.-Pub. Rels.)*
Mary Ann Jones *(Dir.-Customer Rels.)*
Clayton Hollis *(Dir.-Government Rels.)*
H. Edward Crosby *(Dir.-Equip. & Maintenance)*
Ron Miller *(Dir.-Pharmacy)*
J. Earl Andrews *(Dir.-EFTS Presto Network)*
Janis Ferguson *(Dir.-Quality Assurance)*
Grant Booth *(Dir.-Safety)*
Principal(s):

Carol Jenkins Barnett

No. of Mfg. Plants/Facilities: 10

Computer Systems/Hardware:
IBM Systems 3083 & 4381

Outside Service Firm(s):

KPMG Peat Marwick*(Auditors)*
201 N. Franklin St., Ste. 3000
Tampa, FL 33602
Tel.: 813-223-1466
Fax: 813-229-3976

Hartford Life Insurance Co.*(Commercial Insurance Carrier)*
Hartford, CT 06104-2999

Blue Cross & Blue Shield of Florida, Inc.*(Group Insurer)*
532 Riverside
Jacksonville, FL 32231
Tel.: 904-363-5572
Fax: 904-363-5180

Ash, Baursfeld, Burton, Hendrick & Tyrell*(Legal Firm)*
Bethesda, MD

Citibank N.A.*(Major Banking Relationship)*
Corporate Trust Services, 399 Park Ave.
New York, NY 10043
Tel.: 212-559-1605

Peoples Bank*(Major Banking Relationship)*
Lakeland, FL

Divisions:

Publix Super Markets, Inc. **(1)**
P.O. Box 699030
Miami, FL 33269
Tel.: 305-652-2411
Distribution Warehouse
S.I.C.: 4222; 5141
C.L. Newsome *(V.P.)*
Hubert C. Collins *(V.P.-Retail Opers.)*
John Bernard *(Adv. Dir.)*
Dave Swartz *(Dir.-Meat Opers.)*
John Sozio *(Dir.-Produce Opers.)*
Bill Duncan *(Dir.-Dairy/Frozen Foods)*
Thomas O'Connor *(Dir.-Warehouse & Distr.)*

Publix Super Markets, Inc. **(1)**
P.O. Box 2226-F,
Jacksonville, FL 32220
Tel.: 904-781-8600
Warehouse & Distribution
S.I.C.: 4222; 6141
Jesse Benton *(V.P.)*
Danny Sapp *(Dir.-Retail Opers.)*
Robert H. Clayton *(Dir.-Warehousing & Transportation)*
Don Daughtry *(Dir.-Bakery Opers.)*
Clip Hopkins *(Dir.-Meat Opers.)*
Greg Sciullo *(Dir.-Produce Opers.)*

THE PUCKETT GROUP
4818 Washington Ave.
Saint Louis, MO 63108
Tel.: 314-367-3666
Year Founded: 1987
Approx.Billings: $17,450,000
Emp.: 25
Stephen R. Puckett *(Pres. & Creative Dir.)*
Phillip Behnen *(V.P., Chief Fin. Officer)*
Pat Bolling *(Pub. Rels. Dir.)*
Pamela Forbes *(Office Mgr.)*

Computer Systems/Hardware:
Macintosh Network

PUEBLO INTERNATIONAL, INC.
1300 N.W. 22nd St.
Pompano Beach, FL 33069
Tel.: 305-977-2500 DE
Year Founded: 1955
Assets: $301,570,000
Earnings: $9,030,000
Liabilities: $268,178,000
Net Worth: $33,392,000
Approx.Sls.: $1,132,011,000
Emp.: 10,000
Fiscal Year-end: 1/25/92
Import Export
65 Retail Supermarkets & Blockbuster Video Franchises
S.I.C.: 5141; 7841
David W. Morrow *(Chm. Bd., Pres., Chief Exec. Officer & Chief Oper. Officer)*
Jeffrey P. Freimark *(Exec. V.P., Chief Fin. Officer & Gen. Counsel & Sec.)*
Robert Locke *(Sr. V.P.-Plng. & Devel. & Asst. Sec.)*
Marci L. Yunes *(V.P.-Fin. & Treas.)*
Filiberto Berrios *(V.P.-Blockbuster Div.)*
Lawrence Elias *(V.P.-Mngmt. Information Systems)*
Edward A. Gallina *(V.P.-Florida & Virgin Islands)*
Lou Kertesz *(V.P.-Produce Mdsg. & Procurement)*
Robert Silverman *(V.P.-Distr. & Traffic)*
Rafael Torres *(V.P., Controller, Asst. Treas. & Asst. Sec.)*
Beryl Weinstein *(V.P.-Procurement)*
Steven E. Wolf *(V.P.-Human Resources)*

Division:

Pueblo International, Inc.-P.R. Div. **(1)**
Loiza Expwy. Corner of Campo Rico Ave.
Carolina, PR 00630
Tel.: 809-757-3131
Operates Superstores, Conventional Supermarkets & Wholesale Type Food Stores
S.I.C.: 5141; 5411
Hector Quinones *(Pres.)*
Martin Benjamin *(V.P.-Sls. & Mktg.)*
Juan Cogan *(V.P.-Warehouse & Asst. Sec.)*
Antonio Dajer *(V.P.-Human Resources & Asst. Sec.)*
Juan Marrero *(V.P.-Design, Construction & Maintenance)*
Manuel Rodriguez *(V.P.-Grocery & Dairy)*

Subsidiary:

Xtra Super Food Centers, Inc. **(1)**
1300 N.W. 22nd St.
Pompano Beach, FL 33069
Tel.: 305-977-2500 (100%)
Supermarkets
S.I.C.: 5411

PUERTO RICO TOURISM COMPANY
575 Fifth Ave.
New York, NY 10017
Mailing Address:
2 Paseo La Princesa
Old San Juan, PR 00902
Tel.: 212-599-6262
Tel.: 800-223-6530
Fax: 212-818-1866
Year Founded: 1970
Approx.Sls.: $900,000,000
Emp.: 300
Fiscal Year-end: 6/30/90
Tourist Products & Services
S.I.C.: 7389
Miguel A. Domenech *(Exec. Dir.)*
Carlos Diago *(Deputy Dir.)*
Jose A. Rivera *(Comptroller)*
Jaime Rullan *(Dir.-Finance)*
Clarisa Jimencz *(Dir.-Mktg.)*
Meriemil Rodriguez *(Dir.-Communications)*
Jose O. Rolon *(Dir.-Gen. Services)*
Benjamin Van Derdys *(Dir.-Personnel)*

PUGET SOUND PLYWOOD, INC.
P.O. Box 1378
Tacoma, WA 98401
Tel.: 206-627-4111
Year Founded: 1941
Approx.Sls.: $10,000,000
Emp.: 150
Export
Manufacture & Distribute Softwood Plywood
S.I.C.: 2436; 5031
Charles L. Mougey *(Chm. Bd., Treas. & Mgr.-Sls.)*
Leamon J. Bennett *(Pres.)*
Carl Wittenberg *(Controller)*
Morris D. Mortensen *(Sec.)*
Carl R. Wiley *(Gen. Mgr. & Real Estate Officer)*
Carol Benton *(Employee Benefits)*

Computer Systems/Hardware:
IBM

Outside Service Firm(s):

Johnson, Stone, Deaton, Pagano & Co.*(Auditors)*
Tacoma, WA

Gordon, Thomas, Honeywell, Malanca, Peterson & Daheim*(Legal Firm)*
Tacoma, WA

Seafirst Bank*(Major Banking Relationship)*
Seattle, WA

PUGH OIL COMPANY
200 Dodge St.
Racine, WI 53402
Tel.: 414-632-4491
Fax: 414-632-1732
Emp.: 50
Wholesale & Retail Gas, Diesel & Home Fuels
S.I.C.: 5172; 5989; 6719
William Pugh, Jr. *(Chm. Bd. & Pres.)*
Joseph Arvai *(V.P.)*

Computer Systems/Hardware:
IBM PC-XT

Outside Service Firm(s):

Stewart, Payton, Crowford, Tutt*(Legal Firm)*
Racine, WI

Bank One Milwaukee, N.A.*(Major Banking Relationship)*
111 E. Wisconsin Ave.
Milwaukee, WI
Tel.: 414-765-3000

Subsidiaries:

Pugh Marina **(1)**
200 Dodge St.
Racine, WI 53402
Tel.: 414-632-4491

Pugh Oil Company **(1)**
200 Dodge St.
Racine, WI 53402
Tel.: 414-632-4491

White Flash Oil Co. **(1)**
200 Dodge St.
Racine, WI 53402
Tel.: 414-632-4491

PULLIAM MOTOR COMPANY
2800 Two Notch Rd.
Columbia, SC 29204
Tel.: 803-254-4000 DE
Fax: 803-254-4000, Ext. 124
Year Founded: 1930
Approx.Sls.: $26,000,000
Emp.: 122
Fiscal Year-end: 7/31/91
Wholesale & Retail Ford Automobiles & Trucks; Parts & Service
S.I.C.: 5012; 5511
Robert F. Pulliam *(Chm. Bd.)*
Harold Uray *(Pres.)*
Wayne McDaniel *(Controller)*
Bill Childs *(Mgr.-Sls.)*
Ralph Poe *(Mgr.-Service)*
Ann McCallister *(Mgr.-Credit)*

Computer Systems/Hardware:
Datapoint

Outside Service Firm(s):

Ernst & Young*(Auditors)*
P.O. Box 627, 1611 Devonshire Dr.
Columbia, SC 20202
Tel.: 803-254-4700
Fax: 803-252-4090

The McNair Firm*(Legal Firm)*
Columbia, SC

Carolina South Federal Bank*(Major Banking Relationship)*
Columbia, SC

THE PULLMAN COMPANY
(A Co. of Forstmann Little & Co.)
220 S. Orange Ave.
Livingston, NJ 07039
Tel.: 201-535-9522 DE
Fax: 201-535-9837
Assets: $708,415,000
Earnings: $17,632,000
Liabilities: $530,292,000
Net Worth: $178,123,000
Approx.Sls.: $612,627,000
Emp.: 6,500
Manufacture Truck Trailers, Aircraft Seating & Food Service Systems, Provides Engineering Services to the Industry & the Computer Telecommunications & Defense Industries
S.I.C.: 3715; 2531; 8711
William Turner *(Chm. Bd., Pres., Chief Exec. & Chief Oper. Officer)*
Henry S. Lager *(Sr. V.P.-Human Resources)*
Ronald B. Kalich *(Grp. V.P.)*
D. Craig Bowman *(V.P. & Assoc. Gen. Counsel)*

Divisions:

Clevite Elastomers **(1)**
33 Lockwood Rd.
Milan, OH 44846
Tel.: 419-499-2541
Twx: 419-499-2600
Elastomer Products
S.I.C.: 2822; 2824
James B. Gray *(Pres.)*

Imperial Division **(1)**
6300 W. Howard St.
Niles, IL 60648
Tel.: 708-967-4500
Telex: 72 4499
Twx: 910-223-3648
Hydraulic Control Components & Sytems, Hose Assemblies, Tube Fittings & Valves
S.I.C.: 3494
John Higgins *(Pres.)*

Division:

Peabody Engineering Corp. **(2)**
39 Maple St., P.O. Box 2331
Stamford, CT 06906
Tel.: 203-327-7000
S.I.C.: 8711
Frank Lammers *(Pres.)*

Subsidiaries:

Aircraft Products Company **(1)**
12807 Lake Dr.
Delray Beach, FL 33444
Tel.: 407-276-6083
S.I.C.: 3728
E. Ernest Schwartz *(Pres.)*

Aircraft Products Company **(1)**
11710 Central Pkwy.
Jacksonville, FL 32216
Tel.: 904-641-4900
S.I.C.: 3728
Lawrence J. Beard *(V.P. & Gen. Mgr.)*

PTC Aerospace **(1)**
Rte. 202
Bantam, CT 06750
Tel.: 203-567-9441
Aircraft Seats, Gslleys & Food Service Systems
S.I.C.: 2531
Dwayne Woodford *(Pres.)*

PTC Aerospace **(1)**
11752 Markon Dr.
Garden Grove, CA 92641
Tel.: 714-891-3681
S.I.C.: 2531
Donald D. Rutter *(V.P. & Gen. Mgr.)*

The Pullman Company—(Continued)

Peabody Floway, Inc. **(1)**
2494 S. Railroad Ave., P.O. Box 164
Fresno, CA 93707
Tel.: 209-442-4000
S.I.C.: 3561
Raymond W. Dunn *(Pres.)*

Peabody Myers Corp. **(1)**
1621 S. Illinois St.
Streator, IL 61364
Tel.: 815-672-3171
Approx.Sls.: $23,000,000
Emp.: 150
S.I.C.: 3589; 3523
Dennis Sexhus *(Pres.)*
William Aichele *(Controller)*
Barry W. Collins *(Mgr.-Personnel & Adv.)*

Peabody N.E., Inc. **(1)**
P.O. Box 419, 117 Eastman Street
North Easton, MA 02356
Tel.: 617-238-7901
S.I.C.: 1629
John C. Wright *(Pres.)*

Peabody TecTank, Inc. **(1)**
P.O. Box 996,
Parsons, KS 67357
Tel.: 316-421-0200
Mfr. of Bolted Storage Tanks
S.I.C.: 3443
John R. Farris *(Pres.)*

Trailmobile **(1)**
200 E. Randolph
Chicago, IL 60601
Tel.: 312-861-1190
Manufacture Truck Trailers
S.I.C.: 3715
Michael J. Brown *(Pres.)*

Non-U.S. Holdings:

Axios, Ltda. **(1)**
Rua Brasilio Luz, 535 Sto. Amaro 04746,
Sao Paulo, SP Brazil
Tel.: 11-493-3322
M. Telo *(Chief Oper. Officer)*

Barnes de Colombia **(1)**
Apartado 12098, Calle 15 No. 41-17
Bogota, Colombia
Tel.: 268-63-66 (80%)
Pumps for Municipal, Indus., Domestic, Mining/Oil, Construction, Farm/Agricultural & Marine
S.I.C.: 3561
Enrique Bayer *(Pres.)*

Barnes de Mexico **(1)**
Apartado 1774
Monterrey, N.L. Mexico
Tel.: 51-37-37 (20%)
Pumps
S.I.C.: 3561
Enrique Bayer *(Pres.)*

Bi-Metal Bearing **(1)**
c/o Amalgamations Ltd., 861 Anna Salai
Madras, 600 022, India
Bearings
S.I.C.: 3568
A. Krishnamoorthy *(Chief Oper. Officer)*

Clevite de Mexico **(1)**
Monte Caucaso No. 915-6 Piso Lomas de Chapultepec, 11000
Mexico, D.F. Mexico
Tel.: 905-540-0404
Hose Assemblies
S.I.C.: 3494
Jose Alvarez *(Gen. Dir.)*

Clevite SRL **(1)**
Via Bepi Todesca 12 38014
Gardolo, Italy
Tel.: 39-461-990321
Hose Assemblies
S.I.C.: 3494
P. Armanini *(Chief Oper. Officer)*

I-E Proprietary, Ltd. **(1)**
Sydney, N.S.W. Australia
Tel.: 61-02-604-3377
Hose Assemblies, Sub. of Imperial Clevite
S.I.C.: 3494
Kit Carson *(Chief Oper. Officer)*

Imperial Clevite do Brazil **(1)**
Rua Brasilio Luz, 535 Sto. Amaro 04746,
Sao Paulo, Brazil
Tel.: 11-493-3322
Hose Assemblies
S.I.C.: 3494
Manuel Telo *(Chief Oper. Officer)*

Metal Leve S.A. **(1)**
Rua Brasilio Luz, 535 Sto. Amaro 04746,
Sao Paulo, S.P. Brazil
Tel.: 11-522-7011
Mfr. of Pistons for Diesel Engines
S.I.C.: 3592
Wilson Carvalho *(Exec. Dir.)*

Metalurgica Detroit **(1)**
Rua Brasilio Luz, 535 Sto. Amaro 04746,
Sao Paulo, S.P. Brazil
Tel.: 11-445-2118
H. Seabra *(Chief Oper. Officer)*

NDC Co. Ltd. **(1)**
1-687 Mimomi-Cho Narashini-Shi,
Chiba, Ken 275, Japan
Tel.: 0474 72 1121
Y. Nakajima *(Pres.)*

Peabody Holmes Limited **(1)**
Turnbridge
Huddersfield, HD1 6RB, United Kingdom
Tel.: 0484 22222
Air Blowers & Crushers; Mineral & Solid Waste Mngmt. Telex: 51306
S.I.C.: 3564
Ronald J. Cowie *(Dir. & Gen. Mgr.)*

REPCO Bearing Company, Div. of REPCO Ltd. **(1)**
P.O. Box 1088, E. Tamar Highway
Launceston, Tasmania 7250, Australia
Tel.: 0111-61-3-26-1222
Bearings
S.I.C.: 3568
Ivan James *(Gen. Mgr.)*

PULLMAN INDUSTRIES, INC.
25359 Dequindre Rd.
Madison Heights, MI 48071
Tel.: 313-546-4730 **MI**
Fax: 313-546-4735
Year Founded: 1951
Approx.Sls.: $15,000,000
Emp.: 150
Manufacture Automotive Rolled Form Products & Stampings
S.I.C.: 3499; 3465; 3469
Donald D. Carstens *(Chm. Bd.)*
Edwin Matthewson *(Pres. & Chief Exec. Officer)*
Lee Place *(V.P. & Treas.)*
A.G. Rekar *(V.P.-Sls.)*
Joseph Turner *(V.P.-Mfg.)*
William Ott *(Controller)*
Randy Doe *(Dir.-Pur.)*
Principal(s):
Donald D. Carstens

No. of Mfg. Plants/Facilities: 2
No. of U.S. Offices: 3

Computer Systems/Hardware:
IBM AS 400

Outside Service Firm(s):

Price Waterhouse*(Auditors)*
67 W. Michigan Mall
Battle Creek, MI 49017

Massachusetts Mutual Life Insurance Co.*(Group Insurer)*
Troy, MI

Mutual Benefit Life Insurance*(Group Insurer)*
Grand Rapids, MI

Miller, Canfield, Paddock & Stone*(Legal Firm)*
Kalamazoo, MI

Comerica Bank*(Major Banking Relationship)*
211 W. Fort St.
Detroit, MI 48226
Tel.: 313-222-3300

PUMPELLY OIL, INC.
Old Spanish Trail
Westlake, LA 70669
Mailing Address:
P.O. Box 610
Westlake, LA 70669
Tel.: 318-436-3361 **LA**
Fax: 318-433-6327
Approx.Sls.: $15,000,000
Emp.: 40
Gasoline & Oil
S.I.C.: 5171; 5172
Robert J. Pumpelly *(Chm. Bd.)*
R. Glenn Pumpelly *(Pres.)*
Vida Pumpelly *(V.P.)*
Jane Brumby *(Treas.)*
David Brumby *(Sec.)*
Richard Chozen *(Gen. Counsel)*
Principal(s):
Robert J. Pumpelly
R. Glenn Pumpelly
Vida Pumpelly

No. of U.S. Offices: 3

Computer Systems/Hardware:
IBM System 36

Outside Service Firm(s):

Larry Stephenson*(Auditors)*
Lake Charles, LA

Blue Cross & Blue Shield of Louisiana*(Commercial Insurance Carrier)*
Baton Rouge, LA

Continental Insurance*(Group Insurer)*
180 Maiden Lane
New York, NY

Richard Chozen*(Legal Firm)*
Lake Charles, LA

Calcasieu Marine National Bank*(Major Banking Relationship)*
P.O. Box 3402
Lake Charles, LA 70602
Tel.: 318-439-4541

PUNA PLANTATION HAWAII LTD.
50 E. Puainako St.
Hilo, HI 96720
Tel.: 808-959-4575 **HI**
Year Founded: 1916
Approx.Sls.: $67,000,000
Emp.: 475
Supermarkets Chain
S.I.C.: 5411
Hidetoshi Taniguchi *(Chm. Bd.)*
Barry Taniguchi *(Pres.)*
Lon Taniguchi *(V.P. & Sec.)*
Roger Kawasaki *(Treas.)*

Outside Service Firm(s):

Bank of Hawaii*(Major Banking Relationship)*
Honolulu, HI

PURCELL CO., INC.
4402 E. Aloha Dr., Ste. 3
Bay Saint Louis, MS 39520
Tel.: 601-255-7773 **DE**
Fax: 601-255-7930
Year Founded: 1969
Approx.Sls.: $15,000,000
Emp.: 250
Real Estate Devel.; Resort, Municipal & Commercial Operations
S.I.C.: 6552; 6531; 6513; 1531; 6515
Artis E. James, Jr. *(Pres. & Chief Exec. Officer)*
Bill Alexander *(V.P., Treas. & Chief Fin. Officer)*
P. Holcomb Hector *(V.P.)*
George M. McCook *(V.P.-Sls.)*
Carl H. Joffe *(Sec. & Gen. Counsel)*

Divisions:

Diamondhead Div. **(1)**
100 Construction Rd.
Bay Saint Louis, MS 39520
Tel.: 601-255-1236
Emp.: 136
Real Estate Development, Resort & Municipal Operations
S.I.C.: 6531
P. Holcomb Hector *(V.P. & G.M.)*

Lake Arrowhead Div. **(1)**
P.O. Station 20,
Waleska, GA 30183
Tel.: 706-479-5505
Emp.: 80
Real Estate Development, Resort & Municipal Operations
S.I.C.: 6531
Paul G. Snyder *(V.P.)*
John Vest *(Gen. Mgr.)*

Newport Div. **(1)**
P.O. Box 191,
Crosby, TX 77532
Tel.: 713-328-3511
Emp.: 78
Real Estate Devel. & Resort Opers.
S.I.C.: 6531
Jake Bodiford *(Gen. Mgr.)*

Sandpiper Cove Div. **(1)**
P.O. Box 695,
Destin, FL 32541
Tel.: 904-837-8284
Emp.: 8
Real Estate Development
S.I.C.: 6531
George Fontaine *(Gen. Mgr.)*

PURCELL INTERNATIONAL GROUP, INC.
1640 S. Sepulveda Blvd., Ste. 112
Los Angeles, CA 90025
Tel.: 310-477-4433 **DE**
Fax: 310-478-2711
Year Founded: 1969
Approx.Sls.: $28,000,000
Emp.: 145
Employment Agencies
S.I.C.: 7361
Frank Purcell *(Pres. & Chief Exec. Officer)*
Dick Green *(Chief Fin. Officer)*
Robert Abbott *(Sr. V.P.)*
Mike Davis *(Sr. V.P.)*
Jill Sherman *(V.P.-Legal Search Div.)*
Robert Sumpter *(V.P.-Healthcare Search Div.)*

PURITAN BAKERY, INC.
1624 E. Carson St.
Carson, CA 90745
Tel.: 310-830-5451
Fax: 310-830-1164
Approx.Sls.: $12,000,000
Emp.: 100
Manufacture Bakery Products
S.I.C.: 2051
Thomas D. Grimes *(Pres. & Treas.)*
John Markluis *(V.P. & Sec.)*

Outside Service Firm(s):

Ron Hallal*(Auditors)*
Carson, CA

PURITAN/CHURCHILL CHEMICAL COMPANY
916 Ashby St., N. W.
Atlanta, GA 30318
Tel.: 404-875-7331
Fax: 706-876-0116
Year Founded: 1920
Approx.Sls.: $21,000,000
Emp.: 250
Fiscal Year-end: 6/30/91
Export
Polishing Compounds, Soaps, Detergents, Disinfectants, Sanitary & Industrial Maintenance Chemicals, Supplies & Equip.
S.I.C.: 2842; 2841; 2899

John Ashcroft *(Chm. Bd.)*
Tom Reynolds *(Pres.)*
William Keng *(V.P.-Technical)*
Frank Saxton *(V.P.-Mktg. Devel.)*
Regina Crothers *(Controller)*
Richard Kropfl *(Pur. Dir.)*

PURITY DAIRIES INC.
360 Murfreesboro Rd.,
Nashville, TN 37210
Mailing Address:
P.O. Box 100957,
Nashville, TN 37210
Tel.: 615-244-1900 **TN**
Fax: 615-242-8547
Year Founded: 1946
Sales Range: $60-79 Million
Emp.: 290
Manufacturer of Dairy Products
S.I.C.: 2026
F. Miles Ezell, Sr. *(Chm. Bd.)*
John William Ezell *(Pres.)*
Stan Ezell *(V.P. & Sec.)*
John R. Robinson *(V.P. & Treas.)*

Computer Systems/Hardware:
Micro Vax 4000

Outside Service Firm(s):

Guilliams, Wilson & Butler*(Auditors)*
Nashville, TN

First American National Bank*(Major Banking Relationship)*
First American Center
Nashville, TN 37237
Tel.: 615-748-2442

PURITY, INC.
(Formerly Purity Condiments, Inc.)
1800 N.W. 70th Ave.
Miami, FL 33126
Tel.: 305-592-3600
Tel.: 800-654-0235 **DE**
Fax: 305-592-2601
Year Founded: 1935
Approx.Sls.: $22,000,000
Emp.: 84
Fiscal Year-end: 10/31/91
Import Export
Mfr. of Salad Dressings, Mustard, Seasonings, Fruit & Meat Sauces, Syrups & Cleaning Compounds for the Institutional & Foodservice Industries
S.I.C.: 2035; 2087
Carlos C. Fernandez *(Chm., Pres. & Chief Exec. Officer)*
Robert Hooker *(Exec. V.P.-Sls.)*
Michael A. Koven *(Chief Fin. Officer)*
Michael Smith *(Sec.)*
Timothy Knowlton *(Dir.-Quality Control & Res. & Devel.)*
Charles Menezes *(Dlr.-Pur.)*
Marie Diaz *(Mgr.-Export & Import)*

Principal(s):
Carlos C. Fernandez

Outside Service Firm(s):

Deloitte & Touche*(Auditors)*
100 S.E. 2nd St.
Miami, FL 33131-2135
Tel.: 305-538-4141

Liberty Mutual*(Commercial Insurance Carrier)*
8420 NW 52nd St.
Miami, FL 33166
Tel.: 305-592-0370

National Canada Finance Corp.*(Investment Banker)*
Boca Raton, FL

Vedder, Price, Kaufman & Kammholz*(Legal Firm)*
115 S. LaSalle St.
Chicago, IL 60603
Tel.: 312-781-2200

PURITY SUPREME, INC.
2 Billerica Pk., 101 Billerica Ave.
North Billerica, MA 01862
Tel.: 508-663-0750
Food Stores; Angelo's
S.I.C.: 5411
Peter Sodini *(Pres.)*

LAT PURSER & ASSOCIATE
901 S. Kings Dr., Suite #100
Charlotte, NC 28204
Tel.: 704-374-0999
Fax: 704-343-9155
Year Founded: 1961
Sales Range: $100-499 Million
Emp.: 51
Real Estate Developer
S.I.C.: 6552
Lat W. Purser III *(Pres. & Head of Devel.)*
Eric Nichols *(Pres.-Mortgage Co.)*
Arthur T. Townsend *(Chief Fin. Officer & Chief Oper. Officer)*
Linn R. Miller *(Exec. V.P.)*
Robert J. Otten *(Exec. V.P. & Dir. of Prop. Mngmnt.)*
Robert Monaghan *(Controller)*
Steve Horvath *(Dir.-Brokerage)*
Jack Levinson *(Dir.-Leasing)*
Melanie Soles *(Dir.-Mktg.)*

No. of U.S. Offices: 3

Outside Service Firm(s):

Principal Mutual Life Insurance Co.*(Group Insurer)*
711 High St.
Des Moines, IA 50309

Robert Hord*(Legal Firm)*
Charlotte, NC

PUSKAR GIBBON CHAPIN, INC.
3500 Maple Ave., Ste. 900
Dallas, TX 75219
Tel.: 214-528-5400
Fax: 214-521-4538
Year Founded: 1985
Approx.Billings: $47,500,000
Emp.: 47
Consumer Goods & Services
Ross Puskar *(Principal)*
Jim Gibbon *(Principal)*

PUTMAN PUBLISHING CO.
301 E. Erie St.
Chicago, IL 60611
Tel.: 312-644-2020 **DE**
Fax: 312-644-1131
Year Founded: 1938
Approx.Sls.: $21,000,000
Emp.: 140
Trade Journals, Publishing Only; Not Printed On Site
S.I.C.: 2721
Grace E. Cappelletti *(Pres.)*
John M. Cappelletti, Jr. *(V.P.)*
Nicholas G. Cappelletti *(V.P.)*
Bradley J. Hoffman *(Treas.)*

Outside Service Firm(s):

Blackman Kallick Bartelstein*(Auditors)*
300 Riverside Plaza
Chicago, IL 60606
Tel.: 312-207-1040

Carponelli & Krug*(Legal Firm)*
Chicago, IL

Harris Bank*(Major Banking Relationship)*
Chicago, IL

PUTT PUTT GOLF COURSES OF AMERICA, INC.
Putt Putt Bldg., 3007 Ft. Bragg Rd.
Fayetteville, NC 28303
Mailing Address:
P.O. Box 35237
Fayetteville, NC 28303
Tel.: 919-485-7131
Fax: 919-485-1122
Year Founded: 1954
Approx.Sls.: $63,000,000
Emp.: 243
Fiscal Year-end: 6/30/90
Import Export
Franchisor of Miniature Golf & Recreation Complexes
S.I.C.: 7999
E. Don Clayton *(Chm. Bd.)*
David R. Lloyd *(Vice Chm. & Chief Exec. Officer)*
Don S. Clayton *(Pres.)*
Bobby Owens *(V.P.)*
Donna Lloyd *(Sec.)*

Computer Systems/Hardware:
IBM S/36 & P.C.s

Subsidiaries:

Professional Putters Association **(1)**
3007 Fort Bragg Rd.
Fayetteville, NC 28303
Tel.: 919-485-7131
Fax: 919-485-1122
Emp.: 12
Tournament for Professional Putters
S.I.C.: 8611
Don Clayton *(Chm. Bd. & Pres.)*
David R. Lloyd *(Vice Chm., Chief Exec. Officer & Commissioner)*
Joe Aboid *(Natl. Tournament Dir.)*

Southern Golf Distributors, Inc. **(1)**
2913 Ft. Bragg Rd.
Fayetteville, NC 28303
Tel.: 919-485-7131
Fax: 919-484-2213
Import Export
Computer Systems/Hardware:
IBM S/36 & P.C.s
Supply Company for Miniature Golf, Driving Range & Sporting Goods
Larry Lloyd *(Pres.)*
Betty Jo Venrick *(V.P.)*

PUTZMEISTER, INC.
18601 S. Main St.
Gardena, CA 90248
Tel.: 310-769-4500
Fax: 310-516-9820
Year Founded: 1982
Approx.Sls.: $24,000,000
Emp.: 55
Mfr. of Pumps & Pumping Equipment
S.I.C.: 3561
Karl Schlecht *(Chm. Bd.)*
Emile Pilafieis *(Pres.)*
William Burch *(V.P.)*
Al Ettl *(Chief Fin. Officer & Controller)*
Walter Schey *(Sec.)*

THE PYRAMID COMPANIES
The Clinton Exchange, 4 Clinton Sq.
Syracuse, NY 13202
Tel.: 315-422-7000
Fax: 315-422-2717
Emp.: 500
Real Estate Developer
S.I.C.: 6552
Robert J. Congel *(Mng. Partner)*
James A. Tuozzolo *(Chief Exec. Officer)*
David J. Nettina *(Mng. Dir.)*
Timothy Ahearn *(Dir.-Leasing)*

PYRAMID HANDBAGS INC.
100 W. 33rd St., Ste. 800
New York, NY 10001
Tel.: 212-714-2211
Tel.: 800-543-4327
Fax: 212-564-8160
Approx.Sls.: $15,000,000
Mfr. of Backpacks, Handbags, Luggage, Small Leather Goods, Coordinated Rainwear, Umbrellas, Diaper Bags & Totes
S.I.C.: 3171; 3161; 3172; 2385
Henry Fisher *(Pres.)*
Jeffrey Fisher *(V.P.)*
Mitch Cogen *(Mgr.-Sls.)*
Neal Fisher *(Gen. Mgr.)*

Outside Service Firm(s):

Marine Midland Bank*(Major Banking Relationship)*
New York, NY

PYRAMID MOUNTAIN LUMBER
Boy Scout Rd.
Seeley Lake, MT 59868
Mailing Address:
P.O. Box 549
Seeley Lake, MT 59868
Tel.: 406-677-2201 **MT**
Fax: 406-677-2509
Approx.Sls.: $16,000,000
Emp.: 135
Sawmill; Rough, Sawed or Planed Lumber
S.I.C.: 2421
Roger Johnson *(Pres.)*
Douglas Mood *(V.P.)*
Alfred Mood *(Treas. & Sec.)*
Loren Rose *(Dir.-Data Processing & Controller)*

Outside Service Firm(s):

Elmore & Associates*(Auditors)*
Missoula, MT

Garlinton, Lohn & Robinson*(Legal Firm)*
Missoula, MT

Washington Trust Bank*(Major Banking Relationship)*
Spokane, WA

PYROMET, INC.
5 Commerce Dr.
Aston, PA 19014
Tel.: 215-497-1743
Fax: 215-494-3349
Approx.Sls.: $19,000,000
Emp.: 6
Precious Metals
S.I.C.: 3339
Jaydee W. Miller *(Pres.)*
Katherine Miller *(Sec. & Treas.)*

Outside Service Firm(s):

Elko, Fischer, McCabe & Rudman*(Auditors)*
325 Providence Rd.
Media, PA
Tel.: 215-565-3930

PYTTRONIC INDUSTRIES, INC.
422 Stump Rd.
Montgomeryville, PA 18936
Mailing Address:
P.O. Box 1549
Lansdale, PA 79446
Tel.: 215-855-0925
Fax: 215-855-5120
Year Founded: 1966
Sales Range: $10-19 Million
Emp.: 30
Fiscal Year-end: 4/30/92
Electronic Components
S.I.C.: 3679
Morris Schumb *(Chm. Bd.)*
Harry Adams *(Pres., Chief Exec. Officer, & Chief FIn. Officer)*
Robert Juchem *(V.P.-Sls. & Mktg.)*
Louis Narrow *(V.P.-Sls.)*
Ronald Anderson *(Controller)*
John D'Angelo *(Dir.-Sls., Mktg., Purch.)*
Betsy Kolk *(Dir.-Admin./Oper.)*
Joe Hari *(Dir.-Qual. Control)*

Pyttronic Industries, Inc.—(Continued)

Holly Slotter *(Dir.-Data Proc.)*

No. of Mfg. Plants/Facilities: 2

Computer Systems/Hardware:
Prophet 21

Outside Service Firm(s):

Berman, Goldman & Ribakow*(Auditors)*
Baltimore, MD

Blue Cross & Blue Shield Association*(Group Insurance Broker/ Consult)*
Philadelphia, PA

Buchanan, Ingersoll p.c.*(Legal Firm)*
Harrisburg, PA

Maryland National Bank*(Major Banking Relationship)*
10 Light St.
Baltimore, MD 21203
Tel.: 410-244-5000

QEI, INC.
60 Fadem Rd.
Springfield, NJ 07081
Tel.: 201-379-7400
Approx.Sls.: $15,000,000
Emp.: 160
Mfr. Telemetering & Computer Interfacing Equipment
S.I.C.: 3823; 3577; 3663
Edward J. Hall *(Pres.)*
James Krugman *(V.P. & Treas.)*
Stefan Dalyai *(V.P.)*
John Caglione *(Pur. Dir.)*

Non-U.S. Holding:

Quindar Products Ltd. **(1)**
106 Rayette Rd.
Concord, ON L4K 2G3, Canada
Tel.: 416-669-1272
Mfrs. Radio & Television Broadcasting & Communications Equipment
S.I.C.: 3625; 3663
Allan Collins *(V.P.)*

QLM

QLM ASSOCIATES, INC.
470 Wall St.
Princeton, NJ 08540
Tel.: 609-683-1177
Year Founded: 1982
Approx.Billings: $14,000,000
Emp.: 80
Strategic Marketing Plans, Creative Execution,Sales Promotion
W. Robert Lipsky *(Pres.)*
M. Palmer *(Sr. V.P.-Plng.)*
J. A. Mitchell *(V.P.-Plng.)*
Julie MacKee *(Chief Fin. Officer)*
Elizabeth Groome *(Personnel Mgr.)*

QST INDUSTRIES, INC.
231 S. Jefferson
Chicago, IL 60661
Tel.: 312-930-9400
Fax: 312-648-0312
Year Founded: 1880
Approx.Sls.: $165,000,000
Emp.: 300
Textile Manufacture; Converter of Pocketing for Men's Wear; Importer & Exporter
S.I.C.: 2211; 2396; 5131
Ely Lionheart *(Pres.)*
Bill Haber *(Exec. V.P. & Sec.)*
Jeff Carlovatto *(Treas. & Controller)*

Computer Systems/Hardware:
Data General

Outside Service Firm(s):

Prudential Insurance Co. of America*(Group Insurer)*
751 Broad St.
Newark, NJ 07102-3777
Tel.: 201-802-6000

Altheimer & Gray*(Legal Firm)*
10 S. Wacker Dr.
Chicago, IL 60606
Tel.: 312-715-4000

Mid-City National Bank of Chicago*(Major Banking Relationship)*
Chicago, IL

QUACKENBUSH CO. INC.
505 Franklin St.
Buffalo, NY 14202
Tel.: 716-886-4355 **NY**
Fax: 716-883-8277
Year Founded: 1932
Approx.Sls.: $29,900,000
Emp.: 150
Mechanical Contractor; Prefabrication of Pipe Assemblies
S.I.C.: 1711; 3498
David S. Quackenbush *(Pres.)*
Roger H. Blank *(V.P.)*
Ronald R. Daverne *(V.P.)*
R. Fierle *(V.P., Treas. & Sec.)*

Outside Service Firm(s):

KPMG Peat Marwick*(Auditors)*
700 Empire Tower
Buffalo, NY 14202-3786
Tel.: 716-854-1830
Fax: 716-856-8063

Damon & Morey*(Legal Firm)*
1000 Cathedral Plaza
Buffalo, NY
Tel.: 716-856-5500
Fax: 716-856-5510

Manufacturers & Traders Trust Company*(Major Banking Relationship)*
1 M & T Plaza
Buffalo, NY 14240
Tel.: 716-842-4200

QUAD/GRAPHICS, INC.
W224 N3322 Duplainville Rd.
Pewaukee, WI 53072-4195
Tel.: 414-246-9200
Fax: 414-246-6620
Year Founded: 1971
Approx.Sls.: $525,000,000
Emp.: 6,000
Printing & Publishing
S.I.C.: 2752; 2754; 3823; 7319
Corporate Giving Program: The Windhover Foundation Makes Gifts to Charitable Organizations Such as Schools, Hospitals & Cultural Groups
Employee Matching Gifts Program: Co. Will Match Employee Donations in Any Amount to Charities, Schools, Hospitals, etc. of Employees' Choosing. Matching Donations are Made Annually.
H.R. Quadracci *(Chm. Bd.)*
H.V. Quadracci *(Pres. & Chief Exec. Officer)*
Frank M. Arndorfer *(V.P.-Finishing Opers.)*
Carl L. Bennett *(V.P.-Admin.)*
John C. Fowler *(V.P.-Fin.)*
Keith G. Hernke *(V.P.-Prod.)*
Jerry Kirby *(V.P.-Computer Services)*
James P. Melton *(V.P.-Press Opers.)*
Thomas A. Quadracci *(V.P.-Mfg.)*
James J. Ewens *(Treas.)*
Steven Ponto *(Corp. Counsel)*
Jeanne C. Kuelthau *(Corp. Sec.)*
Michael Hall *(Mgr.-Travel)*
Leslie J. Ratay *(Mgr.-Corp. Communications)*
Garda Stanis *(Mgr.-Employee Benefits)*
John Imes *(Environmental Coordinator)*

No. of Mfg. Plants/Facilities: 8
No. of U.S. Offices: 9
No. of Foreign Offices: 2

Outside Service Firm(s):

Arthur Andersen & Co.*(Auditors)*
777 E. Wisconsin Ave., P.O. Box 1215
Milwaukee, WI 53202
Tel.: 414-271-5100
Fax: 414-283-3200

First Wisconsin National Bank*(Major Banking Relationship)*
Sheboygan, WI

Subsidiary:

Quad/West Pre-Press **(1)**
1174 N. Grove, Ste. A.
Anaheim, CA 92806-2198
Tel.: 714-632-0420
Pre-press Film Preparation House
S.I.C.: 2752
Greg Warne *(Admin. Plant Mgr.)*

QUAD SYSTEMS CORPORATION
2 Electronic Dr.
Horsham, PA 19044
Tel.: 215-657-6202
Fax: 215-657-5013
Approx.Sls.: $14,000,000
Emp.: 90
Fiscal Year-end: 9/30/91
Export
Manufacturer of Machines that Produce Electronic Circuits
S.I.C.: 3679
George Crosby *(Chm. Bd.)*
David Smith *(Chief Exec. Officer)*
Anthony R. Drury *(Chief Fin. Officer & V.P.)*
Jack Leonard *(Mgr.-Mktg.)*

No. of Mfg. Plants/Facilities: 1
No. of U.S. Offices: 2

Outside Service Firm(s):

United Jersey Bank*(Major Banking Relationship)*
Cherry Hill, NJ

QUADION CORPORATION
3630 Wooddale Ave.
Minneapolis, MN 55416
Mailing Address:
P.O. Box 1236
Minneapolis, MN 55440
Tel.: 612-927-1400 **MN**
Telex: 882211
Fax: 612-927-1422
Year Founded: 1945
Approx.Sls.: $142,000,000
Emp.: 2,605
Fiscal Year-end: 9/30/90
Import Export
Manufacture Custom Molded Rubber, Plastic & Aluminum Components; Die Casting
S.I.C.: 3069; 3334; 3089
Corporate Giving Program: Through Foundation
Robert W. Carlson, Jr. *(Chm. & Chief Exec. Officer)*
James Lande *(Pres. & Chief Oper. Officer)*
Donald Pyatt *(Exec. V.P.)*
Pete Peterson *(V.P.-Human Resources)*
Jerome L. Posey *(Controller)*
Principal(s):
Robert W. Carlson, Jr.

No. of Mfg. Plants/Facilities: 8
No. of U.S. Offices: 18
No. of Foreign Offices: 2

Computer Systems/Hardware:
IBM System 4341

Outside Service Firm(s):

Copeland Buhl & Co.*(Auditors)*
Wayzata, MN

Marsh & McLennan*(Commercial Insurance Carrier)*
1166 Avenue of the Americas
New York, NY 10036
Tel.: 212-345-6000
Fax: 212-345-3285

Marsh & McLennan*(Group Insurer)*
Minneapolis, MN

Chase Manhattan Bank, N.A.*(International Bank Affiliate)*
One Chase Manhattan Plaza
New York, NY 10081
Tel.: 212-552-2222
Tel.: 800-526-0801
Fax: 212-552-7175

Leonard, Street & Deinard*(Legal Firm)*
150 S. Fifth St., Ste. 2300
Minneapolis, MN 55402
Tel.: 612-335-1500

First National Bank of Minneapolis*(Major Banking Relationship)*
Minneapolis, MN

QUADRANGLE DEVELOPMENT CORPORATION
1001 G St., N.W., Ste. 700 W
Washington, DC 20001
Tel.: 202-393-1999 **DE**
Fax: 202-393-0548
Year Founded: 1965
Sales Range: $100-499 Million
Real Estate Development
S.I.C.: 6552
Robert Gladstone *(Pres.)*
Ernest Davies *(Chief Fin. Officer)*
Christopher Gladstone *(Exec. V.P.)*
Robert J. Knopf *(Sr. V.P.-Development)*
Rex Craven *(V.P.-Property Mngmt.)*
Helen Harley *(V.P.-Leasing)*

Outside Service Firm(s):

Leopold & Linowes*(Auditors)*
Washington, DC

Arent, Fox, Kintner, Plotkin & Kahn*(Legal Firm)*
1815 H St. N.W.
Washington, DC 20006
Tel.: 202-857-6000

Subsidiaries:

Quadrangle Management Company **(1)**
1001 G. St., N.W., Ste. 700 W
Washington, DC 20036
Tel.: 202-393-1999
Rex Craven *(V.P. & Gen. Mgr.)*

Quik Park Inc. **(1)**
1001 G. St., N.W., Ste. 700 W
Washington, DC 20036
Tel.: 202-393-1999
Tom Schlosser *(Gen. Mgr.)*

QUAEL CORP.
1927 Rosa Parks Blvd.
Detroit, MI 48216
Tel.: 313-963-7760 **MI**
Approx.Sls.: $38,000,000
Emp.: 700
Fiscal Year-end: 5/31/90
67 Retail Drug Stores Nationwide: Schettler, Shapero & Crossroads
S.I.C.: 5912
J. Shapero *(Chm. Bd., Pres. & Chief Exec. Officer)*
D. Ray Moss *(V.P.-Opers.)*
Lloyd B. Fisher, Jr. *(Treas.)*
Gloria D. Stalla *(Sec.)*

Computer Systems/Hardware:
IBM PC; ADP Max 8500

Outside Service Firm(s):

Arthur Andersen & Co.*(Auditors)*
400 Renaissance Center
Detroit, MI 48243

Tel.: 313-259-8100

Liberty Mutual*(Commercial Insurance Carrier)*
175 Berkeley St.
Boston, MA

Blue Cross & Blue Shield of Michigan*(Group Insurer)*
Detroit, MI

Happ Insurnace Company*(Group Insurer)*
Detroit, MI

Honigman, Miller, Schwartz & Cohn*(Legal Firm)*
2290 First National Bldg.
Detroit, MI 48226
Tel.: 313-256-7800

N.B.D. Bank, N.A.*(Major Banking Relationship)*
611 Woodward Ave.
Detroit, MI 48226
Tel.: 313-225-1122
Fax: 313-225-3420

Division:

Shapero Stores **(1)**
1927 Rosa Parks Blvd.
Detroit, MI 48216
Tel.: 313-963-7760
Drug Stores Located in Hotels
S.I.C.: 5912
J. Shapero *(Pres.)*
D. Ray Moss *(V.P.-Opers.)*

QUAKER CITY MOTOR PARTS COMPANY
680 North Broad
Middletown, DE 19709
Mailing Address:
P.O. Box 5000
Middletown, DE 19709
Tel.: 302-378-9834 **DE**
Fax: 302-378-0726
Year Founded: 1952
Approx.Sls.: $31,000,000
Emp.: 250
Wholesale Distributor of Automotive Supplies, Parts & Accessories
S.I.C.: 5013; 5531
M.J. Schwartz *(Chm. Bd., Pres. & Chief Exec. Officer)*
James Duckworth *(Exec. V.P.-Fin. & Treas.)*
Joseph T. Brennan *(V.P.-Sls.)*
C.J. McGuire *(V.P.-Opers.)*
Lloyd J. Schumacher *(V.P.)*

Outside Service Firm(s):

First Philadelphia Bank*(Major Banking Relationship)*
Philadelphia, PA

QUAKER FABRIC CORPORATION
941 Grinnell St.
Fall River, MA 02722
Mailing Address:
P.O. Box 2139,
Fall River, MA 02722
Tel.: 508-678-1951 **DE**
Fax: 508-679-2580
Year Founded: 1940
Assets: $87,000,000
Earnings: ($7,474,854)
Liabilities: $30,413,941
Net Worth: $56,586,059
Approx.Sls.: $100,000,000
Emp.: 1,350
Fiscal Year-end: 2/27/90
Upholstery Fabric and Yarn Manufacturer
S.I.C.: 2221
Roberto Pesaro *(Chm. Bd.)*
Larry Liebenow *(Pres. & Chief Exec. Officer)*
Tom Finneran *(Sr. V.P.-Mktg.)*
Paul Kelly *(Chief Fin. Officer & Treas.)*
Jim Dulude *(V.P.-Pur. & MIS)*
Cynthia Gordan *(Legal Counsel)*
Gus Antonucci *(Dir.-Pur.)*
John Brennan *(Dir.-Personnel)*
Joyce E. Costa *(Dir.-Meeting & Plng.)*

Outside Service Firm(s):

Ernst & Young*(Auditors)*
200 Clarendon St., 46th Fl.
Boston, MA 02116
Tel.: 617-266-2000

Hale and Dorr*(Legal Firm)*
60 State St.
Boston, MA 02109-6098
Tel.: 617-526-6000

QUAKER INDUSTRIES LIMITED
90 McMillen Rd.
Antioch, IL 60002
Tel.: 708-395-3300
Fax: 708-395-3305
Year Founded: 1935
Approx.Sls.: $16,000,000
Emp.: 100
Export
Wood, Metal, Hardboard Tray Table Sets, Outdoor Patio Tables, Lawn Spreaders
S.I.C.: 2511
Felix Tarorick *(Pres.)*
Alan Dupuis *(V.P.-Sls. & Mktg.)*
Tony Viola *(Dir.-Mfg.)*

QUALITY BAKERS OF AMERICA COOPERATIVE, INC.
70 Riverdale Ave.
Greenwich, CT 06830
Tel.: 203-531-7100
Fax: 203-531-1406
Year Founded: 1922
Approx.Sls.: $300,000,000
Emp.: 60
Fiscal Year-end: 12/31/90
Bakers Cooperative; Sunbeam Bread, Molenberg Bread
S.I.C.: 2051
C.K. Evers *(Chm. Bd.)*
A. Maier *(Pres.)*
Frank Coffey *(Exec. V.P. & Chief Oper. Officer)*
Don Cummings *(V.P. & Controller)*
Jerry Morano *(V.P.-Mktg. & Sls.)*
E. Stolzer *(V.P.-Mfg.)*
R. Dubow *(V.P. & Gen. Counsel)*
M. Ventura *(Asst. Sec.)*
W. Cooper *(Dir.-Personnel)*
Robert Levengood *(Dir.-Video Services)*
E. Burns *(Dir.-Pur.)*
Michelle Farrell *(Mktg. Coord.)*
J. Robinson *(Mgr.-Mfg.)*
D. Prunella *(Office Mgr.)*

Computer Systems/Hardware:
IBM, Apple, Mac

QUALITY CHEKD DAIRY PRODUCTS ASSOCIATION
1733 Park Place
Naperville, IL 60563
Tel.: 708-717-1110
Fax: 708-717-1126
Year Founded: 1944
Approx.Sls.: $2,600,000,000
Emp.: 14
Fiscal Year-end: 9/30/92
Association of Independent Dairies in the U.S. & Canada
S.I.C.: 8611
H. Lee Richards *(Pres.)*
Mel W. Rapp *(Mng. Dir.)*
Joseph Soehnlen *(V.P.)*
Samuel J. Nichols *(Mktg. Dir.)*

QUALITY CONTROL CORPORATION
7315 W. Wilson Ave.
Harwood Heights, IL 60656
Tel.: 708-867-5400
Fax: 708-867-8854
Approx.Sls.: $18,000,000
Emp.: 220
Precision Metal Components; Mechanical Seals; Electro-Mechanical Assembly & Valves; Connector Accessories; Screw Machine Products
S.I.C.: 3494; 3451
Richard C. Michalek *(Chm. Bd. & Chief Exec. Officer)*
Michael J. Hasley *(Pres.)*
Greg Willard *(V.P.)*
Peter R. Householder *(Treas. & Mgr.-Data Processing)*
Becky Wright *(Pur. Agent)*

Outside Service Firm(s):

Selden Fox & Associates*(Auditors)*
Oak Brook, IL

Coffield, Ungaretti & Harris*(Legal Firm)*
3500 Three First National Plaza
Chicago, IL 60602
Tel.: 312-977-4400

Northwest National Bank*(Major Banking Relationship)*
Chicago, IL

QUALITY FOOD OILS, INC.
87 Pickett District Rd.
New Milford, CT 06776
Tel.: 203-355-9421 **NY**
Fax: 203-354-9672
Year Founded: 1978
Sales Range: $20-39 Million
Emp.: 30
Import Export
Packaging & Distribution of Vegetable & Olive Oils
S.I.C.: 7389; 5149
Anthony Capizzi *(Chm. Bd., Pres. & Chief Exec. Officer)*
Frank Capizzi *(V.P. & Chief Oper. Officer)*
Daniel Lane *(V.P. & Chief Fin. Officer)*
Principal(s):
Anthony Capizzi
Frank Capizzi
Daniel Lane

No. of Mfg. Plants/Facilities: 1
No. of U.S. Offices: 1

Computer Systems/Hardware:
IBM System 36

Outside Service Firm(s):

Greenhaus, Riordan & Company*(Auditors)*
Danbury, CT

Baker & Moots*(Legal Firm)*
New Milford, CT

New Milford Bank & Trust*(Major Banking Relationship)*
New Milford, CT

Subsidiary:

Sunola Food Corp. **(1)**
87 Pickett District Rd.
New Milford, CT 06776
Tel.: 203-355-9417
Fax: 203-354-9672
Emp.: 25
Packaging & Processors of Vegetable Oil
S.I.C.: 5149
Anthony Capizzi *(Pres.)*

QUALITY FOODS INC.
4901 Asher Ave.
Little Rock, AR 72204
Mailing Address:
P.O. Box 4908,
Little Rock, AR 72214
Tel.: 501-568-3141 **AR**
Fax: 501-565-8821
Year Founded: 1932
Assets: $7,750,246
Liabilities: $6,244,198
Net Worth: $1,506,048
Approx.Sls.: $44,000,000
Emp.: 180
Fiscal Year-end: 6/30/90
Wholesale Groceries, Institutional Foods; Cold Storage
S.I.C.: 5141; 5147; 5148; 4222
Don O. Kirkpatrick *(Chm. Bd. & Pres.)*
Carolyn Kirkpatrick *(V.P.)*
Neal Kirkpatrick *(V.P.)*
Philip Tappan *(V.P. & Gen. Mgr.)*
Donna Isom *(Treas. & Sec.)*
Debbie Oldhan *(Controller)*
Mark Briggs *(Dir.-Data Processing)*
Homer Feltner *(Dir.-Pur.)*
Principal(s):
Kirkpatrick Family

No. of Mfg. Plants/Facilities: 1

Computer Systems/Hardware:
Unisys A-6

Outside Service Firm(s):

Yaniger & Mallory*(Auditors)*
Little Rock, AR

Rebsamen Associates*(Commercial Insurance Carrier)*
Little Rock, AR

Friday, Eldridge & Clark*(Legal Firm)*
2000 First Commercial Bldg.
Little Rock, AR 72201
Tel.: 501-376-2011

Union Planters National Bank*(Major Banking Relationship)*
Memphis, TN

The Pension Center*(Pension Manager)*
Little Rock, AR

QUALITY KING DISTRIBUTORS
2060 9th Ave.
Ronkonkoma, NY 11779
Tel.: 516-737-5555
Fax: 516-737-5154
Health & Beauty Aids Distributor
Bernard Nussdorf *(Pres.)*

QUALITY PACKAGING PRODUCTS, INC.
352 W. Britain Ave.
Benton Harbor, MI 49022
Tel.: 616-927-2263
Fax: 616-927-2196
Emp.: 70
Manufacture Corrugated Paper
S.I.C.: 2653
Rhoda Wiesemes *(Pres. & Treas.)*
Kurt Wiesemeses *(V.P.-Mktg. & Sls.)*

Outside Service Firm(s):

Piante & Moran*(Auditors)*
Benton Harbor, MI

QUALITY PETROLEUM CORP.
P.O. Box 3889,
Lakeland, FL 33802-3889
Tel.: 813-687-2682 **FL**
Fax: 813-688-1613
Year Founded: 1971
Assets: $7,513,000
Earnings: $250,000
Liabilities: $3,957,000
Net Worth: $3,556,000
Approx.Sls.: $51,000,000
Emp.: 150
Fiscal Year-end: 9/30/90
Wholesale Petroleum Marketers
S.I.C.: 5172
Ralph W. Weeks *(Pres. & Chief Exec. Officer)*
Stephen Weeks *(V.P.)*
Beverly MacDermott *(Officer Mgr.)*

Outside Service Firm(s):

Carter, Belcourd & Atkinson*(Auditors)*
8th Flr., 500 Florida Ave.
Lakeland, FL 33801

Quality Petroleum Corp.—(Continued)

Tel.: 813-687-4010

Federated Mutual Insurance Co.*(Commercial Insurance Carrier)*
Lakeland, FL

Aetna Life & Casualty*(Group Insurer)*
151 Farmington Avenue
Hartford, CT 06156
Tel.: 203-273-2128
Fax: 203-729-4295

Shelnut & Johnson*(Legal Firm)*
Lakeland, FL

First Florida Bank*(Major Banking Relationship)*
P.O. Box 31265,
Tampa, FL 33631-3265
Tel.: 813-224-1475

A.G. Edwards & Sons*(Pension Manager)*
Port Richey, FL

QUALITY PONTIAC, INC.
1300 Lomas NE
Albuquerque, NM 87125
Tel.: 505-765-1300
Fax: 505-242-3526
Approx.Sls.: $25,000,000
Emp.: 85
Retail Automobiles & Related Parts & Service
S.I.C.: 5511
James E. DiLorenzo *(Chm. Bd., Pres. & Chief Exec. Officer)*
Charles V. DiLorenzo *(V.P.)*
Greg Salberg *(Controller)*

Outside Service Firm(s):

Rogoff, Diamond & Walker*(Auditors)*
Albuquerque, NM

Keleher & McLeod*(Legal Firm)*
P.O. Drawer AA
Albuquerque, NM 87103
Tel.: 505-842-6262

First National Bank Albuquerque*(Major Banking Relationship)*
40 First Plaza
Albuquerque, NM 87102
Tel.: 505-765-4190

QUALITY STORES INC.
1460 Whitehall Rd.
North Muskegon, MI 49445
Mailing Address:
P.O. Box 5200
North Muskegon, MI 49445
Tel.: 616-744-2491 **DE**
Fax: 616-744-2136
Year Founded: 1962
Assets: $53,671,283
Liabilities: $38,401,983
Net Worth: $15,269,300
Approx.Sls.: $197,680,000
Emp.: 1,255
Fiscal Year-end: 2/ 2/92
Import
Chain of Retail, General Merchandise & Farm Stores
S.I.C.: 5261; 5311
John Hilt *(Chm. Bd. & Chief Exec. Officer)*
David Bliss *(Pres.)*
Jim Davis *(Sr. V.P.-Mktg.)*
Dennis W. Byers *(Chief Fin. Officer, V.P.-Fin. & Treas.)*
Andrew W. Baravik *(V.P.-Human Resources & Mngmt. Info. Systems)*
Al Fansler *(V.P.-Store Opers.)*
Wayne E. McCollum *(V.P.-Mdse.)*
Richard McLouth *(Controller)*
Joan Gowell *(Sec.)*
Donald Kettler *(Dir.-Real Estate)*
Gary Gifford *(Mgr.-Personnel Training & Devel.)*
Charles Liddil *(Mgr.-Import)*
James McCamant *(Mgr.-Employee Benefits)*

No. of Mfg. Plants/Facilities: 64
No. of U.S. Offices: 1
No. of Foreign Offices: 1

Computer Systems/Hardware:
IBM 4381

Outside Service Firm(s):

BDO Seidman*(Auditors)*
801 W. Norton
Muskegon, MI 49441
Tel.: 616-739-9441

Culver, Lague & McNally*(Legal Firm)*
P.O. Box 389,
Muskegon, MI 49443

Manufacturers National Bank*(Major Banking Relationship)*
50 Monroe Ave.
Grand Rapids, MI 49503
Tel.: 616-235-2704
Fax: 616-235-2756

QUALITY TECHNOLOGIES CORPORATION
610 N. Mary Ave.
Sunnyvale, CA 94086-2906
Tel.: 408-720-1440
Tel.: 800-533-6786
Fax: 408-720-0848
Year Founded: 1969
Assets: $20,000,000
Earnings: $2,000,000
Liabilities: $10,000,000
Net Worth: $10,000,000
Approx.Sls.: $60,000,000
Emp.: 1,700
Fiscal Year-end: 12/31/90
Import Export
Mfr. LED Lamps; Infrared Emitters; Detectors; Sensors; Displays; Optoisolators; Optocouples; Photo Darlingtons
S.I.C.: 3674
Dr. Ralph Simon *(Pres.)*
Charles Bates *(V.P.-Sls. & Mktg.)*
Edward Miller *(V.P.-Fin.)*
Ella Oakes *(Mgr.-Customer Service)*

Computer Systems/Hardware:
IBM AS400

QUANTIC INDUSTRIES, INC.
990 Commercial St.
San Carlos, CA 94070
Tel.: 415-595-1100
Fax: 415-592-4669
Approx.Sls.: $35,000,000
Emp.: 400
Aerospace Satellite Navigation Systems & Ordnance Devices, Electronic Ordnance Devices, Factory Automation Systems
S.I.C.: 3489; 3812; 3823
Eugene V. Gottlieb *(Pres.)*
Robert M. Valenti *(Pres.-San Carlos Div.)*
Shirley Lathrop *(Mgr.-Personnel)*

Outside Service Firm(s):

KPMG Peat Marwick*(Auditors)*
3 Embarcadero Center
San Francisco, CA 94111
Tel.: 415-951-0100
Fax: 415-397-1129

Cooley, Godward, Castro, Huddleson & Tatum*(Legal Firm)*
5 Palo Alto Square
Palo Alto, CA 94306
Tel.: 415-494-7622
Fax: 415-857-0663

Wells Fargo Bank*(Major Banking Relationship)*
45 Fremont St.
San Francisco, CA 94105

Subsidiary:

Simco/Ramic Corporation **(1)**
P.O. Box 1666
Medford, OR 97501
Tel.: 503-776-9800
James A. Little *(Pres.)*

QUEBEDEAUX PONTIAC, INC.
3566 E. Speedway
Tucson, AZ 85716
Tel.: 602-795-5550 **AZ**
Fax: 602-327-2701
Approx.Sls.: $22,000,000
Emp.: 72
Retail Sales of New & Used Automobiles
S.I.C.: 5511
Thomas Quebedeaux *(Pres.)*
Carol Quebedeaux *(V.P., Sec. & Treas.)*
Leroy Masseth *(Controller)*

Outside Service Firm(s):

First Interstate Bank*(Major Banking Relationship)*
P.O. Box 53441,
Phoenix, AZ 85072-3441
Tel.: 602-229-4049

QUEEN OXYGEN COMPANY
502 Schrock Rd.
Columbus, OH 43229
Mailing Address:
P.O. Box 630,
Worthington, OH 43085
Tel.: 614-846-2211 **OH**
Fax: 614-846-8886
Year Founded: 1975
Earnings: $70,000
Emp.: 18
Fiscal Year-end: 12/31/90
Distribution of Welding Supplies
S.I.C.: 5084
Irene Dugger *(Chm. Bd., Pres., Chief Exec. Officer & Treas.)*
Glenn Dugger *(V.P. & Sec.)*
Barbara Moore *(Dir.-Pur.)*
Jean McCarthy *(Office Mgr.)*

No. of Mfg. Plants/Facilities: 1
No. of U.S. Offices: 1

Computer Systems/Hardware:
UNIX

Outside Service Firm(s):

Michigan Mutual Insurance Co.*(Commercial Insurance Carrier)*
Columbus, OH

Blue Cross of Central Ohio*(Group Insurer)*
Columbus, OH

Campbell, Hornbeck, Chilcoat & Veatch*(Legal Firm)*
Worthington, OH

Fifth Third Bank*(Major Banking Relationship)*
Columbus, OH

QUEENS GROUP, INC.
52-35 Barnett Ave.
Long Island City, NY 11104-1017
Tel.: 718-457-7700 **NY**
Fax: 718-457-9285
Year Founded: 1931
Approx.Sls.: $140,000,000
Emp.: 950
Paperboard, Commercial Printing, Color Separations Design
S.I.C.: 2631; 2759
Jack L. Hecht *(Chm. Bd.)*
Abraham Garde *(Vice Chm.)*
Leonard J. Verebay *(Pres.)*
Jim Stiegelmeyer *(Pres.-Oliver Trucking Co.-Indianapolis, In.)*
Eric Kaltman *(Chief Exec. Officer)*
Julius Brown *(Chief Fin. Officer)*
Richard Roth *(Exec. V.P.-Sls. & Mktg.)*
Manny Ungar *(Exec. V.P.-Mfg.)*
Jack Sims *(Sr. V.P.-Music Sls.)*
Len Hecht *(V.P.-Mktg.)*
Keith Kiedinger *(V.P.-Pkgng. Sls & Natl. Sls. Mgr.)*
Gerald Sanders *(V.P.)*
Joel Weingold *(V.P.-Opers.)*
Max Verebay *(Treas.)*
Martin Kaltman *(Sec.)*
Matthew Lifflander *(Gen. Counsel)*
Julia Sims *(Dir.-Telecommunications)*
Stan Bryan *(Gen. Mgr.-Queens Indiana)*
Dennis Kaltman *(Gen. Mgr.-Queens Group Kentucky)*
Emanual Ungar *(Gen. Mgr.-Queens North Carolina)*
Arthur Valone *(Gen. Mgr.-Queens New Jersey)*
Principal(s):
Leonard J. Verebay
Eric Kaltman
Len Hecht
Gerald Sanders

No. of Mfg. Plants/Facilities: 4
No. of U.S. Offices: 7

Computer Systems/Hardware:
Hewlett Packard

Outside Service Firm(s):

Back, Wax, Streisfeld & Schreiber*(Auditors)*
New York, NY

Tick & Co.*(Group Insurer)*
Lake Success, NY

Townley & Updike*(Legal Firm)*
405 Lexington Ave.
New York, NY 10020
Tel.: 212-682-4567

Marine Midland Bank*(Major Banking Relationship)*
140 Broadway
New York, NY 10015
Tel.: 212-658-1620

Mellon Bank, N.A.*(Major Banking Relationship)*
New York, NY

Subsidiaries:

Queens Group Design **(1)**
120 Wooster St.
New York, NY 10012
Tel.: 212-274-0077
Emp.: 980
Graphic Design Services
Eric Kaltman *(Chief Exec. Officer)*
Julius Brown *(Chief Fin. Officer)*
Richard Roth *(Exec. V.P.-Sls. & Mktg.)*

Queens Group Indiana, Inc. **(1)**
620 S. Belmont Ave.
Indianapolis, IN 46221
Tel.: 317-635-7777
Fax: 317-638-9032
Folding Boxes, Blister Cards, Commercial Printing, Sleeves
S.I.C.: 2759; 2657
Leonard Verebay *(Pres.)*
Emanuel Ungar *(Exec. V.P.-Mfg.)*
Richard Roth *(Exec. V.P.-Sls. & mktg.)*
Richard Dubish *(V.P.-Personnel)*
Vincent Patarino *(V.P.-Customer Service)*

QUEST BUSINESS AGENCY

THE QUEST BUSINESS AGENCY, INC.
2900 N. Loop West, Ste. 1020
Houston, TX 77092
Tel.: 713-956-6569
Tel.: 800-766-6767
Fax: 713-956-2593
Year Founded: 1981
Approx.Billings: $21,370,000
Emp.: 25
Business-to-Business Mktg. Communications Services
Alan D. Vera *(Pres. & Chief Exec. Officer)*

Brian C. Scruby *(Sr. V.P., Dir. Pub. Rels.)*
George Koucouthakis *(V.P., Controller)*
Don Ball *(Mgr., Exhibit Services Div.)*

QUIK PRINT INC.
(Formerly Quik Print Of Kansas, Inc.)
3445 N. Webb Rd.
Wichita, KS 67226
Tel.: 316-636-5666
Fax: 316-636-5678
Year Founded: 1963
Approx.Sls.: $10,000,000
Emp.: 250
Commercial Lithographic Printing, Blueprinting & Photocopying Services
S.I.C.: 2752
D. Wayne Jenkins *(Pres.)*
Johnny Tarrant *(Sr. V.P.)*
Gerald Arnagost *(V.P.)*
Greg R. Perkins *(V.P.-Fin.)*
Vicky Hogan *(Sec.)*
Paul Donham *(Dir.-Pur.)*
Paula Crozier *(Computer Coordinator)*

Outside Service Firm(s):

Allen, Gibbs, Houlik*(Auditors)*
301 N. Main, Ste. 1700
Wichita, KS 67202
Tel.: 316-267-7231

Eberhart & Elkouri*(Legal Firm)*
Wichita, KS

QUIK WOK CORPORATION
4099 McEwen Dr., Ste. 150
Dallas, TX 75244
Tel.: 214-386-0044 IL
Fax: 214-386-0148
Year Founded: 1980
Sales Range: $10-19 Million
Emp.: 200
Fiscal Year-end: 12/31/89
Restaurants
S.I.C.: 5812
Paul M. Lee *(Pres. & Chief Exec. Officer)*
David M. Chan *(V.P. & Chief Fin. Officer)*
Stuart Savitz *(Legal Officer)*
Principal(s):
Paul M. Lee
David M. Chan

Outside Service Firm(s):

Grant Thornton*(Auditors)*
1445 Ross Ave.
Dallas, TX 75202
Tel.: 214-855-7300

Schwartz & Freeman*(Legal Firm)*
401 N. Michigan Ave., Suite 3400
Chicago, IL 60611
Tel.: 312-222-0800

Frost National Bank*(Major Banking Relationship)*
P.O. Box 1600
San Antonio, TX 78296
Tel.: 210-220-4011

QUIKTRIP CORPORATION
901 N. Mingo Rd.
Tulsa, OK 74116
Mailing Address:
P.O. Box 3475,
Tulsa, OK 74101
Tel.: 918-836-8551
Fax: 918-834-4117
Approx.Sls.: $500,000,000
Emp.: 1,500
Fiscal Year-end: 4/30/91
Chain of Convenience Stores in KS, MO, OK, IA & GA
S.I.C.: 5399
Employee Matching Gifts Program: Company Matches Employees Contribution To United Way
Chester Cadieux *(Chm. Bd. & Pres.)*
Al Howerton *(Exec. V.P.-Real Estate)*
Terry Carter *(Sr. V.P.-Fin.)*
Mike Stanford *(Sr. V.P.-Opers.)*
Don Brauns *(V.P.-Opers.)*
Rick Calhoun *(V.P.-Petroleum Services)*
Jim Denny *(V.P.-Human Resources)*
Ron Males *(V.P.-Sls.)*
Wyatt Phillip *(V.P.-Mktg.)*
Dave Reid *(V.P.-Information Services)*
Dale Wilkeson *(Media & Adv. Mgr.)*
Kim Owens *(Mgr.-Benefits)*

Outside Service Firm(s):

Ernst & Young*(Auditors)*
4300 One Williams Ctr.
Tulsa, OK 74142
Tel.: 918-560-3600
Fax: 918-560-3691

Atkins & Wright*(Legal Firm)*
Tulsa, OK

NationsBank Texas*(Major Banking Relationship)*
Dallas, TX

Division:

Quik N Tasty Foods **(1)**
822 Quiktrip Way
Belton, MO 64012
Tel.: 816-331-5508
Emp.: 150
Warehouse & Distributor for Convenience Stores
S.I.C.: 4225
Randy Wright *(Mgr.-Personnel)*

QUILL CORP.
100 Schelter Rd.
Lincolnshire, IL 60069
Tel.: 708-634-6690 DE
Fax: 708-634-6699
Year Founded: 1956
Approx.Sls.: $300,000,000
Emp.: 1,000
Fiscal Year-end: 9/30/90
Import
Mail Order Distributor of Computers and Office Products
S.I.C.: 5112; 5961
Jack Miller *(Pres.)*
Larry Morse *(V.P.-Opers.)*
Robert Worobow *(V.P.-Human Resources)*
Nick Montesano *(V.P.-Sls., Mktg. & Mdse.)*
Arnold Miller *(Treas.)*
Harvey L. Miller *(Sec.)*
Lowell Meyers *(Dir.-Mktg. & Adv.)*
Mark Rosenthal *(Dir.-Mngmt. Information Systems)*
Sheila Hamilton *(Mgr.-Employee Benefits)*
Lin Ivice *(Mgr.-Pub. Rels.)*
Terry Schwarting *(Mgr.-Transportation)*
Lorna Galich *(Coord.-Training & Devel.)*
Susan Klister *(Corp. Travel Planner)*
William Becker *(Pur. Agent)*
Principal(s):
Jack Miller
Arnold Miller
Harvey L. Miller

No. of U.S. Offices: 3

Computer Systems/Hardware:
Sperry/Univac 9100

Outside Service Firm(s):

Kupferberg, Goldberg & Neimark*(Auditors)*
Chicago, IL

American National Bank & Trust Company of Chicago*(Major Banking Relationship)*
33 N. LaSalle St.
Chicago, IL 60602
Tel.: 312-661-5000
Fax: 312-661-6417

QUINCY MUTUAL FIRE INSURANCE COMPANY
57 Washington
Quincy, MA 02169
Tel.: 617-472-8770
Tel.: 800-899-1116
Fax: 617-472-4503
Fax: 800-899-7790
Year Founded: 1851
Approx.Sls.: $102,000,000
Emp.: 150
Fiscal Year-end: 12/31/91
Homeowners, Automobile, Commercial Multi-Peril & Businessowners Insurance
S.I.C.: 6331
Karl L. Briggs *(Chm. Bd.)*
Harold Gerbis, Sr. *(Pres.)*
Roger Brooks *(V.P.-Claims)*
Robert Houghton *(V.P.-Underwriting)*
Kevin Meskell *(V.P. & Mktg. Agent)*
K. Douglas Briggs *(V.P., Treas. & Sec.)*

QUINLAN ADVERTISING
Two Penn Mark Plaza, 11555 N. Meridian
Carmel, IN 46032
Mailing Address:
P.O. Box 1962,
Indianapolis, IN 46206
Tel.: 317-573-5080
Fax: 317-573-5088
Year Founded: 1936
Approx.Billings: $10,000,000
Emp.: 18
Business-to-Business, Industrial & Consumer Adv.
John C. McCaig *(Pres.)*

QUINTANA PETROLEUM CORP.
601 Jefferson St.
Houston, TX 77253
Mailing Address:
P.O. Box 3331
Houston, TX 77253
Tel.: 713-651-8600 TX
Fax: 713-651-8663
Year Founded: 1938
Emp.: 350
Fiscal Year-end: 12/31/91
Petroleum Exploration & Production
S.I.C.: 1311; 1382; 8999
Isaac Arnold, Jr. *(Chm. Bd.)*
H.P. Riley *(Exec. V.P.-Production Opers.)*
James W. Carroll *(V.P.)*
W.H. Drushel, Jr. *(V.P. & Sec.)*
Joe D. McDougald *(Treas.)*
L.R. Stablein *(Controller)*
Rick Giuffre *(Dir.-Real Estate)*
D.J. Harter *(Dir.-Data Processing)*
W. Lunn *(Dir.-Human Resources)*
E.J. Prejean *(Dir.-Pur.)*
Wayne Schneider *(Dir.-Mktg.)*

Outside Service Firm(s):

Arthur Andersen & Co.*(Auditors)*
711 Louisiana, Ste. 1300
Houston, TX 77002-2323
Tel.: 713-237-2793

Vinson & Elkins*(Legal Firm)*
First City Natl. Bank Bldg.
Houston, TX 77001
Tel.: 713-651-2222

Cullen Center Bank & Trust*(Major Banking Relationship)*
Houston, TX

Cullen Center Bank & Trust*(Pension Manager)*
Houston, TX

Subsidiaries:

Quintana Environmental Services, Inc. **(1)**
601 Jefferson, Ste. 3800
Houston, TX 77002
Tel.: 713-651-8600
H.P. Riley *(Pres.)*

Quintana Petroleum Services **(1)**
601 Jefferson
Houston, TX 77002
Tel.: 713-651-8600 (100%)
Petroleum Services
S.I.C.: 1382; 8999
H.P. Riley *(Pres.)*
L.R. Stablein *(V.P. & Treas.)*
J.A. Fox *(V.P.-Mktg.)*

QUINTRON SYSTEMS, INC.
2105 S. Blosser
Santa Maria, CA 93454
Tel.: 805-928-4343
Fax: 805-928-5775
Approx.Sls.: $15,000,000
Emp.: 220
Telecommunications Systems, Telephone Closed Circuit TV Surveillance
S.I.C.: 4899; 1731; 8731
Bryan E. Thompson *(Chm. Bd. & Pres.)*
Elton L. Hammers *(V.P.-Tech. Services)*
James E. McGlothlin *(V.P.-Opers.)*
John Bennett *(Comptroller)*
Christine M. Sullivan *(Pur. Agent)*

Outside Service Firm(s):

Dan Matter & Co.*(Auditors)*
Los Angeles, CA

Daniels, Baratta & Fine*(Legal Firm)*
Santa Maria, CA

Wells Fargo Bank*(Major Banking Relationship)*
420 Montgomery St.
San Francisco, CA 94104

QUOIZEL INC.
325 Kennedy Dr.
Hauppauge, NY 11788
Tel.: 516-273-2700
Fax: 516-231-7102
Approx.Sls.: $30,000,000
Emp.: 160
Import Export
Lamp & Lighting Mfr.
S.I.C.: 3645
Ira H. Phillips *(Pres. & Chief Oper. Officer)*
Todd Phillips *(V.P.)*
Toni Phillips *(Sec.)*
Barbara K. Pearsall *(Dir.-Adv.)*

QUORUM HEALTH GROUP, INC.
(Formerly Quorum Health Resources)
155 Franklin Rd., Ste. 401
Brentwood, TN 37027
Mailing Address:
P.O. Box 24347,
Nashville, TN 37202-4347
Tel.: 615-320-7979
Fax: 615-340-5962
Management Services
S.I.C.: 8741
James Dalton, Jr. *(Pres. & Chief Exec. Officer)*
Robert Huseby *(Pres.-Quorum Health Resources, Inc.)*
Doug Smith *(Vice Chm.-Quorum Health Group Div.)*
Robert A. Yeager *(Chief Fin. Officer)*
Richard Gore *(V.P. & Controller)*
Sandy Anthony *(Dir.-Corp. Communications)*

Quorum Health Group, Inc.—(Continued)

Outside Service Firm(s):

Ernst & Young*(Auditors)*
200 One Commerce Place
Nashville, TN 37239

R & B MACHINE TOOL CO.
118 E. Michigan Ave.
Saline, MI 48176
Mailing Address:
P.O. Box 100
Saline, MI 48176
Tel.: 313-429-9421
Fax: 313-429-9426
Year Founded: 1942
Approx.Sls.: $34,000,000
Emp.: 250
Fiscal Year-end: 12/31/89
Manufacture Special Metal Cutting Machines, Plastics Machinery
S.I.C.: 3541; 3559
Robert D. Redies *(Chm. Bd.)*
Milton Stemen *(Pres.)*
James Corson *(Sr. V.P.-Sls.)*
J. Wyman *(V.P.-Pur.)*
Wilbur K. Pierpont *(Treas.)*
Erik Serr *(Sec. & Gen. Counsel)*

No. of Mfg. Plants/Facilities: 4
No. of U.S. Offices: 1

Outside Service Firm(s):

Deloitte & Touche*(Auditors)*
101 N. Main Street
Ann Arbor, MI 48104-1411
Tel.: 313-769-6200

Trustcorp Bank*(Major Banking Relationship)*
Ann Arbor, MI

Subsidiary:

Saline Investment Co. **(1)**
P.O. Box 100
Saline, MI 48176
Tel.: 313-429-9421
Emp.: 5
Robert Corson *(Pres.)*
R. Edward Redies *(Chief Oper. Officer)*

R & R ADVERTISING
8076 W. Sahara Ave.
Las Vegas, NV 89117
Mailing Address:
P.O. Box 80130,
Las Vegas, NV 89180-0130
Tel.: 702-794-0222
Fax: 702-254-2218
Year Founded: 1974
Approx.Billings: $34,000,000
Emp.: 96
Tourism & Political Adv.
Sig Rogich *(Owner)*
Billy Vassiliadis *(Pres.)*
Ed Rogich *(Exec. V.P.)*
Connie Donohue *(Treas.)*
Rob Powers *(Pub. Rels. Dir.)*

RAIL COMPANY
515 E. Joppa Rd., Ste. 300
Towson, MD 21286
Tel.: 410-583-8990
Fax: 410-583-0672
Year Founded: 1971
Emp.: 185
Management Consulting Firm
S.I.C.: 8742
R.N. Huffman *(Pres. & Treas.)*
W.C. Friese *(V.P.-Engrng.)*
G.H. Reynolds *(V.P.-Corp. Rels.)*
C.J. Speranzella *(V.P.-Bus. Opers.)*
D.A. Nelson *(Controller)*
H.R. Huffman, Jr. *(Gen. Mgr.)*

Computer Systems/Hardware:
IBM PC

Outside Service Firm(s):

Rowles & Co.*(Auditors)*
Baltimore, MD

Lincoln National Life Insurance Co.*(Group Insurer)*
PO Box 208, 1300 S. Clinton
Fort Wayne, IN 46801
Tel.: 219-455-2926
Fax: 219-455-7619

Carson & Jones, Bateman*(Legal Firm)*
Baltimore, MD

Union Trust*(Major Banking Relationship)*
Baltimore, MD

R.A. INDUSTRIES, INC.
Welsh Rd.
Lansdale, PA 19446
Mailing Address:
P.O. Box 247
Lansdale, PA 19446
Tel.: 215-699-8701
Twx: 846117
Fax: 215-699-0370
Approx.Sls.: $15,000,000
Emp.: 200
Manufacture Industrial Hand Trucks, Hydraulic Stockers, Metering Pumps, Chemical Feed Systems Mixes & Faucets
S.I.C.: 3432; 3531; 3537; 3559; 3561
Robert F. Apter *(Chm. Bd.)*
Allen D. Apter *(Pres.)*
Carl P. Apter *(V.P.)*
M. Dowse *(V.P.-Sls.)*
J. Phillipi *(V.P.-Mfg.)*
Lee Albrecht *(Gen. Mgr.)*

Outside Service Firm(s):

Schwartz, Lasson, Harris Ltd.*(Auditors)*
Willow Grove, PA

Cohen, Shapiro, Polisher, Shiekman & Cohen*(Legal Firm)*
PSFS Bldg.
Philadelphia, PA 19107
Tel.: 215-922-1300

Philadelphia National Bank*(Major Banking Relationship)*
5th & Market Sts.
Philadelphia, PA 19101
Tel.: 215-629-3100
Fax: 215-834-2069

R.C.A. RUBBER COMPANY
1833 E. Market St.
Akron, OH 44305
Mailing Address:
P.O. Box 9240,
Akron, OH 44305-0240
Tel.: 216-784-1291 **OH**
Fax: 216-784-2899
Year Founded: 1931
Approx.Sls.: $16,000,000
Emp.: 250
Fiscal Year-end: 6/30/90
Export
Mfr. of Molded Rubber Goods; Rubber Stair Treads
S.I.C.: 3069
Richard T. Reiss *(Pres. & Treas.)*
Eugene D. Rue *(Controller & Mgr.-Credit)*
Clifford E. Reiss II *(Sec. & Asst. To Pres.)*
Karen Mlynar *(Dir.-Data Processing)*
John Spinks *(Dir.-Engrng.)*
Tim Dean *(Mgr.-Production)*
Richard Pinhard *(Mgr.-Sls., Flooring)*
Gordon Schultz *(Mgr.-Sls., Transit)*
William Sloan *(Mgr.-Personnel)*
Richard T. Reiss II *(Pur. Agent)*
Principal(s):
Richard T. Reiss
Clifford E. Reiss II

Computer Systems/Hardware:
IBM

Outside Service Firm(s):

Brott, Kusmits, Maglione, Mardis & Co.*(Auditors)*
Akron, OH

Brouse & McDowell*(Legal Firm)*
500 First National Tower
Akron, OH 4308
Tel.: 216-535-5711

First National Bank of Ohio*(Major Banking Relationship)*
106 S. Main St.
Akron, OH 44308
Tel.: 216-384-7347

Subsidiary:

Pulaski Rubber Co. **(1)**
P.O. Drawer I
Pulaski, TN 38478
Tel.: 615-363-5583

RCM INDUSTRIES
3021 Cullerton Dr.
Franklin Park, IL 60131
Tel.: 708-455-1950
Fax: 708-455-1529
Sales Range: $40-59 Million
Fiscal Year-end: 9/30/91
Holding Company
S.I.C.: 6719
Robert C. Marconi *(Chief Exec. Officer)*

No. of Mfg. Plants/Facilities: 4

Divisions:

AAllied Die Casting Mfg., Inc. **(1)**
3021 Cullerton Dr.
Franklin Park, IL 60131
Tel.: 708-455-1950
Fax: 708-455-1529
Robert C. Marconi *(Pres.)*

AAllied Die Casting Mfg., Inc. **(1)**
P.O. Box 1178
Rutherfordton, NC 28139
Tel.: 704-286-4003
Fax: 704-286-4006
Chuck Hill *(Mgr.)*

Imperial Die Casting **(1)**
Griffin Mill & Brazil Rds.
Easley, SC 29640
Tel.: 803-859-0202
Fax: 803-855-1597
Dennis Freeman *(Chief Fin. Officer)*

Inland Die Casting **(1)**
161 Carpenter Ave.
Wheeling, IL 60090
Tel.: 708-541-2700
Fax: 708-541-7461
Rich Betcher *(Pres.)*

RDI, INC.
1025 W. Thorndale Ave.
Itasca, IL 60143
Tel.: 708-773-2500
Fax: 708-773-3414
Year Founded: 1985
Approx.Sls.: $15,000,000
Emp.: 95
Fiscal Year-end: 9/ 1/91
Export
Manufacture Automation & Process Equipment; Machine Knives; Electrical Panels; Welding Shop; Machinery for Asphalt Roofing Industry; Wrapping and Bundling Machines
S.I.C.: 3569; 3559
Curtis N. Maas *(Chm. Bd. & Chief Exec. Officer)*
Gregg L. Menzies *(Treas.)*
Tom Page *(Sec.)*
Mark Paluch *(Dir.-Opers.)*
Tom Colvin *(Mgr.-Customer Service)*
Gloria Schaible *(Admin. Asst.)*

Outside Service Firm(s):

Grant Thornton*(Auditors)*
700 One Prudential Plaza, 130 East Randolph St.
Chicago, IL 60601
Tel.: 312-856-0200
Fax: 312-565-4719

Benefit Trust & Life*(Group Insurer)*
Chicago, IL

Barack Ferrazzano Kirchbaum & Perlman*(Legal Firm)*
333 W. Wacker Dr., Ste. 2700
Chicago, IL 60606
Tel.: 312-984-3100
Fax: 312-984-3150

Harris Trust & Savings Bank*(Major Banking Relationship)*
111 W. Monroe St.
Chicago, IL 60690
Tel.: 312-461-2265
Tel.: 800-858-0840

Subsidiaries:

Lafayette Precision Products Inc. **(1)**
292 No. Henry St.
Brooklyn, NY 11222
Tel.: 718-383-4545
Fax: 718-383-4658
S.I.C.: 3569
Curtis Maas *(Pres. & Chief Exec. Officer)*
Bill Salvaggio *(Mgr.-Applications)*

Reichel & Drews Inc. **(1)**
1025 W. Thorndale Ave.
Itasca, IL 60143
Tel.: 708-773-2500
Fax: 708-773-3414
Export
S.I.C.: 3569
Curtis Maas *(Pres. & Chief Exec. Officer)*
Gregg Menzies *(Mgr.-Fin.)*
Mike Walton *(Mgr.-Sls.)*
Mike Hardy *(Mgr.-Matls.)*

RHC/SPACEMASTER CORPORATION
(Formerly Reflector-Hardware Corporation)
1400 N. 25th Ave.
Melrose Park, IL 60160
Tel.: 708-345-2500 **IL**
Fax: 708-345-3823
Year Founded: 1901
Approx.Sls.: $102,000,000
Emp.: 1,260
Export
Store, Display & Office Fixtures; Showcases; Commercial, Industrial & Institutional Electric Lighting
S.I.C.: 2542; 2541; 3646
A.R. Umans *(Pres., Chief Exec. Officer & Treas.)*
Arthur H. Bobis *(Pres.-Metal Div.)*
Stanley R. Jewell *(Chief Fin. Officer & V.P.-Fin.)*
Seiji Itahara *(V.P.-Mfg.)*
Craig Umans *(V.P.-Sls.)*
Barbara Jackson *(Controller)*
Dennis Ziegler *(Asst. Sec.)*
Victor Bohlman *(Dir.-Mktg.)*
Linda Lazzaro *(Dir.-Personnel)*
Norbert Mager *(Dir.-Pur.)*
Tim Lynch *(Natl. Sls. Mgr.)*

No. of Mfg. Plants/Facilities: 10
No. of U.S. Offices: 16

Outside Service Firm(s):

Coopers & Lybrand*(Auditors)*
203 N. LaSalle St.
Chicago, IL 60601
Tel.: 312-701-5500

Dann Brothers*(Commercial Insurance Carrier)*
Northbrook, IL

Holleb & Coff, Ltd.*(Legal Firm)*
55 E. Monroe, Suite 4100
Chicago, IL 60603
Tel.: 312-807-4600

The Northern Trust Co.*(Major Banking Relationship)*
50 S. LaSalle St.
Chicago, IL 60675
Tel.: 312-630-6000
Fax: 312-444-7028

Subsidiaries:

Discovery Plastic **(1)**
P.O. Box 330,
Tangent, OR 97389
Tel.: 708-490-5063
Tom Lind *(Pres.)*

Garcy Corporation **(1)**
Piedmont, AL
Tel.: 205-447-9016
Store & Office Fixtures; Fluorescent Lighting Fixtures; Ornamental Lighting Fixtures
S.I.C.: 3646
Joe Kirkland *(Pres.)*
Michael McCullars *(Controller)*

Garcy/SLP **(1)**
Portland, TN

Garcy Specialty Fixtures **(1)**
Lavonia, GA
Manufacturer of Store Fixtures
S.I.C.: 2541
Gary Mayer *(Pres.)*

Goer Manufacturing Co. **(1)**
4500 Mariott Dr., N.
Charleston, SC 29418
Tel.: 803-747-5721
Mfr. of Wood Partitions & Fixtures
S.I.C.: 2541
Ernest J. Goer *(Pres.)*
Randy Goer *(V.P.-Sls.)*
Gary Diamond *(Mgr.-New Directions)*

RHS
15180 Spring Ave.
Santa Fe Springs, CA 90670
Tel.: 310-921-7725
Fax: 310-404-0048
Approx.Sls.: $20,000,000
Emp.: 50
Fiscal Year-end: 4/30/91
Carpet Mfg.; Royalweve
S.I.C.: 2273
Charles E. Coniglio *(Natl. Sls. Mgr.)*
Dennis L. Rodgers *(Dir.-Mktg.)*

RI HOLDINGS
75 Troy Hills Rd.
Whippany, NJ 07891
Tel.: 201-887-0400
Approx.Sls.: $150,000,000
S.I.C.: 3581; 3651; 3578; 5092
James Gang *(Pres.)*

Subsidiary:

Rowe International, Inc. **(1)**
75 Troy Hill Road
Whippany, NJ 07981
Tel.: 201-887-0400 (100%)
Mfrs. Vending Machines, Audio & Video Jukeboxes, Background Music Systems, Bill & Coin Changers
S.I.C.: 3578; 3581; 3651
Bruce K. Coles *(Pres.)*

RII (RICARDS INTERNATIONAL INC.)
1010 Wayne Ave., Ste. 300
Silver Spring, MD 20910
Tel.: 301-565-4020
Fax: 301-565-5112
Year Founded: 1978
Sales Range: $10-19 Million
Emp.: 65
International Marketing & Consulting Firm Specializing in Health, Military & Emergency Management
S.I.C.: 8742
Jose Ricardo *(Chm. Bd. & Chief Exec. Officer)*
Richard Salvatierra *(Pres.)*
Robert Gillette *(V.P.)*
Sharon McIntoch *(Controller)*
Belinda Ransom *(Dir.-Personnel)*
Principal(s):
Jose Ricardo
Richard Salvatierra

No. of U.S. Offices: 2
No. of Foreign Offices: 2

Computer Systems/Hardware:
IBM System 36

Outside Service Firm(s):

Cohen & Associates*(Auditors)*
Washington, DC

M.D.I.P.A.*(Group Insurer)*
Washington, DC

RJO ENTERPRISES, INC.
4500 Forbes Blvd.
Lanham, MD 20706
Tel.: 301-731-3600 **DE**
Fax: 301-731-5391
Year Founded: 1979
Approx.Sls.: $63,000,000
Emp.: 550
Import Export
Information Systems Integration, Telecommunications Network Integration, Electronics Systems Integration, Computer-Aided Logistics Systems, Program Management Services, Software Engineering
S.I.C.: 8711
Corporate Giving Program: Corporate *Charitable Donations are extended to* Worthy Organizations located in the same communities as 1,250 RJO Enterprises, Inc. Operating Facilities
Employee Matching Gifts Program: The Company Matches Employee Charitable Donations of up to $250
Richard J. Otero *(Chm., Pres. & Chief Exec. Officer)*
John Miller *(Chief Fin. Officer, Treas. & Controller)*
John Weldin *(Gen. Counsel)*
Leon Bieri *(Exec. V.P. & Gen. Mgr.)*
Joseph V. Sciortino *(Sr. V.P. & Mgr.-Opers.)*
H. Robert Boehm *(V.P.-Human Resources)*
Joseph F. Spaniol *(V.P.-Contracts & Corp. Sec.)*
John V. Flynn *(Grp. V.P.)*
Greg Brown *(Dir.-Employee Benfits)*
Gary W. Grace *(Dir.-Adv.)*
Wil Pirkey *(Mgr.-Pur.)*
Joseph Gayda *(Corp. Librarian)*
Principal(s):
Leon Bieri
Jeanneine Otero
Richard J. Otero

RK MECHANICAL, INC.
6701 Alameda
Lakewood, CO 80226
Tel.: 303-238-9696
Tel.: 800-783-0075 **NE**
Fax: 303-239-8666
Year Founded: 1981
Assets: $3,718,000
Liabilities: $2,852,579
Net Worth: $865,421
Approx.Sls.: $11,000,000
Emp.: 120
Fiscal Year-end: 7/ 1/90
Plumbing, Sheet Metal, Fire Protection Systems
S.I.C.: 1711; 1799
Ronald L. Kinning *(Chm. Bd. & Chief Exec. Officer)*
Rick L. Kinning *(Pres. & Treas.)*
Gordon Streich *(Chief Fin. Officer)*
Richard Pagel *(Group V.P.)*
Gary Purvis *(V.P.-Pur.)*
Georgia Kinning *(Sec.)*
Walt Downing *(Gen. Counsel)*
Principal(s):
Rick L. Kinning

No. of Mfg. Plants/Facilities: 2
No. of U.S. Offices: 2

Computer Systems/Hardware:
Marathon; IBM

Outside Service Firm(s):

Gary Bayer & Associates*(Auditors)*
Denver, CO

Elrod, Katz, Preeo & Look*(Legal Firm)*
Denver, CO

Littleton National Bank*(Major Banking Relationship)*
Littleton, CO

Subsidiary:

Kinning & Reil of Wyoming **(1)**
6701 West Alameda
Lohewood, CO 80226
Tel.: 303-239-8666
Tel.: 800-783-0075 (100%)
Emp.: 6
Mechanical & Fire Sprinkler Contracting; Inactive
S.I.C.: 5087
Rick Kinning *(Pres.)*
Ronald L. Kinning *(Chief Oper. Officer)*
Gordon Streich *(Chief Fin. Officer)*
Richard Pagel *(V.P.)*
Gary Purvis *(V.P.)*

RMI MARKETING & ADVERTISING
(Corporate Office)
436 Old Hook Rd.
Emerson, NJ 07630
Tel.: 201-261-7000
Year Founded: 1973
Approx.Billings: $18,500,000
Emp.: 20
Marketing, Advertising, Sales Promotion, Incentive/Motivation
Ronald Morgan *(Chm. Bd.)*
Frank K. Sonnenberg *(Pres.)*
Michael JD Haviland *(Exec V.P.)*
Carlo Demetrio *(V.P.)*
Ralph Gonzalez *(V.P.)*
Dick De Rose *(V.P., Western Acct. Services)*

Computer Systems/Hardware:
Apple, IBM

RMS TECHS, INC.
5 Eves Dr.
Marlton, NJ 08053
Tel.: 609-596-5775 **NJ**
Fax: 609-596-0729
Year Founded: 1977
Sales Range: $60-79 Million
Emp.: 981
Nonphyical Commerical Research, Security Systems Services, Software Development
S.I.C.: 8732; 7371; 7382
David Huggins *(Pres. & Chief Exec. Officer)*
V. Thomas Fooks *(Exec. V.P.)*
Harry Kahler *(Sr. V.P.)*
Joseph J. Rita *(V.P.-Fin.)*
Patricia Rogers *(Sec.)*

Outside Service Firm(s):

Coopers & Lybrand*(Auditors)*
Norristown, PA

Continental Bank*(Major Banking Relationship)*
Main & Swede Sts.
Norristown, PA 19401
Tel.: 215-641-8765
Fax: 215-564-7256

RNF MEDIA CORPORATION INC.
9440 Santa Monica Blvd.
Beverly Hills, CA 90210
Tel.: 310-273-2912
Fax: 310-276-8950
Year Founded: 1975
Approx.Billings: $45,000,000
Emp.: 18
Media Buying Service
Brian Fernee *(Pres.)*
Tony Naish *(V.P.)*
Roger Riddell *(V.P.)*
Fernando Vega *(Controller)*

RNL FACILITIES CORPORATION
1225 17th St., Suite 1700
Denver, CO 80202
Tel.: 303-295-1717 **CO**
Fax: 303-292-0845
Year Founded: 1966
Assets: $2,770,000
Liabilities: $2,213,000
Net Worth: $557,000
Sales Range: $10-19 Million
Emp.: 75
Fiscal Year-end: 12/31/92
Holding Company Specializing In Architecture, Interior Design, Urban Planning, Design-build Packaging of Projects, Facility Planning & Management; Software Design & Development
S.I.C.: 6719; 8712; 9532; 7371
Philip H. Goedert *(Pres. & Dir.)*
Richard L. von Luhrte *(Exec. V.P., Sec. & Dir.)*
Stephen C. Newman *(Treas. & Dir.)*
Harold L. Taylor *(Controller)*
Principal(s):
Philip H. Goedert
Richard L. von Luhrte
Stephen C. Newman
John B. Rogers

No. of Mfg. Plants/Facilities: 1
No. of U.S. Offices: 2

Computer Systems/Hardware:
Sun 6810; IBM; Hewlett Packard 7588; Micro Vax II

Outside Service Firm(s):

Gelfand, Houchstadt, Pangborn, Stark & Company*(Auditors)*
Denver, CO

DPIC*(Group Insurer)*
Memphis, TN

Colorado National Bank*(Major Banking Relationship)*
17th & Champa
Denver, CO 80217

First Interstate Bank*(Major Banking Relationship)*
Denver, CO
Tel.: 303-293-5456

Colorado State Bank*(Pension Manager)*
Denver, CO

Subsidiaries:

Design-Build West **(1)**
1225 17th St., Suite 1700
Denver, CO 80205
Tel.: 303-295-1717
Fax: 303-292-0845
Emp.: 4
Design, Construction & Furnishings Procurement
S.I.C.: 7389; 8712
Richard T. Anderson *(Pres.)*
Philip H. Goedert *(Sec./Treas.)*

Interplan **(1)**
1225 17th St., Suite 1700
Denver, CO 80205
Tel.: 303-295-1717
Fax: 303-292-0845
Emp.: 5
Pre-Design Facilities, Planning & Management Systems
S.I.C.: 7373
Philip H. Goedert *(Pres.)*
H. Joshua Gould *(Treas.)*
Richard L. von Luhrte *(Sec.)*

RNL Design **(1)**
1225 17th St., Suite 1700
Denver, CO 80205
Tel.: 303-295-1717
Fax: 303-292-0845
Emp.: 37

RNL Facilities Corporation—(Continued)

Architecture, Design & Urban Planning
S.I.C.: 8712
Philip H. Goedert *(Pres.)*
Richard L. von Luhrte *(Sec.)*
Stephen C. Newman *(Treas.)*

RNL/Interplan **(1)**
221 So. Figueroa, Ste. 200
Los Angeles, CA 90012
Tel.: 213-346-9300
Fax: 213-620-8637
Architecture, Interior Design & Facilities Planning & Management Systems
S.I.C.: 7373; 7389
Philip H. Goedert *(Pres.)*
Richard L. von Luhrte *(Sec.)*
Patrick M. McKelvey *(Treas.)*

RNL Technical Services **(1)**
1225 17th St., Ste. 1700
Denver, CO 80202
Tel.: 303-295-1717
Fax: 303-292-0845
Emp.: 2
Research & Investigation of Building Systems
S.I.C.: 8742
Philip H. Goedert *(Pres.)*
Richard L. von Luhrte *(Sec. & Treas.)*

Space Management Systems **(1)**
1225 17th St., Ste. 1700
Denver, CO 80202
Tel.: 303-295-1717
Fax: 303-292-0845
Emp.: 2
Facilities Software Design & Development
S.I.C.: 7371
Philip H. Goedert *(Pres.)*
Richard L. von Luhrte *(Sec. & Treas.)*

ROC PROPERTIES INC.
6430 South Quebec St.
Englewood, CO 80111
Tel.: 303-741-3707 **DE**
Fax: 303-741-3715
Year Founded: 1986
Assets: $99,359,000
Liabilities: $88,843,000
Net Worth: $10,516,000
Approx.Sls.: $121,151,000
Emp.: 1,300
Manufacture Mobile Homes; Own, Operate & Syndicate Modular/Mobile Home Communities; Sale of Modular/Mobile Homes
S.I.C.: 6719; 6552; 6515; 2451
Gary P. McDaniel *(Chm., Chief Exec. Officer & Sec.)*
James Grange *(V.P.-Fin.)*
Rees F. Davis, Jr. *(V.P.-Acquistions)*

Computer Systems/Hardware:
IBM System 36

Outside Service Firm(s):

Arthur Andersen & Co.*(Auditors)*
717 17th St., Ste. 1900
Denver, CO 80202
Tel.: 303-296-2121

Sherman & Howard*(Legal Firm)*
633 Seventeenth St.
Denver, CO 80202

First Colorado Bank & Trust*(Major Banking Relationship)*
Denver, CO

Plant:

River Oaks Double-Wide Plant **(1)**
Sand Mountain Industrial Park
Boaz, AL 35957
Tel.: 205-593-7040
Manufacture Double-Wide Mobile Homes
S.I.C.: 2451

Subsidiaries:

Inter-Mountain Rentals **(1)**
P.O. Box 1026, 2458 N. 9th St.
Laramie, WY 82070
Tel.: 307-742-6223
Mobile Home Rentals for Oil Drilling Sites
S.I.C.: 7519
Loren Boom *(Mgr.)*

North River Homes, Inc. **(1)**
406 Airport Rd.
Hamilton, AL 35570
Tel.: 205-921-2125
Producer of Manufactured Homes
S.I.C.: 6552
Steve Logan *(Chief Oper. Officer)*

Oak Products, Inc. **(1)**
Sand Mountain Industrial Park
Boaz, AL 35957
Tel.: 205-593-7040
Manufacture Mobile Home Products
S.I.C.: 3431; 3089; 2519
Harold Bridges *(Gen. Mgr.)*

River Oaks Communities, Inc. **(1)**
7395 E. Orchard Rd.
Englewood, CO 80111
Tel.: 303-741-3707
Acquire, Syndicate & Manage Mobile Home Rentals; Developers of Mobile Home Sub-Divisions
S.I.C.: 7519; 6552
Jim Grange *(Gen. Mgr.)*

River Oaks Homes, Inc. **(1)**
Sand Mountain Industrial Park
Boaz, AL 35957
Tel.: 205-593-7040
Manufacture Mobile Homes
S.I.C.: 2451
John E. Jones *(Gen. Mgr.)*

River Oaks Vans, Inc. **(1)**
Sand Mountain Industrial Park.
Boaz, AL 35957
Tel.: 205-593-7040
Van Conversion
S.I.C.: 3713
David Shipp *(Gen. Mgr.)*

RPR & ASSOCIATES, INC.
P.O. Box 11348
Columbia, SC 29211
Tel.: 803-799-1601
Fax: 803-779-0720
Year Founded: 1976
Sales Range: $60-79 Million
General Construction; Construction Management
S.I.C.: 8741
R. Phil Roof *(Pres. & Chief Exec. Officer)*
Ralph Beatty, Jr. *(Exec. V.P.)*
James E. Anderson *(V.P.-Opers.)*
James B. Gambrell *(V.P.-Mktg. & Bus. Devel.)*
Sharon H. Bell *(Controller)*
Edmund F. Strack *(Mgr.-Field Opers.)*
Bennet R. Anderson *(Sr. Project Mgr.)*

Outside Service Firm(s):

Harry B. Gregory & Associates*(Auditors)*
Columbia, SC

South Carolina National Bank*(Major Banking Relationship)*
Columbia, SC

RS ELECTRONICS
34443 Schoolcraft Rd.
Livonia, MI 48150
Tel.: 313-525-1155 **MI**
Fax: 313-525-1184
Approx.Sls.: $40,000,000
Emp.: 160
Import Export
Wholesale Distributor of Electronic Components
S.I.C.: 5065
Winston Stalcup *(Chief Exec. Officer)*
Howard Taxe *(Pres.)*
Syl Biermann *(V.P.-Sls.)*
Ed Gatt *(V.P.-Opers.)*
Michael Simpson *(V.P. Sls.-Southeast Reg.)*
Nancy Gumtow *(Controller)*
Bruce Hoopes *(Dir.-Cash Mngmt.)*
Norm Koloski *(Dir.-Data Processing)*
Dick Miller *(Gen. Sls. Mgr.)*

Divisions:

Fairmont Electronics **(1)**
295 Oser Ave.
Hauppauge, NY 11788
Tel.: 516-231-3313
Sales & Marketing Switches
S.I.C.: 5065
Vincent LaCappra *(Gen. Mgr.)*

Olive Electronics **(1)**
2555 Metro Blvd.
Maryland Heights, MO 63043
Tel.: 314-997-7709
Sales & Marketing Office
S.I.C.: 5065
Syl Biermann *(Gen. Mgr.)*

RTKL ASSOCIATES INC.
400 E. Pratt St.
Baltimore, MD 21202
Tel.: 410-528-8600 **MD**
Fax: 410-385-2455
Year Founded: 1946
Approx.Sls.: $72,000,000
Emp.: 704
Fiscal Year-end: 12/31/90
Export
Architectural & Engineering Services
S.I.C.: 8711; 8712
Harold L. Adams *(Chm. Bd., Pres. & Cheif Exec. Officer)*
Joseph J. Scalabrin *(Vice Chm.)*
David R. Beard *(Sr. V.P.)*
Gary A. Bowden *(Sr. V.P.)*
Robert R. Manfredi *(Sr. V.P.)*
Ted A. Niederman *(Sr. V.P.)*
Donald A. McConnell *(V.P., Treas. & Controller)*

No. of U.S. Offices: 5
No. of Foreign Offices: 2

Outside Service Firm(s):

KPMG Peat Marwick*(Auditors)*
111 S. Calvert St.
Baltimore, MD 21202
Tel.: 410-783-8300

Semmes, Bowen, Semmes*(Legal Firm)*
10 Light Equitable Bldg.
Baltimore, MD 21204
Tel.: 410-296-4400

First National Bank of Maryland*(Major Banking Relationship)*
25 S. Charles St.
Baltimore, MD 21201
Tel.: 410-244-4025

R.T.M. WINNERS
5995 Barfield Rd.
Atlanta, GA 30328
Tel.: 404-256-4900
Fax: 404-847-0284
Emp.: 3,500
Restaurants & Gasoline Service Stations
S.I.C.: 5541; 5812
Russell Umphenour, Jr. *(Chm. Bd., Pres. & Chief Exec. Officer)*
Sharon Barton *(Sr. V.P.)*
Dennis E. Cooper *(Sr. V.P.)*
J. Russell Welch *(V.P.)*

Outside Service Firm(s):

First Atlanta Bank*(Major Banking Relationship)*
Tucker, GA

RTMX-UNIFLEX INC.
800 Eastowne Dr., Ste. 111
Chapel Hill, NC 27514
Tel.: 919-493-1451
Fax: 919-490-2903
Year Founded: 1976
Emp.: 7
Fiscal Year-end: 5/31/91
Export
Advanced Systems Software & Micro-Processors
S.I.C.: 7372
Gary Thomas *(Pres. & Chief Oper. Officer)*
Kenneth R. Lewis *(Treas. & Mgr.-Bus.)*
Randy Lewis *(Dir.-Mktg. & Sls.)*

Computer Systems/Hardware:
Motorola MUME-147, MUME-167; Force CPU-40, CPU-30

Outside Service Firm(s):

Deloitte & Touche*(Auditors)*
Riley, NC

NationsBank Carolinas*(Major Banking Relationship)*
Chapel Hill, NC

RTW, ROGERS TOOL WORKS, INC.
205 N. 13th St.
Rogers, AR 72756
Mailing Address:
P.O. Box 9,
Rogers, AR 72757
Tel.: 501-636-1515
Year Founded: 1952
Approx.Sls.: $40,000,000
Emp.: 980
Fiscal Year-end: 12/31/90
Mfr. of Carbide & Carbide Tipped Cutting Tools
S.I.C.: 3423; 3541
Robert W. Britzke *(Pres.)*
H. Alan King *(V.P.-Sls. & Mktg.)*
Patrick Drake *(Adv. Mgr.)*
Jo Ann Jones *(Pur. Mgr.)*

R.W. ELECTRONICS
206 Andover St.
Andover, MA 01810
Tel.: 508-475-1303
Fax: 508-475-1461
Approx.Sls.: $12,000,000
Emp.: 10
Distribute Electronic Components
S.I.C.: 5065
Peter LeSaffre *(Chm. Bd. & Pres.)*
Robert Benedict *(Chief Exec. Officer, Chief Fin. Officer & V.P.)*
Linda Eastman *(Controller & Office Mgr.)*
Stephen Buckler *(Dir.-Pur.)*
John Lopes *(Gen. Mgr.)*

Computer Systems/Hardware:
MAI Basic Four

Outside Service Firm(s):

Harvey Karll*(Auditors)*
Newburyport, MA

Blue Cross of Massachusetts, Inc.*(Group Insurer)*
Boston, MA

First National Bank of Boston*(Major Banking Relationship)*
P.O. Box 644,
Boston, MA 02102-0644
Tel.: 617-575-2900
Fax: 617-575-2549

RABCO HEALTH SERVICE
444 Madison Ave., Ste. 601
New York, NY 10022
Tel.: 212-688-4500
Fax: 212-888-5025
Holding Company for Health Aids
S.I.C.: 6719; 3842
Ralph Ortiz *(Office Mgr.)*
Principal(s):
Ralph Ortiz
Mr. Gomberg

RACETRAC PETROLEUM, INC.
300 Technology Ct.
Smyrna, GA 30082
Mailing Address:
P.O. Box 105035,
Atlanta, GA 30348
Tel.: 404-431-7600 **GA**
Fax: 404-431-7612
Year Founded: 1959
Approx.Sls.: $506,000,000
Emp.: 2,000
Fiscal Year-end: 12/31/90
Wholesale Petroleum Products; Retail Gasoline & Convenience Stores
S.I.C.: 5541; 5411; 5172
Carl Bolch, Jr. *(Chm. Bd. & Chief Exec. Officer)*
Max V. Lenker *(Pres.)*
Jack Charlesworth *(V.P.-Data Processing)*
Robert J. Dumbacher *(V.P.-Fin. & Treas.)*
John Kopec *(V.P.-Supply & Distr.)*
Robert Stier *(V.P.-Opers.)*
Harriet Landau *(Legal Officer)*
Sue Jackson *(Dir.-Personnel)*

Computer Systems/Hardware:
IBM System 38

Outside Service Firm(s):

KPMG Peat Marwick*(Auditors)*
245 Peachtree Ctr. Ave. N.E., Ste. 1900
Atlanta, GA 30303
Tel.: 404-577-3240

Alston & Bird*(Legal Firm)*
One Atlantic Center, 1201 West Peachtree St.
Atlanta, GA 30309-3424
Tel.: 404-881-7000

Bank South, N.A.*(Major Banking Relationship)*
P.O. Box 4387
Atlanta, GA 30302
Tel.: 404-529-4111

First Atlanta Bank*(Major Banking Relationship)*
Atlanta, GA

RACINE FEDERATED, INC.
2200 South St.
Racine, WI 53404
Tel.: 414-639-6770 **WI**
Fax: 414-639-2267
Year Founded: 1970
Approx.Sls.: $11,000,000
Emp.: 73
Export
Bituminous, Cement & Concrete Related Products & Equipment; Vibrators For Concrete Construction; Flow Instruments, Industrial Process Type
S.I.C.: 3531; 3823
John E. Erskine, Sr. *(Chm. Bd.)*
George B. Miller *(Vice Chm.)*
John E. Erskine, Jr. *(Pres.)*
Anton L. Zeman *(Exec. V.P. & Treas.)*
Thomas G. Nelson *(V.P.)*
Robert Peterson *(V.P.)*
Glenn Coates *(Sec.)*
James Chaplin *(Dir.-Engrng.)*
Willard H. Dalrymple *(Pur. Agent)*

Outside Service Firm(s):

Clifton Gunderson*(Auditors)*
Racine, WI

Bank One Milwaukee, N.A.*(Major Banking Relationship)*
111 E. Wisconsin Ave.
Milwaukee, WI
Tel.: 414-765-3000

Subsidiaries:

Blancett **(1)**
Altus, OK

Hedland **(1)**
2200 South St.
Racine, WI 53404

National Diecasting Machinery **(1)**
Warwick, RI

The Wyco Tool Co. **(1)**
2200 South St.
Racine, WI 53404
Tel.: 414-681-3411
Tel.: 800-233-9926
Fax: 414-639-2267
Approx.Sls.: $6,000,000
Emp.: 35
Fiscal Year-end: 12/31/90
Import Export
Computer Systems/Hardware:
IBM 36
Mfr. Concrete Vibrators, Industrial Flexible Shaft Machines; Hydraulic Strike-Off Extensions for Asphalt Pavers
S.I.C.: 3531; 3546; 3569
A.L. Zeman *(Pres.)*
Kenneth A. Hahn *(V.P.-Sls.)*
Terry Graczyk *(Pur. Agent)*

RADIATOR SPECIALTY COMPANY
1900 Wilkinson Blvd.
Charlotte, NC 28208
Mailing Address:
P. O. Box 34689
Charlotte, NC 28234
Tel.: 704-377-6555
Tel.: 800-438-4532 **NC**
Fax: 800-421-9525
Year Founded: 1924
Approx.Sls.: $137,000,000
Emp.: 700
Fiscal Year-end: 12/31/91
Import Export
Manufacture Automotive, Plumbing & Hardware, Chemical, Rubber & Traffic Control Products
S.I.C.: 5072; 2842; 2819; 2899; 2891; 3053; 3069; 3531
Corporate Giving Program: Handled Through the Blumenthal Foundation
Herman Blumenthal *(Chm. & Chief Exec. Officer)*
Alan Blumenthal *(Pres.)*
M. Thomas Cory *(V.P.-Plumbing Div.)*
James Wells *(V.P.-Chemical Mfg.)*
Terry G. Stokes *(V.P.-Sls., Plumbing Hardware)*
Thomas J. Koval *(Treas. & Controller)*
Ronald Weiner *(Gen. Counsel & Corp. Sec.)*
B.J. Tanner *(Asst. Sec.)*
Ralph Jarrels *(Dir.-Adv.)*
James Rubendall *(Dir.-Data Processing)*
Paul Bell *(Dir.-Pur.)*
Philip L. Joffe *(Mktg. Mgr.)*
John Rae *(Gen. Sls. Mgr.-Automotive)*

Computer Systems/Hardware:
Unibase

Outside Service Firm(s):

Gleiberman, Spears & Shepherd*(Auditors)*
3500 NCNB Plaza
Charlotte, NC 28280

Blue Cross & Blue Shield of North Carolina*(Group Insurer)*
Durham, NC

NationsBank Carolinas*(Major Banking Relationship)*
One NCNB Plaza
Charlotte, NC 28255

Subsidiary:

CRP Hose Division **(1)**
1900 Wilkinson Blvd.
Charlotte, NC 28208
Tel.: 704-377-6555
Tel.: 800-438-4532
Fax: 1-800-845-9883
Import Export
Mfr. & Distributor of Automotive Hose Products
S.I.C.: 3052
L. Kay *(Exec. V.P.)*
T.K. Russell *(Dir.-Adv.)*
Thomas Hayman *(Natl. Sls. Mgr.)*

RADIONICS, INC.
1800 Abbott St.
Salinas, CA 93901
Tel.: 408-757-8877
Fax: 408-757-6831
Year Founded: 1975
Approx.Sls.: $50,000,000
Emp.: 365
Fiscal Year-end: 12/31/91
Import Export
Mfr. of Electronic Security Communications Systems
S.I.C.: 3669
Employee Matching Gifts Program: Match Employee Donation to United Way
G.M. Greer *(Pres.)*
Charles M. Frank *(V.P.-Fin. & Chief Fin. Officer)*
Gary Kallman *(V.P.-Sls.)*
Ken Rolle *(V.P.-Mktg.)*
John G. Pate *(V.P.-Prod. Devel.)*
Terry Winn *(V.P.-Opers.)*
Nancy Belton *(Dir.-Human Resources)*
Rich de La Cruz *(Dir.-Quality Control)*

Outside Service Firm(s):

Ware & Freidenrich*(Legal Firm)*
400 Hamilton Ave.
Palo Alto, CA 94301-1825
Tel.: 415-328-6561
Fax: 415-327-3699

RADIX CORPORATION
4855 Wiley Post Way
Salt Lake City, UT 84116
Tel.: 801-537-1717
Tel.: 800-367-9256 **DE**
Fax: 801-328-3401
Year Founded: 1969
Approx.Sls.: $18,000,000
Emp.: 225
Hand-held Computers, Business Oriented
S.I.C.: 3571; 7372
Alan C. Reed *(Chm. Bd. & Chief Exec. Officer)*
Steven I. Reemer *(Pres. & Chief Oper. Officer)*
Tim Draper *(Chief Fin. Officer)*
James H. Benson *(V.P.-Tech. Opers.)*
Randel L. Wightman *(V.P.-Mktg.)*
Donald E. Johnson *(Dir.-Mktg.)*
Jim Ruff *(Dir.-Engrng.)*
Kris Liacopoulos *(Mgr.-Human Resources)*
Ben Wagnor *(Mgr.-Mktg. & Admin. Opers.)*
Joan C. Elmer *(Supvr.-Travel)*
Patti Nelson *(Buyer)*
Principal(s):
Alan C. Reed

No. of Mfg. Plants/Facilities: 2
No. of U.S. Offices: 4
No. of Foreign Offices: 3

Outside Service Firm(s):

Coopers & Lybrand*(Auditors)*
1700 Benneficial Life Tower
Salt Lake City, UT 84111
Tel.: 801-531-9666

Blue Cross & Blue Shield of Utah*(Group Insurer)*
Salt Lake City, UT

Westone Bank of Utah*(Major Banking Relationship)*
Salt Lake City, UT

RADIX WIRE COMPANY
26260 Lakeland Blvd.
Cleveland, OH 44132
Tel.: 216-731-9191
Fax: 216-731-7082
Year Founded: 1944
Approx.Sls.: $18,000,000
Emp.: 80
Export
Manufacture High Temperature Insulated Wire
S.I.C.: 3357; 3315
R.C. VerMerris *(Chm. Bd. & Pres.)*
R.A. Schordock *(Chief Fin. Officer, Treas. & Controller)*
Peter Thurstone *(Sls. Mgr.)*
Jim Gardner *(Plant Mgr.)*

RADO WATCH COMPANY, INC.
(Div. of SMH U.S. Inc.)
35 E. 21st St.
New York, NY 10010
Tel.: 212-505-4054
Tel.: 212-505-6295
Tel.: 800-283-7236
Fax: 212-505-7256
Approx.Sls.: $18,000,000
Emp.: 20
Fiscal Year-end: 12/31/90
Rado & Diastar Watches
S.I.C.: 3873
John J. Hubacher *(Pres.)*
Joel Potter *(Brand Controller)*
Joy Sapin *(Dir.-Mktg.)*

Computer Systems/Hardware:
IBM PC

RAFFI & SWANSON, INC.
100 Eames St.
Wilmington, MA 01887
Tel.: 508-658-3364 **MA**
Fax: 508-658-3366
Year Founded: 1923
Sales Range: $10-19 Million
Emp.: 110
Coatings, Inks & Adhesives
S.I.C.: 2851; 2893; 2891
Peter M. Jarowey *(Chief Exec. Officer)*
Gabriel Paci *(Chief Oper. Officer & V.P.)*
William Kotek *(Chief Fin. Officer)*
Walter F. Greeley *(Gen. Counsel)*
Barbara Crowell *(Dir.-Personnel)*
Helen Pellerin *(Mgr.-Credit)*

No. of Mfg. Plants/Facilities: 1

C. B. RAGLAND COMPANY
P.O. Box 40587
Nashville, TN 37204
Mailing Address:
P.O. Box 40587,
Nashville, TN 37204
Tel.: 615-259-4622 **TN**
Fax: 615-254-5867
Year Founded: 1917
Assets: $28,000,000
Liabilities: $20,000,000
Net Worth: $8,000,000
Approx.Sls.: $183,000,000
Emp.: 325
Fiscal Year-end: 12/31/90
Wholesaler Grocery Goods
S.I.C.: 5141
J. Michael Hayes *(Pres. & Chief Exec. Officer)*
Robert Agee *(V.P.)*
Edward Tietgens *(V.P.)*
Baker Walker *(Treas., Controller, Sec. & Chief Fin. Officer)*
Ruby Vaughn *(Dir.-Personnel)*

Computer Systems/Hardware:
IBM System 4361

Outside Service Firm(s):

KPMG Peat Marwick*(Auditors)*
1900 Nashville Center, 511 Union St.
Nashville, TN 37219

C. B. Ragland Company—(Continued)

Willis Corroon*(Commercial Insurance Carrier)*
301 Plus Park Blvd.
Nashville, TN 37217
Tel.: 615-367-9702

Farris, Warfield & Kanaday*(Legal Firm)*
Third Natl. Financial Ctr., 424 Church St., Ste. 1900
Nashville, TN 37219
Tel.: 615-244-5200
Fax: 615-726-3185

Third National Bank*(Major Banking Relationship)*
Nashville, TN

New England Mutual Life Insurance Co.*(Pension Manager)*
Boston, MA

T.S. RAGSDALE COMPANY, INCORPORATED
P.O. Box 937
Lake City, SC 29560
Tel.: 803-394-8567 **SC**
Fax: 803-394-8156
Year Founded: 1929
Sales Range: $40-59 Million
Emp.: 278
Fiscal Year-end: 3/31/90
Export
Manufacture Embers Charcoal Briquets & Other Related Products; Tobacco Processor & Redryer; Transportation Brokerage
S.I.C.: 2141; 2999
T. Smith Ragsdale III *(Pres.)*
Shelby J. Kirby *(Chief Fin. Officer, Treas. & Controller)*
S.R. Clayton *(Sr. V.P.-Tobacco Sls.)*
Charles S. Ragsdale *(V.P.)*
Gail Driggers *(Mgr.-Fin. Acctg. Opers.)*
Steve Godwin *(Mgr.-Pur.)*
Eve. G. Lynch *(Mgr.-Opers.)*
Glaze Rollins *(Mgr.-Plant)*
Principal(s):
T. Smith Ragsdale III
Charles S. Ragsdale

No. of Mfg. Plants/Facilities: 2
No. of U.S. Offices: 2
No. of Foreign Offices: 2

Computer Systems/Hardware:
IBM 36; IBM XT

Outside Service Firm(s):

Arthur Andersen & Co.*(Auditors)*
Columbia, SC

Connecticut Mutual*(Group Insurer)*
Hartford, CT

Willcox, Hardee, McLeod, Buyck, Baker & Williams*(Legal Firm)*
Florence, SC

First Union National Bank*(Major Banking Relationship)*
CMG-5, Two First Union Center
Charlotte, NC 28288-1154
Tel.: 704-374-2698
Fax: 704-374-6987

Booke & Co.*(Pension Manager)*
310 W. 4th Street
Winston-Salem, NC 27102
Tel.: 919-748-1120
Fax: 919-748-1120 ext. 462

RAIL EUROPE INC.
226-230 Westchester Ave.
White Plains, NY 10604
Tel.: 914-682-2999
Year Founded: 1991
Approx.Sls.: $130,000,000
Emp.: 200
Fiscal Year-end: 12/31/92
EurailPass, Eurail FlexiPass, Eurail SaverPass, Eurail YouthPass, Eurail Youth FlexiPass, Eurail DrivePass, EurailDrive Pass, Austrian Rabbit Card, Benelux Tourrail Pass, BritFrance RailPass, BritFrance Rail 'n Drive, European East Pass, France RailPass, France Rail 'n Drive, France Rail 'n Fly, France Fly Rail 'n Drive, German FlexiPass, German Rail 'n Drive, Greek Rail Pass, Greek Rail 'n Drive
S.I.C.: 4111
B. Frelat *(Pres.)*
Dag M. Scher *(Exec. V.P.-Corp. Communications)*
A. Van Caneghem *(V.P.-Fin.)*

Computer Systems/Hardware:
DEC

RAIN BIRD SPRINKLER MFG. CORP.
145 N. Grand
Glendora, CA 91740
Tel.: 818-852-7100
Fax: 818-963-4287
Year Founded: 1933
Export
Sprinklers, Valves, Controllers & All Encompassing Automatic Systems; Hose, Portable Sprinklers
S.I.C.: 3432; 3052
A.W. LaFetra *(Pres.)*
Kenneth Mills *(V.P.)*
Bud Terry *(V.P.)*
Arthur Ludwick *(Treas.)*
Kris Freudenthaler *(Dir.-Personnel)*
Carole Allaway Pelton *(Dir.-Adv.)*

RAINBOW APPAREL DISTRIBUTION CENTER
1000 Pennsylvania Ave.
Brooklyn, NY 11207
Tel.: 718-485-3000
Approx.Sls.: $90,000,000
Emp.: 1,500
Fiscal Year-end: 3/ 1/91
Apparel Chain Stores
S.I.C.: 5632
J. Chehebar *(Chief Exec. Officer)*
A. Fallas *(Gen. Mgr.-Mdse.)*
M. Stein *(Gen. Mgr.-Mdse.)*
N. Hoffman *(Fin. Admin.)*
K. Cohen *(Regional Mgr.)*
E. Zarom *(Regional Mgr.)*
L. Laiken *(Controller)*

RAINBOW HOME RENTALS
5414 Youngstown-Warren Rd.
Canfield, OH 44406
Mailing Address:
P.O. Box 9006
Boardman, OH 44512
Tel.: 216-544-2600
Fax: 216-533-4241
Approx.Sls.: $18,000,000
Emp.: 120
Rental of TV's, Appliances & Furniture
S.I.C.: 7359
Wayland Russell *(Pres.)*
Larry Hendricks *(V.P.)*
Michael Vivieros *(V.P.)*
Jason Alford *(Treas. & Sec.)*

RAINFAIR, INC.
3600 S. Memorial Dr.
Racine, WI 53404
Mailing Address:
P.O. Box 1647
Racine, WI 53401
Tel.: 414-554-7000
Tel.: 800-558-5990
Fax: 414-554-6655
Year Founded: 1879
Approx.Sls.: $18,000,000
Emp.: 235
Fiscal Year-end: 4/29/91
Import
Mfr. of Men's Rainwear & Coated Fabrics & Waterproof Footwear
S.I.C.: 2385; 2295
William Mead *(Pres.)*
Bruce Barfelt *(Chief Fin. Officer)*
Sara Vidian *(Dir.-Human Resources)*
Tony Shanine *(Dir.-Data Processing)*

RAINSOFT WATER CONDITIONING CO.
2080 E. Lunt Ave.
Elk Grove Village, IL 60007
Tel.: 708-437-9400
Fax: 708-437-1594
Year Founded: 1953
Approx.Sls.: $25,000,000
Emp.: 126
Fiscal Year-end: 9/30/90
Export
Mfr. Water Softening & Purification Equipment
S.I.C.: 3589
John R. Grayson *(Pres.)*
C. David Cole *(V.P.-Mktg.)*
Robert Ruhstorfer *(Natl. Sls. Mgr.)*
Eric Webb *(Mgr.-Mktg. Services)*

RALEIGH ENTERPRISES, INC.
11444 W. Olympic Blvd.
Los Angeles, CA 90064
Tel.: 310-312-3600 **CA**
Fax: 310-479-3086
Year Founded: 1955
Approx.Sls.: $56,000,000
Emp.: 1,000
Hotels; Studio Property Rental; Motion Picture; Commercial & Industrial Building Operation; Property Operations Of Shopping Centers, Chart & Graph Design; Data Processing Service; Flying Charter Service
S.I.C.: 7011; 7819; 6512; 7336; 7374; 4522
George I. Rosenthal *(Chm. Bd. & Pres.)*
Gabriel Esquibias *(V.P. & Chief Oper. Officer)*
Deborah Rosenthal *(V.P.)*
Mark Rosenthal *(V.P. & Gen. Counsel)*
Anil Sharma *(V.P. & Chief Fin. Officer)*

Outside Service Firm(s):

Mitsui Manufacturers Bank*(Major Banking Relationship)*
Beverly Hills, CA

RALEY'S
500 W. Capital Ave.
West Sacramento, CA 95605
Mailing Address:
P.O. Box 15618,
Sacramento, CA 95852
Tel.: 916-373-3333 **CA**
Fax: 916-444-3733
Year Founded: 1935
Assets: $235,000,000
Liabilities: $155,000,000
Net Worth: $80,000,000
Approx.Sls.: $1,400,000,000
Emp.: 8,500
Fiscal Year-end: 6/30/91
Supermarkets & Drug Stores
S.I.C.: 5411; 5921; 5399; 5912
James E. Teel *(Co-Chm. Bd. & Chief Oper. Officer)*
Joyce N. Teel *(Co-Chm. Bd.)*
Charles L. Collings *(Pres. & Chief Exec. Officer)*
Keith Tronson *(Chief Fin. Officer & Treas.)*
Sam McPherson *(V.P.-Human Resources)*
Kenneth Collings *(Dir.-Personnel)*
Fred Gorath *(Dir.-Plng. & Devel.)*
Frank McMinn *(Mgr.-Adv.)*

Computer Systems/Hardware:
IBM 4381

Outside Service Firm(s):

Coopers & Lybrand*(Auditors)*
Sacramento, CA

Downey, Brand, Seymour & Rohwer*(Legal Firm)*
Sacramento, CA

Bank of America NT&SA*(Major Banking Relationship)*
Sacramento, CA

Prudential Insurance Co. of America*(Pension Manager)*
751 Broad St.
Newark, NJ 07102-3777
Tel.: 201-802-6000

Subsidiary:

Bel Air **(1)**
Sacramento, CA
George Wong *(Pres.)*

RAM GOLF CORPORATION
2020 Indian Boundary Dr.
Melrose Park, IL 60160
Tel.: 708-681-5800
Year Founded: 1948
Approx.Sls.: $40,000,000
Emp.: 600
Mfr. Golf Clubs, Bags, Balls & Clothing
S.I.C.: 3949; 2321; 2325
R.V. Hansberger *(Chm. Bd.)*
James R. Hansberger *(Pres.)*
Allan Hansberger *(V.P.-Mktg.)*
W.L. Hansberger *(V.P.-Mfg.)*
C.R. Schram *(V.P.-Fin.)*
Greg Dinkins *(Sls. Mgr.)*
Fritz Frazier *(Dir.-Mktg.)*

Non-U.S. Holding:

RAM Golf UK **(1)**
Bell Lane Industrial Complex,
Uckfield, East Sussex TN221QL, United Kingdom
Distr. of Golf Equipment
S.I.C.: 5941

RAM GRAPHICS, INC.
State Rd., 9 S.
Alexandria, IN 46001
Mailing Address:
P.O. Box 114,
Alexandria, VA 46001
Tel.: 317-724-7783
Fax: 317-724-7933
Approx.Sls.: $10,000,000
Emp.: 155
Silk Screen Design On Clothing; Trophies
S.I.C.: 5136; 7336; 5094
Ronald Ruby *(Pres.)*
Larry Mercer *(V.P.)*
Patricia Mercer *(Office Mgr.)*
Paulette Ruby *(Gen. Mgr.)*

Outside Service Firm(s):

Jack J. Gray*(Auditors)*
Anderson, IN

Citizens National Bank*(Major Banking Relationship)*
Anderson, IN

RAMA GROUP OF COMPANIES
25 Boxwood Lane
Cheektowaga, NY 14227
Mailing Address:
P.O. Box 211
Buffalo, NY 14225
Tel.: 716-668-5223 **NY**
Fax: 716-668-4526
Year Founded: 1968
Assets: $5,200,000
Liabilities: $3,450,000
Net Worth: $1,750,000
Approx.Sls.: $13,500,000
Emp.: 307

Fiscal Year-end: 12/31/91
Publisher of Metro Community News; Advertising Circular Printing & Distribution; Cold Type Composition & Typesetting
S.I.C.: 2711; 2752; 7319
Richard A. Maussner *(Pres.)*
Kevin M. Murphy *(Chief Fin. Officer & Treas.)*
Lucy Cieply *(Controller & Sec.)*
John Colling *(Dir.-Pur. & Traffic)*
Dale Eichelberber *(Dir.-Mfg.)*
Melissa M. Maussnar *(Dir.-Sls. Promo.)*
Phyllis A. Stevens *(Dir.-Human Resources)*

No. of Mfg. Plants/Facilities: 1

Computer Systems/Hardware:
IBM System 36

Outside Service Firm(s):

Seligman, Eurbach, Kahn & Werlin*(Auditors)*
Amherst, NY

Hurwitz & Fine*(Legal Firm)*
Buffalo, NY

Chase Lincoln First Bank, N.A.*(Major Banking Relationship)*
295 Main St.
Buffalo, NY 14203
Tel.: 716-849-8531

RANCHERS COTTON OIL
2691 S. Cedar Ave.
Fresno, CA 93725
Tel.: 209-443-5270
Emp.: 132
Manufacture Cotton Seed Oil
S.I.C.: 2074
Guido Lombardi *(Chm. Bd.)*
Don Toretta *(Vice Chm.)*
Glen N. Janzem *(Pres. & Chief Exec. Officer)*
K.W. Billings *(Sec. & Treas.)*

Outside Service Firm(s):

Eadie & Payne*(Auditors)*
San Bernardino, CA

Bank of America NT&SA*(Major Banking Relationship)*
San Bernardino, CA

RANCH-WAY, INC.
416 Linden St.
Fort Collins, CO 80521
Tel.: 303-482-1700
Fax: 303-482-6963
Year Founded: 1967
Approx.Sls.: $10,000,000
Emp.: 48
Mfr. of Livestock & Poultry Feeds
S.I.C.: 2048
Phyllis Bixler *(Pres. & Gen. Mgr.)*
Joe Bixler *(V.P.)*
C.K. Bixler *(Treas.)*
Larry Miller *(Dir.-Opers.)*
Bonnie Bixler Szidon *(Sec.)*

RAND
1700 Main St.
Santa Monica, CA 90407-2138
Mailing Address:
P.O. Box 2138
Santa Monica, CA 90407-2138
Tel.: 310-393-0411 **CA**
Fax: 310-393-4818
Year Founded: 1948
Approx.Rev.: $102,200,000
Emp.: 1,100
Fiscal Year-end: 9/30/91
Import Export
Research
S.I.C.: 8731
Lloyd M. Morrisett *(Chm. Bd.)*
James A. Thomson *(Pres. & Chief Exec. Officer)*
Rae W. Archibald *(Chief Fin. Officer & V.P.)*
Lynn E. Davis *(V.P.-Army Research)*
George L. Donohue *(V.P.-Project AIR FORCE)*
Stephen M. Drezner *(V.P.-Research)*
David W. Lyon *(V.P.-Domestic Research)*
Michael D. Rich *(V.P.-Natl. Security Research)*
Barbara R. Williams *(V.P.-Communications)*
Brent D. Bradley *(Deputy V.P.-Fin. & Admin.)*
Vivian J. Arterbery *(Sec.)*
Charles Wolf, Jr. *(Dean-Graduate School)*

Outside Service Firm(s):

Coopers & Lybrand*(Auditors)*
350 S. Grand Ave.
Los Angeles, CA 90071
Tel.: 213-481-1000
Fax: 213-482-6440

Cooley, Godward, Castro, Huddleson & Tatum*(Legal Firm)*
Los Angeles, CA

BankAmerica Corp.*(Major Banking Relationship)*
Anaheim, CA

RAND MCNALLY & COMPANY
8255 N. Central Park
Skokie, IL 60076
Mailing Address:
P.O. Box 7600,
Chicago, IL 60680
Tel.: 708-673-9100 **DE**
Telex: 210041 RMCN UR
Fax: 708-673-0813
Year Founded: 1856
Sales Range: $100-499 Million
Emp.: 3,000
Fiscal Year-end: 12/31/90
Publishers of Maps & Books; Bookbinding & Commercial Lithography; Producers of Airline Tickets & Baggage Tags; Producers of Surface Transportation Tickets & Documents; Publishers of Computerized Mileage & Routing Systems
S.I.C.: 2741; 2731; 2752; 2732; 2789
Andrew McNally III *(Chm. Bd.)*
Andrew McNally IV *(Pres. & Chief Exec. Officer)*
John S. Bakalar *(Exec. V.P. & Treas.)*
Jayne L. Fenton *(V.P.-Map & Atlas Div.)*
Mario Fidanzi *(V.P.-Pur.)*
Donald F. Helm *(V.P.-Personnel & Indus. Rels.)*
Frank Sadorf *(V.P.-Information Services)*
Neil Vill *(V.P.-New Bus. Devel.)*
Russell Voisin *(V.P.-Intl. Sls. Publishing)*
Martin J. Rosinski *(Controller)*
Kurt Stele *(Gen. Counsel)*
Conroy Erickson *(Dir.-Pub. Rels.)*
Cindy Woodyard *(Mgr.-Adv.)*

Computer Systems/Hardware:
National Advance System 9000 DPC; CAD-CAM

Outside Service Firm(s):

Arthur Andersen & Co.*(Auditors)*
33 W. Monroe St.
Chicago, IL 60603-4067
Tel.: 312-580-0033
Fax: 312-507-6748

Metropolitan Life Insurance Co.*(Group Insurer)*
Tampa, FL

Kirkland & Ellis*(Legal Firm)*
200 E. Randolph Dr.
Chicago, IL 60601
Tel.: 312-861-2000
Fax: 312-861-2200

First National Bank of Chicago*(Major Banking Relationship)*
One First National Plaza
Chicago, IL 60670
Tel.: 312-732-9781
Tel.: 312-732-4050
Fax: 312-732-4840
Fax: 312-732-3055

Continental Bank N. A.*(Pension Manager)*
231 S. LaSalle St.
Chicago, IL 60697
Tel.: 312-828-2345
Tel.: 800-426-5754
Telex: 312-828-1783

David J. Greene & Co.*(Pension Manager)*
30 Wall St.
New York, NY
Tel.: 212-344-5180

T. Rowe Price Associates*(Pension Manager)*
100 E. Pratt St.
Baltimore, MD 21202
Tel.: 410-547-2000
Fax: 410-659-0965

Vanguard Group*(Pension Manager)*
Vanguard Financial Ctr., P.O. Box 876
Valley Forge, PA 19482
Tel.: 215-648-6000
Fax: 215-648-6321

Divisions:

Kimball Baggage Tag Division **(1)**
151 Cortland St.
Belleville, NJ 07109
Tel.: 201-759-6500
Twx: 710-990-4967
Telecopier: 201-990-4967, Ext. 250
Product Identification Tags, Transportation Tags & Labels
S.I.C.: 2752
Tom Breen *(Pres.)*

Rand McNally Publishing Group **(1)**
444 N. Michigan Ave.
Chicago, IL 60611
Tel.: 312-321-1751
Publisher of Books, Atlases & Maps
S.I.C.: 2731; 2741; 7379
Henry Feinberg *(Grp. Pres.)*

Rand McNally Publishing Group **(1)**
150 S. Wacker Dr.
Chicago, IL 60606
Tel.: 312-332-2009
S.I.C.: 2741

Subsidiaries:

Rand McNally Book Manufacturing Co. **(1)**
8255 N. Central Park
Skokie, IL 60076
Tel.: 708-673-9100
John Wasson *(Pres.)*

Rand McNally Book & Media Services **(1)**
418 Harding Industrial Dr.
Nashville, TN 37211
Tel.: 615-834-7600
Printing; Computer Software; Graphic Arts
S.I.C.: 2759; 7372; 7336
James Thaden *(Pres.)*

Rand McNalley & Company, d/b/a Champion Map Corp. **(1)**
200 Fentress Blvd.
Daytona Beach, FL 32014
Tel.: 904-258-1270
Publish & Print Maps
S.I.C.: 2741
Robert M. Croasmun *(Gen. Mgr.)*

Rand McNally DocuSystems Group **(1)**
8255 N. Central Park
Skokie, IL 60076
Tel.: 708-673-9100
Tom Breem *(Pres.)*

Rand McNally International **(1)**
8255 N. Central Park
Skokie, IL 60076
Tel.: 708-673-9100

Rand McNally Map Services Co. **(1)**
8255 N. Central Park
Skokie, IL 60076
Tel.: 708-673-9100 (100%)
Retail Map Distribution
S.I.C.: 7389
William Meacham *(V.P.-Travel Products)*

Rand McNally Publishing Group **(1)**
8255 N. Central Park
Skokie, IL 60076
Tel.: 708-673-9100
Henry Feinberg *(Pres.)*

Rand McNally-TDM, Inc. **(1)**
P.O. Box 7600,
Chicago, IL 60680
Tel.: 312-673-9100 (100%)
Transportation Software & On-Line Systems
S.I.C.: 7371; 7372
Jerry M. Ragsdell *(Pres.)*
Diana Baird Ragsdell *(V.P.-Sls.)*

Rand McNally Map Services Company **(1)**
210 S. Fairbanks
Addison, IL 60101
Tel.: 708-543-6277

RANDALL STORES, INC.
1705 N. Main
Mitchell, SD 57301
Mailing Address:
P.O. Box 1200,
Mitchell, SD 57301
Tel.: 605-996-7511 **SD**
Fax: 605-996-1167
Year Founded: 1950
Approx.Sls.: $350,000,000
Emp.: 2,800
Fiscal Year-end: 10/31/89
Grocery Store Chain
S.I.C.: 5411
Ronald F. Randall *(Chm. Bd., Pres. & Chief Exec. Officer)*
William Bell *(Chief Oper. Officer & V.P.)*
Leonard Ellwein *(Chief Fin. Officer & Controller)*
Principal(s):
Ronald F. Randall

Computer Systems/Hardware:
IBM Multi-Sync

Outside Service Firm(s):

McGladrey & Pullen*(Auditors)*
Sioux Falls, SD

Davenport, Evans, Hurwitz & Smith*(Legal Firm)*
Sioux Falls, SD

RANDALL'S FOOD MARKETS, INC.
3663 Briar Park Dr.
Houston, TX 77042
Mailing Address:
PO Box 4506,
Houston, TX 77010-4506
Tel.: 713-268-3500 **TX**
Fax: 713-268-3601
Year Founded: 1980
Approx.Sls.: $675,000,000
Emp.: 8,000
Grocery Stores
S.I.C.: 5411
Corporate Giving Program: Non-Profit Contributions, Gift Certificates, Discounts In-Kind, Sponsorship of Children's Sports Teams
Robert R. Onstead *(Chm. Bd. & Chief Exec. Officer)*
R. Randall Onstead, Jr. *(Pres. & Chief Oper. Officer)*
Ron W. Barclay *(Exec. V.P.-Store Opers.)*
Bob L. Gowens *(Exec. V.P.-Admin. & Fin.)*
Norman P. Frewin, Jr. *(Sr. V.P.-Produce Opers. & Mdse.)*
Joe Livorsi *(Sr. V.P.-Mktg.)*

Randall's Food Markets, Inc.—(Continued)

Robert Hemphill *(V.P.-Data Processing)*
Joe Rollins *(V.P.)*
Kenneth A. Branch *(Sec., Treas. & Controller)*
Lew W. Harpold *(Gen. Counsel)*
R. B. Flores *(Dir.-Print Adv.)*
Cindy Crane Garbs *(Dir.-Public Affairs)*
Jan Gillespie *(Dir.-Human Resources)*

Principal(s):
R. Randall Onstead, Jr.

No. of U.S. Offices: 1

Computer Systems/Hardware:
IBM 4361 & 9377; Tandem 6600; Sperry System 80; Data General; NCR Towers; Cada Data Entry

Outside Service Firm(s):

Arthur Andersen & Co.*(Auditors)*
711 Louisiana, Ste. 1300
Houston, TX 77002-2323
Tel.: 713-237-2793

Industrial Risk Insurers*(Commercial Insurance Carrier)*
Hartford, CT

Kemper Insurance*(Commercial Insurance Carrier)*
Long Grove, IL 60049-0001

Harpold, McDonald, Fitzgerald & Hall*(Legal Firm)*
Houston, TX

Texas Commerce Bank*(Major Banking Relationship)*
600 Travis Street, Suite 1150
Houston, TX 77002
Tel.: 713-236-4865

Texas Commerce Bank*(Pension Manager)*
600 Travis Street, Suite 1150
Houston, TX 77002
Tel.: 713-236-4865

Subsidiaries:

Randall's Warehouse Corporation **(1)**
10700 Telge Rd.
Houston, TX 77095
Tel.: 713-859-6160
R. Randall Onstead, Jr. *(Pres.)*
Jerome W. Pesek *(V.P.)*

Tom Thumb Food & Drugs, Inc. **(1)**
14303 Inwood Rd.
Dallas, TX 75244
Tel.: 214-661-9700
Fax: 214-661-3866
Assets: $240,447,000
Earnings: $18,094,000
Liabilities: $121,369,000
Net Worth: $119,078,000
Approx.Sls.: $1,036,450,000
Emp.: 10,000
Fiscal Year-end: 6/30/89
Supermarkets, Drug Stores & Meat Packing
S.I.C.: 5411; 2011; 5912
Jack Evans, Jr. *(Pres. & Chief Oper. Officer)*
Houston E. Holmes, Jr. *(V.P., Sec. & Legal Counsel)*
James E. Stiles *(V.P. & Chief Fin. Officer)*
Robert B. Cullum, Jr. *(V.P.)*
Mike Chesmore *(Controller)*
David Spafford *(Asst. Controller)*
Jim Dawson *(C.I.S.)*
Sherry Stowe *(Consumer Affairs)*

Subsidiaries:

Culco, Inc. **(2)**
14303 Inwood Rd.
Dallas, TX 75240
Tel.: 214-661-9700 (100%)
Emp.: 4
Distribution Company
S.I.C.: 5411

Cullum Development Co. **(2)**
14303 Inwood Rd.
Dallas, TX 75244
Tel.: 214-661-9700 (100%)
Real Estate Development
S.I.C.: 6552
Houston E. Holmes, Jr. *(Pres. & Chief Opr. Officer)*

Cullum Distribution Center, Inc. **(2)**
14303 Inwood Rd.
Dallas, TX 75240
Tel.: 214-661-9700 (100%)
S.I.C.: 5141

Gooch Packing Co., Inc. **(2)**
P.O. Box 2738,
Abilene, TX 79604
Tel.: 915-673-8223 (100%)
Meat Packing Plant
S.I.C.: 2011
James Garrison *(Chief Oper. Officer)*

Tom Thumb Stores, Inc. **(2)**
14303 Inwood Rd.
Dallas, TX 75234
Tel.: 214-661-9700 (100%)
Supermarkets & Drug Stores
S.I.C.: 5411; 5912
Jack W. Evans, Jr. *(Pres.)*

Division:

Pages Drugs **(3)**
14303 Inwood Rd.
Dallas, TX 75234
Tel.: 214-661-9700 (100%)
Approx.Sls.: $22,000,000
Emp.: 300
Drug Store
S.I.C.: 5912
Jack W. Evans, Jr. *(Pres.)*

RANDOLPH MEDICAL INC.
31742 Enterprise Dr.
Livonia, MI 48150
Tel.: 313-427-4810 **MI**
Fax: 313-425-3085
Approx.Sls.: $55,000,000
Emp.: 225
Wholesale Medical Equipment & Supplies
S.I.C.: 5047
Don L. Randolph *(Pres.)*
John W. Braine *(Exec. V.P.-Fin. & Admin.)*
E. Greenberg *(Exec. V.P.-Sls. & Mktg.)*
Mark G. Blohm *(V.P.-Opers.)*
Ronald Brandt *(V.P.-Data Processing)*
James J. Griffiths *(Dir.-Pur.)*

No. of Mfg. Plants/Facilities: 3

Computer Systems/Hardware:
AS 400 Model 50

Outside Service Firm(s):

Follmer, Rudzewicz & Co.*(Auditors)*
Southfield, MI

Kerr, Russell & Weber*(Legal Firm)*
Detroit, MI

N.B.D. Bank, N.A.*(Major Banking Relationship)*
611 Woodward Ave.
Detroit, MI 48226
Tel.: 313-225-1122
Fax: 313-225-3420

Subsidiaries:

American Hospital Equipment Corp. **(1)**
31742 Enterprise Dr.
Livonia, MI 48150
Tel.: 313-427-4810
Wholesale Distributor of Hospital Equipment
S.I.C.: 5047

Rancare Inc. **(1)**
31742 Enterprise Dr.
Livonia, MI 48150
Tel.: 313-427-4810
Wholesale Distributor of Medical & Surgical Equipment
S.I.C.: 5047

RANDOM CORPORATION
581 Northland Rd.
Cincinnati, OH 45240
Tel.: 513-825-0880
Fax: 513-825-2775
Year Founded: 1960
Approx.Sls.: $10,000,000
Emp.: 150
Mfr. of Laptop Computer Terminals, Medical Equipment & Radon-detection Devices
S.I.C.: 3571; 3829
Ernest J. Timperman *(Pres. & Chief Exec. Officer)*
William M. Stevens *(V.P. & Gen. Mgr.)*
Richard McCoy *(Controller)*

RAND'S INC.
1200 Pike Ave.
North Little Rock, AR 72114
Tel.: 501-376-3881 **AR**
Fax: 501-376-1987
Year Founded: 1925
Approx.Sls.: $55,000,000
Emp.: 147
Wholesale Groceries & Frozen Food
S.I.C.: 5141; 5142
Ben A. Rand, Jr. *(Pres.)*
Frank Hillard *(V.P.-Warehousing)*
Raymond Scroggins *(V.P.-Sls.)*
Sandra Eaton *(Treas.)*

Outside Service Firm(s):

KPMG Peat Marwick*(Auditors)*
Tower Bldg., 11th Fl.,
Little Rock, AR 72201
Tel.: 501-375-3275

Eichenbaum, Scott, Miller, Crockett & Darr*(Legal Firm)*
Tower Bldg.
Little Rock, AR 72201
Tel.: 501-376-4531

Twin City Bank*(Major Banking Relationship)*
N. Little Rock, AR

RANGAIRE & COMPANY
501 So. Wilhite
Cleburne, TX 76031
Mailing Address:
P.O. Box 177
Cleburne, TX 76033
Tel.: 817-556-6500
Tel.: 800-792-2270
Fax: 817-556-6549
Sales Range: $20-39 Million
Emp.: 300
Import Export
Mfr. of Fluorescent Lighting Fixtures, Range Hoods, Compact Freezers
S.I.C.: 3632; 3645; 3646
Joe McKenzie *(Chm. Bd. & Chief Exec. Officer)*
Leon O. Bowen, Jr. *(V.P.-Engrng.)*
J.W. Browder *(V.P.-Natl. Accts.)*
Mike Morris *(V.P.-Mfg.)*
Dan Waldron *(v.P.-Sls. & Mktg.)*
Billie Henderson *(Controller)*
Fred Rogers *(Natl. Sls. Mgr.)*

Outside Service Firm(s):

Jaynes, Reitmeier, Boyd & Therrell, P.C.*(Auditors)*
Waco, TX
Tel.: 817-776-4190

RANGEN, INC.
115 13th Ave., S.
Buhl, ID 83316
Tel.: 208-543-6421 **ID**
Year Founded: 1935
Approx.Sls.: $28,000,000
Emp.: 160
Prepared Foods; Nitrogenous Fertilizers; Bulk Dry Beans
S.I.C.: 2048; 5153
Christopher Rangen *(Chief Exec. Officer)*
Phil Jones *(Pres.)*
Wayne Courtney *(Controller)*

Outside Service Firm(s):

West One Bank*(Major Banking Relationship)*
Buhl, ID

Division:

Rangen Aquaculture Research **(1)**
115 13th Ave., S.
Buhl, ID 83316
Tel.: 208-543-6421
Commercial Physical Research
S.I.C.: 8731
Tim O'Keefe *(Chief Oper. Officer)*

RANIR CORPORATION
4617 E. Paris
Grand Rapids, MI 49508
Mailing Address:
P.O. Box 8547
Grand Rapids, MI 49518
Tel.: 616-698-8880
Fax: 616-698-0820
Year Founded: 1972
Approx.Sls.: $20,000,000
Emp.: 300
Fiscal Year-end: 12/31/91
Import Export
Manufacture Dental Floss, Injection Molding, Travel Toothbrushes, Breath Spray, Travelpacks, etc.
S.I.C.: 2844; 3089; 3843; 5122; 3991
William K. Najjar *(Chm. Bd.)*
Martin Lewkowitz *(Vice Chm.)*
Barry Silverman *(Pres.)*
Marvin Coopersmith *(Exec. V.P.-Opers.)*
Richard Peck *(Exec. V.P.)*
John Carroll *(V.P.-Sls.)*
Gary Hammerlund *(V.P. & Gen. Mgr.)*
Beth Sobel *(V.P.-Sls.)*
Tom Hogan *(Gen. Counsel)*
Joseph Townsend *(Controller)*
Ann Armstrong *(Dir.-Quality Control)*
Linda Hastidt *(Dir.-Pur.)*
Patricia Hazekemp *(Dir.-Human Resources)*

Principal(s):
William K. Najjar
Martin Lewkowitz
Barry Silverman
Marvin Coopersmith
Richard Peck

No. of Mfg. Plants/Facilities: 2

Computer Systems/Hardware:
IBM PC-486

Outside Service Firm(s):

Plante & Moran*(Auditors)*
Grand Rapids, MI

NBD Bank, N.A.*(Major Banking Relationship)*
Grand Rapids, MI

RAO WHOLESALE TIRE CENTERS, INC.
6031 Joy Rd.
Detroit, MI 48204
Tel.: 313-895-1200 **MI**
Fax: 313-834-6330
Year Founded: 1972
Assets: $14,500,000
Liabilities: $13,000,000
Net Worth: $1,500,000
Approx.Sls.: $57,000,000
Emp.: 250
Fiscal Year-end: 6/30/90
Wholesale Tires, Automotive Accessories, Cellular Telephone Systems
S.I.C.: 5014; 5013; 5065
Duane Rao *(Chm. Bd. & Chief Exec. Officer)*
Marc Kahn *(Pres.-RAO-Wholesale Div.)*
Kenneth Rao *(Treas.)*
Elizabeth Rao *(Sec.)*

No. of U.S. Offices: 18

Computer Systems/Hardware:
Data General

Outside Service Firm(s):

Coopers & Lybrand*(Auditors)*
400 Renaissance Center
Detroit, MI 48243
Tel.: 313-446-7100
Fax: 313-446-7117

Carlton Insurance*(Commercial Insurance Carrier)*
Indianapolis, IN

Keller, Thoma, Schwarze, Schwarze, Dubay & Katz*(Legal Firm)*
Detroit, MI

Subsidiaries:

American Tire Reclamation **(1)**
6031 Joy Rd.
Detroit, MI 48204
Tel.: 313-895-1200

Metro Cell, Inc. **(1)**
6031 Joy Rd.
Detroit, MI 48204
Tel.: 313-895-1200

Metro 25 Tire Centers, Inc. **(1)**
6031 Joy Rd.
Detroit, MI 48204
Tel.: 313-895-1200

RAPID ENGINEERING INC.
1100 Seven Mile Rd.
Comstock Park, MI 49321
Mailing Address:
P.O. Box 700,
Comstock, MI 49321
Tel.: 616-784-0500 **MI**
Fax: 616-784-0435
Year Founded: 1962
Approx.Sls.: $16,000,000
Emp.: 150
Fiscal Year-end: 8/31/90
Export
Manufacture Industrial Heating Equipment & Painting Systems
S.I.C.: 3567; 3559
James V. Dirkes *(Pres., Chief Exec. Officer & Treas.)*
Alfred S. Terry *(Sr. V.P.-Mktg.)*
Martin Kuks *(V.P.-Opers.)*
L. Wesorick *(Controller)*
Joanne E. Dirkes *(Sec.)*
Gordon K. Ignasiak *(Mgr.-Pur.)*

No. of Mfg. Plants/Facilities: 2
No. of U.S. Offices: 2

Computer Systems/Hardware:
Prime

Outside Service Firm(s):

Hungerford, Aldrin, Nichols & Carter*(Auditors)*
Grand Rapids, MI

Hartford Life Insurance Co.*(Commercial Insurance Carrier)*
Grand Rapids, MI

Warner, Norcross and Judd*(Legal Firm)*
900 Old Kent Bldg.
Grand Rapids, MI 49503
Tel.: 616-459-6121

Old Kent Bank*(Major Banking Relationship)*
Grand Rapids, MI

Old Kent Bank*(Pension Manager)*
Grand Rapids, MI

Subsidiary:

Bananza Air Management Systems, Inc. **(1)**
5353 52nd St., S.E.
Kentwood, MI 49508
Tel.: 616-698-0500
Fax: 616-784-0435
Emp.: 12
Manufacture Commercial Space Heating Equipment
S.I.C.: 3559
Larry Kensington *(Plant Mgr.)*

RAPID INDUSTRIAL PLASTICS COMPANY
13 Linden Ave., E.
Jersey City, NJ 07305
Tel.: 201-433-5500
Fax: 201-433-4941
Approx.Sls.: $150,000,000
Emp.: 180
Plastic Materials, Injection Molding Of Plastics
S.I.C.: 5162; 3089
Paul Sirotkin *(Pres.)*
Mark Sirotkin *(Treas.)*
Martin Sirotkin *(Sec.)*

Outside Service Firm(s):

Kaback, Ross, Gilman & Company*(Auditors)*
Jersey City, NJ

Chemical Bank*(Major Banking Relationship)*
Brooklyn, NY

RAPID INDUSTRIES, INC.
4003 Oaklawn Dr.
Louisville, KY 40259-0259
Mailing Address:
P.O. Box 19259,
Louisville, KY 40219
Tel.: 502-968-3645 **KY**
Fax: 502-968-6331
Year Founded: 1967
Assets: $6,300,000
Liabilities: $1,300,000
Net Worth: $5,000,000
Approx.Sls.: $20,000,000
Emp.: 148
Fiscal Year-end: 9/30/90
Import
Manufacturer of Industrial Conveyors, Lifts; Structural Steel Erection, Machine & Equipment Demolition, Machine Moving
S.I.C.: 3535; 1791; 3531; 3536; 3537
Walter G. Sheets *(Pres. & Chief Exec. Officer)*
James Burke *(V.P.-Opers.)*
Ken Sheets *(V.P.-Sls. & Mktg.)*
Mary J. Sheets *(Sec. & Treas.)*
F. Donald Carrico *(Controller)*
Tevis Bennett *(Dir.-Pub. Rels.)*
John Palko *(Pur. Agent)*
Principal(s):
Walter G. Sheets
Mary J. Sheets

No. of Mfg. Plants/Facilities: 1
No. of U.S. Offices: 1

Computer Systems/Hardware:
Compaq

Outside Service Firm(s):

Cloyd, Marr, Miller, & Myer*(Auditors)*
Corbin, KY

Continental Insurance*(Commercial Insurance Carrier)*
Louisville, KY

Humana Health Care Plan*(Group Insurance Broker/Consult)*
9300 Shelbyville Rd., Ste. 700
Louisville, KY 40222
Tel.: 502-423-1355

First National Bank of Louisville*(International Bank Affiliate)*
P.O. Box 36000,
Louisville, KY 40233

Merrill Lynch*(Investment Banker)*
Louisville, KY

MacKenzie & Peden*(Legal Firm)*
Louisville, KY

First National Bank of Louisville*(Major Banking Relationship)*
P.O. Box 36000,
Louisville, KY 40233

RAPID MOUNTING & FINISHING CO.
4300 W. 47th St.
Chicago, IL 60632-4476
Tel.: 312-927-5000 **DE**
Fax: 312-927-6446
Year Founded: 1938
Approx.Sls.: $35,000,000
Emp.: 300
Fiscal Year-end: 5/31/92
Import
Mounting & Die Cutting, Cardboard Advertising Displays, Toys & Games, Point of Purchase Advertising
S.I.C.: 3944; 3993; 2675
Earl Abramson *(Chm. Bd. & Pres.)*
David Abramson *(V.P. & Gen. Mgr.)*
Pierre Pype *(V.P.-Sls.)*
George Corich *(V.P.-Mfg.)*
James Poxorn *(V.P.-Pur.)*
James E. Keller *(Treas. & Controller)*
Robert Cooper *(Mgr.-Data Processing)*
Janet Lalas *(Personnel Admin.)*

No. of Mfg. Plants/Facilities: 2
No. of U.S. Offices: 2

Computer Systems/Hardware:
IBM AS/400

Outside Service Firm(s):

Altschuler, Melvoin & Glasser*(Auditors)*
30 S. Wecker Dr.
Chicago, IL 60606
Tel.: 312-207-2800

Travelers Insurance Co.*(Commercial Insurance Carrier)*
1 Tower Square
Hartford, CT 06183
Tel.: 203-222-7821
Fax: 203-222-7813

Blue Cross & Blue Shield Association*(Group Insurer)*
676 N. St. Claire
Chicago, IL 60611

LaSalle National Bank*(Investment Banker)*
120 S. LaSalle St.
Chicago, IL 60603
Tel.: 312-781-8000

Pitler & Mandell*(Legal Firm)*
Chicago, IL

LaSalle National Bank*(Major Banking Relationship)*
120 S. LaSalle St.
Chicago, IL 60603
Tel.: 312-781-8000

Chicago Title & Trust Co.*(Pension Manager)*
111 W. Washington St.
Chicago, IL 60602
Tel.: 312-630-2000
Fax: 312-368-4736

Divisions:

Cadaco **(1)**
4300 W. 47th St.
Chicago, IL 60632-4476
Tel.: 312-927-5000
Mfg. Games
S.I.C.: 3949

Rapid Mounting & Finishing **(1)**
33195 Lewis Ave.
Union City, CA 94587-2201
Tel.: 510-487-0700
Mfg. Cardboard Advertising Displays

RAPID POWER TECHNOLOGIES, INC.
18 Graysbridge Rd.
Brookfield, CT 06804
Tel.: 203-775-0411 **NY**
Fax: 203-775-0666
Year Founded: 1944
Approx.Sls.: $27,000,000
Emp.: 230
Export
Mfr. of Transformers; DC & AC Power Supplies
S.I.C.: 3643; 3612
Ronald J. Viola *(Chm. Bd. & Chief Exec. Officer)*
Riley Wilson *(Pres., Treas., Sec. & Controller)*
Michael Dube *(V.P.-Sls.)*
Nicholas Ciaccia *(Dir.-Mfg.)*
Joseph Kanyik *(Dir.-Engrng.)*
Neil Kurkjy *(Dir.-Sls. & Mktg.)*

Outside Service Firm(s):

Chase Manhattan Bank, N.A.*(Major Banking Relationship)*
Brookfield, CT

RAPTON HONDA-GMC
2820 Fulton Ave.
Sacramento, CA 95821
Tel.: 916-482-5400
Fax: 916-488-8739
Year Founded: 1961
Retail New & Used Automobiles; Service Leasing
S.I.C.: 5511
Mallon Rapton *(Pres.)*
Lois Ann Rapton *(V.P.)*
David S. Segale *(Sec. & Treas.)*

Outside Service Firm(s):

W. J. Pomares & Company*(Auditors)*
Sacramento, CA

Don McMurchie Legal Counsel*(Legal Firm)*
Sacramento, CA

Bank of America NT&SA*(Major Banking Relationship)*
Stockton, CA

ANN RASKAS GOURMET CONFECTIONERS
207 S. 9th St.
Edwardsville, KS 66113
Mailing Address:
P. O. Box 13367,
Edwardsville, KS 66113
Tel.: 913-422-7230
Fax: 913-441-4625
Year Founded: 1978
Approx.Sls.: $15,000,000
Emp.: 50
Fiscal Year-end: 12/31/90
Mfr. & Wholesale Gourmet Hard Candy
S.I.C.: 2064
Joe Jack Merriman *(Chm. Bd.)*
Ernie Simon *(Pres.)*
Robert Simon *(V.P.-Sls.)*
Michael Merriman *(Chief Fin. Officer)*

RAU FASTENERS, INC.
102 Westfield St.
Providence, RI 02907
Tel.: 401-861-7100
Fax: 401-861-1784
Year Founded: 1912
Approx.Sls.: $25,000,000
Emp.: 500
Fiscal Year-end: 9/30/90
Manufacturer of Fasteners, Grommets & Small Metal Stampings
S.I.C.: 3965; 3469
Jack Champagne *(Pres.)*
Frank Basile *(V.P.-Fin.)*
John Conner *(V.P.-Sls.)*
Walter Pierce *(V.P.-Mktg.)*
Joseph Lentin, Jr. *(Chief Fin. Officer)*

RAUB SUPPLY COMPANY
James & Mulberry Streets
Lancaster, PA 17601
Mailing Address:
P.O. Box 3020,
Lancaster, PA 17604-3020
Tel.: 717-397-6221
Fax: 717-397-9669
Year Founded: 1898
Approx.Sls.: $78,000,000
Emp.: 265
Fiscal Year-end: 12/31/91
Wholesale Distribution of Plumbing, Heating, Electrical Industrial Equipment, Appliances & Floor Coverings
S.I.C.: 5074; 5063; 5064; 5023
Joseph C. Schick *(Chm. Bd., Pres., Chief Exec. Officer & Chief Oper. Officer)*
Sam Botte *(Chief Fin. Officer, V.P.-Fin., Treas. & Controller)*
Dennis Schleicher *(V.P.-Mngmt. Information Systems)*
Ralph H. Kline *(Corp. Sec.)*
Robert Halbleib *(Dir.-Leasing)*

Computer Systems/Hardware:
IBM

RAUH, GOOD, DARLO & BARNES ADVERTISING ASSOCIATES, INC.
15425 Los Gatos Blvd.
Los Gatos, CA 95032
Tel.: 408-356-5555
Fax: 408-356-5505
Year Founded: 1969
Approx.Billings: $11,000,000
Emp.: 16
Tourism, Conventions, Hospitality, Business-to-Business, Automotive, Retail
Robert B. Rauh *(Chm. Bd., Pres., Chief Fin. Officer & New Bus. Contact)*
James Barnes *(Exec. V.P., Creative Dir.)*
Darlene A. Rauh *(Sec.)*
Jill Haibeck *(Acctg. Mgr.)*

Computer Systems/Hardware:
Apple, Macintosh

RAULAND-BORG CORPORATION
3450 W. Oakton St.
Skokie, IL 60076-2951
Tel.: 708-679-0900
Tel.: 800-752-7725 **IL**
Fax: 708-679-0625
Year Founded: 1948
Approx.Sls.: $35,000,000
Emp.: 250
Fiscal Year-end: 9/30/91
Import Export
Communication Systems for Health Care, Education & Corrections Fields; Professional Sound Reinforcement Systems
S.I.C.: 3663
William Krucks *(Chm. Bd. & Pres.)*
Kenneth T. James *(Exec. V.P.)*
Norman Kidder *(Sr. V.P.)*
John Gutkneckt *(V.P.-Mfg.)*
Hank Plaisier *(V.P.-Sls. & Mktg.)*
Rich Stalkfleet *(V.P., Controller & Dir.-Engrg.)*
Kenneth R. Krucks *(Asst. Treas.)*
T. Ozanic *(Dir.-Pur.)*
Karen Hyba *(Mgr.-Adv.)*
Carl Bank *(Mgr.-Personnel)*
Principal(s):
William Krucks
Rauland Family

Outside Service Firm(s):

KPMG Peat Marwick*(Auditors)*
Peat Marwick Plaza, 303 E. Wacker Dr.
Chicago, IL 60601
Tel.: 312-938-1000

Alexander & Alexander*(Commercial Insurance Carrier)*
225 N. Michigan Av.
Chicago, IL 60611
Tel.: 312-565-6221

PruCare*(Group Insurer)*
Chicago, IL

Freeborn & Peters*(Legal Firm)*
11 S. LaSalle St.
Chicago, IL 60603
Tel.: 312-750-9500

First National Bank of Chicago*(Major Banking Relationship)*
One First National Plaza
Chicago, IL 60670
Tel.: 312-732-9781
Tel.: 312-732-4050
Fax: 312-732-4840
Fax: 312-732-3055

First National Bank of Chicago*(Pension Manager)*
One First National Plaza
Chicago, IL 60670
Tel.: 312-732-9781
Tel.: 312-732-4050
Fax: 312-732-4840
Fax: 312-732-3055

Subsidiary:

Rauland-Borg (Canada) Inc. **(1)**
6535 Millcreek Dr., Unit 5
Mississauga, ON L5N 2M2, Canada
Tel.: 416-821-2225
Emp.: 6
Sales & Service
S.I.C.: 5065; 7622
William Krucks *(Pres.)*
Kenneth T. James *(Exec. V.P.)*
Rick L. Stalkfleet *(V.P.)*

RAVENSWOOD ALUMINUM CORP.
Rt. 2 South
Ravenswood, WV 26164
Tel.: 304-273-6000
Mfr. Aluminum
S.I.C.: 3334
Greg Davis *(Chm.)*
Bill Hampshire *(Pres.)*
Bob Holiday *(Treas.)*

No. of U.S. Offices: 1

THE RAWLPLUG COMPANY, INC.
Two F.B. Powers Square
New Rochelle, NY 10802
Mailing Address:
P.O. Box 641
New Rochelle, NY 10802
Tel.: 914-235-6300
Fax: 914-633-1981
Year Founded: 1921
Approx.Sls.: $35,000,000
Emp.: 240
Export
Manufacture Plugs, Drills, Drives, Hammer Sets, Toggles, Machine Screw Anchors, Studs, Bolts & Roofing Fasteners
S.I.C.: 3499; 3423; 3451; 3452; 3545
Frederic B. Powers, Jr. *(Chm. Bd. & Pres.)*
George Christensen *(V.P. & Asst. to Pres.)*
Louis Giannuzzi *(V.P.-Engrng.)*
Joseph V. Miressi *(V.P. & Controller)*
Christopher W. Powers *(V.P.-Subsidiary Opers.)*
Jeffrey R. Powers *(V.P.-Mktg.)*
I.W. Powers *(Sec.)*
Wendy A. Hopkins *(Mgr.-Communications)*
Principal(s):
Christopher W. Powers
Frederic B. Powers, Jr.
Jeffrey R. Powers

Subsidiary:

Day Industries **(1)**
3991 Munson Hwy.
Hudson, MI 49247
Tel.: 517-448-8904
Export
S.I.C.: 3499
Jeff Spahr *(Gen. Mgr.)*

RAY-CARROLL COUNTY GRAIN CO-OP
Hwy. 10 West
Richmond, MO 64085
Mailing Address:
P.O. Box 158,
Richmond, MO 64085
Tel.: 816-776-2291 **MO**
Fax: 816-776-3213
Year Founded: 1931
Assets: $18,528,122
Earnings: $1,058,000
Liabilities: $3,545,473
Net Worth: $14,982,649
Approx.Sls.: $57,275,000
Emp.: 120
Fiscal Year-end: 8/31/91
Retail Agricultural Products & Services
S.I.C.: 4221; 5191; 5261; 5541
Arthur Kipping *(Pres. & Chief Exec. Officer)*
Marvin Ritchason *(Chief Oper. Officer & Gen. Mgr.)*
Nelson Heil *(Treas. & Sec.)*
Doug Courtney *(Controller)*
Donald D. Harr *(Office Mgr.)*

Computer Systems/Hardware:
IBM System AS/400

Outside Service Firm(s):

Laird & Kooistra*(Auditors)*
Cedar Rapids, IA

American Bank*(Major Banking Relationship)*
Richmond, MO

RAY COMMUNICATIONS, INC.
179 Lovers Ln.
Elizabeth City, NC 27909
Mailing Address:
P.O. Box 1408,
Elizabeth City, NC 27909
Tel.: 919-335-7294 **VA**
Year Founded: 1965
Emp.: 12
National Satellite Radio Network
S.I.C.: 4832
William S. Ray *(Pres. & Chief Exec. Officer)*
Gregory W. Gingery *(V.P.)*
Scott Fortenberry *(Chief Engineer)*
Lisa D. Ray *(Sls. Coord., Public Rels. & Mktg.)*

Divisions:

Agrinet Farm Radio Network **(1)**
179 Lovers Ln.
Elizabeth City, NC 27909
Tel.: 919-335-7294
Natl., Intl., Reg. & State Agricultural News
S.I.C.: 4832

Ray Satellite Network **(1)**
179 Lovers Ln.
Elizabeth City, NC 27909
Tel.: 919-335-7294
Pro & Collegiate Sports Satellite Distr.; Mobile Satellite Uplink; Broadcast Studio Leasing
S.I.C.: 4899; 7359

Ray Sports Network **(1)**
179 Lovers Ln.
Elizabeth City, NC 27909
Tel.: 919-335-7294
The Atlantic Sports Report, Washington Redskins Football Network, Baltimore Orioles Baseball Network, Philadelphia 76ers
S.I.C.: 4832

RAYCO
(Formerly Ray Co., Inc.)
4800 Fredericksburg Rd.
San Antonio, TX 78229
Tel.: 210-349-1111
Fax: 210-308-1306
Assets: $200,000,000
Net Worth: $200,000,000
Approx.Sls.: $225,000,000
Emp.: 865
Fiscal Year-end: 12/31/90
Single Family Residental Construction, Commercial Property & Land Management & Water Utilities Services
S.I.C.: 1531; 4941; 4952; 6552; 6513; 5031
Ray Ellison *(Chm. Bd. & Pres.)*
Jack H. Williome *(Chief Exec. Officer & V.P.)*
Jack Biegler *(Chief Fin. Officer & V.P.)*
Amy O'Niel *(Controller)*
Jesse Murphy *(Gen. Counsel)*
Martin Polka *(Mgr.-Cash)*

Computer Systems/Hardware:
Nixdorf; IBM

Outside Service Firm(s):

Ernst & Young*(Auditors)*
1900 Frost Bank Tower, 100 W. Houston St.
San Antonio, TX 78205
Tel.: 210-228-9696
Fax: 210-554-0253

Holland-America Insurance Co.*(Group Insurer)*
Los Angeles, CA

Frost National Bank*(Major Banking Relationship)*
P.O. Box 1600
San Antonio, TX 78296

NationsBank Texas*(Pension Manager)*
Austin, TX

Subsidiaries:

Lackland City Water Co. **(1)**
4800 Fredericksburg Rd.
San Antonio, TX 78229
Tel.: 210-349-1111 (100%)

Ray Ellison Homes **(1)**
4800 Fredericksburg Rd.
San Antonio, TX 78229
Tel.: 210-349-1111

Texas Homestead Mortgage Co. **(1)**
4800 Fredericksburg Rd.
San Antonio, TX 78229
Tel.: 210-349-1111 (100%)

RAYMARK FRICTION COMPANY
123 E. Stiegel St.
Manheim, PA 17545
Tel.: 717-665-2211 **CT**
Fax: 717-665-2794
Year Founded: 1929
Sales Range: $20-39 Million
Emp.: 300
Export
Management Services; Friction Automotive Materials-Non-Asbestos
S.I.C.: 3499
Bradley C. Smith *(Pres. & Gen. Mgr.)*
L.D. Serman *(Controller)*
B.E. Lowry *(Dir.-Prod. Development)*
D.F. Tomao *(Dir.-Sls.-Aftermarket & Original Equipment)*
M.A. Geib *(Mgr.-Matls.)*
R.E. Laukhuff *(Mgr.-Human Resources & Sec.)*
C.E. Shank *(Mgr.-Mngmt. Information Services)*
W.F. Stogner *(Mgr.-Opers.)*
J. Walbrecht *(Mgr.-Quality Assurance)*
Principal(s):
Bradley C. Smith

No. of Mfg. Plants/Facilities: 2
No. of U.S. Offices: 2

Outside Service Firm(s):

Grant Thornton*(Auditors)*
605 Third Ave.
New York, NY 10158
Tel.: 212-599-0100
Fax: 212-370-4520

Morgan, Lewis & Bockius*(Legal Firm)*
2000 One Logan Square
Philadelphia, PA 19103
Tel.: 215-963-5000

Fulton County National Bank*(Major Banking Relationship)*
Manheim, PA

RAYMOND AUTOMATION CO., INC.
P.O. Box 5838
Norwalk, CT 06856
Tel.: 203-847-6668
Approx.Sls.: $50,000,000
Emp.: 40
Mfr. Packaging Machinery
S.I.C.: 3565
Paul Dujardin *(Pres.)*

RAYNOR GARAGE DOOR COMPANY
E. River Rd.
Dixon, IL 61021
Mailing Address:
P.O. Box 448
Dixon, IL 61021
Tel.: 815-288-1431
Telex: 27101 RAYUR
Fax: 815-288-7142
Year Founded: 1945
Sales Range: $80-99 Million
Emp.: 650
Fiscal Year-end: 2/28/92
Export
Manufacture Overhead Doors & Door Operators
S.I.C.: 3442; 3699
Ray H. Neisewander, Jr. *(Pres.)*
Tom Kish *(V.P. & Comptroller)*
Jerry O'Brien *(V.P.-Pur.)*
R.A. Smith *(V.P.-Mfg.)*
Frank Hall *(Dir.-Personnel)*
Randall Renne *(Dir.-Sls. & Mktg.)*
Guy Bagger *(Mgr.-Mktg.)*
Terry Lich *(Mgr.-Sls.)*
Terry Martin *(Mgr.-Export)*
Don Silk *(Mgr.-Adv.)*
Thomas Wadsworth *(Mgr.-Communications)*

Computer Systems/Hardware:
IBM AS 400

Outside Service Firm(s):

Arthur Andersen & Co.*(Auditors)*
33 W. Monroe St.
Chicago, IL 60603-4067
Tel.: 312-580-0033
Fax: 312-507-6748

Ward, Murray, Pace & Johnson*(Legal Firm)*
Dixon, IL

Continental Bank N. A.*(Major Banking Relationship)*
231 S. LaSalle St.
Chicago, IL 60697
Tel.: 312-828-2345
Tel.: 800-426-5754
Telex: 312-828-1783

Divisions:

Raynor Distribution Center **(1)**
550 Ryerson Rd.
Lincoln Park, NJ 07035
Tel.: 201-696-7550
Richard Pierro *(Mgr.)*

Raynor Distribution Center **(1)**
3727 Marquis Dr.
Garland, TX 75042
Tel.: 214-276-7300

Raynor Distribution Center **(1)**
10625 E. 51st Ave.
Denver, CO 80239
Tel.: 303-371-1690

RAYOVAC CORPORATION
601 Rayovac Dr.
Madison, WI 53711-2497
Mailing Address:
P.O. Box 44960
Madison, WI 53744-4960
Tel.: 608-275-3340 **WI**
Telex: 190428
Fax: 608-275-4577
Year Founded: 1906
Approx.Sls.: $475,000,000
Emp.: 2,500
Fiscal Year-end: 6/30/92
Import Export
Manufactures Alkaline & Zinc Carbon Round Cell Batteries For Consumer & Industrial Markets; Watch & Hearing Aid Batteries (Button Cells) in Zinc Air, Mercury, Silver Oxide & Lithium Chemical Systems; Magnesium Batteries; Flashlights & Lighting Products for Consumer & Industrial Markets
S.I.C.: 3648; 3692
Thomas F. Pyle *(Chm. Bd., Pres. & Chief Exec. Officer)*
Judith D. Pyle *(Vice Chm. & Sr. V.P.)*
Roger F. Warren *(Exec. V.P. & Gen. Mgr.)*
Gregory A. Brady *(Sr. V.P. & Gen. Mgr.-US Sls.)*
Trygve Lonnebotn *(Sr. V.P.-Opers. & Tech.)*
Marvin G. Siegert *(Sr. V.P. & Chief Fin. Officer)*
Raymond L. Balfour *(V.P.)*
Kenneth V. Biller *(V.P.-Mfg.)*
James Broderick *(V.P. & Gen. Counsel)*
Virgil L. Broering *(V.P.-Distr. & Opers. Support)*
Russ Lefevre *(V.P.-Employee Rels.)*
Glynn M. Rossa *(V.P. & Treas.)*
Dale Tetzlaff *(V.P.-Admin.)*
Gary E. Wilson *(V.P.-Major Acct. Sls.)*
Robert W. Zimmerman *(V.P.-Mktg.)*
Michael G. Thompson *(Corp. Controller)*
John Daggett *(Dir.-Pub. Rels.)*
Darwin Peterson *(Dir.-Matls. Mngmt.)*

No. of Mfg. Plants/Facilities: 6
No. of U.S. Offices: 8
No. of Foreign Offices: 4

Computer Systems/Hardware:
IBM; Compaq

Outside Service Firm(s):

Coopers & Lybrand*(Auditors)*
411 East Wisconsin Bldg.
Milwaukee, WI 53202

Wausau Insurance*(Commercial Insurance Carrier)*
Madison, WI

Foley & Lardner*(Legal Firm)*
777 E. Wisconsin Ave.
Milwaukee, WI 53202
Tel.: 414-271-2400

First National Bank of Chicago*(Major Banking Relationship)*
One First National Plaza
Chicago, IL 60670
Tel.: 312-732-9781
Tel.: 312-732-4050
Fax: 312-732-4840
Fax: 312-732-3055

M & I Marshall & Ilsley Bank*(Pension Manager)*
770 N. Water St.
Milwaukee, WI 53202
Tel.: 414-765-8700

Plants:

RAYOVAC Corporation **(1)**
2600 North Ballard
Appleton, WI 54912
Tel.: 414-731-4151
Fax: 414-731-4151 ext. 53
Mfr. of Dry Cell Batteries & Flashlight Prods.
S.I.C.: 3692; 3648
Richard Cyr *(Plant Mgr.)*

RAYOVAC Corporation **(1)**
P.O. Box 128, 100 Rayovac Court
Fennimore, WI 53809
Tel.: 608-822-3272
Fax: 608-822-3864
Mfr. of Dry Cell Batteries & Flashlight Prods.
S.I.C.: 3692; 3648
Al Roth *(Plant Mgr.)*

RAYOVAC Corporation **(1)**
2851 Portage Rd.
Portage, WI 53901
Tel.: 608-742-5373
Fax: 608-742-6025
Mfr. of Dry Cell Batteries & Flashlight Prods.
S.I.C.: 3692; 3648
Dan Salyard *(Plant Mgr.)*

RAYOVAC Corporation **(1)**
4300 Rouse Rd.
Kinston, NC 28501
Tel.: 919-522-1400
Fax: 919-522-5255
Mfr. of Dry Cell Batteries & Flashlight Prods.
S.I.C.: 3692; 3648
Bill Terry *(Plant Mgr.)*

RAYOVAC Corporation **(1)**
2317 Winnebago St.
Madison, WI 53704
Tel.: 608-246-1000
Fax: 608-246-1025
Mfr. of Dry-Cell Batteries
S.I.C.: 3692
Tom Ward *(Plant Mgr.)*

RAYOVAC Corporation **(1)**
503 Vine St.
Wonewoc, WI 53968
Tel.: 608-464-3121
Fax: 608-464-3121 ext. 145
Mfr. of Dry-Cell Batteries
S.I.C.: 3692
Lee Kucher *(Plant Mgr.)*

RAYOVAC Corporation **(1)**
1100 Dallas St.
Sauk City, WI 53583
Tel.: 608-643-2461
Fax: 608-643-2580
Mfr. of Dry Cell Batteries
S.I.C.: 3692
Don Bye *(Plant Mgr.)*

Non-U.S. Holdings:

RAYOVAC Limited **(1)**
Galleon House, King St.
Maidstone, Kent ME14 1BG, United Kingdom
Tel.: 622-688 331 (100%)
Telex: 622-688331
Fax: 622-685523
Mktg. & Sls. of Batteries & Lighting Prods.
S.I.C.: 5063
Richard Thornley *(European Mgng. Dir.-MP/OEM)*

RAYOVAC UK Limited **(1)**
Stephenson Estate Dist. 12,
Washington, Tyne & Wear NE37 3HW, United Kingdom
Tel.: 91-416-0441
Telex: 53415
Fax: 91-417-8390
Mfr. of Batteries
S.I.C.: 3692
Richard Thornley *(European Mng. Dir.)*

Rayovac/Vidor Limited **(1)**
Galleon House King St.,
Maidstone, Kent ME14 1BG, United Kingdom
Tel.: 622-676699
Fax: 622-676890
Mfr. of Batteries
S.I.C.: 3692
Peter Howard-Jones *(Mng. Dir.)*
Paul Duffy *(Grp. Fin. Dir.)*

RE/MAX INTERNATIONAL, INC.
5445 DTC Pkwy., Ste. 1200
Englewood, CO 80111
Mailing Address:
P.O. Box 3907
Englewood, CO 80155-3907
Tel.: 303-770-5531
Tel.: 800-525-7452 **CO**
Fax: 303-796-3599
Year Founded: 1973
Approx.Sls.: $71,160,000,000
Emp.: 170
Fiscal Year-end: 12/31/91
Master Franchiser of Real Estate & Insurance Brokerages; Relocation & Asset Management Services
S.I.C.: 6531; 6411; 6282; 7389
Dave Liniger *(Chm. Bd.)*
Bob Fisher *(Pres.)*
Mark Roussy *(Pres.-Relocation & Asset Mngmt. Services)*
Gail Liniger *(Chief Exec. Officer)*
John Picon *(Chief Fin. Officer & Treas.)*
Elaine McCain *(Exec. V.P.-Relocation Services)*
Daryl Jesperson *(Sr. V.P.)*
Vinnie Tracey *(Sr. V.P.)*
George Graff *(V.P.-Zone Dir.)*
Joe Reynolds *(V.P.-Fin.)*
Steve Woolley *(V.P.)*
Gary Weil *(Sr. Corp. Counsel)*
John Linton *(Gen. Counsel)*
Bob Brown *(Exec. Dir.-Corp. Image)*
Bob Harple *(Dir.-Mktg.)*
Mike Reagan *(V.P.-Conventions)*
Louise LaMotte *(Mgr.-Human Resources)*
Glynda Tomlinson *(Mgr.-Convention Services)*
Maureen Hardgrove *(Pub. Rels. Coord.)*
Principal(s):
Dave Liniger
Bob Fisher
Gail Liniger
Daryl Jesperson

No. of Foreign Offices: 405

Computer Systems/Hardware:
IBM AS/400

Outside Service Firm(s):

Grant Thornton*(Auditors)*
Englewood, CO

Principal Mutual Life Insurance Co.*(Group Insurer)*
Denver, CO

Division:

RE/MAX Insurance Div. **(1)**
5445 DTC Pkwy., Ste. 1200
Englewood, CO 80111
Tel.: 303-770-5531
Tel.: 800-525-7452
Fax: 303-796-3599
Emp.: 11
Computer Systems/Hardware:
IBM AS400
Franchisor of Insurance Brokerage; Insurance, Brokers & Service
S.I.C.: 6411
Steve Woolley *(Pres.)*

REA MAGNET WIRE COMPANY, INC.
3600 E. Pontiac St.
Fort Wayne, IN 46803
Mailing Address:
P.O. Box 6128,
Fort Wayne, IN 46896-0128
Tel.: 219-424-4252 **DE**
Fax: 219-422-4246
Year Founded: 1933
Approx.Sls.: $140,000,000
Emp.: 650
Manufacture Copper & Aluminum Magnet Wire
S.I.C.: 3357

Rea Magnet Wire Company, Inc.—(Continued)

James M. Vann, Jr. *(Chm. Bd. & Chief Exec. Officer)*
Ronald B. Foster *(Pres.)*
Everett Scherrer *(V.P.-Quality)*
William Schilling *(V.P.-Mfg.)*
William J. Wyatt, Sr. *(V.P.-Fin. & Controller)*
Charles Blake *(Gen. Mgr.-Mktg.)*
Michael Connelly *(Gen. Mgr.-Sls. & Mktg.)*
Kelly Nay *(Gen. Mgr.-Sls.)*

Principal(s):
James M. Vann, Jr.
Ronald B. Foster
William T. Gorman

No. of Mfg. Plants/Facilities: 5

Computer Systems/Hardware:
Hewlett-Packard

Outside Service Firm(s):

Coopers & Lybrand*(Auditors)*
600 Grant St., 35th Fl.
Pittsburgh, PA 15219
Tel.: 412-355-8000
Fax: 412-355-8089

Summit Bank*(Major Banking Relationship)*
P.O. Box 2345,
Fort Wayne, IN 46801-2345
Tel.: 219-427-8333

REACTIVE METALS & ALLOYS CORPORATION (REMACOR)
Rt. 168
West Pittsburg, PA 16160
Mailing Address:
P.O. Box 366
West Pittsburg, PA 16160
Tel.: 412-535-4357 **PA**
Fax: 412-535-7761
Year Founded: 1975
Approx.Sls.: $44,000,000
Emp.: 200
Fiscal Year-end: 6/30/90
Import Export
Manufacture Rare Earth Metals, Alloys & Desulfurization Agents
S.I.C.: 3313; 3339
Joseph R. Jackman *(Chm. Bd., Pres. & Chief Exec. Officer)*
James Young *(Chief Oper. Officer)*
John C. Amer *(V.P.-Fin.)*
Joseph R. Marino *(Gen. Counsel & Sec.)*
Charles Willison *(Treas.)*
Robert Richard *(Dir.-Pur.)*
Joseph Gorski *(Mgr.-Data Processing)*
Eugene Razum *(Mgr.-Human Resources)*

No. of Mfg. Plants/Facilities: 3
No. of U.S. Offices: 3

Computer Systems/Hardware:
MAI Basic Four GPX 440

Outside Service Firm(s):

Arthur Andersen & Co.*(Auditors)*
Five Penn Center, Ste. 2600
Pittsburgh, PA 19103

Pittsburgh National Bank*(Major Banking Relationship)*
Stock Transfer Dept., Fifth & Wood Streets
Pittsburgh, PA 15265

Marsh & McLennan*(Commercial Insurance Carrier)*
Pittsburgh, PA

Prudential Insurance Co. of America*(Group Insurer)*
751 Broad St.
Newark, NJ 07102-3777
Tel.: 201-802-6000

Speith, Bell, McCurdy & Newell*(Legal Firm)*
Cleveland, OH

MMC & P*(Pension Manager)*
Pittsburgh, PA

Subsidiary:

Shaw-Perkins Inc. **(1)**
205 W. Washington St., P.O. Box 1486
New Castle, PA 16103
Tel.: 412-654-1162 (100%)
Approx.Sls.: $3,000,000
Emp.: 40
Steel Fabrication
S.I.C.: 3325

THE READ CORPORATION
25 Wareham St.
Middleboro, MA 02346
Tel.: 508-946-1200
Fax: 508-946-0721
Approx.Sls.: $40,000,000
Emp.: 200
Manufacture Portable Construction Screening Equipment
S.I.C.: 3531
Rod Forter *(Pres.)*
Michael C. Davis *(Chief Fin. Officer)*
Ben Hansbury *(Dir.-Sls. & Mktg.)*

Outside Service Firm(s):

Coopers & Lybrand*(Auditors)*
1 Post Office Square
Boston, MA 02110
Tel.: 617-574-5000
Fax: 617-345-0398

Rivkind & Baker*(Legal Firm)*
Boston, MA

READING ANTHRACITE CO.
200 Mahantongo
Pottsville, PA 17901
Tel.: 717-622-5150
Fax: 717-622-2612
Approx.Sls.: $40,000,000
Emp.: 500
Fiscal Year-end: 12/31/90
Famous Reading Anthracite-The Red Trademarked Coal
S.I.C.: 1231
John W. Rich, Jr. *(Pres.)*
Paul Tornetta *(Sec.)*
James Cantwell *(Pur. Agent)*

Division:

Reading Anthracite Coal Co. **(1)**
200 Mahantongo
Pottsville, PA 17901
Tel.: 717-622-5150
Fax: 717-622-2612
S.I.C.: 1231
R. H. Cairnes *(Pres.)*
Adrian Bethray *(V.P.-Indus. & Export Sls.)*
James J. Muntone *(V.P.-Sls.)*

READING BODY WORKS, INC.
Hancock Blvd. & Gerry St.
Reading, PA 19611
Mailing Address:
P.O. Box 14
Reading, PA 19603
Tel.: 215-775-3301
Tel.: 800-458-2226
Fax: 215-775-3261
Approx.Sls.: $26,000,000
Emp.: 300
Service Line Construction, Stake Bodies, Contractor Bodies Pick-up Caps, Tool Boxes
S.I.C.: 3713; 3714
Irving Suknow *(Pres.)*
Dick Gordon *(Exec. V.P.-Fin.)*
Jack O'Donnell *(V.P.-Sls.)*
Lynn Gordon *(Exec.-Mktg.)*
Bill Rahn *(V.P.-Engrng.)*
Russ Roser *(V.P.-Mfg.)*
Bob Eshleman *(Personnel Dir.)*
Debbie Hartranft *(Mktg. Mgr.)*
Mark Anderson *(Pur. Agent)*

READING EAGLE COMPANY
345 Penn St.
Reading, PA 19603
Tel.: 215-371-5000
Fax: 215-371-5098
Approx.Sls.: $31,000,000
Emp.: 515
Newspaper Publishing; Commercial & Lithographic Book Printing; Radio Broadcasting
S.I.C.: 2711; 2752; 2731; 4832
Myrtle B. Quier *(Chm. Bd., Pres. & Chief Exec. Officer)*
Edith A. Flippin *(Vice Chm.)*
James C. Flippin *(V.P. & Sec.)*
William S. Flippin *(V.P. & Publr.)*
Thomas A. Gannon *(Treas. & Controller)*

Outside Service Firm(s):

Stevens & Lee*(Legal Firm)*
607 Washington St.
Reading, PA 19603
Tel.: 215-376-9781

Hamilton Bank*(Major Banking Relationship)*
515 Penn St.
Reading, PA 19601
Tel.: 215-374-2121

READING TUBE CORP.
Rte. 61
Reading, PA 19605
Mailing Address:
P.O. Box 14026,
Reading, PA 19612-4026
Tel.: 215-926-4141
Fax: 215-926-7317
Year Founded: 1982
Assets: $36,000,000
Net Worth: $36,000,000
Approx.Sls.: $100,000,000
Emp.: 400
Fiscal Year-end: 9/30/90
Manufacture Copper Tubing
S.I.C.: 3351
James A. Lash *(Chm. Bd.)*
James Burton *(Pres. & Chief Oper. Officer)*
Robert R. Erol *(V.P.-Sls. & Mktg.)*
Karen J. Larson *(V.P.-Admin.)*
Patricia Callahan *(Mgr.-Cash)*
Jane Kern *(Mgr.-Personnel)*
Dale Magnuson *(Mgr.-Pur.)*

No. of Mfg. Plants/Facilities: 3

Computer Systems/Hardware:
Wang 85

Outside Service Firm(s):

Price Waterhouse*(Auditors)*
30 S. 17th St.
Philadelphia, PA 19103
Tel.: 215-665-9500

Capital Blue Cross*(Group Insurer)*
Harrisburg, PA

Stevens & Lee*(Legal Firm)*
607 Washington St.
Reading, PA 19603
Tel.: 215-376-9781

Hamilton Bank*(Major Banking Relationship)*
515 Penn St.
Reading, PA 19601
Tel.: 215-374-2121

READY METAL MANUFACTURING COMPANY
4500 W. 47th St.
Chicago, IL 60632
Tel.: 312-376-9700 **IL**
Fax: 312-376-7507
Year Founded: 1947
Approx.Sls.: $35,000,000
Emp.: 350
Mfr. of Office & Store Fixtures, Except Wood; Display or Office Cabinets, Except Wood
S.I.C.: 2542
Edward Radek, Sr. *(Co-Chm. Bd. & Pres.)*
John R. Radek, Sr. *(Co-Chm. Bd.)*
Dennis Radek *(V.P.)*
Robert McKeever *(Dir.-Bus. Admin.)*

Outside Service Firm(s):

LaSalle National Bank*(Major Banking Relationship)*
135 S. LaSalle St.
Chicago, IL 60603
Tel.: 312-443-2440
Fax: 312-443-2819

READY SYSTEMS
470 Potrero Ave.
Sunnyvale, CA 94086
Tel.: 408-736-2600
Tel.: 800-321-2636 **CA**
Fax: 800-228-6023
Year Founded: 1981
Approx.Sls.: $20,000,000
Emp.: 120
Fiscal Year-end: 12/31/91
Export
Mfr. of Real Time Software Engineering Tools
S.I.C.: 7372
Bruce Gregory *(Pres. & Chief Exec. Officer)*
Dan Gaudreau *(Chief Fin. Officer, V.P.-Fin. & Dir.-Opers.)*
James Ready *(Exec. V.P.)*
Jean-Claude Sarnei *(V.P.-Mktg.)*
Dado Vrsalovic *(V.P.-Research & Devel.)*
Ron Workman *(Mgr.-Mktg. Communications)*
Steve Bonelli *(Controller)*
Joyce Moyer *(Dir.-Pur.)*
Deborah Chalmers *(Mgr.-Mktg. Communications)*
Bruce Walton *(Mgr.-Mfg.)*

Principal(s):
James Ready

No. of U.S. Offices: 6
No. of Foreign Offices: 4

Computer Systems/Hardware:
Intel 8086, 80286, 80386, 80960 Family Motorola 68000, 68010, 68020, 68030, 68332; National 32032, 32532; Zilog 280, 28000; AMD 29000, 68040

Outside Service Firm(s):

Ernst & Young*(Auditors)*
55 Almaden Blvd.
San Jose, CA 95115
Tel.: 408-947-5476
Fax: 408-294-2744

Wells Fargo Bank*(Major Banking Relationship)*
420 Montgomery St.
San Francisco, CA 94104

Subsidiary:

Nihon Ready Systems **(1)**
No. 2 Shuukaen Bldg., 2-11-2 Komazawa
Setagayaku
Tokyo, 154, Japan
Sales & Marketing Office
S.I.C.: 5045
Andrei Kobel *(Dir.-Mktg.)*

Non-U.S. Holdings:

Ready Systems, France **(1)**
32 Aveune L'Europe B.T. 87 78143,
Velizy-Villacoublay, Cedex France
Tel.: 1-3946-89-86
Emp.: 105
Mfr. of Real-Time Embedded Microprocessor Software Tools
S.I.C.: 7372

Ready Systems, Germany **(1)**
Arabellastrasse 21-B 8000
Munich, 81, Germany
Tel.: 89-910-10-69
Software Service
S.I.C.: 7372

Ready Systems, U.K. (1)
3rd floor, 33 Queens St.
Maidenhead, Berks SL61 NB, United Kingdom
Tel.: 628-773-100
Software Service
S.I.C.: 7372

REAGAN EQUIPMENT COMPANY, INC.
2550 Belle Chase Hwy.
Gretna, LA 70053
Tel.: 504-368-9760
Fax: 504-368-9768
Approx.Sls.: $42,000,000
Emp.: 195
Wholesale Transportation Equipment & Supplies; Manufacture Pumps, Pumping Equipment Motors & Generator Equipment
S.I.C.: 3561; 3621; 5088
Jeanne L. Reagan *(Chm. Bd.)*
Thomas N. Reagan *(Pres.)*
Harry B. Kelleher *(Sec.)*

Outside Service Firm(s):

A.A. Harmon & Co.*(Auditors)*
Gretna, LA

REAL ESTATE CORP. OF FLORIDA
(d/b/a Landstar Homes)
2533 Boggy Creek Rd.
Kissimmee, FL 34744
Tel.: 407-348-2390
Fax: 407-348-2616
Year Founded: 1978
Approx.Sls.: $46,000,000
Emp.: 140
Residential Developer of Single-Family Homes
S.I.C.: 1531
Rodolfo Stern *(Pres.)*
David Serviansky *(V.P.)*
Edwardo Stern *(Treas.)*
Roberto Horowitz *(Sec.)*
Carl Palmisciano *(Gen. Mgr.)*

Outside Service Firm(s):

Rachlin & Cohen*(Auditors)*
1320 S. Dixie Hwy
Coral Gables, FL 33146

NationsBank Florida*(Major Banking Relationship)*
Orlando, FL

REAL HOLDING MANAGEMENT CORP.
9688 S.W. 24th St.
Miami, FL 33165
Tel.: 305-221-8351
Fax: 305-226-4247
Approx.Sls.: $30,000,000
Emp.: 225
Retail Groceries & Drug Stores
S.I.C.: 5411; 5912
Manuel Herran *(Pres.)*
Armando Guerra *(V.P.)*
Jose Herran *(Treas.)*
Jorge Guerra *(Sec.)*

Outside Service Firm(s):

Ready State Bank*(Major Banking Relationship)*
Miami, FL

REALTY ONE
6000 Rockside Woods Blvd.
Cleveland, OH 44131-2350
Tel.: 216-328-2500
Fax: 216-328-5030
Approx.Sls.: $2,039,811,200
Emp.: 377
Real Estate Agency
S.I.C.: 6513; 6531
Vincent T. Aveni *(Chm. Emeritus)*
Joseph T. Aveni *(Chm. Bd. & Chief Exec. Officer)*
James C. Miller *(Pres.)*
John A. Ludwick *(Chief Oper. Officer & Exec. V.P.)*
Charles Boebinger *(Sr. V.P.)*
Barbara Reynolds *(V.P.-Mktg.)*
Barbara Borazanian *(Treas.)*
Cindy Oney *(Controller)*
J. Terence Burke *(Sec. & Gen. Counsel)*

Outside Service Firm(s):

National City Bank*(Major Banking Relationship)*
Akron, OH

Subsidiary:

Century 21 Kriss & Associates (1)
5473 Warrensville Center Rd.
Maple Heights, OH 44137
Al Kriss *(Pres.)*

RECKSON ASSOCIATES
225 Broadhollow Rd.
Melville, NY 11747
Tel.: 516-694-6900
Year Founded: 1968
Approx.Sls.: $50,000,000
Emp.: 80
Nonresidential Buildings Operators
S.I.C.: 6512
Donald Rechler *(Pres.)*
Roger Rechler *(V.P.)*
Kathy Giamo *(Dir.-Sls. & Mktg.)*

Outside Service Firm(s):

Gary Friedman & Associates*(Auditors)*
Syosset, NY

Block, Hamberger & Amelkin*(Legal Firm)*
Syosset, NY

RECON/OPTICAL, INC.
550 W. Northwest Hwy.
Barrington, IL 60010
Tel.: 708-381-2400
Tel.: 800-323-4975 **DE**
Fax: 708-397-2214
Year Founded: 1922
Approx.Sls.: $60,000,000
Emp.: 520
Fiscal Year-end: 12/31/89
Export
Manufacture Aerospace & Defense Products: Aerial Reconnaissance Cameras, Sighting Systems Military & Industrial Electro-Optical Systems & Precision Optical Lenses, Projection Simulators & Coatings
S.I.C.: 3812; 3825; 3827; 3861
Gordon L. Bourns *(Chm. Bd.)*
William Odems *(Pres. & Chief Exec. Officer)*
Stephen Myskowskio *(Sr. V.P.-Fin.)*
Roy Hacker *(V.P. & Gen. Mgr.-POD Div.)*
Michael Johnson *(V.P.-Human Resources)*
Douglas Smith *(V.P.-Sls. & Bus. Devel.)*
J. Steven *(V.P.-Engrng.)*
Kenneth Jackson *(Gen. Counsel)*
Carl Berry *(Dir.-Pur.)*
Theda Bosio *(Dir.-Employee Benefits & Personnel Training & Devel.)*
Robert Clifford *(Dir.-Mfg.)*
Richard Gillespie *(Dir.-Res. & Devel.)*
Martha Hoult *(Dir.-Pub. Rels.)*
E. Kaszubowski *(Dir.-Intl. Mktg.)*
Craig Scott *(Dir.-Quality Control)*
David Beigel *(Mgr.-Pur.)*
R. Hagen *(Mgr.-Intl. mktg.)*
Gary Wandtke *(Mgr.-Data Processing)*
Principal(s):
Bourns, Inc.

No. of Mfg. Plants/Facilities: 2
No. of U.S. Offices: 2
No. of Foreign Offices: 19

Computer Systems/Hardware:
IBM

Outside Service Firm(s):

KPMG Peat Marwick*(Auditors)*
Peat Marwick Plaza, 303 E. Wacker Dr.
Chicago, IL 60601
Tel.: 312-938-1000

Harris Trust & Savings Bank*(Major Banking Relationship)*
111 W. Monroe St.
Chicago, IL 60690
Tel.: 312-461-2265
Tel.: 800-858-0840

Subsidiaries:

CAI (1)
550 W. Northwest Hwy.
Barrington, IL 60010
Tel.: 708-381-2400
Tel.: 800-323-4975
Fax: 708-381-2214
Ronald J. Kay *(Exec. V.P. & Gen. Mgr.)*
Stephen Myskowski *(Sr. V.P.-Fin.)*
Douglas Smith *(V.P.-Sls. & Mktg.)*
David Beigel *(Mgr.-Pur.)*

Pacific Optical Division (1)
2660 Columbia St.
Torrance, CA 90503
Tel.: 310-328-5840
Fax: 310-320-0550
William Owens *(Sr. V.P. & Gen. Mgr.)*
Anthony DosSantos *(V.P.-Sls. & Mktg.)*
Michael Neill *(Controller)*
Lois Nobile *(Supvr.-Pur.)*

The Record Bar, Inc.
(Name Changed to Super Club Music Corp.)

THE RECORD-JOURNAL PUBLISHING COMPANY
11 Crown St.
Meriden, CT 06450
Tel.: 203-235-1661
Fax: 203-639-0210
Sales Range: $10-19 Million
Emp.: 220
Newspaper Publishing
S.I.C.: 2711
Carter H. White *(Chm. Bd.)*
Barbara C. White *(Vice Chm.)*
Eliot C. White *(Pres., Treas. & Publr.)*
John J. Ausanka, III *(V.P. & Comptroller)*
David T. Lucey *(V.P. & Gen. Mgr.)*
James Smith *(Exec. Editor)*
Paul D. MacKnight *(Sec. & Asst. Treas.)*

Outside Service Firm(s):

DiSanto, Bertoline & Co.*(Auditors)*
Glastonbury, CT

RECORDING & STATISTICAL CORPORATION
40 Richards Ave.
Norwalk, CT 06854
Tel.: 203-855-2452 **DE**
Fax: 208-855-2463
Approx.Sls.: $30,000,000
Emp.: 325
Commercial Printing, Lithographic; Typesetting
S.I.C.: 2752; 2791
Charles Wood *(Chm. Bd.)*
Myron E. Stanton *(Pres.)*
Carl E. Nelson *(Exec. V.P.)*

Outside Service Firm(s):

Coopers & Lybrand*(Auditors)*
1301 Avenue of The Americas
New York, NY 10019
Tel.: 212-536-2000

Milgrim Thomajan Jacobs & Lee, P.C.*(Legal Firm)*
53 Wall St.
New York, NY 10005-2815
Tel.: 212-858-5300

Chemical Bank*(Major Banking Relationship)*
P.O. Box 24935, Church St. Station
New York, NY 10249-4935
Tel.: 212-613-7147
Fax: 212-971-3448

RECREATIONAL EQUIPMENT, INC.
6750 S. 228th
Kent, WA 98032
Mailing Address:
P.O. Box 1938,
Sumner, WA 98390-0800
Tel.: 206-395-3780 **WA**
Twx: 329464
Fax: 206-395-4368
Year Founded: 1938
Approx.Sls.: $258,727,000
Emp.: 4,000
Fiscal Year-end: 12/31/91
Import Export
Wholesale & Retail Sporting Goods & Family Clothing
S.I.C.: 5941; 5699; 5137; 5136
Corporate Giving Program:
Contributions to Areas Focusing on Protection of Public Land, Rivers & Trails for Outdoor Recreation and Programs that Enhance Recreation Opportunities
Ann Ormsby *(Chm. Bd.)*
William G. Britt *(Vice Chm. Bd.)*
Wally Smith *(Pres. & Chief Exec. Officer)*
Dennis Madsen *(Exec. V.P. & Chief Oper. Officer)*
Dan Ducich *(V.P. & Chief Fin. Officer)*
Mark Gappa *(V.P.-Human Resources)*
Robert Korbol *(V.P.-Retail)*
Rod McLeod *(V.P.-Mngmt. Information Systems)*
Kathleen Beemer *(Dir.-Pub. Affairs)*
Sue Brockman *(Dir.-Mktg.)*

No. of Mfg. Plants/Facilities: 3
No. of U.S. Offices: 34

Outside Service Firm(s):

Ernst & Young*(Auditors)*
Kent, WA

First Interstate Bank*(Major Banking Relationship)*
Kent, WA

Bogle & Gates*(Legal Firm)*
Kent, WA

Subsidiaries:

MSR (Mountain Safety Research) (1)
4225 2nd Ave. S.
Seattle, WA 98134
Tel.: 206-624-8573
Mfg. of Mountaineering Equipment
S.I.C.: 3949
Dave Bartholomew *(Pres. & Chief Exec. Officer)*

Thaw, Inc. (1)
1212 1st Ave. So.
Seattle, WA 98134
Tel.: 206-624-4277
Mfg. of Sewen Outdoor Gear & Clothing
S.I.C.: 2329
Will Huisingh *(Pres. & Chief Exec. Officer)*

RED APPLE COMPANIES
823 11th Ave.
New York, NY 10019
Tel.: 212-956-5803 **DE**
Fax: 212-262-4979
Assets: $102,000,000
Liabilities: $82,000,000
Net Worth: $20,000,000
Approx.Sls.: $600,000,000
Emp.: 6,000
Fiscal Year-end: 5/31/90
Supermarket Chain
S.I.C.: 5411
John Catsimatidis *(Chm. Bd., Pres. & Chief Exec. Officer)*
Mike Seltzer *(V.P. & Sec.)*
Stuart Spivak *(Chief Fin. Officer)*

Red Apple Companies—(Continued)

Mike O'Neil *(Gen. Counsel)*
Principal(s):
John Catsimatidis

No. of U.S. Offices: 2

Outside Service Firm(s):

KPMG Peat Marwick*(Auditors)*
345 Park Ave.
New York, NY 10154
Tel.: 212-758-9700
Fax: 212-872-3308

Lowenthal, Landau, Fischer, Ziegler & Bring*(Legal Firm)*
250 Park Ave.
New York, NY 10017
Tel.: 212-986-1116

Continental Bank N. A.*(Major Banking Relationship)*
231 S. LaSalle St.
Chicago, IL 60697
Tel.: 312-828-2345
Tel.: 800-426-5754
Telex: 312-828-1783

Divisions:

Florida Supermarket, Inc. **(1)**
605 S.W. 16th Terrace
Pompano Beach, FL 33069
Tel.: 305-786-3900
Bill Woolley *(Pres.)*

Red Apple Companies Food Group **(1)**
823 11th Ave.
New York, NY 10019
Tel.: 212-956-5803
Charles Criscuolo *(Pres.)*

RED APPLE, INC.
(d/b/a Red Apple Store)
555 S.W. 4th Ave.
Ontario, OR 97914
Mailing Address:
P.O. Box 7308
Boise, ID 83707
Tel.: 208-343-0581
Fax: 208-889-7706
Approx.Sls.: $10,000,000
Emp.: 52
Full Line Food & Variety Store
S.I.C.: 5411
Roger H. Fleenor *(Pres.)*
Sumi Aono *(Treas. & Sec.)*
Dennis Huff *(Mgr.-Store)*

Computer Systems/Hardware:
NCR & BASS & DSAS

Outside Service Firm(s):

Balukoff, Lindstrom & Co.*(Auditors)*
Boise, ID

Sedgwick James*(Commercial Insurance Carrier)*
Boise, ID

IEC Insurance Administrators*(Group Insurer)*
Boise, ID

Eberle, Berlin, Kading, Turnbow & McKlueen*(Legal Firm)*
300 No. Sixth St.
Boise, ID 83701

RED BALL CORPORATION
9750 Third Ave. NE Suite 200
Seattle, WA 98115
Mailing Address:
P.O. Box 1127
Indianapolis, IN 46206 **IN**
Year Founded: 1985
Approx.Sls.: $75,000,000
Emp.: 200
Fiscal Year-end: 12/31/91
Custom Relocation Service, Moving & Storage of Household & Commercial Goods
S.I.C.: 4213
Walter E. Saubert *(Chm. Bd.)*
Melvin D. Duncan, Jr. *(Pres. of American Red Ball Transit & Vice Chm. Red Ball Corp.)*
Micheal W. Duffy *(Exec. V.P. & Gen. Mgr.)*
David W. Hope *(Chief Fin. Officer & V.P. Fin.)*
Walter E. Saubert *(Owner)*
Principal(s):
Melvin D. Duncan, Jr.
Walter E. Saubert

Computer Systems/Hardware:
Sperry Univac Systems 80, PC 200

Outside Service Firm(s):

INB National Bank*(Major Banking Relationship)*
One Indiana Sq.
Indianapolis, IN 46266
Tel.: 317-266-6000

Subsidiaries:

American Red Ball International, Inc. **(1)**
12360 Lake City Way, N.E., Ste. 500
Seattle, WA 98125
Tel.: 206-365-1303 (100%)
Emp.: 20
Unregulated International Freight Forwarder
S.I.C.: 4731
Walter E. Saubert *(Pres.)*

American Red Ball World Wide Movers **(1)**
1335 Sadlier Circle, E. Dr.
Indianapolis, IN 46239
Tel.: 317-353-8331 (100%)
Fax: 317-351-0651
Approx.Sls.: $140,000,000
Emp.: 150
Fiscal Year-end: 12/31/91
Household Goods Mover
S.I.C.: 4213
Melvin D. Duncan, Jr. *(Pres.)*
Michael W. Duffy *(Exec. V.P. & Gen. Mgr.)*
Tom Jackson *(V.P.-Opers.)*
Katrina Blackwell *(V.P.-Sls. & Mktg.)*
David E. Miller *(V.P.-Fin.)*
Russ Seeks *(Dir.-Personnel)*

Red Ball Forwarders, Inc. **(1)**
1335 Sadlier Circle, E. Dr.
Indianapolis, IN 46239
Tel.: 317-352-1651 (100%)
Emp.: 4
Regulated Domestic Freight Forwarder
S.I.C.: 4731
Walter E. Saubert *(Pres.)*
Katrina Blackwell *(V.P. & Gen. Mgr.)*

Red Ball Leasing, Inc. **(1)**
1347 Sadlier Circle, E. Dr.
Indianapolis, IN 46239
Tel.: 317-353-8331 (100%)
Emp.: 2
Purchase, Sell, & Lease Moving Equipment
S.I.C.: 7513
Melvin D. Duncan, Jr. *(Pres.)*

Red Ball Van & Storage, Inc. **(1)**
1347 Sadlier Circle, E. Dr.
Indianapolis, IN 46239
Tel.: 317-353-9101 (100%)
Emp.: 30
Local & Long Distance Household Goods Moving & Storage Agency
S.I.C.: 4214
Melvin D. Duncan, Jr. *(Pres.)*

RED CALLIOPE & ASSOCIATES, INC.
13003 S. Figueroa
Los Angeles, CA 90061
Tel.: 310-516-6100 **CA**
Fax: 310-516-7170
Year Founded: 1969
Approx.Sls.: $10,000,000
Emp.: 45
Manufacture Infant Bedding & Accessories
S.I.C.: 2511; 2515
Stanley Glickman *(Chm. Bd. & Treas.)*
Neal Fohrman *(Pres., Chief Exec. & Chief Fin. Officer & Controller)*
Steve Guyer *(V.P.-Mfg.)*

Computer Systems/Hardware:
Qantel; Digital

Outside Service Firm(s):

Lederman & Co.*(Auditors)*
Los Angeles, CA

Escobar Diversified Services*(Group Insurer)*
Torrance, CA

Mitsui Manufacturers Bank*(Major Banking Relationship)*
Los Angeles, CA

RED CARPET REAL ESTATE SERVICES, INC.
(Sub. of NRS National Real Estate)
P.O. Box 85660,
San Diego, CA 92138
Year Founded: 1986
Approx.Sls.: $2,000,000,000
Emp.: 30
Fiscal Year-end: 6/30/91
Real Estate Franchises & Referral/ Relocations Services; Performance Plus Learning System, Wall to Wall Protection Plan Home Warranty
S.I.C.: 6531
Oswald Jurock *(Chm. Bd. & Chief Exec. Officer)*
Doug Balog *(V.P.)*
Mike Desmarteau *(V.P.-Franchise Sls.)*
John Basar *(Chief Fin. Officer & Controller)*

RED DEVIL INC.
2400 Vauxhall Rd.
Union, NJ 07083
Tel.: 908-688-6900
Tel.: 800-247-3790 **NJ**
Fax: 908-688-8872
Year Founded: 1872
Assets: $22,000,000
Liabilities: $12,000,000
Net Worth: $10,000,000
Approx.Sls.: $50,000,000
Emp.: 350
Fiscal Year-end: 12/31/90
Import Export
Manufacture Painter's Tools, Paint Tinters & Mixers, Caulks & Sealants for Home Repair & Decorating; Electrical Paint Machines
S.I.C.: 3423; 2891
George L. Lee, Jr. *(Chm. Bd.)*
John L. Lee *(Vice Chm.)*
Donald R. MacPherson *(Pres. & Chief Exec. Officer)*
Jack J. Colligan *(Chief Fin. Officer & V.P.-Fin. & Admin.)*
John Fry *(V.P.-Mfg. Opers.)*
George L. Lee III *(V.P.-Plng. & Devel.)*
Mary T. Lee *(V.P.-Customer Rels.)*
Jane T. Lee *(V.P. & Sec.)*
Richard Del Sesto *(V.P.-Sls. & Mktg.)*
Ralph DeLorenzo *(Controller)*
Herbert M. Gannett *(Gen. Counsel)*
John Coff *(Dir.-Data Processing)*
John Primevera *(Mgr.-Intl. Opers.)*
Richard P. Wens *(Mgr.-Mktg. Service)*
Ralph Hansen *(Chief Engineer)*
John Leonard *(Pur. Agent)*
Principal(s):
Lee Family

No. of Mfg. Plants/Facilities: 2
No. of U.S. Offices: 3
No. of Foreign Offices: 1

Computer Systems/Hardware:
AT&T

Outside Service Firm(s):

Grant Thornton*(Auditors)*
9 Campus Dr.
Parsippany, NJ
Tel.: 201-540-0250

Herbert M. Gannet*(Legal Firm)*
Newark, NJ

CoreStates Corporate Trust Services*(Major Banking Relationship)*
P.O. Box 7907,
Philadelphia, PA 19101
Tel.: 215-629-8400

Summit Bank*(Major Banking Relationship)*
Summit, NJ

United Jersey Bank*(Major Banking Relationship)*
Hackensack, NJ

RED ROOF INNS, INC.
4355 Davidson Rd.
Hilliard, OH 43026-2491
Tel.: 614-876-3200
Tel.: 800-THE-ROOF
Fax: 614-771-7838
Year Founded: 1972
Approx.Sls.: $200,000,000
Emp.: 5,000
Motels
S.I.C.: 7011
Barbara Trueman *(Chm. Bd.)*
Jack Van Fossen *(Pres. & Chief Exec. Officer)*
Gary Qualmann *(Chief Fin. Officer & Exec. V.P.)*
John E. Campbell *(Chief Oper. Officer & Exec. V.P.)*
Patricia Dove *(V.P.-Training)*
Raymond Druseikis *(V.P. & Controller)*
John Gordon *(V.P., Gen. Counsel & Sec.)*
Jim Hughes *(V.P.-Real Estate)*
Orlow Wertenberger *(V.P.-Pur.)*
David Wible *(V.P.-Mktg. & Pub. Rels.)*
Jeff Winslow *(V.P.-Mngmt. Information Systems)*
Doug Bruce *(Dir.-Personnel Programs)*
Judie Maiden *(Dir.-EmployeeBenefits)*
Scott Moore *(Dir.-Morgtage Fin.)*
Lee Kleinman *(Mgr.-Telecommunications)*

Computer Systems/Hardware:
Hewlett-Packard 3000

Outside Service Firm(s):

Deloitte & Touche*(Auditors)*
155 E. Broad St.
Columbus, OH 43215
Tel.: 614-221-1000
Fax: 614-229-4647

Porter, Wright, Morris & Arthur*(Legal Firm)*
Huntington Center, 41 S. High St.
Columbus, OH 43215-3406
Tel.: 614-227-2000

The Huntington National Bank*(Major Banking Relationship)*
41 S. High St.
Columbus, OH 43216

RED SPOT PAINT & VARNISH CO.
1016 Columbia
Evansville, IN 47711
Mailing Address:
P.O. Box 418,
Evansville, IN 47703
Tel.: 812-428-9100
Tel.: 800-457-3544
Fax: 812-428-9167
Year Founded: 1903
Approx.Sls.: $70,000,000
Emp.: 440
Fiscal Year-end: 10/31/92
Import Export
Automotive & Industrial Coatings; Paints, Varnishes, Lacquers
S.I.C.: 2851
Milton Z. Thorson *(Chm. Bd.)*
Charles D. Storms *(Pres. & Chief Exec. Officer)*
Mark Lutterbach *(V.P.-Research & Devel.)*
Marc Rhiver *(V.P.-Sls. & Mktg.)*

Peter Ruthenburg *(V.P.-Opers.)*
Howard W. Bootz *(Treas. & Corp. Sec.)*
Steve Halling *(Controller)*
Gene Berkey *(Dir.-Purch.)*
Steve Martin *(Dir.-Personnel)*
Bryan Williams *(Dir.-Intl. Opers.)*
Mike Murphy *(Chief Oper. Officer (MIS))*
June Miller *(Mgr.-Mktg.)*

No. of Mfg. Plants/Facilities: 2
No. of U.S. Offices: 2

Computer Systems/Hardware:
IBM

Outside Service Firm(s):

George S. Olive & Co.*(Auditors)*
20 N.W. Third St., 14th Fl.
Evansville, IN 47708
Tel.: 812-428-6500

Merchants National Bank & Trust Company of Indianapolis*(International Bank Affiliate)*
One Merchants Plaza, Ste. 901E
Indianapolis, IN 46255
Tel.: 317-267-7109

Kahn, Dees, Donovan & Kahn*(Legal Firm)*
Evansville, IN

Old National Bank in Evansville*(Major Banking Relationship)*
P.O. Box 718, 420 Main St.
Evansville, IN 47705
Tel.: 812-464-1200

Verlan, Ltd.*(Commercial Insurance Carrier)*
Washington, DC

Subsidiary:

Red Spot Westland Inc. **(1)**
555 S. Edwin
Westland, MI 48185
Tel.: 313-729-7400
Emp.: 55
Automotive & Industrial Coatings; Paints, Varnishes, Lacquers
S.I.C.: 2851

RED WING PRODUCTS, INC.
190 Express St.
Plainview, NY 11803
Tel.: 516-349-8400
Fax: 516-349-8407
Sales Range: $10-19 Million
Emp.: 15
Plastic Hangers, Tote Bags, Displays, Special Advertising Items
S.I.C.: 3089
Miles A. Coon *(Pres., Chief Oper. Officer & Treas.)*
David Halpert *(V.P.)*
Betty Popp *(Sec. & Controller)*

Outside Service Firm(s):

Anchin, Block & Anchin*(Auditors)*
1375 Broadway
New York, NY 10018

Herrick, Feinstein*(Legal Firm)*
2 Park Ave.
New York, NY 10016
Tel.: 212-684-1400

Chemical Bank*(Major Banking Relationship)*
395 North Service Rd.
Melville, NY 11747

RED WING PUBLISHING COMPANY
433 W. 3rd St.
Red Wing, MN 55066
Tel.: 612-388-8235
Emp.: 69
Newspaper Publishing & Printing
S.I.C.: 2711
Arlin Albrecht *(Pres.)*
Philip N. Duff *(V.P.)*
James Becker *(Treas.)*
Marilyn Albrecht *(Sec.)*

Outside Service Firm(s):

Goodhue County National Bank of Red Wing*(Major Banking Relationship)*
Red Wing, MN

RED WING SHOE CO., INC.
314 Main St.
Red Wing, MN 55066
Tel.: 612-388-8211
Fax: 612-388-7415
Year Founded: 1905
Approx.Sls.: $109,000,000
Emp.: 1,200
Fiscal Year-end: 11/30/90
Export
Manufacture Red Wing Work Shoes, Hunting Boots & Safety Shoes
S.I.C.: 3144; 3143; 3021
William J. Sweasy *(Pres.)*
Glen Dummer *(V.P.-Intl. Div.)*
Joe Goggin *(V.P.-Fin.)*
Craig Livingstone *(Mgr.-Adv.)*

Division:

Red Wing Shoe Vasque Div. **(1)**
314 Main St., Riverfront Center
Red Wing, MN 55066
Tel.: 612-388-8211
Arthur Kenyon *(Mgr.)*

Subsidiary:

S.B. Foot Tanning Co. **(1)**
P.O. Box 73
Red Wing, MN 55066
Tel.: 612-388-4731
Upper Shoe Leather
S.I.C.: 3111
Silas B. Foot, III *(Pres.)*
Robert Kastner *(V.P. & Treas.)*
Ernst Hogen *(V.P.-Opers.)*
Karen Meier *(Sec.)*

REDBURN TIRE COMPANY
3801 W. Clarendon
Phoenix, AZ 85019
Tel.: 602-272-7601 **AZ**
Fax: 602-233-2518
Year Founded: 1979
Approx.Sls.: $27,000,000
Emp.: 140
Wholesale Distribution of Automobile & Truck Tires & Tubes, Rebuilding & Retreading Tires, Tire Repair Shop
S.I.C.: 5014; 7534
J.D. Chastain *(Pres.)*
Donald Leffler *(Treas. & Sec.)*

Outside Service Firm(s):

Citibank N.A.*(Major Banking Relationship)*
Phoenix, AZ

REDCO FOODS, INC.
100 Northfield Dr.
Windsor, CT 06095
Tel.: 203-688-2121
Fax: 203-688-7844
Approx.Sls.: $60,000,000
Emp.: 200
Red Rose & Salada Tea, Black Diamond Cheese, Junket Desserts
S.I.C.: 2099; 2064; 5149
John G. Rigg *(Chm. Bd. & Chief Exec. Officer)*
Gerald Doutre *(Pres.)*
Thomas Burne *(Chief Fin. Officer)*

REDGATE COMMUNICATIONS CORP.
660 Beachland Blvd.
Vero Beach, FL 32963
Tel.: 407-231-6904
Year Founded: 1985
Approx.Billings: $70,000,000
Emp.: 80
Technology, Business-to-Business, Biotechnology & Healthcare
Ted Leonsis *(Chm. Bd., Chief Exec. Officer, Pres. & New Bus. Contact)*
Chuck Clemente *(Chief Oper. Officer)*
Jeff Parsons *(Sr. V.P., Chief Fin. Officer)*

Computer Systems/Hardware:
IBM, Macintosh

REDKEN LABORATORIES, INC.
6625 Variel Ave.
Canoga Park, CA 91303
Tel.: 818-992-2700 **DE**
Fax: 818-884-1156
Year Founded: 1960
Emp.: 879
Fiscal Year-end: 7/31/90
Develops, Manufactures & Markets Hair & Skin Care Products
S.I.C.: 2844
John E. Meehan *(Chm. Bd.)*
John Hammer *(Pres.)*
Paula Kent Meehan *(Chief Exec. Officer)*
Cary Newman *(Sr. V.P.-Worldwide Opers.)*
James W. Griffith *(V.P.-Human Resources)*
Lee D. Hunter, Ph.D. *(V.P.-Research & Devel.)*
W.B. Jones *(V.P.-Admin.)*
Thomas E. McLoughlin *(V.P.-Fin.)*
Christopher J. Meehan *(V.P.-Education)*
D. James Pekin *(V.P., Gen. Counsel & Sec.)*
William E. Peplow *(V.P.-Salon Rels.)*
Richard J. Delia *(Treas.)*
Jim Coffman *(Dir.-Grp. Services)*
Francine Stessel *(Dir.-Communications)*
Kelly Donahue *(Mgr.-Corp. Rels.)*
Kim Kirkland *(Co-Op Adv.)*

Outside Service Firm(s):

Price Waterhouse*(Auditors)*
5950 Canoga Ave.
Woodland Hills, CA 91367
Tel.: 818-704-1117
Fax: 818-704-5354

Towers, Perrin, Forster & Crosby*(Group Insurer)*
1925 Century Park East
Los Angeles, CA 90069
Tel.: 310-556-0330
Fax: 310-551-5859

Bank of America NT&SA*(International Bank Affiliate)*
Tokyo, Japan

Barclays Bank plc*(International Bank Affiliate)*
9 Gracechurch St.
London, EC3V 0BB, United Kingdom
Tel.: 071 623 2266
Telex: 667020
Fax: 071 929 1478

Merrill Lynch*(Investment Banker)*
Los Angeles, CA

Morgan Stanley & Co.*(Investment Banker)*
555 California St.
San Francisco, CA 94104

Latham & Watkins*(Legal Firm)*
633 West Fifth St.
Los Angeles, CA 90071
Tel.: 213-485-1234
Fax: 213-643-9086

Bank of America NT&SA*(Major Banking Relationship)*
555 So. Flower St., 5th Fl.
Los Angeles, CA 90071
Tel.: 213-228-3526
Fax: 213-228-4062

Security Pacific Corporation*(Major Banking Relationship)*
Security Pacific Plaza
Los Angeles, CA 90071
Tel.: 213-345-6211
Fax: 213-625-0809

Union Bank*(Major Banking Relationship)*
445 S. Figueroa St.
Los Angeles, CA 90071
Tel.: 213-236-5076

Morgan Stanley & Co.*(Pension Manager)*
555 California St.
San Francisco, CA 94104

Subsidiaries:

Redken Intl. (Pacific), Inc. **(1)**
6625 Variel Ave.
Canoga Park, CA 91303
Tel.: 818-992-2700 (100%)
S.I.C.: 2844

Redken Laboratories (DISC), Inc. **(1)**
6625 Variel Ave.
Canoga Park, CA 91303
Tel.: 818-992-2700 (100%)
Sales & Mktg.of Hair & Skin Products
S.I.C.: 5122

REDMAN INDUSTRIES, INC.
2550 Walnut Hill Ln., Ste. 200
Dallas, TX 75229
Tel.: 214-353-3600 **DE**
Fax: 214-351-2983
Year Founded: 1937
Approx.Sls.: $400,000,000
Emp.: 4,200
Fiscal Year-end: 3/30/92
Export
Holding Company; Manufacture of Mobile Homes, Aluminum Windows & Doors
S.I.C.: 6719; 2451
Thomas Sturgess *(Pres.)*
Fergus J. Walker *(Exec. V.P.)*
Fred Babb *(V.P.-Admin. & Personnel)*
Paul L. Barrett *(Gen. Counsel & Sec.)*
J. Mark Kirkpatrick *(Treas.)*
Ken Davis *(Dir.-Data Processing)*

Subsidiaries:

Redman Building Products, Inc. **(1)**
2550 Walnut Hill Ln., Ste. 200
Dallas, TX 75229
Tel.: 214-353-3600 (100%)
Approx.Sls.: $100,908,000
Emp.: 1,000
Aluminum Windows & Doors
S.I.C.: 3442
Jack L. Morris *(Pres.)*

Redman Holding Corp. **(1)**
2550 Walnut Hill Ln., Ste. 200
Dallas, TX 75229
Tel.: 214-353-3600
Holding Company
S.I.C.: 6719

Redman Homes, Inc. **(1)**
2550 Walnut Hill Ln., Ste. 200
Dallas, TX 75229
Tel.: 214-353-3600 (100%)
Fax: 214-351-2983
Approx.Sls.: $254,236,000
Emp.: 2,800
Export
Mfr. of Mobile Homes
S.I.C.: 2451
Robert M. Linton *(Pres.)*

Western Homes Corporation **(1)**
2550 Walnut Hill Ln., Ste. 200
Dallas, TX 75229
Tel.: 214-353-3600
Approx.Sls.: $60,491,000
Emp.: 700
Mfr. of MobileHomes
S.I.C.: 2451
F. Gary Edmundson *(Pres.)*

W. C. REDMON CO.
200 Harrison Ave.
Peru, IN 46970
Tel.: 317-473-6683
Fax: 317-473-6686
Year Founded: 1884
Approx.Sls.: $150,000,000
Emp.: 125

W. C. Redmon Co.—(Continued)

Manufacture Clothes Hampers, Bassinettes, Picnic Baskets, Toy Chests
S.I.C.: 2519; 2653; 3944
William L. Redmon *(Chm. Bd.)*
C. Peter Redmon *(Pres. & Mgr.-Adv.)*
Samuel C. Redmon *(Exec. V.P.)*
Elton A. Stuber *(Pur. Agent)*

Principal(s):
Redmon Family

No. of Mfg. Plants/Facilities: 1

Computer Systems/Hardware:
AT&T

Outside Service Firm(s):

Carter, Kirlin & Merrill*(Auditors)*
Indianapolis, IN

Wabash Valley Bank & Trust Co.*(Major Banking Relationship)*
Peru, IN

REDMOND PRODUCTS, INC.
18930 W. 78th St.
Chanhassen, MN 55317
Tel.: 612-934-4868 **MN**
Fax: 612-934-7826
Year Founded: 1979
Approx.Sls.: $115,000,000
Emp.: 250
Fiscal Year-end: 12/31/92
Manufacture Hair Preparations
S.I.C.: 2844
Thomas Redmond, Sr. *(Chm. Bd.)*
Larry Perkins *(Chief Oper. Officer)*
Patricia Redmond Webber *(Pres.)*
Tom Redmond, Jr. *(V.P.-Adv.)*
Frank Reiter *(Controller)*
Ellen Redmond *(Sec.)*
Michael J. Mollerus *(Gen. Counsel)*
Sam Moniaci *(Natl. Sls. Mgr.)*
Sandy Reitsma *(Dir.-Personnel)*
Tim Fitten *(Dir.-Mfg.)*
Steve Storebo *(Dir.-Materials Mngmt.)*
Linda Haning *(Dir.-Tech. Services)*
Lee Edgerly *(Managing Dir.-Intl. Sls.)*

Principal(s):
Thomas Redmond, Sr.

No. of Mfg. Plants/Facilities: 1
No. of U.S. Offices: 2
No. of Foreign Offices: 1

Computer Systems/Hardware:
IBM AS/400

Outside Service Firm(s):

Boeckermann Heimen & Mayer*(Auditors)*
7900 Flying Cloud Dr. #750
Eden Prairie, MN 55344

Northbrook Insurance*(Commercial Insurance Carrier)*
Minneapolis, MN

Kidder, Peabody & Co.*(Investment Banker)*
Minneapolis, MN

Michael J. Mollerus, Ltd.*(Legal Firm)*
Edina, MN

Norwest Bank Minnesota, N.A.*(Major Banking Relationship)*
Hopkins, MN

REECE-CAMPBELL, INC.
1718 Rafston Ave.
Cincinnati, OH 45223
Tel.: 513-542-4600 **OH**
Fax: 513-542-4753
Year Founded: 1983
Approx.Sls.: $34,000,000
Emp.: 50
New Construction of Commercial & Office Buildings; Commercial & Office Buildings Renovation & Repair; Condominium & Apartment Building Construction; Construction Management
S.I.C.: 1542; 1522; 8741
Peter W. Chronis *(Pres.)*

Outside Service Firm(s):

Deloitte & Touche*(Auditors)*
Chiquita Center, 250 E. 5th St., Ste. 1900
Cincinnati, OH 45202
Tel.: 513-784-7100

REED & BARTON CORPORATION
144 W. Britannia
Taunton, MA 02780
Tel.: 508-824-6611 **MA**
Telex: 753535
Fax: 508-822-7269
Year Founded: 1824
Approx.Sls.: $58,000,000
Emp.: 620
Sterling & Silver Plated Flatware & Holloware, Stainless Steel Flatware, Pewter, Wooden Jewelry & Silverware Chests, Silverware & Jewelry Storage Rolls & Bags
S.I.C.: 3914; 3961; 3911; 2499
Sinclair Weeks *(Chm. Bd.)*
Albert D. Krebel *(Pres. & Chief Exec. Officer)*
William Dykstra *(Sr. V.P., Treas. & Investor Rels. Dir.)*
Bryce H. Blair *(V.P.-Retail Sls.)*
A. D. Lachapelle *(V.P.-Mktg.)*
William D. Weeks *(Sec.)*
Arthur Court *(Dir.-Pur.)*
Candace Lofgren *(Dir.-Personnel)*

No. of U.S. Offices: 12

Computer Systems/Hardware:
IBM System 38

Outside Service Firm(s):

Ernst & Young*(Auditors)*
200 Clarendon St., 46th Fl.
Boston, MA 02116
Tel.: 617-266-2000

Blue Shield of Massachusetts, Inc.*(Group Insurer)*
Boston, MA

Sherburne, Powers & Needham*(Legal Firm)*
Boston, MA

First National Bank of Boston*(Major Banking Relationship)*
P.O. Box 644,
Boston, MA 02102-0644
Tel.: 617-575-2900
Fax: 617-575-2549

Divisions:

New England Collectors Society **(1)**
512 Riverside Ave.
Westport, CT 06880
Tel.: 203-226-8010 (100%)
Direct Mail Business
S.I.C.: 5961
Robert Fortin *(Pres.)*

Reed & Barton Giftsources **(1)**
P. O. Box 505,
Yarmouth, ME 04096
Tel.: 207-797-0996 (100%)
Distinctive Gifts & Decorative Accessories
Stanley Cornwall *(Pres.)*

Reed & Barton Housewares **(1)**
144 W. Britannia
Taunton, MA 02780
Tel.: 508-824-6611 (100%)
Distribute Stainless Steel Flatware
S.I.C.: 5094
William Robinson *(Pres.)*

Sheffield Silver Co. **(1)**
144 W. Britannia St.
Taunton, MA 02780
Tel.: 508-824-6611 (100%)
Fax: 508-822-7269
Approx.Sls.: $10,000,000
Emp.: 75
Manufacture Silver Flatware & Holloware
S.I.C.: 3914
Daniel S. Fournier *(Natl. Sls. Mgr.)*
Lisa Perry *(Pub. Rels. Coord.)*

Subsidiaries:

Eureka Manufacturing Co., Inc. **(1)**
47 Elm St.
Norton, MA 02766
Tel.: 508-285-9881 (100%)
Wooden Silverware & Jewelry Chests; Silverware & Jewelry Storage Rolls & Bags
S.I.C.: 2499; 2299
George Gregory *(Pres.)*

Reed & Barton Silversmiths **(1)**
144 W. Britannia
Taunton, MA 02780
Tel.: 508-824-6611
Silversmithing
S.I.C.: 3914
Albert D. Krebel *(Pres.)*

REED EXHIBITION COMPANIES
(A Div. of Reed Publishing (U.S.A.) Inc.)
221 Columbus Ave.
Boston, MA 02116
Mailing Address:
P.O. Box 35,
Boston, MA 02117
Tel.: 617-536-8152
Tel.: 800-525-7585
Fax: 617-536-8719
Year Founded: 1972
Approx.Billings: $22,500,000
Emp.: 72
Trade & Public Shows Advertising
Neil J. Grossman *(Chm. Bd. & Pres.)*
Thomas Caridi *(Sr. V.P., Fin. & Treas.)*
Walter Heithaus *(V.P., Pub. Rels.)*
John Lewinski *(Dir. Adv.)*
Pat Coen *(Data Processing)*
Cindy Gwinn *(Librarian)*

GENE REED CHEVROLET
4001 Dorchester Rd.
Charleston Heights, SC 29405
Tel.: 803-747-9681 **SC**
Fax: 803 554 6285
Approx.Sls.: $40,000,000
Emp.: 112
Automobile Dealerships
S.I.C.: 5511
Gene Reed *(Pres.)*
Charity Chastain *(V.P. & Controller)*
Mike Reed *(V.P.)*

Outside Service Firm(s):

George P. Jones*(Auditors)*
Memphis, TN

Rosen, Rosen & Oberman*(Legal Firm)*
Charleston, SC

South Carolina National Bank*(Major Banking Relationship)*
Charleston, SC

REED GRAIN & BEAN COMPANY
9th & Elm
Buhl, ID 83316
Mailing Address:
P.O. Box 472
Buhl, ID 83316
Tel.: 208-543-4306 **ID**
Emp.: 28
Field Beans; Grains
S.I.C.: 5153
Earl Reed *(Chm. Bd.)*
Carol A. Reed *(Pres.)*
Robert N. Reed *(V.P.)*
Carol O. Reed *(Sec.)*

Outside Service Firm(s):

Benoit & Allen*(Legal Firm)*
Nyssa, OR

First Interstate Bank*(Major Banking Relationship)*
Boise, ID

REED MOTORS, INC.
3776 W. Colonial Dr.
Orlando, FL 32808
Tel.: 407-297-7333 **FL**
Fax: 407-291-7604
Approx.Sls.: $15,000,000
Emp.: 55
New & Used Automobiles
S.I.C.: 5511
John L. Reed *(Pres.)*
Robert H. Reed *(V.P.)*
Raymond Reed *(Treas. & Gen. Sls. Mgr.)*
John J. Reed, Jr. *(Sec. & Gen. Mgr.)*

Outside Service Firm(s):

Sun Bank, N.A.*(Major Banking Relationship)*
200 S. Orange Ave., 8th Fl. SOAB
Orlando, FL
Tel.: 407-237-4141

REEL-O-MATIC SYSTEMS, INC.
6408 S. Eastern
Oklahoma City, OK 73149
Mailing Address:
P.O. Box 95309
Oklahoma City, OK 73143
Tel.: 405-672-0000
Tel.: 800-221-7335
Fax: 405-672-7200
Approx.Sls.: $3,500,000,000
Emp.: 20
Export
Mfr. Of Wire And Cable Handling Equipment To Increase, Re-Spool & Cut All Types Of Flexible Materials. Equipment Manufactured Includes Cable Trailers Re-Spoolers, Pay-out & Take-Up Equipment, Measurers & Coilers. Customized Equipment Is A Speciality
S.I.C.: 3599
John D. Schrott, Jr. *(Chm. Bd., Pres. & Chief Exec. Officer)*
John D. Schrott, Sr. *(V.P.)*
R. Terry Simmons *(V.P. & Adv. Mgr.)*

Computer Systems/Hardware:
IBM

REESE ENTERPRISES, INC.
16350 Asher Ave.
Rosemount, MN 55068
Tel.: 612-423-1126
Fax: 612-423-2662
Approx.Sls.: $15,000,000
Emp.: 125
Weather Strips, Plastic Extrusions, Footmats & Gratings
S.I.C.: 3089; 3069; 3446
Chester W. Ellingson, Jr. *(Chm. Bd., Pres. & Chief Exec. Officer)*
Sarah S. Ellingson *(Chief Fin. Officer & Sec.)*
Bruce A. Senst *(Controller)*

Outside Service Firm(s):

Boyer & Company*(Auditors)*
Burnsvill, MN

Fredrikson & Byron, P.A.*(Legal Firm)*
1100 International Centre, 900 2nd Ave. S.
Minneapolis, MN 55402
Tel.: 612-347-7000

Norwest Bank Minnesota, N.A.*(Major Banking Relationship)*
8th St. & Marquette Ave.
Minneapolis, MN 55479
Tel.: 612-372-8123

Divisions:

Plastic Division **(1)**
16350 Asher Ave.
Rosemount, MN 55068
Tel.: 612-423-1126
Plastic Extrusions
S.I.C.: 3069
Robert T. Ellingson *(Pres.)*
James R. Kinville *(Mgr.)*

Weather Strip Division **(1)**
16350 Asher Ave.
Rosemount, MN 55068
Tel.: 612-423-1126
Weather Strip
S.I.C.: 3089
Chester W. Ellingson III *(Pres.)*
Thomas W. Mangan *(Mgr.)*

REESE FINER FOODS, INC.
300 Broad Acres Dr.
Bloomfield, NJ 07003
Tel.: 201-338-0300
Fax: 201-338-0382
Approx.Sls.: $38,000,000
Emp.: 350
Fiscal Year-end: 5/31/90
Specialty & Imported Foods; Reese, Bonaparte, Ty Ling, Knorr, Sovex, Gunkel, V.I.P., El Rio, Moon Palace, Maurice, London Pub, Francais, Northland Queen, Panni, Grand Duke & Stuart
S.I.C.: 5149
John Beers *(Pres. & Chief Exec. Officer)*
Barry O'Brien *(Chief Fin. Officer)*

REEVE ALEUTIAN AIRWAYS, INC.
4700 W. International Airport Rd.
Anchorage, AK 99502
Tel.: 907-243-1112 **AK**
Fax: 907-249-2317
Year Founded: 1932
Assets: $32,000,000
Liabilities: $11,000,000
Net Worth: $21,000,000
Approx.Sls.: $22,000,000
Emp.: 320
Fiscal Year-end: 12/31/90
Air Transportation
S.I.C.: 4512
Janice M. Reeve *(Chm. Bd.)*
Richard D. Reeve *(Pres.)*
Victor L. Fondy *(V.P.-Opers.)*
Robert L. Hanson *(V.P.-Maintenance)*
David Jensen *(V.P.-Admin.)*
Janice Ogle *(V.P.-Inflight Service)*
Morry Shepard *(Controller)*
Annelise Hansen *(Dir.-Passengers)*

Outside Service Firm(s):

KPMG Peat Marwick*(Auditors)*
Anchorage, AK

National Bank of Alaska*(Major Banking Relationship)*
P.O. Box 100600,
Anchorage, AK 99510-0600

THE REEVES AGENCY, INC.
2219 Maryland Ave.
Baltimore, MD 21218
Tel.: 410-889-6111
Fax: 410-889-6146
Year Founded: 1975
Approx.Billings: $16,000,000
Emp.: 20
Rebecca B. Reeves *(Pres. & New Bus. Contact)*
Alan D. Cohen *(Sr. V.P., Mktg. Services & Devel.)*
John Reeves *(Treas.)*
Karen LeTourneau *(Asst. Comptroller)*

REEVES SOUTHEASTERN CORPORATION
P.O. Box 1968
Tampa, FL 33601
Tel.: 813-626-3191
Fax: 813-623-3401
Year Founded: 1953
Sales Range: $60-79 Million
Emp.: 375
Fiscal Year-end: 10/31/90
Import Export
Manufacture Chain Link Fencing Products & Welded Wire Mesh; Commercial Galvanizing; Access Control Equipment
S.I.C.: 3315; 3479; 5039
Billy G. Sasser *(Chm. Bd., Pres. & Chief Exec. Officer)*
Mike Augello *(V.P.-Mktg. & Adv.)*
Miles L. Lenhart *(V.P.-Fin., Treas. & Sec.)*
Ronald L. Moore *(Dir.-Personnel)*
Principal(s):
Billy G. Sasser
Miles L. Lenhart

No. of Mfg. Plants/Facilities: 2
No. of U.S. Offices: 24

Computer Systems/Hardware:
IBM

Outside Service Firm(s):

Coopers & Lybrand*(Auditors)*
101 E. Kennedy Blvd., Ste. 1500
Tampa, FL 33602
Tel.: 813-229-0221

Liberty Mutual*(Group Insurer)*
Tampa, FL

Trenam, Simmons, Kemker, Scharf, Barkin, Frye & O'Neil*(Legal Firm)*
2700 Barnett Plaza
Tampa, FL 33602
Tel.: 813-223-7474

NationsBank Florida*(Major Banking Relationship)*
400 N. Ashley Dr.
Tampa, FL 33602
Tel.: 813-224-5242

NationsBank Florida*(Pension Manager)*
400 N. Ashley Dr.
Tampa, FL 33602
Tel.: 813-224-5242

REFCO GROUP LTD.
111 W. Jackson
Chicago, IL 60604
Tel.: 312-930-6500
Fax: 312-930-6534
Approx.Sls.: $310,000,000
Emp.: 550
Specialist in Business Risk Management Through the Use of Futures & Options
S.I.C.: 6221
Thomas H. Dittmer *(Chm. Bd.)*
Tone Grant *(Pres.)*
Phillip R. Bennett *(Chief Fin. Officer)*

Division:

Refco Inc. **(1)**
111 W. Jackson
Chicago, IL 60604
Tel.: 312-930-6500
Fax: 312-930-6534
Futures & Options Broker
S.I.C.: 6221
Thomas Dittmer *(Pres.)*

REFERENCE SOFTWARE INTERNATIONAL
330 Townsend St., Ste. 119
San Francisco, CA 94107
Tel.: 415-541-0222
Tel.: 800-872-9933
Fax: 415-541-0509
Year Founded: 1985
Approx.Sls.: $11,000,000
Emp.: 103
Export
Manufactures Software
S.I.C.: 7372
Don Emery *(Pres.)*
Jeff Mallett *(V.P.-Sls. & Mktg.)*
Jerri Brown *(Chief Fin. Officer)*
Lois Tilles *(Mktg. Dir.)*
Sigrid Metson *(Corp. Communications Mgr.)*

REFRIGERATION SUPPLIES DISTRIBUTORS
1201 Monterey Pass Rd.
Monterey Park, CA 91754
Tel.: 213-264-2800 **CA**
Fax: 213-264-9890
Year Founded: 1907
Approx.Sls.: $37,000,000
Emp.: 160
Wholesale Distribution of Refrigeration Equipment & Supplies
S.I.C.: 5078
Henry G. Martin *(Chm. Bd.)*
Brian Martin *(Pres.)*
Jerry Braden *(Sr. V.P. & Gen. Mgr.)*
John Speyer *(V.P.)*

Outside Service Firm(s):

Grant Thornton*(Auditors)*
1000 Wilshire Blvd.
Los Angeles, CA 90017

First Interstate Bank*(Major Banking Relationship)*
P.O.Box 54168, Terminal Annex
Los Angeles, CA 90054-0168
Tel.: 800-522-6645

REGAL MARINE INDUSTRIES INC.
2300 Jetport Dr.
Orlando, FL 32809
Tel.: 407-851-4360 **FL**
Fax: 407-857-1256
Year Founded: 1969
Approx.Sls.: $67,000,000
Emp.: 500
Export
Mfr. Pleasure Boats
S.I.C.: 3732
Paul Kuck *(Pres.)*
Duane Kuck *(Chief Oper. Officer)*
Bill Mudgeft *(V.P.-Sls.)*
David Furlow *(V.P.-Fin. & Admin.)*
Tim Kuck *(V.P.-Mfg.)*
Martin Clement *(Dir.-Pur.)*
Sandra T. Racinski *(Dir.-Data Processing)*
Jim Berkebile *(Dir.-Engrng.)*
Wanda Kenton Smith *(Dir.-Mktg.)*

Outside Service Firm(s):

Forness, Graham & Cottrill*(Auditors)*
Orlando, FL

Sun Bank, N.A.*(Major Banking Relationship)*
200 S. Orange Ave., 8th Fl. SOAB
Orlando, FL
Tel.: 407-237-4141

REGAL WARE, INC.
1675 Reigle Dr.
Kewaskum, WI 53040
Tel.: 414-626-2121 **WI**
Telex: 275402 REGALUR
Fax: 414-626-8565
Year Founded: 1945
Approx.Sls.: $200,000,000
Emp.: 2,000
Fiscal Year-end: 12/31/90
Import Export
Manufactures Cast & Drawn Aluminum Cookware - Silverstone or Teflon II Interiors - Porcelain-Clad & Decorated Exteriors; Stainless Steel Cookware; Portable Electric Appliances; Kitchen Accessories; Giftware; Home Water & Air Filters
S.I.C.: 3634; 3365; 3564
L.N. Peterson *(Co.-Chm. Bd.)*
James D. Reigle *(Co.-Chm. Bd.)*
Jeffrey A. Reigle *(Pres. & Chief Exec. Officer)*
Steven Fraser *(Exec. V.P.-Housewares)*
Robert S. Zarling *(Exec. V.P.-Direct Sls.)*
Allen C. Koepke *(Sr. V.P.-Fin.)*
James G. Moran *(Sr. V.P.-Human Resources)*
Kim T. Peterson *(V.P.-Mktg.)*
Robert F. Branston *(Dir.-Adv.)*
Phillip Ketter *(Dir.-Mktg. Services)*
Adeline A. Halfmann *(Mgr.-Mktg. Communications)*

No. of Mfg. Plants/Facilities: 3
No. of U.S. Offices: 10

Computer Systems/Hardware:
IBM

Outside Service Firm(s):

Ernst & Young*(Auditors)*
111 E. Kilbourn Ave., Ste. 900
Milwaukee, WI 53202
Tel.: 414-273-5900

McDermott, Will & Emery*(Legal Firm)*
227 W. Monroe St.
Chicago, IL 60606-5096
Tel.: 312-372-2000

First Wisconsin National Bank*(Major Banking Relationship)*
777 E. Wisconsin Ave.
Milwaukee, WI 53202
Tel.: 414-765-4321
Fax: 414-355-6903

Division:

Jacksonville Manufacturing Co., Inc. **(1)**
1100 Redmond Rd.
Jacksonville, AR 72076
Tel.: 501-982-0555
Fax: 501-982-0563
Approx.Sls.: $25,000,000
Emp.: 700
Cast Aluminum Cookware, Bakeware & Servingware
S.I.C.: 3365
Hank Craig *(V.P. & Gen. Mgr.)*

REGAN HOLDING CORPORATION
1179 N. McDowell Blvd. N.
Petaluma, CA 94954
Mailing Address:
P.O. Box 7879,
San Francisco, CA 94120-7879
Tel.: 707-778-8638
Holding Company for Life Insurance & Financial Service Companies
S.I.C.: 6311; 6159; 6719
John Regan *(Pres. & Chief Exec. Officer)*
Lynda Regan *(Sr. V.P.-Mktg. Officer)*

Subsidiary:

LifeSurance Corporation **(1)**
1447 Peachtree St.
Atlanta, GA 30309
Tel.: 404-892-8600
Financial Services Holding Company
S.I.C.: 6719
Donnie P. Hester *(Pres.)*
Alice I. Urland *(Asst. Sec.)*

Subsidiary:

Kennesaw Life & Accident Insurance Company **(2)**
1447 Peachtree St. N.E., Ste. 714
Atlanta, GA 30309
Tel.: 404-892-8600
Approx.Sls.: $532,723
Fiscal Year-end: 12/31/89
Mkts. Life Insurance to Employer Groups through Individual Brokers & Agents
S.I.C.: 6411
Donnie P. Hester *(Pres.)*

Regan Holding Corporation—(Continued)

Donald L. Behne *(Treas.)*
Charles D. Agnew *(Sec.)*

REGENCY ASSOCIATES LIMITED PARTNERSHIP
5005 Washington Ave.
Evansville, IN 47715
Mailing Address:
P.O. Box 5189
Evansville, IN 47716
Tel.: 812-477-8893 **IL**
Fax: 812-474-2766
Year Founded: 1982
Sales Range: $10-19 Million
Emp.: 80
Real Estate Investment, Development, Syndication: Apartments & Shopping Centers
S.I.C.: 6798; 6552
Robert Pratten *(Chief Fin. Officer)*
Ronald Miles *(V.P.-Property Mngmt.)*
Gayla J. Gubler *(Dir.-Leasing)*

Principal(s):
Robert Pratten
Ronald Miles
Gayla J. Gubler
David C. Eades
James R. McKinney

Outside Service Firm(s):

McGladrey & Pullen*(Auditors)*
Champaign, IL

Citizens Realty & Insurance*(Commercial Insurance Carrier)*
Evansville, IN

Ward McDonald*(Legal Firm)*
Champaign, IL

National City Bank*(Major Banking Relationship)*
227 Main St.
Evansville, IN
Tel.: 812-464-9668

REGENCY DODGE INC.
9875 Atlantic Blvd.
Jacksonville, FL 32225
Tel.: 904-725-3050 **FL**
Fax: 904-725-3059
Year Founded: 1969
Approx.Sls.: $24,175,000
Emp.: 70
Automobile & Truck Dealership
S.I.C.: 5511
Jack Caruso *(Chm. Bd. & Pres.)*
Deborah Caruso *(V.P.)*
John M. Caruso *(V.P.)*
Laurie E. Caruso *(V.P.)*
Terri L. Michael *(V.P.)*
Kathleen C. Miller *(V.P.)*
Opel Shumate *(V.P.)*
Jo Ann Caruso *(Sec. & Treas.)*

Principal(s):
Jack Caruso

Outside Service Firm(s):

KPMG Peat Marwick*(Auditors)*
One Independent Dr.
Jacksonville, FL 32201

Rogers, Towers, Bailey, Jones, Gay*(Legal Firm)*
Jacksonville, FL

Barnett Banks Trust Company, N.A.*(Major Banking Relationship)*
9000 Southside Blvd., P.O. Box 40200
Jacksonville, FL 32202-0200
Tel.: 904-464-2802

Southeast Bank, N.A.*(Major Banking Relationship)*
Jacksonville, FL

REGENCY GROUP INC.
121 W. Forsyth St.
Jacksonville, FL 32202
Tel.: 904-356-7000
Fax: 904-634-3428
Approx.Sls.: $33,000,000
Emp.: 195
Holding Company; Subdividers & Developers; Real Estate Managers; Mortgage Servicing & Commercial Printing
S.I.C.: 6719; 6552; 6531; 2752; 6163
Joan W. Stein *(Chm. Bd.)*
Martin E. Stein, Jr. *(Pres. & Chief Exec. Officer)*
Robert L. Stein *(Exec. V.P.)*

Outside Service Firm(s):

KPMG Peat Marwick*(Auditors)*
One Independent Dr.
Jacksonville, FL 32201

Barnett Banks Trust Company, N.A.*(Major Banking Relationship)*
9000 Southside Blvd., P.O. Box 40200
Jacksonville, FL 32202-0200
Tel.: 904-464-2802

First Union National Bank*(Major Banking Relationship)*
Jacksonville, FL

REGENCY LINCOLN MERCURY
11810 E. Northwest Hwy.
Dallas, TX 75218
Tel.: 214-328-4371 **TX**
Fax: 214-324-0082
Year Founded: 1982
Assets: $8,500,000
Liabilities: $6,300,000
Net Worth: $2,200,000
Approx.Sls.: $27,500,000
Emp.: 96
Fiscal Year-end: 12/31/91
Automobile Dealership
S.I.C.: 5511
William Y. Tauscher *(Chm. Bd.)*
David A. Williams *(Pres. & Gen. Mgr.)*
Gerald J. Hejnar *(Controller, Sec. & Dir.-Employee Benefits)*
Dale Adams *(Dir.-Sls.)*
David Klingler *(Dir.-Data Processing)*

Principal(s):
William Y. Tauscher
David A. Williams

Computer Systems/Hardware:
Texas Instruments Business System 800

Outside Service Firm(s):

Jack Bewley, C.P.A.*(Auditors)*
Dallas, TX

Subsidiary:

Royale Paint & Body **(1)**
2766 W. Kingsley
Garland, TX 75041
Tel.: 214-278-3002
Emp.: 17
Auto Body Collision Repair
S.I.C.: 7532

REGIAN ADVERTISING & PUBLIC RELATIONS
219 S. Main St.
Fort Worth, TX 76104
Tel.: 817-870-1128
Fax: 817-429-2377
Year Founded: 1981
Approx.Billings: $16,100,000
Emp.: 31
Franchise, Co-op Operations & Public Relations
Greg Regian *(Pres.)*
Julie Wilson *(Exec. V.P.)*
Moiri Brown *(V.P., Fin.)*
Susan Schoolfield *(Pub. Rels. Dir.)*

THE REGINA COMPANY
300 Galleria Pkwy., Ste. 1400
Atlanta, GA 30339
Tel.: 404-988-0122
Approx.Sls.: $85,000,000
Emp.: 1,400
Manufacturer of Regina Elecktrikbroom Vacuum Cleaners, Rug Shampooer/Floor Polishers, Hand Vacs, Steam Vacuum Extractors
S.I.C.: 3635; 3589
Dave Jones *(Pres.)*
Ken Drescher *(Mgr.-Natl. Sls.)*
Keith Fulton *(Dir.-Engrng.)*

Plant:

The Regina Company **(1)**
21180 Johnson Road
Long Beach, MS 39560
Tel.: 601-863-7112
Mfr. of Vacuum Cleaning Products
S.I.C.: 3635; 3589
Leonard Ashby *(Gen. Mgr.)*
John Pugh *(Dir.-Human Resources)*

REGIONAL TRANSPORTATION AUTHORITY (RTA)
One N. Dearborn St., Ste. 1100
Chicago, IL 60602
Tel.: 312-917-0700 **IL**
Fax: 312-917-0846
Year Founded: 1975
Assets: $15,000,000,000
Net Worth: $15,000,000,000
Approx.Sls.: $543,000,000
Emp.: 15,715
Fiscal Year-end: 12/31/90
Public Transportation System Composed of Bus, Rapid Transit, Commuter Rail & Paratransit Services; RTA Maintains Financial Authority Over 3 Autonomous Boards: Suburban Bus Board-Pace, Commuter Rail Service Board-METRA & Chicago Transit Authority-CTA
S.I.C.: 4119; 4111
Gayle M. Franzen *(Chm. Bd.)*
Laura A. Jibben *(Exec. Dir.)*
Toulla Constantinou *(Asst. Exec. Dir.-Plng. & Devel.)*
Marc Hillier *(Asst. Exec. Dir.-Capital Program & Technology)*
Frederick Ollett *(Asst. Exec. Dir.-Fin. & Admin.)*
Becky Nash *(Sec. of the Authority)*
Patricia McGuire *(Treas.)*
Richard J. Bacigalupo *(Gen. Counsel)*
Ben Gattorna *(Sr. Benefits & Compensation Specialist)*
Maxine Berry *(Human Resources Generalist)*
Todd Zarko *(Dir-Mngmt. Information System)*
Vincent Petrini *(Dir.-Communications)*
Barbara A. Hill *(Mgr.-Admin.)*
Terrence Hake *(Inspector General)*

No. of U.S. Offices: 1

Computer Systems/Hardware:
IBM PC-XT & AT; Wang PC; Apple PC

Outside Service Firm(s):

Deloitte & Touche*(Auditors)*
Two Prudential Plaza, 180 N. Stetson
Chicago, IL 60601
Tel.: 312-946-2039

Benefit Trust & Life*(Group Insurer)*

Service Boards:

Chicago Transit Authority **(1)**
Merchandise Mart Plaza,
Chicago, IL 60654
Tel.: 312-664-7200
Local Passenger Transportation
S.I.C.: 4119
Clark Burrus *(Chm. Bd.)*
Alfred Savage *(Exec. Dir.)*
Daniel Leffers *(Deputy Dir.-Fin.)*
Ernest Sawyer *(Deputy Dir.-Admin.)*

Metra, Commuter Rail Service Board **(1)**
547 W. Jackson
Chicago, IL 60606
Tel.: 312-322-6900
Rail Passenger Transportation Within 6 County Regions (Urban & Suburban Commuter)
S.I.C.: 4111
Jeffrey Ladd *(Chm. Bd.)*
James Cole *(Chief Exec. Dir.)*
Richard Tidwell *(Asst. Exec. Dir.-Opers.)*
Frank Racibozynski *(Treas. & Fin.)*
James Bonistalli *(Dir.-Mktg.)*
Robert Ash *(Div. Mgr.-Procurement)*

Pace **(1)**
550 W. Algonquin Rd.
Arlington Heights, IL 60005
Tel.: 708-364-7223
Fax: 708-364-0186
Suburban Transit System
S.I.C.: 4119; 4111
Florence Boone *(Chm. Bd.)*
Joseph DiJohn *(Exec. Dir.)*
Tom McNichols *(Div. Mgr.-Fin. & Admin.)*
Ann Murphy *(Div. Mgr.-Mktg.)*
Larry Bush *(Div. Mgr.-Admin.)*
Ann M. Murphy *(Div. Mgr.-Mktg.)*

REHRIG PACIFIC COMPANY
4010 E. 26th St.
Los Angeles, CA 90023
Tel.: 213-262-5145
Fax: 213-269-8506
Year Founded: 1913
Approx.Sls.: $79,000,000
Emp.: 450
Plastic Cases
S.I.C.: 3089
Michael Doka *(Pres.)*
Brian A. Lynch *(Chief Fin. Officer)*
B.H. Rehrig *(V.P.)*
Muriel Kiser *(Sec.)*

Outside Service Firm(s):

Ernst & Young*(Auditors)*
515 S. Flower St.
Los Angeles, CA 90071
Tel.: 213-621-1666

Pillsbury, Madison & Sutro*(Legal Firm)*
Los Angeles, CA

THE REICH GROUP, INC.
Seven Penn Center, 1635 Market St., Ste. 200
Philadelphia, PA 19103
Tel.: 215-972-1777
Fax: 215-972-1778
Other: 800-331-9316
Year Founded: 1978
Approx.Billings: $35,000,000
Emp.: 390
Direct Marketing
Mort Reich *(Pres. & Chief Exec. Officer)*
Gene Raitt *(Sr. V.P.)*
Michael Brown *(Sr. V.P., Telemarketing Opers.)*
Wendy Weisband *(V.P., Client Services)*

REICHENSTEIN ADVERTISING AGENCY

REICHENSTEIN ADVERTISING AGENCY
187 Mill Lane
Mountainside, NJ 07092
Tel.: 908-232-3200
Fax: 908-232-3272
Fax: 908-232-7249
Year Founded: 1961
Approx.Billings: $24,500,000
Emp.: 26

Marvin Reichenstein *(Chm. Bd. & Pres.)*
Barbara Trent *(V.P., Fin. Dir.)*

REID & O'DONAHUE ADVERTISING, INC.
419 S. Perry St.
Montgomery, AL 31604
Mailing Address:
P.O. Box 1269,
Montgomery, AL 36102
Tel.: 205-263-7812
Fax: 205-264-1127
Year Founded: 1979
Approx.Billings: $18,000,000
Emp.: 18
Retail, Fashion, Political, Package & Tabloid Design
Employee Matching Gifts Program: Non-Qualified Deferred Compensation Plan
Bruce S. Reid *(Chm. Bd. & Chief Exec. Officer)*
Shannon O'Donahue *(Pres.)*
Claudia O'Donahue *(Exec. V.P., Sec. & Treas.)*
Annette Stainback *(Gen. Mgr. & Acctg.)*

Computer Systems/Hardware:
Macintosh

russ reid company

RUSS REID COMPANY, INC.
Two N. Lake Ave., Ste. 600
Pasadena, CA 91101
Tel.: 818-449-6100
Fax: 818-449-6190
Year Founded: 1964
Approx.Billings: $75,000,000
Emp.: 130
Non-Profit Sector: Direct Mail, TV Production & Syndication, Computer Donor Mngmt., Public Relations, Print Brokerage, Media Buying, Telemarketing, Strategic Planning & Research Counsel
Russ Reid *(Chm. Bd. & Chief Exec. Officer)*
Keith Jespersen *(Pres.)*
Terry Cavin *(Sr. V.P., Chief Oper. Officer)*
Gary Evans *(Sr. V.P., TV Production)*
Thomas Harrison *(Sr. V.P., Pub. Rels.)*
Jerry McClun *(Sr. V.P., Media)*
Ernest Wood *(V.P., Devel.)*
Don Haggstrom *(V.P., Finance)*
Susie Collins *(Office Mgr.)*
Stan Bruckheim *(Media Mktg. Mgr.)*

Computer Systems/Hardware:
Novell LAN

REIDBORD BROS., INC.
5000 Baum Blvd.
Pittsburgh, PA 15213
Tel.: 412-687-3000
Fax: 412-687-3005
Approx.Sls.: $10,000,000
Emp.: 9
Men's & Boys' Trousers, Work Shirts & Outerwear Jackets
S.I.C.: 2311; 2325
Murray S. Reidbord *(Pres.)*
Gilda P. Reidbord *(Exec. V.P., Sec. & Treas.)*
Mario J. Frediani *(Comptroller)*

Outside Service Firm(s):

Trosk, Inc.*(Auditors)*
Pittsburgh, PA

F/S REILLY, MEDIA +
3717 Buchanan St.
San Francisco, CA 94123
Tel.: 415-346-1956
Fax: 415-346-0250
Year Founded: 1974
Approx.Billings: $12,500,000
Emp.: 5
Media Planning & Buying
Frank E. Reilly *(Pres.)*
Sharon S. Reilly *(Exec. V.P.)*

REILLY INDUSTRIES, INC.
1510 Market Square Center
Indianapolis, IN 46204
Tel.: 317-638-7531
Fax: 317-248-6472
Year Founded: 1884
Approx.Sls.: $150,000,000
Emp.: 900
Coal-Based Tar Products; Chemicals & Allied Products
S.I.C.: 2865; 2819
Peter C. Reilly *(Chm. Exec. Committee)*
Thomas E. Reilly, Jr. *(Chm. Bd. & Chief Exec. Officer)*
Rolla E. McAdams *(Vice Chm.)*
Robert D. McNeeley *(Pres.)*
Max L. Stinson *(Chief Fin. Officer)*
Robert Polack *(Corp. Counsel & V.P.)*
T.L. Craig *(Mgr.-Data Processing)*

Principal(s):
Reilly Family

Computer Systems/Hardware:
Burroughs

Outside Service Firm(s):

Ernst & Young*(Auditors)*
One Indiana Square, Ste. 3400
Indianapolis, IN 46204
Tel.: 317-236-1100

INB National Bank*(Major Banking Relationship)*
One Indiana Sq.
Indianapolis, IN 46266
Tel.: 317-266-6000

Subsidiaries:

Reilly Chemicals S.A. **(1)**
151 N. Delaware
Indianapolis, IN 46204
Tel.: 317-638-7531
Emp.: 15
S.I.C.: 2819; 2865
Thomas Reilly *(Pres.)*

Reilly Industries Inc. **(1)**
1500 S. Tibbs
Indianapolis, IN 46241
Tel.: 317-247-8141
Emp.: 500
Bob McNeeley *(Pres.)*

Subsidiary:

Morflex, Inc. **(2)**
2110 Highpoint Rd.
Greensboro, NC 27403
Emp.: 100
Produce Citric Acid Esters & DEET
S.I.C.: 2869; 2879
Gary F. Taft *(Pres.)*

REILY ELECTRIC SUPPLY, INC.
3011 Lausat
Metairie, LA 70001
Tel.: 504-853-8888
Fax: 504-837-7320
Wholesale Distributor Electrical Supplies
S.I.C.: 5063
Timothy Reily *(Chm. Bd., Pres. & Chief Exec. Officer)*
Lester Vollenweider *(Treas.)*
Patrick Reily *(Sec.)*

Outside Service Firm(s):

Ernst & Young*(Auditors)*
4200 One Shell Square, 701 Poydras St.
New Orleans, LA 70139
Tel.: 504-581-4200

Whitney National Bank of New Orleans*(Major Banking Relationship)*
P.O. Box 61260,
New Orleans, LA 70161

Subsidiary:

Evans Electric Supply, Inc. **(1)**
1060 Nicholson Dr.
Baton Rouge, LA 70802
Tel.: 504-387-0486
Wholesale Distributor of Electrical Supplies
S.I.C.: 5063
A.D. Womack *(Gen. Mgr.)*

WILLIAM B. REILY & CO., INC.
640 Magazine St.
New Orleans, LA 70130
Tel.: 504-524-6131
Fax: 504-525-8355
Approx.Sls.: $175,000,000
Emp.: 800
Coffee & Tea, Mayonnaise, Vegetable Oil, Salad Dressings & Peanut Butter
S.I.C.: 2034; 2035; 2095; 2099; 2393; 2899
W.B. Reily III *(Pres.)*
J. Leach, Jr. *(V.P.-Fin.)*
Harold Herrmann *(Chief Fin. Officer & Controller)*
Steve Himel *(Human Resources Dir.)*
Bruce Bramen *(Mktg. Dir.)*

Computer Systems/Hardware:
IBM 4341

Outside Service Firm(s):

Arthur Andersen & Co.*(Auditors)*
201 St. Charles Ave., Ste. 4500
New Orleans, LA 70170

Northwestern National Life*(Group Insurer)*
20 Washington Ave. S.
Minneapolis, MN 55401

Monroe & Lemann*(Legal Firm)*
1424 Whitney Bldg.
New Orleans, LA 70130
Tel.: 504-586-1900

First National Bank of Commerce*(Major Banking Relationship)*
New Orleans, LA

Day, Ketterer, Raley, Wright & Rybolt*(Major Banking Relationship)*
800 William R. Day Bldg., 121 Cleveland Ave. So.
Canton, OH 44702
Tel.: 216-455-0173

First Union National Bank*(Major Banking Relationship)*
CMG-5, Two First Union Center
Charlotte, NC 28288-1154
Tel.: 704-374-2698
Fax: 704-374-6987

First Union National Bank*(Pension Manager)*
Two First Union Center
Charlotte, NC 28288-1154
Tel.: 704-374-2698

Divisions:

Caliente Chili, Inc. **(1)**
804 Rio Grande
Austin, TX 78701
Tel.: 512-472-6996
Approx.Sls.: $4,000,000
Emp.: 35
Wick Fowler's 2-Alarm & Family Style Chili Kits, Bean Seasoning, Taco Seasoning, Prepared Rice Dishes & Picante Sauces
S.I.C.: 2035; 2099
Tom Nall *(V.P.-Sls. & Mktg.)*

JFG Coffee Company **(1)**
3434 Mynatt Ave., NW
Knoxville, TN 37919
Tel.: 615-546-2120
Fax: 615-524-8725
Emp.: 150
JFG Special Coffee, JFG Instant Coffee, JFG Sabro Decaffeinated Regular & Instant Coffee, JFG Tea, Mayonnaise, Salad Dressing, Sandwich Spread, Thousand Island Dressing, Cole Slaw Dressing, Peanut Butter
S.I.C.: 2095; 2099
Larry Everett *(Pres. & Gen. Mgr.)*
Ken Canup *(Adv. Mgr.)*
Ken Christopher *(Sls. Mgr.)*
Don Jarnigan *(Pur. Agent)*

Luzianne Blue Plate Foods **(1)**
640 Magazine St.
New Orleans, LA 70130
Tel.: 504-524-6131
Fax: 504-525-8358
Approx.Sls.: $100,000,000
Emp.: 325
Manufacture Coffee, Tea, Mayonnaise & Salad Dressing, Cake Flour, Peanut Butter, Oil; Luzianne, RT, CDM, Herb Magic, Blue Plate Products, Bonus Blend, Red Label, Cajun Creole Dinners
S.I.C.: 2095; 2099; 2035; 2038; 2045
C. James McCarthy *(Pres.)*
W. Steve Frey *(V.P.-Mfg.)*
Michael Campbell *(V.P.-Sls.)*
John Watson *(V.P.-Fin.)*
Bruce B. Bramen *(V.P.-Mktg.)*
Douglas McDougall *(Mgr.-Sls. & Consumer Promotion)*
Steve Himel *(Personnel Mgr.)*
E.P. Randolph *(Pur. Agent)*
Joseph Mattingly *(Brand Mgr.)*

Standard Coffee Service **(1)**
640 Magazine St.
New Orleans, LA 70130
Tel.: 504-831-5341
Coffee Service
S.I.C.: 5963
G. King *(Gen. Mgr.)*

THE JOEY REIMAN AGENCY

THE JOEY REIMAN AGENCY
(Formerly Babbit & Reiman Advertising Inc.)
3060 Peachtree Rd.
Atlanta, GA 30305
Tel.: 404-365-0550
Fax: 404-365-9308
Year Founded: 1986
Approx.Billings: $55,396,000
Emp.: 78
Travel & Lodgings, Packaged Goods, Retail, Restaurants, Automotive, Media, Consumer Services
Joey Reiman *(Chm. Bd. & Chief Exec. Officer)*
Michael Gaffney *(Pres. & Chief Oper. Officer)*
Fred Raimer *(Sr. V.P., Dir. Fin.)*
Lisa White *(Sr. V.P., Acct. Services Dir.)*
Carolyn Davenport *(Sr. Exec. Asst.)*

REIMEL CARTER ADVERTISING, INC.
Academy House, 1420 Locust St.
Philadelphia, PA 19102
Tel.: 215-735-3200
Fax: 215-735-0422/6055
Year Founded: 1962
Approx.Billings: $32,200,000
Emp.: 34
T.L. Reimel *(Pres. & Treas.)*
Edward P. Carter *(Exec. V.P. & Sec.)*
Christopher Posthauer *(V.P., Fin. & Opers.)*

REINALT-THOMAS CORP.
(d/b/a Discount Tire Co.)
903 Airport Dr.
Ann Arbor, MI 48108
Tel.: 313-769-6870 **MI**
Fax: 313-769-6871
Year Founded: 1960
Approx.Sls.: $400,000,000
Emp.: 1,000
Fiscal Year-end: 12/31/90
Retail Auto/Truck Tires; Real Estate Investments
S.I.C.: 5531; 6798
Bruce T. Halle *(Chm. Bd. & Pres.)*
T.R. Von Voightlander *(Exec. V.P.)*
Robert Holman *(V.P.-Fin.)*
Timothy J. Schafer *(Asst. V.P.-Fin.)*
James Silhasek *(Gen. Counsel)*

Computer Systems/Hardware:
IBM AS/400

Outside Service Firm(s):

Deloitte & Touche*(Auditors)*
2901 North Central Ave., Ste. 1200
Phoenix, AZ 85012
Tel.: 602-234-5100
Fax: 602-234-5186

Aetna Life & Casualty*(Group Insurer)*
Fort Wayne, IN

Plattner, Schneidman & Schneider*(Legal Firm)*
Phoenix, AZ

First of America Bank*(Major Banking Relationship)*
Ann Arbor, MI

National Bank of Detroit*(Major Banking Relationship)*
611 Woodward Ave.
Detroit, MI 48226

REINKE MANUFACTURING CO., INC.
101 Reinke Rd.
Deshler, NE 68340
Mailing Address:
P.O. Box 566,
Deshler, NE 68340
Tel.: 402-365-7251
Fax: 402-365-4370
Year Founded: 1954
Approx.Sls.: $40,000,000
Emp.: 150
Export
Agricultural Irrigation Equipment; Steel Tubing & Oil Casing; Truck Trailers
S.I.C.: 3523; 3715; 3449
Ronald Schardt *(Chm. Bd., Chief Exec. Officer & Chief Oper. Officer)*
Willis Kettelhut *(Pres.)*
Victor Johnson *(Chief Fin. Officer, V.P.-Fin. & Treas.)*
Bob Friehe *(Exec. V.P.)*
Lavon O. Bohling *(V.P.-Mktg.)*
Josef Kripal *(V.P. & Dir.-Pur.)*

Computer Systems/Hardware:
IBM

Outside Service Firm(s):

First National Bank*(Major Banking Relationship)*
Omaha, NE

REITMAN INDUSTRIES
10 Patton Dr.
West Caldwell, NJ 07006
Tel.: 201-228-5100
Fax: 201-403-8679
Approx.Sls.: $80,000,000
Emp.: 250
Wholesale & Import Wine & Spirits
S.I.C.: 5182
Margaret R. Carter *(Chm. Bd.)*
Howard Jacobs *(Pres.)*
David C. Lowenstein *(Exec. V.P.)*
S. Leroy Frankel *(Sr. V.P.)*
Dennis A. Resnick *(V.P.-Sls. & Mktg.)*
Dennis M. Portsmore *(V.P., Treas. & Dir.-Data Processing)*

Outside Service Firm(s):

KPMG Peat Marwick*(Auditors)*
150 John F. Kennedy Pkwy.
Short Hills, NJ 07078
Tel.: 201-467-9650

Lowenstein, Sandler, Kohl, Fisher & Boylan*(Legal Firm)*
65 Livingston Ave.
Roseland, NJ 07068
Tel.: 908-992-8700

United Jersey Bank*(Major Banking Relationship)*
Caldwell, NJ

RELA, INC.
6175 Longbow Dr.
Boulder, CO 80301
Tel.: 303-530-2626 **CO**
Fax: 303-520-2866
Year Founded: 1977
Approx.Sls.: $10,000,000
Emp.: 150
Fiscal Year-end: 6/30/92
Export
Integrated Contract Design, Development & Manufacture of Medical Devices, Instruments & Systems
S.I.C.: 3823; 3829
Dean Leffingwell *(Chm. & Chief Exec. Officer)*
John Greenbaum *(Pres. & Chief Oper. Officer)*
Dr. Ammon Balaster *(Exec. V.P.)*
Bruce Arfmann *(Chief Fin. Officer & Treas.)*
Kevin Hocum *(Controller)*
Marc Raizman *(Dir.-Mktg., Intl. Bus.)*
Diana Sadighi *(Mgr.-Human Resources)*
Glenn Scott *(Mgr.-Materials)*
Randel Frazier *(Mgr.-National Sls.)*
Bonnie Norman *(Mgr.-Quality Assurance)*

No. of Mfg. Plants/Facilities: 1

Computer Systems/Hardware:
DEC, Apple, IBM

Outside Service Firm(s):

Deloitte & Touche*(Auditors)*
1560 Broadway, Ste. 1800
Denver, CO 80202-5626
Tel.: 303-837-3000
Fax: 303-825-0567

Chrisman, Bynum & Johnson, P.C.*(Legal Firm)*
1401 Walnut St., Ste. 500
Boulder, CO 80302
Tel.: 303-444-4820

United Bank of Colorado*(Major Banking Relationship)*
Boulder, CO

Divisions:

RELA Manufacturing Division **(1)**
6175 Longbow Dr.
Boulder, CO 80301
Tel.: 303-530-2626
Fax: 303-530-2866
Emp.: 40
Electronic & Electromechanical Assembly
John Greenbaum *(Pres. & Chief Oper. Officer)*
Stephanie Acton *(Mgr.-Mfg.)*
Glenn Scott *(Mgr.-Matls.)*

RELA Model And Machine Shop **(1)**
6175 Longbow Dr.
Boulder, CO 80301
Tel.: 303-530-2626
Capabilites Include Conventional & Computer Numerical-controlled Prototype & Production Machining, Precision Grinding,
S.I.C.: 8734
Glenn Scott *(Gen. Mgr.)*

RELA Product Development Div. (PDD) **(1)**
6175 Longbow Dr.
Boulder, CO 80301
Tel.: 303-530-2626
Fax: 303-530-2866
Approx.Sls.: $10,000,000
Emp.: 75
Fiscal Year-end: 6/30/92
Product Development For Clients in Medical Devices, Instruments, Systems
S.I.C.: 7389; 8734
Dean A. Leffingwell *(Chm. Bd. & Chief Exec. Officer)*
John Greenbaum *(Pres. & Chief Oper. Officer)*
Bruce L. Arfmann *(Chief Fin. Officer)*
Dr. Ammon N. Balaster *(Exec. V.P.)*
Kevin Hocum *(Controller)*
Marc Raizman *(Dir.-Mktg.)*
Diana Sadighi *(Mgr.-Human Resources)*
Glenn Scott *(Mgr.-Matls.)*
Randel Frazier *(Dir.)*
Lief Leirfallom *(Dir.)*
Bill Wood *(Dir.)*

RELIABLE AUTOMATIC SPRINKLER CO., INC.
525 N. MacQuesten Pkwy.
Mount Vernon, NY 10552
Tel.: 914-668-3470
Fax: 914-668-2936
Approx.Sls.: $17,000,000
Emp.: 300
Mfr. of Automatic Fire Sprinkler & Specialty Fire Protection Equipment
S.I.C.: 3569
Frank J. Fee III *(Pres. & Treas.)*
Kevin T. Fee *(Exec. V.P.)*
John A. Beukema *(V.P.-Tech. Services)*
L. Blum *(V.P.-Engrng.)*
Eugene J. Carbine *(V.P.-Fin.)*
Candida M. Fee *(V.P.-Indus. Rels.)*
Michael R. Fee *(V.P.-Sls. Opers.)*
William Kirkpatrick *(V.P.-Mfg.)*
Paul Derounian *(Gen. Counsel)*
Wayne Koppe *(Mgr.-Prod.)*
Tom Wagener *(Mgr.-Pur.)*

Outside Service Firm(s):

Emanuel Colodny & Co.*(Auditors)*
Bronxville, NY

Chemical Banking Corp.*(Major Banking Relationship)*
277 Park Ave.
New York, NY 10041
Tel.: 212-310-6407
Fax: 212-310-4526

RELIABLE CASTINGS CORPORATION
3530 Spring Grove Ave.
Cincinnati, OH 45223
Tel.: 513-541-2627
Fax: 513-541-5696
Year Founded: 1922
Approx.Sls.: $25,000,000
Emp.: 260
Aluminum & Bronze Sand Castings, Aluminum Permanent Mold Castings, Wood & Metal Patterns
S.I.C.: 3365; 3543
R.J. Kuhn *(Pres.)*
Larry Smiley *(Exec. V.P.)*
Tom Barton *(V.P.-Fin. & Admin.)*
C.B. Yellig *(V.P.-Mktg. & Sls.)*
Terry Dean *(Dir.-Pur.)*
Kathy Breeze *(Dir.-Human Resources)*

Outside Service Firm(s):

Fifth Third Bank*(Investment Banker)*
Corporate Trust Services, 38 Fountain Square Plaza
Cincinnati, OH 45263

Graydon, Head & Ritchey*(Legal Firm)*
1900 Fifth Third Center
Cincinnati, OH 45202
Tel.: 513-621-6464

Fifth Third Bank*(Major Banking Relationship)*
Corporate Trust Services, 38 Fountain Square Plaza
Cincinnati, OH 45263

RELIABLE CHEVROLET
800 N. Central Expwy.
Richardson, TX 75080
Mailing Address:
P.O. Box 831240,
Richardson, TX 75083-1240
Tel.: 214-952-1500
Fax: 214-952-8171
Approx.Sls.: $177,000,000
Emp.: 265
27 Automobile Dealerships
S.I.C.: 5511
Cecil Van Tyle *(Owner)*
Darrel McCutcheon *(V.P. & Exec. Mgr.)*

THE RELIABLE CORP.
1001 W. Van Buren St.
Chicago, IL 60607
Tel.: 312-666-1800
Fax: 312-666-6435
Approx.Sls.: $150,000,000
Emp.: 550
Office Products Distribution
S.I.C.: 5112
Merrill Zenner *(Chm. Bd.)*
Gary Rovansek *(Pres.)*
Jim Jones *(Chief Fin. Officer)*

Principal(s):
Merrill Zenner

Outside Service Firm(s):

Arthur Andersen & Co.*(Auditors)*
33 W. Monroe St.
Chicago, IL 60603-4067
Tel.: 312-580-0033
Fax: 312-507-6748

Avery, Hodes, Costello & Burman*(Legal Firm)*
Chicago, IL

American National Bank & Trust Co.*(Major Banking Relationship)*
Chicago, IL

Harris Trust & Savings Bank*(Major Banking Relationship)*
111 W. Monroe St.
Chicago, IL 60690
Tel.: 312-461-2265
Tel.: 800-858-0840

RELIABLE KNITTING WORKS
233 E. Chicago St.
Milwaukee, WI 53202
Mailing Address:
P. O. Box 563
Milwaukee, WI 53201
Tel.: 414-272-5084
Tel.: 800-336-6876
Fax: 414-272-6443
Year Founded: 1911
Emp.: 210
Export
Infants, Childrens, Teens, Misses & Men's Knit Headwear; Scuffie Slippers, Mukluk Slipper Sox; Polar Boots; Knit Golf Club Covers
S.I.C.: 2253; 2252
Isabelle Polacheck *(Pres.)*
Morton Blutstein *(Exec. V.P. & Gen. Mgr.)*
Jerry Polacheck *(Exec. V.P.-Sls.)*
Cindy Evanoff *(V.P.-Admin.)*
Rita Greer *(V.P.-Adv. & Design)*
Al Steinacker *(V.P.-Quality Control)*
Mark Blutstein *(Mgr.-Sls.)*
Mark Zelinski *(Mgr.-Pur.)*
Barbara Blutstein *(Sec.)*

Computer Systems/Hardware:
MAI Basic Four

Outside Service Firm(s):

Ernst & Young*(Auditors)*
111 E. Kilbourn Ave., Ste. 900
Milwaukee, WI 53202
Tel.: 414-273-5900

M & I Northern Bank*(Major Banking Relationship)*
Brookfield, WI

Divisions:

Halper Bros. **(1)**
233 E. Chicago St.
Milwaukee, WI 53201
Tel.: 414-272-5084
Tel.: 800-336-6876
Fax: 414-272-6443
Import Export
High Fashion Ski Accessories
S.I.C.: 2253
Morton Blutstein *(Exec. V.P. & Pur. Mgr.)*
Cynthia Evanoff *(V.P.-Admin.)*
Rita Greer *(V.P.-Design)*
Jerry Polacheck *(V.P.-Sls.)*

Penthouse Knitting Mills **(1)**
233 E. Chicago St.
Milwaukee, WI 53201
Tel.: 414-272-5084
Tel.: 800-336-6876
Fax: 414-272-6443
Export
Computer Systems/Hardware:
MAI Basic Four
Ski Hats, Scarves & Accessories
S.I.C.: 2253
Jerry Polacheck *(V.P.-Sls.)*
Cynthia Evanoff *(V.P.-Admin.)*
Rita Greer *(V.P.-Design)*
Morton Blutstein *(V.P.-Mfg.)*
Mark Zelinski *(Pur. Mgr.)*

RELIABLE STORES, INC.
6301 Stevens Forest Rd.
Columbia, MD 21046
Tel.: 301-381-9650 **DE**
Fax: 301-381-9663
Year Founded: 1900
Assets: $123,812,000
Liabilities: $117,812,000
Net Worth: $6,000,000
Sales Range: $100-499 Million
Emp.: 2,400
Fiscal Year-end: 1/31/91
78 Retail Furniture, Jewelry & Specialty Stores
S.I.C.: 5944; 5712
Jules Ross *(Chm. Bd.)*
Richard M. Barnett *(Pres. & Chief Exec. Officer)*
Thomas R. Guercio *(V.P., Treas. & Chief Fin. Officer)*
Kenneth Luchs *(V.P.-Mktg., Sls. & Adv.)*
W. Ben Ayers *(V.P.-Credit)*
Carmela Leone Bell *(Gen. Counsel & Sec.)*
Howard Erdrich *(Dir.-Msdg. & Pur.)*
Marion Nicholson *(Dir.-Personnel Training & Devel.)*
Robert Amaro *(Dir.-Data Processing)*

Computer Systems/Hardware:
Magnuson; IBM

Outside Service Firm(s):

KPMG Peat Marwick*(Auditors)*
111 S. Calvert St.
Baltimore, MD 21202
Tel.: 410-783-8300

First National Bank of Maryland*(Major Banking Relationship)*
25 S. Charles St.
Baltimore, MD 21201
Tel.: 410-244-4025

Furniture Stores Divisions:

Hub Furniture Co. **(1)**
6301 Stevens Forest Rd.
Columbia, MD 21045
Tel.: 410-997-9650
22 Retail Stores
S.I.C.: 5712
Richard H. Barnett *(Pres. & Chief Exec. Officer)*

The Kline Furniture Co. **(1)**
6301 Stevens Forest Rd.
Columbia, MD 21045
Tel.: 410-997-9650
4 Retail Stores
S.I.C.: 5712
Richard H. Barnett *(Pres. & Chief Exec. Officer)*

Jewelry Stores Divisions:

B&L Jewelry Co. **(1)**
6301 Stevens Forest Rd.
Columbia, MD 21045
Tel.: 410-381-9650
2 Stores
S.I.C.: 5944
Richard M. Barnett *(Pres. & Chief Exec. Officer)*

Barclay & Sons **(1)**
6301 Stevens Forest Rd.
Columbia, MD 21045
Tel.: 410-381-9650
7 Retail Stores
S.I.C.: 5944
Richard M. Barnett *(Pres. & Chief Exec. Officer)*

Barlow & Eaton **(1)**
6301 Stevens Forest Rd.
Columbia, MD 21045
Tel.: 410-997-9650
10 Retail Stores
S.I.C.: 5944
Richard M. Barnett *(Pres. & Chief Exec. Officer)*

Castleberg's **(1)**
6301 Stevens Forest Rd.
Columbia, MD 21045
Tel.: 410-997-9650
3 Retail Stores
S.I.C.: 5944
Richard M. Barnett *(Pres. & Chief Exec. Officer)*

Henebrys **(1)**
6301 Stevens Forest Rd.
Columbia, MD 21046
Tel.: 301-997-9650
6 Retail Stores
S.I.C.: 5944
Richard M. Barnett *(Pres. & Chief Exec. Officer)*

Morton's Jewelry Co. **(1)**
6301 Stevens Forest Rd.
Columbia, MD 21045
Tel.: 410-997-9650
4 Retail Stores
S.I.C.: 5944
Richard M. Barnett *(Pres. & Chief Exec. Officer)*

Relco **(1)**
6301 Stevens Forest Rd.
Columbia, MD 21045
Tel.: 410-997-9650
S.I.C.: 5944

S&N Katz Jewelers **(1)**
6301 Stevens Forest Rd.
Columbia, MD 21045
Tel.: 410-997-9650
10 Retail Stores
S.I.C.: 5944
Richard M. Barnett *(Pres. & Chief Exec. Officer)*

Scott Jewelers **(1)**
6301 Stevens Forest Rd.
Columbia, MD 21045
Tel.: 410-997-9650
5 Retail Stores
S.I.C.: 5944
Richard M. Barnett *(Pres. & Chief Exec. Officer)*

Weiss Jewelers **(1)**
6301 Stevens Forest Rd.
Columbia, MD 21045
Tel.: 410-997-9650
2 Stores
S.I.C.: 5944
Richard M. Barnett *(Pres. & Chief Exec. Officer)*

Distribution Centers:

Hub Furniture Store **(1)**
800 Tidewater Dr.
Norfolk, VA 23504
S.I.C.: 4212
Richard H. Barnett *(Pres. & Chief Exec. Officer)*

Washington Area Distribution Center **(1)**
3400 Pennsy Dr.
Landover, MD 20785
Tel.: 202-624-8600 (100%)
S.I.C.: 4212

RELIANCE ELEVATOR COMPANY
1101 W. Adams St.
Chicago, IL 60607
Tel.: 312-666-4022 **IL**
Fax: 312-666-9285
Approx.Sls.: $11,000,000
Emp.: 136
Fiscal Year-end: 10/31/91
Inspection, Service & Repair Of Elevators; Elevator Installation & Conversion
S.I.C.: 7699; 1796
Thomas Grunnah *(Chm. Bd.)*
Thomas B. LaPorte *(Pres.)*
Don Miller *(V.P.-Opers.)*
Judith Grunnah *(Treas.)*
Henry J. Hofman *(Controller & Sec.)*

Outside Service Firm(s):

Cray Kaiser, Ltd.*(Auditors)*
Oak Brook, IL

Schoenberg, Fisher & Newman, Ltd.*(Legal Firm)*
Chicago, IL

RELIANCE MEDICAL PRODUCTS, INC.
3535 Kings Mills Rd.
Mason, OH 45040
Tel.: 513-398-3937
Year Founded: 1898
Approx.Sls.: $13,000,000
Emp.: 45
Mfr. of Medical & Optical Equipment
S.I.C.: 3841; 3827
J. Morgan Stobie *(V.P.)*
Pam Nelson *(Natl. Sls. Mgr.)*
Ray Grandstaff *(Personnel Mgr.)*
Steven Juenger *(Dir.-Mktg.)*

RELIANCE STEEL & ALUMINUM CO.
2550 E. 25th St.
Los Angeles, CA 90058
Tel.: 213-582-2272 **CA**
Fax: 213-582-2801
Year Founded: 1939
Assets: $146,005,000
Earnings: $9,171,000
Liabilities: $81,400,000
Net Worth: $64,605,000
Approx.Sls.: $371,716,000
Emp.: 950
Fiscal Year-end: 12/31/90
Import
Metal Distribution
S.I.C.: 5051
William T. Gimbel *(Chm. Bd. & Chief Exec. Officer)*
Joe D. Crider *(Pres. & Chief Oper. Officer)*
David H. Hannah *(Chief Fin. Officer & Exec. V.P.)*
Thomas E. Anding *(V.P.)*
Donald M. Hollar *(V.P.)*
Gregg J. Mollins *(V.P.)*
Yvette M. Schiotis *(Sec.)*

No. of Mfg. Plants/Facilities: 18
No. of U.S. Offices: 19

Computer Systems/Hardware:
IBM

Outside Service Firm(s):

Ernst & Young*(Auditors)*
515 S. Flower St.
Los Angeles, CA 90071
Tel.: 213-621-1666

Hartford Life Insurance Co.*(Commercial Insurance Carrier)*
Hartford, CT 06104-2999

Aetna Life & Casualty*(Group Insurer)*
151 Farmington Avenue
Hartford, CT 06156
Tel.: 203-273-2128
Fax: 203-729-4295

Arter, Hadden, Lawler, Felix & Hall*(Legal Firm)*
Los Angeles, CA

Security Pacific Corporation*(Major Banking Relationship)*
Security Pacific Plaza
Los Angeles, CA 90071
Tel.: 213-345-6211
Fax: 213-625-0809

Subsidiary:

Valex Corp. **(1)**
6080 Leland St.
Ventura, CA 93003
Tel.: 805-658-0944
Emp.: 75
Stainless Steel Tubing, Electropolishing & Component Manufacturing
S.I.C.: 3312
Robert Rains *(Pres.)*

RELIEF PRINTING CORPORATION
5160 Rivergrade Rd.
Baldwin Park, CA 91706
Tel.: 818-814-8181
Fax: 818-814-2666
Sales Range: $10-19 Million
Emp.: 165
Business Cards & Quality Stationery
S.I.C.: 2759; 2754
Jerry Bosco *(Pres.)*
Ken Klein *(Gen. Mgr.)*

Outside Service Firm(s):

Sanwa Bank*(Major Banking Relationship)*
Baldwin, CA

REMARKS, INC.
7155 Post Rd.
Dublin, OH 43017
Mailing Address:
P.O. Box 1802
Dublin, OH 43017
Tel.: 614-889-5867 **OH**
Fax: 614-761-1020
Year Founded: 1961
Sales Range: $80-99 Million
Emp.: 270
Fiscal Year-end: 12/31/91
Distributes Fresh, Cured Or Smoked Meats, Dairy Products, Fresh Fish, Seafoods & Packaged Frozen Goods
S.I.C.: 5147; 5143; 5146; 5142
Corporate Giving Program: Corporate Support of United Way
Robert M. Stewart, Sr. *(Chm. Bd. & Chief Exec. Officer)*
Malcom Graves, Jr. *(Pres.)*
Robert Stewart, Jr. *(V.P.)*
Thomas Kottenstette *(V.P.)*
William Davis *(V.P.)*
Emmy Rode *(Treas.)*
Scott E. Hanhart *(Asst. Treas.)*
LouAnn Jones *(Controller)*
Clarence Carrel *(Sec.)*
Principal(s):
Robert M. Stewart, Sr.
Malcom Graves, Jr.
William Davis

No. of Mfg. Plants/Facilities: 4

Computer Systems/Hardware:
Honeywell-Bull

Remarks, Inc.—(Continued)

Outside Service Firm(s):

Haemmerle, Heximer, Harvey & Co.*(Auditors)*
Columbus, OH

Campbell, Hornbeck, Chilcoate & Veach*(Legal Firm)*
Columbus, OH

BancOhio National Bank*(Major Banking Relationship)*
Columbus, OH

Division:

Remarks Co. (1)
P.O. Box 29066
Indianapolis, IN 46229
Tel.: 317-894-1551
Roger Parcels *(V.P. & Gen. Mgr.)*
Scott Dissinger *(Mgr.-Mktg.)*
Dan Stone *(Field Sls. Mgr.)*
Brad McCalla *(Buyer)*

REMCO ENTERPRISES, INC.
10333 Richman Ave., Ste. 300
Houston, TX 77042
Tel.: 713-977-2288
Fax: 713-266-3412
Approx.Sls.: $80,000,000
Emp.: 700
Fiscal Year-end: 10/31/91
TV & Stereo Rental
S.I.C.: 7359
George Fink *(Pres.)*
Cara Brye *(V.P.-Mktg.)*

REMCO TOYS
1107 Broadway, Ste. 808
New York, NY 10010
Tel.: 212-675-3427
Fax: 212-243-4271
Emp.: 80
Manufacture & Distribute Toys
S.I.C.: 3942; 5092
Marvin Azrak *(Owner)*
Ezra Hamway *(Pres.)*
Ed Bachman *(Exec. V.P.)*
Bernie Libou *(V.P.-Sls.)*
Steve Rosenthal *(V.P.-Mktg.)*
Harvey Berlinger *(Controller)*

Subsidiary:

Remco Baby (1)
1107 Broadway, Ste. 808
New York, NY 10010
Tel.: 212-675-3427
Manufacture & Distribute Toys
S.I.C.: 3942; 5092

REMCOR PRODUCTS CO.
500 Regency Dr.
Glendale Heights, IL 60139
Tel.: 708-980-6900
Approx.Sls.: $25,000,000
Emp.: 180
Manufacturing Engineers: Refrigeration Products, Icemakers, Ice Dispensers, Refrigerated Liquid Chillers & Temperature Control Units
S.I.C.: 3585
R.M. Koeneman *(Pres.)*
James P. Barry *(V.P.-Sls. & Mktg.)*
Ben Miller *(V.P.-Engrng.)*
Robert Rzeppa *(Natl. Sls. Mgr.)*
D. Dobbs *(Dir.-Pur.)*

REMINGTON APPAREL, INC.
1217 S. 13th St.
Wilmington, NC 28401
Tel.: 919-763-6543
Approx.Sls.: $15,000,000
Emp.: 250
Mfr. of Men's & Women's Access.
S.I.C.: *2311; 2321; 2322; 2323; 2325; 2331; 2337; 2335; 2342; 2353*
Ron Katzoff *(Chm. Bd.)*
Ray Freeman *(Chief Oper. Officer)*
Terry Cockman *(V.P.-Fin.)*

Division:

Remington Apparel (1)
1217 S. 13th St.
Wilmington, NC 28401
Tel.: 919-763-6543
Men's & Boys' Neckwear
S.I.C.: 2323
Mel Fischkoff *(V.P.)*

REMINGTON PRODUCTS INC.
60 Main St.
Bridgeport, CT 06604
Tel.: 203-367-4400 **DE**
Fax: 203-366-6039
Year Founded: 1979
Approx.Sls.: $250,000,000
Emp.: 1,500
Fiscal Year-end: 9/30/91
Import Export
Manufacture Electric Shavers, Shaving Aids & Air Purifiers; Retailer Knives & Shavers; Lectro Blades, Pool Alarm, Grooming Products
S.I.C.: 3634; 5722; 3822
Victor Kiam II *(Chm. Bd., Pres., Chief Exec. & Chief Oper. Officer)*
Glenn Bell *(V.P.- Adv.)*
Michael J. Duda *(V.P.-Personnel)*
Bruce Gold *(V.P. & Gen. Mgr.)*
Alan Lipson *(V.P. & Gen. Counsel)*
Frank Stack *(V.P.-Sls.)*
Roy Henry *(Chief Acctg. Officer)*
Alex Novak *(Chief Fin. Officer)*

Principal(s):
Victor Kiam II

No. of Mfg. Plants/Facilities: 1
No. of U.S. Offices: 5

Computer Systems/Hardware:
Univac; Prime; Wang

Outside Service Firm(s):

Grant Thornton*(Auditors)*
Stamford, CT

Travelers Insurance Co.*(Commercial Insurance Carrier)*
1 Tower Square
Hartford, CT 06183
Tel.: 203-222-7821
Fax: 203-222-7813

Travelers Insurance Co.*(Group Insurer)*
1 Tower Square
Hartford, CT 06183-2492
Tel.: 203-277-4542
Fax: 203-277-5038

Bank of Montreal*(International Bank Affiliate)*
Toronto, ON Canada

Barclays Bank plc*(International Bank Affiliate)*
300 Galleria Parkway NW, Ste. 800
Atlanta, GA 30339
Tel.: 404-859-2400

Mellon Bank, N.A.*(International Bank Affiliate)*
Mellon Bank Center, 1735 Market St.
Philadelphia, PA 19101-7899

Jones, Day, Reavis & Pogue*(Legal Firm)*
Ste. 3000, 355 S. Grand Ave.
Los Angeles, CA 90071

Mellon Bank, N.A.*(Major Banking Relationship)*
Mellon Bank Center, 1735 Market St.
Philadelphia, PA 19101-7899

Non-U.S. Holdings:

Remington Australia (1)
548 Clayton Rd.
Melbourne, Australia 3168
Tel.: 03 558 0688
Grahm Kimpton *(Chief Oper. Officer)*

Remington Consumer Products, Ltd. (1)
Apex Tower 7 High St.,
New Malden, Surrey KT3 4DL, United Kingdom
Tel.: 011-44-1-942-9361
Geoff Hoddinott *(Mgr.)*

Remington Products (Canada) Inc. (1)
2254 S. Sheridan Way
Mississauga, ON L5J 2M6, Canada
Tel.: 416-822-7222
Harry Calvert *(Mgr.)*

Rempro Trading, Ltd. (1)
GPO Box 4929,
Hong Kong, Hong Kong
Tel.: 825-5-840-1188

REMMELE ENGINEERING, INC.
1211 Pierce Butler Rd.
Saint Paul, MN 55104
Tel.: 612-645-3451
Fax: 612-642-5668
Year Founded: 1949
Approx.Sls.: $60,000,000
Emp.: 435
Import Export
Mfr. of Tools, Dies, Special Machines & Precision Parts
S.I.C.: 3544; 3559
William J. Saul *(Chm. Bd.)*
Thomas R. Moore *(Pres. & Chief Exec. Officer)*
Bert Casper *(V.P.-Mktg.)*
Tom Dolezal *(V.P.)*
Phillip W. Foster *(V.P.-Fin. & Treas.)*
John Herzog *(V.P.-Sls.)*
Bill Iacoe *(V.P.)*
Mike Pudil *(V.P.)*
Charles J. Jungman *(Sec.)*
Mike Bates *(Dir.-Personnel)*
Charles W. Nagle *(Mgr.-Data Processing)*

No. of Mfg. Plants/Facilities: 5

Outside Service Firm(s):

KPMG Peat Marwick*(Auditors)*
4200 Norwest Center, 90 S. 7th St.
Minneapolis, MN 55402
Tel.: 612-341-2222

Dorsey & Whitney*(Legal Firm)*
2200 First Bank Place East
Minneapolis, MN 55402

Midway National Bank*(Major Banking Relationship)*
Minneapolis, MN

RENA-WARE DISTRIBUTORS INC.
8383 158th Ave., N.E.
Redmond, WA 98052
Tel.: 206-881-6171
Fax: 206-882-7500
Approx.Sls.: $100,000,000
Emp.: 1,200
Direct Sales of Cookware & Other Goods
S.I.C.: 5023; 5963
O.W. Zylstra *(Chm. Bd. & Chief Exec. Officer)*
Philip Lindquist *(Pres.)*
Robert Spencer *(Exec. V.P.-Sls.)*
Brad Rich *(V.P.-Opers. & Treas.)*
Mike Mossman *(Controller)*
Rod Jacobson *(Dir.-Data Processing)*

Outside Service Firm(s):

Ernst & Young*(Auditors)*
999 Third Av., Ste. 3500
Seattle, WA 98104
Tel.: 206-621-1800
Fax: 206-682-1234

Bogle & Gates*(Legal Firm)*
Two Union Square, 601 Union St.
Seattle, WA 98101-2322
Tel.: 206-682-5151

Rainier National Bank*(Major Banking Relationship)*
P.O.Box 24407
Seattle, WA 98124

Non-U.S. Holding:

Rena-Ware GmbH (1)
Seftigenstrasse 300B P.O. Box 19, CH-3084
Wabern, Switzerland
Tel.: 031 54 24 16 (100%)
Telex: 912 375
Direct Sales of Cookware & Other Household Goods
S.I.C.: 5963; 5023

RENAISSANCE PUBLISHING CO., INC.
E. 7th
Auburn, IN 46706
Tel.: 219-925-1700
Fax: 219-925-5067
Approx.Sls.: $25,000,000
Emp.: 400
Fiscal Year-end: 12/31/90
Calendars, Funeral Director Service Line, Business Gifts, Promotional Aids, Self Erasing Slates
S.I.C.: 3993; 2741; 3999
Jeffrey Meyer *(Pres.)*
Clair Recker *(V.P.-Mfg.)*
Steve Linham *(V.P.-Sls.)*
Linda Moore Linham *(V.P.-Mktg.)*
John Schimmoller *(Sec. & Treas.)*

RENCO GROUP
45 Rockefeller Plaza
New York, NY 10111
Tel.: 212-541-6000
Fax: 212-541-6197
Approx.Sls.: $1,000,000,000
Steel Production
S.I.C.: 3312; 3316; 2514; 3171; 3496; 5012; 8711
Ira Leon Rennert *(Pres. & Chief Exec. Officer)*
Roger Fay *(V.P.-Fin.)*

Subsidiaries:

AM General Corporation (1)
105 N. Niles Ave.
South Bend, IN 46617-2705
Tel.: 219-237-6222
Supplier of Tactical Wheeled Military Vehicles
S.I.C.: 3711; 5012

AM General Corporation (1)
13200 McInley Hwy.
Mishawaka, IN 46545
Tel.: 219-256-1581
Military Vehicles & Car Bodies
S.I.C.: 3711
Andre Fritz *(V.P.)*

AM General Corporation (1)
1428 W. Henry St.
Indianapolis, IN 46221
Tel.: 317-632-5575
S.I.C.: 3312
Robert A. Moore *(Plant Mgr.)*

AM General Corporation (1)
P.O. Box 728,
Mishawaka, IN 46546
S.I.C.: 3312
Ben Taylor *(Sr. Mgr.)*

AM General Corporation (1)
11900 Hubbard Dr.
Livonia, MI 48150
Tel.: 313-522-4200
Development & Technological Services
S.I.C.: 8711
Fred Oswald *(Mgr.-Admin. Services)*

AM General Corporation (1)
2345 Crystal Dr., Ste. 808
Arlington, VA 22202
Tel.: 703-418-4005
S.I.C.: 5012
J. Paul Gomez *(Dir.-Washington Opers.)*

RENFRO CORP.
661 Linville Rd.
Mount Airy, NC 27030
Tel.: 919-789-5531 **NC**
Year Founded: 1921
Approx.Sls.: $109,000,000
Emp.: 2,250
Import Export
Manufacture & Wholesale Socks
S.I.C.: 2252; 5137; 5136
Robert E. Merritt *(Chm. Bd.)*
W.C. Nichols *(Pres. & Chief Exec. Officer)*
Andrew Kilby *(Chief Fin. Officer & V.P.)*
David Beal *(V.P.-Human Resources)*
Mike Bowman *(V.P.-Opers.)*
Harold Stone, Jr. *(V.P.-Sls. & Mktg.)*

Outside Service Firm(s):

Petree Stockton & Robinson*(Legal Firm)*
1001 W. Fourth St.
Winston-Salem, NC 27101
Tel.: 919-725-2351

NationsBank Carolinas*(Major Banking Relationship)*
One NCNB Plaza T18-7
Charlotte, NC 28255

RENKEN BOAT MANUFACTURING CO.
1750 Signal Point Rd.
Charleston, SC 29412
Tel.: 803-795-1150 **SC**
Fax: 803-795-6854
Year Founded: 1958
Approx.Sls.: $30,000,000
Emp.: 190
Fiscal Year-end: 12/31/91
Import Export
Boat Building & Repairing
S.I.C.: 3732
Carl E. Renken *(Pres. & Chief Exec. Officer)*
Kenny Renken, Jr. *(Exec V.P.)*
Fred Renken *(Plant Mgr.)*
Helen Helms *(Controller)*
Ed Renken *(Dir.-Mktg.)*
William E. Mitchell *(Dir.-Sls.)*
Bob Montgomery *(Dir.-Pur.)*
Mike Kelly *(Quality Control Mgr.)*

Computer Systems/Hardware:
Contel

Outside Service Firm(s):

South Carolina National Bank*(Major Banking Relationship)*
Charleston, SC

RENNOC CORPORATION
3501 Southeast Blvd.
Vineland, NJ 08360-7789
Tel.: 609-327-5400
Fax: 609-825-3583
Sales Range: $20-39 Million
Emp.: 500
Christmas Novelties & Athletic Jackets
S.I.C.: 2329; 2339; 3999
Jean Contravasso *(Gen. Mgr.)*

Outside Service Firm(s):

Hass & Company*(Auditors)*
Philadelphia, PA

Philadelphia National Bank*(Major Banking Relationship)*
Philadelphia, PA

RENOSOL CORP.
1512 Woodland Dr.
Saline, MI 48176
Mailing Address:
P.O. Box 1424
Ann Arbor, MI 48106
Tel.: 313-429-5418
Fax: 313-429-5351
Year Founded: 1981
Approx.Sls.: $30,000,000
Fiscal Year-end: 12/31/91
Export
Manufacture Custom Formulated Vinyl Plastisol & Urethane Parts
S.I.C.: 3069
Warren E. Wright *(Chm Bd.)*
Douglas Peck *(Vice Chm.)*
James Goforth *(Treas.)*

No. of Mfg. Plants/Facilities: 3

Outside Service Firm(s):

Ernst & Young*(Auditors)*
Saline, MI

THE RENOVATOR'S SUPPLY, INC.
Renovator's Old Mill
Millers Falls, MA 01349
Tel.: 413-659-2241 **MA**
Fax: 413-659-3796
Year Founded: 1978
Approx.Sls.: $24,000,000
Emp.: 150
Manufacture Solid Brass Hardware, Lighting, Plumbing & Decorative Accessories for Residential & Commercial Applications
S.I.C.: 3432; 3364; 3645; 3648
Claude Jeanloz *(Chm. Bd.)*
Robert Dodge *(V.P.- Mktg.)*
Robert MacDonald *(V.P.-Fin. Admin.)*
Cynthia Harris *(Dir.-Resource Plnning.)*
Rick Aldrich *(Mgr.)*

Computer Systems/Hardware:
IBM

Outside Service Firm(s):

Coopers & Lybrand*(Auditors)*
1 Post Office Square
Boston, MA 02110
Tel.: 617-574-5000
Fax: 617-345-0398

Bank of New England*(Major Banking Relationship)*
28 State Street
Boston, MA 02109
Tel.: 617-742-4000

Subsidiaries:

Aristera **(1)**
Renovator's Old Mill
Millers Falls, MA 01349
Tel.: 413-659-2211

Country Notebook **(1)**
Renovator's Old Mill
Millers Falls, MA 01349
Tel.: 413-659-2211
Mail-Order Catalog Buisness Supplying Small Home Accessories
S.I.C.: 5961
Brenda Aldrich *(Dir.)*

RENTENBACH ENGINEERING COMPANY
2400 Sutherland Ave.
Knoxville, TN 37919
Mailing Address:
P.O. Box 11087
Knoxville, TN 37919
Tel.: 615-546-2440
Tel.: 800-621-4941 **TN**
Fax: 615-524-1716
Year Founded: 1946
Approx.Sls.: $110,000,000
Emp.: 400
Fiscal Year-end: 9/30/92
General Contractor, Construction Management, Design & Engineering
S.I.C.: 1522; 1541; 1542; 8711
T.J. Rentenbach *(Chm. Bd.)*
T.M. Rentenbach *(Pres. & Chief Exec. Officer)*
Donald W. Freeman *(Sr. V.P.-Bus. Devel.)*
T.C. Walton *(Sr. V.P.-Construction Opers.)*
J.H. Martin *(V.P. & Mgr.-Greensboro Office)*
K.D. Norton *(V.P. & Mgr.-Memphis Office)*
G.A. Ratcliff *(Treas.)*
Principal(s):
T.J. Rentenbach
T.M. Rentenbach

No. of U.S. Offices: 3

Outside Service Firm(s):

Ernst & Young*(Auditors)*
Knoxville, TN

Baker, Worthington, Crossley, Stansberry & Woolf*(Legal Firm)*
Knoxville, TN

First American National Bank*(Major Banking Relationship)*
Knoxville, TN

Subsidiary:

Rentenbach Constructors Incorporated **(1)**
2400 Sutherland Ave.
Knoxville, TN 37919
Tel.: 615-546-2440
General Contractors
S.I.C.: 1522; 1541; 1542
T. M. Rentenbach *(Pres. & Chief Exec. Officer)*

REPCO INCORPORATED
(Filed Chapt. 11 Bankruptcy, Sept. 2, 1992)
2421 N. Orange Blossom Trail
Orlando, FL 32804
Mailing Address:
P.O. Box 7065
Orlando, FL 32854
Tel.: 407-856-1953
Fax: 407-841-0331
Approx.Sls.: $10,000,000
Emp.: 133
Fiscal Year-end: 12/31/90
Mfr. of Two-Way FM Modular Communication Equip. Wireless Long Range Security Systems
S.I.C.: 3669
Andirriya Kostantinidis *(Chm. & Chief Exec. Officer)*
Terry Ferentinos *(Products Line Mgr.)*
James Layne *(Telemetry Products Mgr.)*

REPLACEMENTS, LTD.
P.O. Box 26029,
Greensboro, NC 27420-6029
Year Founded: 1981
Approx.Sls.: $16,500,000
Emp.: 155
Fiscal Year-end: 9/30/91
Import Export
Mail Order House Specializing in Discontinued China, Crystal and Flatware
S.I.C.: 5961
Robert L. Page *(Pres. & Chief Exec. Officer)*
Frank Denny *(V.P.)*
Arthur B. McCarter *(Controller)*
Lea Ann Mills *(Dir.-Sls. & Mktg.)*
Sue Atwell *(Dir.-Human Resources)*
Jim Dunlap *(Dir.-Opers.)*
Sherry Pinendo *(Pur. Mgr.)*

Computer Systems/Hardware:
Data General

REPLOGLE GLOBES, INC.
2801 S. 25th Ave.
Broadview, IL 60153
Tel.: 708-343-0900 **DE**
Telex: 279907
Fax: 708-343-0923
Year Founded: 1930
Sales Range: $10-19 Million
Emp.: 300
Manufacture Replogle World Globes & Sundials
S.I.C.: 3999
William C. Nickels *(Chm. Bd.)*
Robert T. Nickels *(Pres. & Chief Exec. Officer)*
Dan Dillon *(Sr. V.P.-Mktg.)*
Jon E. Hultman *(Sr. V.P.-Mktg.)*
W. John Riemer *(Sr. V.P.-Engrng.)*
Edward J. Dieschbourg *(V.P. & Treas.)*
Harry Bhandari *(V.P.-Mfg.)*
William F. Nickels *(V.P.-Pur.)*
Robert Bytnar *(Dir.-Pur.)*
Jerome Cepa *(Dir.-Data Processing & Office Mgr.)*
Patricia Duncombe *(Dir.-Personnel)*
Ken Jones *(Dir.-Shipping)*
Dan Cepa *(Mgr.-Sls.)*
Pamela Mitacek *(Mgr.-Sls.)*
Katharine Trakselis *(Mgr.-Sls.)*
Lyman S. Betz *(Mgr.-Adv. & Sls. Promo.)*

Principal(s):
William C. Nickels

No. of Mfg. Plants/Facilities: 2
No. of U.S. Offices: 2
No. of Foreign Offices: 2

Computer Systems/Hardware:
IBM System 36

Outside Service Firm(s):

Arthur J. Sabin, P.C.*(Legal Firm)*
Chicago, IL

Subsidiary:

Scan Globe A/S **(1)**
23 Ulvevej DK-4622
Havdrup, Denmark
Tel.: 42 38 54 00 (100%)
Telex: 40275 globes dk
Fax: 42 38 52 70
Mfr. Geographical Globes
S.I.C.: 3999
Per Lund-Hansen *(Mng. Dir.)*

REPUBLIC ALLOYS, INC.
419 Atando Ave.
Charlotte, NC 28206
Tel.: 704-375-5937
Fax: 704-342-3658
Approx.Sls.: $25,000,000
Emp.: 38
Ferrous Metal Scrap & Waste
S.I.C.: 5093
William B. Allen *(Pres.)*
Steven W. Wilson *(V.P.-Admin.)*
Sharon Allen *(Sec.)*

Outside Service Firm(s):

Southern National Bank*(Major Banking Relationship)*
Charlotte, NC

REPUBLIC CONTAINER CORP.
1561 Kennedy Blvd.
Jersey City, NJ 07305
Tel.: 201-333-2564 **NY**
Fax: 201-333-6715
Year Founded: 1935
Assets: $9,000,000
Net Worth: $9,000,000
Approx.Sls.: $23,000,000
Emp.: 175
Manufacture Corrugated Shipping & Mailing Containers, Displays
S.I.C.: 2653; 2655
Ulhas N. Kamat *(Pres.)*
V. Balakrishnan *(Exec. V.P.)*
Paul Koch *(V.P.-Sls.)*

No. of Mfg. Plants/Facilities: 1
No. of U.S. Offices: 1

Outside Service Firm(s):

Zeitlin, Benado & Glickman*(Auditors)*
New York, NY

Republic Container Corp.—(Continued)

National Westminster Bank plc*(Major Banking Relationship)*
175 Water St.
New York, NY 10038-4924
Tel.: 212-602-3364

REPUBLIC CONTRACTING CORP.
869 Pepper St.
Columbia, SC 29209
Tel.: 803-783-4920 **SC**
Fax: 803-783-1623
Sales Range: $40-59 Million
Emp.: 250
Heavy Construction
S.I.C.: 1622; 1623; 1629
J.N. Deirlein *(Pres.)*
Clarence D. Sexton *(V.P.)*

Outside Service Firm(s):

Ernst & Young*(Auditors)*
1300 Huntington Bldg.
Cleveland, OH 44115
Tel.: 216-861-5000

Citizens & Southern National Bank*(Major Banking Relationship)*
Columbia, SC

REPUBLIC DIE & TOOL COMPANY
45000 Van Born Rd.
Belleville, MI 48111
Tel.: 313-699-3400 **MI**
Fax: 313-699-4081
Year Founded: 1947
Assets: $42,177,533
Liabilities: $597,028
Net Worth: $41,580,505
Approx.Sls.: $29,000,000
Emp.: 350
Fiscal Year-end: 8/31/91
Automotive Sheet Metal Stamping Dies
S.I.C.: 3465
John C. Lasko *(Chm. Bd., Pres. & Treas.)*
John Grommes *(V.P. & Chief Oper. Officer)*
Clinton Bair *(Sec. & Controller)*
Mark Prendeville *(Dir.-Personnel)*
Charles Zimmerman *(Dir.-Data Processing)*
Calvin Miller *(Mgr.-Sls.)*
Merle Thomas *(Plant Mgr.)*
Leonard Gaylor *(Pur. Agent)*

Principal(s):
John C. Lasko

No. of Mfg. Plants/Facilities: 1

Outside Service Firm(s):

Curtis, Bailey, Exelby & Sposito*(Auditors)*
Ypsilanti, MI

Cambridge Underwriters Ltd*(Commercial Insurance Carrier)*
Livonia, MI

Michigan Tooling Association*(Group Insurer)*
Dearborn, MI

Dykema, Gossett*(Legal Firm)*
400 Renaissance Ctr., 35th Fl.
Detroit, MI 48243
Tel.: 313-568-6800

Comerica Bank*(Major Banking Relationship)*
211 W. Fort St.
Detroit, MI 48226
Tel.: 313-222-3300

Detroit Tooling Association*(Pension Manager)*
Dearborn, MI

REPUBLIC ENGINEERED STEELS, INC.
410 Oberlin Rd., SW
Massillon, OH 44647
Tel.: 216-837-6000
Year Founded: 1989
Approx.Sls.: $700,000,000
Emp.: 4,900
Cold Finishing of Steel Shapes
S.I.C.: 3316
Russell Maier *(Pres. & Chief Exec. Officer)*
James Riley *(V.P., Chief Fin. Officer & Treas.)*
Marian Carpenter *(Dir.-Adv.)*

REPUBLIC FASTENER PRODUCTS CORP.
671 Waterview Dr.
Great Falls, SC 29055
Tel.: 803-482-2500
Fax: 803-482-2526
Year Founded: 1949
Sales Range: $10-19 Million
Emp.: 15
Manufacture Fasteners, Tools, Cutters, Kits, Hooks & Special Wire Forms
S.I.C.: 3423; 3546; 3965
Daniel F. Barnes *(Chief Exec. Officer)*
Richard A. Barnes *(Pres. & Chief Oper. Officer)*

Computer Systems/Hardware:
Norstar No. 6

Outside Service Firm(s):

Midlantic National Bank*(Major Banking Relationship)*
Fairfield, NJ

Subsidiaries:

Cobar Machine & Tool Co. **(1)**
9 Commerce Rd.
Fairfield, NJ 07006
Tel.: 201-227-1315
S.I.C.: 3423

Nu-Merics Inc. **(1)**
9 Commerce Rd.
Fairfield, NJ 07006
Tel.: 201-227-1812
S.I.C.: 3423

REPUBLIC INDUSTRIES, INC.
7350 W. Wilson Ave.
Harwood Heights, IL 60656
Tel.: 708-867-7400
Fax: 708-867-0291
Approx.Sls.: $15,000,000
Emp.: 325
Manual & Automatic Door Controlling Equipment & Door Hardware Equipment
S.I.C.: 3429; 3498; 3699
J.L. Fox *(Chm. Bd.)*
M.A. Kass *(Pres.)*
H. Froemming *(V.P.-Mfg.)*
Hal Geiser *(V.P.-Tech. Service)*
R. Kniskern *(V.P.-Natl. Mngmt.)*
Wesley Siena *(V.P.-Mngmt. Information Systems)*
L. Slaybaugh *(V.P.-Engrng.)*
J. Stuckert *(V.P.-Mfg.)*
Gilbert Valencia *(V.P.-Electronic Res. & Devel.)*
W. Helmer *(Treas. & Controller)*
Donald A. Straub *(Sec. & Gen. Counsel)*
David Winn *(Pur. Agent)*

Outside Service Firm(s):

KPMG Peat Marwick*(Auditors)*
Peat Marwick Plaza, 303 E. Wacker Dr.
Chicago, IL 60601
Tel.: 312-938-1000

Altheimer & Gray*(Legal Firm)*
10 S. Wacker Dr.
Chicago, IL 60606
Tel.: 312-715-4000

American National Bank & Trust Company of Chicago*(Major Banking Relationship)*
33 N. LaSalle St.
Chicago, IL 60602
Tel.: 312-661-5000
Fax: 312-661-6417

REPUBLIC NATIONAL BANK OF MIAMI
10 N.W. 42nd Ave.
Miami, FL 33126
Tel.: 305-441-7300
Fax: 305-529-0332
Approx.Income: $106,673,000
Emp.: 774
Bank Holding Company
S.I.C.: 6712
Luis Botifoll *(Chm. Bd. & Chief Exec. Officer)*
Roberto Isaias *(Co-Chm.)*
Oscar Bustillo, Jr. *(Pres. & Chief Oper. Officer)*
Roberto Gonzalez-Blanco *(V.P. & Sec.)*
Estefano Isaias *(Treas.)*

Outside Service Firm(s):

Grant Thornton*(Auditors)*
500 E. Broward Blvd.
Fort Lauderdale, FL 33994-3095
Tel.: 305-358-0077

Murai, Wald, Biondo, Matthews & Moreno*(Legal Firm)*
Miami, FL

REPUBLIC STORAGE SYSTEMS COMPANY INC.
1038 Belden Ave., N.E.
Canton, OH 44705
Tel.: 216-438-5800
Tel.: 800-477-1255
Telex: 3266
Fax: 216-454-7772
Year Founded: 1986
Approx.Sls.: $60,000,000
Emp.: 550
Fiscal Year-end: 12/31/90
Mfr. Lockers, Shelving, Metal Cabinets, Storage Racks, Automated Storage Retrieval Systems, Containers
S.I.C.: 2542; 3699; 7299; 5046
Lowell R. Marshall *(Pres. & Chief Exec. Officer)*
John O'Leary *(V.P.-Fin., Treas. & Sec.)*
Richard Raebel *(V.P.-Sls. & Mktg.)*
T.A. Joseph *(Dir.-Engrng.)*
Joan Freeman *(Mgr.-Personnel)*

Outside Service Firm(s):

AmeriTrust Company, N.A.*(Major Banking Relationship)*
P.O. Box 5937, 900 Euclid Ave.
Cleveland, OH 44101-0937

REPUBLIC SUPPLY COMPANY
5646 Milton, Ste. 800
Dallas, TX 75206
Tel.: 214-987-9868 **TX**
Fax: 214-692-7700
Year Founded: 1985
Approx.Sls.: $62,000,000
Emp.: 400
Wholesale Distribution of Oil Well Machinry, Equipment & Supplies; Industrial Supplies; Explosives
S.I.C.: 5084; 5169
Frank M. Late *(Chm. Bd. & Pres.)*
Victor Haesse *(Controller)*

REPUBLIC TELCOM SYSTEMS CORPORATION
6150 Lookout Rd.
Boulder, CO 80301
Tel.: 303-530-8600
Tel.: 800-822-6227
Fax: 303-530-8625
Sales Range: $10-19 Million
Emp.: 125
Manufacture Parts For Communications Equipment
S.I.C.: 3663
Harry Taylor *(Chm. Bd. & Pres.)*
Keith Brue *(Chief Fin. Officer & V.P.)*
Art Schultz *(Sr. V.P.-Sls. & Mktg.)*
Bob Alexander *(V.P.-Customer Service)*
David Hale *(V.P.-Mfg.)*
William J. Hawkins *(V.P.-Mktg.)*
Bob Johnson *(V.P.-Engrng.)*

Outside Service Firm(s):

Colorado National Bank*(Major Banking Relationship)*
17th & Champa
Denver, CO 80217

RESCO PRODUCTS, INC.
1302 Conshohocken Rd.
Conshohocken, PA 19428
Mailing Address:
P.O. Box 108
Norristown, PA 19404
Tel.: 215-279-5010
Telex: 84-6459
Fax: 215-279-6070
Year Founded: 1946
Approx.Sls.: $60,000,000
Emp.: 500
Fiscal Year-end: 12/31/92

Export
Mfr. Refractories, Brick, Ceramic Minerals
S.I.C.: 3255; 3297; 3299
Wm. T. Tredennick *(Pres.)*
R.A. Stephenson *(V.P.)*
William J. Streich *(Treas. & Sec.)*
Donald F. Copeland *(Gen. Counsel)*

Computer Systems/Hardware:
Digital Equipment

Division:

North State Pyrophyllite **(1)**
3514 W. Wendover Ave.
Greensboro, NC 27407
Tel.: 919-299-1441
Emp.: 85
Export
Refractory Mfr.; Paco, Propac
S.I.C.: 3255; 3297; 3299
W.T. Tredennick *(Pres.)*
Gary Hester *(Mgr.-Admin.)*
R.B. Arthur, Jr. *(Mgr.-Mfg.)*
J. Ron Stowers *(Mgr.-Sls.)*

RESEARCH PRODUCTS CORPORATION
1015 E. Washington Ave.
Madison, WI 53703
Mailing Address:
P.O. Box 1467
Madison, WI 53701
Tel.: 608-257-8801
Fax: 608-257-4357
Year Founded: 1939
Approx.Sls.: $30,000,000
Emp.: 275

Import Export
Manufacturer of Aprilaire Evaporative Type Humidifiers; Super E Z Kleen Washable Panel Type Aluminum Air Filters; Space-Gard High Efficiency Air Cleaner (Non Electric); Kleen-Gard Baffle Type Grease Filter
S.I.C.: 3634; 3433
V.J. Hellenbrand *(Chm. Bd. & Pres.)*
Dean E. Pierringer *(V.P.-Sls. & Mktg.)*
R.M. Pasch *(V.P.-Engrng.)*
H.E. Hoveland *(V.P.-Mfg.)*
Dayton A. Jones *(Treas.)*
Harold D. Frank *(Controller)*
Larry A. Olsen *(Gen. Sls. Mgr.)*
Eric E. Swanson *(Adv. Mgr.)*
R.F. Peterson *(Pur. Agent)*

Outside Service Firm(s):

First Wisconsin National Bank*(Major Banking Relationship)*
Madison, WI

RESONEX, INC.
720 Palomar Ave.
Sunnyvale, CA 94086
Tel.: 408-720-8600
Fax: 408-245-1700
Emp.: 120
Magnetic Resonance Imaging Apparatus
S.I.C.: 3826
Gerald Knudson *(Pres. & Chief Exec. Officer)*
Tim Christofferson *(Chief Oper. Officer)*
Alan Lanka *(Chief Fin. Officer)*
Art Marks *(V.P.-Mktg.)*
Dana Squire *(V.P.-Admin.)*

Outside Service Firm(s):

Arthur Andersen & Co.*(Auditors)*
Spear Street Tower, One Market Plaza, Ste. 3500
San Francisco, CA 94105
Tel.: 415-546-8200

Silicon Valley Bank*(Major Banking Relationship)*
3000 Lakeside Dr.
Santa Clara, CA 95054

RESORT CONDOMINIUMS INTERNATIONAL
3502 Woodview Trace
Indianapolis, IN 46268
Mailing Address:
P.O. Box 80260,
Indianapolis, IN 46280
Tel.: 317-871-9500
Fax: 317-871-9744
Year Founded: 1974
Emp.: 2,000
Exchange Service for People Who Own Time Shared Units
S.I.C.: 7389
Christal Dehaan *(Chm. Bd., Pres. & Chief Exec. Officer)*
William F. McConnell *(Chief Oper. Officer)*
Steven Miller *(Chief Fin. Officer, Treas. & Controller)*

Computer Systems/Hardware:
IBM 4381

Outside Service Firm(s):

Arthur Andersen & Co.*(Auditors)*
111 Monument Circle, Ste. 4300
Indianapolis, IN 46204-5143
Tel.: 317-634-3210
Fax: 317-632-3973

Lincoln National Life Insurance Co.*(Group Insurer)*
PO Box 208, 1300 S. Clinton
Fort Wayne, IN 46801
Tel.: 219-455-2926
Fax: 219-455-7619

Bank One, Indianapolis, N.A.*(Major Banking Relationship)*
111 Monument Circle, Ste. 1611
Indianapolis, IN 46204-1611
Tel.: 317-321-8110

Subsidiaries:

EV Services Inc. **(1)**
P.O. Box 80073
Indianapolis, IN 46280
Tel.: 317-871-9500 (100%)
Exchange Service for People with Time Shared Units
S.I.C.: 7389

Endless Vacation Publishing **(1)**
P.O. Box 80073
Indianapolis, IN 46280
Tel.: 317-871-9500
Publisher of a Travel Magazine
S.I.C.: 2721

RCI Travel **(1)**
P.O. Box 80073
Indianapolis, IN 46280
Tel.: 317-871-9500
Travel Agency
S.I.C.: 4724

RCI Quality Services, Inc. **(1)**
P.O. Box 80073
Indianapolis, IN 46280
Tel.: 317-871-9500
Financial & Insurance Service
S.I.C.: 6351

Resort Quality Services, Inc. **(1)**
P.O. Box 80073
Indianapolis, IN 46280
Tel.: 317-871-9500
Exchange Service for People with Time Shared Units
S.I.C.: 7389

RESOURCE, INC.
(Formerly Video Training Corporation)
3825 Henderson Blvd.
Tampa, FL 33629
Tel.: 813-289-7876 **FL**
Fax: 813-289-8057
Year Founded: 1973
Sales Range: $10-19 Million
Emp.: 6
Video Production & Distribution
S.I.C.: 7812
George Resch *(Pres.)*

Computer Systems/Hardware:
Compaq; Wyse

Outside Service Firm(s):

L. O'Neal*(Legal Firm)*
Columbia, SC

RE:SOURCE MARKETING
515 N. Park St.
Columbus, OH 43215
Tel.: 614-621-2888
Year Founded: 1981
Approx.Billings: $18,090,000
Emp.: 40
Channel Marketing, Sales Promotion, Direct Marketing
Nancy Kramer *(Pres.)*
Dick Day *(Tech. Dir.)*
Tim Bell *(Mktg. Dir., New Bus. Contact)*
Janet Eads *(Controller)*
Richard Day *(Tech. Services Dir.)*

Computer Systems/Hardware:
Apple Computer

RESPONSIVE MARKETING COMMUNICATIONS, INC.
1515 Woodfield Rd., Ste. 360
Schaumburg, IL 60173
Tel.: 708-240-1100
Fax: 708-240-1571
Year Founded: 1978
Approx.Billings: $18,080,000
Emp.: 33
Marketing, Planning & Promotion
A.J. Marsiglia *(Chm. & Pres.)*
Marlene Picha *(Sr. V.P., Client Services)*
O'Neal Caliendo *(Sr. V.P., Production Services)*
Lee Pirtle *(V.P., Fin., Sec. & Treas.)*
Nancy Galante *(Dir. Mktg. & Media)*

Computer Systems/Hardware:
Apple Macintosh

RESTAURANT COMPANY, INC.
3500 Water Oak Dr.
Birmingham, AL 35243
Tel.: 205-967-0081
Year Founded: 1989
Approx.Sls.: $10,000,000
Emp.: 30
Fiscal Year-end: 12/31/90
Fast Food Operations
S.I.C.: 5812
James C. Acomb *(Pres. & Chief Exec. Officer)*

RESTAURANT DEVELOPERS CORP.
5755 Granger Rd., Ste. 200
Independence, OH 44131-1410
Tel.: 216-398-1101 **OH**
Fax: 216-398-0707
Year Founded: 1966
Approx.Sls.: $40,000,000
Emp.: 425
Fiscal Year-end: 12/31/90
Operator & Franchisor of Mr. Philly Restaurants
S.I.C.: 6794; 5812
Ronald J. Wolfe *(Pres. & Chief Exec. Officer)*
Jean Sullivan *(V.P.-Mktg.)*
Bill Plautz *(V.P.-Bus. Devel. & Controller)*
William J. Kraus *(Gen. Counsel)*
Joanne Ritner *(Dir.-Personnel)*

No. of U.S. Offices: 3

Computer Systems/Hardware:
DEC

Outside Service Firm(s):

Roulston & Co.*(Investment Banker)*
4000 Chester Ave.
Cleveland, OH 44103
Tel.: 216-431-3000

Central National Bank*(Major Banking Relationship)*
Cleveland, OH

RESTAURANT ENTERPRISES GROUP, INC.
One Park Plaza, Ste. 900
Irvine, CA 92714
Tel.: 714-852-5700 **DE**
Year Founded: 1986
Approx.Sls.: $870,000,000
Emp.: 33,000
Fiscal Year-end: 12/31/91
Family Restaurants, Dinner Houses & Specialty Theme Restaurants, Mexican Style Dinner Houses
S.I.C.: 5812; 5813
J.P. Grace *(Chm. Bd.)*
N.N. Habermann *(Pres. & Chief Exec. Officer)*
M.M. Casey *(Exec. V.P. & Chief Fin. Officer)*
K.L. Harris *(Sr. V.P.-Pur. & Distr.)*
R.T. Trebing *(V.P.-Fin.)*
H. Baray *(V.P. & Gen. Counsel)*
J. Colson *(Sr. V.P.-Fin. & Admin. Services)*
M.E. Malanga *(V.P.-Devel.)*
Robert Gonda *(Treas.)*

Outside Service Firm(s):

Deloitte & Touche*(Auditors)*
Newport Beach, CA

Subsidiaries:

Carrows Restaurants, Inc. **(1)**
One Park Plaza, Ste. 900
Irvine, CA 92714
Tel.: 714-757-7900 (100%)
Approx.Sls.: $100,000,000
Restaurants
S.I.C.: 5812; 5813
D. M. McComas *(Pres.)*

El Torito Restaurants, Inc. **(1)**
2450 White Rd.
Irvine, CA 92714
Tel.: 714-863-6400 (100%)
Approx.Sls.: $380,000,000
Emp.: 10,683
Mexican Style Restaurants
S.I.C.: 5812; 5813
M.M. Casey *(Pres.)*
Dick Butler *(V.P.-Mktg.)*
Randy Metheny *(Dir.-Pur.)*

Far West Concepts, Inc. **(1)**
2701 Alton Parkway
Irvine, CA 92714-5811
Tel.: 714-863-6300
Restaurants
S.I.C.: 5812; 5813

GRC Restaurants, Inc. **(1)**
2701 Alton Parkway
Irvine, CA 92714-5811
Tel.: 714-863-6300
Restaurants
S.I.C.: 5812; 5813

Jojos Restaurants, Inc. **(1)**
2701 Alton
Irvine, CA 92714
Tel.: 714-863-6300
Restaurants

RESTAURANTS UNLIMITED
1818 N. Northlake Way
Seattle, WA 98103
Tel.: 206-634-0550
Fax: 206-632-3533
Year Founded: 1968
Approx.Sls.: $63,000,000
Emp.: 2,000
Owns & Operates Restaurants
S.I.C.: 5812
Richard B. Komen *(Chm. Bd.)*
Raymond W. Lindstrom *(Pres.)*
John D. Byrne *(V.P., Sec. & Treas.)*
Richard W. Giboney *(V.P.-Mktg.)*
John Herman *(V.P.-Opers.)*
James Simonson *(V.P.-Opers.)*
James Welch *(V.P.-Devel.)*
Malcomb Best *(Dir.-Data Processing)*
David Johnson *(Dir.-Pur.)*

Principal(s):
Richard B. Komen

Outside Service Firm(s):

Clark Nuber & Co.*(Auditors)*
Bellevue, WA

Ogden, Ogden & Murphy*(Legal Firm)*
Seattle, WA

The Bank of California, N.A.*(Major Banking Relationship)*
400 California
San Francisco, CA 94104
Tel.: 415-765-0400

RESTONIC CORPORATION
101 N. Wacker
Chicago, IL 60606
Tel.: 312-346-9044
Fax: 312-580-7272
Year Founded: 1938
Approx.Sls.: $150,000,000
Emp.: 10
Fiscal Year-end: 12/31/91
Import Export
Manufacture Mattresses & Liners, Box Springs, Bed Frames, Platform Beds, Waterbeds, Electric Beds, Flotation Beds, Sleep Products & Accessories
S.I.C.: 2392; 2515; 2511; 2514
William Brey *(Pres.)*
Cheryl Prindle *(Controller)*
Allen A. Green *(Dir.-Opers.)*
Arthur Morse *(Dir.-Adv.)*
Thomas Wendorf *(Natl. Sls. Mgr.)*

Computer Systems/Hardware:
IBM

Outside Service Firm(s):

Haight, Hoefeldt, Davis & Jambor*(Legal Firm)*
Chicago, IL

Madison State Bank*(Major Banking Relationship)*
Chicago, IL

RETAIL VENTURES, INC.
150 Thornhill Dr.
Warrendale, PA 15095
Mailing Address:
P.O. Box 788
Warrendale, PA 15095
Tel.: 412-776-4857 PA
Fax: 412-776-6160
Year Founded: 1957
Approx.Sls.: $160,000,000
Emp.: 2,300
Fiscal Year-end: 7/31/91
Import
147 Retail Men's & Ladies' Outdoor Apparel Stores
S.I.C.: 5611; 5699
Jay Schottenstein *(Chm. Bd.)*
Joe Kerin *(Exec. V.P.)*
Bill Lackey *(Exec. V.P.)*
Don Morrison *(Exec. V.P.-Mdse.)*
Gary Geramita *(V.P.-Fin.)*
Michael Foftyk *(V.P.-Stores)*
Jerry Claybaugh *(V.P.-Mnmgt. Information Systems)*
Bill Thatsko *(V.P.-Real Estate)*

Computer Systems/Hardware:
IBM 38

Outside Service Firm(s):

Alpern, Rosenthal & Company*(Auditors)*
Pittsburgh, PA

Sheinberg & Hoover*(Legal Firm)*
Pittsburgh, PA

BancOhio National Bank*(Major Banking Relationship)*
Columbus, OH

REULAND ELECTRIC COMPANY
17969 E. Railroad
City of Industry, CA 91748
Mailing Address:
P.O. Box 1464
City of Industry, CA 91749
Tel.: 818-964-6411
Fax: 818-965-1283
Year Founded: 1930
Emp.: 600
Mfr. of RE Motors; Fluid-Shaft, Electric Motors; Cushion Drive Fluid Coupling; REAP Electric Aluminum Prods.; RTC Soft-Start Motor Control; Dyn Stop-Electronic Brake; Hydraulic Adaptors
S.I.C.: 3621; 3566; 3363; 3625; 3594
Noel Reuland *(Pres.)*
William Kramer, III *(V.P. & Controller)*
Eli Yorba *(V.P.-Corp. Devel.)*
G.R. Stollsteimer *(Mgr.-Sls.)*

Divisions:

Eastern Div. **(1)**
4500 E. Brand River Ave.
Howell, MI 48843
Tel.: 517-546-4400

Foundry Div. **(1)**
17969 E. Railroad St.
City of Industry, CA 91749
Tel.: 818-964-6411

Electronic Control Div. **(1)**
17969 E. Railroad St.
City of Industry, CA 91748
Tel.: 818-964-6411

Motor Div. **(1)**
17969 E. Railroad St.
City of Industry, CA 91748
Tel.: 818-964-6411

REV-A-SHELF
(Sub. of Jones Plastic & Engineering Corp.)
2409 Plantside Dr.
Louisville, KY 40299
Mailing Address:
P.O. Box 99585,
Louisville, KY 40269-0585
Tel.: 502-499-5835
Approx.Sls.: $12,000,000
Emp.: 65
Mfr. of Cabinet & Shelving Hardware & Locks
S.I.C.: 3429
J. Kevin Jones *(Pres.)*

REVCO SCIENTIFIC INC.
275 Aiken Rd.
Asheville, NC 28804
Tel.: 704-658-2711
Tel.: 800-252-7100
Fax: 704-645-3368
Approx.Sls.: $16,000,000
Emp.: 268
Fiscal Year-end: 12/31/90
Export
Refrigerators, Freezers, Ultra-Low Temperature Freezers; Rhem, Revco, Environmental Chambers, Blood Bank Refrigertors, CO2 Incubators, Shakers
S.I.C.: 5078
D.B. Dawley *(Pres.)*

REVCOR, INC.
251 Edwards Ave.
Carpentersville, IL 60110
Tel.: 708-428-4411
Fax: 708-426-4630
Sales Range: $20-39 Million
Fiscal Year-end: 12/31/92
Export
Blower Wheels, Impeller Fans & Housings (Metal & Plastic)
S.I.C.: 3564
John H. Reichwein *(Chm. Bd. & Treas.)*
John H. Reichwein, Jr. *(Pres.)*
Anwar Atalla *(V.P.-Engrng.)*
Edward Murzinski *(V.P.-Mktg. & Sls.)*
Charles Wasinger *(V.P.-Fin.)*
Bruce Wiesley *(V.P.-Mfg.)*
Mary Reichwein *(Sec.)*
Principal(s):
Reichwein Family

No. of Mfg. Plants/Facilities: 2
No. of U.S. Offices: 2

Outside Service Firm(s):

McGladrey & Pullen*(Auditors)*
Schaumburg, IL

American National Bank & Trust Company of Chicago*(Major Banking Relationship)*
33 N. LaSalle St.
Chicago, IL 60602
Tel.: 312-661-5000
Fax: 312-661-6417

REVERE ELECTRIC SUPPLY CO.
2501 W. Washington Blvd.
Chicago, IL 60612
Tel.: 312-738-3636 IL
Fax: 312-738-3675
Year Founded: 1919
Approx.Sls.: $32,500,000
Emp.: 130
Wholesale Electrical Products
S.I.C.: 5063
Thomas A. Eiseman *(Pres.)*
Michael P. Eiseman *(Exec. V.P., Treas. & Information Systems Dir.)*
George Beeson *(V.P. & Comptroller)*
Rob Rooney *(Sls. Mgr.)*
Herb Schrager *(Pur. Dir.)*
Principal(s):
Thomas A. Eiseman
Michael P. Eiseman

Computer Systems/Hardware:
Hewlett-Packard

Outside Service Firm(s):

Arthur Andersen & Co.*(Auditors)*
33 W. Monroe St.
Chicago, IL 60603-4067
Tel.: 312-580-0033
Fax: 312-507-6748

Kamenear Kadison & Anderson*(Legal Firm)*
Chicago, IL

American National Bank & Trust Company of Chicago*(Major Banking Relationship)*
33 N. LaSalle St.
Chicago, IL 60602
Tel.: 312-661-5000
Fax: 312-661-6417

REX LUMBER COMPANY
840 Main St.
Acton, MA 01720-5804
Tel.: 508-263-0055
Fax: 508-263-9806
Approx.Sls.: $48,000,000
Emp.: 310
Lumber & Millwork
S.I.C.: 5031
Lawrence Gagne, Sr. *(Chief Exec. Officer)*
Benjamin Forester *(Pres.)*
William Clark *(V.P.-Fin. & Treas.)*
Stan Dress *(V.P.-Sls. & Mktg.)*
A. Ledyard Smith *(Sec.)*

Outside Service Firm(s):

KPMG Peat Marwick*(Auditors)*
One Boston Place
Boston, MA 02108
Tel.: 617-723-7700

Testa, Hurwitz & Thibeault*(Legal Firm)*
53 State St.
Boston, MA 02109
Tel.: 617-248-7000
Fax: 617-248-7100

Bay Bank Harvard Trust Company*(Major Banking Relationship)*
Boston, MA

REX MARINE CENTER, INC.
144-146 Water St.
Norwalk, CT 06854
Tel.: 203-866-5555 CT
Fax: 203-866-2518
Year Founded: 1968
Approx.Sls.: $13,000,000
Emp.: 50
Boat Dealers
S.I.C.: 5551
William T. Gardella *(Pres.)*
William T. Gardella, Jr. *(V.P.)*
Susan Brown *(Sec.)*
Sandra Mees *(Treas.)*

Outside Service Firm(s):

Macaluso, Nardi & Co.*(Auditors)*
Norwalk, CT

REYCO INDUSTRIES, INC.
600 N. Prospect St.
Springfield, MO 65805
Tel.: 417-862-4343
Sales Range: $10-19 Million
Paul Binds *(Pres.)*

JOHN REYER COMPANY
City Center
Sharon, PA 16146
Tel.: 412-981-2200
Fax: 412-983-8269
Approx.Sls.: $10,000,000
Emp.: 200
Reyer Shoes: Children's, Ladies', Athletic & Men's Shoes & Accessories
S.I.C.: 5661
Harry L. Jubelirer *(Pres.)*
Mark B. Jubelirer *(V.P.)*
Steven W. Jubelirer *(Treas.)*
Natalie Jubelirer *(Sec.)*

Outside Service Firm(s):

Black, Bashor & Porsch*(Auditors)*
Sharon, PA

McDowell National Bank*(Major Banking Relationship)*
Sharon, PA

REYNEN, BARDIS & WINN
9985 Folsom Blvd.
Sacramento, CA 95827
Tel.: 916-366-3665
Fax: 916-369-7128
Year Founded: 1970
Sales Range: $100-499 Million
Emp.: 150
Real Estate Subdivider & Developer
S.I.C.: 6552
Christo D. Bardis *(Pres.)*
John D. Reynen *(Treas. & Sec.)*
Bill Agnell *(Controller)*
Barbara Crossan *(Dir.-Sls.)*
Principal(s):
Christo D. Bardis
John D. Reynen
Thomas Winn

Outside Service Firm(s):

Damore Hamric Schneider, Inc.*(Auditors)*
Sacramento, CA

Elias D. Bardis*(Legal Firm)*
Sacramento, CA

F.T. REYNOLDS COMPANY
1014 W. Towne St.
Glendive, MT 59330
Mailing Address:
P.O. Box 968
Glendive, MT 59330
Tel.: 406-365-2114
Approx.Sls.: $19,000,000
Emp.: 150
Wholesale & Retail Groceries
S.I.C.: 5411; 5149
John K. Reynolds *(Pres.)*
John J. Marman III *(V.P.)*
Charles Marman *(Sec. & Treas.)*

Outside Service Firm(s):

Hu Williamson*(Auditors)*
Glendive, MT

First National Bank*(Major Banking Relationship)*
Glendive, MT

RHEA&KAISER
ADVERTISING, INC.

RHEA & KAISER ADVERTISING, INC.
Naperville Financial Ctr., 400 E. Diehl Rd.
Naperville, IL 60563
Tel.: 708-505-1100
Fax: 708-505-1109
Year Founded: 1978
Approx.Billings: $25,000,000
Emp.: 40
Consumer, Business-to-Business & Agricultural
Stephen L. Rhea *(Pres., New Bus. Contact & Acct. Services Mgr.)*

Van Kaiser *(Exec. V.P., Treas. & Creative Dir.)*
Tony Filipelli *(Sr. V.P., Mktg. Services)*
Curt Ippensen *(V.P., Dir. Strategic Plng.)*
Helen Conroy *(Acctg. Services)*
Sandi Beier *(Office Mgr.)*

RHOADES DEVELOPMENT
1801 C Parkcourt Place
Santa Ana, CA 92701
Tel.: 714-972-9944
Fax: 714-973-0865
Approx.Sls.: $30,000,000
Emp.: 20
Single Family Home Builders
S.I.C.: 1531
Jeffrey P. Rhoades *(Pres.)*
Dennis Dover *(V.P.-Construction)*
Kelly V. Hansen *(V.P.)*

Outside Service Firm(s):

Kenneth Leventhal & Co.*(Auditors)*
Santa Ana, CA

RHODE ISLAND LOTTERY
1425 Pontiac Ave.
Cranston, RI 02920
Tel.: 401-463-6500
Fax: 401-463-5669
Year Founded: 1974
Approx.Sls.: $66,665,237
Emp.: 35
Fiscal Year-end: 6/30/91
State Lottery
S.I.C.: 7999
Peter J. O'Connell *(Exec. Dir.)*
Raymond Grimes *(Deputy Dir.)*

RHODES, INC.
4370 Peachtree Rd., N.E.
Atlanta, GA 30319
Tel.: 404-264-4600 **GA**
Assets: $358,912,000
Earnings: ($12,476,000)
Liabilities: $365,596,000
Net Worth: $6,684,000
Approx.Sls.: $248,813,000
Emp.: 2,050
Fiscal Year-end: 2/28/90
Specialty Retailer of Medium-Priced Home Furnishings
S.I.C.: 5712
Holcombe T. Green, Jr. *(Chm. Bd.)*
Irwin L. Lowenstein *(Pres. & Chief Exec. Officer)*
Joel H. Dugan *(Sr. V.P.-Fin. & Admin.; Sec. & Treas.)*
Joel Lanham *(Exec. V.P.-Field Opers.)*
George G. Harris *(Sr. V.P.-Field Opers.)*
Jack A. Hurst *(Sr. V.P.-Training & Human Resources)*
William Morris *(Sr. V.P.-Mdsg. & Advtg.)*
Richard A. Winans *(V.P.-Credit)*
Barbara Snow *(Controller)*
Jay Tenenbaum *(Dir.-Mktg.)*

Computer Systems/Hardware:
IBM

Subsidiary:

Marks-Fitzgerald Furniture Co. **(1)**
1849 Crestwood Blvd.
Birmingham, AL 35210
Tel.: 205-956-3981
Retail of Home Furniture
S.I.C.: 5712

M. H. RHODES, INC.
99 Thompson Rd.
Avon, CT 06001
Tel.: 203-673-3281
Tel.: 800-548-4637
Fax: 203-673-8633
Year Founded: 1930
Approx.Sls.: $10,000,000
Emp.: 100
Import Export
Mark-Time Timers & Timing Devices, Parking Meters
S.I.C.: 3873; 3625; 3621; 3824
Joseph Morelli *(Chm. Bd., Pres. & Chief Exec. Officer)*
Harold Matles *(V.P.)*
A. Springer *(Controller)*
Richard W. Salvas *(Sls. Mgr.)*

RHODES INTERNATIONAL, INC.
1735 S. Redwood Rd.
Salt Lake City, UT 84105
Mailing Address:
P.O. Box 25487,
Salt Lake City, UT 84125
Tel.: 801-972-0122
Fax: 801-973-0437
Year Founded: 1964
Approx.Sls.: $25,000,000
Emp.: 275
Fiscal Year-end: 6/30/92
Import Export
Mfr. Frozen Bread Dough: Rhodes, Dakota Hearth
S.I.C.: 2051
Ken Farnsworth *(Chm. Bd. & Pres.)*
Darry Campbell *(Opers. Mgr.)*
Johnny Portenier *(Plant Mgr.)*

Subsidiary:

Dakota Bake-N-Serv **(1)**
Hwy. 16 West, P.O. Box 410
West Columbus, WI 53925
Tel.: 414-623-5161
Mfr. Frozen Bread Dough: Rhodes, Dakota Hearth
S.I.C.: 2051

RIBBON NARROW FABRIC COMPANY
565 Winsor Dr.
Secaucus, NJ 07094
Tel.: 201-867-0600
Fax: 201-867-0093
Emp.: 60
Cut Edge Ribbons & Novelty Ribbons
S.I.C.: 2241; 2297
Philip Radus *(Pres. & Treas.)*

Outside Service Firm(s):

Herman J. Dobkin & Co.*(Auditors)*
New York, NY

Midlantic National Bank North*(Major Banking Relationship)*
Secaucus, NJ

RICART FORD INC.
4255 S. Hamilton Rd.
Groveport, OH 43125
Mailing Address:
P.O. Box 27130,
Columbus, OH 43227
Tel.: 614-836-6484
Fax: 614-836-5694
Approx.Sls.: $55,000,000
Emp.: 450
Retail New & Used Automobiles
S.I.C.: 5511
Rhett Ricart *(Pres.)*
Paul F. Ricart, Jr. *(V.P.)*
Brenda Owens *(Chief Fin. Officer)*
Denny Walker *(Gen. Mgr.)*

Outside Service Firm(s):

Schneider, Downs & Company*(Auditors)*
Pittsburgh, PA

Fifth Third Bank*(Major Banking Relationship)*
Columbus, OH

RICCOBON & COMPANY, INC.
13827 Carmenita Rd.
Santa Fe Springs, CA 90670
Tel.: 310-921-7719 **CA**
Fax: 310-921-8456
Year Founded: 1948
Approx.Sls.: $25,000,000
Emp.: 200
Printing of Business Forms; Wholesale Distribution of Office Supplies
S.I.C.: 2752; 5112
Paul J. Riccobon *(Pres.)*
Susan Simon *(Sec.)*

Outside Service Firm(s):

Pacific Western National Bank*(Major Banking Relationship)*
Pico Rivera, CA

Division:

National Computer Supplies **(1)**
13827 Carmenita Rd.
Santa Fe Springs, CA 90670
Tel.: 310-921-7719
Printing of Business Forms
S.I.C.: 2752
Paul J. Riccobon *(Pres.)*

RICE FOOD MARKETS INC.
5333 Gulfton
Houston, TX 77081
Tel.: 713-662-7700 **TX**
Fax: 713-662-7757
Approx.Sls.: $162,000,000
Emp.: 1,600
Grocery Stores; Rental Property Management; Security Services
S.I.C.: 5411; 6531; 7381
Alfred L. Friedlander *(Chm. Bd. & Chief Exec. Officer)*
Joel M. Levy *(Pres.)*
Gary Friedlander *(Sr. V.P.)*
Tom Friedlander *(Sr. V.P.)*
Carl T. Anderson *(V.P.-Store Opers.)*
Joe Mayeux *(V.P.-Grocery)*
Jim Potter *(Controller)*
Rick McCain *(Dir.-Data Processing)*
Kent Milton *(Dir.-Personnel)*

Outside Service Firm(s):

Weinstein, Spira & Co.*(Auditors)*
Houston, TX

Schlanger, Mills, Mayer & Grossberg*(Legal Firm)*
5847 San Felipe, Ste. 1700
Houston, TX 77057
Tel.: 713-785-1700
Fax: 713-785-2091

First City Bank Texas*(Major Banking Relationship)*
Fort Worth, TX

RICE GROWERS ASSOCIATION OF CALIFORNIA
1550 Harbor Blvd.
West Sacramento, CA 95691
Mailing Address:
P.O. Box 958
West Sacramento, CA 95691
Tel.: 916-371-6941 **CA**
Fax: 916-372-7158
Year Founded: 1921
Assets: $41,000,000
Liabilities: $35,000,000
Net Worth: $6,000,000
Sales Range: $20-39 Million
Emp.: 120
Fiscal Year-end: 8/31/91
Export
Rice Milling & Marketing
S.I.C.: 2044; 5153
Larry Grell *(Chm. Bd.)*
David R. Long *(Pres. & Chief Exec. Officer)*
William Ludwig *(Chief Oper. Officer & V.P.)*
Raymond Matsumoto *(Chief Fin. Officer)*
Kaydee Brownlee *(V.P. & Dir.-Human Resources)*
Carl D. Hoff *(Treas. & Controller)*
John W. Kenward *(Sec.)*
Glenn Kohlmiester *(Mgr.-Data Processing)*

Computer Systems/Hardware:
Wang

Outside Service Firm(s):

KPMG Peat Marwick*(Auditors)*
2495 Natomas Park Dr., Ste. 600
Sacramento, CA 95833-2936

EBP, Inc.*(Group Insurer)*
Fresno, CA

New England Mutual Life Insurance Co.*(Group Insurer)*
Boston, MA

Chemical Banking Corp.*(Major Banking Relationship)*
277 Park Ave.
New York, NY 10041
Tel.: 212-310-6407
Fax: 212-310-4526

Sacramento First National Bank*(Major Banking Relationship)*
Sacramento, CA

New England Mutual Life Insurance Co.*(Pension Manager)*
Boston, MA

Subsidiary:

RGA Byproducts **(1)**
P.O. Box 958
Sacramento, CA 95804
Tel.: 916-371-6941

GEORGE RICE & SONS
2001 N. Soto St.
Los Angeles, CA 90032
Tel.: 213-223-2020
Fax: 213-223-3679
Year Founded: 1879
Approx.Sls.: $79,480,000
Emp.: 450
Offset Printing; Annual Reports, Brochures, Posters, Advertising Literature, General Commercial Printing
S.I.C.: 2752
Ewel Grossberg *(Chm. Bd.)*
Randolph K. Ginsberg *(Pres.)*
James F. Clements *(Sr. V.P.)*
James Cooper *(V.P.-Mfg.)*
John Woodlock *(V.P.-Fin.)*
Jack Sherif *(Controller)*

Outside Service Firm(s):

Arthur Andersen & Co.*(Auditors)*
633 W. Fifth St.
Los Angeles, CA 90071
Tel.: 213-614-6500

Armstrong, Hendler & Hirsch*(Legal Firm)*
1888 Century Park East
Los Angeles, CA 90067
Tel.: 310-553-0305

Wells Fargo Bank*(Major Banking Relationship)*
333 S. Grand
Los Angeles, CA 90071
Tel.: 213-253-6836

RICE/SPECTOR INC.
217 S. Hampton Dr.
Venice, CA 90291
Tel.: 310-392-9212
Year Founded: 1979
Approx.Billings: $10,000,000
Emp.: 22
Richard Rice *(Chm. Bd.)*
Don Spector *(Pres.)*
Robert Shand *(Partner)*
Susan York *(Partner)*

RICELAND FOODS, INC.
2120 Park Ave.
Stuttgart, AR 72160
Mailing Address:
P.O. Box 927
Stuttgart, AR 72160
Tel.: 501-673-5500 **AR**
Telex: 536-464
Fax: 501-673-5667
Year Founded: 1921
Assets: $289,827,000
Earnings: $18,634,000
Liabilities: $135,682,000
Net Worth: $154,145,000
Approx.Sls.: $643,904,000
Emp.: 2,000
Fiscal Year-end: 7/31/90

Import Export
Grain Handling & Storage; Rice Milling & Marketing; Soybean Processing; Grain Merchandising
S.I.C.: 2075; 2044; 2079; 0723
Stewart E. Jessup *(Chm. Bd.)*
Richard E. Bell *(Pres. & Chief Exec. Officer)*
Carl. W. Brothers *(Sr. V.P.-Mktg.)*
Michael D. Shook *(Sr. V.P.-Mfg. & Engrng.)*
Harry E. Loftis *(V.P. & Chief Fin. Officer)*
Terry L. Richardson *(V.P.-Admin. & Sec.)*
W. Cary Parker *(V.P.-Food Mktg.)*
Frank T. Orthoefer *(V.P.-Research & Devel.)*
Bill J. Reed *(V.P.-Communications & Pub. Affairs)*
George Vickers *(Asst. V.P.-Human Resources)*
Douglas L. Blohm *(Controller)*
Beverly C. Harlan *(Dir.-Adv.)*
Ben Shelton *(Dir.-Mngmt. Information Systems)*
Bob Longnecker *(Dir.-Telecommunications)*
Jerry A. Delatte *(Gen. Sls. Mgr.-Edible Oils)*
James Borchert *(Mgr.-Pur.)*
Ed Carle *(Prod. Mgr.-Consumer Products)*

Principal(s):
Stewart E. Jessup
Richard E. Bell

No. of Mfg. Plants/Facilities: 35
No. of U.S. Offices: 2

Computer Systems/Hardware:
IBM

Outside Service Firm(s):

Arkwright Mutual Insurance*(Commercial Insurance Carrier)*
225 Wyman St.
Waltham, MA 02254-9198
Tel.: 617-890-9300
Fax: 617-890-0075

Aetna Life & Casualty*(Group Insurer)*
151 Farmington Avenue
Hartford, CT 06156
Tel.: 203-273-2128
Fax: 203-729-4295

Arkwright Mutual Insurance*(Group Insurer)*
225 Wyman St.
Waltham, MA 02254-9198
Tel.: 617-890-9300
Fax: 617-890-0075

Liberty Mutual*(Group Insurer)*
Boston, MA

Sonnenschien, Nath, & Rosenthal*(Legal Firm)*
Washington, DC

Boatmen's Trust Company*(Major Banking Relationship)*
100 North Broadway
St. Louis, MO 63102
Tel.: 314-466-2469

First Tennessee Bank, N.A.*(Major Banking Relationship)*
Memphis, TN

RICH PRODUCTS CORP.
1150 Niagara St.
Buffalo, NY 14213
Mailing Address:
P.O. Box 245,
Buffalo, NY 14240
Tel.: 716-878-8000
Fax: 716-878-8266
Year Founded: 1945
Approx.Sls.: $890,000,000
Emp.: 7,000
Fiscal Year-end: 12/31/91

Import Export
Mfr. Non-Dairy Products, Frozen Foods, Baked Goods & Seafood; Professional Sports; Broadcasting
S.I.C.: 2038; 2099; 7941; 4832; 2092
Robert E. Rich *(Chm. Bd.)*
Robert E. Rich, Jr. *(Pres.)*
Herbert R. Kusche *(Exec. V.P. & Treas.)*
John E. Schaible III *(Sr. V.P.-Opers. & Business Devel.)*
Donald B. Torgersen *(Sr. V.P.-Food Grp.)*
Charles Trego, Jr. *(Sr. V.P. & Chief Fin. Officer)*
Joseph M. Cerra *(V.P.-Mfg.)*
William G. Gisel, Jr. *(V.P.-Intl. Div.)*
J. Sean O'Mahony *(V.P.-Res. & Devel.)*
Edward J. Ryan *(V.P.-Human Resources)*
Dennis J. Wysocki *(V.P.-Mngmt. Information Systems)*
Maureen O. Hurley *(V.P. & Gen. Counsel)*
Dennis Lanning *(Pres.-Bakery & Deli Div.)*
Kevin Malchoff *(Pres.-Food Service Div.)*
John Turner *(Pres.-Consumer Products Div.)*
David R. Rich *(Sec.)*
Gabrielle DeRose *(Dir.-Corp. Communications & Pub. Rels.)*
Jeffrey Kusche *(Dir.-Pur.)*
Lana Lewis *(Dir.-Corp. Benefits)*
Robert Hartung *(Mgr.)*

Principal(s):
Robert E. Rich
Robert E. Rich, Jr.

No. of Mfg. Plants/Facilities: 22
No. of U.S. Offices: 6
No. of Foreign Offices: 4

Computer Systems/Hardware:
IBM

Outside Service Firm(s):

Ernst & Young*(Auditors)*
1400 Key Tower - 50 Fountain Plaza
Buffalo, NY
Tel.: 716-843-5000
Fax: 716-847-6949

Hartford Life Insurance Co.*(Commercial Insurance Carrier)*
Hartford, CT 06104-2999

Arnall, Golden & Gregory*(Legal Firm)*
55 Park Place
Atlanta, GA 30335
Tel.: 404-577-5100

Marine Midland Bank*(Major Banking Relationship)*
P.O. Box 803, 1 Marine Midland Center, 23rd Floor
Buffalo, NY 14203
Tel.: 716-841-2582

Subsidiaries:

Bison Baseball Inc. **(1)**
275 Washington St.
Buffalo, NY 14203
Tel.: 716-846-2000 (100%)
Michael Billoni *(V.P. & Gen. Mgr.)*

Booth Seafood Sales Corp. **(1)**
P.O. Box 667
Saint Simons Island, GA 31522
Tel.: 912-638-5000

Byron's, Inc. **(1)**
West Main St.
Gallatin, TN 37066
Tel.: 615-452-4892
Chuck Charlton *(Pres.)*

Casa Di Bertacchi **(1)**
1910 Gallagher Dr.
Vineland, NJ 08360
Tel.: 609-696-5600
Mfr. of Italian Food Specialties
S.I.C.: 2038
Lawrence Bertacchi *(Pres.)*

S. Gumpert Co., Inc. **(1)**
3200 Riverside Dr.
Columbus, OH 43221
Tel.: 614-486-6631
Approx.Sls.: $10,000,000
Emp.: 125
Fiscal Year-end: 12/31/88
Mfr. Food Items; Gelatine Desserts, Puddings, Cake Mixes
S.I.C.: 2066; 2099
Lee Baker *(Pres.)*
David Dudley *(Exec. V.P.)*
Bert Bruffett *(Dir.-Adv.)*

Rich Fruit Pak Co. **(1)**
19901 S. McHenry Ave.
Escalon, CA 95320
Tel.: 209-838-3564
S.I.C.: 2038

Rich Products Co. **(1)**
4600 N.W. Pkwy.
Hilliard, OH 43026
Tel.: 614-771-1117
Fax: 614-486-9585
Emp.: 16
Non-Dairy Creaming Agents, Vending Powder Soups
S.I.C.: 2034; 2026
Joe Corwin *(Gen. Mgr.)*

Rich Products Dayton **(1)**
521 Kiser St.
Dayton, OH 45404
Tel.: 513-223-8881
Approx.Sls.: $17,000,000
Emp.: 150
Computer Systems/Hardware:
Castle
Mfr. Pies & Cakes
S.I.C.: 2051
Demetri Preonas *(Gen. Mgr.)*
Frank Otway *(V.P.-Sls.)*
J. Maurer *(Sec. & Treas.)*

Rich SeaPak Corp. **(1)**
McKinnon Airport Rd.
Saint Simons Island, GA 31522
Tel.: 912-638-5000
Fax: 912-634-3104
Emp.: 1,200
Frozen Fish, Shrimp, Seafood Specialties, Onion Rings & Vegetables
S.I.C.: 2038; 2037; 2053
Frank W. Holas *(Pres. & Chief Exec. Officer)*
Jim Bailly *(Dir.-Mktg.-Consumer Prods. Div.)*

THE RICHARD & DAVID JACOBS GROUP
25425 Center Ridge Road
Westlake, OH 44145
Tel.: 216-871-4800
Fax: 216-892-2391
Emp.: 1,800
Real Estate Developer
S.I.C.: 6552
Richard E. Jacobs *(Chm. Bd. & Chief Exec. Officer)*
Martin J. Cleary *(Pres. & Chief Oper. Officer)*
David J. Lewanski *(V.P.-Leasing)*
William Fullington *(Dir.-Mktg. Services)*

Computer Systems/Hardware:
IBM

Outside Service Firm(s):

Society National Bank*(Major Banking Relationship)*
900 Euclid Ave., P.O. Box 6477
Cleveland, OH 44101-6477
Tel.: 216-737-5000
Fax: 216-566-8947

RICHARDS BROTHERS OF MOUNTAIN GROVE
P.O. Box 866
Mountain Grove, MO 65711
Tel.: 417-926-4168 **MO**
Year Founded: 1937
Approx.Sls.: $11,000,000
Emp.: 45
Operation of Grocery Stores
S.I.C.: 5141
Wells E. Richards *(Pres.)*
Olive Richards *(V.P. & Sec.)*

Outside Service Firm(s):

Roberts, McKenzie, Morgan & Cummings*(Auditors)*
Springfield, MO

Security Bank of Mountain Grove*(Major Banking Relationship)*
Mountain Grove, MO

THE RICHARDS GROUP, INC.
10000 N. Central Expwy., Ste. 1200
Dallas, TX 75231
Tel.: 214-891-5700
Fax: 214-891-5844
Year Founded: 1957
Approx.Billings: $180,000,000
Emp.: 242
Scott Crockett *(Principal & Mngmt. Supvr.)*
Jan Deatherage *(Principal & Mngmt. Supvr.)*
Jim McGhee *(Principal & Mngmt. Supvr.)*
Dick Murray *(Principal & Mngmt. Supvr.)*
Stan Richards *(Principal & Mngmt. Supvr.)*
Larry Spiegel *(Principal & Media)*
Brad Todd *(Principal & Mngmt. Supvr.)*
Rod Underhill *(Principal & Mngmt. Supvr.)*
Scot Dykema *(Chief Fin. Officer)*

RICHARDSON BROTHERS CO.
Hwy. PP
Sheboygan Falls, WI 53085
Mailing Address:
P.O. Box 907,
Sheboygan Falls, WI 53085
Tel.: 414-467-4631
Fax: 414-467-3850
Year Founded: 1848
Approx.Sls.: $22,000,000
Emp.: 350
Fiscal Year-end: 12/31/91
Mfr. of Dining Room Furniture
S.I.C.: 2511
David Richardson *(Chm. Bd.)*
Joseph Richardson III *(Pres.)*
James Richardson *(V.P.-Natl. Sls.)*
Jerry Loth *(Sec. & Treas.)*
Kirk Heinig *(Pur. Agent)*

RICHARDSON INDUSTRIES, INC.
Rte. 2 Hwy. PP
Shaboygan Falls, WI 53085
Mailing Address:
P.O. Box 907
Sheboygan Falls, WI 53085
Tel.: 414-467-4631 **WI**
Fax: 414-467-3850
Year Founded: 1848
Approx.Sls.: $58,000,000
Emp.: 750

Mfr. of Wooden Dining Room Furniture; Millwork & Lumber; Trusses, Wooden Roof; Laminated Lumber; Wood Moldings, Unfinished & Prefinished; Rough, Dressed & Finished Lumber
S.I.C.: 2511; 5211; 2439; 7389; 2431; 5031; 2491
Joseph Richardson, II *(Chm. Bd.)*
Joseph E. Richardson, III *(Pres.)*
Larry Miller *(V.P.)*
Evelyn Richardson *(V.P.)*
James Richardson *(V.P.)*
Gerald Loth *(Treas. & Sec.)*

Divisions:

Richardson Bros. Co. Div. **(1)**
Rte. 2 Hwy. PP
Sheboygan Falls, WI 53085
Tel.: 414-467-4631
Mfr. of Wooden Household Furniture
S.I.C.: 2511

Richardson Wood Preserving **(1)**
Rte. 2 Hwy. PP
Sheboygan Falls, WI 53085
Tel.: 414-467-4631
Preserving (Creosoting) of Wood
S.I.C.: 2491

RICHARDSON, MYERS & DONOFRIO, INC

RICHARDSON, MYERS & DONOFRIO, INC.
120 W. Fayette St.
Baltimore, MD 21201
Tel.: 410-576-9000
Fax: 410-752-2191
Year Founded: 1964
Approx.Billings: $67,500,000
Emp.: 82
Integrated Communications Programs Involving Public Relations, Advertising, Sales Promotion & Direct Mail
Hal Donofrio *(Pres. & Chief Exec. Officer)*
Clif Aldrich *(Chief Fin. Officer)*
Jamie Rice *(Exec. V.P.)*
Chuck Donofrio *(Exec. V.P.)*
Ken Majka *(Exec. V.P., Creative Dir.)*
Susan Anthony *(Exec. V.P., Pub. Rels.)*
Chris Hartman *(Exec. V.P., Gen. Mgr.-RMD Pub. Affairs)*
Bill Porter *(Sr. V.P., Media Services)*
Paul Field *(Sr. V.P.)*
Nancy Karpinski *(V.P.)*

RICHARDSON STRANG ASSOCIATES
1200 N.W. Front Ave., Ste. 220
Portland, OR 97209
Tel.: 503-226-2721
Fax: 503-226-4854
Year Founded: 1965
Approx.Billings: $12,500,000
Emp.: 16
Charles Richardson *(Pres.)*
Duncan Strang *(Sr. V.P.)*
Robyn Skene *(V.P.)*

RICHCO PLASTICS COMPANY
5825 N. Tripp Ave.
Chicago, IL 60646
Mailing Address:
P.O. Box 804238,
Chicago, IL 60680
Tel.: 312-539-4060
Fax: 312-539-0549
Sales Range: $20-39 Million
Emp.: 250
Manufacture Plastic Installation Hardware
S.I.C.: 3089
James Craig Richardson *(Pres.)*
Jim Fegen *(Exec. V.P. & Gen. Mgr.)*
Burt Pohlmann *(V.P.-Admin. & Affiliated Companies)*
Robert Blackwell *(Dir.-Pur.)*
Sharon Ozimek *(Mgr.-Mktg. Services)*
Ted Pavoris *(Mgr.-Natl. Sls.)*
Al Taylor *(Plant Mgr.)*
Principal(s):
James Craig Richardson

No. of Mfg. Plants/Facilities: 8
No. of U.S. Offices: 6
No. of Foreign Offices: 4

Outside Service Firm(s):

Harris Trust & Savings Bank*(Major Banking Relationship)*
111 W. Monroe St.
Chicago, IL 60690
Tel.: 312-461-2265
Tel.: 800-858-0840

S.D. RICHMAN SONS, INC.
2435 E. Wheatsheaf Lane
Philadelphia, PA 19137
Tel.: 215-535-5100 **PA**
Fax: 215-288-1043
Year Founded: 1901
Sales Range: $10-19 Million
Emp.: 75
Export
Prepared Grades Of Scrap Iron, Steel & Nonferrous Metals
S.I.C.: 5093
David Richman *(Pres.)*
Bruce Richman *(Exec. V.P.)*

Outside Service Firm(s):

A.G. Epstein & Co.*(Auditors)*
Jenkintown, PA

Pelino & Lentz, P.C.*(Legal Firm)*
Packard Bldg.
Philadelphia, PA 19102
Tel.: 215-665-1540

CoreStates First Pennsylvania Bank, N.A.*(Major Banking Relationship)*
16th & Market Sts.
Philadelphia, PA 19101
Tel.: 215-786-8030

RICHMOND MOTOR COMPANY
4600 W. Broad St.
Richmond, VA 23230
Tel.: 804-358-5521
Fax: 804-358-2650
Approx.Sls.: $20,000,000
Emp.: 160
Dealer New & Used Automobiles & Trucks
S.I.C.: 5511
Robert C. King, Sr. *(Pres.)*
Robert C. King, Jr. *(V.P., Gen. Mgr., & Mgr.-Adv. & Mktg.)*
Principal(s):
Robert C. King, Sr.

Outside Service Firm(s):

Deloitte & Touche*(Auditors)*
700 Bldg.,Suite 1800, 700 E. Main St.
Richmond, VA 23219-2619
Tel.: 804-697-1543
Fax: 804-697-1859

Mays & Valentine*(Legal Firm)*
Sovran Center, 1111 E. Main St.
Richmond, VA 23208
Tel.: 804-697-1200

C&S Sovran Bank*(Major Banking Relationship)*
P.O. Box 26904,
Richmond, VA 23261
Tel.: 804-344-1359

Crestar Bank*(Major Banking Relationship)*
P.O. Box 26665,
Richmond, VA 23261
Tel.: 804-782-5995

RICHMOND SCREW ANCHOR COMPANY
7214 Burns St., Richland Hills
Fort Worth, TX 76118
Tel.: 817-284-4981
Fax: 817-284-4504
Year Founded: 1911
Approx.Sls.: $20,000,000
Emp.: 250
Fiscal Year-end: 8/31/92
Export
Engineered Tying Devices, Anchorages & Access. for Concrete Construction
S.I.C.: 3559
C.W. Dishinger *(V.P.)*
John Middleton *(V.P.-Production)*
Gary Tomas *(Controller)*
Harry Lancelot *(Dir.-Engrng.)*
O.W. Secoy *(Mgr.-Adv.)*
A. Gaines *(Mgr.-Natl. Sls.)*

No. of Foreign Offices: 1

RICHMOND TECHNOLOGY INC.
1897 Colton Ave.
Redlands, CA 92374
Tel.: 909-794-2111
Fax: 909-794-4003
Year Founded: 1947
Approx.Sls.: $20,000,000
Emp.: 200
Export
Converted Film & Laminated Products for Aerospace, Electronics, Medical & Food Packaging Applications
S.I.C.: 3089
R.P. Gilbert *(Pres.)*
Dave Gorene *(V.P.-Opers.)*
Charles Hampton *(V.P.-Sls.)*
R. Hauser *(V.P.-Engrng.)*
Debbie Marshall *(Controller)*
Larry Myers *(Mgr.-Pur.)*

Outside Service Firm(s):

Price Waterhouse*(Auditors)*
750 B St.
San Diego, CA 92101
Tel.: 619-231-9830

Stradling, Yocca, Carlson & Rauth*(Legal Firm)*
660 Newport Center Dr., Ste. 1600
Newport Beach, CA 92660
Tel.: 714-640-7035
Fax: 714-725-4100

Wells Fargo Bank*(Major Banking Relationship)*
420 Montgomery St.
San Francisco, CA 94104

RICHTER & RATNER CONTRACTING CORPORATION
55-05 Flushing Ave.
Maspeth, NY 11378
Tel.: 718-497-1600 **NY**
Fax: 718-381-8579
Year Founded: 1912
Assets: $5,550,000
Liabilities: $2,450,000
Net Worth: $3,100,000
Approx.Sls.: $35,000,000
Emp.: 300
Fiscal Year-end: 12/31/91
General Contracting
S.I.C.: 1541; 1542
Charles Ratner *(Chm. Bd.)*
Michael H. Ratner *(Pres.)*
Charles G. Mogul *(Chief Fin. Officer)*
Ronald Weiss *(Mgr.-Construction)*
Principal(s):
Charles Ratner
Michael H. Ratner

No. of Mfg. Plants/Facilities: 2
No. of U.S. Offices: 1

Computer Systems/Hardware:
General Automation Systems & Zebra 6700

Outside Service Firm(s):

Joel Popkin & Co.*(Auditors)*
New York, NY

Frank B. Hall & Co. of New York*(Commercial Insurance Carrier)*
Wall Street Plaza,
New York, NY 10005
Tel.: 212-952-1200
Telex: 125295
Fax: 212-514-6763

Frank B. Hall & Co. of New York*(Group Insurer)*
Wall Street Plaza,
New York, NY 10005
Tel.: 212-952-1200
Telex: 125295
Fax: 212-514-6763

Robinson, Brog & Leinwand*(Legal Firm)*
1345 Ave. of the Americas
New York, NY 10105
Tel.: 212-586-4050

Norstar Bank*(Major Banking Relationship)*
New York, NY

RICO MOTOR COMPANY
501-23 W. Coal
Gallup, NM 87301
Tel.: 505-722-2271
Fax: 505-722-9604
Year Founded: 1971
Approx.Sls.: $36,000,000
Emp.: 82
Retail Sales of New & Used Automobiles
S.I.C.: 5511
T. Howard Menapace *(Pres.)*
Mary Constant *(V.P.)*

Outside Service Firm(s):

Sun West Bank*(Major Banking Relationship)*
Gallup, NM

RIDDLEBERGER BROTHERS, INC.
P.O. Box 27
Mount Crawford, VA 22841
Tel.: 703-434-1731 **VA**
Fax: 703-432-1691
Year Founded: 1946
Approx.Sls.: $15,000,000
Emp.: 190
Mechanical Contractor
S.I.C.: 1711
Hensel D. Riddleberger, Jr. *(Chief Exec. Officer)*
James E. Riddleberger *(Pres.)*
Pablo Cuevas *(Exec. V.P.-Opers.)*
Charles Cline *(V.P.)*
Donald L. Moyers *(Treas., Sec. & Controller)*

Outside Service Firm(s):

McGladrey & Pullen*(Auditors)*
Crawford, VA

Farmers & Merchants Bank*(Major Banking Relationship)*
Long Beach, CA

RIDG-U-RAK, INC.
South Lake St.
North East, PA 16428
Tel.: 814-725-8751
Fax: 814-725-5659
Year Founded: 1942
Approx.Sls.: $32,000,000
Emp.: 275
Designs & Sells Complete Storage Systems; Pallet Storage Racks
S.I.C.: 2452; 5051
John B. Pellegrino *(Pres. & Chief Exec. Offcier)*

Ridg-U-Rak, Inc.—(Continued)

Karen Kaizer *(Sec.)*
Robert A. Johnson *(Dir.-Fin.)*
Richard Winschel *(Mgr.-Personnel)*
John Decker *(Natl. Sls. Mgr.)*

RIDGEVIEW MOTORS, INC.
4025 Mannheim Rd.
Schiller Park, IL 60176
Tel.: 708-678-2300 **IL**
Fax: 708-678-2600
Approx.Sls.: $10,000,000
Emp.: 120
Passenger Car Leasing
S.I.C.: 7515
David Zaransky *(Chm. Bd.)*
Michael Zaransky *(Pres. & Sec.)*
Max Kamm *(V.P.)*
Sylvia Kamm *(V.P.)*
Rosalyn Zaransky *(V.P.)*

Outside Service Firm(s):

Sun Burst*(Major Banking Relationship)*
Baton Rouge, LA

Subsidiary:

Airways Rent A Car **(1)**
4025 N. Mannheim Rd.
Schiller Park, IL 60176
Tel.: 708-678-2300
Fax: 708-678-2600
Approx.Sls.: $28,000,000
Emp.: 50
Fiscal Year-end: 9/30/90
Automobile Rental & Leasing
S.I.C.: 7514
David Zaransky *(Chm. Bd.)*
Michael H. Zaransky *(Pres.)*
Marc Zaransky *(V.P.-Leasing)*
Steve Zaransky *(V.P.-Adv. & Video Systems)*
Pat Pisarski *(Treas.)*
Jamie Goodwin *(Controller)*
Gail Lazzara *(Dir.-Opers.)*
Howard Maybloom *(Dir.-Franchises)*
Rosemary Papas *(Dir.-Training)*
Shirley Schwartz *(Dir.-Personnel)*
Fred Seidner *(Mgr.-Pub. Rels.)*
Jose Yepez *(Service Mgr.)*

RIEMEIER LUMBER COMPANY, INC.
1528 Gest St.
Cincinnati, OH 45203
Tel.: 513-241-3788 **OH**
Fax: 513-241-7883
Year Founded: 1923
Approx.Sls.: $21,000,000
Emp.: 57
Mfr. of Prefabricated Wood Buildings; Millwork & Lumber; Rough, Dressed & Finished Lumber; Trusses; Wooden Roof
S.I.C.: 2452; 5211; 5031; 2439
David A. Luecke *(Pres. & Chief Exec. Officer)*
Kenneth Franke *(V.P. & Treas.)*
Thomas Franke *(V.P. & Sec.)*

Outside Service Firm(s):

Fifth Third Bank*(Major Banking Relationship)*
Corporate Trust Services, 38 Fountain Square Plaza
Cincinnati, OH 45263

RIETH-RILEY CONSTRUCTION CO. INC.
3626 Eckhart Road
Goshen, IN 46526
Mailing Address:
P.O. Box 477
Goshen, IN 46526
Tel.: 219-875-5183
Fax: 219-875-8405
Year Founded: 1916
Assets: $47,667,000
Liabilities: $11,717,000
Net Worth: $35,950,000
Approx.Sls.: $126,313,000
Emp.: 1,000
Fiscal Year-end: 3/31/91
Highway & Heavy Construction
S.I.C.: 1611; 1629
Dale E. Capon *(Chm. Bd. & Pres.)*
Earl J. Hackett *(V.P.-Admin.)*
Robert L. McCormick *(V.P.-Opers.)*
R.A. Franco *(Controller)*
F.J. Gantner *(Gen. Counsel)*
Larry L. Jones *(Treas. & Sec.)*
Jeff Cox *(Dir.-Mngmt. Information Systems)*
L.A. DeWitt *(Mgr.-Bus. Devel.)*
M. Fodor *(Mgr.-Human Resources)*

No. of U.S. Offices: 15

Computer Systems/Hardware:
JD Edwards/IBM

Outside Service Firm(s):

Crowe, Chizek & Co.*(Auditors)*
South Bend, IN

Barnes & Thornburg*(Legal Firm)*
100 N. Michigan., Ste. 600
South Bend, IN 46601
Tel.: 219-233-1171

Midwest Commerce Banking Co.*(Major Banking Relationship)*
Elkhart, IN

RIGGS INDUSTRIES, INC.
Rte. 30 W.
Stoystown, PA 15563
Tel.: 814-629-5621
Fax: 814-629-6588
Year Founded: 1985
Emp.: 350
Structural Steel Erection Contractor; Manufacture Truck Bodies & Trailers, Steel Fabrication Equipment; Rental & Mine Construction
S.I.C.: 1629; 1791; 3713; 3715; 3441
Sidney W. Riggs *(Chm. Bd.)*
S. William Riggs *(V.P.)*
C. Daniel Riggs *(Sec.)*
William Friedline *(Controller)*

Outside Service Firm(s):

Dembo, Jones & Healy*(Auditors)*
Johnstown, PA

Johnstown Bank & Trust Company*(Major Banking Relationship)*
532 - 534 Main St.
Johnstown, PA 15901

Subsidiary:

Somerset Welding & Steel, Inc. **(1)**
P.O. Box 735,
Somerset, PA 15501
Tel.: 814-443-4811
Manufacture Truck Bodies & Trailers; J & J Truck Bodies
S.I.C.: 3713; 3715; 5013; 5082; 5085
Sidney W. Riggs *(Chm. Bd., Sec. & Treas.)*
Guy E. Rush *(V.P.)*
William Friedline *(Controller)*

J. A. RIGGS TRACTOR CO.
9125 Interstate 30
Little Rock, AR 72203
Mailing Address:
P.O. Box 1399,
Little Rock, AR 72203
Tel.: 501-570-3000
Fax: 501-570-3525
Year Founded: 1928
Approx.Sls.: $65,000,000
Emp.: 360
Wholesale Construction Equipment, Engines & Parts
S.I.C.: 5082; 5084
John A. Riggs *(Chm. Bd.)*
Robert G. Cress *(Pres.)*
Jerry L. Griffith *(Sec. & Controller)*

Right Ideas
(See Herbal Enterprises Inc. Listing)

RIGOLI COMMUNICATIONS
2111 Landings Dr.
Mountain View, CA 94043
Tel.: 415-691-1430
Fax: 415-967-1608
Year Founded: 1969
Approx.Billings: $10,000,000
Emp.: 10
Tom Rigoli *(Chm.)*

RIHM MOTOR COMPANY
2108 University Ave.
Saint Paul, MN 55114
Tel.: 612-646-7833
Fax: 612-646-0630
Approx.Sls.: $18,000,000
Emp.: 54
Wholesale Distributor of Trucks & Tractors; General Repair of Trucks
S.I.C.: 5012; 7538
Walter F. Rihm *(Pres.)*
John W. Rihm *(V.P. & Gen. Mgr.)*
Mark Shide *(Controller)*
Pat Duffy *(Mgr.-Parts)*
Mary Foule *(Mgr.-Sls.)*

Outside Service Firm(s):

Bergerson, Booth & Machowicz*(Auditors)*
Minneapolis, MN

Stringer, Courtney & Donnelly*(Legal Firm)*
St. Paul, MN

Midway National Bank*(Major Banking Relationship)*
St. Paul, MN

RIKLIS FAMILY CORPORATION
667 Madison Ave., 12th Flr.
New York, NY 10021
Tel.: 212-735-9500 **DE**
Fax: 212-735-9515
Year Founded: 1980
Approx.Sls.: $2,450,000,000
Emp.: 43,000
Fiscal Year-end: 1/31/90
Import
Holding Company Engaged Through Its Direct & Indirect Subsidiaries & Divisions in Retail Merchandising, Discount Retailing, Manufacturing & Distribution Of Apparel Products
S.I.C.: 5331; 5611; 2329; 2341; 2321; 6719
Meshulam Riklis *(Chm. Bd. & Pres.)*
Paul Weiner *(Treas.)*

No. of Mfg. Plants/Facilities: 40

Computer Systems/Hardware:
IBM

Outside Service Firm(s):

Deloitte & Touche*(Auditors)*
1 World Trade Center
New York, NY 10048
Tel.: 212-669-5000

Equitable Real Estate Investment Managment Inc.*(Group Insurer)*
3414 Peachtree Rd. N.E.
Atlanta, GA 30326-1162

Rubin, Baum, Levin, Constant & Friedman*(Legal Firm)*
645 Fifth Ave.
New York, NY 10022
Tel.: 212-759-2700

Chemical Bank*(Major Banking Relationship)*
450 West 33rd St.
New York, NY 10001
Tel.: 212-613-7197
Fax: 212-947-7628

Security Pacific Corporation*(Major Banking Relationship)*
Security Pacific Plaza
Los Angeles, CA 90071
Tel.: 213-345-6211
Fax: 213-625-0809

Equitable Real Estate Investment Managment Inc.*(Pension Manager)*
3414 Peachtree Rd. N.E.
Atlanta, GA 30326-1162

Chemical Bank*(Pension Manager)*
450 West 33rd St.
New York, NY 10001
Tel.: 212-613-7197
Fax: 212-947-7628

Subsidiaries:

McCrory Corporation **(1)**
667 Madison Ave.
New York, NY 10021
Tel.: 212-735-9500 (100%)
Fax: 212-735-9450
Approx.Sls.: $1,382,000,000
Emp.: 26,100
Fiscal Year-end: 1/31/90
Chain of Retail Variety Stores
S.I.C.: 5331
Meshulam Riklis *(Pres. & Chief Exec. Officer)*
Harold S. Divine *(Exec. V.P.)*
Simona Riklis Akerman *(V.P.)*
Marcia Riklis *(V.P.)*
Ira D. Riklis *(V.P.)*
Paul Weiner *(V.P.)*
Michael J. Magenheim *(Controller)*
Jeff Safchick *(Sec.)*
Phil Weisman *(Dir.-Data Processing)*

Divisions:

McCrory Stores Div. **(2)**
2955 E. Market St.
York, PA 17402
Tel.: 717-757-8181 (100%)
Variety Stores, Restaurant Operations & Franchising
S.I.C.: 5331; 5812; 6794
Robert M. Spenser *(Chm. Bd.)*
Steve Jackel *(Pres. & Chief Oper. Officer)*
Stephen W. Walcavich *(Sr. V.P.-Fin.)*

Subsidiary:

T.G. & Y. Holdings, Inc. **(3)**
2955 E. Market St.
York, PA 17402
Tel.: 717-757-8181 (100%)
Holding Co.
S.I.C.: 6719
Robert Spencer *(Chm. Bd.)*
Steve Jackel *(Pres.)*

Subsidiary:

T.G. & Y. Stores Co. **(4)**
2955 E. Market St.
York, PA 17402
Tel.: 717-757-8181 (100%)
Emp.: 27,000
Department Stores
S.I.C.: 5311
Robert Spencer *(Chm. Bd.)*
Steve Jackel *(Pres.)*

J. J. Newberry Co. **(2)**
667 Madison Ave.
New York, NY 10021
Tel.: 212-735-9500 (100%)
Approx.Sls.: $275,500,000
Emp.: 4,000
Retail Chain of Variety Stores
S.I.C.: 5331

Rapid Distribution Service, Inc. **(1)**
2392 North Du Pont Hwy.
Dover, DE 19901
Tel.: 302-678-3098 (100%)
Trucking Services
S.I.C.: 4212; 4213
Meshulam Riklis *(Pres.)*

SCH Holding Corp. **(1)**
725 Fifth Ave.
New York, NY 10022
Tel.: 212-735-9500 (100%)
Holding Company
S.I.C.: 6719
Meshulam Riklis *(Pres.)*

Subsidiary:

OLT-I Corp. **(2)**
725 Fifth Ave.
New York, NY 10022
Tel.: 212-735-9500 (100%)
Holding Company
S.I.C.: 6719

Non-U.S. Holding:

J. J. Newberry Canadian Ltd. c/o Gault Brothers Div. **(1)**
3960 Jacombs Rd.
Richmond, BC V6V 1X4, Canada
Tel.: 604-273-0441 (100%)
Approx.Sls.: $10,000,000
Emp.: 100
Distr. of Gen. Mdse. to Retail Establishments; Sub. of J. J. Newberry Co.
S.I.C.: 5182
Thomas Whittall *(Chief Oper. Officer)*

RILEY CREEK LUMBER COMPANY
Riley Creek Rd.
Laclede, ID 83841
Mailing Address:
P.O. Box 220
Laclede, ID 83841
Tel.: 208-263-7574 **NV**
Fax: 208-263-9375
Year Founded: 1981
Approx.Sls.: $23,000,000
Emp.: 140
General Sawmills & Paper Mills
S.I.C.: 2421
Marc A. Brinkmeyer *(Pres.)*
Judy Kerns *(Sec.)*

Outside Service Firm(s):

LeMasters & Daniels*(Auditors)*
Spokane, WA

First Security Bank & Trust*(Major Banking Relationship)*
Sandpoint, ID

HAL RINEY & PARTNERS
INCORPORATED

HAL RINEY & PARTNERS, INC.
735 Battery St.
San Francisco, CA 94111
Tel.: 415-981-0950 **CA**
Fax: 415-955-4392
Year Founded: 1986
Approx.Billings: $350,000,000
Emp.: 318
Advertising Agency
S.I.C.: 7311
Hal P. Riney *(Chm. & Chief Exec. Officer)*
James D. Travis *(Pres. & Chief Oper. Officer)*
Lyn Muegge *(Exec. V.P., Chief Fin. Officer)*
Jan Carpenter *(Sr. V.P., Dir. Fin. & Admin.)*
John Yost *(Sr. V.P., Gen. Mgr.)*
Carol Sawyer *(V.P., Personnel Dir.)*

No. of U.S. Offices: 4

Computer Systems/Hardware:
Donovan Data Systems, IMS, IBM, Apple

Outside Service Firm(s):

KPMG Peat Marwick*(Auditors)*
345 Park Ave.
New York, NY 10154
Tel.: 212-758-9700
Fax: 212-872-3308

Frankfurt, Garbus, Klein & Selz*(Legal Firm)*
New York, NY

National Westminster Bank plc*(Major Banking Relationship)*
175 Water St.
New York, NY 10038-4924
Tel.: 212-602-3364

Branches:

Hal Riney & Partners, Inc. **(1)**
54 W. Hubbard
Chicago, IL 60611
Tel.: 312-644-0220
Fax: 312-644-5388
S.I.C.: 7311
Barry Krause *(Sr. V.P., Mng. Dir.)*
Norman Kerr *(V.P., Dir. Mktg.)*

Hal Riney & Partners, Inc. **(1)**
100 East 42nd St.
New York, NY 10017
Tel.: 212-973-2100
Fax: 212-867-2656
S.I.C.: 7311
Jim Travis *(Pres. & Chief Oper. Officer)*
Joe O'Neill *(Exec. V.P., Gen. Mgr. & Chief Creative Officer)*
Tully Plesser *(Sr. V.P., Mkt. Plng. & Res.)*
Doug Seay *(Sr. V.P., Dir. Brdcst. Programming)*
Rochelle Klein *(Sr. V.P., Exec. Creative Dir.)*
Jon Parkinson *(Sr. V.P., Creative Dir.)*
Kathryn Windley *(Sr. V.P., Assoc. Creative Dir.)*

RING SCREW WORKS
31550 Stephenson Hwy.
Madison Heights, MI 48071
Tel.: 313-583-6620
Fax: 313-583-6616
Approx.Sls.: $60,000,000
Emp.: 410
Manufacture Automotive Screws & Bolts, Washers, Specialty Cold-Forged Products
S.I.C.: 3452; 3462; 3463; 3542; 3714
Charles R. O'Brien *(Pres.)*
Richard Gromacki *(V.P.-Opers.)*
Julian Kastleberry *(V.P.-Mfg.)*
Mike Kurko *(V.P.)*
Timothy Gargaro *(Treas.)*

Outside Service Firm(s):

Coopers & Lybrand*(Auditors)*
400 Renaissance Center
Detroit, MI 48243
Tel.: 313-446-7100
Fax: 313-446-7117

N.B.D. Bank, N.A.*(Major Banking Relationship)*
611 Woodward Ave.
Detroit, MI 48226
Tel.: 313-225-1122
Fax: 313-225-3420

RING TECHNOLOGIES, INC.
12901 Stephens Dr.
Warren, MI 48089
Tel.: 313-759-3500
Fax: 313-759-3273
Year Founded: 1941
Emp.: 90
Special Dies, Tools, Jigs & Fixtures
S.I.C.: 3544
George G. Bates *(Gen. Mgr.)*
Dorothy G. Bates *(Sec. & Treas.)*

Outside Service Firm(s):

Steven Fitzpatrick*(Legal Firm)*
Detroit, MI

NBD Bank, N.A.*(Major Banking Relationship)*
P.O. Box 222,
Detroit, MI 48232
Tel.: 313-225-1122

Subsidiary:

JL Tool & Processing, Inc. **(1)**
14080 23 Mile Rd.
Utica, MI 48315
Tel.: 313-566-9700
Mfr. of Prototype Tooling & Vacuum Forming
S.I.C.: 3544
George Bates *(Pres.)*

RINGLING BROS., BARNUM & BAILEY COMBINED SHOWS, INC.
(Sub. of Irvin Feld & Kenneth Feld Productions, Inc.)
8607 Westwood Center Dr.
Vienna, VA 22182
Tel.: 703-448-4000
Fax: 703-448-4100
Emp.: 2,500
Fiscal Year-end: 1/27/91
Circus Operations, Costumes, Ice Shows
S.I.C.: 7999
Kenneth J. Feld *(Pres.)*
Allen J. Bloom *(Exec. V.P.-Mktg & Sls.)*
Charles F. Smith *(Sr. V.P.-Fin. & Treas.)*
Jerome Sowalsky *(Sr. V.P.-Corporate Counsel)*
Susannah G. Smith *(V.P.-Corp. Communications)*

Outside Service Firm(s):

Ernst & Young*(Auditors)*
787 Seventh Ave.
New York, NY 10019
Tel.: 212-773-1243

Wells Fargo Bank*(Major Banking Relationship)*
420 Montgomery St.
San Francisco, CA 94104

Subsidiary:

Ice Follies & Holiday on Ice **(1)**
8607 Westwood Center Dr.
Vienna, VA 22182
Tel.: 703-448-4000
Ice Shows
S.I.C.: 7999
Kenneth Feld *(Pres.)*
Allen J. Bloom *(Sr. V.P.-Mktg. & Sls.)*

RINKE PONTIAC-GMC CO.
27100 Van Dyke
Warren, MI 48093
Tel.: 313-756-5100
Fax: 313-756-5100, Ext. 206
Approx.Sls.: $69,500,000
Emp.: 145
Automobile Dealership
S.I.C.: 5511
Roland Rinke *(Pres., Treas. & Chief Exec. Officer)*
Kevin Rinke *(V.P. & Sec.)*

RIPON FOODS, INC.
420 E. Oshkosh
Ripon, WI 54971
Tel.: 414-748-3151
Fax: 414-748-0233
Year Founded: 1930
Sales Range: $10-19 Million
Emp.: 350
Export
Mfr. of Cookies
S.I.C.: 2051
John E. Bumby *(Chm. Bd.)*
Edward W. Bumby *(Pres.)*
Lowell Dyer *(V.P.-Mktg.)*
Michael J. O'Neill *(V.P.-Sls.)*
Ann Fallon *(Sec.)*
David W. Gerner *(Dir.-Personnel)*
William Otto *(Dir.-Fin.)*
Lee A. Prellwitz *(Dir.-Mfg.)*
Principal(s):
John E. Bumby
Edward W. Bumby

Computer Systems/Hardware:
IBM

Outside Service Firm(s):

Coopers & Lybrand*(Auditors)*
411 East Wisconsin Bldg.
Milwaukee, WI 53202

M & I Ripon State Bank*(Major Banking Relationship)*
Ripon, WI

RIS PAPER COMPANY
45-11 33rd St.
Long Island City, NY 11101
Tel.: 718-392-8100
Fax: 516-742-2585
Approx.Sls.: $500,000,000
Emp.: 725
Fiscal Year-end: 12/31/90
Distributor of Fine Paper Products
S.I.C.: 5111
Thomas Walden *(Chm. Bd. & Chief Fin. Officer)*
Craig Johnson *(Pres. & Chief Oper. Officer)*
William E. Collins *(Pres.-Eastern Reg.)*
Kent L. Carson *(Pres. & Gen. Mgr.-RIS USA)*
Lloyd O. Hoffman *(Pres. & Gen. Mgr.-Washington/Pennsylvania)*
Raymond E. Weaver *(Pres. & Gen. Mgr.-Midwest)*
Peter W. Stropple *(V.P.-Fin. & Sec.)*
Jan A. Herchenroder *(Controller)*
Suzanne J. Cook *(Dir.-Human Resources)*
Arnie Finkelstein *(Dir.-Mngmt. Information Systems)*

No. of U.S. Offices: 24

Computer Systems/Hardware:
IBM System 38

Outside Service Firm(s):

KPMG Peat Marwick*(Auditors)*
345 Park Ave.
New York, NY 10154
Tel.: 212-758-9700
Fax: 212-872-3308

Simpson, Thacher & Bartlett*(Legal Firm)*
425 Lexington Ave.
New York, NY 10017
Tel.: 212-455-2000

National Westminster Bank plc*(Major Banking Relationship)*
Astor Plaza, 1515 Broadway
New York, NY 10036

JOHN RISDALL ADVERTISING
2475 15th St., NW
New Brighton, MN 55112
Tel.: 612-631-1098
Fax: 612-631-2561
Year Founded: 1977
Approx.Billings: $14,200,000
Emp.: 13
Direct Mail & Print Advertising
John Risdall *(Pres.)*

RISH EQUIPMENT COMPANY
Airport Rd. Near U.S. 52
Bluefield, WV 24701
Mailing Address:
P.O. Box 330
Bluefield, WV 24701
Tel.: 304-327-5124
Fax: 304-327-8821
Year Founded: 1985
Sales Range: $40-59 Million
Emp.: 150
Distribute Construction & Mining Machinery, Conveyors, Pumps, Electric Machinery
S.I.C.: 5082
W. Jack Davis *(Chm. Bd.)*
Daniel T. Pochick *(Pres.)*
Wayne E. Thompson *(Chief Oper. Officer)*
D. Steven Hamilton *(Treas.)*
Principal(s):

Rish Equipment Company—(Continued)

W. Jack Davis

No. of U.S. Offices: 8

Outside Service Firm(s):

Brown Edwards & Co.*(Auditors)*
Bluefield, WV

First National Bank of Bluefield*(Investment Banker)*
Bluefield, WV 24701

Richardson, Kemper, Hancock & Davis*(Legal Firm)*
602 Law & Commerce Bldg.
Bluefield, WV 24701
Tel.: 304-327-7158

RISSER OIL CORP.
2863 Executive Center Dr.
Clearwater, FL 34622
Tel.: 813-573-4000
Fax: 813-572-9073
Year Founded: 1960
Assets: $5,800,000
Liabilities: $3,100,000
Net Worth: $2,700,000
Approx.Sls.: $35,000,000
Emp.: 56
Fiscal Year-end: 8/31/90
Wholesale Petroleum Distributor
S.I.C.: 5172
P.N. Risser III *(Pres.)*
Bruce Mitchell *(Mgr.-Opers.)*
Principal(s):
P.N. Risser III

Outside Service Firm(s):

KPMG Peat Marwick*(Auditors)*
St. Petersburg, FL

Federated Mutual Insurance Co.*(Commercial Insurance Carrier)*
Owatonna, MN

Martin, Erroll & Rice*(Legal Firm)*
St. Petersburg, FL

Barnett Banks Trust Company, N.A.*(Pension Manager)*
Tampa, FL

RISSLER & MCMURRY COMPANY
3245 N. Salt Creek Hwy.
Casper, WY 82601
Mailing Address:
P.O. Box 2499,
Casper, WI 82602
Tel.: 307-473-9581 **WY**
Fax: 307-235-0144
Year Founded: 1949
Approx.Sls.: $22,000,000
Emp.: 100
General Contractor, Highway & Street Construction, Paving & Resurfacing
S.I.C.: 1611
W.N. McMurry *(Pres.)*
P.S. Bishop *(Treas. & Sec.)*

Outside Service Firm(s):

Macy & Associates*(Auditors)*
Casper, WY

Wyoming National Bank*(Major Banking Relationship)*
234 E. First St.
Casper, WY 82601

RITCHIE CORPORATION
2020 N. Amidon
Wichita, KS 67203
Mailing Address:
P.O. Box 4048
Wichita, KS 67204
Tel.: 316-838-9301
Fax: 316-832-1343
Year Founded: 1917
Approx.Sls.: $55,000,000
Emp.: 650
Import
Asphalt & Concrete Paving Construction; Ready-Mixed Concrete, Packaged Concrete Mixes, Tennis Court & Track Construction, Sand & Rock Extraction
S.I.C.: 1611; 1442; 1771; 2951; 3272
Hale D. Ritchie, Jr. *(Chm. Bd. & Chief Exec. Officer)*
H.T. Ritchie *(Pres. & Chief Oper. Officer)*
Dave Bucholz *(Chief Fin. Officer)*
J.P. Ritchie *(Sr. V.P.-Opers.)*
Max E. Feaster *(V.P.-Construction)*
Gary Kraisinger *(V.P.-RichMix Products)*
Steve Zuendel *(V.P.-Matls.)*
H.D. Ritchie *(Treas.)*
George Maness *(Controller)*
Ada L. Banks *(Sec.)*
Principal(s):
Hale D. Ritchie, Jr.
H.T. Ritchie

Outside Service Firm(s):

Foulston & Siefkin*(Legal Firm)*
700 Fourth Financial Center
Wichita, KS 67202
Tel.: 316-267-6371

Bank IV*(Major Banking Relationship)*
P.O. Box 1122,
Wichita, KS 67201
Tel.: 316-261-4304

Subsidiaries:

Allen's Concrete, Inc. **(1)**
2020 N. Amidon
Wichita, KS 67203
Tel.: 316-838-9301

Concrete Accessories Company, Inc. **(1)**
2020 N. Amidon
Wichita, KS 67204
Tel.: 316-838-9301

Rich-Mix Products **(1)**
2020 N. Amidon
Wichita, KS 67204
Tel.: 316-838-9301

Ritchie Paving, Inc. **(1)**
2020 N. Amidon
Wichita, KS 67203
Tel.: 316-838-9301

Ritchie Sand Company, Inc. **(1)**
2020 N. Amidon
Wichita, KS 67203
Tel.: 316-838-9301

RITCHIE INDUSTRIES, INC.
120 S. Main
Conrad, IA 50621
Mailing Address:
P.O. Box 730
Conrad, IA 50621
Tel.: 515-366-2525
Year Founded: 1943
Approx.Sls.: $12,000,000
Emp.: 150
Fiscal Year-end: 12/31/90
Mfr. Livestock Fountains & Hydrants
S.I.C.: 3523
Clifford D. Wilson *(Pres. & Chief Exec. Officer)*
Dan Miller *(Sec. & Controller)*
Carla Skramovsky *(Dir.-Pur.)*
Gary Stayskal *(Dir.-Personnel)*
Mike Gerbo *(Dir.-Engrng.)*
Tom Swegle *(Dir.-Mktg.)*
Al Visser *(Mgr.-Mfg.)*
Dee Brown *(Mgr.-Sls.)*
Rich Meester *(Mgr.-Data Processing)*
Jeff Plaehn *(Mgr.-Quality Control)*

Division:

Trojan Specialized Livestock Equip. **(1)**
120 South Main, Box 730
Conrad, IA 50621
Tel.: 515-366-2525
S.I.C.: 3523

RITE-HITE CORPORATION
8900 No. Arbon Dr.
Milwaukee, WI 53223
Mailing Address:
P.O. Box 23043
Milwaukee, WI 53223
Tel.: 414-355-2600
Tel.: 800-456-0600
Year Founded: 1967
Approx.Sls.: $70,000,000
Emp.: 200
Fiscal Year-end: 12/31/90
Mfr. Dok-Lok-Levelers & Safety Prods.; Hydra & Cyclamatic Dock Levelers
S.I.C.: 3599
Arthur K. White *(Chm. Bd.)*
Michael H. White *(Pres. & Chief Exec. Officer)*
Clem Maslowski *(Chief Fin. Officer)*
Morgan P. White *(Exec. V.P.)*
Glenn Manich *(V.P.-Intl. Bus.)*
Terry McGushin *(V.P.-Mktg.)*
Jerry Neumann *(V.P.-Sls.)*
Paul S. Olsen *(V.P.-Rite-Hite Div.)*
Richard Diedrich *(Mgr.-Mktg. Services)*
Anne Sachse *(Mgr.-Adv. & Pub. Rels.)*
Vim Glad *(Corp. Travel Plnr.)*

Subsidiary:

Rite-Hite Corporation (IA) **(1)**
4343 Chavenell Dr.
Dubuque, IA 52001
Tel.: 319-556-2020
Fax: 319-589-2792
Emp.: 350
Export
Computer Systems/Hardware:
IBM/System 400
Mfr. Dock Shelters, Traffic & Powered Doors & Safety Curtains
S.I.C.: 3448
Michael H. White *(Pres.)*
Thomas Semrae *(V.P.-Gen. Mgr. & Chief Exec. Officer)*
Pete Nygarel *(Chief Information Officer (MIS))*
Marilyn Kammiller *(Dir.-Fin. & Acctg.)*
Jon Giuliani *(Dir.-Pur.)*

RITE-WAY, INC.
280 Midland Ave.
Saddle Brook, NJ 07662
Tel.: 201-791-0900
Approx.Sls.: $10,000,000
Emp.: 55
Manufacture Carburetors, Brake Shoes, Generators, Starter Motors, Water Pumps, Distributors, Voltage Regulators, Transmissions
S.I.C.: 3592; 3694; 3714
Thomas C. Devona *(Pres. & Treas.)*
James L. Arbegast *(V.P. & Gen. Mgr.)*
J. Dudas *(Gen. Counsel)*
Harold Cummins *(Mgr.-Prod.)*
Joseph Kozell *(Pur. Agent & Stock Mgr.)*

Outside Service Firm(s):

Charles S. Krantz & Co.*(Auditors)*
Great Neck, NY

National Westminster Bank plc*(Major Banking Relationship)*
2 Montgomery St.
Jersey City, NJ 07302
Tel.: 201-547-7000

RITTENHOUSE INC.
250 S. Northwest Hwy.,
Park Ridge, IL 60068
Tel.: 708-692-9130 **IL**
Fax: 312-318-1712
Year Founded: 1983
Assets: $20,556,210
Liabilities: $11,772,026
Net Worth: $8,784,184
Approx.Sls.: $93,000,000
Emp.: 600
Fiscal Year-end: 3/31/90
Manufacture Paper, Ribbons & Labels for Business Machines
S.I.C.: 2678; 3955
Robert S. Berger *(Chm. Bd.)*
Andrew B. Albert *(Pres. & Co-Chief Exec. Officer)*
Simon J. Blattner, Jr. *(Co-Chief Exec. Officer)*
Simon J. Blattner III *(Chief Fin. Officer)*
John Peterka *(Controller)*
Principal(s):
Andrew B. Albert
Simon J. Blattner, Jr.

No. of Mfg. Plants/Facilities: 8
No. of U.S. Offices: 8
No. of Foreign Offices: 1

Computer Systems/Hardware:
Data General

Outside Service Firm(s):

Joseph Kowalkowski*(Auditors)*
Oak Brook, IL

Cigna*(Commercial Insurance Carrier)*
525 W. Monroe St., Ste. 1900
Chicago, IL 60606
Tel.: 312-648-3742

Cigna*(Group Insurer)*
525 W. Monroe St., Ste. 1900
Chicago, IL 60606
Tel.: 312-648-3742

Jenner & Block*(Legal Firm)*
One IBM Plaza
Chicago, IL 60611
Tel.: 312-222-9350

American National Bank & Trust Company of Chicago*(Major Banking Relationship)*
33 N. LaSalle St.
Chicago, IL 60602
Tel.: 312-661-5000
Fax: 312-661-6417

Simon J. Blattner, III*(Pension Manager)*
Park Ridge, IL

Subsidiary:

Rittenhouse Paper Co. **(1)**
250 S. Northwest Hwy.
Park Ridge, IL 60068
Tel.: 708-692-9130
Manufacture Point Of Sale Expendibles
S.I.C.: 2621
Diana Schultz *(Mgr.)*

RITTER BROS., INC.
1511 N. Cameron St.
Harrisburg, PA 17105
Mailing Address:
P.O. Box 1577,
Harrisburg, PA 17105
Tel.: 717-234-3061 **PA**
Fax: 717-238-7813
Year Founded: 1926
Approx.Sls.: $37,000,000
Emp.: 250
Fiscal Year-end: 12/31/90
General Construction
S.I.C.: 1522; 1541; 1629
William Brightbill *(Pres. & Treas.)*
Steven L. Daniels, AIA *(V.P.-Operations)*
Principal(s):
William Brightbill
Steven L. Daniels, AIA

Computer Systems/Hardware:
IBM

Outside Service Firm(s):

Trout, Ebersole & Groff*(Auditors)*
Harrisburg, PA

Rhoads & Sinon*(Legal Firm)*
Harrisburg, PA

Dauphin Deposit Bank & Trust Co.*(Major Banking Relationship)*
213 Market St.
Harrisburg, PA 17101

Subsidiary:

NORCAM Construction Company **(1)**
1611 N. Cameron St., P.O. Box 2951
Harrisburg, PA 17105
Tel.: 717-232-0370
Fax: 717-232-3523
Emp.: 30
Commercial & Industrial Construction
S.I.C.: 1541
William R. Brightbill *(Pres.)*
Mark Lambdin *(Gen. Mgr.)*

RIVERDALE CHEMICAL CO.
425 W. 194th St.
Glenwood, IL 60425-1584
Tel.: 708-754-3330
Tel.: 800-354-3330
Fax: 708-754-0314
Year Founded: 1941
Approx.Sls.: $18,000,000
Emp.: 48
Import Export
Weedking Compounds 2-4-D & MCPP, and Other Weed Killers & Insecticides
S.I.C.: 2879
James K. Champion *(Pres.)*
Michael J. Champion *(V.P.)*
Marvin R. Moore *(Natl. Sls. Mgr.)*

RIVERS TRAINOR DOYLE & WALSH, INC.
One Catamore Blvd.
Providence, RI 02914
Tel.: 401-434-9200
Fax: 401-434-8912
Year Founded: 1986
Approx.Billings: $10,500,000
Emp.: 27
Health, Pub. Utilities & Energy, Financial, Govt. & Political Adv., Pub. Rels. & Pub. Affairs
Philip R. Rivers *(Pres. & New Bus. Contact)*
Michael M. Doyle *(Exec. V.P., Treas. & Fin.)*
Michael F. Trainor *(Sr. V.P., Adv. Services)*
Robert K. Vincent *(Sr. V.P., Pub. Rels.)*
Thomas E. Walsh *(Sr. V.P., Pub. Rels. Services)*
Grace Quintin *(Office Mgr.)*
Lisa Schaffer *(Sec.)*

RIVERSIDE CENTRAL SERVICES, INC.
521 Main St.
Natchez, MS 39120
Mailing Address:
P.O. Box 1697
Natchez, MS 39121
Tel.: 601-442-3675
Tel.: 601-446-8007 **MS**
Fax: 601-442-3691
Fax: 601-446-8027
Year Founded: 1975
Assets: $11,000,000
Liabilities: $4,000,000
Net Worth: $7,000,000
Approx.Sls.: $2,600,000
Emp.: 25
Warehouse & Trucking Services
S.I.C.: 4226
Larry L. Brown, Sr. *(Pres. & Chief Exec. Officer)*
Allen Brown *(Sec. & Treas.)*
William Gillon *(Controller)*
J. Walter Brown *(Gen. Counsel)*
Larry L. Brown, Jr. *(Dir.-Mktg. & Adv.)*
L. Doughty *(Dir.-Real Estate)*
C. Schuchs *(Dir.-Pur.)*

No. of Mfg. Plants/Facilities: 2
No. of U.S. Offices: 2

Computer Systems/Hardware:
Leading Edge

Outside Service Firm(s):

Gillon & Co.*(Auditors)*
Natchez, MS

Guardian Life Insurance Co.*(Group Insurer)*
New York, NY

Northwestern Mutual*(Group Insurer)*
Milwaukee, WI

United States Fidelity & Guaranty Co.*(Group Insurer)*
100 Light Street
Baltimore, MD 21202
Tel.: 301-547-3000

Deposit Guaranty National Bank*(Investment Banker)*
One Deposit Guaranty Plaza,
Jackson, MS 39201

Brown, Jenkins & Carby*(Legal Firm)*
Natchez, MS

Deposit Guaranty National Bank*(Major Banking Relationship)*
One Deposit Guaranty Plaza,
Jackson, MS 39201

United Mississippi Bank*(Major Banking Relationship)*
Natchez, MS

Harry Edison Associates*(Pension Manager)*
Dallas, TX

RIVERSIDE MANUFACTURING CO.
301 Riverside Dr.
Moultrie, GA 31768
Mailing Address:
P.O. Box 460,
Moultrie, GA 31776
Tel.: 912-985-5210
Tel.: 800-841-8677
Fax: 912-890-2932
Year Founded: 1911
Sales Range: $100-499 Million
Emp.: 1,600
Fiscal Year-end: 6/30/92
Export
Manufacture Business Uniforms & Career Apparel
S.I.C.: 2326; 2321; 2311; 2339
W.J. Vereen *(Pres., Treas., & Chief Exec. Officer)*
H.B. Vereen *(Exec. V.P.)*
Larry Peoples *(Sr. V.P.-Mktg.)*
Barbara B. Vereen *(V.P.-Adv. & Travel)*
Principal(s):
W.J. Vereen

Computer Systems/Hardware:
IBM 3278

Outside Service Firm(s):

Deloitte & Touche*(Auditors)*
100 Peachtree St., Ste. 1700
Atlanta, GA 30303-1943
Tel.: 404-220-1500
Fax: 404-220-1583

MONY*(Group Insurer)*
New York, NY

RIVERSIDE MILLWORK COMPANY, INC.
77 Merrimack St.
Panacook, NH 03303
Tel.: 603-753-6318
Fax: 603-753-6076
Approx.Sls.: $30,000,000
Emp.: 210
Fiscal Year-end: 9/30/91
Manufacture Wholesale & Retail Window & Door Units, Mouldings, Floorings, Plywood & Kitchen Cabinets
S.I.C.: 2431; 2434; 5031; 5211
Andy Connolly *(Pres.)*
Steven Herbert *(Chief Fin. Officer & V.P.)*
Armand Plourde *(V.P.-Opers.)*
Gregory Dow *(V.P.-Sls.)*

Outside Service Firm(s):

Cleveland, Waters & Base*(Legal Firm)*
Concord, NH

Fleet National Bank*(Major Banking Relationship)*
125 Dupont Dr.
Providence, RI 02907-3178
Tel.: 401-278-5335

RIVERSIDE PRESS, INC.
4901 Woodall St.
Dallas, TX 75247
Tel.: 214-631-1150
Fax: 214-951-8035
Approx.Sls.: $38,000,000
Emp.: 380
Commercial Lithography Printing
S.I.C.: 2752
Lloyd M. Gilmore *(Chm. Bd.)*
Garry C. Marsh *(Pres.)*
Harry A. Justiss *(Exec. V.P.)*
Joe Grey, Jr. *(V.P.-Sls.)*
Skip Smith *(V.P.)*
Jackie Walton *(V.P.)*

Outside Service Firm(s):

Bailey, Vaught & Robertson*(Auditors)*
Dallas, TX

Haynes & Boone*(Legal Firm)*
3100 Interfirst Plaza, 901 Main St.
Dallas, TX 75202
Tel.: 214-670-0550

Texas Commerce Bank*(Major Banking Relationship)*
2200 Ross Ave.
Dallas, TX 75266

RIVES CARLBERG
5599 San Felipe, Ste. 1111
Houston, TX 77056
Tel.: 713-965-0764
Fax: 713-965-0135
Year Founded: 1948
Approx.Billings: $36,000,000
W. Charles Carlberg *(Pres. & Chief Exec. Officer)*
Alice Michalec *(Exec. V.P., Gen. Mgr.)*
Tom Adkins *(V.P., Dir. Strategic Planning)*
Cynthia Koplos *(V.P., Dir. Acct. Planning)*
Mark Rice *(V.P., Fin. & Admin.)*
Judi Maddrey *(V.P., Grp. Mngmt. Supvr. & Pub. Rels.)*
Norma Bolton *(Admin. Dir.)*

RIVIANA FOODS INC.
2777 Allen Pkwy.
Houston, TX 77019
Mailing Address:
P.O. Box 2636,
Houston, TX 77252
Tel.: 713-529-3251
Telex: 762623 (OFC HOUSTON)
Fax: 713-529-1661
Sales Range: $100-499 Million
Emp.: 2,400
Fiscal Year-end: 6/30/91
Export
Rice Manufacturer
S.I.C.: 2044
Frank A. Godchaux III *(Chm. Bd.)*
Charles R. Godchaux *(Vice Chm.)*
Joseph A. Hafner *(Pres. & Chief Exec. Officer)*
W. David Hanks *(Exec. V.P. & Asst. Sec.)*
T.M. Forshee *(V.P.-Sls.)*
C.L. Haines *(V.P.-Mktg.)*
Jack M. Nolingberg *(V.P.-Indus. Rels.)*
E. Wayne Ray, Jr. *(V.P.-Fin.)*
Richard F. Vincent *(V.P.-Mfg.)*
R.D. Watts *(V.P.-Industrial & Commodity)*
Elizabeth B. Woodard *(V.P., Gen. Counsel & Sec.)*
John E. Stokes *(Controller)*
Ed S. Crocker, III *(Mgr.)*
Principal(s):
Frank A. Godchaux III
Charles R. Godchaux

Outside Service Firm(s):

Arthur Andersen & Co.*(Auditors)*
711 Louisiana, Ste. 1300
Houston, TX 77002-2323
Tel.: 713-237-2793

Baker & Botts*(Legal Firm)*
3000 One Shell Plaza
Houston, TX 77002
Tel.: 713-229-1789

Texas Commerce Bank*(Major Banking Relationship)*
600 Travis Street, Suite 1150
Houston, TX 77002
Tel.: 713-236-4865

R/K Agri Services, Inc.
(See Riviana Foods Inc.)

RMC Foods
(See Rocky Mountain Company Listing)

ROAD MACHINERY COMPANY
716 S. 7th St.
Phoenix, AZ 85034
Mailing Address:
P.O. Box 4425
Phoenix, AZ 85030
Tel.: 602-252-7121 **AZ**
Fax: 602-253-9690
Year Founded: 1955
Sales Range: $40-59 Million
Emp.: 205
Sales & Rental of Off-Highway Trucks; Servicing & Remanufacturing Components
S.I.C.: 5082; 7699
A.D. Frederickson *(Pres.)*
H.R. Bone, Jr. *(V.P.-Parts & Service)*
R.C. Demorotski *(V.P.-Mining Sls.)*
Jim Frederickson *(V.P.-Admin.)*
A.G. Marr *(V.P.-Mining Sls.)*
Claude Dew *(Gen. Mgr.-Service)*
Patricia Patterson *(Controller)*
Jim Goelzer *(Gen. Parts. Mgr.)*

Computer Systems/Hardware:
DEC

Outside Service Firm(s):

Price Waterhouse*(Auditors)*
100 Cumberland Circle, Ste. 1400
Atlanta, GA 30339

Aetna Life & Casualty*(Group Insurer)*
Phoenix, AZ

Snell & Wilmer*(Legal Firm)*
3100 Valley Ctr.
Phoenix, AZ 85073
Tel.: 602-257-7211

Valley National Bank*(Major Banking Relationship)*
241 North Central Ave., 11th Floor
Phoenix, AZ 85001

ROAD MACHINERY & SUPPLIES CO.
5633 W. Hwy. 13
Savage, MN 55378
Tel.: 612-895-9595

Road Machinery & Supplies Co.—(Continued)

Fax: 612-895-9564
Year Founded: 1926
Approx.Sls.: $45,000,000
Emp.: 220
Wholesale Heavy Construction, Mining & Utility Equipment
S.I.C.: 5082
Michael R. Sill *(Chm. Bd. & Chief Exec. Officer)*
Mitchell J. Sill *(Pres.)*
John Davis *(V.P.-Sls.)*
William T. Holte *(Treas.)*

ROBBINS AUTO PARTS, INC.
110-116 Washington St.
Dover, NH 03820
Tel.: 603-742-2880
Fax: 603-742-3057
Approx.Sls.: $22,000,000
Emp.: 286
Automotive Supplies & Parts
S.I.C.: 5013; 5531
Sidney Robbins *(Chm. Bd.)*
Robert Weisner *(Pres.)*
Richard Robbins *(V.P.)*
Stanley Robbins *(Treas.)*
Steven Cohen *(Sec.)*

Outside Service Firm(s):

Gerald P. Bonder & Co.*(Auditors)*
Boston, MA

Devina, Millmet & Stahl*(Legal Firm)*
Manchester, VT

Bank of New England*(Major Banking Relationship)*
28 State Street
Boston, MA 02109
Tel.: 617-742-4000

ROBBINS, INC.
4777 Eastern Ave.
Cincinnati, OH 45226
Tel.: 513-871-8988 **OH**
Fax: 513-871-7998
Year Founded: 1969
Approx.Sls.: $50,000,000
Emp.: 700
Fiscal Year-end: 10/31/91
Mfr. of Hardwood Flooring Portable Floors & Racquetball Courts, Squash Courts & Residential Wood Block & Parquet Flooring
S.I.C.: 2426
James H. Stoehr, Jr. *(Pres. & Chief Exec. Officer)*
Richard Brian *(Chief Oper. Officer & V.P.-Residential Division)*
Raymond W. Fluegeman *(Chief Fin. Officer, Treas., Controller & Dir.-Data Processing)*
George Riegert *(Controller)*
Jay Seals *(V.P.)*
Jay Cooper *(Dir.-Mktg.)*
Pete Ingram *(Dir.-Admin. & Opers.)*
Peter Meyer *(Dir.-Mngmt. Information Systems)*
David Orewiler *(Mgr.-Human Resources)*
Principal(s):
James H. Stoehr, Jr.

Computer Systems/Hardware:
Honeywell Level 6

Outside Service Firm(s):

Arthur Andersen & Co.*(Auditors)*
425 Walnut St.
Cincinnati, OH 45202
Tel.: 513-381-6900

Graydon, Head & Ritchey*(Legal Firm)*
1900 Fifth Third Center
Cincinnati, OH 45202
Tel.: 513-621-6464

ROBBINS MANUFACTURING COMPANY
Nebraska & 131st. Ave.
Tampa, FL 33612
Mailing Address:
P.O. Box 17939
Tampa, FL 33682
Tel.: 813-971-3030
Fax: 813-972-3980
Approx.Sls.: $40,000,000
Emp.: 230
Lumber Mill; Wood Treating; Wholesale Lumber
S.I.C.: 2421; 2491; 5031
Bruce M. Robbins, Jr. *(Chm. Bd.)*
Laurence W. Hall, Jr. *(Pres.)*
Joseph H. Robbins *(Sr. V.P. & Treas.)*
Rene Huesca *(V.P.-Construction Sls.)*
Jerome G. Robbins *(V.P.)*
William Long, Jr. *(Comptroller)*
Charlie Robbins *(Treas.)*

Outside Service Firm(s):

Rex Meighen & Co.*(Auditors)*
P.O. Box 1790, 509 S. Hyde Park Ave.
Tampa, FL 33601-1790
Tel.: 813-251-1010

Carlton, Fields, Ward, Emmanuel, Smith, Cutler & Kent*(Legal Firm)*
One Harbour Place
Tampa, FL 33602
Tel.: 813-223-5366

First Florida Bank*(Major Banking Relationship)*
P.O. Box 31265,
Tampa, FL 33631-3265
Tel.: 813-224-1475

CHAS ROBERTS AIR CONDITIONING, INC.
9828 N. 19th Ave.
Phoenix, AZ 85021
Tel.: 602-943-7291 **AZ**
Fax: 602-943-3872
Assets: $10,338,529
Liabilities: $4,721,678
Net Worth: $5,616,851
Sales Range: $20-39 Million
Emp.: 325
Heating & Air Conditioning General Contractor
S.I.C.: 1711
Charles Roberts, Jr. *(Chm. Bd. & Pres.)*
Xenia Roberts *(Sec. & Treas.)*
Principal(s):
Charles Roberts, Jr.

No. of Mfg. Plants/Facilities: 1
No. of U.S. Offices: 1

Computer Systems/Hardware:
n/a

Outside Service Firm(s):

KPMG Peat Marwick*(Auditors)*
Phoenix, AZ

Aetna Life & Casualty*(Commercial Insurance Carrier)*
151 Farmington Avenue
Hartford, CT 06156
Tel.: 203-273-2128
Fax: 203-729-4295

Thunderbird Bank*(Investment Banker)*
Phoenix, AZ

Bonn & Anderson*(Legal Firm)*
Phoenix, AZ

Thunderbird Bank*(Major Banking Relationship)*
Phoenix, AZ

F. L. ROBERTS & CO. INC.
93 W. Broad St.
Springfield, MA 01105
Tel.: 413-781-7444
Fax: 413-781-4328
Emp.: 650
Automotive Dealer & Service Stations; Restaurants; Real Estate; Auto Repair Services & Garages
S.I.C.: 5411; 5541; 5171; 5172; 7542; 5812
Abbott S. Roberts *(Chm. Bd.)*
Stephen M. Roberts *(Pres., Chief Exec. Officer & Treas.)*
Seth Roberts *(V.P. & Asst. Treas.)*
Joseph Maggi *(Controller & Chief Fin. Officer)*
Barbara Kuzon *(Dir.-Personnel)*
Kurt Schork *(Dir.)*

Computer Systems/Hardware:
IBM System 36

Outside Service Firm(s):

Aaron Smith Bergman & Gaffney*(Auditors)*
Springfield, MA

Blue Cross of Massachusetts, Inc.*(Group Insurer)*
Boston, MA

Doherty, Wallace, Pillsbury & Murphy*(Legal Firm)*
Springfield, MA

Bank of New England*(Major Banking Relationship)*
Springfield, MA

Subsidiaries:

Broadstreet Plaza **(1)**
511 E. Columbus Ave.
Springfield, MA 01101
Tel.: 413-781-7444

Royal Greenfield Inc. **(1)**
511 E. Columbus Ave.
Springfield, MA 01101
Tel.: 413-781-7444

ROBERTS COMMUNICATIONS INC.
The Piano Works, Ste. 3500, 333 W. Commercial St.
East Rochester, NY 14445
Tel.: 716-381-1000
Tel.: 800-836-7710
Fax: 716-586-2010
Year Founded: 1971
Approx.Billings: $20,240,000
Emp.: 45
Publications, Direct Response & Business-to-Business Adv.
Walter R. Roberts *(Chm. Bd.)*
Paul H. Hudson *(Pres. & Creative Dir.)*
Charles L. Miller *(Sr. V.P., Sec., & Pres.-Publications Div.)*
Diane LaPietra *(V.P., Publications Div.)*
Mike Osborn *(Mng. Dir.-Catalyst Direct)*
Jeff Cleary *(Mng. Dir.-Catalyst Direct)*
Peter LaFauci *(Controller)*
Susan Wells *(Pub. Rels. Dir.)*

JOHN ROBERTS COMPANY
9687 E. River Rd.
Minneapolis, MN 55433
Tel.: 612-755-5500
Fax: 612-755-0394
Year Founded: 1951
Approx.Sls.: $35,000,000
Emp.: 240
Fiscal Year-end: 8/31/91
Commercial Printing & Lithography
S.I.C.: 2752
Robert A. Keene *(Chm. Bd., Sec. & Treas.)*
Michael R. Keene *(Pres.)*
Michael V. Tews *(V.P. & Controller)*
William Culdert *(V.P.-Sls.)*
John Foster *(V.P.-Sls.)*
James Stratton *(V.P.-Sls.)*
Richard W. Olsby *(Dir.-Manufacturing)*

Outside Service Firm(s):

Larsen, Allen, Weishair & Co.*(Auditors)*
Minneapolis, MN

Johnson, Sands, Lizee & Fricker*(Legal Firm)*
Minneapolis, MN

Norwest Bank Minnesota, N.A.*(Major Banking Relationship)*
6th St. & Marquette Ave.
Minneapolis, MN 55479-0065
Tel.: 612-667-8101

ROBERTS FOODS, INC.
1615 W. Jefferson St.
Springfield, IL 62702
Tel.: 217-793-2633 **DE**
Fax: 217-793-3054
Year Founded: 1912
Approx.Sls.: $24,000,000
Emp.: 75
Wholesale Distribution of Packaged Frozen Goods, Groceries & Related Products
S.I.C.: 5142; 5149
Dean E. Robert, Sr. *(Chm. Bd. & Pres.)*
John Steven LaRocca *(Treas. & Sec.)*

Outside Service Firm(s):

Magna Bank of Springfield*(Major Banking Relationship)*
Springfield, IL

J. H. ROBERTS INDUSTRIES INC.
3158 Des Plaines Ave., Ste. 223
Des Plaines, IL 60018
Tel.: 708-699-0080 **DE**
Fax: 708-699-0082
Year Founded: 1982
Assets: $18,600,000
Liabilities: $7,500,000
Net Worth: $11,100,000
Approx.Sls.: $47,400,000
Emp.: 200
Fiscal Year-end: 12/31/90
Import Export
Holding Company
S.I.C.: 6719
John H. Roberts *(Pres. & Chief Exec. Officer)*
Lawrence A. Collins *(Sec. & Treas.)*
Principal(s):
John H. Roberts

No. of Mfg. Plants/Facilities: 8
No. of U.S. Offices: 8

Computer Systems/Hardware:
Compaq

Outside Service Firm(s):

Grant Thornton*(Auditors)*
700 One Prudential Plaza, 130 East Randolph St.
Chicago, IL 60601
Tel.: 312-856-0200
Fax: 312-565-4719

General Casualty Co.*(Commercial Insurance Carrier)*
Chicago, IL

Cigna*(Group Insurer)*
525 W. Monroe St., Ste. 1900
Chicago, IL 60606
Tel.: 312-648-3742

Coffield, Ungaretti & Harris*(Legal Firm)*
3500 Three First National Plaza
Chicago, IL 60602
Tel.: 312-977-4400

McDermott, Will & Emery*(Legal Firm)*
227 W. Monroe St.
Chicago, IL 60606-5096
Tel.: 312-372-2000

American National Bank & Trust Company of Chicago*(Major Banking Relationship)*
33 N. LaSalle St.
Chicago, IL 60602
Tel.: 312-661-5000
Fax: 312-661-6417

Subsidiaries:

Dial Tube Company **(1)**
5133 W. 70th Pl.
Bedford Park, IL 60638
Tel.: 708-594-7576
Tel.: 800-323-2728
Emp.: 25
Steel Service Center
S.I.C.: 5051
Robert J. Stenzel *(Pres.)*
Steve Krautstrunk *(Controller)*
David Stineman *(Mgr.-Matls.)*

Enduro Industries, Inc. **(1)**
136 Commercial Rd.
Addison, IL 60101
Tel.: 708-543-5110
Tel.: 800-323-2529
Emp.: 70
Chrome Plates Steel Bars; Grinding, Polishing,Plating & Induction Hardening
S.I.C.: 3541
G.E. Schulenberg *(Pres.)*
James Segerson *(V.P.-Sls.)*
Bruce Busse *(Dir.-Mktg.)*
Gerry Boe *(Controller)*

Enduro-Niagara Ltd. **(1)**
4750 Christie Dr.
Beamsville, ON L0R 1B4, Canada
Tel.: 416-563-4951
Emp.: 20
Mfr. of Chrome Plated Steel Bars; Grinding, Polishing, Plating & Induction Hardening
S.I.C.: 3541
Andrew Mefine *(Plant Mgr.)*

Mid-West Company **(1)**
100 Tower Dr.
Burr Ridge, IL 60521
Tel.: 708-655-1800
Tel.: 800-323-7224
Emp.: 125
Manufacturing of Cold Drawn Steel Tubing
S.I.C.: 3317
Robert E. Shamburg *(Pres.)*
Fred W. Bolling *(V.P.-Sls.)*
Walt Kretzmann *(Controller)*
John Ferry *(Dir.-Mfg.)*

Moulton Cutting Co. **(1)**
965 So. Lambrecht Rd.
Frankfort, IL 60423
Tel.: 815-469-2711
Emp.: 20
Cutting of Steel Tubing
S.I.C.: 3317
Robert E. Shamburg *(Pres.)*

ROBERTS & RAYMOND ASSOC., INC.
401 City Line Ave., Ste. 209
Bala-Cynwyd, PA 19004
Tel.: 215-667-1502
Fax: 215-667-1455
Year Founded: 1985
Approx.Billings: $24,000,000
Emp.: 22
Pharmaceutical & Healthcare Adv.
Robert Sulpizio *(Pres.)*
Warren A. Dardine *(Exec. V.P.)*
Theresa A. Burke *(Dir., Opers.)*

STANLEY ROBERTS, INC.
65 Industrial Rd.
Lodi, NJ 07644
Tel.: 201-778-5900
Fax: 201-778-8542
Emp.: 145
Manufacturer of Stainless Steel & Gold Flatware & Cutlery
S.I.C.: 3421; 3914
Harold Pomeranz *(Chm. Bd., Treas. & Sec.)*
Edward Pomeranz *(Pres.)*
Leman G. Lane *(Controller)*

Computer Systems/Hardware:
IBM

Outside Service Firm(s):

Glasser & Co.*(Auditors)*
Great Neck, NY

Blodnick, Pomeranz, Schultz & Abramowitz, P.C.*(Legal Firm)*
New York, NY

Midlantic National Bank*(Major Banking Relationship)*
Hackensack, NJ

ROBERTSON FACTORIES, INC.
33 Chandler Ave.
Taunton, MA 02780
Tel.: 508-823-5141 **DE**
Fax: 508-822-8932
Year Founded: 1923
Approx.Sls.: $22,000,000
Emp.: 350
Vogue Ready-Made Curtains & Draperies Creatively Yours - Made-to Measure Lifestyles - Custom Made to Measure Draperies, Top Treatments and Bedspreads; All Custom Products/Accessories; Contract Window/Bedspread & Textile Products
S.I.C.: 2391; 5023
Richard R. Anglin *(Pres. & Chief Exec. & Oper. Officer)*
Philip S. Robertson *(Sr. V.P. & Treas.)*
Robert Corriveau *(V.P. & Controller)*
Charles G. Banyas *(V.P.-Mktg.)*
Benjamin Howes *(V.P.-Mfg.)*
Diana Sullivan *(V.P.-Custom & Made-to-Measure Sls.)*
Carlton Barney *(V.P.-Ready-Made Sls.)*
James P. Whitters III *(Sec.)*
Ellen Hoffman *(Mgr.-Data Processing)*

No. of Mfg. Plants/Facilities: 4

Outside Service Firm(s):

Bay Bank*(Major Banking Relationship)*
Taunton, MA

ROBERTSON MARKETING INC.
803 Pressley Rd., Ste. 104
Charlotte, NC 28217-0971
Tel.: 704-527-5141
Fax: 704-529-5264
Emp.: 13
Manufacture & Distribute Computer Hardware
S.I.C.: 3577; 5045
G. Bruce Robertson *(Pres. & Chief Exec. Officer)*
Ellen Robertson *(V.P.)*
Debbie Salgado *(Office Mgr.)*

Computer Systems/Hardware:
IBM; Memorex Display

Outside Service Firm(s):

Mutual Life*(Group Insurer)*
Charlotte, NC

Branch Banking & Trust Co.*(Major Banking Relationship)*
200 S. Tryon Street
Charlotte, NC 28202
Tel.: 704-342-7039
Fax: 704-342-7048

ROBERTSON'S AUTO SALVAGE
2680 Cranberry Hwy.
Wareham, MA 02571
Mailing Address:
P.O. Box 231
Wareham, MA 02571
Tel.: 508-295-9444
Fax: 508-295-0363
Year Founded: 1970
Approx.Sls.: $10,000,000
Emp.: 27
Fiscal Year-end: 10/31/88
Late Model Auto Salvage
S.I.C.: 5015
Scott V. Robertson *(Pres. & Chief Exec. Officer)*
I. Howard Robertson, Jr. *(Treas. & Chief Fin. Officer)*
Nancy Turgeon *(Sec.)*

Computer Systems/Hardware:
IBM System 36

Outside Service Firm(s):

Creelman Smith*(Auditors)*
Boston, MA

Chubb Life Insurance Co. of America*(Commercial Insurance Carrier)*
Concord, NH

Decas, Murray & Decas*(Legal Firm)*
Marlboro, MA

Shawmut Bank*(Major Banking Relationship)*
Wareham, MA

Subsidiary:

Robertsons Auto Body **(1)**
P.O. Box 231
Wareham, MA 02571
Tel.: 508-295-9200
Automotive Body Shop
S.I.C.: 7532

ROBINHOOD HOMES, INC.
6335 Ferris Sq., Suite G
San Diego, CA 92121
Tel.: 619-558-6335 **CA**
Year Founded: 1973
Sales Range: $10-19 Million
New Single-family Home Construction
S.I.C.: 1521
Barry J. Ross *(Pres.)*
Robert E. Casey Jr. *(Exec. V.P.)*
John D. Casey *(V.P.)*

Outside Service Firm(s):

Imperial Bank*(Major Banking Relationship)*
San Diego, CA

ROBINS ENGINEERS & CONSTRUCTORS, INC.
(A Member of The O&K Orenstein & Koppel AG Group)
7730 E. Belleview Ave.
Englewood, CO 80111
Tel.: 303-770-0808
Fax: 303-770-8233
Year Founded: 1896
Approx.Sls.: $35,000,000
Emp.: 50
Fiscal Year-end: 12/31/91
Import Export
Bulk Material Handling Systems
S.I.C.: 3599
Dr. T. Bahke *(Chm. Bd.)*
J.B. Jeans *(Pres.)*
P. Schlosser *(Sec. & Treas.)*
R. Bumbalo *(Pur. Agent)*

Computer Systems/Hardware:
Autocad II/Micronics 486-25 MHZ W/64 Cache W/MNTH Chip, 8MB 80 NSRAM

ROBINSON BUS SERVICE
1528 Emerson St.
Evanston, IL 60201
Tel.: 708-866-1950
Fax: 708-866-1948
Year Founded: 1968
Approx.Sls.: $10,000,000
Emp.: 550
Bus Service; Transit & School Buses
S.I.C.: 4111; 4141
Leon Robinson, Jr. *(Pres.)*
Roy Robinson *(V.P.)*
Principal(s):
Leon Robinson, Jr.

No. of Mfg. Plants/Facilities: 11
No. of U.S. Offices: 2

Outside Service Firm(s):

First Illinois Bank of Evanston*(Major Banking Relationship)*
800 Davis St.
Evanston, IL 60204
Tel.: 708-866-5500

C. H. ROBINSON CO. INC.
8100 Mitchell Rd., Ste. 200
Eden Prairie, MN 55344
Tel.: 612-937-8500 **DE**
Fax: 612-937-7809
Year Founded: 1905
Sales Range: $500-999 Million
Emp.: 950
Import Export
Trucking & Warehousing
S.I.C.: 5148; 4731; 6719; 4213; 0723
Sid Verdoorn *(Pres., Chief Exec. & Chief Oper. Officer)*
Dale S. Hanson *(Chief Fin. Officer, V.P.-Fin. & Treas.)*
Douglas Berg *(V.P.-Mgmnt. Info. Systems)*
Duane L. McConkey *(V.P.-Admin. & Sec.)*
William Fairbanks *(Controller)*
Owen Gleason *(Gen. Counsel)*

No. of U.S. Offices: 47
No. of Foreign Offices: 2

Computer Systems/Hardware:
IBM

Outside Service Firm(s):

Arthur Andersen & Co.*(Auditors)*
45 S. 7th St.
Minneapolis, MN 55402

Continental Insurance*(Commercial Insurance Carrier)*
180 Maiden Lane
New York, NY

Dorsey & Whitney*(Legal Firm)*
2200 First Bank Place East
Minneapolis, MN 55402

First Bank of St. Paul*(Major Banking Relationship)*
St. Paul, MN

First National Bank of Minneapolis*(Major Banking Relationship)*
Minneapolis, MN

Norwest Bank Minnesota, N.A.*(Major Banking Relationship)*
6th St. & Marquette Av.
Minneapolis, MN 55479
Tel.: 612-667-1234

Investment Advisors Inc.*(Pension Manager)*
1100 Dain Tower, P.O. Box 357
Minneapolis, MN 55440

Norwest Bank of Minneapolis N.A.*(Pension Manager)*
P.O. Box 738, 161 N. Concord Exchange
So. St. Paul, MN 55075-0738
Tel.: 612-450-4064
Fax: 612-450-4078

SWAYNE ROBINSON & COMPANY
214 Main St.
Richmond, IN 47375
Tel.: 317-962-9591
Fax: 317-962-9594
Emp.: 70
Gray Iron Foundry
S.I.C.: 3321
Charles K. Robinson, Jr. *(Pres. & Treas.)*
Jack D. Sickman *(V.P.-Mfg.)*
Charles R. Hyde, Sr. *(Mgr.-Sls.)*
Mike Sickman *(Plant Mgr.)*

Swayne Robinson & Company—(Continued)

Outside Service Firm(s):

Ernst & Young*(Auditors)*
One Indiana Square, Ste. 3400
Indianapolis, IN 46204
Tel.: 317-236-1100

Bank One*(Major Banking Relationship)*
Richmond, IN

ROBINSON HELICOPTER COMPANY, INC.
24747 Crenshaw Blvd.
Torrance, CA 90505
Tel.: 310-539-0508 **CA**
Fax: 310-539-5198
Year Founded: 1973
Approx.Sls.: $55,000,000
Emp.: 500
Fiscal Year-end: 12/31/90
Export
Mfr. of Helicopters
S.I.C.: 3721
Frank Robinson *(Pres.)*
Barbara Robinson *(Chief Fin. Officer & Treas.)*
D. Edward Broman *(V.P.-Procurement)*
P. Wayne Walden *(V.P.-Mfg.)*
Tim Goetz *(Dir.-Mktg.)*
Wayne Walden *(Gen. Mgr.)*
Sherwood Bressler *(Tech. Investigator)*
Tim Gilligan *(Chief Engr.)*

Outside Service Firm(s):

Union Bank*(Major Banking Relationship)*
Torrance, CA

ROBINSON LUMBER & EXPORT COMPANY
4000 Tchoupitoulas St.
New Orleans, LA 70115
Tel.: 504-895-6377
Twx: 6718-445 Roblum
Fax: 504-897-0820
Year Founded: 1893
Assets: $24,690,949
Liabilities: $18,104,409
Net Worth: $6,586,540
Approx.Sls.: $50,000,000
Emp.: 60
Fiscal Year-end: 10/31/91
Import Export
Holding Company
S.I.C.: 6719
Samuel G. Robinson, Sr. *(Chm. Bd.)*
H. Ivens Robinson *(Pres. & Chief Exec. Officer)*
R. Courtney Robinson *(Sec.)*

No. of Foreign Offices: 3

Outside Service Firm(s):

Winston Company*(Auditors)*
New Orleans, LA

Phelps, Dunbar, Marks, Claverie & Sims*(Legal Firm)*
Hibernia Bank Bldg.
New Orleans, LA 70112
Tel.: 504-566-1311

Stone Pigman*(Legal Firm)*
New Orleans, LA

Hibernia National Bank*(Major Banking Relationship)*
New Orleans, LA

Subsidiary:

Robinson Lumber Company **(1)**
4000 Tchoupitoulas St.
New Orleans, LA 70115
Tel.: 504-895-6377
Approx.Sls.: $35,000,000
Emp.: 26
Wholesale Import & Export Lumber, Plywood & Millwork
S.I.C.: 5031
Samuel G. Robinson, Sr. *(Pres.)*
H. Ivens Robinson *(Exec. V.P.-Sls.)*
R. Courtney Robbinson *(Sec.)*

ROBINSON & MAITES, INC.
35 E. Wacker Dr., Ste. 200
Chicago, IL 60601
Tel.: 312-372-9333
Fax: 312-372-0682
Year Founded: 1960
Approx.Billings: $13,000,000
Emp.: 17
Promotional Marketing Services
William A. Robinson *(Mng. Dir.)*
Alan Maites *(Mng. Dir.)*

ROBINSON & ST. JOHN ADVERTISING & PUBLIC RELATIONS, INC.
6650 Southpoint Pkwy., Ste. 200
Jacksonville, FL 32216
Tel.: 904-281-2500
Fax: 904-281-0030
Year Founded: 1984
Approx.Billings: $20,000,000
Emp.: 30
Fiscal Year-end: 6/30/90
Advertising Agency
S.I.C.: 7311
William A. Robinson *(Chm. Bd. & Chief Exec. Officer)*
Dan J. St. John *(Pres.)*
Robert M. Baker *(Chief Fin. Officer & V.P.)*
Karen E. Burdette *(Exec. V.P. & Chief Oper. Officer)*
Connie L. Atkinson *(Dir.-Brdcst. Production)*
Amy Rankin *(Dir.-Pub. Rels.)*
Sandy Chun *(Office Mgr.)*

No. of U.S. Offices: 1

Branch:

Robinson & St. John Advertising & Public Relations, Public Relations Div. **(1)**
6650 Southpoint Pkwy., Ste. 200
Jacksonville, FL 32216
Tel.: 904-281-2500
Fax: 904-281-0030
William A. Robinson *(Chm. Bd. & Chief Exec. Officer)*
Dan J. St. John *(Pres.)*
Amy Rankin *(Pub. Rels. Dir.)*

ROBINSON, YESAWICH & PEPPERDINE
1900 Summit Tower Blvd., Ste. 600
Orlando, FL 32810
Tel.: 407-875-1111
Fax: 407-875-1115
Year Founded: 1983
Approx.Billings: $75,000,000
Emp.: 100
Advertising Agency
S.I.C.: 7311
John E. Robinson, Jr. *(Chm. Bd.)*
Peter C. Yesawich, Ph.D. *(Pres. & Chief Exec. Officer)*
Truman Myers *(Sr. V.P.-Pub. Rels.)*
James Pepperdine *(Sr. V.P.)*

No. of U.S. Offices: 4

Computer Systems/Hardware:
IBM

Branch:

Robinson, Yesawich & Pepperdine **(1)**
104 East 40th St., Ste. 707
New York, NY 10016
Tel.: 212-983-6020
Howard Heinsius *(Pres.-New York)*
Neil Ostergren *(V.P.)*

ROCCO INC.
1 Kratzer Rd.
Harrisonburg, VA 22801
Mailing Address:
Box 549
Harrisonburg, VA 22801
Tel.: 703-568-1400
Fax: 703-568-1401
Year Founded: 1939
Approx.Sls.: $250,000,000
Emp.: 3200
Fiscal Year-end: 12/31/91
Export
Poultry Processing; Feed Mill; Wholesale Building Supplies
S.I.C.: 2015; 2048; 5039
R.H. Strickler *(Chm. Bd.)*
Charles O. Strickler *(Pres.)*
James J. Darazsdi *(Chief Exec. Officer & Sr. V.P.)*
John Williams *(Chief Fin. Officer)*
Chip Christian *(V.P.-Human Res.)*
Robert Walsh *(V.P.-Mktg. & Sls.)*
Harlie Easter *(Dir.-Mngmt. Information Systems)*
Pat May *(Dir.-Pub. Rels.)*
Ron Waters *(Dir.-Res. & Devel.)*
Principal(s):
R.H. Strickler
Charles O. Strickler

No. of Mfg. Plants/Facilities: 8
No. of U.S. Offices: 8

Computer Systems/Hardware:
Sperry

Outside Service Firm(s):

S. B. Hoover & Co.*(Auditors)*
Harrisonburg, VA

Blue Cross & Blue Shield of Virginia*(Group Insurer)*
2015 Staples Mill Rd.
Richmond, VA 23230
Tel.: 804-359-7000
Fax: 804-354-7397

Crestar Bank*(Investment Banker)*
180 E. Market Street
Harrisonburg, VA 22801

Dominion Bank*(Investment Banker)*
Dominion Center
Harrisonburg, VA
Tel.: 703-564-5200

Wharton, Aldhiser & Weaver*(Legal Firm)*
100 S. Mason St.
Harrisonburg, VA
Tel.: 703-434-0316
Fax: 703-434-5502

Crestar Bank*(Major Banking Relationship)*
180 E. Market Street
Harrisonburg, VA 22801

Dominion Bank*(Major Banking Relationship)*
Dominion Center
Harrisonburg, VA
Tel.: 703-564-5200

Subsidiaries:

Rocco Building Supplies Inc. **(1)**
P.O. Box 669
Harrisonburg, VA 22801
Tel.: 703-434-1371
S.I.C.: 5039
Dan Stark *(Chief Oper. Officer)*

Rocco Farm Foods, Inc. **(1)**
Route 3, P.O. Box 370
Edinburg, VA 22824
Tel.: 703-984-4121
S.I.C.: 2048
Ned Kuller *(Chief Oper. Officer)*

Rocco Farms **(1)**
1620 So. Main St.
Harrisonburg, VA 22801
Tel.: 703-434-7394
S.I.C.: 2011; 2015
Ned Kuller *(Chief Oper. Officer)*

Rocco Feeds, Inc. **(1)**
P.O. Box 549
Harrisonburg, VA 22801
Tel.: 703-568-1400

Rocco Further Processing **(1)**
Co-op Drive
Timberville, VA 22853
Tel.: 703-896-7041
Emp.: 250
Processor of Turkey Products
S.I.C.: 2011; 2013; 2015
Tad Pritchett *(Chief Oper. Officer)*
Robert Walsh *(Dir.-Mktg. & Sls.)*
Patricia May *(Dir.-Pub. Rels.)*

Rocco Turkeys, Inc. **(1)**
P.O. Box 158
Dayton, VA 22821
Tel.: 703-879-2521
Approx.Sls.: $215,000,000
Emp.: 1,600
Fiscal Year-end: 12/31/91
Export
Processing of Turkey & Turkey Products
S.I.C.: 2015; 0253
Robert Lauffenburger *(Pres.)*
Rick Chenoweth *(Dir.-Sls.)*
Patricia L. May *(Dir.-Pub. Rels.)*

ROCHE CONSTRUCTORS, INC.
361 71st. Ave.
Greeley, CO 80634
Mailing Address:
P.O. Box 1727
Greeley, CO 80632
Tel.: 303-356-3611 **CO**
Fax: 303-356-3619
Year Founded: 1971
Assets: $12,030,375
Liabilities: $10,038,393
Net Worth: $1,991,982
Sales Range: $40-59 Million
Emp.: 100
Import Export
General Contractor
S.I.C.: 1799
M.B. Roche *(Pres.)*
Pamela A. Ahrens *(Treas.)*
Steven L. Fisbeck *(V.P.)*
Brad L. Pfeifley *(V.P.)*
Thomas J. Roche *(V.P.)*
William F. Sheel *(V.P.)*
Carol G. Wells *(Corp. Sec.)*
Principal(s):
M.B. Roche

No. of U.S. Offices: 5

Computer Systems/Hardware:
IBM PC Compatible

Outside Service Firm(s):

Richard J. Bartels*(Auditors)*
Greeley, CO

Aetna Life & Casualty*(Commercial Insurance Carrier)*
151 Farmington Avenue
Hartford, CT 06156
Tel.: 203-273-2128
Fax: 203-729-4295

Aetna*(Group Insurer)*
% Flood & Peterson Insurance, P.O. Box 578
Greeley, CO 80632

Walker Miller Law Firm*(Legal Firm)*
Greeley, CO

First National Bank of Greeley*(Major Banking Relationship)*
Greeley, CO

ROCHESTER MIDLAND CORPORATION
333 Hollenbeck St.
Rochester, NY 14621
Tel.: 716-336-2200
Fax: 716-467-4406
Year Founded: 1888
Approx.Sls.: $60,000,000
Emp.: 1,200
Export
Mfr. Disinfectants, Liquid & Powder Soaps, Liquid Wax, Insecticides, Soap Dispensers, Water Treatment Chemicals, Industrial Maintenance Products, Sanitary Napkins & Tampons; Distributor of Vending Machines
S.I.C.: 5113; 3999; 2879; 2676; 2841; 2842
Harlan D. Calkins *(Chm. Bd. & Pres.)*
Aram T. Kevorkian *(Sr. V.P.)*
Dirk R. Dunbar *(V.P.-Water Treatment)*
James L. Kerr *(V.P.)*
George Kittredge *(V.P.-Mktg.)*
John O. Luthro *(V.P.-Mfg., Products)*
Frederick D. Singer *(V.P.-Food Div.)*
Dale R. Sloan *(Treas.)*

Outside Service Firm(s):

Harris, Beach, Wilcox, Rubin & Levy*(Legal Firm)*
2 State St.
Rochester, NY 14614
Tel.: 716-232-4440

Chase Lincoln First Bank, N.A.*(Major Banking Relationship)*
One Lincoln First Square
Rochester, NY 14604
Tel.: 716-385-3200

Division:

Rochester-Midland ICL **(1)**
1015 N. 14th St.
Omaha, NE 68102
Tel.: 402-342-4248
Approx.Sls.: $15,000,000
Emp.: 40
Export
Computer Systems/Hardware:
Wang VS 65, NCR PC's
Manufacture Chemicals & Allied Products
S.I.C.: 2841; 2842; 5087
David J. Vivian *(Pres.)*
Richard Gray *(V.P.-Sls. & Mktg.)*
Paul Herrick *(V.P.-Water Chemistry Services)*
Greg Pfeifer *(Treas. & Chief Fin. Officer)*
Marcelline Moon *(Mgr.-Data Processing)*

Subsidiaries:

The C.B. Dolge Co. **(1)**
39 Indian Hill Rd.
Westport, CT 06880
Tel.: 203-454-1993
Approx.Sls.: $1,700,000
Emp.: 10
Manufactures Cleaners, Floor Finishes, Hand Soaps, Disinfectants, Weed-Killers, Insecticides, Janitorial Supplies
S.I.C.: 2879; 2676; 2841; 2842
Alfred K. Dolge *(Pres.)*

Industrial Chemical Laboratories **(1)**
1015 North 14th St.
Omaha, NE 68102
Tel.: 402-342-4248
Mfr. Janitorial Cleaning Supplies & Chemicals
S.I.C.: 2842
D.J. Vivian *(Pres.)*

ROCK HILL MATERIALS COMPANY
339 School St.
Catasauqua, PA 18032
Tel.: 215-264-5586 **PA**
Fax: 215-264-2899
Year Founded: 1947
Sales Range: $10-19 Million
Emp.: 100
Fiscal Year-end: 3/31/91
Ready Mix Concrete
S.I.C.: 3273
Ernest Buskirk *(Pres. & Chief Exec. Officer)*
Glen Buskirk *(Sec. & Treas.)*
Jeffrey Buskirk *(Mgr.-Sls.)*
Robert Short *(Mgr.-Quality Control)*

No. of Mfg. Plants/Facilities: 5
No. of U.S. Offices: 1

Outside Service Firm(s):

Campbell, Rappold & Yurasitz*(Auditors)*
Allentown, PA

Roberts, Traud & Corkery*(Legal Firm)*
Allentown, PA

Bucks County Bank & Trust Company*(Major Banking Relationship)*
Perkasie, PA

ROCK-TENN COMPANY
504 Thrasher St.
Norcross, GA 30091
Mailing Address:
P.O. Box 4098
Norcross, GA 30071
Tel.: 404-448-2193 **GA**
Fax: 404-263-4483
Year Founded: 1936
Approx.Sls.: $515,000,000
Emp.: 4,300
Fiscal Year-end: 9/30/90
Manufacture Recycled & Laminated Recycled Paperboard, Paperboard Packaging, Solid Fiber Partitions, Corrugated Packaging, Plastic Packaging, Folding Cartons & Sorted, Baled Wastepaper
S.I.C.: 2631; 2653; 5093; 2657
A. Worley Brown *(Chm. Bd.)*
Bradley Currey, Jr. *(Pres. & Chief Exec. Officer)*
David Nicholson *(V.P. & Sec.)*
Paul Saari *(Treas. & Asst. Sec.)*
Lever Stewart *(Gen. Counsel & Asst. Sec.)*
Bruce Hendrix *(Dir.-Mngmt. Information Systems)*
G. Martin Shaw *(Dir.-Public Rels.)*
Brad Newman *(Mgr.-Risk)*
Cathy Harris *(Meetings Planner)*

Principal(s):
A. Worley Brown
Bradley Currey, Jr.

No. of Mfg. Plants/Facilities: 56
No. of U.S. Offices: 1

Computer Systems/Hardware:
IBM System 36 & 38

Outside Service Firm(s):

Gulf Life*(Group Insurer)*
Jacksonville, FL

Industrial Risk Insurers*(Group Insurer)*
85 Woodland St.
Hartford, CT 06102
Tel.: 203-520-7300

Kemper Insurance*(Group Insurer)*
Long Grove, IL 60049-0001

King & Spalding*(Legal Firm)*
Trust Co. Tower
Atlanta, GA 30303
Tel.: 404-572-4600

Trust Company Bank*(Major Banking Relationship)*
P.O. Box 4655,
Atlanta, GA 30302

Hutton Capital Management*(Pension Manager)*
New York, NY

Lesesne & Company, Inc.*(Pension Manager)*
Atlanta, GA

Trusco Capital Management*(Pension Manager)*
70 Hurt Plaza, Ste. 1400
Atlanta, GA 30302
Tel.: 404-586-6450

Divisions:

Allforms Packaging Corp. **(1)**
120 Allwood Ave.
Islip, NY 11751
Tel.: 516-582-4710
Manufacture Envelopes
S.I.C.: 2754

Box Innards, Inc. **(1)**
749 N. Poplar
Orange, CA 92668
Tel.: 714-978-3150
Jon Hughes *(Gen. Mgr.)*

Wiregrass Container, Inc. **(1)**
2603 Cottonwood Rd.
Dothan, AL 36301
Tel.: 205-794-7025
Corrugated Board Packaging
S.I.C.: 5113
Stan Jones *(Gen. Mgr.)*

Subsidiaries:

Rock-Tenn Company, Mill Division, Inc. **(1)**
P.O. Box 4098
Norcross, GA 30091
Tel.: 404-448-2193
Collects, Bales & Converts Wastepaper into Paperboard
S.I.C.: 2631; 5093

Rock-Tenn Converting Co. **(1)**
P.O. Box 4098
Norcross, GA 30091
Tel.: 404-448-2193 (100%)
Manufacture Packaging Products from Paperboard, Linerboard, Thermoformed Plastic
S.I.C.: 2653

Winchester Carton Corp. **(1)**
P.O. Box 4098
Norcross, GA 30091
Tel.: 404-448-2193
Manufacture & Distribute Paperboard Packaging Products
S.I.C.: 2657; 5113

ROCKET INDUSTRIES, INC./ EXCEL, THE EXERCISE COMPANY
9935 Beverly Blvd.
Pico Rivera, CA 90660
Tel.: 310-699-0311
Tel.: 800-347-2258 **CA**
Telex: 910-586-4623
Fax: 310-699-6626
Year Founded: 1965
Approx.Sls.: $40,000,000
Emp.: 400
Fiscal Year-end: 5/31/91
Import Export
Manufacture Physical Fitness Equipment; Automotive Steel & Aluminum Road Wheels, Automotive Accessories, Side Exhaust Systems
S.I.C.: 3498; 3949; 3312; 3592
Raymond L. Bleiweis *(Pres.)*
Joe Desens *(Chief Oper. Officer)*
Henry Villamater *(Chief Fin. Officer)*
Mark C. Bleiweis *(V.P.-Sls. Promo. & Adv.)*
Lillian McNulty *(Treas.)*
Bob Bryan *(Dir.-Pur.)*

Computer Systems/Hardware:
Hewlett-Packard 3000 Series 39; IBM

Outside Service Firm(s):

McGladrey & Pullen*(Auditors)*
222 S. Harbor Blvd. #800
Anaheim, CA 92815

First Interstate Bank*(Major Banking Relationship)*
Whittier, CA

RBL&W
ROCKETT, BURKHEAD, LEWIS & WINSLOW

ROCKETT, BURKHEAD, LEWIS & WINSLOW
8601 Six Forks Rd.
Raleigh, NC 27615
Mailing Address:
P.O. Box 18189
Raleigh, NC 27619
Tel.: 919-848-2600
Fax: 919-848-2614
Year Founded: 1985
Approx.Billings: $56,500,000
Emp.: 76

Howard Rockett *(Chm. & Chief Exec. Officer)*
Scott Burkhead *(Exec. V.P., Chief Oper. Officer)*
Lanny P. Bynum *(V.P., Opers. & Fin.)*
Beverly Buck *(Chief Info. Officer & Admin.)*
Catherine Rieger *(Dir., Pub. Rels.)*
Richard French *(V.P., Pub. Rels. Dir.)*
Michael French *(Dir.-FutureWorks Communications)*

ROCKFORD ACROMATIC PRODUCT CO.
611 Beacon St.
Rockford, IL 61130
Tel.: 815-877-7473
Fax: 815-877-0082
Approx.Sls.: $50,000,000
Emp.: 125
Mfr. Screw Machine Prods.; Aircraft Parts; Machinery
S.I.C.: 3728
Dean A. Olson II *(Chm. Bd.)*
James N. Olson *(Pres.)*
Nobel D. Olson *(V.P.-Mktg.)*
Kay J. Mullins *(Treas. & Sec.)*

ROCKFORD PRODUCTS CORP.
707 Harrison Ave.
Rockford, IL 61104
Tel.: 815-397-6000
Fax: 815-229-4326
Year Founded: 1929
Approx.Sls.: $76,000,000
Emp.: 800
Fiscal Year-end: 10/31/90
Import
Manufacture Specialty Fasteners & Cold-Formed Components
S.I.C.: 3452
R. Ray Wood *(Chm., Pres., Chief Exec. & Chief Oper. Officer)*
David Peterson *(Grp. V.P. & Sec.)*
Gerald S. Thain *(V.P.-Fin.)*
Wayne Johnson *(Dir.-Sls.)*
John Waller *(Dir.-Quality)*
Michael Matus *(Mgr.-Mktg.)*
Jerry Norquist *(Mgr.-Safety & Training)*
Tom Smith *(Mgr.-MIS)*

Computer Systems/Hardware:
IBM 3081; Amdal 5890, Model 3005

Outside Service Firm(s):

McGladrey & Pullen*(Auditors)*
Rockford, IL

Vedder, Price, Kaufman & Kammholz*(Legal Firm)*
115 S. La Salle
Chicago, IL 60603
Tel.: 312-781-2200

Amcore Bank*(Major Banking Relationship)*
Rockford, IL

Rockford Products Corp.—(Continued)

Division:

Rockford International Group **(1)**
612 Harrison Avenue
Rockford, IL 61104
Tel.: 815-229-7150
Fax: 815-229-7155
Computer Systems/Hardware:
Amdal 5890,Model 3005
Purchase & Resale of Fasteners Overseas
S.I.C.: 5072
Dick Goff *(Grp. V.P.)*
Rick Wholey *(Dir.-Intl. Sourcing)*
Bill Benson *(Natl. Sls. Mgr.-Automotive After Mkt.)*
Todd Townsend *(Mktg. Service Mgr.)*

ROCKVILLE FABRICS CORPORATION
225 W. 34th St.
New York, NY 10122
Tel.: 212-563-2050 **NY**
Fax: 212-629-0840
Year Founded: 1950
Approx.Sls.: $15,000,000
Emp.: 70
Import Export
Wholesale Distribution of Household Goods; Textile Converters
S.I.C.: 5131; 4213
Walter Levy *(Pres.)*
Peter Levy *(V.P. & Sec.)*

Outside Service Firm(s):

Buchbinder, Stein, Tunick & Platkin*(Auditors)*
One Pennsylvania Plaza
New York, NY 10119-0219

Citibank N.A.*(Major Banking Relationship)*
399 Park Ave.
New York, NY 10043
Tel.: 212-559-1000
Tel.: 800-248-4636

Division:

Active Quilting Div. **(1)**
225 W. 34th St.
New York, NY 10122
Tel.: 212-563-2050
Quilting For The Trade
S.I.C.: 2395

ROCKY MOUNTAIN BANK NOTE COMPANY
10455 W. 6th Ave.
Lakewood, CO 80215
Tel.: 303-233-8080 **CO**
Fax: 303-238-9976
Year Founded: 1907
Approx.Sls.: $84,000,000
Emp.: 1,300
Letterpress & Lithographic Printing, Bank Supplies
S.I.C.: 2752
Chuck Dawson *(Pres.)*
Jim Kinnebrew *(Chief Fin. Officer)*
Anthony Brown *(Dir.-Human Res.)*
Principal(s):
Dr. Russell Scott

Outside Service Firm(s):

Arthur Andersen & Co.*(Auditors)*
717 17th St., Ste. 1900
Denver, CO 80202
Tel.: 303-296-2121

Lentz, Evans & King*(Legal Firm)*
Denver, CO

ROCKY MOUNTAIN COMPANY
(d/b/a RMC Foods)
825 Industrial Rd.
Saint George, UT 84770
Mailing Address:
P.O. Box 338
St. George, UT 84771
Tel.: 801-673-3583
Fax: 801-628-4985
Year Founded: 1941
Approx.Sls.: $30,000,000
Emp.: 175
Wholesale Food Distributorsof Fruit, Vegetables, Seafood, Cheese, Poultry & Poultry Products & Meats
S.I.C.: 5149; 5148; 5143; 5144; 5146; 5147
Principal(s):
Glen Gubler
Stanley Gubler
Ronald Mason
Stanley Ray
H. Bruce Stucki

Outside Service Firm(s):

Zions First National Bank*(Major Banking Relationship)*
St. George, UT

ROCKY MOUNTAIN MECHANICAL, INC.
3412 S.W. Temple
Salt Lake City, UT 84115
Mailing Address:
P.O. Box 65439
Salt Lake City, UT 84165
Tel.: 801-486-3423
Fax: 801-467-1460
Year Founded: 1972
Approx.Sls.: $52,000,000
Emp.: 120
Mechanical, Plumbing & Electrical Contractors & Engineers
S.I.C.: 1711; 1731; 8711
Thomas Petsche *(Chm. Bd. & Pres.)*
Thomas Heward *(V.P.)*
Eva Hammell *(Controller)*
Eva Marie Ingleby *(Pur. Agent-Rocky Mountain)*
Principal(s):
Thomas Petsche

Computer Systems/Hardware:
Wang

Outside Service Firm(s):

Wisan & Smith*(Auditors)*
Salt Lake City, UT

Physicians Health Plan*(Group Insurer)*
Salt Lake City, UT

First Security Bank of Utah*(Major Banking Relationship)*
Salt Lake City, UT

ROCKY ROCOCO CORPORATION
2122 Luann Lane, Ste. 15
Madison, WI 53713
Mailing Address:
P.O. Box 2995,
Madison, WI 53701-2995
Tel.: 608-276-6760
Fax: 608-276-6773
Year Founded: 1974
Approx.Sls.: $30,000,000
Emp.: 600
Fiscal Year-end: 12/31/91
Franchised Pizza Restaurants
S.I.C.: 5812
Thomas P. Hester *(Pres.)*

ROCOR TRANSPORTATION COMPANIES INC.
4350 Will Rogers Pky. Ste. 300 S.
Oklahoma City, OK 73128
Tel.: 405-943-9500 **NV**
Approx.Sls.: $175,000,000
Emp.: 1,200
Fiscal Year-end: 12/31/90
Holding Company; Trucking & Real Estate
S.I.C.: 6719; 4213
David P. Roush *(Chm. Bd., Pres. & Chief Exec. Officer)*
Arthur G. Bortolini *(Sr. V.P.-Fin. & Admin., Treas. & Sec.)*

Computer Systems/Hardware:
IBM System 36

Outside Service Firm(s):

KPMG Peat Marwick*(Auditors)*
2020 No. Central Ave.
Phoenix, AZ 85004
Tel.: 602-253-2000

First Interstate Bank*(Major Banking Relationship)*
P.O. Box 53441,
Phoenix, AZ 85072-3441
Tel.: 602-229-4049

Subsidiaries:

Commercial Parts, Ltd. **(1)**
862 N . 10th St.
San Jose, CA 95112
Tel.: 408-297-0105 (100%)
Auto & Truck Parts Sales
S.I.C.: 5013
Jay Alleman *(Pres.)*

Rocor Properties, Inc. **(1)**
2929 E. Camelback
Phoenix, AZ 85016
Tel.: 602-957-1889 (100%)
Approx.Sls.: $2,000,000
Real Estate Ownership & Leasing
S.I.C.: 6552
David P. Roush *(Chief Opr. Officer)*

RODALE PRESS, INC.
33 E. Minor St.
Emmaus, PA 18098
Tel.: 215-967-5171 **PA**
Fax: 215-967-8963
Year Founded: 1930
Approx.Sls.: $300,000,000
Emp.: 1,000
Fiscal Year-end: 12/31/91
Publish Books & Periodicals
S.I.C.: 2721; 2731
Ardath Rodale *(Chm. Bd. & Chief Exec. Officer)*
Robert J. Teufel *(Pres. & Chief Oper. Officer)*
Placido Corpora *(Pres.-Book Div.)*
John Griffin *(Pres.-Magazine Div.)*
Richard Porter *(Publisher-Prevention)*
Sanford Beldon *(Sr. V.P.)*
John Haberern *(Sr. V.P.)*
Mark Bricklin *(Grp. V.P.)*
James McCullagh *(Grp. V.P.)*
Carolyn Gavett *(V.P.-Assoc. Publisher, Book Division)*
William Gottlieb *(V.P.-Editorial Dir., Book Division)*
George Hirsch *(V.P.-Magazine Div.)*
Thomas Stoneback *(V.P. & Chief Admin. Officer)*
Paul C. Wessel *(V.P. & Chief Fin. Officer)*
Thomas Wolf *(V.P. & Gen. Mgr.)*
Gary D. Pave *(Treas.)*
Tom Storms *(Controller & Dir.-Taxation)*
John Volanski *(Dir.-Personnel)*
Principal(s):
Rodale Family

No. of Mfg. Plants/Facilities: 21
No. of U.S. Offices: 5
No. of Foreign Offices: 1

Outside Service Firm(s):

Grant Thornton*(Auditors)*
2000 Market St.
Philadelphia, PA 19101

Gross, McGinley, LaBarre & Eaton*(Legal Firm)*
Allentown, PA

Bank of Pennsylvania*(Major Banking Relationship)*
Emmaus, PA

W. B. RODDENBERY COMPANY, INC.
(Acquisition by Dean Foods Co. Pending)
17 First Ave., NE
Cairo, GA 31728
Mailing Address:
P.O. Box 60
Cairo, GA 31728
Tel.: 912-377-2102
Fax: 912-377-5797
Year Founded: 1889
Approx.Sls.: $33,000,000
Emp.: 350
Fiscal Year-end: 4/30/91
Manufacture & Export Pickles, Syrups, Peanut Butter & Boiled Peanuts
S.I.C.: 2035; 2099
Julien B. Roddenbery, Jr. *(Pres. & Chief Exec. Officer)*
Ralph J. Roddenbery *(Exec. V.P.-Sls. & Mktg.)*
Julien B. Roddenbery III *(Sr. V.P. & Prod. Sls. Coord.)*
Tom H. Blaydes *(V.P.-Admin.)*
Everett L. Mason *(V.P.-Sls.)*
Jeff Gray *(Dir.-Mktg. & Sls.)*
Principal(s):
Julien B. Roddenbery, Jr.

Computer Systems/Hardware:
IBM

RODEFELD CO., INC.
96 W. Main St.
Richmond, IN 47374
Mailing Address:
P.O. Box 1424,
Richmond, IN 47374
Tel.: 317-935-7626 **IN**
Fax: 317-966-1574
Year Founded: 1900
Approx.Sls.: $20,000,000
Emp.: 130
Fiscal Year-end: 12/31/91
Wholesaler Auto Parts Supplies & Prods.
S.I.C.: 5013
Charles A. Rodefeld *(Pres.)*
James McPherson *(V.P.-Sls.)*
Gary H. Rodefeld *(V.P. & Sec.)*
James Breckenridge *(Controller)*
Principal(s):
Charles A. Rodefeld

Computer Systems/Hardware:
Triad

Outside Service Firm(s):

George S. Olive & Co.*(Auditors)*
Richmond, IN

Harlan, Schussler, Keller, Boston & Bever*(Legal Firm)*
Richmond, IN

Star Bank*(Major Banking Relationship)*
Richmond, IN

RODGERS BUILDERS, INC.
5701 N. Sharon Amity Rd.
Charlotte, NC 28215
Mailing Address:
P.O. Box 18446
Charlotte, NC 28218
Tel.: 704-537-6044 **NC**
Fax: 704-535-0055
Assets: $10,907,023
Liabilities: $9,433,995
Net Worth: $1,473,028
Sales Range: $40-59 Million
Emp.: 175
Fiscal Year-end: 9/30/90
General Contractors
S.I.C.: 1522; 1541; 1542
B.D. Rodgers *(Chm. Bd.)*
Patricia A. Rosamond *(Pres.)*
G.S. Keach *(Sr. V.P.)*
J.B. Dellinger III *(V.P.-Fin.)*

T.E. Hatfield *(V.P.)*
H.G. Canipe, Jr. *(Controller)*

Principal(s):
B.D. Rodgers
Patricia A. Rosamond
J.B. Dellinger III

No. of U.S. Offices: 1

Computer Systems/Hardware:
Texas Instruments

Outside Service Firm(s):

KPMG Peat Marwick*(Auditors)*
Two First Union Center
Charlotte, NC
Tel.: 704-335-5300

St. Paul Fire & Marine Insurance Co.*(Commercial Insurance Carrier)*
385 Washington St.
St. Paul, MN 55102
Tel.: 612-221-7911

Smith, Helms, Mullis & Moore*(Legal Firm)*
227 North Tryon St.
Charlotte, NC 28231

NationsBank Carolinas*(Major Banking Relationship)*
One NCNB Plaza
Charlotte, NC 28255

Subsidiary:

Mid Atlantic Construction, Inc. **(1)**
5701 N. Sharon Amity Rd.
Charlotte, NC 28215
Tel.: 704-537-6044
Fax: 704-535-0055
Emp.: 120
General Contractor
S.I.C.: 1522; 1541; 1542

J.B. RODGERS MECHANICAL CONTRACTORS
2825 W. Thomas Rd.
Phoenix, AZ 85017
Tel.: 602-269-2161
Fax: 602-269-6259
Year Founded: 1946
Approx.Sls.: $20,000,000
Emp.: 300
Mechanical Construction, Industrial Process Piping
S.I.C.: 1711
Ronald Rodgers *(Chm. Bd. & Pres.)*
John Vesely *(V.P.-Construction Div.)*
Mike Wall *(V.P.-Indus. Div.)*
Fred Mason *(Treas., Sec. & Mgr.-Pur.)*

Outside Service Firm(s):

Schultz & Taylor*(Auditors)*
Phoenix, AZ

First Interstate Bank*(Major Banking Relationship)*
P.O. Box 53441,
Phoenix, AZ 85072-3441
Tel.: 602-229-4049

ROESSING BRONZE CO.
Evans City Rd.
Mars, PA 16046
Mailing Address:
P.O. Box 816
Mars, PA 16046
Tel.: 412-538-4000
Fax: 412-538-3956
Approx.Sls.: $16,000,000
Emp.: 100
Manufacture Brass & Bronze Ingots; Continuous Cast Baring Bronze
S.I.C.: 3341; 3351
Alfred R. Barbour *(Chm. Bd.)*
Alfred D. Barbour *(Pres.)*
C. D. Ziel *(V.P.-Sls.)*
Harry H. Libengood, Jr. *(Pur. Agent)*

Principal(s):
Alfred R. Barbour
Alfred D. Barbour

Computer Systems/Hardware:
IBM System 34

Outside Service Firm(s):

Love Scherle & Bauer*(Auditors)*
Pittsburgh, PA

Kirkpatrick & Lockhart*(Legal Firm)*
1500 Oliver Bldg., 535 Smithfield St.
Pittsburgh, PA 15222
Tel.: 412-355-6500
Fax: 412-355-6501

The Union National Bank of Pittsburgh*(Major Banking Relationship)*
Pittsburgh, PA

ROFFE, INC.
808 Howell St.
Seattle, WA 98101
Tel.: 206-622-0456
Fax: 206-623-2462
Year Founded: 1953
Approx.Sls.: $25,000,000
Emp.: 300
Fiscal Year-end: 4/30/90
Roffe Ski-Wear
S.I.C.: 2339; 2329; 2369; 2253
G.R. Jones, Jr. *(Pres.)*
Bob Roffe *(V.P.)*
Sandra L. Andersen *(Controller)*
Mitzi Davies *(Dir.-Adv. & Pub. Rels.)*
Wini Jones *(Dir.-New Prod. Devel.)*
Linda Howe *(Pur. Agent)*

ROGERS & ASSOCIATES ADVERTISING, INC.
3032 Bunker Hill Lane, Ste. 207
Santa Clara, CA 95054
Tel.: 408-496-1112
Fax: 408-496-6704
Year Founded: 1981
Approx.Billings: $29,000,000
Emp.: 65
Recruitment & Business-to-Businesss Adv.
Steven K. Schmidt *(Chm. Bd. & Treas.)*
Curtis K. Rogers *(Pres. & New Bus. Contact)*
Ronni Rogers *(Exec. V.P.-Florida)*
Norm Krieg *(Mktg. Dir.)*

ROGERS GROUP INC.
421 Great Circle Road
Nashville, TN 37228
Mailing Address:
P.O. Box 25250
Nashville, TN 37202
Tel.: 615-242-0585 **IN**
Fax: 615-780-5700
Year Founded: 1908
Approx.Sls.: $200,000,000
Emp.: 2,500
Fiscal Year-end: 3/31/92
Highway & Street Construction; Sand & Gravel Pits; Manufacture Paving Mixtures & Ready-Mixed Concrete; Wholesaler of Construction Materials
S.I.C.: 1611; 1442; 2951; 3273; 5039
Frank M. Warren, Jr. *(Pres. & Chief Exec. Officer)*
Michael McNally *(Sr. V.P.-Plng. & Devel.)*
Kenneth Millsaps *(Sr. V.P.-Central Region Opers.)*
Richard Warden *(Sr. V.P.-Southen Region Opers.)*
Donald R. Williamson *(Sr. V.P.-Fin. & Kentucky Region)*
Alan Coulter *(V.P.-Equipment)*
Gerald J. Kiefer *(V.P.-Human Resources & Safety)*
George Langis *(V.P. & Controller)*
Russell M. Oldfield *(V.P.-Legal & Corp. Sec.)*
Robert Schmidt *(V.P.-Engrng.)*
Chet Foster *(Dir.-Tax & Audit)*
Tom Gmitter *(Dir.-Information Services)*

T. H. ROGERS LUMBER CO. INC.
4545 Lincoln Blvd., Ste. 176
Oklahoma City, OK 73105
Tel.: 405-521-1474 **MO**
Fax: 405-525-8979
Year Founded: 1901
Assets: $11,050,000
Liabilities: $550,000
Net Worth: $10,500,000
Approx.Sls.: $27,000,000
Emp.: 200
Building Materials
S.I.C.: 5211; 5031; 5039
Robert S. Kennedy *(Chm. Bd.)*
John M. Kennedy *(Pres.)*
B.E. Payne *(Exec. V.P. & Chief Oper. Officer)*
Joe N. Myers *(Treas. & Sec.)*
William G. Lindley *(Asst. Treas.)*

Computer Systems/Hardware:
NCR 8230

Outside Service Firm(s):

Rhome & Company*(Auditors)*
Oklahoma City, OK

Pierce, Couch, Hendrickson, Johnston & Baysin*(Legal Firm)*
Oklahoma City, OK

Boatmen's First National Bank of Oklahoma*(Major Banking Relationship)*
P.O. Box 25189,
Oklahoma City, OK 73125

Equitable Life*(Pension Manager)*
1221 Ave. of the Americas
New York, NY 10022
Tel.: 212-382-8038
Fax: 212-382-8089

ROGERS, LUNT & BOWLEN CO.
(d/b/a Lunt Silversmiths)
298 Federal St.
Greenfield, MA 01302
Mailing Address:
P.O. Box 593,
Greenfield, MA 01302
Tel.: 413-774-2774 **MA**
Fax: 413-774-4393
Year Founded: 1902
Approx.Sls.: $20,000,000
Emp.: 290
Fiscal Year-end: 7/31/90
Manufacture & Wholesaler Sterling Silver, Silverplated & Pewter Tableware
S.I.C.: 3914
Denham C. Lunt, Jr. *(Chm. Bd.)*
James H. Lunt *(Pres.)*
Vincent M. Carbone *(V.P.-Mfg.)*
Colby Lunt *(V.P.-Mktg.)*
George C. Lunt II *(V.P.-Sls.)*
David McElhinny *(Treas.)*

Computer Systems/Hardware:
IBM

Outside Service Firm(s):

Coopers & Lybrand*(Auditors)*
2300 Bay Bank Tower, 1500 Main St.
Springfield, MA 01101
Tel.: 413-781-7200

Shawmut Bank*(Major Banking Relationship)*
Greenfield, MA

Subsidiaries:

Heritage Cutlery, Inc. **(1)**
Refinery Rd.
Bolivar, NY 14715
Tel.: 716-928-2500

Lamson and Goodnow Mfg. Co. **(1)**
45 Conway St.
Shelburne Falls, MA 01370
Tel.: 413-625-6331

ROGERS MARKETS INC.
528 W. Washington Blvd.
Fort Wayne, IN 46802
Tel.: 219-423-4376 **IN**
Fax: 219-423-9480
Year Founded: 1944
Approx.Sls.: $115,000,000
Emp.: 1,100
Retail Groceries & Meats
S.I.C.: 5411
William H. Rogers *(Pres.)*
John W. Rogers *(V.P., Treas. & Sec.)*
John Moran *(Controller)*
Roberta Davis *(Dir.-Personnel)*
Richard Gordon *(Dir.-Pur.)*

Outside Service Firm(s):

Shambaugh & Kast*(Legal Firm)*
Fort Wayne, IN

Fort Wayne National Bank*(Major Banking Relationship)*
110 W. Berry St.
Fort Wayne, IN 46802
Tel.: 219-426-0555

ROGERSON AIRCRAFT CORPORATION
2201 Alton Ave.
Irvine, CA 92714
Tel.: 714-660-0666 **CA**
Fax: 714-660-7965
Year Founded: 1975
Assets: $30,000,000
Liabilities: $21,000,000
Net Worth: $9,000,000
Sales Range: $40-59 Million
Emp.: 444
Fiscal Year-end: 11/30/90
Export
Mfr. of Aircraft Fuel Valves & Auxiliary Fuel Tanks, Electronic Flight Instrument Systems, Filament Windings, Laminated Structures, Compression Moldings, Rotor Blades, Floor Beams, Sound Attenuated Structures, Passenger Systems
S.I.C.: 3728; 3812; 3724
Michael Rogerson *(Chm. Bd., Pres. & Chief Exec. Officer)*
H. Cannon Mathews *(V.P.-Fin. & Chief Fin. Officer)*
Joel Fogelson *(V.P.-Mktg.)*

Principal(s):
Michael Rogerson

No. of Mfg. Plants/Facilities: 6
No. of U.S. Offices: 10
No. of Foreign Offices: 5

Computer Systems/Hardware:
DEC Microvax

Outside Service Firm(s):

Deloitte & Touche*(Auditors)*
695 Town Center Dr.
Costa Mesa, CA 92626
Tel.: 714-436-7100

Alexander & Alexander*(Commercial Insurance Carrier)*
Seattle, WA

Jones, Day, Reavis & Pogue*(Legal Firm)*
901 Lakeside Ave.
Cleveland, OH 44114
Tel.: 216-586-3939
Fax: 216-579-0212

Tokai Bank of California*(Major Banking Relationship)*
Los Angeles, CA

Subsidiaries:

Rogerson ATS **(1)**
2201 Alton Ave.
Irvine, CA 92714
Tel.: 714-660-0666
Fax: 714-660-7965
Emp.: 30
Mfr. of Auxiliary Fuel Systems
S.I.C.: 3728

Rogerson Aircraft Corporation—(Continued)

Rogerson Aircraft Controls **(1)**
2201 Alton Ave.
Irvine, CA 92714
Tel.: 714-660-0666
Fax: 213-477-1318
Emp.: 23
Mfr. of Control Valves
S.I.C.: 3728

Rogerson Aircraft Systems **(1)**
2201 Alton Ave.
Irvine, CA 92714
Tel.: 714-660-0666
Fax: 714-660-7965
Emp.: 19
Mfr. of Aircraft Lavatory Systems
S.I.C.: 3728
Stan Balter *(V.P. & Gen. Mgr.)*

Rogerson Hiller Corporation **(1)**
2140 W. 18th St.
Port Angeles, WA 98362
Tel.: 206-452-6891 (100%)
Fax: 206-457-5426
Approx.Sls.: $15,000,000
Emp.: 52
Manufacture Helicopters
S.I.C.: 3721
Gerald Tobias *(Pres.)*
Victor Milner, Jr. *(V.P.-Mktg.)*
Donald Burch *(Dir.-Prod. Support)*
Margi Bistiline *(Sec.)*

Rogerson Kratos **(1)**
403 S. Raymond Ave.
Pasadena, CA 91109
Tel.: 818-449-3090
Fax: 818-795-0322
Emp.: 204
Mfr. of Aircraft Cockpit Instrumentation
S.I.C.: 3728; 3812
Dr. William Firestone *(V.P. & Gen. Mgr.)*
William Wood *(V.P.-Mktg.)*

Non-U.S. Holdings:

Bavaria Avionik Technologie GmbH **(1)**
Kirschastrasse 20 D-8000
Munich, 50, Germany
Tel.: 089 8184 111
Telex: 5215170
Fax: 089 8120 833
Emp.: 85
Mfr. of Aircraft Instrumentation & Test Equipment
S.I.C.: 3812; 3728

Bavaria Cargo Technologie GmbH **(1)**
Kirschastrasse 20 D-8000
Munich, 50, Germany
Tel.: 089 8184 111
Telex: 5215170
Fax: 089 8120 833
Emp.: 5
Mfr. of Aircraft Cargo Loading Systems
S.I.C.: 3535; 3728

Bavaria Keytronic Technologie GmbH **(1)**
Boschstrasse 23 Postfach 50 02 72, D-2000
Hamburg, 50, Germany
Tel.: 040 89 6831
Telex: 213930
Fax: 040 890 3014
Emp.: 115
Manufacture Aircraft Instrumentation
S.I.C.: 3728

ROHRER CORPORATION
717 Seville Rd.
Wadsworth, OH 44281
Mailing Address:
P.O. Box 1009
Wadsworth, OH 44281
Tel.: 216-335-1541 **OH**
Fax: 216-336-5147
Year Founded: 1973
Approx.Sls.: $25,133,000
Emp.: 200
Fiscal Year-end: 5/31/92
Custom Skin & Blister Card Packaging, Paper Spools, Die-Cut Paperboard
S.I.C.: 2671; 2675
John P. Rohrer *(Pres.)*
David W. Rohrer *(V.P.)*
John Comodeca *(Gen. Mgr.)*
Joanne M. Rohrer *(Sec. & Treas.)*

No. of Mfg. Plants/Facilities: 2

Outside Service Firm(s):

First National Bank of Ohio*(Major Banking Relationship)*
106 S. Main St.
Akron, OH 44308
Tel.: 216-384-7347

Plant:

Rohrer Corporation **(1)**
3150 Clinton Court
Norcross, GA 30071
Tel.: 404-476-9077
Emp.: 75

I. ROKEACH & SONS, INC.
South 61 Road
Paramus, NJ 07652
Tel.: 201-587-0024
Fax: 201-587-9273
Approx.Sls.: $27,000,000
Emp.: 150
Fiscal Year-end: 12/31/90
Rokeach Kosher Soups, Borscht, Gefilte Fish, Sauces, Nyafat Shortening, Israeli Fish, Dry Soup Mixes, Coffee-Lite Creamer, Chow Mein Noodles, Candies Imported Soups, Biscuits, Oriental Delicacies, Crackers & Cookies, Candles, Silver Polish, Honey, Mother's Food Products Spices, Pickle Products, Dessert Jels, Pretzels, Soaps & Cleaning Aids
S.I.C.: 2099
Uri Evan *(Pres.)*
Joseph B. Poli *(V.P.-Fin.)*
Irwin Kralstein *(V.P.-Sls.)*
Mitch Halpert *(V.P.)*
Oney Sims *(V.P.-Mfg.)*

Division:

Mother's Food Products **(1)**
80 Ave. K
Newark, NJ 07105
Tel.: 201-589-5297
Emp.: 100
Vacuum Packed Kosher Foods
S.I.C.: 2099
Yuri Ezans *(Pres.)*

Subsidiary:

S.W.B. & Company **(1)**
P.O. Box 264, 28 Cedar St.
Canton, MA 02021
Tel.: 617-828-6710

ROKOP CORPORATION
400 Old Pond Rd.
Bridgeville, PA 15017
Tel.: 412-221-7600
Fax: 412-221-7272
Year Founded: 1971
Approx.Sls.: $16,000,000
Emp.: 20
Import Export
Casting Forms For The Steel Industry
S.I.C.: 3549
Joseph Rokop *(Chm. Bd.)*
Joseph Rokop, Jr. *(Pres.)*
Judith Rokop *(Exec. V.P.-Pur.)*
Nik Rokop *(V.P.-Engrng.)*
Leonard L. Sabo, Jr. *(Dir.-Sls.)*
Principal(s):
Joseph Rokop
Judith Rokop
Nik Rokop
Robert Rokop

Outside Service Firm(s):

Pittsburgh National Bank*(Major Banking Relationship)*
5th Ave. & Wood St.
Pittsburgh, PA 15222
Tel.: 412-355-3000

Eckert, Seamans, Cherin & Mellott*(Legal Firm)*
600 Grant St., 42nd Fl.
Pittsburgh, PA 15219
Tel.: 412-566-6000

ROLAND INTERNATIONAL CORPORATION
3250 Mary Street, Ste. 402
Coconut Grove, FL 33133
Tel.: 305-446-6600 **DE**
Fax: 305-448-7852
Assets: $110,000,000
Liabilities: $75,000,000
Net Worth: $35,000,000
Approx.Sls.: $24,000,000
Emp.: 35
Fiscal Year-end: 12/31/88
Land Development, Investment & Management
S.I.C.: 6552; 6719; 6531
Gerald Robins *(Chm. Bd.)*
Monica Abreu *(V.P.)*
Norva Carrington *(Sec. & Controller)*

No. of U.S. Offices: 4

Computer Systems/Hardware:
Sperry System 80

Outside Service Firm(s):

KPMG Peat Marwick*(Auditors)*
One Biscayne Tower, 2 South Biscayne Blvd., Ste.2900
Miami, FL 33131

Paul, Weiss, Rifkind, Wharton & Garrison*(Legal Firm)*
345 Park Ave.
New York, NY 10022
Tel.: 212-644-8000

Geoffrey Bell & Co.*(Pension Manager)*
New York, NY

ROLL FORMING CORPORATION
Industrial Park, P.O. Box 369
Shelbyville, KY 40065
Tel.: 502-633-4435 **KY**
Fax: 502-633-5824
Year Founded: 1947
Approx.Sls.: $17,000,000
Emp.: 180
Custom Roll Forming
S.I.C.: 3449; 3351; 3353; 3355; 3356; 3442; 3444; 3446; 3728
Barlow W. Brooks, Jr. *(Pres. & Chief Exec. Officer)*
J.W. Brooks *(V.P.)*
James A. Hagan *(V.P. & Treas.)*
Glen Nelson *(V.P.-Sls. & Mktg.)*
Leon Nevers *(V.P.-Mfg.)*
Ivan Schell *(Sec. & Gen. Counsel)*

Outside Service Firm(s):

Cotton & Allen*(Auditors)*
Louisville, KY

Hirn, Reed, Harper & Eisinger*(Legal Firm)*
Louisville, KY

Liberty National Bank & Trust Co.*(Major Banking Relationship)*
416 W. Jefferson St.
Louisville, KY 40202
Tel.: 502-566-2000

ROLLED STEEL PRODUCTS CORPORATION
2187 S. Garfield Ave.
Los Angeles, CA 90040
Tel.: 213-723-8836
Fax: 213-888-9866
Year Founded: 1952
Approx.Sls.: $35,000,000
Emp.: 100
Mfr. & Marketing of Cold Finishing Steel Shapes
S.I.C.: 5051; 3316
Robert Alperson *(Chm. Bd. & Pres.)*
Rozalind Alperson *(V.P.)*
Steven Alperson *(V.P. & Treas.)*
Lorraine Alperson *(Sec.)*
Merril Vodily *(Controller)*
Dora Fernandez *(Mgr.-Credit)*
Karen Smith *(Office Mgr.)*
George Bienefeld *(Pur. Agent)*

Outside Service Firm(s):

Mel Barlon & Associates*(Auditors)*
Los Angeles, CA

Bank of America*(Major Banking Relationship)*
701 S. Western Ave.
Los Angeles, CA 91201

ROLLER DERBY SKATE COMPANY
311 W. Edwards St.
Litchfield, IL 62056
Mailing Address:
P.O. Box 930,
Litchfield, IL 62056-0930
Tel.: 217-324-3961
Year Founded: 1939
Approx.Sls.: $35,000,000
Emp.: 100
Import Export
Mfr. of Roller Skates, Ice Skates & Skateboards
S.I.C.: 3949
Edwin C. Seltzer *(Chm. Bd. & Pres.)*
Walter Frazier *(V.P.-Sls. & Mktg.)*
Jim Scheller *(V.P. & Gen. Mgr.)*
Agatha Seltzer *(Sec.)*
Aleen Watson *(Data Processing)*
Will Marion *(Mgr.-Export)*

Computer Systems/Hardware:
IBM

ROLLERBLADE, INC.
5101 Shady Oak Rd.
Minnetonka, MN 55343
Tel.: 612-930-7000
Fax: 612-930-7100
Year Founded: 1985
Approx.Sls.: $125,000,000
Emp.: 310
Export
Mfr. of In-Line Roller Skates & Parts; Exercise Equipment
S.I.C.: 3949; 5091
Robert O. Naegele, Jr. *(Chm. Bd.)*
Johnson Sundet *(Pres. & Chief Exec. Officer)*
Anthony P. Copa *(V.P.-Fin.)*
Mary Horwath *(V.P.-Mktg. Services & Intl. Mktg.)*
Noel S. Shadko *(V.P.-Mktg. & Strategic Plng.)*

ROLLEX CORPORATION
2001 Lunt Ave.
Elk Grove Village, IL 60007
Tel.: 708-437-3000
Fax: 708-437-7561
Approx.Sls.: $35,000,000
Emp.: 200
Mfr. of Aluminum Building Products
S.I.C.: 3429
Bruce Stevens *(Pres.)*
James L. Brittingham *(V.P.-Sls.)*
Chuck Eary *(V.P.-Mfg.)*
Mort Seelman *(V.P.-Corp. Devel.)*
Bruce Fortelka *(Controller)*

Computer Systems/Hardware:
IBM

Outside Service Firm(s):

Harris, Burman, Sinars & Jiganti*(Legal Firm)*
Chicago, IL

American National Bank & Trust Co.*(Major Banking Relationship)*
Chicago, IL

ROLOCK, INC.
1350 Kings Hwy. E.
Fairfield, CT 06430
Mailing Address:
P.O. Box 250
Fairfield, CT 06430
Tel.: 203-367-8611
Tel.: 800-243-9460 **CT**
Fax: 203-367-9852
Year Founded: 1924
Approx.Sls.: $12,000,000
Emp.: 130
Fiscal Year-end: 12/31/90
Export
Atmosphere Generating & Control Equipment, Pressure Vessels, Chemical Processing Vessels, Fabricated Alloys
S.I.C.: 3325; 3443; 3823; 3599; 3822
David Buennagel *(Chm. Bd.)*
Frank Bergami *(Pres.)*
Don Stover *(Mgr.-Natl. Sls.)*

Outside Service Firm(s):

Ernst & Young*(Auditors)*
New Haven, CT

Siegel, O'Connor, Schiff, Zangari & Kaimen*(Legal Firm)*
Fairfield, CT

Peoples Bank*(Major Banking Relationship)*
Stamford, CT

Subsidiary:

Rolock of California **(1)**
1475 Potrero Ave.
South El Monte, CA 91733
Tel.: 818-579-3230
Fax: 818-401-3740
David Buennagel *(Pres.)*

ROMA HOLDINGS
(Formerly Roma Corporation)
10000 N. Central Expwy.
Dallas, TX 75231
Tel.: 214-891-7600
Fax: 214-696-6321
Year Founded: 1972
Approx.Sls.: $248,000,000
Fiscal Year-end: 3/ 1/91
144 Company-Owned & Franchised Tony Roma Restaurants
S.I.C.: 5812
Kenneth F. Reimer *(Pres. & Chief Exec. Officer)*
Teresa A. Rife *(Chief Fin. Officer & Sr. V.P.)*
Patrick Morris *(Sr. V.P.-Mktg. & Concept Strategic Plng.)*
Paul Lyford *(V.P.-Human Resources)*
Dale Ross *(V.P.-Franchise Devel.)*
David Short *(V.P.-Legal & Gen. Counsel)*
Larry Zimmerman *(V.P.-Restaurant Devel.)*
Peter Letendre *(Controller)*

Computer Systems/Hardware:
IBM System 38

Outside Service Firm(s):

Locke, Purnell, Rain, Harrell*(Legal Firm)*
Republic Natl. Bank Tower
Dallas, TX 75208
Tel.: 214-744-4511

NationsBank of Texas, N.A.*(Major Banking Relationship)*
Dallas, TX

ROMAC INDUSTRIES, INC.
1064 4th Ave. S.
Seattle, WA 98134
Mailing Address:
P.O. Box 3212,
Seatle, WA 98114
Tel.: 206-624-6491
Tel.: 800-426-9341
Fax: 206-624-1971
Year Founded: 1969
Approx.Sls.: $22,000,000
Emp.: 220
Fiscal Year-end: 12/31/90
Export
Pipe Fittings For Water Works Industry
S.I.C.: 3494; 5074; 5085
Manford R. McNeil *(Pres.)*
Joseph M. Warner *(V.P.-Opers.)*
James J. Larkin *(V.P.-Sls.)*
Joan McNeil *(Sec.)*
James M. Treinen *(Controller)*

No. of Mfg. Plants/Facilities: 3
No. of U.S. Offices: 3

Outside Service Firm(s):

Clark, Nuber & Co.*(Auditors)*
Bellevue, WA

The Bank of California, N.A.*(Major Banking Relationship)*
Seattle, WA

Divisions:

Hays Flood Controls **(1)**
P.O. Box 580, 114 Eason Rd.
Dallas, NC 28034-0580
Tel.: 704-922-9565
Tel.: 1-800-354-4297
Fax: 704-922-9595
S.N. Pennell *(Dir.-Sls. & Mktg.)*

Romac Industries, Inc., Hays Division **(1)**
114 Eason Rd.
Dallas, NC 28034-0580
Tel.: 704-922-9565
Tel.: 800-354-4297
Fax: 704-824-1686
Approx.Sls.: $6,000,000
Emp.: 50
Fiscal Year-end: 12/31/90
Import Export
Mfr. of Water Flow & Measurement Products, Brass & Iron Products, Stops, Valves, Fittings for Industry, Plumbing, Heating, Water Meters, Specialized Industrial & Appliance Products Including Solenoid Valves, Flow Control Devices, Strainers & Fitting Assemblies
S.I.C.: 3491; 3824; 3494
J.M. Warner *(Pres.)*
S.N. Pennell *(Dir.-Sls. & Mktg.)*
Edgar Holbrook *(Controller)*
Lisa Burch *(Mgr.-Personnel)*
Hank Nupp *(Quality Control)*

ROMAN ELECTRIC COMPANY, INC.
640 S. 70th St.
Milwaukee, WI 53214
Tel.: 414-771-5400 **WI**
Fax: 414-471-8693
Year Founded: 1929
Approx.Sls.: $21,000,000
Emp.: 200
Electrical Contracting, Panelboard Manufacturing, Appliance Sales
S.I.C.: 1731; 3613; 5064
Gervase R. Rose *(Pres.)*
Thomas W. Pucylowski *(V.P.-Sls.)*
Gregory J. Rose *(V.P.-Opers.)*
Susan T. Rose *(Treas.)*
Paul Wild *(Controller)*
Cathryne G. Rose *(Sec.)*
James Rozewicz *(Pur. Agent)*
Principal(s):
Gervase R. Rose

No. of Mfg. Plants/Facilities: 1

Outside Service Firm(s):

Lincoln State Bank*(Major Banking Relationship)*
Milwaukee, WI

ROMAN, INC.
555 Lawrence Ave.
Roselle, IL 60172
Tel.: 708-529-3000 **IL**
Fax: 708-529-1121
Year Founded: 1963
Approx.Sls.: $37,000,000
Emp.: 145
Import
Wholesaler Of Religious Articles, Collectibles, Christmas Items & Giftware
Ronald T. Jedlinski *(Pres.)*
Lee J. Hanson *(Chief Oper. Officer)*
Anthony P. Jedlinski *(V.P.-Admin.)*
Diane M. Jedlinski *(Sec.)*
Principal(s):
Ronald T. Jedlinski

Outside Service Firm(s):

Ernst & Young*(Auditors)*
233 S. Wacker Dr.
Chicago, IL 60606
Tel.: 312-368-1800
Fax: 312-645-3095

Griffin & Fadden Ltd.*(Legal Firm)*
Chicago, IL

LaSalle National Bank*(Major Banking Relationship)*
120 S. LaSalle St.
Chicago, IL 60603
Tel.: 312-781-8000

ROMAN MEAL COMPANY
2101 S. Tacoma Way
Tacoma, WA 98409
Mailing Address:
P.O. Box 11126
Tacoma, WA 98411
Tel.: 206-475-0964
Fax: 206-475-1906
Emp.: 100
Fiscal Year-end: 6/30/90
Manufacture & Market Cereals, Baker's Mixes, Frozen Waffles & Bakery Goods
S.I.C.: 2038; 2041; 5142
Charles W.H. Matthaei *(Chm. Bd.)*
William L. Matthaei *(Pres. & Chief Exec. Officer)*
Michael Mason *(Chief Admin. Officer)*
Kevin Shiley *(Dir.-Mktg.)*

Outside Service Firm(s):

Allen, Nelson, Turner & Co.*(Auditors)*
955 Tacoma Ave. S. Ste. 210
Tacoma, WA 98402
Tel.: 206-383-4351

ROMANN & TANNENHOLZ ADVERTISING, INC.
420 Lexington Ave.
New York, NY 10017
Tel.: 212-661-8181
Fax: 212-661-8973
Year Founded: 1977
Approx.Billings: $56,000,000
Emp.: 42
Gad Romann *(Pres.)*
Christine Utz *(Sr. V.P., Gen. Mgr.)*
Soad Boutros *(Comptroller)*
Randi Schwartz *(Brdcst. Planner)*
Ron Moreno *(Studio Mgr.)*
Daniel Levine *(Dir., Bus. Devel.)*
Andrea Tongue *(Data Mngmt.)*

ROMANOFF INTERNATIONAL, INC.
Ste. 100, 511111 Carmel Commons Blvd.
Charlotte, NC 28226-3919
Tel.: 704-543-7500
Fax: 704-543-8062
Year Founded: 1989
Emp.: 50
Fiscal Year-end: 12/31/91
Mfr. & Canning of Barbeque Sauce, Specialty Fruits & Condiments, Herring, Caviar, Salad Dressings, Grenadine, Lime Juice, Marinades & Cocktail Mixers
S.I.C.: 2033; 2035; 2091
Jim McCaffrey *(Pres.)*
Henry E. Sieban *(Sr. V.P.-Opers.)*
George S. Hartley *(V.P. & Chief Fin. Officer)*
John R. Randall *(V.P.-Res. & Devel.)*

Outside Service Firm(s):

Deloitte & Touche*(Auditors)*
2000 First Citizens Bank Plaza, 128 S. Tryon St.
Charlotte, NC 28202-5001
Tel.: 704-372-3560

First National Bank of Boston*(Major Banking Relationship)*
P.O. Box 644,
Boston, MA 02102-0644
Tel.: 617-575-2900
Fax: 617-575-2549

ROME CABLE CORPORATION
421 Ridge St.
Rome, NY 13440
Mailing Address:
P.O. Box 71
Rome, NY 13440
Tel.: 315-337-3000
Fax: 315-337-3022
Year Founded: 1936
Approx.Sls.: $150,000,000
Emp.: 550
Fiscal Year-end: 12/31/90
Export
Manufacture Wire & Cable
S.I.C.: 3357
David E. Harvey *(Chm. & Chief Exec. Officer)*
L.S. Beyland *(Pres. & Chief Oper. Officer)*
Stephen Crowley *(V.P.-Mktg. & Sls.)*
Rock E. White *(Chief Fin. Officer & Treas.)*
Mary L. Wuest *(Controller)*
William Sirny *(Dir.-Human Resources)*
Kenneth Fouse *(Dir.-Opers. & Information Systems)*
Marlene Harris *(Supv.-Salary Payroll)*
Kathy Sega *(Mgr.-Pur.)*

No. of Mfg. Plants/Facilities: 1
No. of U.S. Offices: 5

Computer Systems/Hardware:
IBM 4361

Outside Service Firm(s):

KPMG Peat Marwick*(Auditors)*
Syracuse, NY

Liberty Mutual*(Group Insurer)*
175 Berkeley St.
Boston, MA

Jacobs, Persinger & Parker*(Legal Firm)*
70 Pine
New York, NY 10005
Tel.: 212-344-1866

Chase Lincoln First Bank, N.A.*(Major Banking Relationship)*
Syracuse, NY

Bankers Trust Co.*(Pension Manager)*
One Bankers Trust Plaza
New York, NY 10006
Tel.: 212-250-6902

ROME MANUFACTURING CO.
208 E. 2nd Ave.
Rome, GA 30161
Mailing Address:
P.O. Box 191
Rome, GA 30162
Tel.: 706-236-2900 **GA**
Fax: 706-236-2907
Sales Range: $10-19 Million
Emp.: 200
Fiscal Year-end: 10/31/91
Manufacture Men's Casual & Dress Slacks
S.I.C.: 2325
Jerry Crawford *(Chm. Bd.)*
Hugh S. Burnes, Jr. *(Pres.)*
Jean Jones *(Comptroller)*
James Ford *(Sec.)*
Principal(s):
Jerry Crawford
Hugh S. Burnes, Jr.

Rome Manufacturing Co.—(Continued)

No. of Mfg. Plants/Facilities: 1

Outside Service Firm(s):

Ernest J. Rudert & Company*(Auditors)*
Rome, GA

Brinson, Askew, Berry, & Siegler*(Legal Firm)*
Rome, GA

First Union National Bank*(Major Banking Relationship)*
Rome, GA

ROME SENTINEL CO.
333 W. Dominick St.
Rome, NY 13440
Tel.: 315-337-4000 **NY**
Fax: 315-337-4704
Year Founded: 1893
Emp.: 110
Fiscal Year-end: 12/31/89
Publication of Daily Sentinel Newspaper
S.I.C.: 2711
George B. Waters *(Pres. & Publisher)*
Shirley B. Waters *(V.P. & Sec.)*
Stephen Waters *(V.P. & Gen. Mgr.)*
Kenneth Kakaty *(Treas.)*

Outside Service Firm(s):

Coopers & Lybrand*(Auditors)*
One Lincoln Center
Syracuse, NY 13202
Tel.: 315-474-8541
Fax: 315-474-0259

Sullivan & Cromwell*(Legal Firm)*
125 Broad St.
New York, NY 10004
Tel.: 212-558-4000

Norstar Bank, N.A.*(Major Banking Relationship)*
Long Island, NY

ROME STRIP STEEL CO., INC.
530 Henry St.
Rome, NY 13440
Tel.: 315-336-5500
Fax: 315-336-5510
Approx.Sls.: $35,000,000
Emp.: 225
Manufacture Cold Rolled Stripped Steel
S.I.C.: 3316
Kirk Hinman *(Pres., Chief Exec. Officer, Chief Fin. Officer & Treas.)*
Mark Hinman *(V.P., Sec. & Mgr.-Sls.)*
Bill Campbell *(Dir.-Data Processing)*

Computer Systems/Hardware:
NCR

Outside Service Firm(s):

Coopers & Lybrand*(Auditors)*
One Lincoln Center
Syracuse, NY 13202
Tel.: 315-474-8541
Fax: 315-474-0259

McMahon & Grow*(Legal Firm)*
Rome, NY

Marine Midland Bank*(Major Banking Relationship)*
Rome, NY

Marine Midland Bank*(Pension Manager)*
New York, NY

RONALD JAMES DIRECT
11766 Wilshire Blvd., Ste. 310
Los Angeles, CA 90025
Tel.: 310-445-0810
Year Founded: 1986
Approx.Billings: $13,400,000
Emp.: 23
Direct Response
Clare Thain *(Mng. Partner & New Bus. Contact)*

RONCO COMMUNICATIONS & ELECTRONICS INC.
595 Sheridan Dr.
Tonawanda, NY 14150
Tel.: 716-873-0760 **NY**
Fax: 716-879-8198
Year Founded: 1965
Assets: $8,709,380
Liabilities: $4,119,797
Net Worth: $4,589,583
Approx.Sls.: $29,012,704
Emp.: 215
Fiscal Year-end: 12/31/91
Installation of Sound, Power, & Telephone; Wholesale Electrical Equipment & Supplies
S.I.C.: 1731; 5065
Harry A. Ronan *(Chm. Bd. & Pres.)*
Robert Dutschman *(V.P.)*
Thomas R. Lippard III *(V.P.-Fin.)*

Outside Service Firm(s):

Freed, Maxick, Sachs & Murphy*(Auditors)*
Buffalo, NY
Tel.: 716-847-2651

Saperston & Day, P.C.*(Legal Firm)*
1500 Liberty Bank Bldg.
Buffalo, NY 14202
Tel.: 716-856-5400

Manufacturers & Traders Trust Company*(Major Banking Relationship)*
1 M & T Plaza
Buffalo, NY 14240
Tel.: 716-842-4200

RONEY & CO.
One Griswold St.
Detroit, MI 48226
Tel.: 313-963-6700
Year Founded: 1925
Assets: $70,187,997
Liabilities: $56,895,393
Net Worth: $13,292,604
Approx.Sls.: $48,829,203
Emp.: 550
Fiscal Year-end: 9/27/91
Securities Brokers & Investors
S.I.C.: 6211
James A. Richter *(Mng. Partner)*
John C. Avery *(Partner)*
Harry Benjamin *(Partner)*
John J. Burke, Jr. *(Partner)*
Lewis H. Echlin, III *(Partner)*
R.J. Kelly, III *(Partner)*
Walter S. Olsson *(Partner)*
William C. Roney, III *(Partner)*
Andrew R. Spence *(Partner)*
Mark A. Cleland *(Chief Fin. Officer)*
H. Duane Billmeyer *(Dir.-Sls.)*
Sharon L. Paul *(Dir.-Admin. & Opers.)*

Principal(s):
James A. Richter
John C. Avery
Harry Benjamin
John J. Burke, Jr.
Lewis H. Echlin, III
R.J. Kelly, III
Walter S. Olsson
William C. Roney, III
Andrew R. Spence

No. of U.S. Offices: 28

Outside Service Firm(s):

Coopers & Lybrand*(Auditors)*
400 Renaissance Center
Detroit, MI 48243
Tel.: 313-446-7100
Fax: 313-446-7117

Honigman, Miller, Schwartz & Cohn*(Legal Firm)*
2290 First National Bldg.
Detroit, MI 48226
Tel.: 313-256-7800

Manufacturers National Bank N.A.*(Major Banking Relationship)*
38th Fl., 100 Renaissance Center
Detroit, MI 48243
Tel.: 313-222-4227

ROOFING WHOLESALE CO., INC.
1918 W. Grant
Phoenix, AZ 85009
Tel.: 602-258-3794 **AZ**
Fax: 602-254-9416
Sales Range: $40-59 Million
Emp.: 165
Wholesale Roofing & Building Materials
S.I.C.: 5039
Harley Lisherness *(Chm. Bd. & Pres.)*
Stephen K. Rold *(V.P., Treas., Sec. & Controller)*
Bill Dickhoff *(Dir.-Sls., Mktg. & Adv.)*
Mike Oday *(Dir.-Pur. & Opers.)*

Computer Systems/Hardware:
Data General

Outside Service Firm(s):

Vogel & Co.*(Auditors)*
Phoenix, AZ

Ehman, Waldman & Brody*(Legal Firm)*
Phoenix, AZ

Security Pacific Bank Arizona*(Major Banking Relationship)*
Phoenix, AZ

W.A. ROOSEVELT CO.
2727 Commerce St.
La Crosse, WI 54601
Mailing Address:
P.O. Box 1208
La Crosse, WI 54602
Tel.: 608-781-2000 **WI**
Fax: 608-781-3355
Year Founded: 1868
Approx.Sls.: $19,000,000
Emp.: 96
Fiscal Year-end: 12/31/90
Distributor of Plumbing, Heating, Electrical, Air Conditioning & Refrigeration Supplies & Equipment
S.I.C.: 5074; 5075; 5078; 5063
James M. Brindley *(Chm. Bd.)*
Frederick A. Reiman *(Vice Chm.)*
Stephen W. Reiman *(Pres. & Chief Exec. Officer)*
Thomas M. Brindley *(Chief Oper. Officer & Exec. V.P.)*
R.W. Spencer *(Chief Fin. Officer)*
Carol Helgerson *(Dir.-Data Processing)*
Gerald Haas *(Mgr.-Pur.)*
Harold Hemker *(Mgr.-Sls.-Electric)*
Paul Hundt *(Mgr.-Sls.-Refrigeration & Mktg. Coord.)*
James Voshant *(Mgr.-Sls.-Plumbing)*

No. of U.S. Offices: 3

Outside Service Firm(s):

Hawkins, Ash, Baptie & Co.*(Auditors)*
La Crosse, WI

Moen, Sheehan & Meyer*(Legal Firm)*
La Crosse, WI

State Bank of La Crosse*(Major Banking Relationship)*
La Crosse, WI

Branches:

Plover BLFC Branch **(1)**
5680 Plover Rd.
Plover, WI 54467
Tel.: 715-341-5560
Fax: 715-341-6157
Emp.: 7
General Sales
S.I.C.: 5063
M. Dick *(Branch Mgr.)*

Roosevelt Rice Lake Branch **(1)**
310 W. Coleman
Rice Lake, WI 54868
Tel.: 715-234-4370
Fax: 715-234-4176
Emp.: 6
Distributor of Plumbing, Heating, Electrical, Air Conditioning & Refrigeration Supplies & Equipment
S.I.C.: 5063; 5074; 5075; 5078
Mike Beranek *(Branch Mgr.)*

ROOSEVELT PAPER CO.
7601 State Rd.
Philadelphia, PA 19136-3496
Tel.: 215-331-5000
Fax: 215-338-1199
Approx.Sls.: $100,000,000
Emp.: 250
Printing Paper Wholesaler & Converter
S.I.C.: 2679
Irving S. Kosloff *(Chm. Bd.)*
Theodore L. Kosloff *(Pres. & Treas.)*
Curt Wegelius *(V.P.-Sls. & Mktg.)*

No. of U.S. Offices: 3

Outside Service Firm(s):

Price Waterhouse*(Auditors)*
30 S. 17th St.
Philadelphia, PA 19103
Tel.: 215-665-9500

A.I. ROOT COMPANY
623 W. Liberty St.
Medina, OH 44256
Mailing Address:
P.O. Box 588
Medina, OH 44258
Tel.: 216-725-6677 **OH**
Fax: 216-725-5624
Year Founded: 1869
Sales Range: $10-19 Million
Emp.: 200
Fiscal Year-end: 7/31/91
Import Export
Manufacture Beekeeping Supplies; Ecclesiastical & Decorative Candles; Wood Products & Periodical Printing
S.I.C.: 2721; 3999
John A. Root *(Chm. Bd. & Pres.)*
Brad I. Root *(Exec. V.P.)*
Bob Stanners *(Chief Oper. Officer)*
William Fleming *(Treas.)*
Stuart W. Root *(Mgr.-Personnel & Sec.)*
Curtis Brown *(Mgr.-Data Processing)*
Bob Krulik *(Mgr.-Sls., Deco Candles)*
John Holodnak *(Mgr.-Sls., Church Candles)*

No. of Mfg. Plants/Facilities: 2

Outside Service Firm(s):

Deloitte & Touche*(Auditors)*
1717 East Ninth St.
Cleveland, OH 44114
Tel.: 216-589-1300

Laribee, Hertrick & Bougher*(Legal Firm)*
Medina, OH

Society National Bank*(Major Banking Relationship)*
Medina, OH

Division:

A. I. Root Co. **(1)**
529 S. Flores St.
San Antonio, TX 78204
Tel.: 210-492-6143
Emp.: 40
Mfr. Beekeeping Supplies; Ecclesiastical & Decorative Candles; Periodical Printing
S.I.C.: 2499; 2721
Martin Taege *(Mgr.-Opers.)*
Norean Contu *(Mgr.-Sls.)*

ROOT CORPORATION
152 N. Main St.
Mount Wolf, PA 17347
Mailing Address:
P.O. Box 310
Mount Wolf, PA 17347
Tel.: 717-266-5626
Tel.: 800-233-9374 PA
Fax: 800-221-7412
Year Founded: 1888
Approx.Sls.: $35,000,000
Emp.: 380
Fiscal Year-end: 12/31/90
Export
Industrial Wire Cloth; Insect Screening; Fine Wire
S.I.C.: 3315; 3357; 2221; 3496
L.D. Root, Jr. *(Chm. Bd.)*
P.T. Root *(Pres.)*
Frank T. Gaiteri *(V.P.-Engrng.)*
Thomas Murphy *(V.P.-Mfg.)*
Roger P. Pratt *(V.P.-Mktg. & Sls.)*
A.D. Bair *(Treas.)*
Kristy McLain *(Mktg. Coord.)*
Principal(s):
L.D. Root, Jr.
P.T. Root

No. of Mfg. Plants/Facilities: 3
No. of U.S. Offices: 3

Computer Systems/Hardware:
IBM

Outside Service Firm(s):

Seligman, Friedman & Co.*(Auditors)*
York, PA

York Bank & Trust Co.*(Major Banking Relationship)*
York, PA

Divisions:

New York Wire Co., Wire Weaving Mill **(1)**
441 E. Market St.
York, PA 17403
Tel.: 717-854-9571
Insect Screening & Industrial Wire Cloth
B.L. Levisky *(Plant Mgr.)*

New York Wire Co., Textile Mill **(1)**
152 N. Main St.
Mount Wolf, PA 17347
Tel.: 717-266-5626
Insect Screening & Industrial Fabrics (Fiberglass)

New York Wire Co., Wire Drawing Mill **(1)**
Loucks Mill Rd.
York, PA 17403
Tel.: 717-846-4960
Wire, Aluminum, Bronze, Steel
T.R. Gilbert *(Plant Mgr)*

ROPER BROS. LUMBER CO., INC.
130 Pocahontas St.
Petersburg, VA 23803
Mailing Address:
P.O. Box 488,
Colonial Heights, VA 23834
Tel.: 804-748-8141 VA
Fax: 804-774-6870
Year Founded: 1909
Approx.Sls.: $35,000,000
Emp.: 185
Building Materials Home Center
S.I.C.: 5211
Leroy B. Roper *(Chm. Bd.)*
M. Ronald Helms *(Pres. & Chief Exec. Officer)*
Dennis A. Burrows *(Sr. V.P. & Sec.)*
Lawrence Belcher *(V.P.-Sls.)*
Anne W. Pate *(V.P. & Treas.)*
Randy Rogers *(V.P. & Branch Mgr.-Petersburg)*
Patrick Welsh *(V.P. & Branch Mgr.-Fredericksburg)*
Principal(s):
Leroy B. Roper

Computer Systems/Hardware:
IBM AS/400

Outside Service Firm(s):

Ernst & Young*(Auditors)*
One James Center, 901 E. Cary St.,Ste. 1000
Richmond, VA 23219
Tel.: 804-780-0010

Williams, Mullen, Christian & Dobbins*(Legal Firm)*
P.O. Box 1320, United Bank Bldg., 9th & Main
Richmond, VA 23210
Tel.: 804-643-1991

First National Bank of Boston*(Major Banking Relationship)*
P.O. Box 644,
Boston, MA 02102-0644
Tel.: 617-575-2900
Fax: 617-575-2549

ROPPE CORP.
1602-10 N. Union St.
Fostoria, OH 44830
Mailing Address:
P.O. Box X
Fostoria, OH 44830
Tel.: 419-435-8546
Tel.: 800-537-9527 DE
Fax: 419-435-1056
Year Founded: 1955
Approx.Sls.: $45,000,000
Emp.: 300
Fiscal Year-end: 9/30/89
Export
Manufacture Molded & Extruded Rubber Products Including Cove Base, Stair Treads, Stair Nosings, Carpet Installation Accessories & Truck Mud Flaps
S.I.C.: 3061; 3069
Donald P. Miller *(Pres.)*
Doyle G. Dillon *(V.P.-Pur.)*
Frank Kinn *(V.P.-Fin. & Sec.)*
David Miller *(V.P.-Mfg.)*
John Breidenbaugh *(Dir.-Data Proc.)*
Robert Eatmon *(Dir.-Personnel)*

No. of Mfg. Plants/Facilities: 4

Computer Systems/Hardware:
Qantel

Outside Service Firm(s):

Arthur Andersen & Co.*(Auditors)*
Toledo, OH

Baker & Hostetler*(Legal Firm)*
3200 National City Center
Cleveland, OH 44114
Tel.: 216-621-0200
Fax: 216-696-0740

Society Bank*(Major Banking Relationship)*
Fostoria, OH

RB&T Rosanio, Bailets & Talamo
ADVERTISING • MARKETING • PUBLIC RELATIONS

ROSANIO, BAILETS & TALAMO, INC.
12 Executive Campus, Rte. 38
Cherry Hill, NJ 08002
Tel.: 609-488-5500
Year Founded: 1985
Approx.Billings: $16,999,400
Emp.: 45
Healthcare, Travel & Tourism, & Publication Services
Linda Rosanio *(Chm. Bd. & Chief Exec. Officer)*
Jan Talamo *(Vice Chm.)*
Nelson Fellman *(Pres., Sls. Promo.)*
Brian Ablaza *(Chief Information Officer)*
Michael Willmann *(Exec. V.P., Pub. Rels., Mktg. & Res. Dir., New Bus. Contact)*
Lisa Catelli *(Exec. V.P., Opers. & Acct. Services)*
Bridget Szabo *(Sec.)*
Denise Hill *(Pub. Rels. Mgr.)*
Maria Antonelli *(Mktg. Coord.)*
Mary Kay Ward *(Acctg. Mgr.)*

Computer Systems/Hardware:
Macintosh; Diamond Management System; Leading Edge

ROSAUER'S SUPERMARKETS, INC.
W. 1815 Garland
Spokane, WA 99205
Mailing Address:
P.O. Box 9000
Spokane, WA 99209
Tel.: 509-326-8900
Fax: 509-328-2483
Approx.Sls.: $70,000,000
Emp.: 1,250
Supermarkets
S.I.C.: 5411
Larry Geller *(Pres. & Chief Exec. Officer)*
Bill Haraldson *(Chief Oper. Officer & Exec. V.P.-Mktg.)*
C.J. McElderry *(Chief Fin. Officer & V.P.-Fin.)*
Paul Van Gordon *(V.P.-Human Resources)*
Richard Salsbury *(V.P.-Retail Services)*

ROSCO LABORATORIES, INC.
36 Bush Ave.
Port Chester, NY 10573
Tel.: 914-937-1300
Fax: 914-937-5984
Sales Range: $20-39 Million
Emp.: 100
Products For Theater, TV & Film
S.I.C.: 3999; 3648
Stanford Miller *(Pres.)*
Stanley Schwartz *(Exec. V.P.)*
Stuart Streger *(V.P.-Fin.)*

Outside Service Firm(s):

M.R. Wiser & Co.*(Auditors)*
New York, NY

Hahn & Hessen*(Legal Firm)*
350 Fifth Ave., Ste. 3700
New York, NY 10118
Tel.: 212-736-1000

National Westminster Bank plc*(Major Banking Relationship)*
Astor Plaza, 1515 Broadway
New York, NY 10036

ROSCO MANUFACTURING CO.
1001 S.W. 1st St.
Madison, SD 57042
Mailing Address:
P.O. Box B
Madison, SD 57042
Tel.: 605-256-6942 mn
Fax: 605-256-6262
Year Founded: 1928
Approx.Sls.: $15,000,000
Emp.: 110
Fiscal Year-end: 9/30/90
Export
Manufacture Road Maintenance Equipment
S.I.C.: 3531
Employee Matching Gifts Program: United Way
Leroy R. Knuths *(Chm. Bd., Pres. & Chief Exec. Officer)*
Donald Weber *(Chief Fin. Officer)*
Al Rowland *(Pur. Dir.)*
Derek Williams *(Data Processing Dir.)*
Shalmerdean A. Knuths *(Dir.-Admin.)*
Principal(s):
Leroy R. Knuths

No. of Mfg. Plants/Facilities: 1
No. of U.S. Offices: 1

Outside Service Firm(s):

McGladrey & Pullen*(Auditors)*
Sioux Falls, SD

First Bank of Madison*(Major Banking Relationship)*
Madison, SD

May, Johnson, Doyle & Becker*(Legal Firm)*
West 9th St.
Sioux Falls, SD 57117
Tel.: 605-336-2565

ROSE ACRE FARMS
R.R. 5
Seymour, IN 47274
Tel.: 812-497-2557
Fax: 812-497-3311
Year Founded: 1943
Approx.Sls.: $110,000,000
Emp.: 900
Egg Producer
S.I.C.: 0252
Lois Rust *(Pres. & Chief Exec. Officer)*
Ruth Ann Hendericks *(Corp. Sec.)*
Principal(s):
Lois Rust
Ruth Ann Hendericks

Computer Systems/Hardware:
IBM RS 6000

Outside Service Firm(s):

Ernst & Young*(Auditors)*
One Indiana Square, Ste. 3400
Indianapolis, IN 46204
Tel.: 317-236-1100

Baker & Daniels*(Legal Firm)*
300 N. Meridian St., Ste. 2700
Indianapolis, IN 46204
Tel.: 317-237-0300

Rabobank Nederland*(Major Banking Relationship)*
245 Park Ave., 16th Fl.
New York, NY 10167

ROSE ART INDUSTRIES
555 Main St.
Orange, NJ 07050
Tel.: 201-414-1313
Fax: 201-677-9447
Year Founded: 1972
Approx.Sls.: $50,000,000
Emp.: 400
Mfr. of Children's Toys, Crayons, Chalk, Charcoal, Wax & Pastels
S.I.C.: 3944; 3952; 5092
Sydney Rosen *(Chm. Bd.)*
Lawrence Rosen *(Pres.)*
Ed Hertzeberg *(V.P.-Mktg.)*

ROSE PACKING COMPANY
65 S. Barrington Rd.
South Barrington, IL 60010
Tel.: 708-381-5700
Fax: 708-381-9424
Year Founded: 1924
Assets: $18,330,371
Earnings: $1,330,528
Net Worth: $18,330,371
Approx.Sls.: $109,700,000
Emp.: 686
Fiscal Year-end: 7/31/91
Mfr. & Wholesaler of Smoked Meat Products
S.I.C.: 2013
William R. Rose *(Chm. Bd., Pres. & Chief Exec. Officer)*
Henry J. Vandenbergh, Jr. *(Chief Fin. Officer & Treas.)*
Peter W. Rose *(V.P.-Opers.)*
Michael Sheridan *(V.P.-Sls.)*
Dwight Stiehl *(V.P.-Opers.)*

Rose Packing Company—(Continued)

Norman C. Wetherton *(V.P.-Special Sls.)*
Bob Bell *(Asst. Treas. & Controller)*
Charmaine Jeske *(Mgr.-Adv.)*

Computer Systems/Hardware:
IBM System 38 & 4331

Outside Service Firm(s):

Deloitte & Touche*(Auditors)*
Two Prudential Plaza, 180 N. Stetson
Chicago, IL 60601
Tel.: 312-946-2039

Blue Cross & Blue Shield of Illinois*(Group Insurer)*
100 Tower Drive
Burr Ridge, IL 60521
Tel.: 708-323-3666

LaSalle National Bank*(Investment Banker)*
120 S. LaSalle St.
Chicago, IL 60603
Tel.: 312-781-8000

LaSalle National Bank*(Major Banking Relationship)*
120 S. LaSalle St.
Chicago, IL 60603
Tel.: 312-781-8000

ROSE PRINTING COMPANY, INC.
2503 Jackson Bluff Rd.
Tallahassee, FL 32314
Tel.: 904-576-4151
Fax: 904-576-4153
Approx.Sls.: $16,000,000
Emp.: 180
Export
Book Printing & Binding
S.I.C.: 2732; 2789
Charlotte Rosenberg *(Chm. Bd.)*
Charles Rosenberg *(Pres.)*
Karen Haerle *(Mgr.-Sls. & Mktg.)*
Henry Yonkers *(Pur. Agent)*

Outside Service Firm(s):

Betts, Rogers & Sherk*(Auditors)*
Tallahassee, FL

Erwin/Varn*(Legal Firm)*
Tallahassee, FL

First Union National Bank*(Major Banking Relationship)*
Tallahassee, FL

ROSEBURG FOREST PRODUCTS CO.
Old Hwy. 99 S.
Dillard, OR 97432
Tel.: 503-679-3311 **OR**
Fax: 503-679-9683
Approx.Sls.: $687,000,000
Emp.: 4,100
Fiscal Year-end: 3/31/91
Export
Forestry; Lumber & Wood Products
S.I.C.: 2436; 2493; 2421; 5031
Kenneth Ford *(Chm. Bd.)*
William A. Whelan *(Pres. & Chief Exec. Officer)*
Ron C. Parker *(Treas., Sec. & Chief Fin. Officer)*
Bob Erickson *(Dir.-Data Processing)*
William Maule *(Dir.-Pur.)*
Robert K. Wilson *(Dir.-Personnel)*

No. of Mfg. Plants/Facilities: 16
No. of U.S. Offices: 35
No. of Foreign Offices: 1

Computer Systems/Hardware:
IBM 4381

Outside Service Firm(s):

Arthur Andersen & Co.*(Auditors)*
111 S.W. Columbia, Ste. 1400
Portland, OR 97201
Tel.: 503-226-1331

Marsh & McLennan*(Commercial Insurance Carrier)*
1100 Standard Insurance Center
Portland, OR 97204
Tel.: 503-226-9500

U.S. Bancorp*(Major Banking Relationship)*
Portland, OR

ROSELLE PAPER CO., INC.
615 E. First Ave.
Roselle, NJ 07203
Tel.: 908-245-6758
Fax: 908-245-9434
Approx.Sls.: $14,000,000
Emp.: 125
Export
Mfr. of Drawing & Construction Papers, Notebooks, Stationery & Tablets Made From Purchased Materials; Newsprint, Packaging & Mass Merchandising Products
S.I.C.: 2621; 2679
Samuel Lefkovits *(Pres.)*
Bernard Lefkovits *(Treas.)*
Harry Todres *(Controller)*
Eleanor Newallis *(Sec.)*

Outside Service Firm(s):

KPMG Peat Marwick*(Auditors)*
345 Park Ave.
New York, NY 10154
Tel.: 212-758-9700
Fax: 212-872-3308

Summit Bank*(Major Banking Relationship)*
Summit, NJ

ROSEN ASSOCIATES MANAGEMENT CORP.
333 Jericho Turnpike
Jericho, NY 11753
Tel.: 516-822-5350
Fax: 516-433-3821
Year Founded: 1960
Approx.Sls.: $120,000,000
Emp.: 125
Investors, Owners, Developers & Managers of Neighborhood and Community-size Shopping Centers
S.I.C.: 6552; 6531; 6798
Robert A. Rosen *(Pres.)*
Florence Rosen *(Exec. V.P. & Controller)*
David Rosen *(V.P.-Leasing, Mktg. & Adv.)*
Carl Seyfarth *(V.P.-Acquisitions)*
Jay I. Klein *(Sr. Acquisition Analyst)*
Emanuel Zimmer *(Gen. Counsel)*
Rita Fuchs *(Head Bookkeeper)*
Maxine Keir *(Mgr.-Admin.)*
Dolores Miller *(Dir.-Pur.)*
Principal(s):
Robert A. Rosen
Florence Rosen

No. of U.S. Offices: 3

Computer Systems/Hardware:
IBM

RAYMOND ROSEN CO.
15 Colwell Ln.
Conshohocken, PA 19428
Tel.: 215-941-5000
Fax: 215-941-5026
Year Founded: 1927
Assets: $14,000,000
Net Worth: $14,000,000
Approx.Sls.: $100,000,000
Emp.: 208
Fiscal Year-end: 12/31/90
Wholesale Distributor of Appliances & Floor Covering Products, Voice Processing Equipment
S.I.C.: 5023; 5713; 1752; 5064; 3679; 7629
Edward H. Rosen *(Chm. & Chief Exec. Officer)*
Theodore A. Rosen *(Pres. & Chief Oper. Officer)*
Terrence P. Sukalski *(Chief Fin. Officer)*
Charlotte Ott *(Dir.-Personnel)*
John Voitel *(Dir.-Mngmt. Information Systems & Telecommunications)*
Margaret M. Cortese *(Meetings Plng.)*
Principal(s):
Edward H. Rosen
Theodore A. Rosen

No. of U.S. Offices: 2

Computer Systems/Hardware:
Prime 9755 Disc Drive

Outside Service Firm(s):

Connecticut General Life Insurance Co.*(Group Insurer)*
P.O. Box 2975,
Hartford, CT 06104
Tel.: 203-726-6000

Schnader, Harrison, Segal & Lewis*(Legal Firm)*
1600 Market Street
Philadelphia, PA 19103
Tel.: 215-751-2000

Connecticut General Life Insurance Co.*(Pension Manager)*
P.O. Box 2975,
Hartford, CT 06104
Tel.: 203-726-6000

ROSENBERGERS DAIRIES, INC.
847 Forty Foot Rd.
Hatfield, PA 19440
Tel.: 215-855-9074
Fax: 215-855-6486
Approx.Sls.: $10,000,000
Emp.: 140
Wholesale & Retail Milk & Cream
S.I.C.: 2026
William L. Rosenberger *(Pres.)*
Marcus L. Rosenberger *(Treas. & Sec.)*
Robert Nice *(Controller)*

Outside Service Firm(s):

Detweiler & Associates*(Auditors)*
Hatfield, PA

ROSENDIN ELECTRIC, INC.
880 Mabury Rd.
San Jose, CA 95133
Tel.: 408-286-2800 **CA**
Fax: 408-971-7170
Year Founded: 1919
Approx.Sls.: $70,000,000
Emp.: 500
Electrical Contractors
S.I.C.: 1731
Bertha C. Rosendin *(Chm. Bd.)*
Raymond J. Rosendin *(Pres. & Treas.)*
Louis M. Rosendin *(Exec. V.P. & Sec.)*
John R. Coffee *(V.P.-Pur.)*
James Tario *(Gen. Counsel)*
Principal(s):
Bertha C. Rosendin
Raymond J. Rosendin
Louis M. Rosendin

Outside Service Firm(s):

Grant Thornton*(Auditors)*
San Jose, CA

Berliner, Cohen & Biagini*(Legal Firm)*
San Jose, CA

Bank of America NT&SA*(Major Banking Relationship)*
San Jose, CA

RSH&S

ROSENFELD, SIROWITZ, HUMPHREY & STRAUSS, INC.
111 Fifth Ave.
New York, NY 10002
Tel.: 212-505-0200
Fax: 212-505-7309
Year Founded: 1971
Approx.Billings: $100,000,000
Emp.: 120
Leonard Sirowitz *(Co-Chm. Bd. & Creative Dir.)*
Harold L. Strauss *(Co-Chm. Bd. & Opers.)*
Robert G. Mayer *(Sr. Exec. V.P.)*
Fred Brownfeld *(Exec. V.P.)*
Jose Abarquez *(V.P., Controller)*
Carl Langrock *(V.P., Mgr. Information Systems)*
Marie Lemerise *(V.P., Strategic Planning)*
Harry A. Kraus *(Mgr. & Dir. Modular Direct)*

ROSENFIELD/DENTINO, INC.
239 Washington St.
Jersey City, NJ 03702
Tel.: 201-332-1219
Fax: 201-332-4262
Year Founded: 1990
Approx.Billings: $13,000,000
Emp.: 14
Direct Marketing
James R. Rosenfield *(Chm.)*
Karl G. Dentino *(Pres.)*

ROSENS DIVERSIFIED, INC.
1120 Lake Ave.
Fairmont, MN 56031
Tel.: 507-238-4201 **MN**
Fax: 507-238-9966
Year Founded: 1946
Approx.Sls.: $195,000,000
Emp.: 700
Wholesale Distribution of Fertilizer & Fertilizer Materials; Mixing Fertilizers; Buying & Marketing of Cattle; Meat Packing Plants
S.I.C.: 5191; 2011; 2875; 5154
Thomas Rosen *(Pres.)*
Robert A. Hovde *(Treas.)*

Outside Service Firm(s):

First Bank, N.A.*(Major Banking Relationship)*
First Bank Place
Minneapolis, MN 55480

Subsidiaries:

Long Prairie Packing Co. **(1)**
Old Hwy. 71, N.W.
Long Prairie, MN 56347
Tel.: 612-732-2171
Meat Packing Plants
S.I.C.: 2011
Ludwig M. Rosen *(Chm. Bd.)*
William McCallum *(Pres.)*
Elmer H. Rosen *(V.P.)*
Robert Hovde *(Treas.)*
Thomas Rosen *(Sec.)*

Rosens, Inc. **(1)**
1120 Lake Ave.
Fairmont, MN 56031
Tel.: 507-238-4201
Wholesale Distributor of Fertilizer & Fertilizer Materials
S.I.C.: 5191
Ludwig M. Rosen *(Chm. Bd.)*
Elmer Rosen *(Vice Chm. Bd.)*
Thomas Rosen *(Pres.)*
W.B. McCallum *(Exec. V.P.)*
Robert A. Hovde *(Treas.)*

ROSENSHEIN ASSOCIATES
77 Quaker Ridge Road
New Rochelle, NY 10804
Tel.: 914-632-5100
Fax: 914-632-6009
Emp.: 150
Real Estate Developer
S.I.C.: 6552
Bernard J. Rosenshein *(Pres.)*
Lisa Rosenshein *(Dir.-Leasing)*

ROSENTHAL AUTOMOTIVE ORGANIZATION
1550 Wilson Blvd., Suite 700
Arlington, VA 22209
Tel.: 703-522-2300
Fax: 703-527-7392
Year Founded: 1954
Approx.Sls.: $574,000,000
Emp.: 1,200
Retail Sales of New & Used Automobiles
S.I.C.: 5511
Robert M. Rosenthal *(Pres.)*
Mike Charappe *(Exec. V.P.)*
Donald Bavely *(V.P.-Fin.)*

Outside Service Firm(s):

Coopers & Lybrand*(Auditors)*
Washington, DC

Stein, Mitchell & Mezines*(Legal Firm)*
Washington, DC

First Virginia Bank*(Major Banking Relationship)*
Arlington, VA

Subsidiary:

Lane Honda/Hyundai **(1)**
9400 Baltimore Blvd.
College Park, MD 20740
Tel.: 301-441-2900
New & Used Automobile Sales
S.I.C.: 5511
William Lane *(Pres.)*

ROSENTHAL CHEVROLET CO.
3400 Columbia Pike
Arlington, VA 22204
Tel.: 703-920-8700
Fax: 703-553-6422
Approx.Sls.: $450,000,000
Emp.: 1,200
New & Used Retail Automobiles
S.I.C.: 5511
Robert Rosenthal *(Pres.)*
John Adamson *(Gen. Mgr.)*
Donald Bavely *(Treas.)*
Michael Charapp *(Sec.)*

Computer Systems/Hardware:
IBM

Outside Service Firm(s):

Coopers & Lybrand*(Auditors)*
Washington, DC

Blue Cross & Blue Shield of Southwestern Virginia*(Group Insurer)*
Roanoke, VA

ROSEVILLE CHRYSLER PLYMOUTH INC.
25800 Gratiot
Roseville, MI 48066
Tel.: 313-772-0800
Approx.Sls.: $38,500,000
Emp.: 141
Automobile Dealership
S.I.C.: 5511
James E. Riehl Sr. *(Pres.)*
Michael D. Riehl *(V.P.)*
Wayne Andre *(Treas. & Sec.)*
Joe Prantera *(Mgr.-Sls.-Used Cars)*
James A. Simpson *(Gen. Mgr.)*
Jim Voyle *(Mgr.-Sls.-New Cars)*

Outside Service Firm(s):

Goerlich, Richert & Kaiser*(Auditors)*
Port Huron, MI

Dykema, Gossett*(Legal Firm)*
400 Renaissance Ctr., 35th Fl.
Detroit, MI 48243
Tel.: 313-568-6800

Comerica Bank*(Major Banking Relationship)*
211 W. Fort St.
Detroit, MI 48226
Tel.: 313-222-3300

ROSEWOOD PROPERTY COMPANY
500 Crescent Ct., Ste. 300
Dallas, TX 75201
Tel.: 214-871-8600
Fax: 214-871-8616
Approx.Sls.: $260,000,000
Emp.: 1,750
Real Estate Developer & Manager; Hotels; Oil & Gas
S.I.C.: 6552; 6531; 7011
Todd Miller *(Chm. Bd. & Chief Exec. Officer)*
Paul Rowsey, III *(Pres. & Gen. Counsel)*
David Jacobs *(Chief Fin. Officer)*
Jane Mody *(Exec. V.P.-Investments)*

ROSKA DIRECT MARKETING, INC.
1364 Welsh Rd.
North Wales, PA 19454
Tel.: 215-643-9100
Year Founded: 1981
Approx.Billings: $10,500,000
Emp.: 22
Full Service
Jon Roska *(Pres., New Bus. Contact & Creative Dir.)*
Anne Schmidt *(V.P.)*
Chuck McLeester *(V.P.)*
Carmen Franceschino *(Mktg. Dir.)*
Jim Bruno *(Pub. Rels. Dir.)*

ROSS ADVERTISING, INC.
311 N. Lindbergh
Saint Louis, MO 63141
Tel.: 314-567-5200
Tel.: 800-876-1112
Fax: 314-567-4255
Year Founded: 1967
Approx.Billings: $22,000,000
Emp.: 52
Full Service Advertising Agency
Darryl A. Ross *(Chm. Bd. & Pres.)*
Davis L. Morris *(Exec. V.P., Gen. Mgr.)*
Ellen F. Ross *(Dir., Human Resources)*

ROSS BICYCLES USA LTD.
51 Executive Blvd.
Farmingdale, NY 11735
Tel.: 516-249-6000
Fax: 516-249-6015
Approx.Sls.: $55,000,000
Emp.: 450
Import Bicycles
S.I.C.: 3751
Alan Goldmeier *(Pres.)*
Steven Goldmeier *(V.P.)*
Elizabeth Tangen *(V.P.)*
Principal(s):
Alan Goldmeier

Outside Service Firm(s):

Janover & Associates*(Auditors)*
450 7th Ave.
New York, NY 10123
Tel.: 212-695-4355

Norstar Bank, N.A.*(Major Banking Relationship)*
Farmingdale, NY

FRANK B. ROSS CO. INC.
P.O. Box 4085
Jersey City, NJ 07304
Tel.: 201-433-4512 **NJ**
Telex: 710-730-5364 Ross JCTY
Fax: 201-332-3555
Year Founded: 1904
Approx.Sls.: $10,000,000
Emp.: 60
Manufacture Industrial Wax Products
S.I.C.: 2842
Lawrence Houlihan *(Chm. Bd., Pres., Chief Exec. & Chief Fin. Officer, Treas. & Sec.)*
Mary Ann Willemson *(Sec.)*
Carmen Mangan *(Controller)*

Computer Systems/Hardware:
NCR 9300

Outside Service Firm(s):

Danahar & Scott*(Auditors)*
New York, NY

Travelers Insurance Co.*(Group Insurer)*
1 Tower Square
Hartford, CT 06183-2492
Tel.: 203-277-4542
Fax: 203-277-5038

Honnoch, Weisman, Stern, Besser, Berkowitz & Kinne*(Legal Firm)*
Roseland, NJ

ROSS ENGINEERING CO., INC.
104 N. Maple Ave.
Leola, PA 17540
Tel.: 717-656-2095 **PA**
Fax: 717-656-3281
Year Founded: 1962
Approx.Sls.: $23,000,000
Emp.: 165
Mfr. of Boxes For Packing & Shipping; Sheet Metalwork; Automatic Stacking Machines
S.I.C.: 3499; 3444; 3537
Donald E. Speicher *(Pres.)*
George R. Clark, Jr. *(Gen. Mgr.)*
Kevin Wise *(Pur. Agent)*
Cynthia Marburger *(Controller)*
Jim Black *(Mgr.-Personnel)*

Outside Service Firm(s):

Trout, Ebersole & Groff*(Auditors)*
Lancaster, PA

Hartman, Underhill & Brubaker*(Legal Firm)*
Lancaster, PA

Hamilton Bank*(Major Banking Relationship)*
Lancaster, PA

JACK ROSS MOTORS INC.
2700 N. Scottsdale Rd.
Tempe, AZ 85271
Tel.: 602-994-4500
Fax: 602-947-4059
Approx.Sls.: $12,000,000
Emp.: 70
New Automobile Dealership; Real Estate Development
S.I.C.: 5511; 6552
Jack Ross *(Pres.)*
Abe Rodriguez *(V.P.-Parts & Service)*
Thomas Ross *(V.P.-Sls. & Admin.)*
Ron Schultz *(Controller)*
Principal(s):
Jack Ross
Thomas Ross

Computer Systems/Hardware:
IBM PC

Outside Service Firm(s):

Arthur Andersen & Co.*(Auditors)*
Phoenix, AZ

Burch & Cracchiolo*(Legal Firm)*
Phoenix, AZ

First Interstate Bank*(Major Banking Relationship)*
P.O. Box 53441,
Phoenix, AZ 85072-3441
Tel.: 602-229-4049

Ross Roy Group

ROSS ROY GROUP, INC.
100 Bloomfield Hills Pkwy.
Bloomfield Hills, MI 48304
Tel.: 313-433-6000 **MI**
Fax: 313-433-6421
Year Founded: 1926
Approx.Billings: $701,000,000
Emp.: 1,010
Fiscal Year-end: 12/31/91
Holding Company; Advertising
S.I.C.: 6719; 7311
Glen W. Fortinberry *(Chm. & Chief Exec. Officer)*
Chris A. Lawson *(Exec. V.P., Chief Fin. Officer)*
Bruce S. Wagner *(Exec. V.P.)*
Principal(s):
Glen W. Fortinberry

No. of U.S. Offices: 8

Outside Service Firm(s):

Deloitte & Touche*(Auditors)*
200 Renaissance Center, 16th Fl.
Detroit, MI 48243
Tel.: 313-396-3000
Fax: 313-259-8087

Dickinson, Wright, Moon, VanDusen & Freeman*(Legal Firm)*
800 First National Bldg.
Detroit, MI 48226
Tel.: 313-223-3546

Comerica Bank*(Major Banking Relationship)*
211 W. Fort St.
Detroit, MI 48226
Tel.: 313-222-3300

Subsidiaries:

Calet, Hirsch & Ferrell, Inc. **(1)**
250 Park Ave., South
New York, NY 10003
Tel.: 212-777-0666
Fax: 212-777-3261
Emp.: 80
Full Service Agency
S.I.C.: 7311
Ricardo C. Calvillo *(Chm. Bd. & Chief Exec. Officer)*
Donald S. Wergeles *(Pres.)*
Peter Hirsch *(Vice Chm. & Exec. Creative Dir.)*
John F. Ferrell *(Vice Chm. & Exec. Creative Dir.)*
Jane Singer *(Dir., Mktg. & Strategic Plng.)*
Merrill Snyder *(Dir. Mktg. Resources)*

Subsidiaries:

The Bergman Group **(2)**
250 Park Ave., South
New York, NY 10003
Tel.: 212-353-0353
Fax: 212-505-7924
Corporate Identity: Advertising & Collateral
Bill Bergman *(Pres.)*
Sandy Clarkson *(Exec. V.P.)*

Calet, Hirsch & Ferrell, Inc./Florida **(2)**
1321 US 19 South, Ste. 404
Clearwater, FL 34624
Tel.: 813-530-4738
Fax: 813-530-9024
Full Service Agency
Leonard J. Deadman *(Pres.)*

Ross Roy Group, Inc.—(Continued)

The Colligan Group **(2)**
250 Park Ave., South
New York, NY 10003
Tel.: 212-353-0962
Fax: 212-777-3261
Direct Marketing
Richard Colligan *(Pres.)*

The Lipsitt Design Group **(2)**
250 Park Ave., South
New York, NY 10003
Tel.: 212-777-0527
Corporate Identity: Creative Design Services
Martin Lipsitt *(Pres., Dir. Design)*
Elizabeth Jane Pavelle *(Sr. V.P.)*

Ross Roy Communications/N.Y. **(2)**
250 Park Ave., S.
New York, NY 10003
Tel.: 212-777-7077
Full Service Promotion Agency
Ronald-Randolph Wall *(Pres.)*

Anthony M. Franco Inc. **(1)**
400 Renaissance Center, Ste. 600
Detroit, MI 48243
Tel.: 313-567-2300
Fax: 313-567-4486
Emp.: 60
Public Relations
S.I.C.: 7311
Anthony M. Franco *(Chm. & Chief Exec. Officer)*
Michael O. Niederquell *(Exec. V.P.)*
Charles C. Ragains *(Exec. V.P. & Chief Oper. Officer)*
Daniel S. Ponder *(Sr. V.P., Chief Fin. Officer)*
Robert F. Falls *(Pres.-Franco/Griswold, Cleveland)*

Gray & Kilgore, Inc. **(1)**
100 W. Big Beaver Rd., Ste. 300
Troy, MI 48084
Tel.: 313-689-6110
Fax: 313-689-2198
Emp.: 13
S.I.C.: 7311
James F. Eckl *(Pres.)*
Kelly Kane *(Exec. V.P.)*

Griswold, Inc. **(1)**
Landmark Office Towers, 101 Prospect Ave., West
Cleveland, OH 44115
Tel.: 216-696-3400
Fax: 216-696-3405
Emp.: 100
Housewares, Hardware/D.I.Y. & Utility Marketing
S.I.C.: 7311
Jeffery A. Weber *(Exec. V.P. Gen. Mgr.)*
Anthony M. Ciepiel *(Exec. V.P., Chief Fin. Officer)*
Norman E. Olson *(Exec. V.P., Dir., Media Services)*
James G. Fasilis *(Sr. V.P.)*
George W. Cline *(Sr. V.P., Grp. Dir.)*
Mark G. Graf *(Sr. V.P.)*
William E. Day *(V.P.)*
Mary C. DelGreco *(V.P.)*
David J. Gerboc *(V.P.)*
Susan Katz *(V.P.)*
George R. Kestranek *(V.P.)*
Linda M. Konya *(V.P.)*
Robert Marberry *(V.P.)*
Jack Nakel *(V.P.)*
Patricia A. Toncar *(V.P., Dir., Human Resources)*
Stephen A. Walker *(V.P.)*
Monica Wensing *(V.P.)*
Cynthia Williams *(V.P.)*
Lisa M. Woods *(V.P.)*
Evangeline Zervoudis *(V.P., Controller)*

Ross Roy Advertising **(1)**
100 Bloomfield Hills Pkwy.
Bloomfield Hills, MI 48304
Tel.: 313-433-6000
Fax: 313-433-6697
S.I.C.: 7311
Patrick J. Morin *(Pres.)*

Ross Roy Communications **(1)**
100 Bloomfield Hills Pkwy.
Bloomfield Hills, MI 48304
Tel.: 313-433-6000
Fax: 313-433-6330
Emp.: 397
Promotional Marketing, Telemarketing, Teleconferencing, Incentives, Fulfillment, Training, Shows & Meetings, Direct Response, A/V
S.I.C.: 7311
Richard C. Ward *(Pres.)*

Ross Roy Direct **(1)**
100 Bloomfield Hills Pkwy.
Bloomfield Hills, MI 48304
Tel.: 313-433-6000
Fax: 313-433-6417
Emp.: 20
Direct Marketing, Promotional Strategies
Leonard V. Short *(Sr. V.P., Gen. Mgr.)*

Ross Roy Franchise **(1)**
100 Bloomfield Hills Pkwy.
Bloomfield Hills, MI 48304
Tel.: 313-433-6000
Fax: 313-433-6697
Janet C. Muhleman *(Exec. V.P., Gen. Mgr.)*

Ross Roy Inc. **(1)**
100 Bloomfield Hills Pkwy.
Bloomfield Hills, MI 48304
Tel.: 313-433-6000
Fax: 313-433-6421
Emp.: 600
S.I.C.: 7311
Glen W. Fortinberry *(Chm. Bd., Pres. & Chief Exec. Officer)*
John S. Pingel *(Vice Chm.)*
Harry Mellen *(Dir.)*
Patrick J. Morin *(Pres.-Ross Roy Adv.)*
Richard C. Ward *(Pres.-Ross Roy Communications)*
Dick Ward *(Exec. V.P.)*
Jack Frakes *(Exec. V.P., Exec. Creative Dir.)*
Chris A. Lawson *(Exec. V.P., Chief Fin. Officer)*
Janet C. Muhleman *(Exec. V.P.-Ross Roy Franchise)*
Peter C. Vetowich *(Exec. V.P., Dir. Retail Opers.)*
Bruce S. Wagner *(Exec. V.P.-Ross Roy Group)*
Lance L. Aldrich *(Sr. V.P., Assoc. Creative Dir.)*
Julia A. Francke *(Sr. V.P., Grp. Acct. Supvr.)*
David G. Garfield *(Sr. V.P., Dir. Res. & Strategic Planning)*
Pamela A. Getner *(Sr. V.P., Fin.)*
Rita F. Lindholm *(Sr. V.P., Fin.-Partner Co. Opers.)*
Luis Martinez *(Sr. V.P., Grp. Acct. Supvr.)*
Michael A. Pinckes *(Sr. V.P., Grp. Acct. Supvr.)*
Leonard V. Short *(Sr. V.P., Gen. Mgr.-Ross Roy Direct)*
E. Donald Stokes *(Sr. V.P., Dir. Mktg. Plng.)*
Judith A. Toundas *(Sr. V.P., Gen. Mgr., Mktg. Support Services)*
Frank D. Wilberding *(Sr. V.P., Dir. Mktg. Services)*
Robert L. Beatty *(V.P., Dir. Special Markets)*
Barbara P. Celli *(V.P., Gen. Mgr.-RR California)*
Sherri J. Crispin *(V.P., Sr. Project Dir.)*
David C. Heist *(V.P., Grp. Controller)*
Carey Jernigan *(V.P., Admin.)*
Lori Taylor *(V.P., Dir. Human Resources)*
Fred Thomas *(V.P., MIS Dir.)*
Verne C. Hampton, II *(Sec.)*
Joan Sanford *(Controller-Ross Roy, Inc.)*

Ross Roy Productions **(1)**
100 Bloomfield Hills Pkwy.
Bloomfield Hills, MI 48304
Tel.: 313-433-6600
Emp.: 16
Multi-Media Productions with Emphasis on Motion Pictures, Video Tapes, Satellite Telecasts, Live Meeting & Shows
S.I.C.: 7311
William J. Abele *(Sr. V.P., Exec. Producer)*

Ross Roy Retail **(1)**
100 Bloomfield Hills Pkwy.
Bloomfield Hills, MI 48304
Tel.: 313-433-6000
S.I.C.: 7311
Peter C. Vetowich *(Exec. V.P., Dir. Retail Opers.)*

Teledira National Yellow Pages Service **(1)**
Landmark Office Towers, 101 Prospect Ave., West
Cleveland, OH 44115
Tel.: 216-696-5950
Tel.: 800-999-8977
Fax: 216-696-0269
National & Regional Yellow Pages Programs
S.I.C.: 7311
Anthony M. Ciepiel *(Exec. V.P., Chief Oper. Officer)*

Non-U.S. Holdings:

Ross Roy Canada, Ltd. **(1)**
Renaissance Ct., 162 Cumberland St., Ste. 300
Toronto, ON M5R 1A8, Canada
Tel.: 416-968-9472
Fax: 416-968-0246
Emp.: 24
Marketing Communications
S.I.C.: 7311
Peter Bowers *(Pres.)*
Kelly Tolman *(Office Mgr.)*

Ross Roy Communications Canada, Inc. **(1)**
1737 Walker Rd.
Windsor, ON N8Y 4R8, Canada
Tel.: 519-258-7584
Fax: 519-258-4242
Emp.: 80
S.I.C.: 7311
L. Calvin *(Pres.)*

ROSSER FABRAP INTERNATIONAL
524 W. Peachtree St.
Atlanta, GA 30308
Tel.: 404-876-3800 **GA**
Fax: 404-874-3528
Approx.Sls.: $14,000,000
Emp.: 235
Architectural & Engineering Services
S.I.C.: 8712; 8711
Paul C. Rosser *(Chm. Bd.)*
Edward W. Davidson, Jr. *(Pres.)*
Edward F. White *(Exec. V.P.)*
Leon M. Hobbs, Jr. *(Sr. V.P. & Sec.)*
Henry H. Teague *(Sr. V.P.)*
Jack Winter *(V.P.-Fin.)*
Richard K. Little *(Treas.)*

Outside Service Firm(s):

Harris, Deemer, Davidson & Co.*(Auditors)*
Atlanta, GA

ROSSIN GREENBERG SERONICK

ROSSIN GREENBERG SERONICK
181 Newbury St.
Boston, MA 02116
Tel.: 617-267-4949
Fax: 617-267-7322
Year Founded: 1983
Approx.Billings: $18,000,000
Emp.: 25
Jack Rossin *(Chm. & Chief Exec. Officer)*
Ivan Dunmire *(V.P., Opers.)*
Kim Maggio *(Acctg. Mgr.)*
Jennifer Thomas *(Office Mgr.)*
Eileen Corrigan *(Media Supvr.)*
John Young *(Computer Designer)*

Computer Systems/Hardware:
IBM System 36, Macintosh IIfx

BRUCE ROSSMEYER'S TOYOTALAND
(Formerly Longwood Toyota)
2925 N. Hwy. 17-92
Longwood, FL 32750
Tel.: 407-831-9788
Fax: 407-647-3352
Year Founded: 1983
Approx.Sls.: $27,000,000
Emp.: 70
Automobile Dealership
S.I.C.: 5511
Bruce Rossmeyer *(Pres.)*
Max Pearson *(V.P.)*
Principal(s):
Bruce Rossmeyer

Outside Service Firm(s):

Barnett Bank*(Major Banking Relationship)*
Longwood, FL

ROSTONE CORPORATION
2450 Sagamore Pkwy., S.
Lafayette, IN 47905
Tel.: 317-474-2421 **IN**
Fax: 317-474-8785
Year Founded: 1927
Approx.Sls.: $37,000,000
Emp.: 500
Mfr. of Thermoformed Finished Plastic Products
S.I.C.: 3089
Charles Gruner *(Pres.)*
Tom Heier *(V.P.-Fin.)*
Fred Ducharme *(Dir.-Quality Assurance)*
Jim R. Hale *(Dir.-Mfg.)*
Rodney Vanderveer *(Dir.-Human Resources)*
S.J. Hall *(Mgr.-Mfg. Engrng.)*

Outside Service Firm(s):

Ameritrust Company, N.A.*(Major Banking Relationship)*
Ameritrust Center, 525 Vine St., 3rd Fl.
Cincinnati, OH 45202

Rotando Lerch & Iafeliece advertising

ROTANDO LERCH & IAFELIECE ADVERTISING
300 First Stamford Place
Stamford, CT 06902
Tel.: 203-358-2100
Fax: 203-323-1806
Year Founded: 1972
Approx.Billings: $100,100,000
Emp.: 96
Consumer Goods & Services
Lynn Andrew Rotando *(Chm., Pres. & Chief Exec. Officer)*
John A. Lerch *(Vice Chm. & Chief Creative Officer)*
Grant MacDonald *(Sr. V.P., Strategic Plng. & Res.)*
Deborah Sawch *(Sr. V.P., Bus. Devel.)*
Catherine Colucci *(V.P., Comptroller)*
Suzanne Hopkins *(V.P.)*

ROTARY FORMS PRESS, INC.
835 S. High St.
Hillsboro, OH 45133
Tel.: 513-393-3426 **MI**
Fax: 513-393-8473
Year Founded: 1952
Approx.Sls.: $20,216,000
Emp.: 142
Manufacture Custom & Stock Continuous Business Forms
S.I.C.: 2761
Alvin B. Cassner *(Pres. & Chief Exec. Officer)*
Alice E. Cassner *(V.P.)*
Jon H. Cassner *(Sec. & Treas.)*
Ernie Blankenship *(Dir.-Personnel)*
Carol Lovett *(Mgr.-Sls.)*
Richard Vanzant *(Dir.-Pur.)*
John Wright *(Mgr.-Mktg.)*
Curtis B. Cassner *(Accountant)*
John E. Wright *(Corp. Mktg. Mgr.)*
Principal(s):
Alvin B. Cassner
Alice E. Cassner
Jon H. Cassner

No. of Mfg. Plants/Facilities: 4

Computer Systems/Hardware:
ALR POWER 3000

Outside Service Firm(s):

Toukan Smith & Co.*(Auditors)*
Columbus, OH

Feinstein, Crowley Fusco & Mulligan*(Legal Firm)*
Columbus, OH

Fifth Third Bank*(Major Banking Relationship)*
Corporate Trust Services, 38 Fountain Square Plaza
Cincinnati, OH 45263

Divisions:

Computer Stock Forms, Inc. **(1)**
324 S. Washington St.
Greenfield, OH 45123
Tel.: 513-981-7751
Tel.: 800-543-5565
Fax: 513-981-2159
Mfr. Custom & Stock Continuous Business Forms
S.I.C.: 2761
Alvin B. Cassner *(Pres.)*
Robert Cooper *(Plant Mgr.)*

Quality Computer Forms, Inc. **(1)**
402 S.W. 33rd Ave.
Ocala, FL 32674
Tel.: 904-867-0230
Tel.: 800-843-3758
Fax: 904-867-8414
Mfr. Custom & Stock Continuous Business Forms
S.I.C.: 2761
Alvin B. Cassner *(Pres.)*
Delbert Bobbitt *(Plant Mgr.)*

Units Sets, Inc. **(1)**
115 Skimming Dr.
Wilmington, OH 45177
Tel.: 513-382-6981
Fax: 513-382-2480
Mfr. Custom & Stock Continuous Business Forms
S.I.C.: 2761
Alvin B. Cassner *(Pres.)*
Richard Truman *(Plant Mgr.)*

ROTARY MULTIFORMS, INC.
3900 Beaufait
Detroit, MI 48207
Tel.: 313-923-4400
Fax: 313-923-0829
Approx.Sls.: $15,000,000
Emp.: 100
Manufacture Manifold Business Forms
S.I.C.: 2761
Kenneth Vitale *(Pres.)*
Gary Flynn *(Exec. V.P., Treas. & Sec.)*
Peter Frame *(V.P.)*

Outside Service Firm(s):

Comerica Bank*(Major Banking Relationship)*
Dearborn, MI

S. ROTHCHILD & CO., INC.
225 W. 37th St.
New York, NY 10018
Tel.: 212-354-8550 **DE**
Fax: 212-768-2049
Year Founded: 1960
Approx.Sls.: $50,000,000
Emp.: 400
Mfr. of Children's, Women's & Men's Outerwear
S.I.C.: 2369; 2329; 2339
Isidore Friedman *(Chm. Bd.)*
Mark Friedman *(Pres.)*
Paul Friedman *(V.P.)*
William Fuchs *(Treas.)*

Outside Service Firm(s):

Weinick, Sanders & Co.*(Auditors)*
New York, NY

Towne, Dolgin, Sawyler & Horton*(Legal Firm)*
445 Park Ave.
New York, NY 10022
Tel.: 212-371-7000

Meridian Bank*(Major Banking Relationship)*
New York, NY

Divisions:

Galleon Div. **(1)**
225 W. 37th St.
New York, NY 10018
Tel.: 212-354-8550
Consultants, New Products & Services
S.I.C.: 8732
Mark Friedman *(Pres.)*

Junior Concept Div. **(1)**
225 W. 37th St.
New York, NY 10018
Tel.: 212-354-8550
Mfr. of Women's, Children's & Infants Coats
S.I.C.: 2369; 2339
Mark Friedman *(Pres.)*

ROTHSCHILD NORTH AMERICA INC.
One Rockefeller Plaza
New York, NY 10020
Tel.: 212-757-6000 **DE**
Fax: 212-977-3150
Emp.: 150
Fiscal Year-end: 12/31/91
Holding Company & Through Subsidiaries Engages In Investment Banking, Venture Capital, Asset, Trading & Real Estate Management Services
S.I.C.: 8741; 6211; 6531; 6799
David de Rothschild *(Co-Chm.)*
Robert S Pirie *(Co-Chm. Bd.)*
Evelyn de Rothschild *(Chm.-Exec. Committee)*
Gerald Goldsmith *(Pres. & Chief Oper. Officer)*
Robert H. Andrew *(V.P.)*
Peter A. Fried *(Treas. & Sec.)*
Jess L. Belser *(Sr. Mng. Dir.)*

Subsidiary:

Rothschild Inc. **(1)**
One Rockefeller Plaza
New York, NY 10020
Tel.: 212-757-6000
Tel.: 800-753-5151 (100%)
Telex: 422-281
Fax: 212-977-3150
Emp.: 130
Fiscal Year-end: 12/31/90
Investment Banking, Trading & Venture Capital
S.I.C.: 6211; 6799
Robert S. Pirie *(Chm. Bd., Pres. & Chief Exec. Officer)*
Gerald Goldsmith *(Pres. & Chief Oper. Officer)*
D. Pike Aloian *(Sr. V.P.)*
Richard T. Anderson *(Sr. V.P.)*
Lee E. Buchwald *(Sr. V.P.)*
Edwin T. Burton *(Sr. V.P.)*
Craig K. Castilla *(Sr. V.P.)*
Jeffrey S. Hinnel *(Sr. V.P.)*
Robert R. Hussa *(Sr. V.P.)*
Herbert V. Jacobs *(Sr. V.P.)*
Roger P. Marhefka *(Sr. V.P.-Mktg.)*
Edward J. Morris *(Sr. V.P.)*
James J. O'Neill *(Sr. V.P.)*
Salvatore P. Patanio *(Sr. V.P.)*
James E. Quigley III *(Sr. V.P.)*
Martha S. Sproule *(Sr. V.P.)*
John A. Conlon, Jr. *(Mgr. Dir.-Sls.)*

Subsidiaries:

Rothchild Asset Management Inc. **(2)**
One Rockefeller Plaza
New York, NY 10020
Tel.: 212-757-6000 (100%)
Fax: 212-977-3150
Investment Counseling
S.I.C.: 6282
Robert S Pirie *(Chm. Bd.)*
Mark k. Tavel *(Pres. & Chief Investment Officer)*
Edmond Cotty *(Mng. Dir.)*
T. Radey Johnson *(Mng. Dir.)*
George M. Richvalsky *(Mng. Dir.)*
Joseph B. Schwartz *(Mng. Dir.)*
Gregory O. Williams *(Sr. V.P., Sec. & Treas.)*
Richard T. Anderson *(Sr. V.P.)*
Brian Geller *(Asst. V.P.)*
Herbert V. Jacobs *(Asst. Sec.)*

Rothchild Realty Inc. **(2)**
One Rockefeller Plaza
New York, NY 10020
Tel.: 212-757-6000 (100%)
Fax: 212-977-3150
Real Estate
S.I.C.: 6552
John D. McGurk *(Pres.)*

THE ROTOR TOOL COMPANY
26300 Lakeland Blvd.
Cleveland, OH 44132
Tel.: 216-731-8888
Fax: 216-731-0283
Year Founded: 1928
Approx.Sls.: $20,000,000
Emp.: 100
Fiscal Year-end: 9/30/91
Import Export
Portable Pneumatic & High Cycle Electric Tools
S.I.C.: 3546
R.W. Zellner *(Pres.)*
R.C. Smith *(Exec. V.P.)*
Jack E. Shauf *(V.P.-Mfg.)*
J.S. Safran *(V.P.-Engrg.)*
S.C. Bernat *(V.P.-Fin.)*
D.A. Nickel *(Mgr.-Mktg. & Sls.)*

ROTT-KELLER SUPPLY CO.
65 28th St. S.
Fargo, ND 58103-0390
Mailing Address:
P.O. Box 390
Fargo, ND 58107-0390
Tel.: 701-235-0563
Tel.: 800-437-4604 **ND**
Fax: 701-232-7900
Year Founded: 1945
Sales Range: $10-19 Million
Emp.: 35
Fiscal Year-end: 12/31/91
Import Export
Wholesale Distributor of Automobile & Truck Tires & Tubes; Electric Household Appliances; Television Sets; Agricultural & Garden Machinery & Equipment
S.I.C.: 5014; 5064; 5083
Herbert F. Rott, Sr. *(Chm. Bd. & Chief Exec. Officer)*
Herbert Rott, Jr. *(V.P., Sec. & Treas.)*
David Rott *(V.P.)*

Outside Service Firm(s):

Coopers & Lybrand*(Auditors)*
Fargo, ND

State Bank*(Major Banking Relationship)*
Fargo, ND

Subsidiary:

Des Moines Tire **(1)**
120 S.W. 5th St.
Des Moines, IA 50309
Tel.: 515-243-4175
Tel.: 800-437-4188
Emp.: 12
Wholesale Distributor of Tires
S.I.C.: 5014
Herbert F. Rott, Jr. *(Pres.)*

ROTTERDAM VENTURES INC.
(Member of Galesi Group of Companies)
P.O. Box 98
Guilderland Center, NY 12085
Tel.: 518-356-4445 **NY**
Fax: 518-356-5334
Year Founded: 1969
Assets: $312,467,000
Liabilities: $188,610,000
Net Worth: $123,857,000
Approx.Sls.: $110,250,000
Emp.: 450
Fiscal Year-end: 11/30/91
General Warehousing & Storage; Real Property Lessors; Apartment Complexes & Condominium Development; Manufacture Steel Forgings; Manufacture Transportation & Military Equipment; Telecommunications
S.I.C.: 6531; 4225; 6519; 6513; 3443; 3312; 3795; 6552; 4813
Francesco Galesi *(Chm. Bd., Pres. & Chief Exec. Officer)*
David M. Buicko *(Exec. V.P.)*
Robert Sherry *(Sr. V.P.)*
Eugene Ruiz *(Sr. V.P.)*
Gerald J. Hennigan *(Chief Fin. Officer)*
Principal(s):
Francesco Galesi

No. of U.S. Offices: 15

Outside Service Firm(s):

KPMG Peat Marwick*(Auditors)*
74 N. Pearl St.
Albany, NY 12207
Tel.: 518-455-8809

Shearson Lehman Brothers, Inc.*(Investment Banker)*
World Financial Center
New York, NY 10285
Tel.: 212-298-2000

Hodgson, Russ, Andrews, Woods & Goodyear*(Legal Firm)*
Albany, NY

Chemical Banking Corp.*(Major Banking Relationship)*
277 Park Ave.
New York, NY 10041
Tel.: 212-310-6407
Fax: 212-310-4526

Divisions:

Corporate, EDP **(1)**
P.O. Box 98,
Guilderland Center, NY 12085
Tel.: 518-356-4445

Flint River **(1)**
P.O. Box 98,
Guilderland Center, NY 12085
Tel.: 518-356-4445
Farm, Realty Holdings
S.I.C.: 6552

Galesi Enterprises **(1)**
P.O. Box 98,
Guilderland Center, NY 12085
Tel.: 518-356-4445
Office Building
S.I.C.: 6512

Rotterdam Industrial Park **(1)**
P.O. Box 98,
Guilderland Center, NY 12085
Tel.: 518-356-4445
General Warehousing & Storage
S.I.C.: 4225

Subsidiaries:

Distribution Unlimited, Inc. **(1)**
P.O. Box 98,
Guilderland Center, NY 12085
Tel.: 518-861-5107
Fax: 518-356-5334

High Point Ventures, Inc. **(1)**
P.O. Box 98,
Guilderland Center, NY 12085
Tel.: 518-356-4445
372 Unit Apartment Complex, Dallas
S.I.C.: 6513

Jacksonville Ventures, Inc. **(1)**
P.O. Box 98,
Guilderland Center, NY 12085
Tel.: 518-356-4445
334 Unit Apartment Complex, Jacksonville
S.I.C.: 6513

Lake George Ventures, Inc. **(1)**
P.O. Box 98,
Guilderland Center, NY 12085
Tel.: 518-356-4445 (90%)

Rotterdam Ventures Inc.—(Continued)

Condo Development & Sales
S.I.C.: 1531

Subsidiary:

TOW Water Co., Inc. **(2)**
P.O. Box 98,
Guilderland Center, NY 12085
Tel.: 518-356-4445

Mercer Forge, Inc. **(1)**
P.O. Box 98,
Guilderland Center, NY 12085
Tel.: 518-356-4445 (100%)
Metal Forging Mfg.
S.I.C.: 3462

Remington Hill Ventures **(1)**
P.O. Box 98,
Guilderland Center, NY 12085
Tel.: 518-356-4445
440 Unit Apartment Complex, Fort Worth
S.I.C.: 6513

Scotia Industrial Park, Inc. **(1)**
P.O. Box 98,
Guilderland Center, NY 12085
Tel.: 518-356-4445
General Warehousing & Storage
S.I.C.: 4225

Tampa Ventures, Inc. **(1)**
P.O. Box 98,
Guilderland Center, NY 12085
Tel.: 518-356-4445
438 Unit Apartment Complex, Tampa
S.I.C.: 6513

Voorheesville Ventures, Inc. **(1)**
P.O. Box 98,
Guilderland Center, NY 12085
Tel.: 518-356-4445
Real Estate Held for Development
S.I.C.: 6552

Washington Avenue Ventures, Inc. **(1)**
P.O. Box 98,
Guilderland Center, NY 12085
Tel.: 518-356-4445
Operator of Non-Residential Building
S.I.C.: 6512

Winridge Aurora Ventures, Inc. **(1)**
P.O. Box 98,
Guilderland Center, NY 12085
Tel.: 518-356-4445
364 Unit Apartment Complex, Denver
S.I.C.: 6513

Partnership:

Plaza Investment Associates **(1)**
P.O. Box 98,
Guilderland Center, NY 12085
Tel.: 518-356-4445 (50%)
Ownership of Real Estate
S.I.C.: 6798

ROUBINCO, INC.
8550 Lee Hwy.,Ste. 700
Fairfax, VA 22031
Tel.: 703-573-9350 **DE**
Fax: 703-560-3815
Approx.Sls.: $26,000,000
Emp.: 400
Stone Mason Concrete Work; Water, Sewer & Utility Lines; Asphalt Paving Mixtures & Blocks; Industrial Building
S.I.C.: 1741; 1771; 1623; 2951; 1541
Angel S. Roubin *(Pres. & Treas.)*
Jose Roubin *(V.P.)*
Richard Roubin *(V.P. & Sec.)*

Outside Service Firm(s):

Aronson, Fetridge, Weigle & Co.*(Auditors)*
Rockville, MD

First American Bank, N.A.*(Major Banking Relationship)*
McLean, VA

Subsidiary:

Roubin & Janeiro, Inc. **(1)**
8550 Lee Hwy., Ste. 700
Fairfax, VA 22031
Tel.: 703-573-9350
Emp.: 250
Stone Masonry; Resurfacing Contractor; Water, Sewer & Utility Lines
S.I.C.: 1741; 1611; 1623
Angel S. Roubin *(Pres.)*
Robert Moore *(V.P.-Fin. & Sec.)*
Jose A. Roubin *(V.P.)*

ROUGH BROTHERS, INC.
5513 Vine St.
Cincinnati, OH 45216
Mailing Address:
P. O. Box 16010,
Cincinnati, OH 45216
Tel.: 513-242-0310
Tel.: 800-543-7351
Fax: 513-242-0816
Year Founded: 1935
Approx.Sls.: $10,000,000
Emp.: 65
Fiscal Year-end: 12/31/92
Import Export
Mfr. of Commercial & Industrial Greenhouses & Components
S.I.C.: 0181
Albert Reilly *(Pres.)*
Joe Tirschek *(Sls. Mgr.)*

ROUND HILL FOODS, INC.
(Acquisition by WLR Foods Inc. Pending)
South Water St.
New Oxford, PA 17350
Mailing Address:
P.O. Box 38,
New Oxford, PA 17350
Tel.: 717-624-2191
Year Founded: 1974
Approx.Sls.: $60,000,000
Emp.: 575
Turkey Processing
S.I.C.: 2015
Thomas Bross, III *(Chm. Bd.)*
Michael D. Bross *(Pres.)*
Richard Caron *(V.P.-Human Resources)*
Larry Weinstein *(V.P.-Fin.)*
Steve Hauser *(Dir.-Pur.)*
Ed Myers *(Mgr.-Sls.)*

Outside Service Firm(s):

Frost & Co.*(Auditors)*
Little Rock, AR

Wolf & Oyler*(Legal Firm)*
Gettysburg, PA

Mercantile Bank*(Major Banking Relationship)*
York, PA

ROUNDTREE AUTOMOTIVE GROUP
8660 Fern Ave.
Shreveport, LA 71105
Tel.: 318-798-6500
Fax: 318-798-6580
Wholesale & Retail Automobiles
S.I.C.: 5012; 5013; 5511; 5531
Frank Stinson *(Pres.)*

Outside Service Firm(s):

Weems, Wright, Schiempf Associates*(Legal Firm)*
Shreveport, LA

Commercial National Bank*(Major Banking Relationship)*
Shreveport, LA

Subsidiary:

Frontier Chevrolet Co. **(1)**
1617 First Ave., N.
Billings, MT 59101
Tel.: 406-259-5575
Fax: 406-259-4351
Approx.Sls.: $30,000,000
Emp.: 80
Retail Automobiles
S.I.C.: 5511
Dennis Menholt *(Pres.)*

ROUNDY'S, INC.
23000 Roundy Dr.
Pewaukee, WI 53072
Mailing Address:
P.O. Box 473
Milwaukee, WI 53201
Tel.: 414-547-7999 **WI**
Fax: 414-547-4540
Year Founded: 1952
Assets: $390,800,000
Earnings: $6,507,100
Liabilities: $319,900,000
Net Worth: $70,900,000
Approx.Sls.: $2,534,400,800
Emp.: 5,582
Fiscal Year-end: 12/29/91
Import Export
Cooperative; Wholesale Groceries & General Merchandise
S.I.C.: 5141
John R. Dickson *(Pres. & Chief Exec. Officer)*
Robert D. Ranus *(V.P. & Chief Fin. Officer)*
Edward G. Kitz *(V.P. & Treas.)*
Robert G. Turcott *(V.P., Sec. & Gen. Counsel)*
Marion Sullivan *(V.P.-Mktg.)*
John M. Granger *(V.P.-Mngmt. Information Systems)*
Terrence Kapron *(V.P.-Opers.)*
David C. Busch *(V.P.-Human Resources)*
William C. Confer *(V.P.-Industry & Customer Rels.)*
Roger Alsuager *(V.P. Real Estate)*
Lon Behm *(V.P.-Adv.)*
Rich Fox *(V.P.)*

No. of Mfg. Plants/Facilities: 12
No. of U.S. Offices: 12

Computer Systems/Hardware:
IBM

Outside Service Firm(s):

Deloitte & Touche*(Auditors)*
250 E. Wisconsin Ave.
Milwaukee, WI 53202-4283
Tel.: 414-271-3000

Aetna Life & Casualty*(Commercial Insurance Carrier)*
Milwaukee, WI

Blue Cross & Blue Shield United of Wisconsin*(Group Insurer)*
Milwaukee, WI

Whyte & Hirschboeck, S.C.*(Legal Firm)*
111 E. Wisconsin Ave., Ste. 2100
Milwaukee, WI 53202
Tel.: 414-271-8210

Bank One Milwaukee, N.A.*(Major Banking Relationship)*
111 E. Wisconsin Ave.
Milwaukee, WI
Tel.: 414-765-3000

Strong Capital Management*(Pension Manager)*
Milwaukee, WI

Divisions:

Midland Grocery **(1)**
6500 S. US 421
Westville, IN 46391
Tel.: 219-785-4671
Approx.Sls.: $918,000,000
Emp.: 2,700
Wholesale & Retail Grocery Products
S.I.C.: 5141
Mark Mikosz *(Div. Pres.)*
Steve Davis *(Chief Fin. Officer)*
John Gribas *(Dir.-Pur.)*

Roundy's Inc., Milwaukee Div. **(1)**
11300 W. Burleigh St.
Milwaukee, WI 53201
Tel.: 414-453-8200
S.I.C.: 5141
Gerald F. Lestina *(Pres.)*
Ralph Beketic *(Div. V.P.)*

Roundy's Wayco Foods **(1)**
1925 Busse Rd.
Elk Grove Village, IL 60007
Tel.: 708-437-6070
S.I.C.: 5141
Don Twite *(G.M.)*

Subsidiary:

Cedarburg Dairy **(1)**
P.O. Box 287
Cedarburg, WI 53012
Tel.: 414-377-5040
Bob Mathison *(Div. Pres.)*

ROWE CORP.
1123 S. Church St.
Charlotte, NC 28203
Mailing Address:
P.O. Box 33609
Charlotte, NC 28233
Tel.: 704-375-2591 **NC**
Fax: 704-344-8426
Year Founded: 1972
Assets: $30,000,000
Liabilities: $10,000,000
Net Worth: $20,000,000
Approx.Sls.: $80,000,000
Emp.: 1,200
Fiscal Year-end: 10/ 1/90
Holding Company; Manufacture Synthetic Fiber Machinery; Distribute Agriculture Machinery & Products; Electrical, Water, Sewer & Heavy Construction
S.I.C.: 6719; 3552; 5083; 1731; 1629
O. Regan Rowe, Jr. *(Chm. Bd. & Pres.)*
Richard E. Bennion *(V.P.-Fin. & Chief Fin. Officer)*
Richard G. Karriker *(V.P.-Human Resources)*
Carol W. Whiteside *(V.P., Sec. & Treas.)*

Outside Service Firm(s):

Deloitte & Touche*(Auditors)*
2000 First Citizens Bank Plaza, 128 S. Tryon St.
Charlotte, NC 28202-5001
Tel.: 704-372-3560

Grier, Parker, Poe, Thompson, Bernstein, Gage & Preston*(Legal Firm)*
2600 Charlotte Plaza
Charlotte, NC 28244
Tel.: 704-372-9000

NationsBank Carolinas*(Major Banking Relationship)*
One NCNB Plaza T18-7
Charlotte, NC 28255

ROWMAN & LITTLEFIELD PUBLISHERS, INC.
4720 Boston Way
Lanham, MD 20706
Tel.: 301-306-0400 **MD**
Telex: 13-0483
Year Founded: 1949
Business & Economics, Environmental Studies, Geography, Government, Law, Philosophy, Policy Studies, Women's Studies Reference Books
S.I.C.: 2731
James E. Lyons *(Pres.)*
Jonathan Sisk *(Mng. Dir.)*
Lynda Hill *(Promo. & Mktg. Mgr.)*

Divisions:

Barnes & Noble **(1)**
81 Adams Dr.
Totowa, NJ 07512
Tel.: 301-306-0400
Imported Academic Monographs
S.I.C.: 2731

Biblio Distribution Ctr. **(1)**
8705 Bollman Place
Savage, MD 20763
Tel.: 201-306-0400
Book Distribution & Sales
S.I.C.: 5192

Subsidiary:

University Press of America, Inc. **(1)**
4720 Boston Way
Lanham, MD 20706
Tel.: 410-459-3366
College Texts, Scholarly Monographs
S.I.C.: 2731
Raymond Feller *(Pres.)*
James E. Lyons *(V.P. & Publisher)*

ROWTRONICS COMPANY INC.
(d/b/a R.O. Whitesell & Assocs.)
3334 Founders Rd.
Indianapolis, IN 46268
Mailing Address:
P.O. Box 681070,
Indianapolis, IN 46268
Tel.: 317-876-9000 **IN**
Fax: 317-876-8434
Year Founded: 1946
Approx.Sls.: $205,000,000
Emp.: 97
Electronics Manufacturers Representatives
S.I.C.: 8999
Max E. Hinkle *(Chm. Bd., Pres., Chief Exec. Officer & Treas.)*
Stephen M. Underhill *(Chief Fin. Officer, Controller & Dir.-Personnel)*
A. David Meyer *(Gen. Counsel)*
Principal(s):
Max E. Hinkle
William M. Morgan

No. of U.S. Offices: 23

Computer Systems/Hardware:
NEC Astra 350 VS

Outside Service Firm(s):

Ernst & Young*(Auditors)*
One Indiana Square, Ste. 3400
Indianapolis, IN 46204
Tel.: 317-236-1100

Westfield Insurance*(Commercial Insurance Carrier)*
Westfield Center, OH

Key Benefit Administrators*(Group Insurer)*
Indianapolis, IN

A. David Meyer, Esq.*(Legal Firm)*
Indianapolis, IN

AmeriTrust National Bank*(Major Banking Relationship)*
Indianapolis, IN

Michigan Mutual Insurance Co.*(Major Banking Relationship)*
Detroit, MI

McCready & Keene*(Pension Manager)*
Indianapolis, IN

ROYAL CARIBBEAN CRUISES LTD.
1050 Caribbean Way
Miami, FL 33132
Tel.: 305-539-6000
Fax: 305-372-0441
Year Founded: 1970
Approx.Sls.: $800,000,000
Emp.: 1,800
Caribbean Cruises
S.I.C.: 4725
Richard Fain *(Chm. Bd. & Chief Exec. Officer)*
E.W. Stephan *(Pres.)*
R. Glasier *(Chief Fin. Officer)*
Rod McLeod *(Exec. V.P.)*
P. Whelpton *(Exec. V.P.)*
Karine Armstrong *(V.P.-Mktg.)*
Bette Sharp *(Dir.-Mktg. Services)*
Geoff Atack *(Mgr.-Adv.)*
Rich Steck *(Mgr.-Public Rels.)*

THE ROYAL CHINA & PORCELAIN COMPANIES INC.
1265 Glen Ave.
Moorestown, NJ 08057-0912
Tel.: 609-866-2900
Tel.: 800-631-7120
Fax: 609-866-2499
Approx.Sls.: $40,000,000
Emp.: 90
Fiscal Year-end: 12/31/91
Import
Distributes Royal Worcester Fine Bone China, Porcelain & Oven-to-Tableware; Spode Fine Bone China, Fine Stone China & Earthenware, Spode Christmas Tree, RCPC Giftware
S.I.C.: 5023
William H. McKinney *(Pres.)*
William H. Sherman *(V.P.-Fin. & Admin)*
Elizabeth W. Feagans *(V.P.-Mktg. & Communications)*
Harry J. Stone *(V.P.-Sls.)*

ROYAL CRUISE LINE INC.
1 Maritime Plaza, Ste. 1400
San Francisco, CA 94111
Tel.: 415-956-7200
Fax: 415-956-1656
Approx.Sls.: $100,000,000
Emp.: 95
Air/Sea Cruises; M.S. Golden Odyssey, M.S. Crown Odyssey
S.I.C.: 4481; 4512; 4724
Jim Naik, Sr. *(Pres.)*
Carol McRonald *(V.P.-Mktg. & Creative Dir.)*
John Severini *(V.P.-Sls.)*
Jeanne Underwood *(V.P.-Natl. Accts.)*

ROYAL JEEP EAGLE & CHRYSLER PLYMOUTH
485 E. Semoran Blvd.
Casselberry, FL 32707
Tel.: 407-831-2828 **DE**
Fax: 407-339-1914
Year Founded: 1974
Approx.Sls.: $28,000,000
Emp.: 80
Automobile & Jeep Dealership
S.I.C.: 5511
Ray M. Tatum *(Pres.)*
Jo Rogers *(Treas. & Sec.)*
Robert Thomas *(Dir.-Service)*
Charlie Ray *(Sls. Mgr.-Used Cars)*
Richard Shore *(Sls. Mgr.-Used Cars)*
Doug Goodwin *(Mgr.-Gen. Sls.)*

Outside Service Firm(s):

Barnett Banks Trust Company, N.A.*(Major Banking Relationship)*
Orlando, FL

ROYAL OAK ENTERPRISES, INC.
900 Ashwood Pkwy., Ste. 800
Atlanta, GA 30338
Tel.: 404-393-1430
Fax: 404-394-9208
Approx.Sls.: $70,000,000
Emp.: 550
Fiscal Year-end: 9/30/91
Mfr. Charcoal Briquets & Activated Carbons
S.I.C.: 2499; 2819
Bill Reed *(Pres.)*
V. L. Ekedahl *(Exec. V.P.-Mktg.)*
A. R. Sperry *(Sr. V.P. & Sec.)*
Dale Elberg *(Sr. V.P.-Sls. & Mktg.)*
Jerry Peters *(V.P.-Sls.)*
Gayl Gloss *(Mgr.-Mktg.)*

ROYAL OAK FORD INC.
550 N. Woodward
Royal Oak, MI 48067
Tel.: 313-548-4100
Fax: 313-548-0621
Year Founded: 1983
Approx.Sls.: $63,700,000
Emp.: 168
Automobile Dealership
S.I.C.: 5511
John T. McLaughlin *(Pres.)*
Joe Galasso *(Gen. Mgr.)*

ROYAL OLDSMOBILE MAZDA, INC.
3400 Veterans Memorial Blvd.
Metairie, LA 70002
Tel.: 504-888-3400
Fax: 504-889-8447
Approx.Sls.: $33,000,000
Emp.: 130
Retail New & Used Cars
S.I.C.: 5511
John Richardson *(Chm. Bd.)*
A. Vernon Brinson *(Pres.)*
Jim Sanderson *(V.P. & Gen. Mgr.)*
Shirley Holden *(Treas., Sec. & Controller)*

Outside Service Firm(s):

Deloitte & Touche*(Auditors)*
3700 One Shell Square
New Orleans, LA 70139
Tel.: 504-581-2727

Thomas Talifero*(Legal Firm)*
Birmingham, AL

Jefferson Bank & Trust Company*(Major Banking Relationship)*
Metairie, LA

ROYAL PAPER BOX OF CALIFORNIA
1105 S. Maple Ave.
Montebello, CA 90640
Mailing Address:
P.O. Box 458
Montebello, CA 90640
Tel.: 213-728-7041
Fax: 213-722-2646
Year Founded: 1942
Approx.Sls.: $18,000,000
Emp.: 150
Mfr. of Folding Paper Boxes & Displays
S.I.C.: 2657
James R. Hodges *(Pres.)*
Debbie Weaver *(Controller)*
Rolf Peterson *(Plant Mgr.)*
Thomas Roslansky *(Mgr.-Sls.)*

ROYAL WATERBEDS
2440 Adie Rd.
Maryland Heights, MO 63043
Tel.: 314-569-0259
Fax: 314-432-3542
Emp.: 110
Fiscal Year-end: 9/30/91
Distributes & Markets Waterbeds
S.I.C.: 5023
Dennis Boyd *(Pres. & Chief Exec. Officer)*
Mary Bayles *(Sec.)*

Computer Systems/Hardware:
IBM System 34

Outside Service Firm(s):

Boone County National Bank*(Major Banking Relationship)*
Columbia, MO

Citizens & Southern National Bank*(Major Banking Relationship)*
Norcross, GA

ROYLE SYSTEMS GROUP
1000 Cannonball Rd.
Pompton Lakes, NJ 07442
Tel.: 201-839-8118
Telex: 6853520 ROYLEUSA
Fax: 201-839-7327
Approx.Sls.: $13,000,000
Emp.: 100
Rubber & Plastics Extruders, Complete Insulating Systems for the Wire & Cable Industry
S.I.C.: 3357
Justin H. Ramsey *(Chm. Bd.)*
J.C. Ramsey *(Pres.)*
C.E. Ramsey *(V.P.)*
P. Ramsey *(V.P.-Engrng.)*
Greg Ramsey *(V.P.-Sls.)*
William Dvoretsky *(V.P.-Mfg.)*
Vicci Adduce *(Sec.)*
Pat Hazuda *(Pur. Agent)*

ROYTEX, INC.
16 E. 34th St., 17th Floor
New York, NY 10016
Tel.: 212-686-3500
Year Founded: 1965
Approx.Sls.: $19,000,000
Emp.: 125
Distr. of Men's & Boy's Apparel; Robes, Nightwear, Sportswear & Bathing Suits
S.I.C.: 5136
Dennis Mourry *(Chm. Bd. & Chief Exec. Officer)*
David Saginaw *(Pres. & Chief Oper. Officer)*
Charlotte Heintjes *(V.P.-Fin. & Treas.)*
Anthony Patane *(Controller)*

Subsidiary:

Meridian Mfg. Co., Inc. **(1)**
901 D St.
Meridian, MS 39301
Tel.: 601-693-6656
Emp.: 75
Mfr. of Men's & Boy's Apparel; Robes, Nightwear, Bathing Suits, Sportswear
S.I.C.: 2322; 2329
Robert Goodman *(V.P.)*

R. R. & R. R. EVANS COMPANY
(See Roytex, Inc.)

RUBIN EHRENTHAL AND ASSOCIATES

RUBIN EHRENTHAL & ASSOCIATES
100 Ave. of the Americas
New York, NY 10013
Tel.: 212-966-5550
Fax: 212-966-7755
Year Founded: 1987
Approx.Billings: $38,500,000
Emp.: 28
Mel Rubin *(Chm.)*

Rubin Ehrenthal & Associates—(Continued)

Herb Ehrenthal *(Pres.)*
Leo Brandstatter *(V.P., Strategic Planning)*
Rhonda Kelbick *(Gen. Mgr.)*

LILLIE RUBIN AFFILIATES INC.
15705 N.W. 13th Ave.
Miami, FL 33169
Tel.: 305-624-4200 **FL**
Fax: 305-624-9496
Year Founded: 1963
Assets: $21,874,646
Liabilities: $4,838,113
Net Worth: $17,036,533
Approx.Sls.: $55,000,000
Emp.: 600
Import
Retail Women's Apparel
S.I.C.: 5621
Stanley M. Kossoff *(Pres. & Chief Exec. Officer)*
Jim Golden *(Chief Fin. Officer)*
Joseph Serlick *(Exec. V.P.)*
Georgette Rubin *(Treas. & Sec.)*
David Emanuel *(Gen. Counsel)*
Robert Bell *(Dir.-Data Processing)*
Jackie Block *(Dir.-Promo.)*
Principal(s):
Stanley M. Kossoff
Georgette Rubin

Outside Service Firm(s):

Holtz & Co.*(Auditors)*
Ft. Lauderdale, FL

Johnson & Higgins*(Commercial Insurance Carrier)*
Miami, FL

Great-West Life Assurance Co.*(Group Insurer)*
Ft. Lauderdale, FL

David Emanuel Law Firm*(Legal Firm)*
Miami, FL

Sun Bank, N.A.*(Major Banking Relationship)*
Miami, FL 33131

Rubin Postaer and Associates

RUBIN POSTAER & ASSOCIATES
1333 2nd St.
Santa Monica, CA 90401
Tel.: 310-394-4000
Year Founded: 1986
Approx.Billings: $180,700,000
Emp.: 170
Advertising Agency
S.I.C.: 7311
Gerrold R. Rubin *(Pres.)*
Vince Mancuso *(Sr. V.P., Dir. Fin.)*
Lark Baskerville *(V.P., Dir. Human Resources)*
Dave Jenkins *(V.P., Dir.-Honda Auto News Bureau)*
Maria Hinds *(Mgr., Info. Services)*

Branch:

Rubin Postaer and Associates **(1)**
625 Broadway, Ste. 1025
San Diego, CA 92101
Tel.: 619-234-5101

RUBIN RESPONSE SERVICES, INC.
1111 Plaza Dr.
Schaumburg, IL 60173
Tel.: 708-619-9800 **IL**
Fax: 708-619-0150
Year Founded: 1974
Approx.Billings: $21,765,000
Emp.: 51
Fiscal Year-end: 8/31/91
Direct Response Marketing
William S. Rubin *(Chm. Bd. & Pres.)*
Karen L. Gruntman *(V.P.)*
Kenneth Kretschmar *(V.P.)*
Ralph Palmer *(V.P.)*
Arlene Rubin *(V.P., Fin.)*
Marge Ali *(Controller)*
Lynne Decker *(Dir., Mngmt. Opers.)*
Susan Palmer *(Dir., List Mngmt.)*
Judy Rubin-Rotman *(Dir., Adv.)*
Sue Adelmann *(Mgr., Data Processing)*

M. RUBIN & SONS INC.
34-01 38th Ave.
New York, NY 11101
Tel.: 718-361-2800 **NY**
Fax: 718-361-2680
Year Founded: 1944
Approx.Sls.: $12,000,000
Emp.: 50
Import
Manufacturer & Wholesaler of Outerwear, Industrial Parkas & Uniforms, Shirts, Sweaters, Down Vests & Jackets, Leisure Sports Apparel; Designer Licensee Sergio Valente
S.I.C.: 2326; 2329; 5136; 6794
Robert Rubin *(Vice Chm.)*
Donald Rubin *(Pres.)*
Robert Rubin *(Exec. V.P. & Sec.)*
Eric Rubin *(V.P.-Mfg.)*
Phillip Rubin *(V.P.)*
Cliff Korot *(Controller)*

No. of U.S. Offices: 2

Computer Systems/Hardware:
ALPHA Micro

Outside Service Firm(s):

BDO Seidman*(Auditors)*
1430 Broadway
New York, NY
Tel.: 212-765-7500

Fuji Bank Ltd.*(International Bank Affiliate)*
1 World Trade Center
New York, NY

Warshaw, Burstein, Cohen, Schlesinger & Kuh*(Legal Firm)*
55 Fifth Ave.
New York, NY 10017

Chemical Bank*(Major Banking Relationship)*
Long Island City, NY

European American Bank*(Major Banking Relationship)*
Long Island City, NY

Retirement Planning Association*(Pension Manager)*
488 Madison Ave.
New York, NY

RUDEL MACHINERY COMPANY, INC.
P.O. Box 887, 4 Armstrong Rd.
Shelton, CT 06484
Tel.: 203-929-6666 **NY**
Fax: 203-929-0256
Year Founded: 1941
Approx.Sls.: $50,000,000
Emp.: 50
Wholesale Distrubiton of Machine Tools & Accessories
S.I.C.: 5084
Robert W. Gunn *(Pres.)*
John Wendt *(Exec. V.P.)*
Jane B. Garbo *(Exec. Project Mgr.)*
Edwin Woodruff *(V.P.)*
James Ensinger *(Treas. & Sec.)*
Robert Milburn *(Mgr.-Sls. Office)*

Outside Service Firm(s):

Connecticut National Bank*(Major Banking Relationship)*
777 Main St.
Hartford, CT 06115
Tel.: 203-728-2000

RUDER, FINN, INC.
301 East 57th St.
New York, NY 10022
Tel.: 212-593-6400
Telex: 710-581-5271
Fax: 212-593-6397
Year Founded: 1948
Approx.Billings: $34,500,000
Emp.: 300
Public Relations & Corporate Advertising
S.I.C.: 8743; 7311
David Finn *(Chm. Bd. & Chief Exec. Officer)*
Charles Lipton *(Vice Chm.)*
Kathy Bloomgarden *(Pres.)*
Amy Binder *(Pres.-Ruder Finn/NY)*
Peter Finn *(Chief Fin. Officer & Chm. Exec. Committee)*
Abraham Peritz *(Exec. V.P. & Treas.)*
Roz Safrin *(Exec. V.P. & Dir.-Admin.)*
Soraya Elcock *(Librarian)*

Outside Service Firm(s):

Spicer & Oppenheim*(Auditors)*
7 World Trade Center,
New York, NY 10048
Tel.: 212-422-1000

Bressler, Amery & Rothenberg*(Legal Firm)*
90 Broad St
New York, NY 10004
Tel.: 212-425-9300

National Westminster Bank plc*(Major Banking Relationship)*
175 Water St.
New York, NY 10038-4924
Tel.: 212-602-3364

Branches:

Corporate•Technology•Public Affairs **(1)**
301 East 57th St.
New York, NY 10022
Tel.: 212-593-6330
Frank Walton *(Pres.)*

Ruder Finn Consumer Marketing **(1)**
301 East 57th St.
New York, NY 10022
Tel.: 212-593-6395
Jeremy Jacob *(V.P. & Grp. Mgr.)*

Ruder, Finn Field Network **(1)**
301 East 57th St.
New York, NY 10022
Tel.: 212-593-6362
Charles Lipton *(Chm.)*

Ruder Finn Financial Relations **(1)**
301 East 57th St.
New York, NY 10022
Tel.: 212-715-1544
Denis Peters *(Sr. V.P. & Grp. Mgr.)*

Ruder Finn Health Care **(1)**
301 East 57th St.
New York, NY 10022
Tel.: 212-593-6323
M.J. Wyatt *(Pres. & Grp. Mgr.)*

Ruder, Finn, Inc. **(1)**
444 N. Michigan Ave.
Chicago, IL 60611
Tel.: 312-644-8600
Telex: 910-221-5450
Gerald Murray *(Pres.)*
Jim McAvoy *(Pres. & Chief Exec. Officer-Chicago)*

Ruder, Finn, Inc. **(1)**
16027 Ventura Blvd. Ste. 500
Encino, CA 91436-0032
Tel.: 818-382-7700
Fax: 818-783-0032
Saul Warshaw *(Pres.)*

Ruder Finn Lifestyle/Food Marketing **(1)**
301 East 57th St.
New York, NY 10022
Tel.: 212-593-6304
Larry Wilson *(Exec. V.P.)*

Ruder Finn Marketing Communications **(1)**
301 East 57th St.
New York, NY 10022
Tel.: 212-593-6315
Ellen Schaplowsky *(Exec. V.P.)*

Ruder Finn Medical Marketing **(1)**
301 East 57th St.
New York, NY 10022
Tel.: 212-593-6326
Erica Kaplan *(Sr. V.P.)*

Ruder Finn/Washington **(1)**
1516 M St., N.W.
Washington, DC 20036
Tel.: 202-466-7800
Telex: 202-887-0905
Jim McAvoy *(Pres.)*

Ruder, Finn/Raleigh (NC) **(1)**
3600 Glenwood Ave., Ste. 100
Raleigh, NC 27612
Tel.: 919-783-2804
Telecopier: 919-787-0530
Joyce Fitzpatrick *(Sr. V.P. & Group Head)*

Subsidiaries:

Arts & Communications Counselors, Inc., NY **(1)**
301 East 57th St.
New York, NY 10022
Tel.: 212-593-6475
Philippa Polskin *(Pres.)*

Public Relations Productions Co., Inc. **(1)**
301 East 57th St.
New York, NY 10022
Tel.: 212-593-6480
Michael Cannata *(Pres.)*

RF Design Inc. **(1)**
301 East 57th St.
New York, NY 10022
Tel.: 212-593-6429
Michael Schubert *(Dir.)*

Research & Forecasts, Inc. **(1)**
301 East 57th St.
New York, NY 10022
Tel.: 212-593-6429
Nicholas Tortorello *(Chm. Bd.)*
Franklin Walton *(Pres.)*

Ruder Finn Japan Desk **(1)**
301 East 57th St.
New York, NY 10022
Tel.: 212-593-6364
Stephen Wechselblatt *(Dir.)*

Visual Technologies **(1)**
301 East 57th St.
New York, NY 10022
Tel.: 212-751-1500
David Katzive *(Creative Dir.)*

Non-U.S. Holding:

Arts & Communications Counselors, Inc. **(1)**
55 Bloor St., West
Toronto, ON M4W 1A5, Canada
Tel.: 416-966-3421
Fax: 416-966-3088
Nina Wright *(Pres.)*

RUDOLPH FOODS COMPANY
6575 Bellefontaine Rd.
Lima, OH 45804
Mailing Address:
P.O. Box 509
Lima, OH 45802
Tel.: 419-648-3611 **OH**
Fax: 419-648-4087
Year Founded: 1955
Sales Range: $20-39 Million
Emp.: 160

Manufacture Pork Rinds, Cracklings & Extruded Snacks
S.I.C.: 2096
John E. Rudolph *(Pres.)*
Lynn Cline *(Chief Fin. Officer)*
Dale Linet *(V.P.-Sls.)*
James E. Rudolph *(V.P.-Opers.)*
Richard M. Rudolph *(V.P.-Mktg.)*
Principal(s):
John E. Rudolph
Lynn Cline
James E. Rudolph
Richard M. Rudolph
Kathleen A. Rudolph
Mary M. Rudolph
Susan L. Rudolph

No. of Mfg. Plants/Facilities: 2
No. of U.S. Offices: 2

Computer Systems/Hardware:
IBM

Outside Service Firm(s):

Arthur Andersen & Co.*(Auditors)*
Courthouse Plaza SW,
Dayton, OH 45402

Leonard and Leonard*(Legal Firm)*
Lima, OH

Bank One*(Major Banking Relationship)*
Lima, OH

RUDOLPH/LIBBE, INC.
6494 Latcha Rd.
Walbridge, OH 43465
Tel.: 419-241-5000 **OH**
Fax: 418-837-9373
Year Founded: 1955
Approx.Sls.: $110,350,000
Emp.: 350
Fiscal Year-end: 12/31/92
General Contractors-Commercial & Institutional
S.I.C.: 1541; 1542
Corporate Giving Program: Local United Way Agencies Only
Frederick W. Rudolph *(Pres.)*
Frank J. Gianino *(V.P.-Field Oper.)*
Ronald R. Holzman *(V.P.-Human Resources)*
Charles F. Hutchings *(V.P.-Contracts Admin.)*
Scott Wm. Libbe *(V.P.-Sls.)*
Marilyn L. Rudolph *(V.P.-Fin.)*
Phillip J. Rudolph *(V.P.-Bus. & Devel.)*
Robert D. Seeger *(V.P.-Industrial Serv.)*
Allan J. Libbe *(Sec., Treas. & Controller)*
Robert A. Baggs, *(Dir.-Training & Devel.)*

Outside Service Firm(s):

Ernst & Young*(Auditors)*
One Sea Gate
Toledo, OH 43604
Tel.: 419-244-8000

Connelly, Soutar & Jackson*(Legal Firm)*
Toledo, OH

Society National Bank*(Major Banking Relationship)*
Toledo, OH

RUFFIN BUILDING SYSTEMS, INC.
6914 Hwy. 2
Oak Grove, LA 71263-8930
Tel.: 318-428-2305 **LA**
Year Founded: 1971
Approx.Sls.: $20,000,000
Emp.: 180
Prefabricated Metal Buildings; Prefabricated Industrial Buildings
S.I.C.: 3448; 1541
Shelton Ruffin *(Pres.)*
Pat Ruffin *(V.P., Treas. & Sec.)*
Ronney L. Hayes *(Controller)*

Outside Service Firm(s):

West Carroll National Bank*(Major Banking Relationship)*
Oak Grove, LA

RUGBY-DARBY GROUP OF COS.
100 Banks Ave.
Rockville Centre, NY 11570
Tel.: 516-536-3000
Fax: 516-536-8570
Year Founded: 1957
Approx.Sls.: $118,000,000
Emp.: 400
Pharmaceuticals; Kitchen Tools & Utensils; Dentists Professional Supplies; Veterinarians Equipment & Supplies
S.I.C.: 5122; 5023; 5047
Joseph Ashkin *(Pres.)*
Anna Ashkin *(Sec. & Treas.)*

Outside Service Firm(s):

Chemical Bank*(Major Banking Relationship)*
Huntington Station, NY

RUGBY FARMERS UNION ELEVATOR COMPANY
105 E. Dewey St.
Rugby, ND 58368
Tel.: 701-776-5214 **ND**
Fax: 701-776-6437
Year Founded: 1940
Approx.Sls.: $12,000,000
Emp.: 11
Grain Elevators; Wholesale Distribution of Farm Supplies
S.I.C.: 5153; 5191
Duane Johnston *(Gen. Mgr.)*

Outside Service Firm(s):

Norwest Bank Minnesota, N.A.*(Major Banking Relationship)*
Red Wing, MN

RUGG MANUFACTURING COMPANY
105 Newton St.
Greenfield, MA 01301
Mailing Address:
P.O. Box 507
Greenfield, MA 01301
Tel.: 413-773-5471 **MA**
Fax: 413-774-4354
Year Founded: 1842
Approx.Sls.: $12,000,000
Emp.: 80
Import
Mfr. of Steel & Aluminum Snow Shovels, Scoops, Pushers & Lawn Rakes; Retail Lumber Yard & Special Millwork
S.I.C.: 3423; 5211
David H. Fitch *(Chm. Bd.)*
Michael Fritz *(Pres.)*
David Damery *(V.P. & Mgr.-Sls.)*
Stephen E. Peck *(V.P.-Human Resources)*
Jonathan Rugg *(Sec.)*
Thomas R. Finch *(Treas.)*

Outside Service Firm(s):

Bank of New England*(Major Banking Relationship)*
South Deerfield, MA

RUHL COMPANIES, INC.
99 Wall St.
Valhalla, NY 10595
Tel.: 914-761-2600
Fax: 914-761-0405
Approx.Sls.: $10,000,000
Emp.: 70
Holding Company; Mfrs. of Transducers For Machine & Military Aerospace Industries
S.I.C.: 3679; 6719
Frank Ruhl *(Pres. & Chief Exec. Officer)*
David S. Feron *(Sr. V.P.)*
Robert Ruhl *(Controller)*
Harvey Kitay *(Gen. Counsel)*
E. Vesser *(Mgr.-Data Processing)*
Frank Lantz *(Pur. Agent)*

Outside Service Firm(s):

Grant Thornton*(Auditors)*
605 Third Ave.
New York, NY 10158
Tel.: 212-599-0100
Fax: 212-370-4520

Connecticut National Bank*(Major Banking Relationship)*
777 Main St.
Hartford, CT 06115
Tel.: 203-728-2000

Division:

Farrand Controls **(1)**
99 Wall St.
Valhalla, NY 10595
Tel.: 914-761-2600
Mfr. of Transducers For Machine Industry & Military Aerospace Industry
S.I.C.: 3679
Frank Ruhl *(Pres.)*

THE RUHLIN COMPANY
6931 Ridge Rd.
Sharon Center, OH 44274
Mailing Address:
P.O. Box 190,
Sharon Center, OH 44274
Tel.: 216-239-2800
Fax: 216-239-1828
Year Founded: 1918
Approx.Sls.: $96,000,000
Emp.: 885
General Building Contractors; Heavy Construction Contractors; Construction Managers
S.I.C.: 1611; 1541; 1542; 8741
John Ruhlin, Jr. *(Chm. Bd., Pres. & Chief Exec. Officer)*
Russell Gregory *(Chief Fin. Officer & Treas.)*
Terry Lewis *(Controller)*
Michael Stith *(Gen. Counsel)*

Computer Systems/Hardware:
IBM System 38

Outside Service Firm(s):

Coopers & Lybrand*(Auditors)*
P.O. Box 538, 800 Akron Centre Plaza
Akron, OH 44308

Massachusetts Mutual Life Insurance Co.*(Group Insurer)*
Boston, MA

First National Bank of Ohio*(Major Banking Relationship)*
Akron, OH

CHUCK RUHR ADVERTISING
1221 Nicollet Mall, Ste. 600
Minneapolis, MN 55403
Tel.: 612-332-4565
Fax: 612-334-8277
Year Founded: 1964
Approx.Billings: $72,000,000
Emp.: 125
Fiscal Year-end: 10/31/91
Advertising Agency
S.I.C.: 7311
Charles F. Ruhr *(Chm. Bd. & Chief Exec. Officer)*
Robert L. Jones *(Pres., Ruhr-Paragon)*
Louise Scroggins *(Pres.-Chuck Ruhr Advertising)*
Jeff Novak *(V.P., Chief Fin. Officer)*
Lisa Fischburg *(V.P., Admin.-Ruhr/Paragon)*
Rose Larson *(V.P., Plng. & Res.)*
Catherine Marchio *(Mgr., Human Resources)*
Joyce Hovanes *(V.P., Bus. Devel.)*
Principal(s):
Charles F. Ruhr

No. of U.S. Offices: 1

Computer Systems/Hardware:
Burroughs 6820; NBI System 64

Outside Service Firm(s):

Larsen, Allen, Weishair & Co.*(Auditors)*
Minneapolis, MN

RUIZ FOOD PRODUCTS, INC.
501 S. Alta
Dinuba, CA 93618
Mailing Address:
P.O. Box 37,
Dinaba, CA 93618-0037
Tel.: 209-591-5510 **CA**
Fax: 209-688-7629
Year Founded: 1966
Assets: $18,000,000
Earnings: $3,000,000
Liabilities: $11,000,000
Net Worth: $7,000,000
Approx.Sls.: $77,000,000
Emp.: 1,100
Fiscal Year-end: 9/30/91
Manufactures Frozen Mexican Foods
S.I.C.: 2099
Louis Ruiz *(Chm. Bd.)*
Fred Ruiz *(Pres. & Chief Exec. Officer)*
Christopher H. Raborg *(Chief Fin. Officer)*
Thomas Collesberry *(Exec. V.P.)*
David Olson *(V.P. & Controller)*
Luciano Alvarez *(Dir.-Res. & Devel.)*
Robert Duchene *(Dir.-Corp. Devel.)*
Rick McCurry *(Mgr.-Pur.)*
Amy Miller *(Mgr.-Opers.)*
Ernie Morero *(Mgr.-Human Resources)*
Joy Soares *(Mgr.-Mktg.)*
Harry Wright *(Mgr.-Data Processing)*
Principal(s):
Louis Ruiz
Fred Ruiz

No. of Mfg. Plants/Facilities: 1
No. of U.S. Offices: 1

Computer Systems/Hardware:
Altos 3086; 10 PC's

Outside Service Firm(s):

M. Greene & Co.*(Auditors)*
Tulare, CA

Aetna Life & Casualty*(Commercial Insurance Carrier)*
151 Farmington Avenue
Hartford, CT 06156
Tel.: 203-273-2128
Fax: 203-729-4295

Safeco Insurance Co. of America*(Group Insurer)*
Seattle, WA

Kloster, Ruddell, Hornberg & Cochran*(Legal Firm)*
Visalia, CA

Farmers State Bank*(Major Banking Relationship)*
Farmersville, CA

Wells Fargo Bank*(Major Banking Relationship)*
420 Montgomery St.
San Francisco, CA 94104

RUMRILL-HOYT, INC.
60 Corporate Woods
Rochester, NY 14623
Mailing Address:
P.O. Box 1011,
Rochester, NY 14603
Tel.: 716-272-6100
Fax: 716-272-6161
Year Founded: 1933
Approx.Billings: $89,000,000
Emp.: 170
Advertising/Public Relations/ Directory Mngmt. Services
S.I.C.: 8743
Tim Cronin *(Pres. & Chief Exec. Officer)*
Kurt T. Minwell *(V.P., Fin. & Admin.)*

RUMS OF PUERTO RICO
(Div. of Economic Devel. Admin. of the Commonwealth of Puerto Rico)
1290 Ave. of the Americas
New York, NY 10104
Tel.: 212-245-1200
Fax: 212-581-2667
Approx.Sls.: $275,000,000
Emp.: 70
Promote Rums of Puerto Rico
S.I.C.: 8611
Edmundo Bermudez *(Dir.)*
Maria Colon *(Reg. Mgr.)*

RUMSEY ELECTRIC CO.
301 W. Hunting Park Ave.
Philadelphia, PA 19140
Tel.: 215-456-2500 **DE**
Fax: 215-457-1820
Year Founded: 1895
Assets: $19,602,222
Liabilities: $14,436,914
Net Worth: $5,165,308
Approx.Sls.: $74,667,364
Emp.: 160
Fiscal Year-end: 1/31/91
Wholesale Electrical Equipment & Supplies
S.I.C.: 5063
William J. DiBui *(Pres., Chief Exec. & Chief Oper. Officer)*
G. M. Lihota *(V.P. & Mgr.-Utility Sls. Div.)*
Donald A. Brown *(V.P. & Gen. Mgr.-Supply Div.)*
T. L. Chambers *(Sec. & Treas.)*
Jeffrey L. Shisler *(Mgr.-Data Processing)*
George Van Pelt *(Mgr.-Pur.)*
Principal(s):

No. of Mfg. Plants/Facilities: 7
No. of U.S. Offices: 9

Computer Systems/Hardware:
M.A.I. Basic Four

Outside Service Firm(s):

KPMG Peat Marwick*(Auditors)*
1600 Market St.
Philadelphia, PA 19103
Tel.: 215-299-3100

Obermayer, Rebmann, Maxwell & Hippel*(Legal Firm)*
Philadelphia, PA

Philadelphia National Bank*(Major Banking Relationship)*
P.O. Box 13834, Broad & Chestnut Streets
Philadelphia, PA 19101-7618
Tel.: 215-973-8327

CoreStates Financial Corp.*(Major Banking Relationship)*
Philadelphia, PA

RUNDEL PRODUCTS, INC.
1100 N.E. 28th Ave.
Portland, OR 97232
Tel.: 503-284-5511 **OR**
Telex: 282-6759
Fax: 503-282-6759
Year Founded: 1971
Approx.Sls.: $20,000,000
Emp.: 275
Fiscal Year-end: 11/30/92
Import Export
Manufacture Three-Ring Vinyl Notebooks, Custom Index Tabs & Software Packaging
S.I.C.: 2678
C. Dixon Rauch III *(Pres. & Chief Exec. Officer)*
Eric N. Lieberg *(Chief Fin. Officer & Exec. V.P.)*
William Patterson *(Chief Oper. Officer & Sr. V.P.)*
Pam Lockyear *(Controller)*
Terese Tyler *(Asst. Controller)*
Melvin Lester *(Dir.-Communications & Data Processing)*
Kevin Bartholomew *(Mgr.-Pur.)*
Jon Finley *(Mgr.-Mktg. Support)*
Gary L. Scott *(Mgr.-Prod. Scheduling)*
Principal(s):
C. Dixon Rauch III

No. of Mfg. Plants/Facilities: 1
No. of U.S. Offices: 1

Computer Systems/Hardware:
WYSE/AT&T

Outside Service Firm(s):

Mack, Roberts, Hoyle*(Auditors)*
Portland, OR

Willis Corroon*(Group Insurer)*
7 Hanover Square
New York, NY
Tel.: 212-837-0823
Fax: 212-344-8290

Fireman's Fund Insurance Co.*(Group Insurer)*
New York, NY

Unigard Insurance Co.*(Group Insurer)*
1215 Fourth Ave.
Seattle, WA 98161
Tel.: 206-641-4321
Fax: 206-644-2994

United States Fidelity & Guaranty Co.*(Group Insurer)*
100 Light Street
Baltimore, MD 21202
Tel.: 301-547-3000

Dunn, Carney, Allen, Higgins & Tongue*(Legal Firm)*
Portland, OR

United States National Bank of Oregon*(Major Banking Relationship)*
P.O. Box 3850,
Portland, OR 97208
Tel.: 503-275-6111

RUPPMAN NATIONAL YELLOW PAGES SERVICE (RNYPS)
(Div. of Ruppman Marketing Technologies, Inc.)
2001 Ruppman Plaza
Peoria, IL 61614
Tel.: 309-685-5901
Tel.: 800-447-8228
Fax: 309-679-4199
Year Founded: 1963
Approx.Billings: $68,000,000
Emp.: 800
Program Design & Yellow Pages Placement
Charles T. Ruppman *(Chm. Bd. & Chief Exec. Officer)*
Gary Adami *(Exec. V.P., Chief Fin. Officer)*
Michael L. Gregory *(V.P., Corp. Communications)*
Bud Malbon *(V.P., Retail & Fulfillment Distr.)*
Greg Stinson *(V.P., Bus. Devel.)*
Mary Jo Nelson *(V.P., Yellow Pages Services)*
Cherie Thies-Pate *(V.P., Telemarketing Services)*

RURAL ELECTRIC CO-OP
N. Hwy. 76
Lindsay, OK 73052
Mailing Address:
P.O. Box 609,
Lindsay, OK 73052
Tel.: 405-756-3104 **OK**
Fax: 405-756-8957
Year Founded: 1938
Approx.Sls.: $14,000,000
Emp.: 52
Electric Power Transmission
S.I.C.: 4911
Melton Jordon, Jr. *(Pres.)*
Tenys Parr *(V.P.)*
Gary Jones *(Treas. & Sec.)*
Raymond Dew *(Mgr.-Engrng.)*
Dorothy Scoggins *(Mgr.-Data Processing)*
Mike Treadwell *(Gen. Mgr.)*

Outside Service Firm(s):

W.L. Barber*(Legal Firm)*
Lindsay, OK

American Exchange Bank*(Major Banking Relationship)*
Lindsay, OK

RURAL METRO CORPORATION
8401 E. Indian School Rd.
Scottsdale, AZ 85251
Mailing Address:
P.O. Drawer F,
Scottsdale, AZ 85252
Tel.: 602-994-3886 **AZ**
Fax: 602-481-3328
Year Founded: 1948
Assets: $41,000,000
Liabilities: $35,000,000
Net Worth: $6,000,000
Sales Range: $60-79 Million
Emp.: 1,800
Fiscal Year-end: 6/30/88
Manage & Operate Ambulance Services, Fire Departments, Home Health Care Service & Supplies
S.I.C.: 4119; 9224; 7389
Ian Sym-Smith *(Chm. Bd.)*
Robert Manschot *(Pres. & Chief Exec. Officer)*
Mark Liebrer *(Chief Fin. Officer & V.P.)*
James H. Bolin *(Sr. V.P.)*
Robert Edwards *(Sr. V.P. & Gen. Mgr.-Maricopa County)*
Ken Kelley *(V.P.-Mngmt. Information Systems)*
Angela Mavro *(V.P.-Human Resources)*
Sue Brossart *(Dir.-Pub. Rels.)*
Kathy Freiburg *(Dir.-Pur.)*
Cindy Hartzer *(Dir.-Employee Benefits)*
Louis G. Jekel *(Legal Officer)*
Lorraine Tully *(Travel Coord.)*

No. of U.S. Offices: 11

Computer Systems/Hardware:
IBM AS-400

Outside Service Firm(s):

Deloitte & Touche*(Auditors)*
2901 North Central Ave., Ste. 1200
Phoenix, AZ 85012
Tel.: 602-234-5100
Fax: 602-234-5186

St. Paul Fire & Marine Insurance Co.*(Commercial Insurance Carrier)*
385 Washington St.
St. Paul, MN 55102
Tel.: 612-221-7911

Jekel & Howard*(Legal Firm)*
Scottsdale, AZ

RUSCON CORP.
149 E. Bay St.
Charleston, SC 29401
Tel.: 803-723-9861 **SC**
Fax: 803-723-3029
Approx.Sls.: $42,000,000
Emp.: 400
Industrial, Commercial & Residential Building Contractor; Wholesale Construction Equipment
S.I.C.: 1542; 1522; 1541; 5082
Robert B. Russell, Jr. *(Pres.)*
Robert L. Bennett *(Exec. V.P.-Construction)*
James M. Stelling *(Exec. V.P., Treas. & Sec.)*
Edward F. Frederick *(Controller)*

Outside Service Firm(s):

McGuire & Co.*(Auditors)*
Charleston, SC

Buist, Moore, Smythe & McGee*(Legal Firm)*
Charleston, SC

Robertson & Finkler*(Legal Firm)*
Charlston, SC

South Carolina National Bank*(Major Banking Relationship)*
Charleston, SC

RUSH COUNTY FARM BUREAU CO-OP
627 West 3rd St.
Rushville, IN 46173
Tel.: 317-932-3921
Fax: 317-938-1522
Year Founded: 1930
Assets: $4,612,986
Earnings: $227,731
Liabilities: $2,253,163
Net Worth: $2,359,823
Approx.Sls.: $11,661,000
Emp.: 40
Fiscal Year-end: 8/31/90
Agricul. Production; Food & Kindred Prods.; Wholesale Trade-Nondurable Goods
S.I.C.: 5153; 5191; 5072; 5083; 5251; 5211
Joe Leisure *(Chm. & Pres.)*
Mark Webster *(Chief Exec. Officer, Chief Fin. Officer & Gen. Counsel)*

RUSKA INSTRUMENT CORPORATION
3601 Dunvale
Houston, TX 77063
Tel.: 713-975-0547
Fax: 713-975-6338
Approx.Sls.: $12,000,000
Emp.: 130
Instruments To Measure Electricity
S.I.C.: 3825
James E. Lyon *(Chm. Bd. & Chief Exec. Officer)*
E. David Upton *(Exec. V.P.)*
Ronald D. Christ *(V.P.-Fin.)*
J.H. Hinds *(V.P.-Engrng.)*
Marvin Hyatt *(V.P.-Mfg.)*

Outside Service Firm(s):

Childs, Fortenbach, Beck & Guyton*(Legal Firm)*
402 Pierce
Houston, TX 77002
Tel.: 713-659-6681

Bank One*(Major Banking Relationship)*
Houston, TX

Subsidiary:

Ruska Laboratories **(1)**
3601 Dunvale
Houston, TX 77063
Tel.: 713-975-0547
Ray Worden *(Pres.)*

RUSLANDER & SONS, INC.
18 Letchworth St.
Buffalo, NY 14213
Tel.: 716-881-0030 **NY**
Fax: 716-881-6092
Year Founded: 1877
Approx.Sls.: $10,500,000
Emp.: 100
Fiscal Year-end: 12/31/90

Export
Mfr. of Refrigerators & Freezers for Laboratory & Scientific Applications, Morgue & Autopsy Equipment
S.I.C.: 3585
Marshall L. Glickman *(Pres. & Chief Exec. Officer)*
Harold L. Ruslander *(Exec. V.P.-Engrng.)*
Martin Erdei *(V.P.-Human Resources)*
James B. Linehan *(V.P.-Fin.)*

No. of Mfg. Plants/Facilities: 1

Outside Service Firm(s):

KPMG Peat Marwick*(Auditors)*
700 Empire Tower
Buffalo, NY 14202-3786
Tel.: 716-854-1830
Fax: 716-856-8063

Kavinoky & Cook*(Legal Firm)*
120 Delaware Ave.
Buffalo, NY 14202
Tel.: 716-856-9234

Marine Midland Bank*(Major Banking Relationship)*
P.O. Box 803, 1 Marine Midland Center, 23rd Floor
Buffalo, NY 14203
Tel.: 716-841-2582

Subsidiary:

The Jewett Refrigerator Co., Inc. **(1)**
2 Letchworth St.
Buffalo, NY 14213-1098
Tel.: 716-881-0030
Tel.: 800-879-7767
Telex: 646530 JEWETT BUF
Fax: 716-881-6092
Approx.Sls.: $10,500,000
Emp.: 110
Fiscal Year-end: 12/31/91
Import Export
Computer Systems/Hardware:
Wang
Mfr. of Hospital Equipment; Autopsy Tables, Refrigerators & Freezers for Clinical Use
S.I.C.: 3841; 3585; 3821
Marshall L. Glickman *(Pres. & Chief Exec. Officer)*
Harold L. Ruslander *(Sr. V.P. & Treas.)*
Martin Erdei *(V.P.-Mfg.)*
Jeffrey D. Johnston *(V.P.-Intl. Sls. & Mktg.)*
Thomas D. Reider *(V.P.-Sls. & Mktg.)*
James B. Linehan *(V.P.-Fin.)*
Joseph L. Glickman *(Mgr.-Sls.)*

RUSSELL CHEVROLET COMPANY
6100 Landere Rd.
Sherwood, AR 72117
Mailing Address:
P.O. Box 6200
Sherwood, AR 72116
Tel.: 501-835-8300
Fax: 501-835-8300, Ext. 22
Approx.Sls.: $46,000,000
Emp.: 140
Retail New & Used Automobiles
S.I.C.: 5511; 5521; 5531
Bob Russell *(Pres.)*
Richard Russell *(Exec. V.P. & Gen. Mgr.)*
Steve Martin *(Treas. & Sec.)*

Outside Service Firm(s):

One National Bank North Little Rock N.A.*(Major Banking Relationship)*
North Little Rock, AR

The Russell Corporation
(See Russell Chevrolet Company)

H. J. RUSSELL CORP.
504 Fair St. SW
Atlanta, GA 30313
Tel.: 404-330-1000
Fax: 404-688-5179
Approx.Sls.: $143,600,000
Emp.: 450
Building Construction & Real Estate Development
S.I.C.: 1542; 6552
Herman J. Russell *(Chm. Bd. & Chief Exec. Officer)*
Egbert L. Perry *(Pres. & Chief Oper. Officer)*
Joya Johnson *(Gen. Counsel)*

Outside Service Firm(s):

Hulligan, Taylor & Gilbert*(Legal Firm)*
Atlanta, GA

Smith, Gambrell & Russell*(Legal Firm)*
2400 First Atlanta Tower
Atlanta, GA 30383
Tel.: 404-656-1800
Fax: 404-264-2652

NationsBank*(Major Banking Relationship)*
35 Broad St.
Atlanta, GA 30303
Tel.: 404-581-2121
Tel.: 800-848-8198

RUSSELL INDUSTRIES, INC.
555 N. Bell Ave.
Carnegie, PA 15106
Tel.: 412-279-1200
Fax: 412-279-5184
Approx.Sls.: $28,000,000
Emp.: 175
Paving Contractor; Manufacture Paving Materials
S.I.C.: 1611; 2951
Leo P. Russell *(Chm. Bd. & Chief Exec. Officer)*
Stephen P. Russell *(Pres. & Chief Oper. Officer)*
John Russell *(V.P. & Treas.)*

Outside Service Firm(s):

Schneider Downs & Company*(Auditors)*
Pittsburgh, PA

RUSSELL PETROLEUM CORPORATION
3378 Tankview Ct.
Montgomery, AL 36108
Tel.: 205-834-3750 **AL**
Fax: 205-834-3755
Approx.Sls.: $25,000,000
Emp.: 150
Filling Stations; Petroleum Bulk Stations; Independent Kwik Shop Convenience Stores
S.I.C.: 5541; 5171; 5411
E. Wayne Russell, Jr. *(Pres.)*
Gordon L. Heartsell *(Sr. V.P.)*
George Earl Russell *(Treas. & Sec.)*

Outside Service Firm(s):

First Alabama Bank*(Major Banking Relationship)*
Birmingham, AL

RUSSELL-STANLEY CORPORATION
230 Half Mile Rd.
Red Bank, NJ 07701
Tel.: 908-741-6366
Fax: 908-741-4913
Approx.Sls.: $80,000,000
Emp.: 500
Manufacture Industrial Containers
S.I.C.: 3412
William Lima *(Chm. Bd. & Pres.)*
Thomas Comollo *(V.P.-Fin.)*
Greg Robinson *(Controller)*
Louis Gaev *(Dir.-Sls.)*
Phil Bartlett *(Natl. Sls. Mgr.)*

Outside Service Firm(s):

Deloitte & Touche*(Auditors)*
Forrestal Center, 685 College Road East
Princeton, NJ 08540-6691
Tel.: 609-520-2300

Greenbaum, Rowe, Smith, Ravin, Davis & Bergstein*(Legal Firm)*
Metro Corporate Campus 1, P.O. Box 5600
Woodbridge, NJ 07095
Tel.: 908-549-5600

First National Bank of Boston*(Major Banking Relationship)*
P.O. Box 644,
Boston, MA 02102-0644
Tel.: 617-575-2900
Fax: 617-575-2549

Subsidiary:

Russell-Stanley West, Inc. **(1)**
9449 Santa Anita Ave.
Rancho Cucamonga, CA 91730
Tel.: 909-980-7114
Emp.: 75
Industrial Plastic Pails, Drums & Enclosures
S.I.C.: 3089
William Lima *(Pres.)*
John Hunter *(Gen. Mgr.)*
Rick Andersen *(Mgr.-Sls.)*

RUSSELL STOVER CANDIES, INC.
1000 Walnut
Kansas City, MO 64106
Tel.: 816-842-9240 **MO**
Fax: 816-842-7972
Year Founded: 1923
Approx.Sls.: $250,000,000
Emp.: 4,800
Fiscal Year-end: 2/28/91
Mfr., Distributor & Retailer of Candy Stores
S.I.C.: 2064; 2066; 5149; 5441
Louis L. Ward *(Chm. Bd., Pres. & Chief Oper. Officer)*
Thomas S. Ward *(V.P.)*
Robert Maack *(V.P. & Data Processing Dir.)*
Scott H. Ward *(V.P.)*
Jack R. Carr *(Treas.)*
John Lascoe *(Controller)*
Leo Michaelis *(Dir.-Pur.)*
Robinn Weber *(Dir.-Personnel & Employee Benefits)*
Charlene Owings *(Dir.-Creative)*

No. of Mfg. Plants/Facilities: 4
No. of U.S. Offices: 1

Computer Systems/Hardware:
IBM

Outside Service Firm(s):

Deloitte & Touche*(Auditors)*
1010 Grand Ave.
Kansas City, MO 64106-2232
Tel.: 816-474-6180

Lockton Insurance Agency*(Commercial Insurance Carrier)*
Kansas City, MO

LaHood & Associates*(Group Insurer)*
P.O. Box 12170, 6717 W. 63rd St.
Kansas City, KS 66282-2170
Tel.: 913-362-0040
Fax: 913-362-0041

Gage & Tucker*(Legal Firm)*
2345 Grand Ave., 28th Fl.
Kansas City, MO 64108
Tel.: 816-292-2000

Stinson, Mag & Fizzell*(Legal Firm)*
2100 Charter Bank Ctr.
Kansas City, MO 64105

Boatmen's First National Bank of Kansas City*(Major Banking Relationship)*
10th & Baltimore
Kansas City, MO 64183
Tel.: 816-221-2800
Fax: 816-691-7254

Commerce Bank of Kansas City*(Major Banking Relationship)*
10th & Walnut
Kansas City, MO 64141
Tel.: 816-234-2000
Fax: 816-234-2548

Boatmen's Trust Company*(Pension Manager)*
100 North Broadway
St. Louis, MO 63102
Tel.: 314-466-2469

RUSTCO PRODUCTS COMPANY
1485 E. 61st Ave.
Denver, CO 80216
Mailing Address:
P.O. Box 16366,
Denver, CO 80216
Tel.: 303-287-3203
Tel.: 800-592-5655
Fax: 303-287-2203
Year Founded: 1945
Approx.Sls.: $55,000,000
Emp.: 250
Fiscal Year-end: 1/31/91

Export
Mfr. of Cooking Oils, Except Corn; Vegetable Refined; Prepared Flour Mixes & Doughs; Fruit Pie Mixes & Fillings; Testing Laboratories
S.I.C.: 2079; 2045; 2033; 8734
Corporate Giving Program: Supports United Way
Thomas D. Stocks III *(Chm. & Chief Exec. Officer)*
James R. Sponsler *(Pres. & Chief Oper. Officer)*
John R. Ord *(V.P.-Fin. & Admin.)*
Keith A. Sheller *(V.P.-Sls. & Mktg.)*
Bob Burgess *(V.P.-Opers.)*
Rita Ann Carey *(Mgr.-Mktg.)*
Roger Langford *(Mgr.-Data Processing)*
Clay Griffin *(Mgr.-Sls. & Mktg.)*

Outside Service Firm(s):

Colorado National Bank*(Major Banking Relationship)*
17th & Champa
Denver, CO 80217

RUTHMAN PUMP & ENGINEERING CO.
1212 Streng St.
Cincinnati, OH 45223
Tel.: 513-559-1900
Fax: 513-559-0035
Year Founded: 1913
Approx.Sls.: $12,000,000
Emp.: 100

Export
Mfr. Pumps; Rumaco, Gusher
S.I.C.: 3561
T.R. Ruthman *(Pres., Gen. Mgr. & Adv. Dir.)*
Leslie Smith *(Exec. V.P.)*
Russell Daniel *(V.P.)*

Computer Systems/Hardware:
IBM 36

Subsidiary:

Gusher Pumps Inc. **(1)**
Ruthman Dr.
Dry Ridge, KY 41035
Tel.: 606-824-5001
Fax: 606-824-3011

RUTT CUSTOM CABINETRY
P.O. Box 129
Goodville, PA 17528
Tel.: 215-445-6751
Fax: 215-445-9227
Approx.Sls.: $17,000,000
Emp.: 250
Fiscal Year-end: 12/31/90

Rutt Custom Cabinetry—(Continued)

Custom Kitchen Cabinets, Custom Bath Vanities, Office, Den & Bar Furniture; Custom Wood Cabinetry
S.I.C.: 5712
W.R. Wiersma *(Pres.)*
Rus Orban *(V.P.-Mktg.)*
Gerald Hess *(Comptroller)*
Richard Boone *(Human Resources Dir.)*
Don Hess *(Pur. Agent)*
Ted Stone *(Plant Mgr.)*

RYAN HERCO PRODUCTS CORP.
2509 N. Naomi St.
Burbank, CA 91504
Mailing Address:
P. O. Box 588
Burbank, CA 91503
Tel.: 818-841-1141
Fax: 818-842-4488
Year Founded: 1948
Approx.Sls.: $40,000,000
Emp.: 130
Fiscal Year-end: 8/31/90
Import Export
Mfr. & Distr. Plastic Fluid-Handling Systems
S.I.C.: 5162
Brian Bowman *(Chm. Bd. & Chief Fin. Officer)*
Terry O'Brien *(Vice Chm. & Chief Exec. Officer)*
Frank Gibbs *(Pres. & Chief Oper. Officer)*
Ed Glosup *(V.P.-Pur.)*
Bob Sprow *(Sec., Treas. & Controller)*
Larry King *(Dir.-Sls. & Mktg.)*
Fred C. Alexander *(Dir.-Adv.)*

RYAN OLDSMOBILE
324 S. 24th St., W.
Billings, MT 59102
Tel.: 406-656-6200 **MT**
Fax: 406-652-6932
Year Founded: 1951
Approx.Sls.: $10,000,000
Emp.: 42
Retail Sales of New & Used Automobiles
S.I.C.: 5511
Colleen Ryan *(Pres.)*
Phylis Ryan *(V.P.)*
Fred C. Barrett *(Treas. & Sec.)*

Outside Service Firm(s):

Yellowstone Bank*(Major Banking Relationship)*
Billings, MT

RYAN PROPERTIES INC.
700 International Center, 900 2nd Ave. S.
Minneapolis, MN 55402
Tel.: 612-339-9847 **MN**
Fax: 612-337-5552
Year Founded: 1937
Approx.Sls.: $46,000,000
Emp.: 200
Building Operators
S.I.C.: 6512
Pat Ryan *(Pres.)*
Jim Ryan *(Pres.-Ryan Construction Co.)*
Russell R. Ryan *(V.P., Treas. & Sec.)*
Timothy M. Gray *(Controller)*

Outside Service Firm(s):

KPMG Peat Marwick*(Auditors)*
4200 Norwest Center, 90 S. 7th St.
Minneapolis, MN 55402
Tel.: 612-341-2222

First Bank Minneapolis*(Major Banking Relationship)*
Minneapolis, MN

Subsidiaries:

Ryan Construction Company **(1)**
700 International Center, 900 2nd Ave. S.
Minneapolis, MN 55402
Tel.: 612-339-9847
General Contractor Commercial & Industrial Buildings
S.I.C.: 1542; 1541
James R. Ryan *(Pres.)*

Ryan Construction Company Of Minnesota **(1)**
Ryan Building
Hibbing, MN 55746
Tel.: 218-263-6888
General Industrial Buildings Contractor
S.I.C.: 1541
Francis J. Ryan *(Pres.)*
Russell J. Ryan *(V.P.-Sec. & Treas.)*
James R. Ryan *(V.P.)*
Timothy M. Gray *(Comptroller)*

RYDER & SCHILD, INC.
2100 Coral Way, #PH
Miami, FL 33145
Tel.: 305-854-0580
Fax: 305-285-1498
Year Founded: 1961
Approx.Billings: $18,000,000
Emp.: 31
William Ryder *(Chm. & Chief Exec. Officer)*
Alan Dietz *(Pres. & Co-Creative Dir.)*
Richard B. Goldman *(V.P., Media & Mktg. Services)*
Angelina Harris *(Asst. V.P., Fin.)*

RYNONE MANUFACTURING CORPORATION
No. Thomas Ave.
Sayre, PA 18840
Mailing Address:
P.O. Box 128,
Sayre, PA 18840-0128
Tel.: 717-888-5272
Fax: 717-888-1175
Sales Range: $20-39 Million
Emp.: 175
Import Export
Vanities, Marble Tops, Self Edge & Post Form Counter Tops, Counter & Sink Tops, Designer Furniture
S.I.C.: 2514; 3281
Richard T. Rynone *(Pres.)*
Thomas E. Rynone *(Chief Exec. Officer)*
William J. Rynone *(Sec. & Treas.)*
Frank Maguire *(Comptroller)*
Michael Baker *(Mgr.-Sls)*
Andrew Ciavardini *(Mgr.-Pur.)*
Principal(s):
Richard T. Rynone
William J. Rynone

No. of Mfg. Plants/Facilities: 4

Computer Systems/Hardware:
Apple Macintosh II

Outside Service Firm(s):

Martin J. Levenson*(Auditors)*
New York, NY

First National Bank Of Bradford County*(Major Banking Relationship)*
Sayre, PA

Friedlander, Friedlander, Reizes, Jock & Lippman*(Legal Firm)*
Waverly, PA

RYSER BROTHERS INC.
3525 W. Potomac
Chicago, IL 60651
Tel.: 312-342-6400
Fax: 312-342-6408
Year Founded: 1926
Earnings: $332,853
Approx.Sls.: $35,000,000
Emp.: 142
Fiscal Year-end: 2/28/89
Manufacture & Distribute Cheese, Salad Dressing & Horseradish
S.I.C.: 5143; 5142; 5149; 2022; 2035
Frank Ryser *(Chm. Bd., Pres., Chief Exec. Officer & Treas.)*
George Brodzki *(Exec. V.P., Chief Fin. Officer & Controller)*
Donald Tekip *(Dir.-Data Systems)*

No. of U.S. Offices: 2

Computer Systems/Hardware:
IBM System 34

Outside Service Firm(s):

Price Waterhouse*(Auditors)*
200 E. Randolph
Chicago, IL 60601
Tel.: 312-565-1500

Alexander & Alexander*(Commercial Insurance Carrier)*
225 N. Michigan Av.
Chicago, IL 60611
Tel.: 312-565-6221

Lincoln National Life Insurance Co.*(Group Insurer)*
PO Box 208, 1300 S. Clinton
Fort Wayne, IN 46801
Tel.: 219-455-2926
Fax: 219-455-7619

Peterson Ross*(Legal Firm)*
200 E. Randolph Dr.
Chicago, IL

North Shore National Bank*(Major Banking Relationship)*
Chicago, IL

Subsidiary:

Ryser Bros. of Wisconsin **(1)**
105 S. 2nd St.
Mount Horeb, WI 53572
Tel.: 608-437-3051
S.I.C.: 2022; 2035; 5143; 5149

S & A RESTAURANT CORP.
12404 Park Central Dr.
Dallas, TX 75251
Tel.: 214-404-5000
Fax: 214-404-5203
Approx.Sls.: $700,000,000
Emp.: 32,000
384 Restaurants in 32 States
S.I.C.: 5812
Stephen R. Leipsner *(Chm., Pres. & Chief Exec. Officer)*
Nicholas A. Castaldo *(Sr. V.P.-Mktg.)*
Robert M. Hartnett *(Sr. V.P. & Gen. Mgr.-Bennagins)*
Dale Alger *(V.P.-Construction)*
Carolyn A. Dreher *(V.P. & Controller)*

Outside Service Firm(s):

Chemical Banking Corp.*(Major Banking Relationship)*
277 Park Ave.
New York, NY 10041
Tel.: 212-310-6407
Fax: 212-310-4526

Divisions:

Bennigan's **(1)**
12404 Park Central Dr.
Dallas, TX 75251
Tel.: 214-404-5000
Approx.Sls.: $480,000,000
Emp.: 20,000
Fiscal Year-end: 6/30/90
Restaurants & Pubs
S.I.C.: 5812
Robert M. Hartnett *(Sr. V.P. & Gen. Mgr.)*
Bill Watson *(Dir.-Mktg.)*

Steak and Ale Restaurants **(1)**
12404 Park Central Dr.
Dallas, TX 75251
Tel.: 214-404-5000
Restaurants
S.I.C.: 5812

S & C ELECTRIC COMPANY
6601 N. Ridge Blvd.
Chicago, IL 60626-3997
Tel.: 312-338-1000 **DE**
Fax: 312-338-3657
Year Founded: 1911
Approx.Sls.: $250,000,000
Emp.: 1,800
Fiscal Year-end: 12/31/91
Export
Manufacturer of High Voltage Transmission & Primary Distribution Switching & Protection Equipment, Electrical Equipment Fuses, Switchgear & Switches; Molded Epoxy Insulation Components
S.I.C.: 3613; 3625; 3643; 3644
John R. Conrad *(Chm. & Chief Exec. Officer)*
John W. Estey *(Pres. & Chief Oper. Officer)*
R.L. Alworth *(V.P.-Mfg.)*
Vilma M. Bell *(V.P.-Employee Rels.)*
John P. Crain *(V.P.-Information Technology)*
G.A. Guerra *(V.P.-Mfg. Tech.)*
Salvador O. Palafox *(V.P.-Intl.)*
M.L. Redmond *(V.P.-Pur.)*
Stanley F. Slabas *(V.P.-Fin.)*
Thomas J. Tobin *(V.P.-Research & Devel.)*
J.R. West *(V.P.-Sls.)*
J.E. Johann *(Treas.)*
Dorothy A. Skiera *(Corp. Sec.)*
P.C. Thompson *(Controller)*
J.L. Blumenshine *(Dir.-Plant Engrng.)*
Wallace Neuhengen *(Dir.-Quality Control)*
R.C. Sparks *(Dir.-Personnel)*
Brian J. Williams *(Dir.-Information Systems)*
Carey J. Cook *(Mgr.-Engrng. Mktg.)*
J.A. Jones, Jr. *(Mgr.-Personnel)*
M.E. Krause *(Mgr.-Personnel)*
John J. McHugh *(Mgr.-Literature Prod.)*
C.E. Shaw *(Mgr.-Educational Services Mktg.)*
Diane Taylor *(Mgr.-Employee Benefits)*
Thomas D. Anderson *(Assoc. Engrng. Editor)*
W.O. Carlson *(Engrng. Editor)*
J.V. Lapacek *(Patent & Liability Counsel)*

No. of Mfg. Plants/Facilities: 1
No. of U.S. Offices: 40
No. of Foreign Offices: 30

Computer Systems/Hardware:
IBM

Outside Service Firm(s):

Ernst & Young*(Auditors)*
233 S. Wacker Dr.
Chicago, IL 60606
Tel.: 312-368-1800
Fax: 312-645-3095

Kirkland & Ellis*(Legal Firm)*
200 E. Randolph Dr.
Chicago, IL 60601
Tel.: 312-861-2000
Fax: 312-861-2200

First National Bank of Chicago*(Major Banking Relationship)*
One First National Plaza
Chicago, IL 60670
Tel.: 312-732-9781
Tel.: 312-732-4050
Fax: 312-732-4840
Fax: 312-732-3055

Harris Trust & Savings Bank*(Major Banking Relationship)*
111 W. Monroe St.
Chicago, IL 60690
Tel.: 312-461-2265
Tel.: 800-858-0840

LaSalle National Bank*(Major Banking Relationship)*
135 S. LaSalle St., Rm.260
Chicago, IL 60603

Non-U.S. Holding:

S & C Electric Canada Ltd. **(1)**
90 Belfield Rd.
Toronto, ON M9W 1G4, Canada
Tel.: 416-249-9171 (100%)
Fax: 416-249-6051
Emp.: 250
Manufacture High Voltage Fuses & Switches
S.I.C.: 3613
William O. Lowry *(Pres.)*
James Stevenson *(V.P.-Fin. & Acctg.)*
Richard Smith *(V.P.-Mktg. & Sales)*
G. Buchanan *(Dir.-Information Technology)*
D. Patten *(Dir.-Human Resources)*

Joint Venture:

SyC-SELMEC, S.A. de C.V. **(1)**
Calz, Vallejo No. 706A P.O. Box 1338, 06000
Mexico, D.F. Mexico
Tel.: 5-567-8722
Telex: 1771671
Fax: 5-567-2220
Emp.: 250
Mfr. of Electric Controls and Equipment; Joint Venture of S&C and SELMEC S.A.
S.I.C.: 3613
Salvador Palafox *(Mng. Dir.)*

S&D COFFEE INC.
300 U.S. Hwy. 29 S.
Concord, NC 28025
Mailing Address:
P.O. Box 1628
Concord, NC 28026
Tel.: 704-782-3121 NC
Fax: 800-950-4378
Approx.Sls.: $60,000,000
Emp.: 320
Fiscal Year-end: 12/31/91
Manufacture & Distribute Roasted Coffee & Tea Products
S.I.C.: 2095; 2099; 5149
J. Roy Davis, Jr. *(Pres.)*
Gene Luckey *(Exec. V.P.)*
Paul Croom *(Sr. V.P.-Sls.)*
Stephen Cole *(V.P.-Fin.)*
Roy Stamey *(V.P.-Mktg.)*
Luther Barrier *(Comptroller)*
Brenda Horton *(Sec.)*

Outside Service Firm(s):

KPMG Peat Marwick*(Auditors)*
Two First Union Center
Charlotte, NC
Tel.: 704-335-5300

Smith, Helms, Mullis & Moore*(Legal Firm)*
227 North Tryon St.
Charlotte, NC 28231

NationsBank Carolinas*(Major Banking Relationship)*
One NCNB Plaza T18-7
Charlotte, NC 28255

S & P COMPANY
100 Shoreline Dr.
Mill Valley, CA 94941
Tel.: 415-332-0550
Fax: 415-332-0567
Emp.: 2,000
Holding Company; Beer; Aluminum Cans
S.I.C.: 6719; 2082; 3411
Lutz Issleib *(Chm. Bd. & Pres.)*
Bernard Orsi *(Exec. V.P. & Sec.)*
John Schliess *(Controller)*

Outside Service Firm(s):

Price Waterhouse*(Auditors)*
1500 Bank One Plaza, 100 E. Wisconsin Ave.
Milwaukee, WI 53202

San Francisco Agencies*(Commercial Insurance Carrier)*
San Francisco, CA

Hill, Farrer & Burrill*(Legal Firm)*
445 So. Figueroa St., 35th Fl.
Los Angeles, CA 90071

Seafirst Bank*(Major Banking Relationship)*
Vancouver, WA

Seattle First National Bank*(Major Banking Relationship)*
701 Fifth Avenue
Seattle, WA 98104
Tel.: 206-358-3035

C & B Consulting Group*(Pension Manager)*
Fifty Fremont St., 24th Fl.
San Francisco, CA 94105
Tel.: 415-979-0600
Fax: 415-979-0177

Subsidiaries:

General Brewing Company **(1)**
312 W. 8th St.
Vancouver, WA 98660
Tel.: 206-695-3381
Fax: 206-693-4467
Approx.Sls.: $15,000,000
Emp.: 50
Computer Systems/Hardware:
IBM PC-AT
Beer Distributor; Trucking & Warehousing
S.I.C.: 5181; 4225
Lutz Issleib *(Chm. Bd., Pres., Chief Exec. & Chief Oper. Officer)*
John M. Schiess *(Exec. V.P.-Fin. & Controller)*
William M. Bitting *(Gen. Counsel)*
Bernard A. Orsi *(Sec.)*
Gary Damveld *(Dir.-Mktg.)*
Norman Merrill *(Dir.-Data Processing & Office Mgr.)*

Pabst Brewing Co. **(1)**
312 Pearl Pkwy.
San Antonio, TX 78215
Tel.: 210-226-0231
Approx.Sls.: $753,000,000
Emp.: 350
Export
Computer Systems/Hardware:
IBM System 38
Brewery
S.I.C.: 2082; 2083
Lutz E. Issleib *(Chm. Bd. & Pres.)*
Gary Damveld *(Exec. V.P.-Sls.)*
Bernard Orsi *(Exec. V.P.)*
John Schiess *(V.P. & Chief Fin. Officer)*
Ofilia Chavera *(V.P.-Admin.)*
Bud Kempen *(Controller)*
Gene Toler *(Gen. Counsel)*
Robert Stevens *(Corp. Dir.-Indus. Rels.)*
Gary Jansen *(Corp. Dir.-Quality Assurance)*
Gary Lewitzke *(Asst. Corp. Dir.-Indus. Rels.)*
Jack Kratz *(Dir.-Grp. Exec. Mktg.)*
Guenter Ruehle *(Dir.-Pur.)*
Jackie Wegner *(Dir.-Natl. Accts.-Military Sls.)*
Glenn Hardin *(Dir.-Automation Services)*
Paul Kling *(Plant Engineer)*
Val G. Pickett *(Plant Mgr.)*
Keith Hodgins *(Brewing Mgr.)*
Ruth Lewitzke *(Mgr.-Mktg. Services)*
Bob Markwiese *(Mgr.-Packaging)*
Bob Milkovich *(Mgr.-Public Rels.)*
Mark Paulos *(Safety Mgr.)*
William Radtke *(Mgr.-Distr.)*

Pearl Brewing Company **(1)**
312 Pearl Parkway
San Antonio, TX 78215
Tel.: 210-226-0231
Fax: 210-226-2512
Emp.: 500
Fiscal Year-end: 6/30/92
Export
Manufacture Malt Beverages
S.I.C.: 2082
Lutz Issleib *(Chm. Bd. & Pres.)*
Ofilia Chavera *(V.P.-Admin.)*
Barry Harris *(V.P.-Finance)*
Gene Toler *(Gen. Counsel)*
Ed Mueller *(Plant Mgr.)*
Glenn Hardin *(Dir.-Automation Services)*
Syl D. Dew *(Dir.-Safety & Training)*
John C. Kratz *(Dir.-Sls.)*
Ken Tucker *(Quality Control)*

Plants:

Pabst Brewing Co./Milwaukee **(2)**
917 W. Juneau Ave.
Milwaukee, WI 53233
Tel.: 414-223-3500
Export
Brewery
S.I.C.: 2082; 2083

Pabst Brewing Co./Tumwater **(2)**
Schmidt Place & Custer Way
Tumwater, WA 98502
Tel.: 206-754-5000
Fax: 206-754-5258
Emp.: 500
Fiscal Year-end: 6/30/91
Export
Brewing
S.I.C.: 2082
Lutz Issleib *(Pres. & Chief Exec. Officer)*
Ofilia Chavera *(V.P.-Admin.)*
Bernard Orsi *(V.P.)*
Ron Wiepz *(Controller)*
Gary Jansen *(Dir.-Quality Control)*
Barry Baumgarner *(Div. Mgr.-West)*
Roger Haag *(Plant Mgr.)*
Alice Riley *(Mgr.-Personnel)*
Ric L. Berndt *(Mgr.-Quality Assurance)*
Larry Sidor *(Mgr.-Opers.)*
Steve Russell *(Mgr.-Packaging)*
Paul D. Knight *(Brewing Mgr.)*
Donald E. Eckloff *(Plant Engineer)*

Subsidiaries:

Pearl Container Co. **(2)**
245 Newell
San Antonio, TX 78215
Tel.: 210-222-2268
Export
Manufacture Metal Cans
S.I.C.: 3411

Texas Transportation Co. **(2)**
312 Pearl Parkway
San Antonio, TX 78215
Tel.: 210-226-0231
Long-Haul Truck Transportation
S.I.C.: 4213

Affiliate:

Falstaff Brewing Corporation **(2)**
312 W. 8th St.
Vancouver, WA 98660
Tel.: 206-695-3381 (34.6%)
Emp.: 1,750
Falstaff, Narragansett Lager, Krueger Beer, Krueger Pilsner, Krueger Ale, Haffenreffer Lager, Croft Ale, Narragansett Ale, Hanley Pilsner, Boh Beer, Pickwick Ale, Ballantine Beer & Ale
S.I.C.: 5181; 4225
Lutz Isseleib *(Chm., Pres. & Chief Oper. Officer)*
Gary Damveld *(Dir.-Mktg.)*

S & S GRAPHICS, INC.
14880 Sweitzer Lane
Laurel, MD 20707
Tel.: 301-206-7777
Approx.Sls.: $15,000,000
Emp.: 140
Offset Printing
S.I.C.: 2752
George D. Solan *(Pres.)*
Bridget Solan *(V.P.)*
Bob Solan *(Sec.)*
Tom Solan *(Treas.)*

Outside Service Firm(s):

Gelman, Rosenberg & Freedman*(Auditors)*
Bethesda, MD

SAE ENGINEERING, INC.
(Formerly Stanford Applied Engineering, Inc.)
340 Martin Ave.
Santa Clara, CA 95050
Tel.: 408-988-0700
Fax: 408-986-1079
Year Founded: 1963
Assets: $13,500,000
Liabilities: $9,000,000
Net Worth: $4,500,000
Approx.Sls.: $25,000,000
Emp.: 350
Fiscal Year-end: 10/31/90
Electronic Interconnection Components
S.I.C.: 3612
C. Campbell *(Pres.)*
Chuck Sneider *(Chief Fin. Officer)*
Sharon Rosencutter *(Mgr.-Pur.)*
Principal(s):
C. Campbell

No. of Mfg. Plants/Facilities: 4
No. of U.S. Offices: 4
No. of Foreign Offices: 1

Computer Systems/Hardware:
Ultimate 400

Outside Service Firm(s):

Coopers & Lybrand*(Auditors)*
10 Almaden Blvd., Ste. 1600
San Jose, CA 95113
Tel.: 408-295-1020
Fax: 408-292-1382

SAS INSTITUTE INC.
SAS Campus Dr.
Cary, NC 27513-2414
Tel.: 919-677-8000 NC
Fax: 919-677-8123
Year Founded: 1976
Approx.Sls.: $295,100,000
Emp.: 2,300
Fiscal Year-end: 12/31/90
Software Research & Development
S.I.C.: 7372
James H. Goodnight *(Chief Exec. Officer)*
W. Greyson Quarles *(Chief Fin. Officer & V.P.)*
John P. Sall *(Sr. V.P.)*
Charles H. Dunham *(V.P.-Information Systems)*
Barrett Joyner *(Dir.-U.S. Mktg. & Sls.)*
David Russo *(Dir.-Human Resources)*
Theresa Tesh *(Asst. Dir.-Sales & Mktg.)*
Wink Swain *(Mgr.-Mktg. Communications)*
Laura Wilson *(Mgr.-Media & Exhibits)*

No. of U.S. Offices: 6
No. of Foreign Offices: 23

Computer Systems/Hardware:
IBM mainframes, DEC VAX, Data General, Prime, Hewlett-Packard, Sun, IBM PCs, clones, Data General, Solbourne, Apollo, Silicon Graphics, MIPS, NeXT

Outside Service Firm(s):

NationsBank Carolinas*(Major Banking Relationship)*
Raleigh, NC

Regional Offices:

SAS Institute, Inc. **(1)**
Two Prudential Plaza, 180 N. Stetson Ave., 52nd Fl.
Chicago, IL 60601
Tel.: 313-819-6800
Emp.: 40
Software Research & Development
S.I.C.: 7372

SAS Institute, Inc. **(1)**
11920 Wilson Parke Ave.
Austin, TX 78726
Tel.: 512-258-5171
Fax: 512-258-3906
Computer Software-Sales, Research & Development
S.I.C.: 7372
Barbara Barrett *(Gen. Mgr.)*

SAS Institute, Inc. **(1)**
34th Floor, 520 Madison Ave.
New York, NY 10022
Tel.: 212-308-1925
Fax: 212-308-0127
Computer Software Sales & Training
S.I.C.: 7372

Subsidiary:

SAS Consulting Services, Inc. **(1)**
1700 Rockville Pike, Ste. 330
Rockville, MD 20852
Tel.: 301-881-8840
Fax: 301-881-8844
Software Research & Development
S.I.C.: 7372

SAS Institute Inc.—(Continued)

Non-U.S. Subsidiaries:

SAS Institute AB **(1)**
Box 1249, Farogatan 2 164 28,
Kista, Sweden
Tel.: 8-7939030
Fax: 8-793-9030
Software Research & Development
S.I.C.: 7372

SAS Institute Ltd. **(1)**
Beijing Representative Office, Rm. 322,
Kunlun Hotel Chaoyang District,
Beijing, 100004, People's Republic of China
Tel.: 1 5003 388-322
Fax: 1 5003 228

SAS Institute A/S **(1)**
Trollasveien 4 1414
Trollasen, Norway
Tel.: 47-2-805380 (100%)
Fax: 47-2-800703
Software Research & Development
S.I.C.: 7372

SAS Institute GmbH **(1)**
P.O. Box 10 53 07, Neuenheimer Landstr.
28-30 D-6900
Heidelberg, 1, Germany
Tel.: 49-6221-4150
Fax: 49-6221-474850
Software Research & Development
S.I.C.: 7372

SAS Institute Ltd. **(1)**
Room 513-515 Hong Kong Plaza 186-191
Connaught Rd. West,
Hong Kong, Hong Kong
Tel.: 852-5-403160
Telex: 77467 HX
Fax: 852-8582658
Software Research & Development
S.I.C.: 7372

SAS Institute Ltd. (Philippines) **(1)**
Strata 100 Emerald Ave. Oritigas Center
Pasig 1600,
Metro Manila, Philippines
Tel.: 2-632-0628
Fax: 63-2-631-2881
S.I.C.: 7372

SAS Institute (NZ) Ltd. **(1)**
P.O. Box 10-109, The Terrace
Wellington, New Zealand
Tel.: 64-4-4727-595
Telex: NZ31525 MED
Fax: 64-4-4727-055
Software Research & Development
S.I.C.: 7372

SAS Institute Pte. Ltd. **(1)**
510 Thomson Rd., #16-03 Block A SLF
Complex,
Singapore, 1129, Singapore
Tel.: 65-258-6233 (100%)
Telex: RS39402 SASINS
Fax: 65-258-4450
Software Research & Development
S.I.C.: 7372

SAS Institute S.A. **(1)**
Domaine de Gregy Boite Postale 5, 77166
Gregy-sur-Yerres, France
Tel.: 33-1-60-6211-11
Fax: 33-1-60-6211-99
Software Research & Development
S.I.C.: 7372

SAS Institute S.A. (Madrid) **(1)**
Calle Pena Sirio No. 17B Mirasierra, E-28034
Madrid, Spain
Tel.: 34-1-372-1500
Fax: 34-1-372-1689
S.I.C.: 7372

SAS Institute S.A. (Geneve) **(1)**
Ch. des Vergers 4 1208
Geneva, Switzerland
Tel.: 41-22-7358560
Fax: 41-22-7358540
S.I.C.: 7372

SAS Institute Sdn. Bhd. **(1)**
28th Floor Menara Maybank, 100 Jalan Tun
Perak 50050
Kuala Lumpur, Malaysia
Tel.: 60-3-238-3188 (100%)
Fax: 60-3-238-3357
Software Research & Development
S.I.C.: 7372

SAS Institute A/S **(1)**
Kobmagerade 9a 1150
Copenhagen, K, Denmark
Tel.: 45-33-124233 (100%)
Fax: 45-33-116155
Software Research & Development
S.I.C.: 7372

SAS Institute Japan Ltd. **(1)**
Nichirei Akashi-cho Bldg., 6-4 Akashi-cho
Chuo-Ku,
Tokyo, 104, Japan
Tel.: 81-3-5565-8380 (100%)
Fax: 81-3-5565-8389
Software Research & Development
S.I.C.: 7372

SAS Institute Australia Pty. Ltd. **(1)**
Private Bag No. 52
Lane Cove, N.S.W. 2066, Australia
Tel.: 61-2-428-0428 (100%)
Fax: 61-2-418-7211
Software Research & Devel.
S.I.C.: 7372

SAS Institute S.r.l. **(1)**
Via San Martino della Battaglia 17 20122
Milan, Italy
Tel.: 39-2-58300754
Fax: 39-2-58300602
S.I.C.: 7372

SAS Institute B.V. **(1)**
Koninginneweg 31 1217 KR
Hilversum, Netherlands
Tel.: 31-35-284550
Fax: 31-35-217532
S.I.C.: 7372

SAS Institute Oy **(1)**
Sinikalliontie 10 PL 80 02631
Espoo, Finland
Tel.: 358-0-523011
Fax: 358-0-5021198
Softwear Research & Development
S.I.C.: 7372

SAS Institute (Canada) Inc. **(1)**
225 Duncan Mill Rd. Suite 300,
North York, ON M3B 3K9, Canada
Tel.: 416-443-9811
Fax: 416-443-1269
S.I.C.: 7372

SAS Institute NV/SA **(1)**
Interleuvenlaan 10 3001
Heverlee, Belgium
Tel.: 32-16-29-09-30
Fax: 32-16-29-12-69
S.I.C.: 7372

SAS Software, Ltd. **(1)**
Wittington House Henley Rd., Medmenham,
Marlow, SL7 2EB, United Kingdom
Tel.: 44-6284-86933 (100%)
Fax: 44-6284-83203
Software Research & Development
S.I.C.: 7372

SAS Software Korea Ltd. **(1)**
#503 Wonchang Bldg., 26-3 Yoido-Dong
Youngdeungpo-ku,
Seoul, 150-010, Korea
Tel.: 82-2-783-4448
Fax: 82-2-783-4449
S.I.C.: 7372

SAS Software Taiwan Ltd. **(1)**
Sung Chiang Rd., 7F,#261
Taipei, Taiwan R.O.C.
Tel.: 886-2-507-1275
Fax: 886-2-504-1631
S.I.C.: 7372

SB ENTERTAINMENT INC.
121 Chanlon Rd.
New Providence, NJ 07974
Tel.: 908-464-6800
Fax: 908-771-7704
Year Founded: 1988
Assets: $5,562,000
Earnings: ($80,361)
Liabilities: $3,425,000
Net Worth: $2,137,000
Approx.Rev.: $13,172,100
Emp.: 12
Fiscal Year-end: 9/30/92
Production & Distribution of Programs & Films for Cable Television
S.I.C.: 7812
Dean Hollister *(Chm Bd.)*
Thomas M. Bachmann *(Pres. & Chief Exec. Officer)*
Paul Olsewski *(V.P.-Opers. & Corp. Sec.)*
Grace Cede *(Chief Information Officer & V.P.-MIS)*
Michael Wallace *(V.P.-Fin.)*

Computer Systems/Hardware:
IBM

Subsidiary:

Chanlon Video Arts **(1)**
121 Chanlon Rd.
New Providence, NJ 07974
Tel.: 908-344-6700
Music Video Production
S.I.C.: 7812

SBC ADVERTISING

SBC ADVERTISING
707 Park Meadow Rd.
Columbus, OH 43081
Tel.: 614-891-7070
Fax: 614-891-3664
Year Founded: 1969
Approx.Billings: $35,000,000
Emp.: 80
William A. Wickham *(Pres.)*
Richard Adams *(Sr. V.P., Gen. Mgr.)*
David M. Dennis *(Sr. V.P., Chief Fin. Officer & Treas.)*
Brian Harkness *(Sr. V.P., Dir. Pub. Rels.)*

SBN SYSTEM INC.
(Formerly National Business Systems, Inc.)
1530 Progress Rd.
Fort Wayne, IN 46808
Tel.: 416-671-3334
Approx.Sls.: $165,000,000
Emp.: 1,600
Fiscal Year-end: 9/30/90
Credit Card & Credit Related Services
S.I.C.: 7389
Timoth Casgrain *(Pres. & Chief Exec. Officer)*

Division:

Imaging Systems Division **(1)**
1530 Progress Rd.
Fort Wayne, IN 46808
Tel.: 219-484-8611
S.I.C.: 7389
Vincent L. Tofany *(Chief Exec. Officer)*

Subsidiaries:

NBS Imaging Systems, Inc. **(1)**
P.O. Box 8490, 1530 Progress Rd.
Fort Wayne, IN 46898-8490
Tel.: 219-484-8611
Fax: 219-482-2428
S.I.C.: 7389
Vincent L. Tofany *(Pres.)*
Nicholas Denice *(Gen. Mgr.)*

NBS Southern, Inc. **(1)**
11451 S. Belcher Rd.
Largo, FL 34643
Tel.: 813-541-2200
Fax: 813-546-8042
S.I.C.: 7389
Donald O'Neill *(Pres.)*

Applied Holographics, Inc. **(1)**
1530 Progress Rd.
Fort Wayne, IN 46898
Tel.: 219-484-8611
S.I.C.: 7389
Vincent Tofany *(Pres.)*

Card Technology Corporation **(1)**
70 Eisenhower Drive
Paramus, NJ 07652
Tel.: 201-845-7373
Fax: 201-845-3337
S.I.C.: 7389
Harold McNamara *(Gen. Mgr.)*

FundsNet, Inc. **(1)**
385 Nordhoff Pl.
Englewood, NJ 07631
Tel.: 201-569-7764
S.I.C.: 7389
Frederick Galland *(Chief Exec. Officer)*

Non-U.S. Holding:

Card Technology Corp. **(2)**
3198 Orlando Drive
Mississauga, Ontario Canada L4V 1R5
Tel.: 416-678-0411
Fax: 416-678-0430
Harold McNamara *(Gen. Mgr.)*

NBS Card Services, Inc. **(1)**
800 Montrose Ave.
South Plainfield, NJ 07080
Tel.: 908-668-0999
Fax: 908-668-7976
Al Vrancart *(Pres.)*

Non-U.S. Holdings:

NBS Limited-Card Services Division **(1)**
104 Oyster Lane Byfleet, Weybridge,
Surrey, United Kingdom KT14 7HJ
Tel.: 011-44-9323-54242
Fax: 011-44-9232-51380
Hester Havenga *(Fin. Controller)*

NBS Limited-Card Systems Division **(1)**
104 Oyster Lane Byfleet, Weybridge,
Surrey, United Kingdom KT14 7HJ
Tel.: 011-44-9323-51531
Fax: 011-44-9232-51382
Ray Amiri *(Fin. Controller)*

SBN Systems Inc.-Canadian Operations **(1)**
3206 Orlando Drive
Mississauga, Ontario Canada L4V 1R5
Tel.: 416-672-3777
Fax: 416-672-3993
Scott Magnacca *(Mgr.-Sls./Mktg.)*

SBN Systems Inc.-Corporate **(1)**
3220 Orlando Drive
Mississauga, Ontario Canada L4V 1R5
Tel.: 416-671-3334
Fax: 416-671-0690
Michael Knight *(Exec. V.P. & Chief Oper. Officer)*

SBN Systems Inc.-Imprinter Division **(1)**
171 Webster Rd.
Kitchener, Ontario Canada N2C 2E7
Tel.: 519-893-4510
Fax: 519-748-9843
Ian Holland *(Gen. Mgr.)*

SBN Systems Inc.-Montreal **(1)**
5640 Pare Street
Montreal, Quebec Canada H4P 2M1
Tel.: 514-735-1341
Fax: 514-342-9763
Jim Johnson *(Pres.)*

SC COMPANIES, INC.
Stanley Bldg., 225 Iowa Ave.
Muscatine, IA 52761
Tel.: 319-264-6600 **IA**
Fax: 319-264-6658
Year Founded: 1986
Approx.Sls.: $25,000,000
Emp.: 440
Fiscal Year-end: 3/31/92
Holding Company
S.I.C.: 6719; 8711; 8712
Corporate Giving Program: Company Participation is Very Limited
Richard H. Stanley *(Pres.)*
Richard C. Smith *(V.P. & Treas.)*
Ronald E. Barrett *(V.P.)*
Greg G. Thomopulos *(Exec. V.P.)*
Kathleen K. Johnson *(Corp. Sec.)*

Computer Systems/Hardware:
Burroughs 5900

Outside Service Firm(s):

McGladrey & Pullen*(Auditors)*
Davenport, IA

Stanley, Rehling, Lande & VanDerKamp*(Legal Firm)*
300 First Natl. Bank Bldg.
Muscatine, IA 52761
Tel.: 319-264-5000

First National Bank*(Major Banking Relationship)*
Muscatine, IA

Subsidiaries:

Middle West Service Company **(1)**
225 Iowa Ave.
Muscatine, IA 52761
Tel.: 319-264-6600 (100%)
Gas & Electric Rate Consultants
S.I.C.: 8742
Gregs G. Thomopulos *(Chm. Bd. & Pres.)*
Timothy E. Edwards *(V.P.)*
Richard J. Hutmacher *(V.P.)*
Walter D. Jones *(V.P.)*
James F. Lang *(V.P.)*
Robert J. Rusch *(V.P.)*

Stanley Consultants, Inc. **(1)**
Stanley Bldg., 225 Iowa Ave.
Muscatine, IA 52761
Tel.: 319-264-6600 (100%)
Engineering, Architectural & Surveying Services
S.I.C.: 8711; 8712
Richard H. Stanley *(Chm. Bd.)*
Gregs G. Thomopulos *(Pres.)*
Ronald J. Gear *(Sr. V.P.)*
Lloyd J. Larson *(Sr. V.P.)*
Richard A. Marr *(Sr. V.P.)*
Woodrow J. Moore, Jr. *(Sr. V.P.)*
David W. Grounds *(V.P.)*
Walter D. Jones *(V.P.)*
James A. Hollatz *(V.P.)*
Robert Houston *(V.P.)*
Michael E. Hunzinger *(V.P.)*
Kenneth W. Jacobs *(V.P.)*
James F. Lang *(V.P.)*
Richard W. Mettee *(V.P.)*
Charles L. Meyer *(V.P.)*
Herbert R. Ohrt *(V.P.)*
Charles J. Rauch *(V.P.)*
Robert J. Rusch *(V.P.)*
Steven J. Schebler *(V.P.)*
Lowell D. Titus *(V.P.)*
Richard E. Witter *(V.P.)*
Richard C. Smith *(Treas.)*
Kathleen K. Johnson *(Sec.)*

SCC HOLDING CO.
1700 Old Deerfield Rd.
Highland Park, IL 60035
Tel.: 708-831-4800
Fax: 708-831-0421
Assets: $160,000,000
Earnings: $160,000,000
Liabilities: $40,000,000
Net Worth: $120,000,000
Approx.Sls.: $400,000,000
Emp.: 3,500
Fiscal Year-end: 3/31/91
Export
Holding Company for Manufacturers & Distributors of Paper & Plastic Cups
S.I.C.: 6719; 2656; 3086; 5113
Robert L. Hulseman *(Pres.)*
Ronald L. Whaley *(Chief Fin. Officer, V.P. & Treas.)*
Paul F. Hulseman *(Exec. V.P. & Sec.)*
Robert Benstein *(V.P.-Sls. & Mktg.)*
E. Leo Carter *(V.P. & Asst. Sec.)*

Computer Systems/Hardware:
IBM

Outside Service Firm(s):

Fox & Grove*(Legal Firm)*
Chicago, IL

Harris Trust & Savings Bank*(Major Banking Relationship)*
111 W. Monroe St.
Chicago, IL 60690
Tel.: 312-461-2265
Tel.: 800-858-0840

Subsidiaries:

P.R. Solo Cup, Inc. **(1)**
1700 Old Deerfield Rd.
Highland Park, IL 60035
Tel.: 708-831-4800
S.I.C.: 5113

Solo Cup Company **(1)**
1700 Old Deerfield Road
Highland Park, IL 60035
Tel.: 708-831-4800
Emp.: 2,500
Solo Paper & Plastic Cups
S.I.C.: 2656; 3089; 2679
R.L. Hulseman *(Pres.)*
John Hulseman *(Exec. V.P. & Sec.)*
E.L. Carter *(V.P.)*
Ronald L. Whaley *(V.P.)*
D.J. Wolfe *(Dir.-Sls.)*
PeteGleave *(Mgr.-Mktg.)*

SCR, INC.
4550 SW Kruseway, Suite 215
Lake Oswego, OR 97035
Mailing Address:
P.O. Box 1607
Lake Oswego, OR 97035
Tel.: 503-635-1335
Fax: 503-635-3537
Year Founded: 1976
Approx.Sls.: $24,000,000
Emp.: 11
Fiscal Year-end: 5/31/92
Wholesale Forest Products, Plywood
S.I.C.: 5031
James T. Crabtree *(Pres.)*
Terry Crabtree *(V.P.)*
William B. Crabtree *(Sec. & Treas.)*
Principal(s):
James T. Crabtree

Outside Service Firm(s):

Rogers & Amos*(Auditors)*
Lake Oswego, OR

Stoel, Rives, Boley, Jones & Grey*(Legal Firm)*
900 S.W. 5th Ave., 23rd Fl.
Portland, OR 97204
Tel.: 503-224-3380

The Bank of California, N.A.*(Major Banking Relationship)*
Portland, OR

SCS ENGINEERS
3711 Long Beach Blvd.
Long Beach, CA 90807-3315
Tel.: 310-426-9544 **VA**
Fax: 310-427-0805
Year Founded: 1970
Approx.Sls.: $32,000,000
Emp.: 350
Fiscal Year-end: 3/31/92
Consulting Engineers; Solid & Hazardous Waste Management
S.I.C.: 8711
Corporate Giving Program: National organizations whose mission statement or creed includes Environmental Protection or conservation of natural resources (non-religious)
Robert P. Stearns *(Pres.)*
E.T. Conrad *(Exec. V.P.)*
David E. Ross *(Sr. V.P.)*
Anthony J. DiPuccio *(V.P.-Solid Waste Division)*
Miles J. Haven *(V.P.-Electronic Data Processing)*
R. Richard Johnson *(V.P.-Business Devel.)*
William L. Schubert *(V.P.-Fin. & Treas.)*
Christopher G. Ward *(V.P.-Hazardous Waste Division)*
Michael W. McLaughlin *(V.P. & Sec.)*
Robert B. Gardner *(V.P.)*
Henry Gold *(V.P.)*
Kenneth V. LaConde *(V.P.)*
David E. Roberson *(V.P.)*
Thomas Wetherill *(V.P.)*
James J. Walsh *(V.P.)*
John D. Wright *(V.P.)*
Elayne Welch *(Dir.-Human Resources)*

No. of U.S. Offices: 12
No. of Foreign Offices: 1

Outside Service Firm(s):

McGladrey & Pullen*(Auditors)*
222 S. Harbor Blvd. #800
Anaheim, CA 92815

Union Bank*(Major Banking Relationship)*
City of Industry, CA

Subsidiaries:

SCS Analytical Laboratory **(1)**
2860 Walnut Ave.
Long Beach, CA 90806-1834
Tel.: 310-595-9324
Fax: 310-595-6709
Testing Laboratories
S.I.C.: 8734
Lam Van Ho *(V.P.-Analytical Services)*

SCS Field Services **(1)**
4014 Long Beach Blvd.
Long Beach, CA 90807-3315
Tel.: 310-492-6222
Fax: 310-492-6210
Emp.: 40
Environmental Construction Services
S.I.C.: 1799
Galen Petoyan *(V.P.)*

SCT YARNS, INC.
1800 S. Watkins St.
Chattanooga, TN 37404
Mailing Address:
P.O. Box 791
Chattanooga, TN 37401
Tel.: 615-622-3131
Fax: 615-493-1844
Year Founded: 1891
Emp.: 1,200
Manufacture Yarn & Thread
S.I.C.: 2281; 2284
J.W. Thatcher *(Chm. Bd.)*
J. Don Trotter *(Pres. & Chief Exec. Officer)*
D.D. Groves *(V.P. & Chief Fin. Officer)*
Floyd Craig *(V.P.-Human Resources)*
J.C. Farrer *(Dir.-Data Processing)*

Computer Systems/Hardware:
IBM 4381

Outside Service Firm(s):

Deloitte & Touche*(Auditors)*
Chattanooga, TN

Provident Life & Accident Insurance Co.*(Group Insurer)*
P.O. Box 12015
Chattanooga, TN 37401
Tel.: 615-755-7088

Chambliss, Bahner, Crutchfield, Gaston & Irvine*(Legal Firm)*
1000 Tallon Building, 2 Union Square
Chattanooga, TN 37402
Tel.: 615-756-6011

First Tennessee Bank, N.A.*(Major Banking Relationship)*
701 Market St.
Chattanooga, TN 37402

Towers, Perrin, Forster & Crosby*(Pension Manager)*
Chattanooga, TN

SF SERVICES
824 N. Palm St.
North Little Rock, AR 72119
Mailing Address:
P.O. Box 5489,
North Little Rock, AR 72119
Tel.: 501-945-2371 **AR**
Fax: 501-945-7937
Year Founded: 1945
Assets: $138,243,840
Earnings: $8,249,000
Liabilities: $93,867,703
Net Worth: $44,376,137
Approx.Sls.: $316,000,000
Emp.: 800
Fiscal Year-end: 10/31/91
Wholesale Fertilizers, Seeds, Farm Supplies & Crop Protection Suppliers
S.I.C.: 5191; 5172; 5083; 5014; 5013; 2048; 0723
Johnny Wilson *(Chm. Bd.)*
Robert P. Dixon *(Pres. & Chief Exec. Officer)*
John Gaston *(Sr. V.P.-Corp. Services & Chief Fin. Officer)*
Daniel Viator *(Corp. Sec.)*

Computer Systems/Hardware:
IBM

Outside Service Firm(s):

Baird, Kurtz & Dobson*(Auditors)*
Little Rock, AR

Friday, Eldridge & Clark*(Legal Firm)*
2000 First Commercial Bldg.
Little Rock, AR 72201
Tel.: 501-376-2011

SFA, INC.
1401 McCormick Dr.
Landover, MD 20785
Tel.: 301-925-9400 **MD**
Fax: 301-925-8612
Year Founded: 1969
Assets: $11,327,523
Earnings: $903,995
Liabilities: $6,448,523
Net Worth: $4,879,000
Approx.Sls.: $32,980,165
Emp.: 350
Fiscal Year-end: 2/28/91
Export
Research in Physics, Chemistry, Electro-Optics, Fusion & Astronomy; Communications Systems Engineering; Computer Software Development, Tempest, Comsec; Mechanical Engineering; Automation and Robotics
S.I.C.: 8711; 8731
Dr. William C. Moyer *(Chm. Bd., Pres. & Chief Exec. Officer)*
Jerry D. Robinson *(Chief Fin. Officer, V.P. & Treas.)*
Dr. Ted Cohen *(V.P.-Research & Devel.)*
Joan Saidman *(Dir.-Personnel)*
Sandy Woodward *(Dir.-Corp. Communications)*
Donald Nowak *(Mgr.-Telecommunications)*
Pam Mattingly *(Pur. Agent)*
Principal(s):
Dr. William C. Moyer

No. of U.S. Offices: 5

Computer Systems/Hardware:
IBM; Compact; Zenith; Osborne; DEC VAX 11/730; DEC VAX 8350; Sperry-Univac; Multiflow

SFA, Inc.—(Continued)

Outside Service Firm(s):

Canto, Metro, Meyer*(Auditors)*
Bethesda, MD

Comprehensive Benefits*(Group Insurer)*
Philadelphia, PA

Silver, Friedman & Taff*(Legal Firm)*
1735 Eye St., N.W., 11th Fl.
Washington, DC 20006
Tel.: 202-429-6100
Fax: 202-833-3295

Riggs National Bank of Washington, D.C.*(Major Banking Relationship)*
P.O. Box 96206, 1120 Vermont Ave. N.W.
Washington, DC 20090-6206
Tel.: 202-835-4082

Riggs National Bank of Washington, D.C.*(Pension Manager)*
P.O. Box 96206, 1120 Vermont Ave. N.W.
Washington, DC 20090-6206
Tel.: 202-835-4082

SFM MEDIA CORPORATION
1180 Avenue of the Americas • New York, N.Y. 10036
(212) 790-4800

SFM MEDIA CORPORATION
1180 Ave. of the Americas
New York, NY 10036
Tel.: 212-790-4800
Twx: 710-581-2874
Year Founded: 1969
Approx.Billings: $724,000,000
Emp.: 126
Walter Staab *(Chm. & Pres.)*
Stanley Moger *(Pres.-SFM Entertainment Div.)*
Robert Frank *(Pres.-Media Services Div.)*
Jordan Ringel *(Sr. V.P., Bus. Affairs)*
Joseph Gerard *(Sr. V.P., Chief Fin. Officer)*
Malcolm Collins *(Dir., Fin.)*
Susan Hansen *(Dir., Billing & Accts.)*
Patrick Flynn *(Controller)*
Lorraine Hopkins *(Office Mgr.)*
David Merz *(Mgr., Data Processing)*

S-G METALS INDUSTRIES, INC.
2nd & Riverview
Kansas City, KS 66118
Mailing Address:
P.O. Box 2039
Kansas City, KS 66110
Tel.: 913-621-4100 **MO**
Fax: 913-621-4100
Year Founded: 1911
Approx.Sls.: $45,000,000
Emp.: 50
Fiscal Year-end: 10/31/92
Manufacture Aluminum, Brass, Copper & Zinc Ingots, Steel; Distribute Steel Pipe & Tubing
S.I.C.: 3331; 3339; 3334; 5039
Louis G. Galamba, Jr. *(Pres.)*
Erwin R. Sackin *(V.P.)*
L. Homer Orr *(Comptroller & Personnel Dir.)*
K. Wright *(Mgr.-Adv.)*

Computer Systems/Hardware:
Burroughs

Outside Service Firm(s):

Deloitte & Touche*(Auditors)*
1010 Grand Ave.
Kansas City, MO 64106-2232
Tel.: 816-474-6180

Stinson, Mag & Fizzell*(Legal Firm)*
1201 Walnut
Kansas City, MO 64106
Tel.: 816-842-8600

Commerce Bank of Kansas City*(Major Banking Relationship)*
10th & Walnut
Kansas City, MO 64141
Tel.: 816-234-2000
Fax: 816-234-2548

SGD INTERNATIONAL CORP.
(Formerly SGD Holding Corporation)
888 Seventh Ave., Ste. 603
New York, NY 10019
Tel.: 212-265-9000 **DE**
Fax: 212-265-9123
Year Founded: 1982
Approx.Sls.: $215,000,000
Emp.: 40
Fiscal Year-end: 3/31/92

Import Export
International Bartering & Exchange of Services; Import & Export
S.I.C.: 7299; 7389
Jerry Galuten *(Chm. Bd. & Pres.)*
Keith Galuten *(Exec. V.P.)*
Don Duncon *(Grp. V.P.)*
Dick Rogers *(Chief Fin. Officer)*
Sandra L. Galuten *(Treas.)*
Jody Gerber *(Gen. Counsel)*
Milessa Brooks *(Dir.-Admin.)*
Bill Curtis *(Dir.-Adv.)*
Paule Herp *(Dir.-Fin.)*
D. Walker *(Dir.-Data Processing)*
Ian Philips *(Legal Officer)*
Monica Coleman *(Pur. Agent-Services)*
Sandy Jackson *(Pur. Agent-Equipment)*

No. of U.S. Offices: 2
No. of Foreign Offices: 3

Computer Systems/Hardware:
IBM

Outside Service Firm(s):

Shea & Gould*(Legal Firm)*
1251 Avenue of the Americas
New York, NY 10020
Tel.: 212-827-3000

Republic National Bank*(Major Banking Relationship)*
355 Lexington Ave.
New York, NY 10017
Tel.: 212-573-5514

SGI INC.
1471 Elmwood Ave.
Cranston, RI 02910
Tel.: 401-461-0200
Tel.: 1-800-695-7600
Fax: 401-461-0602
Year Founded: 1976
Earnings: $800,000
Approx.Sls.: $30,000,000
Emp.: 70
Fiscal Year-end: 12/31/90

Import
Distributor & Manufacturer of Luggage & Sport Bags
S.I.C.: 3161; 5099
Jeffrey M. Jacober *(Pres. & Chief Exec. Officer)*
Dennis J. Carvalho *(Exec. V.P. & Chief Fin. Officer)*
Paul Oberg *(V.P.)*
Dave Rossi *(V.P.-Mktg.)*
Michael Tobin *(V.P. & Sec.)*
Robert Rainville *(Dir.-Pur.)*
Antone Macedo *(Engineer-Res. & Dev.)*
John Johnson *(Mgr.-Telecommunications)*
Lorraine Manchester *(Admin. Sec.)*

SI HOLDINGS INC.
730 Broadway
New York, NY 10003
Tel.: 212-505-3000 **DE**
Fax: 215-505-3377
Year Founded: 1986
Assets: $143,068,000
Earnings: $3,580,000
Liabilities: $154,346,000
Net Worth: $11,278,000
Approx.Rev.: $299,580,000
Emp.: 1,700
Holding Company; Publisher, Educational Software & Television Features
S.I.C.: 6719; 7812; 2721; 7372
Richard Robinson *(Chm. Bd., Pres. & Chief Exec. Officer)*
Richard Spaulding *(Exec. V.P. & Chief Fin. Officer)*
Frederic J. Bischoff *(V.P. & Chief Fin. Officer)*
Anthony Sacchitelli *(V.P.)*
Katherine Ryden *(V.P.)*
Susan Konn-McCormick *(Treas.)*

Outside Service Firm(s):

Ernst & Young*(Auditors)*
787 Seventh Ave.
New York, NY 10019
Tel.: 212-773-1243

Coudert Brothers*(Legal Firm)*
200 Park Ave.
New York, NY 10166
Tel.: 212-880-4400

United Jersey Bank*(Major Banking Relationship)*
Newark, NJ

Subsidiary:

Scholastic Inc. **(1)**
730 Broadway
New York, NY 10003
Tel.: 212-505-3000 (100%)
Fax: 212-505-3360
Emp.: 1,600
Fiscal Year-end: 12/31/90
Publishing of Scholastic Magazines & Books for School & Home; Educational Computer Software; Educational Television Features
S.I.C.: 2721; 2731; 2741; 7372; 7812
Richard Robinson *(Chm. Bd., Pres. & Chief Exec. Officer)*
Frederic J. Bischoff *(Exec. V.P. & Chief Fin. Officer)*
Barbara Marcus *(Exec. V.P.-Children's Book Pblg.)*
Richard M. Spaulding *(Exec. V.P.-Scholastic, Inc.)*
Ernest Fleishman *(Sr. V.P.-Magazine Grp.)*
David J. Walsh *(Sr. V.P.-Intl.)*
Michele Magazine *(Sr. V.P.-Magazine Grp.)*
Michael Bangs *(Div. V.P.-Information Systems)*
Stephen Bernard *(Div. V.P.-Circulation & Mktg., Magazine Grp.)*
Jean Feiwel *(Div. V.P.-Book Grp.)*
Martin J. Keltz *(V.P.-Scholastic Production)*
Katherine Ryden *(V.P.-Human Resources)*
Frank Grobowski *(V.P.-Book Mfg.)*
Cynthia Harrison *(V.P.-Corp. Communication)*
Peter Kelman *(V.P.-Software Div.)*
Raymond Marchuk *(V.P.-Fin. Opers.)*
Judy Diamond *(V.P.-Field Opers., Book Grp.)*
D. Stertzer *(V.P.-Distr.)*
J. Startz *(V.P.-Scholastic Productions)*
Edward Monagle *(V.P. & Bus. Mgr.-Book Grp.)*
Paul Reiss *(V.P. & Assoc. Publr.-Home Office Computing)*
D. Forte *(V.P.-Scholastic Productions)*
Lynette E. Allison *(V.P.-Gen. Counsel & Sec.)*
Bernadette Gray *(Exec. Editor-Home Office Computing)*
Leslie Lista *(Controller)*
Susan Konn McCormick *(Treas.)*

Divisions:

Scholastic Inc. Information Center **(2)**
1290 Wall St. West
Lyndhurst, NJ 07071
Tel.: 201-939-8050
Computer Services for Company
S.I.C.: 7372
Michael Bangs *(Chief Oper. Officer)*

Scholastic Inc. National Distribution Center **(2)**
P.O. Box 1068,
Jefferson City, MO 65101
Tel.: 314-636-5271
Emp.: 205
Distribution Center
S.I.C.: 2721
Donald R. Stertzer *(V.P. & Chief Oper. Officer)*

Subsidiaries:

California School Book Fairs, Inc. **(2)**
1221 N. Lakeview Ave.
Anaheim, CA 92806
Tel.: 714-970-2700 (80%)
Emp.: 50
Arranges Fairs for Sale of Books
S.I.C.: 5963
James B. Carsky *(Pres.)*

Scholastic Book Fairs, Inc. **(2)**
P.O. Box 178,
Longwood, FL 32750
Tel.: 305-831-9977 (100%)
Emp.: 90
Arranges Fairs for Sale of Books
S.I.C.: 5963
James B. Carsky *(Pres.)*

Scholastic Productions Inc. **(2)**
730 Broadway
New York, NY 10003
Tel.: 212-505-3000 (100%)
Produces Educational Films
S.I.C.: 7812
Martin J. Keltz *(Pres.)*

Non-U.S. Holdings:

Ashton/Scholastic Pty. Ltd. **(1)**
P.O. Box 579
Gosford, N.S.W. 2250, Australia
Tel.: 43-283-555 (100%)
Twx: 79024881-TDNASH
Approx.Sls.: $14,000,000
Emp.: 125
Educational Publishers
S.I.C.: 2731
Ken Jolly *(Mng. Dir.)*

Ashton/Scholastic Pty. Ltd. **(1)**
165 Marua Rd. P.O. Box 12328,
Panmure, Auckland 6, New Zealand
Tel.: 649-596-089 (100%)
Twx: 79121203-ASHCO
Approx.Sls.: $3,900,000
Emp.: 57
Educational Publishers
S.I.C.: 2731
Graham Beattie *(Mng. Dir.)*

Scholastic Publications Ltd. **(1)**
Merlborough House, Holly Walk
Leamington Spa, Warwickshire 33 OJH, United Kingdom
Tel.: 92-681-3910 (100%)
Twx: 312138 SPLS
Approx.Sls.: $10,000,000
Emp.: 110
Publisher-Periodicals
S.I.C.: 2731; 2721
John Cox *(Mng. Dir.)*

Scholastic-Canada, Ltd. **(1)**
123 Newkirk Rd.
Richmond Hill, ON L4C 3G5, Canada
Tel.: 416-883-5300 (100%)
Twx: 610 492-2620
Approx.Sls.: $13,000,000
Emp.: 170
Publisher of Paperback Books for Children
S.I.C.: 2731
F.C.L. Muller *(Pres.)*

SJL OF KANSAS CORP.
833 N. Main
Wichita, KS 67203
Mailing Address:
P.O. Box 333,
Wichita, KS 67201
Tel.: 316-265-3333 **KS**
Fax: 316-292-1197
Year Founded: 1955
Sales Range: $10-19 Million
Emp.: 96
Fiscal Year-end: 12/31/91
Television Broadcasting
S.I.C.: 4833; 4899

George D. Lilly *(Pres. & Treas.)*
Marc Luedtke *(Chief Oper. Officer)*
Robert D. McCurdy *(V.P. & Sec.)*
Allan C. Buch *(V.P. & Gen. Mgr.)*
Georgianna Kurtz *(Chief Fin. Officer & Bus. Mgr.)*
Connie Armstrong *(Dir.-Personnel)*
Michael Hanrahan *(Mgr.-Mktg.)*
James Tellus *(Mgr.-Promo.)*
Anne Harper *(Admin. Asst.)*

Computer Systems/Hardware:
IBM System 36

Outside Service Firm(s):

KPMG Peat Marwick*(Auditors)*
Wichita, KS

Bank IV*(Major Banking Relationship)*
Wichita, KS

Travelers Insurance Co.*(Commercial Insurance Carrier)*
Chicago, IL

Northwestern National Life Insurance Co.*(Group Insurer)*
20 Washington Ave. S.
Minneapolis, MN 55401
Tel.: 612-372-5432
Fax: 612-342-3966

Foulston & Siefkin*(Legal Firm)*
700 Fourth Financial Center
Wichita, KS 67202
Tel.: 316-267-6371

Divisions:

KSNC **(1)**
N. Hwy. 281, P.O. Box 689
Great Bend, KS 67530
Tel.: 316-793-7868
Fax: 316-793-7868
Emp.: 15
Television Broadcasting
S.I.C.: 4833
Mark Nichols *(Station Mgr.)*

KSNG **(1)**
P.O. Box 1076
Garden City, KS 67846
Tel.: 316-275-1101
Fax: 316-275-0576
Emp.: 8
Television Broadcasting
S.I.C.: 4833
Sharolyn Mayfield *(Station Mgr.)*

KSNK **(1)**
P.O. Box 238,
Oberlin, KS 67749
Tel.: 913-475-2248
Fax: 913-475-3944
Emp.: 7
Television Broadcasting
S.I.C.: 4833
Dwayne Detter *(Station Mgr.)*

Subsidiary:

Topeka Television, Corp. **(1)**
6835 N.W. U.S. Hwy. 24
Topeka, KS 66618
Tel.: 913-582-4000 (100%)
Emp.: 60
Television Broadcasting
S.I.C.: 4833
Perry Chester *(V.P. & G.M.)*

Station:

KSNT **(2)**
6835 N.W. U.S. Hwy. 24
Topeka, KS 66618
Tel.: 913-582-4000
Fax: 913-582-5283
Television Broadcasting
S.I.C.: 4833
Perry Chester *(V.P. & G.M.)*

SK HAND TOOL CORP.
3535 W. 47th St.
Chicago, IL 60632
Tel.: 312-523-1300 **IL**
Telex: 756359
Fax: 312-523-2103
Year Founded: 1923
Assets: $24,377,000
Earnings: $2,019,000
Liabilities: $11,320,000
Net Worth: $13,057,000
Approx.Sls.: $43,007,000
Emp.: 382
Fiscal Year-end: 9/30/91
Export
Manufacture & Distribute Mechanics' Hand Tools
S.I.C.: 3423
I.R. Forte *(Pres.)*
Michael D. Miller *(V.P.-Mktg.)*
David W. Fred *(V.P.-Sls.)*
Richard Dowd *(V.P.-Logistics & Control & Controller)*
Leonard D. O'Connell *(Dir.-Personnel)*
Franklin J. Adams *(Dir.-Pur.)*
Dennis D. Vanderplow *(Mgr.-MIS)*
Tim Herrick *(Mgr.-Quality Control)*
Ed Kern *(Mgr.-Export Sls.)*
Frank Adams *(Mgr.-Corp. Pur.)*
Leonard O'Connell *(Mgr.-Corp. Personnel)*
Bill Gardiner *(Plant Mgr.)*
Anthony Bishop *(Plant Mgr.)*

No. of Mfg. Plants/Facilities: 2
No. of U.S. Offices: 2

Computer Systems/Hardware:
Wang VS 85

Outside Service Firm(s):

Cray Kaiser Ltd.*(Auditors)*
Oakbrook Terrace, IL

American National Bank & Trust Company of Chicago*(Major Banking Relationship)*
33 N. LaSalle St.
Chicago, IL 60602
Tel.: 312-661-5000
Fax: 312-661-6417

Arthur J. Gallagher & Co.*(Commercial Insurance Carrier)*
Rolling Meadows, IL

Banque Nationale de Paris*(International Bank Affiliate)*
200 N. Lasalle St.
Chicago, IL 60601
Tel.: 312-977-2200

Parker, Hudson, Rainer & Dobbs*(Legal Firm)*
Atlanta, GA

Nationwide Insurance*(Pension Manager)*
Columbus, OH

SKR RESOURCES, INC.
307 Fifth Ave.
New York, NY 10016
Tel.: 212-545-0015
Fax: 212-779-9879
Year Founded: 1989
Approx.Billings: $23,000,000
Emp.: 11
Exchange of Adv., Goods & Services for Merchandise
Robert J. Richards *(Pres. & Chief Exec. Officer)*
Hal Narotzky *(V.P.)*
Beth I. Shadowitz *(Gen. Counsel)*
George Strangos *(Dir., Remarketing Services)*
Mary Richards *(Billing Mgr.)*
Carol Place *(Office Supvr.)*

S L C GRAPHICS, INC.
50 Rock St.
Pittston, PA 18640
Tel.: 717-655-9681
Approx.Sls.: $24,000,000
Emp.: 200
Fiscal Year-end: 12/31/91
Offset Printing of Publications & Magazines
S.I.C.: 2752
Nick G. Karabots *(Chm. Bd.)*
Thomas Geary *(Sr. V.P.)*
Donald L. Bill *(V.P.-Opers.)*
Robert Davis *(Treas.)*
Charles Huey *(Controller)*
John Walton *(Sec.)*
Helen DeGilio *(Dir.-Pur.)*
Andrea Duloc *(Dir.-Human Resources)*
James Killian *(Dir.-Mktg.)*

No. of Mfg. Plants/Facilities: 1
No. of U.S. Offices: 1

Outside Service Firm(s):

Morgan, Lewis & Bockius*(Legal Firm)*
123 So. Broad St.
Philadelphia, PA 19109
Tel.: 215-875-2500

First Eastern Bank N.A.*(Major Banking Relationship)*
11 West Market St.
Wilkes-Barre, PA 18768
Tel.: 717-826-4603

SLM, INC.
P.O. Box 1070, RDI Patch Rd.
Gloversville, NY 12078
Tel.: 518-725-8101
Fax: 800-725-8155
Approx.Sls.: $200,000,000
Emp.: 300
Export
Mfr. of Buddy L Toys
S.I.C.: 3944
Earl Takefman *(Vice Chm.)*
David Zunenshine *(Chief Exec. Officer)*
Pierre Rochon *(Pres.)*
David Johnson *(Exec. V.P.-Sls.)*
Matt Ludak *(Sr. V.P.-Sls.)*
Harold Price *(V.P.-Sls.)*
Robert Wanke *(V.P.-Mktg.)*
Margie Oyola *(Mgr.-Office)*

Computer Systems/Hardware:
MAI Basic 4

Outside Service Firm(s):

Mann, Judd, Landau*(Auditors)*
New York, NY
Tel.: 212-661-5500

Chubb Group*(Commercial Insurance Carrier)*
P.O. Box 1615,
Warren, NJ 07061
Tel.: 201-580-2000

Finley, Kumble, Wagner, Heine & Underberg*(Legal Firm)*
425 Park Ave.
New York, NY 10022
Tel.: 212-371-5900

Hopgood, Calimafde, Kalil, Blaustein, Judlowe*(Legal Firm)*
New York, NY

SOR INC.
14685 W. 105th St.
Lenexa, KS 66215
Mailing Address:
P.O. Box 15964
Lenexa, KS 66215
Tel.: 913-888-2630
Fax: 913-888-0767
Year Founded: 1967
Assets: $14,162,000
Liabilities: $9,050,000
Net Worth: $5,112,000
Approx.Sls.: $18,000,000
Emp.: 180
Fiscal Year-end: 12/31/90
Import Export
Mfr. of Pressure & Temperature Switches; Static O Ring & SOR; Level & Flow Switches; SOR
S.I.C.: 3822
Roy R. Dunlap *(Chm. Bd.)*
Lew Goetz *(Pres. & Chief Exec. Officer)*
G. David Fisher *(Chief Fin. Officer, V.P. & Controller)*
L. Keith Gann *(Exec. V.P. & Gen. Mgr.)*
David Dunlap *(V.P.)*
Russ Engel *(V.P.)*
Steve K. Highberger *(Dir.-Sls.)*
John Kimbrow *(Dir.-Data Processing)*
Russell Longley *(Dir.-Mktg.)*
Colbert Turney *(Mgr.-Quality Control)*
Jane Peternel *(Nuclear Sls. Coordinator)*
Principal(s):
Roy R. Dunlap

No. of Mfg. Plants/Facilities: 3
No. of U.S. Offices: 2
No. of Foreign Offices: 1

Computer Systems/Hardware:
IBM AS/400

Outside Service Firm(s):

Wolkow, Sharp, Calys & Flint*(Auditors)*
Overland Park, KS

Nationwide Insurance*(Commercial Insurance Carrier)*
One Nationwide Plaza
Columbus, OH 43216
Tel.: 614-249-6488

Shook, Hardy & Bacon*(Legal Firm)*
One Kansas City Place
Kansas City, MO 64105
Tel.: 816-474-6550

Commerce Bank of Kansas City*(Major Banking Relationship)*
10th & Walnut
Kansas City, MO 64141
Tel.: 816-234-2000
Fax: 816-234-2548

Non-U.S. Holding:

SOR Europe, Ltd. **(1)**
2 Star Rd. Partridge Green,
Horsham, Sussex RH13 8RA, United Kingdom (100%)

S.P.C. TRANSPORT
(Formerly S. Prawer & Co.)
150 Read St
Portland, ME 04104
Tel.: 207-775-0223
Fax: 207-775-5170
Year Founded: 1933
Sales Range: $20-39 Million
Emp.: 70
Wholesale Grocery, Dairy, & Non-Food Candy
S.I.C.: 5141; 5143; 5145; 5149
Gilbert Prawer *(Owner)*
Harvey Prawer *(Owner)*
Tod Prawer *(Owner)*

Outside Service Firm(s):

Maine National Bank*(Major Banking Relationship)*
Portland, ME

SPD TECHNOLOGIES
13500 Roosevelt Blvd.
Philadelphia, PA 19116
Tel.: 215-677-4900
Fax: 215-677-1504
Year Founded: 1888
Emp.: 450
Export
Manufacture Military Circuit Breakers & Electrical Protection Equipment
S.I.C.: 3613; 3679
Vice Adm. Earl B. Fowler *(Chm. Bd.)*
Larry A. Colangelo *(Pres. & Chief Exec. Officer)*
John Fleury *(V.P. & Controller)*
Daniel W. Kerkel *(V.P.-Engrg. & Product Assurance)*
Robert R. Seher *(V.P.-Opers.)*
J.R. Slenn *(V.P.-Human Resources)*

SPD Technologies—(Continued)

John Ykema *(V.P. & Chief Technical Officer)*
Dan Schuster *(Dir.-Mktg.)*

Subsidiaries:

Henschel Corp. **(1)**
9 Hoyt Drive
Newburyport, MA 01950
Tel.: 617-462-2400 (100%)
Emp.: 175
Ship Controls & Interior Communication Systems for Commercial Shipping
S.I.C.: 3669
Gunter Waehling *(V.P. & Gen. Mgr.)*
Chas Wagner *(V.P.-Engrg.)*
John Carter *(V.P.-Mktg.)*
Mike Accardi *(V.P.-Fin.)*

Pacord **(1)**
206 W. 35th St.
National City, CA 92050
Tel.: 619-498-5000
Fax: 616-576-1034
Ship Repair
S.I.C.: 3731
Robert Hortsock *(V.P. & Gen. Mgr.)*

SPSS INC.
444 N. Michigan Ave.
Chicago, IL 60611
Tel.: 312-329-3500
Tel.: 800-543-6609 IL
Fax: 312-329-3668
Year Founded: 1975
Approx.Sls.: $36,000,000
Emp.: 250
Fiscal Year-end: 12/31/91
Computer Software
S.I.C.: 7372
Norman H. Nie *(Chm. Bd.)*
Jack Noonan *(Pres. & Chief Exec. Officer)*
Louise Rehling *(Sr. V.P.-Devel.)*
Ed Hamburg *(Sr. V.P.-Bus. Devel.)*
Sue Phelan *(V.P.-Sls.)*
Mark Battaglia *(V.P.-Mktg.)*
Ian Durrell *(V.P.-Intl. Opers.)*
David Pittman *(Sr. Mktg. Assoc.)*
Randy Pitzer *(Mgr.-Mktg. Communications)*

Non-U.S. Holding:

SPSS Europe B.V. **(1)**
P.O. Box 115, 4200 AC
Gorinchem, Netherlands
Tel.: 183036711 (100%)
Computer Software
S.I.C.: 7372

SRI INTERNATIONAL
333 Ravenswood Ave.
Menlo Park, CA 94025-3493
Tel.: 415-326-6200 CA
Telex: 334486
Fax: 415-326-5512
Year Founded: 1946
Approx.Sls.: $300,000,000
Emp.: 3,300
Engineering & Scientific Research; Business Consulting
S.I.C.: 8731; 8742
George M. Keller *(Chm. Bd.)*
James J. Tietjen *(Pres. & Chief Exec. Officer)*
Paul J. Jorgensen *(Chief Oper. Officer)*
John J. Oakson *(Chief Fin. Officer & V.P.)*
Arthur Chait *(Sr. V.P.-Bus. & Policy Grp.)*
Jon K. Clemens *(Sr. V.P.-Sciences & Tech. Grp.)*
John P. McHenry *(Sr. V.P.-Engrng. Res. Grp.)*
J. D. Gleckler *(V.P.-Human Resources)*
David Keaton *(V.P.-Commercial Sls.)*
Donald L. Andrews *(Treas.)*
Harold E. Kruth *(Sec. & Gen. Counsel)*
Peter Valenti *(Controller)*
Tom Little *(Corp. Dir.-Logistics)*

No. of U.S. Offices: 3
No. of Foreign Offices: 10

Computer Systems/Hardware:
Burroughs; DEC VAX; IBM

Outside Service Firm(s):

KPMG Peat Marwick*(Auditors)*
3 Embarcadero Center
San Francisco, CA 94111
Tel.: 415-951-0100
Fax: 415-397-1129

Travelers Insurance Co.*(Group Insurer)*
1 Tower Square
Hartford, CT 06183-2492
Tel.: 203-277-4542
Fax: 203-277-5038

Wells Fargo Bank*(Major Banking Relationship)*
420 Montgomery St.
San Francisco, CA 94104

Teachers Insurance Annuity Association*(Pension Manager)*
New York, NY

Subsidiaries:

David Sarnoff Research Center **(1)**
201 Washington Rd., P.O. Box 5300
Princeton, NJ 08543
Tel.: 609-734-2000
Emp.: 900
S.I.C.: 8731
James E. Carnes *(Pres. & Chief Oper. Officer)*

SRI Development Corp. **(1)**
333 Ravenswood Ave.
Menlo Park, CA 94025
Tel.: 415-326-6200

SRS TECHNOLOGIES
S. Tower, Ste. 402, 3501 Jamboree Rd.
Newport Beach, CA 92660
Mailing Address:
P.O. Box 9219,
Newport Beach, CA 92658-9219
Tel.: 714-854-5400 CA
Fax: 714-854-2300
Year Founded: 1970
Assets: $18,511,000
Earnings: $536,000
Liabilities: $12,175,129
Net Worth: $6,335,871
Approx.Sls.: $37,000,000
Emp.: 380
Defense Electronics Research & Development.; Systems Engineering & Technical Support; Software Development & O/M; Range Support; Test, Evaluation & Training
S.I.C.: 3761; 7372; 7379; 8731; 8711
M.S. Sandhu *(Chm. Bd., Pres. & Chief Exec. Officer)*
James Stovall *(Controller)*
Rick Bruce *(Corp. Sec.)*
Connie Campanile *(Dir.-Personnel)*
Principal(s):
R.O. Conroy
D. Lorinzini
J. Allburn
W. Mead
R.R. Murrel
R.M. Shields

No. of U.S. Offices: 17

Computer Systems/Hardware:
DEC VAX 11/750, 11/780

Outside Service Firm(s):

KPMG Peat Marwick*(Auditors)*
Center Tower, 650 Town Center Drive
Costa Mesa, CA 92626
Tel.: 714-850-4300

Alex. Brown & Sons*(Investment Banker)*
135 E. Baltimore St.
Baltimore, MD 21202
Tel.: 301-727-1700
Fax: 301-783-3197

Sterling, Yocca & Rauth*(Legal Firm)*
Newport Beach, CA

Wells Fargo Bank*(Major Banking Relationship)*
420 Montgomery St.
San Francisco, CA 94104

SSD&W INTEGRATED MARKETING COMMUNICATIONS
350 Main Rd.
Montville, NJ 07045
Tel.: 201-299-8000
Fax: 201-299-7937
Year Founded: 1979
Approx.Billings: $14,000,000
Emp.: 28
Andrew Scelba *(Chm.)*
David F. Scelba *(Chief Exec. Officer)*
Louis DeTitta, Jr. *(Pres., Chief Oper. Officer)*
Stephen Dick *(Exec. V.P., Mktg. Services)*
Edward F. Gardner *(Exec. V.P.)*
Patrick Brightman *(Pub. Rels. Mgr.)*
Carl Ackerman *(Controller)*
Patricia Hardy *(Bookkeeper-A/P)*
Denise Thompson *(Bookkeeper-A/R)*
Frank P. Giarratano, Jr. *(Telecommunications Dir.)*
James C. Callahan *(MIS Dir.)*

S-T INDUSTRIES, INC.
301 Armstrong Blvd. N.
Saint James, MN 56081
Mailing Address:
P.O. Box 29
St. James, MN 56081
Tel.: 507-375-3211 MN
Fax: 507-375-4503
Year Founded: 1983
Assets: $4,800,000
Liabilities: $2,800,000
Net Worth: $2,000,000
Approx.Sls.: $10,000,000
Emp.: 130
Fiscal Year-end: 10/31/90
Import Export
Manufacture Precision Measuring Tools & Optical Comparitors
S.I.C.: 3545; 3423
LeRoy T. Smith *(Chm. Bd., Pres. & Chief Exec. Officer)*
Michael J. Smith *(V.P. & Treas.)*
G. Lillevold *(V.P.-Engrng.)*
J. Koch *(Dir.-Pur.)*
Robert Friesen *(Mgr.-Mktg. & Sls.)*
Martha Miller *(Mgr.-Govt. Sls.)*
Principal(s):
LeRoy T. Smith

No. of Mfg. Plants/Facilities: 1
No. of U.S. Offices: 1

Computer Systems/Hardware:
IBM

Outside Service Firm(s):

KPMG Peat Marwick*(Auditors)*
4200 Norwest Center, 90 S. 7th St.
Minneapolis, MN 55402
Tel.: 612-341-2222

Fireman's Fund Insurance Co.*(Commercial Insurance Carrier)*
San Francisco, CA

Lincoln National Life Insurance Co.*(Group Insurer)*
PO Box 208, 1300 S. Clinton
Fort Wayne, IN 46801
Tel.: 219-455-2926
Fax: 219-455-7619

Fredrikson & Byron, P.A.*(Legal Firm)*
1100 International Centre, 900 2nd Ave. S.
Minneapolis, MN 55402
Tel.: 612-347-7000

S.T. RESEARCH
8419 Terminal Rd.
Newington, VA 22122
Mailing Address:
P.O. Box 1430
Newington, VA 22122-1430
Tel.: 703-550-7000 VA
Fax: 703-550-7470
Year Founded: 1991
Approx.Sls.: $12,000,000
Emp.: 125
Fiscal Year-end: 9/30/91
Export
Research & Development; Manufacture Electronic Equipment
S.I.C.: 3699; 8731
S. Ronald Perrino *(Chm. Bd., Pres. & Chief Exec. Officer)*
Robert R. Bower *(Sr. V.P.)*
Don Reiser *(Sr. V.P.-Engrng.)*
Robert Watson *(Controller)*
Connie Knoernschild *(Human Resources)*
Tony Romero *(MIS)*

Computer Systems/Hardware:
DEC VAX 11750

Outside Service Firm(s):

Ross, Langan & McKendree*(Auditors)*
6829 Elm
McLean, VA 22101
Tel.: 703-893-2660

Long & Foster*(Commercial Insurance Carrier)*
Fairfax, VA

NationsBank*(Major Banking Relationship)*
35 Broad St.
Atlanta, GA 30303
Tel.: 404-581-2121
Tel.: 800-848-8198

STG MARKETING COMMUNICATIONS, INC.
883 Black Rock Turnpike
Fairfield, CT 06430
Tel.: 203-579-1640
Fax: 203-334-6865
Year Founded: 1971
Approx.Billings: $12,225,000
Emp.: 16
George Tibball *(Pres.)*
George Crosby *(V.P.)*
Lorraine Frauenhoffer *(Office Mgr.)*

STS HOLDINGS, INC.
111 Pfingsten Rd.
Northbrook, IL 60062
Mailing Address:
P.O. Box 1009
Northbrook, IL 60062
Tel.: 708-272-6520
Fax: 708-498-2721
Year Founded: 1948
Approx.Sls.: $42,000,000
Emp.: 450
Fiscal Year-end: 12/31/90
Holding Company; Civil Engineering, Hydropower Developers, Insurance, Landfill Developers
S.I.C.: 6719
Clyde N. Baker, Jr. *(Chm. Bd.)*
Michael T. Russell *(Pres.)*
Douglas E. Keats *(Chief Exec. Officer)*
John P. Cross *(Sr. V.P.)*
J. Steven Angell *(Sr. V.P.)*
Mark J. Sundquist *(Sr. V.P.)*

Peter J. Bulandr *(Sr. V.P.)*
William M. Perpich *(Sr. V.P.)*
Daniel T. Stone *(V.P. & Treas.)*
Philip C. Best *(V.P. & Sec.)*

No. of U.S. Offices: 7

Computer Systems/Hardware:
Digital

Outside Service Firm(s):

Arthur Andersen & Co.*(Auditors)*
33 W. Monroe St.
Chicago, IL 60603-4067
Tel.: 312-580-0033
Fax: 312-507-6748

Jenner & Block*(Legal Firm)*
One IBM Plaza
Chicago, IL 60611
Tel.: 312-222-9350

CNA Insurance*(Major Banking Relationship)*
CNA Plaza,
Chicago, IL 60685
Tel.: 312-822-5000

The Northern Trust Co.*(Major Banking Relationship)*
30 S. LaSalle St.
Chicago, IL 60675
Tel.: 312-630-6000

Subsidiary:

STS Consultants, Ltd. **(1)**
111 Pfingsten Rd.
Northbrook, IL 60062
Tel.: 708-272-6520
Fax: 708-498-2721
Civil Consulting Firm Specializing in Geotechnical & Materials Engineering, Geo-Environmental & Water Resources
S.I.C.: 8711; 8741; 4941
Clyde N. Baker, Jr. *(Chm. Bd.)*
Douglas E. Keats *(Pres.)*

S.W. JR. ENTERPRISES, INC.
(d/b/a Wolfe Lumber)
2031 Orchard Dr., Ste. 201
Santa Ana Heights, CA 92707
Mailing Address:
P.O. Box 8751
Newport Beach, CA 92658-8751
Tel.: 714-261-8099 **CA**
Fax: 714-261-5751
Year Founded: 1983
Assets: $5,325,600
Liabilities: $3,300,000
Net Worth: $2,025,600
Approx.Sls.: $36,000,000
Emp.: 10
Retail Lumber
S.I.C.: 5211
Corporate Giving Program:
Percentage of Corporate Profit Returned to Community Charitable Needs in Addition to Yearly Scholarships to a Graduating High School Senior
Sterling H. Wolfe, Jr. *(Pres.)*
Nancy A. Bruss *(Controller)*
Troy Tate *(Gen. Counsel)*
Don Peters *(Dir.-Pur.)*

Outside Service Firm(s):

Sparks & Company*(Auditors)*
Costa Mesa, CA

Tolmam & Wiker Insurance*(Commercial Insurance Carrier)*
Ventura, CA
Tel.: 805-653-7744

Call, Clayton & Jensen*(Legal Firm)*
Newport Beach, CA

Union Bank*(Major Banking Relationship)*
Orange, CA

SABBETH INDUSTRIES LTD
55 N. Industry Court
Deer Park, NY 11729
Mailing Address:
P.O. Box 652
Deer Park, NY 11729
Tel.: 516-242-0303
Telex: 961773
Fax: 516-242-0483
Fax: 516-242-7963
Year Founded: 1961
Approx.Sls.: $83,000,000
Emp.: 200
Fiscal Year-end: 9/30/91
Export
Wholesale Lumber & Forest Products
S.I.C.: 5031
Stephen J. Sabbeth *(Chm. Bd. & Pres.)*
Joseph Paladino *(V.P.-Fin.)*
John Radomski *(Gen. Mgr. & Mgr. Sls.)*

No. of Mfg. Plants/Facilities: 4
No. of U.S. Offices: 4

Outside Service Firm(s):

Margolin, Winer, & Evens*(Auditors)*
Garden City, NY

Gutman & Gutman*(Legal Firm)*
19 Roslyn Rd.
New York, NY 11501

Fleet Bank*(Major Banking Relationship)*
Deer Park, NY 14202

Subsidiaries:

Diversified Wood Products **(1)**
55 N. Industry Ct.
Deer Park, NY 11729
Tel.: 516-242-0303
Fax: 516-242-0483
Wholesale Lumber
S.I.C.: 5031

Sabbeth International Forest Products **(1)**
55 N. Industry Ct.
Deer Park, NY 11729
Tel.: 516-242-0303
Fax: 516-242-0483
Wholesale Lumber; Dry Kiln
S.I.C.: 5031

Sabbeth World Wide Wood Corp. **(1)**
P.O. Box 53
Crystal Springs, PA 15536
Tel.: 814-735-4095
Fax: 814-735-3259
Wholesale Lumber; Dry Kiln
S.I.C.: 5031

Branches:

Atlantic Lumber Company **(2)**
P.O. Box 53
Crystal Springs, PA 15536
Tel.: 814-735-4095
Fax: 814-735-3259
Wholesale Lumber; Dry Kiln
S.I.C.: 5031

Atlantic Lumber Company **(2)**
P.O. Box 503
Waverly, NY 14892
Tel.: 607-565-8136
Fax: 607-565-7002
Sawmill
S.I.C.: 2421

Tebbas Sales Corp. **(1)**
55 N. Industry Ct.
Deer Park, NY 11729
Tel.: 516-242-0303
Fax: 516-242-0483
Wholesale Lumber
S.I.C.: 5031

SABIN ROBBINS PAPER CO.
106 Circle Freeway Dr.
Cincinnati, OH 45246
Tel.: 513-874-5270
Fax: 513-874-5785
Approx.Sls.: $40,000,000
Emp.: 200
Fiscal Year-end: 6/30/92
Paper & Allied Products
S.I.C.: 2621
Thomas P. Price Jr. *(Pres. & Chief Exec. Officer)*
Peter J. Countryman *(Chief Fin. Officer, Treas. & Controller)*
Anthony Scherra *(Mgr.-Data Processing)*

Computer Systems/Hardware:
IBM System 36

Outside Service Firm(s):

Deloitte & Touche*(Auditors)*
Chiquita Center, 250 E. 5th St., Ste. 1900
Cincinnati, OH 45202
Tel.: 513-784-7100

Connecticut General Life Insurance Co.*(Group Insurer)*
P.O. Box 2975,
Hartford, CT 06104
Tel.: 203-726-6000

Graydon, Head & Ritchey*(Legal Firm)*
1900 Fifth Third Center
Cincinnati, OH 45202
Tel.: 513-621-6464

Fifth Third Bank*(Major Banking Relationship)*
Corporate Trust Services, 38 Fountain Square Plaza
Cincinnati, OH 45263

Fifth Third Bank*(Pension Manager)*
Corporate Trust Services, 38 Fountain Square Plaza
Cincinnati, OH 45263

SABRELINER CORP.
18118 Chesterfield Airport Rd.
Chesterfield, MO 63005-1121
Tel.: 314-537-3660 **DE**
Fax: 314-537-9587
Year Founded: 1983
Approx.Sls.: $75,000,000
Emp.: 800
Mfr. & Maintenance of Aircraft, Engines & Parts; Wholesale Aircraft & Petroleum Products
S.I.C.: 3721; 3724; 3728; 5088; 5172
F. Holmes Lamoreux *(Chm. Bd., Pres. & Chief Exec. Officer)*
Robert Dowd *(V.P.-Fin.)*
Susan Seabury Aselage *(V.P. & Sec.)*
Reuben Best *(V.P.-Govt. Opers.)*
Karl R. Childs *(V.P.-Mktg.)*
Jackson Forney *(V.P.-Opers.)*
Bob D. Hanks *(V.P.-Engrng.)*
Gene Harbula *(V.P.-Corp. Devel.)*
Jerry L. Leath *(V.P.-Admin.)*
Allen R. McMahan *(V.P.-Tech. Support)*

Outside Service Firm(s):

Ernst & Young*(Auditors)*
701 Market St.
St. Louis, MO 63101
Tel.: 314-259-1000

Winthrop, Stimson, Putnam & Roberts*(Legal Firm)*
40 Wall St.
New York, NY 10005
Tel.: 212-943-0700

Citibank N.A.*(Major Banking Relationship)*
200 S. Wacker Dr.
Chicago, IL 60631
Tel.: 312-993-3824
Fax: 312-715-1143

SACHNOWITZ & CO.
3410 W. Dallas
Houston, TX 77019
Mailing Address:
P.O. Box 130939,
Houston, TX 77219
Tel.: 713-521-1010
Fax: 713-521-0790
Year Founded: 1940
Approx.Billings: $12,000,000
Emp.: 20
Mktg., Adv., Sls. Promo., Positioning Strategy, Research & Pub. Rels.
Larry Sachnowitz *(Pres. & Sr. Creative Dir.)*
Irv Kauffman *(Sr. V.P.)*

SACHS HOLDING COMPANY
400 Chesterfield Ctr., Ste. 600
Chesterfield, MO 63017
Mailing Address:
P.O. Box 7104
St. Louis, MO 63177
Tel.: 314-537-1000 **IL**
Fax: 908-537-0718
Year Founded: 1967
Sales Range: $60-79 Million
Emp.: 72
Fiscal Year-end: 5/31/92
Real Estate Manager, Developer & Owner of Building Automation
S.I.C.: 6552
Louis S. Sachs *(Chm. Bd. & Pres.)*
Kathy Higgins *(V.P.)*
Anne Frohock *(Dir.-Pub. Rels.)*

Subsidiaries:

Sachs Energy Management Systems **(1)**
16120 Chesterfield Pkwy. S., Ste. 100
Chesterfield, MO 63017
Tel.: 314-532-6000
Facility Automation
S.I.C.: 8741
Alan Kirn *(Pres.)*

Sachs Properties **(1)**
400 Chesterfield Ctr., Ste. 600
Chesterfield, MO 63017
Tel.: 317-537-1000
Real Estate Developer, Owner & Manager
S.I.C.: 6552
Kathy Higgins *(V.P.)*

SACKS & ROSEN, INC. ADVERTISING
305 East 46th St.
New York, NY 10017
Tel.: 212-826-4004
Fax: 212-593-7824
Year Founded: 1964
Approx.Billings: $45,000,000
Emp.: 42
Consumer Adv. & Direct Response Mktg.
Leonard Sacks *(Pres.)*
Michael Rosen *(Exec. V.P., Client Services)*
Bruce Bublick *(Dir., Fin.)*

SACRAMENTO KINGS
1 Sports Pkwy.
Sacramento, CA 95834
Tel.: 916-928-0000
Fax: 916-928-0727
Approx.Sls.: $12,000,000
Emp.: 100
Fiscal Year-end: 6/30/90
Professional Basketball Franchise
S.I.C.: 7941
Gregg Lukenbill *(Owner & Mng. Partner)*
Rick Benner *(Pres.)*
Joe Marsalla *(V.P.-Mktg.)*
Julie Fie *(Dir.-Publicity)*
Phil Hess *(Dir.-Ticket Sls.)*

SACRAMENTO MUNICIPAL UTILITY DISTRICT
6201 "S" St.
Sacramento, CA 95817
Mailing Address:
P.O. Box 15830,
Sacramento, CA 95852-1830
Tel.: 916-452-3211
Fax: 916-732-5940
Year Founded: 1947
Assets: $2,769,461,000
Earnings: $31,079,000

Sacramento Municipal Utility District—(Continued)

Liabilities: $2,619,575,000
Net Worth: $149,886,000
Approx.Sls.: $644,393,000
Emp.: 2400
Fiscal Year-end: 12/31/91
Electric Utility Co.
S.I.C.: 4911
Wendy B. Reid *(Chm. Bd.)*
David S. Freeman *(Chief Exec. Officer & Gen. Mgr.)*
Walter Gaebler, II *(Chief Fin. Officer & Asst. Gen. Mgr.-Fin.)*
Leo Fassler *(Chief Oper. Officer & Asst. Gen. Mgr.)*
Jan Schori *(Gen. Counsel & Corp. Sec.)*
James A. Tracy *(Treas.)*
Noreen Roche Carter *(Asst. Treas.)*
Dorinda Henderson *(Dir.-Personnel Svcs.)*
Hank Dale *(Mngmt. Information Services)*
Mahmud Chaudhry *(Mgr.-Gen. Services)*
Eric Haemer *(Mgr.-Energy Services)*
Gail R. Hullibarger *(Mgr.-Acct. Dept. & Controller)*
Tim Ryan *(Sr. Fin. Analyst)*

Computer Systems/Hardware:
IBM 3270

WILLIAM H. SADLIER, INC.
9 Pine St.
New York, NY 10005
Tel.: 212-227-2120
Tel.: 800221-5175
Fax: 212-312-6080
Year Founded: 1832
Approx.Sls.: $18,000,000
Emp.: 150
Fiscal Year-end: 12/31/90
Publishing
S.I.C.: 2731; 2741
Frank S. Dinger *(Chm. Bd.)*
William S. Dinger *(Pres.)*
Dr. Elinor R. Ford *(Chief Exec. Officer)*
Joseph Brophy *(Exec. V.P.-Sls.)*
Henry Christel *(V.P.-Treas.)*
John Leckie *(V.P.-Prod. & Mfg.)*
Dr. Gerard Baumbach *(V.P.-Publisher)*
John DiSipe *(Exec. Dir.-Mktg.)*
Luke Tursi *(Dir.-Mktg.)*
Kevin O'Donnell *(Natl. Sls. Mgr.)*

Divisions:

Sadlier **(1)**
9 Pine St.
New York, NY 10005
Tel.: 212-227-2120
Tel.: 800-221-5165
Fax: 212-312-6080

W.H. Sadlier Oxford **(1)**
11 Park Pl.
New York, NY 10007
Tel.: 212-227-2120

SAE-PINKERTON & LAWS INC.
(Formerly Pinkerton & Laws Co.)
875 Douglas Rd. N.E.
Atlanta, GA 30342-1410
Tel.: 404-256-1000 **GA**
Fax: 404-256-9339
Year Founded: 1955
Approx.Sls.: $104,000,000
Emp.: 300
Commercial & Industrial Construction
S.I.C.: 1541; 1542
Terry Honan *(Pres. & Chief Exec. Officer)*
W. Jerry Arnold *(Sr. V.P.-Estimating)*
J. Paul Cranmer *(Sr. V.P.-Fin. & Admin.)*
Jeff Jernigan *(Sr. V.P.)*
Jack Shriver *(Sr. V.P.)*
David Simpson *(Sr. V.P.)*

No. of U.S. Offices: 3

Outside Service Firm(s):

Arthur Andersen & Co.*(Auditors)*
Avenue des Arts 56 1040
Brussels, Belgium

Arthur Andersen & Co.*(Auditors)*
133 Peachtree St., N.E.
Atlanta, GA 30303
Tel.: 404-658-1776

Johnson & Higgins*(Commercial Insurance Carrier)*
Washington, DC

SAFE HARBOR WATER POWER CORPORATION
Jointly Owned by Pennsylvania Power & Light Co. & Baltimore Gas & Electric Co.
5093 River Rd.
Conestoga, PA 17516
Mailing Address:
P.O. Box 97
Conestoga, PA 17516-0097
Tel.: 717-872-5441 **PA**
Fax: 717-872-0223
Year Founded: 1930
Assets: $133,990,000
Liabilities: $82,645,000
Net Worth: $51,345,000
Approx.Sls.: $28,000,000
Emp.: 106
Fiscal Year-end: 12/31/92
Generation, Hydro Electric Power
S.I.C.: 4911
Employee Matching Gifts Program: Up to $2,000
Marshall Kaiser *(Pres. & Chief Exec. Officer)*
Steven E. Jones *(V.P.)*
William H. Tonkin *(Treas. & Sec.)*

Outside Service Firm(s):

Price Waterhouse*(Auditors)*
7 St. Paul St.
Baltimore, MD 21202

Chemical Bank*(Major Banking Relationship)*
277 Park Ave.
New York, NY 10172
Tel.: 212-310-6161

SAFEGUARD BUSINESS SYSTEMS, INC.
470 Maryland Dr.
Fort Washington, PA 19034
Tel.: 215-641-5000
Tel.: 800-523-2422 **DE**
Fax: 215-641-6705
Year Founded: 1967
Assets: $235,000,000
Liabilities: $72,000,000
Net Worth: $163,000,000
Sales Range: $100-499 Million
Emp.: 1,600
Fiscal Year-end: 12/31/91
Export
Business Forms & Systems
S.I.C.: 7372
Elvis L. Mason *(Chm. & Chief Exec. Officer)*
Victor K. Nichols *(Pres.)*
James Braun *(Sr. V.P. & Chief Fin. Officer)*
Richard Gommel *(Sr. V.P.-Opers.)*
John Israel *(V.P.-Mktg. & Sls. Support)*
Jeffrey W. Smith *(V.P.-Mngmt. Information Systems)*
Thomas A. Schneider *(Chief Legal Counsel)*
Jon Boettger *(Dir.-Risk Mngmt.)*
John White *(Dir.-Natl. Pur.)*
Donald Lederach *(Dir.-Adv.)*
Bob Miller *(Dir.-Pur.)*
Carol Fox *(Dir.-Meeting Plng. & Corp. Travel Planner)*
John Benson *(Personnel Training & Devel.)*
Bob Connely *(Mgr.-Personnel)*
Susan Davidson *(Cash Mgr.)*
Rudolph Lutterschmidt *(Controller & Safegaurd Int'l.)*

Outside Service Firm(s):

Deloitte & Touche*(Auditors)*
1700 Market St.
Philadelphia, PA 19103
Tel.: 215-246-2322
Fax: 215-569-2441

Fireman's Fund Insurance Co.*(Commercial Insurance Carrier)*
Jersey City, NJ

Industrial Risk Insurers*(Commercial Insurance Carrier)*
85 Woodland St.
Hartford, CT 06102
Tel.: 203-520-7300

Morgan, Lewis & Bockius*(Legal Firm)*
2000 One Logan Square
Philadelphia, PA 19103-6993
Tel.: 215-963-5000
Fax: 215-963-5299

Philadelphia National Bank*(Major Banking Relationship)*
P.O. Box 13834, Broad & Chestnut Streets
Philadelphia, PA 19101-7618
Tel.: 215-973-8327

Subsidiaries:

Accounting Forms Company, Inc. **(1)**
455 Maryland Dr.
Fort Washington, PA 19034
Tel.: 215-641-5000
V. Nichols *(Pres.)*

Safeguard Financial Corp. **(1)**
455 Maryland Dr.
Fort Washington, PA 19034
Tel.: 215-641-5000
Holding Company
S.I.C.: 6719
J. Braun *(Pres.)*

Non-U.S. Holdings:

Safeguard Business Systems Limited **(1)**
420 Britannia Rd. E., Ste. 102
Mississauga, ON L4Z 3L5, Canada
Tel.: 416-890-2400 (100%)
Emp.: 70
Distibutor of Business Systems
C. Aviles *(Pres.)*

Safeguard Europe S.A. **(1)**
ZAC Paris Nord 2 95911
Roissy, Cedex France
Holding Company
A. Haase *(Pres.)*

Safeguard Systems GB, Ltd. **(1)**
Centurion House, Gateway
Crewe, Cheshire CW1 1XJ, United Kingdom
Tel.: 44-270-500921 (100%)
Mfr. & Distibutor of Business Systems
A. Haase *(Pres.)*

SAGE-ALLEN & CO., INC.
900 Main St.
Hartford, CT 06103
Tel.: 203-278-2570 **DE**
Fax: 203-520-5820
Emp.: 1,450
13 Retail Stores in Connecticut & 1 Retail Store in Massachusetts
S.I.C.: 5651; 5311
Lafayette Keeney *(Chm. Bd., Pres. & Chief Exec. Officer)*
David R. Bonney *(Sr. V.P., Treas.)*
Frank Toro *(V.P.-Opers.)*
Rebecca Gilbert *(V.P. & Personnel Dir.)*
Norman Novak *(V.P.-Mngmt. Information Systems)*
Jeffery Albert *(V.P.-Branch Stores)*

SAHARA COAL CO.
3 First National Plaza, Ste. 2000
Chicago, IL 60602
Tel.: 312-782-2690
Fax: 312-782-2690 Ext. 222
Emp.: 140
Bituminous Coal Mining
S.I.C.: 1221; 1222
George Kelm *(Chm. Bd.)*
Charles N. Wheatley *(Pres. & Chief Exec. Officer)*
John Peck *(V.P., Chief Fin. & Admin. Officer)*
Stanley Szymaniak *(Asst. V.P., Admn. & Human Resources Dir.)*

Outside Service Firm(s):

KPMG Peat Marwick*(Auditors)*
Peat Marwick Plaza, 303 E. Wacker Dr.
Chicago, IL 60601
Tel.: 312-938-1000

Hopkins & Sutter*(Legal Firm)*
Three First Natl. Plaza
Chicago, IL 60602
Tel.: 312-558-6600

Harris Trust & Savings Bank*(Major Banking Relationship)*
111 W. Monroe St.
Chicago, IL 60690
Tel.: 312-461-2265
Tel.: 800-858-0840

William Blair & Co.*(Pension Manager)*
135 S. LaSalle St.
Chicago, IL 60603
Tel.: 312-236-1600

ST. CROIX PRESS, INC.
1185 S. Knowles Hwy. 65
New Richmond, WI 54017
Tel.: 715-246-5811
Tel.: 800-826-6622 **WI**
Fax: 715-243-7551
Year Founded: 1971
Approx.Sls.: $20,000,000
Emp.: 200
Fiscal Year-end: 6/30/91
Import Export
Printing Of Periodicals
S.I.C.: 2721; 2791
Edward A. Monette *(Chm., Pres., Chief Exec. & Oper. Officer)*
Glen C. Marlett *(V.P.)*
Ralph Lind *(Corp. Sec. & Controller)*
Dean Lindquist *(Mgr.-Sls.)*
Lowell Johnson *(Mgr.-Plant)*
Deb Ducklow *(Mgr.-Pur.)*
Paulette Butrand *(Mgr.-Systems)*

Principal(s):
Edward A. Monette
Glen C. Marlett
Ralph Lind
Dean Lindquist

No. of Mfg. Plants/Facilities: 2
No. of U.S. Offices: 2

Outside Service Firm(s):

W.J. Bauman Associates Ltd*(Auditors)*
River Falls, WI

First National Bank*(Major Banking Relationship)*
New Richmond, WI

THE ST. GEORGE GROUP, INC.
2600 Centre City Tower
Pittsburgh, PA 15222
Tel.: 412-471-1090
Fax: 412-471-0526
Year Founded: 1982
Approx.Billings: $31,500,000
Emp.: 46
Herbert F. Burger *(Chm. Bd.)*
George E. Garber *(Pres.)*
Stanley Muschweck *(Exec. V.P.)*
Edward Flaherty, III *(Sr. V.P.)*
Michael Koff *(V.P., Pub. Rels. Dir.)*
David Kosick *(V.P., Pub. Rels.-Consumer)*
Bruce R. Downing *(V.P.)*
Martin Giglio *(V.P.)*

ST. JOHNSBURY TRUCKING CO., INC.
119 Jeffrey Ave.
Holliston, MA 01746
Tel.: 508-429-5920
Tel.: 800-767-3300 **DE**
Fax: 508-429-6881
Year Founded: 1921
Assets: $144,824,000
Earnings: $10,097,000
Liabilities: $74,192,000
Net Worth: $70,632,000
Approx.Sls.: $322,075,000
Emp.: 4,600
Fiscal Year-end: 3/31/90
Import Export
Motor Freight Transportation Company
S.I.C.: 4213
William M. Clifford *(Chm., Pres. & Chief Exec. Officer)*
Daniel J. Riley *(Sr. V.P.-Sls., Mktg. & Devel.)*
Donald A. Day *(Sr. V.P.-Fin., Chief Fin. Officer & Sec.)*
Dave Brown *(V.P.-Information Systems)*
Jim Hood *(V.P.-Terminals)*
Richard Cabral *(V.P.-Admin.)*
Ted Lepcio *(V.P.-Corp. Accts.)*
Robert Powers *(V.P.-Maintenance)*
Thomas Wajer *(V.P.-Natl. Accts.)*
Suzanne Carlson *(Mgr.-Employee Benefits)*
Dave Buckley *(Mgr.-Purchasing)*
Allison Williges *(Mgr.-Treasury Opers.)*
Daniel Schur *(Mgr.-Telecommunications)*

No. of Mfg. Plants/Facilities: 68
No. of U.S. Offices: 62
No. of Foreign Offices: 6

Computer Systems/Hardware:
Honeywell 8088

Outside Service Firm(s):

Coopers & Lybrand*(Auditors)*
1 Post Office Square
Boston, MA 02110
Tel.: 617-574-5000
Fax: 617-345-0398

National Union Fire Insurance Co. of Pittsburgh*(Commercial Insurance Carrier)*
2005 Market St., Ste. 2800
Pittsburgh, PA

Lincoln National Life Insurance Co.*(Group Insurer)*
PO Box 208, 1300 S. Clinton
Fort Wayne, IN 46801
Tel.: 219-455-2926
Fax: 219-455-7619

Royal Bank of Canada*(International Bank Affiliate)*
Etobicoke, ON Canada

Kidder, Peabody & Co.*(Investment Banker)*
10 Hanover Square
New York, NY 10005
Tel.: 212-510-3000

Shawmut Bank*(Major Banking Relationship)*
1 Federal St.
Boston, MA 02110
Tel.: 617-292-3715

Frank Russell Company*(Pension Manager)*
909 A St.
Tacoma, WA 98402

ST. LOUIS MUSIC, INC.
1400 Ferguson
Saint Louis, MO 63133
Tel.: 314-727-4512 **MO**
Fax: 314-727-8929
Approx.Sls.: $20,000,000
Emp.: 150
Import Export
Wholesale Musical Instruments & Accessories
S.I.C.: 5099
Eugene Kornblum *(Pres.)*
Don Collins *(Controller)*
Stanley Morgan *(Mgr.-Sls.)*

Outside Service Firm(s):

Gallop, Johnson & Neuman*(Legal Firm)*
101 S. Hanley Rd.
St. Louis, MO 63105
Tel.: 314-862-1200

Commerce Bank of Kansas City*(Major Banking Relationship)*
10th & Walnut
Kansas City, MO 64141
Tel.: 816-234-2000
Fax: 816-234-2548

Subsidiary:

SLM Electronics **(1)**
11880 Borman Dr.
Saint Louis, MO 63146
Tel.: 314-569-0141
Mfrs. Amplifiers & Reinforcements
S.I.C.: 3651

ST. PAUL METALCRAFT, INC.
3737 N. Lexington Ave.
Saint Paul, MN 55126
Tel.: 612-483-6641 **MN**
Fax: 612-483-5618
Year Founded: 1960
Approx.Sls.: $11,000,000
Emp.: 125
Export
Manufacture of Aluminum & Zinc Die Castings & Molds
S.I.C.: 3363; 3369; 3545
John T. Walker *(Chm. Bd., Pres. & Chief Exec. Officer)*
Jim Hinrichs *(V.P.-Opers.)*
Al Mimbach *(V.P.-Fin.)*
Gary T. Walker *(V.P.-Engrng.)*
Paul Engstrom *(Dir.-Pur.)*
Vivian F. Neumann *(Special Projects Coord.)*
Principal(s):
John T. Walker

No. of Mfg. Plants/Facilities: 1
No. of U.S. Offices: 1

Computer Systems/Hardware:
IBM AS400 & Tandy PCs

Outside Service Firm(s):

Grant Thornton*(Auditors)*
500 Pillsbury Center
Minneapolis, MN 55402-1459

American National Bank & Trust of St. Paul*(Major Banking Relationship)*
Fifth & Minnesota Streets
St. Paul, MN 55101
Tel.: 612-298-6000

SAKRETE, INC.
Fischer Ave. & B&O RR
Cincinnati, OH 45217
Mailing Address:
P.O. Box 17087
Saint Bernard, OH 45217
Tel.: 513-242-3644
Tel.: 800-892-5078 **OH**
Fax: 513-242-7845
Year Founded: 1936
Approx.Sls.: $20,000,000
Emp.: 300
Fiscal Year-end: 10/31/90
Manufacture Dry Concrete Mixes
S.I.C.: 3273
Arthur C. Avril *(Pres.)*
Mary J. Avril *(V.P. & Treas.)*
Loraine Jacob *(Sec.)*

Outside Service Firm(s):

Deloitte & Touche*(Auditors)*
Chiquita Center, 250 E. 5th St., Ste. 1900
Cincinnati, OH 45202
Tel.: 513-784-7100

The Central Trust Company, N.A.*(Major Banking Relationship)*
201 E. Fifth
Cincinnati, OH 45202
Tel.: 513-651-8255

Star Bank*(Major Banking Relationship)*
425 Walnut Street
Cincinnati, OH 45202
Tel.: 513-632-4000

SALADMASTER
912 113th St.
Arlington, TX 76010
Tel.: 214-742-2222
Approx.Sls.: $30,000,000
Emp.: 85
Fiscal Year-end: 1/31/90
Cookware; Cutlery; Flatware; China & Crystal
S.I.C.: 3229; 3914
Peter Menke *(Pres.)*
Elton E. Evans *(V.P.-Intl.)*
Wayne Fritz *(V.P.-Sls.)*
Jeff Nelson *(V.P.-Fin.)*
Larry Partridge *(Dir.-Sls. Promo.)*

SALEM NATIONAL CORPORATION
245 Charlois Blvd.
Winston-Salem, NC 27103
Mailing Address:
P.O. Box 2977,
Winston-Salem, NC 27102
Tel.: 919-768-6800 **NC**
Assets: $44,505,000
Liabilities: $40,781,000
Net Worth: $3,724,000
Approx.Sls.: $25,300,000
Emp.: 155
Fiscal Year-end: 6/30/89
Leasing of Truck Tractors & Trailers
S.I.C.: 7513
Kenneth G. Langone *(Chm. Bd. & Chief Exec. Officer)*
Thomas L. Teague *(Pres. & Chief Oper. Officer)*
C. Stephen Dula *(Sec.-Treas. & Chief Fin. Officer)*

Outside Service Firm(s):

Ernst & Young*(Auditors)*
1100 Independence Center
Charlotte, NC 28246
Tel.: 704-372-6300

Petree Stockton & Robinson*(Legal Firm)*
1001 W. Fourth St.
Winston-Salem, NC 27101
Tel.: 919-725-2351

First National Bank of Boston*(Major Banking Relationship)*
P.O. Box 644,
Boston, MA 02102-0644
Tel.: 617-575-2900
Fax: 617-575-2549

Subsidiaries:

Salem Carriers. Inc. **(1)**
245 Charlois Blvd.
Winston-Salem, NC 27103
Tel.: 919-768-6800
Approx.Sls.: $4,000,000
Emp.: 50
Gen. Commodities Common Carrier & Contract Carrier
S.I.C.: 7513
Thomas L. Teague *(Chief Oper. Officer)*

Salem Leasing Corp. **(1)**
245 Charlois Blvd.
Winston-Salem, NC 27103
Tel.: 919-768-6800 (100%)
Approx.Sls.: $21,300,000
Emp.: 150
Leasing of Truck Tractor & Trailers
S.I.C.: 7513
Thomas L. Teague *(Chief Oper. Officer)*

SALLY LOU FASHIONS CORPORATION
1400 Broadway
New York, NY 10018
Tel.: 212-354-9670 **NY**
Fax: 212-719-2942
Year Founded: 1974
Approx.Sls.: $44,000,000
Emp.: 100
Fiscal Year-end: 3/31/92
Mfr. of Women's, Junior's & Missess Dresses
S.I.C.: 2335
Steve Grabow *(Pres.)*
Lester Grayson *(V.P.)*
Barbara Meller *(Controller)*

Outside Service Firm(s):

Blumstein Bond & Company*(Auditors)*
New York, NY

SALT RIVER PROJECT AGRICULTURAL IMPROVEMENT AND POWER DISTRICT
1521 Project Dr.
Tempe, AZ 85281
Mailing Address:
P.O. Box 52025,
Phoenix, AZ 85072-2025
Tel.: 602-236-5900
Fax: 602-236-2505
Year Founded: 1937
Assets: $5,413,303,000
Earnings: $13,192,000
Liabilities: $3,971,806,000
Net Worth: $1,441,497,000
Approx.Sls.: $1,121,935,000
Emp.: 5,400
Fiscal Year-end: 4/30/90
Power & Irrigation Authority
S.I.C.: 4931; 4971
J. R. Lassen *(Pres.)*
C.M. Perkins *(Gen. Mgr.)*
Mark B. Bonsall *(Assoc. Gen. Mgr.)*
John D. Jacobs *(Asst. Gen. Mgr.)*
Paul G. Ahler *(Asst. Gen. Mgr.)*
Richard H. Silverman *(Asst. Gen. Mgr. & Sec.)*
D. S. Wilson *(Assoc. Gen. Mgr.-Plng. & Research)*
J. L. Swartz *(Telecommunications)*

H. SALT SEAFOOD RESTAURANTS
1255 Corp. Center Dr.
Monterey Park, CA 91754
Tel.: 213-264-8766
Fax: 213-264-7262
Year Founded: 1970
Approx.Sls.: $25,000,000
Emp.: 3
Franchised Fast Food Restaurant & Carry Out
S.I.C.: 5812
Leon C. Lin *(Pres.)*
Tim Plodinec *(Chief Oper. Officer)*

SALVATI MONTGOMERY SAKODA, INC.
535 Anton Blvd., Ste. 600
Costa Mesa, CA 92626
Tel.: 714-966-0200
Fax: 714-966-0465
Year Founded: 1981
Approx.Billings: $30,879,485
Emp.: 65
Consumer Products & Services Categories, including Banking, Communications, Food Service & Entertainment
Philip J. Salvati *(Pres. & Chief Exec. Officer)*
Scott Montgomery *(Exec. V.P., Sec. & Creative Dir.)*
Kenneth Sakoda *(Exec. V.P., Treas. & Creative Dir.)*
Karl Lendenmann *(Sr. V.P., Plng. & Res.)*
Dan Pittman *(V.P., Pub. Rels. Dir.)*

Salvati Montgomery Sakoda, Inc.—(Continued)

Greg Smith *(V.P., Admin)*
Rosie Ramirez *(Personnel)*
Michelle Purcell *(Project Supvr.)*
Connie Klosterman *(Office Mgr.)*

Computer Systems/Hardware:
MacIntosh, BCS System, PC

SALWASSER MANUFACTURING COMPANY, INC.
20075 E. Manning
Reedley, CA 93654
Tel.: 209-638-8484
Fax: 209-638-7478
Approx.Sls.: $14,000,000
Emp.: 180
Manufacture Packaging Machines
S.I.C.: 3565
Melvin Salwasser *(Pres.)*
Leslie Salwasser *(Exec. V.P.)*
Dennis Salwasser *(V.P.-Fin. & Real Estate)*
John Loomis *(Gen. Counsel)*
Margaret Salwasser *(Sec. & Treas.)*
Stan Reimer *(Mgr.-Bus.)*
Walter Warren *(Mgr.-Sls. & Mktg.)*
Wally Loewen *(Chief Engr.)*

Outside Service Firm(s):

Just, Nakamura & Martin*(Auditors)*
Reedley, CA

Staniford, Harris & Loomis*(Legal Firm)*
Fresno, CA

Wells Fargo Bank*(Major Banking Relationship)*
Reedley, CA

SALZ LEATHERS, INC.
P.O. Box 1840
Santa Cruz, CA 95061-1840
Tel.: 408-423-4470 **DE**
Fax: 408-425-1626
Year Founded: 1861
Approx.Sls.: $40,000,000
Emp.: 200
Export
Cowhide Side Leather
S.I.C.: 3111
Norman S. Lezin *(Chm. Bd.)*
Jeremy Lezin *(Pres.)*
Burton S. Rees *(V.P. & Treas.)*
Timothy Scopes *(V.P.-Mfg.)*
Pat Martinez *(Dir.-Personnel)*
Michael Mullins *(Mgr.-Sls.)*
Mark Tolaio *(Pur. Agent)*

No. of Mfg. Plants/Facilities: 1
No. of U.S. Offices: 1
No. of Foreign Offices: 10

Outside Service Firm(s):

Dinkelspiel, Donovan & Reder*(Legal Firm)*
1 Embarcadero Center
San Francisco, CA 94111
Tel.: 415-788-1100

The Bank of California, N.A.*(Major Banking Relationship)*
400 California
San Francisco, CA 94104
Tel.: 415-765-0400

SAMELSON-LEON COMPANY, INC.
4280 Concorde
Memphis, TN 38118
Mailing Address:
P.O. Box 18325
Memphis, TN 38181-0325
Tel.: 901-365-3939 **TN**
Fax: 901-795-1611
Year Founded: 1881
Approx.Sls.: $78,000,000
Emp.: 109
Fiscal Year-end: 12/31/89
Wholesale Tobacco, Confectionery & Groceries
S.I.C.: 5141; 5145; 5194
Thomas Scott Fisher *(Chm. Bd. & Chief Exec. Officer)*
Anthony Galler *(Pres. & Chief Oper. Officer)*
Glenn Cofield *(V.P.-Fin.)*
Oscar C. Carr III *(Legal Officer)*
George Martin *(Dir.-Personnel)*
Mike Call *(Mgr.-Sls.)*
Mike Harris *(Mgr.-Data Processing)*

Principal(s):
Thomas Scott Fisher
Anthony Galler

Computer Systems/Hardware:
IBM 38

Outside Service Firm(s):

Gankler, Raines, Brown et al*(Legal Firm)*
One Commerce Sq.
Memphis, TN 38103

First National Bank of Boston*(Major Banking Relationship)*
P.O. Box 644,
Boston, MA 02102-0644
Tel.: 617-575-2900
Fax: 617-575-2549

Subsidiary:

Bluff City Cigarette Service **(1)**
3910 Delp St.
Memphis, TN 38118
Tel.: 901-365-2611
Vending Service
S.I.C.: 5046

SAMMONS ENTERPRISES, INC.
300 Crescent Court, Ste. 700
Dallas, TX 75201
Tel.: 214-855-2800 **DE**
Fax: 214-855-2899
Year Founded: 1938
Assets: $2,482,000
Liabilities: $1,833,000
Net Worth: $649,000
Approx.Sls.: $1,340,000,000
Emp.: 5,100
Fiscal Year-end: 12/31/90
Cable TV; Industrial Equipment & Machinery; Insurance Carriers; Bottled Water; Travel; Hotels
S.I.C.: 6311; 5084; 4899; 5149
E.D. Sammons *(Chm. Bd.)*
Robert W. Korba *(Pres.)*
James N. Whitson *(Exec. V.P. & Chief Oper. Officer)*
Lawrence R. Beach *(Sr. V.P.-Admin.)*
Joseph A. Ethridge *(Sr. V.P.-Fin. & Chief Fin. Officer)*
John H. Washburn *(Sr. V.P.-Legal & Gen. Counsel)*
Diana Cavsey *(Dir.-Pub. Rels.)*
Gayle Brown *(Treas.)*

Computer Systems/Hardware:
IBM PC

Outside Service Firm(s):

Coopers & Lybrand*(Auditors)*
1999 Bryan St., Ste. 3000
Dallas, TX 75201
Tel.: 214-754-5000

Ernst & Young*(Auditors)*
2121 San Jacinto, Ste. 500
Dallas, TX 75201
Tel.: 214-969-8000

Aetna Life & Casualty*(Group Insurer)*
151 Farmington Avenue
Hartford, CT 06156
Tel.: 203-273-2128
Fax: 203-729-4295

Hughes & Luce*(Legal Firm)*
Bank One Center, 1717 Main St.
Dallas, TX 75202
Tel.: 214-651-0477

NationsBank Texas*(Major Banking Relationship)*
901 Main St., 16th Fl.
Dallas, TX 75202
Tel.: 214-922-5000

Subsidiaries:

Briggs Weaver **(1)**
5000 Harry Hines Blvd.
Dallas, TX 75235
Tel.: 214-631-3600
Industrial Supplies; Tools, Fork Lifts, etc.
S.I.C.: 5085; 5084
Homer Denning *(Pres.)*
Gwen Gilbert *(Chief Fin. Officer)*

Health Waters, Inc. **(1)**
282 Hudson St.
Hackensack, NJ 07601
Tel.: 201-489-4700
Approx.Sls.: $2,500,000
Emp.: 12
Fiscal Year-end: 12/31/90
Distributor of Mountain Valley Spring Water
S.I.C.: 5149
Stuart Scott *(Gen. Mgr.)*

Midland National Life Insurance Co. **(1)**
One Midland Plaza
Sioux Falls, SD 57101
Tel.: 605-335-5700
Life Insurance
S.I.C.: 6311; 6411
Jack Watson *(Pres.)*
Alan H. Spencer *(Sr. V.P.-Mktg.)*
Lloyd T. Liken *(V.P.-Fin.)*

Mountain Valley Spring Company **(1)**
150 Central Ave.
Hot Springs, AR 71901
Tel.: 501-623-6671
Tel.: 800-643-1501
Fax: 501-623-5135
Emp.: 100
Export
Bottlers & Distributors of Spring Water
S.I.C.: 5149; 2086
James N. Whitson *(Pres.)*
Thomas Mitchell *(V.P.-Opers. & Gen. Mgr.)*
Craig Ivey *(Dir.-Opers.)*
Donna Merriweather *(Dir.-Human Resources)*
Robert Dwyer *(Mgr.-Sls., S.E.)*
Bruce Kessler *(Mgr.-Sls., N.E.)*
Don Simmons *(Mgr.-Sls., S.W.)*
Steve Taylor *(Mgr.-Sls., Midwest)*

Sammons Communications, Inc. **(1)**
3010 LBJ Frwy., Ste. 800
Dallas, TX 75234
Tel.: 214-484-8888
Cable Television
S.I.C.: 4841
Mark S. Webber *(Pres.)*
Alton Rye *(V.P., Treas. & Controller)*
Sherry Wilson *(V.P.-Mktg.)*

Vinson Supply Co. **(1)**
1323 E. 71st St.
Tulsa, OK 74136
Tel.: 918-481-8770
Fax: 918-481-8614
Approx.Sls.: $400,000,000
Emp.: 500
Import Export
Computer Systems/Hardware:
Unisys 1100-90
Distr. Oil Field & Industrial Supplies
S.I.C.: 5085; 5084
Rob C. Mellor *(Chm., Pres. & Chief Exec. Officer)*
Gerald R. Gray *(Chief Fin. Officer)*

Carolina Mountain Water **(1)**
c/o Mountain Valley Spring Co., P.O. Box 1610
Hot Springs, AR 71902
Tel.: 501-623-6671
Bottlers & Distributors of Spring Water
S.I.C.: 5149
Robert W. Korba *(Pres.)*

SAMPLER PUBLICATIONS INC.
707 Kautz Rd.
Saint Charles, IL 60174
Tel.: 708-377-8000
Fax: 708-377-8194
Year Founded: 1984
Approx.Sls.: $12,050,000
Emp.: 84
Fiscal Year-end: 12/31/91
Publr. of Catalogs
S.I.C.: 2741
Employee Matching Gifts Progra
Mark A. Nickel *(Chief Exec. Officer & Exec. Publr.)*
Denise Boba *(Publr.)*
Margaret B. Kernan *(V.P. & Grp. Publr.)*
Colleen Heitzler *(Mgr.-Accounting)*
Janis Page *(Dir.-Creative Service)*
Terri Landa *(Dir.-Sls.)*
William D. Lowry *(Dir.-Production)*
Steven Slack *(Dir.-Editorial)*

Publication:

Country Sampler **(1)**
707 Kautz Rd.
Saint Charles, IL 60174
Tel.: 708-377-8000
Fax: 708-377-8194
Catalog Publishing
S.I.C.: 2741
Mark A. Nickel *(Chief Exec. Officer)*
Margaret B. Kernan *(Publr.)*
Ann Myers *(Editor)*
Bob Sexton *(Mgr.-Circulation)*
Colleen Heitzler *(Mgr.-Acctg.)*
Terri Landa *(Mgr.-Natl. Sls.)*
Marty Ver Shaw *(Mgr.-Inside Sls.)*
Christine Paulson *(Promotion Coord.)*

SAMSILL CORPORATION
4301 Mansfield Hwy.
Fort Worth, TX 76119
Tel.: 817-536-1906
Fax: 817-535-6900
Year Founded: 1953
Approx.Sls.: $27,000,000
Emp.: 430
Import Export
Manufacture Plastic Products
S.I.C.: 3089
Mark Samsill *(Pres. & Chief Exec. Officer)*
James Adams *(Exec. V.P.)*
Loretta Samsill *(Exec. V.P., Sec. & Treas.)*
James Bankes *(V.P.-Sls. & Mktg.)*
Frank Grady *(Dir.-Personnel)*

Outside Service Firm(s):

Bank One*(Major Banking Relationship)*
Fort Worth, TX

Michner, Swindle, Whitaker & Pratt*(Legal Firm)*
Fort Worth, TX

SAMTEC INC.
810 Progress Blvd.
New Albany, IN 47150
Mailing Address:
P.O. Box 1147
New Albany, IN 47150
Tel.: 812-944-6733 **IN**
Fax: 812-948-5047
Year Founded: 1976
Approx.Sls.: $45,000,000
Emp.: 250
Export
Manufacture Electronic Connectors
S.I.C.: 3678; 3674
Sam M. Shine *(Pres.)*
Dan Tingle *(Controller)*
Mike Hynes *(Natl. Sls. Mgr.)*
Doug Coffman *(Gen. Mgr.)*
Frank Reisert *(Mgr.-Human Resources)*

Outside Service Firm(s):

Monroe, Shine & Co.*(Auditors)*
Louisville, KY

Citizens Fidelity Bank & Trust of Indiana*(Major Banking Relationship)*
New Albany, IN
Tel.: 812-945-2265

MILTON SAMUELS ADVERTISING AGENCY, INC.
31 East 32nd St.
New York, NY 10016
Tel.: 212-532-5151
Fax: 212-532-5499
Year Founded: 1951
Approx.Billings: $32,000,000
Emp.: 32
Consumer Adv., TV & Radio Commercials, Print, Newspapers, Outdoor & Transit, Special Promo., Events, Direct Mail, Brochures & Pub. Rels., Barter, Desktop Pub., Packaging & Sales Promotion
Robert P. Samuels *(Chm. Bd., Chief Exec. Officer)*
Jeffrey M. Ginsberg *(Pres.)*
Ronald Pere *(Chief Oper. Officer, Sr. Creative Dir.)*
Michael Spano *(Chief Fin. Officer)*
Keith Klein *(Dir. of Pub. Rels.)*
Andrea Blau *(Dir. of Business Devel.)*
Scott Ballin *(Dir., Communications)*
Lois Higgins *(Office Mgr.)*

ALLEN SAMUELS CHEVROLET GEO
1625 N. Valley Mills Dr.
Waco, TX 76710
Mailing Address:
P.O. Box 7978
Waco, TX 76714
Tel.: 817-772-8850 **TX**
Fax: 817-776-4560
Approx.Sls.: $28,000,000
Emp.: 100
Retail New & Used Cars & Trucks, Parts, Motor Trailers & Motorcycles
S.I.C.: 5511; 5599; 5571
Allen Samuels *(Pres.)*
Robert W. Steakley, III *(V.P.)*
Russel Kohlscheen *(Sec. & Treas.)*
Principal(s):
Allen Samuels

Computer Systems/Hardware:
Reynolds & Reynolds

Outside Service Firm(s):

Pattillo, Brown & Hill*(Auditors)*
Waco, TX

McNamara & McNamara*(Legal Firm)*
Waco, TX

NationsBank Texas*(Major Banking Relationship)*
Waco, TX

SAN ANGELO ELECTRIC SERVICE COMPANY
P.O. Box 1587, 926-32 Pullman St.
San Angelo, TX 76902
Tel.: 915-653-2336 **TX**
Fax: 915-658-3584
Year Founded: 1932
Emp.: 50
Export
Electrical Equipment Repair, High Voltage, Power Transformers, Electrical Apparatus & Equipment
S.I.C.: 7629; 3612
Corporate Giving Program: The United Way & Christmas for Special Children
J.R. Raines *(Chm. Bd.)*
Vis Thenappan *(Pres. & Chief Exec. Officer)*
Betty Lay *(Sec. & Treas.)*
No. of Mfg. Plants/Facilities: 1
No. of U.S. Offices: 1

Computer Systems/Hardware:
PC's

Outside Service Firm(s):

Drew Holderman*(Auditors)*
San Angelo, TX

Texas Commerce Bank*(Major Banking Relationship)*
San Angelo, TX

SAN DIEGO CHARGERS
9449 Friars Rd.
San Diego, CA 92108
Mailing Address:
P.O. Box 609609,
San Diego, CA 92160-9609
Tel.: 619-280-2111
Fax: 619-280-5569
Year Founded: 1960
Emp.: 135
Professional Football Team
S.I.C.: 7941
Alex G. Spanos *(Chm. Bd. & Pres.)*
Dean Spanos *(Vice Chm.)*
Jeremiah Murphy *(V.P.-Fin.)*
Bill Devaney *(Dir.-Player Personnel)*
Rudy Feldman *(Dir.-Pro Personnel)*
Rich Israel *(Dir.-Mktg.)*
Bill Johnston *(Dir.-Pub. Rels.)*
Joe Scott *(Dir.-Ticket Opers.)*
Bobb Beathard *(Gen. Mgr.)*
Dick Daniels *(Asst. Gen. Mgr.)*
Patrick Curran *(Bus. Mgr.)*

SAN DIEGO ZOO
(Div. of Zoological Society of San Diego)
2920 Zoo Dr.
San Diego, CA 92112
Mailing Address:
P.O. Box 551
San Diego, CA 92103
Tel.: 619-231-1515
Year Founded: 1916
Approx.Sls.: $87,000,000
Emp.: 1,000
Fiscal Year-end: 12/31/91
Zoological Gardens Located in San Diego
S.I.C.: 8422
Arthur C. Risser *(Gen. Mgr.)*
Douglas G. Myers *(Exec. Dir.-Zoological Society)*
Frederick Andrus *(Chief Fin. Officer)*
Martha Baker *(Dir.-Mktg. & Sls.)*
Stan Thompson *(Dir.-Personnel)*

Computer Systems/Hardware:
AS400

Division:

San Diego Wild Animal Park **(1)**
15500 San Pasqual Valley Rd.
Escondido, CA 92027
Tel.: 619-747-8702
Wildlife Preserve
S.I.C.: 8422
Robert McClure *(Gen. Mgr.)*
Frederick Andrus *(Chief Fin. Officer)*
Douglas G. Myers *(Exec. Dir.-Zoological Society)*
Martha Baker *(Dir.-Sls. & Mktg.)*
Stan Thompson *(Mgr.-Personnel)*

SAN FRANCISCO FRENCH BREAD COMPANY
7801 Edgewater Dr.
Oakland, CA 94621
Tel.: 415-568-5511
Fax: 510-562-4830
Year Founded: 1984
Sales Range: $100-499 Million
Emp.: 1,500
Fiscal Year-end: 12/31/90
Manufacture & Wholesale of Bread Products; Operation of Retail Bakeries & Cafes
S.I.C.: 2051; 5149
Louis Giraudo *(Chm. & Co-Chief Exec. Officer)*
Sharon B. Duvall *(Co-Chief Exec. Officer)*
Harry Walsh *(Chief Fin. Officer)*
Fred Groszkruger *(Chief Oper. Officer)*
Steve Giraudo *(Exec. V.P.-Production)*
Pete Sher *(Sec. & Gen. Counsel)*
Jerry Bauer *(Dir.-Mngmt. Information Systems)*
Ralph Bagdonas *(Dir.-Human Resources)*
Ray Friedman *(Dir.-Mktg. Communications)*

Outside Service Firm(s):

Coblentz, Cohen, McCabe & Breyer*(Legal Firm)*
San Francisco, CA

Wells Fargo Bank*(Major Banking Relationship)*
420 Montgomery St.
San Francisco, CA 94104

Subsidiaries:

Andre-Boudin Bakeries, Inc. **(1)**
132 Hawthorne St.
San Francisco, CA 94107
Tel.: 415-882-1849
Approx.Sls.: $5,000,000
Emp.: 90
Bakery; Bread & Rolls
S.I.C.: 2051
Sharon B. Duvall *(Pres. & Chief Exec. Officer)*
Ed Lamperti *(Chief Admin. Officer)*
Tim O'Shea *(Dir.-New Store Devel.)*

Colombo Baking Co. **(1)**
580 Julie Ann Way
Oakland, CA 94621
Tel.: 510-635-4343
Manufacture & Distribution of French Bread
S.I.C.: 2051; 5149
Lou Giraudo *(Pres.)*

Parisian Bakeries **(1)**
1995 Evans Ave.
San Francisco, CA 94124
Tel.: 415-641-1000
Approx.Sls.: $16,000,000
Emp.: 200
Sour Dough Bread
S.I.C.: 2051
Louis Giraudo *(Chm. & Co-Chief Exec. Officer)*
Sharon B. Duvall *(Co-Chief Exec. Officer)*
Fred Groszkruger *(Chief Oper. Officer)*
Harry Walsh *(Chief Fin. Officer)*
Steve Giraudo *(Exec. V.P.-Production)*
Pete Sher *(Sec. & Gen. Counsel)*
Jerry Bauer *(Dir.-Mngmt. Information Systems)*
Ralph Bagdonas *(Dir.-Human Resources)*
Janet Greenlee *(Dir.-Mktg. Communications)*

SAN FRANCISCO GIANTS BASEBALL CLUB
Candlestick Park
San Francisco, CA 94124
Tel.: 415-468-3700
Tel.: 800-SFGIANTS **CA**
Fax: 415-467-0485
Year Founded: 1883
Sales Range: $20-39 Million
Emp.: 112
Major League Baseball Club: The San Francisco Giants
S.I.C.: 7941
Robert A. Lurie *(Chm. Bd.)*
Albert L. Rosen *(Pres. & Gen. Mgr.)*
Corey Busch *(Exec V.P.)*
Patrick J. Gallagher *(Sr. V.P.)*
Jorge Costa *(V.P.-Stadium Opers.)*
Bob Fontaine *(V.P.-Scouting)*
Duffy Jennings *(V.P.-Pub. Rels.)*
Bob Kennedy *(V.P.-Baseball Opers.)*
Arthur Schulze *(V.P.-Tickets)*
John Yee *(V.P.-Finance)*
Michael Shapiro *(Staff Counsel)*
Jeannie Hurley *(Controller)*
Mario Alioto *(Dir.-Mktg.)*
Dave Craig *(Dir.-Community Services)*
Robin Carr Locke *(Dir.-Communications)*
Robert Tolifson *(Dir.-Retail Opers.)*
Mark Ray *(Dir.-Pubs.)*
Principal(s):
Robert A. Lurie

Computer Systems/Hardware:
IBM

SAN JOSE & ASSOCIATES
625 N. Michigan Ave., Ste. 1601
Chicago, IL 60611-3109
Tel.: 312-751-8500
Fax: 312-751-9080
Year Founded: 1981
Approx.Billings: $12,500,000
Emp.: 19
Hispanic Adv.
George L. San Jose *(Pres. & Exec. Creative Dir.)*
Maria Valencia *(V.P., Opers.)*
Carlos C. Seiglie *(Strategic Mktg. Analyst)*
Alfredo Arias *(Pub. Rels. Dir.)*
Glennie Wilding-White *(Client Services)*

SAN MIGUEL (U.S.A.) INC.
1400 Fashion Island Blvd., Ste. 111
San Mateo, CA 94404
Tel.: 415-345-1330
Tel.: 800-247-8739
Telex: 470266 SMI UI
Fax: 415-341-1519
Year Founded: 1946
Approx.Sls.: $10,000,000
Emp.: 18
Fiscal Year-end: 12/31/90
Import
San Miguel Beer, Sun Lik Beer & Exports, Red Horse Malt Liquor & Fruit Purees
S.I.C.: 2082; 2033
Vincent C. Tarroja *(Exec. V.P. & Gen. Mgr.)*
Lola Fullerton *(Chief Fin. Officer)*
Jean Hephinger *(Admin. Mgr.)*

SANBORN MANUFACTURING COMPANY
118 W. Rock St.
Springfield, MN 56087
Mailing Address:
P.O. Box 206
Springfield, MN 56087
Tel.: 507-723-6211
Tel.: 800-448-0152 **MN**
Fax: 507-723-5013
Year Founded: 1963
Emp.: 375
Fiscal Year-end: 12/31/91
Import Export
Manufacture of Portable, Commercial & Industrial Air Compressors, 1/2 - 50 hp.
S.I.C.: 3563
Jerold Kretsch *(Chm. Bd.)*
William C. Besse *(Chief Exec. Officer)*
Steffen I. Magnell *(Pres.)*
Robert Besse *(Sr. V.P.)*
Lonnie Brown *(V.P.-Fin.)*
Tony Everette *(V.P.-Mktg.)*
Jim Graft *(V.P.-Sls.)*
Chuck Kniebel *(V.P.-Engrng.)*
Gary Rolek *(V.P.-Human Resources)*
Jim Batt *(Controller)*
Sue Steinke *(Mgr.-Human Resources)*
Randy Yaeger *(Dir.-Mngmt. Information Systems)*
Scott Ward *(Dir.-Quality Assurance)*
Clayton Kretsch *(Buyer)*
Jan Tallefson *(Exec. Sec.)*

No. of Mfg. Plants/Facilities: 2

Sanborn Manufacturing Company—(Continued)

No. of U.S. Offices: 3

Computer Systems/Hardware:
NCR Systems 10075

Outside Service Firm(s):

Coopers & Lybrand*(Auditors)*
1000 TCF Bldg.
Minneapolis, MN 55402
Tel.: 612-293-2929
Fax: 612-370-9395

Liberty Mutual*(Commercial Insurance Carrier)*
175 Berkeley St.
Boston, MA

Fredrikson & Byron, P.A.*(Legal Firm)*
1100 International Centre, 900 2nd Ave. S.
Minneapolis, MN 55402
Tel.: 612-347-7000

Sanwa Bank*(Major Banking Relationship)*
Chicago, IL

State Bank of Springfield*(Major Banking Relationship)*
Springfield, MN

SANCHEZ & LEVITAN
ADVERTISING / PUBLIC RELATIONS

SANCHEZ & LEVITAN, INC.
1800 S.W. 27th Ave., Ste. 504
Miami, FL 33145
Tel.: 305-442-1586
Fax: 305-442-2598
Year Founded: 1986
Approx.Billings: $10,000,000
Emp.: 12
Hispanic Markets
Fausto H. Sanchez *(Pres. & Creative Dir.)*
Aida Levitan *(Exec. V.P., Pub. Rels. Dir.)*
Angel Castillo *(Gen. Counsel)*
Roberto Lopez *(Controller)*
Allen Brydger *(Dir., Media & Mktg. Services)*

Computer Systems/Hardware:
IBM

SANDERSON PLUMBING PRODUCTS INC.
Tuffy Lane
Columbus, MS 39701
Mailing Address:
P.O. Box 1367,
Columbus, MS 39703
Tel.: 601-328-4000
Fax: 601-329-4362
Year Founded: 1983
Emp.: 600
Export
Beneke, Tuffy & Samaritan Toilet Seats; Sheltering Arms, Toilet Seats with Arms
S.I.C.: 3088
Sandra B. Sanderson *(Pres. & Chief Exec. Officer)*
Ralph Billingsley *(V.P.-Fin.)*
David Morrow *(V.P.-Sls.)*
Sam Sanderson *(Chief Oper. Officer)*

Outside Service Firm(s):

Ernst & Young*(Auditors)*
1400 One Commerce Sq.
Memphis, TN 38103

Threadgill, Smith, Sanders & Jolly*(Legal Firm)*
Columbus, MS

Divisions:

Beneke **(1)**
Tuffy Lane
Columbus, MS 39701
Tel.: 601-328-4000
S.I.C.: 3088

Magnolia Division **(1)**
Tuffy Lane
Columbus, MS 39701
Tel.: 601-328-4000
David Morrow *(V.P.-Sls.)*

SANDLER COMMUNICATIONS INC.
130 Fifth Ave.
New York, NY 10010
Tel.: 212-675-4700
Fax: 212-675-5052
Year Founded: 1984
Approx.Billings: $24,817,750
Emp.: 40
Healthcare
Kenneth B. Sandler *(Pres. & New Bus. Contact)*
Art Mahoney *(Exec. V.P.)*

SANDS INVESTMENTS, INC.
4612 Oleander Dr.
Myrtle Beach, SC 29577
Tel.: 803-449-5286 **SC**
Fax: 803-449-4534
Year Founded: 1974
Approx.Rev.: $28,794,000
Emp.: 1,100
Fiscal Year-end: 1/31/92
Property Management & Public Relations Services
S.I.C.: 6531; 8743
Leslie M. Morris, Jr. *(Pres.)*
Girard M. Blount *(V.P.-Pub. Rels.)*
Thomas E. Baugh, Jr. *(Sec.)*
Paul J. Lohman *(Treas. & Asst. Sec.)*
Principal(s):
Leslie M. Morris, Jr.
Thomas E. Baugh, Jr.

Outside Service Firm(s):

Webster, Rodgers, West, Berry & Grady*(Auditors)*
Myrtle Beach, SC

Puckett, Scheetz & Hogan*(Commercial Insurance Carrier)*
Myrtle Beach, SC

Bellamy Law Firm*(Legal Firm)*
Myrtle Beach, SC

Southern National Bank*(Major Banking Relationship)*
Florence, SC

SANDS MOTOR COMPANY, INC.
5418 N.W. Grand Ave.
Glendale, AZ 85301
Tel.: 602-931-9331 **AZ**
Fax: 602-939-4940
Year Founded: 1938
Approx.Sls.: $60,000,000
Emp.: 140
Fiscal Year-end: 12/31/91
Retail Sales of New & Used Automobiles
S.I.C.: 5511
Louis Sands IV *(Pres.)*
Charles F. Sands *(V.P.)*
Gary R. Long *(Sec.)*

Outside Service Firm(s):

First Interstate Bank*(Major Banking Relationship)*
P.O. Box 53441,
Phoenix, AZ 85072-3441
Tel.: 602-229-4049

Sanel Auto Supply Associates
(See Sands Motor Company, Inc.)

SANFORD & HAWLEY, INC.
1790 Farmington Ave.
Unionville, CT 06085
Tel.: 203-673-3213
Fax: 203-675-9504
Approx.Sls.: $18,000,000
Emp.: 36
Sale of Building Materials; Lumber; Drywall; Hardware; Paint; Plywood; Windows; Doors; Mason Supplies & Roofing
S.I.C.: 5211; 5031; 5033; 5039
Robert P. Sanford *(Pres.)*
Frank W. Sanford *(V.P.-Pur. & Mktg.)*
Edmund E. Sanford *(V.P.-Opers.)*
Robert W. Sanford *(Treas.)*
Clara E. Sanford *(Sec.)*
Mark Lowell *(Gen. Counsel)*
Paul R. Peterson *(Mgr.-Data Processing)*

SANISERV
2020 Production Dr.
Indianapolis, IN 46241
Mailing Address:
P.O. Box 41240
Indianapolis, IN 46241
Tel.: 317-247-0460
Telex: 276064
Fax: 317-247-5130
Approx.Sls.: $20,000,000
Emp.: 70
Fiscal Year-end: 12/31/90
Sani-Serv Soft Ice Cream Machines, Shake Machines, Soft Serv Yogurt Machines, Frozen Liquor Dispensers, Frozen Beverage Dispensers, Gourmet Ice Cream Display & Dipping Cabinets
S.I.C.: 3585
G.E. Aquirre *(Chm. Bd. & Pres.)*
Greg Aguirre *(V.P.-Sls.)*
Kaye Aguirre *(V.P.)*
Gary W. Lucas *(Dir.-Adv.)*

SANTA MONICA FORD COMPANY
1230 Santa Monica Blvd.
Santa Monica, CA 90404
Tel.: 310-451-1588 **CA**
Fax: 310-394-8115
Year Founded: 1948
Approx.Sls.: $400,000,000
Emp.: 85
Fiscal Year-end: 12/31/91
Retail Sales of New & Used Automobiles
S.I.C.: 5511
L. Wayne Harding *(Chm. Bd.)*
Robert Karlin *(Pres.)*
Mark Harding *(V.P.)*
Alex Pangan *(Sec. & Treas.)*

SANTA ROSA STEEL FORMING, INC.
1219 Briggs Ave.
Santa Rosa, CA 95401
Tel.: 707-542-1720 **CA**
Fax: 707-542-1734
Year Founded: 1972
Approx.Sls.: $10,000,000
Emp.: 40
Fiscal Year-end: 12/31/91
Export
Conveyors & Conveying Equipment
S.I.C.: 3535
Bruce Rosemond *(Pres.)*
Jack Gregory *(V.P. & Treas.)*
John McCort *(V.P.-Sls.)*
T. Pilain *(Gen. Mgr.)*
T. Lim *(Pur. Agent)*

Outside Service Firm(s):

Wells Fargo Bank*(Major Banking Relationship)*
420 Montgomery St.
San Francisco, CA 94104

SANTEE PRINT WORKS, INC.
71 W. 35th St.
New York, NY 10001
Tel.: 212-279-0168
Fax: 212-629-8801
Year Founded: 1949
Approx.Sls.: $60,000,000
Emp.: 900
Printing of Cotton Broadwoven Fabrics
S.I.C.: 2261
Martin Barocas *(Pres.)*
Leon Barocas *(V.P., Treas. & Sec.)*

Outside Service Firm(s):

Manufacturers Hanover Trust Co.*(Major Banking Relationship)*
4 New York Plaza
New York, NY 10015
Tel.: 212-633-7938

Subsidiary:

Weilwood Industries, Inc. **(1)**
119 W. 40th St.
New York, NY 10018
Tel.: 212-391-2300
Textile Converters
S.I.C.: 5131
Leon Baracos *(Pres.)*
Marty Baracos *(V.P.)*
Paul Richter *(Controller)*
Victor Baracos *(Sec.)*

THE SANYMETAL PRODUCTS CO., INC.
PO Box 490, Black Oak Industrial Park
Vanceburg, KY 41179
Tel.: 606-796-6711
Fax: 216-446-0085
Approx.Sls.: $20,000,000
Emp.: 300
Fiscal Year-end: 12/31/90
Toilet Partitions; Porcena Porcelain Enameled Partitions; Sanyplastic Plastic Laminated Partitions; Sanyvinyl Vinyl Laminated Partitions & Fast Cycle Laminated Partitions
S.I.C.: 2599
George A. Hommel *(Pres.)*
Steve Perry *(Exec. V.P. & G.M.)*
Frank J. Levstek *(V.P.-Mfg.)*
Robert Pampush *(Treas. & Asst. Sec.)*
Anthony Ruggeri *(Pur. Agent)*

SARATOGA HARNESS RACING, INC.
Nelson Ave.
Saratoga Springs, NY 12866
Mailing Address:
P. O. Box 356
Saratoga Springs, NY 12866
Tel.: 518-584-2110
Fax: 518-583-0995
Year Founded: 1941
Approx.Sls.: $60,000,000
Emp.: 300
Harness Racing Track
S.I.C.: 7948
Joe W. Gerrity, Jr. *(Chm. Bd.)*
William J. Kayo *(V.P.)*
Francis A. Fitzgerald *(V.P.)*
George Wiley *(Controller)*
Frank L. Fernandez *(Treas. & Sec.)*
Warren DeSantis *(Gen. Mgr.)*
George W. Carlson *(Publicity Dir.)*
Helen Casson *(Dir.-Personnel)*
Richard Conte *(Dir.-Telecommunications)*
Frank Della Rocca *(Dir.-Pur.)*

SARGENT-FLETCHER CO.
9400 E. Flair Drive
El Monte, CA 91731
Tel.: 818-443-7171
Fax: 818-579-9183
Year Founded: 1897
Sales Range: $100-499 Million
Emp.: 600

Fiscal Year-end: 3/31/91
Mfr. of In-Flight Refueling Systems, Auxillary Drop Tanks & Pylons; Ground Support Equipment
S.I.C.: 3728
Gordon H. Smith *(Pres.)*
Robert M. Stemmier *(Exec. V.P. & Chief Oper. Officer)*
Chuck Sebastian *(V.P.-Bus. Devel.)*
Joe Beck *(Dir.-Quality Assurance)*
Gregory Catrambone *(Dir.-Fin.)*
Pat Harn *(Dir.-Personnel)*
William Harper *(Mgr.-Pur.)*

Computer Systems/Hardware:
IBM PC

Outside Service Firm(s):

Deloitte & Touche*(Auditors)*
1000 Wilshire Blvd.
Los Angeles, CA 90017-2472
Tel.: 213-688-0800
Fax: 213-688-0100

Massachusetts Mutual Life Insurance Co.*(Group Insurer)*
1295 State St.
Springfield, MA 01111
Tel.: 413-788-8411
Fax: 413-730-6144

McColgan & Vanni*(Legal Firm)*
Los Angeles, CA

Subsidiary:

AJ Industries, Inc. **(1)**
9420 Telstar Ave., Ste. 200
El Monte, CA 91731
Tel.: 818-443-7171
Fax: 818-443-8611
Approx.Sls.: $130,000,000
Emp.: 1,300
Fiscal Year-end: 3/31/90
Export
Bus & Truck Brake Druns & Suspension Systems, Inflight Refueling Systems, Aluminum Aircraft Fuel Tanks & Infra-red Heater Systems
S.I.C.: 3728; 3433; 3714
Gregory Catrambone *(Chm. Bd.)*

SARGENT & GREENLEAF, INC.
1 Security Dr.
Nicholasville, KY 40356
Tel.: 606-885-9411
Fax: 606-885-3063
Approx.Sls.: $30,000,000
Emp.: 200
High Security Locking Devices for Banking, Container & Governmental Industries
S.I.C.: 3429; 3499; 3699
Terry Hershbeger *(Chm. Bd.)*
Jerry Morgan *(Pres. & Chief Oper. Officer)*
Alann Karow *(Sr. V.P.-Fin. & Admin.)*
Ned Urschel *(V.P.-Sls.)*
Maury Andaya *(Data Processing Mgr.)*
Gary Kepler *(Mgr.-Customer Service)*
John Thompson *(Pur. Mgr.)*
Bryan Callihan *(Acctg. Mgr.)*

Subsidiary:

Sargent & Greenleaf International **(1)**
1 Security Dr.
Nicholasville, KY 40356
Tel.: 606-885-9411
Fax: 606-885-3063-

H. E. SARGENT, INC.
101 Bennoch Rd.
Stillwater, ME 04489
Tel.: 207-827-4435
Fax: 207-827-6150
Year Founded: 1926
Approx.Sls.: $45,000,000
Emp.: 350
Heavy Highway Construction & Paving, Roads, Airports, Dams, Industrial Site Preparation, Sewers, Water Treatment Plants, Landfills & Remediation
S.I.C.: 1611; 1623; 1629
John Simpson *(Pres. & Chief Exec. Officer)*
Ken Burrill *(V.P.-Mktg.)*
Richard Martin *(V.P.-Construction)*
Philip Lander *(V.P.-Maintenance)*
George Thomas *(V.P.-Fin.)*
Gerard Tassel *(Treas.)*
Allen Cust *(Pur. Agent)*

Outside Service Firm(s):

KPMG Peat Marwick*(Auditors)*
100 Middle St. Plaza
Portland, ME

KPMG Peat Marwick*(Auditors)*
1211 S.W. Fifth Ave.
Portland, OR 97204

Key Bank*(Major Banking Relationship)*
Bangor, ME

Amerling & Burns*(Legal Firm)*
Portland, ME

Subsidiary:

H. E. Sargent Constructor Inc. **(1)**
145 River Rd.
Lewiston, ME 04241
Tel.: 207-786-4542

SARGENT & LUNDY
55 E. Monroe St.
Chicago, IL 60603
Tel.: 312-269-2000
Telex: 28-0603
Fax: 312-269-3680
Fax: 312-269-3596
Year Founded: 1891
Approx.Sls.: $190,000,000
Emp.: 2,600
Fiscal Year-end: 12/31/91
Consulting Engineers for Design of Nuclear & Fossil Fueled Power Generation Facilities, Transmission Lines & Related Activities for Utility & Industrial Applications
S.I.C.: 8711
Eugene V. Abraham *(Sr. Partner)*
Carmen M. Chiappetta *(Partner & Mgr.-Electrical Dept.)*
George C. Kuhlman *(Partner & Dir.-Engrng.)*
John M. McLaughlin *(Partner & Mgr.-Service Dept.)*
Paul L. Wattelet *(Partner & Mgr.-Mechanical Dept.)*
Donald L. Leone *(Partner & Asst. Mgr.-Mechanical Dept.)*
Donald E. Wolniak *(Partner & Asst. Mgr.-Mechanical Dept.)*
Bryan A. Erler *(Partner & Asst. Mgr.-Structural Dept.)*
William G. Schwartz *(Partner & Asst. Mgr.-Electrical Dept.)*
Alexander Cudzewicz *(Dir.-Fin., Treas. & Chief Fin. Officer)*
J. J. O'Reilly *(Assoc. Head-Computer Srvcs.)*
Gerald A. Boelke *(Head-Employee Rels.)*
Albert Nathan *(Assoc. Head-Contract Procurement)*

No. of U.S. Offices: 5
No. of Foreign Offices: 3

Computer Systems/Hardware:
UNISYS 1100/91, DEC VAXES, & PC LANS

Outside Service Firm(s):

Arthur Andersen & Co.*(Auditors)*
33 W. Monroe St.
Chicago, IL 60603-4067
Tel.: 312-580-0033
Fax: 312-507-6748

Continental Bank N. A.*(Major Banking Relationship)*
231 S. LaSalle St.
Chicago, IL 60697
Tel.: 312-828-2345
Tel.: 800-426-5754
Telex: 312-828-1783

McDermott, Will & Emery*(Legal Firm)*
227 W. Monroe St.
Chicago, IL 60606-5096
Tel.: 312-372-2000

SARGENT & POTRATZ, INC.
250 N. Sunny Slope Rd.
Brookfield, WI 53005
Tel.: 414-789-0900
Fax: 414-789-0757
Year Founded: 1985
Approx.Billings: $15,500,000
Emp.: 24
Agriculture & Industrial Adv.
John W. Sargent *(Pres., Treas., New Bus. Contact, Production & Research Dir.)*
Dean C. Potratz *(Exec. V.P., Sec. & Pub. Rels. Dir.)*
Nancy Sargent *(Office Mgr.)*
Sandy Klotz *(Acctg. Mgr.)*

THE SARGENT-SOWELL COMPANY
(Formerly Sargent Sowell, Inc.)
1185 108th St.
Grand Prairie, TX 75050
Mailing Address:
P.O. Box 534008,
Grand Prairie, TX 75053-9971
Tel.: 214-647-1525
Tel.: 800-527-2450 **TX**
Fax: 214-988-6202
Approx.Sls.: $10,000,000
Emp.: 120
Wholesale Distributor of Law Enforcement Equipment & Supplies; Manufacturer of Signs; Sign Painting Shops
S.I.C.: 5099; 3993
William Montgomery *(Chm. Bd., Pres., & Chief Exec. Officer)*
Don Reed *(Sr. Exec. V.P. & Chief Fin. Officer)*
Rick Cooper *(Exec. V.P.)*
Sherry Johnson *(V.P.-Mktg.)*
Marlene Crisp *(Sec.)*
Parker Fanning *(Controller)*
Bob Burks *(Mgr.-Purch.)*
Gene David *(Mgr.-Mfg.)*

Principal(s):
William Montgomery

SARGENTO INCORPORATED
1 Persnickety Place
Plymouth, WI 53073
Mailing Address:
P. O. Box 350
Plymouth, WI 53073
Tel.: 414-893-8484 **WI**
Fax: 414-893-8399
Year Founded: 1953
Approx.Sls.: $275,000,000
Emp.: 650
Fiscal Year-end: 6/29/91
Mfrs. Cheeses for Sale to Retail & Industrial Users
S.I.C.: 5143; 2022; 6719
Leonard A. Gentine, Sr. *(Chm. Bd.)*
Louis P. Gentine *(Pres. & Chief Exec. Officer)*
Lawrence J. Gentine *(Pres.-Food Service Corp.)*
George H. Hoff *(Exec. V.P. & Chief Fin. Officer)*
Tom Clegg *(V.P.-Mktg.)*
Edward A. Sturzl *(V.P.-Human Resources)*

Principal(s):
Leonard A. Gentine, Sr.
Louis P. Gentine

No. of Mfg. Plants/Facilities: 3
No. of U.S. Offices: 1

Computer Systems/Hardware:
Burroughs A-5F

Outside Service Firm(s):

Price Waterhouse*(Auditors)*
1500 Bank One Plaza, 100 E. Wisconsin Ave.
Milwaukee, WI 53202

Reinhart, Boerner, Van Deuren, Norris & Rieselbach, S.C.*(Legal Firm)*
1000 N. Water St., Ste. 2100
Milwaukee, WI 53202
Tel.: 414-298-1000

First Wisconsin National Bank*(Major Banking Relationship)*
Sheboygan, WI

First Wisconsin National Bank*(Major Banking Relationship)*
777 E. Wisconsin Ave.
Milwaukee, WI 53202
Tel.: 414-765-4321
Fax: 414-355-6903

Subsidiaries:

Duralam, Inc. **(1)**
P.O. Box 862
Appleton, WI 54912
Tel.: 414-734-6698
Emp.: 80
Mfr. Flexible Packaging Matls.
S.I.C.: 2631; 2657
Marv Schneider *(Pres.)*
Dan Baird *(V.P.-Sls.)*
Jeff Lammers *(V.P.-Admin.)*
Gus Marturano *(V.P.-Mfg.)*

Sargento Cheese Co. **(1)**
N. Sunset Dr.
Plymouth, WI 53073
Tel.: 414-893-8484
Distr. Natural Domestic & Imported Cheeses
S.I.C.: 2022; 5143
Leonard A. Gentine, Sr. *(Chm. Bd.)*
Lee Gentine *(Pres. & Chief Exec. Officer)*
Tom Paul *(Controller)*
Ronald E. Begalke *(Exec. V.P.-Opers.)*
Lee M. Gentine *(Exec. V.P.-Mktg.)*
John W. Fernsler *(V.P.-Sls.)*
Mike Gordy *(V.P.-Retail Sls.)*
George H. Hoff *(V.P.-Fin. & Admin.)*
Jerry Robb *(V.P.-Procurement/Prod. Control)*
Edward Sturzl *(V.P.-Personnel)*
Tom Clegg *(Dir.-Adv. & Consumer Promotions)*
Dorothy Farrell *(Dir.-Communications)*
Wayne Casper *(Mgr.-New Prod. Devel.)*
Bredt Wilhelmsen *(Mgr.-Data Processing)*

Sargento Food Service Corp. **(1)**
P.O. Box 390
Plymouth, WI 53073
Tel.: 414-893-8484
Approx.Sls.: $121,000,000
Emp.: 475
Mfr. of Cheeses for Sale to Retail & Indus. Users
S.I.C.: 5143; 2022
Larry Gentine *(Pres.)*
David Lorbecki *(V.P.-Sls.)*
George H. Hoff *(Sec. & Treas.)*

Specialty Foods Group **(1)**
P.O. Box 350,
Plymouth, WI 53073
Tel.: 414-893-8484
S.I.C.: 5143

SASCO GROUP
12900 Alondra Blvd.
Cerritos, CA 90701
Tel.: 310-926-0900 **CA**
Fax: 310-926-1399
Year Founded: 1968
Approx.Sls.: $73,000,000
Emp.: 730
General Electrical Contractor
S.I.C.: 1731
L.H. Smead *(Pres.)*
Scott Eaton *(Sec.)*

Outside Service Firm(s):

BankAmerica Corp.*(Major Banking Relationship)*
Anaheim, CA

Sasco Group—(Continued)

Subsidiaries:

Sasco Electric **(1)**
12900 Alondra Blvd.
Cerritos, CA 90701
Tel.: 310-926-0900
General Electrical Contractor
S.I.C.: 1731
L.H. Smead *(Pres.)*
Milton Greene *(Sec.)*

Sasco/Valley Electric **(1)**
2288 Charleston Rd.
Mountain View, CA 94043
Tel.: 415-967-5728
General Electrical Contractor
S.I.C.: 1731
Richard Yeadon *(Pres.)*
Scott Eaton *(Sec. & Treas.)*
Jeff Tarzwell *(Controller)*

SASS & ASSOCIATES
275 West St., Ste. 300
Annapolis, MD 21401
Tel.: 410-263-8448
Fax: 410-269-0161
Year Founded: 1976
Approx.Billings: $22,000,000
Emp.: 22
Fashion, Consumer Electronics, Yachting, Shopping Centers & Sports Apparel
George G. Sass *(Pres. & Creative Dir.)*
Chris Mushinsky *(Sr. V.P., Gen Mgr.)*
Andrew Perrine *(Research, Dir.)*
Kate Delano *(Pub. Rels.)*

SASSON JEANS FOR MEN
350 5th Ave.
New York, NY 10018
Tel.: 212-629-9209
Fax: 212-629-9147
Approx.Sls.: $25,000,000
Emp.: 600
Mfr. of Men's Jeans
S.I.C.: 2325
Eric Rothfeld *(Pres.)*
Dennis Inqui *(Exec. V.P.)*

SATHERS INC.
Sather Plaza
Round Lake, MN 56167-0028
Mailing Address:
P.O. Box 28
Round Lake, MN 56167
Tel.: 507-945-8343
Fax: 507-945-8343
Year Founded: 1936
Approx.Sls.: $126,000,000
Emp.: 1,040
Fiscal Year-end: 12/31/90
Manufacture, Marketing & Distribution of Confectionery Products
S.I.C.: 5145
Howard E. Kosel *(Chief Exec. Officer)*
William Bradfield *(Pres. & Chief Oper. Officer)*
James Schuller *(V.P.-Fin.)*
Dan Janssen *(Controller)*
Wint Fahrenkrog *(Dir.-Procurement)*
Mike Halverson *(Dir.-Mktg.)*
Doug Pendgraft *(Dir.-Human Resources)*
Steve Luitjens *(Mgr.-Natl. Sls.)*
Tom Warrant *(Mgr.-Information Services)*
Principal(s):
Sather Family

No. of Mfg. Plants/Facilities: 6
No. of U.S. Offices: 6

Computer Systems/Hardware:
IBM ES9000

Outside Service Firm(s):

Friedman, Eisenstein, Raemer & Schwartz*(Auditors)*
Chicago, IL

LaSalle National Bank*(Major Banking Relationship)*
120 S. LaSalle St.
Chicago, IL 60603
Tel.: 312-781-8000

Subsidiary:

Powell's Inc. **(1)**
1707 E. Excelsior Blvd.
Hopkins, MN 55343
General Line Candy Mfr.
S.I.C.: 2064

SAUDER MANUFACTURING CORPORATION
600 Middle St.
Archbold, OH 43502
Tel.: 419-446-9384
Tel.: 800-537-1530
Fax: 419-446-2590
Year Founded: 1934
Approx.Sls.: $21,000,000
Emp.: 2,000
Fiscal Year-end: 12/31/91
Mfr. of Institutional, Office & Church Furniture
S.I.C.: 2521; 2531
Maynard Sauder *(Chm. Bd.)*
Virgil Miller *(Pres.)*
Frank Ulrich *(V.P.-Sls.)*
Ronald Borton *(Sec. & Treas.)*
Jack Spotts *(Mgr.-Production)*
David Schrock *(Plant Engineer)*

SAUDER WOODWORKING CO.
502 Middle St.
Archbold, OH 43502
Tel.: 419-446-2711
Fax: 419-446-2980
Approx.Sls.: $300,000,000
Emp.: 2,000
Fiscal Year-end: 12/31/91
Manufacture Ready To Assemble Fiber Board & Wood Furniture
S.I.C.: 2511; 3083
Erie J. Sauder *(Chm. Bd.)*
Maynard Sauder *(Pres. & Chief Exec. Officer)*
Gene Metz *(V.P.-Sls. & Mktg.)*
Richard Riegsecker *(V.P.-Mfg.)*
Kevin Sauder *(V.P.-Sls. & Mktg.)*
Myrl Sauder *(V.P.-Engr.)*
Elvin D. Yoder *(V.P.-Fin. & Admin & Corp. Sec.)*
Charles Lawrence *(Dir.-Pur.)*
John Yoder *(Dir.-Mktg. & European Sls.)*

Computer Systems/Hardware:
Data General

Outside Service Firm(s):

Krouse & Kern*(Auditors)*
Fort Wayne, IN

Rice, Plassman, Rupp & Hensal*(Legal Firm)*
Archbold, OH

First National Bank of Toledo*(Major Banking Relationship)*
Toledo, OH

SAUER INDUSTRIES, INC.
4960 U.S.X. Tower, 600 Grant St.
Pittsburgh, PA 15219
Tel.: 412-765-8000
Year Founded: 1876
Assets: $22,339,099
Liabilities: $5,809,800
Net Worth: $16,529,299
Approx.Sls.: $41,909,378
Emp.: 200
Fiscal Year-end: 12/31/91
Import Export
William N. Steitz *(Pres.)*
J.P. Sakey *(V.P.)*
Sharon M. Johnson *(Controller & Sec.)*
Joseph J. Yelenic *(Controller-Spec & Voltec)*

Outside Service Firm(s):

Deloitte & Touche*(Auditors)*
2400 One PPG Place
Pittsburgh, PA 15222
Tel.: 412-281-2232

Kirkpatrick & Lockhart*(Legal Firm)*
1500 Oliver Bldg., 535 Smithfield St.
Pittsburgh, PA 15222
Tel.: 412-355-6500
Fax: 412-355-6501

Mellon Bank, N.A.*(Major Banking Relationship)*
P.O. Box 444,
Pittsburgh, PA 15230
Tel.: 412-236-8000
Tel.: 1-800-451-7392
Fax: 412-236-8157

Subsidiaries:

Sauer Holdings **(1)**
715 Kings St., Suite 310
Wilmington, DE 19801

SPEC Group **(1)**
Pleasant Valley Rd., Box 510
Trafford, PA 15085
Tel.: 412-744-3301
Fax: 412-744-0017
Engineering Services
S.I.C.: 8711
Ken Haase *(Chief Oper. Officer)*

Voltec **(1)**
3075 Washington Rd.
McMurray, PA 15317
Tel.: 412-941-5360
Emp.: 25
Relays & Industrial Controls
S.I.C.: 3625
Charles Pitchford *(Exec. V.P. & Gen. Mgr.)*

Concordia Custom Yachts **(1)**
300 Gulf Rd.
South Dartmouth, MA 02748
Tel.: 508-992-9733

THE SAUGATUCK MARKETING GROUP
(Formerly Saugatuck Direct)
18 Kings Hwy. North
Westport, CT 06880
Tel.: 203-226-8166
Fax: 203-227-6667
Year Founded: 1979
Approx.Billings: $53,964,500
Emp.: 43
Direct Response, Sls. Promotion & Mktg. Consulting
Donald J. White *(Pres. & Chief Oper. Officer)*
Jim McAlister *(Exec. V.P.)*

SAUL BROS. & COMPANY, INC.
6500 Peachtree Indus. Blvd.
Norcross, GA 30071
Tel.: 404-417-8000
Fax: 404-417-8008
Year Founded: 1949
Approx.Sls.: $20,000,000
Emp.: 100
Fiscal Year-end: 10/31/91
Manufacture Missy, Junior & Women's Sportswear
S.I.C.: 2339
Harry Gordon *(Chm. Bd. & Controller)*
Robert L. Thomas *(Pres. & Treas.)*
Myra L. Herrin *(V.P.)*
Principal(s):
Harry Gordon
Robert L. Thomas

Outside Service Firm(s):

Savage & Warren*(Auditors)*
Atlanta, GA

Arnall, Golden & Gregory*(Legal Firm)*
55 Park Place
Atlanta, GA 30335
Tel.: 404-577-5100

First National Bank of Boston*(Major Banking Relationship)*
P.O. Box 644,
Boston, MA 02102-0644
Tel.: 617-575-2900
Fax: 617-575-2549

Division:

Habits, Inc. **(1)**
1350 Broadway
New York, NY 10018
Tel.: 212-736-3480
Mfr. of Missy, Junior & Women's Sportswear
S.I.C.: 2339
Richard Schein *(Pres.)*

SAUNDERS BROTHERS
170 Forest St.
Westbrook, ME 04098
Mailing Address:
P.O. Box 1016,
Westbrook, ME 04098
Tel.: 207-854-2551
Tel.: 800-343-0675 **ME**
Fax: 207-854-1243
Year Founded: 1900
Approx.Sls.: $25,000,000
Emp.: 300
Fiscal Year-end: 9/30/90
Import Export
Mfr. Wood Dowels & Turnings, Pool Cues, Wood Furniture Parts, Shelving, Small Furniture & Accessories
S.I.C.: 2499; 2431; 2511; 2541
Bruce T. Saunders *(Chm. Bd.)*
John E. Bowman *(Pres.)*
Clyde Pingree *(Chief Oper. Officer)*
Richard C. Randall *(V.P.-Engrng. Services)*
Robert Webb *(V.P.-Sls. & Mktg.)*

Divisions:

Forest Industries, Inc. **(1)**
18 Fair St.
Fryeburg, ME 04037
Tel.: 207-935-2092
Import Export
Custom Wood Turnings
S.I.C.: 2499
Joel LeTante *(Plant Mgr.)*
Peter Spalding *(Natl. Sls. Mgr.)*

National Wood Products, Co. **(1)**
RFD 1 Box 1575
Oxford, ME 04270
Tel.: 207-343-0675
Import Export
Flatwork; Routing & Shaping
S.I.C.: 2431
Wallace Wall *(Gen. Mgr.)*

Subsidiary:

H. A. Stiles Co. **(1)**
170 Forest St.
Westbrook, ME 04092
Tel.: 207-854-8453
Import Export
Marketing & Sales of Saunders Brothers Products
S.I.C.: 2499; 5046; 5031
Ambrose Berry *(Gen. Mgr.)*

SAUNDERS INCORPORATED
2801 Hwy. 280, Bldg. 1, 3rd Fl.
Birmingham, AL 35223-2407
Tel.: 205-868-6600 **DE**
Fax: 205-868-6536
Year Founded: 1986
Sales Range: $10-19 Million
Emp.: 137
Fiscal Year-end: 12/31/91
Truck Transportation Services
S.I.C.: 4789
Harris Saunders, Jr. *(Chm. Bd.)*
W. Michael Linn *(Asst. Dir. of Bd.)*

Outside Service Firm(s):

Coopers & Lybrand*(Auditors)*
1901 6th Ave. North, Ste. 1600
Birmingham, AL 35203-2602

Bradley, Arant, Rose & White*(Legal Firm)*
1400 Park Place Tower
Birmingham, AL 35203
Tel.: 205-521-8000

SAUNDERS, LUBINSKI & WHITE, INC.
7610 Stemmons Frwy., Ste. 100
Dallas, TX 75247
Tel.: 214-630-6160
Fax: 214-630-4016
Year Founded: 1976
Approx.Billings: $26,000,000
Emp.: 26
Retail, Banking & Mobile Communications
William C. Saunders *(Chm. & Creative Dir.)*
Tracy Griffin *(V.P., Controller)*

SAV-RITE ADVERTISING

2110 Executive Dr.
Salisbury, NC 28145
Tel.: 704-633-8250
Year Founded: 1975
Approx.Billings: $15,000,000
Tom Crabtree *(V.P., Adv.)*

SAVAGE ARMS INC.
Springdale Rd.
Westfield, MA 01085
Tel.: 413-568-7001 **MA**
Fax: 413-562-7764
Year Founded: 1895
Approx.Sls.: $40,000,000
Emp.: 150
Fiscal Year-end: 10/31/91
Import Export
Manufacture Sporting Firearms & Accessories
S.I.C.: 3484
Herman Frietsch *(Chm. Bd.)*
Ronald Coburn *(Pres. & Chief Exec. Officer)*
David H. Tolly *(V.P., Sec. & Gen. Counsel)*
Thomas Humphrey *(V.P.-Fin. & Controller)*
Clayton Pilz *(Mgr.-Sls. & Mktg.)*
Michael Parker *(Pur. Agent)*

No. of Mfg. Plants/Facilities: 1
No. of U.S. Offices: 1

Computer Systems/Hardware:
Prime

SAVE MART SUPERMARKETS
1800 Standiford Ave.
Modesto, CA 95352
Mailing Address:
P.O. Box 4278,
Modesto, CA 95352
Tel.: 209-577-0803
Fax: 209-526-4396
Year Founded: 1952
Approx.Sls.: $1,200,000,000
Emp.: 7,000
Fiscal Year-end: 3/29/92
Supermarket Chain
S.I.C.: 5411
Robert M. Piccinini *(Chm. Bd. & Chief Exec. Officer & Pres.)*
William Kretschmer *(V.P. & Chief Fin. Officer)*
John Bacon *(V.P.-Human Resources)*
Mike Silvera *(Gen. Counsel)*
Ronald Riesenbeck *(Controller)*
Steve Goodman *(Dir.-Personnel)*
Ed Martin *(Dir.-Mngmt. Information Systems)*
Cecil Russell *(Dir.-Mktg.)*
Sally Sanborn *(Dir.-P.R.)*

No. of Mfg. Plants/Facilities: 85

Computer Systems/Hardware:
IBM AS/400

Outside Service Firm(s):

Arthur Andersen & Co.*(Auditors)*
Spear Street Tower, One Market Plaza, Ste. 3500
San Francisco, CA 94105
Tel.: 415-546-8200

Pettit & Martin*(Legal Firm)*
San Jose, CA

Bank of America, N.T. & S.A.*(Major Banking Relationship)*
P.O. Box 37002,
San Francisco, CA 94137

Cutler & Co.*(Pension Manager)*
Los Angeles, CA

Subsidiary:

Yosemite Express Co. **(1)**
4150 N. Golden St. Blvd.
Turlock, CA 95380
Tel.: 209-632-2481
Transportation
S.I.C.: 4731

SAVE MORE FOOD MART, INC.
Rtes. 6 & 51
Hobart, IN 46342
Tel.: 219-942-1108 **IN**
Fax: 219-942-7543
Year Founded: 1927
Sales Range: $20-39 Million
Emp.: 98
Retail Grocery Stores
S.I.C.: 5411
Larry Weiss *(Chm. Bd., Pres., Chief Exec. Officer & Sec.)*
Margaret Weiss *(Controller)*
Principal(s):
Larry Weiss

Computer Systems/Hardware:
Radio Shack Model 12

Outside Service Firm(s):

Deutsch Co.*(Auditors)*
Highland, IN

Kadich & Associates*(Legal Firm)*
Merriville, IN

SAVEMART INC.
332 E. 149th St.
Bronx, NY 10451
Tel.: 718-292-6700
Fax: 718-292-5825
Year Founded: 1950
Approx.Sls.: $100,000,000
Emp.: 250
Consumer Electronics Retailer-TV Sets, Radios, VCRs, Stereos
S.I.C.: 5731
Benjamin Blank *(Chm. & Chief Exec. Officer)*
John Kitzie *(Pres.)*
Romeo Roque *(Treas.)*
John Rossi *(Dir.-Personnel)*
Walter Barnes *(Mgr.-Engrng.)*

Outside Service Firm(s):

Chase Manhattan Bank, N.A.*(Major Banking Relationship)*
One Chase Manhattan Plaza
New York, NY 10081
Tel.: 212-552-2222
Tel.: 800-526-0801
Fax: 212-552-7175

MIKE SAVOIE CHEVROLET INC.
1900 W. Maple Rd.
Troy, MI 48099
Tel.: 313-643-8000 **DE**
Fax: 313-649-3007
Approx.Sls.: $24,000,000
Emp.: 100
Automobile Dealership
S.I.C.: 5511
Michael P. Savoie, Sr. *(Pres.)*
Michael P. Savoie, Jr. *(V.P.)*

Mary Grogg *(Sec. & Treas.)*
Keith Studzinski *(Mgr.-Sls.)*

THE SAVOGRAN COMPANY
259 Lenox St.
Norwood, MA 02062
Mailing Address:
P.O. Box 130
Norwood, MA 02062
Tel.: 617-762-5400
Fax: 617-762-1095
Approx.Sls.: $15,000,000
Emp.: 60
Strypeeze Paint & Varnish Remover; Dirtex Cleaner; Deglosser Compound; LevelBest Spackling Products; Kutzit Liquid Paint Remover; Presto Patch Spackling Compound, H2 Off Remover; Fast Wallpaper Remover; Mintex Waterless Hand Cleaner, Tile Grout Tile Repairer; Crack Filler, Wood Putty, Kwikeeze Brush Cleaner
S.I.C.: 2851
Robert E. Lenk *(Pres.)*
Steve McLean *(V.P.-Sls.)*
John L. Gale *(V.P.-Opers.)*
Mark Monique *(Mgr.-Adv.)*

Affiliate:

Savogran of California **(1)**
3201 Union Pacific Ave.
Los Angeles, CA 90023
Tel.: 213-261-5111
S.I.C.: 2851

SAVOY CONSTRUCTION CO. INC.
3004 McComas Ave.
Kensington, MD 20895
Tel.: 301-942-5200
Fax: 301-942-3008
Sales Range: $10-19 Million
Emp.: 10
General Building Contractors; Construction Management
S.I.C.: 1521; 1522; 1541; 1542
Saul H. Bernstein *(Pres., Chief Exec. Officer & Treas.)*
Edward C. Smith *(Chief Fin. Officer & V.P.)*
Edilio Ursini *(Exec. V.P.-Admin.)*
Alexis Mootoo *(Controller)*

Computer Systems/Hardware:
IBM PC

Outside Service Firm(s):

Max & London*(Auditors)*
Silver Spring, MD

Blue Cross & Blue Shield of the National Capital Area*(Group Insurer)*
Washington, DC

Grossberg, Yochelson, Fox & Beyder*(Legal Firm)*
Baltimore, MD

First Maryland Savings*(Major Banking Relationship)*
Silver Spring, MD

Maryland National Bank*(Major Banking Relationship)*
Baltimore, MD 21202

Maryland National Bank*(Pension Manager)*
Baltimore, MD 21202

Subsidiary:

Ventilating Systems Management **(1)**
3004 McComas Ave.
Kensington, MD 20895
Tel.: 410-942-5200

Sawyer
Riley
Compton
Inc.

SAWYER RILEY COMPTON INC.
1100 Abernathy Rd., Ste. 800
Atlanta, GA 30328
Tel.: 404-393-9849
Fax: 404-393-9953
Year Founded: 1960
Approx.Billings: $33,000,000
Emp.: 50
Business-to-Business
Gordon Sawyer *(Chm. Bd.)*
Franklin Compton *(Pres. & New Bus. Contact)*
Richard Riley *(Exec. V.P.)*
Louis Sawyer *(Exec. V.P.)*
John Schilling *(V.P., Fin. & Admin.)*
S. Craig Plank *(Mktg.)*
Kay Frith *(Exec. Asst.)*

Computer Systems/Hardware:
MacIntosh, NCR

SAXON PAINT & HOME CARE CENTERS INC.
3840 W. Fullerton Ave.,
Chicago, IL 60647
Tel.: 312-252-8100
Fax: 312-252-5850
Year Founded: 1910
Approx.Sls.: $48,000,000
Emp.: 350
Chain of 46 Home Decorating Stores
S.I.C.: 5714; 5719; 5231
Alan Saks *(Pres. & Chief Exec. Officer)*
Sol Bleiweis *(V.P.-Fin.)*
Howard Kraus *(Dir.-Personnel)*
Principal(s):
Alan Saks

Computer Systems/Hardware:
Wang VS 85 & 5

Outside Service Firm(s):

Great-West Life Assurance Co.*(Group Insurer)*
New York, NY

RON SAXON FORD, INC.
225 University Ave.
Saint Paul, MN 55103
Tel.: 612-222-0511
Fax: 612-222-2851
Approx.Sls.: $50,000,000
Emp.: 83
Retail Automobiles
S.I.C.: 5511
Ronald Saxon *(Pres.)*
Natalie Saxon *(V.P.-Fin.)*
Jack Saxon *(Gen. Mgr.)*
Principal(s):
Ronald Saxon

Outside Service Firm(s):

Fox & Company*(Auditors)*
Minneapolis, MN

First Bank, N.A.*(Major Banking Relationship)*
First Bank Place
Minneapolis, MN 55480

CECIL SAYDAH COMPANY
2935 E. 12th St.
Los Angeles, CA 90023
Tel.: 213-263-9321 **CA**
Year Founded: 1970
Approx.Sls.: $25,000,000
Emp.: 350
Mfr. of Linens & Towels
S.I.C.: 2392

Cecil Saydah Company—(Continued)

Richard Saydah *(Pres.)*
John Saydah *(V.P. & Sec.)*
Jeff Zone *(V.P. & Treas.)*
Steven Hall *(Controller)*

Outside Service Firm(s):

Union Bank*(Major Banking Relationship)*
445 S. Figueroa St.
Los Angeles, CA 90071
Tel.: 213-236-5076

SCALAMANDRE, INC.
37-24 24th St.
Long Island City, NY 11101
Tel.: 718-361-8500
Fax: 718-361-8311
Year Founded: 1929
Approx.Sls.: $20,000,000
Emp.: 275
Import Export
Drapery, Upholstery Fabrics, Trimmings, Wall Coverings, Rugs & Carpets
S.I.C.: 2221; 2231; 2269; 2261; 2396; 2273
Edwin W. Bitter *(Chm. Bd.)*
Adriana Scalamandre Bitter *(Pres.)*
E. Ward Bitter *(Exec. V.P.)*
Robert Franco Bitter *(Exec. V.P.)*
Mark J. Bitter *(Exec. V.P.)*
Therese Marie Cook *(Exec. V.P.-A.I.A.)*

Computer Systems/Hardware:
IBM & A.C.S.

SCANGAS BROTHERS HOLDINGS, INC.
326 Lynway
Lynn, MA 01905
Tel.: 617-599-1300 MA
Fax: 617-598-1377
Approx.Sls.: $146,000,000
Emp.: 1,100
Holding Company: Milk Processing, Pasterurizing, Homoganizing, Bottling; Milk, Ultra-High Temperature; Fruit Juices, Ice Milk Packaged; Dairy Products, Except Dried or Canned; Convenience Stores Chain; Dairy Products Stores
S.I.C.: 6719; 2037; 2024; 5143; 5411; 5451; 2026
Angelo N. Scangas *(Chm. Bd.)*
Arthur J. Pappethenasi *(Pres. & Chief Exec. Officer)*
Dick Puricelli *(Chief Fin. Officer)*
Christopher A. Scangas *(Exec. V.P. & Treas.)*
Nicholas A. Scangas *(Exec. V.P.-Mktg. & Sls.)*
James N. Scangas *(Sec.)*

Outside Service Firm(s):

Bank of New England*(Major Banking Relationship)*
One Washington Mall
Boston, MA 02108
Tel.: 617-742-4000

Subsidiaries:

Richdale Dairy Stores, Inc. **(1)**
626 Lynnway
Lynn, MA 01905
Tel.: 617-599-1300
Convenience Stores Chain; Filling Stations; Dairy Products Stores
S.I.C.: 5411; 5541; 5451
Angelo N. Scangas *(Vice Chm.)*

West Lynn Creamery, Inc. **(1)**
626 Lynnway
Lynn, MA 01905
Tel.: 617-599-1300
Milk Processing; Fruit Juices; Ice Cream; Food Preparations; Dairy Products, Except Dried or Canned
S.I.C.: 2026; 2024; 2099; 5143
Angelo N. Scangas *(Chm. Bd.)*

SCHAAKE PACKING COMPANY, INC.
P.O. Box 128
Ellensburg, WA 98926
Tel.: 509-925-5346 WA
Fax: 509-925-5340
Year Founded: 1929
Approx.Sls.: $115,000,000
Emp.: 45
Cattle Feeder
S.I.C.: 0211
Donald E. Schaake *(Pres. & Chief Exec. Officer)*
Paul E. Schaake *(Sec.)*

Outside Service Firm(s):

Ernst & Young*(Auditors)*
999 Third Av., Ste. 3500
Seattle, WA 98104
Tel.: 206-621-1800
Fax: 206-682-1234

Cone, Gillreath & Korte*(Legal Firm)*
Seattle, WA

Security Pacific National Bank*(Major Banking Relationship)*
1301 Fifth Ave.
Seattle, WA 98101
Tel.: 206-621-4530

SCHAD INDUSTRIES, INC.
201 Rue Iberville
Lafayette, LA 70508
Tel.: 318-261-0790 DE
Fax: 318-261-0931
Year Founded: 1894
Approx.Sls.: $100,000,000
Emp.: 200
Fiscal Year-end: 6/30/92
Export
Mfr. of Cottonseed Oil, Refined Not Made In Cottonseed Oil Mills; Peanut Oil, Refined Not Made In Peanut Oil Mills; Soybean Oil, Refined, Not Made In Soybean Oil Mills; Corn Oil, Refined; Coconut Oil; Plain Kernel Oil
S.I.C.: 2079; 2046; 2076
Theodore G. Schad, Jr. *(Chm. Bd., Pres. & Chief Exec. Officer)*
L. Dan Thompson *(Chief Oper. Officer & Sr. V.P.)*
D.W. Place *(V.P.)*
Thomas C. Keller *(Treas. & Sec.)*
R.D. Reed *(Dir.-Fin.)*

No. of Mfg. Plants/Facilities: 1
No. of U.S. Offices: 2

Outside Service Firm(s):

KPMG Peat Marwick*(Auditors)*
Premium Tower,
Baton Rouge, LA

Whitney National Bank of New Orleans*(Major Banking Relationship)*
P.O. Box 61260
New Orleans, LA 70161
Tel.: 504-586-7422

Subsidiaries:

Lou Ana Foods, Inc. **(1)**
731 N. Railroad Ave.
Opelousas, LA 70570
Tel.: 318-948-6561
Mfr. of Vegetable Refined Oils, Cottonseed Oil, Peanut Oil, Soybean Oil, Corn Oil & Coconut Oil
S.I.C.: 2079; 2046
Theodore G. Schad, Jr. *(Chm. Bd., Pres. & Chief Exec. Officer)*
L. Don Thompson *(Chief Oper. Officer & Sr. V.P.)*
James W. Boswell, Jr. *(V.P.-Sls.)*
Don R. Gulley *(V.P.)*
Douglas W. Place *(V.P.)*
Arthur K. House *(V.P.)*
Thomas C. Keller *(Treas. & Sec.)*

Lou Ana Foods Of Texas, Inc. **(1)**
1801 Kingwood, Ste. 200
Kingwood, TX 77339
Tel.: 713-359-7808
Sales & Marketing of Cottonseed, Peanut, Soybean & Vegetable Refined Oils
S.I.C.: 2079; 2046; 2076

Tony Ramos *(Dir.-Food Service Sls.)*

SCHAEDLER BROTHERS, INC.
1030 S. 13th St.
Harrisburg, PA 17104
Tel.: 717-233-1621 PA
Fax: 717-233-1626
Year Founded: 1961
Approx.Sls.: $21,000,000
Emp.: 85
Wholesale Distribution of Electrical Supplies
S.I.C.: 5063
Thomas J. Schaedler, Sr. *(Chm. Bd.)*
James D. Schaedler *(Pres.)*
James Hoffman *(V.P.-Opers.)*
Henry Schaedler *(V.P.-Pur.)*
Jack Smith *(Controller)*
Thomas J. Schaedler, Jr. *(Sec.)*
Arthur Moore *(Mgr.-Sls.)*

Outside Service Firm(s):

Brown, Smith, Wallace, Librach & Gordon*(Auditors)*
Harrisburg, PA

Commonwealth National Bank*(Major Banking Relationship)*
Harrisburg, PA

SCHAEPS ICE CREAM COMPANY
5140 Division St.
Madison, WI 53704
Tel.: 608-249-6411
Fax: 608-249-7900
Year Founded: 1964
Approx.Sls.: $25,000,000
Emp.: 150
Mfr. of Ice Cream
S.I.C.: 2024
Paul A. Thomsen *(Pres.)*
Lester Thomsen *(V.P.)*
Walter L. Thomsen *(Sec. & Treas.)*

S. SCHAFFER GROCERY CORPORATION
27 Weyman Ave.
New Rochelle, NY 10805
Tel.: 914-235-7000
Fax: 914-235-7170
Approx.Sls.: $80,000,000
Emp.: 175
Wholesale Groceries
S.I.C.: 5141
Monroe Schaffer *(Pres.)*
Harvey Finkelstein *(Exec. V.P.)*
Irving Schwartz *(Sec. & Treas.-Intl. Opers.)*

Outside Service Firm(s):

Panfell & Merritt*(Auditors)*
New Rochelle, NY

Bergner & Bergner*(Legal Firm)*
New Rochelle, NY

Chemical Bank*(Major Banking Relationship)*
450 West 33rd St.
New York, NY 10001
Tel.: 212-613-7197
Fax: 212-947-7628

SCHARER ASSOCIATES, INC.
230 Middle Neck Rd.
Great Neck, NY 11021
Tel.: 516-829-8900
Fax: 516-829-8401
Year Founded: 1959
Approx.Billings: $10,360,500
Emp.: 17
Mail Order Adv. & Sales Promotion
Si Scharer *(Pres.)*
Vivian Scharer *(V.P, Chief Exec. Officer)*
Katherine Packard *(Comptroller)*
Joan Shuster *(Chief Info. Officer (MIS))*

SCHARFBERG & ASSOCIATES, LTD. ADV.
911 Benjamin Fox Pavilion
Jenkintown, PA 19046
Tel.: 215-224-2705
Fax: 215-885-8039
Year Founded: 1974
Approx.Billings: $11,050,100
Emp.: 22
Consumer Goods & Services, Entertainment, Radio & Motorcycle Industries
Sheldon Scharfberg *(Pres., Chief Exec. Officer, Treasurer & New Bus. Contact)*
Doug Scharfberg *(Sr. V.P., Sec., Market Res., Telecommunications, Res. & Devel.)*
Marvin Kaufman *(Chief Fin. Officer)*
Louis Marks *(Gen. Counsel)*
Barbara Schimpf *(Controller & Human Resources)*
Pat Mason *(Admin./Opers., Purchasing, Personnel Training & Devel.)*
Tina Isen *(Pub. Rels.)*

Computer Systems/Hardware:
IBM

SCHAWK, INC.
1695 River Rd.
Des Plaines, IL 60018
Tel.: 708-827-9494
Tel.: 800-621-1909
Fax: 708-827-1264
Year Founded: 1953
Approx.Sls.: $98,000,000
Emp.: 850
Fiscal Year-end: 12/31/91
Complete Pre-press Service Incl. Electronic Color Separations, Plates & Proofs for Lithography, Flexography, Gravure & Laser Dies & Visual Pkg. Components
S.I.C.: 2752; 2759; 2796
Clarence W. Schawk *(Chm. Bd. & Chief Exec. Officer)*
David A. Schawk *(Pres.)*
Paul R. Guy *(V.P. & Dir.-Tech.)*
Ann Mulhern *(Chief Information Officer)*
John R. Cragen *(Controller)*
A. Alex Sarkisian *(Sec.)*
Robert E. Drew *(Dir.-Personnel)*
Carrie Scheidemantel *(Dir.-Mktg.)*

No. of Mfg. Plants/Facilities: 10

Computer Systems/Hardware:
General Automation Z-5820

Outside Service Firm(s):

McGladrey & Pullen*(Auditors)*
Chicago, IL

Chubb Group*(Commercial Insurance Carrier)*
Boston, MA

General American Life Insurance Co.*(Group Insurer)*
700 Market
Saint Louis, MO 63101
Tel.: 314-525-5458
Fax: 314-525-3677

Keck, Mahin, Cate & Koehler*(Legal Firm)*
8300 Sears Tower, 233 S. Wacker Dr.
Chicago, IL 60606
Tel.: 312-876-3400

First National Bank of Chicago*(Major Banking Relationship)*
One First National Plaza
Chicago, IL 60670
Tel.: 312-732-9781
Tel.: 312-732-4050
Fax: 312-732-4840
Fax: 312-732-3055

Subsidiaries:

Color Data East **(1)**
5 N. Greenwich Rd.
Armonk, NY 10504
Tel.: 914-273-6665
Fax: 914-273-6889
Printing
S.I.C.: 2752; 2759; 2796
Peter Liter, Jr. *(Gen. Mgr.)*
Carrie Sheidemantel *(Dir.-Mktg.)*

Diemasters **(1)**
1697 W. Imperial Ct.
Mount Prospect, IL 60056
Tel.: 708-981-7788
Tel.: 800-621-1909
Fax: 708-827-1264
Printing
S.I.C.: 2759; 2752; 2796
Tony Klima *(Gen. Mgr.)*
Carrie Sheidemantel *(Dir.-Mktg.)*

Fuzere Manufacturing Company Inc. **(1)**
1237 Birchwood Dr.
Sunnyvale, CA 94089
Tel.: 408-734-4743
Fax: 408-734-9063
Mfr. of Thermoforming Plastic Packaging
S.I.C.: 2671
Donna Fuzere *(Pres.)*
Carrie Scheidemantel *(Mgr.-Mktg.)*

LSI/KALA **(1)**
2325 Burdick St.
Kalamazoo, MI 49007
Tel.: 616-381-3820
Fax: 616-382-9070
Printing
S.I.C.: 2752; 2759; 2796

Litho Colorplate **(1)**
2626 2nd St. N.E., Ste. 100
Minneapolis, MN 55418
Tel.: 612-788-8308
Fax: 612-789-5424
Printing
S.I.C.: 2752; 2759; 2796

Process Color Plate **(1)**
1200 W. Monroe
Chicago, IL 60607
Tel.: 312-243-2216
Tel.: 800-621-1909
Fax: 312-243-2859
Printing
S.I.C.: 2752; 2759; 2796
Pat Netols *(Gen. Mgr.)*
Carrie Sheidemantel *(Dir.-Mktg.)*
Tim Rose *(Sls. Mgr.)*

Robinson Industries **(1)**
11320 E. Main St., P.O. Box 68
Huntley, IL 60142
Tel.: 708-669-5291
Tel.: 800-874-7113
Fax: 708-669-5263
George Colletti *(Gen. Mgr.)*
Carrie Sheidemantel *(Dir.-Mktg.)*
Dan Larson *(Sls. Mgr.)*

Schawkgraphics **(1)**
1600 E. Sherwin Ave.
Des Plaines, IL 60018
Tel.: 708-296-6000
Tel.: 800-621-1909
Fax: 708-296-9466
Printing
S.I.C.: 2752; 2759; 2796
David A. Schawk *(Pres.)*
Carrie Scheidemantel *(Dir.-Mktg.)*
David Raclaw *(V.P.-Sls.)*

Total Reproductions, Inc. **(1)**
6901 Hamlin Ave.
Lincolnwood, IL 60645
Tel.: 708-674-6400
Fax: 708-674-6024
Commercial Printing
S.I.C.: 2752
Dale Salzman *(Gen. Mgr.)*
Carrie Scheidemantel *(Dir.-Mktg.)*

Weston Engraving **(1)**
2626 2nd St. N.E.
Minneapolis, MN 55418
Tel.: 612-789-8514
Fax: 612-789-5424
Printing
S.I.C.: 2752; 2759; 2796

SCHEDULING TECHNOLOGY CORPORATION
42 South St.
Hopkinton, MA 01748
Tel.: 508-435-1001 **CT**
Fax: 538-435-9312
Year Founded: 1979
Earnings: $2,692,000
Sales Range: $10-19 Million
Emp.: 7
Fiscal Year-end: 3/31/92
Export
Licenses & Markets Management Systems Including Software & Media Education
S.I.C.: 7372
G.R. Knipfing *(Chm., Pres. & Chief Exec. Officer)*
Laurie McKew *(Sec.)*
Carol Everett *(Adv. & Public Rels. Exec.)*

Computer Systems/Hardware:
Digital Equipment VAX; IBM, Hewlett Packard, Pc's & Unix

Outside Service Firm(s):

Price Waterhouse*(Auditors)*
160 Federal St.
Boston, MA 02110
Tel.: 617-439-3308
Fax: 617-439-3308

SCHEER ADVERTISING AGENCY
76 S. Orange Ave.
South Orange, NJ 07079
Tel.: 201-762-8100
Fax: 201-762-7968
Year Founded: 1934
Approx.Billings: $33,800,000
Emp.: 35
Retail
Wm. N. Scheer *(Pres.)*
Norman J. Scheer *(Sr. V.P.)*
Steven E. Scheer *(Sr. V.P., Sec. & Treas.)*

SCHEIN/BLATTSTEIN ADVERTISING, INC.
420 Madison Ave.
New York, NY 10017
Tel.: 212-758-1555
Fax: 212-832-8539
Year Founded: 1970
Approx.Billings: $14,000,000
Emp.: 14
Direct Marketing
Eliot DeY. Schein *(Pres.)*

HENRY SCHEIN, INC.
5 Harbor Park Dr.
Port Washington, NY 11050
Tel.: 516-621-4300
Fax: 516-484-7639
Approx.Sls.: $200,000,000
Emp.: 1,000
Sales of Dental, Pharmacuetical & Medical Supplies
S.I.C.: 5047; 5122; 5100
Stanley M. Bergman *(Chm. Bd., Pres. & Chief Exec. Officer)*
Steven Paladino *(V.P.-Fin.)*
Ester Schein *(Sec. & Treas.)*

Outside Service Firm(s):

BDO Seidman*(Auditors)*
1430 Broadway
New York, NY
Tel.: 212-765-7500

Proskauer, Rose, Goetz & Mendelsohn*(Legal Firm)*
1585 Broadway
New York, NY 10036
Tel.: 212-969-3000

Chase Manhattan Bank, N.A.*(Major Banking Relationship)*
Melville, NY

Subsidiaries:

Danbury Pharmacal Inc. **(1)**
12 Stoneleigh Ave.
Carmel, NY 10512
Tel.: 516-625-1700
Emp.: 570
Mfr. of Generic Drugs
S.I.C.: 2834

Schein Pharmaceutical, Inc. **(1)**
26 Harbor Park Dr.
Port Washington, NY 11050
Tel.: 516-625-9000
Fax: 516-625-8648
Assets: $150,000,000
Earnings: $15,000,000
Liabilities: $70,000,000
Net Worth: $80,000,000
Approx.Sls.: $200,000,000
Emp.: 1,200
Fiscal Year-end: 12/31/90
Import Export
Computer Systems/Hardware:
IBM AS/400
Wholesale Distribution of Pharmaceuticals; Manufacturer of Intravenous Solutions
S.I.C.: 5122; 2834
Martin Sperber *(Chm. Bd. & Pres.)*
Stephan Getrare *(Pres.-Retail Div.)*
Jim McGee *(Pres.-Hospital Div.)*
David H. Poe *(Chief Fin. Officer)*
Whit Stearns *(Controller)*

Steris Laboratories, Inc. **(1)**
620 N. 51st Ave.
Phoenix, AZ 85043
Tel.: 602-278-1400
Emp.: 380
Mfr. of Generic Drugs
S.I.C.: 2834

SCHELL/MULLANEY
79 Fifth Ave.
New York, NY 10005
Tel.: 212-366-5300
Year Founded: 1990
Approx.Billings: $25,000,000
Emp.: 25
High Tech, Business-To-Business
Brian Mullaney *(Chm Bd. & New Bus. Contact)*
Michael Schell *(Pres. & Creative Dir.)*

SCHENECTADY CHEMICALS, INC.
10th & Congress St.
Schenectady, NY 12303
Mailing Address:
P.O. Box 1046,
Schenectady, NY 12301
Tel.: 518-370-4200 **NY**
Telex: 145-457
Fax: 518-346-3111
Year Founded: 1906
Approx.Sls.: $180,000,000
Emp.: 500
Fiscal Year-end: 12/31/90
Import Export
Mfr. Varnishes & Resins
S.I.C.: 2851; 2821; 2865
H.D. Wright *(Chm. Bd. & Chief Exec. Officer)*
Wallace A. Graham *(Vice Chm. & Sec.)*
K.C. Petersen *(Pres. & Chief Oper. Officer)*
R. Carr *(V.P.-Chemical Div.)*
K.C. Heckeler *(V.P.-Intl. Div.)*
J.M. Stanton *(V.P.-Electrical Insulation Div.)*
F.F. Wolny *(V.P.-Resin Div.)*
J.C. Obst *(Treas.)*
L.C. Duff *(Corp. Controller)*
A.J. Bourgeois *(Dir.-Pur.)*
Howard Picard *(Information Processing Mgr.)*
J.R. Wyles *(Personnel Mgr.)*
Theodore G. Bosworth *(Acctg. Mgr.)*

No. of Mfg. Plants/Facilities: 5
No. of U.S. Offices: 1

Computer Systems/Hardware:
IBM 4381

Outside Service Firm(s):

KPMG Peat Marwick*(Auditors)*
74 N. Pearl St.
Albany, NY 12207
Tel.: 518-455-8809

Higgins, Roberts, Beyerl & Coan*(Legal Firm)*
Schenectady, NY

Citibank N.A.*(Major Banking Relationship)*
Corporate Trust Services, 399 Park Ave.
New York, NY 10043
Tel.: 212-559-1605

Schenectady Trust Co.*(Major Banking Relationship)*
Schenectady, NY

Schenectady Trust Co.*(Pension Manager)*
Schenectady, NY

Non-U.S. Holdings:

Isomex, S.A. **(1)**
Zettina 16, ZPEM DIAG San Antonio 945-A, Mexico, D.F. 1, Mexico
Tel.: 543-9125
Mfr. Varnishes
S.I.C.: 2851

Nisshoku Schenectady Chemicals, Inc. **(1)**
Osaka, Japan
Mfr. Varnishes
S.I.C.: 2851

Schenectady Chemicals Australia Pty. Ltd. **(1)**
St. Marys, N.S.W. Australia
Mfr. Varnishes
S.I.C.: 2851

Schenectady Chemicals Canada Ltd. **(1)**
319 Comstock Rd.
Scarborough, ON M1L 2H3, Canada
Tel.: 416-757-5136
Paints & Varnishes
S.I.C.: 2821; 2865
Henry Wright *(Pres.)*

Schenectady de France **(1)**
Bethune, France
Mfr. Varnishes
S.I.C.: 2851

Schenectady Iberica S.A. **(1)**
Madrid, Spain
Mfr. Varnishes
S.I.C.: 2851

Schenectady Midland, Ltd. **(1)**
Four Ashes
Wolverhampton, WV10 7BT, United Kingdom
Tel.: 0902-790555
Telex: 339075
Mfr. Varnishes
S.I.C.: 2851

Schenectady Quimica do Brasil Limitada **(1)**
Rue Campos Bicado 52, 04536
Sao Paulo, S.P. Brazil
Tel.: 11-577-6880
Telex: 1122649
Mfr. Varnishes
S.I.C.: 2851

THE JULIUS SCHEPPS CO.
2535 Manana St.
Dallas, TX 75220
Tel.: 214-357-8300
Fax: 214-351-2950
Approx.Sls.: $100,000,000
Emp.: 280
Fiscal Year-end: 8/31/92
Import
Wholesale Liquor, Wine & Beer
S.I.C.: 5182; 5181
Phil J. Schepps *(Chm. Bd.)*
Lee M. Schepps *(Pres.)*
Dennis Barnett *(V.P.-Sls.)*
Gregg Parsons *(V.P.-Fin.)*

The Julius Schepps Co.—(Continued)

Outside Service Firm(s):

Belew, Averitt & Co.*(Auditors)*
Dallas, TX

Johnson & Swanson*(Legal Firm)*
100 Founders Sq., 900 Jackson St.
Dallas, TX 75202
Tel.: 214-977-9000

Kroney, Silverman*(Legal Firm)*
Dallas, TX

Texas Commerce Bank*(Major Banking Relationship)*
2200 Ross Ave.
Dallas, TX 75266

SCHERER BROS. LUMBER COMPANY
9 Ninth Ave., N.E.
Minneapolis, MN 55413
Tel.: 612-379-9633 **MN**
Fax: 612-627-0679
Year Founded: 1930
Assets: $36,580,000
Liabilities: $13,900,000
Net Worth: $22,680,000
Approx.Sls.: $85,000,000
Emp.: 306
Fiscal Year-end: 3/31/92
Import Export
Wholesale & Retail Lumber & Building Materials
S.I.C.: 5031; 5039; 5211
Corporate Giving Program: 5%
Keystone Company
Roger Scherer *(Pres.)*
Mick Frank *(Pres.-Homes)*
Tom Olson *(Pres.-Scherer Financial)*
Gary M. Scherer *(V.P.-Fin.)*
Gregory Scherer *(V.P.-Personnel & Mktg.)*
Michael Scherer *(V.P.-Opers.)*
Bob Heurung *(Controller)*
Pete Scherer *(Sec.)*
Glen Medbery *(Gen. Mgr.-Medbery Yard)*
Joe Anton *(Mgr.-Sls.)*
Don Linn *(Mgr.-Human Resources)*
Tom Myrick *(Mgr.-Mktg.)*

No. of Mfg. Plants/Facilities: 5

Computer Systems/Hardware:
Dataline

Outside Service Firm(s):

Hoffmann & Swintek*(Auditors)*
Minneapolis, MN

Fredrikson & Byron, P.A.*(Legal Firm)*
1100 International Centre, 900 2nd Ave. S.
Minneapolis, MN 55402
Tel.: 612-347-7000

First National Bank of Minneapolis*(Major Banking Relationship)*
P.O. Box A799
Minneapolis, MN 55480
Tel.: 612-370-4606

SCHERER SCIENTIFIC, LTD.
2859 Paces Ferry Rd., Ste. 300
Atlanta, GA 30339
Tel.: 404-333-0066
Fax: 404-333-0068
Year Founded: 1986
Sales Range: $60-79 Million
Emp.: 800
Holding Company; Pharmaceutical Products & Services; Medical Waste
S.I.C.: 5122; 6719; 5100
Robert P. Scherer, Jr. *(Chm. Bd.)*
Robert D. Tucker *(Pres.)*
James E. Brands *(Exec. V.P., Sec. & Treas.)*

No. of U.S. Offices: 1

Computer Systems/Hardware:
IBM

Outside Service Firm(s):

Arthur Andersen & Co.*(Auditors)*
Avenue des Arts 56 1040
Brussels, Belgium

Arthur Andersen & Co.*(Auditors)*
133 Peachtree St., N.E.
Atlanta, GA 30303
Tel.: 404-658-1776

Aetna Life & Casualty*(Investment Banker)*
151 Farmington Avenue
Hartford, CT 06156
Tel.: 203-273-2128
Fax: 203-729-4295

Long, Aldridge & Norman*(Legal Firm)*
1500 Marquis Two Tower, 285 Peachtree Center Ave.
Atlanta, GA 30303-1257
Tel.: 404-527-4000
Fax: 404-527-4198

Trust Company Bank*(Major Banking Relationship)*
Trust Co. Tower
Atlanta, GA 30303
Tel.: 404-588-7963

SCHERING-PLOUGH HEALTHCARE PRODUCTS ADVERTISING CORP.
110 Allen Rd.
Liberty Corner, NJ 07938

Tel.: 908-604-1640
Fax: 908-604-1948
Year Founded: 1990
Approx.Billings: $95,000,000
Emp.: 22
Media Buying & Media Planning
David E. Collins *(Chm. Bd.)*
Russell Elliot *(Pres.)*
Richard Whittaker *(V.P.)*
Maureen Chelius *(V.P.)*
James Lawenda *(Assoc. Dir., Media Pur.)*

SCHIAVONE CONSTRUCTION CO.
1600 Patterson Plank Rd.
Secaucus, NJ 07096
Tel.: 201-867-5070
Fax: 201-866-6132
Year Founded: 1956
Approx.Sls.: $70,000,000
Emp.: 600
Heavy Construction
S.I.C.: 1622; 1623; 1629
Ronald Schiavone *(Pres. & Chief Exec. Officer)*
Raymond J. Donovan *(V.P. & Chief Fin. Officer)*
Gregory M. Vasel *(V.P. & Treas.)*
Morris J. Levin *(Gen. Counsel & Sec.)*

Computer Systems/Hardware:
IBM System 34

Outside Service Firm(s):

Deloitte & Touche*(Auditors)*
1 World Trade Center
New York, NY 10048
Tel.: 212-669-5000

National State Bank*(Major Banking Relationship)*
68 Broad St.
Elizabeth, NJ 07207
Tel.: 908-354-3400

SCHLOSSER FORGE COMPANY
11711 Arrow Rd.
Rancho Cucamonga, CA 91730
Tel.: 909-987-4760
Fax: 909-980-3564
Emp.: 195
Fiscal Year-end: 12/31/91
Forge Rings For Jet Engines
S.I.C.: 3462; 3463
Phillip D. Schlosser *(Chm. Bd.)*
Jeffrey P. Schlosser *(Pres.)*
Dave Richardson *(V.P.-Casting)*
Jack Valasek *(V.P.-Sls.)*
Elaine M. Schlosser *(Treas. & Sec.)*
Mark Poncin *(Controller)*

Outside Service Firm(s):

Bank of America NT&SA*(Major Banking Relationship)*
Rancho Cucamonga, CA

SCHMIDT BAKING CO., INC.
7801 Fitch Lane
Baltimore, MD 21236
Tel.: 410-668-8200
Fax: 410-288-2051
Year Founded: 1786
Approx.Sls.: $12,000,000
Emp.: 1,400
Fiscal Year-end: 12/31/91
Wholesale Bread & Rolls
S.I.C.: 2051
Thomas S. Bowyer, Jr. *(Pres.)*
Charles Bowyer *(Sr. V.P.-Sls.)*
Leonard Bunce *(Sr. V.P.-Fin. & Treas.)*
C. Peter Smith *(Sr. V.P.-Opers.)*
Steve Favazza *(V.P.-Sls./ NorthernDiv.)*
Gerard Sununski *(V.P.-Sls. Southern Div.)*
Donald Hubbard *(Dir.-Indus. Rels.)*

Outside Service Firm(s):

Ernst & Young*(Auditors)*
1 N. Charles St.
Baltimore, MD 21201
Tel.: 410-539-7940
Fax: 410-783-3832

Mercantile-Safe Deposit & Trust Co.*(Major Banking Relationship)*
Baltimore, MD

GEORGE T. SCHMIDT
6151 W. Howard St.
Niles, IL 60648
Tel.: 708-967-6250
Fax: 708-647-7593
Approx.Sls.: $10,000,000
Emp.: 145
Fiscal Year-end: 12/31/90
Mfr. Hand, Pneumatic & Hydraulic Marking Machines & Tools
S.I.C.: 3546
Neil O'Connor *(Pres.)*

THE SCHMIDT/WESTERDAHL GROUP LTD.
700 S.W. Taylor, Ste. 400
Portland, OR 97201
Tel.: 503-279-4000
Fax: 503-279-4066
Year Founded: 1973
Approx.Billings: $23,000,000
Emp.: 30
Edward G. Westerdahl, II *(Pres.)*
Gary Chnstianson *(Pres., Adv. Services)*
Bill Ekse *(Sr. V.P.)*
Laurie Willocks *(V.P., Controller & Gen. Mgr.)*
Martha Crawford Richmond *(V.P., Pub. Rels.)*
Ralph Bender *(Mng. Dir., Recruitment Adv.)*
Mark Forbis *(Bus. Devel. Mgr.)*

SCHMIEDING ENTERPRISES INC.
1411 S. Thompson
Springdale, AR 72765
Tel.: 501-751-4517
Fax: 501-751-6831
Year Founded: 1972
Approx.Sls.: $55,000,000
Emp.: 50
Fiscal Year-end: 12/31/91
Wholesale Fresh Fruits & Vegetables
S.I.C.: 5148
Lawrence H. Schmieding *(Pres.)*
Robby Zink *(Sec.)*

Computer Systems/Hardware:
IBM

Outside Service Firm(s):

Springdale Bank & Trust*(Major Banking Relationship)*
Springdale, AR

PAUL A. SCHMITT MUSIC COMPANY
88 S. 10th St.
Minneapolis, MN 55403
Tel.: 612-339-4811
Fax: 612-339-3574
Approx.Sls.: $27,000,000
Emp.: 325
Retail Musical Merchandise
S.I.C.: 5736
Robert Schmitt *(Chm. Bd.)*
Thomas M. Schmitt *(Pres.)*
Ray E. Hagerman *(V.P.-Fin. & Admin.)*
Curtis J. Karls *(V.P.)*
Wayne Reinhardt *(V.P.)*

Outside Service Firm(s):

KPMG Peat Marwick*(Auditors)*
4200 Norwest Center, 90 S. 7th St.
Minneapolis, MN 55402
Tel.: 612-341-2222

Larson, Allen, Weishair & Co.*(Auditors)*
Minneapolis, MN

Marquette Bank*(Major Banking Relationship)*
777 Marquette Ave.
Minneapolis, MN 55402
Tel.: 612-370-2182

PETER J. SCHMITT HOLDINGS
355 Harlem Rd.
West Seneca, NY 14224
Tel.: 716-825-1111 **DE**
Fax: 716-821-1645
Year Founded: 1988
Approx.Sls.: $1,050,000,000
Emp.: 2,000
Import
Holding Company; General Line Of Groceries
S.I.C.: 5141; 6719
D. Clark Ogle *(Chm. Bd., Pres., Chief Exec. & Chief Oper. Officer)*
Mark Flint *(Sr. V.P. & Chief Fin. Officer)*
Guy Sykes *(Sr. V.P.)*
John R. Balling *(V.P.-Real Estate)*
Paul Lasly *(V.P.-MIS)*
W. Earl McCartney *(V.P. & Treasurer)*
Bruce W. Murray *(V.P. & Controller)*
Francine Nicholas *(Assoc. Counsel)*
Kathy Kreuzer *(Mgr.-Benefits)*
Larry Van Etten *(Mgr.-Telecommunications)*
Louis Will *(Mgr.-Print)*

Computer Systems/Hardware:
IBM 9000-210

Outside Service Firm(s):

Ernst & Young*(Auditors)*
1400 Key Tower - 50 Fountain Plaza
Buffalo, NY
Tel.: 716-843-5000
Fax: 716-847-6949

Jaeckle, Fleischmann & Mugel*(Legal Firm)*
Norstar Building, Twelve Fountain Plaza
Buffalo, NY 14202-2222
Tel.: 716-856-0600

Marine Midland Bank*(Major Banking Relationship)*
P.O. Box 803, 1 Marine Midland Center, 23rd Floor
Buffalo, NY 14203
Tel.: 716-841-2582

Subsidiary:

Peter J. Schmitt Co., Inc. **(1)**
355 Harlem Rd.
West Seneca, NY 14224
Tel.: 716-825-1111
Fax: 716-821-1645
Approx.Sls.: $1,000,000,000
Emp.: 8,700
Fiscal Year-end: 12/29/91
Import
Computer Systems/Hardware:
IBM
Food Wholesale & Retail Co.; Bells Stores, Loblaw Stores, Golden Dawn Stores & Care Discount Drug Stores
S.I.C.: 5141; 5149
D. Clark Ogle *(Pres.)*
Mark A. Flint *(Sr. V.P. & Chief Fin. Officer)*
W. Earl McCartney *(Treas.)*
Bruce Murray *(Controller)*
Francine Nicholas *(Gen. Counsel & Corp. Sec.)*
Jack Mitchell *(Dir.-Personnel)*
Regis Brody *(Sr. V.P.-Retail Opers.)*
Paul Lasly *(V.P.-MIS)*

SCHNADIG CORPORATION
4820 W. Belmont Ave.
Chicago, IL 60641
Tel.: 312-545-2300 **DE**
Fax: 312-545-8898
Year Founded: 1880
Approx.Sls.: $70,000,000
Emp.: 1,000
Fiscal Year-end: 12/31/90
Import Export
Furniture Mfr.
S.I.C.: 2512; 2511
L.K. Schnadig *(Chm. Bd.)*
D.A. Belgrad *(Pres. & Chief Exec. Officer)*
J.L. Schnadig *(Pres.-West Coast Opers.)*
Norman Waxman *(Sr. V.P.)*
Ravi Kumar *(V.P.-Opers.)*
A. Ahlquist *(V.P.-Sls.)*
Robert Cohen *(V.P.-Sls.-East Coast)*
James L. Waters *(V.P.-Employee Rels.)*
C. Weitz *(V.P.-Mktg.-Intl. Tables)*
Dwight Smith *(V.P.-Matls. Mngmt.)*
R. Schnadig *(Sec.)*
David Roadruck *(Mgr.-Adv.)*

No. of Mfg. Plants/Facilities: 6
No. of U.S. Offices: 1

Computer Systems/Hardware:
IBM 4381

Outside Service Firm(s):

KPMG Peat Marwick*(Auditors)*
Peat Marwick Plaza, 303 E. Wacker Dr.
Chicago, IL 60601
Tel.: 312-938-1000

Vedder, Price, Kaufman & Kammholz*(Legal Firm)*
115 S. La Salle
Chicago, IL 60603
Tel.: 312-781-2200

First National Bank of Chicago*(Major Banking Relationship)*
One First National Plaza
Chicago, IL 60670
Tel.: 312-732-9781
Tel.: 312-732-4050
Fax: 312-732-4840
Fax: 312-732-3055

Stein, Roe & Farnham*(Pension Manager)*
One S. Wacker Dr.
Chicago, IL 60606
Tel.: 312-368-7700

Divisions:

International Furniture Div. **(1)**
4820 W. Belmont Ave.
Chicago, IL 60641
Tel.: 312-545-2300
S.I.C.: 2512

International Tables Div. **(1)**
4820 W. Belmont
Chicago, IL 60641
Tel.: 312-545-2300

Karpen Furniture Div. **(1)**
4820 W. Belmont Ave.
Chicago, IL 60641
Tel.: 312-545-2300
S.I.C.: 2512

Plants:

International Tables Corp. **(1)**
U.S. 60 W., Industrial Park, Community D
Henderson, KY 42420
Tel.: 502-826-7250
Wood Household Furniture
S.I.C.: 2511
Stephen Dickerson *(Mgr.-Plant)*

Schnadig Corp. **(1)**
Montoursville, PA 17754
Tel.: 717-368-8693
Uphoistered Household Furniture
S.I.C.: 2512
Robert Rutledde *(Mgr.-Plant)*

Schnadig Corp. **(1)**
P.O. Box 2000, Clarksville Highway, Rte. 2
Cornelia, GA 30531
Tel.: 706-778-7104
Mfrs. Livingroom Furniture Frames
S.I.C.: 2511
James Simmons *(Mgr.-Plant)*

Schnadig Corp. **(1)**
1350 Railroad Ave.
Corona, CA 91720
Tel.: 909-737-5722
Mfr. Upholstered Furniture: Love Seats & Sofas
S.I.C.: 2512
Werner Coppel *(Mgr.-Plant)*

SCHNEIDER COMMERCIAL REAL ESTATE
1915 W. Orangewood, #101
Orange, CA 92668
Tel.: 714-978-8000
Approx.Sls.: $175,000,000
Emp.: 45
Mortgage Banking & Commercial Real Estate
S.I.C.: 6162; 6531
John Snyder *(Pres.)*
Jim Kruse *(V.P.)*
Sutton Roley *(V.P.)*
Al Steward *(V.P.)*
Germaine Fullerton *(Chief Fin. Officer & Controller)*
Bridget Draviczki *(Mgr.-Admin.)*
Jon Kasteler *(Mgr.-Sls.)*

SCHNEIDER MILLS, INC.
462 7th Ave.
New York, NY 10018
Tel.: 212-695-6620
Fax: 212-695-6844
Approx.Sls.: $45,000,000
Emp.: 407
Manufacturer of Destinctive Textiles
S.I.C.: 2221
Isidore Schneider *(Pres. & Chief Exec. Officer)*
Albert Schneider *(V.P.)*
Nathan Lipshitz *(Controller)*
Thomas Murphy *(Treas.)*

Outside Service Firm(s):

Benjamin Nadel & Company*(Auditors)*
New York, NY

Bankers Trust Co.*(Major Banking Relationship)*
P.O. Box 318, Church St. Station
New York, NY 10008
Tel.: 212-454-2212
Fax: 212-454-2783

SCHNEIDER NATIONAL, INC.
3101 S. Packerland Dr.
Green Bay, WI 54304
Mailing Address:
P.O. Box 2545,
Green Bay, WI 54306-2545
Tel.: 414-592-2000
Fax: 414-592-3252
Year Founded: 1938
Approx.Sls.: $960,000,000
Emp.: 12,000
Long Distance Trucking
S.I.C.: 4213
Donald J. Schneider *(Pres.)*
James R. Olson *(Pres.-Van Grp.)*
Larry M. Sur *(Pres.-Special Carriers)*
Carl W. Thiem *(V.P.-Customer Service)*
Robert D. Conway *(Treas. & Sec.)*

Outside Service Firm(s):

Bank One Green Bay*(Major Banking Relationship)*
Green Bay, WI

Chase Manhattan Bank, N.A.*(Major Banking Relationship)*
One Chase Manhattan Plaza
New York, NY 10081
Tel.: 212-552-2222
Tel.: 800-526-0801
Fax: 212-552-7175

SCHNELLER, INC.
6019 Powder Mill Rd.
Kent, OH 44240
Tel.: 216-673-1400
Fax: 216-673-6374
Year Founded: 1964
Approx.Sls.: $14,000,000
Emp.: 170
Import Export
Mfr. of Aircraft Interiors
S.I.C.: 2295; 3083
Robert E. Hopkins *(Chm. & Chief Exec. Officer)*
Don E. Strange *(Pres. & Chief Oper. Officer)*
Jeff Frye *(V.P.-Mfg.)*
Ron L. Burbick *(V.P.-Mktg. & Sls.)*
Donald R. Cardis *(V.P.-Research & Devel.)*
Jerry L. Brubaker *(Sec. & Treas.)*
Marilyn Eisle *(Personnel Mgr.)*

SCHNIEBER FINE FOODS, INC.
2500 State Fair Park Dr.
Lincoln, NE 68504
Tel.: 402-466-3663 **NE**
Fax: 402-466-7352
Approx.Sls.: $12,000,000
Emp.: 48
General Line of Groceries; Packaged Frozen Goods; Janitors' Supplies; Industrial & Personal Service Paper
S.I.C.: 5141; 5142; 5087; 5113
Glenn E. Schnieber *(Pres.)*
Gene Knoche *(V.P.)*
Randall Schnieber *(V.P.)*
Steven G. Schneiber *(V.P.)*
Pamela Boyle *(Treas.)*
Dorothy E. Schnieber *(Sec.)*

Outside Service Firm(s):

Edwin Perry*(Legal Firm)*
Lincoln, NE

National Bank of Commerce*(Major Banking Relationship)*
Lincoln, NE

SCHNITZER STEEL INDUSTRIES, INC.
3200 N.W. Yeon Ave.
Portland, OR 97210
Mailing Address:
P.O. Box 10047
Portland, OR 97210
Tel.: 503-224-9900 **OR**
Telex: 360144
Fax: 503-323-2793
Year Founded: 1906
Approx.Sls.: $300,000,000
Emp.: 750
Fiscal Year-end: 12/31/91
Export
Mfr. of Primary Metals; Environmental Recycling
S.I.C.: 3312
Dr. Leonard Schnitzer *(Chm. Bd. & Chief Exec. Officer)*
Gilbert Schnitzer *(Chm.-Exec. Commitee)*
Robert W. Philip *(Pres.-Schnitzer Steel Industries, Inc.)*
Kenneth M. Novack *(Pres.-Scnitzer Investment Corp.)*
Barry A. Rosen *(V.P., Treas. & Chief Fin. Officer)*

No. of Mfg. Plants/Facilities: 3
No. of U.S. Offices: 10

Outside Service Firm(s):

Price Waterhouse*(Auditors)*
1221 S.W. Morrison, Suite 1800
Portland, OR 97204
Tel.: 503-224-9040

First Interstate Bank*(Major Banking Relationship)*
P.O. Box 3131,
Portland, OR 97208
Tel.: 503-220-4855
Fax: 503-225-7153

U.S. National Bank*(Major Banking Relationship)*
309 S.W. Sixth Ave.
Portland, OR 97208
Tel.: 503-275-4942

Subsidiary:

Cascade Steel Rolling Mills, Inc. **(1)**
3200 No. Hwy. 99 W.
McMinnville, OR 97128
Tel.: 503-472-4181 (100%)
Emp.: 400
Producer of Steel
S.I.C.: 3312
Morton I. Michelson *(Pres.)*

SCHNUCK MARKETS, INC.
11420 Lackland Rd.
Maryland Heights, MO 63043
Mailing Address:
P.O. Box 46928,
St. Louis, MO 63146-6928
Tel.: 314-994-9900
Fax: 314-994-4465
Year Founded: 1952
Approx.Sls.: $1,000,000,000
Emp.: 14,000
Retail Groceries & Pharmaceuticals; Restaurants; Baking
S.I.C.: 5411; 5912; 5812
Craig Schnuck *(Chm. Bd. & Chief Exec. Officer)*
Scott Schnuck *(Pres. & Chief Oper. Officer)*
Todd R. Schnuck *(V.P. & Chief Fin. Officer)*
Mark J. Schnuck *(V.P.-Shopping Development Opers.)*
Gordon Lyons *(V.P.-Super Mkts. Devel.)*
William Jones *(V.P.-Human Resources)*
Frank E. Roeder, Jr. *(V.P.-Facilities)*
Terry Schnuck *(Sec. & Gen. Counsel)*
Gary Meyer *(Controller)*
Susan Gibson *(Communications Specialist)*
Principal(s):
Craig Schnuck
Scott Schnuck

No. of Mfg. Plants/Facilities: 1

Outside Service Firm(s):

Deloitte & Touche*(Auditors)*
One City Centre
St. Louis, MO 63101
Tel.: 314-342-4900
Fax: 314-342-1100

GUY SCHOENECKER, INC.
7630 Bush Lake Rd.
Minneapolis, MN 55439
Tel.: 612-835-4800 **MN**
Fax: 612-835-0394
Year Founded: 1978
Approx.Sls.: $150,000,000
Emp.: 1,000

Guy Schoenecker, Inc.—(Continued)

Wholesale Distributor of Home Furnishings, Furniture, Sporting & Recreation Goods & Electrical Appliances; Manufacturer Of House Slippers & Men's & Boy's Underwear & Nightwear
S.I.C.: 5023; 5021; 5064; 3142; 2322
Guy Schoenecker *(Pres. & Chief Exec. Officer)*
Larry Schoenecker *(Sr. V.P.)*

Outside Service Firm(s):

Park National Bank*(Major Banking Relationship)*
Minneapolis, MN

Subsidiary:

Animal Fair **(1)**
5215 Edina Industrial Blvd.
Edina, MN 55439
Tel.: 612-831-7200
Mfr. of House Slippers, Men's & Boys Underwear & Nightwear; Women's & Children's Pajamas & Bedjackets; Stuffed Toys
S.I.C.: 3142; 2322; 2341; 3942
James Kelly *(V.P., Gen. Mgr. & Controller)*

SCHOENEMAN BROTHERS COMPANY
305 E. 8th St.
Sioux Falls, SD 57102
Tel.: 605-336-2440 **IA**
Fax: 605-336-2529
Year Founded: 1888
Sales Range: $10-19 Million
Emp.: 60
Retail Lumber, Hardware & Building Materials
S.I.C.: 5211; 5251
Herbert M. Schoeneman *(Pres.)*
Cecil Schoeneman *(Treas. & Sec.)*

Outside Service Firm(s):

Williams & Co.*(Auditors)*
Lemars, IA

First National Bank*(Major Banking Relationship)*
Sioux Falls, SD

SCHOOL APPAREL, INC.
4610 Mission St., Ste. 300
San Francisco, CA 94112
Tel.: 415-239-1900
Fax: 415-334-0427
Approx.Sls.: $13,000,000
Emp.: 500
Knit Sweaters & Sweater Coats; Men's, Youths' & Boys Dress Slacks; Men's & Boys Shirts; Blouses
S.I.C.: 2253; 2325; 5136; 5137
Kenneth Knoss *(Pres.)*
Bernice B. Knoss *(Treas.)*
Elizabeth J. Farrah *(Sec.)*

Outside Service Firm(s):

Gary R. Johnston*(Auditors)*
San Francisco, CA

Division:

San Francisco Knitting Mills **(1)**
4610 Mission St., Ste. 300
San Francisco, CA 94112
Tel.: 415-239-1900

SCHOTT BROTHERS, INC.
358 Lehigh St.
Perth Amboy, NJ 08861
Mailing Address:
P.O. Box 506
Perth Amboy, NJ 08861
Tel.: 908-442-2486
Fax: 908-442-6666
Year Founded: 1913
Approx.Sls.: $10,000,000
Emp.: 200
Import Export
Mfr. of Men's & Boys' Leather & Cloth Outerwear & Sheepskin-Lined Clothing
S.I.C.: 2386; 2311; 2329
Melvin Schott *(Pres.)*
Roz Schott *(Exec. V.P.)*
Michael Schott *(V.P.-Production)*
Milton Perlman *(V.P.-Mktg. & Sls.)*
Gail Dorio *(Dir.-Pur.)*

SCHOTT CORPORATION
1000 Parkers Lake Rd.
Wayzata, MN 55391
Tel.: 612-475-1173 **MN**
Fax: 612-475-1786
Year Founded: 1946
Approx.Sls.: $15,000,000
Emp.: 38
Mfr. of Specialty Transformers, Transformer Power Supply
S.I.C.: 3612; 3677
Owen W. Schott *(Pres. & Chief Exec. Officer)*
Wendell Schott *(V.P. & Chief Fin. Officer)*
Janet Woolsten Crost *(Sec.)*

Outside Service Firm(s):

George B. Hanson Company*(Auditors)*
Minneapolis, MN

SCHOTTENSTEIN STORES CORPORATION
3241 Westerville Rd.
Columbus, OH 43224
Tel.: 614-471-4722 **OH**
Fax: 614-478-2253
Assets: $229,465,872
Earnings: $37,096,000
Liabilities: $134,328,521
Net Worth: $95,137,351
Approx.Sls.: $500,000,000
Emp.: 7,000
Fiscal Year-end: 7/31/90
Retail Department Stores & Wholesale Dry Goods
S.I.C.: 5311; 5131; 5136; 5137; 5139
Jay Schottenstein *(Chm. Bd.)*
Saul Schottenstein *(Pres.)*
George Icnano *(Pres.-Dept. Store Div.)*
Emmett Bucklew *(Sr. V.P.-Furniture Dept.)*
George Iacono *(Sr. V.P. & Gen. Mdse. Mgr.-Dept. Store Div.)*
Thomas R. Ketteler *(V.P.-Fin.)*
Herbert E. Minkin *(V.P.-Human Resources)*
Gary Schottenstein *(V.P.)*
Neil Bulman, Jr. *(Sec. & Gen. Counsel)*
Robert Wysinski *(Treas.)*
Ed Arndt *(Dir.-Real Estate)*
Violet Beckman *(Dir.-Adv.- Dept. Store Div.)*
Jerry Kerr *(Dir.-Data Processing)*

Computer Systems/Hardware:
Sperry Univac

Outside Service Firm(s):

Coopers & Lybrand*(Auditors)*
100 E. Broad St.
Columbus, OH 43215

Metropolitan Life Insurance Co.*(Group Insurer)*
One Madison Ave.
New York, NY 10010-3690
Tel.: 215-578-9292

Porter, Wright, Morris & Arthur*(Legal Firm)*
Huntington Center, 41 S. High St.
Columbus, OH 43215-3406
Tel.: 614-227-2000

BancOhio National Bank*(Major Banking Relationship)*
Columbus, OH

Subsidiaries:

G B Stores **(1)**
110 Franklin Sts.
Johnstown, PA 15901
Tel.: 814-536-6633
Fax: 814-539-9070
Assets: $69,618,273
Liabilities: $56,835,283
Net Worth: $12,782,990
Approx.Sls.: $150,000,000
Emp.: 1,800
Fiscal Year-end: 1/31/90
Computer Systems/Hardware:
Burroughs A-9
Holding Co.
S.I.C.: 6719
Tom Zurilla *(Pres. & Chief Exec. Officer)*
John Zimm *(Chief Oper. Officer)*
Lawrence D. Cordek *(Chief Fin. Officer & Corp. Sec.)*
Paul L. Glosser *(Sr. V.P.)*
Harold E. Cooley *(V.P.)*
Andrew Oudish *(Dir.)*
John Bertocchi *(Dir.)*

Subsidiary:

Glosser Brothers, Inc. **(2)**
Franklin & Locust Sts.
Johnstown, PA 15901
Tel.: 814-536-6633
19 Discount Department Stores, 2 Family Apparel Stores, One Dept. Store, One Auto Center, 50 Bargain Stores
S.I.C.: 5311; 5651; 5531
Alvin M. Glosser *(Chm. Bd., Pres. & Chief Exec. Officer)*
Paul L. Glosser *(Sr. V.P.)*
Robert Craighead *(V.P.-Opers.)*
Thomas Zurilla *(Treas. & Chief Fin. Officer)*
W. Louis Coppersmith *(Sec. & Gen. Counsel)*
Phil Rogers *(Personnel Dir.)*
Ken Roslyn *(Data Processing Mgr.)*

Divisions:

Dollar Bargain Stores **(3)**
Franklin & Locust Sts.
Johnstown, PA 15901
Tel.: 814-536-6633 (100%)
S.I.C.: 5311

Gee Bee Department Stores **(3)**
Franklin & Locust Sts.
Johnstown, PA 15901
Tel.: 814-536-6633 (100%)
Emp.: 1,900
Department Stores, Also Located at 13 Stores PA, 2 Stores MD, 1 Store WV
S.I.C.: 5311
Robert E. Craighead *(V.P.-Gen. Mdse. Mgr.)*
Tom Zurilla *(Dir.-Data Processing)*
Tom L. Glosser *(Dir.-Personnel)*

Gee Bee Jr. Family Apparel Store **(3)**
Franklin & Locust Sts.
Johnstown, PA 15901
Tel.: 814-536-6633 (100%)
S.I.C.: 5311

Glosser Bros. Department Store **(3)**
Franklin & Locust Sts.
Johnstown, PA 15901
Tel.: 814-536-6633 (100%)
Department Store
S.I.C.: 5311
Robert E. Craighead *(V.P.-Gen. Mdse. Mgr.)*

Warehouse Outlet Stores **(3)**
Franklin & Locust Sts.
Johnstown, PA 15901
Tel.: 814-536-6633 (100%)
S.I.C.: 5311

Winner's Ladies Off-Price Specialty Store **(3)**
Franklin & Locust Sts.
Johnstown, PA 15901
Tel.: 814-536-6633 (100%)
S.I.C.: 5311

Valley Fair & L.F. Widmann **(1)**
3241 Westerville Rd.
Columbus, OH 43224
Tel.: 614-471-4722

Value City Furniture **(1)**
3421 Westerville Rd.
Columbus, OH 43224
Tel.: 614-471-4722

SCHREIBER FOODS, INC.
425 Pine St.
Green Bay, WI 54301
Mailing Address:
P.O. Box 19010
Green Bay, WI 54307
Tel.: 414-437-7601
Fax: 414-437-7601, Ext. 2200
Approx.Sls.: $801,000,000
Emp.: 3,300
Cheese Processor
S.I.C.: 2022
Robert G. Bush *(Chm. Bd.)*
Jack Meag *(Pres. & Chief Exec. Officer)*
J. Hamann *(V.P.-Mngmt. Information Systems)*
Richard C. Ward *(V.P.-Fin.)*
Rose Hogan *(Corp. Credit Mgr.)*

Computer Systems/Hardware:
IBM

Outside Service Firm(s):

Ernst & Young*(Auditors)*
111 E. Kilbourn Ave., Ste. 900
Milwaukee, WI 53202
Tel.: 414-273-5900

First National Bank of Chicago*(Major Banking Relationship)*
One First National Plaza
Chicago, IL 60670
Tel.: 312-732-9781
Tel.: 312-732-4050
Fax: 312-732-4840
Fax: 312-732-3055

SCHREIER MALTING CO.
704 S. 15th St.
Sheboygan, WI 53081
Mailing Address:
P.O. Box 59
Sheboygan, WI 53082
Tel.: 414-458-6126 **WI**
Telex: 910-264-3889
Fax: 414-458-9034
Year Founded: 1856
Approx.Sls.: $35,000,000
Emp.: 60
Fiscal Year-end: 12/31/88
Processors of Brewers' Malt
S.I.C.: 2083; 2048
Thomas R. Testwuide *(Pres. & Chief Exec. Officer)*
Kurt C. Duecker *(Exec. V.P. & Chief Opers. Officer)*
Kenneth J. Kazmierczak *(Treas., Controller & Sec.)*

No. of Mfg. Plants/Facilities: 2
No. of U.S. Offices: 2

Computer Systems/Hardware:
IBM PC

Outside Service Firm(s):

Grant Thornton*(Auditors)*
Sheboygan, WI

Safeco Insurance Co. of America*(Group Insurer)*
Seattle, WA

Employee Benefit Insurance*(Group Insurer)*
Milwaukee, WI

Federer, Grote, Rohde, Neuses & Dales*(Legal Firm)*
Sheboygan, WI

Godfrey & Kahn*(Legal Firm)*
780 N. Water St.
Milwaukee, WI 53202
Tel.: 414-273-3500
Fax: 414-273-5198

First Wisconsin National Bank*(Major Banking Relationship)*
Sheboygan, WI

First Wisconsin National Bank*(Pension Manager)*
Sheboygan, WI

SCHUCK & SONS CONSTRUCTION CO.
8205 N. 67th Ave.
Glendale, AZ 85302
Tel.: 602-931-3661 **AZ**
Fax: 602-937-3435
Sales Range: $20-39 Million
Emp.: 800
Wholesale Lumber Products; Carpentry; Manufacture Structural Wood Trusses, Doors & Door Frames
S.I.C.: 5031; 1751; 2439; 2431
Jackye Schuck *(Pres.)*
James Liem *(V.P. & Chief Fin. Officer)*
Chuck Winchell *(Controller)*

Computer Systems/Hardware:
IBM

Outside Service Firm(s):

Valley National Bank*(Major Banking Relationship)*
241 North Central Ave., 11th Floor
Phoenix, AZ 85001

SCHUFF STEEL CO.
420 S. 19th Ave.
Phoenix, AZ 85009
Mailing Address:
P.O. Box 39670,
Phoenix, AZ 85069
Tel.: 602-252-7787 **AZ**
Fax: 602-256-0537
Year Founded: 1976
Sales Range: $40-59 Million
Emp.: 350
Fiscal Year-end: 12/31/91
Import
Structural Steel Construction and Fabrication
S.I.C.: 1791
David Schuff *(Pres.)*
Randy J. Eskelson *(V.P.-Comml. Sls.)*
Scott Schuff *(V.P. & Gen. Mgr.)*
Ken Zylstra *(Chief Fin. Officer)*
Phyllis Lowe *(Dir.-Pur.)*
Cathy Nelson *(Dir.-Data Processing)*

No. of Mfg. Plants/Facilities: 1
No. of U.S. Offices: 1

Outside Service Firm(s):

Ernst & Young*(Auditors)*
40 North Central, Ste. 900
Phoenix, AZ 85004
Tel.: 602-258-3366

Security Pacific National Bank*(Investment Banker)*
Phoenix, AZ

GEO. F. SCHULER, INC.
1705 N. Broadway
Stockton, CA 95205
Mailing Address:
P.O. Box 1312
Stockton, CA 95205
Tel.: 209-948-5500 **CA**
Fax: 209-467-4436
Year Founded: 1886
Approx.Sls.: $19,000,000
Emp.: 225
Construction Company
S.I.C.: 1542
William P. Schuler *(Pres.)*
Frances M. Jarvin *(Sec. & Treas.)*
Oscar Hullis *(V.P.)*

Computer Systems/Hardware:
NCR 10000

Outside Service Firm(s):

Rudy Croce & Associates*(Auditors)*
Stockton, CA

Wilson, Haslett, Whitridge*(Legal Firm)*
Stockton, CA

Bank of Stockton*(Major Banking Relationship)*
Stockton, CA

SCHULTZ STEEL COMPANY
5321 Firestone Blvd.
South Gate, CA 90280
Tel.: 213-564-3281
Fax: 213-564-4105
Year Founded: 1946
Approx.Sls.: $25,000,000
Emp.: 250
Fiscal Year-end: 9/30/91
Mfr. of Steel, Titanium & Other Special Metal, Forgings & Rolled Rings
S.I.C.: 3312
Gordon W. Shultz *(Pres.)*
Stephen Shultz *(Exec. V.P.)*
Edward F. Becht *(V.P.-Mktg.)*
Anthony Vinter *(V.P. & Gen. Mgr.)*
Ruth P. Miller *(Treas.)*
Thomas E. Reed *(Controller)*
Peter Nash *(Chief Engr.)*
Douglas E. Talmon *(Pur. Agent.)*

Outside Service Firm(s):

Ernst & Young*(Auditors)*
515 S. Flower St.
Los Angeles, CA 90071
Tel.: 213-621-1666

Donnelly, Clark, Chase & Smiland*(Legal Firm)*
One Bunker Hill, 601 W. 5th St. 12th FL.
Los Angeles, CA 90071
Tel.: 213-891-1010

Wells Fargo Bank*(Major Banking Relationship)*
333 S. Grand
Los Angeles, CA 90071
Tel.: 213-253-6836

SCHULZE & BURCH BISCUIT COMPANY
1133 W. 35th St.
Chicago, IL 60609
Tel.: 312-927-6622
Fax: 312-376-4528
Approx.Sls.: $50,000,000
Emp.: 1,000
Fiscal Year-end: 12/31/90
Cookies, Crackers, Toaster Products & Granola Bars
S.I.C.: 2052; 5149
P.J. Boyle *(Pres.)*
Larry Jefferis *(V.P.-Sls.)*
Paul Langille *(V.P.-Mfg.)*
William Stuart *(V.P.-Mktg. & Sls.)*
Nancy Erickson *(Asst. Mgr.-Mktg.)*

SCHUMACHER-DUGAN CONSTRUCTION
6355 Centre Park Dr.
West Chester, OH 45069
Tel.: 513-777-9800 **OH**
Fax: 513-777-2642
Year Founded: 1964
Approx.Sls.: $26,000,000
Emp.: 80
New Construction of Commercial & Office Buildings; Renovation & Repair; Highway & Street Paving Contractor
S.I.C.: 1542; 1611
Larry Schumacher *(Pres.)*
Harry F. Matheis *(V.P.)*
James Avery *(Treas. & Sec.)*

Outside Service Firm(s):

Ernst & Young*(Auditors)*
1300 Chiquita Center, 250 E. Fifth St.
Cincinnati, OH 45202
Tel.: 513-621-6454

Provident Bank*(Major Banking Relationship)*
One East Fourth St.
Cincinnati, OH 45202
Tel.: 513-579-2732

SCHUMACHER ELECTRIC CORPORATION
7474 N. Rogers Ave.
Chicago, IL 60626
Tel.: 312-973-1600
Tel.: 800-621-5485
Fax: 312-973-7781
Year Founded: 1947
Approx.Sls.: $50,000,000
Emp.: 700
Automotive Battery Chargers & Custom Transformers
S.I.C.: 3629; 3677
Donald Schumacher *(Chm. Bd. & Pres.)*
Ralph Cernahouz *(Chief Fin. Officer & Treas.)*
Bruce Leckie *(Mgr.-Pur.)*

Outside Service Firm(s):

Arthur Andersen & Co.*(Auditors)*
33 W. Monroe St.
Chicago, IL 60603-4067
Tel.: 312-580-0033
Fax: 312-507-6748

American National Bank & Trust Company of Chicago*(Major Banking Relationship)*
33 N. LaSalle St.
Chicago, IL 60602
Tel.: 312-661-5000
Fax: 312-661-6417

F. SCHUMACHER & CO.
79 Madison Ave.
New York, NY 10016-7878
Tel.: 212-213-7900 **NY**
Year Founded: 1889
Approx.Sls.: $250,000,000
Emp.: 1,600
Import Export
Wholesale Distribution & Manufacturing of Home Decorative Fabrics, Wallcoverings, Floorcoverings & Soft Goods
S.I.C.: 5023; 5131; 2211
Philip P. Puschel *(Chm. Bd. & Chief Exec. Officer)*
Michael Landau *(Pres.-FSC Wallcoverings)*
Gerald W. Puschel *(Pres. & Chief Oper. Officer)*
Meri Stevens *(Pres.-Waverly Fabrics)*
Edward Bartolett *(V.P.-Opers.)*
Raymond Chevallier *(V.P.-Mktg.)*
Basil Costantino *(Chief Fin. Officer)*
Robert Gerboth *(Controller)*
Corinne Kevorkian *(Gen. Counsel)*
Joseph Meth *(Treas. & Chief Fin. Officer)*
Margot Nappo *(Asst. Sec.)*
Basil Costantino *(Dir.-Mngmt. Information Systems)*
Jim Hinthorn *(Dir.-Human Resources)*
Ron Myers *(Dir.-Corp. Plng.)*
Arthur Sages *(Managing Dir.-F.S. Contract)*

Computer Systems/Hardware:
IBM

Outside Service Firm(s):

KPMG Peat Marwick*(Auditors)*
345 Park Ave.
New York, NY 10154
Tel.: 212-758-9700
Fax: 212-872-3308

The Bank of New York*(Major Banking Relationship)*
One Wall Street
New York, NY 10286
Tel.: 212-635-6805
Fax: 212-635-3201

Division:

Waverly Fabrics **(1)**
79 Madison Ave.
New York, NY 10016-7878
Tel.: 212-213-7900
Import Export
Computer Systems/Hardware:
IBM
Fabrics, Wallcoverings
S.I.C.: 5023
Meri Stevens *(Pres.)*

SCHUMACHER & FORELLE, INC.
277 Northern Blvd.
Great Neck, NY 11021
Tel.: 516-482-8730 **NY**
Telex: 645904
Fax: 516-482-8725
Year Founded: 1955
Approx.Sls.: $180,000,000
Emp.: 80
Fiscal Year-end: 12/31/90
Export
Planning, Architecture/Engineering & Project Management
S.I.C.: 8712; 8711; 8741; 1542; 7389
James W. Schubauer *(Pres.)*
Kirsten Heinemann *(Dir.-Corp. Plng.)*

No. of U.S. Offices: 5
No. of Foreign Offices: 1

Outside Service Firm(s):

Wind & Wind*(Auditors)*
New York, NY

Chemical Banking Corp.*(Major Banking Relationship)*
277 Park Ave.
New York, NY 10041
Tel.: 212-310-6407
Fax: 212-310-4526

SCHURZ COMMUNICATIONS, INC.
225 W. Colfax Ave.
South Bend, IN 46626
Tel.: 219-287-1001
Year Founded: 1976
Approx.Sls.: $81,000,000
Emp.: 1,000
Holding Company; Daily Newspapers, Radio & TV Broadcasting & Cable TV & Advertising Shoppers
S.I.C.: 6719; 2711; 4832; 4833; 4841
Franklin D. Schurz, Jr. *(Pres.)*
James G. Young, Jr. *(Chief Fin. Officer & Treas.)*
James M. Schurz *(Sr. V.P.)*
E. Berry Smith *(Sr. V.P.-Broadcasting)*
Mary Schurz *(V.P. & Sec.)*
Scott C. Schurz *(V.P.)*
Principal(s):
Franklin D. Schurz, Jr.
James M. Schurz
Mary Schurz
Scott C. Schurz

No. of Mfg. Plants/Facilities: 14

SCHUTTE &COMPANY
Marketing Communications

SCHUTTE & COMPANY
1207 Delaware Ave.
Buffalo, NY 14209
Tel.: 716-884-2120
Year Founded: 1974
Approx.Billings: $42,250,000
Emp.: 72
Marketing, Advertising, Pub. Relations, Sales Promotion & Business-to-Business
Alden F. Schutte *(Pres. & Chief Exec. Officer)*

Schutte & Company—(Continued)

Douglas E. Kellner *(Chief Fin. Officer & Mng. Partner)*
Pamela A. Hobizon *(Controller)*

SCHUTTE LUMBER COMPANY
3001 Southwest Blvd.
Kansas City, MO 64108
Tel.: 816-753-6262
Fax: 816-753-7935
Year Founded: 1880
Approx.Sls.: $11,000,000
Emp.: 59
Distribute Hardwoods & Building Products
S.I.C.: 5031; 5039
Clayton W. Egner *(Pres.)*
James Viani *(Sec.)*
Bill Egner *(Pur. Agent)*
Betty White *(Mgr.-Sls.)*

Principal(s):
Clayton W. Egner

Computer Systems/Hardware:
Ultimate

Outside Service Firm(s):

Deloitte & Touche*(Auditors)*
1010 Grand Ave.
Kansas City, MO 64106-2232
Tel.: 816-474-6180

Stinson, Mag & Fizzell*(Legal Firm)*
2100 Charter Bank Ctr.
Kansas City, MO 64105

Commerce Bank of Kansas City*(Major Banking Relationship)*
10th & Walnut
Kansas City, MO 64141
Tel.: 816-234-2000
Fax: 816-234-2548

SCHWAB CORP.
3000 Main St.
Lafayette, IN 47904
Mailing Address:
P.O. Box 5088
Lafayette, IN 47903
Tel.: 317-447-9470
Tel.: 800-428-7678
Fax: 317-447-8278
Year Founded: 1872
Approx.Sls.: $15,000,000
Emp.: 200
Fiscal Year-end: 12/31/90
Export
Mfr. of Safes & Insulated Filing Cabinets
S.I.C.: 3499; 2522
Peter Neisel *(Chief Exec. Officer)*
John L. Hall *(V.P.-Fin., Treas. & Chief Fin. Officer)*
C. Miller *(Controller)*
Susan Andrews *(Mgr.-Data Processing)*
Jeff McQueen *(Mgr.-Mktg.)*
Janet Pape *(Mktg. Analyst)*

No. of Mfg. Plants/Facilities: 2
No. of U.S. Offices: 1

Computer Systems/Hardware:
AS400

Outside Service Firm(s):

George S. Olive & Co.*(Auditors)*
201 N. Illinois St.
Indianapolis, IN 46204

Dutton & Bailey*(Legal Firm)*
Indianapolis, IN

Merchants National Bank & Trust Company of Indianapolis*(Major Banking Relationship)*
One Merchants Plaza, Ste. 901E
Indianapolis, IN 46255
Tel.: 317-267-7109

S. SCHWAB COMPANY
Upper Potomac Industrial Park
Cumberland, MD 21502
Tel.: 301-729-4488
Fax: 301-729-4057
Year Founded: 1915
Approx.Sls.: $35,000,000
Emp.: 475
Import Export
Manufacturer of Children's Clothing
S.I.C.: 2341; 2369
Richard D. Schwab *(Chm. Bd.)*
Samuel C. Schwab *(Pres. & Chief Exec. Officer)*
Leonard C. Schwab *(Exec. V.P.)*
Mike Armiento *(V.P.-Mfg.)*
Amy Schwab Owens *(V.P.)*
Tadd Schwab *(V.P.)*
Ron Stuart *(Comptroller)*
Doug Schwab *(Sec. & Dir.-Data Processing)*
Pam Ellsworth *(Dir.-Import & Export)*
Lyn Schwab *(Dir.-Mktg.)*
Betsy Hurwitz *(Mgr.-Human Resources)*
Principal(s):
Richard D. Schwab
Samuel C. Schwab

No. of Mfg. Plants/Facilities: 3
No. of U.S. Offices: 24
No. of Foreign Offices: 4

Computer Systems/Hardware:
IBM AS/400; B-40 Model

Outside Service Firm(s):

Wooden & Benson*(Auditors)*
Baltimore, MD

Arent, Fox, Kintner, Plotkin & Kahn*(Legal Firm)*
1815 H St. N.W.
Washington, DC 20006
Tel.: 202-857-6000

Liberty Bank of Maryland*(Major Banking Relationship)*
Cumberland, MD

Richard Fontaine Associates, Inc.*(Pension Manager)*
Baltimore, MD

NWQ Investment Mgr.*(Pension Manager)*
Los Angeles, CA

Shearson Asset Management*(Pension Manager)*
2 World Trade Center, 100th Fl.
New York, NY 10048

SCHWAN'S SALES ENTERPRISES
115 W. College Dr.
Marshall, MN 56258
Tel.: 507-532-3274
Fax: 507-537-8226
Year Founded: 1956
Approx.Sls.: $800,000,000
Emp.: 5,000
Frozen Pizza, Sandwiches & Mexican Foods; Convenience Foods; Ice Cream; Juices; Business Equipment Leasing; Restaurants
S.I.C.: 2032; 2099; 2024; 2033; 5199; 5812
Marvin M. Schwan *(Chm. Bd., Pres. & Chief Exec. Officer)*
Donald Miller *(Controller & Sec.)*
William McCormack *(Gen. Counsel)*
Mark Schwan *(Corp. Counsel)*
Thomas Caron *(Dir.-Mktg.)*
Maynard Coepp *(Dir.-Payroll Mngmt.)*
Larry Gibbs *(Dir.-Personnel)*

Computer Systems/Hardware:
IBM No. 4381; Honeywell DP No. 8

Outside Service Firm(s):

Arthur Andersen & Co.*(Auditors)*
45 S. 7th St.
Minneapolis, MN 55402

Prudential Insurance Co. of America*(Group Insurer)*
751 Broad St.
Newark, NJ 07102-3777
Tel.: 201-802-6000

Christiansen, Stoneberg, Giles & Myuers*(Legal Firm)*
Marshall, MN

Faegre & Benson*(Legal Firm)*
2200 Norwest Ctr., 90 S. 7th St.
Minneapolis, MN 55402-3901
Tel.: 612-336-3000
Fax: 612-336-3026

First National Bank of Minneapolis*(Major Banking Relationship)*
Minneapolis, MN

Norwest Bank Minnesota, N.A.*(Major Banking Relationship)*
Marshall, MN

Investment Advisors Inc.*(Pension Manager)*
1100 Dain Tower, P.O. Box 357
Minneapolis, MN 55440

BEN SCHWARTZ MARKET, INC.
209 W. McClure
Peoria, IL 61604
Tel.: 309-682-6656 **IL**
Year Founded: 1931
Approx.Sls.: $17,000,000
Emp.: 110
Fiscal Year-end: 8/31/91
Retail Supermarkets
S.I.C.: 5411
Joel P. Schwartz *(Pres.)*
Joseph P. Lebau *(Exec. V.P.)*
Cathy Welch *(Sec.)*
Principal(s):
Joel P. Schwartz
Joseph P. Lebau
Cary Schwartz

Outside Service Firm(s):

Landy & Rothbaum*(Auditors)*
Peoria, IL

SCHWARTZ & BENJAMIN, INC.
1370 Ave. of Americas
New York, NY 10019
Tel.: 212-541-9092
Fax: 212-974-0609
Approx.Sls.: $20,000,000
Emp.: 25
Fiscal Year-end: 5/31/90
Imports Footwear
S.I.C.: 5139
Arthur Schwartz *(Pres.)*
Eli Footer *(V.P.-Sls. & Mktg.)*
Phyllis Footer *(V.P.)*
Daniel L. Schwartz *(V.P., Sec. & Treas.)*
Moran Wurdemann *(Controller)*

Computer Systems/Hardware:
IBM System 36

Outside Service Firm(s):

Coles & Bodoin*(Auditors)*
New York, NY

State Street Bank & Trust Co.*(Major Banking Relationship)*
225 Franklin St.
Boston, MA 02110
Tel.: 617-985-8179
Fax: 617-985-9722

JACK SCHWARTZ SHOES, INC.
155 Ave. of the Americas, 9th Fl.
New York, NY 10013
Tel.: 212-691-4700 **NY**
Fax: 212-691-5350
Approx.Sls.: $100,000,000
Emp.: 14
Distributor for British Knights Athletic Footwear
S.I.C.: 5139
Bernard Schwartz *(Chm. Bd.)*
Jack Schwartz *(Pres.)*
Larry Schwartz *(Exec. V.P.)*
Dave Hyle *(V.P.-Sls.)*
Helen Hedges *(Dir.-Mktg.)*
Janet Schwartz *(Dir.-Admin.)*

Outside Service Firm(s):

Brandvein, Kirschner & Pastern*(Auditors)*
New York, NY

Chemical Banking Corp.*(Major Banking Relationship)*
277 Park Ave.
New York, NY 10041
Tel.: 212-310-6407
Fax: 212-310-4526

Subsidiary:

British Knights **(1)**
155 Ave. of the Americas, 9th Fl.
New York, NY 10013
Tel.: 212-691-4700
Athletic Footwear
S.I.C.: 5139
Bernard Schwartz *(Chm. Bd.)*
Jack Schwartz *(Pres.)*

SCHWARZ PAPER COMPANY
8338 N. Austin Ave.
Morton Grove, IL 60053
Tel.: 708-966-2550 **DE**
Fax: 708-966-1271
Year Founded: 1907
Approx.Sls.: $154,000,000
Emp.: 310
Fiscal Year-end: 9/30/92
Paper & Packaging Products; Primary Printer
S.I.C.: 2678; 2679; 2657; 2652
Andrew J. McKenna *(Chm., Pres. & Chief Exec. Officer)*
Christopher Donnelly *(V.P.-Opers.)*
Andrew J. McKenna, Jr. *(V.P.-Sls.)*
Louis De Rose *(V.P. & Chief Fin. Officer)*
Charles A. Rubey, Jr. *(V.P.)*
H. Chukerman *(V.P.-Human Resources)*
Principal(s):
Michael B. McCaskey
Thomas Mints
Arthur J. Decio
Harvey N. Medvin
Edward G. Proctor

Computer Systems/Hardware:
IBM AS400

Outside Service Firm(s):

Arthur Andersen & Co.*(Auditors)*
33 W. Monroe St.
Chicago, IL 60603-4067
Tel.: 312-580-0033
Fax: 312-507-6748

Isham, Lincoln & Beale*(Legal Firm)*
One First Natl. Plaza
Chicago, IL 60603
Tel.: 312-558-7500

SCHWEGMANN GIANT SUPER MARKETS
5300 Gentilly Rd.
New Orleans, LA 70126
Mailing Address:
P.O. Box 26099,
New Orleans, LA 70186
Tel.: 504-947-9921 **LA**
Fax: 504-942-5475
Year Founded: 1869
Approx.Sls.: $450,000,000
Emp.: 4,600
Import
Retail Grocery Stores; Commercial Real Estate Lessors
S.I.C.: 5411; 6512
John Schwegmann *(Chief Exec. Officer & Chm.)*
Sam Levy *(Pres.)*

David Erath *(Chief Fin. Officer)*
Roy Lacoste *(V.P.-Grocery Sls.)*
Marc Robert *(V.P.-Oper.)*
Jorge San Roman *(V.P.-Non-Food Sls.)*
Susan Burge *(Dir.-Pub. Rels.)*
John Detillier *(Dir.-Computer Services)*
Lee Janies *(Dir.-Personnel)*
Richard Reso *(Dir.-Adv.)*
Ron Whitaker *(Dir.-Pur.)*

Principal(s):
John Schwegmann
Sam Levy

Computer Systems/Hardware:
IBM

Outside Service Firm(s):

Deloitte & Touche*(Auditors)*
3700 One Shell Square
New Orleans, LA 70139
Tel.: 504-581-2727

Stone Pigman*(Legal Firm)*
New Orleans, LA

Hibernia National Bank*(Major Banking Relationship)*
New Orleans, LA

SCHWEIZER AIRCRAFT CORPORATION
P.O. Box 147
Elmira, NY 14902
Tel.: 607-739-3821
Fax: 607-796-2488
Approx.Sls.: $37,000,000
Emp.: 550
Export
Airplane Parts & Assemblies, Agricultural Aircraft, Gliders, Light Metal Products, Reconnaissance Aircraft, Helicopters
S.I.C.: 3728; 3499; 3721
Paul H. Schweizer *(Pres. & Treas.)*
M.D. Oakley *(V.P.)*
Leslie Schweizer *(V.P.-Engrng.)*
Kathleen Condon *(Mgr.-Contracts)*
Truman Kosier *(Mgr.-Sls. & Mktg.)*
Thomas Walton *(Mgr.-Personnel)*

Outside Service Firm(s):

Carnevale & Co.*(Auditors)*
Elmira, NY

Sayles, Evans, Brayton, Palmer & Tifft*(Legal Firm)*
New York, NY

Chase Lincoln First Bank, N.A.*(Major Banking Relationship)*
P.O. Box 1250,
Rochester, NY 14603
Tel.: 716-232-5000

SCHWINN BICYCLE COMPANY
217 N. Jefferson St.
Chicago, IL 60661
Tel.: 312-454-7400
Fax: 312-454-7525
Year Founded: 1895
Approx.Sls.: $200,000,000
Emp.: 525
Fiscal Year-end: 12/31/91
Import Export
Manufacturer of Bicycles
S.I.C.: 3751; 6719
E.R. Schwinn, Jr. *(Pres.)*
Al Durelli *(V.P.-Distr.)*
Brian Fiala *(V.P.-Human Resources & MIS)*
Daniel Garramone *(V.P. & Gen. Counsel)*
Michael McNamara *(V.P. & Treas.)*
Ralph D. Murray *(V.P.-Mktg. & Sls. & Chief Oper. Officer)*
Chris Barney *(Controller)*
Robert Keck *(Corp. Sec.)*
Nai-Wen Kiang *(Dir.-Pur.)*
Mike Martinsen *(Dir.-Intl. Mktg.)*
Paul Chess *(Mgr.-Mktg. Communications)*

Computer Systems/Hardware:
IBM Systems 36 & 4381

Outside Service Firm(s):

KPMG Peat Marwick*(Auditors)*
Peat Marwick Plaza, 303 E. Wacker Dr.
Chicago, IL 60601
Tel.: 312-938-1000

Washington National Insurance*(Group Insurer)*
Evanston, IL

Keck, Mahin, Cate & Koehler*(Legal Firm)*
8300 Sears Tower, 233 S. Wacker Dr.
Chicago, IL 60606
Tel.: 312-876-3400

Harris Trust & Savings Bank*(Major Banking Relationship)*
111 W. Monroe St.
Chicago, IL 60690
Tel.: 312-461-2265
Tel.: 800-858-0840

Harris Trust & Savings Bank*(Pension Manager)*
111 W. Monroe St.
Chicago, IL 60690
Tel.: 312-461-2265
Tel.: 800-858-0840

Non-U.S. Holding:

Schwinn (USA)-Csepel Ltd. **(1)**
Gyepson U. 1 1211,
Budapest, Hungary
Mfr. of Bicycles
S.I.C.: 3751
Gyorgy Podolak *(Gen. Mgr.)*

F.J. SCIAME CONSTRUCTION
247 Water St.
New York, NY 10038
Tel.: 212-819-1940
Fax: 212-921-4850
Approx.Sls.: $30,000,000
Emp.: 45
Fiscal Year-end: 4/30/92
Construction Mgrs. & Gen. Contractors
S.I.C.: 1521; 1522; 1531; 1541; 1542
Frank Sciame *(Pres., Treas., Chief Exec. & Chief Fin. Officer)*
Luke Clarizio *(V.P.)*

Outside Service Firm(s):

Joseph Machlin*(Auditors)*
New York, NY

American Health & Life Insurance Co.*(Group Insurer)*
Baltimore, MD

Winston & Strawn*(Legal Firm)*
175 Water St.
New York, NY 10038-4981
Tel.: 212-269-2500

European American Bank*(Major Banking Relationship)*
New York, NY

First Chicago Shareholder Services Trust Co.*(Major Banking Relationship)*
153 West 51st St.
New York, NY 10019
Tel.: 212-791-6422
Fax: 212-385-9798

SCICOM DATA SERVICES, LTD.
10101 Bren Road East
Minnetonka, MN 55343
Tel.: 612-933-4200 **MN**
Fax: 612-936-4132
Approx.Sls.: $19,000,000
Emp.: 235
Fiscal Year-end: 6/30/92
Engaged in Providing Online Data Processing Services to Commercial Customers & Data Entry Services & Graphic Arts & Direct Mail
S.I.C.: 2741; 7331; 7374

Richard A. Walter *(Chm. Bd. & Chief Exec. Officer)*
Steven B. Dille *(Pres. & Chief Oper. Officer)*
Dale Carlson *(Sr. V.P.)*
James G. Bloes *(V.P.)*
John J. Honzl *(V.P. & Chief Fin. Officer)*
Dean G. Iwen *(V.P.)*
Darrel D. Janckila *(V.P.)*
Samuel Le Count *(V.P.)*
Roland R. Lins *(V.P.)*
Edward L. Vick *(V.P.)*
Eileen Davenport *(Controller)*
Thomas R. King *(Sec.)*
Jerry Johnson *(Dir.-Telecommunications)*

Outside Service Firm(s):

House, Nezerka & Froelich*(Auditors)*
Minneapolis, MN

Mutual Benefit Life Insurance*(Group Insurer)*
New York, NY

National Benefit Resources*(Group Insurer)*
St. Louis Park, MN

Century Bank*(Major Banking Relationship)*
Eden Prairie, MN

Merrill Lynch*(Pension Manager)*
P.O. Box 20, World Trade Center
New York, NY 10281
Tel.: 212-449-4843

SCIENCE APPLICATIONS INTERNATIONAL CORPORATION
10260 Campus Point Drive
San Diego, CA 92121-1522
Tel.: 619-546-6000 **DE**
Fax: 619-535-7578
Year Founded: 1969
Assets: $437,253,000
Liabilities: $27,036,000
Net Worth: $410,217,000
Approx.Sls.: $1,285,294,000
Emp.: 14,000
Fiscal Year-end: 1/31/92
Export
High-Tech Research & Development
S.I.C.: 8731
Corporate Giving Program: Company Matches Contributions of a Minimum of $25 to a Maximum of $500 in January for Gifts made the Previous Year on a one to one Basis
J.R. Beyster *(Chm. Bd. & Chief Exec. Officer)*
W.E. Zisch *(Vice Chm.)*
L.A. Kull *(Pres. & Chief Oper. Officer)*
W.A. Roper, Jr. *(Chief Fin. Officer)*
B.A. Schmidt *(Asst. V.P.)*
J.D. Heipt *(Sec.)*
Ward Reed *(Treas.)*
P.A. Sager *(Controller)*
Doug Scott *(Gen. Counsel)*
B.M. Berend *(Dir.-Personnel)*
P.D. Dreesen *(Dir.-Pur.)*
J.E. Russell *(Dir.-Corp. Devel.)*
E.A. Straker *(Dir.-Environment/ Natural Resources)*
J.M. Swartz *(Dir.-Data Processing)*
D. Baldwin *(Mgr.-Real Estate)*
L.E. George *(Mgr.-Training)*
P. Pavlics *(Mgr.-Plng.)*

No. of Mfg. Plants/Facilities: 2
No. of U.S. Offices: 200
No. of Foreign Offices: 2

Computer Systems/Hardware:
Prime 750

Outside Service Firm(s):

Price Waterhouse*(Auditors)*
750 B St.
San Diego, CA 92101
Tel.: 619-231-9830

Prudential Insurance Co. of America*(Group Insurer)*
751 Broad St.
Newark, NJ 07102-3777
Tel.: 201-802-6000

Skadden, Arps, Slate, Meagher & Flom*(Legal Firm)*
Wilmington, DE

Citibank N.A.*(Major Banking Relationship)*
Corporate Trust Services, 399 Park Ave.
New York, NY 10043
Tel.: 212-559-1605

Security Pacific National Bank*(Major Banking Relationship)*
Terminal Annex
Los Angeles, CA 90051
Tel.: 213-613-7641

Subsidiaries:

American Systems Engineering Corporation **(1)**
2829 Guardian Lane, Ste. 200
Virginia Beach, VA 23452
Tel.: 804-463-6666
Fax: 804-463-9100
Emp.: 731
Engineering Services
S.I.C.: 8711
Carl M. Albero *(Pres.)*
Rennee Hunter *(Treas.)*

Bull, Inc. **(1)**
10260 Campus Point Dr.
San Diego, CA 92121
Tel.: 619-552-4710
Fax: 619-552-4705
Stock Broker
S.I.C.: 6211
Anne Maharry *(Pres. & Chief Fin. Officer)*
Karen Johnson *(Chief Oper. Officer)*

Campus Point Realty Corporation **(1)**
10260 Campus Point Drive
La Jolla, CA 92037
Tel.: 619-546-6338
Fax: 619-552-4824
Real Estate Managers
S.I.C.: 6531
D.W. Baldwin *(Pres.)*
Eric Hazard *(Chief Oper. Officer)*
Ward Reed *(Chief Fin. Officer)*

Energy and Technology Management Corporation **(1)**
2021 Century Blvd., 2nd Flr.
Germantown, MD 20874
Tel.: 301-353-8554 (100%)
Fax: 301-353-0265
David Aldrich *(Pres.)*
Gary Amstutz *(Chief Fin. Officer)*

Falcon Associates, Ltd. **(1)**
6862 Elm St., Ste. 430
McLean, VA 22101
Tel.: 703-356-4445
Fax: 703-356-7224
Emp.: 19
Professional Consulting as Applied To Computer Software
S.I.C.: 7371
Thomas H. Neighbors *(Pres. & Chief Oper. Officer)*
John M. Rozea *(Chief Fin. Officer)*

General Sciences Corp. **(1)**
6100 Chevy Chase Dr.
Laurel, MD 20707-2929
Tel.: 301-953-2700 (100%)
Assets: $10,494,061
Earnings: $222,086
Liabilities: $4,310,191
Net Worth: $6,183,870
Approx.Sls.: $15,403,402
Emp.: 211
Fiscal Year-end: 7/31/91
Analysis of Satellite Stability, Orientation & Other Behavior; Severe Storm Research; Processing & Interpretation of Data Form Remote Sensors Such As Satellites & Radar; Development of Computer-Based Models to Analyze The Effects of Toxic Substances On The Environment; Meteorological Satellite Processing Systems
S.I.C.: 8731; 3829; 9511
Jeffrey C. Chen *(Chm. Bd., Pres. & Chief Exec. Officer)*
Dr. Lily C. Chen *(Exec. V.P., Treas. & Chief Fin. Officer)*
Jon C. Chen *(V.P.)*

Science Applications International Corporation—(Continued)

Anthony M. Syntax *(Dir.-Information Sciences Div.)*

Hicks & Associates Inc. **(1)**
230 Palermo
Coral Gables, FL 33134
Tel.: 305-444-7463 (100%)
Approx.Billings: $1,100,000
Emp.: 2
Computer Systems/Hardware:
IBM
Retail & Business-to-Business Adv.
Donald J. Hicks *(Chm. Bd., Pres. & Chief Exec. Officer)*
Daniel Harring *(Acctg.)*

Logistics Systems Architects **(1)**
3800 Watt Ave., Ste. 210
Sacramento, CA 95821
Tel.: 916-974-8800 (100%)
Fax: 916-974-8830
Daniel J. Wagner *(Pres.)*

SAIC Commercial Enterprises, Inc. **(1)**
10260 Campus Point Dr.
San Diego, CA 92121
Tel.: 619-552-4710
High Tech Commercial Applications
S.I.C.: 8711
J.P. Walkush *(Pres.)*
Ronald Suokko *(Chief Fin. Officer)*

SAIC Engineering, Inc. **(1)**
10 Riverside Dr.
Lakeville, MA 02347
Tel.: 508-946-3500
Fax: 508-946-3059
Emp.: 35
Engineering Services
S.I.C.: 8711
Robert S. Cummings *(Pres.)*
Mike Albers *(Chief Fin. Officer)*

Science Applications International Corporation (SAIC Virgin Islands) **(1)**
c/o First Guardian Trust Co., Upper Level Drake Passage
Saint Thomas, VI 00802
Tel.: 809-774-6011 (100%)
Ward Reed *(Pres.)*

Non-U.S. Holdings:

Medecine et Systemes Informatiques Intergres **(1)**
Parc Euromedecine, 95 Rue Pierre Flourens 34090
Montpellier, France
Tel.: 011-33-6775-4983 (100%)
Fax: 011-331-4692-1404
Jean de Kervasdoue *(Pres.)*
Rolf Leprevost *(Chief Oper. Officer)*

SAIC Canada **(1)**
275 Slater St., Ste. 1003
Ottawa, ON K1P 5H9, Canada
Tel.: 613-563-2121
Fax: 613-230-8707
Emp.: 16
Engineering Services
S.I.C.: 8711
Ernest B. Creber *(Pres.)*
Willard Hillegeist *(Chief Fin. Officer)*

SAIC UK Limited **(1)**
Poseidon House, Castle Park
Cambridge, CB3 0RD, United Kingdom
Tel.: 011-44-223-460747
Fax: 011-44-223-315057
Emp.: 2
Engineering Services
S.I.C.: 8711
Andrew Cowan *(Chief Oper. Officer)*

Subsidiary:

Topexpress, Ltd. **(2)**
Poseidon House, Castle Park
Cambridge, United Kingdom CB3 0RD
Tel.: 011-44-223-462121 (100%)
Fax: 011-44-223-315057

Science Applications International, Europe S.A. **(1)**
2 Place de la Defense 92053, LE CNIT WTC1, #209,
Paris, France
Tel.: 011-33-1-46-92-1416 (100%)
Fax: 011-33-1-46-92-1404

SCIENCE & ENGINEERING ASSOCIATES
6100 Uptown Blvd., N.E., Ste. 700
Albuquerque, NM 87110
Tel.: 505-884-2300 **NM**
Fax: 505-884-2991
Year Founded: 1980
Assets: $3,300,000
Liabilities: $1,236,000
Net Worth: $2,064,000
Approx.Sls.: $10,000,000
Emp.: 100
Fiscal Year-end: 4/30/92
Research Services, Except Laboratory
S.I.C.: 8711
James D. Cramer *(Chm. Bd.)*
Gregory R. Woods *(Pres. & Chief Exec. Officer)*
William C. Camp *(Treas. & Chief Fin. Officer)*
Bradley Ross *(Sec.)*

Outside Service Firm(s):

Arthur Andersen & Co.*(Auditors)*
AmericaWest Financial Ctr., 6501 Americas Parkway N.E., Ste. 400
Albuquerque, NM 87110
Tel.: 505-889-4700

William J. Darling & Associates*(Legal Firm)*
Albuquerque, NM

United New Mexico Bank*(Major Banking Relationship)*
Albuquerque, NM

SCIPAR
26 W. Spring St.
Buffalo, NY 14221
Mailing Address:
P.O. Box 400
Buffalo, NY 14231-0400
Tel.: 716-631-3730 **NY**
Fax: 716-631-3799
Year Founded: 1975
Assets: $2,337,000
Earnings: $153,600
Liabilities: $1,467,000
Net Worth: $870,000
Sales Range: $10-19 Million
Emp.: 35
Fiscal Year-end: 2/28/91
Electro-Optical/Image Processing Research & Computer Systems Development
S.I.C.: 8731; 7371; 7373
Robert E. Kinzly *(Pres. & Treas.)*
Walter A. Kammer *(V.P.)*
Henry M. Porter *(Sec. & Gen. Counsel)*
Donald Kwiatkowski *(Mgr.-Pur.)*

No. of Mfg. Plants/Facilities: 1
No. of U.S. Offices: 1

Computer Systems/Hardware:
DEC MicroVAX & VAXStations

Outside Service Firm(s):

Morgan & Beyer C.P.A.*(Auditors)*
Buffalo, NY

Alexander & Alexander*(Commercial Insurance Carrier)*
Buffalo, NY

Alexander & Alexander*(Group Insurer)*
Buffalo, NY

Lippes, Kaminsky, Silverstein, Mathias & Wexler*(Legal Firm)*
Buffalo, NY

Marine Midland Bank*(Major Banking Relationship)*
P.O. Box 803, 1 Marine Midland Center, 23rd Floor
Buffalo, NY 14203
Tel.: 716-841-2582

The Principal Financial Group*(Pension Manager)*
Williamsville, NY

L. M. SCOFIELD COMPANY
6533 Bandini Blvd.
Los Angeles, CA 90040
Tel.: 213-723-5285
Tel.: 800-800-9900
Fax: 213-727-5943
Year Founded: 1932
Approx.Sls.: $15,000,000
Emp.: 100
Fiscal Year-end: 3/31/91
Mfr. Colors & Texturing Systems for Concrete
S.I.C.: 2899; 3272
David Arnold *(Pres.)*
Phillip Arnold *(V.P.)*
Denise D. Kushner *(Mgr.-Communications)*

Division:

Atlanta Mfg. Facility **(1)**
4155 Scofield Rd.
Douglasville, GA 30134
Tel.: 404-920-1200
Fax: 404-920-1827
Mfr. Colors & Texturing Systems for Concrete
S.I.C.: 2899; 3272
Alfred Griffin *(Sls. Mgr.-Western)*
Robert Nussmeier *(Sls. Mgr.-Eastern)*

SCOTCHMAN INDUSTRIES, INC.
180 E. Hwy. 14
Philip, SD 57567
Mailing Address:
P.O. Box 850
Philip, SD 57567
Tel.: 605-859-2542
Fax: 605-859-2499
Year Founded: 1967
Approx.Sls.: $12,000,000
Emp.: 100
Fiscal Year-end: 3/31/92
Import Export
Mfr. of Machine Tools
S.I.C.: 3541
Arthur Kroetch *(Chm. Bd., Pres. & Chief Exec. Officer)*
Jerry Carley *(V.P.-Oper.)*
Gerald Rislov *(V.P.-Dakota Case)*
Jerry Kroetch *(V.P.-Sls. & Mktg.)*
John Hart *(Pur. Dir.)*
Vicki Peterson *(Export Mgr.)*

Computer Systems/Hardware:
NCR

THE SCOTSMAN GROUP, INC.
(d/b/a Williams Mobile Offices)
8211 Town Center Dr.
Baltimore, MD 21236
Tel.: 410-931-6000
Fax: 410-931-6111
Approx.Sls.: $98,000,000
Emp.: 560
Mobile Homes, Prefab Buildings, Office Facilities, Secretarial Service Rental
S.I.C.: 5039; 7389
Barry P. Gossett *(Pres.)*
Simon Dragan *(Exec. V.P.-Scotsman Building Div.)*
Marietta F. Adams *(V.P.-Admin.)*
Steuart A. Kunicki *(V.P.-Mobile Office Div.)*
Peter L. Heumann *(Controller)*

Outside Service Firm(s):

KPMG Peat Marwick*(Auditors)*
111 S. Calvert St.
Baltimore, MD 21202
Tel.: 410-783-8300

First National Bank of Maryland*(Major Banking Relationship)*
25 S. Charles St.
Baltimore, MD 21201
Tel.: 410-244-4025

Subsidiary:

Scotsman Group, Inc. **(1)**
2550 E. 68th St.
Long Beach, CA 90805
Tel.: 213-531-2230
Portable Buildings; Prefabricated Metal; Mobile Buildings For Commercial Use; Prefabricated Buildings, Wood; Equipment & Vehicle Finance Leasing Companies
S.I.C.: 3448; 2451; 2452; 6159
Jim Strode *(V.P.-Mfg.)*
Bob Thomason *(V.P.)*

LOUIS SCOTT ASSOCIATES, INC.
201 W. Passaic St.
Rochelle Park, NJ 07662
Tel.: 201-587-1222
Fax: 201-587-1070
Year Founded: 1969
Approx.Billings: $11,220,000
Emp.: 12
Healthcare & Managed Care Communications
Louis Scott *(Pres.)*
Monique Anastasio *(V.P., Fin.)*

THE SCOTT COMPANY
14111 Scottslawn Rd.
Marysville, OH 43041
Tel.: 513-644-0011
Tel.: 800-543-8873 **DE**
Fax: 513-644-7244
Year Founded: 1870
Approx.Sls.: $380,000,000
Emp.: 1,700
Fiscal Year-end: 9/30/91
Export
Mfr. Lawn Grass Seed, Chemical Fertilizers, Weed & Insect Controls, Mechanical Accessories, Spreaders
S.I.C.: 0181; 2873; 2874; 3523; 5191; 5261
Tadd C. Seitz *(Chm. Bd. & Chief Exec. Officer)*
Theodore J. Host *(Pres. & Chief Oper. Officer)*
Paul D. Yeager *(Chief Fin. Officer & Exec. V.P.)*
Blaine McKinney *(Sr. V.P.-Consumer Bus. Grp.)*
Bernard R. Ford *(V.P.-Strategy & Bus. Devel.)*
Mike Kelty *(V.P.-Res. & Devel.)*
Joe Petite *(V.P.-Consumer Mktg.)*
Richard B. Stahl *(V.P.-Professional Div.)*
Robert A. Stern *(V.P.-Human Resources)*
Craig D. Walley *(V.P. & Legal Counsel)*
Richard Bergum *(Treas.)*
Tom Feusse *(Controller)*
Sargeant V. Chamberlain *(Dir.-Pur.)*
John Wall *(Dir.-Fin. Services)*
David Slaybaugh *(Mgr.-Consumer Pub. Rels.)*
Principal(s):
Tadd C. Seitz

No. of Mfg. Plants/Facilities: 24
No. of U.S. Offices: 24

Computer Systems/Hardware:
Everex 386 SX

Outside Service Firm(s):

Coopers & Lybrand*(Auditors)*
Dayton, OH

McDonough Caperton Insurance Group*(Group Insurer)*
Charleston, WV

SCOTT/LANCASTER/ HERSHFIELD
11111 Santa Monica Blvd., Ste. 1011
Los Angeles, CA 90025
Tel.: 310-445-1522
Fax: 310-445-1523
Approx.Billings: $10,000,000

Steve Scott *(Pres. & Principal)*
Peggy Lancaster *(Principal & Creative Dir.)*
Sam Hershfield *(Principal & Client Services Dir.)*

SCOTT LUMBER COMPANY
253 N. Lincoln Ave.
Bridgeport, OH 43912
Tel.: 614-635-2345
Fax: 614-635-4816
Approx.Sls.: $20,000,000
Emp.: 200
Lumber, Building Materials & Hardware
S.I.C.: 5211; 5251
David B. Turner *(Pres.)*
Sam Seymour *(V.P.)*
Frank Bonacci *(Controller)*

SCOTT PRINTING CORPORATION
190 Baldwin Ave.
Jersey City, NJ 07306
Tel.: 201-795-1200 **DE**
Fax: 201-795-0760
Year Founded: 1925
Fiscal Year-end: 12/31/92
Financial & Commercial Printing
S.I.C.: 2752
Daniel T. Scott *(Pres.)*
Walter Scott, Jr. *(Exec. V.P.)*
Kenneth J. Horowitz *(V.P.-Fin.)*
Jeffrey Kruger *(Controllor)*
Jean Najdzin *(Sec.)*

No. of Mfg. Plants/Facilities: 2
No. of U.S. Offices: 2

Outside Service Firm(s):

Smolin, Lupin & Co.*(Auditors)*
West Orange, NJ

Shanley & Fisher*(Legal Firm)*
131 Madison Ave.
Morristown, NJ
Tel.: 201-285-1000

SCOTT SPECIALTY GASES, INC.
6141 Easton Road
Plumsteadville, PA 18949
Tel.: 215-766-8861
Fax: 215-766-2009
Sales Range: $20-39 Million
Emp.: 425
Import Export
Pure Gases, Gaseous Mixtures, Pure & Mixed Gases In Disposable Containers & Gas Handling Equipment Services
S.I.C.: 2813; 3563; 3569
John Frederick Merz, Jr. *(Chm. Bd., Pres. & Treas.)*
Thomas E. Colman, Ph.D. *(Chief Oper. Officer & Exec. V.P.)*
William Gittler *(V.P.)*
Robert Squires *(V.P.-Fin.)*
Sally R. Michener *(Sec. & Dir.-Personnel & Pub. Rels.)*

SCOTT U.S.A.
110 Lewis St.
Ketchum, ID 83340
Mailing Address:
P.O. Box 2030
Sun Valley, ID 83353
Tel.: 208-622-1000
Fax: 208-622-1005
Emp.: 50
Whlse. Mktg. of Ski & Motorcycle Prods.
S.I.C.: 5091
Ned Post *(Pres.)*
David Stevens *(Comptroller)*
Larry Morton *(Natl. Sls. & Mktg. Mgr.)*

THE SCOULAR COMPANY
The Scoular Building, 2027 Dodge Street
Omaha, NE 68102
Tel.: 402-342-3500 **NE**
Fax: 402-342-4493
Year Founded: 1892
Sales Range: $1 Billion +
Emp.: 260
Fiscal Year-end: 5/31/92
Agricultural Services & Products, Grain Merchandising
S.I.C.: 0723; 5153
Marshall E. Faith *(Chm. Bd. & Chief Exec. Officer)*
Duane Fisher *(Pres.)*
David M. Faith *(Pres.- Scoular Properties, Inc.)*
Ronald D. Nelson *(Chief Fin. Officer & Sec.)*
Tim Regan *(Treas.)*
Larry Maiefski *(Dir.-Mngmt. Information Systems)*

No. of Mfg. Plants/Facilities: 40

Computer Systems/Hardware:
IBM System 38

Outside Service Firm(s):

Coopers & Lybrand*(Auditors)*
1200 Landmark Center
Omaha, NE
Tel.: 402-344-4545

Frank B. Hall*(Commercial Insurance Carrier)*
Omaha, NE

Mutual of Omaha Insurance Company*(Group Insurer)*
Mutual of Omaha Plaza,
Omaha, NE 68175
Tel.: 800-228-7775

Norwest Bank Minnesota, N.A.*(Major Banking Relationship)*
Omaha, NE

Subsidiary:

Scoular Grain Company **(1)**
2027 Dodge
Omaha, NE 68102
Tel.: 402-342-3500
Telex: 484337
Fax: 402-342-4493
Emp.: 500

SCOVILLE PRESS, INC.
14505 27th Ave., N.
Minneapolis, MN 55447
Tel.: 612-553-1400 **MN**
Fax: 612-553-0042
Year Founded: 1974
Sales Range: $20-39 Million
Emp.: 221
Loose Deck Direct Response Postcard Packs & Magazine Reader Service; Subscription Cards Printers, Commercial Printing & Business Forms
S.I.C.: 2752
Jim Rowe *(Chm. Bd.)*
Donald C. Wildman *(Pres.)*
Dan Thornton *(Chief Oper. Officer)*
William Arendt *(V.P.-Human Resources)*
Robert Parsons *(V.P.-Publr. Sls.)*
Frank Saaranen *(V.P.-Fin.)*
Gary Stang *(V.P.-Sls. & Mktg.)*
Rod Sutton *(V.P.-Mfg.)*
Victor P. Seller *(Gen. Counsel)*

No. of Mfg. Plants/Facilities: 2

Outside Service Firm(s):

KPMG Peat Marwick*(Auditors)*
4200 Norwest Center, 90 S. 7th St.
Minneapolis, MN 55402
Tel.: 612-341-2222

First Bank of St. Paul*(Major Banking Relationship)*
St. Paul, MN

SCREW CONVEYOR CORP.
700 Hoffman St.
Hammond, IN 46327
Tel.: 219-931-1450
Fax: 219-931-0209
Approx.Sls.: $17,000,000
Emp.: 300
Export
Conveying Equipment, Truck Dumpers
S.I.C.: 3535; 3532
G.M. Abraham *(Chief Exec. Officer & Gen. Mgr.)*
C.F. Abraham *(Exec. V.P.-Admin.)*
Dwight L. Snow *(V.P.-Sls. & Mktg.)*
Walter Geisler *(V.P.-Engrng.)*
N. Bantsolas *(Mgr.-Sls.)*

SCRIPTO-TOKAI, INC.
11591 Etiwanda Ave.
Fontana, CA 92335
Mailing Address:
P.O. Box 5555
Fontana, CA 92334
Tel.: 909-360-2100
Fax: 909-360-2130
Year Founded: 1926
Approx.Sls.: $125,000,000
Emp.: 627
Scripto Pens, Pencils, Leads, Refills, Erasers & Roller Pens; Disposable Lighters, Butane Fuel & Utility Lighters
S.I.C.: 3951; 3952; 3089; 3999
Keizo Watanabe *(Pres.)*
Hiro Higashiomori *(Sr. V.P.)*
Tim Goeler *(V.P.-Mktg.)*
Norm Merwise *(Mgr.-Natl. Sls.)*

SCRUFARI CONSTRUCTION CO. INC.
3925 Hyde Park Blvd.
Niagara Falls, NY 14305
Tel.: 716-282-1225 **NY**
Fax: 716-282-7699
Year Founded: 1913
Approx.Sls.: $19,000,000
Emp.: 125
General Contractor
S.I.C.: 1522; 1541
Gary Sankes *(Chm. Bd. & Pres.)*
Thomas Warog *(V.P.)*
Principal(s):
Gary Sankes
Thomas Warog
Thomas Warda

Outside Service Firm(s):

Chris Brown*(Auditors)*
Niagara Falls, NY

D. F. Cubello*(Auditors)*
Niagara Falls, NY

Manufacturers & Traders Trust Company*(Major Banking Relationship)*
1 M & T Plaza
Buffalo, NY 14240
Tel.: 716-842-4200

SCUDDER, STEVENS & CLARK, INC.
345 Park Ave.
New York, NY 10154
Tel.: 212-326-6200 **DE**
Fax: 212-751-3451
Year Founded: 1919
Emp.: 1,400
Investment Counseling Firm
S.I.C.: 6722
Daniel Pierce *(Chm. Bd.)*
Edmond D. Villani *(Pres.)*
Stephen R. Beckwith *(Chief Admin. Officer)*
Thomas H. O'Brien *(Treas.)*
Stephen R. Beckwith *(Chief Admin. Officer)*
Juris Padegs *(Sec.)*

SEA ISLAND COMPANY
100 First St.
Sea Island, GA 31561
Mailing Address:
P.O. Box 351
Sea Island, GA 31561
Tel.: 912-638-3611 **GA**
Fax: 912-638-5159
Year Founded: 1928
Approx.Sls.: $52,000,000
Emp.: 1,100
Real Estate Development, Resort Operation, Landscape, Other Business Investments
S.I.C.: 6531; 7011
Alfred W. Jones, Jr. *(Chm. Bd. & Pres.)*
Alfred W. Jones III *(Exec. V.P.)*
J. Dewey Benefield *(V.P.-Real Estate)*
Dennie L. McCrary *(V.P.-Fin. & Sec.)*
E.T. Wright, Jr. *(V.P.-Resort)*
B.R. Gibson *(Dir.-Human Resources & Insurance)*
Harry Kaufmann *(Dir.-Pub. Rels. & Adv.)*

Outside Service Firm(s):

DeLoach & Company*(Auditors)*
Brunswick, GA

Gilbert, Whittle, Harrell, Scarlett & Skelton*(Legal Firm)*
Brunswick, GA

Trust Co. Bank of SE Georgia*(Major Banking Relationship)*
Brunswick, GA

Divisions:

The Cloister **(1)**
Sea Island, GA 31561
Tel.: 912-638-3611
Ted Wright *(V.P. & Mng. Dir.)*

Sea Island Properties, Inc. **(1)**
100 First St.
Sea Island, GA 31561
Tel.: 912-638-5161
Real Estate Developers
S.I.C.: 6531
J. Dewey Benefield *(Exec. V.P.)*

Subsidiary:

Sea Island Services, Inc. **(1)**
100 First St.
Sea Island, GA 31561
Tel.: 912-638-3611
Resort
S.I.C.: 7011
Gibbon McNeely *(Dir.-Securities)*

SEABOARD ELECTRONICS CO.
6986 El Camino Real, Ste. B-205
Carlsbad, CA 92009
Tel.: 619-438-1205
Tel.: 800-637-2346 **NY**
Telex: 646289
Fax: 619-438-8660
Year Founded: 1977
Approx.Sls.: $2,000,000
Emp.: 40
Fiscal Year-end: 7/31/90
Import Export
Design, Sell & Mfr. Data Transmission Systems with Primary Emphasis on Radio Telemetry Technology, Transmitters, Receivers, Repeaters & Radio Alarm Systems; Radio Personal Alarm Systems; Fire Alarm Systems; Wireless Industrial Remote Control Systems; Gasoline Leak Detectors
S.I.C.: 7372; 3661
Joshua Hacker *(Chm. Bd., Pres., Chief Exec. & Chief Fin. Officer)*
Bernie Klempner *(Sr. V.P.-Engrng.)*
Pamela A. Harrell *(Dir.-Mktg.)*

No. of Mfg. Plants/Facilities: 2
No. of U.S. Offices: 2

Seaboard Electronics Co.—(Continued)

Computer Systems/Hardware:
IBM

Outside Service Firm(s):

Bennett Kielson*(Auditors)*
New Rochelle, NY

Global Coverage*(Commercial Insurance Carrier)*
New York, NY

Barclays Bank plc*(International Bank Affiliate)*
75 Wall St.
New York, NY 10265
Tel.: 212-412-4000

Kaiser Permanente*(Group Insurer)*
Portland, OR

Marine Midland Bank*(Investment Banker)*
140 Broadway Ave., 12 Floor
New York, NY 10015
Tel.: 212-440-1000

Ollman & Marcus*(Legal Firm)*
New Rochelle, NY

Barclays Bank plc*(Major Banking Relationship)*
New Rochelle, NY

Branch:

Seaboard Electronics-East Coast Branch **(1)**
70 Church St.
New Rochelle, NY 10805
Tel.: 914-235-8073
Fax: 914-235-8369

SEABOARD FLOUR CORPORATION
200 Boylston St.
Newton, MA 02167
Tel.: 617-332-8492 **DE**
Fax: 617-244-5463
Year Founded: 1948
Approx.Rev.: $450,000,000
Emp.: 3,000
Fiscal Year-end: 12/31/90
Holding Company; Flour Milling & Bakery Products
S.I.C.: 2041; 6719
Harry Bresky *(Pres.)*
Charles Goldman *(Sec.)*
Principal(s):
Harry Bresky

Computer Systems/Hardware:
IBM 3634

Outside Service Firm(s):

KPMG Peat Marwick*(Auditors)*
One Boston Place
Boston, MA 02108
Tel.: 617-723-7700

Widett, Slater & Goldman*(Legal Firm)*
60 State St.
Boston, MA 02109

Division:

Firoillo A. Co. Inc. **(1)**
396 Clark St.
Milldale, CT 06467
Tel.: 1-800-982-3889
Flour Milling & Bakery Products
S.I.C.: 2041

Subsidiary:

Seaboard Corporation **(1)**
200 Boylston St.
Newton, MA 02167
Tel.: 617-332-8492 (75.3%)
Earnings: $21,241,000
Approx.Sls.: $875,874,000
Emp.: 4,693
Fiscal Year-end: 12/31/91
Agri-Processor, Integrated Poultry Processing, Grain Storage, Wholesale Grain Merchandising, Baking; Ship Chartering; Short-Line Railroad Operations; Sales of Spare Parts, Milling Supplies & Equipment to Foreign Affiliates; Owns & Operates Six Flour Mills & Two Feed Mills Located in South America & West Africa
S.I.C.: 2041; 2015; 0913; 5153; 4221; 4011; 2048
H.H. Bresky *(Pres.)*
Richard G. Myers *(Exec. V.P. & Treas.)*
Otto Bresky, Jr. *(Sr. V.P.)*
Donald Robohm *(V.P. & Chief Fin. Officer)*
Jack S. Miller *(V.P.-Opers. & Admin.)*
Charles M. Goldman *(Sec. & Gen. Counsel)*

Divisions:

Seaboard Corporation, Grain Division **(2)**
9000 W. 67th St.
Shawnee Mission, KS 66202
Tel.: 913-676-8800
Grain Storage
S.I.C.: 4221; 5153

Seaboard Farms Division **(2)**
160 Ben Burton Rd.
Bogart, GA 30622
Tel.: 706-543-8700
Wholesale Poultry
S.I.C.: 5144

SEABROOK BROTHERS & SONS, INC.
Finley Road
Seabrook, NJ 08302
Mailing Address:
P.O. Box 5103
Seabrook, NJ 08302
Tel.: 609-455-8080 **NJ**
Fax: 609-455-9282
Year Founded: 1977
Assets: $25,600,000
Liabilities: $14,000,000
Net Worth: $11,600,000
Sales Range: $20-39 Million
Emp.: 500
Fiscal Year-end: 6/ 2/90
Import Export
Frozen Vegetables
S.I.C.: 2037
James M. Seabrook *(Chm. Bd. & Chief Exec. Officer)*
Charles F. Seabrook, II *(Pres.)*
Endel Miido *(V.P.-Fin. & Admin.)*
Brian E. Seabrook *(V.P.-Sls.)*
James M. Seabrook, Jr. *(V.P. & Gen. Mgr.)*
William E. Seabrook *(V.P.-Engrng.)*
Evelyn T. Seabrook *(Sec.)*
Cynthia S. Kramer *(Comptroller & Treas.)*
Principal(s):
James M. Seabrook
Charles F. Seabrook, II
James M. Seabrook, Jr.

Computer Systems/Hardware:
IBM System 38

Outside Service Firm(s):

Deloitte & Touche*(Auditors)*
1700 Market St.
Philadelphia, PA 19103
Tel.: 215-246-2322
Fax: 215-569-2441

Braemer, Ableson & Hitchner*(Legal Firm)*
18th Fl., 1515 Market St.
Philadelphia, PA 19102
Tel.: 215-665-8300

New Jersey National Bank*(Major Banking Relationship)*
Philadelphia, PA

SEABROOK FOODS, INC.
4974 E. Clinton Way
Fresno, CA 93747
Mailing Address:
P.O. Box 8050,
Fresno, CA 93747
Tel.: 209-252-2836
Fax: 209-255-0756
Approx.Sls.: $30,000,000
Emp.: 23
Import Export
Packers of Frozen Fruits & Vegetables
S.I.C.: 2037
Ronald W. Buatte *(Pres. & Gen. Mgr.)*
Takao Yashida *(V.P.-Fin. & Admin.)*
David Blair *(Sec.)*

Outside Service Firm(s):

Deloitte & Touche*(Auditors)*
Fresno, CA

Bank of Fresno*(Major Banking Relationship)*
Fresno, CA

SEABROOK WALLCOVERINGS, INC.
1325 Farmville Rd.
Memphis, TN 38122
Tel.: 901-320-3500
Fax: 901-320-3675
Year Founded: 1978
Approx.Sls.: $87,200,000
Emp.: 550
Fiscal Year-end: 12/31/91
Wholesale & Retail Paint & Wallpaper
S.I.C.: 5198; 5231
James H. Seabrook, Sr. *(Chm. Bd.)*
James H. Seabrook, Jr. *(Pres. & Chief Exec. Officer)*
Larry Cooksey *(V.P.-Fin.)*
James Allen *(Dir.-Corp. Sls.)*
Donna Chastain *(Dir.-Personnel)*
Eddy Meeks *(Mgr.-Data Processing)*
Jerry Hudson *(Mgr.-Mktg.)*

Outside Service Firm(s):

Reynolds, Bone & Greisbeck*(Auditors)*
Memphis, TN

First Tennessee Bank, N.A.*(Major Banking Relationship)*
Memphis, TN

SEALASKA CORPORATION
One Sealaska Plaza, Ste. 400
Juneau, AK 99801-1276
Tel.: 907-586-1512
Tel.: 800-544-2247 **AK**
Fax: 907-586-9214
Year Founded: 1972
Assets: $248,888,000
Liabilities: $98,578,000
Net Worth: $150,310,000
Approx.Sls.: $111,261,000
Emp.: 150
Fiscal Year-end: 3/31/91
Export
Holding Company; Forest Products; Building Materials; Natural Resource Development in Alaska, Portfolio Management, Minerals
S.I.C.: 6719; 6512
Marlene A. Johnson *(Chm. Bd.)*
Bryon I. Mallott *(Pres. & Chief Exec. Officer)*
Robert W. Loescher *(Exec. V.P.-Resource Mngmt.)*
Chris E. McNeil, Jr. *(Exec. V.P. & Gen. Counsel)*
William F. Strafford *(Sr. V.P.-Fin., Treas. & Chief Fin. Officer)*
Edith McHenry *(V.P.-Admin. Services)*
Barbara Searls *(V.P.-Fin.)*
Maxine H. Richert *(Sec.)*
Vikki Mata *(Acting Dir.-Communications)*
Rob Johnson *(Dir.-Data Processing)*
Maxine Richert *(Corp. Sec.)*

Principal(s):
Bryon I. Mallott

No. of Mfg. Plants/Facilities: 1
No. of U.S. Offices: 4

Computer Systems/Hardware:
DEC; IBM; Compaq; MacIntosh

Outside Service Firm(s):

Price Waterhouse*(Auditors)*
1001 Fourth Ave. Plaza
Seattle, WA 98154
Tel.: 206-622-1505

Willis Corroon Corp. of Seattle*(Group Insurance Broker/Consult)*
Seattle, WA

Blue Cross of Washington & Alaska*(Group Insurer)*
Seattle, WA

Birch, Horton, Bittner, Monroe, Peatinger & Anders*(Legal Firm)*
One Sealaska Plaza, Ste. 300
Juneau, AK 99801
Tel.: 907-586-2890

Bank of Tokyo*(Major Banking Relationship)*
1201 3rd Ave., Ste. 1100
Seattle, WA 98101
Tel.: 206-382-6000

National Bank of Alaska*(Major Banking Relationship)*
P.O. Box 100600,
Anchorage, AK 99510-0600

Security Pacific National Bank*(Major Banking Relationship)*
1301 Fifth Ave.
Seattle, WA 98101
Tel.: 206-621-4530

Howard Johnson & Co.*(Pension Manager)*
Portland, OR

Subsidiary:

Sealaska Timber Corporation **(1)**
2030 Sea Level Drive
Ketchikan, AK 99901
Tel.: 907-225-9444

SEALD-SWEET GROWERS, INC.
1991 74th Ave.
Vero Beach, FL 32966
Mailing Address:
P.O. Box 6152,
Vero Beach, FL 32961
Tel.: 407-569-2244
Telex: 807 206
Fax: 407-562-9038
Year Founded: 1909
Approx.Sls.: $145,000,000
Emp.: 60
Fiscal Year-end: 8/31/91
Import Export
Seald-Sweet & Florigold Oranges, Grapefruit, Tangerines, Tangelos & Lemons; Chilled Citrus, Salads & Sections; Georgia & Florida Watermelons; Vidalia Sweet Onions
S.I.C.: 0174; 0161
Philip C. Gates *(Chm. Bd. & Pres.)*
Jay Holford *(Chief Exec. Officer)*
James B. McCranie *(Exec. V.P.-Mktg.)*

SEALING DEVICES INC.
4400 Walden Ave.
Lancaster, NY 14086
Tel.: 716-684-7600
Fax: 716-684-0760
Year Founded: 1964
Approx.Sls.: $14,700,000
Emp.: 90
Fiscal Year-end: 9/30/91
Export
Manufacturer & Distributor Industrial Gaskets, Seals & Sealing Materials
S.I.C.: 3053; 5085
Terry S. Galanis, Sr. *(Chm. Bd.)*
Terry S. Galanis, Jr. *(Pres.)*
Gregory J. DelDuce *(Treas.)*
Marian M. Galanis *(Sec.)*
Wayne K. Carrig *(Mgr.-Sls.)*
Gary Kegler *(Pur. Agent)*

No. of U.S. Offices: 4

Outside Service Firm(s):

Lumsden McCormick & Co.*(Auditors)*
Buffalo, NY

Albrecht, Maguire, Heffern & Gregg*(Legal Firm)*
Buffalo, NY

Marine Midland Bank*(Major Banking Relationship)*
P.O. Box 803, 1 Marine Midland Center, 23rd Floor
Buffalo, NY 14203
Tel.: 716-841-2582

SEALY CORPORATION
c/o Sealy, Inc., 1228 Euclid Ave., 10th Fl.
Cleveland, OH 44115
Tel.: 216-522-1310 DE
Fax: 216-522-1366
Year Founded: 1907
Assets: $1,130,658,000
Earnings: $24,669,000
Liabilities: $1,061,102,000
Net Worth: $69,556,000
Approx.Rev.: $702,350,000
Emp.: 5,500
Fiscal Year-end: 11/30/91
Mfr. of Mattresses, Box Springs, Waterbeds & Waterbed Furniture, Convertible Sleep Sofas
S.I.C.: 2515; 2511
Lymann M. Beggs *(Chm., Pres. & Chief Exec. Officer)*
Douglas R. Schrank *(Chief Fin. Officer & Sr. V.P.)*
Roger James *(Sr. V.P.-Opers.)*
Jeffrey C. Claypool *(V.P.-Human Resources)*
Cynthia Datlund *(V.P.-Mktg)*
Gary Fazio *(V.P.-Sls.)*
John G. Bartik *(Treas.)*
John D. Moran *(Sec. & Gen. Counsel)*
Alicia Arnold *(Dir.-Mktg. Services)*

Outside Service Firm(s):

KPMG Peat Marwick*(Auditors)*
1500 National City Center
Cleveland, OH 44114
Tel.: 216-696-9100

Frederic F. Brace, Jr. Lawyer*(Legal Firm)*
332 So. Michigan Ave.
Chicago, IL 60604
Tel.: 312-347-4400

Sidley & Austin*(Legal Firm)*
One First National Plaza, 42nd Fl.
Chicago, IL 60603
Tel.: 312-853-7000
Fax: 312-853-7036

National City Bank*(Major Banking Relationship)*
P.O. Box 92301, Corp. Trust Dept.
Cleveland, OH 44101
Tel.: 216-575-2000

Subsidiaries:

The Ohio Mattress Company Licensing And Components Group **(1)**
10th Fl., Halle Bldg., 1228 Euclid Ave.
Cleveland, OH 44115
Tel.: 216-522-1310 (100%)
Fax: 216-522-0602
Licensing Services; Mfrs. Spring Units for Mattresses; Testing, Research & Development of New Products
S.I.C.: 6794; 2515
Malcolm Candlish *(Chm. Bd., Pres. & Chief Fin. Officer)*
Douglas R. Schrank *(Sr. V.P. & Chief Fin. Officer)*
Roger J. James *(Sr. V.P.-Opers.)*
R. James Alexy *(Sr. V.P.-Mktg./Sls.)*
William J. McDade *(V.P.-Human Resources)*

Plants:

The Ohio Mattress Company Licensing And Components Group **(2)**
6275 Lake Shore Ct.
Colorado Springs, CO 80915
Tel.: 719-574-6944
Fax: 719-574-2686
Mfr. Spring Units for Mattresses
S.I.C.: 2515
Ronald Miller *(Plant. Super.)*

The Ohio Mattress Company, Licensing And Components Group **(2)**
Majic Industrial Park
Delano, PA 18220
Tel.: 717-467-2721
Fax: 717-467-3147
Mfr. Spring Units for Mattresses
S.I.C.: 2515
Monte Rader *(Plant Mgr.)*

The Ohio Mattress Company Licensing And Componets Group **(2)**
P.O. Box 258, 1132 N. Cullen
Rensselaer, IN 47978
Tel.: 219-866-7181
Fax: 219-866-4504
Mfr. Spring Units for Mattresses
S.I.C.: 2515
Ron Morgan *(Plant Mgr.)*

Sealy, Inc. **(1)**
1228 Euclid Ave., 10th Fl.
Cleveland, OH 44115
Tel.: 216-522-1310 (100%)
Fax: 216-522-0602
Approx.Sls.: $510,000,000
Emp.: 120
Mfr. Of Mattresses & Box Springs
S.I.C.: 2515
Lyman M. Beggs *(Chm., Pres, & Chief Exec. Officer)*
R. James Alexy *(Sr. V.P.-Mktg. & Sls.)*
Roger J. James *(Sr. V.P.-Opers.)*
Douglas R. Schrank *(Sr. V.P. & Chief Fin. Officer)*
William J. McDade *(V.P.-Human Resources)*
Alicia Arnold *(Dir.-Mktg. Services)*

Subsidiaries:

Sealy Mattress Company of Puerto Rico **(2)**
El Commandante Indus. Ctr., #1 San Maracos
Rio Piedras, PR 00924
Tel.: 809-796-0295 (100%)
Fax: 809-750-6190
Mfr. of Mattresses & Box Springs
S.I.C.: 2515
Malcolm Candlish *(Chm. Bd., & Chief Exec. Officer)*
Gustavo Mercier *(Pres.)*
R. James Alexy *(Sr. V.P.-Mktg./Sls.)*
Roger J. James *(Sr. V.P.-Opers.)*
Douglas R. Schrank *(Sr. V.P. & Chief Fin. Officer)*
William J. McDade *(V.P.-Human Resources)*

Ohio-Sealy Mattress Mfg. Co., Inc. **(2)**
One Posturepedic Dr.
Randolph, MA 02368
Tel.: 617-961-1100 (100%)
Fax: 617-963-8766
Mfr. of Mattresses & Box Springs
S.I.C.: 2515
Malcolm Candlish *(Chm. Bd., Pres. & Chief Exec. Officer)*
Douglas R. Schrank *(Sr. V.P. & Chief Fin. Officer)*
Roger J. James *(Sr. V.P.-Opers.)*
R. James Alexy *(Sr. V.P.-Mktg./Sls.)*
William J. McDade *(V.P.-Human Resources)*

Ohio-Sealy Mattress Manufacturing Co.-Fort Worth **(2)**
6550 Wuliger Way
Richland Hills, TX 76180
Tel.: 817-485-8052 (100%)
Fax: 817-581-0160
Mfr. of Mattresses & Box Springs
S.I.C.: 2515
Malcolm Candlish *(Chm. Bd., Pres. & Chief Exec. Officer)*
Douglas R. Schrank *(Sr. V.P. & Chief Fin. Officer)*
Roger J. James *(Sr. V.P.-Opers.)*
R. James Alexy *(Sr. V.P.-Mktg./Sls.)*
William J. McDade *(V.P.-Human Resources)*

Ohio-Sealy Mattress Manufacturing Co.-Houston **(2)**
Hwy. Loop 290, P.O. Box 593
Brenham, TX 77833
Tel.: 409-836-6644 (100%)
Fax: 409-836-1370
Mfr. of Mattresses & Box Springs
S.I.C.: 2515
Malcolm Candlish *(Chm. Bd., Pres. & Chief Exec. Officer)*
Douglas R. Schrank *(Sr. V.P. & Chief Fin. Officer)*
Roger J. James *(Sr. V.P.-Opers.)*
R. James Alexy *(Sr. V.P.-Mktg./Sls.)*
William J. McDade *(V.P.-Human Resources)*

Sealy Mattress Company of Albany, Inc. **(2)**
P.O. Box 5288, 99 Railroad Ave. & Brown Rd.
Albany, NY 12205
Tel.: 518-459-1651 (100%)
Fax: 518-459-1428
Mfr. of Mattresses & Box Springs
S.I.C.: 2515
Malcolm Candlish *(Chm. Bd., Pres. & Chief Exec. Officer)*
Douglas R. Schrank *(Sr. V.P. & Chief Fin. Officer)*
Roger J. James *(Sr. V.P.-Opers.)*
R. James Alexy *(Sr. V.P.-Mktg./Sls.)*
William J. McDade *(V.P.-Human Resources)*

Sealy of Minnesota, Inc. **(2)**
825 Transfer Rd.
Saint Paul, MN 55114
Tel.: 612-645-8143 (100%)
Fax: 612-645-1255
Mfr. of Mattresses & Box Springs
S.I.C.: 2515
Malcolm Candlish *(Chm. Bd., Pres. & Chief Exec. Officer)*
Douglas R. Schrank *(Sr. V.P. & Chief Fin. Officer)*
Roger J. James *(Sr. V.P.-Opers.)*
R. James Alexy *(Sr. V.P.-Mktg./Sls.)*
William McDade *(V.P.-Human Resources)*

Sealy Connecticut, Inc. **(2)**
P.O. 151, 25 Hillside Ave.
Oakville, CT 06779
Tel.: 203-274-9221 (100%)
Fax: 203-274-7873
Mfr. of Mattresses & Box Springs
S.I.C.: 2515
Malcolm Candlish *(Chm. Bd., Pres. & Chief Exec. Officer)*
Douglas R. Schrank *(Sr. V.P. & Chief Fin. Officer)*
Roger J. James *(Sr. V.P.-Opers.)*
R. James Alexy *(Sr. V.P.-Mktg./Sls.)*
William McDade *(V.P.-Human Resources)*

Sealy of Maryland & Virginia, Inc. **(2)**
70-81 Industrial Park
Williamsport, MD 21795
Tel.: 410-223-9700 (100%)
Fax: 410-223-5157
Mfr. of Mattresses & Box Springs
S.I.C.: 2515
Malcolm Candlish *(Chm. Bd., Pres. & Chief Exec. Officer)*
Douglas R. Schrank *(Sr. V.P. & Chief Fin. Officer)*
Roger J. James *(Sr. V.P.-Opers.)*
R. James Alexy *(Sr. V.P.-Mktg./Sls.)*
William J. McDade *(V.P.-Human Resources)*

Sealy Mattress Company of Illinois **(2)**
1030 Fabyan Pkwy.
Batavia, IL 60510
Tel.: 708-879-8011
Fax: 708-879-9105
Mfr. of Mattresses & Box Springs
S.I.C.: 2515
Malcolm Candlish *(Chm. Bd., Pres. & Chief Exec. Officer)*
Douglas R. Schrank *(Sr. V.P. & Chief Fin. Officer)*
Roger J. James *(Sr. V.P.-Opers.)*
R. James Alexy *(Sr. V.P.-Mktg./Sls.)*
William J. McDade *(V.P.-Human Resources)*

Sealy Mattress Company of Kansas City, Inc. **(2)**
3100 Fairfax Traffic Way
Kansas City, KS 66115
Tel.: 913-321-3677 (100%)
Fax: 913-371-7620
Mfr. of Mattresses & Box Springs
S.I.C.: 2515
Malcolm Candlish *(Chm. Bd., Pres. & Chief Exec. Officer)*
Douglas R. Schrank *(Sr. V.P. & Chief Fin. Officer)*
Roger J. James *(Sr. V.P.-Opers.)*
R. James Alexy *(Sr. V.P.-Mktg./Sls.)*
William J. McDade *(V.P.-Human Resources)*

Sealy Mattress Company of Memphis **(2)**
P.O. Box 181112, 4120 Air Trans Rd.
Memphis, TN 38118
Tel.: 901-795-6460 (100%)
Fax: 901-794-9174
Mfr. of Mattresses & Box Springs
S.I.C.: 2515
Malcolm Candlish *(Chm. Bd., Pres. & Chief Exec. Officer)*
Douglas R. Schrank *(Sr. V.P. & Chief Fin. Officer)*
Roger J. James *(Sr. V.P.-Opers.)*
R. James Alexy *(Sr. V.P.-Mktg./Sls.)*
William J. McDade *(V.P.-Human Resources)*

Sealy Mattress Company of Michigan, Inc. **(2)**
21450 Trolley Industrial Dr.
Taylor, MI 48180
Tel.: 313-292-0700 (100%)
Fax: 313-292-2610
Mfr. of Mattresses & Box Springs
S.I.C.: 2515
Malcolm Candlish *(Chm. Bd., Pres. & Chief Exec. Officer)*
Douglas R. Schrank *(Sr. V.P. & Chief Fin. Office)*
Roger J. James *(Sr. V.P.-Opers.)*
R. James Alexy *(Sr. V.P.-Mktg./Sls.)*
William J. McDade *(V.P.-Huamn Resources)*

The Stearns & Foster Bedding Company **(1)**
1228 Euclid Ave.
Cleveland, OH 44115
Tel.: 216-522-0602 (100%)
Mfr. of Mattresses & Box Springs
S.I.C.: 2515
Malcolm Candlish *(Pres.)*
Douglas R. Schrank *(Sr. V.P. & Chief Fin. Offier)*
Roger J. James *(Sr. V.P.-Opers.)*
R. James Alexy *(Sr. V.P.-Mktg./Sls.)*
William J. McDade *(V.P.-Human resources)*

Plant:

The Stearns & Foster Bedding Company **(2)**
200 East Forrer St.
Lockland, OH 45215
Tel.: 513-948-1444
Mfr. of Mattresses & Box Springs
S.I.C.: 2515
Randy Cromer *(Plant Mgr.)*

Subsidiary:

The Stearns & Foster Upholstery Furniture Company **(2)**
10th Fl., Halle Bldg., 1228 Euclid Ave.
Cleveland, OH 44115
Tel.: 216-522-1310 (100%)
Fax: 216-522-0602
Mfr. of Sleep Sofas
S.I.C.: 2515
Malcolm Candlish *(Chm. Bd. & Chief Exec. Officer)*
Douglas R. Schrank *(Sr. V.P. & Chief Fin. Officer)*
Roger J. James *(Sr. V.P.-Opers.)*
R. James Alexy *(Sr. V.P.-Mktg./Sls.)*
William J. McDade *(V.P.-Human Resources)*
Douglas R. Schrank *(Sr. V.P. & Chief Fin. Officer)*

Plants:

Stearns & Foster Upholstery Furniture Co. **(3)**
41995 W. Park Extension
Columbiana, OH 44408
Tel.: 216-482-3395
Fax: 216-482-5496
Mfr. Sofa Beds
S.I.C.: 2515
Malcolm Candlish *(Chm., Pres. & Chief Exec. Officer)*
Douglas R. Schrank *(Sr. V.P. & Chief Fin. Officer)*
Roger J. James *(Sr. V.P.-Opers.)*
R. James Alexy *(Sr. V.P.-Mktg./Sls.)*
William J. McDade *(V.P.-Human Resources)*

Stearns & Foster Upholstery Furniture Co. **(3)**
279 Pontotoc Indus. Pk.
Pontotoc, MS 38863
Tel.: 601-489-7650
Fax: 601-489-7914

Sealy Corporation—(Continued)

Mfrs. Sofa Beds
S.I.C.: 2515
Malcolm Candlish *(Chm., Pres. & Chief Exec. Officer)*
Douglas R. Schrank *(Sr. V.P. & Chief Fin. Officer)*
Roger J. James *(Sr. V.P.-Opers.)*
R. James Alexy *(Sr. V.P.-Mktg./Sls.)*
William J. McDade *(V.P.-Huaman Resources)*

Woodstuff Manufacturing, Inc. **(1)**
1635 S. 43rd Ave.
Phoenix, AZ 85005
Tel.: 602-269-5811 (100%)
Fax: 602-269-5154
Mfr. of Waterbed Furniture
S.I.C.: 2511
Malcolm Candlish *(Chm. Bd. & Chief Exec. Officer)*
Douglas R. Schrank *(Sr. V.P. & Chief Fin. Officer)*
Roger J. James *(Sr. V.P.-Opers.)*
Larry Ragland *(Pres.)*

Non-U.S. Holdings:

Internacional Monterey, S.A. **(1)**
calle Josefina M. Conteras No. 19 col.
Libertad Parte Alta, 22300,
Tijuana, BC Mexico
Tel.: 52-66-82-6661
Mfr. Water Mattresses
S.I.C.: 2515

Sealy Canada, Ltd. **(1)**
14550 112th Ave.
Edmonton, AB T5M 2V1, Canada
Tel.: 403-452-3070
Fax: 403-453-7914
Mfg. Mattresses
S.I.C.: 2515
Larry Rogers *(Pres.)*
Lyman M. Beggs *(Chief Exec. Officer)*
Douglas R. Schrank *(Chief Fin. Officer)*

SEALY MATTRESS COMPANY
(Div. of Ohio Mattress Co.)
4120 Air Trans Rd.
Memphis, TN 38118
Mailing Address:
P.O. Box 181112
Memphis, TN 38118
Tel.: 901-795-6460
Fax: 901-794-9174
Approx.Sls.: $21,000,000
Emp.: 150
Sealy Bedding, Slumber Products, Mattresses
S.I.C.: 2515
John Miller *(V.P.-Mktg.)*
Carl Ollar *(V.P.-Adv. & Mdsg.)*
Jim Morris *(Mgr.-Personnel)*
Gene Trouy *(Pur. Agent)*

SEAMAN FURNITURE CO., INC.
300 Crossways Park Dr.
Woodbury, NY 11797
Tel.: 516-496-9560
Fax: 516-222-0446
Year Founded: 1988
Approx.Sls.: $167,000,000
Emp.: 580
Retail Furniture Stores
S.I.C.: 5712
Alan Rosenberg *(Pres. & Chief Exec. Officer)*
Steven Halper *(Chief Oper. Officer)*
Peter McGeough *(Chief Fin. Officer)*

Outside Service Firm(s):

Ernst & Young*(Auditors)*
395 N. Suce Road
Melville, NY 11747

Shea & Gould*(Legal Firm)*
1251 Ave. of the Americas
New York, NY 10020
Tel.: 212-827-3000

National Westminster Bank plc*(Major Banking Relationship)*
175 Water St.
New York, NY 10038-4924
Tel.: 212-602-3364

SEAMAN-PATRICK PAPER COMPANY
2000 Howard St.
Detroit, MI 48216
Tel.: 313-496-3131
Fax: 313-965-5284
Emp.: 175
Wholesale Fine Paper
S.I.C.: 5111
John Wickett *(Pres.)*
Kim Zuccaro *(Dir.-Personnel)*

SEAMAN TIMBER COMPANY, INC.
P.O. BOx 372
Montevallo, AL 35115
Tel.: 205-665-2536
Approx.Sls.: $15,000,000
Emp.: 170
Pressure Treated Lumber, Timbers, Cross Ties, Poles, Posts, Pallets, Skids & Pallet Lumber
S.I.C.: 2491; 2439; 2448
James D. Seaman *(Pres.)*
Phillip E. Lacey *(V.P.)*
Janet W. Seaman *(Sec. & Treas.)*
Kenneth E. Dailey *(Gen. Mgr.)*

Outside Service Firm(s):

Jamison, Money, Farmer & Co.*(Auditors)*
Tuscaloosa, AL

Tanner, Guin, Ely, Lary & Nieswender, P.C.*(Legal Firm)*
Tuscaloosa, AL

Merchants & Planters Bank*(Major Banking Relationship)*
Tuscaloosa, AL

SEATTLE CITY LIGHT
(Dept. of City of Seattle)
1015 Third Ave.
Seattle, WA 98104
Tel.: 206-625-3000
Year Founded: 1902
Approx.Rev.: $300,000,000
Emp.: 1,907
Municipal Electric Utility; Conservation Loans, Grants & Services
S.I.C.: 4911
Roberta Palm Bradley *(Supt.)*
Shani Taha *(Deputy Supt.)*
John D. Saven *(Deputy Supt.)*
Reg Kaiser *(Deputy Supt.)*
D. Fred Butler *(Chief Engineer)*
Del Mercure *(Dir.-Fin.)*
Jim Fletcher *(Dir.-Oper.)*
May Gerstle *(Dir.-Community Rels.)*
Betty Blair *(Dir.-Customer Service)*
Carole Coe-Hauskins *(Dir.-Admin. Services)*
Kenneth Hunich *(Dir.-Distr.)*
Jim LaCour *(Dir.-Human Resources)*
Alan Green *(Dir.-Information Systems)*
Kirvil Skinnarland *(Dir.-Enviromental Affairs)*
Marya Castillano *(Acting Dir.-Conservation & Solar)*

SEATTLE LIGHTING FIXTURE CO.
222 Second Ave.
Seattle, WA 98104
Tel.: 206-622-1962
Sales Range: $10-19 Million
Mfr. Ceiling Fans
S.I.C.: 3634
John Wratten *(Pres. & Chief Exec. Officer)*

Subsidiary:

Homestead Products **(1)**
1220 Kona Dr.
Compton, CA 90220
Tel.: 310-638-6020
Tel.: 800-229-1326
Fax: 310-635-6545
Approx.Sls.: $14,284,825
Emp.: 50
Computer Systems/Hardware:
Apple Macintosh & Laser Writer
Manufacture Ceiling Fans
S.I.C.: 3634
John Wratten *(Pres. & Chief Exec. Officer)*

SEATTLE PACIFIC INDUSTRIES, INC.
1700 Westlake Ave. North
Seattle, WA 98109
Mailing Address:
P.O. Box 58710
Seattle, WA 98138
Tel.: 206-282-8889
Fax: 206-283-9399
Year Founded: 1981
Sales Range: $100-499 Million
Emp.: 300
Fiscal Year-end: 12/31/90
Import
Designer, Manufacturer and Wholesaler of Men's & Women's Sportswear
S.I.C.: 5136; 5137; 2331; 2339; 2325; 2321; 2329
Douglas Sellin *(Sr. V.P.-Opers. & Fin.)*
Gary Smalley *(Sr. V.P.-Sls. & Mktg.)*
Robert Cash *(V.P. & Treas.)*
Principal(s):
Tony Lau
Brian Leung
Sophia Leung

Computer Systems/Hardware:
Hewlett-Packard

Divisions:

Re-Union Division **(1)**
1700 Westlake Ave. North
Seattle, WA 98109
Tel.: 205-282-8889
Men's Sportswear

Unionbay Division **(1)**
1700 Westlake Ave. North
Seattle, WA 98109
Tel.: 205-282-8889
Young Men's & Young Contemporary Sportswear

SEATTLE PACKAGING CORPORATION
3701 S. Norfolk
Seattle, WA 98118
Tel.: 206-725-3000
Fax: 206-722-5648
Approx.Sls.: $40,000,000
Emp.: 175
Corrugated Containers; Moving & Storage Equipment & Supplies; Fabricated Plastic Forms; Wholesale Printing Papers
S.I.C.: 2653; 2441; 3089; 3412; 5111
Gordon M. Younger *(Pres.)*
Mark Held *(Gen. Mgr.)*
Gilda Jackson *(Dir.-Acctng.)*

Outside Service Firm(s):

Moss Adams*(Auditors)*
Tacoma, WA

Williams, Kastner & Gibbs*(Legal Firm)*
Seattle, WA

U.S. Bank*(Major Banking Relationship)*
Seattle, WA

SEATTLE TIMES COMPANY
1120 John St.
Seattle, WA 98109
Mailing Address:
P.O. Box 70
Seattle, WA 98111
Tel.: 206-464-2111
Fax: 206-464-2905
Year Founded: 1896
Approx.Sls.: $200,000,000
Emp.: 2,000
Newspaper Publisher
S.I.C.: 2711
Frank A. Blethen *(Chm., Chief Exec. Officer & Publr.)*
Mason Sizemore *(Pres. & Chief Oper. Officer)*
John A. Williams *(Exec. V.P.)*
John A. McCall *(V.P. & Circulation Mgr.)*
Carolyn Kelly *(V.P. & Chief Fin. Officer)*
James H. Schafer *(V.P.-Indus. Rels.)*
Marji Ruiz *(V.P.-Adv.)*
William Blethen *(Treas.)*
Frank M. Paiva *(Dir.-Opers.)*
Duane E. Johnson *(Dir.-Labor Rels.)*
Darrell Oldham *(Mgr.-Adv. & Mktg.)*
Roy Schaefer *(Mgr.-Natl. Adv.)*
Mike Lemke *(Mgr.-Classified)*
Greg Bennett *(Mgr.-Retail Majors)*

Outside Service Firm(s):

Deloitte & Touche*(Auditors)*
700 Fifth Ave., Suite 4500
Seattle, WA 98104-5044
Tel.: 206-292-1800

Davis, Wright, Tremaine*(Legal Firm)*
2200 One Union Square
Seattle, WA 98101-1688
Tel.: 206-622-3150

Subsidiary:

Walla-Walla Union Bulletin **(1)**
First & Poplar Sts.
Walla Walla, WA 99362
Tel.: 509-525-3300
Emp.: 70
Sunday & Evening Newspaper, except Saturday
S.I.C.: 2711
Charles Cochrane *(Publr.)*

SEBASTIAN & COOKE
110 Lanidex Plaza
Parsippany, NJ 07054
Tel.: 201-884-0055
Year Founded: 1972
Approx.Sls.: $20,000,000
Emp.: 25
Fiscal Year-end: 8/31/92
Import
Wholesale Appliances & Electronic Products
S.I.C.: 5064; 5065
Samuel Schwartzstein *(Chm. Bd.)*
Daniel Schwartzstein *(Pres.)*
Barbara Sykes *(Treas. & Sec.)*

Outside Service Firm(s):

Gikow, Bierman & Talesnick*(Auditors)*
Roseland, NJ

Gutkin, Miller, Shapiro & Salesner*(Legal Firm)*
Millburn, NJ

United Jersey Bank*(Major Banking Relationship)*
Newark, NJ

SEBASTIAN COTTON & GRAIN CORP.
6th & David Ramirez
Sebastian, TX 78594
Mailing Address:
P.O. Box 310
Sebastian, TX 78594
Tel.: 210-347-3581
Fax: 210-347-5070
Assets: $10,500,000
Net Worth: $10,500,000
Approx.Sls.: $19,500,000
Emp.: 100
Fiscal Year-end: 12/31/90
Agricultural Services; Cotton & Grain
S.I.C.: 5159; 5153; 0723
Tommy Funk *(Pres.)*
Bill Belschner *(V.P.)*
S. Reagan Stone *(Treas.)*

Computer Systems/Hardware:
IBM System 36

Outside Service Firm(s):

Grant Thornton*(Auditors)*
Hare, TX

Pilot Life*(Group Insurer)*
Greensboro, NC

Graham McCollough*(Legal Firm)*
Hadengen, TX

Raymondville State Bank*(Major Banking Relationship)*
Raymondville, TX

Subsidiary:

Aguilares Ranches **(1)**
1-8 Mile West
Sebastian, TX 78594
Tel.: 210-347-3581

SECHRIST INDUSTRIES, INC.
4225 E. La Palma Ave.
Anaheim, CA 92807
Tel.: 714-630-2400
Telex: 752556
Fax: 714-630-8369
Year Founded: 1971
Approx.Sls.: $15,000,000
Emp.: 95
Fiscal Year-end: 12/31/91
Export
Manufacture Medical Products & Industrial Measuring Instruments
S.I.C.: 3823; 3842
David Bush *(Pres.)*
S.J. Bryars *(V.P.-Finance)*
Edwin Winegar *(V.P.-Res. & Devel.)*

Outside Service Firm(s):

Sanwa Bank*(Major Banking Relationship)*
Anaheim, CA

SECO WARWICK CORPORATION
180 Mercer St.
Meadville, PA 16335
Tel.: 814-724-1400
Fax: 814-724-1407
Year Founded: 1984
Approx.Sls.: $25,000,000
Emp.: 200
Export
Mfr. of Industrial Heat Treating Furnaces & Systems; Melting & Holding Equipment for Non Ferrous Metals; Incinerator Systems
S.I.C.: 3567; 3443
Paul Huber *(Pres.)*
Cliff Lohr *(V.P.-Mfg.)*
J.W. Boswell *(V.P.-Sls.)*
Terry Farlik *(Sec. & Treas.)*
D.E. Snyder *(Dir.-Human Resources)*
Doug Glenn *(Mktg. Services Coord.)*

Computer Systems/Hardware:
IBM AS 400

SECURITY ALARMS & FIRE ENGINEERING INC.
4490 S.W. 64th Ave.
Davie, FL 33314
Tel.: 305-791-7233
Year Founded: 1975
Emp.: 12
Installation, Sales & Service of Alarms, Intercoms, CCTV & TV Systems
S.I.C.: 7382
Stuart Glickman *(Chm., Pres. Chief Exec. & Chief Fin. Officer)*
Coral Leonard *(Controller)*

No. of U.S. Offices: 1

Computer Systems/Hardware:
Radio Shack Model II TRS 80

Outside Service Firm(s):

Georgetown Insurance Agency*(Group Insurer)*
Hollywood, FL

Goodman, Pleeter, Webber*(Legal Firm)*
Davie, FL

Barnett Banks Trust Company, N.A.*(Major Banking Relationship)*
Davie, FL

SECURITY MUTUAL LIFE INSURANCE CO. OF NEW YORK
100 Court St.
Binghamton, NY 13901
Mailing Address:
P.O. Box 1625
Binghamton, NY 13902
Tel.: 607-723-3551
Year Founded: 1886
Approx.Sls.: $2,000,000,000
Emp.: 300
Fiscal Year-end: 12/31/90
Life & Group Insurance
S.I.C.: 6311; 6321
Robert W. Byron *(Chm. Bd.)*
Paul H. Pearson *(Pres. & Chief Exec. Officer)*
William W. Atkin *(Exec. V.P. & Chief Fin. Officer)*
Melvin B. Dunn *(Exec. V.P. & Chief Mktg. Officer)*
F. David Mistretta *(V.P., Gen. Counsel & Sec.)*
Daniel P. Foley *(Dir.-Mktg. Svcs.)*
Lauren Weaver *(Mgr.-Sls. Promo. & Pub. Rels.)*
Janet Vanek *(Mgr.-Human Resources)*
John Gal *(Mgr.-Graphics)*

Subsidiary:

Security Equity Life Insurance Co. **(1)**
100 Court St.
Binghamton, NY 13901
Tel.: 607-723-3551
S.I.C.: 6311; 6321

SECURITY PLASTICS, INC.
14427 N.W. 60th Ave.
Miami Lakes, FL 33014
Mailing Address:
P.O. Box 4723,
Miami Lakes, FL 33014
Tel.: 305-823-5440 **FL**
Fax: 305-557-1431
Year Founded: 1955
Approx.Sls.: $40,000,000
Emp.: 400
Fiscal Year-end: 3/31/92
Export
Custom Injection Molder of Engineered, Thermoplastic Components Supplied to the E/E, Automotive, Appliance and Hardware Markets
S.I.C.: 3089
Norman H. Cohan *(Pres. & Chief Exec. Officer)*
Lambert Jacobs *(Exec. V.P.)*
Enidio Gomez *(V.P.-Mfg.)*
Nelson Rodriguez *(V.P.-Sls.)*
Wayne Bower *(Pur. Dir.)*
Nidiam Conesa *(Personnel Supvr.)*
Principal(s):
Norman H. Cohan

No. of Mfg. Plants/Facilities: 2
No. of Foreign Offices: 1

Computer Systems/Hardware:
IBM System AS 400

Outside Service Firm(s):

Arthur Andersen & Co.*(Auditors)*
2100 One Biscayne Tower
Miami, FL 33131
Tel.: 305-374-3700

Greenberg, Traurig, Hoffman, Lipoff, Rosen & Quentel, P.A.*(Legal Firm)*
1221 Brickell Ave.
Miami, FL 33131
Tel.: 305-579-0500

SECURITY VAN LINES, INC.
100 W. Airline Hwy.
Kenner, LA 70062
Mailing Address:
P.O. Box 830,
Kenner, LA 70063
Tel.: 504-468-7711
Fax: 504-464-1818
Year Founded: 1935
Approx.Sls.: $12,000,000
Emp.: 110
Fiscal Year-end: 12/31/90
Moving & Storage of Household Goods; Local Drayage; Convention & Trade Show Drayage; Freight Forwarding
S.I.C.: 4212; 4226; 4731
Donald L. Goldwasser *(Chm. Bd.)*
Charles L. Wolchansky *(Pres.)*
Louise G. Wolchansky *(Sec.)*
Paul McCord, Sr. *(Sls. Mgr.)*

SEESSEL HOLDINGS, INC.
1745 Union
Memphis, TN 38104
Tel.: 901-272-8600 **TN**
Fax: 901-272-8616
Year Founded: 1988
Approx.Sls.: $90,000,000
Emp.: 1,000
Seessel's Supermarket Chain, Delicatessens, Meat Markets Including Freezer Provisioners
S.I.C.: 5411; 5421
Arthur N. Seessel, III *(Pres.)*
Fred Bowman *(V.P. & Chief Fin. Officer)*
Melville J. Seessel *(V.P.)*

Outside Service Firm(s):

First Tennessee Bank, N.A.*(Major Banking Relationship)*
P.O. Box 84
Memphis, TN 38101-0034
Tel.: 901-523-4541

Sefton

SEFTON ASSOCIATES INC.
3351 Claystone, S.E.
Grand Rapids, MI 49546
Tel.: 616-957-0600
Fax: 616-957-2515
Year Founded: 1954
Approx.Billings: $24,000,000
Emp.: 50
David Teater *(Chm. & Chief Exec. Officer)*
Gary Petertyl *(Pres. & Creative Dir.)*
Kenneth Merz *(Exec. V.P. & New Business Contact)*
Linda Water *(V.P. & Sr. Pub. Rels. Consultant)*
Carol Meehan *(Dir., Human Resources)*
Lisa LaCross *(Corp. Sec.)*

THE SEGERDAHL CORP.
1351 S. Wheeling Rd.
Wheeling, IL 60090
Tel.: 708-541-1080
Fax: 708-541-5237
Approx.Sls.: $30,000,000
Emp.: 125
Offset Printing & Binding Text Books, Catalogs, Direct Mail Stuffers
S.I.C.: 2752; 2732; 2759; 2754; 2789; 7331
Earl E. Segerdahl *(Chm. Bd. & Pres.)*
Larry Reimers *(Exec. V.P.)*
John Annel *(V.P.-Sls.)*
Lou Dattomo *(V.P.-Mfg.)*
Gary Kasufkin *(V.P.-Fin.)*
Principal(s):
Earl E. Segerdahl

Computer Systems/Hardware:
Data General

Outside Service Firm(s):

Berg Demarco Lewis & Sawatski*(Auditors)*
Northbrook, IL

American National Bank & Trust Company of Chicago*(Major Banking Relationship)*
33 N. LaSalle St.
Chicago, IL 60602
Tel.: 312-661-5000
Fax: 312-661-6417

SEIBEL & STERN CORP.
112 W. 34th St.
New York, NY 10120
Tel.: 212-563-0326
Fax: 212-564-1434
Year Founded: 1921
Approx.Sls.: $23,000,000
Emp.: 400
Fiscal Year-end: 1/31/91
Children's Dresses
S.I.C.: 5137
Morris H. Seibel *(Chm. Bd.)*
Monroe Seibel *(Pres.)*
Lawrence Davis *(Exec. V.P.)*

SEIGLE'S HOME & BUILDING CENTERS
1331 Davis Rd.
Elgin, IL 60123
Tel.: 708-742-2000
Fax: 708-697-6521
Year Founded: 1895
Approx.Sls.: $100,000,000
Emp.: 600
Retail Home & Building Stores
S.I.C.: 5211; 5251
Harry J. Seigle *(Pres.)*
Scott Hartmann *(V.P.)*
Frank Jaeschke *(V.P.)*
Mark Seigle *(V.P.-Consumer Sales)*
Dan Vahey *(Treas.)*
Rick Mogler *(Dir.-Personnel)*
Principal(s):
Harry J. Seigle

Computer Systems/Hardware:
MAI Basic 4; Data General

Outside Service Firm(s):

Deloitte & Touche*(Auditors)*
Two Prudential Plaza, 180 N. Stetson
Chicago, IL 60601
Tel.: 312-946-2039

Division:

Siegle's Home & Building Centers **(1)**
900 W. North Ave.
Chicago, IL 60622
Tel.: 312-337-6767
Lumberyard
S.I.C.: 5211

SEILER CORPORATION
153 Second Ave.
Waltham, MA 02254
Tel.: 617-890-6200
Fax: 617-890-4694
Approx.Sls.: $350,000,000
Emp.: 2,600
Fiscal Year-end: 8/31/92

Seiler Corporation—(Continued)

Manage & Oper. Food Service Programs & Other Gen. Services in Health Care, Educational. Bus. & Indus. Facilities; Mfr. Bakery Goods
S.I.C.: 8741; 5812; 5962; 2051; 2053
Patrice Douce *(Chm. Bd.)*
Michael Landel *(Pres. & Chief Exec. Officer)*
Gilles Meurice *(Chief Fin. Officer & Treas.)*
Bill Zammer *(Chief Oper Officer)*
David W. Hayes *(V.P.-Personnel & Gen. Counsel)*
Michael Shaw *(Dir.-Mngmt. Information Systems)*

Outside Service Firm(s):

BDO Seidman*(Auditors)*
Boston, MA

Wausau Insurance*(Group Insurer)*
2000 Westwood Dr.
Wausau, WI 54401-7881
Tel.: 715-842-6902
Fax: 715-847-8534

Ropes & Gray*(Legal Firm)*
One International Place
Boston, MA 02110
Tel.: 617-423-6100

State Street Bank & Trust Co.*(Major Banking Relationship)*
P.O. Box 366,
Boston, MA 02101
Tel.: 617-426-5523

Thomas P. Curran & Associates*(Pension Manager)*
Boston, MA

Metropolitan Life Insurance Co.*(Pension Manager)*
One Madison Ave.
New York, NY 10010-3690
Tel.: 215-578-9292

Subsidiary:

Service Supply Corp. **(1)**
153 Second Ave.
Waltham, MA 02254
Tel.: 617-890-6200
Joseph Marchese *(Dir.-Service Supply)*

SEKO-AIR FREIGHT
790 Busse Road
Elk Grove Village, IL 60007
Tel.: 708-806-4800 **IL**
Fax: 708-806-1034
Year Founded: 1976
Sales Range: $80-99 Million
Emp.: 70
Fiscal Year-end: 12/31/91
Air Freight Forwarder
S.I.C.: 4512; 4513
Dan Para *(Pres.)*
Peter G. Baker *(Chief Exec. Officer)*
Gerry Post *(V.P.-Opers.)*
William J. Wascher *(Chief Fin. Officer)*
Mary Sue Kozak *(Admin. Asst.)*

Computer Systems/Hardware:
Prime 9550

Outside Service Firm(s):

Lakeshore National Bank*(Major Banking Relationship)*
Chicago, IL

SELECT SIRES, INC.
11740 U.S. Rt. 42
Plain City, OH 43064
Mailing Address:
P.O. Box 143,
Plain City, OH 43064-0143
Tel.: 614-873-4683 **OH**
Fax: 614-873-5751
Approx.Sls.: $12,242,418
Emp.: 210
Fiscal Year-end: 12/31/91
Export
Livestock Artifical Insemination Services
S.I.C.: 0751
Richard H.L. Chichester *(Chief Exec. Officer & Gen. Mgr.)*
Bill Genasci *(Pres.)*
William Thompson *(V.P.-Mktg. & Devel.)*
Victor J. Williams *(Sec. & Treas.)*

Outside Service Firm(s):

KPMG Peat Marwick*(Auditors)*
Two Nationwide Plaza
Columbus, OH 43215
Tel.: 614-249-2300

The Huntington National Bank*(Major Banking Relationship)*
17 S. High St.
Columbus, OH 43215
Tel.: 614-476-8303

SELECTO-FLASH, INC.
18 Central Ave.
West Orange, NJ 07052
Tel.: 201-677-3500
Fax: 201-674-1529
Sales Range: $10-19 Million
Emp.: 83
Fiscal Year-end: 6/30/92
Graphic Systems For Transportation & Architectural Interiors, Signs & Decals
S.I.C.: 2752; 3993
James Z. Peepas *(Pres.)*
R. Plath *(V.P.-Mktg.)*
F. Russin *(Controller)*
Peter McNab *(Dir.-Admin. & Sls.)*
M. Spangle *(Plant Mgr.)*

Outside Service Firm(s):

Midlantic National Bank*(Major Banking Relationship)*
West Orange, NJ

SELECTONE CORPORATION
23278 Bernhardt St.
Hayward, CA 94545
Tel.: 510-887-1950
Tel.: 800-227-0376 **CA**
Fax: 510-887-4011
Year Founded: 1979
Assets: $900,000
Earnings: $150,000
Liabilities: $300,000
Net Worth: $600,000
Sales Range: $10-19 Million
Emp.: 30
Fiscal Year-end: 3/31/91
Import Export
Manufacture Tone Signaling Equipment for Two-Way Radio Equipment
S.I.C.: 3663
Eliot Terborgh *(Pres. & Chief Exec. Officer)*
John P. Borges *(Chief Oper. Officer)*
James F. Osborne *(Sec.)*
Patricia Hales *(Dir.-Personnel)*

No. of U.S. Offices: 1

Computer Systems/Hardware:
Durango

Outside Service Firm(s):

New York Life*(Group Insurer)*
51 Madison Ave.
New York, NY 10010
Tel.: 212-576-6367
Fax: 212-576-6630

Phoenix Mutual Life Insurance Co.*(Group Insurer)*
Hartford, CT

Wilson, Sonsini, Goodrich & Rosati*(Legal Firm)*
Two Palo Alto Square
Palo Alto, CA 94304
Tel.: 415-493-9300

Silicon Valley Bank*(Major Banking Relationship)*
San Jose, CA

SELIGMAN & ASSOCIATES, INC.
1760 S. Telegraph, Ste.100
Bloomfield Hills, MI 48302
Tel.: 313-334-7300 **DE**
Fax: 313-334-3649
Year Founded: 1954
Assets: $228,907,000
Earnings: $1,009,700
Liabilities: $217,632,700
Net Worth: $11,274,300
Approx.Rev.: $12,500,000
Emp.: 50
Fiscal Year-end: 7/31/91
Home Builders
S.I.C.: 6411; 6531; 1531
Irving R. Seligman *(Chm. Bd. & Treas.)*
Scott J. Seligman *(Pres.)*
Gary Rouse *(V.P.-Property Mngmt.)*
Sarah L. Keiser *(Controller)*
Steve Flaggman *(Gen. Counsel)*
Barbara E. Stewart *(Sec.)*
Patricia Redman *(Dir.-Information Mngmt.)*

Outside Service Firm(s):

Butzel, Keidan, Simon, Myers & Graham*(Legal Firm)*
2490 First National Bldg.
Detroit, MI 48226
Tel.: 313-961-7900

Honigman, Miller, Schwartz & Cohn*(Legal Firm)*
2290 First National Bldg.
Detroit, MI 48226
Tel.: 313-256-7800

Subsidiaries:

Mid-States Mortgage Corp. **(1)**
1760 S. Telegraph #100.
Bloomfield Hills, MI 48302
Tel.: 313-334-7300 (100%)
Mortgage Banking
S.I.C.: 6162
Scott J. Seligman *(Pres.)*

Professional Information Managment **(1)**
24901 Northwestern Hwy., Ste. 400
Southfield, MI 48034
Tel.: 313-355-2400 (100%)
Computer Software Development & Sales
S.I.C.: 7379
Pat Redman *(V.P.)*

Seligman & Assocs. of Michigan **(1)**
1760 S. Telegraph #100
Bloomfield Hills, MI 48302
Tel.: 313-334-7300 (100%)
Single Family Home Building
S.I.C.: 1531

Sterling Savings & Loan **(1)**
28400 Northwestern Hwy., #400
Southfield, MI 48034
Tel.: 313-355-2400 (98%)
Emp.: 110
Savings & Loan
S.I.C.: 6035
Scott J. Seligman *(Pres.)*
Irving R. Seligman *(Treas.)*
Rick Zamojski *(V.P.)*

SELLEN CONSTRUCTION COMPANY
228 9th Ave. N.
Seattle, WA 98109
Tel.: 206-682-7770
Fax: 206-623-5206
Year Founded: 1945
Sales Range: $100-499 Million
Emp.: 250
Fiscal Year-end: 12/31/91
Nonresidential & Industrial Building; General Contractors
S.I.C.: 1541; 1542
Richard C. Redman *(Chm. Bd., Pres. & Chief Exec. Officer)*
Robert E. Barnett *(Exec. V.P.-Opers.)*
Principal(s):
Richard C. Redman

Outside Service Firm(s):

Deloitte & Touche*(Auditors)*
700 Fifth Ave., Suite 4500
Seattle, WA 98104-5044
Tel.: 206-292-1800

Ferguson & Burdell*(Legal Firm)*
Seattle, WA

Seafirst Bank*(Major Banking Relationship)*
Columbia-SeaFirst Center, 701 5th Ave., 11th Flr.
Seattle, WA 98124
Tel.: 206-358-3039
Fax: 206-358-3113

DEAN SELLERS FORD INC.
2600 W. Maple
Troy, MI 48084
Tel.: 313-643-7500 **MI**
Fax: 313-643-7997
Approx.Sls.: $44,000,000
Emp.: 100
Automobile Dealership
S.I.C.: 5511
Thomas D. Sellers *(Pres.)*
John C. Sellers *(V.P.)*
Robert P. Sellers *(Sec. & Treas.)*
Linda Hightower *(Controller)*
Rick Sawicky *(Sls. Mgr.-New Cars)*

BOB SELLERS PONTIAC GMC TRUCK INC.
38000 Grand River
Farmington Hills, MI 48333-2070
Mailing Address:
P.O. Box 2070,
Farmington Hills, MI 48333-2070
Tel.: 313-478-8000 **MI**
Fax: 313-478-0635
Year Founded: 1977
Approx.Sls.: $50,000,000
Emp.: 100
Automobile Dealership
S.I.C.: 5511
Robert B. Sellers *(Pres.)*
Conrad Nason *(Controller)*
Bill Bertera *(Mgr.-Sls.-Pontiac)*

Outside Service Firm(s):

N.B.D. Bank, N.A.*(Major Banking Relationship)*
611 Woodward Ave.
Detroit, MI 48226
Tel.: 313-225-1122
Fax: 313-225-3420

SELLSTROM MANUFACTURING CO.
One Sellstrom Dr.
Palatine, IL 60067
Tel.: 708-358-2000
Tel.: 800-323-7402
Fax: 708-358-8564
Year Founded: 1923
Approx.Sls.: $10,000,000
Emp.: 150
Export
Mfr. of Protective Glasses, Goggles & Helmets
S.I.C.: 3851; 3842
Barbara M. Sellstrom *(Pres.)*
David Peters *(Exec. V.P.)*
James R. Franklin *(V.P.-Sls.)*
Lawrence Schmidt *(V.P. & Treas.)*
Christos Tsakiridis *(V.P.-Mfg.)*
Gerry Adams *(Dir.-Quality Control)*
Madeline Jennings *(Dir.-Mktg.& Communications)*

SELOVER BUICK, INC.
523 N. 29th St.
Billings, MT 59101
Tel.: 406-252-5101
Fax: 406-255-2368
Approx.Sls.: $22,000,000
Emp.: 70

New & Used Automobiles; Passenger Car Leasing
S.I.C.: 5511
George H. Selover *(Pres.)*
Patricia W. Selover *(Sec. & Treas.)*

Outside Service Firm(s):

Tim Janiak *(Auditors)*
Billings, MT

First Bank, N.A. *(Major Banking Relationship)*
Billings, MT

SEMAC INDUSTRIES INC.
County Rd. 407
Millersburg, OH 44654
Mailing Address:
P.O. Box 289
Millersburg, OH 44654
Tel.: 216-674-6080
Tel.: 800-257-3622 **OH**
Fax: 216-674-5629
Year Founded: 1945
Approx.Sls.: $34,000,000
Emp.: 350
Fiscal Year-end: 10/31/91
Export
Manufacture & Wholesale Hardwood Lumber & Related Products
S.I.C.: 2448; 2449; 5031
Archie H. Carpenter *(Chm. Bd.)*
George E. Carpenter *(Pres.)*
Kelly Curren *(V.P.)*

Outside Service Firm(s):

Shaw, Moore, Richardson & Bromund *(Auditors)*
Millersburg, OH

First National Bank of Ohio *(Major Banking Relationship)*
Akron, OH

Subsidiary:

Spartywood Products, Inc. **(1)**
Fairview Rd.
Spartansburg, PA 16434
Tel.: 814-654-7111
Approx.Sls.: $14,000,000
Emp.: 116
Sawmill & Pallet Shop
S.I.C.: 2421; 2448
William Reese *(Pres.)*

SEMBLEX CORPORATION
199 W. Diversey
Elmhurst, IL 60126
Tel.: 708-833-2880
Fax: 708-941-8440
Approx.Sls.: $15,000,000
Emp.: 100
Cold Headed Fasteners
S.I.C.: 3452
Daniel P. Haerther *(Chm. Bd.)*
James Wittersheim *(Pres.)*
James Taylor *(Exec. V.P.)*
Gordon McLeish *(Comptroller)*

Outside Service Firm(s):

Grant Thornton *(Auditors)*
700 One Prudential Plaza, 130 East Randolph St.
Chicago, IL 60601
Tel.: 312-856-0200
Fax: 312-565-4719

Burke, Griffin, Chomicz & Weinke, P.C. *(Legal Firm)*
Chicago, IL

Continental Bank N. A. *(Major Banking Relationship)*
231 S. LaSalle St.
Chicago, IL 60697
Tel.: 312-828-2345
Tel.: 800-426-5754
Telex: 312-828-1783

SEMCO, INC.
13813 Fm 529
Houston, TX 77041
Mailing Address:
P.O. Box 7634
Houston, TX 77270
Tel.: 713-896-1825
Fax: 713-896-1117
Year Founded: 1955
Approx.Sls.: $16,000,000
Emp.: 100
Fiscal Year-end: 3/31/91
Material Handling System
S.I.C.: 3535
Bill Stark *(Chm. Bd. & Pres.)*
Thomas Machann *(Mgr.-Pur.)*

No. of Mfg. Plants/Facilities: 2

Outside Service Firm(s):

Harper & Pearson *(Auditors)*
Houston, TX

Texas Commerce Bank *(Major Banking Relationship)*
717 Travis St.
Houston, TX 77002
Tel.: 713-236-4636
Fax: 713-236-5476

SEMCO INDUSTRIES
90 Hawes Way
Stoughton, MA 02072
Tel.: 617-828-8090
Tel.: 800-441-4500
Fax: 617-344-7936
Year Founded: 1964
Approx.Sls.: $32,000,000
Emp.: 485
Holding Company
S.I.C.: 6719; 2752
Walter F. Gilbert *(Chm. Bd., Pres., Chief Exec. Officer & Treas.)*
Raymond R. Alexander *(Sr. V.P.-Fin.)*

Outside Service Firm(s):

Parent, McLaughlin & Nagle *(Auditors)*
Boston, MA

Palmer & Dodge *(Legal Firm)*
One Beacon St.
Boston, MA 02108
Tel.: 617-573-0100

Shawmut Bank *(Major Banking Relationship)*
One Federal St.
Boston, MA 02211
Tel.: 617-292-2969
Fax: 617-292-4417

Subsidiary:

Spaulding Company, Inc. **(1)**
90 Hawes Way
Stoughton, MA 02072
Tel.: 617-961-3660
Wholesale Commercial Machine & Equipment Business Services, Commercial Printing Letterpress & Screen Blueprinting & Photocopying Service
S.I.C.: 2752
Walter Gilbert *(Chm. Bd.)*

SEMINOLE MANUFACTURING COMPANY
605 17th St. S.
Columbus, MS 39701
Tel.: 601-328-1556 **OK**
Fax: 601-328-1795
Year Founded: 1924
Sales Range: $20-39 Million
Emp.: 800
Export
Mfr. of Men's, Youths' & Boys' Dress Slacks; Men's & Boys' Tailored Dress & Sport Coats & Suits; Men's & Boys' Uniforms
S.I.C.: 2325; 2311
Max Weitzenhoffer *(Chief Exec. Officer)*
Dan W. Berry *(Pres.)*
Kenny J. Pierce *(Sr. V.P.-Mfg.)*
Richard De Sousa *(Sr. V.P.-Sls. & Mdsg.)*
Alfred J. Moeckel *(Sr. V.P.)*
John Rossi *(V.P.-Adv. & Mktg.)*
Vladimer Zea *(V.P.)*
Curtis L. Bray *(V.P.)*

Outside Service Firm(s):

Ernst & Young *(Auditors)*
Jackson, MS

National Bank of Detroit *(Major Banking Relationship)*
611 Woodward Ave.
Detroit, MI 48226

SENATOR FORD
3801 Florin Rd.
Sacramento, CA 95823
Tel.: 916-391-3000
Fax: 916-392-1648
Retail New & Used Motor Vehicles; Passenger Car Rental & Leasing
S.I.C.: 5511; 7515
Robert J. Creedon *(Pres.)*
Joy St. Claire *(Sec.)*
Joe Donaldson *(Mgr.-Business)*
Dave Hellinge *(Gen. Mgr.)*

Outside Service Firm(s):

First Interstate Bank *(Major Banking Relationship)*
Sacramento, CA

SENCORE, INC.
3200 Sencore Dr.
Sioux Falls, SD 57107
Tel.: 605-339-0100
Fax: 605-335-6379
Approx.Sls.: $19,000,000
Emp.: 325
Fiscal Year-end: 12/31/91
Manufacture Electronic Test Equipment
S.I.C.: 3661; 3663
Al Bowden *(Pres. & Chief Exec. Officer)*
Douglas Bowden *(Exec. V.P. & Sec.)*
Bruce Hasche *(Controller)*

Outside Service Firm(s):

Henry Scholten & Co. *(Auditors)*
Sioux Falls, SD

Davenport, Evans, Hurwitz & Smith *(Legal Firm)*
Sioux Falls, SD

Norwest Bank Minnesota, N.A. *(Major Banking Relationship)*
Sioux Falls, SD

SENCORP
One Riverfront Place
Newport, KY 41071
Tel.: 606-292-7000
Fax: 606-292-7047
Approx.Sls.: $180,000,000
Emp.: 2,000
Fabricated Metal Products; Machinery; Trucking & Warehousing
S.I.C.: 3569; 3496; 3315; 6159
William Tillinghast *(Chm. Bd.)*
George Juilfs *(Pres. & Chief Exec. Officer)*
C. L. Garrett *(Sr. V.P.-Fin. & Chief Fin. Officer)*
James H. Racer *(Sr. V.P.)*
Mark Bailey *(V.P. Sec & Gen Counsel)*
Donald C. Bell *(V.P. & Treas.)*
William Clay *(V.P.-Personnel)*
Marilyn Calvert *(Mgr.-Personnel)*

Outside Service Firm(s):

Grant Thornton *(Auditors)*
1600 Atrium One
Cincinnati, OH 45202
Tel.: 513-762-5000

Prudential Insurance Co. of America *(Group Insurer)*
751 Broad St.
Newark, NJ 07102-3777
Tel.: 201-802-6000

Dinsmore & Shohl *(Legal Firm)*
2100 Fountain Square Plaza
Cincinnati, OH 45202-3172
Tel.: 513-977-8200

Bank of Cincinnati *(Major Banking Relationship)*
Cincinnati, OH

The Central Trust Company, N.A. *(Major Banking Relationship)*
201 E. Fifth
Cincinnati, OH 45202
Tel.: 513-651-8255

Star Bank *(Major Banking Relationship)*
425 Walnut Street
Cincinnati, OH 45202
Tel.: 513-632-4000

Fifth Third Bank *(Pension Manager)*
Corporate Trust Services, 38 Fountain Square Plaza
Cincinnati, OH 45263

Subsidiaries:

Senco Products, Inc. **(1)**
8485 Broadwell Rd.
Cincinnati, OH 45244
Tel.: 513-388-2000

Sentron Medical, Inc. **(1)**
8485 Broadwell Rd.
Cincinnati, OH 45244
Tel.: 513-388-2000

SENECA WIRE & MANUFACTURING CO.
S. Vine St.
Fostoria, OH 44830
Mailing Address:
P.O. Box B
Fostoria, OH 44830
Tel.: 419-435-9261
Year Founded: 1905
Approx.Sls.: $60,000,000
Emp.: 500
Import Export
Mfr. of Steel Wire; Industrial & Insect Screening
S.I.C.: 3496
J. Peter McNerney *(Pres.)*
Daniel Richards *(V.P. & G.M.)*
Kevin Shoemaker *(V.P.-Fin., Sec. & Treas.)*
Doug Stearns *(Dir.-Sls. & Mktg.)*

Senn Trucking Co.
(Name Changed To Eastern Flat Bed Systems)

SENNHEISER ELECTRONIC CORP.
6 Vista Dr.
Old Lyme, CT 06371
Mailing Address:
P.O. Box 987,
Old Lyme, CT 06371
Tel.: 203-434-9190
Fax: 203-434-1759
Sales Range: $10-19 Million
Emp.: 32
Import
Distributor Professional Microphones, Headphones & Accessories
S.I.C.: 3651; 3679; 5065
Andrew Brakhan *(Pres.)*
Inge Hieret *(V.P.)*

Computer Systems/Hardware:
IBM System AS/400

Outside Service Firm(s):

Whitman & Ransom *(Legal Firm)*
200 Park Ave.
New York, NY 10166

Sennheiser Electronic Corp.—(Continued)

Tel.: 212-351-3000

Fleet Bank*(Major Banking Relationship)*
New London, CT

Division:

Nuemann (USA) **(1)**
6 Visto Dr.
Old Lyme, CT 00371
Tel.: 203-434-9190
Import
Mfg. of Professional Microphones, Headphones & Accessories
S.I.C.: 3651; 3679

SENSOR DEVELOPMENTS INC.
1050 W. Silverbell Rd.
Orion, MI 48359
Mailing Address:
P.O. Box 290
Lake Orion, MI 48361-0290
Tel.: 313-391-3000 **MI**
Fax: 313-391-0107
Year Founded: 1976
Assets: $1,000,000
Liabilities: $250,000
Net Worth: $750,000
Sales Range: $10-19 Million
Emp.: 70
Fiscal Year-end: 11/30/91
Import Export
Custom Design Strain Gaged Based Sensors To Measure Force or Torque; Service & Repair; Consulting Custom Gaging Services
S.I.C.: 3825
Albert Brendel *(Pres.)*
Carson Boyd *(Mgr.-Opers.)*
James Babiarz *(Mgr.-Sls.)*
Bill Wood *(Mgr.-Mktg.)*
Debbie Bunker *(Buyer)*

Principal(s):
Albert Brendel

No. of Mfg. Plants/Facilities: 1

Computer Systems/Hardware:
PC Network

Outside Service Firm(s):

Roger Duval, P.C.*(Auditors)*
Lathrop Village, MI

Oxford Bank*(Major Banking Relationship)*
Oxford, MI

SENTINEL COMPUTER SERVICES INC.
1010 Jorie Blvd., Ste. 150
Oak Brook, IL 60521
Tel.: 708-990-8060 **IL**
Fax: 708-990-8067
Year Founded: 1982
Approx.Sls.: $22,500,000
Emp.: 280
Fiscal Year-end: 12/31/91
Computer Hardware Maintenance
S.I.C.: 7378
Dennis Hoelzer *(Chm. Bd., Pres. & Chief Exec. Officer)*
James Emmel *(Chief Oper. Officer)*
Timothy Hill *(V.P.-Fin.)*
Brian Osborne *(V.P.-Mktg.)*
Chris Bohne *(Dir.-Personnel)*
Robert Lenartowitz *(Dir.-Data Processing)*
James Scurto *(Dir.-Pur.)*

Computer Systems/Hardware:
IBM/RT

Outside Service Firm(s):

Deloitte & Touche*(Auditors)*
Oak Brook, IL

Blue Cross & Blue Shield of Illinois*(Group Insurer)*
100 Tower Drive
Burr Ridge, IL 60521
Tel.: 708-323-3666

Mesirow Capital*(Investment Banker)*
Chicago, IL

Winston & Strawn*(Legal Firm)*
35 West Wacker, Suite 4700
Chicago, IL 60601
Tel.: 312-558-5600

Harris Trust & Savings Bank*(Major Banking Relationship)*
111 W. Monroe St.
Chicago, IL 60690
Tel.: 312-461-2265
Tel.: 800-858-0840

SENTINEL CONSUMER PRODUCTS, INC.
7750 Tyler Blvd.
Mentor, OH 44060
Tel.: 216-974-8144
Telex: ITT 4332155
Fax: 216-974-0249
Year Founded: 1905
Approx.Sls.: $21,000,000
Emp.: 350
Fiscal Year-end: 6/30/92
Import Export
Health & Beauty Aids; Sentinel First Aids
S.I.C.: 2834; 2844
Michael S. Klein *(Pres.)*
Bert Kovarik *(V.P.-Admin.)*
Harvey Mitchell *(V.P.-Sls.)*
Bob Beebe *(V.P.-Sls.)*
Lanning Bingham *(V.P.-Mfg.)*
Richard Allen *(Asst. V.P./Sr. Controller)*
Donald George *(Dir.-Pur.)*
Diane Ford *(Dir.-Adv.)*
Patrick Ruggles *(V.P.-Mktg.)*
Nick Tozzi *(Mgr.-Quality Assurance)*
Cindy Chadd *(Admin. Asst.)*

Divisions:

Sentinel Consumer Products, Inc. **(1)**
P. O. Box 1417, Freeport Ctr.
Clearfield, UT 84016
Tel.: 801-825-5671
Fax: 801-776-2347
Mfr. of Health & Beauty Aids
S.I.C.: 2834; 2844
Scott Call *(Plant Mgr.)*

Sentinel Consumer Products, Inc. **(1)**
Greenbriar Ind. Park, 100 Sentinel Dr.
Anniston, AL 36201
Tel.: 205-831-8377
Fax: 205-835-2216
Mfr. of Health & Beauty Aids
S.I.C.: 2834; 2844
Lanning Bingham *(Plant Mgr.)*

SENTRY GROUP
900 Linden Ave.
Rochester, NY 14625
Tel.: 716-381-4900
Tel.: 800-828-1438
Fax: 716-381-8559
Year Founded: 1930
Approx.Sls.: $50,000,000
Emp.: 600
Fiscal Year-end: 12/31/91
Export
Manufactures Fire & Theft Resistive Safes, Chests & Files
S.I.C.: 3499
Richard F. Brush *(Chm. Bd.)*
Douglas Brush *(Pres.)*
James Brush *(Exec. V.P.-Sls. & Mktg.)*
Norm Booth *(V.P.-Fin.)*
Virginia Brandreth Canaley *(Mgr.-Mktg. Communications & Dir.-Coop Adv.)*
Bill Gefteas *(Mgr.-Reg. Mkts.)*
Wayne Kokinda *(Mgr.-Materials)*
Debra Maroney *(Mktg. Matls. Mgr.)*
Peter Serron *(Hospitality Sls. Mgr.)*
Bob Urrutia *(Mgr.-Export Sls.)*
Doug Wolk *(Mgr.-Natl. Sls.)*
Terry Marlowe *(Sr. Pur. Agent)*

Outside Service Firm(s):

Coopers & Lybrand*(Auditors)*
2 State St.
Rochester, NY 14614
Tel.: 716-546-5295

Chase Lincoln First Bank, N.A.*(Major Banking Relationship)*
P.O. Box 1250,
Rochester, NY 14603
Tel.: 716-232-5000

Key Bank*(Major Banking Relationship)*
Rochester, NY

SENTRY INSURANCE, A MUTUAL COMPANY
1800 N. Point Dr.
Stevens Point, WI 54481
Tel.: 715-346-6000
Fax: 715-346-7516
Year Founded: 1904
Assets: $3,992,312,000
Earnings: $63,461,000
Liabilities: $3,232,014,000
Net Worth: $760,298,000
Approx.Rev.: $1,530,651,000
Emp.: 4,550
Fiscal Year-end: 12/31/91
Insurance Holding Company
S.I.C.: 6311; 6321; 6331
Larry C. Ballard *(Chm. Bd., Pres. & Chief Exec. Officer)*
John Elsey *(Sr. V.P.-Mktg.)*
Bernard Hlavac *(V.P. & Treas.)*
James Clawson *(V.P.-Legal)*
Caroline E. Fribance *(V.P.-Corp. Services)*
Mario Crocetti *(V.P.-Information Systems)*
Paul A. Verhage *(Chief Fin. Officer)*
Mary Weller *(Dir.-Adv.)*
Dan McGinnity *(Mgr.-Corp. Communications)*
Lil Hanson *(Corp. Conference Mgr.)*

Computer Systems/Hardware:
IBM System 38

Outside Service Firm(s):

KPMG Peat Marwick*(Auditors)*
Peat Marwick Plaza, 303 E. Wacker Dr.
Chicago, IL 60601
Tel.: 312-938-1000

M & I Marshall & Ilsley Bank*(Major Banking Relationship)*
Chicago, IL

Subsidiaries:

Sentry Life Insurance Co. **(1)**
1800 No. Point Dr.
Stevens Point, WI 54481
Tel.: 715-346-6000 (100%)
Life Insurance
S.I.C.: 6311
Peter P. Trapp *(Pres.)*

Sentry Insurance, A Mutual Company **(1)**
1800 No. Point Dr.
Stevens Point, WI 54481
Tel.: 715-346-6000 (100%)
Property, Casualty Insurance Co.
S.I.C.: 6331

Subsidiaries:

Dairyland Insurance Co. **(2)**
9501 E. Shea Blvd.
Scottsdale, AZ 85260
Tel.: 602-860-7800 (100%)
Automobile & Motorcyle Insurance
S.I.C.: 6331
John Elsey *(Pres.)*

Middlesex Insurance Co. **(2)**
34 Monument Sq.
Concord, MA 01742
Tel.: 508-369-8600 (100%)
Fire, Home, Multiple Peril, Auto Insurance
S.I.C.: 6331
Dennis Schwab *(Pres.)*

SEPPALA & AHO CONSTRUCTION COMPANY
Peterboro Road
New Ipswich, NH 03071
Tel.: 603-899-3011
Fax: 603-878-2818
Year Founded: 1952
Approx.Sls.: $100,000,000
Emp.: 400
General Contractor, Commercial & Industrial Buildings, Warehouses, Office & Nonresidential Buildings
S.I.C.: 1541; 1542
Martin Seppala *(Chm. Bd.)*
Samuel R. Seppala *(Pres. & Chief Exec. Officer)*
Thomas M. Luebberman *(V.P. & Treas.)*
Gerald Prunier *(Sec.)*

Outside Service Firm(s):

Arthur Andersen & Co.*(Auditors)*
One Intl. Place, 100 Oliver St.
Boston, MA 02110
Tel.: 617-330-4000
Fax: 617-439-9731

Prunier, Leonard & Bolton*(Legal Firm)*
Nashua, NH

Nashua Trust Company*(Major Banking Relationship)*
Nashua, NH

SEQUENTIA INC.
21819 Royalton Rd.
Strongsville, OH 44136
Mailing Address:
P.O. Box 360530
Strongsville, OH 44136
Tel.: 216-238-2400
Fax: 216-238-0820
Approx.Sls.: $60,000,000
Emp.: 300
Mfr. Fiberglass Reinforced Plastic Panels
S.I.C.: 3089
John F. Doherty *(Pres. & Chief Exec. Officer)*
Don Clark *(Pres.-Division)*
E.C. Billings *(Chief Fin. Officer)*
Joseph E. Kutina *(V.P.-Opers.)*
Cliff J. Peart *(V.P.-Sls.)*

Outside Service Firm(s):

Gomersall & Chester*(Auditors)*
Westlake, OH

Massachusetts Mutual Life Insurance Co.*(Group Insurer)*
1295 State St.
Springfield, MA 01111
Tel.: 413-788-8411
Fax: 413-730-6144

Nicola, Gudbranson & Cooper*(Legal Firm)*
Cleveland, OH

National City Bank*(Major Banking Relationship)*
P.O. Box 92301, Corp. Trust Dept.
Cleveland, OH 44101
Tel.: 216-575-2000

Division:

Sequentia Inc. Reinforced Plastics Div. **(1)**
21819 Royalton Rd.
Strongsville, OH 44136
Tel.: 216-238-2400
Fax: 216-238-0820
Approx.Sls.: $60,000,000
Emp.: 300
Fiscal Year-end: 12/31/90
Alsynite/Structoglas Translucent Glass Fiber Panels
S.I.C.: 3089
John F. Doherty *(Pres. & Chief Exec. Officer)*
D.B. Clark *(Pres.)*
Edwin Billings *(Sec. & Treas.)*

SERFILCO, LTD.
(d/b/a Service Filtration Corp.)
1777 Shermer Rd.
Northbrook, IL 60062
Tel.: 708-559-1777
Tel.: 800-323-5431 **IL**
Telex: 289557 SERFC UR
Fax: 708-559-1995
Year Founded: 1961
Approx.Sls.: $15,000,000
Emp.: 200
Import Export
Mfr. Pumps & Filters, Steam Cleaning Equip. & Hot Pressure Washers
S.I.C.: 3559; 3561; 3569
Jack H. Berg *(Pres. & Chief Exec. Officer)*
Carole L. Berg *(V.P. & Sec.)*
Richard F. Podolski *(V.P.-Sls. & Mktg.)*
James Ringel *(Controller)*
Jerold Swoboda *(Dir.-Data Processing)*
Arthur C. Carlson *(Reg. Mgr.-Sls.)*
Charles Remied *(Reg. Mgr.-Sls.)*
Richard J. Stastny *(Reg. Mgr.-Sls.)*
Clem Traut *(Reg. Mgr.-Sls.)*
Frank Ferraro *(Gen. Mgr.-Opers.)*
James D. Brame *(Mgr.-Adv.)*
James Kempinsky *(Mgr.-Pur.)*

Principal(s):
Jack H. Berg

Outside Service Firm(s):

Ralph Bell*(Auditors)*
Northbrook, IL

Kenneth Swartz*(Legal Firm)*
Morton Grove, IL

Lake Shore National Bank*(Major Banking Relationship)*
605 N. Michigan Ave.
Chicago, IL 60611
Tel.: 312-787-1900

Subsidiary:

A.S.M. Industries **(1)**
1 Lark Ave.
Leola, PA 17540
Tel.: 717-656-2161
Tel.: 800-233-3861
Fax: 717-656-0477
Emp.: 90
Export
Mfr. Pumps, Fittings, Injection Molding, Steam Cleaning Equip.
S.I.C.: 3559; 3561
Jack H. Berg *(Pres.)*

SERIGRAPH, INC.
760 Indiana Ave.
West Bend, WI 53095
Mailing Address:
P.O. Box 438
West Bend, WI 53095
Tel.: 414-335-7200 **DE**
Fax: 414-334-1909
Year Founded: 1949
Approx.Sls.: $64,000,000
Emp.: 800
Fiscal Year-end: 6/30/91
Export
Specialty Offset & Screen Printing: Decals, Decorative Trim
S.I.C.: 2759; 2752
John B. Torinus, Jr. *(Chm. Bd. & Chief Exec. Officer)*
W.R. Grall *(Exec. V.P.)*
R.J. Reis *(Exec. V.P.)*
Richard Erdmann *(Sr. V.P.-Human Resources)*
John Grasse *(Sr. V.P.-Pur. & Quality Control)*
J.H. Hutchison *(Sr. V.P.)*
Alvin L. Curtis *(V.P.-Mktg.)*

Principal(s):
John B. Torinus, Jr.

No. of Mfg. Plants/Facilities: 3

Outside Service Firm(s):

Arthur Andersen & Co.*(Auditors)*
777 E. Wisconsin Ave., P.O. Box 1215
Milwaukee, WI 53202
Tel.: 414-271-5100
Fax: 414-283-3200

serino coyne inc.

SERINO COYNE INC.
1515 Broadway, 36th Fl.
New York, NY 10036
Tel.: 212-626-2700 **NY**
Fax: 212-626-2799
Year Founded: 1977
Assets: $5,518,803
Liabilities: $5,000,412
Net Worth: $518,391
Approx.Billings: $48,560,000
Emp.: 65
Fiscal Year-end: 10/31/91
Advertising Agency
S.I.C.: 7311
Nancy Coyne *(Chm. Bd., Chief Exec. Officer & Dir.-Creative Services)*
Matthew Serino *(Pres.)*
William J. Livolsi, Jr. *(V.P.-Fin.)*
Beth Schefflan *(Office Mgr.)*

Outside Service Firm(s):

Robert A. Goodman & Co.*(Auditors)*
230 Park Ave.
New York, NY 10169

Davis & Gilbert*(Legal Firm)*
850 Third Ave.
New York, NY 10022
Tel.: 212-326-1300

Marine Midland Bank*(Major Banking Relationship)*
250 Park Ave.
New York, NY 10177
Tel.: 212-949-6527

SERONO BAKER DIAGNOSTICS
100 Cascade Dr.
Allentown, PA 18103
Tel.: 215-264-2800
Tel.: 800-345-3127
Telex: 62834124
Fax: 215-266-0184
Year Founded: 1977
Approx.Sls.: $35,000,000
Emp.: 320
Fiscal Year-end: 12/31/90
Import Export
Manufacturer of Medical Instrumentation Systems: Hemotology, Chemistry, Immunology Reagents, Controls, Chemistry & Immunology
S.I.C.: 2835
Jean-Pierre Verhassel *(Pres.)*
Arthur W. Dusseault *(V.P.-Fin.)*
Robert B. Anacone *(V.P.-Mktg. & Sls.)*
David B. Thomas *(V.P.-Quality, Regulatory & Engrng.)*
John Hawkins *(Dir.-Opers.)*
Charles Preston *(Dir.-Tech. Engrng.)*
Donald Wood *(Dir.-Pur.)*
Debby R. Dean *(Dir.-Human Resources)*
Tedd Mishkin *(Dir.-Intl. Support)*
Russel Hock *(Mgr.-Quality Control)*
Carl Isaacs *(Mgr.-Fin. & Leasing)*
Stephanie Warminsky *(Mgr.-Information Systems)*
Ingrid Ulshafer *(Mkt. Services Coord.)*

Computer Systems/Hardware:
IBM AS/400

SERTA, INC.
2800 River Rd.
Des Plaines, IL 60018
Tel.: 708-699-9300 **DE**
Fax: 708-827-0794
Year Founded: 1931
Approx.Sls.: $250,000,000
Emp.: 1,600
Export
Manufacturer Mattresses
S.I.C.: 2515
Ed Lilly *(Pres. & Chief Exec. Officer)*
Edward Scott *(V.P.-Sls. & Mktg.)*
Steve Tipton *(V.P.-Adv.)*

No. of Mfg. Plants/Facilities: 34

Computer Systems/Hardware:
McDonald Douglas 6425

Outside Service Firm(s):

Arthur Andersen & Co.*(Auditors)*
33 W. Monroe St.
Chicago, IL 60603-4067
Tel.: 312-580-0033
Fax: 312-507-6748

Altheimer & Gray*(Legal Firm)*
10 S. Wacker Dr.
Chicago, IL 60606
Tel.: 312-715-4000

American National Bank & Trust Company of Chicago*(Major Banking Relationship)*
33 N. LaSalle St.
Chicago, IL 60602
Tel.: 312-661-5000
Fax: 312-661-6417

SERTA MATTRESS COMPANY
3777 Vaca Valley Pkwy.
Vacaville, CA 95688
Tel.: 707-446-7999 **CA**
Fax: 707-446-8227
Year Founded: 1906
Approx.Sls.: $27,000,000
Emp.: 130
Fiscal Year-end: 12/31/91
Export
Manufacture Mattresses & Box Springs
S.I.C.: 2515
Donald Simon, Sr. *(Chm. Bd.)*
Donald S. Simon, Jr. *(Pres.)*
Steve Alloway *(V.P.-Fin.)*
Dave Puterbaugh *(V.P. & Gen. Mgr.-Serta, Northwest)*
Principal(s):
Donald Simon, Sr.
Donald S. Simon, Jr.

No. of Mfg. Plants/Facilities: 2
No. of U.S. Offices: 2

Computer Systems/Hardware:
IBM

Outside Service Firm(s):

David Kuhner & Co.*(Auditors)*
Orinda, CA

Bank of America NT&SA*(Major Banking Relationship)*
555 California St.
San Francisco, CA 94105
Tel.: 415-622-5120
Fax: 415-622-4585

SERVAAS, INC.
1000 Waterway Blvd.
Indianapolis, IN 46202
Tel.: 317-633-2040
Fax: 317-634-1791
Approx.Sls.: $200,000,000
Emp.: 50
Export
Brass & Bronze Die-Castings, Copper & Copper Alloy Die-Casting; Copper Rolling & Drawing; Cleaning Or Polishing Preparations
S.I.C.: 3364; 3351; 2842
Beurt R. Servaas *(Chm. Bd. & Pres.)*
Gerard W. Golden *(V.P.)*
Clarence Ormsby *(V.P., Sec. & Treas.)*
Cory J. Servaas *(V.P.)*

Outside Service Firm(s):

Klineman, Rose, Wolf & Wallack*(Legal Firm)*
Bethesda, MD

Bank One, Indianapolis, N.A.*(Major Banking Relationship)*
111 Monument Circle, Ste. 1611
Indianapolis, IN 46204-1611
Tel.: 317-321-8110

Subsidiaries:

Carpenter Manufacturing, Inc. **(1)**
1500 W. Main St.
Mitchell, IN 47446
Tel.: 812-849-3131
Fax: 812-849-5727
Approx.Sls.: $45,000,000
Emp.: 400
Fiscal Year-end: 12/31/90
School & Adult Passenger Coaches
S.I.C.: 4151
Timothy S. Durham *(Pres. & Chief Exec. Officer)*
Mike Jones *(V.P.-Fin.)*
D. Pearcy *(V.P.-Sls. & Mktg.)*
Steve Slagel *(V.P.-Engrng.)*
Terry Whitesell *(V.P.-Mktg. & Corp. Devel.)*

Servaas Investments, Inc. **(1)**
1000 Waterway Blvd.
Indianapolis, IN 46202
Tel.: 317-636-1000
Approx.Sls.: $150,000,000
Emp.: 1,000
Brass & Bronze Die-Castings; Copper Rolling Drawing
S.I.C.: 3364
Beurt R. Servaas *(Chm. Bd.)*
Clarence Ormsby *(Sec. & Treas.)*

Servaas Laboratories Inc. **(1)**
1200 Waterway Blvd.
Indianapolis, IN 46202
Tel.: 317-636-7760
Tel.: 800-433-5818
Fax: 317-264-2192
Emp.: 25
Fiscal Year-end: 7/30/91
Mfg. Chemicals; Bar Keepers Friend Cleanser & Polish, Shiny Sinks Plus, Cleanser, Copper Glo & Liquid Copper Glo Cleaners, Just N' Time Spot Remover, Power House Lime Remover & Private Label Cleansers & Lime Removers
S.I.C.: 2842
Gerard W. Golden *(Pres.)*
Tony Patterson *(V.P.-Sls.)*
Lenore E. Terek *(Mgr.-Mktg. Svcs.)*
Donald E. Miller *(Upadvertising/Promo.)*

SERVCO PACIFIC INC.
900 Fort St. Mall Suite 500
Honolulu, HI 96813
Tel.: 808-521-6511
Fax: 808-523-3937
Approx.Sls.: $204,700,000
Emp.: 1,200
Wholesale & Retail Cars & Trucks, Home Appliances, Home Electronics, Laundry Products, Water Heaters, Furniture, Pianos & Organs, Household & Garden Hardware, Clothing; Real Estate; Insurance; Leasing; Advertising; Securities Services
S.I.C.: 5411; 5311; 5012; 5021; 5064; 5099; 5511; 5712; 5731; 5735
George J. Fukunaga *(Chm. Bd. & Chief Exec. Officer)*
Thomas I. Fukunaga *(Pres. & Chief Oper. Officer)*
Gerald K. Harbottle *(Exec. V.P.-Corp. Admin. Opers.)*
Moses Kealoha *(Exec. V.P.-Auto. Retail Sector/Windward Auto Grp.)*
Thomas H. Hatanaka *(Sr. V.P.-Fin. Services Opers.)*
Wallace S. Higashi *(Sr. V.P.-Staff Mngmt.)*
Isaac S. Kinoshita *(Sr. V.P.-Opers. Mgr.)*
Matt N. Masuoka *(Sr. V.P.-Intl. Opers.)*
Jean H. Nakagawa *(Sr. V.P.)*

Servco Pacific Inc.—(Continued)

George S. Sakurai *(Sr. V.P.-Gen. Auto. Opers.)*
Steven S. Hirano *(Grp. V.P.-Hawaiin Adv. & Pub. Rels.)*
Ted A. Kubota *(Grp. V.P.-Sanyo Appliance & Electronic)*
Stanley T. Maebori *(Grp. V.P.)*
Gertrude M. Mori *(Grp. V.P.)*
Charles D. Rivers *(Grp. V.P.-Windward Grp.)*
John Ross *(Grp. V.P.-Wahiawa Grp.)*
Warren Sato *(Grp. V.P.-Marine)*
Roy T. Tokuhisa *(Grp. V.P.-W/S Allied Sls.)*
Patrick D. Ching *(Treas.)*
Edith M. Endo *(Sec.)*

Outside Service Firm(s):

Deloitte & Touche*(Auditors)*
Honolulu, HI

Torkildson, Katz, Jossem, Fonseca & Moore*(Legal Firm)*
Honolulu, HI

Central Pacific Bank*(Major Banking Relationship)*
220 S. King St.
Honolulu, HI 96813
Tel.: 808-544-0500

SERVICE AMERICA CORPORATION
88 Gate House Rd.
Stamford, CT 06904
Mailing Address:
P.O. Box 10203,
Stamford, CT 06904
Tel.: 203-964-5000
Tel.: 800-SAC-NUM1
Fax: 203-964-5018
Year Founded: 1960
Assets: $347,000,000
Liabilities: $542,000,000
Net Worth: $195,000,000
Approx.Sls.: $1,000,000,000
Emp.: 21,000
Fiscal Year-end: 3/31/91
Food & Refreshment Services, Vending Machine Operations, Industrial & Institutional Food Service Concessions
S.I.C.: 5812; 5962
Gary Horvath *(Sr. V.P.-Recreation)*
Tighe Merkert *(Sr. V.P.)*
Peter Petrosian *(Sr. V.P.)*
Jeffrey Alperin *(V.P.-Mngmt. Information Systems)*
Bruce Burnham *(V.P.-Procurement)*
Jeff Flynn *(V.P.-Human Resources)*
Norman Holmes *(V.P.-Sls.)*
Dominic Sartori *(V.P., Controller & Sec.)*
Irene Syrnyk *(V.P. & Counsel)*
Joseph Capute *(Chief Fin. Officer)*
Holly A. Hemphill *(Dir.-Mktg.)*
Jules Mason *(Mgr.-Cash Mngmt.)*

Computer Systems/Hardware:
IBM PC Network

Outside Service Firm(s):

KPMG Peat Marwick*(Auditors)*
345 Park Ave.
New York, NY 10154
Tel.: 212-758-9700
Fax: 212-872-3308

Chemical Bank*(Major Banking Relationship)*
450 West 33rd St.
New York, NY 10001
Tel.: 212-613-7197
Fax: 212-947-7628

Whitman & Ransom*(Legal Firm)*
200 Park Ave.
New York, NY 10166
Tel.: 212-351-3000

Service Control Corp.
(See Service America Corporation)

Service Filtration Corp.
(See Serfilco, Ltd. Listing)

SERVICE MOTOR COMPANY
W. 9614 Hwy. 10
Dale, WI 54931
Mailing Address:
P.O. Box 170
Dale, WI 54931
Tel.: 414-779-4311 **WI**
Fax: 414-667-5330
Year Founded: 1920
Assets: $13,955,117
Earnings: $247,000
Liabilities: $12,684,550
Net Worth: $1,270,567
Approx.Sls.: $20,586,000
Emp.: 70
Fiscal Year-end: 12/31/91
Wholesale Distribution of Farm, Garden, Industrial Machinery & Equipment; Operation of 3 Retail Automotive & Home Supplies Stores
S.I.C.: 3523; 5084; 7359
James Sommer *(Pres., Chief Oper. & Fin. Officer & Treas.)*
Adrian Sommer *(V.P.)*
Nila Sommer *(Sec.)*

No. of Mfg. Plants/Facilities: 4

Computer Systems/Hardware:
IBM System 36

Outside Service Firm(s):

Schumacher & Roman*(Auditors)*
Dale, WI

American Hardware Mutual*(Commercial Insurance Carrier)*
Dale, WI

Travelers Insurance Co.*(Group Insurer)*
Milwaukee, WI

Herling Clark*(Legal Firm)*
Appleton, WI

First State Bank of New London*(Major Banking Relationship)*
New London, WI

Bank One*(Pension Manager)*
111 E. Wisconsin
Neenah, WI 54956

Division:

A & N Leasing **(1)**
Box 132
Dale, WI 54931
Tel.: 414-667-4202
Approx.Sls.: $150,000
Emp.: 1
Leasing
S.I.C.: 7359
Adrian Sommer *(Partner)*
James Sommer *(Partner)*
Nila Sommer *(Partner)*

Branches:

Service Motor Co. **(1)**
N 5560, Hwy. 151
Fond du Lac, WI 54937
Tel.: 414-923-1768
Approx.Sls.: $4,700,000
Emp.: 16
Sls. & Service of Farm & Garden Equipment
S.I.C.: 5083
Clayton Thornber *(Gen. Mgr.)*

Service Motor Co. **(1)**
Hwy. 54 & 57
New Franken, WI 54229
Tel.: 414-468-7700
Approx.Sls.: $2,300,000
Emp.: 11
Retail Sales of Automotive & Home Supplies
S.I.C.: 3523; 5531; 7359
Clair Sommer *(Gen. Mgr.)*

SERVICE PACKING COMPANY
3425 E. Vernon Ave.
Los Angeles, CA 90058
Tel.: 213-588-5286 **CA**
Fax: 213-588-9284
Year Founded: 1957
Approx.Sls.: $210,000,000
Emp.: 350
Fiscal Year-end: 12/31/91
Wholesale Distribution of Meats & Meat Products
S.I.C.: 5147
Sam Cohen *(Pres.)*
Larry Cohen *(Treas.)*
Gary Waldman *(Sec.)*

Outside Service Firm(s):

Sanwa Bank*(Major Banking Relationship)*
Pasadena, CA

SERVICE SUPPLY CO. INC. OF INDIANA
603 E. Washington St.
Indianapolis, IN 46204
Mailing Address:
P.O. Box 732,
Indianapolis, IN 46206
Tel.: 317-638-2424 **IN**
Year Founded: 1948
Assets: $33,000,000
Liabilities: $20,500,000
Net Worth: $12,500,000
Approx.Sls.: $75,000,000
Emp.: 540
Fiscal Year-end: 12/31/90
Distributor Of Fasteners, Nuts, Bolts, Screws
S.I.C.: 5072; 5085; 3452; 3429
Edgar C. Seitz, Jr. *(Chm. Bd. & Exec. V.P.-Pur.)*
Melvin C. Seitz, Jr. *(Pres., Chief Exec. Officer, Chief Oper. Officer & Controller)*
Frank Owings, Jr. *(Exec. V.P., Mng. Dir., Sec. & Treas.)*
Edgar C. Seitz, III *(Exec. V.P.-Pur., Import & Export)*
Charles A. DeLora *(Sr. V.P.-Sls., Mktg., Adv. & Pub. Rels.)*
Jim Weir *(V.P.-Sr. Admin.)*
Frank Owings, Sr. *(V.P.-Special Projects)*
Larry Seitz *(V.P.-Warehousing)*
Harvey Helgason *(V.P.-Sls.)*
Jim Bethel *(Asst. V.P.-Mngmt. Information Services)*
Harry Clore *(Dir.-Data Processing)*
Robert DeLora *(Dir.-Leasing & Real Estate)*
Lee Snider *(Mgr.-Indus.)*
John Causey *(Mgr.-Credit Dept.)*
Blair Prigg *(Mgr.-Acctg.)*
Greg Shaver *(Mgr.-Personnel)*
Paul Modlin *(Mgr.-S/C Devel.)*
Hentry Wheatley *(Mgr.-Quality Control)*

Principal(s):
Edgar C. Seitz, Jr.
Melvin C. Seitz, Jr.
Frank Owings, Jr.
Edgar C. Seitz, III

No. of Mfg. Plants/Facilities: 38
No. of U.S. Offices: 43

Computer Systems/Hardware:
Unisys 1173

Outside Service Firm(s):

Dunbar, Cook Shepard*(Auditors)*
Indianapolis, IN

Prudential Insurance Co. of America*(Group Insurer)*
751 Broad St.
Newark, NJ 07102-3777
Tel.: 201-802-6000

Ice, Miller, Donadio & Ryan*(Legal Firm)*
Indianapolis, IN

INB National Bank*(Major Banking Relationship)*
One Indiana Sq.
Indianapolis, IN 46266
Tel.: 317-266-6000

Merchants National Bank & Trust Company of Indianapolis*(Pension Manager)*
One Merchants Plaza, Ste. 901E
Indianapolis, IN 46255
Tel.: 317-267-7109

SERVICE WEB OFFSET CORPORATION
2500 S. Dearborn St.
Chicago, IL 60616
Tel.: 312-567-7000
Approx.Sls.: $22,000,000
Emp.: 135
Commercial Web Offset Color Printing
S.I.C.: 2759
Joan Vanderbeck *(Pres.)*
Donald Borzak *(V.P.)*
Alan Mitchell *(Sec. & Treas.)*
Seymour Lempert *(Comptroller)*

Outside Service Firm(s):

Altschuler, Melvoin & Glasser*(Auditors)*
30 S. Wecker Dr.
Chicago, IL 60606
Tel.: 312-207-2800

LaSalle National Bank*(Major Banking Relationship)*
120 S. LaSalle St.
Chicago, IL 60603
Tel.: 312-781-8000

SERVISTAR CORPORATION
Servistar Way
East Butler, PA 16029
Mailing Address:
P.O. Box 1510,
Butler, PA 16003-1510
Tel.: 412-283-4567 **PA**
Telex: 5101011585
Fax: 412-284-6320
Year Founded: 1916
Assets: $415,945,000
Earnings: $26,211,000
Liabilities: $320,606,000
Net Worth: $95,339,000
Approx.Sls.: $1,296,033,000
Emp.: 1,270
Fiscal Year-end: 6/30/91
Import Export
Dealer Owned Wholesale Hardware & Lumber
S.I.C.: 5072; 5031; 5198
Peter G. Kelly *(Chm. Bd.)*
Donald Smyth *(Vice Chm.)*
Paul Pentz *(Pres. & Chief Exec. Officer)*
Albert J. Mielcuszny *(Chief Fin. Officer & Sr. V.P.)*
Don Belt *(Sr. V.P.-Mktg.)*
Al Jeveret *(Sr. V.P.-Subsidiaries & New Ventures)*
Jene O'Donnell *(Sr. V.P.-Adv. & Mdsg.)*
Russell Thomas *(Sr. V.P.-Human Resources)*
Donald J. Hoye *(V.P.-Opers.)*
Gary Sease *(V.P.-Data Processing & Inventory Control)*
Carol McCarthy *(Sec.)*
Susanne Quattro *(Controller)*
Jack Villari *(Mgr.-Intl. Accounts)*

No. of Mfg. Plants/Facilities: 6

Computer Systems/Hardware:
IBM 4381 Model 3

Outside Service Firm(s):

Coopers & Lybrand*(Auditors)*
600 Grant St., 35th Fl.
Pittsburgh, PA 15219
Tel.: 412-355-8000
Fax: 412-355-8089

Pittsburgh National Bank*(Investment Banker)*
960 Fort Duquesne Blvd.
Pittsburgh, PA 15265

Springer, Bush & Perry*(Legal Firm)*
Pittsburgh, PA

Pittsburgh National Bank*(Major Banking Relationship)*
Stock Transfer Dept., Fifth & Wood Streets
Pittsburgh, PA 15265

CIGNA*(Pension Manager)*
Los Angeles, CA

Subsidiaries:

Advocate Services, Inc. **(1)**
P.O. Box 1021
Butler, PA 16001
Tel.: 412-283-4567
Emp.: 72
Common Carrier Trucking
S.I.C.: 4213
Mike Postiglione *(Gen. Mgr.)*

Coast to Coast **(1)**
501 S. Cherry St.
Denver, CO 80222
Tel.: 303-377-8400
Wholesale Hardware
S.I.C.: 5072
Ken Hoffman *(Pres. & Chief Exec. Officer)*

Speer Hardware **(1)**
5400 N. 6th St.
Fort Smith, AR 72904
Tel.: 501-782-4901
Emp.: 42
Hardware Distributor
S.I.C.: 5251
Joe Wittenberg *(Gen. Mgr.)*

Total Exposition Concepts **(1)**
P.O. Box 4175
Harrisburg, PA 17111
Tel.: 717-566-9501
Emp.: 18
Trade Show Exhibitor
S.I.C.: 7999
Jan Schofield *(Gen. Mgr.)*

SERVO CORPORATION OF AMERICA
111 New South Road
Hicksville, NY 11801-5259
Mailing Address:
P.O. Box 1490,
Hicksville, NY 11802-1490
Tel.: 516-938-9700 **DE**
Telex: 053-3314
Twx: 510-221-1872
Fax: 516-938-9644
Year Founded: 1946
Approx.Sls.: $20,500,000
Emp.: 150
Fiscal Year-end: 10/31/91
Export
High Technology Manufacturing in Domestic & International Electronics Markets, Computerized Train Inspection Centers for Railroads, Radio Navigation Systems for Airports, Infrared Electro-Optical Devices for Space Satellites, & Meteorological Systems for Military & Commercial Applications & Radio Frequency Receivers & Transmitters
S.I.C.: 3827; 3825; 3669
Stephen A. Barre *(Chm. Bd., Pres., Chief Exec. Officer & Sec.)*
Walter W. Weeden, Jr. *(Sr. V.P.-Transportation Prods. & Gen. Mgr.)*
Robert J. Stalzer *(Sr. V.P. Admin., Fin., Treas. & Asst. Sec.)*
G.F. Tubley *(Dir.-Mktg. Opers. & Programs)*
William H. Krikalo *(Dir.-Data Processing)*

Outside Service Firm(s):

Arthur Andersen & Co.*(Auditors)*
200 Broadhollow Road
Melville, NY 11747

Cullen & Dykman*(Legal Firm)*
177 Montague St.
Brooklyn, NY 11201
Tel.: 718-855-9000

Subsidiary:

Servo International, Inc. **(1)**
69A Kronsprindsens Gade, 3rd Fl.
Saint Thomas, VI 00803 (100%)
Foreign Sales Corp.
S.I.C.: 5065
Robert J. Stalzer *(Pres.)*

Non-U.S. Holding:

Servo Corporation of America **(1)**
3, Chemin du Cap 1006
Lausanne, Switzerland
Tel.: 021/29-98-73
Emp.: 2
Electronic Systems for Airports and Railroad Equip.; Sls. Europe, Middle East and Africa, European Headquarters
S.I.C.: 5065
Vincent Liardet *(Dir.)*

SERVUS FOOTWEAR COMPANY
1136 Second
Rock Island, IL 61201
Mailing Address:
P.O. Box 3610
Rock Island, IL 61204-3610
Tel.: 309-786-7741
Tel.: 800-451-1806
Fax: 309-786-9808
Approx.Sls.: $20,000,000
Emp.: 446
Import Export
Northerner Insulated & Non Insulated Rubber Footwear; Job Designed Indus. & Safety Rubber Footwear; Servus Waterproof Rubber Footwear
S.I.C.: 3021
Mike Cappy *(Chm. Bd.)*
Frank Figge *(Pres.)*
Mary Sculati *(V.P.-Mfg.)*
Bill Lowry *(V.P.-Fin.)*
Arlen Stensrud *(V.P.-Mktg.)*
Bill Moore *(V.P.-Sls.)*
Leon Goold *(Dir.-Pur.)*
Linda Witte *(Mgr.-Human Resources)*
Julie Doltor *(Mgr.-Customer Service)*
Kim Gibson *(Exec. Sec.)*
Julie K. Bollmann *(Mktg. Services Coord.)*
Ron Stone *(Data Processing)*

Computer Systems/Hardware:
IBM

SETCO SALES COMPANY
5880 Hillside Ave.
Cincinnati, OH 45233
Tel.: 513-941-5110
Fax: 513-941-5110
Year Founded: 1912
Approx.Sls.: $12,000,000
Emp.: 140
Fiscal Year-end: 11/30/91
Export
Machine Tool Components; Precision Spindles, Slides & Feeds
S.I.C.: 3545; 3541
H.J. Wagner *(Chm. & Chief Exec. Officer)*
W.A. Ferguson III *(Pres.)*
R.A. Ferguson *(Exec. V.P.)*
M.G. Ferguson *(V.P.-Opers.)*

SETON COMPANY
2500 Monroe Blvd.
Norristown, PA 19403-2325
Tel.: 215-666-9600 **NJ**
Fax: 215-666-1088
Approx.Sls.: $200,000,000
Emp.: 1,050
Fiscal Year-end: 12/31/90
Import Export
Tanning & Finishing of Cattle Hide Leathers; Manufacture & Distribute Chemicals & Coated Fabrics & Health Care Products
S.I.C.: 2295; 3111; 2833; 2834; 2844; 5199; 6512; 5122; 5100
Philip D. Kaltenbacher *(Chm. Bd. & Chief Exec. Officer)*
Paul A. Fertell *(Pres., Chief Oper. & Chief Fin. Officer)*
Robert K. Rothman *(V.P.)*
Robert De Majistre *(V.P. & Sec.)*
Mark Boersma *(Controller)*
Bruce Doherty *(Dir.-Human Resources & Employee Benefits)*
Nick Showich *(Dir.-Mktg.)*
Perry Trechak *(Dir.-Fin.)*
Carl Zipfel *(Dir.-Environmental & Natural Resources)*
Augustus Zangrelli *(Mgr.-Data Processing)*

Outside Service Firm(s):

Crummy, Del Deo, Dolan, Griffinger & Vecchione*(Legal Firm)*
One Riverfront Plaza
Newark, NJ 07102
Tel.: 201-596-4500

Fidelcor*(Major Banking Relationship)*
Mt. Laurel, NJ

Division:

Seton Co. **(1)**
349 Oraton St.
Newark, NJ 07104
Tel.: 201-485-4000
Tanning & Finishing of Cattlehide Leathers
S.I.C.: 3111
Paul A. Fertell *(Chief Oper. Officer)*

Subsidiaries:

A. Mindel & Son, Inc. **(1)**
4200 Creekside Ave.
Toledo, OH 43612
Tel.: 419-476-3535
Hide Wholesalers
S.I.C.: 5199
Bill Davis *(V.P. & Gen. Mgr.)*

Norwood Industries, Inc. **(1)**
57 Morehall Rd.
Frazer, PA 19355
Tel.: 215-647-3500 (100%)
Mfr. of Industrial Tapes, Foams, Films & Laminates; Health Care Products
S.I.C.: 2295

Selco Trucking Co. **(1)**
601 Fifth St. SE
Canton, OH 44702
Tel.: 216-456-3468
Trucking Service
S.I.C.: 4213
William Davis *(V.P.)*

Semex, Inc. **(1)**
57 Morehall Rd.
Malvern, PA 19355
Tel.: 215-647-3500
Mfr., Research, Development & Sales of Health Care Products
S.I.C.: 2834; 5122; 8731; 5100
Paul A. Fertell *(Chief Oper. Officer)*

SETZER FOREST PRODUCTS
2555 Third St.
Sacramento, CA 95818
Tel.: 916-442-2555
Fax: 716-442-4239
Year Founded: 1927
Approx.Sls.: $20,000,000
Emp.: 250
Millwork, Mouldings, Prestologs
S.I.C.: 2431
H.C. Setzer *(Partner)*
G.C. Setzer *(Partner)*
Ron Kangas *(Chief Fin. Officer)*
Mark Kable *(Gen. Mgr.)*
John Campbell *(Sls. Dir.)*
David Stevens *(Prod. Mgr.)*
Scott Setzer *(Personnel Mgr.)*

Outside Service Firm(s):

Deloitte & Touche*(Auditors)*
Sacramento, CA

Downey, Brand, Seymour & Rohwer*(Legal Firm)*
Sacramento, CA

Wells Fargo Bank*(Major Banking Relationship)*
420 Montgomery St.
San Francisco, CA 94104

Plant:

Setzer Forest Products-Oroville Plant **(1)**
1980 Kusel Rd.
Oroville, CA 95966
Tel.: 916-534-8100
Mfg. Millwork
S.I.C.: 2431
Dale Kilpatrick *(Plant Mgr.)*

SEWARD LUGGAGE COMPANY
434 High St.
Petersburg, VA 23803
Tel.: 804-733-5111
Fax: 804-733-8612
Approx.Sls.: $14,000,000
Emp.: 185
Mfr. Luggage, Attaches, Brief Cases, Trunks, Lockers, Bowling Bags
S.I.C.: 3161
Herb Epstein *(Pres.)*
Jim Weir *(V.P.-Opers.)*
Bill Barga *(V.P.-Fin. & Admin.)*

SEWELL VILLAGE CADILLAC CO.
7310 Lemmon Ave.
Dallas, TX 75209
Tel.: 214-350-2000 **TX**
Fax: 214-956-2261
Year Founded: 1957
Approx.Sls.: $96,000,000
Emp.: 295
Retail Sales Of New & Used Automobiles
S.I.C.: 5511
John Griffin *(Pres.)*
J. Carl Sewell, Jr. *(Chief Exec. Officer)*
Richard Clonts *(Chief Fin. Officer, V.P.-Fin. & Sec.)*

Outside Service Firm(s):

Union National Bank*(Major Banking Relationship)*
Dallas, TX

SEXTON CAN CO., INC.
125 Cambridge Park Dr.
Cambridge, MA 02140
Tel.: 617-876-9100 **MA**
Fax: 617-876-1826
Year Founded: 1923
Approx.Sls.: $20,000,000
Emp.: 200
Export
Mfr. of Drawn Metal Containers
S.I.C.: 3411
Edward W. Sexton, Jr. *(Pres. & Chief Exec. Officer)*
Paul A. Goguen *(Exec. V.P., Sec. & Treas.)*
Daniel Casey *(Gen. Mgr.)*
K. Steele *(Mgr.-Sls.)*
J. Barber *(Mgr.-Sls.)*
Wayne Potts *(Pur. Agent)*
Jane Jamet *(Mgr.-Mngmt. Information Systems)*

No. of Mfg. Plants/Facilities: 2
No. of U.S. Offices: 3

Outside Service Firm(s):

Gerald T. Reilly & Co.*(Auditors)*
Milton, MA

Hutchins & Wheeler*(Legal Firm)*
101 Federal St.
Boston, MA 02110
Tel.: 617-725-1500

Sexton Can Co., Inc.—(Continued)

Bay Bank*(Major Banking Relationship)*
Burlington, MA

SEYMOUR MANUFACTURING COMPANY
5th & Broadway
Seymour, IN 47274
Tel.: 812-522-2900 **IN**
Fax: 812-522-6109
Year Founded: 1872
Approx.Sls.: $10,000,000
Emp.: 125
Mfr. of Agricultural Hand Tools, Posthole Diggers, Augers, Weed Cutters, Fireplace Sets, Grass Hooks, Corn Knives, Mason Tools
S.I.C.: 3429; 3496; 3523; 5083; 5191
Clifford A. Birge *(Chm. Bd.)*
Berl Grant *(Pres. & Chief Exec. Officer)*
Roger D. Hackman *(V.P.-Mktg. & Sls.)*
Steven L. Fletcher *(V.P.-Opers.)*
Richard Redmond *(V.P.-Fin.)*

Outside Service Firm(s):

Blue & Co.*(Auditors)*
Seymour, IN

Seymour National Bank*(Major Banking Relationship)*
Seymour, IN

Beck & Harrison, P.C.*(Legal Firm)*
Seymour, IN

SEYMOUR OF SYCAMORE, INC.
917 Crosby Ave.
Sycamore, IL 60178
Tel.: 815-895-9101
Tel.: 800-435-4482
Fax: 815-895-8475
Fax: 800-343-4258
Year Founded: 1949
Approx.Sls.: $28,000,000
Emp.: 115
Fiscal Year-end: 12/31/91
Export
Aerosol Coatings & Chemicals
S.I.C.: 2851
Nancy Seymour Heatley *(Chm. Bd.)*
Sidney Heatley *(Pres.)*
Gus Leep *(V.P.-Res. & Devel.)*
Jack Jachera *(V.P.-Training)*
William Freeman *(V.P.-Treas.)*
John Wilson *(Sls. Mgr.-Indus. Div.)*
Jeanette Hoffman *(Office Mgr.)*
Jerry O'Connell *(Pur. Agent)*
Nancy Ruback *(Mktg. & Sls. Coord.)*

SHADE COMPUTER FORMS CO.
333 Main St.
Green Bay, WI 54301
Mailing Address:
P.O. Box 19730,
Green Bay, WI 54307-9730
Tel.: 414-432-6700 **WI**
Fax: 414-436-2357
Year Founded: 1964
Approx.Sls.: $89,000,000
Emp.: 250
Fiscal Year-end: 3/31/91
Import
Dry Offset Printing: Business Forms
S.I.C.: 2761
James L. Kemerling *(Pres. & Chief Exec. Officer)*
James A. Haggerty *(V.P.-Mfg.)*
Robert E. Krueger *(V.P.-Fin. & Admin.)*
Glen S. Yurjevich *(V.P.-Sls. & Mktg.)*
Robert Rupp *(Dir.-Mktg.)*
Karen Gregg *(Mgr.-Sls. & Mktg. Services)*
Rellen Hayes *(Mgr.-Sls. & Opers.)*
Principal(s):
James L. Kemerling

No. of Mfg. Plants/Facilities: 2
No. of U.S. Offices: 18

Computer Systems/Hardware:
Hewlett Packard

Outside Service Firm(s):

Arthur Andersen & Co.*(Auditors)*
777 E. Wisconsin Ave., P.O. Box 1215
Milwaukee, WI 53202
Tel.: 414-271-5100
Fax: 414-283-3200

Marshall & Ilsley Trust Company*(Major Banking Relationship)*
770 N. Water St.
Milwaukee, WI

Ruder, Ware & Michler, S.C.*(Legal Firm)*
First American Center, 500 3rd St.
Wausau, WI 54402-8050
Tel.: 715-845-4336
Fax: 715-845-2718

SHAFER COMMERCIAL SEATING INC.
4101 E. 48th Ave.
Denver, CO 80216-3298
Tel.: 303-322-7792 **CO**
Fax: 303-393-1836
Year Founded: 1938
Assets: $4,489,774
Liabilities: $1,531,848
Net Worth: $2,957,926
Sales Range: $10-19 Million
Emp.: 139
Import Export
Manufacturer of Commercial Seating; Chairs, Bar Stools, Booths Table Tops & Bases
S.I.C.: 2599
Byron A. Shafer *(Pres. & Chief Exec. Officer)*
Randall J. Shafer *(V.P.-Import & Export)*
Evelyn Shafer *(Sec. & Treas.)*
Jerry Eads *(Controller)*
Richard M. Howard *(Dir.-Mktg.)*
JoAnn Tapia *(Dir.-Human Resources)*
Irwin Suson *(Plant Mgr.)*
Judy Wood *(Office Mgr.)*

No. of Mfg. Plants/Facilities: 4

Outside Service Firm(s):

Smith, Brook, Bolshoun & Company*(Auditors)*
Denver, CO

Alexander & Alexander*(Group Insurance Broker/Consult)*
Denver, CO

Kemper Financial Services*(Investment Banker)*
Denver, CO

Hall & Evans*(Legal Firm)*
717 17th St.
Denver, CO 80202

Colorado National Bank*(Major Banking Relationship)*
17th & Champa
Denver, CO 80217

Berger & Associates*(Pension Manager)*
Denver, CO

SHAKER ADVERTISING AGENCY
The Shaker Bldg., 1100 Lake St.
Oak Park, IL 60301
Tel.: 708-383-5320
Year Founded: 1951
Approx.Billings: $40,000,000
Emp.: 110
Recruitment Adv.
Joseph R. Shaker *(Chm. Bd.)*
Joseph G. Shaker *(Pres.)*
Anthony Shaker *(V.P., Fin.)*
Morris Skall *(V.P., Reg.)*
Catherine Breit *(V.P., Sls.)*
Helen Shaker *(Sec.)*
Jerry DiGani *(Mktg. Res. Dir.)*
Carol Smith *(Librarian)*

SHAKEY'S INCORPORATED
651 Gateway Blvd., Ste. 1200
South San Francisco, CA 94080-7015
Tel.: 415-873-0640
Tel.: 800-444-9268
Fax: 415-737-2191
Year Founded: 1954
Approx.Sls.: $120,000,000
Emp.: 294
Fiscal Year-end: 12/31/91
Franchised Restaurant Chain; Shakey's Pizza/Buffet Restaurants
S.I.C.: 5812
Kay Yew Koh *(Acting Pres. & Chief Fin. Officer)*
James D. Fisher *(V.P.-Mktg.)*

Division:

Monarch Foods, Inc. **(1)**
1024 Andover Park E.
Tukwila, WA 98188
Tel.: 206-575-3716
Franchised Restaurant Chain; Shakey's Pizza/Buffet Restaurants
S.I.C.: 5812
Kay Yew Koh *(Acting Pres. & Chief Fin. Officer)*
Jim Fisher *(V.P.-Mktg.)*

MARK SHALE
500 Joliet Road
Willowbrook, IL 60521
Mailing Address:
P.O. Box 9014,
Willowbrook, IL 60521
Tel.: 708-789-0130
Fax: 708-789-0350
Approx.Sls.: $75,000,000
Emp.: 1,100
Retail Men's & Women's Upscale Traditional Clothing
S.I.C.: 5611; 5621
Shale Baskin *(Chm. Bd.)*
Scott Baskin *(Pres.)*
Rick Anglin *(Chief Fin. Officer)*
Principal(s):
Shale Baskin
Scott Baskin
Brad Baskin
Michael Baskin
Steve Baskin

Computer Systems/Hardware:
IBM

Outside Service Firm(s):

Kupferberg, Goldberg & Neimark*(Auditors)*
Chicago, IL

Sidley & Austin*(Legal Firm)*
One First National Plaza, 42nd Fl.
Chicago, IL 60603
Tel.: 312-853-7000
Fax: 312-853-7036

LaSalle National Bank*(Major Banking Relationship)*
120 S. LaSalle St.
Chicago, IL 60603
Tel.: 312-781-8000

Shamrock Distributing Co.
(See K-J Distributors, Inc. Listing)

SHAMROCK FOODS CO.
2228 N. Black Canyon Hwy.
Phoenix, AZ 85009
Tel.: 602-272-6721
Fax: 602-272-6721
Year Founded: 1924
Approx.Sls.: $253,000,000
Emp.: 948
Fiscal Year-end: 9/30/88
Dairy Products Processing & Food Service Distributor
S.I.C.: 2026; 2024; 2021; 5142; 5149; 5147
Norman P. McClelland *(Chief Exec. Officer)*
Kent McClelland *(Pres.)*
Derrell Fairfield *(Sr. V.P.)*
David B. Hall *(Sr. V.P.)*
Charles Roberts *(V.P.-Human Resources)*
Frances H. McClelland *(Treas., Sec. & Chief Fin. Officer)*
John Hernandez *(Dir.-Data Processing)*
O.C. Stallings *(Chm.-Pens. Comm.)*

Computer Systems/Hardware:
IBM

Outside Service Firm(s):

Anderson & Company*(Auditors)*
Phoenix, AZ

Jennings, Strouss & Salmon*(Legal Firm)*
2 N. Central, Ste. 1600
Phoenix, AZ 85004
Tel.: 602-942-8659

Citibank N.A.*(Major Banking Relationship)*
Phoenix, AZ

Security Pacific Bank Arizona*(Major Banking Relationship)*
Phoenix, AZ

United Bank of Denver*(Major Banking Relationship)*
Denver, CO

Bernstein-Macaulay, Inc.*(Pension Manager)*
New York, NY

Subsidiary:

United Foods Service, Inc. **(1)**
5199 Ivy St.
Commerce City, CO 80022
Tel.: 303-289-4127

SHAMROCK HOLDINGS, INC.
Shamrock Center, 4444 Lakeside Dr.
Burbank, CA 91505
Mailing Address:
P.O. Box 7774
Burbank, CA 91510
Tel.: 818-845-4444
Telex: 5106013464
Fax: 818-842-3142
Holding Company
S.I.C.: 6719
Stanley P. Gold *(Pres.)*
Rudy Reinfrank *(Exec. V.P., Capital Resources Group)*
Mark S. Siegel *(Exec. V.P., Communications & Media Grp.)*
Robert Moskowitz *(Sr. V.P. & Gen. Counsel)*
Bob Avery *(V.P.)*

Outside Service Firm(s):

Price Waterhouse*(Auditors)*
400 S. Hope St.
Los Angeles, CA 90071-2889
Tel.: 213-236-3000

Gang, Tyre, Ramer & Brown*(Legal Firm)*
Burbank, CA

Wells Fargo Bank*(Major Banking Relationship)*
Burbank, CA

Subsidiaries:

Shamrock Broadcasting, Inc. **(1)**
Shamrock Center, 4444 Lakeside Dr.
Burbank, CA 91505
Tel.: 818-845-4444
Telex: 5106013464
Telecopier: 818-845-9718

Radio & Television Broadcasting
S.I.C.: 4832; 4833
William Clark *(Pres.)*
James R. Nixon *(Exec. V.P. & Chief Oper. Officer)*
James R. Fingel *(V.P. & Controller)*
Karen K. Merrell *(V.P.-Admin.)*

Sound Warehouse, Inc. **(1)**
10911 Petal St.
Dallas, TX 75238
Tel.: 214-343-4700
Warehouse & Distribution Record Company
S.I.C.: 7389
Terry Warrell *(Pres.)*

THE SHANE GROUP INC.
250 Industrial Dr.
Hillsdale, MI 49242
Mailing Address:
P.O. Box 765
Hillsdale, MI 49242
Tel.: 517-439-4316 **MI**
Fax: 517-439-1194
Year Founded: 1975
Approx.Sls.: $43,000,000
Emp.: 250
Fiscal Year-end: 12/31/91
Holding Company; Manufacture Playground & Fitness Equipment, Industrial Truck Parts, Screw Machine Products, Athletic Field Lighting, Plumbing Supplies
S.I.C.: 6719; 3949; 3714; 3451; 3648; 3494; 3432
Dwight C. Shaneour, Jr. *(Chm. Bd., Pres. & Chief Exec. Officer)*
Robin Hammel *(V.P. & Asst. Sec.)*
Richard R. Current *(Chief Fin. Officer)*
Alan Dimmers *(Sec.)*
Susan Caulkins *(Controller)*

No. of Mfg. Plants/Facilities: 10

Outside Service Firm(s):

Ernst & Young*(Auditors)*
One Michigan Ave. Bldg., One Michigan Ave.
Lansing, MI 48933
Tel.: 517-487-5000

Alan Dimmers*(Legal Firm)*
Hillsdale, MI

National Bank of Detroit*(Major Banking Relationship)*
611 Woodward Ave.
Detroit, MI 48226

SHANNON & WILSON, INC.
400 N. 34th St., Ste. 100
Seattle, WA 98103-9703
Mailing Address:
P.O. Box 300303
Seattle, WA 98103-9703
Tel.: 206-632-8020 **WA**
Fax: 206-633-6777
Year Founded: 1954
Sales Range: $10-19 Million
Emp.: 175
Geotechnical Consultants, Engineering & Applied Geosciences
S.I.C.: 8711
Earl A. Sibley *(Chm. Bd. & Pres.)*
Rohn D. Abbott *(Sr. V.P.)*
Atef A. Azzam *(Sr. V.P.)*
Raymond P. Miller *(Sr. V.P.)*
J. Ronald Salley *(Sr. V.P.)*

No. of U.S. Offices: 6

Outside Service Firm(s):

Voldal-Wartelle, P.S.*(Auditors)*
Seattle, WA

Tewell & Findlay, Inc.*(Legal Firm)*
Seattle, WA

Seafirst Bank*(Major Banking Relationship)*
Seattle, WA

Security Pacific Bank Washington N.A.*(Major Banking Relationship)*
P.O. Box 3966,
Seattle, WA 98124

Subsidiary:

Arctic Alaska Testing Laboratories **(1)**
2055 Hill Rd., P.O. Box 70843
Fairbanks, AK 99707
Tel.: 907-452-6181
S.I.C.: 8734

SHAPCO, INC.
16340 Roscoe Blvd., Ste. 220
Van Nuys, CA 91406
Tel.: 818-894-5811 **CA**
Fax: 818-894-4642
Year Founded: 1984
Approx.Sls.: $80,000,000
Emp.: 300
Mfr. of Steel Pipe & Tubing; Real Estate
S.I.C.: 3317; 6552
Bernard J. Shapiro *(Chm. Bd.)*
Leonard Shapiro *(Pres.)*
Leonard Gross *(V.P. & Treas.)*
David Shapiro *(V.P.)*
Steven Teller *(V.P.)*

Outside Service Firm(s):

Harris Trust Company of California*(Major Banking Relationship)*
Los Angeles, CA

Division:

Kelly Pipe Div. **(1)**
16340 Roscoe Blvd., Ste. 220
Van Nuys, CA 91406
Tel.: 818-894-5811
Mfr. of Steel Pipe & Tubing
S.I.C.: 3317
Leonard Shapiro *(Pres.)*

SHAPE INC.
Biddeford Industrial Park
Biddeford, ME 04005
Mailing Address:
P.O. Box 366
Biddeford, ME 04005
Tel.: 207-282-6155
Tel.: 800-462-4165 **DE**
Fax: 207-283-9130
Year Founded: 1973
Sales Range: $100-499 Million
Emp.: 1,200
Fiscal Year-end: 4/30/91
Export
Mfr. Audio & Video Cassettes, Compact Disc Packaging & Data Storage Products, Computer Printer Cartridges, RDAT Cassesstes
S.I.C.: 3652
Michael Thomas *(V.P. & Chief Oper. Officer)*
Robert Jensen *(V.P.-Human Resources & Pur.)*
Lindsay Gable *(V.P.-Video Sls.)*
Lloyd Pomber *(V.P.-Audio Sls.)*
Edwin Bisson *(Chief Fin. Officer)*
Kathryn Lunney *(Gen. Counsel)*
Jerry Blayne *(Dir.-Data Processing)*
Robert Payne *(Mgr.-Corp. Acctg.)*
Craig Lovecky *(Mgr.-Research & Devel.)*
Tracy L. Hartman *(Coord.-Mktg. & Adv.)*

No. of Mfg. Plants/Facilities: 6
No. of U.S. Offices: 6

Computer Systems/Hardware:
Hewlett-Packard 3000 Series 7

Subsidiary:

Shape South, Inc. **(1)**
100 Rice Ave., P.O. Box 186
Dadeville, AL 36853
Tel.: 205-825-9298
Fax: 205-825-9298
Emp.: 248
Designs & Mfrs. Precision Prods. for the Computer, Video & Other Magnetic Media Industries
S.I.C.: 3652; 3823
William Stevens *(Gen. Mgr.)*
Betsy Gibson *(Sls. Mgr.)*

SHAPELL INDUSTRIES, INC.
8383 Wilshire Blvd., Ste. 700
Beverly Hills, CA 90211
Tel.: 213-655-7330 **DE**
Fax: 213-651-4349
Year Founded: 1955
Assets: $424,124,000
Net Worth: $424,124,000
Approx.Sls.: $500,000,000
Emp.: 450
Real Estate Developer & Builder
S.I.C.: 6552; 6162; 6512; 1522; 1531; 5712; 6531
Nathan Shapell *(Chm. Bd., Pres. & Chief Exec. Officer)*
David Shapell *(Exec. V.P.)*
Mark Bader *(Sr. V.P.)*
Max Webb *(Sr. V.P.)*
Thomas Zeiger *(Sr. V.P.)*
W. Douglass Harris *(V.P. & Controller)*
Margaret Leong *(V.P.-Fin. Services)*
E. Gerald Sellers *(V.P.-Mktg.)*
Rick Mahan *(Mgr.)*

No. of U.S. Offices: 3

Computer Systems/Hardware:
IBM PC

Outside Service Firm(s):

Price Waterhouse*(Auditors)*
400 S. Hope St.
Los Angeles, CA 90071-2889
Tel.: 213-236-3000

AIC (American Insurance Consultants)*(Group Insurer)*
13245 Riverside Dr.
Sherman Oaks, CA 91413-6011

SHAPSON GERO & SOMMERS, INC.
(Partner in The Worldcom Group)
260 S. Broad St.
Philadelphia, PA 19102
Tel.: 215-545-4300
Fax: 215-546-8510
Year Founded: 1946
Approx.Billings: $10,550,000
Emp.: 21
Print & Broadcast Adv.; Graphic Design; Issue Advocacy/Public Affairs; Crisis Management; Community Relations; Corporate Awareness Programming & Media Relations
Edward M. Shapson *(Pres., Pub. Rels. & New Bus. Contact)*
Robert L. Gero *(Chief Exec. Officer & Creative Dir.)*
Marie Trabold *(Comptroller)*
Connie Garsey *(Human Resources & Office Mgr.)*
Andy Brookman *(Media Buyer)*
Michele Rippman *(Admin. Asst.)*

SHARON CONCEPTS, INC.
1831 Burnet Ave.
Union, NJ 07083
Tel.: 908-964-1900
Fax: 908-964-8421
Year Founded: 1908
Approx.Sls.: $12,000,000
Emp.: 200
Fiscal Year-end: 6/30/92
Export
Mfr. of Framed Mirrors & Pictures
S.I.C.: 2499
Sharon Bezak *(Pres.)*
Stanley M. Cornfield *(Chief Exec. Officer)*
Anthony Spinola *(V.P.-Sls. & Mktg.)*
Jane Cornfield *(Sec.)*
Frank Matino *(Controller)*
Cole Schotz *(Gen. Counsel)*

Outside Service Firm(s):

Mortenson, Fleming, Grizzetti & Boiko*(Auditors)*
340 North Ave.
Cranford, NJ 07016

Maplewood Bank & Trust Co.*(Major Banking Relationship)*
Union, NJ

SHARON-JAY TOGS, INC.
127 W. Rodney French Blvd.
New Bedford, MA 02744
Tel.: 508-999-5252 **MA**
Fax: 508-999-5256
Approx.Sls.: $11,000,000
Emp.: 200
Fiscal Year-end: 4/30/91
Import
Mfr. of Children's Sportswear
S.I.C.: 2339
Samson Segall *(Chm. Bd., Pres. & Treas.)*
Alan Karpas *(Exec. V.P.)*
Steven Hoffman *(V.P.)*
Amos Eisenberg *(V.P.)*
Mary Ann Segall *(Corp. Sec.)*
David Barnett *(Legal)*
Frank Schillman *(Controller)*
David Pearlman *(Mgr.-Sls.)*

Outside Service Firm(s):

Sanders & Daniels Co.*(Auditors)*
New York, NY

Bank of Boston*(Major Banking Relationship)*
New Bedford, MA

SHARON TUBE COMPANY
134 Mill St.
Sharon, PA 16146
Tel.: 412-981-5200
Fax: 412-983-1031
Approx.Sls.: $50,000,000
Emp.: 300
Fiscal Year-end: 12/31/91
Manufacture Pipe & Mechanical Tubing
S.I.C.: 3317
T.R. Levy *(Chm. Bd.)*
Lee Hooper *(Pres.)*
Robert Tookey *(V.P.-Sls.)*
Dennis A. George *(Treas. & Sec.)*

Outside Service Firm(s):

Deloitte & Touche*(Auditors)*
2400 One PPG Place
Pittsburgh, PA 15222
Tel.: 412-281-2232

Eckert, Seamans, Cherin & Mellott*(Legal Firm)*
600 Grant St., 42nd Fl.
Pittsburgh, PA 15219
Tel.: 412-566-6000

McDowell National Bank*(Major Banking Relationship)*
Sharon, PA

Sharp Hartwig

SHARP HARTWIG, INC.
100 W. Harrison Plaza, South Tower, Ste. 500
Seattle, WA 98119
Tel.: 206-282-6242
Fax: 206-283-0547
Year Founded: 1979
Approx.Billings: $15,000,000
Emp.: 20
David L. Sharp *(Pres.)*
Dick Pattison *(Exec. V.P., Opers. & Telecommunications)*
Ann Revell-Pechar *(Pub. Rels. Mgr.)*
Diane Murphy *(Controller)*
Rick Hutter *(Telecommunications)*

SHARP OIL COMPANY
217 N. Main
Anthony, NM 88021
Tel.: 505-882-2512
Fax: 505-882-5677
Year Founded: 1948
Approx.Sls.: $12,000,000
Emp.: 31
Fiscal Year-end: 12/31/91
Petroleum Bulk Stations
S.I.C.: 5171
Jack B. Sharp *(Pres.)*
Jeff Charles *(Gen. Mgr.)*

Outside Service Firm(s):

First National Bank*(Major Banking Relationship)*
Las Cruces, NM

SHAW CREATIONS, INC.
28 W. 20th St.
New York, NY 10011
Tel.: 212-989-6500 **NY**
Fax: 212-645-7215
Year Founded: 1946
Approx.Sls.: $10,000,000
Emp.: 70
Manufacture Umbrellas
S.I.C.: 3999
Morris Shaw *(Pres. & Gen. Mgr.)*
Lawrence Shaw *(Plant Mgr.)*
Marcia Taylor *(Mgr.-Sls.)*

Outside Service Firm(s):

Fred C. Sanders & Co.*(Auditors)*
New York, NY

Chemical Banking Corp.*(Major Banking Relationship)*
277 Park Ave.
New York, NY 10041
Tel.: 212-310-6407
Fax: 212-310-4526

SHEA HOMES
655 Brea Canyon Rd.
Walnut, CA 91789
Tel.: 909-598-1841
Fax: 909-594-0930
Construction Company
S.I.C.: 1531
Roy Humphrey *(Pres.)*

Divisions:

Shea Homes Northern California **(1)**
25 Metro Dr., Ste. 300
San Jose, CA 95110
Tel.: 408-453-3711
S. Reid Gustafson *(Pres.)*

Shea Homes San Diego **(1)**
10721 Treena St., Ste. 200
San Diego, CA 92131-1039
Tel.: 619-549-3156
Mark Brock *(Pres.)*

Shea Homes Southern California **(1)**
655 Brea Canyon Rd.
Walnut, CA 91789
Tel.: 714-598-1841
William York *(Pres.)*

Shea Homes Southwest **(1)**
40 40 E. Camelback Rd., Ste. 200
Phoenix, AZ 85060
Tel.: 602-952-1009
Garth Wieger *(Pres.)*

SHEALY ELECTRICAL WHOLESALERS
25-29 River St.
Greenville, SC 29602
Tel.: 803-242-6880 **SC**
Fax: 803-235-6097
Approx.Sls.: $24,000,000
Emp.: 91
Fiscal Year-end: 12/31/91
Wholesale Electrical Apparatus
S.I.C.: 5063
Frances S. DeLoache *(Chm. Bd.)*
John S. DeLoache *(Pres.)*
Bill DeLoache *(Exec. V.P.)*
Cecil L. Greene *(V.P.-Sls.-Utility Div.)*
Paul Dunn *(Controller)*
Glen Cockerill *(Mgr.-Branch)*

Outside Service Firm(s):

Price Waterhouse*(Auditors)*
Columbia, SC

Leatherwood, Walker, Todd & Mann*(Legal Firm)*
P.O. Box 2248
Greenville, SC 29602
Tel.: 803-242-6440

NationsBank Carolinas*(Major Banking Relationship)*
Spartanburg, SC

SHEARMAN CORPORATION
(d/b/a Lake Charles American Press)
4900 Hwy. 90 E.
Lake Charles, LA 70602
Mailing Address:
P.O. Box 2893,
Lake Charles, LA 70601
Tel.: 318-433-3000 **LA**
Fax: 318-494-4008
Year Founded: 1896
Approx.Sls.: $18,000,000
Emp.: 188
Fiscal Year-end: 3/31/91
Import Export
Publisher Daily Newspaper; Oil Producer
S.I.C.: 2711; 1311
William H. Shearman *(Pres.)*
Thomas B. Shearman, Jr. *(V.P.)*
Maynard Woodhatch *(Sec. & Treas.)*
Sue Beck *(Adv. Sls. Dir.)*
Principal(s):
William H. Shearman

No. of Mfg. Plants/Facilities: 3
No. of U.S. Offices: 3

Computer Systems/Hardware:
HP 3000

Outside Service Firm(s):

McElroy, Quirk & Co.*(Auditors)*
Lake Charles, LA

Woodley, Barnett, Williams, Fenet, Palmer & Pitre*(Legal Firm)*
Lake Charles, LA

Calcasieu Marine National Bank*(Major Banking Relationship)*
P.O. Box 3402
Lake Charles, LA 70602
Tel.: 318-439-4541

SHEEHY, KNOPF & SHAVER, INC.
101 Bullitt Lane, Ste. 107
Louisville, KY 40222
Tel.: 502-426-1314
Fax: 502-426-3755
Year Founded: 1957
Approx.Billings: $17,200,000
Emp.: 25
William J. Sheehy *(Chm. Bd.)*
K. Shaver *(Vice Chm.)*
Paul R. Knopf *(Pres. & Chief Exec. Officer)*
Robert C. Iler *(Sr. V.P.)*
Janet Shaughnessy *(V.P., Admin.)*
Denise Damron *(V.P.)*

SHEFFIELD HARDWARE COMPANY
314 N. Dudley
Americus, GA 31709
Mailing Address:
P.O. Box 1208
Americus, GA 31709
Tel.: 912-924-0331 **GA**
Fax: 912-924-0383
Year Founded: 1947
Approx.Sls.: $12,000,000
Emp.: 65
Wholesale Distribution of Hardware, Farm Equipment Parts & Supplies, Wire Fence, Gates & Accessories, Plumbing & Hydronic Heating Supplies & Paints
S.I.C.: 5072; 5083; 5039; 5074; 5198
John W. Sheffield *(Chm. Bd.)*
John W. Sheffield, Jr. *(Pres.)*
Jean C. Buchanan *(V.P.)*
Walton Grant *(V.P.)*
Langdon C. Sheffield *(V.P. & Treas.)*

Outside Service Firm(s):

J. Dennis Hester*(Auditors)*
Albany, GA

SHEFFIELD STEEL CORPORATION-JOLIET
1 Industry Ave.
Joliet, IL 60434
Mailing Address:
P.O. Box 727,
Joliet, IL 60434
Tel.: 815-723-9335
Fax: 815-740-4907
Approx.Sls.: $60,000,000
Emp.: 200
Fiscal Year-end: 4/30/89
Hot Rolled Steel Bars, Merchant & Special Quality, Special Custom Bar Shapes & Non-Standard Bar Sizes
S.I.C.: 3312
William C. Schwartz *(Pres.)*
Gary Clark Chinski *(Opers. Mgr.)*
John Procik *(Controller)*
Rick Julian *(Mgr.-Human Resources)*
Bob Smith *(Pur. Agent)*
Robert Stager *(Mgr.-Adv.)*

THE SHELBURNE CORPORATION
Rte. 7 S.
Shelburne, VT 05482
Mailing Address:
P.O. Box 158,
Shelburne, VT 05482
Tel.: 802-985-3321 **VT**
Fax: 802-985-8336
Approx.Sls.: $18,000,000
Emp.: 150
Mfr. Ski Prods., Contract Stampings, Hardware & Mechanical, & Electro-Mechanical Assemblies
S.I.C.: 3429; 3949
Mark H. Snelling *(Pres.)*
Michael Grost *(V.P.-Mktg.)*
Andrew P. Snelling *(Treas. & Sec.)*
Bob Finnegan *(Dir.-Pur.)*
Diane Snelling *(Adv.)*
Principal(s):
Mark H. Snelling
Andrew P. Snelling

Computer Systems/Hardware:
Radio Shack 326

Divisions:

Dovre Ski Products **(1)**
Box 339
Shelburne, VT 05482
Tel.: 802-985-3321
Manufacturer of X-Country Ski Bindings
S.I.C.: 3949
Mark Snelling *(Chief Oper. Officer)*

Shelburne Cyclebinding Division **(1)**
Rte. 7, So.
Shelburne, VT 05482

Shelburne Husky Div. **(1)**
P.O. Box 158,
Shelburne, VT 05482
Tel.: 802-985-3321
Emp.: 9
Mfg. Hardware Item
S.I.C.: 3429
Mark H. Snelling *(Pres.)*

Subsidiary:

Barrecrafters **(1)**
Rte. 7, So.
Shelburne, VT 05482
Tel.: 802-985-3321 (100%)
Fax: 802-985-8336
Emp.: 130
Mfr. of Ski Prods.; Racks, Poles & Ski Grabbers
S.I.C.: 3949
Mark H. Snelling *(Pres.)*
Mike Grost *(V.P.-Sls.)*
Diane Snelling *(Adv.)*

SHELBY GROUP INTERNATIONAL, INC.
5321 E. Shelby Dr.
Memphis, TN 38118
Mailing Address:
P.O. Box 171814
Memphis, TN 38187
Tel.: 901-795-5810 **TN**
Fax: 901-365-3660
Year Founded: 1974
Approx.Sls.: $80,000,000
Emp.: 500
Fiscal Year-end: 12/31/90
Imports, Manufactures & Distributes Work Gloves, Dress Gloves, Sunglasses & Rainwear
S.I.C.: 3151; 5136; 3851
Hilliard Crews *(Chm. Bd., Pres., Chief Exec. Officer & Chief Fin. Officer)*
Rick Knox *(Treas. & Controller)*
Cyrus Coleman *(Mgr.-Data Processing)*

No. of Mfg. Plants/Facilities: 4
No. of U.S. Offices: 6

Computer Systems/Hardware:
IBM

Outside Service Firm(s):

Reynolds, Bone & Greisbeck*(Auditors)*
Memphis, TN

Bank of New England*(Major Banking Relationship)*
Memphis, TN

Division:

River City Protective Wear, Inc. **(1)**
5321 E. Shelby Dr.
Memphis, TN 38118
Tel.: 901-794-3321
Rainwear
S.I.C.: 5136; 5137
H.R. Crews *(Pres.)*

SHELBY & SHANE MARKETING COMMUNICATIONS
300 W. Fourth St.
Cincinnati, OH 45202
Tel.: 513-579-8440
Fax: 513-579-1660
Year Founded: 1982
Approx.Billings: $23,365,000
Emp.: 27
Automotive, Healthcare, Communications, Broadcast Promotions, Computer, Sports, Catalogue & Direct Mktg.
Patrick Martin *(Exec. V.P.)*
Terry Burke *(V.P., Mktg. Services)*
John Toole *(V.P., Gen. Mgr.-Catalog & Direct Mktg.)*
Jenny Busam *(Dir., Sports Mktg. & Promo.)*

SHELDONS' INC.
626 Center St.
Antigo, WI 54409-2496
Tel.: 715-623-2382
Tel.: 800-333-4756 **WI**
Fax: 715-623-3001
Year Founded: 1955
Assets: $11,579,840
Liabilities: $2,231,221
Net Worth: $9,348,619

Sales Range: $10-19 Million
Emp.: 90
Fiscal Year-end: 9/30/91
Import
Manufacture Fishing Equipment
S.I.C.: 3949
J.M. Sheldon *(Chm. Bd., Pres. & Chief Exec. Officer)*
A.L. Sheldon *(V.P.)*
Craig A. Blanchard *(Chief Fin. Officer, Treas. & Controller)*
Leone Sheldon *(Sec.)*
Thomas Krautkramer *(Dir.-Employee Benefits)*
Jim Martinsen *(Dir.-Adv. & Pub. Rels.)*
Fred Kohlmeier *(Plant Mgr.)*
Max Morehouse *(Mgr.-Sls.)*
Principal(s):
J.M. Sheldon
A.L. Sheldon
Craig A. Blanchard

No. of Mfg. Plants/Facilities: 3
No. of U.S. Offices: 2
No. of Foreign Offices: 1

Computer Systems/Hardware:
IBM AS400 Y10, Gateway 2000 PC's, IBM PC

Outside Service Firm(s):

Smits, Kilsdonk & Associates*(Auditors)*
Antigo, WI

Travelers Insurance Co.*(Commercial Insurance Carrier)*
Milwaukee, WI

John Alden Insurance Co.*(Group Insurer)*
Dallas, TX

Benefit Trust & Life*(Group Insurer)*
Milwaukee, WI

Societe Generale*(International Bank Affiliate)*
Monte Carlo, Monaco

Foley & Lardner*(Legal Firm)*
777 E. Wisconsin Ave.
Milwaukee, WI 53202
Tel.: 414-271-2400

First Wisconsin National Bank*(Major Banking Relationship)*
777 E. Wisconsin Ave.
Milwaukee, WI 53202
Tel.: 414-765-4321
Fax: 414-355-6903

Strong/Corneliuson Capital Management Inc.*(Pension Manager)*
Milwaukee, WI

Subsidiary:

Mister Twister **(1)**
Drawer 996
Minden, LA 71055
Tel.: 318-377-8818
Emp.: 100
Mfr. Mister Twister Soft Plastic Recreational Fishing Lures
S.I.C.: 3949
Bob Cummings *(Exec. V.P.)*
John Byrd *(V.P.-Fin. & Admin.)*
Pat Metzker *(Sls. Mgr.)*

Non-U.S. Holding:

Mepps S.A. **(1)**
B.P. 09, 06390
Contes, France
Emp.: 100
Mfr. Recreational Fishing Lures
S.I.C.: 3949
Jean Luc Faure *(Gen. Mgr.)*
Pierre Blanchard *(Dir.-Fin. & Admin.)*

SHELTER MUTUAL INSURANCE COMPANY
1817 W. Broadway
Columbia, MO 65218
Tel.: 314-445-8441
Year Founded: 1946
Approx.Rev.: $325,000,000
Emp.: 1,650
Casualty & Life Insurance Company with Branches in 13 States
S.I.C.: 6321; 6311
Gustav J. Lehr *(Chm. Bd. & Chief Exec. Officer)*
John W. Lenox *(Vice Chm. & Exec. V.P.)*
Robert W. Maupin *(Pres. & Chief Oper. Officer)*
James A. Offutt *(Exec. V.P.)*
Donald G. Goodwin *(Sr. V.P.-Info. Svcs.)*
Robert T. Cox *(V.P. & Gen. Counsel)*
Max T. Dills *(V.P.-Actuarial)*
J. Donald Duello *(V.P.-Fin.)*
Vernon Jennings *(V.P.-Gen. Svc.)*
Raymond E. Jones *(V.P.-Admin. & Sec.)*
Donald E. Light *(V.P.-Claims)*
Jean Madden *(V.P.-Comm.)*
Robert Minnick *(V.P. & Treas.)*
Mark E. Zimmer *(V.P.-Mktg.)*

Outside Service Firm(s):

Coopers & Lybrand*(Auditors)*
One Metropolitan Square
St. Louis, MO 63102
Tel.: 314-436-3200

SHENANDOAH LIFE INSURANCE COMPANY
2301 Brambleton Ave., S.W.
Roanoke, VA 24015
Mailing Address:
P.O. Box 12847
Roanoke, VA 24029
Tel.: 703-985-4400
Fax: 703-985-4444
Year Founded: 1914
Approx.Premiums: $121,701,126
Emp.: 224
Fiscal Year-end: 12/31/91
Life Insurance
S.I.C.: 6311
Corporate Giving Program:
Contributions to Social Service & Local Community Activities; Health Care Delivery & Medical Education & Research; Educational Institutions; Education & Research in Fields of Business, Economics & Government; Urban, Social & Environmental Affairs; Arts & Historical Preservation
Employee Matching Gifts Program:
Matches Gifts to any Nonprofit, Public or Private Graduate or Professional School, Junior College, College or University in the U.S., or any Possession of the U.S., which is Accredited by an Appropriate Regional or Professional Accrediting Association
Joseph E. Stephenson *(Pres. & Chief Exec. Officer)*
Charles D. Cox III *(V.P. & Chief Fin. Officer)*
Hartley R. Gaston *(V.P.-Information Systems & Services)*
Pearl H. Gearhart *(V.P.-Admin.)*
James E. Harshaw *(V.P.-Grp.)*
Roger D. Kahle *(V.P.-Mktg.)*
Richard C. Wagner *(V.P.-Individual Insurance Services)*
P. Greggory Williams *(V.P.-Investments & Treas.)*
Willis M. Anderson *(Gen. Counsel & Sec.)*
C. Dale Games *(2nd V.P.-Disability Income)*
David G. Barrett *(2nd V.P.-Individual Sls.)*
Roger W. Johnson *(2nd V.P.-ISS Opers.)*
Michael G. Bell *(2nd V.P. & Actuary)*
Donald M. Kinzer *(2nd V.P.-Investments)*
James B. Cavendish *(2nd V.P.-Group Mktg.)*
Shiu-Shiung Lin *(2nd V.P.-Group Actuary)*
Thomas W. Cecere *(2nd V.P.-Corp. Services)*
Herbert L. Magness *(2nd V.P.-Corp. Actuary)*
Dan A. Chrisman *(2nd V.P. & Chief Underwriter)*
Lois S. Peterson *(2nd V.P.-Admin. Systems)*
Jack W. Cochran *(2nd V.P.-Customer Services)*
Gene F. Sherwood *(2nd V.P.-Human Resources)*
Michael W. Coffman *(Controller)*
Matthew J. Smith *(2nd V.P.-Investment Officer)*
Genevieve C. Henderson *(Asst. Sec.)*

Computer Systems/Hardware:
IBM ES9000-210

Subsidiary:

Old Dominion Life Insurance Co. **(1)**
2301 Brambleton Ave., S.W.
Roanoke, VA 24015
Tel.: 703-985-4400
S.I.C.: 6311
Joseph E. Stephenson *(Pres.)*
Charles D. Cox, III *(V.P. & Actuary)*
Donald M. Kinzer *(Treas.)*
Michael W. Coffman *(Controller)*
Willis M. Anderson *(Gen. Counsel & Sec.)*

SHENANDOAH MFG. CO. INC.
1070 Virginia Ave.
Harrisonburg, VA 22801
Mailing Address:
P. O. Box 839
Harrisonburg, VA 22801
Tel.: 703-434-3838
Tel.: 800-476-7436 **VA**
Fax: 703-434-3068
Year Founded: 1924
Sales Range: $10-19 Million
Emp.: 100
Export
Manufacturer of Poultry & Livestock Equipment; Incinerators; Waste Oil Furnaces; Pet Feeders
S.I.C.: 3523; 3567
Lewis E. Strite *(Chm. Bd. & Chief Exec. Officer)*
L. Gerald Strite *(Pres.)*
Milton W. Heatwole *(Exec. V.P.)*
Richard K. Lantz *(V.P.-Mfg. & Special Sls.)*
Carmen Strite Miller *(Sec.)*
Paul Sauder *(Dir.-Adv.)*

No. of Mfg. Plants/Facilities: 1
No. of U.S. Offices: 1

Computer Systems/Hardware:
IBM System 36

Outside Service Firm(s):

S. B. Hoover & Co.*(Auditors)*
Harrisonburg, VA

Clark & Bradshaw*(Legal Firm)*
Harrisonburg, VA

Dominion Bank*(Major Banking Relationship)*
Dominion Center
Harrisonburg, VA
Tel.: 703-564-5200

SHENANGO FURNACE COMPANY
101 Carnegie Center
Princeton, NJ 08540
Tel.: 609-951-9400
Fax: 412-281-8815
Year Founded: 1906
Assets: $25,000,000
Liabilities: $9,000,000
Net Worth: $16,000,000
Approx.Sls.: $20,000,000
Emp.: 200
Fiscal Year-end: 12/31/90
Export
Primary Metal Industries; Centrifugal Casting
S.I.C.: 3364
G. Whitney Snyder *(Chm. Bd.)*
R. Dixon Hayes *(Pres. & Chief Exec. Officer)*
Robert G. Gardner *(Controller)*
D.L. Ketter *(Sec.)*

No. of Mfg. Plants/Facilities: 4

Outside Service Firm(s):

Ernst & Young*(Auditors)*
2000 Pittsburgh Natl. Bldg.
Pittsburgh, PA 15222
Tel.: 412-644-7800
Fax: 412-644-7419

Pennsylvania Blue Shield*(Group Insurer)*
Camp Hill, PA

Kirkpatrick & Lockhart*(Legal Firm)*
1500 Oliver Bldg., 535 Smithfield St.
Pittsburgh, PA 15222
Tel.: 412-355-6500
Fax: 412-355-6501

Bank One*(Major Banking Relationship)*
Columbus, OH

Mellon Capital Management Corp.*(Pension Manager)*
Pittsburgh, PA

SHEPARD CLOTHING COMPANY
800 Acushnet Ave.
New Bedford, MA 02740
Mailing Address:
P.O. Box 953
New Bedford, MA 02741
Tel.: 508-993-2661
Fax: 508-993-2661, Ext. 133
Approx.Sls.: $47,000,000
Emp.: 874
Men's Apparel
S.I.C.: 2311
Paul D. Kussell *(Pres.)*

Computer Systems/Hardware:
IBM

SHEPARD NILES, INC.
250 N. Genesee St.
Montour Falls, NY 14865
Tel.: 607-535-7111 **NY**
Fax: 607-535-7323
Year Founded: 1878
Approx.Sls.: $32,000,000
Emp.: 350
Fiscal Year-end: 3/30/91
Import Export
Electric Cranes, Hoists, Gantrys, Monorails, Electric Hoists, Molten Metal Carriers, Stacker Cranes, Teleplatforms, Automated/Intergrated Material Handling Systems
S.I.C.: 3536
James Underwood, Jr. *(Pres.)*
Thomas Underwood *(Exec. V.P.)*
Louis Santioni *(V.P.-Sls.)*
William Hobbs *(V.P. & Gen. Mgr.)*
Keith Baumann *(Treas.)*
Howard E. Shumway *(Mgr.-Mktg. Services)*
Marv Geyer *(Mgr.-Plant)*

Outside Service Firm(s):

Deloitte & Touche*(Auditors)*
2400 One PPG Place
Pittsburgh, PA 15222
Tel.: 412-281-2232

Robert P. Lightcap*(Legal Firm)*
Pittsburgh, PA

Chemung Canal Trust Co.*(Major Banking Relationship)*
Elmira, NY

SHEPAUG CORPORATION
54 E. 64th St.
New York, NY 10021
Tel.: 212-751-6633 **DE**
Fax: 212-486-5737
Year Founded: 1969
Emp.: 574

Shepaug Corporation—(Continued)

Holding Co.; Spring & Electrical Devices Mfg.; Real Estate & Publishing; Water Utility
S.I.C.: 6719
Arthur L. Carter *(Pres.)*
Tom Scheinman *(Exec. V.P.)*
Richard S. Wiesenthal *(Sr. V.P. & Chm.-Fin. Committee)*
Vincent Bohn *(Treas.)*
Bernard D. Fischman *(Sec.)*

Outside Service Firm(s):

KPMG Peat Marwick*(Auditors)*
345 Park Ave.
New York, NY 10154
Tel.: 212-758-9700
Fax: 212-872-3308

Chemical Bank*(Major Banking Relationship)*
Albany, NY

Paul, Weiss, Rifkind, Wharton & Garrison*(Legal Firm)*
1285 Avenue of the Americas
New York, NY 10019

Subsidiaries:

Bishopsgate Corp. (1)
54 E. 64th St.
New York, NY 10021
Tel.: 212-751-6633 (100%)
S.I.C.: 6211
Arthur L. Carter *(Pres.)*

Colonial Sand & Stone Co. (1)
54 E. 64th St.
New York, NY 10021
Tel.: 212-751-6633
S.I.C.: 3272

The Nation (1)
72 5th Ave.
New York, NY 10011
Tel.: 212-242-8400
Magazine Publishing
S.I.C.: 2721
David Parker *(Pres.)*

New York Financial Corp. (1)
54 E. 64th St.
New York, NY 10021
Tel.: 212-751-6633 (100%)
S.I.C.: 6141
Richard S. Wiesenthal *(Pres.)*

The New York Observer (1)
54 E. 64th St.
New York, NY 10021
Tel.: 212-755-2400
Newspaper Publishing
S.I.C.: 2711
Gail T. Barker *(Gen. Adv. Mgr.)*

Sunrise Mall Assocs. (1)
635 Madison Ave.
New York, NY 10022
Tel.: 212-355-0600 (50%)
Shopping Center
S.I.C.: 6512

Unimax Holding Corp. (1)
54 E. 64th St.
New York, NY 10021
Tel.: 212-755-8800
Holding Co.
S.I.C.: 2796; 2752; 2754; 2791; 3493
Tom Scheinman *(Pres. & Chief Exec. Officer)*

Utilities & Industries Management Corp. (1)
54 E. 64th St.
New York, NY 10021
Tel.: 212-755-8800 (100%)
S.I.C.: 6211
Arthur L. Carter *(Pres.)*

SHEPHERD CONSTRUCTION CO., INC.
1800 Briarcliff Rd., NE
Atlanta, GA 30329
Tel.: 404-325-9350
Fax: 404-633-5585
Approx.Sls.: $48,000,000
Emp.: 435
Heavy Highway Construction
S.I.C.: 1611
J. Harold Shepherd *(Chief Exec. Officer)*
Dan P. Shepherd *(Chief Oper. Officer)*
Fred W. Crawford, Jr. *(V.P.)*
William Clyde Shepherd, Jr. *(Sec. & Treas.)*
Willard Methany *(Office Mgr.)*

Outside Service Firm(s):

Smith, Adcock & Co.*(Auditors)*
Atlanta, GA

Schreeder, Wheeler & Flint*(Legal Firm)*
Atlanta, GA

Trust Company Bank*(Major Banking Relationship)*
Trust Co. Tower
Atlanta, GA 30303
Tel.: 404-588-7963

SHEPLERS, INC.
6501 W. Kellogg
Wichita, KS 67209
Tel.: 316-946-3838
Fax: 316-946-3730
Year Founded: 1946
Approx.Sls.: $125,000,000
Emp.: 1,200
Fiscal Year-end: 7/28/91
Department Store & Mail Order Apparel
S.I.C.: 5311; 5961
Louis D. Cohen *(Pres. & Chief Exec. Officer)*
John Mosley *(Chief Fin. Officer & Exec. V.P.)*
John Wilcox *(V.P.-Sls. Promo. & Adv.)*

Computer Systems/Hardware:
Unisys

SHERBORNE GROUP, INC.
Park Ave. Tower, 65 E. 55th St.
New York, NY 10022
Tel.: 212-759-6301
Fax: 212-754-9591
Sales Range: $500-999 Million
Emp.: 5,000
Holding Company
S.I.C.: 6719; 3695
Edward Bramson *(Pres.)*
William Fields *(Treas. & Controller)*

Outside Service Firm(s):

Coopers & Lybrand*(Auditors)*
1301 Avenue of The Americas
New York, NY 10019
Tel.: 212-536-2000

Subsidiary:

Ampex Corporation (1)
401 Broadway
Redwood City, CA 94063-3199
Tel.: 415-367-2011
Telex: 910-378-5920
Fax: 415-367-4669
Approx.Sls.: $700,000,000
Emp.: 6,700
Fiscal Year-end: 12/31/90
Mfr. Recorders & Tapes for Industry, Broadcast, CCTV; Instrumentation; Professional Video & Audio Tape & Core Memories for Computer Industry; Video Recorders, Cameras, Switchers, Special Effects, Graphics & Editing Systems; Data Storage Systems
S.I.C.: 3695; 3572; 3651
Ronald J. Ritchie *(Pres. & Chief Exec. Officer)*
Thomas J. Wheeler *(Pres.-Ampex Recording Media Corp.)*
Bob Atchison *(Pres.-Recording Systems)*
George A. Merrick *(Exec. V.P.-Mktg., Sls. & Service)*
Leslie E. Schenk *(V.P. & Chief Fin. Officer)*
Joel D. Talcott *(V.P., Sec. & Gen. Counsel)*
Rob Corrigan *(V.P.-Mktg.)*
C.R. Rhind *(V.P.-Sls.)*
Richard J. Jacquet *(V.P.-Human Resources)*
Rollin Stanford *(V.P.-U.S. Sls.)*
Matthew Doyle *(V.P.-U.S. Service)*
Karen Schweikher *(Dir.-Corp. Communications)*
Al Fisher *(Adv. Mgr.)*

Divisions:

Ampex Computer Products Division (1)
200 N. Nash St.
El Segundo, CA 90245
Tel.: 310-640-0150
Fax: 310-416-1494
Mfr. of Computer Terminals
S.I.C.: 3575
David Chapman *(V.P. & Div. Mgr.)*

Ampex Corporation Marketing, Sales & Service (1)
401 Broadway
Redwood City, CA 94063
Tel.: 415-367-2011
Telex: 348464
Fax: 415-367-2761
Mktg. & Sls. of Ampex Products
S.I.C.: 5099; 5065
Douglas M. Rowan *(V.P. & Gen. Mgr.)*

Ampex Corporation, Video Systems Div. (1)
401 Broadway
Redwood City, CA 94063
Tel.: 415-367-2011
Telex: 348464
Fax: 415-367-2761
Mfrs. Television Equipment
S.I.C.: 3651
George A. Merrick *(V.P. & Div. Mgr.)*

Ampex Magnetic Tape Division (1)
401 Broadway
Redwood City, CA 94063
Tel.: 415-367-2761
Mfr. of Magnetic Tape
S.I.C.: 3695
Thomas J. Wheeler *(V.P. & Div. Mgr.)*

Ampex Recording Systems Division (1)
401 Broadway
Redwood City, CA 94063
Tel.: 415-367-2011
Fax: 415-367-2761
Magnetic Media Storage Peripherals
S.I.C.: 3572
Ronald J. Ritchie *(V.P. & Div. Mgr.)*

THE SHERIDAN GROUP
450 Fame Ave.
Hanover, PA 17331
Tel.: 717-632-3535
Fax: 717-633-8900
Approx.Sls.: $56,000,000
Emp.: 770
Sheet Fed Offset Printing
S.I.C.: 2721; 2731; 2752
R. Champlin Sheridan *(Chm. Bd. & Chief Exec. Officer)*
J.M. Dryden Hall, Jr. *(Sec.)*
Principal(s):
R. Champlin Sheridan

No. of Mfg. Plants/Facilities: 2
No. of U.S. Offices: 1

Outside Service Firm(s):

Coopers & Lybrand*(Auditors)*
217 E. Redwood St.
Baltimore, MD 21202

Hall & Schwartz*(Legal Firm)*
Baltimore, MD

Farmers Bank & Trust Company*(Major Banking Relationship)*
Hanover, PA

Subsidiaries:

Braun-Brumfield, Inc. (1)
100 N. Staebler Rd.
Ann Arbor, MI 48103
Tel.: 313-662-3291
Manufacture Books, Litho Printing
S.I.C.: 2731; 2752
Arnold M. Ziroli *(Pres. & Chief Oper. Officer)*
Karen Atko *(Controller)*

The Sheridan Press, Inc. (1)
Fame Ave.
Hanover, PA 17331
Tel.: 717-632-3535
Sheet Fed Offset Printing
S.I.C.: 2721; 2731; 2752
David L. Horst *(Pres. & Chief Oper. Officer)*
R. Champlin Sheridan *(Chief Exec. Officer)*
Arthur G. Schafer *(V.P.-Fin. & Admin.)*

SHERLEY GRAIN COMPANY
503 Gardner Avenue
Bovina, TX 79009
Tel.: 806-238-1521 **TX**
Fax: 806-238-1414
Year Founded: 1946
Emp.: 9
Agricultural Services; Wholesale Grain Products
S.I.C.: 0723; 5153
G. D. Anderson, Jr. *(Pres. & Chief Exec. Officer)*
Earl Whitten *(Chief Fin. Officer, Treas. & Controller)*

Outside Service Firm(s):

Earl Whitten*(Auditors)*
Bovina, TX

Security State Bank*(Major Banking Relationship)*
Farwell, TX

SHERMAN & REILLY, INC.
400 W. 33rd St.
Chattanooga, TN 37410
Tel.: 615-756-5300
Fax: 615-756-2948
Year Founded: 1927
Emp.: 85
Export
Overhead & Underground Electrical Power Lines, Equipment, Tools & Hardware
S.I.C.: 3612; 3629
F. Ward Reilly, Jr. *(Chm. Bd.)*
James W. Reilly *(Pres.)*
Glenn W. Brown, Jr. *(Exec. V.P.-Sls.)*
John R. Whitt *(V.P.-Sls. & Sec.)*
William Caulkins *(Dir.-Mktg.)*

Outside Service Firm(s):

Miller & Martin*(Legal Firm)*
Chattanooga, TN

First Tennessee Bank, N.A.*(Major Banking Relationship)*
701 Market St.
Chattanooga, TN 37402

SHERMS THUNDERBIRD MARKET
2347 Jacksonville Hwy.
Medford, OR 97501
Mailing Address:
P.O. Box 1400
Medford, OR 97501
Tel.: 503-779-4274 **OR**
Fax: 503-772-6033
Year Founded: 1967
Approx.Sls.: $60,000,000
Emp.: 290
Independent Grocery Stores
S.I.C.: 5411
Sherman Olsrud *(Pres.)*
Wanda J. Olsrud *(Sec.)*

Outside Service Firm(s):

Medford State Bank*(Major Banking Relationship)*
Medford, OR

SHERWOOD FOOD DISTRIBUTORS
(Partnership of Orleans International & Regal Packing Inc.)
18615 Sherwood
Detroit, MI 48234
Tel.: 313-366-3100
Fax: 313-366-3100, Ext. 223
Assets: $29,000,000
Liabilities: $23,000,000
Net Worth: $6,000,000
Approx.Sls.: $350,000,000
Emp.: 225
Fiscal Year-end: 10/31/91
Wholesale Food Distributor
S.I.C.: 5144; 5147
Earl D. Ishbia *(Mng. Partner)*
Larry Tushman *(Mng. Partner)*
Principal(s):
Earl D. Ishbia
Larry Tushman

Computer Systems/Hardware:
IBM 5291

Outside Service Firm(s):

BDO Seidman*(Auditors)*
Detroit, MI

Manufacturers National Bank N.A.*(Major Banking Relationship)*
38th Fl., 100 Renaissance Center
Detroit, MI 48243
Tel.: 313-222-4227

SHERWOOD LUMBER CORPORATION
300 Corporate Plaza
Islandia, NY 11722
Tel.: 516-232-9191
Fax: 516-232-1974
Approx.Sls.: $140,000,000
Emp.: 32
Wholesale Lumber
S.I.C.: 5031
Bernard Goodman *(Chm. Bd. & Treas.)*
Andrew Goodman *(Pres.)*

SHERWOOD & SCHNEIDER ADVERTISING
350 Hudson St.
New York, NY 10014
Tel.: 212-627-8100
Fax: 212-627-8512
Year Founded: 1981
Approx.Billings: $20,500,000
Emp.: 20
Marvin Schneider *(Chm. & Chief Exec. Officer)*
Lew Sherwood *(Pres. & Creative Dir.)*
Marshall Bucci *(Sr. V.P., Grp. Dir.)*
Marvin Davis *(Sr. V.P., Grp. Dir.)*
Robert Nieto *(V.P., Fin.)*

THE SHIDLER GROUP
4 Embarcadero Ctr., Ste. 3150
San Francisco, CA 94111
Tel.: 415-391-4000
Fax: 415-391-1852
Year Founded: 1971
Sales Range: $100-499 Million
Emp.: 183
Real Estate Principals, Investment Firm
S.I.C.: 6798
Jay Shidler *(Pres. & Mng. Partner)*
Don Abbey *(Mng. Partner-Los Angeles/South)*
John Blockey *(Mng. Partner)*
Rob Holman *(Mng. Partner-Corp. Real Estate Acquisitions)*
Paul Lambert *(Mng. Partner-Detroit, St. Louis, Mpls.-St. Paul)*
Ken Livadas *(Mng. Partner-Los Angeles/North)*
Stan Mattison *(Mng. Partner-San Francisco)*
Chip Owen *(Mng. Partner-Phoenix)*
Jim Reynolds *(Mng. Partner-Honolulu & San Diego)*
Mike Tomasz *(Mng. Partner-Chicago)*
Jane Greenblatt *(Partner-New Jersey)*
Fred Ito *(Chief Oper. Officer)*
JoAnne Chun *(Dir.-Personnel)*

No. of U.S. Offices: 13

Computer Systems/Hardware:
IBM System 34 & Macintosh

Outside Service Firm(s):

Arthur Andersen & Co.*(Auditors)*
Honolulu, HI

Cades, Schutte, Fleming & Wright*(Legal Firm)*
P.O. Box 939, 1000 Bishop St.
Honolulu, HI 96813
Tel.: 808-521-9200

First Hawaiian Bank*(Major Banking Relationship)*
165 South King St.
Honolulu, HI 96813
Tel.: 808-525-5876
Fax: 808-525-5791

Subsidiary:

REMark Advertising **(1)**
733 Bishop St., Ste. 2165
Honolulu, HI 96813
Tel.: 808-531-3000
Fax: 808-528-7127
Approx.Billings: $150,000
Comml./Indus. Real Estate
Jay Shidler *(Pres.)*
Ian Killips *(V.P., Chief Mktg. Officer)*
Harriet Stamm *(Creative, Art & Pub. Rel. Dir.)*

SHIELD SECURITY, INC.
200 N. Westmoreland Ave.
Los Angeles, CA 90004
Tel.: 213-387-1221 **CA**
Fax: 213-387-9043
Year Founded: 1964
Approx.Sls.: $16,000,000
Secuirty Guard Service
S.I.C.: 7381
Edward Klosterman *(Pres.)*
John Golden *(V.P.)*
Gregg Evans *(Treas. & Sec.)*

Outside Service Firm(s):

Security Pacific National Bank*(Major Banking Relationship)*
333 S. Hope St.
Los Angeles, CA 90017
Tel.: 213-613-6211

Division:

ESM Tech. **(1)**
1063 Galssele St.
Orange, CA 92667
Tel.: 714-538-3563
Installation of Security Alarms
S.I.C.: 7382
Edward Klosterman *(Pres.)*

SHIFFMAN/FERGUSSON/ STONE ADVERTISING INC.
1 Parker Plaza
Fort Lee, NJ 07024
Tel.: 201-944-9100
Fax: 201-944-3111
Year Founded: 1972
Approx.Billings: $20,500,000
Emp.: 32
Automotive
Milton S. Shiffman *(Pres. & Chief Exec. Officer)*
Rudy Nardelli *(Exec. V.P., Dir. Mktg. Services)*
Tom DiCandia *(V.P., Dir. Opers.)*
Eileen Jackson *(Exec. Sec.)*
Diana Hanas *(Comptroller)*

SHILLCRAFT, INC.
8899 Kelso Drive
Baltimore, MD 21221
Mailing Address:
P.O. Box 7770,
Baltimore, MD 21221
Tel.: 410-682-3060 **MD**
Fax: 410-682-3130
Year Founded: 1923
Approx.Sls.: $10,000,000
Emp.: 25
Fiscal Year-end: 6/30/91
Import Export
Mail Order Crafts; Latch Hook Rugs & Accessories
S.I.C.: 5961
Norman Shillman *(Pres.)*
Joyce Wehberg *(Chief Oper. Officer & Dir.-Pur.)*
Ronald Shillman *(Mgr.-Mktg.)*
Principal(s):
Norman Shillman
Joyce Wehberg

Computer Systems/Hardware:
Hewlett-Packard

Outside Service Firm(s):

Sollins & Stokely*(Auditors)*
Baltimore, MD

Maryland National Bank*(Major Banking Relationship)*
Baltimore, MD 21202

SHIP ANALYTICS, INC.
Rte. 2 & 184, North Stonington Professional Center
North Stonington, CT 06359
Tel.: 203-535-3092 **CT**
Fax: 203-535-0560
Year Founded: 1972
Approx.Sls.: $14,000,000
Emp.: 150
Marine Research & Engingeering Service; Simulation Services; Software Products
S.I.C.: 3829; 7372; 8711; 8731
Alan J. Pesch *(Chm. Bd., Pres. & Chief Exec. Officer)*
Lynda Patnod *(Chief Fin. Officer)*
Francis L. Crowley *(Sec.)*

No. of Mfg. Plants/Facilities: 3
No. of U.S. Offices: 1

Outside Service Firm(s):

Ernst & Young*(Auditors)*
200 Clarendon St., 46th Fl.
Boston, MA 02116
Tel.: 617-266-2000

Fleet National Bank*(Major Banking Relationship)*
Westerly, RI

SHIPLEY OIL COMPANY
550 E. King St.
York, PA 17405
Mailing Address:
P.O. Box 946
York, PA 17405
Tel.: 717-848-4100
Year Founded: 1929
Assets: $13,000,000
Net Worth: $13,000,000
Approx.Sls.: $75,000,000
Emp.: 305
Wholesaler & Retailer of Petroleum Products Including Heating Oil & Gasoline, Heating & A/C Equipment; Installation & Service
S.I.C.: 5172; 5983; 7699
William S. Shipley II *(Chm. Bd., Pres. & Chief Exec. Officer)*
Robert C. Borden, Jr. *(V.P.-Mktg.)*
David E. Wilson *(V.P.-Opers. & Fin.)*
George E. Ioos *(Treas. & Sec.)*
Wyatt F. Morrison *(Asst. Sec. & Dir.)*
Robert Jensenius *(Mgr.-Human Resources)*

Computer Systems/Hardware:
NCR 9300

Outside Service Firm(s):

Ernst & Young*(Auditors)*
212 Locust St.
Harrisburg, PA 17101

Pennsylvania Blue Shield*(Group Insurer)*
Camp Hill, PA

Blakey, Yost, Bupp & Schaumann*(Legal Firm)*
York, PA

Hamilton Bank*(Major Banking Relationship)*
York, PA

Hamilton Bank*(Pension Manager)*
York, PA

SHIVERS TRADING & OPERATING CO.
725 Broad St.
Augusta, GA 30901
Tel.: 706-724-0851
Year Founded: 1981
Approx.Sls.: $210,000,000
Emp.: 3,600
Newspaper Publishing & Printing
S.I.C.: 2711
William S. Morris, III *(Pres.)*
Paul S. Simon *(Exec. V.P.)*
Norman Wilson *(V.P.)*
W.A. Herman, III *(Treas. & Sec.)*

Outside Service Firm(s):

Arthur Andersen & Co.*(Auditors)*
133 Peachtree St., N.E.
Atlanta, GA 30303
Tel.: 404-658-1776

Aetna Life & Casualty*(Group Insurer)*
Charlotte, NC

Hull, Towill, Norman & Barrett*(Legal Firm)*
P.O. Box 1564,
Augusta, GA 30913
Tel.: 706-722-4481

Chase Manhattan Bank, N.A.*(Major Banking Relationship)*
G.P.O. Box 1990,
San Juan, PR 00936
Tel.: 809-753-3625

First Union National Bank*(Major Banking Relationship)*
Jacksonville, FL

Subsidiary:

Morris Corporation **(1)**
P.O. Box 936
Augusta, GA 30913
Tel.: 706-724-0851
Fax: 706-722-7125
Approx.Sls.: $322,000,000
Emp.: 3,400
Computer Systems/Hardware:
IBM 3031
Newspaper Publishing Company, Hartwell Sun & St. Augustine Record; Outdoor Advertising
S.I.C.: 2711; 7312
W.S. Morris, III *(Chm. Bd. & Chief Exec. Officer)*
Paul S. Simon *(Pres. & Chief Fin. Officer)*
Norman Wilson *(V.P.- Investments)*
Joseph E. Kelly III *(V.P.-Computer Services)*
W. A. Herman, III *(Sec. & Treas.)*
Richard Allport *(Dir.-Corp. Support & Devel.)*

SHOE-TOWN, INC.
994 Riverview Dr.
Totowa, NJ 07512
Tel.: 201-785-1900

Shoe-Town, Inc.—(Continued)

Fax: 201-785-8238
Approx.Sls.: $131,000,000
Emp.: 2,300
Retail Shoe Store Chain
S.I.C.: 5661
Irving Beckman *(Pres.)*
Edward D. Solomon *(Chief Exec. Officer)*
Eleanor Kaufman *(V.P.-Adv.)*

Outside Service Firm(s):

Price Waterhouse*(Auditors)*
411 Hackensack Ave.
Hackensack, NJ 07601
Tel.: 201-646-1550

First Fidelity Bank, N.A.*(Major Banking Relationship)*
Totowa, NJ

R. M. SHOEMAKER CO.
One Tower Bridge, 100 Front St.
West Conshohocken, PA 19428
Mailing Address:
P.O. Box 888,
Conshohocken, PA 19428
Tel.: 215-941-5500 **PA**
Fax: 215-941-5526
Year Founded: 1946
Assets: $29,000,000
Liabilities: $22,000,000
Net Worth: $7,000,000
Approx.Sls.: $93,000,000
Emp.: 100
Fiscal Year-end: 9/30/91
General Contractor & Construction Mngmt.
S.I.C.: 1541; 1542; 1522
John H. Ball *(Chm. Bd. & Chief Exec. Officer)*
John K. Ball *(Pres. & Chief Oper. Officer)*
John Bremmer *(V.P.-Estimating & Pur.)*
Wayne Martin *(V.P.-Opers.)*
David R. Strange *(V.P.-Business Devel.)*
Stephen Steelman *(V.P.-Opers.)*
Dale A. Wark *(V.P.-Fin., Chief Fin. Officer, Treas. & Sec.)*
Robert Cubberley *(Controller)*
Thomas Walsh *(Dir.-Data Processing)*

Computer Systems/Hardware:
Texas Instruments Series 600

Outside Service Firm(s):

Pannell, Kerr, Forster*(Auditors)*
1900 Market St., Suite 825
Philadelphia, PA 19103
Tel.: 215-563-5300

Crum & Forster*(Commercial Insurance Carrier)*
Philadelphia, PA

Guardian Life Insurance Co.*(Group Insurance Broker/Consult)*
Philadelphia, PA

Hoyle, Morris & Kerr*(Legal Firm)*
Philadelphia, PA

Philadelphia National Bank*(Major Banking Relationship)*
P.O. Box 13834, Broad & Chestnut Streets
Philadelphia, PA 19101-7618
Tel.: 215-973-8327

SHOFAR KOSHER FOODS, INC.
124 Malvern St.
Newark, NJ 07105
Mailing Address:
P.O. Box 5609
Newark, NJ 07105
Tel.: 201-344-3900
Fax: 201-344-2349
Approx.Sls.: $26,000,000
Emp.: 130
Mfr. of Frankfurters, Knockwurst, Salami, Bologna, Corned Beef, Pastrami & Deli Products
S.I.C.: 2013
Alan Moore *(Pres.)*
George Bell *(V.P.)*
Leonard H. Posnock *(V.P.)*
Michelle Posnock *(Sls. Rep.)*
Norma Fuerst *(Sls. Mgr.)*

Computer Systems/Hardware:
Rexon

SHOGYO INTERNATIONAL CORPORATION
287 Northern Blvd.
Great Neck, NY 11021
Tel.: 516-466-0911 **NY**
Fax: 516-466-0922
Year Founded: 1976
Approx.Sls.: $30,000,000
Emp.: 400
Import Export
Manufacture, Market & Sell Potentrometers, Miniature Lamps, Speakers, Cables, Switches & Plugs
S.I.C.: 3643; 3613; 3645; 3651; 3679; 3823
Mark A. Rubin *(Pres.)*
Howard Rubin *(Exec. V.P.)*
Principal(s):
Mark A. Rubin
Howard Rubin

No. of Mfg. Plants/Facilities: 12
No. of U.S. Offices: 1
No. of Foreign Offices: 12

Computer Systems/Hardware:
IBM

Outside Service Firm(s):

Chase Manhattan Bank, N.A.*(Major Banking Relationship)*
White Plains, NY

SHOKAI FAR EAST LTD.
9 Elena Ct.
Peekskill, NY 10566
Tel.: 914-736-3500
Fax: 914-681-0807
Year Founded: 1960
Approx.Sls.: $20,000,000
Emp.: 35
Mfr. of OEM Components For Industry
S.I.C.: 5065
Michael B. Rubin *(Pres.)*
Joe Weber *(V.P.)*
Larry Koner *(Sls. Mgr.)*

SHONAC CORPORATION
1675 Watkins Rd.
Columbus, OH 43207
Tel.: 614-497-1199
Fax: 614-497-1356
Year Founded: 1969
Sales Range: $100-499 Million
Emp.: 1,500
Retail Shoe Store
S.I.C.: 5661
Stephen Nacht *(Pres.)*
John Rossler *(V.P.-Fin., Treas. & Asst. Sec.)*
Margaret McMahon *(Dir.-Pub. Rels. & Personnel)*
Michael Levison *(Adv. Mgr.)*
Sandra Edmond *(Dir.-Real Estate)*

Computer Systems/Hardware:
IBM System 38

Outside Service Firm(s):

Coopers & Lybrand*(Auditors)*
100 E. Broad St.
Columbus, OH 43215

BancOhio National Bank*(Major Banking Relationship)*
Columbus, OH

SHOOK NATIONAL CORPORATION
225 Lynwood St.
Dayton, OH 45405
Tel.: 513-222-0186 **OH**
Fax: 513-222-0513
Year Founded: 1922
Assets: $36,000,000
Liabilities: $28,000,000
Net Worth: $8,000,000
Approx.Sls.: $101,000,000
Emp.: 300
Fiscal Year-end: 12/31/91
Holding Company
S.I.C.: 6719; 1541; 1542; 1629
Harry F. Gaeke *(Chm. Bd., Chief Exec. & Fin. Officer)*
Clarence J. Bittner *(Pres. & Chief Oper. Officer)*
Hugh E. Wall, Jr. *(Sec.)*

No. of Mfg. Plants/Facilities: 2
No. of U.S. Offices: 1

Outside Service Firm(s):

Deloitte & Touche*(Auditors)*
1700 Courthouse Plaza NE
Dayton, OH 45401
Tel.: 513-223-8821

Bank One*(Investment Banker)*
Kettering Tower
Dayton, OH 45401
Tel.: 513-449-8600

Coolidge, Wall, Womsley & Lombard*(Legal Firm)*
33 W. First St., Ste. 600
Dayton, OH 45402
Tel.: 513-223-8177
Fax: 513-223-6705

Bank One*(Major Banking Relationship)*
Kettering Tower
Dayton, OH 45401
Tel.: 513-449-8600

Harry Van Hopkins*(Pension Manager)*
Dayton, OH

Division:

Shook, Inc. **(1)**
440 Hunter Ave.
Dayton, OH 45404
Tel.: 513-224-8356
Fax: 513-222-0186
Emp.: 300
Construction Company
S.I.C.: 1541; 1542; 1629
Harry F. Gaeke *(Chm. Bd. & Chief Fin. Officer)*
Clarence J. Bittner *(Pres. & Chief Oper. Officer)*
Vincent Corrado *(V.P.)*
James D. Trittschuh *(V.P.)*

SHOPKO STORES, INC.
700 Pilgrim Way
Green Bay, WI 54307-9060
Tel.: 414-497-2211 **MN**
Fax: 414-496-4133
Year Founded: 1962
Approx.Sls.: $1,700,000,000
Emp.: 17,400
Fiscal Year-end: 2/29/92
Import
General Department Store
S.I.C.: 5311
Michael W. Wright *(Chm.)*
William J. Tyrrell *(Vice Chm.)*
Dale Kramer *(Pres. & Chief Exec. Officer)*
Mark Kennedy *(Sr. V.P. & Chief Fin. Officer)*
Tom Hendra *(Sr. V.P.-Mdsg.)*
Gene Bankers *(V.P.-Communications & Investor Rels.)*

SHORELINE PRODUCTS, INC.
921 W. Mayfield Rd.
Arlington, TX 76015
Mailing Address:
P.O. Box 848,
Arlington, TX 76004
Tel.: 817-465-1351
Fax: 817-472-9638
Year Founded: 1985
Emp.: 200
Export
Trailer Mfrs.; Shoreline Boat Trailers, Highlander Small Boat Trailer, Comet Motorcycle, Utility & Snowmobile Trailers
S.I.C.: 3523; 3799; 5012; 5084
Satish Kupta *(Co-Chm. Bd.)*
Denesh Shak *(Co-Chm. Bd.)*
Frank Porco *(Exec. V.P.)*
Dave Ronchetto *(V.P.-Sls. & Adv.)*

Outside Service Firm(s):

KPMG Peat Marwick*(Auditors)*
301 Commerce, Ste. 2500
Ft. Worth, TX 76102
Tel.: 817-335-2655

National Bank*(Major Banking Relationship)*
Arlington, TX

SHOWELL FARMS, INC.
Pitts Rd.
Showell, MD 21862
Mailing Address:
P.O. Box 158,
Showell, MD 21862
Tel.: 410-352-5411
Fax: 401-352-5411, Ext. 221
Year Founded: 1908
Approx.Sls.: $275,000,000
Emp.: 3,900
Fiscal Year-end: 11/30/90
Export
Processor Dressed Poultry
S.I.C.: 2015
Terry Baker *(Chief Exec. Officer)*
Alan Guerrieri *(Pres.)*
Dan McCaigue *(Chief Fin. Officer)*
Michael Guerrieri *(V.P.-Sls. & Mktg.)*
Scott Guerrieri *(V.P.-Further Processed Sls.)*
Curt Hickman *(V.P.-Admin.)*
Marsha Joseph *(Controller)*
Pat Lynch *(Dir.-Pur.)*
Martine Duvall *(Mgr.-Adv. & Public Rels.)*

No. of Mfg. Plants/Facilities: 4

Outside Service Firm(s):

Rose, Feldman, Feinsod & Skehan*(Auditors)*
New York, NY

Chemical Banking Corp.*(Major Banking Relationship)*
277 Park Ave.
New York, NY 10041
Tel.: 212-310-6407
Fax: 212-310-4526

Subsidiaries:

Cookin' Good Distribution Ctr. **(1)**
4712 W. Ohio Ave.
Tampa, FL 33614
Tel.: 813-872-8798

Cookin' Good Distribution Ctr. **(1)**
210 E. Story Rd., Drawer 847
Ocoee, FL 34761
Tel.: 407-656-2631

Showell Farms, Inc. **(1)**
P.O. Box 1040
De Funiak Springs, FL 32433
Tel.: 904-892-3151

Showell Farms, Inc. **(1)**
808 Ross Circle S.E.
Dothan, AL 36303
Tel.: 205-792-4151

Showell Farms, Inc. **(1)**
P.O. Box 8
Staley, NC 27355
Tel.: 919-622-4251

Showell Farms, Inc. **(1)**
P.O. Box 248
Concord, NC 28026
Tel.: 704-788-2403

SHUFORD MILLS, INC.
P.O. Box 2228
Hickory, NC 28603
Tel.: 704-328-2131
Fax: 704-328-8650
Year Founded: 1880
Approx.Sls.: $180,000,000
Emp.: 2,000
Fiscal Year-end: 12/31/91
Import Export
Mfr. Cotton & Synthetic Yarns, Twine & Cord, Pressure Sensitive Tape
S.I.C.: 2281; 2298; 2672
A. Pope Shuford *(Pres. & Chief Exec. Officer)*
Donald L. Cook *(Chief Fin. Officer & Treas.)*
Jerry R. McIntosh *(Chief Admin. Officer)*
Tom Guthrie *(V.P.)*
Bob Harris *(V.P.)*
Glenn Hilton *(V.P.)*
Robert E. Holland *(V.P.-Services)*
W. H. Little, Jr. *(V.P.)*
Charles Shuford *(V.P.)*
Dave Taylor *(V.P.)*
James R. Gibson *(Dir.-Mngmt. Information Systems)*
Principal(s):
A. Pope Shuford

No. of Foreign Offices: 1

Computer Systems/Hardware:
IBM System AS 400

Outside Service Firm(s):

George G. Scott & Co.*(Auditors)*
Hickory, NC

Aetna Life & Casualty*(Group Insurer)*
151 Farmington Avenue
Hartford, CT 06156
Tel.: 203-273-2128
Fax: 203-729-4295

NationsBank Carolinas*(Major Banking Relationship)*
Hickory, NC

First Union National Bank*(Pension Manager)*
Hickory, NC

SHUGART CORPORATION
9292 Jeronimo Rd.
Irvine, CA 92718
Tel.: 714-770-1100 **DE**
Fax: 714-859-4960
Year Founded: 1986
Assets: $60,000,000
Liabilities: $50,000,000
Net Worth: $10,000,000
Sales Range: $80-99 Million
Emp.: 450
Export
Manufacture of Disk Drives, Test Equipment, Terminals & Tape Drives
S.I.C.: 3572; 3575; 3577; 3825
Dennis Narlinger *(Chm., Pres. & Chief Exec. Officer)*
Steven Alvey *(V.P.-Fin. & Opers.)*
Steve Genuser *(V.P.-Mktg. & Sls.)*
Steve Vertun *(V.P.-Sls.)*
Wayne Schrader *(Dir.-Pur.)*
Marty Walchak *(Dir.-Data Processing)*
Farzin Alavi *(Mgr.-Quality Control)*
Uri Kullman *(Mgr.-Res. & Devel.)*
John Woods *(Mgr.-Personnel)*

No. of Mfg. Plants/Facilities: 3
No. of U.S. Offices: 3
No. of Foreign Offices: 3

Computer Systems/Hardware:
Hewlett-Packard

Outside Service Firm(s):

Deloitte & Touche*(Auditors)*
695 Town Center Dr.
Costa Mesa, CA 92626
Tel.: 714-436-7100

BankAmerica Corp.*(Major Banking Relationship)*
Anaheim, CA

McKittrick, Jackson, DeMarco & Peckenpaugh*(Legal Firm)*
Newport Beach, CA

Subsidiary:

Kennedy Company **(1)**
5801 Ayala Ave.
Irwindale, CA 91706
Tel.: 818-334-4333 (100%)
Emp.: 200
Manufacture of Computer Tape Drives
S.I.C.: 3577
Dennis Narlinger *(Pres.)*
Steve Genuser *(V.P.-Mktg. & Sls.)*
Steve Alvey *(Chief Oper. Officer)*
Wayne Schrader *(Dir.-Pur.)*

SHURE BROTHERS INCORPORATED
222 Hartrey Ave.
Evanston, IL 60202-3696
Tel.: 708-866-2200
Tel.: 800-25-SHURE **IL**
Telex: 4330191
Fax: 708-866-2279
Year Founded: 1925
Export
Wired and Wireless Professional Microphones for Sound Reinforcement, Broadcasting, Recording, Hands-Free Cellular, Land Mobile, and Voice Input/Output Applications; Powered and Portable Mixers and Amplifiers for ENG, EFP, and Sound Reinforcement; Teleconferencing Systems; High-fidelity Phonograph Catridges and Styli; AMS Automatic Microphone Mixing Systems; Related Audio Circuitry Components
S.I.C.: 3651; 3675
S.N. Shure *(Chm. Bd.)*
J. Kogen *(Pres.)*
H. Amend *(V.P.-Mfg.)*
T. Burks *(V.P.-Intl. Mktg. & Sls.)*
R. Gilbert *(V.P.-Fin.)*
L. Gunter *(V.P.-Teleconferencing)*
B. Jakobs *(V.P.-Engrng.)*
J. Shea *(V.P.-Personnel)*
J. Furst *(Assoc. V.P.-Total Quality)*
Nancy A. Calvert *(Dir.-Adv. & Pub. Rels.)*
A. Hershner *(Dir.-Sls.)*
H. Morgan *(Dir.-Teleconferencing Mktg. & Sls.)*
M. Pettersen *(Dir.-Mixer Prods.)*
J. Phelan *(Dir.-Intl. Mktg. & Sls.)*
S. Schroeder *(Dir.-Microphone Prods.)*
A. Shirley *(Dir.-Technical Mkts.)*
J. Kontney *(Mgr.-Trade Shows/Artist Rels.)*
F. Rumney *(Mgr.-Domestic Pur.)*

No. of Mfg. Plants/Facilities: 2
No. of U.S. Offices: 1
No. of Foreign Offices: 1

Computer Systems/Hardware:
Hewlett-Packard PC

Outside Service Firm(s):

Continental Bank N. A.*(Major Banking Relationship)*
231 S. LaSalle St.
Chicago, IL 60697
Tel.: 312-828-2345
Tel.: 800-426-5754
Telex: 312-828-1783

Subsidiary:

Shure, GmbH **(1)**
Lohtorstr. 24 7100
Heilbronn, Germany
Tel.: 7131 832 21
Holding Co.
S.I.C.: 6719

SHURFINE-CENTRAL CORP.
2100 N. Mannheim Rd.
Northlake, IL 60164
Tel.: 708-681-2000
Fax: 708-681-5862
Year Founded: 1948
Assets: $29,000,000
Liabilities: $22,200,000
Net Worth: $6,800,000
Approx.Sls.: $640,000,000
Emp.: 150
Fiscal Year-end: 5/31/91
Import Export
Co-op; Procurement, Sale & Merchandising of Private Label Products for Retail Food Distributors
S.I.C.: 5141
Hillar Moore, Jr. *(Chm. Bd.)*
Paul T. Jasper *(Pres. & Chief Exec. Officer)*
Eric Stuhlmann *(V.P. & Chief Fin. Officer)*
David LaPlante *(V.P.-Sls. & Mdse.)*
Wally Struffer *(V.P.-Produce)*
Carole Lemmer *(Controller & Dir.-Human Resources)*
James Champelli *(Dir.-Data Processing)*
Donna DiMaso *(Mgr.-Cust. Rels.)*

No. of Mfg. Plants/Facilities: 1

Computer Systems/Hardware:
IBM System 38

Outside Service Firm(s):

Grant Thornton*(Auditors)*
700 One Prudential Plaza, 130 East Randolph St.
Chicago, IL 60601
Tel.: 312-856-0200
Fax: 312-565-4719

Transamerica Occidental Insurance Co.*(Group Insurer)*
P.O. Box 30253,
Los Angeles, CA 90099

McDermott, Will & Emery*(Legal Firm)*
227 W. Monroe St.
Chicago, IL 60606-5096
Tel.: 312-372-2000

Harris Trust & Savings Bank*(Major Banking Relationship)*
111 W. Monroe St.
Chicago, IL 60690
Tel.: 312-461-2265
Tel.: 800-858-0840

Metropolitan Life Insurance Co.*(Pension Manager)*
One Madison Ave.
New York, NY 10010-3690
Tel.: 215-578-9292

THE SICO COMPANY
15 Mt. Joy St.
Mount Joy, PA 17552
Mailing Address:
P.O. Box 302,
Mount Joy, PA 17552
Tel.: 717-653-1411 **DE**
Fax: 717-653-2302
Year Founded: 1876
Assets: $21,900,000
Earnings: $1,800,000
Liabilities: $12,300,000
Net Worth: $9,600,000
Approx.Sls.: $115,000,000
Emp.: 350
Fiscal Year-end: 5/31/91
Automotive Dealer; Service Stations; Wholesale Gas
S.I.C.: 5983; 5541; 5172
Franklin R. Eichler *(Pres. & Chief Exec. Officer)*
Michael Rees *(V.P.-Mktg.)*
Charles Ricedorf *(V.P.-Admin. & Opers.)*
Craig Herr *(Controller)*
Harrison Diehl, Jr. *(Treas.)*
Darlene F. Halterman *(Asst. Treas. & Sec.)*
Rodney Hershey *(Dir.-Data Processing)*

Computer Systems/Hardware:
Digital

Outside Service Firm(s):

Stockton, Bates & Co.*(Auditors)*
Philadelphia, PA

Travelers Insurance Co.*(Commercial Insurance Carrier)*
One Tower Square
Hartford, CT 06183-6130
Tel.: 203-277-4542
Fax: 203-277-5038

Morgan, Hallgren, Crosswell & Kane*(Legal Firm)*
Lancaster, PA

Hamilton Bank*(Major Banking Relationship)*
Lancaster, PA

Philadelphia National Bank*(Major Banking Relationship)*
P.O. Box 13834, Broad & Chestnut Streets
Philadelphia, PA 19101-7618
Tel.: 215-973-8327

Philadelphia National Bank*(Pension Manager)*
Philadelphia, PA

Subsidiary:

Rollman Supply Company **(1)**
9-15 Mt. Joy St.
Mount Joy, PA 17552
Tel.: 717-653-1411

SICO INC.
7525 Cahill Rd.
Minneapolis, MN 55435
Mailing Address:
P. O. Box 1169
Minneapolis, MN 55440
Tel.: 612-941-1700
Tel.: 800-328-6138
Fax: 612-941-6737
Year Founded: 1951
Approx.Sls.: $29,000,000
Emp.: 150
Export
Mfr. of Space Saving Products; Cafeteria Tables, Stages, Risers & Conference Tables, Portable Dance Floors, Banquet Tables & Fold-In-Wall Beds, Room Service Tables
S.I.C.: 2599
Kermit Wilson *(Chm. Bd.)*
Harold Wilson *(Pres.)*
Andrew J. Shea *(Exec. V.P.)*
Harry Levey *(V.P.-Mfg.)*
Richard Bue *(V.P.-Engrng.)*
Keith Dahlen *(V.P.-Fin.)*
Charles Williamson *(Adv. Mgr.)*

SICOLA MARTIN KOONS FRANK, INC.
6850 Austin Ctr. Blvd., Ste. 270
Austin, TX 78731
Tel.: 512-343-0264
Fax: 512-343-0659
Year Founded: 1982
Approx.Billings: $12,000,000
Emp.: 26
Technology, Food, Packaged Goods, Promo., Direct Mktg., Merchandising, Financial & Healthcare
Tom Sicola *(Chm. Bd., Pres. & New Bus. Contact)*
Steve Martin *(Exec. V.P., Creative Dir.)*
George Frank *(Exec. V.P., Chief Oper. Officer & Treas.)*

Sicola Martin Koons Frank, Inc.—(Continued)

Kathy Field *(Radio & TV Production Dir.)*

Computer Systems/Hardware:
Macintosh

SID TOOL CO. INC.
151 Sunnyside Blvd.
Plainview, NY 11803
Tel.: 516-349-0500
Tel.: 800-645-7270 NY
Fax: 516-349-0265
Year Founded: 1941
Approx.Sls.: $80,000,000
Emp.: 625
Import Export
Wholesale Cutting & Precision Tools, Abrasives, Machinery, Material Handling Equipment & Machine Shop Supplies
S.I.C.: 5084; 5085
Sidney Jacobson *(Chm. Bd.)*
Mitchell Jacobson *(Pres., Treas. & Chief Exec. Officer)*
James Schroeder *(Exec. V.P. & Chief Oper. Officer)*
Barbara Schwartz *(V.P.-Human Resources)*
Thomas Eccleston *(V.P.)*
Steve Harmin *(Mgr.-Sls.)*
Glen Fisher *(Mgr.-Quality Assurance)*
David Gillies *(Mgr.-MIS)*
Jean Haass *(Dir.-Mktg.)*

No. of Mfg. Plants/Facilities: 26
No. of U.S. Offices: 26

Computer Systems/Hardware:
IBM System 38

Outside Service Firm(s):

Arthur Andersen & Co.*(Auditors)*
Melville, NY

Rosenman & Colin*(Legal Firm)*
575 Madison Ave.
New York, NY 10022
Tel.: 212-940-8800

National Westminster Bank plc*(Major Banking Relationship)*
100 Jericho Quadrangle
Jericho, NY 11753

Sidal Aluminum Corp.
(Name Changed To Hoogovens Aluminum Corp.)

SIDDALL, MATUS & COUGHTER, INC. ADVERTISING & PUBLIC RELATIONS
700 Ross Bldg., 801 E. Main St.
Richmond, VA 23219
Tel.: 804-788-8011
Fax: 804-782-9792
Year Founded: 1975
Approx.Billings: $18,000,000
Emp.: 26
National Pub. Rels., Financial Mktg. & Adv., Real Estate Dev., Business-to-Business Communications & Corp. Adv.
John N. Siddall *(Chm. Bd. & Chief Exec. Officer)*
Peter J. Coughter, Jr. *(Pres.)*
Reid P. Carter *(V.P., Mktg. & Research Dir.)*
Elizabeth Longstreet *(V.P., Chief Fin. Officer)*
Bill Hamby *(V.P., Dir. Pub. Rels.)*

Siebel/Mohr

SIEBEL/MOHR, INC.
800 Third Ave.
New York, NY 10022
Tel.: 212-593-0500
Fax: 212-888-7964
Year Founded: 1963
Approx.Billings: $41,000,000
Emp.: 60
Sales Promotion & Graphic Design
Gretchen Siebel *(Pres., Chief Oper. Officer)*
Marc Bressler *(V.P., Dir., Mktg. Services)*
Pam Chan *(Comptroller)*

SIEG COMPANY
400 Main St., Ste.300
Davenport, IA 52801
Tel.: 319-323-3641
Tel.: 800-747-7434 IA
Fax: 319-323-2901
Year Founded: 1912
Assets: $30,400,000
Liabilities: $18,300,000
Net Worth: $12,100,000
Approx.Sls.: $46,300,000
Emp.: 640
Fiscal Year-end: 3/31/92
Wholesale Distribution of Automotive Supplies & Parts; Management of Shopping Centers, Property Operation Only
S.I.C.: 5013; 6512
Madis Sulg *(Chm. Bd. & Chief Exec. Officer)*
Dean Dearking *(V.P.-Admin. & Corp. Sec.)*
Eric Barsness *(V.P. & Div. Gen. Mgr.)*
Steve Brandon *(V.P. & Div. Gen. Mgr.)*
Ken Sorn *(V.P. & Div. Gen. Mgr.)*
Rick BurKamper *(Controller)*
Tom Hanson *(Gen. Counsel)*

Outside Service Firm(s):

Ernst & Young*(Auditors)*
317 6th Ave., Ste. 1100
Des Moines, IA 50309
Tel.: 515-243-2727

Hanson, Bjork & Russell*(Legal Firm)*
1300 Des Moines Bldg.,
Des Moines, IA 50309

Brenton First National Bank*(Major Banking Relationship)*
Davenport, IA

Firstar Bank Davenport, N.A.*(Major Banking Relationship)*
Davenport, IA

Boatmen's National Bank of Des Moines*(Pension Manager)*
Des Moines, IA

Branch:

Sieg Rockford Co. **(1)**
716 N. Madison St.
Rockford, IL 61107
Tel.: 815-964-8631
Wholesale Distribution of Supplies & Parts
S.I.C.: 5013
Ken Sorn *(Mgr.)*

SIEGEL CORP.
2901 Stanley Ave.
Fort Worth, TX 76110
Tel.: 817-921-3081
Fax: 817-921-2572
Manufacture Kitchen Cabinets
S.I.C.: 6719; 2434
Martin D. Siegel *(Pres.)*
Evelyn Siegel *(Sec.)*
Terry Siegel *(Treas.)*

Outside Service Firm(s):

Schreier & Co.*(Auditors)*
Fort Worth, TX

Wynn, Brown, Mack, Renfro & Thompson*(Legal Firm)*
309 W. Seventh St.
Ft. Worth, TX 76102
Tel.: 817-429-0551

First National Bank of Fort Worth*(Major Banking Relationship)*
One Burnett Plaza
Ft. Worth, TX 76102
Tel.: 817-390-6161

Subsidiary:

Legis Corporation **(1)**
2901 Stanley Ave.
Ft. Worth, TX 76109
Tel.: 817-921-3081
Fax: 817-921-2572
Approx.Sls.: $5,000,000
Emp.: 133
Fiscal Year-end: 12/31/90
Mfr. of Kitchen Cabinets
S.I.C.: 2434
Martin D. Siegel *(Pres.)*
Evelyn Siegel *(Sec.)*
Terry Siegel *(Treas.)*

Siegel & Gale

SIEGEL & GALE
1185 Ave. of the Americas
New York, NY 10036
Tel.: 212-730-0101
Fax: 212-730-1462
Approx.Billings: $22,000,000
Adv. Agency Specializing in Corp., Fin. & Issue Adv., Corp. Identity, Language Simplification
S.I.C.: 7311
Alan Siegel *(Chm. & Chief Exec. Officer)*
Ken Morris *(Pres.)*
Peter Swerdloff *(Exec. V.P., Adv. Dir.)*
Charles Reisler *(Sr. V.P., Acct. Mngmt.)*

HENRY I. SIEGEL COMPANY, INC.
1372 Broadway
New York, NY 10018
Tel.: 212-302-6400 NY
Fax: 212-819-9172
Year Founded: 1945
Emp.: 5,000
Women's Wearing Apparel
S.I.C.: 2337; 2331; 2335; 2339
Burton M. Rosenberg *(Pres.)*
Robert Luehrs *(V.P.)*
John Chin *(Treas.)*
Stuart Jaeger *(Controller)*

Computer Systems/Hardware:
IBM 3081

Outside Service Firm(s):

BDO Seidman*(Auditors)*
1430 Broadway
New York, NY
Tel.: 212-765-7500

Divisions:

Women's Clothing Division **(1)**
16 E. 34th St.
New York, NY 10016
Tel.: 212-689-2323
S.I.C.: 2311
Dave Moore *(Chief Opr. Officer)*

Women's Sportswear Division **(1)**
16 E. 34th St.
New York, NY 10016
Tel.: 212-689-2323
S.I.C.: 2337
Robert Luehrs *(Chief Opr. Officer)*

SIEMER MILLING COMPANY
111 W. Main St.
Teutopolis, IL 62467
Mailing Address:
P.O. Box 670,
Teutopolis, IL 62467
Tel.: 217-857-3131
Tel.: 800-826-1065 IL
Fax: 217-857-3092
Year Founded: 1882
Approx.Sls.: $75,000,000
Emp.: 130
Mfr. Soft Wheat Flour
S.I.C.: 2041
Richard C. Siemer *(Pres.)*
Mike Morrissey *(Exec. V.P.)*
Luella Griffin *(V.P.)*
Robert Goldstein *(V.P.-Opers.)*
Harold Kremer *(V.P.-Special Projects)*
Vernon Tegeler *(V.P.-Prod.)*
Constance Barr *(Asst. V.P.-Sls. & Mktg.)*
David Brumleve *(Chief Fin. Officer, Treas., & Sec.)*
Joyce Stock *(Controller)*
Paula Kahrhoff *(Dir.-Pur.)*
Patti Winter *(Dir.-Personnel)*
Principal(s):
Richard C. Siemer

Computer Systems/Hardware:
Compaq PC Network

Outside Service Firm(s):

McGladrey & Pullen*(Auditors)*
Champaign, IL

Millers Mutual Insurance*(Commercial Insurance Carrier)*
Alton, IL

Parker, Siemer, Austin & Resch*(Legal Firm)*
Effingham, IL

FBS Agriculture Credit*(Major Banking Relationship)*
Denver, CO

Subsidary:

Hodgson Mill, Inc. **(1)**
Industrial Park
Gainesville, MO 65655
Tel.: 417-679-4651
Fax: 417-679-4537
Emp.: 30
Whole Grain Mill & Mix Plant
S.I.C.: 2041
Richard C. Siemer *(Pres.)*
David L. Brumleue *(Treas. & Sec.)*
Don Haile *(Gen. Mgr.)*

THE SIERRA CAPITAL COMPANIES
455 Market St., Ste. 1690
San Francisco, CA 941-5
Tel.: 415-543-9009
Fax: 415-543-0660
Year Founded: 1980
Approx.Sls.: $5,000,000
Emp.: 15
Real Estate Asset Management
S.I.C.: 6531
Thomas B. Swartz *(Chm. Bd. & Chief Exec. Officer)*
Dennis R. Konczal *(Pres.)*

Computer Systems/Hardware:
Hewlett-Packard

Outside Service Firm(s):

Arthur Andersen & Co.*(Auditors)*
Spear Street Tower, One Market Plaza, Ste. 3500
San Francisco, CA 94105
Tel.: 415-546-8200

Pettit & Martin*(Legal Firm)*
600 Montgomery St.
San Francisco, CA 94111
Tel.: 415-434-4000

Citibank N.A.*(Major Banking Relationship)*
San Francisco, CA

Subsidiary:

Sierra Capital Realty Services **(1)**
One Kaiser Plaza Ste. 305
Oakland, CA 94612
Tel.: 510 444 3132
Fax: 510 444 3053
Acquisition, Management & Disposition Of Commercial Real Estate
S.I.C.: 6531

SIERRA PACIFIC INDUSTRIES
P.O. Box 496028
Redding, CA 96049
Tel.: 916-275-8812 **CA**
Approx.Sls.: $270,000,000
Emp.: 2,000
Fiscal Year-end: 12/31/90
Lumber & Wood Products, Mouldings
S.I.C.: 2499; 2431; 2421
A.A. Emmerson *(Pres.)*
David Dun *(Sec. & Gen. Counsel)*
Ray Lowry *(Controller)*
Richard L. Smith *(Dir.)*

Outside Service Firm(s):

Ernst & Young*(Auditors)*
555 California St., Ste. 3000
San Francisco, CA 94104
Tel.: 415-951-3000

Divisions:

Sierra Pacific Industries-Arcata Division **(1)**
Samoa Road
Arcata, CA 95521
Tel.: 707-443-3111
Lumber Mfg.
S.I.C.: 2499
Gordon Amos *(Chief Oper. Officer)*

Sierra Pacific Industries-Burney Division **(1)**
Burney, CA 96013
Tel.: 916-335-3788
Lumber Mfg.
Dennis Gomez *(Chief Oper. Officer)*

Sierra Pacific Industries-Hayfork Division **(1)**
Hayfork, CA 96041
Tel.: 916-628-5291
Lumber Mfg.
S.I.C.: 2499
Ken Armstrong *(Plant Mgr.)*

Sierra Pacific Industries-Loyalton Division **(1)**
Loyalton, CA 96118
Tel.: 916-993-4402
Lumber Mfg.
S.I.C.: 2499
Dan Pipkins *(Gen. Mgr.)*

Sierra Pacific Industries-Millwork Division, Red Bluff Plant **(1)**
11400 Reading Rd.
Red Bluff, CA 96080
Tel.: 916-529-5108
Mfrs. Millwork
S.I.C.: 2431
Kendall Pearson *(Gen. Mgr.)*

Sierra Pacific Industries-Millwork Division, Richfield Plant **(1)**
North End of Alameda Rd.
Richfield, CA 96021
Tel.: 916-824-2474
Mfrs. Millwork
S.I.C.: 2431
Mike Schmidt *(Gen. Mgr.)*

Sierra Pacific Industries-Quincy Division **(1)**
1538 Lee Rd.
Quincy, CA 95971
Tel.: 916-283-2820
Lumber Mfg.
S.I.C.: 2499
George Coulter *(Plant Mgr.)*

Sierra Pacific Industries-Redding Division **(1)**
Redding, CA 96001
Tel.: 916-275-1523
Lumber Mfg.
S.I.C.: 2499
George Emerson *(Plant Mgr.)*

Sierra Pacific Industries-Susanville Division **(1)**
End of Sunkist Dr.
Susanville, CA 96130
Tel.: 916-257-2158
Lumber Mfg.
S.I.C.: 2499
Randy Lilburn *(Plant Mgr.)*

SIERRACIN CORPORATION
12780 San Fernando Rd.
Sylmar, CA 91342-3796
Mailing Address:
P.O. Box 9200,
Sylmar, CA 91392-9200
Tel.: 818-362-6802 **DE**
Fax: 818-362-0603
Year Founded: 1952
Assets: $54,584,000
Earnings: $3,116,000
Liabilities: $39,365,000
Net Worth: $15,219,000
Approx.Rev.: $59,280,000
Emp.: 700
Fiscal Year-end: 12/31/90
Import Export
Mfr. of High Technology Glass & Plastic Transparent Products; Precision Servo Motors & Other Components for Aerospace Ground Transportation, Industrial & Commercial Markets
S.I.C.: 3229; 3089; 3728; 2891; 2899; 3621
Christoph Tribull *(Chm. Bd., Pres., Chief Exec. & Chief Oper. Officer)*
Gary Roberts *(Sr. V.P., Chief Fin. Officer, Admin. & Sec.)*
Gary Atkinson *(Controller)*
Patricia A. Sprouse *(Gen. Counsel & Asst. Sec.)*
Eugene Cantreau *(Dir.-Personnel)*

Outside Service Firm(s):

Price Waterhouse*(Auditors)*
5950 Canoga Ave.
Woodland Hills, CA 91367
Tel.: 818-704-1117
Fax: 818-704-5354

California Federal Savings & Loan Association*(Major Banking Relationship)*
5700 Wilshire Blvd
Los Angeles, CA

Divisions:

Harrison Div. **(1)**
3020 Empire Ave.
Burbank, CA 91504
Tel.: 818-842-2131
Mfr. of Metal Seals & Hydraulic Fittings
S.I.C.: 3728
Richard Paul *(Pres.)*
Gary Atkinson *(Controller)*
Jeff Ramclam *(Mgr.-Pur.)*

Magnedyne Div. **(1)**
2258 Rutherford Rd.
Carlsbad, CA 92008
Tel.: 619-438-3321
Mfr. of Electric Motors
S.I.C.: 3621
David Mighdoll *(Pres.)*
Art Barter *(Controller)*
Pam Smith *(Mgr.-Pur.)*

Subsidiary:

Sierracin/Sylmar Corporation **(1)**
12780 San Fernando Rd.
Sylmar, CA 91342
Tel.: 818-362-6711
Flight Deck Windshields; Canopies
S.I.C.: 3728
William Brewer *(Pres.)*
Chas. Morgan *(V.P.-Mktg.)*
Paul Grossman *(V.P.-Controller)*
Barry Schoanvel *(Dir.-Pur.)*

THE SIESEL COMPANY
(Sub. of The Softness Group, Inc.)
381 Park Ave. South, 5th Fl.
New York, NY 10016
Tel.: 212-696-2444
Fax: 212-696-2466
Year Founded: 1927
Approx.Billings: $15,000,000
John Softness *(Chief Exec. Officer)*
Jack Jackness *(V.P.)*
Richard Stewart *(Adv. Dir.)*

SIGAL CONSTRUCTION
3299 K Street N.W.
Washington, DC 20007
Tel.: 202-944-6600
Fax: 203-333-3468
Year Founded: 1977
Approx.Sls.: $100,000,000
Emp.: 75
Full Service Construction Company
S.I.C.: 1629
Gerald R. Sigal *(Chm. Bd.)*
Joseph A. Turner, III *(Pres.)*

Computer Systems/Hardware:
Wang VS 85

Outside Service Firm(s):

Arthur Andersen & Co.*(Auditors)*
1666 K Street, N.W.
Washington, DC 20006

Melrod, Redman, Gartland*(Legal Firm)*
1801 K St., N.W., Ste. 1100
Washington, DC 20006
Tel.: 202-822-5300

Sovran Bank*(Major Banking Relationship)*
Washington, DC

SIGAL/ZUCKERMAN CO.
2 Wisconsin Circle, #800
Chevy Chase, MD 20815
Tel.: 301-657-8300 **MD**
Fax: 301-657-8083
Year Founded: 1981
Approx.Sls.: $84,000,000
Emp.: 100
Fiscal Year-end: 12/31/90
Subdivider & Developer
S.I.C.: 6552
Ellen V. Sigal *(Chief Exec. Officer)*
Shelton Zuckerman *(Pres.)*
Charles A. Gravely *(Sec.)*

SIGALLO, LTD.
14 W. 33rd St.
New York, NY 10001
Tel.: 212-239-1505 **NJ**
Fax: 212-279-2206
Approx.Sls.: $35,000,000
Emp.: 400
Wholesale & Import Men's & Boy's Clothing & Furnishings
S.I.C.: 5136
Steven F. Segal *(Pres.)*
Mark Press *(V.P.-Sls.)*
Alvin H. Loux *(V.P.-Fin.)*
Tracy Cottrell *(Office Mgr.)*

SIGLER & REEVES
3451 N. 34th Ave.
Phoenix, AZ 85017
Mailing Address:
P.O. Box 6630,
Phoenix, AZ 85005
Tel.: 602-272-5541 **NM**
Fax: 602-272-7832
Year Founded: 1969
Sales Range: $40-59 Million
Emp.: 110
Wholesale Heating & Air Conditioning Equipment & Supplies
S.I.C.: 5075
Russell Sigler *(Chm. Bd.)*
Thomas Reeves *(Pres.)*
Jack Sigler *(V.P.)*
Robert Osborn *(Controller)*

Computer Systems/Hardware:
DEC VAX 8200

Outside Service Firm(s):

McGladrey & Pullen*(Auditors)*
Phoenix, AZ

Carson, Messinger, Elliott, Laughlin & Ragan*(Legal Firm)*
Phoenix, AZ

LaSalle National Bank*(Major Banking Relationship)*
135 S. LaSalle St.
Chicago, IL 60690
Tel.: 312-443-2000

SIGMAN MEAT CO. INC.
6000 W. 54th Ave.
Arvada, CO 80002
Mailing Address:
P.O. Box 5292 T.A.
Denver, CO 80217
Tel.: 303-424-5531 **CO**
Fax: 303-420-0760
Year Founded: 1938
Assets: $2,362,000
Earnings: $412,000
Liabilities: $1,355,000
Net Worth: $1,007,000
Approx.Sls.: $18,000,000
Emp.: 120
Fiscal Year-end: 10/31/88
Food & Meat Packers & Processors
S.I.C.: 5147; 2011; 2013
Graig Weisbart *(Chm. Bd.)*
Mehdi Shirazi *(Pres. & Chief Exec. Officer)*
George R. Negomeir *(V.P.-Fin., Treas. & Sec.)*
Larry Barker *(Dir.-Pur.)*
Jack Paison *(Dir.-Mngmt. Information Systems)*
Marcella Lendill *(Mgr.-Meetings Plng.)*
Principal(s):
Graig Weisbart
Mehdi Shirazi

No. of Mfg. Plants/Facilities: 1
No. of U.S. Offices: 1

Computer Systems/Hardware:
Honeywell Level 62

Outside Service Firm(s):

Deloitte & Touche*(Auditors)*
1560 Broadway, Ste. 1800
Denver, CO 80202-5626
Tel.: 303-837-3000
Fax: 303-825-0567

Allendale Mutual Insurance Co.*(Commercial Insurance Carrier)*
1301 Atwood Ave.
Johnston, RI 02919
Tel.: 401-275-3000

James Benefits*(Group Insurer)*
Phoenix, AZ

First Interstate Bank*(Major Banking Relationship)*
Denver, CO
Tel.: 303-293-5456

Lakeside National Bank*(Major Banking Relationship)*
Wheat Ridge, CO

G. A. Walker & Associates*(Pension Manager)*
Arvada, CO 8002

SIGNET INDUSTRIES
17085 Masonic
Fraser, MI 48026
Tel.: 313-296-2000 **MI**

Signet Industries—(Continued)

Fax: 313-296-7483
Approx.Sls.: $33,500,000
Emp.: 500
Manufacture Plastic Automotive Trim & Parts
S.I.C.: 3089; 3465
Charles Bailey *(Pres. & Chief Exec. Officer)*
Charles Bailey, Jr. *(V.P.-Sls.)*
Bill Wong *(Controller)*

Outside Service Firm(s):

Joseph P. Moceri & Co.*(Auditors)*
Detroit, MI

Comerica Bank*(Major Banking Relationship)*
211 W. Fort St.
Detroit, MI 48226
Tel.: 313-222-3300

SIGNIFICS, INC.
28 Prince St.
Rochester, NY 14607
Tel.: 716-271-2622
Fax: 716-442-5079
Year Founded: 1977
Approx.Billings: $12,400,000
Emp.: 20
Healthcare, Photographic & Electronic Imaging, Telecommunications, Financial Services
Douglas U. Baker *(Pres. & Creative Dir.)*
Janice B. Chen *(Exec. V.P.)*

Computer Systems/Hardware:
Novell, IBM, Apple

SILGAN CORPORATION
4 Landmark Sq., Ste. 301
Stamford, CT 06901
Tel.: 203-975-7110
Fax: 203-975-7902
Approx.Sls.: $410,000,000
Emp.: 8
Holding Company; Metal Cans & Plastic Bottles
S.I.C.: 6719; 3411; 3085
D. Greg Horrigan *(Chm. Bd. & Chief Exec. Officer)*
R. Phillip Silver *(Pres.)*
Harley Rankin, Jr. *(Exec. V.P. & Chief Fin. Officer)*
John F. Curley *(V.P.)*
James S. Hoch *(V.P.)*
G. William Sisley *(Sec.)*
Sharon E. Budds *(Dir.-Admin.)*

Outside Service Firm(s):

Ernst & Young*(Auditors)*
Six Landmark Square
Stamford, CT 06901
Tel.: 203-348-3700

Connecticut National Bank*(Major Banking Relationship)*
One Landmark Square
Stamford, CT 06904
Tel.: 203-358-2000

SILICON POWER CUBE CORPORATION
6015 Obispo Ave.
Long Beach, CA 90805
Tel.: 310-634-9390
Fax: 213-630-5338
Approx.Sls.: $26,000,000
Emp.: 400
Manufacture Semiconductor Based Power Devices
S.I.C.: 3674
John Royan *(Pres.)*
Bob Fenton *(V.P.)*
Bob Borawski *(Sec.)*
Wilfred Corrigan *(Treas.)*

Outside Service Firm(s):

Coopers & Lybrand*(Auditors)*
P.O. Box 538, 800 Akron Centre Plaza
Akron, OH 44308

SILICON VALLEY DEVELOPMENT
2620 Augustine Dr., Ste. 101
Santa Clara, CA 95054
Tel.: 408-727-9300
Fax: 408-988-2368
Approx.Sls.: $11,000,000
Emp.: 163
Subdividers & Developers, Machine Tool Attachments & Accessories
S.I.C.: 6552; 3545
David Deardorf *(Chm. Bd.)*
Ted Ringle *(Pres.)*
Carolyn Fellows *(V.P.-Admin.)*
Sue La Cosse *(V.P.-Fin.)*
Don T. Arita *(Treas.)*

Outside Service Firm(s):

Sumitomo Bank*(Major Banking Relationship)*
Cupertino, CA

Subsidiaries:

Idylwild Corporation **(1)**
2620 Augustine Dr., Ste. 120
Santa Clara, CA 95054
Tel.: 408-727-9300
Real Estate Developers
S.I.C.: 6552
Sam Gelpi *(Pres.)*

Servo Products Company **(1)**
433 N. Fair Oaks Ave.
Pasadena, CA 91103
Tel.: 818-796-2460
Manufacture Machine Tools
S.I.C.: 8711
Allen Kaestle *(Pres.)*

SILLCOCKS PLASTICS INTERNATIONAL, INC.
310 Snyder Ave.
Berkeley Heights, NJ 07922
Mailing Address:
P.O. Box 605
Berkeley Heights, NJ 07922
Tel.: 908-665-0300
Tel.: 800-526-4919
Fax: 908-665-9254
Year Founded: 1910
Approx.Sls.: $12,000,000
Emp.: 150
Mfr. Printed Plastic Products
S.I.C.: 3089
John H. Herslow *(Pres.)*
Victor Berkowitz *(Exec. V.P.)*
Hank Oshiro *(Treas.)*
Yvonne Capraun *(Adv. Mgr.)*
Jim Marano *(Natl. Sls. Mgr.)*

Division:

Daylux, Inc. **(1)**
310 Snyder Ave.
Berkeley Heights, NJ 07922
Tel.: 908-665-1555
Tel.: 800-227-7971
Fax: 908-665-1856
J.H. Herslow *(Chm. Bd. & Pres.)*
Victor Berkowitz *(Exec. V.P.)*

SILVER DOLLAR CITY, INC.
Hwy. 76
Branson, MO 65616
Tel.: 417-338-2611
Fax: 417-338-8222
Year Founded: 1957
Approx.Sls.: $60,000,000
Emp.: 4,000
Import
Theme Amusement Parks, Water Parks & Campgrounds
S.I.C.: 7999; 5947; 5812; 7033
Jack Herschend *(Chm. Bd.)*
Peter Herschend *(Vice Chm. & Exec. V.P.)*
Cary Summers *(Pres. & Chief Exec. Officer)*
Ted Reed *(Sr. V.P.-Investments & Treas.)*
Ray Canady *(V.P.-Mktg.)*
Mike Miller *(V.P.-Fin.)*
Rick Todd *(V.P.-Corp. Devel.)*
Rick Baker *(Dir.-Corp. Devel.)*
Beth Etheridge *(Mgr.-Cash Mngmt.)*
Betty Rantz *(Mgr.-Employee Benefits)*
Lisa Rau *(Mgr.-Publicity)*

No. of U.S. Offices: 5

Computer Systems/Hardware:
IBM System 38

Outside Service Firm(s):

Baird, Kurtz & Dobson*(Auditors)*
Springfield, MO

A. Ronald Stewart*(Legal Firm)*
Springfield, MO

Boatmen's Trust Company*(Major Banking Relationship)*
100 North Broadway
St. Louis, MO 63102
Tel.: 314-466-2469

SILVER SPRINGS CITRUS CO-OP
15 S. Kissimmee Ave.
Ocoee, FL 34761
Tel.: 407-656-1122 **FL**
Fax: 407-656-9470
Approx.Sls.: $109,000,000
Emp.: 600
Grower, Harvester & Processor of Citrus Fruits
S.I.C.: 2033; 0174
Earl M. Crittenden *(Pres.)*
Billy C. Youngblood *(Exec. V.P. & Gen. Mgr.)*
Jean Mooney *(V.P.)*
John Rees *(Sec. & Treas.)*

Computer Systems/Hardware:
IBM 36

Outside Service Firm(s):

KPMG Peat Marwick*(Auditors)*
P.O. Box 3031, 111 N. Orange Ave., Suite 1600
Orlando, FL 32802
Tel.: 407-423-3426

SILVER STATE DISPOSAL SERVICE, INC.
(Formerly Silver State Disposal Company)
770 E. Sahara Blvd.
Las Vegas, NV 89104
Mailing Address:
P.O. Box 98508
Las Vegas, NV 89193
Tel.: 702-735-5151 **NV**
Fax: 702-735-1986
Year Founded: 1989
Approx.Sls.: $70,000,000
Emp.: 980
Fiscal Year-end: 9/30/91
Refuse Collection & Disposal Services
S.I.C.: 4953
Alfred Isola *(Chm. Bd. & Pres.)*
Joseph L. Anstett *(Chief Fin. Officer, Exec. V.P. & Sec.)*
Richard Isola *(V.P.-Opers.)*
Thomas Isola *(V.P.-Mktg. & Pub. Rels.)*
Aldo Lippetti *(V.P.-Pur.)*
William J. Anstett *(Controller)*
Shirley Gleeson *(Dir.-Admin.)*
Steve Kalish *(Dir.-Customer Rels.)*
David Kronenberg *(Dir.-Data Processing)*

Computer Systems/Hardware:
Unisys

Outside Service Firm(s):

Piercy, Bowler, Taylor & Kern*(Auditors)*
Las Vegas, NV

Insurance Company of the West*(Commercial Insurance Carrier)*
Las Vegas, NE

PHA Insurance*(Group Insurer)*
Portland, OR

Moran & Weinstock*(Legal Firm)*
Las Vegas, NV

First Interstate Bank*(Major Banking Relationship)*
P.O. Box 98511,
Las Vegas, NV 89193-8511

Fidelity Financial*(Pension Manager)*
Las Vegas, NE

Subsidiary:

Disposal Urban Maintenance Procession Co., Inc. **(1)**
7900 Vegas Valley Rd.
Las Vegas, NV 89122
Tel.: 702-457-5263
Sanitary Landfill Operation
S.I.C.: 4953
Alfred Isola *(Pres.)*
Joseph L. Anstett *(Exec. V.P.)*
Richard Isola *(V.P.-Opers.)*
Aldo Lippetti *(V.P.)*
Thomas Isola *(V.P.)*

Silver Towne Coin Shop
(See Leon Hendrickson d/b/a Silver Towne Coin Shop Listing)

SILVERCREST WESTERN HOME INDUSTRIES CORPORATION
299 North Smith Avenue
Corona, CA 91720
Tel.: 909-734-6610 **CA**
Fax: 714-542-5092
Year Founded: 1969
Emp.: 766
Mfr. Mobile Homes
S.I.C.: 2451
Gary Edmundson *(Pres.)*
Craig Fleming *(V.P.-Sls.)*

Plants:

Silvercrest Western Home Corporation **(1)**
2450 Progress Way
Woodburn, OR 97071
Tel.: 503-981-8808 (100%)
Approx.Sls.: $13,000,000
Emp.: 150
Mfr. Mobile Homes
S.I.C.: 2451
Steve Driscol *(G.M.)*

Silvercrest Western Home Corporation **(1)**
109 County Rd. 101
Woodland, CA 95695
Tel.: 916-662-9156 (100%)
Approx.Sls.: $8,000,000
Emp.: 125
Mfr. Mobile Homes
S.I.C.: 2451
Terry DePaepe *(Gen. Mgr.)*

SILVERMAN PRODUCTS & TEXTILES
205 W. 39th St.
New York, NY 10018
Tel.: 212-944-8200 **NY**
Fax: 212-869-8881
Year Founded: 1977
Approx.Sls.: $30,000,000
Emp.: 35
Import Export
Wholesale Broadwoven Fabrics
S.I.C.: 5131
Morris J. Silverman *(Pres.)*
Alan Silverman *(V.P. & Sec.)*
Lester Silverman *(V.P. & Treas.)*
Glen Silverman *(V.P.)*

Principal(s):
Alan Silverman
Lester Silverman
Glen Silverman

Outside Service Firm(s):

Mendelsohn, Kary, Bell & Natoli*(Auditors)*
New York, NY

Manufacturers Hanover Trust Co.*(Major Banking Relationship)*
P.O. Box 24935, Church St. Station
New York, NY 10249
Tel.: 212-613-7147

SILVER'S INC.
151 W. Fort St.
Detroit, MI 48226
Tel.: 313-963-0000 **MI**
Fax: 313-963-0814
Approx.Sls.: $37,800,000
Emp.: 280
Distributor & Retailer of Office Furniture, Supplies & Gifts
S.I.C.: 5021; 5112; 5943; 5947
Ira Silver *(Chief Exec. Officer)*
Cary Silver *(Pres.)*
Susan S. O'Conner *(V.P. & Sec.)*
Damian Zikakis *(Controller)*

Outside Service Firm(s):

Kleiman, Carney & Greenbaum*(Auditors)*
Farmington Hills, MI

Manufacturers Bank*(Major Banking Relationship)*
P.O. Box 33-400,
Detroit, MI 48226
Tel.: 313-222-7572

SILVERSTONE, ADKINS & BREIT, INC.
1128 Stratford Ave.
Stratford, CT 06497
Tel.: 203-375-2887
Fax: 203-386-1203
Year Founded: 1985
Approx.Billings: $19,300,000
Emp.: 17
Sales Promotion & Merchandising
Bruce T. Silverstone *(Pres. & Creative Dir.)*
Toby L. Breit *(V.P., Dir. Mktg. Services)*
Nancy Johnson *(Mgr., Human Resources)*
Michael Sette *(Pub. Rels. Mgr.)*
Jane Broderick *(Mdse. Fulfillment Coord.)*

Computer Systems/Hardware:
IBM, MacIntosh

SILVESTRI CORP.
2720 N. Paulina St.
Chicago, IL 60614
Tel.: 312-871-5200 **IL**
Fax: 312-871-7058
Year Founded: 1973
Approx.Sls.: $26,000,000
Emp.: 300
Importer & Distributor of Giftware, Christmas Lights & Decorations
S.I.C.: 5199
William Ripley *(Pres.)*
Geoffrey Harris *(Exec. V.P.)*

Principal(s):
Geoffrey Harris

Outside Service Firm(s):

Deloitte & Touche*(Auditors)*
Two Prudential Plaza, 180 N. Stetson
Chicago, IL 60601
Tel.: 312-946-2039

Greenbaum & Gold*(Legal Firm)*
Chicago, IL

Harris Trust & Savings Bank*(Major Banking Relationship)*
111 W. Monroe St.
Chicago, IL 60690
Tel.: 312-461-2265
Tel.: 800-858-0840

SIMKINS INDUSTRIES, INC.
260 East St.
New Haven, CT 06511
Tel.: 203-787-7171 **CT**
Fax: 203-787-5454
Emp.: 1,400
Mfr. of Paper Board & Folding Cartons
S.I.C.: 2631; 2657
L.J. Simkins *(Chm. Bd., Pres., Chief Exec. & Chief Oper. Officer)*
S.F. Gadon *(Sec.)*
James Galvin *(Controller & Chief Acctg. Officer)*
Sal DeFrancesco *(Dir.-Personnel)*

Outside Service Firm(s):

Spector, Cohen, Gadon & Rosen*(Legal Firm)*
1700 Market St.
Philadelphia, PA 19103
Tel.: 215-241-8888

Divisions:

Simkins Carolina Folding Box Div. **(1)**
Landrum, SC 29356
Tel.: 803-457-3361
Mfr. of Boxes
S.I.C.: 2657
H. Byers *(Chief Oper. Officer)*

Simkins Carton Div.-Chicago **(1)**
5701 W. Ogden Ave.
Cicero, IL 60650
Tel.: 708-656-5560
Mfr. of Boxes
S.I.C.: 2657
J. Richter *(Chief Oper. Officer)*

Simkins Carton Div.-Cleveland **(1)**
7275 Wentworth Ave.
Cleveland, OH 44102
Tel.: 216-631-2300
Mfr. of Boxes
S.I.C.: 2657
E. G. McNeil *(Chief Oper. Officer)*

Simkins Carton Div.-Dallas **(1)**
1115 Alma St.
Dallas, TX 75215
Tel.: 214-421-7075
Mfr. of Boxes
S.I.C.: 2657
L. Garfield *(Chief Oper. Officer)*

Simkins Carton Div.-Marietta **(1)**
1069 Atlanta Industrial Dr.
Marietta, GA 30066
Tel.: 404-427-0162
Mfr. of Boxes
S.I.C.: 2657
H. Byers *(Chief Oper. Officer)*

Simkins Maryland Board **(1)**
P.O. Box 3249,
Baltimore, MD 21228
Tel.: 410-747-5100
Paperboard Mills
S.I.C.: 2631
Mark Baisch *(Chief Oper. Officer)*

Simkins New Haven Board **(1)**
259 East St.
New Haven, CT 06511
Mfr. of Paperboard
S.I.C.: 2631
F. P. Camesa *(Chief Oper. Officer)*

Simkins New Haven Carton **(1)**
259 East St.
New Haven, CT 06508
Mfr. of Boxes
S.I.C.: 2657
F. Joslin *(Chief Oper. Officer)*

Subsidiaries:

Beveridge Paper Co. **(1)**
717 W. Washington St.
Indianapolis, IN 46204
Tel.: 317-635-4391 (100%)
Paperboard Mills
S.I.C.: 2631
R. Tarr *(Chief Oper. Officer)*

Lowe Paper Co. **(1)**
Ridgefield, NJ 07657
Tel.: 201-945-4900
Mfr. of Boxes
S.I.C.: 2631

Westfield River Paper Co. **(1)**
Station Rd.
Russell, MA 01071
Tel.: 413-862-3636 (100%)
Mfr. of Boxes
S.I.C.: 2631
F. Fitzpatrick *(Chief Oper. Officer)*

SIMMONS-BOARDMAN PUBLISHING CORP.
345 Hudson St.
New York, NY 10014
Tel.: 212-620-7200 **DE**
Fax: 212-633-1165
Year Founded: 1928
Assets: $4,500,000
Liabilities: $1,500,000
Net Worth: $3,000,000
Approx.Sls.: $10,000,000
Emp.: 110
Fiscal Year-end: 12/31/90
Publisher Trade & Industry Magazines
S.I.C.: 2721
Arthur J. McGinnis, Jr. *(Chm. Bd., Pres., Chief Oper. Officer)*
Arthur J. McGinnis, Sr. *(Chm.-Exec. Committee & Chief Exec. Officer)*
Paul Cocheo *(Controller)*

No. of Mfg. Plants/Facilities: 3
No. of U.S. Offices: 1

Outside Service Firm(s):

Federal Insurance*(Commercial Insurance Carrier)*
Los Angeles, CA

Blue Cross of New York*(Group Insurer)*
New York, NY

Shearson Lehman Brothers, Inc.*(Investment Banker)*
Tower C, World Financial Center
New York, NY 10285
Tel.: 212-298-2000

Marine Midland Bank*(Major Banking Relationship)*
250 Park Ave.
New York, NY 10017
Tel.: 212-503-6642

Equitable Life*(Pension Manager)*
1221 Ave. of the Americas
New York, NY 10022
Tel.: 212-382-8038
Fax: 212-382-8089

Division:

Railway Educational Bureau **(1)**
1809 Capitol Ave.
Omaha, NE 68102
Tel.: 402-346-4300
Mechanical & Maintenance Training for the Railroad Industry Through Correspondence Trade School Utilizing Text & Video
S.I.C.: 8249
Pat Kentner *(Gen. Mgr. & Dir.)*

SIMMONS, DURHAM & ASSOCIATES
906 Olive St.
Saint Louis, MO 63101
Tel.: 314-421-6610
Fax: 314-421-5627
Year Founded: 1985
Approx.Billings: $34,000,000
Emp.: 18
Consumer, Trade, Package Goods
E.C. Simmons, III *(Pres., New Bus. Contact & Creative Dir.)*
B.W. Durham, Jr. *(Exec. V.P., Treas.)*
L.R. Diveley *(V.P., Acct. Services & Mktg. Dir.)*
T.Y. Weidenheimer *(Pres.-V Unit)*
R.K. Bozzay *(V.P.-V Unit)*
L.R. Copeland *(Sec.)*

SIMMONS OIL CORP.
2425 E. Camelback Rd., Ste. 1025
Phoenix, AZ 85016
Tel.: 602-553-2150
Fax: 602-553-2160
Approx.Sls.: $350,000,000
Emp.: 90
Petroleum Wholesale Trading & Refining
S.I.C.: 2911; 5171; 5172
Jerry D. Simmons *(Chm. Bd. & Chief Exec. Officer)*
Randy Garcia *(V.P. & Treas.)*

Computer Systems/Hardware:
IBM

SIMMONS OUTDOOR CORP.
14530 S.W. 119th Ave.
Miami, FL 33186
Tel.: 904-878-5100
Approx.Sls.: $20,000,000
Emp.: 36
Sports Optics
S.I.C.: 3851
Fred Cosper *(Pres.)*
Lynn Andersen *(Treas.)*

SIMMONS UPHOLSTERED FURNITURE, INC.
(Formerly Townhouse Penthouse Industries Inc.)
1314 Hanley Industrial Ct.
Saint Louis, MO 63144
Tel.: 314-968-1818
Fax: 314-968-2371
Sales Range: $100-499 Million
Emp.: 2,000
Manufacture of Upholstered Wood Furniture, Sofa Sleepers
S.I.C.: 6719; 2512
Glenn Rupp *(Pres. & Chief Exec. Officer)*
Andrew Campbell *(Chief Fin. Officer, V.P., Treas. & Sec.)*
David Flesner *(Sr. V.P.-Sls.)*
Edward Flood *(V.P.-Customer Rels.)*
Monte Safron *(V.P.)*

Computer Systems/Hardware:
DEC Digital

Outside Service Firm(s):

Flom & Lapata*(Auditors)*
St. Louis, MO

Greensfelder, Hemker and Gale, P.C.*(Legal Firm)*
1800 Equitable Bldg., 10 S. Broadway
St. Louis, MO 63102
Tel.: 314-241-9090

Bank of St. Louis*(Major Banking Relationship)*
St. Louis, MO

SIMMS & MCIVOR MARKETING COMMUNICATIONS
Branch Estates, 3121 Rte. 22 East
Somerville, NJ 08876-3500
Tel.: 908-722-8777 **NJ**
Fax: 908-722-7833
Year Founded: 1981
Approx.Billings: $12,324,000
Emp.: 25
Medical & General Marketing Communications
S.I.C.: 7311

Simms & McIvor Marketing Communications—(Continued)

Corporate Giving Program: United Way, Orphan Sponsorship
Patrick J. McIvor *(Pres. & Chief Exec. Officer)*

Computer Systems/Hardware:
IBM-PS 2, Mac-II CX, Qume

Outside Service Firm(s):

Brill, Karr, Crane & Tonelli*(Auditors)*
Short Hills, NJ

General Accident Insurance Company of America*(Commercial Insurance Carrier)*
Florham Park, NJ

Garden State Hosp. Plan*(Group Insurer)*
Newark, NJ

Guardian Life Insurance Co.*(Group Insurer)*
Philadelphia, PA

Carton, Witt, Arvanitis & Bariscillo*(Legal Firm)*
Asbury Park, NJ

Chemical Bank*(Major Banking Relationship)*
Whitehouse, NJ

Subsidiary:

Synergetics, Inc. **(1)**
3121 Rte. 22, East
Somerville, NJ 08876
Tel.: 908-722-8777
Fax: 908-722-7833
Emp.: 25
Advertising Operations
S.I.C.: 7311
Patrick J. McIvor *(Pres.)*

SIMON & ASSOCIATES
121 Chanlon Rd.
New Providence, NJ 07974
Tel.: 908-933-3326
Year Founded: 1983
Approx.Billings: $13,500,000
Emp.: 14
Direct Response
Peter Simon *(Pres. & Chief Exec. Officer)*
Marjorie Borman *(Treas.)*

SIMON MARKETING, INC.
(World Headquarters)
1900 Ave. of The Stars, Ste. 400
Los Angeles, CA 90067
Tel.: 310-553-4460
Telex: 910490-2538 SIMON MKTG
Fax: 310-553-6513
Year Founded: 1976
Approx.Billings: $160,000,000
Emp.: 290
Sales Promotion & Mktg. Services
Allan Brown *(Co-Chm. Bd.)*
Eric Stanton *(Co-Chm. Bd.)*
Edwin Rickerson *(Vice-Chm.)*
N.V. (Lito) Domantay *(Exec. V.P., Consumer Products)*
Paul Marcus *(Exec. V.P., Entertainment Mktg.)*
Dan Greenwood *(Exec. V.P., Sports Mktg.)*

MELVIN SIMON & ASSOCIATES
P.O. Box 7033,
Indianapolis, IN 46207
Tel.: 317-636-1600
Fax: 317-685-7221
Sales Range: $10-19 Million
Developers of Shopping Malls
S.I.C.: 1542; 6512
Melvin Simon *(Chief Exec. Officer)*
Principal(s):
Melvin Simon

No. of U.S. Offices: 6

JOSEPH SIMON & SONS, INC.
2202 E. River St.
Tacoma, WA 98421
Tel.: 206-272-9364
Fax: 206-838-1998
Approx.Sls.: $30,000,000
Emp.: 50
Export
Nonferrous Metals Recycling
S.I.C.: 5093
Phillip Simon *(Pres.)*
Norman Simon *(V.P., Sec. & Treas.)*
Mark M. Burley *(Controller)*

Outside Service Firm(s):

Knight, Vale & Gregory*(Auditors)*
Seattle, WA

Seattle First National Bank*(Major Banking Relationship)*
P.O. Box 24186
Seattle, WA 98124

SIMONDS INDUSTRIES INC.
135 Intervale Rd.
Fitchburg, MA 01420-0500
Mailing Address:
P.O. Box 500
Fitchburg, MA 01420-0500
Tel.: 508-343-3731
Fax: 800-541-6224
Year Founded: 1832
Approx.Sls.: $78,000,000
Emp.: 776
Fiscal Year-end: 12/31/91
Manufacturer of Industrial Cutting Tools
S.I.C.: 3545
Charles Doulton *(Chm. Bd.)*
Ross George *(Pres.)*
Joseph Sylvia *(Treas. & Dir.-Fin.)*
George Knepple *(Dir.-Mktg., Metal Prods.)*
Sandra E. LaBree *(Mgr.-Adv. Communications)*

SIMONDS-SHIELDS-THEIS GRAIN CO.
4800 Main St., Ste. 401
Kansas City, MO 64112
Tel.: 816-561-4155 **MO**
Fax: 816-561-5005
Year Founded: 1884
Assets: $8,500,000
Earnings: $200,000
Liabilities: $4,500,000
Net Worth: $4,000,000
Approx.Sls.: $25,000,000
Emp.: 70
Fiscal Year-end: 5/31/88
Commodity Brokers & Services
S.I.C.: 6221; 5153
Willis C. Theis *(Chm. Bd.)*
Stephen Theis *(Pres.)*
Robert Etterling *(Treas. & Sec.)*

Outside Service Firm(s):

Boan & Connealy*(Auditors)*
Kansas City, KS

Mill Mutual*(Commercial Insurance Carrier)*
Kansas City, MO

Morrison & Hecker*(Legal Firm)*
Kansas City, MO

Commerce Bank of Kansas City*(Major Banking Relationship)*
10th & Walnut
Kansas City, MO 64141
Tel.: 816-234-2000
Fax: 816-234-2548

SIMONS MICHELSON ZIEVE, INC.
900 Wilshire Dr.
Troy, MI 48084
Tel.: 313-362-4242 **MI**
Fax: 313-362-2014
Year Founded: 1929
Approx.Billings: $35,000,000
Emp.: 55
Fiscal Year-end: 3/31/91
Advertising Agency
S.I.C.: 7311
Morton Zieve *(Chm. Bd.)*
James A. Michelson *(Pres.)*
Helen Charewych *(V.P.)*
Ron David *(V.P.)*
Lawrence J. Michelson *(V.P.)*
Leonard N. Simons *(V.P.)*
Art Steiber *(V.P.)*
Dennis Zinchook *(V.P.)*

Outside Service Firm(s):

Harvey M. Beim CPA., PC.*(Auditors)*
Southfield, MI

Miro, Miro & Weiner*(Legal Firm)*
500 N. Woodward Ave., Ste. 100
Bloomfield Hills, MI 48013
Tel.: 313-646-2400

Michigan National Bank*(Major Banking Relationship)*
Detroit, MI

SIMPLEX INDUSTRIES, INC.
Simplex Dr.
Scranton, PA 18504
Tel.: 717-346-5113
Tel.: 800-233-4233 **PA**
Fax: 717-346-3731
Year Founded: 1971
Approx.Sls.: $20,000,000
Emp.: 300
Export
Prefabricated Wood Buildings Modulars
S.I.C.: 2452
Frank Fricchione *(Chm. Bd.)*
Henry Fricchione *(Pres.)*
Patrick Fricchione, Sr. *(Chief Exec. Officer)*
Daniel J. Mallon *(Controller)*
J. Michael Zangardi *(Dir.-Sls. & Mktg.)*
Patrick Fricchione, Jr. *(Dir.-Pur.)*
Thomas Basta *(Mgr.-Opers.)*

No. of Mfg. Plants/Facilities: 2

Outside Service Firm(s):

Snyder & Clemente*(Auditors)*
Kingston, PA 18704

First National Community Bank*(Major Banking Relationship)*
Dunmore, PA

Subsidiary:

Simplex Construction Co. Inc. **(1)**
Simplex Dr.
Scranton, PA 18504
Tel.: 717-346-5113
Tel.: 800-233-4233
Emp.: 10
Modular Home Set-up - General Construction Services
S.I.C.: 1521; 1799
Patrick Fricchione Jr. *(Chief Oper. Officer)*
Daniel J. Mallon *(Controller)*
John Pehanich *(Construction Coordinator)*

SIMPLEX TIME RECORDER CO.
Simplex Plaza
Gardner, MA 01441
Tel.: 508-632-2500 **MA**
Fax: 508-632-5632
Assets: $170,000,000
Liabilities: $85,000,000
Net Worth: $85,000,000
Approx.Sls.: $400,000,000
Emp.: 4,000
Fiscal Year-end: 12/31/91
Worldwide Sales and Service of Fire Alarm, Sound, Security, and Other Monitor and Control Systems, as Well as Time and Attendance Recorders, Including Software Based Systems
S.I.C.: 7382
Edward G. Watkins *(Chm. Bd., Pres. & Chief Exec. Officer)*
Thomas A. Curtin *(Exec. V.P. & Chief Fin. Officer)*
Eugene H. Ballard *(V.P. & Gen. Counsel)*
Frank D. Everett *(V.P.-Service Opers.)*
Stephen Lundsted *(V.P.-Mfg.)*
James D. Plante *(V.P.-Field Opers.)*
Joseph H. Griffith *(V.P.-Human Resources & Corp. Services)*
Donald B. Stimer *(V.P. & Treas.)*
John L. Ellis *(V.P.-Mngmt. Opers.)*
Joseph Marzilli *(Asst. Treas.)*
James Lawson *(Dir.-Mngmt. Information Systems)*
Roy M. Janis *(Dir.-Business Plng.)*

Computer Systems/Hardware:
IBM PC

Outside Service Firm(s):

BDO Seidman*(Auditors)*
Boston, MA

Choate, Hall & Stewart*(Legal Firm)*
Exchange Place, 53 State St.
Boston, MA 02109
Tel.: 617-227-5020

First National Bank of Chicago*(Major Banking Relationship)*
One First National Plaza
Chicago, IL 60670
Tel.: 312-732-9781
Tel.: 312-732-4050
Fax: 312-732-4840
Fax: 312-732-3055

Non-U.S. Holdings:

Simplex Intl. Time Equip. Co. Ltd. (Canada) **(1)**
6300 Viscount Rd.
Mississauga, ON Canada L4V 1H3
Tel.: 416-677-7000 (100%)
Sls. & Service of Time Equip.
S.I.C.: 5063

Simplex Intl. Time Equip. Pty. Ltd. **(1)**
32 Cross Street P.O. Box 561
Brookvale, N.S.W. 2100, Australia
(100%)
Sls. & Service of Time Equip.
S.I.C.: 5063

Simplex Management Services, Ltd. **(1)**
Simplex Hse., 284-288 Chase Rd.
Southgate,
London, N14 6HF, United Kingdom
(100%)
Sls. & Service of Time Equip.
S.I.C.: 5063

SIMPLICITY MANUFACTURING, INC.
500 N. Spring St.
Port Washington, WI 53074
Mailing Address:
P.O. Box 997,
Port Washington, WI 53074
Tel.: 414-284-5535
Tel.: 414-284-8669 **DE**
Telex: 510-600-4636
Fax: 414-377-8202
Year Founded: 1922
Approx.Sls.: $100,000,000
Emp.: 550
Fiscal Year-end: 7/31/90
Export
Mfr. Lawn & Garden Equipment; Snowthrowers, Lawn Mowers, Riding Mowers, Garden Tractors
S.I.C.: 3524
Warner Frazier *(Pres. & Chief Exec. Officer)*
J.F. Bracken *(V.P.-Engrng.)*

Carl F. Charles *(V.P.-Fin.)*
G. Chris Covert *(V.P.-Mfg.)*
Conrad Langenberger *(V.P.-N. American Sls. & Mktg.)*
James H. Myers *(V.P.-Intl. Sls. & Product Mngmt.)*
Donald S. Schoonenberg *(Sec. & Controller)*
Don Giageos *(Mgr.-Human Resources)*
William J. Pasbrig *(Mgr.-Systems & Data Processing)*

No. of Mfg. Plants/Facilities: 1
No. of U.S. Offices: 1
No. of Foreign Offices: 1

Computer Systems/Hardware:
Unisys

Outside Service Firm(s):

Price Waterhouse*(Auditors)*
1500 Bank One Plaza, 100 E. Wisconsin Ave.
Milwaukee, WI 53202

Reinhart, Boerner, Van Deuren, Norris & Rieselbach, S.C.*(Legal Firm)*
1000 N. Water St., Ste. 2100
Milwaukee, WI 53202
Tel.: 414-298-1000

First National Bank of Boston*(Major Banking Relationship)*
P.O. Box 644,
Boston, MA 02102-0644
Tel.: 617-575-2900
Fax: 617-575-2549

Subsidiary:

Tornado Products, Inc. **(1)**
500 N. Spring St.
Port Washington, WI 53074
Tel.: 414-284-5535
Mfr. of Chipper/Shredders
S.I.C.: 3524
Don S. Schoonenberg *(Mgr.-Div.)*

J.R. SIMPLOT COMPANY
999 Main St.
Boise, ID 83702
Mailing Address:
P.O. Box 27,
Boise, ID 83707
Tel.: 208-336-2110
Fax: 208-389-7515
Year Founded: 1955
Approx.Sls.: $1,300,000,000
Emp.: 9,000
Fiscal Year-end: 8/31/92
Import Export
Manufactures & Distributes Frozen Potato & Vegetable Products, Fertilizer & Agricultural Chemicals; Farming & Livestock
S.I.C.: 2037; 2873; 2874; 2879; 2875; 0219; 0191
J.R. Simplot *(Chm. Bd.)*
Gordon C. Smith *(Pres., Chief Exec. & Chief Oper. Officer)*
L.E. Costello *(V.P.-Fin. & Chief Fin. Officer)*
Ronald N. Graves *(V.P., Sec. & Gen. Counsel)*
James Crawford *(Treas.)*
Hoyt Blackstock *(Dir.-Mktg.)*
Blaine Jacobson *(Dir.-Mktg.)*
Raymond Sasso *(Dir.-Data Processing)*
Fred Zerza *(Dir.-Pub. Rels. & Adv.)*
Belinda Hofstetter *(Cash Mgr.)*

No. of Mfg. Plants/Facilities: 12
No. of U.S. Offices: 115
No. of Foreign Offices: 2

Computer Systems/Hardware:
Digital Electronics; VAX 2060

Outside Service Firm(s):

Deloitte & Touche*(Auditors)*
101 S. Capitol Blvd.
Boise, ID 83702
Tel.: 208-342-5361

Morgan Stanley & Co.*(Investment Banker)*
1251 Avenue of the Americas
New York, NY 10020
Tel.: 212-703-8447
Fax: 212-703-6476

Hawley, Troxell, Ennis & Hawley*(Legal Firm)*
Boise, ID

Continental Bank N. A.*(Major Banking Relationship)*
231 S. LaSalle St.
Chicago, IL 60697
Tel.: 312-828-2345
Tel.: 800-426-5754
Telex: 312-828-1783

First Security Bank, N.A.*(Major Banking Relationship)*
P.O. Box 2618,
Boise, ID 83701
Tel.: 208-338-2032

Husic Capital Management*(Pension Manager)*
555 California St.
San Francisco, CA 94104
Tel.: 415-398-0800

Olympic Capital Management, Inc.*(Pension Manager)*
Seattle, WA

SEI Associates*(Pension Manager)*
San Francisco, CA

Groups:

J.R. Simplot Co. Food Group **(1)**
P.O. Box 9386
Boise, ID 83707
Tel.: 208-384-8000
Fax: 208-384-8020
S.I.C.: 2037
Hoyt Blackstock *(Pres.)*
Bill Roberts *(V.P.-Mktg. & Sls.)*

J.R. Simplot Co., Minerals & Chemicals Group **(1)**
4122 Yellowstone Ave.
Pocatello, ID 83202
Tel.: 208-238-2700
Fax: 208-238-2760
Emp.: 2,400
Superphosphate Fertilizer & Phosphoric Acid (Wet Process), Ammonium Phosphates Agricultural Chemicals Formulation
S.I.C.: 2874
Don Pottinger *(Pres.)*
Larry Hinderager *(V.P.-Mining & Mfg.)*
John McLeod *(V.P.-Mktg.)*
Sandy Sandoval *(V.P.-Mining & Processing)*
Jerry Mead *(V.P.-Res. & Product Devel.)*
Dan Daniel *(V.P.)*
Ken Maddox *(Dir.-Admin. Services)*
Earl Mapes *(Dir.-Regulation Affair)*
Jacquie Pede *(Sr. Mkt. Analyst)*
Lori Hamann *(Mktg. Services Coord.)*
Jim Driever *(Pur. Agent)*

Subsidiaries:

J.R. Simplot Co.-Agriculture Group **(1)**
HC85, Box 275,
Grand View, ID 83624
Tom Basabe *(V.P. & Gen. Mgr.)*

J.R. Simplot Co.-Diversified Products Group **(1)**
223 Rodeo Ave.
Caldwell, ID 83605
Ray Kaufman *(V.P.)*

J.R. Simplot Co.-Food Group **(1)**
6360 S. Federal Way
Boise, ID 83706-9617
Stephen Beebe *(Pres.)*

J.R. Simplot Co.-Minerals & Chemical Group **(1)**
4122 Yellowstone Ave.
Pocatello, ID 83202
Don Pottinger *(Pres.)*

SIMPSON DURA-VENT CO., INC.
(Div. of Simpson Co.)
902 Aldridge Rd.
Vacaville, CA 95688
Mailing Address:
P.O. Box 1510
Vacaville, CA 95696-1510
Tel.: 707-446-1786
Tel.: 800-227-7374
Approx.Sls.: $20,000,000
Emp.: 190
Fiscal Year-end: 12/31/89
Metal Type B Gas Vent Pipe, All-Fuel Chimneys, Stovepipe, Stainless Steel Chimney Liner, Pellet Vent
S.I.C.: 3444; 3272; 3259
D. Townsend *(Pres. & Gen. Mgr.)*
John Davis *(Dir.-Sls. & Mktg.)*

SIMPSON ELECTRIC CO.
853 Dundee Ave.
Elgin, IL 60120
Tel.: 708-697-2260
Fax: 708-697-2272
Year Founded: 1936
Approx.Sls.: $20,000,000
Emp.: 350
Fiscal Year-end: 9/30/90
Import Export
Mfg. Analog & Digital Test Instrumentation & Panel Meters
S.I.C.: 3825
Michael Allen *(Chm. Bd.)*
Edward M. Herter *(Pres.)*
Donald Anderson *(V.P.-Fin.)*
John Deichl *(V.P.-Mktg. & Sls.)*
John Reich *(V.P.-Research & Devel.)*
Ron Barma *(Mgr.-Adv.)*
Tom Chase *(Mgr.-Personnel)*
Brian P. Gieler *(Western Reg. Sls. Mgr.)*
Saul Mariasis *(Export Mgr.)*
George Oskandy *(Sls. Admin. Mgr.)*
Paul Weber *(Mgr.-Mfg.)*

SIMPSON INVESTMENT CO.
(Sub. of Kamilche Co., a Holding Co.)
1201 Third Ave., Ste. 4900
Seattle, WA 98101-3009
Tel.: 206-224-5000
Fax: 206-224-5060
Year Founded: 1890
Sales Range: $500-999 Million
Emp.: 8,200
Fiscal Year-end: 12/31/91
Import Export
Holding Company; Distribute Wood & Allied Products
S.I.C.: 6719; 2431; 2621; 2611; 2631; 3089; 5031; 2421; 2411; 2436
Corporate Giving Program: The Simpson Fund Foundation Gives to Various Health & Human Service Groups, Education, Cultural Organizations & Other Needs
Employee Matching Gifts Program: 2 for 1 Match up to $1,200 per Employee to Public & Private Secondary Schools & Colleges
William G. Reed, Jr. *(Chm. Bd.)*
F.C. Moseley *(Pres.)*
J. Thurston Roach *(V.P. & Chief Fin. Officer)*
R. James Day *(V.P. & Treas.)*
Joseph Breed *(V.P. & Gen. Counsel)*
Joseph Leitzinger *(V.P.-Pub. Affairs)*
Cynthia P. Sonstelie *(V.P.-Human Resources)*
A.E. Symington *(V.P.-Investments)*
Principal(s):
F.C. Moseley

Computer Systems/Hardware:
IBM 4381

Outside Service Firm(s):

Ernst & Young*(Auditors)*
999 Third Av., Ste. 3500
Seattle, WA 98104
Tel.: 206-621-1800
Fax: 206-682-1234

Lane, Powell, Spears & Lubersky*(Legal Firm)*
1420 Fifth Avenue, Suite 4100
Seattle, WA 98101-2338
Tel.: 206-223-7000

Seattle First National Bank*(Major Banking Relationship)*
701 Fifth Avenue
Seattle, WA 98104
Tel.: 206-358-3035

Frank Russell Company*(Pension Manager)*
909 A St.
Tacoma, WA 98402

RCM Capital Management*(Pension Manager)*
4 Embarcadero Center, Ste. 2900
San Francisco, CA 94111

Operations:

PW Pipe Co. **(1)**
P.O. Box 10049,
Eugene, OR 97440
Tel.: 503-343-0200
Fax: 503-686-9247
Export
S.I.C.: 3089
James K. Rash *(Pres.)*

Simpson Paper Co. **(1)**
One Post St.
San Francisco, CA 94104
Tel.: 415-391-8140 (100%)
Fax: 415-986-4617
Mfr. Of Paper Products
S.I.C.: 2611; 2621; 2631; 2675
John J. Fannon *(Pres.)*

Subsidiaries:

Simpson Tacoma Kraft Co. **(2)**
P.O. Box 2133,
Tacoma, WA 98421
Tel.: 206-572-2150
S.I.C.: 2611; 2621; 2631; 2675
Raymond P. Tennison *(Gen. Mgr.)*

Simpson Plainwell Paper Co., Inc. **(2)**
200 Allegan St.
Plainwell, MI 49080
Tel.: 616-685-5851
Manufactures Coated & Uncoated Papers for Commercial Printing
S.I.C.: 2672; 2674
Roger Huckendubler *(Mgr.-Opers.)*

Simpson Timber Co. **(1)**
3rd & Franklin
Shelton, WA 98584
Tel.: 206-426-3381
Fax: 206-427-8186
Emp.: 2,000
Import Export
Manufacturing: Sawing Rough Lumber; Fir, Hemlock & Redwood Lumber; Plywood Doors
S.I.C.: 5031; 2421; 2431; 2435; 2436; 2499
William G. Reed, Jr. *(Chm. Bd.-SICO)*
F.C. Moseley *(Pres.-SICO)*
Thomas R. Ingham, Jr. *(Pres.-STCO)*
J. Thurston Roach *(V.P., Sec. & Chief Fin. Officer-SICO)*
Robert J. Day *(V.P. & Treas.-SICO)*
J.L. Walker *(V.P.-Land & Timber-STCO)*
J.R. Breed *(V.P. & Gen. Counsel-SICO)*
R.R. Grant *(V.P. & Controller-STCO)*
J.R. Drake *(V.P. & Gen. Mgr.-Northwest-STCO)*
David W. Kaney *(V.P. & Gen Mgr.-SRC)*
James T. Brown *(V.P. & Gen. Mgr.-ARC)*
J.B. Soehnlein *(Environmental & Engrng. Mgr.)*
J.F. Gorman *(Forest Environmental Mgr.)*

Mill:

Simpson Pasadena Paper Co. **(2)**
P.O. Box 872
Pasadena, TX 77501
Tel.: 713-475-6200
S.I.C.: 2611; 2621; 2672; 2674
Henry V. Jones *(Opers. Mgr.)*

SIMUNICO, INC.
301 Rte. 17 N.
Rutherford, NJ 07070
Tel.: 201-507-5800

Simunico, Inc.—(Continued)

Fax: 201-507-5937
Emp.: 400
Fiscal Year-end: 7/31/90
Holding Company; Mfr. of Patient Handling Equipment, Gurnees, Stretchers, Hospital Beds & Juvenile Furniture
S.I.C.: 6719; 2421; 2511; 2599; 3842; 3800; 2500
Al Marchitto *(Chm. Bd. & Chief Exec. Officer)*
Thomas J. Mazza *(Exec. V.P. & Chief Fin. Officer)*
Gaspar Rodriguez *(Asst. Controller)*

Subsidiaries:

Hausted **(1)**
927 Lake Rd.
Medina, OH 44256
Tel.: 216-723-3271
Tel.: 800-428-7833
Fax: 216-725-0505
Emp.: 130
Fiscal Year-end: 7/31/91
Export
Computer Systems/Hardware:
IBM System 36
Mfr. of Patient Handling Equipment; Gurneys, Stretchers, Hospital Beds
S.I.C.: 3842; 2599; 2499; 3800; 2500
John J. Murray *(Pres.)*
Jim Bechtel *(V.P. & Chief Fin. Officer)*
Dennis Daar *(V.P.-Devel.)*
Jerry Silvertooth *(Dir.-Sls. & Mktg.)*
Kate Boland *(Mgr.-Mktg.)*
Al Hemminger *(Mgr.-Pur.)*
Burt Latone *(Mgr.-Plant)*

Simmons Juvenile Products Co., Inc. **(1)**
613 E. Beacon Ave.
New London, WI 54961
Tel.: 414-982-2140
Emp.: 500
Mfr. of Juvenile Furniture
S.I.C.: 2511; 2421
John Moeller *(Pres.)*
Lee Biekkola *(V.P.-Fin. & Admin.)*
G. Charlson *(V.P.-Mfg.)*
J. Lund *(Mgr.-Sls. & Mktg.)*

SINCLAIR OIL CORP.
550 E. South Temple
Salt Lake City, UT 84102
Mailing Address:
P.O. Box 30825,
Salt Lake City, UT 84130
Tel.: 801-363-5100
Fax: 801-524-2848
Sales Range: $1 Billion +
Emp.: 2,500
Fiscal Year-end: 6/30/90
Petroleum Refining & Marketing With Retail Outlets
S.I.C.: 2911; 5541
R. E. Holding *(Pres. & Chief Exec. Officer)*
M. Dale Ensign *(Exec. V.P.-Opers.)*
William Fink *(Sr. V.P.-Supply)*
Charles Barlow *(Treas.)*

No. of Mfg. Plants/Facilities: 3
No. of U.S. Offices: 7

Computer Systems/Hardware:
IBM System 38

Outside Service Firm(s):

Price Waterhouse*(Auditors)*
750 B St.
San Diego, CA 92101
Tel.: 619-231-9830

James Benefits*(Group Insurer)*
Phoenix, AZ

Richards, Bird & Kump*(Legal Firm)*
Salt Lake City, UT

Zions First National Bank*(Major Banking Relationship)*
P.O. Box 30880
Salt Lake City, UT 84130
Tel.: 801-524-4624
Fax: 801-533-0464

Subsidiaries:

Little America Hotels **(1)**
550 E. South Temple
Salt Lake City, UT 84102
Tel.: 801-363-5100
Fax: 801-524-2848
Hotels
S.I.C.: 6513
R. Earl Holding *(Chief Exec. Officer)*
Kenneth Y. Knight *(Pres.)*

Little America Refining **(1)**
550 E. South Temple
Salt Lake City, UT 84102
Tel.: 810-363-5100
Gasoline, Fuel Oils
S.I.C.: 2911
R. Earl Holding *(Pres.)*
Kenneth Y. Knight *(Vice Chm.)*
M. Dale Ensign *(Exec. V.P.)*
Harmon Connell *(V.P.-Refining)*
Richard Cowan *(V.P.-Mktg.)*
Carol Holding *(Treas.)*
Charles Barlow *(Comptroller)*
Lynn S. Richards *(Sec.)*

SINCLAIR PRINTING & LITHO, INC.
4005 Whiteside St.
Los Angeles, CA 90063
Tel.: 213-264-4808
Fax: 213-264-3716
Year Founded: 1929
Approx.Sls.: $19,000,000
Emp.: 176
Multicolor Sheet Fed & Web Offset Lithography Binding
S.I.C.: 2752
Robert J. Sinclair *(Pres.)*
Joy M. Sinclair *(Controller)*
Gary Hawkins *(Plant Mgr.)*
Dan Sinclair *(Sls. Mgr.)*

Outside Service Firm(s):

Deloitte & Touche*(Auditors)*
1000 Wilshire Blvd.
Los Angeles, CA 90017-2472
Tel.: 213-688-0800
Fax: 213-688-0100

Clark & Trevithick*(Legal Firm)*
800 Wilshire Blvd., Ste. 700
Los Angeles, CA 90017
Tel.: 213-629-5700

Sanwa Bank*(Major Banking Relationship)*
Alhambra, CA

SINGERS SUPERMARKETS, INC.
7801 Tonnelle Ave.
North Bergen, NJ 07047
Tel.: 201-854-4400
Fax: 201-854-4413
Approx.Sls.: $135,500,000
Emp.: 2,000
Fiscal Year-end: 6/30/90
Food Stores
S.I.C.: 5411
Sidney Singer *(Chm. Bd. & Chief Exec. Officer)*
Martin Singer *(Pres. & Chief Oper. Officer)*
Sharon Singer *(Chief Fin. Officer & V.P.)*
Lee Cimini *(Controller)*
Richard Geerkem *(Dir.-Opers.)*

Computer Systems/Hardware:
IBM System 34

Outside Service Firm(s):

Guardian Life Insurance Co.*(Group Insurer)*
New York, NY

SINGH INDUSTRIES
6 Saddle Rd.
Cedar Knolls, NJ 07927
Tel.: 201-267-8008
Fax: 201-267-5715
Approx.Sls.: $10,000,000
Emp.: 50
Fiscal Year-end: 9/30/90
Mfr. & Mktr. of Cubic Zirconium; Retail Jewelry
S.I.C.: 5085
Ranjit Singh *(Pres.)*
Shri Singh *(V.P.-Sls.)*
Nomita Kayastha *(Mgr.-Adv.)*
Terry Fearon III *(V.P.-Mfg. Opers.)*

SINTEL, INC.
18437 171st Ave.
Spring Lake, MI 49456 **MI**
Tel.: 616-842-6960
Fax: 616-842-0965
Year Founded: 1947
Assets: $3,900,000
Liabilities: $3,000,000
Net Worth: $900,000
Sales Range: $10-19 Million
Emp.: 60
Fiscal Year-end: 12/31/89
Specialty Sheet Metal Fabricating, Stampings and Production Stampings
S.I.C.: 3444; 3549; 3599
Dennis C. Dornbush *(Pres. & Treas.)*
Gary Speet *(V.P.-Sls.)*
Larry Terwilitiger *(V.P.-Mfg.)*

No. of Mfg. Plants/Facilities: 2
No. of U.S. Offices: 1

Computer Systems/Hardware:
IBM

Outside Service Firm(s):

Maynard & Associates*(Auditors)*
Zeeland, MI

Miller, Johnson, Snell & Cummisky*(Legal Firm)*
Grand Haven, MI

NBD Grand Haven*(Major Banking Relationship)*
Grand Haven, MI

SIOUX FALLS CONSTRUCTION COMPANY
800-810 S. 7th Ave.
Sioux Falls, SD 57101
Tel.: 605-336-1640
Fax: 605-334-9342
Approx.Sls.: $20,000,000
Emp.: 55
Commercial Building, Bridge Elevated Highway, Asphalt Parking Lots, Highway & Street Construction, General Contractor
S.I.C.: 1542; 1622; 1611
Frank L. Boyce *(Chm. Bd.)*
John C. Marshman *(Pres.)*
M.L. Peterson *(V.P.-Bldg.)*
Eugene R. Moser *(Sec. & Treas.)*

Outside Service Firm(s):

Henry Scholten & Co.*(Auditors)*
Sioux Falls, SD

Boyce, Murphy, McDowell & Greenfield*(Legal Firm)*
Sioux Falls, SD

First National Bank*(Major Banking Relationship)*
Sioux Falls, SD

SIOUX HONEY ASSOCIATION
301 Lewis Blvd.
Sioux City, IA 51101
Mailing Address:
P.O. Box 388
Sioux City, IA 51102
Tel.: 712-258-0638
Fax: 712-258-1332
Assets: $40,400,000
Net Worth: $40,400,000
Approx.Sls.: $40,000,000
Emp.: 250
Fiscal Year-end: 6/30/90
Import Export
Honey Processor
S.I.C.: 5149
Gary Evans *(Pres. & Chief Exec. Officer)*
Vic Lund *(V.P.-Fin. & Acctg.)*
Jim Powell *(V.P.-Mktg. & Sls.)*
Ray Draube *(Office Mgr.)*
Renee Logemann *(Mgr.-Data Processing)*

No. of Mfg. Plants/Facilities: 7

Outside Service Firm(s):

Deloitte & Touche*(Auditors)*
2000 First National Center
Omaha, NE 68102
Tel.: 402-346-7788

Washington National Insurance*(Group Insurer)*
Des Moines, IA

Firstar Bank*(Major Banking Relationship)*
Sioux City, IA

Omaha Bank for Co-ops*(Major Banking Relationship)*
Omaha, NE

SIOUX MANUFACTURING CORP.
P.O. Box 400
Fort Totten, ND 58335
Tel.: 701-766-4211
Fax: 701-766-4359
Year Founded: 1973
Approx.Sls.: $61,000,000
Emp.: 470
Fiscal Year-end: 12/31/89
Mfrs. Camouflage & Compression Molding
S.I.C.: 3087; 3842; 3795
Carl McKay *(Pres. & Chief Exec. Officer)*
Terry Johnston *(Controller & Treas.)*
Andy Ecklund *(Mgr.-Human Resources)*
M.J. Duchscherer *(Contract Admin.)*

Outside Service Firm(s):

Charles Bailly & Co.*(Auditors)*
406 Main Ave., Ste. 3000
Fargo, ND 58126-0001
Tel.: 701-239-8500

SIOUX STEEL COMPANY
196 1/2 E. 6th St.
Sioux Falls, SD 57102
Mailing Address:
Box 1265
Sioux Falls, SD 57101
Tel.: 605-336-1750
Fax: 605-336-2528
Year Founded: 1917
Emp.: 200
Fiscal Year-end: 10/31/90
Export
Grain Bins, Galvanized Barnyard Equipment
S.I.C.: 3444; 5039
Phil Rysdon *(Pres.)*
Robert Jensen *(Mgr.-Sls.)*
Dick Klock *(Mgr.-Mktg.)*
Bill Cooper *(Pur. Agent)*

Outside Service Firm(s):

Ernst & Young*(Auditors)*
1400 Pillsbury Center
Minneapolis, MN 55402
Tel.: 612-343-1000

Woods, Fuller, Schultz*(Legal Firm)*
Sioux Falls, SD

Norwest Bank Minnesota, N.A.*(Major Banking Relationship)*
Sioux Falls, SD

Subsidiary:

Koyker Mfg. Co. **(1)**
100 N. Cleveland
Lennox, SD 57039
Tel.: 605-647-2811

Shuttlecraft **(1)**
2803 Murray Rd.
Estherville, IA 51334
Tel.: 712-362-5846

SIOUX VALLEY EMPIRE ELECTRIC ASSOCIATION
1 1/2 Miles W. Of I-29
Colman, SD 57017
Mailing Address:
P.O. Box 216
Colman, SD 57017
Tel.: 605-534-3535 **SD**
Fax: 605-534-3522
Year Founded: 1940
Approx.Sls.: $16,000,000
Emp.: 80
Electrical Power Co-op
S.I.C.: 4911
James Kiley *(Chief Exec. Officer & Gen. Mgr.)*

Outside Service Firm(s):

Eide, Helmeke & Co.*(Auditors)*
Sioux Falls, SD

Alan Glover*(Legal Firm)*
Brookings, SD

Dakota State Bank*(Major Banking Relationship)*
Colman, SD

Subsidiary:

Sioux Valley Rural Television **(1)**
P.O. Box 20,
Colman, SD 57017
Tel.: 605-534-3241
Emp.: 3
Rural Television
S.I.C.: 4833

SIPEX CORPORATION
22 Linnell Circle
Billerica, MA 01821
Tel.: 508-667-8700
Fax: 508-670-9001
Year Founded: 1967
Assets: $23,558,000
Liabilities: $15,918,000
Net Worth: $7,640,000
Approx.Sls.: $27,000,000
Emp.: 300
Fiscal Year-end: 12/31/91
Import Export
Design & Manufacture Analog Signal Processing Components, Dielectrically Isolated or BICMOS Integrated Circuits; Manufacture Dielectrically Isolated Wafers
S.I.C.: 3674; 3676
James Donegan *(Chm. Bd., Pres., Chief Exec. & Oper. Officer)*
Gerald Y. Hattori *(Controller)*
Sanford Cohen *(Sr. V.P.-Technology)*
Frank DiPietro *(Sr. V.P.-Fin. & Chief Fin. Officer)*
Neal Lambert *(Sr. V.P.-Mfg., West Coast)*
Deborah Beaumier *(Dir.-Pur.)*
Peg Coughlin *(Dir.-Human Resources)*
Diane Brownlie *(Human Resources Rep.)*

No. of Mfg. Plants/Facilities: 3
No. of Foreign Offices: 3

Computer Systems/Hardware:
Hewlett Packard 3000 Series 58

Outside Service Firm(s):

Ernst & Young*(Auditors)*
200 Clarendon St., 46th Fl.
Boston, MA 02116
Tel.: 617-266-2000

Sedgwick James*(Commercial Insurance Carrier)*
40 Broad St.
Boston, MA 02109
Tel.: 617-357-6623

Day, Berry & Howard*(Legal Firm)*
Boston, MA

Baybank Boston, N.A.*(Major Banking Relationship)*
Boston, MA

SISTI, ZINBARG & HOWARD, INC.
One Kalisa Way
Paramus, NJ 07652
Tel.: 201-967-1300
Fax: 201-967-0059
Year Founded: 1982
Approx.Billings: $10,450,000
Emp.: 18
Business-to-Business, Consumer Adv., Sales, Promotions & Pub. Rels.
Steven Zinbarg *(Chm. Bd. & Creative Dir.)*
Marvin Howard *(Pres. & New Bus. Contact)*
Michael Sisti *(Chief Exec. Officer)*
Alan Stone *(Exec. V.P.)*
Joe Oliveri *(Exec. V.P.)*
Robin Carley *(Pub. Rels. Dir.)*

SITE OIL CO. OF MISSOURI
50 S. Bemiston Ave.
Clayton, MO 63105
Tel.: 314-725-4321
Fax: 314-725-2381
Year Founded: 1925
Approx.Sls.: $65,000,000
Emp.: 150
Gasoline Stations & Convenience Stores
S.I.C.: 5541; 5411
Alvin Siteman *(Pres.)*
Chris Kemph *(V.P.-Mktg.)*
Eldon Schoeber *(V.P., Sec. & Treas.)*

Outside Service Firm(s):

Arthur Andersen & Co.*(Auditors)*
1010 Market St.
St. Louis, MO 63101

Mercantile Bank N.A.*(Major Banking Relationship)*
Mercantile Tower, One Mercantile Center
Saint Louis, MO 63101
Tel.: 314-425-2525

SITHE ENERGIES, U.S.A., INC.
401 "B" St., Suite 1000
San Diego, CA 92101
Tel.: 619-239-9900 **CA**
Approx.Rev.: $32,000,000
Emp.: 185
Energy Services
S.I.C.: 4931
William Kriegel *(Chm. Bd. & Chief Exec. Officer)*
R.J. Grutsch *(Pres.-Western Division)*
Bruce Wrobel *(Exec. V.P.-Business Devel.)*
Nick Lavin *(Chief Fin. Officer)*
Steven Burton *(Gen. Counsel)*

SIVALLS, INC.
2200 E. 2nd St.
Odessa, TX 79761
Mailing Address:
P.O. Box 2792
Odessa, TX 79760
Tel.: 915-337-3571
Fax: 915-337-2624
Year Founded: 1947
Approx.Sls.: $20,000,000
Emp.: 180
Fiscal Year-end: 10/31/91
Export
Manufacture Oil & Gas Process Equipment
S.I.C.: 3443
C. Richard Sivalls *(Pres. & Chief Exec. Officer)*
Jack A. Zuerker *(Exec. V.P.)*
R.E. Griffin *(Sr. V.P.)*
William J. Lewallen *(V.P.-Engrng.)*
I.R. Nolen *(V.P.-Fin.)*

No. of Mfg. Plants/Facilities: 4
No. of U.S. Offices: 11

Outside Service Firm(s):

Sproles-Woodard & Company*(Auditors)*
Odessa, WA

Texas Commerce Bank*(Major Banking Relationship)*
Odessa, WA

Shafer, Davis, McCollum & Ashley*(Legal Firm)*
Odessa, TX

SKINNER CORP.
1009 N. Lanier Ave.
Lanett, AL 36863
Mailing Address:
P.O. Box 629,
West Point, GA 31833
Tel.: 205-644-2136 **GA**
Fax: 205-644-6895
Assets: $29,778,177
Earnings: $822,629
Liabilities: $11,037,415
Net Worth: $18,740,762
Approx.Sls.: $27,769,988
Emp.: 430
Fiscal Year-end: 6/30/89
Sells Retail Furniture
S.I.C.: 5021; 5712; 5064
Odie G. Skinner *(Chm. Bd. & Chief Exec. Officer)*
Francis S. Reeves *(Co-Chm.)*
Carolyn S. Steele *(Co-Chm.)*
Jack Craft *(Pres.)*
Robert Culbreth *(Chief Fin. Officer, Treas. & Controller)*
Glenn E. Martin *(V.P.)*
Timothy E. McLane *(V.P.-Data Processing)*
Charles M. Reeves *(V.P. & Internal Auditor)*
Daniel McLane *(Asst. V.P.)*
Jefferson G. Steele *(Asst. V.P. & Mgr.-Warehouse)*

Computer Systems/Hardware:
Data General

Outside Service Firm(s):

Grant Thornton*(Auditors)*
Atlanta, GA

Southern Administrative Services*(Group Insurer)*
Columbus, GA

Robinson Humphrey Company, Inc.*(Pension Manager)*
Atlanta, GA

SKOKIE VALLEY BEVERAGE CO.
199 Shepard Ave.
Wheeling, IL 60090
Tel.: 708-541-1500
Fax: 708-541-2059
Year Founded: 1946
Approx.Sls.: $17,000,000
Emp.: 50
Fiscal Year-end: 6/30/90
Wholesale Beverages
S.I.C.: 5149
William P. Schirmang *(Pres., Treas. & Sls. Mgr.)*
Anton T. Schirmang *(V.P.)*
Barbara P. Schirmang *(V.P.)*
Kenneth C. Schirmang *(V.P.-Pur.)*
William A. Schirmang *(V.P.-Data Processing & Sec.)*
John Griffin *(Mgr.-Adv.)*
Principal(s):
William P. Schirmang
Anton T. Schirmang
Barbara P. Schirmang
William A. Schirmang

Outside Service Firm(s):

Wahler & Pecyna*(Legal Firm)*
Chicago, IL

Northbrook Trust & Savings Bank*(Major Banking Relationship)*
Northbrook, IL

SKYWAY FREIGHT SYSTEMS, INC.
225 Westridge Dr.
Watsonville, CA 95076
Mailing Address:
P.O. Box 1810
Santa Cruz, CA 95060-1810
Tel.: 408-722-3133 **CA**
Fax: 408-728-1300
Year Founded: 1977
Assets: $14,360,000
Earnings: ($4,631,000)
Liabilities: $7,071,000
Net Worth: $7,289,000
Approx.Sls.: $63,702,000
Emp.: 750
Fiscal Year-end: 12/31/92
Nationwide Transportation-Line-Haul Trucking, Air Shipments
S.I.C.: 4213; 4513
Employee Matching Gifts Program: One year for employee to be eligible, and then 10% matching.
Robert Baker *(Chief Exec. Officer)*
James F. Watson *(Pres.)*
Dan Gilbertson *(V.P.-Human Resources)*
Stephen E. Holbert *(V.P.)*
Gary Roberts *(V.P.-Info. Systems)*
Doug Thomson *(Dir.-Fin. & Accounting)*
Virginia M. Williams *(Mgr.-Mktg. Services)*
Principal(s):
Robert Baker
James F. Watson

No. of Mfg. Plants/Facilities: 15
No. of U.S. Offices: 15

Computer Systems/Hardware:
Prime 6650

Outside Service Firm(s):

Deloitte & Touche*(Auditors)*
60 S. Market St., Ste. 800
San Jose, CA 95113-2303
Tel.: 408-998-7111
Fax: 408-298-5782

Massachusetts Mutual Life Insurance Co.*(Group Insurer)*
333 Market St., #3120
San Francisco, CA 94105
Tel.: 415-777-3383
Fax: 415-546-7411

Sumitomo Bank*(Major Banking Relationship)*
Los Angeles, CA

Wells Fargo Bank*(Major Banking Relationship)*
420 Montgomery St.
San Francisco, CA 94104

Subsidiary:

Skyway Systems, Inc. **(1)**
225 Westbridge Dr.
Watsonville, CA 95076
Tel.: 408-722-3133

SKYWAY LUGGAGE CO.
10 Wall St.
Seattle, WA 98121
Tel.: 206-441-5300
Fax: 206-441-5306
Year Founded: 1911
Approx.Sls.: $15,000,000
Emp.: 200
Fiscal Year-end: 12/31/90
Luggage Mfg.
S.I.C.: 3161
Henry L. Kotkins *(Chm. Bd.)*
Henry L. Kotkins, Jr. *(Pres.)*
William H. Wilhoit *(Exec. V.P.)*
Larry Clark *(V.P.-Fin. & Admin.)*

Skyway Luggage Co.—(Continued)

Atlas Co. of Boston, Inc. (1)
2121 E. Huntington St.
Philadelphia, PA 19125
Tel.: 215-427-2121
Luggage Mfg.
S.I.C.: 3161

SLANE HOSIERY MILLS, INC.
313-315 S. Centennmial St.
High Point, NC 27260
Tel.: 919-883-4136 **NC**
Fax: 919-886-4543
Year Founded: 1928
Approx.Sls.: $13,000,000
Emp.: 275
Mfr. of Women's Hosiery, Except Socks; Men's, Boys & Girls Hosiery
S.I.C.: 2251; 2252
John C. Slane *(Pres.)*
Ronald Snider *(Exec. V.P.)*
Joe Crowsen *(Mgr.-Plant)*

Outside Service Firm(s):

NationsBank*(Major Banking Relationship)*
High Point, NC

SLANT/FIN CORPORATION
100 Forest Drive
Greenvale, NY 11548
Tel.: 516-484-2600
Fax: 516-484-5921
Year Founded: 1949
Approx.Sls.: $50,000,000
Emp.: 400
Fiscal Year-end: 6/30/91
Export
Fine/Line 30, Fine/Line 15 & Multi-pak 80 Hydronic Baseboards; Fast/Flex Baseboard Connectors; Hydro-Tite Baseboard Expansion Joint; Galaxy, Liberty & Victory Cast Iron Boilers; Caravan Cast Iron Modular Boiler; Monterey JK Air Cooled Pckg. Terminal A/C; JK Heat Pump; Multi/Pak 90 Series Fin-Tube Radiation
S.I.C.: 3433; 3634; 3585; 3822; 3827; 3829
Melvin Dubin *(Chm. Bd. & Pres.)*
Donald Brown *(Exec. V.P. & Treas.)*
Selwyn Steinberg *(Sr. V.P.-Mktg. Services)*
Joseph Durso *(V.P.-Mfg.)*
Jack Kayne *(V.P.-Engrng.)*
Richard Thompson *(Natl. Sls. Mgr.)*
John Svitek *(Controller)*
Delcy Brooks *(Sec.)*
Stephen Gribbin *(Adv. Mgr.)*

Non-U.S. Holding:

Slant-Fin, Ltd./Ltee (1)
6450 Northam Dr.
Mississauga, ON LV4V 1h9, Canada
Tel.: 416-677-8400
Approx.Sls.: $4,000,000
Emp.: 20
Mfr. Heating Equipment
S.I.C.: 3433; 3585
J. Richard Peck *(Pres.)*

SLATER HANFT MARTIN INC

SLATER HANFT MARTIN, INC.
111 Fifth Ave.
New York, NY 10003
Tel.: 212-674-3100
Year Founded: 1981
Approx.Billings: $72,000,000
Emp.: 65
Jerry Martin *(Chm. & Chief Exec. Officer)*
Adam Hanft *(Pres. & Chief Oper. Officer)*
Linda Soro *(V.P., Comptroller)*
Cindy Liebowitz *(Exec. Producer)*
Computer Systems/Hardware:
MacIntosh; IBM System 36

SLEEPECK PRINTING COMPANY
815 S. 25th Ave.
Bellwood, IL 60104
Tel.: 708-544-8900 **IL**
Approx.Sls.: $50,000,000
Emp.: 450
Offset Commercial Printing; Lithographing On Metal
S.I.C.: 2752
William Sleepeck, Jr. *(Chm. Bd.)*
Stanley W. Strotman *(Vice Chm.)*
Michael Sleepeck *(Pres.)*
Robert Kenyon *(Exec. V.P.)*
Robert Gardner *(V.P.-Fin.)*
George Sinka *(V.P.-Mfg.)*

Outside Service Firm(s):

Ernst & Young*(Auditors)*
233 S. Wacker Dr.
Chicago, IL 60606
Tel.: 312-368-1800
Fax: 312-645-3095

Jenner & Block*(Legal Firm)*
Chicago, IL

Continental Bank N. A.*(Major Banking Relationship)*
231 S. LaSalle St.
Chicago, IL 60697
Tel.: 312-828-2345
Tel.: 800-426-5754
Telex: 312-828-1783

Division:

Dixonweb Printing Company (1)
815 S. 25th Ave.
Bellwood, IL 60104
Tel.: 708-544-8900
Commercial Printing
S.I.C.: 2752
Michael Sleepeck *(Pres.)*

SLEEPY'S THE MATTRESS PROFESSIONALS
2 Tri-Harbour Ct.
Port Washington, NY 11050
Tel.: 516-625-1070
Fax: 516-625-1070, Ext. 4149
Emp.: 100
Bedding Retailer
S.I.C.: 5719
David Acker *(Pres.)*
Jack Acker *(V.P.-Sls. & Gen. Mgr.)*
Edward Majepp *(Dir.-Adv.)*

SLOAN VALVE COMPANY
10500 Seymour Ave.
Franklin Park, IL 60131
Tel.: 708-671-4300 **IL**
Fax: 708-671-6944
Year Founded: 1906
Approx.Sls.: $25,000,000
Emp.: 750
Export
Mfr. & Wholesale of Flush Valves, Bedpan Washers, Shower Heads, Hand Dryers, Faucets, Soap Dispensers for Plumbing Industry; Brake Regulators, Retainer Valves, Vacuum Breakers, Angle Cocks for Air Brake Systems of Freight Cars; Non-Ferrous Brass Castings
S.I.C.: 3432; 3743; 5074
Charles S. Allen *(Pres. & Chief Exec. Officer)*
William E. Sloan II *(Exec. V.P., Treas. & Sec.)*
James A. Walsworth *(Chief Fin. Officer)*
Scott Nelson *(Dir.-Personnel)*
C.M. Weege *(Dir.-Mktg.)*
J.R. Coyne *(Mgr.-Western Sls.)*
R.R. Raufeisen *(Mgr.-Adv.)*
F.J. Hawley *(Mgr.-Export & Eastern Sls.)*
Principal(s):
Charles S. Allen
William E. Sloan II
Computer Systems/Hardware:
IBM 4381

Outside Service Firm(s):

Prudential Insurance Co. of America*(Group Insurer)*
751 Broad St.
Newark, NJ 07102-3777
Tel.: 201-802-6000

Divisions:

Sloan Valve, Foundry Div. (1)
Hwy. 33 South
Augusta, AR 72006
Tel.: 501-347-2503
Emp.: 100
Nonferrous Brass Castings
S.I.C.: 3364
Bob Beard *(Foundry Mgr.)*

Sloan Valve, Railroad Products Div. (1)
10500 Seymour Ave.
Franklin Park, IL 60131
Tel.: 708-671-4300
Fax: 708-671-6944
Emp.: 70
Mfr. of Component Parts for Air Brake Systems of Freight Cars
S.I.C.: 3743

Water Control International Inc. (1)
10500 Seymour Ave.
Franklin Park, IL 60131
Tel.: 708-671-4300
Fax: 708-671-6944
Export Sales of Valve Products
S.I.C.: 5074

R & G SLOANE MFG. CO., INC.
7600 N. Clybourn Ave.
Sun Valley, CA 91352
Tel.: 818-767-4726
Approx.Sls.: $75,000,000
Emp.: 700
Mfr. of Plastic Pipe, Fittings & Valves; Engineered Drainage Products; Irrigation Filters; Fire Sprinkler Piping Systems
S.I.C.: 3089
Bill Smith *(Pres.)*
Michael J. Hogan *(V.P.-Mfg.)*
Larry M. Murphy *(V.P.-Sls. & Mktg.)*
Jon Zimmer *(Plant Mgr.)*

SLOANS SUPERMARKETS, INC.
2 Bennett Ave.
New York, NY 10033
Tel.: 212-795-5600
Fax: 212-568-6728
Approx.Sls.: $55,000,000
Emp.: 400
Supermarkets
S.I.C.: 5411
Jules Rose *(Chm. Bd.)*
Stephen E. Karsch *(Sr. Exec. V.P.)*
Martin Weiscott *(V.P.-Fin.)*
Carmine Zappala *(Dir.-Store Opers.)*
Gary Meyer *(Sec. & Treas.)*

Outside Service Firm(s):

Chemical Banking Corp.*(Major Banking Relationship)*
277 Park Ave.
New York, NY 10041
Tel.: 212-310-6407
Fax: 212-310-4526

J.T. SLOCOMB COMPANY
68 Matson Hill Rd.
South Glastonbury, CT 06073
Tel.: 203-633-9485
Fax: 203-633-2388
Sales Range: $60-79 Million
Emp.: 450
Aircraft Engine Parts, Micrometers
S.I.C.: 3545; 3599; 3724
E. John Gregory, Sr. *(Chm. Bd. & Pres.)*
Raymond Charland *(V.P.)*
Edward John Gregory, Jr. *(V.P.)*
Barry Gregory *(V.P.)*
Robert Pastormelo *(V.P.)*
Constantino Tedone *(Sec.)*
Richard Gamble *(Dir.-Sls.)*
Dennis Gareau *(Dir.-Quality)*
Richard Gordon *(Mgr.-Human Resources)*
Harold Kilduff *(Mgr.-Mngmt. Information Systems)*
Ed Ruoff *(Mgr.-Pur.)*
Principal(s):
E. John Gregory, Sr.

No. of Mfg. Plants/Facilities: 4
No. of U.S. Offices: 4

Outside Service Firm(s):

Richard S. Levin*(Auditors)*
Hartford, CT

Leone, Throwe & Nagle*(Legal Firm)*
Hartford, CT

Connecticut Bank & Trust Co., N.A.*(Major Banking Relationship)*
Glastonbury, CT

Divisions:

J.T. Slocomb Co. (1)
235 Interstate Lane
Waterbury, CT 06705
Tel.: 203-754-2995
Emp.: 30

J.T. Slocomb Co. (1)
One Front St.
Cumberland, RI 02864
Tel.: 401-333-3971
Emp.: 30

J.T. Slocomb Company (1)
Wildwood Industrial Park, 901 Industrial Dr.
Wildwood, FL 34785
Tel.: 904-748-5622
Emp.: 30

SMALL PARTS, INC.
600 Humphrey St.
Logansport, IN 46947
Tel.: 219-753-6323
Fax: 219-753-6660
Approx.Sls.: $20,000,000
Emp.: 235
Custom & Pressed Stampings & Springs
S.I.C.: 3495; 3469; 3493
John E. Barnes *(Chief Exec. Officer)*
Michael K. Jordan *(Pres.)*
James P. Bauer *(V.P.-Fin. & Treas.)*
Michael J. Rushinsky *(V.P.-Mfg.)*
James Sampson *(V.P.-Facilities)*

Outside Service Firm(s):

Brink & Brink*(Auditors)*
Logansport, IN

Hanna, Small, Sabatini & Becker*(Legal Firm)*
Logansport, IN

First National Bank of Indiana*(Major Banking Relationship)*
P.O. Box 1247,
New Albany, IN 47151-1247
Tel.: 812-948-4400

SMALL TUBE PRODUCTS CO., INC.
Spring Meadows
Altoona, PA 16603
Mailing Address:
P.O. Box 1674
Altoona, PA 16603
Tel.: 814-695-4491
Fax: 814-696-0702
Approx.Sls.: $65,000,000
Emp.: 275
Manufacture Brass & Copper Tubing
S.I.C.: 3351
James A. Woomer, Jr. *(Pres.)*
Darrell Smith *(Controller)*
Ken Harrington *(Gen. Mgr.-Sls.)*

Outside Service Firm(s):

Deloitte & Touche*(Auditors)*
2400 One PPG Place
Pittsburgh, PA 15222
Tel.: 412-281-2232

Mellon Bank, Central, N.A.*(Major Banking Relationship)*
Altoona, PA

SMARTSTAR CORPORATION
120 Cremona Dr.
Goleta, CA 93117
Mailing Address:
P.O. Box 1950
Goleta, CA 93116-01950
Tel.: 805-685-8000 **CA**
Fax: 805-562-8888
Year Founded: 1977
Sales Range: $10-19 Million
Emp.: 126
Fiscal Year-end: 9/30/89
Export
Software Development & Sales
S.I.C.: 7372
John D. Markel *(Pres., Chief Exec. Officer & Treas.)*
Mike Dion *(V.P.-Engrng.)*
Jose Garcia *(V.P.-Sls.)*
John Otti *(V.P.-Mktg.)*
William A. Robertson *(V.P.-Opers. & Chief Fin. Officer)*
Gary Shenton *(Controller)*
Geraldo Celio *(Mgr.-Systems)*

No. of U.S. Offices: 8

Computer Systems/Hardware:
DEC VAX 8650 & 8700

Outside Service Firm(s):

Ernst & Young*(Auditors)*
21300 Victory Blvd., Ste. 1000
Woodland Hills, CA 91367
Tel.: 818-703-4700

Price, Postel & Parma*(Legal Firm)*
200 E. Carrillo St.
Santa Barbara, CA 93101
Tel.: 805-962-0011

Silicon Valley Bank*(Major Banking Relationship)*
Irvine, CA

SMARTY PANTS N TOPS TOO, INC.
1115 John Reed Ct.
City of Industry, CA 91745
Tel.: 818-369-9811 **CA**
Fax: 818-961-4228
Year Founded: 1960
Approx.Sls.: $28,000,000
Emp.: 650
Retail Sales of Ready-to-Wear Women's Apparel
S.I.C.: 5621
Steven Hyman *(Pres.)*
Helen Hyman *(V.P.)*
David Hyman *(Treas.)*
Susan Hyman *(Sec.)*

Outside Service Firm(s):

Arnold C. Libman*(Auditors)*
City of Industry, CA

Bank of America NT&SA*(Major Banking Relationship)*
City of Industry, CA

SMEAD MANUFACTURING COMPANY
600 E. Smead Blvd.
Hastings, MN 55033
Tel.: 612-437-4111
Fax: 612-437-9134
Year Founded: 1906
Approx.Sls.: $160,000,000
Emp.: 2,600
Fiscal Year-end: 4/30/91
Export
Mfr. Office Paper Filing Supplies
S.I.C.: 2675; 2652
Ebba C. Hoffman *(Chm., Pres., Chief Exec. & Chief Fin. Officer)*
Sharon Avent *(Exec. V.P.)*
David L. Fasbender *(V.P.-Sls.)*
Dale Olson *(Controller)*
Roger Finstad *(Plant Supt.)*
Roland Gilbertson *(Dir.-Mngmt. Information Systems)*
Gordon Goodall *(Dir.-Engng.)*
Dean Schwanke *(Dir.-Human Resources)*
John Welshons *(Dir.-Pur.)*
Principal(s):
Ebba C. Hoffman

No. of Mfg. Plants/Facilities: 5
No. of U.S. Offices: 5

Computer Systems/Hardware:
IBM

Outside Service Firm(s):

KPMG Peat Marwick*(Auditors)*
1600 Meritor Tower, 444 Cedar St.
St. Paul, MN 55102

Travelers Insurance Co.*(Group Insurer)*
1 Tower Square
Hartford, CT 06183-2492
Tel.: 203-277-4542
Fax: 203-277-5038

Norwest Bank Minnesota, N.A.*(Major Banking Relationship)*
6th St. & Marquette Av.
Minneapolis, MN 55479
Tel.: 612-667-1234

ANTON SMIT & CO., INC.
6 Connor Lane
Deer Park, NY 11729
Mailing Address:
P.O. Box 658
Deer Park, NY 11729
Tel.: 516-242-3800
Telex: 9102408645 ANTON AMIT UQ
Fax: 516-242-3023
Sales Range: $10-19 Million
Emp.: 40
Fiscal Year-end: 6/30/91
Mfr. Industrial Diamond Tools, Wheels & Mining Bits
S.I.C.: 3545; 3291
William Verby *(Pres.)*
John Kalabza *(Dir.-Adv.)*
Robert Kertz *(Pur. Agent & Office Mgr.)*

Computer Systems/Hardware:
Kaypro PC

Outside Service Firm(s):

Eidelkind & Levine*(Auditors)*
Plainview, NY

European American Bank*(Major Banking Relationship)*
Commack, NY

WILBUR SMITH ASSOCIATES
Carnation Bank Towers
Columbia, SC 29202
Mailing Address:
P.O. Box 92,
Columbia, SC 29202
Tel.: 803-738-0580
Fax: 803-251-2064
Approx.Sls.: $42,000,000
Emp.: 700
Transportation Consultants, Engineers, Architects, Planners, Economics
S.I.C.: 8748
Robert A. Hubbard *(Chm. Bd. & Pres.)*
Carlos C. Villarreal, Sr. *(Exec. V.P.)*
Norman H. Wuestefeld *(Exec. V.P.)*
John W. Bonnville *(Sr. V.P.)*
Gerald L. Drake *(Sr. V.P.)*
Robert E. Whiteside *(Sr. V.P.-Mktg.)*
James Hardwick *(Admin. Officer)*
Ken Corley *(Controller)*
D.L. Comalander *(Dir.-Data Processing)*
D.A. King *(Dir.-Personnel)*

Outside Service Firm(s):

J. W. Hunt & Co.*(Auditors)*
Middleburg Office Park, 1607 St. Julian Place
Columbia, SC 29202
Tel.: 803-254-8196

South Carolina National Bank*(Major Banking Relationship)*
Columbia, SC

Smith, Badofsky & Raffel, Inc.
Advertising

SMITH, BADOFSKY & RAFFEL, INC. ADVERTISING
325 W. Huron St.
Chicago, IL 60610
Tel.: 312-642-0500
Fax: 312-642-8480
Year Founded: 1980
Approx.Billings: $12,500,000
Emp.: 21
Robert J. Smith *(Pres.)*
William D. Raffel *(Exec. V.P., Treas.)*
Jack Badofsky *(V.P., Creative Dir. & Sec.)*

SMITH BROTHERS FARMS, INC.
27441 68th Ave., S.
Kent, WA 98032
Mailing Address:
P.O. Box 778
Kent, WA 98305
Tel.: 206-852-1000 **WA**
Fax: 206-850-0918
Year Founded: 1920
Approx.Sls.: $55,000,000
Emp.: 210
Fluid Milk Dairy
S.I.C.: 2026
Daniel P. Smith *(Pres.)*
Howard M. Smith *(V.P.)*
Earl M. Davenport *(Treas.)*
Alexis Koester *(Sec.)*

No. of Mfg. Plants/Facilities: 3
No. of U.S. Offices: 1

Outside Service Firm(s):

Moss Adams*(Auditors)*
Tacoma, WA

Mutual of Omaha Insurance Company*(Commercial Insurance Carrier)*
Mutual of Omaha Plaza,
Omaha, NE 68175
Tel.: 800-228-7775

Mutual of Omaha Insurance Company*(Group Insurer)*
Mutual of Omaha Plaza,
Omaha, NE 68175
Tel.: 800-228-7775

Curran & Klewano*(Legal Firm)*
Seattle, WA

Subsidiary:

Smith Tractor & Equipment Co. **(1)**
3607 20th S.E.
Tacoma, WA 98424
Tel.: 206-838-1377
Emp.: 110
Sell Industrial Equipment
S.I.C.: 5084
Scott Highland *(Mgr.)*

PETER W. SMITH & COMPANY, INC.
400 N. Michigan Ave., Ste. 520
Chicago, IL 60611
Tel.: 312-222-0003
Fax: 312-222-0008
Approx.Sls.: $725,000,000
Investment Company
S.I.C.: 6719
Peter W. Smith *(Pres.)*
Alton J. O'Neil *(Mng. Dir.)*
Gail L. Bell *(Corp. Sec.)*

Subsidiaries:

CWT Specialty Stores, Inc. **(1)**
505 Collin St.
South Attleboro, MA 02703
Tel.: 508-399-6000
A Chain of 60 Women's Specialty Stores
S.I.C.: 5632
Gerald Gura *(Pres.)*

Donnelley Marketing, Inc. **(1)**
70 Seaview Ave.
Stamford, CT 06902
Tel.: 203-353-7000 (100%)
Emp.: 2,400
Direct Marketing Service
S.I.C.: 7331; 7375
John A. Cleary *(Pres.)*
Robert K. Sher *(Exec. V.P.)*
Steven R. Snyder *(Exec. V.P.)*
Robert Spillane *(Sr. V.P. & Treas.)*

Subsidiaries:

Carol Wright Sales, Inc. **(2)**
70 Seaview Ave.
Stamford, CT 06904
Tel.: 203-353-7200 (100%)
Telex: 6819243 CRGHT UW
Fax: 203-353-7380
Emp.: 650
Fiscal Year-end: 12/31/90
Import
Computer Systems/Hardware:
IBM 3090-300E
Mail Order Distributor of Gifts, Housewares, Apparel, Decorative Accessories
S.I.C.: 5961
John R. Purcell *(Chm. Bd.)*
Robert I. Ginsberg *(Pres. & Chief Exec. Officer)*
Robert F. Spillane *(Sr. V.P.-Fin.)*
William A. Slater *(V.P. & Gen. Counsel)*
David E. Brace *(V.P.-Opers.)*
Sheryl I. Purcell *(Sec.)*
Norma Zwart *(Controller)*
Donna DiMarco *(Dir.-Mktg.)*

Donnelley Marketing Data Processing Operations **(2)**
70 Seaview Ave
Stamford, CT 06902
Tel.: 203-353-7000
Emp.: 467
Marketing Data On 90 Million Households
S.I.C.: 7375
John A. Cleary *(Pres.)*

Donnelley Marketing Information Services **(2)**
70 Seaview Ave., P.O. Box 10250
Stamford, CT 06904
Tel.: 203-353-7000
Emp.: 100
Demographic & Other Marketing Information Services
S.I.C.: 8732
Gary Hill *(V.P. & Gen. Mgr.)*

Estes Industries, Inc. **(1)**
1295 H St.
Penrose, CO 81240
Tel.: 719-372-6565
Tel.: 800-525-7561
Approx.Sls.: $20,000,000
Emp.: 250
Fiscal Year-end: 8/31/92
Import Export
Computer Systems/Hardware:
DEC VAX, IBM PC/XT
Mfr. & Sale of Kites, Premium/Incentive Items; Model Rockets, Kits, Engines & Supplies
S.I.C.: 3944
Barry Tunick *(Pres. & Gen. Mgr.)*
Troy Carroll *(Controller)*
Dennis Poole *(V.P.-Sls., Rockets & Kites)*
Mary Roberts *(Mgr.-Mktg.)*
M. Payne *(Mgr.-Indus. Rels.)*
George Kale *(Mgr. Mfg.)*
Sneila Scott *(Quality Control)*

Peter W. Smith & Company, Inc.—(Continued)

Mike Dorffler *(Mgr.-Res. & Devel.)*
Norman Bean *(Pur. Agent)*

Flametech Corporation (1)
104 Parker St.
Newburyport, MA 01950
Tel.: 508-462-3163
Mfr. of Feed Screws
S.I.C.: 3452
John Riehl *(Pres.)*

Wedlo, Inc. (1)
3200 2nd Ave.
Birmingham, AL 35202
Tel.: 205-322-4444
Emp.: 350
62-Store SE Jewelry Retailer
S.I.C.: 5944; 5094
Peter Petro *(Pres.)*

Xaloy, Inc. (1)
State Rd. 99
Pulaski, VA 24301
Tel.: 703-980-7560
Mfr. of Pressure Cylinders; Metal Plates & Metal Screws
S.I.C.: 3443; 3452
Walter G. Cox, Jr. *(Pres.)*

J. M. SMITH CORP.
450 Wofford St.
Spartanburg, SC 29301
Tel.: 803-582-1216 **SC**
Fax: 803-591-0333
Year Founded: 1944
Approx.Sls.: $100,000,000
Emp.: 300
Fiscal Year-end: 2/28/91
Wholesale Drugs; Data Processing Services
S.I.C.: 5122; 7374; 5100
Henry Dale Smith *(Chm. Bd.)*
James S. Smith *(Pres.)*
Jimmy Wilson *(Chief Fin. Officer, Treas. & Controller)*
Terry Bagwell *(Dir.-M.I.S.)*
Betty T. Wood *(Sec.)*

Outside Service Firm(s):

Harris, Swain, Brown & Elliott*(Auditors)*
Spartanburg, SC

Gaines & Walsh*(Legal Firm)*
Spartanburg, SC
Fax: 803-591-0333

South Carolina National Bank*(Major Banking Relationship)*
P.O. Box 3128,
Spartanburg, SC 29304
Tel.: 803-596-4200

Divisions:

QS/1 Data Systems Div. (1)
P.O. 6052
Spartanburg, SC 29301
Tel.: 803-578-9455
Bill Cobb *(Pres.)*

Smith Data Processing Div. (1)
P.O. Box 1779
Spartanburg, SC 29304
Tel.: 803-582-1216
A.W. Smith *(Pres.)*

Smith Wholesale Drug Div. (1)
450 Wofford St.
Spartanburg, SC 29301
Tel.: 803-582-1216
B.E. Shelley *(Pres.)*
Ronald G. Bailey *(Dir.-Mktg.)*

SMITH-EDWARDS-DUNLAP COMPANY
Allegheny Ave. at Delaware Expwy.
Philadelphia, PA 19134
Tel.: 215-425-8800 **PA**
Fax: 215-425-9110
Approx.Sls.: $25,000,000
Emp.: 320
Export
Lithographic & Letterpress Printing, Typesetting, Binding; Direct Mail Services; Publishing
S.I.C.: 2759; 2731; 2752; 2789; 2791
Henry K. Lobel *(Chm. Bd. & Pres.)*
Harold Coopersmith *(Exec. V.P.)*
Joseph Scalise *(V.P. & Gen. Mgr.)*
Fred Reed *(V.P.-Fin. & Sec.)*
John Landi *(V.P.-Mfg.)*
Edith Lobel *(Treas.)*
Thomas Dougherty *(Dir.-Personnel)*

Outside Service Firm(s):

Blank, Rome, Comisky & McCauley*(Legal Firm)*
Four Penn Center Plaza
Philadelphia, PA 19103
Tel.: 215-209-3700

Philadelphia National Bank*(Major Banking Relationship)*
P.O. Box 13834, Broad & Chestnut Streets
Philadelphia, PA 19101-7618
Tel.: 215-973-8327

SMITH-EMERY COMPANY
781 E. Washington Blvd.
Los Angeles, CA 90021
Tel.: 213-749-3411 **CA**
Fax: 213-746-7228
Year Founded: 1904
Approx.Sls.: $25,000,000
Emp.: 500
Construction Related Testing & Inspection; Full Service Geotechnical, Chemists, Metallurgists, Window, Wall/Curtain Wall & Specialty Testing
S.I.C.: 8734
George F. Partridge *(Chm. Bd.)*
James E. Partridge *(Pres.)*
Fred Partridge *(Exec. V.P. & Chief Fin. Officer)*
James Duncan *(Controller)*
John W. Hooper *(V.P.-Admin.)*
Principal(s):
George F. Partridge
James E. Partridge
Fred Partridge

Outside Service Firm(s):

Frazer & Torbet*(Auditors)*
City of Industry, CA

First Interstate Bank of California, N.A.*(Major Banking Relationship)*
P.O. Box 3667,
Los Angeles, CA 90051
Tel.: 213-614-4000

Sanwa Bank California*(Major Banking Relationship)*
601 S. Figueroa St.
Los Angeles, CA 90017
Tel.: 213-896-7000

SMITH ENTERPRISES
1953 Langston St.
Rock Hill, SC 29730
Mailing Address:
P.O. Box 12006,
Rock Hill, SC 29731
Tel.: 803-366-7101
Fax: 803-366-1958
Approx.Sls.: $22,000,000
Emp.: 100
Wholesale Filled Easter Baskets; Gourmet Cheese Trays; Plastic Items
S.I.C.: 2022; 5199
Jake Smith *(V.P.-Sls. & Mktg.)*
Michael Sapyta *(Treas.)*
Eloise Anderson *(Pur. Agent)*
Pam Luxon *(Mgr.-Personnel)*
Jim Smith *(Mgr.-Data Processing)*

Outside Service Firm(s):

A. Walt Carpenter*(Auditors)*
Rock Hill, SC

Kennedy, Covington, Lobdell & Hickman*(Legal Firm)*
3300 NCNB Plaza
Charlotte, NC 28282
Tel.: 704-377-6000

First Union National Bank*(Major Banking Relationship)*
Rock Hill, SC

SMITH FARMS, INC.
403 S. Colorado
Flatonia, TX 78941
Tel.: 512-865-3592
Fax: 512-865-3971
Approx.Sls.: $17,000,000
Emp.: 125
Eggs
S.I.C.: 5144
Carl W. Smith *(Pres.)*
Henry Novak *(V.P.)*
Bryan Berger *(Sec. & Treas.)*

Outside Service Firm(s):

Victoria Bank & Trust*(Major Banking Relationship)*
One O'Connor Plaza
Victoria, TX 77902
Tel.: 512-573-5151

KEITH SMITH FARMS, INC.
911 Gaines St.
Hot Springs, AR 71901
Tel.: 501-321-9990 **AR**
Fax: 501-321-2629
Approx.Sls.: $18,000,000
Emp.: 46
Eggs
S.I.C.: 5144
James Keith Smith, II *(Pres.)*
Bill Hunt *(Sec. & Treas.)*

Outside Service Firm(s):

Frost & Co.*(Auditors)*
Little Rock, AR

SMITH FROZEN FOODS, INC.
P.O. Box 68
Weston, OR 97886
Tel.: 503-566-3515
Fax: 503-566-3707
Approx.Sls.: $35,000,000
Emp.: 1,000
Processing of Frozen Peas, Lima & Green Beans, Corn, Carrots, Mixed Vegetables
S.I.C.: 2037
Gordon H. Smith *(Chm. Bd. & Pres.)*
Kelly Brown *(V.P.-Mktg.)*
David H. Jensen *(V.P.-Fin., Opers. & Real Estate)*
Sharon L. Smith *(V.P.)*
Frank Cupp *(Treas.)*
Inez Warnock *(Sec.)*
Russell Crey *(Dir.-Personnel)*
Gerald Brown *(Mgr.-Production)*
Morris Hansen *(Plant Mgr.)*
Corey Zenger *(Pur. Agent)*

Computer Systems/Hardware:
IBM 38

Outside Service Firm(s):

Deloitte & Touche*(Auditors)*
Salem, OR

Smith & Hilbig*(Legal Firm)*
Torrance, CA

U.S. National Bank*(Major Banking Relationship)*
309 S.W. Sixth Ave.
Portland, OR 97208
Tel.: 503-275-4942

SMITH & GILLESPIE ENGINEERS, INC.
1100 Cesery Blvd.
Jacksonville, FL 32211
Mailing Address:
P.O. Box 53138
Jacksonville, FL 32201
Tel.: 904-743-6950 **FL**
Fax: 904-744-6267
Year Founded: 1940
Emp.: 68
Consulting Engineers
S.I.C.: 8711
John M. Colyer *(Chm. Bd. Emeritus)*
James J. Berry *(Chm. Bd.)*
Robert W. Gehrig *(Pres.)*
James C. Williamson, Sr. *(Exec. V.P. & Treas.)*
Harold R. Bridges *(V.P. & Sec.)*
Leona M. Jipp *(Mktg. Coordinator)*

Computer Systems/Hardware:
CAD System

Outside Service Firm(s):

Purvis, Gray & Co.*(Auditors)*
Gainesville, FL

Rogers, Towers, Bailey, Jones, Gay*(Legal Firm)*
Jacksonville, FL

Sun Bank, N.A.*(Major Banking Relationship)*
Jacksonville, FL

SMITH/GREENLAND, INCORPORATED
555 West 57th St.
New York, NY 10019
Tel.: 212-757-3200
Fax: 212-757-7217
Year Founded: 1958
Approx.Billings: $47,000,000
Advertising Agency
S.I.C.: 7311
Leo Greenland *(Chm. & Chief Exec. Officer)*
Drew Greenland *(Exec. V.P.)*
Bert Rosenberg *(Exec. V.P.)*
Oscar H. Haffner *(Sr. V.P., Fin. & Chief Fin. Officer)*
David Schertz *(Controller)*

Computer Systems/Hardware:
IBM

Outside Service Firm(s):

Ernst & Young*(Auditors)*
787 Seventh Ave.
New York, NY 10019
Tel.: 212-773-1243

Davis & Gilbert*(Legal Firm)*
850 Third Ave.
New York, NY 10022
Tel.: 212-326-1300

Chemical Banking Corp.*(Major Banking Relationship)*
277 Park Ave.
New York, NY 10041
Tel.: 212-310-6407
Fax: 212-310-4526

THE SMITH GROUP, INC.
150 W. Jefferson, Ste. 100
Detroit, MI 48226
Tel.: 313-983-3600
Telex: 810-221-9463
Fax: 313-983-3636
Approx.Sls.: $50,100,000
Emp.: 439
Architecture, Engineering, Planning, Construction, Development & Management
S.I.C.: 8712; 8711; 6531; 6552; 8741; 1542
Arnold Mikon *(Pres. & Chief Exec. Officer)*
Joseph B. Uicker *(Sr. V.P.)*
Mike McCuish *(Treas.)*
S.B. Vora *(Sec.)*
Principal(s):
Arnold Mikon
Joseph B. Uicker
S.B. Vora
Fred Moyer
Tim Larsen
Ralph P. Youngren

Computer Systems/Hardware:
Digital

Outside Service Firm(s):

Price Waterhouse*(Auditors)*
200 Renaissance Center, Ste. 3900
Detroit, MI 48243

Berry, Moorman, King, Cook & Hudson*(Legal Firm)*
Detroit, MI

Comerica Bank*(Major Banking Relationship)*
211 W. Fort St.
Detroit, MI 48226
Tel.: 313-222-3300

Subsidiary:

Smith Hinchman Grylls Associates, Inc. **(1)**
150 W. Jefferson Ave., Ste. 100
Detroit, MI 48226
Tel.: 313-964-3000
Emp.: 320
Architectural & Engineering Services
S.I.C.: 8711; 8712
Arnold Mikon *(AIA Pres. & Chief Exec. Officer)*
Andrew A. Vazzano *(AIA Sr. V.P. & Dir.-Mktg.)*

H. B. SMITH CO., INC.
57 Main St.
Westfield, MA 01085
Tel.: 413-568-3148 **MA**
Fax: 413-568-0525
Year Founded: 1853
Approx.Sls.: $30,000,000
Emp.: 350
Manufacture Cast Iron Heating Boilers, Heating Apparatus
S.I.C.: 3443; 3433
Don Ballentine *(Pres.)*
Walter Pawlowski *(Treas. & Controller)*
Peter J. Stasz *(Gen. Counsel)*
David Atkin *(Pur. Agent)*
Edward C. Fila *(Mgr.-Mfg.)*
Chris Jarvis *(Mgr.-Engrng.)*

Outside Service Firm(s):

Grant Thornton*(Auditors)*
53 State St.
Boston, MA 02109
Tel.: 617-723-7900

Bay Bank Boston, N.A.*(Major Banking Relationship)*
Boston, MA

L. B. SMITH, INC.
2001 State Rd.
Camp Hill, PA 17001-8134
Tel.: 717-737-3431 **PA**
Fax: 717-731-8325
Year Founded: 1918
Approx.Sls.: $114,000,000
Emp.: 650
Sales & Repair of Construction Equipment
S.I.C.: 5082; 5511; 6141; 7692
Richard E. Jordan *(Chm. Bd. & Chief Exec. Officer)*
L. L. Light *(Pres. & Chief Oper. Officer)*
R. H. Folk *(Exec. V.P.)*
R. C. Sherwood *(Exec. V.P. & Chief Fin. Officer)*
T.P. Hanlon *(Treas.)*
L. Neilson *(Sec. & Gen. Counsel)*
R. Beecher *(Dir.-Personnel)*
R. Monroe *(Dir.-Pur.)*

No. of Mfg. Plants/Facilities: 1
No. of U.S. Offices: 22

Computer Systems/Hardware:
Mohawk Data Systems

Outside Service Firm(s):

Coopers & Lybrand*(Auditors)*
5 North Fifth Street
Harrisburg, PA 17101

SMITH INDUSTRIES, INC.
2781 Gunter Park Dr. E.
Montgomery, AL 36109
Mailing Address:
P.O. Box 3237
Montgomery, AL 36109
Tel.: 205-277-8520 **AL**
Fax: 205-272-7396
Year Founded: 1926
Approx.Sls.: $42,000,000
Emp.: 480
Export
Mfr. of Plumbing Fixture Fittings & Trim; Firefighting Apparatus; Sprinkler Systems, Fire; Operating Systems Computer Software; Welding Machines & Equipment, Ultrasonic
S.I.C.: 3432; 3569; 7372; 3699
Jay L. Smith *(Pres.)*
O.A. Wilkerson, III *(Sr. V.P. & Treas.)*
Steve C. Chromey *(V.P.-Opers.)*
Arthur W. Samuels *(V.P.)*
Bruce W. Smith *(V.P.-Mktg.)*
Joseph M. Soriano *(V.P.)*
Fraizer Summerall *(Mgr.-Pur.)*

Outside Service Firm(s):

Price Waterhouse*(Auditors)*
100 Cumberland Circle, Ste. 1400
Atlanta, GA 30339

Capell, Howard, Knabe & Cobbs*(Legal Firm)*
Montgomery, AL

Trust Company Bank*(Major Banking Relationship)*
Stock Trans. Dept. P.O.B. 4625, Trust Company of Georgia Bldg.
Atlanta, GA 30302
Tel.: 404-588-7831

Division:

Potter Roemer Div. **(1)**
16833 Edwards
Cerritos, CA 90701
Tel.: 310-404-3753
Mfr. of Firefighting Equipment
S.I.C.: 3569

Subsidiary:

Precision Arc Co. **(1)**
60 Radel St.
Bridgeport, CT 06607
Tel.: 203-378-7397
Mfr. Semi Automatic Welding Machines
S.I.C.: 5084
Donald Thomson *(Pres.)*

EVERETT SMITH INVESTMENT CO. OF DELAWARE
800 N. Marshall St.
Milwaukee, WI 53202
Tel.: 414-273-3421 **DE**
Fax: 414-273-1058
Approx.Sls.: $370,000,000
Emp.: 2,400
Holding Company; Sheet Metal, Tanks, Cabinets, Machine Components
S.I.C.: 6719; 3443; 3444; 3532; 3499
Everett G. Smith *(Pres.)*
Thomas Hauske *(V.P.)*
Alfred G. Janos *(V.P.)*
Anders Segerdahl *(V.P.)*
John Steelman *(V.P.)*
Harry Wallace *(Sec.)*

Outside Service Firm(s):

Price Waterhouse*(Auditors)*
1500 Bank One Plaza, 100 E. Wisconsin Ave.
Milwaukee, WI 53202

Foley & Lardner*(Legal Firm)*
777 E. Wisconsin Ave.
Milwaukee, WI 53202
Tel.: 414-271-2400

First Wisconsin National Bank*(Major Banking Relationship)*
777 E. Wisconsin Ave.
Milwaukee, WI 53202
Tel.: 414-765-4321
Fax: 414-355-6903

Subsidiary:

Sivyer Steel Corporation **(1)**
225 33rd. St.
Bettendorf, IA 52722
Tel.: 319-355-1811
Alloy Steel Castings, Except Investment
S.I.C.: 3325
Everett G. Smith *(Chm. Bd.)*
Claude D. Robinson *(Pres. & Chief Exec. Officer)*
Patricia M. Adrian *(Controller)*

Division:

Riverside Products Div. **(2)**
225 33rd St.
Bettendorf, IA 52722
Tel.: 319-355-1811
Steel; Engineering Services; Research Services, Except Laboratory
S.I.C.: 3325

SMITH, KAPLAN, ALLEN & REYNOLDS, INC.
111 South 108th Ave.
Omaha, NE 68154
Tel.: 402-330-0110
Fax: 402-330-8791
Year Founded: 1949
Approx.Billings: $13,600,000
Emp.: 38
H. Wayne Smith *(Pres. & Treas.)*
Ronald N. Kaplan *(Sr. Exec. V.P., Sec.)*
Mike Furesz *(V.P., Research & Acct. Services)*

SMITH-LEE CO., INC.
537 Fitch
Oneida, NY 13421
Mailing Address:
P.O. Box 330
Oneida, NY 13421
Tel.: 315-363-2500 **NY**
Fax: 315-363-9573
Year Founded: 1898
Sales Range: $10-19 Million
Emp.: 80
Paper Lace & Linen Place Mats, Doilies, Napkins & Tray Covers, Bath Mats, Packaged Merchandise, Serv-Ease Paper Plates, Tray Covers
S.I.C.: 2679
Jonathan M. Groat *(Pres. & Chief Exec. Officer)*
Jack Bailey *(V.P. & Treas.)*
R. C. Cummings *(Sec. & Gen. Counsel)*
Principal(s):
Jonathan M. Groat
Jack Bailey
R. C. Cummings
Thomas Hennessey
Alan A. Mattei

No. of Mfg. Plants/Facilities: 1
No. of U.S. Offices: 1

Computer Systems/Hardware:
IBM System 36

Outside Service Firm(s):

Blue Cross & Blue Shield of Greater Utica, Inc.*(Group Insurer)*
Utica, NY

Liberty Mutual*(Group Insurer)*
Boston, MA

Chase Lincoln First Bank, N.A.*(Investment Banker)*
Oneida, NY

Cummings, McGuire, Dunckel & Co.*(Legal Firm)*
Lowville, NY

J. RICHARD SMITH, LTD.
225 Broad Hollow Rd.
Melville, NY 11747
Tel.: 516-293-8700
Fax: 516-293-8937
Year Founded: 1964
Approx.Billings: $41,435,000
Emp.: 34
Gerald R. Smith *(Chm. Bd. & New Bus. Contact)*
Michael Smith *(Pres., Chief Exec. Officer & Creative Dir.)*
Sandra Smith *(Chief Oper. Officer)*
Rhonda Gastman *(Exec. V.P., Media)*
Rita Almanzo *(Asst. Controller)*

T. L. SMITH MACHINE
7020 Henrietta Rd.
Springville, NY 14141
Mailing Address:
P.O. Box 189
Springville, NY 14141-0189
Tel.: 716-592-2854
Tel.: 800-225-5857
Fax: 716-592-7304
Year Founded: 1902
Approx.Sls.: $10,000,000
Emp.: 100
Fiscal Year-end: 9/30/91
Export
Concrete Transit Mixers
S.I.C.: 3531
Grover Riefler *(Pres.)*
Montie Riefler *(V.P.)*
Art Maracino *(Exec. Vice Pres.)*
Scott Riefler *(Dir.-Sls. & Dir. Mktg./Dir. Response)*
Dick Sarver *(Mgr.-Mfg.)*
Fran Cattone *(Data Processing)*

Computer Systems/Hardware:
ZENIX

Division:

CEM South **(1)**
31800 Progress Rd.
Leesburg, FL 34748
Tel.: 904-728-5988
Export
Computer Systems/Hardware:
IBM P.C.
Concrete Mixers, Parts & Accessories
Grover Riefler *(Pres.)*
Paul Almond *(Sls. Mgr.)*
Laurel Riefler *(Mgr.-Personnel)*

SMITH METAL ARTS COMPANY, INC.
2685 Walden Ave.
Buffalo, NY 14225
Tel.: 716-873-3083 **DE**
Fax: 716-873-3926
Year Founded: 1919
Approx.Sls.: $15,000,000
Emp.: 150
Fiscal Year-end: 12/31/89
Import Export
Manufacture Metal & Plastic Desk Accessories
S.I.C.: 3999; 3089
Daniel R. Donaldson *(Chm. Bd.)*
Cole Bergan *(Pres.)*
John Drenning *(Legal Officer & Sec.)*
Tim Nolan *(Dir.-Pur.)*
Christopher Vogelsang *(Mgr.-Sls.)*

No. of Mfg. Plants/Facilities: 2
No. of U.S. Offices: 2

Computer Systems/Hardware:
PC Network

Outside Service Firm(s):

Johnson, O'Connell & Martino*(Auditors)*
Buffalo, NY

Phillips, Lytle, Hitchcock, Blaine & Huber*(Legal Firm)*
3400 Marine Midland Center
Buffalo, NY 14203
Tel.: 716-847-8400

Key Bank*(Major Banking Relationship)*
Buffalo, NY

Smith Metal Arts Company, Inc.—(Continued)

Subsidiary:

McDonald Products Company (1)
2685 Walden Ave.
Buffalo, NY 14225
Tel.: 716-684-7200
Fax: 716-684-2053
Cole Bergan *(Pres.)*

SMITH MOTORS, INC.
6405 Indianapolis Blvd.
Hammond, IN 46320
Tel.: 219-845-4000 **IN**
Fax: 219-898-7233
Emp.: 62
New & Used Automobiles
S.I.C.: 5511
Jarvis Roper *(Pres.)*
J. Timothy Roper *(V.P.)*
June Springer *(Sec. & Treas.)*

Outside Service Firm(s):

Mercantile National Bank*(Major Banking Relationship)*
Hammond, IN

SMITH PIPE & STEEL CO.
733 N. 19th Ave.
Phoenix, AZ 85009
Mailing Address:
P.O. Box 899,
Phoenix, AZ 85001
Tel.: 602-257-9494 **AZ**
Fax: 602-253-8770
Year Founded: 1938
Sales Range: $40-59 Million
Emp.: 150
Fiscal Year-end: 2/28/90
Import
Steel & Steel Pipe
S.I.C.: 5051
Arnold A. Smith *(Chm. Bd.)*
Herbert Smith *(Pres.)*
Francine M. Murtaugh *(V.P.-Human Res.)*
Steven McNeil *(Treas.)*
Jarril F. Kaplan *(Corp. Sec.)*
Random E. Fodor *(Mgr.-Sls.(Steel Division.))*
Bonnie Payne *(Mgr.-Pur.)*
Francine M. Murtaugh *(Dir.-Personnel)*

No. of Mfg. Plants/Facilities: 2
No. of U.S. Offices: 2

Computer Systems/Hardware:
IBM

Outside Service Firm(s):

Arthur Andersen & Co.*(Auditors)*
Phoenix, AZ

First Interstate Bank*(Major Banking Relationship)*
P.O. Box 53441,
Phoenix, AZ 85072-3441
Tel.: 602-229-4049

SMITH-SHAFER OIL CO.
1639 N. Alpine Rd., Ste. 310
Rockford, IL 61107
Mailing Address:
P.O. Box 680,
Rockford, IL 61105
Tel.: 815-398-8998 **IL**
Year Founded: 1971
Assets: $887,977
Liabilities: $132,546
Net Worth: $755,431
Emp.: 21
Fiscal Year-end: 10/31/89
Retail Petroleum Products
S.I.C.: 5541
Ernst S. Shafer *(Pres., Chief Exec., Chief Oper. & Chief Fin. Officer)*
Linda N. Shafer *(Sec.)*
Terry Nielson *(Office Mgr.)*

No. of U.S. Offices: 1

Computer Systems/Hardware:
Data Point 6860

Outside Service Firm(s):

McGladrey & Pullen*(Auditors)*
Rockford, IL

Alpine Bank*(Major Banking Relationship)*
Rockford, IL

Williams & McCarthy*(Legal Firm)*
Rockford, IL

SMITH & SONS FOODS, INC.
2124 Riverside Dr.
Macon, GA 31208
Tel.: 912-745-4759
Year Founded: 1936
Approx.Sls.: $50,000,000
Emp.: 1,500
Fiscal Year-end: 9/30/90
Restaurants & Cafeterias
S.I.C.: 5812
James A. Smith, Jr. *(Chm. Bd.)*
James A. Smith III *(Pres.)*
Robert A. Smith *(Exec. V.P.)*
R. M. Bennett *(V.P.-Sls. & Mktg.)*
R. E. Douthit *(V.P., Sec. & Treas.)*
David Johnson *(Controller)*

Outside Service Firm(s):

McMullan & McMullan*(Auditors)*
Macon, GA

Sell & Melton*(Legal Firm)*
Macon, GA

Citizens & Southern National Bank*(Major Banking Relationship)*
Macon, GA

Subsidiaries:

S & S Cafeterias (1)
2124 Riverside Dr.
Macon, GA 31208
Tel.: 912-745-4759

S & S Diversified Food Service, Inc. (1)
2124 Riverside Dr.
Macon, GA 31208
Tel.: 912-745-4759

S & S Food Administrators (1)
2124 Riverside Dr.
Macon, GA 31208
Tel.: 912-745-4759

Smith & Sons Catering Co. (1)
2124 Riverside Dr.
Macon, GA 31208
Tel.: 912-745-4759

SMITH SYSTEM MANUFACTURING COMPANY
4184 N. Lexington Ave.
Shoreview, MN 55126
Tel.: 612-482-0260 **DE**
Fax: 612-482-0053
Approx.Sls.: $30,000,000
Emp.: 350
Office Furniture, Except Wood, Sheet Metalwork, School Furniture
S.I.C.: 2522; 3444; 2531
Charles A. Risdall *(Pres.)*
William Risdall *(Exec V.P.)*
Ken Dahlager *(V.P.-Sls. & Mkgt.)*
Herbert H. Taylor *(V.P.)*
Dan Zajac *(Controller)*
Gerald T. Flom *(Sec.)*
John Bathke *(Pur. Agent)*

No. of Mfg. Plants/Facilities: 2

Outside Service Firm(s):

McGladrey & Pullen*(Auditors)*
Minneapolis, MN

Faegre & Benson*(Legal Firm)*
2200 Norwest Ctr., 90 S. 7th St.
Minneapolis, MN 55402-3901
Tel.: 612-336-3000
Fax: 612-336-3026

First Bank Minneapolis*(Major Banking Relationship)*
Minneapolis, MN

SMITH VALVE CORPORATION
One Main St.
Whitinsville, MA 01588
Tel.: 508-234-4611
Fax: 508-234-9568
Approx.Sls.: $30,000,000
Emp.: 300
Forged Steel Gate, Globe & Check Valves, Bronze, Steel Ball Valves
S.I.C.: 3494
Anthony D. Smith *(Chm. Bd.)*
David Eckert *(Co-Pres.)*
Paul Russo *(Co-Pres.)*
Donald W. Bean *(V.P.)*
James J. Hickey *(V.P. & Treas.)*
Howard Y.P. Yang *(V.P.)*

Outside Service Firm(s):

KPMG Peat Marwick*(Auditors)*
Worcester, MA

State Street Bank & Trust Co.*(Major Banking Relationship)*
P.O. Box 366, 225 Franklin St.
Boston, MA 02101
Tel.: 617-786-3000

SMITH'S PERSONNEL SERVICE, INC.
41 E. 42nd St.
New York, NY 10017
Tel.: 212-370-5400
Year Founded: 1936
Approx.Sls.: $350,000,000
Emp.: 6
Executive Recruiters, Permanent & Temporary Employment Agency in Entertainment, Printing & Publishing, Advertising, Graphic Arts
S.I.C.: 7361; 7363
Alayne Spertell *(Pres.)*
Michele Jaloza *(Gen. Mgr.)*
Mara Lynne *(Sls. Dir.)*

SMYTH, BAUER & LEWIS ADVERTISING INC.
201 W. Broad St. Ste. 300
Richmond, VA 23220
Tel.: 804-782-0046
Year Founded: 1991
Approx.Billings: $14,500,000
Emp.: 12
Technical Production Mktg.
Phil Bauer *(Chm. Bd. & Creative Dir.)*
Frederick Smyth *(Pres. & New Bus. Contact)*
Trudi Dickert *(V.P., Controller)*
Robert Metcalf *(Sec. & Treas.)*

H.M. SMYTH CO.
1085 Snelling Ave., N.
Saint Paul, MN 55108
Tel.: 612-646-4544
Fax: 612-646-8949
Year Founded: 1877
Approx.Sls.: $40,000,000
Emp.: 285
Fiscal Year-end: 12/31/91
Labels & Packaging Products
S.I.C.: 2752; 2759; 3086
Paul Trowbridge *(Chm. Bd., Pres. & Chief Exec. Officer)*
Greg Arko *(V.P.)*
David Baumgardner *(V.P.-Fin.)*
William Hickey, III *(V.P.-Mktg. & Sls.)*
Clint Larue *(V.P.-Mfg.)*
Principal(s):
Paul Trowbridge
William Hickey, III
Dan Hickey
Theresa Hickey
John Hickey

No. of Mfg. Plants/Facilities: 3

Outside Service Firm(s):

Carlson, Lundquist & Company*(Auditors)*
St. Paul, MN

Oppenheimer, Wolff & Donnelly*(Legal Firm)*
IDS Ctr., 45 S. Seventh St.
Minneapolis, MN 55402
Tel.: 612-344-9300
Fax: 612-344-9376

Norwest Bank Minnesota, N.A.*(Major Banking Relationship)*
St. Paul, MN

JOHN M. SMYTH CO.
1013 Butterfield Rd.
Downers Grove, IL 60515
Tel.: 708-960-4100 **IL**
Fax: 708-960-3578
Year Founded: 1867
Approx.Sls.: $70,000,000
Emp.: 700
Retailer Home Furnishings & Accessories
S.I.C.: 5712
John M. Smyth *(Chm. Bd.)*
Ken C. Curtis *(Pres.)*
Byron Breems *(V.P.-Fin.)*
Frank Czopek *(V.P.-Opers.)*
Rex Slocum *(V.P.-Personnel)*
Robert W. Smyth *(V.P.)*
Anthony Smyth *(Sec.)*
Gloria Spranza Meyers *(Mgr.-Adv.)*
Principal(s):
John M. Smyth
Robert W. Smyth
Anthony Smyth

Computer Systems/Hardware:
Unysys

Outside Service Firm(s):

Ernst & Young*(Auditors)*
233 S. Wacker Dr.
Chicago, IL 60606
Tel.: 312-368-1800
Fax: 312-645-3095

Mayer, Brown & Platt*(Legal Firm)*
190 S. LaSalle St., Ste. 3900
Chicago, IL 60603
Tel.: 312-782-0600

First National Bank of Chicago*(Major Banking Relationship)*
One First National Plaza
Chicago, IL 60670
Tel.: 312-732-9781
Tel.: 312-732-4050
Fax: 312-732-4840
Fax: 312-732-3055

SNAP-TITE, INCORPORATED
3250 W. Lake Rd.
Erie, PA 16505
Mailing Address:
P.O. Box 8570,
Erie, PA 16505
Tel.: 814-833-6411
Fax: 814-838-6382
Approx.Sls.: $50,000,000
Emp.: 580
Fiscal Year-end: 11/30/90
Import Export
Mfr. of Quick Disconnect Couplings, Hydraulic & Pneumatic Valves; Hoses & Hose Hardware for Industrial & Fire Protection Industries
S.I.C.: 3429; 3494; 3569; 3823; 3492; 7812; 3593; 3052
George A. Clark *(Chm. Bd., Pres. & Chief Exec. Officer)*
Harry West *(Chief Fin. Officer & V.P.)*
Gary L. Clark *(Chief Admin. Officer & V.P.)*
George P. Clark *(V.P. & Treas.)*
John S. Clark *(V.P. & Gen. Mgr.)*
Bob Conway *(V.P. & Gen. Mgr.)*
Harry Martin *(Sec.)*
Dick Sicheri *(Dir.-Human Resources)*
Gene Rejzer *(Mgr.-Information Systems)*

No. of Mfg. Plants/Facilities: 7
No. of U.S. Offices: 6
No. of Foreign Offices: 4

Computer Systems/Hardware:
IBM

Outside Service Firm(s):

Coopers & Lybrand*(Auditors)*
1500 One Cleveland Center, 1375 East 9th Street
Cleveland, OH 44114
Tel.: 216-241-4380
Fax: 216-575-0170

Mellon Bank*(Major Banking Relationship)*
Erie, PA

Elderkin, Martin, Kelly, Messina & Zamboldi*(Legal Firm)*
Erie, PA

Division:

Snap-Tite Ponn **(1)**
217 Titusville Rd.
Union City, PA 16438
Tel.: 814-438-7616
Manufacturer of Hoses
S.I.C.: 3052
Peter Bol *(Gen. Mgr.)*

SNAVELY FOREST PRODUCTS, INC.
P.O. Box 9808
Pittsburgh, PA 15227
Tel.: 412-885-4000 **PA**
Fax: 412-885-6050
Approx.Sls.: $110,000,000
Emp.: 45
Import Export
Lumber & Plywood
S.I.C.: 5031
Christian M. Snavely *(Chm. Bd.)*
Stephen V. Snavely *(Pres.)*
Donald L. Steinhart *(Exec. V.P.)*
John Stockhausen *(Treas.)*
Theresa V. Snavely *(Sec.)*
Andrew P. Duli *(Chief Accountant)*

Outside Service Firm(s):

Kirkpatrick & Lockhart*(Legal Firm)*
1500 Oliver Bldg., 535 Smithfield St.
Pittsburgh, PA 15222
Tel.: 412-355-6500
Fax: 412-355-6501

Branches:

Snavely Forest Products, Inc. **(1)**
2901 Chalbs St.
Baltimore, MD 21226
Tel.: 410-355-7000 (100%)
Lumber & Plywood
S.I.C.: 5031

Snavely Forest Products, Inc. **(1)**
P.O. Box 310,
Freehold, NJ 07728
Tel.: 908-462-2323 (100%)
Lumber & Plywood
S.I.C.: 5031

Snavely Forest Products, Inc. **(1)**
P.O. Box 16107,
Denver, CO 80216
Tel.: 303-287-2591
Sls. of Lumber & Plywood
S.I.C.: 5031
Bill Baugh *(Gen. Mgr.)*

Snavely Forest Products, Inc. **(1)**
302 S. 56th St.
Chandler, AZ 85226
Tel.: 602-961-0978
Wholesale Distr. of Lumber & Plywood
S.I.C.: 5031
Daniel Taylor *(Gen. Mgr.)*

Snavely Forest Products, Inc. **(1)**
P.O. Box 59907,
Dallas, TX 75229
Tel.: 214-358-7541
Lumber & Plywood
S.I.C.: 5031
Robert Starford *(Gen. Mgr.)*

SNOKIST GROWERS
18 W. Mead
Yakima, WA 98902
Mailing Address:
P.O. Box 1587
Yakima, WA 98907
Tel.: 509-453-5631
Fax: 509-457-6417
Year Founded: 1903
Approx.Sls.: $93,000,000
Emp.: 700
Fiscal Year-end: 5/31/91

Export
Packing & Shipping Of Fresh & Canned Fruits
S.I.C.: 2033
James Doornick *(Chm. Bd.)*
Gregory Babock, *(Vice Chm.)*
Jay F. Grandy *(Pres. & Chief Exec. Officer)*
Bernard J. Sims *(V.P.-Fin.)*
Lawrence West *(V.P.-Sls., Processed Fruit)*
Truman Yeager *(V.P.-Sls., Fresh Fruit)*
John Benner *(Pur. Agent)*

Principal(s):
Grower Cooperative

No. of Mfg. Plants/Facilities: 6
No. of U.S. Offices: 2

Outside Service Firm(s):

Moss Adams*(Auditors)*
1001 4th Ave., Ste. 2900
Seattle, WA 98154-1106
Tel.: 206-223-1820

Rainier National Bank*(Major Banking Relationship)*
P.O.Box 24407
Seattle, WA 98124

Franklin & Bersin*(Legal Firm)*
Seattle, WA

SNYDER BROTHERS, INC.
7251 Ohms Lane
Minneapolis, MN 55439
Tel.: 612-830-9033 **MN**
Fax: 612-830-1017
Approx.Sls.: $33,000,000
Emp.: 540
Retail Drug Stores
S.I.C.: 5912
Shirley M. Snyder *(Chm. Bd.)*
Eugene Snyder *(Pres. & Chief Exec. Officer)*
Arvin Cohen *(Exec. V.P. & Treas.)*

Outside Service Firm(s):

Grant Thornton*(Auditors)*
500 Pillsbury Center
Minneapolis, MN 55402-1459

Heck Gene*(Legal Firm)*
Minneapolis, MN

First Bank Minneapolis*(Major Banking Relationship)*
Minneapolis, MN

SNYDER-DIAMOND
1399 Olympic Blvd.
Santa Monica, CA 90404
Tel.: 310-450-1000
Fax: 310-452-7259
Year Founded: 1949
Approx.Sls.: $38,000,000
Emp.: 275
Retail Sales of Plumbing Fixtures & Supplies, Appliances & Decorative Hardware
S.I.C.: 5251; 5072; 5074
Louis H. Snyder *(Chm. Bd. & Chief Exec. Officer)*
Russell W. Diamond *(Pres.)*
Walter S. Diamond *(Sec. & Treas.)*

Outside Service Firm(s):

Ostrow, Bauch, Firestone & Carmody*(Auditors)*
Encino, CA

Staitman, Snyder, Weisman & Tannebaum*(Legal Firm)*
Los Angeles, CA

City National Bank*(Major Banking Relationship)*
8525 W. Pico Blvd.
Los Angeles, CA 90035
Tel.: 310-550-5690

SNYDER INDUSTRIES, INC.
4700 Fremont St.
Lincoln, NE 68504
Mailing Address:
P.O. Box 4583
Lincoln, NE 68504
Tel.: 402-467-5221
Fax: 402-467-3247
Approx.Sls.: $10,000,000
Emp.: 180
Fiscal Year-end: 7/31/90
Polyethylene Applicator & Storage Tanks, Automated Refuse Containers, Custom Engineered Products
S.I.C.: 3443; 3081
Howard Gross *(Chm. Bd. & Chief Exec. Officer)*
Hal Spurrier *(Pres. & Chief Opers. Offcier)*
Bill Anderson *(Mgr.-Sls. & Mktg.)*

SNYDER TANK CORP.
S-3774 Lakeshore Rd.
Buffalo, NY 14219
Tel.: 716-827-5353 **NY**
Fax: 716-827-7903
Year Founded: 1939
Approx.Sls.: $30,000,000
Emp.: 250
Import Export
Manufacture Fuel, Air Tanks & General Metal Fabrication
S.I.C.: 3714
Gerald J. Snyder *(Pres.)*
John Coleman *(V.P. & Gen. Mgr.)*
T. James Snyder *(V.P.)*
David Foster *(Controller)*
Christopher Conboy *(Dir.-Data Processing)*
Fred Domanski *(Dir.-Pur.)*
Robert Jimerson *(Dir.-Engrng.)*

No. of Mfg. Plants/Facilities: 2

Outside Service Firm(s):

Morgan & Beyer C.P.A.*(Auditors)*
Buffalo, NY

Saperston & Day, P.C.*(Legal Firm)*
1500 Liberty Bank Bldg.
Buffalo, NY 14202
Tel.: 716-856-5400

Marine Midland Bank*(Major Banking Relationship)*
P.O. Box 803, 1 Marine Midland Center, 23rd Floor
Buffalo, NY 14203
Tel.: 716-841-2582

SNYDERGENERAL CORPORATION
3219 McKinney Ave.
Dallas, TX 75204-2418
Tel.: 214-754-0500 **MN**
Fax: 214-754-0350
Year Founded: 1982
Approx.Sls.: $850,000,000
Emp.: 6,500
Fiscal Year-end: 12/31/90
Export
Commercial, Industrial, & Institutional Heating, Ventilating, Air-Conditioning & Filtration Products, Systems & Controls & Air Pollution Control Products
S.I.C.: 3585
Richard W. Snyder *(Chm. Bd. & Chief Exec. Officer)*
Bobbi Snyder *(Vice Chm.)*
James F. Brum *(Exec. V.P.-Fin.)*
Bart Bailey *(V.P.-Admin.)*
Dick Driggs *(V.P.-Tech. Support)*
Joe Engle *(V.P.-Pur.)*
Robert L. Snyder *(V.P.-Corp. Devel.)*
Michael B. Caolo *(Sec. & Legal Officer)*
Patrick Noonan *(Corp. Treas.)*
Bruce Hebert *(Corp. Controller)*
William A. Mudge *(Dir.-Corp. Communications)*
Sue Johnson *(Mgr.-Benefits Admin.)*
Stephanie Prescott *(Corp. Communications Supvr.)*

Principal(s):
Richard W. Snyder

No. of Mfg. Plants/Facilities: 15
No. of U.S. Offices: 170
No. of Foreign Offices: 18

Computer Systems/Hardware:
IBM

Outside Service Firm(s):

Ernst & Young*(Auditors)*
2121 San Jacinto, Ste. 500
Dallas, TX 75201
Tel.: 214-969-8000

Aetna Life & Casualty*(Group Insurer)*
151 Farmington Avenue
Hartford, CT 06156
Tel.: 203-273-2128
Fax: 203-729-4295

Michael Caolo & Associates*(Legal Firm)*
Dallas, TX

Citibank N.A.*(Major Banking Relationship)*
Corporate Trust Services, 399 Park Ave.
New York, NY 10043
Tel.: 212-559-1605

SNYDER'S DRUG STORES, INC.
14525 Hwy. 7
Minnetonka, MN 55345
Tel.: 612-935-5441
Fax: 612-936-2512
Year Founded: 1928
Approx.Sls.: $221,000,000
Emp.: 1,758
Fiscal Year-end: 7/25/92
Retail Prescription Drugs & Patent Medicines; Cosmetics; Toiletries; Tobacco & Novelties
S.I.C.: 5912
Donald Beeler *(Chm. Bd., Pres. & Chief Exec. Officer)*
Gary Hawley *(V.P.-Fin. & Chief Fin. Officer)*
Richard F. Oorlog *(V.P.-Human Resources)*
Michael J. Pan *(V.P.-Retail Opers.)*
Philip D. Perkins *(V.P.-Mktg.)*
William J. Vidmar *(V.P.-Wholesale Opers.)*

Principal(s):
Donald Beeler
Gary Hawley

Computer Systems/Hardware:
Honeywell 645

Outside Service Firm(s):

Arthur Andersen & Co.*(Auditors)*
45 S. 7th St.
Minneapolis, MN 55402

Fredrikson & Byron, P.A.*(Legal Firm)*
1100 International Center, 900 Second Av. South
Minneapolis, MN 53402-3397
Tel.: 612-349-6265

General Electric Credit Corp.*(Major Banking Relationship)*
Chicago, IL

SNYDER'S OF HANOVER, INC.
P.O. Box 917,
Hanover, PA 17331
Year Founded: 1924
Approx.Sls.: $40,000,000
Emp.: 500
Fiscal Year-end: 3/31/91
Mfr. & Distributor of Snack Foods
S.I.C.: 2099; 5149
Michael Warehime *(Pres.)*
Charles E. Good *(V.P.-Fin., Sec. & Treas.)*
James Butt *(V.P.-Opers.)*
Dennis Rager *(Controller)*
Pat Monaghan *(Mgr.-Oper.)*
Barry Brooks *(Mgr.-Pur.)*
Bob King *(Mgr.-Quality Assurance, Res. & Devel.)*
Don Kline *(Mgr.-Quality Assurance, Res. & Devel.)*
Judy Willing *(Mgr.-Mktg. Services)*
Rodney Schnurr *(Dir.-Sls. & Mktg.)*
John Vrabel *(Dir.-Mktg.)*
John Lucas *(Dir.-Human Resources)*

No. of Mfg. Plants/Facilities: 3

Outside Service Firm(s):

Harry Ness & Company*(Auditors)*
York, PA

Farmers Bank & Trust Company*(Major Banking Relationship)*
Hanover, PA

SO-LO-FOOD, INC.
4701 Odonnell St.
Baltimore, MD 21224
Tel.: 410-342-3910
Fax: 410-342-6352
Year Founded: 1959
Approx.Sls.: $112,000,000
Emp.: 798
Supermarkets
S.I.C.: 5411
Louis Denrich *(Pres.)*
Stephen Denrich *(Chief Exec. Officer)*
Dena Carmel *(Dir.-Fin.)*
Principal(s):
Louis Denrich
Stephen Denrich

Outside Service Firm(s):

Deloitte & Touche*(Auditors)*
1100 Mercantile Bank Bldg., 2 Hopkins Plaza
Baltimore, MD 21201
Tel.: 410-576-6700

Weinberg & Green*(Legal Firm)*
100 S. Charles St.
Baltimore, MD 21202
Tel.: 410-332-8795

Maryland National Bank*(Major Banking Relationship)*
225 N. Calvert St.
Baltimore, MD 21202
Tel.: 410-244-6565

Subsidiaries:

Civic Food Center, Inc. **(1)**
4701 Odnonnel St.
Baltimore, MD 21224
Tel.: 410-342-3910
Supermarkets
S.I.C.: 5411
Louis Denrich *(Pres.)*

Valu Foods Inc. **(1)**
4701 Odonnell St.
Baltimore, MD 21224
Tel.: 410-342-3910
Approx.Sls.: $11,000,000
Emp.: 165
Supermarkets
S.I.C.: 5411
Louis Denrich *(Pres.)*
Stephen Denrich *(V.P.)*

Soap Opera Digest
(See listing under So-Lo-Food, Inc.)

SOCIETY FOR SAVINGS BANCORP, INC.
31 Pratt St.
Hartford, CT 06145
Mailing Address:
P.O. Box 2200,
Hartford, CT 06145-2200
Tel.: 203-727-5000
Fax: 203-727-5444
Year Founded: 1819
Assets: $2,989,043,000
Earnings: ($64,512,000)
Liabilities: $2,839,631,000
Net Worth: $149,412,000
Approx.Income: $13,500,000
Emp.: 634
Fiscal Year-end: 12/31/91
Bank
S.I.C.: 6029; 6035
Rudolph P. Arnold *(Chm. Bd.)*
Lawrence Connell *(Pres. & Chief Exec. Officer)*
Albert E. Fiacre, Jr. *(Exec. V.P.-Treas & Chief Fin. Officer)*
Robert W. Beggs *(Sr. V.P. & Sec.)*
Peter C. Hickey *(Sr. V.P.-Opers.)*
Frank J. Litwin *(Sr. V.P.-Mktg.)*

Subsidiaries:

Aspenrise Properties, Inc. **(1)**
31 Pratt St.
Hartford, CT 06103
Tel.: 203-727-5000
Real Estate
S.I.C.: 6798

Cleary Lane Associates, Inc. **(1)**
31 Pratt St.
Hartford, CT 06103
Tel.: 203-727-5000
Real Estate
S.I.C.: 6798

Cranston Properties, Inc. **(1)**
31 Pratt St.
Hartford, CT 06103
Tel.: 203-727-5000
Real Estate
S.I.C.: 6798

Fair Harbor Properties, Inc. **(1)**
31 Pratt St.
Hartford, CT 06103
Tel.: 203-727-5000
Real Estate
S.I.C.: 6798

Fidelity Acceptance Corporation **(1)**
79 Towle Bldg., 330 2nd Ave. S.
Minneapolis, MN 55401
Tel.: 612-338-5479
Consumer Finance
S.I.C.: 6141
Florian A. Stang *(Pres.)*

Grinnell Street Associates, Inc. **(1)**
31 Pratt St.
Hartford, CT 06103
Tel.: 203-727-5000
Real Estate
S.I.C.: 6798

Groton Run Properties, Inc. **(1)**
311 Pratt St.
Hartford, CT 06103
Tel.: 203-727-5000

High Point Equities, Inc. **(1)**
31 Pratt St.
Hartford, CT 06103
Tel.: 203-727-5000
Real Estate
S.I.C.: 6798

Kenosia Properties, Inc. **(1)**
31 Pratt St.
Hartford, CT 06103
Tel.: 203-727-5000
Real Estate
S.I.C.: 6798

Master Plans Corporation **(1)**
31 Pratt St.
Hartford, CT 06103
Tel.: 203-727-5000
Real Estate
S.I.C.: 6798

Pennington Corporation **(1)**
31 Pratt St.
Hartford, CT 06103
Tel.: 203-727-5000
Real Estate
S.I.C.: 6798

Society Commercial Properties, Inc. **(1)**
31 Pratt St.
Hartford, CT 06103
Tel.: 203-727-5000
Real Estate
S.I.C.: 6798

Society Mortgage Corporation **(1)**
31 Pratt St.
Hartford, CT 06103
Tel.: 203-727-5000
Mortgage Banking
S.I.C.: 6162

Solar Services, Inc. **(1)**
31 Pratt St.
Hartford, CT 06103
Tel.: 203-727-5000
Computer Services
S.I.C.: 7379

Walker Glen Properties, Inc. **(1)**
31 Pratt St.
Hartford, CT 06103
Tel.: 203-727-5000
Real Estate
S.I.C.: 6798

SOFCO-MEAD, INC.
702 Potential Pkwy. 4
Scotia, NY 12302
Tel.: 518-374-7810
Fax: 518-374-8437
Holding Company
S.I.C.: 6719; 5113; 5087
James V. Gargiulo *(Pres.)*
Peter Marquis *(Exec. V.P.)*
Philip J. Mead *(V.P.)*

Subsidiary:

D. J. Mead-Hubbs & Howe **(1)**
2200 Harlem Rd.
Buffalo, NY 14225
Tel.: 716-895-7900
Fax: 716-895-6684
Approx.Sls.: $44,700,000
Emp.: 200
Fiscal Year-end: 5/31/90
Export
Computer Systems/Hardware:
IBM-AS/400
Wholesale Distributor Of Paper Products & Janitorial Supplies
S.I.C.: 5111; 5113; 5087
James V. Gargiulo *(Pres.)*
Thomas J. Gumkowski *(Chief Oper. Officer)*
Candy Kelley *(Controller)*
Brian Hanley *(Gen. Mgr.)*
Caren Ashkar *(Pur. Agent)*
Pamela Baia *(Mgr.-Human Resources)*
Larry Lloyd *(Supvr.-Data Processing)*

SOFT SHEEN PRODUCTS, INC.
1000 E. 87th St.
Chicago, IL 60619
Tel.: 312-978-0700 **DE**
Fax: 312-978-6185
Year Founded: 1964
Approx.Sls.: $87,900,000
Emp.: 535
Manufacturer of Hair Care Products
S.I.C.: 2844
Edward G. Gardner *(Chm. Bd. & Chief Exec. Officer)*
Betty A. Gardner *(Co-Chm. Bd. & Sec.)*
Gary E. Gardner *(Pres. & Chief Oper. Officer)*
Larry L. Allen *(V.P.-Human Resources)*
Ethan G. Foster *(V.P.-Sls.)*
Denise Gardner *(V.P.-Mktg.)*
Michael V. Roberts *(V.P.-Fin. & Treas.)*
Gladys Taylor *(V.P.-Adv.)*
Alan Wohlman *(V.P.-Res. & Devel.)*
Alice West *(Controller)*
Ronald Delmenico *(Legal Officer)*
Danny O. Clarke *(Dir.-Intl. Fin.)*
William Rohlsen *(Dir.-Data Processing)*
Thurlow W. Simmons *(Dir.-Intl. Bus.)*
Debbie Smith *(Media Dir.)*
Sharon Reed Walker *(Dir.-Plng. & Devel.)*
Donna Wheatley *(Travel Mgr.)*
John Thigpen *(Assoc. Dir.-Pur.)*

Outside Service Firm(s):

Ernst & Young*(Auditors)*
233 S. Wacker Dr.
Chicago, IL 60606
Tel.: 312-368-1800
Fax: 312-645-3095

Continental Bank N. A.*(Major Banking Relationship)*
231 S. LaSalle St.
Chicago, IL 60697
Tel.: 312-828-2345
Tel.: 800-426-5754
Telex: 312-828-1783

SOFTOOL CORPORATION
340 S. Kellogg Ave.
Goleta, CA 93117
Tel.: 805-683-5777
Fax: 805-683-4105
Year Founded: 1977
Sales Range: $10-19 Million
Emp.: 100
Change & Configuration Management Software
S.I.C.: 7371; 7372
Dr. Leon Presser *(Pres.)*
Abe Presser *(Sr. V.P.)*
Rich Hug *(V.P.-IBM Business Unit)*
Kevin Nix *(V.P.-Digital/Unix Business Unit)*
Don Wolfe *(V.P. & Controller)*
Flora Iacchia *(Dir.-Mktg. Communications)*
Laurie Mix *(Mgr.-Sls. Co-ordinating)*

No. of Mfg. Plants/Facilities: 1
No. of U.S. Offices: 3
No. of Foreign Offices: 13

Computer Systems/Hardware:
IBM: Digital, SUN, Hewlett-Packard, Encore

SOKOL & COMPANY
5315 Dansher Rd.
Countryside, IL 60525
Tel.: 708-482-8250
Tel.: 800-EAT-SOLO
Telex: 270051
Fax: 708-482-9750
Year Founded: 1895
Approx.Sls.: $10,000,000
Emp.: 40
Fiscal Year-end: 12/31/90
Solo Cake, Pastry & Dessert Fillings; Fruit Glazes, Ice Cream Toppings; Crunches; Almond Paste
S.I.C.: 2099; 2024
John S. Novak *(Pres.)*
W.B. Dahle *(V.P.-Sls.)*
Edward Randa *(V.P.)*
John S. Novak II *(V.P.-Mfg.)*
Luigi Buffone *(Chief Fin. Officer)*
Mike Daleo *(Pur. Agent)*

SOLAR PRESS, INC.
1120 Frontenac Rd.
Naperville, IL 60563-1799
Tel.: 708-983-1400
Tel.: 800-323-2751 **IL**
Fax: 708-983-6125
Year Founded: 1961
Approx.Sls.: $50,000,000
Emp.: 220
Fiscal Year-end: 12/31/91
Export
Offset Printing
S.I.C.: 2752
Frank C. Hudetz *(Chm. Bd. & Chief Exec. Officer)*

Peter Hudetz *(Pres & Chief Oper. Officer)*
Joseph Hudetz *(Sr. V.P. & Chief Devel. Officer)*
John Dean *(V.P. & Chief Fin. Officer)*
Ron Hatch *(V.P.-Res. & Devel.)*
Mike Hudetz *(V.P.-Quality Assurance)*
David D. Krahn *(V.P.-Bus. Grp.)*
Dr. William Marazano *(V.P.-Education & Training)*
Susan Smith *(V.P.-Mfg.)*
Phil Morris *(Dir.-MIS)*
Tom Rohren *(U.S. Mgr.-Intl. Sls.)*
Connie Bartels *(Mgr.-Corp. Communications)*
Barbara Gunning *(Mgr.-Human Resources)*
Art Gleistein *(Pur. Agent)*

No. of Mfg. Plants/Facilities: 5
No. of U.S. Offices: 6
No. of Foreign Offices: 1

Outside Service Firm(s):

Price Waterhouse*(Auditors)*
200 E. Randolph
Chicago, IL 60601
Tel.: 312-565-1500

First Chicago Bank*(Major Banking Relationship)*
One First National Plaza
Chicago, IL 60670

Subsidiary:

Solar Press, Inc. **(1)**
1205 Corporation Lane
Perryville, MO 63775
Tel.: 314-547-7841
Tel.: 800-359-9210
Emp.: 224
Offset Printing
S.I.C.: 2752

Non-U.S. Holding:

Solar Press, Inc. **(1)**
3 DE Industriezone 9320
Erembodegem, Belgium
Tel.: 011-32-53-83-9010
Emp.: 52

SOLID STATE DEVICES, INC.
14849 Firestone Blvd.
La Mirada, CA 90638
Tel.: 310-921-9660
Fax: 310-921-9216
Approx.Sls.: $13,000,000
Emp.: 210
Semiconductor Circuit Network
S.I.C.: 3674; 3679
Arnold N. Applebaum *(Pres.)*
Marie Williams *(Treas.)*

Outside Service Firm(s):

Jamelson & Watkins*(Auditors)*
Los Alamitos, CA

GEORGE SOLLITT CONSTRUCTION
790 North Central Ave.
Wood Dale, IL 60191
Tel.: 708-860-7333 **IL**
Fax: 708-860-7347
Year Founded: 1838
Assets: $15,000,000
Liabilities: $13,136,000
Net Worth: $1,864,000
Approx.Sls.: $56,000,000
Emp.: 200
Fiscal Year-end: 12/31/88
General Building Contractors
S.I.C.: 1541; 1542; 1522; 1629; 1622
John E. Pridmore *(Chm. Bd.)*
Donald Maziarka *(Pres., Chief Exec. & Chief Oper. Officer)*
A. F. Zabinski, Jr. *(Chief Fin. Officer, Treas. & Controller)*
Bob Polacheck *(Sr. V.P.)*

Computer Systems/Hardware:
NCR

Outside Service Firm(s):

Deloitte & Touche*(Auditors)*
Two Prudential Plaza, 180 N. Stetson
Chicago, IL 60601
Tel.: 312-946-2039

Benefit Trust & Life*(Group Insurer)*
South Bend, IN

Continental Bank N. A.*(Major Banking Relationship)*
231 S. LaSalle St.
Chicago, IL 60697
Tel.: 312-828-2345
Tel.: 800-426-5754
Telex: 312-828-1783

The Northern Trust Co.*(Major Banking Relationship)*
50 S. LaSalle St.
Chicago, IL 60675
Tel.: 312-630-6000
Fax: 312-630-6516

ROBERT SOLOMON & ASSOCIATES ADV. INC.
505 N. Woodward Ave.
Bloomfield Hills, MI 48304
Tel.: 313-540-0660
Fax: 313-540-2124
Year Founded: 1954
Approx.Billings: $28,000,000
Emp.: 34
Robert B. Solomon *(Chm. Bd. & Pres.)*
Shirley Fiorillo *(Exec. V.P.)*
Fred Krause *(V.P.)*
Kenneth Droz *(Promo. & Pub. Rels. Dir.)*

SOLON MANUFACTURING COMPANY
Ferry St.
Solon, ME 04979
Tel.: 207-643-2210
Fax: 207-643-2738
Sales Range: $10-19 Million
Emp.: 230
Ice Cream Sticks, Tongue Depressors, Cotton Tipped Appplicators
S.I.C.: 2499; 3842
Harold V. Tewksbury *(Pres.)*
George LaPointe *(Gen. Mgr.)*
Jim Farley *(Mgr.-Natl. Sls.)*
Gary Bulmer *(Controller)*

SOLVAY PHARMACEUTICALS, INC.
901 Sawyer Rd.
Marietta, GA 30062-2224
Tel.: 404-578-9000
Fax: 404-578-2096
Approx.Sls.: $85,000,000
Emp.: 550
Fiscal Year-end: 12/31/90
Mfr. Pharmaceuticals
S.I.C.: 2834
Jim Warren *(Pres. & Chief Exec. Officer)*
Jesse Coan *(Sr. V.P.-Commercial Opers)*
Larry Muschek *(Sr. V.P.-Scientific Affairs)*
David Powell *(Grp. V.P.-Mfg.)*
Bob Solheim *(Grp. V.P.-Fin. & Admin.)*
Gus Hatfield *(V.P.-Legal Affairs)*
George Mellilo *(V.P.-Sls.)*
Mark Miller *(V.P.-Corp. Rels.)*
Chris Offen *(V.P.-Mktg.)*

SOMERSET PONTIAC GMC INC.
1850 W. Maple Rd.
Troy, MI 48084
Tel.: 313-643-8600 **MI**
Fax: 313-643-6310
Approx.Sls.: $56,000,000
Emp.: 79
Automobile Dealership
S.I.C.: 5511
John B. McMullin, Jr. *(Pres.)*
Victoria Printz *(Sec. & Treas.)*
Richard Grimaldi *(Mgr.-Sls.)*

Outside Service Firm(s):

National Bank of Detroit*(Major Banking Relationship)*
611 Woodward
Detroit, MI 48226
Tel.: 313-225-1000

SOMERSET REFINERY INC.
600 Monticello St.
Somerset, KY 42501
Mailing Address:
P.O. Box 1547,
Somerset, KY 42501
Tel.: 606-679-6301 **IL**
Fax: 606-679-6301, Ext. 247
Year Founded: 1932
Approx.Sls.: $110,500,000
Emp.: 160
Fiscal Year-end: 6/30/91
Independent Refinery Marketer
S.I.C.: 2911; 5172
W. T. Walker *(Pres.)*
T. S. Ballance *(V.P.-Fin. & Treas.)*
Merrel Henderson *(V.P.-Sls.)*
Cy Waddle *(V.P.)*
Joe Howard Claunch *(Sec. & Treas.)*

No. of Mfg. Plants/Facilities: 1
No. of U.S. Offices: 2

Computer Systems/Hardware:
IBM System 36

Outside Service Firm(s):

Klimas & Klimas*(Legal Firm)*
Flossmoor, IL

The Citizens National Bank*(Major Banking Relationship)*
Public Square
Somerset, KY 42501

SOMERSET TECHNOLOGIES, INC.
Weston Canal Rd.
Somerset, NJ 08873
Mailing Address:
P. O. Box 791
New Brunswick, NJ 08903
Tel.: 908-356-6000
Fax: 908-356-0643
Year Founded: 1984
Approx.Sls.: $60,000,000
Emp.: 400
Fiscal Year-end: 12/31/90
Slitters & Rewinders for the Paper & Converting Industries, Book Production Systems, Dehumidification Systems & Humidity Pumps For Food, Beverage, Pharmaceutical, Chemical, Electronic Industries, Hospitals & Other Health Care Facilities, Commercial Buildings, Air Handling Systems, Ovens, Dryers, Coaters, Laminators, Fume Incineration/Regenerative Thermal Oxidation Systems Web & Strip Processing Sys.
S.I.C.: 3585
Francis T. Drury *(Pres.)*
Frank Linsalata *(Chief Exec. Officer)*
E. J. Kurie *(V.P.-Ross Air Systems)*
Ron Rittmann *(V.P.-Fin. & Admin.)*
J. Lemin *(V.P.-Cameron Machine)*
J. Pash *(V.P.-Kathabar Systems)*
F. Pozar *(V.P.-Waldron Converting Machinery)*
Ken Mehrhof *(Adv. & Pub. Rels. Consultant)*

Somma Mattress
(See Echevarria Angel Co., Inc. Listing)

SOMMER & MACA INDUSTRIES, INC.
5501 W. Ogden Ave.
Chicago, IL 60650
Tel.: 312-242-2871
Tel.: 800-323-9200 **IL**
Fax: 312-863-5462
Approx.Sls.: $35,000,000
Emp.: 265
Import Export
Hardware; Glass Making Machinery
S.I.C.: 5072; 3559
Allen Leigh Maca *(Chief Exec. Officer)*
Richard Carroll *(Pres.)*
James P. Johnson *(Exec. V.P.)*
John Davis *(V.P.-Mfg.)*
Jack Hynes *(Controller)*
R. Ford *(Dir.-Engrng.)*
Dick Gabor *(Adv. Mgr.)*

No. of Mfg. Plants/Facilities: 1
No. of U.S. Offices: 5

Computer Systems/Hardware:
IBM SYS 36 & 400

Outside Service Firm(s):

Grant Thornton*(Auditors)*
700 One Prudential Plaza, 130 East Randolph St.
Chicago, IL 60601
Tel.: 312-856-0200
Fax: 312-565-4719

Winston & Strawn*(Legal Firm)*
One 1st Natl. Plaza, No. 5000
Chicago, IL 60603
Tel.: 312-558-5600

American National Bank*(Major Banking Relationship)*
33 North LaSalle St.
Chicago, IL 60690
Tel.: 312-661-6967

Divisions:

Sommer & Maca Industries, Inc.-Concord Division **(1)**
345 Lodi St.
Hackensack, NJ 07601
Tel.: 201-489-0444
Sales & Marketing Of Glazing Supplies
S.I.C.: 3559
G. Kempa *(Reg. V.P.)*

Sommer & Maca Industries, Inc.-Dixie Division **(1)**
309 Fulton Industrial Circle, S.W.
Atlanta, GA 30336
Tel.: 404-691-0250
Sales & Marketing Of Glazing Supplies
S.I.C.: 3559
T. Klein *(Reg. V.P.)*

Sommer & Maca Industries, Inc.-Industrial Machinery Division **(1)**
5501 W. Ogden Ave.
Chicago, IL 60650
Tel.: 312-242-2871
Flat Glass Machinery For Washing, Polishing & Beveling
S.I.C.: 3559
R. Kudel *(Reg. V.P.)*

Sommer & Maca Industries, Inc.-Pacific Division **(1)**
7225 E. Oxford Way
City of Commerce, CA 90040
Tel.: 213-620-0452
Sales & Marketing Of Glazing Supplies
S.I.C.: 3559
M. Graham *(Reg. V.P.)*

Sommer & Maca Industries, Inc.-Texas Division **(1)**
17035 Stemmons Freeway, 1-35
Dallas, TX 75020
Tel.: 214-620-0452
Sales & Marketing Of Glazing Supplies
S.I.C.: 3559
G. Ball *(Reg. V.P.)*

Sommer & Maca Industries, Inc.-Western Division **(1)**
870 Aldo Ave.
Santa Clara, CA 95054
Tel.: 408-988-8700

Sommer & Maca Industries, Inc.—(Continued)

Sales & Marketing Of Glazing Supplies
S.I.C.: 3559
A. Gottesman *(Reg. V.P.)*

SOMMER METALCRAFT CORPORATION
315 Poston Dr.
Crawfordsville, IN 47933
Tel.: 317-362-6200 **IN**
Fax: 317-362-6270
Year Founded: 1931
Approx.Sls.: $15,000,000
Emp.: 300
Fiscal Year-end: 4/30/91
Mfr. Wire Forms & Welded Wire Assembly
S.I.C.: 3496; 3542
Jon W. Sommer *(Pres. & Chief Exec. Officer)*
Jim Reed *(Chief Fin. Officer)*
Robert Hodges *(Pur. Dir.)*
Dale Petrie *(Engrng. Dir. & Prod. Mgr.)*
Lloyd Pettit *(Plant Mgr.)*
Paul M. Moehling *(Gen. Sls. Mgr.)*

Division:

Crown Products Co. **(1)**
315 Poston
Crawfordsville, IN 47933
Tel.: 317-362-6200
Fax: 317-362-6270
Approx.Sls.: $6,000,000
Emp.: 100
Fiscal Year-end: 4/30/90
Mfr. Wire Forms & Welded Assemblies
S.I.C.: 3496; 3471
Jon W. Sommer *(Chm. Bd. & Pres.)*
Paul Moehling *(Sls. Mgr.)*
Lloyd Pattit *(Plant Mgr.)*
Robert Hodges *(Pur. Dir.)*

SON CHIEF ELECTRICS, INC.
41 Meadow St.
Winsted, CT 06098
Tel.: 203-379-2741 **CT**
Fax: 203-379-2742
Year Founded: 1916
Sales Range: $10-19 Million
Emp.: 20
Mfr. Electric Appliances
S.I.C.: 3639
D.F. Fitzgerald *(Pres. & Treas.)*
Hope Fitzgerald *(Sec. & Sls. Admin.)*
Robert M. Fitzgerald, Esq. *(Legal Officer)*
Roland Picard *(Personnel Dir.)*

Computer Systems/Hardware:
Sanyo 55

Outside Service Firm(s):

Moore & Alvord*(Group Insurer)*
Winsted, CT

Connecticut Bank & Trust*(Major Banking Relationship)*
One Constitution Plaza,
Hartford, CT 06115

Divisions:

Black Angus, Inc. **(1)**
41 Meadow St.
Winsted, CT 06098
Tel.: 203-379-2741
Electrical Appliances
S.I.C.: 3639
D. F. Fitzgerald *(Pres.)*

Magic Maid Division **(1)**
41 Meadow St.
Winsted, CT 06098
Tel.: 203-379-2741
Electrical Appliances
S.I.C.: 3639
D. F. Fitzgerald *(Pres.)*

SONICAIR
15150-1 N. Hayden Rd., Suite 200
Scottsdale, AZ 85260
Tel.: 602-483-5700
Tel.: 800-528-6052 **AZ**
Telex: 187164
Fax: 602-483-5770
Year Founded: 1976
Assets: $4,827,572
Liabilities: $2,644,048
Net Worth: $2,183,524
Approx.Sls.: $30,000,000
Emp.: 210
Fiscal Year-end: 12/31/91
Import Export
International Air Courier, Time Sensitive Delivery Service
S.I.C.: 4513
Ray Thurston *(Chm. Bd. & Chief Exec. Officer)*
Dexter B. Hewett *(Pres.)*
James J. Bonen *(Chief Fin. Officer)*
Hal Rabin *(Pres.-Field Support Bank Div.)*
David Toth *(V.P.-International Div.)*
David Marts *(Mgr.-Information Systems)*
Joanne Flachsmann *(Mgr.-Human Resources)*
Kathy Milbauer *(Reg. Mgr.)*
Principal(s):
Ray Thurston
Dexter B. Hewett

No. of U.S. Offices: 12
No. of Foreign Offices: 1

Computer Systems/Hardware:
Motorola & Prime 750

Outside Service Firm(s):

KPMG Peat Marwick*(Auditors)*
2020 No. Central Ave.
Phoenix, AZ 85004
Tel.: 602-253-2000

Citibank N.A.*(Major Banking Relationship)*
Phoenix, AZ

Subsidiary:

Sonic Messenger Service **(1)**
1121 East Missouri Suite 218
Phoenix, AZ 85014
Tel.: 602-234-0686
Emp.: 250
Amy Thurston *(Chief Exec. Officer)*

SONNEVELDT COMPANY
435 Ionia Ave. S.W.
Grand Rapids, MI 49503
Tel.: 616-456-7171 **MI**
Fax: 616-235-1396
Year Founded: 1932
Approx.Sls.: $105,000,000
Emp.: 160
Wholesale Food Service for Fast Food Chains, Paper Products & Frozen/Refrigerated Produce
S.I.C.: 5141; 5113; 5142
John P. Lewis *(Chm. Bd.)*
Gene D. Goulooze *(Vice Chm. & Chief Exec. Officer)*
Fred Hallstedt *(Pres. & V.P-Sls. & Mktg.)*
Jeffrey M. Kowack *(Sr. V.P. & Chief Fin. Officer)*
William Veirs *(V.P.-Sls. & Mktg.)*
David Jacobusse *(V.P.-Purchasing)*
Robert Bootsma *(V.P.-Opers.)*
Leonard Stevens *(V.P.-Mngmt. Information Systems)*

No. of Mfg. Plants/Facilities: 3
No. of U.S. Offices: 1

Computer Systems/Hardware:
Burroughs A9F

Outside Service Firm(s):

Monroe, Sweeirs & Tromp*(Auditors)*
Grand Rapids, MI

Transamerica Occidental Insurance Co.*(Commercial Insurance Carrier)*
P.O. Box 30253,
Los Angeles, CA 90099

Risk Control Insurance*(Group Insurer)*
Grand Rapids, MI

Warner, Norcross & Judd*(Legal Firm)*
Grand Rapids, MI

Great Lakes Federal Savings & Loan*(Major Banking Relationship)*
Grand Rapids, MI

NEL Pension Advisors, Inc.*(Pension Manager)*
Boston, MA

SONOMA MISSION INN & SPA
(Sub. of Rahn Properties, Inc.)
18140 Sonoma Hwy.
Sonoma, CA 95476
Mailing Address:
P.O. Box 1447,
Sonoma, CA 95476
Tel.: 707-938-9000
Year Founded: 1985
Approx.Sls.: $15,000,000
Emp.: 325
Resort
S.I.C.: 7011
Peter Henry *(Gen. Mgr.)*
Jack Burkam *(Dir.-Mktg.)*

SOONER PIPE & SUPPLY CORP.
1000 MidContinent Tower 401 S. Boston
Tulsa, OK 74103
Mailing Address:
P.O. Box 1530
Tulsa, OK 74101
Tel.: 918-587-3391
Fax: 918-587-0863
Emp.: 200
Fiscal Year-end: 7/31/91
Distributor for Oil Tubular Products & General Oil Field Supplies
S.I.C.: 5084
Henry Zarrow *(Pres. & Chief Exec. Officer)*
Jack Zarrow *(Exec. V.P.)*
Jim Arterburn *(V.P. & Controller)*
J. W. Kerby *(V.P.)*
Ray Poiriez *(Asst. V.P.)*
Rebecca Holden *(Dir.-Personnel)*
Beverly McBride *(Coord.-Human Resources)*

Computer Systems/Hardware:
IBM System 4381 & 4341

Outside Service Firm(s):

Ernst & Young*(Auditors)*
4300 One Williams Ctr.
Tulsa, OK 74142
Tel.: 918-560-3600
Fax: 918-560-3691

New England Mutual Life Insurance Co.*(Group Insurer)*
Boston, MA

Sound Playground
(Name Changed to Audio Specialist, Inc.)

SOUND WAREHOUSE, INC.
(Sub. of Shamrock Holdings, Inc.)
10911 Petal Street
Dallas, TX 75238
Tel.: 214-343-4700 **DE**
Fax: 214-343-8608
Year Founded: 1972
Approx.Rev.: $182,000,000
Emp.: 2,500
Fiscal Year-end: 5/31/91
Specialty Retailer of Prerecorded Music, Prerecorded Video Tapes & Other Home Entertainment Software Products; Rental of Prerecorded Video Tapes
S.I.C.: 5735; 7841
Mark S. Siegel *(Chm. Bd.)*
Terry N. Worrell *(Pres. & Chief Exec. Officer)*
Joe N. Malone *(Sr. V.P. & Chief Oper. Officer)*
John E. Vollmer III *(V.P., Chief Fin. Officer & Treas.)*
Robert Moskowitz *(Sec.)*
Nevin St. Romain *(Dir.-Distr. & Pur.)*
Ann Bendalin *(Dir.-Adv.)*
Donna Fiorentino *(Adv. Coord.)*
Robert W. Haggard *(Dir.-Construction)*

SOUNDESIGN

SOUNDESIGN CORPORATION
Harborside Financial Ctr., 400 Plaza 2
Jersey City, NJ 07311
Tel.: 201-434-1050 **DE**
Fax: 201-332-4993
Year Founded: 1956
Assets: $112,304,000
Liabilities: $76,667,000
Net Worth: $35,637,000
Approx.Sls.: $225,000,000
Emp.: 500
Fiscal Year-end: 12/31/90
Import Export
Mfr. of Transistor Radios & Allied Products
S.I.C.: 3651; 5064
Corporate Giving Program:
Advertising Co-op Allowance
Ely Ashkenazi *(Chm. Bd. & Chief Exec. Officer)*
Saul E. Ashkenazi *(Chm.-Exec. Committee)*
M. Franco *(Pres.)*
Robert Winer *(Exec. V.P.-Sls.)*
C. Chraime *(Sr. V.P. & Treas.)*
Harry Franco *(Sr. V.P. & Dir.-Communications)*
Mr. Green *(V.P.-Admin.)*
Albert Hamowy *(V.P.-Domestic Pur.)*
Steve Schleiffer *(V.P. & Controller)*
Gene McConnon *(Asst. V.P.-Mngmt. Information Systems)*

Computer Systems/Hardware:
ADP

Outside Service Firm(s):

Price Waterhouse*(Auditors)*
153 E. 53rd St., 44th Fl.
New York, NY 10022
Tel.: 212-371-2000

Blue Cross of New Jersey*(Group Insurer)*
Newark, NJ

Chemical Bank*(Major Banking Relationship)*
450 West 33rd St.
New York, NY 10001
Tel.: 212-613-7197
Fax: 212-947-7628

Subsidiaries:

Apex Mfg. Co., Inc. **(1)**
107 Trumbull St.
Elizabeth, NJ 07206
Tel.: 908-355-2210 (100%)
Mfr. of Transitor Radios & Allied Products
S.I.C.: 3651

Soundesign Export Corp. **(1)**
34 Exchange Place
Jersey City, NJ 07302
Tel.: 201-434-1050 (100%)
Mfr. & Distr. of Transitor Radios & Allied Products
S.I.C.: 5064

Non-U.S. Holdings:

Soundesign Corp. Hong Kong Ltd. **(1)**
1103 E. Ocean Centre, 98 Granville Rd.
Kowloon, Hong Kong
Approx.Sls.: $5,971,000
Emp.: 50
Radio Sales
S.I.C.: 5065

Soundesign Corp. Japan Ltd. **(1)**
2-chome Hatchobon, Chuo-ku
Tokyo, Japan (70%)
Approx.Sls.: $5,390,000
Emp.: 50
Radio Sales
S.I.C.: 5065
H. Sano *(Chief Oper. Officer)*

SOUTH BEND PLASTICS, INC.
1810 Clover Rd.
Mishawaka, IN 46545
Mailing Address:
P.O. Box 1505
South Bend, IN 46545
Tel.: 219-259-1991 **IN**
Fax: 219-259-7159
Approx.Sls.: $13,000,000
Emp.: 210
Injection Molded Finished Plastic Products
S.I.C.: 3089
W.H. Drinkall *(Chm. Bd. & Chief Exec. Officer)*
Robert Zygulski *(Pres. & Chief Opers. Officer)*
Robert Keuper *(Controller)*
Sue Vicsek *(Corp. Sec.)*
Tim White *(Mgr.-Mfg.)*
Lou Canales *(Mgr.-Pur.)*
Joyce Bartley *(Mgr.-Human Resources)*
David Kelsey *(Mgr.-Q.A.)*

Principal(s):
W.H. Drinkall

No. of Mfg. Plants/Facilities: 2

Computer Systems/Hardware:
IBM 36

Outside Service Firm(s):

McGladrey & Pullen*(Auditors)*
South Bend, IN

Society Bank*(Major Banking Relationship)*
South Bend, IN

SOUTH CENTRAL CO-OP
Hwy. 4, S.
Fairfax, MN 55332
Mailing Address:
P.O. Box E
Fairfax, MN 55332
Tel.: 507-426-8263 **MN**
Fax: 507-426-8266
Year Founded: 1906
Approx.Sls.: $12,000,000
Fiscal Year-end: 12/31/89
Wholesale Grain & Farm Supplies
S.I.C.: 5153; 5191
Chuck Felton *(Gen. Mgr.)*
Richard Graupman *(Dir.)*

Outside Service Firm(s):

Schuetzle Carlson & Company*(Auditors)*
New Ulm, MN

O'Connor Law Firm*(Legal Firm)*
Fairfax, MN

Fidelity State Bank*(Major Banking Relationship)*
Fairfax, MN

SOUTH CHESTER TUBE CO.
(Formerly Southco, Inc.)
(Formerly Southco Inc.)
210 Brinton Lake Rd.
Concordville, PA 19331
Tel.: 215-459-4000
Fax: 215-459-4012
Year Founded: 1899
Emp.: 830
Export
Designers & Mfrs.-Access Hardware for OEM Manufacturers
S.I.C.: 3569
Stephen J. Kelly *(Chm. Bd., Pres. & Chief Exec. Officer)*
C. I. Murphy *(Treas.)*
William Carson *(Controller)*
Thomas G. Fogerty *(Personnel Dir.)*
C. Robert Ganskopp *(V.P.-Sls. & Mktg.)*

No. of Mfg. Plants/Facilities: 7
No. of U.S. Offices: 26
No. of Foreign Offices: 5

Computer Systems/Hardware:
Sperry System 80

Outside Service Firm(s):

Provident Life & Accident Insurance Co.*(Group Insurer)*
Philadelphia, PA

Connecticut General Life Insurance Co.*(Pension Manager)*
P.O. Box 2975,
Hartford, CT 06104
Tel.: 203-726-6000

Provident Capital Management, Inc.*(Pension Manager)*
1700 Market Street, Ste. 1412
Philadelphia, PA 19103-3914

Subsidiary:

Southtec, Inc. **(1)**
1750 N. Broadway
Albany, NY 12204
Tel.: 518-463-4234
Fax: 518-463-0360
Emp.: 200
Industrial Quick-Operating Fasteners
S.I.C.: 5072
Wm. J. Friel *(Chm. Bd.)*
Steven Kelly *(Pres.)*
Steve Krill *(Controller)*
Raymond Canzanese *(Mgr.-Sls.)*
Robt. P. Johnston *(Gen. Mgr.)*

SOUTH DAKOTA LOTTERY
207 E. Capitol, Suite #200
Pierre, SD 57501
Tel.: 605-773-5770
Fax: 605-773-5786
Approx.Sls.: $20,000,000
Emp.: 34
Fiscal Year-end: 6/30/91
State Lottery
S.I.C.: 7999
Susan L. Walker *(Exec. Dir.)*
Andy Comer *(Dir.-Security)*
Curt Everson *(Dir.-Admin.)*
Mark Meyer *(Dir.-Sls.)*
Eileen Dailey Haberling *(Dir.-Adv.)*
Deb Mortensen *(Dir.-Pub. Rels.)*

SOUTH EAST COAL CO.
State Rt. 1840
Irvine, KY 40336
Mailing Address:
P.O. Box 332,
Irvine, KY 40336
Tel.: 606-723-5111
Fax: 606-723-5111, Ext. 217
Approx.Sls.: $75,000,000
Emp.: 565
Fiscal Year-end: 9/30/91
Bituminous Coal Mining
S.I.C.: 1222
Harry Laviers, Jr. *(Pres. & Chief Exec. Officer)*
Chuck Caroll *(Treas., Controller & Chief Fin. Officer)*
Peggy Kayse *(Dir.-Personnel)*

Computer Systems/Hardware:
IBM System 36

Outside Service Firm(s):

Dean, Dorton & Ford*(Auditors)*
Lexington, KY

Bank One*(Major Banking Relationship)*
Columbus, OH

Citizens Fidelity Bank & Trust Co.*(Major Banking Relationship)*
P.O. Box 33000-Citizens Plaza
Louisville, KY 40232
Tel.: 502-581-3381

Continental Bank N. A.*(Major Banking Relationship)*
231 S. LaSalle St.
Chicago, IL 60697
Tel.: 312-828-2345
Tel.: 800-426-5754
Telex: 312-828-1783

Subsidiaries:

South-East Coal Sales Co. **(1)**
P.O. Box 332,
Irvine, KY 40336
Tel.: 606-723-5111

South-East Ohio Coal Co. **(1)**
P.O. Box 332,
Irvine, KY 40336
Tel.: 606-723-5111

SOUTHCO DISTRIBUTING COMPANY
701 Patetown Rd.
Goldsboro, NC 27530
Tel.: 919-735-8012
Fax: 919-735-0097
Approx.Sls.: $82,000,000
Emp.: 130
Wholesale Cigarettes, Confectionery, Notions & Dry Goods
S.I.C.: 5145; 5194
Sherwin Herring *(Pres.)*
Jimmy Shelton *(V.P.-Fin.)*

Principal(s):
David Weil

Outside Service Firm(s):

Thomas R. Howell*(Auditors)*
Goldsboro, NC

SOUTHEASTERN CAPITAL CORPORATION
1873 S. Bellaire St., Ste. 1700
Denver, CO 80222
Tel.: 303-759-8600
Fax: 303-759-3226
Assets: $37,876,367
Liabilities: $29,227,566
Net Worth: $8,648,801
Approx.Sls.: $135,074,235
Emp.: 4
Diversified Holding Co.; Acquisition Co.
S.I.C.: 6719
Jeffrey W. Ross *(Pres.)*
Hein Poulus *(Sr. V.P.)*

SOUTHEASTERN EQUIPMENT COMPANY, INC.
3000 Old Savannah Rd.
Augusta, GA 30906
Mailing Address:
P.O. Box 5438,
Augusta, GA 30916-5438
Tel.: 706-798-4361 **GA**
Fax: 706-798-0348
Year Founded: 1951
Approx.Sls.: $19,000,000
Emp.: 150
Export
Wholesale Distribution of Used Trucks, Tractors & Trailers; Surplus & Salvage Goods; Truck & Automotive Parts & Accessories; Aircraft Equipment & Supplies
S.I.C.: 5521; 5012; 5399; 5013; 5531; 5088
John S. Smith *(Pres.)*
Michael J. Rizner *(Exec. V.P.)*
Tunnie Walden *(Sr. V.P.)*
B. Roy Smith *(V.P.)*
Byron Morris *(Treas.)*
John Smith, Jr. *(Sec.)*

Outside Service Firm(s):

First Union National Bank*(Major Banking Relationship)*
Trust Department, 699 Broad St.
Augusta, GA 30903
Tel.: 706-823-2500

SOUTHEASTERN FREIGHT LINES, INC.
P.O. Box 1691
Columbia, SC 29202
Tel.: 803-794-7300
Tel.: 800-739-5394 **SC**
Year Founded: 1950
Approx.Sls.: $130,000,000
Emp.: 2,400
Common Carrier Trucking
S.I.C.: 4213
W. Tobin Cassels, Jr. *(Chm. Bd.)*
Paul Taylor *(Pres.)*
J. Russell Burleson, Jr. *(V.P.-Fin.)*
Charles A. Pendleton *(V.P.-Mktg.)*

Principal(s):
W. Tobin Cassels, Jr.

No. of Mfg. Plants/Facilities: 27
No. of U.S. Offices: 27

Outside Service Firm(s):

Liberty Mutual*(Commercial Insurance Carrier)*
Boston, MA

Blue Cross & Blue Shield of South Carolina*(Group Insurer)*
1517 Laurel St.
Columbia, SC 29201

Citizens & Southern National Bank*(Major Banking Relationship)*
Columbia, SC

South Carolina National Bank*(Major Banking Relationship)*
Columbia, SC

SOUTHEASTERN INVESTMENT PROPERTIES INC.
933 Lee Rd., Ste. 400A
Orlando, FL 32810
Tel.: 407-629-6660 **FL**
Fax: 407-628-2875
Year Founded: 1978
Approx.Sls.: $80,000,000
Emp.: 32
Commercial Real Estate Broker & Developer
S.I.C.: 6531; 6552
Al Clark *(Chm. Bd. & Pres.)*

Outside Service Firm(s):

William Rippard*(Auditors)*
Altamonte Springs, FL

Bradford & Fletcher*(Legal Firm)*
Orlando, FL

Neduchal & Magee*(Legal Firm)*
Orlando, FL

SOUTHEASTERN MEDEQUIP, INC.
905 N. 3rd St.
Jacksonville Beach, FL 32250
Tel.: 904-246-0333 **FL**
Fax: 904-241-5196
Year Founded: 1973

Southeastern Medequip, Inc.—(Continued)

Earnings: $60,000
Emp.: 9
Fiscal Year-end: 12/31/90
Medical Equipment Supplier To At Home Patients
S.I.C.: 5963
F.W. Fogg *(Pres. & Chief Exec. Officer)*
William Fogg III *(Chief Fin. Officer & Treas.)*

Computer Systems/Hardware:
Texas Instruments

Outside Service Firm(s):

Shaw & Shaw*(Auditors)*
Jacksonville Beach, FL

Lincoln National Life Insurance Co.*(Group Insurer)*
PO Box 208, 1300 S. Clinton
Fort Wayne, IN 46801
Tel.: 219-455-2926
Fax: 219-455-7619

SOUTHEASTERN PENNSYLVANIA TRANSPORTATION AUTHORITY
714 Market St.
Philadelphia, PA 19106
Tel.: 215-580-7840
Year Founded: 1963
Approx.Rev.: $329,500,000
Emp.: 9,500
Fiscal Year-end: 6/30/91
Regional Transportation Authority; Provides Public Transit
S.I.C.: 9621
J. Clayton Undercofler III *(Chm. Bd.)*
Louis J. Gambaccini *(Chief Exec. Officer & Gen. Mgr.)*
James S. Kilcur *(Gen. Counsel)*
Joaquin Bowman *(Dir.-Pub. Rels.)*
Richard Dilullo *(Dir.-Mktg.)*
John Prader *(Dir.-Pur.)*
Jeane Neece *(Dir.-Govt.)*

SOUTHEASTERN STEEL COMPANY
Koppers Rd.
Florence, SC 29503
Mailing Address:
P.O. Box 989,
Florence, SC 29503
Tel.: 803-662-5236
Fax: 803-662-6261
Year Founded: 1945
Approx.Sls.: $19,000,000
Emp.: 225
Fiscal Year-end: 12/31/90
Fabricated Metal Products; Steel Service Center, Machine Shop Facilities
S.I.C.: 5051; 3441
Juanita A. Bulloch *(Pres., Chief Exec. Officer & Treas.)*

Computer Systems/Hardware:
IBM System 34 & 36

Outside Service Firm(s):

Johnson, Stiith, & Assocs.*(Auditors)*
Florence, SC

Provident Life & Accident Insurance Co.*(Group Insurer)*
P.O. Box 12015
Chattanooga, TN 37401
Tel.: 615-755-7088

Bankers Trust Co.*(Major Banking Relationship)*
Charleston, SC

National Bank of South Carolina*(Major Banking Relationship)*
P.O. Box 100526,
Florence, SC 29501-0526
Tel.: 203-667-4000

Subsidiary:

Southeastern Corp. **(1)**
P.O. Box 1069
Florence, SC 29503
Tel.: 803-577-7840
Ernest L. Willis III *(Chief Oper. Officer)*

SOUTHERN AGRICULTURAL INSECTICIDES
7600 Bayshore Rd.
Palmetto, FL 34221
Mailing Address:
P.O. Box 218,
Palmetto, FL 34220
Tel.: 813-722-3285 **FL**
Fax: 812-723-2974
Approx.Sls.: $28,000,000
Emp.: 75
Agricultural Chemicals; Agricultural & Household Pesticides
S.I.C.: 5191; 2879
John J. Diem *(Chm. Bd.)*
John R. Diem *(Pres.)*
Linda L. Diem *(Sec. & Treas.)*

Outside Service Firm(s):

Valdes, McClain, Pratt & Co.*(Auditors)*
Bradenton, FL

SOUTHERN APPAREL CORPORATION
12420 73rd Court
Largo, FL 34643
Tel.: 813-536-8672 **FL**
Fax: 813-539-0752
Emp.: 90
Men's & Boys Shirts & Caps; Retail Jeans Stores
S.I.C.: 5136; 5651
William W. Short, Jr. *(Chm. Bd.)*
Robert Palmiero *(Pres.)*
Allen Flegger *(Treas. & Controller)*

Outside Service Firm(s):

Thomas E. Pease*(Auditors)*
Clearwater, FL

McMullen, Everett & Logan*(Legal Firm)*
Clearwater, FL

SOUTHERN BELLE DAIRY COMPANY, INC.
607 E. Bourne Ave.
Somerset, KY 42501
Tel.: 606-679-1131 **KY**
Year Founded: 1951
Approx.Sls.: $49,000,000
Emp.: 240
Production, Sale & Distribution of Packaged Milk, Milk Products, Ice Cream Mixes & Related Products
S.I.C.: 2026; 5143
Martin P. Shearer *(Pres. & Chief Exec. Officer)*
Al Hamilton *(Chief Oper. Officer & Exec. V.P.)*
Arnold G. Corey *(V.P.-Sls.)*
Max A. Shearer *(V.P.-Opers.)*
Chris Altmaier *(Treas.)*
Welty E. Whitaker *(Dir.-Personnel)*
Dan Hall *(Mgr.-Mngmt. Information Systems)*

Principal(s):
Martin P. Shearer
Max A. Shearer

Computer Systems/Hardware:
IBM System 38

Outside Service Firm(s):

Baird, Kurtz & Dobson*(Auditors)*
Bowling Green, KY

The Citizens National Bank*(Major Banking Relationship)*
Bowling Green, KY

SOUTHERN BEVERAGE PACKERS, INC.
1891 Old Savannah Rd.
Augusta, GA 30914
Tel.: 706-724-2677
Fax: 706-724-5018
Year Founded: 1984
Approx.Sls.: $18,000,000
Emp.: 75
Mfr. of Soft Drinks
S.I.C.: 2086
David M. Byrd *(Pres.)*
Steven Byrd *(V.P.)*
Mary S. Byrd *(Sec.)*

Outside Service Firm(s):

Baird & Company*(Auditors)*
Augusta, GA

SOUTHERN CALIFORNIA BANCORP
310 Broadway
Laguna Beach, CA 92651
Tel.: 714-497-6511 **CA**
Fax: 714-497-5127
Year Founded: 1981
Assets: $34,794,000
Earnings: $2,000
Liabilities: $32,509,000
Net Worth: $2,285,000
Emp.: 43
Fiscal Year-end: 12/31/91
National Bank
S.I.C.: 6021
Ernest George *(Chm. Bd.)*
Jess Barrera *(Pres. & Chief Exec. Officer)*
Richard Cummings *(Chief Fin. Officer)*

Computer Systems/Hardware:
IBM PC

Outside Service Firm(s):

Kenneth Leventhal*(Auditors)*
Costa Mesa, CA

Subsidiary:

First American Capital Bank **(1)**
310 Broadway
Laguna Beach, CA 92651
Tel.: 714-497-6511 (100%)
Fax: 714-497-5127
Emp.: 28
Commercial Bank
S.I.C.: 6021
Ernest George *(Chm.)*
Jess Barrera *(Pres. & Chief Exec. Officer)*

SOUTHERN CASE, INC.
2315 Laurelbrook St.
Raleigh, NC 27604
Mailing Address:
P.O. Box 28147,
Raleigh, NC 27611
Tel.: 919-821-0877
Fax: 919-839-2361
Year Founded: 1974
Approx.Sls.: $20,000,000
Emp.: 240
Export
Mfr. of Plastic Blow-Molded Carry Cases
S.I.C.: 3089
John Reidy *(Chm. Bd.)*
Andrew E. Dembicks *(Pres.)*
J. Louie Yilling *(Chief Fin. Officer)*
R. Stringari *(Gen. Mgr.-Consumer Prods.)*

SOUTHERN CONTAINER CORPORATION
115 Engineers Rd.
Hauppauge, NY 11788
Mailing Address:
P.O. Box 1060
Smithtown, NY 11787
Tel.: 516-231-0400
Fax: 516-231-0174
Year Founded: 1946
Approx.Sls.: $73,000,000
Emp.: 550
Manufacturer of Corrugated Boxes & Products
S.I.C.: 2673; 2674
Louis Grossman *(Chm. Bd.)*
Steven M. Grossman *(Pres.)*
Steven H. Hill *(Sr. V.P., Sec. & Dir.-Fin.)*
Donald L. Kasun *(V.P.)*
Lawrence Wilson *(Controller)*
W. Danek *(Dir.-Data Processing)*
Roberta Saszlow *(Dir.-Pur.)*

Outside Service Firm(s):

KPMG Peat Marwick*(Auditors)*
112 E. Pecan
San Antonio, TX 78205

Bernard Stebel*(Legal Firm)*
Woodbury, NY

Chemical Bank*(Major Banking Relationship)*
450 West 33rd St.
New York, NY 10001
Tel.: 212-613-7197
Fax: 212-947-7628

SOUTHERN ELECTRIC SUPPLY CO., INC.
301 46th Court
Meridian, MS 39301
Tel.: 601-693-4141 **DE**
Fax: 601-693-6225
Year Founded: 1945
Wholesale Electric Supplies & Equipment With Branches Located In Alabama, Florida, Louisiana, Mississippi, Oklahoma & Tennessee
S.I.C.: 5063
Robert Merson *(Pres. & Chief Exec. Officer)*
Guy D. Taylor *(Exec. V.P.)*
James Hopkins *(V.P.-Pur.)*
Judy Mcinnis *(Sec. & Treas.)*

Divisions:

Pyramid Electric Supply Co., Inc. **(1)**
2034 NW Seventh St.
Oklahoma City, OK 73106
Tel.: 405-232-7626
Fax: 706-232-2105
Wholesale Electric Supplies & Equipment
S.I.C.: 5063
Tim Hogan *(Mgr.)*

Wholesale Electric Division **(1)**
420 Press St.
Kingsport, TN 37660
Tel.: 615-246-2900
Fax: 615-378-5548
Wholesale Electric Supplies & Equipment
S.I.C.: 5063
David Byrd *(Mgr.)*

Branches:

Southern Electric Supply Co., Inc. **(1)**
3000 5th Ave. South
Birmingham, AL 35233
Tel.: 205-252-8911
Fax: 205-326-6694
Wholesale Electric Supplies & Equipment
S.I.C.: 5063
Tim Copeland *(Mgr.)*

Southern Electric Supply Co., Inc. **(1)**
1420 Church St., NE
Decatur, AL 35601
Tel.: 205-353-6131
Fax: 205-355-1638
Wholesale Electric Supplies & Equipment
S.I.C.: 5063
Paul Ridgeway *(Mgr.)*

Southern Electric Supply Co., Inc. **(1)**
433 Locust
Gadsden, AL 35902
Tel.: 205-547-6395
Fax: 205-543-7097
Wholesale Electric Supplies & Equipment
S.I.C.: 5063
Larry Isbell *(Mgr.)*

Southern Electric Supply Co., Inc. **(1)**
3307 Moffat Rd.
Mobile, AL 36607
Tel.: 205-479-6000
Fax: 205-479-6039
Wholesale Electric Supplies & Equipment
S.I.C.: 5063
Jim Van Blake *(Mgr.)*

Southern Electric Supply Co., Inc. **(1)**
1141 Holloway Park
Montgomery, AL 36117
Tel.: 205-270-9473
Fax: 205-270-1095
Wholesale Electric Supplies & Equipment
S.I.C.: 5063
Wally Parker *(Mgr.)*

Southern Electric Supply Co., Inc. **(1)**
2006 Tenth Ave.
Tuscaloosa, AL 35402
Tel.: 205-345-2444
Fax: 205-752-5043
Wholesale Electric Supplies & Equipment
S.I.C.: 5063
Thurman Gregory *(Mgr.)*

Southern Electric Supply Co., Inc. **(1)**
4700 NW 15th Ave., Bay a
Ft. Lauderdale, FL 33309
Tel.: 305-491-8188
Fax: 305-491-8511
Wholesale Electric Supplies & Equipment
S.I.C.: 5063
Gail Moore *(Mgr.)*

Southern Electric Supply Co., Inc. **(1)**
3005 SW Williston Rd.
Gainesville, FL 32608
Tel.: 904-335-9175
Fax: 904-335-9095
Wholesale Electric Supplies & Equipment
S.I.C.: 5063
Van Smoak *(Mgr.)*

Southern Electric Supply Co., Inc. **(1)**
500 E. Donegan Ave.
Kissimmee, FL 34744
Tel.: 407-846-1611
Fax: 407-239-6585
Wholesale Electric Supplies & Equipment
S.I.C.: 5063
Harry Boardman *(Mgr.)*

Southern Electric Supply Co., Inc. **(1)**
7401 W. Ellis Rd.
West Melbourne, FL 32904
Tel.: 407-768-0223
Fax: 407-984-7916
Wholesale Electric Supplies & Equipment
S.I.C.: 5063
Mark Harris *(Mgr.)*

Southern Electric Supply Co., Inc. **(1)**
111 S.E. 8th St.
Ocala, FL 32671
Tel.: 904-368-7952
Fax: 904-368-3897
Wholesale Electric Supplies & Equipment
S.I.C.: 5063
Gary Jarrell *(Mgr.)*

Southern Electric Supply Co., Inc. **(1)**
3501 S. Sanford Ave.
Sanford, FL 32773
Tel.: 407-322-0631
Fax: 407-321-4731
Wholesale Electric Supplies & Equipment
S.I.C.: 5063
George Meadows *(Mgr.)*

Southern Electric Supply Co., Inc. **(1)**
672 Old Dixie Hwy.
Vero Beach, FL 32965
Tel.: 407-562-3032
Fax: 407-562-3605
Wholesale Electric Supplies & Equipment
S.I.C.: 5063
David Weaver *(Mgr.)*

Southern Electric Supply Co., Inc. **(1)**
3012 Broadway
Alexandria, LA 71301
Tel.: 318-445-6462
Fax: 318-445-5024
Wholesale Electric Supplies & Equipment
S.I.C.: 5063
Wayne Salard *(Mgr.)*

Southern Electric Supply Co., Inc. **(1)**
8536 S. Choctaw Dr.
Baton Rouge, LA 70815
Tel.: 504-926-3800
Fax: 504-926-4103
Wholesale Electric Supplies & Equipment
S.I.C.: 5063
Melvin Stokes *(Mgr.)*

Southern Electric Supply Co., Inc. **(1)**
Hyw. 171 S.
Leesville, LA 71446
Tel.: 318-238-4400
Wholesale Electric Supplies & Equipment
S.I.C.: 5063
Mike Salard *(Mgr.)*

Southern Electric Supply Co., Inc. **(1)**
5712 Jarvis St.
Harahan, LA 70123
Tel.: 504-733-4844
Fax: 504-736-0159
Wholesale Electric Supplies & Equipment
S.I.C.: 5063
Tony Desselles *(Mgr.)*

Southern Electric Supply Co., Inc. **(1)**
1121 Gardner Blvd.
Columbus, MS 39704
Tel.: 601-328-0625
Fax: 601-328-0822
Wholesale Electric Supplies & Equipment
S.I.C.: 5063
John Lochridge *(Mgr.)*

Southern Electric Supply Co., Inc. **(1)**
610 Kentucky St.
Greenville, MS 38701
Tel.: 601-378-2011
Fax: 601-332-8943
Wholesale Electric Supplies & Equipment
S.I.C.: 5063
Mark Gibson *(Mgr.)*

Southern Electric Supply Co., Inc. **(1)**
1407 Main St.
Greenwood, MS 38930
Tel.: 601-453-8673
Fax: 601-453-2830
Wholesale Electric Supplies & Equipment
S.I.C.: 5063
Lewis Jones *(Mgr.)*

Southern Electric Supply Co., Inc. **(1)**
361 Thomas St.
Grenada, MS 38901
Tel.: 601-226-4071
Fax: 601-226-3785
Wholesale Electric Supplies & Equipment
S.I.C.: 5063
Ronnie Sanders *(Mgr.)*

Southern Electric Supply Co., Inc. **(1)**
1270 28th St.
Gulfport, MS 39501
Tel.: 601-864-5340
Fax: 601-864-9052
Wholesale Electric Supplies & Equipment
S.I.C.: 5063
Steve Shipman *(Mgr.)*

Southern Electric Supply Co., Inc. **(1)**
215 S. Magnolia St.
Laurel, MS 39440
Tel.: 601-425-3107
Wholesale Electric Supplies & Equipment
S.I.C.: 5063
Ken Miller *(Mgr.)*

Southern Electric Supply Co., Inc. **(1)**
912 13th St.
Meridian, MS 39301
Tel.: 601-693-4271
Fax: 601-483-3659
Wholesale Electric Supplies & Equipment
S.I.C.: 5063
Danny McKissack *(Mgr.)*

Southern Electric Supply Co., Inc. **(1)**
607 S. 16th St.
Oxford, MS 38655
Tel.: 601-234-5093
Fax: 601-234-3925
Wholesale Electric Supplies & Equipment
S.I.C.: 5063
Frank Swider *(Mgr.)*

Southern Electric Supply Co., Inc. **(1)**
520 Depot St.
Vicksburg, MS 39180
Tel.: 601-636-1481
Fax: 601-636-1487
Wholesale Electric Supplies & Equipment
S.I.C.: 5063
Guy Sharpe *(Mgr.)*

Southern Electric Supply Co., Inc. **(1)**
3415 W. Andrew Johnson Hwy.
Morristown, TN 37814
Tel.: 615-587-1116
Fax: 615-581-2134
Wholesale Electric Supplies & Equipment
S.I.C.: 5063
Dwayne Cole *(Mgr.)*

Southern Electric Supply Co., Inc. **(1)**
17 Hand Ave.
Bay Minette, AL 36507
Tel.: 205-937-7004
Wholesale electric supplies & equipment
S.I.C.: 5063
Hal Ritchie *(Mgr.)*

Southern Electric Supply Co., Inc. **(1)**
600 NW Peacock Blvd., Ste. 8
Port St. Lucie, FL 34986
Tel.: 407-340-7810
Fax: 407-340-7529
Wholesale electric supplies & equipment
S.I.C.: 5063
David Weaver *(Mgr.)*

SOUTHERN FARM BUREAU CASUALTY INSURANCE COMPANY
P.O. Box 1800,
Ridgeland, MS 39158-1800
Tel.: 601-957-7777 **MS**
Fax: 601-957-4329
Year Founded: 1947
Assets: $562,834,030
Liabilities: $314,540,377
Net Worth: $248,293,653
Approx.Sls.: $562,000,000
Emp.: 1,150
Property & Casualty Insurance
S.I.C.: 6331
S.M. True, Jr. *(Pres.)*
Gerald Garnett *(Exec. V.P. & Chief Exec. Officer)*
Andrew Whisenhunt *(1st V.P.)*
Clark Cavalier *(V.P.-Sls.)*
Sam Cooper *(V.P.)*
Walter Duncan *(V.P.-Legal & Sec.)*
Wynne Jacobs *(V.P. & Treas.)*
Wayne Lee *(V.P.)*
Rod H. Moore *(V.P.-Fin.)*
Mickey Nugent *(V.P.-Opers.)*
John Stenmark *(V.P.-Actuary)*
Thomas Young *(V.P.)*

No. of U.S. Offices: 6

Computer Systems/Hardware:
IBM System 4381

Outside Service Firm(s):

KPMG Peat Marwick*(Auditors)*
One Jackson Place,
Jackson, MS 39201
Tel.: 601-354-3701
Fax: 601-354-3745

Heidelberg, Woodliff & Franks*(Legal Firm)*
Jackson, MI

Trustmark National Bank*(Major Banking Relationship)*
248 E. Capital
Jackson, MS 39201

SOUTHERN FOODS, INC.
3500 Old Battleground Rd.
Greensboro, NC 27410
Mailing Address:
P.O. Box 26801,
Greensboro, NC 27429
Tel.: 919-545-3800 **NC**
Fax: 919-288-4905
Year Founded: 1954
Sales Range: $80-99 Million
Emp.: 354
Meats & Meat Products
S.I.C.: 5147
Victor M. Nussbaum, Jr. *(Pres.)*
James S. Nussbaum *(V.P.)*
R. Michael Nussbaum *(V.P.)*
Patricia Nussbaum *(Sec.)*

Outside Service Firm(s):

Wachovia Bank & Trust Co.*(Major Banking Relationship)*
P.O. Box 21048,
Greensboro, NC 27402

Divisions:

Home Division **(1)**
3500 Old Battleground Rd.
Greensboro, NC 27410
Tel.: 919-288-1441
Deliver Meats To Homes
S.I.C.: 5147

Institutional Division **(1)**
3500 Old Battleground Rd.
Greensboro, NC 27410
Tel.: 919-288-1441
Delivers Meat To Institutions
S.I.C.: 5147

SOUTHERN LEATHER COMPANY
274 Monroe Ave.
Memphis, TN 38103
Mailing Address:
P.O. Box 6
Memphis, TN 38101
Tel.: 901-525-1200
Fax: 901-526-5603
Year Founded: 1912
Fiscal Year-end: 6/30/89
Wholesale Rubber Findings; Ladies' & Men's Shoes, Accessories & Leather Specialty Items
S.I.C.: 5087; 5139; 5199
William A. Loewenberg *(Chm. Bd.)*
William Ira Loewenberg *(Pres.)*
Joel Felt *(Treas.)*
Harry L. Loewenberg *(Dir.-Customer Service)*

Outside Service Firm(s):

Ernst & Young*(Auditors)*
1400 One Commerce Sq.
Memphis, TN 38103

National Bank of Commerce*(Major Banking Relationship)*
Memphis, TN

Union National Bank*(Major Banking Relationship)*
P.O. Box 1541
Little Rock, AR 72203
Tel.: 501-378-4213

SOUTHERN MILLS, INC.
6501 Mall Blvd.
Union City, GA 30291
Mailing Address:
P.O. Box 289
Union City, GA 30291
Tel.: 404-969-1000
Fax: 404-969-6846
Year Founded: 1925
Emp.: 520
Industrial Textiles
S.I.C.: 2299
William D. Ellis *(Chm. Bd. & Chief Exec. Officer)*
Philip S. Vincent *(Pres. & Chief Oper. Officer)*
Robert Bell *(V.P.-Opers.)*
Bob Chiostergi *(V.P.-Mktg. & Sls.)*
Kenneth Collins *(V.P.-Fin.)*
John Gray *(V.P.-Cabletex Div.)*
Mary Jones *(V.P.-Product Engrng.)*
Steve Mitchell *(V.P.-Mfg.)*
Allan Ray *(V.P.-Admin. & Control)*
Joyce Smith *(Pur. Agent)*

No. of Mfg. Plants/Facilities: 6

Southern Mills, Inc.—(Continued)

Outside Service Firm(s):

KPMG Peat Marwick*(Auditors)*
245 Peachtree Ctr. Ave. N.E., Ste. 1900
Atlanta, GA 30303
Tel.: 404-577-3240

Sutherland, Asbill & Brennan*(Legal Firm)*
999 Peachtree St.
Atlanta, GA 30309
Tel.: 404-658-8700

SOUTHERN MINNESOTA BEET SUGAR COOPERATIVE
E. Hwy 212
Renville, MN 56284
Mailing Address:
P.O. Box 500
Renville, MN 56284
Tel.: 612-329-8305
Fax: 612-329-3252
Year Founded: 1972
Approx.Sls.: $111,559,152
Emp.: 250
Fiscal Year-end: 8/31/92
Export
Beet Sugar, Pulp & Molasses
S.I.C.: 2063; 2061
William Rudeen *(Chm. Bd.)*
George Kleven *(Vice Chm.)*
Irvin L. Zitterkopf *(Pres. & Chief Exec. Officer)*
Helmut Doerr *(V.P.-Opers.)*
Jeff Plathe *(V.P.-Fin.)*
Jimmy N. Widner *(V.P.-Agriculture)*
Eugene Schwitters *(Treas.)*
Larry Johnson *(Sec.)*
Dean DeBelly *(Dir.-Pur.)*
Dave Peterson *(Dir.-Personnel)*
Jean-Pierre Monclin *(Mgr.-Technical Services)*

No. of Mfg. Plants/Facilities: 1
No. of U.S. Offices: 1

Computer Systems/Hardware:
NCR

Outside Service Firm(s):

KPMG Peat Marwick*(Auditors)*
4200 Norwest Center, 90 S. 7th St.
Minneapolis, MN 55402
Tel.: 612-341-2222

Dorsey & Whitney*(Legal Firm)*
2200 First Bank Place East
Minneapolis, MN 55402

Bank for Co-ops*(Major Banking Relationship)*
Minneapolis, MN

Subsidiaries:

Midwest Agri-Commodities **(1)**
100 Tamal Plaza, Ste. 180, 200 Tamal Vista Blvd.
Corte Madera, CA 94925

North Central Sugar Marketing Co-Op **(1)**
400 S. Cty Rd. 18, Ste. 250
Saint Louis Park, MN 55426

SOUTHERN OHIO FABRICATORS, INC.
10333 Wayne Ave.
Cincinnati, OH 45215
Tel.: 513-771-1600 **OH**
Fax: 513-771-5490
Year Founded: 1947
Assets: $23,743,000
Liabilities: $12,600,000
Net Worth: $11,143,000
Approx.Sls.: $45,000,000
Emp.: 300
Fiscal Year-end: 6/30/91
Import
Fabricators of Structural Steel Sheets & Plates; Steel Erection
S.I.C.: 3441; 1629; 1791; 3443; 3449
John J. Kling *(Chm. Bd.)*
William H. Worthington *(V.P.)*
Tim J. Gates *(Pres.,Treas. & Dir.-Mngmt. Info. Systems)*
J.T. Nickerson *(V.P.-Mfg.)*
Thomas W. Routledge *(V.P.-Sls.)*
Jim Ludwig *(V.P.-Erection)*
Dan Shaih *(Controller)*
Robert Gillespie *(Pur. Agent)*
Charles Michel *(Dir.-Human Resources)*
Robert Barnes *(Supvr.-Mfg.)*
Principal(s):
John J. Kling
J.T. Nickerson

No. of Mfg. Plants/Facilities: 2
No. of U.S. Offices: 1

Computer Systems/Hardware:
Honeywell

Outside Service Firm(s):

KPMG Peat Marwick*(Auditors)*
1600 Central Trust Ctr., 201 East Fifth St.
Cincinnati, OH 45202
Tel.: 513-421-6430

Dinsmore & Shohl*(Legal Firm)*
2100 Fountain Square Plaza
Cincinnati, OH 45202-3172
Tel.: 513-977-8200

The Central Trust Company, N.A.*(Major Banking Relationship)*
Cincinnati, OH
Tel.: 513-651-8896

SOUTHERN PACIFIC LINES
One Market Plaza, Southern Pacific Bldg.
San Francisco, CA 94105
Tel.: 415-541-1000
Approx.Rev.: $2,412,111,000
Fiscal Year-end: 12/31/90
Railroads, Railroad & Trucking Operations
S.I.C.: 4011
D.M. Mohan *(Pres. & Chief Exec. Officer)*
D.C. Oris *(Sr. V.P.-Mktg. & Sls.)*
Bart Nadeau *(Dir.-Adv.)*

SOUTHERN PIPE & SUPPLY CO., INC.
4330 Hwy. 39 North
Meridian, MS 39301
Mailing Address:
P.O. Box 5738,
Meridian, MS 39301
Tel.: 601-693-2911
Fax: 601-485-0074
Approx.Sls.: $100,000,000
Emp.: 400
Fiscal Year-end: 12/31/90
Wholesale Plumbing & Heating Supplies
S.I.C.: 5074; 5075
Martin Davidson *(Pres. & Chief Exec. Officer)*
James McAllister *(V.P.-Fin.)*
Frank York *(Controller)*
Johnny Dean *(Mgr.-Data Processing)*

Computer Systems/Hardware:
Unisys 80, Model 8

Outside Service Firm(s):

Deloitte & Touche*(Auditors)*
417 No. 20th St., Ste. 1000
Birmingham, AL 35203-3289
Tel.: 205-322-0534

Life Insurance Co. of Georgia*(Group Insurer)*
P.O. Box 105234,
Atlanta, GA 30348-5234
Tel.: 404-980-5100

Berkowicz, Lefkowicz, Isom & Kurshner*(Legal Firm)*
Birmingham, AL
Tel.: 205-328-0480

Deposit Guaranty National Bank*(Major Banking Relationship)*
Meridian, MS

NationsBank*(Major Banking Relationship)*
35 Broad St.
Atlanta, GA 30303
Tel.: 404-581-2121
Tel.: 800-848-8198

SOUTHERN PUMP & TANK CO. INC.
(d/b/a SPATCO)
4800 N. Graham St.
Charlotte, NC 28213
Mailing Address:
P.O. Box 31516
Charlotte, NC 28213
Tel.: 704-596-4373 **NC**
Fax: 704-598-0105
Approx.Sls.: $45,000,000
Emp.: 220
Distribute Liquid & Petroleum Containers, Industrial Pumps & Tanks
S.I.C.: 5084; 5085
Randy Castleberry *(Co-Chm. Bd.)*
Jack Hatcher *(Co-Chm. Bd.)*
Ray Bostian *(Pres.)*
R.E. Arceci *(Sr. V.P.)*
Harold Sloan *(Sr. V.P.)*
Chris Blumberg *(V.P.-Pur.)*
Larry Hunter *(V.P.-Technical Services)*
Steve Irwin *(V.P.-Fin.)*

Outside Service Firm(s):

Deloitte & Touche*(Auditors)*
2000 First Citizens Bank Plaza, 128 S. Tryon St.
Charlotte, NC 28202-5001
Tel.: 704-372-3560

Kennedy, Covington, Lobdell & Hickman*(Legal Firm)*
3300 NCNB Plaza
Charlotte, NC 28282
Tel.: 704-377-6000

NationsBank Carolinas*(Major Banking Relationship)*
One NCNB Plaza T18-7
Charlotte, NC 28255

SOUTHERN RADIO CORPORATION
Mailing Address:
P.O. Box 410667,
Charlotte, NC 28241-0667
Assets: $8,664,000
Liabilities: $4,662,654
Net Worth: $4,001,346
Approx.Sls.: $18,000,000
Emp.: 28
Fiscal Year-end: 12/31/90
Export
Wholesaler & Distributor of Electronics, Furniture, Outdoor Power Equipment & Appliances
S.I.C.: 5064
Thomas J. Jamison *(Chm. Bd. & Chief Exec. Officer)*
R. Kenneth Jamison *(Pres. & Chief Oper. Officer)*
James L. Cole *(V.P.-Sls.)*
Mike Griffith *(Treas. & Sec.)*
Donna Williams *(Dir.-Data Processing)*
Principal(s):
Thomas J. Jamison
R. Kenneth Jamison

No. of Mfg. Plants/Facilities: 1
No. of U.S. Offices: 1

Computer Systems/Hardware:
MAI Basic Four

Outside Service Firm(s):

Deloitte & Touche*(Auditors)*
2000 First Citizens Bank Plaza, 128 S. Tryon St.
Charlotte, NC 28202-5001
Tel.: 704-372-3560

Lincoln National Life Insurance Co.*(Group Insurer)*
PO Box 208, 1300 S. Clinton
Fort Wayne, IN 46801
Tel.: 219-455-2926
Fax: 219-455-7619

NationsBank Carolinas*(Investment Banker)*
One NCNB Plaza T18-7
Charlotte, NC 28255

Kennedy, Covington, Lobdell & Hickman*(Legal Firm)*
3300 NCNB Plaza
Charlotte, NC 28282
Tel.: 704-377-6000

NationsBank Carolinas*(Major Banking Relationship)*
One NCNB Plaza T18-7
Charlotte, NC 28255

NationsBank Carolinas*(Pension Manager)*
One NCNB Plaza T18-7
Charlotte, NC 28255

SOUTHERN STATES COOPERATIVE, INC.
6606 W. Broad St.
Richmond, VA 23230-6234
Mailing Address:
P. O. Box 26234
Richmond, VA 23260
Tel.: 804-281-1000
Telex: 710-956-0165
Fax: 804-281-1141
Year Founded: 1923
Assets: $308,000,000
Earnings: $10,000,000
Liabilities: $179,000,000
Net Worth: $129,000,000
Approx.Sls.: $945,233,969
Emp.: 3,652
Fiscal Year-end: 6/30/92
Import
Wholesale & Retail Feed, Fertilizer, Seed, Petroleum, & Farm, Home & Garden Supplies; Grain Marketing in 5 0f 6 Southern Regional States
S.I.C.: 5983; 5191; 5261; 5171; 5172
Corporate Giving Program: United Way
Galen B. Brubaker *(Chm. Bd.)*
Gene A. James *(Pres. & Chief Exec. Officer)*
M. Terry Ragsdale *(Exec. V.P. & Chief Oper. Officer)*
Jonathan A. Hawkins *(Sr. V.P. & Chief Fin. Officer)*
Gene R. Anderson *(Grp. V.P.-Sls. & Mktg.)*
William M. Smith *(Grp. V.P.-Opers. Services)*
N. Hopper Ancarrow *(V.P. & Gen. Counsel)*
Dr. Joseph D. Coffey *(V.P.-Economics & Plng.)*
C.A. Miller *(V.P.-Information Systems)*
Richard Sherman *(V.P.-Human Resources)*
Robert W. Taylor *(V.P. & Controller)*
John C. Froman *(Asst. Treas.)*
Jerry H. Gass *(Dir.-Communications & Govt. Affairs)*
Edward W. Scharf *(Dir.-Mktg., Adv. & Private Dealer Services)*
Don R. Tindall *(Asst. Dir.-Communications, Sr. Editor & Publr.-Cooperative Pub.)*
Bob Buehler *(Mgr.-Feed Mktg. & Specialty Sls.)*
Paul E. Campbell *(Mgr.-Employee Benefits)*
Turner Gravitt *(Mgr.-Training & Devel.)*
Jeb R. Hockman *(Adv. Mgr.)*
Randye Butcher *(Pur. Agent-Office Supplies)*

Outside Service Firm(s):

Coopers & Lybrand*(Auditors)*
Riverfront Plaza West, 901 E. Byrd St., Ste. 1200
Richmond, VA 23219-4071

Tel.: 804-697-1900

Deloitte & Touche*(Auditors)*
700 Bldg.,Suite 1800, 700 E. Main St.
Richmond, VA 23219-2619
Tel.: 804-697-1543
Fax: 804-697-1859

Booke & Co.*(Group Insurer)*
310 W. 4th Street
Winston-Salem, NC 27102
Tel.: 919-748-1120
Fax: 919-748-1120 ext. 462

Craigie Inc.*(Investment Banker)*
823 Main St.
Richmond, VA 23219
Tel.: 804-649-3900

Wheat First Securities*(Investment Banker)*
Riverfront Plaza, 901 East Byrd St.
Richmond, VA 23219
Tel.: 804-649-2311

C&S Sovran Bank*(Major Banking Relationship)*
P.O. Box 26904,
Richmond, VA 23261
Tel.: 804-344-1359

Crestar Bank*(Major Banking Relationship)*
P.O. Box 26665,
Richmond, VA 23261
Tel.: 804-782-5995

National Bank for Cooperatives*(Major Banking Relationship)*
Baltimore, MD

Brinson Partners, Inc.*(Pension Manager)*
Three First National Plaza, 9th Floor, Ste. 114
Chicago, IL 60602
Tel.: 312-220-7100
Fax: 312-220-7199

Duncan-Hurst*(Pension Manager)*
4365 Exec. Dr., Suite 1520
San Diego, CA 92121
Tel.: 619-597-4800

Phoenix Investment Counsel*(Pension Manager)*
One American Row
Hartford, CT 06115
Tel.: 203-275-5598
Fax: 203-275-5670

Templeton Investment Counsel*(Pension Manager)*
500 E. Broward Blvd., Ste. 2100
Ft. Lauderdale, FL 33394-3091
Tel.: 305-764-7390
Fax: 305-462-1230

Subsidiary:

Wetsel Seed Company **(1)**
P.O. Box 791
Harrisonburg, VA 22801
Tel.: 703-434-6753
Grass & Flower Seeds, Chemical Plant Nutrients
S.I.C.: 0181
Floyd Rigsby *(Gen. Mgr.)*

SOUTHGATE FORD INC.
16501 Fort St.
Southgate, MI 48195
Tel.: 313-282-3636
Fax: 313-282-3636, Ext. 215
Approx.Sls.: $35,000,000
Emp.: 100
New & Used Automobiles Dealership
S.I.C.: 5511
Walter J. Oben, Jr. *(Chm. Bd.)*
Walter J. Oben, Sr. *(Pres.)*
Donna Morgan *(Treas. & Sec.)*
Tom Morse *(Mgr.-Sls.)*

SOUTHLAND FLOORING SUPPLIES OF LOUISVILLE, INC.
1010 Industrial Blvd.
Louisville, KY 40219
Tel.: 502-968-3333 **KY**
Fax: 502-968-1698
Year Founded: 1969
Emp.: 9
Distributor of Flooring Installation Supplies
S.I.C.: 5087
Mike Trick *(Pres.)*
Mark Trick *(V.P.)*

No. of Mfg. Plants/Facilities: 1

Outside Service Firm(s):

Citizens Fidelity Bank & Trust Co.*(Major Banking Relationship)*
P.O. Box 33000-Citizens Plaza
Louisville, KY 40232
Tel.: 502-581-3381

SOUTHLAND INDUSTRIES
1661 E. 32nd St.
Long Beach, CA 90807
Tel.: 310-424-8638 **CA**
Fax: 310-490-0767
Year Founded: 1949
Approx.Sls.: $49,000,000
Emp.: 314
Contractors For Heating & Air Conditioning
S.I.C.: 1711
Michael J. Moore *(Chm. Bd. & Pres.)*
Thomas Egley *(Chief Fin. Officer)*
Andrew Fimiano *(Exec. V.P.)*
William G. Cippinger *(Sr. V.P.)*
David Peters *(Dir.-Engrng.)*
Principal(s):
Michael J. Moore
Andrew Fimiano

Outside Service Firm(s):

Roth, Bookstein & Zaslow*(Auditors)*
Los Angeles, CA

Wells Fargo Bank*(Major Banking Relationship)*
333 S. Grand
Los Angeles, CA 90071
Tel.: 213-253-6836

SOUTHSIDE FORD TRUCK SALES INC.
810 W. Pershing Rd.
Chicago, IL 60609
Tel.: 312-247-4000
Fax: 312-247-8765
Year Founded: 1962
Approx.Sls.: $36,000,000
Emp.: 86
Ford Truck Sales, Service, Rental & Leasing
S.I.C.: 7513
Carl E. Statham *(Pres.)*
W.D. Wendt *(Controller)*
Frank Kilduff *(Gen. Mgr.-Sls.)*
Ron Olson *(Mgr.-Parts)*
Willie Wienhoefer *(Mgr.-Service)*

Outside Service Firm(s):

Corbett & Leukhoff*(Auditors)*
Countryside, IL

Rothschild, Barry & Myers*(Legal Firm)*
2 First Natl. Plz.
Chicago, IL 60603
Tel.: 312-372-2345

Independence Bank of Chicago*(Major Banking Relationship)*
Chicago, IL

SOUTHWARK METAL MANUFACTURING COMPANY
1600 & Washington Ave.
Philadelphia, PA 19146
Tel.: 215-735-3401
Fax: 215-735-0411
Sales Range: $20-39 Million
Emp.: 300
Mfr. of Sheet Metal Products; Galvanized Ducts & Fittings For Heaters
S.I.C.: 3444
Morton L. Spiegel *(Pres. & Treas.)*
William D. Spiegel *(V.P.)*
Gary J. Spiegel *(Sec.)*
Steven Embler *(Mgr.-Opers.)*
Richard D. McGarry *(Mgr.-Sls.)*
Andrew Palestini *(Plant Mgr.)*
David Lazerow *(Pur. Agent)*

Outside Service Firm(s):

BDO Seidman*(Auditors)*
Philadelphia, PA

Mellon Bank, N.A.*(Major Banking Relationship)*
Mellon Independence Center, 7th & Market
Philadelphia, PA 19101-7899

SOUTHWEST FLOOR COVERING INC.
(d/b/a Design for Living)
6965 Consolidated Way
San Diego, CA 92121
Tel.: 619-695-1100 **CA**
Twx: 4990973
Fax: 619-271-9283
Approx.Sls.: $25,000,000
Emp.: 90
Import Export
Flooring Contractor--Sale & Installation of Floor & Window Coverings
S.I.C.: 1752; 1799
Robert D. Motta *(Pres.)*
Mark Fordyce *(V.P.)*
Joseph P. Murphy *(Sec.)*
Principal(s):
Robert D. Motta

No. of Mfg. Plants/Facilities: 3

Outside Service Firm(s):

Brobeck, Phleger & Harrison*(Legal Firm)*
550 West "C", Ste. 1200
San Diego, CA 92101

SOUTHWEST MARINE, INC.
P.O. Box 13308
San Diego, CA 92170
Tel.: 619-238-1000
Fax: 619-238-0934
Year Founded: 1976
Approx.Sls.: $300,000,000
Emp.: 4,000
Export
Government & Commercial Ship Repair
S.I.C.: 3731
Arthur Engel *(Pres. & Chief Exec. Officer)*
James Nakamura *(Chief Fin. Officer & Sr. V.P.)*
Herbert G. Engel *(Exec. V.P. & Chief Oper.Officer)*
Robert M. Bates *(Sr. V.P.)*
David R. Engel *(Sr. V.P.)*
William M. Johnston *(Sr. V.P.)*
Lloyd A. Schwartz *(Sr. V.P. & Gen. Counsel)*

Outside Service Firm(s):

Wells Fargo Bank*(Major Banking Relationship)*
420 Montgomery St.
San Francisco, CA 94104

Subsidiary:

Northwest Marine, Inc. **(1)**
5555 N. Channel Ave., Bldg. 2
Portland, OR 27217
Tel.: 503-285-7557

SOUTHWEST RESEARCH INSTITUTE
6220 Culebra Rd.
San Antonio, TX 78228-0510
Mailing Address:
P.O. Drawer 28510,
San Antonio, TX 78228-0510
Tel.: 210-684-5111 **TX**
Fax: 210-522-3496
Year Founded: 1947
Assets: $155,657,702
Liabilities: $60,963,752
Net Worth: $94,693,950
Approx.Sls.: $180,000,000
Emp.: 2,400
Fiscal Year-end: 9/28/90
Export
Research & Development Company
S.I.C.: 8731
Corporate Giving Program: United Way
Klaus Mai *(Chm. Bd.)*
Martin Goland *(Pres.)*
J. Dan Bates *(Exec. V.P.-Fin.)*
Richard P. Curtin *(Exec. V.P.-Opers.)*
Dr. Robert Bass *(V.P.)*
James Burch *(V.P.)*
Terry Green *(V.P.)*
Amos Holt *(V.P.)*
Donald E. Johnson *(V.P.)*
John Latz *(V.P.)*
Jay Lewallen *(V.P.-Devel.)*
Ulric Lindholm *(V.P.)*
Carl Springer *(V.P.)*
Douglas Travers *(V.P.)*
Gus N. Van Steenberg *(V.P. & Legal Counsel)*
Charles Wood *(V.P.)*
Bill Crumlett *(Dir.-Personnel)*
Joseph S. Kittle *(Dir.-Product Devel.)*

No. of U.S. Offices: 4

Computer Systems/Hardware:
IBM 3270, VAX 8200

Outside Service Firm(s):

Ernst & Young*(Auditors)*
1900 Frost Bank Tower, 100 W. Houston St.
San Antonio, TX 78205
Tel.: 210-228-9696
Fax: 210-554-0253

NationsBank Texas*(Major Banking Relationship)*
430 Soledad
San Antonio, TX 78205
Tel.: 210-225-2511

SOUTHWESTERN/GREAT AMERICAN INC.
2451 Atrium Way
Nashville, TN 37210
Tel.: 615-391-2500
Fax: 615-391-3778
Sales Range: $40-59 Million
Emp.: 425
Holding Co.; Publishers of Books, Educational & Religious Publications
S.I.C.: 6719; 2721; 2731
Spencer Hays *(Chm. Bd.)*
Ralph Mosley *(Vice Chm. & Chief Exec. Officer)*
Jerry Heffel *(Pres.-Southwestern Co.)*
Tom McDow *(Pres.-Great American Opportunities, Inc.)*
Tom Milam *(Pres.-Heritage House)*
Henry Bedford *(Treas.)*
Robert Sircy *(Controller)*
John Moulton *(Dir.-Pur.)*

Computer Systems/Hardware:
IBM System 34

Outside Service Firm(s):

Arthur Andersen & Co.*(Auditors)*
424 Church St.
Nashville, TN 37201
Tel.: 615-726-6000

Stokes & Bartholomew*(Legal Firm)*
Nashville, TN

First American National Bank*(Major Banking Relationship)*
First American Center
Nashville, TN 37237
Tel.: 615-748-2000

SOUTHWESTERN INDUSTRIES, INC.
2605 Homestead Pl.
Rancho Dominguez, CA 90220
Mailing Address:
P.O. Box 9066
Compton, CA 90224-9066
Tel.: 310-608-4422
Approx.Sls.: $10,000,000
Emp.: 100
Import Export
Mfr. of Machine Tool Measurement & Control Products
S.I.C.: 3625
R. W. Leonhard *(Chm. Bd., Pres. & Chief Exec. Officer)*
Stephen F. Pinto *(Mktg. Services Mgr.)*

Computer Systems/Hardware:
CNC

SOUTHWESTERN PETROLEUM CORPORATION
534 N. Main
Fort Worth, TX 76161
Mailing Address:
P.O. Box 961005,
Fort Worth, TX 76161
Tel.: 817-332-2336 **TX**
Fax: 817-877-4047
Approx.Sls.: $20,000,000
Emp.: 325
Export
Industrial Lubricants, Protective Coatings, Paints & Chemical Products
S.I.C.: 2911; 2851; 2992
Arthur J. Dickerson *(Chm. Bd., Pres. & Chief Exec. Officer)*
Robert E. Dickerson *(Exec. V.P.-Lubricants)*
Mike Redmon *(Sr. V.P.-Building Prods.)*
Buddy Thomas *(Sr. V.P.-Export)*
Phillip Frazier *(V.P.-Fin.)*
Rachel Newman *(V.P.-Admin.)*
Patricia Fuller *(Sec.)*
Principal(s):
Arthur J. Dickerson

No. of U.S. Offices: 1
No. of Foreign Offices: 2

Computer Systems/Hardware:
PRIME

Outside Service Firm(s):

Phillips & Welch*(Auditors)*
Fort Worth, TX

Fulbright & Jaworski*(Legal Firm)*
2200 Ross Ave., Ste. 2800
Dallas, TX 75201
Tel.: 214-855-8000
Fax: 214-855-8200

NationsBank Texas*(Major Banking Relationship)*
Ft. Worth, TX

Subsidiary:

Southwestern Petroleum Canada Ltd. **(1)**
P.O. Box 961005
Fort Worth, TX 76161
Tel.: 817-332-2336

Non-U.S. Holding:

N.V. Southwestern Petroleum Europe S.A. **(1)**
Industrial Zone B-2150,
Ostmalle, Belgium

SOUTHWIDE, INC.
60 E. 42nd St.
New York, NY 10165
Tel.: 212-661-2255
Fax: 212-972-6365
Research Development, Production & Marketing, Cotton Planting, Soy Bean Seed, Farming
S.I.C.: 0116; 0131; 5159; 8731
Roger D. Malkin *(Chm. Bd.)*
Melvyn H. Halper *(Sec.)*

Outside Service Firm(s):

Arthur Andersen & Co.*(Auditors)*
165 Madison Ave., Ste. 165
Memphis, TN 38103
Tel.: 901-525-4451

Wien, Malkin & Bettex*(Legal Firm)*
New York, NY

Division:

Southwide, Inc.-Western Div. **(1)**
P.O. Box 1006, Casa Grande Indus. Park
Casa Grande, AZ 85222
Tel.: 602-836-2739
S.I.C.: 0752
Larry Burdett *(Dir.-Western Res.)*
Gary Tollett *(Mgr.-Sls.)*

Subsidiary:

Delta & Pine Land Company **(1)**
P.O. Box 157
Scott, MS 38772
Tel.: 601-742-3351
Fax: 601-742-3350
Approx.Sls.: $20,000,000
Emp.: 200
Seed-Breeders & Producers; D & PL Brand Cotton Seed, Deltapine, Hybrid Corn, D & PL Brand Soybeans; Delta Pine Brand Sorghum
S.I.C.: 0752
Murray Robinson *(Pres.)*
Bill Arnold *(V.P.-Fin.)*
Randy Dismuke *(V.P.-Opers.)*
Clyde Jones *(V.P.-Quality Control)*
Donald L. Kimmel *(V.P.-Mktg.)*
Donald A. Pallin *(V.P.-Intl.)*

SOUTHWIRE COMPANY, INC.
1 S. Wire Dr.
Carrollton, GA 30119
Mailing Address:
P.O. Box 1000,
Carrollton, GA 30119
Tel.: 706-832-4242 **GA**
Telex: 54-2799
Fax: 706-832-4929
Year Founded: 1950
Assets: $415,000,000
Liabilities: $280,000,000
Net Worth: $135,000,000
Approx.Sls.: $1,200,000,000
Emp.: 4,200
Fiscal Year-end: 12/31/88
Manufacturer of Electrical Wire & Cable
S.I.C.: 3357
Roy Richards *(Chief Exec. Officer)*
James C. Richards *(Pres.)*
John Avery *(V.P. & Sec.)*
Frank E. Deems *(V.P.)*
Gary O. Conway *(V.P.)*
Anna Berry *(Treas.)*
Donald W. Baker *(Controller)*
William Hearnburg *(Gen. Counsel)*
Ken Harrison *(Dir.-Data Processing)*
Dewey Teal *(Office Mgr.)*
Michael Wiggins *(Dir.-Employee Rels.)*

No. of Mfg. Plants/Facilities: 11
No. of U.S. Offices: 72

Computer Systems/Hardware:
Burroughs A15

Outside Service Firm(s):

Ernst & Young*(Auditors)*
600 Peachtree St. N.E.
Atlanta, GA 30308
Tel.: 404-874-8300

Kidder, Peabody & Co.*(Investment Banker)*
10 Hanover Square
New York, NY 10005
Tel.: 212-510-3000

Kilpatrick & Cody*(Legal Firm)*
3100 Equitable Bldg., 100 Peachtree St. N.W.
Atlanta, GA 30343
Tel.: 404-572-6500

SOVEREIGN GROUP INC.
8900 Keystone Crossing, Ste. 1150
Indianapolis, IN 46240
Tel.: 317-846-3321 **IN**
Fax: 317-574-9270
Year Founded: 1981
Approx.Sls.: $65,000,000
Emp.: 750
Fiscal Year-end: 12/31/90
Import Export
Financial Services, Locks, Alarms, Combination Vault Locks, Locksmith, Telecommunication Services, Pay Telephones
S.I.C.: 3429; 5072; 3499; 7699; 6159; 4822
J. Fred Risk *(Chm. Bd.)*
O.U. Mutz *(Pres.)*
John Risk *(V.P.)*
Principal(s):
J. Fred Risk
O.U. Mutz
Terry R. Hershberger

No. of Mfg. Plants/Facilities: 5
No. of U.S. Offices: 25
No. of Foreign Offices: 2

Outside Service Firm(s):

Coopers & Lybrand*(Auditors)*
2900 One American Square, Box 82002
Indianapolis, IN 46282
Tel.: 317-639-4161

Subsidiary:

Keystone Group Inc. **(1)**
8900 Keystone Crossing, Ste. 1150
Indianapolis, IN 46240
Tel.: 317-846-3321
Fax: 317-574-9270
Emp.: 4
Investment Banking
S.I.C.: 6211
John T. Risk *(Pres.)*

L.H. SOWLES COMPANY, INC.
2813 Bryant Ave. S.
Minneapolis, MN 55408
Tel.: 612-872-4656
Fax: 612-872-6824
Approx.Sls.: $15,000,000
Emp.: 150
Steel Erection Contractor
S.I.C.: 1791
Lawrence H. Sowles *(Pres.)*
Jack Furst *(V.P.)*
Daniel Sawers *(V.P.)*
S. Berg *(Sec.)*

Outside Service Firm(s):

John A. Knutson & Co.*(Auditors)*
Minneapolis, MN

American National Bank of St. Paul*(Major Banking Relationship)*
St. Paul, MN

SPACE MASTER INTERNATIONAL
1040 Crown Pointe Pkwy., Ste. 900
Atlanta, GA 30338
Tel.: 404-396-1183
Fax: 404-698-0417
Emp.: 75
Wholesale & Lease Prefabricated Portable Buildings
S.I.C.: 5039
Ray A. Wooldridge *(Pres.)*
Doug Alexander *(V.P.)*

Outside Service Firm(s):

Ernst & Young*(Auditors)*
600 Peachtree St. N.E.
Atlanta, GA 30308
Tel.: 404-874-8300

Bank South, N.A.*(Major Banking Relationship)*
P.O. Box 4387
Atlanta, GA 30302
Tel.: 404-529-4111

SPALDING & EVENFLO COMPANIES, INC.
5730A N. Hoover Blvd.
Tampa, FL 33634
Mailing Address:
P.O. Box 30101,
Tampa, FL 33630
Tel.: 813-887-5200 **DE**
Fax: 813-887-5208
Approx.Sls.: $375,000,000
Emp.: 2,600
Evenflo Baby Products, Juvenile Furniture; Recreation Products
S.I.C.: 3944; 2511; 3089; 3949
Ricardo Cisneros *(Chm. Bd.)*
Donald J. Byrnes *(Pres. & Chief Oper. Officer)*
Paul L. Whiting *(Sr. V.P. & Chief Fin. Officer)*
Robert K. Adikes *(V.P., Sec. & Gen. Counsel)*
Stephen J. Dryer *(V.P. & Controller)*
Karen Thomas *(Mgr.-Exec. Admin.)*

Computer Systems/Hardware:
Hewlett-Packard

Outside Service Firm(s):

Deloitte & Touche*(Auditors)*
100 S.E. 2nd St.
Miami, FL 33131-2135
Tel.: 305-538-4141

Willis Corroon*(Commercial Insurance Carrier)*
7 Hanover Square
New York, NY 10004-2594

Prudential Insurance Co. of America*(Group Insurer)*
751 Broad St.
Newark, NJ 07102-3777
Tel.: 201-802-6000

Ohio Citizens Bank*(Pension Manager)*
Toledo, OH

Divisions:

Evenflo Products Co. **(1)**
771 N. Freedom St.
Ravenna, OH 44266
Tel.: 216-296-3465
Mfr. & Mktg. Juvenile & Infant Feeding Products
S.I.C.: 5137; 3069; 3089; 3229
John Kostantaras *(Pres.)*

Evenflo Juvenile Furniture Co. **(1)**
1801 Commerce Dr.
Piqua, OH 45356
Tel.: 513-773-3971
Mfr. & Mktg. Juvenile Furniture
S.I.C.: 2511
George Harris *(Pres.)*
Nick Costides *(V.P.-Opers.)*
Allen Seymour *(V.P.-Sls. & Mktg.)*
Joe Somekh *(Reg. Sls. Mgr.)*
Bill Butler *(Reg. Sls. Mgr.)*
Pat Thomas *(Reg. Sls. Mgr.)*
Mary Sue Webb *(Mgr. Mktg. Services)*
Walt Witwer *(Mktg. Mgr.)*

Spalding **(1)**
P.O. Box 901, 425 Meadow St.
Chicopee, MA 01021
Tel.: 413-536-1200
Athletic Goods
S.I.C.: 5091; 3949
G. Dickerman *(Pres.)*

Division:

Dudley Sports Co. Division **(2)**
P.O. Box 7053, 521 Meadow St.
Chicopee, MA 01021-7053
Tel.: 413-536-1200
Tel.: 800-523-5387
Fax: 413-539-2006
Computer Systems/Hardware:
Hewlett-Packard 950s
Manufacturer & Distributor of Softballs, Baseballs, Bats, Gloves & Related Equipment
S.I.C.: 3949
Tim Voss *(Dir.)*

Non-U.S. Holdings:

Evenflo **(1)**
3/F, Done Narcisa Bldg., 8751 Paseo De Roxas Makati,
Metro Manila, Philippines
Tel.: 86 2022/ 23-86-20-27
Juvenile Feeding Prods.
S.I.C.: 3089; 3229
Arturo Hughes *(Mgr.)*

Evenflo Mexico S.A. **(1)**
Apartado 18939 Delg. Miguel Hidalgo,
Mexico, D.F. 11850, Mexico
Tel.: 905 516-0420 (100%)
Telex: 383-1776309 EMSAME
Juvenile Feeding Prods
S.I.C.: 3089; 3229
Ernesto Luria *(Mng. Dir.)*

Evenflo Products Division **(1)**
121 Roy Blvd.
Brantford, ON N37 5V7, Canada (100%)
Juvenile Feeding Prods.
S.I.C.: 3089; 3229

Spalding Australia Pty. Ltd. **(1)**
P.O. Box 17, 969 Burke Rd.
Camberwell, Victoria Australia 3124
Tel.: (03) 828015 (100%)
Telex: AA 33040 SPALD
Sporting Goods
S.I.C.: 3949; 5091
Jack B. May *(Mgr.)*

Spalding Canada **(1)**
250 Courtland Ave.
Concord, ON L4K 4N3, Canada
Tel.: 416-660-5434 (100%)
Fax: 416-663-7053
Mfr. & Mktg. Sporting Goods
S.I.C.: 3949; 5091
T. Wright *(Chief Oper. Officer)*

Spalding Japan Inc. **(1)**
10F Hibiya Chunichi Bvld. 2-1-4, Urchaiwai-Cho, Chioda-Ku,
Tokyo, 100, Japan
Tel.: 03-3502-4161
Telex: 02226367 Spald J
Sporting Goods
S.I.C.: 3949; 5091
A. T. Ikehata *(Pres.)*

Spalding Japan Inc. **(1)**
Central P.O. Box 2067
Tokyo, 100-91, Japan (100%)
Sporting Goods
S.I.C.: 3949; 5091

SPANG & COMPANY
100 Brugh Ave.
Butler, PA 16001
Mailing Address:
P.O. Box 751,
Butler, PA 16001
Tel.: 412-287-8781 **PA**
Fax: 412-285-4721
Year Founded: 1894
Assets: $102,000,000
Liabilities: $24,000,000
Net Worth: $78,000,000
Sales Range: $100-499 Million
Emp.: 1,000
Import Export
Mfr. of Electric Components, Switchgear & Switchboard Apparatus; Specialty Metals Distribution & Specialty Transformers; Toys & Games
S.I.C.: 3944; 3672; 3613; 3612; 3625; 3341; 3679; 5051
Frank E. Rath *(Chm. Bd.)*
Robert Rath *(Vice Chm.)*
Frank E. Rath, Jr. *(Pres.)*
Charles R. Dorsch *(V.P.-Fin. & Chief Fin. Officer)*
William A. Marsh *(V.P., Sec. & Gen. Counsel)*
Robert A. Rath, Jr. *(V.P.-Engrng. & Specialty Metals)*
Frederick A. Artz *(Treas.)*
Robert K. Brown *(Dir.-Human Resources)*
J.F. Huth, Jr. *(Dir.-Sls.)*
Susan E. Sekscinski *(Dir.-Pur.)*
John M. Jackanic *(Mgr.-Data Processing)*
Principal(s):
Frank E. Rath
Robert Rath
Frank E. Rath, Jr.

No. of Mfg. Plants/Facilities: 7

Computer Systems/Hardware:
IBM 4361, Model 5

Outside Service Firm(s):

Ernst & Young*(Auditors)*
2000 Pittsburgh Natl. Bldg.
Pittsburgh, PA 15222
Tel.: 412-644-7800
Fax: 412-644-7419

Alexander & Alexander*(Commercial Insurance Carrier)*
Pittsburgh, PA

Pittsburgh National Bank*(International Bank Affiliate)*
Stock Transfer Dept., Fifth & Wood Streets
Pittsburgh, PA 15265

Pittsburgh National Bank*(Major Banking Relationship)*
Stock Transfer Dept., Fifth & Wood Streets
Pittsburgh, PA 15265

Union National Bank*(Major Banking Relationship)*
Pittsburgh, PA

Plant:

Spang & Company-Booneville Plant **(1)**
Hwy. 10 E.
Booneville, AR 72927
Tel.: 501-675-4800 (100%)
Mfr. of Magnetic Cores
S.I.C.: 3679

Divisions:

Magnetics **(1)**
P.O. Box 391,
Butler, PA 16003
Tel.: 412-287-8781
Fax: 412-282-6955
Emp.: 700
Mfr. of Broad Range of Magnetic Cores
S.I.C.: 3679
R.A. Rath *(Pres.)*

Spang Power Control **(1)**
P.O. Box 457, Lake St.
Sandy Lake, PA 16145
Tel.: 412-376-7515
Fax: 412-376-2249
Emp.: 100
Produces AC & DC Power Supplies & Transformers
S.I.C.: 3625; 3629; 3679
Lewis N. Martin *(V.P.)*

Spang Specialty Metals **(1)**
P.O. Box 391,
Butler, PA 16003
Tel.: 412-282-3014
Fax: 412-282-4209
Emp.: 50
Produces Magnetic Alloys, Expansion Alloys, Electronic Alloys, Etc.
S.I.C.: 3341

Subsidiary:

Today's Kids **(1)**
Hwy. 10 E.
Booneville, AR 72927
Tel.: 501-675-2000 (100%)
Fax: 501-675-3918
Import Export
Mfr. of Plastic Toys
S.I.C.: 3944

F.E. Rath *(Chm. Bd.)*
F.E. Rath, Jr. *(Pres.)*
C.R. Dorsch *(V.P.-Fin.)*
F.J. Artz *(Treas.)*
W.T. Marsh *(Sec.)*

SPANGLER CANDY COMPANY
P.O. Box 71,
Bryan, OH 43506
Mailing Address:
P.O. Box 71
Bryan, OH 43506
Year Founded: 1906
Approx.Sls.: $30,000,000
Emp.: 400
Fiscal Year-end: 6/30/90
Manufacturer of Candy
S.I.C.: 2064
C. Gregory Spangler *(Pres.)*
Duane Fox *(Sr. V.P.-Mfg.)*
Douglas Taylor *(Sr. V.P.-Sls. & Mktg.)*
Don Rowland *(V.P.-Sls.)*
Gary Tinkel *(V.P.-Mfg.)*
Don Holzhause *(V.P.-Finance)*
William Clark *(Mgr.-Personnel)*
John Holman *(Mgr.-Matls.)*

Computer Systems/Hardware:
IBM

Outside Service Firm(s):

Deloitte & Touche*(Auditors)*
1700 Courthouse Plaza NE
Dayton, OH 45401
Tel.: 513-223-8821

First National Bank of Northwest Ohio*(Major Banking Relationship)*
Dayton, OH

SPANGLER, INC.
2930 S. 44th St.
Kansas City, KS 66106
Tel.: 913-722-4500
Fax: 913-722-3552
Approx.Sls.: $19,300,000
Emp.: 220
Commercial Printing, Lithographic Letterpress, Periodicals & Manufacture Folding Paperboard Boxes & Roll Labels
S.I.C.: 2752; 2721
F. Earl Spangler *(Chm. Bd.)*
Gary Staab *(Pres.)*
Larry V. Pinnick *(Exec. V.P.)*
Chris Pugh *(V.P.-Mfg.)*
Dave Huber *(V.P.-Corp. Quality)*

Outside Service Firm(s):

House, Park & Company*(Auditors)*
Kansas City, KS

Spencer, Fane, Britt & Browne*(Legal Firm)*
106 W. 14th St.
Kansas City, MO 64105
Tel.: 816-474-8100

Commercial National Bank of Kansas City*(Major Banking Relationship)*
Kansas City, MO

A. G. SPANOS DEVELOPMENT, INC.
1341 W. Robinhood Dr.
Stockton, CA 95207
Tel.: 209-478-7954
Fax: 209-478-3309
Approx.Sls.: $390,000,000
Emp.: 875
Apartment Construction & Management
S.I.C.: 1522; 1542; 6513
Alex G. Spanos *(Chm. Bd.)*
Dean A. Spanos *(Pres.)*
Steve Cohen *(Chief Oper. Officer)*
Barry L. Ruhl *(Exec. V.P.)*
Michael A. Spanos *(Exec. V.P.)*
Jeremiah T. Murphy *(V.P.-Fin.)*
George G. Spanos *(Legal Counsel)*
Principal(s):
Alex G. Spanos
Dean A. Spanos
George G. Spanos

Computer Systems/Hardware:
Systel; AT&T

Outside Service Firm(s):

Bowman & Co.*(Auditors)*
Stockton, CA

Alston & Bird*(Legal Firm)*
One Atlantic Center, 1201 West Peachtree St.
Atlanta, GA 30309-3424
Tel.: 404-881-7000

Bank of America NT&SA*(Major Banking Relationship)*
Stockton, CA

SPARKOMATIC CORPORATION
Rte. 6 & 209
Milford, PA 18337
Mailing Address:
P.O. Box 277,
Milford, PA 18337-0277
Tel.: 717-296-6444
Tel.: 800-233-8831 **PA**
Fax: 717-296-6887
Year Founded: 1961
Sales Range: $100-499 Million
Emp.: 550
Fiscal Year-end: 12/31/91
Import Export
Mfr. of Automotive Accessories
S.I.C.: 3651; 3714
Edward Anchel *(Chm. Bd. & Pres.)*
Ronald Dion *(Sr. V.P.-Fin.)*
James Pedranti *(Sr. V.P.)*
Tony Decesare *(V.P.-Opers.)*
Gary Pomes *(V.P.-Sls.)*
John Castagna *(V.P.-Engrng.)*
Andrew Bergstein *(Dir.-Mktg.)*
Annemarie Bray *(Dir.-Personnel)*
Bruce Currie *(Pur. Agent)*

No. of Mfg. Plants/Facilities: 12
No. of U.S. Offices: 5
No. of Foreign Offices: 7

Computer Systems/Hardware:
IBM AS/400

Outside Service Firm(s):

Parente, Randolph, Orlando, Carey & Associates*(Auditors)*
46 Public Square
Wilkes-Barre, PA 18701-2681
Tel.: 717-820-0100
Fax: 717-824-9865

Hourigan, Kluger, Spohrer, Quinn & Myers*(Legal Firm)*
Wilkes-Barre, PA

First Eastern Bank N.A.*(Major Banking Relationship)*
11 West Market St.
Wilkes-Barre, PA 18768
Tel.: 717-826-4603

Divisions:

Kenco **(1)**
P.O. Box 726
Middlebury, IN 46540
Tel.: 219-825-7100
Fax: 219-825-7503
Mfr. Truck & Van Accessories
S.I.C.: 3714
Edward Anchel *(Chm. Bd. & Pres.)*
Jim Pedranti *(Sr. V.P.)*
Tony Decesare *(V.P.-Opers.)*
Gary Pomes *(V.P.-Sls.)*
Ron Dion *(Chief Fin. Officer & Sec.)*
Lori Tremer-Huey *(Treas.)*
Andrew Bergstein *(Dir.-Mktg.)*
Ann Marie Bray *(Dir.-Personnel)*
Steven Klein *(Sls. Coord.)*

Altec Lansing Consumer Products **(1)**
P.O. Box 277
Milford, PA 18337-0277
Tel.: 717-296-4434
Fax: 717-296-2213
Emp.: 55
Import Export

Sparkomatic Corporation—(Continued)

Computer Systems/Hardware:
IBM
Mfr. Home & Car Speakers
S.I.C.: 3651; 3699
Edward Anchel *(Chm. & Pres.)*
Ronald Dion *(Sr. V.P.-Fin.)*
Tony DeCesare *(V.P.-Opers.)*
Paul Tamberelli *(V.P.-Sls.)*
Tommy Freadman *(V.P.-Engrng.)*
Brian McHugh *(Dir.-Mngmt. Information Systems)*
Andrew Bergstein *(Dir.-Mktg.)*
Annemarie Bray *(Dir.-Human Resources)*
Bruce Currie *(Matls. Mgr.)*

SPARTAN INTERNATIONAL
1845 S. Cedar
Holt, MI 48842
Tel.: 517-694-3911
Twx: 229405
Fax: 517-694-7952
Approx.Sls.: $32,000,000
Emp.: 235
Mfr. of Self Adhesives; Vinyl Decorative Trim Products; PVC Moulding Extrusions
S.I.C.: 3083; 2891
Charles H. Krauss *(Pres.)*
Troyl E. Anderson *(V.P.-Fin.)*
Donald J. Clemens *(V.P. & Mgr.-Opers.)*
George L. Robinson *(V.P.-Adv. & Mktg.)*
Jay M. Selvius *(V.P.-Indus. Sls.)*
Helen Krauss *(Sec. & Treas.)*

Outside Service Firm(s):

Campbell, Stanabuck & Company*(Auditors)*
Lansing, MI

Hubbard, Fox, Thomas, White & Bengston*(Legal Firm)*
Lansing, MI

First American Bank, N.A.*(Major Banking Relationship)*
Lansing, MI

Non-U.S. Holding:

Spartan Plastics Canada **(1)**
1015 Green Valley Rd.
London, ON Canada
Tel.: 519-685-3690
Manufactures Side Body Mouldings
S.I.C.: 3089
Ron Webb *(Pres.)*

SPARTAN MILLS
805 Spartan Blvd.
Spartanburg, SC 29301
Mailing Address:
P.O. Box 1658,
Spartanburg, SC 29304
Tel.: 803-574-0211
Fax: 803-587-0291
Approx.Sls.: $270,000,000
Emp.: 5,000
Fiscal Year-end: 11/30/91
Textile Mill Products
S.I.C.: 2211; 2254; 2258; 2269; 6719
Walter S. Montgomery, Sr. *(Chm. Bd.)*
William M. Manning *(Vice Chm.)*
Walter S. Montgomery, Jr. *(Pres., Treas., Chief Exec. & Chief Fin. Officer)*
Mitchell Allen *(V.P.)*
H. Richard Baldwin *(V.P.-Admin. & Controller)*
George Bannerman *(V.P.-Fin.)*
Harold Thompson *(V.P.-Indus. Rels.)*
Perry Conley *(Controller)*
Eugene McTeer *(Dir.-Mngmt. Information Systems)*

Computer Systems/Hardware:
Burroughs Systems 812 & 783

Outside Service Firm(s):

Ernst & Young*(Auditors)*
787 Seventh Ave.
New York, NY 10019
Tel.: 212-773-1243

Provident Life & Accident Insurance Co.*(Group Insurer)*
P.O. Box 12015
Chattanooga, TN 37401
Tel.: 615-755-7088

Citizens & Southern National Bank*(Major Banking Relationship)*
Columbia, SC

Southern National Bank*(Major Banking Relationship)*
Spartanburg, SC

Wachovia Bank & Trust Co.*(Major Banking Relationship)*
Charlotte, NC

SPARTAN OIL CORP.
419 Spring St.
Lansing, MI 48912
Mailing Address:
P.O. Box 18218,
Lansing, MI 48901
Tel.: 517-485-2285
Fax: 517-485-0605
Approx.Sls.: $27,000,000
Emp.: 105
Fiscal Year-end: 4/30/91
Refining & Wholesale Trade-Petroleum
S.I.C.: 5171; 6512; 5014; 5013; 1711; 5983
Bruce J. Maguire *(Chm. Bd.)*
James H. Smit *(Pres. & Chief Exec. Officer)*
Mark Jennings *(Controller)*

Computer Systems/Hardware:
NCR 920

Outside Service Firm(s):

Foster, Swift, Collins & Smith*(Legal Firm)*
Lansing, MI

First America Bank*(Major Banking Relationship)*
Lansing, MI

SPARTAN STORES INC.
850 76th St., SW
Grand Rapids, MI 49518
Mailing Address:
P.O. Box 8700,
Grand Rapids, MI 49518
Tel.: 616-878-2000 **MI**
Fax: 616-878-2775
Year Founded: 1917
Assets: $329,285,455
Earnings: $2,041,278,293
Net Worth: $329,285,455
Approx.Sls.: $2,042,298,399
Emp.: 2,200
Fiscal Year-end: 3/28/92
Import
Merchandiser of Food & Non-Food Products
S.I.C.: 5141; 5142; 5147; 5148; 5143; 5199
Donald J. Koop *(Chm. Bd.)*
Patrick M. Quinn *(Pres., Chief Exec. Officer & Chief Oper. Officer)*
James B. Meyer *(Chief Fin. Officer & Sr. V.P.)*
Charles B. Fosnaugh *(V.P.-Mkt. Devel.)*
William E. May *(V.P.-Mngmt. Information Systems)*
Robert Morse *(V.P.-Human Resources)*
Joseph Smoliga, Jr. *(V.P.-Plymouth Opers.)*
Kenneth W. Wagar *(V.P.-Mktg.)*
L. George Williams, Jr. *(V.P.-Grand Rapids Opers.)*
Mary Dechow *(Mgr.-Communication & Govt. Affairs)*
Lou Hall *(Gen. Mgr.-Pur.)*
Peter Lima *(Mgr.-Transportation)*
Jann McKellar *(Mgr.-Adv.)*

Computer Systems/Hardware:
IBM 3083

Outside Service Firm(s):

Deloitte & Touche*(Auditors)*
Grand Rapids, MI

Miller, Canfield, Paddock & Stone*(Legal Firm)*
150 W. Jefferson Ave.
Detroit, MI 48226
Tel.: 313-963-6420

Michigan National Bank*(Major Banking Relationship)*
77 Monroe Center
Grand Rapids, MI 49501
Tel.: 616-451-7600

Michigan National Bank*(Pension Manager)*
77 Monroe Center
Grand Rapids, MI 49501
Tel.: 616-451-7600

Subsidiaries:

Capistar, Inc. **(1)**
4147 Keller Rd.
Holt, MI 48842
Tel.: 517-699-3555 (100%)
Fax: 517-699-3570
Wholesale Grocer
S.I.C.: 5141
Thomas Beckett *(Pres.)*

L & L/Jiroch Distributing Co. **(1)**
5075 Clay Ave., S.W.
Grand Rapids, MI 49548
Tel.: 616-530-6600
Fax: 616-530-6677
Emp.: 180
Michael B. Alexander *(Chief Oper. Officer)*

Market Development Co. **(1)**
5296 Eastern Ave.
Kentwood, MI 49508
Tel.: 616-530-4500
Fax: 616-530-4561
Charles B. Fosnaugh *(Chief Oper. Officer)*

Shield Insurance **(1)**
3900 Sparks Dr., S.E.
Grand Rapids, MI 49518
Tel.: 616-285-4800
Fax: 616-285-4842
R. Scott Hummel *(Chief Oper. Officer)*

United Wholesale Inc. **(1)**
850 76th St., S.W.
Grand Rapids, MI 49501
Tel.: 616-878-2000
Charles Losey *(Chief Oper. Officer)*

SPATZ & CO.
3175 Commercial Ave., Ste. 203
Northbrook, IL 60062
Tel.: 708 559 7900 **IL**
Fax: 708 559 8015
Year Founded: 1970
Assets: $30,702,508
Liabilities: $16,255,812
Net Worth: $14,446,696
Sales Range: $20-39 Million
Emp.: 150
Real Estate Investment Firm; Developer; Commercial Real Estate Broker; Shopping Center Management
S.I.C.: 6153; 6552
William Spatz *(Chm. Bd. & Chief Exec. Officer)*
Barry E. Herring *(Pres. & Chief Oper. Officer)*
Judith Haines *(Sr. V.P.-Human Resources)*
Wendy Spatz *(V.P.-Design & Promo.)*
Stan Staszak *(Controller)*
Steven Peck *(Gen. Counsel)*
Betty Jensen *(Mgr.-Leasing)*
Principal(s):
Barry E. Herring
Wendy Spatz

Outside Service Firm(s):

Miller, Cooper & Co.*(Auditors)*
Northbrook, IL

Zurich American Insurance Co.*(Commercial Insurance Carrier)*
New York, NY

Health Plan Administrators*(Group Insurer)*
Rockford, IL

Sherfsky, Saitlin & Froelich*(Legal Firm)*
Chicago, IL

Amro Bank*(Major Banking Relationship)*
Amsterdam, Netherlands

NBD Bank, N.A.*(Major Banking Relationship)*
Highland Park, IL

Subsidiaries:

River Bend, Inc. **(1)**
3175 Commercial Ave., Ste. 203
Northbrook, IL 60062
Tel.: 708 559 7900
Fax: 708 559 8015
Real Estate Operations
S.I.C.: 6552

S & C Maintenance Corp. **(1)**
3175 Commercial Ave., Ste. 203
Northbrook, IL 60062
Tel.: 708 559 7900
Fax: 708 559 8015
Maintenance Operations
S.I.C.: 7349

Spatz Centers, Inc. **(1)**
3175 Commercial Ave., Ste. 203
Northbrook, IL 60062
Tel.: 708 559 7900
Fax: 708-559-8015
Shopping Centers Management
S.I.C.: 8741; 6552

Spatz & Co. Development **(1)**
3175 Commercial Ave., Ste. 203
Northbrook, IL 60062
Tel.: 708 559 7900
Fax: 708 559 8015
Real Estate Development
S.I.C.: 6552

SPAULDING & SLYE COMPANY
25 Burlington Mall Rd.
Burlington, MA 01803
Tel.: 617-523-8000
Telex: 229-7709
Fax: 617-523-8001
Year Founded: 1966
Assets: $74,544,000
Earnings: $2,630,000
Liabilities: $51,116,000
Net Worth: $23,428,000
Sales Range: $40-59 Million
Emp.: 210
Fiscal Year-end: 12/31/91
Commercial Real Estate Services Firm
S.I.C.: 6531
Corporate Giving Program: United Way of Massachusetts Bay
Peter M. Small *(Chm. Bd.)*
James B. Karman *(Pres.)*
David A. Neskey *(Chief Fin. Officer & Sr. V.P.-Fin.)*
Robert K. Lemons *(Sr. V.P.-Property Mgmt.)*
Andrew M. Nesvet *(V.P. & Treas.)*
Paul D. Potash *(V.P. & Controller)*
Susan C. Ash *(Asst. V.P. & Mgr.-Benefits & Risk)*

Computer Systems/Hardware:
IBM System 36

Outside Service Firm(s):

Arthur Andersen & Co.*(Auditors)*
One Intl. Place, 100 Oliver St.
Boston, MA 02110
Tel.: 617-330-4000

Fax: 617-439-9731

Kemper Insurance*(Commercial Insurance Carrier)*
Long Grove, IL 60049-0001

Northwestern National Life*(Group Insurer)*
20 Washington Ave. S.
Minneapolis, MN 55401

Hale and Dorr*(Legal Firm)*
60 State St.
Boston, MA 02109-6098
Tel.: 617-526-6000

First National Bank of Boston*(Major Banking Relationship)*
P.O. Box 644,
Boston, MA 02102-0644
Tel.: 617-575-2900
Fax: 617-575-2549

Subsidiary:

Spaulding & Slye Construction **(1)**
25 Burlington Mall
Burlington, MA 01803
Tel.: 617-270-9595

SPEAKMAN COMPANY
301 E. 30th
Wilmington, DE 19802
Mailing Address:
P.O. Box 191
Wilmington, DE 19899
Tel.: 302-764-7100
Fax: 302-764-1956
Year Founded: 1869
Emp.: 300
Speakman Showers, Brass Plumbing, Decorative Brass Plumbing Fittings & Safety Equipment
S.I.C.: 3432
W.A. Speakman III *(Pres. & Chief Exec. Officer)*
W.A. Denham *(V.P.-Mfg.)*
David C. Bailey *(Treas.)*
J.O. Stanaland *(Dir.-Sls.)*
Denise A. Pitts *(Coordinator of Mktg.)*

Outside Service Firm(s):

KPMG Peat Marwick*(Auditors)*
Wilmington, DE

Richards, Layton & Finger*(Legal Firm)*
Wilmington, DE

SPECIALIZED MEDIA SERVICES, INC.
741 Kenilworth Ave., Ste. 204
Charlotte, NC 28204
Mailing Address:
P.O. Box 37171,
Charlotte, NC 28237
Tel.: 704-333-3111
Fax: 704-332-7466
Year Founded: 1982
Approx.Billings: $10,000,000
Emp.: 10
Media Planning & Buying
Darlene S. Jones *(Pres.)*
Richard M. Apfel *(V.P.)*

SPECIALTY EQUIPMENT COMPANIES INC.
6581 Revlon Dr.
Belvidere, IL 61008
Tel.: 815-544-5111
Fax: 815-544-5151
Approx.Sls.: $300,000,000
Fiscal Year-end: 1/31/91
Export
Mfr. of Restaurant Equipment & Supplies; Dryers for Hands & Hair
S.I.C.: 3589; 3799; 3821
James B. Knoll *(Pres. & Chief Exec. Officer)*
Donald K. McKay *(Exec. V.P.-Fin.)*
Jeff P. Rhodenbaugh *(Dir.-Mktg.)*

Outside Service Firm(s):

KPMG Peat Marwick*(Auditors)*
2211 York Rd.
Oak Brook, IL 60521
Tel.: 708-954-3700

Divisions:

Beverage-Air Co. **(1)**
P.O. Box 5932
Spartanburg, SC 29304
Tel.: 803-582-8111
William W. Robertson *(Pres.)*
Paul Corden *(Dir.-Mktg.)*

Bloomfield Industries **(1)**
4546 W. 47th St.
Chicago, IL 60632
Tel.: 312-254-7600
Approx.Sls.: $40,000,000
Emp.: 350
Manufacture Restaurant Equipment & Supplies, Coffee Brewing Equipment Beverage Systems & Related Supplies
S.I.C.: 3589; 3444; 3469; 3471; 7692
Gregory J. Ziols *(Pres.)*
John Kominsky *(Pur. Dir.)*
Christoper Stern *(Dir.-Mktg.)*

Ice Craft **(1)**
750 N. Blackhawk Blvd.
Rockton, IL 61072
Tel.: 815-624-7776
Jim Knoll *(Pres.)*

Market Forge Company **(1)**
35 Garvey St.
Everett, MA 02149
Tel.: 617-387-4100
Emp.: 500
Commercial Cooking Equipment, Storage Racks
S.I.C.: 3589; 3496
Hal Hamilton *(Pres.)*
Jack Kenny *(Controller)*
Lou Rotando *(Mfg. Mgr.)*
Steve Powers *(Pur. Agent)*

Taylor Company **(1)**
750 N. Blackhawk Blvd.
Rockton, IL 61072
Tel.: 815-624-8333
Commercial Ice Cream, Milk Shakes, Frozen Confection, Slush
S.I.C.: 3556
Clark Wangaard *(Pres.)*
Dan Johnston *(V.P.)*
John Curtis *(Comptroller)*
Debra E. Sweger *(Dir.-Mktg.)*

Wells Manufacturing Company **(1)**
2 Eric Circle
Verdi, NV 89439
Tel.: 702-345-0444
Fax: 702-345-0569
Emp.: 200
Fiscal Year-end: 1/31/91
Manufacturer of Commercial Cooking Equipment
S.I.C.: 3589
Donald Folgner *(Pres.)*
Edward Mungcal *(Controller)*
J.D. Lambert *(Mgr.-Pur.)*
Anita Thomas *(Mgr.-Human Resources)*
Barbara Young *(Mgr.-MIS)*
Glenn Kress *(Mgr.-Mfg. & Engrng.)*
Sherre Compton *(Supvr.-Mktg.)*

World Dryer Corp. **(1)**
5700 McDermott Dr.
Berkeley, IL 60163
Tel.: 708-449-6950
Tel.: 800-323-0701
Fax: 708-449-6958
Approx.Sls.: $12,000,000
Emp.: 55
Export
Computer Systems/Hardware:
IBM 32
World Hand Dryers & World Hair Dryers
S.I.C.: 3634
Randy M. Cordova *(Pres.)*
Tom Vic *(V.P.-Fin. & Controller)*
Thomas Landy *(V.P.-Sls. & Mktg.)*
John Potts *(Mfg. Mgr. & Pur. Dir.)*
Linda Kilbrydg *(Personnel Mgr.)*
Nancy Mullen *(Data Processing Dir.)*
Cathy Sibley *(Export Mgr.)*

Non-U.S. Holding:

Bloomfield Industries Canada Ltd. **(1)**
5850 Keaton Crescent
Mississauga, ON L5R 3K2, Canada
Tel.: 416-507-1700 (100%)

Wholesale Distr. of Food Service Equipment, Coffeemaking Equipment
S.I.C.: 5046
Tom Warne *(Gen. Mgr.)*
G. Mackinnon *(Mgr.-Sls.)*

SPECIALTY INDUSTRIES, INC.
120 N. Charles St.
Red Lion, PA 17356
Tel.: 717-246-1661
Fax: 717-246-1660
Approx.Sls.: $36,000,000
Emp.: 250
Corrugated Packaging Materials
S.I.C.: 2653
Carl W. Cheek *(Chm. Bd.)*
Chris Mehiel *(Pres.)*
Robert M. Jenkins *(V.P.-Fin.)*
Ronald L. McKinney *(V.P.-Sls.)*
Jeffrey Grove *(Mgr.-Mfg.)*

No. of Mfg. Plants/Facilities: 7

Outside Service Firm(s):

KPMG Peat Marwick*(Auditors)*
111 S. Calvert St.
Baltimore, MD 21202
Tel.: 410-783-8300

Hamilton Bank*(Major Banking Relationship)*
Red Lion, PA

Piper & Marbury*(Legal Firm)*
36 S. Charles St.
Baltimore, MD 21202
Tel.: 410-835-8000

Divisions:

Westreet Industries **(1)**
8901 Kelso Dr.
Baltimore, MD 21221
Tel.: 410-686-8400
C. Burkhardt *(Gen. Mgr.)*

Westreet Industries **(1)**
6301 B. Seaforth
Baltimore, MD 21224
Tel.: 410-633-7050
Dick Ealing *(Gen. Mgr.)*

Subsidiaries:

Allied Container Corp. **(1)**
901 N. Newkirk St.
Baltimore, MD 21205
Tel.: 410-675-7000
Ronald L. McKinney *(Gen. Mgr.)*

Krafcor Unlimited **(1)**
6301 B. Seaforth
Baltimore, MD 21224
Tel.: 410-633-4320
Richard Ealing *(Gen. Mgr.)*

SPECIALTY MANUFACTURING COMPANY
5858 Centerville Rd.
St. Paul, MN 55127
Tel.: 612-653-0599
Emp.: 140
Mfr. of Lawn & Garden Products, Plastic Injection Molding, Metal Stampings, Product Development, Contract Manufacturing
S.I.C.: 3524; 3089; 3469; 3491
Bruce A. Lawin *(Pres.)*
Mark Nosbush *(V.P.)*
Bruce Helland *(Mgr.-Mktg. & Sls., Garden Div.)*
Forest Holmes *(Mgr.-Mktg. & Sls., Valves Div.)*
Kevin Carlson *(Pur. Agent)*
Paul R. Dyndiuk *(Mgr.-Mfg.)*
Terry Nelson *(Chief Engr.)*

Outside Service Firm(s):

Broeker Hendrickson & Co.*(Auditors)*
St. Paul, MN

First Bank Security*(Major Banking Relationship)*
St. Paul, MN

SPECIALTY PAPERBOARD INC.
Brudies Rd.
Brattleboro, VT 05302
Mailing Address:
P.O. Box 498
Brattleboro, VT 05302
Tel.: 802-257-0365
Tel.: 800-451-4378 **DE**
Fax: 802-257-5973
Emp.: 365

Export
Specialty Paperboard; Reinforced Fiber Materials For Cut Gasket Fabrication; Cover Materials
S.I.C.: 2631
K. Peter Norrie *(Chm. Bd.)*
Alex Kwader *(Pres., Chief Exec. Officer & Gen. Mgr.)*
Bruce Moore *(Chief Fin. Officer & V.P.)*
Fred Bliss *(Chief Information Officer & Dir.-Data Processing)*
David Allen *(Dir.-Human Resources, Employee Benefits & Govt. Affairs)*
Jack Kondos *(Dir.-Sls., Sls. Promo. & Adv.)*
Dennis Lively *(Dir.-Quality Control)*
Mick Mundell *(Dir.-Pur.)*
David Y. Parker *(Dir.-Import & Export)*
Stephen Steidle *(Dir.-Sls.)*
David Spokowkski *(Treas.)*
Paul Street *(Gen. Counsel)*
Mary Larsen *(Sec.)*
S. Steidle *(Dir.-Sls.)*
James Barker *(Mgr.-Human Resources)*
Hanspeter Gattiker *(Mgr.-Intl.)*
Peter Gendreau *(Mgr.-Technical)*
J. Kondos *(Mgr.-Mktg.)*
Mick Mundell *(Mgr.-Matls.)*
Eric Wolinsky *(Gen. Mgr.-Latex Fiber Products Div.)*

Outside Service Firm(s):

Moffatt, Thomas, Barrett, Rock & Fields*(Legal Firm)*
911 W. Idaho St., Ste. 300
Boise, ID 83701

SPECIALTY RESTAURANTS CORPORATION
4155 E. LaPalma Ave., Ste. 250
Anaheim, CA 92807
Tel.: 714-634-0300 **CA**
Fax: 714-634-3869
Year Founded: 1958
Assets: $125,000,000
Earnings: $2,000,000
Liabilities: $78,500,000
Net Worth: $46,500,000
Approx.Sls.: $178,000,000
Emp.: 7,000
Fiscal Year-end: 6/29/89
Operates Restaurants
S.I.C.: 5812; 5813
David C. Tallichet, Jr. *(Chm. Bd., Pres. & Chief Exec. Officer)*
John T. Kenny *(Exec. V.P.-Fin. & Oper.)*
Robert P. Wahlstrom *(V.P.-Pur.)*
Fred Polivka *(V.P. & Controller)*
Alan Carreco *(V.P. & Legal Counsel)*
Joyce Johnson *(Controller-West Region)*
Howard Bell *(Controller-Florida Region)*
Ken Kern *(Dir.-Leasing)*
Simon Vojidani *(Dir. of Opers-West Region)*
Mark Thompson *(Dir. of Opers. East Region)*
Bill Rozinski *(Dir. of Opers.-S. Central Region)*
Dan Van Norden *(Dir. of Opers.-Florida Region)*

Computer Systems/Hardware:
IBM System 38

Specialty Restaurants Corporation—(Continued)

Outside Service Firm(s):

Ernst & Young*(Auditors)*
515 S. Flower St.
Los Angeles, CA 90071
Tel.: 213-621-1666

California Federal Savings & Loan Association*(Major Banking Relationship)*
5700 Wilshire Blvd
Los Angeles, CA

Restaurants:

Alabama:

Birmingham Hill Restaurant Corp. **(1)**
2033 Golden Crest Dr.
Birmingham, AL 35209
Tel.: 205-324-1501
Operates Baby Doe's Matchless Mine Restaurant
S.I.C.: 5812

Alaska:

Mall Entertainment USA **(1)**
Northway Mall, Ste. J-10, Penland Parkway
Anchorage, AK 99504
Tel.: 907-272-1479
Operates Chubby Chuckles Restaurant
S.I.C.: 5812

California:

Berkeley Marina Restaurant Corp. **(1)**
199 Seawall Dr.
Berkeley, CA 94710
Tel.: 415-843-2733
Operates His Lordships Restaurant
S.I.C.: 5812

Candlestick Waterfront Rest. Corp. **(1)**
30 Jack London Sq.
Oakland, CA 94607
Tel.: 510-839-8333
Operates Shenanigan's Restaurant
S.I.C.: 5812

Casuda Canyon Restaurant Corp. **(1)**
3500 Ramona Blvd.
Monterey Park, CA 91754
Tel.: 213-268-4177
Operates Luminarias Restaurant
S.I.C.: 5812

Coyote Restaurant Corp. **(1)**
Coyote Point Dr.
San Mateo, CA 94401
Tel.: 415-347-1027
Operates Castaway Restaurant
S.I.C.: 5812

Del Rey Restaurant Corp. **(1)**
13813 Fiji Way
Marina Del Rey, CA 90291
Tel.: 310-823-4522
Operates Shaghai Red's
S.I.C.: 5812

Mission Hills Restaurant Corp. **(1)**
15600 Odyssey Dr.
Granada Hills, CA 91344
Tel.: 818-366-6444
Operates Odyssey Restaurant
S.I.C.: 5812

94th Aero Squadron of San Jose, Inc. **(1)**
1160 Coleman Ave.
San Jose, CA 95110
Tel.: 408-287-6150
S.I.C.: 5812

94th Aero Squadron of Torrance, Inc. **(1)**
2780 Skypark
Torrance, CA 90505
Tel.: 310-539-6203
Operates Doolittle's Raiders Restaurant
S.I.C.: 5812

Orange Hill Restaurant Corp. **(1)**
PO Box 2307, 6410 E. Chapman
Orange, CA 92669
Tel.: 714-997-2910
Operates Orange Hill Restaurant
S.I.C.: 5812

Ports O'Call Restaurant Corp. **(1)**
Berth 76
San Pedro, CA 90731
Tel.: 310-833-3553
Operates Port O'Call Restaurant
S.I.C.: 5812

Runway Two Five Corporation **(1)**
11022 Aviation Blvd.
Los Angeles, CA 90045
Tel.: 310-670-3093
Operates Proud Bird Restaurant
S.I.C.: 5812

Specialty Restaurant Corporation **(1)**
3700 Ramona Blvd.
Monterey Park, CA 91754
Tel.: 213-264-8426
S.I.C.: 5812

Specialty Restaurants Corp **(1)**
8885 Balboa Ave.
San Diego, CA 92123
Tel.: 619-560-6771
S.I.C.: 5812

Stockton Restaurant Corp. **(1)**
321 W. Weber St.
Stockton, CA 95203
Tel.: 209-466-2866
Operates Castaway Restaurant
S.I.C.: 5812

Stockton Chili Pepper, Inc. **(1)**
235 N. Center Rd.
Stockton, CA 95203
Tel.: 209-467-3636
Operates Chili Pepper Restaurant
S.I.C.: 5812

Van Nuys Airport Restaurant Corp. **(1)**
16320 Raymer Ave.
Van Nuys, CA 91406
Tel.: 818-994-7437
Operates 94th Aero Squadron Restaurant
S.I.C.: 5812

Verdugo Restaurant Corp. **(1)**
1250 Harvard Rd.
Burbank, CA 91503
Tel.: 818-848-6691
Operates Castaway Restaurant
S.I.C.: 5812

Walnut Creek Restaurant Corp. **(1)**
3800 Valle Vista
Walnut Creek, CA 94598
Tel.: 818-848-6691
Operates Boundary Oak Restaurant
S.I.C.: 5812

Yankee Whaler Company **(1)**
Berth 75
Oakland, CA 90731
Tel.: 310-831-0181
Operates Yankee Whaler Restaurant
S.I.C.: 5812

Colorado:

Colorado Air Restaurant Corp. **(1)**
10081 E. 25th Ave.
Aurora, CO 80010
Tel.: 303-344-4614
94th Aero Squadron
S.I.C.: 5812

Denver Baby Doe's Rest. Corp. **(1)**
2530 23rd Ave.
Denver, CO 80211
Tel.: 303-433-3386
Operates Baby Doe's Matchless Mine
S.I.C.: 5812

Denver Freeway Restaurant Corp. **(1)**
2150 Bryant St.
Denver, CO 80211
Tel.: 303-433-8406
Operates Chili Pepper Restaurant
S.I.C.: 5812

El Paso Restaurant Corp. **(1)**
230 Point of the Pines Dr.
Colorado Springs, CO 80907
Tel.: 709-599-8550
Operates Sunbird Restaurant
S.I.C.: 5812

Mall Entertainment USA **(1)**
Southwest Plaza 2-B-735, 8501 W. Bowles Ave.
Littleton, CO 80123
Tel.: 303-973-6334
Operates Chubby Chuckles Restaurant
S.I.C.: 5812

North Denver Hill Corp. **(1)**
9350 Grant St.
Thornton, CO 80229
Tel.: 303-433-8406
Operates Brittany Hill Restaurant
S.I.C.: 5812

Delaware:

Specialty Restaurants Corp **(1)**
143 N. DuPont Hwy.
New Castle, DE 19720
Tel.: 302-328-3527
S.I.C.: 5812

Florida:

Chili Pepper of Rocky Point, Inc. **(1)**
2425 Rocky Point Dr.
Tampa, FL 33607
Tel.: 813-887-1943
Operates Rusty Pelican Restaurant
S.I.C.: 5812

Jacksonville Crawdaddy Corp. **(1)**
1643 Prudential Dr.
Jacksonville, FL 32207
Tel.: 904-396-3546
Operates Crawdady's Restaurant
S.I.C.: 5812

94th Aero Squadron of Pinellas County, Inc. **(1)**
94th Fairchild Dr.
Clearwater, FL 34620
Tel.: 813-536-0409
Operates 94th Aero Squadron
S.I.C.: 5812

94th Aero Squadron Restaurant, Inc. **(1)**
2500 NW 62nd St.
Fort Lauderdale, FL 33309
Tel.: 305-491-4595
Operates the 95th Bomb Group Restaurant
S.I.C.: 5812

94th Aero Squadron of Miami, Inc. **(1)**
1395 NW 57th Ave.
Miami, FL
Tel.: 305-898-4251
Operates 95th Aero Squadron Restaurant
S.I.C.: 5812

94th Aero Squadron of Orlando, Inc. **(1)**
494 Rickenbacker Dr.
Orlando, FL 32803
Tel.: 407-898-4251
Operates the 4th Fighter Group
S.I.C.: 5812

94th Aero Squadron of Sarasota, Inc. **(1)**
8301 N. Tamiami Trail
Sarasota, FL 34243
Tel.: 813-355-8591
Operates the 306th Bomb GroupRestaurant
S.I.C.: 5812

94th AS of West Palm Beach, Inc. **(1)**
3989 Southern Blvd.
West Palm Beach, FL 33406
Tel.: 305-683-3919
Operates 391st Bomb Group Restaurant
S.I.C.: 5812

Pinellas Crabcooker, Inc. **(1)**
16100 Fairchild Dr.
Clearwater, FL 34620
Tel.: 813-536-6541
Operates Dockside Broiler Restaurant
S.I.C.: 5812

Pinellas Farmhouse, Inc. **(1)**
15481 49th St. N.
Clearwater, FL 34622
Tel.: 813-530-9771
Operates Las Fontanas Restaurant
S.I.C.: 5812

Rocky Point Village Corp. **(1)**
2500 Rocky Point Dr.
Tampa, FL 33607
Tel.: 813-885-7407
Operates Crawdaddy's Restaurant
S.I.C.: 5812

Specialty Restaurants Corp. **(1)**
South Point Pk., #1 Washington Ave.
Miami Beach, FL 33139
Tel.: 305-673-1708
Operates Crawdady'sRestaurant
S.I.C.: 5812

Georgia:

Atlanta Hill Restaurant Corp. **(1)**
2239 Powers Ferry Rd.
Marietta, GA 30067
Tel.: 404-955-3637
Operates Baby Doe's Matchless Mine Restaurant
S.I.C.: 5812

57th Fighter Group of Atlanta, Inc. **(1)**
3829 Clairmont Rd.
Atlanta, GA 30341
Tel.: 404-457-7757
Operates the 57th Fighter Group Restaurant
S.I.C.: 5812

Specialty Restaurants Corp. **(1)**
3300 Northlake Parkway
Atlanta, GA 30345
Tel.: 404-952-4487
Restaurant
S.I.C.: 5812

Illinois:

94th Aero Squadron of Palwaukee, Inc. **(1)**
1070 S. Milwaukee Ave.
Wheeling, IL 60090
Tel.: 708-459-3700
Operates 94th Aero Squadron Restaurant
S.I.C.: 5812

Louisiana:

New Orleans Waterfront Rest. Corp. **(1)**
Bermuda St. Wharf, 2 Bermuda St.
New Orleans, LA 70114
Tel.: 504-362-2981
Operates Algiers Landing Restaurant
S.I.C.: 5812

Maryland:

94th of College Park, Inc. **(1)**
5240 Calvert Rd.
College Park, MD 20740
Tel.: 301-699-9400
Operates 94th Aero Squadron Restaurant
S.I.C.: 5812

Michigan:

Specialty Restaurants Corp **(1)**
201 W. Atwater St.
Detroit, MI 48226
Tel.: 313-259-6801
Restraurant
S.I.C.: 5812

Missouri:

Ninety-Fourth of St. Louis, Inc. **(1)**
5933 McDonnel Blvd.
Saint Louis, MO 63134
Tel.: 314-731-3300
Operates 94th Aero Squadron of St. Louis
S.I.C.: 5812

New Jersey:

North Pier Associates **(1)**
Pier D-T, Lincoln Harbour
Weehawken, NJ 07087
Tel.: 201-348-6628

Operates Shanghai Red's Restaurant
S.I.C.: 5812

Specialty Restaurants Corp. **(1)**
195 Passaic Ave.
Fairfield, NJ 07006
Tel.: 201-882-5660
Restaurant
S.I.C.: 5812

New York:

Buffalo Waterfront Restaurant Corp. **(1)**
2 Templeton Terrace
Buffalo, NY 14202
Tel.: 716-856-9191
Operates Crawdaddy's Restaurant
S.I.C.: 5812

56th Fighter Group of Long Island, Inc. **(1)**
Republic Airport-Gate 1, Route 110
East Farmingdale, NY 11735
Tel.: 516-694-8280
Operates 56th Fighter Group Restaurant
S.I.C.: 5812

Specialty Restaurants Corp. **(1)**
100 Amherst Villa Rd.
Cheektowaga, NY 14229
Tel.: 716-631-3465
S.I.C.: 5812

Specialty Restaurants Corp. **(1)**
377 River St.
Troy, NY 12180
Tel.: 518-273-2244
Restaurant
S.I.C.: 5812

Ohio:

94th Aero Squadron of Columbus, Inc. **(1)**
Port Columbus Intl. Airport, 5030 Sawyer Rd.
Columbus, OH 43219
Tel.: 614-237-9093 (100%)
S.I.C.: 5812

Specialty Restaurants Corp. **(1)**
2379 W. 5th St.
Columbus, OH 43204
Tel.: 614-486-6463
S.I.C.: 5812

Specialty Restaurants Corporation **(1)**
679 W. Spring St.
Columbus, OH 43215
Tel.: 614-224-0000
S.I.C.: 5812

Specialty Restaurants Corp. **(1)**
20000 Brookpark Rd.
Cleveland, OH 44135
Tel.: 216-267-1010
S.I.C.: 5812

356th Fighter Group **(1)**
Akron-Canton Airport, 2787 Mt. Pleasant Rd.
North Canton, OH 44720
Tel.: 216-494-3500
S.I.C.: 5812

Oregon:

Port Center Restaurant Corp. **(1)**
4575 N. Channell Ave.
Portland, OR 97217
Tel.: 503-289-0966
S.I.C.: 5812

Pennsylvania:

Moshulu, Inc. **(1)**
Chestnut St. at Penn's Landing
Philadelphia, PA 19106
Tel.: 215-925-3237
S.I.C.: 5812

94th Aero Squadron of Philadelphia, Inc. **(1)**
No. Philadelphia Airport, 2750 Red Lion Rd.
Philadelphia, PA 19154
Tel.: 215-671-9400
S.I.C.: 5812

Tennessee:

Nashville Crawdaddy, Inc. **(1)**
14 Oldham St.
Nashville, TN 37213
Tel.: 615-255-5434
S.I.C.: 5812

94th AS of Memphis, Inc. **(1)**
2561 Democrat Rd.
Memphis, TN 38118
Tel.: 901-346-1260
S.I.C.: 5812

94th Aero Squadron of Nashville, Inc. **(1)**
1362-A Murfreesboro Rd.
Nashville, TN 37217
Tel.: 615-361-4212
S.I.C.: 5812

Texas:

Baby Doe's, Inc. **(1)**
3305 Harry Hines Blvd.
Dallas, TX 75201
Tel.: 214-871-7310
S.I.C.: 5812

Baby Doe's, Inc. **(1)**
8505 Cypress St.
Houston, TX 77012
Tel.: 713-928-9921
S.I.C.: 5812

Toll Road Restaurant Corp. **(1)**
1900 Ben St.
Fort Worth, TX 76103
Tel.: 817-534-4908
S.I.C.: 5812

Washington:

Renton Waterfront Restaurant Corp. **(1)**
1011 W. Perimeter Rd.
Renton, WA 98055
Tel.: 206-235-6330
S.I.C.: 5812

Wisconsin:

Castaways of Wisconsin, Inc. **(1)**
550 N. Harbor Dr.
Milwaukee, WI 53202
Tel.: 414-271-0597
S.I.C.: 5812

SPECIALTY RETAILERS, INC.
10201 S. Main
Houston, TX 77025
Mailing Address:
P.O. Box 35167
Houston, TX 77235
Tel.: 713-669-2674
Holding Company
S.I.C.: 6719; 5311
Bernard Fuchs *(Chm. Bd., Pres. & Chief Exec. Officer)*

Outside Service Firm(s):

Price Waterhouse*(Auditors)*
1700 Pacific Ave., Ste. 1400
Dallas, TX 75201-4698
Tel.: 214-922-8040

Texas Commerce Bank*(Major Banking Relationship)*
717 Travis St.
Houston, TX 77002
Tel.: 713-236-4636
Fax: 713-236-5476

Subsidiaries:

Fashion Bar Inc. **(1)**
401 S. Buckley Rd.
Aurora, CO 80017
Tel.: 303-695-7979
Fax: 303-695-3224
Approx.Sls.: $98,000,000
Emp.: 1,400
Retail Womens & Mens Wear
S.I.C.: 5611; 5621
Bernard Fuchs *(Pres. & Chief Exec. Officer)*

Three Beall Brothers 3, Inc. **(1)**
1237 E. Rusk St.
Jacksonville, TX 75766
Tel.: 903-586-9823
Junior Department Store Chain
S.I.C.: 5311
Jay Ivia *(Controller)*

SPECTRONICS CORPORATION
956 Brush Hollow Rd.
Westbury, NY 11590
Mailing Address:
P.O. Box 483
Westbury, NY 11690
Tel.: 516-333-4840
Tel.: 800-274-8888
Fax: 516-333-4859
Year Founded: 1955
Sales Range: $10-19 Million
Emp.: 150

Export
Ultraviolet Light Sources, X-Ray Cassettes, Laboratory Instruments, Banking, Security, Air Conditioning & Refrigeration & Vehicle/Industrial Leak Detectors
S.I.C.: 3641; 3648; 3844; 3674; 3826
William Cooper *(Pres.)*
Jonathan Cooper *(V.P.-Sls. & Mktg.)*
Les Davis *(Dir.-Adv., Copr. Communications & Data Processing)*
Barbara Heslin *(Dir.-Personnel)*
Ken Guidorizzi *(Mgr.-Quality Control)*
Gary Naftaly *(Mgr.-Sls.)*
Ujjal Sen *(Mgr.-Res. & Devel.)*
David Taub *(Mgr.-Intl. Sls.)*
Eileen Brown *(Corp. Travel Planner)*
K.C. Leighley *(Chief Engr.)*
Art Lowe *(Pur. Agent)*

No. of Mfg. Plants/Facilities: 1
No. of U.S. Offices: 1

SPECTRULITE CONSORTIUM, INC.
1001 College Ave.
Madison, IL 62060-0258
Tel.: 618-452-5190 **DE**
Fax: 618-452-7929
Year Founded: 1986
Sales Range: $100-499 Million
Emp.: 430
Magnesium& Magnesium Alloy Bars, Shapes, Sheets, etc.; Aluminum Plates
S.I.C.: 3356; 3353
William Barnes *(Pres. & Chief Exec. Officer)*
Patrick Knoll *(V.P. & Chief Fin. Officer)*
Phyllis Barnes *(Corporate Sec.)*

Outside Service Firm(s):

Coopers & Lybrand*(Auditors)*
203 N. LaSalle St.
Chicago, IL 60601
Tel.: 312-701-5500

SPECTRUM COLOR CENTER
6275 Joyce Dr.
Golden, CO 80403
Tel.: 303-425-0400
Fax: 303-425-0655
Emp.: 80
Color Separations & Custom Stripping
S.I.C.: 2816
Erwin B. Eckstein *(Chm. Bd., Pres. & Chief Exec. Officer)*
Helene Eckstein *(Chief Fin. Officer, Treas., Sec. & Mktg. Coord.)*
S. J. McDonald *(Controller & Systems Mgr.)*
Amy Cody *(Dir.-Data Processing & Systems Mgr.)*

Computer Systems/Hardware:
Kenex

Outside Service Firm(s):

Nationwide Insurance*(Commercial Insurance Carrier)*
Hartford, CT

Lincoln National Life Insurance Co.*(Group Insurer)*
PO Box 208, 1300 S. Clinton
Fort Wayne, IN 46801
Tel.: 219-455-2926
Fax: 219-455-7619

Charles F. Molling*(Legal Firm)*
Denver, CO

First Interstate Bank*(Major Banking Relationship)*
Golden, CO

SPECTRUM INDUSTRIES, INC.
1600 Johnson St.
Chippewa Falls, WI 54729
Tel.: 715-723-6750
Fax: 715-723-9002
Approx.Sls.: $15,000,000
Emp.: 285
Manufacture Wood Furniture; Prepress Services
S.I.C.: 2511; 2521; 2791
David Hancock *(Pres.)*
Patrick E. McKeon *(Exec. V.P.-Sls. & Mktg.)*
Richard J. Stevens *(V.P.)*
Donald E. Stumpf *(Mgr.-Personnel)*
Bernard J. Sokup *(Pur. Agent)*

Outside Service Firm(s):

Wipfli, Ullrich, Bertleson*(Auditors)*
Eau Claire, WI

Foley & Lardner*(Legal Firm)*
777 E. Wisconsin Ave.
Milwaukee, WI 53202
Tel.: 414-271-2400

Norwest Bank Minnesota, N.A.*(Major Banking Relationship)*
Eau Claire, WI

Subsidiary:

Media Graphics **(1)**
427 S. LaSalle St.
Chicago, IL 60605
Tel.: 312-922-6800
Typesetting & Pre-Press Services
S.I.C.: 2791
John Matyiasck *(V.P. & Gen. Mgr.)*

SPEEDLING INCORPORATED
4300 Old U.S. Hwy 41
Sun City, FL 33586
Mailing Address:
P.O. Box 7220
Sun City, FL 33586
Tel.: 813-645-3221
Fax: 813-645-8123
Year Founded: 1968
Approx.Sls.: $24,000,000
Emp.: 250
Fiscal Year-end: 9/30/92
Import Export
Vegetables, Melons, Ornamental Nursery Products, Farm Supplies, Tobacco
S.I.C.: 0181; 0161; 5191; 3089; 5194
Dr. Berl M. Thomas *(Pres.)*
David Roach *(Controller)*
F. Edward Fouse *(Dir.-Data Processing)*
Clark Mayer *(Dir.-Human Resources)*

Computer Systems/Hardware:
IBM AS 400

SPEEDRACK PRODUCTS GROUP, LTD.
1015 Nine Mile Rd., N.W.
Sparta, MI 49345
Tel.: 616-887-0002
Tel.: 800-752-7352
Fax: 616-887-2693
Approx.Sls.: $25,000,000

Speedrack Products Group, Ltd.—(Continued)

Emp.: 250
Industrial Boltless, Adjustable, Tubular and Structural Steel Storage Racks, Selective Rack; Drive-In Rack; Rack Supported Buildings; Cantilever Rack; Stacker Rack; Reverse Gravity Flow Rack
S.I.C.: 3496; 2542; 2541
J. Becker *(Pres.)*
Phil Belisle *(Exec. V.P.)*

SPEER, YOUNG & HOLLANDER, INC.
3580 Wilshire Blvd., Ste. 2020
Los Angeles, CA 90010
Tel.: 213-487-2363
Fax: 213-487-0072
Year Founded: 1949
Approx.Billings: $10,000,000
Emp.: 20
Business-to-Business
Barton Young *(Pres.)*
Charles Bartleson *(Exec. V.P.)*
Richard Kozak *(V.P.)*
Dennis Washburn *(V.P.)*
John Dillon *(V.P., Pub. Rels.)*
Christel Beard *(Pub. Rels. Assoc.)*
Marie Domingo *(Pub. Rels. Coord.)*
Michele Richardson *(Bus. Mgr.)*

Computer Systems/Hardware:
IBM, Apple, MacIntosh

SPENCER COMPANIES INC.
120 Woodson St. N.W.
Huntsville, AL 35801
Mailing Address:
P.O. Box 18128,
Huntsville, AL 35804
Tel.: 205-533-1150
Tel.: 800-633-2910 (adj. to AL)
AL
Fax: 205-535-2910
Year Founded: 1923
Assets: $14,960,424
Earnings: $136,781
Liabilities: $10,332,434
Net Worth: $4,627,990
Approx.Sls.: $49,076,241
Emp.: 350
Fiscal Year-end: 5/31/92
Wholesale & Retail Gasoline, Motor Oil & Lubricants; Convenience Stores; Manufacturer & Wholesaler of Ice
S.I.C.: 5172; 5541; 2097; 5199; 5411
Guy J. Spencer, Jr. *(Chm. Bd., Pres. & Chief Exec. Officer)*
W.L. Standridge *(Chief Fin. Officer, Treas. & Sec.)*
Robert E. Adams *(Exec. V.P. & Chief Oper. Officer)*
Sarah S. Chappell *(Sr. V.P.-Personnel)*
W. A. Fred Henderson *(Sr. V.P.)*
Fred C. Reid *(V.P.)*
Guy J. Spencer III *(V.P.)*
Randall G. Birdsong *(Controller)*

Principal(s):
Guy J. Spencer, Jr.
Sarah S. Chappell
Guy J. Spencer III

No. of Mfg. Plants/Facilities: 82
No. of U.S. Offices: 16

Computer Systems/Hardware:
IBM

Outside Service Firm(s):

Dudley, Hopton-Jones, Sims & Freeman*(Auditors)*
Huntsville, AL

Your Insurance Man, Inc.*(Commercial Insurance Carrier)*
Decatur, AL

Blue Cross & Blue Shield of Alabama*(Group Insurance Broker/Consult)*
450 Riverchase Pkwy. East
Birmingham, AL 35298
Tel.: 205-988-2245

Lange, Simpson, Robinson & Somerville*(Legal Firm)*
Huntsville, AL 35804

Third National Bank*(Major Banking Relationship)*
Nashville, TN

Divisions:

MidSouth Ice Co. **(1)**
120 Woodson St. N.W.
Huntsville, AL 35801
Tel.: 205-533-1150
Tel.: 800-633-2910
Fax: 205-535-2910
Manufacturer & Wholesaler of Ice
S.I.C.: 2097; 5199
Robert E. Adams *(Pres. & Chief Exec. Officer)*

Spencer Oil Company **(1)**
120 Woodson St. N.W.
Huntsville, AL 35801
Tel.: 205-533-1150
Sarah S. Chappell *(Pres.)*

Divisions:

Alabama Oil Company **(2)**
120 Woodson St. N.W.
Huntsville, AL 35801
Tel.: 205-533-1150
Tel.: 800-633-2910
Fax: 205-535-2910
Distributors for Amoco Gasoline
S.I.C.: 5172
Guy J. Spencer III *(V.P. & Gen. Mgr.)*

MidSouth Oil Co. **(2)**
P.O. Box 583
Fairfield, AL 35064
Tel.: 205-744-0020
Fax: 205-744-0038
Distributors for Citgo Gasoline
S.I.C.: 5172
Fred Reid *(V.P. & Gen. Mgr.)*

SPENCER INDUSTRIES, INC.
120 Albany St. Plaza, 6th Fl.
New Brunswick, NJ 08903-2629
Tel.: 908-745-9009
Approx.Sls.: $60,000,000
Emp.: 2,500
Spencer, Casual & Webster Slacks; Tailfeather & Manhandler Jeans
S.I.C.: 2325; 2329
G.W. Spencer *(Pres.)*
J.M. Quinn *(Exec. V.P.)*
Liz Dowdle *(V.P.-Mktg., Mdsg. & Adv.)*
Larry Newman *(V.P.-Sls.)*
J. O'Connell *(V.P.-Fin.)*
Robert Dreyling *(Controller)*

Subsidiary:

Casual Sportswear Co., Inc. **(1)**
901 Keystone Industrial Park
Dunmore, PA 18512
Tel.: 717-346-0701
Emp.: 60
Mfr. of Men's & Boy's Slacks, Jeans & Walk Shorts
S.I.C.: 2325; 2253; 2329; 2254
Gordon W. Spencer *(Chm. Bd.)*
James Quinn *(Exec. V.P.)*
Joseph O'Connell *(V.P.-Fin.)*
Jim Burgener *(V.P.-Sls.)*
Charles Grochowski *(V.P.-Distr.)*
Liz Dowdle *(V.P.-Mktg., Mdsg. & Adv.)*
Robert Dreyling *(Controller)*

SPENCER PRESS, INC.
90 Spencer Dr.
Wells, ME 04090
Tel.: 207-646-9926
Fax: 207-646-5021
Year Founded: 1947
Approx.Sls.: $45,000,000
Emp.: 500

Commercial Offset Printing
S.I.C.: 2752
John Spenlinhauer, III *(Pres.)*
Eugene Sullivan *(Chief Fin. Officer)*
Stephen Spenlinhauer *(V.P.-Mktg.)*
William Vecchio *(V.P.-Opers.)*

Outside Service Firm(s):

Harvey & Parent*(Auditors)*
North Andover, MA

SPENCER TURBINE CO.
600 Day Hill Rd.
Windsor, CT 06095
Mailing Address:
P.O. Box 587
Windsor, CT 06095
Tel.: 203-688-8361
Tel.: 800-232-4321 CT
Fax: 203-688-0098
Emp.: 270
Import Export
Manufacture Air & Gas Moving Equipment, Air Filters, Motor Mufflers, Turbo Compressors, Vortex Blowers, Vacuum Cleaning Systems, Tubing & Fittings, Pneumatic, Furnace & Sewage Treatment Blowers
S.I.C.: 3564; 3498; 3535; 3569; 3589
Frank F. Wilson *(Chm. Bd.)*
Robert G. Rayve *(Pres. & Chief Exec. Officer)*
Frederick B. Barclay *(Chief Fin. Officer & V.P.)*
John C. Broadwell *(V.P.-Mfg.)*
Richard G. Hajec *(V.P.-Engrng.)*
John P. Kinel, Jr. *(V.P.-Industrial Sls.)*
Robert V. Kmon *(V.P.-Special Prods.)*
Richard L. Edwards *(Treas.)*
Barbara C. Klenke *(Sec.)*
Jim McCool *(Mgr.-Pur.)*

Outside Service Firm(s):

Ernst & Young*(Auditors)*
Goodwyn Sq., 225 Asylum St.
Hartford, CT 06103
Tel.: 203-247-3100

Robinson & Cole*(Legal Firm)*
Hartford, CT

Fleet National Bank*(Major Banking Relationship)*
Hartford, CT

SPENCER'S INC.
238 Willow St.
Mount Airy, NC 27030
Tel.: 919-789-9111
Fax: 919-789-6824
Year Founded: 1926
Approx.Sls.: $60,000,000
Emp.: 2,000
Mfr. Infants' & Children's Sleepwear & Underwear, Paperboard Set-Up Boxes
S.I.C.: 2341; 2652
James H. Crossingham, Jr. *(Chm. Bd. & Pres.)*
John Weddle *(Exec. V.P.)*
Helen C. Rowe *(V.P.-Quality Control)*
Burton Slate *(V.P.-Mfg.)*
Rex O'Neal *(Treas.)*
Thomas M. Faw *(Sec.)*
James Ayers *(Dir.-Pur.)*
Jamye C. Benik *(Dir.-Adv.)*
Carlis Mabry *(Dir.-Personnel)*
Robert Caldwell *(Natl. Sls. Mgr.)*

Outside Service Firm(s):

Apple, Bell, Johnson & Co.*(Auditors)*
Burlington, NC

First Union National Bank*(Major Banking Relationship)*
P.O. Box 21965,
Greensboro, NC 27420

SPERLING
1001 Loyola Ave.
New Orleans, LA 70113
Tel.: 504-522-2478
Fax: 504-522-2482
Year Founded: 1973
Approx.Billings: $11,610,000
Emp.: 21
Gay Sperling *(Pres. & New Bus. Contact)*
Jack Boasberg *(V.P., Sec.)*
Jac Sperling *(V.P., Treas.)*
J.H. Dunbar *(V.P., Dir. Human Resources)*
Al Boudreaux *(Comptroller)*
Kathleen Brown *(Natl. Pub. Rels. Mngmt.)*
Kelly Swords *(Opers. Mgr.)*
Elissa Cohen *(Mktg. Dir. & Acct. Supvr.)*
Eve Boasberg *(Pub. Rels. Mgr.)*
Michele DuBos *(Computer Opers.)*
Sherry Smith *(Pub. Rels. Dir.)*

SPIEGEL MEATS, INC.
8020A N.W. 60th St.
Miami, FL 33166
Mailing Address:
P.O. Box 521023
Miami, FL 33152
Tel.: 305-592-7797 FL
Fax: 305-593-7017
Year Founded: 1969
Approx.Sls.: $27,000,000
Emp.: 56
Wholesale Fresh Meats & Provisions
S.I.C.: 5147
Marcel Croteau *(Pres.)*
Edmond Croteau *(V.P.)*
Mary Fawkes *(Controller)*
Nick Pupello *(Mgr.-Pur.)*

No. of Mfg. Plants/Facilities: 1

Outside Service Firm(s):

Spear Safer Harmoun & Co.*(Auditors)*
Miami, FL

Michael Gettlemen*(Legal Firm)*
Miami, FL

Sun Bank, N.A.*(Major Banking Relationship)*
Miami, FL 33131

Division:

RealCold Storage **(1)**
8020 N.W. 60th St.
Miami, FL 33166
Tel.: 305-592-7797 ext. 54
Emp.: 4
Warehouse Facility
S.I.C.: 4222
Pedro Lugo *(Mgr.)*
Mary Fawkes *(Controlller)*

FRANKLIN SPIER, INC.
650 First Ave.
New York, NY 10016
Tel.: 212-679-4441
Fax: 212-685-0812
Year Founded: 1929
Approx.Billings: $30,679,000
Emp.: 45
Book Adv. & Promotion
Alix Nelson *(Chm. & Chief Exec. Officer)*
David M. Cathers *(Pres. & Chief Oper. Officer)*
Robert Adler *(Exec. V.P., Fin. & Admin)*
Kathleen Kelly *(Personnel & Office Mgr.)*

I. SPIEWAK & SONS, INC.
505 Eighth Ave.
New York, NY 10018
Tel.: 212-695-1620
Tel.: 800-223-6850 **NY**
Fax: 212-629-4803
Year Founded: 1904
Approx.Sls.: $50,000,000
Emp.: 450
Fiscal Year-end: 1/31/92
Import Export
Manufacture of Outerwear & Uniforms; Operation of Trade Shows; Leasing of Automobiles
S.I.C.: 2329; 2326; 2339; 5699; 7389; 7515
Gerald Spiewak *(Chm. Bd.)*
Michael Spiewak *(Pres. & Chief Exec. Officer)*
David Anderson *(V.P.-Mfg.)*
Robert Spiewak *(Treas.)*
Roy Spiewak *(Controller & Import Mgr.)*
Jeffery Novick *(Legal Officer)*
Scott Dishman *(Dir.-Mktg. & Adv.)*
Seymour Kaufman *(Dir.-Personnel & Data Processing)*
Howard Warmflash *(Dir.-Pur.)*
Sol Jacobs *(Mgr.-Natl. Sls.)*
Lynn Walkerbrod *(Export Mgr.)*
Principal(s):
Gerald Spiewak
Michael Spiewak

No. of U.S. Offices: 4
No. of Foreign Offices: 3

Computer Systems/Hardware:
IBM System 36/PC Network

Outside Service Firm(s):

Greenberg & Levy*(Auditors)*
New York, NY

Chemical Banking Corp.*(Major Banking Relationship)*
277 Park Ave.
New York, NY 10041
Tel.: 212-310-6407
Fax: 212-310-4526

Division:

Golden Fleece Outerwear Co. **(1)**
505 8th Ave.
New York, NY 10018
Tel.: 212-695-1620
Fax: 212-629-4803
Manufacture & Sales of Mens & Boys Outerwear
S.I.C.: 2329
Gerald Spiewak *(Chief Oper. Officer)*

Subsidiaries:

TSE Leasing Co. **(1)**
505 8th Ave.
New York, NY 10018
Tel.: 212-695-1620 (100%)
Leasing of Machinery & Automobiles
S.I.C.: 7359; 7515
Robert Spiewak *(Chief Oper. Officer)*

Division:

Trade Show Enterprises **(2)**
505 8th Ave.
New York, NY 10018
Tel.: 212-695-1620
Operation of Trade Shows; Leasing of Machinery, Equipment & Automobiles
S.I.C.: 7389; 7515
Robert Spiewak *(Chief Oper. Officer)*

Division:

M.W.O.S. Trade Show **(3)**
505 8th Ave.
New York, NY 10018
Tel.: 212-695-1637
Tel.: 800-223-6850
Operation of Trade Shows
S.I.C.: 7389
Gerald Spiewak *(Chief Oper. Officer)*

Trappings Co. **(1)**
505 8th Ave.
New York, NY 10018
Tel.: 212-695-1624 (100%)
Fashion Outerwear for Men
S.I.C.: 2329
Gerald Spiewak *(Chief Oper. Officer)*

SPINNAKER SOFTWARE CORPORATION
201 Broadway St.
Cambridge, MA 02139
Tel.: 617-494-1200
Tel.: 800-323-8088
Fax: 617-494-1219
Year Founded: 1982
Approx.Sls.: $30,016,979
Emp.: 145
Fiscal Year-end: 6/30/92
Application Software; Publisher's Computer Software
S.I.C.: 7372
C. David Seuss *(Chm., Pres., Chief Exec. Officer & Treas.)*
Lynn Weiss *(Exec. V.P. & Chief Oper. Officer)*
Milton H. Bunker, Jr. *(V.P.-Opers.)*
Julie Wainwright *(V.P.-Intl. Sls. & Mktg.)*
Pricilla A. Seuss *(V.P.-Sls.)*
David Thurman *(V.P.-Sls.-Plus Div.)*
Cindy Sweetser *(V.P.-Mktg.-PSF Div.)*
Howard Rosenblum *(Sec.)*
Linda Fisher *(Sr. Mgr.-Channel Mktg.)*
Maura Jones *(Mgr.-Mktg. Communications)*

SPINNERIN YARN CO., INC.
30 Wesley St.
South Hackensack, NJ 07606
Tel.: 201-343-5900
Fax: 201-343-6988
Approx.Sls.: $20,000,000
Emp.: 350
Fiscal Year-end: 12/31/90
Sales Yarns & Commission Dyeing; Spinnerin
S.I.C.: 5199; 2211
Kurt O. Trueb *(Chm. Bd.)*
Wesley Edwards *(Pres. & Chief Exec. Officer)*
William Rabadan *(V.P.-Mktg.)*
Doug Hamilton *(Controller & Treas.)*

SPIRES RESTAURANTS INC.
1544 W. Yale Ave.
Orange, CA 92667
Tel.: 714-282-7092 **CA**
Fax: 714-282-8081
Year Founded: 1965
Approx.Sls.: $33,000,000
Emp.: 1,200
Restaurant Chain, 25 Locations in Southern CA
S.I.C.: 5812
John Haretakis *(Pres.)*
Paul Escalera *(V.P.-Opers.)*
Jim Learakos *(V.P.-Food Services)*
Paul Strathman *(Controller)*
Principal(s):
John Haretakis

Computer Systems/Hardware:
IBM PC Jr.

Outside Service Firm(s):

Deloitte & Touche*(Auditors)*
Anaheim, CA

Bank of America*(Major Banking Relationship)*
701 S. Western Ave.
Los Angeles, CA 91201

SPIRIT CRUISES
501 Front St.
Norfolk, VA 23510
Tel.: 804-627-2900 **VA**
Fax: 804-640-9315
Year Founded: 1972
Approx.Sls.: $55,000,000
Emp.: 150
Fiscal Year-end: 8/31/92
Operates Cruise, Dining & Entertainment Vessels; Travel Arrangements
S.I.C.: 4481; 4729
Robert Shaw *(Pres.)*
Patrick Hermier *(Chief Fin. Officer)*
Joseph Gold *(Sr. V.P.)*
Doug Porter *(V.P.-Mktg.)*
Chuck Johnson *(V.P.-Sls.)*
Chris Hendricks *(V.P.)*
Theresa Bannon *(Dir.-Mktg. & Adv.)*

No. of U.S. Offices: 35

Outside Service Firm(s):

Goodman & Co.*(Auditors)*
Newport News, VA

Payne, Gates & Farthing*(Legal Firm)*
One Commercial Pl.
Norfolk, VA 23510
Tel.: 804-622-3611

United Virginia Bank*(Major Banking Relationship)*
Norfolk, VA

SPIRITE INDUSTRIES, INC.
150 S. Dean St.
Englewood, NJ 07631
Tel.: 201-871-4910 **NY**
Fax: 201-871-9790
Assets: $5,000,000
Liabilities: $3,000,000
Net Worth: $2,000,000
Approx.Sls.: $20,000,000
Emp.: 60
Fiscal Year-end: 12/31/91
Import
Mfr. of Women's Under Garments Including Brassieres, Girdles & Panties
S.I.C.: 2342
Fred N. Kronfeld *(Chief Exec. & Chief Fin. Officer & Treas.)*
Harvey Bernstein *(Pres. & Sec.)*
Andrew S. Kornfeld *(Grp. V.P.)*
Gary H. Kronfeld *(Sr. V.P.)*
H. Spar *(Gen. Counsel)*
J. Garcia *(Pur. Agent)*
Samuel Belsky *(Dir.-Personnel & Controller)*

Outside Service Firm(s):

Anchin, Block & Anchin*(Auditors)*
1375 Broadway
New York, NY 10018

Midlantic National Bank*(Major Banking Relationship)*
Metro Park Plaza,
Edison, NJ 08818
Tel.: 908-321-8000

SPIROL INTERNATIONAL CORP.
965 N. Main St.
Danielson, CT 06239
Mailing Address:
P.O. Box 179
Danielson, CT 06239
Tel.: 203-774-8571 **CT**
Fax: 203-774-0487
Year Founded: 1952
Approx.Sls.: $30,000,000
Emp.: 300
Fiscal Year-end: 9/30/91
Import Export
Mfr. Engineered Fasteners, Including Pins, Inserts, Spacers & Other Tubular Products, as well as Shims, Pin & Insert Assembly Equipment & Parts Feeding Systems
S.I.C.: 3498; 3469; 3452; 3629
Hans H. Koehl *(Chm. Bd. & Chief Exec. Officer)*
James C. Shaw *(Pres.)*
William Hunt *(Chief Fin. Officer)*
Pamela M. Bonneville *(V.P.-Admin.)*
David R. Dryfuse *(V.P.-Ohio Opers.)*
Richard Snider *(V.P.-Canadian Opers.)*
Guenther C. Wexler *(V.P.-Production Tech.)*
Phyllis R. Racine *(Sec.)*

Divisions:

C.E.M. Div. Spirol Intl. Corp. **(1)**
99 Rock Ave.
Danielson, CT 06239
Tel.: 203-774-8571
Fax: 203-774-0487
Approx.Sls.: $8,000,000
Emp.: 150
C.E.M. Spirol Pins, Spacers, Connectors, Self-Tapping Inserts & Assembly Equip., Pin Inserters, Insert Drivers, Rivets, Knurled Nuts, Heat/Ultrasonic Inserts, Heat Insert Drivers, Expansion Inserts
S.I.C.: 3452
Hans H. Koehl *(Chm. Bd.)*
James C. Shaw *(Pres.)*
William Hunt *(V.P. & Treas.)*
Mark Coakley *(Mgr.-Sls.)*

Spirol West **(1)**
15121 Golden West Circle
Westminster, CA 92683
Tel.: 714-894-1111
S.I.C.: 3452
James C. Shaw *(Pres.)*

Non-U.S. Holdings:

Spirol Ind. Ltd. **(1)**
3103 St. Etienne Blvd.
Windsor, ON N8W 5B1, Canada
Tel.: 519-974-3334 (100%)
Fax: 519-974-6550
Emp.: 17
Indus. Fasteners/Stampings; Assembly Equip.
S.I.C.: 3452; 3629
James C. Shaw *(Pres.)*

Spirol Ind. Ltd. **(1)**
Princewood Rd., Carlstrees Ind. Estate NN17 2ET
Corby, Northants United Kingdom
Tel.: 0536-67634 (100%)
Fax: 0536-203415
Emp.: 50
Indus. Fasteners; Assembly Equip.
S.I.C.: 3452; 3629
Michael Harris *(Mng. Dir.)*

Spirol S.A. **(1)**
2, Rue Charles Cros -ZAE- B.P. No. 40, 95322
Saint-Leu-la-Foret, France
Tel.: 1-39-60-47-72 (51%)
Fax: 1-39-60-55-73
Emp.: 4
Indus. Fasteners
S.I.C.: 3452

SPLENDOR FORM INTERNATIONAL INC.
29-10 Thomson
Long Island City, NY 11101
Tel.: 718-392-6600 **DE**

Splendor Form International Inc.—(Continued)

Fax: 718-392-6613
Year Founded: 1954
Assets: $14,000,000
Liabilities: $4,000,000
Net Worth: $10,000,000
Approx.Sls.: $20,000,000
Emp.: 400
Mfr. Ladies' Undergarments
S.I.C.: 2342; 2341
Jacob J. Delman *(Chm. Bd. & Chief Oper. Officer)*
Jack Desperak *(Pres. & Chief Exec. Officer)*
Richard Delman *(Chief Fin. Officer, Treas., Sec. & Controller)*
Burton Singer *(Dir.-Pur.)*
Ethel Singer *(Dir.-Personnel)*
Seymour Goldfeld *(Legal Officer)*

Principal(s):
Jacob J. Delman
Jack Desperak

No. of Mfg. Plants/Facilities: 2
No. of U.S. Offices: 2
No. of Foreign Offices: 1

Computer Systems/Hardware:
MAI Basic 4 210

Outside Service Firm(s):

Bernard Katz*(Auditors)*
Eastchester, NY

Empire Blue Cross & Blue Shield*(Group Insurer)*
New York, NY

Chase Manhattan Bank, N.A.*(Investment Banker)*
One Chase Manhattan Plaza
New York, NY 10081
Tel.: 212-552-2222
Tel.: 800-526-0801
Fax: 212-552-7175

Seymour Goldfeld*(Legal Firm)*
Long Island City, NY

Division:

Splendor Form Brassiere, Inc. **(1)**
29-10 Thomson Ave.
Long Island City, NY 11101
Tel.: 212-392-6600 (100%)
Approx.Sls.: $20,000,000
Emp.: 1,000
Mfg. Ladies' Undergarments
S.I.C.: 2342
Steven Delman *(Chief Oper. Officer)*

THE SPOHN CORPORATION
1775 E. 45th St.
Cleveland, OH 44103
Tel.: 216-431-8070 **OH**
Fax: 216-431-6924
Approx.Sls.: $37,000,000
Emp.: 350
Warm Air Heating & Air Conditioning Contractor; Plumbing, Ventilation & Duct Work Contractor; Water, Sewer & Utility Lines
S.I.C.: 1711; 1623
David K. Nachman *(Pres. & Chief Exec. Officer)*
George W. Spohn, III *(V.P.)*
David T. Spohn *(Treas.)*
Dennis A. Spohn *(Sec.)*

Outside Service Firm(s):

Ciulla Stephens & Company*(Auditors)*
Cleveland, OH

T.L. Jacobs*(Legal Firm)*
Cleveland, OH

National City Bank*(Major Banking Relationship)*
P.O. Box 92301, Corp. Trust Dept.
Cleveland, OH 44101
Tel.: 216-575-2000

SPORLAN VALVE COMPANY
7525 Sussex Ave.
Saint Louis, MO 63143
Tel.: 314-647-2775
Fax: 314-647-1714
Year Founded: 1934
Approx.Sls.: $50,000,000
Emp.: 300
Fiscal Year-end: 12/31/89
Export
Manufacture Refrigeration & Air Conditioning Controls & Components
S.I.C.: 3822
K.A. Ohlemeyer *(Pres.)*
J.D. Boing *(Sr. V.P.-Pur. & Production)*
A.J. Schelich *(V.P.-Mfg.)*
D.E. Chura *(Gen. Mgr.-Sls.)*
J.E. Grimm *(Mgr.-Sls.-OEM)*
R.L. Siebert *(Mgr.-Adv.)*

Computer Systems/Hardware:
IBM System 36

Outside Service Firm(s):

Deloitte & Touche*(Auditors)*
One City Centre
St. Louis, MO 63101
Tel.: 314-342-4900
Fax: 314-342-1100

Alexander & Alexander*(Commercial Insurance Carrier)*
St. Louis, MO

SPORTO CORP.
2 Midway St.
Boston, MA 02210
Tel.: 617-426-2121
Fax: 617-423-4160
Approx.Sls.: $30,000,000
Emp.: 390
Holding Co.; Women's Fashion Athletic/Leisure Footwear, Cold Weather Boots
S.I.C.: 6719; 3143; 3144; 3149; 5139
David Brilliant *(Pres.)*
James Brilliant *(Chief Exec. Officer)*
Steve Brilliant *(V.P.)*
Greg Rager *(V.P.-Sls. & Mktg.)*

THE SPORTSMAN'S GUIDE, INC.
900 Apollo Rd.
Eagan, MN 55121
Tel.: 612-686-9000 **MN**
Fax: 612-546-9332
Year Founded: 1977
Assets: $5,237,142
Earnings: $212,157
Liabilities: $4,699,856
Net Worth: $537,286
Approx.Sls.: $32,000,000
Emp.: 200
Fiscal Year-end: 1/ 1/93
Import
Mail Order Outdoor Hunting & Sporting Goods
S.I.C.: 5961
Len Paletz *(Chm., Pres., Chief Exec. & Chief Oper. Officer)*
Jim Gorczycki *(Controller & Human Resources Dir.)*
Ralph Heyman *(Gen. Counsel)*
Gary Olen *(Sec. & Exec. V.P.)*
Alan Mattis *(Dir.-Data Processing)*
Ro Finnegan *(Dir.-Adv.)*
Joe Friebe *(Dir.-Mktg.)*
Jackie McFarland *(Mgr.-Pur.)*

Computer Systems/Hardware:
IBM

SPOTNAILS INC.
1100 Hicks Rd.
Rolling Meadows, IL 60008
Tel.: 708-259-1620
Fax: 708-259-9236
Approx.Sls.: $12,000,000
Emp.: 150
Automated Systems, Pneumatic Tools & Fasteners, Carton Closers, Spotnails, Spotstaples, Spotbrads, Spotpins
S.I.C.: 3823
Mark Wilson *(Pres.)*
J. Kisiazek *(V.P.-Mfg.)*
James Lee *(Controller)*
Charles Chartier *(Mgr.-Sls.)*
L. Bettencourt *(Plant Mgr.)*

Outside Service Firm(s):

Ernst & Young*(Auditors)*
233 S. Wacker Dr.
Chicago, IL 60606
Tel.: 312-368-1800
Fax: 312-645-3095

LaSalle National Bank*(Major Banking Relationship)*
135 S. La Salle St.
Chicago, IL 60690

SPRAYING SYSTEMS CO.
North Ave. at Schmale Rd.
Wheaton, IL 60188
Mailing Address:
P.O. Box 7900,
Wheaton, IL 60189-7900
Tel.: 708-665-5000
Fax: 708-260-0842
Year Founded: 1937
Sales Range: $10-19 Million
Export
Mfr. & Sales of Spray Nozzles & Related Accessories
S.I.C.: 3499
James Bramsen *(Pres.)*
Phillip Larsen *(V.P.-Fin.)*
Martin Hynes *(Controller)*
Ken Kasperski *(Dir.-Intl. Sls.)*
Dave Lantz *(Dir.-Telecommunications)*

Computer Systems/Hardware:
IBM

Outside Service Firm(s):

Gary Wheaton Bank*(Major Banking Relationship)*
Wheaton, IL

Non-U.S. Holdings:

Spraying Systems Co. Far East **(1)**
Dai Ichi Iwata Bldg., 8f-5-10-18, Higashi Gotanda Schinagawa-Ku,
Tokyo, 141, Japan
Tel.: 03-3445-6031
Emp.: 100
Mfr. & Sales of Spray Nozzles
S.I.C.: 3499; 5074
Dr. Mikio Yamada *(Mng. Dir.)*

Spraying Systems Deutschland GmbH **(1)**
Grossmoorring 9 D-2100
Hamburg, 90, Germany
Tel.: 40-76-60-010 (100%)
Emp.: 200
Mfr. & Sales of Spray Nozzles
S.I.C.: 3499; 5074
Ernst Schrader *(Mng. Dir.)*

SPRECKLES INDUSTRIES, INC.
4234 Hacienda Dr.
Pleasanton, CA 94566
Tel.: 510-460-0840
Fax: 510-460-0953
Year Founded: 1987
Approx.Sls.: $400,000,000
Emp.: 3,000
Sugar & Industrial Manufacturing
S.I.C.: 2063
George A. Lamberth *(Pres.)*
Robert L. Schmalz *(V.P., Sec. & Gen. Counsel)*
Donald C. Roof *(Chief Fin. Officer, Treas. & Comptroller)*
Mary Terwilliger *(Dir.-Acctg. & Pur.)*

Outside Service Firm(s):

Arthur Andersen & Co.*(Auditors)*
Spear Street Tower, One Market Plaza, Ste. 3500
San Francisco, CA 94105
Tel.: 415-546-8200

Pillsbury, Madison & Sutro*(Legal Firm)*
235 Montgomery St.
San Francisco, CA 94104
Tel.: 415-983-1000

Citibank N.A.*(Major Banking Relationship)*
Corporate Trust Services, 399 Park Ave.
New York, NY 10043
Tel.: 212-559-1605

Wells Fargo Bank*(Major Banking Relationship)*
420 Montgomery St.
San Francisco, CA 94104

Subsidiaries:

Carbidie Corporation **(1)**
Arona Rd.
Irwin, PA 15642
Tel.: 412-864-5900
Sales Range: $10-19 Million
Emp.: 165
Carbide Preforms, Die Parts, Tungsten Carbide Die & Wear Parts
S.I.C.: 3544
P.J. Waslis *(Pres.)*
Edward S. Cline *(Sls. Mgr.)*
H.O. Logan *(Plant Mgr.)*

Duff-Norton **(1)**
9415 Pioneer Ave.
Charlotte, NC 28217
Tel.: 704-588-0510
Fax: 704-588-8180
Approx.Sls.: $55,000,000
Emp.: 1,500
Mfr. Duff-Norton Lifting Jacks, Coffing Hoists, Electric Wire Rope & Coil Chain, Hand Chain & Lever Hoists, Rotating Joint, Duff Lynx Hoist & Pullers
S.I.C.: 3423; 3494; 3536; 3566; 3569
James E. Boyd *(Pres.)*
Larry Kalsoukis *(V.P.-Fin.)*
Raymond A. Davies *(V.P.-Sls. & MKtg.)*
Edward Cummings *(V.P.-Mfg.)*
Michael G. Miller *(Dir.-Engrng.)*
Curtis R. Sanborn *(Adv. Mgr.)*
Betty Martin *(Dir.-Human Resources)*

THE SPRING AIR COMPANY
2980 River Rd.
Des Plaines, IL 60018
Tel.: 708-297-5577 **IL**
Fax: 708-299-0195
Year Founded: 1926
Approx.Sls.: $239,000,000
Emp.: 1,260
Fiscal Year-end: 12/31/91
Mfr. Mattresses & Matching Foundations
S.I.C.: 2515
Earl Kluft *(Chm. Bd.)*
Donald P. Pellegrini *(Pres. & Chief Exec. Officer)*
James Tobin *(Sr. V.P.-Sls. & Mktg.)*
Elaine M. Nissen *(V.P.-Fin.)*
LeRoy Simon *(V.P.-Mfg.)*
Linda A. Baer *(Dir.-Communications)*
Bernie Pilchen *(Natl. Dir.-Mktg.)*
Principal(s):
Donald P. Pellegrini

No. of Mfg. Plants/Facilities: 36
No. of U.S. Offices: 29

Computer Systems/Hardware:
Lan Novell 386, SBT

Outside Service Firm(s):

Deloitte & Touche*(Auditors)*
Two Prudential Plaza, 180 N. Stetson
Chicago, IL 60601
Tel.: 312-946-2039

Group Administration Agency*(Commercial Insurance Carrier)*
20 N. Wacker Dr.
Chicago, IL 60606

Benefit Trust & Life Insurance*(Group Insurer)*
P.O. Box 7915,
Lake Forest, IL

Merrill Lynch*(Investment Banker)*
141 W. Jackson Blvd.
Chicago, IL 60604

McBride, Baker & Coles*(Legal Firm)*
500 W. Madison St., 40th Fl.
Chicago, IL 60606
Tel.: 312-715-5700

American National Bank*(Major Banking Relationship)*
33 North LaSalle St.
Chicago, IL 60690
Tel.: 312-661-6967

Principal Mutual Life Insurance Co.*(Pension Manager)*
Mason City, IA

SPRING ARBOR DISTRIBUTORS
10885 Textile Rd.
Belleville, MI 48111
Tel.: 313-481-0900 **MI**
Fax: 313-483-9560
Year Founded: 1978
Approx.Sls.: $125,000,000
Emp.: 620
Wholesale Distribution of Books
S.I.C.: 5192
Corporate Giving Program:
Evangelical Christian Charities
Thomas Murphy, Sr. *(Chm. Bd.)*
James Carlson *(Vice Chm.)*
Richard Pigott *(Pres.)*
Jerry Rode *(Sr. V.P. & Chief Information Officer)*
Joel Manby *(Sr. V.P.-Mktg. & Sls.)*
Timothy Williams *(V.P., Treas. & Sec.)*
David Dykhouse *(V.P.-Mktg. Devel.)*
Sheila Dornan *(V.P.-Human Resources)*

No. of U.S. Offices: 6

Outside Service Firm(s):

N.B.D. Bank, N.A.*(Major Banking Relationship)*
611 Woodward Ave.
Detroit, MI 48226
Tel.: 313-225-1122
Fax: 313-225-3420

SPRING ENGINEERS, INC.
9740 Tanner Rd.
Houston, TX 77040
Mailing Address:
P.O. Box 40446
Houston, TX 77240
Tel.: 713-690-9488
Tel.: 800-899-9488 **TX**
Fax: 713-686-9600
Fax: 713-690-1199
Year Founded: 1966
Approx.Sls.: $10,000,000
Emp.: 85
Export
Manufacture Mechanical Springs Wire Forms, Fabrications Metal Stampings & Machinery
S.I.C.: 3469; 3495; 3599
Kevin Grace *(Pres. & Chief Oper. Officer)*
John R. Grace *(Chief Exec. Officer)*
Theodore Combs *(Controller)*
R.J. Jasken *(Mgr.-Sls.)*
Principal(s):
John R. Grace

No. of Mfg. Plants/Facilities: 2
No. of U.S. Offices: 2

Computer Systems/Hardware:
Hewlett Packard

Outside Service Firm(s):

White Petrov McHone*(Auditors)*
Houston, TX

Jim Stephenson*(Legal Firm)*
Houston, TX

Park National Bank*(Major Banking Relationship)*
Houston, TX

SPRING-GREEN LAWN CARE CORPORATION
11927 Spaulding School Dr.
Plainfield, IL 60544
Tel.: 815-436-8777
Tel.: 800-435-4051
Year Founded: 1977
Approx.Sls.: $14,500,000
Emp.: 200
Fiscal Year-end: 1/31/90
Professional Lawn & Tree Care Service; Franchises Available
S.I.C.: 0782
Thomas W. Hofer *(Pres.)*
Barry Matthews *(V.P.-Franchise Support)*
William Ticknor *(Dir.-Franchise Devel. & Mktg.)*

SPRING, O'BRIEN & CO. INC.
220 Fifth Ave.
New York, NY 10001
Tel.: 212-213-4133
Fax: 212-213-4139
Year Founded: 1982
Approx.Billings: $12,080,000
Emp.: 16
Mktg. & Communication Services
S.I.C.: 7311; 7812; 8743
Chris Spring *(Pres.)*
Procter Lippincott *(Sr. V.P., Acct. Dir. & Pub. Rels.)*
Sharon Fischer *(Fin. & Controller)*

Computer Systems/Hardware:
IBM, MacIntosh

SPRINGBORN LABORATORIES, INC.
One Springborn Center
Enfield, CT 06082
Tel.: 203-749-8371 **DE**
Fax: 203-749-8234
Fax: 203-749-7533
Year Founded: 1944
Assets: $22,000,000
Earnings: $1,700,000
Liabilities: $11,000,000
Net Worth: $11,000,000
Approx.Sls.: $31,000,000
Emp.: 400
Fiscal Year-end: 12/31/91
Export
International Network of Independent Contract Laboratories Providing Engineering, Research & Development, Testing & Quality Assurance, Consulting & Publishing Services for Industry, Government & Trade Associations
S.I.C.: 8734; 8711; 8731; 8748
Corporate Giving Program: Annual Contribution to United Way.
Robert C. Springborn *(Chm. Bd., Pres. Chief Exec. Officer)*
Arthur J. Karszes *(Exec. V.P. & Pres.-Applied Physical Sciences Div.)*
Frederick G. Crocker, Jr. *(V.P. & Chief Fin. Officer & Treas.)*
Robert B. Foster *(V.P. & Pres.-Applied Environmental Sciences Div.)*
Dean E. Rodwell *(V.P. & Pres.-Applied Life Science Div.)*
James P. Galica *(Dir.-Material Sciences Div.)*
John F. Gual *(Dir.-General Consumer Merchandise)*
Thomas D. Vitro *(Dir.-Data Processing & Controller)*
Carol A. Dyjak *(Mgr.-Bus. Admin. & Human Resources)*
Principal(s):
Robert C. Springborn

No. of Mfg. Plants/Facilities: 8
No. of U.S. Offices: 4
No. of Foreign Offices: 4

Computer Systems/Hardware:
Qantel 45; Hewlett Packard; IBM PC & Compatibles

Outside Service Firm(s):

Coopers & Lybrand*(Auditors)*
2300 Bay Bank Tower, 1500 Main St.
Springfield, MA 01101
Tel.: 413-781-7200

Palmer Goodell Insurance Agency*(Group Insurer)*
Springfield, MA

UNUM Corporation*(Group Insurer)*
2211 Congress St.
Portland, ME 04122
Tel.: 207-770-2211
Fax: 207-770-4387

BayBank Valley Trust Company*(Investment Banker)*
BayBank Tower, 1500 Main St.
Springfield, MA 01115
Tel.: 413-781-7575
Fax: 413-734-7252

Cummings & Lockwood*(Legal Firm)*
P.O. Box 120, City Place I - 36th Fl.
Hartford, CT 06103
Tel.: 203-275-6700

BayBank Valley Trust Company*(Major Banking Relationship)*
BayBank Tower, 1500 Main St.
Springfield, MA 01115
Tel.: 413-781-7575
Fax: 413-734-7252

BayBank Valley Trust Company*(Pension Manager)*
BayBank Tower, 1500 Main St.
Springfield, MA 01115
Tel.: 413-781-7575
Fax: 413-734-7252

Divisions:

Mammalian Toxicology Division **(1)**
553 N. Broadway
Spencerville, OH 45887
Tel.: 419-647-4196
Fax: 419-647-6560
Approx.Sls.: $5,000,000
Emp.: 90
Applied Research into the Toxicological Effects of Chemicals & Chemical Mixtures on Biological Systems. Complete Support Facilities (Pathology, Clinical, Analytical). Specialty Areas: Teratology, Combustion, Sensitization, & Regulatory
S.I.C.: 8734
Dean E. Rodwell *(Pres.)*

Springborn Environmental Sciences Division **(1)**
790 Main St.
Wareham, MA 02571
Tel.: 508-295-2550
Fax: 508-295-8107
Approx.Sls.: $10,000,000
Emp.: 170
Environmental Fate & Aquatic Toxicological Testing & Consulting Services to Govt. Agencies & Industries; Leading Supplier of Testing Services to Measure Toxic Effects of Chemicals & Indus. Wastes on Aquatic Organisms; Lab & Field Investigations Pertaining to Inland Estuarine & Offshore Aquatic Environments
S.I.C.: 7389; 8734
Robert B. Foster *(Pres.)*

Springborn Laboratories-Materials Science Division **(1)**
Ten Springborn Center
Enfield, CT 06082
Tel.: 203-749-8371
Telex: 4436041
Fax: 203-749-7533
Approx.Sls.: $2,500,000
Emp.: 20
Applied & Product Oriented Research in Analytical Sciences; Drug & Clinical Analysis; Development of Polymeric Materials, Products, Process & Systems; Engineering Applications & Converting; Energy Research & Development; Environmental Research; Physical & Life Sciences; Informational Analysis; Analogy Testing of Rubber & Plastic; Regulatory Services: Product Registration & Notification
S.I.C.: 8731; 8734

Springborn Laboratories-Testing & QA Division **(1)**
One Springborn Center
Enfield, CT 06082
Tel.: 203-749-8371
Telex: 4436041
Fax: 203-749-7533
Approx.Sls.: $10,000,000
Emp.: 110
Materials & Product Testing, Inspection & Quality Assurance Services; Coordinates Efforts of Sister Laboratories Located in Taiwan, Hong Kong & Switzerland
S.I.C.: 8734
Arthur J. Karszes *(Pres.)*
John Gual *(Dir.-Mktg.)*

Non-U.S. Holdings:

Springborn Laboratories (Europe) AG **(1)**
Seestrasse 21 CH-9326
Horn, Switzerland
Tel.: 413612
Telex: 881536
Fax: 418630
Approx.Sls.: $1,650,000
Emp.: 23
Testing, Analysis Quality Control Laboratory for Textiles, Polymers, Toys, Household Supply, Electrical & Electronic Products; European Headquarters
S.I.C.: 8734
Anton Falk *(Adm. Leader)*

Springborn Laboratories (Hong Kong) Ltd. **(1)**
1004, 10th Fl. Star Centre, 443-451 Castle Peak Rd.
Kwai Chung, N.T. Hong Kong
Tel.: 4233092 (100%)
Telex: 49832
Fax: 4805436
Approx.Sls.: $2,300,000
Emp.: 60
Laboratory for Testing & Inspection of Consumer Products
S.I.C.: 8734
W. H. Kwok *(Lab. Dir.)*

Springborn (Taiwan) Ltd. **(1)**
3F-1, No. 135, Roosevelt Rd. Sec. 3
Taipei, Taiwan R.O.C.
Tel.: 2 391-2391 (100%)
Fax: 2 392-5411
Approx.Sls.: $415,000
Emp.: 12
Laboratory for Testing & Inspection of Consumer Products
S.I.C.: 8734
Sam Kam *(Lab. Dir.)*

SPRINGER SCHMID GROUP
24800 Chagrin Blvd., Ste. 300
Beachwood, OH 44122
Tel.: 216-292-3760
Fax: 216-464-4230
Approx.Sls.: $60,000,000
Emp.: 2,500
Hotel Development & Management
S.I.C.: 6513; 7011
George E. Springer *(Chm. Bd.)*
Al Schmid *(Sr. V.P.)*
Walter A. Miller *(V.P.-Opers.)*
Alberto Chia *(Gen. Mgr.)*

Springwall®

THE SPRINGWALL MATTRESS CO.
(Div. of Schubert Industries Inc.)
1510 Bauer Blvd.
Akron, OH 44305
Tel.: 216-733-8302
Fax: 216-733-5140
Approx.Sls.: $12,000,000

The Springwall Mattress Co.—(Continued)

Emp.: 120
Springwall & Chiropractic Mattresses & Box Springs
S.I.C.: 2515
J.R. Schubert *(Pres.)*
Dick Mankamyer *(Mktg. & Sls.)*

SPROTT OIL CO., INC.
P.O. Drawer 1332
Manning, SC 29102
Tel.: 803-435-8809 **SC**
Fax: 803-435-8549
Year Founded: 1929
Assets: $1,884,152
Liabilities: $761,483
Net Worth: $1,122,669
Approx.Sls.: $10,000,000
Emp.: 23
Fiscal Year-end: 9/30/92
Wholesale Petroleum
S.I.C.: 5172; 5015
H.B. Sprott, Jr. *(Pres. & Chief Exec. Officer)*
H.B. Sprott III *(V.P. & Sec.)*
Jayne Bagnal *(Controller)*
Principal(s):
H.B. Sprott, Jr.

Computer Systems/Hardware:
CADO

Outside Service Firm(s):

Chellis, Mitchum & Co.*(Auditors)*
Summerville, SC

Federated Mutual Insurance Co.*(Commercial Insurance Carrier)*
Owatonna, MN

Blue Cross & Blue Shield of South Carolina*(Group Insurer)*
1517 Laurel St.
Columbia, SC 29201

Coffey, Cooper, Chandler, Du Rant*(Legal Firm)*
Manning, SC

National Bank of South Carolina*(Major Banking Relationship)*
Manning, SC

SPURGEON MERCANTILE COMPANY
822 W. Washington Blvd.
Chicago, IL 60607
Tel.: 312-738-5400
Fax: 312-728-5437
Emp.: 1,700
Junior Department Stores
S.I.C.: 5311
Donald Schumacher *(Pres. & Chief Exec. Officer)*
Eric Anderson *(Controller & Treas.)*
Jeff Olson *(Dir.-Data Processing)*

SQUIRE-COGSWELL COMPANY
3411 Commercial Ave.
Northbrook, IL 60062
Tel.: 708-272-8900
Tel.: 800-448-0770 **IL**
Fax: 708-272-7410
Year Founded: 1916
Approx.Sls.: $20,000,000
Emp.: 120
Fiscal Year-end: 2/28/91
Import Export
Mfr. & Wholesale Distributor of Oil-free Air Compressors & Vacuum Pumps
S.I.C.: 3563; 3821; 5075; 5084
Yvonne Schifter *(Chm. Bd. & Chief Exec. Officer)*
Craig R. Schifter *(Pres.)*
Carol D. Lewis *(Exec. V.P.)*
Greg Pas *(V.P., Chief Fin. Officer & Treas.)*
John Castanes *(Sec.)*
H. Kaht *(Chief Engr.)*
Eric Baum *(Dir.-Pur.)*
Don Dahm *(Dir.-Sls.)*
Martin Jindra *(Dir.-Mktg.)*

Outside Service Firm(s):

American National Bank*(Major Banking Relationship)*
33 North LaSalle St.
Chicago, IL 60690
Tel.: 312-661-6967

Kavathas & Castanes*(Legal Firm)*
Chicago, IL

Subsidiary:

Aeros Instruments, Inc. **(1)**
3411 Commercial Ave.
Northbrook, IL 60062
Tel.: 708-564-8020
Emp.: 65
Import Export
Mfr. of Portable Medical Suction Devices
S.I.C.: 3841
Craig R. Schifter *(Pres.)*
Carol D. Lewis *(Exec. V.P.)*
Jim Koppa *(Gen. Mgr.)*
Martin Jindra *(Dir.-Mktg.)*
Dan Van Arsdale *(Dir.-Sls.)*
Ron Walker *(Dir.-Pur.)*

STABLER COMPANIES, INC.
635 Lucknow Rd.
Harrisburg, PA 17110
Tel.: 717-234-3106
Fax: 717-234-2016
General Contractor; Highway & Street Construction, Manufacture Asphalt Paving Mixtures, Crushed & Broken Limestone
S.I.C.: 3999; 2951; 1422; 1611
Donald B. Stabler *(Chm. Bd.)*
Cyril C. Dunmire, Jr. *(Pres.)*
Burt Crawford *(V.P.-Construction)*
Douglas B. Danko *(Sec.)*
Thomas M. Minori *(Asst. Sec.)*
Richard D. Saiers *(Mgr.-Data Processing)*

Outside Service Firm(s):

KPMG Peat Marwick*(Auditors)*
Canton, OH

Rhoads & Sinon*(Legal Firm)*
Harrisburg, PA

Dauphin Deposit Bank & Trust Co.*(Major Banking Relationship)*
213 Market St.
Harrisburg, PA 17101

Subsidiary:

Stabler Construction Company **(1)**
635 Lucknow Rd.
Harrisburg, PA 17110
Tel.: 717-234-3106
Highway Construction & Reconstruction
S.I.C.: 1611
Donald B. Stabler *(Chm. Bd. & Pres.)*

STACKIG, SANDERSON & WHITE, INC.
7680 Old Springhouse Rd.
McLean, VA 22102
Tel.: 703-734-3300
Fax: 703-760-9734
Year Founded: 1960
Approx.Billings: $46,600,000
Emp.: 70
Business-to-Business, High-Tech, Government & Financial
David Pogue *(Chm. Bd. & Chief Exec. Officer)*
Laurence Rosenfeld *(Pres.)*
David Swanston *(Pres.-Pub. Rels. Div.)*
Walt Rossbach *(Sr. V.P., Pres.-Aerospace/Defense Grp.)*
Deborah League *(V.P., Pres.-Recruitment)*
Ann Marie Avellino *(V.P., Controller)*
Bernie Fitzgerald *(V.P., Gen. Mgr.-FL)*
Tim Letzkus *(V.P.)*
Dr. David Smith *(V.P.)*
Bill Lane *(V.P.)*
Gary Harris *(V.P.)*
Joan Garber *(V.P.)*
Catherine Tolson *(Asst. Dir., Human Resources)*

THE STACKPOLE CORPORATION
133 Federal St., 9th Fl.
Boston, MA 02110
Tel.: 617-423-3520
Fax: 617-350-7263
Year Founded: 1906
Approx.Sls.: $105,000,000
Emp.: 1,900
Fiscal Year-end: 12/31/91
Export
Mfr. of Carbon & Graphite Specialties, Rare Metal Compositions, Rotating Seal Discs for Water Pumps Packing Gland Seals, Ceramic Parts, Permanent Magnets & Powder Metal Products
S.I.C.: 3624
L.G. Hall, Jr. *(Chm. Bd.)*
J.S. Parkhill *(Pres.)*
William W. Teeple *(V.P., Chief Fin. Officer & Treas.)*
Dr. W.T. Brydges *(V.P.-Bus. Devel.)*
A.C. Bailey *(Sec.)*
Robert J. Coffey *(Controller)*
Robyn M Hunter *(Mgr.-Fin.)*
J.I. Saalfield *(Mgr.-Real Estate)*
Jean-Marie Ingeni *(Asst. V.P.)*

Outside Service Firm(s):

Deloitte & Touche*(Auditors)*
2400 One PPG Place
Pittsburgh, PA 15222
Tel.: 412-281-2232

Division:

Pure Carbon Company **(1)**
441 Hall Ave.
St. Marys, PA 15857
Tel.: 814-781-1573
Mfr. of Carbon Graphite Specialties
S.I.C.: 3624
J.D. Quinn *(Pres. & Gen. Mgr.)*

Stackpole Magnet Division **(1)**
700 Elk Ave.
Kane, PA 16735
Tel.: 814-837-7000
Fax: 814-837-7000 x054
Import
Mfr. of Magnets
S.I.C.: 3499
D.L. Williams *(Gen. Mgr.)*

Non-U.S. Holding:

Stackpole Limited **(1)**
550 Evans Ave.
Toronto, ON M8W 2V6, Canada
Tel.: 516-252-9411
Carbon Graphite Specialties
S.I.C.: 3624

STADELMAN FRUIT INC.
314 S. 2nd Ave.
Yakima, WA 98902
Mailing Address:
P.O. Box 1323
Yakima, WA 98907
Tel.: 509-452-8571
Tel.: 800-541-0394 **WA**
Fax: 509-457-6137
Year Founded: 1952
Assets: $13,270,429
Liabilities: $10,277,610
Net Worth: $2,992,819
Approx.Sls.: $11,965,420
Emp.: 650
Fiscal Year-end: 4/31/88
Export
Wholesale Fruit Distributor
S.I.C.: 5148
Pete Stadelman *(Pres., Chief Exec. & Fin. Officer)*
Bob Knight *(Chief Fin. Officer, Controller & Sec.)*
Bill Little *(V.P.)*
Rob Stewart *(Dir.-Sls.)*
Craig Lancaster *(Dir.-Quality Control)*
Perry Menard *(Dir.-Export)*
Larry Lembeck *(Office Mgr.)*
Principal(s):
Pete Stadelman
Mary Little

No. of Mfg. Plants/Facilities: 5
No. of U.S. Offices: 4

Computer Systems/Hardware:
IBM

Outside Service Firm(s):

Moss Adams*(Auditors)*
Yakima, WA

New York Life*(Group Insurer)*
51 Madison Ave.
New York, NY 10010
Tel.: 212-576-6367
Fax: 212-576-6630

Velikanje, Moore& Shore*(Legal Firm)*
Yakima, WA

Bank of California*(Major Banking Relationship)*
Seattle, WA

Equitable Real Estate Investment Managment Inc.*(Pension Manager)*
3414 Peachtree Rd. N.E.
Atlanta, GA 30326-1162

Metropolitan Life Insurance Co.*(Pension Manager)*
One Madison Ave.
New York, NY 10010-3690
Tel.: 215-578-9292

Affiliate:

H & S Fruit Co. **(1)**
Cheyne Rd.
Zillah, WA 98953
Fruit Storage

RUSSELL STADELMAN & COMPANY
3059 Forest Hill Rd.
Germantown, TN 38138
Tel.: 901-755-1391
Fax: 901-754-4672
Year Founded: 1976
Approx.Sls.: $40,440,000
Emp.: 26
Fiscal Year-end: 6/30/91
Import
Importers of Wholesale Hardwoods
S.I.C.: 5031
Russell C. Stadelman, Sr. *(Chm. Bd. & Treas.)*
Russell C. Stadelman II *(Pres.)*
Michael Heitzman *(V.P.-Sls.)*
Shirley M. Stadelman *(Sec.)*
Scott Vanderburg *(Controller)*
Principal(s):
Russell C. Stadelman, Sr.
Russell C. Stadelman II
Shirley M. Stadelman

No. of U.S. Offices: 1
No. of Foreign Offices: 4

Computer Systems/Hardware:
Digital

Outside Service Firm(s):

BDO Seidman*(Auditors)*
2500 Commerce Tower
Memphis, TN 38103-2545
Tel.: 901-523-2303
Fax: 901-525-7478

Sedgwick James*(Commercial Insurance Carrier)*
Memphis, TN

Johnson, Grusin, Kee & May*(Legal Firm)*
Memphis, TN

LaSalle National Bank*(Major Banking Relationship)*
120 S. LaSalle St.
Chicago, IL 60603
Tel.: 312-781-8000

STAHMANN FARMS, INC.
P.O. Box 550
Las Cruces, NM 88005
Tel.: 505-526-2453 **NM**
Fax: 505-526-5160
Approx.Sls.: $20,000,000
Emp.: 450
Pecan Grove
S.I.C.: 0173
William J. Stahmann *(Chm. Bd.)*
Wayne R. Stahmann *(Pres.)*
Deane F. Stahmann, Jr. *(V.P.)*
Ophelia Archer *(Treas. & Sec.)*

Outside Service Firm(s):

KPMG Peat Marwick*(Auditors)*
Las Cruces, NM

STAINLESS INCORPORATED
One Stainless Plaza
Deerfield Beach, FL 33441-4798
Tel.: 305-421-4290
Tel.: 800-877-5177 **MI**
Fax: 305-421-4464
Approx.Sls.: $30,000,000
Emp.: 180
Fiscal Year-end: 3/31/92
Export
Mfr. Custom Stainless Steel Prods. for Construction, Architectural & Food Service Industries
S.I.C.: 2599; 3421; 3446; 3499
Gregory E. Kassab *(Chm. Bd. & Chief Exec. Officer)*
Robert L. Kassab *(Vice Chm., Pres. & Chief Oper. Officer)*
Thomas Kassab *(Exec. V.P.-Mktg.)*
Michael G. Perez *(Sr. V.P.)*
Carol L. Reno *(Sec.)*
Anthony Asher *(Gen. Counsel)*
Maureen Harlan *(Treas.)*
Nestor Ibraham *(Dir.-Pur.)*
David J. Lawler *(Dir.-Data Processing)*
Michael Reno *(Dir.-Sls.)*
Karen L. Hansen *(Corp. Travel Planner)*

No. of Mfg. Plants/Facilities: 3
No. of U.S. Offices: 7
No. of Foreign Offices: 1

Computer Systems/Hardware:
Honeywell

Outside Service Firm(s):

O'Brien, Patroske & Co.*(Auditors)*
Southfield, MI

Manufacturers National Bank N.A.*(Investment Banker)*
38th Fl., 100 Renaissance Center
Detroit, MI 48243
Tel.: 313-222-4227

Sullivan, Wade, Bone, Tyler & Asher*(Legal Firm)*
Southfield, MI

Manufacturers National Bank N.A.*(Major Banking Relationship)*
38th Fl., 100 Renaissance Center
Detroit, MI 48243
Tel.: 313-222-4227

Subsidiary:

Charter House Incorporated **(1)**
4660 136th Ave.
Holland, MI 49424
Tel.: 616-399-6000
Emp.: 50
Mfr. of Wood Products
S.I.C.: 2491
Michael G. Perez *(V.P.)*
Darryl Sult *(Gen. Mgr.)*
Andrea Lyon *(Mgr.-Pur.)*

STAKMORE INC.
Elm St.
Owego, NY 13827
Mailing Address:
P.O. Box 309
Owego, NY 13827
Tel.: 607-687-1616
Fax: 607-687-0049
Year Founded: 1922
Emp.: 90
Export
Manufacturer of Stakmore Folding Furniture
S.I.C.: 2512
David A. Niermeyer *(Pres.)*

Computer Systems/Hardware:
IBM System 36

Outside Service Firm(s):

Anchin, Block & Anchin*(Auditors)*
1375 Broadway
New York, NY 10018

Chemical Banking Corp.*(Major Banking Relationship)*
277 Park Ave.
New York, NY 10041
Tel.: 212-310-6407
Fax: 212-310-4526

STAMCO INDUSTRIES INC.
26650 Lakeland Blvd.
Euclid, OH 44132-2644
Tel.: 216-731-9333
Fax: 216-731-9338
Year Founded: 1983
Approx.Sls.: $12,000,000
Emp.: 95
Fiscal Year-end: 12/31/90
Contract Metal Stampings & Dies Medium to Heavy Gauge
S.I.C.: 3469; 3465
W.E. Sopko *(Pres.)*
L. Reber *(Controller)*
W.F. Hotchkin *(Dir.-Mktg. & Sls.)*
D. Humphreys *(Dir.-Human Resources)*
T. Medved *(Dir.-Quality Assurance)*
F.E. Stanonik *(Plant Mgr.)*
J. Lewandowski *(Chief Engr.)*

Computer Systems/Hardware:
Hewlett-Packard

STAMLER CORPORATION
(An Oldenburg Group Company)
Main & Stamler Sts.
Millersburg, KY 40348
Tel.: 606-484-3431
Year Founded: 1953
Approx.Sls.: $25,000,000
Emp.: 150
Export
Mfr. of Mining & Materials Handling Equipment
S.I.C.: 3532; 3531; 3535
Charles M. Anderson *(Pres. & Chief Oper. Officer)*
James C. Wilson *(Controller)*
Edward H. Ratcliff, Jr. *(Dir.-Engrng.)*

STANBEE COMPANY, INC.
70 Broad St.
Carlstadt, NJ 07072
Mailing Address:
P.O. Box 436
Carlstadt, NJ 07072
Tel.: 201-933-9666
Telex: 7985
Fax: 201-933-7985
Year Founded: 1949
Approx.Sls.: $10,000,000
Emp.: 75
Fiscal Year-end: 12/31/90
Import Export
Mfr. Shoe Components
S.I.C.: 3131
Howard Berkson *(Pres.)*
Stanley Berkson *(Sec. & Treas.)*
Ed Spirko *(Controller)*
Michael Berkson *(Eastern Reg. Mgr.)*
John Walker *(Western Reg. Mgr.)*
Charles Tomesko *(Plant Mgr.)*
Benard Eisenberg *(Technical Dir.)*

STANCHEM INC.
401 Berlin St.
East Berlin, CT 06023
Tel.: 203-828-0571 **CT**
Fax: 203-828-3297
Year Founded: 1969
Assets: $4,000,000
Liabilities: $2,000,000
Net Worth: $2,000,000
Sales Range: $10-19 Million
Emp.: 100
Import Export
Manufacturer of Fire Retardant Paints & Fire Proofing Coatings
S.I.C.: 2851; 2899
W.G. West *(Pres.)*
John C. Lukman *(Exec. V.P.)*
David L. Porter *(V.P.-Fin.)*
W. Casey West *(V.P.-Sls. & Mktg.)*
John R. Abraham *(Controller)*

No. of Mfg. Plants/Facilities: 1
No. of U.S. Offices: 1
No. of Foreign Offices: 1

Computer Systems/Hardware:
NCR

Outside Service Firm(s):

Coopers & Lybrand*(Auditors)*
280 Trumbull St.
Hartford, CT 06103

Robinson, Robinson & Cole*(Legal Firm)*
799 Main St.
Hartford, CT 06103
Tel.: 203-278-0700

Connecticut National Bank*(Major Banking Relationship)*
777 Main St.
Hartford, CT 06115
Tel.: 203-728-2000

Divisions:

Albi Manufacturing Division **(1)**
401 Berlin St.
East Berlin, CT 06023
Tel.: 203-828-0571
Fax: 203-828-3297

Polymer & Specialty Coatings Division **(1)**
401 Berlin St.
East Berlin, CT 06023
Tel.: 203-828-0571
Fax: 203-828-3297

STANCO METAL PRODUCTS, INC.
2101 168th Ave.
Grand Haven, MI 49417-0307
Mailing Address:
P.O. Box 307
Grand Haven, MI 49417
Tel.: 616-842-5000
Fax: 616-842-9080
Approx.Sls.: $17,000,000
Emp.: 110
Auto Hardware, Bathroom Fixtures, Reflector Pans For Electric & Gas Stoves, Splatter Shields
S.I.C.: 3714; 3431; 3444
Warren H. Stansberry, Jr. *(Chm. Bd.)*
Warren H. Stansberry, III *(Pres. & Treas.)*
Gerald L. Slagel *(V.P.-Engrng.)*
Richard Fenske *(Controller & Office Mgr.)*
Nancy Mills *(Mgr.-Personnel)*
Ted Reinecke *(Pur. Agent)*

Outside Service Firm(s):

BDO Seidman*(Auditors)*
Grand Haven, MI

Old Kent Bank & Trust Co.*(Major Banking Relationship)*
Grand Haven, MI

STANDARD ADVERTISING AGENCY
7100 Service Merchandise Dr.
Brentwood, TN 37027
Tel.: 615-660-7980
Fax: 615-660-7912
Year Founded: 1980
Approx.Billings: $15,000,000
Emp.: 12
Retail Adv.
Raymond Zimmerman *(Chm. Bd.)*
Peter Braud *(Chief Fin. Officer)*
Bill Cress *(Operating V.P., Adv. & Mktg.)*

STANDARD BRANDS OF AMERICA, INC.
2199 W. Atlantic Blvd.
Pompano Beach, FL 33069
Tel.: 305-973-6100 **FL**
Fax: 305-971-2561
Year Founded: 1977
Approx.Sls.: $100,000,000
Emp.: 230
Fiscal Year-end: 6/30/90
Retail Televisions, Stereos, Video Cassette Recorders & Household Appliances
S.I.C.: 5731; 5722
Edward H. McCluskey *(Chm. Bd.)*
Edward V. McCluskey *(Pres.)*
Dawn Jenny *(Sec.)*
Matthew Cohen *(Controller)*

STANDARD CANDY CO., INC.
715 Massman Dr.
Nashville, TN 37210-3787
Mailing Address:
P.O. Box 101025,
Nashville, TN 37224-1025
Tel.: 615-889-6360 **TN**
Fax: 615-889-6365
Approx.Sls.: $25,000,000
Emp.: 250
Fiscal Year-end: 6/30/92
Export
Manufacture Candy
S.I.C.: 2064
James M. Fischer, Jr. *(Chm. Bd.)*
James W. Spradley, Jr. *(Pres. & Chief Exec. Officer)*
Michael H. MacDonald *(V.P. & Gen. Mgr.)*
Raymond Peters *(V.P.-Opers.)*
Sharon Jones *(Dir.-Personnel)*
Neil Spradley *(Mgr.-Export)*
Principal(s):
James M. Fischer, Jr.
James W. Spradley, Jr.
James W. Spradley, Sr.

No. of Mfg. Plants/Facilities: 2

Computer Systems/Hardware:
Texas Instruments

Outside Service Firm(s):

Deloitte & Touche*(Auditors)*
424 Church St., Ste. 2400
Nashville, TN 37219-2396

Tune, Entrekin & White*(Legal Firm)*
Nashville, TN

First American National Bank*(Major Banking Relationship)*
First American Center
Nashville, TN 37237
Tel.: 615-748-2000

STANDARD CHLORINE CHEMICAL COMPANY
1015-25 Belleville Tpke.
Kearny, NJ 07032
Tel.: 201-997-1700
Fax: 201-998-4953

Standard Chlorine Chemical Company—(Continued)

Approx.Sls.: $35,000,000
Emp.: 210
Process Chlorinated Benzenes
S.I.C.: 2865
Louis P. Wiener *(Pres.)*
Al Lifson *(V.P.-Sls. & Mktg.)*
Maureen Walsh *(Office Mgr.)*

Outside Service Firm(s):

Samuel Klein & Co.*(Auditors)*
Newark, NJ

Fidelity Bank*(Major Banking Relationship)*
Broad & Walnut St.
Philadelphia, PA 19109

STANDARD COMMUNICATIONS CORPORATION
108 W. Victoria
Carson, CA 90746
Mailing Address:
P.O. Box 92151
Los Angeles, CA 90009-2151
Tel.: 310-532-5300
Telex: 67-7173
Fax: 310-515-7197
Year Founded: 1969
Emp.: 225
Import Export
Manufacturer of Two-Way Communication Equipment & Desalinators
S.I.C.: 3661; 3559
Mark Thomas *(Pres. & Chief Exec. Officer)*
Donald K. Ebeling *(Mgr.-Adv.)*
Lisa Jones *(Mgr.-Personnel)*

Computer Systems/Hardware:
IBM

Outside Service Firm(s):

John Hancock Mutual Life Insurance Co.*(Group Insurer)*
One Financial Center, 44th Floor
Boston, MA 02111
Tel.: 617-348-3707
Fax: 617-350-0305

Bank of America NT&SA*(Major Banking Relationship)*
555 So. Flower St., 5th Fl.
Los Angeles, CA 90071
Tel.: 213-228-3526
Fax: 213-228-4062

First Interstate Bank of California, N.A.*(Major Banking Relationship)*
P.O. Box 3667,
Los Angeles, CA 90051
Tel.: 213-614-4000

STANDARD CORPORATION
455 23rd St.
Ogden, UT 84401
Mailing Address:
P.O. Box 951,
Ogden, UT 84401
Tel.: 801-394-7711
Tel.: 800-234-5505 **NV**
Fax: 801-625-4508
Year Founded: 1888
Approx.Sls.: $67,000,000
Emp.: 600
Television Broadcasting Stations; Newspspers Publishing & Printing, Standard Examiner Daily Newspaper
S.I.C.: 4833; 2711
Wilda G. Hatch *(Pres.)*
George C. Hatch *(Treas.)*
James Barclay *(Dir.-Adv.)*
Patti Woolman *(Dir.-Promo.)*
Blaine Thurgood *(Mgr.-Data Processing)*
Randall C. Hatch *(Publr.)*
Principal(s):
Wilda G. Hatch

Outside Service Firm(s):

First Security Bank of Utah*(Major Banking Relationship)*
2404 Washington Blvd.
Ogden, UT 84401
Tel.: 801-621-0700

STANDARD DUPLICATING MACHINES CORP.
10 Connector Rd.
Andover, MA 01810
Tel.: 508-470-1920
Tel.: 800-526-4774
Fax: 508-470-0819
Year Founded: 1910
Approx.Sls.: $35,000,000
Emp.: 85
Fiscal Year-end: 12/31/91
Import Export
Spirit Duplicating Machines, Digital Duplicators, Friction & Vacuum Collating Systems, Perfect Binders, Paper Cutters, Folding Machines, Numbering Machines, Spine Tapers, Bookletmakers, Heavy Duty Staplers, Drills, Counters, On & Off-Line Laserprint Finishing Equipment
S.I.C.: 3579
L. Guy Reny *(Chm. Bd. & Pres.)*
Timothy G. Reny *(Exec. V.P.)*
Douglas E. Reny *(V.P.-Tech. Services & Distr.)*
Robert M. Blanck *(V.P.-Mktg.)*
David Reny *(V.P.-Sls.)*
Russell Graham *(Treas.)*
Stan Boothby *(Pur. Dir.)*
Bob Comyns *(Mktg. Services Mgr.)*
Neal Swanson *(Mktg. Communications Mgr.)*
John Doherty *(Natl. Sls. Mgr.-Finishing)*
Steven Reny *(Natl. Sls. Mgr.-Reprographics)*

Computer Systems/Hardware:
LAN/Compaq

Division:

Standard Roneo **(1)**
10 Connector Rd.
Andover, MA 01810
Tel.: 508-470-1920
Fax: 508-470-0819

STANDARD ELECTRONICS, INC.
215 John Glenn Dr.
Amherst, NY 14228
Tel.: 716-691-3061
Fax: 716-691-3170
Year Founded: 1946
Approx.Sls.: $38,000,000
Emp.: 68
Wholesale Electronic Parts & Consumer Products
S.I.C.: 5065
Leonard A. Dopkins *(Chm. Bd., Treas. & Sec.)*
William L. Humston *(Pres.)*
Marcy A. DeGain *(Controller)*

Outside Service Firm(s):

BDO Seidman*(Auditors)*
Buffalo, NY

Manufacturers & Traders Trust Company*(Major Banking Relationship)*
1 M & T Plaza
Buffalo, NY 14240
Tel.: 716-842-4200

STANDARD GARMENT COMPANY, INC.
48 W. 37th St.
New York, NY 10018
Tel.: 212-594-0116 **PA**
Year Founded: 1961
Approx.Sls.: $14,000,000
Emp.: 305
Mfr. of Women's, Juniors' & Misses' Dresses, Slacks & T-shirts & Tops Made From Purchased Materials
S.I.C.: 2335; 2331; 2339
Stanley Schwartz *(Pres.)*
Albert Josephs *(V.P. & Treas.)*

Outside Service Firm(s):

Sanders & Daniels Co.*(Auditors)*
New York, NY

Manufacturers Hanover Trust Co.*(Major Banking Relationship)*
P.O. Box 24935, Church St. Station
New York, NY 10249
Tel.: 212-613-7147

STANDARD GRAVURE CORP./ SHEA COMMUNICATIONS
2849 Paces Ferry Rd., Ste. 100
Atlanta, GA 30339
Tel.: 404-431-9077 **KY**
Fax: 404-431-9348
Year Founded: 1922
Sales Range: $100-499 Million
Emp.: 400
Fiscal Year-end: 12/31/90
Offset Printer Specializing in Retail Advertising Supplements
S.I.C.: 2759; 2754; 2752
Michael D. Shea *(Pres.)*
Donald M. McCall *(Exec. V.P.)*
C. David Carley, III *(V.P.-Fin.)*
James Mitchell *(V.P.-Sls.)*
Linda Smith *(Corp. Controller & Sec.)*
Principal(s):
Michael D. Shea

No. of Mfg. Plants/Facilities: 1
No. of U.S. Offices: 5

Computer Systems/Hardware:
IBM AS 400 & 36

Outside Service Firm(s):

BDO Seidman*(Auditors)*
235 Peachtree St. N.E., Ste. 700
Atlanta, GA
Tel.: 404-688-6841

Citizens Fidelity Bank & Trust Co.*(Major Banking Relationship)*
P.O. Box 33000-Citizens Plaza
Louisville, KY 40232
Tel.: 502-581-3381

Divisions:

Standard Gravure d/b/a Oklahoma Graphics **(1)**
5400 N.W. 5th St.
Oklahoma City, OK 73127
Tel.: 405-945-6200
Fax: 405-945-6277
Offset Printers, Mail Order Catalogs & Advertising Supplements
S.I.C.: 2752; 2759
Vernon Rothenberger *(V.P.-Opers.)*
Patrick A. Flynn *(Mgr.-Sls.)*
Cindell Smith *(Dir.-Mfg.)*

STANDARD INDUSTRIES, INC.
3500 S. West Temple
Salt Lake City, UT 84115
Tel.: 801-263-3339
Fax: 801-261-1952
Approx.Sls.: $16,000,000
Emp.: 75
Wholesale Restaurant Equipment
S.I.C.: 5046
Ellery Kingston *(Pres.)*
Rhoda Kingston *(V.P.)*
Rachel O. Young *(Sec.)*

Outside Service Firm(s):

West One Bank*(Major Banking Relationship)*
Salt Lake City, UT

Subsidiaries:

Standard Restaurant Equipment Co. **(1)**
2922 E. McDowell Rd.
Phoenix, AZ 85008
Tel.: 602-275-8550
Emp.: 35
Retail/Wholesale Restaurant Equipment
S.I.C.: 5046
Lewis Lafontaine *(Gen. Mgr.)*
Becky Perry *(Mgr.-Sls.)*

Standard Restaurant Equipment Co. **(1)**
5675 S. Valley View Dr.
Las Vegas, NV 89118-2411
Tel.: 702-798-3998
Emp.: 10
Retail/Wholesale Restaurant Equipment
S.I.C.: 5046
Alan Warenski *(Gen. Mgr.)*
Kim Nelso *(Mgr.-Sls.)*

STANDARD-KNAPP, INC.
127 Main St.
Portland, CT 06480
Tel.: 203-342-1100
Fax: 203-342-0783
Sales Range: $10-19 Million
Emp.: 250
Manufacture Automatic Packaging Equipment
S.I.C.: 3565; 3569
Arthur A. Tanner *(Pres.)*
Barton Bauers, Jr. *(V.P.-Fin.)*
A. John Lorenze *(V.P.-Mktg.)*
John L. Raudat *(V.P.-Engrng.)*
Robert L. Reynolds *(V.P.-Mfg.)*

STANDARD LAFARGE
6715 Tippecanoe Rd.
Canfield, OH 44406
Mailing Address:
P.O. Box 1378
Youngstown, OH 44501
Tel.: 216-533-3338 **OH**
Fax: 216-533-0922
Year Founded: 1914
Approx.Sls.: $40,000,000
Emp.: 800
Fiscal Year-end: 12/31/89
Manufacture Blast Furnace Slag, Sand & Gravel, Limestone & Iron Ore
S.I.C.: 3295; 6719; 1442; 1011; 1499; 2951
D.B. Beart *(Pres. & Chief Exec. Officer)*
R.I. Dillon *(Exec. V.P. & Treas.)*
J.A. Lewis *(Sr. V.P.-Fin.)*
P.S. Ratcliff *(Sr. V.P.-Sls. & Opers.)*
J.D. Beeghly *(V.P.)*
T.G. Brown *(V.P.-Sls.)*
R.E. Loesch *(V.P.-Human Resources)*
P. Sacripanti *(Controller)*
R. Hendrickson *(Gen. Counsel)*
H.A. Gunn *(Dir.-Pur.)*
Barbara L. McNany *(Dir.-Employee Benefits)*
F.R. Ference *(Mgr.-Data Processing)*

No. of Mfg. Plants/Facilities: 20

Computer Systems/Hardware:
IBM System 38

Outside Service Firm(s):

Equitable Real Estate Investment Managment Inc.*(Pension Manager)*
3414 Peachtree Rd. N.E.
Atlanta, GA 30326-1162

Subsidiary:

The Cleveland Builders Supply Co. **(1)**
2100 W. 3rd St.
Cleveland, OH 44113
Tel.: 216-621-4300
Fax: 216-621-2651
Approx.Sls.: $40,000,000
Emp.: 150
Fiscal Year-end: 12/31/90
Mfr. & Distr. of Hard Building Materials; C.B.S.
S.I.C.: 3292; 3272; 5039
Jack Whitlinger *(V.P.-Sls.)*

Bob Pacholewski *(Gen. Mgr.)*
R.J. Mares *(Pur. Agent)*

STANDARD LOCKNUT & LOCKWASHER
1212 S. Rangeline Rd.
Carmel, IN 46032
Mailing Address:
P.O. Box 1900
Carmel, IN 46032
Tel.: 317-846-4231
Tel.: 800-783-6887 **IN**
Fax: 317-573-5515
Year Founded: 1946
Approx.Sls.: $11,500,000
Emp.: 140
Export
Mfr. of Bearings Accessories
S.I.C.: 3549
Robert F. Waddell *(Chm. Bd.)*
R. Scott Waddell *(Pres. & Treas.)*
H. Richard Goddard *(V.P.-Opers.)*
James A. Brown *(V.P.-Sls.)*
Greg Perkins *(V.P.-Systems)*
Edward M. Wetzel *(Controller)*
Joe Weir *(Sr. Mfg. Engr.)*
Chuck Wittum *(Mgr.-Pur.)*

No. of Mfg. Plants/Facilities: 2

Computer Systems/Hardware:
Unisys; Bamcs

Outside Service Firm(s):

K. B. Parrish*(Auditors)*
Indianapolis, IN

Williams & Associates*(Legal Firm)*
Indianapolis, IN

Merchants National Bank & Trust Company of Indianapolis*(Major Banking Relationship)*
One Merchants Plaza, Ste. 901E
Indianapolis, IN 46255
Tel.: 317-267-7109

STANDARD MANIFOLD COMPANY, INC.
4020 N. Tripp Ave.
Chicago, IL 60641
Tel.: 312-282-9600 **IL**
Approx.Sls.: $12,000,000
Emp.: 44
Computers & Accessories; Personal & Home Entertainment; Office Supplies; Wood Office Furniture
S.I.C.: 5045; 5112; 2521
Howard J. MacKenzie *(Chm. Bd.)*
David Fleischmann *(Pres.)*
William Burgman *(V.P.-Mktg.)*
Thomas J. Kreiniker *(Sec. & Controller)*

Outside Service Firm(s):

Altschuler, Melvoin & Glasser*(Auditors)*
30 S. Wecker Dr.
Chicago, IL 60606
Tel.: 312-207-2800

American National Bank & Trust Company of Chicago*(Major Banking Relationship)*
33 N. LaSalle St.
Chicago, IL 60602
Tel.: 312-661-5000
Fax: 312-661-6417

STANDARD MANUFACTURING COMPANY
750 Second Ave.
Troy, NY 12182
Tel.: 518-235-2200
Fax: 518-235-2668
Sales Range: $20-39 Million
Emp.: 600
Mfr. of Men's & Boys' Outerwear
S.I.C.: 2329
George H. Arakelian *(Chm. Bd. & Pres.)*
Richard Brazeau *(V.P. & Controller)*
Dorothy J. Arakelian *(Treas. & Sec.)*

Outside Service Firm(s):

Shutt & Dembo*(Auditors)*
Schenectady, NY

Lombardi, Reinhard, Walsh & Harrison*(Legal Firm)*
Albany, NY

First American Bank, N.A.*(Major Banking Relationship)*
Albany, NY

STANDARD MEDICAL IMAGING, INC.
9002 Red Branch Rd.
Columbia, MD 21045
Tel.: 301-997-1500
Tel.: 800-952-9729 **MD**
Fax: 301-992-9729
Year Founded: 1954
Approx.Sls.: $40,000,000
Emp.: 111
Fiscal Year-end: 12/31/90
Retail Sales, Installation & Repair of X-Ray Equipment, X-Ray Film, Supplies, Accessories & All Medical Imaging Equipment
S.I.C.: 5047; 7629
Martin S. Himeles *(Chm. Bd. & Chief Exec. Officer)*
Roger C. Norden *(Pres.)*
James F. Krieger *(Sr. V.P.)*
Wayne L. Smith *(V.P.-Service & Engrng.)*
Katherine Langenfelder *(Sec.)*
Arthur J. Ostroff *(Treas. & Controller)*
Bill Sanly *(Mgr.-Quality Control)*
Ken Snyder *(Mgr.-Costing)*

No. of U.S. Offices: 4

Outside Service Firm(s):

Berman, Goldman & Ribakow*(Auditors)*
Columbia, MD

Weinberg & Green*(Legal Firm)*
100 S. Charles St.
Baltimore, MD 21202
Tel.: 410-332-8795

NationsBank*(Major Banking Relationship)*
Baltimore, MD

STANDARD PLYWOOD, INC.
Old Laurens Road
Clinton, SC 29325
Tel.: 803-833-6250
Fax: 803-833-6664
Approx.Sls.: $12,000,000
Emp.: 300
Fiscal Year-end: 12/31/90
Mfr. Hardwood, Veneer & Plywood
S.I.C.: 2421
Robert W. Anderson *(Chm. Bd.)*
Donald Finkell *(Pres. & Chief Exec. Officer)*
Harleigh J. Mangum *(V.P.-Fin.)*
Deanna M. Gates *(Sec.)*

STANDARD SHOE COMPANY
1000 S. LaBrea
Inglewood, CA 90301
Tel.: 310-330-3666
Fax: 310-673-5951
Year Founded: 1948
Approx.Sls.: $31,000,000
Emp.: 500
Retail Shoes & Handbags
S.I.C.: 5661; 5632
Larry Schwartz *(Pres.)*
Marvin Martin *(Chief Fin. Officer)*
Bob Sanders *(V.P.)*
Christine Copp *(Controller)*
Don Carr *(Mgr.-Adv.)*

Outside Service Firm(s):

Buchalter, Nemer, Fields & Younger*(Legal Firm)*
601 S. Figueroa St., Ste. 2500
Los Angeles, CA 90017-5704
Tel.: 213-891-0700

First Business Bank*(Major Banking Relationship)*
Los Angeles, CA

STANDARD SUPPLY & HARDWARE
832 Tchoupitoulas St.
New Orleans, LA 70130
Tel.: 504-586-8400
Fax: 504-525-6030
Year Founded: 1909
Approx.Sls.: $50,000,000
Emp.: 275
Wholesale Mill Supplies, Machinery & Hardware
S.I.C.: 5072; 5084; 5085
E.M. Hadden *(Pres.)*
Ron Cancienne *(Mgr.-Sls.)*

Outside Service Firm(s):

Jones, Walker, Waechter, Poitevent, Carrere & Denegre*(Legal Firm)*
Place St. Charles, 201 St. Charles Ave.
New Orleans, LA 70112
Tel.: 504-582-8000

Whitney National Bank of New Orleans*(Major Banking Relationship)*
P.O. Box 61260
New Orleans, LA 70161
Tel.: 504-586-7422

STANDARD TEXTILE CO., INC.
1 Knollcrest Dr.
Cincinnati, OH 45222
Mailing Address:
P.O. Box 371805,
Cincinnati, OH 45222-1805
Tel.: 513-761-9255 **OH**
Telex: 214670
Year Founded: 1940
Approx.Sls.: $200,000,000
Emp.: 1,200
Import Export
Manufacture & Distribute Health Care Textiles & Apparel
S.I.C.: 2311; 2211
Paul Heiman *(Chm. Bd. & Chief Exec. Officer)*
Gary Heiman *(Pres. & Chief Oper. Officer)*
Ernst D. Frankel *(Chief Fin. Officer, Treas., Controller & Sec.)*
Chris Bopp *(Chief Information Officer)*
Mark Heiman *(Exec. V.P.)*
Edward M. Frankel *(V.P. & Gen. Counsel)*
Norman Frankel *(V.P.-Sls. & Mktg.)*
Anthony Tedesco *(V.P.-Mktg. & Fantagraph Div.)*
Jerry Fick *(Sec.)*
Barbara Beuke *(Dir.-Meetings Plng.)*
Jeffrey Taylor *(Dir.-Research & Devel.)*
Principal(s):
Paul Heiman
Mark Heiman

No. of Mfg. Plants/Facilities: 7
No. of U.S. Offices: 4
No. of Foreign Offices: 3

Computer Systems/Hardware:
Honeywell

Outside Service Firm(s):

Deloitte & Touche*(Auditors)*
Chiquita Center, 250 E. 5th St., Ste. 1900
Cincinnati, OH 45202
Tel.: 513-784-7100

Strauss & Troy*(Legal Firm)*
201 E. 5th St., Ste. 2100
Cincinnati, OH 45202
Tel.: 513-621-2120

Fifth Third Bank*(Major Banking Relationship)*
Corporate Trust Services, 38 Fountain Square Plaza
Cincinnati, OH 45263

Provident National Bank*(Major Banking Relationship)*
4140 Hamilton Ave.
Cincinnati, OH
Tel.: 513-681-3900

STANDARD-THOMSON CORPORATION
152 Grove St.
Waltham, MA 02254
Tel.: 617-894-7310 **DE**
Telex: 923448
Fax: 617-894-2235
Year Founded: 1922
Approx.Sls.: $35,000,000
Emp.: 350
Fiscal Year-end: 12/31/91
Import Export
Manufacture Auto & Truck Thermostats, Temperature & Pressure Controls, Bellows
S.I.C.: 3823; 3714; 3599
David R. Paridy *(Pres. & Chief Exec. Officer)*
David J. Nenno *(Exec. V.P. & Gen. Mgr.)*
Peter E. Manzon *(V.P. & Chief Fin. Officer)*
John Peacock *(V.P.-Personnel)*
M. Migliozzi *(Mgr.-Procurement)*
Doris Compton *(Admin. Asst.)*

Computer Systems/Hardware:
Hewlett Packard

Outside Service Firm(s):

Deloitte & Touche*(Auditors)*
Two Prudential Plaza, 180 N. Stetson
Chicago, IL 60601
Tel.: 312-946-2039

STANDARD TOOL & MANUFACTURING COMPANY
738 Schuyler Ave.
Lyndhurst, NJ 07071
Tel.: 201-939-5500
Fax: 201-939-0289
Year Founded: 1910
Approx.Sls.: $20,000,000
Emp.: 200
Fiscal Year-end: 3/31/91
Design & Manufacture Synchronous & Non-Synchronous Transfer Lines & Dial Type Machinery for Assembly & Machining Operations
S.I.C.: 3699; 3599; 3559
Bernard K. Crawford *(Chm. Bd.)*
William F. Crawford *(Pres.)*
Joseph L. Bodnar *(Chief Fin. Officer & Treas.)*
Joseph Coffey *(V.P.-Data Processing)*
Richard George *(V.P.-Sls.)*
William Koons *(Dir.-Indus. Rels.)*
Peter Richardson *(Dir.-Mktg. & Adv.)*
Jane Gemmel *(Pur. Agent)*
Principal(s):
Bernard K. Crawford
William F. Crawford

No. of Mfg. Plants/Facilities: 1

Computer Systems/Hardware:
IBM System 36; CADAM

Outside Service Firm(s):

KPMG Peat Marwick*(Auditors)*
150 John F. Kennedy Pkwy.
Short Hills, NJ 07078
Tel.: 201-467-9650

Fireman's Fund Insurance Co.*(Group Insurer)*
New York, NY

Massachusetts Mutual Life Insurance Co.*(Group Insurer)*
1295 State St.
Springfield, MA 01111
Tel.: 413-788-8411
Fax: 413-730-6144

Shearman & Sterling*(Legal Firm)*
599 Lexington Ave.
New York, NY 10022

Standard Tool & Manufacturing Company—(Continued)

Tel.: 212-848-4000

Skadden, Arps, Slate, Meagher, & Flom*(Legal Firm)*
New York, NY

National Community Bank*(Major Banking Relationship)*
24 Park Ave.
Rutherford, NJ 07070

The Principal Financial Group*(Pension Manager)*
711 High St.
Des Moines, IA 50309
Tel.: 515-247-4593
Tel.: 800-543-4015

STANDARD WELDERS SUPPLY CO.
363 Walnut
Memphis, TN 38126
Tel.: 901-525-6821 **TN**
Fax: 901-525-6821, Ext. 775
Year Founded: 1950
Approx.Sls.: $23,000,000
Emp.: 180
Wholesale Distribution of Welding Machinery & Equipment; Industrial Gases; Oxygen; Hospital Equipment & Supplies
S.I.C.: 5084; 5169; 5047
Robert Q. McEniry *(Chm. Bd.)*
Robert G. McEniry *(Pres.)*
William Vaughan, Jr. *(Exec. V.P.)*
Michael B. Dlugach *(V.P.)*
Barbara D. Faulk *(Asst. Sec.)*

Outside Service Firm(s):

National Bank of Commerce*(Major Banking Relationship)*
Memphis, TN

STANDCO INDUSTRIES, INC.
2701 Clinton Drive
Houston, TX 77020
Mailing Address:
P.O. Box 87
Houston, TX 77001
Tel.: 713-224-6311
Fax: 713-229-9312
Year Founded: 1912
Approx.Sls.: $20,000,000
Emp.: 170
Fiscal Year-end: 10/31/90

Import Export
Mfr. Industrial Products-Stand-Cote Industrial Coating, Gaskets, Oilfield Brake Blocks, Bolts, Primary Flow Elements, API Ring Joint Gaskets, Washpipe
S.I.C.: 3053; 3069; 3452; 3498; 3533
Minor Peeples *(Pres. & Chief Exec. Officer)*
Donald Givens *(V.P.-Mktg. & Sls.)*
Pete Paul *(Admin. Services Mgr.)*

Divisions:

Export Services **(1)**
P.O. Box 87
Houston, TX 77001
Tel.: 713-224-6311
Fax: 713-229-9312
S.I.C.: 3452
Lynn Kennerly *(Export Rep.)*

K&W, A Div. of Standco Industries, Inc. **(1)**
2701 Clintor Dr.
Houston, TX 77020
Tel.: 713-224-6311
Fax: 713-229-9312
Import Export
Mfr. of Metal Gaskets
S.I.C.: 3053
Jim Heath *(Gen. Mgr.)*

Stand-Cote Industrial Coatings Div. **(1)**
P.O. Box 87
Houston, TX 77001
Tel.: 713-224-6311
Fax: 713-229-9312
Specialty Coatings
S.I.C.: 3053; 3069
George Schamberger *(Gen. Mgr.)*

Standco Oilfield Products Div. **(1)**
2701 Clinton Dr.
Houston, TX 77020
Tel.: 713-224-6311
Fax: 713-229-9312
Import Export
Mfr. of Oilfield Related Prods.
S.I.C.: 3533
B. McCrary *(Gen. Mgr.)*

Sterling Rubber & Gasket **(1)**
P.O. Box 87
Houston, TX 77001
Tel.: 713-224-6311
Fax: 713-229-9312
Mfr. of Rubber, Metal & Gasket Prods.
S.I.C.: 3053
Thomas Ahlschier *(Gen. Mgr.)*

STANDUN, INC.
15854 Ornelas St.
Irwindale, CA 91706
Tel.: 818-960-5051 **CA**
Fax: 818-338-1630
Year Founded: 1968
Approx.Sls.: $38,000,000
Emp.: 350
Fiscal Year-end: 12/31/91

Export
Auto Bumpers for Trucks & Industrial Tools
S.I.C.: 3546; 3714
David L. Sharp *(Pres. & Chief Oper. Officer)*
Jay M. Allsup *(Chief Fin. Officer & Treas.)*
Paul W. Westerhoff *(Sec.)*
Terry Karst *(Controller)*

No. of Mfg. Plants/Facilities: 4

Computer Systems/Hardware:
IBM PC

Outside Service Firm(s):

Ernst & Young*(Auditors)*
515 S. Flower St.
Los Angeles, CA 90071
Tel.: 213-621-1666

Smith & Malmrose*(Legal Firm)*
Los Angeles, CA

Security Pacific Corporation*(Major Banking Relationship)*
Security Pacific Plaza
Los Angeles, CA 90071
Tel.: 213-345-6211
Fax: 213-625-0809

Pacific Mutual*(Pension Manager)*
Los Angeles, CA

Operating Units:

Fey Mfg. Co., Inc. **(1)**
15854 Ornelas
Irwindale, CA 91706
Tel.: 818-960-5051
Approx.Sls.: $26,000,000
Emp.: 200
Motor Vehicle Parts & Accessories
S.I.C.: 3714
David L. Sharp *(Pres.)*
Jay Allsup *(Chief Fin. Officer)*
Sherman Ray *(Mgr.-Sls.)*

Sigma Plating Co., Ltd. **(1)**
1040 Otterbein
La Puente, CA 91748
Tel.: 818-965-2561
Approx.Sls.: $1,500,000
Emp.: 55
Electroplating
S.I.C.: 3471
Paul Westerhoff *(Pres.)*

Zephyr Mfg. Co. **(1)**
201 S. Hindry Ave.
Inglewood, CA 90307
Tel.: 213-776-7600
Approx.Sls.: $10,000,000
Emp.: 175
Export
Cutting Tools
S.I.C.: 3545
Bernard Kersulis *(Pres.)*

STANLEY FASTENING SYSTEMS
149 Washington
Worcester, MA 01610
Tel.: 508-795-0909
Fax: 508-752-0138
Year Founded: 1909
Approx.Sls.: $50,000,000
Emp.: 600
Fiscal Year-end: 12/31/90
Import Export
Stanley Fastening Tools & Handtools, Parker/Trojan Power Tool Accessories
Employee Matching Gifts Program: Colleges & Universities 2 for 1; Culture & Arts 1 for 1
Bruce Behnke *(Pres. & Chief Exec. Officer)*
Donald Baldocei *(Exec. V.P.-Opers.)*
Rick Wontka *(Exec. V.P.-Human Resources)*
Ronald Blythe *(V.P.-Consumer Sls.)*
Rick Goff *(Natl. Sls. Mgr.)*

Computer Systems/Hardware:
Hewlett-Packard

STANLEY KNIGHT CORPORATION
3604 Glendora Rd.
New Troy, MI 49119
Tel.: 616-426-4444
Fax: 616-426-4448
Approx.Sls.: $10,000,000
Emp.: 120
Mfr. of Soda Fountain & Food Service Equipment
S.I.C.: 3585; 3556; 3589
Donald J. Badtke *(Chm. Bd. & Pres.)*
John Archer *(V.P. & Controller)*
Bruce E. Nitz *(V.P.-Sls. & Mktg.)*
Al Weisser *(V.P.-Mfg. & Supvr.-Plant)*

Outside Service Firm(s):

Kenefick, Gilmore & Bergerson*(Legal Firm)*
New Troy, MI

Old Kent Bank*(Major Banking Relationship)*
Michigan City, IN

STANLEY STEEMER INTERNATIONAL, INC.
5500 Stanley Steemer Pkwy.
P.O. Box 156
Dublin, OH 43017
Tel.: 614-764-2007
Fax: 614-764-1506
Year Founded: 1947
Approx.Sls.: $100,000,000
Emp.: 250
Fiscal Year-end: 12/31/91
Franchiser of Residential & Commercial Carpet & Upholstery Cleaning Services
S.I.C.: 7217; 3589
Wesley Bates *(Chm. Bd. & Pres.)*
Peter A. Bonfini *(V.P. & Treas.)*
John Hassey *(V.P.-Mktg.)*
Philip P. Ryser *(V.P. & Legal Counsel)*

STANLEY STORES INC.
1400 8th St.
Bay City, TX 77414
Tel.: 409-245-6355 **TX**
Fax: 409-245-1032
Approx.Sls.: $219,000,000
Emp.: 1,250
Supermarkets
S.I.C.: 5411
Olin B. Stanley *(Chm. Bd.)*
Fred C. Stanley *(Pres.)*
Larry Fountain *(V.P.)*
John C. Hancock *(Treas. & Sec.)*
Russell Law *(Gen. Counsel)*
Ron Owens *(Dir.-Pur.)*
Bobby Williams *(Dir.-Data Processing)*
Raymond Matura *(Produce Buyer)*

Outside Service Firm(s):

First State Bank*(Major Banking Relationship)*
Bay City, TX

STAPLE COTTON COOPERATIVE ASSOCIATION
214 W. Market St.
Greenwood, MS 38930
Mailing Address:
P.O. Box 547
Greenwood, MS 38930
Tel.: 601-453-6231
Tel.: 1-800-844-6231 **TN**
Fax: 601-453-6274
Year Founded: 1921
Assets: $44,646,535
Liabilities: $8,170,196
Net Worth: $36,476,339
Approx.Sls.: $517,091,697
Emp.: 157
Fiscal Year-end: 8/31/91

Export
Cooperative for 2,400 Cotton Farmers; Cotton Marketing & Warehousing; Agricultural Financing
S.I.C.: 5159; 4221; 6159
Aven Whittington *(Chm. Bd.)*
Woods E. Eastland *(Pres. & Chief Exec. Officer)*
M.L. Alford *(V.P. & Treas.)*
R.E. Dilatush, Jr. *(V.P. & Sec.)*
Meredith Allen *(V.P.-Mktg.)*
Jimmy C. Garrett *(V.P.-Warehousing)*
Lawrence A. Gnemi *(V.P.-Systems & Controls)*
Virginia White *(V.P. & Asst. Sec.)*
Barry K. Bond *(Mgr.-Data Processing)*
Sterling Jones *(Div. Mgr.-Cotton Services)*
Leo Williams *(Pur. Agent)*

No. of Mfg. Plants/Facilities: 2
No. of U.S. Offices: 9
No. of Foreign Offices: 7

Computer Systems/Hardware:
IBM 4381 & IBM Pc's

Outside Service Firm(s):

Deloitte & Touche*(Auditors)*
Jackson, MS

United States Fidelity & Guaranty Co.*(Commercial Insurance Carrier)*
100 Light Street
Baltimore, MD 21202
Tel.: 301-547-3000

Benmark*(Group Insurer)*
Jackson, MS

Hartford Life Insurance Co.*(Group Insurer)*
Hartford, CT 06104-2999

Lincoln National Life Insurance Co.*(Group Insurer)*
116 E. Berry
Ft. Wayne, IN 46802
Tel.: 219-423-6111

State Mutual Life Assurance Co. of America*(Group Insurer)*
440 Lincoln St.
Worcester, MA 01605
Tel.: 508-852-1000

Whittington, Brock, Swayze & Dale*(Legal Firm)*
Greenwood, MS

CoBank-National Bank for Cooperatives*(Major Banking Relationship)*
Jackson, MS

Deposit Guaranty National Bank*(Major Banking Relationship)*
One Deposit Guaranty Plaza,
Jackson, MS 39201

Nationwide Insurance*(Pension Manager)*
Columbus, OH

Subsidiaries:

Staple Cotton Cooperative Association/Itta Bena **(1)**
P.O. Box 547
Greenwood, MS 38930
Tel.: 601-254-6344
Cotton Storage
S.I.C.: 4225
Jimmy C. Garrett *(V.P.-Warehousing)*

Staple Cotton Discount Corporation **(1)**
P.O. Box 547
Greenwood, MS 38930
Tel.: 601-453-6231
Emp.: 11
Agricultural Lending
S.I.C.: 6159
Jerry Hoover *(V.P. & Chief Oper. Officer)*

STAR BRONZE COMPANY
803 Mahoning St.
Alliance, OH 44601
Mailing Address:
P.O. Box 2206
Alliance, OH 44601
Tel.: 216-823-1550
Year Founded: 1932
Approx.Sls.: $10,000,000
Emp.: 34
Fiscal Year-end: 7/31/90
Manufactures Zip-Strip Paint & Varnish Remover, Zip-Guard Urethane Clear Wood Finish; Pleasuretone Touch-Up Enamel; Zip-Kleen Brush Cleaner; Zip-Sander Liquid Paint Sander; Zip-Strip Liquid Refinisher & Remover; Water Rinsable Paint & Varnish Remover Real-Wood Exterior Wood Preservative; The Wood Preserver Clear Wood Preservative; Zip-Guard Interior Wood Stain; Zip-Guard Environmental Wood Finish
S.I.C.: 2851
R.D. Lytle *(Chm. Bd., Pres. & Chief Exec. Officer)*
Brian W. Miller *(Treas.)*
Harold Barker *(V.P.-Pur.)*
F.H. McGary *(V.P.-Mfg.)*
James A. Raber *(Sec.)*
Carolyn Sutton *(Dir.-Adv.)*
Fred Connelly *(Dir.-Technical)*
Deb Boyd *(Sls. Coord. & Travel Planner)*
Dean Russ *(Pur. Agent)*

Computer Systems/Hardware:
IBM

STAR CHILDREN'S DRESS COMPANY, INC.
112 W. 34th St.
New York, NY 10120
Tel.: 212-279-1524 **NY**
Fax: 212-594-7532
Year Founded: 1953
Assets: $8,400,000
Liabilities: $5,600,000
Net Worth: $2,800,000
Approx.Sls.: $30,000,000
Emp.: 65
Fiscal Year-end: 2/28/91
Export
Mfr. of Girls, Childrens & Infants Dresses
S.I.C.: 2361
Jerome Rosen *(Chm. Bd.)*
Edward Rosen *(Pres.)*
Hermine Rosen *(Sec.)*
Peter Sands *(Controller)*

No. of Mfg. Plants/Facilities: 3

Computer Systems/Hardware:
Wang 5060, VS 65, VS 6

Outside Service Firm(s):

Goldstein, Golub, Kessler & Co.*(Auditors)*
New York, NY

Vogel, Kamay & Spiegler*(Legal Firm)*
New York, NY

Republic National Bank*(Major Banking Relationship)*
355 Lexington Ave.
New York, NY 10017
Tel.: 212-573-5514

Subsidiary:

Virginia Apparel Manufacturing Co., Inc. **(1)**
Rte. 681
Amelia Court House, VA 23002
Tel.: 804-561-5061
Emp.: 90
Mfg. & Processing
S.I.C.: 2361
Jerome Rosen *(Chm. Bd.)*
Edward Rosen *(Pres.)*

STAR CUTTER CO.
23461 Industrial Park Dr.
Farmington Hills, MI 48335
Tel.: 313-474-8200
Fax: 313-474-9518
Approx.Sls.: $35,000,000
Emp.: 450
Import Export
Manufacture Metal Cutting Tools
S.I.C.: 3541
Norman B. Lawton *(Pres.)*
Bradley L. Lawton *(Exec. V.P.)*
Howard C. Didier *(V.P.-Personnel)*
Boyd Moilanen *(V.P.-Fin.)*
Richard McLeod *(V.P.)*
Martin Woodhouse *(V.P.)*
Anthony Ferrante *(Pur. Agent)*
Principal(s):
Norman B. Lawton
Bradley L. Lawton

Computer Systems/Hardware:
Digital

Outside Service Firm(s):

Moore, Smith & Dale*(Auditors)*
23800 W. Ten Mile Rd.
Southfield, MI 48034

Chiro Herrinton Runstadler & Thomas*(Legal Firm)*
2833 Crooks Rd.
Troy, MI 40875

Comerica Bank*(Major Banking Relationship)*
211 W. Fort St.
Detroit, MI 48226
Tel.: 313-222-3300

STAR EXPANSION COMPANY
Pleasant Hill Rd.
Mountainville, NY 10953
Tel.: 914-534-2511
Tel.: 800-247-8274 **NY**
Fax: 914-534-2510
Year Founded: 1903
Sales Range: $20-39 Million
Emp.: 500
Import Export
Mfr. Specialty Anchors & Fasteners for Hollow Wall, Concrete/Masonry & Metal Applications
S.I.C.: 3452
H. Peter Stern *(Chm. Bd.)*
Roland G. Nasser *(Pres.)*
James F. Flynn *(V.P.-Fin.)*
Edward S. Sims *(V.P.-Sls.)*
Spencer L. Koslan *(Sec.)*
Francis X. Fabiano *(Mgr.-Intl. Mktg.)*
D. Bruce Kerr *(Mgr.-Personnel)*
Barry Leach *(Mgr.-Natl. Field Sls.)*
Peter J. Pluger *(Mgr.-Natl. Sls.)*
Ronald Trent *(Supvr.-Opers.)*
Principal(s):
H. Peter Stern

Computer Systems/Hardware:
IBM

Outside Service Firm(s):

Ernst & Young*(Auditors)*
787 Seventh Ave.
New York, NY 10019
Tel.: 212-773-1243

Chemical Banking Corp.*(Major Banking Relationship)*
277 Park Ave.
New York, NY 10041
Tel.: 212-310-6407
Fax: 212-310-4526

Non-U.S. Subsidiaries:

Star Expansion Industries, Ltd. **(1)**
6680 Excelsior Ct.
Mississauga, ON L5T 2J2, Canada
Tel.: 416-564-0586
Fax: 416-0593
Mfr. of Metal Fasteners
S.I.C.: 3452
James Branagh *(Gen. Mgr.)*

Star Expansion Shields Ltd. **(1)**
6680 Excelsior Ct.
Mississauga, ON L5T 2J2, Canada
Tel.: 416-564-0586
Fax: 416-564-0593
Mfrs. Metal Fasteners
S.I.C.: 3452
James Branaugh *(Gen. Mgr.)*

STAR FOOD PROCESSING, INC.
3444 E. Commerce
San Antonio, TX 78220
Tel.: 210-223-4553
Tel.: 800-882-MEAL
Fax: 210-226-7447
Year Founded: 1983
Approx.Sls.: $87,000,000
Emp.: 500
Fiscal Year-end: 12/31/90
Export
Mfr. of Meals-Ready-to-Eat for the Government
S.I.C.: 2099
William Allan *(Chm. Bd.)*
L.C. Robbins *(Pres. & Chief Exec. Officer)*
Clifford Lowe *(Treas. & Sec.)*
Tom Garrett *(V.P.)*
Alan Koerber *(V.P.-Pur.)*

STAR FOOD PRODUCTS, INC.
727 S. Spring St.
Burlington, NC 27215
Tel.: 919-227-4079 **NC**
Fax: 919-227-2109
Year Founded: 1963
Approx.Sls.: $10,000,000
Emp.: 78
Mfr. & Wholesale Distribution of Sausage & Other Prepared, Smoked & Cured Meats
S.I.C.: 2013; 5147
Louise Bell Caudie *(Pres.)*
George L. Bell *(V.P. & Sec.)*
Hugh P. Bell *(V.P.)*

Outside Service Firm(s):

Gilliam, Coble & Moser*(Auditors)*
Burlington, NC

FirstSouth Bank*(Major Banking Relationship)*
Burlington, NC

STAR LIQUOR DEALERS
345 Underhill Blvd.
Syosset, NY 11791
Tel.: 516-921-9300
Fax: 516-921-9038
Year Founded: 1933
Approx.Sls.: $200,000,000
Emp.: 500
Liquor Distributors & Importers
S.I.C.: 5182
Martin Silver *(Pres., Chief Fin. Officer & Treas.)*

No. of Mfg. Plants/Facilities: 1
No. of U.S. Offices: 1

Computer Systems/Hardware:
IBM 4361

Outside Service Firm(s):

Gassman, Rebhun & Co., P.C.*(Auditors)*
New York, NY

Liberty Mutual*(Group Insurer)*
175 Berkeley St.
Boston, MA

National Westminster Bank plc*(Major Banking Relationship)*
West Hempstead, NY

National Westminster Bank plc*(Pension Manager)*
West Hempstead, NY

STAR LUMBER & SUPPLY COMPANY, INC.
325 S. West St.
Wichita, KS 67213
Mailing Address:
P.O. Box 7712,
Wichita, KS 67277
Tel.: 316-942-2221 **KS**
Fax: 316-941-0134
Year Founded: 1939
Approx.Sls.: $62,500,000
Emp.: 485
Fiscal Year-end: 1/31/92
Retail Building Materials
S.I.C.: 5211
Corporate Giving Program: Goebel Family
William J. Goebel *(Co-Chm. Bd.)*
Robert L. Goebel *(Co-Chm. Bd.)*
Christopher J. Goebel *(Pres., Chief Exec. Officer & Chief Oper. Officer)*
Michael G. Goebel *(Exec. V.P.-Mdsg.)*
Roger Voge *(V.P.-Fin)*
Mary Ann Cravens *(V.P.-Admin. & Sec.)*
Steve Briggs *(Controller)*
Pat Doehrer *(Dir.-Mktg.)*
Dave Gregory *(Dir.-Mdsg. & Adv.)*
Don Steiner *(Dir.-Human Resources)*

No. of Mfg. Plants/Facilities: 4

Computer Systems/Hardware:
IBM AS/400

Outside Service Firm(s):

Allen, Gibbs, Houlik*(Auditors)*
301 N. Main, Ste. 1700
Wichita, KS 67202
Tel.: 316-267-7231

Triplett, Woolf & Garretson*(Legal Firm)*
151 N. Main
Wichita, KS 67202
Tel.: 316-265-5700

Bank IV*(Major Banking Relationship)*
P.O. Box 1122,
Wichita, KS 67201
Tel.: 316-261-4304

STAR-PARTS INC.
P.O. Box 160, 125 Butler Dr.
Hazleton, PA 18201
Tel.: 717-455-7548 **NJ**
Fax: 717-454-1477
Year Founded: 1954
Sales Range: $10-19 Million
Emp.: 30
Export

Star-Parts Inc.—(Continued)

Manufacture Commercial Graphic Arts Equipment
S.I.C.: 3861; 3599
S. C. Wilcox *(Pres.)*
William Brior *(Mgr.-Admin.)*
Nancy M. Andrasko *(V.P.-Sls. & Pur.)*
Joseph Peterko *(Dir.-Mfg.)*
Bill Brior *(Dir.-Mktg.)*

No. of Mfg. Plants/Facilities: 1

Computer Systems/Hardware:
IBM PC/AT

Outside Service Firm(s):

Blue Cross of Northeastern Pennsylvania*(Group Insurer)*
Wilkes-Barre, PA

STAR SALES CO., INC.
1803 N. Central
Knoxville, TN 37917
Tel.: 615-524-0771 **TN**
Fax: 615-524-4889
Year Founded: 1988
Approx.Sls.: $14,000,000
Emp.: 90
Wholesale Distrubtion of Notions; Druggists' Sundries; Toys; Florists' Supplies; Artifical Flowers; Automotive Supplies
S.I.C.: 5131; 5122; 5092; 5193; 5013
Neil Foster *(Pres. & Chief Exec. Officer)*
Kenneth Apple *(V.P.)*
Bill Guffey *(V.P.)*
J.C. Ridenour *(V.P.)*

Outside Service Firm(s):

Perry Hamilton & Co.*(Auditors)*
Knoxville, TN

First Tennessee Bank, N.A.*(Major Banking Relationship)*
Knoxville, TN

STAR VIDEO ENTERTAINMENT, L.P.
550 Grand St.
Jersey City, NJ 07302
Tel.: 201-333-4600
Fax: 201-333-1609
Year Founded: 1979
Assets: $25,000,000
Liabilities: $20,000,000
Net Worth: $5,000,000
Approx.Sls.: $60,000,000
Emp.: 180
Distribute Pre-Recorded Video Cassettes
S.I.C.: 5099
Bernard Herman *(Pres.)*
Bach Arthur *(V.P.)*
Richard Goffman *(V.P.)*
Steven Lam *(V.P.-Fin.)*
Fran Stevens *(Controller)*

Computer Systems/Hardware:
Qantel 64

Outside Service Firm(s):

Bloom, Hochberg & Co.*(Auditors)*
New York, NY

Travelers Insurance Co.*(Group Insurer)*
1 Tower Square
Hartford, CT 06183
Tel.: 203-222-7821
Fax: 203-222-7813

Budd Larner*(Legal Firm)*
Short Hills, NJ

STARCRAFT AUTOMOTIVE CORP.
2703 College Ave.
Goshen, IN 46526
Mailing Address:
P.O. Box 1903,
Goshen, IN 46526
Tel.: 219-533-1105 **DE**
Fax: 219-533-7180
Year Founded: 1903
Sales Range: $100-499 Million
Emp.: 600
Fiscal Year-end: 12/31/90
Export
Manufacture of Starcraft Van Conversions, Specialized Vehicles
S.I.C.: 3716
Kelly L. Rose *(Chm. Bd.)*
Richard A. Newberry *(Pres. & Chief Oper. Officer)*
Rikki F. Kain *(V.P.-Fin.)*
Joseph G. Martin *(V.P.-Pur.)*
Greg B. Hardin *(V.P.-Sls.)*
David Hildebrandt *(V.P.-Intl. Sls.)*
Bradley Lemler *(Controller)*
Frank Ermeti *(Dir.-Human Resources)*

No. of Mfg. Plants/Facilities: 6
No. of U.S. Offices: 5
No. of Foreign Offices: 1

Computer Systems/Hardware:
Burroughs

Outside Service Firm(s):

Arthur Andersen & Co.*(Auditors)*
33 W. Monroe St.
Chicago, IL 60603-4067
Tel.: 312-580-0033
Fax: 312-507-6748

Kemper Insurance*(Commercial Insurance Carrier)*
Atlanta, GA

Northwestern National Life*(Group Insurer)*
20 Washington Ave. S.
Minneapolis, MN 55401

Salomon Brothers*(Investment Banker)*
Chicago, IL

Barnes & Thornburg*(Legal Firm)*
100 N. Michigan., Ste. 600
South Bend, IN 46601
Tel.: 219-233-1171

Citibank N.A.*(Major Banking Relationship)*
Corporate Trust Services, 399 Park Ave.
New York, NY 10043
Tel.: 212-559-1605

INB Bank*(Pension Manager)*
Indianapolis, IN

STARCREST PRODUCTS OF CALIFORNIA
3660 Brennan Ave.
Perris, CA 92370
Tel.: 909-943-2011 **DE**
Fax: 909-943-2971
Year Founded: 1971
Approx.Sls.: $140,000,000
Emp.: 750
Fiscal Year-end: 12/31/91
Mail Order House
S.I.C.: 5961
T.M. Calandra *(Pres.)*
M. Donnelly *(V.P.)*
Betty Abramson *(Dir.-Personnel & Acctg.)*

Computer Systems/Hardware:
IBM 4341 & 4381

Outside Service Firm(s):

Lincoln National Life Insurance Co.*(Group Insurer)*
San Mateo, CA

City National Bank*(Major Banking Relationship)*
Newport Beach, CA

Divisions:

Handsome Rewards **(1)**
3660 Brennan Ave.
Perris, CA 92370
Tel.: 909-943-2011
Fax: 909-943-2971
Mail Order House
S.I.C.: 5961
T.M. Calandra *(Pres.)*
M. Donnelly *(V.P.)*
Betty Abramson *(Dir.-Personnel & Acctg.)*

Signatures **(1)**
3660 Brennan Ave.
Perris, CA 92370
Tel.: 909-943-2011
Fax: 909-943-2971
Computer Systems/Hardware:
IBM 4341 & 4381
Mail Order House
S.I.C.: 5961
T.M. Calandra *(Pres.)*
M. Donnelly *(V.P.)*
Betty Abramson *(Dir.-Personnel & Acctg.)*

Starcrest of California **(1)**
3660 Brennan Ave.
Perris, CA 92370
Tel.: 909-943-2011
Fax: 909-943-2971
Computer Systems/Hardware:
IBM 4341 & 4381
Mail Order House
S.I.C.: 5961
T.M. Calandra *(Pres.)*
M. Donnelly *(V.P.)*
Betty Abramson *(Dir.-Personnel & Acctg.)*

STARKEY LABORATORIES, INC.
6700 Washington Ave. S.
Eden Prairie, MN 55344
Mailing Address:
P.O. Box 9457
Eden Prairie, MN 55344
Tel.: 612-941-6401 **MN**
Fax: 612-828-9262
Year Founded: 1968
Approx.Sls.: $225,000,000
Emp.: 2,325
Fiscal Year-end: 12/31/91
Import Export
Mfr. & Repair of Custom In-The-Ear Hearing Aids
S.I.C.: 3842; 7699; 3800
William F. Austin *(Pres., Sec. & Treas.)*
Jim Bremer *(V.P.-Credit)*
Cindy Dawson *(V.P.-Professional Rels.)*
Mike Jones *(V.P.-Intl.)*
Jerry Ruzicka *(V.P.-Mfg.)*
Dale Thorstad *(V.P.-Opers.)*

No. of Mfg. Plants/Facilities: 22
No. of U.S. Offices: 13
No. of Foreign Offices: 9

Computer Systems/Hardware:
Unisys

Branch:

NuEar Electronics **(1)**
10070 Mesa Rim Rd.
San Diego, CA 92121
Tel.: 619-450-9972
Mfr. of Hearing Aids
S.I.C.: 3842; 3800
Roy Bain *(Managing Dir.)*

J-STARR INDUSTRIES, INC.
801 Janesville Ave.
Fort Atkinson, WI 53538
Tel.: 414-563-5521
Tel.: 800-325-8595
Fax: 414-563-5521 Ext. 398
Approx.Sls.: $28,000,000
Emp.: 200
Mfr. Barn Cleaners, Mechanical Cattle Feeders, Volumaster Silo Unloaders, Big Jim Silo System for Loading & Unloading Silos, Feed Mixers, Scales, Manure Handling Equip.
S.I.C.: 3523
John Neil *(Pres.)*
Mike Phelps *(Controller)*
Dean Hanke *(Adv. Mgr.)*
Bill Stevens *(Personnel Mgr.)*

STARR SEIGLE MCCOMBS, INC.
Pacific Tower, 19th Fl., 1001 Bishop St.
Honolulu, HI 96813
Tel.: 808-524-5080
Fax: 808-523-7443
Year Founded: 1956
Approx.Billings: $35,500,000
Emp.: 90
Jack M. Seigle *(Chm. & Chief Exec. Officer)*
Stewart W. McCombs *(Pres.)*
John Lochridge *(Sr. V.P., Acct. Service)*
John Sutton *(Sr. V.P., Fin.)*

STARVING STUDENTS, INC.
8525 W. Pico Blvd., 2nd Floor
Los Angeles, CA 90035
Mailing Address:
P.O. Box 351206,
Los Angeles, CA 90035
Tel.: 310-854-4464 **CA**
Fax: 310-854-6913
Year Founded: 1973
Assets: $2,778,358
Net Worth: $2,778,358
Approx.Sls.: $15,000,000
Emp.: 400
Fiscal Year-end: 12/31/91
Moving & Storage
S.I.C.: 4212; 4225
Ethan Harold Margalith *(Chm. Bd., Chief Exec. Officer & Treas.)*
Mark A. Ciccone *(V.P.-Opers.)*
Steven Levan *(V.P.-Fin. & Admin.)*
Tony Schaffer *(V.P.-Mktg.)*
Suzanne Conley *(Controller)*
Glenn Heald *(Dir.-Mktg.)*
Principal(s):
Ethan Harold Margalith

No. of U.S. Offices: 25

Outside Service Firm(s):

Duitch & Franklin*(Auditors)*
Los Angeles, CA

Move-Pak*(Commercial Insurance Carrier)*
Los Angeles, CA

MetLife HealthCare Network of California, Inc.*(Group Insurer)*
Long Beach, CA

Hirschtick, Chenen, Lemon & Curtis*(Legal Firm)*
Los Angeles, CA

Bank of America*(Major Banking Relationship)*
701 S. Western Ave.
Los Angeles, CA 91201

STATE ELECTRIC SUPPLY CO.
210 20th St.
Huntington, WV 25703
Tel.: 304-523-7491 **WV**
Approx.Sls.: $70,000,000
Emp.: 350
Wholesale Electrical Supplies
S.I.C.: 5063
Arthur Weisberg *(Chm. Bd.)*
John Spoor *(Pres.)*
Clarence Martin *(Exec. V.P., Treas. & Sec.)*
Shirley Blake *(V.P.-Sls.-Dunbar)*
Richard Jeffrey *(V.P.-Sls.-Parkersburg)*

Arnold Moore *(Mgr.-Sls. & Mktg.)*
Principal(s):
Arthur Weisberg

Outside Service Firm(s):

Hayflich & Steinberg*(Auditors)*
Huntington, WV

R. M. Levy*(Legal Firm)*
Huntington, WV

Twentieth Street Bank*(Major Banking Relationship)*
Huntington, WV

STATE FARM MUTUAL AUTOMOBILE INSURANCE COMPANY
One State Farm Plaza
Bloomington, IL 61710
Tel.: 309-766-2311 **IL**
Fax: 309-766-1783
Year Founded: 1922
Assets: $42,676,020,049
Liabilities: $22,954,919,948
Net Worth: $19,721,100,101
Approx.Sls.: $19,592,725,473
Emp.: 58,113
Fiscal Year-end: 12/31/91
Casualty Insurance
S.I.C.: 6331; 6311
Edward B. Rust, Jr. *(Chm. Bd., Pres. & Chief Exec. Officer)*
Vincent J. Trosino *(Chief Oper. Officer & Exec. V.P.)*
Roger Joslin *(Sr. V.P. & Treas.)*
Charles Wright *(V.P.-Agency)*
Bruce Callis *(V.P.)*
Alan Curry *(V.P. & Actuary)*
Cranford A. Ingham *(V.P. & Gen. Counsel)*
Roger Lehman *(V.P.)*
Daniel F. McNertney *(V.P.-Adv.)*
James E. Rutrough *(V.P.-Personnel)*
Laura P. Sullivan *(V.P. & Sec.)*
Don Bittner *(Dir.-Adv.)*
R.S. Bugajski *(Dir.-Adv.)*
Robert L. Denny *(Dir.-Agency Sls., Devel. & Promo. Services)*
Laura Garrett *(Librarian)*

No. of Foreign Offices: 1

Computer Systems/Hardware:
IBM; Hewlett-Packard

Outside Service Firm(s):

Coopers & Lybrand*(Auditors)*
203 N. LaSalle St.
Chicago, IL 60601
Tel.: 312-701-5500

State Farm Mutual Automobile Insurance Co.*(Group Insurer)*
Bloomington, IL

Common Management Companies:

State Farm County Mutual Insurance Co. of Texas **(1)**
17301 Preston Rd.
Dallas, TX 75379
Tel.: 214-250-5000 (100%)
Casualty Insurance
S.I.C.: 6331
Phil Able *(Div. Mgr.-W. Texas)*
Tom Larson *(Div. Mgr.-E. Texas)*
Harry Ostrom *(Div. Mgr.-Dallas)*
Lloyd Parker *(Div. Mgr.-Ft. Worth)*

State Farm Lloyds, Inc. **(1)**
17301 Preston Rd.
Dallas, TX 75379
Tel.: 214-250-5000 (100%)
Property Insurance
S.I.C.: 6331
Harold D. Covey *(V.P. & Chief Admin. Officer)*

Subsidiaries:

State Farm Fire and Casualty Co. **(1)**
112 E. Washington St.
Bloomington, IL 61701
Tel.: 309-766-2311 (100%)
Approx.Sls.: $6,351,426,184
Emp.: 11,104
Property Insurance
S.I.C.: 6331
Harold D. Covey *(Exec. V.P., Treas. & Chief Admin. Officer)*

State Farm General Insurance Co. **(1)**
112 E. Washington St.
Bloomington, IL 61701
Tel.: 309-766-2311 (100%)
Property Insurance
S.I.C.: 6331
Harold D. Covey *(Exec. V.P., Treas. & Chief Admin. Officer)*

State Farm Life Insurance Co. **(1)**
One State Farm Plaza
Bloomington, IL 61710
Tel.: 309-766-2311 (100%)
Approx.Sls.: $1,992,185,378
Emp.: 1,936
Life Insurance
S.I.C.: 6311
Marvin D. Bower *(Chm. Bd.)*
Glenn A. Britt *(Exec. V.P.)*
C.R. Charlson *(V.P. & Sec.)*

State Farm Life and Accident Assurance Co. **(1)**
One State Farm Plaza
Bloomington, IL 61710
Tel.: 309-766-2311 (100%)
Life Insurance
S.I.C.: 6311
Glen A. Britt *(Exec. V.P. & Treas.)*

STATE INDUSTRIES INC.
500 Bypass Rd.
Ashland City, TN 37015
Tel.: 615-792-4371
Tel.: 800-365-0024
Telex: 78-6510
Fax: 800-365-3298
Assets: $100,000,000
Net Worth: $100,000,000
Approx.Sls.: $325,000,000
Emp.: 1,500
Fiscal Year-end: 10/31/90
Export
Manufactures Waterheaters & Pump Tanks
S.I.C.: 3639; 3561
John Lindahl *(Chm. Bd. & Chief Exec. Officer)*
Herbert W. Lindahl *(Pres. & Chief Oper. Officer)*
Joseph V. Lanier *(Chief Fin. Officer & V.P.-Fin.)*
John Lindahl, Jr. *(V.P.-Sls.)*
Phil Loughrey *(V.P.-Mktg.)*
Jim Raymer *(V.P.-Pur.)*
Hilda Wilsdorf *(V.P.-Customer Service)*
Michael Lalor *(Treas.)*
T. R. Gainer *(Controller)*
Stan Hahn *(Mgr.-Export)*
Roy Paul *(Mgr.-Data Processing)*
Principal(s):
John Lindahl
Herbert W. Lindahl

Computer Systems/Hardware:
IBM 4381

Outside Service Firm(s):

Lattimore, Black, Morgan & Cain*(Auditors)*
Nashville, TN

King & Spalding*(Legal Firm)*
Trust Co. Tower
Atlanta, GA 30303
Tel.: 404-572-4600

Bankers Trust Co.*(Major Banking Relationship)*
Nashville, TN

Merrill Lynch*(Pension Manager)*
P.O. Box 20, World Trade Center
New York, NY 10281
Tel.: 212-449-4843

Sovran Bank*(Pension Manager)*
One Commerce Place M-B
Nashville, TN 37219
Tel.: 615-749-4113

Subsidiary:

Apcom Inc. **(1)**
Hwy. 49 South
Ashland City, TN 37015
Tel.: 615-792-4371

STATE VOLUNTEER MUTUAL INSURANCE CO. INC.
101 W. Park Dr.
Brentwood, TN 37027
Mailing Address:
P.O. Box 1065
Brentwood, TN 37024
Tel.: 615-377-1999
Fax: 615-377-9192
Year Founded: 1975
Assets: $268,274,000
Liabilities: $221,691,000
Net Worth: $46,583,000
Approx.Sls.: $59,000,000
Emp.: 46
Fiscal Year-end: 12/31/89
Medical Malpractice, Property & Casualty Insurance
S.I.C.: 6321; 6331; 6351
Dr. Allen S. Edmonson *(Chm. Bd.)*
Dr. William H. Edwards *(Pres.)*
Steven C. Williams *(Chief Exec. Officer)*
Harold R. Burch *(Sr. V.P.-Claims)*
John M. Gilbert *(Sr. V.P.-Mktg.)*
Terry R. Blankenship *(V.P.-Mngmt. Information Systems)*
David R. Cole *(V.P.-Loss Prevention)*
Steven C. Williams *(Chief Oper. Officer)*
Robert P. Boren *(Chief Fin. Officer)*

Computer Systems/Hardware:
Hewlett-Packard 3000

Outside Service Firm(s):

Arthur Andersen & Co.*(Auditors)*
Third Natl. Fin. Cntr., 424 Church St., Ste. 1100
Nashville, TN 37219

First American Bank, N.A.*(Major Banking Relationship)*
Nashville, TN

STATE-WIDE CAPITAL CORP.
152 EAB Plaza, W. Tower 7th Fl.
Uniondale, NY 11556-0152
Tel.: 516-683-9500 **NY**
Emp.: 35
Licensed Mortgage Bankers in NY, NJ & CT
S.I.C.: 6162
Stephen A. Sobin *(Pres.)*
Mark S. Rubin *(Exec. V.P.)*
Leon Schenker *(Controller)*

Outside Service Firm(s):

Empire Blue Cross & Blue Shield*(Group Insurer)*
New York, NY

Guardian Life Insurance Co.*(Group Insurer)*
New York, NY

Lawrence Rigie, Esq.*(Legal Firm)*
White Plains, NY

Chemical Bank*(Major Banking Relationship)*
Great Neck, NY

Pension Service, Inc.*(Pension Manager)*
New York, NY

STATES, INC.
300 N. Breckenridge Ave.
Breckenridge, TX 76024
Mailing Address:
P.O. Box 911
Breckenridge, TX 76424
Tel.: 817-559-3355 **TX**
Fax: 817-559-3220
Year Founded: 1984
Emp.: 100
Fiscal Year-end: 2/28/91
Oil & Gas Production
S.I.C.: 1311
Lester Clark *(Chm. Bd.)*
John H. Connally *(Pres.)*
Fred F. Dueser *(Chief Exec. Officer)*
O.H. Reaugh *(Sr. V.P. & Asst. Sec.)*
E. Bruce Street *(V.P.)*
M. Boyd Street *(V.P.)*
Conner Stamper *(Treas.)*
C. R. Anderson *(Gen. Counsel)*
Ronald L. Holloway *(Sec.)*
Paul Prater *(Dir.-Real Estate)*
Jerry Robison *(Dir.-Data Processing)*
Grady R. Ware *(Dir.-Personnel)*
Eileen Speer *(Corp. Records Administrator)*

No. of U.S. Offices: 1

Computer Systems/Hardware:
IBM AS/400

Outside Service Firm(s):

General American Life Insurance Co.*(Group Insurer)*
Dallas, TX

Gulf Insurance Co.*(Commercial Insurance Carrier)*
Dallas, TX

Thompson & Knight*(Legal Firm)*
Republic National Bank
Dallas, TX 75201
Tel.: 214-655-7500

First National Bank*(Major Banking Relationship)*
P.O. Box 2260
Ft. Worth, TX 76101
Tel.: 817-390-6779

Team Bank*(Major Banking Relationship)*
P.O. Box 2604,
Fort Worth, TX 76113
Tel.: 817-884-4614

Subsidiary:

Breck Operating Corp. **(1)**
300 N. Breckenridge Ave.
Breckenridge, TX 76424
Tel.: 817-559-3355
Fax: 817-559-3220
Emp.: 90
Oil & Gas Properties
S.I.C.: 6519
Fred F. Dueser *(Chief Exec. Officer)*

STATLER INDUSTRIES
300 Middlesex Ave.
Medford, MA 02155
Tel.: 617-395-7770 **MA**
Year Founded: 1968
Approx.Sls.: $70,000,000
Emp.: 600
Export
Manufacture & Distribute Paper, 100% Recycled Sanitary Paper Products; Paper Napkins, Towels, Bath Tissues, Facial Tissues
S.I.C.: 2621; 2676
Leonard Sugarman *(Chm. Bd., Pres. & Chief Exec. Officer)*
Edward Minchello *(V.P.- Mfg.)*
Paul Sugarman *(Treas.)*
Steve Freed *(Controller)*
Harris Baseman *(Sec.)*
G.A. Parlee *(Dir.-Human Resources)*

Computer Systems/Hardware:
IBM

Outside Service Firm(s):

KPMG Peat Marwick*(Auditors)*
One Boston Place
Boston, MA 02108
Tel.: 617-723-7700

Blue Cross of Massachusetts, Inc.*(Group Insurer)*
Boston, MA

Statler Industries—(Continued)

Bernkopf, Goodman & Baseman*(Legal Firm)*
Boston, MA

U.S. Trust Co.*(Major Banking Relationship)*
30 Court St.
Boston, MA 02108

Subsidiary:

Doeskin Co. **(1)**
300 Middlesex Ave.
Medford, MA 02155
Tel.: 617-395-7770
Paper Prods.
S.I.C.: 2621

STATTON FURNITURE MANUFACTURING COMPANY
504 E. First St.
Hagerstown, MD 21740
Tel.: 301-739-0360
Fax: 301-739-8421
Year Founded: 1926
Approx.Sls.: $12,000,000
Emp.: 198
Manufacture Wood Furniture
S.I.C.: 2511; 2512
Philip J. Statton *(Pres.)*
Thomas H. Hardinge, III *(V.P.-Sls. & Mktg., Treas. & Sec.)*
David B. Statton *(Sls. Rep.)*
Thomas M. Statton *(Plant Mgr.)*

Outside Service Firm(s):

Keller Zanger Company*(Auditors)*
Frederick, MD

Lacy Wright*(Legal Firm)*
Martinsburg, MD

First National Bank of Maryland*(Major Banking Relationship)*
25 S. Charles St.
Baltimore, MD 21201
Tel.: 410-244-4025

STAUCH VETROMILE & MITCHELL ADVERTISING, INC.
55 S. Brow St.
East Providence, RI 02914
Tel.: 401-438-0614
Fax: 401-438-9140
Year Founded: 1971
Approx.Billings: $11,500,000
Emp.: 17
Business-to-Business Adv., Mktg. & Pub. Rels.
Manfred R. Stauch *(Pres. & Adv.)*
Robert W. Vetromile *(Pres., Pub. Rels. & Creative Dir.)*
Molla Lavett *(V.P., Controller)*
Cynthia Pennoyer *(Asst. Controller)*
Suzanne Vetromile *(Admin.)*

STAUFFER COMMUNICATIONS, INC.
616 Jefferson St.
Topeka, KS 66607
Tel.: 913-295-1111 **DE**
Fax: 913-295-1198
Fax: 913-295-1144
Year Founded: 1930
Assets: $113,995,226
Earnings: $5,030,604
Liabilities: $43,694,680
Net Worth: $70,300,546
Approx.Sls.: $133,609,505
Emp.: 2,300
Fiscal Year-end: 12/31/91
Import Export
Newspaper Publishers; Radio & TV
S.I.C.: 2711; 4832; 4833
John H. Stauffer *(Chm. Bd. & Pres.)*
Frank H. Shepherd *(Exec. V.P. & Chief Oper. Officer)*
Kenneth C. Bronson *(V.P.-Newspapers)*
E. Van Anderson *(V.P.-National Media)*
Gerald N. Holley *(V.P.-Television)*
William D. Duckworth *(V.P., Corp. Treas. & Asst. Sec.)*
Robert D. Fromme *(V.P.-Radio)*
David A. Beliles *(V.P.-Newspapers)*
Thomas H. Collinson *(Asst. V.P.-Newapapers)*
Peter W. Stauffer *(Asst. V.P.-Newspapers)*
Donald R. Keating *(Asst. V.P.-Natl. Media)*
Rockford E. Smith *(Asst. V.P.-Computer Sls.)*
Debra G. Turner *(Asst. V.P.-Human Resources)*
Darrel K. Fry *(Controller)*
John H. Stauffer, Jr. *(Gen. Counsel & Corp. Sec.)*

Newspaper Operations:

The Ardmore Daily Ardmoreite **(1)**
117 W. Broadway
Ardmore, OK 73402
Tel.: 405-223-2200 (100%)
Fax: 405-226-2363
Emp.: 46
Newspaper
S.I.C.: 2711
William H. Stauffer *(Publr.)*
Barbara Winkler *(Adv. Mgr.)*
Kathy Worley *(Bus. Mgr.)*
Jim Hefley *(Mgr.-Circulation)*

The Arkansas City Daily Traveler **(1)**
P.O. Box 988, 5th Ave. & A St.
Arkansas City, KS 67005
Tel.: 316-442-4200 (100%)
Fax: 316-442-7438
Emp.: 22
Newspaper
S.I.C.: 2711
Kim M. Benedict *(Publr.)*
Carol Kincaid *(Bus. Mgr.)*
Shari Redd *(Mgr.-Circulation)*

Auburndale Star **(1)**
213 E. Lake Ave., Box 126
Auburndale, FL 33823
Tel.: 813-967-4134
Fax: 813-967-2707
Newspaper
S.I.C.: 2711
Larry Beasley *(Publr.)*
Mary Schaal *(Bus. Mgr.)*
Jim Johnson *(Mgr.-Circulation)*
Pam Breuggeman *(Mgr.-Adv.)*

Blue Springs Examiner **(1)**
P.O. Box 1057, 500 W. R.D. Mize Rd.
Blue Springs, MO 64013
Tel.: 816-229-9161 (90%)
Fax: 816-224-2806
Emp.: 12
Newspaper
S.I.C.: 2711
Daniel S. Collinson *(Publr.)*
Irene Baltrusaitis *(Adv. Mgr.)*
Becky Ely *(Bus. Mgr.)*
Kevin Kampman *(Mgr.-Circulation)*

Brainerd Daily Dispatch **(1)**
506 James St. Box D
Brainerd, MN 56401
Tel.: 218-829-4705 (100%)
Fax: 218-829-7735
Emp.: 55
Newspaper
S.I.C.: 2711
Terry J. McCollough *(Publr.)*
Joe Smart *(Mgr.-Adv.)*
Joyce Caughey *(Mgr.-Bus.)*
Greg Guenin *(Mgr.-Circulation)*

Dodge City Daily Globe **(1)**
705 Second St., Box 820
Dodge City, KS 67801
Tel.: 316-225-4151
Fax: 316-225-4154
Newspaper
S.I.C.: 2711
Peter J. Esser, III *(Publr.)*
Susan Conrardy *(Bus. Mgr.)*
Terry Cochran *(Mgr.-Circulation & Adv.)*

Dodge City Shopper's Weekly **(1)**
316 W. Wyatt Earp
Dodge City, KS 67801
Tel.: 316-225-1114
Fax: 316-225-0014
Shopper News Publication
S.I.C.: 2711
Peter J. Esser, III *(Publr.)*
Judy Stand *(Gen. Sls. Mgr.)*

Glenwood Post **(1)**
P.O. Box 550, 2014 Grand Ave.
Glenwood Springs, CO 81602
Tel.: 303-945-8515 (100%)
Fax: 303-945-4487
Emp.: 26
Newspaper
S.I.C.: 2711
Robb L. Krecklow *(Publr.)*
Tammie Sherman *(Bus. Mgr.)*
Mike Igo *(Mgr.-Circulation)*
Fred Martin *(Mgr.-Adv.)*

The Grand Island Daily Independent **(1)**
P.O. Box 1208, 1st & Cedar Sts.
Grand Island, NE 68801
Tel.: 308-382-1000 (100%)
Fax: 308-382-8129
Emp.: 76
Newspaper
S.I.C.: 2711
David A. Beliles *(Publr.)*
Kent Thomas *(Gen. Mgr.)*
Molly Holcher *(Bus. Mgr.)*
Mark Chaney *(Mgr.-Circulation)*
Gary Loftus *(Adv. Mgr.)*

Haines City Herald & Ridge Shopper **(1)**
11 C St., Box 1596
Haines City, FL 33844
Tel.: 813-422-8683
Fax: 813-422-5442
Newspaper
S.I.C.: 2711
Larry Beasley *(Publr.)*
Mary Schaal *(Bus. Mgr.)*
Jim Johnson *(Mgr.-Circulation)*
Dennis Wilkinson *(Adv. Mgr.)*

The Hannibal Courier-Post **(1)**
P.O. Box A, 200 N. 3rd St.
Hannibal, MO 63401
Tel.: 314-221-2800 (100%)
Fax: 314-221-1568
Emp.: 40
Newspaper
S.I.C.: 2711
John D. Goossen *(Publr.)*
Carolyn Taylor *(Bus. Mgr.)*
Joann Franklin *(Mgr.-Circulation)*
Donald Smith *(Adv. Mgr.)*

Hillsdale Daily News **(1)**
P.O. Box 287, 33 McCollum
Hillsdale, MI 49242
Tel.: 517-437-7351 (100%)
Fax: 517-437-3963
Emp.: 27
Newspaper
S.I.C.: 2711
William K. Turner *(Publr.)*
David Holcomb *(Bus. Mgr.)*
Tim Blankenship *(Mgr.-Circulation)*
Judy Gabriele *(Mgr.-Adv.)*

The Holland Sentinel **(1)**
54-56 W. 8th St.
Holland, MI 49423
Tel.: 616-392-2311 (100%)
Fax: 616-392-3526
Emp.: 65
Newspaper
S.I.C.: 2711
Clay W. Stauffer *(Publr.)*
David Miedema *(Bus. Mgr.)*
Stephen Knape *(Mgr.-Circulation)*
Margaret Van Sant *(Adv. Mgr.)*

The Independence Examiner **(1)**
P.O. Box 458, 410 S. Liberty
Independence, MO 64051
Tel.: 816-254-8600 (90%)
Fax: 816-836-3805
Emp.: 65
Newspaper
S.I.C.: 2711
Ben F. Weir, Jr. *(Publr.)*
Becky Ely *(Bus. Mgr.)*
Kevin Kampman *(Mgr.-Circulation)*
Irene Baltrusaitis *(Adv. Mgr.)*

Lake Wales Daily Highlander **(1)**
33 W. Orange Ave., Box 872
Lake Wales, FL 33859-0872
Tel.: 813-676-2571
Fax: 813-678-1309
Emp.: 27
Newspaper
S.I.C.: 2711
Larry Beasley *(Publr.)*
Mary Schaal *(Bus. Mgr.)*
Jim Johnson *(Mgr.-Circulation)*
Rick Etzkorn *(Mgr.-Adv.)*

The Newton Kansan **(1)**
P.O. Box 268, 121 W. 6th St.
Newton, KS 67114
Tel.: 316-283-1500 (100%)
Fax: 316-283-2471
Emp.: 25
Newspaper
S.I.C.: 2711
Douglas J. Anstaett *(Publr.)*
Janice Nesser *(Bus. Mgr.)*
Larry Sadowski *(Mgr.-Circulation)*
Dennis Garrison *(Adv. Mgr.)*

The Oak Ridger **(1)**
785 Oak Ridge Turnpike
Oak Ridge, TN 37830
Tel.: 615-482-1021
Fax: 615-482-7834
Emp.: 55
Newspaper
S.I.C.: 2711
Lawrence E. Weil *(Publr.)*
Pip Pippen *(Bus. Mgr.)*
Miriam McFadden *(Mgr.-Circulation)*
Cecil Burnette *(Mgr.-Adv.)*

Pittsburg Morning Sun **(1)**
P.O. Box H, 701 N. Locust
Pittsburg, KS 66762
Tel.: 316-231-2600 (100%)
Fax: 316-231-0645
Emp.: 43
Newspaper
S.I.C.: 2711
Thomas H. Collinson *(Publr.)*
LeAnn Pipkin *(Bus. Mgr.)*
Billie Casella *(Mgr.-Circulation)*
John Maddox *(Adv. Mgr.)*

Shawnee News-Star **(1)**
P.O. Box 1688, 215 N. Bell
Shawnee, OK 74801
Tel.: 405-273-4200 (100%)
Fax: 405-273-4207
Emp.: 54
Newspaper
S.I.C.: 2711
John L. Tucker *(Publr.)*
Jeri McEntire *(Bus. Mgr.)*
Roy Greenlee *(Mgr.-Circulation)*
Sherry Wilkins *(Adv. Mgr.)*

Shopper Publishing Group **(1)**
2901 W. Memorial Blvd., Drawer 1110
Lakeland, FL 33802
Tel.: 813-688-8500
Fax: 813-686-7079
Newspaper
S.I.C.: 2711
Larry Beasley *(Publr.)*
Mary Schaal *(Bus. Mgr.)*
Jim Johnson *(Mgr.-Circulation)*

The Topeka Capital-Journal **(1)**
616 Jefferson St.
Topeka, KS 66607
Tel.: 913-295-1111
Tel.: 800-777-7171 (100%)
Fax: 913-295-1198
Emp.: 276
Newspaper
S.I.C.: 2711
Peter W. Stauffer *(Publr.)*
Randy Magee *(Bus. Mgr.)*
Carolyn Terhune *(Dir.-Mktg.)*
Garran Allison *(Mgr.-Adv.)*
William M. Osborne *(Adv. Mgr.)*

The Yankton Press & Dakotan **(1)**
P.O. Box 56, 319 Walnut
Yankton, SD 57078
Tel.: 605-665-7811 (100%)
Fax: 605-665-1721
Emp.: 28
Newspaper
S.I.C.: 2711
Robert C. Helsley *(Publr.)*
Larry Benson *(Bus. Mgr.)*
John Stine *(Mgr.-Circulation)*

The York News-Times **(1)**
P.O. Box 279, 327 Platte Ave.
York, NE 68467
Tel.: 402-362-4478 (100%)
Fax: 402-362-6748
Emp.: 22
Newspaper
S.I.C.: 2711
Dan Collin *(Publr.)*
Jackie Regier *(Bus. & Circulation Mgr.)*
David Sjuts *(Adv. Mgr.)*

Winter Haven News Chief **(1)**
650 Sixth St., S.W.
Winter Haven, FL 33880
Tel.: 813-294-7731
Fax: 813-294-2008
Newspaper
S.I.C.: 2711
Larry Beasley *(Publr.)*
Mary Schaal *(Bus. Mgr.)*
Jim Johnson *(Mgr.-Circulation)*
Janice Saunders *(Adv. Mgr.)*

Broadcasting Operations:

KGFF-AM **(1)**
MacArthur & Bryan Sts.
Shawnee, OK 74802-0009
Tel.: 405-273-4390 (100%)
Fax: 405-273-4350
Emp.: 8
Radio Broadcasting
S.I.C.: 4832
Richard Carter *(Gen. Mgr.)*

KGNC-AM & FM **(1)**
P.O. Box 710,
Amarillo, TX 79189
Tel.: 806-355-9801 (100%)
Fax: 806-354-8779
Emp.: 23
Radio Broadcasting
S.I.C.: 4832
Robert F. Russell *(Gen. Mgr.)*
Shirley Brinkley *(Bus. Mgr.)*
Larry Vanover *(Mgr.-Promo.)*
Doug Sullens *(Mgr.-Sls.)*

KGWN-TV **(1)**
2923 E. Lincolnway
Cheyenne, WY 82001
Tel.: 307-634-7755
Fax: 307-635-8604
Emp.: 45
Television Broadcasting
S.I.C.: 4833
Carl J. Occhipinti *(Gen. Mgr.)*
Bert Grant *(Bus. Mgr.)*
Steve Vancourt *(Mgr.-Promo.)*
Dusty Thein *(Mgr.-Sls.)*

KMIZ-TV **(1)**
501 Business Loop, 70 East
Columbia, MO 65201
Tel.: 314-449-0917 (100%)
Fax: 314-875-7078
Emp.: 40
Television Broadcasting
S.I.C.: 4833
Carlos Fernandez *(Gen. Mgr.)*
Gary Peel *(Bus. Mgr.)*
Pat Dalbey *(Mgr.-Sls.)*

KTVS-TV **(1)**
P.O. Box 432, 224 N. Third
Sterling, CO 80751
Tel.: 303-522-5743
Fax: 303-522-7813
Emp.: 13
Sattelite to KGWN-TV
S.I.C.: 4833
Gene L. Huston *(Resident Mgr.)*
Fran Davis *(Mgr.-Sls.)*

KCOY-TV **(1)**
1211 McCoy Lane
Santa Maria, CA 93455
Tel.: 805-925-1200 (100%)
Fax: 805-922-9830
Emp.: 65
Television Station
S.I.C.: 4833
Charles S. Stauffer *(Gen. Mgr.)*
Debbi Johnson *(Bus. Mgr.)*
Wendy Eisele *(Mgr.-Promo.)*
Joe Marcoe *(Mgr.-Sls.)*

KSTF-TV **(1)**
P.O. Box 1619, 1402 First Ave.
Scottsbluff, NE 69361
Tel.: 308-632-6107
Fax: 308-632-3470
Sattelite to KGWN-TV
S.I.C.: 4833
Bon Olsen *(Gen. Mgr.)*
Doug Fitzgerald *(Mgr.-Sls.)*

KGWC-TV **(1)**
304 N. Center
Casper, WY 82602
Tel.: 307-234-1111
Fax: 307-234-2835
Television Broadcasting
S.I.C.: 4833
Alan Nicksic *(Gen. Mgr.)*
Gale Peterson *(Bus. Mgr.)*
Jeremy Patey *(Mgr.-Promo.)*
Tim Swanson *(Mgr.-Sls.)*

Kansas City Royals Radio Network **(1)**
P.O. Box 419969,
Kansas City, MO 64141
Tel.: 816-921-6122 (100%)
Fax: 816-921-7423
Emp.: 2
Broadcasting Network
S.I.C.: 4832
Robert D. Fromme *(Gen. Mgr. & V.P.-Radio Div.)*
Beverly Anderson *(Bus. Mgr.)*
Bob Stiegler *(Mgr.-Sls.)*

Kansas Information Network **(1)**
5600 W. 6th St.
Topeka, KS 66606
Tel.: 913-272-3456
Emp.: 4
Radio Network
S.I.C.: 4832
Gerald N. Holley *(Gen. Mgr.)*

Kansas Agriculture Network **(1)**
5600 W. 6th St.
Topeka, KS 66606
Tel.: 913-272-2199
Emp.: 2
Radio Network
S.I.C.: 4832
Al Lobeck *(Gen. Mgr.)*

Wildcat Sports Network **(1)**
5600 W. 6th St.
Topeka, KS 66606
Tel.: 913-272-3456 x-357
Emp.: 1
Radio Network For The Kansas State Wildcats
S.I.C.: 4832
Gerald N. Holley *(Gen. Mgr.)*

WIBW-TV AM & FM **(1)**
5600 W. 6th St.
Topeka, KS 66606
Tel.: 913-272-3456 (100%)
Fax: 913-272-0117
Emp.: 135
Broadcasting
S.I.C.: 4832; 4833
Alexander Lobeck *(Gen. Mgr.-AM & FM Radio)*
Beverly Anderson *(Bus. Mgr.)*
Craig Colboch *(Mgr.-Sls.)*

National Media Operations:

Capper's **(1)**
616 Jefferson St.
Topeka, KS 66607
Tel.: 913-295-1101 (100%)
Emp.: 85
Periodical
S.I.C.: 2721
Don Keating *(Gen. Mgr.)*
Leah Reichert *(Mgr.-Bus.)*
Dianne Graves *(Mgr.-Circulation)*
Keith Chartier *(Mgr.-Adv.)*

Capper's Insurance Service, Inc. **(1)**
616 Jefferson St.
Topeka, KS 66607
Tel.: 913-295-1101 (100%)
Emp.: 20
Ins. Agency
S.I.C.: 6411
John M. Fries *(G.M.)*

Grit Printing Co. **(1)**
1 Maynard Street
Williamsport, PA 17701
Tel.: 717-326-1771 (100%)
Fax: 717-323-8538
Emp.: 75
Commercial Printing
S.I.C.: 2752
E. Van Anderson *(V.P.)*
Robert C. Kessler *(Plant Mgr.)*

Grit Publishing Company **(1)**
208 W. 3rd St.
Williamsport, PA 17701
Tel.: 717-326-1771 (100%)
Fax: 717-326-6940
Approx.Sls.: $29,900,000
Emp.: 60
Publishing; Commercial Printing; Marketing Services
S.I.C.: 2721
E. Van Anderson *(V.P.)*
John D. Brockway *(Dir.-Adv.)*

Other Operations:

Communications & Signaling, Inc. **(1)**
Bank IV Tower, 6th & Kansas
Topeka, KS 66603
Tel.: 913-232-6396 (80%)
Fax: 913-232-3758
Emp.: 17
Security
S.I.C.: 7382
Thomas W. Gorrell *(Gen. Mgr.)*

The Computer Patch of Joplin **(1)**
3316 E. 32nd, Box 1330
Joplin, MO 64802
Tel.: 417-782-0285
Fax: 417-782-1282
Retail Computer Store
S.I.C.: 5734
Rockford Smith *(Asst. V.P.-Computer Sls. Div.)*
Lucille Hurst *(Bus. Mgr.)*
James Allman *(Mgr.-Sls. & Mktg.)*

Stauffer Media Systems, Inc. **(1)**
3316 East 32nd Street
Joplin, MO 64802
Tel.: 417-782-0283 (50.5%)
Fax: 417-782-1282
Emp.: 4
Computer Software & Hardware
S.I.C.: 7372
Rockford E. Smith *(Asst. V.P.-Computer Sls. Div.)*

STAVELEY SENSORS, INC.
91 Prestige Park Circle
East Hartford, CT 06108
Tel.: 203-289-5428
Telex: 643778
Fax: 203-289-3189
Approx.Sls.: $10,000,000
Emp.: 107
Import Export
Mfr. of Ultrasonic Accessories; Transducers
S.I.C.: 3679; 3699
Joseph Zarrelli *(Gen. Mgr. & Controller)*
Anthony Ruiz *(Sls. Mgr.)*
Larry Schuck *(Dir.-Pur.)*
James C. Harris *(Dir.-Mngmt. Information Systems)*
Scott Benson *(Mktg. Mgr.)*
George Lewis *(Dir.-Engrng.)*

STEADLY COMPANY
200 River St.
Carthage, MO 64836
Mailing Address:
2530 Grand Ave., P.O. Box 419
Carthage, MO 64836
Tel.: 417-358-6011
Fax: 417-358-3400
Year Founded: 1907
Approx.Sls.: $42,000,000
Emp.: 650
Fiscal Year-end: 12/31/90
Export
Springs for Bedding & Furniture Indus.
S.I.C.: 3495
William J. Cheney *(Chm. Bd., Pres. & Chief Exec. Officer)*
Thomas E. Jones, Jr. *(Chief Oper. & Chief Fin. Officer)*
Michael J. McPherson *(Sec. & Controller)*
Volly W. Fullerton *(Dir.-Pur.)*
T. Robert Jones *(Mgr.-Information Services)*
Glenda R. Jones *(Mgr.-Employee Benefits & Cash Mngmt.)*
James E. Bane *(Mgr.-Research & Devel.)*

Computer Systems/Hardware:
IBM AS-400

STEAKLEY CHEVROLET SUBARU INC.
6411 E. Northwest Hwy.
Dallas, TX 75231
Mailing Address:
P.O. Box 821508,
Dallas, TX 75382-1508
Tel.: 214-363-8341 **TX**
Fax: 214-691-2918
Year Founded: 1962
Approx.Sls.: $83,000,000
Emp.: 205
Fiscal Year-end: 5/31/92
Retail New & Used Automobiles
S.I.C.: 5511
John W. Steakley *(Pres.)*
Michael E. Reeder *(V.P.)*
Arvel H. Rodgers *(V.P. & Gen. Mgr.)*
Kelly L. McCrory *(Sec. & Treas.)*
Principal(s):
John W. Steakley

Computer Systems/Hardware:
ADP

Outside Service Firm(s):

Spicer & Oppenheim *(Auditors)*
Dallas, TX

North Park National Bank *(Major Banking Relationship)*
Dallas, TX

STEARNS ENTERPRISES, INC.
410 W. Vine St.
Lexington, KY 40507
Tel.: 606-231-7878 **DE**
Fax: 606-233-2192
Year Founded: 1902
Sales Range: $10-19 Million
Emp.: 9
Real Estate Developers & Investors
S.I.C.: 6552; 6798
Robert E. Gable *(Chm. Bd.)*
Frank C. Thomas *(Vice Chm.)*
Thomas R. Zinn *(Pres. & Sec.)*
Valerie J. Dahl *(V.P. & Asst. Sec.)*
Principal(s):
Robert E. Gable

Computer Systems/Hardware:
IBM PC

Outside Service Firm(s):

Deloitte & Touche *(Auditors)*
333 W. Vine St., Ste 1200
Lexington, KY 40507
Tel.: 606-233-4035

Citizens Fidelity Bank & Trust Co.-Lexington *(Major Banking Relationship)*
163 W. Short St.
Lexington, KY 40507
Tel.: 606-233-0400

Buckley & Co., Inc. *(Group Insurer)*
Lexington, KY

Greenebaum, Doll & McDonald *(Legal Firm)*
Louisville, KY

STEBBINS ENGINEERING & MFG. CO.
363 Eastern Blvd.
Watertown, NY 13601
Tel.: 315-782-3000
Fax: 315-782-0481
Sales Range: $40-59 Million
Emp.: 1,500
Export
Mfr. & Installs Reinforced Tile and Linings
S.I.C.: 1799
A.E. Calligaris *(Chm. Bd., Pres. & Chief Exec. Officer)*
William M. Rohloff *(Chief Fin. Officer, Treas. & Sec.)*
R. Battista *(V.P.-Personnel)*
F.W. Blum *(V.P.-Pur.)*
Stephen D. Crane *(V.P.)*

Stebbins Engineering & Mfg. Co.—(Continued)

J.E. MacAleese *(V.P.)*
Joseph Macsuga *(V.P.)*
Robert J. Storms *(V.P.)*
Andrew J. Weiss *(V.P.-Sls. & Mktg.)*
J.P. Alteri *(Dir.-Data Processing)*

Computer Systems/Hardware:
IBM System 36

Outside Service Firm(s):

Deloitte & Touche*(Auditors)*
1 World Trade Center
New York, NY 10048
Tel.: 212-669-5000

Willmott, Wisner, Scanlon, Saunders & Haas*(Legal Firm)*
Watertown, NY

Key Bank*(Major Banking Relationship)*
Watertown, NY

Non-U.S. Holding:

Canadian Stebbins Engineering & Mfg. Co. Ltd. **(1)**
2700 Lancaster Rd.
Ottawa, ON K1B 4T7, Canada
Tel.: 613-523-8093
Export
Mfr. & Installation of Reinforced Tile Tank & Linings
S.I.C.: 1799
Alonzo LeCouffe *(V.P. & Gen. Mgr.)*

STEEL, INC.
6245 Clermont St.
Commerce City, CO 80022
Tel.: 303-287-0331 **CO**
Fax: 303-287-0338
Approx.Sls.: $12,000,000
Emp.: 62
Metal Sheets; Iron Or Steel Structural Shapes
S.I.C.: 5051
John L. McCallin *(Chm. Bd.)*
Daniel J. McCallin *(Pres.)*
David Carr *(V.P.)*
Harold V. Tepoorten *(Treas. & Sec.)*
Dan Schlaegel *(Dir.-Engrng.)*

Outside Service Firm(s):

John M. Hanson & Co.*(Auditors)*
Denver, CO

Gorsuch & Kirgis*(Legal Firm)*
Denver, CO

Central Bank*(Major Banking Relationship)*
Denver, CO

Steelcase

STEELCASE INC.
901 44th St. SE
Grand Rapids, MI 49508
Mailing Address:
P.O. Box 1967,
Grand Rapids, MI 49501
Tel.: 616-247-2710 **MI**
Fax: 616-246-4041
Year Founded: 1912
Approx.Sls.: $1,900,000,000
Emp.: 14,300
Fiscal Year-end: 2/28/91
Metal & Wood Office Furniture & Systems
S.I.C.: 2521; 2522
Robert C. Pew *(Chm. Bd.)*
David D. Hunting, Sr. *(Vice Chm.)*
William P. Crawford *(Pres.-Stow & Davis)*
Jerry K. Myers *(Pres. & Chief Exec. Officer)*
Robert Pew III *(Exec. V.P.-S/C Opers.)*
Paul H. Witting *(Sr. V.P. & Gen. Sls. Mgr.)*
Jack V. Stegmier *(Sr. V.P.-Opers.)*
Duane E. Bucklin *(Sr. V.P.-Admin. Services)*
Roger Choquette *(V.P. & Gen. Sls. Mgr.-Southern Area)*
Thomas G. Cleland *(V.P. & Gen. Sls. Mgr.-Eastern Area)*
Russ Coyner *(V.P.-Mktg.)*
David H. Donnelly *(V.P. & Gen. Sls. Mgr.-Western Area)*
Gerald Donnelly *(V.P.)*
David S. Fry *(V.P., Sec. & Gen. Counsel)*
Gerard Hekker *(V.P.-Mfg.)*
William Heyne *(V.P. & Gen. Sls. Mgr.-Central Area)*
Robert E. Hubling *(V.P. & Treas.)*
Lawrence F. Leete, Jr. *(V.P.-Natl. & Intl. Accts.)*
Alvin P. Lehnerd *(V.P.-Prod. Devel.)*
Roger L. Martin *(V.P.-Human Resources & Community Rels.)*
Ted Matthews *(V.P.-Sls., Southern Area)*
John T. Munroe *(V.P.-Sls. Services & Physical Distr.)*
James E. Stievater *(V.P. & Controller)*
Karen VanGorder *(V.P.-Training & Devel.)*
Peter M. Wege *(V.P. & Sec.)*
John R. Klein *(Dir.)*

Computer Systems/Hardware:
IBM

Outside Service Firm(s):

BDO Seidman*(Auditors)*
99 Monroe Ave. NW, Ste. 800
Grand Rapids, MI 49503
Tel.: 616-774-7000
Fax: 616-451-2096

Old Kent Bank*(Major Banking Relationship)*
Grand Rapids, MI

Divisions:

Details **(1)**
379 W. Broadway
New York, NY 10012
Tel.: 212-334-9100
Manufacturer of Personalized Desk Accessories
S.I.C.: 3999
Jack Cottrell *(Pres.)*

Steelcase Inc./International Div. **(1)**
901 44th St. S.E.
Grand Rapids, MI 49508
Tel.: 616-246-9465
Emp.: 15
Metal and Wood Office Furniture & Systems
S.I.C.: 2521; 2522
John Klein *(Gen. Mgr.)*

Steelcase Inc./Stow & Davis Carolina Div. **(1)**
P.O. Box 1389, Cane Creek Indus. Pk.
Fletcher, NC 28732
Tel.: 704-684-2241 (100%)
Emp.: 719
Wood Office Furniture & Systems
S.I.C.: 2521
John R. Ruhl *(Gen. Mgr.)*

Steelcase Inc./Western Div. **(1)**
1123 Warner Ave.
Tustin, CA 92680
Tel.: 714-259-8000 (100%)
Emp.: 982
Metal and Wood Office Furniture & Systems
S.I.C.: 2521; 2522
Robert A. Ballard *(V.P. & Gen. Mgr.)*

Steelcase Wood Div. **(1)**
4300 44th St. S.E.
Kentwood, MI 49508
Tel.: 616-246-4000
Emp.: 790
Fiscal Year-end: 2/28/91
Wood Office Furniture, Open Plan Systems, Seating
S.I.C.: 2521; 2541
John Ruhl, Sr. *(Gen. Mgr.)*
Bob Crain *(Dir.-Mktg. & Sls.)*

Vecta **(1)**
1800 S. Great Southwest Pkwy.
Grand Prairie, TX 75051
Tel.: 214-641-2860 (100%)
Fax: 214-660-1746
Emp.: 246
Fiscal Year-end: 2/28/91
Wood Office Furniture, Tables & Area Seating
S.I.C.: 2521; 2522
James Welch *(Pres.)*
Doris Todd *(Communications. Mgr.)*
Debra Strandberg *(Communications Asst.)*

Affiliate:

Attwood Corporation **(1)**
1016 N. Monroe St.
Lowell, MI 49331
Tel.: 616-897-9241 (100%)
Fax: 616-897-8358
Sales Range: $20-39 Million
Emp.: 364
Fiscal Year-end: 2/00/93
Import Export
Marine Hardware/Plastic Injected Moldings
S.I.C.: 3429; 3089
Donald Rocheleau *(Pres.)*
Lew Haeck *(V.P.-Opers.)*
Steve Taugher *(V.P.-Sls.)*
Bruce Haveman *(Fin. Dir.)*
Beverly Wickman *(Dir.-Pur.)*
Steve Rogal *(Dir.-Mktg.)*
John Boot *(Mktg. Communications Mgr.)*
Tom Powell *(Personnel Mgr.)*
Pat Thelen *(Data Processing)*
John Seevers *(Quality Control)*

Plant:

Steelcase, Inc./Athens Plant **(1)**
214 Durham Dr.
Athens, AL 35611
Tel.: 205-232-8112
Emp.: 526
Metal Office Furniture (Panel Systems)
S.I.C.: 2522
James M. Waybright *(Plant Mgr.)*

Subsidiaries:

Brayton International Inc. **(1)**
255 Swathmore Ave.
High Point, NC 27264
Tel.: 919-434-4151
Emp.: 270
Mfr. Wood Office Furniture
S.I.C.: 2521
Paul Brayton *(Pres.)*

Hedberg Data Systems, Inc. **(1)**
Hartford Executive Pk., One Hartfield Blvd.
East Windsor, CT 06088
Tel.: 203-627-7025
Emp.: 36
Computer Software Development & Services
S.I.C.: 7372
David N. Auth *(Pres.)*

Metropolitan Furniture Corporation **(1)**
245 E. Harris Ave.
South San Francisco, CA 94080
Tel.: 415-871-6222 (100%)
Emp.: 209
Custom Contract Wood Office Furniture
S.I.C.: 2521
Edmund White *(Pres.)*

Steelcase Financial Services, Inc. **(1)**
901 44th St. S.E.
Grand Rapids, MI 49508
Tel.: 616-245-4468
Steelcase Dealer Financing
Robert C. Pew *(Chm.)*

Stow & Davis Furniture Co. **(1)**
4300 44th St., S.E.
Kentwood, MI 49508
Tel.: 616-246-4000
Emp.: 549
Wood Office Furniture & Systems
S.I.C.: 2521
William P. Crawford *(Pres.)*

Non-U.S. Holdings:

Steelcase Canada Ltd. **(1)**
7200 Woodbine Ave.
Toronto, ON Canada M3C 2R7
Tel.: 416-495-6333 (100%)
Mfrs. Office Furniture & Equipment
S.I.C.: 2522; 2521

Steelcase Kurogane Ltd. **(1)**
25-8 Ishizunaka-Mashi, Neyagawa FH1
Osaka, 572, Japan (50%)
Mfrs. Office Furniture & Equipment
S.I.C.: 2522; 2521

Steelcase-Strafor S.A. **(1)**
132-57400 Zone Industrielle
Farrebourg, France
Tel.: 88-299013 (50%)
Mfrs. Office Furniture & Equipment
S.I.C.: 2522; 2521
Edward Cory *(Chief Exec. Officer)*

Subsidiary:

Steelcase Strafor (U.K.) Ltd. **(2)**
120 Moorgate
London, United Kingdom EC2
Tel.: 071-586-5933 (100%)
Mfrs. Office Furniture & Equipment
S.I.C.: 2522; 2521

Non-U.S. Joint Venture:

Pohlschroder & Co. KG **(1)**
Steinbrinkstrasse 61 4600
Dortmund, Germany
Tel.: 0231-2187-0 (50%)
Mfr. of Office Furniture & Equipment; Joint Venture of Steelcase Inc. & Financiere Strasor S.A.
S.I.C.: 2521; 2522

STEELITE, INC.
1010 Ohio River Blvd.
Pittsburgh, PA 15202
Tel.: 412-734-2600
Fax: 412-734-2608
Year Founded: 1957
Approx.Sls.: $20,000,000
Emp.: 83
Import Export
Mfr. of Metal Clad Building Materials, Wall & Roof Panels, Industrial Ventilation Equipment
S.I.C.: 3448; 3585
LeRoy Thompson, Jr. *(Chm. & Chief Exec. Officer)*
Robert Leighton *(Pres.)*
Edward Mullin *(Exec. V.P.)*
Harbaugh Miller *(Sec.)*
Joseph Urso *(Mgr.-Sls.)*
Tom Horensky *(Mgr.-Pur.)*
Jamie Berdine *(Mktg. Coord.)*

STEELOX SYSTEMS, INC.
(Formerly Building Technologies Corporation)
2412 Courseview, Dr., Ste. 300
Mason, OH 45040
Mailing Address:
P.O. Box 8181,
Mason, OH 45040-8000
Tel.: 513-573-5200 **DE**
Fax: 513-573-5299
Approx.Sls.: $43,000,000
Emp.: 250
Fiscal Year-end: 12/31/91
Export
Mfr. of Fabricated Commercial & Industrial Building Systems
S.I.C.: 3448
T.A. Naritoni *(Chm. Bd.)*
Frank B. Chapman *(Pres.)*
Edwin D. McQueen *(Exec. V.P.-Sls.)*
Richard W. Layding *(V.P.-Engrng.)*
Shinsure Hoh *(Chief Fin. Officer)*
John J. DiPretro *(Gen. Mgr.-Mfg.)*
Robert J. Huff *(Gen. Mgr.-Pur.)*
Charles E. Praeger *(Gen. Mgr.-Roofing)*
Frank L. McKain *(Mgr.-Human Resources)*
R.C. Ruble *(Mgr.-Res. & Devel.)*

Computer Systems/Hardware:
IBM AS/400 B50

Outside Service Firm(s):

Thompson, Hine & Flory*(Legal Firm)*
Cincinnati, OH

American National Bank*(Major Banking Relationship)*
Cincinnati, OH

STEENBERG HOMES, INC.
300 Rolling Meadows Dr.
Fond du Lac, WI 54936-1257
Mailing Address:
P.O. Box 1257,
Fond du Lac, WI 54936-1257
Tel.: 414-922-3166 **WI**
Fax: 414-922-5148
Year Founded: 1952
Assets: $7,703,053
Earnings: $205,950
Liabilities: $5,543,053
Net Worth: $2,160,000
Approx.Sls.: $20,000,000
Emp.: 150
Fiscal Year-end: 12/31/90
Retail Mobile & Modular Homes
S.I.C.: 5271
W.D. Steenberg *(Chm. Bd. & Pres.)*
Thomas R. Huettl *(Sr. V.P., Chief Oper. Officer, Treas. & Sec.)*
James A. Reitzner *(V.P.-Mktg.)*

Computer Systems/Hardware:
Burroughs

Outside Service Firm(s):

KPMG Peat Marwick*(Auditors)*
777 E. Wisconsin Ave.
Milwaukee, WI 53202
Tel.: 414-276-4200

Great-West Life Assurance Co.*(Group Insurer)*
135 S. LaSalle St.
Chicago, IL 60603
Tel.: 312-782-3753

Sager & Pavlick*(Legal Firm)*
Fond du Lac, WI

Steffen Dairy Foods Co., Inc.
(See listing under Steenberg Homes, Inc.)

STEGNER FOOD PRODUCTS CO.
5 Chili Hill Drive
Cincinnati, OH 45238
Mailing Address:
P.O. Box 58643
Cincinnati, OH 45258
Tel.: 513-922-1125
Approx.Sls.: $20,000,000
Emp.: 90
Export
Stegner's Shelf Stable, Microwaveable Bowls (Quick Delight) Spaghetti w/Meatballs, Lasagna, Fettucini Marinara, Beef Ravioli, Beef Stew, Macaroni & Cheese, Noodles w/Chicken, ABC's Pasta, Chili Mac & Chili w/ Beans
S.I.C.: 2032; 2099
Edward J. Stegner *(Chm. Bd. & Chief Exec. Officer)*
Donald L. Ottke *(Pres.)*
Bob Pasucci *(V.P.-Sls. & Mktg.)*

STEIN, KILLPATRICK & ROGAN ADVERTISING
15 West 26th St.
New York, NY 10010
Tel.: 212-213-1112
Fax: 212-779-7305
Year Founded: 1983
Approx.Billings: $11,000,000
Emp.: 15
Business-to-Business & Consumer Adv., Publishing, Electronic Info. Services, Childrens/Parents Prods., Brdcst. & Telecommunications, Travel
Thomas Stein *(Pres & New Bus. Contact)*

Computer Systems/Hardware:
MacIntosh

STEIN ROBAIRE HELM, INC.
11911 San Vicente Blvd., Ste. 324
Los Angeles, CA 90049
Tel.: 310-471-4333
Fax: 310-207-4493
Year Founded: 1988
Approx.Billings: $45,000,000
Emp.: 35
Greg J. Helm *(Chief Exec. Officer)*
Caroline Beck *(Exec. V.P. & Dir., Strategic Plng.)*

Computer Systems/Hardware:
Macintosh

STEINBACH
535 Old Tarrytown Rd.
White Plains, NY 10603
Tel.: 914-683-1360
Fax: 914-428-3147
Approx.Sls.: $225,000,000
Emp.: 4,000
Fiscal Year-end: 1/27/91
Department Store
S.I.C.: 5311
Anthony Veziris *(Pres.)*
Frank Traendly *(Sr. V.P.-Fin.)*
Louis Bodosksky *(V.P.-Mdse. Info.)*
Don Shaffer *(V.P.-Human Resources)*
Stan Berger *(Controller)*
Fred Bunnel *(Dir.-Data Processing)*
Bob Gaines *(Dir.-Personnel)*
Edward J. Pestovic *(Adv. Dir.)*
Greg Johnson *(Mgr.-Pur.)*

STEINER/BRESSLER ADVERTISING
100 Brookwood Place, Ste. 400
Birmingham, AL 35209
Tel.: 205-871-8211
Fax: 205-879-5044
Year Founded: 1968
Approx.Billings: $13,000,000
Emp.: 27
Retail, Package Goods & Financial Adv.
Cy Steiner *(Pres., Admin. & Acct. Services)*
Harry Bressler *(Exec. V.P., Creative)*
Judy Vaughn Fraser *(Dir., Res. & Plng.)*
Gene McKay *(Dir., Automotive Mktg. Grp.)*

Computer Systems/Hardware:
MacIntosh

STEINER & COMPANY
715 S. Washington St.
Milford, DE 19963
Mailing Address:
P.O. Box 354,
Milford, DE 19963
Tel.: 302-422-4519 **DE**
Fax: 302-422-9655
Approx.Sls.: $10,000,000
Emp.: 260
Reprocess Textile Waste Fibers
S.I.C.: 5093
Edward S. Steiner *(Pres.)*
B.B. Butler *(V.P.)*
Leonard Donohue *(Treas. & Sec.)*

Outside Service Firm(s):

Central Fidelity Bank*(Major Banking Relationship)*
Halifax, VA

Subsidiary:

Clover Yarns, Inc. **(1)**
P.O. Box B-8
Clover, VA 24534
Tel.: 804-572-1120
Reprocess Textile Waste Fibers
S.I.C.: 5093
B.B. Butler *(Plant Mgr.)*

STEINER CORPORATION
505 E. S. Temple St.
Salt Lake City, UT 84102
Mailing Address:
P.O. Box 2317,
Salt Lake City, UT 84110
Tel.: 801-328-8831 **NV**
Fax: 801-363-5680
Year Founded: 1889
Approx.Sls.: $219,691,000
Emp.: 7,000
Linen Supply; Food Canning; Leasing
S.I.C.: 7213; 7359; 2033
Richard R. Steiner *(Pres. & Chief Exec. Officer)*
Kevin K. Steiner *(V.P.-Fin. & Treas.)*
Timothy Weiler *(Sec.)*
John Bishoff *(Controller)*
William R. Shepard *(Dir.-Data Processing)*

Computer Systems/Hardware:
IBM 4331

Outside Service Firm(s):

Ernst & Young*(Auditors)*
50 S. Main, Ste. 1400
Salt Lake City, UT 84144
Tel.: 801-538-2500

Fabian Clendenin*(Legal Firm)*
Salt Lake City, UT

First Interstate Bank*(Major Banking Relationship)*
2nd South & Main
Salt Lake City, UT 84101

Divisions:

Change-O-Matic/Wesco **(1)**
1266 S. Orchard Rd.
Aurora, IL 60507
Tel.: 708-897-8458
Garment Services
S.I.C.: 7219
Robert L. Steiner *(Pres.)*

Farm Store No. 1 **(1)**
1414 Grove St., P.O. Box 9076
Boise, ID 83707
Tel.: 208-343-6681
Other Stores Located at Nampa & Caldwell, ID
Les Bishop *(Mgr.)*

Steiner Foreign Linen Division **(1)**
505 E. S. Temple St.
Salt Lake City, UT 84110
Tel.: 801-328-8831
Subs. Located in Canada, Mexico, Brazil, Argentina, Italy, W. Germany, So. Africa, & Australia
S.I.C.: 7213

Steiner U.S. Linen Div. **(1)**
505 E. S. Temple St.
Salt Lake City, UT 84110
Tel.: 801-328-8831
District Offices Located at AZ, ID, NV, UT, OR, WA, CA, HI, IL, WI, CO, MT, WY, NM
S.I.C.: 7213
Marvin S. Priske *(V.P.)*

Plant:

American Fine Foods, Inc. (Nyssa Plant) **(1)**
100 E. Locust St.
Nyssa, OR 97913
Tel.: 503-372-2271
S.I.C.: 2033
Duke Wilson *(Prod. Opers.)*

Subsidiaries:

American Fine Foods, Inc. **(1)**
25 N. 6th St., P.O. Box 460
Payette, ID 83661
Tel.: 208-642-9061
Meat & Vegetable Products
S.I.C.: 2033
Robert B. Moss *(Pres.)*

American Industrial Services **(1)**
505 E.S. Temple St.
Salt Lake City, UT 84102 (100%)
Richard R. Steiner *(Pres.)*

Affiliate:

American Uniform Co. **(1)**
Parker St. N.E.
Cleveland, TN 37311
Tel.: 615-476-6561
Fax: 615-339-3702
Mfr. of Industrial Work Clothing and Linen Apparel; Uniform Rental
S.I.C.: 2311; 2337
Gary K. Smith *(Pres.)*
John P. Ward *(V.P.-Fin. & Sec.)*
T. Roy Jones *(V.P.-Sls.)*
Reggie Suits *(Sls. Mgr.)*

STEINER ELECTRIC CO.
1250 Touhy Ave.
Elk Grove Village, IL 60007
Tel.: 708-228-0400
Fax: 708-228-1352
Approx.Sls.: $74,000,000
Emp.: 230
Distribute Electrical & Electronic Supplies
S.I.C.: 5063; 5065
Harold M. Kerman *(Pres.)*
Robert Beckmann *(Dir.-Sls.)*
Richard Kerman *(Dir.-Mktg.)*

Computer Systems/Hardware:
Hewlett Packard 3070

Outside Service Firm(s):

American National Bank*(Major Banking Relationship)*
33 North LaSalle St.
Chicago, IL 60690
Tel.: 312-661-6967

STEINERT & ASSOCIATES, INC.
260 Madison Ave. 20th. Floor
New York, NY 10016
Tel.: 212-889-5000
Year Founded: 1987
Approx.Billings: $30,000,000
Emp.: 32
Direct Response
Jan Allan Steinert *(Pres. & Chief Exec. Officer)*
Pierre Madacsi *(V.P., Chief Fin. Officer)*

STEINWAY MUSICAL PROPERTIES, INC.
800 South St.
Waltham, MA 02154
Tel.: 617-894-9770
Fax: 617-894-9803
Holding Company: Pianos
S.I.C.: 6719; 3931

Steinway Musical Properties, Inc.—(Continued)

Bruce A. Stevens *(Pres.)*
Leo Spellman *(Dir.-Adv. & Pub. Rels.)*
Sanford G. Woodard *(Gen. Mgr.-Quality Assurance & Engrng.)*

Outside Service Firm(s):

First Fidelity Bank, N.A.*(Major Banking Relationship)*
New York, NY

Subsidiary:

Steinway & Sons **(1)**
Steinway Place
Long Island City, NY 11105
Tel.: 718-721-2600
Tel.: 800-366-1853
Fax: 718-932-4332
Emp.: 1,000
Export
Piano Manufacturer
S.I.C.: 3931
Bruce A. Stevens *(Pres.)*
Sanford G. Woodard *(Sr. V.P. & Gen. Mgr.)*
Daniel Koenig *(V.P.-Mfg.)*
Frank Mazurco *(V.P.-Sls. & Mktg.)*
Dennis J. Tortora *(Controller & Asst. Treas.)*
Leo Spellman *(Dir.-Adv. & Pub. Rels.)*

THE STELLAR GROUP INC.
2900 Hartley Rd.
Jacksonville, FL 32257
Tel.: 800-488-2900 **FL**
Fax: 904-260-2088
Year Founded: 1985
Assets: $12,689,768
Liabilities: $10,835,547
Net Worth: $1,854,221
Approx.Sls.: $100,000,000
Emp.: 275
Fiscal Year-end: 6/30/91
General Contractor Industrial & Commercial Buildings, Industrial Refrigeration
S.I.C.: 1541; 1542
Ronald H. Foster *(Pres.)*
George J. Albertelli *(Sr. V.P. & Sec.)*
H. Bobby Cothren *(Sr. V.P.)*
Walter Foster *(Sr. V.P.)*
Emma Lee Carpenter *(V.P.-Employee Benefits)*
Michael Greene *(V.P.-Pur.)*
Rogers Towers *(V.P. & Gen. Counsel)*
Ernest Veale *(V.P.-Sls., Mktg., Mdse. & Adv.)*
Gabriel Bove *(Dir.-Plng. & Devel.)*
Lamar Nash *(Dir.-Real Estate)*
Diane Puckett *(Dir.-Data Processing)*
Linda Sedwick *(Dir.-Human Resources)*
Keri Scott *(Corp. Travel Planner)*
Principal(s):
Ronald H. Foster
George J. Albertelli
H. Bobby Cothren

No. of U.S. Offices: 1

Outside Service Firm(s):

Gunn, Patterson, Spaulding & Bohn*(Auditors)*
Jacksonville, FL

Construction Insurance*(Commercial Insurance Carrier)*
Jacksonville, FL

Jefferson Pilot*(Group Insurer)*
Jacksonville, FL

Sun Bank, N.A.*(Investment Banker)*
Jacksonville, FL

Rogers, Towers, Bailey, Jones, Gay*(Legal Firm)*
Jacksonville, FL

Sun Bank, N.A.*(Major Banking Relationship)*
Jacksonville, FL

STEPHAN & BRADY, INCORPORATED
1850 Hoffman St.
Madison, WI 53701
Tel.: 608-241-4141 **WI**
Fax: 608-241-4246
Year Founded: 1952
Approx.Billings: $30,580,500
Emp.: 52
Fiscal Year-end: 9/30/90
Advertising Agency
S.I.C.: 7311
Jack Ragel *(Chm., Pres. & Chief Exec. Officer)*
Frank Fueger *(Vice Chm. & Exec. V.P.)*
Katherine Johnson-Becklin *(Sr. V.P., Acct. Dir.)*
George Whitely *(Sr. V.P., Acct. Dir.)*
Pamela Black *(Sr. V.P., Pub. Rels.)*
Jeanette Riechers *(V.P., Pub. Rels.)*
Steve Forsyth *(V.P., Pub. Rels. Dir.)*
Jeanette Riechers *(Acct. Supvr., Pub. Rel.)*

Computer Systems/Hardware:
DEC VAC

Outside Service Firm(s):

Morton Nehls & Tierney*(Auditors)*
Madison, WI

Wisconsin Physicians Service*(Group Insurer)*
Madison, WI

Stolper, Koritzinsky, Brewster & Neider, S.C.*(Legal Firm)*
Madison, WI

Valley National Bank*(Major Banking Relationship)*
Madison, WI

STEPHEN ASSOCIATES, INC.
60 East 42nd St.
New York, NY 10165
Tel.: 212-867-3880
Tel.: 800-722-7007
Fax: 212-867-0494
Year Founded: 1959
Approx.Billings: $12,000,000
Emp.: 8
Stephen Pliss *(Pres.)*
Ken Howser *(V. P., Sec.)*
Bruce Colwin *(Assoc. Media Dir.)*

STEPHENSON, INC.
5731 General Washington Dr.
Alexandria, VA 22312
Tel.: 703-642-9000
Fax: 703-354-0384
Approx.Sls.: $19,000,000
Emp.: 155
Sheetfed & Web Lithography & Color Separations
S.I.C.: 2752
G.W. Stephenson, Jr. *(Pres. & Treas.)*
Joseph Richards *(Pur. Agent)*

Outside Service Firm(s):

Becker & Company*(Auditors)*
Washington, DC

Tucker, Flyer & Lewis*(Legal Firm)*
1615 C St., N.W., Ste. 400
Washington, DC 20036
Tel.: 202-429-3200

The Riggs National Bank*(Major Banking Relationship)*
P.O. Box 2651
Washington, DC
Tel.: 202-624-2628

STEPHENS, INC.
111 Center Street
Little Rock, AR 72201
Mailing Address:
P.O. Box 3507,
Little Rock, AR 72203
Tel.: 501-374-4361 **AR**
Telex: 536-248
Fax: 501-374-1324
Year Founded: 1933
Assets: $396,650,000
Liabilities: $267,471,000
Net Worth: $129,179,000
Approx.Rev.: $126,132,000
Emp.: 531
Fiscal Year-end: 12/27/91
Investment Banking Services
S.I.C.: 6211; 6289
Jackson T. Stephens *(Chm. Bd.)*
Warren A. Stephens *(Pres. & Chief Exec. Officer)*
C. Ray Gash *(Chief Fin. Officer, Sr. V.P., Treas. & Sec.)*
I.E. Butler *(Exec. V.P.)*
J.E.M. Jacoby *(Exec. V.P.)*
Ellen M. Gray *(Sr. V.P.-Admin. Services & Dir.-Human Resources)*
Zoe Hines *(Sr. V.P. & Controller)*
David A. Knight *(Sr. V.P. & Gen. Counsel)*
Phil Shellabarger *(Sr. V.P. & Compliance Officer)*
J.D. Simpson III *(Sr. V.P.)*
Ted Cashion *(V.P.-Systems Coordinator)*
Dale Aclin *(Mgr.-Real Estate)*
Rick Alexander *(Mgr.-Data Proc.)*
Bob Egendoerfer *(Mgr.-Cash)*
Melva Robinson *(Mgr.-Telecommunications)*
Rick Turner *(Mgr.-Corp. Acctg.)*
Principal(s):
Warren A. Stephens
J.E.M. Jacoby

No. of U.S. Offices: 1

Computer Systems/Hardware:
Tandem TNS II

Outside Service Firm(s):

Arthur Andersen & Co.*(Auditors)*
111 Center St.
Little Rock, AR 72201

Union Life Insurance Co.*(Group Insurer)*
Little Rock, AR

Arnold, Grobmyer & Haley*(Legal Firm)*
Little Rock, AR

Chemical Bank*(Major Banking Relationship)*
450 West 33rd St.
New York, NY 10001
Tel.: 212-613-7197
Fax: 212-947-7628

First National Bank of Chicago*(Major Banking Relationship)*
One First National Plaza
Chicago, IL 60670
Tel.: 312-732-9781
Tel.: 312-732-4050
Fax: 312-732-4840
Fax: 312-732-3055

Worthen National Bank of Arkansas*(Major Banking Relationship)*
P.O. Box 1681, 200 W. Capitol
Little Rock, AR 72201
Tel.: 501-378-1209
Fax: 501-378-1062

Wyatt Co.*(Pension Manager)*
2121 San Jacinto St., #2400
Dallas, TX
Tel.: 214-978-3400

Subsidiaries:

SD Leasing Company **(1)**
2201 Brookwood, Ste. 114
Little Rock, AR 72201
Tel.: 501-666-5600 (100%)
Emp.: 87
Leases Office Equip.
S.I.C.: 7359

Stephens Holding Company, Inc. **(1)**
111 Center St.
Little Rock, AR 72201
Tel.: 501-374-4361 (100%)
Emp.: 3
Investment in Operating Subsidiaries
S.I.C.: 6719

Stephens Overseas Services, Inc. **(1)**
111 Center St.
Little Rock, AR 72201
Tel.: 501-374-4361 (100%)
S.I.C.: 6289
Warren A. Stephens *(Chief Oper. Officer)*

JOHN STERLING CORPORATION
11600 Sterling Pkwy.
Richmond, IL 60071
Mailing Address:
P.O. Box 469
Richmond, IL 60071
Tel.: 815-678-2031
Fax: 815-678-4360
Approx.Sls.: $10,000,000
Emp.: 100
Import Export
Sterling Hardware for Sliding & Folding Doors, Hardware & Housewares Products
S.I.C.: 3429; 3446
John R. Sterling *(Pres.)*
Nick Stavros *(Natl. Sls. Mgr.)*

Computer Systems/Hardware:
IBM RISC 9000

STERLING ELECTRIC, INC.
16752 Armstrong Ave.
Irvine, CA 92714
Mailing Address:
P.O. Box 25070
Santa Ana, CA 92799
Tel.: 714-474-0520
Tel.: 800-654-6220 **DE**
Fax: 714-474-0543
Year Founded: 1927
Approx.Sls.: $15,000,000
Emp.: 85
Fiscal Year-end: 11/30/90
Import Export
Variable Speed Drives, Gearmotors, AC Motors, Right Angle Gear Motors, Right Angle & Parallel Reducers
S.I.C.: 3621
Corporate Giving Program: United Way
Raymond E. Helton *(Pres. & Chief Exec. Officer)*
Walter Mashburn *(Mgr.-Adv.)*

Computer Systems/Hardware:
Unisys

STERLING HEIGHTS DODGE, INC.
40111 Van Dyke
Sterling Heights, MI 48313
Tel.: 313-939-3900
Fax: 313-939-3220
Emp.: 70
Retail New & Used Automobiles
S.I.C.: 5511
Anthony J. Viviano *(Pres.)*
Philip Viviano *(V.P.)*
Betty Tyll *(Treas. & Sec.)*

Outside Service Firm(s):

NBD Bank, N.A.*(Major Banking Relationship)*
611 Woodward Ave.
Detroit, MI 48226
Tel.: 313-225-1122

STERLING HOMES CORP.
871 East Glendale Ave.
Sparks, NV 89431
Tel.: 702-331-1104 **CA**
Year Founded: 1976
Assets: $228,180,000
Liabilities: $193,202,000
Net Worth: $34,978,000
Approx.Sls.: $100,000,000
Emp.: 100
Fiscal Year-end: 12/31/89
Holding Company
S.I.C.: 6719
Robert H. Lintz *(Chm. Bd.)*
R.V. Mendoza *(Pres. & Chief Exec. Officer)*
William F. Dohr *(V.P.-Opers.)*
Maxine L. Bridges *(Sec., Treas. & Dir.-Personnel & Investor Rels.)*
Robert Burton *(Sls. & Mktg. Dir.)*

Principal(s):
Robert H. Lintz
Susan Lintz Dohr

No. of U.S. Offices: 1

Computer Systems/Hardware:
IBM at Mini Network

Outside Service Firm(s):

Kenneth Leventhal & Co.*(Auditors)*
Ste. 800, 660 Newport Center Dr.
Newport Beach, CA 92660
Tel.: 714-640-5000

Nationwide Insurance*(Commercial Insurance Carrier)*
Orange, CA

Blue Cross of California*(Group Insurer)*
Anaheim Hills, CA

Gibson, Dunn & Crutcher*(Legal Firm)*
800 Newport Center Dr.
Newport Beach, CA 92660
Tel.: 714-451-3800

Bank of America NT&SA*(Major Banking Relationship)*
Costa Mesa, CA

Subsidiaries:

Sterling Builders, Inc. **(1)**
19762 MacArthur Blvd.
Irvine, CA 92715
Tel.: 714-253-3352
Fax: 714-752-0271
Emp.: 36
Land Development & Home Builder
S.I.C.: 6552; 1521
Harvey R. Mendoza *(Pres.)*
Barbara Jennings *(Controller)*
Robert Burton *(Dir.-Sls. & Mktg.)*

Sterling Savings & Loan **(1)**
19752 MacArthur Blvd.
Irvine, CA 92715
Tel.: 714-253-3340
Fax: 714-752-5823
Emp.: 37
Financial Institution
S.I.C.: 6035
Robert K. Parker *(Pres.)*
Mark W. Child *(Exec. V.P.)*
Marty Yuen *(V.P.)*

STERLING, INC.
5200 W. Clinton Ave.
Milwaukee, WI 53223
Tel.: 414-354-0970
Fax: 414-354-6421
Emp.: 230
Mfr. of Packaged Temperature Control Systems, Condensation Pumps, Control Valves, Hydraulic Presses, Granulators, Automatic Parts Removal Equipment, Automatic Handling & Processing Equipment
S.I.C.: 3822; 3494; 3542; 3559; 3714; 3561
Gil King *(Pres.)*
Horst O. Sieben *(Chief Fin. Officer)*
Richard Rocke *(V.P.)*

Computer Systems/Hardware:
IBM

Outside Service Firm(s):

Coopers & Lybrand*(Auditors)*
411 East Wisconsin Bldg.
Milwaukee, WI 53202

M & I Marshall & Ilsley Bank*(Major Banking Relationship)*
770 N. Water St.
Milwaukee, WI 53202
Tel.: 414-765-8700

Subsidiary:

AEC, Inc. **(1)**
801 AEC Drive
Wood Dale, IL 60191
Tel.: 708-595-1060
Telex: 28-7426
Fax: 708-595-8924
Assets: $27,514,463
Liabilities: $15,276,365
Net Worth: $12,238,098
Approx.Sls.: $65,899,000
Emp.: 600
Fiscal Year-end: 10/31/90
Mfr. of Water Cooling, Water Recovery & Energy Recapture Products & Systems; Automated Parts, Material Reclaim Systems; Automated Material Handling Systems, Conveyance Systems; Robots
S.I.C.: 3823; 3559; 3535; 3536
Frank Reed *(Pres.)*
Richard Stewart *(V.P. & G.M.)*
Kathy Butzan *(Pur. Dir.)*
Robert Zega *(Personnel Dir.)*
Bruce Boyd *(Adv. & Mktg. Mgr.)*

Subsidiaries:

Application Engineering Corporation **(2)**
801 AEC Drive
Wood Dale, IL 60191
Tel.: 708-595-1060 (100%)
Approx.Sls.: $27,000,000
Mfr. of Water Cooling, Water Recovery & Energy Recapture Products & Systems
S.I.C.: 3823; 3559
Richard Stewart *(V.P. & G.M.)*
Vin Berger *(Dir.-Sls.)*

Application Automation, Inc. **(2)**
801 AEC Drive
Wood Dale, IL 60191
Tel.: 708-595-1060 (100%)
Approx.Sls.: $5,000,000
Emp.: 35
Mfr. of Robotics
S.I.C.: 3559
James Healy *(Gen. Sls. Mgr.)*

Nelmor Co., Inc. **(2)**
Rivulet St.
No. Uxbridge, MA 01538
Tel.: 508-278-5584 (100%)
Approx.Sls.: $14,000,000
Emp.: 215
Mfr. of Material Reclaim Systems; Granulating & Size Reduction Machinery
S.I.C.: 3541; 3559
Peter Lothes *(V.P. & G.M.)*
Ed Ronca *(V.P.-Sls.)*
Richard Bacon *(Finance Mgr.)*
Ray Sotek *(Pur. Dir.)*

Whitlock, Inc. **(2)**
801 AEC Dr.
Wood Dale, IL 60191
Tel.: 708-595-1060
Approx.Sls.: $18,000,000
Emp.: 230
Mfr. of Automated Material Handling Systems, Conveyance Systems; Drying, Storage & Blending Systems
S.I.C.: 3535; 3559; 3536
Richard Stewart *(V.P. & G.M.)*
Vincent Berger *(Gen. Sls. Mgr.)*

STERLING JEWELRY & DISTRIBUTING CO.
5801 E. Northwest Hwy.
Dallas, TX 75231
Tel.: 214-363-4551 **TX**
Fax: 214-363-5177
Wholesale Distributors and some Mail Order Business
S.I.C.: 5311
Howard Donsky *(Pres.)*
Ervin Donsky *(Chief Exec. Officer)*
Jeff Borovay *(Sr. V.P.)*
Abe H. Donsky *(Sr. V.P.)*
Nathan Donsky *(Sr. V.P.)*
Andrew Solomon *(Sr. V.P.)*

Outside Service Firm(s):

Philip Vogel & Co.*(Auditors)*
Dallas, TX

Bank One Texas, N.A.*(Major Banking Relationship)*
1717 Main St.
Dallas, TX 75201
Tel.: 214-290-7915
Fax: 214-290-7959

STERLING LUMBER & INVESTMENT CO.
7000 N. Broadway
Denver, CO 80221
Tel.: 303-427-9661 **CO**
Fax: 303-427-4326
Year Founded: 1909
Approx.Sls.: $20,000,000
Emp.: 90
Holding Company; Lumber & Other Building Materials; Investment Company
S.I.C.: 5211; 6719
Herbert H. Vandermoer *(Chm. Bd.)*
Marvin Steele *(Pres.)*
Willard H. Marsh *(V.P.)*
Roger L. Segerson *(Treas. & Controller)*
S.K. Hodge *(Sec.)*
Buryl Carringer *(Mgr.-Opers.)*

Outside Service Firm(s):

United Bank of Denver*(Major Banking Relationship)*
P.O. Box 5247
Denver, CO 80217
Tel.: 303-861-8811

STERLING PAPER CO.
2155 E. Castor Ave.
Philadelphia, PA 19134
Tel.: 215-744-5350
Fax: 215-533-9577
Approx.Sls.: $11,000,000
Emp.: 80
Fiscal Year-end: 1/31/91
Mfr. of Paperboard Cartons, Pails, Plates & Specialties
S.I.C.: 2657
Martin Stein *(Pres. & Treas.)*
Suzanne S. Faigen *(V.P.)*
Elizabeth Chamberlin *(Controller)*
John H.L. Paul *(Sec.)*

Outside Service Firm(s):

Benen, Saidel & Co.*(Auditors)*
Philadelphia, PA

Schulman & Schulman*(Legal Firm)*
Philadelphia, PA

Philadelphia National Bank*(Major Banking Relationship)*
5th & Market Sts.
Philadelphia, PA 19101
Tel.: 215-629-3100
Fax: 215-834-2069

STERLING SUPPLY COMPANY, INC.
4900 Lincoln Ave.
Lisle, IL 60536
Tel.: 708-969-8600
Fax: 708-969-3271
Approx.Sls.: $20,000,000
Emp.: 35
Fiscal Year-end: 12/31/90
Wholesale Plumbing Supplies
S.I.C.: 5074
Bernice Samson *(Chm. & Pres .)*
Roger Samson *(Exec. V.P.-Personnel)*
Steve Cook *(Dir.-Adv. & Sls. Promo.)*
Jennifer Liu-Grushka *(Dir.-Data Processing)*
Larry Weiland *(Dir.-Sls.)*

STERLITE CORPORATION
198 Main St.
Townsend, MA 01469
Tel.: 508-597-8702 **MA**
Fax: 508-597-5911
Approx.Sls.: $60,000,000
Emp.: 400
Mfr. of Plastic Kitchenware, Tableware & Houseware
S.I.C.: 3089
Albert Stone *(Pres. & Chief Exec. Officer)*
Bruce M. Garvin *(V.P.-Fin. & Controller)*
Martin Shaevel *(V.P.-Sls.)*
Conrad Stone *(V.P.-Personnel)*
David M. Stone *(V.P.-Mktg.)*
Edward Bloomstein *(Natl. Sls. Mgr.)*

Outside Service Firm(s):

KPMG Peat Marwick*(Auditors)*
One Boston Place
Boston, MA 02108
Tel.: 617-723-7700

Hale and Dorr*(Legal Firm)*
60 State St.
Boston, MA 02109-6098
Tel.: 617-526-6000

Merchants National Bank*(Major Banking Relationship)*
Leominster, MA

STERN ADVERTISING, INC.
29125 Chagrin Blvd.
Pepper Pike, OH 44122
Tel.: 216-464-4850
Fax: 216-464-7859
Year Founded: 1954
Approx.Billings: $36,000,000
Emp.: 70
Consumer, Retail Mktg. & Adv.
Nelson M. Stern *(Chm.)*
William J. Stern *(Pres.)*
Bruce M. Stern *(Exec. V.P.)*
Terri Dutton Drohan *(Dir., Pub. Rels.)*

M.L. STERN & COMPANY, INC.
8350 Wilshire Blvd.
Beverly Hills, CA 90211
Tel.: 213-650-4001 **CA**
Fax: 213-654-4422
Year Founded: 1980
Approx.Sls.: $25,000,000
Emp.: 170
Security Brokers
S.I.C.: 6211
M.L. Stern *(Pres.)*
Paul H. White *(Exec. V.P.)*
Steve Kempa *(V.P. & Controller)*
H. David Longthorne *(V.P. & Asst. Controller)*
Maxine E. Stern *(Sec.)*

Outside Service Firm(s):

Gursey, Schneider & Co.*(Auditors)*
Los Angeles, CA

Security Pacific National Bank*(Major Banking Relationship)*
333 S. Hope St.
Los Angeles, CA 90017
Tel.: 213-613-6211

JACOB STERN & SONS, INC.
1464 E. Valley Rd.
Santa Barbara, CA 93108
Mailing Address:
P.O. Box 50740
Santa Barbara, CA 93150
Tel.: 805-565-1411
Fax: 805-565-1415
Approx.Sls.: $100,000,000
Emp.: 100
Manufacture Tallow, Grease, Vegetable Oils, Animal Feed, Fats & Fatty Acids
S.I.C.: 2077; 2048; 2843; 2899
Philip L. Bernstein *(Pres.)*
John Lindquist *(V.P.-Texas)*

Jacob Stern & Sons, Inc.—(Continued)

Jeffrey Peeler *(V.P.)*
H. Peeters *(V.P.)*
Richard L. Sheffer *(V.P.)*
Jerome Weisberg *(V.P. & Sec.)*

STERN & STERN INDUSTRIES INC.
708 Third Ave.
New York, NY 10017
Tel.: 212-972-4040
Fax: 212-818-9230
Year Founded: 1889
Approx.Sls.: $10,000,000
Emp.: 125
Manufacture Industrial Fabrics
S.I.C.: 2296; 2211
Lawrence D. Glaubinger *(Chm. Bd.)*
Peter B. Thornton *(Pres.)*
Stanley Cone *(V.P.-Mfg.)*
Lee Kessler *(Sec. & Controller)*

Outside Service Firm(s):

Hertz, Herson & Company*(Auditors)*
New York, NY

Chemical Bank*(Major Banking Relationship)*
450 West 33rd St.
New York, NY 10001
Tel.: 212-613-7197
Fax: 212-947-7628

STERNHEIMER BROTHERS INC.
5501 Ferncroft Rds.
Sandston, VA 23150
Tel.: 804-226-1324 **VA**
Fax: 804-222-4894
Year Founded: 1868
Approx.Sls.: $40,000,000
Emp.: 300
Fiscal Year-end: 12/31/90
Import
Retail Chain Stores
S.I.C.: 5331
Mark A. Sternheimer *(Pres.)*
Ross Sternheimer *(Treas. & Sec.)*
Art Klein *(Mgr.-Adv.)*

Computer Systems/Hardware:
IBM Series 1, IBM PCs

Outside Service Firm(s):

McGladrey & Pullen*(Auditors)*
P.O. Box 1276,
Richmond, VA 23210
Tel.: 804-644-4525

Crestar Bank*(Major Banking Relationship)*
Box 26665
Richmond, VA 23261
Tel.: 804-782-7302

STERN'S MIRACLE-GRO PRODUCTS, INC.
800 Port Washington Blvd.
Port Washington, NY 11050
Tel.: 516-883-6550
Fax: 516-883-6563
Approx.Sls.: $75,000,000
Emp.: 30
Import Export
Miracle-Gro & Miracid All Purpose Plant Food
S.I.C.: 2873; 2874
John Kenlon *(Pres.)*
Horace Hagedorn *(Chief Exec. Officer)*
Lee Reichart *(Dir.-Adv.)*

STEUART INVESTMENT CO.
4646 40th St. NW
Washington, DC 20016
Tel.: 202-537-8940
Fax: 202-244-4518
Approx.Sls.: $400,000,000
Emp.: 800
Petroleum Storage & Marketing; Property Leasing; Seafood; Transportation
S.I.C.: 5171; 5172; 4922; 4731; 5146
Curtis Steuart *(Chm. Bd.)*
John Johnson *(Pres.)*
John E. Baker *(Chief Fin. Officer, Treas. & Controller)*
Leonard P. Steuart, II *(V.P.)*
John R. Clark *(Gen. Counsel)*

Outside Service Firm(s):

Price Waterhouse*(Auditors)*
1801 K. Street, N.W.
Washington, DC 20006
Tel.: 202-296-0800

Aetna Life & Casualty*(Group Insurer)*
151 Farmington Avenue
Hartford, CT 06156
Tel.: 203-273-2128
Fax: 203-729-4295

American Trust Security*(Major Banking Relationship)*
Washington, DC

Riggs National Bank of Washington, D.C.*(Major Banking Relationship)*
P.O. Box 96206, 1120 Vermont Ave. N.W.
Washington, DC 20090-6206
Tel.: 202-835-4082

Subsidiaries:

Steuart Petroleum Company **(1)**
4646 40th St. N.W.
Washington, DC 20016
Tel.: 202-537-8900
Emp.: 650
Petroleum Terminaling & Mktg. Co.
S.I.C.: 5171
Leonard P. Steuart *(Chm. Bd. & Chief Exec. Officer)*
Giorgio Bianconi *(Vice Chm.)*
John C. Johnson *(Pres. & Chief Oper. Officer)*
W. Woodruff *(V.P.-Personnel)*

Steuart Seafoods **(1)**
4646 40th St. N.W.
Washington, DC 20016
Tel.: 202-537-8940
Wholesale Seafoods
S.I.C.: 5146

Steuart Transportation Co. **(1)**
Lighthouse Rd.
Pine Point, MD 20674
Tel.: 301-870-3360
S.I.C.: 4731

STEUART PETROLEUM COMPANY
4646 40th St. NW
Washington, DC 20016
Tel.: 202-537-8900
Telex: 904-279
Fax: 202-537-0392
Year Founded: 1905
Assets: $112,645,000
Earnings: ($1,539,000)
Liabilities: $79,001,000
Net Worth: $33,644,000
Approx.Sls.: $361,921,000
Emp.: 915
Fiscal Year-end: 12/31/91
Petroleum Terminaling & Marketing Company
S.I.C.: 5171
Leonard P. Steuart *(Chm. Bd.)*
Giorgio Bianconi *(Co-Chief Exec. Officer)*
John C. Johnson *(Co-Chief Exec. Officer)*
James N. Schwarz *(Sec. & Gen. Counsel)*
Jerry A. Waggoner *(Treas.)*
Melody Barackman *(Controller)*
Doug Ridge *(Mgr.-Mngmt. Information Systems)*

STEVEDORING SERVICES OF AMERICA
3415 11th Ave. SW
Seattle, WA 98134
Tel.: 206-623-0304
Fax: 206-623-0179
Year Founded: 1954
Emp.: 9,000
Stevedoring Services
S.I.C.: 4491
John Heningway *(Pres.)*
John Price *(V.P.)*
Charles Sadoski *(Controller)*

Outside Service Firm(s):

Security Pacific National Bank*(Major Banking Relationship)*
1301 Fifth Ave.
Seattle, WA 98101
Tel.: 206-621-4530

DAVID G. STEVEN, INC.
663 Fifth Ave.
New York, NY 10022
Tel.: 212-593-0444
Fax: 212-371-9280
Emp.: 90
Fiscal Year-end: 12/31/92
Mfr. Watches
S.I.C.: 3873
Benjamin Kaiser *(Pres.)*
Steven Kaiser *(V.P.-Mktg.)*
Ethel Kleinman *(Dir.-Adv.)*

Computer Systems/Hardware:
MAI Basic 4

Outside Service Firm(s):

Friedman, Alpren & Green*(Auditors)*
New York, NY

National Westminster Bank plc*(Major Banking Relationship)*
Astor Plaza, 1515 Broadway
New York, NY 10036

STEVENS-LEE COMPANY
1600 Xenium Lane N.
Minneapolis, MN 55441
Tel.: 612-553-1881 **MN**
Fax: 612-552-1209
Approx.Sls.: $10,000,000
Emp.: 100
Export
Manufacturer of Milk Dispensers & Refrigerated Food Service Equipment
S.I.C.: 3585; 3523; 3556; 3589; 3632
Harold R. Rubin *(Pres. & Chief Exec. Officer)*
Paul A. Beneson *(V.P.-Pur.)*
Raymond Bishop *(V.P.-Mktg.)*
Michael E. Rodich *(V.P.-Mfg.)*
Stuart A. Rubin *(V.P.-Opers.)*
Benjamin H. Rubin *(Sec. & Treas.)*
Arnold Dobrin *(Dir.-Pur.)*

Outside Service Firm(s):

Apple & Apple*(Auditors)*
Minneapolis, MN

Leonard, Street & Deinard*(Legal Firm)*
150 S. Fifth St., Ste. 2300
Minneapolis, MN 55402
Tel.: 612-335-1500

First Bank Minneapolis*(Major Banking Relationship)*
Minneapolis, MN

MICHAEL STEVENS LTD.
One Nixon Lane
Edison, NJ 08837
Tel.: 908-248-9070 **NJ**
Sales Range: $20-39 Million
Emp.: 200
Distribution Company
Michael Agresta *(Pres.)*

Outside Service Firm(s):

Leipziger & Breskin*(Auditors)*
New York, NY

Bernard Rackear, P.C.*(Legal Firm)*
New York, NY

National Westminster Bank plc*(Major Banking Relationship)*
Astor Plaza, 1515 Broadway
New York, NY 10036

Subsidiary:

Dover Handbag Co., Inc. **(1)**
20 W. 33rd St., Eighth Flr.
New York, NY 10001
Tel.: 212-563-7055
Fax: 212-239-9031
Approx.Sls.: $25,000,000
Emp.: 75
Mfr. of Handbags
S.I.C.: 3171
Evelyn Hester *(Pres.)*

STEVES & SONS
P.O. Drawer S
San Antonio, TX 78211
Tel.: 210-924-5111
Fax: 210-924-0470
Approx.Sls.: $15,000,000
Emp.: 250
Doors & Frames, Wood, Steel, Folding & Fire Door Units
S.I.C.: 2431; 3442
Marshall T. Steves, Sr. *(Chm. Bd.)*
Edward Galt Steves *(Vice Chm. & Chief Exec. Officer)*
Sam Bel Steves, II *(Pres. & Chief Oper. Officer)*
John J. Straff *(Chief Fin. Officer)*
Stephen C. Julian *(Controller)*

Outside Service Firm(s):

Burnside & Rishebarger*(Auditors)*
San Antonio, TX

Texas Commerce Bank*(Major Banking Relationship)*
San Antonio, TX

STEWART'S ICE CREAM CO., INC.
P.O. Box 435
Saratoga Springs, NY 12866
Tel.: 518-581-1000
Fax: 518-584-0160
Approx.Sls.: $240,000,000
Emp.: 1,600
Mfr. Ice Cream & Soda; Operate Retail Convenience Stores
S.I.C.: 2024; 2086; 5411
William P. Dake *(Pres.)*
Richard Dunn *(V.P.-Plant Opers.)*
Leo Scheone *(V.P.-Fin.)*
Nancy Trimbur *(V.P.-Constr. & Maintenance)*
William Stack *(Mgr.-Data Processing)*

STIEFEL LABORATORIES, INC.
2801 Ponce De Leon
Coral Gables, FL 33134
Tel.: 305-443-3807
Year Founded: 1945
Approx.Sls.: $50,000,000
Emp.: 30
Import Export
Mfr. of Dermatological Pharmaceuticals
S.I.C.: 2834
W.K. Stiefel *(Chm. & Pres.)*
C.W. Stiefel *(Vice Chm., Exec. V.P., Gen. Counsel & Corp. Sec.)*
R.I. Fried *(Chief Fin. Officer)*
Jon A. Jungquist *(V.P. & G.M.)*

Division:

Stiefel Laboratories, Inc., Oak Hill **(1)**
Route 145
Oak Hill, NY 12460
Tel.: 518-239-6901
Approx.Sls.: $35,000,000
Emp.: 300
Fiscal Year-end: 3/30/91
Mfr. of Dermatological Pharmaceuticals
S.I.C.: 2834
W.K. Stiefel *(Pres. & Chief Exec. Officer)*
Charles W. Stiefel *(Exec. V.P.)*
Herbert A. Stiefel *(V.P.)*
Richard Fried *(Treas.)*

Michael Martinolich *(Mgr.-Medical Adv. & Promotion)*

City National Bank*(Major Banking Relationship)*
400 Roxbury Dr.
Beverly Hills, CA 90212

Affiliate:

Computer Service Company **(1)**
P.O. Box 74901,
Los Angeles, CA 90004
Tel.: 213-382-2331
Emp.: 40
Manufacture of Traffic Signals
S.I.C.: 3669

SWB
STIEGLER, WELLS & BRUNSWICK, INC

STIEGLER, WELLS & BRUNSWICK, INC.
3865 Adler Place
Bethlehem, PA 18017
Tel.: 215-866-0611
Fax: 215-866-8650
Year Founded: 1969
Approx.Billings: $17,500,000
Emp.: 35
Industrial & Financial Adv.
Daniel C. Wells *(Chm. & Chief Exec. Officer)*
Paul E. Brunswick *(Pres. & Chief Oper. Officer)*
Ernie R. Stiegler, Jr. *(Sr. Exec. V.P., Chief Admin. Officer)*
Lawrence C. Feldman *(V.P., Fin.)*
Henry R. Raab *(V.P., Pub. Rels.)*
Thomas Roth *(V.P., Mktg.)*

Computer Systems/Hardware:
Placintosh IIfx Graphics Computer with Work Stations; Compugraphics 8400

STEINY & COMPANY, INC.
221 N. Ardmore Ave.
Los Angeles, CA 90004
Mailing Address:
P.O. Box 74901,
Los Angeles, CA 90004
Tel.: 213-382-2331
Fax: 213-381-6781
Year Founded: 1953
Assets: $30,000,000
Liabilities: $18,000,000
Net Worth: $12,000,000
Approx.Sls.: $95,000,000
Emp.: 400
Fiscal Year-end: 9/30/90
Electrical Contractor
S.I.C.: 1731
John O. Steiny *(Chm. Bd.)*
Susan Steiny *(Pres.)*
R.H. Alston *(V.P.)*
Jay Perry *(Sec., Treas. & Controller)*

Principal(s):
John O. Steiny
Susan Steiny
John T. Steiny
Nancy Steiny Borris
Julia Steiny Johnson

No. of Mfg. Plants/Facilities: 5
No. of U.S. Offices: 5

Computer Systems/Hardware:
HCR

Outside Service Firm(s):

Hutchinson & Bloodgood*(Auditors)*
420 N. Brand Blvd., Ste. 600
Glendale, CA 91203

Alexander & Alexander*(Commercial Insurance Carrier)*
Los Angeles, CA

Gill & Baldwin*(Legal Firm)*
144 N. Brand Blvd.
Glendale, CA 91203

Bank of America NT&SA*(Major Banking Relationship)*
555 So. Flower St., 5th Fl.
Los Angeles, CA 90071
Tel.: 213-228-3526
Fax: 213-228-4062

THE STIFFEL COMPANY
700 N. Kingsbury
Chicago, IL 60610
Tel.: 312-664-9200
Fax: 312-664-3873
Year Founded: 1932
Sales Range: $20-39 Million
Emp.: 500
Import Export
Mfr. of Lamps & Shades
S.I.C.: 3645; 2295
Jim Snodgrass *(Chm. Bd. & Pres.)*
Steve Lindblad *(Vice Chm.)*
Don Rogalski *(V.P.-Fin. & Admin. & Treas.)*
John A. Passini *(V.P.-Sls.)*
James Cunningham *(V.P.-Mfg.)*
Michael McNally *(V.P.-Human Resources)*
Sophie Melko *(Dir.-Mktg.)*
Hank Cogan *(Mgr.-Pur.)*

Computer Systems/Hardware:
AS/400

Outside Service Firm(s):

Ernst & Young*(Auditors)*
233 S. Wacker Dr.
Chicago, IL 60606
Tel.: 312-368-1800
Fax: 312-645-3095

Continental Bank N. A.*(Major Banking Relationship)*
231 S. LaSalle St.
Chicago, IL 60697
Tel.: 312-828-2345
Tel.: 800-426-5754
Telex: 312-828-1783

STIHL INC.
(Sub. of Stihl International, Germany)
536 Viking Dr.
Virginia Beach, VA 23452
Tel.: 804-486-9100
Fax: 804-486-9288
Year Founded: 1926
Emp.: 400
Fiscal Year-end: 12/31/90
Import Export
Mfr. Chain Saws, Grass Trimmers, Brush Cutters & Outdoor Power Equipment
S.I.C.: 3546; 5084; 5083
Hans Peter Stihl *(Chm. Bd.)*
Fred Whyte *(Pres.)*
Peter Mueller *(Exec. V.P.-Mfg.)*
Manfred Schwarz *(Exec. V.P.-Fin.)*
Tom Burris *(Mgr.-Export Sls.)*
Jackson D'Armond *(Mgr.-Adv. & Sls. Promo.)*
Jack H. Guthrie *(Mgr.-Mktg. Services)*
Monica Mills *(Mgr.-Human Resources)*
Terry Richards *(Mgr.-Sls.)*
Roger Simons *(Mgr.-Engrng. Services)*
Letha Marquez *(Travel Coord. & Meetings Plng. Dir.)*

Computer Systems/Hardware:
IBM

Stihl Parts, Inc. **(1)**
520 Viking Dr.
Virginia Beach, VA 23452
Tel.: 804-486-9244
Fax: 804-486-9197
Import Export

Computer Systems/Hardware:
IBM
Distr. of Machinery
S.I.C.: 5084
George Cruz *(Gen. Mgr.)*

Non-U.S. Holding:

Stihl Eastern Canada Ltd. **(1)**
579 Ave. Godin
Ville Vanier, PQ G1M 3G7, Canada
Tel.: 418-683-1717 (100%)
Mfr. of Chainsaws & Accessories
S.I.C.: 3546
J. Saillant *(Pres.)*

STILES CORPORATION
6400 N. Andrews Ave.
Fort Lauderdale, FL 33309
Tel.: 305-776-9300
Fax: 305-771-0416
Approx.Sls.: $55,000,000
Emp.: 200
Industrial Buildings & Warehouses Nonresidential Construction; Real Estate Brokers; Landscaping Contractors
S.I.C.: 0781; 1541; 1542; 1731; 6531
Terry Stiles *(Pres.)*
Bill Young *(Exec. V.P.)*
Trish Schlegel *(Controller)*
Diane G. Diamantis *(Dir.-Mktg. Communications)*

Outside Service Firm(s):

Madsen, Sapp, Mena, Rodriguez & Co., PA*(Auditors)*
Fort Lauderdale, FL

Chase Manhattan Bank, N.A.*(Major Banking Relationship)*
One Chase Manhattan Plaza
New York, NY 10081
Tel.: 212-552-2222
Tel.: 800-526-0801
Fax: 212-552-7175

STILLMAN & HOAG, INC.
386 Grand Ave.
Englewood, NJ 07631
Tel.: 201-871-6126
Fax: 201-569-6319
Approx.Sls.: $167,000,000
Emp.: 410
Retail, Rent & Lease New & Used Automobiles & Recreational Vehicles
S.I.C.: 5511; 7519
Walter R. Stillman *(Chm. Bd. & Pres.)*
John C. Stillman *(Exec. V.P. & Sec.)*

Outside Service Firm(s):

Weidenbaum, Ryder & Co.*(Auditors)*
Englewood Cliffs, NJ

Lebson & Prigoff*(Legal Firm)*
Englewood, NJ

Midlantic National Bank*(Major Banking Relationship)*
Hackensack, NJ

STILLMAN SEAL
6020 Avenida Encinas
Carlsbad, CA 92009
Tel.: 619-438-1011
Fax: 619-438-7536
Approx.Sls.: $11,000,000
Emp.: 175
Mfr. Still-Seal Gaskets, Permadized Seals, Molded Specialty Seals, Diaphragms, Specialized Rubber Compounding, Specialty Self-Lubricating
S.I.C.: 3053; 3061; 3562
G.I. Haight *(Div. Mgr.)*
R. Kazmarex *(Controller)*
D. Seach *(Product Mgr.)*

EDWIN B. STIMPSON COMPANY, INC.
900 Sylvan Ave.
Bayport, NY 11705
Tel.: 516-472-2000 **NY**
Telex: 4972370
Fax: 516-472-2425
Year Founded: 1852
Sales Range: $20-39 Million
Emp.: 613
Fiscal Year-end: 12/31/90
Export
Manufacture Eyelets, Metal Snap Fasteners, Grommets & Washers, Terminals, Metal Stampings & Attaching Machines
S.I.C.: 3131; 3452; 3469; 3643; 3644; 3965; 3559
Howard C. Rau *(Chm. Bd.)*
Edward J. Sheridan *(Pres. & Chief Exec. Officer)*
George A. Fortmuller *(Chief Fin. Officer, Treas. & Sec.)*
R. E. Rau, Jr. *(Exec. V.P.)*
James E. Cuenin *(V.P.)*
John H. Rau *(V.P.)*
William G. Rauss *(Dir.-Sls. & Mktg.)*
E. J. DeWalters *(Mgr.-Sls.)*

Principal(s):
Howard C. Rau
Edward J. Sheridan

No. of Mfg. Plants/Facilities: 2

Computer Systems/Hardware:
Unisys V340

Outside Service Firm(s):

KPMG Peat Marwick*(Auditors)*
1 Jericho Plaza
Jericho, NY 11753
Tel.: 516-822-9100

Aetna Life & Casualty*(Group Insurer)*
151 Farmington Avenue
Hartford, CT 06156
Tel.: 203-273-2128
Fax: 203-729-4295

Chemical Bank*(Major Banking Relationship)*
395 North Service Rd.
Melville, NY 11747

Chase Manhattan Bank, N.A.*(Major Banking Relationship)*
One Chase Manhattan Plaza
New York, NY 10081
Tel.: 212-552-2222
Tel.: 800-526-0801
Fax: 212-552-7175

STINSON SEAFOOD COMPANY
Route 186
Prospect Harbor, ME 04669
Mailing Address:
HCR60 Box 17,
Prospect Harbor, ME 04669
Tel.: 207-963-7331
Year Founded: 1927
Approx.Sls.: $30,000,000
Emp.: 800
Import Export
Canned & Cured Sardines, Frozen Fillets, Fish Steaks, Ground Fish
S.I.C.: 2091; 2092
Roland Chabot *(Chief Fin. Officer)*
Richard Klingaman *(Export Consultant)*

STOCK YARDS PACKING CO., INC.
340 N. Oakley Blvd.
Chicago, IL 60612
Tel.: 312-733-6050
Tel.: 800-621-1119
Tel.: 800-621-3687 **DE**
Fax: 312-733-0738
Year Founded: 1893
Approx.Sls.: $65,000,000
Emp.: 98
Fiscal Year-end: 4/30/92
Export
Meat & Meat Products for Restaurants, Institutions, Airlines, Hospitals, Homes; Holiday Meat Gift Packages
S.I.C.: 2011; 5961; 5147; 5421

Stock Yards Packing Co., Inc.—(Continued)

Dan Pollack *(Pres.)*
Harry Katz *(Exec. V.P.-Sls. & Sec.)*
Stanley Katz *(V.P.-Adv. & Treas.)*
Dan Rost *(Mgr.-Mktg.)*
William Kramp *(Buyer)*

No. of U.S. Offices: 3

Computer Systems/Hardware:
Digital; Adds

Outside Service Firm(s):

Greenberg, Keele, Lunn & Aronberg*(Legal Firm)*
One IBM Plaza
Chicago, IL 60611
Tel.: 312-828-9600

Continental Bank N. A.*(Major Banking Relationship)*
231 S. LaSalle St.
Chicago, IL 60697
Tel.: 312-828-2345
Tel.: 800-426-5754
Telex: 312-828-1783

STOCKER & YALE, INC.
133 Brimbol Ave.
Beverly, MA 01915
Mailing Address:
P.O. Box 494,
Beverly, MA 01915
Tel.: 508-927-3940
Tel.: 800-843-8011
Fax: 508-937-8756
Year Founded: 1946
Approx.Sls.: $15,000,000
Emp.: 160
Fiscal Year-end: 12/31/90
Export
Mfr. Optical Instruments: Scanners, Compactors, Illuminators; Machine Tool Accessories, Material Handling Equipment, Watches, Compases & Chart Recorders
S.I.C.: 3827; 3544; 3535; 3543; 3599; 3812; 3829; 3873
Mark Blodgett *(Chm. Bd.)*
James Bickman *(Pres. & Treas.)*
Susan Hojer *(Chief Fin. Officer)*
Dwayne Hillman *(Dir.-Mktg.)*
Mike Lavey *(Sls. Mgr.)*
Greg Theokas *(Mktg. Mgr.)*
R. Richards *(Pur. Agent)*

Computer Systems/Hardware:
AS 400 Marketing System

Division:

MFE Instruments **(1)**
133 Brimbal Ave.
Beverly, MA 01915
Tel.: 508-921-9104
Tel.: 800-472-4633
Telex: 953145 EasyLink
Fax: 508-921-9110
Approx.Sls.: $5,000,000
Emp.: 50
Fiscal Year-end: 12/31/90
Export
Mfr. of OEM Oscillographic Recorders-Single Thru 8 Channel, AC & DC Powered, Pen Motors & Recorder Supplies, Digital Casette Recorders & Data Loggers, Thermal Printers
S.I.C.: 3825; 3823; 3826; 3829; 3577
Mark W. Blodgett *(Chm. Bd.)*
James Bickman *(Pres.)*
Susan Hojer *(Chief Fin. Officer, Controller & Mgr.-Personnel)*
Don R. Riley *(Gen. Mgr.)*
Dwayne Hillman *(Dir.-Mktg.)*
Nelson Gauthier *(Dir.-Pur.)*
John Lepore *(Mktg., Sls. & Adv. Mgr.)*
Michael P. Kiley *(Mgr.-Quality Assurance & Prod. Mgr.)*
John Powers *(Mgr.-Mfg.)*
Mark Greenfield *(Tech. Services)*
James Amnott *(Quality Control)*

STOCKHAM VALVES & FITTINGS, INC.
4000 10th Ave. N.
Birmingham, AL 35212
Mailing Address:
P.O. Box 10326
Birmingham, AL 35202
Tel.: 205-592-6361
Fax: 205-591-1300
Fax: 205-592-4665
Emp.: 1,600
Manufacture Flow Control Devices, Fittings, Valves & Couplings
S.I.C.: 3494
Larry Kinderman *(Chm. Bd.)*
Herbert Stockham *(Pres. & Chief Exec. Officer)*
John Cantlin *(V.P.-Fin.)*

Outside Service Firm(s):

Ernst & Young*(Auditors)*
Harbert Plaza, 1900 AmSouth
Birmingham, AL 35243

Allendale Mutual Insurance Co.*(Commercial Insurance Carrier)*
1301 Atwood Ave.
Johnston, RI 02919
Tel.: 401-275-3000

Home Life Insurance Co.*(Commercial Insurance Carrier)*
New York, NY

IRI*(Commercial Insurance Carrier)*
New York, NY

Southeast Health Plan*(Group Insurer)*
Birmingham, AL

Bradley, Arant, Rose & White*(Legal Firm)*
1400 Park Place Tower
Birmingham, AL 35203
Tel.: 205-521-8000

SouthTrust Bank*(Major Banking Relationship)*
Birmingham, AL
Tel.: 205-254-5068

Whitney National Bank of New Orleans*(Major Banking Relationship)*
P.O. Box 61260
New Orleans, LA 70161
Tel.: 504-586-7422

Subsidiaries:

Accu-Cast, Inc. **(1)**
4000 10th Ave. North
Birmingham, AL 35202
Tel.: 205-592-6361

Aliceville Casting Co. **(1)**
4000 10th Ave. North
Birmingham, AL 35202
Tel.: 205-592-6361

Atlas Pattern Works **(1)**
4000 10th Ave. North
Birmingham, AL 35202
Tel.: 205-592-6361

Marlan Valves Co. **(1)**
4000 10th Ave. North
Birmingham, AL 35202
Tel.: 205-592-6361

Rockingham Stainless Steel **(1)**
4000 10th Ave. North
Birmingham, AL 35202
Tel.: 205-592-6361

St. Clair Manufacturing Co. **(1)**
4000 10th Ave. North
Birmingham, AL 35202
Tel.: 205-592-6361

Southwestern Foundries **(1)**
4000 10th Ave. North
Birmingham, AL 35202
Tel.: 205-592-6361

SWB
Stockton·West·Burkhart, Inc.

STOCKTON WEST BURKHART INC.
401 E. Court St.
Cincinnati, OH 45202
Tel.: 513-381-5600
Fax: 513-381-0434
Year Founded: 1936
Approx.Billings: $20,000,000
Emp.: 31
Bertrand A. Schloemer *(Chm. Bd.)*
Jay B. Schloemer *(Pres.)*
Dottie Warner *(Controller)*

THE STOGEL COMPANIES INC.
19 W. 44th St.
New York, NY 10036
Tel.: 212-302-5500 **NY**
Fax: 212-302-5512
Year Founded: 1963
Approx.Billings: $8,500,000
Emp.: 10
Fiscal Year-end: 1/31/91
Advertising Agency
S.I.C.: 7311
Philip Stogel *(Chm.)*
Lawrence Stogel *(Pres.)*
Yale Stogel *(Sr. V.P.)*
Florence S. Stogel *(Treas.)*
Laura Panzarino *(Corp. Sec.)*
George Gilbert *(Dir.-Mktg. Res. & Acct. Services)*
Chuck Stoael *(Sports Editor/Writer)*

Outside Service Firm(s):

The Bank of New York*(Major Banking Relationship)*
One Wall Street
New York, NY 10286
Tel.: 212-635-6805
Fax: 212-635-3201

STOLPER-FABRALLOY CO.
115 N. Janecek Rd.
Waukesha, WI 53186
Tel.: 414-786-3400 **WI**
Fax: 414-786-9249
Year Founded: 1908
Approx.Sls.: $15,000,000
Emp.: 150
Export
Mfr. of Parts for Turbines
S.I.C.: 3511
Lloyd A. Gerlach *(Chm. Bd.)*
Jan Wedel *(Pres.)*
G. Felhofer *(Treas.)*

Outside Service Firm(s):

KPMG Peat Marwick*(Auditors)*
777 E. Wisconsin Ave.
Milwaukee, WI 53202
Tel.: 414-276-4200

First Wisconsin National Bank*(Major Banking Relationship)*
777 E. Wisconsin Ave.
Milwaukee, WI 53202
Tel.: 414-765-4321
Fax: 414-355-6903

F.H. STOLTZE LAND & LUMBER COMPANY
219 N. Main St.
Stillwater, MN 55082
Mailing Address:
P.O. Box 439
Stillwater, MN 55082
Tel.: 612-439-2200 **MT**
Fax: 612-439-5917
Year Founded: 1912
Approx.Sls.: $33,000,000
Emp.: 200
Fiscal Year-end: 12/31/91
Sawmill
S.I.C.: 2421
Daniel W. O'Brien *(Pres.)*
Rem Kohrt *(V.P. & Gen. Mgr.)*
Greg A. Johnson *(Treas. & Controller)*

No. of Mfg. Plants/Facilities: 3
No. of U.S. Offices: 4

Outside Service Firm(s):

Ernst & Young*(Auditors)*
St. Paul, MN

Doherty, Rumble & Butler*(Legal Firm)*
2800 Minnesota World Trade Center
St. Paul, MN 55101-4999
Tel.: 612-291-9333

First Bank of St. Paul*(Major Banking Relationship)*
St. Paul, MN

Subsidiary:

Stoltze-Conner Lumber Co. **(1)**
P.O. Box 410
Darby, MT 59289
Tel.: 406-821-3242
Emp.: 75
Sawmill
S.I.C.: 2421
Michael Lingholm *(Mgr.)*

STONCO
2345 Vauxhall Rd.
Union, NJ 07083
Tel.: 908-964-7000
Year Founded: 1947
Approx.Sls.: $40,000,000
Emp.: 200
Import Export
Outdoor Commercial & Industrial Lighting; Incandescent & H.I.D. (High Intensity Discharge)
S.I.C.: 3646
G. Gulden *(V.P. & Gen. Mgr.)*
Phil Henry *(Reg. Sls. Mgr.)*

Computer Systems/Hardware:
HP3000

STONE ADVERTISING
821 Broadway
New York, NY 10003
Tel.: 212-353-0494
Fax: 212-673-4303
Year Founded: 1987
Approx.Billings: $11,500,000
Emp.: 9
Consumer Adv.
Roger Stone *(Pres.)*

Computer Systems/Hardware:
Macintosh, Apple

DON STONE ASSOCIATES INC.
P.O. Box 198,
Mamaroneck, NY 10543
Tel.: 914-698-5063
Year Founded: 1983
Approx.Billings: $10,275,000
Emp.: 5
Don Stone *(Pres.)*
H. Hagedorn *(Treas.)*

STONE, AUGUST, BAKER COMMUNICATIONS COMPANIES
1301 W. Long Lake Rd.
Troy, MI 48098
Tel.: 313-641-0400
Fax: 313-641-0425
Year Founded: 1956
Approx.Billings: $31,787,000
Emp.: 55
Advertising Agency
S.I.C.: 7311
Ronald I. Stone *(Chm.)*

James M. August *(Pres.)*
James Grossman *(V.P., Pub. Rels.)*
Roy Barnes *(V.P., Pub. Rels.)*
Kelly Neill *(Sr. V.P., Dir. Consumer/ Retail Client Services)*
Gilbert A. Testa *(V.P.)*

Outside Service Firm(s):

Zalenko & Associates*(Auditors)*
Southfield, MI

Republic Hogg Robinson*(Commercial Insurance Carrier)*
Southfield, MI

UNUM Life Insurance Company*(Group Insurer)*
P.O. Box 9500,
Portland, ME 04104
Tel.: 800-521-9750

Silver, Gould, Eizelman, Zoller & Jackier*(Legal Firm)*
1533 N. Woodward
Bloomfield Hills, MI 48304

Michigan National Bank*(Major Banking Relationship)*
Southfield, MI

Subsidiary:

R. J. Baker Advertising, Inc. **(1)**
1301 W. Long Lake Rd.
Troy, MI 48098
Tel.: 313-641-0400
Fax: 313-641-0425
S.I.C.: 7311
James M. August *(Pres.)*
Gilbert A. Testa *(V.P.)*
Roy Barnes *(V.P., Pub. Rels.)*

Subsidiaries:

H. G. Productions **(2)**
1301 W. Long Lake Rd.
Troy, MI 48098
Tel.: 313-641-0400
Harry Goldberg, Jr. *(Pres.)*

Stone August Baker Public Relations **(2)**
1301 W. Long Lake Rd., Ste. 350
Troy, MI 48098
Tel.: 313-641-0400
Approx.Billings: $828,000
Emp.: 8
Computer Systems/Hardware:
IBM; Apple MacIntosh
Media Rels., Special Events, Crisis Communications, Pub. Opinion Research, Newsletters & Collateral, Continuity Mailing Programs, Industrial & Business-to-Business Communications
Ron Stone *(Pres.)*
James Grossman *(V.P., Pub. Rels., Promo. & Special Events)*
Roy Barnes *(V.P.)*

The Strategy Company **(2)**
1301 W. Long Lake Rd.
Troy, MI 48098
Tel.: 313-641-0400
James M. August *(Pres.)*

STONE MANUFACTURING COMPANY, INC.
1500 Poinsett Hwy.
Greenville, SC 29609
Tel.: 803-242-6300
Fax: 803-242-6300 ext.413
Approx.Sls.: $75,000,000
Emp.: 2,000
Men's & Boys' Underwear & Athletic Uniforms & Juniors Athletic Clothing; Family Clothing Stores
S.I.C.: 2322; 2329; 5651
Eugene E. Stone, III *(Chm. Bd.)*
Eugene E. Stone, IV *(Chief Exec. Officer)*
Charles Rivers Stone *(Pres.)*
John J. Brausch *(V.P.-Fin.)*

Outside Service Firm(s):

Ernst & Young*(Auditors)*
C & S Bank Tower, Two Shelter Centre, Ste. 800
Greenville, SC 29603

Haynsworth, Marion, McKay & Guerard*(Legal Firm)*
75 Beattie Place, 2 Shelter Centre 11th Fl
Greenville, SC 29601
Tel.: 803-240-3300

South Carolina National Bank*(Major Banking Relationship)*
Columbia, SC

STONE & SIMONS ADVERTISING, INC.
24245 Northwestern Hwy.
Southfield, MI 48075
Tel.: 313-358-4800 **MI**
Fax: 313-358-0128
Year Founded: 1956
Assets: $2,238,800
Liabilities: $1,465,847
Net Worth: $772,953
Approx.Billings: $32,000,000
Emp.: 45
Fiscal Year-end: 4/30/92
Advertising Agency
S.I.C.: 7311
Corporate Giving Program: United Way
Charles G. Stone *(Chm., Pres. & Chief Exec. Officer)*
Howard Dembs *(V.P. & Acct. Grp. Suprvr.)*
Christopher Gaffield *(V.P. & Dir.-Mktg.)*
Larry Steinberg *(V.P., Assoc. Group Supvr., & Dir.-Creative)*
Ellis Veech *(V.P. & Dir.-Media)*
Sarah Martin *(Treas.)*
Rose Szwed *(Dir.-Pub. Rels.)*
Paula Huttula *(Mgr.-Office)*

No. of U.S. Offices: 1

Computer Systems/Hardware:
IBM System 36, Zeos, Compac & IBM PC's

Outside Service Firm(s):

Kleiman, Carney & Greenbaum*(Auditors)*
Farmington Hills, MI

CNA Insurance*(Commercial Insurance Carrier)*
CNA Plaza,
Chicago, IL 60685
Tel.: 312-822-5000

Blue Cross & Blue Shield of Michigan*(Group Insurer)*
Detroit, MI

Butzel Long*(Legal Firm)*
Madden Bldg., 150 W. Jefferson, Ste. 900
Detroit, MI 48226-4430
Tel.: 313-225-7000
Fax: 313-225-7080

Comerica Bank*(Major Banking Relationship)*
211 W. Fort St.
Detroit, MI 48226
Tel.: 313-222-3300

Subsidiary:

Stone & Simons Advertising, Inc. **(1)**
701 Congressional Blvd., Ste. 120
Carmel, IN 46032
Tel.: 317-571-1114
Fax: 317-571-1245
Advertising Agency
S.I.C.: 7311
Jim Buckley *(Mgr.)*

STONE & THOMAS
1030 Main St.
Wheeling, WV 26003
Tel.: 304-232-3344 **WV**
Year Founded: 1847
Approx.Sls.: $100,000,000
Emp.: 2,500
Department Stores
S.I.C.: 5311
Edward C. Armbrecht, Jr. *(Chm. Bd. & Co-Chief Exec. Officer)*
Wilbur S. Jones, Jr. *(Pres. & Co-Chief Exec. Officer)*
Stephen D. Frome *(V.P.-Mngmt. Information Systems)*
William E. Maxwell *(V.P. & Controller)*
Kenneth L. Morgan *(V.P.-Personnel)*
J. Morrison *(V.P.-Reg. Mgr., Northern Stores)*
John R. Terrill *(V.P.-Credit & Internal Audit)*

Outside Service Firm(s):

Deloitte & Touche*(Auditors)*
2400 One PPG Place
Pittsburgh, PA 15222
Tel.: 412-281-2232

Security National Bank*(Major Banking Relationship)*
Wheeling, WV

Divisions:

Stone & Thomas Merchandising Offices **(1)**
Lee & Dickinson Sts.
Charleston, WV 25326
Tel.: 304-346-0981
S.I.C.: 5311
S.P. Roemer *(Exec. V.P. & Gen. Mktg. Mgr.)*
Sophia Pappas *(V.P-Reg. Mgr.)*

Stone & Thomas Advertising & Visual Offices **(1)**
208 Hale St.
Charleston, WV 25326
Tel.: 304-345-7930
Lewis Soulsby *(V.P.-Adv.)*
Doug Holmstrom *(Mgr.-Visual Mdsg.)*

STONECUTTER MILLS CORP.
Dallas Street
Spindale, NC 28160
Mailing Address:
P.O. Box 157,
Spindale, NC 28160
Tel.: 704-286-2341
Year Founded: 1920
Mfr. of Yarn & Woven Textile Products; Dyeing, Finish Cloth
S.I.C.: 2211; 2221; 2261; 2262; 2281
James R. Cowan *(Chm. Bd. & Chief Exec. Officer)*
Adin H. Rucker, Jr. *(Pres. & Treas.)*
T.P. Walker *(Sr. V.P. & Sec.)*
S.G. Gabriel *(Dir.-Personnel)*
Tom Harris *(Dir.-Pur.)*
Norman Hardin *(Mgr.-Data Processing)*

Subsidiaries:

Mitchell Co. **(1)**
400 Spindale
Spindale, NC 28160
Tel.: 704-286-2511
S.I.C.: 2211; 2221; 2262; 2261; 2281

Henson Timber Products Corp. **(1)**
Duke Street
Forest City, NC 28043
Tel.: 704-245-4241
S.I.C.: 5099

Rutherford Warehouse Corp. **(1)**
P.O. Box 157,
Spindale, NC 28160
S.I.C.: 4225

Stonecutter Trucking Co. **(1)**
P.O. Box 157,
Spindale, NC 28160
S.I.C.: 4213

STONES, INC.
524 Webster St.
Bainbridge, GA 31717
Tel.: 912-246-1444 **GA**
Fax: 912-246-9083
Year Founded: 1959
Approx.Sls.: $12,000,000
Emp.: 110
Home Centers; Wholesale Distribution of Exterior & Interior Building Materials
S.I.C.: 5211; 5031
James W. Stone *(Chm. Bd.)*
Joe Higdon *(Pres.)*
Victor H. Dickenson *(V.P.)*
Laura Bridges *(Treas.)*
Bruce W. Kirbo *(Sec.)*

Outside Service Firm(s):

Dickson & Hilburn*(Auditors)*
Bainbridge, GA

STONHARD

STONHARD, INC.
One Park Ave.
Maple Shade, NJ 08052
Tel.: 609-779-7500
Tel.: 800-257-7953 **DE**
Telex: 710-892-0769
Fax: 609-779-0638
Year Founded: 1922
Earnings: $700,000
Approx.Sls.: $95,000,000
Emp.: 700
Fiscal Year-end: 12/31/91
Import Export
Mfr. & Installation of Industrial & Commercial Polymer-Base Floors, Coatings & Linings.
S.I.C.: 1752; 2851
H. Donald Stork *(Chm. Bd.)*
J.M. Stork *(Pres.)*
Donald Zikmund *(V.P.-Sls.)*
Gary Moran *(V.P.-Admin.)*
Peggy Fynan *(V.P.-Mktg.)*
James Hamer *(V.P.-Opers.)*
Frederick A. Pfaff *(V.P.-Research & Devel.)*
David P. Reif *(Chief Fin. Officer)*
Pam Russel *(Dir.-Employee Benefits)*
Kendall Ellis *(Adv. Mgr.)*
Principal(s):
H. Donald Stork

No. of Mfg. Plants/Facilities: 3
No. of U.S. Offices: 5
No. of Foreign Offices: 3

Computer Systems/Hardware:
Prime System 9955

Outside Service Firm(s):

Haefle Van Sciver & Co.*(Auditors)*
Haddonfield, NJ

Crum & Forster*(Commercial Insurance Carrier)*
Philadelphia, PA

Great-West Life Assurance Co.*(Group Insurer)*
8505 East Orchard Rd.
Englewood, CO 8011
Tel.: 800-537-2033

Dechert, Price & Rhoads*(Legal Firm)*
4000 Bell Atlantic Tower, 1717 Arch St.
Philadelphia, PA 19103
Tel.: 215-994-4000
Tel.: 2000

Fidelity Bank*(Major Banking Relationship)*
Broad & Walnut St.
Philadelphia, PA 19109

Non-U.S. Holdings:

Stonhard Latin America **(1)**
Los Juarez No. 26 Colonia San Jose, D3900 Insurgentes,
Mexico, D.F. Mexico
Tel.: 525-563-9900 (49%)
Fax: 525-598-4614
Approx.Sls.: $4,250,000
Emp.: 10
Install Epoxy Based Industrial & Commercial Floor Resurfacing
S.I.C.: 1752; 3531; 3996; 2891; 2851
Ing. Javier F. Maldonado *(Chief Oper. Officer)*

Stonhard, Inc.—(Continued)

Stonhard, Europe **(1)**
143 Woluwelaan 1831
Diegem, Belgium
Tel.: 02 720-8982
Telex: 2241 MVALU LU
Fax: 322/720-4727
Approx.Sls.: $12,000,000
Emp.: 45
Manufacture & Install Epoxy-Based Indus. & Comml. Floor Resurfacing Material
S.I.C.: 1752; 3531
James Baldino *(Chief Oper. Officer)*

Stonhard, Ltd. **(1)**
95 Sunray St.
Whitby, ON L1N 9C9, Canada
Tel.: 416-430-3333
Fax: 416-430-3056
Approx.Sls.: $14,500,000
Manufacture of Industrial & Commercial Floor Resurfacing Material
S.I.C.: 1752; 3531
Alan Brooks *(Chief Oper. Officer)*

STOP SHOP SAVE
770 W. North Ave.
Baltimore, MD 21217
Tel.: 410-225-7900 **MD**
Fax: 301-523-1403
Year Founded: 1986
Approx.Sls.: $50,000,000
Emp.: 300
Grocery Store Chain
S.I.C.: 5411
Henry T. Baines *(Pres.)*
Edith M. Baines *(Sec.)*

Outside Service Firm(s):

Signet Bank*(Major Banking Relationship)*
P.O. Box 1077, 7 St. Paul St.
Baltimore, MD 21203

STORM PRODUCTS COMPANY, INC.
112 S. Glasgow Ave.
Inglewood, CA 90301
Tel.: 213-776-8141 **CA**
Fax: 213-645-6701
Year Founded: 1957
Approx.Sls.: $28,000,000
Emp.: 360
Import Export
Wholesale & Manufacture Electronic Wire Cable & Assemblies
S.I.C.: 3357; 3643
John A. Storm *(Pres.)*
Ray Noble *(V.P.)*
June Storm *(V.P., Sec. & Treas.)*

Outside Service Firm(s):

John Baretta*(Auditors)*
Santa Monica, CA

David J. Dealey*(Legal Firm)*
Santa Monica, CA

MetroBank*(Major Banking Relationship)*
Los Angeles, CA

STOWE-PHARR MILLS, INC.
100 Main St.
McAdenville, NC 28101
Mailing Address:
P.O. Box 1939,
McAdenville, NC 28101
Tel.: 704-824-3551
Fax: 704-824-0072
Year Founded: 1939
Assets: $195,000,000
Liabilities: $122,000,000
Net Worth: $73,000,000
Approx.Sls.: $350,000,000
Emp.: 4,000
Fiscal Year-end: 3/31/92
Export
Mfr. Textile Yarns
S.I.C.: 2281; 2269; 0181
J.M. Carstarphen *(Chm. Bd., Pres. & Chief Exec. Officer)*
James H. Howard *(Chief Fin. Officer & Corp. Sec.)*
J.J. Chamberlain *(Exec. V.P.)*
Charles N. Stegall *(Controller)*
Kenneth C. Botts *(Dir.-Mfg.)*
Greg Peeler *(Dir.-Cash Mgmnt.)*
Don O. Spangler *(Dir.-Employee Benefits)*
Gene Thompson *(Dir.-Human Resources)*

Computer Systems/Hardware:
IBM

Outside Service Firm(s):

Deloitte & Touche*(Auditors)*
2000 First Citizens Bank Plaza, 128 S. Tryon St.
Charlotte, NC 28202-5001
Tel.: 704-372-3560

Liberty Mutual*(Commercial Insurance Carrier)*
175 Berkeley St.
Boston, MA

Johnston, Taylor, & Allison*(Legal Firm)*
Charlotte, NC

First Wachovia Bank & Trust Co.*(Major Banking Relationship)*
Atlanta, GA

NationsBank Carolinas*(Major Banking Relationship)*
One NCNB Plaza T18-7
Charlotte, NC 28255

New England Mutual Life Insurance Co.*(Pension Manager)*
Boston, MA

STRACHAN SHIPPING CO.
6002 Commerce Blvd.
Garden City, GA 31408
Mailing Address:
P.O. Box 3147,
Savannah, GA 31402
Tel.: 912-966-5200
Fax: 912-966-6967
Approx.Sls.: $67,000,000
Emp.: 630
Terminal Operations; Agents & Stevedores for Ship Owners
S.I.C.: 4491
J. R. McPhearson, Jr. *(Pres.)*
E. L. Ennis *(Chief Fin. Officer, Treas. & Controller)*
Vernon Cawthon *(Asst. V.P.-Fin.)*
Peter M. Grier *(Asst. V.P.-Data Processing)*

Computer Systems/Hardware:
IBM 4341

Outside Service Firm(s):

Price Waterhouse*(Auditors)*
Savannah, GA

Home Life Insurance Co.*(Commercial Insurance Carrier)*
New York, NY

Citizens & Southern Trust Company, Inc.*(Investment Banker)*
Savannah, GA

Adams, Gardner & Ellis*(Legal Firm)*
Savannah, GA

Citizens & Southern Trust Company, Inc.*(Major Banking Relationship)*
Savannah, GA

First Union National Bank*(Major Banking Relationship)*
Savannah, GA

Jamison, Eaton & Wood*(Pension Manager)*
Chatham, NJ

Meinus & Co.*(Pension Manager)*
Savannah, GA

Subsidiary:

Oceanic Shipping Co. **(1)**
6002 Commerce Blvd.
Garden City, GA 31408
Tel.: 912-238-2000

STRAFCO, INC.
1964 S. Alamo
San Antonio, TX 78204
Mailing Address:
P.O Box 600,
San Antonio, TX 78292
Tel.: 210-226-0101 **TX**
Fax: 210-271-7495
Year Founded: 1870
Approx.Sls.: $109,000,000
Emp.: 1,130
Fiscal Year-end: 12/31/90
Wholesale & Retail Auto Parts, Tires
S.I.C.: 5013; 5014; 5531
David J. Straus *(Chm. Bd. & Chief Exec. Officer)*
Joseph Straus, Jr. *(Vice Chm.)*
Jack Trawick *(Pres.)*
Huey J. Rhudy *(Treas. & Sec.)*
Murray Betts, Jr. *(Dir.-Personnel)*
Bob Morley *(Pur. Dir.-Tire Div.)*
Harrell Tipton *(Pur. Dir.-Automotive Div.)*
Karl Kuykendall *(Mgr.-Data Processing)*

No. of U.S. Offices: 108

Computer Systems/Hardware:
Sperry Univac

Outside Service Firm(s):

KPMG Peat Marwick*(Auditors)*
112 E. Pecan
San Antonio, TX 78205

Frost National Bank*(Major Banking Relationship)*
P.O. Box 1600
San Antonio, TX 78296

Sanger & Altgelt*(Commercial Insurance Carrier)*
P.O. Box 12365,
San Antonio, TX

Prudential Insurance Co. of America*(Group Insurer)*
751 Broad St.
Newark, NJ 07102-3777
Tel.: 201-802-6000

Lang, Ladon, Green, Coghlan & Fisher*(Legal Firm)*
San Antonio, TX

STRAHMAN VALVES, INC.
3 Vreeland Rd.
Florham Park, NJ 07932-1590
Tel.: 201-377-4900 **NJ**
Twx: 136497
Fax: 201-822-1819
Year Founded: 1921
Approx.Sls.: $13,000,000
Emp.: 70
Fiscal Year-end: 3/31/91
Export
Manufacture Mixing Units & Hose Stations; Ram Type Drain Valves; Piston Type Sampling Valves; Liquid Level Gauges
S.I.C.: 3494; 3823; 3829
Herman Strahman, Jr. *(Chm. Bd. & Pres.)*
Richard D. Strahman *(V.P. & Treas.)*
Donald W. Van Hook *(Controller)*
William R. Pascoe *(Gen. Mgr.)*
Donald J. Abrams *(Mgr.-Sls., Drain Valves)*
Kevin Carroll *(Mgr.-Sls.)*
Philip Traversi *(Mgr.-Acctg.)*
Dan Mariani *(Pur. Agent)*

No. of Mfg. Plants/Facilities: 1
No. of U.S. Offices: 1

Outside Service Firm(s):

KPMG Peat Marwick*(Auditors)*
Stamford, CT

KPMG Peat Marwick*(Auditors)*
150 John F. Kennedy Pkwy.
Short Hills, NJ 07078
Tel.: 201-467-9650

Ribis, McCluskey & Sweeney*(Legal Firm)*
Short Hills, NJ

Midlantic National Bank*(Major Banking Relationship)*
West Orange, NJ

STRAIGHT ARROW PUBLISHERS, INC.
1290 Ave. of the Americas
New York, NY 10104
Tel.: 212-484-1616
Fax: 212-767-8205
Publisher of Periodicals & Books
S.I.C.: 2721; 2741
Jann S. Wenner *(Chm. Bd.)*
Kent Brownridge *(Sr. V.P. & Gen. Mgr.)*
Dana Fields *(V.P. & Grp. Publr.)*
Robert Wallace *(V.P. & Exec. Editor)*
Les Zeifman *(V.P.-Sls.)*
Tracy T. Britton *(Dir.-Promos.)*

Outside Service Firm(s):

Ernst & Young*(Auditors)*
787 Seventh Ave.
New York, NY 10019
Tel.: 212-773-1243

Subsidiaries:

Rolling Stone Magazine **(1)**
1290 Ave. of the Americas
New York, NY 10104
Tel.: 212-484-1616
Fax: 212-767-8209
Approx.Sls.: $55,000,000
Emp.: 125
Publr. of Periodicals & Books; Rolling Stone Magazine; Distributor of Rolling Stone Goods
S.I.C.: 2731
Jann S. Wenner *(Chm. Bd.)*
Kent Brownridge *(Sr. V.P. & Gen. Mgr.)*
Les Zeifman *(V.P. & Grp. Publr.)*
Robert Wallace *(V.P. & Exec. Editor)*
Dana Fields *(V.P. & Assoc. Publr.)*
Karen Johnston *(Sr. Editor)*
Stuart Zakim *(Dir.-Publicity)*
Nancy Amigron *(Promo. Dir.)*
Julie Arkin *(Mgr.-Eastern Reg. Adv.)*
David Rheins *(Mgr.-Fashion Adv.)*

Us Magazine **(1)**
1290 Ave. of the Americas
New York, NY 10104
Tel.: 212-484-1616
Fax: 212-767-8205
Approx.Sls.: $30,000,000
Emp.: 75
Fiscal Year-end: 12/31/90
Magazine Publishing
S.I.C.: 2721
Ian Birch *(Editor)*
Dan Sullivan *(Gen. Mgr.)*
Alen Rosenbloom *(Adv. Dir.)*

Men's Journal **(1)**
745 Fifth Ave.
New York, NY 10151
Tel.: 212-758-3800
Men's Magazine
S.I.C.: 2721

STRANG COMMUNICATIONS COMPANY
600 Rinehart Rd.
Lake Mary, FL 32746
Tel.: 407-333-0600
Fax: 407-333-9753
Approx.Sls.: $12,000,000
Emp.: 90
Fiscal Year-end: 12/31/91
Christian Retailing & Charisma Ministries Today
S.I.C.: 8661; 2721
Stephen E. Strang *(Pres. & Publisher)*
Tim Gilmour *(Asst. Publr.)*

Robert Walker *(Editor)*

STRATEGIC DISTRIBUTION INC.
165 Mason St.
Greenwich, CT 06830
Ted Rieple *(Pres.)*

Subsidiary:

SafetyMaster Corporation **(1)**
12 Garden Ave.
Billings, MT 59101
Tel.: 406-248-8098
Fax: 406-252-8199
Approx.Sls.: $25,000,000
Emp.: 120
Wholesale Industrial Fire Safety Equipment
S.I.C.: 5087
Ted Rieple *(Pres.)*
Brent Johnson *(V.P. & Gen. Mgr.)*
John Horning *(Controller)*
Wendy Capron *(Dir.-Personnel Training & Devel.)*
Kent Mason *(Dir.-Data Processing)*
Ron Niebauer *(Dir.-Mktg. & Direct Mktg.)*
David Sheets *(Dir.-Pur.)*

Subsidiary:

Coluson Technologies **(2)**
12 Garden Ave.
Billings, MT 59107
Tel.: 406-248-8098
Emp.: 15
Specialized Safety Services
Harvey Schock *(Gen. Mgr.)*

STRATMAR★
★STRAT for strategic MAR for marketing

STRATMAR SYSTEMS, INC.
109 Willett Ave.
Port Chester, NY 10573
Tel.: 914-937-7171
Fax: 914-937-6045
Year Founded: 1969
Approx.Sls.: $15,000,000
Emp.: 140
Fiscal Year-end: 12/31/90
Mktg. Services Including Couponing & Demonstrations, Rebates & Premium Fulfillment, Detailing & Merchandising
S.I.C.: 7389
Dr. Dan Ailloni-Charas *(Chm. Bd.)*
Carmine Iouse *(Pres.)*
Marsha Gruen *(V.P.-Trade Relation)*
Walter Murray *(V.P.-Fulfillment)*
Cecil Farmer *(Controller)*
Nicholas J. Angell *(Dir.-Mktg.)*
Ethan Charas *(Dir.-Sls. Admin.)*

Computer Systems/Hardware:
Nouelle/LAN

Subsidiaries:

Space Control Corp. **(1)**
1255 W. Broad St.
Stratford, CT 06497
Tel.: 203-378-1113

Stratmar Fulfillment Corp. **(1)**
1255 E. Broad St.
Stratford, CT 06497
Tel.: 203-378-1113
Computer Systems/Hardware:
IBM AS/400
S.I.C.: 7389
Nicholas J. Angell *(Dir.-Mktg. & Adv.)*

Stratmar Research Corp. **(1)**
Woodland Dr.
Rye Brook, NY 10573
Tel.: 914-937-7171
S.I.C.: 7389

Stratmar Resources, Inc. **(1)**
Woodland Dr.
Rye Brook, NY 10573
Tel.: 914-937-7171

STRATTON CORP.
Stratton Mountain
South Londonderry, VT 05155
Tel.: 802-297-2200
Approx.Sls.: $30,000,000
Emp.: 250
Ski Lodge
S.I.C.: 7011
Hans Geier *(Pres.)*
Ralph W. Rawson *(Sr. V.P.-Govt. Rels.)*
Dallas Carey *(Mgr.-Adv. & Mktg.)*

STRATTON MANAGEMENT COMPANY
Plymouth Meeting Exec. Campus, 610 W. Germantown Pike, Ste. 361
Plymouth Meeting, PA 19462
Tel.: 215-941-0888 **MD**
Fax: 215-941-0330
Year Founded: 1972
Approx.Assets: $500,000,000
Emp.: 24
Fiscal Year-end: 12/30/90
Advisory Service, Manages Two Funds
S.I.C.: 6722; 6282
James W. Stratton *(Chm. Bd., Pres. & Chief Exec. Officer)*
John A. Affleck *(Sr. V.P.)*
Gerard E. Heffernan *(Sr. V.P.)*
James Van Dyke Quereau *(Sr. V.P.)*
Michael J. Siano *(Controller)*
Arlene E. Stratton *(Treas.)*
Charles Hopkins *(Dir.-Mktg.)*

Computer Systems/Hardware:
Hewlett-Packard 250 & IBM PC

Outside Service Firm(s):

Drinker, Biddle & Reath*(Legal Firm)*
1000 Westlakes Dr., Ste. 300
Berwyn, PA 19312
Tel.: 215-993-2200
Fax: 215-993-8585

National Westminster Bank plc*(Pension Manager)*
1 Exchange Place
Jersey City, NJ 07303
Tel.: 201-547-7000

Subsidiaries:

Stratton Growth Fund, Inc. **(1)**
Plymouth Meeting Exec. Campus, 610 W. Germantown Pike, Ste. 361
Plymouth Meeting, PA 19462
Tel.: 215-941-0255
Tel.: 800-634-5726 (100%)
Approx.Assets: $24,000,000
Open-End Investment Company with the Objective of Long Term Growth Invested Primarily in Common Stocks
S.I.C.: 6722
James W. Stratton *(Chm. Bd. & Chief Exec. Officer)*
John A. Affleck *(Pres.)*
Gerard E. Heffernan *(V.P.)*
Patricia L. Sloan *(Sec. & Treas.)*
John L. Grieco *(Dir.-Mktg.)*

Stratton Monthly Dividend Shares, Inc. **(1)**
Plymouth Meeting Exec. Campus, 610 W. Germantown Pike, Ste. 361
Plymouth Meeting, PA 19462
Tel.: 215-941-0255
Tel.: 800-634-5726 (100%)
Approx.Assets: $31,200,000
Open-End Investment Company, Specializing in Income-Oriented Common Stocks
S.I.C.: 6722
James W. Stratton *(Chm. Bd. & Chief Exec. Officer)*
Gerard E. Heffernan *(Pres.)*
John A. Affleck *(V.P.)*
Patricia L. Sloan *(Sec. & Treas.)*
John L. Grieco *(Dir.-Mktg.)*

R & S STRAUSS, INC.
9A Brick Plant Rd.
South River, NJ 08882-1098
Mailing Address:
P.O. Box 532
Union, NJ 07083
Tel.: 908-390-9000
Year Founded: 1919
Approx.Sls.: $122,000,000
Emp.: 1,500
Fiscal Year-end: 1/31/91
Import
Auto Parts Accessories & Service Chain
S.I.C.: 5531
Alfred Woods *(Pres.)*
Bill Polzin *(V.P.-Fin.)*
Carol Fernandez *(Controller)*
Dave Perrin *(V.P., MIS)*
Gary Hunt *(V.P.-Mdsg. & Distr.)*

STRAW HAT COOPERATIVE CORP.
6400 Village Pkwy.
Dublin, CA 94568
Tel.: 510-829-1500
Year Founded: 1987
Approx.Sls.: $30,000,000
Emp.: 2,225
Franchised Pizza Restaurants
S.I.C.: 5812; 6794
Art Fletcher *(Chm. Bd.)*
Jack T. Wood *(Pres. & Chief Exec. Officer)*

Computer Systems/Hardware:
Paradox 3.5

STREAMLIGHT INC.
1030 W. Germantown Pike
Norristown, PA 19403
Tel.: 215-631-0600
Year Founded: 1973
Approx.Sls.: $10,000,000
Emp.: 100
Export
Mfr. of Portable Lighting Equipment
S.I.C.: 3648
C. Brad Penney *(Pres. & Chief Exec. Officer)*
Ray Sharrah *(Sr. V.P.-Opers.)*
George Collier *(V.P.-Fin. & Personnel Mgr.)*
Lori Hare *(V.P.-Sls. & Mktg.)*
Carm Growcott *(Sec.)*
Edward Tasca *(Dir.-Systems)*
Terry C. Detwiler *(Plant Mgr.)*
Charles Craft *(Mgr.-Engrng.)*
Ron DelBuono *(Mgr.-Matls.)*
Cindy Law *(Sr. Sls. Rep. & Export Mgr.)*
MaryEllen Giangiulio *(Mktg. Services Coord. & Corp. Travel Planner)*

STREECH ELECTRIC COMPANY
3870 E. Eagle Dr.
Anaheim, CA 92807
Tel.: 714-632-6780 **CA**
Fax: 714-630-3735
Approx.Sls.: $11,000,000
Emp.: 75
Electrical Contractor
S.I.C.: 1731; 5063
Clark Robinson *(Pres. & Treas.)*
Norman Edson *(Sec.)*

Outside Service Firm(s):

Robert McCorkle*(Auditors)*
Anaheim, CA

Sun West Bank*(Major Banking Relationship)*
Santa Fe, NM

J. D. STREETT & CO., INC.
144 Weldon Pkwy.
Maryland Heights, MO 63043
Tel.: 314-432-6600
Fax: 314-432-4248
Year Founded: 1884
Assets: $8,920,522
Liabilities: $6,719,397
Net Worth: $2,201,125
Approx.Sls.: $60,000,000
Emp.: 120
Fiscal Year-end: 12/31/90
Petroleum Prods. Distr. & Retail
S.I.C.: 5172; 5541
Newell A. Baker *(Chm. Bd.)*
Kenneth A. Baker *(Vice Chm.)*
Darrel Huisinga *(Pres. & Treas.)*
Newell A. Baker, Jr. *(Exec. V.P. & Corp. Sec.)*
James A. Schuering *(Controller)*
Dan Scheetz *(Gen. Mgr.-Lubes)*
Bob Ward *(Gen. Mgr.-Retail)*
Lee Rochnagel *(Mgr.-Info. Systems)*
E.J. Keitel *(Mgr.-Private Pkgng.)*

Computer Systems/Hardware:
Burroughs

Outside Service Firm(s):

Ernst & Young*(Auditors)*
701 Market St.
St. Louis, MO 63101
Tel.: 314-259-1000

Boatmen's Trust Company*(Major Banking Relationship)*
100 North Broadway
St. Louis, MO 63102
Tel.: 314-466-2469

O. J. STROBEL OIL & TIRE CO., INC.
1101 N. Main St.
Summerville, SC 29483
Tel.: 803-873-4660
Fax: 803-873-8012
Approx.Sls.: $17,000,000
Emp.: 68
Wholesale Petroleum & Petroleum Products, Tires & Tubes
S.I.C.: 5172; 5014
Oren J. Strobel *(Pres. & Treas.)*
Lula Z. Strobel *(Sec.)*

Outside Service Firm(s):

McKnight, Frampton & Company*(Auditors)*
Charleston, SC

South Carolina National Bank*(Major Banking Relationship)*
700 Main St.
Columbia, SC 29201

THE STROH BREWERY COMPANY
100 River Place
Detroit, MI 48207
Tel.: 313-446-2000 **AZ**
Fax: 313-446-2223
Year Founded: 1850
Approx.Sls.: $1,300,000,000
Emp.: 2,600
Fiscal Year-end: 3/31/92
Export
Manufacture of Beer & Liquor
S.I.C.: 2082
Corporate Giving Program: Individual Case-By-Case Basis
Peter W. Stroh *(Chm. Bd. & Chief Exec. Officer)*
William L. Henry *(Pres. & Chief Oper. Officer)*
James R. Avery *(Sr. V.P.-Opers. Plng. & Control)*
Joseph Franzem *(Sr. V.P.-Sls. & Admin.)*
George E. Kuehn *(Sr. V.P., Sec. & Gen. Counsel)*
Christopher Sortwell *(Sr. V.P. & Chief Fin. Officer)*
Walter R. Hintz *(V.P. & Controller)*
Steve Anderson *(V.P.-Quality Assurance)*
John Curtin *(V.P.-Matls. Mngmt.)*
Joseph D. Hertrich *(V.P.-Brewing)*
Robert Pitcole *(V.P.-Information Systems & Services)*

The Stroh Brewery Company—(Continued)

Michael C. Porter *(V.P.-Mktg.)*
Norman P. Swanson *(V.P.-Sls.)*
Vincent Abetamarco *(Treas.)*
Jovan Jovanovski *(Dir.-Sls. & Intl. Mktg.)*
Lacey Logan *(Dir.-Communications & Pub. Rels.)*

No. of Mfg. Plants/Facilities: 7
No. of U.S. Offices: 7

Computer Systems/Hardware:
IBM 3033

Outside Service Firm(s):

Deloitte & Touche*(Auditors)*
200 Renaissance Center, 16th Fl.
Detroit, MI 48243
Tel.: 313-396-3000
Fax: 313-259-8087

Connecticut General Life Insurance Co.*(Group Insurer)*
P.O. Box 2975,
Hartford, CT 06104
Tel.: 203-726-6000

Butzel Long*(Legal Firm)*
Madden Bldg., 150 W. Jefferson, Ste. 900
Detroit, MI 48226-4430
Tel.: 313-225-7000
Fax: 313-225-7080

STROMBECKER CORPORATION
600 N. Pulaski Rd.
Chicago, IL 60624
Tel.: 312-638-1000 **IL**
Fax: 312-638-3679
Year Founded: 1876
Sales Range: $20-39 Million
Emp.: 450
Fiscal Year-end: 12/31/90
Import Export
Mfr. of Metal, Plastic and Wooden Toys & Novelties; Plastic Molding; Soap Bubbles
S.I.C.: 3944; 3089
Myron B. Shure *(Chm. Bd.)*
Daniel B. Shure *(Pres.)*
Alan Brouilette *(Chief Fin. Officer)*
John Schutz *(Exec. V.P.)*
James A. Fink *(V.P.-Sls.)*
Joseph O'Brien *(V.P.)*
Thomas Romano *(V.P.)*
Elliot P. Rossen *(V.P.-Mktg.)*
M.P. Glickman *(Treas.)*
Thomas Goldblatt *(Gen. Counsel)*
Andrew Coshand *(Mgr.-Mngmt. Information Systems)*

No. of Mfg. Plants/Facilities: 4
No. of U.S. Offices: 5
No. of Foreign Offices: 1

Computer Systems/Hardware:
IBM System 34

Outside Service Firm(s):

Grant Thornton*(Auditors)*
700 One Prudential Plaza, 130 East Randolph St.
Chicago, IL 60601
Tel.: 312-856-0200
Fax: 312-565-4719

Holleb & Coff, Ltd.*(Legal Firm)*
55 E. Monroe, Suite 4100
Chicago, IL 60603
Tel.: 312-807-4600

Continental Bank N. A.*(Major Banking Relationship)*
231 S. LaSalle St.
Chicago, IL 60697
Tel.: 312-828-2345
Tel.: 800-426-5754
Telex: 312-828-1783

Divisions:

Strombecker Chemtoy Division **(1)**
600 North Pulaski Rd.
Chicago, IL 60624
Tel.: 312-638-1000
Mfr. of Toys, Soap Bubbles, Jump Robes Snow Spray, Christmas Decorations
S.I.C.: 3944

Tootsietoy Division **(1)**
600 No. Pulaski Rd.
Chicago, IL 60624
Tel.: 312-638-1000
Mfr. of Metal Car Toys
S.I.C.: 3944

Division:

Tootsietoy Preschool Products Div. **(2)**
600 N. Pulaski
Chicago, IL 60624
Tel.: 312-638-1000
Mfr. of Wooden Toys
S.I.C.: 3944

Subsidiaries:

Durant Electronics, Inc. **(1)**
2200 Arkansas Ave.
Durant, OK 74701
Tel.: 405-924-5100 (100%)
Mfr. of Custom Thermoforming Plastic Components
S.I.C.: 3089; 3944
Harlan Monk *(Gen. Mgr.)*

Esquire Novelty Co. **(1)**
Forest Ave.
Amsterdam, NY 12010
Tel.: 518-843-3000 (100%)
Mfr. of Toys
S.I.C.: 3944
J. Gorecki *(Gen. Mgr.)*

Joy Toy, Co. **(1)**
200 5th Ave.
New York, NY 10010
Tel.: 212-675-3857
Mfr. of Toys
S.I.C.: 3944

Non-U.S. Holdings:

Esquire Canada, Inc. **(1)**
125 South Street North
Port Robinson, ON L0S 1J0, Canada
Tel.: 416-384-2228
Fax: 416-384-2544
Mfr. of Toy Caps
S.I.C.: 2899
Charles Bradley *(Gen. Mgr.)*

Strombecker (HK) Ltd. **(1)**
926-7 East Wing, New World Office Bldg.
24 Salisbury Rd., Tsimshatsui, Kowloon, Hong Kong
Tel.: 37245466
Toy Mfg., Buying & Selling
S.I.C.: 3944; 3089
Daniel Shure *(Mng. Dir.)*

STROMBERG-CONNORS COMMUNICATIONS
62 Bowman Ave.
Rye Brook, NY 10573
Tel.: 914-939-4080
Year Founded: 1989
Approx.Billings: $10,500,000
Emp.: 17
Direct Marketing Programs
Hank Stromberg *(Pres.)*

Computer Systems/Hardware:
Macintosh, IBM

STRONGHEART PRODUCTS, INC.
300 S. 55th St.
Kansas City, KS 66106
Mailing Address:
P.O. Box 2009
Kansas City, KS 66110
Tel.: 913-621-4909
Fax: 913-621-2627
Year Founded: 1931
Approx.Sls.: $23,000,000
Emp.: 100
Fiscal Year-end: 8/31/91
Export
Canned Dog & Cat Food, Dry Dog Food
S.I.C.: 2047
Robert Terlip *(Chm. Bd.)*
John Anasto *(Pres., Chief Exec. & Chief Oper. Officer)*
Jon Dahlquist *(Sr. V.P.-Opers.)*
Gary Pingree *(Treas.)*

STROUDS
780 So. Nogales St.
City of Industry, CA 91748
Tel.: 818-912-2866
Fax: 818-913-4841
Year Founded: 1979
Approx.Sls.: $145,000,000
Emp.: 1,100
Fiscal Year-end: 3/ 1/91
Retail Stores; Specializing in Bed, Bath & Tabletop Linens
S.I.C.: 5719; 5712
Bill Stroud *(Chm. Bd. & Chief Exec. Officer)*
Wayne P. Selness *(Pres.)*
Joseph A. Imbrogulio *(Sr. V.P.)*
Steven R. Kerkstra *(V.P.-Fin.)*
Mark Grand *(V.P.-Stores)*
Roberta Chavance *(V.P.-Personnel)*
Joyce Stroud *(V.P.)*
Ken Rushworth *(Dir.-Adv.)*
Linda McNamara *(Controller)*

THE STROUSE, ADLER COMPANY
78 Olive
New Haven, CT 06507
Tel.: 203-777-3484
Approx.Sls.: $11,000,000
Emp.: 300
Fiscal Year-end: 8/31/90
Smoothie Foundation Garments
S.I.C.: 2342
Alfred A. Kniberg *(Chief Exec. Officer)*
Paul McDonald *(V.P.-Fin.)*

STROUSE GREENBERG

Tel.: 215-985-1100
Fax: 215-732-1527
Emp.: 100
Real Estate Investment; Development; Commercial Real Estate Broker
S.I.C.: 6153; 6552
Joseph Straus, Jr. *(Chm. Bd.)*
Albert Eisen *(Vice Chm.)*
Samuel Switzenbaum *(Pres. & Chief Exec. Officer)*
Steven Kessler *(Chief Oper. & Chief Fin. Officer)*
Joseph Egan *(Exec. V.P.)*
Harvey Levitt *(Sec.)*
John K. Kaiser *(Dir.-Mktg.)*
Joy Largent *(Dir.-Human Resources)*

STRUCTURAL FOAM PLASTICS, INC.
P.O. box 5208,
North Branch, NJ 08876
Year Founded: 1967
Assets: $7,400,000
Liabilities: $4,600,000
Net Worth: $2,800,000
Approx.Sls.: $19,130,000
Emp.: 250
Fiscal Year-end: 9/30/91
Export
Mfr. of Plastic Structural Molding Foam & Molds; Plastics Work Machinery
S.I.C.: 3089; 3544
William S. Rosania *(Pres.)*
John Rosania *(Treas. & Sec.)*
Sal Sessanta *(Controller)*
Dan Carey *(Mgr.-Pur.)*
Jeff W. Rosania *(Mgr.-Engrng.)*
Carl A. Rosania *(Mgr.-Sls.)*

No. of Mfg. Plants/Facilities: 3

Outside Service Firm(s):

Amper, Politziner & Mattia*(Auditors)*
Edison, NJ

Morris, McLaughlin & Marcus*(Legal Firm)*
Somerville, NJ

United Jersey Bank*(Major Banking Relationship)*
Princeton, NJ

Affiliates:

Structural Foam Plastics **(1)**
Cherry St.
Liberty Center, OH 43532
Tel.: 419-533-2811
Emp.: 55
Plastic Injection Molding
S.I.C.: 3089
Michael Rosania *(Gen. Mgr.)*

Structural Foam Plastics **(1)**
1400 Northwest Ave.
West Chicago, IL 60185
Tel.: 708-231-7400
Plastic Injection Molding
S.I.C.: 3089
Ernest Holdridge *(Gen. Mgr.)*

STRUCTURAL INDUSTRIES, INC.
96 New South Rd.
Hicksville, NY 11801
Tel.: 516-822-5200
Fax: 516-822-5207
Sales Range: $10-19 Million
Emp.: 135
Mfr. of Picture Frames
S.I.C.: 2499
Stanley Hirsch *(Pres.)*
Jamie Hirsch *(V.P.-Mfg. & Pur.)*
Judy Vietneer *(Controller)*

Outside Service Firm(s):

Richard Kandel*(Auditors)*
Lynbrook, NY

Bank of New York*(Major Banking Relationship)*
Hicksville, NY

PAUL STUART, INC.
Madison Ave. & 45th St.
New York, NY 10017
Tel.: 212-682-0320
Tel.: 800-678-8278
Fax: 212-983-2742
Year Founded: 1939
Approx.Sls.: $40,000,000
Emp.: 250
Fiscal Year-end: 1/31/91
Retail Apparel Specialty Store
S.I.C.: 5699
Clifford Grodd *(Pres.)*
Paul Stuart Ostrove *(V.P.)*
Jack Donahue *(Chief Fin. Officer)*
James Trier *(Controller)*
Julie Oddy *(Public Rels. Dir.)*
William Redpath *(Dir.-Adv.)*
David Rosen *(Mgr.-Personnel)*

STUART-IRONSIDES, INC.
7575 Plaza Court
Willowbrook, IL 60521
Tel.: 708-655-4595
Fax: 708-655-1088
Approx.Sls.: $70,000,000
Emp.: 300
Fiscal Year-end: 12/31/90
Cutting Fluids & Lubricants: Thredkut, Superkool, Dascolene, Excelene Cutting & Grinding Oils: Dasco Water-Mix Coolant Concentrate; Dasco Kleen Cleaner; Kleenkut,

Solvol Emulsion Soluble Oils; Codol Semi- Synthetic Coolant; Hi-D & Dascool Synthetic Coolants; Rol Kleen Rolling Oils; Sturaco Gear Lubricants; Drawsol Drawing Compound; Thermex Hot Die & Forging Compounds
S.I.C.: 2992
Jim Castle *(Pres.)*
C.D. Summers *(V.P. & Controller)*
W.S. Scheu *(V.P.-Export Sls.)*
C.E. Santangelo, Jr. *(V.P.-Ironsides Div.)*
J. Barthel *(Mgr.-Tech.)*
R.F. Coit *(Pur. Agent)*
Patricia Wiemeler *(Mgr.-Personnel)*

Subsidiaries:

Stuart-Ironsides, Inc. **(1)**
6715 McKinley Ave.
Los Angeles, CA 90001
Tel.: 213-758-3181
Fax: 213-778-0030
S.I.C.: 2992

Stuart-Ironsides, Inc. **(1)**
4346 Tacony St.
Philadelphia, PA 19124
Tel.: 215-744-5858
Fax: 215-289-4417
S.I.C.: 2992

STUHR ENTERPRISES INC.
403 W. First St.
Wilton, IA 52778
Tel.: 319-732-3878
Fax: 319-732-3869
Emp.: 150
Manufacture Wood Handles & Wood Trimmings; Wooden Toys; Turned & Shaped Parts
S.I.C.: 2499; 3944
Ed Stuhr *(Pres.)*
Gene Boswell *(V.P. & Plant Mgr.)*

Outside Service Firm(s):

Carver Michales, Taylor, Reese & Lambert*(Auditors)*
Muscatine, IA

STURGIS IRON & METAL COMPANY, INC.
70675 S. Centerville Rd.
Sturgis, MI 49091
Mailing Address:
P.O. Box 579
Sturgis, MI 49091
Tel.: 616-651-7851
Fax: 616-651-4189
Year Founded: 1950
Approx.Sls.: $44,000,000
Emp.: 300
Fiscal Year-end: 8/31/91
Ferrous Metal Scrap & Waste; Truck Parts & Accessories
S.I.C.: 5093; 5013
Ralph Levin *(Pres.)*
Bob Driver *(Chief Fin. Officer)*
Delmer Richmond *(Sec. & Treas.)*
Ed Arenstein *(Non-Ferrous Mktg.)*
Joe Turpin *(Pur. Agent)*
Mia Levin *(Asst. to the Pres.)*

Principal(s):
Ralph Levin

No. of Mfg. Plants/Facilities: 5

Outside Service Firm(s):

Deloitte & Touche*(Auditors)*
Sturgis, MI

Dresser Law Offices*(Legal Firm)*
Sturgis, MI

AmeriTrust National Bank*(Major Banking Relationship)*
Elkart, IN

Subsidiaries:

South Bend Scrap & Processing **(1)**
1305 Prairie Ave.
South Bend, IN 46680
Tel.: 219-287-3311
S.I.C.: 5093
Cary Levin *(V.P.)*

Sturgis Metals Division, Elkhart **(1)**
P.O. Box 4537, 1514 W. Lusher Ave.
Elkhart, IN 46515
Tel.: 219-295-0155
S.I.C.: 5093
Starr Levin *(V.P.)*

Three Rivers Iron & Metal **(1)**
206 E. Broadway
Three Rivers, MI 49093
Tel.: 616-278-1785
S.I.C.: 5093
Ralph Levin *(Pres.)*

Kalamazoo Scrap & Processing **(1)**
2900 Miller Rd.
Kalamazoo, MI 49001
Tel.: 616-381-7277
S.I.C.: 5093
Ralph Levin *(Pres.)*

Liberty Auto Parts **(1)**
2900 Miller Rd.
Kalamazoo, MI 49001
Tel.: 616-385-2900
S.I.C.: 5013
Ralph Levin *(Pres.)*

THE STURM COMMUNICATIONS GROUP, INC.
737 N. Michigan Ave., Ste. 1400
Chicago, IL 60611
Tel.: 312-943-1881
Fax: 312-943-2346
Year Founded: 1980
Approx.Billings: $18,218,520
Emp.: 25
Healthcare
Arthur C. Sturm, Jr. *(Chm. Bd. & Pres.)*
Robert C. Rosenberg *(V.P., Corp. Devel.)*
Lynn Benzing *(V.P., Dir. Strategic Services)*
Mike Cafferata *(V.P., Creative Dir.)*
Donna King *(Office Mgr.)*
Gary Reznick *(Controller)*

STUSSER ELECTRIC COMPANY
660 S. Andover St.
Seattle, WA 98108
Tel.: 206-624-8770 **WA**
Fax: 206-623-6234
Year Founded: 1919
Approx.Sls.: $70,000,000
Emp.: 230
Fiscal Year-end: 12/31/91
Wholesale Electrical Parts & Equipment to Construction Industry
S.I.C.: 5063
Herbert C. Stusser *(Chm. Bd.)*
Leslie E. Stusser *(Pres.)*
Philip Davis *(V.P.-Sls. & Mktg.)*
Stephen J. Wimbush *(V.P.-Fin. & Opers.)*
Lonnie Thelan *(Dir.-Data Processing)*
Richard Krabel *(Mgr.-Inventory Control)*
Robert Lowy *(Mgr.-Human Resources)*

Principal(s):
Stusser Family

No. of Mfg. Plants/Facilities: 11
No. of U.S. Offices: 11

Computer Systems/Hardware:
Data General

Outside Service Firm(s):

Price Waterhouse*(Auditors)*
1001 Fourth Ave. Plaza
Seattle, WA 98154
Tel.: 206-622-1505

Bogle & Gates*(Legal Firm)*
Two Union Square, 601 Union St.
Seattle, WA 98101-2322
Tel.: 206-682-5151

Rainier National Bank*(Major Banking Relationship)*
P.O.Box 24407
Seattle, WA 98124

STYLE AUTO
7100 Sophia Ave.
Van Nuys, CA 91406
Tel.: 818-988-5300 **CA**
Fax: 818-988-3742
Year Founded: 1977
Approx.Sls.: $12,000,000
Emp.: 18
Importer & Distributor of Apparel
S.I.C.: 5136; 5137; 5139
Steven F. Gilman *(Chm. Bd., Pres, & Chief Exec. Officer)*
Mark H. Friedman *(Exec. V.P., Treas. & Chief Fin. Officer)*
Liz Thorner *(Dir.-Pur.)*
Robert Ezra *(Gen. Counsel)*
Richard Gilman *(Consultant)*

No. of U.S. Offices: 3
No. of Foreign Offices: 1

Computer Systems/Hardware:
ADDS System Mentor 2000

Outside Service Firm(s):

Stonefield & Josephson*(Auditors)*
Los Angeles, CA

Blue Cross & Blue Shield of Nebraska*(Group Insurer)*
Omaha, NE

Robert Ezra, Esq.*(Legal Firm)*
Encino, CA

Mercantile National Bank*(Major Banking Relationship)*
Los Angeles, CA 90067

SUBURBAN COMMUNICATIONS CORP.
36251 Schoolcraft Rd.
Livonia, MI 48150
Tel.: 313-591-2300 **MI**
Year Founded: 1974
Approx.Sls.: $37,000,000
Emp.: 700
Holding Company; Publisher of Community Newspapers; Printing Plants
S.I.C.: 6719; 2711
Philip H. Power *(Chm. Bd.)*
Richard D. Aginian *(Pres. & Chief Exec. Officer)*
Richard Brady *(V.P.-Mktg.)*
David Karapetian *(V.P.-Human Resources)*
Charles A. Paukstis *(V.P.-Fin. & Treas.)*
J. Reddy *(V.P.-Editorial)*
C.S. Wood *(V.P.-Mfg.)*
John A. Wise, Jr. *(Sec.)*

Outside Service Firm(s):

Arthur Andersen & Co.*(Auditors)*
400 Renaissance Center
Detroit, MI 48243
Tel.: 313-259-8100

Wise & Marsac*(Legal Firm)*
Detroit, MI

Michigan National Bank*(Major Banking Relationship)*
Livonia, MI

SUBWAY FRANCHISEE ADVERTISING FUND TRUST
325 Bic Drive
Milford, CT 06460
Tel.: 203-877-4281
Tel.: 800-888-4848
Fax: 203-876-6687
Year Founded: 1990
Sales Range: $60-79 Million
Emp.: 30
Fiscal Year-end: 12/31/90
Sandwiches & Salads Franchisee Advertising Fund Trust for Subway Fast Food Restaurants
S.I.C.: 6794
Frederick DeLuca *(Pres.)*
Cindy Eadie *(Exec. Dir.)*
Thomas W. Hislop *(Controller)*
Kathy Charbonneau *(Mgr.-Communications)*
Donna Powell *(Mgr.-Adv.)*
Perry Schwartz *(Production Assistant)*

Outside Service Firm(s):

Robbins, Greene, Horowitz, Rochlin, Lester & Levitan*(Auditors)*
New York, NY

Farren & King*(Legal Firm)*
New Haven, CT

First Bank, N.A.*(Major Banking Relationship)*
New Haven, CT

Affiliate:

Franchise World Headquarters **(1)**
325 Bic Drive
Milford, CT 06460
Tel.: 203-877-4281
Fred DeLuca *(Pres.)*
Dick Pilchen *(V.P.-Mktg.)*
Millie Shinn *(V.P.-Opers.)*

THE SUDDATH COMPANIES
5266 Highway Ave.
Jacksonville, FL 32205
Mailing Address:
P.O. Box 60069
Jacksonville, FL 32254
Tel.: 904-781-7100
Fax: 904-783-0189
Year Founded: 1978
Assets: $37,000,000
Liabilities: $25,000,000
Net Worth: $12,000,000
Approx.Sls.: $73,000,000
Emp.: 416
Fiscal Year-end: 12/31/88
Import Export
Long Distance Moving & Freight Forwarding
S.I.C.: 4213; 4214
Stephen M. Suddath *(Chm. Bd.)*
A. Quinn Bell *(Pres. & Chief Exec. Officer)*
Robert J. Price *(V.P., Treas. & Pur. Mgr.)*
Barbara S. Strickland *(Gen. Counsel)*
Steven Carson *(Dir.-Telecommunications)*
Ralph Cooper *(Dir.-Data Processing)*
Joyce Russell *(Dir.-Pur.)*
Elizabeth Spradley *(Dir.-Personnel)*

Principal(s):
Stephen M. Suddath

No. of Mfg. Plants/Facilities: 1
No. of U.S. Offices: 20

Computer Systems/Hardware:
IMB AS400; TI990 Business Systems

The Suddath Companies—(Continued)

Outside Service Firm(s):

KPMG Peat Marwick*(Auditors)*
One Independent Dr.
Jacksonville, FL 32201

Vanliner Insurance Company*(Commercial Insurance Carrier)*
Fenton, MO

Blue Cross & Blue Shield of Florida, Inc.*(Group Insurer)*
532 Riverside
Jacksonville, FL 32231
Tel.: 904-363-5572
Fax: 904-363-5180

Merrill Lynch*(Investment Banker)*
Jacksonville, FL

Michael E. Demont*(Legal Firm)*
Jacksonville, FL

First Union National Bank*(Major Banking Relationship)*
Jacksonville, FL

Robert J. Price*(Pension Manager)*
Jacksonville, FL

Subsidiaries:

Air Land Forwarders, Inc. **(1)**
P.O. Box 37977
Jacksonville, FL 32254
Tel.: 904-781-7100
Michael C. Richardson *(Pres.)*

Bellcrest Holding Co., Inc. **(1)**
206 Magnolia St.
Millen, GA 30442
Tel.: 912-982-4000

Caribbean Moving & Storage, Inc. **(1)**
P.O. Box 60069
Jacksonville, FL 32254
Tel.: 904-744-9270

Data Storage Center **(1)**
P.O. Box 6367
Jacksonville, FL 32254
Tel.: 904-783-0260

General Commercial Packaging, Inc. **(1)**
P.O. Box 420572
Kissimmee, FL 34742-0572
Tel.: 407-870-7646

Sudco Development Co., Inc. **(1)**
P.O. Box 60069
Jacksonville, FL 32254
Tel.: 904-781-7100

Suddath Moving Systems, Inc. **(1)**
P.O. Box 61802
Jacksonville, FL 32254
Tel.: 904-781-7100

Suddath Transportation Service **(1)**
P.O. Box 60069
Jacksonville, FL 32254
Tel.: 904-781-7600

Suddath Van Lines **(1)**
P.O. Box 60069
Jacksonville, FL 32254
Tel.: 904-781-7100

Summit Commercial Property, Inc. **(1)**
6622 Southpoint Dr., S., Ste. 400
Jacksonville, FL 32216
Tel.: 904-739-8000

Withers/Suddath Van Lines, Inc. **(1)**
6900 N.W. 74th Ave.
Miami, FL 33152
Tel.: 305-885-8161

SUES, YOUNG & BROWN INC.
5151 Commerce Dr.
Baldwin Park, CA 91706
Tel.: 818-338-3800
Fax: 818-338-1967
Year Founded: 1946
Approx.Sls.: $10,000,000
Emp.: 22
Wholesaler Electrical Appliances
S.I.C.: 5064
Richard F. Young *(Chm. Bd., Pres. & Chief Exec. Officer)*
James P. Converse *(V.P. & Gen. Sls. Mgr.)*
Linda Laybourne *(Treas. & Chief Fin. Officer)*
Jeanette A. Roe *(Dir.-Data Processing)*
Principal(s):
Richard F. Young

Computer Systems/Hardware:
IBM PC-AT

Outside Service Firm(s):

Schwartz & Kaler*(Auditors)*
Beverly Hills, CA

Schwartz & Bloom*(Legal Firm)*
Beverly Hills, CA

Bank of America, N.T. & S.A.*(Major Banking Relationship)*
P.O. Box 37002,
San Francisco, CA 94137

Bank of America NT&SA*(Major Banking Relationship)*
City of Commerce, CA

SUGAR CANE GROWERS COOPERATIVE OF FLORIDA
Airport Road, P.O. Box 666
Belle Glade, FL 33430
Tel.: 407-996-5556
Fax: 407-996-4747
Approx.Sls.: $65,000,000
Emp.: 1,000
Cooperative; Raw Sugar & Molasses
S.I.C.: 2061
George H. Wedgworth *(Pres.)*
Enrique R. Arias *(Exec. V.P.)*
Robert D. Apelgren *(V.P.)*
Tony Contreras *(V.P.-Mktg.)*
William L. Kramer *(V.P. & Gen. Mgr.)*
Walter J. Kautz *(Sec. & Treas.)*
Jeff Ward *(Gen. Counsel)*
John Gray *(Comptroller & Asst. Sec.-Treas.)*
Raymond Campbell *(Dir.-Personnel)*
John Pitts *(Pur. Agent)*

Outside Service Firm(s):

KPMG Peat Marwick*(Auditors)*
P.O. Box 3031, 111 N. Orange Ave., Suite 1600
Orlando, FL 32802
Tel.: 407-423-3426

Bank of Belle Glade*(Major Banking Relationship)*
Belle Glade, FL

SUGAR CREEK PACKING CO.
3476 Irwin-Simpson Rd. Ste. 119
Mason, OH 45040
Tel.: 513-459-8355 **OH**
Fax: 513-459-8595
Emp.: 150
Bacon Processor
S.I.C.: 2013
John S. Richardson *(Pres., Chief Exec. & Chief Fin. Officer)*
Teresa Wilson *(Controller)*

Computer Systems/Hardware:
Radio Shack

Outside Service Firm(s):

Allstate Insurance*(Group Insurer)*
Northbrook, IL

Altschuler, Melvoin & Glasser*(Group Insurer)*
30 S. Wecker Dr.
Chicago, IL 60606
Tel.: 312-207-2800

BancOhio National Bank*(Major Banking Relationship)*
Washington Court House, OH

SUISSA/MILLER
3015 Main St., Ste. 300
Santa Monica, CA 90405
Tel.: 310-392-9666
Fax: 310-392-2625
Year Founded: 1985
Approx.Billings: $35,000,000
Emp.: 30
David Suissa *(Chm.)*
Bruce Miller *(Pres.)*
Mary Porper *(V.P., Finance)*

SUITT CONSTRUCTION COMPANY, INC.
1400 Cleveland St.
Greenville, SC 29607
Mailing Address:
P.O. Box 8858,
Greenville, SC 29604-9986
Tel.: 803-250-5000
Fax: 803-250-5037
Year Founded: 1968
Approx.Sls.: $200,000,000
Emp.: 2,000
Fiscal Year-end: 3/31/90
General Contractors of Non-Residential & Industrial Buildings
S.I.C.: 1542; 1541
T. Howard Suitt *(Pres. & Chief Exec. Officer)*
T.H. Suitt, Jr. *(V.P. & Treas.)*
D.G. Warren *(V.P.-Opers.)*
Hilda Suitt *(Sec.)*
J.T. Decembrino *(Dir.-Admin.)*
R. Whaley *(Dir.-Pur.)*

No. of U.S. Offices: 5

Computer Systems/Hardware:
IBM AS 400; IBM PC

Outside Service Firm(s):

Ernst & Young*(Auditors)*
C & S Bank Tower, Two Shelter Centre, Ste. 800
Greenville, SC 29603

Lincoln National Life Insurance Co.*(Group Insurer)*
Hartford, CT

Wausau Insurance*(Group Insurer)*
Hartford, CT

South Carolina National Bank*(Major Banking Relationship)*
7515 Northside Dr.
Greenville, SC
Tel.: 803-577-8280

SULLIVAN & BROWNELL, INC.
P.O. Box 450, 1 Kingwood, Rte. 66
Randolph, VT 05060
Tel.: 802-728-3300
Fax: 802-728-3309
Year Founded: 1973
Approx.Billings: $10,100,610
Emp.: 7
Paul J. Sullivan *(Pres.)*
Debra Becker *(Sec.)*

Computer Systems/Hardware:
IBM System 36; Mac 11ci; Mac IILX

SULLIVAN & COZART INC.
822 W. Kentucky St.
Louisville, KY 40203
Mailing Address:
P.O. Box 953
Louisville, KY 40201
Tel.: 502-584-4213 **KY**
Fax: 502-584-4236
Year Founded: 1933
Approx.Sls.: $60,000,000
Emp.: 340
General Contractor, Construction Management of Multi-Family & Commercial Buildings, Hospitals
S.I.C.: 1522; 1542
Dan J. Sullivan, Jr. *(Pres.)*
Michael A. Thorp *(V.P.)*
Robert A. Lawrence *(Treas.)*

SULLIVAN HAAS COYLE
One Capital City Plaza, 3350 Peachtree Rd., Ste. 950
Atlanta, GA 30326
Tel.: 404-231-1661
Fax: 404-264-1723
Year Founded: 1982
Approx.Billings: $10,200,000
Emp.: 20
Jerry Sullivan *(Principal & Co-Creative Dir.)*
Bob Coyle *(Principal & Mktg. Dir.)*
Merrell Calhoun *(Pres.-Pub. Rels.)*

SULLIVAN HIGDON & SINK INCORPORATED
801 E. Douglas
Wichita, KS 67202
Mailing Address:
P.O. Box 11009,
Wichita, KS 67202
Tel.: 316-263-0124
Fax: 316-263-3978
Fax: 316-263-7017
Year Founded: 1971
Approx.Billings: $40,884,583
Emp.: 58
Advertising, Public Relations & Marketing
Allan K. Higdon *(Chm.)*
B. Vaughn Sink *(Pres.)*
Samuel M. Williams *(V.P., Chief Fin. Officer)*
Janis M. Friesen *(Dir., Pub. Rels.)*
Lynell Stucky *(Mktg. Dir.)*
Peggy Caine *(Acctg. Mgr.)*
Donna Montgomery *(Office Mgr.)*

Computer Systems/Hardware:
Data General MV5600

SULLIVAN HOLDING COMPANY
100 Winners Circle
Brentwood, TN 37027
Tel.: 615-377-0377
Fax: 615-377-0370
Holding Company
S.I.C.: 6719; 2796; 2759
James Sullivan *(Chm. Bd., Pres. & Chief Exec. Officer)*
Brian Richardson *(V.P. & Chief Fin. Officer)*

Outside Service Firm(s):

KPMG Peat Marwick*(Auditors)*
1900 Nashville Center, 511 Union St.
Nashville, TN 37219

Davis, Graham & Stubbs*(Legal Firm)*
370 Seventeenth St., Ste. 4700
Denver, CO 80202
Tel.: 303-892-9400

Chase Manhattan Bank, N.A.*(Major Banking Relationship)*
One Chase Manhattan Plaza
New York, NY 10081
Tel.: 212-552-2222
Tel.: 800-526-0801
Fax: 212-552-7175

Subsidiaries:

American Color **(1)**
2340 E. Polk St.
Phoenix, AZ 85006
Tel.: 602-275-4347
Fax: 606-244-1467
Emp.: 735
Pre-Press Service House For Printing, Publishing & Advertising Industries
S.I.C.: 2796

Douglas Brazell *(Pres.)*
Frank Benham *(V.P.)*
Gary Kessler *(Controller)*
Rick Claxton *(Dir.-Human Resources)*

Sullivan Graphics **(1)**
100 Winners Circle
Brentwood, TN 37027
Tel.: 615-377-0377
Emp.: 45
Printers Of Magazines, Newspaper Inserts, Comics
S.I.C.: 2759
Stephen Dyott *(Pres.)*
James Sullivan *(Chm. Bd.)*
Brian Richardson *(Chief Fin. Officer)*

SULLIVAN LONG & HAGERTY, INC.
801 5th Ave., N.
Birmingham, AL 35203
Tel.: 205-251-6261
Fax: 205-251-1409
Approx.Sls.: $50,000,000
Emp.: 500
General Contractors
S.I.C.: 1521; 1522
Charles A. Long, Jr. *(Chm. Bd. & Pres.)*
Wm. A. Cobb *(Exec. V.P.)*
Joe Hill *(Sr. V.P.)*
Wm. J. Long *(Sr. V.P.)*
Hiram Y. McKinney *(Sr. V.P., Sec., Treas. & Controller)*
Joseph D. Morris *(Sr. V.P.)*

Outside Service Firm(s):

Pearce, Bevill, Leland, Leesburg & Moore*(Auditors)*
Birmingham, AL

Cabaniss, Johnston, Gardner, Dumas & O'Neal*(Legal Firm)*
Birmingham, AL

AmSouth Bank N.A.*(Major Banking Relationship)*
P.O. Box 11426
Birmingham, AL 35202
Tel.: 205-326-5321

SULLIVAN OIL COMPANY
2773 N. Flannery
Baton Rouge, LA 70814
Tel.: 504-273-0170 **LA**
Fax: 504-273-3743
Year Founded: 1966
Approx.Sls.: $24,000,000
Emp.: 121
Fiscal Year-end: 12/31/90
Wholesale Petroleum & Retail Convenience Stores
S.I.C.: 5172; 5411
Kenneth R. Sullivan *(Pres. & Chief Exec. Officer)*
Glenda D. Sullivan *(Sec.)*
Daisy L. Holden *(Controller)*
Earl Vickry *(Gen. Mgr.)*
Jeff Floyd *(Mgr.-Comml. Sls.)*
Denice Harrington *(Mgr.-Automated Fueling Sls.)*
Clay Tuschoff *(Mgr.-Retail Sls.)*
Principal(s):
Kenneth R. Sullivan
Glenda D. Sullivan

No. of U.S. Offices: 1

Computer Systems/Hardware:
IBM

Outside Service Firm(s):

Pulliam & Tullieau*(Auditors)*
Baton Rouge, LA

Gulf Insurance Co.*(Commercial Insurance Carrier)*
Dallas, TX

Associated Health of Louisiana*(Group Insurer)*
New Orleans, LA

Aaron & Turner*(Legal Firm)*
Baton Rouge, LA

Guaranty Bank & Trust*(Major Banking Relationship)*
Baton Rouge, LA

New York Life*(Pension Manager)*
New York, NY

Subsidiary:

Express 1 Stop **(1)**
2773 N. Flannery Rd.
Baton Rouge, LA 70814
Tel.: 504-273-0170
Emp.: 59
Convenience Store & Gasoline Outlet
S.I.C.: 5311
Forrest Hawkins *(Chief Oper. Officer)*

SULLIVAN PAPER COMPANY
P.O. Box 88, 61 Progress Ave.
West Springfield, MA 01090
Tel.: 413-734-3107
Fax: 413-731-7515
Year Founded: 1941
Sales Range: $40-59 Million
Emp.: 110
Fiscal Year-end: 12/31/91
Import Export
Converted Papers, Gift Wrap, Fine Papers For Printers
S.I.C.: 2679; 3577
Richard S. Sullivan *(Chm. Bd.)*
Thomas C. Sullivan *(Pres. & Chief Fin. Officer)*
James E. Wagner *(Exec. V.P.)*
Roy Britten *(V.P.-Mfg.)*
Richard Bryant *(V.P.-Mfg.)*
Paul Fortini *(V.P.-Sls.)*
Raymond Scott *(V.P.-Pur.)*
Edward Sullivan *(V.P.-Human Resources)*
George R. Sullivan *(V.P.-Sls.)*
Rick Cowles *(Controller)*
Donald V. Gasparini *(Mgr.-Sls. Promo.)*
Principal(s):
Richard S. Sullivan
Thomas C. Sullivan

No. of U.S. Offices: 1

Outside Service Firm(s):

Roan Mallows & Company*(Auditors)*
Springfield, MA

Murray, Disanti, Schubert & Fitzgerald*(Legal Firm)*
Springfield, MA

Multibank*(Major Banking Relationship)*
Springfield, MA

Affilatiates:

Little Falls Color Print **(1)**
Riverside Industrial Park,
Little Falls, NY 13365
Emp.: 55
Gravure Printing & Converting
S.I.C.: 3577
Donald Matthias *(Pres.)*

Sulpaco West **(1)**
600 E. Hancock St.
Appleton, WI 54912
Tel.: 414-749-2140
Gravure Printing & Converting
S.I.C.: 3577
Michaeel Sullivan *(V.P.)*

SUMMA CORPORATION
(A General Partner of Howard Hughes Properties Limited Partnership)
3800 Howard Hughes Pkwy.
Las Vegas, NV 89109
Mailing Address:
P.O. Box 14000
Las Vegas, NV 89114
Tel.: 702-791-4000 **NV**
Fax: 702-791-4385
Year Founded: 1929
Emp.: 135
Real Estate Investment & Development
S.I.C.: 6531; 6552
William R. Lummis *(Chm. Bd.)*
John L. Goolsby *(Pres. & Chief Exec. Officer)*
M. Rex Baird *(Sr. V.P., Treas. & Chief Fin. Officer)*
Ronald C. Brooks *(Sr. V.P.)*
Mark L. Fine *(Sr. V.P.)*
Robert E. Morrison *(Sr. V.P.)*
Michael C. Niarchos *(Sr. V.P., Gen. Counsel & Sec.)*
Vernon C. Olson *(Sr. V.P.)*
Stephen I. Reinstein *(Sr. V.P.)*
Kevin T. Orrock *(V.P.)*
T. Mark Paris *(V.P.)*
Dennis Sizemore *(V.P. & Controller)*

No. of U.S. Offices: 2

Outside Service Firm(s):

Deloitte & Touche*(Auditors)*
3800 Howard Hughes Pkwy., Ste. 1600
Las Vegas, NV 89109
Tel.: 702-791-1000
Fax: 702-369-1736

Johnson & Higgins*(Commercial Insurance Carrier)*
2029 Century Park East
Los Angeles, CA
Tel.: 310-552-9665

Andrews & Kurth*(Legal Firm)*
4200 Texas Commerce Tower
Houston, TX 77002
Tel.: 713-220-4200

Bank of America NT&SA*(Major Banking Relationship)*
555 So. Flower St.
Los Angeles, CA 90071
Tel.: 213-683-3868

SUMMA FOUR, INC.
25 Sundail Aee.
Manchester, NH 03103-7251
Tel.: 603-625-4050
Tel.: 800-544-3440 **DE**
Fax: 603-668-4491
Year Founded: 1976
Earnings: $989,000
Sales Range: $10-19 Million
Emp.: 100
Fiscal Year-end: 3/31/91
Export
Manufacture Specialty Telecommunications Switching Systems
S.I.C.: 3669
Barry R. Gorsun *(Pres. & Chief Exec. Officer)*
Daniel J. Hoy *(V.P. & Chief Oper. Officer)*
Mark Tubinus *(V.P. & Chief Technologist)*
Phyllis Hoffman *(V.P.-Sls. & Mktg.)*
Edward M.A. Mier *(V.P.-European Opers.)*
George Matz *(Natl. Dir.-Field Opers.)*
Martha Boissonneault *(Dir.-Corp. Communications)*
Joanne Hyde *(Dir.-Human Resources)*
Charles Kolbenson *(Dir.-Engrng.)*
John Shaw *(Dir.-Mktg.)*
Paul DeMello *(Mgr.-Quality Control)*
Kathi Goelzenleuchter *(Mgr.-Acctg.)*
Kathy Bolduc *(Supvr.-Pur.)*
Paul Semple *(Legal Officer)*

No. of Mfg. Plants/Facilities: 1
No. of U.S. Offices: 5
No. of Foreign Offices: 1

Computer Systems/Hardware:
Sunmicro Systems-Development Platform; Macola-Administrative Software

Outside Service Firm(s):

Coopers & Lybrand*(Auditors)*
Manchester, NH

Alexander & Alexander*(Commercial Insurance Carrier)*
225 N. Michigan Av.
Chicago, IL 60611
Tel.: 312-565-6221

Willis Caroon*(Group Insurer)*
Rochester, NH

McSwiney, Semple, Bowers & Wise*(Legal Firm)*
Concord, NH

Fleet National Bank*(Major Banking Relationship)*
Corporate Trust Dept., 125 Dupont Dr.
Providence, RI 02907
Tel.: 617-426-9555

First NH Bank, N.A.*(Major Banking Relationship)*
Manchester, NH

Non-U.S. Holding:

Summa Four Limited **(1)**
246 Bedford Ave.
Slough, Berkshire SL1 4RJ, United Kingdom
Tel.: 753 517789
Sales & Marketing
S.I.C.: 5063; 5065
Edward M.A. Mier *(V.P.-European Opers.)*

SUMMERFIELD TRUCK CO. INC.
5900 Southport Rd.
Portage, IN 46368
Tel.: 219-763-7227
Tel.: 1-800-676-PETE **IN**
Year Founded: 1960
Approx.Sls.: $25,000,000
Emp.: 85
Truck & Parts Sales, Service, Leasing & Financing
S.I.C.: 5012; 6159; 7538
Arthur E. Summerfield, Jr. *(Chm. Bd. & Pres.)*
Stephen Buha *(V.P., Gen. Mgr. & Chief Exec. Officer)*
Maxine Summerfield *(Treas.)*
Judy Widener *(Controller)*
Diane Baroevich *(Chief Fin. Officer)*
Robert Buha *(Dir.-Leasing)*
Principal(s):
Arthur E. Summerfield, Jr.

Computer Systems/Hardware:
Display Data

Outside Service Firm(s):

Crowe, Chizek & Co.*(Auditors)*
P.O. Box 3687,
Oak Brook, IL 60822
Tel.: 708-954-7408
Fax: 708-799-1299

CNA Insurance*(Commercial Insurance Carrier)*
CNA Plaza,
Chicago, IL 60685
Tel.: 312-822-5000

Singleton, Levy, Crist & Johnson*(Legal Firm)*
Highland, IN

Gainer Bank*(Major Banking Relationship)*
Gary, IN

Genesee Bank*(Pension Manager)*
Number One East First St.
Flint, MI

SUMMIT COMMUNICATIONS, INC.
115 Perimeter Center Pl., Suite #1150
Atlanta, GA 30346
Tel.: 404-394-0707
Fax: 404-394-9778
Approx.Sls.: $76,000,000
Emp.: 700
Radio Broadcasting & Cable TV
S.I.C.: 4832; 4841; 4899

Summit Communications, Inc.—(Continued)

James W. Wesley *(Pres.)*
James Strawn *(Exec. V.P.)*
Owen Weber *(Exec. V.P.-Radio)*
Bernard Gray *(Sr. V.P.-Devel. & Sec.)*
Nannette N. Allen *(V.P.-Fin. & Admin.)*
Roger Heffelfinger *(Treas.)*
Sarah Pattison *(Controller)*

Outside Service Firm(s):

Womble, Carlyle, Sandridge & Rice*(Legal Firm)*
Wachovia Bldg.
Winston Salem, NC 27102
Tel.: 919-721-3600

SUMMIT CORPORATION OF AMERICA
1430 Waterbury Rd.
Thomaston, CT 06787
Tel.: 203-283-4391
Fax: 203-283-4010
Sales Range: $80-99 Million
Emp.: 250
Electroplating
S.I.C.: 3471
L.B. Foster *(Chm. Bd.)*
R.A. Fumire *(Pres.)*
W. Zura *(Controller)*
John F. Bessozzi, Jr. *(Gen. Counsel)*
Charles F. Bradley *(Mgr.-Personnel)*
Ernest LeClair *(Gen. Mgr.)*
Principal(s):
L.B. Foster

Outside Service Firm(s):

Deloitte & Touche*(Auditors)*
Hartford, CT

Connecticut National Bank*(Major Banking Relationship)*
777 Main St.
Hartford, CT 06115
Tel.: 203-728-2000

SUMMIT ENVIRONMENTAL GROUP
115 Dewalt Ave. N.W.
Canton, OH 44702
Tel.: 216-455-7333
Fax: 216-455-8134
Ted Savastomo *(Chief Exec. Officer)*

Subsidiary:

WW Engineering & Science Inc. **(1)**
5555 Glenwood Hills Pkwy. S.E.
Grand Rapids, MI 49512
Tel.: 616-942-9600
Fax: 616-942-6499
Assets: $43,500,000
Liabilities: $24,200,000
Net Worth: $19,300,000
Approx.Sls.: $56,000,000
Emp.: 800
Fiscal Year-end: 6/30/92
Computer Systems/Hardware:
DEC-VAX; HP-3000
Consulting Engineers & Scientists
S.I.C.: 8741; 8711; 8731; 7379
Corporate Giving Program: United Way
S.S. Saless *(Pres.-WWES)*
W.J. Cretens *(Pres.-WWOS)*
Gary M. Kienzle *(Exec. V.P. & Chief Fin. Officer)*
D.J. Gebben *(Sr. V.P.)*
R.C. Johr *(Sr. V.P.)*
S.L. Kubas *(Sr. V.P.)*
R.R. Rediske *(Sr. V.P.)*
Ralph Berner *(V.P.)*
R. Phillips *(V.P.-Corp. Admin.)*
Paul Verbrugge *(Controller)*
Judy D. Boonstra *(Dir.-Data Processing)*
Ted J. Cline *(Dir.-Human Resources)*
Douglas A. Smith *(Dir.-Corp. Graphic Systems & Telecommunications)*
William Jackson *(Mgr.-Personnel Admin.)*

Division:

J.W. Welsch & Associates **(2)**
6435 Castleway W. Dr.
Indianapolis, IN 46250-1940
Tel.: 317-842-7033
Fax: 317-576-6549
Rick Gelinas *(V.P.)*

Summit Holdings Corporation
(See Listing Under Louis Padnos Iron & Metal Co., Name Changed To Padnos-Summit Div.)

SUN BULB COMPANY, INC.
Hwy. 17, S.
Arcadia, FL 33821
Mailing Address:
P.O. Drawer 698
Arcadia, FL 33821
Tel.: 813-494-4022
Fax: 813-494-7568
Year Founded: 1956
Sales Range: $10-19 Million
Emp.: 30
Fiscal Year-end: 6/30/92
Import Export
Growers & Distributors of Flower Bulbs, Bromeliads, Orchids & Ferns
S.I.C.: 0181; 5193
Rodney Hollingsworth *(Pres.)*
Tom Hollingsworth *(V.P.)*
Linda Hollingsworth *(Sec. & Treas.)*

Computer Systems/Hardware:
IBM System 36

Outside Service Firm(s):

Sun Bank, N.A.*(Major Banking Relationship)*
Arcadia, FL

Divisions:

The Orchid Center **(1)**
P.O. Box 1116
Arcadia, FL 33821
Tel.: 813-494-5896
Robert Palmer *(Gen. Mgr.)*

Sun Chemical Company, Inc. **(1)**
P.O. Box 309
Arcadia, FL 33821
Tel.: 813-494-5896
Mike Provau *(Gen. Mgr.)*

SUN COMPUTERS, INC.
One Civic Plaza, Ste. 600
Carson, CA 90745
Tel.: 310-538-8338
Tel.: 800-640-4786 **CA**
Fax: 310-538-3959
Year Founded: 1980
Approx.Sls.: $85,000,000
Emp.: 230
Wholesale Distributor & Retail Sales of Computers & Accessories; Personal & Home Entertainment; Personal Computers
S.I.C.: 5045; 5734
David Sun *(Pres. & Chief Exec. Officer)*
Betty Lee Sun *(Exec. V.P.)*
Betty Krusiewicz *(V.P.-Mktg.)*
Dan Cho *(Dir.-Fin.)*
David Graham *(Dir.-Opers.)*
Bob Holmes *(Dir.-Human Resources)*
Dana Hoopingarner *(Dir.-Branch Sls.)*
Reginald Sims *(Dir.-Corp. Sls.)*
Zygmunt Sczepanski *(Dir.-Educational Sls.)*
Rick Stace *(Dir.-Pur.)*

SUN DATA INC.
1300 Oakbrook Drive
Norcross, GA 30093
Mailing Address:
P.O. Box 5250,
Norcross, GA 30091-5250
Tel.: 404-449-6116
Tel.: 800-241-9882 **GA**
Fax: 404-448-7726
Year Founded: 1976
Approx.Sls.: $120,000,000
Emp.: 201
Fiscal Year-end: 6/30/92
Import Export
Lease & Wholesale of New & Pre-Owned Mid-Range Computers and Peripherals
S.I.C.: 7379; 5044; 6159
Corporate Giving Program: Company Chosen Charities by our Contributions Committee
John H. Crilly *(Pres. & Chief Exec. Officer)*
Eric Prockow *(V.P. & Chief Fin. Officer)*
William Collyer *(V.P. & Gen. Counsel)*
Art Kimicata *(V.P.-Sls. & Mktg.)*
Macon Collyer *(V.P. & Gen. Counsel)*

No. of U.S. Offices: 14

Computer Systems/Hardware:
System 3X & AS/400

Outside Service Firm(s):

Arthur Andersen & Co.*(Auditors)*
133 Peachtree St., N.E.
Atlanta, GA 30303
Tel.: 404-658-1776

Page & Bacek*(Legal Firm)*
Atlanta, GA
Tel.: 404-365-9900

Powell, Goldstein, Frazer & Murphy*(Legal Firm)*
191 Peachtree St. NE, 16th Fl.
Atlanta, GA 30303
Tel.: 404-572-6700
Fax: 404-572-5958

Trust Company Bank*(Major Banking Relationship)*
Trust Co. Tower
Atlanta, GA 30303
Tel.: 404-588-7963

SUN DIAMOND GROWERS OF CALIFORNIA
5568 Gibraltar Dr.
Pleasanton, CA 94588
Mailing Address:
P.O. Box 9024
Pleasanton, CA 94566
Tel.: 510-463-8200
Telex: 171317
Fax: 510-463-7492
Year Founded: 1980
Assets: $32,010,800
Earnings: $42,166,000
Liabilities: $17,552,400
Net Worth: $14,458,400
Approx.Sls.: $581,700,000
Emp.: 2,100
Fiscal Year-end: 7/31/91
Export
Farmer Cooperative; Processing & Marketing of Walnuts, Pecans, Filberts, Brazil Nuts & Almonds, Prunes, Raisins, Dried Figs, Cut Dried Fruits, Apricots, Peaches, Pears, Apples, Mixtures of Dried Fruits & Nuts, Fruit Juices, Dried Fruit Paste & Animal Feed
S.I.C.: 0179; 0723; 2034; 5149; 0173; 0175; 2068; 2084
William Hosie *(Chm. Bd.)*
Larry D. Busboom *(Pres. & Chief Fin. Officer)*
Richard Douglas *(Sr. V.P.-Corp. Affairs)*
Robert Beckwith *(V.P.-Intl. Sls.)*
Anthony Kluge *(Chief Info. Officer)*
George O. Petty *(Sec.)*
Nick Tummers *(Controller)*
Michael Strambi *(Asst. Treas.)*
W.P. Beaton *(Dir.-Employee Benefits)*

Computer Systems/Hardware:
Burroughs

Outside Service Firm(s):

KPMG Peat Marwick*(Auditors)*
3 Embarcadero Center
San Francisco, CA 94111
Tel.: 415-951-0100
Fax: 415-397-1129

Chemical Bank*(Major Banking Relationship)*
50 California St.
San Francisco, CA 94111
Tel.: 415-954-9500
Tel.: 800-647-4273

Divisions:

Diamond Walnut Growers, Inc. **(1)**
1050 S. Diamond St.
Stockton, CA 95205
Tel.: 209-467-6000
Growers of Walnuts
S.I.C.: 0179; 0723; 5149
William Hosie *(Chm.)*
William Cuff *(Pres.)*

Hazelnut Growers of Oregon **(1)**
401 N. 26th Ave.
Cornelius, OR 97113
Tel.: 503-648-4176
Growers of Hazelnut
S.I.C.: 0179; 0723; 5149
Don W. Jossy *(Chm.)*
Larry Holden *(Gen. Mgr.)*

Sun-land Products of California **(1)**
5568 Gibraltar Dr.
Pleasanton, CA 94588
Tel.: 510-463-8200
Growers of Raisins & Related Products
S.I.C.: 0723; 5149
Earl Giacolini *(Chm.)*
Larry D. Busboom *(Pres.)*

Sun-Maid Growers of California **(1)**
13525 S. Bethel Ave.
Kingsburg, CA 93631
Tel.: 209-896-8000
Tel.: 800-272-4746
Telex: 984644
Fax: 209-897-2362
Approx.Sls.: $175,000,000
Emp.: 500
Fiscal Year-end: 7/31/92
Export
Computer Systems/Hardware:
Burroughs
Packing & Distribution of Raisins, Dried Apricots, Peaches, Mixed Cut Fruit, Raisin Juice Concentrate, Dried Pears, Animal Feed & Gift Packs
S.I.C.: 0179; 0723; 2034; 5149
Pete J. Penner *(Chm. Bd.)*
Barry F. Kriebel *(Pres.)*
Richard Emde *(V.P.-Fin.)*
Frank Ferraris *(V.P.-Mktg.)*
James Henderson *(V.P.-Opers.)*
Bruce Conley *(Dir.-Industrial Rels.)*
Teresa Freeto *(Dir.-Quality Assurance)*
Harold Hilker *(Dir.-Industrial Sls.)*
Rod Stephens *(Dir.-Pur. & Production Plng.)*
Steve Marcus *(Mgr.-MIS)*
John Slinkard *(Mgr.-Human Resources)*

Sunsweet Growers Inc. **(1)**
901 Walton Ave.
Yuba City, CA 95991
Tel.: 916-674-5010
Export
Growers of Prunes & Related Products
S.I.C.: 0179; 0723; 2034; 5149
Earl Giacolini *(Chm.)*
Harold W. Jackson *(Pres.)*

Valley Fig Growers **(1)**
2028 S. 3rd.
Fresno, CA 93718
Tel.: 209-237-3893
Growers of Figs
S.I.C.: 0179; 0723; 2034; 5149
Robert M. McAuley *(Chm.)*
Jennifer M. Mathis *(Pres.)*

SUN FINANCIAL GROUP, INC.
2502 Rocky Pt. Dr., Ste. 375
Tampa, FL 33607
Tel.: 813-289-7000 **MI**
Fax: 813-281-1919
Year Founded: 1981
Approx.Sls.: $28,000,000
Emp.: 55
Import Export
Leasing Commercial Equipment
S.I.C.: 7359
Clay M. Biddinger *(Pres. & Chief Exec. Officer)*
David Cardew *(V.P.-Fin.)*
John Ellett *(V.P.)*
Michael J. O'Donnell *(V.P.-Asset Mngmt.)*

Outside Service Firm(s):

Price Waterhouse*(Auditors)*
400 N. Ashley, Ste. 2800
Tampa, FL 33602
Tel.: 813-223-7577

Holland & Knight*(Legal Firm)*
P.O. Box 1288
Tampa, FL 33601
Tel.: 813-223-1621

NationsBank Florida*(Major Banking Relationship)*
600 Florida Ave.
Tampa, FL 33602
Tel.: 813-224-5151

SUN HILL INDUSTRIES
48 Union St.
Stamford, CT 06906
Tel.: 203-324-7550
Fax: 203-356-9233
Approx.Sls.: $8,000,000
Emp.: 22
Development, Manufacturing & Marketing of Holiday Products: Easter Egg Dyes, Halloween & Christmas Decorations
S.I.C.: 3999
Benson Zinbarg *(Pres., Chief Exec. & Chief Fin. Officer & Treas.)*
Anita Dembiczak *(V.P.-Pur.)*
Alan Sleath *(Controller)*
Judy Aronin *(Mgr.-Natl. Sls.)*
Saul Feit *(Mgr.-Natl. Sls., Retail Div.)*
Barbara Fortin *(Mgr.)*
Kathy Bond *(Bookkeeper)*

Computer Systems/Hardware:
Qantel

Outside Service Firm(s):

Bregman & Co.*(Auditors)*
Stamford, CT

Metropolitan Life Insurance Co.*(Group Insurer)*
One Madison Avenue
New York, NY 10010-3690

SUN LAKES MARKETING
25612 E. J. Robson Blvd.
Sun Lakes, AZ 85248
Tel.: 602-895-9600
Fax: 602-895-0136
Assets: $99,000,000
Liabilities: $39,000,000
Net Worth: $60,000,000
Sales Range: $40-59 Million
Emp.: 125
Real Estate Development, Land & Home Sales
S.I.C.: 6531; 6552
Edward J. Robson *(Chm. Bd.)*
Steve Robson *(Pres.)*
Jim Hubbard *(Chief Fin. Officer)*
Richard Koenig *(V.P.-Sls.)*
Mike Osborn *(V.P.-Mktg.)*

Computer Systems/Hardware:
IBM System 36

Outside Service Firm(s):

G. Bernard Berry Ltd.*(Auditors)*
Phoenix, AZ

Security Pacific Bank Arizona*(Major Banking Relationship)*
Phoenix, AZ

SUN PROCESS CONVERTING COMPANY
505 Bonnie Lane
Elk Grove Village, IL 60007
Tel.: 708-593-0447
Tel.: 800-323-0697
Fax: 708-593-0115
Year Founded: 1970
Approx.Sls.: $15,000,000
Emp.: 185
Fiscal Year-end: 5/31/91
Export
Manufacture Pressure Sensitive Decorative Appliques
Michael Moore *(Pres.)*
Ronald Weingardt *(Exec. V.P.)*
Mary Woods *(Mgr.-Sls.)*
Lisa Spike *(Supvr.-Mktg.)*
Principal(s):
Michael Moore
Ronald Weingardt

No. of Mfg. Plants/Facilities: 3

Outside Service Firm(s):

Glenview State Bank*(Major Banking Relationship)*
Glenview, IL

SUNBEAM-OSTER COMPANY, INC.
One Citizen's Plaza, 6th Fl.
Providence, RI 02903
Tel.: 401-831-0050 **PA**
Fax: 401-831-0389
Approx.Sls.: $885,600,000
Fiscal Year-end: 12/29/91
Import Export
Small Electric Kitchen Appliances, Patio Furniture, Outdoor Grills, Clocks & Weather Instruments, Bathroom Scales, Hair Dryers, Automatic Blankets
S.I.C.: 3634; 3822; 3825; 3524; 3356; 3494
Paul Kazarian *(Chm. & Mng. Dir.)*
Robert Setrakiann *(Treas.)*
Michael G. Lederman *(Gen. Counsel & Sec.)*
Henry Rauzi *(Controller)*

Major Operating Units:

Allegheny International Credit Corp. **(1)**
Two Oliver Plaza, Ste. 880
Pittsburgh, PA 15222
Commercial Finance Company
S.I.C.: 6159
Charles C. Maupin *(Pres.)*

Sunbeam Casual Furniture Co. **(1)**
Victor Reiter Pkwy.
Portland, TN 37148
Tel.: 615-325-9283
Fax: 910-380-2855
Emp.: 600
Aluminum Lawn & Patio Furniture
S.I.C.: 2519
Earle W. Maxwell, Jr. *(Pres.)*
John L. McDaniel *(V.P.-Sls. & Mktg.)*
Andrew C. Hill *(Mktg. Dir.)*
Andy Hill *(Dir.-Mktg. & Adv.)*
Jacquelyn M. Schroeder *(Exec. Sec.)*

Sunbeam-Oster Household Products **(1)**
1501 Woodfield Rd., Ste. 400N
Schaumburg, IL 60173
Tel.: 708-995-8900
Approx.Sls.: $400,000,000
Emp.: 100
Fiscal Year-end: 9/30/91
Import Export
Small Appliances
S.I.C.: 3634; 3069; 2392
James Clegg *(Pres.)*
Richard Boynton *(V.P.-Sls.)*
Doug Everitt *(V.P.-Fin.)*
Mark A. Porter *(V.P.-Mktg.-Bedding)*
Michael Matthews *(Dir.-Mktg.)*

Divisions:

Sunbeam Home Comfort **(2)**
Hwy. 45 North, Box 38
Shubuta, MS 39360
Tel.: 601-687-1531
Fax: 601-687-1380
Approx.Sls.: $30,000,000
Emp.: 350
Fiscal Year-end: 10/31/90
Hanson Scales-Postal, Bathroom, Clinical & Kitchen; Stationery, Healthcare, Shower Massagers
S.I.C.: 3596; 3829; 3842
George Stewart *(Pres.)*
William Zador *(V.P.-Sls. & Mktg.)*
Billy Boone *(Controller)*
Mary Adams *(Mgr.-Customer Service)*
Claudie Johnson *(Mgr.-Matls.)*
John Shirley *(Mgr.-Human Resources)*

Springfield Instrument Company **(2)**
76 Passaic St.
Wood-Ridge, NJ 07075
Tel.: 201-777-2900
Measuring & Controlling Devices
S.I.C.: 3829
Jack McEvily *(Pres.)*

Sunbeam Appliance Company **(2)**
2001 S. York Rd.
Oak Brook, IL 60521
Tel.: 708-719-5000
Sales Office Sunbeam Products
S.I.C.: 5064

Sunbeam Outdoor Products Co. **(2)**
4101 Howard Bush Dr.
Neosho, MO 64850
Tel.: 417-451-4550
Fax: 417-451-7921
Approx.Sls.: $200,000,000
Export
Manufacture Outdoor Grills & Camping Equipment
S.I.C.: 3631; 3949
Rick Davidson *(Pres.)*
William King *(Exec. V.P.)*
Rob Johnson *(V.P.-Sls. & Mktg.)*
Sal Vaccaro Jr. *(V.P.-Mktg.)*
Bill Edwards *(V.P.-Finance & Controller)*
Andy Hill *(Dir.-Mktg.)*
Gary Brattin *(Pur. Mgr.)*
Mike Franks *(Sls. Promo. Mgr.)*

Non-U.S. Holdings:

Eriez Products Magneticos e Metalurgicos, Ltda. **(1)**
Caixa Postall 2632 01000
Sao Paulo, Brazil
Tel.: 55-11-257-4217
Produces Magnetic Materials & High-Alloy Castings for the Automotives Farm Machinery & Constructed Equip.
S.I.C.: 3499

Oster de Venezuela S.A. **(1)**
Edificie Principal No. 2, Pis 2 3 ra Tra Los Ruices,
Caracas, Venezuela
Tel.: (02) 239-5780
Mfr. Household Appliances
S.I.C.: 3639
George E. Barry *(Chief Oper. Officer)*

Sofedem S.A. **(1)**
46 Rue Arago
Puteaux, 92801, France
Gernard Vehlhaber *(Chief Oper. Officer)*

Sunbeam Consumer Products Far East, Ltd. **(1)**
Room 1505 Tai Sang Commercial Bldg., 24-
Hong Kong, Hong Kong
Tel.: (5) 283624
David Brakes *(Chief Oper. Officer)*

Sunbeam Corporation (Canada) Limited **(1)**
1040 Islington Ave.
Toronto, ON Canada M87 4R58
Tel.: 416-236-2481
Fax: 416-236-2481
Household Appliances Sales & Marketing, Repair
S.I.C.: 5046; 7629
M.R. Morrow *(Pres. & Gen. Mgr.)*
B.R. Coles *(V.P.-Sls.)*
S. Howell *(V.P.-Service)*
Michael Andrews *(Chief Fin. Officer)*

Sunbeam del Peru S.A. **(1)**
Casilla Postal 5673
Lima, 100, Peru
Tel.: 52-9353
Telex: 26034 pe sunbeam
Fax: 14-52-8420
Approx.Sls.: $10,000,000
Emp.: 200
Household & Personal Appliances
S.I.C.: 3634
Jesus M. Morales *(Pres.)*
Franz A. Schmid *(Pres & Gen Mgr)*

Sunbeam Div. **(1)**
103 rue La Fayette
Paris, 75481, France
Jacques Lebert *(Chief Oper. Officer)*

Sunbeam Iberica S.A. **(1)**
Rambla De Cataluna No. 98, 7th Flr.
Barcelona, 8, Spain
Tel.: 310.09.60
John Bloxcidge *(Chief Oper. Officer)*

Sunbeam Intercontinental Ltd. **(1)**
Georgetown, Cayman Islands
George Lucero L. *(Chief Oper. Officer)*

Sunbeam Mexicana S.A. de C.V. **(1)**
A.V. Dr. Gustavo Baz No. 180 Apartado Postale,
Tlalnepantla, Mexico
Tel.: 397-56-99
Mfr. Appliances
S.I.C.: 3634
Fernando Lopez B. *(Chief Oper.Officer)*

Sunbeam Vertriebsgesellschaft mbH **(1)**
Waldstrasse 256 6050
Offenbach/Main, Germany
Tel.: (0611) 85-3011
Hans Goetsch *(Chief Oper. Officer)*

Tube Turns de Mexico, S.A. **(1)**
K.M. 22.5 Carretera Federal Mex-Puebla
Chicoloapan, Edo. de Mexico Mexico
Tel.: 905-510-0610

SUNCLIPSE, INC.
1610 S. Greenwood Ave.
Montebello, CA 90640
Mailing Address:
P.O. Box 2052,
Montebello, CA 90640
Tel.: 213-721-2132
Fax: 213-725-0775
Year Founded: 1948
Assets: $90,000,000
Net Worth: $90,000,000
Approx.Sls.: $240,000,000
Emp.: 1,500
Fiscal Year-end: 10/31/88
Paper & Allied Products
S.I.C.: 5113; 2679; 2653
Phillip Shelton *(Chm. Bd. & Pres.)*
William Dodds *(Chief Fin. Officer & Sec.)*
Darryl Abotomey *(V.P. & Controller)*
Charles Mason *(V.P.-Human Resources)*
Curt Thomas *(Gen. Counsel)*
Stephen Huntington *(Mgr.-Data Processing)*

Computer Systems/Hardware:
IBM Systems 36 & 38

Outside Service Firm(s):

Deloitte & Touche*(Auditors)*
21550 Oxnard St., Ste. 800
Woodland Hills, CA 91367-7100
Tel.: 818-593-4800
Fax: 818-347-4278

Smith Barney, Harris Upham & Company, Inc.*(Investment Banker)*
1345 Avenue of the Americas
New York, NY
Tel.: 212-698-6559
Fax: 212-698-5735

Bank of America NT&SA*(Major Banking Relationship)*
555 S. Flower St., 5th Fl.
Los Angeles, CA 90071
Tel.: 213-228-3868

First Interstate Bank of California, N.A.*(Major Banking Relationship)*
P.O. Box 3667,
Los Angeles, CA 90051
Tel.: 213-614-4000

SUNDAY RIVER SKIWAY CORPORATION
Sunday River Rd.
Bethel, ME 04217
Mailing Address:
P.O. Box 450,
Bethel, ME 04217
Tel.: 207-824-2187 **ME**

Sunday River Skiway Corporation—(Continued)

Fax: 207-824-2111
Year Founded: 1958
Sales Range: $20-39 Million
Ski Resort & Real Estate Development
S.I.C.: 6552
Leslie B. Otten *(Pres. & Treas.)*

SUNDOWN VITAMIN CO., INC.
4031 N.E. 12th Terrace
Fort Lauderdale, FL 33334
Tel.: 305-565-3566
Fax: 305-565-1918
Year Founded: 1976
Approx.Sls.: $55,000,000
Emp.: 280
Fiscal Year-end: 12/31/91
Import Export
Mfr. & Distributor of Vitamins, Food Supplements & Over-the-Counter Pharmaceuticals
S.I.C.: 2834; 2099; 5122
Employee Matching Gifts Progra
Carl DeSantis *(Pres.)*
Gary Cotton *(Chief Fin. Officer)*
Damon DeSantis *(Exec. V.P.)*
Richard Wisely *(Sr. V.P.)*
Dean DeSantis *(V.P.-Opers.)*
Nick Palin *(V.P.-Whlse. Sls.)*
Principal(s):
Carl DeSantis
Damon DeSantis

Computer Systems/Hardware:
Wang

Outside Service Firm(s):

Richard Burton & Associates*(Legal Firm)*
Ft. Lauderdale, FL

First Union National Bank*(Major Banking Relationship)*
100 N.E. 3rd Av.
Fort Lauderdale, FL 33301-1155
Tel.: 305-467-5531

Division:

Rexall Inc. Consumer Products Div. **(1)**
4031 N.E. 12th Terrace
Fort Lauderdale, FL 33334
Tel.: 305-561-2187
Fax: 305-568-0928
Mfr. of Pharmaceuticals
S.I.C.: 2834
Armend Szmulewitz *(Chief Exec. Officer)*

Subsidiaries:

Rexall Group **(1)**
4031 N.E. 12th Terrace
Fort Lauderdale, FL 33334
Tel.: 305-561-2187
Fax: 305-568-0928
Sales Range: $10-19 Million
Emp.: 400
Computer Systems/Hardware:
Wang 5754
Mfr., Distribution & Marketing of Branded & Private Label Vitamins & Nutritional Products, Over-The-Counter Drugs & Health & Beauty Aids
S.I.C.: 2834; 5122; 5100
Carl DeSantis *(Pres.)*
Armend Szmulewitz *(Chief Exec. Officer)*
John Little *(Dir.-Mktg.)*

Thompson Nutritional Products **(1)**
4031 N.E. 12th Terrace
Fort Lauderdale, FL 33334
Tel.: 305-565-3566
Fax: 305-565-1918
Approx.Sls.: $19,500,000
Emp.: 200
Mfr. of Vitamins, Mineral Products & Nutritional Supplements
S.I.C.: 2833; 2844
Carl DeSantis *(Pres.)*

SUNDT CORP.
4101 E. Irvington Rd.
Tucson, AZ 85714
Mailing Address:
P.O. Box 26685,
Tucson, AZ 85726
Tel.: 602-748-7555 **AZ**
Fax: 602-747-9673
Year Founded: 1890
Assets: $88,913,000
Liabilities: $64,223,000
Net Worth: $24,690,000
Approx.Sls.: $379,245,000
Emp.: 1,500
Fiscal Year-end: 9/30/91
Commercial & Industrial Transportation Construction
S.I.C.: 1522; 1541; 1542; 1611; 1622; 1623; 1629
H. Wilson Sundt *(Chm. Bd. & Chief Exec. Officer)*
C. Richard Fedrick *(Vice Chm.)*
J. Doug Pruitt *(Pres.)*
Raymond C. Bargull *(Exec. V.P.-Real Estate Officer & Chief Fin. Officer)*
Dave Crawford *(Exec. V.P.-Bldg. Grp.)*
Lonnie Brenick *(Sr. V.P.)*
E. Peter Johnson *(Sr. V.P. & Gen. Counsel)*
Albert I. Schifano *(Sr. V.P.-Personnel)*
Charles A. Boyd *(V.P.)*
Mary Descoteaux *(V.P. & Controller)*
Carol Peabody *(V.P. & Treas.)*
Robert J. Vint *(V.P.-Data Processing)*
C.E. Collins *(Group Exec. V.P.-Special Projects)*
R. Steve Lewis *(Group Exec. V.P.-Heavy Construction)*
Sandie Merilott *(Dir.-Pur.)*
Wayne Oliver *(Dir.-Personnel Training & Devel.)*
Principal(s):
C. Richard Fedrick
Raymond C. Bargull
E. Peter Johnson
Albert I. Schifano
Cornell E. Collins
Doug Pruitt
Dean N. Ninteman
R. Steve Lewis

No. of Mfg. Plants/Facilities: 1
No. of U.S. Offices: 9
No. of Foreign Offices: 1

Computer Systems/Hardware:
IBM 4341 & PC; Hewlett-Packard 1000; Compaq PC

Outside Service Firm(s):

Crable, Parsons & Dooley*(Auditors)*
Tucson, AZ

Molloy, Jones & Donahue*(Legal Firm)*
Tucson, AZ

Valley National Bank*(Major Banking Relationship)*
Tucson, AZ

Subsidiaries:

C. R. Fedrick, Inc. **(1)**
P.O. Box 688,
Novato, CA 94948
Tel.: 415-892-0848
Constuction Dams, Utilities, Pipeline Construction
S.I.C.: 1623; 1629
C. Richard Fedrick *(Chief Exec. Officer)*
Dee Fedrick *(Pres.)*

Ninteman Construction Company, Inc. **(1)**
4375 Jutland Dr., #200
San Diego, CA 92138
Tel.: 619-490-6800
Fax: 619-490-6818
Construction Industrial Buildings, Warehouses and other Non-Residential Buildings.
S.I.C.: 1541; 1542
Dean N. Ninteman *(Director Emeritus)*
J. Doug Pruitt *(Chm. & Chief Exec. Officer)*
Thomas Remensperger *(Pres. & Chief Oper. Officer)*

Sundt Products, Inc. **(1)**
4798 S. Julian Ave.
Tucson, AZ 85714
Tel.: 602-748-7555
Manufacture Tanks, Ducts & Scrubbers for Industrial Applications
S.I.C.: 3443; 3444; 3589
Robert Musser *(Pres.)*
Jerry Allen *(V.P. & Chief Oper. Officer)*

SUNFLOWER ELECTRIC POWER CORPORATION
301 W. 13th St.
Hays, KS 67601
Mailing Address:
P.O. Box 980
Hays, KS 67601
Tel.: 913-628-2845 **KS**
Fax: 913-628-3260
Year Founded: 1957
Approx.Rev.: $84,480,213
Emp.: 230
Fiscal Year-end: 12/31/91
Cooperative; Generation & Transmission of Electric Power
S.I.C.: 4911
Perry Rubart *(Chm. Bd.)*
John Tracy *(Vice Chm.)*
L. Christian Hauck *(Pres. & Chief Exec. Officer)*
Sid Severson *(Chief Fin. Officer & Sr. V.P.)*
Jims Hanks *(V.P.-Employee Benefits & Human Resources)*
Jerry Kempf *(V.P.-External Affairs)*
L. Earl Watkins, Jr. *(Gen. Counsel & Sec.)*
Caroll Waggoner *(Treas.)*
Jerry Herman *(Mgr.-Data Processing)*
Jana Horsfall *(Mgr.-Pur.)*

No. of U.S. Offices: 3

Computer Systems/Hardware:
IMB System 38

Outside Service Firm(s):

KPMG Peat Marwick*(Auditors)*
707 17th St.
Denver, CO 80202
Tel.: 303-296-2323
Fax: 303-295-8829

Watkins, Calcara & Rondeau*(Legal Firm)*
Hays, KS

Rural Electrification Administration*(Major Banking Relationship)*
Kansas City, MO

Plants:

Garden City Complex **(1)**
P.O. BOx 1649
Garden City, KS 67846
Tel.: 316-275-0161
Electric Generation & Transmission Utility
S.I.C.: 4911
L. Christian Hauck *(Pres. & Chief Exec. Officer)*

Holcomb Station **(1)**
#1 Holcomb Lane
Holcomb, KS 67851
Tel.: 316-277-2590
Fax: 316-277-2598
Emp.: 230
Electric Generation & Transmission Utility
S.I.C.: 4911
L. Christian Hauck *(Pres. & Chief Exec. Officer)*
Sid Severson *(Chief Fin. Officer)*
Carroll Waggoner *(Dir.-Mktg.)*
Jana Horsfall *(Dir.-Pur.)*

the Sunflower Group

THE SUNFLOWER GROUP
(A Div. of Dennis Garberg & Associates)
10895 Lowell, Ste. 300
Overland Park, KS 66210
Tel.: 913-451-2125
Tel.: 800-288-5085
Fax: 913-345-2640
Year Founded: 1978
Approx.Billings: $55,000,000
Emp.: 140
Cents-Off Coupon & R-O-P Creative Concept, Production & Ad Placement in Newsp., Reg. & Local Mktg., Competitive Promo. Tracking
Dennis Garberg *(Chm. Bd. & Chief Exec. Officer)*
Elaine Stansfield *(Pres. & Chief Oper. Officer)*
Marty Wilson *(Pres.-AdTracking Div.)*
Linda Tate *(Chief Fin. Officer)*
Chuck Chowins *(V.P., Opers.)*
Tom Lantz *(V.P., Natl. Sales Mgr.)*
Tom Butler *(V.P., Sales)*
Tom Roberts *(V.P., Sales)*
Tom Reddy *(Dir., Newsp. Rels.)*

SUNGLASS HUT CORPORATION
120 SW 8th St.
Miami, FL 33130
Tel.: 305-858-5990
Fax: 305-858-0013
Approx.Sls.: $75,000,000
Emp.: 1,400
Wholesale & Retail Sunglasses
S.I.C.: 5199; 5999
Jack Chadsey *(Pres., Chief Exec. & Oper. Officer)*
Walter Krysevig *(V.P. & Chief Fin. Officer)*

Outside Service Firm(s):

Arthur Andersen & Co.*(Auditors)*
2100 One Biscayne Tower
Miami, FL 33131
Tel.: 305-374-3700

NationsBank Florida*(Major Banking Relationship)*
P.O. Box 02-5337 DT MIA 4-3, 150 SE 3rd Ave.
Miami, FL 33102-5337

SUNKIST GROWERS, INC.
14130 Riverside Dr.
Sherman Oaks, CA 91423-2392
Mailing Address:
P.O. Box 7888,
Van Nuys, CA 91409-7888
Tel.: 818-986-4800 **CA**
Telex: 651467 SUNKISTLSA
Fax: 818-379-7204
Year Founded: 1893
Earnings: $796,807,000
Approx.Sls.: $1,033,000,000
Emp.: 1,200
Fiscal Year-end: 10/31/91
Import Export
Distr. of Citrus Fruits
S.I.C.: 2037; 5148
Thomas N. Dungan *(Chm. Bd.)*
Russell L. Hanlin *(Pres., Chief Exec. & Chief Oper. Officer)*
Dale Cunningham *(Sr. V.P. & Gen. Counsel)*
H.B. Flach *(V.P.-Fin. & Admin.)*
Curtis W. Anderson *(V.P.-Member & Pub. Rels.)*
William G. Anderson *(V.P.-Processed Products)*
Owen W. Belletto *(V.P.-Research, Diagonal Tech. Services)*
David P. Bernstein *(V.P.-Fresh Fruit Mktg.)*

W.K. Quarles *(V.P.-Govt. Affairs)*
William P. Quarrels, Jr. *(V.P.-Govt. Affairs)*
R.G. French *(Treas. & Controller)*
Eileen H. Fowler *(Sec.)*
Charles C. Marshall *(Dir.-Information Resources)*
Gene J. Sass *(Dir.-Mktg. & Intl. Mktg. Services)*
R.J. Mead *(Dir.-Export Mktg. Services)*
C.V. Romero *(Pur. Agent)*
John R. McGovern *(Mgr.-Employee Benefits & Human Resources)*
M.S. Gillmore *(Mgr.-Telecommunications)*
G. Winands *(Mgr.-Domestic Adv.)*
Sharon Drabeck *(Mgr.-Corp. Cash Mngmt.)*
Paul Jensen *(Mgr.-Sunkist Real Estate)*
D.A. Goodwin *(Mgr.-Fin. Analysis & Investments)*
T.E. Gaddis *(Mgr.-Conferences & Special Events)*

No. of Mfg. Plants/Facilities: 2
No. of U.S. Offices: 32
No. of Foreign Offices: 6

Computer Systems/Hardware:
IBM 4381; IBM AS/400

Outside Service Firm(s):

Deloitte & Touche*(Auditors)*
1000 Wilshire Blvd.
Los Angeles, CA 90017-2472
Tel.: 213-688-0800
Fax: 213-688-0100

Nationwide Insurance*(Commercial Insurance Carrier)*
One Nationwide Plaza
Columbus, OH 43216
Tel.: 614-249-6488

Travelers Insurance Co.*(Group Insurer)*
1 Tower Square
Hartford, CT 06183
Tel.: 203-222-7821
Fax: 203-222-7813

Bank of America NT&SA*(International Bank Affiliate)*
555 So. Flower St.
Los Angeles, CA 90071
Tel.: 213-228-3868

Goldman, Sachs & Co.*(Investment Banker)*
85 Broad St.
New York, NY 10004
Tel.: 212-902-1000
Fax: 212-902-4451

Tuttle & Taylor Inc.*(Legal Firm)*
355 S. Grand Ave.
Los Angeles, CA 90071
Tel.: 213-683-0600

First Interstate Bank of California, N.A.*(Major Banking Relationship)*
P.O. Box 3667,
Los Angeles, CA 90051
Tel.: 213-614-4000

Collins Associates*(Pension Manager)*
Newport Beach, CA

Divisions:

Sunkist Growers, Inc.-Central Division (1)
P.O. Box 4650,
Overland Park, KS 66204
Tel.: 913-888-1831
S.I.C.: 5148
D.F. Kerschbaum *(Mgr.)*

Sunkist Growers, Inc.-Eastern Division (1)
Two University Plaza
Hackensack, NJ 07601
Tel.: 201-488-0774
S.I.C.: 5148
P.W. Lee *(Mgr.)*

Sunkist Growers, Inc.-Southern Division (1)
North Center Office, Room 217, 4319 Covington Hwy.
Decatur, GA 30035
Tel.: 404-284-0214
Approx.Sls.: $700,000,000
Emp.: 1,500
Fresh Sunkist Oranges, Lemons, Grapefruit, Tangerines
S.I.C.: 5148
D.A. Vorderlondwehr *(Mgr.)*

Sunkist Grower, Inc.-Western Division (1)
6055 E. Washington Blvd., Ste. 929
Los Angeles, CA 90040
Tel.: 213-724-6122
S.I.C.: 5148
J.J. Payne *(Mgr.)*

Sunkist Growers, Processed Products (1)
720 E. Sunkist
Ontario, CA 91761
Tel.: 909-983-9811
Fax: 909-983-3461
Approx.Sls.: $200,000,000
Emp.: 550
Fiscal Year-end: 10/31/91
Import Export
Computer Systems/Hardware:
DEC/VAX
Processed Citrus & Other Fruit Ingredients for the Food, Beverage, Confectionary, Health and Beauty Aid, Flavoring and Fragrance Industries; Products Include Citrus and Fruit Juices, Concentrates, Purees, Beverage Bases, Citrus Oils, Aromatics and Flavorings, Dry Flavoring Ingredients, Pectin, Pharmaceutical Ingredients; Also Retail & Foodservice Packaged Juices, Juice Drinks, Juice Concentrates, & Be
S.I.C.: 5149
Russel L. Hanlin *(Pres. & Chief Exec. Officer)*
James Anderson *(Dir.-Sls.)*
Michael H. Loudon *(Dir.-Mktg.)*
Jim Gass *(Personnel Mgr.)*

Subsidiary:

SunMac Hawaii, Ltd. (1)
P.O. Box 2720, 972 So. Queen St.
Honolulu, HI 96803
Tel.: 808-536-0851 (51%)
Fax: 808-537-1216
Approx.Sls.: $390,000
Emp.: 6
Warehousing & Packing of Fruit
S.I.C.: 4221; 4783
R.L. Hanlin *(Pres.)*

Non-U.S. Holdings:

International Agricultural Market Development Co. (1)
Avenue Louise 416 Bte. 15, 1050
Brussels, Belgium
Tel.: 02-648-1905 (100%)
Telex: 84663576
Emp.: 3
Citrus Marketing Cooperative
S.I.C.: 2037; 5148

Sunkist (Europe) S.A. (1)
Rue du Valentin 29 CH-1004
Lausanne, Switzerland
Tel.: 021 22.48.04 (100%)
Citrus Marketing Cooperative
S.I.C.: 0174; 5148; 2037

Sunkist (Far East) Promotion, Ltd. (1)
Swire House, 11 Chater Rd., 12th Fl.
Hong Kong, Hong Kong
Tel.: 5 249219 (100%)
Telex: 80736 Sunfe HX
Citrus Marketing Cooperative
S.I.C.: 5148

Sunkist Pacific, Ltd. (1)
5-19, Akasaka 4-chome Minato-ku, Tokyo, 107, Japan
Tel.: 03-3586-8137 (100%)
Telex: J 24632 SHNIHON
Emp.: 21
Citrus Marketing Cooperative
S.I.C.: 5148
Ryo Shimizu *(Rep. Dir.)*

SUNLINE COACH CO., INC.
245 S. Muddy Creek Rd.
Denver, PA 17517
Tel.: 215-267-2858 **PA**
Fax: 215-267-0527
Year Founded: 1964
Sales Range: $10-19 Million
Emp.: 200
Export
Travel Trailers & Campers
S.I.C.: 3792
Employee Matching Gifts Progra
John Zimmerman *(Chm. Bd.)*
W. Larry Lawernce Jr. *(Pres. & Chief Exec. Officer)*
Louis Martin *(Exec. V.P.)*
Dan Hagy *(V.P.-Oper.)*
Rich Zimmerman *(Dir.-MIS)*
Gary Schafer *(Mgr.-Sls.)*

Outside Service Firm(s):

Trout, Ebersole & Groff*(Auditors)*
Lancaster, PA

SUNNEN PRODUCTS COMPANY
7910 Manchester Ave.
Saint Louis, MO 63143
Tel.: 314-781-2100
Tel.: 800-325-3670 **DE**
Fax: 314-781-1533
Year Founded: 1927
Approx.Sls.: $53,000,000
Emp.: 630
Fiscal Year-end: 12/31/91
Import Export
Industrial Honing Machines & Auto Engine Rebuilding Equipment; Precision ID Gages
S.I.C.: 3541
James K. Berthold *(Chm. Bd. & Pres.)*
Remi L. Wrona *(Pres.-Intl. Sls.)*
Richard J. Ruth *(V.P.-Employee Rels.)*
C. Diane Boulware *(Sec.)*
Paul E. Slaten *(Treas.)*
Ronald S. Suchanek *(Dir.-Corp. Admin.)*
Walter Black *(Mgr.-Natl. Sls.)*
Robert Davis *(Mgr.-Mktg. Communications)*
Allan Hopkins *(Dir.-Mktg.)*
Frank Michaels *(Mgr.-Plant Engrng.)*
Jean Miller *(Mgr.-Employee Benefits)*
Carl Pelech *(Mgr.-Res. & Devel.)*

No. of Mfg. Plants/Facilities: 1
No. of U.S. Offices: 1
No. of Foreign Offices: 1

Computer Systems/Hardware:
Unisys

Outside Service Firm(s):

Grace & Co.*(Auditors)*
St. Louis, MO

Barclays Bank plc*(International Bank Affiliate)*
St. Thomas, Virgin Islands

Bryan, Cave, McPheeters & McRoberts*(Legal Firm)*
One Metropolitan Sq.
St. Louis, MO 63102
Tel.: 314-259-2000

Pioneer Bank & Trust Co.*(Major Banking Relationship)*
St. Louis, MO

Paul E. Slaten*(Pension Manager)*
St. Louis, MO

SUNNILAND CORPORATION
P.O. Box 1697
Sanford, FL 32771
Tel.: 407-322-2421 **DE**
Fax: 407-330-0122
Year Founded: 1884
Assets: $11,625,104
Liabilities: $6,725,147
Net Worth: $4,899,957
Approx.Sls.: $44,596,253
Emp.: 175
Fiscal Year-end: 12/31/90
Wholesale Roofing Materials & Supplies; Fertilizer Pesticides; Garden Supplies
S.I.C.: 5039; 5191
Lee P. Moore *(Chm..)*
Thomas W. Moore *(Pres.)*
Delbert Abney *(V.P. & Sec.)*
Charles C. Ward, Jr. *(Treas.)*
Helen Kelly *(Dir.-Personnel)*
Thomas J. Wallace *(Dir.-Mktg.)*
Bill Stonestreet *(Mgr.-Sls.)*
Robert B. Simonds *(Programmer)*

Computer Systems/Hardware:
IBM System 36

Outside Service Firm(s):

Greene, Dycus & Co.*(Auditors)*
Sanford, FL

William Hutchinson*(Legal Firm)*
Sanford, FL

Barnett Bank*(Major Banking Relationship)*
Sanford, FL

SUNNYLAND FOODS, INC.
(Sub. of Bongrain S.A., France)
603 Cassidy Rd.
Thomasville, GA 31792
Tel.: 912-226-1611 **GA**
Fax: 912-225-3752
Year Founded: 1934
Assets: $27,000,000
Liabilities: $16,000,000
Net Worth: $11,000,000
Approx.Sls.: $190,000,000
Emp.: 900
Fiscal Year-end: 12/31/90
Processed Meats Manufacturer
S.I.C.: 2011
Lyndell Bisbee *(Gen. Mgr.)*
Phillip Meadows *(Dir.-Sls.)*
Brian Gresham *(Dir.-Fin. Services)*
Gary Albright *(Pur. Agent)*
Thomas Little *(Dir.-Human Resources)*
Principal(s):
Lyndell Bisbee

No. of Mfg. Plants/Facilities: 2

Computer Systems/Hardware:
NCR 8565

Outside Service Firm(s):

Arthur Andersen & Co.*(Auditors)*
Avenue des Arts 56 1040
Brussels, Belgium

Arthur Andersen & Co.*(Auditors)*
133 Peachtree St., N.E.
Atlanta, GA 30303
Tel.: 404-658-1776

American Heritage Life Insurance Co.*(Group Insurer)*
Thomasville, GA

Altman & McGraw*(Legal Firm)*
Thomasville, GA

NationsBank*(Major Banking Relationship)*
35 Broad St.
Atlanta, GA 30303
Tel.: 404-581-2121
Tel.: 800-848-8198

Subsidiaries:

Brooks County Packing Co. (1)
North Hyland
Quitman, GA 31643
Tel.: 912-263-4111
Emp.: 35
Whole Hog Sausage Manufacturer
S.I.C.: 2011
Steve Twedell *(Gen. Mgr.)*

Sunnyland Foods, Inc.—(Continued)

Premium Pork Processors **(1)**
P.O. Box 729
Moultrie, GA 31768
Tel.: 912-985-3400
Emp.: 269
Hog Slaughter
S.I.C.: 2011
Jim Paquin *(Pres.)*

SUNOX, INC.
4236 Statesville Rd.
Charlotte, NC 28269
Mailing Address:
P.O. Box 33871,
Charlotte, NC 28233
Tel.: 704-596-6262
Fax: 704-596-1081
Year Founded: 1957
Sales Range: $60-79 Million
Emp.: 375
Fiscal Year-end: 12/31/90
Wholesale Welding Materials
S.I.C.: 5084
John King *(Chm. & Chief Exec. Officer)*
Jim King *(Pres. & Chief Oper. Officer)*
Jerry Ballard *(V.P.-Sls. & Mktg.)*
Doug Crayton *(V.P.-Opers.)*
Clayton T. Rumble *(V.P.-Fin. & Chief Fin. Officer)*
Jay Jacobs *(Controller)*
Kennedy Covington *(Gen. Counsel)*

Principal(s):
John King
Jim King

No. of U.S. Offices: 17

Computer Systems/Hardware:
IBM AS400

Outside Service Firm(s):

Ernst & Young*(Auditors)*
Charleston, WV

First Union National Bank*(Major Banking Relationship)*
CMG-5, Two First Union Center
Charlotte, NC 28288-1154
Tel.: 704-374-2698
Fax: 704-374-6987

Nations Bank*(Major Banking Relationship)*
Charlotte, NC

SUNRISE NISSAN OF ORANGE PARK
1565 Wells Rd.
Orange Park, FL 32073
Tel.: 904-269-9400 **FL**
Fax: 904-264-6334
Year Founded: 1976
Approx.Sls.: $24,000,000
Emp.: 77
Automobile Dealership
S.I.C.: 5511
J. Stephen Risley, Jr. *(Pres.)*
Dorothy L. Risley *(V.P.)*
Pat Nicholson *(Treas.)*
Hal Lynch *(Sec.)*

Principal(s):
J. Stephen Risley, Jr.
Hal Lynch

Outside Service Firm(s):

James V. Knutzen*(Auditors)*
Jacksonville, FL

Gable, Taylor, Deese*(Legal Firm)*
Jacksonville, FL

Barnett Banks Trust Company, N.A.*(Major Banking Relationship)*
9000 Southside Blvd., P.O. Box 40200
Jacksonville, FL 32202-0200
Tel.: 904-464-2802

SUNROC CORPORATION
300 S. Pennell Rd.
Media, PA 19063
Tel.: 215-459-1100
Fax: 215-459-1063
Year Founded: 1922
Approx.Sls.: $25,000,000
Emp.: 300
Fiscal Year-end: 3/31/91
Import Export
Water Coolers & Security Devices
S.I.C.: 3585; 3669
Anthony Salamone *(Pres.)*
Peter Lindley *(V.P.-Sls. & Mktg.)*
Russ Waters *(Treas.)*
Michael Abrams *(Dir.-Matls.)*
Hal Wenner *(Mgr.-Mfg.)*
Gerald P. Joyce *(Mgr.-Pur.)*
Joseph Kontuly *(Mgr.-Adv.)*

Outside Service Firm(s):

Coopers & Lybrand*(Auditors)*
2400 Eleven Penn Center
Philadelphia, PA 19103-2962
Tel.: 215-963-8000

Pepper, Hamilton & Scheetz*(Legal Firm)*
123 S. Broad
Philadelphia, PA 19109
Tel.: 215-893-3000

Philadelphia National Bank*(Major Banking Relationship)*
5th & Market Sts.
Philadelphia, PA 19101
Tel.: 215-629-3100
Fax: 215-834-2069

Subsidiaries:

Maid-O-Mist **(1)**
3217 N. Pulaski Rd.
Chicago, IL 60641
Tel.: 312-685-7300
Fax: 312-685-7332
Emp.: 50
Fiscal Year-end: 3/31/91
Export
Mfr. of Heating Specialties
S.I.C.: 3433
James N. Nielsen *(Gen. Mgr.)*
William J. Robinson *(Mgr.-Mktg.)*

Telkee Inc. **(1)**
300 S. Pennell Rd.
Media, PA 19063
Tel.: 215-459-1100
Fax: 215-459-1063
Emp.: 200
Fiscal Year-end: 3/31/90
Manufacture & Distribute Telkee Key Control Systems & Key File Systems
S.I.C.: 3669
Anthony A. Salamone *(Pres.)*
Peter M. Lindley *(V.P.-Sls. & Mktg.)*
Russ Waters *(Treas.)*
M.C. Abrams *(Dir.-Materials)*
Jerry Joyce *(Pur. Agent)*
J.J. Kontuly *(Adv. Mgr.)*

SUNSTATES REALTY GROUP INC.
(Sub. of Acton Corporation)
4600 Marriott Dr., Ste. 200
Raleigh, NC 27612
Mailing Address:
P.O. Box 30043,
Raleigh, NC 27622
Tel.: 919-781-5611 **FL**
Assets: $106,551,255
Liabilities: $63,475,259
Net Worth: $43,075,996
Approx.Sls.: $66,707,075
Emp.: 463
Real Estate Devel. Mngmt. & Sales
S.I.C.: 6552; 6531
Richard Leonard *(Pres.)*

Subsidiaries:

National Development Co., Inc. **(1)**
2711 LBJ Freeway, Suite 1044
Dallas, TX 75234
Tel.: 214-620-1100 (100%)
Emp.: 102
Real Estate Devel., Mngmt. & Sls.
S.I.C.: 6531; 6552
Robert J. Sabinske *(Pres.)*

Sunstates Properties, Inc. **(1)**
4600 Marriott Dr., Suite 200
Raleigh, NC 27612
Tel.: 919-781-5611 (100%)
Emp.: 42
Real Estate Devel., Mngmt. & Sls.
S.I.C.: 6531; 6552
Richard A. Leonard *(Admin. V.P.)*

Treco Communities, Inc. **(1)**
1325 San Marco Blvd.
Jacksonville, FL 32207
Tel.: 904-396-1600 (100%)
Emp.: 235
Real Estate Development
S.I.C.: 6531; 6552
Paul H. Albritton, Jr. *(Pres.)*

Treco Property Services, Inc. **(1)**
1325 San Marco Blvd.
Jacksonville, FL 32207
Tel.: 904-399-1600 (100%)
Real Estate Mngmt., Leasing & Sales of Comm. Income Properties
S.I.C.: 6531
John M. Joyce *(Pres.)*

Treco Realty Group, Inc. **(1)**
1325 San Marco Blvd.
Jacksonville, FL 32207
Tel.: 904-396-1600 (100%)
Mortage Banking & Real Estate Sls. & Syndications & Investment Mngmt.
S.I.C.: 6162; 6722; 6531
John Joyce *(Pres.)*

SUNTEC INDUSTRIES INC.
2210 Harrison Ave.
Rockford, IL 61125
Mailing Address:
P.O. Box 7010
Rockford, IL 61125
Tel.: 815-226-3700
Fax: 815-226-3848
Year Founded: 1984
Approx.Sls.: $50,000,000
Emp.: 240
Fiscal Year-end: 5/31/91
Import Export
Designer & Mfr. Of Fuel Oil Pumps
S.I.C.: 3561; 3566; 3568
Milton Brown *(Pres.)*
David Bippus *(V.P.-Opers.)*

Computer Systems/Hardware:
DEC

Division:

Cotta Transmission Company **(1)**
2210 Harrison Ave.
Rockford, IL 61104
Tel.: 815-394-7400
Fax: 815-226-3848
Fiscal Year-end: 5/31/91
Export
Transmissions & Gear Boxes-Custom/ Special Design & Manufacturing
S.I.C.: 3714
David L. Zierke *(Mgr.-Mktg. & Sls.)*

SUNWEAVE LINEN CORPORATION
1040 Sixth Ave.
New York, NY 10018
Tel.: 212-869-0801
Fax: 212-921-9679
Sales Range: $20-39 Million
Emp.: 100
Tableclothes, Napkins, Runners & Placemats
S.I.C.: 2392
Joseph A. Cohen *(Chm. Bd. & Pres.)*
Ezra Cohen *(V.P., Sec. & Treas.)*

Outside Service Firm(s):

Herman Wolfson & Company*(Auditors)*
New York, NY

Hofheimer, Gartlir & Gross*(Legal Firm)*
633 Third Ave.
New York, NY 10017
Tel.: 212-818-9000

The Bank of New York*(Major Banking Relationship)*
One Wall Street
New York, NY 10286
Tel.: 212-635-6805
Fax: 212-635-3201

SUPER CLUB MUSIC CORP.
(Formerly The Record Bar, Inc.)
2151 Northwest Pkwy.
Marietta, GA 30067
Tel.: 404-988-9805
Tel.: 800-226-5000 **NC**
Fax: 404-951-8480
Approx.Sls.: $100,000,000
Emp.: 1,300
Fiscal Year-end: 1/31/90
Retail Records, Tapes & Videos
S.I.C.: 5735
Daryl Baldwin *(Acting Pres.)*
Robert Perkins *(V.P.-Fin. & Chief Fin. Officer)*
Joe Martin *(Dir.-Adv.-Super Club)*

No. of Mfg. Plants/Facilities: 130

Computer Systems/Hardware:
Prime Systems 9750 & 9950

Outside Service Firm(s):

Prudential Health Care Plan*(Group Insurer)*
Greensboro, NC

Maxwell & Hutson*(Legal Firm)*
Durham, NC

SUPER D DRUG STORES
4695 Outland Center Dr., Ste. 101
Memphis, TN 38118
Tel.: 901-366-1144
Approx.Sls.: $125,000,000
Emp.: 1,140
Fiscal Year-end: 12/31/90
Discount Drug Stores; Hyde Park Health & Beauty Aid Prods.
S.I.C.: 5912
Henry Beattie *(Pres.)*
Jerry Treece *(V.P.)*
Bob Billings *(Sr. V.P.-Pharmacy)*
Doug Radant *(V.P.-Opers.)*
Carl Wheeler *(V.P.-Pur.)*
Philip Stevenson *(Mgr.-Adv.)*

SUPER 8 MOTELS, INC.
Box 4090, 1910 8th Ave. N.E.
Aberdeen, SD 57401
Tel.: 605-225-2272
Tel.: 800-800-8000
Telex: 798336
Fax: 605-226-3728
Year Founded: 1974
Emp.: 487
Economy Motel Chain
S.I.C.: 7011
Ron Rivett *(Chm. Bd.)*
Loren Steele *(Vice Chm., Chief Exec. Officer & Pres.)*
Harvey Jewett *(Chief Oper. Officer)*
Brad Brummond *(Chief Fin. Officer & Treas.)*
Mike Kistner *(Exec. V.P.-Opers.)*
Dale Susen *(Exec. V.P.- Sls.)*
Linda Cummings *(V.P.-Human Resources)*
Jon Kennedy *(V.P.-Mktg. & Adv.)*
Paul Petit *(V.P.-Franchise Advisory Serv.)*
Jerry Skaare *(V.P.-Mngmt. Information Systems)*
Flo Allen *(Asst. V.P.-Training)*
Dennis Shawd *(Asst. V.P.-Quality Assurance)*
Bill Bowen *(Gen. Counsel & V.P.)*
Maryanne Hagemann *(Controller)*
Joe Ronge *(V.P.-Central Pur.)*
Jan Fenner *(Dir.-Corp. Travel)*
Jeff Stockert *(Dir.-Corp. Fin.)*

No. of U.S. Offices: 1

Computer Systems/Hardware:
Data General MV-10,000

Outside Service Firm(s):

Schector, Dokken, Kantor Andrews & Selcer*(Auditors)*
Aberdeen, SD

Frank B. Hall*(Commercial Insurance Carrier)*
Minneapolis, MN

Norwest Bank Minnesota, N.A.*(Major Banking Relationship)*
204 S. 1st. St.
Aberdeen, SD

Siegel, Barnett & Schutz*(Legal Firm)*
Aberdeen, SD

Principal Mutual*(Pension Manager)*
Aberdeen, SD

Subsidiaries:

Midwest Motel Supply **(1)**
1910 8th Ave., N.E.
Aberdeen, SD 57401
Tel.: 605-225-2272
Emp.: 24
Suppliers of Furniture, Fixtures & Equipment
S.I.C.: 5021
Dave Blackmon *(Pres.)*
Dan Jarman *(Sr. V.P. of Phone Div.)*
Todd Heintzman *(V.P. of Sign Div.)*
Bob Sundling *(V.P.-Furnishings)*

Super 8 Management, Inc. **(1)**
1910 8th Ave., N.E.
Aberdeen, SD 57401
Tel.: 605-225-2272
Emp.: 17
Motel Management
S.I.C.: 8741
Richter Clay *(Pres.)*

SUPERBA, INC.
1735 S. Santa Fe Ave.
Los Angeles, CA 90021
Mailing Address:
P.O. Box 21805
Los Angeles, CA 90021
Tel.: 213-688-7970 **CA**
Telex: 673407
Fax: 213-623-3226
Year Founded: 1873
Emp.: 700
Fiscal Year-end: 12/31/91
Import Export
Manufacture Men's Neckwear
S.I.C.: 2323; 5611; 5136
Louis Wiley *(Chm. Bd.)*
Mervyn Mandelbaum *(Pres. & Chief Exec. Officer)*
Peter Straus *(Exec. V.P.)*
Richard Taussig *(Sr. V.P.-Sls.)*
John J. Trabold *(V.P.-Fin.)*

No. of Mfg. Plants/Facilities: 2
No. of U.S. Offices: 4
No. of Foreign Offices: 1

Outside Service Firm(s):

Gumbiner, Savett, Friedman & Rose, Inc.*(Auditors)*
Santa Monica, CA

LSW Insurance Services*(Commercial Insurance Carrier)*
Los Angeles, CA

First Unum Life Insurance Co.*(Group Insurer)*
Elmsford, NY

Buchalter, Nemer, Fields & Younger*(Legal Firm)*
601 S. Figueroa St., Ste. 2500
Los Angeles, CA 90017-5704
Tel.: 213-891-0700

Subsidiary:

Octavio, Inc. **(1)**
P.O. Box 6189, State Rd. #1, KM 124.0
Ponce, PR 00733
Tel.: 809-844-2525

SUPERIOR AUCTIONEERS & MARKETING, INC.
12002 Huebner Rd., Ste. 200
San Antonio, TX 78230
Mailing Address:
P.O. Box 786001
San Antonio, TX 78278-6001
Tel.: 210-697-0700
Fax: 210-697-9744
Year Founded: 1984
Approx.Sls.: $80,000,000
Emp.: 37
Fiscal Year-end: 4/30/91
Auction Co.; Appraisals & Private Sales
S.I.C.: 7389; 5999
Daniel J. Kruse *(Chm. Bd.)*
Gary C. Bergman *(Pres.)*
Bill J. Brewington *(Exec. V.P. & Gen. Mgr.)*
Gary T. Young *(V.P. & Dir.-Mktg.)*
Steve Noel *(Controller)*
Carroll Hall *(Sls. Dir.-RTC)*
Allen Hughes *(Dir.-Sls.)*

SUPERIOR CONTAINER, INC.
4500 Emery Industrial Pkwy.
Warrensville, OH 44128
Tel.: 216-831-3700 **OH**
Fax: 216-831-3709
Year Founded: 1961
Sales Range: $20-39 Million
Emp.: 250
Fiscal Year-end: 4/30/91
Corrugated Boxes
S.I.C.: 2653
Loren W. Houston *(Chm. Bd. & Pres.)*
John J. Tomick *(V.P.)*
Jeanne A. Houston *(Treas.)*
Andrew G. Hanes *(Controller & Sec.)*
Principal(s):
Loren W. Houston

No. of Mfg. Plants/Facilities: 4
No. of U.S. Offices: 4

Computer Systems/Hardware:
Datapoint; IBM

Outside Service Firm(s):

Pecsak, Rea & Demarchi*(Auditors)*
Cleveland, OH

Republic Hogg Robinson*(Commercial Insurance Carrier)*
Cleveland, OH

Berteh, Fludine, Millean & O'Malley Co. L.P.A.*(Legal Firm)*
Cleveland, OH

National City Bank*(Major Banking Relationship)*
P.O. Box 92301, Corp. Trust Dept.
Cleveland, OH 44101
Tel.: 216-575-2000

Subsidiary:

Modern Packaging Corp. **(1)**
506 Huber Dr.
Monroe, MI 48161
Tel.: 313-242-4014
Emp.: 80
Manufacture Folding Cartons
S.I.C.: 2653
Dennis Heindel *(V.P. & Gen. Mgr.)*

SUPERIOR DAIRY, INC.
4719 Navarre Rd. S.W.
Canton, OH 44706
Mailing Address:
P.O. Box 80995, Station C
Canton, OH 44708
Tel.: 216-477-4515
Fax: 216-477-5908
Year Founded: 1922
Approx.Sls.: $50,000,000
Emp.: 300
Fiscal Year-end: 12/31/90
Processors of Milk & Dairy Products
S.I.C.: 2026; 2021; 2022; 2023; 2024
Leo Soehnlen *(Chm. Bd.)*
Daniel Soehnlen *(Pres.)*
Thomas Soehnlen *(V.P.-Sls.)*
Emil Soehnlen *(V.P.)*
Jim Innes *(Controller)*

SUPERIOR FAST FREIGHT
600 E. Live Oak Ave.
Irwindale, CA 91706
Tel.: 818-357-9800
Tel.: 800-841-4188 **CA**
Fax: 818-305-2188
Year Founded: 1955
Approx.Sls.: $25,000,000
Emp.: 180
Freight Forwarding
S.I.C.: 4731
Dorothy L. Castro *(Chm. Bd. & Chief Exec. Officer)*
Richard Castro *(Pres. & Chief Oper. Officer)*
Dorothy Castro *(Sr. V.P., Treas. & Sec.)*

SUPERIOR FEDERAL BANK
5000 Rogers Ave.
Fort Smith, AR 72903
Tel.: 501-452-8900 **AR**
Year Founded: 1934
Approx.Sls.: $63,850,000
Emp.: 239
Mutual Savings Bank
S.I.C.: 6035
Bruce McNeill *(Chm. Bd., Pres. & Chief Exec. Officer)*
Art Allen *(Exec. V.P.-Admin. Div.)*
Joseph Edwards *(Sr. V.P. & Chief Fin. Officer)*
Gordon Frank *(Sr. V.P.-Retail Banking)*
Louis Garr *(Sr. V.P.-Lending Div.)*
Jim Gray *(Treas.)*
Alan Hill *(Controller)*

Outside Service Firm(s):

Deloitte & Touche*(Auditors)*
Little Rock, AR

Federal Home Loan Bank*(Major Banking Relationship)*
Irving, TX

SUPERIOR GRAPHITE COMPANY
120 S. Riverside Plaza
Chicago, IL 60606
Tel.: 312-559-2999 **IL**
Fax: 212-559-9064
Year Founded: 1917
Approx.Sls.: $40,000,000
Emp.: 250
Fiscal Year-end: 12/31/91
Import Export
Ground, Pulverized, Refined or Blended Natural Graphite, Advanced Ceramic Materials, Lubricants, Graphite Electrodes
S.I.C.: 3295; 3548; 2992
Peter Roy Carney *(Pres.)*
William A. Bagot *(V.P.-Mktg.)*
Joseph E. Doninger *(V.P.-Mfg.)*
William M. Goldberger *(V.P.-Research & Devel.)*
Wes Kreuger *(Treas.)*
Ron Pawelko *(Sec.)*

No. of Mfg. Plants/Facilities: 3
No. of U.S. Offices: 5
No. of Foreign Offices: 2

Outside Service Firm(s):

Ernst & Young*(Auditors)*
233 S. Wacker Dr.
Chicago, IL 60606
Tel.: 312-368-1800
Fax: 312-645-3095

American National Bank & Trust Company of Chicago*(Major Banking Relationship)*
33 N. LaSalle St.
Chicago, IL 60602
Tel.: 312-661-5000
Fax: 312-661-6417

SUPERIOR INDUSTRIES OF NEBRASKA, INC.
5217 S. 132nd St.
Omaha, NE 68137
Mailing Address:
P.O. Box 37447,
Omaha, NE 68137
Tel.: 402-895-2292 **NE**
Fax: 402-895-5539
Year Founded: 1964
Approx.Sls.: $20,000,000
Emp.: 100
Fiscal Year-end: 12/31/90
Cold Storage Insulation; Contractor Designing & Building Cold Storage Facilities
S.I.C.: 1742; 1799; 1541; 5211
Charles C. Myers *(Pres.)*
Clayton K. Bowker *(V.P.-Fin.)*
Ron A. Callahan *(V.P.-Gen. Construction)*
Michael J. Connerley *(V.P.-Opers.)*
Scott A. McLain *(V.P.-Natl. Sls. & Mktg.)*
Linda Rukes *(Mgr.)*

Computer Systems/Hardware:
Altos System

Outside Service Firm(s):

Arthur Andersen & Co.*(Auditors)*
1700 Farnam
Omaha, NE 68102
Tel.: 402-348-0123

Fraser, Stryker, Veach, Vaughn, Meusey, Olson, Boyer*(Legal Firm)*
409 S. 17th
Omaha, NE

North & Black, P.C.*(Legal Firm)*
Omaha, NE

FirsTier Bank*(Major Banking Relationship)*
Omaha, NE

SUPERIOR LABEL SYSTEMS, INC.
11405 Grooms Rd.
Cincinnati, OH 45242
Mailing Address:
P.O. Box 42415
Cincinnati, OH 45242
Tel.: 513-489-3800 **OH**
Fax: 513-489-2416
Year Founded: 1970
Assets: $8,468,000
Liabilities: $4,972,000
Net Worth: $3,496,000
Approx.Sls.: $28,000,000
Emp.: 250
Fiscal Year-end: 12/31/91
Flexographic Printing
S.I.C.: 2759
Kenneth Kidd *(Chm. Bd. & Pres.)*
Robert Tenhover *(Chief Oper. Officer)*
Jim Gettlefinger *(V.P.)*
Thomas Braig *(Sec.)*
Walter F. Zeek, Jr. *(Controller)*
Earl Gettlefinger *(Treas.)*
Robert C. White *(Dir.-Mktg.)*
Randy Barlow *(Dir.-Opers.)*

No. of Mfg. Plants/Facilities: 3

Outside Service Firm(s):

Grant Thornton*(Auditors)*
1600 Atrium One
Cincinnati, OH 45202
Tel.: 513-762-5000

Provident Bank*(Major Banking Relationship)*
One E. Fourth St.
Cincinnati, OH 45202
Tel.: 513-579-2731

Superior Label Systems, Inc.—(Continued)

Subsidiary:

Superior Machine Systems **(1)**
11405 Grooms Rd.
Cincinnati, OH 45242
Tel.: 513-489-3800
Emp.: 15
Mfr. of Packaging Machinery
S.I.C.: 3565
Troy Hall *(Mgr.-Mktg.)*

SUPERIOR LINEN & DRAPERY COMPANY
385 Prospect St.
Hackensack, NJ 07601
Tel.: 201-343-3300 **NJ**
Fax: 201-343-0602
Year Founded: 1920
Approx.Sls.: $49,000,000
Emp.: 100
Wholesale Distribution of Linens & Towels
S.I.C.: 5023
David A. Lieberman *(Chm. Bd.)*
Paul J. Lieberman *(Pres.)*
Arthur Zucker *(Chief Fin. Officer)*

Outside Service Firm(s):

Goldstein, Golub, Kessler & Co.*(Auditors)*
New York, NY

Manufacturers Hanover Trust Co.*(Major Banking Relationship)*
4 New York Plaza
New York, NY 10015
Tel.: 212-633-7938

SUPERIOR MACHINE COMPANY OF SOUTH CAROLINA, INC.
P.O. Box 5419
Florence, SC 29502
Tel.: 803-664-3001 **SC**
Fax: 803-664-3007
Year Founded: 1963
Sales Range: $20-39 Million
Emp.: 300
Heavy Industrial Machinery Manufacturing & Repair
S.I.C.: 3554; 3599
J.R. Bryan Jackson *(Pres.)*
Hans K. Laufer *(V.P.-Opers.)*
James M. Odom *(V.P.-Fin. & Admin.)*
Wayne F. Walker *(V.P.-Sls., Steel Industry)*
Gary W. Gardner *(Mgr.-Pulp & Paper Industry Sls.)*
Wayne M. Pipkin *(Mgr.-Matls.)*
Principal(s):
J.R. Bryan Jackson
Hans K. Laufer

No. of Mfg. Plants/Facilities: 2
No. of U.S. Offices: 2

Outside Service Firm(s):

Cherry, Bekaert & Holland*(Auditors)*
Florence, SC

Marsh & McLennan*(Group Insurer)*
Charlotte, NC

Willcox, Hardee, McLeod, Buyck, Baker & Williams*(Legal Firm)*
Florence, SC

NationsBank Carolinas*(Major Banking Relationship)*
One NCNB Plaza T18-7
Charlotte, NC 28255

First Union National Bank of North Carolina*(Pension Manager)*
Stock Transfer Dept., First Union Plz.
Charlotte, NC 28288
Tel.: 704-374-6161
Fax: 704-374-6987

Division:

Marion Machine Company Division **(1)**
P.O. Box 1169
Marion, NC 28752
Tel.: 704-652-6141
Tel.: 800-627-1639
Emp.: 66
Rock Crusher Repair Facility; Machine Shop; Fabrication & Repair of Steel Mill Equipment
S.I.C.: 3559; 3599
Elwood L. Cunningham *(V.P. & Gen. Mgr.)*
Harold L. Huskins *(Mgr.-Sls.)*

SUPERIOR OIL CO. INC.
400 W. Regent St.
Indianapolis, IN 46225
Tel.: 317-781-4400
Fax: 317-781-4401
Year Founded: 1932
Approx.Sls.: $47,600,000
Emp.: 98
Wholesale Solvents, Chemicals, Gasoline & Industrial Oils
S.I.C.: 5169; 5172
Gary S. Johnson *(Pres. & Chief Exec. Officer)*
Ray Roemke *(V.P.)*
Robert W. Anderson *(Sec., Treas. & Comptroller)*

Outside Service Firm(s):

Dunbar, Cook Shepard*(Auditors)*
Indianapolis, IN

SUPERIOR REPROGRAPHICS
1933 5th Ave.
Seattle, WA 98101
Tel.: 206-443-6900
Tel.: 800-542-7835
Fax: 206-441-8390
Year Founded: 1909
Assets: $2,328,008
Liabilities: $1,255,588
Net Worth: $1,072,420
Sales Range: $10-19 Million
Emp.: 98
Fiscal Year-end: 10/31/91
Reprographics, Photo, Printing & Copying
S.I.C.: 7389
Frank B. Talmage *(Chm. Bd. & Chief Exec. Officer)*
Bobbie Lee *(Pres.)*
Peter Judd *(Gen. Counsel)*
Dennis LaPorte *(Dir.-Sls.)*
Principal(s):
Frank B. Talmage

No. of Mfg. Plants/Facilities: 4
No. of U.S. Offices: 4

Outside Service Firm(s):

Ken Wall & Company*(Auditors)*
Seattle, WA

Hurley, Atkins & Stewart*(Commercial Insurance Carrier)*
Seattle, WA

Pacific NW Bank*(Investment Banker)*
Seattle, WA

Pacific NW Bank*(Major Banking Relationship)*
Seattle, WA

SUPERIOR TUBE COMPANY
Germantown Pike & Cross Keys Rd.
Collegeville, PA 19426
Mailing Address:
P.O. Box 159,
Collegeville, PA 19426
Tel.: 215-489-5200
Fax: 215-489-5252
Year Founded: 1934
Emp.: 600
Import Export
Manufacturer of Small Diameter Metal Tubing
S.I.C.: 3317
Paul E. Kelly, Sr. *(Chm. Bd.)*
Donald C. Reilly *(Pres.)*
Vincent T. Dolan *(Chief Fin. Officer)*
P.C. Howse *(Treas.)*
James V. Fergus *(Dir.-Personnel)*
Sharon P. Jackson *(Mgr.-Mktg. Services)*

Computer Systems/Hardware:
IBM System 38

Outside Service Firm(s):

Provident National Bank*(Major Banking Relationship)*
Collegeville, PA

SUPERMARKETS GENERAL CORPORATION
301 Blair Rd.
Woodbridge, NJ 07095
Mailing Address:
P.O. Box 5301,
Woodbridge, NJ 07095-0915
Tel.: 908-499-3000 **DE**
Fax: 908-499-4072
Year Founded: 1966
Assets: $1,736,156,000
Liabilities: $2,203,144,000
Net Worth: $466,988,000
Approx.Sls.: $5,729,601,000
Emp.: 32,249
Fiscal Year-end: 2/ 1/92
Retail Chain Supermarkets, Home Centers & Drug Stores
S.I.C.: 5211; 5411; 5912
Jack Futterman *(Chm. Bd., Pres. & Chief Exec. Officer)*
Anthony Cuti *(Chief Fin. Officer)*
Jules Borshadel *(Sr. V.P.)*
Robert Joyce *(Sr. V.P.-Human Resources)*
Joseph W. Adelhardt *(V.P. & Controller)*
Marc Strassler *(Sec. & Gen. Counsel)*
Bud Green *(Dir.-Pur.)*
Harvey Gutman *(Dir.-Real Estate & Res. & Devel.)*
Joe Lacko *(Dir.-Mngmt. Information Systems)*
John Marques *(Dir.-Leasing)*
Rick McFeeley *(Dir.-Employee Benefits)*
Maureen McGurl *(Dir.-Pension Admin.)*
Michael Pignatello *(Dir.-Personnel Training & Devel.)*
James Teufel *(Dir.-Cash Mngmt. & Investor Rels.)*
Larry Salinas *(Corp. Grants Contact)*

Computer Systems/Hardware:
IBM 3083

Outside Service Firm(s):

Deloitte & Touche*(Auditors)*
Newark, NJ

Merrill Lynch*(Investment Banker)*
P.O. Box 20, World Trade Center
New York, NY 10281
Tel.: 212-449-4843

Sherman & Sterling*(Legal Firm)*
153 E. 53rd St.
New York, NY 10022
Tel.: 212-940-3269

Bankers Trust Co.*(Major Banking Relationship)*
130 Liberty St., 20th Fl.
New York, NY 10006
Tel.: 212-250-2737

Chemical Bank*(Major Banking Relationship)*
270 Park Ave.
New York, NY 10017
Tel.: 212-270-4872

CoreStates First Pennsylvania Bank, N.A.*(Major Banking Relationship)*
Philadelphia, PA

First Fidelity Bank*(Major Banking Relationship)*
765 Broad Street
Newark, NJ 07101

Divisions:

Pathmark **(1)**
301 Blair Rd.
Woodbridge, NJ 07095
Tel.: 908-499-3000
Fax: 908-499-3072
Approx.Sls.: $4,050,000,000
Emp.: 27,936
Fiscal Year-end: 2/ 2/91
Computer Systems/Hardware:
IBM
139 Supermarkets
S.I.C.: 5411
Corporate Giving Program:
Contributions of Less Than $100 to Over 10,000 Local Religious, Educational, Youth & Community Groups Throughout our Five-State Trading Area
Jack Futterman *(Chm. Bd., Pres. & Chief Exec. Officer)*
Anthony J. Coti *(Exec. V.P. & Chief Fin. Officer)*
Isadore Lemmerman *(Exec. V.P.-Mdsg.)*
Jerome Katcher *(Sr. V.P.-Fin. & Admin.)*
Richard Kenny *(Sr. V.P.-Eastern Div.)*
Robert Joyce *(Sr. V.P.-Admin.)*
Bernard Kenny *(Sr. V.P.-Southern Div.)*
Donald Firth *(Sr. V.P.-Logistics)*
Robert Paton *(Sr. V.P.-Central Div.)*
Isadore Zalkin *(Sr. V.P.-Labor Rels.)*
Bill Bodmer *(Sr. V.P.-Adv. & Sls.)*
Harvey Gutman *(V.P.-Retail Devel.)*
Maureen McGurl *(V.P.-Human Resources)*
Joseph Lacko *(V.P.-Systems Devel. & Telecommunications)*
Joseph Adelhardt *(V.P. & Controller)*
Marc Strassler *(Sec. & Gen. Counsel)*
Betty Greitzer *(Dir.-Pub. Affairs)*
Walter Roberts *(Dir.-Quality Assurance)*
Brendan Brennan *(Dir.-Pur.)*
Terri Illes *(Mgr.-Adv.)*

Rickel Home Centers **(1)**
200 Helen St.
South Plainfield, NJ 07080
Tel.: 908-668-7000
Approx.Sls.: $478,000
Emp.: 4,595
49 Do-It-Yourself Home Centers
S.I.C.: 5211
Moshe Meidar *(Chm. Bd., Pres. & Chief Exec. Officer)*

SUPERSHUTTLE INTERNATIONAL
7001 W. Imperial Hwy.
Los Angeles, CA 90045
Tel.: 310-417-8427 **DE**
Fax: 213-337-7270
Year Founded: 1983
Approx.Sls.: $48,000,000
Emp.: 1,700
Airport Transportation Services
S.I.C.: 4111
Mitchell Rouse *(Chm. Bd. & Chief Exec. Officer)*
John Goss *(Pres. & Chief Oper. Officer)*
David Koscielak *(Chief Fin. Officer)*

No. of Mfg. Plants/Facilities: 4
No. of U.S. Offices: 4

Outside Service Firm(s):

Tokai Bank of California*(Major Banking Relationship)*
Los Angeles, CA

SUPPORT SYSTEMS ASSOCIATES, INC.
1300 Veterans Memorial Hwy.
Hauppauge, NY 11788
Tel.: 516-231-8998
Fax: 516-231-1140
Approx.Sls.: $50,000,000
Emp.: 650
Engineering Service
S.I.C.: 7372; 7379
John Zoltak *(Pres.)*
Thomas Reilly *(Exec. V.P.)*
Richard Keats *(V.P.)*

Outside Service Firm(s):

Norstar Bank, N.A.*(Major Banking Relationship)*
Melville, NY

SURCO PRODUCTS, INC.
Odomaster Industrial Park, 8th & Pine Aves.
Braddock, PA 15104
Mailing Address:
P.O. Box 777,
Braddock, PA 15104
Tel.: 412-351-7700
Tel.: 800-556-0111
Fax: 412-351-7701
Year Founded: 1946
Approx.Sls.: $10,000,000
Emp.: 40
Fiscal Year-end: 9/30/91
Import Export
Air Fresheners, Deodorants, Odor Control Systems, Perfume Compounds
S.I.C.: 2842; 2844; 3429; 3634; 2899; 3564; 3699
Arnold Zlotnik *(Pres.)*
Cliff Zlotnik *(Exec. V.P.)*
Judee Godshall *(Controller)*
Jack Austin *(Gen. Mgr.)*
Susan Rupert *(Mgr.-Adv.)*

Subsidiaries:

Air-Scent International **(1)**
215-225 Eighth Ave., P.O. Box 1000
Braddock, PA 15104
Tel.: 412-351-2100
Tel.: 800-247-0770
Fax: 412-351-7701
S.I.C.: 2842; 2844
Arnold Zlotnik *(Chief Oper. Officer)*

Unsmoke International **(1)**
1135 Braddock Ave.
Braddock, PA 15104
Tel.: 412-351-8686
Tel.: 800-332-6037
Fax: 412-351-1394
S.I.C.: 2842; 2844
Cliff Zlotnik *(Chief Oper. Officer)*
Judy Zlotnik *(Chief Fin. Officer)*

Non-U.S. Holding:

Odomaster Canada **(1)**
994 Westport Crescent Unit A-7,
Mississauga, ON L5T 1G1, Canada
Tel.: 416-671-1010
Fax: 412-351-7701
Approx.Sls.: $2,500,000
Emp.: 12
Mfr. of Air Fresheners, Fragrances, Fan Deodorizers, Odor Control Systems, Perfume Bases
S.I.C.: 2844
A. Zlotnik *(Pres.)*
Judee Godshall *(Controller)*

SURGICAL APPLIANCE INDUSTRIES, INC.
3960 Rosslyn Dr.
Cincinnati, OH 45209
Tel.: 513-271-4594 **OH**
Fax: 513-271-4594
Approx.Sls.: $42,000,000
Emp.: 600
Mfr. of Surgical Appliances & Supplies; Orthopedic Appliances; Braces; Elastic & Support Hosiery
S.I.C.: 3842; 3800
Leslie T. Applegate *(Chm. Bd. & Chief Exec. Officer)*
L. Thomas Applegate *(Pres. & Chief Oper. Officer)*

Outside Service Firm(s):

Ernst & Young*(Auditors)*
1300 Chiquita Center, 250 E. Fifth St.
Cincinnati, OH 45202
Tel.: 513-621-6454

Graydon, Head & Ritchey*(Legal Firm)*
1900 Fifth Third Center
Cincinnati, OH 45202
Tel.: 513-621-6464

The Central Trust Company, N.A.*(Major Banking Relationship)*
201 E. Fifth
Cincinnati, OH 45202
Tel.: 513-651-8255

Subsidiary:

Theradyne Corporation **(1)**
21730 Hanover Ave.
Lakeville, MN 55044
Tel.: 612-469-4404
Tel.: 800-328-4014
Fax: 612-469-2200
Approx.Sls.: $20,000,000
Emp.: 165
Export
Computer Systems/Hardware:
IBM
Mfr. of Wheelchairs for Hospitals & Nursing Homes; Home Health Care Equipment
S.I.C.: 2599; 3842; 3800; 2500
David L. Douma *(Chm. Bd. & Pres.)*
Peter Holst *(Controller & Dir.-Data Processing)*
Donald Roberson *(Dir.-Mktg. & Sls.)*
Rose Ullmann *(Pur. Agent)*

SURGICAL SPECIALTIES
40 S. Museum Rd.
Reading, PA 19607
Mailing Address:
P.O. Box 310
Reading, PA 19607
Tel.: 215-777-1949
Fax: 215-777-1949
Emp.: 180
Mfr. of Surgical & Medical Instruments
S.I.C.: 3841
Rolf D. Schmidt *(Chm. Bd.)*
Paul A. Krupa *(Pres.)*
Barry Ewald *(Controller)*
Aileen Kranford *(Mgr.-Personnel)*
James Bracher *(Dir.-Mktg.)*
Richard Bond *(Pur. Agent.)*

Outside Service Firm(s):

Price Waterhouse*(Auditors)*
30 S. 17th St.
Philadelphia, PA 19103
Tel.: 215-665-9500

Philadelphia National Bank*(Major Banking Relationship)*
5th & Market Sts.
Philadelphia, PA 19101
Tel.: 215-629-3100
Fax: 215-834-2069

SUSQUEHANNA PFALTZGRAFF
140 E. Market St.
York, PA 17401
Mailing Address:
P.O. Box 1069,
York, PA 17405
Tel.: 717-848-5500 **DE**
Fax: 717-771-1440
Approx.Sls.: $250,000,000
Emp.: 4,200
Fiscal Year-end: 12/31/91
Mfr. of Ceramic Dinnerware & Giftware; Radio & Cable TV Stations
S.I.C.: 3269; 3263; 4832; 4841
Louis J. Appell, Jr. *(Pres.)*
Craig W. Bremer *(Sec.)*
Clair J. Bange *(Dir.-Mngmt. Information Service)*

Outside Service Firm(s):

Philip R. Friedman & Assoc.*(Auditors)*
York, PA

York Bank & Trust Co.*(Major Banking Relationship)*
York, PA

Subsidiaries:

Casco Cable Television Inc. **(1)**
Fort Andross, 14 Main St., Ste. 111
Brunswick, ME 04011
Tel.: 207-729-2624 (100%)
Cable Television
S.I.C.: 4841

Judy Hausmann *(Gen. Mgr.)*

The Pfaltzgraff Co. **(1)**
140 E. Market St.
York, PA 17401
Tel.: 717-848-5500
Fax: 717-846-1133
Emp.: 1,800
Fiscal Year-end: 12/31/91
Export
Mfr. of Stoneware, Dinnerware, Glassware & Accessories
S.I.C.: 3263; 3269; 3229; 3262
L.J. Appell, Jr. *(Chm. Bd.)*
William H. Simpson *(Pres., Pfaltzgraff Group)*
David Lengyel *(Pres., Pfaltzgraff Consumer Prod. Div.)*

Radio Indianapolis, Inc. **(1)**
8120 Knue Rd.
Indianapolis, IN 46250
Tel.: 317-842-9550 (100%)
Modern Country Music Broadcasting; WFMS-FM
S.I.C.: 4832
A.W. Carlson *(Pres.)*
Monte Maupin *(Gen. Mgr.)*

Radio Metroplex Inc. **(1)**
3500 Maple Ave., Ste. 1600
Dallas, TX 75219-3906
Tel.: 214-526-2400 (100%)
KPLX-FM, Modern Country Music
S.I.C.: 4832
Arthur W. Carlson *(Pres.)*
Dan Halyburton *(V.P. & Gen. Mgr.)*

Susquehanna Radio Corp. **(1)**
Pembroke One Bldg., 281 Independence Blvd., Ste. 101
Virginia Beach, VA 23462
Tel.: 804-497-1310 (100%)
WGH-AM Sports Radio; WGH-FM Contemporary Radio
S.I.C.: 4832
Bill Whitlow *(Gen. Mgr.)*

Syracuse China Corp. **(1)**
2900 Court St.
Syracuse, NY 13221
Tel.: 315-455-5671 (100%)
Emp.: 1,200
Fiscal Year-end: 12/31/90
Mfr. of Commercial Chinaware
S.I.C.: 3262
Louis Appell Jr. *(Chm. Bd.)*
Charles S. Goodman *(Pres.)*
William Fenn *(Sr. V.P.)*
Judson Shepherd *(V.P.-Sls.)*
Jere Riggs *(Chief Fin. Officer)*
Virginia McMahon *(Pur. Agent)*

WARM Broadcasting Co. **(1)**
Wilkes Barre Scranton Hwy., Box 590
Avoca, PA 18641
Tel.: 717-346-5222 (100%)
Adult Contemporary Radio Broadcasting
S.I.C.: 4832
Arthur W. Carlson *(Pres.)*
Charles T. Morgan *(Supervising Exec.)*
Philip P. Condron *(Gen. Mgr.)*

WSBA AM/FM **(1)**
Box 910
York, PA 17405
Tel.: 717-764-1155 (100%)
AM Station Featuring Conservative Contemporary Music; FM Station Featuring Soft Rock
S.I.C.: 4832
Chris J. Huber *(V.P. & Station Mgr.)*

THE SUSSMAN/ZICCARDI GROUP
221 West 41st St.
New York, NY 10036
Tel.: 212-398-9970 **NY**
Fax: 212-398-1885
Year Founded: 1944
Approx.Billings: $18,000,000
Emp.: 26
S.I.C.: 7311
Donald P. Ziccardi *(Pres. & Chief Exec. Officer)*
Seymour Wagner *(Exec. V.P.)*
Allyn Salpeter *(V.P., Dir. Fin.)*
Jacqueline Wein *(Asst. to Pres.)*

SUTTER HOME WINERY, INC.
277 St. Helena Hwy. S.
Saint Helena, CA 94574
Mailing Address:
P.O. Box 248,
St. Helena, CA 94574
Tel.: 707-963-3104
Fax: 707-963-8532
Year Founded: 1890
Approx.Sls.: $100,000,000
Emp.: 225
Fiscal Year-end: 6/30/91

Export
Winery
S.I.C.: 2084
Louis Trinchero *(Chm. & Chief Exec. Officer)*
Roger J. Trinchero *(Pres.)*
Jim Miller *(Exec. V.P.-Sls. & Mktg.)*
Alex Morgan *(V.P.-Mktg.)*
Anthony R. Torres *(V.P.-Admin.)*
Vera Trinchero Torres *(Sec. & Treas.)*
Stanley Hock *(Dir.-Pub. Rels.)*

Outside Service Firm(s):

Shurtz & Dowis*(Auditors)*
St. Helena, CA

Broad, Shultz, Larson & Wineburg*(Legal Firm)*
St. Helena, CA

Wells Fargo Bank*(Major Banking Relationship)*
St. Helena, CA

SUTTER/MARTIN, INC.
165 Arlington Heights Rd.
Buffalo Grove, IL 60089
Tel.: 708-537-0003
Fax: 708-537-0757
Year Founded: 1976
Approx.Billings: $12,000,000
Emp.: 23
Healthcare, High-Tech Business-to-Business Adv.
Lynn R. Sutter *(Chm. Bd. & Pres.)*
Edward K. Martin *(Exec. V.P.)*
H.A. Bizzell *(V.P.)*
Ron Wietlispach *(V.P.-EduTrain Div.)*
Charlotte Mankowsky *(V.P., Admin./ Opers.)*

SUZANNAH FARMS
9105 Burrough Dover Lane
Pennsauken, NJ 08110
Tel.: 609-663-3240
Fax: 609-665-7959
Emp.: 200
Canned Hams, Luncheon Meats, Sausage
S.I.C.: 2013
Susan Fletcher *(Chm. Bd. & Pres.)*
Elvis Hicks *(V.P.-Opers.)*
Karen Koerwer *(V.P.-Fin.)*
Charles Boyer *(Sls. Coord.)*

SVERDRUP CORPORATION
13723 Riverport Dr.
Maryland Heights, MO 63043
Tel.: 314-436-7600 **MO**
Twx: 910-761-1085
Fax: 314-298-0045
Year Founded: 1928
Approx.Sls.: $598,261,000
Emp.: 4,600
Fiscal Year-end: 12/31/91
Complete Project Delivery, Including Development, Planning, Design, Construction, Construction Management, Program Management, Design/build Start-up & Operations in the Market Areas of Advanced

Sverdrup Corporation—(Continued)

Technology, Architecture, Environmental, Industrial, Public Works & Transportation for Private Government Clients
S.I.C.: 1522; 1541; 1542; 1611; 1622; 1623; 6512; 6552; 7371; 7372; 7373; 7374; 7376; 8711; 8712; 8713; 8731; 8733; 8734; 8741; 8742; 8744
B.R. Smith, Jr. *(Chm. Bd. & Chief Exec. Officer)*
G.E. Roesenkoetter *(Vice Chm.)*
J.D. Whitfield *(Pres.)*
L.F. White *(Chief Fin. Officer & V.P.)*
R.E. Beumer *(Exec. V.P.)*
J.C. Uselton *(Exec. V.P.)*
A.L. Baer *(Sr. V.P. & Gen. Mgr., Southern Grp.)*
R.W. Butler *(Sr. V.P.-Advanced Tech. Mkt.)*
J.L. Haack *(Sr. V.P.-Architecture Mkt.)*
K.G. Kreikemeier *(Sr. V.P. & Gen. Mgr., Central Grp.)*
C.N. LeTellier *(Sr. V.P. & Gen. Mgr., Capital Grp.)*
S.R. Pate *(Sr. V.P.)*
G.R. Pennington *(Sr. V.P.-Trans. & Public Works Mkts.)*
H.G. Schwartz, Jr. *(Sr. V.P.-Environmental Mkt.)*
D.N. Weisstuch *(Sr. V.P. & Gen. Mgr., Eastern Grp.)*
G.E. Woley *(Sr. V.P. & Gen. Mgr., Western Grp.)*
J.C. Franke *(V.P. & Dir.-Human Resources)*
J.L. Moore *(V.P. & Dir.-Admin. & Audits)*
A.S. Morrisson *(V.P., Sec. & Gen. Counsel)*
J.J. Roth *(V.P.-Food & Bev. Mkt.)*
T.E. Wehrle *(Treas.)*
G.J. Howell *(Controller)*
J.L. Bryan *(Dir.-Communications & Pub. Rels.)*
M.C. Hannigan *(Dir.-Corp. Mktg.)*
Carol Rodney *(Asst. Treas.)*

Principal(s):
Employee-Owned

No. of U.S. Offices: 30

Computer Systems/Hardware:
VAX 11/785; VAX 11/751; VAX 6310; VAX 8530; DEC VAX 6420; VAX Station 2000; MicroVAX II/GPX; MicroVAX 3300; Micro VAX 3100; VAX Station 4000; VAX Stateion 3100; IBM PC & Compatibles; Macintosh

Outside Service Firm(s):

Ernst & Young*(Auditors)*
701 Market St.
St. Louis, MO 63101
Tel.: 314-259-1000

Aetna Life & Casualty*(Commercial Insurance Carrier)*
St. Louis, MO

CNA Insurance*(Group Insurer)*
Chevy Chase, MD

General American Life Insurance Co.*(Group Insurer)*
700 Market
Saint Louis, MO 63101
Tel.: 314-525-5458
Fax: 314-525-3677

Boatmen's National Bank of St. Louis*(Major Banking Relationship)*
One Boatmen's Plaza, 800 Market St.
St. Louis, MO 63101
Tel.: 314-466-6000

First Union National Bank*(Major Banking Relationship)*
CMG-5, Two First Union Center
Charlotte, NC 28288-1154
Tel.: 704-374-2698
Fax: 704-374-6987

Mercantile Bank N.A.*(Major Banking Relationship)*
Mercantile Tower, One Mercantile Center
Saint Louis, MO 63101
Tel.: 314-425-2525

Union Bank of Switzerland*(Major Banking Relationship)*
30 S. Wacker Dr.
Chicago, IL 60606

Subsidiaries:

Sverdrup Building Corporation **(1)**
1836 Lackland Hill Pkwy.
Saint Louis, MO 63146
Tel.: 314-997-0300
Fax: 314-997-6092
General Contracting, Construction Management & Design/Build of Capital Facilities
S.I.C.: 1522; 1541; 1542; 8711; 8712; 8741; 8742
K.R. Whitaker *(Pres.)*

Sverdrup Environmental Inc. **(1)**
801 N. Eleventh St.
Saint Louis, MO 63101
Tel.: 314-436-7600
Fax: 314-421-1935
Professional Services For Complete Project Delivery Including Planning, Permitting, Design, Construction, Start-up & Operations, Construction Management & Design/Build In Areas of Air Quality, Water Supply & Treatment, Industrial & Municipal Wastewater, Treatment, High Purity Water Treatment Processes & Hazardous Waste Management
S.I.C.: 1541; 1542; 8711; 8712; 8713; 8741; 1623
H.G. Schwartz, Jr. *(Pres.)*

Sverdrup Investments, Inc. **(1)**
13723 Riverport Dr.
Maryland Heights, MO 63043
Tel.: 314-436-7600
Fax: 314-298-1850
Real Estate Development, Marketing, Financing, Ownership, Management & Operation
S.I.C.: 6512; 6531; 6552; 7011; 8741
B.R. Smith, Jr. *(Chm. Bd.)*
J.C. Uselton *(Pres.)*

Sverdrup Southern Constructors, Inc. **(1)**
1900 Summit Tower Blvd., Ste. 300
Orlando, FL 32810
Construction Contractors: Bridges, Highways, Streets & Tunnels
S.I.C.: 1611; 1622; 1623
A.L. Baer *(Pres.)*

Sverdrup Technology, Inc. **(1)**
600 William Northern Blvd., P.O. Box 884
Tullahoma, TN 37388
Tel.: 615-455-6400
Fax: 615-393-6212
Advanced Technology Engineering Services; Design/Build of Test Facilities; Scientific, Engineering & Operation & Maintenance Support Services; Scientific & Engineering Support For Weapons Systems Programs
S.I.C.: 7371; 7372; 7373; 7374; 7376; 8711; 8733; 8734; 8741; 8744
S.R. Pate *(Pres.)*

SWALLEN'S, INC.
5533 Fair Ln.
Cincinnati, OH 45227
Tel.: 513-527-6700 **OH**
Fax: 513-527-6888
Sales Range: $100-499 Million
Emp.: 1,300
Retail Discount Store Chain in Ohio & Kentucky
S.I.C.: 5311
Donald Swallen *(Chm. Bd., Pres.& Chief Exec. Officer)*
Robert A. Davis *(Chief Oper. Officer & Sec.)*
Dale Swallen *(V.P.-Warehousing)*
Sharad N. Buddhdev *(Chief Fin. Officer & Asst. Sec.)*
Bruce Swallen *(Treas.)*
Richard Craft *(Dir.-Pur.)*
John Konerman *(Dir.-Personnel)*
Principal(s):
Swallen Family

No. of Mfg. Plants/Facilities: 9

Computer Systems/Hardware:
Data General; Novell PC Gateway; MV2000 Network

Outside Service Firm(s):

Deloitte & Touche*(Auditors)*
Chiquita Center, 250 E. 5th St., Ste. 1900
Cincinnati, OH 45202
Tel.: 513-784-7100

Stanley Mathews Company*(Legal Firm)*
Cincinnati, OH

The Huntington National Bank*(Major Banking Relationship)*
Cincinnati, OH

Provident National Bank*(Major Banking Relationship)*
4140 Hamilton Ave.
Cincinnati, OH
Tel.: 513-681-3900

SWANER HARDWOOD COMPANY, INC.
5 W. Magnolia Blvd.
Burbank, CA 91502
Tel.: 213-849-6761 **CA**
Fax: 818-846-3662
Year Founded: 1967
Approx.Sls.: $35,000,000
Emp.: 250
Wholesale Distributor of Treated Wood Millwork; Mfr. of Plywood; Bed Frames, Except Waterbed; Bedside Stands; Wood Dressers
S.I.C.: 5031; 2511; 2491
Keith Swaner *(Chief Exec. Officer)*
Gary Swaner *(Pres.)*
Stephen Haag *(V.P. & Treas.)*
Beverly Swaner *(Sec.)*

Outside Service Firm(s):

King, King & Aleman*(Auditors)*
Burbank, CA

Holstead, Baker & Olson*(Legal Firm)*
Los Angeles, CA

Community Bank*(Major Banking Relationship)*
Burbank, CA

SWANSON RUSSELL ASSOCIATES
1222 P. St.
Lincoln, NE 68508
Tel.: 402-475-5191
Fax: 402-475-6135
Year Founded: 1962
Approx.Billings: $18,000,000
Emp.: 55
Business-to-Business, Agri-Business, Outdoor, Recreation, Consumer Products & Services
W.M. "Gus" Swanson *(Chm.)*
Steven Russell *(Pres.)*
Mick Sibbel *(Exec. V.P., Chief Oper. Officer)*
Parker Stoner *(V.P., Media & Mktg. Devel.)*
Jeff Patterson *(Pub. Rels. Spec.)*

THE SWANSON COMPANY MANUFACTURERS
3747 W. Buckeye Rd.
Phoenix, AZ 85009
Mailing Address:
P.O. Box 6570
Phoenix, AZ 85005
Tel.: 602-269-5161 **AZ**
Fax: 602-269-7625
Year Founded: 1948
Approx.Sls.: $16,000,000
Emp.: 89
Fiscal Year-end: 9/30/90
Export
Plastic & Fabricated Pipe; Irrigation Equipment
S.I.C.: 3084
Frank Keery *(Chm. Bd. & Chief Exec. Officer)*
Wilmer Ostermeier *(Pres.)*
Jim Janzen *(V.P.)*
Ron Parisi *(V.P.)*
Stephen Beans *(Treas.)*
Marlin Steele *(Mgr.-Quality Control)*
Audrey G. Jedinak *(Dir.-Personnel)*
Ray Moore *(Plant Mgr.)*

Outside Service Firm(s):

Arthur Andersen & Co.*(Auditors)*
Phoenix, AZ

Schimmel, Hill, Bishop & Gruender*(Legal Firm)*
Phoenix, AZ

Security Pacific National Bank*(Major Banking Relationship)*
Phoenix, AZ

SWEDE SPORTSWEAR COMPANY, INC.
1675 S. Alameda St.
Los Angeles, CA 90021
Tel.: 213-749-8261
Fax: 213-749-3710
Approx.Sls.: $20,000,000
Emp.: 190
Women's Sportswear
S.I.C.: 2339
George Wiley *(Pres.)*
Judi Wiley *(V.P.)*
Anthony Jeremiah *(Controller)*

Outside Service Firm(s):

Bitticks & Co.*(Auditors)*
Los Angeles, CA

Bank of America*(Major Banking Relationship)*
701 S. Western Ave.
Los Angeles, CA 91201

E.A. SWEEN COMPANY
(d/b/a Deli Express)
16101 W. 78th St.
Eden Prairie, MN 55344
Tel.: 612-937-9440
Fax: 612-937-0186
Approx.Sls.: $44,000,000
Emp.: 400
Sandwiches
S.I.C.: 5149
Tom Sween *(Chm. Bd. & Chief Exec. Officer)*
Rolf Engstrom *(Sr. V.P.-Mktg. & Admin.)*
Robert Linner *(Sr. V.P.-Prod. Sls. Opers.)*
Lester W.B. Moore *(Sr. V.P., Sec. & Sls.-Fast Food Service)*
Larry Youngblood *(Sr. V.P.)*
Stephen Hoese *(Controller)*
Richard Johnson *(Dir.-Admin.)*
Ruth Vickerman *(Dir.-Pur. Agent)*
Gerry Cieminski *(Mgr.-Data Processing)*

Outside Service Firm(s):

Deloitte & Touche*(Auditors)*
250 E. Wisconsin Ave.
Milwaukee, WI 53202-4283
Tel.: 414-271-3000

Dorsey & Whitney*(Legal Firm)*
2200 First Bank Place East
Minneapolis, MN 55402

Marquette Bank, N.A.*(Major Banking Relationship)*
Sixth & Marquette
Minneapolis, MN 55402
Tel.: 612-341-5651

JAKE SWEENEY AUTO LEASING INC.
8276 Vine St.
Cincinnati, OH 45216
Tel.: 513-761-8310 **OH**
Fax: 513-761-1486
Year Founded: 1956
Sales Range: $10-19 Million
Emp.: 16
Automobile Rental & Leasing
S.I.C.: 7515; 7514
Mary S. Sweeney *(Pres. & Dir.-Adv.)*
Susan Kreuzmann *(V.P.)*
Joseph A. Grathwohl *(Treas.)*
Joseph Feldkamp *(Sec.)*
Tammy Garrett *(Dir.-Personnel)*
Principal(s):
Jacob B. Sweeney

Computer Systems/Hardware:
IBM

Outside Service Firm(s):

Munninghoff Lange & Co.*(Auditors)*
Cincinnati, OH

Joseph F. Feldkamp, Jr.*(Legal Firm)*
Cincinnati, OH

Fifth Third Bank*(Major Banking Relationship)*
Corporate Trust Services, 38 Fountain Square Plaza
Cincinnati, OH 45263

JAKE SWEENEY AUTOMOTIVE INC.
33 W. Kemper Rd.
Cincinnati, OH 45246
Tel.: 513-782-2800 **OH**
Fax: 513-782-2884
Year Founded: 1971
Assets: $26,837,033
Liabilities: $23,618,184
Net Worth: $3,218,849
Sales Range: $100-499 Million
Emp.: 330
Fiscal Year-end: 12/31/88
New & Used Auto Sales & Service; Jake Sweeney Chevrolet, Inc., Jake Sweeney Mazda, Inc., Jake Sweeney BMW, Inc., Jake Sweeney Chrysler Plymouth, Inc.
S.I.C.: 5511
Jacob B. Sweeney, Jr. *(Pres.)*
Gregory Sweeney *(V.P.)*
Joseph A. Grathwohl *(Treas.)*
James Clark *(Dir.-Adv.)*
Fred Mangold *(Dir.-Sls.)*
Principal(s):
Jacob B. Sweeney, Jr.

Outside Service Firm(s):

Munninghoff Lange & Co.*(Auditors)*
Cincinnati, OH

Joseph F. Feldkamp, Jr.*(Legal Firm)*
Cincinnati, OH

Fifth Third Bank*(Major Banking Relationship)*
Corporate Trust Services, 38 Fountain Square Plaza
Cincinnati, OH 45263

Division:

Jake Sweeney Auto Leasing, Inc. **(1)**
8276 Vine St.
Cincinnati, OH 45216
Sales Range: $10-19 Million
Emp.: 16
Mary S. Sweeney *(Pres. & Dir.-Adv.)*
Susan Kreuzmann *(V.P.)*
Joseph A. Grathwohl *(Treas.)*
Joseph Feldkamp *(Sec.)*
Tammy Garrett *(Dir.-Personnel)*

Subsidiary:

Jake Sweeney Jeep Eagle, Inc. **(1)**
11535 McGillard St.
Cincinnati, OH 45246
Tel.: 513-782-2800
New Car Dealer
S.I.C.: 5511
Jacob B. Sweeney, Jr. *(Pres.)*

SWEETHEART CUP CO., INC.
7575 S. Kostner Ave.
Chicago, IL 60652
Tel.: 312-767-3300
Fax: 312-767-9652
Approx.Sls.: $800,000,000
Emp.: 10,000
Mfr. of Sweetheart, Jazz, Touch of Spring, Appeal, Silent Service, Simple Elegance, Guildware Paper & Plastic Cups, Plates, Bowls, Straws & Containers, Munchie Cups, Gallery Souvenir Cups
S.I.C.: 2657; 3089; 2052
Phil Silver *(Chief Exec. Officer)*
Phillip White *(Pres.)*
Dean Jacobsen *(V.P.-Mktg.)*
Roger Cregg *(V.P.-Fin.)*
William Haas *(V.P.-Sls.)*
Richard Horneck *(V.P.-Mfg.)*
Richard O'Reilly *(V.P.-Human Recources)*
Vincent Truant *(V.P.-Natl. Acct. Sls.)*
Paul Pretko *(Mgr.-Customer Service)*
David Meyers *(Dir.-Bus. Devel.)*
Cathy Fitzmaurice *(Adv. Coord.)*

Division:

Sweetheart Cup Co., Inc. **(1)**
10100 Reisterstown
Owings Mills, MD 21117
Tel.: 410-363-1111
S.I.C.: 2052

Subsidiaries:

Sweetheart Corporation **(1)**
905 Southern Way
Sparks, NV 89431
Tel.: 702-359-7466
Mfr. of Disposable Containers
S.I.C.: 2657; 3089
Richard Gregoire *(Plant Mgr.)*

Sweetheart Cup Corporation **(1)**
400 Gay St.
Manchester, NH 03103
Tel.: 603-668-2200
Mfr. of Disposable Containers
S.I.C.: 2657; 3089
Walter Daw *(Plant Mgr.)*

Sweetheart Cup Corporation **(1)**
1 Burlington Ave.
Wilmington, MA 01887
Tel.: 617-666-8100
Mfr. of Disposable Containers
S.I.C.: 2657; 3089
Dave Canavera *(Plant Mgr.)*

Sweetheart Cup Corporation **(1)**
30 Inner Belt Rd.
Somerville, MA 02143
Tel.: 617-666-8100
Mfr. of Disposable Containers & Folding Paperboard Boxes
S.I.C.: 2656; 3086; 2657
Jack Hynes *(Plant Mgr.)*

Sweetheart Cup Corporation **(1)**
951 Glenwood Ave.
Atlanta, GA 30316
Tel.: 404-622-1731
Mfr. of Folding Paperboard Boxes
S.I.C.: 2657
Ed Diaz *(Plant Mgr.)*

Sweetheart Cup Corporation **(1)**
1550 Wrightsboro Rd.
Augusta, GA 30904
Tel.: 706-737-7000
Mfr. of Folding Paperboard Boxes & Plastic Products
S.I.C.: 2657; 3089
Ron Winkowski *(Plant Mgr.)*

Sweetheart Cup Corporation **(1)**
1455 Hwy. 138
Conyers, GA 30207
Tel.: 404-483-9556
Mfr. of Disposable Containers
S.I.C.: 2657; 3089
Steve Liakos *(Plant Mgr.)*

Sweetheart Cup Corporation **(1)**
7575 S. Kostner Ave.
Chicago, IL 60652
Tel.: 312-767-3300
Mfr. of Disposable Containers
S.I.C.: 2657; 3089
Donn Gea *(Plant Mgr.)*

Sweetheart Cup Corporation **(1)**
4425 Mitchell St.
North Las Vegas, NV 89030
Tel.: 702-644-0980
Mfr. of Disposable Containers
S.I.C.: 2657; 3089
Russ Martin *(Production Mgr.)*

Sweetheart Cup Corporation **(1)**
1100 N.Glenstone
Springfield, MO 65801
Tel.: 417-862-2744
Mfr. of Disposable Containers
S.I.C.: 2657; 3089
Dimitrios Koukoulomatis *(Plant Mgr.)*

Sweetheart Cup Corporation **(1)**
4444 W. Ledbetter
Dallas, TX 75236
Tel.: 214-339-3131
Mfr. of Disposable Containers
S.I.C.: 2656; 2657; 3086
Chuck Campbell *(Plant Mgr.)*

SWEETLIFE FOODS, INC.
1120 Harvey Lane
Suffield, CT 06078
Mailing Address:
P.O. Box 385,
Windsor Locks, CT 06096
Tel.: 203-623-1681 **MO**
Fax: 203-627-5076
Year Founded: 1924
Approx.Sls.: $975,000,000
Emp.: 3,000
Import Export
Wholesale Suppliers for Supermarkets
S.I.C.: 5141
Julian Leavitt *(Chm. Bd., Pres., Chief Exec. Officer & Treas.)*
D. Katz *(V.P.)*
Joel Leavitt *(V.P.)*
J. Rosenfield *(V.P., Controller & Chief Fin. Officer)*
K. Dumond *(Dir.-Data Processing)*
E. Hammett *(Dir.-Employee Rels.)*

Computer Systems/Hardware:
IBM 4381

Outside Service Firm(s):

Ernst & Young*(Auditors)*
Goodwyn Sq., 225 Asylum St.
Hartford, CT 06103
Tel.: 203-247-3100

Bank of New England*(Major Banking Relationship)*
28 State Street
Boston, MA 02109
Tel.: 617-742-4000

CIGNA*(Pension Manager)*
Los Angeles, CA

Subsidiary:

Springfield Sugar & Prod. Co. **(1)**
P.O. Box 385,
Windsor Locks, CT 06096
Tel.: 203-623-1681
Emp.: 2,000
Julian Leavitt *(Pres.)*

SWELL-WEAR, INC.
350 Fifth Ave.
New York, NY 10118
Mailing Address:
1350 Broadway
New York, NY 10018
Tel.: 212-736-7420 **NY**
Fax: 212-736-7435
Year Founded: 1960
Sales Range: $10-19 Million
Emp.: 31
Import
Mfr. of Plastic & Rubberized Rainwear, Nylon Jackets & Shirts & Sportswear
S.I.C.: 2385; 2321; 2329; 2331; 2339
Shirley Bren *(Pres.)*
Joel Bren *(V.P.)*

Outside Service Firm(s):

Putterman, Rush & Shapiro*(Auditors)*
New York, NY

Danow, McMullan & Panoff*(Legal Firm)*
New York, NY

Israel Discount Bank*(Major Banking Relationship)*
511 Fifth Ave.
New York, NY 10017

SWEPCO TUBE CORPORATION
One Clifton Blvd.
Clifton, NJ 07015
Tel.: 201-778-3000
Year Founded: 1949
Approx.Sls.: $25,000,000
Emp.: 150
Fiscal Year-end: 11/ 1/90
Swepco Pipe Tubing
S.I.C.: 3494
P.A. Tobelmann *(Chm. Bd. & Chief Exec. Officer)*
A. Ridella *(Pres. & Chief Oper. Officer)*
Charles Nichols *(V.P.-Sls.)*
K. Shultz *(Dir.-Field Sls.)*
Steve Oberhelman *(Controller)*
Ted Taylor *(Dir.-Mktg.)*
T. Schlicting *(Dir.-Pur.)*

SWIFT-COR TOOL ENGINEERING
344 W. 157th St.
Gardena, CA 90248
Tel.: 310-329-1129
Fax: 310-323-2029
Approx.Sls.: $10,000,000
Emp.: 200
Metal Parts & Assemblies
S.I.C.: 3444; 3728
Ralph D. Scriba *(Chm. Bd. & Chief Exec. Officer)*
Lance Rich *(V.P.-Mfg.)*
John C. Sernay *(V.P.-Engrng.)*
Jerry Soldner *(V.P.-Sls.)*
Chuck Miller *(Comptroller)*

Outside Service Firm(s):

First Business Bank*(Major Banking Relationship)*
Torrance, CA

SWIFT DODGE ROLLS ROYCE INC.
6250 Florin Rd.
Sacramento, CA 95823
Tel.: 916-422-4300
Tel.: 800-933-3254 **CA**
Fax: 916-422-3447
Year Founded: 1966
Approx.Sls.: $84,000,000
Emp.: 145
Fiscal Year-end: 12/31/90
New & Used Vehicle Sales, Parts & Service
S.I.C.: 5511
Corporate Giving Program: United Way
Charles O. Swift *(Chm. Bd. & Pres.)*
Robert P. Swift *(Exec. V.P. & Treas.)*
Jennifer Mayo *(V.P. & Chief Fin. Officer)*
Randy Crump *(V.P.-Sls.)*
Jerry Shaver *(V.P.-Parts)*
Roxanne Daneri *(Sec. & Gen. Counsel)*
Dan Heill *(Fleet Mgr.)*
Principal(s):
Charles O. Swift

Swift Dodge Rolls Royce Inc.—(Continued)

Computer Systems/Hardware:
Automatic Data Processing

Outside Service Firm(s):

W. J. Pomares & Company*(Auditors)*
Sacramento, CA

Chrysler Insurance*(Commercial Insurance Carrier)*
P.O. Box 5168,
Southfield, MI

Foundation Health*(Group Insurer)*
Sacramento, CA

Miller & Daneri*(Legal Firm)*
Sacramento, CA

Bank of America NT&SA*(Major Banking Relationship)*
Rancho Cordova, CA

SWIFT INSTRUMENTS, INC.
952 Dorchester Ave.
Dorchester, MA 02125
Tel.: 617-436-2960
Tel.: 1-800-446-1116
Fax: 617-436-3232
Year Founded: 1926
Emp.: 50
Fiscal Year-end: 12/31/90
Import Export
Importers & Mfrs. of Binoculars, Field Glasses, Astronomical Telescopes, Barometers, Thermometers, Hygrometers Specialty Magnifiers, Spotting Scopes, Microscopes & Accessories, Riflescopes; Aerolite & Swift
S.I.C.: 3851; 3827; 3829
Humphrey H. Swift *(Pres. & Adv. Mgr.)*
Harold B. Mercer *(Exec. V.P. & Treas.)*
Stephen H. Swift *(Sr. V.P.)*
James G. Mercer *(Asst. Treas.)*
Bruce K. Mercer *(Mgr.-Natl. Sls.)*

Outside Service Firm(s):

State Street Bank & Trust Co.*(Major Banking Relationship)*
225 Franklin St.
Boston, MA 02101
Tel.: 617-786-3000

Goodwin, Procter & Hoar*(Legal Firm)*
Exchange Place
Boston, MA 02109-2881
Tel.: 617-570-1000

Division:

Technical Instruments Div. **(1)**
P.O. Box 562
San Jose, CA 95106
Tel.: 408-293-2380
Fax: 408-292-7967
Teaching & Research Microscopes
S.I.C.: 3827
Takashi Komatsuzaki *(Div. & Branch Mgr.)*
Harold B. Mercer *(Treas.)*
Fred Gerlach *(Mgr.-Natl. Sls.)*
Alison C. Swift *(Asst. Sls. Mgr.)*

M. SWIFT & SONS INC.
10 Love Lane
Hartford, CT 06141
Mailing Address:
P.O. Box 150,
Hartford, CT 06141
Tel.: 203-522-1181
Tel.: 800-682-0380
Fax: 203-249-5934
Emp.: 70
Export
Fabricated Metal Products; Gold Leafing
S.I.C.: 3449; 5051
M. Allen Swift *(Chm. Bd., Pres. & Treas.)*
A. Keith Wells *(Chief Fin. Officer & Controller)*
Jane E. Gurka *(Mgr.-Personnel & Sec.)*

Outside Service Firm(s):

Deloitte & Touche*(Auditors)*
New Haven, CT

Fireman's Fund Insurance Co.*(Commercial Insurance Carrier)*
Hartford, CT

Hartford Life Insurance Co.*(Commercial Insurance Carrier)*
Hartford, CT 06104-2999

Aetna Life & Casualty*(Group Insurer)*
151 Farmington Avenue
Hartford, CT 06156
Tel.: 203-273-2128
Fax: 203-729-4295

Murtha, Cullina, Richter & Pinney*(Legal Firm)*
City Place 1 185 Asylum St.
Hartford, CT 06103-3469
Tel.: 203-240-6000
Fax: 2032406150

Fleet National Bank*(Major Banking Relationship)*
Hartford, CT

Subsidiary:

M. Swift & Sons Canada Inc. **(1)**
1801 Favard
Montreal, PQ H3K 1Y3, Canada
Tel.: 514-935-2479 (100%)
Gold Stamping
S.I.C.: 3449

SWINERTON & WALBERG CO.
580 California St.
San Francisco, CA 94104
Tel.: 415-421-2980 **CA**
Fax: 415-984-1384
Year Founded: 1888
Assets: $105,000,000
Liabilities: $90,000,000
Net Worth: $15,000,000
Approx.Sls.: $500,000,000
Emp.: 1,200
Fiscal Year-end: 12/31/89
Import
General Building; Heavy Construction; Construction Services
S.I.C.: 1542; 1541; 1629; 1623
Milo S. Gates *(Chm. Bd. & Chief Exec. Officer)*
David H. Grubb *(Pres. & Chief Oper. Officer)*
Donald W. Leyman *(Exec. V.P.)*
James R. Gillette *(Sr. V.P.-Fin., Treas. & Chief Fin. Officer)*
Gordon W. Marks *(Sr. V.P.)*
Larry Duggan *(V.P.)*
Louis P. Gerhardy *(V.P.)*
Salvatore Bossio *(Corp. Sec.)*
Luke Argilla *(Corp. Counsel)*
Michael Re *(Controller)*
Linda Carlson *(Dir.-Personnel)*
Michael Ford *(Dir.-Mktg.)*
Paul Holmes *(Dir.-Data Processing)*
Robert Rehme *(Dir.-Pur.)*

No. of U.S. Offices: 6

Computer Systems/Hardware:
IBM PC; Prime

Outside Service Firm(s):

KPMG Peat Marwick*(Auditors)*
3 Embarcadero Center
San Francisco, CA 94111
Tel.: 415-951-0100
Fax: 415-397-1129

Mutual of New York*(Group Insurer)*
New York, NY

Hassard, Bonnington, Rogers & Huber*(Legal Firm)*
San Francisco, CA

Wells Fargo Bank*(Major Banking Relationship)*
420 Montgomery St.
San Francisco, CA 94104

Wyatt Co.*(Pension Manager)*
345 California St.
San Francisco, CA 94104
Tel.: 415-986-6568

SWIRL, INC.
8 W. 38th St.
New York, NY 10018
Tel.: 212-302-6540
Approx.Sls.: $20,000,000
Emp.: 500
Mfrs. of Models Coat, Alternatives, Oscar de la Renta, Swirl Directions
S.I.C.: 2384; 2339
Joseph Santarlasci *(Chm. Bd.)*
Anthony Gosson *(Pres.)*
Gene Young *(Controller)*

Subsidiaries:

Easley Textile **(1)**
508 Greenville Rd.
Easley, SC 29640
Tel.: 803-859-3256

Models Coat **(1)**
508 Greenville Rd.
Easley, SC 29640
Tel.: 803-859-2400

Affiliate:

Swirl Sales, Inc. **(1)**
8 West 38th St.
New York, NY 10018
Tel.: 212-302-6540

THE SWISS COLONY
1112-7th Ave.
Monroe, WI 53566
Tel.: 608-328-8400
Fax: 608-328-8457
Year Founded: 1926
Approx.Sls.: $100,000,000
Emp.: 1,200
Fiscal Year-end: 12/31/90
Import Export
Swiss Colony Cheese, Meats, Pastries, Candies, Fruits, Nuts, Gift Packs, Retail Operations, Dining Facilities
S.I.C.: 2022; 2011; 2013; 2051; 2064; 2066; 2033; 2087; 2035; 2068; 5812; 5411
John Baumann *(V.P.-Mktg.)*

SWISS-M-TEX, L.P.
(Formerly Emb-Tex Corp.)
(d/b/a M-Tex)
Hwy. 25
Travelers Rest, SC 29690
Mailing Address:
P.O. Box 968
Travelers Rest, SC 29690
Tel.: 803-834-7281 **SC**
Fax: 803-834-5587
Approx.Sls.: $20,000,000
Emp.: 350
Manufacture Schiffli Machine Embroidery
S.I.C.: 2397
Richard Wassmer *(Pres.)*
Robert Ross *(Chief Exec. Officer)*
Pat Barton *(V.P.-Fin.)*
H.A. Linn *(Controller)*
Peter Girard *(Dir.-Sls.)*
Lynda Wallace *(Dir.-Personnel)*

Outside Service Firm(s):

Arthur Andersen & Co.*(Auditors)*
2300 Charlotte Plaza
Charlotte, NC 28244
Tel.: 704-332-0092

Deloitte & Touche*(Auditors)*
Columbia, SC

Leatherwood, Walker, Todd & Mann*(Legal Firm)*
P.O. Box 2248
Greenville, SC 29602
Tel.: 803-242-6440

NationsBank Carolinas*(Major Banking Relationship)*
Spartanburg, SC

SWIVELIER CO., INC.
33 Route 304
Nanuet, NY 10954
Tel.: 914-623-3471 **NY**
Fax: 914-623-1861
Year Founded: 1947
Emp.: 100
Fiscal Year-end: 1/31/92
Import Export
Manufacture Adjustable Lighting Fixtures, Track Lighting & Recessed Lighting Fixtures for Commercial, Institutional & Residential Use
S.I.C.: 3646; 3645
N.R. Schwartz *(Chm. Bd.)*
M.I. Schwartz *(Pres.)*
G. Phelan *(V.P.-Mfg.)*
L. Cafarchio *(Sec. & Controller)*
I. Schucker *(Mgr.-Sls.)*
J. Blasucci *(Pur. Agent)*
T. Hanlon *(Mgr.-Personnel)*

No. of Mfg. Plants/Facilities: 1
No. of U.S. Offices: 1

Computer Systems/Hardware:
Qantel; IBM; Compaq; Leading Edge; CompuAdd

Outside Service Firm(s):

Schwaeber & Sloane*(Auditors)*
Great Neck, NY

Marine Midland Bank*(Major Banking Relationship)*
140 Broadway
New York, NY 10015
Tel.: 212-658-1620

Division:

Point Electric **(1)**
33 Route 304
Nanuet, NY 10954
Tel.: 914-623-3471
Fax: 914-623-1861
Import Export
Mfr. Adjustable Lighting Products for Do-It-Yourself Installation
S.I.C.: 3645
M.I. Schwartz *(Pres.)*
I. Schucker *(Sls. Mgr.)*
J. Blasucci *(Pur. Agent)*

SWOPE AUTOMOTIVE GROUP, INC.
10 Louisville Auto Center
Louisville, KY 40299
Tel.: 502-499-5000 **KY**
Fax: 502-499-5019
Year Founded: 1952
Approx.Sls.: $53,000,000
Emp.: 169
Automobile Dealership
S.I.C.: 5511
Samuel G. Swope *(Chm. Bd.)*
Richard S. Swope *(Pres.)*
Mark St. Hudson *(Chief Fin. Officer)*
Harry T. Haffner, Jr. *(V.P.-Sls.)*
John M. Winkler *(V.P.)*

Outside Service Firm(s):

Coopers & Lybrand*(Auditors)*
Louisville, KY 46201

Liberty National Bank & Trust Co.*(Major Banking Relationship)*
416 W. Jefferson St.
Louisville, KY 40202
Tel.: 502-566-2000

SYAR INDUSTRIES, INC.
2301 Napa Vallejo Hwy.
Napa, CA 94558
Mailing Address:
P.O. Box 2540,
Napa, CA 94558
Tel.: 707-252-8711
Fax: 707-257-2630
Year Founded: 1933
Approx.Sls.: $34,000,000

Emp.: 320
Sales-Stone, Clay, Rock, Sand & Gravel Products for Construction Industry
S.I.C.: 5032
C.M. Syar *(Chm. Bd.)*
James M. Syar *(Pres. & Chief Oper. Officer)*
John M. Jonas *(Chief Fin. Officer, V.P. & Sec.)*
Ralph Locke *(V.P.-Mktg.)*
Dave Ross *(Asst. to Pres.)*
Bob Grignon *(Dir.-Data Processing)*
Pete Tvilborg *(Dir.-Personnel)*

Computer Systems/Hardware:
IBM System 38

Outside Service Firm(s):

Cal-Surance Group*(Commercial Insurance Carrier)*
Torrance, CA

Kaiser Insurance*(Group Insurer)*
Oakland, CA

New York Life*(Group Insurer)*
New York, NY

SYBEX GROUP
2021 Challenger Dr.
Alameda, CA 94501
Tel.: 510-523-8233
Fax: 510-523-2373
Year Founded: 1976
Sales Range: $60-79 Million
Emp.: 65
Publisher of Introductory & Professional Books on Computers
S.I.C.: 2731
Rodnay Zaks *(Pres. & Chief Exec. Officer)*
Alan J. Oakes *(Exec. V.P. & Natl. Sls. Mgr.)*
Roger Squier *(V.P.-Fin. & Opers.)*
Isabella Zagane *(Mgr.-Acctg.)*

Computer Systems/Hardware:
IBM

Outside Service Firm(s):

Arthur Andersen & Co.*(Auditors)*
Berkeley, CA

Lincoln National Life Insurance Co.*(Group Insurer)*
Lincoln, NE

SYCON CORPORATION
959 Cheney Ave.
Marion, OH 43302
Tel.: 614-382-5771
Fax: 614-383-6254
Approx.Sls.: $18,000,000
Emp.: 175
Export
Manufactures Truck & Bus Accessories
S.I.C.: 3714
Arnold B. Seimer *(Pres.)*
Clyde R. Forbes *(V.P. & Treas.)*
Myron Crowell *(Controller)*
Paul Kestler *(Opers. Mgr.)*
R.D. Wearn *(Gen. Mgr.)*
Jeanne Black *(Pur. Agent)*
Anne Greashaber *(Mgr.-Adv.)*

Divisions:

Acragage **(1)**
959 Cheney Ave.
Marion, OH 43302
Tel.: 614-382-5771
Mfr. Process Gages for Trucks
S.I.C.: 3714

Air-O-Matic Power Steer Co. **(1)**
959 Cheney Ave.
Marion, OH 43302
Tel.: 614-382-5771
Fax: 614-383-6254
Emp.: 150
Export
Computer Systems/Hardware:
IBM PC AT
Truck & Automotive Equipment
S.I.C.: 3714
A.B. Siemer *(Pres.)*
C. Fobes *(V.P.-Fin.)*
Anna Greashaber *(Mgr.-Adv. & Mktg.)*
J. Parady *(Sls. Mgr.)*
R.D. Wearn *(Gen. Mgr.)*
J. Black *(Pur. Agent)*

Beacon Gage **(1)**
959 Cheney Ave.
Marion, OH 43302
Tel.: 614-382-5771
Mfr. Special Pressure Gages for Railroads
S.I.C.: 3714

Cyclo-Gard **(1)**
959 Cheney Ave.
Marion, OH 43302
Tel.: 614-382-5771
Mfrs. Air Dryer for Larger Trucks
S.I.C.: 3714

Digitec **(1)**
959 Cheney Ave.
Marion, OH 43302
Tel.: 614-387-3444
Fax: 614-383-6254
Approx.Sls.: $8,000,000
Emp.: 100
Export
Computer Systems/Hardware:
IBM-486
Manufacturer of Electronic Test Equipment; DigiTec-Digital Panel Meters, Printers & Dataloggers
S.I.C.: 3825
A.B. Siemr *(Chm. Bd.)*
M. Crowell *(Controller)*
R.D. Wearn *(Gen. Mgr.)*
A. Greashaber *(Mgr.-Adv. & Mktg.)*
B. Poplin *(Mgr.-Sls.)*
J. Black *(Pur. Agent)*

LevelAc **(1)**
959 Cheney Ave.
Marion, OH 43302
Tel.: 614-382-5771
Mfr. Switches for Trucks
S.I.C.: 3714

Meco **(1)**
959 Cheney Ave.
Marion, OH 43302
Tel.: 614-382-5771
Mfr. Motor Vehicle Parts
S.I.C.: 3714

ServiceRecorder **(1)**
959 Cheney Ave.
Marion, OH 43302
Tel.: 614-382-5771
Mfr. Time Mngmt. Clocks for Trucks
S.I.C.: 3714

StarMaster **(1)**
959 Cheney Ave.
Marion, OH 43302
Tel.: 614-382-5771
Mfr. Parts for Trucks & Buses
S.I.C.: 3714

WestCon **(1)**
959 Cheney Ave.
Marion, OH 43302
Tel.: 614-382-5771
Digital Thermal & Electronic Devices for Motor Vehicles
S.I.C.: 3714

SYMMONS INDUSTRIES INC.
31 Brooks Dr.
Braintree, MA 02184
Tel.: 617-848-2250 **MA**
Fax: 617-843-3849
Year Founded: 1938
Approx.Sls.: $30,000,000
Emp.: 175
Fiscal Year-end: 12/31/91
Import Export
Pressure Balanced Safety Shower Systems
S.I.C.: 3494; 3432
William B. O'Keefe *(Chm. Bd.)*
Albert G. Fehrm *(Pres.)*
Kevin V. Symmons *(Exec. V.P.)*
John L. Diohep *(V.P.-Sls.)*
Dennis R. Murphy *(V.P.-Fin. & Chief Fin. Officer)*
Colin ManDonald *(Chief Engr.)*
James J. Galvin *(Dir.-Mktg.)*
K.J. Chisholm *(Pur. Agent)*

Computer Systems/Hardware:
DEC Vax 6310

Outside Service Firm(s):

Darmody, Merlino & Company*(Auditors)*
Boston, MA

Lyne, Woodworth & Evarts*(Legal Firm)*
Boston, MA

First National Bank of Boston*(Major Banking Relationship)*
P.O. Box 644,
Boston, MA 02102-0644
Tel.: 617-575-2900
Fax: 617-575-2549

SYMONS CORPORATION
251 S. Lake Ave., Ste. 606
Pasadena, CA 91101
Tel.: 213-684-1800
Approx.Sls.: $85,000,000
Emp.: 1,000
Concrete Forms; Sheet Metal
S.I.C.: 3444
Merrill L. Nash *(Pres.)*
Kevin Combs *(Treas., Chief Fin. Officer & Sec.)*

Outside Service Firm(s):

Ernst & Young*(Auditors)*
515 S. Flower St.
Los Angeles, CA 90071
Tel.: 213-621-1666

Security Pacific Corporation*(Major Banking Relationship)*
Security Pacific Plaza
Los Angeles, CA 90071
Tel.: 213-345-6211
Fax: 213-625-0809

Divisions:

Richmond Screw Anchor Division **(1)**
17051 E. Green Drive
City of Industry, CA 91716
Tel.: 818-964-8890
Bolts, Nuts, Rivets & Washers; Construction Machinery
S.I.C.: 5072; 5082

Steel Form Division **(1)**
251 S. Lake Ave., Ste. 606
Pasadena, CA 91101
Tel.: 213-684-1800
Concrete Block & Brick; Concrete Products
S.I.C.: 3444

Subsidiary:

Symons Corporation **(1)**
200 E. Touhy Ave.
Des Plaines, IL 60018
Tel.: 708-298-3200
Telex: 5101010497 DSP CGO
Fax: 708-635-9287
Approx.Sls.: $100,000,000
Emp.: 600
Fiscal Year-end: 8/30/92
Import Export
Computer Systems/Hardware:
IBM
Pre-engineered Concrete Forming Systems & Access. for Walls, Columns, & Decks, Custom Forms including Forms & Support Equip. for Underground Construction; Fiberglass Column Forms; Flying Systems & Shoring; Form Release, Curing, Hardening & Sealing Chemicals
S.I.C.: 3444; 2899
Raymond E. Bartholomae *(Exec. V.P. & G.M.)*
Brian Johnson *(V.P.-Admin.)*
Jim Benka *(Controller)*
Richard Wolter *(Dir.-Personnel)*
Robert Flathau *(Dir.-New Prod. Devel.)*
Ken Kozlowski *(Mgr.-Natl. Sls.)*
Clark A. Springman *(Mgr.-Adv.)*
Joe Colado *(Mgr.-Plant)*
Robert Taylor *(Mgr.-Pur.)*
Ken Remus *(Mgr.-Prod.)*
Manny Lopez *(Mgr.-Prod.)*
Chuck Hornaday *(Mgr.-Prod.)*
Chuck Podgurski *(Mgr.-Prod.)*
Kevin Smith *(Mgr.-Mngmt. Information System)*
Mike Norkus *(Mgr.-Quality Control)*
Mike Miller *(Mgr.-Corp. Engrng.)*

SYMPLEX COMMUNICATIONS CORP.
5 Research Dr.
Ann Arbor, MI 48103
Tel.: 313-995-1555
Fax: 313-995-1564
Year Founded: 1983
Approx.Sls.: $10,000,000
Emp.: 63
Designs, Manufactures & Sells Data Communications Equipment
S.I.C.: 3661; 3823; 5045; 7373
George Brostoff *(Chm. Bd. & Treas.)*
Jeff Jacobowitz *(Pres.)*
Cyrus Azar *(Sec.)*
Principal(s):
George Brostoff
Jeff Jacobowitz
Cyrus Azar

SYNDET PRODUCTS, INC.
201 Boston Turnpike
Bolton, CT 06040
Tel.: 203-646-0172
Fax: 203-645-6070
Wholesale Chemicals & Allied Products
S.I.C.: 2851; 5198
William Gorra *(Pres.)*
Michele O'Neil *(V.P.)*

Outside Service Firm(s):

Bay Bank Harvard Trust Company*(Major Banking Relationship)*
Boston, MA

Schatz, Schwartz & Fenton*(Legal Firm)*
Springfield, MA

Subsidiary:

Chemical Specialties Corp. **(1)**
54 Waltham Ave.
Springfield, MA 01109
Tel.: 413-788-0896
Wholesale Chemicals & Allied Products
S.I.C.: 2851; 5198
George M. Gorra *(Chm. Bd.)*
William Gorra *(Pres. & Chief Exec. & Chief Fin. Officer)*

SYNDICATE SYSTEMS, INC.
250 E. 96th St., Ste. 415
Indianapolis, IN 46240
Mailing Address:
P.O. Box 40789
Indianapolis, IN 46240
Tel.: 317-581-4444
Year Founded: 1976
Approx.Sls.: $60,000,000
Emp.: 500
Holding Company; Manufacture Store Fixtures, Metal Partitions
S.I.C.: 6719; 5087
Glenn Swisher *(Chm. Bd. & Chief Exec. Officer)*
Jerry L. Burris *(Pres.)*
Robert Hagemier *(Sec.)*

SYNERGISM, INC.
712 E. Evelyn Ave.
Sunnyvale, CA 94086
Tel.: 408-739-5000 **CA**
Fax: 408-730-0144
Year Founded: 1954
Approx.Sls.: $75,000,000
Emp.: 400
Holding Company
S.I.C.: 6719
Eugene A. Ravizza *(Chm. Bd. & Pres.)*
James S. Ryley *(Vice Chm.)*
Claranne R. Long *(Chief Fin. Officer)*
Principal(s):
Eugene A. Ravizza

Synergism, Inc.—(Continued)

Outside Service Firm(s):

Boitano, Sargent & Lawrence*(Auditors)*
San Jose, CA

Bernard Vogel*(Legal Firm)*
San Jose, CA

Bank of America NT&SA*(Major Banking Relationship)*
San Jose, CA

Subsidiaries:

A.D. Controls **(1)**
791 Nuttman St.
Santa Clara, CA 95054
Tel.: 408-988-3571
Norman Haas *(Chief Exec. Officer)*

Cascade Controls, Inc. **(1)**
712 E. Evelyn Ave.
Sunnyvale, CA 94086
Tel.: 408-245-1000
Ray Pfeifer *(Chief Exec. Officer)*

Certronics, Inc. **(1)**
775 Commercial St.
San Jose, CA 95112
Tel.: 408-452-5000
Aaron Colton *(Chief Exec. Officer)*

Cupertino Electric, Inc. **(1)**
714 E. Evelyn Ave.
Sunnyvale, CA 94086
Tel.: 408-991-1000
Approx.Sls.: $39,000,000
Emp.: 260
Electrical Contracting
S.I.C.: 1731
James S. Ryley *(Pres.)*

D.M.A. Associates **(1)**
712 E. Evelyn Ave.
Sunnyvale, CA 94086
Tel.: 408-991-1005
Claranne Long *(Chief Exec. Officer)*

A SIGN OF SERVICE

SYRACUSE SUPPLY COMPANY
5921 Court St. Rd.
Syracuse, NY 13221
Mailing Address:
P.O. Box 4814,
Syracuse, NY 13221
Tel.: 315-463-9511 **NY**
Fax: 315-463-9831
Year Founded: 1885
Assets: $97,268,000
Earnings: $586,000
Liabilities: $75,061,000
Net Worth: $22,207,000
Approx.Rev.: $109,965,000
Emp.: 460
Fiscal Year-end: 12/31/90
Sales, Servicing & Leasing of Construction-Type Equipment, Industrial Engines, Machine Tools; Material Handling Systems, Industrial Supplies, Over-the-Highway Trucks; Computer Hardware & Peripherals
S.I.C.: 5082; 5084; 5045; 5085; 7352; 7353; 7359; 7513
H. Douglas Barclay *(Chm. Bd.)*
Stephen J. Suhowatsky *(Pres. & Chief Exec. Officer)*
Addison L. Everett *(V.P. & Chief Fin. Officer)*
George S. Deptula *(Sec.)*
James M. Snyder *(Controller)*
Del Wayne *(Admin. Mgr.)*

No. of Mfg. Plants/Facilities: 10

Computer Systems/Hardware:
IBM System 38

Outside Service Firm(s):

KPMG Peat Marwick*(Auditors)*
Syracuse, NY

Hancock & Estabrook*(Legal Firm)*
Mony Tower 1, P.O. Box 4976
Syracuse, NY 13221

Groups:

Industrial Lift Trucks **(1)**
4381 Walden Ave.
Lancaster, NY 14086
Tel.: 716-684-9040
Mfr. of Quality Lift Trucks & Related Equipment; Provides Parts & Service Support, Applications Engineering to Adapt Standard Machines to Specific Needs & Conducts Extensive Customer Training Programs
S.I.C.: 3536
Norm Borgocell *(Mgr.)*

Syracuse Supply Construction & Equipment Division **(1)**
Colvin Station 294, P.O. Box 37
Syracuse, NY 13205
Tel.: 315-476-9981
Marketing of Construction Equipment, Engines & Over-the-Highway Trucks
S.I.C.: 5082

Syracuse Supply Industrial Products Division **(1)**
5921 Court St. Rd.
Syracuse, NY 13201
Tel.: 315-463-9511
Mktg. of Machine Tools, Pumps & Compressors; Industrial Computer Hardware & Software
S.I.C.: 5084; 5045
Matty Perry *(Chief Oper. Officer)*

Subsidiaries:

New York Systems Exchange Corp. **(1)**
150 Broad Hollow Rd.
Melville, NY 11747
Tel.: 516-673-3830 (100%)
Fax: 516-673-3845
Emp.: 12
Retail of New & Used Computer Systems & Peripheral Packages Nationally
S.I.C.: 5734; 7377
Stephen C. Zaleski *(Pres.)*
Robert Stevenson *(Exec. V.P.)*
Howard A. Stabile *(V.P.)*

Primacare Health Resources, Inc. **(1)**
5921 Court St. Rd.
Syracuse, NY 13221
Tel.: 315-463-7000
Rental, Sales & Service of Durable Medical Equipment, Respirators, Oxygen Concentrators, Infant Monitoring Systems; Sales & Rental of Wheel Chairs, Hospital Beds & other Durable Hospital Supplies
S.I.C.: 7352; 5047
Stephen J. Suhowatsky *(Pres. & Chief Exec. Officer)*
Howard R. Phipps *(V.P. & Chief Fin. Officer)*
James R. McVety *(Sec.)*

Subsidiaries:

At Home Respiratory and Medical, Inc. **(2)**
6-102nd St.
Troy, NY 12180
Tel.: 518-235-0800
Rental, Sales & Service of Durable Medical Equipment
S.I.C.: 7352; 5047
William D. Dessingue, Sr. *(Pres.)*
William D. Dessingue, Jr. *(V.P.)*

Atlantic Health Care Resources, Inc. **(2)**
P.O. Box 58, 69 Main St.
Cherry Valley, MA 01611
Tel.: 508-892-1135
Rental, Sales & Service of Durable Medical Equipment
S.I.C.: 7352; 5047; 7699
Steven K. Niland *(Pres.)*

Metro Medical Resources, Inc. **(2)**
264 St. John St.
Portland, ME 04102
Tel.: 207-775-1318
Rental, Sales & Service of Durable Medical Equipment
S.I.C.: 7352; 5047; 7699
James A. Berryman *(Pres.)*

Mountaineer Medical/Primacare I.V. **(2)**
6810 MacCorkle Ave. SE
Charleston, WV 25304
Tel.: 304-925-6675
Fax: 304-925-2199
Emp.: 17
Rental, Sales & Service of Durable Medical Equipment
S.I.C.: 7352; 5047; 7629; 7699
James J. Monroe *(Pres.)*

Penn Medical Services, Inc. **(2)**
159 Morgantown
Uniontown, PA 15401
Tel.: 412-439-9696
Rental, Sales & Service of Durable Medical Equipment
S.I.C.: 7352; 5047; 7699
John C. Lish *(Pres.)*

Syracuse Supply Leasing Co., Inc. **(1)**
5921 Court St. Rd., P.O. Box 4945
Syracuse, NY 13221
Tel.: 315-463-9511
Flexible Leasing & Rental Plans
S.I.C.: 7513

SYRATECH CORPORATION
175 McClellan Hwy.
East Boston, MA 02128
Tel.: 617-569-2200 **DE**
Fax: 617-561-8484
Year Founded: 1986
Assets: $50,000,000
Earnings: $4,000,000
Liabilities: $24,000,000
Net Worth: $26,000,000
Approx.Sls.: $75,000,000
Emp.: 700
Fiscal Year-end: 12/31/90
Holding Company
S.I.C.: 6719
Leonard Florence *(Chm. Bd., Pres. & Chief Exec. Officer)*
E. Merle Randolph *(Chief Fin. Officer)*
Faye A. Florence *(Gen. Counsel)*
Tim Burke *(Dir.-Human Resources)*
Melvin L. Levine *(Dir.-Pur.)*
Jayson Score *(Mgr.-Opers.)*

Outside Service Firm(s):

Coopers & Lybrand*(Auditors)*
One Lincoln Center
Syracuse, NY 13202
Tel.: 315-474-8541
Fax: 315-474-0259

Paul, Weiss, Rifkind, Wharton & Garrison*(Legal Firm)*
345 Park Ave.
New York, NY 10022
Tel.: 212-644-8000

United States Trust Company of New York*(Major Banking Relationship)*
Boston, MA

Subsidiaries:

Syroco Inc. **(1)**
7528 State Fair Blvd.
Baldwinsville, NY 13027
Tel.: 315-635-9911 (100%)
Fax: 315-635-1047
Emp.: 400
Syroco Decorative Accessories, Clocks, Plaques, Mirrors, Tables, Wood/Metal Framed Prints, Resin Furniture
S.I.C.: 2499; 3873; 3231; 3089; 3999
Frank Deramo *(Exec. V.P.)*
Charles McCarthy *(V.P.-Sls. & Mktg.)*
Ray Carrock *(Fin. Officer)*

Wallace International Silversmiths, Inc. **(1)**
175 McClellan Hwy.
East Boston, MA 02128
Tel.: 617-561-2200
Fax: 617-569-8484
Approx.Sls.: $30,000,000
Emp.: 250
Import Export
Mfr. of Sterling & Silverplated Flatware; Holloware Giftware
S.I.C.: 3914
Leonard Florence *(Pres.)*
E. Merle Randolph *(V.P. & Chief Fin. Officer)*
Scott Bial *(V.P.-Sls. & Mktg.)*
Melvin Levine *(V.P.-Pur.)*

Wallace Silversmiths **(1)**
175 McClellan Hwy.
East Boston, MA 02128
Tel.: 617-561-2200 (100%)
Fax: 617-561-8484/0275
Emp.: 300
Mfr. of Flatware & Holloware
S.I.C.: 3914
Leonard Florence *(Chief Oper. Officer)*

SYSTEM PLANNING CORP.
1500 Wilson Blvd.
Arlington, VA 22209
Tel.: 703-351-8200 **DE**
Fax: 703-841-3668
Year Founded: 1970
Assets: $14,412,000
Earnings: $1,758,000
Net Worth: $14,412,000
Approx.Sls.: $45,000,000
Emp.: 395
Fiscal Year-end: 3/31/90
Export
Scientific Research; Engineering Design Services; Manufacture of Instrumentation Radars & Electronic Equipment
S.I.C.: 8731; 3812; 3663
Ronald L. Easley *(Chm. Bd., Pres. & Chief Exec. Officer)*
Charles F. Hengels *(Chief Fin. Officer)*
Maurice N. Schriber *(Chief Oper. Officer)*
Sayre Stevens *(Chief Scientist)*
Dov Zakheim *(V.P.)*
Heinz Lenzen *(Controller)*
Nicholas Mercury *(Corp. Librarian)*
Principal(s):
Ronald L. Easley

No. of Mfg. Plants/Facilities: 1
No. of U.S. Offices: 4

Computer Systems/Hardware:
Data General; MV 8000; MV 4000

Outside Service Firm(s):

Arthur Andersen & Co.*(Auditors)*
1666 K Street, N.W.
Washington, DC 20006

Hartford Life Insurance Co.*(Commercial Insurance Carrier)*
Hartford, CT 06104-2999

Lincoln National Life Insurance Co.*(Group Insurer)*
PO Box 208, 1300 S. Clinton
Fort Wayne, IN 46801
Tel.: 219-455-2926
Fax: 219-455-7619

Caplan, Wechsler & Selzen*(Legal Firm)*
Bethesda, MD

Maryland National Bank*(Pension Manager)*
Baltimore, MD 21202

Subsidiaries:

SPC International Corp. **(1)**
1500 Wilson Blvd.
Arlington, VA 22209
Tel.: 703-841-2800
S.I.C.: 8748
Dr. Dou S. Zakheim *(Chief Exec. Officer)*

TriData Inc. **(1)**
1500 Wilson Blvd.
Arlington, VA 22209
Tel.: 703-841-2800
Emp.: 7
Fire Prevention Studies; Local Government Analyses
S.I.C.: 9224

Philip Schaenman *(Pres.)*

SYSTEMS ENGINEERING & MANUFACTURING CORP.
44 Campanelli Pkwy.
Stoughton, MA 02072
Mailing Address:
P.O. Box 507
Stoughton, MA 02072
Tel.: 617-344-1700 **DE**
Fax: 617-341-1713
Year Founded: 1949
Assets: $13,570,000
Liabilities: $12,313,000
Net Worth: $1,257,000
Emp.: 150
Fiscal Year-end: 9/30/90
Mfr., Designing & Engineering of Automated Plating & Wetprocessing Systems, Wastewater Treatment & Metal Recovery Equipment, Solution Filtration Systems for Metal Finishing & Printed Circuit Board Industries
S.I.C.: 3559
Walter E. Guertler, Jr. *(Chm. Bd., Pres., Chief Exec. Officer)*
Stuart Raifman *(Asst. Sec.)*
James Cobis *(Pur. Agent)*
Gretchen Devery *(Coord.-Personnel)*
Richard Haskell *(Controller)*

Outside Service Firm(s):

Ernst & Young*(Auditors)*
One Old Stone Square
Providence, RI 02903
Tel.: 401-331-7000

State Street Bank & Trust Co.*(Major Banking Relationship)*
P.O. Box 366,
Boston, MA 02101
Tel.: 617-426-5523

Foley, Hoag & Eliot*(Legal Firm)*
One Post Office Square
Boston, MA 02210
Tel.: 617-482-1390

Divisions:

Baker Bros. de Puerto Rico **(1)**
P.O. Box 14
Las Piedras, PR 00671
Tel.: 809-733-8585
Emp.: 6
Mfr. Filters
S.I.C.: 3559
Steve Baker *(Chief Oper. Officer)*

Baker Brothers/Micro-Plate **(1)**
12200 34th St. North
Clearwater, FL 34622
Tel.: 813-577-7777
Emp.: 26
Mfr. of Automated Plating & Wet Processing Linen Wastewater-Treatment & Metal Recovery Systems, Plating Solution Filtration Systems
S.I.C.: 3559

Non-U.S. Holding:

Systems Engineering & Mfg. Nederlands B.V. **(1)**
Magnesiumweg 2 P.O. Box 92,
Heerenveen, Netherlands
Tel.: 31-5130-319-55 (100%)
Emp.: 23
Mfrs. Filter Pumps
S.I.C.: 3561
Hans Huizynea *(Mng. Dir.)*

SYSTEMS PARKING, INC.
918 E. Green St.
Pasadena, CA 91106
Tel.: 818-792-7275
Fax: 818-568-9666
Approx.Sls.: $50,000,000
Emp.: 1,500
Automated Parking; Real Estate
S.I.C.: 7521; 6531
Tom Kanngiesser *(Pres.)*
Duane H. Cameron *(Exec. V.P.)*
Lydia Byrne *(V.P.-Admin.)*
Ada Miyar *(V.P.-Fin.)*
John Gernert *(Treas.)*
Donald Sachs *(Sec.)*

Outside Service Firm(s):

Ernst & Young*(Auditors)*
515 S. Flower St.
Los Angeles, CA 90071
Tel.: 213-621-1666

Kindel & Anderson*(Legal Firm)*
555 S. Flower, Ste. 2600
Los Angeles, CA 90071
Tel.: 213-680-2222

Bank of America*(Major Banking Relationship)*
701 S. Western Ave.
Los Angeles, CA 91201

SYSTEMS RESEARCH AND APPLICATIONS CORPORATION
2000 15th St. N.
Arlington, VA 22201
Tel.: 703-558-4700 **VA**
Fax: 703-558-4723
Year Founded: 1978
Assets: $29,000,000
Liabilities: $20,400,000
Net Worth: $8,600,000
Approx.Sls.: $49,000,000
Emp.: 580
Fiscal Year-end: 6/30/91
Computer Related Systems Engineering; Computer Software Systems Analysis & Design, Custom Computer Software Development
S.I.C.: 7373
William K. Brehm *(Chm. Bd.)*
Dr. Ernst Volgenau *(Pres.)*
Edward Legasey *(Exec. V.P.)*
Gary Nelson *(Exec. V.P.)*

Outside Service Firm(s):

Crestar Bank*(Major Banking Relationship)*
Box 26665
Richmond, VA 23261
Tel.: 804-782-7302

SYSTECH COMPUTER CORPORATION
6465 Nancy Ridge Dr.
San Diego, CA 92121
Tel.: 619-453-8970
Fax: 619-453-0238
Approx.Sls.: $20,000,000
Emp.: 160
Mfr. Computer Interface Equipment
S.I.C.: 3577
Mark Fowler *(Pres.)*
Trevor Constable *(V.P.-Sls. & Mktg.)*
Jack H. Hetzell, II *(V.P.-Fin.)*
Tim Hathaway *(Dir.-Engng.)*

Outside Service Firm(s):

Deloitte & Touche*(Auditors)*
701 "B" St., Ste. 1900
San Diego, CA 92101-8198

Bank of America NT&SA*(Major Banking Relationship)*
San Diego, CA

DAVE SYVERSON LINCOLN MERCURY
2310 E. Main St.
Albert Lea, MN 56007
Tel.: 507-373-1438 **MN**
Fax: 507-373-3063
Year Founded: 1967
Approx.Sls.: $40,000,000
Emp.: 65
Wholesale & Retail Service of New & Used Automobiles & Trucks; Repair Shops; Truck Leasing
S.I.C.: 5511; 5012; 7538; 7513
David B. Syverson *(Pres.)*
Lowell Bruns *(Mgr.-Opers.)*
Susan Bjerke *(Office Mgr.)*

Principal(s):
David B. Syverson

Outside Service Firm(s):

Eide Helmeke & Co.*(Auditors)*
Minneapolis, MN

First Bank, N.A.*(Major Banking Relationship)*
Albert Lee, MN

Subsidiary:

Dave Syverson Truck Center, Inc. **(1)**
6300 S. 63 Highway
Rochester, MN 55904
Tel.: 507-289-3357
Emp.: 25
Truck Sales & Service
S.I.C.: 5511
David B. Syverson *(Chief Exec. Officer)*
Patrick Pettey *(Pres.)*

T & R ELECTRIC SUPPLY COMPANY, INC.
Hwy. 34 W.
Colman, SD 57017
Tel.: 605-534-3555
Fax: 605-534-3861
Approx.Sls.: $11,000,000
Emp.: 140
Wholesale New & Used Electrical Equipment & Line Materials
S.I.C.: 5063
James R. Thompson *(Pres.)*
Kenneth E. Ross *(V.P.)*
Janice Ross *(Treas.)*

Outside Service Firm(s):

Dakota State Bank*(Major Banking Relationship)*
Colman, SD

TAD TECHNICAL SERVICES CORP.
639 Massachusetts Ave.
Cambridge, MA 02139
Tel.: 617-868-1650 **MA**
Fax: 617-492-1432
Year Founded: 1956
Approx.Sls.: $500,000,000
Emp.: 15,000
Fiscal Year-end: 12/31/90
Engineering, Architectural & Surveying Services
S.I.C.: 8711; 8712; 8713
David J. McGrath, Jr. *(Pres. & Chief Exec. Officer)*
Eugene N. Christopher *(Sr. V.P.)*
Norman Wirtz *(V.P.-Fin. & Chief Fin. Officer)*
William F. Katter *(V.P.-Admin.)*
Edward Bonadio *(V.P.-Phoenix)*
Edward J. Brennan *(V.P.-Washington, DC)*
E. David Conner *(V.P.-Los Angeles)*
James W. Davis *(V.P.-Chicago)*
Malcolm High *(Controller)*

No. of U.S. Offices: 175
No. of Foreign Offices: 1

Outside Service Firm(s):

Theodore Samet & Co.*(Auditors)*
Boston, MA

Ropes & Gray*(Legal Firm)*
One International Place
Boston, MA 02110
Tel.: 617-423-6100

Fleet National Bank*(Major Banking Relationship)*
28 State St.
Boston, MA 02109

TBWA
ADVERTISING, INC.

TBWA ADVERTISING, INC.
TBWA House, 292 Madison Ave.
New York, NY 10017
Tel.: 212-725-1150
Fax: 212-213-2869
Year Founded: 1977
Approx.Billings: $300,000,000
Emp.: 300
Fiscal Year-end: 12/31/90
Advertising
S.I.C.: 7311
William G. Tragos *(Founder, Chm. & Chief Exec. Officer-WW)*
Richard N. Costello *(Pres. & Chief Oper. Officer)*
Arnold Arlow *(Exec. V.P., Co-Creative Dir.-U.S.)*
Peter Lubalin *(Exec. V.P., Co-Creative Dir.-U.S.)*
S. Murray Gaylord *(Exec. V.P., Dir. Acct. Services)*
James H. Quest *(Exec. V.P., Dir. Grp. Devel.)*
Geoff Hayes *(Exec. V.P., Exec. Art Dir.)*
Claude Fromm *(Exec. V.P., Media Dir.)*
Stuart Loss *(Exec. V.P., Chief Fin. Officer)*
Patricia Cameron *(Exec. V.P., Dir. Planning & Research)*
Grant Castle *(Exec. V.P., Dir. Mktg. Services)*
Steve Feldman *(Sr. V.P., Sr. Art Dir.)*
Robert Nelson *(Sr. V.P., Dir. Brdcst. Production)*
Maria Beltrametti *(Sr. V.P., Mngmt. Supvr.)*
Robert Rosenthal *(Sr. V.P., Mngmt. Supvr.)*
Richard Lewis *(Sr. V.P., Mngmt. Supvr.)*
Richard Goldman *(Sr. V.P., Controller)*
Steve Wakeen *(V.P., Mngmt. Supvr.)*
Cynthia Rhea *(V.P., Acct. Dir.)*
Marianne Frawley *(V.P., Acct. Dir.)*
Tom McManus *(V.P., Sr. Art Dir.)*
David Warren *(V.P., Sr. Copywriter)*
Jeff Linder *(V.P., Sr. Copywriter)*
Harry Woods *(V.P., Sr. Copywriter)*
Alan Levine *(V.P., Copywriter)*
Reatha Braxton *(V.P., Assoc. Media Dir.)*
Richard Lefkowitz *(V.P., Assoc. Media Dir.)*
Judy Sullivan *(V.P., Assoc. Media Dir.)*
William Bradford *(V.P., Plng. & Res.)*
Matthew Tokatlian *(V.P., Bus. Affairs)*
Bonnie Varela *(V.P., Traffic Dir.)*
Kaaren Varchetto *(V.P., Office Mgr.)*

Computer Systems/Hardware:
Hewlett Packard

Subsidiaries:

Beisler & Associates, Inc. **(1)**
292 Madison Ave.
New York, NY 10017
Tel.: 212-725-1250
Fax: 212-679-4651
Approx.Billings: $2,000,000
Emp.: 6
Sales Promotion
S.I.C.: 7389
Edward J. Beisler *(Pres.)*

TBWA Kerlick Switzer **(1)**
TBWA House, 1000 St. Louis Union Station
Saint Louis, MO 63103
Tel.: 314-241-4656
Fax: 314-241-4927
Advertising
S.I.C.: 7311
Michael G. Switzer *(Chm.)*
Robert E. Johnson *(Pres.-Entertainment Div.)*
Arthur Gramer *(Exec. V.P., Dir. Acct. Services)*
Lloyd Wolfe *(Exec. V.P., Creative Dir.)*
Coleman Steele *(Exec. V.P., Media Dir.)*
Dave Christoff *(Exec. V.P., Production Dir.)*
Mark Kushner *(Exec. V.P., Fin.)*
Kelly L. Hoskins *(Sr. V.P., Entertainment Div.)*

TBWA Advertising, Inc.—(Continued)

Non-U.S. Holdings:

A4 Reklamcilik **(1)**
Turizm ve Seyahat Ltd.Sti, Tesvikiye Cad
No 137 5-809-200 Nisantasi,
Istanbul, Turkey
Tel.: 1305348
Fax: 1311596
Emine Keyder *(Pres.)*

Artplan Publicidade **(1)**
Rua Fonta de Daudade 329 Loga,
Rio de Janeiro, Brazil
Tel.: 21-2867340
Fax: 21-2667156
S.I.C.: 7311
Maurice Cohen *(Mng. Dir.)*

Austria III **(1)**
Daringergasse 6 A-1190
Vienna, Austria
Tel.: 327-5500
Fax: 237-55013
Advertising
S.I.C.: 7311
Horst Wilfinger *(Mng. Dir.)*

De TBWA Groep B.V. **(1)**
Dr. Willem Dreesweg 2 1185 VB
Amsterdam, 443714, Netherlands
Tel.: 20-656-2400
Telex: 10478
Fax: 20-647-4844
Advertising
S.I.C.: 7311
Roland van Kralingen *(Chm.)*

EPG/TBWA **(1)**
Rua Marques de Fronteira 4A 3 Esq., 1000
Lisbon, Portugal
Tel.: 545221
Fax: 525831
S.I.C.: 7311
Jose Carlos Botelho Moniz *(Mng. Dir.)*

J. N. Leoussis Advertising & Marketing S.A. **(1)**
4, Kartalist 11528
Athens, Greece
Tel.: 1-7752616
Telex: 218807 leou gr
Fax: 1-7713700
Approx.Billings: $6,530,900
Emp.: 38
S.I.C.: 7311
Nicos J. Leoussis *(Mng. Dir.)*
M. Maripa *(Acct. Planner)*
Dimitra Charatzi *(Public Rels. Dir.)*

Multicom TBWA Advertising B.V. **(1)**
Dillenburgstraat 5A P.O. Box 7006, 5652 Am
Eindhoven, Netherlands
Tel.: 40-526499
Fax: 40-550671
Tom Klosters *(Mng. Dir.)*

TBWA **(1)**
Corso Garibaldi, 18 35100
Padova, Italy
Tel.: 49-8751565
Albino Ponchio *(Mng. Dir.)*

TBWA **(1)**
Avda. Diagonal, 604 08021 Atico,
Barcelona, Spain
Tel.: 3-2022188
Telex: 81143
Fax: 3-2009940
Pepe Guerrero *(Mng. Dir.)*

TBWA **(1)**
Via Cusani 5 20121
Milan, Italy
Tel.: 885-91
Telex: 311488
Fax: 869-3308
Advertising
S.I.C.: 7311
Alberto Levi *(Chm. Bd. & Mng. Dir.)*

TBWA **(1)**
Hansaallee 30/32 D-6000
Frankfurt/Main, 1, Germany
Tel.: 69-15210
Telex: 412173
Fax: 152-1192
Advertising
S.I.C.: 7311
Mike Camesasca *(Mng. Dir.)*

TBWA **(1)**
Lowenstrasse 29 8021
Zurich, Switzerland
Tel.: 211-1050
Telex: 813547
Fax: 211-7714
Advertising
S.I.C.: 7311
Bruno Zanola *(Mng. Dir.)*

TBWA **(1)**
Avenue Louise 326 (BTE 123) 1050
Brussels, Belgium
Tel.: 538-5051
Telex: 61201
Fax: 538-1726
Advertising
S.I.C.: 7311
Andre Duval *(Mng. Dir.)*

TBWA **(1)**
Via Kenia 66/A 00144
Rome, Italy
Tel.: 591-6724
Telex: 611197
Advertising
S.I.C.: 7311
Anders Weinar *(Mng. Dir.)*

TBWA Dusseldorf GmbH **(1)**
Immermannstr. 40 4000
Dusseldorf, 1, Germany
Tel.: 211-367060
Telex: 17-211 42 68
Fax: 211-3670618
Emp.: 27
S.I.C.: 7311
Meinolf Winkelmeyer *(Mng. Dir.)*

TBWA de Plas **(1)**
25 rue du Pont-Neuf 75001
Paris, France
Tel.: 40 41 58 59
Telex: 670222
Fax: 40 26 62 50
Approx.Billings: $124,740,000
Emp.: 90
Advertising
S.I.C.: 7311
Uli Wiesendanger *(Founder)*
Claude Bonnange *(Founder)*
Pierre de Plas *(Pres. & Gen. Mgr.)*
Jean-Pierre Baudais *(Chief Fin. Officer & Corp. Sec.)*

TBWA Espana S.A. **(1)**
Profesor Waksman, 14 28036
Madrid, Spain
Tel.: 457-3008
Telex: 45221
Fax: 259-9872
Advertising
S.I.C.: 7311
Frutos Moreno *(Mng. Dir.)*

TBWA Hamburg GmbH **(1)**
Neuer Wall 50 2000
Hamburg, 36, Germany
Tel.: 040-369-0700
Telex: 17-403337
Fax: 040-369-07111
Emp.: 29

TBWA Holmes Knight Ritchie **(1)**
8 Crinan St.
London, WC2E 9DQ, United Kingdom
Tel.: 833-5544
Fax: 833-8751
Advertising
S.I.C.: 7311
Dick Knight *(Chm. Bd.)*
Alsadair Ritchie *(Mng. Dir.)*
Keith Smith *(Deputy Mng. Dir.)*
Jamie Davenport *(Deputy Mng. Dir.)*

T C MANUFACTURING COMPANY, INC.
1527 Lyons St.
Evanston, IL 60204
Tel.: 708-869-2320 **DE**
Fax: 708-866-8695
Year Founded: 1941
Assets: $39,000,000
Liabilities: $21,400,000
Net Worth: $17,600,000
Approx.Sls.: $63,000,000
Emp.: 450
Fiscal Year-end: 10/31/90
Export
Mfr. of Miscellaneous Plastic Products, Flexible Film Packaging, Laminating & Adhesive Coatings; Corrosion Prevention Products & Pharmaceuticals; Packaging Products
S.I.C.: 2834; 2899
Shiro F. Shiragao *(Chm. Bd., Pres. & Chief Exec. Officer)*
Herbert L. Stern, Jr. *(Chm.-Exec. Committee & Sec.)*
Peter Clemens *(V.P. & Chief Fin. Officer)*
Sally Claasen *(V.P.-Mfg.)*
Ernest Heplen *(V.P.-Engrng.)*
Sherrill MacDonald *(V.P.-Admin.)*
Richard Dokmo *(V.P.)*

Computer Systems/Hardware:
DEC

Outside Service Firm(s):

KPMG Peat Marwick*(Auditors)*
Peat Marwick Plaza, 303 E. Wacker Dr.
Chicago, IL 60601
Tel.: 312-938-1000

Gottlieb & Schwartz*(Legal Firm)*
69 Washington
Chicago, IL 60602
Tel.: 312-726-2122

LaSalle National Bank*(Major Banking Relationship)*
135 S. LaSalle St.
Chicago, IL 60603
Tel.: 312-443-2440
Fax: 312-443-2819

Divisions:

Pak-Sher Co. **(1)**
2500 N. Longview
Kilgore, TX 75662
Tel.: 903-984-8596
Fax: 903-984-1524
Mfrs. Plastic Bags
S.I.C.: 3089
William Mishkind *(Chief Oper. Officer)*
Gary Thompson *(Mgr.-Sls.)*
Gorgas E. Paulsen *(Mgr.-Sls.)*

Tape Coat Division **(1)**
1527 Lyon St.
Evanston, IL 60204
Mfr. of Corrosion Protection Tapes
S.I.C.: 2672
Richard C. Dokmo *(Pres.)*
John Blitstien *(V.P.-Engng.)*
George Harris *(V.P.-Pipeline Sls.)*
Jack Maki *(V.P.-Sls.)*

UDL Laboratories, Inc. **(1)**
1718 Northrock Court
Rockford, IL 61103-1201
Tel.: 815-282-1201
Tel.: 800-435-5272
Fax: 815-282-9391
Emp.: 200
Fiscal Year-end: 10/00/92
Computer Systems/Hardware:
IBM System 36
Distribute a Full Line of Generic Pharmaceuticals: Solid Orals & Liquid Dosage Form Designed for Institutional Use
S.I.C.: 5122
Michael Reicher *(Pres.)*
John Ford *(V.P.-Mktg. & Sls.)*
Tim Wait *(Controller)*
Dan Weist *(Dir.-Mktg.)*
Hal Korman *(Natl. Sls. Mgr.)*
Jackie Champion *(Mgr.-Pur.)*
Jan Meyers *(Mgr.-Personnel)*

TCC
3250 Mary St.
Miami, FL 33133
Tel.: 305-445-2493
Fax: 305-445-4255
Emp.: 12,000
Hotels & Office Buildings; Management & Land Developers
S.I.C.: 1522; 7011
Donald Lafton *(Co-Chm. Bd.)*
Sherwood M. Weiser *(Co-Chm. Bd. & Chief Exec. Officer)*
Tomas F. Hewitt *(Pres.)*
Peter Temling *(Chief Fin. Officer & Exec. V.P.-Fin.)*
Irving Zeldman *(Sr. Exec. V.P.)*
Kenneth J. Gaudet *(Sr. V.P.)*
Jeffrey J. Springer *(Sr. V.P.-Devel.)*
Peter Sibley *(V.P.)*

Outside Service Firm(s):

Mallah, Furman & Co.*(Auditors)*
Miami, FL

Greenberg, Traurig, Hoffman, Lipoff, Rosen & Quentel, P.A.*(Legal Firm)*
1221 Brickell Ave.
Miami, FL 33131
Tel.: 305-579-0500

Jefferson National Bank*(Major Banking Relationship)*
300 - 41st. Street
Miami Beach, FL 33140

TCH INDUSTRIES INC.
3040 Charlevoix Dr. S.E.
Grand Rapids, MI 49546
Tel.: 616-942-0505 **MI**
Year Founded: 1982
Approx.Sls.: $50,000,000
Emp.: 471
Manufacture Custom Zinc & Aluminum Die Castings
S.I.C.: 3363; 3364
Theodore Hohman *(Pres.)*
James A. Weston *(V.P.-Fin.)*
Principal(s):
Theodore Hohman

Outside Service Firm(s):

Coopers & Lybrand*(Auditors)*
161 Ottawa Ave., N.W.
Grand Rapids, MI 49503
Tel.: 616-458-7700

Law, Weathers & Richardson*(Legal Firm)*
Grand Rapids, MI

First Michigan Bank*(Major Banking Relationship)*
Grand Rapids, MI

TDA
(Formerly Telephone Directory Advertising, Inc.-Atlanta)
8399 Dunwoody Place
Atlanta, GA 30350
Tel.: 404-993-3222
Fax: 404-587-4765
Sales Range: $10-19 Million
Advertising Agency
S.I.C.: 7311
Gene Ray *(Pres.)*

TD INDUSTRIES INC.
13850 Diplomat Dr.
Dallas, TX 75234
Tel.: 214-888-9500 **TX**
Fax: 214-888-9507
Year Founded: 1946
Assets: $37,000,000
Liabilities: $25,900,000
Net Worth: $11,100,000
Approx.Sls.: $130,000,000
Emp.: 1,100
Mechanical Contractor; Wholesale Air Conditioning, Heating, Plumbing & Refrigeration Supplies, Equipment & Services
S.I.C.: 1711; 5074; 5075; 5078; 7623
J.B. Lowe, Jr. *(Chm. Bd., Pres. & Chief Exec. Officer)*
Mike Fitzpatrick *(Chief Fin. Officer & V.P.)*

No. of Mfg. Plants/Facilities: 1
No. of U.S. Offices: 8

Computer Systems/Hardware:
DEC-VAX

Outside Service Firm(s):

KPMG Peat Marwick*(Auditors)*
1601 Elm St., Ste. 1600
Dallas, TX 75201
Tel.: 214-754-2000
Fax: 214-754-2297

Liberty Mutual*(Commercial Insurance Carrier)*
175 Berkeley St.
Boston, MA

Locke, Purnell, Rain, Harrell*(Legal Firm)*
Republic Natl. Bank Tower
Dallas, TX 75208
Tel.: 214-744-4511

Team Bank*(Major Banking Relationship)*
P.O. Box 35207,
Dallas, TX 75235

TH&M ADVERTISING, INC.
2600 Michelson Dr., Ste. 1500
Irvine, CA 92715
Tel.: 714-756-8326
Fax: 714-756-2517
Year Founded: 1971
Approx.Billings: $18,000,000
Emp.: 20
Retail, Real Estate, High Tech & Business-to-Business
Jim Hughes *(Chm., Pres. & Creative Dir.)*
Judy Higashi *(Dir.-Opers.)*
Lisa Zwick *(Dir.-Pub. Rels.)*

Computer Systems/Hardware:
Macintosh

TIC UNITED CORPORATION
4645 North Central Expressway
Dallas, TX 75205
Tel.: 214-559-0580 **DE**
Fax: 214-559-9510
Approx.Sls.: $163,000,000
Emp.: 2,000
Fiscal Year-end: 12/31/91
Fabricated Metal Products; Agriculture Machinery; Transportation Equipment
S.I.C.: 3443; 3511; 3711; 4212
Stratton Georgoulis *(Chm. Bd., Pres. & Chief Exec. Officer)*
David R. Mayle *(V.P., Sec. & Gen. Counsel)*
Dean Marcy *(V.P.-Fin.)*
Karen Longtin *(Asst. Treas.)*
Randy S. Williams *(Asst. Corp. Controller)*
Thomas Baird *(Dir.-Employee Benefits)*
Barry Tonenholtz *(Tax Mgr.)*

No. of Mfg. Plants/Facilities: 13
No. of U.S. Offices: 1

Computer Systems/Hardware:
IBM AS/400, HP Spectrum 950, IBM System 36

Outside Service Firm(s):

Ernst & Young*(Auditors)*
2121 San Jacinto, Ste. 500
Dallas, TX 75201
Tel.: 214-969-8000

Northwestern National Life*(Group Insurer)*
20 Washington Ave. S.
Minneapolis, MN 55401

First City Bank, Texas-Dallas*(Major Banking Relationship)*
1401 Elm
Dallas, TX 75283
Tel.: 214-939-8000

Division:

Western Metal Finishing Division **(1)**
P.O. Box 1399, 10647 S. Garfield Ave.
South Gate, CA 90280
Tel.: 213-773-4210
Approx.Sls.: $6,000,000
Emp.: 20
Electroplating, Plating, Polishing, Anodizing & Coloring; Coating, Engraving & Allied Services; Aircraft Parts & Auxiliary Equipment
S.I.C.: 3471; 3479; 3728
John Didun *(Gen. Mgr.)*
Jeri Peterson *(Controller)*
John Stock *(Sls. Mgr.)*

Subsidiaries:

Atlas Foundry & Machine Co. **(1)**
3021 S. Wikeson St.
Tacoma, WA 98409
Tel.: 206-475-4600
Steel Castings, Alloy Steel Castings, Stainless Steel
S.I.C.: 3325
Jim Reder *(Pres.)*
Terry L. Snider *(V.P. & Comptroller)*

Hutchinson Wil-Rich Manufacturing Co. **(1)**
4645 N. Central Expwy.
Dallas, TX 75205
Tel.: 214-559-0580
Mfrs. Farm Machinery & Equipment
S.I.C.: 3523
William Corbett *(Chm. & Chief Exec. Officer)*

Subsidiaries:

Blumhardt Manufacturing Company **(2)**
W. Hwy 13
Wahpeton, ND 58075
Tel.: 214-559-9593
Mfrs. Farm Equip.
S.I.C.: 3523

Wil-Rich Noble Company **(2)**
W. Hwy 13
Wahpeton, ND 58075
Tel.: 214-559-9593
Mfrs. Farm Equip.
S.I.C.: 3523

Lone Star Forge Company **(1)**
4645 NorthCentral Expressway
Dallas, TX 75205
Tel.: 214-559-0580 (100%)
Metal Products Fabrication
S.I.C.: 3728; 3421; 3463

Subsidiary:

Kropp Forge Co. **(2)**
5301 W. Roosevelt Rd.
Chicago, IL 60650
Tel.: 312-652-6666
Approx.Sls.: $35,000,000
Emp.: 220
Aircraft Parts & Aux. Equip.; Nonferrous Forgings; Iron & Steel Forgings
S.I.C.: 3728; 3462; 3463
Nick Ruggiero *(Gen. Mgr.)*
Robert Kowske *(Sls. Dir.)*
Jim Pohl *(Controller)*

Nebraska Engineering Co. **(1)**
P.O. Box 12277,
Omaha, NE 68112
Tel.: 402-453-6912
Mfr. of Grain Handling Equipment
S.I.C.: 3523
Bill Hiltgen *(Chief Oper. Officer)*

TIC Investment Corp. **(1)**
4645 N. Central Expwy.
Dallas, TX 75205
Tel.: 214-559-0580
Venture Capitol
S.I.C.: 6799
Bill Hiltgen *(Gen. Mgr.)*

T. J. CINNAMONS LTD.
(Operation of Signature Foods, Inc.-A Holding Co.)
1010 W. 39th St.
Kansas City, MO 64111
Tel.: 816-931-9341 **MO**
Fax: 816-931-1446
Year Founded: 1985
Assets: $2,550,000
Liabilities: $2,565,000
Net Worth: $15,000
Approx.Sls.: $50,000,000
Emp.: 240
Fiscal Year-end: 12/31/90
Specialty Food Stores Franchisor; Cinnamon Rolls
S.I.C.: 5812
Ted Rice *(Chm. Bd. & Co-founder)*
Bill Teel *(Pres.)*
Sam Rice *(Exec. V.P. & Chief Oper. Officer)*
Joyce Rice *(V.P.-Training & Co-founder)*
David Stein *(V.P.-Fin., Chief Fin. Officer & Controller)*
Karen Jackson *(V.P.-Mktg. & Adv.)*
Debbie Buzick *(Franchise Coord.)*

Principal(s):
Ted Rice
Bill Teel
Joyce Rice

No. of Mfg. Plants/Facilities: 225
No. of U.S. Offices: 1

Computer Systems/Hardware:
IBM PC Network

Outside Service Firm(s):

Deloitte & Touche*(Auditors)*
1010 Grand Ave.
Kansas City, MO 64106-2232
Tel.: 816-474-6180

Fireman's Fund Insurance Co.*(Commercial Insurance Carrier)*
Kansas City, MO

Lincoln National Life Insurance Co.*(Group Insurer)*
Kansas City, MO

Smith, Gill, Fisher & Butts*(Legal Firm)*
One Kansas City Place, 35th Fl, 1200 Main St.
Kansas City, MO 64105
Tel.: 816-474-7400

Boatmen's First National Bank of Kansas City*(Major Banking Relationship)*
10th & Baltimore
Kansas City, MO 64183
Tel.: 816-221-2800
Fax: 816-691-7254

TLC BEATRICE INTERNATIONAL HOLDINGS INC.
9 West 57th St., 48th Fl.
New York, NY 10019
Tel.: 212-756-8900 **DE**
Fax: 212-888-3093
Earnings: $45,600,000
Approx.Rev.: $1,540,000,000
Emp.: 4,500
Fiscal Year-end: 12/31/91
Marketer of Ice Cream Products, Grocery Distributor, Grocery Stores, Broker of Dairy Products, Marketer of Food Processing Equipment, Producer of Soft Drinks & Beverages, Producer of Snack Foods
S.I.C.: 5141; 5084; 5149; 5142; 5143; 5145; 2086; 2099
Dumas M. Simeus *(Pres. & Chief Oper. Officer)*
John F. Sipple-Asher *(Pres.-Eur. Grocery Prods. Div.)*
Daniel Jux *(Pres.-Food Distr. Div.)*
Mark J. Thorne *(Chief Fin. Officer & V.P.-Fin.)*
Everett L. Grant, III *(Sr. V.P.-Spec. Asst. to Chm.-Fin.)*
Dennis P. Jones *(Sr. V.P.-Bus. Plng. & Devel.)*
Carl Brody *(V.P.-Dir. of Taxes)*
Randolph A.K. Cabban *(V.P.-Fin. Dir., Eur. Grocery Prods.)*
Rene S. Meily *(V.P.-Dir. of Communications)*
David A. Guarino *(V.P.-Controller)*
W. Kevin Wright *(V.P.-Gen. Counsel & Asst. Sec.)*
Charles Clarkson *(Sec.)*
N.S. Molberger *(Asst. Sec.)*

No. of Foreign Offices: 15

Outside Service Firm(s):

Deloitte & Touche*(Auditors)*
1633 Broadway
New York, NY 10019

Subsidiaries:

Adams International **(1)**
8948 N.W. 24th Terrace
Miami, FL 33172
Tel.: 305-592-3337
Markets Food Processing Machinery for the Snack Food Industry
S.I.C.: 5084
Roy Culver *(Pres.)*

Mantecados Payco **(1)**
113 Chardon Ave., Box 908
Hato Rey, PR 00919
Tel.: 809-758-9000
Markets Ice Cream under the Payco and Lady Richmond Brands
S.I.C.: 5143
Dennis Jones *(Gen. Mgr.)*

Non-U.S. Subsidiary:

Artic N.V. S.A. **(1)**
G. Huysmanspin 1 Lot 2000
Brussels, Belgium
Tel.: 378 1075 (100%)
Ice Cream & Desserts
S.I.C.: 2024

TMP Worldwide

TMP WORLDWIDE, INC.
1633 Broadway, 33rd Fl.
New York, NY 10019
Tel.: 212-977-4200
Fax: 212-956-2142
Year Founded: 1967
Approx.Billings: $397,000,000
Emp.: 1207
Advertising Agency Specializing in Planning & Placement Of Yellow Pages Advertising For National Advertisers
S.I.C.: 7311
Andrew J. McKelvey *(Chm. & Pres.)*
David Hosokawa *(Chief Exec. Officer)*
Paul M. Camara *(Sr. V.P.)*
Thomas G. Collison *(Sr. V.P. & Chief Fin. Officer)*
Harold L. Levy *(Sr. V.P.-Sls. & Mktg. & New Bus. Contact)*
Bernice Hazell *(V.P.-Customer Service)*
Robert Lamb *(V.P.- Mktg./Strategic Plng.)*
Frank J. Troise *(V.P.-Oper.)*
Nancy Cheppo *(Dir.-Human Resources)*

Branches:

ADS/TMP Worldwide **(1)**
4719 Hampden Lane
Bethesda, MD 20814
Tel.: 301-654-8560
Fax: 301-654-6201
S.I.C.: 7311
Chris Stimac *(Divisional Pres.)*

BTD/TMP Worldwide **(1)**
13252 Garden Grove Blvd., Ste. 100
Garden Grove, CA 92643
Tel.: 714-971-9930
Tel.: 800-621-4905
Fax: 714-971-9931
Approx.Billings: $13,300,000
Emp.: 39
National Yellow Pages Adv.
S.I.C.: 7311; 7211
Joan D. Olsen *(Pres.)*
Connie Shellenberger *(Agency Opers. Mgr.)*
Sondra Nash *(Data Processing Mgr.)*

Branch:

BTD/TMP Worldwide **(2)**
9708 Skillman, Ste. 101
Dallas, TX 75243
Tel.: 214-349-0001
Tel.: 800-527-0252
S.I.C.: 7311
Donna Shields *(Agency Supvr.)*

TMP Worldwide, Inc.—(Continued)

Communications Planning Corporation/TMP Worldwide **(1)**
2801 Townsgate Rd., Ste. 215
Westlake Village, CA 91361
Tel.: 818-991-5400
Fax: 818-991-5482
Approx.Billings: $75,000,000
Emp.: 32
National Yellow Pages Advertising & Media Buying
Ron Plotkin *(Pres.)*

Communications Planning Corporation/TMP Worldwide **(1)**
3880 RFD
Long Grove, IL 60047-7676
Tel.: 708-726-7300
Fax: 708-726-1333
Advertising
S.I.C.: 7311
Ron Plotkin *(Div. Pres.)*
Harvey Stein *(Sr. V.P.)*

Damart/TMP Worldwide **(1)**
7700 France Ave., South
Minneapolis, MN 55435
Tel.: 612-830-2286
Fax: 612-830-2567
Approx.Billings: $6,400,000
Emp.: 14
Yellow Page Adv.
Gerda Carlson *(Div. Exec. V.P.)*

Directory Data Management **(1)**
2514 So. 102nd St.
West Allis, WI 53227
Tel.: 414-546-6759
Fax: 414-546-6759
S.I.C.: 7311
Marty Felde *(Pres.)*

Douglas Bewick Associates/TMP Worldwide **(1)**
117 Park Ave.
West Springfield, MA 01089
Tel.: 413-781-3682
Fax: 413-731-8617
Approx.Billings: $3,000,000
Emp.: 8
Yellow Pages Adv.
Rose Hopkinson *(Div. V.P.)*
Lori Crane *(V.P., Admin.)*

DSI/TMP Worldwide **(1)**
P.O. Box 1067
Danville, IL 61834-1067
Tel.: 217-443-6255
Tel.: 800-621-5518
Fax: 217-443-6020
Emp.: 20
S.I.C.: 7311
Joe Glick *(Div. Pres.)*
Shirley L. Glick *(Branch Mgr. & Dir., Opers.)*

National Media Services, Inc. **(1)**
One Premier Plaza, 600 Morgan Falls Rd., Suite 125
Atlanta, GA 30350
Tel.: 404-551-5930
S.I.C.: 7311
Mark Church *(Pres.)*

TMP Worldwide, Inc. **(1)**
10700 Meridian Ave., No., Ste. 201
Seattle, WA 98133
Tel.: 206-361-6977
Fax: 206-361-9595
S.I.C.: 7311
Lance Willis *(Div. Pres.)*

Telephone Directory Advertising, Inc.-Cincinnati **(1)**
2260 Park Ave.
Cincinnati, OH 45206-2710
Tel.: 513-221-3206
Fax: 513-221-8708
S.I.C.: 7311
Bill Frank *(Pres.)*

TMP Worldwide, Inc. **(1)**
3785 N.W. 82nd Ave., Ste. 408
Miami, FL 33166
Tel.: 305-599-2513
Fax: 305-592-8748
S.I.C.: 7311
Dave Myer *(Dir., Mktg. Services)*

TMP Worldwide, Inc. **(1)**
3880 RFD
Long Grove, IL 60047
Tel.: 708-726-7770
Fax: 708-726-7797
S.I.C.: 7311
Lance Johnson *(Div. Sr. V.P.)*

TMP Worldwide, Inc. **(1)**
12800 Riverside Dr.
North Hollywood, CA 91607
Tel.: 818-762-3033
Fax: 818-766-9243
S.I.C.: 7311

TMP Worldwide, Inc. **(1)**
The TMP Bldg., 125 Hopping Brook Rd.
Holliston, MA 01746
Tel.: 508-429-8331
Fax: 508-429-7561
S.I.C.: 7311

TMP Worldwide, Inc. **(1)**
500 Turtle Cove Blvd., Ste. 150
Rockwall, TX 75087
Tel.: 214-722-2020
Fax: 214-722-2033
S.I.C.: 7311
Bruce Oppermann *(Div. V.P.)*

TMP Worldwide, Inc. **(1)**
6800 France Ave. South, Ste. 500
Edina, MN 55435
Tel.: 612-922-2300
Fax: 612-922-1028
S.I.C.: 7311
Alfred M. Cady *(Div. Pres.)*

TMP Worldwide, Inc. **(1)**
International Trade Center, 600 International Dr.
Mount Olive, NJ 07828
Tel.: 201-347-1357
Fax: 201-347-2654
S.I.C.: 7311
Ron Pearl *(Div. V.P.)*

TMP Worldwide, Inc. **(1)**
889 Ridge Lake Blvd., Ste. 210
Memphis, TN 38120
Tel.: 901-680-0112
Fax: 901-680-0125
S.I.C.: 7311
Susie Simon *(Dir., Opers.)*

TMP Worldwide, Inc. **(1)**
38C Grove St.
Ridgefield, CT 06877
Tel.: 203-438-0427
Fax: 203-431-3176
S.I.C.: 7311
R.W. (Bill) Grech *(Div. Pres.)*

TMP Worldwide, Inc. **(1)**
3425 Tatting Rd.
Matthews, NC 28105
Tel.: 704-846-1061
Fax: 704-846-1061
S.I.C.: 7311
Karen Cook *(Acct. Exec.)*

Telephone Marketing Programs, Inc. **(1)**
12800 Riverside Dr.
North Hollywood, CA 91607
Tel.: 818-980-2000
Fax: 818-980-1294
S.I.C.: 7311
Bud Kanne *(Pres.)*

YPMS/TMP Worldwide, Inc. **(1)**
10144 N. Port Washington Rd.
Mequon, WI 53092
Tel.: 414-241-8600
Fax: 414-241-3269
Approx.Billings: $48,503,000
Emp.: 141
Fiscal Year-end: 11/30/88
Computer Systems/Hardware:
Nixdorf
National Yellow Pages Advertising
S.I.C.: 7311
Ron Plotkin *(Chm. Bd.)*
Richard C. Miller *(Pres. & Chief Exec. Officer)*
James F. Ponce *(Div. Pres., Sec. & Gen. Mgr.)*
Robert B. Kennedy *(Exec. V.P.)*
Rudy N. Magnolia *(Sr. V.P.)*
David J. Madison *(Sr. V.P.)*
Mark O. Brown *(V.P., Dir. Analytical & Tech. Services)*
Helen B. Harper *(V.P., Human Resources)*
Kathleen L. Smith *(V.P., Publr. Info. Center)*
R.M. Tuchalski *(V.P., Chief Fin. Officer, Controller)*
George R. Boehm *(V.P., Dir. Media & Mkt. Research)*
Richard B. Miller *(Mktg. Services Mgr.)*
Tim Dittloff *(Mgr., Telemarketing)*

Branches:

TMP Worldwide, Inc. **(2)**
614 Superior Ave. W., Ste. 1120
Cleveland, OH 44113-1398
Tel.: 216-241-3650
Fax: 216-241-4668
A. J. Kosack *(Dir., Opers.)*

Yellow Pages Marketing Services, Inc.-Kansas City **(2)**
7301 Mission Rd., Ste. 107
Prairie Village, KS 66208
Tel.: 913-831-4300
Fax: 913-831-2348
Laura Hawkins *(Branch Mgr.)*

Yellow Pages Marketing Services, Inc.-Los Angeles **(2)**
18919 Nordhoff St., Ste. 4
Northridge, CA 91324
Tel.: 818-772-0077
Fax: 818-772-0250
Rudy Magnolia *(Sr. V.P.)*
Marilyn Magnolia *(Office Mgr.)*

Yellow Pages Marketing Services, Inc.-San Francisco **(2)**
232 Bay Vista Circle, Ste. 100
Sausalito, CA 94965
Tel.: 415-332-9484
Fax: 415-332-5748
Marilyn G. Young *(V.P., District Mgr.)*

Yellow Pages Marketing Services, Inc.-New York **(2)**
600 International Dr.
Mount Olive, NJ 07828
Tel.: 201-347-1357
Fax: 201-347-2654
David J. Madison *(Sr. V.P.)*
C.M. Attanasio *(Office Mgr.)*

Subsidiaries:

Bekins Group **(1)**
12800 Riverside Dr., 2nd Floor
North Hollywood, CA 91607
Tel.: 818-980-2000
Fax: 818-766-9243
Robert (Bud) Kane *(Div. Pres.)*

DDM/TMP Worldwide **(1)**
10144 N. Port Washington Rd.
Mequon, WI 53092
Tel.: 414-241-8608
Tel.: 800-558-6223
Fax: 414-241-3269
Martin Felde *(Div. Pres.)*

DSIC/TMP Worldwide **(1)**
1250 Fourteen Mile Rd.
Clawson, MI 48017
Tel.: 313-288-2266
Fax: 313-288-2268
Steve Snyder *(Chm.)*
Ed Albertson *(Pres.)*

DSI/TMP Worldwide **(1)**
Pointe Inverness Office Park, 7030 Pointe Inverness Way, Ste. 200
Fort Wayne, IN 46804
Tel.: 219-432-0948
Fax: 219-436-0307
Mark Church *(Div. Pres.)*

TMP Worldwide, Inc. **(1)**
7400 N. Shadeland Ave., Ste. 125
Indianapolis, IN 46250
Tel.: 317-594-3100
Fax: 317-594-3106
B.J. Ray *(Gen. Mgr.)*

TMP Worldwide, Inc. **(1)**
12825 Flushing Meadow Dr.
Saint Louis, MO 63131
Tel.: 314-965-0454
Fax: 314-965-7237

Non-U.S. Holdings:

Japan Directory Advertising Company, Ltd. (JDAC) **(1)**
303 Yotsuya Mansion, 1-22 Arakicho, Shinjuku-ku
Tokyo, 160, Japan
Tel.: 81-33-358-2441
Fax: 81-33-358-2866
Planning & Placement of Yellow Pages Advertising
Ken Takahashi *(Pres.)*

NAP-Ltd. **(1)**
131 Jarvis St., Ste. 202
Toronto, ON M5C 2H6, Canada
Tel.: 416-864-1990
Fax: 416-864-1897
John Yocom *(Pres.)*

NDAP/TMP Worldwide **(1)**
184 Front St. East, Ste. 201
Toronto, ON M5A4N3, Canada
Tel.: 416-864-1990
Fax: 416-864-1897
Approx.Billings: $10,000,000
Emp.: 22
National Yellow Pages Programs
John Yocom *(Div. Pres.)*
Gina Rocha *(Dir.-Opers.)*
Alan Levin *(V.P.-Sls.)*
Sam Tang *(Controller)*
Rosemary Beach *(Mktg. Mgr.)*

Programmes Marketing Annuaires (PMA) **(1)**
91 Avenue de la Republique 75011
Paris, France
Tel.: 33-1-48058600
Fax: 48052313
Michel Datchary *(Chm.)*
Jean-Marie Guille *(Mng. Dir.)*

Telephone Marketing Programs-SMET **(1)**
Via P. Coletta, 59 20137
Milan, Italy
Tel.: 39-2 546-5168
Tel.: 39-2 551-95460
Fax: 39-2 551-81976
Dr. Giuliano Frascari *(Mng. Dir.)*

TMP Ltd. **(1)**
Palmsaa House, Uphall Rd.,
Ilford, Essex United Kingdom IGI 2JS
Tel.: 44-81-514-1072
Fax: 44-81-514-4633
Brian Devine *(Mng. Dir.)*

TMP/Telephone Marketing Programs, Ltd. **(1)**
Palmsaa House, Uphall Rd.
Ilford, Essex IGI 2JS, United Kingdom
Tel.: 44-81-514-1072
Fax: 44-81-514-4633
Approx.Billings: $5,000,000
Emp.: 17
Yellow Pages Advertising
Brian Devine *(Mng. Dir.)*
Jerry Smythe *(Dir., Sales & Mktg.)*
Paul Devine *(Dir., Opers.)*

T O PLASTICS, INC.
2901 E. 78th St.
Minneapolis, MN 55425
Tel.: 612-854-2131 **MN**
Fax: 612-854-2154
Approx.Sls.: $13,000,000
Emp.: 170
Manufacture Plastic Products
S.I.C.: 3089
Robert A. Beech *(Pres. & Chief Exec. Officer)*
Charles Goers *(Gen. Mgr.)*
John E. Daubney *(Sec.)*
Dorothy Leffler *(Treas.)*

No. of Mfg. Plants/Facilities: 4

Computer Systems/Hardware:
Wang

Outside Service Firm(s):

Wilkerson, Guthmann & Johnson *(Auditors)*
Minneapolis, MN

TPS, Incorporated
(Name Changed to Carquest)

T & S BRASS & BRONZE WORKS, INC.
2 Saddlebrook Ct.
Travelers Rest, SC 29690
Tel.: 803-834-4102 DE
Fax: 803-834-3518
Year Founded: 1947
Approx.Sls.: $25,000,000
Emp.: 225
Fiscal Year-end: 12/31/89
Import Export
Plumbing Products; Faucets, Valves & Fittings For Commercial, Industrial & Institutional Projects
S.I.C.: 3432; 3494
Claude I. Theisen *(Pres. & Chief Exec. Officer)*
Craig Ashton *(V.P.-Mfg.)*
Dennis Bazzy *(V.P.-Engrng., Research & Devel.)*
Clifford R. Theisen *(V.P.-Fin. & Dir.-Data Processing)*
Joan L. Theisen *(Sec.)*
Rick Skelton *(Controller)*
Steve Abercrombie *(Dir.-Pur.)*
Carolyn Helderman *(Dir.-Personnel)*
Richard Goughneour *(Mgr.-Mfg. Services)*

No. of Mfg. Plants/Facilities: 1
No. of U.S. Offices: 1
No. of Foreign Offices: 1

Computer Systems/Hardware:
IBM

Outside Service Firm(s):

Ernst & Young*(Auditors)*
C & S Bank Tower, Two Shelter Centre, Ste. 800
Greenville, SC 29603

Hannoch, Weisman, Stern, Besser, Berkowitz & Kinne*(Legal Firm)*
Union, NJ

Bancorporation, Inc.*(Major Banking Relationship)*
Greenville, SC

TSC INDUSTRIES, INC.
320 Plus Park Blvd.
Nashville, TN 37217
Tel.: 615-366-4600 DE
Fax: 615-366-4650
Year Founded: 1938
Assets: $99,642,000
Earnings: $3,600,000
Liabilities: $82,379,000
Net Worth: $17,263,000
Approx.Sls.: $215,895,000
Emp.: 1,500
Fiscal Year-end: 12/28/91
Retail Chain of Auto & Home Supply Stores, Stocking Products for the Do-It-Yourself & Farm Markets
S.I.C.: 5399; 5251; 5531
Thomas J. Hennesy *(Chm. Bd. & Chief Exec. Officer)*
Joseph Scarlett *(Pres. & Chief Oper. Officer)*
Don Corwin *(Chief Information Officer)*
Gerry Newkirk *(Exec. V.P.)*
Thomas Flood *(V.P.-Admin. & Fin. & Treas.)*
Lee Haberer *(V.P.-Real Estate)*
Joseph D. Maxwell *(V.P.-Mktg.)*
John Pearson *(V.P.-Mdsg.)*
Dan Wright *(V.P.-Mngmt. Information Systems)*
Mike Kincaid *(Controller)*
Gwen Herald *(Sec.)*
Brad Schramek *(Dir.-Human Resources)*
Larry Witte *(Mgr.-Systems & Progressions)*
Principal(s):
Thomas J. Hennesy
Joseph Scarlett
Gerry Newkirk
Thomas Flood
Joseph D. Maxwell

No. of Mfg. Plants/Facilities: 146
No. of U.S. Offices: 1

Computer Systems/Hardware:
IBM AS 400

Outside Service Firm(s):

Price Waterhouse*(Auditors)*
4400 Harding Rd.
Nashville, TN 37205
Tel.: 615-292-5000

Alexander & Alexander*(Commercial Insurance Carrier)*
3319 West End Ave.
Nashville, TN 37202
Tel.: 615-383-9539

J. W. Carrell*(Group Insurer)*
Nashville, TN

First National Bank of Boston*(Investment Banker)*
P.O. Box 644,
Boston, MA 02102-0644
Tel.: 617-575-2900
Fax: 617-575-2549

Richard O'Neill & Allegart*(Legal Firm)*
885 Third Ave.
New York, NY 10022
Tel.: 212-207-1200
Fax: 212-750-9022

First National Bank of Boston*(Major Banking Relationship)*
P.O. Box 644,
Boston, MA 02102-0644
Tel.: 617-575-2900
Fax: 617-575-2549

Sovran Bank*(Pension Manager)*
Memphis, TN

TSI INDUSTRIES, INC.
8507 Rainswood Dr.
Landover, MD 20785
Tel.: 301-322-5577
Fax: 301-341-1121
Approx.Sls.: $15,000,000
Emp.: 115
Manufacture Aluminum Window Systems, Glass & Glazing Services
S.I.C.: 1793; 3442
Victor Cornellier *(Pres.)*
Kevin Moran *(Treas. & Sec.)*

Outside Service Firm(s):

Grant Thornton*(Auditors)*
Two Hopkins Plaza
Baltimore, MD 21201
Tel.: 410-685-4000

TSR, INC.
201 Sheridan Spring Rd.
Lake Geneva, WI 53147
Mailing Address:
P.O. Box 756,
Lake Geneva, WI 53147
Tel.: 414-248-3625
Fax: 414-248-0389
Year Founded: 1976
Approx.Sls.: $25,000,000
Emp.: 120
Fiscal Year-end: 6/30/90
Produces & Distributes Role Playing Games, Board Games; Magazine Publisher
S.I.C.: 3944; 2721; 5092
Lorraine Williams *(Pres.)*
Willard Martens *(V.P.-Fin., Treas. & Chief Oper. Officer)*
Michael Martin *(V.P.-New Prod. Devel.)*
John McCory, Jr. *(V.P.-Sls.)*
Richard Behling *(V.P.-Mktg.)*
Cindy Rick *(Adv. Coord.)*

Computer Systems/Hardware:
IBM

Outside Service Firm(s):

KPMG Peat Marwick*(Auditors)*
Peat Marwick Plaza, 303 E. Wacker Dr.
Chicago, IL 60601
Tel.: 312-938-1000

Hartford Life Insurance Co.*(Commercial Insurance Carrier)*
Hartford, CT 06104-2999

Provident Life & Accident Insurance Co.*(Group Insurer)*
P.O. Box 12015
Chattanooga, TN 37401
Tel.: 615-755-7088

Chadwell, Kayser, Ltd.*(Legal Firm)*
35 West Wacker Dr., Ste. 3300
Chicago, IL 60601-1698
Tel.: 312-419-7500

TST/IMPRESO, INC.
652 Southwestern Blvd.
Coppell, TX 75019
Mailing Address:
P.O. Box 506
Coppell, TX 75019
Tel.: 214-462-0100
Fax: 214-462-7764
Year Founded: 1976
Approx.Sls.: $75,000,000
Emp.: 250
Fiscal Year-end: 8/31/91
Import Export
Manufacture Manifold Business Forms
S.I.C.: 2761
Marshall Sorokwasz *(Pres. & Chief Exec. Officer)*
Richard Bloom *(Exec. V.P.)*
John Graves *(V.P.-Mfg.)*
Charles Edwin Meador *(V.P.-Fin.)*
Jacob Schmidt *(V.P.-Mktg.)*
Robert Kopitke *(Treas.)*
Donald E. Jett *(Sec.)*
Dan Berman *(Dir.-Sls. & Mktg.)*
John Lynch *(Dir-Exports)*

No. of U.S. Offices: 12

Computer Systems/Hardware:
IBM 34

Outside Service Firm(s):

Arthur Andersen & Co.*(Auditors)*
901 Main St., Ste. 5600
Dallas, TX 75202
Tel.: 214-741-8300

TTX CO.
101 N. Wacker Dr.
Chicago, IL 60606
Tel.: 312-853-3223 DE
Fax: 312-984-3790
Year Founded: 1955
Assets: $1,621,134,000
Liabilities: $1,105,283,000
Net Worth: $515,851,000
Approx.Sls.: $621,468,000
Emp.: 1,400
Fiscal Year-end: 12/31/91
Supplies Specialty & Standardized Freightcars to Railroads
S.I.C.: 4741
Raymond C. Burton, Jr. *(Pres. & Chief Exec. Officer)*
H.V. Logan *(Sr. V.P.-Fleet Mngmt.)*
R.S. Hulick *(V.P.-Equip.)*
Robert J. Williams *(V.P. & Gen. Counsel)*
R.E. Zimmerman *(V.P. & Chief Fin. Officer)*
T.D. Marion *(Treas.)*
F.J. Previti *(Controller)*
W.F. Todd *(Sec.)*

No. of Mfg. Plants/Facilities: 4
No. of U.S. Offices: 1

Computer Systems/Hardware:
IBM

Outside Service Firm(s):

KPMG Peat Marwick*(Auditors)*
Peat Marwick Plaza, 303 E. Wacker Dr.
Chicago, IL 60601
Tel.: 312-938-1000

TV HOST INC.
3935 Jonestown Rd.
Harrisburg, PA 17109
Mailing Address:
P.O. Box 1665,
Harrisburg, PA 17105
Tel.: 717-657-1700
Fax: 717-657-2921
Year Founded: 1966
Approx.Sls.: $25,000,000
Emp.: 125
Fiscal Year-end: 4/30/91
Customized Cable Publication for Major Cable System Operators
S.I.C.: 2721
David Stefanic *(Pres. & Chief Exec. Officer)*
Robert Newell *(Chief Oper. Officer)*
Nick Hughes *(Chief Fin. Officer, Treas. & Controller)*
Frank Dillahey *(Exec. V.P.)*
John Morthanos *(Dir.-Mktg.)*
Lou Pirnik, Jr. *(Adv. Dir.)*

Divisions:

TV Host Central, Inc. **(1)**
3201 N.E. Loop 820, Ste. 150
Fort Worth, TX 76137
Tel.: 817-847-1773
Anna Addison *(Gen. Mgr.)*

TV Host West, Inc. **(1)**
529 S.W. Third Ave., Ste. 200
Portland, OR 97204
Tel.: 503-241-9099
Fax: 503-299-6487
Curt Jantz *(Gen. Mgr.)*

TV Preview, Inc. **(1)**
201 King St.
Chappaqua, NY 10514
Tel.: 914-238-8481
Ron Ceisler *(Pres.)*

TVESCO, INC.
296 Adams Ave.
Memphis, TN 38101
Tel.: 901-525-4751
Fax: 901-525-0400
Approx.Sls.: $75,000,000
Emp.: 75
Holding Company; Electrical Apparatus & Equipment
S.I.C.: 5063; 6719
John L. Salmon *(Chm. Bd., Sec. & Treas.)*
Jack D. Liles *(Pres.)*
H.R. Baker III *(V.P.)*
J.E. Bryant, Jr. *(V.P.-Data Processing)*
William R. Lambert *(V.P.)*
Michael McNeely *(V.P.)*
David H. Williams *(V.P.-Fin.)*

Outside Service Firm(s):

Rhea & Ivy*(Auditors)*
Memphis, TN

Boone, Wellford, Clark, Langschmidt & Apperson*(Legal Firm)*
One Commerce Sq.
Memphis, TN 38103
Tel.: 901-523-0311

Commerce Union Bank*(Major Banking Relationship)*
Memphis, TN

TAB CHEMICALS, INC.
4801 S. Austin
Chicago, IL 60638
Tel.: 312-586-2000 IL
Approx.Sls.: $59,000,000
Emp.: 42
Fiscal Year-end: 12/31/91
Import Export
Food Additives & Preservatives; Industrial Chemicals & Surface Active Agents
S.I.C.: 5169
Thomas J. Turriff *(Chm. Bd., Pres. & Treas.)*

Tab Chemicals, Inc.—(Continued)

James M. Griffin *(Exec. V.P. & Gen. Mgr.)*
Patricia Turriff *(Sec.)*
Eric Frazier *(Dir.-Sls.)*
Frank McGrail *(Mgr.-Mktg. & Quality Control)*
Stella Schubert *(Intl. Coord.)*

Computer Systems/Hardware:
LAN

Outside Service Firm(s):

Terrell Weiss & Sugar Ltd.*(Auditors)*
Chicago, IL

American National Bank*(Major Banking Relationship)*
Chicago, IL

TABS ASSOCIATES
2904 Emmorton Rd.
Abingdon, MD 21009
Mailing Address:
P.O. Box 805,
Abingdon, MD 21009
Tel.: 410-515-7755
Fax: 410-515-7759
Emp.: 502
Presort Mail Service
S.I.C.: 7331
James Ford *(Pres.)*
Fred Ford *(Chief Exec. Officer)*
Paul White *(Exec. V.P.)*

Computer Systems/Hardware:
IBM

Outside Service Firm(s):

Lebson Tanputson*(Auditors)*
Baltimore, MD

Stump, Harvey & Cook*(Commercial Insurance Carrier)*
Hunt Valley, MD

Stump, Harvey & Cook*(Group Insurer)*
Hunt Valley, MD

White, Mendal, & Clark*(Legal Firm)*
Baltimore, MD

Maryland National Bank*(Major Banking Relationship)*
Baltimore, MD 21202

TACA INTERNATIONAL AIRLINES, S. A.
P.O. Box 20047
New Orleans, LA 70141
Tel.: 504-468-5202
Fax: 504-468-5231
Year Founded: 1931
Approx.Sls.: $80,000,000
Emp.: 1,150
Fiscal Year-end: 12/31/92
Passenger & Cargo Airline
S.I.C.: 4512
Enrique Borgo *(Chm. Bd.)*
Federico Bloch *(Pres. & Chief Exec. Officer)*
William Handal *(V.P. & Gen. Mgr.)*
Joaquin Palomo *(V.P.-Corp. Fin.)*
Alfredo Schildknecht *(V.P.-Technical)*
Antonio Carbonero *(Dir.-Govt. Affairs)*
Daniel Sternfels *(Dir.-Passenger Service)*
Enrique Luna *(Dir.-Fin.)*
Jaime Avila *(Dir.-Cargo)*
Jaime Gonzalez *(Dir.-Technical)*
Julio Flores *(Dir.-Corp. Planning)*
Mauricio Sol *(Dir.-Mktg. & Sls.)*
Carlos Alfaro *(Mgr.-Adv.)*
Alfredo Pasada *(Mgr.-Data Processing)*
Billy Barraza *(Mgr.-Sls.)*

Divisions:

Taca International Airlines **(1)**
P.O. Box 20047
New Orleans, LA 70141
Tel.: 504-468-5202
Peter J. Messina *(U.S. Regional Mgr.)*

Taca International Airlines, S. A. **(1)**
4299 N. W. 36th St.
Miami, FL 33166
Tel.: 305-358-0066
Fax: 305-871-2554
Eric Calzado *(Div. Mgr.)*

TACO INC.
1160 Cranston St.
Cranston, RI 02920
Tel.: 401-942-8000
Fax: 401-942-2360
Approx.Sls.: $35,000,000
Emp.: 400
Fiscal Year-end: 12/31/90
Pumping, Heat Transfer, Hydronic Control & Solar Equip.
S.I.C.: 3561; 3443; 3625
John Hazen White *(Pres.)*
Tom Lawrence *(Sr. V.P.-Sls. & Mktg.)*
John Ricottilli, Jr. *(Sr. V.P.-Opers.)*
Glen Graham *(Treas. & Controller)*

Affiliate:

Unipas, Inc. **(1)**
1142 Cranston St.
Cranston, RI 02920
Tel.: 401-942-8000
S.I.C.: 3561

TACO JOHN'S INTERNATIONAL, INC.
P.O. Box 1589,
Cheyenne, WY 82003-1589
Year Founded: 1969
Approx.Sls.: $137,000,000
Emp.: 4,500
Fiscal Year-end: 12/31/91
Taco John's Mexican Fast Food Franchised Restaurants
S.I.C.: 5812
Corporate Giving Program: Require Written Request for Donations. Do Not Give to Causes Benefitting Single Individuals. Priority Given to Health, Education, Child Welfare & Fitness
Harold Holmes *(Co-Chm. Bd.)*
James Woodson *(Co-Chm. Bd.)*
Pieter Roelofs *(Pres. & Chief Exec. Officer)*
Jeri Williams *(Chief Info. Officer)*
Regina Fitzgerald *(V.P.-Human Resources)*
Mike Gent *(V.P.-Franchise Development)*
Wayne Lutz *(V.P.-Corp. Affairs)*
Barry Sims *(V.P. & Chief Fin. Officer)*
Greg Thomas *(V.P.-Mktg.)*
Gary Wofford *(V.P.-Opers.)*
Steve Giersch *(Mgr.-Training & Devel.)*
Renee Middleton *(Mgr.-Mktg. & Production)*
Monica Miller *(Mgr.-Pub. Rels. & Res.)*
Rick Scharf *(Mgr.-Research & Devel.)*
Penny Olive *(Exec. Sec.)*
Stephanie Gooden *(Office Mgr./H.R. Administrator)*

Principal(s):
Harold Holmes
James Woodson

No. of U.S. Offices: 1

Computer Systems/Hardware:
IBM AS/400 System B20

Outside Service Firm(s):

McGladrey & Pullen*(Auditors)*
320 W. 25th
Cheyenne, WY
Tel.: 307-634-2151

Key Bank*(Major Banking Relationship)*
Cheyenne, WY

TACONY CORPORATION
1760 Gilsinn Lane
Fenton, MO 63026
Tel.: 314-349-3000 **MO**
Fax: 314-349-2333
Approx.Sls.: $40,000,000
Emp.: 125
Electric & Household Fans; Electric Household Sewing Machines; Vacuum Cleaners; Household Appliance Parts
S.I.C.: 5064
Kenneth Tacony *(Pres.)*
H. William Hinderer, III *(Chief Fin. Officer & V.P.-Fin. & Admin.)*
Emily Tacony *(Treas.)*

Outside Service Firm(s):

Coopers & Lybrand*(Auditors)*
One Metropolitan Square
St. Louis, MO 63102
Tel.: 314-436-3200

Julius H. Berg*(Legal Firm)*
St. Louis, MO

TACT HOLDING
538 Mission St.
South Pasadena, CA 91030
Tel.: 818-441-1177 **CA**
Fax: 818-441-9573
Year Founded: 1958
Approx.Sls.: $250,000,000
Emp.: 830
Holding Company; Grocery & Liquor Stores
S.I.C.: 5411; 5921; 6719
John Shields *(Pres. & Chief Exec. Officer)*
Eugene Pemberton *(V.P.)*
Leroy Watson *(V.P.)*
David Yoda *(V.P. & Sec.)*

Outside Service Firm(s):

KPMG Peat Marwick*(Auditors)*
725 S. Figueroa St.
Los Angeles, CA 90017
Tel.: 213-972-4000

Subsidiary:

Trader Joes Co. **(1)**
538 Mission St.
South Pasadena, CA 91030
Tel.: 818-441-1177
Grocery Chain & Liquor Stores
S.I.C.: 5411; 5921
John Shields *(Chm. Bd., Pres. & Chief Exec. Officer)*
Michael Parker *(Sr. V.P.)*
Eugene Pemberton *(V.P.)*
Leroy Watson *(V.P.)*
David Yoda *(Sec. & Treas.)*

TAGSONS PAPERS, INC.
99 Broadway
Albany, NY 12201
Mailing Address:
P.O. Box 1999
Albany, NY 12201
Tel.: 518-462-0200 **NY**
Fax: 518-462-9717
Year Founded: 1930
Emp.: 300
Import Export
Mfr. of Paper Products: Toweling, Textile Papers, Groundwood Disposables & Tissues
S.I.C.: 2621; 2676
Eugene J. Galante *(Pres. & Treas.)*
Nicholas T. Galante III *(Exec. V.P.)*
Thomas A. Galante II *(Exec. V.P.)*
Gary J. Boyea *(V.P.-Mfg.)*
Frances M. Galante *(V.P.)*
Violet A. Galante *(V.P.)*
Thomas J. Nash *(V.P.-Admin. & Controller)*
Joyce M. Galante *(Sec. & Legal Counsel)*
Harlene S. Palmieri *(Asst. Sec.)*
Ray Holoboski *(Dir.-Indus. Rels.)*
Shirley Duchesne *(Mgr.-Benefits)*
Jeff Ellis *(Mgr.-Pur.)*
Norman Ryskoski *(Resident Mgr.)*
Barbara Stanton *(Mgr.-Customer Service)*

Outside Service Firm(s):

KPMG Peat Marwick*(Auditors)*
74 N. Pearl St.
Albany, NY 12207
Tel.: 518-455-8809

Marine Midland Bank*(Major Banking Relationship)*
Albany, NY

TAJ INTERNATIONAL HOTELS
1315 16th St., N.W.
Washington, DC 20036
Tel.: 202-332-0711 **DE**
Fax: 202-332-6257
Approx.Sls.: $13,000,000
Emp.: 260
Hotels
S.I.C.: 7011
Lionnel Coulter *(Pres.)*
Leo Fernandes *(V.P.)*
Deepak Panjabi *(Sec.)*

Subsidiaries:

Canterbury Hotel **(1)**
1733 N Street N.W.
Washington, DC 20036
Tel.: 202-393-3000
Fax: 202-785-9581
S.I.C.: 7011
B. Ann Molloy *(Gen. Mgr.)*

Georgetown Marbury Hotel **(1)**
3000 'M' Street N.W.
Washington, DC 20007
Tel.: 202-726-5000
Fax: 202-337-4250
S.I.C.: 7011

Hampshire Hotel **(1)**
1310 New Hampshire Ave.
Washington, DC 20036
Tel.: 202-296-7600
Fax: 202-293-2476
S.I.C.: 7011
V. Barthwal *(Gen. Mgr.)*

Quality Hotel Downtown **(1)**
1315 16th St. N.W.
Washington, DC 20036
Tel.: 202-232-8000
Fax: 202-667-9827
S.I.C.: 7011
S. Segal *(Gen. Mgr.)*

Ramada Inn Downtown **(1)**
1430 Rhode Island Ave. N.W.
Washington, DC 20036
Tel.: 202-462-7777
Fax: 202-332-3519
S.I.C.: 7011
S. Vohra *(Gen. Mgr.)*

TAKATTA INC.
(Formerly Takatta/Gateway Industries, Inc.)
19900 Governors Dr.
Olympia Fields, IL 60461
Tel.: 708-957-4400 **DE**
Fax: 708-481-5013
Approx.Sls.: $80,000,000
Emp.: 1,250
Fiscal Year-end: 12/31/90
Manufacture Automobile Seatbelts
S.I.C.: 2399; 3714
James Takatta *(Chm. Bd.)*
Elmar Stanley *(Pres.)*
Frank J. Frick *(Chief Oper. & Chief Exec. Officer & Sec.)*
Alan C. Kromer *(Chief Fin. Officer & Controller)*
Shoji Uenishi *(Treas.)*
Andrew Dean *(Dir.-Pur.)*
John Martin *(Dir.-Data Processing)*
Doyle Brown *(Mgr.-Sls.)*
Esther Puszkiewicz *(Mgr.-Personnel)*
Don Crotty *(Sls.& Cost Analyst)*

Computer Systems/Hardware:
IBM System 38

Outside Service Firm(s):

Ernst & Young*(Auditors)*
233 S. Wacker Dr.
Chicago, IL 60606
Tel.: 312-368-1800
Fax: 312-645-3095

Home Life Insurance Co.*(Commercial Insurance Carrier)*
Chicago, IL

Arvey, Hodes, Costello & Burman*(Legal Firm)*
180 N. LaSalle St.
Chicago, IL 60601
Tel.: 312-855-5000

Harris Trust & Savings Bank*(Major Banking Relationship)*
111 W. Monroe St.
Chicago, IL 60690
Tel.: 312-461-2265
Tel.: 800-858-0840

Divisions:

DLS Div. **(1)**
222 E. 2nd St.
Bremen, IN 46506
Tel.: 219-546-4717
Approx.Sls.: $3,500,000
Emp.: 100
Manufacture Electrical Wire Harness
S.I.C.: 3679
Wayne Dickerhoff *(V.P.)*

Gateway Safety Systems Co. **(1)**
1990 Governors Dr.
Olympia Fields, IL 60461
Tel.: 708-957-5013 (100%)

Non-U.S. Holding:

Equipo Automotriz Americana S.A. de C.V. **(1)**
Calle 13 N625 Agua Prieta,
Sonora, Mexico
Tel.: 46-81401 (100%)
Emp.: 500
Automotive Seat Belts
S.I.C.: 2399
William K. Conway *(Chief Opr. Officer)*

TAL INC.
3645 W. Lake Rd.
Erie, PA 16505
Tel.: 814-838-4505
Fax: 814-838-6242/4276
Year Founded: 1974
Approx.Billings: $11,000,000
Emp.: 23
M. Tal Hindson *(Chm. & Chief Exec. Officer)*
Evan R. James *(Pres. & Chief Oper. Officer)*

TALK-A-PHONE CO.
5013 N. Kedzie Ave.
Chicago, IL 60625
Tel.: 312-539-1100
Fax: 312-539-1241
Export
Talk-A-Phone Intercom System for Office, Industrial & Apartment Use, Fast Food Drive Thru Systems, Self-Service Gas Station Systems& Americans with Disabilities Act Complaint Communication Systems & Hands-Free Emergency Phones (ADA Compliant)
S.I.C.: 3663; 3669
Abraham Shanes *(Chm. Bd. & Treas.)*
Z. Liberman *(Pres.)*
Samuel Shanes *(Exec. V.P. & Sec.)*
Dan F. Kagan *(Mgr.-Sls.)*

Computer Systems/Hardware:
Macintosh

Tallant LaPointe & Partners, Inc.
San Francisco • Denver

TALLANT LAPOINTE & PARTNERS, INC.
825 Battery St.
San Francisco, CA 94111
Tel.: 415-398-1940
Tel.: 800-875-7515
Fax: 415-398-4899
Year Founded: 1958
Approx.Billings: $10,000,000
Emp.: 11
Scientific, Healthcare, Biotech, Environmental, Chemical, Computer & Software, Electronics & Semiconductor Adv. & Mktg.
Corporate Giving Program: Charities
Robert E. LaPointe *(Chm. & Chief Exec. Officer)*
Buddy Hovatter *(Pres. & Creative Dir.)*

Computer Systems/Hardware:
MacIntosh, Hyundai Electronics America

TALLAPOOSA RIVER ELECTRIC CO-OP
Hwy. 431
South Lafayette, AL 36862
Mailing Address:
P.O. Box 675
South Lafayette, AL 36862
Tel.: 205-864-9331 **AL**
Fax: 205-864-0817
Year Founded: 1934
Approx.Sls.: $12,000,000
Emp.: 63
Distribution of Electric Power
S.I.C.: 4911
Jack Green *(Pres.)*
Lafayette Fuller *(V.P.)*
Bobby Jones *(Gen. Mgr.)*
Dorsey Hill *(Treas. & Sec.)*

Outside Service Firm(s):

Farmers & Merchants Bank*(Major Banking Relationship)*
Lafayette, AL

TALLGRASS TECHNOLOGIES CORP.
11100 W. 82nd St.
Overland Park, KS 66214
Tel.: 913-492-6002 **KS**
Fax: 913-492-2465
Year Founded: 1981
Assets: $7,000,000
Liabilities: $3,400,000
Net Worth: $3,600,000
Sales Range: $20-39 Million
Emp.: 140
Fiscal Year-end: 6/30/90
Disc & Tape Drives
S.I.C.: 3572
Ernest Wassman *(Chm. Bd.)*
Gary D. Bosnak *(Chief Fin. Officer)*

No. of Mfg. Plants/Facilities: 1
No. of U.S. Offices: 1
No. of Foreign Offices: 5

Computer Systems/Hardware:
IBM System 36

Outside Service Firm(s):

KPMG Peat Marwick*(Auditors)*
1000 Walnut St.
Kansas City, MO 64106

CIGNA*(Group Insurer)*
Los Angeles, CA

Connecticut General Life Insurance Co.*(Group Insurer)*
Seattle, WA

Watson, Ess, Marshall & Enggas*(Legal Firm)*
Grand Ave.
Kansas City, MO 64106
Tel.: 816-842-3132

Commerce Bank of Kansas City*(Major Banking Relationship)*
10th & Walnut
Kansas City, MO 64141
Tel.: 816-234-2000
Fax: 816-234-2548

TALON, INC.
626 Arch St.
Meadville, PA 16335
Tel.: 814-337-1281
Telex: 91-4497
Fax: 1-800-242-2566
Year Founded: 1893
Sales Range: $40-59 Million
Emp.: 900
Zephyr, Channel-Zip, Omni, Talon Slide Fasteners & Zippers, Apparel & Textiles
S.I.C.: 2399; 2389; 3965
Steven Zambito *(Pres. & Chief Exec. Officer)*
Larry L. Crawford *(V.P.-Fin. & Treas.)*
Andrew G. Himes *(V.P.-Admin. & Sec.)*
Daniel Larkin *(V.P.-Mfg.)*
James Thornley *(V.P.-Mktg. & Sls.)*
John Powell *(Controller)*
Richard Osborne *(Dir.-Mngmt. Information Systems)*
Charles Jenkins *(Mgr.-Pur.)*
Jeffrey Stevenson *(Mktg. & Adv. Mgr.)*

No. of Mfg. Plants/Facilities: 7
No. of U.S. Offices: 3

Computer Systems/Hardware:
IBM System 4341

Outside Service Firm(s):

Coopers & Lybrand*(Auditors)*
600 Grant St., 35th Fl.
Pittsburgh, PA 15219
Tel.: 412-355-8000
Fax: 412-355-8089

General American Life Insurance Co.*(Group Insurer)*
700 Market
Saint Louis, MO 63101
Tel.: 314-525-5458
Fax: 314-525-3677

Edwards & Angell*(Legal Firm)*
2700 Hospital Trust Twr.
Providence, RI 02903
Tel.: 401-274-9200

Continental Bank N. A.*(Major Banking Relationship)*
231 S. LaSalle St.
Chicago, IL 60697
Tel.: 312-828-2345
Tel.: 800-426-5754
Telex: 312-828-1783

Pennbank*(Pension Manager)*
Meadville, PA

TAMAQUA CABLE PRODUCTS CORPORATION
Willow St.
Schuylkill Haven, PA 17972
Mailing Address:
P.O. Box 347,
Schuylkill Haven, PA 17972
Tel.: 717-385-4381 **PA**
Twx: 834573
Fax: 717-385-1092
Year Founded: 1969
Approx.Sls.: $50,000,000
Emp.: 135
Import Export
Manufacture Electrical Cables
S.I.C.: 3351
William H. Combs *(Chm. Bd.)*
William H. Combs III *(Pres.)*
George Combs *(V.P.-Mktg.)*
Mike Home *(V.P.-Mfg.)*
Andrew Pavick *(V.P.-Fin.)*
John Sullivan *(V.P.-Matls.)*

Outside Service Firm(s):

Deloitte & Touche*(Auditors)*
Ste. 200, Two Windsor Dr., 7540 Windsor Dr.
Allentown, PA 18195
Tel.: 215-366-5100

Dechert, Price & Rhoads*(Legal Firm)*
4000 Bell Atlantic Tower, 1717 Arch St.
Philadelphia, PA 19103
Tel.: 215-994-4000
Tel.: 2000

Pennsylvania National Bank*(Major Banking Relationship)*
Pottsville, PA

TAMAROFF BUICK INC.
28585 Telegraph Rd.
Southfield, MI 48034
Tel.: 313-353-1300 **DE**
Fax: 313-353-7058
Year Founded: 1969
Assets: $15,775,000
Liabilities: $9,900,000
Net Worth: $5,875,000
Approx.Sls.: $65,000,000
Emp.: 150
Fiscal Year-end: 6/30/90
Automobile Dealership
S.I.C.: 5511
Marvin Tamaroff *(Pres.)*
Anthony Jerome *(V.P.)*
Susan Deeb *(Sec. & Treas.)*

Outside Service Firm(s):

Plante & Moran*(Auditors)*
Detroit, MI

Hoffert, Litt & Solway*(Legal Firm)*
Southfield, MI

National Bank of Detroit*(Major Banking Relationship)*
611 Woodward
Detroit, MI 48226
Tel.: 313-225-1000

Security Bank & Trust Co.*(Major Banking Relationship)*
Southgate, MI

Subsidiary:

Tamaroff Leasing Co. **(1)**
28585 Telegraph Rd.
Southfield, MI 48034
Tel.: 313-353-1300
Car Rental & Leasing
S.I.C.: 7514; 7515
Marvin Tamaroff *(Pres.)*
William Wurst *(Sec. & Treas.)*
Anthony Jerome *(Gen. Mgr.)*

THE TANEY CORPORATION
5130 Allendale Lane
Taneytown, MD 21787
Tel.: 410-756-6671 **MD**
Fax: 410-756-4103
Year Founded: 1962
Approx.Sls.: $20,000,000
Emp.: 220
Mfr. of Wood Stairs & Wood Stair Parts
S.I.C.: 2431
Eric E. Glass *(Pres.)*
Audrey Glass *(V.P.)*
Brian Glass *(V.P.)*
Jeff Glass *(V.P.)*
Ralph E.F. May *(Controller)*

Outside Service Firm(s):

McLean, Koeler, Sparks & Hammond*(Auditors)*
Westminster, MD

Levan, Schimel, Richman & Belman*(Legal Firm)*
Baltimore, MD

The Taney Corporation—(Continued)

Signet Bank*(Major Banking Relationship)*
P.O. Box 1077, 7 St. Paul St.
Baltimore, MD 21203

TANG INDUSTRIES INC.
1965 Pratt Blvd.
Elk Grove Village, IL 60007
Tel.: 708-806-7600 **DE**
Telex: 28-0576 TANGIND
Fax: 708-806-7220
Year Founded: 1961
Approx.Rev.: $775,000,000
Emp.: 2,000
Fiscal Year-end: 12/31/91
Import Export
Holding Company; Metal Industries
S.I.C.: 6719
Cyrus Tang *(Chm. Bd., Pres., & Chief Exec. Officer)*
Michael Tang *(Exec. V.P.)*
F.D. Sove *(V.P.)*
Robert Burke *(Gen. Counsel)*
Bertrand Chung *(Mgr.-Mngmt. Information Systems)*
Guy Sisto *(Mgr.-Insurance Services & Credit Dept.)*
Norine Yesulis *(Mgr.-Personnel)*
Kurt R. Swanson *(Asst. to the Pres.)*

Computer Systems/Hardware:
IBM 4341

Outside Service Firm(s):

Ernst & Young*(Auditors)*
233 S. Wacker Dr.
Chicago, IL 60606
Tel.: 312-368-1800
Fax: 312-645-3095

Continental Bank N. A.*(Major Banking Relationship)*
231 S. LaSalle St.
Chicago, IL 60697
Tel.: 312-828-2345
Tel.: 800-426-5754
Telex: 312-828-1783

Subsidiaries:

National Material Limited Partnership **(1)**
1965 Pratt Blvd.
Elk Grove Village, IL 60007
Tel.: 708-806-7600 (100%)
Steel Service Center
S.I.C.: 5051

Subsidiaries:

National Lamination Co. **(2)**
555 Santa Rosa Dr.
Des Plaines, IL 60010
Tel.: 708-298-7676 (100%)
Electrical Steel Laminations
S.I.C.: 3399
R. Del Boccio *(Gen. Mgr.)*

National Metal Products Co. **(2)**
100 Leland Ct., P.O. Box 827
Bensenville, IL 60106
Tel.: 708-766-9050 (100%)
Steel Stampings
S.I.C.: 3469
Jack Garvey *(Chief Oper. Officer)*

Scrap Corporation of America **(2)**
1965 Pratt Blvd.
Elk Grove Village, IL 60007
Tel.: 708-806-7600 (100%)
Steel & Non-Ferrous Metals Processing
S.I.C.: 3356; 3312
Howard Foster *(Chief Oper. Officer)*

Tower Metal Products **(2)**
301 N. Hill
Fort Scott, KS 66701
Tel.: 316-223-1215
Secondary Aluminum & Ingot
S.I.C.: 3341
Audie Tang *(Chief Oper. Officer)*

Taber Metals, Inc. **(1)**
P.O. Drawer 1418
Russellville, AR 72801
Tel.: 501-968-1021
Custom Aluminum Extrusions & Billet
S.I.C.: 3341
M.E. Rains *(Gen. Mgr.)*

TANNER CO. INC.
Oak Springs Rd.
Rutherfordton, NC 28139
Mailing Address:
P.O. Box 1139
Rutherfordton, NC 28139
Tel.: 704-287-4205 **NC**
Fax: 704-287-7771
Fax: 704-286-2072
Year Founded: 1931
Approx.Sls.: $55,000,000
Emp.: 750
Fiscal Year-end: 5/31/90
Import
Manufacture Women's Dresses & Sportswear
S.I.C.: 2335; 2331; 2337
Simpson B. Tanner III *(Chm. Bd.)*
James T. Tanner *(Pres. & Chief Exec. Officer)*
Chap Johnston *(Chief Oper. Officer)*
Al Andrews *(Pres.-Retail & Tanner Div.)*
Al Joyner *(Pres.-Mfg.)*
Joan Ussery *(Pres.-Doncaster Div.)*
Michael S. Tanner *(Exec. V.P.)*
Donald Crawford *(V.P.-Private Labels)*
Tom Downs *(V.P.-Corp. Plng. & Human Resources)*
J. Richard Wilkins *(V.P.-Admin.-Wholesale Div.)*
Scott Womack *(V.P. & Chief Fin. Officer)*
James H. Baughman *(Dir.-Data Processing)*
Sherry Owens *(Dir.-Personnel)*
Principal(s):
Simpson B. Tanner III
James T. Tanner
Michael S. Tanner

No. of Mfg. Plants/Facilities: 3

Outside Service Firm(s):

McGladrey & Pullen*(Auditors)*
Charlotte, NC

Fleming, Robinson, Bradshaw & Hinson, P.A.*(Legal Firm)*
First Union Plz.
Charlotte, NC 28801
Tel.: 704-377-2536

NationsBank Carolinas*(Major Banking Relationship)*
One NCNB Plaza T18-7
Charlotte, NC 28255

TANNING RESEARCH LABS., INC.
(d/b/a Hawaiian Tropic Advertising)
1190 U.S. 1 North
Ormond Beach, FL 32174
Mailing Address:
P.O. Box 5111,
Daytona Beach, FL 32118-5111
Tel.: 904-677-9559
Tel.: 800-874-4844
Fax: 904-677-9595
Year Founded: 1969
Emp.: 190
Manufacture Hawaiian Tropic, Ski Pro & Ultra Sun Formula Skin Care Products
S.I.C.: 2844
Ronald J. Rice *(Pres.)*
Larry L. Adams *(V.P. & Gen. Counsel)*
Stephen Hickey *(V.P.)*
William Jenning *(V.P.-Fin.)*
Jack Surrette *(V.P.-Mktg. & Product Devel.)*
Shelly Coluccio *(Dir.-Mktg.)*
Jeff Lalanne *(Dir.-Adv.)*

Outside Service Firm(s):

Price Waterhouse*(Auditors)*
Orlando, FL

NationsBank Florida*(Major Banking Relationship)*
Jacksonville, FL

TAPCO PRODUCTS COMPANY
45657 Port St.
Plymouth, MI 48170-6010
Tel.: 313-451-8272
Fax: 313-451-0702
Approx.Sls.: $20,000,000
Emp.: 20
Sheet Metalworking Machines, Plastic Shutters, Construction Materials
S.I.C.: 3542; 3089; 5039
Walter G. Marsh *(Chief Exec. Officer)*
Richard MacLeod *(Pres.)*
Leonard M. Visosky *(V.P. & Sec.)*
Jack Wallace *(Gen. Mgr.)*

Outside Service Firm(s):

Comerica Bank*(Major Banking Relationship)*
211 W. Fort St.
Detroit, MI 48226
Tel.: 313-222-3300

TAPEMARK
(Formerly Tapemark Company)
150 E. Marie Ave.
West St. Paul, MN 55118
Tel.: 612-455-1611 **MN**
Fax: 612-450-8428
Year Founded: 1955
Approx.Sls.: $36,000,000
Emp.: 280
Import Export
Mfr. of Pressure Sensitive Label Products; Medical Products, Die Cutting & Automatic Labelling Systems
S.I.C.: 2672; 2675
Corporate Giving Program: 1991- 5.2% of income given to charitable causes in areas of education, social issues, poverty, hunger & the creative arts. Sponsor an annual golf tournament and all proceeds go to charity.
Robert C. Klas *(Chm. Bd.)*
Robert C. Klas, Jr. *(Pres.)*
James T. Burmeister *(V.P. & Chief Fin. Officer)*
Donald M. Weber *(V.P.-Corp. Plng.)*
William L. Klas *(Sec. & Treas.)*
Robert Couture *(Dir.-Personnel)*
Thomas Yetter *(Mgr.-Sls.)*
Charles Von Hinueber *(Pur. Agent)*

No. of Mfg. Plants/Facilities: 5
No. of U.S. Offices: 8

Computer Systems/Hardware:
NCR

TARACORP, INC.
3490 Piedmont Rd., Ste. 1311
Atlanta, GA 30305
Tel.: 404-233-1971 **GA**
Fax: 404-233-4536
Year Founded: 1884
Assets: $15,000,000
Liabilities: $5,000,000
Net Worth: $10,000,000
Approx.Sls.: $50,000,000
Emp.: 350
Import Export
Manufacture Solders, X-ray & Nuclear Shielding, Plumbing Products, Lead Shot
S.I.C.: 3356
Louis J. Taratoot *(Chm., Pres. & Chief Exec. Officer)*
Stanton Sobel *(Vice Chm. & Treas.)*
R. Kim Taratoot *(Exec. V.P.)*
Mark Taylor *(Sr. V.P.)*
Larry Durben *(Controller)*
Virginia Murphy *(Mgr.-Human Res.)*

No. of Mfg. Plants/Facilities: 4

Computer Systems/Hardware:
IBM System 36

Outside Service Firm(s):

Deloitte & Touche*(Auditors)*
100 Peachtree St., Ste. 1700
Atlanta, GA 30303-1943
Tel.: 404-220-1500
Fax: 404-220-1583

Prudential/Pru-Care*(Group Insurer)*
Jacksonville, FL

Bank South, N.A.*(Major Banking Relationship)*
P.O. Box 4387
Atlanta, GA 30302
Tel.: 404-529-4111

Trust Company Bank*(Major Banking Relationship)*
P.O. Box 4655,
Atlanta, GA 30302

William M. Mercer Incorporated*(Pension Manager)*
Atlanta, GA

Subsidiaries:

Taracorp Evans, Inc. **(1)**
740 Lambert Dr.
Atlanta, GA 30324
Tel.: 404-233-1971

Taracorp Imaco, Inc. **(1)**
P.O. Box S-Salem Station
Winston-Salem, NC 27107
Tel.: 919-777-8600

Taracorp Industries, Inc. **(1)**
16th & Cleveland Blvd.
Granite City, IL 62040
Tel.: 618-451-4400

TARCO
P.O. Box 17875
North Little Rock, AR 72117
Tel.: 501-945-4506
Fax: 501-945-7718
Year Founded: 1977
Sales Range: $20-39 Million
Emp.: 100
Manufacture Roofing Materials
S.I.C.: 2952; 3272; 3259; 3444; 3281
David Snowden *(Pres. & Chief Exec. Officer)*
David Snowden Jr. *(Controller)*
Darla Sherry *(Mgr.-Office)*

Computer Systems/Hardware:
IBM System 23

Outside Service Firm(s):

Rasco, Burris & Winter*(Auditors)*
Little Rock, AR

Arkansas Blue Cross & Blue Shield, Inc.*(Group Insurer)*
Little Rock, AR

Griffith Smith*(Legal Firm)*
N. Little Rock, AR

One Bank*(Major Banking Relationship)*
N. Little Rock, AR

Subsidiary:

Tarco of Texas, Inc. **(1)**
2403 E. 6th St.
Belton, TX 76513
Tel.: 817-939-3775
Glen Passmore, Jr. *(Gen. Mgr.)*

TAREN HOLDINGS, INC.
6040 Bandini Blvd.
Los Angeles, CA 90040
Tel.: 213-726-1262
Fax: 213-726-7975
Year Founded: 1989
Approx.Sls.: $200,000,000
Emp.: 6,430
Import Export

Holding Company; Women's, Misses' & Juniors' Apparel
S.I.C.: 2339; 2331; 2337; 2369; 2361; 5632; 6719
Michael C. Proies *(Pres.)*
William Bussiere *(Chief Fin. Officer)*
Jerry Crosby *(V.P.-Intl. Licensing)*
Tom Lesinski *(V.P.-Mktg.)*
Paul L. Coyne *(Treas.)*

Outside Service Firm(s):

Citibank N.A.*(Major Banking Relationship)*
Corporate Trust Services, 399 Park Ave.
New York, NY 10043
Tel.: 212-559-1605

Subsidiaries:

Catalina **(1)**
6040 Bandini Blvd.
Los Angeles, CA 90040
Tel.: 213-726-1262
Fax: 213-726-7975
Emp.: 1,500
Fiscal Year-end: 12/31/90
Design & Manufacture Catalina Swimsuits & Sportswear
S.I.C.: 2389
Michael C. Proies *(Pres.)*
June Wylie *(Adv. Dir.)*

Cole of California **(1)**
2615 Fruitland Ave.
Los Angeles, CA 90058
Tel.: 213-587-3112
Fax: 213-581-3908
Approx.Sls.: $80,000,000
Emp.: 700
Fiscal Year-end: 7/31/90
Export
Mfr. of Ladies Swimwear
S.I.C.: 2389
Terry Allen *(Pres.-Swimwear/Taren)*
Mike Proiss *(Chief Exec. Officer/Taren)*
Bill Bussier *(Chief Fin. Officer/Taren)*
Anne Cole *(Sr. V.P.)*
Tom Lesinski *(V.P.-Mktg./Taren)*
Bill Singletary *(Controller)*
Kellie Lovejoy *(Dir.-Adv. & Pub. Rels.)*
Martha Ramos *(Dir.-Quality Control)*
Sally O'Hare *(Dir.-Human Resources/Taren)*
Andy Beattie *(Mgr.-Natl. Sls.)*
Amelia DeCastro *(Mgr.-Export)*

TARGET ENTERPRISES LTD.
3375 Barham Blvd.
Hollywood, CA 90068
Tel.: 213-462-1234
Year Founded: 1975
Approx.Billings: $28,500,000
Emp.: 12
Media Buying & Planning
David L. Bienstock *(Pres.)*
Kathy McNabb *(V.P., Dir. Opers.)*

TARGET SPORTSWEAR, INC.
1290 Ave. of the Americas, Ste. 1800
New York, NY 10104
Tel.: 212-541-6800
Fax: 212-586-2815
Emp.: 1,200
Men's Clothing; Ladies' Apparel
S.I.C.: 2311; 2339; 5136; 5137
Robert Bayer *(Pres.)*
H.T. Roy *(Sr. V.P.-Admin.)*
Jerry Heidelberg *(Controller)*
Robert Fitzmaurice *(Mgr.-Indus. Rel.)*

Outside Service Firm(s):

Joseph Herbert & Co.*(Auditors)*
330 Seventh Ave.
New York, NY 10001

Hyde Point Fashions **(1)**
485 Seventh Ave., 5th Fl.
New York, NY 10018
Tel.: 212-594-4321

John Peel Ltd. **(1)**
1290 Ave. of the Americas
New York, NY 10104
Tel.: 212-541-6800

TARGET STAMPED PRODUCTS CORP.
8091 State Rte. 5
Kinsman, OH 44428
Mailing Address:
P.O. Box L,
Kinsman, OH 44428
Tel.: 216-876-4511
Fax: 216-876-4632
Year Founded: 1948
Approx.Sls.: $12,000,000
Emp.: 175
Fiscal Year-end: 5/30/92
Mfr. of Steel Stampings & Dies
S.I.C.: 3469; 3544
Harvey H. Haynam *(Chm. & Chief Exec. Officer)*
Roy W. Van Kanegan, Jr. *(Pres., Treas. & Sec.)*
Dan Moore *(Mgr.-Sls.)*
Bruce Betts *(Pur. Agent)*

Computer Systems/Hardware:
IBM 36

Targetcom INC

TARGETCOM, INC.
The North Pier Terminal, 401 E. Illinois, Ste. 525
Chicago, IL 60611
Tel.: 312-822-1100
Year Founded: 1988
Approx.Billings: $10,700,000
Emp.: 8
Direct Response
Jay Miller *(Pres.)*
Roger Sinnes *(V.P.-EnviroCom Div. & New Bus. Contact)*

Computer Systems/Hardware:
Macintosh

TARLOW ADVERTISING
950 Third Ave.
New York, NY 10022
Tel.: 212-826-0399
Fax: 212-308-6176
Fax: 212-308-8708
Year Founded: 1988
Approx.Billings: $160,000,000
Emp.: 74
Dick Tarlow *(Pres., New Bus. Contact & Creative Dir.)*
Russell Gilsdorf *(Exec. V.P., Creative Dir. & Media Dir.)*
John DeAngelis *(Sr. V.P., Chief Fin. Officer)*
Maria Curran *(V.P., Acct. Supvr.)*
Douglas Soraci *(V.P., Acct. Supvr.)*
Jane Wheatley *(V.P., Acct. Supvr.)*

TARLTON CORPORATION
5500 W. Park Ave.
Saint Louis, MO 63110-1898
Tel.: 314-647-6000 **MO**
Fax: 314-647-1940
Year Founded: 1946
Assets: $23,000,000
Liabilities: $19,050,000
Net Worth: $3,950,000
Approx.Sls.: $60,000,000
Emp.: 250
Fiscal Year-end: 12/31/90
Contractors for Commercial, Industrial & Institutional Utilities & Health Care Markets
S.I.C.: 1629; 1541; 1623
Robert P. Elsperman, P.E. *(Chm. Bd. & Chief Exec. Officer)*
Robert D. Siess, P.E. *(Pres. & Chief Oper. Officer)*
George Biderman *(V.P.-Mktg.)*
Gary D. Cervanka, P.E. *(V.P.)*
Daniel E. Frisbee, P.E. *(V.P.)*
John J. Fisher *(Controller & Asst. Sec.)*
John Hale *(Sec.)*
Nadine Gremler *(Corp. Lib. & Sec.)*
David Moore *(Dir.-Mngmt. Information Systems)*
Ron Webelhuth *(Dir.-Purch. & Construction Res.)*
Patricia A. Allers *(Mgr.-Personnel)*
Principal(s):
Robert P. Elsperman, P.E.

No. of U.S. Offices: 1

Computer Systems/Hardware:
IBM System 36

Outside Service Firm(s):

Deloitte & Touche*(Auditors)*
One Cascade Plaza, Ste. 1600
Akron, OH 44303-1187
Tel.: 216-253-2022

Home Life Insurance Co.*(Commercial Insurance Carrier)*
New York, NY

Fireman's Fund Insurance Co.*(Group Insurer)*
San Francisco, CA

General American Life Insurance Co.*(Group Insurer)*
700 Market
Saint Louis, MO 63101
Tel.: 314-525-5458
Fax: 314-525-3677

Evans & Dixon*(Legal Firm)*
St. Louis, MO

Commerce Bank of Kansas City*(Major Banking Relationship)*
10th & Walnut
Kansas City, MO 64141
Tel.: 816-234-2000
Fax: 816-234-2548

Commerce Bank of Kansas City*(Pension Manager)*
10th & Walnut
Kansas City, MO 64141
Tel.: 816-234-2000
Fax: 816-234-2548

TARRANT SERVICE AGENCY, INC.
1830 Cargo Ct.
Louisville, KY 40299
Mailing Address:
P.O. Box 99586,
Louisville, KY 40269
Tel.: 502-491-2511
Fax: 502-491-2717
Earnings: $250,000
Sales Range: $10-19 Million
Emp.: 30
Fiscal Year-end: 12/31/90
Distributor of Trane HVAC Replacement Parts
S.I.C.: 5075
R. Lane Tarrant *(Chm. Bd., Pres. & Chief Exec. Officer)*
Joseph W. Grom *(V.P.)*
Jo Campbell *(Corp. Sec. & Office Mgr.)*

Computer Systems/Hardware:
Qantel System 40

Outside Service Firm(s):

Ray Strothman & Co.*(Auditors)*
Louisville, KY

Citizens Fidelity Bank & Trust Co.*(Major Banking Relationship)*
Citizens Plaza, P.O. Box 3300
Louisville, KY 40232
Tel.: 502-581-3389

New York Life*(Pension Manager)*
51 Madison Ave.
New York, NY 10010
Tel.: 212-576-6367
Fax: 212-576-6630

SARKES TARZIAN, INCORPORATED
205 N. College Ave.
Bloomington, IN 47401
Mailing Address:
P.O. Box 62
Bloomington, IN 47402
Tel.: 812-332-7251
Fax: 812-331-4575
Sales Range: $20-39 Million
Emp.: 250
Fiscal Year-end: 6/30/91
Radio & TV Broadcasting
S.I.C.: 4832; 4833
Thomas Tarzian *(Chm. Bd.)*
Valerie Carney *(Sr. V.P. & Gen. Counsel)*
Thomas Tolar *(Sr. V.P.)*
Geoffrey Vargo *(Sr. V.P.)*
Robert W. Davis II *(Sr. V.P.-Acct. & Fin. & Treas.)*
Candace Wendling *(V.P.)*
C.B. Dutton *(Sec.)*
Principal(s):
Thomas Tarzian
Pat Tarzian

No. of U.S. Offices: 5

Outside Service Firm(s):

Bank One, Indianapolis, N.A.*(Major Banking Relationship)*
111 Monument Circle, Ste. 1611
Indianapolis, IN 46204-1611
Tel.: 317-321-8110

TASA CORPORATION
Two Gateway Center, Ste. 990
Pittsburgh, PA 15222
Tel.: 412-391-2141 **PA**
Fax: 412-391-2147
Year Founded: 1917
Approx.Sls.: $8,000,000
Emp.: 5
Fiscal Year-end: 12/31/91
Export
Natural Resources & Real Estate Holdings
S.I.C.: 6552; 5052
R.E. Dougherty, Jr. *(Pres. & Treas.)*
William S. Smith *(Sec. & Gen. Counsel)*
R.L. Smith *(Asst. Treas.)*
Russell F. Steele *(Asst. Sec.)*

No. of U.S. Offices: 1

Computer Systems/Hardware:
Compaq 286 + Network

Outside Service Firm(s):

Deloitte & Touche*(Auditors)*
2400 One PPG Place
Pittsburgh, PA 15222
Tel.: 412-281-2232

Pittsburgh National Bank*(Major Banking Relationship)*
Stock Transfer Dept., Fifth & Wood Streets
Pittsburgh, PA 15265

Seubert & Associates, Inc.*(Commercial Insurance Carrier)*
Sewickley, PA

Pennsylvania Blue Shield*(Group Insurer)*
Camp Hill, PA

Pietragallo, Bosick & Gordon*(Legal Firm)*
Pittsburgh, PA

TASCO
7600 N.W. 26th St.
Miami, FL 33122
Mailing Address:
P.O. Box 520080,
Miami, FL 33152-0080
Tel.: 305-591-3670

Tasco—(Continued)

Telex: 441128
Fax: 305-592-5895
Fax: 305-592-9516
Year Founded: 1954
Approx.Sls.: $90,000,000
Emp.: 200
Fiscal Year-end: 12/31/90
Import Export
Manufacture & Distribute Binoculars, Opera Glasses, Telescopes, Rifloscopes, Pistolscopes, Microscopes, & Sports Glasses
S.I.C.: 5091; 5048; 5049; 3827
George Rosenfield *(Pres.)*
Sheryl Rosenfield *(Exec. V.P.)*
Estelle Rosenfield *(Treas.)*
Lea Barnette *(Sec.)*
Greg Bland *(Dir.-Sls.)*
Dan Cavanah *(Dir.-Opers.)*
Christopher D. Garbow *(Dir.-Fin.)*
Scott Helmer *(Dir.-Mktg.-Sports Optics)*
Barbara Kogan *(Dir.-Human Resources)*
Elvia Roche *(Mgr.-Acctg.)*
Roger Vallecorse *(Mgr.-Quality Control)*
Eileen Torres *(Buyer)*
Randi Vega *(Buyer)*
Cathy Vosekas *(Buyer)*
Principal(s):
George Rosenfield
Sheryl Rosenfield
Estelle Rosenfield

No. of Mfg. Plants/Facilities: 2
No. of U.S. Offices: 2

Computer Systems/Hardware:
AS/400

Outside Service Firm(s):

Kaufman & Rossin*(Auditors)*
Miami, FL

Liberty Mutual*(Commercial Insurance Carrier)*
8420 NW 52nd St.
Miami, FL 33166
Tel.: 305-592-0370

Hartford Life Insurance Co.*(Group Insurer)*
99 NW 183rd St.
Miami, FL 33169
Tel.: 305-653-5330

Therrel Baisden & Meyer Weiss*(Legal Firm)*
1111 Lincoln Rd. MB
Miami, FL 33139
Tel.: 305-672-1921

NationsBank Florida*(Major Banking Relationship)*
P.O. Box 02-5337 DT MIA 4-3, 150 SE 3rd Ave.
Miami, FL 33102-5337

Equitable Life*(Pension Manager)*
6701 SW 72nd St. SM
Miami, FL 33143
Tel.: 305-661-6201

TASH, INC.
450 E. Jarvis Ave.
Des Plaines, IL 60018
Tel.: 708-296-8880
Tel.: 800-397-8274 **DE**
Fax: 708-296-2963
Year Founded: 1988
Approx.Sls.: $100,000,000
Emp.: 400
Wholesale Distribution of Toys, School Supplies, Hair Accessories & General Merchandise, Non-Durable
S.I.C.: 5092; 5049; 5131; 5199
Ralph Tash *(Chm. Bd.)*
Ron Grove *(Pres.)*
Henry G. Wisniewski *(Exec. V.P. & Treas.)*
James Tulley *(V.P. & Gen. Mgr.-Midwest)*
Ron Jones *(V.P. & Gen. Mgr.-West)*
Rich Johnson *(Controller)*

Outside Service Firm(s):

Lakeshore National Bank*(Major Banking Relationship)*
Chicago, IL

Branch:

Tash, Inc. **(1)**
12681 Pala Dr.
Garden Grove, CA 92641
Tel.: 714-373-4500
Fax: 714-739-2671

TASSANI COMMUNICATIONS
515 N. State St.
Chicago, IL 60610-4320
Tel.: 312-644-2400
Fax: 312-644-1504
Year Founded: 1978
Approx.Billings: $21,000,000
Emp.: 45
Advertising Agency Specializing In Integrated Communications Services
S.I.C.: 8748
Sally M. Tassani *(Pres. & Chief Exec. Officer)*
James A. Paglia *(Exec. V.P., Chief Oper. Officer)*
David A. Pierce *(V.P.)*
Suzanne LaCroix *(Dir.-Opers.)*
Suzanne Dewosky *(Mgr.-Human Resources)*
Margaret E. Eich *(Mgr.-Acctg.)*
Mary E. Hartman *(Mgr.-Mktg. Devel.)*
Steven R. LaCroix *(Mgr.-Computer Design)*
Frank Dietrich *(Supervisor-Pub. Rels.)*

TATE ACCESS FLOORS, INC.
7510 Montevideo Rd.
Jessup, MD 20794
Tel.: 410-799-4200
Fax: 410-799-4207
Year Founded: 1963
Approx.Sls.: $80,000,000
Emp.: 470
Import Export
Manufacture Access Floor Systems
S.I.C.: 2426
R.L. Tate *(Chm. Bd., Sec. & Treas.)*
Daniel Baker *(Pres. & Chief Exec. Officer)*
Victor Sainato *(V.P.-Sls.-Contracting)*
Dennis O'Brien *(V.P. & Chief Fin. Officer)*

Outside Service Firm(s):

Price Waterhouse*(Auditors)*
7 St. Paul St.
Baltimore, MD 21202

Piper & Marbury*(Legal Firm)*
36 S. Charles St.
Baltimore, MD 21202
Tel.: 410-835-8000

Mercantile-Safe Deposit & Trust Co.*(Major Banking Relationship)*
Baltimore, MD

TATUM FARMS
Rte. 3 & Hwy. 136 N.
Dawsonville, GA 30534
Tel.: 706-265-3211
Fax: 706-265-2378
Approx.Sls.: $12,000,000
Emp.: 100
Poultry Breeding Stock, Hatching Eggs
S.I.C.: 0254; 5144
W.L. Tatum *(Pres.)*
Rick Tatum *(Exec. V.P.)*
Ray Oliver *(V.P.-Opers. & Pur. & Comptroller)*

Outside Service Firm(s):

Kidd & Rich*(Auditors)*
Atlanta, GA

Thompson, Fox & Hardmans*(Legal Firm)*
Gainesville, GA

Dawson County Bank*(Major Banking Relationship)*
Dawsonville, GA

TATUM TOOMEY & WHICKER
1820 Eastchester Dr.
High Point, NC 27265
Tel.: 919-889-3009
Fax: 919-889-3007
Year Founded: 1983
Approx.Billings: $22,000,000
Emp.: 30
Richard Toomey *(Partner)*
Roger Tatum *(Partner)*
Burton Whicker *(Partner)*
Jynne Rich *(Exec. Sec. & Librarian)*

TAUBER OIL COMPANY
55 Waugh Dr., Ste. 700
Houston, TX 77007
Mailing Address:
P.O. Box 4645
Houston, TX 77210
Tel.: 713-869-8700 **TX**
Fax: 713-869-8069
Year Founded: 1953
Assets: $93,346,220
Earnings: $1,646,000
Liabilities: $79,647,761
Net Worth: $13,698,459
Approx.Sls.: $1,232,000,000
Emp.: 50
Fiscal Year-end: 9/30/90
Wholesale Petroleum Products Marketing
S.I.C.: 5172; 5169; 5171
Orner J. Tauber, Jr. *(Pres. & Chief Exec. Officer)*
David Tauber *(Exec. V.P.)*
Richard Tauber *(Exec. V.P.)*
J. Patrick O'Neal *(V.P.-Fin.)*
Joe Sassin *(Controller)*
Principal(s):
Orner J. Tauber, Jr.
David Tauber
Richard Tauber

Computer Systems/Hardware:
Compaq

Outside Service Firm(s):

Mohle, Adams, Till, Guidry & Wallace*(Auditors)*
Houston, TX

First City National Bank*(Major Banking Relationship)*
Houston, TX

TAUSCHE MARTIN LONSDORF
1315 Peachtree St., N.E.
Atlanta, GA 30309
Tel.: 404-881-8080
Fax: 404-874-7739
Year Founded: 1979
Approx.Billings: $21,730,860
Emp.: 31
Russell V. Umphenour *(Chm. Bd.)*
Margaret Ann Martin *(Vice Chm.)*
Joseph C. Lonsdorf *(Pres.)*
H. Daniel Lovern, Jr. *(V.P., Fin.)*

TAWIL ASSOCIATES INC.
(d/b/a Mayfair Infants Wear)
100 Wesley White Dr.
Carteret, NJ 07008
Mailing Address:
P.O. Box 67,
Carteret, NJ 07008
Tel.: 908-382-4055 **NJ**
Fax: 908-382-1918
Approx.Sls.: $35,000,000
Emp.: 100
Manufacture Infants' & Children's Clothing
S.I.C.: 2369
Morris E. Tawil *(Pres.)*
Isaac Tawil *(Exec. V.P.)*
Jack Tawil *(V.P.)*
Fred Tawil *(Sec.)*
Theodore Tawil *(Treas.)*
Principal(s):
Morris E. Tawil

Outside Service Firm(s):

Greenbaum, Rowe, Smith, Ravin, Davis & Bergstein*(Legal Firm)*
900 Third Ave., 34th Flr.
New York, NY 10022
Tel.: 212-755-0606

Israel Discount Bank*(Major Banking Relationship)*
511 Fifth Ave.
New York, NY 10017

TAYLOR ADVERTISING, INC.
33 N. Stone Ave., Ste. 1000
Tucson, AZ 85701
Tel.: 602-624-0100
Fax: 602-624-9238
Year Founded: 1954
Approx.Billings: $11,208,000
Emp.: 16
Jay Taylor *(Pres. & Creative Dir.)*
Tony Basche *(Sr. V.P., Mktg. & Acct. Services)*
David Stubson *(V.P., Fin. & Admin.)*
David Trumble *(V.P., Pub. Rels.)*
Tina Sandovail *(Asst. V.P., Admin.)*

NELSON A. TAYLOR CO., INC.
10 W. 9th Ave.
Gloversville, NY 12078
Tel.: 518-725-0681
Fax: 518-725-4335
Year Founded: 1947
Approx.Sls.: $50,000,000
Emp.: 500
Fiscal Year-end: 9/30/91
Accessories For Boats; Windshields, Mirrors, Flags, Tempered Glass, Portable Toilets For RV & Marine, Air Conditioning & Refrigeration For Boats; Awnings
S.I.C.: 3231; 3999; 2399; 3089
William F. Jones *(Chm. Bd.)*
James W. Taylor *(Pres. & Chief Exec. Officer)*
J. Schulte *(Chief Fin. Officer & V.P.)*
John E. Taylor *(Treas.)*
David Trumbull *(Mgr.-Pur.)*
Patrick VanderVeen *(Mgr.-Engrng.)*
Principal(s):
J. Schulte

Outside Service Firm(s):

City National Bank of New York*(Major Banking Relationship)*
Gloversville, NY

Division:

Taylor Made Products **(1)**
167 N. Main St.
Gloversville, NY 12078
Tel.: 518-725-2624
Mfr. of Awnings
S.I.C.: 3089
Ira Morris *(Gen. Mgr.)*

Subsidiaries:

Taylor Made, Indiana **(1)**
P.O. Box 157
Kendallville, IN 46755
Tel.: 219-347-1368
Mfr. of Windshields & Tops For Boats
S.I.C.: 3231
Peter Atkin *(Pres.)*

Taylor Products, Inc. **(1)**
P.O. Box 77
Payne, OH 45880
Tel.: 419-262-2313
Glass Tempering
S.I.C.: 3231

Larry Mawer *(Pres.)*

Affiliates:

Marine Air Systems, Inc. **(1)**
2000 N. Andrews Ave. Ext.
Pompano Beach, FL 33069
Tel.: 305-973-2477
Mfr. of Air Conditioning & Refrigeration Units For Boats
S.I.C.: 3585
Mason Heydt *(Pres.)*

SeaLand Technology **(1)**
9030 Township Rd. 1043, 4th St.
Big Prairie, OH 44611
Tel.: 216-496-3211
Mfr. of Marine & RV Toilets
S.I.C.: 3431
Edward McKiernan *(Pres.)*

TAYLOR CORPORATION
1725 Roe Crest Dr.
Mankato, MN 56001
Mailing Address:
P.O. Box 3728,
North Mankato, MN 56001
Tel.: 507-625-2828 **MN**
Fax: 507-625-2988
Year Founded: 1948
Approx.Sls.: $250,000,000
Emp.: 5,000
Import
Printing; Electronics; Banking
S.I.C.: 2752; 2759; 6022; 3674
Glen A. Taylor *(Chm. Bd. & Chief Exec. Officer)*
Bradley Schreier *(Pres. & Chief Oper. Officer)*
Albert Fallenstein *(Exec. V.P.)*
Ed Alvarez *(V.P.-West Coast Opers.)*
Ron Bleess *(V.P.)*
Bob Hoffman *(V.P.-Sls.)*
Duane Jergenson *(V.P.-Opers.)*
William Kozitska *(V.P.-Fin.)*
Larry Lorenzen *(V.P.-Corp. Devel.)*
Monte McCoy *(V.P.-Intl. Opers.)*
Glenn Miller *(V.P.-Mngmt. Information Systems)*
John Schmitt *(V.P. & Gen Mgr.-Thermography Imprinting Div.)*
Larry Taylor *(V.P.-Engrng.)*
Gary Zellmer *(V.P.-Mktg.)*
Greg Jackson *(Gen. Counsel)*

No. of Mfg. Plants/Facilities: 32
No. of U.S. Offices: 31
No. of Foreign Offices: 1

Computer Systems/Hardware:
IBM

Outside Service Firm(s):

Wolf-Etter*(Auditors)*
Mankato, MN

Regan, Regan & Meyer*(Legal Firm)*
Mankato, MN

Valley National Bank*(Major Banking Relationship)*
North Mankato, MN

Subsidiaries:

A & E Business Products **(1)**
4424 Haines Rd.
Duluth, MN 55811
Tel.: 218-722-0594
Fax: 218-722-2076
Emp.: 95
Wholesale & Retail Office Supplies, Machines & Furniture
S.I.C.: 5112
Tom Holmstrom *(Pres. & Chief Exec. Officer)*

Tax Forms Printing **(1)**
943 Flynn Rd.
Camarillo, CA 93012
Tel.: 805-484-8081
Tel.: 800-482-9367
Fax: 805-484-7723
Sales Range: $10-19 Million
Emp.: 70
Computer Systems/Hardware:
Basic/4 730
Mfr. of Rotary Forms
S.I.C.: 2761

Ron Hoffmeyer *(Gen Mgr.)*
Don Prouty *(Mgr.-Natl. Accts.)*
Annette Hebert *(Admin. Asst.)*

TAYLOR DRUG STORES, INC.
4010 Crittenden Dr.
Louisville, KY 40209
Tel.: 502-368-6541
Fax: 502-368-6541 Ext. 444
Year Founded: 1879
Approx.Sls.: $110,000,000
Emp.: 1000
Fiscal Year-end: 4/30/91
Drug Store Chain
S.I.C.: 5912
William H. Harrison, Jr. *(Chm. Bd. & Chief Exec. Officer)*
Samuel R. Boulton *(Pres. & Chief Oper. Officer)*
Thomas W. O'Bryan *(Sr. V.P. & Chief Fin. Officer)*
William Cahaney *(V.P.-Real Estate)*
Robert G. Mayer *(V.P.-Data Processing)*
Lynn Oates *(V.P.-Mktg.)*
Tom Weisert *(V.P.-Pharmacy Opers.)*
James Hudson *(Controller)*
Bill Robertson *(Dir.-Adv.)*
Connie Adams *(Mgr.-Human Resources)*

Outside Service Firm(s):

Deloitte & Touche*(Auditors)*
510 W. Broadway
Louisville, KY 40202
Tel.: 502-562-2000

ED TAYLOR CONSTRUCTION CO.
5175 S. Royal Atlanta Dr.
Tucker, GA 30084
Mailing Address:
P.O. Box 48489
Atlanta, GA 30362
Tel.: 404-939-8200 **GA**
Fax: 404-939-9920
Year Founded: 1973
Assets: $10,205,653
Liabilities: $6,399,204
Net Worth: $3,806,449
Sales Range: $60-79 Million
Emp.: 250
Fiscal Year-end: 10/31/90
Commercial Construction
S.I.C.: 1542; 1541
Donal Kieran O'Neill *(Chm. Bd., Pres. & Chief Exec. Officer)*
Larry Cobb *(V.P.-Fin., Treas. & Sec.)*
William L. Kizer *(V.P.-Georgia Interior Construction Div.)*
H. E. Lovelace *(V.P.-Mktg.)*
Jim Marcan *(V.P.-Florida Construction Div.)*
Maureen Richardson *(Dir.-Personnel)*
Tench Coxe *(Legal Officer)*

Principal(s):
Donal Kieran O'Neill
William L. Kizer

No. of U.S. Offices: 3

Computer Systems/Hardware:
Wang

Outside Service Firm(s):

Deloitte & Touche*(Auditors)*
100 Peachtree St., Ste. 1700
Atlanta, GA 30303-1943
Tel.: 404-220-1500
Fax: 404-220-1583

Fidelity & Deposit Co. of Maryland*(Commercial Insurance Carrier)*
Atlanta, GA

Troutman, Sanders, Lockerman & Ashmore*(Legal Firm)*
600 Peachtree St., Ste. 5200
Atlanta, GA 30308-2216
Tel.: 404-885-3000

Trust Company Bank*(Major Banking Relationship)*
Stock Trans. Dept. P.O.B. 4625, Trust Company of Georgia Bldg.
Atlanta, GA 30302
Tel.: 404-588-7831

Smith Barney, Harris Upham & Company, Inc.*(Pension Manager)*
Atlanta, GA

TAYLOR-EVANS SEED CO.
(Sub. of Agri Genetics)
505 S. Hwy. 87
Tulia, TX 79088
Mailing Address:
P.O. Box 68,
Tulia, TX 79088
Tel.: 806-995-4111
Fax: 806-995-4159
Approx.Sls.: $10,000,000
Emp.: 43
Fiscal Year-end: 8/31/90
Golden Acres Hybrid Grain Sorghums, Hybrid Forage Sorghums, Hybrid Sorghums Sudan, Hybrid Corns
James Allison *(Pres. & Dir.-Res. & Devel.)*
C.W. Hall *(Controller)*
Bob Oldham *(Mgr.-Sls.)*

TAYLOR-GORDON/WIDMANN & CO., INC.
292 Madison Ave.
New York, NY 10017
Tel.: 212-683-3700
Fax: 212-532-1528
Year Founded: 1970
Approx.Billings: $30,000,000
Emp.: 30
Anthony Widmann *(Chm. & Chief Exec. Officer)*
Elaine Taylor-Gordon *(Pres.)*
John F. Shima *(Sr. V.P., Mktg. & Media)*
Lucy Rogenstein *(Sr. V.P.)*
Phyllis DeLuise *(V.P., Opers. & Traffic Mgr.)*
Yolanda Salazar *(Controller)*

TAYLOR MACHINE WORKS, INC.
650 North Church Ave.
Louisville, MS 39339
Tel.: 601-773-3421
Fax: 601-773-9646
Year Founded: 1927
Approx.Sls.: $70,000,000
Emp.: 750
Fiscal Year-end: 12/31/90
Export
Manufacture Fork Lift Trucks 11,500-120,000 Lbs. Capacity with Options & Attachments; Container Handling Equipment; Pulpwood Loaders (Sling-Type & Grapple); Log Stackers
S.I.C.: 3537
W.A. Taylor, Jr. *(Chm. Bd.)*
W.A. Taylor III *(Pres.)*
N.P. Autry *(Sr. V.P.-Fin.)*
Richard Ballard *(Gen. Counsel)*
Hal Robison *(Controller)*
Joe Boykin *(Dir.-Data Processing)*
Ken Collins *(Dir.-Materials)*
Don Ellis *(Dir.-Communications)*
Doug Hulse *(Dir.-Intl. Mktg.)*
William Metts *(Dir.-Mktg.)*
J.T. Monk *(Dir.-Engrng.)*
Jack Pearson *(Sls. Mgr.-Dealers)*
Bobby Triplett *(Mgr.-Mktg. Services)*
Dean Watkins *(Mgr.-Human Resources)*
Don Woodruff, Jr. *(Mgr.-Sls.-Dealers)*
Davis Kelley *(Pur. Agent)*

Outside Service Firm(s):

KPMG Peat Marwick*(Auditors)*
One Jackson Place,
Jackson, MS 39201
Tel.: 601-354-3701
Fax: 601-354-3745

Wells, Wells, Marble & Hurst*(Legal Firm)*
Louisville, MS

National Bank of Commerce*(Major Banking Relationship)*
Memphis, TN

TAYLOR MEDICAL INC.
2155 IH 10 E.
Beaumont, TX 77704
Mailing Address:
P.O. Box 4904,
Beaumont, TX 77704
Tel.: 409-835-5021 **TX**
Year Founded: 1986
Approx.Sls.: $100,000,000
Emp.: 580
Wholesale Distr. of Medical Equipment & Supplies
S.I.C.: 5047
R. Craig Christopher *(Chm. Bd.)*
Todd Christopher *(Pres.)*
Gene Humphrey *(Chief Fin. Officer)*
Jim Hayes *(Chief Information Officer)*
Gene Crisman *(Gen. Mgr.)*
Gary Hedge *(Dir.-Mktg.)*

Subsidiaries:

DH Medical Supply Inc. **(1)**
203 Sedgwick Rd.
West Hartford, CT 06107
Tel.: 203-828-4034
Approx.Sls.: $6,000,000
Emp.: 8
Wholesale Distribution of Medical Equipment
S.I.C.: 5047
Chuck Souder *(Pres.)*

Desert Medical Supply Inc. **(1)**
3740 E. LaSalle
Phoenix, AZ 85040
Tel.: 602-437-9200
Approx.Sls.: $8,000,000
Emp.: 40
Wholesale Distribution of Medical Equipment
S.I.C.: 5047
John G. Power *(Pres.)*

Taylor Home Health Inc. **(1)**
2865 Laurel
Beaumont, TX 77702
Tel.: 409-838-9173
Rental & Sales of Medical & Hospital Equipment
S.I.C.: 7352; 5047; 5990
Willie Hall *(Pres.)*

Taylor Medical of LA **(1)**
2155 IH 10 E.
Beaumont, TX 77701
Tel.: 409-835-5021
Wholesale Distribution of Medical Equipment
S.I.C.: 5047
John W. Road *(Pres.)*

TAYLOR-MORLEY, INC.
1227 Fern Ridge Pkwy., Ste. 1224, 3rd fl
Saint Louis, MO 63141
Tel.: 314-434-9000 **MO**
Fax: 314-434-1390
Year Founded: 1952
Approx.Sls.: $95,000,000
Emp.: 250
Residential Builder & Developer
S.I.C.: 1521; 1522; 6513; 6552
Benton E. Taylor *(Chm. Bd.)*
Harry T. Morley *(Pres. & Chief Exec. Officer)*
William Taylor *(Sr. V.P. & Treas.)*
James G. Brennan *(V.P.-Fin. & Construction)*
Robert P. Brinson *(V.P. & Controller)*

Outside Service Firm(s):

Aselage & Kieffer*(Auditors)*
St. Louis, MO

Taylor-Morley, Inc.—(Continued)

Rubin Brown Gornstein & Co.*(Auditors)*
230 S. Bemiston Ave.
St. Louis, MO 63105
Tel.: 314-727-8150

Susman, Schermer, Rimmel, Shifrin*(Legal Firm)*
St. Louis, MO

American Bank*(Major Banking Relationship)*
St. Louis, MO

Boatmen's Trust Company*(Major Banking Relationship)*
100 North Broadway
St. Louis, MO 63102
Tel.: 314-466-2469

Commerce Bank of Kansas City*(Major Banking Relationship)*
10th & Walnut
Kansas City, MO 64141
Tel.: 816-234-2000
Fax: 816-234-2548

First Bank, N.A.*(Major Banking Relationship)*
St. Louis, MO

Landmark First National Bank*(Major Banking Relationship)*
St. Louis, MO

Mark Twain St. Louis Bank*(Major Banking Relationship)*
1630 S. Lindbergh Blvd.
St. Louis, MO 63131

TAYLOR OIL CO. INC.
110 Oakwood Dr.
Winston-Salem, NC 27103
Mailing Address:
P.O. Box 5195,
Winston-Salem, NC 27113
Tel.: 919-725-9531
Fax: 919-722-8372
Approx.Sls.: $66,000,000
Emp.: 250
Fiscal Year-end: 12/31/88
Automotive Dealer & Service Stations
S.I.C.: 5171; 5541
John A. Taylor *(Chm. Bd.)*
Philip Ryan *(Pres.)*
Allen Denny *(V.P.)*
Mark McCuiston *(V.P.)*
Anderson Taylor *(V.P.)*

Computer Systems/Hardware:
IBM System 36

Outside Service Firm(s):

Blue Cross & Blue Shield of North Carolina*(Group Insurer)*
Durham, NC

Southern National Bank*(Major Banking Relationship)*
Winston-Salem, NC

TAYLOR • SMITH GROUP

TAYLOR-SMITH GROUP
2000 West Loop South, 16th Fl.
Houston, TX 77027
Tel.: 713-877-1220
Fax: 713-877-1672
Year Founded: 1983
Approx.Billings: $38,000,000
Emp.: 64
Advertising, Marketing, Media & Public Relations
Larry Taylor *(Chm. Bd.)*
Dick Smith *(Exec. V.P.)*
John Fosdick *(Dir., Res. & Plng.)*

Computer Systems/Hardware:
AdAid, Media Mngmt. Plus, MacIntosh, IBM, Simmons Choices

TEACHERS INSURANCE AND ANNUITY ASSOCIATION-COLLEGE RETIREMENT EQUITIES FUND
730 Third Ave.
New York, NY 10017
Tel.: 212-490-9000 **NY**
Year Founded: 1918
Approx.Assets: $104,300,000,000
Emp.: 3,800
Fiscal Year-end: 12/31/91

Import Export
Life, Pensions/Retirement Annuities, Group Life & Total Disability, Long-Term Care Insurance
S.I.C.: 6311
Clifton R. Wharton, Jr. *(Chm. Bd. & Chief Exec. Officer)*
John H. Biggs *(Pres. & Chief Oper. Officer)*
Thomas W. Jones *(Exec. V.P.-Fin. & Plng.)*
John A. Putney, Jr. *(Exec. V.P.-Opers. Support)*
Charles H. Stamm *(Exec. V.P. & Gen. Counsel)*
Don W. Harril *(Exec. V.P.)*
Matina S. Horner *(Exec. V.P.)*
J. Daniel Lee, Jr. *(Exec. V.P.)*
James S. Martin *(Exec. V.P.)*
John J. McCormack *(Exec. V.P.)*
Thomas G. Walsh *(Exec. V.P.)*
Peter C. Clapman *(Sr. V.P. & Chief Counsel-Investments)*
David B. Bullett *(Sr. V.P.)*
Virgil H. Cumming *(Sr. V.P.)*
George Francomano *(Sr. V.P.)*
Larry D. Hershberger *(Sr. V.P.)*
Ronald P. McPhee *(Sr. V.P.)*
C. Oscar Morong, Jr. *(Sr. V.P.)*
John A. Somers *(Sr. V.P.)*
Peter A. Trikaminas *(Sr. V.P.)*
James A. Wolf *(Sr. V.P.)*
Richard J. Adamski *(V.P. & Treas.)*
Robert G. Gilmore *(V.P. & Chief Counsel-Corp. Fin.)*
Louis R. Garcia *(V.P. & Chief Ombudsman)*
Herbert B. Gordon *(V.P. & Chief Counsel-Govt. Rels.)*
Harry I. Klaristerfeld *(V.P. & Actuary)*
Jean Cullinan Ray *(V.P. & Chief Counsel-Insurance)*
Betty B. Robbins *(V.P. & Chief Counsel-Mortgage & Real Estate)*
Albert J. Wilson *(V.P., Sec. & Chief Counsel)*
Diane M. Axelrod *(V.P.)*
James F. Blair *(V.P.)*
Bruce L. Boyd *(V.P.)*
Douglas A. Dial *(V.P.)*
Kirk L. Dorn *(V.P.)*
Peter J. Farley *(V.P.)*
Michael Fegan *(V.P.)*
Eric E. Fisher *(V.P.)*
Richard L. Gibbs *(V.P.)*
Linda H. Lamel *(V.P.)*
Diane Oakley *(V.P.)*
Mary Ann Werner *(V.P.)*
Susan P. Young *(V.P.)*
Kathleen M. Nelson *(Mng. Dir.-Closing & Mortgage Loan Admin.)*
Carol D. Nichols *(Mng. Dir.-Mortgage & Real Estate Investments)*
Daniel J. Sullivan *(Mng. Dir.-Mortgage & Real Estate Investments)*

Outside Service Firm(s):

Ernst & Young*(Auditors)*
787 Seventh Ave.
New York, NY 10019
Tel.: 212-773-1243

TEACHERS MANAGEMENT & INVESTMENT CORPORATION
#6 Upper Newport Plaza
Newport Beach, CA 92660
Mailing Address:
P.O. Box 2500,
Newport Beach, CA 92660
Tel.: 714-955-9100
Fax: 714-955-9109
Year Founded: 1968
Emp.: 435
Real Estate Principals, Brokers & Developers; Investment Services for Educators
S.I.C.: 6531; 6552; 6211
James Boyden *(Pres. & Chief Exec. Officer)*
Hughie Hong *(Chief Fin. Officer)*

Computer Systems/Hardware:
Wang VS 100

Outside Service Firm(s):

KPMG Peat Marwick*(Auditors)*
725 S. Figueroa St.
Los Angeles, CA 90017
Tel.: 213-972-4000

Capital Bank of California*(Major Banking Relationship)*
Los Angeles, CA

TEAM BANCSHARES, INC.
3300 Oak Lawn
Dallas, TX 75219
Mailing Address:
P.O. Box 190667,
Dallas, TX 75219-0667
Tel.: 214-521-4171 **TX**
Year Founded: 1988
Assets: $5,664,933,000
Liabilities: $5,341,797,000
Net Worth: $323,136,000
Approx.Income: $35,033,000
Emp.: 2,882
Fiscal Year-end: 12/31/91
Bank Holding Company
S.I.C.: 6712
Ronald G. Steinhart *(Chm. Bd. & Chief Exec. Officer)*
Bayard H. Friedman *(Sr. Chm.)*
Robert H. Stewart III *(Vice Chm.)*
Terry Kelley *(Pres. & Chief Oper. Officer)*
Robert F. Lehman, Jr. *(Pres.-FAMCO)*
William E. Abraham *(Exec. V.P. & Dir.-Credit Policy)*
Robert C. Ammons *(Exec. V.P. & Dir.-Human Resources)*
Jerry W. Bevers *(Exec. V.P.-Dir. of Retail Banking)*
Gary W. Cage *(Exec. V.P. & Chief Fin. Officer)*
Susan W. Miller *(Exec. V.P. & Dir.-Opers.)*
Bruce Petty *(Exec. V.P.-Trust)*
H. David Taylor *(Exec. V.P. & Dir.-Processing Services)*
Mike Ballases *(Chm.-Houston Region)*
Martin C. Bowen *(Chm.-Ft. Worth Region)*
L.O. Brightbill, III *(Vice Chm.-Ft. Worth Region & Mgr.-Correspondent Banking)*
Jeffrey M. Washington *(Sr. V.P.-Mktg.)*
Rhodes Baker *(Sr. V.P. & Gen. Counsel)*
Robert Lohman *(Dir.-Facilities)*
Patricia A. Steele *(Mktg. Communications)*
David L. Perdue *(Chm.-Dallas Region & Mgr.-Comml. Banking)*
John B. Roach, Jr. *(Exec. V.P. & Metroplex Region Retail Mgr.)*
Tim A. Loudermilk *(Exec. V.P. & Reg. Mgr.-Real Estate Lending)*
Craig F. Hartberg *(Sr. V.P. & Reg. Mgr.-Private Banking)*
Linda M. Salton *(Sr. V.P. & Reg. Mgr.-Trust Banking)*
David G. Wilson *(Sr. V.P. & Grp. Mgr.-Comml. Banking)*
Paul C. Koch *(V.P. & Grp. Mgr.-Comml Banking)*

Banking Subsidiary:

Team Bank **(1)**
P.O. Box 2050
Fort Worth, TX 76113
Tel.: 817-884-4000 (100%)
Banking Services
S.I.C.: 6021
Terry Kelley *(Pres. & Chief Oper. Officer)*
Gary W. Cage *(Exec. V.P. & Chief Fin. Officer)*
Jerry Bevers *(Exec. V.P.-Sls.)*
Judith Schultz *(Exec. V.P.-Mktg.)*
Bob Allen *(Dir.-Pur.)*

Branches:

Team Bank/Amarillo **(2)**
P.O. Box 231
Amarillo, TX 79182
Tel.: 806-378-3100
Banking Services
S.I.C.: 6021
Larry D. Trantham *(Pres.)*

Team Bank/Dallas **(2)**
P.O. Box 35207
Dallas, TX 75235
Tel.: 214-353-8100
Banking Services
S.I.C.: 6021
David L. Perdue *(Chm.-Dallas Region)*

TECA CORPORATION
Three Campus Dr.
Pleasantville, NY 10570
Tel.: 914-769-5900
Tel.: 800-GET-TECA
Approx.Sls.: $15,000,000
Emp.: 100
Fiscal Year-end: 12/31/90
Mfr. & Distributor of Diagnostic Medical Equipment
S.I.C.: 3841
Clive Snowdon *(Chm. Bd.)*
Lewis Rosenblum *(Pres.)*
Michael Pattinson *(Chief Fin. Officer)*
Deidre Thorp-Batbera *(Dir.-Acctg.)*
Robert Drabik *(Dir.-Sls.)*
Simon Griffin *(Dir.-Mktg., Instruments)*
Alan Schaefer *(Dir.-Mktg., Accessories)*
Jennifer Freedman *(Dir.-Mktg. Communications)*
Donna Ellis *(Dir.-Personnel)*

THE TECH GROUP
14677 N. 74th St.
Scottsdale, AZ 85260
Tel.: 602-483-3000 **AZ**
Fax: 602-951-3065
Year Founded: 1967
Sales Range: $60-79 Million
Emp.: 550
Fiscal Year-end: 6/30/91
Holding Company for Thermoplastics Manufacturers
S.I.C.: 6719; 3089
Steve Uhlmann *(Pres.)*
Thom Niemiec *(Treas. & Sec.)*

Computer Systems/Hardware:
Apple Macintosh

Outside Service Firm(s):

Toback & Company*(Auditors)*
Phoenix, AZ

Security Pacific Bank Arizona*(Major Banking Relationship)*
Phoenix, AZ

Subsidiaries:

Star Container, Inc. **(1)**
Addinburg, IN
Tel.: 812-526-8000

Star Container, Inc. **(1)**
2525 E. Magnolia
Phoenix, AZ 85034
Tel.: 602-275-3000
Hal Tashman *(Chief Exec. Officer)*
Jim Hughes *(V.P.-Sls. & Mktg.)*

Selma Femenia *(Controller)*

Tech CBI **(1)**
Caguas, PR
Tel.: 809-747-7900

Tech Medical Inc. **(1)**
640 S. Rockford Dr.
Tempe, AZ 85281
Tel.: 602-894-9128
Mfr. of Plastic Products
S.I.C.: 3089
Frank Mead *(Gen. Mgr.)*
Mark McGaffin *(Controller)*

Tech Mold, Inc. **(1)**
1735 W. 10th St.
Tempe, AZ 85281
Tel.: 602-968-8691
Bill Kushmaul *(Chief Oper. Officer)*
Mike Wade *(Controller)*

Tech Plastics **(1)**
1415 S. McClintock
Tempe, AZ 85281
Tel.: 602-966-7283
Mfr. of Plastic Products
S.I.C.: 3089
Don Miller *(V.P. & Gen. Mgr.)*
Mark McGaffin *(Controller)*

Tech Poulson, Inc. **(1)**
14677 N. 74th St.
Scottsdale, AZ 85260
Tel.: 602-948-6130
Mfr. of Plastic Products
S.I.C.: 3089
Steve Uhlman *(Pres.)*
Mark McGaffin *(Controller)*
Tom Pudesta *(Mgr.-Sls.)*

Top-Seal Corp. **(1)**
2236 E. University Dr.
Phoenix, AZ 85034
Tel.: 602-275-5577
Phil Owens *(Pres. & Chief Oper. Officer)*
Thom Niemiec *(Treas.)*

TECH INDUSTRIES, INC.
85 Fairmount St.
Woonsocket, RI 02895
Mailing Address:
P.O. Box J
Woonsocket, RI 02895
Tel.: 401-765-0600
Fax: 401-766-4742
Year Founded: 1965
Sales Range: $40-59 Million
Emp.: 450
Plastic Packaging Components
S.I.C.: 3089
Herbert Wang *(Chm. Bd.)*
David Wang *(Pres.)*
Dan Carter *(V.P.-Sls.)*
Jim Carria *(V.P.-Fin.)*
Richard Van Hine *(Dir.-Human Resources)*
William Anderson *(Mgr.-Pur.)*

Outside Service Firm(s):

Ernst & Young*(Auditors)*
One Old Stone Square
Providence, RI 02903
Tel.: 401-331-7000

Adler, Pollock & Sheehan, Inc.*(Legal Firm)*
Providence, RI

Rhode Island Hospital Trust National Bank*(Major Banking Relationship)*
Hospital Trust Tower
Providence, RI

TECHNIC INCORPORATED
One Spectacle St
Cranston, RI 02910
Mailing Address:
P.O. Box 9650,
Providence, RI 02940
Tel.: 401-781-6100
Fax: 401-781-2890
Year Founded: 1944
Assets: $10,000,000
Earnings: $415,000
Liabilities: $4,000,000
Net Worth: $6,000,000
Approx.Sls.: $68,000,000
Emp.: 149
Fiscal Year-end: 12/31/90
Import Export
Manufacture Chemical & Metallurgical Products
S.I.C.: 2819; 2899; 3559; 3341
A.A. Weisberg *(Chm. Bd. & Treas.)*
H. Shoushaniao *(Pres.)*
Louis J. Hirbour *(V.P.)*
David D. Weisberg *(V.P. & Sec.)*
George F. David *(Chief Fin. Officer)*
Harry Brack *(Dir.-Adv.)*
J. Maxon *(Dir.-Mktg.)*
R. Weisberg *(Dir.-Pub. Rels.)*
Sook Yin *(Dir.-Sls. & Gen. Sls. Mgr.)*
S. Verkauf *(Mgr.-Export)*
Laslo Y. Urachez *(Pur. Agent)*

No. of Mfg. Plants/Facilities: 4
No. of U.S. Offices: 4
No. of Foreign Offices: 3

Computer Systems/Hardware:
NCR

Outside Service Firm(s):

Christiansen & Co.*(Auditors)*
Providence, RI

Farthingale, Frothingham, Foster, Ltd.*(Investment Banker)*
Cranston, RI

Hinkley, Allen, Snyder & Comen*(Legal Firm)*
1500 Fleet Ctr.
Providence, RI 02903
Tel.: 401-274-2000

Fleet National Bank*(Major Banking Relationship)*
125 Dupont Dr.
Providence, RI 02907-3178
Tel.: 401-278-5335

Division:

Technic Incorporated-Equipment Div. **(1)**
120 Maryland Ave.
Pawtucket, RI 02860
Tel.: 401-728-7081
Fax: 401-278-2890
Emp.: 186
Import Export
Manufacture Precious Metal Chemicals & Equipment for Electroplating
S.I.C.: 3559; 3339
H. Shoushaniao *(Pres.)*

TECHNICAL AID CORPORATION
109 Oak St.
Newton Upper Falls, MA 02164
Tel.: 617-969-3100 **MA**
Fax: 617-969-5470
Year Founded: 1969
Temporary Help Supply Services
S.I.C.: 7363
Salvatore Balsamo *(Chm. Bd., Pres. & Chief Exec. Officer)*
Michael Iandoli *(Exec. V.P.)*
Kenneth Reisman *(V.P., Gen. Counsel & Sec.)*
Vincent Santosuosso, Jr. *(Dir.-Personnel)*

Computer Systems/Hardware:
IBM 4341

Outside Service Firm(s):

Coopers & Lybrand*(Auditors)*
1 Post Office Square
Boston, MA 02110
Tel.: 617-574-5000
Fax: 617-345-0398

Bank of New England*(Major Banking Relationship)*
Randolph, MA

Maccabees Mutual Life Insurance Co.*(Commercial Insurance Carrier)*
Boston, MA

Blue Cross of Massachusetts, Inc.*(Group Insurer)*
Boston, MA

Maccabees Mutual Life Insurance Co.*(Group Insurer)*
Boston, MA

American Fiduciary Corp.*(Pension Manager)*
Newton, MA

Division:

Tech/Aid **(1)**
109 Oak St.
Newton Upper Falls, MA 02164
Tel.: 617-969-3100
Approx.Sls.: $88,000,000
Emp.: 3,190
Supplies Top-Level Contract Engineers, Designers, Drafters & Technicians
S.I.C.: 7363

Subsidiaries:

Computer Enterprises, Inc. **(1)**
109 Oak St.
Newton Upper Falls, MA 02164
Tel.: 617-969-3100 (100%)
Approx.Sls.: $814,000
Emp.: 40
Provides Data Entry Services & Processing
S.I.C.: 7363
Joseph Fabiano *(Chief Oepr. Officer)*

EDP/TEMPS Inc. **(1)**
109 Oak St.
Newton Upper Falls, MA 02164
Tel.: 617-969-3100 (100%)
Approx.Sls.: $24,000,000
Emp.: 580
Contract MIS Professionals
S.I.C.: 7363

Home Care p.r.n., Inc. **(1)**
109 Oak St.
Newton Upper Falls, MA 02164
Tel.: 617-969-3100 (100%)
Approx.Sls.: $237,000
Emp.: 30
Home Health Care Services
S.I.C.: 7363; 8082

MicroTemps Systems & Programming **(1)**
109 Oak St.
Newton Upper Falls, MA 02164
Tel.: 617-969-3100 (100%)
Approx.Sls.: $16,000,000
Emp.: 175
Supplies Professional Contractors for Systems & Applications Software
S.I.C.: 7363

Systems Management & Development **(1)**
109 Oak St.
Newton Upper Falls, MA 02164
Tel.: 617-969-3100 (100%)
Approx.Sls.: $877,000
Emp.: 4
Specialized Expertise in Software Design & Devel. and Hardware & Software Maintenance
S.I.C.: 7363
Robert Feeney *(Chief Oper. Officer)*

TAC/Medical Services Inc. **(1)**
109 Oak St.
Newton Upper Falls, MA 02164
Tel.: 617-969-3100 (100%)
Approx.Sls.: $4,000,000
Emp.: 376
Nursing & Health Care Professional Supply Services
S.I.C.: 7363; 8082

TAC/TEMPS Inc. **(1)**
109 Oak St.
Newton Upper Falls, MA 02164
Tel.: 617-969-3100 (100%)
Approx.Sls.: $32,000,000
Emp.: 2,400
Supplies Temporary Office, Light Industrial & Assembly Personnel
S.I.C.: 7363

TECHNICARBON COMPANY, INC.
89 Guian St.
Springfield, MA 01104
Tel.: 413-781-7696
Fax: 413-788-9860
Year Founded: 1945
Approx.Sls.: $33,000,000
Emp.: 150
Mfr. of Carbon Paper For Typewriters; Sales Book; Manifold Business Forms; Coated Paper Except Photographic
S.I.C.: 3955; 2761; 2672
George Hano *(Chm. Bd.)*
Frank Hano *(Pres. & Chief Exec. Officer)*
Phillip Hano *(V.P. & Treas.)*
Donald G. Upton *(V.P.-Opers.)*
Wayne Marek *(Controller)*
Phillip Hano, III *(Sec.)*

Outside Service Firm(s):

Lester Halpern & Co.*(Auditors)*
Holyoke, MA

Ely, King & Corcoran*(Legal Firm)*
Springfield, MA

TECHNOGRAPHICS, INC.
P.O. Box 1106
Stratton, PA 18501
Tel.: 717-347-2035
Fax: 717-347-2507
Approx.Sls.: $60,000,000
Emp.: 280
Special & Technical Papers
S.I.C.: 5113
John Grado *(Chm. Bd. & Chief Exec. Officer)*
Eugene Sorbo *(Pres.)*

Subsidiary:

Fitchburg Coated Products Inc. **(1)**
P. O. Box 1106
Scranton, PA 18501
Tel.: 717-347-2035
Approx.Sls.: $50,000,000
Emp.: 300
Mfr. Coated Papers
S.I.C.: 2891
Brian Kelly *(Pres.)*
Pat Burke *(V.P.-Prod. Devel.)*
Dave Devino *(V.P.-Mfg.)*
Nick Nichols *(V.P.-Personnel)*
Mike Marjeoti *(Controller)*
Joe Orr *(Natl. Sls. Mgr.)*
Ron Smith *(Pur. Agent)*

TECHNOLOGY APPLICATIONS, INC.
6101 Stevenson Ave.
Alexandria, VA 22304
Tel.: 703-461-2000 **DE**
Fax: 703-461-2420
Year Founded: 1977
Assets: $23,395,553
Liabilities: $17,358,386
Net Worth: $6,037,167
Approx.Sls.: $57,994,439
Emp.: 800
Fiscal Year-end: 4/30/90
Information Technology, High Performance Computing, Systems and Logistics Engineering, C 3 I, Ship Alteration and Installation Services, Scientific/Technology Support, Simulator Operation/Maintenance, Weapons Systems and Environmental Science
S.I.C.: 3571; 3724; 3728; 3731; 3761; 3764; 3769; 8731
Corporate Giving Program: Matches up to $5,000 of Employee Contribution to Nonprofit Organizations Approved in Advance by the Company & Collected During the Annual Fund Drive Period as Established by the Company
James I. Chatman *(Chm. Bd. & Pres.)*
John R. Register *(Sr. V.P., Chief Fin. Officer & Treas.)*
Michael Carey *(Comptroller)*

Technology Applications, Inc.—(Continued)

Dale H. Dumas *(Sec.)*

No. of Mfg. Plants/Facilities: 36

Outside Service Firm(s):

Arthur Andersen & Co.*(Auditors)*
1666 K Street, N.W.
Washington, DC 20006

Crestar Bank*(Major Banking Relationship)*
Washington, DC 20005

Subsidiary:

TAI Services, Inc. **(1)**
6101 Stevenson Ave.
Alexandria, VA 22304
Tel.: 703-461-2000

TECHNOLOGY FOR ENERGY CORPORATION
10737 Lexington Dr.
Knoxville, TN 37932
Mailing Address:
P.O. Box 22996,
Knoxville, TN 37933
Tel.: 615-966-5856 **TN**
Fax: 615-675-1241
Year Founded: 1975
Approx.Sls.: $12,600,000
Emp.: 59
Fiscal Year-end: 12/31/89
Provides Energy Production & Consumption Industries with Innovative Products & Services Aimed at Improvements in Productivity, Quality, Cost Containment, Safety & Plant Life
S.I.C.: 3823; 3829; 3822
Ronald D. Brenner *(Pres. & Chief Exec. Officer)*
Donald Sidlowski *(Dir.-Industrial Prod. Sls.)*
Principal(s):
Ronald D. Brenner
James C. Robinson

No. of Mfg. Plants/Facilities: 1
No. of U.S. Offices: 1

Computer Systems/Hardware:
DEC VAX 11/780; 8Mb Memory; 6250 BPI; Tape Drive; VT 100's & VT200's; Line Printers, Terminals, IBM PC's & Macintosh SE's

TECHNOLOGY TRANSFER INSTITUTE
741 10th St.
Santa Monica, CA 90402
Tel.: 310-394-8305
Telex: 494-8322
Fax: 310-451-2104
Year Founded: 1976
Approx.Sls.: $6,500,000
Emp.: 25
Fiscal Year-end: 10/31/89
Educational Seminars & Conferences; Consulting in Computer Technology
S.I.C.: 7379; 8243
Dr. Leonard Kleinrock *(Chm. Bd. & Chief Exec. Officer)*
John Phillips *(Pres.)*
Tony Shaw *(V.P.-Mktg.)*
Dr. John Silvester *(Dir.-Consulting)*

Computer Systems/Hardware:
IBM PC

Outside Service Firm(s):

Cohen, England, Whitfield & Osburne*(Legal Firm)*
Oxnard, CA

TECKNIT
129 Dermody St.
Cranford, NJ 07016
Tel.: 908-272-5500
Approx.Sls.: $25,000,000
Emp.: 419
Fiscal Year-end: 12/31/90
EMI Shielding & Conductive Materials
S.I.C.: 3679
Paul D. Beck *(Pres. & Chief Exec. Officer)*
Tom Mc Creery *(Sls. Dir.)*
Steve Ferrie *(Mktg. Dir.)*
James L. Pean *(Mgr.-Adv.)*

TECON PACIFIC
1980 S. River Rd. W.
Sacramento, CA 95691
Tel.: 916-371-0305
Fax: 916-372-0323
Year Founded: 1967
Manufacture Architectural, Pre-Cast Concrete Products
S.I.C.: 3272
James Clark *(Pres.)*
Jack Casper *(Comptroller)*

Outside Service Firm(s):

Gordon Odom Davis*(Auditors)*
Sacramento, CA

Wells Fargo Bank*(Major Banking Relationship)*
Sacramento, CA

TECOT ELECTRIC SUPPLY COMPANY
55 Lukens Dr.
New Castle, DE 19720
Tel.: 302-429-9100
Fax: 302-429-6268
Approx.Sls.: $27,000,000
Emp.: 135
Electrical Supplies & Construction Materials
S.I.C.: 5063
Stephen L. Tecot *(Chm. Bd.)*
Vincent P. Sanzone *(Pres.)*
Scott M. Cutler *(V.P.-Fin.)*

Outside Service Firm(s):

Price Waterhouse*(Auditors)*
1220 N. Market St.
Wilmington, DE 19801

Bank of Delaware*(Major Banking Relationship)*
Wilmington, DE

A. TEICHERT & SON, INC.
3500 American River Dr.
Sacramento, CA 95864
Mailing Address:
P.O. Box 15002
Sacramento, CA 95851
Tel.: 916-484-3011
Fax: 916-484-6506
Year Founded: 1887
Approx.Sls.: $115,000,000
Emp.: 1,300
Fiscal Year-end: 3/31/88
Heavy Engineering Contractors & Building Materials Producers
S.I.C.: 3272; 1611
Louis V. Riggs *(Pres. & Chief Exec. Officer)*
Charles M. Alexander *(Exec. V.P. & Chief Oper. Officer)*
Norman E. Eilert *(Sr. V.P. & Chief Fin. Officer)*

Outside Service Firm(s):

KPMG Peat Marwick*(Auditors)*
2495 Natomas Park Dr., Ste. 600
Sacramento, CA 95833-2936

McDonnell, Holland & Allen*(Legal Firm)*
Sacramento, CA

Wells Fargo Bank*(Major Banking Relationship)*
420 Montgomery St.
San Francisco, CA 94104

Subsidiaries:

Henningsen & Sons, Inc. **(1)**
600 Placerville Dr.
Placerville, CA 95667
Tel.: 916-622-3825
Redi-Mix Concrete
S.I.C.: 5032
Chet Gibson *(Plant Mgr.)*

Teichert Land Co. **(1)**
3500 American River Dr.
Sacramento, CA 95864
Tel.: 916-484-3011 (100%)
Fred Teichert *(Chief Oper. Officer)*

TEKNI-PLEX, INC.
68 35th St.
Brooklyn, NY 11232
Tel.: 718-788-2108 **DE**
Fax: 718-788-2353
Year Founded: 1967
Assets: $12,320,220
Liabilities: $7,847,263
Net Worth: $4,472,957
Approx.Sls.: $31,732,571
Emp.: 257
Export
Manufacture Food, Cosmetics & Pharmaceutical Packaging Materials
S.I.C.: 3089
Tom Y.C. Tang *(Pres.)*
John Hrenyo *(V.P.)*
Carl Mazzone *(V.P.)*
Jane Y. Tang *(Treas. & Corp. Sec.)*
William Kaplan *(Controller)*
Edwin Landis, Esq. *(Gen. Counsel)*
Don Oswall *(Mgr.-Mktg.)*
James Chu *(Mgr.-Mfg.)*
Stanley Mozade *(Dir.-Engrng.)*
Craig Jones *(Dir.-Data Processing)*
Randy Stefanchik *(Pur. Agent)*
Principal(s):
Tom Y.C. Tang

No. of Mfg. Plants/Facilities: 2
No. of U.S. Offices: 2

Outside Service Firm(s):

Rich, Baker, Berman & Company*(Auditors)*
Maplewood, NJ

Meyner & Landis*(Legal Firm)*
Newark, NJ

First National Bank*(Major Banking Relationship)*
Bridgewater, NJ

Subsidiary:

Tekni-Plex, Inc. **(1)**
201 Industrial Pkwy.
Somerville, NJ 08876
Tel.: 908-722-4800
Emp.: 250
Manufacture Packaging Materials
S.I.C.: 3089

TEKNOR APEX COMPANY
505 Central Ave.
Pawtucket, RI 02861
Tel.: 401-725-8000
Fax: 401-725-8095
Approx.Sls.: $200,000,000
Emp.: 1,300
Nylon Resins; Thread, Rubber, Garden Hose, Plasticizers; Window Sheeting
S.I.C.: 2821; 3069; 3052; 2869; 3083
Norman M. Fain *(Chm. Bd.)*
Victor J. Baxt *(Pres.)*
Herbert Malin *(Exec. V.P. & Sec.)*
Jonathan D. Fain *(Sr. V.P.)*

Outside Service Firm(s):

Price Waterhouse*(Major Banking Relationship)*
50 Kennedy Plaza
Providence, RI 02903
Tel.: 401-421-0501

TEKRA CORPORATION
16700 W. Lincoln Ave.
New Berlin, WI 53151
Tel.: 414-784-5533
Tel.: 800-448-3572 **WI**
Telex: 880393 TEKRA UD
Fax: 414-797-3276
Year Founded: 1938
Approx.Sls.: $50,000,000
Emp.: 150
Fiscal Year-end: 1/31/91
Import Export
Wholesale Distributor of Plastic Films, Adhesive Tapes, Laminating Adhesives Hardcoated Plastics & Printable Topcoated Films
S.I.C.: 5113; 2295
William N. Godfrey *(Chm. Bd., Pres. & Chief Exec. Officer)*
Nick Argeroudis *(V.P.-Sls. & Mktg., Distr.)*
Bill Beyer *(V.P.-Opers.)*
Mike Kolman *(V.P.-Res. & Devel.)*
Richard Martin *(V.P.-Sls. & Mktg., C&L)*
Jerry Webb *(V.P.-Fin.)*
Ralph Giammarco *(Dir.-Mktg.)*
Tom Gehl *(Mgr.-Pur.)*
Sheila Goodson *(Mgr.-Quality Control)*
Olga Micic *(Mgr.-Communications)*
Kevin Kelly *(Mgr.-Intl. Sls.)*
Steve Koepke *(Mgr.-Mngmt. Information Systems)*
Karen Vetta *(Mgr.-Human Resources)*

No. of Mfg. Plants/Facilities: 4
No. of U.S. Offices: 4

Computer Systems/Hardware:
Unisys A5 F Mainframe

Outside Service Firm(s):

Arthur Andersen & Co.*(Auditors)*
777 E. Wisconsin Ave., P.O. Box 1215
Milwaukee, WI 53202
Tel.: 414-271-5100
Fax: 414-283-3200

Robertson-Ryan*(Commercial Insurance Carrier)*
Milwaukee, WI
Tel.: 414-277-5591

Alta Health Strategies*(Group Insurer)*
Milwaukee, WI 53201

First Wisconsin Financial Services*(Major Banking Relationship)*
Milwaukee, WI
Tel.: 608-868-6000

M & I Marshall & Isley Bank*(Pension Manager)*
Milwaukee, WI

Divisions:

Tekra Corp., East Coast Div. **(1)**
23 Bridle Ln.
Westboro, MA 05181
Tel.: 508-898-3151
Tel.: 800-448-3572
Fax: 808-898-0150

Tekra Corp., Southeast Div. **(1)**
10900-D S. Commerce Blvd.
Charlotte, NC 28273
Tel.: 704-588-9992
Tel.: 800-248-3572
Fax: 704-588-9992

Tekra Corp., West Coast Div. **(1)**
540 Porter Way
Placentia, CA 92670
Tel.: 714-579-0435
Tel.: 800-448-3572
Fax: 704-579-0435

TELE-COM PRODUCTS, INC.
1070 Hamilton Rd.
Duarte, CA 91010
Tel.: 818-303-1183 **CA**
Fax: 818-358-8485
Year Founded: 1977
Approx.Sls.: $20,000,000

Emp.: 35
Fiscal Year-end: 3/31/92

Import Export
Distribute Electronic & Telephone Products to Retailers Interconnect Companies, Phone Companies, Nationwide
S.I.C.: 5064
Dennis J. Awad *(Pres., Chief Exec. & Fin. Officer & Treas.)*
John Awad *(Exec. Vice Pres. & Dir.-Opers.)*
Carmen Awad *(Dir.-Personnel)*
Hans Smarius *(Dir.-Sls.)*
Tony DeAlmieda *(Mgr.-Data Processing)*
Jackie Largent *(Sec.)*

Principal(s):
Dennis J. Awad

No. of U.S. Offices: 1

Computer Systems/Hardware:
Rexon

Outside Service Firm(s):

Booth & Booth*(Auditors)*
Pasadena, CA

Booth & Booth*(Legal Firm)*
Pasadena, CA

Sanwa Bank*(Major Banking Relationship)*
Pasadena, CA

Mutual Benefit Life Insurance*(Pension Manager)*
520 Broad St.
Newark, NJ 07102-3184
Tel.: 201-481-8000

TELECHRON, INC.
101 Union St.
Ashland, MA 01721
Tel.: 508-881-2500
Fax: 508-881-1466
Year Founded: 1916
Approx.Sls.: $10,000,000
Emp.: 125
Fiscal Year-end: 12/31/90

Export
Electric Timers, Timer Motors & Synchronous Motors
S.I.C.: 3873; 3625
R. Laine *(Pres., Chief Fin. Officer & Treas.)*
B. Beregascazy *(V.P.-Mfg.)*
T. Jones *(V.P.-Tech./Customer Service)*
R. Dunnirvine *(Controller)*
R. Herlihy *(Dir.-Mktg.)*
S. Cormier *(Dir.-Res. & Devel.)*
J. Salvia *(Mgr.-Quality Assurance)*
J. Gresian *(Pur. Agent)*

TELESCIENCES CO. SYSTEMS INC.
351 New Albany Rd.
Moorestown, NJ 08057
Tel.: 609-866-1000 **NJ**
Fax: 609-866-0185
Year Founded: 1987
Assets: $46,000,000
Earnings: $1,022,868
Liabilities: $33,000,000
Net Worth: $13,000,000
Approx.Sls.: $70,000,000
Emp.: 275
Fiscal Year-end: 6/30/90
Telecommunications Equipment, Computer-Controlled Telephone Support Equipment
S.I.C.: 3825; 3661
Howard Oringer *(Chm. Bd. & Chief Exec. Officer)*
James Poynter *(Pres.)*
Steve Cotton *(V.P.-Engrng.)*
Terry Stavropoulos *(V.P.-Opers.)*
Robert Onraet *(Chief Fin. Officer)*
Mark Kadish *(Controller)*

Subsidiary:

Telescience Transmission Systems, Inc. **(1)**
48761 Kato Rd.
Fremont, CA 94538
Tel.: 510-661-0300 (100%)
Approx.Sls.: $45,000,000
Emp.: 400
Mfrs. & Distributes Microwave Radios
S.I.C.: 3663

TELESCOPE CASUAL FURNITURE, INC.
85 Church St.
Granville, NY 12832
Mailing Address:
P.O. Box 299,
Granville, NY 12832
Tel.: 518-642-1100 **NY**
Fax: 518-642-2536
Year Founded: 1903
Approx.Sls.: $26,000,000
Emp.: 300

Import Export
Mfr. Aluminum, Wood & Casual Furniture
S.I.C.: 2511; 2512; 2514
Henry J.W. Vanderminden, Jr. *(Chm. Bd.)*
Henry J.W. Vanderminden III *(Pres.)*
Robert D. Vanderminden, Sr. *(Chief Exec. Officer)*
Raymond Scribner *(Sr. V.P.)*
Kathy Rathbun *(V.P. & Dir.-Human Resources)*
R. Vanderminden, Jr. *(V.P. & Mgr.-Plant)*
Rick Doyle *(Controller)*
John Perkins *(Dir.-Data Processing)*
Griff Thomas *(Dir.-Sls. & Customer Service)*
Pete Didio *(Mgr.-Adv.)*
Barbara Goodspeed *(Mgr.-Employee Benefits)*
Bruce Rathbun *(Mgr.-Quality Control)*
Robert Urlwin *(Mgr.-Mktg.)*
Henry Vanderminden IV *(Mgr.-Sls.)*
Richard Chapman *(Pur. Agent)*

No. of Mfg. Plants/Facilities: 1
No. of U.S. Offices: 1

Computer Systems/Hardware:
IBM System 34

Outside Service Firm(s):

LaGuardia & Petrella*(Auditors)*
Fort Lee, NJ

Manning & Napier*(Investment Banker)*
Rochester, NY

Everett, Johnson & Breckinridge*(Legal Firm)*
New York, NY

John E. Fitzgerald, Esq.*(Legal Firm)*
Glen Falls, NY

Chase Lincoln First Bank, N.A.*(Major Banking Relationship)*
Albany, NY

Norstar Bank, N.A.*(Major Banking Relationship)*
Albany, NY

George Buck Associates*(Pension Manager)*
Two Pennsylvania Plaza
New York, NY 10001
Tel.: 212-330-1050

Subsidiaries:

Mettowee Lumber & Plastic Co., Inc. **(1)**
85 Church St.
Granville, NY 12832
Tel.: 518-642-1100 (100%)
Emp.: 15
Plastic Extrusions & Lumber
S.I.C.: 3089; 2421
Henry J. Vanderminden, Jr. *(Chm. Bd.)*
Robert D. Vanderminden *(Pres. & Treas.)*
Henry J.W. Vanderminden III *(Exec. V.P. & Sec.)*
John Freed *(Mgr.-Sls.)*

Affiliate:

Telegraphics Printing **(1)**
85 Church St.
Granville, NY 12832
Tel.: 518-642-1100
Commercial Printing
S.I.C.: 2752
James Urch *(Mgr.-Adv.)*

TELESENSORY
455 N. Bernardo Ave.
Mountain View, CA 94039
Mailing Address:
P.O. Box 7455
Mountain View, CA 94043
Tel.: 415-960-0920
Tel.: 800-227-8418 **CA**
Fax: 415-969-9064
Year Founded: 1970
Approx.Sls.: $30,000,000
Emp.: 200
Fiscal Year-end: 12/31/91

Export
Mfr. of Electromedical/Electro Theraputic Apparatus, specifically, Electronic Products for the Blind and Visually Impaired
S.I.C.: 3845
Corporate Giving Program:
Corporative Giving is Limitied to Gifts that Support and Encourage the Visually Handicapped and Blind
John G. Linvill *(Chm. Bd.)*
James C. Bliss *(Pres. & Chief Exec. Officer)*
William S. Schwarz *(Exec. V.P. & Chief Fin. Officer)*
Paul J. Lewis *(V.P.-Sls. & Mktg.)*
R. Savoie *(V.P.-Engrng.)*
Natan Saad *(V.P.-Mfg.)*
Barbara Sorensen *(Dir.-Materials)*
Rose Marie Wildsmith *(Dir.-Human Relations)*
Charles Harrison *(Mgr.-Prod.)*

No. of Mfg. Plants/Facilities: 3
No. of U.S. Offices: 1
No. of Foreign Offices: 2

Outside Service Firm(s):

Deloitte & Touche*(Auditors)*
60 S. Market St., Ste. 800
San Jose, CA 95113-2303
Tel.: 408-998-7111
Fax: 408-298-5782

Thoits Insurance Service*(Commercial Insurance Carrier)*
Palo Alto, CA

CIGNA*(Group Insurer)*
101 California St., Ste. 1930
San Francisco, CA 94111
Tel.: 415-954-1387
Fax: 415-954-1385

Wilson, Sonsini, Goodrich & Rosati*(Legal Firm)*
2 Palo Alto Square, Ste. 900
Palo Alto, CA 94306
Tel.: 415-493-9300
Fax: 415-493-6811

Plaza Bank of Commerce*(Major Banking Relationship)*
Sunnyvale, CA

TELEX COMMUNICATIONS, INC.
9600 Aldrich Ave. S.
Minneapolis, MN 55420
Tel.: 612-884-4051 **DE**
Fax: 612-884-0043
Year Founded: 1936
Approx.Sls.: $115,000,000
Emp.: 1,800
Fiscal Year-end: 3/31/92

Export
Manufacture & Market Electronic Audio Communication Devices & Antennas
S.I.C.: 3679
John Hale *(Chm. Bd. & Pres.)*
Phillip Phelon *(Exec. V.P.)*
Darrell Dyer *(V.P. & Treas.)*
Dan Dantzler *(V.P.-Corp. Devel.)*
Michael L. Olinger *(V.P.-Intl. Mktg.)*
Kathy Curran *(Dir.-Human Resources)*
Ronald B. Taylor *(Mgr.-Adv. & Mktg.)*

Computer Systems/Hardware:
Audio/Video Presentation Equipment, Professional Audio, Communication Equipment

Outside Service Firm(s):

First Bank Minneapolis*(Major Banking Relationship)*
P.O. Box A700, 120 S. Sixth St.
Minneapolis, MN 55480
Tel.: 612-370-4141

Divisions:

RTS Systems **(1)**
9600 Aldrich Ave., S.
Minneapolis, MN 55420
Tel.: 612-884-4051
Manufacture Intercoms & Audio Equipment
S.I.C.: 3669
John Hale *(Pres.)*

Telex Hy-gain Div. **(1)**
8601 E. Cornhusker Hwy.
Lincoln, NE 68505
Tel.: 402-467-5321
Emp.: 290
Manufacture & Market Antennas
S.I.C.: 3679
Jim Roths *(Mktg. Mgr.)*

TELL CITY CHAIR CO.
417 Seventh St.
Tell City, IN 47586
Mailing Address:
P.O. Box 369,
Tell City, IN 47586
Tel.: 812-547-3491 **IN**
Fax: 812-547-6977
Year Founded: 1865
Approx.Sls.: $30,000,000
Emp.: 500
Mfr. of American Traditional Furniture
S.I.C.: 2511
Douglas Fenn *(Pres.)*
Dick Yargis *(V.P.-Sls.)*
William N. Smith *(Treas. & Sec.)*
Mark McMahon *(Pur. Agent)*

Outside Service Firm(s):

Citizens Fidelity Bank & Trust*(Major Banking Relationship)*
Tell City, IN

TELSCO INDUSTRIES
3301 W. Kingsley Rd.
Garland, TX 75041
Mailing Address:
P.O. Box 180205,
Dallas, TX 75218
Tel.: 214-278-6131
Fax: 214-271-5710
Year Founded: 1945
Approx.Sls.: $12,000,000
Emp.: 150
Fiscal Year-end: 9/30/92

Export
Manufactures Underground Sprinkler Systems
S.I.C.: 3432
L.O. Snoddy *(Chm. Bd. & Pres.)*
Bob Anderson *(Sec. & Treas.)*
Karen Mitchell *(Dir.-Pur.)*
Don Thompson *(Dir.-Mktg. & Sls.)*
H. Gene Johnson *(Mgr.-Adv. & Sls. Promo.)*

Principal(s):
L.O. Snoddy

No. of Mfg. Plants/Facilities: 1
No. of U.S. Offices: 9
No. of Foreign Offices: 1

Telsco Industries—(Continued)

Computer Systems/Hardware:
Hewlett Packard/PC

Outside Service Firm(s):

Connecticut General Life Insurance Co.*(Group Insurer)*
Dallas, TX

Gardere & Wynne*(Legal Firm)*
3000 Thanksgiving Tower, 1601 Elm St.
Dallas, TX 75201-4761
Tel.: 214-999-3000

InterFirst Bank*(Major Banking Relationship)*
P.O. Box 83000
Dallas, TX 75283
Tel.: 214-744-8000

Division:

Weather-Matic Div. **(1)**
3301 W. Kingsley Rd.
Garland, TX 75041
Tel.: 214-278-6131

TEMKIN & TEMKIN
(Formerly The Schram Advertising Company)
Bldg. 800, 450 Skokie Blvd.
Northbrook, IL 60062
Tel.: 708-498-1700 **IL**
Fax: 708-498-3162
Year Founded: 1945
Sales Range: $10-19 Million
Emp.: 12
Sales Promo., Business-to-Business, Direct Mail, Creative & Production Services
S.I.C.: 7311
Ira P. Weinstein *(Chm. Bd.)*
Steven Temkin *(Pres.)*
Laura W. Temkin *(Co-Pres.)*
Wallace Mason *(V.P., Sec. & Chief Fin. Officer)*

Computer Systems/Hardware:
IBM PC

Outside Service Firm(s):

Ostrow, Reisin, Berk, & Abrams, Ltd.*(Auditors)*
Chicago, IL

Seyfarth, Shaw, Fairweather & Geraldson*(Legal Firm)*
Chicago, IL

Harris Trust & Savings Bank*(Major Banking Relationship)*
111 W. Monroe St.
Chicago, IL 60690
Tel.: 312-461-2265
Tel.: 800-858-0840

TEMP-CONTROL MECHANICAL CORP.
4800 N. Channel
Portland, OR 97217
Mailing Address:
P.O. Box 11065
Portland, OR 97211
Tel.: 503-285-9851
Fax: 503-285-9978
Approx.Sls.: $15,000,000
Emp.: 100
Fiscal Year-end: 12/31/91
Mechanical Contractors
S.I.C.: 1711
James F. Culbertson, Jr. *(Pres.)*
Kevin E. Busch *(Controller)*
Principal(s):
James F. Culbertson, Jr.

Computer Systems/Hardware:
Bidtek

Outside Service Firm(s):

The Emberland Co.*(Auditors)*
Portland, OR

TEMPEL STEEL COMPANY
5215 Old Orchard Rd.
Skokie, IL 60077-1076
Tel.: 708-581-9400 **IL**
Fax: 708-581-9025
Year Founded: 1945
Approx.Sls.: $200,000,000

Import Export
Manufacture Magnetic Steel Laminations for Electric Motors, Generators, Ballasts & Transformers
S.I.C.: 3612; 3621; 3677; 3679
Vincent Buonanno *(Pres.)*
Ron Bailitz *(V.P.-Fin.)*
Stephen A. Foerster *(V.P.-Corp. Plng.)*
Joe Pargulski *(Mgr.-Data Processing)*
Arthur Canning *(Dir.-Personnel)*

No. of Mfg. Plants/Facilities: 3
No. of U.S. Offices: 4
No. of Foreign Offices: 2

Outside Service Firm(s):

Ernst & Young*(Auditors)*
233 S. Wacker Dr.
Chicago, IL 60606
Tel.: 312-368-1800
Fax: 312-645-3095

Pedersen & Houpt*(Legal Firm)*
Chicago, IL

Continental Bank N. A.*(Major Banking Relationship)*
231 S. LaSalle St.
Chicago, IL 60697
Tel.: 312-828-2345
Tel.: 800-426-5754
Telex: 312-828-1783

Subsidiary:

Portage Tool Company **(1)**
2045 Pratt Blvd.
Elk Grove Village, IL 60007
Tel.: 708-569-3860
Manufacture Carbide Dies
S.I.C.: 2819

TEMPERATURE EQUIPMENT CORPORATION
2000 N. Ruby St.
Melrose Park, IL 60160
Tel.: 708-681-6220
Fax: 708-681-0041
Distr. of Warm Air Heating Equipment, Air Conditioning Equipment
S.I.C.: 5075; 5078
Frank Mungo *(Pres.)*
R.F. Toland *(Exec. V.P.)*
Robert Mungo *(V.P. & Treas.)*
Raymond F. Mungo *(V.P.)*
Grant Gregory *(V.P.)*
Kelly Fooch *(Sec.)*

Divisions:

The Harry Alter Company **(1)**
5940 N. Northwest Hwy.
Chicago, IL 60631
Tel.: 312-775-5552
Fax: 312-775-7082
Approx.Sls.: $6,000,000
Emp.: 23
Fiscal Year-end: 12/31/90
National Distributor of Refrigeration, Air Conditioning & Heating Supplies
S.I.C.: 5075; 5078
Todd Allen *(Pres.)*
Art Novacek *(Mgr.-Opers. & Mktg.)*
Greg Liades *(Mgr.-Data Processing)*

Bryant Mungo Division **(1)**
17725 Volbrecht Rd.
Lansing, IL 60438
Tel.: 708-418-0900
Distr. of Bryant Air Conditioning Products
S.I.C.: 5075; 5078
Frank Mungo *(Pres.)*

TEMPLETON, KENLY & CO., INC.
2525 Gardner Rd.
Broadview, IL 60153
Tel.: 708-865-1500 **IL**
Fax: 708-865-0894
Year Founded: 1901
Assets: $15,000,000
Liabilities: $10,000,000
Net Worth: $5,000,000
Approx.Sls.: $18,000,000
Emp.: 200
Fiscal Year-end: 12/31/91
Import Export
Manufacture Mechanical & Hydraulic Jacks, Hydraulic Cylinders & Accessories
S.I.C.: 3569
John Templeton *(Chm. Bd.)*
Robert Spath *(Pres.)*
Arnold Decker *(V.P.-Engrng.)*
Richard R. Kuhr *(V.P.-Mfg.)*
William A. Stepenson *(V.P.-Sls.)*
Robert J. Alberts *(Corp. Sec. & Treas.)*

No. of Mfg. Plants/Facilities: 6
No. of U.S. Offices: 5
No. of Foreign Offices: 3

Computer Systems/Hardware:
IBM

Outside Service Firm(s):

Price Waterhouse*(Auditors)*
200 E. Randolph
Chicago, IL 60601
Tel.: 312-565-1500

Winston & Strawn*(Legal Firm)*
One 1st Natl. Plaza, No. 5000
Chicago, IL 60603
Tel.: 312-558-5600

The Northern Trust Co.*(Major Banking Relationship)*
50 S. LaSalle St.
Chicago, IL 60675
Tel.: 312-630-6000
Fax: 312-630-6516

TEMPORARIES, INCORPORATED
400 N. Sam Houston Pkwy E., Ste. 820
Houston, TX 77060
Tel.: 713-445-5200
Fax: 713-447-3358
Year Founded: 1969
Assets: $8,000,000
Net Worth: $8,000,000
Approx.Sls.: $36,000,000
Emp.: 15,000
Fiscal Year-end: 10/31/89
Temporary Office Help to Business & the Medical Industry, Specializing in Word Processing, Data Processing, & Clerical Help
S.I.C.: 7363
Stacy Noel *(Pres.)*

No. of U.S. Offices: 35

Computer Systems/Hardware:
IBM-PC

TEMPS & COMPANY
3325 M. St., N.W.
Washington, DC 20007
Tel.: 202-463-1556 **GA**
Fax: 202-333-5639
Emp.: 100
Temporary Help Service
S.I.C.: 7363
Steven Etteridge *(Pres.)*
Timothy Etteridge *(Sec. & Treas.)*

Outside Service Firm(s):

Century National Bank*(Major Banking Relationship)*
Washington, DC

Division:

Temps & Co. **(1)**
655 15th St. N.W.
Washington, DC 20005
Tel.: 202-463-8686
Accounting Office For Temporary Service
S.I.C.: 7363
Steven Ettridge *(Pres.)*

TENAX CORPORATION
4 Old Newtown Rd.
Danbury, CT 06810
Tel.: 203-792-8400
Fax: 203-744-6817
Year Founded: 1966
Approx.Sls.: $30,000,000
Emp.: 300
Fiscal Year-end: 6/30/90
Export
Mfr. of Custom Molded Plastic Parts for Health Care & Electronic Industry
S.I.C.: 3089
Michael Rich *(Pres.)*
F. Donald Ek *(Exec. V.P.)*
Antony D'Amico *(V.P.-Fin.)*
Peter Arentzen *(V.P.-Sls.)*
Paul Ford *(Dir.-Pur.)*
Joan Carpenter *(Personnel Dir.)*

TENCARVA MACHINERY CO., INC.
3409 W. Wendover Ave.
Greensboro, NC 27407
Mailing Address:
P.O. Box 7267
Greensboro, NC 27407
Tel.: 919-852-1043 **DE**
Fax: 919-852-0689
Year Founded: 1978
Approx.Sls.: $31,000,000
Emp.: 76
Fiscal Year-end: 12/31/91
Wholesale & Service Machinery, Machine Tools & Industrial Equipment
S.I.C.: 5084
John S. Miller *(Pres. & Chief Exec. Officer)*
Henry V. Cashwell *(Sec. & Treas.)*
Principal(s):
Henry V. Cashwell

No. of U.S. Offices: 14

Computer Systems/Hardware:
IBM System 36

Outside Service Firm(s):

Price Waterhouse*(Auditors)*
1800 One Triad Plaza
Winston-Salem, NC 27101
Tel.: 919-725-0691
Fax: 919-725-5022

Nationwide Insurance*(Commercial Insurance Carrier)*
Greensboro, NC

Mid-South Insurance Co.*(Group Insurer)*
Fayetteville, NC

Schell, Bray, Aycock, Abel & Livingston*(Legal Firm)*
P.O. Box 21847, 230 N. Elm St.
Greensboro, NC 27401
Tel.: 919-370-8800
Fax: 919-370-8830

NationsBank Carolinas*(Major Banking Relationship)*
Greensboro, NC

Sterling Capital Management Co.*(Pension Manager)*
1770 Independence Center
Charlotte, NC 28246
Tel.: 704-372-8670

Divisions:

Tencarva Machinery Company **(1)**
4108 Park Rd, Ste. 215
Charlotte, NC 28209
Tel.: 704-521-9400
Fax: 704-521-8988
Wholesale Machine Tools
S.I.C.: 5084
C.J. Pearce *(Mgr.)*

Tencarva Machinery Co. **(1)**
3508 Overlook Circle
Knoxville, TN 37919
Tel.: 615-588-7674
Fax: 615-588-7676
Wholesale Machine Tools
S.I.C.: 5084
D.F. Hubbard *(Mgr.)*

Tencarva Machinery Co. **(1)**
321 E. Trinity Lane
Nashville, TN 37207
Tel.: 615-227-6770
Fax: 615-227-6772
Wholesale Machine Tools
S.I.C.: 5084
N.W. Hicks *(V.P. & Mgr.)*

Tencarva Machinery Co. **(1)**
153 Business Park, Warehouse #2, Bay 10
Chattanooga, TN 37421
Tel.: 615-892-8928
Fax: 615-892-8929
Wholesale Machine Tools
S.I.C.: 5084
J.W. Wilson *(Mgr.)*

Tencarva Machinery Co. **(1)**
3725 Getwell Cove
Memphis, TN 38118
Tel.: 901-794-7570
Fax: 901-794-7593
S.I.C.: 5084
W.B. Strong *(Mgr.)*

Tencarva Machinery Co. **(1)**
2831 E. Oakland Ave.
Johnson City, TN 37602
Tel.: 615-282-5455
Fax: 615-282-3204
Wholesale Machine Tools
S.I.C.: 5084
J.R. Smith *(Mgr.)*

Tencarva Machinery Co. **(1)**
1405 Old Dairy Road
Columbia, SC 29201
Tel.: 803-256-8100
Fax: 803-256-8102
Wholesale Machine Tools
S.I.C.: 5084
W.F. Wannamaker *(V.P.)*
W.H. Crawford, Jr. *(Mgr.)*

Tencarva Machinery Co. **(1)**
Pelham Industrial Pk.
Greer, SC 29651
Tel.: 803-297-6464
Fax: 803-297-6466
Wholesale Machine Tools
S.I.C.: 5084
H.D. George *(Mgr.)*

Tencarva Machinery Co. **(1)**
1244 B. Executive Blvd., Ste. 114
Chesapeake, VA 23320
Tel.: 804-548-0400
Fax: 804-548-2408
Wholesale Machine Tools
S.I.C.: 5084
R.M. Lee *(Mgr.)*
J.T. Smith *(V.P.)*

Tencarva Machinery Co. **(1)**
3646 Aerial Way Dr., Suite 1
Roanoke, VA 24018
Tel.: 703-343-6978
Fax: 703-343-6981
Wholesale Machine Tools
S.I.C.: 5084
D.A. Wirth *(Mgr.)*

Tencarva Machinery Co. **(1)**
2231 E. Belt Blvd.
Richmond, VA 23224
Tel.: 804-231-6266
Fax: 804-231-9265
Wholesale Machine Tools
S.I.C.: 5084
W.S. Tatum *(Mgr.)*

Tencarva Machinery Co. **(1)**
3409 W. Wendover Ave., Ste. 101
Greensboro, NC 27407
Tel.: 919-852-1040
Fax: 919-852-0689
Wholesale Machine Tools
S.I.C.: 5084
H.S. Muse, Jr. *(Mgr.)*

Tencarva Machinery Co. **(1)**
108 N. Kerr Ave., Ste.A1
Wilmington, NC 28405
Tel.: 919-799-8800
Fax: 919-799-8801
Wholesale Machine Tools
S.I.C.: 5084
R.W. Tayloe *(V.P. & Mgr.)*

Tencarva Machinery Co.-Asheville **(1)**
230-6 Rutledge Road
Fletcher, NC 28732-9325
Tel.: 704-684-2896
Fax: 704-684-2897
Wholesale Machine Tools
S.I.C.: 5084
K.D. Love *(Mgr.)*

Tencarva Machinery Company **(1)**
2460 Remount Rd., Suite 107
North Charleston, SC 29418
Tel.: 803-747-1173
Fax: 803-747-1174
Wholesale Machine Tools
S.I.C.: 5084
D.S. Lee *(Mgr.)*

Tencarva Machinery Co. **(1)**
P.O. Box 16312,
Baltimore, MD 21210
Tel.: 301-235-9302
Fax: 301-467-4629
Wholesale Machine Tools
S.I.C.: 5084

A. TENENBAUM CO. INC.
4500 W. Bethany Rd.
North Little Rock, AR 72117
Tel.: 501-945-0881 **AR**
Fax: 501-945-3865
Year Founded: 1890
Approx.Sls.: $98,000,000
Emp.: 212
Wholesale Scrap Metal & Steel
S.I.C.: 5093; 5051
Joseph M. Tenenbaum *(Chm. Bd.)*
Harold Tenenbaum *(Pres.)*
R.J. Wills *(Sec. & Treas.)*

Outside Service Firm(s):

Dobbs, Albright & Co.*(Auditors)*
Little Rock, AR

Eichenbaum, Scott, Miller, Crockett & Darr*(Legal Firm)*
Tower Bldg.
Little Rock, AR 72201
Tel.: 501-376-4531

Worthen National Bank of Arkansas*(Major Banking Relationship)*
P.O. Box 1681, 200 W. Capitol
Little Rock, AR 72201
Tel.: 501-378-1209
Fax: 501-378-1062

Subsidiary:

Arkansas Aluminum Alloys **(1)**
P.O. Box 1410
Hot Springs, AR 71902
Tel.: 501-262-3420
Wholesale Scrap Metal
S.I.C.: 5093

TENNELEC/NUCLEUS, INC.
(Sub. of Oxford Instruments Group, plc, Oxford, U.K.)
601 Oak Ridge Turnpike
Oak Ridge, TN 37830
Mailing Address:
P.O. Box 2560,
Oak Ridge, TN 37831-2560
Tel.: 615-482-4041 **TN**
Fax: 615-483-5891
Year Founded: 1968
Assets: $7,000,000
Earnings: $1,110,000
Liabilities: $2,500,000
Net Worth: $4,500,000
Approx.Sls.: $15,250,000
Emp.: 178
Fiscal Year-end: 3/31/91
Import Export
Manufacture of Electronic Instrumentation
S.I.C.: 3829; 3679
David Coffey *(Chm. Bd.)*
John Hearn *(Pres. & Chief Exec. Officer)*
Coley Pardue *(V.P.-Fin.)*
Judy Voght *(V.P.-Personnel & Human Resources & Sec.)*
C. Eugene Lawson *(Controller)*
Gil El Sayad *(Mgr.-Export)*

Outside Service Firm(s):

Willard L. Carr, CPA*(Auditors)*
P.O. Box 3521,
Oak Ridge, TN 37851

Third National Bank*(Major Banking Relationship)*
Oak Ridge, TN

TENNESSEE DRESSED BEEF COMPANY
50 Van Buren St.
Nashville, TN 37208
Tel.: 615-742-5800 **TN**
Fax: 615-742-5814
Approx.Sls.: $100,000,000
Emp.: 95
Fresh Meats; Beef Products From Beef Slaughtered On Site
S.I.C.: 5147; 2011
Richard N. Hall, Sr. *(Pres.)*
William A. Hall *(Sec. & Treas.)*

Outside Service Firm(s):

Arthur Andersen & Co.*(Auditors)*
Third Natl. Fin. Cntr., 424 Church St., Ste. 1100
Nashville, TN 37219

Sovran Bank*(Major Banking Relationship)*
One Commerce Place M-B
Nashville, TN 37219
Tel.: 615-749-4113

Division:

Action Commodities Corporation **(1)**
P.O. Box 1384
Loganville, GA 30249
Tel.: 404-466-6302
Meat Brokers
S.I.C.: 6163
John Denney *(Gen. Mgr.)*

TENNESSEE FARMERS CO-OP
200 Waldron
La Vergne, TN 37086
Mailing Address:
P.O. Box 3003,
La Vergne, TN 37086
Tel.: 615-793-8011
Telex: 810 380 4303
Fax: 615-793-8343
Year Founded: 1945
Assets: $100,000,000
Earnings: $2,100,000
Liabilities: $54,000,000
Net Worth: $46,000,000
Approx.Sls.: $290,000,000
Emp.: 585
Fiscal Year-end: 7/31/91
Agricultural Production & Services; Manufacture Agricultural Chemicals
S.I.C.: 2048; 2873; 2874; 5072; 2879; 5172; 2047
Kenneth Nixon *(Chm. Bd.)*
Bobby Warren *(Vice Chm.)*
Philip R. Walker *(Pres. & Chief Exec. Officer)*
Charles Reeves *(Chief Fin. Officer & Treas.)*
Bob Cunningham *(Gen. Counsel & Sec.)*
Charles Atkins *(V.P.-Sls.)*
Herbert Groce *(V.P.)*
Allen Pogue *(V.P.)*
Ray Wilson *(V.P.)*
William Davis *(Dir.-Personnel, Human Resources & Employee Benefits)*
David Martin *(Dir.-Safety)*
Marshall Anderson *(Mgr.-Data Processing)*
Charles Cunningham *(Mgr.-Personnel Training & Devel.)*
Jerry Kirk *(Mgr.-Adv.)*

No. of Mfg. Plants/Facilities: 9

Computer Systems/Hardware:
PC Wide Area LAN System

Outside Service Firm(s):

KPMG Peat Marwick*(Auditors)*
1900 Nashville Center, 511 Union St.
Nashville, TN 37219

NationsBank of Tennessee*(Commercial Insurance Carrier)*
One Sovran Plaza
Nashville, TN 37219
Tel.: 615-749-3333

Nationwide Insurance*(Commercial Insurance Carrier)*
Columbus, OH

Wausau Insurance*(Commercial Insurance Carrier)*
Atlanta, GA

Equitable Real Estate Investment Managment Inc.*(Group Insurer)*
3414 Peachtree Rd. N.E.
Atlanta, GA 30326-1162

Southeastern Advisory Services*(Investment Banker)*
Atlanta, GA

Sovran Bank*(Investment Banker)*
One Commerce Place M-B
Nashville, TN 37219
Tel.: 615-749-4113

Reinhart, Boerner, Van Deuren, Norris & Rieselbach, S.C.*(Legal Firm)*
1000 N. Water St., Ste. 2100
Milwaukee, WI 53202
Tel.: 414-298-1000

Commerce Union*(Major Banking Relationship)*
Nashville, TN

Subsidiary:

Dyer-Lauderdale Farmers Co-op **(1)**
Dyersburg, TN (100%)
Emp.: 26
Retail Farm Supplies
S.I.C.: 3523
Stanley Anderson *(Chief Oper. Officer)*

TENNESSEE RESTAURANT CORP.
One Pierce Pl., Ste. 100E
Itasca, IL 60143
Tel.: 708-250-0471
Holding Company
S.I.C.: 6719; 5812; 5451
Donald Smith *(Chm. Bd.)*
Rick Arras *(Pres.)*

Subsidiaries:

Friendly Ice Cream Corp. **(1)**
1855 Boston Rd.
Wilbraham, MA 01095
Tel.: 413-543-2400
Fax: 413-543-3966
Approx.Sls.: $500,000,000
Emp.: 37,000
Mfr. of Ice Cream; Restaurant Chain Company Operating Over 700 Retail Restaurants
S.I.C.: 2024; 5812
Donald N. Smith *(Pres.)*
Joseph A. O'Shaughnessy *(Sr. Exec. V.P.)*
Larry W. Browne *(Sr. V.P., Corp. Fin. Officer, & Gen. Counsel)*
William R. Fraser *(V.P.-Pur.)*
Michael D. Kelly *(V.P.-Mktg.)*

Tennessee Restaurant Corp.—(Continued)

David Young *(Dir.-Human Resources Devel.)*

Division:

Food Service Division **(2)**
1855 Boston Rd.
Wilbraham, MA 01095
Tel.: 413-543-2400
Gerald Sinsigalli *(Pres.)*

Perkins Family Restaurants **(1)**
6075 Poplar Ave., Ste. 800
Memphis, TN 38119
Tel.: 901-766-6400
Fax: 901-766-6482
Assets: $119,095,000
Earnings: $15,184,000
Liabilities: $54,166,000
Net Worth: $64,929,000
Approx.Rev.: $180,512,000
Emp.: 6,900
Restaurants
S.I.C.: 5812
Donald N. Smith *(Chm. & Chief Exec. Officer)*
Richard K. Arras *(Pres. & Chief Oper. Officer)*
Dan G. Esmond *(Exec. V.P.-Opers.)*
Larry Brown *(Sr. V.P.-Corp. Fin.)*
Susan E. Henderson-Hernandez *(V.P.-Mktg.)*
James Barrasso *(V.P.-Pur.)*
Joe Colonnetta, Jr. *(V.P.-Corp. Fin.)*
Michael P. Donahoe *(V.P., Chief Fin. Officer & Treas.)*
Joe Gillette *(V.P.-Opers.)*
Norman J. Hill *(V.P.-Human Resources)*
Jack W. Willingham *(V.P.-Corp. Devel.)*
Donald F. Wiseman *(V.P., Gen. Counsel & Sec.)*
L. Wayne Drury *(Controller)*
Paul Freeman *(Dir.-Research & Devel.)*
Phil Joyner *(Dir.-Mngmt. Information Systems)*
John King *(Dir.-Mktg.)*
Bob Winters *(Dir.-Training)*
Margaret Hancock *(Dir.-Telecommunications)*
Dodie Goldsmith *(Mgr.-Employee Benefits)*
Louis Jeml *(Mgr.-Gen. Acctg.)*
Karen Larson *(Mgr.-Plng. & Devel.)*

TENNESSEE VALLEY AUTHORITY
400 W. Summitt Hill Dr.
Knoxville, TN 37902-1499
Tel.: 615-632-2101
Fax: 615-632-6783
Year Founded: 1933
Assets: $27,672,000,000
Earnings: ($387,000,000)
Liabilities: $23,073,000,000
Net Worth: $4,599,000,000
Approx.Sls.: $5,339,000,000
Emp.: 27,000
Fiscal Year-end: 9/30/90
Resource Development & Electric Power Production & Wholesale Distribution in the Tennessee Valley--Tennessee, Parts of Alabama, Georgia, Mississippi, Kentucky, North Carolina & Virginia
S.I.C.: 4911
Corporate Giving Program:
Participates in Combined Federal Campaign
Marvin T. Runyon *(Chm. Bd.)*
William F. Willis *(Sr. Exec. V.P.)*
William F. Malec *(Sr. V.P. & Chief Fin. Officer)*
Mary L. Cartwright *(Sr. V.P.-Communications & Employee Devel.)*
Robert C. Steffy, Jr. *(Sr. V.P. & Chief Quality Officer)*
Robert L. Yates *(V.P. & Treas.)*
Edward S. Christenbury *(V.P. & Gen. Counsel)*
Tony Creswell *(V.P.-Minority Resources)*
Louis S. Grande *(V.P.-Information Services)*
James W. McCarter *(V.P.-Pur.)*
Norman A. Zigrossi *(Inspector Gen.)*
Michael E. Draper *(Controller)*
Terrell Burkhart *(Mgr.-Treas. Services)*
Richard C. Crawford *(Mgr.-Transmission & Customer Services)*
Larry H. Edwards *(Mgr.-Retirement Services)*
John J. O'Donnell *(Mgr.-Facilities Services)*
Daniel B. Shaver *(Mgr.-Telecommunications)*
Kathy J. White *(Mgr.-Fin. Dept.)*
H. Reid Campbell *(Specialist-Customer Services)*
Oliver D. Kingsley, Jr. *(Pres.)*
Joseph W. Dickey *(Sr. V.P.-Fossil & Hydro Generations)*
Dan Nauman *(Sr. V.P.-Nuclear Generation)*
Joseph R. Bynum *(V.P.-Nuclear Opers.)*
John H. Garrity *(V.P.-Watts Bar Nuclear Plant)*
Nicholas C. Kazanas *(V.P.-Completion Assurance)*
William Kuh *(V.P.-Employee Rels. & Devel.)*
H. Fred McCluskey *(V.P.-Browns Ferry Restart)*
Mark O. Medford *(V.P.-Nuclear Assurance, Licensing & Fuels)*
William Museler *(V.P.-Belefonte)*
John W. Thompson *(V.P.-Fuels)*
Tom Williams *(V.P.-Fossil Opers.)*
Jack L. Wilson *(V.P.-Sequoyah Nuclear Plant)*
O.J. Zeringue *(V.P.-Browns Ferry Nuclear)*
Frank Adkins *(Acting V.P.-Hydro Opers.)*
Bob Wernly *(Quality Officer)*
Mary Sharpe Hayes *(Pres.)*
Jimmy L. Cross *(V.P.-Customer Plng.)*
Glenn E. Parrish *(V.P.-Customer Service E. & W.)*
Richard L. Tallant *(V.P.-Customer Service N. & S.)*
Steve G. Whitley *(V.P.-Transmission)*
W.F. Willis *(Pres.)*
Billy J. Bond *(V.P.-River Basin Opers.)*
John T. Shields *(Sr. V.P.-Natl. Fertilizer & Environmental Res. Center)*
John G. Stewart *(V.P.-Valley Resources)*

Computer Systems/Hardware:
IBM Mainframe and Personal Computers

TENNESSEE WHOLESALE DRUG COMPANY
200 Cumberland Bend
Nashville, TN 37228
Tel.: 615-244-8110 **TN**
Fax: 615-254-1565
Wholesaler of Drugs
S.I.C.: 5122; 5100
J.E. Richard *(Chm. Bd. & Chief Oper. Officer)*
Pauline Hohlfeld *(Pres.)*

Subsidiary:

Alabama Wholesale Drug Co. **(1)**
822 James Record Rd.
Huntsville, AL 35824
Tel.: 205-772-7150 (100%)
Wholesale Drug Distributor
S.I.C.: 5122; 5100
Charles Nix *(Gen. Mgr.)*

TENNSCO CORPORATION
201 Tennsco Dr.
Dickson, TN 37055
Mailing Address:
P.O. Box 1888
Dickson, TN 87056
Tel.: 615-446-8000
Tel.: 800-251-8184
Fax: 615-446-7224
Year Founded: 1962
Approx.Sls.: $55,000,000
Emp.: 545
Fiscal Year-end: 3/31/91
Import
Office Cabinets
S.I.C.: 2522
Lester D. Speyer *(Chm. Bd.)*
Stuart W. Speyer *(Pres.)*
Joe F. Youree *(Exec. V.P.)*
Jerry B. Estes *(V.P.)*
Hal McCalla *(V.P.-Sls.)*
Roy L. Stinson *(V.P.)*
Robert Speyer *(Treas.)*
Mickey Self *(Pur. Agent)*

Principal(s):
Lester D. Speyer
Stuart W. Speyer

No. of Mfg. Plants/Facilities: 6
No. of U.S. Offices: 1

Computer Systems/Hardware:
DEC

Outside Service Firm(s):

Mayes & Wolters CPA*(Auditors)*
308 E. College St.
Dickson, TN

Liberty Mutual*(Commercial Insurance Carrier)*
P.O. Box 300, Three Maryland Farms, Ste. 230
Brentwood, TN 37027-0300
Tel.: 615-373-9555

Bass, Berry & Sims*(Legal Firm)*
27th Fl., First American Ctr.
Nashville, TN 37238
Tel.: 615-244-5370

Third National Bank*(Major Banking Relationship)*
201 4th Ave. No., Uptown Sta., Box 2844
Nashville, TN 37167
Tel.: 615-748-4742

The Principal Financial Group*(Pension Manager)*
711 High St.
Des Moines, IA 50309
Tel.: 800-543-4015

TENSION ENVELOPE CORP.
819 E. 19th St.
Kansas City, MO 64108-1781
Tel.: 816-471-3800
Fax: 816-283-1498
Year Founded: 1886
Approx.Sls.: $180,000,000
Emp.: 1,500
Fiscal Year-end: 9/30/91
Mfr. of Custom Envelopes
S.I.C.: 2677
E. Bertram Berkley *(Chm. Bd.)*
Walter Hiersteiner *(Vice Chm.)*
William Berkley *(Pres. & Chief Exec. Officer)*
Larry R. Denton *(V.P.-Fin.)*
Richard Kranz *(V.P.-Production)*
Gary Surbaugh *(V.P.-Natl. Sls.)*
Richard L. Berkley *(Sec. & Treas.)*
Robert McGowan *(Dir.-Pur.)*
William Sharp *(Dir.-Personnel)*
Bernard Klein *(Mgr.-Mktg. Devel.)*
Andrew Weed *(Mgr.-Gen. Sls.)*
Dan Imler *(Mgr.-Mtg. Communications)*
Karl Dahlquist *(Mgr.-Data Processing)*

No. of Mfg. Plants/Facilities: 11
No. of U.S. Offices: 39

Computer Systems/Hardware:
IBM

Outside Service Firm(s):

Arthur Andersen & Co.*(Auditors)*
1500 Commerce Tower, 911 Main St.
Kansas City, MO 64105
Tel.: 816-221-4200
Fax: 816-221-7693

Margolin & Kirwin*(Legal Firm)*
Kansas City, MO

Commerce Bank of Kansas City*(Major Banking Relationship)*
10th & Walnut
Kansas City, MO 64141
Tel.: 816-234-2000
Fax: 816-234-2548

TERRAL-NORRIS SEED CO., INC.
604 Ninth St.
Lake Providence, LA 71254
Mailing Address:
P.O. Box 826
Lake Providence, LA 71254
Tel.: 318-559-2840
Year Founded: 1950
Approx.Sls.: $15,000,000
Emp.: 50
Export
Distribution of Seed, Soybeans, Rice, Wheat, Oats & Corn
S.I.C.: 5153; 5191
Thomas F. Terral *(Pres. & Chief Exec. Officer)*
Larry J. Mullen *(V.P.-Sls., Sec. & Treas.)*

TERMINAL GRAIN CORP.
518 8th St.
Sioux City, IA 51101
Mailing Address:
P.O. Box 3809
Sioux City, IA 51102
Tel.: 712-258-6596
Fax: 712-258-6590
Assets: $12.000,000
Net Worth: $12,000,000
Approx.Sls.: $40,000,000
Emp.: 70
Fiscal Year-end: 6/30/88
Agricultural Services
S.I.C.: 5153; 5191
Douglas E. Palmer *(Pres. & Chief Fin. Officer)*
Frank Boeshart *(V.P., Treas. & Controller)*

Computer Systems/Hardware:
IBM PC

Outside Service Firm(s):

AMC-Melewar Zecha Communications Sdn. Bhd.*(Auditors)*
No.1, Wisma AMC, Jalan Sri Semantan
Satu 50490 Damansara Heights,
Kuala Lumpur, Malaysia
Tel.: 3-254-5000
Telex: MA 31832 MZC
Fax: 03-255-0558/9826

Klass, Whitcher, & Mishne*(Legal Firm)*
Sioux City, IA

Security National Bank*(Major Banking Relationship)*
Sioux City, IA

TERMINIX SERVICE, INC.
3618 Fernandino Rd.
Columbia, SC 29210
Mailing Address:
P.O. Box 2627
Columbia, SC 29202
Tel.: 803-772-1783 **SC**
Fax: 803-772-1845
Year Founded: 1947
Approx.Sls.: $20,000,000
Emp.: 475
Fiscal Year-end: 12/31/90
Pest Control, Repairs, Moisture Control
S.I.C.: 7342
T.P. Knox, Jr. *(Chm. Bd.)*
Marion A. Knox, Sr. *(Vice Chm.)*
Thomas N. Fortson, Jr. *(Pres.)*
Marion A. Knox, Jr. *(V.P., Treas. & Sec.)*

Principal(s):
T.P. Knox, Jr.
Marion A. Knox, Sr.
Thomas N. Fortson, Jr.
Marion A. Knox, Jr.

Computer Systems/Hardware:
IBM AS-400

Outside Service Firm(s):

Rogers Montgomery & Co., P.A.*(Auditors)*
Columbia, SC

Belser, Lewis, Bruce & Rogers*(Legal Firm)*
Columbia, SC

NationsBank*(Major Banking Relationship)*
Columbia, SC

TERRE HILL CONCRETE PRODUCTS, INC.
Rte. 897 S.
Terre Hill, PA 17581
Tel.: 215-445-6736 **PA**
Fax: 215-445-7724
Year Founded: 1917
Sales Range: $20-39 Million
Emp.: 180
Import Export
Mfr. of Concrete Blocks & Precast Concrete Products
S.I.C.: 3272; 3271
E.G. Smith *(Chm. Bd.)*
Robert Lazarchick *(Pres.)*
John Glass *(V.P.)*
A. Martin, Jr. *(V.P.-Opers.)*
Dale Wiest *(Controller)*
Klara Smith *(Sec.)*

Outside Service Firm(s):

Meridian Bank*(Major Banking Relationship)*
One Meridian Plaza, 36th Fl.
Philadelphia, PA
Tel.: 215-854-3900

TERUYA BROS., LTD.
1276 Young St.
Honolulu, HI 96814
Tel.: 808-521-6946
Fax: 808-536-8517
Holding Company; Supermarkets
S.I.C.: 6719; 5411
Raymond Teruya *(Chm. Bd. & Chief Exec. Officer)*
Wallace Teruya *(Vice Chm.)*

Outside Service Firm(s):

Bank of Hawaii*(Major Banking Relationship)*
Honolulu, HI

Subsidiary:

Times Super Market Ltd. **(1)**
2153 N. King St.
Honolulu, HI 96819
Tel.: 808-847-0811
Fax: 808-841-5283
Approx.Sls.: $187,000,000
Emp.: 1,000
Supermarket Chain
S.I.C.: 5411
George Miura *(Pres.)*
Wayne Teruya *(Exec. V.P.-Fin.)*

TETKO, INC.
333 S. Highland Ave.
Briarcliff Manor, NY 10510
Tel.: 914-941-7767 **NY**
Fax: 914-762-8498
Sales Range: $40-59 Million
Emp.: 150
Fiscal Year-end: 12/31/91
Export
Synthetic Silk Fabrics, Wire Meshes & Supplies
S.I.C.: 2221; 3496
Peter Lohaus *(Pres.)*
Patrick Callaghan *(V.P.-Fin.)*
Richard Antes *(Comptroller)*
Ed Greger *(Mgr.- Div.)*
Al Guercio *(Mgr.- Div.)*

Outside Service Firm(s):

Deloitte & Touche*(Auditors)*
1 World Trade Center
New York, NY 10048
Tel.: 212-669-5000

Cuddy & Fedder*(Legal Firm)*
White Plaines, NY

Chase Manhattan Bank, N.A.*(Major Banking Relationship)*
One Chase Manhattan Plaza
New York, NY 10081
Tel.: 212-552-2222
Tel.: 800-526-0801
Fax: 212-552-7175

Division:

Tetko Inc., Depew Operations **(1)**
P.O. Box 346
Lancaster, NY 14086
Tel.: 716-683-4050
Emp.: 65
Chuck Wait *(V.P. & Gen. Mgr.)*

Teton International
(See B & B Homes Corporation Listing)

TEXAS COMMERCE BANCSHARES, INC.
712 Main St.
Houston, TX 77002
Mailing Address:
P.O. Box 2558,
Houston, TX 77252
Tel.: 713-236-4865 **DE**
Year Founded: 1886
Assets: $18,215,000,000
Earnings: $104,000,000
Liabilities: $17,241,000,000
Net Worth: $974,000,000
Approx.Sls.: $711,000,000
Emp.: 7,800
Fiscal Year-end: 12/31/90
Bank Holding Company
S.I.C.: 6021; 6712
Marc J. Shapiro *(Chm. Bd.)*
John L. Adams *(Vice Chm.)*
Robert C. Hunter *(Vice Chm.)*
Alan R. Buckwalter III *(Pres.)*
H. Worth Burke *(Exec. V.P.-Capital Markets)*
Frank T. Carnella *(Exec. V.P. - Technology)*
Donald L. Hawk *(Exec. V.P.-Admin.)*
Stephen H. Field *(Exec. V.P.-Real Estate Banking)*
David W. Mooney *(Exec. V.P.-Consumer Banking)*
Keith D. Oldfield *(Exec. V.P.-Loan Admin.)*
Larry L. Shryock *(Exec. V.P.-Comml. Banking)*
Kenneth L. Tilton *(Exec. V.P. & Controller)*
Marshall C. Tyndall *(Exec. V.P.-Mktg.)*
Michael H. Tyson *(Exec. V.P.-Trust)*
Gary K. Wright *(Exec. V.P.-Corp. Banking)*
Steven M. Youts *(Exec. V.P.-Investment Banking)*
Beverly H. McCaskill *(Sr. V.P., Chief Admin. Officer & Sec.)*
Ann V. Rogers *(Sr. V.P.-Human Resources)*
Shelby R. Rogers *(Sr. V.P. & Gen. Counsel)*
David Senior *(Sr. V.P.-Real Estate)*
C. Richard Summers *(Sr. V.P.-Plng. & Devel.)*
Sarah H. Peterson *(V.P.-Pub. Rels.)*
D. Glenn Baird *(Mktg. Officer)*

Banking Subsidiaries:

Stone Fort National Bank **(1)**
300 E. Main St.
Nacogdoches, TX 75961
Tel.: 713-564-4624 (100%)
Banking
S.I.C.: 6021
Gary Godfrey *(Chm.)*

Texas Commerce Bank-Amarillo **(1)**
2201 Civic Circle
Amarillo, TX 79109
Tel.: 806-355-9661 (100%)
Banking
S.I.C.: 6021
George C. Sell *(Chm.)*

Texas Commerce Bank-Austin **(1)**
700 Lavaca
Austin, TX 78701
Tel.: 512-476-6611 (100%)
Banking
S.I.C.: 6021
W. Merriman Morton *(Chm.)*

Texas Commerce Bank-Beaumont **(1)**
510 Park
Beaumont, TX 77704
Tel.: 409-838-0234 (100%)
Banking
S.I.C.: 6021
Dan Hallmark *(Chm.)*

Texas Commerce Bank-Rio Grande Valley **(1)**
1034 E. Levee St.
Brownsville, TX 78520
Tel.: 210-546-2461 (100%)
Banking
S.I.C.: 6021
Robert M. Duffey, Jr. *(Chm.)*

Texas Commerce Bank-Corpus Christi **(1)**
802 N. Carancau
Corpus Christi, TX 78403
Tel.: 512-883-3621 (100%)
Banking
S.I.C.: 6021
Mike Nogueira *(Chm.)*

Texas Commerce Bank-National Association **(1)**
2200 Ross
Dallas, TX 75201
Tel.: 214-922-2300 (100%)
Banking
S.I.C.: 6021
John L. Adams *(Chm. & Chief Exec. Officer)*

Texas Commerce Bank-Houston **(1)**
712 Main St.
Houston, TX 77002
Tel.: 713-236-4865 (100%)
S.I.C.: 6021
Marc Shapiro *(Chm.)*

Texas Commerce Bank-Longview **(1)**
213 N. Fredonia
Longview, TX 75601
Tel.: 903-753-5511 (100%)
Banking
S.I.C.: 6021
Leland Camp *(Chm.)*

Texas Commerce Bank-Lubbock **(1)**
1701 W. Hwy. 83
Lubbock, TX 79408
Tel.: 806-763-3471
Banking
S.I.C.: 6021
Tommie Stevens *(Chm.)*

Texas Commerce Bank-New Braunfels **(1)**
111 W. San Antonio St.
New Braunfels, TX 78130
Tel.: 210-625-7541 (100%)
Banking
S.I.C.: 6021
Bob Smith *(Chm.)*

Texas Commerce Bank-Odessa **(1)**
620 N. Grant
Odessa, TX 79760
Tel.: 915-337-5261 (100%)
Banking
S.I.C.: 6021
Ron Fancher *(Chm.)*

Texas Commerce Bank-San Angelo **(1)**
301 W. Beauregard
San Angelo, TX 76901
Tel.: 915-653-5911 (100%)
Banking
S.I.C.: 6021
Dal Dewees *(Pres.)*

Texas Commerce Bank-San Antonio **(1)**
1020 N.E. Loop 410
San Antonio, TX 78209
Tel.: 210-829-6100 (100%)
Banking
S.I.C.: 6021
Joe McKinney *(Chm. & Chief Exec. Officer)*

TEXAS ELECTRIC COOPERATIVES, INC.
8140 Burnet Rd.
Austin, TX 78758
Tel.: 512-454-0311
Fax: 512-454-4221
Approx.Sls.: $16,000,000
Emp.: 170
Manufacture Power Line Poles, Electrical Transformers; Trade Association Activities & Engineering Consulting
S.I.C.: 2491; 2741; 8711
Henry UnSheid *(Pres.)*
James A. Morris *(Exec. V.P.)*
Pat McAlester *(Sec. & Treas.)*
Bill Lewis *(Editor)*
Neal Johnson *(Dir.-Govt. Rels.)*
Joe Anthony *(Mgr.-Pole Treating Div.)*
Wilburn Neyland *(Mgr.-Transformer Div.)*

Outside Service Firm(s):

John A. Drew & Associates*(Auditors)*
Dallas, TX

McGinnis, Lochridge & Kilgore*(Legal Firm)*
Austin, TX

Team Bank*(Major Banking Relationship)*
Austin, TX

TEXAS METAL WORKS, INC.
937 Pine St.
Beaumont, TX 77701
Mailing Address:
P.O. Box 3607
Beaumont, TX 77704
Tel.: 409-833-5601
Fax: 409-833-0285
Approx.Sls.: $10,000,000
Emp.: 85
Forged Pine Flanges
S.I.C.: 3494
Harry Lynch *(Chm. Bd.)*
Mark M. Moore *(Pres.)*
George B. Morgan III *(V.P.-Prod. Engrng.)*
Wayne Sanders *(V.P.-Sls.)*
Sherry Scott *(Sec. & Treas.)*

Outside Service Firm(s):

Cook & McClelland*(Auditors)*
Beaumont, TX

Moore, Landrey, Garth & Jones*(Legal Firm)*
Beaumont, TX

First City National Bank*(Major Banking Relationship)*
Beaumont, TX

TEXAS OLEFINS CO.
8707 Katy Fwy., Ste. 300
Houston, TX 77024
Tel.: 713-461-2223 **TX**
Fax: 713-461-1029
Approx.Sls.: $260,000,000
Emp.: 280
Wholesale Petrochemicals
S.I.C.: 5169; 5172
Dave C. Swalm *(Chm. Bd. & Chief Exec. Officer)*
John Shelton *(Pres.)*
Gene Bohny *(Exec. V.P.)*
La Nell Cooke *(Sec.)*

Outside Service Firm(s):

Coopers & Lybrand*(Auditors)*
1100 Louisiana, Ste. 4100
Houston, TX 77002
Tel.: 713-757-5200
Fax: 713-757-5249

TEXAS REFINERY CORP.
One Refinery Place, 840 N. Main St.
Fort Worth, TX 76106
Mailing Address:
P.O. Box 711
Ft. Worth, TX 76101
Tel.: 817-332-1161
Tel.: 800-827-0711 **TX**
Fax: 817-332-2340
Year Founded: 1922
Approx.Sls.: $30,000,000
Emp.: 475
Fiscal Year-end: 10/31/92
Export
Mfr. of Protective Roof Coatings & Lubricants; Big Red Industrial Cleaner
S.I.C.: 2952; 2992; 2891; 2842
Sebert L. Pate *(Chm. Bd.)*
C. Patrick Pate *(Vice Chm.)*
A.M. Pate III *(Vice Chm.)*
Jerry W. Hopkins *(Pres. & Chief Oper. Officer)*
Garvin Cox *(Sr. V.P.)*
Ron Hinds *(V.P.-Credits & Collections)*
Vincent L. Lawson *(V.P.-Res. & Devel.)*
Barbara Main *(V.P.-Pur.)*
Jim E. Peel *(V.P.)*
D.R. Taylor *(V.P.-Production)*
Vivian A. Sharp *(Sec. & Treas.)*
Janet May *(Dir.-Personnel)*
Pamela A. Bell *(Mgr.-Adv.)*

Computer Systems/Hardware:
Prime

Outside Service Firm(s):

Crumley, Murphy & Shrull*(Legal Firm)*
Ft. Worth, TX

First Republic Bank Ft. Worth*(Major Banking Relationship)*
Ft. Worth, TX

Lincoln National Life Insurance Co.*(Group Insurer)*
PO Box 208, 1300 S. Clinton
Fort Wayne, IN 46801
Tel.: 219-455-2926
Fax: 219-455-7619

Brown, Herman, Scott, Dean & Miles*(Legal Firm)*
P.O. Box 1350
Fort Worth, TX 76101
Tel.: 817-284-9321

The Northern Trust Co.*(Major Banking Relationship)*
30 S. LaSalle St.
Chicago, IL 60675
Tel.: 312-630-6000

TEXAS STEEL CO., INC.
3901 Hemphill Rd.
Fort Worth, TX 76110
Mailing Address:
P.O. Box 2976,
Fort Worth, TX 76113
Tel.: 817-923-4611 **TX**
Fax: 817-927-5350
Year Founded: 1907
Assets: $10,900,000
Liabilities: $7,000,000
Net Worth: $3,900,000
Approx.Sls.: $26,200,000
Emp.: 383
Fiscal Year-end: 12/31/91
Import Export
Steel Foundry & Machining Operation
S.I.C.: 3599
John H. James *(Chm. Bd.)*
T.K. Armstrong, Jr. *(Pres. & Chief Oper. Officer)*
Diane Hoeller *(Controller)*
E. Frank Laminack *(V.P.-Indus. Rels.)*
J. Brown *(Dir.-Pur.)*
L. Cranford *(Dir.-Data Processing)*
Principal(s):
John H. James
T.K. Armstrong, Sr.

No. of Mfg. Plants/Facilities: 1
No. of U.S. Offices: 1

Computer Systems/Hardware:
IBM System 38, PC Network

Outside Service Firm(s):

Coopers & Lybrand*(Auditors)*
301 Commerce, Suite 1900
Fort Worth, TX 76102
Tel.: 817-332-2243

Marsh & McLennan*(Commercial Insurance Carrier)*
Fort Worth, TX

TEXTILE RUBBER & CHEMICAL COMPANY
1400 Tiarco Dr.
Dalton, GA 30720
Tel.: 706-277-1300 **GA**
Fax: 706-277-1111
Year Founded: 1954
Sales Range: $100-499 Million
Emp.: 400
Import Export
Wholesale & Manufacture Rubber Products
S.I.C.: 3069; 5199
F. Harvey Howalt, Jr. *(Pres. & Chief Exec. Officer)*
Ray N. Taylor *(Exec. V.P.)*
Neil E. Tillotson *(Treas.)*
Grafton J. Corbett III *(Sec.)*
E.F. Canler *(Mgr.-Intl.)*
Chang B. Yim *(Mgr.-Intl.)*

Outside Service Firm(s):

Edward E. Piaisted*(Auditors)*
Boston, MA

First National Bank*(Major Banking Relationship)*
Boston, MA

Subsidiary:

Lewallyn Engineering **(1)**
1803 Abuttmew Rd.
Dalton, GA 30722
Tel.: 706-226-1534
Engineering Services
S.I.C.: 8711
Michael Lewallyn *(Pres.)*

TEXTILEASE CORPORATION
10733 Tucker St
Beltsville, MD 20705
Tel.: 301-937-4555
Fax: 301-937-1274
Year Founded: 1947
Approx.Sls.: $50,000,000
Emp.: 950
Rental & Cleaning Garments, Uniforms; Retail Apparel & Accessories
S.I.C.: 7218
Gerald L. Stempler *(Chm. Bd.)*
Regis Larkin *(Vice Chm.)*
S. Denis Thomas *(Pres.)*
Michael P. Flynn *(V.P.-Fin.)*
Gary Meliker *(V.P.-Human Resources)*
Deana Stempler *(Sec.)*
Ramsey Taweel *(Dir.-Mktg.)*

Outside Service Firm(s):

Grabush, Newman & Co.*(Auditors)*
Baltimore, MD

Weinberg & Green*(Legal Firm)*
100 S. Charles St.
Baltimore, MD 21202
Tel.: 410-332-8795

Crestar Bank*(Major Banking Relationship)*
Greenbelt, MD

THE TEXWIPE CO., INC.
650 E. Crescent Ave.
Upper Saddle River, NJ 07458
Tel.: 201-327-9100
Tel.: 800-284-5577
Fax: 201-327-5945
Sales Range: $40-59 Million
Emp.: 320
Export
Manufacture Cleanroom & Laboratory Wiping Cloths, Presaturated Pads, Solvents and Specialty Electronics and Computer Cleaning Kits
S.I.C.: 2842
Edward Paley *(Pres.)*
Richard Crimmins *(Chief Oper. Officer)*
Douglas Paley *(Exec. V.P.-Sls.)*
Steven Paley *(Exec. V.P.-Res. & Devel.)*
William Paley *(Exec. V.P.-Mktg.)*
Florence Paley *(Sr. V.P.)*
Michael Kobylarz *(V.P. & Controller)*
Michael Schuetz *(Dir.-Corp. Communications)*
Brenda Fegelein *(Mgr.-Human Resources)*

Outside Service Firm(s):

BDO Seidman*(Auditors)*
Paramus, NJ

Shanley & Fisher*(Legal Firm)*
131 Madison Ave.
Morristown, NJ
Tel.: 201-285-1000

United Jersey Bank*(Major Banking Relationship)*
Westwood, NJ

THEOCHEM LABS., INC.
7373 Rowlett Park Dr.
Tampa, FL 33610
Tel.: 813-237-6463
Tel.: 800-237-2591 **FL**
Fax: 813-237-2059
Year Founded: 1962
Approx.Sls.: $35,000,000
Emp.: 150
Export
Manufacture Cleaning & Maintenance Products
S.I.C.: 2841; 2842
Steve P. Theofilos *(Chm. Bd., Pres. & Chief Exec. Officer)*
John S. Theofilos *(Exec. V.P.)*
Maria Callas *(Sr. V.P.)*
Kathy S. Theofilos *(Treas.)*
Angie Harder *(Controller)*
Cynthia Smith *(Sec.)*
Randy Frazier *(Gen. Mgr.)*
Dr. G. Churchill *(Dir.-Govt. Affairs & Quality Control)*
Joe Maceda *(Dir.-Pur.)*
Lenny Wydotis *(Dir.-Opers.)*
Tom Vizzina *(Dir.-Sls. & Mktg., Mgr.-Natl. Sls.)*
Cynthia Smith *(Exec. Sec.)*
Principal(s):
Steve P. Theofilos

No. of Mfg. Plants/Facilities: 4
No. of U.S. Offices: 4

Computer Systems/Hardware:
MAI Systems

Outside Service Firm(s):

Baumann & Co., P.A.*(Auditors)*
Tampa, FL

Carlton, Fields, Ward, Emmanuel, Smith, Cutler & Kent*(Legal Firm)*
One Harbour Place
Tampa, FL 33602
Tel.: 813-223-5366

First Union National Bank*(Major Banking Relationship)*
Tampa, FL

Divisions:

Pyramid Chemical Company, Inc. **(1)**
1008 N. Raleigh St.
Greensboro, NC 27405
Tel.: 919-274-1715
Fax: 919-274-1715
Emp.: 10
Export
Computer Systems/Hardware:
AS/400
Mfr. & Distributor of Specialty Chemicals
S.I.C.: 2841; 2842
Randy Frazier *(Gen. Mgr.)*

Time Products, Inc. **(1)**
3780 Browns Mill Rd. S.E.
Atlanta, GA 30354
Tel.: 404-767-7526
Fax: 404-767-7010
Emp.: 50
Export
Computer Systems/Hardware:
AS/400
Spray Dried Products, Warewash, Laundry & Institutional Food Brokers
S.I.C.: 2841; 2842
Chris Callas *(Chief Oper. Officer & Dir.-Sls. & Mktg.)*
Pam Colker *(Dir.-Pur.)*

Affiliate:

Apollo Industries **(1)**
1850 S. Cobb Industrial Blvd.
Smyrna, GA 30082
Tel.: 404-433-0210
Fax: 404-433-0132
Export
Computer Systems/Hardware:
AS/400
Speciality Cleaning
S.I.C.: 2842
Maria Theo-Callas *(Chief Oper. Officer)*
Jeff Colker *(Dir.-Sls. & Mktg.)*

Theradyne Corporation
(See listing under Theochem Labs., Inc.)

THERAPEDIC ASSOCIATES, INC.
1801 Clint Moore Rd., Ste. 103
Boca Raton, FL 33487
Mailing Address:
P.O. Box 4026,
Linden, NJ 07036
Tel.: 407-241-3541
Fax: 407-241-4318
Year Founded: 1960
Approx.Sls.: $120,000,000
Emp.: 34
Fiscal Year-end: 12/31/91
Mfr. of Mattresses
S.I.C.: 2515; 3069
Martin Galex *(Pres. & Chief Exec. Officer)*
Gerald Gershaw *(Pres.-Intl. Div.)*
Stanley Goldstein *(Chief Fin. Officer)*

THERM, INC.
P.O. Box 310
Ithaca, NY 14850
Tel.: 607-272-8500 **NY**
Year Founded: 1944
Approx.Sls.: $38,000,000
Emp.: 350
Mfr. of Machine Parts, Stamped or Pressed Metal
S.I.C.: 3469
Robert R. Sprole, II *(Chm. Bd. & Pres.)*
Ken Parker *(Pres.)*
John Nichols *(V.P.-Mfg.)*
Peter Stoneman *(V.P.-Engrng.)*
Terry Bowen *(Treas.)*
Richard Grossman *(Sec.)*
George Miller *(Mgr.-Pur.)*

Outside Service Firm(s):

Key Bank*(Major Banking Relationship)*
2nd S. Warren
Syracuse, NY 13202
Tel.: 315-470-5000

THERMA-TRU CORP.
1684 Woodlands Dr., Ste. 150
Maumee, OH 43537
Tel.: 419-891-7400
Fax: 419-891-7411
Year Founded: 1962
Approx.Assets: $80,000,000
Emp.: 500
Fiscal Year-end: 12/31/90
Mfr. of Building Materials; Therma Tru Insulated Steel & Fiberglass Door Systems, French Patio Door Systems, Blabel Fire Doors & Steel Frames, Custom Vinyl Windows
S.I.C.: 3442; 2431
D.K. Welles, Sr. *(Founder & Chm.)*
D.K. Welles, Jr. *(Pres. & Chief Exec. Officer)*
Stephen J. Bores *(Exec. V.P. & Chief Oper. Officer)*
Ron Wiles *(V.P.-Sls. & Mktg.)*
David D. Haddix *(Treas.)*

Divisions:

Therma-Tru Indiana Mfg. Opers. **(1)**
108 Mutzfield Rd.
Butler, IN 46721
Tel.: 219-868-5811
Mfr. Of Fiber Glass & Steel Door Entry Systems
S.I.C.: 3429

Therma-Tru Western Mfg. Opers. **(1)**
Industrial Park Rd.
Van Buren, AR 72956
Tel.: 501-474-7011
Mfr. Of Door Entry Systems
S.I.C.: 3429

THERMAL AMERICAN FUSED QUARTZ CO.
1600 W. Lee St.
Louisville, KY 40201
Mailing Address:
P.O. Box 740009
Louisville, KY 40201
Tel.: 302-856-7741
Fax: 302-856-2436
Year Founded: 1954
Approx.Sls.: $10,000,000
Emp.: 60
Import Export
Mfr. of Fused Quartz & Silica
S.I.C.: 3295
Thomas Larkin *(Pres.)*
Glenn A. Miller *(Dir.-Mktg. & Sls.)*
G. Kanter *(Controller)*

THERMAL TECHNOLOGY INDUSTRIES
1321 Burlington
N. Kansas City, MO 64116
Tel.: 816-221-1640 **MO**
Fax: 816-221-7550
Year Founded: 1977
Emp.: 45
Wholesale Distribution of Plastic Window Frames & Sash
S.I.C.: 3089
Daniel J. Fioroni *(Chm. Bd.)*
Doug Campbell *(Pres.)*
Craig Bouise *(Treas. & Controller)*
Marilyn S. Moody *(Sec.)*

Branch:

Forest Siding Supply, Inc. **(1)**
50 N. May
Oklahoma City, OK 73107
Tel.: 405-235-2400
Sales & Marketing of Siding, Except Wood; Insulation, Thermal
S.I.C.: 5033
Sonya McKinney *(Gen. Mgr.)*

THERMALLOY, INC.
2021 W. Valley View
Farmers Branch, TX 75334-8993
Mailing Address:
P.O. Box 810839
Dallas, TX 75381-0839
Tel.: 214-243-4321
Fax: 214-241-4656
Year Founded: 1958
Approx.Sls.: $22,000,000
Emp.: 265
Fiscal Year-end: 12/31/90
Export
Mfrs. & Exporters of Semiconductor Accessories
S.I.C.: 3674
W.D. Jordan *(Pres.)*
B.B. Shipp *(Exec. V.P. & Chief Fin. Officer)*
L.W. Tucker *(V.P.-Sls. & Mktg.)*
Gary Gameson *(V.P.-Mfg.)*
Howard Hinshaw *(V.P.-Engrng.)*
Chris Hallmark *(Dir.-Personnel & Plant Mgr.)*
David Barnes *(Mktg. Communications Mgr.)*
Katherine Callohan *(Admin. Asst.)*

THERMO ELECTRIC CO., INC.
109 N. Fifth St.
Saddle Brook, NJ 07662
Tel.: 201-843-5800 **NJ**
Fax: 201-843-7144
Year Founded: 1941
Approx.Sls.: $50,000,000
Emp.: 500
Fiscal Year-end: 6/30/91
Export
Manufactures Industrial Temperature Controls, Pyrometers, Thermocouples, Thermo Couplewire & Cable, Connectors, Switches & Panels, Thermowells, Temperature Indicators, Temperature Sensors
S.I.C.: 3823; 3357
Paul F. Walter *(Chm. Bd., Pres. & Chief Exec. Officer)*
Douglas E. Frank *(V.P. & Gen. Mgr.)*
Daniel J. Mahon *(V.P.-Fin.)*
Anna C. Walter *(V.P. & Sec.)*
Claudia Bergan *(Mgr.-Export)*
Joanne F. Carroccio *(Mgr.-Personnel)*
Dennis Gloede *(Mgr.-Adv.)*
Fred Stote *(Mgr.-Mfg.)*
Ted Wang *(Mgr.-Quality Control)*

Outside Service Firm(s):

Ernst & Young*(Auditors)*
Park 80 West - Plaza One
Saddle Brook, NJ 07662

Apruzzese, McDermott, Mastro & Murphy*(Legal Firm)*
P.O. Box 112, 25 Independence Blvd.
Liberty Corner, NJ 07938

United Jersey Bank*(Major Banking Relationship)*
192 Paterson Plank Rd.
Carlstadt, NJ 07072

Divisions:

Thermo Electric (Southeast Region) **(1)**
3440 Oakcliff Rd.
Atlanta, GA 30340
Tel.: 404-451-3733
Mfr. of Thermocouples, Temperature & Process Controllers & Indicators
S.I.C.: 3357; 3823

Thermo Electric (Southwest Region) **(1)**
12503 Exchange Dr.
Stafford, TX 77477
Tel.: 713-240-1330
Mfr. of Thermocouples, Temperature & Process Controllers & Indicators
S.I.C.: 3357; 3823; 3822

Thermo Electric (Central Region) **(1)**
5261 W. 161st St.
Cleveland, OH 44142
Tel.: 216-433-4510
Mfr. of Thermocouple Connectors & Accessories, Themperature & Process Controllers & Indicators
S.I.C.: 3823; 3822

Thermo Electric (Western Region) **(1)**
7061 Vineland Ave.
North Hollywood, CA 91605
Tel.: 818-765-5276
Mfr. of Thermocouple Connectors & Accessories, Temperature & Process Controller & Indicators
S.I.C.: 3823

Wire & Cable Div. **(1)**
109 Fifth St.
Saddle Brook, NJ 07662
Tel.: 201-843-5800
S.I.C.: 3357

Non-U.S. Holdings:

Thermo Electric (Canada) Ltd. **(1)**
12 Rutherford Rd. So.
Brampton, ON L6W 3J2, Canada
Tel.: 416-451-0813 (100%)
Telex: 069-7664
Fax: 416-451-4606
Mfrs. Temperature Controls & Sensors
S.I.C.: 3357; 3823

Thermo Electric GmbH **(1)**
Postfach 900 406, Neue Eiler Str. 36 5000 Cologne, 90, Germany
Tel.: 02203/32063 (100%)
Telex: 887-3514
Mfrs. Temperature Controls & Sensors
S.I.C.: 3357; 3823
M. Hausberg *(Chief Oper. Officer)*

Thermo Electric Intl. B.V. **(1)**
P.O. Box 65 2360 AB
Warmond, Netherlands
Tel.: 1711-19206 (100%)
Telex: 884-39-212
Fax: 01711-11653
Mfrs. Temperature Controls & Sensors
S.I.C.: 3357; 3823
G. J. D. de Graaff *(Chief Oper. Officer)*

Thermo Electric Intl. Ltd. **(1)**
P.O. Box 10
Sittingbourne, Kent ME10 3RN, United Kingdom
Tel.: 795-79-481 (100%)
Telex: 96-50-49
Fax: 795-22174
Mfrs. Temperature Controls & Sensors
S.I.C.: 3357; 3823
R.A. Flint *(Chief Oper. Officer)*

Thermo Electric S.A. **(1)**
26 Rue Pasteur 94456
Limiel Brevannes, France
Tel.: 1-45 993145 (100%)
Telex: 261176
Fax: 1-45992596
S.I.C.: 3357; 3823
B. Drouilly *(Chief Oper. Officer)*

THERMO INDUSTRIES INC.
4300 Golf Acres Dr.
Charlotte, NC 28208
Mailing Address:
P.O. Box 668109
Charlotte, NC 28266
Tel.: 704-394-7311
Year Founded: 1953
Approx.Sls.: $45,000,000
Emp.: 98
Distributor of Heating & Cooling Equipment
S.I.C.: 5075; 5074
E.C. Hunt, Jr. *(Chm. Bd. & Chief Exec. Officer)*
Robert M. Teague *(Pres. & Chief Exec. Officer)*
James A. Anderson *(Sr. V.P.)*
Edmund S. Mann *(Treas. & Corp. Sec.)*

No. of U.S. Offices: 2

Outside Service Firm(s):

NationsBank Carolinas*(Major Banking Relationship)*
One NCNB Plaza,
Charlotte, NC 28255
Tel.: 704-374-5000

THERMON MANUFACTURING COMPANY
100 Thermon Dr.
San Marcos, TX 78666
Mailing Address:
P. O. Box 609,
San Marcos, TX 78667
Tel.: 512-396-5801 **TX**
Fax: 512-396-3627
Year Founded: 1954
Assets: $20,100,000
Earnings: $1,150,000
Liabilities: $7,000,000
Net Worth: $13,100,000
Approx.Sls.: $33,000,000
Emp.: 250
Fiscal Year-end: 3/31/91
Export
Manufacturing, Engineering & Installation of Steam & Electric Heat Tracing Products
S.I.C.: 3087; 3357; 3433; 3823
Corporate Giving Program: Local Non-Profit Entries; Dollar for Dollar
Richard L. Burdick *(Chm., Pres., Chief Exec. & Chief Oper. Officer)*
P. Kenneth Pitzer *(V.P.-Fin.)*
George Alexander *(V.P.-Sls. & Mktg.)*
Kenneth G. Downing *(V.P.-Opers.)*
Ben Johnson *(V.P.-Engrng.)*
R. Knox Pitzer *(V.P.-Admin. & Sec.)*
Roy Barth *(V.P.-Res. & Devel.)*
David Ralph *(Controller)*
Peter Baen *(Dir.-Mktg. & Corp. Video Systems)*
Sandy Michaelwicz *(Dir.-Telecommunications)*
Principal(s):
Richard L. Burdick

No. of Mfg. Plants/Facilities: 11
No. of U.S. Offices: 3
No. of Foreign Offices: 8

Computer Systems/Hardware:
Hewlett Packard Series 70

Outside Service Firm(s):

Ernst & Young*(Auditors)*
1221 McKinney, Ste. 2400
Houston, TX 77010
Tel.: 713-750-1200

Marsh & McLennan*(Commercial Insurance Carrier)*
San Antonio, TX

Aetna Life & Casualty*(Group Insurer)*
San Antonio, TX

NationsBank Texas*(Investment Banker)*
Austin, TX

Patterson, Boyd, Lowery & Aderholt*(Legal Firm)*
Houston, TX

NationsBank Texas*(Major Banking Relationship)*
Austin, TX

NationsBank Texas*(Pension Manager)*
Austin, TX

Subsidiaries:

Curlee Manufacturing Div. **(1)**
13639 Alding Westfield
Houston, TX 77039
Tel.: 713-449-6271 (90%)
Telex: 77-6461
Approx.Sls.: $6,500,000
Emp.: 90
Mfr. of Heat Transfer Materials
S.I.C.: 3443
John Willis *(Pres.)*

Thermon Manufacturing Company—(Continued)

Eneron Co. **(1)**
100 Therman Dr.
San Marcos, TX 78666
Tel.: 512-396-5801 (100%)
Telex: 77-6461
Fax: 512-392-5884
Approx.Sls.: $100,000
Emp.: 4
Engineering Services
S.I.C.: 8711

Indeco Packaging Div. **(1)**
2410 Barnes Dr.
San Marcos, TX 78667
Tel.: 512-396-5814 (20%)
Telex: 77-6461
Emp.: 10
Mfr. of Strapping and Packaging Systems, Polyester Meat Slings
S.I.C.: 3565
Danny Springs *(Pres.)*

Non-U.S. Holdings:

Manufacturera Thermon de Mexico, S.A. **(1)**
Edif. Santos Despacho 415 Apdo. Postal 539, Suc. "K",
Monterrey, Nuevo Leon Mexico
Tel.: 52 46 39 80 (36%)
Approx.Sls.: $50,000
Emp.: 20
Mfr. of Heat Tracing Systems
S.I.C.: 3443
Armando Buentello *(Gen. Mgr.)*

Thermon Australia **(1)**
Private Bag 32, P.O. Box Bayswater 3153
30 London Dr.,
Bayswater, 3153, Australia
Tel.: 03-762-6900 (85%)
Telex: AA 38445
Fax: 03 762-9519
Approx.Sls.: $800,000
Emp.: 7
Mfr. of Heat Tracing Systems, Engineering & Sales
S.I.C.: 3443; 5084
Peter Band *(Mng. Dir.)*

Thermon Benelux **(1)**
Korteweg 1 P.O. Box 205, 2640 AE
Pijnacker, Netherlands
Tel.: 1736-6741 (90%)
Telex: 38032
Approx.Sls.: $3,000,000
Emp.: 40
Mfr. of Heat Tracing Systems, Electrical Cables
S.I.C.: 3443
Hans Stoutjesdijk *(Mng. Dir.)*

Thermon Canada **(1)**
Blue Heron Dr. P.O. Box 89,
Hyde Park, ON N0M 1Z0, Canada
Tel.: 519-657-3400 (40%)
Telex: 064 5800
Approx.Sls.: $3,000,000
Emp.: 35
Mfr. of Heat Tracing Systems; Engineering & Sales
S.I.C.: 3443
Frank Heizer *(Mng. Dir.)*

Thermon Far East **(1)**
2-17-1 Tsuruya-cho Kanadawa-Ku,
Yokohama, 221, Japan
Tel.: 045-314-8814 (100%)
Telex: 3822-030
Fax: 45-314-8817
Approx.Sls.: $1,250,000
Emp.: 12
Holding Co.; Heat Tracing Systems, Cables, Panels Accessories, Instrumentation, Engineering & Sales
S.I.C.: 3443; 5084
John Beene *(Mng. Dir.)*

Thermon France **(1)**
91 Boulevard d'Alsace Lorraine Batiment C, 93110
Rosny-sous-Bois, France
Tel.: 01-854-36-60 (89%)
Telex: 240154F
Fax: 1-854-3680
Approx.Sls.: $3,000,000
Emp.: 27
Mfr. of Heat Tracing Cables, Panels, Accessories, Instrumentation, Engineering and Sales
S.I.C.: 3443
Paul Irwin *(Mng. Dir.)*

Thermon International Services SA **(1)**
14, Grand Places P.O. Box 937, 1701
Fribourg, 1, Switzerland
Tel.: 037 22 41 41 (35%)
Telex: 942563 TAC CH
Approx.Sls.: $800,000
Emp.: 2
Sales of Heat Transfer Products
S.I.C.: 5084

Thermon U.K. (Ltd.) **(1)**
18 Tower Rd. Glover West,
Washington, Tyne & Wear NE37 2SH,
United Kingdom
Tel.: 091 4177836 (35%)
Fax: 091 4150632
Approx.Sls.: $3,000,000
Emp.: 34
Mfr. of Heat Tracing Cables, Panels, Accessories, Instrumentation, Engineering & Sales
S.I.C.: 3443; 5084
Neil Cunningham *(Mng. Dir.)*

THERMWELL PRODUCTS CO., INC.
150 E. Seventh St.
Paterson, NJ 07524
Tel.: 201-684-5000
Fax: 201-278-2105
Year Founded: 1930
Approx.Sls.: $50,000,000
Emp.: 1,000
Fiscal Year-end: 4/30/91
Mfrs. of Frost King Do-It-Yourself Packaged Consumer Products
S.I.C.: 3442; 3069; 2431
David B. Gerstein *(Pres.)*
Mel Gerstein *(Treas. & Dir.-Mktg., Adv. & Pub. Rels.)*
Irving Gerstein *(V.P.)*

Subsidiaries:

Filmco Industries Inc. **(1)**
100 5th Ave.
Paterson, NJ 07524
Tel.: 201-684-5000
S.I.C.: 3442

Lever Mfg. Corp. **(1)**
150 E. Seventh St.
Paterson, NJ 07524
Tel.: 201-684-5000
Fax: 201-742-8722
Approx.Sls.: $6,000,000
Emp.: 100
Mfg. Machinery (Slitting, Winding & Biasing)
S.I.C.: 3549; 3552
Irving Gerstein *(Pres.)*
L. Robert Cohen *(Exec. V.P.)*
Mel Gerstein *(V.P.-Mktg. & Adv.)*

THIELE KAOLIN CO.
Kaolin Rd.
Sandersville, GA 31082
Mailing Address:
P.O. Box 1056
Sandersville, GA 31082
Tel.: 912-552-3951 **GA**
Fax: 912-552-4105
Year Founded: 1946
Approx.Sls.: $93,000,000
Emp.: 519
Fiscal Year-end: 12/31/91
Export
Open Pit Kaolin Mining for Paper Filler & Paper Coating
S.I.C.: 1455
Paul F. Thiele *(Chm. Bd. & Chief Exec. Officer)*
William H. Wiggins *(Pres. & Chief Oper. Officer)*
David R. Ginn *(Exec. V.P.)*
Martina J. Hodges *(V.P.-Sls.)*
Lynne S. Sheppard *(Treas.)*
John S. Barton *(Corp. Sec.)*
Alex Cawthon *(Dir.-Human Resources)*
William Page *(Dir.-Pur.)*
Charles Byrne *(Mgr.-Data Processing)*

No. of Mfg. Plants/Facilities: 2
No. of U.S. Offices: 1

Computer Systems/Hardware:
NCR; IBM PC

Outside Service Firm(s):

Bricker & Rooks*(Auditors)*
Norcross, GA

United States Fidelity & Guaranty Co.*(Commercial Insurance Carrier)*
100 Light Street
Baltimore, MD 21202
Tel.: 301-547-3000

Life Insurance Co. of Georgia*(Group Insurer)*
P.O. Box 105234,
Atlanta, GA 30348-5234
Tel.: 404-980-5100

Anderson, Walker & Reichert*(Legal Firm)*
Macon, GA

Wachovia Bank of Georgia, N.A.*(Major Banking Relationship)*
191 Peachtree St. N.E.
Atlanta, GA 30303

George D. Warthen Bank*(Major Banking Relationship)*
Sandersville, GA

The Principal Financial Group*(Pension Manager)*
711 High St.
Des Moines, IA 50309
Tel.: 515-247-4593
Tel.: 800-543-4015

Subsidiaries:

Piedmont Minerals **(1)**
P.O. Box 1056
Sandersville, GA 31082
Tel.: 912-552-3951
Kaolin Mining & Processing
S.I.C.: 1455

Villa South Inc. **(1)**
South Harris St.
Sandersville, GA 31082
Tel.: 912-552-1234
Emp.: 57
Motel
S.I.C.: 7011; 5812
Ellen Askew *(Mgr.)*

THINKING MACHINES CORPORATION
245 First St.
Cambridge, MA 02142
Tel.: 617-234-1111
Fax: 617-234-4444
Year Founded: 1983
Approx.Sls.: $45,000,000
Emp.: 360
Export
Mfr. of Mainframe Computers
S.I.C.: 3571
Sheryl Handler *(Pres. & Chief Exec. Officer)*
Fred Butler *(V.P.-Fin.)*
Richard J. Clayton *(V.P.)*
Marvin Denicoff *(V.P.)*
Mirza Mehdi *(V.P.)*
Paul Brountas *(Sec.)*

TED THOMAS ASSOCIATES INC., ADVERTISING
210 W. Washington Square
Philadelphia, PA 19106-3512
Tel.: 215-592-7500 **PA**
Fax: 215-592-4287
Year Founded: 1953
Approx.Billings: $46,077,800
Emp.: 63
Advertising Agency Specializing in Professional Promotion to Health Service Market
S.I.C.: 7311
Robert D. Ritchie *(Pres.)*
Beverly F. Wernette *(Exec. V.P.)*
Donald J.M. Phillips *(Sr. V.P.)*
E. Michael Scott *(Sr. V.P.)*
Christine C. Ciuryla *(V.P. & Supvr. Accts.)*
Carol D. Rominiecki *(V.P.-Opers.)*
David B. Vogelsang *(V.P. & Dir.-Creative-Copy)*

No. of U.S. Offices: 2

Computer Systems/Hardware:
IBM

Branch:

TTA/Newport, Inc. **(1)**
4440 Von Karman, Ste. 220
Newport Beach, CA 92660
Tel.: 714-851-9563
Fax: 714-851-5091
Emp.: 14
Pharmaceutical Ad Agency
S.I.C.: 7311
Timothy J. Friday *(Exec. V.P., Gen. Mgr.)*
Stacey Howman *(Pub. Rels. Dir.)*
Christina Rodriques *(Client Services Dir.)*

Division:

CoMed Communications Division **(1)**
210 W. Washington Square
Philadelphia, PA 19106
Tel.: 215-592-1363
Fax: 215-592-9085
Advertising Agency
S.I.C.: 7311
Michael D. Scott *(Chief Oper. Officer & Creative Dir.)*
Brian P. Russell *(V.P. & Dir.)*
Amy Neilsen Smith *(Dir.-Meeting & Program Services)*
Ann F. Hale *(Mgr.-Opers. & Production)*
Susan Dobrowolski *(Mgr.-Program Services)*
Maryann Orndorff *(Mgr.-Special Events & Meeting Services)*
Brenda Frank *(Editor)*
Tara M. Ryan *(Medical Writer)*

IRA THOMAS ASSOCIATES, INC.
20 Ohltown Rd.
Youngstown, OH 44515
Tel.: 216-793-3000
Fax: 216-793-7469
Year Founded: 1937
Approx.Billings: $16,300,000
Emp.: 61
Business-to-Business, Consumer & Public Relations
Ira D. Thomas *(Pres.)*
Richard W. Gunn *(Exec. V.P.)*
Cornelius A. Murray *(Sr. V.P.)*

Computer Systems/Hardware:
Admark, Data General, Complete Mini-Mainframe MV3500, Incorp. Word Processing & Electronic Mail

CHARLIE THOMAS AUTO WORLD
12215 Gulf Fwy.
Houston, TX 77207
Mailing Address:
P.O. Box 266407,
Houston, TX 77207
Tel.: 713-948-5722
Fax: 713-947-8758
Approx.Sls.: $482,000,000
Emp.: 1,200
Automobile Dealership
S.I.C.: 5511
Charles F. Thomas *(Chm. Bd.)*
Lawrence E. Gerdis *(Pres.)*

Outside Service Firm(s):

Ernst & Young*(Auditors)*
1 Houston Ctr., 1200 McKinney
Houston, TX 77002
Tel.: 713-750-1500

Enterprise Bank*(Major Banking Relationship)*
Houston, TX

THOMAS BUILT BUSES, INC.
1408 Courtesy Rd.
High Point, NC 27260
Mailing Address:
P.O. Box 2450,
High Point, NC 27261
Tel.: 919-889-4871
Fax: 919-889-2589
Year Founded: 1916
Sales Range: $100-499 Million
Emp.: 1,100
Fiscal Year-end: 9/30/91
Import Export
Mfr. of School & Commercial Buses
S.I.C.: 3713
John W. Thomas, Jr. *(Chm. Bd. & Chief Exec. Officer)*
John W. Thomas III *(Pres.)*
Larry C. Bannon *(V.P.-Export Sls.)*
Roger Chilton *(V.P.-Domestic Sls.)*
Willis P. Duncan, Jr. *(V.P.-Fin. & Treas.)*
Doug Harrison *(V.P.-Mfg.)*
Ronald Holzhauser *(V.P.-Engrng.)*
Gene Saunders *(Controller)*
Ted Clayton *(Mgr.-Natl. School Bus. Sls.)*
Mickey Fox *(Mgr.-Adv.)*
John Millard *(Mgr.-MIS)*
Ron Moore *(Mgr.-Mktg.)*
Bob Price *(Mgr.-Comml. Sls.)*
Ed Swaim *(Mgr.-Saf-T-Liner Sls.)*
Terry Darr *(Reg. Mgr.)*
Ken Hedgecock *(Reg. Mgr.)*
Curt Kiser *(Reg. Mgr.)*
Chris Thomas *(Reg. Mgr.)*
Rick Holbert *(Dir.-Human Res.)*
Ken McDonell *(Dir.-Specialty Prod. Sls.)*
Bob Simonds *(Financing Coordinator)*
Brad Thomas *(Pur. Agent)*
Principal(s):
John W. Thomas, Jr.

No. of U.S. Offices: 1
No. of Foreign Offices: 2

Computer Systems/Hardware:
IBM 400

Outside Service Firm(s):

Deloitte & Touche*(Auditors)*
Greensboro, NC

Womble, Carlyle, Sandridge & Rice*(Legal Firm)*
Wachovia Bldg.
Winston Salem, NC 27102
Tel.: 919-721-3600

North Carolina National Bank*(Major Banking Relationship)*
Charlotte, NC

Non-U.S. Holding:

Thomas Built Buses of Canada, Ltd. **(1)**
P.O. Box 580,
Woodstock, ON N4S 7Z5, Canada
Tel.: 519-539-1226
Emp.: 350
Mfr. School & Commercial Buses
S.I.C.: 3711; 3713

THOMAS CONVEYOR COMPANY
555 I-35 South
Burleson, TX 76028
Mailing Address:
P.O. Box 2916,
Ft. Worth, TX 76101
Tel.: 817-295-7151
Tel.: 800-433-2217
Fax: 817-447-3840
Approx.Sls.: $20,000,000
Emp.: 255
Fiscal Year-end: 12/31/90
Export
Mfrs. of Bulk Material Conveyors; Screw Conveyors; Bucket Elevators & Drag Conveyors
S.I.C.: 3523
B.J. Hinterlong *(Pres. & Gen. Mgr.)*
Mark Osborn *(Sls. Mgr.)*

THOMAS ENGINEERING INC.
575 W. Central Rd.
Hoffman Estates, IL 60195
Tel.: 708-358-5800
Fax: 708-358-5817
Approx.Sls.: $22,000,000
Emp.: 100
Fiscal Year-end: 4/30/92
Distribute Pharmaceutical Tablet Presses, Design & Manufacture Tablet Coating Equipment, Coders, Marking & Printing Devices, Punches & Dies
S.I.C.: 3559; 3549; 3565; 3596; 3699
Thomas J. Casey *(Chm. Bd.)*
Brian T. Casey *(Pres.)*
Pam Giese *(Controller)*
Roy Thompson *(Mgr.-Purch.)*

Outside Service Firm(s):

Altschuler, Melvoin & Glasser*(Auditors)*
30 S. Wecker Dr.
Chicago, IL 60606
Tel.: 312-207-2800

Schiff, Hardin & Waite*(Legal Firm)*
7200 Sears Tower, 233 S. Wacker Dr.
Chicago, IL 60606
Tel.: 312-876-1000

Harris Bank of Barrington*(Major Banking Relationship)*
201 S. Grove Ave.
Barrington, IL 60010
Tel.: 708-381-4000

Subsidiaries:

Teko Realty Corporation **(1)**
575 W. Central Rd.
Hoffman Estates, IL 60195
Tel.: 708-358-5800
Fax: 708-358-5817

Triangle Metals, Inc. **(1)**
2500 Harrison Ave.
Rockford, IL 61108
Tel.: 815-398-0280
Fax: 815-398-6988

THOMAS & HOWARD
P.O. Box 947
Columbia, SC 29202
Tel.: 803-788-5520
Fax: 803-799-9097
Approx.Sls.: $165,000,000
Emp.: 580
Wholesale Groceries
S.I.C.: 5141
David R. Clark *(Pres.)*
John White *(V.P. & Div. Pres.)*
Thomas T. Perkins *(Sec. & Treas.)*

Outside Service Firm(s):

J. W. Hunt & Co.*(Auditors)*
Middleburg Office Park, 1607 St. Julian Place
Columbia, SC 29202
Tel.: 803-254-8196

McCutchen, Doyle, Brown & Emerson*(Legal Firm)*
Columbia, SC

Citizens & Southern National Bank*(Major Banking Relationship)*
Charleston, SC

THOMAS & PERKINS

THOMAS & PERKINS
1451 Larimer Square, Ste. 300
Denver, CO 80202
Tel.: 303-573-4911
Year Founded: 1985
Approx.Billings: $15,000,000
Emp.: 30
Bryan Thomas *(Chm. Bd., Pres. & New Bus. Contact)*
Tom Botelho *(V.P., Acct. Services & Mktg. Dir.)*
Nancy Long *(V.P., Mktg. & Res. Dir.)*
Cheryl Cotten *(V.P., Opers.)*
James Czupor *(V.P., Pub. Rels.)*
Denise Rasser *(Office Mgr.)*

THOMAS PIPE & STEEL, INC.
P.O. Box 53187
Baton Rouge, LA 70805
Tel.: 504-356-9822
Fax: 504-357-6960
Year Founded: 1984
Assets: $12,500,000
Liabilities: $8,650,000
Net Worth: $3,850,000
Approx.Sls.: $36,000,000
Emp.: 80

Import Export
National Pipe Distributor & Steel Service Center
S.I.C.: 1791
J.L. Mallett *(Pres.)*
Jill Mallett *(Mgr.-Sls.)*
Jay Mallett *(Mgr.-Steel Div.)*

Principal(s):
J.L. Mallett

No. of Mfg. Plants/Facilities: 1
No. of U.S. Offices: 1

Outside Service Firm(s):

Hawthorn, Waymouth & Carroll*(Auditors)*
Baton Rouge, LA
Tel.: 504-923-3000

THOMAS PUBLISHING CO.
One Penn Plaza
New York, NY 10119
Tel.: 212-695-0500
Year Founded: 1898
Emp.: 350

Export
Publishers of Thomas Register American Manufacturers, Industrial Equipment News, American Export Register, Managing Automation, Thomas Food Industry Register
S.I.C.: 2741; 2721
Jose E. Andrade *(Chm. Bd.)*
Carl T. Holst-Knudsen *(Pres.)*
R.E. Ahrensdorf *(V.P.-Intl. Opers.)*
R.E. Andersen *(V.P.-Plng.)*
H. Vance Crawford *(V.P.-Opers.)*
E.V. Dillon *(V.P.-Mktg.)*
Donald MacPherson *(V.P.-Fin.)*
Barbara Hanson *(Dir.-Mktg.)*
Ruth Hurd *(Publr.)*
R. Duchaine *(Editor)*
Tina Gattney *(Mgr.-Mktg. Services)*
R.E. Richardson *(Grp. Publr.)*
James Vick *(Publr.)*
Mark Devlin *(Editor)*
Richard Cherichella *(Bus. Mgr.)*
Stephanie Fox-Morris *(Dir.-Mktg.)*
James Morris *(Publr.)*
Robert Malone *(Editor)*
Irene Berger *(Mgr.-Publication)*
Rick Sauter *(Mgr.-Ad Sls.)*

Outside Service Firm(s):

Manufacturers Hanover Trust Co.*(Major Banking Relationship)*
4 New York Plaza
New York, NY 10015
Tel.: 212-623-3232

Divisions:

American Export Register **(1)**
One Penn Plaza
New York, NY 10119
Tel.: 212-695-0500
Publishers of American Export Register Books
S.I.C.: 2721
Irene Berger *(Mgr.-Publication)*
Rick Sauter *(Mgr.-Ad Sls.)*

American Literature Review **(1)**
One Penn Plaza
New York, NY 10119
Tel.: 212-695-0500
Publishers of American Literature Review Books
S.I.C.: 2721
Irene Berger *(Mgr.-Publication)*
Rick Sauter *(Mgr.-Ad Sls.)*

Industrial Equipment News **(1)**
One Penn Plaza
New York, NY 10199
Tel.: 212-695-0500
Publishers of Industrial Equipment News Magazine
S.I.C.: 2721
R.E. Richardson *(Grp. Publr.)*
James Vick *(Publr.)*
Mark Devlin *(Editor)*
Richard Cherichella *(Mgr.-Bus.)*
Margaret Wormley *(Dir.-Mktg.)*

Managing Automation **(1)**
One Penn Plaza
New York, NY 10119
Tel.: 212-695-0500
Publishers of Managing Automation Magazine
S.I.C.: 2721
James Morris *(Publr.)*
Robert Malone *(Editor)*

Thomas Register **(1)**
One Penn Plaza
New York, NY 10119
Tel.: 212-695-0500
Publishers of Thomas Register
S.I.C.: 2721
Ruth Hurd *(Publr.)*
R. Duchaine *(Editor)*
Rita Lieberman *(Mgr.-Promos.)*
Mary Jean Barnes *(Mgr.-Sls. Services)*

THOMAS & SKINNER, INC.
1120 E. 23rd St.
Indianapolis, IN 46206
Mailing Address:
P.O. Box 150 B
Indianapolis, IN 46206
Tel.: 317-923-2501 **IN**
Fax: 317-923-5919
Year Founded: 1903
Approx.Sls.: $22,000,000
Emp.: 300
Fiscal Year-end: 12/31/90
Export
Mfr. of Permanent Magnets & Permanent Magnet Assemblies; Silicon Iron Electric Laminations
S.I.C.: 3679; 3499
Jas C. Skinner *(Chm. Bd.)*
Norris E. Krall *(Pres.)*
Thomas E. Kolish *(V.P. & Treas.)*
Vernon A. Detlef *(Chief Exec. Officer & V.P.-Opers)*
Mike O'Connell *(Chief Fin. Officer & Comptroller)*
Carl R. Tufts *(Mgr.-Sls. & Mktg.)*
Dr. Achuta Rao *(Mgr.-Engineering & Quality Control)*
Patsy Davenport *(Mgr.-Pur.)*

No. of Mfg. Plants/Facilities: 4
No. of U.S. Offices: 5

Outside Service Firm(s):

Coopers & Lybrand*(Auditors)*
2900 One American Square, Box 82002
Indianapolis, IN 46282

Thomas & Skinner, Inc.—(Continued)

Tel.: 317-639-4161

One Bank*(Major Banking Relationship)*
Indianapolis, IN

Division:

Laminations Div. **(1)**
1120 E. 23rd St.
Indianapolis, IN 46206
Tel.: 317-923-2501
Fax: 317-923-5919
Silicon Iron Electronic Laminations
S.I.C.: 3679
Doyle D. Mink *(Gen. Mgr.)*

THOMAS STEEL STRIP CORP.
Delaware Ave. NW
Warren, OH 44485
Tel.: 216-841-6111
Fax: 216-841-6320
Year Founded: 1974
Sales Range: $100-499 Million
Emp.: 700
Fiscal Year-end: 12/31/89
Steel Manufacturers
S.I.C.: 3316; 3325; 3315; 3312
Jurgen Thumann *(Chm. Bd. & Chief Exec. Officer)*
M.T. Schmader *(Pres.)*
A.W. Skrobola *(Sr. V.P.-Fin., Sec. & Treas.)*
W.C. Helbley *(Dir.-Pur.)*
Charlie Van Horn *(Dir.-Human Resources)*

Computer Systems/Hardware:
IBM 4381

Outside Service Firm(s):

Blue Cross & Blue Shield in Eastern Ohio*(Group Insurer)*
Youngstown, OH

Connecticut General Life Insurance Co.*(Group Insurer)*
P.O. Box 2975,
Hartford, CT 06104
Tel.: 203-726-6000

Bank of New England*(Major Banking Relationship)*
28 State Street
Boston, MA 02109
Tel.: 617-742-4000

European American Bank*(Major Banking Relationship)*
New York, NY

Pittsburgh National Bank*(Pension Manager)*
Stock Transfer Dept., Fifth & Wood Streets
Pittsburgh, PA 15265

I. C. THOMASSON ASSOCIATES, INC.
2120 Eighth Ave., So.
Nashville, TN 37204
Mailing Address:
P.O. Box 40527
Nashville, TN 37204
Tel.: 615-383-6821 **TN**
Fax: 615-297-7505
Year Founded: 1942
Sales Range: $10-19 Million
Emp.: 65
Fiscal Year-end: 9/30/91
Mechanical & Electrical Consulting Engineering Services
S.I.C.: 8711; 8742
Joseph J. Wimberly, III *(Chm. Bd. & Pres.)*
George Bratton *(V.P.)*
Carol W. Chambliss *(V.P.)*
Bill Martin *(Treas. & Sec.)*
Bruce Mason *(Controller)*

No. of U.S. Offices: 1

Outside Service Firm(s):

Arthur Andersen & Co.*(Auditors)*
Third Natl. Fin. Cntr., 424 Church St., Ste. 1100
Nashville, TN 37219

Bolt Cummings Connor & Berry*(Legal Firm)*
Nashville, TN

Third National Bank*(Major Banking Relationship)*
Nashville, TN

THOMPSON ADVERTISING PRODUCTIONS, INC.
31690 W. 12 Mile Rd.
Farmington Hills, MI 48334
Tel.: 313-553-4566
Fax: 313-553-2138
Year Founded: 1974
Approx.Billings: $12,000,000
Emp.: 23
Automotive, Marine & Industrial Markets
John R. Thompson *(Pres.)*
Zachary Thompson *(Pres.-Competition Graphics Div.)*
Clay Thompson *(V.P., Gen. Mgr.)*
John Cerrito *(Gen. Mgr.-Competition Graphics Div.)*
Jerry McCabe *(Dir.-Mktg. Services)*
Caroline Hodge *(Dir., Electronic Composition)*
Peggy Taylor *(Media & Communications Coord.)*
Scott Harris *(Computer Services)*
Keri Haworth *(Pub. Rel. Asst.)*

THOMPSON & COMPANY
Cotton Exchange Bldg., 65 Union Ave., 8th Fl.
Memphis, TN 38103
Tel.: 901-527-8000
Fax: 901-527-3697
Year Founded: 1981
Approx.Billings: $12,000,000
Emp.: 22
Michael H. Thompson *(Pres. & Creative Dir.)*
Robert Vornbrock *(Chief Oper. Officer & Acct. Supvr.)*
Carolyn Boyd *(Comptroller)*
Barbara Drabowicz *(Mgr., Pub. Rels.)*

THOMPSON ENTERPRISES INC.
12201 Minnetonka Blvd.
Minnetonka, MN 55343
Tel.: 612-933-2521 **MN**
Fax: 612-933-3662
Year Founded: 1964
Approx.Sls.: $65,000,000
Emp.: 500
General Residential Contractor; Plumbing, Heating & Air Conditioning; Electrical Work; Wholesale Construction Materials; Retail Lumber & Building Materials, Home Furnishings
S.I.C.: 1521; 1711; 1731; 5039; 5211; 5719
Dennis O. Thompson *(Chm. Bd.)*
Scott Thompson *(Pres.)*
Michael Greengard *(V.P., Sec. & Treas.)*

Computer Systems/Hardware:
Control Data

Outside Service Firm(s):

Lurie, Besikof, Lapidus & Co.*(Auditors)*
Minneapolis, MN

THE THOMPSON GROUP COMPANIES
(Div. of Thompson International)
5840 Airline Rd.
Henderson, KY 42420
Mailing Address:
P.O. Box 656
Henderson, KY 42420
Tel.: 502-826-3751
Tel.: 800-626-7054
Telex: 20-4297
Year Founded: 1951
Approx.Sls.: $15,000,000
Emp.: 150
Fiscal Year-end: 2/28/92
Export
Mfr. Rotary Drilling Tools for Mining, Waterwell, Shaft & Construction & Blast Hole
S.I.C.: 3541; 3545
Susie Givens *(Pres. & Chief Exec. Officer)*
Elizabeth Thompson *(Exec. V.P.)*
Hugh Gardner *(Chief Fin. Officer)*
Cliff Thompson *(V.P.-Opers.)*
Don Thompson Jr. *(V.P.-Sls.)*
Ruth Raley *(Sec. & Treas.)*
Lupe Padilla *(Dir.-Sls. Intl.)*
Teresa Carrier *(Pur. Agent)*
Jack McDonald *(Dir.-Mktg.)*
Mike Skaggs *(Dir.-Human Resources)*
Doug Black *(Dir.-N. American Sls.)*
Jim Hunter *(Sls. Coord.)*
Dave King *(Plant Mgr.-Tool Tech)*
Martha Floyd *(Telemarketing)*
Jack Patterson *(Engrng./Tech. Service)*
Mike Bays *(Engrng. & Quality Control)*
Bernie Schaar *(Product Engr.)*
Jeff Osborne *(Quality Control)*
Ginny Greenwell *(Export Mgr.)*

Computer Systems/Hardware:
IBM Mainframe

C.F. THOMPSON GROUP, INC.
752 Bloomfield Ave.
Windsor, CT 06095
Tel.: 203-688-7281
Fax: 203-688-6225
Year Founded: 1955
Approx.Billings: $16,125,000
Emp.: 62
Adv. & Mktg. Communications
Frank Thompson *(Pres. & Treas.)*
Richard Giangreco *(Exec. V.P., Controller)*
Bill Duncan *(V.P., Gen. Mgr. & Sls.)*
Sam Frenis *(V.P., Adv.)*
Mark McCrackin *(Dir., Mktg.)*
Glenn Thompson *(Pur. Dir.)*
Dan Willett *(Opers. Mgr.)*

Computer Systems/Hardware:
Apple, MS-DOS

THOMPSON/MARINCE ADVERTISING
70 N.E. Loop, Ste. 610
San Antonio, TX 78216
Tel.: 210-349-9925
Year Founded: 1976
Approx.Billings: $19,200,000
Emp.: 24
Consumer, Retail, Banking, Healthcare & Package Goods
Corporate Giving Program: United Way
Kenneth W. Thompson *(Chm. Bd. & Pres.)*
William C. Ault *(Exec. V.P.)*
Gale Thompson *(Chief Fin. Officer & Corp. Sec.)*
Stella de la Garza *(Sec.)*

Computer Systems/Hardware:
IBM, MacIntosh

THOMPSON-MCCULLY CO.
5905 Belleville Rd.
Belleville, MI 48111
Tel.: 313-397-2050 **MI**
Fax: 313-397-8480
Approx.Sls.: $35,000,000
Emp.: 300
Highway & Street Construction; Ready-Mixed Asphalt & Concrete
S.I.C.: 1611; 2951; 3273
Robert M. Thompson *(Pres. & Chief Exec. Officer)*
Rollin A. Jones *(V.P.)*
Larry R. Carroll *(Sec.)*
Robert O. Cain *(Controller)*

Outside Service Firm(s):

Michigan National Bank*(Major Banking Relationship)*
Clawson, MI

Subsidiary:

Thompson-McCully Asphalt Paving Co. **(1)**
5905 Belleville Rd.
Belleville, MI 48111
Tel.: 313-397-2050
Asphalt Paving Contractors
S.I.C.: 1611; 2951
Robert Thompson *(Pres.)*

THOMPSON MEDICAL COMPANY, INC.
222 Lakeview Ave., 17th Fl.
West Palm Beach, FL 33401-6112
Tel.: 407-820-9900
Fax: 407-832-2297
Year Founded: 1947
Approx.Sls.: $125,000,000
Emp.: 100
Fiscal Year-end: 11/30/91
Export
Markets & Sell Health Care Products
S.I.C.: 2834; 5122; 2099; 5149
Dan Rodgers *(Chm. Bd. & Pres.)*
Greg Shaban *(Sr. V.P.-Sls.)*
Joseph Librizzi *(V.P. & Treas.)*
Charles T. Noonan *(V.P.-Opers.)*
Thomas A. Vater *(Controller & Sec.)*
Elise Donahue *(Dir.-Sls. Devel.)*
John Jordan *(Dir.-Mngmt. Information Systems)*
Bob Poline *(Dir.-Opers.)*
Alex Terranova *(Dir.-Quality Control)*
Tia Zimmermann *(Mgr.-Adv.)*
Peter Ellis *(Librarian)*
Joanne Richelson *(Mktg. Dept.)*

No. of U.S. Offices: 1
No. of Foreign Offices: 2

Outside Service Firm(s):

Arthur Andersen & Co.*(Auditors)*
1345 Ave. of the Americas
New York, NY 10105
Tel.: 212-708-4000

Bankers Trust Co.*(Major Banking Relationship)*
P.O. Box 9050, Church St. Station
New York, NY 10008
Tel.: 212-250-6037

THOMPSON STEEL CO., INC.
120 Royall St.
Canton, MA 02021
Tel.: 617-828-8800

Fax: 617-828-5082
Year Founded: 1922
Approx.Sls.: $90,000,000
Emp.: 500
Import Export
Primary Metal Industries
S.I.C.: 3316; 5051; 3398
George T. Ryan *(Chief Exec. Officer)*
Mary L. Ryan *(Chief Fin. Officer & V.P.)*
Brendan K. McCormick *(Exec. V.P.)*
Frederick F. Conway *(Treas.)*
T. Kevin O'Connor *(Mgr.-EDP)*

No. of Mfg. Plants/Facilities: 7

Computer Systems/Hardware:
IBM System 4231

Outside Service Firm(s):

KPMG Peat Marwick*(Auditors)*
One Boston Place
Boston, MA 02108
Tel.: 617-723-7700

Paul Revere Life Insurance Co.*(Group Insurer)*
Worcester, MA

U.S. Healthcare*(Group Insurer)*
Boston, MA

Shawmut Bank*(Major Banking Relationship)*
1 Federal St.
Boston, MA 02110
Tel.: 617-292-3715

Subsidiary:

Arrow Thompson Metals **(1)**
6880 Troost Ave.
North Hollywood, CA 91605
Tel.: 818-765-0522
Emp.: 50
Stainless Steel
S.I.C.: 5051
Hank Williams *(Plant Mgr.)*

THOMPSON TRACTOR COMPANY
2401 Pinson Hwy.
Birmingham, AL 35202
Mailing Address:
P.O. Box 10367
Birmingham, AL 35202
Tel.: 205-841-8601
Tel.: 800-547-0760
Fax: 205-849-4287
Year Founded: 1957
Emp.: 700
Fiscal Year-end: 12/31/90
Selling & Servicing of Heavy Machinery
S.I.C.: 5082; 5083; 5084
Michael D. Thompson *(Pres. & Chief Exec. Officer)*
Tom McGough *(Treas.)*
Donald L. Sample *(Controller & Sec.)*
Frank Wright *(Dir.-Human Resources)*

Computer Systems/Hardware:
IBM System 38

Outside Service Firm(s):

Warren, Averett, Kimbrough & Marino*(Auditors)*
Birmingham, AL

Bradley, Arant, Rose & White*(Legal Firm)*
1400 Park Place Tower
Birmingham, AL 35203
Tel.: 205-521-8000

Central Bank*(Major Banking Relationship)*
Birmingham, AL

SouthTrust Bank*(Major Banking Relationship)*
Birmingham, AL
Tel.: 205-254-5068

SouthTrust Bank*(Pension Manager)*
Birmingham, AL
Tel.: 205-254-5068

THOMSON MACCONNELL CADILLAC, INC.
2820 Gilbert Ave.
Cincinnati, OH 45206
Tel.: 513-221-5600
Fax: 513-221-1048
Approx.Sls.: $43,000,000
Emp.: 76
Fiscal Year-end: 12/31/90
Auto Sales, Service & Leasing; Retail Automotive Supplies
S.I.C.: 5531; 5511; 7515
Christopher J. MacConnell *(Pres.)*
Daniel R. MacConnell *(V.P.-Sls.)*
Timothy J. MacConnell *(Treas.)*
Karen Martin *(Controller)*
Principal(s):
Christopher J. MacConnell

Computer Systems/Hardware:
IBM PC-XT

Outside Service Firm(s):

Spaeth & Batterberry*(Auditors)*
Cincinnati, OH

Clark & Eyrich*(Legal Firm)*
525 Vine St.
Cincinnati, OH 45202

Star Bank*(Major Banking Relationship)*
425 Walnut Street
Cincinnati, OH 45202
Tel.: 513-632-4000

THORNTON OIL CORP.
10101 Linn Station Rd., Ste. 200
Louisville, KY 40223
Tel.: 502-425-8022 **De**
Fax: 502-425-8022, Ext. 150
Year Founded: 1972
Approx.Sls.: $132,000,000
Emp.: 950
Gasoline Service Stations & Convenience Stores
S.I.C.: 5541; 5411
James H. Thornton *(Chm. Bd.)*
Paul J. Perconti *(Pres. & Chief Exec. Officer)*
David Brauckmann *(V.P.-Fin.)*
Bob Iezzi *(V.P.-Mktg.)*
Michael Kapfhammer *(V.P.-Opers.)*
Richard Snider *(V.P.-Corp. Affairs)*
Brenda M. Stackhouse *(V.P.-Pur.)*
Alex Campbell *(Sec.)*

Outside Service Firm(s):

Monroe, Shine & Co.*(Auditors)*
Louisville, KY

Wyatt, Tarrant, Combs, Gilbert & Milom*(Legal Firm)*
28th Fl., Citizens Plaza
Louisville, KY 40202
Tel.: 502-589-5235

Citizens Fidelity Bank & Trust Co.*(Major Banking Relationship)*
P.O. Box 33000-Citizens Plaza
Louisville, KY 40232
Tel.: 502-581-3381

THOROUGHBRED SOFTWARE INTERNATIONAL, INC.
19 School House Rd.
Somerset, NJ 08875
Tel.: 908-560-1377
Tel.: 800-524-0430 **NJ**
Fax: 908-560-1594
Year Founded: 1982
Assets: $5,200,000
Earnings: $1,500,000
Liabilities: $3,900,000
Net Worth: $1,300,000
Approx.Sls.: $10,000,000
Emp.: 78
Fiscal Year-end: 11/30/91
Export
Computer Software Developer
S.I.C.: 7372
Corporate Giving Program: Junior & College Level for 4GL & Accounting Software, Business Basic Products; Requests must be from the Professor & on School Letterhead; Will Provide one Full Complement of 4GL Environment, IDOL-IV & Solution IV Accounting; Demonstration & Training
John L. Johnson *(Chm. Bd. & Pres.)*
Carmen T. Randazzo *(Chief Oper. Officer)*
Lynn E. Alexander *(V.P.-Mktg. & Sales)*
E. Terrance Bradunas *(V.P.-Consulting Services)*
Martin R. Flower *(V.P.-European Opers.)*
Roger D. Sparks *(V.P.-Advanced Applications)*
Kathleen M. Johnson *(Corp. Sec.)*
Patrick J. O'Neil *(Gen. Counsel)*
Anne C. Fritz *(Dir.-Human Resources)*
Kathleen Kennedy *(Dir.-Opers.)*
Lenore Luberoff *(Dir.-Meetings Planning)*
Charles Gilman *(Mgr.-Tech. Services)*
Donna Milito *(Mgr.-Telemarketing)*

No. of Mfg. Plants/Facilities: 1
No. of U.S. Offices: 4
No. of Foreign Offices: 3

Computer Systems/Hardware:
DEC 486

Outside Service Firm(s):

M.R. Weiser & Co.*(Auditors)*
99 Wood Ave. S.
Iselin, NJ 08830
Tel.: 908-549-2800

Chubb Group*(Commercial Insurance Carrier)*
Rte. 78
Basking Ridge, NJ

Guardian Life Insurance Co.*(Group Insurer)*
P.O. Box 5633
Bethlehem, PA

Continental Bank, N.A.*(Major Banking Relationship)*
1500 Market St.
Philadelphia, PA 19102
Tel.: 215-564-7475

Connecticut General Life Insurance Co.*(Pension Manager)*
P.O. Box 2975,
Hartford, CT 06104
Tel.: 203-726-6000

Non-U.S. Holdings:

Thoroughbred Europe Ltd. **(1)**
Abacus House, 68 a North St.
Romford, Essex RM 1 1DA, United Kingdom
Tel.: 7 08766988 (100%)
Emp.: 8
Sales & Marketing
S.I.C.: 7372; 5045
Martin Flower *(V.P.-Opers.)*
Jenny Read *(Mgr.-Acctg.)*
Barry Pastel *(Regional Sls. Mgr., UK & Spain)*
Ben Vlaeminck *(Regional Sls. Mgr., Benelux & France)*
Daniel Dornbierer *(Regional Sls. Mgr., Australia, Switzerland & Germany)*

Thoroughbred RD-COM GmbH **(1)**
Nufringer Strasse 17A D-7033
Herrenberg, Germany
Tel.: 7032 31020/31029
Fax: 7032 34955
Import Export
Computer Systems/Hardware:
PC 286 & 386 Based Intel & UNIX
Software Services
S.I.C.: 7372
Lothar Rosner *(Mng. Dir.)*
Lothar Jaus *(Pur. Dir.)*

Thoroughbred/Quark **(1)**
c/o Quark Informatica, Carlet, 3 E-03007
Alicante, Spain
Tel.: 3461512 3220
Fax: 346522 7804
Software Services; Holdings in Mexico, Caracas, Venezuela and Santiago, Chile; 20%-Owned by Thoroughbred Software International, Inc.
S.I.C.: 5045
Roberto Dale *(Mgr.)*

THRALL ENTERPRISES, INC.
181 W. Madison St., Fl. 47
Chicago, IL 60602
Tel.: 312-621-8200
Fax: 312-621-4549
Approx.Sls.: $200,000,000
Emp.: 850
Industrial Supplies, Printing Ink
S.I.C.: 5085; 2893
Jerome A. Thrall *(Chm. Bd.)*
Stanley D. Christianson *(Pres. & Chief Exec. Officer)*
Jerome Jeffrey Thrall *(Exec. V.P. & Sec.)*
Nancy G. McAfee *(V.P., Treas. & Controller)*
James Randall Thrall *(V.P.)*
Marilynn L. Thrall *(V.P.)*

Outside Service Firm(s):

Arthur Andersen & Co.*(Auditors)*
33 W. Monroe St.
Chicago, IL 60603-4067
Tel.: 312-580-0033
Fax: 312-507-6748

Carroll, Hartigan & McCauley*(Legal Firm)*
Chicago, IL

American National Bank*(Major Banking Relationship)*
33 North LaSalle St.
Chicago, IL 60690
Tel.: 312-661-6967

Subsidiary:

Naz-Dar Company **(1)**
1087 N. North Branch St.
Chicago, IL 60622
Tel.: 312-943-8338
Silk Screen Process Inks, Equipment & Supplies
S.I.C.: 2893
J. Jeffrey Thrall *(Chm. Bd. & Chief Exec. Officer)*
Michael P. Fox *(Pres.)*
James Walsh *(Exec. V.P.)*
Kent A. Schnese *(V.P.-Sls. & Mktg.)*
Jay Loprest *(Asst. V.P.-Mfg. & Purchasing)*

THRIFTWAY, INC.
4901 Hunt Rd.
Cincinnati, OH 45242
Tel.: 513-984-0500
Fax: 513-984-8644
Year Founded: 1959
Approx.Sls.: $350,000,000
Emp.: 3,500
Chain of Supermarkets & Drug Stores
S.I.C.: 5411; 5912
Richard E. Lindner, Sr. *(Chm. Bd.)*
Richard E. Lindner, Jr. *(Pres.)*
Robert E. Bailey *(Exec. V.P.-Adv. & Mktg.)*
Walter Dietz *(V.P. & Treas.)*
Thomas P. Robbins *(V.P.)*
Sam Gilardi *(Dir.-Opers.)*
Joel Pugh *(Mgr.-Data Processing)*

Outside Service Firm(s):

George S. Olive & Co.*(Auditors)*
Cincinnati, OH

Keating, Muething & Klekamp*(Legal Firm)*
1 E. Fourth St.
Cincinnati, OH 45202
Tel.: 513-579-6400

Thriftway, Inc.—(Continued)

Provident Bank*(Major Banking Relationship)*
One E. Fourth St.
Cincinnati, OH 45202
Tel.: 513-579-2731

THRIFTY DRUG STORES, INC.
(d/b/a Thrifty-White Stores)
8441 Wayzata Blvd.
Minneapolis, MN 55426
Mailing Address:
10700 Hwy. 55, Ste. 300
Minneapolis, MN 55441
Tel.: 612-545-2234 **MN**
Fax: 612-545-3832
Assets: $27,024,068
Liabilities: $19,134,654
Net Worth: $7,889,414
Approx.Sls.: $89,706,000
Emp.: 1,100
Fiscal Year-end: 4/30/89
Retail Drugs & Sundries
S.I.C.: 5912
Douglas A. Stark *(Chm. Bd. & Chief Exec. Officer)*
Cliff Wallace *(Pres.)*
Richard C. Hayes *(V.P.-Pharmacy)*
Leroy E. Moore *(Sec. & Treas.)*
Curt Renneke *(Dir.-MIS)*
Mark Basco *(Dir.-Fin.)*
Robert Narveson *(Dir.-Opers.)*
Robert Schirber *(Mgr.-Acctg.)*
Lee Osborn *(Mgr.-Mktg.)*
Gordy Bentson *(Asst. Mgr.-Mktg.)*
Cindy Kim *(Adv. Coord.)*
Robert Reynolds *(Payroll & Benefits Supv.)*
Margaret McLain *(Cosmetics Coord.)*
Vickie Kellogg *(Exec. Asst.)*

No. of U.S. Offices: 1

Outside Service Firm(s):

McGladrey & Pullen*(Auditors)*
Minneapolis, MN

Marquette Bank*(Major Banking Relationship)*
777 Marquette Ave.
Minneapolis, MN 55402
Tel.: 612-370-2182

Fredrikson & Byron, P.A.*(Legal Firm)*
1100 International Centre, 900 2nd Ave. S.
Minneapolis, MN 55402
Tel.: 612-347-7000

Subsidiary:

White Drug Enterprises, Inc. **(1)**
8441 Wayzata Blvd.
Minneapolis, MN 55426
Tel.: 612-545-2234
Retail Drugs & Sundries
S.I.C.: 5912
Clifford Wallace *(Pres.)*
Mark Basco *(Dir.-Fin.)*

THRIFTY OIL COMPANY
10000 Lakewood Blvd.
Downey, CA 90240
Tel.: 310-923-9876 **CA**
Fax: 310-869-9739
Year Founded: 1963
Emp.: 1,000
Gasoline & Petroleum Refining
S.I.C.: 2911
Ted Orden *(Chm. Bd. & Pres.)*
Barry Berkett *(Exec. V.P.-Retail Opers. & Sec.)*
John E. Elgin *(Sr. V.P. & Chief Fin. Officer)*
Robert T. Flesh *(Sr. V.P.)*
Van Tarver *(Sr. V.P.-Retail)*
Jerry L. Haight *(V.P.-Mktg.)*
Jack Vernie *(V.P.-Fin., Refining)*
Mike Hewell *(Retail Controller)*
Barbara Buler *(Legal Officer)*
Fred Adler *(Dir.-Pur.)*
Pat Killian *(Dir.-Data Processing, Refining)*

No. of Mfg. Plants/Facilities: 1

No. of U.S. Offices: 2

Outside Service Firm(s):

Deloitte & Touche*(Auditors)*
21550 Oxnard St., Ste. 800
Woodland Hills, CA 91367-7100
Tel.: 818-593-4800
Fax: 818-347-4278

First Interstate Bank of California, N.A.*(Major Banking Relationship)*
P.O. Box 3667,
Los Angeles, CA 90051
Tel.: 213-614-4000

Subsidiary:

Golden West Refining Company **(1)**
13539 E. Foster Rd.
Santa Fe Springs, CA 90670
Tel.: 310-921-3581
Oil Refining
S.I.C.: 2911
Ted Orden *(Pres.)*

Thrifty-White Stores
(See Thrity Drug Stores, Inc. Listing)

THRUWAY FASTENERS INC.
2910 Niagara Falls Blvd.
North Tonawanda, NY 14120
Tel.: 716-694-1434 **NY**
Fax: 716-694-3865
Year Founded: 1959
Approx.Sls.: $29,000,000
Emp.: 182
Fiscal Year-end: 12/31/91
Distribute Hardware & Adhesives
S.I.C.: 5072
Paul G. Lemke, Sr. *(Chm. Bd. & Pres.)*
P. Jenkins *(V.P.)*
Paul G. Lemke, Jr. *(V.P.)*
M. Jenkins *(Treas.)*
Diane Brennan *(Sec. & Controller)*

Computer Systems/Hardware:
Basic Four 4000

Outside Service Firm(s):

Joseph Mitchell*(Auditors)*
Buffalo, NY

Bank of New York*(Major Banking Relationship)*
Tonawanda, NY

THUNDERBIRD STEEL CORPORATION
4300 2nd, N.W.
Albuquerque, NM 87107
Tel.: 505-345-7866 **TX**
Fax: 505-345-7866
Emp.: 26
Wholesale Distribution of Building Materials, Steel & Painting Products
S.I.C.: 5051; 5198; 5023; 5032; 5162
James R. Quillen *(Pres.)*
Michael Taylor *(Sec.)*

Outside Service Firm(s):

Pulakos & Alongi Ltd.*(Auditors)*
Albuquerque, NM

First National Bank Albuquerque*(Major Banking Relationship)*
40 First Plaza
Albuquerque, NM 87102
Tel.: 505-765-4190

THUNDERLINE CORPORATION
8707 Samuel Barton Dr.
Belleville, MI 48111
Mailing Address:
P.O. Box 309,
Belleville, MI 48111
Tel.: 313-397-5000
Fax: 313-397-2955
Approx.Sls.: $20,000,000
Emp.: 210

Export
Manufacture Automotive Rubber Molding
S.I.C.: 3499
Robert J. Gignac *(Chm. Bd.)*
Kurt Pederson *(Pres.)*
Graham G. Barton *(Sec.)*
Frank Barnard *(Controller)*

Outside Service Firm(s):

Manufacturers National Bank N.A.*(Major Banking Relationship)*
38th Fl., 100 Renaissance Center
Detroit, MI 48243
Tel.: 313-222-4227

THYBONY WALL COVERINGS CO.
3720 N. Kedzie Ave.
Chicago, IL 60618
Tel.: 312-463-3005
Fax: 312-463-8988
Approx.Sls.: $19,000,000
Emp.: 120
Fiscal Year-end: 12/31/91
Wholesale Wall Coverings
S.I.C.: 5198
James D. Thybony *(Pres.)*
Ed Bochniak *(V.P. & Controller)*
Mary Norton *(V.P.-Mktg.)*
Matthew White *(V.P.-Sls.)*
John Zeleniak *(V.P.-Opers.)*

TICKETMASTER CORPORATION
3701 Wilshire Blvd., 7th Fl.
Los Angeles, CA 90010
Tel.: 213-381-2000
Fax: 213-386-1244
Emp.: 150
Computerized Ticket Services; Ticketmaster
S.I.C.: 7922; 3579
Frederick D. Rosen *(Chm. Bd.)*
Robert Leonard *(Pres.)*
Terry Barnes *(Gen. Mgr.-Chicago Opers.)*

TICOR TITLE GUARANTEE CO.
39 Broadway
New York, NY 10006
Tel.: 212-509-6000
Approx.Sls.: $20,000,000
Emp.: 600
Title Insurance, Abstracts of Title
S.I.C.: 6361
Michael A. Lewis *(Pres. & Chief Exec. Officer)*
Bernard Rifkin *(Exec. V.P. & Sec.)*
Kenneth C. Kohen *(Sr. V.P. & Mktg. Dir.)*

TIDELANDS OIL PRODUCTION CO.
301 East Ocean, Ste. 300
Long Beach, CA 90802
Mailing Address:
P.O. Box 1330
Long Beach, CA 90801
Tel.: 213-436-9918
Fax: 213-495-1950
Year Founded: 1989
Approx.Sls.: $45,000,000
Emp.: 245
Crude Oil Production
S.I.C.: 1311
W.T. Smith *(Pres. & Gen. Mgr.)*
Donald E. Burns *(V.P.-Fin.)*
Mark Kapelke *(V.P.-Engrg.)*
Jim Quay *(V.P.-Opers.)*
Joanne P. Rivera *(V.P.-Human Resources)*
A. van Os *(V.P.-Gas Processing)*
Don Foster *(Controller)*
Jerry Snow *(Dir.-Safety)*
Catherine Hill *(Pension Admin.)*
Jim Connolly *(Dir.-Pur.)*

Computer Systems/Hardware:
DEC Micro-VAX 2; VAX 8600

Outside Service Firm(s):

Deloitte & Touche*(Auditors)*
1000 Wilshire Blvd.
Los Angeles, CA 90017-2472
Tel.: 213-688-0800
Fax: 213-688-0100

Lloyds Bank Plc*(Commercial Insurance Carrier)*
Lime Street
London, United Kingdom
Tel.: 01-283-4026

Blue Cross of California*(Group Insurer)*
21555 Oxnard St.
Woodland Hills, CA 91367
Tel.: 818-703-2345

Connecticut General Life Insurance Co.*(Group Insurer)*
P.O. Box 2975,
Hartford, CT 06104
Tel.: 203-726-6000

Guardian Life Insurance Co.*(Group Insurer)*
New York, NY

Grisham & Cannon*(Legal Firm)*
Long Beach, CA

Union Bank*(Major Banking Relationship)*
445 S. Figueroa St.
Los Angeles, CA 90071
Tel.: 213-236-5076

Equitable Life*(Pension Manager)*
1221 Ave. of the Americas
New York, NY 10022
Tel.: 212-382-8038
Fax: 212-382-8089

TIERNAY METALS, INC.
2600 Marine Ave.
Redondo Beach, CA 90278
Tel.: 213-676-0184 **CA**
Fax: 213-679-0223
Year Founded: 1956
Approx.Sls.: $45,000,000
Emp.: 150

Export
Distributor of Aluminum Extrusions to the Aerospace Industry
S.I.C.: 5051
William A. Steinmetz *(Chm. Bd.)*
Robert P. Keehn *(Pres.)*
Barbara Carr *(V.P. & Sec.)*
Thomas Rasmussen *(V.P. & Treas.)*
Charles Steinmetz *(V.P.)*

Outside Service Firm(s):

Ernst & Young*(Auditors)*
515 S. Flower St.
Los Angeles, CA 90071
Tel.: 213-621-1666

TIFFANY EXTRUDERS, INC.
155 Sherman Ave.
Paterson, NJ 07502
Tel.: 201-956-1300 **NJ**
Fax: 201-956-1609
Year Founded: 1971
Approx.Sls.: $18,000,000
Emp.: 50

Export
Plastic Bags, LDC & Apparel
S.I.C.: 2673
Carl Gurgold *(Pres.)*
Alan Silverman *(V.P.)*
Steven Gurgold *(Dir.-Sls.)*
Todd Rubzin *(Dir.-Mktg.)*

No. of Mfg. Plants/Facilities: 2

Outside Service Firm(s):

J.M. Levy & Company*(Auditors)*
New York, NY

Cole, Schotz, Bernstein, Meisel & Forman*(Legal Firm)*
Hackensack, NJ

First Fidelity Bank, N.A.*(Major Banking Relationship)*
Hackensack, NJ

Subsidiary:

Power Plastics Inc. **(1)**
155 Sherman Ave.
Paterson, NJ 07502
Tel.: 800-932-0482
Emp.: 12
Small Bags
S.I.C.: 2759
Steven Gurgold *(Chief Oper. Officer)*
Todd Rubzin *(Chief Fin. Officer)*

TIFFANY INDUSTRIES, INC.
1015 Corporate Sq. Dr., Ste. 105
Saint Louis, MO 63132
Tel.: 314-991-1700 **MO**
Mfr. of Office Furniture & Agricultural Equipment
S.I.C.: 2522; 2521; 3523
Joe Simpkins *(Chm. Bd. & Chief Exec. Officer)*
Frank Leber *(V.P.)*

Subsidiaries:

Tiffany Industries Americas Corp. **(1)**
9666 Olive Blvd., Ste. 750
St. Louis, MO 63132
Tel.: 314-991-1700
Exporters of Agricultural Equip. & Srvs.
S.I.C.: 5083
Frank Leber *(V.P.)*

Tiffany Stand & Furniture Company **(1)**
1015 Corporate Sq., Ste. 105
St. Louis, MO 63132
Tel.: 314-991-1700
Approx.Sls.: $24,000,000
Emp.: 400
Fiscal Year-end: 12/31/90
Mfr. Office Machine Stands; Word Processing Furniture
S.I.C.: 2522
David Ridgway *(Pres.)*
John Dorato *(V.P.-Sls.)*

TIFFIN MOTOR HOMES, INC.
502 4th St., N.W.
Red Bay, AL 35582
Tel.: 205-356-8661 **AL**
Fax: 205-356-8219
Year Founded: 1972
Approx.Sls.: $91,000,000
Emp.: 227
Travel Trailers & Campers; Mobile Homes Transport
S.I.C.: 3792; 4213
Robert A. Tiffin, Jr. *(Pres.)*
David S. Tiffin *(V.P.)*
R. Alex Tiffin, Sr. *(Treas. & Sec.)*

Outside Service Firm(s):

Hardwick, Von Stoy & Sparks*(Auditors)*
Red Bay, AL

TIGER ELECTRONICS, INC.
980 Woodlands Pkwy.
Vernon Hills, IL 60061
Tel.: 708-913-8100
Fax: 708-913-8118
Approx.Sls.: $18,000,000
Emp.: 25
Sales & Distribution of Tiger Electronic Toys Learning Aids, Video Software
S.I.C.: 5092
R. O. Rissman *(Pres.)*
Roger Shiffman *(Exec. V.P.)*
William Dohrmann *(V.P.-Mktg.)*
Lori Grupp *(V.P.-Mktg.)*
Scott Forester *(Chief Fin. Officer)*
Lianue Czirjak *(Dir.-Mktg.)*

TIGHE INDUSTRIES, INC.
P.O. Box 251A, E. Prospect Rd.
York, PA 17406
Tel.: 717-252-1578 **PA**
Fax: 717-252-4685
Year Founded: 1969
Sales Range: $10-19 Million
Emp.: 45
Costumes; Women's, Misses' and Juniors' Bathing Suits and Leotards
S.I.C.: 2389; 2339
Leroy A. King Jr. *(Chm Bd. & Chief Exec. Officer)*
Delaine Zimmer *(Exec. V.P. & Chief Oper. Officer)*
Al Berryman *(Dir.-Sls.)*
Robert McCreary *(Dir.-Adv..)*
Robert Niedziekski *(Dir.-Human Resources)*
Vivian Poff *(Mgr.-Prod.)*
Raeann Almoney *(Mgr.-Mfg. Serv.)*
Patsy Bigler *(Personnel Admin.)*
Gary M. Gilbert *(Asst. Sec.)*

No. of Mfg. Plants/Facilities: 3

Computer Systems/Hardware:
System 38 400

Outside Service Firm(s):

Miller & Company*(Auditors)*
York, PA

York Bank & Trust Co.*(Major Banking Relationship)*
York, PA

TILCON, INC.
Black Rock Ave.
New Britain, CT 06052
Mailing Address:
P.O. Box 1357
New Britain, CT 06050
Tel.: 203-223-3651
Fax: 203-225-1865
Approx.Sls.: $100,000,000
Emp.: 1,500
Manufacture Concrete & Asphalt Building Materials
S.I.C.: 5039; 2951; 1611; 1622; 3241
Joseph B. Kittederg *(Pres. & Exec. Oper. Officer)*
Angelo Tomasso, Jr. *(Chief Exec. Officer)*
Charles McDonald *(Chief Fin. Officer)*
Peter Lohne *(V.P.)*
Anthony P. Germano *(Controller)*

Outside Service Firm(s):

KPMG Peat Marwick*(Auditors)*
Stamford Square, 3001 Summer St.
Stamford, CT 06905
Tel.: 203-356-9800

Marks, Murase & White*(Legal Firm)*
400 Park Ave.
New York, NY 10022
Tel.: 212-832-3333

European American Bank*(Major Banking Relationship)*
New York, NY

Chemical Banking Corp.*(Pension Manager)*
277 Park Ave.
New York, NY 10041
Tel.: 212-310-6407
Fax: 212-310-4526

The Principal Financial Group*(Pension Manager)*
711 High St.
Des Moines, IA 50309
Tel.: 515-247-4593
Tel.: 800-543-4015

TILLAMOOK COUNTY CREAMERY ASSN.
4175 Hwy. 101 N.
Tillamook, OR 97141
Mailing Address:
P. O. Box 313
Tillamook, OR 97141
Tel.: 503-842-4481
Fax: 503-842-3102
Year Founded: 1909
Assets: $59,700,000
Earnings: $2,000,000
Liabilities: $36,900,000
Net Worth: $22,800,000
Approx.Sls.: $100,000,000
Emp.: 300
Fiscal Year-end: 12/31/91
Dairy Cooperative
S.I.C.: 2022; 2026; 5143; 2024
Edward Myers *(Chm. Bd. & Pres.)*
Dale Buck *(Vice Chm.)*
Bruce Lundquist *(Controller)*
D. R. Sutton *(Sec.)*
Harold Schild *(Dir.)*
Gary Sauriol *(Mgr.-Sls. & Mktg.)*

Computer Systems/Hardware:
MAI Basic 4

TIMBER PRODUCTS COMPANY, LP
305 S. 4th St.
Springfield, OR 97477
Tel.: 503-747-3321
Fax: 503-747-0390
Year Founded: 1967
Approx.Sls.: $220,000,000
Emp.: 900
Rough, Dressed & Finished Lumber; Hardwood or Hardwood Faced Plywood; Softwood Plywood; Veneer Stock, Softwood, Particleboard Products
S.I.C.: 5031; 2435; 2436; 2493
Wayne R. Atwood *(Gen. Partner)*
Lawrence J. Moore *(Gen. Partner)*

Outside Service Firm(s):

United States National Bank of Oregon*(Major Banking Relationship)*
P.O. Box 3850,
Portland, OR 97208
Tel.: 503-275-6111

TIME OIL COMPANY
2737 W. Commodore Way
Seattle, WA 98199
Tel.: 206-285-2400
Fax: 206-283-8036
Approx.Sls.: $225,000,000
Emp.: 115
Filling Stations, Gasoline, Fuel Oil, Diesel Fuel & Lubricating Oils & Greases
S.I.C.: 5541; 5172
Edward Miller *(Chm. Bd.)*
H. Roger Holiday *(Pres.)*
Terrill Henderson *(V.P.-Fin.)*

Outside Service Firm(s):

Ernst & Young*(Auditors)*
515 S. Flower St.
Los Angeles, CA 90071
Tel.: 213-621-1666

Subsidiaries:

Time Oil Co. **(1)**
5150 Wilshire Blvd.
Los Angeles, CA 90036
Tel.: 213-938-7151
Sale & Marketing of Oil & Oil Products
S.I.C.: 5172
Robert Redd *(V.P.-Sls.-Refinery Products)*
Ben Tsuchida *(V.P. & Sec.)*
William Kitto *(V.P.-Crude Oil Pur.)*

U.S. Oil & Refining Co. **(1)**
3001 Marshall Ave.
Tacoma, WA 98421
Tel.: 206-383-1651
Petroleum Refining
S.I.C.: 2911
Thomas C. Temple *(Pres.)*
Al Cabodi *(V.P.-Refinery Opers.)*
Sterlin Parrish *(Treas.)*

TIME SYSTEMS, INC.
5353 N. 16th St., Ste. 400
Phoenix, AZ 85016
Tel.: 602-265-3220
Tel.: 800-562-6441 **AZ**
Fax: 602-264-6607
Year Founded: 1978
Approx.Sls.: $17,500,000
Emp.: 179
Fiscal Year-end: 12/31/91
Import Export
Time Management & Productivity Training Company
S.I.C.: 8741
Ron Huber *(Chm. Bd., Pres. & Chief Exec. Officer)*
Judy Huber *(Exec. V.P., Treas. & Sec.)*
David Hall *(Sr. V.P.-Sls. & Mktg.)*
Debra Larson *(V.P.-Mktg. & Training)*
James A. Hieronymus *(Chief Fin. Officer)*
Joseph Schnurr *(Controller)*
Kim Corson *(Gen. Counsel)*
Ralph Hicks *(Mgr.-Pur. & Inventory)*
Pam Korzon *(Mgr.-Organization Devel.)*
Sharon Snow *(Mgr.-Management Info. Systems)*
Kent Sowers *(Mgr.-Production)*
David Weiss *(Mgr.-Tech.)*
Judy Williams *(Mgr.-Human Resources)*
David Cazel *(Graphics Coordinator)*
Anita Silmser *(Mktg. Analyst)*
Principal(s):
Ron Huber
Judy Huber

No. of Mfg. Plants/Facilities: 1
No. of U.S. Offices: 14
No. of Foreign Offices: 3

Computer Systems/Hardware:
DRC/Hewlet Packard

Outside Service Firm(s):

Gallant, Farrow & Hensley*(Auditors)*
Phoenix, AZ

Reliance Insurance Co.*(Commercial Insurance Carrier)*
Phoenix, AZ

Blue Cross & Blue Shield of Arizona, Inc.*(Group Insurer)*
Phoenix, AZ

Lewis & Roca*(Legal Firm)*
Phoenix, AZ

Valley National Bank*(Major Banking Relationship)*
241 North Central Ave., 11th Floor
Phoenix, AZ 85001

IDS Trust*(Pension Manager)*
Phoenix, AZ

Subsidiary:

Time Index, Inc. **(1)**
825 East University
Phoenix, AZ 85034
Tel.: 602-495-9233
Tel.: 800-899-9233
Emp.: 16
Design & Manufacture of Custom Index Tabbing
S.I.C.: 2621
Ron Huber *(Chm. Bd., Pres. & Chief Exec. Officer)*
James Hieronymus *(Chief Fin. Officer)*
Alex Jiminez *(Mgr.-Time Index)*

TIMEC COMPANY
155 Corporate Pl.
Vallejo, CA 94590
Tel.: 707-642-2222
Fax: 707-648-2719
Year Founded: 1971
Sales Range: $40-59 Million

Timec Company—(Continued)

Emp.: 800
Fiscal Year-end: 12/31/90
Refinery & Oilfield Maintenance; Equipment Manufacturer
S.I.C.: 3533; 2911
R.B. Wood *(Pres. & Treas.)*
Gary L. French *(V.P.)*

No. of Mfg. Plants/Facilities: 20

Computer Systems/Hardware:
IBM System 36

Outside Service Firm(s):

American General Group Insurance Co.*(Group Insurer)*
16130 Ventura Blvd.
Los Angeles, CA
Tel.: 213-872-0473

McCabe, Swartz, Evans, Levy & Dawe*(Legal Firm)*
Concord, CA

Bank of America NT&SA*(Major Banking Relationship)*
555 So. Flower St., 5th Fl.
Los Angeles, CA 90071
Tel.: 213-228-3526
Fax: 213-228-4062

TIMEMED LABELING SYSTEMS, INC.
144 Tower Dr.
Burr Ridge, IL 60521
Tel.: 708-986-1800
Tel.: 800-323-4840
Fax: 708-986-0016
Approx.Sls.: $27,000,000
Emp.: 200
Export
Manufacture Pressure-Sensitive Tapes & Labels Including Computer Labeling Systems and Barcoding for Hospital, Laboratory, Research & Industrial Fields, Time Tape Pressure Sensitive Tape, Flo-Meters Labels, Instromark Tape for Surgical Instruments, Labels for Patient Charges; The Health Coder System for Thermal Bar Code Labeling
S.I.C.: 2672
John Nerad *(Chm. Bd.)*
Jerry Nerad *(Pres.)*
Vic Robertson *(V.P.-Sls. & Mktg.)*
Charles Johnson *(Controller)*
Nancy Finigan *(Dir.-Mktg.)*
Robert Fines *(Mgr.-Natl. Sls.)*
Thomas Nelson *(Mgr.-Personnel)*
Randy Zehr *(Mgr.-Mktg. & Communications)*
Greta Goldman *(Pur. Agent)*
Principal(s):
Jerry Nerad

No. of Mfg. Plants/Facilities: 3

Outside Service Firm(s):

Hutton, Nelson & McDonald*(Auditors)*
Oakbrook, IL

McDermott, Will & Emery*(Legal Firm)*
227 W. Monroe St.
Chicago, IL 60606-5096
Tel.: 312-372-2000

Standard Chartered Bank*(Major Banking Relationship)*
Chicago, IL

Divisions:

TimeMed Labeling Systems, Inc. **(1)**
9566 Vassar Ave.
Chatsworth, CA 91311
Tel.: 818-882-8463
Fax: 818-882-9416

TimeMed Labeling Systems, Inc. **(1)**
2808 McGowan St.
Dallas, TX 75203
Tel.: 214-833-2533
Fax: 214-942-5046

THE TIMES-PICAYUNE PUBLISHING CORP.
3800 Howard Ave.
New Orleans, LA 70140
Tel.: 504-826-3279
Fax: 504-826-3636
Emp.: 900
Newspaper Publishing
S.I.C.: 2711
Ashton Phelps, Jr. *(Pres. & Publr.)*
Beth Adams *(V.P. & Mgr.-Personnel)*
Wayne Benjamin *(V.P. & Pur. Agent)*
Crawford Carroll *(V.P. & Mktg. Services Dir.)*
Earl Cobb *(V.P. & Bus. Mgr.)*
Linda Dennery *(V.P. & Gen. Mgr.)*
Robert G. O'Neill *(V.P. & Adv. Dir.)*
Morris Schneider *(V.P. & Dir.-Circulation)*
Hiram Torres *(V.P. & Credit Mgr.)*
Jim Amoss *(Editor)*
Lester S. Key *(Mgr.-Gen. Adv.)*

Computer Systems/Hardware:
IBM

Outside Service Firm(s):

Paul Scherer & Co.*(Auditors)*
New York, NY

Hibernia National Bank*(Major Banking Relationship)*
New Orleans, LA

National Bank of Commerce*(Major Banking Relationship)*
New Orleans, LA

TIMES PRINTING COMPANY, INC.
453 5th St.
Random Lake, WI 53075
Mailing Address:
P.O. Box 325, 453 Fifth St.
Random Lake, WI 53075-0325
Tel.: 414-994-4396 **WI**
Fax: 414-994-2088
Year Founded: 1918
Assets: $12,000,000
Liabilities: $9,500,000
Net Worth: $2,500,000
Approx.Sls.: $25,000,000
Emp.: 250
Fiscal Year-end: 10/31/91
Import Export
Commercial Offset Printing
S.I.C.: 2752
Ray Scholler *(Pres.)*
John Scholler *(V.P.-Prod.)*
Gordon Clausing *(V.P.-Mktg. & Sls.)*
Judy Mueller *(Dir.-Opers.)*
James Scholler *(Dir.-Pur.)*
Bernice Scholler *(Sec. & Treas.)*
Lester Miller *(Controller)*
Jean Vetter *(Mgr.-Data Processing)*
Dave Sanchez *(Dir.-Telecommunications)*
Principal(s):
Ray Scholler
John Scholler
Judy Mueller
James Scholler
Bernice Scholler
Jean Vetter

No. of Mfg. Plants/Facilities: 2
No. of U.S. Offices: 4

Computer Systems/Hardware:
IBM Compatible

Outside Service Firm(s):

Dippold, Cooper & Nelson*(Auditors)*
Sheboygan, WI

Ansay Insurance*(Commercial Insurance Carrier)*
Port Washington, WI

EBC Insurance*(Group Insurer)*
Milwaukee, WI

First Wisconsin National Bank*(Investment Banker)*
777 E. Wisconsin Ave.
Milwaukee, WI 53202
Tel.: 414-765-4321
Fax: 414-355-6903

Rhode, Neuses & Dales*(Legal Firm)*
Sheboygan, WI

First Wisconsin National Bank*(Major Banking Relationship)*
777 E. Wisconsin Ave.
Milwaukee, WI 53202
Tel.: 414-765-4321
Fax: 414-355-6903

Ray Scholler*(Pension Manager)*
Random Lake, WI

TIMESAVERS INC.
5270 Hanson Ct.
Minneapolis, MN 55429-3161
Mailing Address:
P.O. Box 22190
Minneapolis, MN 55422-0190
Tel.: 612-537-3611
Fax: 612-537-9247
Approx.Sls.: $30,000,000
Emp.: 320
Fiscal Year-end: 6/30/91
Mfrs. of Wide Abrasive Sanding & Grinding Machines; Wide Belt Sanding Machinery; Coated Abrasive Machinery; CNC Routers; Vibratory Finishing Equip.
S.I.C.: 3553
G.L. Schuster *(Chm. Bd.)*
R.S. Vold *(Pres.)*
Tom Bishop *(Buyer)*

TIMEX CORPORATION
Park Rd. Extension
Middlebury, CT 06762
Mailing Address:
P.O. Box 310,
Middlebury, CT 06762
Tel.: 203-573-5000 **DE**
Fax: 203-573-6901
Year Founded: 1857
Approx.Sls.: $600,000,000
Emp.: 10,000
Fiscal Year-end: 12/31/90
Mfr. of Watches, Timing Instruments
S.I.C.: 3873; 3829; 3625
Fred Olsen *(Chm. Bd.)*
James Binns *(Pres. & Chief Exec. Officer)*
C.M. Jacobi *(V.P.-Sls. & Mktg.-World Wide)*
Muhammad Saleh *(V.P.-Human Res.)*
Rudy DeAngelis *(V.P.-Fin.)*
F. Sherer *(V.P. & Gen. Counsel)*
D. Rahilly *(Dir.-Mktg. & Sls.-U.S.A.)*
Ronald Sok *(Mgr.-Adv. & Pub. Rels.)*
Rose Spires *(Mktg. Coord.)*
Principal(s):
Fred Olsen

No. of U.S. Offices: 1

Computer Systems/Hardware:
IBM 3081

Outside Service Firm(s):

KPMG Peat Marwick*(Auditors)*
City Place II
Hartford, CT 06103-4103
Tel.: 203-522-3200
Fax: 203-297-5555

Aetna Life & Casualty*(Group Insurer)*
151 Farmington Avenue
Hartford, CT 06156
Tel.: 203-273-2128
Fax: 203-729-4295

Chase Manhattan Bank, N.A.*(Major Banking Relationship)*
One Chase Manhattan Plaza
New York, NY 10081
Tel.: 212-552-2222
Tel.: 800-526-0801
Fax: 212-552-7175

Chemical Banking Corp.*(Major Banking Relationship)*
277 Park Ave.
New York, NY 10041
Tel.: 212-310-6407
Fax: 212-310-4526

TIMPTE INDUSTRIES, INC.
1290 Broadway, Ste. 500
Denver, CO 80203
Tel.: 303-839-1900 **DE**
Fax: 303-839-1111
Sales Range: $100-499 Million
Emp.: 700
Fiscal Year-end: 3/31/90
Holding Company; Manufacture Truck Trailers, Tank Trailers & Aluminum Recreational Boats
S.I.C.: 6719; 3713; 3715; 3732; 3443
James E. Lakin *(Chm. Bd.)*
Thomas W. Gamel *(Pres.)*
David Benbow *(V.P.)*
Doug Walliser *(V.P.)*
Principal(s):
James E. Lakin
Thomas W. Gamel
David Benbow
Doug Walliser

No. of Mfg. Plants/Facilities: 5
No. of U.S. Offices: 15

Computer Systems/Hardware:
IBM Systems 36 & 38

Outside Service Firm(s):

KPMG Peat Marwick*(Auditors)*
1600 FirsTier Bank Bldg., 13th & M Streets, Ste. 1600
Lincoln, NE 68508
Tel.: 402-476-1216

Fairfield & Woods*(Legal Firm)*
Denver, CO

Subsidiary:

Timpte, Inc. **(1)**
2801 23rd Ave.
Council Bluffs, IA 51501
Tel.: 712-328-8651
Emp.: 500
Fiscal Year-end: 3/31/87
Manufacture Over-the-Road Truck Trailers
S.I.C.: 3715; 3713; 3443
James C. Remick *(Pres.)*
Ken Alred *(Exec. V.P.)*

TINGLEY RUBBER CORPORATION
200 South Ave.
South Plainfield, NJ 07080
Mailing Address:
P.O. Box 100
South Plainfield, NJ 07080
Tel.: 908-757-7474
Tel.: 800-631-5498
Fax: 908-757-9239
Year Founded: 1896
Approx.Sls.: $25,000,000
Emp.: 200
Fiscal Year-end: 8/31/91
Import Export
Molded Rubber Footwear; Protective Clothing, Over the Sock Protective Footwear
S.I.C.: 3069
James McCollum *(Chm. Bd.)*
David Rand *(Pres.)*
Bruce McCollum *(Exec. V.P.)*
Rosemarie Fisher *(Controller)*
George Apgar *(Dir.-Tech. Services)*
Lorraine Pulley *(Dir.-Personnel)*
Lori Wolff *(Dir.-Govt. Affairs)*

Outside Service Firm(s):

Trien, Rosenberg, Felix, Rosenberg, Barr & Weinberg*(Auditors)*
Morristown, NJ

National State Bank of New Jersey*(Major Banking Relationship)*
Springfield, NJ

TINIUS OLSEN TESTING MACHINE CO., INC.
1065 Easton Rd.
Willow Grove, PA 19090
Mailing Address:
P.O. Box 429,
Willow Grove, PA 19090
Tel.: 215-675-7100
Fax: 215-441-0899
Year Founded: 1889
Approx.Sls.: $10,000,000
Emp.: 115
Import Export
Mfr. Testing & Balancing Machines, Instruments & Equipment
S.I.C.: 3825
John A. Milane *(Pres.)*
C. Robert Tait, Jr. *(V.P.-Mfg.)*
John T. Murray *(Treas. & Sec.)*
Joseph M. Sherlock *(Mgr.-Sls. & Adv.)*
Frank E. Geary *(Pur. Agent)*

Outside Service Firm(s):

Mathieson, Aitken & Co.*(Auditors)*
Plymouth Meeting, PA

Obermayer, Rebmann, Maxwell & Hippel*(Legal Firm)*
Philadelphia, PA

Provident National Bank*(Major Banking Relationship)*
1000 Westlakes Dr.
Berwyn, PA 19312

TINSLEY ADVERTISING
2660 Brickell
Miami, FL 33129
Tel.: 305-856-6060 **FL**
Fax: 305-858-3877
Year Founded: 1974
Approx.Billings: $60,000,000
Emp.: 75
Fiscal Year-end: 12/31/91
Import Export
Advertising Agency
S.I.C.: 7311
Sandra C. Tinsley *(Chm. Bd.)*
James P. Flanagan *(Pres. & Dir.-Client Services)*
Richard W. Kelsey *(Exec. V.P.)*
Joseph G. Albonetti *(Sr. V.P. & Dir.-Hispanic & Intl. Mktg.)*
Douglas Cooper *(V.P. & Dir.-Yellow Pages)*
Principal(s):
Sandra C. Tinsley

Computer Systems/Hardware:
Apple Macintosh, IBM PC

Outside Service Firm(s):

Southeast Bank, N.A.*(Major Banking Relationship)*
One Southeast Financial Center
Miami, FL 33131

Subsidiaries:

Conceptos International **(1)**
2660 Brickell
Miami, FL 33129
Tel.: 305-856-6060
Advertising Operations
S.I.C.: 7311
Joseph Albonetti *(Sr. V.P.)*

Tinsley Public Relations **(1)**
2660 Brickell
Miami, FL 33129
Tel.: 305-856-6060
Advertising Operations
S.I.C.: 7311
Joe Abrell *(Managing Dir.)*

Tinsley Sports Network **(1)**
2660 Brickell
Miami, FL 33129
Tel.: 305-856-6060
Advertising Operations
S.I.C.: 7311
Jim Flanagan *(Gen. Mgr.)*

Tinsley Yellow Page Services **(1)**
2660 Brickell
Miami, FL 33129
Tel.: 305-856-6060
Advertising Operations
S.I.C.: 7311
Douglas Cooper *(V.P.)*

TIPPINS INCORPORATED
435 Butler St.
Pittsburgh, PA 15223
Mailing Address:
P.O. Box 9547,
Pittsburgh, PA 15223
Tel.: 412-781-7600 **PA**
Telex: 86-6615
Fax: 412-781-7612
Year Founded: 1958
Sales Range: $40-59 Million
Emp.: 270
Export
Designer of Rolling Mills for Ferrous & Non-Ferrous Producers
S.I.C.: 3547; 3549
Corporate Giving Program: United Way & Selected Organizations
George W. Tippins *(Chm. Bd.)*
John E. Thomas *(Pres. & Chief Exec. Officer)*
Richard S. Connolly *(Exec. V.P.)*
Charles K. Pine *(V.P.-Opers.)*
Anthony Wilson *(V.P.-Sls. & Mktg.)*
Ernest A. Carpenter *(V.P.-Admin. & Gen. Counsel)*
Sidney Snitkin *(V.P.-Controls)*
Michael G. Smarto *(Controller)*
Robert Crooks *(Dir.-Pur.)*
Lawrence E. Scott *(Mgr.-Mngmt. Information Systems)*
Richard W. Little *(Maintenance Mgr.)*
Gary L. Gent *(Cash Mngmt.)*
Principal(s):
George W. Tippins
John E. Thomas

No. of Mfg. Plants/Facilities: 2

Computer Systems/Hardware:
Prime

Outside Service Firm(s):

Ernst & Young*(Auditors)*
2000 Pittsburgh Natl. Bldg.
Pittsburgh, PA 15222
Tel.: 412-644-7800
Fax: 412-644-7419

Kirkpatrick & Lockhart*(Legal Firm)*
1500 Oliver Bldg., 535 Smithfield St.
Pittsburgh, PA 15222
Tel.: 412-355-6500
Fax: 412-355-6501

Subsidiaries:

International Mill Construction, Inc. **(1)**
435 Butler St., P.O. Box 9525
Pittsburgh, PA 15223
Tel.: 412-781-3340
C.K. Pine *(Pres.)*

International Mill Construction, Inc. **(1)**
435 Butler St., P.O. Box 925
Pittsburgh, PA 15223
Tel.: 412-781-3340 (100%)
International Mill Construction
S.I.C.: 1629
Charles K. Pine *(Pres.)*
Sheldon Jones III *(V.P.)*

TISHMAN REALTY & CONSTRUCTION CO.
666 5th Ave.
New York, NY 10103
Tel.: 212-399-3600
Fax: 212-397-1316
Construction & Development
S.I.C.: 1541; 1522; 8741; 6552
John L. Tishman *(Chm.)*
Larry Schwartzwalder *(Pres.)*
Kathy Kotown *(Sec.)*
Principal(s):
John L. Tishman

No. of U.S. Offices: 6
No. of Foreign Offices: 2

TITAN INDUSTRIAL CORP.
555 Madison Ave.
New York, NY 10022
Tel.: 212-421-6700
Fax: 212-421-6708
Approx.Sls.: $300,000,000
Emp.: 250
International Steel Marketing
S.I.C.: 5051
Jerome Siegel *(Chm. Bd.)*
Michael S. Levin *(Pres. & Chief Exec. Officer)*
George Cady *(Chief Fin. Officer)*
Steven A. Levy *(Exec. V.P. & Treas.)*
Thomas A. Potter *(Gen. Counsel)*
Richard Blumberg *(Controller)*

Computer Systems/Hardware:
IBM System 36

Outside Service Firm(s):

Weil, Gotshal & Manges*(Legal Firm)*
767 5th Ave.
New York, NY 10153
Tel.: 212-310-8000

National Westminster Bank plc*(Major Banking Relationship)*
Astor Plaza, 1515 Broadway
New York, NY 10036

E. H. TITCHENER & COMPANY
1 Titchener Place
Binghamton, NY 13905
Mailing Address:
P.O. Box 1706
Binghamton, NY 13902
Tel.: 607-772-1161
Fax: 607-771-0264
Approx.Sls.: $7,000,000
Emp.: 180
Manufacture Custom-Fabricated Wire, Welded Wire Assemblies, Tubing, Sheet Metal & Stampings
S.I.C.: 3496; 3444
Carlton J. Conrad, Sr. *(Chm. Bd.)*
Carlton J. Conrad, Jr. *(Pres. & Chief Exec. Officer)*
Al Brazinski *(Chief Fin. Officer)*
Ralph Barnhart *(V.P.-Engrng.)*
Donald E. Young *(V.P.-Mktg. & Sls.)*

TOBACCO SUPPLY
2411 Industrial Dr.
Springfield, TN 37172
Tel.: 615-384-2421 **TN**
Fax: 615-384-7767
Year Founded: 1944
Approx.Sls.: $18,000,000
Emp.: 60
Export
Buying & Selling of Tobacco Leaf; Tobbacco Auctioning & Warehousing
S.I.C.: 5159
Paul Keith *(Pres.)*
Ed Alexander *(V.P.)*
Bertha Jenkins *(Sec.)*

Outside Service Firm(s):

Wentworth & Olson*(Auditors)*
Springfield, TN

Sovran Bank*(Major Banking Relationship)*
Springfield, TN

TOBER INDUSTRIES, INC.
1520 Washington Ave.
Saint Louis, MO 63103
Tel.: 314-421-2030 **MO**
Telex: 684-1013 TOBEX
Fax: 314-621-3064
Year Founded: 1905
Sales Range: $10-19 Million
Emp.: 18
Import
Footwear Importer
S.I.C.: 5139
Lester V. Tober *(Pres. & Chief Exec. Officer)*
Irvin E. Tober *(Vice Chm.)*
Bennett E. Frelich *(Exec. V.P.)*
Thompson Mitchell *(Gen. Counsel)*
Gerald Bernatz *(Gen. Mgr.)*

Computer Systems/Hardware:
IBM System 36

Outside Service Firm(s):

Thompson & Mitchell*(Legal Firm)*
One Mercantile Center
St. Louis, MO 63101
Tel.: 314-231-7676

Mercantile Bank*(Major Banking Relationship)*
Saint Louis, MO

Division:

World Import Co. **(1)**
1520 Washington Ave.
Saint Louis, MO 63103
Tel.: 314-421-2030

TOBERMAN
5100 Oakland Ave.
Saint Louis, MO 63110
Tel.: 314-533-2490
Year Founded: 1925
Approx.Sls.: $45,000,000
Emp.: 25
Wholesale Grain & Feed
S.I.C.: 5153; 5191
Walter I. Toberman *(Pres.)*
Allen Toberman *(V.P.)*
David Toberman *(Treas. & Sec.)*
Principal(s):
Walter I. Toberman
David Toberman

Outside Service Firm(s):

Burt Allison Co.*(Auditors)*
Belleview, MO

Lowenhaupt, Chasnoff, Armstrong & Mellitz*(Legal Firm)*
St. Louis, MO

Mark Twain St. Louis Bank*(Major Banking Relationship)*
1630 S. Lindbergh Blvd.
St. Louis, MO 63131

TOC Retail
(Acquired by E-Z Serve Corp.)

THE TODD-AO CORPORATION
172 Golden Gate Ave.
San Francisco, CA 94102
Tel.: 415-928-3200
Fax: 415-673-3329
Assets: $33,416,000
Earnings: $2,645,000
Liabilities: $9,538,000
Net Worth: $23,878,000
Approx.Rev.: $29,000,000
Emp.: 175
Fiscal Year-end: 8/31/91
Sound Recording for Motion Pictures & Television
S.I.C.: 7812
Marshall Naify *(Chm. Bd.)*
Robert A. Naify *(Pres.)*
Chris Jenkins *(V.P.)*
Ronald Zimmerman *(Chief Fin. Officer)*
Silas R. Cross *(Controller)*
Dan Malstrom *(Sec.)*
J.R. DeLang *(Dir.-Sls. & Mktg.)*

Subsidiary:

Todd-AO/East **(1)**
254 W. 54th St.
New York, NY 10019
Tel.: 212-265-6225
Sound Recording
S.I.C.: 7812

J. L. TODD AUCTION CO.
531 Broad St.
Rome, GA 30161
Tel.: 706-291-7007
Tel.: 800-241-7591
Fax: 706-291-0335
Year Founded: 1917
Approx.Sls.: $25,000,000
Emp.: 12
Fiscal Year-end: 12/31/90
Auctioneers of Real Estate
S.I.C.: 7389
J. L. Todd *(Chm. Bd. & Pres.)*
Joe Tarpley *(Sr. V.P.)*
John Conn *(Sr. V.P.)*
John Todd *(V.P.)*
Randy Lang *(V.P.)*
Doris Todd *(Treas.)*
Carolyn Brock *(Sec.)*
Linda Fletcher *(Mgr.-Adv.)*

A.M. TODD COMPANY
1717 Douglas Ave.
Kalamazoo, MI 49007
Mailing Address:
P.O. Box 711
Kalamazoo, MI 49005
Tel.: 616-343-2603
Twx: 224416
Fax: 616-343-4913
Year Founded: 1869
Approx.Sls.: $130,000,000
Emp.: 275
Manufacture Essential Oils, Animal Feed Products & Food Ingredients
S.I.C.: 2048; 2899
A.J. Todd III *(Pres.)*
James S. Todd *(Exec. V.P.)*
Ian D. Blair *(V.P. & Treas.)*
Donald E. Cole *(V.P.-Pur.-Northwest)*
Donald E. Rutherford *(V.P. & Controller)*
R.D. Webb *(V.P.-Sls.-Eastern)*
David B. Daughtery *(Dir.-Intl. Fin.)*
Argyle Stevens *(Mgr.-Mgmt. Information Systems)*

Outside Service Firm(s):

Ernst & Young*(Auditors)*
1100 Old Kent Bank Bldg.
Kalamazoo, MI 49007
Tel.: 616-349-6671

Howard & Howard*(Legal Firm)*
400 Kalamazoo Bldg.
Kalamazoo, MI 49007
Tel.: 616-382-1483
Fax: 616-382-1568

First National Bank of Chicago*(Major Banking Relationship)*
One First National Plaza
Chicago, IL 60670
Tel.: 312-732-9781
Tel.: 312-732-4050
Fax: 312-732-4840
Fax: 312-732-3055

Subsidiaries:

Flavorite Laboratories **(1)**
5980 Hurt Rd.
Horn Lake, MS 38671
Tel.: 601-393-3610
Approx.Sls.: $30,000,000
Emp.: 200
Manufacture Food Seasonings
S.I.C.: 2099
John F. Garner *(Pres.)*

Zink & Triest **(1)**
111 Commerce Dr.
Montgomeryville, PA 18936
Tel.: 215-362-1100
Vanilla Bean Importer
S.I.C.: 5149
David B. Daugherty *(Pres.)*

TODD PIPE & SUPPLY HAWTHORNE
4828 W. 145th St.
Hawthorne, CA 90251
Tel.: 310-970-0007 CA
Fax: 310-970-0005
Year Founded: 1966
Plumbing Fittings & Supplies
S.I.C.: 5074
Karl McMillen *(Pres.)*
Steve Owen *(V.P.)*
Gary Michel *(Treas. & Sec.)*

Outside Service Firm(s):

Imperial Bank*(Major Banking Relationship)*
Inglewood, CA

Division:

Todd Pipe & Supply Garden Grove **(1)**
13591 Harbor Blvd.
Garden Grove, CA 92643
Tel.: 714-638-4442
Wholesale Distributor of Plumbing & Hydronic Heating Supplies
S.I.C.: 5074
Karl McMillen *(Pres.)*

TODD & SARGENT, INC.
620 Arrasmith Trail
Ames, IA 50010-9022
Tel.: 515-232-0442 IA
Fax: 515-232-0682
Year Founded: 1961
Assets: $7,337,214
Liabilities: $5,316,049
Net Worth: $2,021,165
Approx.Sls.: $32,000,000
Emp.: 200
Fiscal Year-end: 12/31/90
New Construction Of Industrial Buildings; Millwright
S.I.C.: 1541; 1796
Warren B. Sargent *(Chm. Bd.)*
Lee M. Sargent *(Pres. & Chief Exec. Officer)*
Phillip B. Sargent *(Exec. V.P.-Admin.)*
Clint Steele *(V.P.-Mktg.)*
Fred Fairchild *(V.P.-Engrng.)*
Art Jenison *(V.P.-Opers.)*
Paul Sondgeroth *(V.P.)*
Tom Larsen *(Treas.)*
Jean Sargent *(Sec.)*

No. of Mfg. Plants/Facilities: 1
No. of U.S. Offices: 3

Computer Systems/Hardware:
Prime & Macintosh

Outside Service Firm(s):

Reese & Company*(Auditors)*
Ames, IA

First National Bank*(Major Banking Relationship)*
Ames, IA

Subsidiary:

PMI **(1)**
620 Arrasmith Trail
Ames, IA 50010
Tel.: 515-232-2595
Emp.: 75
Millwright Services
S.I.C.: 1541
Gary Sondgereth *(V.P.)*

Todds Enterprises
(See Cornucopia, Inc. Listing)

THE TOG SHOP
Lester Square
Americus, GA 31710
Tel.: 912-924-8801
Year Founded: 1955
Approx.Sls.: $40,000,000
Emp.: 325
Mail Order & Retail Women's Apparel
S.I.C.: 5961; 5621; 2339
Richard Hewitt *(Pres.)*
Dan Eberhart *(V.P.)*
Carl Tott *(V.P.)*
James Yawn *(V.P.)*
Roy Fricks *(Controller)*
Catherine Moody *(Sec.)*
Clayton Freeman *(Dir.-Data Processing)*

Computer Systems/Hardware:
IBM System AS/400

Outside Service Firm(s):

Hodges, Wallis & Allen*(Auditors)*
Americus, GA

Citizens Bank of Americus*(Major Banking Relationship)*
Americus, GA

TOLLESON LUMBER COMPANY, INC.
903 Jernigan St.
Perry, GA 31069
Tel.: 912-987-2105
Fax: 912-987-5773
Year Founded: 1919
Approx.Sls.: $73,000,000
Emp.: 325
Manufacture Lumber & Southern Pine Wood Treatment
S.I.C.: 2421; 2491
W.G. Wood *(Pres.)*
Grady Davis *(V.P.-Sls. & Mktg.)*
Clarence Montgomery *(V.P.-Opers.)*
Edwin Pierce *(Treas. & Mgr.-Pur.)*
John D. Erwin *(Sec.)*

Outside Service Firm(s):

George A. Pennington & Company*(Auditors)*
Atlanta, GA

Ted Moore*(Legal Firm)*
Atlanta, GA

Bank South*(Major Banking Relationship)*
Macon, GA

TOLLMAN/HUNDLEY HOTELS
100 Summit Lake Dr., 3rd. Fl.
Valhalla, NY 10595
Tel.: 914-747-3636
Fax: 914-747-1937
Fax: 914-747-1938
Year Founded: 1978
Approx.Sls.: $325,000,000
Emp.: 20,000
Fiscal Year-end: 12/31/90
Hotel Holding Co.
S.I.C.: 7011
Stanley S. Tollman *(Chm. Bd.)*
Monty D. Hundley *(Pres.)*
Victor Appledy *(Exec. V.P.-Sls. & Mktg.)*
Thomas W. Aro *(Exec. V.P.)*
Sanford Freedman *(Exec. V.P. & Gen. Counsel)*
Brett G. Tollman *(Exec. V.P.)*
Jim Cutler *(Sr. V.P.-Leasing & Risk Mngmt.)*
Tom Damewood *(V.P.-Human Resources)*
Charlie Goldman *(V.P.-Pur.)*
Kathy Stephens *(V.P. & Controller)*
Simon Vermooten *(V.P.-Mngmt. Information Systems)*
Thomas Wilson *(V.P.-Sls.)*
Patti Marino *(Admin. Asst.)*

Computer Systems/Hardware:
HIS/Lodgistix Front & Back Office Software IBM/Compatible Hardware

Subsidiary:

Days Inns of America, Inc. **(1)**
2751 Bufford Hgwy., N.E.
Atlanta, GA 30324
Tel.: 404-325-4000 (49%)
Approx.Rev.: $136,315,000
Owns, Operates & Franchises Economy Motels
S.I.C.: 7011
John Snodgrass *(Pres.)*
Kevin Jeter *(Exec. V.P.-Sls. & Mktg.)*
Richard Smith *(Sr. V.P.-Admin.)*
Douglas Collins *(Chief Fin. Officer)*
Roger Treadaway *(Dir.-Pur.)*

Subsidiary:

Days Inns of America, Inc. **(2)**
339 Jefferson Rd.
Parsippany, NJ 07054
Tel.: 201-428-9700 (100%)
Fax: 201-428-6057
Approx.Sls.: $1,300,000,000
Emp.: 5,950
Owns & Operates 1000 Hotels & Motels in 50 States, the District of Columbia & 4 Other Countries
S.I.C.: 7011
John Russell *(Pres.)*
Richard A. Smith *(Sr. V.P.-Admin.)*
Robert McGrail *(Sr. V.P.-Mktg.)*
Keith Linde *(V.P.-Mktg. Services)*
Vicky Kenyon Caruso *(Dir.-Mktg. Services)*
Penzie Finetto *(Dir.-Adv. & Promo.)*

TOLLYCRAFT YACHTS CORP.
2200 Clinton Ave.
Kelso, WA 98626
Tel.: 206-423-5160
Tel.: 800-536-5160
Fax: 206-423-2607
Year Founded: 1936
Approx.Sls.: $20,000,000
Emp.: 200
Fiscal Year-end: 8/31/92
Export
Inboard Motor Yachts & Cruisers
S.I.C.: 5551
Randall Bogrand *(Pres. & Chief Exec. Officer)*
George Moorehead *(V.P. & Chief Oper. Officer)*
Monica Osborne *(V.P. & Chief Fin. Officer)*
Pat Bachman *(Sr. V.P.-Customer Rels.)*
Mona Fox *(Sls. Admin.)*

TOM Software, Inc.
(See Listing Under Kennedy Associates; Name Changed To APPX)

CHARLES TOMBRAS ADVERTISING, INC.
630 Concord St.
Knoxville, TN 37919
Mailing Address:
P.O. Box 15151,
Knoxville, TN 37901
Tel.: 615-524-5376
Fax: 615-524-5667
Year Founded: 1944
Approx.Billings: $20,000,000
Emp.: 45
Charles P. Tombras, Jr. *(Chm. Bd. & Pres.)*
Geraldine Bailey *(Chief Fin. Officer)*

TOMCO AUTO PRODUCTS, INC.
(d/b/a Tomco Carburetor Company)
4330 E. 26th St.
Vernon, CA 90023
Tel.: 213-268-4830
Tel.: 800-858-3458 CA
Fax: 213-269-4148
Year Founded: 1946
Assets: $18,500,000
Liabilities: $16,200,000
Net Worth: $2,300,000
Approx.Sls.: $26,800,000
Emp.: 500
Fiscal Year-end: 9/30/91
Export
Remanufacture of Domestic, Import & Truck Carburetors & TBI Units
S.I.C.: 3592
Donald Maltzman *(Chm. Bd.)*
Victor Moss *(Pres. & Sec.)*
Richard Schoenfeld *(Treas.)*
Bob Miller *(Dr.-Sls.)*
Principal(s):
Donald Maltzman
Victor Moss

No. of Mfg. Plants/Facilities: 1

Outside Service Firm(s):

Levine, Cooper, Spiegel & Co.*(Auditors)*
Los Angeles, CA

Willis Corroon*(Commercial Insurance Carrier)*
Santa Ana, CA

Cooper, Epstein & Hurewitz*(Legal Firm)*
Beverly Hills, CA

City National Bank*(Major Banking Relationship)*
8525 W. Pico Blvd.
Los Angeles, CA 90035
Tel.: 310-550-5690

TOM'S FOODS
900 8th St.
Columbus, GA 31994
Tel.: 706-323-2721
Fax: 706-328-8231
Approx.Sls.: $230,000,000
Emp.: 1,900
Fiscal Year-end: 12/31/91
Tom's Toasted Peanuts, Candy, Peanut Butter Sandwiches, Potato Chips, Cookies & Snacks
S.I.C.: 2099; 2068
Mike Dillon *(Chm. Bd. & Pres.)*
Paul Serff *(Chief Exec. Officer & Sr. V.P.-Human Resources)*
Lyn Anderson *(Chief Fin. Officer)*
Bruce Bowman *(Sr. V.P.-Mfg.)*
Bill Britenbach *(V.P.-Sls. & Mktg.)*
Don Dakin *(V.P.-Contract Sls.)*
Al Davis *(V.P.-Reg. Sls. & Gen. Mgr.)*
R. Mac Johnson *(V.P.-Mktg.)*
Jerry Killough *(V.P.-Reg. Sls. & Gen. Mgr.)*
Shenee Williams *(Controller)*
Tim Campbell *(Dir.-Personnel)*
Jim Davis *(Dir.-Quality Control)*
Sam Faulkner *(Dir.-Pur.)*
Kathy Ellis *(Mgr.-Benefits & Admin.)*

No. of Mfg. Plants/Facilities: 7

Outside Service Firm(s):

Arthur Andersen & Co.*(Auditors)*
Columbus, GA

Hatcher Stubbs Land Hollis & Rothchild*(Legal Firm)*
Columbus, GA

First Union National Bank*(Pension Manager)*
Columbus, GA

Divisions:

Delimatic Refreshment Services **(1)**
900 8th St.
Columbus, GA 31902
Tel.: 706-323-2721
S.I.C.: 2099; 2068

Tom's Snax Co. **(1)**
900 8th St.
Columbus, GA 31902
Tel.: 706-323-2721
S.I.C.: 2099; 2068
Andy Robinson *(V.P.-Mfg.)*

Subsidiary:

Tom's Distributing Inc. **(1)**
900 8th St.
Columbus, GA 31902
Tel.: 706-323-2721
Peanut Butter Sandwiches, Cookies & Snacks
S.I.C.: 2099; 2068

TONE COMMANDER SYSTEMS
4370 150th NE
Redmond, WA 98073-9739
Mailing Address:
P.O. Box 97039
Redmond, WA 98073-9739
Tel.: 206-883-3600
Tel.: 800-524-0024
Fax: 206-881-7179
Year Founded: 1972
Approx.Sls.: $4,000,000
Emp.: 42
Import Export
Manufacture Telephone Systems
S.I.C.: 3661
Stephen R. Hill *(Chm. & Pres.)*
Richard Lee *(Dir.-Mktg.)*
Norton Lovold *(Dir.-Sls.)*
Mark Morris *(Dir.-Mfg.)*
Hilve Shuey *(Dir.-Fin. & Admin.)*

No. of Mfg. Plants/Facilities: 1
No. of U.S. Offices: 1

Outside Service Firm(s):

Benson & McLaughlin*(Auditors)*
Seattle, WA

TOOL KING
2492 W. 2nd Ave.
Denver, CO 80223
Tel.: 303-922-5551
Fax: 303-934-3696
Emp.: 50
Specialty Retail Franchisers
S.I.C.: 5251
Donald Cohen *(Chm. Bd., Pres., Chief Exec. Officer & Chief Fin. Officer)*
Lawrence Fantich *(Treas. & Sec.)*

Computer Systems/Hardware:
IBM System 34 & PC

Outside Service Firm(s):

Citizens Bank Westminister*(Major Banking Relationship)*
Westminister, CO

TOP BILLING INC.
1222 16th Ave., S., Suite #24
Nashville, TN 37212
Mailing Address:
P.O. Box 121089
Nashville, TN 37212
Tel.: 615-327-1133
Fax: 615-327-1199
Approx.Sls.: $10,000,000
Emp.: 12
Fiscal Year-end: 12/31/90
Personnel Management/Booking Agency
S.I.C.: 7361
Tandy Rice, Jr. *(Chm. Bd. & Chief Exec. Officer)*
Debbie Green *(Office Mgr.)*

TOP FLIGHT, INC.
1300-06 Central Ave.
Chattanooga, TN 37408
Tel.: 615-266-8171
Tel.: 800-777-3740 **TN**
Fax: 615-266-6857
Year Founded: 1920
Approx.Sls.: $26,000,000
Emp.: 250
Import Export
Manufacture School Supplies & Envelopes
S.I.C.: 5943; 2754
Harry T. Robinson, Jr. *(Chm. Bd. & Sec.)*
E. Montogmery Robinson *(Pres. & Treas.)*
Charles Beasley *(V.P.-Pur.)*
Dan Robinson *(Dir.-Mktg.)*
Dewitt Dunn *(Mgr.-Data Processing)*
Grace Pratt *(Office Mgr.)*
Curtis Robinson *(Sls. Mgr.-Envelopes)*
George Robinson *(Natl. Sls. Mgr.)*
Harry T. Robinson III *(Plant Mgr.)*
Principal(s):
Harry T. Robinson, Jr.
E. Montogmery Robinson

No. of Mfg. Plants/Facilities: 1
No. of U.S. Offices: 1

Computer Systems/Hardware:
IBM AS/400

Outside Service Firm(s):

Petty & Landis*(Auditors)*
Chattanooga, TN

Blue Cross & Blue Shield of Tennessee*(Group Insurer)*
Chattanooga, TN

American Bank*(Major Banking Relationship)*
Chattanooga, TN

First Tennessee Bank, N.A.*(Pension Manager)*
701 Market St.
Chattanooga, TN 37402

TOPA EQUITIES LTD, INC.
1800 Ave. of the Stars, Ste. 1400
Los Angeles, CA 90067
Tel.: 310-203-9199
Fax: 310-557-1837
Year Founded: 1962
Emp.: 274
Loan Brokers
S.I.C.: 6163
John E. Anderson *(Pres. & Treas.)*
Therese D. Curtis *(Sec.)*

Outside Service Firm(s):

Arthur Andersen & Co.*(Auditors)*
633 W. Fifth St.
Los Angeles, CA 90071
Tel.: 213-614-6500

Musick, Peeler & Garrett*(Legal Firm)*
One Wilshire Blvd.
Los Angeles, CA 90017
Tel.: 213-629-7600

First Interstate Bank of California, N.A.*(Major Banking Relationship)*
P.O. Box 3667,
Los Angeles, CA 90051
Tel.: 213-614-4000

Subsidiaries:

Topa Insurance Company **(1)**
1800 Ave. of the Stars, Ste. 200
Los Angeles, CA 90067
Tel.: 310-201-0451
Emp.: 65
Insurance Brokers
S.I.C.: 6411
John E. Anderson *(Owner)*
Harry Degner *(Chm. Bd.)*
Harry Petru *(Pres.)*
William Leone *(Sr. V.P. & Treas.)*
Thomas Dean *(V.P.)*
John Small *(V.P.)*

Topa Savings Bank **(1)**
1800 Ave. of the Stars
Los Angeles, CA 90067
Tel.: 310-785-0606
Savings Bank
S.I.C.: 6035
John E. Anderson *(Chm. Bd.)*
Robert R. Hallman *(Chief Exec. Officer)*
Richard B. Young *(Pres.)*
Michael E. Taylor *(Sr. V.P.)*
Charles J. Siegel *(V.P. & Chief Fin. Officer)*
Michael C. Maloney *(V.P.)*

Topa Thrift & Loan Association **(1)**
1800 Ave. of the Stars
Los Angeles, CA 90067
Tel.: 310-553-4900
Emp.: 250
Industrial Loan Banks & Companies; Consumer Finance, Not a Deposit Bank
S.I.C.: 6141
Richard D. Young *(Pres. & Chief Exec. Officer)*
Gary L. Barnes *(Sr. V.P.)*
Robert W. Graves *(Sr. V.P.)*
Douglas G. Housley *(Sr. V.P.)*
Joe Alexander *(V.P.)*
Charles J. Siegel *(Chief Fin. Officer & Treas.)*

TOPCO ASSOCIATES, INC.
7711 Gross Point Rd.
Skokie, IL 60077-2697
Tel.: 708-676-3030 **WI**
Telex: 72-4441
Fax: 708-676-4949
Year Founded: 1948
Assets: $165,025,000
Liabilities: $149,208,000
Net Worth: $15,817,000
Approx.Sls.: $2,875,000,000
Emp.: 390
Fiscal Year-end: 3/31/92
Import
Co-operative Procurement of Trade Goods
S.I.C.: 5141; 5142
John Beggs *(Pres. & Chief Exec. Officer)*
Steven Rubow *(Exec. V.P.)*
William Reego *(Sr. V.P.-Fin. & Chief Fin. Officer)*
Frank Mayes *(Sr. V.P.-Plng. & Devel.)*
Daniel Mazur *(Sr. V.P.-Branded Goods)*
Ronald Ficks *(V.P.-Personnel & Admin. Services)*
Neil Kelly *(V.P.-Produce Opers.)*
Douglas Mohler *(V.P.-Tech. Services)*
James Wisner *(V.P.-Mktg.)*
Russ Wolfe *(V.P.-Meat Opers.)*
Jack Zrecny *(V.P.-Support Services)*
Brian Sato *(Controller)*
Jonathan Buchbinder *(Mgr.-Fin.)*
Margaret Mantle *(Mgr.-Trng.)*

Computer Systems/Hardware:
IBM 4381/AS 400

Outside Service Firm(s):

KPMG Peat Marwick*(Auditors)*
Peat Marwick Plaza, 303 E. Wacker Dr.
Chicago, IL 60601
Tel.: 312-938-1000

Liberty Mutual Insurance Group/Boston*(Commercial Insurance Carrier)*
Chicago, IL

Prudential Insurance Co. of America*(Group Insurer)*
751 Broad St.
Newark, NJ 07102-3777
Tel.: 201-802-6000

Bell, Boyd & Lloyd*(Legal Firm)*
Three First National Plaza
Chicago, IL 60602
Tel.: 312-372-1121

Harris Trust & Savings Bank*(Pension Manager)*
111 W. Monroe St.
Chicago, IL 60690
Tel.: 312-461-2265
Tel.: 800-858-0840

Subsidiary:

Kingston Marketing Co. **(1)**
7711 Gross Point Rd.
Skokie, IL 60076
Tel.: 708-674-9878
Import
Food, Drugs, Beauty Aids & Household Products
S.I.C.: 5141; 5142

TOPCOR FINANCIAL CORPORATION
1555 W. 44th St.
Chicago, IL 60609
Tel.: 312-376-9400 **TX**
Fax: 312-376-9348
Year Founded: 1981
Approx.Sls.: $27,000,000
Emp.: 800
Exposition Operation
S.I.C.: 7999
Anne Murchison *(Pres.)*
John D. O'Connell *(Exec. V.P.)*
Ruth Woodward *(V.P.)*
Scott Bradley *(Sec.)*
William S. Seiden *(Treas.)*

Topcor Financial Corporation—(Continued)

Outside Service Firm(s):

Arthur Andersen & Co.*(Auditors)*
33 W. Monroe St.
Chicago, IL 60603-4067
Tel.: 312-580-0033
Fax: 312-507-6748

Subsidiary:

United Exposition Service Company **(1)**
1555 W. 44th St.
Chicago, IL 60609
Tel.: 312-376-9400
Emp.: 450
Exposition Operation
S.I.C.: 7999
C.W. Murchison *(Chm. Bd.)*
John D. O'Connell *(Pres.)*
William S. Selden *(Exec. V.P. & Treas.)*
George Mudry *(Controller)*

TOPFLIGHT CORP.
160 E. 9th Ave.
York, PA 17404
Mailing Address:
P.O. Box 2847,
York, PA 17405
Tel.: 717-843-9901
Fax: 717-845-6087
Year Founded: 1944
Approx.Sls.: $20,000,000
Emp.: 275
Fiscal Year-end: 6/30/90
Printed Pressure-Sensitive Adhesive Materials for Electronic Switches, Labels & Nameplates
S.I.C.: 3679; 2759; 3993; 2891
E. W. Huber *(Chm. Bd.)*
Patrick F. Masterson *(Pres.)*
Richard Amspacher *(V.P.-Fin.)*
Jerry Anderson *(V.P. & Gen. Mgr.-Switch Div.)*
James Danser *(V.P.-Sls. & Mktg.)*
G. Sciamgula *(Dir.-Quality Control)*
Robert Spahr *(Dir.-Engrng.)*
Jerry Dyer *(Mgr.-Adv.)*
Steve Nicholas *(Pur. Agent)*

No. of U.S. Offices: 2
No. of Foreign Offices: 13

Computer Systems/Hardware:
Wang

Outside Service Firm(s):

Kochenour, Earnest, Smyser & Burg*(Auditors)*
York, PA

Budding, Boddington & Kehm*(Legal Firm)*
York, PA

York Bank & Trust Co.*(Major Banking Relationship)*
York, PA

Subsidiary:

Adhesive Research, Inc. **(1)**
P.O. Box 100
Glen Rock, PA 17327
Tel.: 717-235-7979
Mfr. of Adhesives
S.I.C.: 2891
Erwin H. Huber *(Pres.)*

TOPLINE ADVERTISING
111 Gary Way
Ronkonkoma, NY 11779
Tel.: 516-588-5900
Fax: 516-588-1039
Year Founded: 1977
Approx.Billings: $14,000,000
Emp.: 20
Retail Adv.
Robert Williams *(Pres.)*
Jeanne Fontana *(Chief Exec. Officer)*

TOPLINE IMPORTS, INC.
3625 132nd Ave. S.E., 4th Fl.
Bellevue, WA 98006
Tel.: 206-643-3003
Fax: 206-643-3846
Year Founded: 1980
Approx.Sls.: $60,000,000
Emp.: 40
Fiscal Year-end: 6/30/91
Import
Wholesale Shoes
S.I.C.: 5139
William F. Snowden *(Chm. Bd., Pres. & Chief Exec. Officer)*
Richard A. Philby *(Chief Fin. Officer & V.P.-Fin.)*
Kyle Kittoe *(Dir.-Data Processing)*
Principal(s):
William F. Snowden

Outside Service Firm(s):

Arthur Andersen & Co.*(Auditors)*
Norton Building, 801 2nd Ave.
Seattle, WA 98104
Tel.: 206-623-8023
Fax: 206-386-8675

American States Insurance Co.*(Commercial Insurance Carrier)*
500 N. Meridian St.
Indianapolis, IN 46204-1275
Tel.: 317-262-6262
Fax: 317-262-6290

King County Medical Blue Shield*(Group Insurer)*
P.O. Box 21267
Seattle, WA 98111
Tel.: 206-464-3958
Fax: 206-622-7959

Karr Tuttle*(Legal Firm)*
Bellevue, WA

U.S. Bank*(Major Banking Relationship)*
Seattle, WA

TOPSY'S INTERNATIONAL INC.
221 W. 74th Terrace
Kansas City, MO 64114
Tel.: 816-523-5555
Fax: 816-523-4747
Approx.Sls.: $13,915,133
Emp.: 427
Fiscal Year-end: 7/26/90
Food Service & Franchise Co.; Topsy's Shoppes Popcorn Franchise
S.I.C.: 6794
Robert Ramm *(Pres.)*

TORCO OIL
111 E. Wacker Dr., Ste. 1300,
Chicago, IL 60601
Tel.: 312-616-1700
Fax: 312-616-9388
Year Founded: 1961
Approx.Sls.: $275,000,000
Emp.: 160
Import
Petroleum Products & Natural Gas Distribution; Automotive Dealerships
S.I.C.: 4924; 5172
Anthony M. Tortoriello *(Chm. Bd. & Pres.)*
William S. Johnson *(Vice Chm.)*
Michael J. Tassi *(Chief Fin. Officer & Treas.)*
Julie T. Vainisi *(Exec. V.P.-Gas. Div.)*
Helen T. Kennedy *(V.P.-Personnel)*

Computer Systems/Hardware:
Tandy 6000; IBM PC XT

Outside Service Firm(s):

KPMG Peat Marwick*(Auditors)*
Peat Marwick Plaza, 303 E. Wacker Dr.
Chicago, IL 60601
Tel.: 312-938-1000

Katten, Muchin & Zavis*(Legal Firm)*
525 W. Monroe St., Ste. 1600
Chicago, IL 60661-3693
Tel.: 312-902-5200

Division:

Torco Oil Automotive Division **(1)**
800 E. Roosevelt Rd.
Wheaton, IL 60187
Tel.: 708-668-1500
Automobile Dealership
S.I.C.: 5511
G. Anthony Schnurr *(Pres.)*

TORCON, INC.
214 E. Grove St.
Westfield, NJ 07090-1608
Mailing Address:
P.O. Box 609
Westfield, NJ 07091
Tel.: 908-232-8900 **NJ**
Fax: 908-232-2044
Year Founded: 1965
Approx.Sls.: $220,000,000
Emp.: 150
Fiscal Year-end: 11/30/91
Construction Management, General Construction & Project Consultants
S.I.C.: 1542; 1541; 1629; 8742
Benedict Torcivia *(Chm. Bd. & Chief Exec. Officer)*
Benedict Torcivia, Jr. *(Exec. V.P.)*
Joseph A. Torcivia *(Exec. V.P.)*
Louis Dolci *(Sr. V.P.)*
Eugene W. Lloyd *(Sr. V.P.)*
Leon Sculti *(Sr. V.P.)*
Philip A. Centineo *(V.P.-Construction)*
Frank S. Hlavenka *(V.P.-Construction)*
Philip Fischer *(Treas. & Sec.)*

Computer Systems/Hardware:
MAI Basic 4

Outside Service Firm(s):

Wiss & Company*(Auditors)*
Livingston, NJ

Fidelity Union Trust Co.*(Major Banking Relationship)*
765 Broad St.
Newark, NJ 07101
Tel.: 201-430-4000

TORINO FASHIONS, INC.
462 7th Ave.
New York, NY 10018
Tel.: 212-868-8080 **NY**
Fax: 212-268-6523
Year Founded: 1971
Approx.Sls.: $19,000,000
Emp.: 60
Mfr. of Women's, Juniors' & Missess' Dresses
S.I.C.: 2335
Bernard Tobin *(Pres.)*
Frank Iorio *(V.P., Treas. & Sec.)*
Marty Bond *(Accountant)*

Outside Service Firm(s):

Bloomstein, Bond & Co.*(Auditors)*
New York, NY

Chemical Banking Corp.*(Major Banking Relationship)*
277 Park Ave.
New York, NY 10041
Tel.: 212-310-6407
Fax: 212-310-4526

TORK, INC.
One Grove St.
Mount Vernon, NY 10550
Tel.: 914-664-3542 **DE**
Telex: 131447
Fax: 914-664-5052
Year Founded: 1922
Assets: $7,893,000
Earnings: $322,000
Liabilities: $1,626,000
Net Worth: $6,267,000
Approx.Sls.: $14,177,000
Emp.: 185
Fiscal Year-end: 7/31/91
Time Controls; Photoelectric Controls; Programmable Controllers & Signaling Devices
S.I.C.: 3674; 3669; 3822; 3829
Dorset White *(Chm. Bd.)*
R. Sam Shankar *(Pres.)*
Carmen M. Caputo *(Chief Fin. Officer, V.P.-Fin. & Treas.)*
Leonard Caponigro *(V.P.-Mfg. & Personnel & Dir.-Pur.)*
Joel Berson *(Sec. & Gen. Counsel)*
Elliot Mintzer *(Mgr.-Mktg. Services, Corp. Video Systems & Telecommunications)*

Non-U.S. Holding:

Tork Electro Sistemas S.A. **(1)**
Calle Hortensia #97, Local 2, Col. Los Angeles Femina Delg. Ixtapalapa, C.P. 09830
Mexico, D.F. Mexico
Tel.: 905-691-6857 (100%)
Mfr. Time Controls, Photoelectric Controls
S.I.C.: 3625
Javier Tecocoatzi *(Mgr.)*

TORKE COFFEE COMPANY, INC.
3455 Paine Ave.
Sheboygan, WI 53081
Tel.: 414-458-4114
Fax: 414-458-0488
Emp.: 19
Torke Coffee; Roast & Manufacture Fresh Brewed Coffee
S.I.C.: 2095
Elwood F. Torke *(Pres.)*
Allen R. Berchem *(V.P.-Fin. & Pur.)*
Ward J. Torke *(V.P.-Sls., Mktg. & Personnel Dir.)*
Marcella B. Torke *(Sec. & Treas.)*

Outside Service Firm(s):

Schenk & Associates*(Auditors)*
Appleton, WI

Rohde, Neuses & Dales*(Legal Firm)*
Sheboygan, WI

First Wisconsin National Bank*(Major Banking Relationship)*
Sheboygan, WI

TORRANCE NISSAN, INC.
20710 Hawthorne Blvd.
Torrance, CA 90503
Tel.: 310-370-7401 **CA**
Fax: 310-371-2861
Year Founded: 1968
Approx.Sls.: $50,000,000
Emp.: 95
Retail Sales of New & Used Automobiles
S.I.C.: 5511
William J. Adkins *(Pres.)*
J. Alflen *(Treas. & Sec.)*
Jerry Heuer *(Gen. Mgr.)*

Outside Service Firm(s):

Bank of America*(Major Banking Relationship)*
701 S. Western Ave.
Los Angeles, CA 91201

TOTAL COMMUNICATIONS GROUP
122 East 42nd St.
New York, NY 10168
Tel.: 212-949-3400
Fax: 212-949-7534
Year Founded: 1981
Approx.Billings: $10,000,000

Emp.: 10
Planning & Buying Radio, TV, Cable, Network & Local, Sports Marketing
Jerry Wolff *(Pres.)*
Sandra Crystal *(V.P.)*
Walter Seidel *(V.P.)*

TOTEM RESOURCES CORPORATION
1100 Olive Way, Ste. 1100
Seattle, WA 98101
Tel.: 206-628-4343 **AK**
Fax: 206-628-9245
Year Founded: 1982
Approx.Sls.: $80,000,000
Emp.: 155
Holding Company; Intercoastal Transportation, Freight
S.I.C.: 6719; 4424
Robert B. McMillen *(Pres. & Chief Exec. Officer)*
Jim Gauntt *(V.P.-Fin.)*
Robert P. Magee *(V.P.)*
Jack J. Martin *(V.P.)*
Leonard H. Shapiro *(V.P.)*
Everett W. Trout *(V.P.-Opers.)*

Outside Service Firm(s):

Puget Sound Bank*(Major Banking Relationship)*
Seattle, WA

Subsidiary:

Totem Ocean Trailer Express **(1)**
1100 Olive Way, Ste. 1100
Seattle, WA 98101
Tel.: 206-628-4343
Fax: 206-628-9245
Intercoastal Transportation, Freight
S.I.C.: 4424
Robert B. McMillen *(Pres. & Chief Exec. Officer)*

TOTER INCORPORATED
841 Meacham Rd.
Statesville, NC 28677
Mailing Address:
P.O. Box 5338
Statesville, NC 28677
Tel.: 704-872-8171
Tel.: 800-772-0071 **NC**
Fax: 704-878-0734
Year Founded: 1983
Emp.: 243
Export
Mfr. of Plastic Industrial Containers; Plastic Municipal Trash Systems
S.I.C.: 3089
David R. Grogan *(Chm., Pres. & Chief Exec. Officer)*
William W. Henning *(Sr. V.P.-Sls.)*
Larry Boppe *(Chief Fin. Officer & V.P.-Opers.)*
Bill Cagle *(V.P.-Res. & Devel.)*
Harold G. Karn, Jr. *(V.P.-Mktg.)*
Ralph Lynn *(V.P.-Western Reg. Sls.)*
William Pope *(Sec.)*

No. of Mfg. Plants/Facilities: 3
No. of U.S. Offices: 3

Computer Systems/Hardware:
IBM AS/400

Outside Service Firm(s):

Ernst & Young*(Auditors)*
1100 Independence Center
Charlotte, NC 28246
Tel.: 704-372-6300

NationsBank Carolinas*(Major Banking Relationship)*
One NCNB Plaza T18-7
Charlotte, NC 28255

TOTES INCORPORATED
10078 E. Kemper Rd.
Loveland, OH 45140
Tel.: 513-583-2300 **OH**
Fax: 513-683-4765
Year Founded: 1924
Emp.: 1,000
Fiscal Year-end: 2/29/92
Import Export
Manufacture Rainwear & Umbrellas
S.I.C.: 3021; 3999; 2385
Bradford E. Phillips *(Chm.)*
Ron Best *(Pres. & Chief Exec. Officer)*
Norman Kronenberg *(Sr. V.P.-Sls.)*
Dan Murphy *(V.P.-Mktg. & Prod. Devel.)*
Sheldon A. Kopin *(V.P.-Retail Opers.)*
Donald E. Olinger *(V.P.-Procurement)*
Linda G. Schmidt *(V.P.-Human Resources)*

No. of Mfg. Plants/Facilities: 2
No. of U.S. Offices: 3
No. of Foreign Offices: 2

Computer Systems/Hardware:
IBM System 38

Outside Service Firm(s):

Arthur Andersen & Co.*(Auditors)*
425 Walnut St.
Cincinnati, OH 45202
Tel.: 513-381-6900

Star Bank*(Major Banking Relationship)*
425 Walnut Street
Cincinnati, OH 45202
Tel.: 513-632-4000

Plant:

Totes Incorporated **(1)**
260 Centerville Rd.
Lancaster, PA 17603
Tel.: 717-291-1828
Manufacture Raingear
S.I.C.: 3021
Bill Shoenberger *(Plant Mgr.)*

Subsidiary:

Jones Optical Company **(1)**
P.O. Box 3096
Boulder, CO 80307
Tel.: 303-447-8727
Approx.Sls.: $2,000,000
Emp.: 25
Fiscal Year-end: 6/30/90
Mfr. & Distr. of Sport Fashion & Sport Action Eyewear; Ski, Motorcycle & Military Goggles & Accessories
S.I.C.: 3851
Bradford E. Phillips *(Pres. & Chief Exec. Officer)*
Chester Zukowski *(Gen. Mgr.)*

Non-U.S. Holdings:

Totes Canada Ltd. **(1)**
77 Brown's Line
Etobicoke, ON M8W 4X5, Canada
Tel.: 416-503-0359
Mktg. & Dist. Of Rainwear & Umbrellas
S.I.C.: 5136; 5137
Don Wilson *(Mng. Dir.)*

Totes Europe **(1)**
Sulzburgstrasse 144 5000
Cologne, 41, Germany
Tel.: 221 476 0621
Distr. of Rainwear
S.I.C.: 5136; 5137

Totes U.K. Limited **(1)**
Eastman House, Radford Crescent
Billericay, Essex CM12 0DN, United Kingdom
Tel.: 277-630-277
Fax: 277-630-276
Mktg. & Dist. Of Rainwear & Umbrellas
S.I.C.: 5136; 5137
Michael Bate *(Mng. Dir.)*

TOTSY MANUFACTURING COMPANY, INC.
1 Bigelow St.
Holyoke, MA 01040
Mailing Address:
P.O. Box 509
Holyoke, MA 01041
Tel.: 413-536-0510 **MA**
Fax: 413-532-9804
Year Founded: 1930
Sales Range: $10-19 Million
Emp.: 100
Fiscal Year-end: 12/31/90
Dolls, Doll Clothing & Accessories
S.I.C.: 3942
Shefford S. Goldband *(Chm. Bd.)*
Steven M. Feldman *(Pres.)*
Barry Schulman *(V.P.)*
John L. Sullivan *(Treas., Sec. & Controller)*
Stan Borke *(Mgr.-Sls.)*

No. of Mfg. Plants/Facilities: 1
No. of U.S. Offices: 2
No. of Foreign Offices: 1

Computer Systems/Hardware:
Wang

Outside Service Firm(s):

Coopers & Lybrand*(Auditors)*
2300 Bay Bank Tower, 1500 Main St.
Springfield, MA 01101
Tel.: 413-781-7200

Cooley, Shrair P.C.*(Legal Firm)*
Springfield, MA

BayBank Valley Trust Co.*(Major Banking Relationship)*
1500 Main St.
Springfield, MA 01101
Tel.: 413-781-7575

TOTTEN TUBES, INC.
1555 Los Palos St.
Los Angeles, CA 90023
Tel.: 213-268-1871 **CA**
Fax: 213-269-4140
Year Founded: 1955
Approx.Sls.: $22,000,000
Emp.: 53
Marketing of Steel Pipe & Tubbing
S.I.C.: 5051
Marvin Totten *(Chm. Bd.)*
David Totten *(Pres.)*
Jeffrey Totten *(V.P. & Treas.)*
Tracy Totten *(V.P.-Sls. & Mktg.)*

Outside Service Firm(s):

Brown, Lloyd & Stevenson*(Auditors)*
Los Angeles, CA

Union Bank*(Major Banking Relationship)*
3810 Wilshire Blvd.
Los Angeles, CA 90051
Tel.: 213-480-6500

TOURNEAU INC.
500 Madison Ave.
New York, NY 10022
Tel.: 212-758-3265
Fax: 212-593-0236
Approx.Sls.: $15,000,000
Emp.: 60
Fiscal Year-end: 12/31/90
Mfr. & Retail Tourneau Watches, Clocks, Jewelry
S.I.C.: 3873; 5944
David Wexler *(Pres.)*
Robert Wexler *(Gen. Mgr.)*

TOWERS, PERRIN, FORSTER & CROSBY, INC.
245 Park Ave.
New York, NY 10167
Tel.: 212-309-3400
Fax: 212-309-3857
Approx.Sls.: $600,000,000
Emp.: 5,000
Management Consultants; Reinsurance Brokerage
S.I.C.: 8742; 7389; 6311
John Lynch *(Chm. & Pres.)*
David W. Weiss *(Treas.)*

No. of U.S. Offices: 30
No. of Foreign Offices: 28

Computer Systems/Hardware:
IBM

Outside Service Firm(s):

Arthur Andersen & Co.*(Auditors)*
1601 Market St.
Philadelphia, PA 19103
Tel.: 215-241-7300

Dechert, Price & Rhoads*(Legal Firm)*
4000 Bell Atlantic Tower, 1717 Arch St.
Philadelphia, PA 19103
Tel.: 215-994-4000
Tel.: 2000

CoreStates First Pennsylvania Bank, N.A.*(Major Banking Relationship)*
Center Sq. West Tower, 15th & Market Streets
Philadelphia, PA 19101

ROBERT TOWERS ADVERTISING, INC.
345 Park Ave S., 8th Fl.
New York, NY 10010
Tel.: 212-685-0737
Fax: 212-696-0909
Approx.Billings: $13,400,000
Robert Solon *(Pres.)*
Dora Goziker *(Controller)*

TOWN & COUNTRY FOOD MARKETS, INC.
1522 S. Florence St.
Wichita, KS 67209
Mailing Address:
P.O. Box 17087,
Wichita, KS 67217
Tel.: 316-942-7940
Fax: 316-942-0216
Approx.Sls.: $489,000,000
Emp.: 800
Retail Groceries & Gas Stations; Non Residential Building Operators; Wholesale Oil & Gasoline
S.I.C.: 5411; 5541; 6512
Phillip G. Ruffin *(Pres.)*
Ron Kroeger *(V.P. & Treas.)*
Lynne Ruffin *(V.P.)*
Eugene C. Coombs *(Sec. & Gen. Counsel)*
Tammy White *(Dir.-Personnel)*
Pat Ruffin *(Gen. Mgr.)*

Outside Service Firm(s):

KPMG Peat Marwick*(Auditors)*
Wichita, KS

Kahrs Nelson, Fanning Hite & Kellogg*(Legal Firm)*
Wichita, KS

Bank IV*(Major Banking Relationship)*
P.O. Box 1122,
Wichita, KS 67201
Tel.: 316-261-4304

TOWN & COUNTRY FORD INC.
6015 Preston Hwy.
Louisville, KY 40219
Tel.: 502-964-8131
Fax: 502-964-0268
Approx.Sls.: $60,000,000
Emp.: 337
Automobile Dealerships
S.I.C.: 5511
William Hays, Sr. *(Pres. & Chief Exec. Officer)*
William Hays, Jr. *(V.P.)*
Gloria A. Hays *(Treas.)*
J. Dan Bouchillon *(Sec.)*

TOWN & COUNTRY SUPERMARKET
(d/b/a Price Chopper Foods)
Main St.
Hardy, AR 72542
Mailing Address:
P.O. Box 88
Hardy, AR 72542
Tel.: 501-856-3269
Fax: 501-856-2529
Approx.Sls.: $74,000,000
Emp.: 650

Town & Country Supermarket—(Continued)

Grocery
S.I.C.: 5411
Robert W. Clay *(Pres.)*
Carl McMillan *(Treas. & Gen. Mgr.)*

TOWN PUMP, INC.
600 S. Main St.
Butte, MT 59701
Tel.: 406-782-9121
Fax: 406-723-9533
Approx.Sls.: $65,000,000
Emp.: 600
Filling Stations; Gasoline; Convenience Stores; Independent Family Restaurants; Commercial & Industrial Building Operators; Motels
S.I.C.: 5541; 5411; 5812; 6512; 7011
Thomas F. Kenneally, Sr. *(Pres. & Chief Exec. Officer)*
Thomas P. Kenneally *(V.P.)*
Mary Kenneally *(Treas. & Sec.)*

Outside Service Firm(s):

Arthur Andersen & Co.*(Auditors)*
45 S. 7th St.
Minneapolis, MN 55402

Bozworth & Slivka*(Legal Firm)*
Denver, CO

First Interstate Bank*(Major Banking Relationship)*
Billings, MT

TOWN SQUARE FURNITURE, INC.
402 Hawkins
Hillsboro, TX 76645
Tel.: 817-582-7444
Fax: 817-582-7623
Approx.Sls.: $11,000,000
Emp.: 170
Wood Household Furniture
S.I.C.: 2511
James Hodges *(Chm. Bd.)*
Wendell Hodges *(Pres.)*
Bobby Hodges *(V.P.)*
Teresa Hodges *(Sec.)*

Outside Service Firm(s):

Citizens National Bank*(Major Banking Relationship)*
Hillsboro, TX

TOWNE PROPERTIES
1055 St. Paul Pl.
Cincinnati, OH 45202
Tel.: 513-381-8696
Fax: 513-784-9358
Year Founded: 1961
Approx.Sls.: $60,000,000
Emp.: 500
Real Estate Development & Management
S.I.C.: 6531; 6552
Marvin Rosenberg *(Chm. Bd. & Sec.)*
Phil Montanus *(Pres.-Devel.)*
Bob Wehlke *(Pres.-Towne Properties Asset Management Co.)*

Principal(s):
Marvin Rosenberg
Phil Montanus
Neil K. Bortz

Computer Systems/Hardware:
Datapoint, IBM Personal

Outside Service Firm(s):

Flagel, Huber, Flagel & Co.*(Auditors)*
Dayton, OH

Provident National Bank*(Major Banking Relationship)*
4140 Hamilton Ave.
Cincinnati, OH
Tel.: 513-681-3900

TSR
Towne, Silverstein, Rotter Inc.

TOWNE, SILVERSTEIN, ROTTER INC.
411 Lafayette St.
New York, NY 10003
Tel.: 212-353-1700 **NY**
Fax: 212-353-9881
Year Founded: 1965
Approx.Billings: $83,000,000
Emp.: 35
Advertising Agency
S.I.C.: 7311
Steve H. Rotter *(Chm. Bd.)*
Richard L. Flaxman *(Pres.)*
Binnie J. Levin *(Chief Fin. Officer & Sr. V.P.)*
Rosemarie Miksis-Zivic *(Sr. V.P. & Assoc. Dir.-Creative)*
Debbie Sutton *(Sr. V.P.-Acct. Services)*
Albert Wilcox *(Asst. Comptroller, Office Mgr.)*

Townhouse Penthouse Industries Inc.
(See Towne, Silverstein, Rotter Inc.)

THE TOWNSEND AGENCY, LTD.
9700 Higgins Rd., Ste. 600
Rosemont, IL 60018
Tel.: 708-318-9010
Fax: 708-318-9036
Year Founded: 1979
Approx.Billings: $15,365,084
Emp.: 25
Integrated Direct Response & Adv.
Gary Tillery *(Chm. Bd. & Sec.)*
Philip S. Walkenshaw *(Pres., Chief Exec. Officer & Treas.)*
David Ives *(Exec. V.P., Gen. Mgr.)*
Sandra Stanard *(Dir., Admin.)*

TOWNSEND & BOTTUM, INC.
2245 S. State St.
Ann Arbor, MI 48104
Mailing Address:
P.O. Box 1368,
Ann Arbor, MI 48106
Tel.: 313-761-3440 **MI**
Fax: 313-761-1607
Year Founded: 1908
Earnings: $1,000,000
Approx.Sls.: $50,000,000
Emp.: 60
Fiscal Year-end: 12/31/90
General Building & Heavy Construction Contractors
S.I.C.: 1629; 1541; 1542; 1771; 1791; 1794; 1796; 1799
C.E. Bottum *(Chm. Bd.)*
John Gassman *(Pres., Chief Exec. Officer & Chief Fin. Officer)*
Vicki Steck *(Controller)*
Joan Kellerman *(Mgr.-Pur. & Contracts)*
Barbara M. Wolcott *(Mgr.-Human Res.)*

No. of U.S. Offices: 1

Computer Systems/Hardware:
IBM PC's

Outside Service Firm(s):

Michigan Mutual Insurance Co.*(Commercial Insurance Carrier)*
Lansing, MI

Aetna Life & Casualty*(Group Insurer)*
151 Farmington Avenue
Hartford, CT 06156
Tel.: 203-273-2128
Fax: 203-729-4295

National Bank of Detroit*(International Bank Affiliate)*
Ann Arbor, MI

National Bank of Detroit*(Investment Banker)*
Ann Arbor, MI

Pear, Sperling, Egan & Muskovitz*(Legal Firm)*
Ann Arbor, MI

National Bank of Detroit*(Major Banking Relationship)*
Ann Arbor, MI

TOWNSEND ENGINEERING CO.
2425 Hubbell Ave.
Des Moines, IA 50317
Mailing Address:
P.O. Box 1433
Des Moines, IA 50305
Tel.: 515-265-8181
Fax: 515-263-3344
Emp.: 100
Townsend Fish, Pork-Cut, Bacon & Poultry Skinner; Townsend Frank-A-Matic; Townsend Injector
S.I.C.: 3599
Ray T. Townsend *(Chm. Bd.)*
Ted Townsend *(Pres.)*
Tom Hooker *(V.P.-Opers. & Treas.)*
Al Larson *(V.P.)*
Nick Neumann *(Pur. Agent)*

Outside Service Firm(s):

Ernst & Young*(Auditors)*
317 6th Ave., Ste. 1100
Des Moines, IA 50309
Tel.: 515-243-2727

TOWNSEND & O'LEARY, INC.
23282 Mill Creek Dr., #300
Laguna Hills, CA 92653
Tel.: 714-855-7870
Fax: 714-855-8790
Year Founded: 1983
Approx.Billings: $15,400,000
Emp.: 26
Franchise Adv.
Ramon Townsend *(Chm. Bd.)*
Stephen E. O'Leary *(Pres.)*
Patricia O'Leary *(Controller)*

TOY BIZ, INC.
333 E. 38th St.
New York, NY 10016
Tel.: 212-682-4700
Fax: 212-682-5317
Year Founded: 1988
Emp.: 25
Import
Manufacture & Distribute Toys
S.I.C.: 3942; 3944
Lou Schwartz *(Pres.)*
Roseann Costa *(Sls. & Mktg. Admin.)*

Outside Service Firm(s):

Ernst & Young*(Auditors)*
787 Seventh Ave.
New York, NY 10019
Tel.: 212-773-1243

Chemical Banking Corp.*(Major Banking Relationship)*
277 Park Ave.
New York, NY 10041
Tel.: 212-310-6407
Fax: 212-310-4526

TRACE PRODUCTS
1040 E. Brokaw Ave.
San Jose, CA 95131
Tel.: 408-441-8040 **DE**
Telex: 466462
Assets: $13,924,000
Earnings: $4,931,000
Liabilities: $5,161,000
Net Worth: $8,763,000
Approx.Sls.: $20,200,000
Emp.: 120
Fiscal Year-end: 2/29/88
Technology, Production & Mktg. of Systems for Automated, High-Volume Duplication of Computer Software & Data on Floppy Disks
S.I.C.: 7379; 3577
Dennis P. McDonnell *(Pres. & Chief Exec. Officer)*
Paul Chesterman *(V.P., Chief Fin. Officer & Sec.)*
Kevin J. McDonnell *(V.P.-Engrng.)*
Craig L. McHugh *(V.P.-Sls.)*
Georgette Psaris *(V.P.-Mktg.)*
Al Sadler *(V.P.-Opers.)*

Outside Service Firm(s):

Coopers & Lybrand*(Auditors)*
10 Almaden Blvd., Ste. 1600
San Jose, CA 95113
Tel.: 408-295-1020
Fax: 408-292-1382

Pillsbury, Madison & Sutro*(Legal Firm)*
333 W. Santa Clara St.
San Jose, CA 95113
Tel.: 408-947-4000

Non-U.S. Holding:

Trace U.K., Ltd. **(1)**
Valley House, Spring Valley Business Centre Porters Wood,
Saint Albans, Hertfordshire AL3 6PP, United Kingdom
Tel.: 727 66155 (100%)
Telex: 265259
Software Duplication
S.I.C.: 7379

TRACO ADVERTISING, INC.
P. O. Box 3286,
Tulsa, OK 74101
Tel.: 918-495-6381
Fax: 918-495-7388
Approx.Billings: $10,000,000
Walter H. Richardson *(Gen. Mgr.)*
Mark Swadener *(Treas.)*
Jeanne Alcott *(Sec.)*

TRACOR, INC.
6500 Tracor Ln.
Austin, TX 78725-2000
Tel.: 512-926-2800 **DE**
Telex: 776410
Fax: 512-929-2257
Year Founded: 1955
Assets: $165,000,000
Liabilities: $90,000,000
Net Worth: $75,000,000
Emp.: 3,694
Fiscal Year-end: 12/31/91
Import Export
Research, Development & Manufacture of Technological Products & Services for Government & Commercial Markets
S.I.C.: 3471; 3483; 3728; 3769; 3823; 3721; 3677; 3679
Corporate Giving Program: Health, Welfare, Civic, Art, Cultural & Educational Organizations
Employee Matching Gifts Program: Matches 1 for 1 Donations for Financial Assistance to Educational Institutions
James B. Skaggs *(Chm. Bd., Pres. & Chief Exec. Officer)*
Robert K. Floyd *(V.P.-Fin. & Chief Fin. Officer)*

Russell E. Painton *(V.P., Gen. Counsel & Sec.)*
Jack Rock *(V.P.-Advanced Programs)*
Murray Shaw *(V.P.-Human Resources)*
Woody P. Endsley *(V.P. & Treas.)*
Roger Sadler *(V.P.-Bus. Devel.)*
Thomas V. Talbott *(V.P. & Controller)*
Joe DiDonato *(Pur. Dir.-Aerospace)*
Bill Gandy *(Dir.-Data Processing)*
Bill Miller *(Dir.-Telecommunications)*
Bill McClellan *(Dir.-Information Systems-Aerospace)*
Marian Kelley *(Mgr.-Pub. Rels.)*
Holly Brannon *(Mgr.-Pension Admin.)*

Computer Systems/Hardware:
Sperry-Univac

Outside Service Firm(s):

Ernst & Young*(Auditors)*
1221 McKinney, Ste. 2400
Houston, TX 77010
Tel.: 713-750-1200

National Union Fire Insurance of Houston*(Commercial Insurance Carrier)*
Houston, TX

Prudential Insurance Co. of America*(Group Insurer)*
Prudential Tower Suite 450, 800 Boylston St.
Boston, MA 02119

Childs, Fortenbach, Beck & Guyton*(Legal Firm)*
402 Pierce
Houston, TX 77002
Tel.: 713-659-6681

Bank of America, N.T. & S.A.*(Major Banking Relationship)*
P.O. Box 37002,
San Francisco, CA 94137

Alliance Capital Management*(Pension Manager)*
Dallas, TX

Fayez Sarofim & Co.*(Pension Manager)*
Two Houston Center, Suite 2907
Houston, TX 77010
Tel.: 713-654-4484
Fax: 713-654-8184

Investment Advisors Inc.*(Pension Manager)*
1100 Dain Tower, P.O. Box 357
Minneapolis, MN 55440

Subsidiaries:

Tracor Aerospace, Inc. **(1)**
6500 Tracor Ln.
Austin, TX 78725-2070
Tel.: 512-926-2800 (100%)
Fax: 512-929-2241
Approx.Sls.: $80,000,000
Emp.: 1,160
Computer Systems/Hardware:
Sperry Univac
Design & Manufacture of Electronic Systems & Advanced Electronic Devices for Military & Commercial Customers
S.I.C.: 3669; 3728
George R. Melton *(Pres.)*
Dick Williamson *(V.P.-Fin. & Grp. Controller)*
Gerald L. Neely *(V.P.-Bus. Devel.)*
Joseph DiDonato *(Dir.-Procurement)*

Division:

Tracor Aerospace, Inc. Expendables Division **(2)**
Bollinger Canyon Rd.
San Ramon, CA 94583
Tel.: 415-837-7201 (100%)
Telex: 171235
Fax: 415-820-5772
Emp.: 124
Engineering & Administration of Advanced Countermeasures Development Programs
S.I.C.: 2899; 3483; 3663; 3728
Martin C. Hughes *(Division V.P.)*

Subsidiaries:

Tracor ELSIN **(2)**
540 Oakmead Pkwy.
Sunnyvale, CA 94086
Tel.: 408-733-3900 (100%)
Fax: 408-749-8612
Approx.Sls.: $4,700,000
Emp.: 47
Development of High Performance Receivers & Signal Processing Equipment
S.I.C.: 3669
Charles Willingham *(Pres.)*
J. Reimers *(V.P.-Fin. & Admin. Div.)*
J. Bohn *(Mktg. Dir.)*

Tracor GIE **(2)**
Provo Research Park, 1652 W. 820 N.
Provo, UT 84601
Tel.: 801-377-9090
Devel. & Production of Advanced Countermeasures, Paints & Coatings to Modify the Signatures of Aircraft, Ground Vehicles & Other Military Hardware from Multispectral Systems
S.I.C.: 3471
Bill Wallace *(Pres.)*

Tracor Applied Sciences Inc. **(1)**
1601 Research Blvd.
Rockville, MD 20850
Tel.: 301-279-4200 (100%)
Fax: 301-279-4597
Emp.: 2,437
Research & Development, Ocean Technology
S.I.C.: 3823; 8742
K. Bruce Hamilton *(Pres.)*
Thomas V. Talbott *(V.P.-Fin. & Grp. Controller)*

Divisions:

Tracor Applied Sciences, Analysis & Applied Research Div. **(2)**
6500 Tracor Ln.
Austin, TX 78725
Tel.: 512-929-2053
Fax: 512-929-2241
Research & Development for Defense Industry
S.I.C.: 3761
Homer Wieland *(V.P.)*

Tracor Applied Sciences, Electronic Systems Div. **(2)**
402 Cottonwood Pkwy.
California, MD 20619
Tel.: 301-862-9300
Fax: 301-862-9330
Defense Contractor
S.I.C.: 3769
Bob Weiland *(V.P.)*

Tracor Applied Sciences, Systems Technology Div. **(2)**
1601 Research Blvd.
Rockville, MD 20850
Tel.: 301-279-4200
Fax: 301-279-4504
Engineering & Technical Support Services to Defense Industry
S.I.C.: 8711
Tom Cass *(V.P.)*

Subsidiary:

Tracor Technology Resources, Inc. **(2)**
1601 Research Blvd.
Rockville, MD 20850
Tel.: 301-984-2800 (100%)
Fax: 301-279-4597
Approx.Sls.: $5,100,000
Emp.: 78
Provides Systems Engineering & Scientific, Technical, Informational & Program Management Services in Toxicology & Chemistry to Federal Government Agencies
S.I.C.: 8742
Gilbert Maton *(Pres.)*

Tracor Flight Systems, Inc. **(1)**
6500 Tracor Ln.
Austin, TX 78725
Tel.: 512-929-2870
Fax: 512-929-4818
Approx.Sls.: $25,000,000
Emp.: 340
Performs, Programs & Builds Systems in Areas of Flight Testing, Electronic Warfare Training & Testing & Military Aircraft Modification
S.I.C.: 3812
Donald L. Fagan *(Pres.)*
Ray Barker *(V.P.-Business Devel.)*
Bert Robles *(Dir.-Opers.)*

Subsidiary:

Tracor Ultron **(2)**
540 Oakmead Pkwy.
Sunnyvale, CA 94086
Tel.: 408-733-5393 (100%)
Fax: 408-733-5392
Approx.Sls.: $4,200,000
Emp.: 10
Enciphered Communications, Cryptographic Products & Services
S.I.C.: 3669
Charles M. Willingham *(Pres.)*

TRADEHOME SHOE STORES, INC.
429 Prior Ave. N.
Saint Paul, MN 55104
Tel.: 612-646-1345 MN
Fax: 612-646-2705
Assets: $8,851,593
Liabilities: $3,300,387
Net Worth: $5,551,206
Sales Range: $20-39 Million
Emp.: 250
Fiscal Year-end: 1/31/92
Import Export
Retail Shoes; Tradehome Shoes
S.I.C.: 5661
Donald A. Mains *(Pres. & Treas.)*
Harold J. Smith *(V.P. & Sec.)*
Donald J. Kos *(Controller)*

Outside Service Firm(s):

Coopers & Lybrand*(Auditors)*
1000 TCF Bldg.
Minneapolis, MN 55402
Tel.: 612-293-2929
Fax: 612-370-9395

Winthrop & Weinstine*(Legal Firm)*
444 Cedar Street
St. Paul, MN 55101

Norwest Bank Minnesota, N.A.*(Major Banking Relationship)*
P.O. Box 738, 161 North Concord Exchange
St. Paul, MN 55075
Tel.: 612-450-4046

TRADERS SUPERMARKETS, INC.
P.O. Box 158
Berrien Springs, MI 49103
Tel.: 616-471-2471 MI
Assets: $1,616,000
Liabilities: $499,000
Net Worth: $1,117,000
Approx.Sls.: $10,000,000
Emp.: 85
Supermarkets
S.I.C.: 5411
Kenneth W. Sink *(Pres. & Treas.)*
Barbara J. Sink *(V.P., Sec. & Dir.-Personnel)*
Principal(s):
Kenneth W. Sink
Barbara J. Sink

No. of Mfg. Plants/Facilities: 2

Computer Systems/Hardware:
IBM PC-XT & AT

Outside Service Firm(s):

Dumke & Associates*(Auditors)*
St. Joseph, MI

Hartwig & Crow*(Legal Firm)*
St. Joseph, MI

Old Kent Bank*(Major Banking Relationship)*
Saint Johns, MI

TRADING PORT, INC.
North Manning Blvd. & Prospect Ave.
Albany, NY 12206
Mailing Address:
P.O. Box 6249
Albany, NY 12206
Tel.: 518-489-2501
Fax: 518-489-0140
Approx.Sls.: $33,000,000
Emp.: 210
Bi Lo Grocery; Wholesale & Retail Groceries
S.I.C.: 5141; 5411
Avrum Tabachneck *(Pres.)*
Eli Benno *(V.P., Treas. & Sec.)*

Outside Service Firm(s):

Key Bank*(Major Banking Relationship)*
Albany, NY

TRAFALGAR/GHURKA
349 Connecticut Ave.
Norwalk, CT 06854
Tel.: 203-853-4747
Tel.: 800-245-4368
Fax: 203-853-2361
Year Founded: 1969
Approx.Assets: $15,000,000
Emp.: 200
Export
Mgr. of Luxury Luggage & Handbags; Belts, Wallets
S.I.C.: 3161; 3171; 3172; 3199
Marley Hodgson *(Chm. Bd. & Pres.)*
Robert Olsen *(Controller)*

TBC
TRAHAN, BURDEN & CHARLES, INC.
ADVERTISING AND PUBLIC RELATIONS

TRAHAN, BURDEN & CHARLES, INC.
1030 N. Charles St.
Baltimore, MD 21201
Tel.: 410-347-7500
Fax: 410-547-1135
Year Founded: 1974
Approx.Billings: $66,000,000
Emp.: 106
Robert Matz *(Pres.)*
Thomas L. Burden *(Exec. V.P. & Pres.-TBC Direct)*
Allan Charles *(Exec. V.P., Creative Dir.)*
Mark Allen *(Exec. V.P., Dir. Acct. Services)*
Sandra S. Hillman *(Exec. V.P., Pub. Rels. Dir.)*
Cynthia Ciccone-Scott *(Exec. V.P., Mngmt. Supvr.)*
E. Manny Klein *(Exec. V.P., Media Services Dir.)*
Edith House *(V.P., Pub. Rels.)*
Bonnie Mach *(V.P., Admin.)*
Ellie Waite *(V.P., Fin.)*

Trailer Train Co.
(Name Changed To TTX Co.)

TRAILER WHEEL & FRAME COMPANY
8222 North Freeway
Houston, TX 77037
Mailing Address:
P.O. Box 38904,
Houston, TX 77338-8904
Tel.: 713-931-2910
Fax: 713-931-2909
Emp.: 84

Trailer Wheel & Frame Company—(Continued)

Wholesale & Retail Truck Trailers & Accessories, Parts & Pick-Up Accessories
S.I.C.: 5013; 5531; 5599
Bernard Vlahakis *(Pres. & Chief Exec. Officer)*
Glenda Vlahakis *(Sec. & Treas.)*
David Naff *(Acctg. Mgr.)*

Outside Service Firm(s):

Curtis Cloud & Company*(Auditors)*
Houston, TX

First State Bank*(Major Banking Relationship)*
Brazoria, TX

TRAINER WORTHAM & COMPANY INCORPORATED
845 Third Ave., 6th Fl.
New York, NY 10022
Tel.: 212-759-7755
Telex: 697 3038 bil nw
Fax: 212-826-2198
Year Founded: 1924
Emp.: 25
Investment Counselors
S.I.C.: 6282
Charles V. Moore *(Pres.)*
Alexander A. Arnold *(Mng. Dir.)*
David P. Como *(Mng. Dir.)*
George B. Dornblaser *(Mng. Dir.)*
H. Williamson Ghriskey, Sr. *(Mng. Dir.)*
H. Williamson Ghriskey, Jr. *(Mng. Dir.)*
Patricia D. Riley *(Mng. Dir.)*
Sonny DeGady *(Controller)*

TRAK INTERNATIONAL, INC.
369 W. Western Ave.
Port Washington, WI 53074
Tel.: 414-284-5571
Fax: 414-284-4955
Year Founded: 1923
Approx.Sls.: $80,000,000
Emp.: 250
Fiscal Year-end: 8/31/92

Export
Mfr. of Fork-Lifts & Skid-Steer Loaders
S.I.C.: 3531
Dean R. Axtell *(Chm. Bd. & Dir.-Intl. Sls.)*
P. Enoch Stiff *(Pres. & Chief Exec. Officer)*
Robert Colvin *(V.P.-Govt.)*
Paul W. Freedy *(V.P.-Engrng.)*
Curtis J. Laetz *(V.P.-Mktg.)*
Clyde Maki *(V.P.-Tech. Services)*
Robert D. Melin *(V.P.-Mfg.)*
Allan J. Jablonsky *(Treas. & Controller)*
Michelle Larson *(Gen. Counsel)*
Terry W. Mahoney *(Sec.)*
Wendell Moss *(Dir.-Sls.-SCAT TRAK Loaders)*
Judy Thomas *(Dir.-Telecommunications)*
Steve Follstad *(Mgr.-Human Resources)*
Mike Furlott *(Natl. Service Mgr.)*
Kevin Grady *(Mgr.-Credit & Asst. Treas.)*
Hank Knaub *(Mgr.-Pur.)*
E. Jean Morrell *(Mgr.-Mktg. Services)*
Mary Morris *(Mgr.-Quality Control)*
Dave Olson *(Mgr.-Mngmt. Information Systems)*
Paul D. Roblee *(Natl. Sls. Mgr.)*
Michael Weber *(Mgr.-Tech. Publications)*

No. of Mfg. Plants/Facilities: 1
No. of U.S. Offices: 1

Computer Systems/Hardware:
IBM AS400

Outside Service Firm(s):

Price Waterhouse*(Auditors)*
1500 Bank One Plaza, 100 E. Wisconsin Ave.
Milwaukee, WI 53202

TRAMMELL CROW COMPANY
3500 Trammell Crow Center, 2001 Ross Ave.
Dallas, TX 75201
Tel.: 214-979-5100
Telex: 551646
Fax: 214-979-6058
Year Founded: 1948
Assets: $8,200,000,000
Sales Range: $1 Billion +
Emp.: 2,600
Fiscal Year-end: 12/31/91
Commercial Real Estate Development, Leasing & Management & Investment
S.I.C.: 6531; 6552; 6798
Trammell Crow *(Chm. Bd.)*
Charlie Brindell *(Pres. & Chief Exec. Officer)*
Michael B. Decker *(Chief Fin. Officer)*
Tom Green *(Gen. Counsel)*
Steve LaVer *(Dir.-Opers.)*
Sandra Seamans *(Mgr.-Communications)*

No. of U.S. Offices: 80

Computer Systems/Hardware:
IBM System 38

Subsidiaries:

Trammell Crow Interests **(1)**
3500 Trammell Crow Center, 2001 Ross Ave.
Dallas, TX 75201
Tel.: 214-979-5100 (100%)
Harlan Crow *(Mng. Partner)*

Trammell Crow Residential **(1)**
3500 Trammell Crow Center, 2001 Ross Ave.
Dallas, TX 75201
Tel.: 214-979-5100 (100%)

Outside Service Firm(s):

Jones, Day, Reavis & Pogue*(Legal Firm)*
901 Lakeside Ave.
Cleveland, OH 44114
Tel.: 216-586-3939
Fax: 216-579-0212

TRANS NATIONAL TRAVEL
2 Charlesgate West
Boston, MA 02215-3552
Tel.: 617-262-0123
Fax: 617-638-3445
Approx.Sls.: $125,000,000
Emp.: 200
Fiscal Year-end: 12/31/90
Travel Agency; Special Membership Services
S.I.C.: 4724
Steve Belkin *(Chm. Bd. & Pres.)*
Douglas Furbush III *(Chief Fin. Officer)*
Earl Schwartz *(Treas.)*

Divisions:

Financial Division **(1)**
2 Charlesgate West
Boston, MA 02215-3552
Tel.: 617-262-0123

Insurance Division **(1)**
2 Charlesgate West
Boston, MA 02215-3552
Tel.: 617-262-0123

Member Awareness Division **(1)**
2 Charlesgate West
Boston, MA 02215-3552
Tel.: 617-262-0123

Travel Division **(1)**
2 Charlesgate West
Boston, MA 02215-3352
Tel.: 617-262-0123

TRANSAMERICAN REFINING CORPORATION
140 Cypress Station, Ste. 200
Houston, TX 77090
Tel.: 713-444-1199 **TX**
Fax: 713-444-1147
Year Founded: 1966
Assets: $469,000,000
Liabilities: $528,900,000
Net Worth: $59,900,000
Emp.: 1,400
Fiscal Year-end: 7/31/91
Export
Petroleum Refinery
S.I.C.: 5172
John R. Stanley *(Chm. Bd. & Pres.)*
Ed Donahue *(V.P.-Tax & Treasury)*
Mike Greenlee *(V.P.-Exploration)*
R. Craig Shepherd *(V.P.)*
Jim Roberts *(Treas.)*
George Wright *(Controller)*
Joseph Speelman *(Gen. Counsel)*
David Traylor *(Dir.-Gas Mktg.)*
Tom Vasquez *(Dir.-Mngmt. Information Systems)*
Rod DeVersa *(Pur. Agent)*

No. of U.S. Offices: 3

Computer Systems/Hardware:
Digital Equipment 1170

Outside Service Firm(s):

Coopers & Lybrand*(Auditors)*
1100 Louisiana, Ste. 4100
Houston, TX 77002
Tel.: 713-757-5200
Fax: 713-757-5249

AIG (American International Group)*(Group Insurer)*
Houston, TX

Gardere & Wynne*(Legal Firm)*
3000 Thanksgiving Tower, 1601 Elm St.
Dallas, TX 75201-4761
Tel.: 214-999-3000

Continental Illinois*(Major Banking Relationship)*
231 So. LaSalle St.
Chicago, IL
Tel.: 312-828-2345

Continental Bank N. A.*(Major Banking Relationship)*
231 S. LaSalle St.
Chicago, IL 60697
Tel.: 312-828-2345
Tel.: 800-426-5754
Telex: 312-828-1783

Subsidiary:

TransAmerican Refining Corp. **(1)**
2992 River Rd.
New Sarpy, LA 70078
Tel.: 504-764-8611
Emp.: 140
Refining Assets
S.I.C.: 5172
Gary Karr *(Gen. Mgr.)*

TRANSAMMONIA INC.
350 Park Ave.
New York, NY 10022
Tel.: 212-223-3200
Tel.: 800-221-2267
Fax: 212-759-1410
Year Founded: 1971
Sales Range: $500-999 Million
Emp.: 188
Wholesale of Fertilizers, Liquid Petroleum Gases, Petrochemicals; Deep Sea Foreign Transportation & Countertrading Operations
S.I.C.: 5191; 5172; 4449
Ronald Stanton *(Chm. Bd. & Chief Exec. Officer)*
Elias R. Gonzalez *(Vice Chm.)*
Elias Gonzalez *(Chief Fin. Officer)*
Edward L. Gleason *(Pres.)*
Fred Lowenfels *(Sr. V.P. & Gen. Counsel)*
James Benfield *(Treas.)*
Lawrence Berman *(Controller)*
Marguerite Danheiser *(Dir.-Human Resources)*
Jay Shroades *(Mgr.-Data Processing)*

Computer Systems/Hardware:
IBM PC

Outside Service Firm(s):

Arthur Andersen & Co.*(Auditors)*
1345 Ave. of the Americas
New York, NY 10105
Tel.: 212-708-4000

Massachusetts Mutual Life Insurance Co.*(Group Insurer)*
1295 State St.
Springfield, MA 01111
Tel.: 413-788-8411
Fax: 413-730-6144

Chase Manhattan Bank, N.A.*(Major Banking Relationship)*
One Chase Manhattan Plaza
New York, NY 10081
Tel.: 212-552-2222
Tel.: 800-526-0801
Fax: 212-552-7175

Chemical Bank*(Major Banking Relationship)*
450 West 33rd St.
New York, NY 10001
Tel.: 212-613-7197
Fax: 212-947-7628

Chemical Banking Corp.*(Major Banking Relationship)*
277 Park Ave.
New York, NY 10041
Tel.: 212-310-6407
Fax: 212-310-4526

First Chicago Shareholder Services Trust Co.*(Major Banking Relationship)*
153 West 51st St.
New York, NY 10019
Tel.: 212-791-6422
Fax: 212-385-9798

Irving Trust Co.*(Major Banking Relationship)*
New York, NY

Kidder, Peabody & Co.*(Pension Manager)*
10 Hanover Square
New York, NY 10005
Tel.: 212-510-3000

Non-U.S. Holding:

Transammonia AG **(1)**
Bellariastrasse 51 8038
Zurich, Switzerland
Tel.: 01/482 8383
Telex: 815 969
Telecopier: 01/481 6222
Emp.: 12
Trading in Fertilizer and Fertilizer Raw Materials, European Headquarters
S.I.C.: 5191
Peter Baumann *(Pres.)*

TRANSCO INC.
55 E. Jackson Blvd.
Chicago, IL 60604
Tel.: 312-427-2818 **DE**
Telex: 25-6134
Fax: 312-427-4975
Year Founded: 1936
Assets: $19,700,000
Earnings: $800,000
Liabilities: $3,550,000
Net Worth: $16,150,000
Approx.Sls.: $26,000,000
Emp.: 500
Fiscal Year-end: 3/31/92
Import Export
Manufacture & Installation of Prefabricated Insulation; Insulation Contracting; Fire Protection Products; Corrosion Resistant Coatings; Sound Attenuation Products; Railcar Modification, Repair & Refurnishing; Contract Steel Fabrications; Structural Fireproofing; Insulation Pads; Material Handling Devices Manufacturing & Repair
S.I.C.: 3296; 3743; 3499; 4011; 3479; 4789
Employee Matching Gifts Program: Contributions to Higher Education
Howard S. Goss *(Chm., Chief Exec. Officer & Treas.)*
Robert M. Goss *(Pres., Chief Oper. Officer)*
Robert C. Anderson *(V.P. & Pur. Agent)*
Ellen M. Smith *(Chief Fin. Officer & Comptroller)*
Jay S. Berlinsky *(Sec.)*
Peggy Damm *(Asst. Comptroller)*
Principal(s):
Howard S. Goss

No. of Mfg. Plants/Facilities: 13
No. of U.S. Offices: 5

Computer Systems/Hardware:
IBM System 36

TRANSCO INC.
35005 Michigan Ave.
Wayne, MI 48184
Tel.: 313-729-9500
Fax: 313-729-9789
Approx.Sls.: $80,000,000
Emp.: 900
Truck & Trailer Leasing, Retail Petroleum Products & Tires
S.I.C.: 7513; 5541; 5531
Anthony C. LaBue *(Pres.)*
Donald C. Hayden *(Chief Exec. Officer)*
Paul P. Maise *(Chief Fin. Officer & Treas.)*
T. Kuehn *(Controller)*
Principal(s):
Donald C. Hayden

Computer Systems/Hardware:
IBM System 36

Outside Service Firm(s):

Coopers & Lybrand*(Auditors)*
203 N. LaSalle St.
Chicago, IL 60601
Tel.: 312-701-5500

Ernst & Young*(Auditors)*
One Detroit Center, 500 Woodward, Ste. 1700
Detroit, MI 48243
Tel.: 313-259-9600

Alexander & Alexander*(Commercial Insurance Carrier)*
225 N. Michigan Av.
Chicago, IL 60611
Tel.: 312-565-6221

Lincoln National Pension Insurance*(Pension Manager)*
Fort Wayne, IN

Hartford Life Insurance Co.*(Commercial Insurance Carrier)*
Hartford, CT 06104-2999

RMSCO Management*(Group Insurer)*
Chicago, IL

Greenburger Krause & Jacobs*(Legal Firm)*
Chicago, IL

Rudnick & Wolfe*(Legal Firm)*
Chicago, IL

American National Bank & Trust Company of Chicago*(Major Banking Relationship)*
33 N. LaSalle St.
Chicago, IL 60602
Tel.: 312-661-5000
Fax: 312-661-6417

LaSalle National Bank*(Major Banking Relationship)*
120 S. LaSalle St.
Chicago, IL 60603
Tel.: 312-781-8000

Harris Associates, L.P.*(Pension Manager)*
Two North LaSalle St.
Chicago, IL 60606-3790
Tel.: 312-621-0600

Subsidiaries:

National Thermal Insulation **(1)**
55 E. Jackson Blvd.
Chicago, IL 60604
Tel.: 312-427-2818 (100%)
Fax: 312-427-4975
Insulation Contractor
S.I.C.: 1742
Robert M. Goss *(Pres.)*
August Benesh *(V.P.)*

Transco Products Inc. **(1)**
55 E. Jackson Blvd.
Chicago, IL 60604
Tel.: 312-427-2818 (100%)
Fax: 312-427-4975
Insulation Contractor; Structural Fire Proofing-Fire Protection Products
S.I.C.: 1742; 3499
E.L. Avery *(Pres. & Chief Exec. Officer)*

Transco Railway Products Inc. **(1)**
820 Hopley St.
Bucyrus, OH 44820
Tel.: 419-562-1031 (100%)
Fax: 419-562-3684
Railcar Modification
S.I.C.: 3743
I.A. Thompson *(Chief Exec. Officer)*
David Kenealy *(V.P. & Chief Oper. Officer)*

Transco Realty Inc. **(1)**
55 E. Jackson Blvd.
Chicago, IL 60604
Tel.: 312-427-2818 (100%)
Fax: 312-427-4975
Robert M. Goss *(Chief Exec. Officer)*

Advance Thermal Corp. **(1)**
544 York Rd.
Bensenville, IL
Joseph Pirogovsky *(Pres.)*

TRANSCOASTAL MORTGAGE COMPANY
10900 N.E.Fourth, Ste. 2350
Bellevue, WA 98004-5841
Tel.: 206-453-2270
Fax: 206-453-2275
Mortgage Banking
S.I.C.: 6162
John W. Delaney *(Pres. & Chief Exec. Officer)*

TRANSILWRAP COMPANY, INC.
2828 N. Paulina St., Ste. 100
Chicago, IL 60657-4098
Tel.: 312-296-1000
Fax: 312-296-2007
Year Founded: 1931
Sales Range: $10-19 Million
Emp.: 100
Fiscal Year-end: 6/30/91
Import Export
Manufacturing, Conversion & Distribution of Plastics
S.I.C.: 3089; 3081; 2821; 3952
Morton D. Minkus *(Pres.)*
Michael Hels *(Chief Fin. Officer)*
Herbert M. Drower *(V.P.)*
Bob Beilfuss *(V.P.-Human Resources & Admin.)*
Joe Mitchell *(Dir.-Data Processing)*
Michael J. Berry *(Mktg. Mgr.)*
Principal(s):
Morton D. Minkus
Herbert M. Drower

Computer Systems/Hardware:
IBM System AS 400

Outside Service Firm(s):

BDO Seidman*(Auditors)*
111 E. Wacker Dr.
Chicago, IL 60601

Chatman & Roin*(Legal Firm)*
Chicago, IL

Division:

Sealtron Corporation **(1)**
2615 N. Paulina St.
Chicago, IL 60614
Tel.: 312-528-8000
Jack Klisiewicz *(Div. Mgr.)*

Subsidiaries:

Plastic Products of Indiana **(1)**
300 Industrial Park
Richmond, IN 47374
Tel.: 317-935-1520 (100%)
Manufacturing, Conversion & Distribution of Plastics
S.I.C.: 3089
Paul Volkringer *(Div. Mgr.)*

Transilwrap Co., Inc. **(1)**
3616 McCall Pl.
Atlanta, GA 30340
Tel.: 404-458-8121 (100%)
Manufacturing, Conversion & Distribution of Plastics
S.I.C.: 3089
Jim McConnell *(Div. Mgr.)*

Transilwrap Co., Inc. **(1)**
4700 Manufacturing Rd.
Cleveland, OH 44135
Tel.: 216-676-0600 (100%)
Manufacturing, Conversion & Distribution of Plastics
S.I.C.: 3089
James Carlin *(Div. Mgr.)*

Transilwrap Co., Inc. **(1)**
6635 Nineteen Mile Rd.
Sterling Heights, MI 48078
Tel.: 313-731-1700 (100%)
Manufacturing, Conversion & Distribution of Plastics
S.I.C.: 3089
Chuck Kohn *(Div. Mgr.)*

Transilwrap Co., Inc. **(1)**
4231 E. 75th Terrace
Kansas City, MO 64132
Tel.: 816-363-7600 (100%)
Manufacturing, Conversion & Distribution of Plastics
S.I.C.: 3089
Linda Haley *(Div. Mgr.)*

Transilwrap Co. of Philadelphia **(1)**
320 Camer Dr.
Bensalem, PA 19020
Tel.: 215-245-7878 (100%)
Manufacturing, Conversion & Distribution of Plastics
S.I.C.: 3089
Dave Badgley *(Div. Mgr.)*

Transilwrap Company, Inc. **(1)**
615 Daniels Rd.
Nazareth, PA 18064
Tel.: 201-460-1800 (100%)
Manufacturing, Conversion & Distribution of Plastics
S.I.C.: 3089
John Brolsma *(Div. Mgr.)*

Transilwrap Company, Inc. **(1)**
11875 Burke St.
Santa Fe Springs, CA 90670
Tel.: 310-945-1942 (100%)
Manufacturing, Conversion & Distribution of Plastics
S.I.C.: 3089
Rich Draude *(Div. Mgr.)*

Transilwrap Company, Inc. **(1)**
One West Lake St.
Northlake, IL 60164
Tel.: 708-562-8201 (100%)
Manufacturing, Conversion & Distribution of Plastics
S.I.C.: 3089
Dan Modlinski *(Div. Mgr.)*

Divisions:

Transilwrap Co., Inc. **(2)**
1299 Eagan Industrial Rd.
Eagan, MN 55121
Tel.: 612-454-8411
Manufacture, Convert & Distribute Plastics
S.I.C.: 3089
David Youngren *(Div. Mgr.)*

Transilwrap Company, Inc. **(2)**
1118 Quaker St.
Dallas, TX 75207
Tel.: 214-630-1417
Manufacture, Convert & Distribute Plastics
S.I.C.: 3089
John Sakelaris *(Div. Mgr.)*

TRANSISTOR DEVICES, INC.
85 Horsehill Rd.
Cedar Knolls, NJ 07927
Tel.: 201-267-1900
Year Founded: 1961
Approx.Sls.: $28,000,000
Emp.: 200
Mfr. of Electronic Power Supplies & Related Equipment; Transformers; PC Boards
S.I.C.: 3679; 3677; 3825
John H. Bickford *(Chm. Bd. & Treas.)*
Richard F. Blake *(Pres.)*
James A. Gilson *(V.P.-Sls. & Adv.)*
Robert A. Rath *(V.P.-Fin.)*
George M. Duff, Jr. *(Sec.)*
Peter R. Duerre *(Controller & Personnel Dir.)*

TRANSMET CORPORATION
4290 Perimeter Dr.
Columbus, OH 43228
Tel.: 614-276-5522
Fax: 614-276-3299
Year Founded: 1979
Export
Manufacture Metal Products
S.I.C.: 3399
Dr. Sherwood Fawcett *(Chm. Bd.)*
P. Doug Shull *(Pres.)*

No. of Mfg. Plants/Facilities: 1

Outside Service Firm(s):

Weaver & Evans*(Auditors)*
Columbus, OH

Simmons, Meiers & Kort*(Legal Firm)*
Columbus, OH

The Huntington National Bank*(Major Banking Relationship)*
41 S. High St.
Columbus, OH 43216

TRANSNATIONAL MOTORS INC.
(d/b/a Mazda Distributors Great Lakes)
618 Kenmoor
Grand Rapids, MI 49546
Mailing Address:
P.O. Box 2008
Grand Rapids, MI 49501
Tel.: 616-949-7570
Fax: 616-949-7828
Approx.Sls.: $425,000,000

Transnational Motors Inc.—(Continued)

Emp.: 130
Wholesale Automobile Parts & Supplies
S.I.C.: 5012; 5013
Peter C. Cook *(Chm. Bd.)*
Robert L. Hooker *(Pres.)*
Max D. Boersma *(V.P. & Treas.)*
Thomas Claus *(V.P.-Fin.)*
Cal Verduin *(V.P.-Sls.)*
Gordon Quist *(Sec.)*
James Fouts *(Dir.-Human Resources)*
Ted Andriese *(Mgr.-Pub. Rels.)*
Larry Goff *(Mgr.-Mktg.)*

TRANSPO ELECTRONICS, INC.
2150 Bringle Ave.
Orlando, FL 32808
Tel.: 407-298-4563 **FL**
Fax: 407-298-4519
Emp.: 160
Manufacture & Market Automotive Voltage Regulators, Supplies & Parts
S.I.C.: 3694; 5013
Frank Oropeza *(Pres.)*
Anne Oropeza *(V.P. & Sec.)*
Frank Oropeza, Jr. *(V.P.)*
Mike Deverall *(V.P.)*

Outside Service Firm(s):

First Union National Bank*(Major Banking Relationship)*
Orlando, FL

TRANSUS INC.
2090 Jonesboro Rd., SE
Atlanta, GA 30315
Mailing Address:
P.O. Box 6944
Atlanta, GA 30315
Tel.: 404-627-7331
Tel.: 800-241-2458 **GA**
Fax: 404-627-3978
Year Founded: 1928
Approx.Sls.: $81,200,000
Emp.: 1,200
Fiscal Year-end: 12/31/91
Motor Freight Carrier
S.I.C.: 4213
Patricia C. Winship *(Chm. Bd.)*
Blanton C. Winship *(Pres. & Chief Exec. Officer)*
W.D. Croft *(V.P.-Container Div.)*
Randy J. Hudson *(V.P.-Sls. & Mktg.)*
Jack C. Murdock *(V.P.-Fin., Sec. & Treas.)*
H.L. Spring, Jr. *(V.P.-Opers.)*
H. Dillon Winship, III *(V.P.-Equip. & Maintenance)*
Norman W. Jaros *(Dir.-Personnel)*
J.W. Tarleton *(Dir.-Loss Prevention & Security)*
Ronald O. Williams *(Dir.-Pur. & Property)*
H. David Harris *(Asst. Treas. & Controller)*
Margaret M. Morris *(Asst. Sec.)*
Thurman Davis *(Mgr.-Mngmt. Information Systems)*
Principal(s):
Blanton C. Winship

No. of Mfg. Plants/Facilities: 48
No. of U.S. Offices: 48

Computer Systems/Hardware:
IBM 4381

Outside Service Firm(s):

Arthur Andersen & Co.*(Auditors)*
133 Peachtree St., N.E.
Atlanta, GA 30303
Tel.: 404-658-1776

Protective Life Insurance*(Commercial Insurance Carrier)*
Indianapolis, IN

Southern Administrative Services*(Group Insurer)*
Columbus, GA

Trust Company Bank*(Investment Banker)*
Trust Co. Tower
Atlanta, GA 30303
Tel.: 404-588-7963

Long, Aldridge & Norman*(Legal Firm)*
1500 Marquis Two Tower, 285 Peachtree Center Ave.
Atlanta, GA 30303-1257
Tel.: 404-527-4000
Fax: 404-527-4198

NationsBank*(Major Banking Relationship)*
35 Broad St.
Atlanta, GA 30303
Tel.: 404-581-2121
Tel.: 800-848-8198

TRAPP FAMILY LODGE, INC.
42 Trapp Hill Rd.
Stowe, VT 05672
Tel.: 802-253-8511
Tel.: 800-826-7000 **VT**
Fax: 802-253-8511
Year Founded: 1962
Sales Range: $10-19 Million
Emp.: 200
Resort Hotel; Cross Country Ski Area; Ski & Gift Shop; Restaurant & Bar
S.I.C.: 5812; 5947; 7011
Johannes von Trapp *(Pres.)*
George von Trapp *(V.P. & Treas.)*
Christopher Ludington *(Controller)*
James Boyce *(Mgr.-Sls.)*
Peter McHugh *(Mgr.-Property & Pur. Agent)*
Eldon Towle *(Chief Engr.)*

Outside Service Firm(s):

Levitsky & Berney*(Auditors)*
Woodbridge, CT

Adams, Darby & Laundon*(Legal Firm)*
Stowe, VT

Vermont National Bank*(Major Banking Relationship)*
Stowe, VT

TRAUTH DAIRY INC.
16 E. 11th St.
Newport, KY 41071
Mailing Address:
P.O. Box 1770
Newport, KY 41071
Tel.: 606-431-7553 **KY**
Fax: 606-431-0349
Year Founded: 1920
Approx.Sls.: $50,000,000
Emp.: 155
Fiscal Year-end: 9/30/91
Wholesale Dairy Products Including: Ice Cream, Cultured Dairy Products such as Cottage Cheese, Sour Cream, & Buttermilk
S.I.C.: 5143
Louis J. Trauth, Jr. *(Chm. Bd.)*
David E. Trauth, Jr. *(Pres. & Chief Exec. Officer)*
Andrew Trauth *(V.P.-Engrng.)*
Steven A. Trauth *(V.P.-Prod. & Sec.)*
Gary Sparks *(Controller)*
Doug Sipes *(Mgr.-Quality Control)*
Dan Smith *(Mgr.-Milk Div. Sls.)*
Pete Vaughn *(Mgr.- Ice Cream Div. Sls.)*
Principal(s):
Louis J. Trauth, Jr.
David E. Trauth, Jr.
Andrew Trauth
Steven A. Trauth

No. of Mfg. Plants/Facilities: 1

TRAVELING SOFTWARE INC.
18702 N. Creek Pkwy. S.
Bothell, WA 98011
Tel.: 206-483-8088
Tel.: 800-343-8080
Fax: 206-487-1284
Year Founded: 1981
Approx.Sls.: $15,000,000
Emp.: 95
Mfr. of Prepackaged Software
S.I.C.: 7372
Mark Eppley *(Chm. & Chief Exec. Officer)*
Dan Crane *(Pres.)*
David Payne *(V.P.-Fin.)*
Jonathan Scott *(V.P.-Sls.)*

TRAYER PRODUCTS, INC.
541 E. Clinton St.
Elmira, NY 14902
Tel.: 607-734-8124
Fax: 607-732-1387
Approx.Sls.: $23,000,000
Emp.: 270
Mfr. Automobile Shackles, Pins & Bolts, Shock Absorber & Stabilizer Links
S.I.C.: 3714
William A. Tryon II *(Chm. Bd.)*
Joseph C. Gaver *(Pres.)*
Timothy P. Sommer *(Mgr.-Mktg.)*

Computer Systems/Hardware:
IBM 38

Outside Service Firm(s):

KPMG Peat Marwick*(Auditors)*
600 Clinton Square
Rochester, NY 14604

Sayles, Evans, Brayton, Palmer & Tifft*(Legal Firm)*
New York, NY

Chemung Canal Trust Co.*(Major Banking Relationship)*
Elmira, NY

TRAYLOR BROTHERS, INC.
835 N. Congress Ave.
Evansville, IN 47715
Mailing Address:
P.O. Box 5165
Evansville, IN 47715
Tel.: 812-477-1542 **IN**
Fax: 812-474-3223
Year Founded: 1946
Assets: $85,000,000
Liabilities: $47,000,000
Net Worth: $38,000,000
Approx.Sls.: $210,000,000
Emp.: 1,500
Export
Bridge, Tunnel, Heavy Construction & Commercial Buildings
S.I.C.: 1622; 1542; 1629
William F. Traylor *(Chm. Bd.)*
Thomas W. Traylor *(Pres.)*
R.C. Ingram *(V.P. & Sec.)*
J.H. Hummel *(V.P.)*
Glen R. Traylor *(V.P.)*
Dennis Schmidt *(Treas.)*
Principal(s):
Family-Owned

No. of U.S. Offices: 4

Outside Service Firm(s):

George S. Olive & Co.*(Auditors)*
20 N.W. Third St., 14th Fl.
Evansville, IN 47708
Tel.: 812-428-6500

Citizens National Bank*(Major Banking Relationship)*
20 NW Third St.
Evansville, IN 47739-0001
Tel.: 812-464-3400

TRAYLOR CHEMICAL & SUPPLY CO.
1911 Traylor Blvd.
Orlando, FL 32804
Mailing Address:
P.O. Box 547937
Orlando, FL 32854-7937
Tel.: 407-422-6151
Fax: 407-423-5316
Approx.Sls.: $19,000,000
Emp.: 48
Wholesale Agricultural Chemicals
S.I.C.: 5169; 5191
W. Leroy Traylor, Sr. *(Chm. Bd.)*
W. Leroy Traylor, Jr. *(Pres. & Chief Exec. Officer)*
William E. Comer *(Exec. V.P.-Fin.)*
John D. Cadmus *(V.P.)*
R. Eldred Carpenter, Jr. *(V.P.)*
Larry Skelton *(Pur. Agent)*

Outside Service Firm(s):

KPMG Peat Marwick*(Auditors)*
P.O. Box 3031, 111 N. Orange Ave., Suite 1600
Orlando, FL 32802
Tel.: 407-423-3426

NationsBank Florida*(Major Banking Relationship)*
Orlando, FL

TREADWELL CORPORATION
341 Railroad St.
Thomaston, CT 06787
Tel.: 203-283-8251
Fax: 203-283-0569
Year Founded: 1906
Emp.: 49
Fiscal Year-end: 12/31/90
Mfr. Oxygen Generators for Use in the U.S. Navy Submarines
S.I.C.: 3621
F.R. Curry *(Vice Chm.)*
J.A. Johnson *(Pres.)*
R. Gould *(V.P.-Mfg.)*
R.F. Olson *(V.P., Treas. & Sec.)*

No. of Mfg. Plants/Facilities: 1
No. of U.S. Offices: 2

Outside Service Firm(s):

Ernst & Young*(Auditors)*
787 Seventh Ave.
New York, NY 10019
Tel.: 212-773-1243

Dornbush, Mensch, Mandelstam & Schaeffer*(Legal Firm)*
747 Third Ave.
New York, NY 10017
Tel.: 212-759-3300

Marine Midland Bank*(Major Banking Relationship)*
140 Broadway
New York, NY 10015
Tel.: 212-658-1620

Subsidiary:

Elometa Corporation **(1)**
85 Oxford Dr.
Moonachie, NJ 07074
Tel.: 201-440-8872
Emp.: 375
Holding Company; Special Electro Chemical Machinery
S.I.C.: 6719; 3621
J.A. Johnson *(Pres.)*
Richard F. Olson *(Sec. & Treas.)*

TREASURE CHEST ADVERTISING CO., INC.
511 W. Citrus Edge
Glendora, CA 91740
Tel.: 818-914-3981 **DE**
Fax: 818-852-3054
Year Founded: 1967
Approx.Sls.: $530,000,000
Emp.: 3,200
Fiscal Year-end: 6/30/91
Offset Printing: Advertising Circulars, Newspaper Magazines, Newspaper Comics, Newspaper TV Magazines, Special Newspaper Supplements, Publications, Catalogs
S.I.C.: 2752
Robert E. Milhous *(Chm. Bd.)*
Paul B. Milhous *(Vice Chm.)*
Sanford G. Scheller *(Pres. & Chief Exec. Officer)*
Kenneth B. Erickson *(Sr. V.P. & Chief Fin. Officer)*

Richard B. Olerich *(Sr. V.P.-Sls. & Mktg.)*
Donald E. Roland *(Sr. V.P.-Opers.)*
Donald L. Brumfield *(V.P.-Pur. & Engrng.)*
Verne Lockard *(V.P. & Treas.)*
Landis MacIntosh *(V.P.-Information Systems)*
Robert E. Mason *(V.P. & Controller)*
Robert J. Turner *(V.P.-Human Resources)*

No. of Mfg. Plants/Facilities: 14
No. of U.S. Offices: 25

Computer Systems/Hardware:
IBM PC

Outside Service Firm(s):

Arthur Andersen & Co.*(Auditors)*
633 W. Fifth St.
Los Angeles, CA 90071
Tel.: 213-614-6500

TREASURE ISLAND FOODMARTS INC.
3460 N. Broadway
Chicago, IL 60657
Tel.: 312-327-4265
Fax: 312-327-6337
Year Founded: 1964
Approx.Sls.: $100,000,000
Emp.: 700
Retail Grocery Chain
S.I.C.: 5411
Chris Kamberos *(Chm. Bd., Pres. & Chief Oper. Officer)*
Frank Kamberos *(V.P.)*
Robert Johnson *(Controller & Dir.-Data Processing)*

Principal(s):
Chris Kamberos
Frank Kamberos

Computer Systems/Hardware:
Sorbus

Outside Service Firm(s):

Wellington Insurance*(Commercial Insurance Carrier)*
Chicago, IL

Prudential HMO*(Group Insurer)*
Chicago, IL

North Community Bank*(Major Banking Relationship)*
Chicago, IL

TREATY CO.
501 Gray Ave.
Greenville, OH 45331
Mailing Address:
P.O. Box 40
Greenville, OH 45331
Tel.: 513-548-2181
Fax: 513-547-0124
Approx.Sls.: $30,000,000
Emp.: 170
Wholesale Jobber of Plumbing & Heating Supplies, Utility Products, Industrial Supplies
S.I.C.: 5074
Mead Montgomery *(Chm. Bd. & Chief Exec. Officer)*
R.H. Lear *(Pres.)*
David L. Watts *(Exec. V.P.)*
C.W. Drehs *(V.P.-Credit)*
Don Thornhill *(V.P.-Data Processing)*
David R. Shelton *(Sec.)*
M.L. Tinka *(Controller)*

Computer Systems/Hardware:
IBM System 38

Outside Service Firm(s):

Deloitte & Touche*(Auditors)*
1700 Courthouse Plaza NE
Dayton, OH 45401
Tel.: 513-223-8821

Keck, Mahin, Cate & Koehler*(Legal Firm)*
8300 Sears Tower, 233 S. Wacker Dr.
Chicago, IL 60606
Tel.: 312-876-3400

Society National Bank*(Major Banking Relationship)*
Dayton, OH

TREE TOP, INC.
220 E. 2nd Ave.
Selah, WA 98942
Mailing Address:
P.O. Box 248
Selah, WA 98942-0248
Tel.: 509-697-7251 **WA**
Fax: 509-697-0421
Year Founded: 1960
Assets: $139,600,000
Liabilities: $108,600,000
Net Worth: $31,000,000
Approx.Sls.: $247,000,000
Emp.: 1,225
Fiscal Year-end: 7/31/91
Export
Apple Sauce, Frozen Apples, Apple Juice, Dried Fruit Prods. & Pure Fruit Juice Blends
S.I.C.: 2033; 2034
Roger Strand *(Chm. Bd.)*
Frank Elsener *(Pres. & Chief Exec. Officer)*
Richard W. Bailey *(V.P.-Fin. & Chief Fin. Officer)*
Ron Flagg *(V.P.-Human Resources)*
Ed Reinhart *(V.P.-Sls.)*
Ed Russell *(V.P.-Mktg.)*
Thomas P. Stokes *(V.P.-Opers.)*
Melinda G. Kile *(Controller)*
Robert E. Graham *(Dir.-Mktg.)*

No. of Mfg. Plants/Facilities: 5
No. of U.S. Offices: 1

Computer Systems/Hardware:
AS/400

Outside Service Firm(s):

Deloitte & Touche*(Auditors)*
3900 U.S. Bancorp Tower
Portland, OR 97204
Tel.: 503-222-1341
Fax: 503-224-2172

Pettit-Morry Co.*(Commercial Insurance Carrier)*
Seattle, WA

Pettit-Morry Co.*(Group Insurer)*
Seattle, WA

Halverson & Applegate*(Legal Firm)*
Yakima, WA

Seattle First National Bank*(Major Banking Relationship)*
Seattle, WA 98154

J. TREFFILETTI & SONS, INC.
4 N. Ferry St.
Albany, NY 12207
Tel.: 518-434-3106
Fax: 518-438-8151
Year Founded: 1979
Approx.Sls.: $26,000,000
Emp.: 44
Wholesale Groceries
S.I.C.: 5141
Carmen D. Treffiletti *(Pres.)*
John P. Treffiletti *(V.P.)*
Anthony J. Treffiletti *(Sec. & Treas.)*
Joseph Treffiletti *(Pur. Agent)*

Outside Service Firm(s):

Teal, Becker & Chiaramonte*(Auditors)*
Albany, NY

Key Bank*(Major Banking Relationship)*
Albany, NY

TREMONT CORPORATION
(42%-Owned by Valhi)
1999 Broadway
Denver, CO 80202
Tel.: 303-296-5600 **DE**
Fax: 303-296-5650
Assets: $337,053,000
Earnings: ($1,500,000)
Liabilities: $104,735,000
Net Worth: $232,318,000
Approx.Rev.: $170,100,000
Fiscal Year-end: 12/31/91
Import Export
Holding Company for Manufacture of Titanium Metals
S.I.C.: 6719; 3339; 3356
J. Landis Martin *(Chm. Bd., Pres. & Chief Exec. Officer)*
Kirby C. Adams *(V.P.)*
Susan E. Alderton *(V.P.-Fin. & Treas.)*
David B. Garten *(V.P. & Gen. Counsel)*
Steven L. Watson *(V.P. & Sec.)*
Frank B. Wright, Jr. *(V.P.)*

Subsidiaries:

Bentonite Corporation **(1)**
1999 Broadway
Denver, CO 80202
Tel.: 303-296-5600
Fax: 303-296-5650
Export
Mining & Processing of Bentonite
S.I.C.: 1459
Frank B. Wright, Jr. *(Pres. & Chief Exec. Officer)*

Titanium Metals Corporation **(1)**
1999 Broadway
Denver, CO 80202
Tel.: 303-296-5600
Fax: 303-296-5650
Approx.Sls.: $230,604,000
Emp.: 1,300
Manufacturer of Titanium Metals
S.I.C.: 3339; 3356
Kirby Adams *(Pres. & Chief Exec. Officer)*
Jan G. Barkman *(V.P.-Intl.)*
Donald E. Cooper *(V.P.-Technology)*
Daniel G. DePuydt *(V.P.-Human Resources)*
Dennis P. Kelly *(V.P. & Chief Fin. Officer)*
John P. Monahan *(V.P.-Sls.)*
Robert E. Musgraves *(V.P. & Gen. Counsel)*
Thomas A. Buck *(V.P.-Mfg.)*
E.E. Mild *(Dir. Mktg. Devel.)*

TREMONT FOODS
703 Nursery Rd.
Linthicum Heights, MD 21090
Tel.: 410-636-1400 **MD**
Fax: 410-636-5608
Year Founded: 1953
Approx.Sls.: $14,000,000
Emp.: 57
Wholesale Refrigerated & Frozen Foods, Dry Specialties
S.I.C.: 5142; 5143; 5149
Robert Pruitt *(Chm. Bd. & Pres.)*
Cheryl Pruitt *(Exec. V.P. & Treas.)*
Paul R. Richter *(V.P.-Sls.)*
Mike Metzbower *(V.P.-Mktg.)*
Barbara Fiscus *(Controller)*
Scott Mattingly *(Mgr.-Opers.)*

Principal(s):
Robert Pruitt

Outside Service Firm(s):

Barry Glass*(Auditors)*
Baltimore, MD

The Carrollton Bank of Baltimore*(Major Banking Relationship)*
Baltimore, MD

TREND LINE CORPORATION
4400 River Oaks Dr.
Jackson, MS 39208
Tel.: 601-932-8668 **MS**
Fax: 601-932-8321
Year Founded: 1972
Approx.Sls.: $38,000,000
Emp.: 1,200
Contract Food Services; Cold & Hot Drinks, Soup, Candy & Snacks Vending Machines
S.I.C.: 5812; 5962
William T. Hogg, Jr. *(Chm. Bd.)*
Noreen Hogg Bordelon *(Pres.)*

Outside Service Firm(s):

Deposit Guaranty National Bank*(Major Banking Relationship)*
One Deposit Guaranty Plaza,
Jackson, MS 39201

Sunburst Bank*(Major Banking Relationship)*
Jackson, MS

Subsidiary:

Valley Innovative Management Service **(1)**
4400 River Oaks Dr.
Jackson, MS 39208
Tel.: 601-932-3925
Contract Food Services; Hot & Cold Drinks, Soup, Candy & Snack Food Vending Machines
S.I.C.: 5812; 5962
Ronald J. Cockayne *(Chm. Bd.)*
Marilyn Collins *(Pres. & Chief Exec. Officer)*
Mark Harkey *(Treas.)*
Betty Cole *(Sec.)*

TREND OFFSET PRINTING SERVICES
3722 Catalina St.
Los Alamitos, CA 90720
Tel.: 310-598-2446
Fax: 310-430-2373
Approx.Sls.: $55,000,000
Emp.: 375
Offset Printing, Bookbinding & Related Work
S.I.C.: 2752; 2789
Brooks Iwakiri *(Chm. Bd.)*
Anthony Lienau *(Chief Exec. Officer)*
Robert Lienau, Jr. *(Pres.)*
Munir Ahmed *(V.P.-Fin.)*
Ronald Labowe *(Sec. & Treas.)*
Paul Finie *(Gen. Mgr.)*

No. of Mfg. Plants/Facilities: 1
No. of U.S. Offices: 1

Computer Systems/Hardware:
Kenes/Profitrack

Outside Service Firm(s):

Labowe, Labowe & Hoffman*(Legal Firm)*
Los Angeles, CA

Bank of America NT&SA*(Major Banking Relationship)*
555 So. Flower St.
Los Angeles, CA 90071
Tel.: 213-228-3868

TRENDWAY CORPORATION
13467 Quincy St.
Holland, MI 49424
Tel.: 616-399-3900
Tel.: 800-748-0234 **MI**
Fax: 616-399-5099
Year Founded: 1968
Approx.Sls.: $48,000,000
Emp.: 300
Fiscal Year-end: 12/31/91
Export
Mfr. of Open Office Furniture, Floor to Ceiling Moveable Partitions & Seating
S.I.C.: 2542; 2522
Donald G. Heeringa *(Chm. Bd. & Pres.)*
James P. Heeringa *(Exec. V.P.-Sls.)*
Doug Dinkins *(V.P.-Opers.)*
David Field *(V.P.-Sls. & Mktg.)*
Al Hoffman *(V.P.-Engrng.)*
Harlan Sprik *(V.P.-Fin., Treas. & Sec.)*
Julie Berghoef *(Dir.-Adv.)*
John Kibiloski *(Dir.-Pur.)*
Marlene Serne *(Dir.-Personnel)*
David VanderKooi *(Dir.-Govt. Sls.)*
Jay Vruggink *(Mgr.-Production)*

Trendway Corporation—(Continued)

Pat Wygant *(Mktg. Administrator & Corp. Travel Planner)*

Outside Service Firm(s):

Coopers & Lybrand*(Auditors)*
Grand Rapids, MI

Varnum, Riddering, Schmidt & Howlett*(Legal Firm)*
800 Prime Bank Bldg., Pearle & Monroe, NW
Grand Rapids, MI 49503
Tel.: 616-459-4186

Old Kent Bank*(Major Banking Relationship)*
Grand Rapids, MI

H.O. TRERICE COMPANY
12950 W. Eight Mile Rd.
Oak Park, MI 48237
Tel.: 313-399-8000
Fax: 313-399-7246
Year Founded: 1923
Approx.Sls.: $19,000,000
Emp.: 210
Export
Dial & Digital Pressure Gauges, Temperature Instruments
S.I.C.: 3823
Allan Feys *(Pres.)*
William E. Wright *(Chief Exec. Officer)*
Mario Reyes *(V.P.)*
Robert L. Farmer *(Controller)*
Stuart Saari *(Dir.-Pur.)*
Owen P. Reynolds *(Dir.-Engrng.)*

No. of Mfg. Plants/Facilities: 2
No. of U.S. Offices: 14
No. of Foreign Offices: 3

Outside Service Firm(s):

Fitzgerald, Peters, Dakmak, & Miller*(Legal Firm)*
Detroit, MI

Manufacturers Hanover Trust Co.*(Major Banking Relationship)*
Detroit, MI

TRERICE TOSTO INTERNATIONAL
32100 Telegraph Road, Ste. 100
Bingham Farms, MI 48010
Tel.: 313-540-1000
Fax: 313-540-1038
Year Founded: 1925
Approx.Sls.: $125,000,000
Real Estate Brokerage & Development
S.I.C.: 6531
Byron W. Trerice, Jr. *(Chm. Bd. & Chief Exec. Officer)*
Leo R. Tosto *(Pres.)*
Jack Roznowski *(V.P.-Fin. & Controller)*
Principal(s):
Byron W. Trerice, Jr.
Leo R. Tosto

Computer Systems/Hardware:
IBM PC/XT/AT

Outside Service Firm(s):

Deloitte & Touche*(Auditors)*
200 Renaissance Center, 16th Fl.
Detroit, MI 48243
Tel.: 313-396-3000
Fax: 313-259-8087

Cross, Wrock, Miller, Dieson*(Legal Firm)*
Detroit, MI

Honigman, Miller, Schwartz & Cohn*(Legal Firm)*
2290 First National Bldg.
Detroit, MI 48226
Tel.: 313-256-7800

Subsidiaries:

Trerice Development Co. **(1)**
32100 Telegraph Road, Ste. 100
Birmingham, MI 48010
Tel.: 313-540-1000 (100%)
Emp.: 6
Real Estate & Land Developers
S.I.C.: 6531
Leo R. Tosto *(Pres.)*

Trerice Management Co. **(1)**
32100 Telegraph Road, Ste. 100
Birmingham, MI 48010
Tel.: 313-540-1000 (100%)
Emp.: 5
Commercial, Industrial & Apartment Property Management
S.I.C.: 6531
Leo R. Tosto *(Pres.)*

Trerice/Tosto Investment Services Co. **(1)**
32100 Telegraph Road, Ste. 100
Birmingham, MI 48010
Tel.: 313-540-1000 (100%)
Security Syndications
S.I.C.: 6211
Leo R. Tosto *(Pres.)*

TRESSA, INC.
2711 Circleport Dr.
Erlanger, KY 41018
Tel.: 606-525-1300
Fax: 606-525-0326
Year Founded: 1969
Emp.: 500
Hair-care Preparations
S.I.C.: 2844
Connie Forbriger *(Pres.)*
Bill Forbriger *(V.P.)*
Mary Jo Madden *(Treas.)*

Trettco, Inc.
(See Tressa, Inc.)

TRI-CHEM, INC.
1 Cape May St.
Harrison, NJ 07029
Tel.: 201-482-5500 **DE**
Fax: 201-482-0002
Year Founded: 1948
Assets: $15,500,000
Earnings: $500,000
Net Worth: $15,500,000
Approx.Sls.: $18,000,000
Emp.: 250
Manufacture Fabric Paints, Silk Screened Fabric and Molded Plastic
S.I.C.: 3952; 2297; 3089
Andrew D. McKnight *(Chm. Bd. & Chief Exec. Officer)*
Walter E. Powers *(Pres.)*
R.Y. Keegan *(Treas.)*
Walter J. Wilkens *(Controller)*

Outside Service Firm(s):

KPMG Peat Marwick*(Major Banking Relationship)*
Harrison, NJ

United Jersey Bank*(Major Banking Relationship)*
Newark, NJ

TRI-CITY ELECTRICAL CONTRACTORS INC.
430 West Dr.
Altamonte Springs, FL 32714
Mailing Address:
P.O. Box 160849
Altamonte Springs, FL 32716
Tel.: 407-788-3500 **FL**
Fax: 407-682-7353
Year Founded: 1958
Approx.Sls.: $50,000,000
Emp.: 900
Fiscal Year-end: 12/31/91
Electrical Contractor
S.I.C.: 1731
Helmuth L. Eidel *(Pres.)*
Paula Eidel *(Exec. V.P.)*
David Beasley *(V.P.-Opers.)*
Charles J. Eidel *(V.P.-Sls.)*
James Hineman *(Dir.-Pur.)*
Wanda Tempest *(Benefits Mgr.)*
Principal(s):
Helmuth L. Eidel
Paula Eidel

No. of U.S. Offices: 3

Computer Systems/Hardware:
Texas Instrument

Outside Service Firm(s):

Cuthill & Eddy*(Auditors)*
Orlando, FL

Liberty Mutual*(Commercial Insurance Carrier)*
175 Berkeley St.
Boston, MA

Humana Health Care Plan*(Group Insurer)*
Orlando, FL

Dempsey & Goldsmith, P.A.*(Legal Firm)*
Orlando, FL

First Union National Bank*(Major Banking Relationship)*
Orlando, FL

Branch Offices:

Tri-City Electrical Contractors Inc. **(1)**
9942 Currie Davis Dr., Ste. D-7
Tampa, FL 33619
Tel.: 813-622-7180
Fax: 813-628-0732
Electrical Contractors
S.I.C.: 1731

Tri-City Electrical Contractors Inc. **(1)**
2118 Corporate Dr.
Boynton Beach, FL 33426
Tel.: 407-369-8490
Fax: 407-369-8493
Electrical Contractors
S.I.C.: 1731

Tri-City Electrical Contractors Inc. **(1)**
Airport Woods, 12296 Matterhorn Rd., Ste. 3A
Fort Myers, FL 33913
Tel.: 813-768-5566
Fax: 813-768-2336
Electrical Contractors
S.I.C.: 1731

Tri-City Electrical Contractors Inc. **(1)**
P.O. Box 22927,
Lake Buena Vista, FL 32830
Tel.: 407-827-5357
Fax: 407-827-5359
Electrical Contractors; Disney Office
S.I.C.: 1731

TRI-CITY OLDSMOBILE INC.
3920 Dutchmans Lane
Louisville, KY 40207
Tel.: 502-897-6541 **KY**
Fax: 502-896-0952
Year Founded: 1936
Assets: $7,771,097
Liabilities: $3,563,381
Net Worth: $4,207,716
Approx.Sls.: $32,000,000
Emp.: 126
Fiscal Year-end: 12/31/90
Automobile Dealership
S.I.C.: 5511
Charles H. Dishman *(Pres. & Chief Exec. Officer)*
Kenneth Wood *(Mgr.-Sls.)*

Outside Service Firm(s):

Coopers & Lybrand*(Auditors)*
Louisville, KY 46201

Stites & Harbison*(Legal Firm)*
600 West Main St.
Louisville, KY 40202
Tel.: 502-587-3400

Liberty National Bank & Trust Co.*(Major Banking Relationship)*
416 W. Jefferson St.
Louisville, KY 40202
Tel.: 502-566-2000

TRI-K INDUSTRIES, INC.
27 Bland St.
Emerson, NJ 07630
Tel.: 201-261-2800
Fax: 201-261-1432
Approx.Sls.: $14,000,000
Emp.: 18
Fiscal Year-end: 12/31/92
Distributor of Cosmetic Ingredients
S.I.C.: 2844
Reno Del Dotto *(Pres.)*
Joe Krasinski *(Controller)*
Ray Lyons *(Gen. Counsel)*
Diana Davis *(Dir.-Pur.)*
Maria Smith *(Dir.-Res. & Devel.)*

TRI-MARK METAL CORP.
10106 Grinnell
Detroit, MI 48213-1192
Tel.: 313-925-4900 **MI**
Fax: 313-925-6751
Year Founded: 1973
Approx.Sls.: $50,000,000
Emp.: 100
Fiscal Year-end: 12/31/89
Import Export
Industrial Contractor with Engineering, Manufacturing & Installation Capabilities Specializing in Paint Finishing & Pollution Control Systems for the Automotive Industry
Robert A. Krueger *(Pres., Chief Exec. Officer & Treas.)*
Sylvia J. Kalinowski *(Chief Oper. Officer & Controller)*
James M. Dixon *(Exec. V.P.)*
Donald R. Fegert *(V.P.)*
Lawrence M. Fegert *(Dir.-Pur.)*
Gus Zabel *(Dir.-Engrng.)*
Principal(s):
Robert A. Krueger
Donald R. Fegert

No. of Mfg. Plants/Facilities: 3
No. of U.S. Offices: 1

Computer Systems/Hardware:
Wang; IBM; Hewett Packard

Outside Service Firm(s):

Paul V. Engstrom & Co.*(Auditors)*
Southfield, MI

Regan & Stevens*(Legal Firm)*
Detroit, MI

Manufacturers National Bank N.A.*(Major Banking Relationship)*
38th Fl., 100 Renaissance Center
Detroit, MI 48243
Tel.: 313-222-4227

TRI-STATE ARMATURE ELECTRIC WORKS
330 E. Calhoun Ave.
Memphis, TN 38126
Tel.: 901-527-8412 **TN**
Fax: 901-521-1065
Approx.Sls.: $19,000,000

Emp.: 150
Wholesale Distribution of Electric Motors & Electrical Supplies; General Electrical Contractor; Rebuilding Motors, Except Automotive
S.I.C.: 5063; 1731; 7694
Fritz Weigandt *(Chm. Bd.)*
David Mayhall *(Pres.)*
Larry Boyd *(V.P.)*

Outside Service Firm(s):

BDO Seidman*(Auditors)*
2500 Commerce Tower
Memphis, TN 38103-2545
Tel.: 901-523-2303
Fax: 901-525-7478

TRI-STATE MACK DISTRIBUTORS
494 E.H. Crump Blvd.
Memphis, TN 38126
Tel.: 901-774-2211 **TN**
Fax: 901-775-2328
Year Founded: 1946
Approx.Sls.: $42,000,000
Emp.: 160
Commercial Trucks, New & Used Trucks, Tractors & Trailers
S.I.C.: 5012; 5511
Fontaine A. Maddox, Jr. *(Pres.)*
James D. Maddox *(V.P.)*
Rodney A. Maddox *(V.P.)*
Robert M. Myers *(Treas.)*

Outside Service Firm(s):

First American National Bank*(Major Banking Relationship)*
Nashville, TN

TRI-STATE MOTOR TRANSIT CO.
E. 7th Street Rd. & Business I-44
Joplin, MO 64802
Mailing Address:
P.O. Box 113,
Joplin, MO 64802
Tel.: 417-624-3131 **DE**
Fax: 417-624-3131 x463
Assets: $49,194,000
Earnings: $1,057,000
Liabilities: $30,251,000
Net Worth: $18,943,000
Approx.Sls.: $111,373,000
Emp.: 815
Fiscal Year-end: 12/31/90
Transportation-Common Carrier
S.I.C.: 4213
Michael Lawrence *(Chm. Bd.)*
Henry P. Hoffman *(Chief Exec. Officer)*
Gary Hartter *(Pres.)*
Daryl Deel *(Exec. V.P. & Treas.)*
C. Gerald Hendren *(Sr. V.P.-Fin. & Admin.)*
Henry Hoffman *(Sr. V.P.)*
William Wiley *(Sr. V.P.)*
Siamek Azmoudeh *(V.P.-MIS)*
Terry Taylor *(V.P.-Fin.)*
Edward A. Vrooman *(Gen. Counsel & Sec.)*
Ronald L. Atkinson *(Controller)*
Donald E. Bassett *(Dir.-Cash Mngmt.)*
P. I. Farinacci *(Personnel Dir.)*
Bob D. Oglesby *(Dir.-Maintenance)*

Subsidiary:

Aero Body & Truck Equipment, Inc. **(1)**
E. 7th St. Rd. Bus. I-44
Joplin, MO 64801
Tel.: 417-624-3131 (100%)
Emp.: 10
Body Repairs; Commercial-Sleeper Berths
S.I.C.: 7538
Michael Lawrence *(Chm. Bd. & Pres.)*

TRI-STATE WHOLESALE ASSOCIATED GROCERS
1000 Hawkins
El Paso, TX 79915
Mailing Address:
P.O. Box 9938,
El Paso, TX 79990
Tel.: 915-774-6400 **TX**
Fax: 915-774-6443
Year Founded: 1952
Approx.Sls.: $240,000,000
Emp.: 325
Fiscal Year-end: 1/31/92
Full Line Grocery, Produce, Meats, Frozen Foods, Dairy, HBA & Non-Foods
S.I.C.: 5141; 5122; 5142; 5149
Stanton L. Irvin *(Pres. & Gen. Mgr.)*
Maxine Hixon *(V.P.-Fin.)*
Ronald N. McCrobie *(V.P.-Procurement)*
Jose Mora, Jr. *(V.P.-Distr.)*
Carey Prather *(V.P.-Safety & Training)*
P. Michael Kennedy *(Dir.-Data Processing)*
Christeen Wade *(Dir.-Personnel)*
Allison Groenwoldt *(Exec. Admin.)*

No. of Mfg. Plants/Facilities: 3
No. of U.S. Offices: 1

Computer Systems/Hardware:
IBM AS400-B60

Outside Service Firm(s):

KPMG Peat Marwick*(Auditors)*
The Cortez, 310 N. Mesa St., Ste. 1000
El Paso, TX 79901
Tel.: 915-532-3665

Tri-State Insurance Agency*(Group Insurer)*
El Paso, TX

Kemp, Smith, Duncan & Hammond*(Legal Firm)*
2000 MBank Plaza
El Paso, TX 79901
Tel.: 915-533-4424

Citicorp Industrial Credit*(Major Banking Relationship)*
Atlanta, GA

Texas Commerce Bank*(Major Banking Relationship)*
El Paso, TX

Maxine Hixon*(Pension Manager)*
El Paso, TX

TRI VALLEY GROWERS INC.
1255 Battery St.
San Francisco, CA 94120
Mailing Address:
P.O. Box 7114,
San Francisco, CA 94120-7114
Tel.: 415-445-1600 **CA**
Fax: 415-445-1628
Year Founded: 1932
Assets: $505,220,000
Earnings: $39,953,000
Liabilities: $354,634,000
Net Worth: $150,586,000
Approx.Sls.: $746,000,000
Emp.: 3,000
Fiscal Year-end: 1/31/90
Import Export
Fruit & Vegetable Production & Canning; Fork Lift Distributor; Manufacture Sanitary Cans
S.I.C.: 2033; 0161; 0179; 0172; 0175; 2035; 3411
James Saras *(Chm. Bd. & Chief Exec. Officer)*
Travis Mullinex *(Pres. & Chief Oper. Officer)*
Donald Schulak *(Exec. V.P. & Chief Fin. Officer)*
Peter Thor *(Exec. V.P.-Mktg.)*
Paul McGinty *(Exec. V.P.-Sls.)*
Richard Norona *(Sr. V.P.-Opers.)*
James Spitze *(Sr. V.P.-Information Systems)*
A. Lynn French *(V.P.-Quality Assurance & Tech. Sls.)*
Edward Miller *(V.P.-Human Resources)*
Robert Parodi *(V.P.-Tech. Services)*
Paul Schaefer *(V.P.-Human Resources)*
Terry Witzel *(V.P.-Corp. Relations)*
James Salisbury *(Treas. & Asst. Sec.)*
Jean Faris *(Corp. Sec.)*
Dave Hash *(Controller)*
Cliff Nagle *(Dir.-Pur.)*
Scott Powers *(Dir.-Data Processing)*
Paul Vantress *(Dir.-Leasing)*
Robert Burns *(Mgr.-Sls. Promotion & Food Service Mktg.)*
Suzanne Coffey *(Mgr.-Public Relations)*
Ed Miller *(Mgr.-Employee Benefits)*
Ed Parker *(Mgr.-Res. & Devel.)*
Dan Thornton *(Mgr.-Mktg. Services)*
Paul Vantress *(Mgr.-Real Estate)*

No. of Mfg. Plants/Facilities: 11
No. of U.S. Offices: 5

Computer Systems/Hardware:
DEC VAX 11/780

Outside Service Firm(s):

Deloitte & Touche*(Auditors)*
50 Fremont St.
San Francisco, CA 94105-2230
Tel.: 415-393-4300
Fax: 415-227-0452

Nationwide Insurance*(Commercial Insurance Carrier)*
Walnut Creek, CA

Dewey Ballantine*(Legal Firm)*
333 S. Hope St.
Los Angeles, CA 90071

Bank of America, N.T. & S.A.*(Major Banking Relationship)*
P.O. Box 37002,
San Francisco, CA 94137

Security Pacific National Bank*(Major Banking Relationship)*
Modesto, CA

Ashland Management Inc.*(Pension Manager)*
New York, NY

Divisions:

S & W Fine Foods **(1)**
1827 Walden Office Sq.
Schaumburg, IL 60195
Tel.: 708-303-0220
S.I.C.: 5149
Ed Baniewicz *(Mgr.)*
Don Bayma *(Reg. Mgr.)*

S & W Fine Foods **(1)**
4900 Hopyard Rd., Ste. 285
Pleasanton, CA 94566
Tel.: 510-734-9750
S.I.C.: 5411
Tom Terry *(Div. Mgr.)*

S & W Fine Foods **(1)**
5201 N. 19th Ave.
Phoenix, AZ 85016
Tel.: 602-242-3087
S.I.C.: 2033
Paul Getzelman *(Division Mgr.)*

S & W Fine Foods **(1)**
P.O. Box 296, 10755 S. E. Jennifer St.
Clackamas, OR 97015
Tel.: 503-656-9941
S.I.C.: 2033
Bob Heiney *(Division Mgr.)*

S & W Fine Foods **(1)**
1578 W. 17th South
Salt Lake City, UT 84104
Tel.: 801-974-0219
S.I.C.: 5149
Paul Sutherland *(Mgr.)*

S & W Fine Foods **(1)**
P.O. Box 58550, 551 Strander Blvd.
Tukwila, WA 98199
Tel.: 206-575-3600
S.I.C.: 2033
Vic Reed *(Div. Mgr.)*

S & W Fine Foods **(1)**
5010 Loma Vista Ave.
Los Angeles, CA 90058
Tel.: 213-588-3141
S.I.C.: 2033
Ken Boyle *(Division Mgr.)*

S & W Fine Foods, Inc. **(1)**
3160 Crow Canyon Rd.
San Ramon, CA 64583-0587
Tel.: 510-866-4500
Fax: 510-866-1343
Import Export
Computer Systems/Hardware:
Dec VAX
Norman L. Correia *(Pres.)*
Dick Fink *(V.P.-Mktg.)*
Doug Ripley *(V.P.-Sls.)*
Pete McKewen *(V.P.-Opers.)*
Paula Schiff *(Mgr.-Personnel)*

Tri Valley Growers Container Division, Inc. **(1)**
41099 Boyce Rd.
Fremont, CA 94538-2498
Tel.: 510-656-8800
Emp.: 310
Manufacture Sanitary Cans for Canning Operations
S.I.C.: 3411
Dick Dickson *(Mgr.)*

Valley Fork Lift Co. **(1)**
P.O. Box 577440, 140 Riverside
Modesto, CA 95357
Tel.: 209-572-5440
Emp.: 65
Fork Lift Distributors
S.I.C.: 5012
Paul Kennedy *(Gen. Mgr.)*
Walt Berris *(Mgr.-Opers.)*

TRIAN GROUP
900 3rd Ave., 31st Fl.
New York, NY 10022
Tel.: 212-230-3000
Fax: 212-230-3023
Year Founded: 1988
Emp.: 40
Fiscal Year-end: 12/31/91
Holding Company
S.I.C.: 6719
Nelson Peltz *(Chm. & Chief Exec. Officer)*
Peter W. May *(Pres. & Chief Oper. Officer)*

Subsidiaries:

Brandt, Inc. **(1)**
1750 Woodhaven Dr.
Bensalem, PA 19020
Tel.: 215-638-3600 (100%)
Fax: 215-638-1188
Approx.Sls.: $70,000,000
Emp.: 700
Fiscal Year-end: 12/31/91
Import Export
Computer Systems/Hardware:
DEC RISC Computers with Ultrix Application Software
Mfr. of Coin Changing, Paying & Sorting Equipment, Currency & Document Processing Machinery
S.I.C.: 3569; 3578; 3579
Douglas C. Rattray *(Pres.)*
Barry Astrowsky *(V.P.-Fin.)*
Gary Wilkins *(V.P.-Mktg.)*

Triangle PWC, Inc. **(1)**
P.O. Box 711,
New Brunswick, NJ 08903
Approx.Sls.: $169,000,000
Mfr. of Electrical Steel Conduit
S.I.C.: 3644
Bruce K. Cowles *(Pres.)*

TRIANGLE DISTRIBUTING COMPANY
12065 Pike St.
Santa Fe Springs, CA 90670
Tel.: 310-699-3424 **CA**

Triangle Distributing Company—(Continued)

Fax: 310-699-2318
Year Founded: 1957
Approx.Sls.: $89,000,000
Emp.: 200
Wholesale Distributor of Beer & Other Fermented Malt Liquors
S.I.C.: 5181
James B. Fleming *(Pres.)*
Michael J. Crow *(V.P.)*
Lavern Faiester *(V.P.)*
Preston G. Heimark *(V.P.)*
Craig Ewing *(Mgr.-Human Resources)*
Milo Ramirez *(Mgr.-Sls.)*

Outside Service Firm(s):

Deloitte & Touche*(Auditors)*
Santa Fe Springs, CA

First Interstate Bank*(Major Banking Relationship)*
Santa Fe Springs, CA

TRIANGLE ELECTRIC COMPANY
29787 Stephenson Hwy.
Madison Heights, MI 48071
Tel.: 313-399-2200
Fax: 313-399-2612
Year Founded: 1983
Approx.Sls.: $35,000,000
Emp.: 150
Electrical Contractor
S.I.C.: 1731
Roy C. Martin, Sr. *(Chief Exec. Officer & Sec.)*
Jimmie R. Palmer *(Pres.)*
Roy C. Martin, Jr. *(V.P.-Fin. & Treas.)*
John A. McFeely, Jr. *(V.P.-Engrng. & Estimating)*
Earl Riske *(V.P.-Opers.)*

Outside Service Firm(s):

Doeren & Mayhew*(Auditors)*
Troy, MI

Kerr, Russell & Weber*(Legal Firm)*
Detroit, MI

National Bank Of Detroit*(Major Banking Relationship)*
NBD Financial Tower, 900 Tower Dr., 14th Fl.
Troy, MI 48098
Tel.: 313-828-6900

TRIANGLE MAINTENANCE CORPORATION
71 S. Central Ave.
Valley Stream, NY 11580
Tel.: 516-561-1700
Fax: 516-872-1599
Approx.Sls.: $50,000,000
Emp.: 3,400
Provides Complete Building Maintenance Services; Installs, Operates, Maintains & Repairs Production Equipment In Plants & Warehouses
S.I.C.: 7349; 0782; 1711; 1721; 1731; 1751; 7342; 8744; 7699
Ralph Fine *(Chm. Bd.)*
Lonnie Fine *(Pres.)*
William Beckfeld *(V.P.-Regional)*
Jerry Gilbert *(V.P.-Opers.)*
Robert Abreu *(Dir.-Human Resources)*
Carmine Gesevle *(Gen. Mgr.-Aviation)*
Perry Fine *(Mgr.-Projects & Dir.-Mngmt. Information Systems)*
Irina Goldenstein *(Mgr.-Data Processing)*
Joanne Schickler *(Pur. Agent)*

Outside Service Firm(s):

Rifkin, Levin & Lebowitz*(Auditors)*
New York, NY

Citibank N.A.*(Major Banking Relationship)*
Corporate Trust Services, 399 Park Ave.
New York, NY 10043
Tel.: 212-559-1605

TRIANGLE MARKETING CORP.
32 Bleecker St.
New York, NY 10012
Tel.: 212-966-0100 **NY**
Year Founded: 1958
Assets: $19,000,000
Liabilities: $4,000,000
Net Worth: $15,000,000
Approx.Sls.: $50,000,000
Emp.: 150
Fiscal Year-end: 12/31/90
Export
Converter & Distribute Printing, Publishing & Packaging Paper & Board
S.I.C.: 5111
Lawrence Diamond *(Chm. Bd., Pres., Chief Exec. & Chief Oper. Officer & Dir.-Pur.)*
Sam Marks *(Exec. V.P., Corp. Sec. & Dir.-Pur.)*
Gary Damiano *(Chief Fin. Officer & Controller)*
David Applebaum *(V.P.-Mfg.)*
I. Stephen Genkin *(Treas.)*
Craig Shields, Esq. *(Gen. Counsel)*
Principal(s):
Lawrence Diamond
Sam Marks
David Applebaum
I. Stephen Genkin

No. of Mfg. Plants/Facilities: 1
No. of U.S. Offices: 2

Outside Service Firm(s):

Feldman, Herbstman & Braverman*(Auditors)*
Great Neck, NY

National Westminister Bank U.S.A.*(Major Banking Relationship)*
175 Water St.
New York, NY 10038
Tel.: 212-602-4000

Divisions:

Garden State Converters **(1)**
32 Bleecker St.
New York, NY 10012
Tel.: 212-966-0100
Emp.: 100
Converters
S.I.C.: 3621

Newbrook Paper **(1)**
32 Bleecker St.
New York, NY 10012
Tel.: 212-966-0100
Emp.: 100
Paper Merchants
S.I.C.: 5111

TRIANGLE PACIFIC CORPORATION
16803 Dallas Pkwy.
Dallas, TX 75248
Mailing Address:
P.O. Box 660100
Dallas, TX 75266
Tel.: 214-931-3000 **NY**
Fax: 214-931-3000 x415
Approx.Sls.: $352,600,000
Emp.: 4,100
Import Export
Mfr. of Kitchen Cabinets & Hardwood Flooring
S.I.C.: 2434; 2426
Eli Jacobs *(Chm. Bd. & Chief Exec. Officer)*
Floyd Sherman *(Pres. & Chief Oper. Officer)*
M. Joseph McHugh *(Sr. Exec. V.P.-Fin., Admin. & Treas.)*
Joseph Nussbaum *(Exec. V.P. & Pres.-Cabinet Div.)*
Darryl T. Marchand *(V.P., Gen. Counsel & Sec.)*
John G. Conklin *(V.P.-Mfg.)*
Charles A. Engle *(V.P.-Sls.)*
James T. Fidler *(V.P.-Data Processing)*
Michael Kearins *(V.P.-Sls.)*
Alan M. Kurzman *(V.P.-Mktg.)*
Allan Silver *(V.P.-Mfg.)*
Robert J. Symon *(V.P. & Controller)*
Debbie Wetterlin *(Dir.-Personnel)*
George Kaplan *(Dir.-Corp. Acctg.)*

Outside Service Firm(s):

Arthur Andersen & Co.*(Auditors)*
901 Main St., Ste. 5600
Dallas, TX 75202
Tel.: 214-741-8300

Provident Life & Accident Insurance Co.*(Group Insurer)*
P.O. Box 12015
Chattanooga, TN 37401
Tel.: 615-755-7088

Miller, Singer, Raives & Brandes, P.C.*(Legal Firm)*
One Rockefeller Plaza
New York, NY 10020
Tel.: 212-582-6700

Chemical Bank*(Major Banking Relationship)*
450 West 33rd St.
New York, NY 10001
Tel.: 212-613-7197
Fax: 212-947-7628

First National Bank of Boston*(Major Banking Relationship)*
P.O. Box 644,
Boston, MA 02102-0644
Tel.: 617-575-2900
Fax: 617-575-2549

NationsBank Texas*(Major Banking Relationship)*
P.O. Box 225961
Dallas, TX 75265
Tel.: 214-653-5000

NationsBank Texas*(Pension Manager)*
P.O. Box 225961
Dallas, TX 75265
Tel.: 214-653-5000

Divisions:

Bruce Hardwood Floors **(1)**
16803 Dallas Pkwy.
Dallas, TX 75248
Tel.: 214-931-3000
Fax: 214-931-3100 Ext. 430
Approx.Sls.: $70,000,000
Emp.: 1,400
Export
Mfr. of Hardwood Floors
S.I.C.: 2426
Floyd Sherman *(Pres.)*
Mike Kearins *(V.P.-Sls.)*
Bob Barrch *(Dir.-Mktg.)*

Cabinets Div. **(1)**
16803 Dallas Pkwy.
Dallas, TX 75248
Tel.: 214-931-3000
Approx.Sls.: $173,000,000
Emp.: 1,800
Mfr. of Kitchen & Bathroom Cabinets
S.I.C.: 2434

Classic Bath Products **(1)**
16803 Dallas Pkwy.
Dallas, TX 75248
Tel.: 214-931-3000
Mfr. of Bathroom Cabinets
S.I.C.: 2434

Del Mar Div. **(1)**
16803 Dallas Pkwy.
Dallas, TX 75248
Tel.: 214-931-3000
Mfr. of Kitchen & Vanity Cabinets
S.I.C.: 2434

IXL Furniture **(1)**
16803 Dallas Pkwy.
Dallas, TX 75248
Tel.: 214-931-3000
Approx.Sls.: $20,000,000
Emp.: 600
IXL Kitchen & Bathroom Cabinets, Wall Systems & Hutches
S.I.C.: 2514; 2434
Floyd Sherman *(Pres.)*
Joseph McHugh *(Sr. Exec. V.P.)*
Joseph Nussbaum *(Exec. V.P.)*
Charles Engle *(V.P.-Sls.)*
Dave Hickman *(Dir.-Mktg.)*

Manufacturing Building Products Div. **(1)**
P.O. Box 167,
Beltsville, MD 20705
Tel.: 301-937-5000
Mfr. of Wood Kitchen Cabinets
S.I.C.: 2434

Tri-Pac Div. **(1)**
16803 Dallas Pkwy.
Dallas, TX 75248
Tel.: 214-931-3000
Mfr. of Kitchen & Vanity Cabinets
S.I.C.: 2434

U.S. Slate & Marble Co. **(1)**
16803 Dallas Pkwy.
Dallas, TX 75248
Tel.: 214-931-3000
Mfr. of Table & Cabinet Tops
S.I.C.: 2434

TRIBBLE & STEPHENS CO.
10610 Haddington
Houston, TX 77043
Tel.: 713-465-8550 **TX**
Fax: 713-973-7107
Year Founded: 1968
Approx.Sls.: $160,000,000
Emp.: 240
Fiscal Year-end: 10/31/90
General Contractor; Commercial & Industrial Construction
S.I.C.: 1542; 1541
James L. Tribble *(Chm. Bd. & Chief Exec. Officer)*
James H. Stephens *(Pres.)*
Ken Brown *(Sr. V.P.-Opers.)*
Barbara Thomas *(Sr. V.P.)*
Jay Tribble *(Corp. Sec.)*

No. of Foreign Offices: 6

Outside Service Firm(s):

Harold F. Huff, CPA*(Auditors)*
Houston, TX

Texas Commerce Bank*(Major Banking Relationship)*
600 Travis Street, Suite 1150
Houston, TX 77002
Tel.: 713-236-4865

TRIBORO ELECTRIC CORP.
539 Jacksonville Rd.
Warminster, PA 18974
Tel.: 215-345-6000
Fax: 215-443-7697
Year Founded: 1934
Approx.Sls.: $40,000,000
Emp.: 950
Mfr. of Electrical Wiring Devices, Insulated Wire & Lamp Wire, Power Supply Cord Sets
S.I.C.: 3699; 3357; 3645
Murray B. Yarmark *(Pres.)*
Martin J. Yarmark *(Exec. V.P.)*
Harold Yarmark *(V.P.)*
John J. Zecca *(V.P.-Mfg.)*
Gerald Malone *(Chief Engineer)*
Nick Dilnnel *(Pur. Agent)*
Principal(s):
Murray B. Yarmark
Martin J. Yarmark

Computer Systems/Hardware:
Qantel

Outside Service Firm(s):

Rudolph, Palitz & Co.*(Auditors)*
Philadelphia, PA

Industrial Valley Bank*(Major Banking Relationship)*
Philadelphia, PA

TRIBUNE REVIEW PUBLISHING CO.
622 Cabin Hill Dr.
Greensburg, PA 15601
Tel.: 412-834-1151
Fax: 412-838-5170

Approx.Sls.: $20,000,000
Emp.: 280
Newspaper Publisher; Tribune Review
S.I.C.: 2711
Edward H. Harrell *(Pres.)*
George A. Beidler *(Exec. V.P.-Editor)*
Richard M. Scaife *(Dir.-Pub.Rels.)*
Robert Alp *(Controller)*
Kraig Cawley *(Dir.-Adv.)*
Charles Fry *(Dir.-Circulation)*

Outside Service Firm(s):

Here, Kramer, Connell, Murphy, & Goldknap, P.C.*(Auditors)*
Horsham, PA

Pittsburgh National Bank*(Major Banking Relationship)*
P.O. Box 548,
Pittsburgh, PA 15230-0548
Tel.: 412-236-8000

Subsidiary:

T-R Printing & Publishing **(1)**
P.O. Box280,
Irwin, PA 15642
Tel.: 412-863-3601
Commercial Printing
S.I.C.: 2711
Vic Ketchman *(Chief Oper. Officer)*

TRICO ELECTRIC CO-OP
5100 W. Ina Rd.
Tucson, AZ 85743
Tel.: 602-744-2944 **AZ**
Fax: 602-744-2329
Year Founded: 1945
Approx.Sls.: $21,000,000
Emp.: 60
Distribution of Electric Power
S.I.C.: 4911
George P. Davies *(Chm. Bd. & Pres.)*
Edward L. Anway *(V.P.)*
Marv Athey *(Gen. Mgr.)*
L. Nick Buckelew *(Treas.)*
Barbara Stockwell *(Sec.)*

TRICON INDUSTRIES, INC.
2325 Wisconsin Ave.
Downers Grove, IL 60515
Tel.: 708-964-2330 **DE**
Fax: 708-964-5179
Year Founded: 1944
Assets: $10,470,000
Liabilities: $6,570,000
Net Worth: $3,900,000
Approx.Sls.: $25,000,000
Emp.: 360
Fiscal Year-end: 12/31/91
Import Export
Mfr. Custom Switches & Connectors, Insert Molding Products, Electrical Contact Assemblies, Preforms, Bulkwire Pstrip, Copper, Silver & Nickel Paste & Fluxes
S.I.C.: 3679; 2899; 3089; 3499; 3613; 3678; 5085
Theodore R. Boedeker *(Pres.)*
Pat Grandle *(Mgr.-Mktg. & Sec.)*
Susan Grandle *(Mgr.-Human Resources & Treas.)*

No. of Mfg. Plants/Facilities: 4
No. of U.S. Offices: 4

Computer Systems/Hardware:
Texas Instruments 990

Outside Service Firm(s):

Price Waterhouse*(Auditors)*
Oak Brook, IL

Arthur J. Gallagher & Co.*(Commercial Insurance Carrier)*
150 S. Walker Dr. #100
Chicago, IL 60606

Northwestern National Life*(Group Insurer)*
Lake Forest, IL

Coffield, Ungaretti & Harris*(Legal Firm)*
3500 Three First National Plaza
Chicago, IL 60602
Tel.: 312-977-4400

Lake Shore National Bank*(Major Banking Relationship)*
605 N. Michigan Ave.
Chicago, IL 60611
Tel.: 312-787-1900

Divisions:

Tricon Brazing Alloys & Chemical Products Div. **(1)**
5000 Chase St.
Downers Grove, IL 60515
Tel.: 708-963-0220
Tel.: 800-654-6850
Emp.: 21
Mfr. of Chemicals & Fabricated Metal Products
S.I.C.: 2899; 3499
T.R. Boedeker *(Pres.)*
Rosalie Gartner *(Mgr.-Sls.)*
Jim Hansen *(Mgr.-Mfg.)*
Cullen Kline *(Mgr.-Materials)*

Tricon Electromechanical Div. **(1)**
2325 Wisconsin Ave.
Downers Grove, IL 60615
Tel.: 708-964-2330
Emp.: 339
Mfr. of Plastic Products, Connectors For Electronic Application, Switchgear & Switchboard & Electronic Components
S.I.C.: 3089; 3678; 3613; 3679
Ralph W. Grandle *(Exec. V.P.)*
Robert Stevens *(Mgr.-Sls.)*
Leonard Lucchesi *(Mgr.-Materials)*
Donald Paul *(Dir.-Tech. Services)*
John Cieplak *(Mgr.-Mfg.)*

Plant:

Tricon Electromechanical Plant **(2)**
5402 Janes Ave.
Downers Grove, IL 60515
Tel.: 708-241-0972

TRIDENT FINANCIAL CORPORATION
4601 Six Forks Rd.
Raleigh, NC 27609
Tel.: 919-781-8900
Approx.Sls.: $21,000,000
Emp.: 32
Financial Institution Investment Banking
S.I.C.: 6282
William M. Moore, Jr. *(Chm. Bd. & Pres.)*
Timothy E. Lavelle *(Sr. V.P. & Mng. Dir.)*
Michael A. Murphy *(Sr. V.P. & Mng. Dir.)*

TRIDENT SEAFOOD CORPORATION
5303 Shilshole Ave., NW
Seattle, WA 98107
Tel.: 206-783-3818
Fax: 206-782-7246
Year Founded: 1973
Approx.Sls.: $300,000,000
Emp.: 400
Process Crabs & Frozen Fish
S.I.C.: 6719; 2092
Charles Bundrant *(Pres.)*
Kaare Ness *(V.P.)*
Ed Perry *(V.P.)*
Larry Geraghty *(Treas.)*

Outside Service Firm(s):

Deloitte & Touche*(Auditors)*
Seattle, WA

Seattle First National Bank*(Major Banking Relationship)*
Seattle, WA 98154

WM. S. TRIMBLE COMPANY, INC.
2200 Atchley St.
Knoxville, TN 37920
Tel.: 615-573-1911
Fax: 615-573-5239
Approx.Sls.: $10,000,000
Emp.: 49
Mfr. Metal Doors & Frames, Finish Hardware, Folding Partitions, Overhead Doors, Wood Doors, Building Specialties
S.I.C.: 3442; 2431; 2541; 3429
James Sieber *(Chm. Bd.)*
William S. Trimble, Jr. *(Pres.)*
R. V. Souder *(V.P.)*
Jay Earl Rainwater *(Sec. & Legal Counsel)*

Computer Systems/Hardware:
IBM 3600

Outside Service Firm(s):

Hamilton, Gilbert & Perry*(Auditors)*
Knoxville, TN

Rainwater, Humble & Vowell*(Legal Firm)*
Knoxville, TN

Third National Bank*(Major Banking Relationship)*
Nashville, TN

TRIMFIT, INC.
10450 Drummond Rd.
Philadelphia, PA 19154
Tel.: 215-632-3000
Fax: 215-632-6430
Approx.Sls.: $39,000,000
Emp.: 1,600
Fiscal Year-end: 12/31/91
Mfr. Socks, Hosiery, Tights & Stretchwear
S.I.C.: 2251; 2252
Martin B. Kramer *(Chm. Bd.)*
Arnold A. Kramer *(Pres. & Chief Exec. Officer)*
Harry Schultz *(Controller)*

Computer Systems/Hardware:
IBM 4341

Outside Service Firm(s):

Gardner, Waschler, Goldman & Co.*(Auditors)*
New York, NY

Provident National Bank*(Major Banking Relationship)*
1000 Westlakes Dr.
Berwyn, PA 19312

Non-U.S. Holding:

Trimfit Company Limited **(1)**
375 Rexdale Blvd.
Rexdale, ON M9W 1S1, Canada
Tel.: 416-743-5363 (100%)
Emp.: 65
Mfrs. Women's Hosiery
S.I.C.: 2251; 2252
Arnold J. Kramer, Jr. *(Pres.)*

TRIMTEX CO. INC.
400 Park Ave.
Williamsport, PA 17701
Tel.: 717-326-9135
Fax: 717-326-4250
Year Founded: 1919
Approx.Sls.: $15,000,000
Emp.: 305
Fiscal Year-end: 12/31/91
Import Export
Trimtex Braided, Knitted & Woven Trimmings & Tapes; Functional Braids, Specification Tapes, Braids; Coatings & Finishing of Trims
S.I.C.: 2241
Kurt Stahel *(Pres.)*
William Henderson *(V.P.-Home Furnishing)*
Eric K. Hall *(V.P.-Mfg.)*
Doris E. Stevens *(Controller)*
Helen Eck *(Dir.-Personnel)*
Kenneth Brown *(Mgr.-Sls.)*

Computer Systems/Hardware:
AS 400

TRINA, INC.
Ace St.
Fall River, MA 02722
Mailing Address:
P.O. Box 1431
Fall River, MA 02722
Tel.: 508-678-7601
Telex: 200245
Fax: 508-672-3058
Approx.Sls.: $20,000,000
Emp.: 500
Manufacture Travel Kits, Gift Items, Travel & Home Accessories
S.I.C.: 2392; 2676; 2842; 3171; 3172; 2844; 2515
David Manasco *(Pres. & Chief Exec. Officer)*
Roger R. Rouleau *(Mgr.-Adv. & Design)*

Computer Systems/Hardware:
Wang

Outside Service Firm(s):

Meyer, Regan & Wilner*(Auditors)*
Fall River, MA

Marine Midland Bank*(Major Banking Relationship)*
140 Broadway Ave., 12 Floor
New York, NY 10015
Tel.: 212-440-1000

TRINIDAD/BENHAM CORPORATION
P.O. Box 22139
Denver, CO 80222
Tel.: 303-220-1400 **DE**
Fax: 303-220-1490
Year Founded: 1978
Approx.Sls.: $115,000,000
Emp.: 450
Wholesale Dried Beans, Lentils, Peas, Rice, Popcorn & Aluminum Foil
S.I.C.: 5153
Wayne Van Vleet *(Chm. Bd.)*
Carl C. Hartman *(Pres., Chief Oper. & Chief Exec. Officer)*
Charles W. Meiers Jr. *(Chief Fin. Officer & V.P.)*
Linda Walmsley *(Dir.-Human Resources)*

Computer Systems/Hardware:
Honeywell

Outside Service Firm(s):

Price Waterhouse*(Auditors)*
950 17th St., Ste. 2600
Denver, CO 80202
Tel.: 303-893-8100

Fairfield & Woods*(Legal Firm)*
Denver, CO

Sherman & Howard*(Legal Firm)*
633 17th St.
Denver, CO 80202
Tel.: 303-297-2900

Team Bank*(Major Banking Relationship)*
P.O. Box 2604,
Fort Worth, TX 76113
Tel.: 817-884-4614

Wells Fargo Bank*(Major Banking Relationship)*
420 Montgomery St.
San Francisco, CA 94104

Trinidad/Benham Corporation—(Continued)

Subsidiaries:

D & D Bean Company **(1)**
P.O. Box 22139
Denver, CO 80222
Tel.: 303-368-7200

Ed J. Lyng Company **(1)**
P.O. Box 22139
Denver, CO 80222
Tel.: 303-368-7200

Food Oils Corporation **(1)**
145 Grant St.
Carlstadt, NJ 07072
Tel.: 201-935-7888
Fax: 201-935-7266
Approx.Sls.: $22,000,000
Emp.: 36
Corn, Vegetable Oils & Shortenings
S.I.C.: 2046; 2079
William Stewart *(Gen. Mgr.)*

Phoenix Industries **(1)**
P.O. Box 22139
Denver, CO 80222
Tel.: 303-368-7200

Sabine Trucking, Inc. **(1)**
P.O. Box 22139
Denver, CO 80222
Tel.: 303-368-7200

Trinidad Bean & Elevator Co. **(1)**
P.O. Box 22139
Denver, CO 80222
Tel.: 303-368-7200

Westlam Foods **(1)**
P.O. Box 22139
Denver, CO 80222
Tel.: 303-368-7200

TRINKLE SALES, INC.
1010 Haddonfield-Berlin Rd.
Cherry Hill, NJ 08034
Mailing Address:
P.O. Box 5320,
Cherry Hill, NJ 08034
Tel.: 609-795-4200 **NJ**
Fax: 609-795-9364
Year Founded: 1931
Approx.Sls.: $44,200,000
Emp.: 25
Manufacturers Representative for Electronic Components
S.I.C.: 5065
Robert C. Trinkle *(Pres.)*
Betty L. Trinkle *(Treas.)*
Neila Jayne *(Sec.)*
Principal(s):
Robert C. Trinkle

Computer Systems/Hardware:
IBM System 36 & IBM PC

Outside Service Firm(s):

D'Amico, Caglioti & Co.*(Auditors)*
Pennsauken, NJ 08109

Parker, McCay & Criscuolo*(Legal Firm)*
Cherry Hill, NJ

First Fidelity Bank, N.A.*(Major Banking Relationship)*
Morristown, NJ

TRIO PRODUCTS INC.
250 Warden Ave.
Elyria, OH 44035
Tel.: 216-323-5457 **OH**
Fax: 216-323-3247
Year Founded: 1960
Approx.Sls.: $10,000,000
Emp.: 130
Mfr. Extrusion Blow & Injection Blow Molded Plastic Containers & Custom Molded Parts; Extruded Sheeting
S.I.C.: 3083; 3089
Joseph Bennett *(Pres.)*
Charles Daane *(Treas.)*
Ridley Watts, Jr. *(Dir.-Opers.)*
J. Charles Derringer *(Mgr.-Natl. Sls.)*
Principal(s):
Joseph Bennett

No. of Mfg. Plants/Facilities: 2
No. of U.S. Offices: 3

Outside Service Firm(s):

Hausser & Taylor*(Auditors)*
Cleveland, OH

Weston, Hurd, Fallon, Paisley & Howley*(Legal Firm)*
Cleveland, OH

Society National Bank*(Major Banking Relationship)*
900 Euclid Ave., P.O. Box 6477
Cleveland, OH 44101-6477
Tel.: 216-737-5000
Fax: 216-566-8947

TRIPLE A SPECIALTY COMPANY
4953 W. 66th St.
Bedford Park, IL 60638
Tel.: 708-458-7200 **IL**
Fax: 708-458-9583
Approx.Sls.: $15,000,000
Emp.: 90
Manufacture Auto & Marine Original Equipment & Replacement Electrical Parts, Maintenance & Test Equipment, Battery Chargers, Booster Cables, Ignition Wire, MIG Welders, Armature Analyzers, Plasma Metal Cutters
S.I.C.: 3519; 3429; 3694; 3612; 3629; 3699; 3825
I. Robert Bernes *(Pres.)*
William E. Berendt *(Exec. V.P. & Chief Oper. Officer)*
Lee Hamilton *(Sls. Mgr.)*
Joe Gaske *(Data Processing Dir.)*
Dan Flynn *(Prod. & Catalog Mgr.)*
Principal(s):
I. Robert Bernes

No. of Mfg. Plants/Facilities: 1
No. of U.S. Offices: 1
No. of Foreign Offices: 1

Outside Service Firm(s):

Rome & Associates*(Auditors)*
Chicago, IL

Lincoln National Life Insurance Co.*(Group Insurer)*
PO Box 208, 1300 S. Clinton
Fort Wayne, IN 46801
Tel.: 219-455-2926
Fax: 219-455-7619

American National Bank & Trust Company of Chicago*(Major Banking Relationship)*
33 N. LaSalle St.
Chicago, IL 60602
Tel.: 312-661-5000
Fax: 312-661-6417

TRIPLE F, INC.
10104 Douglas Ave.
Des Moines, IA 50322
Mailing Address:
P.O. Box 3600
Des Moines, IA 50322
Tel.: 515-254-1200 **IA**
Fax: 515-254-1351
Year Founded: 1961
Assets: $16,000,000
Liabilities: $6,000,000
Net Worth: $10,000,000
Approx.Sls.: $40,000,000
Emp.: 460
Fiscal Year-end: 9/30/90
Holding Company; Livestock Feeds, Vitamins & Trace Mineral Premixes; Manufacture Equipment for Producing Animal Feeds
S.I.C.: 6719; 0119; 2834; 3556
Wayne F. Fox *(Chm. Bd. & Chief Exec. Officer)*
Dr. Leroy Hanson *(Pres. & Chief Oper. Officer)*
Jed Harms *(V.P.-Mktg. & Sls.)*
Jim VonBon *(Treas.)*
Stephen W. Roberts *(Sec.)*
Janice Miller *(Communications Coord.)*
Principal(s):
Wayne F. Fox
Dr. Leroy Hanson

No. of Mfg. Plants/Facilities: 11
No. of U.S. Offices: 8
No. of Foreign Offices: 3

Computer Systems/Hardware:
IBM

Outside Service Firm(s):

KPMG Peat Marwick*(Auditors)*
2500 Ruan Center
Des Moines, IA 50309
Tel.: 515-288-7465

Davis, Hockenberg, Wine, Brown, Koehn & Shors*(Legal Firm)*
Des Moines, IA

Valley National Bank*(Major Banking Relationship)*
Des Moines, IA

Subsidiaries:

Insta-Pro International, Ltd. **(1)**
10301 Dennis Dr.
Des Moines, IA 50322
Tel.: 515-254-1260 (100%)
Mfr. of Extruder Machines
S.I.C.: 3542

Meta Farm **(1)**
10215 Dennis Dr.
Des Moines, IA 50322
Tel.: 515-254-1280
Mfr. of Additives For Animal Feed
S.I.C.: 2047; 2048
Mark Richards *(Mng. Dir.)*

TRIPLE S TECHNOLOGIES, INC.
14320 S. Portage Rd.
Vicksburg, MI 49097
Tel.: 616-649-0545
Fax: 616-649-3427
Approx.Sls.: $20,000,000
Emp.: 175
Fiscal Year-end: 12/31/90
Injection Molding of Plastics; Industrial Molds
S.I.C.: 3089; 3544
Daniel B. Canavan *(Chm. Bd.)*
Victor V. Valentine *(Pres.)*
Jim Lamb *(V.P.-Engrng.)*
Bill Stewart *(V.P.-Mfg.)*

Outside Service Firm(s):

Arizona Bank*(Major Banking Relationship)*
Phoenix, AZ

Subsidiaries:

Triple S Plastics, Inc. **(1)**
14320 S. Portage Rd.
Vicksburg, MI 49097
Tel.: 616-649-0545
Approx.Sls.: $12,000,000
Emp.: 160
Injection Molded Finished Plastic Products, Industrial Molds
S.I.C.: 3089; 3544
Daniel B. Canavan *(Pres.)*
Allan P. Lawson *(V.P.-Mfg.)*
Doug Clary *(Pur. Agent)*
Edie Smith *(Dir.-Personnel)*

Triple S Plastics Southwest **(1)**
6680 S. Country Club Rd.
Tucson, AZ 85706
Tel.: 602-573-0440
Injection Molding
S.I.C.: 3089
Alan Lawson *(Pres.)*

TRIPLETT ELECTRICAL INSTRUMENT CORPORATION
1 Triplett Drive
Bluffton, OH 45817
Tel.: 419-358-5015
Tel.: 800-TRI-PLET
Fax: 419-358-7956
Year Founded: 1904
Emp.: 240
Electrical/Electronic Test Instruments & Process Control Equipment
S.I.C.: 3625; 3629; 3823; 3825; 3829
Warren J. Hess *(Pres.)*
Terry L. Florence *(Mgr.-Product)*
Ted Suever *(Mgr.-Adv.)*
Joel Weldy *(Mgr.-Sls.)*
Anthony Armlay *(Pur. Agent)*

TRISTATE ELECTRICAL SUPPLY CO., INC.
1741 Dual Hwy.
Hagerstown, MD 21740
Tel.: 301-733-1212
Tel.: 301-733-7225
Fax: 301-733-7225
Approx.Sls.: $60,000,000
Emp.: 302
Distribute Electrical Products
S.I.C.: 5063
John M. Waltersdorf *(Pres.)*
John G. Waltersdorf *(Exec. V.P.-Sls.)*
Robert B. Witt *(Sr. V.P.)*
Grayson W. Oldfather *(Exec. V.P.-Corp. Services & Chief Fin. Officer)*
R.E. Johnson *(V.P.-Reg. Baltimore)*
William Malcolm *(V.P.-Pur.)*
Scott A. McDowell *(V.P.-Reg. York, PA)*
William Smith *(V.P.-Reg. Salisbury)*
Roy G. Stotler *(V.P.-Reg. Hagerstown)*
Shana K. Wolfe *(Controller)*
Margaret S. Waltersdorf *(Sec.)*

Outside Service Firm(s):

Coopers & Lybrand*(Auditors)*
217 E. Redwood St.
Baltimore, MD 21202

Weinberg & Green*(Legal Firm)*
100 S. Charles St.
Baltimore, MD 21202
Tel.: 410-332-8795

Maryland National Bank*(Major Banking Relationship)*
Baltimore, MD 21202

Triton Corporation
(Name Changed To RII, Ricards International Inc.)

TRITON INC.
4267 Winters Chapel Rd.
Doraville, GA 30360
Tel.: 404-457-7271
Fax: 404-457-0652
Year Founded: 1955
Approx.Sls.: $92,000,000
Emp.: 300
Owns & Operates Chain of Gasoline & Convenience Stores
S.I.C.: 5411; 5541
T.V. Patton *(Chm. Bd.)*
Jim Richardson *(Pres.)*
L.E. Bluebaugh *(V.P.-Stores)*
Melvin Seligman *(V.P.)*
James Gaffney *(Controller)*

Computer Systems/Hardware:
IBM System 36

TRITON INDUSTRIES, INC.
1020 N. Kolmar Ave.
Chicago, IL 60651
Tel.: 312-384-3700
Fax: 312-384-8748
Approx.Sls.: $12,000,000
Emp.: 100
Export

Mfr. of Metal Stampings & Fabrications
S.I.C.: 3469; 3499
Brent Wortell *(Pres.)*
Tony Fuss *(Controller)*
Mark Ferdinand *(Gen. Counsel)*
Louis Shapiro *(Gen. Counsel)*

TRIUMPH*LOR, INC.
15710 John F. Kennedy Blvd., Ste. 150
Houston, TX 77032
Tel.: 713-987-8111 **LA**
Telex: 798718 TRILORHOU
Fax: 713-987-2628
Year Founded: 1985
Assets: $31,000,000
Liabilities: $16,000,000
Net Worth: $15,000,000
Approx.Sls.: $22,000,000
Emp.: 175
Fiscal Year-end: 12/31/90
Import Export
Mfr., Sale & Lease of Oilfield Drilling Equipment
S.I.C.: 3533; 7359; 5084
Howard B. Myers *(Pres. & Chief Exec. Officer)*
Charles E. Crass *(V.P.-Fin. & Chief Fin. Officer)*
William Schock *(V.P.-Engrng.)*
Richard Werner *(V.P.-Opers.)*
Larry Bourque *(Dir.-Pur.)*
Ken Brock *(Mgr.-Window Cutting)*
Tommy P. Grimes *(Mgr.-Admin.)*
Charles Joubert *(Mgr.-Domestic Opers.)*
Frank Parish *(Mgr.-Export Sls.)*
Craig Spencer *(Mgr.-Mktg.)*
Patti Wisnewski *(Intl. Sls. Coordinator)*
Ray Lopez *(Intl. Sls. Rep.)*
Dan Nichol *(Intl. Sls. Rep.)*

No. of U.S. Offices: 8
No. of Foreign Offices: 1

Outside Service Firm(s):

Ernst & Young*(Auditors)*
4200 One Shell Square, 701 Poydras St.
New Orleans, LA 70139
Tel.: 504-581-4200

Sedgwick James*(Group Insurer)*
New Orleans, LA

First Interstate Bank*(International Bank Affiliate)*
First Interstate Plaza
Houston, TX 77210
Tel.: 713-224-6611

Milling, Benson, Woodward, Hillyer, Pierson & Miller*(Legal Firm)*
909 Poydras St., Ste. 2300
New Orleans, LA 70112
Tel.: 504-569-7000

Manufacturing & Engineering Headquarters:

Triumph-LOR, Inc. **(1)**
212 Southpark Rd.
Lafayette, LA 70508
Tel.: 318-837-2743
Telex: 586682 TRILORAF
Fax: 318-837-5219
Mfg. & Engineering of Oilfield Equipment
S.I.C.: 3533
Joe Albarado *(Plant Mgr.)*

Divisions:

Triumph/LOR, Inc. **(1)**
6922 LaPaseo
Houston, TX 77087
Tel.: 713-643-3159
Fax: 713-643-2318
Houston Rentals
S.I.C.: 7359
Ron Richardson *(Area Mgr.)*

Triumph/LOR, Inc. **(1)**
P.O. Drawer A, 720 Cantwell
Corpus Christi, TX 78469
Tel.: 512-883-6271
Fax: 512-883-2327
Wholesale Distr. of Oilfield Machinery
S.I.C.: 5084
Philip Jackson *(Sls. Rep.)*

Triumph/LOR, Inc. **(1)**
1333 S. E. 25th St.
Oklahoma City, OK 73129
Tel.: 405-677-2464
Fax: 405-677-0240
Wholesale Distr. of Oilfield Machinery
S.I.C.: 5084
Ross Farris *(Area Mgr.)*
Orval Bagley *(Sls. Rep.)*

Triumph/LOR, Inc. **(1)**
P.O. Box 2161,
Laurel, MS 39440
Tel.: 601-649-1302
Sales & Leasing of Oilfield Equipment
S.I.C.: 7359; 5084
John T. Patterson *(District Sls. Mgr.)*

Triumph-Lor, Inc. **(1)**
305 Baronne, Suite 500
New Orleans, LA 70112
Tel.: 504-524-9157
Wholesale Distr. of Oilfield Machinery
S.I.C.: 5084
Jim Porter *(Sls. Rep.)*

Triumph-Lor, Inc. **(1)**
15333 Drummet, Suite 210
Houston, TX 77032
Tel.: 713-999-8111
Fax: 713-987-2628
International Sales
S.I.C.: 5084
Frank Parish *(Export Sls. Mgr.)*
Dan Nichol *(Intl. Acct. Rep.)*
Ray Lopez *(Intl. Acct. Rep.)*
Joyce Coker *(Inside Sls. Supvr.)*

Triumph-LOR, Inc. **(1)**
P.O. Box 51246, 212 Southpark Rd.
Lafayette, LA 70505
Tel.: 318-837-9871
Telex: 586682 TRILORAF
Fax: 318-837-5219
Wholesale Distr. of Oilfield Machinery
S.I.C.: 5084
Charlie Joubert *(Area Mgr.)*
Malcolm Bearb *(Sls. Mgr.-Lafayette District)*
Don Bernard *(Mgr.-Service Dept.)*

Triumph-LOR, Inc. **(1)**
606 Glendale Ave.
Houma, LA 70360
Tel.: 504-876-5519
Wholesale Distr. of Oilfield Machinery
S.I.C.: 5084
Howard Oubre *(Sls. Rep.)*

Triumph-LOR, Inc. **(1)**
P.O. Box 157, Rt. 2,Box 327-A
Spiro, OK 74959
Tel.: 918-436-2468
Wholesale Distr. of Oilfield Machinery
S.I.C.: 5084
Kent Benge *(Sls. Rep.)*
Billy Crandell *(Sls. Rep.)*

Non-U.S. Holding:

Triumph/LOR Oilfield Services Ltd. **(1)**
Kirkhill Industrial Estates, Dyce
Aberdeen, United Kingdom
Tel.: 224-724646 (100%)
Telex: 73551 TRILORAB
Emp.: 16
Sale & Leasing of Oilfield Equipment
S.I.C.: 5084; 7359
John Berry *(Mgr.-North Sea Opers.)*

TRIUMPH PET INDUSTRIES, INC.
4th St. & Rt. 59
Hillburn, NY 10931
Tel.: 914-357-6666
Fax: 914-357-6804
Approx.Sls.: $18,000,000
Emp.: 100
Dog & Cat Food
S.I.C.: 2047
Isadore Gittelman *(Pres.)*
Milton Gittelman *(V.P, Treas. & Sec.)*

Outside Service Firm(s):

Ginsberg & Grill*(Auditors)*
Suffern, NY

Joe Deutsch*(Legal Firm)*
New York, NY

The Bank of New York*(Major Banking Relationship)*
Suffern, NY

TRIZEC PROPERTIES, INC.
(Wholly-owned Sub. of Trizec Corp. Ltd., Calgary, Canada)
15760 Ventura Blvd., Ste. 500
Encino, CA 91436
Tel.: 818-783-0660 **CA**
Fax: 818-783-2108
Assets: $1,700,000,000
Liabilities: $1,100,000,000
Net Worth: $600,000,000
Approx.Sls.: $200,000,000
Emp.: 1,800
Developers of Shopping Centers & Commercial Real Estate
S.I.C.: 6512; 1542
Harold Milavsky *(Chm. Bd. & Pres.)*
Robert Forrest *(V.P.-Opers.)*
Mark Hazan *(Controller)*

Subsidiary:

The Hahn Co. **(1)**
4350 La Jolla Villiage Dr., Ste. 700
San Diego, CA 92122
Tel.: 619-546-1001 (100%)
Approx.Sls.: $140,000,000
Emp.: 1,500
Developers of Shopping Centers
S.I.C.: 6512; 1542
John M. Gilchrist, Jr. *(Pres. & Chief Exec. Officer)*

TROJAN STEEL CO.
1414 McCorkle Ave., S.W.
Charleston, WV 25303
Mailing Address:
P.O. Box 2426
Charleston, WV 25329
Tel.: 304-746-1200 **WV**
Fax: 304-746-1243
Year Founded: 1927
Approx.Sls.: $12,000,000
Emp.: 140
Mfr. Fabricated Structural Steel & Plate Work, Chutes, Hoppers for the Coal & Chemical Industries; Steel Warehouse
S.I.C.: 3441; 3443; 5051
Carroll L. Ash *(Co-Chm., Pres. & Chief Exec. Officer)*
Richard M. Venable, Jr. *(Co-Chm. & V.P.)*
Mary Jane Toothman *(Sec.)*
Gary W. Paxton *(Controller)*
Preston B. King *(Dir.-Pur.)*

No. of Mfg. Plants/Facilities: 2

Computer Systems/Hardware:
PC Network

Outside Service Firm(s):

Devan & Co.*(Commercial Insurance Carrier)*
Charleston, WV

Payne, Loeb & Ray*(Legal Firm)*
Charleston, WV

One Valley Bank*(Major Banking Relationship)*
Charleston, WV

TRONCALLI MOTORS, INC.
1625 Church St.
Decatur, GA 30033
Tel.: 404-292-3853
Fax: 404-297-0332
Sales Range: $40-59 Million
Emp.: 160
Sales & Service of Automobiles & Parts
S.I.C.: 5012; 5013; 5511; 5531
Samuel Troncalli *(Chm. Bd.)*
Charles D. Troncalli *(Pres.)*
Katherine Brown *(Treas. & Sec.)*

Computer Systems/Hardware:
ADP Max 8500

Outside Service Firm(s):

Mordt, Davis & Co.*(Auditors)*
Decatur, GA

Simmons, Warren & Sczcecko*(Legal Firm)*
Decatur, GA

Citizens & Southern National Bank*(Major Banking Relationship)*
Decatur, GA

TRONE ADVERTISING INC.

TRONE ADVERTISING, INC.
P.O. Box 35565,
Greensboro, NC 27425
Tel.: 919-886-1622
Fax: 919-886-4242
Year Founded: 1982
Approx.Billings: $68,500,000
Emp.: 101
Consumer Products, Business to Business, Local Leverage Marketing, Data Base Marketing
Oliver S. (Lee) Trone, III *(Pres.)*
Mark K. Herpel *(Pres.-Compel Mktg. Promotions)*
Thomas A. Mooth *(Exec. V.P.)*
W. Donald White *(Exec. V.P.)*
Earle Bower *(V.P.)*
Joe Bucci *(V.P.)*
Angelyn M. Honton *(V.P., Controller)*
Dixon Johnston *(V.P., New Acct. Devel.)*
Jim Doyle *(V.P.)*
Doug Barton *(V.P.)*
Natalie Perkins *(V.P.)*
Walter D. Sowinski *(Mng. Dir.-SDA Design Services)*
Anne Wemhoff *(Mgr.-Pub. Rels.)*

Computer Systems/Hardware:
IBM, MacIntosh, Novell Net, Ad Aid

TROPAR MFG. CO., INC.
5 Vreeland Rd.
Florham Park, NJ 07932
Mailing Address:
P.O. Box 215
Florham Park, NJ 07932
Tel.: 201-822-2400
Fax: 201-822-2891
Year Founded: 1959
Approx.Sls.: $10,000,000
Emp.: 90
Import Export
Mfr. of Trophies, Plaques & Gift Awards; Bronze Tablets, Medals, Emblematic Jewelry, Clocks
S.I.C.: 3499; 3873
Peter V. Ilaria *(Chm. Bd. & Pres.)*
Murray Mintz *(Chief Fin. Officer)*
Gregory Della Badia *(Dir.-Admin.)*
Peter E. Ilaria *(Dir.-Mktg. & Sls.)*
Anthony Primavera *(Dir.-Data Processing)*
Alex Cilentro *(Mgr.-Mfg.)*
Thomas Fitzgerald *(Mgr.-Pur.)*
Christine Marcello *(Mgr.-Human Resources)*

Computer Systems/Hardware:
ULTIMATE 1425

Outside Service Firm(s):

United States Fidelity & Guaranty Co.*(Commercial Insurance Carrier)*
100 Light Street
Baltimore, MD 21202
Tel.: 301-547-3000

Tropar Mfg. Co., Inc.—(Continued)

Blue Cross of New Jersey*(Group Insurer)*
Newark, NJ

First Fidelity Bank, N.A.*(Major Banking Relationship)*
Atlantic City, NJ

Divisions:

Tropar Mfg. Co., Inc. **(1)**
2313 N. Preston St.
Ennis, TX 75119
Tel.: 214-875-5831
Fax: 214-875-4701
Import Export
Computer Systems/Hardware:
Ultimate 1410
S.I.C.: 3499
C. Yowell *(Div. Mgr.)*

Tropar Mfg. Co., Inc. **(1)**
3306 Bloomingdale
Melrose Park, IL 60160
Tel.: 708-343-3200
Fax: 708-343-4551
Computer Systems/Hardware:
Ultimate 1410
S.I.C.: 3499

TROPICAL GARMENT MANUFACTURING COMPANY
2508 Ivy St.
Tampa, FL 33607
Mailing Address:
PO BOX 885,
Tampa, FL 33601
Tel.: 813-877-7511 **FL**
Fax: 813-874-8448
Year Founded: 1927
Approx.Sls.: $70,000,000
Emp.: 700
Fiscal Year-end: 9/30/91
Mfr. & Marketing of Boys', Men's & Women's Sportswear
S.I.C.: 2325
William Compton *(Pres., Chief Exec. Officer & Chief Oper. Officer)*
Michael Kagan *(Exec. V.P. & Chief Fin. Officer)*
Paul Anders *(Sr. V.P.-Mngmt. Information Systems)*
D. Andy Hilton *(Sr. V.P.-Sls. & Mktg.)*
Jerry Pickett *(Sr. V.P.-Plng., Pur. & Distr.)*
Jerry Yates *(Sr. V.P.-Opers.)*
Sharon Perdue *(Controller)*
Jerry Pickett *(V.P.-Pur.)*
Vicki Cortez *(Dir.-Human Resources)*
Principal(s):
William Compton
Michael Kagan

Outside Service Firm(s):

Ernst & Young*(Auditors)*
787 Seventh Ave.
New York, NY 10019
Tel.: 212-773-1243

NationsBank Florida*(Major Banking Relationship)*
600 Florida Ave.
Tampa, FL 33602
Tel.: 813-224-5151

TROPITONE FURNITURE CO. INC.
1401 Commerce Blvd.
Sarasota, FL 34243
Mailing Address:
P.O. Box 3197
Sarasota, FL 34230
Tel.: 813-355-2715
Fax: 813-355-2692
Approx.Sls.: $40,000,000
Emp.: 500
Summer & Casual Furniture
S.I.C.: 2519
Douglas Baker *(Pres.)*
George Dunn *(V.P.-Mktg.)*
Bob Manhard *(Dir.-Data Processing)*
Principal(s):
Douglas Baker
No. of Mfg. Plants/Facilities: 2

Outside Service Firm(s):

NationsBank*(Major Banking Relationship)*
35 Broad St.
Atlanta, GA 30303
Tel.: 404-581-2121
Tel.: 800-848-8198

Subsidiary:
Tropitone Furniture **(1)**
5 Marconi
Irvine, CA 92718
Tel.: 714-951-2010
Andy Harper *(Pres.)*

Veneman **(1)**
P.O. Box 3197
Sarasota, FL 34230
Tel.: 813-355-2715

ALBERT TROSTEL PACKINGS, LTD.
901 Maxwell St.
Lake Geneva, WI 53147
Tel.: 414-248-4481
Fax: 414-248-4821
Approx.Sls.: $27,000,000
Emp.: 330
Custom Seals & Precision Moldings; Polyurethane Products
S.I.C.: 3089; 3053
Everett G. Smith *(Chm. Bd.)*
Robert Gamache *(Pres.)*
Charles Krull *(Treas.)*
Harry Wallace *(Sec.)*
Paul Elliot *(Pur. Agent)*

Subsidiary:

Albert Trostel & Sons Co. **(1)**
10201 W. Lincoln Ave., Ste. 207
West Allis, WI 53227
Tel.: 414-327-4870
Fax: 414-327-3054
Approx.Sls.: $230,000,000
Emp.: 1,000
Fiscal Year-end: 11/30/90
Manufacture Automotive & Furniture Upholstery & Leather, Precision Molded Rubber Products, Oil Seals, Cast Urethane
S.I.C.: 3111; 2822; 3053; 3069
Everett G. Smith *(Pres.)*
Anders Segerdahl *(V.P.)*
Thomas Somodi *(Controller)*
Charles D. Krull *(Treas.)*

ALBERT TROSTEL & SONS COMPANY
10201 W. Lincoln Ave., Ste. 405
Milwaukee, WI 53227
Tel.: 414-327-4870 **WI**
Fax: 414-327-3054
Approx.Sls.: $175,000,000
Emp.: 900
Export
Leather Tanneries; Upholstery & Mechanical Leather
S.I.C.: 3111
Anders Segerdahl *(Pres.)*
Charles D. Krull *(V.P. & Treas.)*
Harry L. Wallace *(Sec.)*

Outside Service Firm(s):

Price Waterhouse*(Auditors)*
1500 Bank One Plaza, 100 E. Wisconsin Ave.
Milwaukee, WI 53202

Continental Bank N. A.*(Major Banking Relationship)*
231 S. LaSalle St.
Chicago, IL 60697
Tel.: 312-828-2345
Tel.: 800-426-5754
Telex: 312-828-1783

Division:

Eagle-Ottawa Leather Co. **(1)**
200 N. Beechtree St.
Grand Haven, MI 49417
Tel.: 616-842-4000
Leather Tanning
S.I.C.: 3111
Anders Segerdahl *(Pres.)*

Subsidiary:

Albert Trostel Packings Ltd. **(1)**
901 Maxwell St.
Lake Geneva, WI 53147
Tel.: 414-248-4481
Approx.Sls.: $27,000,000
Emp.: 350
Gaskets Packing & Sealing Devices; Packing Rubber; Mechanical Rubber Goods; Synthetic Rubber
S.I.C.: 3053; 3061; 2822
Everett G. Smith *(Chm. Bd.)*
Robert Gamache *(Pres.)*

TROUT INC.
Chelan Falls Rd.
Chelan, WA 98816
Mailing Address:
P.O. Box 669
Chelan, WA 98816
Tel.: 509-682-2591
Fax: 509-682-2651
Approx.Sls.: $30,000,000
Emp.: 200
Export
Packers & Shippers of Export Apples
S.I.C.: 0175; 5148
Al Marclar *(Pres.)*
Larry T. Lundberg *(Gen. Mgr. & Sec.)*
Richard Easley *(Mgr.-Sls.)*

Outside Service Firm(s):

Latreel & Co.*(Auditors)*
Wenatchee, WA

Central Washington Bank*(Major Banking Relationship)*
Chelan, WA

TROY CORPORATION
72 Eagle Rock Ave.
East Hanover, NJ 07936
Mailing Address:
P.O. Box 366
East Hanover, NJ 07936-0366
Tel.: 201-884-4300
Fax: 201-884-4317
Year Founded: 1950
Approx.Sls.: $50,000,000
Emp.: 175
Import Export
Mfr. Industrial Fungicides, Bactericides, Specialty Chemicals for Paints, Inks, Adhesives, Caulks, Sealants
S.I.C.: 2851; 2879
Daryl D. Smith *(Pres. & Chief Exec. Officer)*
Thomas V. Gilboy *(Chief Fin. Officer & V.P.-Fin.)*
Dr. Rudi Moerck *(V.P.-Mktg. & Sls.)*
William Rudlof *(V.P.-Opers.)*
William Singer *(V.P.-Res. & Devel.)*
Scott Gonge *(Sec.)*
Bernard Papa *(Controller)*
Al M. Gerardo *(Dir.-Personnel)*
Bill Hughs *(Dir.-Pur.)*
Tim Savage *(Mgr.-Natl. Sls.)*
Robert Zussman *(Mgr.-Quality Control)*

Computer Systems/Hardware:
IBM-AS 400

Outside Service Firm(s):

Lowenstein, Sandler, Kohl, Fisher & Boylan*(Legal Firm)*
744 Broad St.
Newark, NJ 07102
Tel.: 201-624-4600

First National Bank of Boston*(Major Banking Relationship)*
P.O. Box 644,
Boston, MA 02102-0644
Tel.: 617-575-2900
Fax: 617-575-2549

TROY

TROY MILLS, INC.
18 Monadnock St.
Troy, NH 03465
Tel.: 603-242-7711
Tel.: 800-362-7289
Telex: 710 364-1692
Fax: 603-242-3026
Year Founded: 1865
Approx.Sls.: $40,000,000
Emp.: 500
Fiscal Year-end: 10/31/92
Export
Mfr. of Automotive Interior Fabrics, Industrial Filtration Media, Nonwoven Fabrics, Apparel Fabrics, Acoustical Wall Covering Fabrics
S.I.C.: 2299; 2297; 3089
F. Fuller Ripley *(Chm. Bd.)*
Barrett F. Ripley *(Pres. & Chief Exec. Officer)*
Martin Ballen *(V.P.-Auto Sls.)*
Frank H. Hodgman III *(V.P. & Treas.)*
Robert A. Parsons *(V.P.-Res. & Devel.)*
Brent E. Ruediger *(V.P.-Mktg.)*
James A. Cuddy *(Dir.-Mfg.)*
Ken A. Smith *(Dir.-Material Control)*
Joanne Moose *(Mgr.-Adv.)*
Donald Parpan *(Mgr.-Human Resources)*

Computer Systems/Hardware:
IBM

Outside Service Firm(s):

Coopers & Lybrand*(Auditors)*
1 Post Office Square
Boston, MA 02110
Tel.: 617-574-5000
Fax: 617-345-0398

Goodnow, Arwe, Ayer, Prigge & Wrigley*(Legal Firm)*
Boston, MA

Bank of New England*(Major Banking Relationship)*
28 State Street
Boston, MA 02109
Tel.: 617-742-4000

Division:

Troy Mills, Inc. **(1)**
625 N. Pennsylvania Ave.
Harrisville, WV 26362
Tel.: 304-643-2972
Fax: 304-643-2149
Export
Trunk Padding for Cars
S.I.C.: 2396
Dick Bruerton *(Gen. Mgr.)*
Richard A. Kerns *(Plant Mgr.)*

THE TROY SAVINGS BANK
Second & State
Troy, NY 12180
Tel.: 518-270-3200
Year Founded: 1823
Approx.Sls.: $560,000,000
Emp.: 200
Fiscal Year-end: 12/31/91
Checking, Savings Accounts, Loans, Mortgages, Certificates, of Deposit Life Insurance, Investments, Commercial Loans
S.I.C.: 6035
Daniel J. Hogarty Jr. *(Pres. & Chief Exec. Officer)*
Ronald E. Campbell *(Sr. V.P.)*
William L. Kneissl *(Sr. V.P., Sec. & Treas.)*
Kevin M. O'Bryan *(Sr. V.P.)*
Harry J. Robinson *(Sr. V.P.)*
William J. Biggins *(V.P. & Dir.-Life Insurance Products)*

Allan J. Costello *(V.P.-Auditor)*
Peter D. Cureau *(V.P. & Dir.-Commercial Mortgage Lending)*
Gary L. Ebeltoft *(V.P. & Dir.-Plng.)*
Nedwin Emerson *(V.P. & Dir.-Adv. & Pub. Rels.)*
Pamela J. Hayner *(V.P. & Dir. Residential Mortgage Lending)*
Peter C. Knapp *(V.P. & Dir.-Human Resources)*
Michael C. Mahar *(V.P. & Dir.-Commercial Lending)*
Tracey A. McKeough-Olender *(V.P. & Dir.-Branch Admin. & Training & Education)*
Paul R. Vergoni *(V.P. & Dir.-Branch Oper.)*
Jane K. Cordts *(V.P.-Data Processing)*
Edward M. Maziejka Jr. *(V.P.-Fin. Admin.)*
Michael R. Lyons *(Dir.-Fin. Plng.)*
Margaret C. Fitzgerald *(Human Resource Opers. Mgr.)*

Divisions:

Troy Savings Bank **(1)**
Broadway & 16th St.
Watervliet, NY 12189
Tel.: 518-274-1402

Troy Savings Bank-Clifton Park **(1)**
Rtes. 9 & 146
Clifton Park, NY 12065
Tel.: 518-371-2330

Troy Savings Bank-East Greenbush **(1)**
615 Columbia Tpke.
East Greenbush, NY 12061
Tel.: 518-477-7911

Troy Savings Bank-Glens Falls **(1)**
Aviation Mall
Glens Falls, NY 12801
Tel.: 518-798-3333

Troy Savings Bank-Hudson Valley Plaza **(1)**
Vandenburgh Ave.
Troy, NY 12180
Tel.: 518-272-0032

Troy Savings Bank-Latham **(1)**
Troy-Schenectady Rd. & Sunset Dr.
Latham, NY 12110
Tel.: 518-783-9586

Troy Savings Bank-Schenectady **(1)**
1626 Union St.
Schenectady, NY 12309
Tel.: 518-346-0402

Troy Savings Bank-Whitehall **(1)**
184 Broadway
Whitehall, NY 12887
Tel.: 518-499-2200

Subsidiaries:

TS Capital Corp. **(1)**
Second & State
Troy, NY 12180
Tel.: 518-270-3200
A Corporation Created to Provide Equity in Real Estate Projects

The Family Insurance Agency, Inc. **(1)**
Second & State
Troy, NY 12180
Tel.: 518-270-3200
Life Insurance Products & Annuities

The Family Investment Services Co., Inc. **(1)**
Second & State
Troy, NY 12180
Tel.: 518-270-3200
Brokerage & Investment Advice

The Family Mortgage Banking Co., Inc. **(1)**
Second & State
Troy, NY 12180
Tel.: 518-270-3200
Residential Mortgages

Troy SB Real Estate Co., Inc. **(1)**
Second & State
Troy, NY 12180
Tel.: 518-270-3200
Real Estate, Special Projects & Commercial Loan Brokerage

TRU-FIT PRODUCTS CORP.
460 Lake Rd.
Medina, OH 44256
Mailing Address:
P.O. Box 702
Medina, OH 44258
Tel.: 216-725-7741
Fax: 216-725-0161
Year Founded: 1928
Approx.Sls.: $10,000,000
Emp.: 175
Mfr. Special Cold Headed Fasteners & Bolts, Weld Studs & Equipment
S.I.C.: 3452; 3548
C.E. Workman *(Chm. Bd. & Chief Exec. Officer)*
R.E. Workman *(Pres.)*
R.L. Law *(V.P.-Sls.)*
Steve Kern *(Dir.-Data Processing)*
Principal(s):
C.E. Workman
R.E. Workman

Outside Service Firm(s):

Norman, Jones, Enlow & Co.*(Auditors)*
Lancaster, OH

The Old Phoenix National Bank*(Major Banking Relationship)*
Medina, OH

TRU-WELD GRATING, INC.
2000 Corporate Dr.
Wexford, PA 15090
Mailing Address:
P.O. Box 1238
Wexford, PA 15090
Tel.: 412-934-5320
Fax: 412-934-5348
Year Founded: 1983
Sales Range: $10-19 Million
Emp.: 130
Import Export
Mfr. Steel Grating
S.I.C.: 3312; 3446
Martin M. Shaffer *(Pres.)*
Donald L. Firestone *(V.P. & Treas.)*
Robert J. Roth *(V.P. & Sec.)*
M. Todd Shaffer *(Dir.-Pur. & Mfg. Services)*
Michele Paulos *(Dir.-Human Resources)*

No. of Mfg. Plants/Facilities: 2

Outside Service Firm(s):

Hill, Barth & King*(Auditors)*
Wexford, PA

Goehring, Rutter & Boehm*(Legal Firm)*
Pittsburgh, PA

TRUCCHIS MARKETS
1062 Broadway
Raynham, MA 02767
Tel.: 508-824-7515
Fax: 508-824-7576
Year Founded: 1928
Approx.Sls.: $30,000,000
Emp.: 400
Fiscal Year-end: 12/31/88
Wholesale Food Stores; Owner Retail Supermarkets
S.I.C.: 5411; 5141
David Truchi *(Pres. & Chief Exec. Officer)*
James Truchi *(Chief Fin. Officer, Treas. & Controller)*
William Truchi *(V.P.)*

Computer Systems/Hardware:
IBM 5251

Outside Service Firm(s):

Blue Cross of Massachusetts, Inc.*(Group Insurer)*
Boston, MA

Bank Of New England South*(Major Banking Relationship)*
Brockton, MA

TRUCK WORLD INC.
1610 Thomas Rd.
Hubbard, OH 44425
Mailing Address:
P.O. Box 248,
Hubbard, OH 44425
Tel.: 216-448-2210
Fax: 216-448-4241
Approx.Sls.: $136,000,000
Emp.: 105
Wholesale Gasoline, Fuel Oils, Lubricants & Bulk Petroleum Products; Full Service Truck Stop
S.I.C.: 5171; 5172; 5541
J. Gary Burke *(Pres.)*
Robert E. Israel *(Exec. V.P.)*
Jeffrey Patterson *(Controller)*

Outside Service Firm(s):

Cohen & Associates*(Auditors)*
Washington, DC

Mahoning National Bank*(Major Banking Relationship)*
Youngstown, OH

TRUE COMPANIES
895 W. River Cross Rd.
Casper, WY 82602
Mailing Address:
P.O. Drawer 2360
Casper, WY 82602
Tel.: 307-237-9301
Telex: 318-042
Fax: 307-266-0252
Year Founded: 1948
Sales Range: $100-499 Million
Emp.: 500
Oil & Gas Extraction & Distribution; Trucking & Warehousing; Oil Pipelines
S.I.C.: 1311; 4212; 4213; 4226; 5172; 4612; 4613
H.A. True, Jr. *(Pres. & Chief Exec. Officer)*
Dwain S. Park *(Controller)*
L. Stanley Lowe *(Gen. Counsel)*
Ron Severson *(Dir.-Personnel)*
A.K. Martin *(Mgr.-Credit)*
Principal(s):
H.A. True, Jr.

Computer Systems/Hardware:
HP 3000

Outside Service Firm(s):

McGladrey & Pullen*(Auditors)*
Casper, WY

Blue Cross & Blue Shield of Wyoming*(Group Insurer)*
Cheyenne, WY

Standard Life Insurance Co.*(Group Insurer)*
Portland, OR

Hilltop National Bank*(Major Banking Relationship)*
Casper, WY

Subsidiaries:

Belle Fourche Pipeline Co. **(1)**
895 W. River Cross Rd.
Casper, WY 82602
Tel.: 307-237-9301
S.I.C.: 4612; 4613

Black Hills Trucking Co. **(1)**
895 W. River Cross Rd.
Casper, WY 82602
Tel.: 307-237-9301
S.I.C.: 4212; 4213

Eighty Eight Oil Co. **(1)**
895 W. River Cross Rd.
Casper, WY 82602
Tel.: 307-237-9301

True Drilling Co. **(1)**
P.O. Box 2360
Casper, WY 82602
S.I.C.: 1311

True Oil Co. **(1)**
895 W. River Cross Rd.
Casper, WY 82602
Tel.: 307-273-9301
S.I.C.: 1311

True Ranches **(1)**
895 W. River Cross Rd.
Casper, WY 82602
Tel.: 307-273-9301

TRUMBULL CORPORATION
1020 Lebanon Rd.
West Mifflin, PA 15122
Mailing Address:
P.O. Box 98100,
Pittsburgh, PA 15227
Tel.: 412-462-9300
Fax: 412-462-2588
Approx.Sls.: $72,000,000
Emp.: 112
Heavy Construction Contractors
S.I.C.: 1629; 1794; 2951; 2952
Louise H. Dick *(Chm. Bd.)*
Michael J. Rago *(Pres.)*
Robert Hecht *(Chief Exec. Officer)*
Steven Clark *(Exec. V.P.-Fin.)*
Clifford R. Rowe *(Exec. V.P.)*
Chuck Pryor *(Dir.-Bus. Devel.)*
Diane Check *(Mgr.-Data Processing)*

Computer Systems/Hardware:
IBM PC

Outside Service Firm(s):

McCrory & McDowell*(Auditors)*
Pittsburgh, PA

Liberty Mutual*(Commercial Insurance Carrier)*
Boston, MA

Guardian Life Insurance Co.*(Group Insurer)*
New York, NY

Buchanan, Ingersoll p.c.*(Legal Firm)*
600 Grant St., 57th Flr.
Pittsburgh, PA 15219
Tel.: 412-562-8800

Subsidiary:

Trumbull Investments, Inc. **(1)**
P.O. Box 98100
Pittsburgh, PA 15227
Tel.: 412-462-9300

THE TRUMP GROUP
767 Fifth Ave., 50th Fl.
New York, NY 10153
Tel.: 212-838-1000 **DE**
Fax: 212-759-4708
Sales Range: $1 Billion +
Emp.: 10,000
Holding Co.; Real Estate
S.I.C.: 6719; 6512; 6513; 6552
Julius Trump *(Chm. Bd. & Chief Exec. Officer)*
Eddie Trump *(Pres.)*
James Bazlen *(Sr. V.P.-Mergers & Acquisitions)*
James Lieb *(Sr. V.P.)*
Principal(s):
Julius Trump
Eddie Trump

The Trump Group—(Continued)

Computer Systems/Hardware:
IBM PC; AT&T PC; Apple Macintosh PC

Subsidiary:

Northern Pacific Corporation **(1)**
767 Fifth Ave.
New York, NY 10153
Tel.: 212-838-1000 (100%)
Auto & Home Supply Stores
S.I.C.: 5531
Julius Trump *(Chm.)*
Eddie Trump *(Pres.)*

Division:

Northern Automotive Corporation **(2)**
645 E. Missouri
Phoenix, AZ 85012
Tel.: 602-265-9200
Fax: 602-234-0936
Emp.: 10,000
Import
Computer Systems/Hardware:
IBM AS/400
Automotive Supplies
S.I.C.: 5013; 5531
Julius Trump *(Chm. Bd.)*
James Bazlen *(Vice Chm.)*
Art Hicks *(Exec. V.P.)*
Bill Stapleton *(Sr. V.P.-Mngmt. Information Systems)*
Beric Christiansen *(Sr. V.P.-Distr. & Real Estate)*
Dave LaBau *(V.P.-Legal)*
Don Watson *(Controller)*

TRUMP ORGANIZATION
725 Fifth Ave.
New York, NY 10022
Tel.: 212-832-2000
Real Estate Holding Company
S.I.C.: 6552; 6512; 7011
Donald J. Trump *(Pres.)*
Harry Geruldsen *(V.P., Pur.-Real Estate)*
Janine Repa *(Dir.-Pub. Rels.)*

Operations:

Trump's Castle Casino Resort **(1)**
Huron Ave. & Brigantine Blvd.
Atlantic City, NJ 08401
Tel.: 609-441-2000
Tel.: 800-777-1177
Fax: 609-345-2021
Emp.: 3,300
Gaming Casino & Resort
S.I.C.: 7999
Roger P. Wagner *(Pres. & Chief Oper. Officer)*
William Dayton *(Sr. V.P.-Mktg.)*
Barry Cregan *(V.P.-Hotel Opers.)*
Jeanine Repa *(Exec. Dir.-Adv. & Pub. Rels.)*

Trump Plaza of the Palm Beaches **(1)**
525 S. Flagler Dr.
West Palm Beach, FL 33401
Tel.: 407-655-2555
Condominium Residences, Penthouses & Grand Penthouses
S.I.C.: 6513

The USAir Shuttle **(1)**
75-20 Astoria Blvd.
Jackson Heights, NY 11370
Tel.: 718-397-6000
Tel.: 800-247-8786
Fax: 718-397-6020
Emp.: 1,000
Scheduled Shuttle Airline Service Between Boston, New York & Washington, DC
S.I.C.: 4512
Donald J. Trump *(Chm. Bd.)*
Terry Hallcom *(Pres.)*
Robert L. Sharak *(Dir.-Mktg.)*
Randall Smith *(Dir.-Sls.)*
Amy E.B. Fisher *(Dir.-Adv. & Res.)*
Dave Shippley *(Pub. Rels.)*

Trump Towers **(1)**
725 Fifth Ave.
New York, NY 10022
Tel.: 212-832-2929
Residential Properties
S.I.C.: 6512; 6513

TRUMPF INC.
Hyde Rd., Farmington Industrial Park
Farmington, CT 06032 **CT**
Tel.: 203-677-9741
Fax: 203-678-1704
Year Founded: 1967
Approx.Sls.: $50,000,000
Emp.: 210
Fiscal Year-end: 6/30/91
Export
Wholesale Metalworking Machinery
S.I.C.: 5084
Berthold Leibinger *(Chm. Bd.)*
Daniel Dechamps *(Pres. & Treas.)*
James Bento *(Exec. V.P.)*
Rainer Hundsdorfer *(V.P.-Mktg. & Sls.)*
David B. Murray *(Dir.-Adv.)*
John Radziewicz *(Dir.-Pur.)*

TRUNK & ASSOCIATES, INC.
98 Park St.
Montclair, NJ 07042
Tel.: 201-746-8400
Fax: 201-746-1367
Year Founded: 1983
Approx.Billings: $10,000,000
Emp.: 16
Healthcare Adv.
de Paul Trunk *(Pres.)*
Kevin Collins *(Dir., Fin. & Admin.)*
Anita Shum *(Studio Mgr.)*

TUBULAR STEEL INC.
1031 Executive Pkwy.
Saint Louis, MO 63141
Tel.: 314-851-9200
Fax: 314-851-9336
Year Founded: 1953
Approx.Sls.: $125,000,000
Emp.: 300
Steel Distribution
S.I.C.: 5051
John M. Hauck *(Chm. Bd.)*
John C. Hauck *(Pres.)*
Al J. Rakers *(Sr. V.P.)*
Duane Boyce *(V.P.)*
T.L. Erwin *(V.P.-Opers.)*
Hugh C. McLaughlin *(V.P.-Sls.)*
James A. Morgan *(V.P.-Fin. & Sec.)*
Stan Mueller *(Dir.-Data Processing)*

No. of Mfg. Plants/Facilities: 4
No. of U.S. Offices: 5
No. of Foreign Offices: 3

Outside Service Firm(s):

Ernst & Young*(Auditors)*
701 Market St.
St. Louis, MO 63101
Tel.: 314-259-1000

Greensfelder, Hemker and Gale, P.C.*(Legal Firm)*
1800 Equitable Bldg., 10 S. Broadway
St. Louis, MO 63102
Tel.: 314-241-9090

Boatmen's Trust Company*(Major Banking Relationship)*
100 North Broadway
St. Louis, MO 63102
Tel.: 314-466-2469

TUCKER ROCKY DISTRIBUTING
2424 N.E. Riverside Way
Portland, OR 97211
Tel.: 503-288-6621
Approx.Sls.: $18,000,000
Emp.: 100
Distributor of Motorcycle Parts & Accessories
S.I.C.: 3751
Karl Frank *(Gen. Mgr.)*

TUCKER WAYNE/LUCKIE & COMPANY
600 Luckie Dr.
Birmingham, AL 35223
Tel.: 205-879-2121
Fax: 205-877-9729
Year Founded: 1922
Approx.Billings: $150,000,000
Emp.: 207
Advertising Agency
S.I.C.: 7311
Robert E. Luckie, Jr. *(Chm. Bd.)*
Matthew Connor *(Chm.-Exec. Committee)*
Frank M. Lee *(Vice Chm.)*
C. Knox Massey, Jr. *(Pres.)*
H. Thomas Fuller *(Chief Fin. Officer & Sr. V.P.)*
Sidney L. Smith *(Exec. V.P. & Pres.-Atlanta)*

Branches:

Tucker Wayne/Luckie & Company **(1)**
1100 Peachtree St., NE, Ste. 1800
Atlanta, GA 30309
Tel.: 404-347-8700
Fax: 404-347-8800
Approx.Billings: $150,000,000
Sidney L. Smith *(Pres.)*
William H. Zuspan *(Sr. V.P., Media & Info. Research)*
Edwin N. Hinckley *(Sr. V.P.)*
Mark Kirkpatrick *(Sr. V.P.)*
A. Carlton Malcolm, Jr. *(Sr. V.P.)*
Richard McReynolds *(Sr. V.P.)*
James S. Reeder, Jr. *(Sr. V.P.)*
Mike Butler *(V.P.)*
Charles Cooper *(V.P.)*
Sylvan L. Harris *(V.P.)*
Carroll T. Harris *(V.P.)*
Mike Kane *(V.P.)*
Tom Luckie *(V.P.)*
Earl McNulty *(V.P.)*
Karen Stephens *(V.P.)*
John L. Wheeler *(V.P.)*
Markay Wiley *(V.P.)*
Ken Yarbrough *(V.P.)*
Ann Lally *(V.P., Communications)*
Elizabeth Shanklin *(V.P., Bus. Devel.)*
Angela Cooper *(Mgr., Data Processing)*
Dora VanRy *(Mgr., Office Services)*
Cathy Richards *(Controller)*

Tucker Wayne/Luckie & Company **(1)**
600 Luckie Dr.
Birmingham, AL 35223
Tel.: 205-879-2121
Fax: 205-877-9729
Frank M. Lee *(Pres.)*
Bob Luckie, III *(Sr. V.P.)*
Mike Murphy *(Sr. V.P.)*
Jim Andrews *(Sr. V.P., Opers.)*
Laura Doumont *(V.P.)*
Ronnie Grillo *(V.P.)*
Ed Mizzell *(V.P.)*
Jane Mantooth *(Dir., Fin. & Office Services)*
Ken Morgan *(Dir., Mktg. & Research)*

TUCKERMAN OPTICAL CO.
64 E. Broad St.
Columbus, OH 43215
Tel.: 614-221-0515
Year Founded: 1972
Sales Range: $10-19 Million
Emp.: 275
Retail Optical Stores
S.I.C.: 5995
Dr. Steven A. Tuckerman *(Pres.)*
Peg Emptage *(V.P.-Opers.)*
Howard Task *(V.P.-Adv.)*
Gary Peters *(Controller)*

Principal(s):
Dr. Steven A. Tuckerman

Computer Systems/Hardware:
Lanier Word Processor

Outside Service Firm(s):

Coopers & Lybrand*(Auditors)*
100 E. Broad St.
Columbus, OH 43215

Pilot Life*(Group Insurer)*
Greensboro, NC

Banc One*(Major Banking Relationship)*
Columbus, OH

The Optical Shops **(1)**
64 E. Broad St.
Columbus, OH 43215
Tel.: 614-221-0515

Divisions:

Le Cirque Optique **(1)**
649 Broad St.
Columbus, OH 43215
Tel.: 614-221-0515

TUCSON REALTY & TRUST CO.
1890 E. River Rd.
Tucson, AZ 85718
Tel.: 602-577-7000 **AZ**
Fax: 602-577-5571
Year Founded: 1911
Approx.Sls.: $350,000,000
Emp.: 350
Fiscal Year-end: 12/31/90
Property Management, Relocation Residential & Commercial Real Estate
S.I.C.: 6531
George H. Amos, Jr. *(Chm. Bd.)*
George H. Amos III *(Pres.)*
Mike Ashurst *(Sr. V.P.-Comml. Div. Head)*
Dan McEvoy *(Sr. V.P.-Residental)*
Martin O'Shea *(Sr. V.P.-Fin.)*
Dick Anderson *(V.P.-Property Mngmt.)*
Pamela J. Price *(V.P. & Sec.)*
John Riley *(V.P.)*
John Durso *(Dir.-Recruiting & Training)*
Principal(s):
Amos Trust

No. of U.S. Offices: 6

Computer Systems/Hardware:
Wang; IBM PC

Outside Service Firm(s):

Coopers & Lybrand*(Auditors)*
Tucson, AZ

Royal Insurance Co.*(Commercial Insurance Carrier)*
New York, NY

Royal Insurance Co.*(Group Insurer)*
New York, NY

Waterfall, Economidis, Hanshaw & Villamana*(Legal Firm)*
Tucson, AZ

Security Pacific Bank Arizona*(Major Banking Relationship)*
Tucson, AZ

Subsidiary:

Preferred Properties **(1)**
1890 E. River Rd.
Tucson, AZ 85718

TUDOR INC.
P.O. Box 7917
Alexandria, LA 71306
Approx.Sls.: $20,000,000
Emp.: 300
Commercial & Industrial Construction
S.I.C.: 1541; 1542
Robert B. Tudor, Jr. *(Pres.)*
Bill J. Johnson *(V.P.)*
John M. Tudor *(V.P.)*
Michael S. Tudor *(Sec. & Gen. Counsel)*

Principal(s):
Robert B. Tudor, Jr.
Michael S. Tudor

Computer Systems/Hardware:
IBM Compatibles

Outside Service Firm(s):

Adler & Pias *(Auditors)*
Alexandria, LA

Premier Bank *(Major Banking Relationship)*
P.O. Box 1511
Baton Rouge, LA 70821

TUFFY ASSOCIATES CORP.
1414 Baronial Plaza Dr.
Toledo, OH 43615
Tel.: 419-865-6900
Fax: 419-865-7343
Year Founded: 1972
Approx.Sls.: $45,000,000
Emp.: 25
Fiscal Year-end: 12/31/90
Quality Under Car Service Franchisor Exhaust, Brakes, Suspension, Front End
S.I.C.: 7533
Roger Slotkin *(Chm. Bd.)*
Keenan Moran *(Pres.)*
Jon Strole *(Accountant)*
Robert Bresler *(Dir.-Real Estate)*
Bill Claus *(Dir.-Oper. & Training)*
Mike Koontz *(Dir.-Mktg. & Adv.)*

TULIP CORPORATION
3211 E. 26th St.
Los Angeles, CA 90023
Tel.: 213-263-9001 **CA**
Fax: 213-261-42281
Year Founded: 1974
Approx.Sls.: $73,000,000
Emp.: 850
Export
Mfr. of Plastic Containers, Except Foam; Injection Molded Finished Plastic Products; Presses; Hydraulic & Pneumatic, Mechanical & Manual
S.I.C.: 3089; 3542
Fred Teshinsky *(Pres.)*
Don Uchiyama *(Exec. V.P. & Sec.)*
Al Schmidt *(V.P.-Mktg. & Sls.)*

Divisions:

P.H.I. Division **(1)**
14955 E. Salt Lake Ave.
City of Industry, CA 91746
Tel.: 818-968-9686
Emp.: 100
Fred Teshinsky *(Plant Mgr.)*

Tulip Corp., Milwaukee Div. **(1)**
714 E. Keefe Ave.
Milwaukee, WI 53215
Tel.: 414-445-5555
Mfr. of Plastic Products
S.I.C.: 3089
Neal Wills *(Plant Mgr.)*

Tulip Corp., Niagara Falls Div. **(1)**
3125 Highland Ave.
Niagara Falls, NY 14305
Tel.: 716-282-1261
Mfr. of Custom Injection Molded Plastics
S.I.C.: 3083
John Signare *(Plant Mgr.)*

TULLEY BUICK-PONTIAC COMPANY, INC.
147 Daniel Webster Hwy. S
Nashua, NH 03061
Tel.: 603-888-0550
Fax: 603-888-5040
Year Founded: 1957
Approx.Sls.: $55,000,000
Emp.: 141
Retail New & Used Automobiles & Trucks
S.I.C.: 5511
Vincent F. Tulley *(Chm. Bd.)*
John E. Tulley *(Pres.)*
Mark M. Tulley *(Treas.)*

Outside Service Firm(s):

Downey & Co. *(Auditors)*
Braintree, MA

Hamblett & Kerrigan *(Legal Firm)*
Nashua, NH

First NH Bank, N.A. *(Major Banking Relationship)*
Manchester, NH

TUNMORE OLDSMOBILE INC.
2677 Delaware Ave.
Buffalo, NY 14216
Tel.: 716-877-1500 **NY**
Fax: 716-877-9603
Year Founded: 1923
Approx.Sls.: $18,000,000
Emp.: 72
Automobile Dealership
S.I.C.: 5511
Edward E. Tunmore *(Chm. Bd. & Treas.)*
E. Roger Tunmore *(Pres. & Sec.)*
Anthony Otaviano *(Dir.-Sls.)*
William Schlau *(Dir.-Data Processing)*

Outside Service Firm(s):

Gould & Swanson *(Auditors)*
Buffalo, NY

Myron Siegel *(Legal Firm)*
Kenmore, NY

Manufacturers & Traders Trust Company *(Major Banking Relationship)*
1 M & T Plaza
Buffalo, NY 14240
Tel.: 716-842-4200

TUPMAN THURLOW CO. INC.
Cedar Plaza, 20 Cedar St.
New Rochelle, NY 10801
Tel.: 914-633-0777 **NY**
Fax: 914-633-9876
Year Founded: 1915
Approx.Sls.: $250,000,000
Emp.: 50
Fiscal Year-end: 12/31/89
Import
Importer & Wholesaler of Food Products
S.I.C.: 5141; 5142
David J. Jackson *(Pres. & Chief Exec. Officer)*
Paul Blakeley *(V.P.-Fin.)*
Dennis McGee *(Sec.)*
Robert Bucci *(Controller)*

No. of U.S. Offices: 3

Computer Systems/Hardware:
IBM System 36

Outside Service Firm(s):

KPMG Peat Marwick *(Auditors)*
345 Park Ave.
New York, NY 10154
Tel.: 212-758-9700
Fax: 212-872-3308

Connecticut General Life Insurance Co. *(Group Insurer)*
P.O. Box 2975,
Hartford, CT 06104
Tel.: 203-726-6000

Cadwalader Wickersham & Taft *(Legal Firm)*
100 Maiden Lane
New York, NY 10038
Tel.: 212-504-6000

Brown Brothers, Harriman & Co. *(Major Banking Relationship)*
59 Wall St.
New York, NY 10005-2818
Tel.: 212-493-8029

National Westminster Bank plc *(Major Banking Relationship)*
Astor Plaza, 1515 Broadway
New York, NY 10036

Massachusetts Mutual Life Insurance Co. *(Pension Manager)*
1295 State Street
Springfield, MA 01111
Tel.: 413-788-8411

Turf Irrigation & Water Works Supply
(Name Changed To Flori Corp., d/b/a Turf Irrigation & Water Works Supply)

TURNBULL ENTERPRISES, INC.
3635 Benson Ave.
Baltimore, MD 21227
Tel.: 410-644-8282
Fax: 301-644-0439
Approx.Sls.: $10,000,000
Emp.: 155
Export
Shipboard Furniture For U.S. Navy, Coast Guard & Maritime Services
S.I.C.: 2599
Louis S. Esposito *(Pres.)*
Melvin E. Roloff *(Gen. Mgr.)*
Wayne Bienvenu *(Sec.)*
Lance Bobroski *(Pur. Agent)*
Jerome Henry Fuller *(Shop Mgr.)*

Outside Service Firm(s):

Leonard J. Miller *(Auditors)*
Baltimore, MD

Whiteford, Taylor & Preston *(Legal Firm)*
Baltimore, MD

Maryland National Bank *(Major Banking Relationship)*
10 Light St.
Baltimore, MD 21203
Tel.: 410-244-5000

TURNER DAIRIES, INC.
653 Dairy Lane
Covington, TN 38019
Tel.: 901-476-2643
Fax: 901-476-2761
Approx.Sls.: $75,000,000
Emp.: 415
Mfr. Wholesale & Retail Milk, Cottage Cheese, Sour Cream, Ice Cream & Ice Cream Novelties
S.I.C.: 2024; 2026; 5143; 5451
Peter Alexander Turner *(Pres.)*
Steve Turner *(V.P.-Mktg. & Adv.)*
Darrell Rogers *(Treas. & Sec.)*
Ed Fleming *(Dir.-Sls.)*
Judy Wilson *(Dir.-Personnel)*
Bob Burrack *(Mgr.-Plant)*

Outside Service Firm(s):

DelBrocco & Associates *(Auditors)*
Memphis, TN

G. Michael Acree Law Firm *(Legal Firm)*
Covington, TN

First Tennessee Bank, N.A. *(Major Banking Relationship)*
P.O. Box 101
Memphis, TN 38101
Tel.: 901-523-4555

Subsidiary:

Forest Hill Dairy **(1)**
2040 Maidson Ave.
Memphis, TN 38174
Tel.: 901-272-5200
Dairy
S.I.C.: 0241
Dave Simmler *(Plant Mgr.)*

THE TURNER & SEYMOUR MFG. COMPANY
100 Lawton St.
Torrington, CT 06790
Mailing Address:
P.O. Box 358,
Torrington, CT 06790
Tel.: 203-489-9214 **CT**
Fax: 203-482-3197
Year Founded: 1848
Approx.Sls.: $20,000,000
Emp.: 175
Fiscal Year-end: 12/31/90
Export
Manufacture Chains, Upholstery Nails & Tacks, Furniture Glides, Iron Castings
S.I.C.: 3315; 3495; 3321; 2514
Allen M. Sperry *(Chm. Bd.)*
Thomas Pretak *(Pres.)*
Kenneth A. Rizzi *(Controller)*
Frank Silano *(Gen. Mgr.)*
George Binette *(Mgr.-Prod.)*
Carol Soliani *(Mgr.-Personnel)*

No. of Mfg. Plants/Facilities: 3
No. of U.S. Offices: 1
No. of Foreign Offices: 2

Computer Systems/Hardware:
IBM System 36

Outside Service Firm(s):

Ernst & Young *(Auditors)*
Goodwyn Sq., 225 Asylum St.
Hartford, CT 06103
Tel.: 203-247-3100

Bank of Boston *(Major Banking Relationship)*
81 W. Main St.
Waterbury, CT 06702
Tel.: 203-574-7000

TURNER SUPPLY COMPANY
250 N. Royal St.
Mobile, AL 36602
Tel.: 205-438-5581 **AL**
Fax: 205-432-3216
Year Founded: 1968
Approx.Sls.: $15,000,000
Emp.: 100
Wholesale Distributor of Industrial Machine Parts & Electrical Supplies
S.I.C.: 5084; 5063
Howard M. Schramm, Jr. *(Chm. Bd. & Pres.)*
Hoyt R. Foster *(V.P.)*
Bruce M. Reagan *(V.P.)*
Lloyd J. Keuler *(Treas. & Sec.)*

Outside Service Firm(s):

Ernst & Young *(Auditors)*
1200 1st National
Mobile, AL 36652
Tel.: 205-438-6158

AmSouth Bank, N.A. *(Major Banking Relationship)*
Mobile, AL

TURTLE & HUGHES, INC.
1900 Lower Rd.
Linden, NJ 07036
Tel.: 908-574-3600 **NJ**
Fax: 908-574-3723
Approx.Sls.: $86,000,000
Emp.: 160
Export
Wholesale Distributor of Electrical Supplies
S.I.C.: 5063
Suzanne T. Millard *(Chm. Bd. & Pres.)*
Frank W. Millard *(Exec. V.P.)*
Jack G. Sinagra *(Sr. V.P. & Asst. Treas.)*
Trevor N. Barnett *(V.P.-Fin.)*
Norman S. Blumenthal *(V.P.)*
Jack Justilian *(V.P.)*
Terry Miller *(V.P.)*
John E. Rothe *(V.P. & Sec.)*

Turtle & Hughes, Inc.—(Continued)

Charles H. Wright *(V.P.)*
Terence R. Wright *(V.P.)*
Principal(s):
Suzanne T. Millard

Outside Service Firm(s):

Arthur Andersen & Co.*(Auditors)*
P.O. Box 221, 101 Eisenhower Pkwy.
Roseland, NJ 07068
Tel.: 201-403-6100
Fax: 201-403-0579

Lowenstein, Sandler, Kohl, Fisher & Boylan*(Legal Firm)*
65 Livingston Ave.
Roseland, NJ 07068
Tel.: 908-992-8700

United Jersey Bank*(Major Banking Relationship)*
Roseland, NJ

Division:

Douglaston Electric **(1)**
P.O. Box 348, Rte. 303
West Nyack, NY 10994
Tel.: 914-358-6966
Fax: 914-358-6565
Wholesale Electrical Distributor
S.I.C.: 5063
Kevin Ensor *(Chief Oper. Officer)*

TURTLE WAX, INC.
5655 W. 73rd St.
Chicago, IL 60638
Tel.: 708-563-3600
Fax: 312-563-3833
Approx.Sls.: $115,000,000
Emp.: 325
Fiscal Year-end: 10/31/91
Export
Turtle Wax Car Care Products
S.I.C.: 2842; 2891; 2899
Sondra A. Healy *(Chm. Bd.)*
Denis J. Healy *(Pres.)*
Charles A. Tornabene *(Pres.-Consumer Prods. Div.)*
Harvey Kornhaber *(Grp. V.P.-Res. & Devel.)*
Matthew Broderick *(V.P.-Mktg.)*
Philip R. Donegan *(V.P.-Opers. & Gen. Mgr.-Indus. Prods. Div.)*
Thomas B. Walsh *(V.P. & Chief Fin. Officer)*
Raymond P. Kolodziej *(V.P.-Corp. Controller & Treas.)*
Randall D. Boitz *(Dir.-Pur.)*
Twyla Stephenson *(V.P.-Human Resources)*
Ed Kusek *(Dir.-Mktg.)*
John Dippel *(Mgr.-Mktg.-Household Prods.)*
Barbara Edwards *(Admin. Asst.-Consumer Prods. Div.)*
Principal(s):
Sondra A. Healy
Denis J. Healy

Computer Systems/Hardware:
IBM System 38

Outside Service Firm(s):

Arthur Andersen & Co.*(Auditors)*
33 W. Monroe St.
Chicago, IL 60603-4067
Tel.: 312-580-0033
Fax: 312-507-6748

Corroon & Black*(Commercial Insurance Carrier)*
Chicago, IL

Harris Trust & Savings Bank*(Major Banking Relationship)*
111 W. Monroe St.
Chicago, IL 60690
Tel.: 312-461-2265
Tel.: 800-858-0840

Non-U.S. Holding:

Turtle Wax Manufacturing Ltd. **(1)**
P.O. Box 102, Gillibrands Road
Skelmersdale, Lancs. WN8 9TX, United Kingdom
Tel.: 695-22161 (100%)
Dressings, Polishes, Cleaners
S.I.C.: 2842
Roy Line *(Gen. Mgr.)*

TURTLEDOVE CLEMENS, INC.
111 S.W. Front Ave.
Portland, OR 97204
Tel.: 503-226-3581
Fax: 503-273-4277
Year Founded: 1941
Approx.Billings: $11,000,000
Emp.: 25
Strategic Planning, Marketing, Adv. & Pub. Rels.
Jay Clemens *(Pres. & Chief Exec. Officer)*
Barbara Bratsberg *(V.P.)*

TUSCARORA YARNS INC.
8760 E. Franklin St.
Mount Pleasant, NC 28124
Tel.: 704-436-6527
Fax: 704-436-9461
Year Founded: 1899
Approx.Sls.: $60,000,000
Emp.: 900
Mfr. Acrylic, Polyester, Cotton & Rayon Yarns
S.I.C.: 2281
Martin B. Foil, Jr. *(Chm. Bd. & Chief Exec. Officer)*
Jim Fry *(Pres. & Chief Oper. Officer)*
Bill Flanary *(V.P.-Personnel)*
John Riddle *(V.P.-Sls.)*
Alan Hayes *(Sec.)*

Outside Service Firm(s):

Ernst & Young*(Auditors)*
1100 Independence Center
Charlotte, NC 28246
Tel.: 704-372-6300

NationsBank Carolinas*(Major Banking Relationship)*
One NCNB Plaza,
Charlotte, NC 28255
Tel.: 704-374-5000

TUTHILL CORPORATION
908 N. Elm St.
Hinsdale, IL 60521
Tel.: 708-655-2266 **DE**
Fax: 708-655-2297
Year Founded: 1927
Approx.Sls.: $129,000,000
Emp.: 1,120
Fiscal Year-end: 12/13/91
Export
Mfr. of Industrial Pumps & Blowers, Quick Connective Couplings, Control Linkage Components & Push-Pull Cables
S.I.C.: 3496; 3561; 3728; 3429; 3564; 3499; 3492
James G. Tuthill, Jr. *(Pres. & Chief Exec. Officer)*
Glen R. Ostdiek *(Sec. & Treas.)*
Garry D. Johnson *(Dir.-Data Processing)*

Outside Service Firm(s):

Deloitte & Touche*(Auditors)*
Two Prudential Plaza, 180 N. Stetson
Chicago, IL 60601
Tel.: 312-946-2039

Schiff, Hardin & Waite*(Legal Firm)*
7200 Sears Tower, 233 S. Wacker Dr.
Chicago, IL 60606
Tel.: 312-876-1000

Harris Trust & Savings Bank*(Major Banking Relationship)*
111 W. Monroe St.
Chicago, IL 60690
Tel.: 312-461-2265
Tel.: 800-858-0840

Divisions:

Cablecraft Inc. **(1)**
4401 S. Orchard St.
Tacoma, WA 98411
Tel.: 206-475-1080
Twx: 910-441-2625
Fax: 206-474-1623
Mfr. of Push-Pull Cable Assemblies, Manual Transmission Shift Systems, Levers & Related Cable Hardware
S.I.C.: 3496; 3714; 3728
K.K. Clarno *(Pres.)*

Fill-Rite Division **(1)**
4204 Ferguson Rd.
Fort Wayne, IN 46809
Tel.: 219-747-7524
Telex: 272915 TUTFR UR
Fax: 219-747-3159
Mfr. of Electric & Hand-Operated Gasoline Pumps, Meters & Electronic Fuel Control Systems
S.I.C.: 3586; 3829
George P. Jenkins *(Pres.)*
Ron Bullock *(V.P.-Mktg.)*
Hal Pawlowsky *(Mgr.-Engrng.)*

Hansen Coupling Division **(1)**
4050 W. 150th St.
Cleveland, OH 44135
Tel.: 216-252-3880
Fax: 216-252-1529
Mfr. of Quick Connective Fluid Line Couplings
S.I.C.: 3492
John Weston *(Pres.)*
Stanley Hunter *(V.P.-Mktg.)*

Hansen Plastics Division **(1)**
2050 Sunnydale Blvd.
Clearwater, FL 34625
Tel.: 813-446-8593
Fax: 813-446-8595
Mfr. of Injection Molded Plastics
S.I.C.: 3089
John Hartley *(Gen. Mgr.)*

Superior Linkage Division **(1)**
2110 Summit St.
New Haven, IN 46774
Tel.: 219-749-5105
Fax: 219-493-2387
Mfr. of Ball Joints, Mechanical Linkages & Spherical Rod End Ball Joints for Automotive, Agricultural, Industrial & Marine Use
S.I.C.: 3568; 3714
F.S. Galssini *(Pres.)*
Tom Shubat *(Mgr.-Mktg.)*
Tim O'Connell *(Mgr.-Engrng.)*

Tuthill Pump Company of California **(1)**
5143 Port Chicago Hwy.
Concord, CA 94520
Tel.: 415-676-8000
Telex: 753 639
Fax: 415-676-8151
Mfr. of Seal-Less Magnetically Coupled Gear Pumps
S.I.C.: 3561
D.S. Londahl *(Pres.)*

Tuthill Pump **(1)**
12500 S. Pulaski Rd.
Alsip, IL 60658
Tel.: 708-389-2500
Fax: 708-388-0869
Emp.: 200
Import Export
Mfr. of Rotary Pumps & Rotary Process Pumps, Quick Seal Test Plugs, Fill-Rite Hand Electric Gasoline Pumps
S.I.C.: 3561; 3586
H.H. Flock *(Pres.)*
T. Jeffery *(V.P.-Mfg.)*
M. Santori *(Mgr.-Mktg.)*
M. Mulcahy *(Mgr.-Engrng.)*

Subsidiaries:

J.J. Tourek Co. **(1)**
1800 Touhy Ave.
Elk Grove Village, IL 60007
Tel.: 708-640-1700
Mfr. of Mechanical Handling Equipment; Screw Machine Products & Ball Joints
S.I.C.: 3567; 3714; 3568; 3451
Peter J. Hoag *(Gen. Mgr.)*

MD Pneumatics, Inc. **(1)**
4840 W. Kearney
Springfield, MO 65803
Tel.: 417-865-8715 (100%)
Fax: 417-865-2950
Emp.: 100
Import Export
Mfr. of Positive Displacement Blowers & Vacuum Pumps
S.I.C.: 3564
Robert Gossman *(Pres.)*
James Ashcraft *(Comptroller)*
Carl R. Coles *(Mgr.-Mktg.)*
Michael Stone *(Mgr.-Engrng.)*
Carlos Neal *(Mgr.-Prod.)*

TUTOR-SALIBA CORPORATION
15901 Olden St.
Sylmar, CA 91342
Tel.: 818-362-8391 **CA**
Fax: 818-367-5379
Year Founded: 1973
Assets: $132,018,000
Liabilities: $96,053,000
Net Worth: $35,965,000
Approx.Sls.: $265,000,000
Emp.: 750
New Construction of Commercial & Office Buildings; Subway Construction
S.I.C.: 1542; 1629
Ronald N. Tutor *(Pres. & Chief Exec. Officer)*
Kenneth Burk *(Chief Fin. Officer & V.P.)*
Naseeb M. Saliba *(Exec. V.P. & Sec.)*
Albert G. Tutor *(Exec. V.P. & Treas.)*
Bruce E. Dennis *(Mgr.-Corp. Risk Mngmt.)*
Principal(s):
Ronald N. Tutor
Naseeb M. Saliba
Albert G. Tutor

Outside Service Firm(s):

Fuhler, Baker & Co.*(Auditors)*
Sherman Oaks, CA

Bank of America*(Major Banking Relationship)*
701 S. Western Ave.
Los Angeles, CA 91201

Joint Venture:

Perini Corp. **(1)**
390 Main St.
San Francisco, CA 91342
Tel.: 415-541-5395
Commercial Heavy Construction
S.I.C.: 1629

R.C. TWAY COAL COMPANY
2601 S. Third St.
Louisville, KY 40208
Tel.: 502-637-2551 **KY**
Fax: 502-635-1314
Approx.Sls.: $46,000,000
Emp.: 400
Truck Trailers
S.I.C.: 3715
Robert C. Tway, Jr. *(Chm. Bd.)*
Robert C. Tway, III *(Pres.)*
Glenn Dobrick *(Exec. V.P.)*
Thomas L. Elder *(V.P. & Treas.)*
Larry Hartog *(Sec. & Asst. Treas.)*

Outside Service Firm(s):

Deloitte & Touche*(Auditors)*
510 W. Broadway
Louisville, KY 40202
Tel.: 502-562-2000

Citizens Fidelity Bank & Trust Co.*(Major Banking Relationship)*
P.O. Box 33000-Citizens Plaza
Louisville, KY 40232
Tel.: 502-581-3381

TWEDDLE LITHO COMPANY
24000 Harper Ave.
St. Clair Shores, MI 48080
Tel.: 313-371-3300 **MI**
Fax: 313-771-0311
Year Founded: 1954
Approx.Sls.: $24,000,000
Emp.: 80
Fiscal Year-end: 7/31/91
Lithography & Photocomposition
S.I.C.: 2752; 2791
Michael E. Tweddle *(Chm. Bd. & Pres.)*
Carl Zuckero *(Sr. V.P.-Pur.)*
Jim Foster *(V.P.-Sls. & Mktg.)*
Tom Dupont *(V.P.)*
Zachary M. Davies *(Controller & Sec.)*

No. of Mfg. Plants/Facilities: 1
No. of U.S. Offices: 3

Outside Service Firm(s):

Plante & Moran*(Auditors)*
Southfield, MI

Manufacturers National Bank N.A.*(Major Banking Relationship)*
38th Fl., 100 Renaissance Center
Detroit, MI 48243
Tel.: 313-222-4227

TWENTIETH CENTURY COMPANIES
4500 Main St., Ste. 1500
Kansas City, MO 64111
Tel.: 816-531-5575 **MD**
Fax: 816-932-4203
Year Founded: 1984
Approx.Sls.: $67,000,000
Emp.: 530
Investment Advisory Service; Data Processing Service
S.I.C.: 6282; 7374
James E. Stowers *(Pres.)*
Irving Kuraner *(V.P.)*
Robert Puff, Jr. *(V.P.)*
James Stowers, III *(V.P.)*
Dennis Von Wadden *(V.P.)*
Ronald A. Neville *(Treas.)*
Wendy Welte *(Sec.)*

Outside Service Firm(s):

Baird, Kurtz & Dobson*(Auditors)*
Commerce Tower, 911 Main, Ste. 1900
Kansas City, MO
Tel.: 816-221-7544

Subsidiaries:

Twentieth Century Investors **(1)**
4500 Main St., Ste. 1500
Kansas City, MO 64111
Tel.: 816-531-5575
Emp.: 6
Security Brokers & Dealers
S.I.C.: 6211
James E. Stowers *(Pres.)*
Dennis Von Wadden *(V.P. & Sec.)*
Irving Kuraner *(V.P.)*
Ron Neville *(V.P.)*
Robert Puff, Jr. *(V.P.)*
James E. Stowers, III *(V.P.)*
Marianne Roepkey *(Treas.)*

Twentieth Century Investors, Inc. **(1)**
4500 Main St.
Kansas City, MO 64111
Tel.: 816-531-5575
Approx.Assets: $5,030,000,000
Emp.: 400
Dealers of Mutual Funds
S.I.C.: 6211
James E. Stowers *(Pres.)*
Irving Kuraner *(Exec. V.P.)*
Robert M. Bigley *(V.P.-Oper.)*
Dave Dilley *(V.P.-Information Systems)*
Charles M. Duboc *(V.P.-Investments)*
Ronald A. Neville *(Treas.)*
Dennis C. Von Wadden *(Sec.)*

Twentieth Century Services **(1)**
4500 Main
Kansas City, MO 64111
Tel.: 816-531-5575
Approx.Sls.: $50,000,000
Emp.: 530
Data Processing Service; Administrative Management
S.I.C.: 7374; 8741
James E. Stowers *(Pres.)*
Dennis Von Wadden *(V.P. & Sec.)*
Robert Puff, Jr. *(V.P.)*
James Stowers, III *(V.P.)*

21 INTERNATIONAL HOLDINGS, INC.
153 E. 53 St., Ste. 5900
New York, NY 10022
Tel.: 212-230-0400
Fax: 212-593-1363
Approx.Sls.: $1,000,000,000
Emp.: 5,000
Import Export
Holding Company
S.I.C.: 6719
Marshall S. Cogan *(Chm. Bd., Pres. & Chief Exec. Officer)*
Fred Marcus *(Exec. V.P.)*
Robert Nelson *(Chief Fin. Officer)*
Barry Zimmerman *(Mng. Dir.)*

Outside Service Firm(s):

J. H. Cohn & Co.*(Auditors)*
Newark, NJ

Shonwald, Haber, Shaffzin & Mullman*(Legal Firm)*
New York, NY

Chemical Bank*(Major Banking Relationship)*
450 West 33rd St.
New York, NY 10001
Tel.: 212-613-7197
Fax: 212-947-7628

Subsidiaries:

Curon **(1)**
P.O. Box 188
Cornelius, NC 28031
Tel.: 704-892-8081
Emp.: 700
Polyurethane Foam for Cushions, Mattresses, Furniture Cushioning, Carpet Cushioning, Clothing Interlining & Various Industrial Applications
S.I.C.: 3086
John Current *(Pres.)*

Foam Product Corporation **(1)**
1500 E. Secont St.
Eddystone, PA 19013
Tel.: 215-876-2551
Mfr. of Prime Polyurethane Foam Carpet Cushion
S.I.C.: 3069
Robert J. Hay *(Pres. & Chief Oper. Officer)*
Kenneth R. Fuette *(V.P. & Controller)*
Paul A. Haslanger *(V.P.-Mfg.)*

Plants:

Scotfoam Corp. **(2)**
1705 A Rockdale Industrial Blvd.
Conyers, GA 30207
Tel.: 404-922-0100
Polyurethane Foam Mfr.
S.I.C.: 3069
Clint McBuffee *(Plant Mgr.)*

Scotfoam Corp. **(2)**
3210 Curtis Blvd.
Mesquite, TX 75149
Tel.: 214-288-7655
Foam Manufacturing Plant
S.I.C.: 3069
Jack Snyder *(Plant Mgr.)*

Scotfoam Corp. **(2)**
3005 Commercial Rd.
Fort Wayne, IN 46809
Tel.: 219-747-7485
Polyurethane Foam Manufacturer
S.I.C.: 3069
J. W. Darlington *(Plant Mgr.)*

Scotfoam Corp. **(2)**
1400 A East Victoria Ave.
San Bernardino, CA 92406
Tel.: 909-824-8981
Mfr. Plastics & Rubber & Polyurethane Foam
S.I.C.: 3069
D. C. Dobratc *(Plant Mgr.)*

Foamex L.P. **(1)**
823 Waterman Ave.
East Providence, RI 02914
Tel.: 401-438-0900
Prime & Bonded Urethane
S.I.C.: 2821
Robert J. Hay *(Pres. & Chief Exec. Officer)*
R. J. Vanaria *(V.P.-Fin., Treas. & Sec.)*
John A. Lembree *(V.P.-Mktg.)*
William H. Bundy *(V.P.-Mfg.)*

Hollytex **(1)**
Park 80 Plaza West One
Saddle Brook, NJ 07662
Tel.: 201-843-0900
Approx.Sls.: $210,000,000
Emp.: 1,100
Mfr. Carpets, Carpet Cushioning
S.I.C.: 2299; 5023
Peter J. Cohen *(Exec. V.P.)*
Terry J. Kall *(V.P.-Sls. & Mktg.)*
John J. Byrne *(V.P.-Mfg.)*
Robert Herzog *(V.P.-Indus. Rels.)*
Paul Nunno *(V.P.-Data Processing)*
James G. Thompson *(Treas.)*
Gary A. Schonwald *(Sec. & Legal Officer)*

Plants:

General Felt, Fairless Hills **(2)**
259 Canal Rd.
Fairless Hills, PA 19030
Tel.: 215-736-8611
Foam Rubber Carpet Pads
S.I.C.: 3069
John Noon *(Plant Mgr.)*
Nick Petro *(Plant Supt.)*

General Felt Industries, Inc. **(2)**
8320 Rex Rd.
Pico Rivera, CA 90660
Tel.: 310-728-0151
Mfg. Plant for Sponge Rubber Underlay; Bonded Urethane
S.I.C.: 3069
Pratap Dholakia *(Plant Mgr.)*

General Felt Industries, Inc. **(2)**
2772 Depot St.
Sanford, FL 32771
Tel.: 305-321-5812
Mfg. Plant for Bonded Urethane
S.I.C.: 2821
Harishanker Rajgor *(Plant Mgr.)*

General Felt Industries, Inc. **(2)**
2121 E. Wheatsheaf Ln.
Philadelphia, PA 19137
Tel.: 215-744-4444
Mfg. Plant for Indoor, Outdoor Carpet, Felt Underlay, Synthetic Grass
S.I.C.: 3069; 2273
Louis Melillo *(Plant Mgr.)*

General Felt Industries, Inc. **(2)**
10726 Doric St.
Dallas, TX 75220
Tel.: 215-350-6611
Mfg. Plant for Bonded Polyurethane Underlay
S.I.C.: 3069
George De La Garza *(Plant Supt.)*

General Felt Industries, Inc. **(2)**
1936 East St.
Trenton, NJ 08619
Tel.: 609-587-5800
Sponge Rubber Underlay
S.I.C.: 3069
Hank D'Andrea *(Plant Mgr.)*

Divisions:

Hollytex-Central Div. **(2)**
13-150 Merchandise Mart
Chicago, IL 60654
James B. Liddle *(V.P.)*

Hollytex-Western Div. **(2)**
6025 E. Randolph St.
Los Angeles, CA 90040
Tel.: 213-728-0151
Robert Howard *(V.P.)*

Subsidiary:

Focus Carpet Co. **(2)**
1627 Abutment Rd.
Dalton, GA 30720
Tel.: 706-278-1234
Approx.Sls.: $13,000,000
Floor Coverings
S.I.C.: 2273
Paul Reznikoff *(Exec. V.P.)*

Knoll International, Inc. **(1)**
655 Madison Ave.
New York, NY 10021
Tel.: 212-826-2400
Holding Company; Mfr. Office Furniture
S.I.C.: 6719
Marshall S. Cogan *(Chm. Bd. & Chief Exec. Officer)*
Mel Silver *(Pres. & Chief Oper. Officer)*
Peter Cohen *(Pres. & Chief Oper. Officer-North American Opers.)*
Ronald Kass *(Sr. V.P.-Mktg.)*
Lewis Singer *(Sr. V.P.-Sls.)*
James T. Wakeling *(Sr. V.P.-Opers.)*
Frank M. Pope *(Sr. V.P.-Fin.)*
William H. Oler *(V.P.-Corp. Accts. & Plng.)*

Plant:

Knoll Intl., Inc. **(2)**
P.O. Box 157, Water St.
East Greenville, PA 18041
Tel.: 215-679-7991
Mfr. Plant for Furniture
S.I.C.: 2521; 2522
James T. Wakeling *(Sr. V.P.-Opers.)*
Richard Jordan *(V.P.-Data Processing)*
David G. Culp *(Controller)*

The "21" Club, Inc. **(1)**
21 W. 52nd St.
New York, NY 10019
Tel.: 212-582-7200 (100%)
Approx.Sls.: $12,000,000
Emp.: 300
Restaurant
S.I.C.: 5812
Kenneth Aretsky *(Chm. & Chief Oper. Officer)*
Brian McGuire *(V.P. & Chief Financial Officer)*

Non-U.S. Holdings:

Color Your World, Inc. **(1)**
10 Carson St.
Toronto, ON M8W 3R5, Canada
Tel.: 416-259-3251
Retail Paint, Wall Coverings & Related Products
S.I.C.: 5231; 5713
Bruce Strongman *(Pres.)*

Concorco Lda. **(1)**
Sociedade Corticeira Concoroco Lda.
Santa Marta de Corroios, Portugal
Tel.: Lisbon 249-0231 (80%)
Cork & Cork-Rubber Prods.
S.I.C.: 2499; 3069
Paul Schobert *(Gen. Mgr.)*

Establissement Mesnel, S.A. **(1)**
9-11 rue de la Riviere 78420
Carrieres-sur-Seine, France (60%)
Automotive Window Sealing Systems
S.I.C.: 3069
Francois Mesnel *(Gen. Mgr.)*

Knoll International Italia S.p.A. **(1)**
11, v. M.te Napoleone 20121
Milan, Italy
Tel.: 2 78 4151

KnollOffice, Inc. **(1)**
160 Pears Ave.
Toronto, ON M5R 1T2, Canada
Tel.: 416-960-9819 (100%)
Fax: 416-960-3625
Distr. of Furniture
S.I.C.: 5021; 5712
Eberhard von Huene *(Pres.)*

Leece-Neville de Mexico S.A. de C.V. **(1)**
Ave. Alvara Obregon y Claveles. H
Matamoros, Tamps Mexico
Tel.: Matamoros 2-25-55 (100%)
Emp.: 755
Assembly of Fractional Horsepower DC Motors
S.I.C.: 3621
William J. Hughes *(V.P. & Gen. Mgr.)*

Mo-Car Internacional, S.A. **(1)**
Apartado, Postal 5259-K
Monterrey, N.L. Mexico
Tel.: 541-207 (40%)
Starter Drives & Batteries
S.I.C.: 3691
Roosevelt Guerra *(Chief Oper. Officer)*

TWIN CITY DIE CASTINGS CO.
1070 33rd Ave. S.E.
Minneapolis, MN 55414
Tel.: 612-645-3611
Fax: 612-645-0724
Year Founded: 1919
Approx.Sls.: $18,000,000
Emp.: 180
Fiscal Year-end: 9/30/92
Export
Mfr. of Aluminum & Zinc Die Castings
S.I.C.: 3363; 3364; 3365; 3369
Corporate Giving Program: Contributes to United Way
James D. Harmon *(Chm. Bd.)*
Steven J. Harmon *(Pres. & Chief Exec. Officer)*
Ernest L. Peterson *(V.P.-Opers.)*
Douglas Harmon *(V.P.-Fin.)*
Alvin W. Pfingsten *(Dir.-Quality Assurance)*
Richard I. Burton *(Dir.-Sls. & Mktg.)*
Mark A. Harmon *(Mgr.-Human Resources)*
T.J. Heider *(Chief Engr.)*
George R. Johnson *(Asst. Sec. & Gen. Counsel)*

Computer Systems/Hardware:
IBM System 38

Subsidiary:

Twin City Die Castings Co. **(1)**
122 Cessna St. N.W.
Watertown, SD 57201
Tel.: 605-886-9448
Fax: 605-886-2489
Export
Mfr. Of Zinc & Aluminum Die Castings
S.I.C.: 3363
John Neyssen *(Plant Mgr.)*

TWIN CITY FOODS, INC.
P.O. Box 699
Stanwood, WA 98292
Tel.: 206-629-2111
Fax: 206-629-3533
Year Founded: 1945
Assets: $75,000,000
Approx.Sls.: $103,000,000
Emp.: 1,000
Processors of Frozen Vegetables
S.I.C.: 2037
Arne T. Lervick *(Chm. Bd. & Chief Exec. Officer)*
Rodger O. Lervick *(Pres.)*
Ronald H. Keolker *(Chief Fin. Officer, V.P., Treas. & Controller)*
David Miller *(Mgr.-Data Processing)*

Computer Systems/Hardware:
IBM

Outside Service Firm(s):

Williams & Nulle*(Auditors)*
Mount Vernon, WA

Imperial Life*(Group Insurer)*
Toronto, ON Canada

Standard Life Insurance Co.*(Group Insurer)*
Portland, OR

Davis, Tremaine & Co.*(Legal Firm)*
Seattle, WA

Security Pacific National Bank*(Major Banking Relationship)*
Stanwood, WA

TWIN COUNTY GROCERS, INC.
145 Talmadge Rd.
Edison, NJ 08818
Tel.: 908-287-4600
Fax: 908-287-6027
Year Founded: 1944
Sales Range: $500-999 Million
Emp.: 1,000
Wholesale Grocery Cooperative
S.I.C.: 5141; 5142; 5431; 5149; 5143; 5147
Calvin Bell *(Chm. Bd.)*
James A. Burke *(Pres.)*
Victor Bonini *(Chief Fin. Officer & V.P.-Fin.)*
Joseph Casamento *(V.P.-Human Resources)*
Satish Juneja *(V.P.-Mngmt. Information Systems)*
Mike Stolarz *(V.P.-Sls. & Adv.)*
William Michas *(Treas.)*
Thomas S. Cummiskey *(Controller)*

No. of U.S. Offices: 1

Computer Systems/Hardware:
IBM

Outside Service Firm(s):

Twinco Services, Inc.*(Group Insurer)*
Edison, NJ

Shearson Lehman Brothers, Inc.*(Investment Banker)*
World Financial Center
New York, NY 10285
Tel.: 212-298-2000

Wilentz, Goldman & Spitzer*(Legal Firm)*
Woodbridge, NJ

Sullivan, Morrissey & Mickel Capital Management*(Pension Manager)*
New York, NY

Subsidiaries:

Twinco Services, Inc. **(1)**
145 Talmadge Rd.
Edison, NJ 08818
Tel.: 908-287-4600
Insurance Services
S.I.C.: 6311; 6321; 6324
James A. Burke *(Chief Oper. Officer)*

Twinco Trucking Co., Inc. **(1)**
145 Talmadge Rd.
Edison, NJ 08818
Tel.: 908-287-4600
James A. Burke *(Chief Oper. Officer)*

TWINCRAFT, INC.
P.O. Box 186
Winooski, VT 05404
Tel.: 802-655-2200
Fax: 802-655-3874
Year Founded: 1978
Approx.Sls.: $26,000,000
Emp.: 200
Soap Manufacturer
S.I.C.: 2841
Robert Asch *(Chm. Bd.)*
Peter Asch *(Pres. & Chief Exec. Officer)*
David Asch *(Exec. V.P.-Treas. & Sec.)*
Mark Pritchard *(V.P. & Gen. Mgr.)*
Pamela Simpson *(Mgr.-Personnel)*

No. of U.S. Offices: 4

Computer Systems/Hardware:
Wang VS 85

Outside Service Firm(s):

Gallagher & Flynn*(Auditors)*
Boston, MA

CIGNA*(Group Insurer)*
Hartford, CT
Tel.: 203-726-6000

TYLAN GENERAL, INC.
9577 Chesapeake Drive
San Diego, CA 92123
Tel.: 619-571-1222
Fax: 619-576-1703
Year Founded: 1979
Assets: $12,500,000
Earnings: $1,600,000
Liabilities: $930,000
Net Worth: $11,570,000
Approx.Sls.: $35,000,000
Emp.: 250
Fiscal Year-end: 10/31/91
Export
Manufacture of Vacuum & Electronic Flow Controllers
S.I.C.: 3825
David J. Ferran *(Pres. & Chief Exec. Officer)*
David Stone *(Chief Fin. Officer & Treas.)*
Ric Erdman *(V.P.-Opers.)*
Michal Chick *(Dir.-Human Resources)*
Michael A. Grandinetti *(V.P.-Sls. & Mktg.)*
Cindy Stewart *(Mktg. & Adv. Admin.)*

Division:

Tylan General, Inc.-Flow Division **(1)**
359 Van Ness Way
Torrance, CA 90501
Tel.: 310-212-5533
Fax: 310-212-5311
Mfr. of Proprietary Precision Components, Subsystems & Systems Used by the Semiconductor Industry to Process Silicon Wafers
S.I.C.: 3669; 3825
Rick Erdman *(Gen. Mgr.-Mfg.)*

Non-U.S. Holdings:

Tylan GmbH **(1)**
Kirchhoffstrasse 8 D-8057
Eching, Germany
Tel.: 81 653701 (100%)
Semiconductor Equipment
S.I.C.: 3825
Kurt Henche *(Mng. Dir.)*

Tylan SARL **(1)**
7-8 Place de L'Europe Zone Industrial de Chesnes, F-38296
La Verpilliere, France
Tel.: 33 79 3615 808 (100%)
Telex: 310259
Fax: 33 74 955 750
Semiconductor Equipment
S.I.C.: 3825

Tylan (UK) Ltd. **(1)**
Unit 19, Westmead Industrial Estate
Westlea,
Swindon, United Kingdom
Tel.: 793 615808 (100%)
Telex: 444462
Fax: 44 793 671 442
Sls. & Service
S.I.C.: 5065
Jim Hurley *(Mng. Dir.)*

TYLER ELEVATOR PRODUCTS, INC.
6161 Halle Dr.
Valley View, OH 44125
Tel.: 216-524-0100
Approx.Sls.: $10,000,000
Emp.: 170
Mfr. of Elevator Cabs & Entrances
S.I.C.: 3534
R.E. Vinciquerra *(Pres.)*
Clarence J. Bordelon *(V.P.-Sls. & Admin.)*
Bill Lovell *(Controller)*
Steve King *(Dir.-Pur.)*
Thomas Holloran *(Dir.-Engrng.)*

TYLER LIMITED PARTNERSHIP
P.O. Box 249, East Highway 12
Benson, MN 56215
Tel.: 612-843-3333 **MN**
Fax: 612-843-2467
Approx.Sls.: $15,000,000
Emp.: 100
Import Export
Fertilizer Equipment, Lift Trucks
S.I.C.: 3523; 3531
Donald E. McGrath *(Pres.)*
Ivan Bowen, III *(V.P.-Opers.)*
Charles Alsip *(V.P.-Engrng.)*
William J. Luzum *(V.P. & Treas.)*
Elaine Mitteness *(Sec.)*

Outside Service Firm(s):

Arthur Andersen & Co.*(Auditors)*
45 S. 7th St.
Minneapolis, MN 55402

Avery, Hodes, Costello & Burman*(Legal Firm)*
Chicago, IL

Continental Bank, N.A.*(Major Banking Relationship)*
Minneapolis, MN

TYNDALE HOUSE PUBLISHERS, INC.
351 Executive Drive
Carol Stream, IL 60188
Mailing Address:
P.O. Box 80
Wheaton, IL 60189
Tel.: 708-668-8300
Fax: 708-668-9092
Year Founded: 1962
Approx.Sls.: $27,000,000
Emp.: 210
Fiscal Year-end: 4/30/91
Export
Publishers of Bibles, Religious Books, Videos & Periodicals
S.I.C.: 2731; 2721; 7812
Corporate Giving Program: United Way
Kenneth N. Taylor *(Chm. Bd.)*
Mark D. Taylor *(Pres. & Chief Exec. Officer)*
Ron Beers *(V.P. & Editor-in-Chief)*
Doug Knox *(V.P.-Mktg. & Assoc. Publisher)*
Cliff Johnson *(V.P.-Sls.)*
Paul Matthews *(V.P. & Asst. Sec.)*
Deborah Copelin *(Sec.)*

Computer Systems/Hardware:
Data General Mainframe, Novell Network

UC INDUSTRIES, INC.
3 Century Dr.
Parsippany, NJ 07054
Tel.: 201-267-1605
Fax: 201-267-1495
Approx.Sls.: $50,000,000
Emp.: 274
Mfr. of Extruded Polystyrene Insulation Board, Residential & Comml. Roofing Insulation Board
S.I.C.: 3086; 3089
R.S. Schaffler *(Chm. Bd.)*
Jerry L. Weinstein *(Pres.)*
G. Vilarin *(V.P.-Fin.)*
W.A. Pond *(V.P.-Sls.)*
F. Sydlowski *(V.P.-Mfg.)*
Wayne Gersch *(Dir.-Mktg.)*
John Calton *(Mgr.-Mktg. Services)*
Nicole Gagnon *(Mktg. Services Coord.)*

UDT SENSORS, INC.
12525 Chadron Ave.
Hawthorne, CA 90250
Tel.: 310-978-0516
Fax: 310-644-1727
Year Founded: 1967
Approx.Sls.: $22,000,000
Emp.: 300
Fiscal Year-end: 6/30/91
Export
Designs, Develops, Manufactures & Markets High Performance Light Sensor Products
S.I.C.: 3829
Deepak Chopra *(Chm. Bd., Pres. & Chief Exec. Officer)*
Ajay Mehra *(Sec., Treas. & Controller)*
Verna Jacobs *(Personnel Dir.)*
Bob Perry *(Natl. Sls. Mgr.)*
Narayan Taneja *(Dir.-Res. & Devel.)*

Subsidiary:

Akra Tool **(1)**
1135 S. Airport Circle
Euless, TX 76040
Tel.: 817-571-5420
Fax: 817-545-0112
S.I.C.: 3829

UES, INC.
4401 Dayton-Xenia Rd.
Dayton, OH 45432
Tel.: 513-426-6900
Fax: 513-429-5413
Year Founded: 1973
Assets: $5,700,000
Earnings: $34,937
Liabilities: $3,100,000
Net Worth: $2,600,000
Approx.Sls.: $16,000,000
Emp.: 190
Fiscal Year-end: 9/30/90
Research & Development Company
S.I.C.: 8731
Krishan K. Joshi *(Pres. & Chief Exec. Officer)*
Larry E. Clay *(Exec. V.P. & Chief Fin. Officer)*
Ross L. Morgan *(Sr. V.P.)*
Rodney C. Darrah *(V.P.-Treas.)*
Robert G. Ferguson *(V.P.-Bus. Devel.)*
John J. Gruenwald *(Comptroller)*
Imogene J. Hoffer *(Dir.-Publications)*
Barbara L. Vincent *(Dir.-Pur. & Security Officer)*
Deborah E. Yount *(Dir.-Personnel)*
Principal(s):
Krishan K. Joshi

No. of Mfg. Plants/Facilities: 1
No. of U.S. Offices: 5

Computer Systems/Hardware:
Wang

Outside Service Firm(s):

Battelle & Battelle*(Auditors)*
3400 South Dixie Dr.
Dayton, OH 45402

General American Life Insurance Co.*(Group Insurer)*
Dublin, OH

Cox & Ginger*(Legal Firm)*
Dayton, OH

First National Bank of Dayton*(Major Banking Relationship)*
1 First National Plaza
Dayton, OH 45402
Tel.: 513-226-2000

First National Bank of Dayton*(Pension Manager)*
1 First National Plaza
Dayton, OH 45402
Tel.: 513-226-2000

UFE INCORPORATED
1850 S. Greeley St.
Stillwater, MN 55082-0007
Mailing Address:
P.O. Box 7
Stillwater, MN 55082-0007
Tel.: 612-439-1561 **MN**
Fax: 612-439-0511
Year Founded: 1953
Assets: $21,000,000
Liabilities: $10,000,000
Net Worth: $11,000,000
Approx.Sls.: $43,000,000
Emp.: 640
Fiscal Year-end: 3/31/91
Export
Manufacture Precision Plastic Parts
S.I.C.: 3089
Employee Matching Gifts Program: Gifts Above $15 and Up to $500 Per Non-profit Matched
Orville D. Johnson *(Chm. Bd. & Chief Exec. Officer)*
Martin N. Kellogg *(Pres., Chief Oper. Officer & Corp. Sec.)*
George R. Frost *(Chief Fin. Officer & Treas.)*
Lelan M. Jamison *(V.P.-Mktg.)*
Robert J. Williams *(V.P.-Opers.)*
Kathleen G. Sundquist *(Dir.-Personnel)*
Joseph F. Vossen *(Dir.-Business Systems)*
Principal(s):
Orville D. Johnson
Martin N. Kellogg

No. of Mfg. Plants/Facilities: 4
No. of Foreign Offices: 1

Computer Systems/Hardware:
Unisys

Outside Service Firm(s):

KPMG Peat Marwick*(Auditors)*
1600 Meritor Tower, 444 Cedar St.
St. Paul, MN 55102

Faegre & Benson*(Legal Firm)*
2200 Norwest Ctr., 90 S. 7th St.
Minneapolis, MN 55402-3901
Tel.: 612-336-3000
Fax: 612-336-3026

First Bank, N.A.*(Major Banking Relationship)*
First Bank Place
Minneapolis, MN 55480

Subsidiary:

UFE Pte Ltd **(1)**
No. 5 Joo Koon Way
Singapore, Singapore
Tel.: 8620252
Mfg. Precision Plastic Parts
S.I.C.: 3089
Dr. Phillip Adams *(Mng. Dir.)*

Affiliate:

UFE Cal Tec Inc. **(1)**
1125 Beacon St.
Brea, CA 92621-2937
Tel.: 714-671-2600
Emp.: 130
Mfr. Precision Plastic Parts
S.I.C.: 3089
James Heaton *(Pres.)*
Patrick Brennan *(Controller)*

UIS, INC.
600 5th Ave.
New York, NY 10020
Tel.: 212-581-7660 **NY**
Fax: 212-581-7517
Year Founded: 1945
Approx.Sls.: $630,000,000
Emp.: 6,700
Import Export
Mfr. of Auto Parts; Industrial Equipment; Drop Forgings; Iron Castings
S.I.C.: 3714; 3463; 3462
Harry Lebensfeld *(Chm. Bd. & Chief Exec. Officer)*
Andrew G. Pietrini *(Pres.)*
Joseph F. Arrigo *(V.P., Treas. & Sec.)*

No. of Foreign Offices: 5

Computer Systems/Hardware:
IBM PC

Outside Service Firm(s):

Grant Thornton*(Auditors)*
605 Third Ave.
New York, NY 10158
Tel.: 212-599-0100
Fax: 212-370-4520

Spangler Carlson*(Legal Firm)*
New York, NY

First National Bank of Boston*(Major Banking Relationship)*
P.O. Box 644,
Boston, MA 02102-0644
Tel.: 617-575-2900
Fax: 617-575-2549

First National Bank of Boston*(Pension Manager)*
P.O. Box 644,
Boston, MA 02102-0644
Tel.: 617-575-2900
Fax: 617-575-2549

Wertheim Asset Mgmt. Services*(Pension Manager)*
New York, NY

Divisions:

Airtex Products **(1)**
407 W. Main St.
Fairfield, IL 62837
Tel.: 618-842-2111
Fax: 618-842-4069
Approx.Sls.: $60,000,000
Emp.: 1,050
Import Export
Mfr. of Automotive Replacement Parts
S.I.C.: 3714
Dimitri Monge *(Pres. & Chief Oper. Officer)*
Alan Kemp *(Controller)*
Dennis Brant *(Matls. Mgr.)*
Nelson Kirkwood *(Sls. Mgr.)*

Union Forging Co. **(1)**
506 North St.
Endicott, NY 13760
Tel.: 607-785-9975
Fax: 607-785-1927
Mfr. of Drop Forgings
S.I.C.: 3462
Joseph Sack *(Chief Oper. Officer)*

Subsidiaries:

Champion Laboratories, Inc. **(1)**
4th & Walnut Sts.
Albion, IL 62806
Tel.: 618-445-2395 (100%)
Fax: 618-456-2260
Fax: 618-445-4040
Emp.: 1,700
Mfr. of Automotive Oil & Air Filters
S.I.C.: 3714
Thomas Mowatt *(Chief Oper. Officer)*
David J. Arosteguy *(Exec. V.P.-Mktg. Admin.)*
Gerald Fields *(V.P.-Engrng & OEM Sls.)*
Charles Casaleggi *(V.P.-Opers.)*
Lesa Matthes *(Controller)*
John A. Evans *(Natl. Sls. Mgr.)*
William A. Lear *(Pur. Agent)*

Subsidiaries:

Luber-Finer, Inc. **(2)**
P.O. Box 8,
Albion, IL 62806
Tel.: 618-445-3686 (100%)
Fax: 618-445-3063
Mfr. of Automotive Filters; Off Road Equipment & Industrial Engines
S.I.C.: 3714
Thomas Mowatt *(Chief Oper. Officer)*

The Sacks Electrical Supply Co. **(2)**
711 Johnston St.
Akron, OH 44306
Tel.: 216-253-2141 (100%)
Fax: 216-253-1055
Wholesale & Distribution of Electrical Supplies
S.I.C.: 5063
Melvin D. Sacks *(Chief Oper. Officer)*

HKM of Delaware Corp. **(1)**
600 Fifth Ave.
New York, NY 10020
Tel.: 212-581-7660 (100%)
Distribution of Automotive Brake Parts
S.I.C.: 5013
Andrew G. Pietrini *(Chief Oper. Officer)*

Subsidiary:

HKM of California Corp. **(2)**
3171 East 12th St.
Los Angeles, CA 90023
Tel.: 213-269-0572 (100%)
Fax: 213-269-2686
Mfr. of Automotive Brake Products
S.I.C.: 3714
William Axelrod *(Chief Oper. Officer)*

Hurd Millwork Company, Inc. **(1)**
520 S. Whelen Ave.
Medford, WI 54451
Tel.: 715-748-2011
Fax: 715-748-6043
Approx.Sls.: $75,000,000
Emp.: 800
Mfr. & Wholesale of Millwork Products; Wood Windows & Patio Doors
S.I.C.: 2431; 5031
Kenneth Hallgren *(Pres. & Chief Oper. Officer)*
Roy Doering *(V.P.-Sls. & Mktg.)*
Michael V. Geisler *(Gen. Acctg. Mgr.)*

Mid-South Mfg. Co. **(1)**
P.O. Box 278,
Marked Tree, AR 72365
Tel.: 501-358-3473 (100%)
Fax: 501-358-3473
Mfr. of Automobile Water Pumps
S.I.C.: 3714
Don Wilson *(Chief Oper. Officer)*

Neapco, Inc. **(1)**
Queen & Bailey St.
Pottstown, PA 19464
Tel.: 215-323-6000
Tel.: 800-821-2374 (100%)
Fax: 215-326-3857
Approx.Sls.: $50,000,000
Emp.: 450
Import Export
Computer Systems/Hardware:
Unysis
Mfr. of Auto Parts
S.I.C.: 3714
Ronald H. Vaughn *(Pres.)*
F.H. Rocca *(V.P.-Mktg. & Sls.)*
William Patterson *(Treas.)*
Edward Hollander *(Mgr.-Opers.)*
Nina Slaybaugh *(Mgr.-Personnel)*
Richard Snyder *(Mgr.-Quality Assurance)*
K.L. Sheffey *(Mgr.-Export)*
Bob Jones *(Pur. Agent)*

New England Confectionery Co. **(1)**
254 Massachusetts Ave.
Cambridge, MA 02139
Tel.: 617-876-4700 (100%)
Fax: 617-876-2356
Emp.: 400
Export
Mfr. of Candy
S.I.C.: 2064
Domenic M. Antonellis *(Pres. & Chief Oper. Officer)*
John A. Boggia *(V.P.-Opers.)*
Stanley W. Byerly *(Chief Fin. Officer)*
Lawrence J. Finn *(Treas.)*
Charles Blood *(Dir.-Sls. Admin.)*
David Sullivan *(Reg. Sls. Mgr.-Midwest)*
Walter Marshall *(Mktg. Mgr.)*
George W. Chadwick *(Natl. Sls. Mgr.)*

Subsidiary:

Stark Candy Company **(2)**
Candy Lane & Hickory
Pewaukee, WI 53072
Tel.: 414-691-0600
Fax: 414-691-2947
Approx.Sls.: $25,000,000
Emp.: 200
Fiscal Year-end: 12/31/91
Mfr. of Candy
S.I.C.: 2064
Domenic Antonellis *(Pres.)*
John Boggia *(V.P.-Opers.)*
Hans Becher *(V.P.-Sls.)*
Larry Finn *(Treas.)*
Shelley Von Haden *(Controller)*
Patricia Raap *(Mgr.-Facilities)*
Barbara Anderson *(Mgr.-Personnel)*
Kathy Stewart *(Pur. Agent)*
Walter Marshall *(Coord.)*

Divisions:

Stark Candy Company **(3)**
254 Massachusetts Ave.
Cambridge, MA 02139
Tel.: 617-876-4700
Fax: 617-876-2356
Mfr. of Candy
S.I.C.: 2064

Stark Candy Company **(3)**
100 Candy Lane
Thibodaux, LA 70301
Tel.: 504-446-1354
Mfr. of Candy
S.I.C.: 2064

Three States Supply Co., Inc. **(1)**
666-E. H. Crump Blvd.
Memphis, TN 38216
Tel.: 901-948-8651 (100%)
Fax: 901-948-2454
Wholesale of Hardware
S.I.C.: 5072
Charles Brejot *(Chief Oper. Officer)*

UIS Export Corporation **(1)**
600 5th Ave.
New York, NY 10020
Tel.: 212-581-7660 (100%)
Export Sales for the Automotive Industry
S.I.C.: 5013
Andrew G. Pietrini *(Chief Oper. Officer)*

UIS, Inc.—(Continued)

Wells Mfg. Corp. **(1)**
P.O. Box 70
Dond Du Lac, WI 54935
Emp.: 800
Fiscal Year-end: 12/31/91
Import Export
Computer Systems/Hardware:
DEC
Mfr. of Automotive Ignition Parts
S.I.C.: 3714; 3694
William A. Allen *(Pres.)*
Jack Barbeau *(V.P.-Mfg.)*
Kenneth Brooks *(V.P.-Fin.)*
Robert L. Jacobs *(V.P.-Human Resources)*
William Ricketts *(V.P.-Opers.)*
Gavin Spence *(V.P.-Sls.)*
Ward Trastek *(Mgr.-Information Systems)*
Gene Langenecker *(Sls. Admin. Mgr.)*
T.L. Zuehlke *(Mgr.-Pur.)*

Non-U.S. Holdings:

Automotive Accessory Co., Ltd. **(1)**
771 Main St.
Winnipeg, MB R2W 3NS, Canada
Tel.: 204-942-2514 (100%)
Mfr. of Automotive Fuel & Water Pumps
S.I.C.: 3714; 3586
Gustan Hillius *(Pres.)*

Flexible Lamps Ltd. **(1)**
Rubbolite House, Centre Dr.,
Epping, Essex CM16 4JJ, United Kingdom
Tel.: 378 74550 (100%)
Mfr. of Lighting Components for the Automotive Industry
S.I.C.: 3714; 3647
Robert L. Groves *(Chief Oper. Officer)*

Luber-Finer, Europe, N.V./S.A. **(1)**
Waterwilgweg, 4 2050
Antwerp, Belgium
Tel.: 3-2197777 (100%)
Fax: 3-2197653
Mfr. of Motor Vehicle Parts & Accessories
S.I.C.: 3714
Thomas Mowatt *(Chief Oper. Officer)*

Wells Manufacturing Canada Ltd. **(1)**
1080 Meyerside Dr.
Mississauga, ON L5T 1J4, Canada
Tel.: 416-670-9419 (100%)
Fax: 416-670-9419
Mfr. & Wholesale of Ignition Products
S.I.C.: 3714; 5013
Raymond Datt *(Pres.)*

Wells Manufacturera de Mexico S.A. de C.V. **(1)**
Carretera Laredo, Km. 9 Parque Industrial Maquil Park,
Reynosa, Tamps. Mexico
Tel.: 40-512-630-4310 (100%)
Mfr. of Automotive Ignition Parts
S.I.C.: 3714
William A. Allen *(Chief Oper. Officer)*

ULLICO INC.
111 Massachusetts Ave., N.W.
Washington, DC 20001
Tel.: 202-682-0900 **MD**
Fax: 202-682-4911
Year Founded: 1927
Assets: $2,077,799,000
Liabilities: $2,056,711,000
Net Worth: $21,088,000
Sales Range: $500-999 Million
Emp.: 645
Fiscal Year-end: 12/31/89
Insurance Holding Company
S.I.C.: 6719; 6311; 6321
Corporate Giving Program: United Fund
Robert A. Georgine *(Chm., Pres. & Chief Exec. Officer)*
John F. Gentleman *(Pres.)*
William L. Cross *(Chief Fin. Officer & Sr. V.P.)*
Joseph Carabillo *(Chief Legal Officer & V.P.)*
James W. Luce *(Exec. V.P.)*
Charles R. Sormani *(Sr. V.P.-Insurance Opers.)*
Carole Assante *(V.P.-Human Resources)*
Thomas B. Bowling *(V.P.-Actuary)*
Kenneth E. Holmes *(V.P.-Mngmt. Information Systems)*
Mark A. Maloney *(V.P.-Mktg.)*
Lester H. Null, Sr. *(Treas. & Sec.)*

No. of U.S. Offices: 45

Computer Systems/Hardware:
IBM 3090-Model 200

Outside Service Firm(s):

Price Waterhouse*(Auditors)*
1801 K. Street, N.W.
Washington, DC 20006
Tel.: 202-296-0800

Citibank N.A.*(Major Banking Relationship)*
Corporate Trust Services, 399 Park Ave.
New York, NY 10043
Tel.: 212-559-1605

Subsidiaries:

The Union Labor Life Insurance Co. **(1)**
111 Massachusetts Ave., N.W.
Washington, DC 20001
Tel.: 202-682-0900 (100%)
Fax: 202-682-4911
Insurance
S.I.C.: 6311; 6321
Robert A. Georgine *(Pres. & Chief Exec. Officer)*

Zenith Administrators, Inc. **(1)**
111 Massachusetts Ave., N.W.
Washington, DC 20001
Tel.: 202-682-0900 (100%)
Fax: 202-682-4911
Administrative Services
S.I.C.: 8741
James Luce *(Pres.)*

Subsidiary:

Zenith Administrators of Texas **(2)**
4600 Gulf Frwy., Ste. 300
Houston, TX 77023
Tel.: 713-926-2422
Fund Administrators
S.I.C.: 6733
William A. Rhodes, Jr. *(V.P.-Opers.)*

U.R.M. STORES, INC.
N. 7511 Freya
Spokane, WA 99207
Mailing Address:
P.O. Box 3365
Spokane, WA 99220
Tel.: 509-467-2620 **WA**
Fax: 509-467-3689
Year Founded: 1921
Assets: $119,400,000
Liabilities: $98,100,000
Net Worth: $21,300,000
Approx.Sls.: $468,900,000
Emp.: 2,000
Fiscal Year-end: 7/31/89
Cooperative; Wholesale Grocery Distributor; Retail Grocery Services
S.I.C.: 5141; 5149; 7311; 5411
A.M. Akins *(Chm. Bd.)*
J. Steve Herbison *(Pres. & Chief Exec. Officer)*
Dick Goodnight *(V.P.-Data Processing)*
B. Miller *(V.P.-Transportation)*
B.E. Shelby *(V.P.-Store Devel.)*
Ron Vawter *(V.P.-Opers.)*
P.B. Cerutti *(Legal Counsel)*
Dennis Horan *(Sec. & Treas.)*
Linda Wilson *(Dir.-Personnel)*

No. of Mfg. Plants/Facilities: 1
No. of U.S. Offices: 1

Computer Systems/Hardware:
Burroughs; IBM

Outside Service Firm(s):

Coopers & Lybrand*(Auditors)*
Seafirst Financial Center,
Spokane, WA 99204

Safeco Insurance Co. of America*(Group Insurer)*
Seattle, WA

C. Underwood, Campbell, Brock & Cerutti*(Legal Firm)*
Spokane, WA

West One Bank*(Major Banking Relationship)*
101 S. Capitol Blvd.
Boise, ID 83701
Tel.: 208-383-7947
Fax: 208-383-3870

The Principal Financial Group*(Pension Manager)*
711 High St.
Des Moines, IA 50309
Tel.: 515-247-4593
Tel.: 800-543-4015

Subsidiaries:

Merchants Insurance Agency **(1)**
North 7511 Freya
Spokane, WA 99220
Tel.: 509-467-2620
Emp.: 6
Insurance Agency
S.I.C.: 6311; 6331
Larry Geller *(Pres.)*

Peirone Produce Company **(1)**
524 Trent
Spokane, WA 99202
Tel.: 509-838-3515
Distributor of Fresh Produce
S.I.C.: 5149
Pat Davidson *(Pres.)*

U.R.M. Development Corp. **(1)**
North 7511 Freya
Spokane, WA 99220
Tel.: 509-467-2620
Emp.: 2
Loan Company
S.I.C.: 6141
Steve Herbison *(Chief Exec. Officer)*

USA PETROLEUM CORPORATION
2701 Ocean Park Blvd., Ste. 210
Santa Monica, CA 90405
Tel.: 310-452-6200
Telex: 652332
Fax: 310-450-4020
Year Founded: 1957
Assets: $73,149,999
Earnings: $1,029,000
Net Worth: $73,149,999
Approx.Sls.: $220,500,000
Emp.: 1,800
Warehousing, Automotive Dealer & Service Stations
S.I.C.: 4225; 5541; 5599
John J. Moller *(Pres. & Chief Exec. Officer)*
Mark Conant *(Exec. V.P.)*
Lyle Schlyer *(Gen. Counsel)*
Jennifer Welch *(Dir.-Personnel & Insurance)*

Computer Systems/Hardware:
IBM

Outside Service Firm(s):

Deloitte & Touche*(Auditors)*
1000 Wilshire Blvd.
Los Angeles, CA 90017-2472
Tel.: 213-688-0800
Fax: 213-688-0100

Allstate Insurance*(Group Insurer)*
Northbrook, IL

Wells Fargo Bank*(Major Banking Relationship)*
420 Montgomery St.
San Francisco, CA 94104

USA NETWORK
(A Joint Venture of MCA Inc. & Paramount Pictures Corp.)
1230 Ave. of the Americas
New York, NY 10020
Tel.: 212-408-9100
Fax: 212-408-8863
Year Founded: 1980
Approx.Sls.: $200,000,000
Emp.: 201
Fiscal Year-end: 12/31/90
Advertiser-Supported Entertainment Basic Cable Network; Joint Venture of MCA, Inc. and Paramount Pictures Corp., Sub. of Paramount Communications
S.I.C.: 4833
Kay Koplovitz *(Pres. & Chief Exec. Officer)*
John Silvestri *(Exec. V.P.-Adv. Sls.)*
David Kenin *(Exec. V.P.-Programming)*
Stephen Brenner *(Sr. V.P.-Bus. Affairs & Opers.; Gen. Counsel)*
Douglas Holloway *(Sr. V.P.-Affiliate Rels.)*
Andrew Besch *(Sr. V.P.-Mktg.)*
Douglas Hamilton *(V.P.-Admin. & Chief Fin. Officer)*
Mary Lou O'Callaghan *(V.P.-Media Rels.)*

Branches:

USA Network **(1)**
401 No. Michigan Ave.
Chicago, IL 60611
Tel.: 312-644-1522
Advertiser Supported Cable Network
S.I.C.: 4833

USA Network **(1)**
2049 Century Park East
Los Angeles, CA 90067
Tel.: 310-277-0199
Advertiser Supported Cable Network
S.I.C.: 4833
Bruce Braun *(V.P.-Western Region)*

USA Network **(1)**
1230 6th Ave.
New York, NY 10020
Tel.: 212-408-9100
Sydney Cuinsberg *(Dir.-Eastern Region)*
Barry Frey *(Mng. Dir.-Intl. Sls.)*
Lou Fazio *(Supvr.-Program Admin.)*

USA Network **(1)**
2000 Town Center, Ste. 2460
Southfield, MI 48075
Tel.: 313-353-1200
Advertiser Supported Cable Network
S.I.C.: 4833
Steve Van Ophuijsen *(V.P.)*

USA Network Control Center **(1)**
300 New Highway
Hauppauge, NY 11788
Tel.: 212-408-9100
Advertiser Supported Cable Network
S.I.C.: 4833

UVP, INC.
5100 Walnut Grove
San Gabriel, CA 91776
Mailing Address:
P.O. Box 1501
San Gabriel, CA 91778
Tel.: 818-285-3123
Fax: 818-285-2940
Year Founded: 1932
Approx.Sls.: $10,000,000
Emp.: 100
Export
Blak-Ray Long Wave Lamps; Mineralight Short Wave Lamps; Chromato-Vue Viewing Cabinets; Light-Wryter Transfer Paper; Pen-Ray Calibration Lamps; Fixtures; Memorase Eprom Erasing Units, UV Ozone Cleaning Unit, Germicidal Lamps, UV Curing; Leak Detection Systems
S.I.C.: 3641; 3648; 2679
Paul B. Warren *(Chm. Bd. & Pres.)*
Bob Hannah *(Controller)*
Bob Cosgrove *(Dir.-Opers.)*
Ronald Meyer *(Dir.-Engrng.)*

Outside Service Firm(s):

Deloitte & Touche*(Auditors)*
1000 Wilshire Blvd.
Los Angeles, CA 90017-2472
Tel.: 213-688-0800
Fax: 213-688-0100

UVP North (1)
825 E. Evelyn
Sunnyvale, CA 94086
Tel.: 408-245-4111

KEITH UDDENBERG, INC.
7520 Soundview Dr.
Gig Harbor, WA 98335
Mailing Address:
P.O. Box 444
Gig Harbor, WA 98335
Tel.: 206-851-6688 **WA**
Fax: 206-851-6554
Year Founded: 1955
Approx.Sls.: $250,000,000
Emp.: 1,300
Grocery Stores
S.I.C.: 5411
A. Keith Uddenberg *(Pres.)*
Wayne Ormiston *(Chief Oper. Officer)*
Lori Dee Schacht *(V.P.)*
R. Keith Uddenberg *(V.P.)*
Doug Henken *(Mgr.-Mktg.)*
Signo Uddenberg *(Mgr.-Retail Opers.)*
Mike Gastineau *(Dist. Mgr.-Thriftway Stores)*
Ed Nelson *(Dist. Mgr.-Stock Market Foods)*
Patricia Maldon *(Office Mgr.)*
Jolene T. Greeley *(Controller)*
Eugenia M. Uddenberg *(Sec. & Treas.)*
Principal(s):
A. Keith Uddenberg
R. Keith Uddenberg
Eugenia M. Uddenberg

Outside Service Firm(s):

Deloitte & Touche*(Auditors)*
700 Fifth Ave., Suite 4500
Seattle, WA 98104-5044
Tel.: 206-292-1800

McGavick, Graves, Beale & McNerthney*(Legal Firm)*
Tacoma, WA

Puget Sound Bank*(Major Banking Relationship)*
GIG Harbor, WA

UGLY DUCKLING RENT-A-CAR
(Sub. of Duck Ventures, Inc.)
2425 E. Camelback Rd., Ste. 650
Phoenix, AZ 85016
Tel.: 602-381-8459
Tel.: 1-800-THE-DUCK **AZ**
Fax: 602-553-7070
Year Founded: 1977
Approx.Sls.: $10,000,000
Emp.: 7
Fiscal Year-end: 12/31/91
Franchise Automobile Rentals
S.I.C.: 7514
William Don Gray *(Pres.)*
Robert D. Holt *(Sr. V.P.)*
Pam Grand *(Admin.)*
Jerry Hochevar *(V.P. & Gen. Mgr.)*

No. of Mfg. Plants/Facilities: 135
No. of U.S. Offices: 200

Computer Systems/Hardware:
Digital; AB Dick; IBM

GEORGE UHE CO., INC.
12 Rte. 17 N.
Paramus, NJ 07652
Mailing Address:
P.O. Box 970
Paramus, NJ 07653
Tel.: 201-843-4000 **NY**
Telex: ITT-421086
Fax: 201-843-7517
Year Founded: 1921
Sales Range: $100-499 Million
Emp.: 30
Fiscal Year-end: 12/31/91
Import Export
Brokers & Agents for Essential Oil & Aromatic Chemicals, Chemical/ Pharmaceutical Intermediates, Spices
S.I.C.: 5122; 5169; 5199; 5100
Karl M. Poehlmann *(Pres. & Chief Exec. Officer)*
Larry N. Maslow *(V.P. & Sec.)*
David S. Cookson *(V.P.)*
Alan H. Cohen *(Chief Fin. Officer & Treas.)*
Bernhard E. Holzapfer *(V.P.)*
Chris K. Diaz *(Asst. V.P.)*
Principal(s):
Karl M. Poehlmann

No. of U.S. Offices: 1

Computer Systems/Hardware:
IBM LAN Network

Outside Service Firm(s):

Deloitte & Touche*(Auditors)*
2 Hilton Court
Parsippany, NJ 07054
Tel.: 201-631-6700

Haskell Brokerage*(Commercial Insurance Carrier)*
New York, NY

Chubb Life America*(Group Insurer)*
8 Sylvan Way
Parsippany, NJ

Cole, Schotz, Bernstein, Meisel & Forman*(Legal Firm)*
Hackensack, NJ

Price, Raffer, & Brown*(Pension Manager)*
Los Angeles, CA

THE UHLMANN CO.
1009 Central
Kansas City, MO 64105
Mailing Address:
P.O. Box 419410
Kansas City, MO 64141
Tel.: 816-221-8200
Fax: 816-221-5504
Approx.Sls.: $13,000,000
Emp.: 20
Fiscal Year-end: 12/31/90
Ceresota & Heckers Unbleached Naturally White & Whole Wheat Flour
S.I.C.: 2041
Paul Uhlmann, Jr. *(Chm. Bd.)*
R. Hugh Uhlmann *(Chm.-Exec. Committee)*
John W. Uhlmann *(Pres.)*
Paul Uhlmann III *(Pres.-Grocery Products Div.)*
J.A. Rasmussen *(V.P. & Dir.-Mktg.)*
Stanley P. Cyphers *(Comptroller)*
Joe Williams *(Dir.-Sls. & Mktg.)*
John Steele *(Dir.-Pur.)*

ULBRICH STAINLESS STEELS & SPECIAL METALS, INC.
57 Dodge Ave.
North Haven, CT 06473
Tel.: 203-239-4481 **CT**
Telex: 160110
Fax: 203-239-7479
Year Founded: 1924
Approx.Sls.: $100,000,000
Emp.: 425
Fiscal Year-end: 12/31/90
Import Export
Manufacture of Rerolled Stainless Steel Strip & Special Metal Strip, Round & Flat Shaped Wire
S.I.C.: 3315; 3316
Frederick C. Ulbrich, Jr. *(Chm. Bd., Pres. & Chief Exec. Officer)*
Richard J. Ulbrich *(Vice Chm.)*
Frederick C. Ulbrich III *(Pres.-Service Ctr. Grp.)*
Jay J. Cei *(V.P.-Fin.)*
Chris L. Durlach *(V.P.-Mktg. & Intl. Div.)*
J. Bulyk *(V.P.-Corp. Devel.)*
Mike Petro *(Dir.-Human Resources)*
John Miller *(Dir.-Pur.)*
Principal(s):
Frederick C. Ulbrich, Jr.
Richard J. Ulbrich
Frederick C. Ulbrich III

No. of Mfg. Plants/Facilities: 6

Computer Systems/Hardware:
IBM 9221

Outside Service Firm(s):

Aetna Life & Casualty*(Group Insurer)*
151 Farmington Avenue
Hartford, CT 06156
Tel.: 203-273-2128
Fax: 203-729-4295

Subsidiary:

Ulbrich Wire, Inc. (1)
55 Defco Park Ave.
North Haven, CT 06473
Tel.: 203-239-4481 (100%)
Fax: 203-239-7479
Import
Stainless Steel & Nickel Alloy Wire
S.I.C.: 3315; 3356
Fredrick C. Ulbrich, Jr. *(Chm. Bd. & Chief Exec. Officer)*
Jay Cei *(Pres. & Chief Oper. Officer)*

Affiliates:

Ulbrich of California, Inc. (1)
5455 E. Home Ave.
Fresno, CA 93727
Tel.: 209-456-2316
Fax: 209-456-2321
Warehousing & Distribution of Stainless Steel & Nickel Alloy Wire
S.I.C.: 5051
Greg Boucher *(Gen. Mgr.)*

Ulbrich of Georgia, Inc. (1)
1465 Beaver Ruin Rd.
Norcross, GA 30093
Tel.: 404-921-3100
Fax: 404-923-3225
Warehousing & Distribution of Stainless Steel & Nickel Alloy Wire
S.I.C.: 5051
Ed Brandt *(Gen. Mgr.)*

Ulbrich of Illinois, Inc. (1)
12340 S. Laramie
Alsip, IL 60658
Tel.: 708-568-7500
Fax: 708-371-1802
Warehousing & Distribution of Stainless Steel & Nickel Alloy Wire
S.I.C.: 5051
Dale Blouin *(Gen. Mgr.)*

ULLENBERG CORP.
420 Bell Ave.
Chattanooga, TN 37405
Mailing Address:
P.O. Box 4157,
Chattanooga, TN 37405
Tel.: 615-266-7758
Fax: 615-266-8733
Approx.Sls.: $22,000,000
Emp.: 250
Whlsle. Rings & Pendants; Forever Yours & Rings & Things
S.I.C.: 5094
Thomas H. Ullenberg *(Chm. Bd.)*
Ronald T. Ullenberg *(Pres.)*
Norman Sprinz *(V.P.)*
Charles Soule *(Chief Fin. Officer)*
Sam Crig *(Sec.)*
Donna Laster *(Adv. Mgr.)*
Wes Gilliand *(Sls. Mgr.)*

ULTIMO LTD.
114 E. Oak St.
Chicago, IL 60611
Tel.: 312-787-0906 **IL**
Fax: 312-787-3904
Year Founded: 1969
Emp.: 55
Wholesale Distribution of Men's & Boys Accessories; Retail Sales of Women's Ready-to-Wear Apparel
S.I.C.: 5611; 5621
Joan Weinstein *(Pres.)*
Armand Poteshman *(Asst. Sec.)*

Outside Service Firm(s):

Poteshman, Grossman & Associates*(Auditors)*
Chicago, IL

ULTRA TOOL & PLASTICS, INC.
155 Pineview Dr.
Amherst, NY 14228
Tel.: 716-691-6223 **NY**
Fax: 716-691-7888 **PLANT II**
Year Founded: 1964
Approx.Sls.: $21,385,000
Emp.: 400
Plastic Injection Molding
S.I.C.: 3544; 3089
Robert Ljungberg *(Chm. Bd., Pres., Chief Exec. & Chief Oper. Officer)*
Susan L. Ljungberg *(Exec. V.P. & Gen. Mgr.)*
Don Jankowski *(Chief Info. Officer)*
Maryanne Ljungberg *(Treas.)*
Craig Sampson *(Dir.-Training & Devel.)*
Brian J. Stocker *(Dir.-Human Resources)*
Terry O'Neil *(Mgr.-Indus. Engrng.)*
John McGee *(Mgr.-Sls.)*
Tony Crook *(Mgr.-Sls.)*
William Wright *(Mgr.-Prod.)*
Richard Krawczyk *(Mgr.-Quality Assurance)*
Ronald Wright *(Mgr.-Warehouse)*
George Hake *(Mgr.-Sls. & Cost Analysis)*
Denny Hinman *(Mgr.-Plant)*
Mike Newton *(Tooling Engineer)*
Susan L. Ljungberg *(Gen. Mgr.)*
John Daily *(Controller)*
Principal(s):
Robert Ljungberg

No. of Mfg. Plants/Facilities: 2
No. of U.S. Offices: 2

Outside Service Firm(s):

Lawler, Kersten & Witkowski*(Auditors)*
Williamsville, NY

Blair & Roach*(Legal Firm)*
Buffalo, NY

Manufacturers & Traders Trust Company*(Major Banking Relationship)*
1 M & T Plaza
Buffalo, NY 14240
Tel.: 716-842-4200

UNCAS MANUFACTURING COMPANY
623 Atwells Ave.
Providence, RI 02909-2413
Mailing Address:
P.O. Box 966
Providence, RI 02901-0966
Tel.: 401-421-0680
Fax: 401-272-2530
Year Founded: 1911
Approx.Sls.: $20,000,000
Emp.: 300
Fiscal Year-end: 12/31/90
Import Export
Mfr. Costume Jewelry
S.I.C.: 3911
Stanley L. Sorrentino *(Chm. Bd., Chief Exec. Officer & Treas.)*
John M. Corsini *(Pres. & Chief Oper. Officer)*
Thomas R. Conti *(V.P.-Opers.)*
Richard L. Yale *(V.P.-Fin.)*
Robert J. Calvano *(Gen. Sls. Mgr.)*

Division:

Curtman Division (1)
623 Atwells Ave.
Providence, RI 02909-2413
Tel.: 401-421-0680
Telex: 929480 UNCAS PVD
Fax: 401-272-2530

UNDERGROUND CONSTRUCTION COMPANY, INC.
5145 Industrial Way
Benicia, CA 94510
Mailing Address:
P.O. Box 2000
Benicia, CA 94510
Tel.: 707-746-8800
Fax: 707-746-1314
Year Founded: 1936
Approx.Sls.: $50,000,000
Emp.: 400
Heavy Construction, Water Sewer & Utility Lines; General Engineering Contractors; General Contractors of Non-Residential & Industrial Buildings & Warehouses
S.I.C.: 1541; 1542; 1622; 1623
Richard E. Hall *(Chm. Bd. & Chief Exec. Officer)*
J.G. Siler *(Pres.)*
Lynn E. Barr *(V.P. & Chief Oper. Officer)*
T.K. McManus, Jr. *(V.P.-Fin.)*
Neil Parrish *(Treas. & Project Mgr.)*
Barry P. Evergettis *(Sec.)*
James Curry *(Dir.-Personnel)*

Outside Service Firm(s):

S. J. Gallina & Co.*(Auditors)*
Sacramento, CA

Turner & Franzoia*(Legal Firm)*
Oakland, CA

Bank of America NT&SA*(Major Banking Relationship)*
P.O. Box 37002,
San Francisco, CA 94137
Tel.: 415-624-2486

Subsidiary:

M.G.C. Company **(1)**
5145 Industrial Way
Benicia, CA 94510
Tel.: 707-746-8900
Emp.: 30
General Constractors of Non-Residential & Industrial Buildings & Warehouses
S.I.C.: 1541; 1542
Barry P. Evergettis *(Pres.)*

UNEX CONVEYING SYSTEMS, INC.
10 Progress Rd.
Jackson, NJ 08527
Tel.: 908-928-2800
Approx.Sls.: $10,000,000
Emp.: 110
Mfr. of Conveyors & Conveying Systems
S.I.C.: 3535
Frank Neuwirth *(Chm. Bd. & Pres.)*
Hal Pfeiffer *(V.P.)*
Doug Shore *(Dir.-Pur.)*
Carol Ann Neuwirth *(Adv. Mgr.)*

UNGER COMPANY
12401 Berea Rd.
Cleveland, OH 44111
Tel.: 216-252-1400 **OH**
Fax: 216-252-1427
Year Founded: 1920
Approx.Sls.: $12,000,000
Emp.: 40
Import Export
Wholesale Distribution of Boxes & Containers
S.I.C.: 5113
Paul A. Unger *(Chm. Bd.)*
Gerald F. Unger *(Pres. & Chief Exec. Officer)*
Thomas Zimmerman *(Chief Fin. Officer & V.P.)*
Sonja F. Unger *(Sec.)*
Ruth Vincent *(Mgr.-Adv.)*

Outside Service Firm(s):

Meaden & Moore*(Auditors)*
Cleveland, OH

Weston, Hurd, Fallon & Paisley*(Legal Firm)*
Cleveland, OH

Huntington National Bank*(Major Banking Relationship)*
Cleveland, OH

UNICOVER CORPORATION
One Unicover Center
Cheyenne, WY 82008
Tel.: 307-634-5911
Fax: 307-771-3134
Approx.Sls.: $32,000,000
Emp.: 260
Philatelist Stamps; Mail Order House; Porcelain Enameled Products & Utensils; Paper Coated or Laminated For Packaging
S.I.C.: 5999; 5961; 5092; 3469; 2671
James A. Helzer *(Pres. & Chief Exec. Officer)*
James A. Willnis *(Exec. V.P.)*
Robert S. Hahn *(V.P.)*
H. Albert Helzer *(Treas.)*

Outside Service Firm(s):

Wyoming National Bank*(Major Banking Relationship)*
Cheyenne, WY

UNIFAX, INC.
1065 Hwy. 315, Ste. 203
Wilkes-Barre, PA 18702
Tel.: 717-822-0902
Fax: 717-822-0909
Salad Dressing; Oleomargarine; Condiments; Packaged Frozen Goods
S.I.C.: 5149; 5142
Frank Bevevino *(Chm. & Chief Exec. Officer)*
Thomas McMullen *(Pres. & Chief Oper. Officer)*
David McAnally *(Chief Fin. Officer)*
Philip Morgan *(Dir.-Mktg.)*

Outside Service Firm(s):

KPMG Peat Marwick*(Auditors)*
4905 Tildgman St.
Allentown, PA 18104
Tel.: 215-391-6380

Subsidiary:

Kings Foodservice **(1)**
269 S. Center Dr.
Alcoa, TN 37701
Tel.: 615-982-8100
Salad Dressing; Oleomargarine; Condiments; Packaged Frozen Foods
S.I.C.: 5149; 5142
John Purvis *(Pres.)*

UNIFLEX, INC.
383 W. John St.
Hicksville, NY 11802
Mailing Address:
P.O. Box 96
Hicksville, NY 11801
Tel.: 516-932-2000
Tel.: 800-223-0564
Year Founded: 1963
Approx.Sls.: $22,000,000
Emp.: 300
Fiscal Year-end: 1/31/91
Export
Mfrs. of Polyethylene Products, Plastic Shopping Bags; Hand-L Bag, Uni-Tote, Econo-Tote, Uni-Cord, Econo-Cord, Budget-Tote, All American Shopper, Uni-Box, Cut-Out Tote, Texture-Flex, Mailing Envelopes, Freight Courier Pouches, Specigard Disposable Specimen Bags, Protex-ray Disposable Cassette Covers, Medical Supply Items
S.I.C.: 3089
Warner Heuman *(Chm. Bd.)*
H. Barry *(Pres. & Dir.-Sls.)*
Jay Warner *(Exec. V.P.)*
Robert K. Semel *(Exec. V.P.)*
M. Heuman *(Sr. V.P. & Treas.)*
Erich Vetter *(Sr. V.P. & Sec.)*
Martin Brownstein *(V.P.-Sls. & Adv. Specialty)*
Melissa Cantor *(V.P.-Opers.)*
R. Gugliotta *(V.P.-Fin.)*
Howard Samuels *(V.P.-Production)*
Kurt Vetter *(V.P.-Res. & Devel.)*
Hy Brownstein *(Dir.-Mktg.)*
Lee Cantor *(Natl. Sls. Mgr.)*

UNIFLOW MANUFACTURING CO.
1525 E. Lake Rd.
Erie, PA 16512
Tel.: 814-453-6761
Fax: 814-455-6336
Approx.Sls.: $28,000,000
Emp.: 260
Fiscal Year-end: 12/31/90
Manufacture Automatic Ice Cube Machines, Ice Storage Bins, Ice Crushers & Dispensers
S.I.C.: 3585; 3632
Thomas E. Kuebler *(Chm. Bd.)*
J. Clark Kuebler *(Pres.)*
Thomas O. Martin *(V.P.-Admin.)*
Brad Phillips *(Chief Fin. Officer)*
Chirs Kuebler *(Mgr.-Engrng.)*
Vince Campanelli *(Mgr.-Adv. & Sls. Promo.)*
Kris Malee *(Pur. Supvr.)*

UNIFOIL CORPORATION
217 Brook Ave.
Passaic, NJ 07055
Tel.: 201-365-2000
Twx: 134651
Fax: 201-365-0924
Approx.Sls.: $35,000,000
Emp.: 99
Mfr. of Aluminum Coated Paper & Paperboard
S.I.C.: 2671
Edward J. Alois *(Pres.)*
William Boehler *(V.P.)*
Joel M. Holzberg *(V.P.-Mktg. & Sls.)*
Thomas S. Calderone *(Treas.)*

Outside Service Firm(s):

Goovearts & Kedersha*(Auditors)*
Hasbrouck Heights, NJ

Waldman, Renda & McKinney*(Legal Firm)*
Hawthorne, NJ

Citizens First National Bank*(Major Banking Relationship)*
Passaic, NJ

UNIGROUP, INC.
One United Dr.
Fenton, MO 63026
Tel.: 314-326-3100
Year Founded: 1947
Approx.Rev.: $789,000,000
Emp.: 950
Fiscal Year-end: 12/31/91
Holding Company: Household Goods Transportation
S.I.C.: 6719; 4212; 4213
Maurice Greenblatt *(Chm. Bd.)*
Gerald P. Stadler *(Vice Chm.)*
Robert J. Baer *(Pres.)*
Douglas H. Wilton *(Chief Fin. Officer)*
Charles R. Childers *(Chief Information Officer)*
Clyde H. Springer *(Treas.)*
Charles G. McDaniel *(Sec.)*
Morton I. Golder *(Gen. Counsel)*
Sherry Fagin *(Dir.-Human Resources)*
John Howard *(Dir.-Cash Mngmt.)*
Cliff Saxton *(Dir.-Pub. Rels.)*
William Beard *(Mgr.-Leasing)*
Mel Beauchamp *(Mgr.-Pur.)*
Arthur Coffey *(Mgr.-Real Estate)*
Ann Gebhard *(Mgr.-Benefits)*
Richard Sullivan *(Mgr.-Intl.)*
Sandra Offerman *(Mgr.)*

Computer Systems/Hardware:
IBM

Outside Service Firm(s):

Arthur Andersen & Co.*(Auditors)*
1010 Market St.
St. Louis, MO 63101

Goldman, Sachs & Co.*(Investment Banker)*
St. Louis, MO

Boatmen's Bank of St. Louis*(Major Banking Relationship)*
1 Boatmen's Plaza
St. Louis, MO

Subsidiaries:

United Capital Services, Inc. **(1)**
One United Dr.
Fenton, MO 63026
Tel.: 314-326-3100
Robert J. Baer *(Pres.)*

United Leasing, Inc. **(1)**
One United Dr.
Fenton, MO 63026
Tel.: 314-343-9333
Truck & Trailer Leasing
S.I.C.: 7513
William F. Beard, Jr. *(Exec. V.P.)*

United Van Lines, Inc. **(1)**
One United Dr.
Fenton, MO 63026
Tel.: 314-326-3100
Earnings: $2,890,000
Approx.Sls.: $789,200,000
Emp.: 950
Fiscal Year-end: 12/31/91
Transportation of Household Goods
S.I.C.: 4213; 4212
Maurice Greenblatt *(Chm. Bd.)*
Gerald P. Stadler *(Vice Chm.)*
Robert J. Baer *(Pres.)*
James L. Wilson *(Exec. V.P.)*
Clyde H. Springer *(Treas.)*
Charles G. McDaniel *(Sec.)*
Morton I. Golder *(Gen. Counsel)*

Vanliner Group, Inc. **(1)**
One United Dr.
Fenton, MO 63026
Tel.: 314-326-3100
Insurance
S.I.C.: 6399
Daniel E. Yates *(Exec. V.P.)*

UNIHEALTH AMERICA
4100 W. Alameda
Burbank, CA 91505
Tel.: 818-566-6301
Earnings: $18,952,000
Approx.Sls.: $2,141,640,000
Emp.: 12,000
Fiscal Year-end: 9/30/91
Health Care Services
S.I.C.: 8099
Paul Teslow *(Pres. & Chief Exec. Officer)*
Gary Leary *(Exec. V.P. & Chief Oper. Officer)*
Karen Cockrell *(Sec.)*
Dennis Strom *(Sr. V.P.)*
Paul Aleala *(Chief Info. Officer & Pres.-CaseCare)*
Eric Benveniste *(Chief Fin. Officer)*
Stephen Adams *(V.P.-Fin.)*
Tom Bria *(V.P.-Compensation & Benefits)*
Stan Croonquist *(V.P.-Human Resources)*
Dennis Eder *(V.P.-Treasury)*
Linda McKenzie *(Sec.)*
Don Crane *(Gen. Counsel)*
Jim Baker *(Dir.-Pur.)*
Tony Cox *(Dir.-Telecommunications)*

Computer Systems/Hardware:
AS400

Outside Service Firm(s):

Ernst & Young*(Auditors)*
515 S. Flower St.
Los Angeles, CA 90071
Tel.: 213-621-1666

In-House*(Commercial Insurance Carrier)*

In-House*(Group Insurance Broker/ Consult)*

Musick, Peeler & Garrett*(Legal Firm)*
One Wilshire Blvd.
Los Angeles, CA 90017
Tel.: 213-629-7600

Bank of America*(Major Banking Relationship)*
Los Angeles, CA

Subsidiaries:

Glendale Memorial Hospital and Medical Center **(1)**
Central and Los Feliz
Glendale, CA 91225-7036
Tel.: 818-502-1900

La Palma Intercommunity Hospital **(1)**
7901 Walker St.
La Palma, CA 90623-1764
Tel.: 714-670-7400

Lindsay Hospital Medical Center **(1)**
740 Sequoia Ave.
Lindsay, CA 93247-1423
Tel.: 209-562-4955

Long Beach Community Hospital **(1)**
1720 Termino Ave.
Long Beach, CA 90804-2180
Tel.: 213-498-1000

Martin Luther Hospital **(1)**
P.O. Box 3304, 1830 W. Romneya Dr.
Anaheim, CA 92801-1854
Tel.: 714-491-5200

Meadowlands Hospital Medical Center **(1)**
Meadowlands Parkway
Secaucus, NJ 07094-2912
Tel.: 201-392-3100

PacifiCare Health Systems, Inc. **(1)**
5995 Plaza Dr.
Cypress, CA 90630
Tel.: 714-952-1121 (65%)
Assets: $322,328,000
Earnings: $25,702,000
Liabilities: $222,650,000
Net Worth: $99,678,000
Approx.Rev.: $1,242,357,000
Emp.: 1,900
Fiscal Year-end: 9/30/91
Computer Systems/Hardware:
Digital Equipment Corp.
Health Care Co.
S.I.C.: 6311; 6324
Corporate Giving Program: Gifts are Subject to Review by the Pacificare Foundation, a Non-profit, Charitable Corporation
Samuel J. Tibbitts *(Chm. Bd.)*
Frank R. McDougall *(Vice Chm.)*
Terry Hartshorn *(Pres. & Chief Exec. Officer)*
Alan Hoops *(Exec. V.P., Chief Oper. Officer & Sec.)*
Wayne Lowell *(Sr. V.P., Chief Fin. Officer & Treas.)*
Richard Lipeles *(Sr. V.P. & Pres.-Pacificare California)*
John Siefker *(Sr. V.P.)*
Lucy Meyer Cunningham *(V.P. & Pres.-Pacificare Foundation)*
Debby Iacunato *(V.P.-Corp. Communications)*
Richard Kislowski *(V.P.-Information Services)*
Carmen Ness *(V.P.-Govt. Rels.)*
John Ninomiya *(V.P.-Health Data Analysis)*
Fred Ryder *(V.P. & Controller)*
C. William Wood *(V.P.-Human Resources)*
Joseph S. Konowiecki *(Gen. Counsel & Asst. Sec.)*
Kathy Reid *(Dir.-Admin. Services)*
Ellen Erickson *(Corp. Travel Planner)*

Subsidiaries:

Columbia General Life Insurance Co. **(2)**
23282 Mill Creek, Ste. 1300
Laguna Hills, CA 92653
Tel.: 714-859-7920 (100%)
Emp.: 40
Life Insurance & Managed Care
S.I.C.: 6311
Richard Lindstrom *(Pres.)*
Len Whyte *(Chief Fin. Officer)*

PacifiCare of California **(2)**
5796 Corporate Ave.
Cypress, CA 90630
Tel.: 714-236-5555 (100%)
Emp.: 825
Health Maintenance Organization
S.I.C.: 6324
Richard Lipeles *(Pres.)*
David Barr *(Chief Fin. Officer)*
Michael Lombardi *(V.P.-Mktg.)*

PacifiCare of Oklahoma Inc. **(2)**
7134 S. Yale Ave., Ste. 700
Tulsa, OK 74136
Tel.: 918-496-1200 (100%)
Emp.: 115
David Kibbe *(Pres.)*
Ron Waetzman *(Chief Fin. Officer)*

PacifiCare of Oregon, Inc. **(2)**
Five Centerpointe Dr., Ste. 600
Lake Oswego, OR 97035
Tel.: 503-620-9324 (100%)
Emp.: 130
Health Maintenance Organization
S.I.C.: 6324
David Hallock *(Pres.)*
Gary Hubbard *(V.P.-Sls. & Mktg.)*
Pat Feyen *(Chief Fin. Officer)*

Execu-Fit Health Programs, Inc. **(2)**
One Lombard St.
San Francisco, CA 94111
Tel.: 415-981-0111
Health & Wellness Program
S.I.C.: 8099
Karen Behnke *(Pres.)*

San Gabriel Valley Medical Center **(1)**
218 S. Santa Anita Ave.
San Gabriel, CA 91776-1137
Tel.: 818-289-5454

Santa Monica Hospital Medical Center **(1)**
1250 16th St.
Santa Monica, CA 90404-1200
Tel.: 213-319-4000

Valley Hospital **(1)**
1410 N. Garey Ave.
Pomona, CA 91767-3810
Tel.: 909-623-8388

THE UNIMAX CORPORATION
54 E. 64th St.
New York, NY 10021
Tel.: 212-755-8800 **DE**
Fax: 212-486-5737
Year Founded: 1965
Assets: $24,053,800
Earnings: ($672,700)
Liabilities: $22,363,700
Net Worth: $1,690,100
Approx.Sls.: $24,755,000
Emp.: 312
Fiscal Year-end: 3/31/91
Mfr. of Industrial Controls & Steel Springs
S.I.C.: 3493; 3625
Arthur L. Carter *(Chm. Bd.)*
Tom Scheinman *(Pres. & Chief Exec. Officer)*
Richard S. Wiesenthal *(Exec. V.P. & Chief Fin. Officer)*
John D. Sicher, Jr. *(V.P. & Gen. Counsel)*
Peter G. Giosa *(V.P.)*
Carol Bacic *(Controller)*
Vincent A. Bohn *(Treas.)*
Fred Ravine *(Dir.-Risk Mngmt.)*
John Volk *(Dir.-Data Processing)*

No. of Mfg. Plants/Facilities: 6
No. of U.S. Offices: 3
No. of Foreign Offices: 1

Computer Systems/Hardware:
IBM PC

Outside Service Firm(s):

KPMG Peat Marwick*(Auditors)*
345 Park Ave.
New York, NY 10154
Tel.: 212-758-9700
Fax: 212-872-3308

Liberty Mutual*(Commercial Insurance Carrier)*
Boston, MA

State Mutual Life Assurance Co. of America*(Group Insurer)*
440 Lincoln St.
Worcester, MA 01605
Tel.: 508-852-1000

Chemical Banking Corp.*(Investment Banker)*
277 Park Ave.
New York, NY 10041
Tel.: 212-310-6407
Fax: 212-310-4526

Paul, Weiss, Rifkind, Wharton & Garrison*(Legal Firm)*
1285 Avenue of the Americas
New York, NY 10019

Chemical Banking Corp.*(Major Banking Relationship)*
277 Park Ave.
New York, NY 10041
Tel.: 212-310-6407
Fax: 212-310-4526

State Mutual Life Assurance Co. of America*(Pension Manager)*
440 Lincoln St.
Worcester, MA 01605
Tel.: 508-852-1000

Division:

Lee Spring Company **(1)**
1462 62nd St.
Brooklyn, NY 11219
Tel.: 718-236-2222
Approx.Sls.: $18,500,000
Emp.: 240
Mfr. of Springs
S.I.C.: 3495
P. Giosa *(Chief Oper. Officer)*

Subsidiary:

Ward Leonard Electric Company, Inc. **(1)**
31 South St.
Mount Vernon, NY 10550
Tel.: 914-664-1000 (100%)
Approx.Sls.: $4,000,000
Emp.: 50
Mfr. of Motor Controls
S.I.C.: 3625
J. Carter *(Pres.)*
Bernie McCamish *(V.P.-Sls. & Mktg.)*
William Collins *(Controller)*
Myron Moroz *(Mgr.-Engrng.)*
Ron Powers *(Dir.-Personnel & Pub. Rels.)*
Lois Beatty *(Dir.-Pub.)*

Non-U.S. Holding:

Lee Spring Co., Ltd. **(1)**
Wokingham, SL67DF, United Kingdom
Tel.: 0628-32646 (100%)
Approx.Sls.: $1,000,000
Emp.: 5
Springs
S.I.C.: 3493

THE UNION OF ARKANSAS CORP.
124 W. Capitol
Little Rock, AR 72201
Mailing Address:
P.O. Box 1541
Little Rock, AR 72203
Tel.: 501-378-4000 **NY**
Fax: 501-375-8823
Year Founded: 1933
Approx.Sls.: $66,000,000
Emp.: 500
Bank Holding Company
S.I.C.: 6712
Herbert H. McAdams II *(Chm. Emeritus & Chief Exec. Officer)*
H. Hall McAdams, III *(Chm. Bd.)*
Robert C. Connor *(Pres.)*

Principal(s):
H. Hall McAdams, III
Robert C. Connor
Walter A. DeRoeck

Outside Service Firm(s):

Frost & Co.*(Auditors)*
Little Rock, AR

Smith & Nixon*(Legal Firm)*
Little Rock, AR

Subsidiaries:

Union National Bank of Arkansas **(1)**
Capitol at Louisiana
Little Rock, AR 72201
Tel.: 501-378-4000
National Bank
S.I.C.: 6021

Union National Bank of Austin **(1)**
Capitol at Louisiana
Little Rock, AR 72201
Tel.: 501-378-4000
S.I.C.: 6021

Union National Bank of Oklahoma **(1)**
Capitol at Louisiana
Little Rock, AR 72201
Tel.: 501-378-4000
S.I.C.: 6021

THE UNION CENTRAL LIFE INSURANCE CO.
1876 Waycross Rd.
Cincinnati, OH 45240
Mailing Address:
P.O. Box 179,
Cincinnati, OH 45201
Tel.: 513-595-2200
Tel.: 800-825-1551 **OH**
Fax: 513-595-2918
Year Founded: 1867
Assets: $3,207,833,000
Earnings: $16,042,951
Liabilities: $3,016,246,000
Net Worth: $191,587,000
Approx.Sls.: $540,193,000
Emp.: 790
Fiscal Year-end: 12/31/91
Insurance Company
S.I.C.: 6311; 6321
Corporate Giving Program: Offers Financial Support to Qualified Tax-Exempt Organizaitons, Particularly in the Greater Cincinnati Area
Employee Matching Gifts Program: Matches Dollar-For-Dollar Employees' Personal Gifts-From a Minimum of $25 per Gift up to a Maximum of $500 a Year-to Accredited Public & Private American Colleges & Universities
Larry R. Pike *(Chm. Bd., Pres. & Chief Exec. Officer)*
Lothar A. Vasholz *(Exec. V.P. & Corp. Mktg. Officer)*
Stephen R. Hatcher *(Sr. V.P.-Admin. & Chief Fin. Officer)*
Carl B. Wright *(Sr. V.P.)*
Donna Sanders *(V.P.-Human Resources)*
David F. Westerbeck *(V.P., Sec. & Gen. Counsel)*
William G. Brenner *(Treas.)*
Marilyn R. Mitchell *(Comptroller)*
Lois Butt *(Dir.-Pur.)*

No. of U.S. Offices: 250

Computer Systems/Hardware:
Siera 3090

Outside Service Firm(s):

Price Waterhouse*(Auditors)*
2200 Chemed Center, 255 E. 5th St.
Cincinnati, OH 45202-4798
Tel.: 513-621-1900

The Union Central Life Insurance Co.—(Continued)

Subsidiaries:

Manhattan Life Insurance Company (1)
1876 Waycross Rd.
Cincinnati, OH 45240
Life Insurance
S.I.C.: 6311
Daniel J. Fischer *(Chief Oper. Officer)*

Manhattan National Corporation (1)
P. O. Box 5353,
Cincinnati, OH 45201
Tel.: 513-595-5400
Insurance, Investments & Pension Services Company
S.I.C.: 6282; 6311
James J. Breen *(Sr. V.P. & Chief Oper. Officer)*

UNION CITY BODY COMPANY, INC.
350 W. Deerfield Rd.
Union City, IN 47390
Mailing Address:
P.O. Box 190
Union City, IN 47390
Tel.: 317-964-3121
Tel.: 800-428-6650 **IN**
Fax: 317-964-3763
Year Founded: 1898
Approx.Sls.: $92,000,000
Emp.: 1,000
Fiscal Year-end: 8/31/92
Import Export
Mfr. Truck Bodies
S.I.C.: 3713
Alan T. Nolan *(Chm. Bd.)*
Steven L. Adelsperger *(Pres.)*
Mark A. Heistand *(Chief Fin. Officer)*
John W. Adelsperger *(Sr. V.P.)*
Jerry A. Cox *(Sr. V.P.)*
Joseph A. Snyder *(Sr. V.P.)*
John E. Halpin *(V.P.)*
L.A. Hindsley *(V.P. & Chief Engineer)*
Robert C. Weimer *(V.P. & Controller)*
L. C. Wright *(V.P.-Sls. & Mktg.)*
Marcelyn Vaupel *(Treas.)*
Lisa Spille *(Sec.)*
T.K. Puderbaugh *(Dir.-Pur.)*
Jerry Osborne *(Plant Mgr.)*
A. Wayne Lahman *(Indus. Rels. Mgr.)*
Jim Van Skyock *(Dir.-Personnel)*
Principal(s):
Adelsperger Family

Computer Systems/Hardware:
IBM AS/400

Outside Service Firm(s):

Coopers & Lybrand*(Auditors)*
400 Renaissance Center
Detroit, MI 48243
Tel.: 313-446-7100
Fax: 313-446-7117

United of Omaha*(Group Insurer)*
Mutual of Omaha Plaza
Omaha, NE 68175
Tel.: 800-327-8871

Union Equity Cooperative Exchange
(Acquired by Farmland Industries, Inc., name changed to Union Equity)

THE UNION FORK & HOE CO.
500 Dublin Ave.
Columbus, OH 43215
Mailing Address:
P. O. Box 1940
Columbus, OH 43216
Tel.: 614-222-4400
Fax: 614-221-8397
Year Founded: 1890
Approx.Sls.: $225,000,000
Emp.: 700
Fiscal Year-end: 7/31/91
Import Export
Lawn, Garden, Farm & Indus. Hand Tools
S.I.C.: 3523; 3524; 3423
Gabe Midaly *(Pres.)*
Jim Farland *(V.P.-Sls. & Mktg.)*
R. Speer *(Chief Fin. Officer)*
R.D. Saxton *(Controller)*
David A. Durell *(Mktg. Dir.)*
Harold Bauer *(Adv. Mgr.)*
B. Wolford *(Credit Mgr.)*
Jim Lytle *(Mgr.-Pur.)*

UNION HOLDINGS, INC.
30 Rockefeller Plaza, Ste. 4314
New York, NY 10112
Tel.: 212-649-5990
Year Founded: 1984
Approx.Sls.: $1,500,000,000
Emp.: 2,700
Holding Co. for Natural Gas & Propane Utilities, Meat Packing, Trucking & Processed Foods
S.I.C.: 4924; 6719; 4923; 2011
Ezra Zilkha *(Chm. Bd.)*
Anthony Geller *(Pres. & Chief Exec. Officer)*
Donald Zilkha *(V.P. & Asst. Sec.)*
Cecile Zilkha *(Sec.)*
Judith Geller *(Treas. & Asst. Sec.)*
Principal(s):
Ezra Zilkha

Computer Systems/Hardware:
IBM System 38

Outside Service Firm(s):

KPMG Peat Marwick*(Auditors)*
One Williams Center, Ste. 1600
Tulsa, OK 74172

Shea & Gould*(Legal Firm)*
New York, NY

Citibank N.A.*(Major Banking Relationship)*
Corporate Trust Services, 399 Park Ave.
New York, NY 10043
Tel.: 212-559-1605

National Westminster Bank plc*(Major Banking Relationship)*
Astor Plaza, 1515 Broadway
New York, NY 10036

Subsidiary:

Idle Wild Foods (1)
72 Cambridge St.
Worcester, MA 01603
Tel.: 508-757-7761 (100%)
Approx.Sls.: $1,200,000,000
Emp.: 2,500
Process & Wholesale Meat
S.I.C.: 2011; 5147
Anthony Geller *(Chief Exec. Officer)*
Jeffrey Geller *(Exec. V.P.)*

Subsidiaries:

Central Realty Corp. (2)
P.O. Box 1358,
Liberal, KS 67901
Tel.: 316-624-1851 (100%)
Real Estate
S.I.C.: 6531

Subsidiary:

Red L Foods (3)
150 Searles Rd.
Pomfret Center, CT 06259
Tel.: 203-928-2711
Tel.: 800-243-1185
Fax: 203-928-0351
Approx.Sls.: $5,000,000
Export
Mfr. Frozen Hors d'Oeuvres & Quiche Lorraine
S.I.C.: 2038; 5142
P. Fasino *(Chief Fin. Officer & Controller)*
T.B. Phillips *(Managing Dir.)*
Wm. Mahone *(Gen. Counsel)*
M. Benhase *(Mgr.-Mfg.)*

Idle Wild Management Corporation (2)
256 Franklyn St.
Worcester, MA 01604
Tel.: 508-757-7761
Emp.: 12
Robert Carlson *(Data Processing Dir.)*
Herbert L. Daitch *(Controller)*

National Beef Packing Company (2)
P.O. Box 978,
Liberal, KS 67901
Tel.: 316-624-1851 (100%)
Meat Packing
S.I.C.: 5146
Rod White *(V.P. & Gen. Mgr.)*
Victor Manke *(Controller)*
John Piper *(Data Processing Dir.)*
Robert Hill *(Purchasing Dir.)*
Cynthia Stecker *(Personnel Dir.)*

Subsidiaries:

Liberal By-Products (3)
P.O. Box 978,
Liberal, KS 67901
Tel.: 316-624-1851 (100%)
Meat Packaging
S.I.C.: 5146

LISC Management Services (3)
P.O. Box 978,
Liberal, KS 67901
Tel.: 316-624-1851 (100%)
S.I.C.: 8741

Subsidiary:

Liberal International Sales Corp. (4)
P.O. Box 978,
Liberal, KS 67901
Tel.: 316-624-1851 (100%)
Sales
S.I.C.: 5146

Liberal International Sales V.I. Inc. (3)
P.O. Box 978,
Liberal, KS 67901
Tel.: 316-624-1851 (100%)
Approx.Sls.: $150,000,000
S.I.C.: 5146
Jim Mc Carty *(Gen. Mgr.)*

Southwestern Equipment Co. (3)
P.O. Box 978,
Liberal, KS 67901
Tel.: 316-624-1851 (100%)
Auto & Home Supply Store
S.I.C.: 5531

National Carriers, Inc. (2)
P.O. Box 1358
Liberal, KS 67901
Tel.: 800-835-2097 (100%)
Trucking Co.
S.I.C.: 4214
John Jacobsen Jr. *(Chief Oper. Officer)*
Jim Mc Carty *(Gen. Mgr.)*
Jim Wills *(Opers. Mgr.)*
John Piper *(Data Processing Dir.)*
Tom Michael *(Controller)*

Supreme Feeders, Inc. (2)
P.O. Box 708,
Liberal, KS 67901
Tel.: 316-624-6296
Approx.Sls.: $56,000,000
Emp.: 78
Custom Feedlot
S.I.C.: 0211
John Oringderf *(Gen. Mgr.)*
Ron Heeke *(Contr.)*

Divisions:

Cimaron Grain Co. (3)
P.O. Box 708,
Liberal, KS 67901
Tel.: 316-624-1836 (100%)
Grain
S.I.C.: 5153
John Oringderf *(Gen. Mgr.)*

Supreme Cattle Co. (3)
P.O. Box 708,
Liberal, KS 67901
Tel.: 316-624-6296 (100%)
Cattle Feeding
S.I.C.: 0211
John Oreingderf *(Gen. Mgr.)*

UNION INDUSTRIES, INC.
10 Admiral St.
Providence, RI 02908
Mailing Address:
P.O. Box 6025
Providence, RI 02940
Tel.: 401-274-7000
Tel.: 800-556-6454 **RI**
Fax: 401-331-1910
Year Founded: 1954
Approx.Sls.: $20,000,000
Emp.: 175
Printers & Converters of Flexible Packaging
S.I.C.: 2673
H. Alan Frank *(Pres., Chief Fin. Officer & Treas.)*
Thomas F. McCabe *(Exec. V.P.)*
Harley Frank *(V.P. & Sec.)*
Edward S. Goldin *(Legal Officer)*
Ron Beauregard *(Controller)*
Jeff Brandenburg *(Tech. Dir.)*
William Moniz *(Gen. Mgr.)*
Michael Sugerman *(Pur. Mgr.)*
Principal(s):
H. Alan Frank
Harley Frank

No. of Mfg. Plants/Facilities: 1
No. of U.S. Offices: 1

Computer Systems/Hardware:
Wang

Outside Service Firm(s):

Newton B. Cohn*(Auditors)*
Providence, RI

Liberty Mutual*(Commercial Insurance Carrier)*
Providence, RI

Pucci & Goldin*(Legal Firm)*
123 Dyer St.
Providence, RI 02909
Tel.: 401-861-7400

Subsidiaries:

Admiral Packaging, Inc. (1)
10 Admiral St.
Providence, RI 02940
Tel.: 401-274-7000
Tel.: 800-262-0027
Fax: 401-521-9470
Approx.Sls.: $5,000,000
Mfr. Plastic Envelopes
S.I.C.: 3089
H. Alan Frank *(Chief Exec. Officer)*
Thomas McCabe *(Pres.)*
Harley Frank *(V.P.)*
Lynn Wise *(V.P.-Sls.)*
Carol Bienenfeld *(Sls. & Mktg. Admin.)*

Union Paper Co. (1)
10 Admiral St.
Providence, RI 02908
Tel.: 401-274-7000
Fax: 401-331-1910
Approx.Sls.: $3,000,000
Mfr. Paper, Polyethylene & Cellophane Bags, Plain & Printed
S.I.C.: 2673; 3089
H. Alan Frank *(Chief Exec. Officer)*

UNION PEN COMPANY
777 W. Putnam Ave.
Greenwich, CT 06836
Mailing Address:
P.O. Box 5010,
Greenwich, CT 06836
Tel.: 203-531-4240
Fax: 203-531-8297
Approx.Sls.: $15,000,000
Emp.: 140
Mfr. of Writing Instruments, Unipeco, Fine-Riter, Flex-A-Matic; Advertising Specialties
S.I.C.: 3951; 3952; 3993
Morton Tenny *(Pres.)*
Robert Rosenthal *(V.P.-Fin.)*
Florence Silagi *(Dir.-Admin.)*
Steve Richman *(Dir.-Mktg.)*

UNION PUMP COMPANY
4600 Dickman Rd.
Battle Creek, MI 49015
Tel.: 616-966-4600 **MI**
Telex: 3750182
Fax: 616-962-3534
Year Founded: 1885
Approx.Sls.: $52,500,000
Emp.: 355
Export
Mfr. Pumps & Valves
S.I.C.: 3561; 3491
Peter S. Ordway *(Chm., Pres. & Chief Exec. Officer)*
William P. Winslow *(V.P.-Opers.)*
James R. Rossen *(V.P.-Fin. & Treas.)*
David Dempsey *(Dir.-Sales & Mktg.)*
Donald D. Kuenzel *(Asst. Treas. & Sec.)*
David J. Hoover *(Mgr.-Pur.)*
Thomas A. Gossard *(Mgr.-Human Resources)*
Joseph S. Allmond *(Mgr.-Data Processing & Telecommunications)*
Paul D. Woods *(Mgr.-Quality Control)*
Kathy M. Barker *(Intl. Acct. Specialist)*

Outside Service Firm(s):

BDO Seidman*(Auditors)*
99 Monroe Ave. NW, Ste. 800
Grand Rapids, MI 49503
Tel.: 616-774-7000
Fax: 616-451-2096

Warner, Norcross & Judd*(Legal Firm)*
One Vandenberg Center
Grand Rapids, MI 49502
Tel.: 616-459-6121

Zions First National Bank*(Major Banking Relationship)*
One South Main St.
Salt Lake City, UT 84111
Tel.: 801-582-4812

Non-U.S. Holding:

Union Pump (Canada) Ltd. **(1)**
4211 Mainway Dr.
Burlington, ON L7L 5N9, Canada
Tel.: 416-335-2580 (100%)
Telex: 618978
Mfr. Pumps
S.I.C.: 3561
Doug J. Lunam *(V.P. & Gen. Mgr.)*

UNION STEEL PRODUCTS, INCORPORATED
509 N. Albion St.
Albion, MI 49224
Mailing Address:
P.O. Box 60,
Albion, MI 49224
Tel.: 517-629-2181
Tel.: 800-543-5193
Fax: 517-629-9009
Year Founded: 1903
Approx.Sls.: $12,000,000
Emp.: 150
Fiscal Year-end: 12/31/91
Export
Material Handling Equip., Contract Mfg. & Finishing Of Steel & Wire Products, Bakery & Food Service Equip.; Wire & Sheet Metal Fabrication
S.I.C.: 5084; 5046; 3312
Donald Carsten *(Chm. Bd.)*
David H. Delger *(Pres.)*
Joe Battles *(Controller)*
Charles Lasater *(Mgr.-Quality Control)*

UNION SWITCH & SIGNAL INC.
5800 Corporate Dr.
Pittsburgh, PA 15237
Mailing Address:
P.O. Box 420,
Pittsburgh, PA 15230-0420
Tel.: 412-366-2400
Tel.: 800-351-1520
Telex: 086-6448
Fax: 412-369-2399
Year Founded: 1881
Approx.Sls.: $85,000,000
Emp.: 650
Fiscal Year-end: 12/31/90
Export
Mfr. Railroad & Rail Rapid Transit Signal & Communication Products & Systems
S.I.C.: 3743
Arthur W. Ticknor *(Chm. Bd.)*
Walter Alessandrini *(Pres. & Chief Exec. Officer)*
Werner Philipp *(V.P. & Chief Fin. Officer)*
A.A. Florence *(V.P.-Communications & Plng.)*
Jeff Gaudio *(V.P.-Mktg. Opers.)*
Louis D. Kopsa *(V.P.-Human Resources)*
Robert A. Peterson *(V.P.-Res. & Devel.)*
Kevin E. Riddett *(V.P.-Mfg.)*
Mike Pracht *(V.P.-Projects)*
Charles E. Stipancic *(Dir.-Sls. Headquarters-Transit)*
Allen F. O'Rourke *(Dir.-Sls. Headquarters-Railroad)*
John E. Midili *(Dir.-Sls.-Western Region)*
George W. Rvdge *(Dir.-Sls.-Eastern Region)*
Gregory Babicz *(Supvr.-Mktg. Communications)*

UNIPHASE CORPORATION
163 Baypointe Pkwy.
San Jose, CA 95134
Tel.: 408-434-1800
Fax: 408-433-3838
Approx.Sls.: $22,000,000
Emp.: 209
Laser Systems & Equipment
S.I.C.: 3699
Dale E. Crane *(Chm. Bd.)*
Kevin Kalkhoven *(Pres.)*
Daniel R. Heibel *(V.P.-Opers.)*
Richard Johnson *(V.P.-Res. & Devel.)*
David Osborne *(V.P.-Sls. & Mktg.)*
Dan Pettit *(V.P.-Fin.)*

Outside Service Firm(s):

Silicon Valley Bank*(Major Banking Relationship)*
3000 Lakeside Dr.
Santa Clara, CA 95054

UNIROYAL CHEMICAL COMPANY, INC.
World Headquarters
Middlebury, CT 06749
Tel.: 203-573-2000
Fax: 203-573-3079
Year Founded: 1904
Approx.Sls.: $830,000,000
Emp.: 2,800
Fiscal Year-end: 9/30/92
Chemical Company
S.I.C.: 2879; 2869
Robert J. Mazaika *(Chm. Bd., Pres. & Chief Exec. Officer)*
Joseph B. Eisenberg *(V.P. & Gen. Mgr.-Chemicals & Polymers)*
Gerald H. Fickenscher *(V.P. & Chief Fin. Officer)*
Edward L. Hagen *(V.P.-Bus. Devel.)*
Neil A. Melore *(V.P.-Human Resources)*
Michael M. Powers *(V.P. & Gen. Mgr.-Intl. Opers.)*
William A. Stephenson *(V.P. & Gen. Mgr.-Specialties)*
Frank Manganella *(Treas.)*

Outside Service Firm(s):

Skadden, Arps, Slate, Meagher & Flom*(Legal Firm)*
919 3rd Ave.
New York, NY 10022
Tel.: 212-371-6000
Fax: 212-735-2000

Citibank N.A.*(Major Banking Relationship)*
Corporate Trust Services, 399 Park Ave.
New York, NY 10043
Tel.: 212-559-1605

Sales Offices:

Uniroyal Chemical Co., Inc, **(1)**
1530 E. Shaw, Ste. 105
Fresno, CA 93710
Tel.: 209-224-8910
Western Regional Sales Office
S.I.C.: 5169
James Ford *(Sales Mgr.)*

Uniroyal Chemical Co., Inc. **(1)**
158 Wind Chime Ct.
Raleigh, NC 27609
Tel.: 919-848-9675
Fax: 919-870-7624
Sales Office
S.I.C.: 5169

Uniroyal Chemical Co., Inc. **(1)**
1745 Merriman Rd.
Akron, OH 44313
Tel.: 216-864-2145
Fax: 216-867-4720
Sales Office
S.I.C.: 5169

Uniroyal Chemical Co., Inc. **(1)**
P.O. Box 460,
Painesville, OH 44077
Tel.: 216-357-7574
Sales Office
S.I.C.: 5169

Uniroyal Chemical Co., Inc. **(1)**
1 Metro Villa Creek Dr., Ste. 285
Dallas, TX 75234-7311
Tel.: 214-243-7553
Sales Office
S.I.C.: 5169

Subsidiaries:

Gustafson, Inc. **(1)**
1400 Preston Rd., Ste. 40
Plano, TX 75903
Tel.: 214-985-8877 (100%)
Mfr. Pesticides & Fungicides
S.I.C.: 2879
William Donwen *(Pres.)*

Uniroyal Chemical Co., Inc. **(1)**
P.O. Box 147, Highway 225
Bay Minette, AL 36507
Tel.: 205-937-2400
Mfr. of Weed Killer
S.I.C.: 2879

Uniroyal Chemical Co., Inc. **(1)**
Elm St.
Naugatuck, CT 06770
Tel.: 203-723-3000
S.I.C.: 2869; 2879

Uniroyal Chemical Co., Inc. **(1)**
1701 48th St., Ste. 102
Des Moines, IA 50265
Tel.: 515-224-4700

Uniroyal Chemical Co., Inc. **(1)**
P.O. Box 397, Highway 30
Geismar, LA 70734
Tel.: 504-673-8871
S.I.C.: 2869; 2879

Uniroyal Chemical Co., Inc. **(1)**
214 West Ruby St.
Gastonia, NC 28054
Tel.: 704-864-3411
S.I.C.: 2869; 2879

Uniroyal Chemical Co., Inc. (Leffingwell) **(1)**
P.O. Box 1880, 111 So. Berry St.
Brea, CA 92622
Tel.: 714-529-3973 (100%)
Mfr. Fertilizer
S.I.C.: 2879
J.R. Zinn *(Mgr.)*

Joint Venture:

Rubicon Inc. **(1)**
P.O. Box 517,
Geismar, LA 70734
Tel.: 504-673-6141
Joint Venture of I.C.I. and Uniroyal
S.I.C.: 2869; 2879

Non-U.S. Holdings:

Hannaford Seedmaster Services Australia (Pty) Ltd. **(1)**
52 East Avenue
Beverly, 5009, Australia
Tel.: 8-340-0366
Fax: 8-340-0774
S.I.C.: 5169

Premier Chemical Co., Ltd. **(1)**
Bank Tower, Ste. 704, 205, Tun Hwa North Rd.
Taipei, Taiwan
Tel.: 2 713 1790/3
Fax: 2 713 3708
S.I.C.: 5169

Premier Chemical Plant **(1)**
3-1 Hsing Kung Rd. Ta She Industrial Zone, Kaohsiung, Taiwan
Tel.: 7-351-4121
Fax: 7-351-2051
S.I.C.: 2869; 2879

Uniroyal Chemical Co., Inc. (Singapore) **(1)**
Cathay Building, 11, Dhoby Ghaut #07-01
Singapore, 0922, Singapore
Tel.: 338-5028
Telex: 78623253
Fax: 338-6509
S.I.C.: 5169

Uniroyal Chemical Company Limited **(1)**
West Sunrise Highway
Freeport, Bahamas
Tel.: 352-7861
Fax: 352-3136
S.I.C.: 2869; 2879

Uniroyal Chemical Japan **(1)**
Parkside Annex, 5th Fl., Banchi, Sanbancho, Chiyoda-ku
Tokyo, Japan
Tel.: 3-5276-2241
Fax: 3-5276-2245
Business Office

Uniroyal Chemical Ltd. **(1)**
25 Erb St.
Elmira, ON Canada N3B 3A2
Tel.: 519-669-1671 (100%)
Telex: 3696955421
Fax: 519-669-1679
Agricultural & Industrial Chemicals
S.I.C.: 2879; 2869; 5169

Uniroyal Chemical Ltd. **(1)**
P.O. Box 1120,
Guelph, ON N1H 6N3, Canada
Tel.: 519-822-3790
Fax: 519-821-1956
S.I.C.: 2819

Uniroyal Chemical Ltd. **(1)**
Kennet House, 4 Langley Quay Waterside Drive,
Slough, Berks SL3 6EH, United Kingdom
Tel.: 753-580888
Telex: 849940
Fax: 753-591350
Business Center

Uniroyal Chemical Pty. Ltd. **(1)**
3 Bowen Crescent
Melbourne, 3004, Australia
Tel.: 3-267-2811
Telex: 79036821
Fax: 3-267-2835
S.I.C.: 5169

Uniroyal Chemical Pty. Ltd. **(1)**
Unit 2, 13 Stanton Rd.
Seven Hills, N.S.W. 2147, Australia
Tel.: 2-838-7800
Fax: 2-838-7852
S.I.C.: 5169

Uniroyal Chemical Company, Inc.—(Continued)

Uniroyal Chimica, S.P.A. **(1)**
Viale Delle Industrie, 40 Casella Postale 13, 04013
Latina Scalo, Italy
Tel.: 773 43605/6/7/8
Fax: 773 438141
S.I.C.: 2879; 2869

Uniroyal Quimica, S.A. **(1)**
Avenida Morumbi, 7 029 CEP 05650, 0100
Caixa Postal 30 380,
Sao Paulo, SP, Brazil
Tel.: 11 533 0222
Fax: 11 542 4476
S.I.C.: 2879; 2869

Uniroyal Quimica, S.A. **(1)**
Avenida Brasil,5333 Caixa Postal 202,
Rio Claro, SP Brazil
Tel.: 195-343600
Fax: 195-343955
S.I.C.: 2869; 2879

Non-U.S. Joint Ventures:

Hahn Jung Chemical, Inc. **(1)**
Soh Jin Building, 6th Fl., #237-10 Non
Hyon-Dong Kangnam-Ku,
Seoul, 130-010, Korea
Tel.: 2-548-5701
Telex: HANNONG K 22991
Fax: 2-542-3656

Novaquim S.A. de C.V. **(1)**
Insurgentes Sur, 1106 Col. Nochebuena
Mexico, 03720, Mexico
Tel.: 5-575-6460
Telex: 3831771818
Fax: 5-575-6700

Orchem (Pty) Ltd. (Plant) **(1)**
Sunsen St. P.O. Box 19,
Sasolburg, 9570, South Africa
Tel.: 16-760200
Fax: 16-731411

Unikor Chemical, Inc. **(1)**
#433 Moknaedong
Ansan City, Kyungki-Do 425-100, Korea
Tel.: 345-495-3511
Fax: 345-495-3510

UNISON INDUSTRIES
7575 Baymeadows Way
Jacksonville, FL 32256
Tel.: 904-739-4000
Approx.Sls.: $60,000,000
Emp.: 500
Mfr. of Aircraft Ignition Equipment for Piston, Turbine & Jet Engines
S.I.C.: 3724
Frederick B. Sontag *(Pres.)*
Bradley D. Mottier *(Sr. V.P.)*
Bart Calkins *(V.P.-Fin.)*
John R. Frus *(V.P.-Engrng. & Res.)*
Larry C. Huetsch *(V.P.-Mfg.)*
William E. Nielsen *(V.P.-Admin.)*
John Pillman *(V.P.-Opers.)*
Dan Ryan *(V.P.-Mktg.)*

Subsidiaries:

Slick Aircraft Products **(1)**
530 Blackhawk Park Ave.
Rockford, IL 61104

Unison Industries **(1)**
7575 Baymeadows Way
Jacksonville, FL 32256
Tel.: 904-739-4000
Approx.Sls.: $60,000,000
Emp.: 500
Mfr. of Aircraft Ignition Equipment for Piston, Turbine & Jet Engines
S.I.C.: 3724
Frederick B. Sontag *(Pres.)*
Bradley D. Mottier *(Sr. V.P.)*
Bart Calkins *(V.P.-Fin.)*
John R. Frus *(V.P.-Engrng. & Res.)*
Larry C. Huetsch *(V.P.-Mfg.)*
William E. Nielsen *(V.P.-Admin.)*
John Pillman *(V.P.-Opers.)*
Dan Ryan *(V.P.-Mktg.)*

UNISTRUT CORPORATION
3971 South Research Park Dr.
Ann Arbor, MI 48108
Tel.: 313-930-0030
Fax: 313-930-0290
Approx.Sls.: $74,000,000
Emp.: 570
Fiscal Year-end: 12/31/90
Unistrut Metal Framing & Space Frame Systems; Telespar Tubing
S.I.C.: 3441; 3444; 3446
Mark Malfese *(Pres.)*
Ed Cady *(Sr. V.P.-Fin.)*
Tim Condit *(Sr. V.P.-Space Frame Grp.)*
Ron Jones *(Sr. V.P.-Distr.)*
Ruthanne Kelly *(Sr. V.P.-Human Resources)*
Richard Snyder *(Sr. V.P.-Mktg.)*
Millicent A. Fisher *(Mktg. Coord.)*

Computer Systems/Hardware:
IBM System 38

Outside Service Firm(s):

Coopers & Lybrand*(Auditors)*
400 Renaissance Center
Detroit, MI 48243
Tel.: 313-446-7100
Fax: 313-446-7117

Liberty Mutual*(Commercial Insurance Carrier)*
175 Berkeley St.
Boston, MA

Travelers Insurance Co.*(Group Insurer)*
1 Tower Square
Hartford, CT 06183-2492
Tel.: 203-277-4542
Fax: 203-277-5038

Dykema, Gossett*(Legal Firm)*
400 Renaissance Ctr., 35th Fl.
Detroit, MI 48243
Tel.: 313-568-6800

National Bank of Detroit*(Major Banking Relationship)*
Ann Arbor, MI

UNISYSTEMS, INC.
155 E. 55th St.
New York, NY 10022
Tel.: 212-826-0850 **DE**
Fax: 212-759-9069
Year Founded: 1969
Approx.Sls.: $16,000,000
Emp.: 27
Publisher & Distributor of Children's Coloring, Activity & Story Books; Adult Puzzle & Game Books; Toys
S.I.C.: 3944
Lawrence Steinberg *(Pres. & Chief Exec. Officer)*
Warren Cohen *(V.P., Sec. & Treas.)*
Edward Lenk *(V.P.)*
Jill Steinberg *(V.P.)*

Outside Service Firm(s):

Deloitte & Touche*(Auditors)*
1633 Broadway
New York, NY 10019

Reid & Priest*(Legal Firm)*
40 W. 57th St.
New York, NY 10022
Tel.: 212-603-2000

State Street Bank & Trust Co.*(Major Banking Relationship)*
New York, NY

UNITED ACQUISITION CORPORATION
823 11th Ave.
New York, NY 10019
Tel.: 212-580-6805
Fax: 212-262-4979
Approx.Sls.: $850,000,000
Emp.: 2,180
Holding Company; Retail Gas; Petroleum Refining
S.I.C.: 6719; 2911; 5541
John Catsimatidis *(Chm. Bd.)*

Outside Service Firm(s):

KPMG Peat Marwick*(Auditors)*
1 Mellon Bank Ctr.
Pittsburgh, PA 15219
Tel.: 412-391-9710

Lowenthal, Landau, Fischer, Ziegler & Bring*(Legal Firm)*
250 Park Ave.
New York, NY 10017
Tel.: 212-986-1116

United Acquisition Corporation*(Major Banking Relationship)*
823 11th Ave.
New York, NY 10019
Tel.: 212-580-6805
Fax: 212-262-4979

Subsidiaries:

United Refining Company **(1)**
15 Bradley St.
Warren, PA 16365
Tel.: 814-723-1500
Twx: 5106954781
Approx.Sls.: $566,000,000
Emp.: 2,100
Refines Petroleum Products
S.I.C.: 2911; 2951; 5541
John A. Catsimatidis *(Chm. Bd. & Pres.)*
Thomas C. Covert *(Exec. V.P.-Opers.)*
Myron Turfitt *(Exec. V.P.-Fin.)*
L. Loughlin *(Sr. V.P.-Personnel)*
Marshal Stauton *(V.P. & Counsel)*
Ashton L. Ditka *(V.P.-Mktg. & Sls.)*
Donald E. Sobina *(V.P. & Controller)*
Dennis E. Bee *(Treas.)*

United Refining Inc. **(1)**
15 Bradley St.
Warren, PA 16365
Tel.: 814-723-1500
Twx: 5106954781
Approx.Sls.: $570,000,000
Emp.: 2,160
Refines & Markets Petroleum Products
S.I.C.: 2911
John A. Catsimatidis *(Pres. & Treas.)*

Vulcan Asphalt Refining Company **(1)**
P.O. Box 388
Cordova, AL 35550
Tel.: 205-483-9262
Fax: 205-483-7065
Mfr. Asphalt
S.I.C.: 2911
Tom Covert *(Exec. V.P.)*

UNITED A G CO-OP, INC.
7401 "F" St.
Omaha, NE 68127-1874
Mailing Address:
P.O. Box 1131,
Omaha, NE 68101
Tel.: 402-339-7300 **NE**
Fax: 402-339-9153
Year Founded: 1933
Assets: $42,569,134
Liabilities: $26,151,308
Net Worth: $16,417,826
Approx.Sls.: $278,372,357
Emp.: 324
Fiscal Year-end: 2/ 3/90
Wholesale Grocery Distributor
S.I.C.: 5141
Harold Cooperman *(Chm. Bd.)*
T. W. Olsen *(Pres. & Chief Exec. Officer)*
Dennis Schulte *(Chief Fin. Officer & V.P.-Fin.)*
Glenn Tyletki *(V.P.-Mktg.)*
Wm. J. Wiedemeyer *(V.P.-Distr.)*
Janet Larson *(Treas. & Sec.)*
Dale Williamsen *(Dir.-Data Processing)*

No. of Mfg. Plants/Facilities: 1
No. of U.S. Offices: 1

Computer Systems/Hardware:
IBM 4381

Outside Service Firm(s):

Deloitte & Touche*(Auditors)*
2000 First National Center
Omaha, NE 68102
Tel.: 402-346-7788

Central States Health & Welfare Insurance*(Group Insurer)*
Des Plaines, IL

United Retailers Benefit Trust*(Group Insurer)*
Omaha, NE

Erickson & Sederstrom*(Legal Firm)*
Omaha, NE

First National Bank of Omaha*(Pension Manager)*
One First National Center
Omaha, NE 68102

Subsidiaries:

United Financial Resources **(1)**
6211 "L" St.
Omaha, NE 68117
Tel.: 402-734-1250
Emp.: 350

United Retailers Insurance Corp. **(1)**
6211 "L" St.
Omaha, NE 68117
Tel.: 402-339-7300

UNITED AIR SPECIALISTS, INC.
4440 Creek Rd.
Cincinnati, OH 45242
Tel.: 513-891-0400
Fax: 513-891-4171
Approx.Sls.: $30,000,000
Emp.: 232
Export
Mfr. of Air Cleaners & Heat Exchangers
S.I.C.: 3564; 3443
William A. Cheney *(Chm. Bd.)*
Durwood G. Rorie, Jr. *(Pres.)*
Brian Colls *(V.P.-European Sls.)*
James Simmons *(V.P.-Sls.)*
John Wiegel *(V.P.-Engrng.)*
John Blight *(V.P.-Fin. & Admin.)*
Paige George *(Mktg. Specialist)*
William M. Rehl III *(Controller)*

UNITED ALUMINUM CORPORATION
100 United Dr.
North Haven, CT 06473
Mailing Address:
P.O. Box 215,
North Haven, CT 06473
Tel.: 203-239-5881
Tel.: 800-243-2515
Fax: 203-239-4441
Year Founded: 1185
Approx.Sls.: $15,000,000
Emp.: 90
Import Export
Aluminum Coiled Sheet & Strip; Brazing Sheet
S.I.C.: 3353
Robert E. Lapides *(Chm.)*
John S. Lapides *(Pres.)*
James A. Lapides *(V.P.-Mktg. & Opers)*
N. James Norlie *(V.P.-Sls.)*
William McCullom *(Mgr.-Sls.)*
Frank Mascia *(Mgr.-Human Resources)*
Campbell Buchanan *(Mgr.-Technology & Quality Control)*
Brian Gray *(Mgr.-Sls./Intl. Sls. & Exports)*
William Hall *(Mgr.-Pur.)*
Frederick R. Jones *(Dir.-Adv.)*

No. of Mfg. Plants/Facilities: 1

Outside Service Firm(s):

Connecticut National Bank*(Major Banking Relationship)*
North Haven, CT

UNITED ARTISTS THEATRE CIRCUIT, INC.
9110 E. Nichols Ave, Ste. 200
Englewood, CO 80112
Tel.: 303-792-3600
Fax: 303-790-8907
Approx.Rev.: $697,000,000
Emp.: 12,000
Theatre Exhibition Company
Stuart Blair *(Chm. Bd.)*
Peter Warzell *(Pres.)*
Arvey, Hodes, Costello & Burman*(Legal Firm)*
180 N. LaSalle St.
Chicago, IL 60601
Tel.: 312-855-5000

LaSalle National Bank*(Major Banking Relationship)*
120 S. LaSalle St.
Chicago, IL 60603
Tel.: 312-781-8000

UNITED BROADCASTING INC.
4733 Bethesda Ave., Ste. 808
Bethesda, MD 20814
Tel.: 301-652-7707
Fax: 301-652-4614
Year Founded: 1944
Approx.Sls.: $30,000,000
Emp.: 325
Radio Broadcasting Co.; WJZE-FM, Washington, D.C.; WJMO, Cleveland Hghts., OH; KSOL, San Mateo, CA; KALI, San Gabriel, CA; WINX, Rockville, MD; WKDM, New York, NY; United Cable Co. of N.H., Manchester, NH; G. O. Enterprises, VT; WJMO-FM, Cleveland Hghts, OH; WERQ-AM-FM, Baltimore, MD
S.I.C.: 4832
Gerald Hroblak *(Chief Exec. Officer & Pres.)*
William Parris *(V.P.-Brdcst.)*
Stewart Young *(V.P.-Legal Affairs)*
Arthur Rawson *(Treas.)*
Mark Day *(Controller)*
Betsy Peisach *(Dir.-Natl. Promotions)*

Outside Service Firm(s):

Buchanan & Mitchell*(Auditors)*
Bethesda, MD

Erik, Fox, Kintner, Plottkin & Kahn*(Legal Firm)*
Washington, DC

American Security Bank, N.A.*(Major Banking Relationship)*
1501 Pennsylvania Ave. N.W.
Washington, DC 20013
Tel.: 202-624-4000

Subsidiary:

92 Q WERQ AM/FM **(1)**
111 Park Ave.
Baltimore, MD 21201
Tel.: 410-523-6900
Fax: 410-669-2127
Radio Stations
S.I.C.: 4832
Scott Fey *(Gen. Mgr.)*

UNITED COATINGS, INC.
2850 Festival Dr.
Kankakee, IL 60901
Tel.: 815-935-1200
Fax: 815-935-1322
Approx.Sls.: $150,000,000
Emp.: 500
Mfr. of Latex Paints
S.I.C.: 2851
Jules F. Knapp *(Chm. Bd., Pres. & Chief Exec. Officer)*
Jim Perry *(Sr. V.P.)*
Tony Janus *(V.P.-Fin.)*
Joy Knapp *(V.P.-Mktg.)*
F. Schaffer *(V.P.-Sls.)*
T. Tukiendorf *(Comptroller)*
Principal(s):
Jules F. Knapp

No. of Mfg. Plants/Facilities: 6
No. of U.S. Offices: 7

Computer Systems/Hardware:
Wang VS

Outside Service Firm(s):

Friedman, Eisenstein, Raemer & Schwartz*(Auditors)*
Chicago, IL

THE UNITED COMPANY
P.O. Box 1280, 1005 Glenway Ave.
Bristol, VA 24203
Tel.: 703-466-3322
Fax: 703-466-3322
Approx.Sls.: $360,000,000
Emp.: 1,200
Coal Mining, Oil Drilling, Real Estate & Financial Services; Manufacture Movable Walls
S.I.C.: 5052; 1222
James W. McGlothlin *(Chm. Bd. & Pres.)*
Bill Miller *(Dir.-Pub. Rels.)*
Principal(s):
James W. McGlothlin

Computer Systems/Hardware:
Hewlett Packard 3000/68-48

Outside Service Firm(s):

Price Waterhouse*(Auditors)*
Johnson City, TN

Dominion Bank*(Major Banking Relationship)*
P.O. Box 13327,
Roanoke, VA
Tel.: 703-563-7851
Fax: 703-563-7696

NationsBank Carolinas*(Major Banking Relationship)*
One NCNB Plaza
Charlotte, NC 28255

UNITED DAIRY FARMERS, INC.
3955 Montgomery Rd.
Cincinnati, OH 45212
Tel.: 513-396-8700
Fax: 513-396-8736
Approx.Sls.: $100,000,000
Emp.: 2,300
Chain of Convenience Stores; Milk Processing, Cottage Cheese, Ice Cream & Ices; Frozen Dairy Desserts
S.I.C.: 5411; 5141; 2026; 5143
Robert D. Linder, Sr. *(Chm. Bd.)*
Robert D. Lindner, Jr. *(Pres.)*
Alan B. Lindner *(Exec. V.P.)*
Paul Brunner *(Chief Fin. Officer)*
Phyllis McCoy *(Corp. Sec.)*
Ann Fehring *(Controller)*
Bill Cullen *(Adv. Dir.)*

Outside Service Firm(s):

Provident Bank*(Major Banking Relationship)*
One E. Fourth St.
Cincinnati, OH 45202
Tel.: 513-579-2731

UNITED DAIRYMEN OF ARIZONA
2008 Hardy Dr.
Tempe, AZ 85282
Mailing Address:
P.O. Box 26877
Tempe, AZ 85282
Tel.: 602-275-6264
Fax: 602-829-7491
Approx.Sls.: $250,000,000
Emp.: 125
Fiscal Year-end: 9/30/90
Company Markets Milk & Manufactures Other Milk Products
S.I.C.: 5143
Conrad Gingg *(Pres. & Chief Exec. Officer)*
James Tappan *(Chief Fin. Officer & Treas.)*
Joseph Lambros *(Controller)*
Annette Baynes *(Dir.-Data Processing)*

Computer Systems/Hardware:
IBM System 34

Outside Service Firm(s):

Eadie & Payne*(Auditors)*
San Bernardino, CA

Continental Insurance*(Group Insurer)*
180 Maiden Lane
New York, NY

Doherty, Rumble & Butler*(Legal Firm)*
2800 Minnesota World Trade Center
St. Paul, MN 55101-4999
Tel.: 612-291-9333

First Interstate Bank*(Major Banking Relationship)*
P.O. Box 53441,
Phoenix, AZ 85072-3441
Tel.: 602-229-4049

UNITED DESIGN
P.O. Box 1200
Noble, OK 73068
Tel.: 405-872-3468 **OK**
Fax: 405-360-4442
Year Founded: 1975
Approx.Sls.: $30,000,000
Emp.: 700
Mfr. Giftware Figures
S.I.C.: 3449; 3269
Gary Clinton *(Chm. Bd., Pres. & Chief Exec. Officer)*
Jean M. Clinton *(Chief Oper. Officer)*
Robert Clinton *(V.P.-Fin.)*
Rene Cook *(Office Mgr.)*
Larry Ferree *(Dir.-Personnel)*
Tracy Sperry *(Dir.-Pur.)*
Steve Younge *(Dir.-Data Processing)*

No. of Mfg. Plants/Facilities: 1
No. of U.S. Offices: 1

Computer Systems/Hardware:
MAI Basic 4

Outside Service Firm(s):

Arthur Andersen & Co.*(Auditors)*
20 W. Broadway, Ste. 1200
Oklahoma City, OK 73109
Tel.: 405-236-1491

Liberty National Bank & Trust Co.*(Major Banking Relationship)*
P.O. Box 25848,
Oklahoma City, OK 73125-0848
Tel.: 405-231-6000

UNITED ENGINE & MACHINE COMPANY
4909 Goni Rd.
Carson City, NV 89706
Tel.: 702-882-7790 **CA**
Fax: 702-882-7773
Approx.Sls.: $28,000,000
Emp.: 400
Piston & Piston Rings
S.I.C.: 3592
Ray R. Sulprizio *(Pres.)*
Deuta Sulprizio *(V.P. & Treas.)*
Vatinia Yraceburu *(Sec.)*
Frank Rudin *(Mgr.-Pur.)*
Principal(s):
Ray R. Sulprizio
Deuta Sulprizio
Vatinia Yraceburu

Outside Service Firm(s):

Ernst & Young*(Auditors)*
Reno, NV

Valley Bank of Nevada*(Major Banking Relationship)*
300 S. Fourth St.
Las Vegas, NV 89101

UNITED ENGINES, INC.
5555 W. Reno
Oklahoma City, OK 73127
Tel.: 405-947-3321 **DE**
Fax: 405-947-3406
Year Founded: 1939
Approx.Sls.: $28,000,000
Emp.: 160

Export
Wholesale Distributor of Industrial Machinery
S.I.C.: 5084
Jerry W. Morton *(Chm. Bd.)*
Jay W. Morton *(Pres. & Chief Exec. Officer)*

Outside Service Firm(s):

Quail Creek Bank, N.A.*(Major Banking Relationship)*
Oaklahoma City, OK

UNITED ENVELOPE COMPANY, INC.
525 W. 52nd St., 2nd Fl.
New York, NY 10019
Tel.: 212-246-2500
Fax: 212-974-0449
Approx.Sls.: $36,000,000
Emp.: 110

Export
Envelopes, Lithographic Commercial Printing
S.I.C.: 2677; 2752
Joseph Schlanger *(Chm. Bd.)*
Harry Fishbein *(Pres.)*
Robert Fishbein *(Exec. V.P. & Treas.)*
Richard Schlanger *(Exec. V.P. & Sec.)*

Outside Service Firm(s):

Hertz, Herson & Company*(Auditors)*
New York, NY

National Westminster Bank plc*(Major Banking Relationship)*
Astor Plaza, 1515 Broadway
New York, NY 10036

UNITED FARM BUREAU FAMILY LIFE INSURANCE CO.
130 E. Washington
Indianapolis, IN 46204
Mailing Address:
P.O. Box 1250
Indianapolis, IN 46206
Tel.: 317-263-7200
Fax: 317-263-7350
Year Founded: 1935
Approx.Premiums: $575,000,000
Emp.: 1,500
Fiscal Year-end: 12/31/90
Multiple Line Insurance
S.I.C.: 6311; 6331
Harry Pearson *(Pres.)*
Don Henderson *(Exec. V.P. & Chief Exec. Officer)*
Joe Hanna *(Sr. V.P.-Mktg.)*
John C. Hand *(Sr. V.P., Gen. Counsel & Corp. Sec.)*
Alice Kroll *(Sr. V.P., Life Co. & Casualty)*
Jerry L. Foster *(V.P.)*
Joseph M. Dugan *(V.P.-Data Processing Services)*
Barbara Sinclair *(Mgr.-Corp. Communications)*
Earl Nahre *(Pur. Agent)*
Burtis G. Taylor *(Exec. Asst.)*

Subsidiary:

United Farm Bureau Life Insurance Co. **(1)**
130 E. Washington St.
Indianapolis, IN 46204
Tel.: 317-263-7200

UNITED FARM TOOLS, INC.
113 W. Public Sq., 4th Fl.
Glasgow, KY 42141
Mailing Address:
P.O. Box 1599,
Glasgow, KY 42142
Tel.: 502-651-7121 **WV**
Fax: 502-651-7384
Year Founded: 1976
Assets: $17,484,849
Liabilities: $4,345,909
Net Worth: $13,138,940
Approx.Sls.: $45,000,000
Emp.: 200
Fiscal Year-end: 10/31/91
Export
Mfr. Stalk Shredders, No-Til Drills, Sugar Beet Defoilators, Potato Deviners, Edible Bean Cutters, Sugarcane Shredder, Grain Drills, Grain Carts, Dump Wagons, Ditchers, Rotary Cutters, Levee Plows, Cultivators, Augers, Bale Grinders, Fertilizer Spreader, Row Crop & Field Cultivators, Seeder Spreader, Rip-N-Plant, Peanut Inverter
S.I.C.: 3523
Sam Lawson *(Pres. & Chief Exec. Officer)*
Joe Curtis *(V.P.-Sls. & Mktg.)*
Smitty Moore *(V.P.-Opers.)*
Ralph Risimini *(V.P.-Mfg.)*
Mark Brown *(Controller)*
Gene Frazier *(Dir.-Pur.)*
Jim Tharaldson *(Chief Engineer)*
Roberta Bryant *(Adv.)*

No. of Mfg. Plants/Facilities: 2
No. of U.S. Offices: 3

Divisions:

United Farm Tools, Mohawk **(1)**
Drawer 967
Fitzgerald, GA 31750
Tel.: 912-423-9371
Fax: 912-423-3980
Approx.Sls.: $3,000,000
Emp.: 30
Farm Machinery
S.I.C.: 3523
Joe Curtis *(V.P.-Sls. & Mktg.)*
Steve Smith *(Pur. Agent)*
Thomas Spivey *(Sales Mgr.)*
John Lawson *(Plant Mgr.)*

United Farm Tools, Kentucky Div. **(1)**
P.O. Box 1599
Glasgow, KY 42142
Tel.: 502-651-7121
Approx.Sls.: $1,000,000
Emp.: 12
Export
Farm Machinery
S.I.C.: 3523
Sam Lawson *(Chm. Bd.)*
Smitty Moore *(V.P.-Opers.)*
Joe Curtis *(V.P.-Sls. & Mktg.)*
John Lawson *(Mgr.-Plant; Paulk, GA)*
Tommy Spivey *(Mgr.-Regional Sls.; GA Plant)*
Mark Brown *(Controller)*
Jim Tharaldson *(Chief Engineer & IA Plant Mgr.)*

United Farm Tools Speedy Mfg. Div. **(1)**
RR 2, Box CP 24
Oelwein, IA 50662
Tel.: 319-283-5451
Approx.Sls.: $12,000,000
Emp.: 100
Fiscal Year-end: 10/30/88
Mfr. Speedy Stalk Shredders, Sugar Beet Defoliators, Potato Deviners, Edible Bean Cutters & Grain Drills
S.I.C.: 5191; 3523
Robert E. Kammer *(Pres.)*
James Tharaldson *(V.P.)*

Subsidiary:

United Farm Tools, Inc., Oelwein **(1)**
Speedy City Park Rd., P.O. Box 311
Oelwein, IA 50662
Tel.: 319-283-5451
Fax: 319-283-5454
S.I.C.: 3523
Loren Fawns *(Plant Mgr.)*
Tex Kohlmeyer *(Sls. Mgr.)*
Larry Winkey *(Pur. Agent)*

UNITED FEEDS, INC.
4310 W. State Rd. 38
Sheridan, IN 46069
Mailing Address:
P.O. Box 108
Sheridan, IN 46069
Tel.: 317-758-4495 **IN**
Year Founded: 1956
Approx.Sls.: $70,000,000
Emp.: 240
Livestock Feeds, Farm Supplies, Swine Production
S.I.C.: 2048; 0213
John R. Swisher *(Pres. & Chief Exec. Officer)*
Phil Shafer *(V.P.-Sls.)*
Marshall Adkins *(Sec. & Treas.)*
Norma Goodnight *(Dir.-Data Processing)*
Principal(s):
John R. Swisher
Phil Shafer
Marshall Adkins
Tom Bache
Dan Wawrzyniak

Outside Service Firm(s):

Bagley, Hoage & Harrison*(Auditors)*
Indianapolis, IN

Kappes, Fuller & Eads*(Legal Firm)*
Indianapolis, IN

Summit Bank*(Major Banking Relationship)*
Ligonier, IN

UNITED FOAM PLASTICS CORPORATION
172 E. Main St.
Georgetown, MA 01833
Tel.: 508-352-2200 **MA**
Twx: 710-347-0315
Fax: 508-352-7169
Year Founded: 1963
Approx.Sls.: $24,800,000
Emp.: 225
Fiscal Year-end: 12/31/91
Import Export
Mfr. Foam Plastics
S.I.C.: 3083; 3086
William H. Shaw *(Pres. & Chief Exec. Officer)*
Richard L. Bailly *(Exec. V.P.)*
Paul J. Greenler *(V.P.-Fin.)*
R. Jeffrey Bailly *(Dir.-Pur.)*
Jane Doucette *(Dir.-Data Processing)*
Jack Nagy *(Dir.-Mktg.)*
Kay Wantman *(Dir.-Personnel)*
Wayne G. Williams *(Dir.-Project Devel. & Tech. Res.)*

No. of Mfg. Plants/Facilities: 9
No. of U.S. Offices: 7

Computer Systems/Hardware:
IBM

Outside Service Firm(s):

KPMG Peat Marwick*(Auditors)*
One Boston Place
Boston, MA 02108
Tel.: 617-723-7700

Lynch, Brewer, Hoffman & Sands*(Legal Firm)*
101 Federal St.
Boston, MA 02110
Tel.: 617-951-0800

Gloucester Bank & Trust*(Major Banking Relationship)*
Gloucester, MA

UNITED FOOD SERVICE DISTRIBUTORS, INC.
875 Broadway
Albany, NY 12207
Tel.: 518-463-2111
Fax: 518-463-0290
Approx.Sls.: $30,000,000
Emp.: 125
Food Service Distributor
S.I.C.: 5812
Frank Crisafulli *(Pres.)*
Dennis Cagain *(V.P.)*
Eugene Crisafulli *(V.P.)*
Patricia Houle *(Sec.)*
Frank Carraziolo *(Treas.)*

Outside Service Firm(s):

Teal, Becker & Chiaramonte*(Auditors)*
Albany, NY

First American Bank, N.A.*(Major Banking Relationship)*
Albany, NY

UNITED GILSONITE LABORATORIES
P.O. Box 70
Scranton, PA 18501
Tel.: 717-344-1202
Tel.: 800-UGL-LABS
Fax: 717-969-7634
Year Founded: 1932
Approx.Sls.: $20,000,000
Emp.: 140
Fiscal Year-end: 12/31/90
Export
Cement Paints, Glazing & Caulking Compounds, Wall Patching Materials, Paint Sundries, Clear Finishes, Drylok Masonry Waterproofing Decorating Products; Zar Clear Finishes for Wood; Zar Interior Wood Stain; Zar Rain Stain Exterior Wood Stain; Temproo f Stove & Fireplace Maintenance Products
S.I.C.: 2851
M.C. MacKinnon *(Pres.)*
Frank Balish *(V.P.-Mfg.)*
Frank E. John III *(V.P.-Sls.)*
James J. Bohn *(Treas.)*
Joseph M. McGraw *(Dir.-Adv. & Pub. Rels.)*
W. Phillips *(Pur. Agent)*

Outside Service Firm(s):

Robert T. Kelly & Co.*(Auditors)*
Scranton, PA

Third National Bank*(Major Banking Relationship)*
Scranton, PA

Divisions:

United Gilsonite Laboratories **(1)**
30290 Road 76
Visalia, CA 93277
Tel.: 209-651-1061
Cement Paints, Glazing & Caulking Compounds, Wall Patching Materials, Paint Sundries, Clear Finishes, Drylok Masonry, Waterproofing, Decorating Products, Zar Clear Finishes for Wood; Zar Interior Wood Stain; Zar Rain Stain Exterior Wood Stain; Temproff Stove & Fireplace Maintenance Products
S.I.C.: 2851

United Gilsonite Laboratories **(1)**
330 W. Lafayette St.
Jacksonville, IL 62656
Tel.: 217-243-7878
Cement Paints, Glazing & Caulking Compounds, Wall Patching Materials, Paint Sundries, Clear Finishes, Drylok Masonry Waterproofing, Decorating Products, Zar Clear Finishes for Wood; Zar Interior Wood Stain; Zar Rain Stain Exterior Wood Stain; Temproff Stove & Fireplace Maintenance Products

UNITED GRAPHICS, INC.
(Sub. of Cairn Capital, Inc., Don Mills, Canada)
1401 Broadway
Seattle, WA 98122
Tel.: 206-325-4400
Fax: 206-328-3797
Year Founded: 1904
Approx.Sls.: $16,000,000
Emp.: 85
Lithographic Commercial Printing
S.I.C.: 2752
Charles B. Steeley *(Pres. & Chief Exec. Officer)*
Wayne Mitchell *(V.P.-Mfg.)*
James J. Curtis *(V.P.-Sls. & Mktg.)*
Steve Wilson *(V.P.-Fin.)*
Jo Powers *(Dir.-Personnel)*

Outside Service Firm(s):

Deloitte & Touche*(Auditors)*
700 Fifth Ave., Suite 4500
Seattle, WA 98104-5044
Tel.: 206-292-1800

Perkins, Coie*(Legal Firm)*
Washington Mutual Tower, 1201 3rd Ave., 40th Flr.
Seattle, WA 98101-3099
Tel.: 206-583-8888
Fax: 206-583-8500

U.S. Bank*(Major Banking Relationship)*
Seattle, WA

UNITED GROCERS INC.
P.O. Box 22187, 6433 SE Lake Road
Portland, OR 97222
Tel.: 503-653-6330
Fax: 503-652-7358
Year Founded: 1915
Assets: $248,246,000
Earnings: $12,060,000
Liabilities: $211,815,000
Net Worth: $36,431,000
Approx.Sls.: $882,000,000
Emp.: 1,150
Fiscal Year-end: 9/30/91
Import Export
Wholesale Grocers
S.I.C.: 5411
Raymond Nidiffer *(Chm. Bd.)*
Alan C. Jones *(Pres., Chief Exec. Officer & Sec.)*
John W. White *(Chief Fin. Officer & Asst. Treas.)*
Mark Bloom *(Dir.-Corp. Fin.)*
Keith Miller *(Dir.-Pur.)*
Susan Weber *(Dir.-Human Resources)*
George Fleming *(Mgr.-Store Fin.)*
Jack Smith *(Mgr.-Projects)*
Joe Sunderland *(Mgr.-Data Processing)*
Mary Jenness *(Asst. Mgr.-Personnel)*
Lyman R. Brown *(Controller)*

UNITED HARDWARE DISTRIBUTING CO.
5005 Nathan Lane
Plymouth, MN 55442
Mailing Address:
P.O. Box 410
Minneapolis, MN 55440
Tel.: 612-559-1800 **MN**
Fax: 612-557-2799
Year Founded: 1945
Assets: $61,031,771
Earnings: ($649,611)
Liabilities: $46,325,393
Net Worth: $14,706,378
Approx.Sls.: $132,649,901
Emp.: 365
Fiscal Year-end: 11/30/91
Wholesale Hardware
S.I.C.: 5072
Gordon Schafer *(Chm. Bd.)*
Stan Severson *(Vice Chm.)*
David Heider *(Pres. & Chief Exec. Officer)*
Frank Lewendowski *(Chief Info. Officer)*
John Nitsche *(Chief Fin. Officer, V.P. & Treas.)*
Robert Branton *(V.P.-Sls. & Mktg.)*
Scott Buss *(Controller)*
Robert Korstad *(Sec.)*
Keith Kock *(Dir.-Trustworthy Stores Program)*
Gary Lindemen *(Mgr.-Opers.)*

Computer Systems/Hardware:
IBM 4381

Outside Service Firm(s):

McGladrey & Pullen*(Auditors)*
1800 Town Square, 445 Minnesota St.
St. Paul, MN 55101

Moss & Barnett*(Legal Firm)*
4800 Norwest Center, 90 S. Seventh St.
Minneapolis, MN 55402
Tel.: 612-347-0300
Fax: 612-339-6686

Marquette Bank*(Major Banking Relationship)*
777 Marquette Ave.
Minneapolis, MN 55402
Tel.: 612-370-2182

Subsidiary:

Farwell, Ozmun, Kirk & Co. **(1)**
5005 Nathan Lane
Plymouth, MN 55442
Tel.: 612-559-1800
Wholesale Hardware
S.I.C.: 5072
David Heide *(Pres. & Chief Exec. Officer)*

UNITED HEALTH PLAN
3405 W. Imperial Hwy.
Inglewood, CA 90303
Tel.: 310-671-3465 **CA**
Fax: 310-673-9176
Year Founded: 1967
Assets: $33,595,000
Earnings: $4,624,000
Liabilities: $26,982,000
Net Worth: $6,613,000
Approx.Sls.: $120,000,000
Emp.: 650
Fiscal Year-end: 12/31/90
Health Maintenance Organization
S.I.C.: 8071; 8011; 8611
B. Wyatt *(Chm. Bd.)*
Steve Shean *(Chief Fin. Officer)*
Dr. Clyde W. Oden *(Pres. & Chief Exec. Officer)*
Dave A. Petteway *(Chief Oper. Officer & Exec. V.P.)*
M. Owens *(Exec. V.P.)*
Martin Hartman *(V.P.-Mktg.)*
Charles Wood *(V.P.-Admin.)*
Brainard Simpson *(Treas.)*
Renato DeGuzman *(Controller)*
Alma Graham *(Gen. Counsel)*
Ron Bolding *(Dir.-Mdsg. & Pur.)*
Delilah Camarillo *(Dir.-Mngmt. Information Systems)*
Sidney Gibson *(Dir.-Plng. & Devel.)*
Madria Marshall *(Dir.-Personnel)*
Jemela Swift *(Mgr.-Telecommunications)*

Outside Service Firm(s):

Arthur Andersen & Co.*(Auditors)*
633 W. Fifth St.
Los Angeles, CA 90071
Tel.: 213-614-6500

Iris Rideau & Associates*(Commercial Insurance Carrier)*
Culver City, CA

Golconda Financial*(Investment Banker)*
El Monte, CA

Munger, Tolles & Rickershauser*(Legal Firm)*
606 Southhill
Los Angeles, CA 90014
Tel.: 213-626-1491

Imperial Bank*(Major Banking Relationship)*
Inglewood, CA

Union Mutual Life Insurance Co.*(Pension Manager)*
Portland, ME

UNITED LABORATORIES, INC.
955 Hawthorn
Itasca, IL 60143
Mailing Address:
P.O. Box 389,
Addison, IL 60101
Tel.: 708-773-0252
Tel.: 800-323-2594 **DE**
Fax: 708-773-0595
Year Founded: 1964
Assets: $9,244,052
Liabilities: $4,952,307
Net Worth: $4,291,745
Approx.Sls.: $23,000,000
Emp.: 140
Fiscal Year-end: 7/31/91
Wholesale Specialty Chemicals; Manufacture Specialty Cleaning, Polishing & Sanitation Preparations
S.I.C.: 2842; 5169
N.J. Savaiano *(Chm. Bd. & Pres.)*
D.S. Brown *(Chief Fin. Officer, V.P., Treas. & Gen. Counsel)*
R.G. Difino *(V.P.-Mktg. Services)*
Sheryl Farley *(Controller)*
J. O'Connor *(Dir.-Mngmt. Information Systems)*

Principal(s):
N.J. Savaiano

No. of Mfg. Plants/Facilities: 4
No. of U.S. Offices: 4
No. of Foreign Offices: 1

Computer Systems/Hardware:
MAI Basic Four 8000 Series

Outside Service Firm(s):

Warady & Davis*(Auditors)*
Chicago, IL

Travelers Insurance Co.*(Group Insurer)*
200 W. Madison St., Ste. 2100
Chicago, IL 60606
Tel.: 312-750-2800

The Northern Trust Co.*(Major Banking Relationship)*
50 S. LaSalle St.
Chicago, IL 60675
Tel.: 312-630-6000

UNITED MCGILL CORP.
One Mission Park
Groveport, OH 43125
Mailing Address:
P.O. Box 7,
Groveport, OH 43125
Tel.: 614-836-9981 **OH**
Fax: 614-836-9843
Year Founded: 1951
Assets: $24,000,000
Liabilities: $10,000,000
Net Worth: $14,000,000
Approx.Sls.: $60,000,000
Emp.: 615
Fiscal Year-end: 12/31/91

Export
Fabricated Steel Products: Sheet Metal Duct & Fittings, Acoustical Products, Pressure Vessel, Vacuum & Heat Recovery Systems, Air Pollution Control Systems
S.I.C.: 3564; 3443; 3448; 3444
James D. McGill *(Pres.)*
Wayne W. Custer *(V.P.)*
Jayne F. McGill *(Sec.)*
Norman L. Boyer *(Dir.-Fin. & Acct.)*
Kathleen P. Cauley *(Dir.-Personnel)*
Henry Phillips *(Dir.-Adv.)*
Linda S. Ward *(Dir.-Computer Services)*

No. of Mfg. Plants/Facilities: 8
No. of U.S. Offices: 25

Computer Systems/Hardware:
Hewlett-Packard

Outside Service Firm(s):

Price Waterhouse*(Auditors)*
41 South High Street
Columbus, OH 43215

Metropolitan Life Insurance Co.*(Group Insurer)*
Columbus, OH

The Huntington National Bank*(Major Banking Relationship)*
41 S. High St.
Columbus, OH 43216

UNITED METAL FABRICATORS, INC.
409 Eisenhower Blvd.
Johnstown, PA 15904
Tel.: 814-266-8726
Tel.: 800-638-5322
Fax: 814-266-1870
Year Founded: 1955
Approx.Sls.: $20,000,000
Emp.: 130

Export
Mfr. of Physicians & Hospital Furniture
S.I.C.: 2599
Raymond DiBattista *(Pres. & Chief Exec. Officer)*
Stephen Costantino *(V.P.-Mfg.)*
Arthur Costanzo *(Sec.)*

UNITED PARCEL SERVICE OF AMERICA, INC.
400 Perimeter Center,
Terraces North
Atlanta, GA 30346
Tel.: 404-913-6000 **DE**
Fax: 404-913-6619
Year Founded: 1907
Assets: $8,858,561,000
Earnings: $700,170,000
Liabilities: $4,985,409,000
Net Worth: $3,873,152,000
Approx.Sls.: $15,019,830,000
Emp.: 256,000
Fiscal Year-end: 12/31/91
Nationwide Parcel Delivery Services; Nationwide Air Express Services; International Air Express Services
S.I.C.: 4215; 4513
Kent C. Nelson *(Chm. Bd. & Chief Exec. Officer)*
John W. Alden *(Sr. V.P.-Bus. Devel.)*
John J. Kelly *(Sr. V.P.-Human Resources)*
Joseph Moderow *(Sr. V.P. & Sec., Legal & Public Affairs)*
Donald W. Layden *(Sr. V.P.-Intl. Opers.)*
James P. Kelly *(Sr. V.P.-Labor Rels.)*
Edwin A. Jacoby *(Sr. V.P. & Treas.)*
J.R. Peterson *(Sr. V.P. & Sec.)*
Francis J. Erbick *(Sr. V.P.-Info. Services)*
Donald Fischer *(Sr. V.P.-Intl. Systems)*
James P. Kelly *(St. V.P. & Chief Oper. Officer)*
Richard O. Oehme *(Sr. V.P.-Air Opers.)*
Charles L. Schaffer *(Sr. V.P.-Engrng.)*
Calvin E. Tyler *(Sr. V.P.-Opers.)*
Clinton L. Yard *(Sr. V.P.-Opers.)*
Sam Lockwood *(V.P.-Real Estate)*
Ken Schellie *(V.P.-Corp. Communications)*
Peter W. Fredo *(V.P.-Customer Communications & Adv.)*
Frank Erbrick *(Dir.-Info. Services)*
Paul Meyer *(Mgr.-Natl. Adv.)*
Lawrence Bloomenkranz *(Mgr.-Intl. Adv.)*
Bob Clanin *(Mgr.-Treasury)*
Len Theis *(Mgr.-Strategic Cost Analysis)*
J.Stein *(Mgr.-Fin. Res.)*

Computer Systems/Hardware:
IBM

Outside Service Firm(s):

Deloitte & Touche*(Auditors)*
1600 Summer St.
Stamford, CT 06905-5121
Tel.: 203-351-4600

Aetna Life & Casualty*(Group Insurer)*
151 Farmington Avenue
Hartford, CT 06156
Tel.: 203-273-2128
Fax: 203-729-4295

Empire Blue Cross & Blue Shield*(Group Insurer)*
New York, NY

Salomon Brothers*(Investment Banker)*
7 World Trade Center
New York, NY 10048
Tel.: 212-783-7000

Schnader, Harrison, Segal & Lewis*(Legal Firm)*
1600 Market Street
Philadelphia, PA 19103
Tel.: 215-751-2000

Bankers Trust Co.*(Major Banking Relationship)*
P.O. Box 318, Church St. Station
New York, NY 10008
Tel.: 212-454-2212
Fax: 212-454-2783

Chemical Banking Corp.*(Major Banking Relationship)*
277 Park Ave.
New York, NY 10041
Tel.: 212-310-6407
Fax: 212-310-4526

Citibank N.A.*(Major Banking Relationship)*
Corporate Trust Services, 399 Park Ave.
New York, NY 10043
Tel.: 212-559-1605

Bankers Trust Co.*(Pension Manager)*
One Bankers Trust Plaza
New York, NY 10006
Tel.: 212-250-6902

Sanford C. Bernstein & Co., Inc.*(Pension Manager)*
767 Fifth Ave.
New York, NY 10153
Tel.: 212-756-4383
Fax: 212-756-4405

Chemical Bank*(Pension Manager)*
450 West 33rd St.
New York, NY 10001
Tel.: 212-613-7197
Fax: 212-947-7628

Equitable Real Estate Investment Managment Inc.*(Pension Manager)*
3414 Peachtree Rd. N.E.
Atlanta, GA 30326-1162

Investment Advisors Inc.*(Pension Manager)*
1100 Dain Tower, P.O. Box 357
Minneapolis, MN 55440

Metropolitan Life Insurance Co.*(Pension Manager)*
One Madison Ave.
New York, NY 10010-3690
Tel.: 215-578-9292

J. P. Morgan Investment Management, Inc.*(Pension Manager)*
522 Fifth Ave.
New York, NY 10036
Tel.: 212-837-2300
Fax: 212-819-1871

Non-U.S. Holdings:

UPS/Alimondo **(1)**
Via Fantoli 15/2 20138
Milan, Italy
Tel.: 02 50791
Courier Services
S.I.C.: 4513; 4512

United Parcel Service of Canada **(1)**
3195 Airway Dr.
Mississauga, ON H8T 3T2, Canada
Tel.: 416-676-6030 (100%)
Parcel Delivery Services
S.I.C.: 4215; 4513

United Parcel Service of America, Inc.—(Continued)

Glenn C. Smith *(Pres.)*

UNITED PARKING, INC.
100 Peachtree St., Ste. 335
Atlanta, GA 30303
Tel.: 404-658-9053 TN
Fax: 404-658-9053
Year Founded: 1961
Approx.Sls.: $17,000,000
Emp.: 300
Parking Garage; Parking Lots; Real Estate Brokers & Agents
S.I.C.: 7521; 6531
Robert F. Dennis *(Chm. Bd.)*
Samuel T. Wadsworth *(Pres.)*
Roy Burdett *(V.P.-Devel.)*

Outside Service Firm(s):

Smith Adcock & Co.*(Auditors)*
Atlanta, GA

Trust Company Bank*(Major Banking Relationship)*
P.O. Box 4625, 25 Park Place
Atlanta, GA 30302
Tel.: 404-588-7815

UNITED PIECE DYE WORKS, LP
14 Washington Rd., Bldg. 1
Rear Entrance
Princeton Junction, NJ 08550
Mailing Address:
CN 5269,
Princeton, NJ 08853
Tel.: 609-799-6707 DE
Fax: 609-275-6164
Year Founded: 1989
Approx.Sls.: $55,000,000
Emp.: 550
Fiscal Year-end: 12/31/91
Export
Dyeing & Finishing of Manmade Fiber & Silk Fabrics; Finishing Plants; Cotton, Broadwoven Fabric Mills
S.I.C.: 2262; 2261; 2231
Harold C. Summerford *(Chm. Bd.)*
Keith E. Johnson *(Pres.)*
Ernest S. Knighton *(Chief Exec. Officer)*
James E. Landry *(Chief Fin. Officer, Exec. V.P. & Sec.)*
Donald G. Simms *(Controller)*
Lewis Cassell *(Dir.-Sls.)*
George Hill *(Dir.-Mktg.)*

No. of Mfg. Plants/Facilities: 2
No. of U.S. Offices: 2

Computer Systems/Hardware:
IBM AS/400

Outside Service Firm(s):

Richard A. Eisner & Co.*(Auditors)*
575 Madison Ave.
New York, NY 10022
Tel.: 212-355-1700

Otterbourg, Steindler, Houston & Rosen*(Legal Firm)*
230 Park Ave.
New York, NY 10017
Tel.: 212-661-9100

UNITED POWER ASSOCIATION
P.O. Box 800
Elk River, MN 55330
Tel.: 612-441-3121 MN
Fax: 612-241-2366
Year Founded: 1963
Assets: $845,670,000
Liabilities: $809,662,000
Net Worth: $36,008,000
Approx.Sls.: $168,174,000
Emp.: 417
Fiscal Year-end: 12/31/88
Electric Utility Cooperative
S.I.C.: 4911
Philip Tideman *(Chm. Bd., Pres. & Chief Exec. Officer)*
Philip O. Martin *(Chief Oper. Officer & Gen. Mgr.)*
John R. Wright, Jr. *(Chief Fin. Officer)*
Lowell Hultgren *(V.P.)*
Gerald Richards *(Treas.)*
E. S. Knickerbocker *(Sec.)*
Kenneth Skogquist *(Asst. Sec.)*

Outside Service Firm(s):

Arthur Andersen & Co.*(Auditors)*
45 S. 7th St.
Minneapolis, MN 55402

Levander, Glenn, Miller, Anderson, Kuntz*(Legal Firm)*
S. St. Paul, MN

Norwest Bank of Minneapolis N.A.*(Major Banking Relationship)*
P.O. Box 738, 161 N. Concord Exchange
So. St. Paul, MN 55075-0738
Tel.: 612-450-4064
Fax: 612-450-4078

UNITED PRODUCERS & CONSUMERS CO-OP
1821 E. Jackson St.
Phoenix, AZ 85034
Tel.: 602-254-5644 AZ
Fax: 602-254-5644, Ext. 14
Year Founded: 1934
Approx.Sls.: $10,000,000
Emp.: 60
Wholesale Distribution of Hardware; Feed & Farm Supply
S.I.C.: 5251; 5999
Emil Rovey *(Pres.)*
Lyle Riggs *(V.P.)*
Pauline McInerney *(Gen. Mgr.)*
Ralph Ashby *(Treas. & Sec.)*

Outside Service Firm(s):

Richard B. Berkland*(Auditors)*
Phoenix, AZ

First Interstate Bank*(Major Banking Relationship)*
P.O. Box 53441,
Phoenix, AZ 85072-3441
Tel.: 602-229-4049

UNITED REFRIGERATED SERVICES
2964 Peachtree Rd., NW, Ste. 700
Atlanta, GA 30305
Tel.: 404-261-6691
Fax: 404-261-0344
Approx.Sls.: $90,000,000
Emp.: 1,500
Public Refrigerated Warehousing
S.I.C.: 4222
Maury A. Klumok *(Vice Chm.)*
Ralph Quinn *(Pres.)*
Hal Justice *(Exec. V.P.-Mktg.)*
Tom Ryan *(Exec. V.P.-Opers.)*
Allen L. Shulman *(Exec. V.P.-Admin.)*
Gail A. Adams *(V.P. & Sec.)*

Outside Service Firm(s):

Deloitte & Touche*(Auditors)*
100 Peachtree St., Ste. 1700
Atlanta, GA 30303-1943
Tel.: 404-220-1500
Fax: 404-220-1583

Arnall, Golden & Gregory*(Legal Firm)*
Atlanta, GA

First National Bank of Atlanta*(Major Banking Relationship)*
2 Peachtree Street N.W.
Atlanta, GA 30383

UNITED SERVICES AUTOMOBILE ASSOCIATION (USAA)
USAA Bldg.,
San Antonio, TX 78288
Tel.: 210-498-2211 TX
Fax: 210-498-9940
Year Founded: 1922
Assets: $7,353,000,000
Liabilities: $4,185,000,000
Net Worth: $3,168,000,000
Approx.Rev.: $3,449,000,000
Emp.: 13,000
Fiscal Year-end: 12/31/91
Property & Casualty Insurance; Personal Financial Service Products Including Life Insurance, Mutual Funds, Real Estate Limited Partnerships & Personal Banking Services
S.I.C.: 8611; 6331; 6311; 6211; 6282; 8742; 6531; 6099
Gen. Robert McDermott *(Chm. Bd. & Chief Exec. Officer)*
Gen. Robert Herres *(Pres. & Chief Oper. Officer)*
Herbert E. Emanuel *(Exec. V.P. & Chief Admin. Officer)*
George H. Ensley *(Chief of Staff)*
William McCrae *(Sr. V.P. & Gen. Counsel)*
Alfred Ray Otte *(Sr. V.P & Controller)*
William J. Regan *(Sr. V.P. & Treas.)*

Outside Service Firm(s):

KPMG Peat Marwick*(Auditors)*
112 E. Pecan
San Antonio, TX 78205

Division:

Property & Casualty Insurance **(1)**
USAA Bldg.,
San Antonio, TX 78288
Tel.: 210-498-2211
S.I.C.: 6331
M. Staser Holcomb *(Pres.)*

Subsidiaries:

USAA Buying Service **(1)**
USSA Bldg.,
San Antonio, TX 78288
Tel.: 210-498-8905
S.I.C.: 8611

USAA Federal Savings Bank **(1)**
USAA Bldg.,
San Antonio, TX 78288
Tel.: 210-498-2265
S.I.C.: 6035

USAA Investment Management Co. **(1)**
USAA Bldg.,
San Antonio, TX 78288
Tel.: 210-498-8000
S.I.C.: 6211

USAA Life Insurance Co. **(1)**
USAA Bldg.,
San Antonio, TX 78288
Tel.: 210-498-8000
S.I.C.: 6311

USAA Satellite Communications **(1)**
USAA Bldg.,
San Antonio, TX 78288
Tel.: 210-498-2211
Donald R. Lasher *(Pres.-Info. Services Div.)*

USAA Travel Agencies **(1)**
USAA Bldg.,
San Antonio, TX 78288
Tel.: 210-498-8356
S.I.C.: 4724
Richard A. Goertz *(Asst. V.P.)*

UNITED STATES BAKERY
315 N.E. 10th Ave.
Portland, OR 97232
Mailing Address:
P.O. Box 14769,
Portland, OR 97214
Tel.: 503-232-2191
Fax: 503-731-5680
Year Founded: 1906
Approx.Sls.: $100,000,000
Emp.: 1,400
Fiscal Year-end: 12/31/90
Distribute Breads, Buns & Related Products
S.I.C.: 5149
Murrey R. Albers *(Chm. Bd. & Pres.)*
Jerry Boness *(Chief Fin. Officer)*
Ron McKnight *(Exec. V.P.-Sls.)*
John R. Rader *(Exec. V.P.-Opers.)*
Tom Powers *(V.P.-Fleet)*
John Duwe *(Sec. & Treas.)*
Steve Mayer *(Mgr.-Human Resources)*
Ken Waltos *(Mgr.-Personnel)*

Outside Service Firm(s):

Deloitte & Touche*(Auditors)*
3900 U.S. Bancorp Tower
Portland, OR 97204
Tel.: 503-222-1341
Fax: 503-224-2172

Tonkon, Torp, Galen, Marmaduke & Booth*(Legal Firm)*
1600 Pioneer Tower, 888 S.W. Fifth Ave.
Portland, OR 97204
Tel.: 503-221-1440

First Interstate Bank*(Major Banking Relationship)*
P.O. Box 3131,
Portland, OR 97208
Tel.: 503-220-4855
Fax: 503-225-7153

Divisions:

Franz Bakery **(1)**
P.O. Box 14769,
Portland, OR 97214
Tel.: 503-232-2191
Distributes Breads, Buns & Related Products
S.I.C.: 5149
Ron McKnight *(Exec. V.P.-Adv.)*

Snyder Bakery **(1)**
P.O. Box 305
Spokane, WA 99210
Tel.: 509-535-7726
Distributes Breads, Buns & Related Products
S.I.C.: 5149
Barry Ware *(Gen. Mgr.)*

Snyder Bakery **(1)**
16 N. Third Ave.
Yakima, WA 98902
Tel.: 509-453-8223
Distributes Breads, Buns & Related Products
S.I.C.: 5149
Ernie Wiggins *(Reg. Sls. Mgr.)*

William's Bakery **(1)**
P.O. Box 1375,
Eugene, OR 97440
Tel.: 503-485-8211
Distributes Breads, Buns & Related Products
S.I.C.: 5149
Bob Mitchell *(Gen. Mgr.)*

UNITED STATES BRONZE POWDERS, INC.
Route 202
Flemington, NJ 08822
Mailing Address:
P.O. Box 31
Flemington, NJ 08822
Tel.: 908-782-5454
Telex: 83-3488
Fax: 908-782-3489
Approx.Sls.: $14,600,000
Emp.: 135
Export
Metallic Powders & Pigments; Venus Aluminum, Brass, Bronze, Copper, Infiltrants & Stainless Steel
S.I.C.: 3399
K.C. Ramsey *(Pres.)*
V.J. Vaccaro *(V.P.-Fin.)*
N.L. Nielson *(V.P.-Opers.)*
W.J. Cwieka *(V.P.-Sls.)*
P.E. Matthews *(V.P.-Technical)*
R.A. Foster *(Treas./Controller)*
R.J. Kraemer *(Dir.-Pur.)*
V.S. Diehl *(Mgr.-Personnel)*
E. Fabula *(Mgr.-Data Processing)*
Les Minnerly *(Mgr.-Quality Control)*
Veronica Diehl *(Mgr.-Adv.)*

Computer Systems/Hardware:
IBM

U.S. CAN COMPANY
900 Commerce Dr., Ste. 302
Oak Brook, IL 60521
Tel.: 708-571-2500 **DE**
Fax: 708-572-1439
Year Founded: 1983
Approx.Sls.: $400,000,000
Emp.: 2,000
Fiscal Year-end: 12/31/91
Export
Metal Containers for Aerosol, Paint & Specialty Products
S.I.C.: 3411
William J. Smith *(Chm. Bd., Pres. & Chief Exec. Officer)*
Frank J. Galvin *(Exec. V.P.)*
T.W. Stonich *(Sr. V.P.-Fin. & Chief Fin. Officer)*
Gerald A. Vaughan *(Sr. V.P.-Mfg. & Tech.)*
P.J. Andres *(V.P. & Treas.)*
J.R. McGowan *(V.P. & Controller)*
B.C. Brock *(V.P.-Human Resources)*
P.J. Carrier *(V.P.-Mngmt. Information Systems)*
J.W. Healy *(V.P. & Grp. Exec.-US Can West)*
Martin A. Roth *(V.P.-Opers. Plng. & Research)*
T J. Yurco *(V.P.-Matls. Mngmt. & Logistics)*
Annelle Paschal *(Dir.-Human Resources & Pub. Rels.)*
Robert Jacobsen *(Gen. Mgr.-Mktg.)*

No. of Mfg. Plants/Facilities: 14
No. of U.S. Offices: 9

Computer Systems/Hardware:
IBM

Division:

D & H Tool and Die **(1)**
10505 Sandyville Rd. S.E.
East Sparta, OH 44626
Tel.: 216-866-3975 or 866-3981
Emp.: 12
Tools & Dies
S.I.C.: 3544
Dave Reader *(Chief Oper. Officer)*

Subsidiaries:

Romany Ceramics Inc. **(1)**
East Sparta, OH 44626
Tel.: 216-866-5531 (100%)
Emp.: 180
Ceramic Wall Tile
S.I.C.: 3253
Richard Falbo *(V.P. & Gen. Mgr.)*

Sparta Mosaic, Inc. **(1)**
East Sparta, OH 44626
Tel.: 216-866-5531 (100%)
Emp.: 210
Ceramic Mosaic Floor Tile
S.I.C.: 3253
Richard Falbo *(V.P. & Gen. Mgr.)*

UNITED STATES CERAMIC TILE CO.
10233 Sandyville Rd., SE
East Sparta, OH 44626
Mailing Address:
P.O. Box 338,
East Sparta, OH 44626
Tel.: 216-866-5531
Tel.: 800-321-0684 **DE**
Fax: 216-866-5340
Year Founded: 1913
Approx.Sls.: $37,000,000
Emp.: 500
Fiscal Year-end: 2/28/91
Import Export
Ceramic Floor & Wall Tile; Ceramic Dies & Tooling
S.I.C.: 3253
Robert E. Schlemmer *(Pres. & Chief Exec. Officer)*
Donald Olsen *(Exec. V.P.-Sls. & Mktg.)*
Larry Hay *(V.P.-Fin.)*
James Speakman *(V.P.-Sls.)*
Jeff Raper *(Controller)*
Glen Johnstone *(Dir.-Pur.)*
Matthew C. Smith *(Mgr.- Mktg.)*

No. of Mfg. Plants/Facilities: 3

Computer Systems/Hardware:
IBM

Outside Service Firm(s):

Coopers & Lybrand*(Auditors)*
P.O. Box 538, 800 Akron Centre Plaza
Akron, OH 44308

United of Omaha*(Commercial Insurance Carrier)*
Mutual of Omaha Plaza
Omaha, NE 68175
Tel.: 800-327-8871

UNITED STATES COLD STORAGE, INC.
(Sub. of J S & S Holdings, Inc.)
100 Dobbs Ln., Ste. 102
Cherry Hill, NJ 08034
Tel.: 609-354-8181
Fax: 609-354-8199
Approx.Sls.: $90,000,000
Emp.: 800
Fiscal Year-end: 12/31/90
Manufacture & Sell Ice; Refrigerated Warehouses
S.I.C.: 2097; 4222; 5199
Edward Scott *(Chm. Bd.)*
David F. Beauchamp *(Pres.)*
John Omps *(Sr. V.P.-Fin.)*
Pat Fitzpatrick *(Sr. V.P.-California Region)*
Gerald Nelson *(Sr. V.P.-Southern Region)*
Bill D. Tackett *(Sr. V.P.-Northern Region)*
Gerard F. Maron *(Sr. V.P.-Mid-Atlantic Region)*
David M. Harlan *(V.P.-Natl. Sls. & Mktg.)*
Gerald Boyle *(Mgr.-Data Processing)*

Computer Systems/Hardware:
IBM Systems 34 & 36

Outside Service Firm(s):

KPMG Peat Marwick*(Auditors)*
1600 Market St.
Philadelphia, PA 19103
Tel.: 215-299-3100

Mellon Bank, N.A.*(Legal Firm)*
P.O. Box 444,
Pittsburgh, PA 15230
Tel.: 412-236-8000
Tel.: 1-800-451-7392
Fax: 412-236-8157

Subsidiary:

United States Cold Storage of Calif. **(1)**
2003 S. Cherry St.
Fresno, CA 93718
Tel.: 209-237-6145
Fax: 209-237-0719

U.S. COMMUNICATIONS CORPORATION
901 Marquette Ave. S. 17th Fl.
Minneapolis, MN 55402
Tel.: 612-373-3000
Twx: 3062
Year Founded: 1975
Approx.Billings: $96,000,000
Emp.: 101
Integrated Marketing Services
Terence Graunke *(Chm. Bd. & Pres.)*
Carolyn Maduza *(Sr. V.P., Chief Fin. Officer)*

U.S. COMPUTER SERVICES
(d/b/a Cabledata)
11020 Sun Center Dr.
Rancho Cordova, CA 95670
Tel.: 916-636-4500
Fax: 916-636-5645
Year Founded: 1965
Approx.Sls.: $80,000,000
Emp.: 1,025
Cable Television Information Systems
S.I.C.: 7372
Jim Castle *(Chm. Bd. & Chief Exec. Officer)*
Arthur O. Hawkins *(V.P., Chief Fin. Officer & Treas.)*
Chuck Clupper *(V.P.-Electrical Design)*
Patricia A. George *(V.P.-Human Resources)*
Raymond W. Matteson *(V.P.-New Bus. Devel. & Mktg.)*
Gerald S. Knapp *(V.P.-Opers.)*
Maggie Wilderotter *(V.P.-Sls.)*

Outside Service Firm(s):

Coopers & Lybrand*(Auditors)*
Sacramento, CA

Gray & Thurn*(Legal Firm)*
Sacramento, CA

The Bank of California, N.A.*(Major Banking Relationship)*
400 California
San Francisco, CA 94104
Tel.: 415-765-0400

U.S. CONSTRUCTION CO., INC.
P.O. Box 211429,
Columbia, SC 29221
Tel.: 803-731-9146 **SC**
Fax: 803-798-6214
Approx.Sls.: $31,000,000
Emp.: 200
Road & Highway Construction
S.I.C.: 1611
James K. Ewart, III *(Pres. & Chief Exec. Officer)*
Thomas O. Cook *(Dir.-Opers.)*
Ed Alexander *(Dir.-Pur.)*
Patrick Kistler *(Dir.-Fin. & Data Processing)*
Charles Leath *(Dir.-Engrng.)*
Kenneth W. Palm *(Dir.-Personnel)*

Outside Service Firm(s):

Keels & Hughes*(Auditors)*
Columbia, SC

Cooper, Coffas & Heizer*(Legal Firm)*
Columbia, SC

Citizens & Southern National Bank*(Major Banking Relationship)*
Columbia, SC

U.S. CREATIVE, INC.
901 S. MoPac Expwy., Barton Oaks Plaza II, Ste. 595
Austin, TX 78746
Tel.: 512-328-2040
Year Founded: 1985
Approx.Billings: $12,000,000
Emp.: 19
Retail, Fast Food, & Maturity Mktg.
Candice Medlin *(Pres.)*
Jean Chandler *(V.P.)*
Lloyd Sheep *(V.P., Mktg.)*
Randall House *(Sec. & Treas.)*

U.S. DIVERS CO., INC.
3323 W. Warner Ave.
Santa Ana, CA 92799
Mailing Address:
P.O. Box 25018
Santa Ana, CA 92799
Tel.: 714-540-8010 **CA**
Fax: 714-432-9340
Approx.Sls.: $33,600,000
Emp.: 400
Under Water Diving Equipment, Life Support Equipment For Fire Fighting & Industrial Safety
S.I.C.: 3569; 3949
Capt. J. Y. Cousteau *(Chm. Bd.)*
Michael M. Chapman *(Exec. V.P. & Co-Chief Oper. Officer)*
Frank Muller *(Exec. V.P. & Co-Chief Oper. Officer)*
Normand Couturier *(V.P.-Fin.)*

Division:

U.S. Divers **(1)**
3323 W. Warner Ave.
Santa Ana, CA 92799
Tel.: 714-540-8010
Larry Chisholm *(Natl. Sls. Mgr.)*

U.S. ENGINEERING COMPANY
3433 Roanoke Rd.
Kansas City, MO 64111
Tel.: 816-753-6969 **MO**
Fax: 816-931-5773
Year Founded: 1893
Approx.Sls.: $70,000,000
Emp.: 675
Mechanical Contractors: Heating, Ventilating, Air Conditioning, Process Piping, Plumbing, Sheet Metal Fire Protection, Specialty Piping Installation
S.I.C.: 1711; 1761; 1799
Henry Nottberg, III *(Chm. Bd., Pres. & Chief Exec. Officer)*
Max E. Singer *(Chief Fin. Officer, V.P. & Treas.)*
Dwight Brinkman *(V.P.-Western Region)*
William F. Daniels *(V.P.-Corp. Mktg.)*
Joe Finegan *(V.P.-Maintenance & Service)*
Gregory B. Gillam *(V.P.)*
Curtis Hunter *(V.P.-Eastern Region)*
J. Daniel Oxler, Jr. *(V.P.-Kansas City Region)*
Paul T. Russell, Jr. *(V.P.-Gen. Mgr. Eastern Region)*
Dennis Simonich *(V.P.-Mktg.-Western Region)*

Outside Service Firm(s):

Baird, Kurtz & Dobson*(Auditors)*
Commerce Tower, 911 Main, Ste. 1900
Kansas City, MO
Tel.: 816-221-7544

Continental Insurance*(Commercial Insurance Carrier)*
180 Maiden Lane
New York, NY

Lincoln National Life Insurance Co.*(Group Insurer)*
PO Box 208, 1300 S. Clinton
Fort Wayne, IN 46801
Tel.: 219-455-2926
Fax: 219-455-7619

Watson, Ess, Marshall & Enggas*(Legal Firm)*
Grand Ave.
Kansas City, MO 64106
Tel.: 816-842-3132

United Missouri Bank*(Major Banking Relationship)*
P.O. Box 226
Kansas City, MO 64141
Tel.: 816-556-7000

Branch:

U.S. Engineering Co. **(1)**
729 S.E. 8th Street
Loveland, CO 80539
Tel.: 303-669-1666
Fax: 303-663-0685

U.S. ENERTEK, INC.
4901 E. Main St.
Farmington, NM 87402
Tel.: 505-326-1151
Fax: 505-325-0317
Approx.Sls.: $31,000,000
Emp.: 200
Fiscal Year-end: 6/30/91

U.S. Enertek, Inc.—(Continued)

Manufactures Gas & Oil Production Equipment, Olman Heath Products; Oilfield Service & Rentals; Cranes & Water Blasters; Oilfield Power Equipment; Custom Machining
S.I.C.: 3559
Rodney Heath *(Pres. & Chief Exec. Officer)*
Al Dean *(Prod. Mgr.-E.C.I. Controls & Instruments)*
Bob Jones *(Reg. Sls. Mgr.-Rocky Mt. North)*
Jack Weatherford *(Reg. Sls. Mgr.-Rocky Mt. South)*
Dwayne Howle *(Reg. Sls. Mgr.-Mid Continent)*
Ken Henley *(Reg. Sls. Mgr.-Gulf Coast)*

U.S. FOOD PRODUCTS, INC.
1200 N. Ashland, Rm. 610
Chicago, IL 60622
Tel.: 312-342-7210
Fax: 312-347-7933
Approx.Sls.: $13,000,000
Emp.: 5
Fiscal Year-end: 12/31/90
Krakus Imported Polish Ham; Danish Kitchen Imported Hams
S.I.C.: 5147
Timothy R. Piech *(Pres. & Adv. Mgr.)*

U.S. FURNITURE INDUSTRIES, INC.
1200 Surrett Dr.
High Point, NC 27260
Mailing Address:
P.O. Box 2127
High Point, NC 27261
Tel.: 919-884-7375 **NC**
Fax: 919-884-7000
Approx.Sls.: $57,000,000
Emp.: 615
Fiscal Year-end: 12/31/91
Mfr. Wood & Metal Household & Office Furniture
S.I.C.: 2511; 2512; 2514; 2521; 2522
Stanley R. Taylor *(Chm. Bd.)*
Ronald L. Hundey *(Pres.)*
David Beaston *(V.P.)*
Dwight Bumgarner *(V.P.)*
John McCarthy *(V.P.)*
Ed Cornwell *(Treas. & Asst. Sec.)*

Outside Service Firm(s):

Arthur Andersen & Co.*(Auditors)*
One Southern Life Center
Greensboro, NC 27401
Fax: 919-378-1445

U.S. GRAPHITE, INC.
1621 E. Holland Ave.
Saginaw, MI 48601
Tel.: 517-755-0441
Fax: 517-755-0445
Sales Range: $10-19 Million
Emp.: 150
Mfr. of Mechanical Carbon Graphite Parts
S.I.C.: 3624
Allan Vandail *(Chm. Bd.)*
Ronald J. Kovel *(V.P.-Engrng.)*
Hal Richards *(V.P.-Fin.)*
Richard H. Stroebel *(V.P.-Mfg.)*
Evelyn Vogel *(Pur. Agent)*

Outside Service Firm(s):

Rehmann, Robson & Co., P.C.*(Auditors)*
Saginaw, MI

Comerica Bank*(Major Banking Relationship)*
Saginaw, MI

UNITED STATES LUGGAGE COMPANY
400 Wireless Blvd.
Hauppauge, NY 11788
Mailing Address:
P.O. Box 969,
Smithtown, NY 11787
Tel.: 516-434-7070
Fax: 516-434-7326
Approx.Sls.: $15,000,000
Emp.: 35
Fiscal Year-end: 12/31/90
Import
Leather Attache & Portfolio
S.I.C.: 3161
Lawrence Krulik *(Chm. Bd.)*
Richard Krulik *(Vice Chm.)*
Bernard D. Sadow *(Pres.)*
Lew Levy *(Exec. V.P.)*
Carol Schnall *(V.P. & Chief Fin. Officer)*
Alan Friedgood *(Dir.-Sls.)*

Computer Systems/Hardware:
IBM 36

Affiliate:

Dunston Leathers, Inc. **(1)**
400 Wireless Blvd.
Hauppauge, NY 11788
Tel.: 516-434-7070
Fax: 516-434-7326
S.I.C.: 3161

U.S. MANUFACTURING CORP.
30855 Little Mack Ave.
Roseville, MI 48066
Tel.: 313-293-8744 **MI**
Fax: 313-293-8908
Year Founded: 1964
Assets: $28,000,000
Liabilities: $15,000,000
Net Worth: $13,000,000
Approx.Sls.: $62,000,000
Emp.: 540
Fiscal Year-end: 12/31/88
OEM Manufacture & Supply Automotive Products, Machined Castings & Forgings, Metal Extrusions, Weldments
S.I.C.: 3549; 3499
Joseph A. Simon, Sr. *(Chm. Bd., Pres. & Chief Exec. Officer)*
George A. Simon *(Exec. V.P.)*
William K. Cooksey *(V.P.-Sls. & Mktg.)*
Robert L. Peltier *(V.P.-Fin.)*
Joseph Simon, Jr. *(V.P.-Engrng.)*
Richard B. Lorenz *(Controller)*
Albert Kanakri *(Dir.-Data Processing)*

No. of Mfg. Plants/Facilities: 4

Outside Service Firm(s):

Godfrey, Hammel & Daniels*(Auditors)*
St. Clair Shores, MI

Michigan National Bank*(Major Banking Relationship)*
Detroit, MI

U.S. Metal Container Company
(See U.S. Manufacturing Corp.)

U.S. METALSOURCE CORPORATION
200 Corporate Center Dr., Ste. 200
Coraopolis, PA 15108
Tel.: 412-264-7280
Fax: 412-264-4813
Year Founded: 1986
Approx.Sls.: $350,000,000
Emp.: 950
Fiscal Year-end: 9/30/90
Primary Metal Industries-Steel, Aluminum & Titanium Metal
S.I.C.: 5051; 5039
David Hopton *(Pres. & Chief Exec. Officer)*
Thomas M. Brandt, Jr. *(Chief Fin. Officer)*
Connie Howard *(Controller)*
Bruce Nagle *(Mgr.-Human Resources)*
Holland Donaldson *(Mgr.-Pur.)*

Outside Service Firm(s):

Deloitte & Touche*(Auditors)*
1 World Trade Center
New York, NY 10048
Tel.: 212-669-5000

Arkwright Mutual Insurance*(Commercial Insurance Carrier)*
225 Wyman St.
Waltham, MA 02254-9198
Tel.: 617-890-9300
Fax: 617-890-0075

Aetna Life & Casualty*(Group Insurer)*
151 Farmington Avenue
Hartford, CT 06156
Tel.: 203-273-2128
Fax: 203-729-4295

The Principal Financial Group*(Group Insurer)*
Des Moines, IA

Prudential Insurance Co. of America*(Group Insurer)*
751 Broad St.
Newark, NJ 07102-3777
Tel.: 201-802-6000

Weil, Gotshal & Manges*(Legal Firm)*
767 5th Ave.
New York, NY 10153
Tel.: 212-310-8000

Chemical Bank*(Major Banking Relationship)*
450 West 33rd St.
New York, NY 10001
Tel.: 212-613-7197
Fax: 212-947-7628

U.S. MUSIC CORPORATION
2885 S. James Dr.
New Berlin, WI 53151
Tel.: 414-784-8388
Fax: 414-784-9258
Manufacture Electric & Acoustical Guitars
S.I.C.: 3931
Charles Faaf *(Pres.)*

Outside Service Firm(s):

M & I Marshall & Isley Bank*(Major Banking Relationship)*
Milwaukee, WI

Subsidiary:

Guild Music Corporation **(1)**
60 Industrial Dr.
Westerly, RI 02891
Tel.: 401-596-0141
Manufacture Electric & Acoustical Guitars
S.I.C.: 3931
George Stafleos *(Gen. Mgr.)*

U.S. NEWS & WORLD REPORT
1290 Avenue of the Americas
New York, NY 10104
Tel.: 212-830-1500
Fax: 212-830-1560
Year Founded: 1933
Approx.Sls.: $140,000,000
Emp.: 500
Publishers of Weekly News Magazine
S.I.C.: 2721
Mortimer B. Zuckerman *(Chm. Bd. & Editor-in-Chief)*
Fred Drasner *(Pres. & Chief Exec. Officer)*
Alice Rogoff *(Sr. V.P.-Fin. & Chief Fin. Officer)*
Thomas R. Evans *(Sr. V.P.)*
K.C. Forward *(V.P.-Adv. Sls.)*
Patrick K. Hagerty *(V.P.-Adv. Sls.)*
William M.C. Miller *(V.P.-Adv. Sls.)*
Suzan Nanfeldt *(V.P.-Mktg.)*
Dudley F. Wing *(V.P.-Adv. Sls.)*
Merrill McLoughlin *(Co-Editor)*
Michael Ruby *(Co-Editor)*
David Gergen *(Editor-at-Large)*

Computer Systems/Hardware:
Data General

Outside Service Firm(s):

Coopers & Lybrand*(Auditors)*
Washington, DC

Liberty Mutual*(Commercial Insurance Carrier)*
175 Berkeley St.
Boston, MA

Aetna Life & Casualty*(Group Insurer)*
151 Farmington Avenue
Hartford, CT 06156
Tel.: 203-273-2128
Fax: 203-729-4295

Salomon Brothers*(Investment Banker)*
7 World Trade Center
New York, NY 10048
Tel.: 212-783-7000

Shaw, Pittman, Potts & Trowbridge*(Legal Firm)*
2300 N St. N.W.
Washington, DC 20037
Tel.: 202-663-8000

Chemical Banking Corp.*(Major Banking Relationship)*
277 Park Ave.
New York, NY 10041
Tel.: 212-310-6407
Fax: 212-310-4526

Subsidiaries:

Applied Graphics Technologies **(1)**
15 Neil Court
Oceanside, NY 11572
Tel.: 516-766-4111
Sales Range: $20-39 Million
Emp.: 270
Color Separation For Publishing Industry
S.I.C.: 2752; 7335; 7336
Peter Faucetta *(Chm. Bd., Pres. & Chief Exec. Officer)*
Eric Bernstein *(V.P.-Mfg.)*
Louis Conetta *(V.P. & Gen. Mgr.)*
Nat Buonfiglio *(Treas.)*
Douglas Shaka *(Controller)*
Robert Grimm *(Mgr.-Sls.)*

Applied Graphics Technology **(1)**
463 Barrell Ave.
Carlstadt, NJ 07072
Tel.: 201-935-3200
Printing
S.I.C.: 2721

THE UNITED STATES PLAYING CARD COMPANY
Beech & Park St.
Cincinnati, OH 45212
Tel.: 513-396-5700
Fax: 513-396-5879
Approx.Sls.: $80,000,000
Emp.: 500
Playing Cards, Games & Playing Cards Accessories
S.I.C.: 5092; 3944
Ronald C. Rule *(Pres. & Chief Exec. Officer)*
Robert M. LeFevre *(Sr. V.P.-Mktg. & Sls.)*
Charles R. Zunk *(V.P.-Opers.)*
Louis B. Eichhold *(V.P.-Human Resources & Indus.)*
Ellen S. Young *(Mgr.-Mktg.)*
Elmer Koenig *(Pur. Agent)*

Subsidiary:

Arrco Playing Card Co. **(1)**
Beech St. & Park Ave.
Cincinnati, OH 45212
Tel.: 513-396-5700
Fax: 513-396-5879
Approx.Sls.: $5,000,000
Emp.: 40
Fiscal Year-end: 9/30/90

21 Poker, Club Casino, Streamline, Duratone, Midway & Pla-Mor Playing Cards, Poker Chips, Dice & Accessories, Safety Town Children's Games, Mystic Wizard Magic Cards
S.I.C.: 5092
Ellen Young *(Mktg. Mgr.)*
Mary L Kazanski *(Mgr.-Casino)*

UNITED STATES REALTY & INVESTMENT CO.
1160 Raymond Blvd.
Newark, NJ 07102
Tel.: 201-622-5959 **NJ**
Fax: 201-622-5964
Investment Properties
S.I.C.: 6531; 6799; 6141; 6512
Ivor Braka *(Chm. Bd.)*
Charles Darwish *(Pres.)*
Steven Krieger *(V.P.)*
Mindy Kleinberg *(Chief Fin. Officer)*

Outside Service Firm(s):

J. H. Cohn & Co.*(Auditors)*
75 Eisenhower Pkwy.
Roseland, NJ 07068-1697
Tel.: 201-228-3500

Subsidiary:

Lehman Associates, Inc. **(1)**
909 Broad St.
Newark, NJ 07102
Tel.: 201-622-5959 (100%)
Fax: 201-622-5964
Emp.: 16
Real Estate Brokerage
S.I.C.: 6531
Lester E. Lehman *(Pres.)*

U.S. REDUCTION COMPANY
9200 Calumet Ave.
Munster, IN 46321
Tel.: 219-836-0555
Fax: 219-836-0058
Year Founded: 1984
Approx.Sls.: $200,000,000
Emp.: 463
Fiscal Year-end: 5/31/91
Secondary Smelter & Refinery of Non-Ferrous Metals; Manufacture Aluminum Ingots & Master Alloys
S.I.C.: 3334
Lawrence Liebman *(Chm. Bd.)*
Richard S. Neufeld *(Pres.)*
K. D. Killin *(V.P.-Engrng.)*
Bob Baader *(Dir.-Data Processing)*
Andy Campbell *(Plant Mgr.)*
Mark Dunbar *(Plant Mgr.)*
Mark Matusick *(Plant Mgr.)*
Al Reinhart *(Plant Mgr.)*
Herb Kocher *(Mgr.-Credit)*

Computer Systems/Hardware:
IBM System 36

Outside Service Firm(s):

Deloitte & Touche*(Auditors)*
Two Prudential Plaza, 180 N. Stetson
Chicago, IL 60601
Tel.: 312-946-2039

Adams, Fox, Adelstein & Rosen*(Legal Firm)*
208 So. LaSalle St.
Chicago, IL 60604
Tel.: 312-368-1900

Congress Financial Corp.*(Major Banking Relationship)*
Chicago, IL

U.S. REPEATING ARMS COMPANY
275 Winchester Ave.
New Haven, CT 06511
Tel.: 203-789-5000
Fax: 203-789-5071
Approx.Sls.: $55,000,000
Emp.: 620
Mfr. Firearms
S.I.C.: 3484
Donald Global *(Pres.)*
Fred Angelone *(Chief Fin. Officer)*
Hardy Merrill *(V.P.-Mfg.)*
George Rockwell *(V.P.-Mktg.)*
Richard Whalen *(V.P.-Admin.)*
Alan Paul *(Mgr.-Data Processing)*

Outside Service Firm(s):

Manufacturers Hanover Trust Co.*(Major Banking Relationship)*
4 New York Plaza
New York, NY 10015
Tel.: 212-623-4444

UNITED STATES SAVINGS BONDS DIVISION, TREASURY DEPARTMENT
800 K St. NW
Washington, DC 20001
Mailing Address:
Treasury Dept. Savings Bond Division
Washington, DC 20226
Tel.: 202-377-7710
Approx.Sls.: $11,000,000,000
Emp.: 250
Fiscal Year-end: 9/30/92
United States Savings Bonds
S.I.C.: 9311
Thomas E. Anfinson *(Exec. Dir.)*
Richard Schneebeli *(Deputy Exec. Dir.-Sls. & Mktg.)*
William Deaver *(Dir.-Adv. & Promo.)*
David J. Starck *(Adv. Mgr.)*

UNITED STATES SUGAR CORPORATION
111 Ponce de Leon Ave.
Clewiston, FL 33440
Mailing Address:
P.O. Drawer 1207,
Clewiston, FL 33440
Tel.: 813-983-8121 **DE**
Fax: 813-983-4802
Assets: $307,656,000
Earnings: $4,114,000
Liabilities: $270,754,000
Net Worth: $36,902,000
Approx.Sls.: $305,323,000
Emp.: 2,550
Grows Sugar Cane & Extracts Raw Sugar
S.I.C.: 2061; 0212
William S. White *(Chm. Bd.)*
J. Nelson Fairbanks *(Pres.)*
A.R. Mayo *(Sr. V.P.-Sugar Houses)*
James E. Terrill *(V.P.-Admin.)*
Robert H. Buker, Jr. *(V.P.-Legal Affairs)*
R.C. Lee *(V.P.-Personnel & Community Affairs)*
R.A. Miller *(V.P.-Engrng.)*
Frank L. Polhill *(V.P.-Agriculture)*
Frank D. Teets *(V.P.-Vegetable Opers.)*
Bob Muraro *(Gen. Counsel)*
Stephen V. Goffman *(Controller)*

Outside Service Firm(s):

Coopers & Lybrand*(Auditors)*
5959 Blue Lagoon Dr.
Miami, FL 33126
Tel.: 305-263-8200

Mershon, Sawyer, Johnston, Dunwody & Cole*(Legal Firm)*
1600 First National Bank Bldg.
Miami, FL 33131
Tel.: 305-358-5100

Chemical Banking Corp.*(Major Banking Relationship)*
277 Park Ave.
New York, NY 10041
Tel.: 212-310-6407
Fax: 212-310-4526

Essex Invest. Mgmt. Co.*(Pension Manager)*
Boston, MA

National Bank of Detroit*(Pension Manager)*
611 Woodward
Detroit, MI 48226
Tel.: 313-225-1000

Plants:

Bryant Sugar House **(1)**
111 Ponce de Leon Ave.
Clewiston, FL 33440
Tel.: 813-983-8121
Sugar Production
S.I.C.: 2061

Clewiston Sugar House **(1)**
111 Ponce de Leon Ave.
Clewiston, FL 33440
Tel.: 813-983-8121
Sugar Production
S.I.C.: 2061

Subsidiaries:

South Bay Growers, Inc. **(1)**
P.O. Box 56,
South Bay, FL 33493
Tel.: 305-996-2085 (100%)
Growing & Selling Vegetables
S.I.C.: 0161

United States Corrulite Corporation **(1)**
P. O. Box 2307,
Clewiston, FL 33440
Tel.: 813-983-8121 (100%)
Emp.: 100
Cattle Ranch & Mfr. of Plastic Boxes
S.I.C.: 0212; 3089
John B. Boy *(Pres.)*

U.S. TURBINE CORPORATION
7685 S. State Rte. 48
Maineville, OH 45039
Tel.: 513-683-6100
Year Founded: 1974
Approx.Sls.: $20,000,000
Emp.: 100
Export
Mfr. of Gas Turbine Generator & Compressor Sets
S.I.C.: 3511
Larry D. Davis *(Pres.)*
Alan R. Wenzel *(V.P.)*
Tom Smith *(V.P.-Mktg.)*
Thomas J. Mergy *(Chief Fin. Officer)*
Carl J. Tallmadge *(Dir.-Engrng.)*

UNITED STEEL & WIRE CO.
4909 Wayne Rd.
Battle Creek, MI 49015
Mailing Address:
P.O. Box 256,
Battle Creek, MI 49016
Tel.: 616-962-5571
Tel.: 800-227-7887
Fax: 616-962-5577
Year Founded: 1982
Approx.Sls.: $25,000,000
Emp.: 425
Export
Mfr. of Wire Shelving, Shopping Carts, Racks, Cases & Carriers
S.I.C.: 3496
Donald Carstens *(Chief Exec. Officer)*
Matthew Carstens *(Pres.)*
Frank G. Craig *(V.P.)*
Tom Myers *(V.P.-Mngmt. Information Systems)*

Outside Service Firm(s):

Price Waterhouse*(Auditors)*
67 W. Michigan Mall
Battle Creek, MI 49017

UNITED STORES
P.O. Box 903
Bay City, MI 48707-0903
Tel.: 517-892-5593 **MI**
Fax: 517-892-3723
Year Founded: 1908
Approx.Sls.: $111,000,000
Emp.: 200
Wholesale Groceries & Frozen Foods
S.I.C.: 5141; 5142
Robert G. Koffman *(Pres. & Chief Exec. Officer)*
Don Miller *(Exec. V.P.)*
Gerald H. Blumenau *(Sr. V.P.-Opers.)*
John R. Van Laan *(Sr. V.P.-Fin.)*
Gary H. Adelman *(Dir.-Adv.)*
David H. Straub *(Dir.-Data Processing)*

Computer Systems/Hardware:
IBM

Outside Service Firm(s):

First of America Bank*(Major Banking Relationship)*
Bay City, MI

Subsidiary:

Saginaw Meat & Produce Company **(1)**
P.O. Box 3304
Saginaw, MI 48605
Tel.: 517-755-5331

UNITED TECTONIC INDUSTRY
7201 Paxton St.
Harrisburg, PA 17111
Tel.: 717-564-3434 **PA**
Fax: 717-564-7580
Year Founded: 1969
Approx.Sls.: $23,000,000
Emp.: 87
General Construction Equipment & Machinery; Masonry Equipment & Supplies; Cranes; Heavy Construction Equipment Rental & Repair
S.I.C.: 5082; 7353; 7699
Paul W. Stephenson *(Chm. Bd.)*
James A. Penman *(Pres.)*
Donald E. Minnich *(Sr. V.P. & Treas.)*
Richard W. Cleckner *(Sec.)*

Outside Service Firm(s):

KPMG Peat Marwick*(Auditors)*
Harrisburg, PA

Fulton Bank*(Major Banking Relationship)*
110 Penn Sq.
Lancaster, PA 17602
Tel.: 717-291-2411

UNITED THERMAL CORPORATION
560 Lexington Ave., 9th Fl.
New York, NY 10022
Tel.: 212-826-8600
Emp.: 250
Utility Providing Steam Service
S.I.C.: 4961
Peter J. Fagan *(Pres.)*
Glen A. Swinehart *(Sr. V.P.-Opers.)*
William Gendron *(Asst. Controller)*

Outside Service Firm(s):

Ernst & Young*(Auditors)*
1300 Huntington Bldg.
Cleveland, OH 44115
Tel.: 216-861-5000
Fax: 303-291-6234

The Bank of New York*(Major Banking Relationship)*
One Wall Street
New York, NY 10286
Tel.: 212-635-6805
Fax: 212-635-3201

Subsidiary:

Catalyst Energy Corporation **(1)**
560 Lexington, 9th Fl.
New York, NY 10022
Tel.: 212-826-8600
Fax: 212-826-8740
Emp.: 600
Alternative Producer Of Electric & Steam Energy
S.I.C.: 4911

United Van Lines, Inc.
(See listing under United Thermal Corporation)

UNIVERSAL BUILDERS SUPPLY, INC.
216 S. Terrace Ave.
Mount Vernon, NY 10550
Tel.: 914-699-2400 **DE**
Fax: 914-699-2609
Assets: $25,000,000
Liabilities: $3,000,000
Net Worth: $22,000,000
Approx.Sls.: $25,000,000
Emp.: 200
Import Export
Building & Maintenance Equipment, Aluminum Scaffolding, Shoring, Material & Personnel Hoists & Towers Forming Shoring Products & Architectural Woodwork
S.I.C.: 3429; 3531; 3536; 3537
Kevin O'Callaghan *(Pres.)*
R.A. O'Callaghan *(Chief Exec. Officer)*
Alan Shalders *(Sr. V.P.-Engrng.)*
Tom Flynn *(V.P.-Architectural Woodwork)*
Craig O'Callaghan *(Gen. Superintendant)*
Cal O'Callaghan *(Dir.-Safety & E.E.O. Coordinator)*
Lois Johnson *(Office Mgr.)*
Bob Siegal *(Controller)*
James Connors *(Gen. Counsel)*
Allan Shorley *(Mgr.-Overseas)*

No. of Mfg. Plants/Facilities: 1
No. of U.S. Offices: 2
No. of Foreign Offices: 1

Outside Service Firm(s):

BDO Seidman*(Auditors)*
White Plains, NY

Manufacturers Hanover Trust Co.*(Major Banking Relationship)*
4 New York Plaza
New York, NY 10015
Tel.: 212-623-4444

UNIVERSAL COMPANIES, INC.
2801 E. Beltline N.E.
Grand Rapids, MI 49505
Tel.: 616-364-6161 **MI**
Fax: 616-364-5558
Year Founded: 1955
Assets: $89,000,000
Liabilities: $54,400,000
Net Worth: $34,600,000
Approx.Sls.: $400,000,000
Emp.: 2,300
Fiscal Year-end: 12/26/90
Wholesale Softwoods; Restaurant Opers.
S.I.C.: 5031; 5812
William G. Currie *(Chm. Bd., Pres., Chief Exec. & Chief Oper. Officer)*
Michael G. Maxfield *(Exec. V.P.)*
Douglas Honholt *(Exec. V.P.-Mktg.)*
James Overbeek *(V.P.)*
Philip Boggiano *(Dir.-Data Processing)*
Jeff Davis *(Dir.-Communications)*

No. of Mfg. Plants/Facilities: 48

Computer Systems/Hardware:
IBM

Outside Service Firm(s):

Deloitte & Touche*(Auditors)*
Grand Rapids, MI

Michigan National Bank*(Major Banking Relationship)*
77 Monroe Center
Grand Rapids, MI 49501
Tel.: 616-451-7600

Subsidiaries:

Universal Forest Products, Inc. **(1)**
2801 East Beltline, N.E.
Grand Rapids, MI 49505
Tel.: 616-364-6161
Emp.: 1,700
Manufacture & Wholesale Softwoods & Treaded Products
S.I.C.: 5031
R. Dale Lausch *(Pres.)*

Universal Restaurants, Inc. **(1)**
2801 E. Beltline N.E.
Grand Rapids, MI 49505
Tel.: 616-364-6161
Emp.: 1,100
Restaurants
S.I.C.: 5812
Jim Webb *(Pres.)*

UNIVERSAL CONSTRUCTION COMPANY
29 Greystone Ave.
Kansas City, KS 66103
Mailing Address:
P.O. Box 3248,
Kansas City, KS 66103
Tel.: 913-342-1150 **MO**
Fax: 913-342-1151
Approx.Sls.: $30,000,000
Emp.: 125
General Contractor
S.I.C.: 1542; 1541
Archie W. Smith, III *(Chm. Bd.)*
Steven N. Smith *(Pres.)*
Douglas Niedens *(Sec. & Treas.)*

Outside Service Firm(s):

Baird, Kurtz & Dobson*(Auditors)*
Commerce Tower, 911 Main, Ste. 1900
Kansas City, MO
Tel.: 816-221-7544

Boatmen's First National Bank of Kansas City*(Major Banking Relationship)*
10th & Baltimore
Kansas City, MO 64183
Tel.: 816-221-2800
Fax: 816-691-7254

UNIVERSAL COOPERATIVES, INC.
7801 Metro Pkwy.
Minneapolis, MN 55425
Mailing Address:
P.O. Box 460,
Minneapolis, MN 55440
Tel.: 612-854-0800 **MN**
Telex: RCA 229-731
Fax: 612-854-5744
Year Founded: 1972
Assets: $70,000,000
Earnings: $2,000,000
Liabilities: $35,000,000
Net Worth: $35,000,000
Approx.Sls.: $200,000,000
Emp.: 485
Fiscal Year-end: 7/31/92
Import Export
International Farm Supply Cooperative; Agricultural Chemicals, Animal Health Products, Livestock Equipment, Lubricating Oils, Twine, Tires, Automotive Accessories, Feed Additives, Import/Broker Bird Seed & Jute
S.I.C.: 2298; 2879; 3011; 3523; 5072; 5083; 5172; 2992; 5191; 3085
Stanley Nielsen *(Chm. Bd.)*
George Winstead *(Vice Chm.)*
Patrick M. Finley *(Pres. & Gen. Mgr.)*
Terrance Bohman *(V.P.-Fin.)*
William Cubbage *(V.P.-Animal Health & Nutrition)*
Robert Ellis *(V.P.-Mfg. & Distr.-Lawn, Farm & Garden Chemicals)*
L. Bryan Morrison *(V.P.-Human Resources)*
Pete Nicas *(V.P.-Mktg. & Sls.-Security Prods.)*
Robert Ramsdell *(V.P.-Mktg. & Sls.-Lawn, Farm & Garden)*
Leon Westbrock *(Sec. & Treas.)*
Loyal Leitgen *(Dir.-Intl. Mktg.)*

No. of Mfg. Plants/Facilities: 7
No. of U.S. Offices: 1

Computer Systems/Hardware:
NCR Mainframe & IBM PC

Outside Service Firm(s):

KPMG Peat Marwick*(Auditors)*
4200 Norwest Center, 90 S. 7th St.
Minneapolis, MN 55402
Tel.: 612-341-2222

Allendale Mutual Insurance Co.*(Commercial Insurance Carrier)*
1301 Atwood Ave.
Johnston, RI 02919
Tel.: 401-275-3000

Mutual Service Life Insurance Co.*(Group Insurer)*
Arden Hills, MN

Doherty, Rumble & Butler*(Legal Firm)*
2800 Minnesota World Trade Center
St. Paul, MN 55101-4999
Tel.: 612-291-9333

First National Bank of Minneapolis*(Major Banking Relationship)*
Minneapolis, MN

Saint Paul Bank for Cooperatives*(Major Banking Relationship)*
Saint Paul, MN

Mutual Service Life Insurance Co.*(Pension Manager)*
Arden Hills, MN

Subsidiaries:

Security Products Company of Delaware, Inc. **(1)**
7801 Metro Pkwy.
Minneapolis, MN 55425
Tel.: 612-854-6223 (100%)
Approx.Sls.: $13,000,000
Emp.: 20
Mfr. Lawn & Garden Prods.
S.I.C.: 2873; 2879
Pat Finley *(Pres.)*
Terry Bohman *(V.P.-Fin.)*
Robert Ellis *(V.P.-Mfg.)*
Anthony Nicas *(V.P.-Sls. & Mktg.)*
Tom Alden *(Mgr.-Oper. & Mfg.)*
Michael Parks *(Mgr.-Mktg.)*

Security Products Company **(1)**
7801 Metro Pkwy.
Minneapolis, MN 55425
Tel.: 612-854-6223 (100%)
Fax: 612-854-5571
Computer Systems/Hardware:
NCR Mainframe & IBM PC
Mfr. of Lawn & Garden Products
S.I.C.: 2879; 2873; 2874
Pete Nicas *(V.P.-Sls. & Mktg.)*
Michael Parks *(Mgr.-Mktg.)*

UNIVERSAL DYNAMICS INC.
13600 Dabney Rd.
Woodbridge, VA 22191
Mailing Address:
P.O. Drawer X,
Woodbridge, VA 22194-0396
Tel.: 703-491-2191 **MN**
Fax: 703-690-6535
Year Founded: 1972
Approx.Sls.: $14,000,000
Emp.: 176
Fiscal Year-end: 7/31/92
Import Export
Diversified Holding Company
S.I.C.: 6719
Ernest N. May Jr. *(Chm. Bd.)*
Donald Rainville *(Pres. & Chief Oper. Officer)*
Dewey Rainville *(Chief Exec. Officer)*
Beverly Giroux *(V.P. & Chief Fin. Officer)*
William R. Lukaszyk *(V.P.-Material Handling Sls.)*
Liam Nolan *(Controller)*
Ronald Bankos *(Dir.-Sls.)*
Cynthia Graham *(Dir.-Quality Control)*
Janice Harcharek *(Dir.-Human Resources & Sec.)*
Terry May *(Dir.-Data Processing)*
Robert Crawford *(Mgr.-Engineering)*
Louis Hurst *(Mgr.-Pur.)*
Hal Taylor *(Mgr.-Prod.)*

Computer Systems/Hardware:
IBM Compatables

Division:

Universal Dynamics Inc. **(1)**
46 Pearl St.
North Plainfield, NJ 07076
Tel.: 908-757-5900 (100%)
Fax: 908-757-5898
Emp.: 9
Marketing & Engineering of Material Handling Systems for the Plastics Industry
S.I.C.: 5084
Dewey Rainville *(Chief Exec. Officer)*
Beverly Giroux *(Chief Fin. Officer)*
Donald Rainville *(Chief Oper. Officer)*

Subsidiary:

Universal Dynamics, Inc. **(1)**
13600 Dabney Rd.
Woodbridge, VA 22191
Tel.: 703-491-2191 (100%)
Fax: 703-690-6535
Mfr. of Machinery for the Plastics Industry
S.I.C.: 3559
Dewey Rainville *(Chief Exec. Officer)*
Donald Rainville *(Pres. & Chief Oper. Officer)*
Beverly Giroux *(V.P.-Fin.)*
Janice Harcharek *(Sec.)*
Louis Hurst *(Mgr.-Pur.)*

UNIVERSAL FOLDING BOX COMPANY, INC.
Madison & 13th Sts.
Hoboken, NJ 07030
Tel.: 201-659-7373 **NY**
Fax: 201-798-4126
Year Founded: 1910
Approx.Sls.: $14,000,000
Emp.: 175
Folding Paper Boxes & Display Containers
S.I.C.: 2652; 2657
Sanford L. Batkin *(Pres. & Treas.)*
Frank Pauza *(V.P. & Gen. Mgr.)*
Ruth Vernick *(V.P. & Sec.)*
Richard Berkey *(V.P.-Mfg.)*
Irwin Greenbert *(V.P.-Natl. Acct. Sls.)*
Paul Lehman *(V.P.-Quality Assurance)*
Joan Scherb *(V.P.-Pur. & Plng.)*
Sheldon Weill *(V.P.-Mktg. & Sls.)*
Brent Rance *(V.P.)*

Outside Service Firm(s):

Edward Isaacs & Co.*(Auditors)*
New York, NY

Herrick, Feinstein*(Legal Firm)*
2 Park Ave.
New York, NY 10016
Tel.: 212-684-1400

Midlantic National Bank*(Major Banking Relationship)*
Newark, NJ
Tel.: 908-321-8188

United Jersey Bank*(Major Banking Relationship)*
Hackensack, NJ

UNIVERSAL LIFE INSURANCE COMPANY
480 Linden Ave., P.O. Box 241
Memphis, TN 38126
Tel.: 901-525-3641 **TN**
Fax: 901-528-8266
Year Founded: 1923
Sales Range: $20-39 Million
Emp.: 800
Accident, Health & Life Insurance
S.I.C.: 6311; 6321
A. Maceo Walker, Sr. *(Chm. Bd. & Chief Exec. Officer)*
G.T. Howell *(Pres. & Chief Oper. Officer)*
Frances M. Hassell *(Sr. V.P. & Sec.)*
Eldridge M. Williams *(Sr. V.P.)*
Howard B. Chandler *(1st. V.P. & Chief Fin. Officer)*
James Hawkins *(V.P. & Assoc. Agency Dir.)*

Harold R. Shaw, Sr. *(V.P.-Underwriting)*

Outside Service Firm(s):

Brown & Evans*(Legal Firm)*
Memphis, TN

First National Bank*(Major Banking Relationship)*
Birminghan, AL

UNIVERSAL MOLDING COMPANY
10807 Stanford Ave.
Lynwood, CA 90262
Tel.: 213-636-0721 **CA**
Fax: 213-632-7775
Year Founded: 1948
Approx.Sls.: $38,000,000
Emp.: 250
Export
Aluminum Rolling & Drawing
S.I.C.: 3355
Cliff W. Pratt *(Pres. & Treas.)*
Syd Sossin *(Exec. V.P.)*
Dorothea Gary *(V.P.-Sec.)*
Jim Lease *(Mgr.-Pur.)*

Outside Service Firm(s):

James J. Smith*(Auditors)*
Los Angeles, CA

UNIVERSAL OVERALL COMPANY
1060 W. Van Buren St.
Chicago, IL 60607
Tel.: 312-226-3336 **DE**
Fax: 312-226-1986
Approx.Sls.: $16,000,000
Emp.: 110
Work Uniforms; Overalls & Coveralls
S.I.C.: 2326
Sanford Eckerling *(Pres. & Treas.)*
Robert Northern *(V.P.)*
Gerald Festenstein *(Controller)*
Jack Feinstein *(Dir.-Sls., Pur. & Adv.)*
Principal(s):
Sanford Eckerling

Outside Service Firm(s):

Rome & Associates*(Auditors)*
Chicago, IL

Oak Brook Bank*(Major Banking Relationship)*
Oak Brook, IL

UNIVERSAL PHOTONICS, INC.
495 W. John St.
Hicksville, NY 11801
Tel.: 516-935-4000
Tel.: 800-645-7173
Approx.Sls.: $25,000,000
Emp.: 150
Mfr. & Distribution of Abrasives, Polishing Compounds, Machinery & Supplies for the Optical Industries
S.I.C.: 3291; 2842; 3541
Alan C. Ritter *(Pres.)*
Walter DeTour *(V.P.-Mktg.)*
John Sheridan *(V.P.-Fin.)*
Alice Durkin *(Sec.)*
Martin Lerner *(Gen. Counsel)*
Neil Johnson *(Opers. Mgr.)*
Ed Weingarten *(Pur. Agent)*

Universal Roofers, Inc.
(Name Changed To Bryant Universal Roofers Inc.)

UNIVERSAL SECURITIES CORPORATION
1050 Financial Center, 505 20th Street N.
Birmingham, AL 35203
Tel.: 205-323-8794 **DE**
Fax: 205-324-0728
Year Founded: 1959
Approx.Assets: $10,000,000
Emp.: 13
Discount Security Broker
S.I.C.: 6211
Samuel T. Nash, Jr. *(Pres.)*
Amelia J. Nash *(Exec. V.P.)*
Kerry S. Davidson *(V.P.)*
Rene C. Thompson *(Treas.)*
Kay F. Hughes *(Sec.)*

No. of U.S. Offices: 1

Computer Systems/Hardware:
IBM PC

Outside Service Firm(s):

Blue Cross & Blue Shield of Alabama*(Group Insurer)*
450 Riverchase Pkwy. East
Birmingham, AL 35298
Tel.: 205-988-2245

Sirote, Permutt, Friend, Friedman, Held & Apolinsky*(Legal Firm)*
2222 Arlington Ave. South
Birmingham, AL 35205
Tel.: 205-933-7111

Samuel T. Nash, Jr.*(Pension Manager)*
Birmingham, AL

UNIVERSITY BOOK STORE
711 State St.
Madison, WI 53703
Tel.: 608-257-3784
Fax: 608-257-9479
Year Founded: 1892
Approx.Sls.: $17,000,000
Emp.: 110
College Book Stores; School Supplies
S.I.C.: 5942; 5943
John H. Epple *(Pres.)*

Outside Service Firm(s):

Grant Thornton*(Auditors)*
Madison, WI

First Wisconsin National Bank*(Major Banking Relationship)*
Madison, WI

UNIVEX CORPORATION
3 Old Rockingham Rd.
Salem, NH 03079
Tel.: 603-893-6191
Fax: 800-356-5614
Approx.Sls.: $13,000,000
Emp.: 95
Fiscal Year-end: 12/31/90
Mfg. Food Preparing Machines; Univex
S.I.C.: 3639
James Papadinis *(Chm. Bd.)*
Phil Pappas, Jr. *(Pres.)*
James Williams *(V.P.-Sls.)*
Richard Pereira *(V.P.-Mfg.)*
Tom Lanard *(Pur. Agent)*

UniWorld Group,Inc.

UNIWORLD GROUP, INC.
100 Ave. of the Americas
New York, NY 10013
Tel.: 212-219-1600
Fax: 212-274-8565
Year Founded: 1969
Approx.Billings: $62,500,000
Emp.: 75
African-American & Hispanic Adv.
Byron E. Lewis *(Chm. & Chief Exec. Officer)*
Josefina Penzes *(Sr. V.P., Chief Fin. Officer)*
Cecilia Foster *(Sr. V.P., Human Resources)*
Lester McClurg *(Pur.)*

UP-RIGHT, INC.
1775 Park St.
Selma, CA 93662
Mailing Address:
P.O. Box 560,
Selma, CA 93662
Tel.: 209-896-5150 **CA**
Fax: 209-896-9012
Year Founded: 1947
Approx.Sls.: $100,000,000
Emp.: 740
Fiscal Year-end: 6/30/91
Export
Mfr. of Aluminum Scaffolds, Air Telescoping Work Platforms, Elevating Platforms, Grape Harvesters, Pipe Fittings, Self-Propelled Scissor Lifts & Boom Lifts, Portable Towers
S.I.C.: 3523; 5082; 5083; 3446; 3441; 7353; 3499; 3531; 7359
George M. Strmotich *(Chm. Bd.)*
David K. Sargent *(Pres.)*
James T. Dillon *(V.P.-Fin.)*
Michael Murnin *(V.P.-Sls. & Mktg.)*
Michael D. Ream *(V.P.-Engrng.)*
Armen S. George *(Legal Officer)*
Tom M. Thompson *(U.S. Mgr.-Harvesters)*
Jack Harwood *(Customer Service Mgr.)*
Irene Gonzalez *(Mgr.-Human Resources)*
David Melton *(Mgr.-Mngmt. Info. Systems)*

Outside Service Firm(s):

Arthur Andersen & Co.*(Auditors)*
1800 Harrison St., Ste. 1800
Oakland, CA 94612
Tel.: 510-465-6333

Lincoln National Life Insurance Co.*(Group Insurer)*
PO Box 208, 1300 S. Clinton
Fort Wayne, IN 46801
Tel.: 219-455-2926
Fax: 219-455-7619

Siebel Capital Management Co.*(Investment Banker)*
Marin, CA

Orrick, Herrington & Sutcliffe*(Legal Firm)*
Old Federal Reserve Bank Bldg., 400 Sansome St.
San Francisco, CA 95814
Tel.: 415-392-1122

The Bank of California, N.A.*(Major Banking Relationship)*
400 California
San Francisco, CA 94104
Tel.: 415-765-0400

Divisions:

Harvester Division **(1)**
1775 Park St.
Selma, CA 93662
Tel.: 209-896-5150
Approx.Sls.: $6,000,000
Emp.: 160
Grape Harvesting Machinery
S.I.C.: 3523
S. Pat Nelson *(Plant Mgr.)*
Tom M. Thompson *(Harvester Mgr.)*

Up-Right Work Platforms Division **(1)**
1775 Park St.
Selma, CA 93662
Tel.: 209-896-5150
Aluminum Scaffolding & Portable Lifts
S.I.C.: 3446; 3534
Pat Nelson *(Plant Mgr.)*
Theodore S. Ockels *(Pres., Chief Exec. Officer, Chief Fin. Officer & Treas.)*
Thomas M. Thompson *(Contr., Asst. Treas.)*
Lee Genet *(Systems Mgr.)*
Donald Reichert *(V.P. Admn.)*
James O. Hartman *(Gen. Couns., Sec.)*
Barbara Davis *(Acctg. Mgr.)*

Non-U.S. Holdings:

Access Equipment Ltd. **(1)**
Audley Ave.
Newport, Shropshire TF10 7DP, United Kingdom
Tel.: 0952815815
Telex: 851 35610 ACCESS G
S.I.C.: 3531; 3537
David Sargent *(Mng. Dir.)*

Instant S.R.L. **(1)**
Via Montanari 7, S. Martino Siccomario
Pavia, Italy
Tel.: (0382) 49 8860 (100%)
Telex: 843-312818 Instan I
Portable Aluminum Scaffolds
S.I.C.: 3537
Carlo Bacchiega *(Dir.)*

John Rusling Ltd. **(1)**
Old Hall, Station Rd.
Newport, Shropshire TF10 7DP, United Kingdom
Tel.: (0952) 811779 (100%)
Telex: 851 35207 Ruslin G
Scaffolds
S.I.C.: 3537
David K. Sargent *(Mng. Dir.)*

Up-Right (Far East) Ltd. **(1)**
Unit 243, Ubi Ave. 4 Intrepid Warehouse Complex,
Singapore, 1440, Singapore
Tel.: 745-8777 (100%)
Telex: 786 39229 INSCAF RS
S.I.C.: 3537
Vincent Wee *(Chief Oper. Officer)*

Up-Right (Ireland) Ltd. **(1)**
Pottery Rd. Dun Laoire Co.,
Dublin, Ireland
Tel.: (353) 1-853333 (100%)
Telex: 852 30201 UPRT EI
Emp.: 150
Scaffolds, Work & Elevating Platforms, Scissor Lifts
S.I.C.: 3537
Reinold Visser *(Mfg. Mgr.)*

Up-Right Scaffolds Ltd. **(1)**
108 Industrial Dr.
Whitby, ON L1N 5Z8, Canada
Tel.: 416-668-7701 (100%)
Telex: 06981395 UPRIGHT WTBY CA
Emp.: 20
S.I.C.: 3537

N.V. Vectur S.A. **(1)**
1243 Chaussee de Haecht 1130
Brussels, Belgium
Tel.: 02/2154 652 (100%)
Telex: 846 64050 LOCHAF B
Emp.: 30
Scaffolds, Work & Elevating Platforms, Lifts
S.I.C.: 3537
Paul Robeys *(Mng.)*

Vectur Aluminumstallningar **(1)**
Baldersbaekrej 33 2635
Ishoj, Denmark
Tel.: (02) 525052 (100%)
Telex: 855 33653 VECTUR DK
Emp.: 15
Scaffolds, Work & Elevating Platforms, Lifts
S.I.C.: 3537
Erik Brandi *(Mgr.)*

Vectur GmbH **(1)**
Voelklinger Landstr. 80 D-4000
Dusseldorf, 1, Germany
Tel.: 49 211/30.60.81-84 (100%)
Telex: 84108588448 VEC D
Emp.: 50
Scaffolds, Work & Elevating Platforms, Lifts
S.I.C.: 3537
Claus-Detlef Hadenfeldt *(Mng. Dir.)*

Vectur B.V. **(1)**
Zwolsweg 335 7300 AH Apeldoorn,
Apeldoorn, Netherlands
Tel.: (055) 551 969
Telex: 844/36367 VEC NL
S.I.C.: 3537
Jan Koldenhof *(Mng. Dir.)*

Vectur S.A. **(1)**
CH-1041
Bottens, sur Lausanne Switzerland
Tel.: (021) 831 344
Telex: 846 64050 LOCHAF B
S.I.C.: 3537

UPPCO, INC.
5610 W. Bloomingdale
Chicago, IL 60639
Tel.: 312-622-7010
Fax: 312-622-6587
Approx.Sls.: $21,000,000
Emp.: 400
Sub Fractional Horse Power Motors
S.I.C.: 3621
Jerome Joseph *(Chm. Bd., Pres. & Treas.)*
Justin Joseph *(Mgr.-Sls.)*
Mark Joseph *(Mgr.-Engrng. & Sec.)*
Ed Burback *(Pur. Agent)*

Outside Service Firm(s):

Ostrow, Reisin, Berk, & Abrams, Ltd.*(Auditors)*
Chicago, IL

Cowan & Minetz*(Legal Firm)*
Chicago, IL

LaSalle National Bank*(Major Banking Relationship)*
120 S. LaSalle St.
Chicago, IL 60603
Tel.: 312-781-8000

THE UPPER DECK COMPANY
5909 The Otter Place
Carlsbad, CA 92008
Tel.: 619-929-6500
Fax: 619-929-6548
Year Founded: 1988
Approx.Sls.: $24,000,000
Emp.: 250
Mfr. of Basketball & Baseball Trading Cards & Posters
S.I.C.: 2759
Boris Korbel *(Chm. Bd.)*
Richard McWilliam *(Pres.)*
Paul Sumner *(Sr. V.P.)*
Don Bodow *(V.P.-Mktg.)*
Jay McCracken *(V.P.-Sls.)*

UPPER MIDWEST INDUSTRIES, INC.
732 30th Ave., S.E.
Minneapolis, MN 55414
Tel.: 612-331-2566
Fax: 612-331-1250
Approx.Sls.: $21,000,000
Emp.: 275
Export
Mfr. Expanded Metals, Precision Electronic & Close Tolerance Sheet Metal Work, Rotational Molding Plastic Components, Plastic Fertilizer Storage Tanks & Cash Drawers
S.I.C.: 3449; 3444; 2821; 3443
David R. Carlsen *(Chm. Bd., Sec. & Legal Counsel)*
Charles Carlsen *(Pres. & Chief Oper. Officer)*
Craig Swanson *(Treas.)*

Outside Service Firm(s):

Price Waterhouse*(Auditors)*
3100 Multifoods Tower, 33 S. Sixth St.
Minneapolis, MN 55402

Marquette Bank*(Major Banking Relationship)*
777 Marquette Ave.
Minneapolis, MN 55402
Tel.: 612-370-2182

Divisions:

APG Division **(1)**
1601 67th Ave. No.
Brooklyn Center, MN 55430
Tel.: 612-560-1440
Metal Stamping
S.I.C.: 3469

Atlas Manufacturing Division **(1)**
732 30th Ave. S.E.
Minneapolis, MN 55414
Tel.: 612-331-2566
Manufacture Sheet Metal Work
S.I.C.: 1761

Solar Plastics-Minneapolis **(1)**
732 30th Ave. S.E.
Minneapolis, MN 55414
Tel.: 612-331-8636
Manufacture Plastics Materials
S.I.C.: 2821

Solar Plastics-Quad Cities **(1)**
1924 Comenitz Dr.
Davenport, IA 52802
Tel.: 319-323-7924
Manufacture Plastics Materials
S.I.C.: 2821

Solar Plastics-Sioux City Division **(1)**
1658 riverside Blvd.
Sioux City, IA 55109
Tel.: 712-233-1496
Manufacture Plastics Materials
S.I.C.: 2821

Spantek Division **(1)**
1520 So. 5th St.
Hopkins, MN 55343
Tel.: 612-331-8636
Manufacture Metal Work
S.I.C.: 5084

UPSTATE MILK COOPERATIVES INC.
7115 W. Main St.
Le Roy, NY 14482
Tel.: 716-768-2247
Fax: 716-768-2089
Year Founded: 1971
Sales Range: $10-19 Million
Emp.: 600
Producer, Wholesale Distributor & Retailer of Dairy Products
S.I.C.: 2023; 5143; 5451; 5963
Herbert Nobles *(Treas.)*
Herb Binsack *(Gen. Mgr.)*
Gary Evans *(Dir.-Information Services)*
Stewart Hempel *(Dir.-Personnel)*
Greg Knapp *(Dir.-Fin.)*
Joe Vr *(Dir.-Sls. & Mktg.)*

Computer Systems/Hardware:
IBM PC-XT

Outside Service Firm(s):

KPMG Peat Marwick*(Auditors)*
700 Empire Tower
Buffalo, NY 14202-3786
Tel.: 716-854-1830
Fax: 716-856-8063

Blue Cross of Western New York, Inc.*(Group Insurer)*
P.O. Box 828, 275 Oak St.
Buffalo, NY 14240

Springfield Bank for Co-operatives*(Major Banking Relationship)*
Springfield, MA

Division:

Bison Foods Company **(1)**
196 Scott St.
Buffalo, NY 14204
Tel.: 716-854-8400
Fax: 716-855-3063
Approx.Sls.: $25,000,000
Emp.: 130
Fiscal Year-end: 6/30/91
Mfr. & Distr. of Cultured Dairy Products; Bison Natural Yogurts, Cottage Cheese, Sour Cream & Chip Dips
S.I.C.: 5143; 5149; 2024; 2026; 2022; 2099
Herbert Binsack *(Pres.)*
Joseph Ur *(Dir.-Sls. & Mktg.)*

URSCHEL LABS INC.
2503 Calumet Ave.
Valparaiso, IN 46383
Tel.: 219-464-4811 **IN**
Fax: 219-462-3879
Approx.Sls.: $34,000,000
Emp.: 335
Machinery For Cutting, Chopping, Grinding & Mixing; Chemical Milling Machines; Subdividers & Developers; Data Processing Service
S.I.C.: 3556; 3541; 6552; 7374
Joe R. Urschel *(Chm. Bd.)*
Robert R. Urschel *(Pres.)*
Charles Parsons *(V.P.)*
Dave Steider *(V.P.-Sls.)*
Elena V. Urschel *(V.P. & Sec.)*
Gerald W. Urschel *(V.P.)*
Ralph A. Burns *(Treas.)*
Richard Miller *(Dir.-Pur.)*
Eugene Cole *(Mgr.-Engrng.)*
Steve Nusso *(Mgr.-Data Processing)*

Outside Service Firm(s):

Continental Bank N. A.*(Major Banking Relationship)*
231 S. LaSalle St.
Chicago, IL 60697
Tel.: 312-828-2345
Tel.: 800-426-5754
Telex: 312-828-1783

USIBELLI COAL MINE, INC.
3 Miles Nenana River Rd.
Healy, AK 99743
Tel.: 907-683-2226 **AK**
Fax: 907-683-2253
Year Founded: 1964
Approx.Sls.: $34,000,000
Emp.: 110
Strip Mining; Bituminous Coal
S.I.C.: 1221
Joseph E. Usibelli *(Chm. Bd. & Chief Fin. Officer)*
Joseph E. Usibelli, Jr. *(Pres.)*
Rosalie Abel Whyel *(V.P.)*
A. Kirk Lanterman *(Treas. & Sec.)*

Outside Service Firm(s):

Key Bank*(Major Banking Relationship)*
Healy, AK

FRED USINGER, INC.
1030 N. Old World Third St.
Milwaukee, WI 53203
Tel.: 414-276-9100
Tel.: 800-558-9997 **TX**
Fax: 414-291-5277
Year Founded: 1880
Approx.Sls.: $15,000,000
Emp.: 150
Fiscal Year-end: 2/28/91
Export
Mfr. of Sausages
S.I.C.: 2013; 5421
Frederick D. Usinger *(Chm. Bd.)*
Fritz Usinger *(Pres.)*
Jon Gabe *(V.P.-Sls. & Mktg.)*
Hans Prehn *(V.P.-Mfg.)*
Allen Weidler *(V.P.-Fin. & Sec.)*
Tim Lamers *(Controller)*
Cathy Heying *(Mgr.-Human Resources)*

Computer Systems/Hardware:
IBM

Outside Service Firm(s):

Ernst & Young*(Auditors)*
111 E. Kilbourn Ave., Ste. 900
Milwaukee, WI 53202
Tel.: 414-273-5900

M & I Marshall & Isley Bank*(Major Banking Relationship)*
Milwaukee, WI

UTICA BOILERS INC.
2201 Dwyer Ave.
Utica, NY 13501
Mailing Address:
P.O. Box 4729
Utica, NY 13504
Tel.: 315-797-1310
Fax: 315-797-3762
Year Founded: 1950
Approx.Sls.: $14,000,000
Emp.: 75
Cast Iron Heating Boilers
S.I.C.: 3433
Robert E. Reed *(Chm. Bd.)*
E.C. Reed *(Pres. & Sec.)*
Richard H. Hilton *(Treas.)*
Donald Sedar *(Mgr.-Pur.)*

Principal(s):
Robert E. Reed
E.C. Reed

Outside Service Firm(s):

Barone, Howard & Hilton*(Auditors)*
Utica, NY

Evans, Severn, Bankert & Peet*(Legal Firm)*
Utica, NY

Norstar Bank, N.A.*(Major Banking Relationship)*
Utica, NY

UTICA MUTUAL INSURANCE COMPANY
180 Genesee St.
New Hartford, NY 13413
Mailing Address:
P.O. Box 530
Utica, NY 13503
Tel.: 315-734-2000 **NY**
Telex: 5101007611
Fax: 315-734-2680
Year Founded: 1914
Assets: $1,354,055,484
Earnings: $29,000,000
Liabilities: $1,138,622,784
Net Worth: $215,432,700
Approx.Premiums: $458,133,230
Emp.: 1,350
Fiscal Year-end: 12/31/91
Fire, Property, Liability & Multiple Lines Casualty Insurance
S.I.C.: 6331
W. Craig Heston *(Chm. & Chief Exec. Officer)*
Wallace H. Watkins *(Pres.)*
John R. Zapisek *(Sr. V.P., Chief Fin. Officer & Treas.)*
Richard B. Griswold *(Sr. V.P.-Plng. & Information Research)*
John G. Di Liberto *(Sr. V.P.-Claims)*
Vincent J. Looney *(Sr. V.P. & Reg. Office Admin.)*
Albert A. Ritchie *(Sr. V.P.-Data Processing/Services)*
J. Douglas Robinson *(Sr. V.P.-Mktg.)*
Thomas P. Bonaros *(V.P. & Gen. Counsel)*
Robert W. Dicks, Jr. *(V.P. & Gen. Auditor)*
Anthony Paolozzi *(V.P. & Controller)*
George T. Dodd *(V.P.-Actuary)*
Clark Peterson *(V.P.-Human Resources)*
Edward Smith *(V.P.-Data Processing)*
George Wardley *(Sec.)*
Michael Austin *(Dir.-Corp. Communications & Asst. Sec.)*
Kim Baker *(Dir.-Organizational Devel.)*
F. William Gaw *(Dir.-Employee Benefits)*
Mark Wilkins *(Dir.-Cash Mngmt.)*
Holly Foster *(Asst. Dir.-Corp. Communications)*
Richard J. Karpinski *(Asst. V.P.-H.O. Services)*

No. of U.S. Offices: 15
No. of Foreign Offices: 1

Computer Systems/Hardware:
IBM

Outside Service Firm(s):

Coopers & Lybrand*(Auditors)*
One Lincoln Center
Syracuse, NY 13202
Tel.: 315-474-8541
Fax: 315-474-0259

Bond, Schoeneck & King*(Legal Firm)*
One Lincoln Center
Syracuse, NY 13202
Tel.: 315-422-0121

Marine Midland Bank*(Major Banking Relationship)*
Syracuse, NY

Subsidiaries:

Republic Franklin Insurance Co. **(1)**
2500 Corporate Exchange Drive
Columbus, OH 43229
Tel.: 614-891-1767
Fax: 614-891-6834
Keith W. Jones *(Pres.)*

UNI-Service Operations Corporation **(1)**
P.O. Box 530
Utica, NY 13503
Tel.: 315-734-2000

Utica Lloyds of Texas **(1)**
Ste. M-1188, 8350 N. Central Expwy.
Dallas, TX 75206
Tel.: 214-691-8800
S.I.C.: 6331

Utica National Insurance Co. of Texas **(1)**
Ste. M-1188, 8350 N. Central Expwy.
Dallas, TX 75206
Tel.: 214-691-8800
S.I.C.: 6331

Utica National Insurance Group **(1)**
180 Genesee St.
New Hartford, NY 13413
Tel.: 315-735-3321
Multiple-Line Property, Casualty & Life Insurance
W. Craig Heston *(Chm. & Chief Exec. Officer)*

Utica National Life Insurance Company **(1)**
P.O. Box 530
Utica, NY 13503
Tel.: 315-734-2000
S.I.C.: 6311

UTILITIES CONSTRUCTION CO., INC. OF SOUTH CAROLINA
1890 Milford St.
Charleston, SC 29405
Mailing Address:
P.O. Box 20485
Charleston, SC 29413
Tel.: 803-722-0161 **SC**
Fax: 803-722-4006
Year Founded: 1947
Approx.Sls.: $28,000,000
Emp.: 360
Power Line Construction; Electrical Contractor; Wholesale Electrical Apparatus & Tools
S.I.C.: 1623; 1731; 5063
James C. Murray *(Pres. & Chief Exec. Officer)*
A.L. Lofton, Jr. *(V.P. & Treas.)*
Brian Sledge *(Controller)*
Russell W. Lamb *(Mgr.-Human Resources)*

Outside Service Firm(s):

McKnight, Frampton & Company*(Auditors)*
Charleston, SC

Nationsbank*(Major Banking Relationship)*
Charleston, NC

Subsidiary:

Line Equipment Sales Co., Inc. **(1)**
551 Meeting St.
Charleston, SC 29403
Tel.: 803-722-3306
Emp.: 10
Wholesale Electrical Apparatus & Equipment
S.I.C.: 5063
John I. Hagan *(Pres.)*
Donna McNeil *(Sec.)*

UTILITY TRAILER MANUFACTURING CO.
17295 E. Railroad St.
City of Industry, CA 91749
Mailing Address:
P.O. Box 1299
City of Industry, CA 91749
Tel.: 818-965-1541
Telex: 67-0443
Fax: 818-965-2790
Year Founded: 1914
Approx.Sls.: $220,000,000
Emp.: 1,800
Fiscal Year-end: 12/31/90
Import Export
Mfr. Truck-Trailers
S.I.C.: 3715
Paul F. Bennett *(Chm. Bd. & Chief Exec. Officer)*
Harold C. Bennett *(Pres.)*
Arthur L. Goolsbee *(Chief Fin. Officer)*
Craig Bennett *(Chief Oper. Officer & V.P.-Sls. & Mktg.)*
J.C. Bennett *(V.P.)*
Walter Bennett *(V.P.)*
Michael Blum *(Controller)*
Jack L. Foate *(Dir.-Pur.)*
Fon Koot *(Dir.-Distribution Systems)*
John J. Stanton *(Dir.-Indus. Rels.)*
Tim Dunlop *(Mgr.-Mktg.)*

No. of Mfg. Plants/Facilities: 4

Computer Systems/Hardware:
IBM System 38

Outside Service Firm(s):

KPMG Peat Marwick*(Auditors)*
725 S. Figueroa St.
Los Angeles, CA 90017
Tel.: 213-972-4000

Allstate Insurance*(Group Insurer)*
Northbrook, IL

Altschuler, Melvoin & Glasser*(Group Insurer)*
30 S. Wecker Dr.
Chicago, IL 60606
Tel.: 312-207-2800

First Interstate Bank*(Major Banking Relationship)*
City of Industry, CA

UVEX SAFETY, INC.
(Formerly Uvex Winter Optical, Inc.)
10 Thurber Blvd.
Smithfield, RI 02917
Tel.: 401-232-1200
Fax: 401-232-1830
Approx.Sls.: $25,000,000
Emp.: 200
Fiscal Year-end: 7/31/91
Import Export
Mfr. Plastic Eye Protection; Ophthalmic Accessories; Motorcycle Goggles; Ski Goggles & Sunglasses; X Uvex Goggles/Spectacles
S.I.C.: 3851; 3841
Walter Stephan *(Pres. & Chief Exec. Officer)*
Jim Hall *(Exec. V.P.)*
Steven P. Tolisano *(V.P.-Fin.)*
Ray Baker *(V.P.-Mfg.)*
Harry Neff *(V.P.-Sls. & Mktg.)*
Joyce L. McCarthy *(Mgr.-Mktg. Services)*

Computer Systems/Hardware:
IBM

VATEX AMERICA, INC.
(Formerly VATEX Corporation)
2395 Hermitage Rd.
Richmond, VA 23220
Mailing Address:
P.O. Box 5247,
Richmond, VA 23220
Tel.: 804-353-9010
Fax: 804-353-8939
Year Founded: 1976
Assets: $5,300,000
Earnings: $500,000
Liabilities: $3,600,000
Net Worth: $1,700,000
Approx.Sls.: $5,000,000
Emp.: 90
Screen Printers, Advertising Specialties, Wholesale Monograms & Sportwear Imprinting
S.I.C.: 2759
Jerry Gorde *(Chm. Bd. & Chief Exec. Officer)*
Ben Kutner *(Chief Fin. Officer, Treas. & Sec.)*

Computer Systems/Hardware:
Alpha Micro

Outside Service Firm(s):

Goodman & Co.*(Auditors)*
Newport News, VA

Crestar Bank*(Major Banking Relationship)*
P.O. Box 26665,
Richmond, VA 23261
Tel.: 804-782-5995

VCA TELETRONICS INC.
500 Willow Tree Rd.
Leonia, NJ 07605
Tel.: 201-947-6450 **DE**
Fax: 201-947-0448
Year Founded: 1968
Approx.Sls.: $30,000,000
Emp.: 275
Video Production/Post-Production, Duplication & Fulfillment
S.I.C.: 7812; 7819
Stefan Romaniuk *(V.P.-Fin. & Sec.)*

Outside Service Firm(s):

Northbrook Property & Casualty*(Commercial Insurance Carrier)*
South Barrington, IL

Gilbert & Davis*(Legal Firm)*
New York, NY

National Westminster Bank USA*(Major Banking Relationship)*
175 Water St.
New York, NY 10038
Tel.: 212-602-4000
Fax: 212-602-2279

Mangam Agency*(Pension Manager)*
Newark, NJ

Noble Lowndes*(Pension Manager)*
East Orange, NJ

Divisions:

Video Production/Post Production Div. **(1)**
231 E. 55th St.
New York, NY 10022
Tel.: 212-355-1600

Video Program Duplicating Div. **(1)**
500 Willow Tree Rd.
Leonia, NJ 07605
Tel.: 201-947-6450

V.F. ENERGIES, INC.
295 S. Main St.
Madisonville, KY 42431
Mailing Address:
P.O. Box 815
Madisonville, KY 42431
Tel.: 502-821-6950
Fax: 502-825-8012
Year Founded: 1987
Assets: $1,500,000
Liabilities: $100,000
Net Worth: $1,400,000
Approx.Sls.: $45,000,000
Emp.: 3
Fiscal Year-end: 12/31/91
Import
Coal Sales
S.I.C.: 5052
Vicky L. Foley *(Chm. Bd. & Pres.)*
Eloise G. Foley *(V.P.)*
Flem Gordon *(Treas.)*
Cecil E. Foley, Jr. *(Dir.-Special Projects)*
Kay Ashby *(Gen. Mgr.)*
Ricky D. Foley *(Mgr.-Sls. Promo. & Pub. Rels.)*

Principal(s):
Vicky L. Foley

Outside Service Firm(s):

Bruce & Company*(Auditors)*
Madisonville, KY

Employers Health Group*(Group Insurer)*
Madison, WI

Farmers Bank & Trust Co.*(Investment Banker)*
Madisonville, KY

Liberty National Bank & Trust Co.*(Investment Banker)*
Louisville, KY

Flem Gordon*(Legal Firm)*
N. Main St.
Madisonville, KY 42431

Farmers Bank & Trust Co.*(Major Banking Relationship)*
Madisonville, KY

Divisions:

Triple F Limousin Cattle **(1)**
295 S. Main St.
Madisonville, KY 42431
Tel.: 502-821-6950
Emp.: 3
Breeder of Limousin Cattle
S.I.C.: 0212
Vicky L. Foley *(Chief Oper. Officer)*
Larry Verhey *(Mgr.-Cattle)*
Ricky Foley *(Mgr.-Farm)*
Cecil Foley *(Mgr.-Farm)*

Triple F Limousin Cattle **(1)**
Paris, KY 40361
Tel.: 502-821-6950
Cattle
S.I.C.: 0212
Vicky L. Foley *(Pres.)*

V.G.S. CORP. D/B/A SOUTHLAND OIL COMPANY
5170 Galaxie Dr.
Jackson, MS 39206
Mailing Address:
P.O. Box 13609,
Jackson, MS 39236
Tel.: 601-981-4151
Fiscal Year-end: 12/31/90
Petroleum Refining & Marketing
S.I.C.: 2911; 5172
Charles W. Else *(Chm. Bd.)*
Roger G. McGrath *(Pres. & Chief Exec. Officer)*
James D. Bennett *(Chief Fin. Officer & Treas.)*
Daisy S. Blackwell *(Sec.)*
Harold G. Voelkel *(Controller)*

Computer Systems/Hardware:
IBM System S/38

Outside Service Firm(s):

Deloitte & Touche*(Auditors)*
1 World Trade Center
New York, NY 10048
Tel.: 212-669-5000

Trustmark National Bank*(Major Banking Relationship)*
248 E. Capital
Jackson, MS 39201

Trustmark National Bank*(Pension Manager)*
248 E. Capital
Jackson, MS 39201

VJ GROWERS, INC.
500 W. Orange Blossom Trail
Apopka, FL 32712
Tel.: 407-886-5555 DE
Fax: 407-880-1722
Assets: $9,000,000
Liabilities: $3,000,000
Net Worth: $6,000,000
Approx.Sls.: $26,000,000
Emp.: 95
Fiscal Year-end: 12/31/90
Horticulture Supplies
S.I.C.: 5099; 5199
Bryam E. Dickens *(Chm. Bd.)*
Walter Sullivan *(Pres.)*
Dennis Brinkman *(V.P.)*
C.W. Christopher *(V.P.)*
Charles Ticehurst *(V.P.-Fin. & Admin.)*
David Helfer *(Controller)*
Tom Benson *(Dir.-Devel.)*
J. Voithofer *(Pur. Agent)*

Computer Systems/Hardware:
Hewlett Packard

Outside Service Firm(s):

Continental Bank N. A.*(Major Banking Relationship)*
231 S. LaSalle St.
Chicago, IL 60697
Tel.: 312-828-2345
Tel.: 800-426-5754
Telex: 312-828-1783

VMC FIBERGLASS PRODUCTS INC.
(d/b/a Tri-Glas Industries)
Industrial Park, 3 Barnes St.
Daleville, AL 36322
Mailing Address:
P.O. Box 1088,
Daleville, AL 36322
Tel.: 205-598-2422 AL
Telex: 205-598-8017
Fax: 205-598-8017
Year Founded: 1973
Assets: $5,000,000
Earnings: $1,500,000
Net Worth: $5,000,000
Approx.Sls.: $15,000,000
Emp.: 200
Fiscal Year-end: 12/31/89
Mfr. of Fiberglass Products
S.I.C.: 3713
Corporate Giving Program: Company Gives to the United Way on a 50% Match Basis
John Watson *(Chm. Bd.)*
Bob Ostendorf *(Pres. & Chief Exec. Officer)*
John D. Steel *(V.P. & Sec.)*
Larry King *(Controller)*
Frank Mitchell *(Dir.-Opers.)*
Terri Knox *(Dir.-Personnel)*
Paul Thomas *(Dir.-Research & Devel.)*
Wayne Wood *(Dir.-Pur.)*
Darlene Wright *(Dir.-Meetings Planning)*

No. of Mfg. Plants/Facilities: 10
No. of U.S. Offices: 1

Computer Systems/Hardware:
IBM Network

Outside Service Firm(s):

Carpenter, Wiggins, Jordan & Thomas*(Auditors)*
Dothan, AL

Johnston, Hinesley & Flowers*(Legal Firm)*
Dothan, AL

South Trust First National Bank*(Major Banking Relationship)*
Dothan, AL

VSI FASTENERS, INC.
12362 Beach Blvd.
Stanton, CA 90680
Tel.: 714-891-8400 CA
Fax: 714-894-0279
Year Founded: 1956
Approx.Sls.: $50,000,000
Emp.: 400
Import
Fasteners
S.I.C.: 5072
Arnold Scribner *(Pres. & Chief Exec. Officer)*
Dennis Blake *(V.P.-Sls.)*
Derwyn Cugley *(V.P.-Mktg.)*
Norma Hart *(Mgr.-Data Processing)*
Victor Triana *(Mgr.-Natl. Sls.)*
Steven Ho *(Pur. Agent)*

Outside Service Firm(s):

KPMG Peat Marwick*(Auditors)*
Center Tower, 650 Town Center Drive
Costa Mesa, CA 92626
Tel.: 714-850-4300

Citibank N.A.*(Major Banking Relationship)*
Los Angeles, CA

V.T. INC.
8500 Shawnee Mission Pkwy.
Merriam, KS 66202
Mailing Address:
P.O. Box 795
Shawnee Mission, KS 66201
Tel.: 913-432-6400 MO
Fax: 913-789-1039
Year Founded: 1973
Approx.Sls.: $1,266,746,349
Emp.: 3,300
Fiscal Year-end: 12/31/91
Holding Co.; Automobile Dealerships
S.I.C.: 6719; 5511
Cecil L. Van Tuyl *(Chm. Bd., Pres. & Chief Exec. Officer)*
John A. Morford *(V.P. & Chief Fin. Officer)*
Robert J. Holcomb *(Sec. & Treas.)*
Bradford Pittenger *(Legal Officer)*
Daniel Mattox *(Dir.-Data Processing)*
Principal(s):
Cecil L. Van Tuyl
Larry Van Tuyl

No. of U.S. Offices: 28

Computer Systems/Hardware:
IBM; Reynolds & Reynolds; ADP

Outside Service Firm(s):

Coopers & Lybrand*(Auditors)*
Kansas City, MO

Travelers Ins. Co.*(Commercial Insurance Carrier)*
Kansas City, MO

Woodsmall Benefit Services*(Group Insurer)*
Kansas City, MO

Clyde G. Meise*(Legal Firm)*
Kansas City, MO

Southgate Bank & Trust*(Major Banking Relationship)*
Prairie Village, KS

VV PUBLISHING CORP.
(Sub. of Stern Publications)
36 Cooper Square
New York, NY 10003
Tel.: 212-475-3300
Fax: 212-460-1400
Year Founded: 1955
Sales Range: $10-19 Million
Emp.: 200
Publisher of Village Voice Weekly Newspaper
S.I.C.: 2711
Leonard N. Stern *(Chm. Bd.)*
David Schneiderman *(Pres.)*
William Dwyer *(V.P.-Fin.)*
Alan Levin *(Controller)*
Averyl Smart *(Sec.)*
Pat Pagano *(Dir.-Opers.)*
Ava Seave *(Dir.-Circulation)*
Pete Weinberger *(Dir.-Display Adv.)*
Theresa West *(Dir.-Personnel)*
Donna Bates *(Mgr.-Systems)*
Kathy Thornton *(Mgr.-Classifieds)*
Jonathan Z. Larsen *(Editor)*
David Schneiderman *(Publisher)*

Computer Systems/Hardware:
IBM 3081

VAAGEN BROTHERS LUMBER, INC.
565 W. 5th
Colville, WA 99114
Tel.: 509-684-5071
Fax: 509-684-2168
Year Founded: 1950
Approx.Sls.: $57,000,000
Emp.: 475
Sawmills & Planing Mills; Wholesale Lumber
S.I.C.: 2421; 5031
Duane Vaagen *(Pres.)*
Wayne A. Vaagen *(V.P.)*
Dave Hallan *(Dir.-Fin.)*
Dennis E. Vaagen *(Mgr.-Sls. & Mktg.)*

Outside Service Firm(s):

BDO Seidman*(Auditors)*
Spokane, WA

Lukins & Annis*(Legal Firm)*
Spokane, WA

Security Pacific National Bank*(Major Banking Relationship)*
1301 Fifth Ave.
Seattle, WA 98101
Tel.: 206-621-4530

THE VAGABOND INNS
(Formerly Northview Corporation)
5405 Moorehouse Dr., Ste. 200
San Diego, CA 92121
Mailing Address:
P.O. Box 85011
San Diego, CA 92138
Tel.: 619-455-1800
Tel.: 800-522-1555
Fax: 619-535-0396
Emp.: 60
Owns & Manages The Vagabond Inns
S.I.C.: 7011
Tom Evans *(Pres.)*
Les Biggins *(V.P.-Fin.)*
Jerry Murphree *(V.P.-Opers.)*
Laurie Woodruff *(V.P.-Devel. & Mktg.)*
Cathleen Hunters *(Coord.-Sls. & Mktg.)*

Outside Service Firm(s):

Stutman, Treister & Glatt*(Legal Firm)*
Los Angeles, CA

Bank of America NT&SA*(Major Banking Relationship)*
San Diego, CA

Subsidiary:

The Vagabond Inns **(1)**
5405 Morehouse Dr., Ste. 200
San Diego, CA 92121
Tel.: 619-455-1800
Fax: 619-552-8214
Emp.: 900
Fiscal Year-end: 1/31/91
Operates & Owns Motor Inns
S.I.C.: 7011
Thomas D. Evans *(Pres.)*
Les Biggins *(V.P.-Fin.)*
Patrick Dyer *(V.P. & Gen. Counsel)*
Jerry Murphree *(V.P.-Oper.)*
Laurie Woodruff *(V.P.-Mktg.)*
Rollie Ayers *(Dir.-Sls.)*
Nora Miller *(Dir.-Pur.)*
Marianne Dowdy *(Mgr.-Personnel)*

VALCOR ENGINEERING CORP.
2 Lawrence Rd
Springfield, NJ 07081
Tel.: 201-467-8400
Fax: 201-467-8382
Year Founded: 1941
Approx.Sls.: $50,000,000
Emp.: 275
Fiscal Year-end: 12/31/90
Export
Solenoid & Manual Valves, Metering Pumps, Fluid Control Components, Pressure Regulators, Accumulators, Electromagnetic & Electronic Devices
S.I.C.: 3492
George Landberg *(Chief Oper. Officer)*
Bruce Friedman *(Chief Fin. Officer)*
Leigh Walters *(Gen. Counsel)*
Ed Pruzinsky *(Adv. Mgr.)*
J. Stuart *(Pur. Agent)*

Subsidiary:

Electroid Corp. **(1)**
45 Fadem Rd.
Springfield, NJ 07081
Lauri Paporello *(Mgr.-Adv.)*

VALENTINE-RADFORD, INC.
(A VR Communications Company)
1100 Commerce Towers
Kansas City, MO 64105
Mailing Address:
P.O. Box 13407, 911 Main Street
Kansas City, MO 64199
Tel.: 816-842-5021 MO
Fax: 816-421-2636
Year Founded: 1947
Assets: $10,595,112
Liabilities: $9,168,768
Net Worth: $1,426,344
Approx.Billings: $63,726,760
Emp.: 200
Fiscal Year-end: 11/30/89
Import Export
Advertising Agency
S.I.C.: 7311
Robert C. Lang *(Chm. Bd.)*
Chuck Curtis *(Chief Exec. Officer & Pres.)*
Nancy Johnson *(V.P., Yellow Pages Dir.)*
Susan Spaulding *(V.P., Direct Mktg. Dir.)*
Ernie Capobianco *(V.P., Chief Fin. Officer)*
Ken Davenport *(MIS Mgr.)*
Jeff McClure *(Controller)*
Cindy Kitchen *(Office Mgr.)*

No. of U.S. Offices: 1

Computer Systems/Hardware:
IBM AS400, Apple MacIntosh Network, Novell PC Network & C. Itoh Network

Outside Service Firm(s):

Donnelly, Meiners & Jordan*(Auditors)*
4600 Madison Ste. 1100
Kansas City, MO 64112
Tel.: 816-753-3000

Alexander & Alexander*(Commercial Insurance Carrier)*
1000 Walnut
Kansas City, MO 64105

Alexander & Alexander*(Group Insurer)*
1000 Walnut
Kansas City, MO 64105

Commerce Bank of Kansas City*(Investment Banker)*
10th & Walnut
Kansas City, MO 64141
Tel.: 816-234-2000
Fax: 816-234-2548

Commerce Bank of Kansas City*(Major Banking Relationship)*
10th & Walnut
Kansas City, MO 64141
Tel.: 816-234-2000
Fax: 816-234-2548

Branches:

Boasberg Valentine-Radford, Inc. **(1)**
4600 Madison Ave., Ste. 1300
Kansas City, MO 64112
Tel.: 816-531-2100
Fax: 816-756-1471
Emp.: 25
Public Relations
Howard Boasberg *(Chm. Bd. & Chief Exec. Officer)*
Gerald Schleicher *(Sr. V.P.)*
Eric Morgenstern *(V.P.)*

Market Directions, Inc. **(1)**
300 Commerce Tower
Kansas City, MO 64105
Tel.: 816-842-0020
Approx.Billings: $4,700,000
Emp.: 13
Market Research
Susan Spaulding *(Pres.)*

Rice & Rice Inc. **(1)**
Thresher Square, Ste. 100, 700 South Third St.
Minneapolis, MN 55415
Tel.: 612-342-2890
Fax: 612-342-2188
Approx.Billings: $6,670,000
Emp.: 7
Consumer Brands, Corporate Image, Business-to-Business, Trade, Sales & Promotion & Direct Marketing
S.I.C.: 7311
Charles L. Curtis *(Chief Exec. Officer)*
Ron Counton *(Pres.)*
William D. Calkins *(Sec.)*

VALK MANUFACTURING COMPANY
66 E. Main St.
New Kingstown, PA 17072
Mailing Address:
P. O. Box 218,
Carlisle, PA 17013
Tel.: 717-766-0711 **PA**
Fax: 717-697-6297
Year Founded: 1954
Sales Range: $10-19 Million
Emp.: 100
Fiscal Year-end: 4/30/91
Export
Mfr. of Snow Plows & Replacement Cutting Edges
S.I.C.: 3531; 3523
Richard Valk *(Chm. Bd.)*
Ted P. Valk *(Pres.)*
James F. Hay *(Chief Fin. Officer & V.P.)*
Tom Disinger *(V.P.)*
Robert Lang *(V.P.)*
Kenneth C. Sherry *(Sec. & Controller)*

Computer Systems/Hardware:
IBM System 23

Outside Service Firm(s):

Herman, Gross & Co.*(Auditors)*
Allentown, PA

Blank, Rome, Comisky & McCauley*(Legal Firm)*
Four Penn Center Plaza
Philadelphia, PA 19103
Tel.: 215-209-3700

Dauphin Deposit Bank & Trust Co.*(Major Banking Relationship)*
213 Market St.
Harrisburg, PA 17101

VALLERIE'S TRANSPORT SERVICE, INC.
465 Connecticut Ave.
Norwalk, CT 06851
Tel.: 203-838-4751 **CT**
Fax: 203-855-9311
Year Founded: 1923
Approx.Sls.: $29,000,000
Emp.: 375
Trucking, Except Local
S.I.C.: 4213
Donald E. Vallerie, Sr. *(Pres.)*
Doug Doyle *(Controller)*

Outside Service Firm(s):

Thomas F. Ryan*(Auditors)*
Norwalk, CT

DePanfilis & Vallerie*(Legal Firm)*
Norwalk, CT

Union Trust*(Major Banking Relationship)*
637 West Avenue
Norwalk, CT 06856

VALLET FOOD SERV INC.
1230 E. 12th St.
Dubuque, IA 52001
Tel.: 319-588-2346 **IA**
Fax: 319-588-0632
Emp.: 40
Fiscal Year-end: 12/31/90
Wholesale Poultry & Poultry Products; Groceries; Fresh Fruits & Vegetables; Frozen Foods
S.I.C.: 5144; 5141; 5149; 5148
Ed White *(Pres.)*
Cal Buss *(V.P., Sec. & Treas.)*

Outside Service Firm(s):

First National Bank*(Major Banking Relationship)*
Dubuque, IA

VALLEY ASPHALT CORPORATION
11641 Mosteller Rd.
Cincinnati, OH 45241
Tel.: 513-771-0820
Fax: 513-771-2678
Approx.Sls.: $17,000,000
Emp.: 500
General Contractors Highway & Street Construction; Manufacture Asphalt & Tar Paving Mixtures
S.I.C.: 1611; 2951
James P. Jurgensen *(Pres.)*
James A. King *(Chief Fin. Officer & V.P.)*
B. C. Lykins *(V.P.-Sls.)*

Computer Systems/Hardware:
Unisys

Outside Service Firm(s):

Grant Thornton*(Auditors)*
1600 Atrium One
Cincinnati, OH 45202
Tel.: 513-762-5000

Benjamin, Faulkner, Tepe & Sack*(Legal Firm)*
Cincinnati, OH

Subsidiary:

John R. Jurgensen Co. **(1)**
11641 Mosteller Rd.
Cincinnati, OH 45241
Tel.: 513-771-0820
Emp.: 400
Heavy Highway Construction
S.I.C.: 1611
John C. Jurgensen *(Pres.)*

VALLEY DETROIT DIESEL ALLISON
13644 E. Nelson
City of Industry, CA 91746
Tel.: 818-333-1243 **CA**
Fax: 818-369-7096
Year Founded: 1948
Approx.Sls.: $60,000,000
Emp.: 205
Export
Wholesale Distributor of Diesel Engines & Parts
S.I.C.: 5084
H. Clark Lee *(Pres.)*
Robert K. Humphreys *(Sec. & Treas.)*
Gloria Reck *(Exec. Coord.)*

No. of U.S. Offices: 5

Outside Service Firm(s):

Wells Fargo Bank*(Major Banking Relationship)*
333 S. Grand
Los Angeles, CA 90071
Tel.: 213-253-6836

VALLEY FORGE ASSOCIATES
(House Agency)
Liberty Park
Valley Forge, PA 19493
Tel.: 215-648-5000
Approx.Billings: $15,500,000
Direct Response Ins.
Norman Phelps *(Pres. & Chief Exec. Officer)*

VALLEY ISLE PRODUCE, INC.
90 Amala Pl.
Kahului, HI 96732
Tel.: 808-877-5055 **HI**
Fax: 808-877-4960
Year Founded: 1950
Approx.Sls.: $43,000,000
Emp.: 140
Wholesale Distribution of Packaged Frozen Goods; Fresh Fruits & Vegetables; General Line of Groceries; Fresh Meats
S.I.C.: 5142; 5148; 5141; 5147
Roy H. Okumura *(Chief Exec. Officer)*
Nelson Okumura *(Pres.)*
Lorrane Okumura *(Treas.)*

Outside Service Firm(s):

First Hawaiian Bank*(Major Banking Relationship)*
165 South King St.
Honolulu, HI 96813
Tel.: 808-525-5876
Fax: 808-525-5791

VALLEY PONTIAC BUICK GMC, INC.
3104 Auburn Way N.
Auburn, WA 98002
Mailing Address:
P.O. Box 129
Auburn, WA 98071
Tel.: 206-833-2420 **WA**
Fax: 206-939-4571
Year Founded: 1969
Approx.Sls.: $22,000,000
Emp.: 63
Retail Automobiles
S.I.C.: 5511
Frank Lee *(Chm. Bd.)*
Ronald C. Claudon, Sr. *(Pres. & Chief Oper. Officer)*
Floyd H. Miller *(Sec. & Treas.)*

Outside Service Firm(s):

Peterson & Sullivan*(Auditors)*
Seattle, WA

Mike Reynolds*(Legal Firm)*
Seattle, WA

Puget Sound National Bank*(Major Banking Relationship)*
P.O. Box 11500
Tacoma, WA 98411
Tel.: 206-383-2871

VALLEYDALE PACKERS INC.
1119 Commonwealth Ave.
Bristol, VA 24201
Mailing Address:
P.O. Box 1479,
Bristol, VA 24203
Tel.: 703-669-3112
Year Founded: 1933
Approx.Sls.: $250,000,000
Emp.: 1,100
Fiscal Year-end: 1/ 2/88
Meat Packers
S.I.C.: 2011
James H. Neuhoff *(Chm. Bd., Pres. & Chief Exec. Officer)*
James E. Barefoot *(Chief Fin. Officer & Controller)*
William N. O'Dell *(V.P.-Admin.)*
Allen Smith *(Sec.)*
Phil Ferguson *(Pur. Agent)*

No. of Mfg. Plants/Facilities: 3

Computer Systems/Hardware:
Burroughs 900

Outside Service Firm(s):

Brown Edwards & Co.*(Auditors)*
Roanoke, VA

Blue Cross & Blue Shield of Tennessee*(Group Insurer)*
Chattanooga, TN

McGuire, Woods, Battle & Boothe*(Legal Firm)*
One James Ctr., 801 E. Main St.
Richmond, VA 23220
Tel.: 804-644-4131

Dominion Bank*(Major Banking Relationship)*
Bristol, VA

Dominion Bank*(Pension Manager)*
Bristol, VA

Subsidiary:

Neuhoff Farms, Inc. **(1)**
2149 Electric Rd. SW
Roanoke, VA 24018
Tel.: 703-989-6414

VALU DISCOUNT, INC.
3916 Dupont Square S.
Louisville, KY 40207
Tel.: 502-895-9533 **MN**
Fax: 502-895-1273
Year Founded: 1978
Sales Range: $40-59 Million
Emp.: 350
Fiscal Year-end: 2/28/91
Supermarket Stores
S.I.C.: 5411
Frank G. Neumann *(Pres.)*
Eugene R. Dummer *(V.P.)*
Janet Neumann *(Treas.)*
Barbara Dimmer *(Sec.)*
Margaret Kopatz *(Sr. Corp. Accountant)*
Principal(s):
Frank G. Neumann
Eugene R. Dummer

Computer Systems/Hardware:
Compac 386 System

Outside Service Firm(s):

Deloitte & Touche*(Auditors)*
510 W. Broadway
Louisville, KY 40202
Tel.: 502-562-2000

Liberty National Bank & Trust Co.*(Investment Banker)*
416 W. Jefferson St.
Louisville, KY 40202
Tel.: 502-566-2000

Valu Discount, Inc.—(Continued)

Goldberg & Simpson, PSC*(Legal Firm)*
Louisville, KY

Liberty National Bank & Trust Co.*(Major Banking Relationship)*
416 W. Jefferson St.
Louisville, KY 40202
Tel.: 502-566-2000

VAN CLEEF & ARPELS, INC.
744 Fifth Ave., 2nd Fl.
New York, NY 10019
Tel.: 212-644-9500
Fax: 212-355-5697
Approx.Sls.: $28,000,000
Emp.: 75
Jewelry Stores
S.I.C.: 5094; 5944
Philippe Arpels *(Pres. & Chief Oper. Officer)*
Carol Bahdaw *(Dir.-Mktg. & Pub. Rels.)*

VAN DYNE-CROTTY, INC.
903 Brandt St.
Dayton, OH 45401
Mailing Address:
P.O. Box 442
Dayton, OH 45401
Tel.: 513-236-1500
Fax: 513-233-9397
Year Founded: 1935
Approx.Sls.: $45,000,000
Emp.: 700
Fiscal Year-end: 9/30/91
Import
Textile Leasing & Maintenance Service; Industrial Launderers
S.I.C.: 7218
L. William Crotty *(Chm., Pres. & Chief Exec. Officer)*
Richard A. Maurer *(V.P. & Treas.)*
James F. Stangle *(V.P.-Admin.)*
Robert S. Crotty *(V.P. & Dir.-Mktg.)*
Kenneth Fisher *(Dir.-Systems)*
Dan Montgomery *(Dir.-Mktg. & Adv.)*
Dan Studebaker *(Mgr.-Mdsg. & Pur.)*

Computer Systems/Hardware:
Data General

VAN LEUNENS INC.
621 Wilmer Ave.
Cincinnati, OH 45226
Tel.: 513-533-2700 **OH**
Fax: 513-321-5884
Year Founded: 1954
Approx.Sls.: $85,000,000
Emp.: 1,100
Retail Department Stores
S.I.C.: 5311
A. Stanley Johnson *(Chm. Bd., Pres. & Chief Exec. Officer)*
Jack D. Emerson *(Exec. V.P.)*
Charles E. Holland *(V.P.-Opers.)*
Edward Niewahner *(Treas.)*
C. Jackson Cromer *(Sec. & Gen. Counsel)*
Richard Englert *(Dir.-Adv.)*
James L. Large *(Dir.-Personnel)*
Principal(s):
A. Stanley Johnson
Employees

Computer Systems/Hardware:
IBM System 36

Outside Service Firm(s):

Thompson, Hine & Flory*(Legal Firm)*
Cincinnati, OH

Bank One*(Major Banking Relationship)*
Milford, OH

Provident Bank*(Major Banking Relationship)*
One East Fourth St.
Cincinnati, OH 45202
Tel.: 513-579-2732

Divisions:

All About Sports **(1)**
621 Wilmer Ave.
Cincinnati, OH 45226
Tel.: 513-533-2700
Sporting Goods Stores
S.I.C.: 5941
A. Stanley Johnson *(Pres.)*

Pets-N-Such **(1)**
621 Wilmer Ave.
Cincinnati, OH 45226
Tel.: 513-533-2700
Pet Stores
S.I.C.: 5999
A. Stanley Johnson *(Pres.)*

THE VAN METRE COMPANIES
5252 Lyngate Ct.
Burke, VA 22015
Tel.: 703-425-2600 **VA**
Fax: 703-239-0395
Year Founded: 1955
Assets: $200,000,000
Liabilities: $63,000,000
Net Worth: $137,000,000
Approx.Sls.: $89,147,000
Emp.: 300
Fiscal Year-end: 12/31/91
Operative Builder Developer & Property Manager
S.I.C.: 1531; 6531; 6552
Albert G. Van Metre, Sr. *(Chm. & Pres.)*
Richard J. Rabil *(Chief Exec. Officer & Exec. V.P.)*
M. Kledzik *(V.P.-Sls.)*
Kenneth Ryan *(V.P.-Fin.)*
John Regan *(Controller)*
Gaye Vaughan *(Sec.)*
Kathy Ault *(Dir.-Data Processing)*
Clinton A. Britt *(Dir.-Res. & Devel.)*
D. Keith Kretzinger *(Dir.-Mktg.)*
Cheryl Salter *(Dir.-Human Resources)*
Gerald A. Clement *(Mgr.-Pur.)*
Principal(s):
Albert G. Van Metre, Sr.

Outside Service Firm(s):

Samson & Stern*(Auditors)*
Washington, DC

Melrod, Redman, Gartland*(Legal Firm)*
1801 K St., N.W., Ste. 1100
Washington, DC 20006
Tel.: 202-822-5300

First American Bank, N.A.*(Major Banking Relationship)*
McLean, VA

VAN PELT CORPORATION
13700 Sherwood
Detroit, MI 48212
Tel.: 313-365-3600
Fax: 313-365-2828
Approx.Sls.: $30,000,000
Emp.: 100
Wholesale Steel Tubing
S.I.C.: 5051
David B. Van Pelt, Sr. *(Chm. Bd. & Chief Exec. Officer)*
James M. Sutika *(Pres. & Treas.)*
R. Schlau *(V.P.-Opers.)*

Outside Service Firm(s):

KPMG Peat Marwick*(Auditors)*
Suite 1200, 150 W. Jefferson
Detroit, MI 48226

Dickinson, Wright, Moon, VanDusen & Freeman*(Legal Firm)*
800 First National Bldg.
Detroit, MI 48226
Tel.: 313-223-3546

Michigan National Bank*(Major Banking Relationship)*
Detroit, MI

VAN SON HOLLAND INK CORP. OF AMERICA
92 Union St.
Mineola, NY 11501
Tel.: 516-294-8811
Fax: 516-294-8608
Year Founded: 1953
Approx.Sls.: $34,500,000
Emp.: 150
Importing & Distribution of Printing Inks
S.I.C.: 5049; 5085
Karl V. Anton, Jr. *(Pres.)*
Robert Langer *(Exec. V.P.)*
Joseph Bendowski *(V.P.)*
John A. Burns *(V.P.)*
Robert Korrow *(V.P.)*
Margaret V. Markiewicz *(Treas.)*
William Janofsky *(Controller)*

Computer Systems/Hardware:
Digital

Outside Service Firm(s):

The Bank of New York*(Major Banking Relationship)*
One Wall Street
New York, NY 10286
Tel.: 212-635-6805
Fax: 212-635-3201

VAN WINKLE & ASSOCIATES, INC.
1819 Peachtree St. N.W., Ste. 315
Atlanta, GA 30309
Tel.: 404-355-0126
Year Founded: 1984
Approx.Billings: $12,000,000
Emp.: 14
Fritz Van Winkle *(Chm. Bd. & Pres.)*
Joy Dillingham *(Asst. to Pres.)*
Elina Mabe *(V.P.)*
Richard Maddox *(V.P.)*
Dinorah Jallouk *(Office Services Mgr.)*

VANCE INDUSTRIES, INC.
7401 W. Wilson Ave.
Chicago, IL 60656
Tel.: 708-867-6000 **DE**
Fax: 708-867-5601
Year Founded: 1955
Approx.Sls.: $8,500,000
Emp.: 110
Fiscal Year-end: 12/31/90
Export
Manufacturer of Stainless Steel Sinks, Brass Bar Sinks, Sink Frames, Tempered Glass Food Preparation Surfaces & Assorted Kitchen Accessories
S.I.C.: 3231; 3432
Wayne E. Toussaint *(Chm. Bd.)*
William M. Rapp *(Pres.)*
Andrew S. Vavasis *(Exec. V.P. & Chief Oper. Officer)*
Debby Barry *(Controller)*
Daniel Mayer *(Gen. Mgr.-Wholesale Div.)*
James Schleiter *(Gen. Mgr.-Retail Mkts. Div.)*
Andrej A.B. Remec *(Mgr.-Opers.)*
Frank O'Connor *(Mgr.-Materials Procurement & Pur.)*
Janet Bain *(Mgr.-Quality Control)*
Sophie A. Melko *(Mgr.-Mktg. Services)*
Sandy Viso *(Mgr.-Data Processing)*
Lisa Walker *(Mktg. Serv. Coord.)*

No. of Mfg. Plants/Facilities: 1
No. of U.S. Offices: 1

Computer Systems/Hardware:
IBM System AS/400

Outside Service Firm(s):

Borgeson & Grant*(Auditors)*
Park Ridge, IL

Mid-City*(Major Banking Relationship)*
Chicago, IL

Kemper Insurance*(Commercial Insurance Carrier)*
Long Grove, IL 60049-0001

Blue Cross & Blue Shield of Illinois*(Group Insurer)*
100 Tower Drive
Burr Ridge, IL 60521
Tel.: 708-323-3666

Continental Bank N. A.*(International Bank Affiliate)*
231 S. LaSalle St.
Chicago, IL 60697
Tel.: 312-828-2345
Tel.: 800-426-5754
Telex: 312-828-1783

Vedder, Price, Kaufman & Kammholz*(Legal Firm)*
Chicago, IL

VANCE PUBLISHING CORPORATION
400 Knightsbridge Parkway
Lincolnshire, IL 60069
Tel.: 708-634-2600 **NY**
Fax: 708-634-4379
Approx.Sls.: $38,000,000
Emp.: 340
Publish & Print Trade Journals; Trade Show Arrangements
S.I.C.: 2721; 7389
William C. Vance *(Chm. Bd. & Chief Exec. Officer)*
John B. O'Neil *(Vice Chm.)*
John Berry *(V.P.)*
W.E.P. Coon *(V.P.)*
Walter A. Kay *(V.P. & Treas.)*
Warren Morse *(V.P.)*

Outside Service Firm(s):

Wildman, Harrold, Allen & Dixon*(Legal Firm)*
225 W. Wacker Dr.
Chicago, IL 60606
Tel.: 312-222-0400

American National Bank*(Major Banking Relationship)*
33 North LaSalle St.
Chicago, IL 60690
Tel.: 312-661-6967

R. T. VANDERBILT COMPANY, INC.
30 Winfield St.
Norwalk, CT 06855
Tel.: 203-853-1400
Fax: 203-853-1452
Year Founded: 1916
Approx.Sls.: $170,000,000
Emp.: 620
Fiscal Year-end: 12/31/90
Export
Mfr. & Distributor of Chemicals & Minerals
S.I.C.: 5052
H.B. Vanderbilt *(Chm. Bd. & Chief Exec. Officer)*
H.B. Vanderbilt, Jr. *(Vice Chm.)*
G.L. Fiederlein *(Pres. & Chief Oper. Officer)*
J. Lathrop *(Exec. V.P.-Admin.)*
D. Gorman *(Exec. V.P.-Sls.)*
J. Denaro *(V.P., Chief Fin. Officer & Treas.)*
R. Ohm *(V.P.-Devel.)*
R. Price *(V.P.-Rubber Chemicals & Mineral Grp.)*
P. Vanderbilt *(V.P.-Environmental & Sec.)*
H. Gartland *(Controller)*

Computer Systems/Hardware:
IBM 400s

VANDERGRIFF CHEVROLET GEO
901 E. Division
Arlington, TX 76010
Tel.: 817-265-8231
Fax: 817-274-6942
Approx.Sls.: $50,000,000
Emp.: 100
Automobile Sales, Rental & Leasing
S.I.C.: 5511; 7514; 7515
Victor Vandergriff *(Pres.)*

Computer Systems/Hardware:
EDS

Outside Service Firm(s):

KPMG Peat Marwick*(Auditors)*
301 Commerce, Ste. 2500
Ft. Worth, TX 76102
Tel.: 817-335-2655

Northwest National Bank of Arlington*(Major Banking Relationship)*
Arlington, TX
Tel.: 817-860-2061

VANDINE, HUMPHREY, HERBERT, ALBER & MANGES, INC.
322 Blvd. of the Allies
Pittsburgh, PA 15222
Tel.: 412-261-4611
Fax: 412-261-3741
Year Founded: 1969
Approx.Billings: $13,000,000
Emp.: 20
Alan VanDine *(Chm.)*
Richard Herbert *(Pres., Chief Exec. & Fin. Officer)*
Susan L. Boyle *(V.P.)*
Stephen A. Alber *(Sec.)*
Michael Geraci *(Pub. Rels. Dir.)*

Computer Systems/Hardware:
Apple, MacIntosh

VANGUARD ENERGY CORP.
1111 North Loop W.
Houston, TX 77008
Tel.: 713-880-8750 **TX**
Telex: 774648
Fax: 713-880-9311
Approx.Sls.: $388,000,000
Emp.: 27
Wholesale Natural Gas, Pipe Lines, Liquified Petroleum Gas Production & Distr.
S.I.C.: 4924; 4612; 1311; 4925
Phillip Trotter *(Pres. & Chief Exec. Officer)*
Tom Garner *(V.P.)*
John Kelly, Jr. *(V.P. & Sec.)*

Outside Service Firm(s):

Ernst & Young*(Auditors)*
1 Houston Ctr., 1200 McKinney
Houston, TX 77002
Tel.: 713-750-1500

Young & Brooks*(Legal Firm)*
Houston, TX

First City, Texas-Houston, N.A.*(Major Banking Relationship)*
P.O. Box 809,
Houston, TX 77001
Tel.: 713-658-6011

THE VANGUARD GROUP, INC.
1300 Morris Dr.
Wayne, PA 19087
Mailing Address:
P.O. Box 876
Valley Forge, PA 19482
Tel.: 215-648-6000
Fax: 215-648-6322
Approx.Assets: $40,000,000,000
Emp.: 1,700
Holding Company For Mutual Funds
S.I.C.: 6719; 6282
John J. Brennan *(Pres.)*
Raymond J. Klapinsky *(Sr. V.P. & Sec.)*
Karen E. West *(V.P. & Controller)*
Richard Hyland *(Treas.)*

Outside Service Firm(s):

Price Waterhouse*(Auditors)*
30 S. 17th St.
Philadelphia, PA 19103
Tel.: 215-665-9500

Stradley, Ronon, Stevens & Young*(Legal Firm)*
2600 Commerce Sq.
Philadelphia, PA 19103
Tel.: 215-564-8000

First National Bank of Boston*(Major Banking Relationship)*
P.O. Box 644,
Boston, MA 02102-0644
Tel.: 617-575-2900
Fax: 617-575-2549

VANGUARD PLASTICS, INC.
831 N. Vanguard
McPherson, KS 67460
Mailing Address:
P.O. Box 346,
McPherson, KS 67460
Tel.: 316-241-6369
Fax: 316-241-2123
Year Founded: 1977
Approx.Sls.: $20,000,000
Emp.: 120
Fiscal Year-end: 10/31/89
Mfr. of Polybutylene Piping Systems
S.I.C.: 3084
Keith Swinehart, Sr. *(Chm. Bd., Chief Exec. Officer & Chief Fin. Officer)*
Keith Swinehart, II *(Pres.)*
Bill Seiler *(Gen. Counsel)*
John Frasier *(Dir.-Mktg.)*
Dan Brace *(Gen. Mgr.)*
Roger Burris *(Gen. Mgr.-Plant)*

No. of Mfg. Plants/Facilities: 3

Computer Systems/Hardware:
NCR

Outside Service Firm(s):

Emery, Pearman & Stuart*(Auditors)*
McPherson, KS

Insurance Management Assoc.*(Commercial Insurance Carrier)*
Wichita, KS

Breymer & Wise*(Legal Firm)*
McPherson, KS

Home State Bank*(Major Banking Relationship)*
McPherson, KS

VANPORT MANUFACTURING, INC.
28590 S.E. Wally Rd.
Boring, OR 97009
Tel.: 503-663-4466 **OR**
Fax: 503-663-1516
Year Founded: 1967
Approx.Sls.: $94,000,000
Emp.: 175
Rough, Sawed Or Planed Lumber
S.I.C.: 2421; 5099
Adolf Hertrich *(Chm. Bd.)*
Edward Harris *(V.P.)*
Debe Proudfit *(Sec. & Treas.)*

Outside Service Firm(s):

Roger Meyer*(Legal Firm)*
Portland, OR

Key Bank*(Major Banking Relationship)*
Gresham, OR

VANTAGE COMPANIES
2777 Stemmons Fwy.
Dallas, TX 75207
Tel.: 214-631-0600 **TX**
Fax: 214-689-2206
Year Founded: 1959
Approx.Sls.: $510,000,000
Emp.: 1,500
Real Estate Operators
S.I.C.: 6512
John F. Eulich *(Chm. Bd. & Chief Exec. Officer)*
C. Huston Bell *(Pres.)*
Mark Collop *(Exec. V.P.)*
William B. Beste *(Sr. V.P.-Fin.)*

Computer Systems/Hardware:
IBM System 38

Outside Service Firm(s):

Akin, Gump, Hauer & Feld*(Legal Firm)*
4100 First City Center
Dallas, TX 75201

NationsBank Texas*(Major Banking Relationship)*
901 Main St., 16th Fl.
Dallas, TX 75202
Tel.: 214-922-5000

VARAT ENTERPRISES, INC.
58 S. Burty Rd.
Piedmont, SC 29673
Mailing Address:
P.O. Box 8793
Greenville, SC 29604
Tel.: 803-277-2693
Fax: 803-299-3228
Approx.Sls.: $28,000,000
Emp.: 440
Wholesale Women's Maternity Uniforms, Sleepwear, Apparel & Sportswear
S.I.C.: 2335; 2337; 2339; 2341; 5137
Joshua E. Varat *(Pres. & Chief Exec. Officer)*
Leith A. Smith *(V.P.-Fin. & Dir.-Data Processing)*
Jo Evans *(Dir.-Personnel)*

No. of Mfg. Plants/Facilities: 4

Outside Service Firm(s):

KPMG Peat Marwick*(Auditors)*
One Shelter Place, Box 10529
Greenville, SC 29603

Haynsworth, Marion, McKay & Guerard*(Legal Firm)*
75 Beattie Place, 2 Shelter Centre 11th Fl
Greenville, SC 29601
Tel.: 803-240-3300

First Union National Bank*(Major Banking Relationship)*
Two First Union Center CMG-5-1154
Charlotte, NC 28288-1154
Tel.: 704-374-6250

VAREL MANUFACTURING CO.
9230 Denton Dr.
Dallas, TX 75235
Mailing Address:
P.O. Box 540157,
Dallas, TX 75354
Tel.: 214-351-6487
Fax: 214-351-6438
Approx.Sls.: $60,000,000
Emp.: 1,375
Fiscal Year-end: 7/31/90
Mfr. Drilling Bits
S.I.C.: 5084
Daniel W. Varel *(Chm. Bd., Pres. & Gen. Mgr.)*
Mark Varel *(Sr. V.P.)*
Bill Hayes *(V.P.-Fin.)*
Steve Hodges *(Sec. & Treas.)*
Ray Hughes *(Adv. Mgr. & Communications Dir.)*
Donna Trotman *(Personnel Dir.)*
Daniel Varel, Jr. *(Pur. Dir.)*

VARI TRONICS COMPANY, INC.
2745 E. Huntington Dr.
Duarte, CA 91010
Tel.: 818-359-8321
Fax: 818-358-4564
Approx.Sls.: $12,000,000
Emp.: 190
Telephone Connector & Data Cables, Wiring Harnesses, Connectorized Block Assemblies, Backfields, Digital Signal Interconnects, Universal Card Shelves, Digital Interface Panels, Backboards & Refurbishment Services
S.I.C.: 3661; 3679; 3699; 3823
E.C. Rothenberger *(Pres.)*
Yvonne Bartlebaugh *(V.P.)*
Eva Rothenberger *(Sec. & Treas.)*
R. Gatchel *(Controller)*
L. Bogut *(Mgr.-Mktg.)*
Marshall Hall *(Mgr.-Prod.)*

Outside Service Firm(s):

Swenson & Clark*(Auditors)*
Covina, CA

Hill, Farrer & Burrill*(Legal Firm)*
445 So. Figueroa St., 35th Fl.
Los Angeles, CA 90071

Sanwa Bank*(Major Banking Relationship)*
601 S. Figueroa St.
Los Angeles, CA 90017
Tel.: 213-896-7817
Fax: 213-489-1977

VARIED INVESTMENTS, INC.
1600 Oregon St.
Muscatine, IA 52761
Tel.: 319-264-4211
Fax: 319-264-4216
Sales Range: $100-499 Million
Holding Company; Grain Processing
S.I.C.: 6719
J.H. Kent *(Pres.)*

Computer Systems/Hardware:
IBM System 38

Outside Service Firm(s):

McGladrey & Pullen*(Auditors)*
221 3rd Ave., Ste. 300
Cedar Rapids, IA 52401
Tel.: 319-366-2791

The Northern Trust Co.*(Major Banking Relationship)*
50 S. LaSalle St.
Chicago, IL 60675
Tel.: 312-630-6000
Fax: 312-630-6516

Pacific Investment Management*(Pension Manager)*
P.O. Box 9000, 840 Newport Center Dr.
Newport Beach, CA 92660
Tel.: 714-640-3347

Division:

Evergreen Mills Inc. **(1)**
221 N. Rennie
Ada, OK 74820
Tel.: 405-332-6611
Tel.: 800-654-3909
Fax: 405-332-1956
Approx.Sls.: $30,000,000
Emp.: 100
Fiscal Year-end: 9/28/91
Evergreen Feeds
S.I.C.: 2048
Keith Hultquist *(Chm. Bd.)*
Bob Waller *(Pres.)*
Art Dean *(Exec. V.P. & G.M.)*
Lee Murphy *(V.P. & Sls. Mgr.)*
Gerald Brady *(V.P.-Mfg. & Distr.)*
Bob Nanney *(Pur. Agent)*

Subsidiaries:

Grain Processing Corp. **(1)**
1600 Oregon St.
Muscatine, IA 52761
Tel.: 319-264-4211
Fax: 319-264-4216
Sales Range: $100-499 Million

Varied Investments, Inc.—(Continued)

Emp.: 1,428
Grain Processing
S.I.C.: 2046; 2065; 2819
J.T. Kautz *(Chm. Bd. & Chief Exec. Officer)*

Kent Feeds Inc. (1)
1600 Oregon St.
Muscatine, IA 52761
Tel.: 319-264-4211
Emp.: 1,000
Computer Systems/Hardware:
IBM System AS400
Mfr. Livestock Feed
S.I.C.: 2047; 2048
R.C. Kautz *(Co-Chm. Bd.)*
J.H. Kent *(Co-Chm. Bd.)*
R.H. Severson *(Pres.)*
Glen A. Mente *(Sr. V.P.-Nutrition)*
Fred Miller *(Sr. V.P.-Mktg.)*
Kenneth A. Gregersen *(Sr. V.P.-Adv.)*
Chris J. Zogg *(Sec. & Gen. Counsel)*

VARIETY WHOLESALERS, INC.
3401 Greshams Lake Rd.
Raleigh, NC 27615
Tel.: 919-876-6000
Fax: 919-790-9572
Emp.: 2,250
Variety Department Stores
S.I.C.: 5331
John W. Pope, Sr. *(Pres.)*
Jack W. Bonds *(Sr. V.P.)*
James Arthur Pope *(V.P. & Gen. Counsel)*

Outside Service Firm(s):

NationsBank Carolinas*(Major Banking Relationship)*
Raleigh, NC

VARITYPER, INC.
11 Mt. Pleasant Ave.
East Hanover, NJ 07936
Tel.: 201-887-8000
Fax: 201-887-0731
Year Founded: 1881
Approx.Sls.: $85,000,000
Emp.: 550
Fiscal Year-end: 12/31/91
Export
Supplier of Electronic, Professional Composition and Imagesetting Systems
S.I.C.: 3579
Robert Trenkamp *(Pres. & Chief Exec. Officer)*
Mike Dillon *(V.P.-Sls.)*
James Marlow *(Sr. V.P. & Chief Fin. Officer)*
Ed Fortier *(Dir.-Customer Service)*
Susan Webb *(Dir.-Sls. Support & Mktg.)*

VASA INSURANCE GROUP, INC.
(Subsidiary of WASA Insurance Company Limited, Stockhom Sweden)
525 S. Meridian St.
Indianapolis, IN 46225
Mailing Address:
P.O. Box BAI
Greenwood, IN 46142
Tel.: 317-238-5500 **IN**
Fax: 317-238-5788
Year Founded: 1972
Assets: $115,000,000
Earnings: $1,252,000
Liabilities: $91,400,000
Net Worth: $23,600,000
Approx.Rev.: $53,640,000
Emp.: 200
Fiscal Year-end: 12/31/91
Insurance
S.I.C.: 6311; 6321; 6331
Corporate Giving Program: Program Directed Toward Upgrading Public Education & Health Issues; Assist With Select Overall Community Development
Rune Hallaker *(Chm. Bd.)*
Lars Casteborn *(Pres.)*
Don W. Blackwell *(Chief Fin. Officer, V.P. & Treas.)*
John B. Bridge *(V.P.-Real Estate, Sec. & Gen. Counsel)*
Denise J. Davis *(V.P.-Information Systems)*
Mark E. Hershman *(V.P.-Corp. Communications & Admin. Services)*
F. James Mohl *(V.P. & Actuary)*
Robert G. Mallison *(Asst. V.P. & Actuary)*
William T. Ryan *(Controller)*
Sandy Hudson *(Dir.-Pur.)*
Judy Jenings *(Dir.-Personnel Training & Devel.)*
Corliss White *(Dir.-Human Resources)*

Subsidiaries:

Brougher Agency, Inc. (1)
525 S. Meridian St.
Indianapolis, IN 46225
Tel.: 317-238-5678 (100%)
Fax: 317-238-5787
Emp.: 1
Life Insurance Brokerage
S.I.C.: 6411
Lars Casteborn *(Chm. Bd.)*
Eric Olson *(Pres.)*
John B. Bridge *(V.P., Gen. Counsel & Sec.)*
Don W. Blackwell *(Treas.)*

VASA Brougher, Inc. (1)
525 S. Meridian St.
Indianapolis, IN 46225
Tel.: 317-238-5600 (100%)
Fax: 317-238-5748
Approx.Sls.: $85,000,000
Emp.: 96
Life & Health Insurance
S.I.C.: 6411
Lars Casteborn *(Chm. Bd.)*
Eric Olson *(Pres.)*
Lanny R. Green *(Sr. V.P.-Mktg.)*
John B. Bridge *(V.P. & Sec.)*
Arlene Cayetano *(V.P.-Grp. Opers.)*
Patricia Freeman Dorson *(V.P. & Gen. Counsel)*
Patricia A. Redding *(V.P.-Information Systems)*
John R. Retz *(V.P.-Mkt. Devel.)*
Patty J. Smith *(Asst. V.P.-Fin. & Treas.)*

VASA Life Insurance Co. (1)
525 S. Meridian St.
Indianapolis, IN 46206
Tel.: 317-238-5955
Life & Health Insurance
S.I.C.: 6411
Lars Casteborn *(Chm. Bd.)*

VASA North Atlantic Insurance Company (1)
525 S. Meridian St.
Indianapolis, IN 46225
Tel.: 317-238-5800 (100%)
Approx.Sls.: $43,900,000
Emp.: 69
Fiscal Year-end: 12/31/90
Professional Liability
S.I.C.: 6411
Lars Casteborn *(Chm. Bd.)*
G. Thomas Folds *(Pres.)*
Jack A. Hewett *(Sr. V.P.-Admin., Chief Fin. Officer & Treas.)*
Jon Whiteman *(V.P. & Treas.)*
John B. Bridge *(V.P. & Sec.)*
Kathryn McGlothlin *(V.P.-Claims)*
F. James Mohl *(V.P. & Actuary)*
Jeff Sharp *(V.P.-Opers.)*
Jeff Ellis *(V.P.-Personal Lines)*

VECTURA GROUP, INC.
4 PPG Place, Ste. 300
Pittsburgh, PA 15222
Tel.: 412-434-4730
Fax: 412-434-1799
Approx.Sls.: $300,000,000
Emp.: 900
Marine Towing Services; Stevedoring; Contract Bending & Shaping
S.I.C.: 4492; 4491
Joseph J. Kappel *(Pres. & Chief Exec. Officer)*
H. James McKnight *(V.P. & Sec.)*
John J. Cronin, Jr. *(Controller)*

Subsidiary:

National Marine, Inc. (1)
400 Poydras St.
New Orleans, LA 70130
Tel.: 504-529-8600
Fax: 504-529-8643
Water Transportation
S.I.C.: 4424
Dominic J. Verona *(Pres.)*

VEDA INTERNATIONAL, INC.
11 Canal Center Plaza
Alexandria, VA 22314
Tel.: 703-684-8005 **DE**
Fax: 703-684-8102
Year Founded: 1962
Sales Range: $60-79 Million
Emp.: 1,100
Export
Holding Company
S.I.C.: 6719
Carl R. Varblow *(Chm. Bd. & Chief Fin. Officer)*
Marc S. Ross *(Pres. & Chief Exec. Officer)*
Phyllis D. Seidler *(Admin. Services Mgr.)*

Outside Service Firm(s):

Arthur Andersen & Co.*(Auditors)*
1666 K Street, N.W.
Washington, DC 20006

Hartford Life Insurance Co.*(Commercial Insurance Carrier)*
Hartford, CT 06104-2999

Golden, Freda & Schraub*(Legal Firm)*
Washington, DC

Spriggs & Hollingsworth*(Legal Firm)*
Washington, DC

Riggs National Bank of Washington, D.C.*(Major Banking Relationship)*
P.O. Box 96206, 1120 Vermont Ave. N.W.
Washington, DC 20090-6206
Tel.: 202-835-4082

Subsidiaries:

Chameleon Technologies Incorporated (1)
Ste. 11, Canal Center Plaza, Ste. 300
Alexandria, VA 22314
Tel.: 703-684-8005
Fax: 703-684-8102
Develops & Markets Simulation Products For Entertainment Industry
Marc S. Ross *(Chief Exec. Officer)*
Dale R. Roberts *(Pres.)*
Carl R. Varblow *(Chief Fin. Officer)*

Veda Design Group (1)
1800 N. Beauregard St.
Alexandria, VA 22311
Tel.: 703-998-8332
Approx.Billings: $790,000
Industrial Adv.
S.I.C.: 7311
Dale Roberts *(V.P., Mktg.)*
Chuck Mitchell *(V.P., Program Devel.)*
Jim Victor *(V.P., Opers.)*
Steve Beauch *(Sec. & Treas.)*

Veda Incorporated (1)
Ste. 300, 11 Canal Center Plaza
Alexandria, VA 22314
Tel.: 703-684-8005
Fax: 703-684-8102
Sales Range: $60-79 Million
Emp.: 1,100
Professional Engineering & Technical Support Services; Systems Engineering & Analysis; Program Planning & Finance Management; Test & Evaluation; Logistics Engineering; Software Engineering
S.I.C.: 7371; 7373; 7379; 8711; 8742
Carl R. Varblow *(Chm. Bd. & Chief Fin. Officer)*
Marc S. Ross *(Pres. & Chief Exec. Officer)*
Thomas F. Bennett *(Legal Counsel)*
Frankie F. Darden *(Controller)*
S.R. Beauch *(Fin. Dir.)*
Dale R. Roberts *(Mktg. Dir.)*
Douglas W. Redmond *(Admin. Dir.)*
Gary L. Palonen *(Tech. Dir.)*

Veda Systems, Incorporated (1)
6 Pecan Ct., Ste A.
California, MD 20619
Tel.: 301-737-1558
Fax: 301-863-2744
Developes, Markets & Manufactures Telemetry Systems & Aircraft Simulation Products
S.I.C.: 3823
David E. Butler *(Pres.)*
Marc S. Ross *(Chief Exec. Officer)*
Carl R. Varblow *(Chief Fin. Officer)*

VEECO INSTRUMENTATIONS, INC.
Terminal Dr.
Plainview, NY 11803
Tel.: 516-349-8300 **NY**
Emp.: 250
High Vacuum Equipment, Leak Detection Systems, Ion Milling, Ion Implantation, Photoresist Processing Equip., Automated Wafer Fab Systems
S.I.C.: 3812; 3669; 3674; 3679; 3825
Edward H. Braun *(Pres.)*
Walter Scherr *(V.P. & G.M.)*
Mary Anne Barrise *(Mgr.-Mktg. & Communications)*

Subsidiaries:

Sloan Technology (1)
602 E. Montecito St.
Santa Barbara, CA 93103
Tel.: 805-963-4431
Fax: 805-965-0522
Emp.: 75
Fiscal Year-end: 5/ 2/91
Export
Mfr. of Instruments
S.I.C.: 5065
Ed Braun *(Pres. & Chief Exec. Officer)*
Tom Kern *(V.P. & G.M.)*
Bob Germain *(V.P.-Mktg.)*
Terry Walker *(Dir.-Mfg.)*
John Jamieson *(Dir.-Engrng.)*
Kat Marin *(Dir.-Personnel)*
Don Johnson *(Pur. Dir.)*
Tim Ballinger *(Mgr.-Mktg. Communications)*

Veeco UPA Technology Inc. (1)
60 Oak Dr.
Syosset, NY 11791
Tel.: 516-364-1080
Mfr. of Instruments
S.I.C.: 3825
Walter Scherr *(V.P. & Gen. Mgr.)*

Non-U.S. Holdings:

Veeco GmbH (1)
P.O. Box 81 8000
Munich, 45, Germany
Tel.: 89 311-76-49 (100%)
Mktg. & Sls.
S.I.C.: 5065; 5084

Veeco Instruments Ltd. (1)
Abbey Barn Road
High Wycombe, Bucks United Kingdom
Tel.: 04-494-36386 (100%)
Mktg. & Sls.
S.I.C.: 5065; 5084

Veeco K.K. (1)
Denpa Bldg. 1-11-15 Higiashigotanda, Shinagawa-Ku,
Tokyo, Japan
Provides Sls., Service & Application Support for Semiconductor Equip. & Instrumentation Prods.
S.I.C.: 5065; 5084
R. Madarame *(Chief Oper. Officer)*

VELCON FILTERS, INC.
1750 Rogers Ave.
San Jose, CA 95112
Mailing Address:
P.O. Box 6828
San Jose, CA 95150
Tel.: 408-436-6525
Twx: 346482
Fax: 415-436-7612
Approx.Sls.: $25,000,000
Emp.: 200
Mfr. of Filtration Equipment
S.I.C.: 3569

Lucian W. Taylor *(Chm. Bd.)*
David Taylor *(Pres.)*
R.B. Taylor *(V.P.-Sls. & Mktg.)*
Kajetan Nowacki *(Sec. & Treas.)*

Outside Service Firm(s):

Wilson, Sonsini, Goodrich & Rosati*(Legal Firm)*
Two Palo Alto Square
Palo Alto, CA 94304
Tel.: 415-493-9300

Bank of America NT&SA*(Major Banking Relationship)*
San Jose, CA

VELSICOL CHEMICAL CORPORATION
10400 W. Higgins Rd.
Rosemont, IL 60018
Tel.: 708-298-9000
Tel.: 800-233-0836 **DE**
Telex: 3730755
Fax: 708-298-9014
Year Founded: 1940
Approx.Sls.: $100,000,000
Emp.: 400
Export
Mfr. Industrial Chemicals, Pesticides
S.I.C.: 2819; 2869; 2879; 2865
Arthur R. Sigel *(Chm. Bd., Pres. & Chief Exec. Officer)*
Lawrence M. Hartman *(Chief Fin. Officer & Exec. V.P.)*
David M. Frederick *(V.P.-International)*
Charles Hanson *(V.P.-Environmental)*
Dennis Leu *(V.P.-Mktg. & Sls.)*
James D. Groszek *(Controller)*
Lyndon Whitlock *(Sec. & Gen. Counsel)*
Ronald L. Bonato *(Dir.-Employee Benefits)*
Guillermo Bonet *(Dir.-Intl. Business)*
Richard E. Davis *(Dir.-Mngmt. Information Systems)*
Jerry Graybosch *(Dir.-Intl. Fin.)*
Gerald Jaffe *(Dir.-Matls. Mngmt.)*
Donna Jennings *(Dir.-Communications)*
Neal Netzel *(Dir.-Quality Control)*
Renee Hammond *(Mgr.-Human Resources)*
Principal(s):
Arthur R. Sigel
Lawrence M. Hartman
David M. Frederick
Charles Hanson
Dennis Leu

No. of Mfg. Plants/Facilities: 3
No. of U.S. Offices: 2
No. of Foreign Offices: 4

Computer Systems/Hardware:
IBM System 36; Compaq PC

Outside Service Firm(s):

Deloitte & Touche*(Auditors)*
Two Prudential Plaza, 180 N. Stetson
Chicago, IL 60601
Tel.: 312-946-2039

Johnson & Higgins*(Group Insurer)*
500 W. Madison
Chicago, IL 60606
Tel.: 312-648-4200

Sidley & Austin*(Legal Firm)*
One First National Plaza, 42nd Fl.
Chicago, IL 60603
Tel.: 312-853-7000
Fax: 312-853-7036

Harris Trust & Savings Bank*(Major Banking Relationship)*
111 W. Monroe St.
Chicago, IL 60690
Tel.: 312-461-2265
Tel.: 800-858-0840

The Northern Trust Co.*(Pension Manager)*
50 S. LaSalle St.
Chicago, IL 60675
Tel.: 312-630-6000
Fax: 312-630-6516

Non-U.S. Holdings:

Velsicol Australia Limited **(1)**
10 William St. P.O. Box 349,
Turramurra, N.S.W. 2074, Australia
Tel.: 2 488 9011
Fax: 2 488 9717

Velsicol Chemical Corporation **(1)**
4th Floor, Marsman Building, Buendia Ave. & Washington St. Makati,
Metro Manila, Philippines
Tel.: 2 815 0792

Velsicol Chemical Limited **(1)**
Worting House,
Basingstoke, Hampshire RG23 8PY, United Kingdom
Tel.: 256-817640
Fax: 256-811876

Velsicol Overseas Corporation **(1)**
33 Multiadou St. Glyfada, 166 75
Athens, Greece
Tel.: 1 962 9553
Fax: 1 962 9682

VENCHURS PACKAGING, INC.
800 Liberty St.
Adrian, MI 49221
Tel.: 517-263-8937 **MI**
Fax: 517-265-7468
Year Founded: 1973
Assets: $13,500,000
Liabilities: $7,100,000
Net Worth: $6,400,000
Approx.Sls.: $36,000,000
Emp.: 100
Fiscal Year-end: 9/30/91
Packaging & Labeling Services
S.I.C.: 7389
John W. Wyatt *(Pres.)*
Ronald Reeves *(V.P. & Gen. Mgr.)*
V.M. Brown *(V.P.-Opers.)*
Edward F. Palisin *(V.P.-Mktg.)*
John Chandler *(Dir.-Personnel)*
K.R. Powell *(Mgr.-Materials)*
R. Robertson *(Mgr.-Pur.)*

Outside Service Firm(s):

Schippers, Kinter & Robertson*(Auditors)*
Adrian, MI

Ohio Citizens Bank*(Major Banking Relationship)*
Toledo, OH

The Venet Companies, Inc.

THE VENET COMPANIES, INC.
465 Chestnut St.
Union, NJ 07083
Tel.: 908-687-1313
Fax: 908-964-3913
Year Founded: 1954
Approx.Billings: $95,500,000
Emp.: 130
Retail, Consumer, Business-to-Business, & Banking
Zal Venet *(Chm. Bd., Pres. & Chief Exec. Officer)*
Barbara Hamilton *(Controller)*

VENGROFF WILLIAMS & ASSOCIATES, INC.
93 Centershore Rd.
Centerpoint, NY 11721
Tel.: 516-757-5100 **NY**
Fax: 516-754-5117
Year Founded: 1964
Sales Range: $500-999 Million
Emp.: 250
Fiscal Year-end: 12/31/90
Collection Agency
S.I.C.: 7322
Harvey Vengroff *(Chm. Bd. & Chief Exec. Officer)*
Robert Williams *(Pres.)*
Robert Hirsch *(V.P.-Sls.)*
Joel Vengroff *(V.P.)*
Mark Vengroff *(V.P.)*

No. of Mfg. Plants/Facilities: 15
No. of U.S. Offices: 14

Computer Systems/Hardware:
IBM System 200

Outside Service Firm(s):

Ziedman & Lackowitz*(Auditors)*
Syosset, NY

National Westminister Bank Plc*(Major Banking Relationship)*
Greenlawn, NY

Subsidiary:

Vengroff Williams Realty Management **(1)**
109 Centerline Rd.
Centerpoint, NY 11721
Tel.: 516-754-4300
Real Estate Management & Investment
S.I.C.: 6531; 6798
Harvey Vengroff *(Chief Exec. Officer)*

VENTA INC.
1055 Aurora Pkwy., Ste. 100
Denver, CO 80204
Tel.: 303-892-7171
Fax: 303-893-6505
Year Founded: 1969
Sales Range: $80-99 Million
Emp.: 325
Wholesaler of Petroleum Products; Retail Convenience Food Stores
S.I.C.: 5411; 5712
H.G. Arnold *(Chm. Bd. & Chief Fin. Officer)*
R.W. Hagmeyer *(Pres.)*
D.L. Quam *(Controller)*
E.E. Kingham *(Dir.-Mktg.)*
Gary Wetzbarger *(Mgr.-Admin.)*
Principal(s):
H.G. Arnold
R.W. Hagmeyer

No. of U.S. Offices: 1

Outside Service Firm(s):

Smith, Brooks, Bolshoun*(Auditors)*
Denver, CO

Sherman & Howard*(Legal Firm)*
633 17th St.
Denver, CO 80202
Tel.: 303-297-2900

VENTRE PACKING COMPANY, INC.
6050 Court St. Rd.
Syracuse, NY 13206-1730
Tel.: 315-463-2384
Fax: 315-463-5897
Year Founded: 1938
Approx.Sls.: $15,000,000
Emp.: 50
Fiscal Year-end: 12/31/91
Import Export
Enrico Spaghetti Sauces, Institutional Foods & Private Label Packing, Michelini Spaghetti Sauce, Mexican Sauces, Mexican Picante & Cooking Sauces, Seafood Cocktail Sauces, Cajun Creole Sauce, BBQ Sauces, Taco Salsa, Enchilada Salsa, Ketchup
S.I.C.: 2099; 2035
John Ventre, Jr. *(Chm. Bd. & Chief Exec. Officer)*
Martin Ventre *(Pres.)*
Jacki Papai *(Chief Fin. Officer, Sec. & Treas.)*
Frank Ventre Jr. *(Gen. Counsel)*
Alfred D. Marco *(Controller)*
Hugh Keegan *(Dir.-Mktg.)*
James Williamson *(Dir.-Sls.)*
Joe Yaeger *(Dir.-Quality Control)*
Steve Weinstein *(Natl. Sls. Mgr.)*
James Faivre *(Mgr.-Mfg.)*
Tom Renna *(Mgr.-Export)*

Computer Systems/Hardware:
IBM

VENTURA ASSOCIATES, INC.
1211 Ave. of the Americas, 26th Floor
New York, NY 10036
Tel.: 212-302-8277
Fax: 212-302-2587
Year Founded: 1971
Approx.Billings: $24,750,000
Emp.: 25
Prize Promotions, Including Sweepstakes, Contests & Games, Sports Mktg., Incentive Program, Direct Mktg. & Fulfillment
Ken Fehskens *(Pres. & Chief Exec. Officer)*
Marla Altberg *(V.P., Sls. & Mktg.)*
Al Wester *(Dir., Opers.)*
Nigel Morgan *(Chief Fin. Officer)*

VENTURA COASTAL CORPORATION
2325 Vista Del Mar
Ventura, CA 93002
Mailing Address:
P.O. Box 69
Ventura, CA 93002
Tel.: 805-653-7000
Fax: 805-653-7777
Processing of Citrus Products
S.I.C.: 2033
Dean Ulrich *(Pres.)*
Bill Borges *(V.P.-Sls. & Mktg.)*
Don Grace *(V.P.-Fin.)*
Maxine Gould *(Controller)*

Outside Service Firm(s):

Deloitte & Touche*(Auditors)*
Woodland Hills, CA

Best, Best & Krieger*(Legal Firm)*
P.O. Box 1028
Riverside, CA 92502
Tel.: 909-686-1450

Wells Fargo Bank*(Major Banking Relationship)*
Ventura, CA

VENTURA TRAVELWARE, INC.
32-33 47th Ave.
Long Island City, NY 11101
Tel.: 718-392-6200
Telex: 427149 VENWAR
Fax: 718-937-8158
Year Founded: 1936
Approx.Sls.: $10,000,000
Emp.: 225
Fiscal Year-end: 12/31/90
Import Export
Mfr. of Luggage
S.I.C.: 3161
Richard Epstein *(Pres.)*
Walter Bialo *(Chief Exec. Officer)*
Irwin Davidson *(V.P.-Mktg.)*
Col. Malcolm Farnsworth *(V.P.-Premium Div.)*
B. White *(V.P.-Sls.)*
Sally Richards *(Dir.-Public Rels.)*
Gunther Schnell *(Dir.-Engrng. Services)*
Sam Ward *(Dir.-Acct. Services)*
Mason Edwards, Jr. *(Mgr.-Customer Rels.)*
Sally Anne Schiano *(Mgr.-Exports)*

No. of Mfg. Plants/Facilities: 2
No. of U.S. Offices: 2

Computer Systems/Hardware:
AT & T

Outside Service Firm(s):

Mendlowitz & Weitsen*(Auditors)*
New York, NY

Ventura Travelware, Inc.—(Continued)

Bankers Trust Co.*(Major Banking Relationship)*
P.O. Box 318, Church St. Station
New York, NY 10008
Tel.: 212-454-2212
Fax: 212-454-2783

Division:

Ventura Travelware, Inc.-International Div. **(1)**
32-33 47th Ave.
Long Island City, NY 11101
Tel.: 718-392-6200
B. White *(V.P.)*

VENTUREDYNE, LTD.
10201 W. Lincoln Ave., Ste. 400
Milwaukee, WI 53227
Tel.: 414-327-2211 **WI**
Approx.Sls.: $100,000,000
Emp.: 1,400
Mfr. Industrial Machinery, Material Handling Equipment, Environmental Test Chambers
S.I.C.: 3532; 3585; 3829; 3559
Brian L. Nahey *(Pres. & Chief Exec. Officer)*
Bruce A. Beda *(V.P., Treas., Chief Fin. Officer & Sec.)*

Outside Service Firm(s):

Deloitte & Touche*(Auditors)*
250 E. Wisconsin Ave.
Milwaukee, WI 53202-4283
Tel.: 414-271-3000

Michael, Best & Friedrich*(Legal Firm)*
100 East Wisconsin Avenue
Milwaukee, WI 53202
Tel.: 414-271-6560

First Wisconsin National Bank*(Major Banking Relationship)*
777 E. Wisconsin Ave.
Milwaukee, WI 53202
Tel.: 414-765-4321
Fax: 414-355-6903

Divisions:

Advanced Detection Systems **(1)**
4740 W. Electric Ave.
Milwaukee, WI 53219
Tel.: 414-672-7830
S.I.C.: 3669

Chisholm, Boyd & White Co. **(1)**
4101 W. 126th St.
Alsip, IL 60658
Tel.: 708-597-7550
Compaction Presses & Machinery for Refractories & Processing Indus.
S.I.C.: 3297

Climet Instruments Co. **(1)**
1320 W. Colton Ave.
Redlands, CA 92374
Tel.: 909-793-2788
Electronic Pollution Monitoring Equip. & Meteorological Devices
S.I.C.: 3812

Dings Dynamics Co. **(1)**
4740 W. Electric Ave.
Milwaukee, WI 53219
Tel.: 414-672-7830
Magnetic Motor Brakes & Clutches
S.I.C.: 3568

Dings Magnetic Co. **(1)**
4740 W. Electric Ave.
Milwaukee, WI 53219
Tel.: 414-672-7830
Magnetic Separation, Purification, Material Handling & Process Protection Equip.
S.I.C.: 3532

Scientific Dust Collectors **(1)**
4740 W. Electric Ave.
Milwaukee, WI 53219
Tel.: 414-672-7830
Dust Collecting Equip.
S.I.C.: 3589

Sound Creation **(1)**
900 John Nolen Drive, 130B
Madison, WI 53713
Tel.: 608-256-3646
Emp.: 6
Research & Development
S.I.C.: 8731
Ray Taborshak *(V.P.-Research & Devel.)*

Thermotron Industries, Inc. **(1)**
Kollen Park Dr.
Holland, MI 49423
Tel.: 616-392-1491
Environmental Test Chambers
S.I.C.: 3812

Subsidiary:

Carnes Company, Inc. **(1)**
10210 W. Lincoln Ave.
Milwaukee, WI 53227
Tel.: 414-327-2211
Air Distribution Equipment
S.I.C.: 3564; 3585
Brian L. Nahey *(Pres. & Chief Exec. Officer)*
Bruce A. Beda *(V.P. & Treas. & Chief Fin. Officer)*

VERMEER MANUFACTURING COMPANY
New Sharon Rd.
Pella, IA 50219
Mailing Address:
P.O. Box 200
Pella, IA 50219
Tel.: 515-628-3141
Telex: 478-309
Fax: 515-628-3614
Sales Range: $100-499 Million
Emp.: 1,200
Fiscal Year-end: 10/31/91
Export
Mfr. of Industrial Ditchers, Stump Cutters, Rock Cutters, Cable Plows, Tree Spades, Brush Chippers, Large Round Hay Balers, & Rakes
S.I.C.: 3523
Gary J. Vermeer *(Founder)*
Robert Vermeer *(Chm. Bd. & Chief Exec. Officer)*
Mary Andringa *(Pres. & Chief Oper. Officer)*
Jarrett Cowden *(V.P.-Mktg.)*
Nelson Nikkel *(V.P.-Vermeer Underground)*
Pat Weiler *(V.P.-Vermeer Underground)*
Larry McCarthy *(Gen. Mgr.-Vermeer AT)*
Arlie Vander Hoek *(Gen. Mgr.-Vermeer OEM)*
Kent Rotert *(Mgr.-Mktg. Communications)*
Denny Vos *(Natl. Sls. Mgr.)*

Outside Service Firm(s):

Norwest Bank Iowa N.A.*(Major Banking Relationship)*
666 Walnut
Des Moines, IA

VERMONT LOTTERY COMMISSION
South Barre, P.O. Box 420
Barre, VT 05670
Tel.: 802-828-2274
Fax: 802-476-6347
Year Founded: 1978
Approx.Sls.: $51,000,000
Emp.: 19
Fiscal Year-end: 6/30/91
State Lottery
S.I.C.: 7999
Fredrick R. McGibney *(Dir.)*
Harry W. Seal *(Business Mgr.)*
Stanley Roberts *(Mgr.-Sls.)*
Bethany Bishop *(Mgr.-Mktg.)*

VERNAY LABORATORIES, INC.
120 E. S. College St.
Yellow Springs, OH 45387
Mailing Address:
P.O. Box 310
Yellow Springs, OH 45387
Tel.: 513-767-7261
Telex: 212956
Fax: 513-767-7913
Year Founded: 1945
Approx.Sls.: $50,000,000
Emp.: 800
Import Export
Mfr. Precision Molded Rubber Parts
S.I.C.: 3069; 3714; 3845; 3061
Stephen W. Stephens *(Chm. Bd.)*
Bob Nagy *(Pres. & Chief Exec. Officer)*
Serge Vernet *(Exec. V.P.-Investor Rels.)*
Dennis Loyer *(V.P.-Fin.)*
Paul Grahm *(V.P.-Research & Chief Chemist)*
Bill Lightsey *(V.P.-Human Res.)*
Dennis Bell *(Controller & Treas.)*
Frank Beafore *(Dir.-Marketing)*
George Stillablower *(Dir.-Sls.)*
Gerard Stello *(Dir.-International Sales & Prod. Dev.)*
Eric Jones *(Mgr.-Personnel)*
Rick Gudorf *(Mgr.-Data Proc.)*
Sam Walden *(Mgr.-Materials)*
Mary Snyder *(Exec. Asst.)*

Computer Systems/Hardware:
Micro Term PC, IBM & Apple Macintosh

Outside Service Firm(s):

Battelle & Battelle*(Auditors)*
3400 South Dixie Dr.
Dayton, OH 45402

Prudential Insurance Co. of America*(Group Insurer)*
751 Broad St.
Newark, NJ 07102-3777
Tel.: 201-802-6000

Martin, Brown, Hull*(Legal Firm)*
Springfield, OH

Star Bank*(Major Banking Relationship)*
425 Walnut Street
Cincinnati, OH 45202
Tel.: 513-632-4000

The Prudential Asset Management Company*(Pension Manager)*
751 Broad St., 19th Fl.
Newark, NJ 07102-3777
Tel.: 201-802-8400
Fax: 201-802-8456

Star Bank*(Pension Manager)*
425 Walnut Street
Cincinnati, OH 45202
Tel.: 513-632-4000

VERNELL'S CANDY COMPANY
11959 Northrup Way
Bellevue, WA 98005
Tel.: 206-827-3855
Tel.: 800-425-7638
Fax: 206-455-8450
Approx.Sls.: $35,000,000
Emp.: 275
Fiscal Year-end: 6/30/90
Candy Manufacturer
S.I.C.: 2064; 2066
Ray Kiely *(Pres.)*
Doug Carroll *(Controller)*
Ken Avedisian *(Fin. Dir.)*
Mike Ahlstrom *(Dir.-Mktg.)*
Larry Widman *(Gen. Mgr.-Export)*

THE VERNON COMPANY
604 W. 4th N.
Newton, IA 50208
Tel.: 515-792-9000
Fax: 515-792-6901
Year Founded: 1902
Approx.Sls.: $56,300,000
Emp.: 1,000
Fiscal Year-end: 2/28/92
Import
Manufactures Ad Specialties, Calendars, Gifts, Signs, Premiums, Incentives, Sales Promotion Programs, Caps, Jackets, Cutlery; Business Gifts; Awards, Premiums, Incentives
S.I.C.: 2752; 2754; 2771; 3993; 7389; 2326; 2339; 3421; 2353
Corporate Giving Program:
Community Betterment Projects
Employee Matching Gifts Program:
United Way
W.F. Vernon *(Chm. Bd.)*
Joe Geneser *(Pres.)*
Joe Pugel *(V.P.-Mfg.)*
George Riley *(V.P.-Sls.)*
Dan Stevenson *(V.P.-Fin.)*
Chris Vernon *(Dir.-Product Lines)*
Dave Gildenzopf *(Dir.-Pressure Sensitive Markings & Training)*
Donald J. Costanzo *(Dir.-Mktg.)*
Maurice Phillips *(Dir.-Personnel)*
Harry Holmes *(Mgr.-Sls.)*
Lee Atkinson *(Mgr.-Data Processing)*
Joe Street *(Mgr.-Mfg.)*
Bill Wright *(Pur. Agent)*

Computer Systems/Hardware:
IBM & Macintosh

Divisions:

Dunlop Manufacturing Co. **(1)**
P.O. Box 248,
Unionville, MO 63665
Tel.: 816-947-2455
Import
Mfr. Advertising Specialties
S.I.C.: 3993
D. Davis *(Mgr.-Sls.)*

Gee Cee Cap Company **(1)**
Old Hwy. 169 N.
Grant City, MO 64456
Tel.: 800-433-2277
Mfr. Caps
S.I.C.: 2353
Scott Hoak *(Mgr.-Sls.)*

T Shirt Graphics **(1)**
111 11th St.
Des Moines, IA 50309-4214
Tel.: 515-282-4745
Fax: 515-282-4611
Wearables for Men & Women
S.I.C.: 5136; 5137
Allen Veck *(Mgr.-Sls.)*

VSM
VERNON•SASSOS•McGILL, Inc.

VERNON SASSOS MCGILL, INC.
156 Fifth Ave.
New York, NY 10010
Tel.: 212-645-0900
Year Founded: 1988
Approx.Billings: $47,500,000
Emp.: 10
Media Planning, Buying & Analysis
Thomas P. Sassos *(Pres.)*
Joanne McGill *(Exec. V.P.)*
Susan Acocella *(Controller)*

VERYFINE PRODUCTS, INC.
210 Littleton Rd.
Westford, MA 01886
Mailing Address:
P.O. Box 670,
Westford, MA 01886
Tel.: 508-692-0030
Fax: 508-692-9481
Year Founded: 1865
Approx.Sls.: $200,000,000
Emp.: 400
Fiscal Year-end: 12/31/90
Export

Manufacturer of Apple Juice, Drinks & Sauce
S.I.C.: 2037; 2033; 2035
James R. Rowse, Sr. *(Chm. Bd.)*
Sam B. Rowse *(Pres.)*
Dennis Dakin *(V.P.-Sls.-Vending & Food Service)*
Robert Littlefield *(V.P.-Retail Sls.)*
Steven Rowse *(V.P.-Mktg.)*
Donald Smallwood *(V.P.-Opers.)*
Mark O'Day *(Dir.-Mktg. Communications)*
Joel Turnbull *(Dir.-Retail Sls.)*
Louisa Attenborough *(Mgr.-Pub. Rel.)*
Ann Sharpe *(Mgr.-Mktg. Services)*
Nancy Beach *(Corp. Meeting Planner)*

Computer Systems/Hardware:
IBM

Outside Service Firm(s):

Indian Head Bank*(Major Banking Relationship)*
Nashua, NH

VESCO OIL CORP.
16055 W. 12 Mile Rd.
Southfield, MI 48076
Tel.: 313-557-1600
Fax: 313-557-2236
Approx.Sls.: $10,000,000
Emp.: 100
Petroleum Products
S.I.C.: 5172
Richard Epstein *(Chm. Bd., Pres. & Chief Exec. Officer)*
Steve Mcisaac *(Controller)*

Computer Systems/Hardware:
Point 4

Outside Service Firm(s):

Parker, Wittus & Co.*(Auditors)*
Southfield, MI

Travelers Insurance Co.*(Group Insurer)*
1 Tower Square
Hartford, CT 06183-2492
Tel.: 203-277-4542
Fax: 203-277-5038

Sommer, Schwartz, Silver, Schwartz*(Legal Firm)*
Southfield, MI

N.B.D. Bank, N.A.*(Major Banking Relationship)*
611 Woodward Ave.
Detroit, MI 48226
Tel.: 313-225-1122
Fax: 313-225-3420

VESS BEVERAGES, INC.
2525 Schuetz Rd.
Maryland Heights, MO 63043
Tel.: 314-567-1300
Fax: 314-569-0930
Approx.Sls.: $33,000,000
Emp.: 140
Soft Drinks in Bottles & Cans
S.I.C.: 2086
Don R. Schneeberger *(Pres. & Treas.)*
Roger Placke *(V.P. & Sec.)*
Melvin L. Edwards *(Comptroller)*
John Valleroy *(Mktg. & Adv. Dir.)*

VIBRA SCREW INC.
755 Union Blvd.
Totowa, NJ 07511
Tel.: 201-256-7410
Fax: 201-256-7567
Approx.Sls.: $10,000,000
Emp.: 130
Fiscal Year-end: 12/31/90
Dry Materials Feeders, Bin Activators, Continuous Blenders; Screens
S.I.C.: 3523
Eugene A. Wahl *(Chm. Bd.)*
Eugene R. Wahl *(Pres.)*
Rich Wahl *(V.P.-Adv.)*
Ellen Wahl *(Treas.)*
Wayne Sweeney *(Pur. Agent)*

Outside Service Firm(s):

Grant Thornton*(Auditors)*
9 Campus Dr.
Parsippany, NJ
Tel.: 201-540-0250

Ramapa Bank*(Major Banking Relationship)*
Wayne, NJ

VIC MANUFACTURING
1620 Central Ave., N.E.
Minneapolis, MN 55413
Tel.: 612-781-6601
Tel.: 800-669-8777
Telex: 821260
Fax: 612-781-8559
Year Founded: 1938
Approx.Sls.: $12,000,000
Emp.: 70
Fiscal Year-end: 12/31/90
Import Export
Dry Cleaning Equip., Coin-Op Dry Cleaners & Vapor Absorption Systems; Air Pollution
S.I.C.: 3582
Walter Wilkie *(Chm. Bd.)*
Ronald E. Lewis *(Pres.)*
Brad Billison *(Controller)*
Raymond Menard *(Dir.-Mktg. & Prod.)*
Mary Vukonich *(Mgr.-Personnel)*
Tony Nelson *(Pur. Agent)*

Computer Systems/Hardware:
IBM System 36

Division:

Imparts **(1)**
1620 Central Ave. NE
Minneapolis, MN 55413-2556
Tel.: 612-781-6601
Import
Mfr. of Dry Cleaning Equipment
S.I.C.: 3582
William McManus *(Gen. Mgr.)*
Raymond Menard *(Dir.-Mktg.)*

VICTAULIC COMPANY OF AMERICA
4901 Kesslersville Rd.
Easton, PA 18042
Mailing Address:
P.O. Box 31,
Easton, PA 18044-0031
Tel.: 215-559-3300
Telex: 18044-0031
Fax: 215-250-8817
Year Founded: 1925
Emp.: 1,400
Fiscal Year-end: 9/30/91
Import Export
Manufactures Pipe Couplings, Fittings & Valves, Accessories & Tools
S.I.C.: 3494; 3322
George F. Naumann *(Chm. Bd. & Chief Exec. Officer)*
Joseph M. Trachtenberg *(Pres. & Chief Oper. Officer)*
David S. Bugby *(V.P.-Mfg.)*
Thomas M. Kiley *(V.P.-Sls.)*
Maurice J. Webb *(V.P.-Special Projects)*
Wayne Barefoot *(Treas.)*
Patricia Fisher *(Sec.)*
Beverly Yelpo *(Controller)*
Brian P. Bissey *(Gen. Counsel)*
William Buss *(Dir.-Human Resources)*
Thomas J. Conroy *(Dir.-Data Processing)*
Louis Hayden *(Dir.-Procurement)*
Maryellin Treacy *(Dir.-Employee Benefits)*
Miles Berkow *(Mgr.-Cash Mngmt.)*
John R. Diamant *(Mgr.-Intl. Division)*
Douglas Dole *(Mgr.-Res. & Devel.)*
Alec Gorsky *(Mgr.-Govt. Sls.)*
Gilbert K. Greene *(Mgr.-Mktg. Services)*
Dina Manoway *(Mgr.-Mfg.)*

No. of Mfg. Plants/Facilities: 6
No. of U.S. Offices: 21
No. of Foreign Offices: 6

Computer Systems/Hardware:
IBM System 38 & IBM AS/400

Outside Service Firm(s):

Deloitte & Touche*(Auditors)*
Ste. 200, Two Windsor Dr., 7540 Windsor Dr.
Allentown, PA 18195
Tel.: 215-366-5100

Brown Brothers, Harriman & Co.*(Major Banking Relationship)*
59 Wall St.
New York, NY 10005-2818
Tel.: 212-493-8029

Subsidiaries:

Apex Galvanizing Corp. **(1)**
New Village, Edison Rd., RD#1
Stewartsville, NJ 08886
Tel.: 908-859-0085 (100%)
Emp.: 70
Hot Dip & Centrifugal Galvanizing
S.I.C.: 3494
Ronald Eroh *(Chief Oper. Officer)*

Victaulic International **(1)**
4901 Kesslerville Rd.
Easton, PA 18042
Tel.: 215-559-3300 (100%)
Fax: 215-250-8817
Emp.: 12
Exports Plumbing Supplies & Equipment
S.I.C.: 5074
George F. Naumann *(Chief Exec. Officer)*
Richard M. Klain *(Mgr.-Latin American Sls.)*
Brooke Amiss *(Dir.-Mktg.)*
Russ Carlson *(Dir.-Sls.)*
Kathy Twiss *(Mgr.-Adv.)*
John R. Diamont *(Mgr.-International Div.)*

Victaulic Tool Company **(1)**
P.O. Box 31,
Easton, PA 18042
Tel.: 215-559-3300 (100%)
Emp.: 15
Pipe Preparation Tool Sales & Leasing
S.I.C.: 5074; 7359
S. Karl Sellers *(Mgr.-Tool Div.)*

TBV, Inc. **(1)**
P.O. Box 72, 103 Worcester-Providence Road
Millbury, MA 01527
Tel.: 508-865-6918
Tel.: 508-528-7500 (100%)
Emp.: 50
Corrosion Resistant and Cryogenic Valves
S.I.C.: 3494
David C. Putnam *(Pres.)*

Non-U.S. Holdings:

Victaulic Company of Canada Limited **(1)**
65 Worcester Road
Rexdale, ON M9W 5N7, Canada
Tel.: 416-675-5729 (100%)
Telex: 06-989158
Fax: 416-675-5729
Emp.: 150
Mfr. of Pipe Couplings; Fittings & Valves
S.I.C.: 3494; 3322
Richard N. Cope *(V.P. & Gen. Mgr.)*
Donald R. Jones *(Mktg.)*

N.V. Pipeco, S.A. **(1)**
Ambachstraat 6 P.O. Box 58, Industrial Park,
Landerzeel, Belgium
Tel.: 52-30-4611
Fax: 52-30-4619
Emp.: 8
S.I.C.: 3494
David K. Sharkey *(Gen. Mgr.)*
William Ashworth *(Adm. Supv.)*

VICTOR CORPORATION
618 Main St.
West Warwick, RI 02893
Mailing Address:
P.O. Box 1001,
West Warwick, RI 02893
Tel.: 401-821-1700
Fax: 401-821-7040
Approx.Sls.: $42,000,000
Emp.: 650
Primary Metal Industries; Electric & Electronic Equipment; Manufacture Wire & Cable Products
S.I.C.: 3315; 3629
John Libera *(Chm. Bd. & Chief Exec. Officer)*
E. M. Colafanto *(V.P.)*
Allan Zenofsky *(Controller)*
Jack Walsh *(Mgr.-Indus. Rels.)*

Computer Systems/Hardware:
IBM

Outside Service Firm(s):

KPMG Peat Marwick*(Auditors)*
600 Fleet Center
Providence, RI 02903
Tel.: 401-421-6600

Blue Cross & Blue Shield of Rhode Island*(Group Insurer)*
Providence, RI

Edwards & Angell*(Legal Firm)*
2700 Hospital Trust Twr.
Providence, RI 02903
Tel.: 401-274-9200

First National Bank of Boston*(Major Banking Relationship)*
P.O. Box 644,
Boston, MA 02102-0644
Tel.: 617-575-2900
Fax: 617-575-2549

Fleet National Bank*(Major Banking Relationship)*
125 Dupont Dr.
Providence, RI 02907-3178
Tel.: 401-278-5335

VICTORIA PACKING CORPORATION
443 E. 100th St.
Brooklyn, NY 11236
Tel.: 718-927-3000 **NY**
Fax: 718-649-7069
Year Founded: 1929
Approx.Sls.: $30,000,000
Emp.: 175
Import Export
Condiments, Specialty Foods, Spices
S.I.C.: 2035; 2099
Joseph Aquilina *(Chm. Bd.)*
Benjamin Aquilina *(Pres.)*
Gerald Aquilina *(V.P.-Personnel)*
Barry Gold *(Controller)*
Rosemarie Cardinale *(Dir.-Sls. Promo.)*
B. Savino *(Mgr.-Sls.)*

No. of Mfg. Plants/Facilities: 4
No. of U.S. Offices: 1

Outside Service Firm(s):

Bisectti Grassi*(Auditors)*
Brooklyn, NY

European American Bank*(Major Banking Relationship)*
Brooklyn, NY

VICTORIA STATION INCORPORATED
200 Broad St.
Stamford, CT 06901
Tel.: 203-967-4003 **CA**
Fax: 203-967-4229
Assets: $67,625,000
Liabilities: $47,683,000
Net Worth: $19,942,000
Approx.Sls.: $18,000,000
Emp.: 680
Fiscal Year-end: 9/30/91
11 Restaurants in 5 States
S.I.C.: 5812

Outside Service Firm(s):

Pillsbury, Madison & Sutro*(Legal Firm)*
225 Bush
San Francisco, CA 94104
Tel.: 415-983-1000

Victoria Station Incorporated—(Continued)

Operating Company:

Victoria Station Incorporated, A California Corp. **(1)**
Wood Island
Larkspur, CA 94939
Tel.: 415-461-4550 (100%)
S.I.C.: 5812

Subsidiaries:

Bonkers, Inc. **(1)**
Wood Island
Larkspur, CA 94939
Tel.: 415-461-4550
Restaurants
S.I.C.: 5812

Euston Station, Inc. **(1)**
Wood Island
Larkspur, CA 94939
Tel.: 415-461-4550
S.I.C.: 5812

Railhead Restaurants, Inc. **(1)**
Wood Island
Larkspur, CA 94939
Tel.: 415-461-4550
S.I.C.: 5812

Victoria Station of Arizona, Inc. **(1)**
Wood Island
Larkspur, CA 94939
Tel.: 415-461-4550
S.I.C.: 5812

Victoria Station of Atlanta, Inc. **(1)**
Wood Island
Larkspur, CA 94939
Tel.: 415-461-4550
S.I.C.: 5812

Victoria Station of Colorado, Inc. **(1)**
Wood Island
Larkspur, CA 94939
Tel.: 415-461-4550
S.I.C.: 5812

Victoria Station of Louisiana, Inc. **(1)**
Wood Island
Larkspur, CA 94939
Tel.: 415-461-4550
S.I.C.: 5812

Victoria Station of Virginia, Inc. **(1)**
Wood Island
Larkspur, CA 94939
Tel.: 415-461-4550
S.I.C.: 5812

Victoria Station of Washington, Inc. **(1)**
1880 Fairview E.
Seattle, WA 98102
Tel.: 206-323-5935 (100%)
S.I.C.: 5812

Victoria Station of Wisconsin, Inc. **(1)**
Wood Island
Larkspur, CA 94939
Tel.: 415-461-4550
S.I.C.: 5812

Affiliate:

Victoria Station of Texas, Inc. **(1)**
Wood Island
Larkspur, CA 94939
Tel.: 415-461-4550
S.I.C.: 5812

VICTORY FINANCIAL GROUP, INC.
3115 6th St.
Metairie, LA 70002
Tel.: 504-837-2230 **DE**
Fax: 504-522-0493
Approx.Assets: $523,543,834
Fiscal Year-end: 12/31/90
Life Insurance Holding Co.
S.I.C.: 6311; 6719
Louis J. Roussel, Jr. *(Chm. Bd., Pres. & Chief Exec. Officer)*

Principal(s):
Louis J. Roussel, Jr.

Computer Systems/Hardware:
Point Four

Outside Service Firm(s):

Self-Insured*(Group Insurer)*

Subsidiaries:

LifeSurance Corporation **(1)**
1447 Peachtree St., N.E.
Atlanta, GA 30309
Tel.: 404-892-8600 (57.8%)
Life Insurance
S.I.C.: 6311
Michael R. Kruger *(Pres.)*

Louisiana National Life Insurance Company **(1)**
1501 American Bank Bldg.
New Orleans, LA 70130
Tel.: 504-524-5321 (100%)
Holding Co.; Life Insurance
S.I.C.: 6311; 6719

Subsidiaries:

Guaranty Savings Insurance Company **(2)**
1501 American Bank Bldg.
New Orleans, LA 70130
Tel.: 504-524-5321 (100%)
S.I.C.: 6311

National Savings Life Insurance Company **(2)**
Hwy. 231 S., P.O. Box 1338
Murfreesboro, TN 37133
Tel.: 615-896-1502 (100%)
Approx.Sls.: $32,000,000
Emp.: 575
Life, Annuities, Accident & Health Insurance
S.I.C.: 6311; 6321
Donnie P. Hester *(Pres.)*
Charles D. Agnew *(V.P.-Pur. & Sec.)*
Don Behne *(V.P. & Treas.)*
Ray Gosnell *(V.P. & Mktg. Mgr.)*

Victory Life Insurance Company **(2)**
300 W. 8th Ave.
Topeka, KS 66603
Tel.: 913-357-6151 (100%)
S.I.C.: 6311
Craig F. Kammen *(Chm. Bd., Pres. & Chief Exec. Officer)*

Mutual Savings Life Insurance Company **(1)**
2801 Hwy. 31 S.
Decatur, AL 35601
Tel.: 205-552-7011 (56.3%)
Emp.: 1,050
Life, Accident & Health Insurance
S.I.C.: 6311; 6321
Louis J. Roussel, Jr. *(Chm. Bd. & Pres.)*
Benny L. Frady *(Exec. V.P.)*
Lotuce L. Hamm, Jr. *(Sr. V.P. & Treas.)*
Benjamin S. Gravolet *(V.P. & Sec.)*

Subsidiaries:

First Pyramid Life Insurance Company of America **(2)**
650 Shackleford Rd., Ste. 400
Little Rock, AR 72211
Tel.: 501-224-8900 (100%)
Emp.: 81
Life Insurance
S.I.C.: 6311
Archie R. Dykes *(Chm. Bd.)*
John A. Hartnedy *(Pres.)*
Charles Linklater *(Sr. V.P.-Admin.)*
Cleo Murphy *(Sr. V.P.-Mktg.)*
Harry Lapham *(V.P.-Fin. Services)*
Liz Oswald *(V.P.-Computer Services)*
Betty Wineland *(V.P.-Communications)*
Roger Viola *(Sec.)*

Mutual Savings Fire Insurance Company **(2)**
P.O. Box 2222
Decatur, AL 35602
Tel.: 205-552-7011 (100%)
Fire Insurance
S.I.C.: 6331

Southern United Life Insurance Company **(2)**
P.O. Box 2222
Decatur, AL 35602
Tel.: 205-552-7011 (100%)
Life Insurance
S.I.C.: 6311

Subsidiaries:

Southern United Fire Insurance Company **(3)**
P.O. Box 2222
Decatur, AL 35602
Tel.: 205-552-7011 (100%)
Fire Insurance
S.I.C.: 6331

SUL Corporation **(3)**
1500 American Bank Bldg.
New Orleans, LA 70130
Tel.: 504-524-0711 (100%)
Holding Co.
S.I.C.: 6712

Subsidiary:

Southern United Corporation **(4)**
1500 American Bank Bldg.
New Orleans, LA 70130
Tel.: 504-524-0711 (82.3%)
Life Insurance
S.I.C.: 6311

VICTORY MARKETS INC.
54 E. Main St.
Norwich, NY 13815
Tel.: 607-335-4711 **NY**
Fax: 607-335-4727
Assets: $172,845,000
Liabilities: $153,737,000
Net Worth: $19,108,000
Approx.Sls.: $500,000,000
Emp.: 5,000
Fiscal Year-end: 12/31/90
87 Retail Food Stores in NY & PA
S.I.C.: 5411; 2051; 5541; 6512
Aaron Malinsky *(Pres. & Chief Exec. Officer)*
Eugene B. Kulakosky *(Sr. V.P.-Grocery & Non-Food Buying)*
Donald A. Dosch *(V.P. & Corp. Controller)*
William Cushing *(V.P.-Deli/Bakery Opers.)*
Donald J. Hayes *(V P.-Video Opers. & Labor Control)*
Joseph V. Scotto *(V.P.-Produce Opers.)*
Patricia Philips *(Mgr.-Employee Rels.)*

Computer Systems/Hardware:
IBM 4381

Outside Service Firm(s):

KPMG Peat Marwick*(Auditors)*
Syracuse, NY

Willkie, Farr & Gallagher*(Legal Firm)*
One Citicorp Ctr., 153 E. 53rd St.
New York, NY 10022
Tel.: 212-935-8000

National Bank & Trust Co. of Norwich*(Major Banking Relationship)*
52 S. Broad St.
Norwich, NY 13815
Tel.: 607-334-2231

Operating Units:

Food King, Inc. **(1)**
54 E. Main St.
Norwich, NY 13815
Tel.: 607-335-4711 (100%)
Wholesale Franchisor
S.I.C.: 6794
Darryl R. Gregson *(Chief Oper. Officer)*

Great American Food Stores, Inc. **(1)**
54 E. Main St.
Norwich, NY 13815
Tel.: 607-335-4711 (100%)
Retail Food Chain
S.I.C.: 5411
Darryl R. Gregson *(Pres. & Chief Exec. Officer)*

Divisions:

Carl's Drug Company, Inc. **(1)**
P.O. Box 203, Success Drive
Rome, NY 13440
Tel.: 315-336-1080
Tod Bogan *(Pres.)*
Rich Hodaica *(Dir.-Adv.)*

Food King Independent Supermarkets **(1)**
54 E. Main St.
Norwich, NY 13815
Tel.: 607-355-4704
S.I.C.: 5411

Victory Discount Beverage Center **(1)**
54 E. Main St.
Norwich, NY 13815
Tel.: 607-355-4711
S.I.C.: 5411

Victory Video Inc. **(1)**
54 E. Main St.
Norwich, NY 13815
Tel.: 607-335-4711
Emp.: 500
Oper. & Franchisor of Video Rental Stores
S.I.C.: 6794; 7841
Darryl R. Gregson *(Pres. & Chief Exec. Officer)*

Village Markets **(1)**
54 E. Main St.
Norwich, NY 13815
Tel.: 607-335-4704
S.I.C.: 5411

U Pump 'Em **(1)**
54 E. Main St.
Norwich, NY 13815
Tel.: 607-335-4711 (100%)
Emp.: 45
Gasoline Stations
S.I.C.: 5541
Darryl R. Gregson *(Chief Oper. Officer)*

Affiliates:

Dunco Realty & Equip. Corp. **(1)**
54 E. Main St.
Norwich, NY 13815
Tel.: 607-335-4711 (100%)
Real Estate
S.I.C.: 6512
Darryl R. Gregson *(Chief Oper. Officer)*

Norwich Recycling Corp. **(1)**
Woods Corners
Norwich, NY 13815
Tel.: 607-335-4711 (100%)
Emp.: 30
Salvage of Containers
S.I.C.: 5093
Darryl R. Gregson *(Chief Oper. Officer)*

VIDEO PRODUCTS DISTRIBUTORS, INC.
6051 S. Watt Ave.
Sacramento, CA 95829
Tel.: 916-386-2220 **DE**
Fax: 916-386-9780
Year Founded: 1980
Sales Range: $100-499 Million
Emp.: 160
Wholesaler of Pre-recorded Videotapes & Accessories
S.I.C.: 7822
Robert Cummins *(Chm. Bd.)*
Tim Shannahan *(Pres. & Chief Exec. Officer)*
Robert Wittenberg *(Sr. V.P.-Sls., Mktg. & Pur.)*
Russ Frazier *(V.P.-Sls.)*
Hans Lange *(V.P.-Fin.)*
David Sedin *(Controller)*
Janie Fisher *(Dir.-Telecommunications)*
Jake Jacobs *(Dir.-Opers.)*
James Roberts *(Dir.-Mngmt. Information Systems)*
Shelley Heberle *(Mgr.-Mktg.)*
Celeste Rasmussen *(Personnel Admin.)*

Principal(s):
Tim Shannahan
The Vista Group

No. of U.S. Offices: 6

Computer Systems/Hardware:
DEC/VAX Cluster of an 8530/8300/785

Outside Service Firm(s):

Arthur Andersen & Co.*(Auditors)*
300 Capitol Mall
Sacramento, CA 95814

Nationwide*(Commercial Insurance Carrier)*
Sacramento, CA

Health Plan of America*(Group Insurer)*
Sacramento, CA

Hill, Wynne, Troop & Meisinger*(Legal Firm)*
10940 Wilshire Blvd.
Los Angeles, CA 90024
Tel.: 310-824-7000
Fax: 310-443-7599

Union Bank*(Major Banking Relationship)*
Sacramento, CA

Pension Specialists*(Pension Manager)*
Rancho Cordora, CA

VIDICOM, L.D. BEVAN COMPANY, INC.
1125 Business Center Circle
Thousand Oaks, CA 91320
Tel.: 805-375-3750
Tel.: 800-843-4266 **CA**
Fax: 805-375-2777
Year Founded: 1976
Sales Range: $10-19 Million
Emp.: 50
Export
Vidicom: Teleconferencing Systems Integration, Design, Manufacturing, Installation & Support
S.I.C.: 3669
L. Darrell Bevan *(Pres. & Chief Exec. Officer)*
Phillip L. Gantt *(Dir.-Sls. & Mktg.)*
Kelly Albinger *(Mgr.-Mktg. Services)*
Marc Benrey *(Mgr.-Intl. Sls.)*
Jeff Kagan *(Mgr.-Pur.)*
Brett J. Lukes *(Mgr.-Materials)*
William C. Notthoff *(Gen. Mgr.)*
Phyllis A. White *(Office Mgr.)*
Principal(s):
L. Darrell Bevan
Patricia F. Bevan

No. of Mfg. Plants/Facilities: 1
No. of U.S. Offices: 6
No. of Foreign Offices: 1

Outside Service Firm(s):

Coopers & Lybrand*(Auditors)*
Thousand Oaks, CA

VIENNA SAUSAGE MFG. CO.
2501 N. Damen
Chicago, IL 60647
Tel.: 312-278-7800 **IL**
Year Founded: 1893
Assets: $22,600,000
Net Worth: $22,600,000
Approx.Sls.: $100,000,000
Emp.: 750
Fiscal Year-end: 4/29/91
Food Processor & Distributor Of Delicatessen, Beef, Desserts & Pickles
S.I.C.: 2013; 2035; 5147
James Eisenberg *(Chm. Bd. & Chief Exec. Officer)*
James W. Bodman *(Pres. & Chief Oper. Officer)*
Thomas Pierce *(Exec. V.P.)*
Bill Hamati *(Sr. V.P.-Branch Sls.)*
George Sklenicka *(Sr. V.P.-Admin. & Controller)*
Dennis Wilson *(Sr. V.P.-Opers.)*
Terry Billings *(V.P.-Data Processing)*
Jamie Eisenberg *(V.P.-Human Resources)*
Bill Magri *(V.P.-Sls. Los Angeles Div.)*
Tom McGlade *(V.P.-Chicagoland Sls.)*
James McGlone *(V.P.-Acctg.)*
Carl Morgan *(V.P.-Credit)*
Richard Mueller *(V.P.-Engrng.)*
Donna Overacker *(V.P.-Pur.)*
Robert Schwartz *(V.P.-Natl. Sls.)*
Jeff Walser *(V.P.-Clearwater Div.)*

No. of Mfg. Plants/Facilities: 20
No. of U.S. Offices: 12
No. of Foreign Offices: 2

Computer Systems/Hardware:
IBM System 38

Outside Service Firm(s):

Price Waterhouse*(Auditors)*
200 E. Randolph
Chicago, IL 60601
Tel.: 312-565-1500

Connecticut General Life Insurance Co.*(Group Insurer)*
P.O. Box 2975,
Hartford, CT 06104
Tel.: 203-726-6000

Aaron, Schimberg, Hess, Rusnak, Deutsch & Gilbert*(Legal Firm)*
55 W. Monroe St.
Chicago, IL 60603
Tel.: 312-726-5700

First National Bank of Chicago*(Pension Manager)*
One First National Plaza
Chicago, IL 60670
Tel.: 312-732-9781
Tel.: 312-732-4050
Fax: 312-732-4840
Fax: 312-732-3055

Subsidiaries:

Big Foot Cattle Co. **(1)**
11511 Rte. 14
Harvard, IL 60033
Tel.: 815-943-7906
Abattoir
S.I.C.: 2011
Hy Ramis *(Pres.)*

Bistro Soups, Ltd. **(1)**
2501 N. Damen
Chicago, IL 60647
Tel.: 312-278-7800
S.I.C.: 2032

Chipico Pickles **(1)**
2501 N. Damen
Chicago, IL 60647
Tel.: 312-278-7800
Emp.: 650
Processing & Distr. Beef Prods. & Other Specialty Foods
S.I.C.: 2013; 5147
James Bodman *(Pres.)*
Howard Schnepper *(Sls. & Mktg. Mgr.)*

Pie Piper Products, Ltd. **(1)**
2501 N. Damen
Chicago, IL 60647
Tel.: 312-278-7800
Emp.: 40
Baking of Deli Style Food Prods.
S.I.C.: 2051
Bob Johnston *(Pres.)*

Sula Supply **(1)**
837 N. California
Chicago, IL 60622
Tel.: 312-278-7711
Mfr. Paper Supplies
S.I.C.: 2675; 2678
John Zigmond *(Pres.)*

Vienna Beef, Ltd. **(1)**
2501 N. Damen
Chicago, IL 60647
Tel.: 312-278-7800

VIKING GRAPHICS
4027 N. Kedzie Ave.
Chicago, IL 60618
Tel.: 312-588-4300
Fax: 312-588-7453
Year Founded: 1966
Approx.Sls.: $17,500,000
Emp.: 155
Fiscal Year-end: 6/30/90
Prepress Color Communications Services; Color Separator; Electronic Color Imaging
S.I.C.: 7336; 2796
Warren Hanssen *(Pres.)*
Bruce Hanssen *(Exec. V.P. & Gen. Mgr.)*
Jerry Cacciatore *(Production Mgr.)*

Division:

Vectron Datagraphics **(1)**
9815 W. Foster Ave.
Schiller Park, IL 60176
Tel.: 708-678-1234
Fax: 708-678-8318
S.I.C.: 2796

Subsidiary:

Viking Color Corporation **(1)**
742 Ponce De Leon Place, N.E.
Atlanta, GA 30306
Tel.: 404-875-7821
Fax: 404-875-1553
S.I.C.: 2796
Ron Fletcher *(Gen. Mgr.)*

VIKING RANGE CORP.
111 Front St.
Greenwood, MS 38930
Mailing Address:
P.O. Drawer 956,
Greenwood, MS 38930
Tel.: 601-455-1200 **MS**
Fax: 601-453-7939
Year Founded: 1984
Sales Range: $10-19 Million
Emp.: 110
Export
Manufacture Gas Cooking Stoves
S.I.C.: 3631
Fred Carl, Jr. *(Chm. Bd., Pres. & Chief Exec. Officer)*
Listor Durden *(V.P.-Mktg. & Sls.)*
Joel Ferriss *(V.P.-Fin.)*
Jim Hurley *(V.P.-Engrng.)*
Tawana Thompson *(V.P.-Opers.)*
John R. Helms, Jr. *(Dir.-Mktg.)*
Dale Persons *(Mgr.-Natl. Sls.)*

No. of Mfg. Plants/Facilities: 1
No. of U.S. Offices: 1

Computer Systems/Hardware:
IBM Compatible

Outside Service Firm(s):

Deloitte & Touche*(Auditors)*
Jackson, MS

Gerald & Brand*(Legal Firm)*
Jackson, MS

VIKING YACHT CO.
Rte. #9
New Gretna, NJ 08224
Tel.: 609-296-6000 **NJ**
Fax: 609-296-3956
Year Founded: 1964
Approx.Sls.: $60,000,000
Emp.: 500
Export
Mfr. Pleasure Yachts
S.I.C.: 3732; 5091
Robert T. Healey *(Chm. Bd.)*
William J. Healey *(Pres. & Chief Exec. Officer)*
Gerard Straub *(Exec. V.P.)*
Thomas S. Carroll *(Exec. V.P.)*
Kathy MacCausland *(Adv. Mgr.)*
Principal(s):
Robert T. Healey
William J. Healey

No. of Mfg. Plants/Facilities: 1
No. of U.S. Offices: 1
No. of Foreign Offices: 1

Outside Service Firm(s):

Price Waterhouse*(Auditors)*
30 S. 17th St.
Philadelphia, PA 19103
Tel.: 215-665-9500

Deutsche Credit Corporation*(Major Banking Relationship)*
2333 Waukegan Rd.
Deerfield, IL 60015
Tel.: 708-948-7272
Fax: 708-948-5088

VILE-GOLLER, FINE ART PRINTING & LITHOGRAPHY
101 Greystone
Kansas City, KS 66103
Tel.: 913-342-1393 **MO**
Fax: 913-621-4856
Approx.Sls.: $21,000,000
Emp.: 200
Commercial Printing & Lithography
S.I.C.: 2752
Joel D. Vile *(Chm. Bd. & Pres.)*
Joe Fagan *(V.P.-Sls.)*
Randy Umscheid *(V.P.-Fin.)*
Lyle Van Vieet *(V.P.-Mfg.)*
Bella Vile *(Sec.)*

Outside Service Firm(s):

DeWitt & Zeldin*(Legal Firm)*
Kansas City, MO

Security Bank*(Major Banking Relationship)*
Kansas City, MO

VILLAGE CAR COMPANY
(d/b/a Bean & Conquest)
40-44 Summer St.
Bangor, ME 04401
Tel.: 207-945-9401
Fax: 207-945-0065
Approx.Sls.: $28,000,000
Emp.: 55
Chevrolet Dealership
S.I.C.: 5511; 7513
John E. Quirk *(Pres. & Chief Exec. Officer)*
Bill Deering *(Mgr.-Sls.)*

Computer Systems/Hardware:
TeleVideo

Outside Service Firm(s):

Rudman & Winchell*(Legal Firm)*
84 Harlow St.
Bangor, ME 04401
Tel.: 207-947-4501

VILLAGE FORD INC.
23535 Michigan Ave.
Dearborn, MI 48124
Tel.: 313-565-3900 **DE**
Approx.Sls.: $49,000,000
Emp.: 126
Automobile Dealership
S.I.C.: 5511
James Seavitt *(Pres.)*
Dipak Shah *(Sec. & Treas.)*
Chuck Brainard *(Mgr.-Sls.)*

VILLAUME INDUSTRIES, INC.
2926 Lone Oak Circle
Saint Paul, MN 55121
Tel.: 612-454-3610
Tel.: 800-488-3610 **MN**
Fax: 612-454-8556
Fax: 612-454-8123
Year Founded: 1882
Assets: $12,000,000
Liabilities: $8,000,000
Net Worth: $4,000,000
Sales Range: $10-19 Million
Emp.: 160
Fiscal Year-end: 10/31/91
Export
Industrial Wood Products; Wood Fuel Pellets, Wood Boxes, Crates, Trusses; Sawmill Products, Lumber & Chips; Building Components & Specialty Products
S.I.C.: 2439; 2441; 2448; 2449; 2452; 2499
Robert M. Linsmayer *(Chm. Bd.)*

Villaume Industries, Inc.—(Continued)

J. Nicholas Linsmayer *(Pres.)*
James A. Luzum *(Chief Fin. Officer, Treas. & Controller)*
C.J. McMahon *(Sr. V.P.)*
Isaac Ganz *(V.P.)*
Charles E. Meyerding *(Sec.)*
Dan O'Brien *(Gen. Counsel)*

No. of Mfg. Plants/Facilities: 3
No. of U.S. Offices: 2

Computer Systems/Hardware:
IBM

Outside Service Firm(s):

Sands, Lee & Anderson*(Auditors)*
St. Paul, MN

Doherty, Rumble & Butler*(Legal Firm)*
2800 Minnesota World Trade Center
St. Paul, MN 55101-4999
Tel.: 612-291-9333

American National Bank & Trust of St. Paul*(Major Banking Relationship)*
Fifth & Minnesota Streets
St. Paul, MN 55101
Tel.: 612-298-6000

Subsidiary:

Valley Forest Resources Co. **(1)**
P.O. Box 27,
Marcell, MN 56657
Tel.: 612-454-3610
Tel.: 800-488-3610
Emp.: 120
Manufacture Fuel Pellets & Wood Products
S.I.C.: 3482
F.M. Hovarter *(V.P.)*
Lawrence Paulson *(Chief Fin. Officer)*
John Fisher *(Dir.-Sls.)*

VILLAZON COMPANY INC.
3104 N. Armenia Ave.
Tampa, FL 33607
Mailing Address:
P.O. Box 22625
Tampa, FL 33622
Tel.: 813-879-2291
Fax: 813-878-2446
Approx.Sls.: $18,000,000
Emp.: 250
Fiscal Year-end: 12/31/90
Cigar Mfrs.; Bances, Hoyo de Monterrey Punch
S.I.C.: 2121
Frank Llaneza *(Pres.)*
Sherwin Seltzer *(V.P.-Gen. Sls. Mgr., Adv. Mgr., Sls. Promo. Mgr. & Pub. Rels.)*
C. Gonzalez *(Sec., Treas. & Pur. Agent)*

VILTER MANUFACTURING CORPORATION
2217 S. First St.
Milwaukee, WI 53207
Tel.: 414-744-0111 **WI**
Telex: 201325
Fax: 414-744-3483
Year Founded: 1867
Approx.Sls.: $40,000,000
Emp.: 350
Fiscal Year-end: 12/31/91

Export
Industrial Refrigeration, Heat Exchange & Air Conditioning Equipment
S.I.C.: 5078; 3585
A.A. Silverman *(Chm. Bd., Pres. & Chief Exec. Officer)*
R.A. Hall *(V.P.-Sls. & Gen. Mgr.)*
P.G. Szymaszek *(Exec. V.P.-Engrng.)*
E. Husmann *(Dir.-Personnel)*
Frank Vanoss *(Dir.-Pur.)*
Mark Richfield *(Asst. Dir.-Mktg.)*
D. Collodel *(Export Mgr.)*

Subsidiaries:

Filbert Corp. **(1)**
251 Altamonte Commerce Blvd., Ste. #1410
Altamonte Springs, FL 32714
Tel.: 407-862-1011 (100%)
Sales & Installation of Industrial Refrigeration, Air Conditioning & Dairy Equipment
S.I.C.: 5078
Ken Johnson *(Gen. Mgr.)*

Filbert Corp. (Main Office) **(1)**
7218 N.W. 56th St.
Miami, FL 33166
Tel.: 305-884-1212 (100%)
Fax: 305-884-2299
Export
Sales & Installation of Industrial Refrigeration, Air Conditioning & Dairy Equipment
S.I.C.: 5078

Gebhardt Industrial Refrigeration, Inc. **(1)**
3625 W. Elm St.
Milwaukee, WI 53209
Tel.: 414-352-2800
Fax: 414-352-8033
Sale of Refrigeration & Air Condition Equipment
S.I.C.: 5078
Tom Collins *(Gen. Mgr.)*

Vilter Export Corp. **(1)**
2217 S. First St.
Milwaukee, WI 53207
Tel.: 414-744-0111 (100%)
Sale of Industrial & Air Conditioning Equipment Outside U.S.
S.I.C.: 3585
Dino Collodel *(Chief Oper. Officer)*

VINCENNES STEEL CORP.
2007 Oliphant Dr.
Vincennes, IN 47591
Tel.: 812-882-4550
Approx.Sls.: $12,000,000
Emp.: 148
Steel Fabrication
S.I.C.: 3441
Joseph P. Day *(Pres.)*

VINCENT FOOD INDUSTRIES, INC.
135 S. LaSalle St.
Chicago, IL 60603
Tel.: 312-782-1838 **DE**
Fax: 312-782-1841
Year Founded: 1956
Approx.Sls.: $12,000,000
Emp.: 100
Holding Company for Manufacturers of Specialty Food Products
S.I.C.: 2034; 2035; 2087; 7389; 6719
Burton J. Vincent *(Chm. Bd, Pres. & Chief Exec. Officer)*
Alan J. Marek *(Treas. & Chief Fin. Officer)*
John K. O'Connor *(Sec.)*
Patricia L. Tujo *(Asst. Corp. Sec.)*

Outside Service Firm(s):

Ernst & Young*(Auditors)*
233 S. Wacker Dr.
Chicago, IL 60606
Tel.: 312-368-1800
Fax: 312-645-3095

Lord, Bissell & Brook*(Legal Firm)*
115 S. LaSalle St.
Chicago, IL 60603
Tel.: 312-443-0700

Divisions:

Dale Foods **(1)**
1501 N. 31st Ave.
Melrose Park, IL 65801
Tel.: 312-343-8997 (100%)
Mfr. Specialty Foods Primarily Dry Soups & Bases, Desserts, Sauces & Entree Mixes, Fruit Drink Concentrates, Contact Packaging & Formulation
S.I.C.: 2034; 2035; 2087; 7389
James J. Piccione *(Pres.)*

J.L. DeGraffenreid & Sons, Inc. **(1)**
1301 W. Webster
Springfield, MO 65801
Tel.: 314-862-9411 (100%)
Emp.: 35
Mfr. Pickles & Relishes for Food Service Indus.
S.I.C.: 2035
Jonathan Gallo *(Pres.)*

Gage Food Products Company **(1)**
1501 N. 31st Ave.
Melrose Park, IL 60160
Tel.: 312-626-3171 (100%)
Emp.: 50
Specialty Food Distr. to Schools, Health Care Indus., Summer Camps, State & County Facilities
S.I.C.: 2023; 2033; 2034; 2043; 2099
James J. Piccione *(Pres.)*

VINDICATOR CORPORATION
3001 Beecave Rd.
Austin, TX 78746
Tel.: 512-328-8080
Fax: 512-314-1270
Approx.Sls.: $10,000,000
Mfr. Security Systems
S.I.C.: 3661
Jay G. Ford *(Pres.)*
James Summerlin *(V.P.-Sls.)*
William Regan *(Controller)*

VINTNERS INTERNATIONAL COMPANY, INC.
P.O. Box 780
Gonzales, CA 93926
Tel.: 408-675-2481
Fax: 408-675-2611
Year Founded: 1987
Approx.Sls.: $260,000,000
Emp.: 850
Fiscal Year-end: 7/31/90
Sales & Distr. of Wines & Champagne
S.I.C.: 5182
Paul M. Schlem *(Chm. Bd.)*
Frank Jerant *(Pres.)*
Michael Gerdes *(Exec. V.P. & Chief Fin. Officer)*

VINYL THERM, INC.
321 W. 83rd St.
Bloomington, MN 55420
Tel.: 612-884-4329 **MN**
Fax: 612-884-1231
Assets: $51,000,000
Liabilities: $35,000,000
Net Worth: $16,000,000
Sales Range: $20-39 Million
Emp.: 150
Fiscal Year-end: 12/31/88
Wood Windows
S.I.C.: 2431
Bruce K. Hoyt *(Chm. Bd.)*
Steven B. Hoyt *(Pres.)*
Mitch Speicher *(Chief Fin. Officer)*
Brad Hoyt *(Mgr.-Plng. & Devel.)*
Denise Hoyt *(Dir.-Mngmt. Information Systems)*

Principal(s):
Bruce K. Hoyt
Steven B. Hoyt

No. of Mfg. Plants/Facilities: 1
No. of U.S. Offices: 1

Computer Systems/Hardware:
IBM System 36

Outside Service Firm(s):

Boulay, Heutmaker, Zibell & Co.*(Auditors)*
Edina, MN

Travelers Insurance Co.*(Group Insurer)*
1 Tower Square
Hartford, CT 06183-2492
Tel.: 203-277-4542
Fax: 203-277-5038

Popham, Haik, Schnobrich Ltd.*(Legal Firm)*
Minneapolis, MN

First Trust Company, Inc.*(Pension Manager)*
First Trust Center, 180 E. Fifth St.
St. Paul, MN 55164

Subsidiaries:

The Hoyt Company **(1)**
8300 Grand Ave. S.
Bloomington, MN 55420
Tel.: 612-884-4338
Fax: 612-884-1231
Assets: $51,000,000
Liabilities: $35,000,000
Net Worth: $16,000,000
Sales Range: $20-39 Million
Emp.: 150
Fiscal Year-end: 12/31/88
Window Manufacturer; Commericial & Industrial Real Estate Development
S.I.C.: 2431; 6552
Bruce K. Hoyt *(Chief Oper. Officer)*
Mitch Speicher *(Chief Fin. Officer)*

Hoyt Construction **(1)**
8300 Grand Ave., S.
Bloomington, MN 55420
Tel.: 612-292-0525
S.I.C.: 6552
Bruce K. Hoyt *(Chief Oper. Officer)*

Hoyt Development **(1)**
13400 15th Ave., Suite F
Plymouth, MN 55441
Tel.: 612-941-8200
S.I.C.: 6552
Brad Hoyt *(Chief Oper. Officer)*

HARRY VIOLA ADVERTISING

125 Chubb Ave.
Lyndhurst, NJ 07071
Tel.: 201-460-3828
Year Founded: 1972
Approx.Billings: $12,000,000
Emp.: 11
Advertising Agency
S.I.C.: 7311
Harry Viola *(Pres.)*
Steven Tonelli *(Computer Graphics)*

VIRGINIA DEPARTMENT OF ECONOMIC DEVELOPMENT TOURISM DEVELOPMENT GROUP
1021 E. Cary St.
Richmond, VA 23219
Tel.: 804-786-2051
Fax: 804-786-1919
Approx.Rev.: $6,900,000,000
Emp.: 70
Promotes Tourism to Virginia
S.I.C.: 7389
Patrick McMahon *(Dir.)*
David Sheatsley *(Dir.-Adv. & Res.)*
Martha Steger *(Dir.-Pub. Rels.)*

VIRGINIA HOT SPRINGS, INC.
U.S. Rte. 220
Hot Springs, VA 24445
Tel.: 703-839-5500
Fax: 703-839-7656
Year Founded: 1902
Approx.Sls.: $23,866,000
Emp.: 1,000
Resort & Baths
S.I.C.: 7011; 7999
Daniel H.H. Ingalls, Sr. *(Chm. Bd.)*
Daniel H.H. Ingalls, Jr. *(Pres.)*
Joseph F. Tuning *(V.P.-Fin.)*
Tim Bugas *(Dir.-Sls.)*
Steve Harrison *(Resident Mgr.)*
Brenda Hite *(Personnel Mgr.)*
Harvey Hackett *(Dir.-Personnel)*
John M. Gazzola, Jr. *(Pub. Rels. Mgr.)*

VIRGINIA METAL INDUSTRIES, INC.
12314 Old Gordonsville Rd.
Orange, VA 22960
Mailing Address:
P.O. Box 709,
Orange, VA 22960
Tel.: 703-672-2800
Tel.: 800-553-9255
Fax: 703-672-3158
Year Founded: 1976
Approx.Sls.: $12,000,000
Emp.: 150
Fiscal Year-end: 12/31/90
Export
Mfr. of Movable Metal Partitions
S.I.C.: 2542; 3446
James W. McGlothlen *(Chm. Bd.)*
David P. Hoyt *(Pres. & Chief Exec. Officer)*
John N. Gianakos *(V.P.-Opers. & Controller)*
John C. Paisley *(V.P.-Sls.)*
Wayne L. Bell *(V.P. & Sec.)*
Lois A. Clarke *(Treas.)*
Peggie Thompson *(Dir.-Personnel & Adv.)*
Carolyn L. Sharp *(Dir.-Corp. Plng.)*

Computer Systems/Hardware:
IBM

VIRGINIA STATE LOTTERY DEPARTMENT
2201 W. Broad St.
Richmond, VA 23220
Mailing Address:
P.O. Box 4689,
Richmond, VA 23220
Tel.: 804-367-9130
Tel.: 800-243-5825
Fax: 804-367-9261
Year Founded: 1988
Approx.Sls.: $725,000,000
Emp.: 292
Fiscal Year-end: 7/ 1/90
State Lottery
S.I.C.: 7999
Kenneth W. Thorson *(Dir.)*
Larry J. Gray, Jr. *(Dir.-Deputy)*
James L. Nulph *(Dir.-Mktg.)*
Brent Pennington *(Dir.-Sls.)*
Paula Otto *(Dir.-Pub. Info.)*
Dennis Shaw *(Dir.-Security)*
Patricia Taylor *(Dir.-Personnel)*
Lou Stafford *(Internal Audit)*
Sean Athey *(Adv. Specialist)*

Computer Systems/Hardware:
IBM AS400

THE VIRTUAL GROUP
2950 Waterview Dr.
Rochester Hills, MI 48309
Tel.: 313-853-6000
Year Founded: 1983
Sales Range: $10-19 Million
Emp.: 70
Computer Rebuilding, Sales & Service
S.I.C.: 5045; 7378
Michael Dolik *(Pres.)*
D. Mark Ratliff *(V.P.)*

VISA U.S.A. INC.
3155 Clearview Way
San Mateo, CA 94402
Mailing Address:
P.O. Box 8999,
San Francisco, CA 94128
Tel.: 415-570-3200
Fax: 415-378-8100
Year Founded: 1970
Approx.Sls.: $85,000,000,000
Emp.: 800
Fiscal Year-end: 9/30/90
Import Export
Visa Payment Cards & Travelers Cheques & Travel Vouchers
S.I.C.: 6153
H. Robert Heller *(Pres.)*
Charles T. Russell *(Chief Exec. Officer)*
Brad Morgan *(Exec. V.P.-Mktg.)*
Roger L. Pierce *(Exec. V.P.)*
Wesley C. Tallman *(Exec. V.P.)*
John Van Aken *(Sr. V.P.-Human Resources)*
John H. Bennett *(Sr. V.P.-Mktg.)*
Rob Robins *(Sr. V.P.)*
Janet L. Soderstrom *(Sr. V.P.-Adv. & Promo.)*
David L. Roberts *(Dir.-Mktg. Admin.)*
David Brancoli *(Dir.-Pub. Rels.)*
Liz Silver *(Dir.-Adv.)*

VISIBLE CHANGES
1303 Campbell Rd.
Houston, TX 77055
Tel.: 713-984-8800
Fax: 713-984-2632
Year Founded: 1977
Approx.Sls.: $25,000,000
Emp.: 420
Fiscal Year-end: 6/30/90
Chain of Hair Cutting Salons
S.I.C.: 7231
John McCormack *(Chm. Bd.)*
Maryanne McCormack *(Pres.)*
Esther Wu *(Chief Fin. Officer, Treas. & Controller)*
Wilhelmina Castillo *(Chief Admin. Officer)*
Sandi Morton *(V.P.-Opers.)*
Sharon Ensminger *(Dir.-Pur.)*
Linda Jianto *(Sr. Dir.-Prog.)*

Computer Systems/Hardware:
IBM

Outside Service Firm(s):

Stoval, Grandy & Whatley*(Auditors)*
Fort Worth, TX

Allstate Insurance*(Group Insurer)*
Northbrook, IL

Great-West Life Assurance Co.*(Group Insurer)*
8505 East Orchard Rd.
Englewood, CO 8011
Tel.: 800-537-2033

Bear Stearns & Co.*(Investment Banker)*
245 Park Ave.
New York, NY 10167

Texas Commerce Bank*(Major Banking Relationship)*
600 Travis Street, Suite 1150
Houston, TX 77002
Tel.: 713-236-4865

Subsidiaries:

VC Management Services **(1)**
1303 Campbell Rd.
Houston, TX 77055
Tel.: 713-984-8800

Visible Changes of Austin **(1)**
6001 Airport
Austin, TX 78752
Tel.: 512-467-2102
Hair Styling
S.I.C.: 7231

Visible Changes of Texas **(1)**
7400 San Pedro
San Antonio, TX 78216
Tel.: 210-349-1581
Hair Styling
S.I.C.: 7231

VISIRECORD SYSTEMS, INC.
345 Wilson Ave.
South Norwalk, CT 06854
Mailing Address:
P.O. Box 568
South Norwalk, CT 06856
Tel.: 203-853-2722
Telecopier: 203-854-0655
Year Founded: 1987
Sales Range: $10-19 Million
Emp.: 30
Mfr. VisiRecord Business Systems & Equipment, Filing Equipment & Accessories
S.I.C.: 2522
R. Stumpf *(Gen. Mgr.)*

Outside Service Firm(s):

R. DeTenflis*(Auditors)*
Norwalk, CT

VITA FOOD PRODUCTS, INC.
2222 W. Lake St.
Chicago, IL 60612
Tel.: 312-738-4500 **IL**
Fax: 312-738-3215
Year Founded: 1928
Approx.Sls.: $30,000,000
Emp.: 150
Fiscal Year-end: 8/31/90
Export
Processors of Herring & Smoked-Fish Products
S.I.C.: 2091
Stephen Rubin *(Pres.)*
Clark Feldman *(Exec. V.P.)*
Robert Ramirez *(Controller)*
Louis Lyrla *(Dir.-Pur.)*
Ken Molfese *(Mgr.-Quality Control)*

Computer Systems/Hardware:
Unisys

Outside Service Firm(s):

Grant Thornton*(Auditors)*
700 One Prudential Plaza, 130 East Randolph St.
Chicago, IL 60601
Tel.: 312-856-0200
Fax: 312-565-4719

New England Mutual Life Insurance Co.*(Group Insurer)*
New York, NY

VITA-MILK DAIRY, INC.
427 N.E. 72nd St.
Seattle, WA 98115
Tel.: 206-524-7070 **WA**
Fax: 206-522-0844
Year Founded: 1937
Approx.Sls.: $44,000,000
Emp.: 95
Fiscal Year-end: 9/30/91
Mfr. Dairy Products
S.I.C.: 2026
Edwin A. Teel *(Chm. Bd.)*
E. Gerald Teel *(Pres. & Chief Oper. Officer)*
Daryl L. Vander Pol *(V.P., Treas. & Sec.)*

Computer Systems/Hardware:
IBM AS400

Outside Service Firm(s):

Bowen Weeks & Company*(Auditors)*
Seattle, WA

Karr Tuttle & Koch*(Legal Firm)*
Seattle, WA

Key Bank*(Major Banking Relationship)*
Seattle, WA

VITATECH INTERNATIONAL, INC.
2832 Dow Ave.
Tustin, CA 92680
Tel.: 714-832-9700
Fax: 714-731-8482
Approx.Sls.: $11,000,000
Emp.: 54
Vitamin Preparations
S.I.C.: 2834
Thomas T. Tierney *(Pres.)*
Dr. Michael F. Nassar *(V.P.)*
Elizabeth C. Tierney *(V.P.)*
Janet Peterson *(Controller)*
Candace M. Mathews *(Dir.-Pur.)*

Outside Service Firm(s):

Little & Gray*(Auditors)*
Irvine, CA

C.J. VITNER & CO., INC.
4202 W. 45th St.
Chicago, IL 60632
Tel.: 312-523-7900
Fax: 312-523-9143
Year Founded: 1928
Approx.Sls.: $25,000,000
Emp.: 285
Fiscal Year-end: 9/30/90
Mfr. Snack Products
S.I.C.: 5149; 2096
James C. Vitner *(Chm. Bd.)*
William A. Vitner *(Pres.)*
Robert Anderson *(V.P.-Pur. Opers.)*
Edward Cepa *(V.P.-Opers.)*
Terry M. Cook *(V.P.-Sls.)*
Tom Slawson *(V.P.-Mktg.)*
Richard Loritz *(Gen. Counsel)*
Patrick Hudgin *(Controller)*

Computer Systems/Hardware:
Basic IV/Norand

Vitt Media International, Inc
Media Planning and Buying Professionals

VITT MEDIA INTERNATIONAL, INC.
1114 Ave. of the Americas
New York, NY 10036
Tel.: 212-921-0500
Fax: 212-575-4709
Year Founded: 1969
Approx.Billings: $441,650,000
Emp.: 131
Fiscal Year-end: 8/31/89
Media Planning, Buying, Syndication; Marketing & Media Research
S.I.C.: 7319; 8732
Sam B. Vitt *(Chm. Emeritus)*
Roy A. Muro *(Chm. & Chief Exec. Officer)*
Robert Calandruccio *(Pres. & Chief Oper. Officer)*
E.T. Reynolds *(Pres.-Vitt/Reynolds, Toronto)*
Max Buck *(Exec. V.P.)*
Robert Heide *(Exec. V.P.)*
David R. Williams *(Exec. V.P., Mngmt. Rep. & Pres.-David R. Williams, Inc.)*
Alan Hyman *(Sr. V.P., Los Angeles)*
John Power *(Sr. V.P., Mngmt. Rep. & Communications Mgr.)*
John Sharman *(Sr. V.P.)*
Ronald Shapiro *(Sr. V.P., Comptroller)*
Adriaen Ito *(Grp. V.P.)*
Audrey Blauner *(V.P., Dir. Office Services)*
Delana Browner *(V.P., Dir. Computer Opers.)*
Ruth Koehler *(V.P., Sr. Assoc.)*
Kenny Veale *(V.P., Mgr. Fin. Services)*
Yolande Vicari *(V.P., Dir. Quality Control)*
Diane Chan *(V.P.)*
Carole Edwards *(V.P.)*
Mike Lopez *(V.P.)*
Holly Wexler *(V.P.)*
Christine Barros *(Assoc. V.P.)*
Adam Batt *(Assoc. V.P.)*
Robert Ekizian *(Assoc. V.P.)*
Barbara Heinrichs *(Assoc. V.P.)*
Stu Marcus *(Assoc. V.P.)*
Judy Merrifield *(Assoc. V.P.)*
Carole Richman *(Assoc. V.P.)*
Kathy Whalen *(Assoc. V.P.)*
Theresa Whalen *(Assoc. V.P.)*

Vitt Media International, Inc.—(Continued)

John J. Cooper *(Sr. Assoc.)*
H. Kaplan *(Sr. Assoc., Corp.)*
E. Robbins *(Sr. Assoc., Corp.)*
H. Baldwin *(Reg. Dir.-St. Paul, MN)*
J.A. Beaton *(Reg. Dir.-PR & Virgin Islands)*
Robert Cress *(Reg. Dir.)*
Carmine Iorio *(Reg. Dir.-Washington, DC)*
Robert Morin *(Reg. Dir.-Midwest)*
H. Land *(Dir., Plng.)*
Roy A. Muro *(Chm.)*
Max Buck *(Exec. V.P.)*
John Sharman *(Sr. V.P.)*
Delana Browner *(Assoc. V.P., Dir. Computer Opers.)*
Jacqueline Hector *(Data Processing Mgr.)*
Ronald Shapiro *(Sr. V.P., Comptroller)*
Yolande Vicari *(V.P., Dir. Quality Control)*
Kenny Veale *(V.P., Mgr. Financial Services)*
Harry Murcott *(Grp. V.P.)*
Robert Calandruccio *(Pres.)*
Harry Murcott *(Grp. V.P.)*

No. of U.S. Offices: 2
No. of Foreign Offices: 1

Computer Systems/Hardware:
IBM PC; Sperry PC; EXXON 500; Vydec

Outside Service Firm(s):

Ernst & Young*(Auditors)*
787 Seventh Ave.
New York, NY 10019
Tel.: 212-773-1243

Union Mutual Life Insurance Co.*(Commercial Insurance Carrier)*
Portland, ME

Hall, Dickler, Lawler, Kent & Friedman*(Legal Firm)*
460 Park Ave.
New York, NY 10017
Tel.: 212-838-4600

Skadden, Arps, Slate, Meagher & Flom*(Legal Firm)*
913 Third Ave.
New York, NY 10022
Tel.: 212-371-6000

Chemical Banking Corp.*(Major Banking Relationship)*
277 Park Ave.
New York, NY 10041
Tel.: 212-310-6407
Fax: 212-310-4526

Noble Lowndes*(Pension Manager)*
East Orange, NJ

Branches:

Advertiming Inc. **(1)**
85 Thorndike St.
Arlington, MA 02174
Tel.: 617-371-1902
Tel.: 212-221-6541
Fred Ward *(Pres.)*
Cynthia Poe *(Exec. V.P.)*
John Power *(Grp. V.P.)*

Vitt Media Direct **(1)**
1114 Ave. of the Americas
New York, NY 10036
Tel.: 212-921-0500
Fax: 212-768-0049
Sheldon Kawer *(Exec. V.P.)*
Robert Heide *(Exec. V.P.)*
Anthony Cerrato *(Sr. V.P.)*
Joseph D'Alto *(Grp. V.P.)*

Vitt Media International, Inc. - Los Angeles **(1)**
12400 Wilshire Blvd., Ste. 610
Los Angeles, CA 90025
Tel.: 213-820-4003
Fax: 213-826-4814
Alan Hyman *(Sr. V.P.)*
Sam Randazzo *(V.P.)*
Robert Ekizian *(Assoc. V.P.)*
Adriaen Ito *(Grp. V.P.)*
Christopher Camu *(Assoc.)*
Gary Sherfey *(Assoc.)*

Vitt/Reynolds Media International Limited **(1)**
26 Soho St., Ste. 380
Toronto, ON M5T 1Z7, Canada
Tel.: 416-599-7078
Telex: 06983639
Fax: 416-599-7087
Strategic Media Planning/Buying/Syndication for All Media; Marketing/Media Research Analysis
E. Thomas Reynolds *(Pres.)*

David R. Williams, Inc. **(1)**
1114 Ave. of the Americas
New York, NY 10036
Tel.: 212-921-0500
David R. Williams *(Pres.)*
Sheldon Kawer *(Exec. V.P.)*

Subsidiary:

David R. Williams, Inc. **(1)**
1114 Ave. of the Americas
New York, NY 10036
Tel.: 212-921-0500
S.I.C.: 7319
David R. Williams *(Pres.)*

VITUS ELECTRICAL SUPPLY COMPANY
2358 W. 7th Place
Eugene, OR 97402
Mailing Address:
P.O. Box 2789,
Eugene, OR 97402-2603
Tel.: 503-484-6337 **OR**
Fax: 503-484-4124
Year Founded: 1947
Approx.Sls.: $12,000,000
Emp.: 38
Wholesale Distributor of Computers, Disk Drivers; Electrical Supplies
S.I.C.: 5045; 5063
Maurice Vitus, Jr. *(Pres.)*
Felicia J. Vitus *(V.P., Sec. & Treas.)*

Outside Service Firm(s):

Centennial Bank, Inc.*(Major Banking Relationship)*
Eugene, OR

VIVIAN MILLWORKS
61 Elizabeth St.
Forty Fort, PA 18704
Tel.: 717-288-0492
Fax: 717-283-1162
Approx.Sls.: $13,000,000
Emp.: 60
Wood Panels, Lumber Millwork, Hardware, Plywood
S.I.C.: 2431; 2436
H. Melvin Vivian, Jr. *(Chm. Bd.)*
Harry M. Vivian *(Pres.)*

Outside Service Firm(s):

Hanover Bank of Pennsylvania*(Major Banking Relationship)*
Wilkes Barre, PA

THE VOGEL COMMUNICATIONS GROUP
11835 Olympic Blvd., Ste. 800
Los Angeles, CA 90064
Tel.: 310-444-5244
Fax: 310-444-5246
Year Founded: 1987
Approx.Billings: $12,500,000
Emp.: 14
William C. Vogel *(Pres. & New Bus. Contact)*
Howard Wallman *(Exec. V.P.)*
Robin Whitney *(V.P.)*

VOGLER MOTOR COMPANY, INC.
1170 E. Main
Carbondale, IL 62901
Tel.: 618-457-8135 **IL**
Fax: 618-529-3010
Year Founded: 1923
Approx.Sls.: $22,000,000
Emp.: 80
Retail Sales of New & Used Automobiles, Pickups & Vans
S.I.C.: 5511
Frank C. Black *(Pres.)*
Donald C. Vogler *(V.P.)*

Outside Service Firm(s):

First National Bank & Trust Co.*(Major Banking Relationship)*
Carbondale, IL

HENRY VOGT MACHINE CO.
1000 W. Ormsby Ave.
Louisville, KY 40210
Mailing Address:
P.O. Box 1918
Louisville, KY 40201
Tel.: 502-634-1500
Telex: 204-230
Fax: 502-637-7344
Year Founded: 1880
Sales Range: $100-499 Million
Emp.: 1,500
Fiscal Year-end: 8/31/91
Export
Mfr. Valve & Pipe Fittings, Steam Boilers, Refrigeration & Ice Making Equipment, Petroleum Refinery & Chemical Plant Equipment, Heat Recovery Equipment
S.I.C.: 3433; 3585; 3494; 3559; 3443
Henry Heuser *(Chm. Bd.)*
Henry V. Heuser, Jr. *(Pres. & Chief Exec. Officer)*
Leland D. Schlegel, Jr. *(Exec. V.P.)*
W. Douglas Glass *(V.P. & Mgr.-Valves & Fittings)*
David G. White *(V.P.-Opers.)*
W. Kent Oyler III *(Treas.)*
Margaret S. Culver *(Sec.)*
Mark Cain *(Mgr.-Personnel)*
Jerry Looney *(Mgr.-Adv.)*
Carl E. Douglas *(Pur. Agent)*

Outside Service Firm(s):

Coopers & Lybrand*(Auditors)*
Louisville, KY 46201

Wyatt, Tarrant, Combs, Gilbert & Milom*(Legal Firm)*
28th Fl., Citizens Plaza
Louisville, KY 40202
Tel.: 502-589-5235

Citizens Fidelity Bank & Trust Co.*(Major Banking Relationship)*
P.O. Box 33000-Citizens Plaza
Louisville, KY 40232
Tel.: 502-581-3381

Divisions:

Boiler & Heat Exchange Div. **(1)**
P.O. Box 1918
Louisville, KY 40201
Tel.: 502-634-1500
Export

Tube-Ice Div. **(1)**
P.O. Box 1918
Louisville, KY 40201
Tel.: 502-634-1500
Export

Turbo Refrigerating **(1)**
P.O. Box 396
Denton, TX 76202
Tel.: 817-387-4301
S.I.C.: 3585
James F. Tucker II *(Chief Oper. Officer)*
Kyle Pierce *(Dir.-Corp. Communication)*

Valve & Fitting Div. **(1)**
P.O. Box 1918
Louisville, KY 40201
Tel.: 502-634-1500
Export

VOGUE & BODY SHOPS, INC.
(Formerly Vogue Shops, Inc.)
6225 Powers Ave.
Jacksonville, FL 32217
Tel.: 904-737-0811
Fax: 904-737-6509
Year Founded: 1950
Approx.Sls.: $94,403,000
Emp.: 2,100
Fiscal Year-end: 12/31/90
Retail Ready-To-Wear Clothing
S.I.C.: 5621
Jerrold Rosenbaum *(Chm. Bd.)*
Ronnie Rosenbaum *(Pres.)*
Curtis V. Hill *(V.P. & Controller)*
Harvey Kaplan *(V.P. & Gen. Mgr.)*
Lillian Friedman *(Treas.)*
Judy Anderson *(Asst. Controller & Dir.-Personnel)*

Outside Service Firm(s):

Joseph Hartman & Associates*(Auditors)*
Jacksonville, FL

Pappas & Metcalf*(Legal Firm)*
Jacksonville, FL

First Union National Bank*(Major Banking Relationship)*
Jacksonville, FL

Vogue Coach Company
(Name Changed to Mitchell Coach Manufacturing)

VOIT CORP.
1451 Pittsford-Victor Rd.
Fairport, NY 14450
Tel.: 716-385-2390
Fax: 716-385-8701
Approx.Sls.: $27,000,000
Emp.: 150
Fiscal Year-end: 12/31/90
Exercise Equipment, Inflatables, Underwater Sports Gear, Bowling Bags & Golf Bags
S.I.C.: 3949
David H. Goldman *(Pres.)*
David M. Pender *(V.P.-Fin.)*
Bernard A. Frank *(V.P.)*
Theodore Ellenoff *(Sec. & Treas.)*

VOIT SPORTS, INC.
100 Willowbrook Office Park,
1451 Pittsford-Victor Rd.
Fairport, NY 14450
Tel.: 716-385-2390
Fax: 716-385-8701
Approx.Sls.: $33,000,000
Emp.: 200
Fiscal Year-end: 12/31/90
Voit Sports Equipment
S.I.C.: 3949
David H. Goldman *(Pres.)*
David Pender *(V.P.-Fin.)*
Richard N. Bethel *(V.P.-Mktg. & Adv.)*
Bernard A. Frank *(V.P.)*
Theodore Ellenoff *(Treas. & Sec.)*

THE JOHN VOLK COMPANY
676 St. Clair
Chicago, IL 60611
Tel.: 312-787-7117
Fax: 312-787-7315
Year Founded: 1974
Approx.Billings: $13,300,000
Emp.: 15
Marketing Communications
John Volk *(Pres.)*
Mary Kowalczyk *(Dir., Pub. Affairs)*

THE VOLLRATH COMPANY INC.
1236 N. 18th St.
Sheboygan, WI 53082
Mailing Address:
P.O. Box 611,
Sheboygan, WI 53082
Tel.: 414-457-4851
Fax: 414-459-6570
Year Founded: 1874
Approx.Sls.: $120,000,000
Emp.: 1,200
Fiscal Year-end: 12/31/90
Import Export
Vollrath Stainless Steel Food Service Utensils & Equipment, Holloware; Plastic Serving Utensils, Stainless Steel & Plastic Medical Products, Castings & Deep-Drawn Components
S.I.C.: 3312; 3469
Thomas G. Belot *(Pres.)*
Marty Crneckiy *(Exec. V.P.-Fin.)*
Mike Carpenter *(V.P.-Sls. & Mktg.)*
Steve Rahn *(Dir.-Pur.)*
Steven Karrasch *(Mgr.-Mktg. Services)*

Outside Service Firm(s):

Arthur Andersen & Co.*(Auditors)*
777 E. Wisconsin Ave., P.O. Box 1215
Milwaukee, WI 53202
Tel.: 414-271-5100
Fax: 414-283-3200

Foley & Lardner*(Legal Firm)*
777 E. Wisconsin Ave.
Milwaukee, WI 53202
Tel.: 414-271-2400

M & I Marshall & Ilsley Bank*(Major Banking Relationship)*
770 N. Water St.
Milwaukee, WI 53202
Tel.: 414-765-8700

Subsidiaries:

Leyse **(1)**
23 Kilbourn St.
Kewaunee, WI 54216
Tel.: 414-388-3111 (100%%)
Mfr. of Cookware Products
S.I.C.: 3631
Charley Klein *(Gen. Mgr.)*
Dick Forsythe *(Controller)*
Robert Behnke *(Sls. Mgr.)*
Joe Novak *(Pur. Agent)*

Vollrath Refrigeration Inc. **(1)**
719 St. Croix
River Falls, WI 54022
Tel.: 715-425-6741
Commercial Refrigerated Equipment; Walk-in Coolers; Freezers & Insulated Structures
S.I.C.: 3585
George Harvey *(Pres.)*

VOLVO SALES & SERVICE CENTER
4375 Lincoln Ave.
Lile, IL 60532
Tel.: 708-852-7200 **IL**
Fax: 708-852-0464
Year Founded: 1962
Approx.Sls.: $70,000,000
Emp.: 215
Retail Sales of New & Used Automobiles
S.I.C.: 5511
Horst Korallus *(Pres.)*
Guenther, Korallus *(V.P. & Sec.)*

Outside Service Firm(s):

Harris Bank Naperville*(Major Banking Relationship)*
503 N. Washington St.
Naperville, IL 60566
Tel.: 708-420-3500

G. VON HAMM TEXTILES, INC.
916 Kaahi Place
Honolulu, HI 96817
Tel.: 808-847-4411 **HI**
Fax: 808-847-1688
Approx.Sls.: $12,000,000
Emp.: 55
Wholesale Distributor of Textiles
S.I.C.: 5131
Gunther Von Hamm *(Pres. & Treas.)*
James Byrne *(Sr. V.P.)*
James Pell *(V.P.)*

Outside Service Firm(s):

Rosenberg & Hong*(Auditors)*
Honolulu, HI

Bendet, Fidell & Sakai*(Legal Firm)*
Honolulu, HI

Bank of Hawaii*(Major Banking Relationship)*
Honolulu, HI

VON HOUSEN MOTORS
1810 Howe Ave.
Sacramento, CA 95825
Tel.: 916-924-8000 **CA**
Fax: 916-924-6718
Year Founded: 1961
Assets: $37,800,000
Liabilities: $27,000,000
Net Worth: $10,800,000
Approx.Sls.: $71,000,000
Emp.: 265
Fiscal Year-end: 5/31/91
Import
Retail & Service Of New & Used Cars, Wholesale & Retail Automotive Parts
S.I.C.: 5013; 5511; 5531; 7538
George Grinzewitsch *(Chm. Bd. & Pres.)*
George Grinzewitsch, Jr. *(V.P.)*
Jim Pomares *(Sec., Treas. & Personnel Mgr.)*

Outside Service Firm(s):

W. J. Pomares & Company*(Auditors)*
Sacramento, CA

Farmers Insurance*(Commercial Insurance Carrier)*
Sacramento, CA

Bank of America NT&SA*(Major Banking Relationship)*
555 California St.
San Francisco, CA 94105
Tel.: 415-622-5120
Fax: 415-622-4585

Subsidiary:

Von Housen Auto Parts **(1)**
11057 Mills Station Rd.
Sacramento, CA 95827
Tel.: 916-362-0691
Auto Parts
S.I.C.: 5013
Robert Neely *(Chief Oper. Officer)*

VOSS INDUSTRIES, INC.
2168 W. 25th St.
Cleveland, OH 44113
Tel.: 216-771-7655 **OH**
Fax: 216-771-2887
Year Founded: 1954
Approx.Sls.: $11,000,000
Emp.: 150
Fiscal Year-end: 9/30/91
Export
Mfr. of Clamps & Couplings; Hose; Heat Exchangers; Condensers & Components; Mechanical Power Transmission Equipment
S.I.C.: 3429; 3443; 3452
William J. Voss *(Pres.)*
Marianne Voss *(Treas. & Sec.)*

Outside Service Firm(s):

Deloitte & Touche*(Auditors)*
1717 East Ninth St.
Cleveland, OH 44114
Tel.: 216-589-1300

Society National Bank*(Major Banking Relationship)*
Cleveland, OH

VOYAGER EMBLEMS, INC.
3707 Lockport Rd.
Sanborn, NY 14132-9705
Tel.: 716-731-4121
Tel.: 800-828-1603
Fax: 716-731-4365
Year Founded: 1921
Approx.Sls.: $10,000,000
Emp.: 210
Fiscal Year-end: 9/30/91
Import Export
Manufactures Swiss Embroidered Emblems & Caps
S.I.C.: 2395; 2399; 2353
Donald B. Grant *(Chm. Bd.)*
David Grant *(Pres.)*
D.G. Turner *(V.P.-Sls.)*
Michael P. Conroy *(Chief Fin. Officer)*
Gloria Hildebrandt *(Mgr.-Admin. & Opers.)*
George Swiger *(Mgr.-Retail Sls.)*
Wayne Goetz *(Mgr.-Natl. Sls.)*
James Rash *(Mgr.-Oper.)*
H. Ghobrial *(Mgr.-Production)*

Computer Systems/Hardware:
IBM

VULCAN IRON WORKS, INC.
12700 Lyndon
Detroit, MI 48227
Tel.: 313-491-0810 **MI**
Fax: 313-934-7469
Assets: $7,700,000
Liabilities: $5,500,000
Net Worth: $2,200,000
Approx.Sls.: $14,000,000
Emp.: 100
Fiscal Year-end: 12/31/90
Structural Iron Work
S.I.C.: 1791
Jimmie R. Edwards *(Pres.)*
Michael John *(Chief Fin. Officer & V.P.)*
Boris Volchoff *(V.P.-Engrng.)*

Outside Service Firm(s):

Grant Thornton*(Auditors)*
Detroit, MI

Fitzgerald, Peters, Dakmak, & Miller*(Legal Firm)*
Detroit, MI

Manufacturers National Bank N.A.*(Major Banking Relationship)*
38th Fl., 100 Renaissance Center
Detroit, MI 48243
Tel.: 313-222-4227

W-B SUPPLY CO.
111 N. Naida
Pampa, TX 79065
Mailing Address:
P.O. Drawer 2479
Pampa, TX 79065
Tel.: 806-669-1103 **TX**
Fax: 806-665-0453
Year Founded: 1971
Assets: $2,620,000
Earnings: ($330,000)
Liabilities: $1,250,000
Net Worth: $1,370,000
Approx.Sls.: $16,400,000
Emp.: 45
Fiscal Year-end: 3/31/91
General Oil Supplies
S.I.C.: 5084
Mike Deaver *(Chm. Bd.)*
Ronald G. Hess *(Pres.)*
Terry Gaines *(V.P.-Fin.)*
Alan Lotman *(V.P. & Controller)*
Steven Swaze *(Sec.)*
Ray White *(Dir.-Pur.)*
Kay Swart *(Office Mgr.)*

No. of U.S. Offices: 9

Computer Systems/Hardware:
IBM System 36

Outside Service Firm(s):

Deloitte & Touche*(Auditors)*
1400 Lincoln Plaza, LB-4
Dallas, TX 75201-3302
Tel.: 214-220-8000

Travelers Insurance Co.*(Commercial Insurance Carrier)*
1 Tower Square
Hartford, CT 06183
Tel.: 203-222-7821
Fax: 203-222-7813

BMA Insurance Agency*(Group Insurer)*
Kansas City, MO

Whittenburg, Whittenburg & Schachter*(Legal Firm)*
Amarillo, TX

W&F MANUFACTURING CORPORATION, INC.
(Sub. of Pepsi-Cola Buffalo Bottling Corp.)
2299 Kenmore Ave.
Buffalo, NY 14207-1311
Tel.: 716-874-5850
Tel.: 800-365-0808
Fax: 716-874-5976
Year Founded: 1926
Approx.Sls.: $20,000,000
Emp.: 300
Mfr. Scented Candles, Scented Pomanders, Scented Wax Air Fresheners, Canning Wax, Paste-up Wax, Scented Wax Chipsm Wax Confections & Taffy
S.I.C.: 3999
Irwin Pastor *(Pres. & Chief Exec. Officer)*
Scott Pastor *(Vice Chm.)*
Todd Pastor *(Pres.)*
Sydney Pastor *(Exec. V.P.)*
Michael Brown *(Sr. V.P.)*
Jerry Cooper *(Sr. V.P.)*
Peter M. Guerra *(Grp. V.P.)*
Daniel Tantalo *(Chief Fin. Officer)*
David Streamer *(Controller)*
Jane Crossan *(Gen. Counsel)*
Walter Burkard *(Dir.-Personnel)*
Randy Brodsky *(Opers. Coordinator)*
Kristin Adamson *(Mkt. Res. Analyst & Sls. Co-ordinator)*

THE WBDC GROUP
50 Monroe Pl. N.W.
Grand Rapids, MI 49503
Tel.: 616-235-6000 **MI**
Fax: 616-235-6132
Year Founded: 1960
Approx.Sls.: $18,000,000
Emp.: 210
Export
Mechanical, Electrical & Civil Engrng. & Architectural Services
S.I.C.: 8711; 8712
Paul D. Bowers, Jr. *(Chm. Bd.)*
Charles Gaskill *(Pres.)*
Harold O. Sibley *(Exec. V.P.)*
William J. Bont *(V.P.-Sls.)*
John H. Edison *(V.P.-Real Estate)*
Paul A. Hahka *(V.P.)*
Robert E. Self *(V.P.)*
John W. Weiss *(V.P.-Mktg. & Adv.)*
Lucinda Gezon *(Treas.)*
Joanne Jullehe *(Controller)*
Dan Sardie *(Dir.-Human Resources)*
Alan Bedell *(Corp. Trainer)*
Penelope Richardson *(Corp. Librarian)*
Principal(s):
Paul D. Bowers, Jr.
Charles Gaskill
Harold O. Sibley
Robert E. Self

No. of U.S. Offices: 4

WBH INDUSTRIES, INC.
3016 Avenue E.
Arlington, TX 76011
Tel.: 817-649-5700 **TX**

WBH Industries, Inc.—(Continued)

Fax: 817-649-5701
Approx.Sls.: $13,000,000
Emp.: 100
Wholesale Distributor of Hardware & Millwork; Manufacturer of Metal Doors, Sash & Trim
S.I.C.: 5072; 3442; 5031
Harley D. Webb *(Chm. Bd. & Pres.)*
Jack Gray *(Exec. V.P.)*
Charles Happel *(Exec. V.P.)*
Larry Harrell *(V.P.)*
Margaret Smith *(Sec.)*

Outside Service Firm(s):

Rylander, Clay & Opety*(Auditors)*
Dallas, TX

Hughes & Luce*(Legal Firm)*
Bank One Center, 1717 Main St.
Dallas, TX 75202
Tel.: 214-651-0477

Subsidiary:

W B H International, Inc. **(1)**
3016 Avenue E.
Arlington, TX 76011
Tel.: 817-272-7301
Approx.Sls.: $2,000,000
Emp.: 6
Wholesale Distributor of Exterior & Interior Building Materials; Doors & Door Frames
S.I.C.: 5039; 5031
Harley D. Bebb *(Pres.)*

WDP, INC.
211 E. 43rd St., Ste. 1005
New York, NY 10017
Tel.: 212-557-7625 **DE**
Year Founded: 1973
Approx.Sls.: $12,500,000
Emp.: 125
Steel Mill Rolls
S.I.C.: 3547
Duane Wilder *(Chm. Bd., Pres. & Treas.)*
Amelia R. Dempster *(Sec.)*

Outside Service Firm(s):

Ernst & Young*(Auditors)*
2000 Pittsburgh Natl. Bldg.
Pittsburgh, PA 15222
Tel.: 412-644-7800
Fax: 412-644-7419

Kirkpatrick & Lockhart*(Legal Firm)*
1500 Oliver Bldg., 535 Smithfield St.
Pittsburgh, PA 15222
Tel.: 412-355-6500
Fax: 412-355-6501

Equibank*(Major Banking Relationship)*
Two Oliver Plz.
Pittsburgh, PA 15222
Tel.: 412-288-5000

WEN PRODUCTS, INC.
5810 Northwest Hwy.
Chicago, IL 60631
Tel.: 312-763-6060
Year Founded: 1951
Approx.Sls.: $25,000,000
Emp.: 450
Import Export
Electric Hand Power Tools, Soldering Guns, Electric Chain Saws, Bench Products
S.I.C.: 3546; 3423
Nick Anton *(Pres.)*
Bill Anton *(V.P.-Mktg.)*
Larry Shapiro *(V.P.-Sls.)*
Keith Wright *(Chief Fin. Officer)*
Charles Shields *(Controller)*
Marty Krough *(Dir-Pur)*
Dan DePaolis *(Natl. Sls. Mgr.)*
Albert A. Pioch *(Mgr.-Sls. & Mktg.)*
Don Hendrich *(Data Processing)*

W F I, INC.
4407 Haygood
Houston, TX 77022
Mailing Address:
P.O. Box 7303,
Houston, TX 77248
Tel.: 713-695-3633
Fax: 713-695-3528
Approx.Sls.: $12,000,000
Emp.: 187
Ferrous & Nonferrous Machinery Forgings
S.I.C.: 3462; 3463
Robert Schraeder *(Pres.)*
Ivan Dupont *(V.P.-Fin.)*
Michael Billot *(Gen. Sls. Mgr.)*
John Cotes *(Mgr.-Nuclear & Military Sls.)*

Outside Service Firm(s):

Bank One Milwaukee, N.A.*(Major Banking Relationship)*
111 E. Wisconsin Ave.
Milwaukee, WI
Tel.: 414-765-3000

WGM/HYDRO
(Div. of Norsk Hydro A/S, Oslo, Norway)
270 Lawrence Ave.
South San Francisco, CA 94080
Tel.: 415-871-1770 **CA**
Fax: 415-873-1471
Year Founded: 1850
Approx.Sls.: $200,000,000
Emp.: 80
Agricultural & Industrial Chemicals
S.I.C.: 5169; 5199; 5191; 5052
Tom Consoli *(Exec. V.P.)*
Dr. Bob Millaway *(Adv. Dir. & Prod. Mgr.-Hydro)*

Outside Service Firm(s):

KPMG Peat Marwick*(Auditors)*
3 Embarcadero Center
San Francisco, CA 94111
Tel.: 415-951-0100
Fax: 415-397-1129

St. Paul Insurance Companies*(Group Insurer)*
St.Paul, MN

Brobeck, Phleger & Harrison*(Legal Firm)*
Spear St. Tower, One Market Plaza
San Francisco, CA 94105
Tel.: 415-442-0900

Wells Fargo Bank*(Major Banking Relationship)*
420 Montgomery St.
San Francisco, CA 94104

Martin Sosnoff Assocs.*(Pension Manager)*
New York, NY

WGM SAFETY CORPORATION
205 Washington St.
Reading, PA 19603
Mailing Address:
P.O. Box 622
Reading, PA 19603-622
Tel.: 215-376-8566 **DE**
Fax: 215-371-7740
Sales Range: $60-79 Million
Emp.: 450
Fiscal Year-end: 12/31/90
Mfr. of Safety Products, Fall Protection, Head, Hearing, Eye & Respiratory Protection
S.I.C.: 3851
John A. Casey *(Chm. Bd.)*
V.D. McCroskey *(Pres. & Chief Exec. Officer)*
Edward B. Kern *(Treas.)*
Roger Gehring *(Sr. V.P.)*
Rodney Fogelman *(Dir.-Human Resources)*
R. Fogelman *(Dir.-Personnel)*

Principal(s):
Christian Dalloz S.A.

Outside Service Firm(s):

Coopers & Lybrand*(Auditors)*
2400 Eleven Penn Center
Philadelphia, PA 19103-2962
Tel.: 215-963-8000

Bankers Trust Co.*(Major Banking Relationship)*
Philadelphia, PA

WICO CORPORATION
6400 W. Gross Point Rd.
Niles, IL 60714-4508
Tel.: 708-647-7500
Tel.: 800-367-9426
Fax: 708-647-8526
Year Founded: 1940
Approx.Sls.: $40,000,000
Emp.: 500
Import Export
Mfr. & Distributor of Amusement & Vending Supplies; Manufacturer of Controls For Home Video Games & Computers
S.I.C.: 3699
Edward G. Sokolofski *(Pres.)*
Bob Emmrich *(V.P.-Penn Ray)*
Nolan L. Lameka *(V.P.-Fin.)*
Dave Ruber *(V.P.-Opers.)*
Mike Rudowicz *(V.P.-Sls.)*
Ed Brooks *(Dir.-Mfg.)*
Rich Santercola *(Dir.-Adv. & Mktg.)*
Vartkes Sinanian *(Mgr.-Export)*

WRM, INC.
144 Whitestick St.
Mabscott, WV 25871
Tel.: 304-255-1457 **WV**
Fax: 304-255-1498
Approx.Sls.: $17,000,000
Emp.: 75
Strip Mining, Bituminous Coal Mining
S.I.C.: 1221
Tracy W. Hylton *(Pres.)*
John Bruens *(Treas. & Sec.)*
Principal(s):
Betty Jo Hylton

Outside Service Firm(s):

Raleigh County National Bank*(Major Banking Relationship)*
Beckley, WV

Subsidiary:

Perry & Hylton, Inc. **(1)**
144 Whitestick St.
Mabscott, WV 25871
Tel.: 304-255-1457
Fax: 304-255-1498
Strip Mining, Bituminous Coal Mining
S.I.C.: 1221
Tracy W. Hylton *(Pres.)*

W S HOLDING COMPANY
400 Fuller-Wiser Rd.
Euless, TX 76039
Mailing Address:
P.O. Box 61920
Dallas, TX 75261-9120
Tel.: 817-283-5444 **DE**
Fax: 817-283-0393
Emp.: 1,800
General Line of Groceries
S.I.C.: 5141
Ronald E. Elmquist *(Chm. Bd. & Chief Exec. Officer)*
Peter Smith *(Pres. & Chief Oper. Officer)*
William J. Bayer *(V.P. & Treas.)*
Rudy Zinsmeister *(V.P.)*

Outside Service Firm(s):

Ernst & Young*(Auditors)*
500 Throckmorton St.
Fort Worth, TX 76102
Tel.: 817-335-1900
Fax: 817-335-2728

Bank of Nova Scotia*(Major Banking Relationship)*
Houston, TX

Subsidiary:

White Swan, Inc. **(1)**
400 Fuller-Wiser Rd.
Euless, TX 76039
Tel.: 817-283-5444
Fax: 817-283-0393
Approx.Sls.: $600,000,000
Emp.: 1,850
Fiscal Year-end: 12/31/90
Institutional Food Distributor
S.I.C.: 5141
Ronald E. Elmquist *(Chm. & Chief Exec. Officer)*
Peter Smith *(Pres. & Chief Oper. Officer)*
William J. Beyer *(Sr. V.P. & Chief Fin. Officer)*
Homer Forsythe *(V.P.-Opers.)*
Rudy Zinsmeister *(V.P.-Human Resources)*
Jim McMahon *(V.P.-Natl. Accounts)*
Bob Cogswell *(V.P.-Mdsg. & Mktg.)*

Division:

Watson Food Service Industries **(2)**
3712 Haggar Way
Dallas, TX 75209
Tel.: 214-350-3561
Approx.Sls.: $22,000,000
Emp.: 125
R.L. Watson, Jr. *(Pres.)*
William Burris *(V.P.-Sls.)*
Ron Carlson *(V.P.-Fin.)*

WSF INDUSTRIES, INC.
7 Hackett Dr.
Tonawanda, NY 14150
Mailing Address:
P.O. Box 400/Kenmore Branch,
Buffalo, NY 14217
Tel.: 716-692-4930 **NY**
Fax: 716-692-4135
Year Founded: 1942
Sales Range: $10-19 Million
Emp.: 90
Fiscal Year-end: 12/31/90
Import Export
Manufacturer of Processing Equipment
S.I.C.: 3479; 3565; 3567; 3443
John L. Hettrick *(Chm. Bd. & Chief Exec. Officer)*
Henry J. Piegza *(Pres.)*
Martin Schwab *(V.P.-Sls.)*
John L. Hettrick, Jr. *(Gen. Mgr. & Asst. to the Chm. Bd.)*
James Ruffing *(Mgr.-Sls.)*
Curtis L. Smith *(Mgr.-Quality Control)*
Joseph Wroblewski *(Mgr.-Mfg.)*
Gary R. Fornasiero *(Chief Engr.)*
Robert C. Eckam *(Pur. Agent)*

No. of Mfg. Plants/Facilities: 1
No. of U.S. Offices: 1

Computer Systems/Hardware:
IBM PC

Outside Service Firm(s):

Dopkins & Co*(Auditors)*
Amherst, NY

Hodgson, Russ, Andrews, Woods & Goodyear*(Legal Firm)*
1800 One M & T Plaza
Buffalo, NY 14203
Tel.: 716-856-4000

WTTW (CHANNEL 11)
5400 N. St. Louis
Chicago, IL 60625
Tel.: 312-583-5000
Fax: 312-583-3046
Emp.: 250
Television Station
S.I.C.: 4833
William J. McCarter *(Pres. & Chief Exec. Officer)*
John Rahmann *(Exec. V.P.)*
David Buehrer *(Sr. V.P.-Fin. & Admin. Services)*

Richard Bowman *(Sr. V.P.-WTTW/ Channel Broadcast Center)*
C. Patterson Denny *(Sr. V.P.-The Television Production Center)*
Bruce T. Marcus *(Sr. V.P.-Corp. Mktg. & Communications)*
Larry Ocker *(Sr. V.P.-Engrng. & Video Services)*
Tessa Burton *(V.P.-Viewer Mktg.)*
John Grace *(V.P.-Chicago Program Mktg.)*
Jerry Hanna *(V.P.-Engrng. & Video Services)*
Katherine Lauderdale *(V.P.-Gen. Counsel)*
Reese Marcusson *(V.P.-Controller)*
Martin J. McLaughlin *(V.P.-Corp. Affairs)*
Paul Nebenzahl *(V.P.-Development)*
Melissa Wohl *(V.P.-Intl. Sls. & Co-Prod.)*
Tanya Neimark *(Dir.-Corp. Communications)*

Outside Service Firm(s):

Harris Trust & Savings Bank*(Major Banking Relationship)*
111 W. Monroe St.
Chicago, IL 60690
Tel.: 312-461-2265
Tel.: 800-858-0840

WWF PAPER CORPORATION
2 Bala Plaza
Bala-Cynwyd, PA 19004
Tel.: 215-667-9210
Tel.: 800-345-1305 **PA**
Fax: 215-667-1663
Fax: 215-667-2691
Year Founded: 1922
Sales Range: $500-999 Million
Emp.: 500
Import Export
Wholesale Converted Paper
S.I.C.: 5111; 5113
Edward Furlong, Jr. *(Pres. & Chief Exec. Officer)*
Stewart S. Furlong *(Pres.-WWF Book Publishing)*
George Sergio *(Exec. V.P. & Chief Fin. Officer)*
Donald H. Palmer *(Sr. V.P. & Dir.-Exports & Imports)*
J. Adelsberger *(V.P.-Mngmt. Information Systems)*
Gloria Gregg *(V.P.-Admin.)*
Robert Keeler *(V.P.-Mktg.)*
Vincent F. Basile *(Controller)*
Kenneth Staff *(Gen. Counsel)*
Doug Powell *(Mgr.-Corp. Credit)*
Principal(s):
Edward Furlong, Jr.

No. of Mfg. Plants/Facilities: 10
No. of U.S. Offices: 15
No. of Foreign Offices: 1

Computer Systems/Hardware:
Burroughs A-9

Outside Service Firm(s):

Coopers & Lybrand*(Auditors)*
P.O. Box 538, 800 Akron Centre Plaza
Akron, OH 44308

Johnson & Higgins*(Group Insurer)*
125 Broad St.
New York, NY 10004-2424
Tel.: 212-574-7000
Fax: 212-574-8988

Duane, Morris & Heckscher*(Legal Firm)*
One Liberty Place
Philadelphia, PA 19103
Tel.: 215-979-1800

Subsidiaries:

Forest Atwood Paper Company **(1)**
1150 Lively Blvd.
Elk Grove Village, IL 60007
Tel.: 708-593-7500
Fax: 708-593-7956
Fine Paper Sls., Converting
S.I.C.: 5111
Thomas O'Brien *(Pres.)*

Forest Atwood Paper Company-New York **(1)**
185 Madison Ave.
New York, NY 10016
Tel.: 212-545-1488
Fax: 212-545-1491
Harry Hoover *(V.P.)*
Fran Boytano *(Dir.-Pur.)*

Miami Paper Company **(1)**
9771 NW 91st. Ct.
Medley, FL 33178
Tel.: 305-887-0707
Fax: 305-887-0420
Paper Merchants; Printing Papers
S.I.C.: 5111
Al Kaplan *(Pres.)*

WWF International Limited **(1)**
71 Arch St.
Greenwich, CT 06830
Tel.: 203-661-9091
Fax: 203-661-9461
Paper Brokers
S.I.C.: 5111
John Curtin *(Co-Gen. Mgr.)*
Allan Chapman *(Co-Gen. Mgr.)*

WWF National **(1)**
529 Main St.
Boston, MA 02129
Tel.: 617-242-7003
Fax: 617-241-5991
Fine Paper Sales
S.I.C.: 5111
Bill Deford *(Gen. Mgr.)*

WWF Paper Corporation - N.E. **(1)**
45 Belden St.
East Hartford, CT 06108
Tel.: 203-289-9324
Tel.: 800-631-8895
Fax: 203-282-9575
Paper Distributors
S.I.C.: 5111
John Patenaude *(Gen. Mgr.)*

Communications Paper Divison **(1)**
2 Bala Plaza
Bala-Cynwyd, PA 19004
Tel.: 215-667-9210
Paper Distributors
S.I.C.: 5111
Robert D. Simone, Jr. *(Exec. V.P.)*

WWF Paper Corp.-New England **(1)**
290 Beaver St.
Franklin, MA 02038
Tel.: 508-520-3305
Tel.: 800-225-5580
Fax: 508-520-0220
Fine Paper Sls.
S.I.C.: 5111
Philip Pietrafetta *(Reg. Mgr.)*

WWF Paper Corporation - West (California) **(1)**
2727 Workman Mill Rd.
City of Industry, CA 91746
Tel.: 310-699-0391
Fax: 310-692-7890
Paper Distributos
S.I.C.: 5111
Manvil Mgrublian *(Pres.)*

WWF/Royal Paper Company **(1)**
185 Madison Ave., 12th Fl.
New York, NY 10016
Tel.: 212-684-1200
Tel.: 800-232-5503
Fax: 212-679-5532
Fine Paper Sls.
S.I.C.: 5111
Robert Spinosa *(Exec. V.P. & Gen. Mgr.)*

Wilcox-Walter-Furlong Paper Co. **(1)**
P.O. Box 44105, 5255 Fulton Industrial Blvd.
Atlanta, GA 30336
Tel.: 404-696-8900
Tel.: 800-282-9116
Fax: 404-696-2914
Fine Paper Sales
S.I.C.: 5111
Doug Invester *(Gen. Mgr.)*

Wilcox-Walter-Furlong Paper Co. **(1)**
54th & Grays Ave.
Philadelphia, PA 19143
Tel.: 215-724-0500
Tel.: 800-523-2653
Fax: 215-724-2080
Fine Paper Sales
S.I.C.: 5111
Lorraine Iwanicka *(Pres.)*

Wilcox-Walter-Furlong Paper Co. **(1)**
4245 Carolina Ave.
Richmond, VA 23261
Tel.: 804-321-1210
Fax: 804-321-6154
Fine Paper Sls.
S.I.C.: 5111
John Lowery *(Gen. Mgr.)*

Wilcox-Walter-Furlong Paper Co. of Washington **(1)**
8750 Larkin Rd.
Savage, MD 20763
Tel.: 410-792-8666
Tel.: 800-222-9522
Fax: 410-792-0548
Fine Paper Sales
S.I.C.: 5111
Elmer Williams *(Pres.)*
Robert Worthington *(V.P.)*
Maureen Cassidy *(V.P.)*

Non-U.S. Subsidiary:

WWF Paper Sales U.K., Ltd. **(1)**
Claire House, Bridge St.
Leatherhead, Surrey KT222 8HY, United Kingdom
Tel.: 372-3761333
Fax: 372 386366
Fine Paper Sales
S.I.C.: 5111
Roger Spikesman *(Mng. Dir.)*

WYO-BEN, INC.
3044 Hesper Rd.
Billings, MT 59102
Mailing Address:
P.O. Box 1979
Billings, MT 59103
Tel.: 406-652-6351 **MT**
Fax: 406-656-0748
Year Founded: 1952
Approx.Sls.: $15,000,000
Emp.: 110
Export
Bentonite Clay, Drilling Fluid Chemicals & Materials
S.I.C.: 1459; 2899
Alfred Keith Brown *(Chm. Bd.)*
David S. Brown *(Pres.)*
David L. Auer *(Exec. V.P.)*
Rockwood Brown *(Sr. V.P., Sec. & Gen. Counsel)*
Douglas A. Buckingham *(Treas. & Controller)*
Robert Stichman *(Dir.-Sls.)*

No. of Mfg. Plants/Facilities: 3
No. of U.S. Offices: 1

Outside Service Firm(s):

KPMG Peat Marwick*(Auditors)*
1000 1st. Interstate Center, 401 N. 31st. St.
Billings, MT 59103

Anderson, Brown, Gerbase, Cebull etal*(Legal Firm)*
Billings, MT

First Bank Billings*(Major Banking Relationship)*
Billings, MT

TOM WADE CO.
405 Maple Heights
Kenton, TN 38233
Mailing Address:
P.O. Box 263
Kenton, TN 38233
Tel.: 901-749-5305 **TN**
Fax: 901-749-0076
Year Founded: 1920
Approx.Sls.: $35,000,000
Emp.: 42
Fiscal Year-end: 12/31/90
Agricultural Services; Grain Elevators; Cotton Ginning; Farming; Strawberries
S.I.C.: 0724; 0171; 5153; 5191
Tom W. Wade, Jr. *(Chm. Bd. & Chief Exec. Officer)*
Principal(s):
Tom W. Wade, Jr.

No. of Mfg. Plants/Facilities: 4
No. of U.S. Offices: 5

Computer Systems/Hardware:
IBM; Compaq

Outside Service Firm(s):

Carmichael, Enoch & Associates*(Auditors)*
Dyersburg, TN

Union City Insurance Agency*(Commercial Insurance Carrier)*
Union City, TN
Tel.: 901-749-5305
Fax: 901-749-0076

First State Bank*(Major Banking Relationship)*
Kenton, TN

Subsidiaries:

Como Grain Co. **(1)**
Hwy. 54
Como, TN 38223
Tel.: 901-642-4889
Emp.: 4
Grain Elevator
S.I.C.: 5153

Dyer Grain Co. **(1)**
Hwy. 45
Dyer, TN 38330
Tel.: 901-692-2389
Emp.: 11
Grain Elevator
S.I.C.: 5153

Kenton Grain Co. **(1)**
405 Maple Heights
Kenton, TN 38233
Tel.: 901-749-5421
Emp.: 9
Grain Elevator
S.I.C.: 5153

Wade Gin Co. **(1)**
105 E. Taylor St.
Kenton, TN 38233
Tel.: 901-749-5305
Emp.: 9
Cotton Ginning
S.I.C.: 0724

Wade Land Co. **(1)**
405 Maple Heights
Kenton, TN 38233
Tel.: 901-749-5305
Emp.: 4

WAFFLE HOUSE, INC.
5986 Financial Dr.
Norcross, GA 30071
Tel.: 404-447-4488
Approx.Sls.: $80,000,000
Emp.: 6,000
Short-Order Restaurants
S.I.C.: 5812
Joe Rogers, Sr. *(Chm. Bd.)*
Joe W. Rogers, Jr. *(Pres.)*
Thomas F. Forkner *(Vice Chm.)*
Charles L. Julian *(Exec. V.P.-Oper.)*
Michael McCarthy *(Exec. V.P.)*
Corwin McKay *(V.P.-Data Processing)*
Principal(s):
Joe W. Rogers, Jr.
Thomas F. Forkner

Computer Systems/Hardware:
IBM System 38

Outside Service Firm(s):

Arthur Andersen & Co.*(Auditors)*
133 Peachtree St., N.E.
Atlanta, GA 30303
Tel.: 404-658-1776

Waffle House, Inc.—(Continued)

Alston & Bird*(Legal Firm)*
One Atlantic Center, 1201 West Peachtree St.
Atlanta, GA 30309-3424
Tel.: 404-881-7000

NationsBank*(Major Banking Relationship)*
35 Broad St.
Atlanta, GA 30303
Tel.: 404-581-2121
Tel.: 800-848-8198

WAGGONER CORP.
1400 Rochester Rd.
Troy, MI 48083
Mailing Address:
P.O. Box 4210,
Troy, MI 48099
Tel.: 313-588-2121
Fax: 313-588-8199
Year Founded: 1946
Approx.Sls.: $50,000,000
Emp.: 500
Metal Stampings & Assemblies
S.I.C.: 3469; 3465
Donald E. Waggoner *(Chm. Bd.)*
Donald E. Waggoner, Jr. *(Chief Exec. Officer)*
William Waggoner *(Pres. & Treas.)*
Mitch Simon *(V.P.-Opers.)*
Peter Waggoner *(Dir.-Personnel)*
John Blevins *(Plant Mgr.)*
Kenneth Fox *(Mgr.-Quality Control)*
F.I. Keywell, III *(Accountant)*
Peggy Perrone *(Pur. Agent)*
Principal(s):
Donald E. Waggoner
William Waggoner

No. of Mfg. Plants/Facilities: 2

Outside Service Firm(s):

Dubrinsky, Einstandig, Heilbrunn & Beckwith*(Auditors)*
Southfield, MI

Keywell & Rosenfeld*(Legal Firm)*
Troy, MI

Michigan National Bank*(Major Banking Relationship)*
Troy, MI

E.R. WAGNER MFG. CO.
WAGNER PRODS. DIV.
331 Riverview Dr.
Hustisford, WI 53034
Mailing Address:
P.O. Box 405,
Hustisford, WI 53034
Tel.: 414-349-3271
Fax: 414-349-3487
Approx.Sls.: $15,000,000
Emp.: 100
Fiscal Year-end: 12/31/90
Wagner Casters
S.I.C.: 3429
Dr. Frank Sterner *(Pres.)*
Dale Ballard *(Gen. Mgr.)*
Allen Stubbe *(Mgr.-Sls. & Mktg.)*
Richard Wick *(Pur. Agent)*

WAGNER MILLS INC.
P.O. Box 545
Schuyler, NE 68661
Tel.: 402-352-2471 **NE**
Year Founded: 1942
Assets: $5,300,000
Liabilities: $85,000
Net Worth: $5,215,000
Approx.Sls.: $12,300,000
Emp.: 18
Fiscal Year-end: 12/31/91
Grain Mill
S.I.C.: 5153
LeRoy Trofholz *(Pres. & Chief Exec. Officer)*
B.T. Friedrichsen *(Sec. & Treas.)*

Computer Systems/Hardware:
Burroughs

Outside Service Firm(s):

KPMG Peat Marwick*(Auditors)*
1600 FirsTier Bank Bldg., 13th & M Streets, Ste. 1600
Lincoln, NE 68508
Tel.: 402-476-1216

Norwest Bank Minnesota, N.A.*(Major Banking Relationship)*
Omaha, NE

Alexander & Alexander*(Commercial Insurance Carrier)*
P.O. Box 82515
Lincoln, NE 68501-2515

WAGNER SPRAY TECH CORP.
1770 Fernbrook Lane
Minneapolis, MN 55447
Mailing Address:
P.O. Box 9362,
Minneapolis, MN 55440
Tel.: 612-553-0759
Fax: 612-553-7288
Approx.Sls.: $130,000,000
Emp.: 200
Fiscal Year-end: 12/31/90
Mfr. Paint Spraying Equipment
S.I.C.: 3563; 5084
Sean James *(Pres.)*
Tom Craig *(V.P.-Fin. & Treas.)*
Carl Cooper *(V.P.-Mktg.)*
Richard Swenson *(V.P.-Sls.)*
Kenneth R. Ester *(V.P.-Mfg. & Engrng.)*
Terry Peterson *(Customer Services Mgr.)*

WAGSTAFF INC.
(Formerly Wagstaff Engineering, Inc.)
N. 3910 Flora Rd.
Spokane, WA 99216
Tel.: 509-922-1404 **WA**
Fax: 509-924-0241
Year Founded: 1946
Approx.Sls.: $20,000,000
Emp.: 160
Export
Mfg. Extrusion Dies for Ingots
S.I.C.: 3544
William G. Wagstaff *(Pres.)*
Frank E. Wagstaff *(V.P.)*
Robert H. Lee *(Sec. & Treas.)*
Steve Usher *(Dir.-Mktg.)*

Outside Service Firm(s):

Washington Trust Bank*(Major Banking Relationship)*
Spokane, WA

Subsidiary:

Wagstaff Eastern **(1)**
4657 Northbend
Hebron, KY 41048
Tel.: 606-689-5400
Mfg. of Extrusion Dies for Ingots
S.I.C.: 3544
W. Wagstaff *(Pres.)*

WAHL CLIPPER CORP.
2900 N. Locust
Sterling, IL 61081
Tel.: 815-625-6525 **1919**
Fax: 815-625-1193
Emp.: 400
Mfr. of Hair Clippers, Trimmers, Shavers & Massagers
S.I.C.: 3999; 3634; 3421
Robert L. Wahl *(Chm. Bd.)*
John F. Wahl *(Pres. & Chief Exec. Officer)*
Jim Wahl *(V.P.-Sls.)*
William B. Burke *(Treas. & Chief Fin. Officer)*
Lee Baty *(Gen. Counsel)*
Patrick Anello *(Dir.-Mktg.)*
Tom Britton *(Dir.-Data Processing)*
Bob Thurber *(Dir.-Consumer Sls.)*
Richard Harding *(Mgr.-Plant)*
Alan Corrigan *(Mgr.-Pur.)*

No. of Mfg. Plants/Facilities: 1
No. of U.S. Offices: 1
No. of Foreign Offices: 1

Computer Systems/Hardware:
IBM System 36

Outside Service Firm(s):

Lindgren, Callahan, Weaver, Van Osdol*(Auditors)*
Sterling, IL

Central National Bank of Sterling*(Major Banking Relationship)*
Sterling, IL

WAHL INSTRUMENTS
5750 Hannum Ave.
Culver City, CA 90231
Tel.: 213-641-6931
Tel.: 800-421-2853 **CA**
Fax: 213-670-2840
Year Founded: 1953
Sales Range: $10-19 Million
Emp.: 49
Fiscal Year-end: 2/28/90
Export
Industrial Process Temperature
S.I.C.: 3823
William Wahl, Sr. *(Pres.)*
John Reed *(V.P. & Sec.)*
Dave Sweener *(V.P.-Opers.)*
Stu Brown *(Mgr.-Sls.)*
Maria Galindo *(Mgr.-Pur.)*
Jeff Sampson *(Mgr.-Adv.)*
Ken Junkert *(Consulting Engineer)*

No. of Mfg. Plants/Facilities: 1

Outside Service Firm(s):

Mitsui Manufacturers Bank*(Major Banking Relationship)*
Los Angeles, CA

WAKEFERN FOOD CORPORATION
600 York St.
Elizabeth, NJ 07207
Tel.: 908-527-3300
Fax: 908-527-3397
Assets: $307,000,000
Liabilities: $274,000,000
Net Worth: $33,000,000
Approx.Sls.: $2,400,000,000
Emp.: 3,400
Fiscal Year-end: 9/28/90
Wholesale Groceries
S.I.C.: 5141
Thomas P. Infusino *(Chm. Bd.)*
Jerome D. Yaguda *(Pres. & Chief Exec. Officer)*
Robert W. Campbell *(Exec. V.P.-Fin. & Admin.)*
Jack Dreyer *(V.P.-Human Resources)*
D.V. Romano *(Treas.)*
Laurence Inserra *(Sec.)*
Thomas Drogaris *(Controller)*
James Watson *(Gen. Counsel)*
James Smith *(Dir.-Mngmt. Information Systems)*
Steve Korcius *(Mgr.-Real Estate)*

Computer Systems/Hardware:
IBM 3090-200

Outside Service Firm(s):

Victor Goldblat & Co.*(Auditors)*
Irvington, NY

Prudential Insurance Co. of America*(Group Insurer)*
751 Broad St.
Newark, NJ 07102-3777
Tel.: 201-802-6000

Weil, Gotshal & Manges*(Legal Firm)*
767 5th Ave.
New York, NY 10153
Tel.: 212-310-8000

Segal Association*(Pension Manager)*
New York, NY

Subsidiaries:

Food Haulers, Inc. **(1)**
600 York St.
Elizabeth, NJ 07207
Tel.: 908-527-3300
S.I.C.: 4212

National Transport Services Co. **(1)**
600 York St.
Elizabeth, NJ 07207
Tel.: 908-527-3300
S.I.C.: 4213

RSI **(1)**
600 York St.
Elizabeth, NJ 07207
Tel.: 908-527-3300

Shop-Rite of Bensalem Inc. **(1)**
600 York St.
Elizabeth, NJ 07207
Tel.: 908-527-3300
S.I.C.: 5411

Shop-Rite Beverages, Inc. **(1)**
600 York St.
Elizabeth, NJ 07207
Tel.: 908-527-3300
S.I.C.: 5141

Shop-Rite Cigarettes (CT) **(1)**
600 York St.
Elizabeth, NJ 07207
Tel.: 908-527-3300
S.I.C.: 5194

Shop-Rite Supermarkets, Inc. **(1)**
600 York St.
Elizabeth, NJ 07207
Tel.: 908-527-3300
Supermarkets
S.I.C.: 5411

TRR Carriers, Inc. **(1)**
600 York St.
Elizabeth, NJ 07207
Tel.: 908-527-3300
S.I.C.: 4212

Wakefern Finance Co. **(1)**
600 York St.
Elizabeth, NJ 07207
Tel.: 908-527-3300
S.I.C.: 5141

WALBRIDGE ALDINGER COMPANY
613 Abbott St.
Detroit, MI 48226-2521
Tel.: 313-963-8000
Telex: 810-242-1457
Fax: 313-963-8150
Year Founded: 1916
Assets: $107,649,258
Liabilities: $80,000,207
Net Worth: $27,649,051
Approx.Sls.: $300,000,000
Emp.: 1,357
Fiscal Year-end: 12/31/90
Gen. Contractors/Construction Mgrs.
S.I.C.: 1541; 1542
John Rakolta, Sr. *(Chm. Bd. & Sec.)*
John Rakolta, Jr. *(Pres., Chief Exec. Officer & Treas.)*
Richard J. Haller *(Exec. V.P.)*
Ronald L. Hausmann *(Exec. V.P.)*
Michael R. Haller *(Sr. V.P.)*
Michael W. Carroll *(Grp. V.P. & Chief Fin. Officer)*
Gerald Kelly *(Grp. V.P.)*
Cyril S. Klimes *(Grp. V.P.)*
Gary Brown *(V.P.-Opers.)*
E.G. Clawson *(V.P.-Opers.)*
William Gruebnau *(V.P.-Opers.)*
David Hamilton *(V.P.-Opers.)*
Terry Merritt *(Asst. Corp. Sec. & Pub. Rels. Coord.)*
Kevin Martin *(Dir.-Mktg.)*
Bill Nosseck *(Dir.-Mngmt. Information Systems)*
Jerry Rolfsmeyer *(Dir.-Human Resources)*

A. Gary Gauger *(Mgr.-Sls.)*
James Tessmer *(Chief Estimator)*
Eric Twigg *(Chief Estimator)*

No. of U.S. Offices: 2
No. of Foreign Offices: 2

Computer Systems/Hardware:
IBM System 36; Hewlett Packard 6000

Outside Service Firm(s):

Doeren & Mayhew*(Auditors)*
Troy, MI

Manufacturers National Bank N.A.*(Major Banking Relationship)*
38th Fl., 100 Renaissance Center
Detroit, MI 48243
Tel.: 313-222-4227

Wayne Oakland Agency*(Commercial Insurance Carrier)*
Livonia, MI

Manufacturers National Bank N.A.*(Investment Banker)*
38th Fl., 100 Renaissance Center
Detroit, MI 48243
Tel.: 313-222-4227

Honigman, Miller, Schwartz & Cohn*(Legal Firm)*
2290 First National Bldg.
Detroit, MI 48226
Tel.: 313-256-7800

Subsidiaries:

Darin & Armstrong, Inc. **(1)**
38099 Schoolcraft
Livonia, MI 48150
Tel.: 313-591-6000 (100%)
Gen. Contractors; Construction Mgrs.
S.I.C.: 1541; 1542
John Rakolta, Jr. *(Pres. & Chief Exec. Officer)*

Gulf Constructors International, Inc. **(1)**
P.O. Drawer 4256
Sarasota, FL 34230
Tel.: 813-366-2552 (100%)
Emp.: 350
S.I.C.: 1542; 1522
Daniel E. Whiteman *(Chief Oper. Officer)*

WALCO-LINCK COMPANY
1234 Route 46
Clifton, NJ 07015
Tel.: 201-471-1070
Tel.: 800-338-2329
Fax: 201-471-5574
Approx.Sls.: $10,000,000
Emp.: 25
Fiscal Year-end: 12/31/90
Import Export
Mfr. Glitter Prods., Insecticides, Laundry Bluing
S.I.C.: 2879; 2842
William L. Burge *(Pres.)*
R.E. Bozzo *(V.P.)*

Subsidiary:

Gaston Johnston **(1)**
1234 Rt. 46
Clifton, NJ 07013
Tel.: 201-471-1070
Fax: 201-471-5574
Emp.: 25
Fiscal Year-end: 12/31/91
Johnson's No-Roach & Hadabug Insecticides
S.I.C.: 2879
Bill Burge *(Pres.)*
Richard Bozzo *(V.P.-Opers.)*

WALDBILLIG & BESTEMAN, INC.
6225 University Ave.
Madison, WI 53705
Tel.: 608-238-4767
Tel.: 800-395-4767
Year Founded: 1963
Approx.Billings: $20,540,000
Emp.: 26
Sls. Promo., Financial & High Tech Adv.
William J. Waldbillig *(Pres. & Chief Exec. Officer)*
David A. Genschaw *(Exec. V.P., Chief Fin. Officer)*
Michael Mowbray *(Mktg. Dir.)*
Maryann Jerred *(Pur. Mgr.)*
Philip Davis *(Pub. Rels. Dir.)*
Tracy Garvens *(Data Processing Mgr.)*

Computer Systems/Hardware:
Mini Mainframe AT&T, Apple MacIntosh, IBM, AGFA Imagesetter

WALDES TRUARC, INC.
500 Memorial Dr.
Somerset, NJ 08875
Mailing Address:
P.O. Box 6723
Somerset, NJ 08875
Tel.: 908-469-7999
Fax: 908-469-2532
Approx.Sls.: $30,000,000
Emp.: 101
Fiscal Year-end: 12/31/91
Import Export
Mfr. of Retaining Rings, Assembly Tools, Recessing Tools & Gages
S.I.C.: 3545
Ronald M. England *(Pres.)*
Virgil L. Metcalf *(V.P.-Sls. & Mktg.)*
Frank Vitale *(Treas.)*
Thomas G. Punzo, Jr. *(Sls. Admin.)*
Jerry Fernee *(Mgr.-Quality)*

D. WALDNER COMPANY, INC.
125 Rte. 110
Farmingdale, NY 11735
Tel.: 516-694-1522
Fax: 516-694-1812
Year Founded: 1939
Approx.Sls.: $47,000,000
Emp.: 140
Import Export
Retail Office Furniture
S.I.C.: 5712; 5999
Daniel Waldner *(Chm. Bd.)*
Stephen Waldner *(Chief Exec. Officer)*
John P. Gallivan *(Pres.)*
Art Ravella *(V.P.-Opers.)*
Ruth Borgeson *(Mgr.-Pur.)*
Principal(s):
Stephen Waldner
John P. Gallivan
Jeffrey Waldner

No. of U.S. Offices: 3

Computer Systems/Hardware:
Hedberg/Digital Microyax

Outside Service Firm(s):

Extebank*(Major Banking Relationship)*
Melville, NY

WALDO BROS. COMPANY
202 Southampton St.
Boston, MA 02118
Tel.: 617-445-3000 **MA**
Fax: 617-427-5691
Year Founded: 1869
Sales Range: $10-19 Million
Emp.: 35
Marketing of a General Line of Building Materials
S.I.C.: 5211
Paul Colgan *(Chm. Bd. & Pres.)*
Paul L. Driscoll *(V.P.)*
Richard Davis *(Sec.)*

Outside Service Firm(s):

Ray D. Anderson*(Auditors)*
Boston, MA

State Street Bank & Trust Co.*(Major Banking Relationship)*
225 Franklin St.
Boston, MA 02101
Tel.: 617-328-5000

Subsidiary:

Waldo Bros. Company **(1)**
595 Nutmeg Rd., N.
South Windsor, CT 06074-2461
Tel.: 203-289-9500
Emp.: 4
Marketing of a General Line of Building Materials
S.I.C.: 5211
Scott Hamer *(Gen. Mgr.)*

WALDORF CORPORATION
2250 Wabash Ave.
Saint Paul, MN 55114
Tel.: 800-328-6861
Telex: 612-641-4791
Year Founded: 1985
Sales Range: $100-499 Million
Emp.: 2,100
Mfr. of Recycled Paperboard, Recycled Corrugated Medium and Folding Cartons
S.I.C.: 2657
Employee Matching Gifts Program:
Company Matches Employee Contributions To Local United Way.
Eugene U. Frey *(Chm. Bd. & Chief Exec. Officer)*
Richard E. O'Leary *(Vice Chm.)*
Donald H. Swan *(Pres.)*
Bob Bellafronto *(Sr. V.P.-Folding Carton Opers.)*
Jack Greenshields *(Sr. V.P.-Mill Opers.)*
Tom Cardinal *(V.P.-Quality Assurance & Tech.)*
Brian Kovalchuk *(V.P.-Fin.)*
Lawrence J. Larsen *(V.P.-Personnel)*
Tom Mortimer *(V.P.-Planning & Devel.)*
Jerry Phillips *(V.P. & Gen. Mgr.-F/C Opers. St. Paul)*
Anita M. Bertelsen *(Sec.)*
Robert Gorman *(Mgr.-Mngmt. Information Systems)*
Tom Kalbrener *(Mgr.-Benefits & Compensation)*
Susan Lewis *(Mgr.-Fin. Services & Treas.)*
Bruce Wilson *(Mgr.-Procurement & Transportation)*
JoAnne Heywood *(Telecommunications Specialist)*
Kathy Kubes *(Sec. to the Chm.)*
Principal(s):
Eugene U. Frey
Anita M. Bertelsen
John E. Byrne
Richard E. O'Leary

No. of Mfg. Plants/Facilities: 7
No. of U.S. Offices: 12

Computer Systems/Hardware:
IBM Systems 38 & 36

Outside Service Firm(s):

Price Waterhouse*(Auditors)*
3100 Multifoods Tower, 33 S. Sixth St.
Minneapolis, MN 55402

Dorsey & Whitney*(Legal Firm)*
2200 First Bank Place East
Minneapolis, MN 55402

Towers, Perrin, Forster & Crosby*(Pension Manager)*
8300 Norman Center Drive, Ste. 600
Minneapolis, MN 55437-1097

WALK, HAYDEL & ASSOCIATES, INC.
600 Carondelet St.
New Orleans, LA 70130
Tel.: 504-586-8111 **LA**
Telex: 587302
Fax: 504-522-0554
Year Founded: 1959
Sales Range: $20-39 Million
Emp.: 560
Fiscal Year-end: 5/31/91
Export
Engineering Services; Construction Management
S.I.C.: 8711; 8741
Frank H. Walk *(Co-Chm. Bd. & Chief Exec. Officer)*
Gerald M. Haydel *(Co-Chm. Bd. & Chief Exec. Officer)*
Peter R. Quirk *(Pres. & Chief Oper. Officer)*
E.T.L. Borie *(Sr. V.P.-Process & Environmental)*
Richard A. Van Wooten *(Sr. V.P.)*
Waldemar Stopkey *(V.P.-Admin.)*
W.E. Read *(V.P.-Bus. Devel.)*
Agatha M. Haydel *(Treas.)*
Frank H. Walk, Jr. *(Legal Officer)*
Consuelo F. Walk *(Sec.)*
Donna R. Morris *(Dir.-Investor Rels., Asst. Sec. & Treas.)*
William Clarke *(Dir.-Corp. Video Systems & Telecommunications)*
Elmo Soignier *(Dir.-Personnel)*
Joseph Landwehr *(Dir.-Pur.)*
Principal(s):
Frank H. Walk
Gerald M. Haydel
Agatha M. Haydel
Consuelo F. Walk

No. of U.S. Offices: 4

Outside Service Firm(s):

KPMG Peat Marwick*(Auditors)*
One Shell Center, Ste. 3500
New Orleans, LA 70139

Whitney National Bank of New Orleans*(Major Banking Relationship)*
P.O. Box 61260,
New Orleans, LA 70161

Henican, James & Cleveland*(Legal Firm)*
New Orleans, LA

WALKER & ASSOCIATES, INC.
1100 Morgan Keegan Tower
Memphis, TN 38103
Tel.: 901-522-1100 **TN**
Fax: 901-522-1101
Year Founded: 1965
Approx.Billings: $18,000,000
Emp.: 40
Fiscal Year-end: 12/31/90
Advertising Agency
S.I.C.: 7311
Deloss Walker *(Chm. Bd. & Pres.)*
Mark McMullen *(Exec. V.P.-Mktg. Services)*
Don Sherman *(Exec. V.P.-Mktg. Res.)*
Ceil T. Walker *(Exec. V.P.-Opers.)*
Earl Farrell *(V.P.-Pub. Rels.)*
Marcia Stewart *(Controller)*

No. of U.S. Offices: 2

Computer Systems/Hardware:
IBM System AS400

WALKER & ASSOCIATES, INC.
P.O. Box 1029
Welcome, NC 27374
Tel.: 704-731-6391
Fax: 800-822-1058
Approx.Sls.: $72,000,000
Emp.: 100
Distribute Telephone & Telecommunications Products
S.I.C.: 5065
M. Chris Walker *(Chief Exec. Officer)*
Alva M. Stokes, III *(Pres.)*
Fred Pope *(Chief Fin. Officer & Controller)*
Tim Lawing *(V.P. & Gen. Mgr.)*
Chris Walker *(Treas.)*
Virginia M. Walker *(Sec.)*
Mark Whitley *(Dir.-Fin.)*

Outside Service Firm(s):

Reynolds, Bone & Greisbeck*(Auditors)*
Memphis, TN

Walker & Associates, Inc.—(Continued)

McGladrey & Pullen*(Auditors)*
Winston-Salem, NC

Brown & Associates*(Commercial Insurance Carrier)*
Memphis, TN

Petree, Stockton & Robinson*(Legal Firm)*
3500 One First Union Center, 302 So. College St.
Winston Salem, NC 28202
Tel.: 919-725-2351

Central Benefits Life*(Group Insurer)*
Memphis, TN

First Union National Bank*(Major Banking Relationship)*
Winston-Salem, NC

Leake & Rothman*(Legal Firm)*
Memphis, TN

First Tennessee Bank, N.A.*(Pension Manager)*
Memphis, TN

Branch:

Walker & Associates, Inc. **(1)**
10800 Financial Center Pkwy., Ste. 370
Little Rock, AR 72211
Tel.: 501-221-1894
Fax: 501-227-0703
Brianne Bush *(V.P.)*

WALKER DIE CASTING, INC.
1125 Higgs St.
Lewisburg, TN 37091
Mailing Address:
P.O. Box 1189
Lewisburg, TN 37091
Tel.: 615-359-6206 **TN**
Fax: 615-359-8030
Year Founded: 1958
Approx.Sls.: $40,000,000
Emp.: 300
Zinc Aluminum Die Castings
S.I.C.: 3363
Robert H. Walker *(Pres. & Treas.)*
John R. Walker *(V.P.)*
Kenneth Attkisson *(Gen. Mgr.)*
Elizabeth Cochran *(Sec.)*

No. of Mfg. Plants/Facilities: 1
No. of U.S. Offices: 1

Outside Service Firm(s):

John L. Wallace*(Legal Firm)*
Lewisburg, TN

First National Bank*(Major Banking Relationship)*
Lewisburg, TN

WALKER MAGNETICS GROUP, INC.
17 Rockdale St.
Worcester, MA 01606
Tel.: 508-853-3232 **MA**
Approx.Sls.: $50,000,000
Emp.: 590
Import Export
Machine Tool Attachments & Accessories; Laboratory Apparatus & Furniture; Industrial Instruments Measurement Display/Control Process Variable; Electromedical Equipment; Conveyors & Conveying Equipment
S.I.C.: 3545; 3821; 3823; 3845; 3535; 3549
John N. Engelsted *(Chm. Bd. & Chief Exec. Officer)*
Hendric J.M. Los *(Pres.)*
Charles Alesi *(Exec. V.P.)*
Eric Engelsted *(V.P.)*
Warren C. Lane, Jr. *(Sec.)*

Outside Service Firm(s):

Deloitte & Touche*(Auditors)*
125 Summer St.
Boston, MA 02110
Tel.: 617-261-8000
Fax: 617-261-8111

Lane, Greene, Murtha & McGee*(Legal Firm)*
Worcester, MA

Mechanics Bank*(Major Banking Relationship)*
Worcester, MA

Divisions:

O.S. Walker Co., Inc. **(1)**
17 Rockdale St.
Worcester, MA 01606
Tel.: 508-853-3232
Electromagnetic & Permanent Magnetics; Chucks & Lifting Magnets & Demagnetizers; Laboratory Magnets & Power Supplies
S.I.C.: 3536; 3499; 3545; 3825
Charles Alesi *(Pres.)*

Walker National, Inc. **(1)**
P.O. Box 18155
Columbus, OH 43218
Tel.: 614-481-0007
Mfr. & Repair of Heavy Lifting Magnets for Steel & Scrap Industries
S.I.C.: 3825; 7699
Paul A. Bean *(V.P. & Gen. Mgr.)*

Walker Scientific **(1)**
17 Rockdale St.
Worcester, MA 01606
Tel.: 508-852-3674
Instruments & Measuring Devices
S.I.C.: 3825
Charles Alesi *(Pres.)*

O. S. WALKER CO. INC.
Rockdale St.
Worcester, MA 01606
Tel.: 508-853-3232
Fax: 508-852-8649
Approx.Sls.: $12,000,000
Emp.: 150
Fiscal Year-end: 9/31/91
Import Export
Magnetic Chucks, Lift Magnets & Instruments; Ceramax; Separation Equipment
S.I.C.: 3545
J.N. Engelsted *(Chm. Bd.)*
Charles Alesi *(Pres.)*
Steven Powers *(V.P.-Engrng.)*
John Bernard *(Dir.-Mfg.)*

WALKER-PIONEER MOSS
460 W. 34th St.
New York, NY 10001
Tel.: 212-947-1800
Fax: 212-967-4630
Approx.Sls.: $10,000,000
Emp.: 110
Graphic Arts; Photography
S.I.C.: 7336; 7335
Harry Nichols *(Pres.)*
Hachik Basmajian *(V.P.)*
John Eggers *(V.P.)*
Charles Divin *(Controller)*

Outside Service Firm(s):

Back, Wax, Streisfeld & Schreiber*(Auditors)*
New York, NY

Becker, Goldstein, Graff*(Legal Firm)*
New York, NY

Chemical Bank*(Major Banking Relationship)*
450 West 33rd St.
New York, NY 10001
Tel.: 212-613-7197
Fax: 212-947-7628

M.S. WALKER, INC./ SEACOAST
20 Third Ave.
Somerville, MA 02143
Tel.: 617-776-6700
Fax: 617-776-5808
Year Founded: 1929
Approx.Sls.: $55,000,000
Emp.: 200
Kennedy's Scotch Whiskey & Imports, Allen's Flavored Brandies, Don Cossack Vodka, Cossack Vodka & Gin, Ron Roberto Rum, Casalini Liqueurs, Allen's Liqueurs, Costa do Sol Rose Wine, Karl Von Stetter German Wine
S.I.C.: 2085; 5182
Robert Shaw *(Chm. Bd.)*
Harvey Allen *(Pres. & Chief Exec. Officer)*
Michael Brady *(V.P.-Sls. & Mktg.)*
Scott Allen *(Mktg. Dir.)*
William Livingstone *(Gen. Sls. Mgr.)*

WALKER WIRE & STEEL COMPANY
660 E. Ten Mile Rd.
Ferndale, MI 48220
Tel.: 313-399-4800
Fax: 313-399-7881
Year Founded: 1944
Approx.Sls.: $54,000,000
Emp.: 200
Steel Wire Drawing
S.I.C.: 3315
John D. King *(Pres.)*
Paul R. Goodale *(Exec. V.P.)*
Richard Bare *(V.P.-Fin.)*
William D. McMachon *(Treas. & Sec.)*

No. of Mfg. Plants/Facilities: 3

Outside Service Firm(s):

National Bank of Detroit*(Major Banking Relationship)*
611 Woodward
Detroit, MI 48226
Tel.: 313-225-1000

WALL COLMONOY CORP.
30261 Stephenson Hwy.
Madison Heights, MI 48071
Tel.: 313-585-6400
Fax: 313-585-7960
Year Founded: 1938
Approx.Sls.: $21,100,000
Emp.: 381
Export
Mfr. of Hard Facing Alloys
S.I.C.: 3369; 3724; 3728; 3398; 3399; 3548
William P. Clark *(Chm. Bd.)*
Joseph Maria *(Pres.)*
W.P. Clark, Jr. *(V.P.-Sls. & Mktg.)*
S.C. DuBois *(V.P.-Research & Devel.)*
Robert L. Peaslee *(V.P.)*
Joseph Drobot *(Treas.)*

Outside Service Firm(s):

Coopers & Lybrand*(Auditors)*
400 Renaissance Center
Detroit, MI 48243
Tel.: 313-446-7100
Fax: 313-446-7117

WALLA WALLA GRAIN GROWERS, INC.
P.O. Box 310
Walla Walla, WA 99362
Tel.: 509-525-6510 **WA**
Year Founded: 1929
Approx.Sls.: $49,700,000
Emp.: 22
Fiscal Year-end: 5/31/92
Grain Storage; Storage Co-Op & Marketing Feed & Seed
S.I.C.: 4221; 5153
Craig Buchanan *(Pres.)*
Donald O. Schmidt *(Gen. Mgr., Treas. & Sec.)*
Bruce Bond *(Mgr.-Admin.)*
Jerry Lightfoot *(Mgr.-Opers.)*

Outside Service Firm(s):

Blodgett, Mickelsen & Naef*(Auditors)*
Kennewick, WA

Seattle First National Bank*(Major Banking Relationship)*
Walla Walla, WA

WALLACE CO. INC.
5757 Oates Rd.
Houston, TX 77078
Mailing Address:
P.O. Box 2597
Houston, TX 77252
Tel.: 713-675-2661
Fax: 713-672-5848
Approx.Sls.: $90,000,000
Emp.: 230
Import Export
Distribute Pipe Valves & Fittings
C.S. Wallace, Sr. *(Chm. Bd.)*
C.S. Wallace, Jr. *(Pres.)*
John W. Wallace *(Chief Exec. Officer)*
Bala Nathan *(Chief Fin. Officer)*
Tanya Webb *(Dir.-Personnel)*

Computer Systems/Hardware:
IBM 3031

Outside Service Firm(s):

KPMG Peat Marwick*(Auditors)*
Westchester Financial Ctr., 11 Martine Ave.
White Plains, NY 10606

Texas Commerce Bank*(Major Banking Relationship)*
717 Travis St.
Houston, TX 77002
Tel.: 713-236-4636
Fax: 713-236-5476

Connecticut General Life Insurance Co.*(Pension Manager)*
P.O. Box 2975,
Hartford, CT 06104
Tel.: 203-726-6000

WALLACE LEISURE PRODUCTS, INC.
31 & Jefferson Sts.
Philadelphia, PA 19121
Tel.: 215-232-9900
Fax: 215-235-0570
Approx.Sls.: $25,000,000
Emp.: 150
Manufacture & Import Metal Beds, Folding Tables & Other Furniture
S.I.C.: 2514; 5021
Jerome Robins *(Chm. Bd.)*
Alan Robins *(Pres.)*
Harry Richards *(Controller)*
Phil Lassman *(Mgr.-Pur.)*
Michael Wright *(Mgr.-Engrng.)*

Outside Service Firm(s):

Fishbein & Co.*(Auditors)*
Elkins Park, PA

Meridian Bank*(Major Banking Relationship)*
One Meridian Plaza, 36th Fl.
Philadelphia, PA
Tel.: 215-854-3900

WALLACE & WALLACE FUEL OIL
200-33 Linden Blvd.
St. Albans, NY 11412
Tel.: 718-528-6000
Approx.Sls.: $10,000,000
Emp.: 10
Integrated Oil Company
S.I.C.: 2911; 1311; 1381
Juanita Wallace *(Pres., Chief Fin. Officer, Treas. & Sec.)*

Computer Systems/Hardware:
IBM System 3

Outside Service Firm(s):

St. Paul Insurance Companies*(Commercial Insurance Carrier)*
St.Paul, MN

Empire Blue Cross & Blue Shield*(Group Insurer)*
New York, NY

WALLE CORPORATION
600 Elmwood Park Blvd.
Jefferson, LA 70123
Tel.: 504-734-8000
Fax: 504-733-2513
Approx.Sls.: $14,000,000
Emp.: 140
Lithograph Printing
S.I.C.: 2752
Cecil M. Keeney *(Chief Exec. Officer)*
Michael D. Keeney *(Pres.)*
Robert Riecke *(Treas. & Sec.)*

Outside Service Firm(s):

Hibernia National Bank*(Major Banking Relationship)*
Jefferson, LA

WALLED LAKE DOOR COMPANY
4527 N. 16th St.
Phoenix, AZ 85016
Mailing Address:
P.O. Box 32458
Phoenix, AZ 85064
Tel.: 602-266-4244
Fax: 602-234-2797
Approx.Sls.: $25,000,000
Emp.: 400
Flush Doors, Embossed, Printed Hardboard Doors
S.I.C.: 2431
Edward Quinif *(Chm. Bd. & Pres.)*
Owen Tengelly *(Treas. & Controller)*

Principal(s):
Edward Quinif

Outside Service Firm(s):

Deloitte & Touche*(Auditors)*
2901 North Central Ave., Ste. 1200
Phoenix, AZ 85012
Tel.: 602-234-5100
Fax: 602-234-5186

Citizens & Southern National Bank*(Major Banking Relationship)*
Phoenix, AZ

WALLICH LUMBER CO.
10701 Lyndon
Detroit, MI 48238
Tel.: 313-491-5151
Fax: 313-491-5140
Approx.Sls.: $24,200,000
Emp.: 15
Retail & Wholesale Lumber & Building Materials
S.I.C.: 5031; 5211
Markham Heid *(Pres.)*
James Osebold *(Exec. V.P. & Gen. Mgr.)*
Corey Epstein *(Sec./Treas.)*
Michael Mahoney *(Mgr.- Sls.)*

Outside Service Firm(s):

Doeren & Mayhew*(Auditors)*
Troy, MI

Michigan National Bank*(Major Banking Relationship)*
Ann Arbor, MI

Muller, Muller, Richmond & Harns*(Legal Firm)*
Detroit, MI

W.W. WALLWORK, INC.
4001 W. Main
Fargo, ND 58107
Tel.: 701-282-2350
Tel.: 800-937-3003 **ND**
Fax: 701-282-2350, Ext. 273
Year Founded: 1921
Approx.Sls.: $55,000,000
Emp.: 170
Fiscal Year-end: 12/31/90
Export
Wholesale & Retail Cars, Trucks & Parts, Truck Trailers Service & Repair
S.I.C.: 5012; 5013; 5511; 5531; 7539
W.W. Wallwork, III *(Pres.)*
R. Gourde *(Gen. Mgr. & Sec.)*
John Hajospek *(Controller)*
Dewey McLaren *(Mgr.-Leasing)*
Leo Silbernagel *(Mgr.-Service & Parts)*
Principal(s):
W.W. Wallwork, III

Computer Systems/Hardware:
ADP

Outside Service Firm(s):

Eide Helmeke & Co.*(Auditors)*
500 Dakota Bank Building
Fargo, ND 58102

Dakota Bank & Trust Co. Of Fargo*(Major Banking Relationship)*
Fargo, ND

WALMAN OPTICAL COMPANY
801 12th Ave. N.
Minneapolis, MN 55411
Tel.: 612-520-6000
Tel.: 800-873-9256 **MN**
Year Founded: 1915
Approx.Sls.: $50,000,000
Emp.: 720
Fiscal Year-end: 11/30/91
Mfr. Eyeglasses & Contact Lenses
S.I.C.: 3851
Robert C. Morrow *(Chm. Bd.)*
Charles Patterson *(Pres., Chief Exec. Officer & Chief Oper. Officer)*
Gala Helmke *(Dir.-Data Processing)*
Rose Van Moer *(Dir.-Personnel)*
Emory Solie *(Legal Officer)*

No. of Mfg. Plants/Facilities: 37
No. of U.S. Offices: 37

Computer Systems/Hardware:
Datapoint & Convergent Tech.

ED WALPERT & ASSOCIATES
69-930 Hwy. 111, Ste. 209 & 210
Rancho Mirage, CA 02270
Tel.: 619-770-9200
Fax: 619-770-9761
Year Founded: 1974
Approx.Billings: $15,000,000
Emp.: 10
Sales Promotion, Merchandising & Incentive Travel
H.E. Walpert *(Chm. Bd., Pres. & Chief Exec. Officer)*
S.L. Walpert *(Vice Chm.)*
Margaret King *(V.P., Admin.)*
Helen Nielsen *(Chief Fin. Officer)*

WALPOLE WOODWORKERS, INC.
767 East Street
Walpole, MA 02081
Mailing Address:
P.O. Box 151
Walpole, MA 02081
Tel.: 508-668-2800
Approx.Sls.: $13,000,000
Emp.: 300
Cedar Fencing, Furniture & Small Buildings, Chain Link
S.I.C.: 2499; 2452; 2451; 3496
Samuel D. DeForest *(Pres.)*
Louis A. Maglio *(V.P.-Sls.)*
Robert E. Warrington *(V.P.-Opers.)*
James E. Loer, Jr. *(Treas.)*
Marion Welch *(Mgr.-Admin.)*

Outside Service Firm(s):

Bower Bonanno & Company*(Auditors)*
Needham, MA

Warner & Stackpole*(Legal Firm)*
Needham, MA

Shawmut Bank*(Major Banking Relationship)*
Needham, MA

WALSER AUTOMOTIVE CORPORATION
2100 W. 78th St.
Richfield, MN 55423
Tel.: 612-866-9122
Fax: 612-869-3723
Year Founded: 1956
Approx.Sls.: $170,000,000
Emp.: 525
Auto Selling & Leasing
S.I.C.: 5511; 7514; 7513
Robert J. Walser *(Chm. Bd.)*
Mike Schrank *(Pres.)*
Gelaine Scholz *(Treas. & Sec.)*

Outside Service Firm(s):

Norwest Bank Minnesota, N.A.*(Major Banking Relationship)*
Minneapolis, MN

Subsidiaries:

Walser Ford Inc. **(1)**
3555 S. Hwy. 100
Saint Louis Park, MN 55416
Tel.: 612-925-5500
Automobile Dealership
S.I.C.: 5511

Walser Leasing Inc. **(1)**
317 Main St.
Hopkins, MN 55343
Tel.: 612-933-3083
Automobile & Light Truck Leasing
S.I.C.: 7514; 7515

WALSH CONSTRUCTION CO. OF ILLINOIS
292 W. Adam
Chicago, IL 60607
Tel.: 312-563-5400 **IL**
Fax: 312-927-9813
Year Founded: 1898
Assets: $47,830,033
Liabilities: $37,763,411
Net Worth: $10,066,622
Approx.Sls.: $200,000,000
Emp.: 500
Fiscal Year-end: 12/31/89
General Contractors
S.I.C.: 1542
Mathew Walsh, Jr. *(Chm. Bd.)*
Daniel J. Walsh *(Pres.)*
Larry J. Kibbon *(Treas. & Sec.)*
Rita Curtis *(Dir.-Data Processing)*
Patrick M. Donley *(Dir.-Bus. Devel.)*
Principal(s):
Mathew Walsh, Jr.
Daniel J. Walsh

No. of U.S. Offices: 3

Computer Systems/Hardware:
VS 75 Wang

Outside Service Firm(s):

Wolf & Company*(Auditors)*
Elmhurst, IL

O'Brien, O'Rourke, Hogan & McNulty*(Legal Firm)*
Chicago, IL

Harris Trust & Savings Bank*(Major Banking Relationship)*
111 W. Monroe St.
Chicago, IL 60690
Tel.: 312-461-2265
Tel.: 800-858-0840

WALSWORTH PUBLISHING COMPANY, INC.
306 N. Kansas
Marceline, MO 64658
Tel.: 816-376-3543
Fax: 816-258-7798
Approx.Sls.: $40,000,000
Emp.: 1,000
Yearbook Representative & Distributor
S.I.C.: 2731
Don O. Walsworth *(Pres. & Chief Exec. Officer)*
Richard Mull *(Exec. V.P. & Mgr.-Sls.)*
Joseph Cupp *(V.P.-Opers.)*
Victor Eaton *(V.P.-Yearbook Sls.)*
Joel Bronell *(Treas.)*
George W. Kurten *(Sec. & Dir.-Personnel)*
David Schattgen *(Mgr.-Comml. Printing Sls.)*

Outside Service Firm(s):

Mayer, Hoffman & McCann*(Auditors)*
Marceline, MO

WALTER INDUSTRIES, INC.
1500 N. Dale Mabry Hwy.
Tampa, FL 33607
Tel.: 813-871-4811 **DE**
Fax: 813-871-4360
Year Founded: 1946
Assets: $3,276,211,000
Earnings: $14,462,000
Liabilities: $3,529,493,000
Net Worth: $253,282,000
Approx.Sls.: $1,326,397,000
Emp.: 8,104
Fiscal Year-end: 5/31/91
Import Export
Mfr. of Pressure Pipe & Fittings, Underground Mining, Bituminous; Production of Coke, Chemicals & Allied Products; Various Building Materials & Industrial Products; New Construction of Single Family Homes
S.I.C.: 6719; 1222; 1521; 2999; 3321; 5169
James W. Walter *(Chm. Bd.)*
G.R. Durham *(Pres. & Chief Exec. Officer)*
Kenneth J. Matlock *(Exec. V.P. & Chief Fin. Officer)*
Robert W. Michael *(Sr. V.P. & Grp. Exec.)*
William N. Temple *(Sr. V.P. & Grp. Exec.)*
William H. Weldon *(Sr. V.P.-Fin.)*
Donald M. Kurucz *(V.P. & Treas.)*
Gerald W. Hermann *(V.P.-Employee Rels.)*
David L. Townsend *(V.P.-Pub. Rels.)*
John F. Turbville *(V.P.-Legal & Sec.)*
Perry Golkin *(V.P.)*
Michael T. Tokarz *(V.P.)*
F.A. Hult *(Controller)*
Stephen H. Foxworth *(Asst. Treas.)*
Thomas G. Ketcham *(Asst. Controller)*
Eric McCarthy *(Dir.-Corp. Communications)*
Mary C. Snow *(Asst. Sec.)*

Computer Systems/Hardware:
Amdahl

Outside Service Firm(s):

Price Waterhouse*(Auditors)*
400 N. Ashley, Ste. 2800
Tampa, FL 33602
Tel.: 813-223-7577

Aetna Life & Casualty*(Group Insurer)*
151 Farmington Avenue
Hartford, CT 06156
Tel.: 203-273-2128
Fax: 203-729-4295

Merrill Lynch*(Investment Banker)*
P.O. Box 20, World Trade Center
New York, NY 10281
Tel.: 212-449-4843

Walter Industries, Inc.—(Continued)

Shackleford, Farrior, Stallings & Evans, P.A.*(Legal Firm)*
501 E. Kennedy Blvd., Ste. 1400
Tampa, FL 33602
Tel.: 813-273-5000

Bankers Trust Co.*(Major Banking Relationship)*
280 Park Ave.
New York, NY 10017
Tel.: 212-454-2647

Manufacturers Hanover Trust Co.*(Major Banking Relationship)*
Tampa, FL

Scudder, Stevens & Clark*(Pension Manager)*
345 Park Av.
New York, NY 10154

Sterling Capital Management Co.*(Pension Manager)*
1770 Independence Center
Charlotte, NC 28246
Tel.: 704-372-8670

Subsidiaries:

Best Insurors, Inc. **(1)**
1500 N. Dale Mabry Hwy.
Tampa, FL 33607
Tel.: 813-871-4671 (100%)
Home & General Insurance Services
S.I.C.: 6411
Dana Synder *(Pres.)*
Lee Voss *(V.P.-Fin.)*

Cardem Insurance Co., Ltd. **(1)**
1500 N. Dale Mabry
Tampa, FL 33607
Tel.: 813-871-4811 (100%)
Approx.Sls.: $12,700,000
Reinsurance for Customer Property & Credit Life Insurance
S.I.C.: 6411
Kenneth J. Matlock *(Pres.)*

Dixie Building Supplies, Inc. **(1)**
1500 N. Dale Mabry Hwy.
Tampa, FL 33607
Tel.: 813-871-4718 (100%)
Approx.Sls.: $14,200,000
Emp.: 9
Wholesale Building Supplies
S.I.C.: 5031
R.W. Michael *(Pres.)*

Division:

Mining Div. **(2)**
P.O. Box 133, Rte. 1, Hwy. 216
Brookwood, AL 35444
Tel.: 205-556-6000
Mining
S.I.C.: 1221
William Carr *(Pres.)*
James M. Sims *(V.P., Chief Fin. & Chief Acctg. Officer)*

Hamer Properties, Inc. **(1)**
1500 N. Dale Mabry Hwy.
Tampa, FL 33607
Tel.: 813-871-4811
Property Leasing
S.I.C.: 6519
William N. Temple *(Pres.)*

J. W. Walter, Inc. **(1)**
1500 N. Dale Mabry Hwy.
Tampa, FL 33607
Tel.: 813-871-4811
Property Leasing
S.I.C.: 6519
William N. Temple *(Pres.)*

J.W. Window Components, Inc. **(1)**
1500 N. Dale Mabry Hwy.
Tampa, FL 33607
Tel.: 813-871-4014
Approx.Sls.: $31,000,000
Emp.: 380
Screens & Components, Window Spacers, Weather stripping, & Sash Balances
S.I.C.: 2431
Robert Rudolph *(Pres. & Chief Oper. Officer)*
Frank J. Palladini *(V.P. & Treas.)*
Edmund W. Lanctot, Jr. *(V.P.-Sls. & Mktg.)*

Mid-State Homes, Inc. **(1)**
1500 N. Dale Mabry Hwy.
Tampa, FL 33607
Tel.: 813-871-4621 (100%)
Approx.Sls.: $210,000,000
Emp.: 60
Mortgage Financing for Jim Walter Homes Customers
S.I.C.: 6141
Sam J. Salario *(Pres.)*
W.N. Weldon *(V.P.-Chief Fin. officer)*

Sloss Industries Corporation **(1)**
3500 35th Ave. N.
Birmingham, AL 35207
Tel.: 205-254-7803
Approx.Sls.: $72,000,000
Emp.: 400
Mfr. of Furnace & Foundry Coke, Mineral Wool & Specialty Chemicals
S.I.C.: 3312; 3296
Lee C. Houlditch *(Pres.)*
R. Lee Vinzant *(V.P. & Treas.)*

Southern Precision Div. **(1)**
1500 Georgia Rd.
Birmingham, AL 35210
Tel.: 205-956-3556
Approx.Sls.: $11,000,000
Emp.: 90
Foundry & Plastic Tooling, Numerical Control Machining & Resin-Coated Sand
S.I.C.: 3543; 2821
Earl E. Case *(Pres.)*
Harold F. Bailey *(V.P.)*

United States Pipe & Foundry Company **(1)**
3300 First Ave. N.
Birmingham, AL 35222
Tel.: 205-254-7000 (100%)
Approx.Sls.: $313,000,000
Emp.: 2,700
Water & Waste Water Transmission Products; Industrial Castings
S.I.C.: 3321; 3325; 3491; 3499
Dorrance R. Wedell *(Pres. & Chief Oper. Officer)*
E.J. Mize, Jr. *(V.P.-Fin., Treas., Chief Fin. & Acctg. Officer)*
Joseph T. Donahue *(V.P.-Mktg.)*
William E. Fleck *(V.P.-Mfg.)*
S.M. Boswell *(Dir.-Employee Rels.)*
R.N. Swanson *(Pur. Agent)*

Divisions:

Pipe Div. **(2)**
3300 1st Ave. N.
Birmingham, AL 35202
Tel.: 205-254-7000
Ductile Iron Pressure Pipe, Valve & Fittings, Drain, Waste & Vent Pipe & Fittings
S.I.C.: 3321
Dorrance R. Wedell *(Pres. & Chief Oper. Officer)*
J.T. Donahue *(V.P.-Mktg.)*
W.E. Fleck *(V.P.-Mfg.)*
G.J. Bogs *(Sls. Promo. & Adv. Mgr.)*
H.L. Ransom *(Sls. Mgr.-Pipe)*

U.S. Castings Div. **(2)**
P.O. Box 788,
Anniston, AL 36201
Metal Castings
S.I.C.: 3321
Clarence Parris *(Pres.)*

Vestal Manufacturing **(1)**
South Main St.
Sweetwater, TN 37847
Tel.: 615-337-6125
Approx.Sls.: $13,000,000
Emp.: 190
Production of Iron & Steel Products for the Home, Industrial & Commercial Applications; Fireplace Dampers, Ash Dumps, Clean Out Doors & Various Fireplace Accessories
S.I.C.: 3441
David Vestal *(Pres.)*
Clyde Wells *(Controller & Treas.)*
Keith E. Shope *(V.P.-Opers.)*
Clyde L. Wells *(Controller & Treas.)*

Jim Walter Computer Services, Inc. **(1)**
1500 N. Dale Mabry Hwy.
Tampa, FL 33607
Tel.: 813-871-4242 (100%)
Emp.: 30
Data Processing Services
S.I.C.: 7374
Kenneth J. Matlock *(Pres.)*

Jim Walter Homes, Inc. **(1)**
1500 N. Dale Mabry Hwy.
Tampa, FL 33607
Tel.: 813-871-4611 (100%)
Approx.Sls.: $177,000,000
Emp.: 1,000
Contractor of Single Family Homes
S.I.C.: 1521
Robert W. Michael *(Pres. & Chief Oper. Officer)*
D. Wayne Hornsby *(Exec. V.P.)*
W. Kendall Baker *(V.P., Treas., Chief Fin. & Acctg. Officer)*

Walter Land Co. **(1)**
1500 N. Dale Mabry Hwy.
Tampa, FL 33607
Tel.: 813-871-4472 (100%)
Devel. of Real Estate
S.I.C.: 6552
William N. Temple *(Pres.)*

Jim Walter Resources, Inc. **(1)**
Rte. 1, Hwy. 16
Brookwood, AL 35444
Tel.: 205-556-6000 (100%)
Approx.Sls.: $416,000,000
Emp.: 2,800
Coal Mining; Methane Gas
S.I.C.: 1221
Willaim Carr *(Pres., Chief Oper. Officer)*
James M. Sims *(V.P., Chief Fin. & Acctg. Officer)*
Charles C. Pierce *(V.P.)*

WALTON MONROE MILLS, INC.
119 First St.
Monroe, GA 30655
Mailing Address:
P.O. Box 1046,
Monroe, GA 30655
Tel.: 706-267-9411
Fax: 706-267-9411, Ext. 288
Year Founded: 1895
Approx.Sls.: $505,000,000
Emp.: 5,000
Manufacture Textiles
S.I.C.: 2211; 2281
G. Steven Felker *(Pres., Chief Exec. Officer & Treas.)*
Robert G. Nelson *(Exec. V.P.)*
Marvin S. Bonner *(V.P.-Opers.)*
Mickey Lankford *(V.P.-Mktg.)*
B. Coleman Pannell *(V.P.-Admin. & Sec.)*
Eugene Ash *(Asst. Sec. & Dir.-Indus. Rels.)*

Computer Systems/Hardware:
NCR

Outside Service Firm(s):

Ernst & Young*(Auditors)*
600 Peachtree St. N.E.
Atlanta, GA 30308
Tel.: 404-874-8300

First National Bank of Atlanta*(Major Banking Relationship)*
2 Peachtree Street N.W.
Atlanta, GA 30383

Trust Company Bank*(Major Banking Relationship)*
P.O. Box 4655,
Atlanta, GA 30302

Subsidiary:

Avondale **(1)**
119 First St.
Monroe, GA 30655
Tel.: 706-267-2626
Mfr. of Textiles
S.I.C.: 2211; 2281
Steven Felker *(Chief Oper. Officer)*

WALWORTH COMPANY
10190 Harwin Dr.
Houston, TX 77036
Tel.: 713-777-7788
Approx.Sls.: $25,000,000
Emp.: 240
Fiscal Year-end: 10/31/90
Mfr. Bronze, Iron, Cast Steel, LPV Indus. Valves, Pipeline Gate & Bail Valves
S.I.C.: 3069; 3494; 3492; 3491
Juan Correa *(Pres.)*
Joe Heinrich *(V.P.-Sls.)*

WANG'S INTERNATIONAL, INC.
4250 E. Shelby Dr.
Memphis, TN 38118
Tel.: 901-362-2111 **TN**
Fax: 901-362-2292
Year Founded: 1976
Approx.Sls.: $140,000,000
Emp.: 975
Fiscal Year-end: 4/30/92
Import Export
Wholesale Distributor of Arts & Craft Equipment & Supplies
S.I.C.: 5021; 5719; 5199; 5399
Robert Wang *(Pres.)*
Susie Wang *(Exec. V.P.)*
James Smith *(Chief Fin. Officer)*
Larry Davis *(V.P.-Opers.)*
Bernie Kelley *(V.P.-Sls.)*

ASHLEY F. WARD, INC.
2530 Spring Grove Rd.
Cincinnati, OH 45214
Tel.: 513-381-1943
Fax: 513-381-2029
Approx.Sls.: $23,000,000
Emp.: 100
Mfr. Screw Machine Products, Lighters; Real Estate Development
S.I.C.: 3451; 3999; 6553
Ashley F. Ward *(Chm. Bd.)*
William Ward *(Pres.)*
Eugene P. Ruehlmann *(Sec.)*

Principal(s):
Ashley F. Ward
William Ward

Computer Systems/Hardware:
Burroughs

Outside Service Firm(s):

Strauss & Troy*(Legal Firm)*
Cincinnati, OH

The Central Trust Company, N.A.*(Major Banking Relationship)*
Cincinnati, OH
Tel.: 513-651-8896

THE WARD MACHINERY COMPANY
10615 Beaver Dam Rd.
Cockeysville, MD 21030
Tel.: 410-584-7700
Fax: 410-771-8406
Year Founded: 1962
Approx.Sls.: $51,300,000
Emp.: 425
Fiscal Year-end: 5/31/91
Export
Mfr. Corrugated Container Machinery
S.I.C.: 3554
W.F. Ward, Jr. *(Chm. Bd.)*
Thomas M. Scanlan, Jr. *(Pres. & Chief Exec. Officer)*
David M. Annon *(V.P.-Fin.)*
Thomas C. Davis *(V.P.-Sls. & Mktg.)*
Fred D. Miller *(V.P.-Mfg.)*
Douglas R. Munro *(V.P.-Engrng.)*
W. Lee Thomas *(Gen. Counsel)*
William A. Hopp *(Controller)*
Dwayne Schrader *(Mgr.-Adv.)*

Principal(s):
Thomas M. Scanlan, Jr.

No. of Mfg. Plants/Facilities: 2
No. of U.S. Offices: 4
No. of Foreign Offices: 2

Computer Systems/Hardware:
IBM

Outside Service Firm(s):

Grant Thornton*(Auditors)*
Two Hopkins Plaza
Baltimore, MD 21201
Tel.: 410-685-4000

Maryland National Bank*(Major Banking Relationship)*
10 Light St.
Baltimore, MD 21203
Tel.: 410-244-5000

WARD MANUFACTURING, INC.
115 Gulick St.
Blassburg, PA 16912
Mailing Address:
P.O. Box 9
Blassburg, PA 16912
Tel.: 717-638-2131
Fax: 717-638-3385
Sales Range: $20-39 Million
Emp.: 610
Mfr. of Malleable & Gray Iron Ductile Castings, Fittings Pipe Hangers & Connectors
S.I.C.: 3321; 3322; 3494
Doyne Chartreau *(Pres.)*
Maurice L. Harman *(V.P.-Fin.)*
Mark L. Meyer *(Dir.-Mktg.)*
Ike Campbell *(Pur. Agent)*

Outside Service Firm(s):

Citizens & Northern Bank*(Major Banking Relationship)*
Wellsboro, PA

WARD PRODUCTS CORPORATION
633 Nassau St.
New Brunswick, NJ 08903
Mailing Address:
P.O. Box 1327,
New Brunswick, NJ 08903
Tel.: 908-873-2200
Fax: 908-846-2261
Approx.Sls.: $10,000,000
Emp.: 500
Mfr. of Automobile Antennas & CB Radios
S.I.C.: 3679; 3663
J.B. Cejka *(Pres.)*
E.J. Milazzo *(Exec. V.P.)*
Frank Heeder *(V.P.)*
F.V. Cejka *(Treas. & Sec.)*

Outside Service Firm(s):

United Jersey Bank*(Major Banking Relationship)*
Princeton, NJ

WARD TRUCKING CORP.
2nd Ave. & 7th St.
Altoona, PA 16602
Mailing Address:
P.O. Box 1553,
Altoona, PA 16603
Tel.: 814-944-0803 **PA**
Fax: 814-944-0803, Ext. 316
Year Founded: 1933
Assets: $19,648,000
Liabilities: $6,629,000
Net Worth: $13,019,000
Approx.Sls.: $45,750,000
Emp.: 656
Fiscal Year-end: 12/31/91
Import Export
Transportation of General Commodities
S.I.C.: 4213
G. William Ward *(Chm. Bd.)*
David K. Ward *(Pres.)*
Michael E. Ward *(Exec. V.P.)*
James L. Burns *(V.P.-Oper.)*
Michael Johns *(V.P.-Mktg.)*
Thomas J. Mowers *(V.P.-Mngmt. Info. Systems)*
David K. Ward *(V.P.-Admin.)*
Robert C. Giuler *(Controller)*
J. Richard Ward *(Sec. & Treas.)*
William T. Ward *(Mgr.)*
James Boito *(Mgr.)*

Principal(s):
G. William Ward
David K. Ward
Michael E. Ward

No. of Mfg. Plants/Facilities: 14
No. of U.S. Offices: 14

Computer Systems/Hardware:
AS/400

Outside Service Firm(s):

Young, Oakes, Brown & Co.*(Auditors)*
Altoona, PA

ITT Hartford*(Group Insurer)*
200 W. Madison
Hartford, CT

Blue Cross of Western Pennsylvania*(Group Insurance Broker/Consult)*
One Smithfield St.
Pittsburgh, PA 15222
Tel.: 1-800-242-6425

WARDROP MURTAUGH TEMPLE
333 N. Michigan Ave.
Chicago, IL 60601
Tel.: 312-750-9200
Fax: 312-750-1322
Year Founded: 1970
Approx.Billings: $10,200,000
Emp.: 20
Jack Wardrop *(Pres.)*
Phil Murtaugh *(Sr. V.P.)*
Robert Milhizer *(V.P., Chief Fin. Officer)*

WARDS COVE PACKING COMPANY
88 E. Hamlin St.
Seattle, WA 98109
Mailing Address:
P.O. Box 5030 University Station
Seattle, WA 98105
Tel.: 206-323-3200 **AK**
Year Founded: 1928
Approx.Sls.: $100,000,000
Emp.: 2,000
Fiscal Year-end: 12/31/91
Export
Wholesale Canned Salmon, Fresh & Frozen Salmon, Frozen King Crab, Frozen Opilio Crab, Frozen Black Cod, Fresh & Frozen Halibut, Shrimp, Salmon Caviar
S.I.C.: 5149
A.W. Brindle *(Pres.)*
Harold A. Brindle *(V.P. & Sec.)*
Peter Gasca *(Treas.)*
Patrick J. Douglas *(Mgr.-Sls.)*
Principal(s):
A.W. Brindle
Harold A. Brindle

No. of Mfg. Plants/Facilities: 7
No. of U.S. Offices: 1

Computer Systems/Hardware:
Datapoint

Outside Service Firm(s):

Ernst & Young*(Auditors)*
999 Third Av., Ste. 3500
Seattle, WA 98104
Tel.: 206-621-1800
Fax: 206-682-1234

Reed, McClure, Moceri, Thonn & Moriarty*(Legal Firm)*
3600 Columbia Center, 701 5th Ave.
Seattle, WA 98104
Tel.: 206-292-4900

Subsidiaries:

Alaska Boat Co. **(1)**
P.O. Box 5030 University Station
Seattle, WA 98105
Tel.: 206-323-3200
Operates Boats used for Fishing
S.I.C.: 7999

Seafresh Inc. **(1)**
P.O. Box 5030 University Station
Seattle, WA 98105
Tel.: 206-323-3200
Marketing of Company's Products
S.I.C.: 5149; 5146; 5142

WAREHOUSE HOME FURNISHINGS DISTRIBUTOR
711 Bellevue Ave.
Dublin, GA 31021
Mailing Address:
P.O. Box 1140
Dublin, GA 31040
Tel.: 912-275-3150
Tel.: 800-333-5819 **GA**
Fax: 912-275-6145
Year Founded: 1949
Assets: $90,768,338
Liabilities: $72,731,980
Net Worth: $18,036,358
Approx.Sls.: $115,000,000
Emp.: 1,120
Fiscal Year-end: 1/31/91
Farmers Furniture Company; Wholesale & Retail Furniture
S.I.C.: 5021; 5712
Sherwin Glass *(Chm. Bd.)*
Ronald G. Payne *(Pres. & Chief Exec. Officer)*
Tom Hersman *(Chief Information Officer & Dir. Tele.)*
Phillip Faircloth *(V.P. & Chief Fin. Officer)*
Baker Morgan *(V.P.-Store Opers.)*
Gary Carter *(V.P.)*
Robert Garrett *(V.P.)*
Raymond Couch *(Dir.-Res. & Devel.)*
Mary Ann Darby *(Dir.-Mktg.)*
Steven Sheffield *(Dir.-Human Resources)*
Todd Shingleton *(Dir.-Data Processing)*
Sam Moore *(Controller)*
Bill Danner *(Mgr.-Sls. & Training)*
Tommy Dyson *(Mgr.-Adv.)*
Herman G. Haggard *(Mgr.-Audits & Risk Mgmt.)*
Tom Turner *(Mgr.-Sls. Training)*
Principal(s):
Sherwin Glass

No. of U.S. Offices: 105

Computer Systems/Hardware:
Honeywell/Pick System

Outside Service Firm(s):

Ernst & Young*(Auditors)*
600 Peachtree St. N.E.
Atlanta, GA 30308
Tel.: 404-874-8300

NationsBank*(Major Banking Relationship)*
35 Broad St.
Atlanta, GA 30303
Tel.: 404-581-2121
Tel.: 800-848-8198

Palmer & Cay/Carswell, Inc.*(Commercial Insurance Carrier)*
Savannah, GA

Jones, Hill & Mercer*(Group Insurer)*
P.O. Box 9888
Savannah, GA

Kidder, Peabody & Co.*(Investment Banker)*
Atlanta, GA

Arnall, Golden & Gregory*(Legal Firm)*
55 Park Place
Atlanta, GA 30335
Tel.: 404-577-5100

Subsidiary:

J & J Furniture Co, Inc. **(1)**
703 Oglethorpe Ave.
Albany, GA 31021
Furniture Sales
S.I.C.: 5021
Jerry Sweat *(Pres.)*

WAREMART INC.
8590 Fairview Ave.
Boise, ID 83704
Tel.: 208-377-0110
Fax: 208-377-0474
Year Founded: 1967
Approx.Sls.: $190,000,000
Emp.: 960
Retail Grocery
S.I.C.: 5411
William D. Long *(Chm. Bd. & Pres.)*
Dave Goodwin *(V.P.-Adv. & Pur.)*
Lee Gull *(V.P.-Retail Opers.)*
Gary Piva *(V.P.-Fin.)*
Robert Richins *(V.P.-Properties)*
Jerry Rule *(V.P.-Data Processing)*
Mel Thomas *(V.P.-Meat)*
Millie Newton *(Sec.)*
Principal(s):
Employee-Owned

Outside Service Firm(s):

Deloitte & Touche*(Auditors)*
101 S. Capitol Blvd.
Boise, ID 83702
Tel.: 208-342-5361

Norwest Bank of Minneapolis N.A.*(Investment Banker)*
P.O. Box 738, 161 N. Concord Exchange
So. St. Paul, MN 55075-0738
Tel.: 612-450-4064
Fax: 612-450-4078

Sedgwick James*(Group Insurer)*
Minneapolis, MN

Holland & Hart*(Legal Firm)*
P.O. Box 8749
Denver, CO 80201
Tel.: 303-575-8000

Norwest Bank of Minneapolis N.A.*(Major Banking Relationship)*
P.O. Box 738, 161 N. Concord Exchange
So. St. Paul, MN 55075-0738
Tel.: 612-450-4064
Fax: 612-450-4078

Division:

Waremart Inc. **(1)**
8005 Humziker Rd.
Tigard, OR 97223
Tel.: 503-620-2587
Grocery Store
S.I.C.: 5411
Scott Preece *(V.P.)*

WARING & LAROSA, INC.
909 Third Ave.
New York, NY 10022
Tel.: 212-755-0700
Fax: 212-644-6980
Year Founded: 1968
Approx.Billings: $85,000,000
Emp.: 80
Advertising
S.I.C.: 7311
Joseph LaRosa *(Chm. & Co-Chief Exec. Officer)*
Saul Waring *(Vice Chm. & Co-Chief Exec. Officer)*
Morton Grossman *(Chief Fin. Officer & Treas.)*
Larry Weisberg *(Pres. & Chief Oper. Officer)*
Jim Dragoumis *(Exec. V.P./Dir. Mktg. Services)*
Clancy Cherry *(Sr. V.P., Finance)*
Rosanne DeLuca *(Dir., Bus. Devel. & Pub. Rels.)*
Roberta Tucker *(Personnel Mgr.)*

WARM BROTHERS CONSTRUCTION COMPANY
2335 Florence Ave.
Cincinnati, OH 45206
Tel.: 513-961-3787 **OH**

Warm Brothers Construction Company—(Continued)

Fax: 513-961-1189
Year Founded: 1977
Approx.Sls.: $17,000,000
Emp.: 85
New Construction of Warehouses, Commercial & Office Buildings & Hospitals; Commercial & Inudstrial Building Operation
S.I.C.: 1541; 1542; 6512
Alexander D. Warm *(Chm. Bd.)*
James E. Kelley *(Pres.)*
Stuart Warm *(Exec. V.P. & Treas.)*
Donald L. Rice *(V.P. & Sec.)*

Outside Service Firm(s):

Arthur Andersen & Co.*(Auditors)*
425 Walnut St.
Cincinnati, OH 45202
Tel.: 513-381-6900

Taft, Stettinius & Hollister*(Legal Firm)*
First Natl. Bank Center
Cincinnati, OH 45202
Tel.: 513-381-2838

Fifth Third Bank*(Major Banking Relationship)*
Corporate Trust Services, 38 Fountain Square Plaza
Cincinnati, OH 45263

WARMINGTON HOMES
3090 Pullman Ave., Ste. A
Costa Mesa, CA 92626
Tel.: 714-557-5511
Year Founded: 1972
Approx.Sls.: $61,000,000
Emp.: 200
Speculative Builder; Single Family Homes, Commercial & Office Buildings, Renovation & Repair, Interior Design
S.I.C.: 1531; 1542; 7389
Edward G. Warmington *(Chm. Bd.)*
James P. Warmington *(Pres.)*
Larry Riggs *(Sr. V.P.-Sls. & Mktg.)*
William Kreisle *(Sr. V.P.)*
Timothy P. Hogan *(V.P.)*

WARN INDUSTRIES, INC.
13270 S.E. Pheasant Court
Milwaukie, OR 97222
Tel.: 503-659-8750
Tel.: 800-543-9276
Fax: 503-654-3438
Year Founded: 1948
Approx.Sls.: $69,000,000
Emp.: 450
Fiscal Year-end: 7/30/91
Import Export
Mfr. Battery Driven Winches, Selective Drive Hubs, Fender Flares, Running Boards & Auxiliary Lights
S.I.C.: 3531; 3714
Michael T. Warn *(Pres. & Chief Exec. Officer)*
Scot Davidson *(Aftermarket Mgr.)*
Tom Dunlap *(OEM Mgr.)*
Barbara O'Donnell *(Mgr.-Adv.)*

No. of Mfg. Plants/Facilities: 2
No. of U.S. Offices: 1

Computer Systems/Hardware:
Hewlett-Packard 3000 Series 70 & 42

Outside Service Firm(s):

Deloitte & Touche*(Auditors)*
700 Fifth Ave., Suite 4500
Seattle, WA 98104-5044
Tel.: 206-292-1800

Rainier National Bank*(Major Banking Relationship)*
Seattle, WA

Lasher & Johnson*(Legal Firm)*
Seattle, WA

WARNER, BICKING, MORRIS & PARTNERS, INC.
866 United Nations Plaza
New York, NY 10017
Tel.: 212-759-7900
Fax: 212-759-8087
Year Founded: 1964
Approx.Billings: $29,500,000
Emp.: 30
Fiscal Year-end: 5/31/90
Advertising Agency
S.I.C.: 7311
John E. Warner *(Chm. Bd., Chief Exec. Officer & Creative Dir.)*
Andrew Morris *(Pres. & Chief Oper. Officer)*
Ron Plummer *(Pres.-The Plummer Group)*
Bradley Kabhash *(Pres.-The High Technology Group)*
John F. Bicking *(Dir.-Fin.)*
Carol Romeo *(Dir.-Pub. Rels.)*

No. of U.S. Offices: 1

Branch:

The Plummer Group **(1)**
866 United Nations Plaza
New York, NY 10017
Tel.: 212-759-7900
Fax: 212-759-8087
S.I.C.: 7311
Ron Plummer *(Pres.)*

WARNER CANDY COMPANY, INC.
2954 W. Lawrence Ave.
Chicago, IL 60625
Tel.: 312-539-0400
Fax: 312-539-0804
Year Founded: 1936
Approx.Sls.: $15,000,000
Emp.: 160
Wholesale Distributor of Candy, Salted or Roasted Nuts; Novelties
S.I.C.: 5145; 5199
Philip Kesler *(Pres.)*
Robert Douglas *(V.P. & Sec.)*
Wylie B. Douglas *(V.P.)*
Ruth Douglas *(Treas.)*

Outside Service Firm(s):

Albany Bank*(Major Banking Relationship)*
Chicago, IL

WARNER PRESS, INC.
1200 E. 5th St.
Anderson, IN 46018
Mailing Address:
P.O. Box 2499
Anderson, IN 46018
Tel.: 317-644-7721
Tel.: 800-347-7721
Fax: 317-649-3664
Year Founded: 1881
Assets: $15,495,239
Liabilities: $10,385,336
Net Worth: $5,109,903
Approx.Sls.: $22,000,000
Emp.: 249
Fiscal Year-end: 12/31/91
Religious Publishers; Sunshine Line
S.I.C.: 2731
Donald McCall *(Chm. Bd.)*
Robert G. Rist *(Pres. & Chief Exec. Officer)*
James D. Tanner *(Chief Oper. Officer & Sr. V.P.)*
John Blise *(V.P.-Product Mngmt.)*
Michael G. Hupp *(V.P.-Mktg. & Sls.)*
Ervin Rockhill *(Controller)*
Steve Freeman *(Dir.-Pur.)*
Susan Hare *(Dir.-Mktg.)*
Robert Harvey *(Dir.-Pur.)*
Cheryl Heberling *(Dir.-Pension Admin.)*
Bob Nealeigh *(Dir.-Sls.)*
Stephen Beverly *(Mgr.-Pub. Rels.)*
Steve Brogan *(Mgr.-Personnel)*
James R. Friend *(Mgr.-Data Processing)*
Sandra Hall *(Personnel Asst.)*

Computer Systems/Hardware:
Honeywell/Bull

Outside Service Firm(s):

KPMG Peat Marwick*(Auditors)*
135 N. Pennsylvania St.
Indianapolis, IN 46204
Tel.: 317-636-5592
Fax: 317-635-3314

Busby, Austin, Cooper & Farr*(Legal Firm)*
Indianapolis, IN

Anderson Banking Co.*(Major Banking Relationship)*
Anderson, IN

Divisions:

Commercial Service Printing **(1)**
1200 E. 5th St.
Anderson, IN 46018
Tel.: 317-644-7721

Warner Press Publishers **(1)**
1200 E. 5th St.
Anderson, IN 46018
Tel.: 317-644-7721

WARNER VINEYARDS
706 S. Kalamazoo St.
Paw Paw, MI 49079
Mailing Address:
P.O. Box 269
Paw Paw, MI 49079
Tel.: 616-657-3165
Fax: 616-657-4443
Year Founded: 1938
Approx.Sls.: $10,000,000
Emp.: 100
Fiscal Year-end: 8/31/91
Production & Packaging of Juice & Wine
S.I.C.: 2084; 2037; 2033
James J. Warner *(Pres.)*
Lynne Warner *(Treas. & Sec.)*

Outside Service Firm(s):

KPMG Peat Marwick*(Auditors)*
Peat Marwick Plaza, 303 E. Wacker Dr.
Chicago, IL 60601
Tel.: 312-938-1000

Old Kent Bank*(Major Banking Relationship)*
Kalamazoo, MI

GEORGE E. WARREN CORP.
605 17th St.
Vero Beach, FL 32960
Tel.: 407-778-7100 **MA**
Fax: 407-778-7171
Year Founded: 1908
Assets: $93,702,000
Liabilities: $85,683,000
Net Worth: $8,019,000
Approx.Sls.: $868,267,000
Emp.: 20
Fiscal Year-end: 12/31/91
Import Export
Wholesale Distributor of Petroleum Products
S.I.C.: 5172
Thomas L. Corr *(Pres. & Chief Exec. Officer)*
Cole J. Buckner *(V.P.-Mktg.)*
Jonathan W. Taylor *(Treas.)*
C. David Goldman *(Sec. & Clerk)*
Michael George *(Controller)*

No. of U.S. Offices: 2

Computer Systems/Hardware:
Fujitsu

Outside Service Firm(s):

Arthur Andersen & Co.*(Auditors)*
One Intl. Place, 100 Oliver St.
Boston, MA 02110
Tel.: 617-330-4000
Fax: 617-439-9731

Frank B. Hall*(Commercial Insurance Carrier)*
99 High St.
Boston, MA 02110-3271
Tel.: 617-482-3100

Brenner, Saltzman, Wallman & Goldman*(Legal Firm)*
271 Whitney Ave.
New Haven, CT 06511
Tel.: 203-772-2600
Fax: 203-562-2098

Chase Manhattan Bank, N.A.*(Major Banking Relationship)*
One Chase Manhattan Plaza
New York, NY 10081
Tel.: 212-552-2222
Tel.: 800-526-0801
Fax: 212-552-7175

WARREN DISTRIBUTING CORP.
226 Glenwood Ave.
Raleigh, NC 27603
Tel.: 919-828-9100
Fax: 919-828-8896
Approx.Sls.: $20,000,000
Emp.: 36
Fiscal Year-end: 3/00/90
Household Electrical Appliances
S.I.C.: 5064
Robert S. Warren, Jr. *(Pres.)*
James Finch *(Controller)*
Robert S. Warren III *(Sec. & Treas.)*
Ricky Cooper *(Mgr.-Data Processing)*
Charles Odom *(Gen. Mgr.-Personnel)*

WARREN DISTRIBUTION, INC.
727 S. 13th St.
Omaha, NE 68102
Tel.: 402-341-9397
Fax: 402-341-0494
Approx.Sls.: $68,000,000
Emp.: 150
Fiscal Year-end: 12/31/90
Wholesale Indus. Oils & Greases, Anti-Freeze & Automotive Accessories
S.I.C.: 5172; 5169; 2899
Robert Schlott *(Pres.)*
Chuck Downey *(Chief Fin. Officer)*
John Schluter *(Treas.)*
Jack Schlott *(Dir.)*
Jack Van Orman *(Dir.-Data Processing)*
Thelma Schlott *(Corp. Sec.)*

WARREN EQUITIES INC.
10 E. 53rd St.
New York, NY 10022
Tel.: 212-751-8100
Fax: 212-758-1798
Sales Range: $500-999 Million
Emp.: 1,600
Petroleum Investment, Convenient Stores & Management Consultants
S.I.C.: 5172
Warren Alpert *(Chm. Bd.)*
Edward M. Cosgrove *(Pres.)*
Herbert M. Kaplan *(Exec. V.P.)*
John Dziedzic *(Treas.)*
Richard Sawicki *(Comptroller)*
Thomas Palumbo *(Dir.-Personnel)*
Principal(s):
Warren Alpert

Computer Systems/Hardware:
IBM System 36-NCR Tower Series

Outside Service Firm(s):

KPMG Peat Marwick*(Auditors)*
600 Fleet Center
Providence, RI 02903
Tel.: 401-421-6600

Citibank N.A.*(Major Banking Relationship)*
Corporate Trust Services, 399 Park Ave.
New York, NY 10043
Tel.: 212-559-1605

State Street Bank & Trust Co.*(Major Banking Relationship)*
P.O. Box 366,
Boston, MA 02101
Tel.: 617-426-5523

Alpert & Eastman*(Legal Firm)*
Providence, RI

Subsidiaries:

Drake Petroleum Company, Inc. **(1)**
P.O. Box 2616, Elmwood Station
Providence, RI 02907
Tel.: 401-461-5500
Fax: 401-941-2050
Emp.: 460
Wholesale & Retail Gasoline Operation
S.I.C.: 2911
Alfred J. Letizia *(Pres.)*
James F. Ahern *(V.P.)*
Richard J. Sawicki *(Treas.)*

Kenyon Oil Company, Inc. **(1)**
P.O. Box 866, 221 Quinebaug Rd.
North Grosvenordale, CT 06255
Tel.: 203-974-1400
Fax: 203-923-2173
Emp.: 597
Retail Gasoline & Convenience Store Operation
S.I.C.: 2911; 5411
Francis K. La Forge *(Pres.)*
David Preble *(V.P.)*
John Nagle *(V.P.)*
Ernest Wilk *(Treas.)*

Mid-Valley Oil Company, Inc. **(1)**
1 S. Water St.
New Windsor, NY 12550
Tel.: 914-561-4019
Fax: 914-562-4500
Emp.: 239
Wholesale & Retail Gasoline & Fuel Oil Operation
S.I.C.: 2911; 5983
Dennis Ryley *(Pres.)*
Edward Cosgrove *(V.P.)*
Francis K. La Forge *(V.P.)*
Ernest J. Wilk *(Treas.)*

Mid-Valley Petroleum Corporation **(1)**
1 S. Water St.
Newburgh, NY 12550
Tel.: 914-561-4000
Fax: 914-562-4500
Emp.: 23
Terminaling Operations
Herbert M. Kaplan *(Pres.)*
Edward M. Cosgrove *(V.P.)*
Cosmo A. Scianna *(V.P.)*
John T. Dziedzic *(Treas.)*

Puritan Oil Company, Inc. **(1)**
1 S. Black Horse Pike
Bellmawr, NJ 08030
Tel.: 609-931-3700
Fax: 609-931-5651
Emp.: 73
Wholesale & Retail Gasoline Operation
S.I.C.: 2911
Francis K. LaForge *(Pres.)*
Edward M. Cosgrove *(V.P.)*
Herbert M. Kaplan *(V.P.)*
Richard J. Sawicki *(Treas.)*

Warex Petroleum Corporation **(1)**
355 Allens Ave.
Providence, RI 02905
Tel.: 401-461-5500
Fax: 401-941-2570
Emp.: 17
Wholesale Gasoline & Fuel Oil Trading
S.I.C.: 2911
Herbert M. Kaplan *(Pres.)*
Edward M. Cosgrove *(V.P.)*
August Schiesser *(V.P.)*
John Dziedzic *(Treas.)*

Warren Oil Company **(1)**
355 Allens Ave.
Providence, RI 02905
Tel.: 401-461-5500
Fax: 401-941-2050
Emp.: 46
Wholesale & Retail Fuel Oil Operation
S.I.C.: 2911
Alfred J. Letizia *(Pres.)*
Edward M. Cosgrove *(V.P.)*

Charles S. Jean *(V.P.)*
Richard J. Sawicki *(Treas.)*

WARREN PROPERTIES
(Formerly Frank Raymond Warren)
6134 La Granada
Rancho Santa Fe, CA 92067
Mailing Address:
P.O. Box 915
Rancho Santa Fe, CA 92067
Tel.: 619-756-3711
Year Founded: 1945
Approx.Sls.: $38,000,000
Emp.: 700
Apartment Building, Motel & Hotel Construction; Motel & Hotel Management
S.I.C.: 1522; 7011
Frank Raymond Warren *(Pres.)*
John Sparduto *(Controller)*

Outside Service Firm(s):

Price Waterhouse*(Auditors)*
750 B St.
San Diego, CA 92101
Tel.: 619-231-9830

Rayburn, Moon & Smith, P.A.*(Major Banking Relationship)*
P.O. Box 37389, 217 N. Tryon St.
Charlotte, NC 28237
Tel.: 704-334-0891
Fax: 704-377-1897

WARREN TOOL GROUP
11900 Winrock Rd.
Hiram, OH 44234
Mailing Address:
P.O. Box 68
Hiram, OH 44234
Tel.: 216-569-3224
Fax: 1-800-543-3225
Approx.Sls.: $44,000,000
Emp.: 600
Heavy Hand Tools, Vises, Levels, Clamps, Chisels, Punches & Striking Tools
S.I.C.: 3423
Alexander Pendleton *(Chm. Bd. & Chief Exec. Officer)*
Scott C. Meyer *(V.P.)*

WARREN/KREMER/CMP/ADVERTISING/INC.
Two Park Ave.
NY NY 10016
212-686-2914
Fax 686-5652

WARREN/KREMER/CMP/ADVERTISING/INC.
2 Park Ave.
New York, NY 10016
Tel.: 212-686-2914
Fax: 212-686-5652
Year Founded: 1974
Approx.Billings: $30,000,000
Emp.: 40
Herbert Cohen *(Chm. Bd.)*
Peter Warren *(Pres.)*
John H. Pollok *(Exec. V.P.)*
Robert Paino *(Exec. V.P.)*
Alfonse Marino *(Sr. V.P., Creative Dir.)*
Irving Binder *(Sr. V.P., Sls. Promo.)*
Abraham Kremer *(Sr. V.P.)*
Peter Parisi *(Sr. V.P.)*
Phil Growick *(Sr. V.P.)*
Sy Lipton *(Sr. V.P.)*
Carol McCrone *(Sr. V.P.)*
Brenda Massy *(V.P., Controller)*

WARRENS WALLER PRESS
339 Harbor Way
South San Francisco, CA 94080
Tel.: 415-589-6262 **CA**
Fax: 415-589-0578
Year Founded: 1937
Assets: $11,576,000
Liabilities: $6,683,000
Net Worth: $4,893,000
Approx.Sls.: $15,000,000
Emp.: 110
Fiscal Year-end: 12/31/91
Commercial Lithographic Printing
S.I.C.: 2752
Betty J. Tipton *(Chm. Bd.)*
Lynne Mertens *(Pres.)*
Richard Jankowski *(Chief Exec. Officer)*
Frank Brunini *(V.P.-Mfg.)*
Stephen Hart *(V.P.)*
Leslie Schmidt *(Sec. & Treas.)*
Heinz Mertens *(Plant Mgr.)*

Outside Service Firm(s):

Harris & Margolis*(Auditors)*
Philadelphia, PA

Jackson, Petty Cole & Black*(Legal Firm)*
650 California St.
San Francisco, CA 94108
Tel.: 415-433-1950

Bank of America NT&SA*(Major Banking Relationship)*
555 California St.
San Francisco, CA 94105
Tel.: 415-622-5120
Fax: 415-622-4585

Subsidiary:

Reliable Graphics **(1)**
San Rafael, CA
Printing
S.I.C.: 2752
Robert Davies *(Pres.)*

WARWICK BAKER & FIORE INC
ADVERTISING
A PARTNER IN ALLIANCE INTERNATIONAL

WARWICK BAKER & FIORE INC.
100 Ave. of the Americas
New York, NY 10013
Tel.: 212-941-4200
Fax: 212-941-4277
Approx.Billings: $170,000,000
Emp.: 160
Advertising
S.I.C.: 7311
John P. Warwick *(Hon. Chm.)*
Wilder D. Baker *(Chm. & Chief Exec. Officer)*
Robert J. Fiore *(Pres., Chief Oper. Officer & Creative Dir.)*
Ronald S. Fierman *(Exec. V.P., Gen. Mgr.)*
Susan Small-Weil *(Exec. V.P., Chief Plng. Officer)*
Tony Isidore *(Exec. V.P., Creative Dir.)*
Paul Paulson *(Exec. V.P.)*
Karen Mortenson *(Sr. V.P., Mgr. New Bus. Devel.)*
Ann Demeri *(V.P., Personnel)*

WASCO PRODUCTS, INC.
Pioneer Ave.
Sanford, ME 04073
Mailing Address:
P.O. Box 351
Sanford, ME 04073
Tel.: 207-324-8060
Fax: 207-324-8377
Approx.Sls.: $25,000,000
Emp.: 250
Roof Windows, Skylights, Heat & Smoke Vents
S.I.C.: 3444; 3442
Merle Taylor *(Pres.)*
Arthur P. Jentoft *(Exec. V.P.)*
Donald G. White *(Treas.)*
Bart Moffer *(Gen. Mgr.-Residential Div.)*
Merle E. Taylor *(Gen. Mgr.-Comml. Div.)*
Gilbert N. L'Heureux *(Pur. Agent)*

Outside Service Firm(s):

MacDonald, Page & Company*(Auditors)*
Portland, ME

Pierce, Atwood, Scribner, Allen, Smith & Lancaster*(Legal Firm)*
Portland, ME

Fleet National Bank*(Major Banking Relationship)*
Portland, ME

WASHERS, INC.
33375 Glendale Ave.
Livonia, MI 48150
Tel.: 313-523-1000 **MI**
Fax: 313-425-1297
Emp.: 170
Mfr. Metal Washers & Bolts
S.I.C.: 3452
George Strumbos *(Pres.)*
John D. Donahue *(Sec.)*

Outside Service Firm(s):

NBD Bank, N.A.*(Major Banking Relationship)*
611 Woodward Ave.
Detroit, MI 48226
Tel.: 313-225-1122

Subsidiary:

Alpha Bolt Company **(1)**
1524 E. Fourteen Mile Rd.
Madison Heights, MI 48071
Tel.: 313-585-6050
Approx.Sls.: $21,000,000
Emp.: 75
Mfr. Metal Bolts
S.I.C.: 3452
John Kantgias *(Pres.)*
George Strumbos *(V.P. & Treas.)*
Bernard Thiteca *(V.P.)*
John D. Donahue *(Sec.)*

WASHINGTON BEEF COMPANY
1300 Mercantile Lane, Ste. 100 J
Landover, MD 20785
Tel.: 301-925-2777
Fax: 301-925-4536
Year Founded: 1940
Approx.Sls.: $30,000,000
Emp.: 135
Wholesale Fresh Meats & Allied Products
S.I.C.: 5147
Gaylen Nickey *(Pres.)*

Outside Service Firm(s):

KPMG Peat Marwick*(Auditors)*
Bethesda, MD

Adelberg, Rudow, Hendler & Sameth*(Legal Firm)*
10 Light St.
Baltimore, MD 21202
Tel.: 410-539-5195

First American Bank, N.A.*(Major Banking Relationship)*
Washington, DC

WASHINGTON CORPORATION
101 International Way
Missoula, MT 59801
Tel.: 406-523-1300
Fax: 406-721-4794
Approx.Sls.: $500,000,000
Emp.: 3,000
Heavy Construction, Mining & Public Utilities
S.I.C.: 1623; 6719
Dennis Washington *(Chm. Bd.)*
Dorn Parkinson *(Pres.)*
Leroy Wilkes *(V.P.)*
Helen B. Miller *(Treas. & Sec.)*
Greg Rutherford *(Controller)*
William Murphy *(Gen. Counsel)*

Washington Corporation—(Continued)

Outside Service Firm(s):

American National Bank & Trust of St. Paul*(Major Banking Relationship)*
Fifth & Minnesota Streets
St. Paul, MN 55101
Tel.: 612-298-6000

WASHINGTON HOMES, INC.
1802 Brightseat Rd., 6th Fl.
Landover, MD 20785-4235
Tel.: 301-772-8900 **MD**
Fax: 301-772-1380
Year Founded: 1965
Approx.Sls.: $95,000,000
Emp.: 170
Fiscal Year-end: 7/31/91
Home Builders
S.I.C.: 1521
Geaton A. DeCesaris, Sr. *(Chm. Bd.)*
Geaton A. DeCesaris, Jr. *(Pres. & Chief Exec. Officer)*
Clayton Miller *(Chief Fin. Officer)*
Paul Sukalo *(Sr. V.P.)*
Robert Yeatman *(Sr. V.P.)*
John Zwirecki *(Sr. V.P.)*
Thomas Connelly *(Sec.)*
Jackie Lozier *(Treas.)*
Rose Kerr *(Asst. Controller)*

Outside Service Firm(s):

Deloitte & Touche*(Auditors)*
Alexandria, VA

Signet Bank*(Major Banking Relationship)*
Bethesda, MD

Hopkins & Sutter*(Legal Firm)*
888 16th St., N.W.
Washington, DC 20006

Subsidiaries:

All-Seasons, Inc. **(1)**
1802 Brightseat Rd.
Largo, MD 20785-4235
Tel.: 410-772-8900 (100%)
General Contractor
S.I.C.: 1521

Citadel Land, Inc. **(1)**
1802 Brightseat Rd.
Largo, MD 20785-4235
Tel.: 410-772-8900 (100%)
General Contractor
S.I.C.: 1521

Consultants Corp. **(1)**
1802 Brightseat Rd.
Largo, MD 20785-4235
Tel.: 410-772-8900 (100%)
General Contractor
S.I.C.: 1521

Designed Contracts, Inc. **(1)**
1802 Brightseat Rd.
Largo, MD 20785-4235
Tel.: 410-772-8900 (100%)
General Contractor
S.I.C.: 1521

Housing-Home Sales, Inc. **(1)**
1802 Brightseat Rd.
Largo, MD 20785-4235
Tel.: 410-772-8900 (100%)
General Contractor
S.I.C.: 1521

The Southampton Corp. **(1)**
1802 Brightseat Rd.
Largo, MD 20785-4235
Tel.: 410-772-8900 (100%)
General Contractor
S.I.C.: 1521

Washington Homes Financial Corporation **(1)**
1802 Brightseat Rd.
Largo, MD 20785-4235
Tel.: 410-772-8900 (100%)
Credit Institutions
S.I.C.: 6141

Washington Homes Financial Corporation, II **(1)**
1802 Brightseat Rd.
Largo, MD 20785-4235
Tel.: 410-772-8900 (100%)
Credit Institutions
S.I.C.: 6141

Washington Homes Financial Corporation, III **(1)**
1802 Brightseat Rd.
Largo, MD 20785-4235
Tel.: 410-772-8900
Credit Institutions
S.I.C.: 6141

Washington Homes, Inc. of Virginia **(1)**
1802 Brightseat Rd.
Largo, MD 20785-4235
Tel.: 410-772-8900 (100%)
General Contractors
S.I.C.: 1521

The Washington Savings Bank, FSB **(1)**
P.O. Box 220, Charles County Plaza
Waldorf, MD 20604
Tel.: 301-843-7200
Approx.Assets: $100,000,000
Savings Institutions
S.I.C.: 6035

WASHINGTON MUTUAL SAVINGS BANK
1201 Third Ave.
Seattle, WA 98101
Tel.: 206-461-2000 **WA**
Year Founded: 1889
Assets: $7,117,800,000
Liabilities: $6,558,100,000
Net Worth: $559,700,000
Approx.Income: $4,801,800,000
Fiscal Year-end: 12/31/91
State Chartered Stock Savings Bank
S.I.C.: 6036
Kerry K. Killinger *(Chm. Bd., Chief Exec. Officer & Pres.)*
William A. Longbrake *(Sr. Exec. V.P. & Chief Fin. Officer)*
Lee D. Lannoye *(Exec. V.P.)*
Craig E. Tall *(Exec. V.P.)*
Michael D. Towers *(Exec. V.P.)*
S. Liane Wilson *(Exec. V.P.)*
Larry R. Bond *(Sr. V.P.)*
Jack A. Cornick *(Sr. V.P.)*
Alan J. Dorman *(Sr. V.P.)*
Lindy J. Friedlander *(Sr. V.P.)*
Steven J. Freimuth *(Sr. V.P.)*
Robert J. Flowers *(Sr. V.P.)*
Marc R. Kittner *(Sr. V.P. & Corp. Counsel)*
Robert J. Mathison *(Sr. V.P.)*
David G. Murphy *(Sr. V.P.)*
Deanna W. Oppenheimer *(Sr. V.P.)*
M. Lynn Ryder *(Sr. V.P.)*
Norman H. Swick *(Sr. V.P.)*
Douglas G. Wisdorf *(Sr. V.P. & Controller)*
William L. Lynch *(V.P. & Sec.)*

Subsidiaries:

Washington Mutual Federal Savings Bank **(1)**
1201 Third Ave.
Seattle, WA 98101
Tel.: 206-461-2000
Federal Savings Bank
S.I.C.: 6035

Subsidiaries:

Columbia Services, Inc. **(2)**
1201 Third Ave.
Seattle, WA 98101
Tel.: 206-461-2000
Insurance Agents
S.I.C.: 6411

First Columbia Escrow, Inc. **(2)**
1201 Third Ave.
Seattle, WA 98101
Tel.: 206-461-2000
S.I.C.: 6531

Mill Maple Properties, Inc. **(2)**
1201 Third Ave.
Seattle, WA 98101
Tel.: 206-461-2000
S.I.C.: 6531

Mill Plain One, Inc. **(2)**
1201 Third Ave.
Seattle, WA 98101
Tel.: 206-461-2000
Real Estate
S.I.C.: 6531

Mill Plain Two, Inc. **(2)**
1201 Third Ave.
Seattle, WA 98101
Tel.: 206-461-2000
Real Estate
S.I.C.: 6531

Mill Plain Three, Inc. **(2)**
1201 Third Ave.
Seattle, WA 98101
Tel.: 206-461-2000
Real Estate
S.I.C.: 6531

Mill Plain Four, Inc. **(2)**
1201 Third Ave.
Seattle, WA 98101
Tel.: 206-461-2000
Real Estate
S.I.C.: 6531

North American Acceptance Corporation **(2)**
1201 Third Ave.
Seattle, WA 98101
Tel.: 206-461-2000
S.I.C.: 6531

SS Service Corporation **(2)**
1201 Third Ave.
Seattle, WA 98101
Tel.: 206-461-2000
Loan Insurance
S.I.C.: 6411

VanFed Appraisal Company **(2)**
1201 Third Ave.
Seattle, WA 98101
Tel.: 206-461-2000
Appraisal Company
S.I.C.: 6531

VanFed Investment Service, Inc. **(2)**
1201 Third Ave.
Seattle, WA 98101
Tel.: 206-461-2000
Investment Advisory Service
S.I.C.: 6282

VanFed Mortgage Company **(2)**
1201 Third Ave.
Seattle, WA 98101
Tel.: 206-461-2000
S.I.C.: 6162

WM Financial, Inc. **(1)**
1201 Third Ave.
Seattle, WA 98101
Tel.: 206-461-2000
Investment Services Advisors; Company Intermediary Between Parent & Subsidiaries
S.I.C.: 6282

Subsidiaries:

Benefit Service Corporation **(2)**
1201 Third Ave., 12th Fl.
Seattle, WA 98101
Tel.: 206-461-2000
Pension & Retirement Plan Consultants
S.I.C.: 6411

Subsidiary:

Benefit Service Corporation of Alaska **(3)**
4300 B St., Ste. 104
Anchorage, AK 99503
Pension & Retirement Plan Consultants
S.I.C.: 6411

Composite Research & Management Company **(2)**
1201 Third Ave.
Seattle, WA 98101
Tel.: 206-461-2000
Investment Advisory Company
S.I.C.: 6282

Murphy Favre, Inc. **(2)**
1201 Third Ave.
Seattle, WA 98101
Tel.: 206-461-2000
Securities Brokers
S.I.C.: 6211

Subsidiary:

Murphy Favre Securities Services, Inc. **(3)**
601 Riverside Ave., Fl. 9
Spokane, WA 99201
Investment Advisory Service
S.I.C.: 6282

Murphy Favre Properties, Inc. **(2)**
1191 2nd Ave.
Seattle, WA 98101
Manage Real Estate Limited Partnerships
S.I.C.: 6531

Subsidiary:

Murphy Favre House Managers, Inc. **(3)**
1201 Third Ave., 3rd Fl.
Seattle, WA 98101
Tel.: 206-461-2000
As Special Limited Partner In Real Estate Partnerships
S.I.C.: 6531

Mutual Travel, Inc. **(2)**
1201 Third Ave., 18th Fl.
Seattle, WA 98101
Tel.: 206-461-2000
Full-Service Travel Agency
S.I.C.: 4724

Subsidiaries:

Kawaguchi Travel Services, Inc. **(3)**
1201 Third Ave., 18th Fl.
Seattle, WA 98101
Tel.: 206-461-2000
Travel Agency Specializing In Business, Group & Incentive Travel
S.I.C.: 4724

Signature Travel, Inc. **(3)**
1201 Third Ave., 18th Fl.
Seattle, WA 98101
Tel.: 206-461-2000
Travel Agency
S.I.C.: 4724

Subsidiaries:

General Travel Services, Inc. **(4)**
1201 Third Ave., 18th Fl.
Seattle, WA 98101
Tel.: 206-461-2000
Travel Agency
S.I.C.: 4724

Holiday House, Inc. **(4)**
1201 Third Ave., 18th Fl.
Seattle, WA 98101
Tel.: 206-461-2000
Travel Agency
S.I.C.: 4724

WM Life Insurance Company **(2)**
1203 Third Ave., 6th Fl.
Seattle, WA 98101
Tel.: 206-461-2000
Capital Life Insurance Company
S.I.C.: 6311

Subsidiary:

Empire Life Insurance Company **(3)**
1203 Third Ave., 6th Fl.
Seattle, WA 98101
Tel.: 206-461-2000
Life Insurance Company
S.I.C.: 6311

WM Trust Company **(2)**
1201 Third Ave.
Seattle, WA 98101
Tel.: 206-461-2000

Washington Mutual Life Insurance Services **(2)**
1201 Third Ave.
Seattle, WA 98101
Tel.: 206-461-2000
Life & Health Insurance Company
S.I.C.: 6321; 6311

Preston Ridge Financial Services Corporation **(1)**
1201 Third Ave.
Seattle, WA 98101
Tel.: 206-461-2000
Financial Service Company
S.I.C.: 6282

Subsidiaries:

Preston Properties of Arizona, Inc. **(2)**
1201 Third Ave.
Seattle, WA 98101
Tel.: 206-461-2000
S.I.C.: 6531

Preston Properties of California, Inc. **(2)**
1201 Third Ave.
Seattle, WA 98101
Tel.: 206-461-2000
S.I.C.: 6531

Preston Properties Texas, Inc. **(2)**
1201 Third Ave.
Seattle, WA 98101
Tel.: 206-461-2000
S.I.C.: 6531

Preston Property Management Company **(2)**
1201 Third Ave.
Seattle, WA 98101
Tel.: 206-461-2000
S.I.C.: 6531

WASHINGTON STATE DAIRY PRODUCTS COMMISSION
1107 N.E. 45th, Ste. 205
Seattle, WA 98105
Tel.: 206-545-6763
Fax: 206-545-6666
Year Founded: 1939
Approx.Sls.: $1,200,000,000
Emp.: 7
Fiscal Year-end: 6/30/90
Adv. & Promo. Milk Prods.
S.I.C.: 8611
Liz Anderson *(Chm. Bd.)*
Stephen Matzen *(Gen. Mgr.)*
Steve Malloch *(Mgr.-Adv. & Promo.)*
Amy Carr *(Communications Specialist)*

WASSERSTROM COMPANY
477 S. Front St.
Columbus, OH 43215
Tel.: 614-228-6526 **OH**
Fax: 614-228-6525, Ext. 306
Approx.Sls.: $51,000,000
Emp.: 250
Export
Office Furniture & Supplies
S.I.C.: 5087; 5021; 5046; 5112
Rodney Wasserstrom *(Pres. & Chief Exec. Officer)*
Frank Fancelli *(Exec. V.P. & Chief Opers. Officer)*
Robert Stone *(Exec. V.P.)*
Dennis Blank *(Sr. V.P.-Fin.)*
Tom Rush *(Dir.-Data Processing & Ass't. V.P.)*
William Voigt *(Mgr.-Distr. & Ass't. V.P.)*
Ursula Vermillion *(V.P.)*
Ernest Lang *(Ass't. V.P.-Pur.)*
Shelly Myers *(Ass't. V.P.-Human Resources)*
Debbie Rabe *(Controller)*
Alan Wasserstrom *(Treas.)*

Outside Service Firm(s):

Coopers & Lybrand*(Auditors)*
100 E. Broad St.
Columbus, OH 43215

BancOhio National Bank*(Major Banking Relationship)*
Columbus, OH

Wasserstrom & Soltis*(Legal Firm)*
Columbus, OH

WATERLOO SERVICE COMPANY
1402 Logan
Waterloo, IA 50703
Mailing Address:
P.O. Box 300,
Waterloo, IA 50704
Tel.: 319-233-4232 **IA**
Fax: 319-233-5134
Year Founded: 1935
Assets: $3,194,987
Liabilities: $811,764
Net Worth: $2,383,223
Approx.Sls.: $35,173,655
Emp.: 24
Fiscal Year-end: 8/31/91
Petroleum Co-operative
S.I.C.: 5171
Bruce Kitzinger *(Pres.)*
Stephen Hinman *(V.P.)*
Clair W. Randall *(Gen. Mgr.)*
Gerald Staebell *(Sec.)*

No. of Mfg. Plants/Facilities: 3
No. of U.S. Offices: 1

Outside Service Firm(s):

Meriwether, Wilson & Co.*(Auditors)*
1200 35th St., Ste. 400
Des Moines, IA 50265

Farmland Insurance*(Commercial Insurance Carrier)*
1963 Bell Ave.
Des Moines, IA 50315

Associated Benefits Corp.*(Group Insurer)*
2929 Westown Pkwy.
Des Moines, IA 50265

Redfern Mason Dieter Larsen & Moore*(Legal Firm)*
315 Clay St.
Cedar Falls, IA 50613

Waterloo Savings Bank*(Major Banking Relationship)*
Waterloo, IA

National Bank of Waterloo*(Pension Manager)*
Trust Department, P.O. Box 5300
Waterloo, IA 50704

WATKINS ASSOCIATED INDUSTRIES INC.
1958 Monroe Dr. NE
Atlanta, GA 30324
Tel.: 404-872-3841
Fax: 404-872-2812
Emp.: 51
Diversified Holding Company
S.I.C.: 6719
Bill Watkins *(Chm. Bd.)*
William A. Freeman *(Pres.)*
John F. Watkins, Jr. *(V.P.)*
W. B. Watkins IV *(V.P.)*
George W. Ready *(Treas. & Sec.)*

Computer Systems/Hardware:
IBM System 34

Subsidiaries:

Land Span Inc. **(1)**
6270 McDonough Dr.
Norcross, GA 30093
Tel.: 404-441-2990
Emp.: 60
Common Carrier Long Distance Trucking
S.I.C.: 4213
Peter C. Monti *(Pres.)*

Navajo Western Land Co. **(1)**
502 W. 7th
Walsenburg, CO 81089
Tel.: 719-738-3043
Approx.Sls.: $683,000,000
Emp.: 6
Real Estate Subdividers & Developers
S.I.C.: 6552
William A. Freeman *(Pres.)*

Watkins Associated Developers **(1)**
1958 Monroe Dr. NE
Atlanta, GA 30301
Tel.: 404-872-3841
Emp.: 11
Non-Residential Property Operator
S.I.C.: 6512
William A. Freeman *(Pres.)*

WATKINS INCORPORATED
P.O. Box 5570,
Winona, MN 55987-0570
Fax: 507-452-6723
Year Founded: 1868
Approx.Sls.: $40,000,000
Emp.: 300
Import Export
Extracts, Spices, Health & Beauty Aids, Household Aids, Insecticides, Medicines, Food Specialties, Farm Supplies
S.I.C.: 2082; 2099; 2879; 5191
Irwin L. Jacobs *(Chm. Bd.)*
Richard C. Wantock *(Pres.)*
Duane R. Evans *(V.P.-Fin.)*
James R. Yenish *(V.P.-Admin. & Treas.)*
Terri Lieder *(Art Dir.)*
Merlyn Von Bargen *(Pur. Agent)*

WATKINS SYSTEM INC.
Rte. 202
Concordville, PA 19331
Mailing Address:
P.O. Box 4000
Concordville, PA 19331
Tel.: 215-358-3400 **PA**
Fax: 215-459-0224
Approx.Sls.: $56,000,000
Emp.: 200
Retail Truck Sales & Leasing; Fleet Maintenance Services; Skilled Labor Services
S.I.C.: 5511; 7363; 7513
Dwain J. Watkins *(Chm. Bd.)*
Robert G. Watkins, Jr. *(Vice Chm. & Co-Pres.)*
George E. Watkins *(Co-Pres.)*
Donald R. Shipengrover *(Treas. & Sec.)*
Joe Watkins *(Asst. Treas.)*
Henrietta Stafford *(Mgr.-Personnel)*

WATLOW ELECTRIC MANUFACTURING COMPANY
12001 Lackland Rd.
Saint Louis, MO 63146
Tel.: 314-878-4600 **MO**
Fax: 314-878-6814
Year Founded: 1922
Emp.: 1,500
Fiscal Year-end: 12/31/91
Export
Designs & Manufactures Electric Heating Units, Temperature Controls & Sensors, Power Switching Devices & Controls for Industrial & Commercial Machinery & Equipment
S.I.C.: 3823; 3822; 3567
George B. Desloge *(Chm. Bd.)*
Louis Desloge, Jr. *(Vice Chm.)*
Gary M. Neal *(Pres. & Chief Exec. Officer)*
Gene Kalhorn *(Sr. V.P.)*
George Marklin *(Sr. V.P.)*
Worth A. Kramer *(V.P., Treas. & Corp. Sec.)*
Keith Laken *(V.P. & Div. Gen. Mgr.)*
Ray Kunz *(Controller)*
Tom Weiss *(Div. Gen. Mgr.)*
William F. Ott, Jr. *(Dir.-Mktg.)*
Elmer Moore *(Dir.-Human Resources)*
Monica Green *(Dir.-Compensation & Benefits)*
J. Michael Mason *(Dir.-Information Systems)*
Paul Horn *(Dir.-Total Quality)*
Donna Rosenberg *(Mgr.-Corp. Admin.)*
Judith H. Simms-Brown *(Mgr.-Adv. Services)*
Tim Crnko *(Mgr.-Natl. Sls.)*

No. of Mfg. Plants/Facilities: 10
No. of Foreign Offices: 6

Computer Systems/Hardware:
UNISYS 2200

Outside Service Firm(s):

KPMG Peat Marwick*(Auditors)*
1010 Market St.
Saint Louis, MO 63101
Tel.: 314-444-1400

Mark Twain Bank*(Major Banking Relationship)*
12375 St. Charles Rock Rd.
Bridgeton, MO 63044

Greensfelder, Hemker and Gale, P.C.*(Legal Firm)*
1800 Equitable Bldg., 10 S. Broadway
St. Louis, MO 63102
Tel.: 314-241-9090

Subsidiaries:

Chesterfield Industrial Park, Inc. **(1)**
12001 Lackland Rd.
St. Louis, MO 63146
Tel.: 314-878-4600
Real Estate Holding Company
S.I.C.: 3567; 6512; 6719

Claud S. Gordon Company **(1)**
5710 Kenosha St.
Richmond, IL 60071
Tel.: 815-678-2211 (100%)
Fax: 815-678-3961
Emp.: 250
Mfr. Industrial Instruments for Measurement, Display & Control of Process Variables & Related Products
S.I.C.: 3823
Dennis Studley *(Dir.-Opers.)*
G.L. Wells *(Dir.-Sls. & Mktg.)*

Pacific Heater Corporation **(1)**
115 Flier Dr.
Pacific, MO 63069
Tel.: 314-257-6166
Fax: 314-257-6184
Mfr. of Cartridge Heaters
S.I.C.: 3567
Drew Dubray *(Gen. Mgr.)*

Watlow Aov, Inc. **(1)**
4545 E. La Palma Ave.
Anaheim, CA 92807
Tel.: 714-779-2252
Fax: 714-777-9626
Export
Mfr. of Electric Heating Elements
S.I.C.: 3567
Joe Riley *(Gen. Mgr.)*

Watlow Batavia, Inc. **(1)**
1310 Kingsland Dr.
Batavia, IL 60510
Tel.: 708-879-2696 (100%)
Fax: 708-879-1101
Mfr. of Cast-in Heaters
S.I.C.: 3567
Pat Kinane *(Gen. Mgr.)*

Watlow Columbia, Inc. **(1)**
2101 Pennsylvania Dr.
Columbia, MO 65202
Tel.: 314-474-9402 (100%)
Fax: 314-474-5859
Mfr. of Flexible & Ceramic Fiber Heaters
S.I.C.: 3567
Charles Baughman *(Gen. Mgr.)*

Watlow Winona, Inc. **(1)**
1241 Bundy Blvd.
Winona, MN 55987
Tel.: 507-454-5300
Mfr. of Electronics
S.I.C.: 3823
Keith Laken *(Gen. Mgr.)*

Watlow Electric Manufacturing Company—(Continued)

Division:

Watlow Infrared Company **(2)**
Freeport Industrial Pk.
Decorah, IA 52101
Tel.: 319-382-8446 (100%)
Fax: 319-382-2418
Mfr. of Infrared Instruments
S.I.C.: 3823
Randy Buschling *(Gen. Mgr.)*

Watlow Electric Company of California **(1)**
12001 Lackland Rd.
St. Louis, MO 63146
Tel.: 314-878-4600
Real Estate Holding Company
S.I.C.: 6512; 6719

Watlow Electric Foreign Sales Corporation **(1)**
12001 Lackland Rd.
St. Louis, MO 63146
Tel.: 314-878-4600
Foreign Sales Corporation
S.I.C.: 5084

Watlow Industries, Inc. **(1)**
6 Industrial Loop Dr.
Hannibal, MO 63401
Tel.: 314-221-2816
Fax: 314-221-3723
Mfr. of Electric Heating Units, Temperature Controls & Thermocouples for Industrial & Commercial Machinery & Equipment
S.I.C.: 3567
Allan Wideman *(Gen. Mgr.)*
Steve Rhoads *(Sls. Mgr.)*

Division:

Watlow Process Systems, Inc. **(2)**
300-A Industrial Dr.
Troy, MO 63379
Tel.: 314-528-7676
Fax: 314-528-7091
Electric Heating Units
S.I.C.: 3567
Rob Bohn *(Gen. Mgr.)*

Watlow St. Louis, Inc. **(1)**
12001 Lackland Rd.
St. Louis, MO 63146
Tel.: 314-878-4600
Fax: 314-878-6814
Electric Heating Units
S.I.C.: 3567
Tom Weiss *(Gen. Mgr.)*

Non-U.S. Holdings:

Watlow Electric Mfg. Co. GmbH **(1)**
Industriegebiet Heidig, Lauchwasenstrasse
1 Postfach 1165, D-7521
Kronau, Germany
Tel.: 49 7253 890 (100%)
Fax: 7253 8999
Emp.: 50
Mfr. of Heating Elements
S.I.C.: 3567
Michael Glynn *(Gen. Mgr.)*

Watlow France S.A.R.L. **(1)**
Immeuble Somag, Z.I. Rue Ampere 95300
Pontoise, France
Tel.: 33 1 3073 24 25 (100%)
Fax: 33 1 3073 28 75
Emp.: 4
Sales & Marketing Office
S.I.C.: 5064
Jose Desloge *(Gen. Mgr.)*

Watlow Italy **(1)**
Via Adige 13 20135
Milan, Italy
Tel.: 2 5518 5161 (100%)
Telex: 316419
Fax: 11 39 2 5519 1596
Emp.: 4
Sales & Marketing Office
S.I.C.: 5084
Andrea Fabiano *(Gen. Mgr.)*

Watlow Korea **(1)**
Samsung Bldg., St. 302, 945-3 Daechi-Dong, Kangham-ku
Seoul, Korea
Tel.: 011 82 2 563 5777
Fax: 011 82 2 563 5779
Emp.: 2
Sales & Marketing Office
S.I.C.: 5084
Kim Kye Su *(Gen. Mgr.)*

Watlow Limited **(1)**
Thornfield Industrial Estate, Hooton St.
Nottingham, NG3 2NJ, United Kingdom
Tel.: 602 691 418444 (100%)
Fax: 602 413954
Emp.: 30
Mfr., Sales & Marketing of Heating Elements
S.I.C.: 3567; 5075; 5084
Peter Wilson *(Gen. Mgr.)*

Watlow Singapore Pte. Ltd. **(1)**
Ayer Rajah Industrial Estate, 55 Ayer Rajah Crescent #03-19 to #03-23,
Singapore, 0513, Singapore
Tel.: 65-777 5488
Fax: 65-778 0323
Emp.: 3
Sales & Marketing Office
S.I.C.: 5075; 5084
Watson Ng *(Gen. Mgr.)*

Watlow Taiwan **(1)**
10F-1 No. 189 Chi-Sen 2nd Road,
Kaohsiung, Taiwan
Tel.: 7 216 5891
Fax: 7 216 5892
Emp.: 2
Sales & Marketing Office
S.I.C.: 5084; 5063
Andy Yeh *(Gen. Mgr.)*

WATSON ELECTRIC SUPPLY INC.
320 S. Walton
Dallas, TX 75226
Mailing Address:
P.O. Box 159002,
Dallas, TX 75315
Tel.: 214-742-8441
Fax: 214-741-4811
Year Founded: 1947
Approx.Sls.: $25,000,000
Emp.: 250
Fiscal Year-end: 9/30/88
Wholesaler of Electrical Appliances & Supplies
S.I.C.: 5063; 5064; 5065; 5084
Houston B. Watson *(Chm. Bd., Chief Exec. Officer, Chief Fin. Officer & Treas.)*
Austin B. Watson *(Vice Chm.)*
Malcolm Lee Watson *(Pres.)*
Anthony Watson *(V.P. & Asst. Sec.)*

Computer Systems/Hardware:
IBM System 36

Outside Service Firm(s):

Weaver & Tidwell*(Auditors)*
Fort Worth, TX

Life Insurance Co. of the Southwest*(Group Insurer)*
Dallas, TX

NationsBank Texas*(Major Banking Relationship)*
901 Main St., 16th Fl.
Dallas, TX 75202
Tel.: 214-922-5000

NationsBank Texas*(Pension Manager)*
901 Main St., 16th Fl.
Dallas, TX 75202
Tel.: 214-922-5000

WATSON'S QUALITY TURKEY PRODUCTS, INC.
Black Horse Pike
Turnersville, NJ 08012
Mailing Address:
P.O. Box 215
Turnersville, NJ 08012
Tel.: 609-227-0594
Fax: 609-228-6756
Approx.Sls.: $20,000,000
Emp.: 150
Processed Turkey
S.I.C.: 2015
Albert O. Watson *(Pres.)*
Vince Bond *(Mgr.-Sls.)*

WATT INDUSTRIES
2716 Ocean Park Blvd.
Santa Monica, CA 90405
Tel.: 310-450-0779
Fax: 310-452-9134
Year Founded: 1959
Approx.Sls.: $622,000,000
Emp.: 800
Real Estate Company
S.I.C.: 6531
Raymond A. Watt *(Chm. Bd.)*
Theodore Cox *(Pres.)*
James Maginn *(Chief Fin. Officer & Sr. V.P.)*
Judith Hain Leimert *(Sr. V.P.-Fin.)*
Ryoko Takata *(Controller)*

Outside Service Firm(s):

Kenneth Leventhal & Co.*(Auditors)*
Century City, CA

Bank of America NT&SA*(Major Banking Relationship)*
555 So. Flower St.
Los Angeles, CA 90071
Tel.: 213-683-3868

Watt, Roop & Co.

WATT, ROOP & CO.
1100 Superior Ave., 13th Fl.
Cleveland, OH 44114
Tel.: 216-566-7019
Fax: 216-566-0857
Year Founded: 1981
Approx.Billings: $29,800,000
Emp.: 32
Public Relations & Marketing
Ronald W. Watt *(Chm. & Chief Exec. Officer)*
James J. Roop *(Pres. & Chief Oper. Officer)*
Howard Cleveland *(Pres.-WRC Mktg. Group)*
Michael Zimmerman *(Sr. V.P.)*
Andy Opila *(Sr. V.P.)*
Pamela S. Barr *(Sr. V.P.)*

WAUKESHA FOUNDRY INC.
1300 Lincoln Ave.
Waukesha, WI 53186
Tel.: 414-542-0741
Fax: 414-549-8440
Year Founded: 1914
Approx.Sls.: $20,000,000
Emp.: 180
Export
Stainless Steel, Corrosion & Heat Resistant, High Alloy Steel, Waukesha Metal, Brass & Aluminum Castings
S.I.C.: 3561; 3363; 3366; 3325
B. Kerwin *(Pres.)*
G. Evans *(V.P.-Sls. & Mktg.)*
J. Richter *(V.P.-Fin.)*
Diane Konkel *(Mgr.-Indus. Rels.)*
K. VanzenBergen *(Pur. Agent)*

Outside Service Firm(s):

Arthur Andersen & Co.*(Auditors)*
777 E. Wisconsin Ave., P.O. Box 1215
Milwaukee, WI 53202
Tel.: 414-271-5100
Fax: 414-283-3200

WAUSAU HOMES, INC.
Hwy. 51 South
Rothschild, WI 54474
Mailing Address:
P.O. Box 8005
Wausau, WI 54402
Tel.: 715-359-7272
Fax: 715-359-2867
Year Founded: 1960
Approx.Sls.: $80,000,000
Emp.: 325
Fiscal Year-end: 12/31/91
Wausau Homes
S.I.C.: 1522
Marvin Schuette *(Pres. & Chief Exec. Officer)*
Frank Opatik *(V.P. & Dir.-Engrng.)*
Tom Schuette *(V.P.)*
Jim Von Rueden *(Chief Fin. Officer & Controller)*
Pat Brady *(Gen. Counsel)*
Tom Mason *(Dir.-Sls. & Mktg.)*
Glen Schilling *(Dir.-Mfg.)*
Madonna McMahan *(Mgr.-Mktg. Services)*
Duane Peterson *(Mgr.-Personnel)*
Jim Hamann *(Pur. Agent)*

WAVETEK CORPORATION
9045 Balboa Ave.
San Diego, CA 92123
Mailing Address:
P.O. Box 85265
San Diego, CA 92138
Tel.: 619-279-2200 **DE**
Fax: 619-450-0325
Year Founded: 1963
Earnings: $19,000
Approx.Sls.: $90,605,000
Emp.: 970
Fiscal Year-end: 9/30/91
Designing, Developing, Mfg. & Marketing World Wide General & Special Purpose Electronic Test & Measurement Equipment & Related Products
S.I.C.: 3825; 3829; 5049
Terrance Gooding *(Pres. & Chief Exec. Officer)*

Outside Service Firm(s):

Deloitte & Touche*(Auditors)*
701 "B" St., Ste. 1900
San Diego, CA 92101-8198

Gray, Cary, Ames & Frye*(Legal Firm)*
2100 Union Bank Bldg.
San Diego, CA 92101
Tel.: 619-699-2700

Divisions:

Wavetek Communications Div. **(1)**
5808 Churchman Bypass
Indianapolis, IN 46203-6109
Tel.: 317-788-9351 (100%)
Telex: 684-2041
Fax: 317-788-5999
Emp.: 273
Fiscal Year-end: 9/27/91
Export
Computer Systems/Hardware:
Prime
Designs, Mfr. & Mkts. Signal Generators, CATV Test Equip. & Calibration Instruments
S.I.C.: 3825
Dr. Terence Gooding *(Pres.)*
John Dwight *(V.P. & Gen. Mgr.)*
Janet Gearns *(Controller)*
Shirlee Ewell *(Sec.)*
Ron Jent *(Mgr.-Mfg.)*
Glenn Meyer *(Mgr.-Pur.)*
Steve Zug *(Mgr.-Human Resources)*
Jim Pletcher *(Mgr.-Mngmt. Info. Systems)*
Erney Nikov *(Mgr.-Quality Control)*
Jay Smith *(Mgr.-Engnrg.)*
Russ Byrd *(Mgr.-Mktg.)*
Jack Webb *(Mgr.-Mktg.)*

Wavetek Microwave, Inc. **(1)**
488 Tosman Dr.
Sunnyvale, CA 94089
Tel.: 408-734-5780
S.I.C.: 3825

Subsidiary:

Wavetek San Diego Inc. **(1)**
P.O. Box 85265, 9045 Balboa Ave.
San Diego, CA 92123
Tel.: 619-279-2200 (100%)
Fax: 619-565-9558
Emp.: 321
Mfr. of Function Generators, Sweep & Phase Meters
S.I.C.: 3825
Darrell Johnson *(Gen. Mgr.)*

Non-U.S. Holdings:

Wavetek Datron **(1)**
Hurricane Way, Norwich Airport
Norwich, NR6 6JB, United Kingdom
Tel.: 0603-404824
Fax: 0603-483670
Mfr. of Precision Digital Multimeters, Calibrators & Calibration Equipment
S.I.C.: 3825
Paul Stevenson *(Gen. Mgr.)*

Wavetek Electronics GmbH **(1)**
Hans-Pinsel Strasse 9-10 8013
Munich, Germany
Tel.: 089-465062/66 (100%)
Sls. & Mfr. of Electronic Test & Measurement Equipment
S.I.C.: 3825; 5065
Achim Methline *(European Sls. Dir.)*

Wavetek Electronics Ltd. **(1)**
Kingfisher Works, Tag Lane Hare Hatch, Reading, Berkshire RG10 9LT, United Kingdom
Tel.: 073-522-2124 (100%)
Mfr. & Sls. of Electronic Test Equipment
S.I.C.: 3825; 5065
Brian Malin *(Gen. Mgr.)*

WAWA, INC.
Red Roof, Baltimore Pike
Wawa, PA 19063
Tel.: 215-358-8000 **NJ**
Fax: 215-358-8777
Year Founded: 1865
Approx.Sls.: $463,814,000
Emp.: 7,800
Fiscal Year-end: 12/31/90
Convenience Stores
S.I.C.: 5411
Richard P. Wood, Jr. *(Pres.)*
Donald H. Price *(Exec. V.P.)*
Vincent P. Anderson *(Sr. V.P. & Legal Officer)*
Ed Chambers *(Sr. V.P. & Chief Fin. Officer)*
Howard Stoeckel *(V.P.-Mktg.)*
Carolyn Bratten *(Legal Sec.)*

No. of Mfg. Plants/Facilities: 1
No. of U.S. Offices: 9

Computer Systems/Hardware:
Digital

Outside Service Firm(s):

Deloitte & Touche*(Auditors)*
1700 Market St.
Philadelphia, PA 19103
Tel.: 215-246-2322
Fax: 215-569-2441

Montgomery, McCracken, Walker & Rhoads*(Legal Firm)*
3 Parkway
Philadelphia, PA 19103
Tel.: 215-563-0650

Philadelphia National Bank*(Major Banking Relationship)*
P.O. Box 13834, Broad & Chestnut Streets
Philadelphia, PA 19101-7618
Tel.: 215-973-8327

WAYN-TEX INC.
901 S. Belphine Ave.
Waynesboro, VA 22980
Tel.: 703-946-4200
Mfr. of Carpet Backing Fabrics
S.I.C.: 2299
Bill Rion *(Pres. & Chief Oper. Officer)*

WAYNE CORPORATION
(Filed Chapter 11 Bankrptcy-August 12, 1992)
Industries Rd.
Richmond, IN 47374-8447
Mailing Address:
P.O. Box 1448,
Richmond, IN 47374
Tel.: 317-962-7511 **DE**
Fax: 317-962-5729
Year Founded: 1837
Sales Range: $80-99 Million
Emp.: 556
Fiscal Year-end: 1/31/91
Export
Manufacture Commercial, School & Special Buses
S.I.C.: 3711
Jack H. DeKruif *(Chm. Bd. & Chief Exec. Officer)*
Paul E. Hartge *(V.P.-Sls. & Mktg.)*
Phillip C. Williams *(Dir.-Regional Sls. & Mktg.)*
Wayne Roselius *(Dir.-Engrng.)*
Tony LaCalamita *(Mgr.-Regional Sls. & Mktg.)*
Jerry Basuk *(Mgr.-Opers.)*
Ken Neverman *(Mgr.-Regional Sls. & Mktg.)*

No. of Mfg. Plants/Facilities: 1
No. of U.S. Offices: 1

Computer Systems/Hardware:
IBM 4331-2 & PS2/30, IBM PC-XT

Outside Service Firm(s):

Arthur Andersen & Co.*(Auditors)*
111 Monument Circle
Indianapolis, IN 46204
Tel.: 317-634-3210

Star Bank*(Major Banking Relationship)*
Richmond, IN

Associated Agencies*(Commercial Insurance Carrier)*
Morrisville, PA

John Hancock Mutual Life Insurance Co.*(Group Insurer)*
Columbus, OH

James V. Looby, Esq.*(Legal Firm)*
Glendale, CA

WAYNE STEEL, INC.
1070 W. Liberty St. Extn.
Wooster, OH 44691
Tel.: 216-264-8416 **OH**
Fax: 216-264-8420
Approx.Sls.: $55,000,000
Emp.: 110
Steel Service Center
S.I.C.: 5051
Thomas J. Shapiro *(Pres.)*
Robert L. Stauffer *(V.P.-Fin.)*
Brian L. Schmidt *(Controller)*
Tom Pacek *(Mgr.-Materials)*

Outside Service Firm(s):

Meaden & Moore*(Auditors)*
Cleveland, OH

Buckingham, Doolittle & Burroughs L.P.A.*(Legal Firm)*
50 S. Main St., P.O. Box 1500
Akron, OH 44309
Tel.: 216-376-5300

WAYNE WIRE CLOTH PRODUCTS, INC.
10 Dresden St.
Kalkaska, MI 49646
Tel.: 616-258-9187 **MI**
Fax: 616-258-5504
Year Founded: 1943
Approx.Sls.: $16,000,000
Emp.: 300
Mfr. of Industrial Filters & Strainers, Screw Machine Products & Stampings
S.I.C.: 3569
Carl Miller, Jr. *(Chm. Bd.)*
Edward Goossens *(Pres.)*
Dale Lantzer *(Comptroller)*
Mike Brown *(Mgr.-Sls.)*
Norman Groner *(Mgr.-Prod.)*
Thomas Ropers *(Chief Engr.)*

Outside Service Firm(s):

R.J. Johnson*(Auditors)*
Traverse City, MI

Farmers & Merchants Bank*(Major Banking Relationship)*
Hillman, MI

Division:

Hillman Division **(1)**
P.O. Box 156
Hillman, MI 49746
Tel.: 517-742-4591
Mfr. of Hardware Cloth, Woven Wire, Mewtal Stampings, Welding Repair
S.I.C.: 3496
G. Thomas *(Gen. Mgr.)*

WALTER H. WEABER SONS, INC.
RD #4 Box 1255
Lebanon, PA 17042
Tel.: 717-867-2212
Fax: 717-867-1711
Year Founded: 1941
Approx.Sls.: $32,000,000
Emp.: 340
Export
Rough, Sawed & Planed Lumber; Kiln Drying Of Lumber
S.I.C.: 2421
Galen G. Weaber *(Pres.)*
Nicholas Georgells *(V.P.-Sls.)*
Rodney J. Graeff *(V.P.-Fin. & Treas.)*
Larry E. Shuman *(V.P. & Sec.)*
Stanley Templin *(V.P.)*

Outside Service Firm(s):

Knisley & Associates*(Auditors)*
Harrisburg, PA

Egli, Reilly, Walfson, Sheffy & Shrum*(Legal Firm)*
Lebanon, PA

Midlantic National Bank*(Major Banking Relationship)*
744 Broad St.
Newark, NJ 07101
Tel.: 201-266-8295

WEASLER ENGINEERING INC.
Hwy. 45 N.
West Bend, WI 53095
Mailing Address:
P.O. Box 558
West Bend, WI 53095
Tel.: 414-338-2161 **WI**
Fax: 414-338-3709
Year Founded: 1951
Approx.Sls.: $20,000,000
Emp.: 220
Fiscal Year-end: 12/31/88
Mfr. Drive Lines, Universal Joints, Shock Absorbing Flexible Couplings, Torque Limiting & Over-Running Clutches
S.I.C.: 3568
Anthony V. Weasler *(Chm. Bd.)*
James T. Hawkins *(Pres.)*
Ben Reak *(Sr. V.P.-Corp. Devel.)*
Thomas R. Crowley *(V.P.-Opers.)*
James N. Gennrich *(V.P.-Fin.)*
George L. Goering *(V.P.-Pur.)*
Roger Mayhew *(V.P.-Res. & Devel.)*
Principal(s):
Anthony V. Weasler

Computer Systems/Hardware:
DEC PDP 11/83

Outside Service Firm(s):

Zeigert, Smaler, Kaminski & Freyberg*(Auditors)*
Milwaukee, WI

M & I Marshall & Ilsley Bank*(Major Banking Relationship)*
West Bend, WI

Division:

AG Components Div. **(1)**
Hwy. 45 N.
West Bend, WI 53095
Tel.: 414-338-2161
Richard D. Preston *(Vice Pres.)*

WEATHERBY, INC.
2781 Firestone Blvd.
South Gate, CA 90280
Tel.: 213-569-7186
Fax: 213-569-5025
Year Founded: 1945
Approx.Sls.: $20,000,000
Emp.: 80
Fiscal Year-end: 12/31/90
Import Export
Mfr. Weatherby Rifles, Shotguns, Scopes & Ammunition
S.I.C.: 3484
Ed Weatherby *(Chm. Bd. & Pres.)*
Patrick Bell *(Chief Fin. Officer)*
Paul Shepard *(Gen. Counsel)*
Brad Ruddell *(Dir.-Mktg.)*

WEATHERLY FINANCIAL GROUP
(Formerly The Weatherly Companies)
20 Exchange Place, 23rd Fl.
New York, NY 10005
Tel.: 212-809-2920 **DE**
Fax: 212-363-4788
Year Founded: 1982
Investment Banking
S.I.C.: 6719; 6799
Tom McFall *(Chm., Pres. & Chief Exec. Officer)*

Outside Service Firm(s):

Price Waterhouse*(Auditors)*
30 S. 17th St.
Philadelphia, PA 19103
Tel.: 215-665-9500

Weatherly Private Capital, Inc.*(Investment Banker)*
New York, NY

Citibank N.A.*(Major Banking Relationship)*
Los Angeles, CA

Division:

Weatherly Consumer Products, Inc. **(1)**
101 Prosperous Place, Ste. 200
Lexington, KY 40509
Tel.: 606-263-3633
Fax: 606-263-3669
Mfr. Jobe's & Ross Brand Horticulture & Plant Care Accessories
S.I.C.: 0781; 0181
James R. Hills *(Pres.)*
Graig Schuster *(Chief Fin. Officer)*
Thomas Bensberg *(Dir.-Mfg.)*

Subsidiaries:

Hamburger Hamlets Inc. **(1)**
14156 Magnolia Blvd.
Sherman Oaks, CA 91423-1119
Tel.: 818-995-7333
Fax: 818-783-1525
Assets: $34,025,000
Earnings: ($992,000)
Liabilities: $11,971,000
Net Worth: $22,054,000
Approx.Sls.: $53,012,000
Fiscal Year-end: 12/29/91
Holding Co.; 19 Restaurants in CA; 4 in Washington, DC; 1 in Chicago, IL
S.I.C.: 5812; 6719
Thomas McFall *(Chm. & Chief Exec. Officer)*
Paul M. Brockman *(Pres.)*
David Fox *(Exec. V.P.)*
Barry Crater *(V.P.-Food & Beverage)*
Joseph Lordon *(V.P.-Human Resources)*
Fran Pomerantz *(V.P.-Human Devel.)*
Jon Richards *(V.P.-Construction & Devel.)*

Weatherly Capital Corp. **(1)**
20 Exchange Place, 23rd Fl.
New York, NY 10005
Tel.: 212-809-2920
Investment Consultants
S.I.C.: 6799

Weatherly Financial Group—(Continued)

Weatherly Frozen Foods Group, Inc. **(1)**
1000 118th Ave., N.
St. Petersburg, FL 33702
Tel.: 813-577-1500
Fax: 813-576-8971
Manufacture & Distribute Frozen Desserts & Frozen Novelties
S.I.C.: 2024
Thomas G. Dixcy *(Pres.)*
William Fagot *(Chief Fin. Officer)*

Weatherly Private Capital, Inc. **(1)**
20 Exchange Place, 23rd Fl.
New York, NY 1005
Tel.: 212-809-2920
Fax: 212-363-4788
Investment Banking Services
S.I.C.: 6211
Thomas A. McFall, Jr. *(Pres. & Chief Exec. Officer)*

Weatherly Securities Corp. **(1)**
20 Exchange Place, 23rd Fl.
New York, NY 10005
Tel.: 212-809-2920
Fax: 212-363-4788
Broker/Dealer Of Listed & Unlisted Securities
S.I.C.: 6211
Michael E. Recca *(Pres.)*

C. WEAVER CHEVROLET, INC.
Commercial Dr.
New York Mills, NY 13417
Mailing Address:
P.O. Box 100
New York Mills, NY 13417
Tel.: 315-736-0151
Fax: 315-736-0157
Approx.Sls.: $12,000,000
Emp.: 43
Car & Truck Sales, Service, Parts & Leasing
S.I.C.: 5511; 7515; 7513; 7538; 7539; 7537
Joseph V. Cooper *(Chm. Bd. & Pres.)*
David Cooper *(Exec. V.P.)*
Richard Mallory *(Treas. & Sec.)*
John Balzano *(Gen. Counsel)*
Jim Robinson *(Mgr.-Sls.)*

Computer Systems/Hardware:
NCR

Outside Service Firm(s):

Stegmeier, Smith & Cyphert*(Auditors)*
Alden, NY

Savings Bank of Utica*(Major Banking Relationship)*
Utica, NY

W.H. WEAVER CONSTRUCTION CO.
P.O. Box 26040-604
Greensboro, NC 27420
Tel.: 919-275-9600
Fax: 919-275-2241
Approx.Sls.: $30,000,000
Emp.: 175
General Contractors
S.I.C.: 1541; 1542
Michael Weaver *(Chm. Bd.)*
Roy J. Maness *(Pres.)*
Douglas A. George *(V.P.-Sls.)*
Robert G. Kelley *(V.P.-Fin.)*
Allen Leach *(Controller)*

Outside Service Firm(s):

Arthur Andersen & Co., S.C.*(Auditors)*
1345 Avenue of the Americas
New York, NY 10019
Tel.: 212-708-4000

McGladrey & Pullen*(Auditors)*
Drawer G-2, 230 N. Elm St.
Greensboro, NC 27402
Tel.: 919-273-4461

Brooks, Pierce, McLendon, Humphrey & Leonard*(Legal Firm)*
2000 Renaissance Plaza
Greensboro, NC 27402
Tel.: 919-373-8850

First Union National Bank*(Major Banking Relationship)*
P.O. Box 21965,
Greensboro, NC 27420

WEAVER POPCORN COMPANY, INC.
130 E. Main St.
Van Buren, IN 46991
Mailing Address:
P.O. Box 395,
Van Buren, IN 46991
Tel.: 317-934-2101 **IN**
Fax: 317-934-4052
Year Founded: 1928
Approx.Sls.: $85,000,000
Emp.: 250
Fiscal Year-end: 9/30/90
Export
Mfr. & Package Popcorn
S.I.C.: 2096; 5145
Welcome I. Weaver *(Chm. Bd.)*
Michael E. Weaver *(Pres., Chief Exec. Officer & Chief Oper. Officer)*
Bradley Egbert *(Chief Fin. Officer)*
Richard P. Lintner *(Sr. V.P.)*
Cathy Karporal *(Dir.-Consumer Affairs)*
Ed O'Neil *(Dir.-Res. & Devel.)*
Teresa A. Flaugher *(Mgr.-Mktg. Services)*
James Labas *(Mgr.-Export)*
Hal Taylor *(Mgr.-Natl. Sls.-Retail)*
Rebecca Weaver *(Mgr.-Human Resources)*
Principal(s):
Weaver Family

No. of Mfg. Plants/Facilities: 2

WEB FOOD PRODUCTS CORP.
144-06 94th Ave.
Jamaica, NY 11435
Tel.: 718-291-4000
Fax: 718-658-4510
Approx.Sls.: $21,500,000
Emp.: 100
Fiscal Year-end: 3/31/91
Krauss, Trunz & Farmer Boy Tasty Meats
S.I.C.: 2011; 2013
R. Romeo *(Pres.)*
Guy Sieome *(Controller)*

JERVIS B. WEBB COMPANY
34375 West 12 Mile Rd.
Farmington Hills, MI 48331
Tel.: 313-553-1000
Telex: 211892 jwebb ur
Fax: 313-553-1253
Year Founded: 1919
Approx.Sls.: $275,000,000
Approx.Assets:$130,000,000
Emp.: 2,200
Fiscal Year-end: 12/31/91
Import Export
Mfr. of Custom-Designed Material Handling Systems, Conveyors
S.I.C.: 3625; 3535; 3462; 1731
Jervis C. Webb *(Chm. Bd. Emeritus)*
George H. Webb *(Chm. Bd.)*
Jervis H. Webb *(Asst. Chm. Bd.)*
Joseph M. Hammond *(Pres. & Chief Exec. Officer)*
Chris Webb *(V.P. & Gen. Counsel)*
Robert Pierson *(V.P.-Sls. & Mktg.)*
Keith Scrutton *(V.P.-Personnel)*
John S. Sobczyk *(V.P.-Fin. & Chief Fin. Officer)*
Brian G. Stewart *(V.P.-Engrng.)*
David C. Clark *(V.P. & Treas.)*
Ed Duczkowski *(Dir.-Quality Control)*
Michael Loux *(Dir.-Mkt. Research)*
Joseph J. Pietrangeli *(Dir.-Pur.)*
Anthony H. Allen *(Mgr.-Plant)*
Paul Hopersberger *(Mgr.-Mktg.)*
Principal(s):
Jervis C. Webb
George H. Webb

No. of Mfg. Plants/Facilities: 15
No. of U.S. Offices: 23
No. of Foreign Offices: 19

Computer Systems/Hardware:
IBM 9121

Outside Service Firm(s):

Coopers & Lybrand*(Auditors)*
400 Renaissance Center
Detroit, MI 48243
Tel.: 313-446-7100
Fax: 313-446-7117

Northern Group Services, Inc.*(Group Insurer)*
P.O. Box 7676,
St. Clair Shores, MI 48080
Tel.: 313-779-7676

Bodman, Longley & Dahling*(Legal Firm)*
100 Renaissance Center
Detroit, MI 48243
Tel.: 313-259-7777

N.B.D. Bank, N.A.*(Major Banking Relationship)*
611 Woodward Ave.
Detroit, MI 48226
Tel.: 313-225-1122
Fax: 313-225-3420

National Bank of Detroit*(Pension Manager)*
611 Woodward Ave.
Detroit, MI 48226

Divisions:

Ann Arbor Computer **(1)**
1201 E. Ellsworth
Ann Arbor, MI 48104
Tel.: 313-973-7875
Roger Buiten *(Gen. Mgr.)*

Bulk Systems **(1)**
560 Webb Industrial Dr. N.E.
Marietta, GA 30062
Tel.: 404-426-3900

Unibilt **(1)**
34375 W. Twelve Mile Rd.
Farmington Hills, MI 48331
Tel.: 313-553-1232
Ted Tylman *(Gen. Mgr.)*

Webb-Materials Handling Equip. **(1)**
560 Webb Industrial Dr., N.E.
Marietta, GA 30062
Tel.: 404-426-3900
Daniel Korach *(V.P. & Gen. Mgr.)*

Webb-Norfolk Conveyor **(1)**
155 King St. (Rte. 3A)
Cohasset, MA 02025
Tel.: 617-383-9400
Jim Ogburn *(Gen. Mgr.)*

Subsidiaries:

Webb Electric Co. **(1)**
24420 Indoplex Circle
Farmington Hills, MI 48335
Tel.: 313-553-1246
Fax: 313-478-2020
Electrical Contractors
S.I.C.: 1731
Jimmy Vaughan *(V.P. & Gen. Mgr.)*

Webb-Triax Company **(1)**
215 Fifth Ave.
Chardon, OH 44024
Tel.: 216-285-4630
Automated Storage & Retrieval Systems
S.I.C.: 3535; 3537
Harry E. Smith *(V.P. & Gen. Mgr.)*

Affiliates:

Control Engineering Co. **(1)**
8212 Harbor Springs Rd.
Harbor Springs, MI 49740
Tel.: 616-347-3931

Jervis B. Webb Co. of California **(1)**
4550 Seville Ave.
Los Angeles, CA 90058
Tel.: 213-588-8271
John Marshman *(V.P. & Gen. Mgr.)*

Jervis B. Webb Co. of Georgia **(1)**
560 Webb Industrial Dr., N.E.
Marietta, GA 30062
Tel.: 404-426-3900
Dan Korach *(V.P. & Gen. Mgr.)*

Webb Forging **(1)**
P.O. Box 400
Carlisle, SC 29031
Tel.: 803-427-8421
Fax: 803-427-8421
Fax: Ext. 41
Close Tolerance Forgings & Machining
S.I.C.: 3312; 3462
Richard Canada *(V.P. & Gen. Mgr.)*

Non-U.S. Holdings:

Jervis B. Webb Company Ltd. **(1)**
Dawson Road Mount Farm,
Milton Keynes, MK1 1QY, United Kingdom
Tel.: 0908 270222 (100%)
Fax: 0908 270014
Mktg. & Sales of Automated Computer Controls
S.I.C.: 5049

Jervis B. Webb Company of Canada Ltd. **(1)**
1647 Burlington St., East
Hamilton, ON L8H 7M5, Canada
Tel.: 416-547-0411 (100%)
Fax: 416-549-3798
Designs, Builds, Installs & Maintains Computer Controls for Automated Material Handling & Manufacturing Systems
S.I.C.: 3823

FRED WEBB INC.
N. Green St.
Greenville, NC 27834
Mailing Address:
P.O. Box 158
Greenville, NC 27835
Tel.: 919-758-2141 **NC**
Fax: 919-830-3672
Year Founded: 1948
Approx.Sls.: $55,000,000
Emp.: 50
Fiscal Year-end: 4/30/89
Feed Grain Merchandising & Storage
S.I.C.: 5153; 4221
J. Fred Webb *(Pres. & Chief Exec. Officer)*
Jim A. King *(Chief Fin. Officer)*
Jeff Edwards *(V.P.)*
Elizabeth Monday *(Controller)*

No. of Mfg. Plants/Facilities: 8
No. of U.S. Offices: 1

Outside Service Firm(s):

Durham, Martin, Jenkins & Co.*(Auditors)*
Raleigh, NC

NationsBank Carolinas*(Major Banking Relationship)*
One NCNB Plaza T18-7
Charlotte, NC 28255

Subsidiaries:

Leco Feed Mills, Inc. **(1)**
609 Brite St.
Kinston, NC 28501
Tel.: 919-758-2141
Grain Elevator
S.I.C.: 4221; 5153

Wakelon Agri-Products, Inc. **(1)**
P.O. Box 676
Zebulon, NC 27597
Tel.: 919-269-6116
Grain Elevator
S.I.C.: 4221; 5153

WEBB, MURRAY & ASSOCIATES
608 No. 14th St.
La Porte, TX 77571
Tel.: 713-471-8104
Fax: 713-471-1854
Emp.: 49
Install & Service Safety & Fire Protection Systems; Engineering & Construction
S.I.C.: 1799; 8711; 1731
R.M. Webb *(Pres. & Chief Exec. Officer)*
R.W. Murray *(Chief Fin. Officer, Sr. V.P., Treas., Controller & Sec.)*

Computer Systems/Hardware:
IBM PCs

DEL WEBB'S COVENTRY
(Formerly Coventry Financial, Inc.)
4550 N. Black Canyon Hwy.
Phoenix, AZ 85017
Tel.: 602-433-5280 **AZ**
Fax: 602-433-5298
Year Founded: 1980
Assets: $100,000,000
Liabilities: $80,000,000
Net Worth: $20,000,000
Sales Range: $80-99 Million
Emp.: 90
Holding Company
S.I.C.: 6719; 1521
Joseph Contadino *(Chm. Bd., Pres. & Treas.)*
Richard Day *(V.P.-Fin. & Data Processing)*
David Schreiner *(V.P.-Sls., Adv. & Mktg.)*

Computer Systems/Hardware:
Prime

Outside Service Firm(s):

Ernst & Young*(Auditors)*
40 North Central, Ste. 900
Phoenix, AZ 85004
Tel.: 602-258-3366

Winston & Strawn*(Legal Firm)*
Phoenix, AZ

Mera Bank*(Major Banking Relationship)*
Phoenix, AZ

Subsidiaries:

Coventry Homes of Colorado **(1)**
6915 Ashely Dr.
Colorado Springs, CO 80922
Tel.: 303-637-0048
General Contractor Single Family Homes
S.I.C.: 1521

Design Center **(1)**
3040 N. 44th St., Ste. 201
Phoenix, AZ 85018
Tel.: 602-957-1954
Retail Carpet & Tile
S.I.C.: 5713

Fairmount Mortgage, Inc. **(1)**
Black Kenyon Blvd.
Phoenix, AZ 85018
Tel.: 602-957-1954
Lender to Home Buyers
S.I.C.: 6141

Universal Homes, Inc. **(1)**
3875 N. 44th St.
Phoenix, AZ 85018
Tel.: 602-840-8300
General Contractor Single Family Homes
S.I.C.: 1521

WEBCRAFT TECHNOLOGIES, INC.
Route 1 & Adams Station Rd.
North Brunswick, NJ 08902
Mailing Address:
P.O. Box 185
North Brunswick, NJ 08902-6023
Tel.: 908-297-5100
Tel.: 800-955-0545 **De**
Telex: 701-480-3822
Fax: 908-821-3010
Year Founded: 1969
Approx.Sls.: $260,000,000
Emp.: 1,775
Fiscal Year-end: 12/31/90
Import
Direct Response Printing Specialists, Catalog & Magazine Inserts, Billing Stuffers & Instant Lottery Tickets
S.I.C.: 2752; 7331
Thomas Cochill *(Pres. & Chief Exec. Officer)*
Michael Goldman *(Pres.-Comml. Grp.)*
Robert Okin *(Chief Fin. Officer)*
John H. Jones *(Exec. V.P.-Sls.)*
Duane E. Kaisand *(Exec. V.P.)*
Stanford B. Silverschotz *(V.P.-Technical Services)*
Joe Hegarty *(Treas.)*
Ira Horowitz *(Gen. Counsel)*
Robert Madison *(Dir.-Pur.)*
Mark Mehler *(Dir.-Personnel)*
Nancy Krosner *(Mgr.-Adv.)*
Kim Smith *(Mgr.-Adv. Project)*
Ben Wax *(Mgr.-Corp. Facilities)*

No. of Mfg. Plants/Facilities: 6
No. of U.S. Offices: 17

Computer Systems/Hardware:
IBM

Outside Service Firm(s):

Ernst & Young*(Auditors)*
202 Carnegie Center
Princeton, NJ 08640
Tel.: 609-243-0303
Fax: 609-243-9322

Aetna Life & Casualty*(Group Insurer)*
151 Farmington Avenue
Hartford, CT 06156
Tel.: 203-273-2128
Fax: 203-729-4295

Lowenstein, Sandler, Kohl, Fisher & Boylan*(Legal Firm)*
65 Livingston Ave.
Roseland, NJ 07068
Tel.: 908-992-8700

United Jersey Bank*(Major Banking Relationship)*
Franklin Park, NJ

Subsidiary:

Webcraft Games, Inc. **(1)**
205 N. Center Dr.
North Brunswick, NJ 08902
Tel.: 908-297-5100
Tel.: 800-955-0545 (100%)
Fax: 201-422-2828
Print Instant Scratch-off Lottery Tickets
S.I.C.: 2752
John Carson *(Pres.)*

WEBER COHN & RILEY, INC.
444 N. Michigan Ave.
Chicago, IL 60611
Tel.: 312-527-4260
Fax: 312-527-4273
Year Founded: 1960
Approx.Billings: $16,000,000
Emp.: 31
Ronald I. Cohn *(Chm.)*
James V. Riley *(Pres.)*
Joseph Marconi *(Exec. V.P.)*
Marc Michaelson *(V.P., Pub. Rels. Dir.)*
Ginny LaVone *(V.P.)*

FRED WEBER INC.
2320 Creve Coeur Mill Rd.
Maryland Heights, MO 63043
Mailing Address:
P.O. Box 2501
Maryland Heights, MO 63043-8501
Tel.: 314-344-0070 **MO**
Fax: 314-344-0970
Year Founded: 1928
Emp.: 650
Fiscal Year-end: 1/31/90
Heavy Highway & Building Construction
S.I.C.: 1629
Thomas P. Dunne *(Chm. Bd. & Chief Exec. Officer)*
William K. Powell *(Pres.)*
William R. Gaines, Jr. *(Exec. V.P.)*
John W. Maupin *(V.P.-Gen. Counsel & Sec.)*
David L. Poe *(V.P.-Asphalt Opers.)*
Charles E. Ray *(V.P.-Quarry Opers.)*
John D. Wunderlich *(V.P.-Fin.)*
Richard H. Travers *(Treas.)*

Outside Service Firm(s):

Deloitte & Touche*(Auditors)*
One City Centre
St. Louis, MO 63101
Tel.: 314-342-4900
Fax: 314-342-1100

Boatmen's National Bank*(Major Banking Relationship)*
800 Market St.
St. Louis, MO 63166
Tel.: 314-554-6000

WEBER MARKING SYSTEMS, INC.
711 W. Algonquin Rd.
Arlington Heights, IL 60005
Tel.: 708-364-8500
Tel.: 800-225-0883 **IL**
Fax: 708-364-8575
Approx.Sls.: $70,000,000
Emp.: 650
Fiscal Year-end: 12/31/90
Export
All-Mark Marking Ink for Metals, Continu-Matic Continuous Form Stencils, Mini-Graph Card Duplicator, Stenmark Stencil Cutting Machine, Tab-On Marking Stencils Legitronic Electronic Label Printer, Label Printing Machines, Label Applicators, Custom Printed Labels, Bar Code Scanners
S.I.C.: 2899; 2761; 3579; 2759; 2675; 3577; 3953; 3955
Joseph A. Weber, Sr. *(Chm. Bd.)*
Joseph A. Weber, Jr. *(Pres.)*
N. Drucker *(V.P.-Fin., Treas. & Sec.)*
D.P. McGrath *(V.P.-Mktg.)*
Brad Weber *(V.P.-Mfg.)*
Douglas D. Weber *(V.P.-Intl.)*
R.J. Stake *(Mgr.-Mktg. Communications)*
D. Figler *(Pur. Agent)*

Outside Service Firm(s):

First Chicago Bank*(Major Banking Relationship)*
Mt. Prospect, IL

Subsidiaries:

Ink Specialties Co. **(1)**
1436 E. Davis St.
Arlington Heights, IL 60005
Tel.: 708-394-5494
Manufactures Ink
S.I.C.: 2899
R.D. Mann *(Pres.)*

Tape & Label Engineering **(1)**
2950 47th Ave. N.
Saint Petersburg, FL 33714
Tel.: 813-527-6686
Manufactures Pressure Sensitive Labels
S.I.C.: 2759
Lee Paul *(Pres.)*

Non-U.S. Holdings:

Weber Marking Systems Canada ltd. **(1)**
6180 Danville Rd.
Mississauga, ON L5T 2H7, Canada
Tel.: 416-564-6881 (100%)
Mfr. of Marking Supplies, Labels, Labeling Machines, Hand Stampers, Stencils, Duplicating Ink
S.I.C.: 3953; 2679
Colin Stanley *(Plant Mgr.)*

Weber Marking Systems (Far East) Co. Ltd. **(1)**
3-6-1 chome Tsukiji Chuo-ku
Tokyo, 104, Japan
Tel.: 03-3543-5021 (100%)
Marking Systems, Labels
S.I.C.: 3953; 2679

Weber Marking Systems Ltd. **(1)**
Cavendish 7, 8 & 9, Litchfield Rd. Industrial Estate
Tamworth, Staffs. B79 7UL, United Kingdom
Tel.: 0827 311110 (100%)
Telex: 342504
Fax: 0827 310527
Mfr. of Marking Sytems
S.I.C.: 3953

Weber Marking Systems Ltd. **(1)**
MacMerry Industrial Estates
Trenent, East Lothian EH33 1HD, United Kingdom (100%)
Mfr. of Marking Sytems
S.I.C.: 3953

WEBER-STEPHEN PRODUCTS
200 E. Daniels Rd.
Palatine, IL 60067
Tel.: 708-934-5700
Fax: 708-934-0291
Sales Range: $60-79 Million
Emp.: 450
Fiscal Year-end: 9/30/91
Mfr. Barbecue Kettles; Insect Killers
S.I.C.: 3631
George Stephen, Sr. *(Pres.)*
Michael Kempster *(Sr. V.P.-Sls. & Mktg.)*
Len Gryn *(Exec. V.P.)*
Jim Forbes *(V.P.-Sls.)*
George A. Stephen, Jr. *(V.P.-Pur.)*
James Stephen *(V.P.-Mfg.)*
Jennifer Davidoff *(Dir.-Mktg.)*
Betty A. Hughes *(Dir.-Consumer Affairs)*
Joe Moore *(Dir.-Human Resources)*
Bill Krieger *(Mgr.-Data Processing)*
Principal(s):
George Stephen, Sr.

Computer Systems/Hardware:
IBM System 38

Outside Service Firm(s):

Ernst & Young*(Auditors)*
233 S. Wacker Dr.
Chicago, IL 60606
Tel.: 312-368-1800
Fax: 312-645-3095

Frisch & Frisch*(Legal Firm)*
Chicago, IL

Continental Bank N. A.*(Major Banking Relationship)*
231 S. LaSalle St.
Chicago, IL 60697
Tel.: 312-828-2345
Tel.: 800-426-5754
Telex: 312-828-1783

WEBSTER INDUSTRIES INC.
325 Hall St.
Tiffin, OH 44883
Tel.: 419-447-8232
Tel.: 800-243-9327
Fax: 419-448-1618
Year Founded: 1876
Assets: $9,800,000
Liabilities: $3,300,000
Net Worth: $6,500,000
Approx.Sls.: $28,000,000
Emp.: 325

Webster Industries Inc.—(Continued)

Fiscal Year-end: 12/31/91
Export
Mfr. Conveying & Engineering Chains, Malleable Iron Castings
S.I.C.: 3535; 3462; 3322
Fredric C. Spurck *(Pres. & Chief Exec. Officer)*
James F. Riedel *(V.P.-Mktg. & Adv.)*
George K. Tolford *(V.P.)*
Chris English *(Chief Fin. Officer & Treas.)*
Patty Kauffman *(Sec.)*
G. Turner *(Dir.-Personnel)*
Mike Kuhn *(Dir.-Data Processing)*

No. of Mfg. Plants/Facilities: 3
No. of U.S. Offices: 3

Computer Systems/Hardware:
IBM System 38

Outside Service Firm(s):

Groner, Boyle & Quillin*(Auditors)*
Columbus, OH

CIGNA*(Group Insurer)*
Los Angeles, CA

Tomb & Hering*(Legal Firm)*
Tiffin, OH

The Huntington National Bank*(Major Banking Relationship)*
41 S. High St.
Columbus, OH 43216

Divisions:

Portland Chain Mfg. Co. **(1)**
12475 S.W. Herman Rd.
Tualatin, OR 97062
Tel.: 503-692-4818
Fax: 503-692-8268
Mfr. of Welded Steel Chain
S.I.C.: 3496

Webster Mfg. Co. **(1)**
325 Hall St.
Tiffin, OH 44883
Tel.: 419-447-8232
Tel.: 800-243-9327
Fax: 419-448-1618
Export
Computer Systems/Hardware:
IBM System
Conveyors, Elevators & Components, Material Handling Equip.
S.I.C.: 3535

Subsidiaries:

Stacy Equipment Co. **(1)**
325 Hall St.
Tiffin, OH 44883
Tel.: 419-447-8232
Fax: 419-448-1618
Distributor of Power Transmission Equipment
S.I.C.: 5063

Webster-Portalloy Chains, Inc. **(1)**
3800 Second St., P.O. Box 1747
Meridian, MS 39302
Tel.: 601-482-0183
Fax: 601-693-5918
Export
Computer Systems/Hardware:
IBM System
Malleable & Welded Steel Chain
S.I.C.: 3496

WECHCO, INC.
1000 Herrontown Rd.
Princeton, NJ 08540
Tel.: 609-921-0501 **NY**
Export
Holding Company
S.I.C.: 6719
Elwood W. Phares II *(Chm. Bd. & Pres.)*
Bruce D. Muretta *(Treas.)*
Miles M. Glantz *(Sec. & Corp. Counsel)*

Outside Service Firm(s):

Weber Lipshie & Company*(Auditors)*
1430 Broadway
New York, NY
Tel.: 212-382-3400

Rogers & Wells*(Legal Firm)*
200 Park Ave.
New York, NY 10166
Tel.: 212-878-8000

United Jersey Bank*(Major Banking Relationship)*
Hackensack, NJ

Subsidiary:

West Chemical Products, Inc. **(1)**
1000 Herrontown Rd.
Princeton, NJ 08540
Tel.: 609-921-0501
Fax: 609-924-4308
Approx.Sls.: $23,000,000
Emp.: 130
Fiscal Year-end: 11/30/91
Export
Computer Systems/Hardware:
Data Point; IBM PC
Mfr. of Insecticides & Specialty Chemicals
S.I.C.: 2819; 2879; 2869; 2899; 2842; 2841
Elwood W. Phares II *(Chm. Bd., Pres. & Chief Exec. Officer)*
Michael E. Jalbert *(Exec. V.P.-Opers.)*
Gulab Dhole *(Chief Fin. Officer & Controller)*
Miles M. Glantz *(Gen. Counsel & Sec.)*
Johannes Larsen *(Dir.-Mktg.)*
John Pollack *(Dir.-Pur.)*
Kimberly A. Lyons *(Dir.-Human Resources)*
Micheal Gagliardi *(Export Mgr.)*
Dr. Phillip Figdore *(Mgr.-Res. & Devel.)*

Subsidiary:

Penetone Corp. **(2)**
74 Hudson Ave.
Tenafly, NJ 07670
Tel.: 201-567-3000
Tel.: 800-631-1652 (100%)
Fax: 201-569-5340
Approx.Sls.: $15,000,000
Emp.: 58
Fiscal Year-end: 11/30/92
Export
Computer Systems/Hardware:
IBM
Mfr. & Sales of Chemicals
S.I.C.: 2819; 5169; 2842; 2899
Elwood W. Phares II *(Chm. Bd.)*
Michael E. Jalbert *(Pres.)*
Gulab S. Dhole *(V.P.-Fin. & Admin.)*
John Baine *(V.P.-Sls.)*
John Larsen *(V.P.-Intl.)*
Michel Gagliardi *(Sls. Coordinator-Intl. Div.)*
Jocelyne Rouleau *(Adv. Coordinator)*
Johannes Larsen *(V.P.-Mktg.)*
John Pollack *(Dir.-Pur.)*
Ralph Andino *(Dir.-Opers. N. America)*
Maurice Cohen *(Dir.-Mktg.)*
Michael Pleus *(Govt. Regulatory Affairs Supervisor)*
Phil Figdore *(Dir.-Technical)*
Kimberly Lyons *(Mgr.-Human Resources)*

Subsidiary:

Petron Corporation **(3)**
16700 Glendale Dr.
New Berlin, WI 53151
Tel.: 414-797-4680
Tel.: 800-992-8226
Fax: 414-796-1080
Emp.: 16
Mfr. of Specialty Lubricants & Greases
S.I.C.: 2992
Elwood W. Phares *(Chm. Bd.)*
Michael E. Jalbert *(Pres.)*
Arthur J. Klenner *(V.P.-Sls.)*
Gulab Dhole *(Treas.)*

Plant:

Penetone Corporation **(3)**
6014 South Eastern Ave.
Los Angeles, CA 90040
Tel.: 213-726-1579
Tel.: 800-421-6211
Fax: 213-726-0141
Office & Warehouse
S.I.C.: 2842
Bob Boyle *(Mgr.)*

Non-U.S. Holding:

West Pentone Inc. **(1)**
10900 Secant St.
Ville d'Anjou, PQ Canada H1J 1S5
Tel.: 514-355-4660
Tel.: 800-361-8927 (100%)
Fax: 514-355-2319
Emp.: 65
Mfr. of Specialty Chemicals; Degreasers, Agricultural Sanitizers/Disinfectants, Specialty Oils & Greases
S.I.C.: 2842; 2841; 2992
Elwood W. Phares *(Chm. Bd.)*
Michael E. Jalbert *(Pres.)*
Gulab S. Dhole *(V.P.-Fin. & Admin. & Controller)*
Johannes Larsen *(V.P.-Mktg.)*

WECHSLER COFFEE CORP.
10 Empire Blvd.
Moonachie, NJ 07074
Tel.: 201-440-1700
Fax: 201-440-5380
Year Founded: 1903
Approx.Sls.: $80,000,000
Emp.: 411
Fiscal Year-end: 9/30/90
Coffee & Food Products
S.I.C.: 2095; 5149
Elaine Slater *(Chm. Bd.)*
Michael Slater *(Pres.)*
Frank Osusky *(Chief Fin. Officer & V.P.-Fin.)*
Ira Block *(V.P., Gen. Counsel & Sec.)*
John D'Amico *(V.P. & Controller)*
Lloyd Bosca *(Dir.-Pension Admin.)*
Frank Serino *(Mgr.-Data Processing)*
Rita Weissblatt *(Mgr.-Personnel)*

Computer Systems/Hardware:
IBM System 38; IBM PC

Outside Service Firm(s):

KPMG Peat Marwick*(Auditors)*
345 Park Ave.
New York, NY 10154
Tel.: 212-758-9700
Fax: 212-872-3308

Aetna Life & Casualty*(Group Insurer)*
425 Fifth Ave.
New York, NY 10018
Tel.: 212-512-0777

Dornbush, Mensch, Mandelstam & Schaeffer*(Legal Firm)*
747 Third Ave.
New York, NY 10017
Tel.: 212-759-3300

Bankers Trust Co.*(Major Banking Relationship)*
P.O. Box 318, Church St. Station
New York, NY 10008
Tel.: 212-454-2212
Fax: 212-454-2783

First National Bank of Chicago*(Major Banking Relationship)*
One First National Plaza
Chicago, IL 60670
Tel.: 312-732-9781
Tel.: 312-732-4050
Fax: 312-732-4840
Fax: 312-732-3055

Midlantic National Bank*(Major Banking Relationship)*
Newark, NJ
Tel.: 908-321-8188

United Jersey Bank*(Major Banking Relationship)*
Moonachie, NJ

Subsidiaries:

In-Office Coffee Company **(1)**
2143 Rt. 4
Fort Lee, NJ 07024
Tel.: 201-592-8970
S.I.C.: 5149

Richheimer Food **(1)**
10 Empire Blvd.
Moonachie, NJ 07074
Tel.: 201-440-1700
S.I.C.: 5149

WEGMANS FOOD MARKETS, INC.
1500 Brooks Ave.
Rochester, NY 14692-0844
Mailing Address:
P.O. Box 844
Rochester, NY 14692
Tel.: 716-328-2550 **NY**
Fax: 716-328-4626
Year Founded: 1917
Approx.Sls.: $1,191,000,000
Emp.: 16,000
Fiscal Year-end: 12/31/88
Retail Supermarkets; 45 Stores in NY Only
S.I.C.: 5411
Robert B. Wegman *(Chm. Bd., Chief Exec. Officer & Treas.)*
Daniel R. Wegman *(Pres.)*
James J. Leo *(Corp. Controller)*
Paul S. Speranza *(Gen. Counsel & Sec.)*
Mary Ellen Burris *(Dir.-Consumer Affairs)*
Mark G. Kindig *(Dir.-Fin.)*
Gerard Pierce *(Dir.-Human Resources)*
Donald R. Reeve *(Dir.-Mngmt. Information Systems)*

Computer Systems/Hardware:
IBM

Outside Service Firm(s):

Arthur Andersen & Co.*(Auditors)*
Ste. 1500, One Marine Midland Plaza
Rochester, NY 14604

Chase Lincoln First Bank, N.A.*(Major Banking Relationship)*
P.O. Box 1250,
Rochester, NY 14603
Tel.: 716-232-5000

WEHCO MEDIA, INC.
115 E. Capitol St.
Little Rock, AR 72203
Tel.: 501-378-3400
Fax: 501-378-3908
Year Founded: 1973
Approx.Sls.: $64,000,000
Emp.: 800
Holding Company; Newspapers, Radio, TV & Cable Systems
S.I.C.: 6719; 2711; 4832; 4833; 4841
Walter E. Hussman, Jr. *(Chm. Bd., Pres. & Publr.)*
Betty P. Hussman *(V.P.)*
Allen W. Berry *(Controller)*
Terrel P. Davenport *(Mgr.-Data Processing Systems)*

Outside Service Firm(s):

Ernst & Young*(Auditors)*
425 W. Capitol, Ste. 3600
Little Rock, AR 72201
Tel.: 501-372-5443
Fax: 501-372-6288

Rose Law Firm*(Legal Firm)*
720 W. 3rd St.
Little Rock, AR 72201
Tel.: 501-375-9131

First Commercial Bank*(Major Banking Relationship)*
P.O. Box 1331,
Little Rock, AR 72201

Union National Bank*(Major Banking Relationship)*
P.O. Box 1541
Little Rock, AR 72203
Tel.: 501-378-4213

Subsidiary:

Wehco Video Inc. **(1)**
115 E. Capitol St.
Little Rock, AR 72203
Tel.: 501-378-3400
Cable Television Operators
S.I.C.: 4841
Walter E. Hussman, Jr. *(Pres.)*

WEHR CONSTRUCTORS INC.
2517 Plantside Dr.
Louisville, KY 40299
Tel.: 502-491-9250 **KY**
Fax: 502-491-3540
Year Founded: 1946
Assets: $7,200,000
Liabilities: $5,400,000
Net Worth: $1,800,000
Approx.Sls.: $34,000,000
Emp.: 280
Fiscal Year-end: 3/31/89
General Contractor Commercial & Industrial Buildings
S.I.C.: 1541; 1542
Claude A. Berry, Jr. *(Chm. Bd. & Pres.)*
Claude A. Berry, III *(Exec. V.P.)*
Dale R. Berry *(V.P.)*
Edward M. Berry *(V.P.)*
Charles J. Sullivan *(V.P.-Fin.)*

Outside Service Firm(s):

Deloitte & Touche*(Auditors)*
510 W. Broadway
Louisville, KY 40202
Tel.: 502-562-2000

Liberty National Bank & Trust Co.*(Major Banking Relationship)*
Louisville, KY

WEIBEL VINEYARDS
1250 Stanford Ave.
Mission San Jose, CA 94539
Mailing Address:
P.O. Box 3398,
Mission San Jose, CA 94539
Tel.: 415-656-2340
Fax: 415-656-0109
Year Founded: 1945
Approx.Sls.: $18,000,000
Emp.: 130
Fiscal Year-end: 6/30/90
Producers of Wine & Champagne; Weibel
S.I.C.: 2084
Fred E. Weibel *(Pres.)*
Fred E. Weibel, Jr. *(Exec. V.P., Sec. & Treas.)*
Richard Casqueiro *(V.P.-Wine Maker)*
Cary Daste *(V.P.-Mktg.)*

WEICHERT COMPANY
1625 State Hwy. 10
Morris Plains, NJ 07950
Tel.: 201-267-7777
Sales Range: $1 Billion +
Full Service Real Estate Company
S.I.C.: 6531
James M. Weichert *(Pres.)*

Subsidiary:

Weichert Realty, Inc. **(1)**
Station Center, 1700 Diagonal Rd.
Alexandria, VA 22314
Tel.: 703-739-3100
Fax: 703-739-0276
Approx.Sls.: $3,000,000,000
Emp.: 2,700
Full Service Real Estate Company
S.I.C.: 6531
W. Howard Rooks *(Pres.)*
Bruce L. Green *(Sr. V.P. & Gen. Mgr.)*
Ann King *(Dir.-Mktg.)*
Sandra Walthen *(Dir.-Personnel)*

Subsidiaries:

Weichert Insurance Agency, Inc. **(2)**
1700 Diagonal Rd.
Alexandria, VA 22314
Tel.: 703-739-3100

Weichert Realty Career Development **(2)**
1700 Diagonal Rd.
Alexandria, VA 22314
Tel.: 703-739-3100
Career Training
S.I.C.: 8249

WEIDER HEALTH & FITNESS
21100 Erwin St.
Woodland Hills, CA 91367
Tel.: 818-884-6800 **CA**
Fax: 818-704-5734
Year Founded: 1936
Sales Range: $500-999 Million
Emp.: 350
Import Export
Food Supplements, Exercise Equip. & Fitness Magazines
S.I.C.: 2721; 2834; 3949
Joseph Weider *(Chm. Bd.)*
Gerald Wasserman *(Pres. & Chief Exec. Officer)*
Eric Weider *(Pres. & Chief Exec. Officer-Equipment Division)*
Richard Bizzaro *(Pres. & Chief Exec. Officer-Food Division)*
Michael T. Carr *(Pres. & Chief Exec. Officer-Publishing Division)*
Ronald Novak *(Chief Fin. Officer)*
Kim Spenchian *(Chief Info. Officer)*
Leon Katz *(V.P.-Fin.)*
Bernard Cartoon *(Gen. Counsel)*
Amy Causing *(Dir.-Pub. Rels. & Publ.)*
Sandra Schulman *(Dir.-Mktg.)*
Janet Jurkowski *(Dir.-Human Resources)*
David Obey *(Dir.-Circulation & Publ.)*
Principal(s):
Joseph Weider

No. of Mfg. Plants/Facilities: 3
No. of U.S. Offices: 3
No. of Foreign Offices: 4

Computer Systems/Hardware:
IBM PC

Subsidiary:

Schiff Products, Inc. **(1)**
1911 S., 3850 W.
Salt Lake City, UT 84104
Tel.: 801-972-0300 (100%)
Fax: 801-972-6532
Emp.: 27
Manufacture & Marketing of Health Foods, Nutritional Supplements, Vitamins & Personal Care Products
S.I.C.: 5122; 2834; 2833
David Mastroianni *(Dir.-Mktg.)*

WEIGHTMAN

THE WEIGHTMAN GROUP
1818 Market St.
Philadelphia, PA 19103
Tel.: 215-561-6100 **PA**
Fax: 215-496-9195
Year Founded: 1948
Approx.Billings: $114,000,000
Emp.: 165
Advertising Agency
S.I.C.: 7311
Charles Coffey *(Chm.)*
Dave Jordan *(Vice Chm.)*
John Goodchild *(Pres. & Chief Exec. Officer)*
David S. Culver *(Pres.-Weightman Pub. Rels.)*
Mark Plamondon *(Exec. V.P.)*
James Saunders *(Sr. V.P., Chief Fin. Officer)*
George Erickson *(V.P., Admin.)*
Ann Turco *(V.P., Controller)*
Cindi Probst *(Yellow Pages Mgr.)*

No. of U.S. Offices: 2

Computer Systems/Hardware:
IBM System 36

Outside Service Firm(s):

KPMG Peat Marwick*(Auditors)*
Princeton, NJ

Boardman Hamilton*(Group Insurer)*
Philadelphia, PA

Wolf, Block, Schorr & Solis-Cohen*(Legal Firm)*
Packard Bldg.
Philadelphia, PA 19102
Tel.: 215-977-2000

Travelers Insurance Co.*(Pension Manager)*
1 Tower Square
Hartford, CT 06183
Tel.: 203-222-7821
Fax: 203-222-7813

Subsidiaries:

Weightman Advertising, Inc. **(1)**
1818 Market St.
Philadelphia, PA 19103
Tel.: 215-561-6100
Fax: 215-496-9195
John Goodchild *(Pres. & Chief Exec. Officer)*
Mark Plamondon *(Exec. V.P.)*

Weightman Public Relations **(1)**
1818 Market St.
Philadelphia, PA 19103
Tel.: 215-561-6100
Fax: 215-496-9194
Emp.: 25
Full Service Public Relations Agency
S.I.C.: 7311
John Goodchild *(Chm.)*
David S. Culver *(Pres.)*

Weightman Research **(1)**
1818 Market St.
Philadelphia, PA 19103
Tel.: 215-561-9094
Fax: 215-496-9194
Full Service Mktg. & Research Firm
S.I.C.: 7311
Elaine Walker *(Info. Services Mgr.)*

WEIL BROTHERS COTTON INC.
4444 Park Blvd.
Montgomery, AL 36116
Mailing Address:
P.O. Box 20100
Montgomery, AL 36120-0100
Tel.: 205-244-1800 **DE**
Fax: 205-271-4238
Year Founded: 1878
Emp.: 100
Cotton Merchant
S.I.C.: 5159
Adolph Weil, Jr. *(Chm. Bd.)*
Robert S. Weil, Sr. *(Chm.-Executive Committee)*
Robert S. Weil, II *(Pres.)*
Adolph Weil, III *(Exec. V.P.)*
James E. McGee *(Chief Fin. Officer, Treas. & Controller)*

No. of U.S. Offices: 6
No. of Foreign Offices: 2

Computer Systems/Hardware:
IBM System 36

Outside Service Firm(s):

The Principal Financial Group*(Group Insurer)*
Des Moines, IA

First Alabama Bank*(Major Banking Relationship)*
P.O. Box 5260
Montgomery, AL 36103
Tel.: 205-832-8011

First Alabama Bank*(Pension Manager)*
Montgomery, AL

WEINBRENNER SHOE COMPANY, INC.
108 So. Polk St.
Merrill, WI 54452
Tel.: 715-536-5521
Tel.: 800-826-0002
Fax: 715-536-1172
Year Founded: 1892
Approx.Sls.: $30,000,000
Emp.: 500
Fiscal Year-end: 9/31/90
Import Export
Uniform, Work, Safety, Outdoor/ Casual Boots & Shoes
S.I.C.: 3143; 3144
Corporate Giving Program: 50/50 5% of Purchases
James V. Greenlee *(Chm. Bd.)*
Lance Nienow *(Chief Oper. Officer)*
Dennis Black *(V.P.-Mktg.)*
Dave Gissleman *(Chief Fin. Officer & Controller)*
Dave Finanger *(Sec.)*

Computer Systems/Hardware:
AS 400

WEINERS ENTERPRISES, INC.
6005 Westview
Houston, TX 77055
Mailing Address:
P.O. Box 2612
Houston, TX 77252
Tel.: 713-688-1331 **TX**
Fax: 713-688-1396
Year Founded: 1926
Approx.Sls.: $200,000,000
Emp.: 2,000
Holding Co.; Department Stores
S.I.C.: 6719; 5311
Leon Weiner *(Chm. Bd. & Chief Exec. Officer)*
Sol B. Weiner *(Pres.)*
Robert Shapiro *(Sec. & Controller)*

Outside Service Firm(s):

Deloitte & Touche*(Auditors)*
333 Clay St., Ste. 2300
Houston, TX 77002
Tel.: 713-756-2000

Texas Commerce Bank*(Major Banking Relationship)*
600 Travis Street, Suite 1150
Houston, TX 77002
Tel.: 713-236-4865

Subsidiary:

Weiners Stores Inc. **(1)**
6005 Westview
Houston, TX 77055
Tel.: 713-688-1331
Department Stores
S.I.C.: 5311
Sol B. Weiner *(Pres.)*

SJ WEINSTEIN ASSOCIATES INC.
100 Fifth Ave.
New York, NY 10011
Tel.: 212-206-0222
Fax: 212-645-2538
Year Founded: 1979
Approx.Billings: $30,000,000
Emp.: 30
Healthcare Products
Stephen J. Weinstein *(Chm. Bd., Chief Exec. Officer & Creative Dir.)*
Barry R. Frankel *(Pres., Chief Oper. Officer & New Bus. Contact)*
Brian Boyle *(Chief Fin. Officer)*
Mel H. Getzoff *(Exec. V.P., Mngmt. Supvr.)*
Sondra Levine *(Controller)*
Garfield Davis *(Studio Asst.)*

Computer Systems/Hardware:
Macintosh, NCR

WEINSTEIN OTTERMAN & ASSOCIATES
137 Fifth Ave.
New York, NY 10010
Tel.: 212-505-5650
Fax: 212-505-7990
Year Founded: 1978
Approx.Billings: $14,200,000
Emp.: 23
Banking, Financial Services, Publishing, Communications & Travel
Stephen Weinstein *(Pres.)*

Weinstein Otterman & Associates—(Continued)

M. Gura *(V.P., Dir., Special Mktg.)*
L. Auerhan *(Research Dir.)*

WEINSTOCK, WHITE & ASSOCIATES
7500 Capital Dr.
Memphis, TN 38138
Tel.: 901-755-0077
Fax: 901-755-0045
Year Founded: 1985
Approx.Billings: $18,000,000
Emp.: 37
Ronald D. Weinstock *(Pres.)*

WEINTRAUB AND ASSOCIATES, INC.
11756 Borman Dr., Ste. 150
Saint Louis, MO 63146
Tel.: 314-991-5800
Fax: 314-991-3577
Year Founded: 1953
Approx.Billings: $18,000,000
Emp.: 20
Retail Adv., Trade Assn. Mngmt.
Lawrence Weintraub *(Chm.)*
Robert Weintraub *(Pres. & Creative Dir.)*

Computer Systems/Hardware:
Unix Environment, MAC IIci's

WEISER MINKUS WALEK COMMUNICATIONS, INC.
160 N. Wacker Dr.
Chicago, IL 60606
Tel.: 312-368-1500
Fax: 312-368-1545
Year Founded: 1979
Approx.Billings: $12,996,500
Emp.: 20
Michael Weiser *(Chm. Bd.)*

WEISS PACKING CO., INC.
Turkey Hollow Rd.
Donora, PA 15033
Tel.: 412-379-5500
Fax: 412-379-5807
Sales Range: $20-39 Million
Emp.: 137
Meat Packing, Frozen & Canned Meats & Poultry
S.I.C.: 2011; 2013; 2015
Selwyn M. Weiss *(Chm. Bd. & Treas.)*
Wilfred A. Weiss *(Pres.)*
Seymour Weiss *(V.P. & Sec.)*
David Duvall *(Gen. Mgr.)*
Melvin Levy *(Gen. Counsel)*

Outside Service Firm(s):

Love Scherle & Bauer*(Auditors)*
Pittsburgh, PA

Irwin Bank & Trust*(Major Banking Relationship)*
Irwin, PA

WEISS SHEET METAL COMPANY
1715 W. 135th St.
Gardena, CA 90249
Tel.: 213-770-1700
Fax: 213-327-5952
Year Founded: 1962
Emp.: 100
Roofing & Sheet Metal Work
S.I.C.: 1761
Jim D. Cockayne *(Pres.)*

Andre Sarai *(V.P., Treas. & Sec.)*
Albert Sakharoff *(V.P.-Sls. & Mktg.)*

Outside Service Firm(s):

Lee Anthony & Associates*(Auditors)*
Los Angeles, CA

Brown & Altshuler*(Legal Firm)*
Los Angeles, CA

MetroBank*(Major Banking Relationship)*
Los Angeles, CA

WEISS, WHITTEN, CARROLL, STAGLIANO INC.
96 Morton St.
New York, NY 10014
Tel.: 212-255-3900
Fax: 212-255-6347
Year Founded: 1991
Approx.Billings: $40,000,000
Emp.: 34
Tom Carroll *(Pres. & New Bus. Contact)*
Adam Stagliano *(Dir., Acct. Plng.)*
Jay Oranowitz *(Controller)*
Kathleen Roth *(Office Mgr.)*

CARL WEISSMAN & SONS, INC.
P.O. Box 1609
Great Falls, MT 59403
Tel.: 406-761-4848 **MT**
Fax: 406-761-4848, Ext. 251
Year Founded: 1915
Approx.Sls.: $20,000,000
Emp.: 225
Fiscal Year-end: 12/31/89
Wholesale Distributor of Hardware, Electrical & Plumbing Supplies, Steel Warehouse Products, Automotive Parts, Industrial Power Transmission Products
S.I.C.: 5051; 5013; 5063; 5072; 5074; 5085; 5093
Jerrold Weissman *(Pres.)*
Thomas Howard *(V.P. & Sec.)*
Leonard Weissman *(V.P.)*
Donald Armstrong *(Treas.)*
Michael Hannula *(Pur. Agent)*

Computer Systems/Hardware:
IBM AS-400

Outside Service Firm(s):

Douglas Wilson & Co.*(Auditors)*
Great Falls, MT

Jardine, Stephenson, Blewett & Weaver*(Legal Firm)*
Great Falls, MT

National Canada Finance Corp.*(Major Banking Relationship)*
New York, NY

Subsidiaries:

National-General Supply, Inc. **(1)**
410 14th St., S.W., P.O. Box 2288
Great Falls, MT 59403
Tel.: 406-761-6861
Emp.: 30
Hardware Sales to the U.S. Air Force
S.I.C.: 5072
Jerrold Weissman *(Pres.)*
Andrew Marshall *(Exec. V.P.)*

Northwest Fence Products Co. **(1)**
P.O. Box 1204, 226 2nd Ave., So.
Great Falls, MT 59403
Tel.: 406-453-4632
Emp.: 15
Fence Erection; Commercial & Residential
S.I.C.: 1799
Jerrold Weissman *(Pres.)*
Jess Wilson *(V.P.)*

THE WEITZ-COHEN CONSTRUCTION CO.
800 Second Ave.
Des Moines, IA 50309
Tel.: 515-246-4700
Fax: 515-246-4799
Year Founded: 1952
Sales Range: $60-79 Million
Emp.: 300
Fiscal Year-end: 3/31/91
General Contractor of Commercial & Industrial Construction
S.I.C.: 1541; 1542
Fred Weitz *(Chm. Bd. & Chief Exec. Officer)*
Glenn H. De Stigter *(Pres. & Chief Oper. Officer)*
Rick H. Poppe *(V.P.-Bus. Acquisitions)*
Arthur V. Neis *(Treas.)*
David S. Strutt *(Sec.)*
Jennifer K. Hays *(Mktg. Coord.)*

Outside Service Firm(s):

KPMG Peat Marwick*(Auditors)*
2500 Ruan Center
Des Moines, IA 50309
Tel.: 515-288-7465

Isaacson, Rosenbaum, Woods, Levy & Snow*(Legal Firm)*
Denver, CO

Norwest Bank Minnesota, N.A.*(Major Banking Relationship)*
Des Moines, IA

Branches:

Weitz-Cohen Construction Company **(1)**
899 Logan St., Ste. 600
Denver, CO 80203
Tel.: 303-860-6600
Fax: 303-860-6698
General Contractor of Commercial & Industrial Construction
S.I.C.: 1541
Donald E. Thorpe *(Pres.)*

Weitz-Cohen Construction Company **(1)**
2255 N. 44th St., Ste. 125
Phoenix, AZ 85008
Tel.: 602-225-0225
General Contractor Of Commercial & Industrial Construction
S.I.C.: 1541
Larry Mohr *(Pres.)*

Weitz-Cohen Construction Company **(1)**
560 Village Blvd., Ste. 120
West Palm Beach, FL 33409
Tel.: 407-686-3511
General Contractor Of Commercial & Industrial Construction
S.I.C.: 1541
Jim Koepnick *(Pres.)*

THE WEITZ CORPORATION
800 2nd Ave.
Des Moines, IA 50309
Tel.: 515-245-7600
Fax: 515-245-7609
Year Founded: 1855
Approx.Sls.: $225,000,000
Emp.: 400
Fiscal Year-end: 3/31/92
General Contractors & Real Estate Developers
S.I.C.: 1541; 6552
Corporate Giving Program: Charitable *Investments are Directed Towards* Cultural Programs and Activities, Education, and Human Services
Employee Matching Gifts Program: Educational Programs, Within Prescribed Dollar Limits, Employee Gifts to Colleges, Universities and Graduate School Programs.
Fred W. Weitz *(Chm. Bd. & Pres.)*
Darlene A. Bradner *(V.P.-Human Resources)*
James M. Brandl *(V.P.)*
David Strutt *(V.P. & Sec.)*
Arthur V. Neis *(Treas.)*
Principal(s):
Fred W. Weitz

Computer Systems/Hardware:
Digital VAX Equipment

Outside Service Firm(s):

KPMG Peat Marwick*(Auditors)*
2500 Ruan Center
Des Moines, IA 50309
Tel.: 515-288-7465

Davis, Hockenberg, Wine, Brown, Koehn & Shors*(Legal Firm)*
Des Moines, IA

Norwest Bank Minnesota, N.A.*(Major Banking Relationship)*
Des Moines, IA

Subsidiaries:

Life Care Services Corporation **(1)**
800 Second Ave.
Des Moines, IA 50309
Tel.: 515-245-7650
Fax: 515-245-7650
Development & Management Of Retirement Communities
S.I.C.: 6531; 6552
Fred W. Weitz *(Chm. Bd. & Chief Exec. Officer)*
Stan G. Thurston *(Pres.)*
Arthur V. Neis *(Chief Fin. Officer & Treas.)*

The Weitz Company, Inc. **(1)**
800 2nd Ave.
Des Moines, IA 50309
Tel.: 515-245-7600
Fax: 515-245-7609
Construction Management; Engineering Services
S.I.C.: 1541; 8711
Fred W. Weitz *(Chm. Bd. & Chief Exec. Officer)*
Glenn DeStigter *(Pres. & Chief Oper. Officer)*

WEITZMAN//LIVINGSTON, INC.
4709 Montgomery Ln.
Bethesda, MD 20814
Tel.: 301-951-4900
Fax: 301-657-7950
Year Founded: 1970
Approx.Billings: $20,800,000
Emp.: 30
Alan R. Weitzman *(Pres. & Chief Exec. Officer)*

WEKSLER INSTRUMENTS CORP.
80 Mill Rd.
Freeport, NY 11520
Mailing Address:
P.O. Box 808
Freeport, NY 11520
Tel.: 516-623-0100
Fax: 516-623-0128
Year Founded: 1925
Approx.Sls.: $15,000,000
Emp.: 220
Import Export
Manufacture Scientific Instruments for Temperature, Pressure & Humidity
S.I.C.: 3823
Peter Marks *(Chm. Bd. & Pres.)*
Kenneth Shavelson *(Chief Fin. Officer, Exec. V.P., Dir.-Intl. Fin. & Treas.)*
John Carnival *(V.P. & Dir.-Sls., Mktg., Direct Mktg., Adv. & Media)*
Saul Rosenblatt *(V.P.-Engrng.)*
Russell Alpert *(Dir.-Quality Control)*
Edith Gerhard *(Dir.-Import)*
Daniel Harren *(Dir.-Data Processing)*
Regina Kohan *(Dir.-Pur.)*
Elsie Lovejoy *(Dir.-Export)*
Joseph Moriarty *(Dir.-Mfg.)*
Peter Marks *(Contact-Mergers & Acquisitions & Dir.-Plng. & Devel.)*
Principal(s):
Peter Marks

No. of Mfg. Plants/Facilities: 1
No. of U.S. Offices: 1

Outside Service Firm(s):

KPMG Peat Marwick*(Auditors)*
1 Jericho Plaza
Jericho, NY 11753
Tel.: 516-822-9100

O'Reilly & Marsh, PC*(Legal Firm)*
1505 Kellum Pl.
Mineola, NY 11501

Chemical Bank*(Major Banking Relationship)*
Jericho, NY

WELCO LUMBER COMPANY
P.O. Box 125
Marysville, WA 98270
Tel.: 206-659-1261
Fax: 206-659-1261, Ext. 61
Approx.Sls.: $20,000,000
Emp.: 150
Western Red Cedar Lumber
S.I.C.: 2421
E.P. Garrett *(Pres.)*
Gary D. LaMarche *(Treas. & Controller)*
Robert E. Crunkilpon *(Gen. Mgr.)*
Garrett Eddy *(Asst. Treas.)*
Gene Baker *(Mgr.-Sls.)*
Bob Davenport *(Mgr.-Production)*

Computer Systems/Hardware:
Ultimate

Outside Service Firm(s):

Harper, Bancroft & Angel*(Auditors)*
Seattle, WA

Davis, Wright, Tremaine*(Legal Firm)*
2200 One Union Square
Seattle, WA 98101-1688
Tel.: 206-622-3150

Seattle First National Bank*(Major Banking Relationship)*
701 Fifth Avenue
Seattle, WA 98104
Tel.: 206-358-3035

WELDON, WILLIAMS & LICK, INC.
711 N. A St.
Fort Smith, AR 72902
Tel.: 501-783-4113
Fax: 501-783-7050
Approx.Sls.: $21,000,000
Emp.: 279
Specialty Printing
S.I.C.: 2759
Seaborn W. Jackson, Jr. *(Chm. Bd.)*
James D. Wolcott, Jr. *(Pres.)*
Jerry P. Hendricks *(V.P.-Sls.)*
Robert Marion *(V.P.-Prod.)*
Tracey Geren *(Treas. & Sec.)*

Outside Service Firm(s):

Tracey Geren*(Auditors)*
Fort Smith, AR

Dailey Law Firm*(Legal Firm)*
Fort Smith, AR

First National Bank*(Major Banking Relationship)*
Fort Smith, AR

WELLENS & CO., INC.
6600 France Ave., S.
Minneapolis, MN 55435
Tel.: 612-925-4600
Fax: 612-925-1851
Approx.Sls.: $25,000,000
Emp.: 7
Merchandiser-Animal Feed Ingredients
S.I.C.: 5159
Leroy Wellens *(Chm. Bd., Pres., Chief Exec. & Chief Fin. Officer & Treas.)*
Brian Lund *(Controller)*

Computer Systems/Hardware:
IBM PC XT

Outside Service Firm(s):

Ernst & Young*(Auditors)*
1400 Pillsbury Center
Minneapolis, MN 55402
Tel.: 612-343-1000

Blue Cross & Blue Shield of Minneapolis*(Group Insurer)*
Minneapolis, MN

Daniels & Daniels*(Legal Firm)*
Minneapolis, MN

Norwest Bank Minnesota, N.A.*(Major Banking Relationship)*
6th St. & Marquette Av.
Minneapolis, MN 55479
Tel.: 612-667-1234

Weller & O'Sullivan
ADVERTISING

WELLER & O'SULLIVAN ADVERTISING
5757 Wilshire Blvd., Penthouse
Los Angeles, CA 90036
Tel.: 213-937-0823
Fax: 213-937-1510
Year Founded: 1984
Approx.Billings: $10,000,000
Emp.: 8
Tom O'Sullivan *(Pres. & Partner)*
Jim Weller *(Partner & Creative Dir.)*

WELLINGTON INDUSTRIES INC.
52 Courtland St.
Paterson, NJ 07503
Tel.: 201-278-2222
Fax: 201-278-2222
Approx.Sls.: $69,000,000
Emp.: 1,700
Fiscal Year-end: 6/30/91
Mfr. Lawn Furniture, Grill Covers, Umbrellas, Table Cloths; Swimming Pool & Patio Prods.; Water Skiing & Boating Equip.
S.I.C.: 2514; 2392; 3949; 3999
Richard Wellington *(Pres.)*
Andy Postnicks *(Chief Fin. Officer)*
John Massengale *(Sec.)*

Subsidiary:

Wellington Home Products **(1)**
52 Courtland St
Paterson, NJ 07503
Tel.: 201-278-6300
Fax: 201-278-2222
Emp.: 350
Wellington Fiberglass & Polypropylene Webbings, Polypropylene Webbing Kits & Rolls, Vinyl Outdoor Covers for Furniture, Grills, Insulated Picnic Bags, Re-Usable Ice Packs, Christmas Stockings, Tree Skirts, Replacement Cushions For Lawn Furniture
S.I.C.: 2241; 3081; 2392; 3631; 3086
Richard Wellington *(Pres.)*
Andy Postnicks *(Chief Fin. Officer)*
John Massengale *(Sec.)*

WELLMADE INDUSTRIES, INC.
131 West 33rd Street
New York, NY 10001
Tel.: 212-564-3526
Fax: 212-465-8169
Approx.Sls.: $15,000,000
Emp.: 9
Lean Jeans: Girls & Childrens Slacks
S.I.C.: 2369
Dennis Spitalnick *(Pres.)*
Andrea Spitalnick *(Sec. & Treas.)*

Outside Service Firm(s):

Rashba & Polkart*(Auditors)*
New York, NY

Merchants Bank*(Major Banking Relationship)*
New York, NY

WELLS ALUMINUM CORP.
300 S. St. Louis Blvd.
South Bend, IN 46601
Mailing Address:
P.O. Box 77
South Bend, IN 46624
Tel.: 219-234-8100
Fax: 219-232-7471
Year Founded: 1943
Assets: $130,000,000
Net Worth: $130,000,000
Approx.Sls.: $210,000,000
Emp.: 1,321
Fiscal Year-end: 12/31/89
Aluminum Extrusions
S.I.C.: 3354
Edward R. Heiser *(Pres. & Chief Exec. Officer)*
Donald R. Wolfgang *(Chief Fin. Officer & V.P.)*
David Larson *(V.P.-Sls. & Mktg.)*
John Smail *(V.P.-Human Resources)*
T.N. Holmes *(Dir.-Data Processing)*

No. of Mfg. Plants/Facilities: 7
No. of U.S. Offices: 9

Computer Systems/Hardware:
IBM System 34

Outside Service Firm(s):

KPMG Peat Marwick*(Auditors)*
135 N. Pennsylvania St.
Indianapolis, IN 46204
Tel.: 317-636-5592
Fax: 317-635-3314

Aetna Life & Casualty*(Group Insurer)*
151 Farmington Avenue
Hartford, CT 06156
Tel.: 203-273-2128
Fax: 203-729-4295

Barnes & Thornburg*(Legal Firm)*
100 N. Michigan., Ste. 600
South Bend, IN 46601
Tel.: 219-233-1171

National Bank of Detroit*(Major Banking Relationship)*
Detroit, MI 48226

WELSBACH ELECTRIC CORP.
19-49 42nd St.
Long Island City, NY 11105
Tel.: 718-274-4200
Fax: 718-274-7427
Approx.Sls.: $30,000,000
Emp.: 250
Fiscal Year-end: 12/31/90
Construction & Maintenance of Street Lights, Traffic Lights & Parking Meters
S.I.C.: 1731; 1799
Fredric Goodman *(V.P.-Fin.)*
Keith Carney *(V.P.-Engrng.)*
Edward Geyer *(V.P.-Opers.)*
Thomas Crotty *(Controller)*

Affiliate:

Jamaica Water Properties **(1)**
410 Lakeville Rd.
Lake Success, NY 11042
Tel.: 516-488-4600

WELSCO INC.
9006 Crystal Hill Rd.
North Little Rock, AR 72113
Mailing Address:
P.O. Box 1058,
North Little Rock, AR 72115
Tel.: 501-771-1204 **AR**
Fax: 501-771-4062
Year Founded: 1941
Assets: $4,500,000
Net Worth: $4,500,000
Sales Range: $10-19 Million
Emp.: 100
Fiscal Year-end: 12/31/90
Manufacture & Sell Industrial Gases & Welding Supplies
S.I.C.: 5084; 2813; 3548
Stephen Harrison *(Chm. & Chief Exec. Officer)*
Bill Layton, Jr. *(Pres. & Chief Oper. Officer)*
Gladys Martin *(Chief Fin. Officer, Treas., Sec. & Dir.-Personnel)*
David Cagle *(V.P.-Inventory & Distr.)*
Brian Harrison *(V.P.-Industrial Gases)*
Gerald Perrier *(V.P.-Mktg.)*
Robert Boshears *(Mgr.-Sls.)*

No. of Mfg. Plants/Facilities: 2

Computer Systems/Hardware:
Data General CS 200

Outside Service Firm(s):

L. Cotton Thomas, CPA's*(Auditors)*
Little Rock, AR

Arkansas Blue Cross & Blue Shield, Inc.*(Group Insurer)*
Little Rock, AR

Rose Firm*(Legal Firm)*
Little Rock, AR

First Commercial Bank*(Major Banking Relationship)*
P.O. Box 1331,
Little Rock, AR 72201

WELSH COMPANY
1535 S. 8th
Saint Louis, MO 63104
Tel.: 314-231-8822
Fax: 314-621-6056
Year Founded: 1929
Sales Range: $20-39 Million
Emp.: 550
Import
Mfr. of Juvenile Products; Toys, Furniture; Wire Display Racks, Powder Coatings, Chrome Plating, Bend & Punch Tubing
S.I.C.: 2514; 2519; 2512; 2511; 3942; 3069; 2542; 3479; 3469; 3471
A.D. Welsh, Jr. *(Pres.)*
Dana Connon *(Grp. V.P.)*
Mark Thomson *(Chief Fin. Officer)*
Ed Greensfelder *(Gen. Counsel)*
Bill Birkenmeier *(Mgr.-Sls.)*
Tom Burgher *(Mgr.-Sls.)*
B. Nenninger *(Mgr.-Pub. Rels.)*
Charles Loose *(Pur. Agent)*
Principal(s):
A.D. Welsh, Jr.
Dana Connon

No. of Mfg. Plants/Facilities: 4
No. of U.S. Offices: 4

Computer Systems/Hardware:
IBM

Outside Service Firm(s):

Bloom Rones & Co.*(Auditors)*
St. Louis, MO

Alexander & Alexander*(Commercial Insurance Carrier)*
St. Louis, MO

Great-West Life Assurance Co.*(Group Insurer)*
St. Louis, MO

Greensfelder, Hemker and Gale, P.C.*(Legal Firm)*
1800 Equitable Bldg., 10 S. Broadway
St. Louis, MO 63102
Tel.: 314-241-9090

Mark Twain St. Louis Bank*(Major Banking Relationship)*
1630 S. Lindbergh Blvd.
St. Louis, MO 63131

WELSH FARMS, INC.
55 Fairview Ave.
Long Valley, NJ 07853
Tel.: 908-876-3131 **DE**
Fax: 908-876-5083
Sales Range: $20-39 Million
Emp.: 300

Welsh Farms, Inc.—(Continued)

Milk, Ice Cream, Ice Cream Mixes, Fruit Drinks & Orange Juice
S.I.C.: 2024; 2026
E. Holsapple *(Chm. Bd.)*
Frank J. Hood *(Pres. & Chief Exec. Officer)*
Robert J. Smith *(Sec.)*

Outside Service Firm(s):

Deloitte & Touche*(Auditors)*
2 Hilton Court
Parsippany, NJ 07054
Tel.: 201-631-6700

Saiber, Schlesinger, Satz & Goldstein*(Legal Firm)*
Newark, NJ

WELSH GRAPHICS
2181 E. Foothill Blvd.
Pasadena, CA 91107
Tel.: 818-449-1600 **CA**
Fax: 818-304-4296
Year Founded: 1948
Approx.Sls.: $30,000,000
Emp.: 225
Color Lithographing
S.I.C.: 2752
Robert J. Welsh *(Pres.)*
Leslie J. Welsh *(V.P.)*
Fraukh Bashir *(Controller)*

Outside Service Firm(s):

Nazar Ashjian*(Auditors)*
Pasadena, CA

Community Bank*(Major Banking Relationship)*
Pasadena, CA

WEMCO, INC.
966 S. White St.
New Orleans, LA 70125
Tel.: 504-822-3700
Fax: 504-821-1088
Approx.Sls.: $50,000,000
Emp.: 750
Men's Neckwear, Shirts & Trousers
S.I.C.: 2323; 2321; 2325
Sidney C. Pulitzer *(Chm. Bd. & Chief Oper. Officer)*
Arthur C. Pulitzer *(Pres.)*
W.F. Matthew *(V.P. & Treas.)*

Outside Service Firm(s):

Deloitte & Touche*(Auditors)*
3700 One Shell Square
New Orleans, LA 70139
Tel.: 504-581-2727

Bronfin, Heller, Steinberg & Berins*(Legal Firm)*
New Orleans, LA

Whitney National Bank of New Orleans*(Major Banking Relationship)*
P.O. Box 61260
New Orleans, LA 70161
Tel.: 504-586-7422

WENCZEL TILE CO.
200 Enterprise Ave.
Trenton, NJ 08638
Mailing Address:
P.O. Box 5308
Trenton, NJ 08638
Tel.: 609-599-4503
Fax: 609-989-8548
Year Founded: 1929
Approx.Sls.: $30,000,000
Emp.: 455
Fiscal Year-end: 12/31/90
Mfr. Ceramic Wall & Floor Tile; Countertop Tile
S.I.C.: 3253
Gary Papp *(Pres.)*
James R. Greathouse *(Exec. V.P.-Oper.)*
Eduardo Angolo *(V.P.-Engrng.)*
Gerald C. Mueller *(Dir.-Sls. & Mktg.)*
Arthur R. Wenczel *(Sec.)*
Joseph A. Hannawacker *(Dir.-Mktg.)*
Rita Mathias *(Dir.-Pur.)*
John Heaney *(Dir.-Fin.)*
Douglas Wurzler *(Mgr.-Personnel)*
Barbara Abbott *(Mgr.-Pub. Rels.)*

Subsidiaries:

Wenczel Tile Company **(1)**
6608 S. Westshore Blvd.
Tampa, FL 33616
Tel.: 813-839-5301
Fax: 813-831-5305

Wenczel Tile Distributing Company **(1)**
2016 Alden Rd.
Orlando, FL 32803
Tel.: 305-898-7741

Wenczel Tile Distributing Company **(1)**
2040 Weaver Park Dr.
Clearwater, FL 33575
Tel.: 813-446-1114

Wenczel Tile Distributing Company **(1)**
1931 13th Ave.
Sarasota, FL 34236
Tel.: 813-955-3394

Wenczel Tile Distributing Company **(1)**
1410 N. Himes Ave.
Tampa, FL 33607
Tel.: 813-876-2483

Wenczel Tile Distributing Company **(1)**
14516 U.S. Hwy. 19
Hudson, FL 34667
Tel.: 813-869-2566

Wenczel Tile Distributing Company **(1)**
1518 State Ave.
Daytona Beach, FL 34625
Tel.: 904-677-0470

Wenczel Tile Distributing Company **(1)**
5870-A Oakbrook Pkwy.
Norcross, GA 30093
Tel.: 404-448-5630
Fax: 404-446-5916

Wenczel Tile Distributing Company **(1)**
1691 B-Enterprise Way
Marietta, GA 30067
Tel.: 404-956-1833

Wenczel Tile Distributing Company **(1)**
1288 S. Perimeter Hwy.
College Park, GA 30349
Tel.: 404-997-2590

Wenczel Tile Distributing Company **(1)**
925 Twin Elms Court
Nashville, TN 37210
Tel.: 615-244-0038

WENDT ADVERTISING, INC.
P.O. Box 2129,
Great Falls, MT 59403
Tel.: 406-452-8581
Fax: 406-771-0603
Year Founded: 1929
Approx.Billings: $12,500,000
Emp.: 31
Stanley F. Meyer *(Chm. & Chief Exec. Officer)*
Mary Tietjen *(Pres.)*

Computer Systems/Hardware:
Admark "Agency" Software/Data General, Macintosh, Media Mgmt. Plus/PC's

WENGER CORPORATION
555 Park Dr.
Owatonna, MN 55060
Tel.: 507-455-4100 **MN**
Telex: 263-228-WNGR UR
Fax: 507-455-4258
Year Founded: 1946
Approx.Sls.: $30,000,000
Emp.: 330
Fiscal Year-end: 12/31/91
Import Export
Mfr. Music Chairs, Music Stands, Lighting & Sound Systems, Standard & Custom Stages, Risers, Acoustical Shells & Music Software for Computers
S.I.C.: 3999; 3446; 3646; 3648; 1799; 7372
Jerry Wenger *(Chm. Bd. & Pres.)*
Ken Pizel *(Chief Fin. Officer & Treas.)*
Phillip Martin *(Sec.)*
James E. Brunner *(Dir.-Fin. Services & Investor Rels.)*
Jan Clementsan *(Dir.)*
Carole Haughton *(Dir.-Mngmt. Information Systems)*
Dale Kuyper *(Dir.-Pur.)*
James H. McCormick *(Dir.-Personnel)*
Kari Wenger *(Mgr.-Adv.)*
Principal(s):
Jerry Wenger

No. of Mfg. Plants/Facilities: 1

Computer Systems/Hardware:
IBM

Outside Service Firm(s):

Deloitte & Touche*(Auditors)*
900 Pillsbury Ctr.
Minneapolis, MN 55402
Tel.: 612-332-2301
Fax: 612-375-5418

Federated Mutual Insurance Co.*(Group Insurer)*
Owatonna, MN

Norwest Bank Minnesota, N.A.*(Investment Banker)*
6th St. & Marquette Av.
Minneapolis, MN 55479
Tel.: 612-667-1234

Dorsey & Whitney*(Legal Firm)*
2200 First Bank Place East
Minneapolis, MN 55402
Tel.: 612-340-2600
Fax: 612-340-2600

First National Bank of Owatonna*(Major Banking Relationship)*
Owatonna, MN

Norwest Bank Minnesota, N.A.*(Pension Manager)*
6th St. & Marquette Av.
Minneapolis, MN 55479
Tel.: 612-667-1234

WERTHAN PACKAGING, INC.
1400 8th Ave. N.
Nashville, TN 37202
Mailing Address:
P.O. Box 1310
Nashville, TN 37202
Tel.: 615-259-9331 **TN**
Fax: 615-726-1093
Year Founded: 1898
Sales Range: $40-59 Million
Emp.: 500
Mfr. Paper Multiwall, Consumer & Textile Bags, Polyethylene Film & Indus. Shipping Sacks
S.I.C.: 2393; 2674; 2759
Bernard Werthan, Jr. *(Pres. & Chief Exec. Officer)*
Morris Profitt *(Chief Fin. Officer & V.P.)*
Earl Chance *(V.P.-Pur.)*
Scott Shaw *(V.P.-Personnel)*
Bart Schwartz *(Legal Officer)*
Ron Brown *(Dir.-Data Processing)*
Earl Chance *(Dir.-Pur.)*
Principal(s):
Bernard Werthan, Jr.

No. of Mfg. Plants/Facilities: 4
No. of U.S. Offices: 1

Computer Systems/Hardware:
Honeywell

Outside Service Firm(s):

KPMG Peat Marwick*(Auditors)*
1900 Nashville Center, 511 Union St.
Nashville, TN 37219

Trabue, Sturdivant & DeWitt*(Legal Firm)*
Life & Casualty Tower
Nashville, TN 37219
Tel.: 615-327-0772

First American Bank, N.A.*(Major Banking Relationship)*
Nashville, TN

WESBAR CORPORATION
4201 County Hwy. P
West Bend, WI 53095
Mailing Address:
P.O. Box 577
West Bend, WI 53095
Tel.: 414-334-2381 **WI**
Fax: 414-677-4737
Year Founded: 1934
Sales Range: $100-499 Million
Emp.: 100
Fiscal Year-end: 12/31/91
Export
Mfr. of Marine, Agricultural & Industrial Trailer Components; Lights, Wire Harnesses, Hub & Grease Caps, Trailer Jacks & Boat Ladders
S.I.C.: 3523; 3715
M.A. Nielsen *(Pres., Chief Exec. Officer & Treas.)*
T.J. Aceto *(V.P.-Opers., Metal Products Div.)*
S. Johnston *(V.P.-Mktg.)*
C.I. Nielsen, III *(V.P.-Sls.)*
E.G. Paffrath *(V.P.-Opers., Electrical Products Div.)*
J. Perry *(Mgr.-Pur.)*

No. of Mfg. Plants/Facilities: 1
No. of U.S. Offices: 1

Computer Systems/Hardware:
IBM System 36

Outside Service Firm(s):

Arthur Andersen & Co.*(Auditors)*
777 E. Wisconsin Ave., P.O. Box 1215
Milwaukee, WI 53202
Tel.: 414-271-5100
Fax: 414-283-3200

WEST CENTRAL CO-OP
P.O. Box 68
Ralston, IA 51459
Tel.: 712-667-3200
Fax: 712-667-3215
Approx.Sls.: $96,622,440
Emp.: 125
Agricultural Services; Food Products
S.I.C.: 5153; 2075; 2048
Wayne Seaman *(Chief Exec. Officer & Gen. Mgr.)*
Janie Hertel *(Controller)*
Charles Haberer *(Dir.)*
Roger Wessling *(Dir.)*
Thomas Feldmann *(Mgr.-Mktg.)*

Computer Systems/Hardware:
IBM System 36

Outside Service Firm(s):

Gardiner & Co.*(Auditors)*
Des Moines, IA

Mutual Service Life Insurance Co.*(Group Insurer)*
Arden Hills, MN

Gerkin & Schwarzkopf*(Legal Firm)*
Des Moines, IA

Home State Bank*(Major Banking Relationship)*
Jefferson, IA

Omaha Bank for Co-ops*(Major Banking Relationship)*
Omaha, NE

AGRI Industries*(Pension Manager)*
Des Moines, IA

Subsidiaries:

Redeco Industries **(1)**
P.O. Box 68
Ralston, IA 51459
Tel.: 712-667-3200 (100%)

W.C. Commodities **(1)**
P.O. Box 68
Ralston, IA 51459
Tel.: 712-667-3200 (100%)

WEST COAST GROWERS & PACKERS, INC.
1445 Nebraska
Selma, CA 93662
Mailing Address:
P.O. Box 119
Selma, CA 93662
Tel.: 209-896-2140
Fax: 209-896-4304
Approx.Sls.: $45,000,000
Emp.: 200
Fiscal Year-end: 12/31/90
Export
Cinderella Seedless Raisins & Currants, Blondie Golden Seedless Raisins
S.I.C.: 2034; 0171
S. W. Schuman, Jr. *(Chm. Bd. & Pres.)*
D. A. Martens *(V.P.-Sls. & Mktg.)*
Don Kilgore *(V.P.-Opers.)*
Jerry Geiger *(Controller)*

WEST COAST NATIONAL VIDEO
(Formerly West Coast Video Ltd.)
9990 Global Rd.
Philadelphia, PA 19115
Tel.: 215-677-1000
Fax: 215-677-5804
Year Founded: 1982
Approx.Sls.: $25,000,000
Emp.: 500
Rental of Prerecorded Videotapes; Retail Video Accessories
S.I.C.: 7841
Harold Stone *(Chm. Bd.)*
Elliot Stone *(Pres.)*
Richard Abt *(Exec. V.P.)*
Karen Owens *(Dir.-Adv.)*
David Waxler *(Controller)*

Outside Service Firm(s):

Philadelphia National Bank*(Major Banking Relationship)*
P.O. Box 13834, Broad & Chestnut Streets
Philadelphia, PA 19101-7618
Tel.: 215-973-8327

Subsidiaries:

National Video, Inc. **(1)**
9990 Global Rd.
Philadelphia, PA 19115
Tel.: 215-677-1000
Fax: 215-677-5804
Approx.Sls.: $83,000,000
Emp.: 30
Fiscal Year-end: 3/31/91
Franchised Video Rental Stores
S.I.C.: 7841
Elliot Stone *(Pres. & Chief Exec. Officer)*
Karin Owens *(V.P.-Adv. & Admin.)*

Princeton Partners, Inc. **(1)**
2 Research Way, Princeton Forrestal Center
Princeton, NJ 08540
Tel.: 609-452-8500
Fax: 609-452-7212
Approx.Billings: $10,500,000
Emp.: 17
Consumer, Financial & Healthcare
Catherine A. Mathis *(Pres.)*
Thomas Sullivan *(Exec. V.P.)*

WEST & COMPANY

WEST & COMPANY MARKETING & ADVERTISING
401 E. Jackson St., Ste. 3600
Tampa, FL 33602
Tel.: 813-224-9378 **FL**
Fax: 813-223-9871
Year Founded: 1966
Approx.Billings: $65,000,000
Emp.: 91
Advertising Agency
S.I.C.: 7311
Benjamin B. West *(Pres. & Chief Exec. Officer)*
Michael Edmeades *(Chief Oper. Officer)*
Bill Bender *(V.P., Gen. Mgr.)*
Luke Greene *(Controller)*

No. of U.S. Offices: 4

WEST DAIRIES, INC.
P.O. Box 169, W. Bridge St., Stoney Run
Spring City, PA 19475
Tel.: 215-948-8300
Fax: 215-948-7879
Year Founded: 1943
Approx.Sls.: $19,000,000
Emp.: 150
Vending Machine Sale of Milk; Wholesale Milk
S.I.C.: 5143; 5451; 5962
Hanlon Harris Jr. *(Pres.)*
James Phillip West *(Exec. V.P.)*
Kenneth Lahner *(Controller)*
Elsie M. West *(Sec.)*

No. of Mfg. Plants/Facilities: 1
No. of U.S. Offices: 3

Outside Service Firm(s):

Ed Roberts*(Auditors)*
Hatboro, PA

Harrison & Demcisak*(Legal Firm)*
Hatboro, PA

Continental Bank, N.A.*(Major Banking Relationship)*
Norristown, PA

WEST LUMBER CO.
280 Westminster Dr., NE
Atlanta, GA 30309
Tel.: 404-875-4745
Fax: 706-876-5076
Approx.Sls.: $325,000,000
Emp.: 2,100
Manufacture Lumber
S.I.C.: 2421; 5211; 5031
Charles B. West *(Chm. Bd.)*
G. Vincent West *(Pres.)*
Edward A. Crosta *(Sr. V.P. & Treas.)*
Howard Ashworth *(V.P. & Corp. Plng.)*
Don Williams *(Controller)*
Principal(s):
Charles B. West

Computer Systems/Hardware:
IBM System 36

Outside Service Firm(s):

Coopers & Lybrand*(Auditors)*
1155 Peachtree St.
Atlanta, GA 30309
Tel.: 404-870-1309

Bank South, N.A.*(Major Banking Relationship)*
P.O. Box 4387
Atlanta, GA 30302
Tel.: 404-529-4111

WEST MILL CLOTHES, INC.
57-07 31st Ave.
Woodside, NY 11377
Tel.: 718-204-6640
Fax: 718-204-6658
Year Founded: 1917
Sales Range: $20-39 Million
Emp.: 450
Fiscal Year-end: 6/30/91
Mfr. Men's Formal Wear
S.I.C.: 2311
Harvey Weinstein *(Pres.)*
Murray Westreich *(Exec. V.P., Sec. & Treas.)*
Bernard Farber *(Sr. V.P.-Mktg. & Sls.)*
Farokh Hirji *(Controller)*
Marvin Arno *(Dir.-Data Processing)*
Clifford Goodman *(Dir.-Personnel)*
Kathryn S. Hyland *(Dir.-Adv.)*
Principal(s):
Harvey Weinstein
Murray Westreich

No. of Mfg. Plants/Facilities: 1
No. of U.S. Offices: 1

Computer Systems/Hardware:
IBM

Outside Service Firm(s):

Louis Sturz & Co.*(Auditors)*
New York, NY

KBS*(Commercial Insurance Carrier)*
New Rochelle, NY

Cowan, Liebowitz & Latman*(Legal Firm)*
New York, NY

Chemical Bank*(Major Banking Relationship)*
450 West 33rd St.
New York, NY 10001
Tel.: 212-613-7197
Fax: 212-947-7628

Chemical Banking Corp.*(Major Banking Relationship)*
277 Park Ave.
New York, NY 10041
Tel.: 212-310-6407
Fax: 212-310-4526

Divisions:

Pierre Cardin Formal Wear **(1)**
57-07 31st Ave.
Woodside, NY 11377
Tel.: 718-204-6640
S.I.C.: 2311

West Mill Clothes, H.M.C. Div. **(1)**
57-07 31st Ave.
Woodside, NY 11377
Tel.: 718-204-6640
S.I.C.: 2311

West Mill Clothes, Tuxacco Accessories Div. **(1)**
Keystone Industrial Park, 257 Rittenhouse Circle
Bristol, PA 19007
Tel.: 215-785-2300
Formal Shirts & Accessories
S.I.C.: 2321
Clement Crystal *(Pres.)*

WEST, PAUSBACK & VAUGHAN, INC.
3101 Petty Rd., Ste. 1000
Durham, NC 27707
Tel.: 919-489-0929
Fax: 919-489-8469
Year Founded: 1985
Approx.Billings: $18,550,000
Emp.: 24
William K. West *(Pres. & Creative Dir.)*
Delaine Womack *(Acctg. Mgr.)*

Computer Systems/Hardware:
MacIntosh Network

WEST PUBLISHING CO.
610 Opperman Dr.
Eagan, MN 55123
Tel.: 612-687-7000 **MN**
Fax: 612-228-7081
Year Founded: 1876
Approx.Sls.: $395,000,000
Emp.: 5,200
Printing & Publishing-Legal, Educational & Electronic
S.I.C.: 2731; 2732; 2741
Dwight D. Opperman *(Pres. & Chief Exec. Officer)*
Grant E. Nelson *(Chief Fin. Officer)*
G.L. Cafesjian *(V.P.)*
L.J. Culligan *(V.P.)*
Charles C. Cunningham *(V.P.)*
Jerrol Tostrud *(V.P.)*

Computer Systems/Hardware:
IBM PC

Outside Service Firm(s):

Arthur Andersen & Co.*(Auditors)*
30 E. Seventh Street
St. Paul, MN 55101
Tel.: 612-291-1211

First Bank of St. Paul*(Major Banking Relationship)*
St. Paul, MN

Subsidiary:

West Services, Inc. **(1)**
610 Opperman Dr.
Eagan, MN 55123
Tel.: 612-687-7000
Dwight D. Opperman *(Pres.)*

WEST UNION CORP.
35 Union
Memphis, TN 38103
Mailing Address:
P.O. Box 3177
Memphis, TN 38173
Tel.: 901-529-5700
Approx.Sls.: $100,000,000
Emp.: 900
Wholesale Hardware
S.I.C.: 5072; 5023
Joseph Orgill, III *(Chm. Bd.)*
Michael McDonnell *(Pres. & Chief Exec. Officer)*
Robert E. Hawkins *(Chief Fin. Officer, Treas., Controller & Sec.)*
Charles Epperson *(V.P.-Human Resources)*

Computer Systems/Hardware:
IBM 4341

Outside Service Firm(s):

Deloitte & Touche*(Auditors)*
Memphis, TN

Armstrong, Allen, Prewitt, Gentry, Johnson & Holmes*(Legal Firm)*
1900 One Commerce Sq.
Memphis, TN 38103
Tel.: 901-523-8211

First Tennessee Bank, N.A.*(Major Banking Relationship)*
Memphis, TN

Goldman, Sachs & Co.*(Pension Manager)*
85 Broad St.
New York, NY 10004
Tel.: 212-902-1000
Fax: 212-902-4451

West Union Corp.—(Continued)

Subsidiary:

Orgill Brothers & Company, Inc. (1)
2100 Latham St.
Memphis, TN 38103
Tel.: 901-946-3381
Approx.Sls.: $90,000,000
Emp.: 600
Joseph Orgill, III *(Chm. Bd. & Sec.)*
William M. Fondren, Jr. *(Pres.)*

WEST VIRGINIA LOTTERY
312 MacCorkle S.E.
Charleston, WV 25314
Mailing Address:
P.O. Box 2067
Charleston, WV 25327
Tel.: 304-558-0500
Tel.: 800-WVA-CASH
Fax: 800-982-2274
Year Founded: 1985
Approx.Sls.: $90,000,000
Emp.: 30
Fiscal Year-end: 6/30/92
State Lottery
S.I.C.: 7999
E. E. Bryan *(Dir.)*
Robert Wilhelm *(Deputy Dir.-Fin. & Admin.)*
Tamara L. Gunnoe *(Deputy Dir.-Mktg.)*
Bill Woodford *(Chief of Security & Computer Services)*

Computer Systems/Hardware:
G Tech

WESTAIR HOLDING INC.
5570 Air Terminal Dr.
Fresno, CA 93727
Tel.: 209-294-6915 **CA**
Year Founded: 1982
Assets: $78,984,000
Earnings: $7,184,000
Liabilities: $62,534,000
Net Worth: $16,450,000
Approx.Rev.: $239,068,000
Emp.: 1544
Fiscal Year-end: 12/31/91
Regional Airline System
S.I.C.: 4512
Timothy P. Flynn *(Chm. Bd. & Chief Exec. Officer)*
Maurice J. Gallagher, Jr. *(Pres.)*
Craig Belmondo *(V.P. & Chief Oper. Officer-WestAir Commuter Airlines, Inc.)*
Bryan K. Bedford *(V.P. & Chief Fin. Officer)*
Ronald B. Booth *(V.P.-Fin. & Admin./ WestAir Commuter Airlines, Inc.)*
Gary Ellmer *(V.P.-Tech. Services/ WestAir Commuter Airlines)*
Mark Peterson *(V.P.-Corp. Affairs)*

WESTAT INC.
1650 Research Blvd.
Rockville, MD 20850
Tel.: 301-251-1500
Fax: 301-294-2040
Year Founded: 1963
Approx.Sls.: $87,200,000
Emp.: 1,500
Fiscal Year-end: 12/31/91
Statistical Survey Research
S.I.C.: 8732
Joseph Waksberg *(Chm. Bd.)*
Joseph A. Hunt *(Pres.)*
Michael Beck *(Sr. V.P.-Fin.)*
Thomas McKenna *(Sr. V.P. & Corp. Sec.)*
James Smith *(V.P.-Data Processing)*
Thomas Jones *(V.P.-Telecommunications)*
Patricia Smith *(Dir.-Personnel Admin.)*
Maureen Stadwick *(Librarian)*
Nancy King *(Corp. Travel Planner)*

WESTCHESTER LACE, INC.
3901 Liberty Ave.
North Bergen, NJ 07047
Tel.: 201-864-2150
Fax: 201-864-2116
Year Founded: 1976
Sales Range: $10-19 Million
Emp.: 125
Export
Mfr. of Raschel Lace
S.I.C.: 2258
Gerald J. Scher *(Chm. Bd., Treas. & Sec.)*
L. Edelson *(Pres.)*

Outside Service Firm(s):

Hudson United Bank*(Major Banking Relationship)*
Union City, NJ

WESTCO PRODUCTS, INC.
7351 Crider Ave.
Pico Rivera, CA 90660
Tel.: 310-949-1054 **CA**
Fax: 310-949-1257
Year Founded: 1928
Approx.Sls.: $190,000,000
Emp.: 450
Import Export
Prepared Flour Mixes & Doughs; Bakery Products, Fruit Fillings & Icings
S.I.C.: 2045; 5149
Allen S. Ziegler *(Chm. Bd.)*
Ronald L. Ziegler *(Pres.)*
Joe D. Castor *(V.P.)*
Douglas Ziegler *(Sec. & Treas.)*
Carl Wertz *(Controller)*
Steve Mosier *(Gen. Mgr.-Sls.)*
Principal(s):
Allen S. Ziegler
Ronald L. Ziegler
Douglas Ziegler

No. of Mfg. Plants/Facilities: 4
No. of U.S. Offices: 10

Computer Systems/Hardware:
Digital VAX

Outside Service Firm(s):

Transamerica Occidental Insurance Co.*(Commercial Insurance Carrier)*
P.O. Box 30253,
Los Angeles, CA 90099

Transamerica Occidental Insurance Co.*(Group Insurer)*
P.O. Box 30253,
Los Angeles, CA 90099

First Business Bank*(Major Banking Relationship)*
Los Angeles, CA

Divisions:

Standard Flour Co. (1)
2425 Saybrook Ave.
City of Commerce, CA 90040
Tel.: 213-726-2228
Distributors of Flour
S.I.C.: 5149
Andy Van Schalk *(Mgr.)*

Westco Food Service (1)
827 N. Main St.
Las Vegas, NV 89101
Tel.: 702-382-5622
Wholesale Food Service
S.I.C.: 5149
Don Roby *(Mgr.)*

Westco Products/Bay Area (1)
32621 Central Ave.
Union City, CA 94587
Tel.: 510-487-8188
Wholesale Bakery Supplies
S.I.C.: 5149
Tim Thompson *(Mgr.)*

Westco Products/Intermountain (1)
805 W. 2500 South
Salt Lake City, UT 84119
Tel.: 801-972-1131
Tom Smith *(Mgr.)*

Branches:

Westco Products/North Nevada (2)
475 Nugget Ave.
Sparks, NV 89431
Tel.: 702-359-0532
Wholesale Bakery Supplies
S.I.C.: 5149
Robert Kern *(Mgr.)*

Westco Products/Northwest (2)
6555 S.W. 111th St.
Beaverton, OR 97005
Tel.: 503-643-9401
Wholesale Bakery Supplies
S.I.C.: 5149
Fred Meyer *(Mgr.)*

Westco Products/Phoenix (2)
5720 W. Jefferson St.
Phoenix, AZ 85043
Tel.: 602-272-0444
Wholesale Bakery Supplies
S.I.C.: 5149
Claude Herbison *(Mgr.)*

Westco Products/Sacramento (1)
521 N. 10th St.
Sacramento, CA 95814
Tel.: 916-442-4321
Wholesale Bakery Supplies
S.I.C.: 5149
Ron Marion *(Mgr.)*

Westco Products/Seattle (1)
9883 40th Ave. So.
Seattle, WA 98118
Tel.: 206-721-5559
Wholesale Bakery Supplies
S.I.C.: 5149
John Cartwright *(Mgr.)*

NELSON WESTERBERG, INC.
1500 Arthur Ave., Ste. 200 W
Elk Grove Village, IL 60007
Tel.: 708-437-2080
Fax: 708-437-2199
Approx.Sls.: $11,000,000
Emp.: 342
Household Goods Transport & Warehousing
S.I.C.: 4213; 4226
John R. Westerberg *(Pres.)*
Alan S. Mileski *(Exec. V.P.)*
Gordon R. Borske *(V.P.)*
Grant D. Erickson *(Sec.)*

Outside Service Firm(s):

Midlantic National Bank*(Major Banking Relationship)*
Metro Park Plaza,
Edison, NJ 08818
Tel.: 908-321-8000

The Northern Trust Co.*(Major Banking Relationship)*
50 S. LaSalle St.
Chicago, IL 60675
Tel.: 312-630-6000
Fax: 312-444-7028

Subsidiary:

Nelson Westerberg Of New Jersey (1)
1500 Arthur Ave., Ste. 200 W
Elk Grove Village, IL 60007
Tel.: 708-437-7050
Household Goods Transport & Warehousing
S.I.C.: 4213; 4226
John R. Westerberg *(Pres.)*

WESTERN CO-OP ELECTRIC UTILITY ASSOCIATION
P.O. Box 278
Wakeeney, KS 67672
Tel.: 913-743-5561 **KS**
Fax: 913-743-2717
Year Founded: 1946
Approx.Sls.: $10,000,000
Emp.: 22
Electric Power Distribution
S.I.C.: 4911
Larry J. Evans *(Pres.)*
Donald L. Schultz *(V.P.)*
David L. Schneider *(Gen. Mgr.)*

Outside Service Firm(s):

Bernard Ebbert*(Auditors)*
Wakeeney, KS

Trego Wakeeney State Bank*(Major Banking Relationship)*
Wakeeney, KS

WESTERN CONTROLS
526 North 400 West
North Salt Lake, UT 84054
Mailing Address:
P.O. Box 540508,
North Salt Lake, UT 84054
Tel.: 801-292-5900
Fax: 801-292-5954
Distribute Electrical & Electronic Industrial Automatic Controls, Including Process Controls
S.I.C.: 5063; 5065
Roger Turner *(Pres., Chief Exec. & Fin. Officer)*

Computer Systems/Hardware:
IBM; Qantel

Outside Service Firm(s):

Tebbs, Smith*(Auditors)*
Salt Lake City, UT

Sessions & Moore*(Legal Firm)*
Salt Lake City, UT

First Interstate Bank*(Major Banking Relationship)*
2nd South & Main
Salt Lake City, UT 84101

WESTERN DAIRYMEN COOPERATIVE, INC.
12450 N. Washington St.
Thornton, CO 80241
Mailing Address:
P.O. Box 33120,
Thornton, CO 80233-0120
Tel.: 303-451-0422
Fax: 303-452-5484
Year Founded: 1987
Sales Range: $100-499 Million
Milk Marketing Cooperative
S.I.C.: 5143
James P. Camerlo, Jr. *(Chm. Bd. & Pres.)*
Lee W. Mortensen *(Chief Fin. Officer)*
Leland M. Anderson *(Exec. V.P. & Gen. Mgr.)*
Gregory G. Yando *(V.P.-Mktg.)*
Lynn Cottrell *(V.P.-Admin. & Dir.-Personnel)*
John Cleland *(Treas.)*
Dale W. Bleck *(Controller-Denver)*
Scott Brown *(Controller-Salt Lake City)*

No. of Mfg. Plants/Facilities: 7
No. of U.S. Offices: 2

Outside Service Firm(s):

McDonald, Holligan & McPherson*(Auditors)*
Pueblo, CO

Holme Roberts & Owen*(Legal Firm)*
1701 Lincoln St., Ste. 4100
Denver, CO 80202
Tel.: 303-861-7000

First Security Bank of Utah*(Pension Manager)*
Salt Lake City, UT

WESTERN DATA SYSTEMS
26707 Agoura Rd.
Calabasas, CA 91302
Tel.: 818-880-0800 **CA**
Fax: 818-880-1424
Year Founded: 1977
Sales Range: $10-19 Million
Emp.: 100

Fiscal Year-end: 1/31/90
Export
Computer MRPII Software & Services
S.I.C.: 7372; 7371; 7378
Anton Roddie *(Pres.)*
Emmett Burns *(Chief Exec. Officer)*
Steve Heinrichs *(Chief Fin. Officer)*
Peggy Biddison *(V.P.-Mktg.)*
Allan Wilson *(V.P.-Sls. & Cust. Service)*
Richard Pardi *(Controller)*
Jim Cutler *(Dir.-Contracts)*
Jodi Sacco *(Dir.-Mktg. Communications)*
Susan Christman *(Mgr.-Office Services)*
Principal(s):
Anton Roddie

No. of Mfg. Plants/Facilities: 1
No. of U.S. Offices: 7
No. of Foreign Offices: 1

Computer Systems/Hardware:
Hewlett Packard; IBM; DEC

Outside Service Firm(s):

KPMG Peat Marwick*(Auditors)*
Woodland Hills, CA

T. Rowe Price Associates*(Pension Manager)*
100 E. Pratt St.
Baltimore, MD 21202
Tel.: 410-547-2000
Fax: 410-659-0965

WESTERN DEVELOPMENT CORPORATION
3000 K St. N.W., Suite 200
Washington, DC 20007
Tel.: 202-965-3600
Fax: 202-298-5111
Year Founded: 1967
Approx.Sls.: $71,400,000
Emp.: 300
Real Estate Developer; Commercial, Residential & Retail
S.I.C.: 6552
Herbert Miller *(Chm. Bd. & Chief Exec. Officer)*
Richard L. Kramer *(Vice Chm.)*
David Lick *(Chief Fin. Officer & Sr. V.P.)*
Tom Kehoe *(Exec. V.P.-Devel.)*
Harry Nick *(Exec. V.P.)*
John Penn *(Exec. V.P.)*
Patience O'Connor *(Sr. V.P.-Mktg.)*
Ronald Salerno *(Sr. V.P.)*
Joan E. Wallace *(Dir.-Opers.)*
Brenda Hudson *(Mgr.-Mngmt. Information Systems)*

WESTERN DIESEL SERVICES INC.
1424 Ashby Rd.
Saint Louis, MO 63132
Tel.: 314-429-2131 **MO**
Fax: 314-429-2355
Year Founded: 1929
Approx.Sls.: $60,000,000
Emp.: 400
Diesel Drivetrain Sales & Service
S.I.C.: 5084; 7538
John Costello *(Pres.)*
Tom Palmer *(Pres.)*
Hugh Scott, III *(Chief Exec. Officer)*
Don Campbell *(V.P. & Controller)*
Phyllis Davidson *(V.P.)*
Charles Turner *(V.P.-Opers.)*
Rex Walker *(V.P.)*
Steve Maedge *(Dir.-Data Processing)*
Principal(s):
Hugh Scott, III

Outside Service Firm(s):

Arthur Andersen & Co.*(Auditors)*
1010 Market St.
St. Louis, MO 63101

Edward Murphy*(Legal Firm)*
Clayton, MO

Barnett Banks Trust Company, N.A.*(Major Banking Relationship)*
9000 Southside Blvd., P.O. Box 40200
Jacksonville, FL 32202-0200
Tel.: 904-464-2802

Wells Fargo Bank*(Major Banking Relationship)*
San Francisco, CA

Subsidiary:

Detroit Diesel Allison Co. **(1)**
500 S. Lombard
Addison, IL 60101
Tel.: 708-620-2000
Fax: 708-620-0287
Mfr. & Distribute Diesel & Gas Turbine Generating Equipment
S.I.C.: 3621; 3511; 5084
Thomas Palmer *(Pres.)*
C. Lambert *(Mgr.-Data Processing)*

WESTERN EXTRUSIONS
1735 Sandy Lake Rd.
Carrollton, TX 75006
Mailing Address:
P.O. Box 810219
Dallas, TX 75381
Tel.: 214-245-7515
Year Founded: 1979
Sales Range: $20-39 Million
Emp.: 222
Aluminum Extrusions
S.I.C.: 3341
A.P. McEvoy, Jr. *(Pres.)*
Charles McEvoy *(Exec. V.P.)*
Walt Taylor *(V.P.-Mfg.)*
Lyle Williams *(V.P.-Mktg.)*
Arthur D. Myer *(Controller)*
Pat Lenaberg *(Mgr.-Data Processing)*
Morgan Conley *(Pur. Agent)*
Principal(s):
A.P. McEvoy, Jr.

Computer Systems/Hardware:
Tandy PC Model 6000, Model 16V using the Xenix Operating System

Outside Service Firm(s):

Altschuler, Melvoin & Glasser*(Commercial Insurance Carrier)*
30 S. Wecker Dr.
Chicago, IL 60606
Tel.: 312-207-2800

Allstate Insurance*(Commercial Insurance Carrier)*
Northbrook, IL

MBank Dallas*(Major Banking Relationship)*
1900 Pacific
Dallas, TX 75265

WESTERN FEDERAL SAVINGS & LOAN ASSOCIATION
13160 Mindanao Way
Marina Del Rey, CA 90292
Mailing Address:
P.O. Box 9959
Marina Del Rey, CA 90295
Tel.: 310-306-6500
Year Founded: 1896
Approx.Sls.: $112,677,000
Emp.: 1,000
Fiscal Year-end: 12/30/90
Savings and Loan Association
S.I.C.: 6035
Hugh Evans, Jr. *(Chm. Bd.)*
James E. Bethel *(Pres. & Chief Exec. Officer)*
Mark Nussbaum *(Chief Fin. Officer)*
Gregory Oliver *(Sr. V.P.-Mktg.)*
Diana C. Berrones *(V.P.-Adv.)*
Patricia Briggs *(V.P.-Loan Origination)*

Computer Systems/Hardware:
MISER

WESTERN GRAIN, INC.
Colorado Derby Bldg., 202 W. 1st St., Ste. 403
Wichita, KS 67202
Tel.: 316-263-1219
Approx.Sls.: $12,500,000
Emp.: 25
Buy & Sell Grain
S.I.C.: 5153
Darwin L. Sampson *(Chm. Bd.)*
John Severe *(Pres. & Gen. Mgr.)*
Jim Sampson *(Treas.)*

Outside Service Firm(s):

William Johnson & Company*(Auditors)*
Wichita, KS

Merkel Chartered*(Legal Firm)*
Wichita, KS

First National Bank of Wichita*(Major Banking Relationship)*
Box One
Wichita, KS 67201
Tel.: 316-268-1201

THE WESTERN GROUP
1637 N. Warson Rd.
Saint Louis, MO 63132
Mailing Address:
P.O. Box 32407,
St. Louis, MO 63132
Tel.: 314-427-6733 **MO**
Fax: 314-427-6199
Year Founded: 1915
Approx.Sls.: $104,374,000
Emp.: 215
Fiscal Year-end: 3/31/91
Waterproofing Contractors
S.I.C.: 1799
Benjamin M. Bishop *(Chm. & Chief Exec. Officer)*
William L. Bishop *(Pres. & Chief Oper. Officer)*
David Brisk *(Exec. V.P.-Opers.)*
Michael E. Harmon *(Chief Fin. Officer)*

Outside Service Firm(s):

Price Waterhouse*(Auditors)*
One Boatmen's Plaza
St. Louis, MO 63101
Tel.: 314-425-0500

Mercantile Bank St. Louis*(Major Banking Relationship)*
P.O. Box 321
St. Louis, MO 63166
Tel.: 314-425-2755

Subsidiaries:

Brisk Waterproofing **(1)**
720 Grand Ave.
Ridgefield, NJ 07657
Tel.: 201-945-0210
Waterproofing Contractors
S.I.C.: 1799

Western Waterproofing Company of America, Inc. **(1)**
1637 N. Warson
Saint Louis, MO 63132
Tel.: 314-427-6733
Emp.: 400
Specialty Contractor
S.I.C.: 1799

Western Waterproofing Company, Inc. **(1)**
1637 N. Warson
Saint Louis, MO 63132
Tel.: 314-427-6733
Emp.: 800

WESTERN INDUSTRIES, INC.
1211 N. 62nd St.
Milwaukee, WI 53213
Tel.: 414-771-7700
Fax: 414-771-7371
Approx.Sls.: $120,000,000
Emp.: 1,100
Export
Metal & Plastic Stampings & Fabrications
S.I.C.: 3441; 3469
Jack F. Kellner *(Chm. Bd.)*
G. Ronald Morris *(Pres. & Chief Exec. Officer)*

Outside Service Firm(s):

KPMG Peat Marwick*(Auditors)*
777 E. Wisconsin Ave.
Milwaukee, WI 53202
Tel.: 414-276-4200

Foley & Lardner*(Legal Firm)*
777 E. Wisconsin Ave.
Milwaukee, WI 53202
Tel.: 414-271-2400

M & I Marshall & Ilsley Bank*(Major Banking Relationship)*
770 N. Water St.
Milwaukee, WI 53202
Tel.: 414-765-8700

WESTERN INTERNATIONAL MEDIA

WESTERN INTERNATIONAL MEDIA CORPORATION
8544 Sunset Blvd.
Los Angeles, CA 90069
Tel.: 310-659-5711
Year Founded: 1970
Approx.Billings: $1,100,000,000
Emp.: 790
Advertising Agency
S.I.C.: 7311
Dennis F. Holt *(Pres. & Chief Exec. Officer)*
Roar Sinstad *(Chief Info. Officer)*
Mark Dodge *(Exec. V.P. & Gen. Counsel)*
William Croasdale *(Pres.-Network Brdcst. Div.)*
Juan Carlos Nieto del Rio *(Pres.-Spanish Comm. Corp.)*
Ronald Glazer *(Pres.-Syndication Div.)*
Bruce Hoenig *(Pres.-Entertainment Div.)*
Elaine Kaplan *(Pres.-Spot TV Div.)*
Leon Rosen *(Pres.-T.V. Mktg.)*
Olga Mardirossian *(Sr. V.P. & Controller)*
Tom Mullins *(Sr. V.P.)*
Bill Overlock *(Sr. V.P. & Chief Fin. Officer)*
Jim Vouvakis *(Sr. V.P.-Yellow Pages)*
Joan Geller *(Dir.-Admin.)*
Sue Inkrot *(Brdcst. Services Admin.)*
William Croasdale *(Pres., Network)*
Dawn Imber *(Sr. Network Negotiator)*
Kristen Starble *(Sr. Network Negotiator)*
Ann Lange *(V.P.)*
Chris Hart *(Dir., Distr.)*
Sharon Goodrich *(Office Mgr.)*
Pat Keating *(Sr. V.P., Dir. Plng. & Print)*
Connie Robinson *(Assoc. Dir., Plng.)*
Nadia Pidhajecky *(Assoc. Dir., Plng.)*
Peggy Walsh *(Plng. Supvr.)*
Susan Montgomery *(Sr. Planner)*
Teriann Link *(Sr. Planner)*
Christina Chiella *(Print Buyer)*
Patrice Danielsen *(Exec. Asst.)*
Wendy Storch *(Dir.)*
Beth Lowry *(Office Mgr.)*
Michael Cox *(Sr. V.P., Mngmt. Information Systems)*
Fernanado de Gasperis *(Micro Comp. Analyst)*
Charlotte Harris *(Project Mgr.)*
Kira Roessler *(Project Leader)*
Bryan Andrews *(Sr. Tech. Mgr.)*
Mauro Bordovsky *(PC Mgr.)*
Curt Levis *(Sr. Program Analyst)*
Sunchai Mektrakarn *(Sr. Program Analyst)*

Western International Media Corporation—(Continued)

Ken McFadden *(Sr. Program Analyst)*
John Wu *(Sr. Program Analyst)*
David Wulf *(Oper. Mfr.)*
Robby Hicks *(Opers. Tech.)*
Scott Mouden *(Program Analyst)*

Branches:

Motivational Incentives Group **(1)**
8544 Sunset Blvd.
Los Angeles, CA 90069
Tel.: 310-659-5711
Dwight Case *(Mng. Dir.)*

Networks America **(1)**
8981 Sunset Blvd.
Los Angeles, CA 90069
Tel.: 310-854-7500
Dwight Case *(Pres.)*

Outdoor Media Inc. **(1)**
8544 Sunset Blvd.
Los Angeles, CA 90069
Tel.: 310-659-5711
Dave Bryman *(V.P.)*

Outdoor Services, Inc. **(1)**
15315 Magnolia Blvd.
Sherman Oaks, CA 91403
Tel.: 818-501-8299
Mark Barnes *(Pres.)*
Don Robinson *(Gen. Mgr.)*

Patriot Direct Dial Systems **(1)**
8544 Sunset Blvd.
Los Angeles, CA 90069
Tel.: 310-854-7509
Doug Livingston *(Pres.)*
John Phee *(V.P., Tech. Services)*
Dan Sager *(Dir., Mktg.)*
Sherry Catchpole *(Dir., Client Services)*
Kim Mairorino *(Sales Acct. Rep.)*
Laura Menge *(Admin. Asst.)*

Promotional Broadcast Services **(1)**
8544 Sunset Blvd.
Los Angeles, CA 90069
Tel.: 310-659-5711
Steve Berger *(Pres.)*
Sheryl Ansen *(Program Scheduler)*

SMS Audio & Video Duplicating **(1)**
8544 Sunset Blvd.
Los Angeles, CA 90069
Tel.: 310-854-7535
Andy Gilbert *(Acct. Exec.)*

Spanish Communications Corp. **(1)**
8544 Sunset Blvd.
Los Angeles, CA 90069
Tel.: 310-659-5711
Juan Carlos Nieto del Rio *(Pres.)*

Sports Call, Inc. **(1)**
8544 Sunset Blvd.
Los Angeles, CA 90069
Tel.: 310-659-5711
Dennis Holt *(Pres.)*

U.S. Yellow Pages **(1)**
401 E. Illinois St., Ste. 430
Chicago, IL 60611
Tel.: 312-645-0711
Shelly Stern *(Reg. Mgr.)*

U.S. Yellow Pages **(1)**
8544 Sunset Blvd.
Los Angeles, CA 90069
Tel.: 310-854-4859
Jim Vouvakis *(Sr. V.P.)*
Teri Delehanty *(Opers. Mgr.)*

U.S. Yellow Pages **(1)**
440 Pacific Ave.
San Francisco, CA 94133
Tel.: 415-788-7711
Larry Schenfeld *(Sr. V.P.)*
Sandi Jones *(Supvr.)*
Craig Flores *(Admin. Asst.)*

U.S. Yellow Pages **(1)**
455 University Ave., Ste. 270
Sacramento, CA 95825
Tel.: 916-447-1172
Carole Brennan *(Reg. Mgr.)*

U.S. Yellow Pages **(1)**
2711 N. Haskell Ave., Ste. 2105
Dallas, TX 75204
Tel.: 214-821-2711
Barbara Mead *(Acct. Exec.)*

Western International Media Corporation **(1)**
500 S. Buena Vista Rd., #118
Burbank, CA 91504
Tel.: 818-560-7693
Kristy Frudenfeld *(V.P., Assoc. Dir. Plng.)*
Joan Baker *(Brdcst. Dir.)*

Western International Media Corporation **(1)**
1270 Ave. of the Americas
New York, NY 10020
Tel.: 212-332-1711
Dennis F. Holt *(Chief Exec. Officer)*
Michael Keenan *(Sr. V.P., Mng. Dir.)*
Joe Weber *(V.P., Syndication)*
Ronald Bassknight *(Mngmt. Information Systems Mgr.)*
Keisha Shiver *(Sr. Analyst Res.)*
Mary Leal Brady *(Admin. Asst.)*
Diana Cofresi *(Office Mgr.)*
Eva Dolan *(Admin. Asst.)*

Western International Media Corporation **(1)**
401 E. Illinois St., Ste. 430
Chicago, IL 60611
Tel.: 312-645-0711
Dan Zifkin *(V.P., Syndication)*
Robert Cohen *(Plng. Asst.)*
Stephen Allsteadt *(Print Asst.)*
Kathy Quinn *(Admin. Asst.)*

Western International Media Corporation **(1)**
440 Pacific Ave.
San Francisco, CA 94133
Tel.: 415-788-7711
David Babbitz *(Sr. V.P., Mng. Dir.)*
Mickey Taylor *(Office Mgr.)*

Western International Media Corporation **(1)**
7 Piedmont Center, Ste. 300
Atlanta, GA 30305
Tel.: 404-261-1307
Lynne Baker *(Sr. V.P., Mng. Dir.)*
Angie Garrison *(Admin. Asst.)*
Errol Davis *(Program Devel. Resources)*

Western International Media Corporation **(1)**
2711 N. Haskell Ave. Ste. 2150
Dallas, TX 75204
Tel.: 214-821-2711
Frank Nichols *(Mng. Dir.)*

Western International Media Corporation **(1)**
1200 17th St., Ste. 2620
Denver, CO 80202
Tel.: 303-623-7711
Bonnie Blitz *(Reg., Media Dir.)*

Western International Media Corporation **(1)**
Maccabees Center, 25800 Northwestern Hwy., Ste. 882
Southfield, MI 48075
Tel.: 313-352-6711
Carol Briolat *(Media Dir.)*

Western International Media Corporation **(1)**
1601 E. Flamingo Rd., #18
Las Vegas, NV 89119
Tel.: 702-794-0711
Jim Johnston *(V.P., Acct. Services)*

Western International Media Corporation **(1)**
10 S. Fifth St., Ste. 315
Minneapolis, MN 55402
Tel.: 612-333-7711
Karen Neumann *(Sr. V.P., Mng. Dir.)*
Robyn Campbell *(V.P., Assoc. Dir.)*

Western International Media Corporation **(1)**
4000 Westerly Pl., Ste. 150
Newport Beach, CA 92660
Tel.: 714-752-7114
John Vrba *(V.P., Mng. Dir.)*
Becky Vejar *(Admin. Asst.)*

Western International Media Corporation **(1)**
1930 E. Marlton Pike
Cherry Hill, NJ 08003
Tel.: 609-424-4711
John DeSanto *(V.P., Client Services)*
Linda Wied *(Admin. Asst.)*

Western International Media Corporation **(1)**
4041 N. Central C 200
Phoenix, AZ 85012
Tel.: 602-650-1711
Kathy Crawford *(Sr. V.P., Mng. Dir.)*
Judi Vochatzer *(Dir. of Direct Response, Billing Supvr.)*
Pam Cardy *(Office Mgr.)*

Western International Media Corporation **(1)**
6915 S.W. Macadam, Ste. 100
Portland, OR 92701
Tel.: 503-245-7775

Western International Media Corporation **(1)**
1325 Airmotive Way, Ste. 175-T
Reno, NV 89502
Tel.: 702-329-2993
Roy Powers *(V.P., Mng. Dir.)*

Western International Media Corporation **(1)**
455 University Ave., Ste. 270
Sacramento, CA 95825
Tel.: 916-447-1172
Marian Miller *(Sr. V.P., Mng. Dir.)*

Western International Media Corporation **(1)**
215 S. State St., Ste. 550
Salt Lake City, UT 84111
Tel.: 801-363-5711
Craig Hulet *(Sr. V.P., Reg. Dir.)*
Paige Porter *(Admin. Asst.)*

Western International Media Corporation **(1)**
610 W. Ash, Ste. 810
San Diego, CA 92101
Tel.: 619-696-1520
Dan Miller *(Exec. V.P.)*
Chris Du Charme *(Mng. Dir.)*
Debra Cavatio *(Asst. Buyer)*

Western International Media Corporation **(1)**
720 Olive Way, Ste. 1500
Seattle, WA 98101
Tel.: 206-343-7711
Alan Fraback *(Sr. V.P., Mng. Dir.)*

Western International Media Corporation **(1)**
7700 Leesburg Pike, #229
Falls Church, VA 22043
Tel.: 708-385-3229
Frank Becker *(Mng. Dir.)*

Western International Media Corporation **(1)**
1949 E. Sunshine, Corp. Center Two, Ste. 1-112
Springfield, MO 65804
Tel.: 417-887-9711
Valerie Diggons *(Sr. V.P., Mng. Dir.)*

Western International Media Corporation **(1)**
30 St. Clair Ave., Ste. 1201
Toronto, ON M4V 3A1, Canada
Tel.: 416-924-4711
Dick Berndt *(Sr. V.P., Mng. Dir.)*

Western International Merchandising **(1)**
8544 Sunset Blvd.
Los Angeles, CA 90069
Tel.: 310-659-5711
Dennis F. Holt *(Chm., Chief Exec. Officer)*
Armand La Pointe *(Pres.)*

Western International Premiums **(1)**
8544 Sunset Blvd.
Los Angeles, CA 90069
Tel.: 310-659-4711
Dennis F. Holt *(Chm., Chief Exec. Officer)*
Dwight Case *(Mng. Dir.)*

WESTERN LINEN CORP.
(Formerly Service Control Corp.)
4131 N. 24th St., Ste. A200
Phoenix, AZ 85016
Tel.: 602-957-4411 **AZ**
Fax: 602-954-6163
Year Founded: 1977
Sales Range: $80-99 Million
Emp.: 2,500
Fiscal Year-end: 9/28/90
Industrial Launderer & Occupational Linen Supplier
S.I.C.: 7218; 7213
George E. McFall *(Pres. & Chief Exec. Officer)*
Bobby Rice *(Chief Fin. Officer)*
Roberta Rice *(V.P., Treas. & Sec.)*
Bill Flatcher *(Controller)*

No. of Mfg. Plants/Facilities: 15

Computer Systems/Hardware:
Compaq-Xenix-Operating System

Outside Service Firm(s):

Price Waterhouse*(Auditors)*
3300 North Central
Phoenix, AZ 85012
Tel.: 602-274-0550

Congress Financial Corp.*(International Bank Affiliate)*
Los Angeles, CA

Drexel, Burnham, Lambert*(Investment Banker)*
Beverly Hills, CA

Greenberg & Glusker*(Legal Firm)*
1900 Ave. of the Stars
Los Angeles, CA 90064
Tel.: 310-553-3610

WESTERN PACIFIC DATA SYSTEMS
7373 Engineer Rd.
San Diego, CA 92111
Tel.: 619-292-7205 **CA**
Fax: 619-292-5156
Year Founded: 1979
Assets: $5,500,000
Liabilities: $4,500,000
Net Worth: $1,000,000
Approx.Sls.: $20,000,000
Emp.: 100
Fiscal Year-end: 12/31/91
Export
Computers, Peripherals & Software
S.I.C.: 5045
Neil Hadfield *(Chm. Bd., Chief Fin. Officer & Sec.)*
Margaret Jackson *(Pres.)*
Principal(s):
Neil Hadfield
Margaret Jackson

No. of U.S. Offices: 11

Computer Systems/Hardware:
Texas Instrument

Outside Service Firm(s):

Chubb Group*(Auditors)*
San Diego, CA

Steres, Alpert & Carne*(Auditors)*
1901 First Ave.
San Diego, CA 92101

First National Bank of San Diego*(Major Banking Relationship)*
San Diego, CA

Subsidiary:

Western Pacific Data Systems **(1)**
1601 Capital Ave.
Plano, TX 75074
Tel.: 214-423-5944

Distributors of Computer Hardware & Software
S.I.C.: 5045
Don Yong *(Gen. Mgr.)*

WESTERN PETROLEUM COMPANY
9531 W. 78th St.
Eden Prairie, MN 55344
Tel.: 612-941-9090 **MN**
Telex: 29-0758
Year Founded: 1969
Assets: $2,300,000
Liabilities: $17,900,000
Net Worth: $15,600,000
Approx.Sls.: $266,800,000
Emp.: 40
Fiscal Year-end: 12/31/91
Import
Wholesale Petroleum Products
S.I.C.: 5171; 5172
James W. Emison *(Pres.)*
Michael T. Budd *(Sr. V.P.)*
Richard W. Carthaus *(Sr. V.P. & Sec.)*
Leland R. Granlund *(V.P., Treas. & Chief Fin. Officer)*
Don R. Green *(V.P.)*
Richard S. Neville *(V.P.-Mktg.)*
Principal(s):
James W. Emison

No. of U.S. Offices: 2

Computer Systems/Hardware:
IBM System 36

Outside Service Firm(s):

McGladrey & Pullen*(Auditors)*
1800 Town Square, 445 Minnesota St.
St. Paul, MN 55101

WESTERN REGIONAL OFF TRACK BETTING
700 Ellicott St.
Batavia, NY 14020
Tel.: 716-343-1423 **NY**
Fax: 716-343-6873
Year Founded: 1973
Assets: $13,691,799
Earnings: $8,438,294
Liabilities: $7,397,284
Net Worth: $6,294,515
Approx.Sls.: $199,800,000
Emp.: 400
Fiscal Year-end: 12/31/90
Pari-Mutual Off-Track Wagering
S.I.C.: 7999
Robert J. Kane *(Chm. Bd.)*
Martin C. Basinait *(Pres. & Chief Exec. Officer)*
Richard F. Mackey *(Exec. V.P.-Admin.)*
George W. Wagner *(Chief Fin. Officer & Comptroller)*
Timothy McCarthy *(Sec. & Gen. Counsel)*
Ed Carney *(Dir.-Pub. Rels.)*
Arnold Kelly *(Dir.-Purchasing)*
Marsha McColl *(Dir.-Data Processing)*
Patrick Murphy *(Dir.-Human Resources)*
Kenneth Krotz *(Mgr.-Cash Mgmt.)*
Joann Wolcott *(Mgr.-Real Estate)*
Principal(s):
Robert J. Kane

No. of U.S. Offices: 52

Computer Systems/Hardware:
Control Data

Outside Service Firm(s):

Deloitte & Touche*(Auditors)*
One Lincoln First Square
Rochester, NY 14604
Tel.: 716-232-1200

Marine Midland Bank*(Major Banking Relationship)*
140 Broadway Ave., 12 Floor
New York, NY 10015
Tel.: 212-440-1000

Security Northstar*(Major Banking Relationship)*
New York, NY

WESTERN REINSURANCE BROKERS, INC.
(d/b/a Western Re/Managers)
3435 Wilshire Blvd., Ste. 123
Los Angeles, CA 90010
Tel.: 213-487-7161
Fax: 213-380-7634
Year Founded: 1972
Approx.Sls.: $27,690,154
Emp.: 20
Managing General Agents For Insurance & Reinsurance
S.I.C.: 6411
Milton B. Buettner *(Chm. Bd.)*
Donald W. Grant *(Pres. & Mgr.-Sls.)*
Lon Varnadore *(Exec. V.P.)*
Clay R. Braatz *(Sr. V.P.-Personnel)*
Edward Dziadkowicz *(V.P.)*
Betty Hagopian *(Comptroller)*
Margy Gabory *(Pur. Agent)*
Principal(s):
Milton B. Buettner
Donald W. Grant
Lon Varnadore
Clay R. Braatz
Edward Dziadkowicz

Outside Service Firm(s):

K.C. Miller, CPA*(Auditors)*
San Dimas, CA

Sanwa Bank*(Major Banking Relationship)*
601 S. Figueroa St.
Los Angeles, CA 90017
Tel.: 213-896-7817
Fax: 213-489-1977

Western-Southern Life

WESTERN & SOUTHERN LIFE INSURANCE CO.
400 Broadway
Cincinnati, OH 45202
Tel.: 513-629-1800
Tel.: 800-333-5152 **OH**
Fax: 513-629-1081
Year Founded: 1888
Assets: $6,110,000,000
Net Worth: $6,110,000,000
Approx.Sls.: $1,269,000,000
Emp.: 6,199
Fiscal Year-end: 12/31/91
Life Insurance
S.I.C.: 6311
William J. Williams *(Chm. Bd. & Chief Exec. Officer)*
John F. Barrett *(Pres. & Chief Oper. Officer)*
James N. Clark *(Exec. V.P.)*
Carroll R. Hutchinson *(Sr. V.P. & Chief Actuary)*
William F. Ledwin *(Sr. V.P. & Chief Investment Officer)*
J.J. Miller *(Sr. V.P. & Chief Mktg. Officer)*
Kenneth A. Palmer *(Sr. V.P.-Information Services)*
Robert A. Bodeker *(V.P.)*
Herbert R. Brown *(V.P.-Community Affairs)*
James W. Carpenter *(V.P. & Sr. Counsel)*
Keith T. Clark, M.D. *(V.P. & Medical Dir.)*
David G. Ennis *(V.P. & Auditor)*
Robert M. Gutzwiller *(V.P.)*
Noreen J. Hayes *(V.P.-Human Resources)*
Edward S. Heenan *(V.P. & Comptroller)*
James A. Helms *(V.P.)*
Dale P. Hennie *(V.P.)*
Donald W. Kaplan *(V.P. & Actuary)*
Turner E. Kirby *(V.P.-Pension Admin.)*
J. Thomas Lancaster *(V.P. & Treas.)*
John F. Letscher *(V.P.)*
Harold V. Lyons *(V.P. & Actuary)*
Paul J. Nerone *(V.P.)*
Mario J. San Marco *(V.P.-Real Estate Investments & Services)*
Gene H. Schellpeper *(V.P.)*
Thomas M. Stapleton *(V.P.-Real Estate Devel.)*
Robert H. Starnes *(V.P.-Adv. & Public Rels.)*
Richard K. Taulbee *(V.P.)*
Donald J. Wuebbling *(V.P. & Gen. Counsel)*
Edward J. Babbitt *(2nd V.P. & Legislative Counsel)*
William J. Davis *(2nd V.P. & Dir.-Data Processing Opers.)*
Mark A. Hester *(2nd V.P. & Dir.-Sls. Service)*
Ronald K. Humphrey *(2nd V.P. & Dir. Admin. Services)*
Robert E. Murphy *(2nd V.P. & Dir.-Property Mngmt.)*
Raymond J. Noschang *(2nd V.P., Asst. Sec. & Dir.-Real Estate Services)*
John J. O'Connor *(2nd V.P. & Sr. Portfolio Mgr.-Special Investment Fin.)*
Robert A. Dressman *(Dir.-Cash Mngmt.)*
Elaine M. Reuss *(Asst. Cash Mgr.)*
Ruth M. Mairose *(Travel Agent-Public Rels.)*
Lorraine A. Dufour *(Librarian)*
Margaret A. Parks *(Sec.)*
Kim R. Chiodi *(Mgr.-Training & Personnel Research)*

No. of U.S. Offices: 257

Computer Systems/Hardware:
IBM 3090

Outside Service Firm(s):

Coopers & Lybrand*(Auditors)*
203 N. LaSalle St.
Chicago, IL 60601
Tel.: 312-701-5500

The Central Trust Company, N.A.*(Major Banking Relationship)*
Cincinnati, OH
Tel.: 513-651-8896

Subsidiaries:

Columbus Life Insurance Co. **(1)**
303 East Broad St.
Columbus, OH 43215
Tel.: 614-221-5875 (100%)
Emp.: 2,303
Life Insurance
S.I.C.: 6311
Paul H. Amato *(Pres.)*

Continental General Corporation **(1)**
8901 Indian Hills Dr.
Omaha, NE 68114
Tel.: 402-397-3200 (100%)
Herman E. Myers, Jr. *(Pres.)*

Fort Washington Investment Advisors, Inc. **(1)**
550 E. Fourth St.
Cincinnati, OH 45202
Tel.: 513-651-2900 (100%)
Asset Management
S.I.C.: 6282
William F. Ledwin *(Pres.)*
E. James Roche *(V.P. & Mng. Dir.)*
James B. McGuire *(V.P.)*

IFS Financial Services, Inc. **(1)**
318 Broadway
Cincinnati, OH 45202
Tel.: 513-684-1400
Investment Services
S.I.C.: 6282
Edward G. Harness *(Pres.)*

IFS Systems, Inc. **(1)**
1130 N. Chase Pkwy., Ste. 200
Marietta, GA 30067
Tel.: 404-952-4721
Fax: 404-952-9882
Financial Planning Software
S.I.C.: 7372
Linda Grace *(V.P.)*

WESTERN STATES ENVELOPE CO.
4480 N. 132nd St.
Butler, WI 53007
Mailing Address:
P.O. Box 2048,
Milwaukee, WI 53201
Tel.: 414-781-5540
Year Founded: 1908
Approx.Sls.: $43,000,000
Emp.: 465
Fiscal Year-end: 4/30/91
Envelope Products
S.I.C.: 2677
Geo. French Moss *(Pres.)*
Glenn W. Carlton *(Sr. V.P.-Mfg.)*
Gordon E. Westphal *(Sr. V.P. & Treas.)*
Mark Lemberger *(V.P.-Sls.)*
E. John Ellis *(Sec.)*
Russell Golomski *(Dir.-Human Resources)*
Charles Ego *(Mgr.-Mktg.)*
Thomas Ibach *(Pur. Agent)*

WESTERN STATES MACHINE CO.
1798 Fairgrove Ave.
Hamilton, OH 45012
Tel.: 513-863-4758
Fax: 513-863-3846
Year Founded: 1917
Approx.Assets: $16,000,000
Emp.: 150
Fiscal Year-end: 1/31/91
Export
Mfr. of Centrifugals & Accessories for the Sugar, Chemical & Pollution Industries
S.I.C.: 3569
Charles O'Neile *(Pres.)*
O. Wood Moyle III *(V.P.)*
Charles A. Duersch *(Treas.)*
Donald J. Asplan *(Sec.)*
Roger Fair *(Gen. Sls. Mgr.)*
Richard Sloneker *(Dir.-Personnel)*
John Madaffari *(Dir.-Pur.)*
William Budd *(Mgr.-Data Processing)*
Wesely Flannery *(Production Mgr.)*
Joseph Bange *(Dir.-Engrng.)*

Computer Systems/Hardware:
Unisys

WESTERN STATES PETROLEUM INC.
450 S. 15th Ave.
Phoenix, AZ 85007
Tel.: 602-252-0404 **AZ**
Fax: 602-340-9621
Emp.: 66
Wholesale Petroleum, Retail Gas Service Stations & Farm Supplies
S.I.C.: 5171; 5191; 5541
Robert F. Kec *(Pres.)*
Janet Kec *(Sec. & Treas.)*

Computer Systems/Hardware:
Wang

Outside Service Firm(s):

Thunderbird Bank*(Major Banking Relationship)*
Phoenix, AZ

Western
TEMPORARY SERVICES®

WESTERN TEMPORARY SERVICES, INC.
301 Lennon Lane
Walnut Creek, CA 94598-2404
Mailing Address:
P.O. Box 9280,
Walnut Creek, CA 94598-2404
Tel.: 510-930-5300 **CA**
Fax: 510-934-5489
Year Founded: 1948
Sales Range: $100-499 Million
Emp.: 1,020
Temporary Help Service; 350 Offices World-Wide
S.I.C.: 7361; 7363
W. Robert Stover *(Chm. Bd. & Chief Exec. Officer)*
Harvey L. Maslin *(Pres. & Chief Oper. Officer)*
Paul A. Norberg *(Chief Fin. Officer & Exec. V.P.)*
Gregg E. Plummer *(Chief Information Officer & V.P.)*
Robin A. Herman *(V.P. & Gen. Counsel)*
Stephen J. Russo *(Treas.)*
Dirk Sodestrom *(Controller)*
Stephen H. Clark *(Dir.-Creative & Mgr.-Adv.)*

No. of U.S. Offices: 300
No. of Foreign Offices: 30

Computer Systems/Hardware:
DEC

Outside Service Firm(s):

Price Waterhouse*(Auditors)*
Walnut Creek, CA

Smith & Granberg*(Legal Firm)*
3474 Wells Fargo Bldg., 44 Montgomery
San Francisco, CA 94104
Tel.: 415-391-0900

First Interstate Bank*(Pension Manager)*
345 California St., 8th Flr.
San Francisco, CA 94104
Tel.: 415-773-7801

Divisions:

Marketing Services Div. **(1)**
301 Lennon Lane
Walnut Creek, CA 94598-2404
Tel.: 510-930-5300
Fax: 510-935-1217
Marketing Personnel
S.I.C.: 7363

Santa Div. **(1)**
301 Lennon Lane
Walnut Creek, CA 94598-2404
Tel.: 510-930-5300
Fax: 510-935-1217
Santa Services
S.I.C.: 7363

Western Industrial Div. **(1)**
301 Lennon Lane
Walnut Creek, CA 94598-2404
Tel.: 510-930-5300
Fax: 510-934-5489
Temporary Help Service
S.I.C.: 7363

Western Photo Service Div. **(1)**
301 Lennon Lane
Walnut Creek, CA 94598-2404
Tel.: 510-930-5300
Fax: 510-935-1217
Permanent Placement Agency
S.I.C.: 7363

Western Temporary Services Office Div. **(1)**
301 Lennon Lane
Walnut Creek, CA 94598-2404
Tel.: 510-930-5300
Fax: 510-934-5489
Temporary Help Service
S.I.C.: 7363

Subsidiaries:

Western Permanent Services Agency, Inc. **(1)**
301 Lennon Lane
Walnut Creek, CA 94598-2404
Tel.: 510-930-5300 (100%)
Permanent Placement Agency
S.I.C.: 7363
W. Robert Stover *(Chm. Bd. & Chief Exec. Officer)*

Western Temporary Services (USA), Inc. **(1)**
301 Lennon Lane
Walnut Creek, CA 94598-2404
Tel.: 510-930-5300 (100%)
Fax: 510-934-5489
Temporary Help Supply Services
S.I.C.: 7363
W. Robert Stover *(Chm. & Chief Exec. Officer)*

Divisions:

Western Medical Services Div. **(2)**
301 Lennon Lane
Walnut Creek, CA 94598-2404
Tel.: 510-930-5300
Fax: 510-934-5489
Temporary Medical Personnel Services
S.I.C.: 7363; 8082
Michael J. Nicholson *(Pres.)*

Western Technical Div. **(2)**
800 Roosevelt Rd., Ste. 310, Bldg. B
Glen Ellyn, IL 60137
Tel.: 708-469-0250
Fax: 708-469-0350
Technical Contract Personnel
S.I.C.: 7363
Lorrance S. Entwistle *(Pres.)*

Subsidiary:

Western Video Images, Inc. **(2)**
600 Townsend Street, Suite 300W
San Francisco, CA 94103
Tel.: 415-252-6000 (100%)
Fax: 415-621-6780
Videotape Post Production Services
S.I.C.: 7812
Michael Cunningham *(Pres.)*

Non-U.S. Holdings:

Kontorservice Inc. **(1)**
Eyvind Lyches vei 13 B 1301
Sandvika, Norway
Tel.: 2 549141
Fax: 2 518102
Help Supply Services
S.I.C.: 7363
Erik Thorud *(Mng. Dir.)*

Western Personnel Services Pty. Ltd. **(1)**
88 Albert Rd.
South Melbourne, Victoria 3205, Australia
Tel.: 3-696-5500 (100%)
Fax: 3 696 5451
Temporary Help Services; Regional Office for Australia & New Zealand
S.I.C.: 7363
Ian Chisholm *(Mng. Dir.)*

Western Service A/S **(1)**
54 Kobmagergade 1150
Copenhagen, Denmark
Tel.: 33-123900 (100%)
Fax: 42 967768
Temporary Help Services; Regional Office for Denmark
S.I.C.: 7361; 7363
Mogens Larsen *(Mng. Dir.-Contl. Europe)*

Western Service, Inc. **(1)**
Marketgasse 56 3011
Bern, Switzerland
Tel.: 31-228846
Fax: 31 213661
Temporary Help Service
S.I.C.: 7361; 7363
Erik Thorud *(Mng. Dir.)*

Western Staff Services (NZ) Ltd. **(1)**
Level 2, Quay Tower, CNR Customs & Albert Sts. P.O. Box 4333,
Auckland, New Zealand
Tel.: 9-3096685 (100%)
Fax: 9-3089299
Temporary Help Service
S.I.C.: 7361; 7363

Western Staff Services (U.K.) Ltd. **(1)**
46/50 Southgate St.
Gloucester, GL1 2DR United Kingdom
Tel.: 452-304177
Fax: 452-300332
Temporary Help Service
S.I.C.: 7361; 7363
Janet Crispin *(Mng. Dir.)*

WESTERN TRAILER EQUIPMENT & MANUFACTURING CO.
1110 E. Hwy. 80
Abilene, TX 79601
Mailing Address:
P.O. Box 994
Abilene, TX 79604
Tel.: 915-673-8311
Fax: 915-673-2963
Emp.: 12
Heavy Duty Truck Specialists; Sales, Parts & Service
S.I.C.: 7538
Henry L. King *(Chm. Bd.)*
Tommy King *(Pres. & Chief Exec. Officer)*

Computer Systems/Hardware:
Parts Plus

Outside Service Firm(s):

Larry Barnes*(Auditors)*
San Angelo, TX

First National Bank of Abilene*(Major Banking Relationship)*
400 Pine St., P.O. Box 701
Abilene, TX 79604
Tel.: 915-675-7000

WESTFALL GMC TRUCK INC.
811 Atlantic
North Kansas City, MO 64116
Tel.: 816-421-7262 **MO**
Fax: 816-234-0201
Approx.Sls.: $230,000,000
Emp.: 150
Retail New & Used Trucks
S.I.C.: 5511
Pearl E. Westfall *(Chm. Bd.)*
Jane O'Dell *(Pres. & Treas.)*
Ervin E. O'Dell *(Exec. V.P.)*
William C. Westfall *(Sec.)*
Mark O'Dell *(Dir.-Data Processing)*

Computer Systems/Hardware:
NCR

Outside Service Firm(s):

Francis A. Wright & Co.*(Auditors)*
Kansas City, MO

John Crossette*(Legal Firm)*
Excelsior Springs, MO

Boatmen's Bank of Excelsior Springs*(Major Banking Relationship)*
218 South St.
Excelsior Springs, MO 64024
Tel.: 816-637-3133

WESTFIELD COMPANIES
1 Park Circle
Westfield Center, OH 44251
Mailing Address:
P.O. Box 5001
Westfield Center, OH 44251-5001
Tel.: 216-887-0101 **OH**
Fax: 216-887-0840
Year Founded: 1848
Assets: $1,058,036,371
Liabilities: $719,675,833
Net Worth: $338,360,538
Approx.Sls.: $475,212,097
Emp.: 1,580
Fiscal Year-end: 12/31/91
Diversified Insurance Companies
S.I.C.: 6331; 6351; 6311
R. Cary Blair *(Pres. & Chief Exec. Officer)*
T. H. Pickering *(Sr. V.P. & Sec.)*
Otto Bosshard *(Sr. V.P. & Treas.)*
Barbara R. Cochran *(V.P. & Controller)*

Computer Systems/Hardware:
IBM

Outside Service Firm(s):

KPMG Peat Marwick*(Auditors)*
Two Nationwide Plaza
Columbus, OH 43215
Tel.: 614-249-2300

Vorys, Sater, Seymour & Pease*(Legal Firm)*
52 E. Gay St.
Columbus, OH 43215
Tel.: 614-464-6400

Old Phoenix National Bank*(Major Banking Relationship)*
Medina, OH

WESTGATE FABRICS, INC.
1000 Fountain Parkway
Grand Prairie, TX 75053
Tel.: 214-647-2323 **TX**
Fax: 214-660-7096
Approx.Sls.: $22,000,000
Emp.: 143
Wholesale Distributor of Home Furnishings; Screen Printing
S.I.C.: 5023; 2261
Reese B. Davis *(Chm. Bd.)*
Barry Witt *(Pres.)*
Sungho Park *(Chief Fin. Officer)*
Ben M. Jones *(V.P. & Gen. Mgr.)*
John P. Stenger *(V.P.-Pur.)*
Lauris H. Gibson *(Sec.)*
Kathy Brown *(Dir.-Design)*
Phyllis Isbell *(Dir.-Personnel)*
Steve Tate *(Mgr.-Credit)*
J.C. Wright *(Mgr.-Opers.)*

Outside Service Firm(s):

KPMG Peat Marwick*(Auditors)*
301 Commerce, Ste. 2500
Ft. Worth, TX 76102
Tel.: 817-335-2655

Texas American Bank*(Major Banking Relationship)*
Fort Worth, TX

WESTGATE INC.
1355 Beaulieu Ln.
Port Allen, LA 70767
Mailing Address:
P.O. Box 1948
Baton Rouge, LA 70821
Tel.: 504-749-2635 **LA**
Fax: 504-749-2638
Year Founded: 1974
Approx.Sls.: $14,000,000
Emp.: 400
Electrical/Instrumentation/Maintenance/Construction Contractor
S.I.C.: 1731
John C. Thigpen *(Pres. & Chief Oper. Officer)*
Diane Muscarello *(Sec. & Treas.)*
Carey Boudreaux *(Dir.-Data Processing)*
Joseph Hall *(Dir.-Pur.)*
Carl M. Hughes *(Dir.-Personnel/Construction)*
Sidney Mabile *(Dir.-Personnel/Maintenance)*
Barbara S. Gill *(Mgr.-Human Resources)*
Charles G. Marceaux *(Mgr.-Sls.)*
Martha S. Thigpen *(Mgr.-Mktg.)*
Principal(s):
John C. Thigpen

No. of Mfg. Plants/Facilities: 1
No. of U.S. Offices: 1

Computer Systems/Hardware:
IBM Compatible PC's

Outside Service Firm(s):

Hawthorn, Waymouth & Carroll*(Auditors)*
Baton Rouge, LA
Tel.: 504-923-3000

USF & G*(Commercial Insurance Carrier)*
Baltimore, MD

New York Life*(Group Insurer)*
New York, NY

Taylor, Porter, Brooks & Phillips*(Legal Firm)*
Baton Rouge, LA

City National Bank*(Major Banking Relationship)*
Baton Rouge, LA

Merl J. Schexnaildre*(Pension Manager)*
Baton Rouge, LA

WESTIN, INC.
4727 Center St.
Omaha, NE 68106
Tel.: 402-553-3363 **NE**
Fax: 402-553-1932
Approx.Sls.: $40,000,000
Fiscal Year-end: 12/31/91
Import
Holding Company; Manufactures & Distributes Food Products
S.I.C.: 2033; 2037; 5141; 6719
Richard S. Westin *(Chm. Bd., Pres. & Chief Exec. Officer)*
John W. Hurley *(Exec. V.P. & Sec.)*
Loretta Eenhuis *(Treas. & Data Processing Dir.)*

Outside Service Firm(s):

Deloitte & Touche*(Auditors)*
2000 First National Center
Omaha, NE 68102
Tel.: 402-346-7788

First National Bank of Omaha*(Major Banking Relationship)*
One First National Center
Omaha, NE 68102

Subsidiary:

Great American Breaded Vegetable Co. **(1)**
2910 E. Harcourt St.
Rancho Dominguez, CA 90221-5502
Tel.: 310-638-9969 (100%)
Fax: 310-638-1219
Mfr. of Frozen Food Processors
S.I.C.: 2037
Bernie Goldman *(Mgr.)*

Non-U.S. Holding:

InterOliva **(1)**
Calle Las Cruces s/n, Dos Hermanos
Seville, Spain
Tel.: 54-720-400 (100%)
Approx.Sls.: $20,000,000
Emp.: 450
Olive Processing & Packaging
S.I.C.: 2033; 2079
Carlos Jimenez Diaz *(Pres.)*

WESTLAKE HARDWARE, INC.
15501 W. 99th St.
Shawnee Mission, KS 66219
Tel.: 913-888-0808
Fax: 913-888-2153
Year Founded: 1905
Approx.Sls.: $113,000,000
Emp.: 1,100
Hardware; Commercial & Industrial
S.I.C.: 5251; 6512
Howard W. Elsberry *(Chm., Pres. & Chief Exec. Officer)*
Richard Masinton *(Sr. V.P.-Fin. & Chief Fin. Officer)*
Doug Burton *(Sr. V.P.-Mktg.)*
Tom Terrell *(Sr. V.P.-Opers.)*
Cynthia Mason *(V.P.)*
Robert A. O'Neill *(V.P.)*
Paul Francis *(Controller)*

WESTLIE MOTOR COMPANY
500 S. Broadway
Minot, ND 58701
Mailing Address:
P.O. Box 548,
Minot, ND 58701
Tel.: 701-852-1354 **ND**
Year Founded: 1947
Approx.Sls.: $27,000,000
Emp.: 100
Retail Sales of New & Used Automobiles, Pickups & Vans; Rent-a-Car Service; Truck Leasing Without Drivers; Automotive Supplies & Parts; Automotive Repair Shops
S.I.C.: 5511; 7514; 7513; 5013; 7539
Charles Westlie *(Chm. Bd.)*
Charles R. Marshall *(Pres. & Gen. Mgr.)*
Darek Zaun *(Chief Fin. Officer)*
James H. Westlie *(Treas. & Sec.)*

WESTON PAPER & MANUFACTURING CO.
2001 No. 19th St.
Terre Haute, IN 47804
Mailing Address:
P.O. Box 238
Terre Haute, IN 47808
Tel.: 812-232-0521 **OH**
Fax: 812-232-0529
Year Founded: 1949
Approx.Sls.: $142,000,000
Emp.: 1,650
Mfr. of Corrugated Shipping Containers, Corrugated Materials & Paperboard
S.I.C.: 2653; 2631
Edward T. Turner, Jr. *(Chm. Bd. & Pres.)*
Paul H. Granzow *(Sr. V.P.)*
Charles E. Beaman *(Group V.P.-Container Opers.)*
Ronald R. Hanks *(V.P. & Gen Mgr.-Lexington Plant)*
Ronald P. Holmes *(V.P.-Sls.)*
William F. Jones *(V.P. & Gen Mgr.-Chicago Box Plant)*
Donald L. Miller *(V.P.-Fin. & Treas.)*
David J. Moreno *(V.P. & Gen Mgr.-Fort Wayne Plant)*
Gary W. Schomer *(V.P. & Gen Mgr.-Terre Haute Plant)*
David L. Robinson *(V.P. & Mill General Mgr.)*
Steven E. Messmer *(Controller)*
Julia A. Hoffman *(Sec.)*
Dwight McKay *(Asst. Treas.)*

No. of Mfg. Plants/Facilities: 5

Outside Service Firm(s):

Coopers & Lybrand*(Auditors)*
2900 One American Square, Box 82002
Indianapolis, IN 46282
Tel.: 317-639-4161

Subsidiaries:

Wabash Fibre Box Co.-South **(1)**
4401 Sarah
Jonesboro, AR 72401
Tel.: 501-932-0600
Fax: 501-935-2478
Corrugated Packaging
S.I.C.: 2653
Scott Moon *(V.P. & Gen. Mgr.)*

Plants:

Wabash Fibre Box Co.-Terre Haute Plant **(2)**
2000 N. 19th St.
Terre Haute, IN 47804
Tel.: 812-232-0521
Fax: 812-232-9110
Corrugated & Solid Fibre Boxes
S.I.C.: 2653
Gary W. Schomer *(V.P. & Gen. Mgr.)*

Wabash Fibre Box Co.-Chicago Plant **(2)**
6850 W. 62nd St.
Chicago, IL 60638
Tel.: 312-586-3200
Fax: 312-586-3210
Corrugated & Solid Fibre boxes
S.I.C.: 2653
William F. Jones *(V.P. & Gen. Mgr.)*

Wabash Fibre Box Co.-Fort Wayne Plant **(2)**
Baer Field, Baer Field - Box #9310
Fort Wayne, IN 46899
Tel.: 219-747-9111
Fax: 219-747-3888
Corrugated & Solid Fibre Boxes
S.I.C.: 2653
David J. Moreno *(V.P. & Gen. Mgr.)*

Wabash Fibre Box Co.-Lexington Plant **(2)**
2575 Palumbo Dr.
Lexington, KY 40509
Tel.: 606-269-8877
Fax: 606-266-2543
Corrugated & Solid Fibre Boxes
S.I.C.: 2653
Ronald R. Hanks *(V.P. & Gen. Mgr.)*

Wabash Fibre Box Co.-South **(1)**
127 Interstate Dr.
Richland, MS 39218
Tel.: 601-932-3050
Fax: 601-939-4584
Corrugated Packaging
S.I.C.: 2653
Joe F. Cockroft *(V.P. & Gen. Mgr.)*

Wabash Fibre Box Co.-South **(1)**
1571 16th St. Circle
Mobile, AL 36615
Tel.: 205-432-4300
Fax: 205-433-2159
Corrugated Packaging
S.I.C.: 2653
Doug Graham *(Gen. Mgr.)*

Wabash Fibre Box Co.-South **(1)**
947 Washington Ferry Rd., Route 5, Box 852A
Prattville, AL 36067
Tel.: 205-361-1755
Fax: 205-361-1664
Corrugated Packaging
S.I.C.: 2653
Jack T. Taylor *(Gen. Mgr.)*

Division:

Gibson Continer Divison **(2)**
Industrial Park South
Verona, MS 38879
Tel.: 601-566-8900
Fax: 601-566-7603
Waymon Gibson *(V.P. & Gen. Mgr.)*

Wabash Pioneer Container Corp. **(1)**
N143 W6049 Pioneer Rd.
Cedarburg, WI 53012-0045
Tel.: 414-377-2442
Fax: 414-377-1951
Emp.: 264
Mfr. of Corrugated Containers
S.I.C.: 2653
James A. Woodard *(Pres.)*

WETSEL-OVIATT LUMBER COMPANY
P.O. Box 910
Folsom, CA 95763
Tel.: 916-933-6684
Fax: 916-933-3473
Year Founded: 1939
Approx.Sls.: $22,000,000
Emp.: 155
Sawmill; Manufacturer of Wooden Box Tops
S.I.C.: 2421; 2449
Cecil Wetsel, Jr. *(Pres. & Treas.)*
John Jacino *(1st V.P.-Sls. & Mktg.)*
William Kerfoot *(2nd V.P. & Controller)*
Sandra Senne *(Sec.)*

Outside Service Firm(s):

Grant Bennett Accountants*(Auditors)*
Sacramento, CA

Charles M. Asbury*(Legal Firm)*
Sacramento, CA

Wells Fargo Bank*(Major Banking Relationship)*
Sacramento, CA

WEXNER & JACOBSON, INC.
117 1/2 Union Ave.
Memphis, TN 38103
Mailing Address:
P.O. Box 3834,
Memphis, TN 38173
Tel.: 901-523-0769
Twx: 5911150
Fax: 901-525-1887
Year Founded: 1930
Emp.: 350
Retail Womens Shoes & Accessories Chain
S.I.C.: 5661
Alfred B. Wexner *(Pres.)*
Hugh N. Jacobson *(Exec. V.P.-Treas.)*
William Cruse *(Controller)*

Outside Service Firm(s):

BDO Seidman*(Auditors)*
2500 Commerce Tower
Memphis, TN 38103-2545
Tel.: 901-523-2303
Fax: 901-525-7478

Hanover, Walsh, Jalenak & Blair*(Legal Firm)*
219 Adams Avenue
Memphis, TN 38103

Union Planters National Bank*(Major Banking Relationship)*
P.O. Box 387,
Memphis, TN 38147
Tel.: 901-523-6865
Fax: 901-523-6490

WHALING INDUSTRIES, INC.
387 Quarry St.
Fall River, MA 02723
Tel.: 508-678-9061
Fax: 508-678-9061, Ext. 221
Approx.Sls.: $30,000,000
Emp.: 485
Fiscal Year-end: 1/31/91
Import
Holding Company; Manufacture Rainwear & Outerwear
S.I.C.: 2253; 2385; 6719
James S. Pavao *(Pres.)*
William Cassano *(V.P.-Mktg. & Sls.)*
Joe Medieros *(V.P.-Opers.)*
Joseph L. Pavao *(V.P.)*
Donald Raposa *(Controller)*
Grace Oliverre *(Dir.-Personnel)*
Deborah Sousa *(Mgr.-Data Processing)*
Daciano Stone *(Mgr.-Pur.)*
Manuel Pavao *(Engr.)*

Outside Service Firm(s):

Murphy & Company*(Auditors)*
Providence, RI

Sahady, Entin & Entin*(Legal Firm)*
Fall River, MA

First National Bank of Boston*(Major Banking Relationship)*
P.O. Box 644,
Boston, MA 02102-0644
Tel.: 617-575-2900
Fax: 617-575-2549

Subsidiary:

Whaling Manufacturing Company, Inc. **(1)**
387 Quarry St.
Fall River, MA 02732
Tel.: 617-678-9061
Mfr. Rainwear & Outerwear
S.I.C.: 2253; 2385

Whaling Industries, Inc.—(Continued)

James S. Pavao *(Pres.)*

WHARFSIDE RESTAURANTS, INC.
Der Buro Komplex, 4201-A Mannheim Road
Jasper, IN 47546-9618
Tel.: 812-482-3212 **IN**
Fax: 812-482-4013
Year Founded: 1971
Approx.Sls.: $56,000,000
Emp.: 2,800
Fiscal Year-end: 12/31/91
Fast Food Restaurant Chain
S.I.C.: 5812
Robert Ruckriegel *(Pres.)*
David G. Buehler *(V.P.)*
Lovella Ruckriegel *(Treas.)*
Judith Stetter Buehler *(Sec.)*
Larry Freyberger *(Controller)*
Jim Crumpacker *(Dir.-Mktg. & Adv.)*
William F. Martin *(Dir.-Real Estate)*
Ed Olberding *(Dir.-Data Processing)*
Jane Persohn *(Dir.-Employee Benefits)*
Donald J. Sullivan *(Dir.-Pur. & Personnel Training & Devel.)*

Principal(s):
Robert Ruckriegel
David G. Buehler
Lovella Ruckriegel
Judith Stetter Buehler

Outside Service Firm(s):

Noffsinger, Price, Bradley & Shively*(Legal Firm)*
4201-N Mannheim Road
Jasper, IN 47546

National City Bank*(Major Banking Relationship)*
227 Main St.
Evansville, IN
Tel.: 812-464-9668

WHATABURGER, INC.
4600 Parkdale Dr.
Corpus Christi, TX 78411
Mailing Address:
P.O. Box 6220
Corpus Christi, TX 78411
Tel.: 512-878-0650
Fax: 512-878-0682
Approx.Sls.: $180,000,000
Emp.: 6,000
Fast Food-Hamburgers
S.I.C.: 5812
Grace Dobson *(Chm. Bd.)*
Jim L. Peterson *(Pres. & Chief Exec. Officer)*
Willis D. Coston *(Exec. V.P.-Sls.)*
Alan J. Stoner *(Sr. V.P.-Opers.)*
Carl J. Chatelain *(Sr. V.P.-Fin. Plng.)*
Peter Opel *(V.P.-Human Resources)*
Thomas E. Dobson *(V.P.-Franchise & Contract Div.)*
Joseph A. Middendorf *(V.P.-Real Estate & Franchise Devel.)*
R. Bruce Able *(V.P. & Controller)*
Jim Holder *(V.P.-Construction)*

WHEAT, FIRST SECURITIES INC.
901 E. Byrd St.
Richmond, VA 23219
Tel.: 804-649-2311
Year Founded: 1934
Approx.Sls.: $190,000,000
Emp.: 1,800
Fiscal Year-end: 3/31/91
Investment Banker & Broker
S.I.C.: 6211
John L. McElroy, Jr. *(Chm. Bd.)*
Marshall B. Wishnack *(Pres.)*
Ralston L. Brooke *(Sr. V.P.-Mktg. & Adv.)*

Subsidiary:

Butcher & Singer **(1)**
2 Logan Square, 18th & Arch St.
Philadelphia, PA 19103
Tel.: 215-496-7300
Approx.Sls.: $40,000,000
Emp.: 450
Fiscal Year-end: 3/31/91
Security Dealers
S.I.C.: 6211
McBee Butcher *(Chm. & Chief Exec. Officer)*
Thomas D. Zoidis *(Pres.)*

WHEATLAND TUBE COMPANY
900 Haddon Ave.
Collingswood, NJ 08108
Tel.: 609-854-5400
Fax: 609-854-0616
Approx.Sls.: $200,000,000
Emp.: 400
Export
Mfr. of Steel Pipe, Electric Weld Steel Tubing, Rigid Steel Conduit & Steel Fittings
S.I.C.: 3084; 3089; 3317
James E. O'Donnell *(Chm. Bd., Pres. & Chief Exec. Officer)*
James E. Feeney *(Sr. V.P.-Mfg.)*
C. Richard Wahl *(Sr. V.P., Treas. & Sec.)*
Peter S. Dooner, Jr. *(V.P.-Electrical Sls.)*
Edwin Hopkinson *(V.P.-Pipe Sls.)*
Archibald G. Struthers *(V.P.-Credit & Asst. Sec.)*
Henry Weiss *(V.P.-Mktg.)*
James Dunn *(Controller)*

Outside Service Firm(s):

Ernst & Young*(Auditors)*
1800 John F. Kennedy Blvd.
Philadelphia, PA 19103-7499
Tel.: 215-864-3300

Philadelphia National Bank*(Major Banking Relationship)*
Collingswood, NJ

WHEATON INC.
(Formerly Wheaton Industries)
1101 Wheaton Ave.
Millville, NJ 08332
Tel.: 609-825-1400 **NJ**
Fax: 609-825-0146
Year Founded: 1888
Approx.Sls.: $500,000,000
Emp.: 5,000
Manufacture Glass & Plastics; Bottles, Closures, Decorative Glassware & Machinery
S.I.C.: 3089; 3229; 3499; 4213; 4225
Robert I. Veghte *(Pres. & Chief Exec. Officer)*
David Slack *(V.P.-Admin.)*
James Gutknecht *(Sec.)*
Dan Replogle *(Treas.)*
Eileen Basho *(Mgr.-Information Systems)*

Computer Systems/Hardware:
IBM 4341

Outside Service Firm(s):

Arthur Andersen & Co.*(Auditors)*
1601 Market St.
Philadelphia, PA 19103
Tel.: 215-241-7300

Aetna Life & Casualty*(Group Insurer)*
151 Farmington Avenue
Hartford, CT 06156
Tel.: 203-273-2128
Fax: 203-729-4295

Blue Cross of New Jersey*(Group Insurer)*
Newark, NJ

Heritage Bank*(Major Banking Relationship)*
Millville, NJ

Bankers Trust Co.*(Pension Manager)*
One Bankers Trust Plaza
New York, NY 10006
Tel.: 212-250-6902

Divisions:

General Machinery Co. **(1)**
N. Tenth St.
Millville, NJ 08332
Tel.: 609-825-7500
S.I.C.: 3499
John Glowacki *(V.P. & Gen. Mgr.)*

Wheaton Cartage **(1)**
1101 Wheaton Ave.
Millville, NJ 08332
Tel.: 609-825-1400
S.I.C.: 4213; 4225

Wheaton Coated Products **(1)**
Rte. 40
Mays Landing, NJ 08330
Tel.: 609-625-2291
S.I.C.: 3229
A. Joseph Richter *(V.P. & Gen. Mgr.)*

Wheaton Glass Co. **(1)**
3rd & "G" Sts.
Millville, NJ 08332
Tel.: 609-825-1400
S.I.C.: 3229
Glenn Gies *(Pres.)*
C.E. Snider *(V.P.-Fin. & Admin.)*
Michael Mossburg *(V.P.-Sls.)*
James Slough *(Dir.-Pur.)*

Wheaton Injection Molding **(1)**
Sharp St.
Millville, NJ 08332
Tel.: 609-825-1400
S.I.C.: 3089
Geoffrey DeRohan *(V.P. & Gen. Mgr.)*

Wheaton Instruments **(1)**
No. Tenth St.
Millville, NJ 08332
Tel.: 609-825-1400
S.I.C.: 3229
Donald Fauerbach *(V.P. & Gen. Mgr.)*

Wheaton International **(1)**
1101 Wheaton Ave.
Millville, NJ 08332
Tel.: 609-825-1400
Mfr. of Glass & Plastics
S.I.C.: 3089; 3229
Michael T. Zee *(V.P. & Gen. Mgr.)*

Wheaton Plastic Containers **(1)**
Mill St. & Weymouth Rd.
Mays Landing, NJ 08330
Tel.: 609-625-4811
S.I.C.: 3089
Charles Minarik *(Pres.)*

Wheaton Safety Container Co. **(1)**
Rte. 40
Mays Landing, NJ 08330
Tel.: 609-625-2291
Mfr. of Plastic Containers
S.I.C.: 3089
A. Joseph Richter *(V.P. & Gen. Mgr.)*

Wheaton Scientific **(1)**
N. Tenth St.
Millville, NJ 08332
Tel.: 609-825-1400
S.I.C.: 3229
Edward C. Wheaton *(Pres.)*

Wheaton Tubing Products **(1)**
N. Tenth St.
Millville, NJ 08332
Tel.: 609-825-1400
S.I.C.: 3229
George H. Bartels *(V.P. & Gen. Mgr.)*

Non-U.S. Holding:

Wheaton do Brazil **(1)**
Caixa Postal 1461
Sao Paulo, 01051, Brazil
Mfrs. of Glass & Plastic Specialties
S.I.C.: 3221; 3089

WHEATON VAN LINES, INC.
8010 Castleton Rd.
Indianapolis, IN 46250
Mailing Address:
P.O. Box 50800
Indianapolis, IN 46250
Tel.: 317-849-7900 **IN**
Fax: 317-849-3718
Year Founded: 1945
Assets: $26,396,000
Liabilities: $8,376,526
Net Worth: $18,019,474
Approx.Sls.: $60,000,000
Emp.: 136
Fiscal Year-end: 12/31/91
Coast-to-Coast Moving of Household Goods
S.I.C.: 4213
E.S. Wheaton *(Chm. Emeritus)*
Stephen F. Burns *(Chm. Bd., Pres. & Chief Exec. Officer)*
W.E. Sterrett *(Exec. V.P. & Treas.)*
J.W. McCormack *(V.P.-Sls.)*
Sidney J. Luckett *(V.P.-Quality Control)*
Donna Keating *(Dir.-Personnel)*
Gary Shuman *(Dir.-Data Processing)*
Edward Benz *(Asst. Treas. & Controller)*

No. of U.S. Offices: 4

Computer Systems/Hardware:
IBM AS/400

Outside Service Firm(s):

Ernst & Young*(Auditors)*
One Indiana Square, Ste. 3400
Indianapolis, IN 46204
Tel.: 317-236-1100

Bank One, Indianapolis, N.A.*(Major Banking Relationship)*
111 Monument Circle, Ste. 1611
Indianapolis, IN 46204-1611
Tel.: 317-321-8110

WHEELER BROTHERS GRAIN CO.
501 W. Russworm
Watonga, OK 73772
Mailing Address:
P.O. Box 29
Watonga, OK 73772
Tel.: 405-623-7223
Fax: 405-623-2686
Approx.Sls.: $30,000,000
Emp.: 45
Grain Storage & Railroad Operation
S.I.C.: 5153; 4011
E.O. Wheeler *(Chm. Bd.)*
Steve Smola *(Pres. & Chief Exec. Officer)*
Mike Mahoney *(V.P.)*
Richard Cowan *(Sec., Treas., Controller & Chief Fin. Officer)*

Computer Systems/Hardware:
Wang

Outside Service Firm(s):

Price Waterhouse*(Auditors)*
Colcord Bldg., 15 N. Robinson, Ste. 400
Oklahoma City, OK 73102
Tel.: 405-272-9251

Blue Cross & Blue Shield of Oklahoma*(Group Insurer)*
Tulsa, OK

Commerce Bank of Kansas City*(Major Banking Relationship)*
10th & Walnut
Kansas City, MO 64141
Tel.: 816-234-2000
Fax: 816-234-2548

Watonga State Bank*(Major Banking Relationship)*
Watonga, OK

Subsidiaries:

AT&L Railroad **(1)**
P.O. Box 29
Watonga, OK 73772
Tel.: 405-623-7223 (100%)
Short Line Railroad
S.I.C.: 4011

Wheeler Bros. Grain Co. **(1)**
420 Santa Fe
Alva, OK 73717
Tel.: 405-327-0141
Grain & Kindred Products
S.I.C.: 4221; 5191; 5261
Dean Goll *(Mgr.)*

WHEELOCK INC.
273 Branchport Ave.
Long Branch, NJ 07740
Tel.: 908-222-6880
Fax: 908-222-8707
Year Founded: 1923
Approx.Sls.: $10,000,000
Emp.: 200
Fiscal Year-end: 12/31/90
Electromechanical & Electronic Audible & Visual Signals, Transducers, Strobe/Horns, Strobe/Chimes, Bells, Horns, Strobe Speakers, Chimes for Fire Alarm Systems or General Purpose Signals & Telephone Ringing Relays & Signals, Explosion-Proof Bells & Relays, Voice Paging
S.I.C.: 3669; 3661; 3679; 3663
Peter W. Tarlton *(Pres.)*
Douglas E. Phillips *(V.P.-Opers)*
Joseph P. Henry *(V.P.-Fin. & Admin.)*
Stephen W. Andrews *(V.P.-Engrng.)*
William L. Goldstein *(V.P.-Mktg. & Sls.)*

Wheels, Inc.
(See Frank Consolidated Enterprises Inc. Listing)

BUFF WHELAN CHEVROLET & GEO, INC.
40445 Van Dyke Ave.
Sterling Heights, MI 48313
Tel.: 313-939-7300 MI
Fax: 313-939-3060
Approx.Sls.: $89,600,000
Emp.: 113
Automobile Dealership, Leasing & Repair Services; Wholesale & Retail Automotive Parts
S.I.C.: 5511; 7515; 7538; 5013; 5531
Robert Whelan *(Pres.)*
Kirk Miller *(Treas.)*
William Studebaker *(Gen. Mgr.)*
Virginia Villaire *(Office Mgr.)*

Outside Service Firm(s):

Deloitte & Touche*(Auditors)*
2 Ruan Center
Des Moines, IA 50309
Tel.: 515-288-1200

Stewart, Lasce, Nowak, Macmi, Flynn*(Legal Firm)*
Detroit, MI

Comerica Bank*(Major Banking Relationship)*
211 W. Fort St.
Detroit, MI 48226
Tel.: 313-222-3300

WHIBCO, INC.
River Rd.
Leesburg, NJ 08327
Mailing Address:
P.O. Box 259
Leesburg, NJ 08327
Tel.: 609-785-2090
Fax: 609-785-0444
Year Founded: 1841
Approx.Sls.: $12,000,000
Emp.: 175
Import Export

Industrial Sands & Foundry Products
S.I.C.: 1446; 1442; 3295; 3559; 5032
Walter R. Sjogren, Sr. *(Chm. Bd.)*
Wade R. Sjogren *(Pres.)*
Walter R. Sjogren, Jr. *(V.P.-Opers.)*
Loriann Sjogren *(V.P. & Sec.)*
Carl V. Stott *(V.P.-Fin.)*

Outside Service Firm(s):

Klatzkin & Company*(Auditors)*
Trenton, NJ

Norris, McCaughlin & Marcus*(Legal Firm)*
Somerville, NJ

United Jersey Bank*(Major Banking Relationship)*
Cherry Hill, NJ

WHIPPS
38 S. Main
Athol, MA 01331
Mailing Address:
P.O. Box 1058,
Athol, MA 01331
Tel.: 508-249-7924
Fax: 508-249-3072
Emp.: 20
Manufacture Water-Waste Treatment Plant Equipment
S.I.C.: 3829; 3594; 3543
Pauline Whipps *(Pres.)*
George Whipps *(V.P. & Chief Fin. Officer)*

Computer Systems/Hardware:
IBM

Outside Service Firm(s):

Kuman, Kashuk & Stevens*(Auditors)*
Worcester, MA

Paul Revere Life Insurance Co.*(Group Insurer)*
Worcester, MA

Bank of New England*(Major Banking Relationship)*
28 State Street
Boston, MA 02109
Tel.: 617-742-4000

WHISPER SOFT MILLS INC.
111 W. 40th St.
New York, NY 10018
Tel.: 212-921-9177
Fax: 212-921-3771
Year Founded: 1971
Approx.Sls.: $20,000,000
Emp.: 180
Fiscal Year-end: 12/31/90
Mfr. of Home Furnishings- Luxury Satin Beddings & Accessories
S.I.C.: 2392
D.T. Thompson *(Chm. Bd.)*
R.E. Gehl *(Pres.)*
Sara Gangitano *(Sec.)*
Marge Padgett *(Designer)*

WHITE CASTLE SYSTEM, INC.
555 W. Goodale
Columbus, OH 43215
Mailing Address:
P.O. Box 1498,
Columbus, OH 43216
Tel.: 614-228-5781 DE
Fax: 614-464-0596
Year Founded: 1921
Approx.Sls.: $305,000,000
Emp.: 9,500
Fiscal Year-end: 12/31/91
259 Fast Food Hamburger Specialists Located Throughout the Midwest
S.I.C.: 5812
Employee Matching Gifts Program: Submit Requests to the Chairman of the Contributions Committee, Jack L. Trador
E.W. Ingram, Jr. *(Chm. Bd.)*
E.W. Ingram III *(Pres. & Chief Exec. Officer)*
Tim Murrin *(Pres.-Pur.)*
J.W. Bricker *(V.P. & Treas.)*
G. Roger Post *(V.P., Sec. & Gen Counsel)*
Jack L. Trador *(V.P. & Asst. Sec.)*
Russell J. Meyer *(Controller)*
Nicholas W. Zuk *(Legal Officer)*
Mark I. Gelderloos *(Sr. Dir.-Engrng. Construction)*
Fred G. Gunderson *(Dir.-Human Resources)*
Richard D. Randall *(Dir.-Risk Mngmt.)*
John J. Ransom *(Dir.-Mngmt. Information Systems)*
Dave Rister *(Dir.-Plng. & Devel.)*
Kim K. Bartley *(Dir.-Mktg.)*
James F. Sipp *(Dir.-Intl.)*

Computer Systems/Hardware:
IBM

Outside Service Firm(s):

Ernst & Young*(Auditors)*
One Columbus, 10 W. Broad St.
Columbus, OH 43215
Tel.: 614-224-5678

Porter, Wright, Morris & Arthur*(Legal Firm)*
Huntington Center, 41 S. High St.
Columbus, OH 43215-3406
Tel.: 614-227-2000

Bank One*(Major Banking Relationship)*
Columbus, OH

Loomis, Sayles & Co., Inc.*(Pension Manager)*
One Financial Center
Boston, MA 02111
Tel.: 617-482-2450
Fax: 617-482-1985

Subsidiaries:

PSB Co. **(1)**
555 W. Goodale St.
Columbus, OH 43215
Tel.: 614-228-5781 (100%)
Fax: 614-221-9398
Approx.Sls.: $6,307,200
Emp.: 100
Mfr. of Steel, Lawn Spreaders, Powder Painting, Versa Hangers, No Guess Lawn Spreader Markers, Job Shop Orders
S.I.C.: 3444
Tim Murrin *(Dir.-Pur.)*
F.G. Gunderson *(Dir.-Personnel)*
Louis Hill *(Dir.-Mktg.)*
Bob Johns *(Gen. Mgr.)*

White Castle Distributing, Inc. **(1)**
555 W. Goodale St.
Columbus, OH 43216
Tel.: 614-228-5781
Fax: 614-464-0596
259 Fast Food Hamburger Specialists Located Throughout the Midwest
S.I.C.: 5812
William A. Blake *(V.P.)*

E JAMES WHITE Co
Integrated Marketing Services
151 Spring Street • Suite 300 • Herndon, VA 22070
703 318 8000 • FAX 703 318 8540

E. JAMES WHITE COMPANY
151 Spring St., Ste. 300
Herndon, VA 22070
Tel.: 703-318-8000
Fax: 703-318-8540
Year Founded: 1975
Approx.Billings: $18,000,000
Emp.: 30
Travel, Leisure, Tourism, Healthcare, Business & Publishing
E. James White *(Chm. Bd. & Pres.)*
David Whitmore *(Gen. Counsel & Controller)*

Computer Systems/Hardware:
MacIntosh

WHITE COUNTY FARM BUREAU CO-OP ASSOCIATION
210 W. Harrison St.
Monticello, IN 47960
Mailing Address:
P.O. Box 387
Monticello, IN 47960
Tel.: 219-583-7656 IN
Fax: 219-583-6975
Year Founded: 1927
Approx.Sls.: $19,000,000
Emp.: 35
Wholesale Distribution of Grains; Grain Elevators; Petroleum Bulk Stations; Farm Supplies
S.I.C.: 5153; 5171; 5191
Jim Wagner *(Pres.)*
William Schroeder *(V.P.)*
Ron Larew *(Gen. Mgr.)*
Robert Sanbloom *(Sec.)*

Outside Service Firm(s):

Bank of Reynolds*(Major Banking Relationship)*
Reynolds, IN

WHITE ELECTRICAL CONSTRUCTION CO.
1730 Chattahoochee Ave.
Atlanta, GA 30318
Mailing Address:
P.O. Box 19629
Atlanta, GA 30325
Tel.: 404-351-5740
Fax: 404-355-5823
Year Founded: 1910
Approx.Sls.: $20,000,000
Emp.: 300
Fiscal Year-end: 9/30/90
Electrical Construction
S.I.C.: 5063
E.R. DuBose *(Chm. Bd.)*
S.I. DuBose *(Pres.)*
Mike Taylor *(Sec. & Treas.)*

WHITE, GOOD & CO.
ADVERTISING

WHITE, GOOD & CO.
418 Chestnut St.
Lebanon, PA 17042
Tel.: 717-274-8301
Fax: 717-274-8305
Year Founded: 1981
Approx.Billings: $10,000,000
Emp.: 12
Robert F. Good *(Chm. Bd.)*
Ann S. White *(Pres.)*
Susan Baronowski *(Pub. Rels.)*

WHITE HEN PANTRY, INC.
660 Industrial Dr.
Elmhurst, IL 60126
Tel.: 708-833-3100 DE
Fax: 708-833-7034
Year Founded: 1965
Approx.Sls.: $340,000,000
Emp.: 400
Fiscal Year-end: 2/ 1/92
Convenience Food Stores
S.I.C.: 5399
Robert G. Robertson *(Pres. & Chief Exec. Officer)*
George S. Bovis *(Sr. V.P.-Mktg. Devel. & Growth Plng.)*
Allen S. Davis *(Sr. V.P.-Opers.)*
Douglas J. Fritsch *(V.P. & Gen. Mgr.-Midwest Reg.)*
Robert B. Knight *(Sr. V.P.-Admin. & Treas.)*
Robert C. Smith *(Sr. V.P., Sec. & Gen. Counsel)*
Fred J. Sulich *(Controller)*

White Hen Pantry, Inc.—(Continued)

David A. Crackel *(Dir.-Real Estate)*
Eugene F. Lang *(Dir.-Oper. Services)*
Ronald F. Revell *(Dir.-Mdsg.)*
Richard J. Ruzecki *(Dir.-Information Systems)*
James J. Walz *(Dir.-Franchising & Training)*
Principal(s):
Robert G. Robertson
George S. Bovis
Allen S. Davis
Robert B. Knight
Robert C. Smith

No. of U.S. Offices: 3

Computer Systems/Hardware:
Wang VS 300

Outside Service Firm(s):

Arthur Andersen & Co.*(Auditors)*
33 W. Monroe St.
Chicago, IL 60603-4067
Tel.: 312-580-0033
Fax: 312-507-6748

CNA Insurance*(Commercial Insurance Carrier)*
CNA Plaza,
Chicago, IL 60685
Tel.: 312-822-5000

Blue Cross & Blue Shield of Illinois*(Group Insurer)*
100 Tower Drive
Burr Ridge, IL 60521
Tel.: 708-323-3666

McDermott, Will & Emery*(Legal Firm)*
227 W. Monroe St.
Chicago, IL 60606-5096
Tel.: 312-372-2000

American National Bank & Trust Company of Chicago*(Major Banking Relationship)*
33 N. LaSalle St.
Chicago, IL 60602
Tel.: 312-661-5000
Fax: 312-661-6417

American National Bank*(Pension Manager)*
33 North LaSalle St.
Chicago, IL 60690
Tel.: 312-661-6967

THE WHITE LILY FOODS CO.
P.O. Box 871
Knoxville, TN 37901
Tel.: 615-546-5511
Fax: 615-521-7725
Approx.Sls.: $50,000,000
Emp.: 160
Manufacturer of White Lily Flour, Mixes & Corn Meal
S.I.C.: 2041
Ted A. Pedas *(Pres. & Chief Oper. Officer)*
Lloyd L. Montgomery *(V.P.-Mktg.)*
J. Charles Smiddy *(V.P.-Consumer Sls.)*
J.W. Stamper *(V.P.-Pur. & Distr.)*

WHITE MOP WRINGER COMPANY
10702 N. 46th St.
Tampa, FL 33617
Mailing Address:
P.O. Box 16647,
Tampa, FL 33687
Tel.: 813-971-2223
Fax: 813-971-6090
Year Founded: 1893
Approx.Sls.: $40,000,000
Emp.: 450
Fiscal Year-end: 3/31/91
Export
Mfr. of Industrial Cleaning Equipment
S.I.C.: 3589; 2392; 3089; 3411; 3635; 3639
Robert R. Schneider *(V.P.-Sls. & Mktg.)*
Tom Halluska *(V.P.-Fin.)*
Judy Jadwin *(Mgr.-Adv.)*

Outside Service Firm(s):

Ernst & Young*(Auditors)*
1800 One Mony Plaza,
Syracuse, NY 13202
Tel.: 315-425-8011

Jones, Day, Reavis & Pogue*(Legal Firm)*
Tampa, FL

NationsBank Florida*(Major Banking Relationship)*
600 Florida Ave.
Tampa, FL 33602
Tel.: 813-224-5151

Divisions:

Piedmont-White Mop Co. **(1)**
321 Atando Ave.
Charlotte, NC 28201

White/Mipro Receptables **(1)**
Corporation Park
Scotia, NY 12302
Tel.: 518-372-5486
Distribute Garbage Cans
S.I.C.: 5085

Subsidiary:

Pullman/Holt Corp. **(1)**
10702 46th St.
Tampa, FL 33617
Tel.: 813-971-2223
Tel.: 800-237-7582
Commercial Vacuum Cleaners, Floor & Rug Care Machines
S.I.C.: 3589
Bob Eukovich *(V.P.)*
Judy Jadwin *(Dir.-Adv.)*

WHITE ROCK DISTILLERIES INC.
21 Saratoga St.
Lewiston, ME 04240
Mailing Address:
P.O. Box 1829
Lewiston, ME 04241-1829
Tel.: 207-783-1433 **ME**
Fax: 207-783-8409
Approx.Sls.: $40,000,000
Emp.: 63
Import Export
Holding Company; Manufacturer & Wholesaler of Lawrence Beverages, Poland Spring Distilled Gin & Gold Crown Liquors, Cordials &Cocktails, Fairview Liquors; Federal Distillers--Nuyens Liquors, Maui Schnapps, Ice Box Cordials, Regal Club Liquors & Cordials
S.I.C.: 2084; 2085; 5182; 6719
Raymond R. Coulombe *(Chm. & Chief Exec. Officer)*
Cecile J. Coulombe *(Pres., Treas. & Sec.)*
Janet M. Bishop *(V.P.-Human Resources)*
Dennis N. Coulombe *(V.P.-Opers.)*
Paul G. Coulombe *(V.P.-Mktg.)*
Roland Coulombe *(V.P.-Adv.)*
Joseph P. McGovern *(Chief Tech. Advisor)*
Roger Gelinas *(Controller)*
Principal(s):
Raymond R. Coulombe
Cecile J. Coulombe

No. of Mfg. Plants/Facilities: 1
No. of U.S. Offices: 1

Outside Service Firm(s):

Gervais*(Auditors)*
Lewiston, ME

Skelton, Taintor & Abbott*(Legal Firm)*
95 Maine St.
Auburn, ME 04210
Tel.: 207-784-3200

Fleet National Bank*(Major Banking Relationship)*
Bangor, ME

Division:

Fairview Wine Co. **(1)**
21 Saratoga St.
Lewiston, ME 04240
Tel.: 207-783-1433
Emp.: 65
Manufacturing of Liquor
S.I.C.: 2085
Raymond Coulombe *(Chief Exec. & Chief Oper. Officer)*
Cecile J. Coulombe *(Pres.)*
Paul Coulombe *(V.P.-Mktg.)*
Roland Coulombe *(V.P.-Adv.)*
Dennis Coulombe *(V.P.-Opers.)*
Janet Bishop *(V.P.)*

Subsidiaries:

Federal Distillers **(1)**
21 Saratoga St.
Lewiston, ME 04240
Tel.: 207-783-1433
Manufacturing of Liquor
S.I.C.: 2085

Lawrence & Company **(1)**
21 Saratoga St.
Lewiston, ME 04240
Tel.: 207-783-1433 (100%)
Fax: 207-783-8409
Ready-To-Serve Highballs & Beverages
S.I.C.: 2085
Raymond R. Coulombe *(Chief Exec. Office)*
Cecile J. Coulombe *(Pres.)*
Paul Coulombe *(V.P.-Mktg.)*
Dennis Coulombe *(V.P.-Opers.)*
Roland L. Coulombe *(V.P.-Adv. & Opers.)*
Janet Bishop *(V.P.)*

Maine Bottlers **(1)**
21 Saratoga St.
Lewiston, ME 04240
Tel.: 207-783-1433
Fax: 207-783-8409
Manufacturing of Liquor
S.I.C.: 2085
Raymond R. Coulombe *(Chief Exec. Officer)*
Cecile J. Coulombe *(Pres.)*
Paul Coulombe *(V.P.-Mktg.)*
Dennis Coulombe *(V.P.-Opers.)*
Roland L. Coulombe *(V.P.-Adv. & Oper.)*
Janet Bishop *(V.P.)*

Nuyens Liquor Importing, Inc. **(1)**
40 Underhill Blvd.
Syosset, NY 11791
Tel.: 516-921-3377 (100%)
Importers
S.I.C.: 5182
Raymond R. Coulombe *(Pres.)*
Cecile J. Coulombe *(V.P. & Treas.)*

WHITE ROCK PRODUCTS CORP.
16-16 White Stone Expwy.
White Stone, NY 11357
Tel.: 718-746-3400
Fax: 718-767-0413
Approx.Sls.: $30,000,000
Emp.: 200
White Rock Sparkling Water & Flavored Beverages, Natural Mineral Water, Cardinal Beer, Moussy Non Alcoholic Malt Beverage, Aseptic Juice & Drinks & Famous Amos Diet Chocolate Drinks
S.I.C.: 2086; 2037; 2082
Alfred Y. Morgan, Jr. *(Pres.)*
William Indyk *(V.P.-Sls.)*
Barclay H. Griffiths *(Chief Fin. Officer)*

WHITE STAG MANUFACTURING COMPANY
7915 Haskell Ave.
Van Nuys, CA 91409
Tel.: 818-782-7568
Fax: 818-375-1695
Approx.Sls.: $50,000,000
Emp.: 800
Fiscal Year-end: 1/ 3/91
White Stag Skiwear for Men, Boys, Women & Girls
S.I.C.: 2339; 2329; 2369
Chris Staff *(Pres.)*
Roger Williams *(V.P., Treas. & Controller)*

Division:

Edelweiss **(1)**
5700 S.E. Harvey Dr.
Portland, OR 97206
Tel.: 503-777-1711
Mfrs. Skiwear
S.I.C.: 2337
Thomas J. Bienemann *(Pres.)*

WHITE STORAGE & RETRIEVAL SYSTEMS, INC.
30 Boright Ave.
Kenilworth, NJ 07033
Tel.: 201-272-6700
Fax: 201-272-5920
Approx.Sls.: $50,000,000
Emp.: 400
Conveyor Systems & Storage; Retrieval Systems
S.I.C.: 3535
Donald Weiss *(Pres.)*
Ray Mattes *(V.P.-Fin.)*
Hubert Eichenlaub *(Pur. Agent)*

Outside Service Firm(s):

Manheim, Kosson & Novick*(Auditors)*
Millburn, NJ

United Jersey Bank*(Major Banking Relationship)*
Newark, NJ

WHITEHAWK PARTNERSHIP
155 S. El Molino Ave.
Pasadena, CA 91101
Tel.: 818-792-7976
Fax: 818-577-1340
Year Founded: 1982
Emp.: 25
General Contractors; New Construction of Single Family Homes & Multi-Family Dwellings
S.I.C.: 1521; 1522
James Oates *(Pres. & Partner)*
Lawrence R. Schield, Jr. *(Partner)*
The Whitehead Co., Inc. *(Partner)*

Outside Service Firm(s):

David Arrit*(Auditors)*
Pasadena, CA

Sanwa Bank*(Major Banking Relationship)*
Pasadena, CA

WHITEMYER ADVERTISING, INC.
Fourth St.
Zoar, OH 44697
Tel.: 216-874-2432
Year Founded: 1971
Approx.Billings: $10,000,000
Emp.: 18
Donald E. Whitemyer *(Pres.)*
Mark Spaner *(Exec. V.P.)*
Tom Simmelink *(V.P., Pub. Rels.)*
Lisa Geers *(Dir. Media & Mktg.)*

R. O. Whitesell Assoc.
(See Rowtronics Company Inc. Listing)

WHITESTAR GRAPHICS, INC.
P.O. Box 278,
Spring Grove, IL 60018
Mailing Address:
P.O. Box 278,
Spring Grove, IL 60018
Year Founded: 1965
Approx.Rev.: $30,000,000
Emp.: 300
Fiscal Year-end: 8/31/92
Export
Mfr. of Custom Business Forms; Editorial & Pre-Press Functions for Textbook Publishers
S.I.C.: 6719; 2761; 2791
Corporate Giving Program: United Way

Employee Matching Gifts Program: United Way-Company Matches Employees Contributions
William White *(Chm. Bd.)*
Ben L. McSwiney *(Pres. & Chief Exec. Officer)*
Ed Welch *(Pres.-Clarinda Co.)*
Scot M. McCormick *(Chief Fin. Officer)*

Computer Systems/Hardware:
IBM System 38; LAN's

Outside Service Firm(s):

Ernst & Young*(Auditors)*
317 6th Ave., Ste. 1100
Des Moines, IA 50309
Tel.: 515-243-2727

Kirkland & Ellis*(Legal Firm)*
200 E. Randolph Dr.
Chicago, IL 60601
Tel.: 312-861-2000
Fax: 312-861-2200

Harris Trust & Savings Bank*(Major Banking Relationship)*
111 W. Monroe St.
Chicago, IL 60690
Tel.: 312-461-2265
Tel.: 800-858-0840

Subsidiaries:

The Clarinda Company **(1)**
220 No. 1st St.
Clarinda, IA 51632
Tel.: 712-542-5131
Tel.: 800-831-5821 (100%)
Fax: 712-542-5059
Typesetting Services
S.I.C.: 2791
Ed Welch *(Pres.)*

Division:

The Clarinda Company Color Division **(2)**
1780 W. 7th St.
Saint Paul, MN 55116
Tel.: 612-699-2771
Tel.: 800-522-5018 (100%)
Fax: 612-699-9008
Emp.: 45
Color Separation
S.I.C.: 2796
Paul Raymond *(Gen. Mgr.)*

Forms Corporation Of America **(1)**
3106 N. Rte. 12
Spring Grove, IL 60081
Tel.: 815-675-2392
Tel.: 815-675-2477
Tel.: 800-435-4382 (100%)
Approx.Sls.: $30,000,000
Emp.: 220
Fiscal Year-end: 8/31/91
Export
Mfr. of Business Forms
S.I.C.: 2761
Rose Principe *(V.P.-Mktg. & Sls.)*
Sonny Erickson *(V.P.-Opers.)*
Ben L. McSwiney *(Pres. & Chief Oper. Officer)*
Dan Peterson *(Mgr.-Pur.)*
Julie Hughey *(Mgr.-Distributor Sls.)*
Ellie McEwen *(Mgr.-Human Resources)*

WHITFIELD FOODS, INC.
1101 N. Court St.
Montgomery, AL 36104
Mailing Address:
P.O. Box 791
Montgomery, AL 36101-0791
Tel.: 205-263-2541
Tel.: 800-633-8790 **AL**
Fax: 205-262-4203
Year Founded: 1906
Approx.Sls.: $12,000,000
Emp.: 175
Fiscal Year-end: 9/30/90
Table Syrups; Alaga & Yellow Label, Tastee, Plow Boy, Red Hill, Whitfield
S.I.C.: 2061; 2099
L. B. Whitfield III *(Chm. Bd.)*
Frank G. Whitfield *(Pres. & Chief Exec. Officer)*
Joe McNair *(Exec. V.P.-Fin.)*
Les Massey *(Controller)*
Tommy Mancuso *(Gen. Counsel)*
Wes Shanks *(Dir.-Data Processing)*
Don Wheeler *(Dir.-Quality Control)*
Tom Curry *(Plant Mgr.)*
Steve Handlon *(Mgr.-Sls.)*
Principal(s):
L. B. Whitfield III
Frank G. Whitfield

Computer Systems/Hardware:
UNISYS

Outside Service Firm(s):

Jackson Thornton*(Auditors)*
Montgomery, AL

Massachusetts Mutual Life Insurance Co.*(Group Insurer)*
1295 State Street
Springfield, MA 01111
Tel.: 413-788-8411

Rushton, Stakely, Johnston & Garrett*(Legal Firm)*
P.O. Box 270
Montgomery, AL 36195
Tel.: 205-834-8480

WHITIN ROBERTS CO.
109 N. McNeil Rd.
Sanford, NC 27330
Mailing Address:
P.O. Box 250,
Sanford, NC 27330
Tel.: 919-775-7321
Tel.: 800-432-6601
Tel.: 800-438-3348
Telex: 6843007
Fax: 919-776-0121
Year Founded: 1831
Approx.Sls.: $11,000,000
Emp.: 300
Fiscal Year-end: 12/31/90
Textile Preparatory Machinery & Parts; Recycling Equip.
S.I.C.: 3552; 3569
Derrick A.M. Smith *(Pres.)*
M.J. Deshaies *(V.P.-Engrng.)*
David Palmer *(V.P.-Sls.)*
Dewey Averitt *(Chief Fin. Officer)*
Kathi Smith *(Treas.)*
Jim Collins *(Controller)*
Joe Williams *(Sec.)*
Terry Clemmer *(Dir.-Pur.)*
David Ainsworth *(Dir.-Quality Control)*
Lynn Poe *(Gen. Mgr.)*
Wayne Williams *(Mgr.-Personnel)*
W.R. Harris *(Mgr.-Import & Export)*
Bobby Brown *(Mgr.-Mfg.)*

Division:

Whitin Roberts Mfg. Div. **(1)**
Sanford, NC 27330
Tel.: 919-775-7321
Tel.: 800-432-6601
Tel.: 800-438-3348
Telex: 6843007 WHITI UW
Fax: 919-776-9121
Mfr. Textile Machinery & Replacement Parts
S.I.C.: 3552
Derrick A.M. Smith *(Chm. Bd.)*
Dewey Averitt *(Chief Fin. Officer)*
Bruce J. Morris *(Sls. Dir.)*
Terry Clemmer *(Pur. Dir.)*

Subsidiary:

Mauldin Mfg. Co., Inc. **(1)**
2499 Rutherford Rd.
Greenville, SC 29608
Tel.: 803-244-5007
Manufacture of Road Paving Equipment
S.I.C.: 3531
Dan McWilliams *(Gen. Mgr.)*
Bob Sang *(Sls. Mgr.)*

WHITING CORPORATION
15700 Lathrop Ave.
Harvey, IL 60426
Tel.: 708-331-4000
Tel.: 312-468-9400 **IL**
Fax: 312-785-0755
Year Founded: 1884
Approx.Sls.: $50,000,000
Emp.: 400
Fiscal Year-end: 12/31/91
Export
Mfr. Material Handling Equipment
S.I.C.: 3536; 3569; 3743; 3559; 3441; 3443; 3567; 8711
W.J. Saxonmeyer *(Chm. Bd.)*
Raymond E. Gibson *(Pres.)*
Jeffrey L. Kahn *(Exec. V.P. & Chief Fin. Officer)*
John F. Fisher *(V.P.-Opers.)*
Casey J. Skorpinski *(V.P.-Customer Service, Sls. & Mktg.)*
Michael D. Burge *(Controller)*
Catherine L. Collins *(Treas.)*
Costas T. Bourtsos *(Dir.-Intl. Mktg. & Export)*
Gary Cervak *(Mgr.-Information Systems)*
Peter S. Hammond *(Mgr.-Adv.)*
Mary Ann Kuebler *(Mgr.-Human Resources)*
Edward A. Scully *(Mgr.-Pur.)*

Computer Systems/Hardware:
IBM 4331, IBM AS 400, Prime 850

Outside Service Firm(s):

Grant Thornton*(Auditors)*
700 One Prudential Plaza, 130 East Randolph St.
Chicago, IL 60601
Tel.: 312-856-0200
Fax: 312-565-4719

The Northern Trust Co.*(International Bank Affiliate)*
50 S. LaSalle St.
Chicago, IL 60675
Tel.: 312-630-6000
Fax: 312-630-6516

Winston & Strawn*(Legal Firm)*
One 1st Natl. Plaza, No. 5000
Chicago, IL 60603
Tel.: 312-558-5600

The Northern Trust Co.*(Major Banking Relationship)*
50 S. LaSalle St.
Chicago, IL 60675
Tel.: 312-630-6000
Fax: 312-630-6516

Non-U.S. Holding:

Whiting Equipment Canada, Inc. **(1)**
350 Alexander St.
Welland, ON L3B 5P4, Canada
Tel.: 416-732-7585 (100%)
Emp.: 60
Mfr. of Material Handling Equipment
S.I.C.: 3441; 3443; 3535; 3536; 3554; 3559; 3567; 3569; 3743
Harold Lee *(Pres.)*
William Paterson *(Sec.)*
Florian Guriel *(Asst. Sec. & Treas.)*
Ernie Hamilton *(Mgr.-Sls.)*

WHITING MANUFACTURING CO., INC.
9999 Carver Rd.
Cincinnati, OH 45242
Tel.: 513-791-9100
Fax: 513-791-9101
Approx.Sls.: $30,000,000
Emp.: 400
Manufacture Comforters, Bedspreads, Draperies, Bed Pillows, Bed Ruffles, Pillow Shams, Day Bed Sets, Sleeping Bags
S.I.C.: 2392; 2391
C. Ross Whiting *(Chm. Bd.)*
Richard T. Whiting *(Pres. & Chief Exec. Officer)*
Valeria Good *(V.P.-Fin.)*
Jerry Momper *(V.P.-Natl. Sls.)*
Emmet Winslow *(Dir.-Mfg. & Personnel)*
Gale Scott *(Mgr.-Data Processing)*
Principal(s):
C. Ross Whiting
Richard T. Whiting

Outside Service Firm(s):

Harry W. Tenkotte*(Auditors)*
Cincinnati, OH

Frost & Jacobs*(Legal Firm)*
2500 Central Trust Ctr.
Cincinnati, OH 45202
Tel.: 513-651-6800

Star Bank*(Major Banking Relationship)*
425 Walnut Street
Cincinnati, OH 45202
Tel.: 513-632-4000

Whiting-Patterson Co.
(Acquired by CC Industries, Inc., name changed to American Envelope of Philadelphia)

WHITING-TURNER CONTRACTING CO.
300 E. Joppa Rd.
Baltimore, MD 21286
Tel.: 301-821-1100 **MD**
Fax: 301-337-5770
Year Founded: 1909
Approx.Sls.: $320,000,000
Emp.: 1,250
General Construction & Construction Management
S.I.C.: 1622; 1629
Willard Hackerman *(Pres. & Treas.)*
Charles A. Irish *(Exec. V.P.)*
Edward D. Burger *(Sr. V.P.)*
Stuart H. Dobson *(Sr. V.P.)*
Stephen Duffy *(Sr. V.P.)*
Karen Lucas *(Mktg. Coord.)*

No. of U.S. Offices: 6

Computer Systems/Hardware:
IBM

Outside Service Firm(s):

Merchantile Safe Deposit & Trust*(Major Banking Relationship)*
Baltimore, MD

WHITMIRE DISTRIBUTION
81 Blue Ravine Rd.
Folsom, CA 95630
Tel.: 916-985-5180
Fax: 916-985-5016
Sales Range: $10-19 Million
Pharmaceutical Distributor
S.I.C.: 2834
Steve Devine *(Dir.-Mktg.)*
Principal(s):
Steve Devine

WHITTAKER, CLARK & DANIELS, INC.
1000 Coolidge St.
South Plainfield, NJ 07080
Tel.: 908-561-6100
Tel.: 800-732-0562
Fax: 908-757-3488
Fax: 800-833-8139
Year Founded: 1890
Approx.Sls.: $60,000,000
Emp.: 180
Fiscal Year-end: 12/31/91
Import Export
Minerals, Colors & Chemicals
S.I.C.: 5169; 2816; 2819; 2865; 2899
George J. Dippold *(Chm. Bd. & Pres.)*
Michael Argyelan *(Exec. V.P.)*
Edwin Davenport *(Sr. V.P.-Opers.)*
Theodore Hubbard *(Sr. V.P.-Sls.)*
Vin Cronen *(Sec. & Treas.)*

Computer Systems/Hardware:
Hewlett-Packard

Outside Service Firm(s):

KPMG Peat Marwick*(Auditors)*
150 John F. Kennedy Pkwy.
Short Hills, NJ 07078
Tel.: 201-467-9650

WHITTENBERG CONSTRUCTION CO.
4774 Allmond Ave.
Louisville, KY 40209
Mailing Address:
P.O. Box 9429
Louisville, KY 40209
Tel.: 502-361-8891 **KY**
Fax: 502-368-9192
Year Founded: 1925
Assets: $3,000,000
Liabilities: $2,300,000
Net Worth: $700,000
Approx.Sls.: $15,000,000
Emp.: 150
Fiscal Year-end: 12/31/91
Import Export
General Contractor
S.I.C.: 1542; 1541
Pat Noonan *(Pres.)*
Bruce Jones *(V.P.)*

Outside Service Firm(s):

Chilton & Medley*(Auditors)*
Louisville, KY

Smith & Smith*(Legal Firm)*
Louisville, KY

First National Bank*(Major Banking Relationship)*
Louisville, KY

WHOLESALE ELECTRONIC SUPPLY
2809 Ross Ave.
Dallas, TX 75201
Tel.: 214-969-9400 **TX**
Fax: 214-969-0773
Year Founded: 1950
Approx.Sls.: $14,000,000
Emp.: 80
Wholesale Distributor of Television Sets; Video Cassette Recorders & Accessories; Radios; Communication Equipment For Education & Duplicating Fields
S.I.C.: 5064; 5065
John N. Leedom, Sr. *(Chm. Bd.)*
Melinda Woodson *(Pres.)*
Sally Cooper *(Sr. V.P.-C&E Group)*
John N. Leedom, Jr. *(Sr. V.P.)*
Doris Jewell *(V.P.-Fin, Treas. & Sec.)*

Outside Service Firm(s):

Compass Bank*(Major Banking Relationship)*
Richardson, TX

Division:

Electronic Center **(1)**
2809 Ross Ave.
Dallas, TX 75201
Tel.: 214-969-9400
Tel.: 800-880-9400
Florists
S.I.C.: 5992
Melinda Woodson *(Pres.)*

WICK BUILDING SYSTEMS
404 Walter Rd.
Mazomanie, WI 53560
Mailing Address:
P. O. Box 490,
Mazomanie, WI 53560
Tel.: 608-795-4281
Fax: 608-795-2740
Year Founded: 1958
Assets: $13,000,000
Earnings: $1,009,000
Net Worth: $13,000,000
Approx.Sls.: $70,000,000
Emp.: 700
Fiscal Year-end: 12/31/91
Mfr. Specializing in Mobile Homes, Panelized Homes & Pole Barns
S.I.C.: 2451; 2452; 3448; 1521; 1522
John F. Wick *(Chm. Bd. & Chief Exec. Officer)*
Jeff Wick *(Pres. & Chief Oper. Officer)*
Darrell Kolsted *(V.P.-Fin. & Oper.)*
O. Lynn Bybee *(Treas. & Controller)*
Wayne Jansen *(Mgr.-Data Processing)*

No. of Mfg. Plants/Facilities: 3
No. of U.S. Offices: 4

Computer Systems/Hardware:
IBM

Outside Service Firm(s):

Ernst & Young*(Auditors)*
111 E. Kilbourn Ave., Ste. 900
Milwaukee, WI 53202
Tel.: 414-273-5900

Winthrop & Weinstine*(Legal Firm)*
444 Cedar Street
St. Paul, MN 55101

First Wisconsin National Bank*(Major Banking Relationship)*
Madison, WI

Subsidiary:

Wick Bldg. Systems Inc. Manufactured Homes Div. **(1)**
2301 E. 4th St.
Marshfield, WI 54449
Tel.: 715-387-2551
Fax: 715-387-2931
Approx.Sls.: $75,000,000
Emp.: 350
Marshfield, Artcraft & Rollohome Mobile Homes
S.I.C.: 2451
Harris Berg *(V.P. & Gen. Mgr.)*
Ray Porter *(Gen. Sls. Mgr.)*
Richard Voigt *(Controller)*

WICKER PARK L.P.
2300 Wabansia Ave.
Chicago, IL 60647
Tel.: 312-384-1200
Approx.Sls.: $50,000,000
Emp.: 1,500
Fiscal Year-end: 12/31/90
Mfr. Women's Dresses & Sportswear
S.I.C.: 2335; 2339
Jerome Smoler *(Chm. Bd.)*
Irwin Smoler *(Pres.)*
Thomas Moore *(V.P. & Chief Fin. Officer)*
Leonard Smoler *(V.P.)*

WICKES LUMBER CO.
706 Deerpath Dr.
Vernon Hills, IL 60061
Tel.: 708-367-3400 **DE**
Fax: 708-367-3750
Approx.Rev.: $850,000,000
Emp.: 5,000
Fiscal Year-end: 12/29/90
Retailer of Lumber & Building Supplies
S.I.C.: 5211
William Hensler *(Chm. Bd.)*
J. Steven Wilson *(Chief Exec. Officer)*
John Morgrette *(Sr. V.P. & Chief Fin. Officer)*

No. of Mfg. Plants/Facilities: 196

Outside Service Firm(s):

Coopers & Lybrand*(Auditors)*
203 N. LaSalle St.
Chicago, IL 60601
Tel.: 312-701-5500

Schiff, Hardin & Waite*(Legal Firm)*
7200 Sears Tower, 233 S. Wacker Dr.
Chicago, IL 60606
Tel.: 312-876-1000

Bankers Trust Co.*(Major Banking Relationship)*
P.O. Box 318, Church St. Station
New York, NY 10008
Tel.: 212-454-2212
Fax: 212-454-2783

Continental Bank N. A.*(Major Banking Relationship)*
231 S. LaSalle St.
Chicago, IL 60697
Tel.: 312-828-2345
Tel.: 800-426-5754
Telex: 312-828-1783

WICKLAND CORPORATION
1765 Challenge Way
Sacramento, CA 95815
Mailing Address:
P.O. Box 13648,
Sacramento, CA 95853-3648
Tel.: 916-921-1100
Fax: 916-921-3408
Year Founded: 1960
Approx.Sls.: $400,000,000
Emp.: 925
Holding Company: Wholesale Petroleum Products
S.I.C.: 5541; 5172; 6719
J.A. Wickland, Jr. *(Chm. Bd. & Chief Exec. Officer)*
John A. Wickland III *(Pres.)*
Robert Byrum *(V.P.-Intl. Supply & Distr.)*
Robert Sanz *(V.P.-Supply & Distr.)*

Outside Service Firm(s):

Coopers & Lybrand*(Auditors)*
Sacramento, CA

Capital Bank Of Commerce*(Major Banking Relationship)*
Sacramento, CA

Subsidiary:

Wickland Oil Company, Inc. **(1)**
1765 Challenge Way
Sacramento, CA 95815
Tel.: 916-921-1100
Wholesale Petroleum Products
S.I.C.: 5172; 5541
Roy Wickland *(Pres.)*

WIEDEN & KENNEDY
320 Southwest Washington · Portland, Oregon 97204
Telephone: 503·228·4381 Telefax: 503·226·0512

WIEDEN & KENNEDY, INC.
320 S.W. Washington
Portland, OR 97204
Tel.: 503-228-4381
Fax: 503-295-6631
Year Founded: 1982
Approx.Billings: $200,000,000
Emp.: 205
David F. Kennedy *(Chm. Bd. & Creative Dir.)*
Dan G. Wieden *(Pres. & Creative Dir.)*
Joe Naporano *(Chief. Fin. Officer)*
Jackie Follett *(Dir.-Admin.)*
Chris Riley *(Dir.-Acct. Plang.)*
Kathy Brooks *(Mgr.-Broadcast Business)*
Mark Barden *(Acct. Planning Supvr.)*
Mary Normand *(Creative Sec.)*

Computer Systems/Hardware:
Macintosh

E.M. WIEGMANN & COMPANY, INC.
501 Douglas
Freeburg, IL 62243
Tel.: 618-539-3193
Fax: 618-539-5794
Approx.Sls.: $12,000,000
Emp.: 240
Junction Boxes, Electric
S.I.C.: 3644
Sue Wiegmann Agne *(Pres.)*
Virginia Baumgarte *(Sec. & Treas.)*
Kenneth Nagel *(Dir.-Engrng.)*
Leroy H. Weber *(Pur. Agent)*

Outside Service Firm(s):

Robert L. Marti*(Auditors)*
Belleville, IL

Magna Bank*(Major Banking Relationship)*
Belleville, IL

JOHN WIELAND HOMES INC.
1950 Sullivan Rd.
Atlanta, GA 30337
Tel.: 404-996-1400 **GA**
Fax: 404-991-6670
Year Founded: 1971
Assets: $92,000,000
Liabilities: $64,000,000
Net Worth: $28,000,000
Sales Range: $100-499 Million
Emp.: 360
Fiscal Year-end: 12/31/91
Single-Family Residential Construction
John F. Wieland *(Chm. Bd., Pres. & Chief Exec. Officer)*
Richard A. Bacon *(Sr. V.P. & Gen. Counsel)*
John B. Gillespie *(Sr. V.P.)*
Robert M. Pope, Jr. *(Sr. V.P.-Fin.)*
Norman S. Cohen *(V.P.)*
Daniel V. Fincher *(V.P.)*
Lawrie O. Horst *(V.P.-Mktg.)*
Rodney A. Johnson *(V.P.)*
S. Victoria Parker *(V.P.-Corp. Rels. & Human Resources)*
Steven E. Romeyn *(V.P.)*
Lawrence J. Pelkowski *(Treas.)*
Marcia J. Ratka *(Broker)*
Principal(s):
John F. Wieland

No. of U.S. Offices: 1

Computer Systems/Hardware:
IBM AS/400

Outside Service Firm(s):

Birnbrey, Minsk & Minsk*(Auditors)*
Atlanta, GA

Marsh & McLennan*(Commercial Insurance Carrier)*
1166 Avenue of the Americas
New York, NY 10036
Tel.: 212-345-6000
Fax: 212-345-3285

Blue Cross & Blue Shield of Georgia, Inc.*(Group Insurer)*
Atlanta, GA

Altman, Kritzer & Levick*(Legal Firm)*
6400 Powers Ferry Rd.
Atlanta, GA 30339

Cashin, Norton & Mullins*(Legal Firm)*
Atlanta, GA

Trust Company Bank*(Major Banking Relationship)*
Stock Trans. Dept. P.O.B. 4625, Trust Company of Georgia Bldg.
Atlanta, GA 30302
Tel.: 404-588-7831

Trust Company Bank*(Pension Manager)*
P.O. Box 4625, 25 Park Place
Atlanta, GA 30302
Tel.: 404-588-7815

Affiliates:

Residential Support Services, Inc. **(1)**
19450 Sullivan Rd.
Atlanta, GA 30337
Tel.: 404-996-1400
Building Materials
S.I.C.: 5211
John Wieland *(Chief Oper. Officer)*
Robert M. Pope, Jr. *(Sr. V.P.-Fin.)*
Rod Johnson *(V.P.)*

Wieland Financial Services, Inc. **(1)**
1950 Sullivan Rd.
Atlanta, GA 30337
Tel.: 404-996-1425
Emp.: 14
Mortgage Company
S.I.C.: 7389
Robert M. Pope, Jr. *(Sr. V.P.-Fin.)*
Jean Butterworth *(V.P.)*
Brad Cornwell *(Asst. V.P.)*
Dave Sander *(Asst. V.P.)*

Jean Fitzgerald *(Asst. Sec. & Loan Officer)*
Wayne Black *(Loan Officer)*
Larry Carlisle *(Loan Officer)*
Ken Cartwright *(Loan Officer)*
Bret Hoggard *(Loan Officer)*
Danny Howell *(Loan Officer)*
Steve Knoll *(Loan Officer)*
Jim Messer *(Loan Officer)*
Marty Patterson *(Loan Officer)*

John Wieland Homes of Charleston, Inc. **(1)**
443-H Longpoint Rd.
Mount Pleasant, SC 29464
Tel.: 803-849-8787
Emp.: 1
Residential Construction
S.I.C.: 1531
Robert M. Pope, Jr. *(Sr. V.P.-Fin.)*
Larry Pelkowski *(Treas.)*

John Wieland Homes of Charlotte, Inc. **(1)**
8349-K Arrowridge Blvd.
Charlotte, NC 28273
Tel.: 704-522-9200

John Wieland Homes of Jacksonville, Inc. **(1)**
5151 Sunbeam Rd., Ste. 19
Jacksonville, FL 32257
Tel.: 904-636-9617

Wieland Realty Associates, Inc. **(1)**
124 Johnson Ferry Road
Atlanta, GA 30328
Tel.: 404-843-8474
Emp.: 8
Real Estate
S.I.C.: 6531
Marcia Ratka *(Pres. & Broker)*
John Wieland *(Chief Oper. Officer)*
Robert M. Pope, Jr. *(Sr. V.P.-Fin.)*
Roberta Hanson *(Mgr.-Sls.)*
Beverly Pike *(Mgr.-Sls.)*
Ed Stolz *(Mgr.-Sls.)*

WIGAND CORPORATION
850 Elkton Dr.
Colorado Springs, CO 80907
Tel.: 719-599-8887 **OH**
Fax: 719-599-8828
Year Founded: 1958
Approx.Sls.: $22,000,000
Emp.: 250
Mfr. of Planing Mill, Millwork
S.I.C.: 2431; 2491
Emeric Wigand *(Pres.)*
Emeric Wigand, Jr. *(Exec. V.P.)*
Delroy Johnson *(V.P.-Fin.)*

Outside Service Firm(s):

Deloitte & Touche*(Auditors)*
P.O. Box 938,
Colorado Springs, CO 80901
Tel.: 719-636-5126

First National Bank*(Major Banking Relationship)*
Colorado Springs, CO

WIGWAM MILLS, INC.
3402 Crocker Ave.
Sheboygan, WI 53081
Mailing Address:
P.O. Box 818,
Sheboygan, WI 53082-0818
Tel.: 414-457-5551
Tel.: 800-558-7760
Fax: 414-457-0311
Year Founded: 1905
Approx.Sls.: $30,000,000
Emp.: 400
Export
Sports & Athletic Socks & Knit Headwear
S.I.C.: 2252; 2253
R.E. Chesebro *(Chm. Bd.)*
R.E. Chesebro, Jr. *(Pres.)*
Gene Oeschger *(Sr. V.P.-Sls. & Mktg.)*
Robert Wickhan *(Treas. & Sec.)*
Jeff Kortes *(Dir.-Human Resources)*
Hary Higgins *(Mgr.-Prod. Devel.)*

Computer Systems/Hardware:
IBM AS400

Outside Service Firm(s):

Deloitte & Touche*(Auditors)*
250 E. Wisconsin Ave.
Milwaukee, WI 53202-4283
Tel.: 414-271-3000

Employer's Health Insurance*(Group Insurer)*
Green Bay, WI

WIL-FREDS CONSTRUCTION, INC.
274 E. Indian Trail
Aurora, IL 60505
Tel.: 708-897-4000 **DE**
Fax: 708-897-4444
Approx.Sls.: $40,263,846
Emp.: 125
Fiscal Year-end: 12/31/90
General Contractor
S.I.C.: 1541; 1542; 1522
W. William Luxion *(Chm. Bd. & Chief Exec. Officer)*
W.T. Luxion *(Pres.)*
Sylvester Kanzler *(Sr. V.P.-Estimating)*
Robert M. Stone *(Treas. & Chief Fin. Officer)*
Judith A. Sanders *(Sec.)*
Clifford A. Luxion *(Mgr.-Business Devel.)*

Outside Service Firm(s):

McDonald & Doherty*(Auditors)*
Barrington, IL

Querrey & Harrow Ltd.*(Legal Firm)*
Chicago, IL

Harris Bank Naperville*(Major Banking Relationship)*
503 N. Washington St.
Naperville, IL 60540
Tel.: 708-420-3500

WILBUR-ELLIS COMPANY & CONNELL BROTHERS COMPANY
(Formerly Wilbur-Ellis Company)
320 California St.
San Francisco, CA 94104
Mailing Address:
P.O. Box 7454,
San Francisco, CA 94120
Tel.: 415-772-4000 **CA**
Fax: 415-772-4011
Year Founded: 1923
Approx.Sls.: $800,000,000
Emp.: 1,800
Distributors of Agricultural Chemicals & Animal Foodstuffs; Exporters of Industrial Chemicals to Far East
S.I.C.: 5169
Carter P. Thacher *(Chm. Bd.)*
Brayton Wilbur, Jr. *(Pres. & Chief Exec. Officer)*
Frank M. Brown *(V.P.)*
Don Thompson *(V.P.)*
Robert T. Pantzer *(Controller)*
Ingrid Kroneberg *(Sec.)*
Herbert B. Tully *(Treas.)*
John C. Hannon *(Asst. Treas.)*
Donald Blois *(Dir.-Personnel)*

Computer Systems/Hardware:
IBM PC-AT & XT

Outside Service Firm(s):

Hood & Strong*(Auditors)*
San Francisco, CA

Aetna Life & Casualty*(Group Insurer)*
151 Farmington Avenue
Hartford, CT 06156
Tel.: 203-273-2128
Fax: 203-729-4295

Thatcher, Albrecht & Rutcliffe*(Legal Firm)*
San Francisco, CA

The Bank of California, N.A.*(Major Banking Relationship)*
550 So. Flower St.
Los Angeles, CA 90071

Non-U.S. Holdings:

Connell Brothers Company Ltd. **(1)**
#19-07 Orchard Towers, 400 Orchard Rd.
Singapore, 0923, Singapore
Tel.: 734-4677
Telex: RS2170 Connell
Fax: 235-6304

Connell Brothers Co. Philippines Inc. **(1)**
P.O. Box 42,
Makati, Metro Manila Philippines
Tel.: 63 81 71 15 48 (100%)
Distr. of Chemicals
S.I.C.: 5169

Connell Brothers (Hong Kong) Ltd. **(1)**
601, 6/F Stanhope House, 738 Kings Rd.
Hong Kong, Hong Kong
Tel.: 565 5123 (100%)
Telex: 73768 CONEL HX
Fax: 811-1010
Distr. of Machinery, Goods & Food
S.I.C.: 5084; 5131; 5149

Wilbur-Ellis Company of Canada **(1)**
Ste. 310 15 Dartmouth Road,
Bedford, NS B4A 3X6, Canada
Tel.: 902-835-5544 (100%)
Fax: 902-835-6555
Distr. & Mktg. of Fish Meal & Fish Produce
S.I.C.: 5146
Casey Lynch *(Mgr.)*

WILDER MANAGEMENT ASSOCIATES
950 Winter St., Ste. 4300
Waltham, MA 02154
Tel.: 617-890-3500
Fax: 617-890-1999
Emp.: 70
Real Estate Investment & Development
S.I.C.: 6552
Joel B. Wilder *(Chm. Bd.)*
David J. Mallen *(Chief Fin. Officer & Sr. V.P.-Employee Benefits)*
Andrew T. LaGrega *(Sr. V.P.-Sls., Mktg., Adv. & Human Resources)*
Thomas Wilder *(V.P.)*

WILD'S BAKING COMPANY
214 S. Dean St.
Englewood, NJ 07631
Tel.: 201-567-4700
Year Founded: 1932
Approx.Sls.: $20,000,000
Emp.: 100
Import Export
Mfr. Baked Goods; European Style Bread
S.I.C.: 2051; 2052
Dennis Norberg *(Chm.)*
J. Wilcha *(Pres.)*

Computer Systems/Hardware:
NEC 386 SX

WILEN MANUFACTURING COMPANY, INC.
3760 Southside Industrial Pkwy.
Atlanta, GA 30354
Tel.: 404-366-2111 **GA**
Fax: 404-361-8832
Year Founded: 1939
Approx.Sls.: $25,000,000
Emp.: 260
Export
Mfr. of Floor & Dust Mops & Plain Polishing Cloths
S.I.C.: 2392
Joseph Wilen *(Pres.)*
David W. Shivers *(V.P.-Opers.)*
Mike Baker *(V.P.-Fin.)*

Outside Service Firm(s):

First Atlanta Bank*(Major Banking Relationship)*
Atlanta, GA

F.A. WILHELM CONSTRUCTION CO., INC.
3914 Prospect St.
Indianapolis, IN 46203
Mailing Address:
P.O. Box 516,
Indianapolis, IN 46206
Tel.: 317-359-5411
Fax: 317-359-8346
Year Founded: 1923
Approx.Sls.: $171,000,000
Emp.: 355
General Contractor; Construction Management
S.I.C.: 1541; 1542; 8741
James M. Wilhelm *(Pres. & Chief Exec. Officer)*
Paul R. O'Connor *(Sec., Treas. & Chief Fin. Officer)*
Brian J. Sullivan *(Dir.-Mktg. & Adv.)*
Principal(s):
James M. Wilhelm

Computer Systems/Hardware:
NCR 9300

Outside Service Firm(s):

George S. Olive & Co.*(Auditors)*
201 N. Illinois St.
Indianapolis, IN 46204

Fireman's Fund Insurance Co.*(Commercial Insurance Carrier)*
New York, NY

Donley, Horan*(Group Insurer)*
6330 E. 75th Ste. 106
Indianapolis, IN 46250
Tel.: 317-849-3282

Wood, Mercer*(Legal Firm)*
Indianapolis, IN

Merchants National Bank & Trust Company of Indianapolis*(Major Banking Relationship)*
One Merchants Plaza, Ste. 901E
Indianapolis, IN 46255
Tel.: 317-267-7109

WILKATA PACKAGING CORPORATION
300 Hoyt St.
Kearny, NJ 07032
Mailing Address:
P.O. Box 521
Kearny, NJ 07032
Tel.: 201-991-4800
Fax: 201-997-2514
Approx.Sls.: $12,500,000
Emp.: 150
Mfr. of Folding Cartons, Boxes & Displays
S.I.C.: 2657; 2652; 2653
Robert C. Wolf *(Pres.)*
John Visco *(V.P.)*
John Furbush *(V.P.-Fin.)*
Gene Giordano *(V.P.-Sls.)*
Joseph Sestilio *(Plant Mgr.)*

Outside Service Firm(s):

Ernst & Young*(Auditors)*
Metropark, 99 Wood Ave., S.
Iselin, NJ 08830
Tel.: 908-906-3211

Bank of Baltimore*(Major Banking Relationship)*
Baltimore, MD

Wilkins Outdoor Network, Inc.—(Continued)

Wilkins Outdoor Network

WILKINS OUTDOOR NETWORK, INC.
600 Morgan Falls Rd., Ste. 205
Atlanta, GA 30350
Tel.: 404-804-1818
Fax: 404-804-0029
Year Founded: 1965
Approx.Billings: $16,000,000
Emp.: 15
Out of Home Media, Planning, Contracting, Production & Consolidated Billing
W.N. (Bill) Wilkins *(Pres.)*
Lisa Weaver *(V.P.)*
Robert Oliver *(Chief Fin. Officer)*
Heidi Gura *(Contract Services)*
Marie Gilliland *(Admin.)*

WILKINS-ROGERS INCORPORATED
27 Frederick Rd.
Ellicott City, MD 21043
Mailing Address:
P.O. Box 308,
Ellicott City, MD 21041
Tel.: 410-465-5800
Fax: 410-750-0163
Year Founded: 1913
Approx.Sls.: $30,000,000
Emp.: 125
Fiscal Year-end: 12/31/90
Export
Family Flours, Bakers Flours, Corn Meal, Prepared Baking Mixes, Bread & Cake; Washington Brand, Indian Head
S.I.C.: 2041
S.H. Rogers, Jr. *(Chm. Bd.)*
Richard A. Rogers *(Pres.)*
Leon R. Gleaves *(V.P.-Mktg. & Sls.)*
Michael S. Everett *(V.P. & Chief Oper. Officer)*

Subsidiary:

Spangles' Flour Mills of Mt. Joy **(1)**
Mount Joy, PA 17552
Tel.: 717-653-1403
Flour Mill
S.I.C.: 2041

WILL & BAUMER INCORPORATED
Old Liverpool & Buckley Rd.
Liverpool, NY 13088
Mailing Address:
P.O. Box 4880,
Syracuse, NY 13221
Tel.: 315-451-1000
Tel.: 800-733-7337
Fax: 315-451-0120
Year Founded: 1855
Approx.Sls.: $10,000,000
Emp.: 120
Fiscal Year-end: 6/30/91
Import Export
Church, Restaurant, Institutional, Gift, Florist Candles & Accessories
S.I.C.: 3999
Howard J. Nybo *(Pres.)*
Marshall Ciccone *(Exec. V.P.-Fin.)*
Robert J. Schefter *(V.P.-Mktg.)*

Computer Systems/Hardware:
MAI Basic 4

Outside Service Firm(s):

Richard Eisner*(Auditors)*
New York, NY

Manufacturers Hanover Trust Co.*(Major Banking Relationship)*
270 Park Ave.
New York, NY 10017
Tel.: 212-286-3229

THE WILL-BURT COMPANY
169 S. Main
Orrville, OH 44667
Mailing Address:
P.O. Box 900
Orrville, OH 44667
Tel.: 216-682-7015
Fax: 216-684-1190
Year Founded: 1918
Approx.Sls.: $24,000,000
Emp.: 300
Export
Will-Burt Stoker, Combustioneer #77, Solid Fuel Central Furnaces, Pneumatic Telescoping Masts
S.I.C.: 3433
Harry Featherstone *(Pres.)*

WILLAMETTE-WESTERN CORPORATION
(Filed Chapt. 11 Bankruptcy, Dec. 5, 1991)
4555 N. Channel Av.
Portland, OR 97217
Mailing Address:
P.O. Box 3220
Portland, OR 97217
Tel.: 503-285-9111
Fax: 503-283-2602
Year Founded: 1937
Approx.Sls.: $100,000,000
Emp.: 1,000
Heavy Construction Contractors; Water Transportation; Pile Driving & Foundations, Dreding, Security
S.I.C.: 1499; 1629; 4489
Arthur A. Reidel *(Chm. Bd. & Chief Exec. Officer)*
G. F. Nelson *(Pres.)*
Wm. V. Spicer *(Sr. Exec. V.P. & Chief Fin. Officer)*
Ralph Mauro *(Corp. Sec.)*
Walter Swanson *(Dir.-Employee Benefits)*
Irene Jordan *(Mngmt. Info. Systems Dir.)*
Bob Hawes *(Purchasing Mgr.)*
John Schenk *(Real Estate Mgr.)*
Paul H. Brown, Jr. *(Controller)*
Bill Cox *(Corp. Counsel)*

Computer Systems/Hardware:
Prime

WILLARD GRAIN & FEED, INC.
104 Ash
Celina, TX 75009
Tel.: 214-382-2367 **TX**
Approx.Sls.: $55,000,000
Emp.: 170
Fertilizer & Fertilizer Materials; Wheat; Corn
S.I.C.: 5191; 5153
Jane Willard *(Pres.)*
Charles S. Goodell *(V.P.)*
Brenda Goodell *(Sec.)*
Kathy Willard *(Treas.)*

Outside Service Firm(s):

Pingleton & Associates*(Auditors)*
Dallas, TX

Abernathy, Roeder, Robertson & Joplin*(Legal Firm)*
101 E. Davis
McKinney, TX 75069
Tel.: 214-238-9657

WILLERT HOME PRODUCTS, INC.
4044 Park Ave.
Saint Louis, MO 63110
Tel.: 314-772-2822
Fax: 314-772-3506
Approx.Sls.: $19,000,000
Emp.: 200
Mfr. Household Insecticides & Deodorants
S.I.C.: 2879; 2842; 3469
August W. Willert, Jr. *(Chm. Bd.)*
William D. Willert *(Pres. & Treas.)*
Susan Hantak *(Exec. V.P. & Controller)*
T.P. Gleason *(V.P.-Sls.)*
Willimae C. Willert *(V.P. & Sec.)*
C. Ackridge *(Mgr.-Data Processing)*
J. Nehrt *(Chief Engineer)*
Principal(s):
August W. Willert, Jr.
William D. Willert
Willimae C. Willert

Computer Systems/Hardware:
IBM

Outside Service Firm(s):

KPMG Peat Marwick*(Auditors)*
1010 Market St.
Saint Louis, MO 63101
Tel.: 314-444-1400

Armstrong, Teasdale, Schlafly, Davis & Dicus*(Legal Firm)*
One Metropolitan Square
St. Louis, MO 63102
Tel.: 314-621-5065
Fax: 314-621-5065

Boatmen's Trust Company*(Major Banking Relationship)*
100 North Broadway
St. Louis, MO 63102
Tel.: 314-466-2469

R.C. WILLEY HOME FURNISHINGS
2301 S. 300 W.
Salt Lake City, UT 84115
Tel.: 801-461-3900
Fax: 801-461-3990
Year Founded: 1933
Approx.Sls.: $130,000,000
Emp.: 800
Furniture Stores; Electric Household Appliances; High Fidelity Stereo Equipment
S.I.C.: 5712; 5722; 5731
William H. Child *(Chm. Bd. & Chief Exec. Officer)*
Sheldon F. Child *(Pres.)*
Richard R. Turnbow *(V.P.-Fin.)*
Scott L. Hymas *(Treas.)*
Patricia Child *(Sec.)*

Outside Service Firm(s):

Arthur Andersen & Co.*(Auditors)*
36 South State St., Ste. 1600
Salt Lake City, UT 84111
Tel.: 801-533-0820
Fax: 801-534-0550

Snow, Christensen & Martineau*(Legal Firm)*
Salt Lake City, UT

Key Bank*(Major Banking Relationship)*
Salt Lake City, UT

JOHN WILLIAMS & ASSOCIATES, LTD.
180 Harbor Dr., Ste. 228
Sausalito, CA 94965
Tel.: 415-332-3333
Fax: 415-331-8235
Year Founded: 1983
Approx.Billings: $22,645,900
Emp.: 15
Direct Response Lead Generation & Marketing Database Development
John F. Williams *(Chm. Bd., Pres. & New Bus. Contact)*
David Angelvich *(Controller)*
Don Lanman *(V.P., Dir. Database Mktg.)*
Julie LaPlant *(Accountant)*

Computer Systems/Hardware:
Macintosh, IBM

DON E. WILLIAMS CO.
7920 14th St. W.
Rock Island, IL 61201
Tel.: 309-787-8160 **IL**
Fax: 309-787-6886
Year Founded: 1948
Assets: $5,490,286
Liabilities: $2,274,160
Net Worth: $3,216,126
Approx.Sls.: $19,953,474
Emp.: 70
Fiscal Year-end: 12/31/90
Import Export
Distribute Industrial Supplies
S.I.C.: 5085
Don E. Williams *(Chm. Bd., Pres. & Chief Exec. Officer)*
Steve Doellinger *(Exec. V.P.)*
Randall A. Emerson *(V.P.-Mngmt. Information Systems)*
Carl O. Kiefer *(V.P.-Fin., Sec. & Treas.)*
David Schmitz *(V.P.)*
Marvin L. Schrager *(Gen. Counsel)*
Lavern Balk *(Controller)*
Dan Lyphout *(Quality Process Mgr.)*
Principal(s):
Don E. Williams

No. of Mfg. Plants/Facilities: 2
No. of U.S. Offices: 4

Computer Systems/Hardware:
IBM

Outside Service Firm(s):

McGladrey & Pullen*(Auditors)*
Peoria, IL

Molyneaux Insurance, Inc.*(Commercial Insurance Carrier)*
Davenport, IA

Blackwood, Nowinski & Swanson*(Legal Firm)*
Rock Island, IL

MetroBank*(Major Banking Relationship)*
East Moline, IL

Division:

Dewco Milwaukee Sales **(1)**
6235 Industrial Court
Greendale, WI 53129
Tel.: 414-421-2650
Emp.: 15
S.I.C.: 5085

WILLIAMS COMPANY OF ORLANDO, INC.
2301 Silver Star Rd.
Orlando, FL 32804
Tel.: 407-295-2530
Fax: 407-297-0459
Approx.Sls.: $22,000,000
Emp.: 200
General Contractor & Construction Manager
S.I.C.: 1522; 1542; 5039
Bruce E. Williams *(Pres., Chief Exec. Officer & Treas.)*
Adrian G. Hammond *(V.P.)*
Paul L. Jenny *(V.P.)*
H. Jack Judy *(V.P.)*
Alan R. Williams *(V.P. & Sec.)*

Outside Service Firm(s):

Riggs & Cox*(Auditors)*
Orlando, FL

Dean, Mead, Egerton, Bloodworth*(Legal Firm)*
Orlando, FL

Atico Savings Bank*(Major Banking Relationship)*
Orlando, FL

WILLIAMS DISTRIBUTING COMPANY
658 Richmond N.W.
Grand Rapids, MI 49504
Mailing Address:
P.O. Box 2585
Grand Rapids, MI 49504
Tel.: 616-456-1613
Fax: 616-456-8091
Approx.Sls.: $20,000,000
Emp.: 54
Distributor Wholesale Household Appliances, Video Games
S.I.C.: 5064
Robert T. Williams *(Chm. Bd.)*
James C. Williams *(Pres.)*
Robert T. Williams, Jr. *(V.P.-Opers.)*
Michael Koster *(Treas.)*
Principal(s):
Robert T. Williams
James C. Williams
Robert T. Williams, Jr.

Computer Systems/Hardware:
Qantel

Outside Service Firm(s):

Kregel, Raterink, Kingman & Co.*(Auditors)*
Grand Rapids, MI

Damon & Damon*(Legal Firm)*
Grand Rapids, MI

Old Kent Bank*(Major Banking Relationship)*
Grand Rapids, MI

WILLIAMS FOODS INC.
13301 W. 99th St.
Lenexa, KS 66215
Tel.: 913-888-4343
Fax: 913-888-4955
Year Founded: 1937
Approx.Sls.: $18,000,000
Emp.: 60
Fiscal Year-end: 6/30/91
Food Mfg., Seasonings, Sauces, Gravy Mixes, Spices, Fruit Pectin, Indus. Blending of Seasonings
S.I.C.: 2033; 2035; 2099
Conrad Hock, Jr. *(Chm. Bd. & Pres.)*
Jack Sauer *(V.P.-Devel.)*
Edward M. Cox *(Sec.)*

WILLIAMS INTERNATIONAL
2280 W. Maple Rd.
Walled Lake, MI 48390
Mailing Address:
P.O. Box 200
Walled Lake, MI 48088
Tel.: 313-624-5200
Fax: 313-669-1577
Year Founded: 1955
Approx.Sls.: $140,000,000
Emp.: 1,200
Manufacture Jet Engines & Gas Turbines
S.I.C.: 3724
Sam B. Williams *(Pres. & Chief Exec. Officer)*
E. L. Klein *(Exec. V.P. & Chief Oper. Officer)*
Leonard D. Frescoln *(V.P.-Fin. & Admin.)*
Donald Dumas *(Dir.-Indus. Rels.)*

Computer Systems/Hardware:
IBM

Outside Service Firm(s):

Deloitte & Touche*(Auditors)*
200 Renaissance Center, 16th Fl.
Detroit, MI 48243
Tel.: 313-396-3000
Fax: 313-259-8087

N.B.D. Bank, N.A.*(Major Banking Relationship)*
611 Woodward Ave.
Detroit, MI 48226
Tel.: 313-225-1122
Fax: 313-225-3420

WILLIAMS INTERNATIONAL INDUSTRIES, INC.
P.O. Box 1116
Richmond, VA 23208
Year Founded: 1964
Emp.: 125
Holding Company; Heavy Rigging & Hauling; Crane & Construction Equipment Rentals
S.I.C.: 6719; 1629; 7353
John D. Williams, Jr. *(Pres.)*
Gloria A. Martin *(Sec. & Treas.)*

Computer Systems/Hardware:
Prime

Outside Service Firm(s):

Christian, Barton, Epps, Brent & Chappell*(Legal Firm)*
1200 Mutual Bldg.
Richmond, VA 23219
Tel.: 804-644-7851

Subsidiary:

Williams Crane & Rigging, Inc. **(1)**
938 E. 4th St.
Richmond, VA 23208
Tel.: 804-233-9221
Heavy Rigging & Hauling; Crane & Contruction Equip. Rentals
S.I.C.: 1629; 7353
John D. Williams, Jr. *(Pres.)*
Donald D. Nolan, Jr. *(Exec. V.P.)*

MARTINWILLIAMS
ADVERTISING INCORPORATED

MARTIN WILLIAMS ADVERTISING INC.
10 S. Fifth St.
Minneapolis, MN 55402
Tel.: 612-340-0800
Fax: 612-342-9700
Year Founded: 1948
Approx.Billings: $119,000,000
Emp.: 152
David Floren *(Chm. & Chief Exec. Officer)*
Tom Weyl *(Pres. & Chief Creative Officer)*
Dan Woodbury *(Sr. V.P., Dir. Mktg. Services)*
Tim Frojd *(V.P., Chief Fin. Officer)*

WILLIAMS PATENT CRUSHER AND PULVERIZER CO.
2701 N. Broadway
Saint Louis, MO 63102
Tel.: 314-621-3348
Fax: 314-436-2639
Year Founded: 1872
Approx.Sls.: $10,000,000
Emp.: 130
Fiscal Year-end: 4/30/91
Export
Mfr. of Crushing and Grinding Machinery
S.I.C.: 3569
Robert M. Williams *(Pres. & Treas.)*
Robert M. Williams, Jr. *(V.P.)*
David Lambeth *(Supt.)*
Joan Stoecklin *(Mgr.-Adv.)*
Carl Rehmer *(Gen. Mgr.-Sls.)*
Rick Beckett *(Pur. Agent)*

WILLIAMS & ROCKWOOD
307 West 200 South, Ste. 3005
Salt Lake City, UT 84101
Tel.: 801-364-9136
Year Founded: 1987
Approx.Billings: $12,000,000
Emp.: 30
Tim J. Williams *(Pres.)*
Dave Cole *(V.P., Gen. Mgr.)*
Erni Armstrong *(Bus. Mgr.)*

Computer Systems/Hardware:
MacIntosh, NEC PCs, Novell Network

WILLIAMS STEEL & HARDWARE COMPANY
60 28th Ave., N.
Minneapolis, MN 55440-0540
Mailing Address:
P.O. Box 540
Minneapolis, MN 55440-0540
Tel.: 612-588-9800
Fax: 612-588-9875
Year Founded: 1860
Approx.Sls.: $25,000,000
Emp.: 140
Fiscal Year-end: 12/31/90
Import Export
Distribution Of Steel & Industrial Supplies
S.I.C.: 5051; 5085
Corporate Giving Program: Contact Directly for Guidelines
William R. Winter *(Chm. Bd.)*
Kenneth E. Puffer *(Vice Chm.)*
Michael W. McCarthy *(Chief Exec. Officer & Treas.)*
William R. Winter, Jr. *(Pres. & Chief Oper. Officer)*
Jack A. Ocenasek *(Exec. V.P.-Opers.)*
James T. Hess *(V.P.-Sls.)*
Mark Koenig *(Controller)*

Outside Service Firm(s):

Coopers & Lybrand*(Auditors)*
1000 TCF Bldg.
Minneapolis, MN 55402
Tel.: 612-293-2929
Fax: 612-370-9395

Gray, Plant, Mooty, Mooty & Bennett*(Legal Firm)*
3400 City Center, 33 So. 6th St.
Minneapolis, MN 55402
Tel.: 612-343-2800
Fax: 612-830-0270

Norwest Bank Minnesota, N.A.*(Major Banking Relationship)*
6th St. & Marquette Av.
Minneapolis, MN 55479
Tel.: 612-667-1234

Subsidiaries:

Williams Fastener & Supply Co. **(1)**
P.O. Box 74678
Cedar Rapids, IA 52407
Tel.: 319-366-7461
Distributors of Steel Fasteners
S.I.C.: 5072
Deb Hilleshiem *(Mgr.)*

Williams Steel & Supply **(1)**
124 East 24th St.
Dickenson, ND 58601
Tel.: 701-225-4458
Rick Scheeler *(Mgr.)*

WILLIAMS TELEVISION TIME, INC.
1630 21st St.
Santa Monica, CA 90404
Tel.: 213-828-8600
Year Founded: 1987
Approx.Billings: $50,000,000
Emp.: 85
Direct Response Advertising Agency
Kathleen Williams *(Pres. & Chief Exec. Officer)*
Darrell Griffin *(Chief Oper. Officer & Chief Fin. Officer)*
Danny Anz *(Chief Information Officer (Mngmt. Information Systems))*
Steve Howard *(Exec. V.P., Mktg.)*
Louann Stafford *(Sr. V.P., Acct. Services)*
Dana Merola *(Controller)*
Kathy Dellinger *(Dir.-Human Resources)*
Laura Fox *(Dir.-Pub. Rels. & Mktg.)*

WILLIAMS, WHITE & COMPANY
600 Third Ave.
Moline, IL 61265
Tel.: 309-797-7650 **IL**
Fax: 309-797-7655
Year Founded: 1854
Approx.Sls.: $13,000,000
Emp.: 129
Fiscal Year-end: 9/30/90

Export
Machine Hydraulic & Mechanical Presses, Bulldozers, Punches, Shears

S.I.C.: 3542; 3553; 3593; 3599
William A. Getz *(Chm. Bd.)*
Michael V. Cornell *(Pres.)*
David L. Ellis *(V.P.-Engrng.)*
David Thomas *(V.P.-Mfg.)*
Thomas G. Getz *(Treas.)*
Linda K. Wolbers *(Controller)*
Robert C. Crane *(Mgr.-Mktg.)*
Fred E. Morrison *(Mgr.-Sls.)*
David Schnackel *(Mgr.-Estimating)*
John L. Stutz *(Mgr.-Plant)*
Richard Hibrant *(Pur. Agent)*

No. of Mfg. Plants/Facilities: 1
No. of U.S. Offices: 1

Outside Service Firm(s):

Davis, Butterfield & Company*(Auditors)*
Moline, IA

Bozeman, Patton, Neighbour & Noe*(Legal Firm)*
Moline, IA

First National Bank Of Moline*(Major Banking Relationship)*
Moline, IA

WILLIAMS WHITTLE ASSOCIATES, INC.
711 Princess St.
Alexandria, VA 22314
Tel.: 703-836-9222
Fax: 703-836-9267
Year Founded: 1967
Approx.Billings: $20,000,000
Emp.: 27
Healthcare, Real Estate, Automotive, Banking, Retail & Agriculture
S.I.C.: 7311
D. Anderson Williams *(Chm. Bd.)*
Robert L. Whittle *(Pres.)*
Joy Nathan *(Sr. V.P., Pub. Rels.)*
Catherine Seay *(Sr. V.P., Creative Dir.)*
Pam Goodnow *(V.P., Fin & Admin.)*
Jackie Tison *(Dir., Mktg. Services)*

Outside Service Firm(s):

Bruner, Kane & McCarthy*(Auditors)*
Alexandria, VA

Williams Whittle Associates, Inc.—(Continued)

Holden & Co.*(Commercial Insurance Carrier)*
Alexandria, VA

Peter Yelverton, Inc.*(Group Insurer)*
Alexandria, VA

Blankingship & Keith*(Legal Firm)*
Fairfax, VA

First American of Virginia*(Major Banking Relationship)*
Alexandria, VA

Merrill Lynch*(Pension Manager)*
Washington, DC

WILLIAMSON-DICKIE MFG. CO.
319 Lipscomb
Fort Worth, TX 76104
Mailing Address:
P.O. Box 1779,
Ft. Worth, TX 76101
Tel.: 817-336-7201
Fax: 817-336-5183
Year Founded: 1922
Assets: $200,000,000
Liabilities: $140,000,000
Net Worth: $60,000,000
Approx.Sls.: $356,000,000
Emp.: 4,000
Fiscal Year-end: 12/31/90
Import Export
Dickies Clothes for Men & Boys; Apparel Rental; Plastic Film; Laundries
S.I.C.: 2326; 7299
Gail P. Williamson *(Chm. Bd.)*
R. Stephen Lefler *(Pres. & Chief Exec. Officer)*
Hal Bynum *(V.P.-Mfg.)*
C.M. Crane *(V.P.-Sls.)*
Jack L. Marr *(V.P.-Admin.)*
Philip Williamson *(V.P.-Opers.)*
Frank E. Brock *(Sec. & Treas.)*
John K. Morgan *(Controller)*
Kirby Morgan *(Dir.-Data Processing)*
Karina Siepert *(Mgr.-Pur.)*
Caron Nicklas *(Mgr.-Adv.)*

Computer Systems/Hardware:
IBM

Outside Service Firm(s):

Ernst & Young*(Auditors)*
500 Throckmorton St.
Fort Worth, TX 76102
Tel.: 817-335-1900
Fax: 817-335-2728

Division:

Williamson-Dickie Apparel Mfg. Co. **(1)**
509 W. Vickery Blvd.
Fort Worth, TX 76101
Tel.: 800-336-7201
Men's & Boys' Apparel
S.I.C.: 2326; 7299
Gail P. Williamson *(Chm. Bd.)*
R. Stephen Lefler *(Pres.)*

Subsidiaries:

Blessings Corp. **(1)**
45 Knightsbridge Rd.
Piscataway, NJ 08854
Tel.: 908-457-0330
Earnings: $5,644,100
Approx.Sls.: $101,798,200
Fiscal Year-end: 12/31/89
Ivan Becker *(Pres.)*

Dickies Industrial Ware **(1)**
509 W. Vickery Blvd.
Fort Worth, TX 76101
Tel.: 817-336-7941

Ropa Sultana, Inc. **(1)**
KM 183.3 Barrio Algarroba
Mayaguez, PR 00709
Tel.: 809-832-0246

SetloWear, Inc. **(1)**
Indian River Rd.
Orange, CT 06477
Tel.: 203-795-5601
Fax: 203-795-5607

T.D. WILLIAMSON, INC.
8506 E. 61st St.
Tulsa, OK 74133
Mailing Address:
P.O. Box 2299,
Tulsa, OK 74101
Tel.: 918-254-9400 OK
Telex: 49-7494
Fax: 918-254-9474
Year Founded: 1933
Assets: $47,000,000
Liabilities: $19,000,000
Net Worth: $28,000,000
Approx.Sls.: $72,000,000
Emp.: 515
Fiscal Year-end: 12/29/91
Export
Mfg. & Maintenance of Engineered Pipeline Equipment & Plant Piping Systems
S.I.C.: 3494; 3533
A.B. Steen *(Chm Bd.)*
Richard B. Williamson *(Pres. & Chief Exec. Officer)*
Michael J. Hall *(Sr. V.P., Treas., Chief Fin. & Admin. Officer)*
Wade J. Wnuk *(Sr. V.P. & Gen. Mgr.-Western Hemisphere & Asia)*
John L. Hatheway *(Sr. V.P. & Gen. Mgr.-Global Pipeline Services)*
Cornelis Boshuizen *(V.P. & Dir.-Quality Assurance)*
John C. Hamilton *(V.P. & Dir.-Corp. Res. & Devel.)*
Barbara K. Bucholtz *(Sec.)*
Steve Johnson *(Dir.-Corp. Benefits & Risk Mgr.)*
David R. Miller *(Dir.-Human Resources)*
Don Thompson *(Dir.-Personnel)*
Jean-Paul Van Schandevijl *(Mgr.-Belgium)*
Kim R. Stover *(Mgr.-Mktg.)*
Ronald S. Whatley *(Mgr.-Data Processing)*
Robert Shafer *(Pur. Agent)*
Gerald Culhane *(Corp. Accountant & Mgr.-Fin.)*

No. of Mfg. Plants/Facilities: 4
No. of U.S. Offices: 10
No. of Foreign Offices: 4

Outside Service Firm(s):

Coopers & Lybrand*(Auditors)*
1400 Mid-Continent Tower
Tulsa, OK 74103
Tel.: 918-596-8200
Fax: 918-596-8300

Johnson & Higgins*(Commercial Insurance Carrier)*
Tulsa, OK

Hall, Estill, Hardwick, Gable, Golden & Nelson*(Legal Firm)*
One Williams Center, 4100 Bank of Oklahoma Tower
Tulsa, OK 74172
Tel.: 918-588-2400

The Fourth National Bank of Tulsa*(Major Banking Relationship)*
Tulsa, OK

Texas Commerce Bank*(Major Banking Relationship)*
2200 Ross Ave.
Dallas, TX 75266

Dalton, Greiner, Hartman, Maher & Co.*(Pension Manager)*
630 Fifth Ave., Ste. 3425
New York, NY 10111
Tel.: 212-459-0500

Division:

Urethane Products **(1)**
10727 E. 55th Place
Tulsa, OK 74145
Tel.: 918-664-7070
Fax: 918-664-7091
Emp.: 14
Export
Manufacturer of Urethane Products
S.I.C.: 2821
Doug Reiss *(Mgr.-Piping Systems)*

Subsidiaries:

TDW Building Corporation **(1)**
8506 E. 61st St.
Tulsa, OK 74133
Tel.: 918-254-9400 (100%)
Fax: 918-254-9474
Corporate TDW Building
S.I.C.: 6512
Richard B. Williamson *(Pres.)*

TDW Foreign Sales Corp. **(1)**
1A Gallows Bay
Christiansted, VI 00820
Tel.: 809-778-8588 (100%)
Foreign Sales Corp.
S.I.C.: 5051
Richard B. Williamson *(Pres.)*

TDW Services, Inc. **(1)**
6801 S. 65th West Ave.
Tulsa, OK 74101
Tel.: 918-446-1941 (100%)
Fax: 918-446-0398
Emp.: 67
Maintenance & Inspection of Pipeline & Plant Piping Systems; Corporate Management Office
S.I.C.: 1389
John L. Hatheway *(Gen. Mgr.)*

Plants:

Mid-South Service Center **(2)**
13419 S. Choctaw
Baton Rouge, LA 70815
Tel.: 504-272-3021
Emp.: 6
Services for Maintenance & Inspection of Pipeline & Plant Piping Systems
S.I.C.: 1389
Steve M. Jacob *(Mgr.)*

Concord Service Ctr. **(2)**
2322-K Bates Ave.
Concord, CA 94524
Tel.: 415-687-2484
Fax: 415-687-8346
Emp.: 8
Services for Maintenance & Inspection of Pipeline & Plant Piping Systems
S.I.C.: 1389
Tom Harmon *(Mgr.)*

Denver Service Center/INTEC **(2)**
1805 East 58th Ave., Unit J
Denver, CO 80216
Tel.: 303-292-9662
Emp.: 2
S.I.C.: 1389

East Coast Service Ctr. **(2)**
250 Corporate Blvd., Suite D
Newark, DE 19702
Tel.: 302-733-0974
Fax: 302-733-0975
Emp.: 1
Services for Maintenance & Inspection of Pipeline & Plant Piping Systems
S.I.C.: 1389
Gary W. Bishop *(Mgr.)*

Florida Service Center **(2)**
P.O. Box 559
Perry, FL 32347-9998
Tel.: 904-584-8686
Emp.: 1
S.I.C.: 1389

Indiana Service Center/Satellite Location **(2)**
4325 N. Mayflower Rd., South Lake Center, Ste. 105
South Bend, IN 46628
Tel.: 219-272-1768
Emp.: 8
Services for Maintenance & Inspection of Pipeline & Plant Piping Systems
S.I.C.: 1389
John Montgomery *(Mgr.-Mid Continent Opers.)*

Gulf Coast Service Center **(2)**
P.O. Box 1429, 2308 W. Fairmont Pkwy.
La Porte, TX 77572
Tel.: 713-470-0791
Fax: 713-470-2282
Emp.: 10
Services for Maintenance & Inspection of Pipeline & Plant Piping Systems
S.I.C.: 1389
John L. Montgomery *(Mgr.)*

Global Pipeline Surveys **(2)**
2929 W. 21st St.
Tulsa, OK 74107
Tel.: 918-592-0535
Fax: 918-582-1423
Emp.: 16
Internal Inspection of Pipelines
S.I.C.: 1389
John L. Hatheway *(Mgr.)*
Joe L. Bartlett *(Mgr.-Kaliper Services)*
Jack Rankin *(Mgr.-FLAWSONIC Corrosion Inspection Services)*
Michael M. Goodson *(Mgr.-Opers.)*

Mid-Continent Service Center **(2)**
6801 S. 65th West Ave.
Tulsa, OK 74131
Tel.: 918-446-1941
Fax: 918-446-0398
Emp.: 15
Services for Maintenance & Inspection of Pipeline & Plant Piping Systems
S.I.C.: 1389
John L. Montgomery *(Mgr.)*

TDW Delaware, Inc. **(1)**
1100 N. Market St., Ste. 780
Wilmington, DE 19809
Tel.: 302-651-8079
Business Services
S.I.C.: 7389
A. B. Steen *(Pres.)*

TDW Trading, Inc. **(1)**
1100 N. Market St., Ste.780
Wilmington, DE 19801
Business Services
S.I.C.: 7389
A. B. Steen *(Pres.)*

Williamson International Corp. **(1)**
8506 E. 61st St.
Tulsa, OK 74133
Tel.: 918-254-9400
Fax: 918-254-9474
Emp.: 17
Coordinates Intl. Activities
S.I.C.: 8742
Richard B. Williamson *(Pres.)*

Non-U.S. Holdings:

T.D. Williamson S.A. **(1)**
6 rue du Travail 1400
Nivelles, Brabant Belgium
Tel.: 32-67/21-08-21 (100%)
Telex: 57403
Fax: 32-67/21-08-28
Approx.Sls.: $12,000,000
Emp.: 91
Mfr. Engineered Pipeline Equipment; Maintenance & Inspection of Pipeline & Plant Piping Systems
S.I.C.: 3494
Alain M. Roussel *(Plant Mgr.)*

T.D. Williamson (U.K.) Ltd. **(1)**
Faraday Rd., Dorcan Way
Swindon, Wiltshire SN3 5HF, United Kingdom
Tel.: 44-793/24971 (100%)
Telex: 851-449-351
Fax: 44-793/514971
Approx.Sls.: $4,000,000
Emp.: 33
Mfr. Engineered Pipeline Equipment; Maintenance & Inspection of Pipeline & Plant Piping Systems
S.I.C.: 1389; 3494

WILLIS CASE HARWOOD, INC.
3411 Office Park Dr.
Dayton, OH 45439
Tel.: 513-299-7394
Fax: 513-299-9290
Year Founded: 1918
Approx.Billings: $12,000,000
Emp.: 24
Lewis M. Bonadies *(Pres. & Chief Exec. Officer)*

Larry E. Furrow *(Sr. V.P., Dir.-Bus. Opers.)*
Deborah Sibert *(V.P., Dir.-Pub. Impressions)*
Patricia Butler *(Controller)*

WILLMAR MANUFACTURING
Industrial Park
Willmar, MN 56201
Mailing Address:
P.O. Box 957
Willmar, MN 56201
Tel.: 612-235-0767
Fax: 612-235-2516
Approx.Sls.: $10,000,000
Emp.: 150
Mfr. of Bulk Fertilizer Equipment; Bulk Feed Bodies; Salt & Sand Spreaders for Ice Control
S.I.C.: 3523
L. Faber *(Pres.)*
Rex Guthaund *(Gen. Sls. Mgr.)*

Subsidiary:

Henderson Mfg. **(1)**
P.O. Box 40
Manchester, IA 52057
Tel.: 319-927-2828
S.I.C.: 3523
Julian L. Pugh *(Gen. Mgr.)*

WILLOUGHBY'S
110 W. 32nd St., 6th & 7th Aves.
New York, NY 10001
Tel.: 212-564-1600
Fax: 212-790-1921
Year Founded: 1989
Approx.Sls.: $25,514,000
Emp.: 120
Fiscal Year-end: 1/31/91
Retail Cameras, Binoculars, Camera Accessories, Audio Equipment & Home & Business Computers
S.I.C.: 5946; 5999; 5734; 5731; 5043
Haim Anfankar *(Pres. & Gen. Mgr.)*
John Stiles *(V.P., Admin. & Controller)*
Steven Welbo *(Dir.-Pur.)*

WILLS AND EVANS
280 Madison Ave.
New York, NY 10016
Tel.: 212-340-3800
Fax: 212-725-1276
Year Founded: 1983
Approx.Billings: $47,380,000
Emp.: 43
Integrated Advertising Programs both in the U.S. and Internationally
R. Scott Wills *(Pres.)*
Benjamin Evans *(Exec. V.P. & Creative Dir.)*
Richard Dale *(Exec. V.P. & Mng. Dir.)*
Neil Levine *(Controller)*

WILLS GROUP, INC.
U.S. Rte. 301
La Plata, MD 20646
Mailing Address:
P.O. Box E
La Plata, MD 20646
Tel.: 301-934-8101
Fax: 301-932-3668
Emp.: 800
Petroleum Products, Convenience Store Products
S.I.C.: 5172; 5149
J. Blacklock Wills *(Chm. Bd.)*
J. Blacklock Wills, Jr. *(Pres.)*
Charles F. Boyers *(Sr. V.P., Admin. & Sec.)*

Outside Service Firm(s):

Coopers & Lybrand*(Auditors)*
Washington, DC

Mudd, Mudd, & Fitzgerald*(Legal Firm)*
La Plata, MD

Mercantile-Safe Deposit & Trust Co.*(Major Banking Relationship)*
Baltimore, MD

WILLSON SAFETY PRODUCTS
2nd & Washington Sts.
Reading, PA 19601
Mailing Address:
P.O. Box 622,
Reading, PA 19603-0622
Tel.: 215-376-6161
Approx.Sls.: $24,000,000
Emp.: 200
Fiscal Year-end: 12/31/92
Export
Willson Personal Safety Equipment For Eye, Hearing & Head Protection
S.I.C.: 3851; 3842
V. Donald McCroskey *(Pres.)*
Roger W. Gehring *(Sr. V.P. & Gen. Mgr.)*
Rodney M. Fogelman *(Personnel Dir.)*
John C. Gillespie *(Mktg. Dir.)*
Joseph J. Reimer *(Dir.-Sls.)*
Carl Annas *(Consumer Sls. Mgr.)*
Ingemar Olsson *(Indus. Sls. Mgr.)*
Christine B. Ciabattoni *(Mktg. Services Supvr.)*

WILMORITE INC.
1265 Scottsville Rd.
Rochester, NY 14624
Tel.: 716-464-9400
Fax: 716-328-1784
Real Estate Developer
S.I.C.: 6552
William F. Wilmot *(Chm. Bd.)*
Vincent J. Maida *(Vice Chm.)*
Thomas C. Wilmot *(Pres. & Chief Exec. Officer)*
James Backus *(V.P.-Engrng. & Construction)*
Albert E. Cashette *(V.P.-Leasing)*
David M. Jacobstein *(V.P.-Fin.)*
Ronald A. Cocquyt *(Sec. & Treas.)*
John R. Kraus *(Dir.-Mktg.)*

WILSEY BENNETT CO.
2351 Powell St., Ste. 500
San Francisco, CA 94133
Mailing Address:
P.O. Box 3532,
San Francisco, CA 94119
Tel.: 415-391-4150 **CA**
Fax: 415-433-0690
Sales Range: $100-499 Million
Real Estate Development & Investment, Floral Transportation
S.I.C.: 6719; 6552; 4213
Michael W. Wilsey *(Chm. Bd. & Pres.)*
William Anderson *(V.P. & Treas.)*
Doug Toovey *(Controller)*
Alfred S. Wilsey, Jr. *(Sec.)*

Computer Systems/Hardware:
IBM System 34

Outside Service Firm(s):

Deloitte & Touche*(Auditors)*
50 Fremont St.
San Francisco, CA 94105-2230
Tel.: 415-393-4300
Fax: 415-227-0452

O'Melveny & Myers*(Legal Firm)*
San Francisco, CA

Divisions:

Air Fresh Trucking **(1)**
2351 Powell St.
San Francisco, CA 94133
Tel.: 415-391-4150
Transport of Fresh Cut Flowers Nationwide
S.I.C.: 4213
Michael W. Wilsey *(Pres.)*

Wilsey Bennett Real Estate Division **(1)**
2351 Powell St.
San Francisco, CA 94133
Tel.: 415-391-4150
Real Estate Development & Investment
S.I.C.: 6552
Alfred S. Wilsey, Jr. *(Pres.)*

Subsidiary:

Wilsey Foods, Inc. **(1)**
633 S. Mission
Los Angeles, CA 90023
Tel.: 213-265-7100
S.I.C.: 2079
Jack Davis *(Pres.)*

WILSHIRE NEWPORT INC.
4002 W. Burbank Blvd.
Burbank, CA 91505
Tel.: 818-845-6200
Year Founded: 1980
Approx.Billings: $18,600,000
Emp.: 39
High Tech & Financial Services
John Mooers *(Pres.)*
Robert Mooers *(Exec. V.P.)*
Martin Olivero *(Sr. V.P., Client Services & Acct. Exec.)*
Stella Atkinson *(Pub. Rels.)*
Stephanie Tapp *(Librarian)*

JIM WILSON & ASSOCIATES
4121 Carmichael Rd., Ste. 501
Montgomery, AL 36106
Mailing Address:
P.O. Box 4480
Montgomery, AL 36103-4480
Tel.: 205-260-2500
Year Founded: 1975
Sales Range: $100-499 Million
Emp.: 3,000
Holding Company; Real Estate Development; 15 Malls in the United States
S.I.C.: 6552; 6719
Jim Wilson *(Pres.)*
Jim Wilson, III *(Exec. V.P.)*
Carl Bartlett *(V.P.)*

Outside Service Firm(s):

KPMG Peat Marwick*(Auditors)*
1200 Financial Center
Birmingham, AL 35203
Tel.: 205-324-2495

Subsidiary:

Diversified Products Corporation **(1)**
309 Williamson Ave.
Opelika, AL 36803
Tel.: 205-749-9001
Approx.Sls.: $150,000,000
Emp.: 1,635
Mfr. & Distr. Physical Fitness Equip., Sporting Goods
S.I.C.: 3949; 5091
Stephen J. O'Brien *(Pres. & Chief Exec. Officer)*
Dick Jenkins *(Sr. V.P.-Fin.)*
Ira Silberman *(Sr. V.P.)*
Paul Chamblee *(V.P.-Mfg.)*
Rick Himmer *(V.P.-Trucking)*
Michael Murphy *(V.P.-Personnel)*
Jim England *(Dir.-Mktg. & Sls.)*
Gerald Nix *(Mgr.-Mktg. Services)*

THE H. W. WILSON CO.
950 University Ave.
Bronx, NY 10452
Tel.: 718-588-8400
Tel.: 800-367-6770
Fax: 718-538-2716
Year Founded: 1898
Approx.Sls.: $25,000,000
Emp.: 520
Fiscal Year-end: 4/30/91
Publishers Indexes & Reference Works
S.I.C.: 2731; 2741
Leo M. Weins *(Pres. & Treas.)*
Bruce R. Carrick *(V.P. & Editor Gen. Publications)*
George I. Lewicky *(V.P. & Dir.-Indexing Services)*
Frank W. Miller *(V.P.-Mktg. & Sls.)*
Harold Regan *(V.P.-Personnel & Admin.)*
James Phelan *(Controller)*
Nancy Schwartz *(Dir.-Adv. & Promo.)*
Carol Unger *(Asst. Dir.-Personnel Admin.)*

Outside Service Firm(s):

Sullivan & Cromwell*(Legal Firm)*
125 Broad St.
New York, NY 10004
Tel.: 212-558-4000

Chase Manhattan Bank, N.A.*(Major Banking Relationship)*
One Chase Manhattan Plaza
New York, NY 10081
Tel.: 212-552-2222
Tel.: 800-526-0801
Fax: 212-552-7175

Subsidiary:

The H.W. Wilson Co. **(1)**
955 Massachusetts Ave.
Cambridge, MA 02139
Tel.: 617-492-0800
S.I.C.: 2731; 2741

WILSON, HORNE, MCCLELLAND & GRAY, INC.
400 Interstate North Pkwy., Ste. 900
Atlanta, GA 30339
Tel.: 404-984-9464
Year Founded: 1982
Approx.Billings: $12,075,000
Emp.: 15
Business-to-Business, Healthcare & Consumer Adv.
Steve Sherry *(Pres.)*
Bob Martinez *(Controller)*

WILSON INDUSTRIES INC.
1301 Conti St.
Houston, TX 77002
Mailing Address:
P.O. Box 1492
Houston, TX 77251
Tel.: 713-237-3700 **TX**
Fax: 713-237-8539
Year Founded: 1921
Assets: $111,200,000
Liabilities: $40,200,000
Net Worth: $71,000,000
Approx.Sls.: $300,000,000
Emp.: 736
Fiscal Year-end: 12/31/90
Export
Distributor of Fabricated Metal Products & Machinery
S.I.C.: 3533; 3561; 3593; 5084; 7359
Wallace S. Wilson *(Chm. Bd., Pres. & Chief Exec. Officer)*
R.W. Barefield *(Sr. V.P.)*
Robert Brown *(V.P.-Fin.)*
G.W. Gist *(V.P.-Admin.)*
Humberto G. Kuhn *(Sec. & Legal Counsel)*
Gary Nelson *(Controller)*
Elizabeth Ann Gray *(Dir.-Personnel)*
James E. Musgrove *(Gen. Mgr.-Intl. Dept.)*

Wilson Industries Inc.—(Continued)

Walter Lueck *(Mgr.-Data Processing)*
Bill D. Peterson *(Mgr.-Quality Control)*

No. of U.S. Offices: 56
No. of Foreign Offices: 3

Computer Systems/Hardware:
Burroughs 1990

Outside Service Firm(s):

Arthur Andersen & Co.*(Auditors)*
711 Louisiana, Ste. 1300
Houston, TX 77002-2323
Tel.: 713-237-2793

Connecticut General Life Insurance Co.*(Group Insurer)*
P.O. Box 2975,
Hartford, CT 06104
Tel.: 203-726-6000

First City National Bank*(Major Banking Relationship)*
Houston, TX

Texas Commerce Bank*(Major Banking Relationship)*
P.O. Box 2558
Houston, TX 77001
Tel.: 713-236-4646

Subsidiary:

Houston Engineers **(1)**
P.O. Box 567, 1710 Burnett St.
Houston, TX 77026
Tel.: 713-237-3050
Fax: 713-228-4227
Emp.: 158
Fishing Jars for Drilling
S.I.C.: 3533
Dwight E. Beach *(Pres.)*
John D. Crooks *(V.P.-Intl.)*
Richard Killingsworth *(V.P.-Domestic Opers.)*
William J. Roberts *(V.P.-Mktg.)*

Non-U.S. Holding:

Wilson Supply International (U.K.) Ltd. **(1)**
Oak House, London Rd.
Sevenoaks, Kent TN13 1BL, United Kingdom
Tel.: 0732 459011 (100%)
Telex: 95638 WILSON G
Fax: 0732-457340
Roy Airey *(Gen. Mgr.)*

Branches:

Wilson Supply International (U.K.) Ltd. **(2)**
Great Yarmouth Marine Base South Denes Rd.,
Yarmouth, Norfolk United Kingdom
Tel.: 0493 57344

Wilson Supply International (U.K.) Ltd. **(2)**
40 Abbotswell Rd. Tulles,
Aberdeen, United Kingdom
Tel.: 0224 872811

KEMMONS WILSON COMPANIES
1629 Winchester Rd.
Memphis, TN 38116
Tel.: 901-346-8800
Fax: 901-396-3570
Year Founded: 1977
Emp.: 3,600
General Contractor of Small Office Buildings & Shopping Complexes; Developer, Owner & Manager of Commercial & Residential Properties; Hotel Properties, Operates Commercial Real Estate, Banking
S.I.C.: 1541; 6512; 6552; 6513; 6035
Kemmons Wilson, Sr. *(Chm. Bd. & Owner)*
Spence Wilson *(Pres.)*
Robert Wilson *(Exec. V.P.)*
Kemmons Wilson, Jr. *(Exec. V.P.)*
John Pettey *(Treas. & Chief Fin. Officer)*
R.E. Wallin *(Gen. Counsel)*
Bill Batt *(Controller)*

Outside Service Firm(s):

Scott, Branim & Blythe*(Auditors)*
Memphis, TN

Martin, Tate, Morrow & Marston, P.C.*(Legal Firm)*
Union Planters Natl. Bank Bldg.
Memphis, TN 38103
Tel.: 901-525-5881

Union Planters National Bank*(Major Banking Relationship)*
P.O. Box 387,
Memphis, TN 38147
Tel.: 901-523-6865
Fax: 901-523-6490

Subsidiary:

Federal Savings Bank **(1)**
524 Garrison Ave.
Fort Smith, AR 72901
Tel.: 501-782-8901
Fax: 501-782-0094
Emp.: 130
Savings & Loan Association
S.I.C.: 6035
Jerry Vest *(Pres.)*
Dean Hudson *(Sr. V.P. & Treas.)*
Rick Haggard *(Sr. V.P.-Comml. Loans)*
Randy McCullers *(V.P. & Controller)*
Riley Jackson *(V.P.-Mktg., Pur. & Adv.)*
Gary Newton *(V.P.-Consumer Loans)*

WILSON PRODUCTS CO.
1811 W. 1700 So.
Salt Lake City, UT 84104
Tel.: 801-972-5633
Fax: 801-975-0915
Approx.Sls.: $12,000,000
Emp.: 150
Fiscal Year-end: 10/31/91
Export
Mfr. & Distributor Mexican Foods; Lynn Wilson's
S.I.C.: 2032
Lynn R. Wilson *(Chm. Bd.)*
David Wilson *(Pres. & Gen. Mgr.)*
Larry Kramer *(V.P.-Sls. & Adv. Mgr.)*
Brad Spence *(Sec.)*
Clara Hickam *(Mgr.-Personnel)*
John Holton *(Mgr.-Mfg.)*
Fonda Sperry *(Mgr.-Quality Control)*
Trent Bake *(Dir.-Pur.)*

Computer Systems/Hardware:
ATT WS386-25

WILSON PUGH INC.
Highway 165 South
Portland, AR 71663
Tel.: 501-737-2251
Fax: 501-737-2335
Approx.Sls.: $100,000,000
Emp.: 15
Cotton Gin & Fertilizer Plant
S.I.C.: 0724
George Pine *(Chm. Bd.)*
Craig Shackelford *(Pres. & Chief Exec. Officer)*
Gay Tipps *(Treas. & Chief Fin. Officer)*

Computer Systems/Hardware:
IBM System 36

Outside Service Firm(s):

Ralph McQueen & Co.*(Auditors)*
Dermot, AR

Arkansas Blue Cross & Blue Shield, Inc.*(Group Insurer)*
Little Rock, AR

Wilmot State Bank*(Major Banking Relationship)*
Wilmot, AR

RALPH C. WILSON ENTERPRISES
400 Renaissance Center, Ste. 2140
Detroit, MI 48243
Tel.: 313-259-9100
Fax: 313-259-9101
Emp.: 1,300
Television Broadcasting Stations, Manufactured General Hardware, General Contractor, Highway, Street & Airport Runway Construction
S.I.C.: 1381; 4833; 6411; 3429; 1611
Ralph C. Wilson, Jr. *(Chm. Bd. & Pres.)*
Jeffrey C. Littmann *(Chief Fin. Officer & V.P.)*
David N. Olsen *(Exec. V.P.)*
P. Jane Wright *(Sec.)*

Outside Service Firm(s):

Arthur Andersen & Co.*(Auditors)*
One Intl. Place, 100 Oliver St.
Boston, MA 02110
Tel.: 617-330-4000
Fax: 617-439-9731

Comerica Bank*(Major Banking Relationship)*
211 W. Fort St.
Detroit, MI 48226
Tel.: 313-222-3300

Subsidiaries:

Highwood Service, Inc. **(1)**
400 Renaissance Court
Detroit, MI 48243
Tel.: 313-259-9100
Boarding Services For Racing & Non-racing Horses, Automotive Stampings, Television Translator Station
S.I.C.: 0752; 3465; 4833
Ralph C. Wilson, Jr. *(Chm. Bd. & Pres.)*
David N. Olsen *(Exec. V.P.)*
Jeffrey C. Littman *(Chief Fin. Officer)*
P. Jane Wright *(Sec.)*

Inland Tool & Manufacturing, Inc. **(1)**
20263 HooverRd.
Detroit, MI 48205
Tel.: 313-372-1400
Approx.Sls.: $35,000,000
Emp.: 400
Original Auto Parts
S.I.C.: 3714
Daniel Kass *(Acting Pres.)*
J.M. Swink *(Controller)*

WILSON SCULLEY ASSOCIATES
12400 Olive Blvd., Ste. 545
Saint Louis, MO 63141
Tel.: 314-434-1870
Fax: 314-434-1219
Year Founded: 1983
Approx.Billings: $15,000,000
Emp.: 14
Direct Mktg. & Sls. Promo.
Valarie M. Wilson *(Chm. & Chief Exec. Officer)*

WILTEL COMMUNICATIONS SYSTEMS, INC.
(Div. of Williams Telecommunications Group, Inc.)
8665 New Trails Dr.
The Woodlands, TX 77381
Tel.: 713-364-5000
Fax: 713-364-5956
Approx.Sls.: $280,000,000
Emp.: 1,700
Fiscal Year-end: 12/31/91
Telecommunications Equipment Sales & Service
S.I.C.: 5065
Ed Lavin, Jr. *(Chief Exec. Officer)*
Henry C. (Harry) Hirsch *(Pres. & Chief Oper. Officer)*
Tom Elliott *(Sr. V.P.-Sls. & Mktg.)*
Gary Woodrow *(Dir.-Mktg.)*

WILTON CORPORATION
300 S. Hicks
Palatine, IL 60067
Tel.: 708-934-6000
Fax: 708-934-6730
Approx.Sls.: $65,000,000
Emp.: 475
Fiscal Year-end: 4/30/91
Import Export
Mfr. Vises, C-Clamps, Work Positioner Tools, Metalworking & Woodworking Machinery, Packaging Products
S.I.C.: 3423; 3429; 3541; 3546; 3549; 3553; 5072; 5084; 3523; 2672; 3569
Alex J. Vogl *(Chm. Bd. & Pres.)*
Charles Vogl *(V.P., Treas. & Pres.-Winchester Grp.)*
James Falduto *(V.P. & Gen. Mgr.-Tools)*
Ernest E. Torkilsen *(V.P. & Gen. Mgr.-Machinery Div.)*
Walter Guyer *(V.P.-Fin.)*
John T. Sisul *(V.P.-Human Resources)*
James Kulbeda *(Dir.-Mktg.-Indus. Prods. Group)*
John J. Cimaglia *(Adv. Mgr.-Indus. Prods. Group)*

Computer Systems/Hardware:
IBM

Outside Service Firm(s):

KPMG Peat Marwick*(Auditors)*
Peat Marwick Plaza, 303 E. Wacker Dr.
Chicago, IL 60601
Tel.: 312-938-1000

Lord, Bissell & Brook*(Legal Firm)*
115 S. LaSalle St.
Chicago, IL 60603
Tel.: 312-443-0700

LaSalle National Bank*(Major Banking Relationship)*
135 S. LaSalle St., Rm.260
Chicago, IL 60603

Divisions:

Anderson Products **(1)**
1040 Southbridge St.
Worcester, MA 01610
Tel.: 508-755-6100
Fax: 508-755-4694
Emp.: 100
Fiscal Year-end: 4/30/91
Export
Mfr. Industrial Power Brushes, Saws & Abrasives
S.I.C.: 3624; 3291; 3425; 3991; 3541; 3553
Scott H. Curtis *(Product Application Mgr.)*
Michael C. Pervier *(Plant Supt.)*
Joseph Lavin *(Pur. Agent)*
Lenice Martel *(Human Resources Admin.)*

Wilton Engineered Products Div. **(1)**
300 S. Hicks Rd.
Palatine, IL 60067
Tel.: 708-934-6000

Wilton Machinery Div. **(1)**
300 S. Hicks Rd.
Palatine, IL 60067
Tel.: 708-934-6000

Wilton Packaging Div. **(1)**
300 S. Hicks Rd.
Palatine, IL 60067
Tel.: 708-934-6000

Wilton Tool Div. **(1)**
300 S. Hicks Rd.
Palatine, IL 60067
Tel.: 708-934-6000
James Falduto *(Gen. Mgr.)*

WILTON INDUSTRIES, INC.
2240 W. 75th St.
Woodridge, IL 60517
Tel.: 708-963-7100 **DE**
Fax: 708-963-7299
Approx.Sls.: $90,000,000
Emp.: 500
Fiscal Year-end: 7/31/91

Import
Import, Manufacture & Distribution of Consumer Products; Baking & Decorating Products: Copco & Rowoco Fashion Cookware & Kitchenware; The Weston Gallery: Upscale Picture Frames; Operation of Let Them Eat Cake Bakeries
S.I.C.: 5023; 5961; 2051
Vincent A. Naccarato *(Chm. Bd., Pres. & Chief Exec. Officer)*
Ronald P. Zenner *(Exec. V.P. & Chief Oper. Officer)*
Bruce A. Campbell *(Chief Fin. Officer)*
Marvin G. Oakes *(V.P.-Mktg.)*
Zella Junkin *(Dir.-Pub. Rels.)*
Ruth Ann Miller *(Dir.-Personnel Training & Devel.)*
Robert Ory *(Dir.-Pur.)*

Outside Service Firm(s):

Deloitte & Touche*(Auditors)*
Two Prudential Plaza, 180 N. Stetson
Chicago, IL 60601
Tel.: 312-946-2039

Coffield, Ungaretti & Harris*(Legal Firm)*
3500 Three First National Plaza
Chicago, IL 60602
Tel.: 312-977-4400

American National Bank & Trust Company of Chicago*(Major Banking Relationship)*
33 N. LaSalle St.
Chicago, IL 60602
Tel.: 312-661-5000
Fax: 312-661-6417

Bankers Trust Co.*(Major Banking Relationship)*
233 S. Wacker Dr., Ste. 5200
Chicago, IL 60606

Subsidiaries:

Copco **(1)**
2240 W. 75th St.
Woodridge, IL 60517
Tel.: 708-963-7100
Mfr. of Cookware & Kitchenware
S.I.C.: 3269; 3469

Let Them Eat Cake **(1)**
4900 W. 25th
Cicero, IL 60650
Tel.: 708-863-4200
Bakery Stores
S.I.C.: 2051; 5461
Stephen Miller *(Pres.)*

Rowoco **(1)**
2240 W. 75th St.
Woodridge, IL 60517
Tel.: 708-963-7100
Mfr. of Cookware & Kitchenware
S.I.C.: 3263; 3269; 3469
Vincent Naccarato *(Pres.)*

Weston Gallery **(1)**
2240 W. 75th St.
Woodridge, IL 60517
Tel.: 708-963-7100
Mfr. of Upscale Metal & Wood Picture Frames
S.I.C.: 2499

WINCHELL MARKETING
1315 Cherry St.
Philadelphia, PA 19107
Tel.: 215-568-1770
Fax: 215-496-3721
Year Founded: 1968
Approx.Billings: $11,350,000
Emp.: 12
Business-to-Business Adv.
Al Spiotta *(Admin. & Art Dir.)*

WINCUP
(Formerly Scott Containers Products Group, Inc.)
7980 W. Buckeye Rd.
Phoenix, AZ 85043
Tel.: 800-292-2877
Fax: 800-628-1070
Sales Range: $10-19 Million
Manufacturing Plastic Products
S.I.C.: 2676; 3086
Michael Kennedy *(Pres.)*
Andy Farina *(Chief Fin. Officer)*
Don Drushel *(Dir.-Pur.)*
Rich Husinger *(Dir.-Sls.)*
John McKelvey *(Dir.-Human Resources)*
Mark Suihus *(Dir.-Data Processing)*

WINDART HOLDING INC.
9101 Perkins St.
Pico Rivera, CA 90660
Tel.: 213-723-6301 **DE**
Fax: 310-949-1386
Year Founded: 1989
Import Export
Holding Company
S.I.C.: 6719
Allen J. Osherow *(Chm. Bd. & Pres.)*

Outside Service Firm(s):

Clumeck, Stern, Phillips & Schwartz*(Auditors)*
15910 Ventura Blvd., Ste. 1633
Encino, CA 91436

Sander A. Kessler & Associates*(Commercial Insurance Carrier)*
Los Angeles, CA

Al Gundell*(Group Insurer)*
Bel Air, CA

Security Pacific Corporation*(Major Banking Relationship)*
Security Pacific Plaza
Los Angeles, CA 90071
Tel.: 213-345-6211
Fax: 213-625-0809

Subsidiary:

Windsor Art Products, Inc. **(1)**
9101 Perkins St.
Pico Rivera, CA 90660
Tel.: 310-723-6301
Fax: 310-949-1386
Approx.Sls.: $22,000,000
Emp.: 250
Fiscal Year-end: 1/ 1/91
Import Export
Computer Systems/Hardware:
HP 3000
Framed Pictures & Mirrors
S.I.C.: 3999
Allen J. Osherow *(Chm. Bd. & Pres.)*
Morris Waldman *(Controller)*
Kathy Skoien *(Pur. Agent)*
Peter Globerson *(Sec.)*
Pauline Rashella *(Mgr.-Design)*
John Jansen *(Plant Mgr.)*

WINDEMULLER ELECTRIC INC.
4685 Spartan Industrial Dr.
Grandville, MI 49418
Mailing Address:
P.O. Box 933,
Grandville, MI 49468-0933
Tel.: 616-538-6440 **MI**
Fax: 616-538-5885
Year Founded: 1954
Assets: $4,300,000
Liabilities: $2,200,000
Net Worth: $2,100,000
Approx.Sls.: $15,000,000
Emp.: 135
Fiscal Year-end: 12/31/88
Electrical Contractor
S.I.C.: 1731
Edward Windemuller *(Pres.)*
Mark Windemuller *(V.P.)*
Michael Windemuller *(V.P.)*
J. Lee Murphy *(Sec.)*
Charles Alles *(Treas.)*

Outside Service Firm(s):

Kregel, Raterink, Kingman & Co.*(Auditors)*
Grand Rapids, MI

Miller, Johnson, Snell & Cummisky*(Legal Firm)*
Grand Rapids, MI

Byron Center State Bank*(Major Banking Relationship)*
2475-84th St.
Byron Center, MI 49315

WINDERMERE COMMUNICATIONS, INC.
301 City Line Ave.
Bala-Cynwyd, PA 19004
Tel.: 215-664-5550
Fax: 215-664-1436
Year Founded: 1976
Approx.Billings: $17,400,000
Emp.: 23
Pharmaceutical & Healthcare Communications
Louis E. Starr, Jr. *(Pres.)*

THE WINDHAM COMPANY
627 E. Government St.
Pensacola, FL 32501
Mailing Address:
P.O. Box 12587,
Pensacola, FL 32573
Tel.: 904-433-4693 **FL**
Fax: 904-433-4777
Year Founded: 1973
Approx.Sls.: $39,500,000
Emp.: 27
Motel, Hotel, & Condominium Development & Management
S.I.C.: 7011
Robert T. Windham, Sr. *(Chm. Bd., Pres. & Chief Exec. Officer)*
LaJuan Redman *(Exec. V.P.-Admin.)*

No. of U.S. Offices: 1

Computer Systems/Hardware:
IBM System 34 & 2100

Outside Service Firm(s):

Frank Hughes*(Auditors)*
Pensacola, FL

Shell, Fleming Davis & Menge*(Legal Firm)*
Pensacola, FL

Bank of Pensacola*(Major Banking Relationship)*
Pensacola, FL

WINDMILL HOLDINGS CORP.
801 Montgomery St.
San Francisco, CA 94133
Tel.: 415-982-3019 **CA**
Holding Company: Food Processing, Flour & Grains, Mixes & Pet Food
S.I.C.: 2083; 6719; 2041
Ian R. Wilson *(Chm. Bd., Pres., & Chief Exec. Officer)*
Ray Chung *(Exec. V.P., Chief Fin. Officer & Treas.)*
Lyn Hollon *(Dir.-Admin. & Corp. Sec.)*
M. Laurie Cummings *(Controller & Asst. Treas.)*

Subsidiary:

Windmill Corp. d/b/a Martha White Foods, Inc. **(1)**
Two Maryland Farms, Ste. 340
Brentwood, TN 37027
Tel.: 615-377-4961
Fax: 615-377-0867
Approx.Sls.: $134,000,000
Emp.: 520
Flour, Corn Meal, Dog Food, Cake Mixes
S.I.C.: 2041; 2045
Robert V. Dale *(Pres.)*
Dennis Dahl *(V.P.-Mktg.)*
F. Don Cowan *(V.P.-Opers.)*
Vaughn Oakley *(V.P.-Sls.)*
Ed Alexander *(Chief Fin. Officer)*

Subsidiaries:

Barry-Carter Milling Co. **(2)**
P.O. Box 369,
Lebanon, TN 37087
Tel.: 615-444-0841
Flour & Meal
S.I.C.: 2041
Dale Nunnery *(Gen. Mgr.)*

Frozen Specialties, Inc. **(2)**
601 McArthur
Archbold, OH 43502
Tel.: 419-445-9015
Produces Private Label & Branded Frozen Pizza
S.I.C.: 2038

Keco Milling Co. **(2)**
Old Hwy. 22
McKenzie, TN 38201
Tel.: 901-352-3396
Pet Food
S.I.C.: 2048
M.S. Lucero *(Gen. Mgr.)*

Martha White Mills of W.Va., Inc. **(2)**
P.O. Box 346,
Huntington, WV 25708
Tel.: 304-529-3351
Flour & Meal
S.I.C.: 2041
David Colbert *(Gen. Mgr.)*

Model Mill Co. **(2)**
P.O. Box 609,
Jackson, TN 38302
Tel.: 901-424-3535
Flour, Meal & Grits
S.I.C.: 2041
Paul Hampton *(Gen. Mgr.)*

Roush Products Co., Inc. **(2)**
1000 Wenig Rd., NE
Cedar Rapids, IA 52406
Tel.: 319-365-9423
Milling
S.I.C.: 2041
Vincent J. Noce *(Pres.)*

WINDSOR FASHIONS
3901 S. Broadway
Los Angeles, CA 90037
Tel.: 213-232-8121
Fax: 213-234-3970
Year Founded: 1956
Approx.Sls.: $18,700,000
Emp.: 350
Fiscal Year-end: 9/30/91
Retail Ladies Ready-To-Wear Shoes & Accessories
S.I.C.: 5621; 5661; 5632
Maurice Zekaria *(Pres.)*
Fortunate Dallal *(V.P.-Personnel & Treas.)*
Alice Zekaria *(Sec. & Mgr.-Gen. Mdse.)*
Odille Hansen *(Dir.-Opers.)*
Teresa Silva *(Dir.-Human Resources & Sls. Supvr.)*
Curtis Rose *(Mgr.-Data Processing)*
Lourdes Martinez Burson *(Supvr.-Mktg.)*
Tracy Penoncello *(Buyer-Adv.)*

Outside Service Firm(s):

Leibowitz Wasser & Co.*(Auditors)*
Los Angeles, CA

Bank of America NT&SA*(Major Banking Relationship)*
City of Industry, CA

WINDSOR INDUSTRIES, INC.
1351 W. Stanford Ave.
Englewood, CO 80110
Tel.: 303-762-1800 **CO**
Fax: 303-762-0817
Year Founded: 1970
Approx.Sls.: $17,000,000
Emp.: 105
Import Export
Mfr. of Commercial Floor Cleaning Machines
S.I.C.: 3589
Thomas M. Francis *(Pres.)*

Windsor Industries, Inc.—(Continued)

Mark Betker *(Exec. V.P.)*
Charles Haper *(Sr. V.P.)*
T. Sanford Francis *(Mgr.-Mktg.)*

Outside Service Firm(s):

Deloitte & Touche*(Auditors)*
1560 Broadway, Suite 1800
Denver, CO 80202

Holland & Hart*(Legal Firm)*
P.O. Box 8749
Denver, CO 80201
Tel.: 303-575-8000

Norwest Bank*(Major Banking Relationship)*
Denver, CO

WINDSOR PUBLICATIONS, INC.
21827 Nordhoff St.
Chatsworth, CA 91311
Mailing Address:
P.O. Box 2500
Chatsworth, CA 91313
Tel.: 818-700-0200
Tel.: 800-678-2574 **IL**
Fax: 818-701-6649
Approx.Sls.: $20,000,000
Emp.: 250
Fiscal Year-end: 6/30/90
Books, Directories & Guides Publishing
S.I.C.: 2731; 2741; 2721
Elliot Martin *(Chm. Bd., Pres. & Chief Exec. Officer)*
James L. Fish *(Chief Oper. Officer)*
Joel Katz *(Exec. V.P.)*
William McAllister *(V.P.)*
Terry Pender *(Controller)*
Bella Goldberg *(Mgr.-Human Resources)*
Carolyn Martin *(Travel Coordinator)*

Outside Service Firm(s):

Grant Thornton*(Auditors)*
1000 Wilshire Blvd.
Los Angeles, CA 90017

Security Pacific Natl. Bank*(Major Banking Relationship)*
P.O. Box 60228, Terminal Annex
Los Angeles, CA 90060
Tel.: 213-613-7641

WINDSOR SERVICE, INC.
2415 Kutztown Rd.
Reading, PA 19605
Mailing Address:
P.O. Box 13787,
Reading, PA 19612-3787
Tel.: 215-929-0716
Fax: 215-929-4825
Approx.Sls.: $19,000,000
Emp.: 100
Paving Contractor & Manufacture Asphalt Products
S.I.C.: 1611; 2951; 2952
George A. Walborn *(Pres.)*
John A. Demartino *(V.P.-Data Processing & Fin.)*
Randy O. Good *(V.P.-Sls.)*
Earl J. Walborn *(V.P. & Sec.)*

Outside Service Firm(s):

Ernst & Young*(Auditors)*
Wyomissing Professional Center, 875 Berkshire Blvd.
Reading, PA 19610

Fry & Golden*(Legal Firm)*
Reading, PA

Bank of Pennsylvania*(Major Banking Relationship)*
Reading, PA

WINDSOR SHADE TOBACCO COMPANY, INC.
158-166 Woodland St.
Hartford, CT 06105
Tel.: 203-522-1153 **CT**
Fax: 203-524-5567
Approx.Sls.: $25,000,000
Emp.: 10
Tobacco Warehousing & Storage
S.I.C.: 4221
Oliver Thrall *(Pres.)*
Calvin Arnold *(V.P.)*
Raymond Garcia *(Asst. V.P.)*
Hubbell H. Brown *(Treas.)*
Gilbert S. Arnold *(Sec.)*

Outside Service Firm(s):

Connecticut National Bank*(Major Banking Relationship)*
777 Main St.
Hartford, CT 06115
Tel.: 203-728-2000

WINE & SCHULZ INC.
3939 Produce Rd.
Louisville, KY 40218
Mailing Address:
P.O. Box 36248
Louisville, KY 40233
Tel.: 502-964-1981 **KY**
Fax: 502-964-1981
Approx.Sls.: $18,000,000
Emp.: 123
Wholesale Specialty Food Items
S.I.C.: 5149
Lee Alan *(Chm. Bd.)*
Norman Lee Wine *(Pres. & Chief Exec. Officer)*
Norman F. Wine *(Exec. V.P.)*
Lee A. Schulz *(Sec. & Treas.)*

WING INDUSTRIES, INC.
11999 Plano Rd.
Dallas, TX 75243
Mailing Address:
P.O. Box 38347
Dallas, TX 75238
Tel.: 214-699-9900
Year Founded: 1924
Approx.Sls.: $50,000,000
Emp.: 475
Mfr. of Wood Louvered Products
S.I.C.: 2431
Sam A. Wing, Jr. *(Chm. Bd., Pres. & Chief Exec. Officer)*
Tom Cox *(Exec. V.P. & Chief Fin. Officer)*
Robert Mickle *(V.P.-Sls. & Mktg.)*
Spurgeon Peaden *(V.P.-Mfg.)*
Lonnie Duke *(Dir.-Human Resources)*
Wayne Keel *(Dir.-Mngmt. Information)*
Karen Kozuba *(Mgr.-Corp. Personnel)*

Divisions:

Wing Industries North Central **(1)**
775 Belden Ave. #D
Addison, IL 60101
Tel.: 708-543-1199
Fax: 708-543-9862
S.I.C.: 5031
John Lamden *(Mgr.)*

Wing Industries Northeastern **(1)**
60 Progress Dr., Bldg. 4
Manchester, CT 06040
Tel.: 203-643-1525
Fax: 203-649-5708
S.I.C.: 5031
Roy Serrell *(Mgr.)*

Wing Industries South Central **(1)**
6202 Industrial Drive
Greenville, TX 75401
Tel.: 903-455-1200
Fax: 903-470-9304
Mfr. of Interior Doors
S.I.C.: 2431
Red Ferrell *(Plant Mgr.)*

Wing Industries Southeastern **(1)**
3353 La Salle
Charlotte, NC 28216
Tel.: 704-391-9464
Fax: 704-392-2906
S.I.C.: 5031
Ronald Watts *(Gen. Mgr.)*

Wing Industries Western **(1)**
1516 S. Archibald
Ontario, CA 91761
Tel.: 909-923-7596
Fax: 909-947-3587
S.I.C.: 5031

BILL WINK CHEVROLET & GEO
10700 Ford Rd.
Dearborn, MI 48126
Tel.: 313-582-5400 **MI**
Fax: 313-582-0282
Approx.Sls.: $199,300,000
Emp.: 86
Automobile Dealership
S.I.C.: 5511
William J. Wink, III *(Pres.)*
Sandra Harrison *(Sec. & Treas.)*
Jerrold Johnston *(Gen. Mgr.)*
Tom Kelly *(Mgr.-Sls.)*

WINKLER MCMANUS
150 Spear St., 16th Fl.
San Francisco, CA 94105
Tel.: 415-957-0242
Year Founded: 1973
Approx.Billings: $22,100,000
Emp.: 24
Agnieszka Winkler *(Pres.)*

WINKO-MATIC SIGNAL CO./ MULTISONICS CORP.
6301 Best Friend Rd.
Norcross, GA 30071
Tel.: 404-662-5400
Fax: 404-263-8353
Manufacture Sign & Indicator
S.I.C.: 3714
Donald Griffin *(Pres.)*

Subsidiary:

American Sign & Indicator Corporation **(1)**
N. 2310 Fancher Way
Spokane, WA 99212
Tel.: 509-536-6400
Manufacture Sign & Indicator
S.I.C.: 3714
Donald Griffin *(Pres.)*

FRANK W. WINNE & SON, INC.
44 N. Front St.
Philadelphia, PA 19106
Tel.: 215-627-3313
Fax: 215-627-6555
Approx.Sls.: $50,000,000
Emp.: 140
Manufacture & Distribute Textile Mill Products
S.I.C.: 2211; 5131
J. Douglas Coath, Sr. *(Pres. & Chief Exec. Officer)*
Tom Bitzer *(V.P.)*
J. Douglas Coath, Jr. *(V.P.)*
George Hollenbach *(V.P.)*
Rob Aoelizzi *(Comptroller)*

Outside Service Firm(s):

Rainer Associates*(Auditors)*
New Town, PA

Blue Cross & Blue Shield Association*(Group Insurer)*
Hartford, CT

Provident National Bank*(Major Banking Relationship)*
1000 Westlakes Dr.
Berwyn, PA 19312

WINNER COMMUNICATIONS, INC.
37 Union Square West
New York, NY 10003
Tel.: 212-206-0111
Fax: 212-627-9874
Year Founded: 1972
Approx.Billings: $75,000,000
Martin Feinberg *(Pres.)*
Robert Seibel *(V.P.)*
Jay Silman *(Controller)*
Barbara French *(Opers. Dir.)*

WINONA KNITS
1200 Storr's Pond Rd.
Winona, MN 55987
Mailing Address:
P.O. Box 5400
Winona, MN 55987
Tel.: 507-454-3240 **MN**
Fax: 507-454-6058
Year Founded: 1977
Assets: $3,348,703
Liabilities: $2,027,210
Net Worth: $1,321,493
Approx.Sls.: $11,793,000
Emp.: 125
Fiscal Year-end: 1/31/91
Retail Clothing
S.I.C.: 5611; 5621; 5651
Corporate Giving Program:
Contributions to United Way & Loon Watch
Pat Woodworth *(Chm. Bd., Pres. & Chief Exec. Officer)*
Mike Pulk *(Exec. V.P.)*
Bud Bachler *(V.P.-Mktg./ Communications)*
Shirley Benedict *(V.P.-Fin.)*
Linda Carothers *(V.P.-Info. Systems)*

Computer Systems/Hardware:
IBM A/S 400

Outside Service Firm(s):

Harris Trust & Savings Bank*(Major Banking Relationship)*
111 W. Monroe St.
Chicago, IL 60690
Tel.: 312-461-2265
Tel.: 800-858-0840

Merchants Bank of Winona*(Major Banking Relationship)*
Winona, MN

WINONA KNITTING MILLS, INC.
902 E. Second St.
Winona, MN 55987
Tel.: 507-454-4381 **MN**
Fax: 507-457-5750
Year Founded: 1943
Approx.Sls.: $20,000,000
Emp.: 500
Manufactures Knitted Men's & Women's Sweaters And Markets Them Through National Wholesale Mail-order & Retail Companies
S.I.C.: 2253
L.R. Woodworth *(Chm. Bd.)*
Peter Woodworth *(Pres.)*
Rich Christenson *(V.P.-Mktg.)*
Ken Deml *(V.P.)*
Kevin Mahoney *(V.P.)*
Everett Mueller *(V.P.)*
Jerry Saslow *(V.P.)*

No. of Mfg. Plants/Facilities: 2

No. of U.S. Offices: 1

Computer Systems/Hardware:
IBM

Outside Service Firm(s):

McGladrey & Pullen*(Auditors)*
Mesa, AZ

Benson & Merchlerwitz*(Legal Firm)*
Winona, MN

Merchants Bank of Winona*(Major Banking Relationship)*
Winona, MN

WINROCK ENTERPRISES, INC.
2101 Brookwood Dr.
Little Rock, AR 72202
Tel.: 501-663-5340 **AR**
Fax: 501-663-4456
Year Founded: 1955
Approx.Sls.: $35,000,000
Emp.: 150
Manufacture Plastic Pipe, Water Well Fittings; Land Development
S.I.C.: 3084; 3494; 6552
Russell B. McDonough, Jr. *(Chm. Bd., Pres. & Chief Exec. Officer)*
Gary Catlett *(Controller & V.P.)*

Outside Service Firm(s):

KPMG Peat Marwick*(Auditors)*
Tower Bldg., 11th Fl.,
Little Rock, AR 72201
Tel.: 501-375-3275

Shults, Ray & Kurrus*(Legal Firm)*
Little Rock, AR

The Northern Trust Co.*(Major Banking Relationship)*
30 S. LaSalle St.
Chicago, IL 60675
Tel.: 312-630-6000

Worthen National Bank of Arkansas*(Major Banking Relationship)*
P.O. Box 1681, 200 W. Capitol
Little Rock, AR 72201
Tel.: 501-378-1209
Fax: 501-378-1062

HARRY WINSTON, INC.
718 5th Ave.
New York, NY 10019
Tel.: 212-245-2000
Fax: 212-489-0016
Emp.: 300
Jeweler
S.I.C.: 5094; 5944
Ronald Winston *(Pres.)*
Robert Benvenuto *(Exec. V.P.)*
Bridgette Devine *(Dir.-Pub. Rels. & Adv.)*

Computer Systems/Hardware:
DEC 1170

Outside Service Firm(s):

Empire Blue Cross & Blue Shield*(Group Insurer)*
New York, NY

Bankers Trust Co.*(Major Banking Relationship)*
P.O. Box 318, Church St. Station
New York, NY 10008
Tel.: 212-454-2212
Fax: 212-454-2783

WINSTON STEEL PRODUCTS CO.
2700 W. Warren Ave.
Detroit, MI 48208
Tel.: 313-894-3300 **MI**
Fax: 313-894-0551
Sales Range: $20-39 Million
Import Export
Steel Service Center
S.I.C.: 5051
Harry P. Walts *(Pres. & Chief Exec. Officer)*
James Raiskin *(V.P.-Mktg. & Sls.)*
Stephanie Jones *(Dir.-Data Processing)*

Outside Service Firm(s):

Grant Thornton*(Auditors)*
Southfield, MI

Manufacturers National Bank N.A.*(Major Banking Relationship)*
38th Fl., 100 Renaissance Center
Detroit, MI 48243
Tel.: 313-222-4227

WINSTON TIRE COMPANY
900 W. Alameda
Burbank, CA 91506
Tel.: 818-843-7311 **CA**
Fax: 818-954-9433
Year Founded: 1962
Assets: $39,685,000
Liabilities: $29,305,000
Net Worth: $10,380,000
Approx.Sls.: $150,000,000
Emp.: 1,500
Fiscal Year-end: 9/30/91
Retail Tire & Automotive Services
S.I.C.: 5531
Sam Winston *(Chm. Bd. & Chief Exec. Officer)*
Thomas Bonburg *(Pres.)*
George Grismer *(Chief Fin. Officer & Exec. V.P.)*
Jacques Hunter *(Sr. V.P.-Real Estate)*
Russ Smith *(Sr. V.P. & Sls. Mgr.)*
Dwight Hansen *(V.P.-Prod. Distr. & Whlsle.)*
Lauren Smith *(V.P.-Human Resources)*
Vartan Bavougian *(Treas.)*
Joseph Marino *(Controller)*
Bob Donnelly *(Dir.-Adv.)*
Principal(s):
Sam Winston

Computer Systems/Hardware:
Hewlett-Packard 3000 Series 958

Outside Service Firm(s):

Ernst & Young*(Auditors)*
515 S. Flower St.
Los Angeles, CA 90071
Tel.: 213-621-1666

Bank of America*(Major Banking Relationship)*
701 S. Western Ave.
Los Angeles, CA 91201

WINTER VOLVO & LINCOLN MERCURY
3805 Florin Rd.
Sacramento, CA 95823
Tel.: 916-421-3400
Fax: 916-421-1329
Year Founded: 1948
Approx.Sls.: $30,000,000
Emp.: 90
Retail New & Used Automobiles
S.I.C.: 5511
Dale Vaira *(V.P. & Gen. Mgr.)*

Outside Service Firm(s):

Heather Sanguinetti Caminata & Sakai, Inc.*(Auditors)*
Stockton, CA

Bank of America NT&SA*(Major Banking Relationship)*
Rancho Cordova, CA

WINTERKORN LILLIS INC.
400 Euclid Bldg., Midtown Plaza
Rochester, NY 14604
Tel.: 716-454-1010
Fax: 716-454-1575
Year Founded: 1975
Approx.Billings: $14,000,000
Emp.: 31
Business-to-Business, Consumer, Trade, Medical, Science, Food Services Adv. & Pub. Rels.
William J. Lillis *(Pres. & Chief Exec. Officer)*
Wendy Nelson *(Exec. V.P., Opers.)*
Elaine Dilcango-Crowel *(V.P., Pub. Rels.)*

WINTERS WELDING WORKS, INC.
Hwy. 83
Winters, TX 79567
Tel.: 915-754-5418
Fax: 915-754-4129
Year Founded: 1953
Emp.: 15
Welding Contractor; Pipeline Construction; Manufacture Oil Field Storage Vessels
S.I.C.: 1623; 1799; 3443
C.R. Pinkerton *(Pres. & Chief Exec. Officer)*
Tim Meyer *(Sec.)*

Outside Service Firm(s):

Tom Haimner*(Auditors)*
Winters, TX

Grindstaff Slimp*(Legal Firm)*
Winters, TX

Security State Bank*(Major Banking Relationship)*
Wingate, TX

WINTHROP PRINTING COMPANY, INC.
235 Old Colony Ave.
Boston, MA 02127
Tel.: 617-268-9660
Fax: 617-268-6735
Approx.Sls.: $19,000,000
Emp.: 205
Sheet Fed & Webb Offset Printing
S.I.C.: 2752; 2759
John H. Orral *(Chm. Bd.)*
Roy E. Orrall *(Pres.)*
Arthur Fusco *(V.P.-Tech.)*
Anders Moestue *(V.P.-Mfg.)*
John F. Orrall *(V.P.-Mktg.)*
Catherine St. Saveur *(V.P.)*
James Hoole *(Controller)*
J. Peter Orrall *(Treas.)*

Outside Service Firm(s):

Petersen & Hoaglund*(Auditors)*
Babson Park, MA

Fleet Bank*(Major Banking Relationship)*
Boston, MA

WIRE ROPE CORP. OF AMERICA, INC.
609 N. 2nd St.
Saint Joseph, MO 64501
Mailing Address:
P.O. Box 288
St. Joseph, MO 64502
Tel.: 816-233-0287 **CT**
Fax: 816-233-2072
Year Founded: 1931
Approx.Sls.: $75,000,000
Emp.: 950
Mfr. of High Carbon Steel Wire, Wire Rope and Allied Products
S.I.C.: 3496; 3315
James E. Josendale *(Chm. Bd.)*
John P. Barclay, Jr. *(Pres. & Chief Exec. Officer)*
C.W. Salanski *(Chief Oper. Officer)*
Stephen D. Wurtzler *(Treas. & Chief Fin. Officer)*
Eugene Lager *(Mgr.-Data Processing)*
O. L. Ellis *(Mgr.-Personnel)*

Computer Systems/Hardware:
IBM 4361

Outside Service Firm(s):

Gray, Hunter & Stenn*(Auditors)*
Quincy, IL

General American Life Insurance Co.*(Group Insurer)*
700 Market
Saint Louis, MO 63101
Tel.: 314-525-5458
Fax: 314-525-3677

Hoskins, King, McGannon, Hahn & Hurwitz*(Legal Firm)*
Commerce Bank Bldg., 922 Walnut, Ste. 1100
Kansas City, MO 64106
Tel.: 816-221-2416

Norstar Bank, N.A.*(Major Banking Relationship)*
Albany, NY

The Northern Trust Co.*(Major Banking Relationship)*
50 S. LaSalle St.
Chicago, IL 60675
Tel.: 312-630-6000
Fax: 312-630-6516

Team Bank*(Major Banking Relationship)*
P.O. Box 2604,
Fort Worth, TX 76113
Tel.: 817-884-4614

Norstar Investment*(Pension Manager)*
Rochester, NY

Reimer & Koger Assocs.*(Pension Manager)*
Mission, KS

Subsidiary:

Leschen Wire Rope **(1)**
609 N. 2nd
Saint Joseph, MO 64501
Tel.: 816-233-2563
Fax: 816-233-2072
Emp.: 750
Leschen Red Strand Wire Rope, Wire Rope Slings, Synthetic Web Slings, Alloy Chain Slings, Structural Strand
S.I.C.: 3496; 3315
James Josendale *(Chm. Bd.)*
John P. Barclay, Jr. *(Pres.)*
C.W. Salanski *(Chief Oper. Officer)*
Stephen Wurtzler *(Chief Fin. Officer)*
Richard Kessler *(V.P.-Mfg.)*
O.L. Ellis *(Mgr.-Personnel)*
Gene Lager *(Mgr.-Data Processing)*
Frank Napolitano *(Mgr.-Sls.)*
C.R. Wheeler *(Mgr.-Res. & Devel.)*

THE WIREMOLD COMPANY
60 Woodlawn St.
West Hartford, CT 06133
Tel.: 203-233-6251 **CT**
Fax: 203-232-2062
Approx.Sls.: $87,000,000
Emp.: 900
Oil Field Wireline Contractor; Surface Metal Raceways & Fittings for Electric Light & Power & Telephone Wiring; Flexible Air Conduits & Ducts
S.I.C.: 3644; 3643; 3646; 3648
John Davis Murphy *(Chm. Bd.)*
Robert H. Murphy *(Vice Chm.)*
Arthur Byrne *(Pres.)*
Orest J. Fiume *(V.P. & Fin. Administrator)*
Gary L. Grenter *(V.P.-Opers.)*
R.P. Ryan *(V.P.-Sls.-Electric Div.)*
Stephen C. Atwood, Jr. *(Dir.-Production)*
Charles A. Whitney *(Dir.-Research & Devel.)*

Outside Service Firm(s):

Coopers & Lybrand*(Auditors)*
280 Trumbull St.
Hartford, CT 06103

Connecticut National Bank*(Major Banking Relationship)*
777 Main St.
Hartford, CT 06115
Tel.: 203-728-2000

WISCONSIN DAIRIES COOPERATIVE
Hwy. 12 W.
Baraboo, WI 53913
Mailing Address:
Box 111,
Baraboo, WI 53913
Tel.: 608-356-8316
Fax: 608-356-9005
Approx.Sls.: $465,000,000
Emp.: 900
Dairy Cooperative
S.I.C.: 2026; 2023; 2022; 2021
Ed Brooks *(Chm. Bd.)*
Donald Storhoff *(Pres.)*
Duaine Kamenick *(Chief Fin. Officer & V.P.-Fin.)*
John Murphy *(V.P.-Personnel)*
John Helt *(Treas.)*
J. Judkins *(Controller)*

Computer Systems/Hardware:
Honeywell DPS #7

Outside Service Firm(s):

Price Waterhouse*(Auditors)*
1500 Bank One Plaza, 100 E. Wisconsin Ave.
Milwaukee, WI 53202

Blue Cross & Blue Shield United of Wisconsin*(Group Insurer)*
Milwaukee, WI

LaRowe & Gerlach*(Legal Firm)*
Reedsburg, WI

M & I Marshall & Ilsley Bank*(Major Banking Relationship)*
770 N. Water St.
Milwaukee, WI 53202
Tel.: 414-765-8700

Saint Paul Bank for Cooperatives*(Major Banking Relationship)*
Saint Paul, MN

First Wisconsin National Bank*(Pension Manager)*
777 E. Wisconsin Ave.
Milwaukee, WI 53202
Tel.: 414-765-4321
Fax: 414-355-6903

Subsidiary:

Dairy Technology Ltd. **(1)**
Route #3 Highway 12 West
Baraboo, WI 53913
Tel.: 608-356-8316

WISCONSIN LABEL CORPORATION
1102 Jefferson St.
Algoma, WI 54201
Tel.: 414-487-3424 **WI**
Fax: 414-487-5644
Year Founded: 1966
Approx.Sls.: $25,000,000
Emp.: 210
Fiscal Year-end: 5/31/91
Paper Products, Converted Pressure Sensitive Materials
S.I.C.: 2679
Terrance Fulwiler *(Chief Exec. Officer)*
Dennis Bell *(Pres.)*
David Groessl *(Sr. V.P.)*
Daniel Fulwiler *(V.P.)*
Jay Tomekeck *(V.P. & Treas.)*
Robert Cummings *(Dir.-Sls. & Mktg.)*

No. of Mfg. Plants/Facilities: 3

Outside Service Firm(s):

First Wisconsin National Bank*(Major Banking Relationship)*
Manitowoc, WI

WISDOM IMPORTS SALES CO. INC.
17401 Eastman
Irvine, CA 92714
Mailing Address:
P.O. Box 18348
Irvine, CA 92713
Tel.: 714-261-5533
Fax: 714-262-5539
Year Founded: 1933
Approx.Sls.: $70,000,000
Emp.: 75
Fiscal Year-end: 12/31/90
Import
General Agents for Premium Imported Beers & Beverages
S.I.C.: 5181
Corporate Giving Program: Company Sponsors Wheelchair Tennis Tornaments
Francisco Sada *(Pres.)*
John J. Lennon *(V.P.-Mktg.)*
Johnny Moore *(V.P.-Sls.)*
Jesus Romero *(V.P.-Fin.)*

No. of U.S. Offices: 8

WITCHER CONSTRUCTION COMPANY
3601 Minnesota Dr., Ste. 650
Minneapolis, MN 55435
Tel.: 612-830-9000 **MN**
Fax: 612-830-1365
Year Founded: 1945
Approx.Sls.: $35,000,000
Emp.: 100
Fiscal Year-end: 12/31/90
General Contractor; Construction Management; Design & Build Commercial Buildings & Multiple Housing Complexes
S.I.C.: 1522
Michael W. Redmond *(Pres.)*
Frederick M. Furland *(V.P.)*
Kenneth W. Styrlund *(V.P.)*

Principal(s):
Michael W. Redmond

No. of U.S. Offices: 1

Computer Systems/Hardware:
IBM

WITT COMPANY
4454 Steel Pl.
Cincinnati, OH 45209
Tel.: 513-871-5700
Tel.: 800-543-7417
Fax: 513-871-7452
Year Founded: 1887
Approx.Sls.: $20,000,000
Emp.: 225
Fiscal Year-end: 12/31/90
Import Export
Galvanized Metal Receptacles, Dispense-A-Liner Vinyl Liners, Metal Wastebaskets, Push Door Receptacles, Ash Urns, Spacecube Storage Boxes, Security Receptacles, Job Galvanizing
S.I.C.: 3469; 3479; 3412; 3499
Mary Witt Wydman *(Chm. Bd. & Chief Exec. Officer)*
Marcy Wydman *(Pres.)*
Tim Harris *(Exec. V.P.-Products)*
J.E. Powers *(V.P.-Mktg. & Sls.)*
Gregg Battaglia *(Controller)*
Pat Haskell *(Dir.-Personnel & Benefits)*
Shirley Bennett *(Mgr.-Pur. & Traffic)*

No. of U.S. Offices: 2

Outside Service Firm(s):

Santen & Hughes*(Legal Firm)*
Cincinnati, OH

Divisions:

Muncie Division **(1)**
2415 S. Walnut St.
Muncie, IN 47302
Tel.: 317-289-3427
Joe Wendel *(Gen. Mgr.)*

Witt Galvanizing Division **(1)**
4454 Steel Pl.
Cincinnati, OH 45209
Tel.: 513-871-5700
Kevin Lax *(Exec. V.P.)*

Witt Products Division **(1)**
4454 Steel Pl.
Cincinnati, OH 45209
Tel.: 513-871-5700
Tim Harris *(Exec. V.P.)*

BILL WOESTE DEALER GROUP
8667 Beechmont Ave.
Cincinnati, OH 45254
Mailing Address:
P.O. Box 54366
Cincinnati, OH 45255
Tel.: 513-388-3700 **OH**
Fax: 513-388-3723
Year Founded: 1980
Approx.Sls.: $154,000,000
Emp.: 205
Fiscal Year-end: 12/31/91
Auto Dealerships; Sales & Service of New & Used Toyota, Chevrolet, Volvo, Geo, Lotus, Porsche, Audi & Lincoln Mercury Cars
S.I.C.: 5511
Bill F. Woeste, Jr. *(Pres. & Dir.-Pur.)*
Shirley Weeks *(Chief Fin. Officer & Dir.-Data Processing)*
Margo L. Wueste *(V.P.)*
Cynthia Woeste *(V.P. & Sec.)*
Cynthia S. MacConnell *(Sec. & Treas.)*
Chris Hahn *(Gen. Mgr.)*
Principal(s):
Bill F. Woeste, Jr.
Cynthia Woeste

No. of Mfg. Plants/Facilities: 5
No. of U.S. Offices: 1

Computer Systems/Hardware:
Reynolds & Reynolds

Outside Service Firm(s):

Rippie & Kingston*(Auditors)*
Cincinnati, OH

Art Hauser Ins. Co.*(Commercial Insurance Carrier)*
Cincinnati, OH

Nationwide*(Group Insurer)*
Cincinnati, OH

Coors, Bassett, Kohlhepp, Holloren Moren*(Legal Firm)*
Cincinnati, OH

Provident National Bank*(Major Banking Relationship)*
4140 Hamilton Ave.
Cincinnati, OH
Tel.: 513-681-3900

Provident Bank*(Pension Manager)*
One East Fourth St.
Cincinnati, OH 45202
Tel.: 513-579-2732

Subsidiaries:

Cincinnati Limousine Service Inc. **(1)**
8639 Beechmont Ave.
Cincinnati, OH 45255
Tel.: 513-388-3723
Emp.: 2
Limousine and Van Rental Service
S.I.C.: 4119
Cynthia S. MacConnell *(Chief Oper. Officer)*

Tom Moser Porsche Audi **(1)**
Beechmont Ave.
Cincinnati, OH 45230
Tom Moser *(Chief Exec. Officer)*

WOHLERT CORP.
708-12 E. Grand River Ave.
Lansing, MI 48906
Mailing Address:
P.O. Box 20217
Lansing, MI 48901
Tel.: 517-485-3750 **MI**
Fax: 517-485-0501
Year Founded: 1943
Assets: $14,000,000
Liabilities: $12,000,000
Net Worth: $2,000,000
Approx.Sls.: $30,000,000
Emp.: 350
Fiscal Year-end: 5/31/90
Import Export
Mfr. of Flexplates, Flywheels, Aircraft and Commercial Welded Rings & Ring Gears
S.I.C.: 3728
Kenneth E. Patenge *(Chm., Pres. & Chief Exec. Officer)*
Mark S. Reister *(Chief Oper. Officer & Sec.)*
James Barnes *(V.P., Treas. & Chief Fin. Officer)*
Barry Biscombe *(Mgr.-Outside Sls.)*
Sherry Linskens *(Mgr.-Matls.)*
Principal(s):
Kenneth E. Patenge
James Barnes

No. of Mfg. Plants/Facilities: 3
No. of U.S. Offices: 2

Computer Systems/Hardware:
IBM System 38

Outside Service Firm(s):

Maner, Costerian & Ellis*(Auditors)*
Lansing, MI

CNA Insurance*(Commercial Insurance Carrier)*
CNA Plaza,
Chicago, IL 60685
Tel.: 312-822-5000

WOLCOTT & LINCOLN, INC.
4800 Main St., Ste. 565
Kansas City, MO 64112
Tel.: 816-753-6750 **MO**
Fax: 816-753-0146
Year Founded: 1926
Assets: $16,830,079
Liabilities: $13,816,101
Net Worth: $3,013,978
Sales Range: $10-19 Million
Emp.: 70
Wholesale Grain & Commodity Futures
S.I.C.: 5153; 4221; 6221
David W. Gibson *(Chm. Bd.)*
Daniel Gibson *(Pres.)*
Richard Williams *(V.P.)*
Cynthia Gibson *(Sec.)*
Frank P. Hoffman *(Treas.)*
Principal(s):
Daniel Gibson

Computer Systems/Hardware:
IBM Systems 34 & 36

Outside Service Firm(s):

John Merra*(Auditors)*
Kansas City, MO

Mill Mutual*(Commercial Insurance Carrier)*
Kansas City, MO

Polsinelli, White & Vardiman*(Legal Firm)*
Kansas City, MO

Commerce Bank of Kansas City*(Major Banking Relationship)*
10th & Walnut
Kansas City, MO 64141
Tel.: 816-234-2000
Fax: 816-234-2548

First National Bank of Kansas City*(Pension Manager)*
10th & Baltimore
Kansas City, MO 64105
Tel.: 816-221-2800

LELAND A. WOLF & ASSOCIATES
100 Foster City Blvd.
Foster City, CA 94404
Tel.: 415-573-8041
Fax: 415-574-8226
Year Founded: 1979
Sales Range: $40-59 Million
Emp.: 120
Employee Benefit Plan Services
S.I.C.: 6324
Leland A. Wolf *(Pres. & Chief Exec. Officer)*
Sally Wolf *(Chief Oper. Officer & V.P.)*
Lisa Wolf Klain *(Dir.-Personnel)*

Computer Systems/Hardware:
DEC VAX; PC Network

Outside Service Firm(s):

Ernst & Young*(Auditors)*
555 California St., Ste. 3000
San Francisco, CA 94104
Tel.: 415-951-3000

First Interstate Bank*(Major Banking Relationship)*
Foster City, CA

WOLF, BLOCK, SCHORR & SOLIS-COHEN
Packard Bldg., 12th Fl., 15th & Chestnut Sts.
Philadelphia, PA 19102
Tel.: 215-977-2000
Fax: 215-977-2334
Year Founded: 1903
Approx.Billings: $51,500,000
Emp.: 230
Law Firm
S.I.C.: 8111
Robert Segal *(Chm. Exec. Committee & Mng. Partner)*
Charles G. Kopp *(Chief Exec. Officer)*
Patricia Wyatt *(Dir.-Library Services)*
John Duckett *(Librarian)*

WOLF BLUMBERG KRODY INC.
19 Garfield Place
Cincinnati, OH 45202
Tel.: 513-784-0066
Fax: 513-784-0986
Year Founded: 1979
Approx.Billings: $40,000,000
Emp.: 65
Healthcare, Consumer Products , Home Builders, Products & Appliances, Business to Business, Products & Services, Product Package Design
Dale Wolf *(Pres.)*
Jim Lewis *(Exec. V.P., Fin.)*
Linda Cornell *(Sr. V.P., Chief Oper. Officer)*
Joe Obermeyer *(Sr. V.P., Grp. Head)*
Jesse Taggart *(V.P.-Eastern Region)*
Linnea Lose *(V.P., Pub. Rels. Dir.)*
Barron Krody *(V.P., Grp. Head)*

WOLF MANUFACTURING COMPANY
18th & Waco Dr.
Waco, TX 76707
Tel.: 817-753-7301
Year Founded: 1947
Emp.: 400
Fiscal Year-end: 12/31/91
Leisurewear, Fleecewear & Sportswear
S.I.C.: 2329
Mark E. Wolf *(Pres.)*

Outside Service Firm(s):

Texas National Bank*(Major Banking Relationship)*
Waco, TX

WOLFBERG, ALVAREZ & ASSOCIATES INC.
5960 S.W. 57th Ave.
Miami, FL 33143
Tel.: 305-666-5474
Fax: 305-666-4994
Emp.: 80
Architecture & Engineering Firm
S.I.C.: 8711; 8712
Julio Alvarez *(Pres.)*
David A. Wolfberg *(Sr. V.P.)*
Jose A. Mola *(V.P.-Opers.)*
Marcel Morlote *(V.P.-Architecture)*
Ramon Duran *(Controller)*

Computer Systems/Hardware:
Calcomp; IBM

Outside Service Firm(s):

Ernst & Young*(Auditors)*
2700 One Biscayne Tower
Miami, FL

Hartford Life Insurance Co.*(Group Insurer)*
Hartford, CT 06104-2999

Southeast Bank, N.A.*(Major Banking Relationship)*
1 Southeast Financial Center
Miami, FL 33131
Tel.: 305-666-5656

WOLFER PRINTING COMPANY
6670 E. Flotilla St.
City of Commerce, CA 90040
Tel.: 213-721-5411
Fax: 213-720-1245
Year Founded: 1913
Approx.Sls.: $25,000,000
Emp.: 90
Publisher & Contract Lithographic Printing
S.I.C.: 2741; 2752
Robert W. Good *(Pres.)*
George Moffett *(Chief Oper. Officer)*
John Colston *(V.P.-Fin.)*
Mike Wellman *(V.P.-Sls. & Mktg.)*
Carolyn Haywood *(Sls. Admin.)*

Outside Service Firm(s):

City National Bank*(Major Banking Relationship)*
8525 W. Pico Blvd.
Los Angeles, CA 90035
Tel.: 310-550-5690

WOLFF ASSOCIATES, INC.
The Wolff Bldg., 500 East Ave.
Rochester, NY 14607
Tel.: 716-461-8300
Fax: 716-461-0835
Year Founded: 1935
Approx.Billings: $11,483,000
Emp.: 21
Print, Radio & TV, Direct Response, Special Events, Promo. Matls., Dealer Programs, Presentaions & Mdsg. Aids
Raymond Del Monte *(Pres. & Chief Exec. Officer)*
Joanne Holter *(Dir., Admin.)*
Kathy Stuewe *(Dir., Fin.)*
Jim Grabowski *(Assoc. Controller)*

WOLFF & MUNIER, INC.
50 Broadway
Hawthorne, NY 10532
Tel.: 718-562-5600
Fax: 914-741-1100
Year Founded: 1919
Approx.Billings: $58,000,000
Emp.: 300
Fiscal Year-end: 12/31/89
Mechanical Contractors & Engineers
S.I.C.: 1711; 8711
Emile H. Munier *(Chm. Bd.)*
Alan E. Fidellow *(Pres.)*
Robert S.C. Munier *(Exec. V.P. & Treas.)*

Outside Service Firm(s):

Chemical Banking Corp.*(Major Banking Relationship)*
277 Park Ave.
New York, NY 10041
Tel.: 212-310-6407
Fax: 212-310-4526

WOLFINGTON BODY COMPANY
Route 100
Exton, PA 19341
Tel.: 215-458-8501
Fax: 215-458-0293
Approx.Sls.: $40,000,000
Emp.: 140
Export
Distribution of School Buses, Ambulances & Funeral Cars
S.I.C.: 4151; 5012
Harry A. Wolfington *(Chm. Bd.)*
John F. Wolfington *(Pres.)*
James E. Wolfington *(Exec. V.P. & Sec.)*
Richard I. Wolfington *(V.P.)*
Robert H. Wolfington *(V.P.)*
Nancy Baird *(V.P.-Admin.)*

WOLLIN PRODUCTS, INC.
4295 N. Rooisevelt
Stevensville, MI 49127
Tel.: 616-429-3201 **MI**
Year Founded: 1957
Sales Range: $20-39 Million
Emp.: 300
Mfr. of Injection Molded Plastics
S.I.C.: 3089
Ewald Lechmann *(Pres. & Chief Exec. Officer)*
Randy Lueth *(V.P.-Fin. & Admin.)*
Robert Howell *(V.P.-Sls. & Mktg.)*

Outside Service Firm(s):

Glabensky, Gleiss, Bittner & Hyrns*(Legal Firm)*
St. Joseph, MI

Inter City Bank*(Major Banking Relationship)*
Stevensville, MI

WOLVERINE MASSACHUSETTS CORPORATION
(Formerly Wolverine Corporation)
51 E. Main St.
Merrimac, MA 01860
Tel.: 508-346-4541
Fax: 508-346-4213
Sales Range: $10-19 Million
Emp.: 100
Mfr. of Industrial Dryers, Roasters & Air Pollution Control Equipment
S.I.C.: 3564; 3567
Deepak Kulkarni *(Chm. Bd.)*
Philip Constable *(Chief Oper. Officer)*
Donald D. Taylor *(Sr. V.P.-Sls.)*
Edward J. Hines *(V.P., Treas. & Sec.)*

Outside Service Firm(s):

Arthur Andersen & Co.*(Auditors)*
1 International Place, Fort Hill Square
Boston, MA 02110
Tel.: 617-330-4000

Varet, Marcus, Fink*(Legal Firm)*
Boston, MA

Hansalls, Osake, Pankki*(Major Banking Relationship)*
New York, NY

WOLVERINE PACKING CO.
1340 Winder
Detroit, MI 48207
Tel.: 313-259-7500
Fax: 313-568-1909
Approx.Sls.: $160,000,000
Emp.: 145
Fiscal Year-end: 12/31/91
Wholesale Meat Packer & Distributor
S.I.C.: 5147
A. James Bonahoom, Jr. *(Pres. & Sec.)*
Roger Bonahoom *(V.P. & Treas.)*
Brian Bartis *(Controller)*

Outside Service Firm(s):

Doyle, Litt & Co.*(Auditors)*
Troy, MI

Dykema, Gossett*(Legal Firm)*
400 Renaissance Ctr., 35th Fl.
Detroit, MI 48243
Tel.: 313-568-6800

Michigan National Bank*(Major Banking Relationship)*
Detroit, MI

WOMETCO ENTERPRISES, INC.
3195 Ponce de Leon Blvd.
Coral Gables, FL 33134
Tel.: 305-529-1400
Fax: 305-529-1466
Approx.Sls.: $112,000,000
Emp.: 2,850
Fiscal Year-end: 6/30/92
Movie Theaters, Seaquarium, Automatic Vending & Industrial Feeding Operators; Food Services; Ice Cream Stores
S.I.C.: 8422; 7832; 5451; 3581; 5812
Arthur Hertz *(Chm. Bd. & Chief Exec. Officer)*
Michael S. Brown *(Pres.)*
Andrew Weston *(V.P.-Fin.)*
Principal(s):
Arthur Hertz
Michael S. Brown

Computer Systems/Hardware:
IBM PC

Outside Service Firm(s):

Deloitte & Touche*(Auditors)*
100 S.E. 2nd St.
Miami, FL 33131-2135
Tel.: 305-538-4141

Steel Hector & Davis General Counsel*(Legal Firm)*
Southeast 1st Natl. Bank Bldg.
Miami, FL 33131
Tel.: 305-577-2800

National Westminster Bank plc*(Major Banking Relationship)*
Astor Plaza, 1515 Broadway
New York, NY 10036

PETER WONG & ASSOCIATES, INC.
200 E. Cary St.
Richmond, VA 23219
Tel.: 804-648-1900
Fax: 804-780-2416
Year Founded: 1980
Approx.Billings: $14,000,000
Emp.: 16
Transportation, Business-to-Business & Intl. Adv.
Peter Wong *(Pres.)*
Jennifer Wong *(Treas. & Controller)*
Mike Blackburn *(Dir., Pub. Rels.)*
Shelly Blackstone *(Mktg. Mgr.)*

THE W.B. WOOD COMPANY
150 Floral Ave.
New Providence, NJ 07974
Tel.: 908-771-9000 **NJ**
Fax: 908-655-6500
Year Founded: 1905
Assets: $12,859,000
Earnings: $162,000
Liabilities: $10,826,000
Net Worth: $2,033,000
Approx.Sls.: $55,000,000

The W.B. Wood Company—(Continued)

Emp.: 170
Fiscal Year-end: 12/31/90
Office Furnishings Contractor; Interior Designer
S.I.C.: 5999; 8742
David W. Kopelman *(Chm. Bd.)*
W. Barton Wood III *(Pres.)*
Robert F. Blau *(Chief Oper. Officer)*
M. Peretz *(Exec. V.P.-Sls.)*
Stewart Bradway *(V.P.-Fin.)*
Denise Baime *(V.P.)*

No. of U.S. Offices: 4

Computer Systems/Hardware:
Honeywell

Outside Service Firm(s):

J. H. Cohn & Co.*(Auditors)*
75 Eisenhower Pkwy.
Roseland, NJ 07068-1697
Tel.: 201-228-3500

Genex, Inc.*(Commercial Insurance Carrier)*
Roslyn, NY

Garden State Insurance*(Group Insurer)*
Perth Amboy, NJ

National Community Bank*(Investment Banker)*
24 Park Ave.
Rutherford, NJ 07070

Feinberg, Feinberg & Tritsch*(Legal Firm)*
Rahway, NJ

WOODBURY BUSINESS FORMS, INC.
101 Lukken Industrial Dr. E.
La Grange, GA 30240
Tel.: 706-882-2977
Fax: 706-882-1837
Approx.Sls.: $11,000,000
Emp.: 180
Custom Business Forms, Snapout & Continuous
S.I.C.: 2761
Joe L. Bradfield *(Pres.)*
Gerald O. Phillips *(V.P.)*
J.K. Boatwright, III *(Treas.)*
T.E. Duncan *(Sec.)*

Outside Service Firm(s):

J.K. Boatwright & Co.*(Auditors)*
La Grange, GA

Duncan, Thomasson & Acree*(Legal Firm)*
LaGrange, GA

Trust Company Bank*(Major Banking Relationship)*
La Grange, GA

WOODCRAFT INDUSTRIES, INC.
525 Lincoln Ave., SE
Saint Cloud, MN 56304
Tel.: 612-252-1503 **MN**
Fax: 612-252-1504
Assets: $12,365,601
Liabilities: $6,473,222
Net Worth: $5,892,379
Approx.Sls.: $31,000,000
Emp.: 425
Fiscal Year-end: 12/31/91
Export
Manufacture Hardwood Dimensions; Cabinet components
S.I.C.: 2426
Corporate Giving Program: Selected Charities by Management Group are Supported Financially & With Volunteers.
Employee Matching Gifts Program: We Match All Gifts Given to Our Local United Way.
Thomas A. Ritsche *(Chief Exec. Officer)*
Lewis R. Walker *(Pres.)*
Dennis Gregory *(V.P.-Fin. & Chief Fin. Officer)*
Steven Wilhelm *(Dir.-Mktg. & Resources)*
Jerome Braner *(Mgr.-Division)*
Stephen Jacobs *(Mgr.-Division)*
Sheila Krogmer *(Mgr.-Human Resources)*
Donald Swanstrom *(Mgr.-Division)*
Jon Knudson *(Buyer-Lumber)*

No. of Mfg. Plants/Facilities: 3
No. of U.S. Offices: 1

Computer Systems/Hardware:
IBM System 36
PC Network-IBM Compatible

Outside Service Firm(s):

McMahon, Hartmann & Amundson*(Auditors)*
St. Cloud, MN

Indiana Lumberman's Insurance*(Commercial Insurance Carrier)*
Indianapolis, IN

Ronke T. Noonan*(Legal Firm)*
Norwest Center, Suite 700
St. Cloud, MN

First Bank, N.A.*(Major Banking Relationship)*
Saint Cloud, MN

Investment Advisors, Inc.*(Pension Manager)*
P.O. Box 357, 3700 First Bank Pl.
Minneapolis, MN 55440

WOODFIN HOLDING CORPORATION
9255 Towne Center Dr., Ste. 900
San Diego, CA 92121
Tel.: 619-450-1833
Fax: 619-450-9497
Holding Company
S.I.C.: 6719; 8741; 7011
Samuel A. Hardage *(Chm. Bd.)*

Outside Service Firm(s):

Pannell, Kerr, Forster*(Auditors)*
Chicago, IL

Hill, Wynne, Troop & Meisinger*(Legal Firm)*
10940 Wilshire Blvd.
Los Angeles, CA 90024
Tel.: 310-824-7000
Fax: 310-443-7599

Union Bank*(Major Banking Relationship)*
8155 Mercury Ct., P.O. Box 2529
San Diego, CA 92112

Subsidiaries:

Woodfin Hotel Management, Inc. **(1)**
9255 Towne Center Dr., Ste. 900
San Diego, CA 92121
Tel.: 619-450-1833
Hotel Management
S.I.C.: 7011; 8741
Roger C. Royce *(Pres.)*

Woodfin Suites, Inc. **(1)**
9255 Towne Center Dr., Ste. 900
San Diego, CA 92121
Tel.: 619-450-1833
Hotels
S.I.C.: 6513; 7011
Roger C. Royce *(Pres.)*

WOODFIN-SMITH PONTIAC, INC.
300 Wooddale Blvd.
Baton Rouge, LA 70806
Mailing Address:
P.O. Box 66558,
Baton Rouge, LA 70896
Tel.: 504-926-7171 **LA**
Fax: 504-926-7171, Ext. 242
Year Founded: 1951
Assets: $4,539,877
Liabilities: $3,413,764
Net Worth: $1,126,113
Approx.Sls.: $40,647,927
Emp.: 81
Fiscal Year-end: 12/31/91
Import
Retail New & Used Automobiles
S.I.C.: 5511
Ira J. Woodfin *(Pres.)*
John M. Carnahan *(Sec. & Treas.)*
Ken Fischer *(Dir.-Fin.)*
Randy Dominue *(Mgr.-Sls.)*
B. J. Martin *(Mgr.-Office)*
Principal(s):
Ira J. Woodfin
John M. Carnahan

Outside Service Firm(s):

Seale, Smith & Phelps*(Legal Firm)*
Baton Rouge, LA

Hancock Bank*(Major Banking Relationship)*
Baton Rouge, LA

Hibernia National Bank*(Major Banking Relationship)*
Baton Rouge, LA

WOODMEN ACCIDENT & LIFE CO.
1526 K St
Lincoln, NE 68508
Mailing Address:
P.O. Box 82288
Lincoln, NE 68501
Tel.: 402-476-6500
Fax: 402-437-4392
Year Founded: 1890
Approx.Sls.: $124,000,000
Emp.: 700
Fiscal Year-end: 12/31/90
Life, Group, Disability & Health Insurance
S.I.C.: 6311; 6321
John Haessler *(Pres. & Chief Exec. Officer)*
W. Orr *(Sr. V.P. & Dir.-Agencies)*
Fred Rickers *(Sr. V.P.-Ins. Opers.)*
Gary Moerer *(2nd V.P.-Admin.)*
Rich Peters *(2nd V.P.-Mktg. Services & Pub. Rels.)*

WOODRUFF ELECTRICAL CO-OP
3190 N. Washington
Forest City, AR 72335
Mailing Address:
P.O. Box 1619
Forest City, AR 72335
Tel.: 501-633-2262 **AR**
Fax: 501-633-0629
Year Founded: 1937
Approx.Sls.: $18,000,000
Emp.: 70
Distribution of Electric Power
S.I.C.: 4911
Wayne Beadles *(Chm. Bd. & Pres.)*
Glynn H. Carpenter *(Gen. Mgr.)*
J. Wampler *(Sec.)*

Outside Service Firm(s):

First National Bank of Eastern Arkansas*(Major Banking Relationship)*
Forest City, AR

JOE E. WOODS, INC.
65 E. Main St., Ste. 401
Mesa, AZ 85201
Tel.: 602-964-4560 **AZ**
Fax: 602-969-8304
Year Founded: 1977
Assets: $15,399,003
Liabilities: $12,608,296
Net Worth: $2,790,707
Sales Range: $60-79 Million
Emp.: 100
Fiscal Year-end: 11/30/92
General Contractor; Commercial & Industrial Construction
S.I.C.: 1542; 1541
Joe E. Woods *(Pres.)*
David James *(V.P.-Fin. & Treas.)*
Jay Janiga *(V.P.)*
W. David Jansen *(V.P.)*
Raymond M. Nitti *(V.P.)*
Nina Jo Woods *(Sec.)*

Outside Service Firm(s):

Deloitte & Touche*(Auditors)*
2901 North Central Ave., Ste. 1200
Phoenix, AZ 85012
Tel.: 602-234-5100
Fax: 602-234-5186

Alexander & Alexander*(Commercial Insurance Carrier)*
P.O. Box A
Albuquerque, NM 87103
Tel.: 505-889-6700
Fax: 505-884-7831

The Principal Financial Group*(Group Insurer)*
Ames, IA

Roberts, Ellsworth & Rowley*(Legal Firm)*
Mesa, AZ

Zions First National Bank of Arizona*(Major Banking Relationship)*
Phoenix, AZ

Subsidiary:

Price Woods, Inc. **(1)**
63 E. Main St., Ste. 601
Mesa, AZ 85201
Tel.: 602-948-9451
Emp.: 16
General Contractor, Custom Homes, Tenant Improvements
S.I.C.: 1541
Jeffrey D. Price *(Pres.)*
Craig Porter *(V.P.)*
David James *(Sec. & Treas.)*

T.B. WOOD'S SONS COMPANY
440 N. Fifth Ave.
Chambersburg, PA 17201
Tel.: 717-264-7161
Fax: 717-264-6420
Year Founded: 1857
Approx.Sls.: $74,000,000
Emp.: 635
Fiscal Year-end: 12/31/90
Export
Mfr. Industrial Power Transmission Equipment & SCR Drive Controls
S.I.C.: 3321; 3568
Thomas C. Foley *(Chm. Bd.)*
Michael L. Hurt *(Pres. & Chief Oper. Officer)*
David Halleen *(V.P.-Fin.)*
Don Michaels *(V.P.-Mfg.)*
John B. Mitchell *(V.P.-Engrng.)*
C.W. Ewing *(Dir.-Personnel)*
Allen W. Fortna *(Mgr.-Distr. Sls.)*
Mike Leatherman *(Mgr.-Data Processing)*

Computer Systems/Hardware:
IBM System 4381

Outside Service Firm(s):

Arthur Andersen & Co.*(Auditors)*
133 Peachtree St., N.E.
Atlanta, GA 30303
Tel.: 404-658-1776

New England Mutual Life Insurance Co.*(Group Insurer)*
Boston, MA

Pennsylvania Blue Shield*(Group Insurer)*
Camp Hill, PA

WOODWARD-CLYDE GROUP, INC.
4582 S. Ulster St., Ste. 600
Denver, CO 80237
Tel.: 303-740-2600
Tel.: 800-776-3296 **DE**
Fax: 303-740-2650
Year Founded: 1950
Assets: $86,000,000
Liabilities: $56,000,000
Net Worth: $30,000,000
Approx.Sls.: $233,000,000
Emp.: 2,300
Fiscal Year-end: 12/31/91
Engineering, Environmental & Earth Science Consulting Firm
S.I.C.: 8711; 8742
Frank Waller *(Chm. Bd.)*
Jean-Yves Perez *(Pres. & Chief Exec. Officer)*
R.K. Wilson *(Chief Fin. & Chief Admin. Officer)*
D.R. Gaboury *(Chief Oper. Officer)*
Paul J. Sanner *(Sr. V.P. & Gen. Counsel)*
J. David Dean *(Sr. V.P.-Mktg.)*
Walter Dutko *(V.P.-Fin. Opers. & Admin.)*
David J. Dimick *(V.P.-Fin. & Acctg.)*
Alan M. Jaramillo *(V.P.-Human Resources)*
John H. Lovejoy *(V.P.-Information Systems)*
Charles Wahtola *(V.P.-Corp. Devel.)*
Marilyn Brewer *(Dir.-Corp. Communications)*

Outside Service Firm(s):

Ernst & Young*(Auditors)*
555 California St., Ste. 3000
San Francisco, CA 94104
Tel.: 415-951-3000

Aetna Life & Casualty*(Group Insurer)*
San Francisco, CA

Bronson, Bronson & McKinnon*(Legal Firm)*
555 California St.
San Francisco, CA 94104

Bank of America, N.T. & S.A.*(Major Banking Relationship)*
P.O. Box 37002,
San Francisco, CA 94137

BankAmerica Investment Mngmt. Corp (BAIMCO)*(Pension Manager)*
San Francisco, CA

Affiliates:

Woodward-Clyde Consultants **(1)**
4582 S. Ulster St., Ste. 600
Denver, CO 80237
Tel.: 303-740-2600
Tel.: 800-776-3296
Fax: 303-740-2650
Consultants
S.I.C.: 8742
Charles Wahtola *(Pres. & Chief Exec. Officer)*

Woodward-Clyde International **(1)**
4584 S. Ulster St., Ste. 600
Denver, CO 80237
Tel.: 303-740-2600
Tel.: 800-776-3296
Fax: 303-740-2650
Engineering, Environmental, Geotechnical & Waste Management Services
S.I.C.: 8711; 8742
Jean-Yves Perez *(Pres. & Chief Exec. Officer)*

Woodward-Clyde Federal Services **(1)**
4584 S. Ulster St., Ste. 600
Denver, CO 80237
Tel.: 410-309-0800
Emp.: 59
Engineering, Environmental, Geotechnical & Waste Management Consulting Services for the Government
S.I.C.: 8711; 8742
Charles Wahtola *(Pres.)*

WOODWARD DIRECT, INC.
8001 Lincoln Ave.
Skokie, IL 60077
Tel.: 708-677-5500
Year Founded: 1947
Approx.Billings: $25,000,000
Emp.: 85
National Yellow Pages Adv.
J.F. Woodward *(Chm. Bd.)*
James Woodward, Jr. *(Pres.)*
Robert A. Scott *(V.P., Fin. Services)*

WOODWARD & LOTHROP/ JOHN WANAMAKER
(Formerly Woodward & Lothrop Incorporated)
1025 F St. N.W.
Washington, DC 20013
Tel.: 202-879-8000 **VA**
Fax: 202-879-8136
Year Founded: 1880
Approx.Sls.: $900,000,000
Emp.: 14,000
Fiscal Year-end: 1/31/90
32 Fashion Deptartment Stores in WA, MD, VA, PA, NJ, NY & DE
S.I.C.: 5311
Arnold Aronson *(Chm. Bd. & Chief Exec. Officer)*
Robert J. Mulligan *(Vice Chm. & Chief Admin. Officer)*
Robert B. Mang *(Pres. & Chief Oper. Officer)*
Ron Ackerman *(Sr. V.P.-Mngmt. Info. Services)*
Gerry Barnett *(Sr. V.P.-Real Estate)*
Joe Culver *(Sr. V.P.-Personnel)*
Kai Frost *(Sr. V.P.-Mktg.)*
Joseph F. Gallucci *(Chief Fin. Officer)*
Joel Nichols *(V.P.-Adv.)*
Judith Pickering *(Sec. & Legal Counsel)*
John Novak *(Controller)*
Debra Miller *(Pub. Rels., Fashion & Special Events)*

Principal(s):
Arnold Aronson
Robert J. Mulligan

Computer Systems/Hardware:
IBM System 3033

Outside Service Firm(s):

Arthur Andersen & Co.*(Auditors)*
1666 K Street, N.W.
Washington, DC 20006

Subsidiary:

John Wanamaker, Philadelphia **(1)**
1300 Market St.
Philadelphia, PA 19101
Tel.: 215-422-2000 (100%)
Emp.: 8,000
Fiscal Year-end: 12/31/90
Department Store
S.I.C.: 5311
Arnold Aronson *(Chm. Bd. & Chief Exec. Officer)*
Joseph Gallucci *(Chief Fin. Officer & Sr. V.P.)*
James R. Wells *(Exec. V.P. & Gen. Mgr)*
Elaine Bauer *(Sr. V.P. & Gen. Mdsg. Mgr.-RTW)*
Joseph Culver *(Sr. V.P.-Human Resources)*
Kathy Fraizer *(Sr. V.P. & Gen. Mgr.-Accessories)*
David Prensky *(Sr. V.P. & Gen. Mgr.-Men's)*
Adrian Rice *(Sr. V.P. & Gen. Mgr.-Home Store)*
Donald Godfrey *(V.P.-Stores)*

WOODWORK CORPORATION OF AMERICA
1432 W. 21st St.
Chicago, IL 60608
Tel.: 312-226-4800
Fax: 312-226-3619
Year Founded: 1913
Approx.Sls.: $30,000,000
Emp.: 350
Import Export
Mfr. of Architectural Woodwork, Store Fixtures, Cabinet Work, Bank Fixtures, Special Woodwork, Custom Furniture, Fitting Rooms
S.I.C.: 2541; 2421; 2431; 2434; 2511; 2521
Robert F. Kay *(Pres.)*
Clarence Kamba *(Exec. V.P.)*
A. Bezouska *(V.P.-Architectural Sls.)*
R. Heilman *(V.P.-Mktg.)*
M. Korkosz *(V.P. & Sls. Mgr.)*
Bruce Stulik *(Treas.)*
Richard Siebel *(Sec.)*
Dan Owczarski *(Dir.-Pur.)*

WOOLPERT CONSULTANTS
409 E. Monument Ave.
Dayton, OH 45402
Tel.: 513-461-5660
Fax: 513-461-0743
Year Founded: 1911
Approx.Sls.: $36,000,000
Emp.: 530
Consulting Engineer; Civic Engineering; Sanitary Engineers; Photogrammetic Engineering; Architectural Engineering
S.I.C.: 8711; 8713; 8712
Wallace E. Smith *(Chm. Bd. & Partner)*
James A. Herman *(Chief Oper. Officer, Chm. Exec. Comm., & Ptnr.)*
Robert Geeding *(Chief Fin. Officer & Ptnr.)*
Rex W. Cowden *(Partner)*
Bruce E. Davidson *(Partner)*
Donald Ernst *(Partner)*
William Farno *(Partner)*
Dale Flaherty *(Partner)*
Robert F. Grimes *(Partner)*
Paul W. Gruner *(Partner)*
Mark Lawner *(Partner)*
William Love, Jr. *(Partner)*
Ralph E. Norman, Jr. *(Partner)*
Gary L. Stewart *(Partner)*
Michael Weddle *(Partner)*

Outside Service Firm(s):

Battelle & Battelle*(Auditors)*
3400 South Dixie Dr.
Dayton, OH 45402

WOOLRICH, INC.
Mill St.
Woolrich, PA 17779
Tel.: 717-769-6464 **PA**
Fax: 717-769-6469, Ext. 387
Year Founded: 1830
Sales Range: $100-499 Million
Emp.: 2,076
Fiscal Year-end: 12/31/91
Import Export
Mfr. Men's & Women's Sportswear & Outerwear, Upholstery & Panel Fabrics, Blankets
S.I.C.: 2231; 2329; 5399; 4941; 2339; 2337
Roswell Brayton, Sr. *(Chm. Bd.)*
S. Wade Judy *(Pres. & Chief Exec. Officer)*
Peter D. Culbertson *(Sr. V.P.-Mktg. & Mdsg.)*
Larry F. Little *(Sr. V.P.-Opers. & Sourcing)*
Roswell Brayton, Jr. *(V.P.-Fin.)*
James Haymes *(V.P.-Admin.)*
Richard J. Holcombe *(V.P.-Mktg.)*
James Lawrence *(V.P.-Piece Goods Sls.)*
William J. Peterson, Jr. *(V.P.-Ailey Div.)*
Doris Jodun *(Sec.)*
Sharon Masters *(Asst. Sec.)*
George J. Panko, Jr. *(Asst. Treas.)*
Clair Mattas *(Pur. Agent)*

Computer Systems/Hardware:
4 IBM AS 400's

Outside Service Firm(s):

Stockton Bates & Co.*(Auditors)*
Lancaster, PA

Allendale Mutual Insurance Co.*(Commercial Insurance Carrier)*
Livingston, NJ

Blue Cross & Blue Shield Association*(Group Insurer)*
Wilkes-Barre, PA

Mellon Bank*(Major Banking Relationship)*
State College, PA

William M. Mercer Incorporated*(Pension Manager)*
Philadelphia, PA

Divisions:

Down Products Div. **(1)**
P.O. Box 343,
Broomfield, CO 80020
Tel.: 303-469-3391
Mfr. of Men's & Women's Sprotswear & Outerwear, Upholstery & Panel Fabrics, Blankets
S.I.C.: 2329; 2337; 2339; 2231
Ed Taylor *(Plant Mgr.)*

Woolrich Store Co. **(1)**
4432 Austin Bluffs Pkwy.
Colorado Springs, CO 80918
Tel.: 719-594-0081
Mill Outlet Store
S.I.C.: 5399
Gareth Bishop *(Sr. Mgr.-Western Stores)*

Woolrich Store Co. **(1)**
P.O. Box 680,
Alliance, NE 69301
Tel.: 308-762-4231
Mill Outlet Store
S.I.C.: 5399
Gary Thompson *(Mgr.)*

Woolrich Store Div. **(1)**
Mill St.
Woolrich, PA 17779
Tel.: 717-769-6469
Mill Outlet Store
S.I.C.: 5399
Dean Brubaker *(Gen. Mgr.)*

Subsidiaries:

The Chatham Water Co. **(1)**
Mill St.
Woolrich, PA 17779
Tel.: 717-769-6464 (100%)
Approx.Sls.: $196,000
Emp.: 4
Water Utility
S.I.C.: 4941
John E. Rich, Jr. *(Gen. Mgr.)*

John Rich & Sons **(1)**
900 Market St.
Wilmington, DE 19801
Tel.: 302-421-7432

Non-U.S. Holdings:

Woolcan **(1)**
1880 32nd Ave.
Lachine, PQ S8T 3J7, Canada
Mfr. of Men's & Women's Sportswear & Outerwear, Upholstery & Panel Fabrics, Blankets
S.I.C.: 2231; 2329; 2339; 2337
Buster Leger *(Pres.)*

Woolkong, Ltd. **(1)**
907-8 Po Lung Centre 11 Wang Chiu Rd., Kowloon Bay, Kowloon Hong Kong

Woolkong Ltd. **(1)**
Tower 1 Metroplaza No. 223, Units 2513-19
Level 25, Hing Fong Road
Kwai Fong, New Territories Hong Kong
Mfr. of Men's & Women's Sportswear & Outerwear, Upholstery & Panel Fabrics, Blankets
S.I.C.: 2231; 2337; 2329; 2339

WOOLVERTON OLDSMOBILE-G.M.C. TRUCK, INC.
1325 Cassat Ave.
Jacksonville, FL 32205
Tel.: 904-387-6511 **DE**

Woolverton Oldsmobile-G.M.C. Truck, Inc.—(Continued)

Fax: 904-387-3717
Year Founded: 1935
Sales Range: $10-19 Million
Emp.: 60
Automobile & Truck Dealership
S.I.C.: 5511
Fred T. Woolverton, Jr. *(Pres.)*
Thomas E. Booth *(Sec. & Treas.)*
Principal(s):
Fred T. Woolverton, Jr.

THE WOOSTER BRUSH COMPANY
604 Madison Ave.
Wooster, OH 44691
Mailing Address:
P.O. Drawer B
Wooster, OH 44691
Tel.: 216-264-4440
Tel.: 800-392-7246 **OH**
Telex: 986355
Fax: 216-263-0495
Year Founded: 1851
Approx.Sls.: $55,000,000
Emp.: 520
Fiscal Year-end: 4/30/90
Import Export
Manufacture of Paint Brushes & Roller Applicators
S.I.C.: 3991; 3423
Woodrow J. Zook *(Chm. Bd.)*
Stanley R. Welty, Jr. *(Pres.)*
David A. Rowekamp *(Sr. V.P.-Sls. & Mktg.)*
Thomas W. Zook *(V.P.-Admin, Asst. Treas. & Asst. Sec.)*
Richard J. Crowell *(V.P.-Mfg.)*
Robert Fravel *(V.P.-Natl. Accts.)*
Jack Kane *(V.P.-Mktg.)*
Jon Rose *(V.P.-Sls.)*
Allan K. Rodd *(Treas. & Asst. Sec.)*
William Fagert *(Asst. Treas.)*
Mike Palmer *(Mgr.- Human Resources)*
Robert Ricksecker *(Mgr.-Adv.)*
Scott Rutledge *(Mgr.-Mktg.)*
James L. Riggs *(Pur. Agent)*

Outside Service Firm(s):

Card, Palmer, Sibbison & Co.*(Auditors)*
Cleveland, OH

Allendale Mutual Insurance Co.*(Commercial Insurance Carrier)*
1301 Atwood Ave.
Johnston, RI 02919
Tel.: 401-275-3000

Metropolitan Life Insurance Co.*(Group Insurer)*
One Madison Ave.
New York, NY 10010-3690
Tel.: 215-578-9292

Bank One*(Major Banking Relationship)*
Wooster, OH

Bank One*(Major Banking Relationship)*
Kettering Tower
Dayton, OH 45401
Tel.: 513-449-8600

Continental Bank N. A.*(Major Banking Relationship)*
231 S. LaSalle St.
Chicago, IL 60697
Tel.: 312-828-2345
Tel.: 800-426-5754
Telex: 312-828-1783

Chicago Asset Management Co.*(Pension Manager)*
11 S. LaSalle
Chicago, IL 60603

Continental Bank N. A.*(Pension Manager)*
231 S. LaSalle St.
Chicago, IL 60697
Tel.: 312-828-2345
Tel.: 800-426-5754
Telex: 312-828-1783

Division:

Wooster Magikoter West Division **(1)**
1960 Joule St.
Reno, NV 89703
Tel.: 702-786-1950
Fax: 702-786-2004
Household Or Industrial Brushes; Paint Rollers
S.I.C.: 3991
Charles Sharkey *(Plant Mgr.)*

WORDPERFECT CORPORATION
1555 N. Technology Way
Orem, UT 84057
Tel.: 801-222-5000
Tel.: 800-451-5151
Telex: 820618
Fax: 801-222-5077
Year Founded: 1979
Approx.Sls.: $532,000,000
Emp.: 2,758
Fiscal Year-end: 12/31/91
Export
Mfr. of Computer Software
S.I.C.: 7372; 7371; 3695
Corporate Giving Program: Company Offers a Software Donation Program. Charitable Donations Remain within the State & Go to Non-Profit Organizations & Educational & Awareness Campaigns
Bruce W. Bastian *(Chm. Bd.)*
Alan C. Ashton *(Pres.)*
Dan Lunt *(Sr. V.P.)*
R. Duff Thompson *(V.P. & Gen. Counsel)*
Greg Blackham *(V.P.-Software Devel.)*
Brent Done *(V.P.-Sls.)*
John Lewis *(V.P.-International)*
Andre Peterson *(V.P.)*
Clive Winn *(V.P.-Mktg.)*
Freida Childs *(Sec.)*
McKay Matthews *(Controller)*
Jeff Acerson *(Dir.-Corp. Communications)*
Newton Andrus *(Dir.-Pur. & Property Services)*
Claire Averett *(Dir.-Personnel)*
Kerri Brock *(Dir.-Channel Mktg.)*
Greg Butterfield *(Dir.-Govt. Accts. Div.)*
Royce Bybee *(Dir.-DataPerfect)*
Kal Farr *(Dir.-Security)*
Mike Grayson *(Dir.-Publications)*
Don Harris *(Dir.-Mktg., Latin America)*
Kris Johnson *(Dir.-ABP Devel.)*
John Lockwood *(Dir.-Telecommunications)*
David Pearson *(Dir.-Intl. PC Product Mktg.)*
Pam Pyle *(Dir.-Adv.)*
Ann McCallistar *(Mgr.-Employee Benefits)*
Lesa Roberts *(Production Coord.)*

Principal(s):
Bruce W. Bastian
Alan C. Ashton

No. of Mfg. Plants/Facilities: 1
No. of U.S. Offices: 1
No. of Foreign Offices: 44

Computer Systems/Hardware:
IBM; DEC VAX, Macintosh, Next, DG, IBM System 370, Unix

Outside Service Firm(s):

Price Waterhouse*(Auditors)*
Salt Lake City, UT

Davis, Hoxie, Faithfull & Hapgood*(Legal Firm)*
New York, NY

First Security Bank of Utah*(Major Banking Relationship)*
Orem, UT

Subsidiary:

Wordperfect Manufacturing **(1)**
510 W. 510 S.
Lindon, UT 84057
Tel.: 801-221-5000
Tel.: 800-526-6215
Emp.: 700
Production/Copy Plant; Packaging & Labeling Services for WordPerfect Products
S.I.C.: 7389

WORLD AEROSPACE CORPORATION
8625 Monticello Lane, N.
Maple Grove, MN 55369
Tel.: 612-424-8999
Fax: 612-424-1419
Fax: 612-424-3599
Year Founded: 1946
Assets: $16,936,593
Liabilities: $6,202,263
Net Worth: $10,734,330
Sales Range: $20-39 Million
Emp.: 120
Fiscal Year-end: 12/31/91
Machining Parts & Components For Jet Engines & Aircraft For Both Commercial & Defense Application
S.I.C.: 3724
Isaac E. Phelps *(Pres. & Chief Exec. Officer)*
Isaac E. Phelps, II *(V.P.)*
Gary L. Hadley *(Treas. & Chief Exec. Officer)*
Kimberly Campbell *(Sec.)*
Jim Barth *(Mgr.-Sls.)*
I.E. Phelps, II *(Mgr.-Mfg. Engrng.)*

Outside Service Firm(s):

Larson, Ludwig, Stokes, Pecoraro, Combs & Bohne*(Auditors)*
San Diego, CA

Larson, Allen, Weishair & Co.*(Legal Firm)*
Minneapolis, MN

Mackall, Crounse & Moore*(Legal Firm)*
1600 TCF Tower
Minneapolis, MN 55402
Tel.: 612-333-1341

First Bank, N.A.*(Major Banking Relationship)*
Minneapolis, MN

WORLD CARPETS, INC.
One World Plaza
Dalton, GA 30722
Mailing Address:
P.O. Box 1448,
Dalton, GA 30722
Tel.: 706-278-8000
Tel.: 800-241-4900 **GA**
Telex: 6827148 WORLD UW
Fax: 706-278-9454
Year Founded: 1954
Approx.Sls.: $225,000,000
Emp.: 2,090
Fiscal Year-end: 6/30/92
Export
Textile Mill Products; Carpets& Custom Rugs
S.I.C.: 2273; 2392

John Shaheen *(Chm. Bd.)*
David Shaheen *(Vice Chm. & Chief Exec. Officer)*
Piera Shaheen *(Vice Chm.)*
David Polley *(Pres.)*
Martha A. McCorkle *(Chief Fin. Officer & V.P.-Fin.)*
Charles Mitchell *(V.P.-Mfg.)*
Bill Waters *(V.P.-Mktg.)*
Ronny Williams *(V.P.-Information Services)*
Ken Beaudoin *(Dir.-Personnel)*
Jim Carrier *(Dir.-Pur.)*
Principal(s):
John Shaheen
David Shaheen
Piera Shaheen

No. of Mfg. Plants/Facilities: 7
No. of U.S. Offices: 13

Computer Systems/Hardware:
IBM 3083

Outside Service Firm(s):

Goodson-Decosimo & Company*(Auditors)*
Dalton, GA

Travelers Insurance Co.*(Group Insurer)*
1 Tower Square
Hartford, CT 06183-2492
Tel.: 203-277-4542
Fax: 203-277-5038

King & Spalding*(Legal Firm)*
Trust Co. Tower
Atlanta, GA 30303
Tel.: 404-572-4600

Hardwick Bank*(Major Banking Relationship)*
Dalton, GA

Alex. Brown & Sons*(Pension Manager)*
Boston, MA

WORLD COMPUTER CORP.
985 W. Entrance Dr.
Auburn Hills, MI 48326
Tel.: 313-377-4840 **MI**
Fax: 313-377-2024
Approx.Sls.: $35,000,000
Emp.: 280
Design & Manufacture Integrated Computer Systems for Financial Institutions
S.I.C.: 7373; 7372
William J. Devers *(Chm. Bd.)*
Donn Schulte *(Pres. & Chief Exec. Officer)*
Gerald Campbell *(Chief Fin. Officer)*
Dave Selina *(Sr. V.P.-Mktg. & Sls.)*
Ken Sucher *(Sr. V.P.)*

Outside Service Firm(s):

Price Waterhouse*(Auditors)*
200 Renaissance Center, Ste. 3900
Detroit, MI 48243

Lakeshore National Bank*(Major Banking Relationship)*
Chicago, IL

WORLD JAI-ALAI
(Sub. of WJA Realty Limited Partnership)
3500 N.W. 37th Ave.
Miami, FL 33142
Tel.: 305-633-6400 **DE**
Fax: 305-634-7013
Approx.Sls.: $36,241,000
Emp.: 1,355
Jai-Alai
S.I.C.: 7941
Richard P. Donovan *(Pres., Chief Exec. & Fin. Officer)*
H. Paul Rico *(V.P.)*
Rudy Angulo *(Controller)*
Daniel J. Licciardi *(Gen. Mgr.)*
David Lemmon *(Dir.-Pub. Rels. & Adv.)*
Gerald Robinson *(Mgr.-Data Processing)*

No. of U.S. Offices: 4

Computer Systems/Hardware:
IBM System 36 & IBM PC

Outside Service Firm(s):

Bingham, Dana & Gould*(Legal Firm)*
150 Federal St.
Boston, MA 02110
Tel.: 617-951-8000
Fax: 617-951-8736

Divisions:

Fort Pierce Jai-Alai **(1)**
Kings Hwy. at Peco's Rd.
Fort Pierce, FL 34950
Tel.: 305-633-6400
Approx.Sls.: $4,603,000
Emp.: 135
Oper. of Jai-Alai
S.I.C.: 7941
Bill Diaz *(Gen. Mgr.)*

Miami Jai-Alai **(1)**
3500 N.W. 37th Ave.
Miami, FL 33142
Tel.: 305-633-6400
Emp.: 500
Opr. of Jai-Alai
S.I.C.: 7941
Richard P. Donovan *(Chief Exec. Officer)*
R. Paul Rico *(V.P. & G.M.)*
David Lemmon *(Dir.-Pub. Rels.)*

Ocala Jai-Alai **(1)**
P.O. Box 548,
Orange Lake, FL 32681
Tel.: 305-633-6400
Emp.: 130
Opr. of Jai-Alai
S.I.C.: 7941
Richard P. Donovan *(Chief Exec. Officer)*
Tom Contreras *(Gen. Mgr.)*

Tampa Jai-Alai **(1)**
5125 S. Dale, Mabry Hwy.
Tampa, FL 33611
Tel.: 305-633-6400
Emp.: 360
Opr. of Jai-Alai
S.I.C.: 7941
Richard P. Donovan *(Chief Exec. Officer)*
Giles Ellis, Jr. *(V.P. & G.M.)*
M. Mark Beiro *(Dir.-Pub. Rels.)*

World Jai-Alai Players **(1)**
3500 N.W. 37th Ave.
Miami, FL 33142
Tel.: 305-633-6400
Emp.: 165
Supplier of Jai-Alai Players to Other Divs.
S.I.C.: 7941
Richard P. Donovan *(Chief Exec. Officer)*

Non-U.S. Holding:

Guernica Espectaculos & Turismo, S.A. **(1)**
Carlos Gangoiti 14
Guernica, Vizcaya Spain
Tel.: 011-344-685-0200 (50%)
S.I.C.: 7941
Francisco Aldimiz *(Chief Oper. Officer)*

WORLD OIL COMPANY
9302 Garfield
South Gate, CA 90280
Tel.: 213-560-8801
Fax: 213-928-5623
Year Founded: 1948
Approx.Sls.: $310,000,000
Emp.: 400
Petroleum Refining & Marketing
S.I.C.: 2911; 5172
Bernard B. Roth *(Chm. Bd. & Chief Exec. Officer)*
Robert S. Roth *(Pres.)*
Mark A. Snell *(Exec. V.P.)*
Toshiko Chan *(Office Mgr.)*

Principal(s):
Bernard B. Roth
Robert S. Roth

Outside Service Firm(s):

KPMG Peat Marwick*(Auditors)*
725 S. Figueroa St.
Los Angeles, CA 90017
Tel.: 213-972-4000

Bank of America NT&SA*(Major Banking Relationship)*
555 So. Flower St., 5th Fl.
Los Angeles, CA 90071
Tel.: 213-228-3526
Fax: 213-228-4062

WORLD PUBLISHING COMPANY
(Formerly Newspaper Printing Corp. Inc.)
315 S. Boulder
Tulsa, OK 74103
Mailing Address:
P.O. Box 1770,
Tulsa, OK 74102
Tel.: 918-583-2161
Fax: 918-582-0415
Year Founded: 1941
Emp.: 860
Newspaper Printing & Publishing
S.I.C.: 2711; 2759; 6719
Robert Lorton *(Chm.)*
Kenneth Fleming *(Pres. & Chief Oper. Officer)*
Robert Lorton III *(V.P.-Admin. & Opers.)*
Richard Major *(Mgr.-Business Systems)*

Computer Systems/Hardware:
DEC

Outside Service Firm(s):

Connecticut General Life Insurance Co.*(Group Insurer)*
P.O. Box 2975,
Hartford, CT 06104
Tel.: 203-726-6000

Boone, Smith, Davis & Hurst*(Legal Firm)*
Tulsa, OK

Farmers & Merchants Bank*(Major Banking Relationship)*
Tulsa, OK

WORLD SHIPPING, INC.
11740 Clifton Blvd.
Lakewood, OH 44107
Tel.: 216-228-7676 **OH**
Fax: 216-228-5921
Year Founded: 1962
Approx.Sls.: $25,000,000
Emp.: 200
Fiscal Year-end: 2/28/91
Import Export
International Shipping Agency
S.I.C.: 4729; 4731
Corporate Giving Program: United Way
Jack E. Hunger *(Chm. Bd. & Pres.)*
Richard Coleman *(Exec. V.P.)*
Russell Graef *(Sr. V.P.)*
Steve D. Hossa *(V.P.-Liner Div.)*
Hugh Goldie *(V.P.-Opers.)*
John E. Hunger *(Chief Fin. Officer & Treas.)*
Douglas Denny *(Sec.)*
Fred M. Hunger *(Dir.-Corp. Devel.)*
Principal(s):
Jack E. Hunger

No. of U.S. Offices: 16

Computer Systems/Hardware:
IBM AS/400

Outside Service Firm(s):

Coopers & Lybrand*(Auditors)*
1500 One Cleveland Center, 1375 East 9th Street
Cleveland, OH 44114
Tel.: 216-241-4380
Fax: 216-575-0170

Marsh & McLennan*(Commercial Insurance Carrier)*
1 Cleveland Center, Ste. 2500, 1375 E. 9th St.
Cleveland, OH 44114
Tel.: 216-241-0908

Massachusetts Mutual Life Insurance Co.*(Group Insurer)*
Boston, MA

Calfee, Halter & Griswold*(Legal Firm)*
800 Superior Ave., Ste. 1800
Cleveland, OH 44115-2688
Tel.: 216-622-8200
Fax: 216-241-0816

Society National Bank*(Major Banking Relationship)*
Cleveland, OH

Society National Bank*(Pension Manager)*
Cleveland, OH

Subsidiary:

Container Port Group **(1)**
1340 Depot St., Ste. 103
Cleveland, OH 44116
Tel.: 216-333-1330
Tel.: 800-448-2742
Emp.: 130
Marine Container Repair & Storage; Inland Transportation
S.I.C.: 4212; 7699; 4449; 4213
Jack E. Hunger *(Pres.)*
Richard C. Coleman *(Exec. V.P.)*
Russell Graef *(Sr. V.P.)*
John E. Hunger *(Chief Fin. Officer)*

WORLD TITLE COMPANY
7530 N. Glenoaks Blvd.
Burbank, CA 91504
Tel.: 818-767-2800 **CA**
Fax: 818-771-1367
Year Founded: 1980
Emp.: 595
Real Estate Title Insurance
S.I.C.: 6361
Mike Lowther *(Chm. Bd. & Pres.)*
Harold Humphrey *(Vice Chm. Bd.)*
Blaine Osburn *(Mgr.-Human Resources)*

WORLD'S FINEST CHOCOLATE, INC.
4801 S. Lawndale Ave.
Chicago, IL 60632
Tel.: 312-847-4600 **DE**
Fax: 312-847-4006
Year Founded: 1938
Approx.Sls.: $100,000,000
Emp.: 600
Fiscal Year-end: 12/31/90
Mfr. Chocolate & Cocoa Products
S.I.C.: 2066
Edmond Opler, Jr. *(Chm. Bd., Pres. & Chief Exec. Officer)*
Thomas F. Morris *(Exec. V.P. & Chief Fin. Officer)*
Donald Mann *(Sr. V.P.)*
Chester M. Klos *(V.P.)*
George Bullwinkel *(Gen. Counsel)*
Joseph McGinnis *(Dir.-Mktg.)*
Paul Snyder *(Dir.-Data Processing)*
R. Schumann *(Dir.-Quality Control)*
Senn Gee *(Mgr.-Pur.)*
H. Schmidt *(Mgr.-Direct Mktg.)*
Greg Serratore *(Mgr.-Personnel)*
Pam Shields *(Mgr.-Mktg.)*
J. Zombek *(Mgr.-Corp. Travel Planner)*
Principal(s):
Edmond Opler, Jr.

Computer Systems/Hardware:
IBM System 38

Outside Service Firm(s):

Schwartz, Cooper, Kolb & Gaynor*(Legal Firm)*
Chicago, IL

First National Bank of Chicago*(Major Banking Relationship)*
One First National Plaza
Chicago, IL 60670
Tel.: 312-732-9781
Tel.: 312-732-4050
Fax: 312-732-4840
Fax: 312-732-3055

Non-U.S. Holdings:

World's Finest Chocolate Australia Pty. Ltd. **(1)**
8 Bridge Rd.
Stanmore, N.S.W. 2048, Australia
Tel.: 02-550-1633 (100%)
Mfrs. Chocolate Products
S.I.C.: 2066
Luke Nadj *(Mng. Dir.)*
Andrew Janiszewski *(Controller)*
David Nance *(Sls. Mgr.)*
Donald Jarmen *(Dir.-Pur.)*

World's Finest Chocolate Canada Ltd. **(1)**
Second Street
Campbellford, ON K0L 1L0, Canada
Tel.: 705-653-3590 (100%)
Mfrs. Cocoa & Chocolate Products
S.I.C.: 2066
Karl Howse *(V.P. & Gen. Mgr.)*
Milt Neuman *(Sls. Mgr.)*

Subsidiary:

Cook Chocolate Canada Ltd. **(2)**
Second St.
Campbellford, ON K1L 1L0, Canada
Tel.: 705-653-3590 (100%)
Mfrs. Cocoa Products
S.I.C.: 2066
Karl Howse *(V.P. & Gen. Mgr.)*

THE WORNICK COMPANY
500 Airport Blvd., Ste. 442
Burlingame, CA 94010
Mailing Address:
P.O. Box 1700,
Burlingame, CA 94011
Tel.: 415-342-6558 **DE**
Fax: 415-342-0833
Approx.Sls.: $91,600,000
Emp.: 700
Food Processing & Packaging
S.I.C.: 2032; 2099,
Ronald C. Wornick *(Chm. Bd. & Pres.)*

No. of Mfg. Plants/Facilities: 3
No. of U.S. Offices: 3

Outside Service Firm(s):

KPMG Peat Marwick*(Auditors)*
3 Embarcadero Center
San Francisco, CA 94111
Tel.: 415-951-0100
Fax: 415-397-1129

Alexander & Alexander*(Commercial Insurance Carrier)*
McAllen, TX

General American Life Insurance Co.*(Group Insurer)*
700 Market
Saint Louis, MO 63101
Tel.: 314-525-5458
Fax: 314-525-3677

Gary Thomasson, Paul, Marks*(Legal Firm)*
Corpus Christi, TX

Bank of America NT&SA*(Major Banking Relationship)*
Burlingame, CA

McAllen State Bank*(Major Banking Relationship)*
McAllen, TX

The Pacific Bank*(Major Banking Relationship)*
San Francisco, CA

Texas State Bank*(Major Banking Relationship)*
McAllen, TX

Subsidiaries:

Right Away Foods Corporation **(1)**
200 N. First St.
McAllen, TX 78502
Tel.: 210-687-9401

Shelf Stable Foods, Inc. **(1)**
1201 N. Stockwell Rd.
Evansville, IN 47715
Tel.: 812-477-5361

Wornick Properties, Inc. **(1)**
500 Airport Blvd., Ste. 442, P.O. Box 1700
Burlingame, CA 94011
Tel.: 415-342-6558

WORRELL ENTERPRISES, INC.
1450 S. Dixie Hwy.
Boca Raton, FL 33432
Mailing Address:
P.O. Box 820
Deerfield Beach, FL 33403
Tel.: 407-338-3298
Fax: 804-296-3621
Sales Range: $100-499 Million
Emp.: 1,300
Newspaper Publishing
S.I.C.: 2711
Thomas E. Worrell, Jr. *(Chm. Bd. & Pres.)*
Ed Freakley *(Exec. V.P.)*

Principal(s):
Thomas E. Worrell, Jr.

Computer Systems/Hardware:
AT&T; Compaq

Outside Service Firm(s):

Price Waterhouse*(Auditors)*
919 E. Main St.
Richmond, VA 23219
Tel.: 804-648-9281

McGuire, Woods, Battle & Boothe*(Legal Firm)*
One James Ctr., 801 E. Main St.
Richmond, VA 23220
Tel.: 804-644-4131

First National Bank of Chicago*(Major Banking Relationship)*
One First National Plaza
Chicago, IL 60670
Tel.: 312-732-9781
Tel.: 312-732-4050
Fax: 312-732-4840
Fax: 312-732-3055

WORSLEY COMPANIES INC.
10 Cardinal Dr.
Wilmington, NC 28403
Mailing Address:
P.O. Box 3227,
Wilmington, NC 28406
Tel.: 919-395-5300 **NC**
Fax: 919-395-6691
Year Founded: 1941
Approx.Sls.: $170,000,000
Emp.: 1,575
Fiscal Year-end: 6/30/90
Wholesale Petroleum Products & Convenient Stores
S.I.C.: 5171; 5411
Walter C. Worsley, Jr. *(Chm. Bd. & Pres.)*
William A. Ambrose *(Exec. V.P., Treas. & Dir.-Investor Rels.)*
Walter C. Worsley, III *(V.P.)*
Julius Moore *(Dir.-Human Resources)*
Joel Bailey *(Dir.-Pur.)*
Don Quinn *(Mgr.-Environmental Services)*
Roger D. Teague *(Sec. & Controller)*

Principal(s):
Walter C. Worsley, Jr.
Walter C. Worsley, III

No. of U.S. Offices: 18

Computer Systems/Hardware:
IBM System 36

Outside Service Firm(s):

Cherry, Bekaert & Holland*(Auditors)*
Wilmington, NC

Lanier, Whaley & Company*(Auditors)*
Wilmington, NC

Harold W. Wells & Son*(Commercial Insurance Carrier)*
Wilmington, NC

Woodbury & Co.*(Group Insurer)*
Wilmington, NC

Branch Banking & Trust Company*(Investment Banker)*
Wilmington, NC

Murchison, Taylor, Kendrick, Gibson & Davenport*(Legal Firm)*
Wilmington, NC

Branch Banking & Trust Company*(Major Banking Relationship)*
Wilmington, NC

Branch Banking & Trust Company*(Pension Manager)*
Wilmington, NC

WORZALLA PUBLISHING CO., INC.
3535 Jefferson St.
Stevens Point, WI 54481
Mailing Address:
P.O. Box 307,
Stevens Point, WI 54481
Tel.: 715-344-9600
Tel.: 800-873-6655 **WI**
Fax: 715-344-2578
Year Founded: 1892
Assets: $21,277,325
Liabilities: $16,273,175
Net Worth: $5,004,150
Approx.Sls.: $31,215,609
Emp.: 352
Fiscal Year-end: 3/31/92
Export
Juvenile & Text Books, Sheetfed & Web Printing Plus Binding
S.I.C.: 2732; 2789
Charles W. Nason *(Chm. Bd. & Pres.)*
Frank Anderko *(V.P.-Mfg. & Sec.)*
Cedric Burroughs *(V.P.-Admin.)*
William Little *(V.P.-Treas. & Controller)*
John Prais *(V.P.-Sls.)*
Cheri Karch *(Dir.-Corp. Rels.)*
Sam Crockett *(Supvr.-Acctg.)*
Bill Mansur *(Supvr.-Data Processing)*
Jerry Rockman *(Supvr.-Education, Safety & Training)*
Mary Zurawski *(Supvr.-Pur.)*
Ron Blaha *(Mgr.-Quality Assurance)*
Marianne Schiefer *(Mgr.-Human Resources)*

Principal(s):
Employee-Owned

No. of Mfg. Plants/Facilities: 1
No. of U.S. Offices: 8

Computer Systems/Hardware:
Unisys

Outside Service Firm(s):

Cottingham & Butler*(Commercial Insurance Carrier)*
Dubuque, IA

Foley & Lardner*(Legal Firm)*
777 E. Wisconsin Ave.
Milwaukee, WI 53202
Tel.: 414-271-2400

Bank One Milwaukee, N.A.*(Major Banking Relationship)*
111 E. Wisconsin Ave.
Milwaukee, WI
Tel.: 414-765-3000

WOTCO INC.
(Formerly Western Oil Tool & Manufacturing Company)
415 First St.
Mills, WY 82602
Mailing Address:
P.O. Box 260
Casper, WY 82601
Tel.: 307-235-1591
Fax: 307-265-8554
Approx.Sls.: $21,000,000
Emp.: 154
Iron Or Steel Expansion Joints
S.I.C.: 3532
Richard A. Jahn *(Pres.)*
Harold "Bud" Allison *(V.P.-Opers.)*
Ted M. Atchley *(V.P.-Mktg.)*
Steve Shellenberger *(V.P.-Fin.)*

Outside Service Firm(s):

Macy & Associates*(Auditors)*
Casper, WY

Brown, Drew, Apostolos & Massey*(Legal Firm)*
512 Petroleum Bldg.
Casper, WY 82601

Division:

Double Diamond Dist. Inc. (1)
3400 E. Yellowstone Hwy.
Casper, WY 82609
Tel.: 307-234-4646
Distribution
S.I.C.: 3532
Donald Swanstrom *(Mgr.-Sls.)*

WOZNIAK INDUSTRIES, INC.
Two Mid America Plaza, Ste. 706
Oakbrook Terrace, IL 60181
Tel.: 708-954-3400 **IL**
Fax: 708-954-3605
Year Founded: 1985
Approx.Sls.: $85,000,000
Emp.: 800
Metal Stampings; Injection Molding of Plastics; Iron & Steel Forgings; Electroplating of Metals or Formed Products
S.I.C.: 3469; 3089; 3462; 3471
Edward F. Wozniak *(Pres. & Chief Exec. Officer)*
Anthony Vastaris *(Chief Fin. Officer & V.P.)*
Alexis Stadt *(Mgr.-Pur.)*

Outside Service Firm(s):

American National Bank & Trust Co. of Chicago*(Major Banking Relationship)*
33 N. LaSalle St.
Chicago, IL 60690
Tel.: 312-661-5000
Telex: 190066
Fax: 312-853-0290

WRAY-WARD-LASETER ADVERTISING
1100 E. Morehead St.
Charlotte, NC 28204
Tel.: 704-332-9071
Fax: 704-375-5971
Year Founded: 1977
Approx.Billings: $11,000,000
Emp.: 24
Fiscal Year-end: 12/31/90
Media Advertising, Direct Marketing, Public Relations & Promotions
S.I.C.: 7311
Robert L. Ward *(Pres.)*
James F. Laseter, III *(Exec. V.P.)*
Katherine Wentz *(V.P., Controller)*
Phil Whitesell *(Dir., Pub. Rels.)*

Outside Service Firm(s):

Wachovia Bank & Trust Co.*(Major Banking Relationship)*
Charlotte, NC

CAROLE WREN, INC.
75 Ninth Ave., 3rd Fl.
New York, NY 10011
Tel.: 212-675-7023 **NY**
Fax: 212-989-6707
Year Founded: 1946
Approx.Sls.: $20,000,000
Emp.: 60
Mfr. of Women's & Children's Sportswear
S.I.C.: 2339; 2369
Martin J. Leff *(Pres.)*
Jeffrey Leff *(V.P.-Sls.)*
Norman Wolf *(Sec. & Treas.)*

Outside Service Firm(s):

Irving Kaufman & Company*(Auditors)*
New York, NY

Chemical Banking Corp.*(Major Banking Relationship)*
277 Park Ave.
New York, NY 10041
Tel.: 212-310-6407
Fax: 212-310-4526

WRIGHT BRAND FOODS, INC.
2310 McGhee St.
Vernon, TX 76384
Mailing Address:
P.O. Box 1779,
Vernon, TX 76385
Tel.: 817-553-1811
Fax: 817-552-2912
Year Founded: 1965
Emp.: 425
Smoked Meat Processor
S.I.C.: 2013
Robert L. Wright *(Pres.)*
Bob Williamson *(Chief Fin. Officer)*
W. Dan Wright *(V.P.)*
William E. Wright *(Sec.)*

Outside Service Firm(s):

Wagner National Bank*(Major Banking Relationship)*
Vernon, TX
Fax: 817-552-2912

F.B. WRIGHT CO.
9999 Mercier Ave.
Dearborn, MI 48121
Tel.: 313-843-8250 **MI**
Telex: 23-5753
Fax: 313-843-8450
Year Founded: 1938
Approx.Sls.: $35,000,000
Emp.: 160
Fiscal Year-end: 12/31/88
Import Export
Wholesale Rubber & Plastic Industrial Supplies
S.I.C.: 5085
William J. Reno *(Chm. Bd., Pres. & Chief Exec. Officer)*
Jack A. Doerr *(Chief Fin. Officer, V.P. & Treas.)*
John L. King *(Legal Officer)*
Richard Pitts *(Dir.-Pur.)*
Richard Steffes *(Dir.-Data Processing)*

Principal(s):
William J. Reno

No. of Mfg. Plants/Facilities: 5
No. of U.S. Offices: 5

WRIGHT-SCHUCHART, INC.
425 Pontiuf Ave. North
Seattle, WA 98109
Mailing Address:
P.O. Box 3764,
Seattle, WA 98124
Tel.: 206-447-7545
Fax: 206-447-7535
Year Founded: 1885
Assets: $68,000,000
Liabilities: $53,000,000
Net Worth: $15,000,000
Approx.Sls.: $470,000,000
Emp.: 3,000
Contractors
S.I.C.: 1541; 1542; 1629; 1711; 1731
Bruce Connor *(Pres.)*
Maureen Israel *(Chief Exec. Officer & Controller)*
Daniel McDougall *(Sr. V.P.)*
Paul Myhre *(V.P. & Treas.)*
Goerge S. Schuchart, Jr. *(V.P.)*
Richard Bangert *(V.P.)*
Larry Worth *(Controller)*
Tom Hughes *(Dir.-Data Processing)*
Robert Helsell *(Dir.)*

Computer Systems/Hardware:
IBM System 38 Model 40

Outside Service Firm(s):

Deloitte & Touche*(Auditors)*
700 Fifth Ave., Suite 4500
Seattle, WA 98104-5044
Tel.: 206-292-1800

Blue Cross of Washington & Alaska*(Group Insurer)*
Seattle, WA

Foster, Pepper & Shefelman*(Legal Firm)*
1111 3rd Ave. Bldg.
Seattle, WA 98101
Tel.: 206-447-4400

Rainier National Bank*(Major Banking Relationship)*
Seattle, WA

Seattle First National Bank*(Major Banking Relationship)*
701 Fifth Avenue
Seattle, WA 98104
Tel.: 206-358-3035

Rainier National Bank*(Pension Manager)*
Seattle, WA

G.F. WRIGHT STEEL & WIRE COMPANY
243 Stafford
Worcester, MA 01603
Tel.: 508-754-6824
Fax: 508-755-3243
Approx.Sls.: $12,000,000
Emp.: 125
Mesh, Netting & Woven Wire Made From Purchased Wire; Hardware Cloth
S.I.C.: 3496
Merrill W. Wright, Jr. *(Chm. Bd. & Pres.)*
John A. Ritacco *(V.P. & Treas.)*
Francis A. Capalbo *(V.P.-Sls.)*

Outside Service Firm(s):

KPMG Peat Marwick*(Auditors)*
One Boston Place
Boston, MA 02108
Tel.: 617-723-7700

Bowditch & Dewey*(Legal Firm)*
Boston, MA

State Street Bank & Trust Co.*(Major Banking Relationship)*
P.O. Box 366,
Boston, MA 02101
Tel.: 617-426-5523

WM. E. WRIGHT LIMITED PARTNERSHIP
South St.
West Warren, MA 01092
Tel.: 413-436-7732 DE
Fax: 413-436-9785
Year Founded: 1897
Emp.: 400
Wrights Tapes & Braids, Laces & Trims, & Decorator Trims, Bondex, Ribbon, Thread
S.I.C.: 2396; 3965; 5131; 2241
John J. Lynch *(Pres.)*
Michael D. Fuss *(Chief Fin. Officer & V.P.)*
Patricia DeSantis *(V.P.-Natl. Accts.)*
Jack Matsen *(V.P.-Sls., Western Region)*
Douglas J. Rains *(V.P.-Natl. Accts.)*
Stanley White *(V.P.-Sls./Eastern Reg.)*
Paul A. Willer *(V.P.-Sls.)*
Joseph Gotta *(Dir.-Systems & Distribution)*
Frank DeGray *(Mgr.-Pur.)*

Outside Service Firm(s):

Price Waterhouse*(Auditors)*
200 E. Randolph
Chicago, IL 60601
Tel.: 312-565-1500

Altheimer & Gray*(Legal Firm)*
10 S. Wacker Dr.
Chicago, IL 60606
Tel.: 312-715-4000

Division:

Boye Needle **(1)**
4343 N. Ravenswood Ave.
Chicago, IL 60613
Tel.: 312-472-0354
Fax: 312-472-9377
Emp.: 70
Fiscal Year-end: 12/31/90
Import Export
Art Needlework & Sewing Notions; Knitting Needles & Crochet Hooks
S.I.C.: 3496
John J. Lynch *(Pres.)*
Michael Fuss *(Chief Fin. Officer)*
Don Bodziak *(Dir.-Opers.)*
Jan Ryan *(Mgr.-Employee Rels.)*

WROUGHT WASHER MFG., INC.
2100 S. Bay St.
Milwaukee, WI 53207
Tel.: 414-744-0771 WI
Fax: 414-482-0144
Year Founded: 1887
Approx.Sls.: $35,000,000
Emp.: 350
Export
Mfr. Washers & Stampings
S.I.C.: 3452; 3469
E.G. Pruim *(Chm. Bd., Pres. & Chief Exec. Officer)*
John C. Allen *(V.P.-Sls. & Mktg.)*
Anthony Dicola *(V.P.-Mfg.)*
Paul J. Schulz *(V.P.-Fin. & Controller)*
J.H. Kringel *(Sec.)*
Kenneth Krzykowski *(Dir.-Pur.)*
James Otto *(Mgr.-Human Resources)*
D. Zupancic *(Mgr.-Quality Control)*
Principal(s):
E.G. Pruim
R.W. Allsop & Assoc.

No. of Mfg. Plants/Facilities: 3

Outside Service Firm(s):

Deloitte & Touche*(Auditors)*
250 E. Wisconsin Ave.
Milwaukee, WI 53202-4283
Tel.: 414-271-3000

Michael, Best & Friedrich*(Legal Firm)*
100 East Wisconsin Avenue
Milwaukee, WI 53202
Tel.: 414-271-6560

Subsidiary:

Frankulin Tool & Mfg. Co. **(1)**
16680 W. Cleveland Ave.
New Berlin, WI 53151
Tel.: 414-782-4524
Fax: 414-782-5546
Emp.: 25
Tool & Die Design & Mfg.
S.I.C.: 3544
R. Franklin *(Pres. & Chief Oper. Officer)*

WUNDA WEVE CARPET CO.
1221 Batesville Rd.
Greenville, SC 29650
Mailing Address:
P.O. Box 167
Greenville, SC 29602
Tel.: 803-879-8000
Approx.Sls.: $90,000,000
Export
Mfr. of Wunda Weave Carpets
S.I.C.: 2273
Lester Hudson *(Chm. Bd.)*
David Holt *(Pres.)*
Brian W. Warren *(V.P.-Opers.)*
Carroll E. Caldwell *(Mgr.-Adv. & Sls. Promo.)*
Tim Gilmore *(Mgr.-Mktg. & Mdse.)*

Plant:

Wunda Weve Carpet Yarn Plant **(1)**
White, GA 30184
Tel.: 706-382-5665
Mfr. of Carpet Yarn
S.I.C.: 2273
C.L. Chastain *(Plant Mgr.)*

WURZBURG, INC.
710 S. Fourth St.
Memphis, TN 38126
Mailing Address:
P.O. Box 710,
Memphis, TN 38101
Tel.: 901-525-1441
Fax: 901-578-2610
Approx.Sls.: $75,000,000
Emp.: 300
Packaging & Shipping Supplies, Materials, Handling Equipment, Tape & Label Printers, Die Cut Cushioning Products, Business Forms & Systems
S.I.C.: 2653; 2672; 2761; 2675; 3569
B. Lapides *(Co-Chm. Bd.)*
Warren Wurzburg, Sr. *(Co-Chm. Bd.)*
Richard Wurzburg *(Pres.)*
Reginald Wurzburg *(Chief Exec. Officer)*
George Walters *(V.P.-Sls.)*
Edgar Wilkinson *(V.P.-Labels Production)*
Warren S. Wurzburg, Jr. *(V.P.-Labels Sls.)*
Clayton H. Saap *(Sec. & Controller)*
John Lewis *(Dir.-Personnel)*
Ken Draffin *(Pur. Agent)*
R.W. Fisher *(Pur. Agent)*
Cathy Meeks *(Pur. Agent)*
Billy Roberson *(Pur. Agent)*
Principal(s):
Richard Wurzburg
Reginald Wurzburg

Computer Systems/Hardware:
NCR 9822

Outside Service Firm(s):

Deloitte & Touche*(Auditors)*
Memphis, TN

WYANDOT INC.
135 Wyandot Ave.
Marion, OH 43302
Tel.: 614-383-4031
Tel.: 1-800-992-6368 OH
Fax: 614-382-5584
Year Founded: 1936
Approx.Sls.: $65,000,000
Emp.: 500
Fiscal Year-end: 12/31/91
Export
Corn Based Snack Foods for Food Service & Retail Sales
S.I.C.: 2099; 5149
D. Warren Brown *(Pres. & Chief Exec. Officer)*
Raymond D. Moloney *(Exec. V.P.)*
Robert J. Schmidt *(Sr. V.P.-Fin. & Admin.)*
Dick Mault *(V.P.-Marion Division)*
Jeffrey D. Bury *(V.P.-Bus. Devel.)*
Gary Haugsby *(V.P.-Sls.)*
Rick Leibold *(V.P.-Matls.)*
Don Mount *(V.P.-Opers.)*
Rex Parrott *(V.P.-Human Resources)*
Roger Washburn *(V.P.-Information Systems)*
Rudy Schneider *(Dir.-Pur.)*
David H. Brown *(Sec.)*
Principal(s):
D. Warren Brown

No. of Mfg. Plants/Facilities: 2
No. of U.S. Offices: 1

Computer Systems/Hardware:
IBM AS400

Outside Service Firm(s):

Holbrook, Manter, Nichols & Rogers*(Auditors)*
Marion, OH

McDonald & Company*(Investment Banker)*
Columbus, OH

Emens, Kegler, Brown, Hill & Ritter*(Legal Firm)*
65 E. State St.
Columbus, OH 43215
Tel.: 614-462-5400

Society National Bank*(Major Banking Relationship)*
Columbus, OH

Subsidiary:

Wayandot, Inc. **(1)**
125 Peacely St.
Jeffersonville, IN 47130
Tel.: 812-283-3528
John Land *(V.P.)*

WYATT CAFETERIAS INC.
10726 Plano Rd.
Dallas, TX 75238
Tel.: 214-349-0060 TX
Fax: 214-553-5645
Year Founded: 1931
Sales Range: $100-499 Million
Fiscal Year-end: 12/31/91
Cafeterias
S.I.C.: 5812
Richard M. Gozia *(Chm. & Chief Exec. Officer)*
Debra L. Tippett *(Sr. V.P.-Mktg.)*
Nancy Schuerr *(V.P.-Human Resources)*
Matt Peiffer *(Treas.)*
Dan Jones *(Controller)*
Danny Tutle *(Dir.-Mktg.)*
Jennifer Maloney *(Mgr.-Adv.)*

Outside Service Firm(s):

Ernst & Young*(Auditors)*
2121 San Jacinto, Ste. 500
Dallas, TX 75201
Tel.: 214-969-8000

Texas Commerce Bank*(Major Banking Relationship)*
2200 Ross Ave.
Dallas, TX 75266

WYATT INC.
Wyatt Executive Bldg., 322 E. Main St.
Branford, CT 06405
Tel.: 203-483-4400 CT
Fax: 203-624-2336
Year Founded: 1935
Approx.Sls.: $320,000,000
Emp.: 83
Fiscal Year-end: 10/31/92
Import
Wholesale Fuel Distributor
S.I.C.: 5171
Kirk F. Blanchard *(Chm. Bd.)*
Dennis T. Meagher *(Pres.)*
Margaret Klein *(Chief Exec. Officer & Chief Fin. Officer)*
Donald B. Craft *(Exec. V.P.)*
Raymond J. Gincauage *(Sr. V.P.)*
Frank A. Rinaldi *(Grp. V.P.)*
Greg Bonenberger *(Gen. Counsel & Corp. Sec.)*
Stuart English *(Controller)*
Principal(s):
Kirk F. Blanchard
Donald B. Craft

No. of Mfg. Plants/Facilities: 6
No. of U.S. Offices: 4

Computer Systems/Hardware:
Data General; IBM PC

Outside Service Firm(s):

KPMG Peat Marwick*(Auditors)*
City Place II
Hartford, CT 06103-4103
Tel.: 203-522-3200
Fax: 203-297-5555

Aetna Life & Casualty*(Commercial Insurance Carrier)*
425 Fifth Ave.
New York, NY 10018
Tel.: 212-512-0777

Wyatt Inc.—(Continued)

Morgan Stanley & Co.*(Investment Banker)*
1251 Avenue of the Americas
New York, NY 10020
Tel.: 212-703-8447
Fax: 212-703-6476

Wiggin & Dana*(Legal Firm)*
195 Church St.
New Haven, CT 06508
Tel.: 203-789-1511

Bank Brussels Lambert*(Major Banking Relationship)*
New York, NY

Bank Of Boston*(Major Banking Relationship)*
New Haven, CT

NMB Post Bank Groep, n.v.*(Major Banking Relationship)*
New York, NY

Wyckoff Company
(Name Changed To Pacific Sound Resources)

JEFF WYLER DEALER GROUP, INC.
829 Eastgate South Dr.
Cincinnati, OH 45245
Tel.: 513-752-7450 **OH**
Fax: 513-752-1923
Approx.Sls.: $60,000,000
Emp.: 105
Retail Automobile Dealership
S.I.C.: 5511
Jeff Wyler *(Pres.)*
Charles Adomitis *(Exec. V.P.)*
Carrie Lakes *(Dir.-Mktg.)*

Principal(s):
Jeff Wyler

Subsidiaries:

Jeff Wyler Chevrolet Dealership **(1)**
1117 Rte. 32
Batavia, OH 45103
Tel.: 513-752-3447
Automobile Dealership
S.I.C.: 5511
Jim Hadley *(Gen. Mgr.)*

Jeff Wyler Nissan Dealership **(1)**
1117 Rte 32
Batavia, OH 45103
Tel.: 513-753-6688
Automobile Dealership
S.I.C.: 5511
Michael Gelter *(Gen. Mgr.)*

WYOMING MACHINE COMPANY
5300 W. Old Yellowstone
Casper, WY 82604
Mailing Address:
P.O. Box 2335,
Casper, WY 82602
Tel.: 307-472-1000 **UT**
Fax: 307-472-1002
Year Founded: 1980
Approx.Sls.: $48,000,000
Emp.: 220
General Construction Machinery & Equipment
S.I.C.: 5082
Richard Wheeler *(Pres.)*
Linda S. Wheeler *(V.P.)*
Robert Chynoweth *(Treas. & Sec.)*

Outside Service Firm(s):

Norwest Bank of Casper Wyoming*(Major Banking Relationship)*
Casper, WY

WYSE ADVERTISING, INC.
24 Public Square
Cleveland, OH 44113
Tel.: 216-696-2424
Fax: 216-621-2950
Year Founded: 1951
Approx.Billings: $139,000,000
Emp.: 185
Fiscal Year-end: 12/31/91
Advertising & Public Relations
S.I.C.: 7311
Marc A. Wyse *(Chm. & Chief Exec. Officer)*
James B. Rucker, Jr. *(Vice Chm.)*
Lois Wyse *(Pres.)*
James Pockmire *(Exec. V.P., Fin. & Admin.)*
Adeline Gasparelli *(Sec. & Treas.)*

No. of U.S. Offices: 2

Computer Systems/Hardware:
Datatrak Systems

Branches:

Catcher **(1)**
1140 Terminal Tower
Cleveland, OH 44113
Tel.: 216-696-1619
Fax: 216-771-6486
Paul Rector *(Pres.)*

Market Wyse **(1)**
1140 Terminal Tower
Cleveland, OH 44113
Tel.: 216-696-2424
Fax: 216-771-6486
Steve Verba *(Pres.)*

North Coast Behavioral Research **(1)**
945 Terminal Tower
Cleveland, OH 44113
Tel.: 216-861-5780
Fax: 216-861-3572
Julia Wargo *(Pres.)*

Pinnacle Media **(1)**
1140 Terminal Tower
Cleveland, OH 44113
Tel.: 216-696-3660
Fax: 216-771-6486
Rick Koehler *(Pres.)*

Wyse Advertising/Cleveland **(1)**
24 Public Square
Cleveland, OH 44113
Tel.: 216-696-2424
Fax: 216-621-2950
Carl Camden *(Co-Pres.)*
Michael Marino *(Co-Pres.)*

Wyse Advertising/New York **(1)**
79 Fifth Ave., 11th Fl.
New York, NY 10003
Tel.: 212-242-0200
Fax: 212-242-0415
John Lippmann *(Exec. V.P.)*

Wyse Direct **(1)**
1140 Terminal Tower
Cleveland, OH 44113
Tel.: 216-696-2427
Fax: 216-771-6486
Paul Rector *(Pres.)*

Wyse-Landau Public Relations **(1)**
1140 Terminal Tower
Cleveland, OH 44113
Tel.: 216-696-1686
Fax: 216-771-6486
Howard Landau *(Pres.)*

X-A CABINET CORPORATION
16930 Valley View Ave.
La Mirada, CA 90638
Tel.: 310-926-1331
Fax: 213-926-1365
Emp.: 200
Manufacture Household Cabinets
S.I.C.: 2511
Richard N. Anderson *(Pres.)*
Michael J. Anderson *(V.P.)*
Gary Anderson *(Treas. & Sec.)*
Gary Patterson *(Controller)*
Marc Anderson *(Plant Mgr.)*

Outside Service Firm(s):

Muller, King & Mathys*(Auditors)*
Downey, CA

Bear, Kotob, Ruby & Gross*(Legal Firm)*
Downey, CA

Community Bank*(Major Banking Relationship)*
Huntington Park, CA

Subsidiary:

Andys Rental Inc. **(1)**
16930 Valley View Ave.
La Mirada, CA 90638
Tel.: 213-773-8711
Approx.Sls.: $12,000,000
Emp.: 3
Machinery & Equipment Rental
S.I.C.: 7359
Frank Anderson *(Pres.)*
Michael J. Anderson *(V.P.-Opers. & Pur.)*
Betty Jo Anderson *(Sec.)*

XEBEC CORPORATION
5612 Brighton Terrace
Kansas City, MO 64130
Tel.: 816-444-9700
Fax: 816-444-9737
Approx.Sls.: $40,000,000
Emp.: 400
Fiscal Year-end: 12/31/90
Circuit Analyzers
S.I.C.: 3629
F.L. Thompson *(Chm. Bd.)*
R.K. Thompson *(Pres.)*
John Fitzsimmons *(V.P.-Sls.)*
Robert P. Lyons *(Sec.)*
Mary Lynn O'Connor *(Adv. & Mktg.)*

Subsidiary:

DIT-MCO Intl. **(1)**
5612 Brighton Terrace
Kansas City, MO 64130
Tel.: 816-444-9700
Approx.Sls.: $30,000,000
Emp.: 300
Mfr. Electronic Test Equip.
S.I.C.: 3679
F.L. Thompson *(Chm. Bd.)*
Richard K. Thompson *(Pres.)*
John Fitzsimmons *(Dir.-Mktg.)*
Mike Mathews *(Mktg. Mgr.)*
Robert Schmitz *(Mktg. Communications)*

XERXES CORPORATION
7901 Xerxes Ave. S.
Minneapolis, MN 55431
Tel.: 612-887-1890
Fax: 612-887-1870
Year Founded: 1979
Approx.Sls.: $60,000,000
Emp.: 500
Manufacture Fiberglass Storage Tanks & Air Pollution Control Products
S.I.C.: 3089; 3564
Rodney P. Burwell *(Chm. Bd.)*
Al Dorris *(Pres. & Chief Exec. Officer)*
Robin L. Berg *(Sr. V.P.-Research & Devel.)*
Ronald M. Bachmeier *(V.P.-Fin., Chief Fin. Officer & Treas.)*
Jeff Russell *(V.P.-Mktg. & Sls.)*
Craig D. Peterson *(Gen. Counsel & Sec.)*
Harry Holland *(Pur. Agent)*
Terry Jensen *(Mgr.-Mktg. Services)*

Computer Systems/Hardware:
PRIME 6150

Outside Service Firm(s):

Coopers & Lybrand*(Auditors)*
1000 TCF Bldg.
Minneapolis, MN 55402
Tel.: 612-293-2929
Fax: 612-370-9395

Moss & Barnett*(Legal Firm)*
4800 Norwest Center, 90 S. Seventh St.
Minneapolis, MN 55402
Tel.: 612-347-0300
Fax: 612-339-6686

First National Bank of Boston*(Major Banking Relationship)*
150 Royall St.
Canton, MA 02021
Tel.: 617-575-2900
Tel.: 800-442-2001

XTEK, INC.
P.O. Box 415701,
Cincinnati, OH 45241
Year Founded: 1909
Assets: $37,000,000
Liabilities: $26,000,000
Net Worth: $11,000,000
Approx.Sls.: $50,000,000
Emp.: 340
Fiscal Year-end: 12/31/91
Export
Mfrs. Hardened Steel Machine Components
S.I.C.: 3531; 3532; 3547; 3559; 3566
James D. Kiggen *(Chm. Bd., Pres. & Chief Exec. Officer)*
Robert C. Wood *(Chief Fin. Officer, Treas. & Sec.)*
Karl H. Hoelmer *(V.P.)*
Jeffrey A. Rowe *(V.P.)*
Paul W. Bridge, Jr. *(Controller)*
S. Craig Fowler *(Mgr.-Human Resources)*
Stephen A. Hart *(Mgr.-Data Processing)*
William S. Nicholson *(Mgr.-Matls.)*
Jennifer G. King *(Asst. Mgr.-Human Resources)*

Computer Systems/Hardware:
IBM 4381

Outside Service Firm(s):

Price Waterhouse*(Auditors)*
2200 Chemed Center, 255 E. 5th St.
Cincinnati, OH 45202-4798
Tel.: 513-621-1900

Thompson, Hine & Flory*(Legal Firm)*
Cincinnati, OH

Fifth Third Bank*(Major Banking Relationship)*
Corporate Trust Services, 38 Fountain Square Plaza
Cincinnati, OH 45263

Fifth Third Bank*(Pension Manager)*
Corporate Trust Services, 38 Fountain Square Plaza
Cincinnati, OH 45263

Division:

XTEK/Arizona Division **(1)**
1710 W. Broadway, P.O. Box 27288
Tempe, AZ 85282
Tel.: 602-968-6141 (100%)
Emp.: 40
S.I.C.: 3532
George Corfield *(Gen. Mgr.)*

Non-U.S. Holding:

Xtek Canada, Ltd. **(1)**
1344 Martingrove Rd.
Rexdale, ON M9W 4X3, Canada
Tel.: 416-743-8217
Mfrs. Wheels for Cranes
S.I.C.: 3312; 3559
Richard Harding *(Mgr.)*

YRJ CORPORATION
5711 Hillcroft
Houston, TX 77036
Mailing Address:
P.O. Box 36150,
Houston, TX 77236
Tel.: 713-782-8580 **TX**
Fax: 713-952-4618
Year Founded: 1978
Assets: $23,210,931
Earnings: $606,922
Liabilities: $16,343,280
Net Worth: $6,867,651
Approx.Sls.: $59,397,060
Emp.: 883
Fiscal Year-end: 3/31/91
Holding Company, Reprographic & Printing Services, Architectural Supplies, Blueprinting & Photocopying, Manufacture Photographic Equipment
S.I.C.: 6719; 3861
Yandell Rogers, Jr. *(Pres. & Gen. Counsel)*
Elvin Geisselbrecht *(Treas. & Sec.)*
Leslie Rogers *(Chief Info. Officer)*
Maureen Farany *(Mgr.-Employee Benefits)*

Computer Systems/Hardware:
DEC System 5780

Outside Service Firm(s):

NationsBank Texas*(Major Banking Relationship)*
Austin, TX

Subsidiaries:

Ridgway's, Inc. **(1)**
5711 Hillcroft Ave.
Houston, TX 77036
Tel.: 713-782-8580 (100%)
Fax: 713-952-4618
Emp.: 558
Reprographic & Printing Services
S.I.C.: 3861
Y. Rogers, Jr. *(Pres.)*

Universal Blueprint Paper Co. **(1)**
327 Bryan Ave.
Fort Worth, TX 76104
Tel.: 817-332-9259 (100%)
Fax: 817-332-5120
Emp.: 148
Coating & Converting Mill Roll Paper Base Paper Stock
S.I.C.: 3861; 2672
George Springer *(Pres.)*

YSD INDUSTRIES
3710 Henricks Rd.
Youngstown, OH 44515
Tel.: 216-792-6521 **OH**
Fax: 216-792-2422
Year Founded: 1924
Emp.: 185
Produces Discharge Gates, Sides, Roofs, Doors For Railroad Freight Cars & Custom Steel & Aluminium Fabrications
S.I.C.: 3743
William D. Mundinger *(Pres.)*
William H. Peters *(V.P.-Sls.)*
Stanley W. Cosky *(Controller)*
Dane L. Carder, Sr. *(Dir.-Mfg.)*
John Golubic *(Dir.-Pur.)*
Sue Sidell *(Mgr.-Admin.)*

Outside Service Firm(s):

Ernst & Young*(Auditors)*
1300 Huntington Bldg.
Cleveland, OH 44115
Tel.: 216-861-5000

YSI INCORPORATED
1725 Brannum Lane
Yellow Springs, OH 45387
Tel.: 513-767-7241
Telex: 205437
Fax: 513-767-9353
Year Founded: 1948
Approx.Sls.: $35,000,000
Emp.: 300
Export
Mfr. Electronic Scientific Instruments & Transducers
S.I.C.: 3823; 3825; 3829; 3826
Malte von Matthiessen *(Chm. Bd. & Chief Exec. Officer)*
Basil Zabek *(Exec. V.P.)*
Lee Erdman *(V.P. Fin. & Treas.)*
N.M. Harshaw *(V.P. Human Res. & Sec.)*
P. Nelson *(V.P.-Corp. Quality Assurance)*
Jim Smith *(V.P.-Mktg.)*
Chris Kowal *(Controller)*

Computer Systems/Hardware:
IBM System 38 & IBM PC

Outside Service Firm(s):

Deloitte & Touche*(Auditors)*
1700 Courthouse Plaza NE
Dayton, OH 45401
Tel.: 513-223-8821

Connecticut General Life Insurance Co.*(Group Insurer)*
P.O. Box 2975,
Hartford, CT 06104
Tel.: 203-726-6000

Star Bank*(Major Banking Relationship)*
425 Walnut Street
Cincinnati, OH 45202
Tel.: 513-632-4000

YAFFE & CO.
First Center Office Plaza,
26913 Northwestern Hwy., Ste. 500
Southfield, MI 48034
Tel.: 313-262-1700
Fax: 313-262-1701
Year Founded: 1959
Approx.Billings: $52,400,000
Emp.: 58
Fred Yaffe *(Chm. Bd. & Chief Exec. Officer)*
John Cassidy *(Sr. V.P., Opers.)*

YALE INDUSTRIAL TRUCKS OF SOUTHERN CALIFORNIA
2615 Pellissier
City of Industry, CA 91742
Mailing Address:
P.O. Box 1231,
City of Industry, CA 91749
Tel.: 310-699-0501
Fax: 310-692-6678
Approx.Sls.: $15,000,000
Emp.: 80
Sale & Service of Fork Lifts
S.I.C.: 7699; 7359
Frank A. Higgins *(Pres.)*
Andrew Frontzak *(V.P.)*

Outside Service Firm(s):

Union Bank*(Major Banking Relationship)*
City of Industry, CA

Subsidiary:

Yale Industrial Trucks **(1)**
2411 E. Winston
Anaheim, CA 92806
Tel.: 714-956-9656
Frank A. Higgins *(Pres.)*

YALE UNIVERSITY PRESS
302 Temple St.
New Haven, CT 06511
Mailing Address:
Box 92A, Yale Station
New Haven, CT 06520
Tel.: 203-432-0960
Telex: 963531
Fax: 203-432-0948
Year Founded: 1907
Approx.Sls.: $14,000,000
Emp.: 100
Fiscal Year-end: 6/30/91
Book Publisher
S.I.C.: 2731
John G. Ryden *(Dir.)*
Tina C. Weiner *(Assoc. Dir. & Mktg. Mgr.)*
Susan Donnelly *(Sls. Mgr.)*
Ruth Sachs *(Adv. Mgr.)*
Sarah F. Clark *(Assoc. Mktg. Dir.)*
Dennis Danaher *(Asst. to the Dir.)*

Computer Systems/Hardware:
Vista

YANKEE PUBLISHING INCORPORATED
Main St.
Dublin, NH 03444
Tel.: 603-563-8111 **NH**
Fax: 603-563-8252
Year Founded: 1935
Approx.Sls.: $40,000,000
Emp.: 110
Fiscal Year-end: 6/30/91
Publisher of Yankee Magazine, Calendars & Travel Guides
S.I.C.: 2721; 2741
Joseph B. Meagher *(Pres. & Chief Exec. Officer)*
Judson D. Hale, Sr. *(Sr. V.P.)*
David J. Noonan *(V.P.)*
Brian Piani *(V.P.-Fin. & Treas.)*
Joseph R. Timko *(V.P.-Mktg. & Circulation)*
James H. Fishman *(V.P.-Sls.)*
John B. Pierce *(V.P.-Editorial)*
Judith H. Allen *(Sec.)*
Gordon Hale *(Controller)*
Kathleen Pek *(Dir.-Human Resources)*
Martha Cavanaugh *(Mgr.-Mktg. Services)*
Principal(s):
Judson D. Hale, Sr.

No. of U.S. Offices: 5

Computer Systems/Hardware:
IBM AS/400

Outside Service Firm(s):

Coopers & Lybrand*(Auditors)*
Manchester, NH

Kendall Insurance Co.*(Commercial Insurance Carrier)*
P.O. Box 1840, 90 South Main Street
Rochester, NH 03867
Tel.: 603-332-5800
Telex: 94-4406

Brighton, Fernald, Taft & Falby*(Legal Firm)*
Peterborough, NH

State Street Bank & Trust Co.*(Major Banking Relationship)*
P.O. Box 366,
Boston, MA 02101
Tel.: 617-426-5523

Subsidiary:

Alaska Publishing Properties, Inc. **(1)**
808 E. St., Ste. 200
Anchorage, AK 99501
Tel.: 907-272-6070
Magazine Publishers
S.I.C.: 2721
Joseph B. Meagher *(Pres. & Chief Exec. Officer)*
Dave Noonan *(Publisher)*
Brian Piani *(Chief Fin. Officer)*

YARDNEY TECHNICAL PRODUCTS, INC.
82 Mechanic St.
Pawcatuck, CT 06379-2154
Tel.: 203-599-1100
Fax: 203-599-3903
Year Founded: 1944
Approx.Sls.: $18,000,000
Emp.: 250
Fiscal Year-end: 9/30/91
Export
Primary & Secondary Silver & Nickel, Battery Systems, Portable Rechargeable High Intensity Lights, Solid State Chargers & Voltage Scanners, Seawater Batteries, Lithium Batteries
S.I.C.: 3692; 3648; 3691; 3629
R.M. Scibelli *(Pres. & Chief Exec. Officer)*
Ken Avery *(Sr. V.P.-Finance)*
Peter A. Karpinski *(Sr. V.P.-Engrng.)*
Maureen Smith *(V.P.-Human Rels.)*
L.R. Magnarella *(V.P.-Contracts & Mktg.)*
Dave Cryer *(Contorller)*
A.M. Aretakis *(Mgr.-Mktg. & Sls.)*
J. Gulluscio *(Mfg. Mgr.)*
Paul Cryan *(Mgr.)*
Ben Lazev *(Dir.-Pur.)*
Dawn Landsiedel *(Mgr.)*
Joe Pacheco *(Quality Control)*
Maureen Holland *(Corp. Librarian)*
Heather Ballastrini *(Administrator)*
Franz Goebel *(Dir.)*

Computer Systems/Hardware:
HP3000

YATES ENTERPRISES INC.
602 W. Falvey
Texarkana, TX 75504
Mailing Address:
P.O. Box 1426
Texarkana, TX 75504
Tel.: 903-832-6502 **TX**
Fax: 903-832-7903
Approx.Sls.: $160,000,000
Emp.: 1,500
Convenience Store Chain
S.I.C.: 5411
Jim E. Yates *(Pres.)*
Tom Coleman *(V.P.)*
Sonja Hubbard *(Treas. & Sec.)*

No. of U.S. Offices: 342

Computer Systems/Hardware:
IBM System 36

Outside Service Firm(s):

Grier, Reeves & Lawley*(Auditors)*
Texarkana, TX

Eric Bishop*(Legal Firm)*
Ashdown, AR

First Bank, N.A.*(Major Banking Relationship)*
Texarkana, TX

YAZOO INVESTMENT CORPORATION
711 W. Capital St.
Jackson, MS 39203
Tel.: 601-961-6877 **MS**
Fax: 601-961-6995
Year Founded: 1983
Approx.Sls.: $193,000,000
Emp.: 2
Holding Company for Gas Transmission & Distribution
S.I.C.: 4923; 6719
Roger B. Oresman *(Chm. Bd.)*
Matthew Holleman *(Pres.)*
Daisy S. Blackwell *(Treas. & Sec.)*

Outside Service Firm(s):

Deloitte & Touche*(Auditors)*
Jackson, MS

AEGIS*(Commercial Insurance Carrier)*
Harborside Financial Center, 700 Plaza Two
Jersey City, NJ 07311
Tel.: 201-915-7200
Fax: 201-451-3472

Overstreet, Kuykendall, Sumners & Hughes*(Legal Firm)*
Jackson, MS

Deposit Guaranty National Bank*(Major Banking Relationship)*
One Deposit Guaranty Plaza,
Jackson, MS 39201

Yazoo Investment Corporation—(Continued)

Trustmark National Bank*(Major Banking Relationship)*
248 E. Capital
Jackson, MS 39201

Trustmark National Bank*(Pension Manager)*
248 E. Capital
Jackson, MS 39201

Subsidiary:

Mississippi Valley Gas Co. **(1)**
711 W. Capitol St.
Jackson, MS 39203
Tel.: 601-961-6900
Fax: 601-961-6995
Assets: $110,429,771
Liabilities: $81,369,475
Net Worth: $29,060,296
Approx.Sls.: $168,645,157
Emp.: 603
Fiscal Year-end: 9/30/90
Computer Systems/Hardware:
IBM System 4361
Natural Gas Distribution
S.I.C.: 4924
Roger B. Oresman *(Chm. Bd.)*
Edmund R. Butler *(Pres. & Chief Exec. Officer)*
Matthew L. Holleman *(Exec. V.P & Treas.)*
Thomas H. Bowen, Jr. *(V.P.-Admin. Services)*
Joe J. Powell, Jr. *(V.P.-Tech. Services)*
Walter R. Wilder *(V.P.-Public & Govt. Rels.)*
W.K. Rogers *(V.P.-Rates & Industrial Mktg.)*
H.F. Langley *(Controller)*
Richard W. Wise *(Legal Officer)*
T.L. Keyes *(Asst. Treas. & Admin. Asst.)*
Jack Tyler *(Dir.-Data Processing)*
Henry Burge *(Dir.-Pur.)*

Subsidiary:

Mississippi Energies, Inc. **(2)**
711 W. Capitol St., P.O. Box 3348
Jackson, MS 39203
Tel.: 601-961-6900
Gas Distribution Utility
S.I.C.: 4924
Edmund R. Butler *(Chief Oper. Officer)*

YENKIN-MAJESTIC PAINT CORPORATION
1920 Leonard Ave.
Columbus, OH 43219
Tel.: 614-253-8511
Fax: 614-224-1641
Year Founded: 1920
Approx.Sls.: $45,000,000
Emp.: 160
Mfr. Paints, Resins, Varnishes & Enamels
S.I.C.: 2851
Bernard K. Yenkin *(Chm. Bd.)*
Merom Brachman *(Pres.)*
Martin Hassell *(V.P.-Sls.)*
Chester W. Stahl *(V.P.-Tech.)*
Chester Hauck *(V.P.-Indus. Sls.)*
Jerry Askew *(V.P.-Associated Services)*
Michael W. Aurnou *(Treas.)*
John Gerhold *(Mgr.-Pur.)*

YERGER BROS., INC.
520 Front St.
Lititz, PA 17543
Mailing Address:
P.O. Box 1200
Lititz, PA 17543
Tel.: 717-626-2145
Fax: 717-627-4600
Year Founded: 1916
Sales Range: $10-19 Million
Emp.: 200
Import
Mfr. of Point of Purchase Displays, Store Fixtures; Home & Office Furniture; Cut-to-size Parts & Packaging Products
S.I.C.: 3993; 2499; 2511; 2521; 2541; 2671
John R. Yerger *(Chm. Bd. & Pres.)*
William E. Forster *(V.P. & Gen. Mgr.)*
Dale L. Overly *(V.P.-Opers. & Treas.)*
Ralph J. Rosen *(V.P.-Sls. & Mktg.)*
Theodore V. Konas *(Controller & Asst. Treas.)*
Paul R. Diehm *(Dir.-Human Resources)*
Edward E. Eisenhooth *(Mgr.-Pur.)*
Earl A. Furman *(Mgr.-Mfg. & Quality Control)*
Arthur L. Kress *(Mgr.-Engrng.)*
Daniel McGlothin *(Mgr.-Information Services)*

Outside Service Firm(s):

Buehler, Falk & Company*(Auditors)*
Lancaster, PA

Barley, Snyder, Cooper & Barber*(Legal Firm)*
Lancaster, PA

Dauphin Deposit Bank & Trust*(Major Banking Relationship)*
Lancaster, PA

YOAKUM PACKING COMPANY
P.O. Box 192
Yoakum, TX 77995
Tel.: 512-293-3541
Fax: 512-293-2261
Approx.Sls.: $10,000,000
Emp.: 50
Meat Processors; Beef, Pork, Poultry & Private Label
S.I.C.: 2013
James E. Pietsch *(Pres.)*
Russell Obelgoner *(V.P. & Treas.)*
Sheri Kusak *(Sec.)*
Glen Kusak *(Plant Mgr.)*

Outside Service Firm(s):

Roloff, Hanatek & Co.*(Auditors)*
Victoria, TX

Kvinta & Kvinta*(Legal Firm)*
Yoakum, TX

First State Bank*(Major Banking Relationship)*
Yoakum, TX

YODER OIL COMPANY INC.
2204 California Rd.
Elkhart, IN 46514
Mailing Address:
P.O. Box 10
Elkhart, IN 46515
Tel.: 219-264-2107 **IN**
Fax: 219-264-1475
Year Founded: 1937
Assets: $4,310,000
Liabilities: $1,798,000
Net Worth: $2,512,000
Sales Range: $20-39 Million
Emp.: 180
Fiscal Year-end: 6/30/90
Distributor of Petroleum; Operate Convenience Stores, Carwash & Quick Oil Change Facilities
S.I.C.: 5172; 5399; 5983; 5541
G.L. Yoder *(Chm. Bd.)*
Kent Yoder *(Pres., Chief Exec. Officer, Chief Fin. Officer & Treas.)*
Donald Steiner *(Controller)*

No. of U.S. Offices: 13

Computer Systems/Hardware:
Unisys

Outside Service Firm(s):

Coopers & Lybrand*(Auditors)*
Elkhart, IN
Tel.: 219-294-7441

Benefit Trust & Life*(Group Insurer)*

Prudential-Bache*(Investment Banker)*
9 West 57th St.
New York, NY 10019
Tel.: 212-415-5800
Fax: 212-415-5885

Daniels, Sanders & Pianowski*(Legal Firm)*
Elkhart, IN

AmeriTrust National Bank*(Major Banking Relationship)*
Elkart, IN

YORK BARBELL CO., INC.
3300 Board Rd.
York, PA 17402
Mailing Address:
PO Box 1707,
York, PA 17405
Tel.: 717-767-6481
Fax: 717-764-0044
Year Founded: 1932
Approx.Sls.: $12,000,000
Emp.: 140
Fiscal Year-end: 12/31/91
Import Export
Mfr. of Food Supplements; Physical Fitness Equipment
S.I.C.: 2834; 3949
John B. Terpak, Sr. *(Chm. Bd.)*
Victor J. Standish *(Pres. & Treas.)*
Alda Ketterman *(Exec. V.P.)*
John Terpak, Jr. *(V.P.-Sls.)*
David Fortney *(Controller)*
George McDonald *(Gen. Counsel)*

Computer Systems/Hardware:
UNISYS

Outside Service Firm(s):

Miller & Company*(Auditors)*
York, PA

CoreStates Corporate Trust Services*(Major Banking Relationship)*
Hamilton, PA

YORK BUILDING PRODUCTS CO., INC.
1020 N. Hartley St.
York, PA 17405
Mailing Address:
P.O. Box 1708,
York, PA 17405-1708
Tel.: 717-848-2831
Fax: 717-854-9156
Approx.Sls.: $20,000,000
Emp.: 150
Mfr. of Building Blocks; Quarrying; Processes Asphalt
S.I.C.: 3281; 1442; 3271
Robert H. Steward, Jr. *(Pres.)*
Gary Stewart *(V.P.)*
Terrence Stewart *(V.P.)*
Rick Werner *(Controller)*
Wade H. Paramore *(Mgr.-Sls.)*
Edwin I. Myers *(Pur. Agent)*
Donald Park *(Chief Engr.)*

Outside Service Firm(s):

Dorgan & Stambaugh*(Auditors)*
York, PA

Laucks & Monroe*(Legal Firm)*
York, PA

Drovers & Mechanics Bank*(Major Banking Relationship)*
York, PA

York Bank & Trust Co.*(Major Banking Relationship)*
York, PA

YORK WALLCOVERINGS INC.
750 Linden Ave.
York, PA 17404
Mailing Address:
P.O. Box 5166
York, PA 17405
Tel.: 717-846-4456
Fax: 717-843-5624
Approx.Sls.: $10,000,000
Emp.: 137
Roomates, Whisper Prints, Sun Shower, Ginger Tree, Peppermill
S.I.C.: 3089; 2679; 2621
C.J. Vizzi *(Pres.)*
R.L. Henneman *(V.P.-Opers.)*
R.C. Redding *(V.P.-Design)*
S.A. Thomas *(Asst. Sec. & Controller)*
Bill Burget *(Mgr.-Mktg.)*

YORKTOWN TOOL & DIE CORPORATION
104 E. Smith
Yorktown, IN 47396
Tel.: 317-759-7767
Fax: 317-759-9834
Approx.Sls.: $15,000,000
Emp.: 150
Export
Design & Build Special Machinery, Tools, Jigs, Fixtures, Plastic, Aluminum Injection Molds& engineering Design Services
S.I.C.: 3544
John A. Bratt *(Chm. Bd.)*
Jerry Dunn *(Pres.)*
Wilma Shoul *(Controller)*
Brian King *(Dir.-Mfg.)*
Stan Musselman *(Dir.-Engrng.)*
Robert Peterson *(Pur. Agent)*
Principal(s):
John A. Bratt

Outside Service Firm(s):

The Indiana National Bank*(Major Banking Relationship)*
One Indiana Sq.
Indianapolis, IN 46266
Tel.: 317-266-6000

YORKTOWNE, INC.
100 Redco Ave.
Red Lion, PA 17356
Mailing Address:
P.O. Box 231
Red Lion, PA 17356-0231
Tel.: 717-244-4011
Fax: 717-244-5497
Year Founded: 1908
Approx.Sls.: $40,000,000
Emp.: 700
Fiscal Year-end: 9/30/92
Mfr. Kitchen Cabinets, Vanities, Countertops & Specialty Furniture
S.I.C.: 2434
Dick Beckman *(V.P.-Fin.)*
W. Ted Fetner *(V.P. & Exec. Asst.)*
Garth Hoffman *(V.P.-Human Resources)*
Robert Shoemaker *(V.P.-Sls. & Mktg.)*
John Stephenson *(V.P.-Mktg.)*
Charles Taylor *(Mgr.-Pur.)*
Dee Uttermohlen *(Mktg. Service Coord.)*

YORKTOWNE PAPER MILLS, INC.
1001 Loucks Mill Rd.
York, PA 17405
Tel.: 717-843-8061
Fax: 717-843-3426
Year Founded: 1940
Approx.Sls.: $23,000,000
Emp.: 350
Manufacture Paperboard Die-Cut Paperboard Fiber Tubes & Cores
S.I.C.: 2655
Daniel J. Sparler *(Chm. Bd., Pres. & Chief Exec. Officer)*
Milton V. Oakley *(Vice Chm. & Sec.)*

D. John Sparler *(Exec. V.P. & Treas.)*
John Kennedy *(Sr. V.P.)*
Larry D. Brenneman *(V.P.-Human Resources)*
Philip B. Jones *(V.P.-Tube Core Opers.)*
John W. Welsh *(V.P.-Mktg.)*
Fred Merck *(Dir.-Engrng.)*
Russell E. Yoas *(Mgr.-Pur. & Production)*

Outside Service Firm(s):

Stockton, Bates & Co.*(Auditors)*
Philadelphia, PA

Stock & Leader*(Legal Firm)*
York, PA

Drovers & Mechanics Bank*(Major Banking Relationship)*
York, PA

Divisions:

The Columbia Corporation **(1)**
Rte. 295
Chatham, NY 12037
Tel.: 518-392-4000
Recycled Paperboard & Paperboard Products, Mat & Illustration Boards
S.I.C.: 2631; 2675
James L. Salerno *(V.P. & Gen. Mgr.)*
George N. Hoover, III *(Controller)*
George R. Cartwright *(Mgr.-Mktg.)*
Thomas M. Cummings *(Mgr.-Sls.)*
Henry M. Greenhouse *(Dir.-Res. & Devel.)*
Joseph Litsermeier *(Chief Engnr.)*
Kenneth H. Wilber *(Pur. Agent)*

Mercer Paper Tube Co. **(1)**
River Rd.
South Gardener, ME 04345
Tel.: 207-582-3400
S.I.C.: 2631; 2655
Robert Hurd *(Gen. Mgr.)*

Mercer Paper Tube Co. **(1)**
1700 Calhoun St.
Trenton, NJ 00638
Tel.: 609-695-5451
S.I.C.: 2631; 2655

Mercer Paper Tube Co. **(1)**
State St., P.O. Box 391
Ludlow, MA 01056
Tel.: 413-583-5123
S.I.C.: 2631; 2655
Jerry Jones *(Gen. Mgr.)*

Mercer Paper Tube Co. **(1)**
P.O. Box 29 Arlington Rd.
Greenville, PA 16125
Tel.: 412-646-1234
S.I.C.: 2631; 2655
Jay Hartman *(Mgr.)*

Mercer Paper Tube Co. **(1)**
91 Glenn St.
Lawrence, MA 01843
Tel.: 508-687-0303
S.I.C.: 2631; 2655
Jerry Jones *(Gen. Mgr.)*

Yorktowne Paper Mills of Maine **(1)**
721 Water St.
Gardener, ME 04345
Tel.: 207-582-3230
S.I.C.: 2631; 2655
Joe Emerson *(Gen. Mgr.)*

Yorktowne Paper Mills of ME **(1)**
1001 Loucks Mill Rd.
York, PA 17405
Tel.: 717-843-8061
Approx.Sls.: $7,000,000
Emp.: 230
Manufacture Recycled Paperboards, Tubes & Cores
S.I.C.: 2631; 2655
Daniel J. Sparler *(Chm. Bd., Pres. & Chief Exec. Officer)*

YOUNG AUTOMOTIVE GROUP
3210 E. 96th St.
Indianapolis, IN 46240
Mailing Address:
P.O. Box 40319,
Indianapolis, IN 46240-0319
Tel.: 317-573-8488 **IN**
Fax: 317-573-8497
Year Founded: 1966
Approx.Sls.: $191,000,000
Emp.: 502
Retail Automotive Sales & Service
S.I.C.: 5511
Dan E. Young *(Chm. Bd.)*
Alan V. Young *(Pres. & Chief Exec. Officer)*
Conway M. Anderson *(Chief Oper. Officer)*
Jan R. Chenoweth *(Chief Fin. Officer)*
William A. Young *(V.P.)*
Andrew Lee Fonacier *(Asst. Controller)*
Principal(s):
Dan E. Young
Alan V. Young
William A. Young

YOUNG ELECTRIC SIGN COMPANY
336 S. 400 W.
Salt Lake City, UT 84101
Tel.: 801-363-8900 **UT**
Fax: 801-467-3447
Year Founded: 1918
Approx.Sls.: $50,000,000
Emp.: 810
Mfr. of Neon & Electric Signs; Sign Rental, Installation & Maintenance
S.I.C.: 3993; 7359; 1799
Thomas Young, Jr. *(Chm. Bd.)*
Michael T. Young *(Pres.)*
Ben F. Jones *(Sr. V.P. & Gen. Mgr.)*
D. Duane Wardle *(V.P.-Fin. & Treas.)*
Jeffrey S. Young *(Sec.)*

Outside Service Firm(s):

Deloitte & Touche*(Auditors)*
50 S. Main St., Ste. 1800
Salt Lake City, UT 84144
Tel.: 801-328-4706

First Interstate Bank*(Major Banking Relationship)*
P.O. Box 53441,
Phoenix, AZ 85072-3441
Tel.: 602-229-4049

Divisions:

Young Electric Sign Boise Div. **(1)**
416 E. 41st
Boise, ID 83714
Tel.: 208-345-2982
Mfr. of Signs not Made in Custom Sign Painting Shops; Sign Installation & Maintenance; Signs, Except Electric
S.I.C.: 5099; 3993
R.W. Williams *(Pres.)*

Young Electric Sign Denver Div. **(1)**
3660 E. 40th Ave.
Denver, CO 80205
Tel.: 303-329-3726
Mfr. of Signs
S.I.C.: 3993

Young Electric Sign Las Vegas Div. **(1)**
5119 S. Cameron St.
Las Vegas, NV 89118
Tel.: 702-876-8080
Mfr. of Signs
S.I.C.: 3993

Young Electric Sign Phoenix Div. **(1)**
201 S. 26th St.
Phoenix, AZ 85034
Tel.: 602-275-5791
Mfr. of Signs not Made in Custom Sign Painting Shops
S.I.C.: 3993
Jake Winkleplech *(Mgr.)*

R.S. YOUNG EXCAVATING, INC.
G-5305 N. Dort Hwy.
Flint, MI 48505
Tel.: 313-789-7511
Fax: 313-789-3606
Year Founded: 1979
Assets: $1,782,881
Liabilities: $1,041,987
Net Worth: $740,894
Sales Range: $10-19 Million
Emp.: 25
Underground Excavating Contractor; Installation, Repair & Replacement Of Watermains & Sewer Lines
S.I.C.: 1794
Robert S. Young *(Pres.)*
Mary G. Young *(Treas.)*
Fred Wilson *(Dir.-Personnel)*

No. of U.S. Offices: 1

Subsidiary:

R.S. Young Environmental Clean Up **(1)**
G 5305 N. Dort Hwy.
Flint, MI 48505
Tel.: 313-789-7511
Refuse Clean Up
S.I.C.: 4953

YOUNG & FRANKLIN, INC.
942 Old Liverpool Rd.
Liverpool, NY 13088
Tel.: 315-457-3110
Year Founded: 1908
Approx.Sls.: $10,000,000
Emp.: 80
Import
Mfr. of Specialty Fluid Control Valves for Land-Based Gas Turbines, Aircraft & Marine Applications
S.I.C.: 3494
Dudley Johnson *(Pres.)*
Lawrence Mitter *(V.P.-Engrng.)*
Jean Argus *(Mgr.-Pur.)*
Craig Froelich *(Mgr.-Sls.)*
Michael Yates *(Mgr.-Mktg.)*

DANIEL F. YOUNG, INC.
17 Battery Pl. 8th Fl.
New York, NY 10004
Tel.: 212-248-1700 **NY**
Fax: 212-809-9896
Year Founded: 1903
Approx.Sls.: $400,000,000
Emp.: 400
Import Export
Freight Forwarding; Customhouse Brokers
S.I.C.: 4731
Joseph G. Kearns *(Chief Exec. Officer)*
Robert J. Lanigan *(Pres.)*
Thomas A. Madden *(Exec. V.P.)*
Quentin C. Biegen *(V.P.)*
John V. Keenan *(V.P.)*
Edward P. Walsh *(V.P.)*
Albert Wichertch, Jr. *(V.P.)*
Rita P. Bentley *(Treas.)*
John V. Corcoran *(Sec.)*

Outside Service Firm(s):

Chase Manhattan Bank, N.A.*(Major Banking Relationship)*
One Chase Manhattan Plaza
New York, NY 10081
Tel.: 212-552-2222
Tel.: 800-526-0801
Fax: 212-552-7175

JACK YOUNG ASSOCIATES
100 E. Diamond Ave.
Hazleton, PA 18201-0522
Mailing Address:
P.O. 522
Hazleton, PA 18201
Tel.: 717-455-7706 **NJ**
Fax: 717-455-9399
Year Founded: 1961
Sales Range: $10-19 Million
Emp.: 150
Fiscal Year-end: 12/31/89
Export
Manufacturer of Men's & Ladies' Sweaters
S.I.C.: 2329; 2253
Jack Young *(Chm. Bd., Pres., Chief Exec. & Chief Fin. Officer)*
Julius Waltzer *(V.P. & Treas.)*
Principal(s):
Jack Young
Julius Waltzer

No. of Mfg. Plants/Facilities: 1

Computer Systems/Hardware:
IBM XT; Apple Macintosh

Outside Service Firm(s):

Irving Kaufman & Company*(Auditors)*
New York, NY

Hyman & Lazaar*(Commercial Insurance Carrier)*
Queens, NY

Guardian Life Insurance Co.*(Group Insurer)*
New York, NY

Peoples Trust Company*(Investment Banker)*
Hazleton, PA

Laputka, Bayless, Ecker & Cohn*(Legal Firm)*
2 E. Broad St.
Hazleton, PA 18201

Peoples First National Bank*(Major Banking Relationship)*
Hazleton, PA

Division:

Pocono Knits, Inc. **(1)**
100 E. Diamond
Hazleton, PA 18201
Tel.: 717-455-7706
Mfr. of Men's & Ladies' Sweaters
S.I.C.: 2253; 2329
Jack Young *(Chief Exec. Officer)*
Todor Sekosan *(Pres.)*
Julius Waltzer *(Treas.)*

YOUNG & LARAMORE
310 E. Vermont St.
Indianapolis, IN 46204
Tel.: 317-264-8000
Year Founded: 1983
Approx.Billings: $25,300,000
Emp.: 24
David Young *(Chm. Bd. & Pres.)*
Jeff Laramore *(Exec. V.P., Sec.)*
David Clifton *(Treas. & Chief Fin. Officer)*
Doyia Chadwick *(Pub. Rels. Dir.)*
Cecelia Brennan *(Acctg. Mgr.)*

Computer Systems/Hardware:
Macintosh

YOUNG PECAN SHELLING CO., INC.
1200 Pecan St.
Florence, SC 29501
Mailing Address:
P.O. Drawer 5779,
Florence, SC 29502
Tel.: 803-664-2330
Tel.: 800-829-6864 **SC**
Fax: 803-664-2344
Year Founded: 1959
Approx.Sls.: $50,000,000
Emp.: 150
Import Export
Wholesale Shelled Pecans
S.I.C.: 5145
J. Givens Young *(Chm. Bd. & Pres.)*
Thomas J. Howard *(Exec. V.P.-Specialty Sls.)*
James W. Swink *(Exec. V.P. & Sec.)*
Murray L. Garber *(V.P.-Fin.)*
Florence H. Young *(V.P.)*
Jo Cobb *(Dir.-Data Processing)*
Joey Hawkins *(Dir.-Pur.)*

No. of Mfg. Plants/Facilities: 3
No. of U.S. Offices: 3
No. of Foreign Offices: 1

Computer Systems/Hardware:
IBM System 36

Young Pecan Shelling Co., Inc.—(Continued)

Outside Service Firm(s):

Ernst & Young*(Auditors)*
P.O. Box 627, 1611 Devonshire Dr.
Columbia, SC 20202
Tel.: 803-254-4700
Fax: 803-252-4090

Wright, Powers & McIntosh*(Legal Firm)*
Columbia, SC

South Carolina National Bank*(Major Banking Relationship)*
Columbia, SC

Subsidiary:

Young Pecan Company West, Inc. **(1)**
2211 E. Missouri, Ste. E 102
El Paso, TX 79903
Tel.: 915-534-7484
Emp.: 4
Operation Base for Mexican Plant
S.I.C.: 8741; 5159

YOUNG-PHILLIPS SALES CO.
3250 Healy Dr.
Winston-Salem, NC 27103
Mailing Address:
P.O. Box 25288,
Winston-Salem, NC 27114
Tel.: 919-768-0110
Fax: 919-765-7866
Year Founded: 1953
Assets: $14,500,000
Liabilities: $9,700,000
Net Worth: $4,800,000
Approx.Sls.: $68,000,000
Emp.: 171
Distributor of Graphic Arts & Professional Photographic Supplies & Equipment & Office Products
S.I.C.: 5199; 5043; 5044
John B. Phillips, Jr. *(Chm. Bd.)*
Richard M. Blair *(Pres.)*
Sam Hancock *(V.P.-Fin. & Admin.)*
Mary C. Phillips *(Sec. & Treas.)*

Computer Systems/Hardware:
Data General MV 15000, Model 10

Outside Service Firm(s):

Cannon & Co.*(Auditors)*
Winston-Salem, NC

Argus Group*(Commercial Insurance Carrier)*
Winston-Salem, NC

Blue Cross & Blue Shield of North Carolina*(Group Insurer)*
Durham, NC

Wachovia Bank & Trust Co.*(Investment Banker)*
P.O. Box 3001,
Winston-Salem, NC 27102
Tel.: 800-633-4236

YOUNG RADIATOR COMPANY
2825 Four Mile Rd.
Racine, WI 53404
Tel.: 414-639-1010 **WI**
Telex: 26-4435
Fax: 414-639-1013
Year Founded: 1927
Approx.Sls.: $50,000,000
Emp.: 600
Fiscal Year-end: 12/31/90
Import Export
Manufacturer of Standard & Customed Designed Radiators, Air-Cooled & Water Cooled; Shell & Tube Heat Exchangers; Charge Air Coolers; Compressor Aftercoolers & Unit Heaters
S.I.C.: 3714; 3433
F.M. Young, Jr. *(Pres.)*
Harry Gant *(Chief Fin. Officer, Treas. & Sec.)*
R.J. Dezek *(Dir.-Sls. & Mktg.)*
D.O. Klompmaker *(Mgr.-Sls.-Automotive Div.)*
Roger Slater *(Mgr.-Mktg. Services)*
E.J. Smerchek *(Mgr.-Sls.-Indus. Div.)*
Principal(s):
F.M. Young, Jr.

No. of Mfg. Plants/Facilities: 3
No. of U.S. Offices: 1

Computer Systems/Hardware:
Unisys U-430

Outside Service Firm(s):

Arthur Andersen & Co.*(Auditors)*
777 E. Wisconsin Ave., P.O. Box 1215
Milwaukee, WI 53202
Tel.: 414-271-5100
Fax: 414-283-3200

Bank One Milwaukee, N.A.*(Major Banking Relationship)*
111 E. Wisconsin Ave.
Milwaukee, WI
Tel.: 414-765-3000

First National Bank of Chicago*(Pension Manager)*
One First National Plaza
Chicago, IL 60670
Tel.: 312-732-9781
Tel.: 312-732-4050
Fax: 312-732-4840
Fax: 312-732-3055

YOUNG REFINING CORP.
7982 Huey Road
Douglasville, GA 30134
Mailing Address:
P.O. Box 796
Douglasville, GA 30133
Tel.: 404-942-2343 **DE**
Fax: 404-942-3850
Year Founded: 1971
Sales Range: $20-39 Million
Emp.: 70
Fiscal Year-end: 3/31/90
Manufacture Petroleum Products
S.I.C.: 2911
Dr. C.B.F. Young *(Chm. Bd. & Pres.)*
John K. Hudson *(Chief Fin. Officer)*
James T. Young *(Exec. V.P.)*
J.E. Jordan, Jr. *(Treas.)*
Principal(s):
Dr. C.B.F. Young

No. of Mfg. Plants/Facilities: 1
No. of U.S. Offices: 2

Computer Systems/Hardware:
IBM System 34

Outside Service Firm(s):

BDO Seidman*(Auditors)*
235 Peachtree St. N.E., Ste. 700
Atlanta, GA
Tel.: 404-688-6841

State Mutual Life Assurance Co. of America*(Group Insurer)*
Atlanta, GA

Hurt, Richardson, Garner, Todd & Cudenhead*(Legal Firm)*
Atlanta, GA

First American Bank, N.A.*(Major Banking Relationship)*
Atlanta, GA

YOUNG & ROEHR, INC.
28 S.W. First, Ste. 500
Portland, OR 97204
Tel.: 503-222-0626
Fax: 503-222-0154
Year Founded: 1968
Approx.Billings: $18,000,000
Emp.: 19
Business-to-Business Adv.
Lois Leonard *(Chm. Bd. & Pres.)*
Brian D. Mount *(Exec. V.P., Creative Dir., Sec. & Treas.)*

Y&R
Young & Rubicam Inc.
285 Madison Avenue
New York, New York 10017-6486

YOUNG & RUBICAM INC.
285 Madison Ave.
New York, NY 10017
Tel.: 212-210-3000 **NY**
Twx: 710-581-3607
Fax: 212-490-9073
Year Founded: 1923
Approx.Billings: $7,800,000,000
Emp.: 10,000
Advertising Agency; Public Relations, Package Design, Sales Promotion & Direct Advertising
S.I.C.: 7311
Alex Kroll *(Chm. & Chief Exec. Officer)*
Peter A. Georgescu *(Pres.-Y&R Inc.)*
John McGarry *(Exec. V.P., Pres. & Chief Exec. Officer-No. America)*
R. John Cooper *(Exec. V.P., Gen. Counsel & Sec.)*
David Greene *(Exec. V.P., Chief Fin. Officer)*
Joseph E. De Deo *(Exec. V.P., Chief Creative Officer)*
Larry Snoddon *(Exec. V.P., Pres. & Chief Exec. Officer-Burson Marsteller)*
Alan J. Sheldon *(Exec. V.P., Gen. Mgr.)*
Satish Korde *(Exec. V.P., Dir., Consumer Res.-WW)*
Margaret Mark *(Exec. V.P., Dir., Res.)*
Steve Heyer *(Exec. V.P.)*
John Sanders *(Exec. V.P.)*
Stan Stefanski *(Exec. V.P., Dir., Bus. Affairs-WW)*
Steven Heyer *(Exec. V.P.)*
Kathleen Ancuta *(Sr. V.P., Corp. Fin.)*
Eileen Balaban *(Sr. V.P., Dir., Client Compensation)*
Ann Hesselink *(Sr. V.P., Dir. Taxes)*
Richard McGowan *(Sr. V.P., Dir. Communications)*
Rosemary Nelson *(Sr. V.P., Gen. Counsel & Asst. Sec.)*
Lawrence Miller *(Sr. V.P., Deputy Gen. Counsel & Asst. Sec.)*
John W. Rindlaub *(Sr. V.P., Dir. Govt. & Industry Rels.)*
Stephen Messana *(Sr. V.P., Dir. Human Resources-WW)*
Nicholas Rudd *(Sr. V.P., Chief Info. Officer-Y&R Inc.)*
Daniel Visneaskus *(Sr. V.P., Internal Audit)*
Nancy R. Wynne *(Sr. V.P., Dir. Real Estate)*
Ingo Krauss *(Vice Chm. & Chm.-Europe Exec. Committee)*
John McGarry *(Vice Chm., Pres. & Chief Exec. Officer-No. America)*
Frank Anfield *(Pres. & Chief Exec. Officer Y&R New York)*
Tim Pollak *(Vice Chm.-WW & Dir., Client Services)*
Stan Stefanski *(Exec. V.P., Dir. Bus. Affairs-WW)*
Fernan Montero *(Exec. V.P., Area Dir.-Latin America)*
Phil Asche *(Exec. V.P., Dir.-Y&R Adv., Area Dir.-Australia/New Zealand)*
Mary Alice Kennedy *(V.P. Dir. Coord.)*

Outside Service Firm(s):

Price Waterhouse*(Auditors)*
153 E. 53rd St., 44th Fl.
New York, NY 10022
Tel.: 212-371-2000

Metropolitan Life Insurance Co.*(Group Insurer)*
One Madison Ave.
New York, NY 10010-3690
Tel.: 215-578-9292

First Chicago Shareholder Services Trust Co.*(Major Banking Relationship)*
153 West 51st St.
New York, NY 10019
Tel.: 212-791-6422
Fax: 212-385-9798

Metropolitan Life Insurance Co.*(Pension Manager)*
One Madison Ave.
New York, NY 10010-3690
Tel.: 215-578-9292

Pacific Investment Management*(Pension Manager)*
P.O. Box 9000, 840 Newport Center Dr.
Newport Beach, CA 92660
Tel.: 714-640-3347

Subsidiaries:

The Bravo Group **(1)**
11 West 42nd St., 2nd Fl.
New York, NY 10036
Tel.: 212-575-1280
Approx.Billings: $55,000,000
Emp.: 81
Hispanic Mktg.
Daisy Exposito *(Pres. & Chief Creative Officer)*

Burson-Marsteller **(1)**
230 Park Ave. South
New York, NY 10003-1566
Tel.: 212-614-4000
Fax: 212-614-4262
Public Relations
S.I.C.: 7311
Harold Burson *(Founder & Chm.)*
James H. Dowling *(Chm. Bd.)*
Larry E. Snoddon *(Pres. & Chief Exec. Officer)*
Thomas D. Bell, Jr. *(Vice Chm. & Chief Operating Officer Worldwide (Washington))*
Thomas J. Mosser *(Vice Chm. & Chief Oper. Officer Worldwide (London))*
Joseph C. Benway *(Exec. V.P., Chief Fin. Officer)*
Robert S. Leaf *(Chm.-Intl./London)*
James B. Lindheim *(Chm., Burson Marsteller/Europe (Paris))*
Elias Buchwald *(Vice Chm.)*
Angus Maitland *(Vice Chm., Corp. Communications (London))*
Stan Sauerhaft *(Vice Chm.-Mergers & Acquisitions)*
Albert Tortorella *(Vice Chm., Media)*
Geoffrey Nightingale *(Exec. V.P., Pres.-Synergenics)*
Wayne Pines *(Exec. V.P., Dir. Medical Issues (Washington))*
Barbara Smith *(Exec. V.P., Creative Dir.)*
Gregory Waldron *(Sr. V.P., Worldwide Dir., Human Resources)*

CYB Yasumura Design **(1)**
11 West 42nd St.
New York, NY 10036
Tel.: 212-768-5000
Fax: 212-768-5126
Emp.: 33
Computer Systems/Hardware:
Macintosh Based Systems
Brand Identity Development, Packaging Design, Corporate Identity Development, Environmental Design
Muts Yasumura *(Chm. & Exec. Design Dir.)*
Joy Greene *(Pres. & Chief Oper. Officer)*
Christopher Nunes *(Sr. V.P., Grp. Dir.)*

Cato Johnson-New York **(1)**
675 6th Ave., 3rd Fl.
New York, NY 10010-5104
Tel.: 212-941-3700
Fax: 212-627-8342
Approx.Billings: $50,000,000
Advertising Agency
S.I.C.: 7311
John Burke *(Pres. & Chief Exec. Officer)*
Stephen Zammarchi *(Chief Oper. Officer)*
Nick Becce *(Sr. V.P., Mngmt. Supvr.)*
Leslie Beck *(Bus. Affairs Mgr.)*

Cato Johnson Worldwide **(1)**
675 6th Ave., 3rd Fl.
New York, NY 10010
Tel.: 212-941-3700
Fax: 212-627-8342
Approx.Billings: $350,000,000
Advertising Agency
S.I.C.: 7311
Jean-Paul Lafaye *(Pres. & Chief Exec. Officer-Worldwide)*
Brian Harris *(Chief Fin. Officer-Worldwide)*

Chapman Direct Advertising (1)
230 Park Ave., South
New York, NY 10003
Tel.: 212-614-3880
Fax: 212-614-3888
Approx.Billings: $115,000,000
Emp.: 125
Computer Systems/Hardware:
MacIntosh
Direct Marketing
William P. Sutherland *(Pres. & Chief Exec. Officer)*
Jane Ames *(Gen. Mgr.)*
Michael Moore *(Exec. V.P., Acct. Services)*
Janet Falvo *(Sr. V.P., Fin. Services)*
Barry Kessel *(Sr. V.P., Exec. Creative Dir.)*
Leonard Ross *(Sr. V.P., Production)*

(1)
Tel.: 319-395-6500
Fax: 319-395-6575
Approx.Billings: $95,000,000
Emp.: 200
Advertising Agency
S.I.C.: 7311
F.C. "Buzz" Baker *(Pres. & Chief Exec. Officer)*
James E. Meeks *(Sr. V.P., Acctg. Dir., Special Projects)*
William J. Fultz *(Chm.)*
David A. Brazier *(V.P., Dir. Bus. Affairs)*
Edward C. Mertens *(V.P., Dir. Acctg.)*
Gerald L. Anderson *(Sr. V.P., Dir. Signal Grp.)*
Robert E. Buckley *(Sr. V.P., Dir. Signal Grp.)*
Robert N. Cline *(Sr. V.P., Acct. Grp. Dir.)*
Michael A. Curless *(Sr. V.P., Dir.-Tech. & Training)*
Michael A. Curless *(Sr. V.P., Dir. Tech. Services)*
Richard Damrow *(Sr. V.P., Grp. Dir.)*
Ronald D. Howes *(Sr. V.P., Grp. Supvr.)*
Robert M. Kays *(Sr. V.P., Acct. Grp. Dir.)*
Mark R. Lunde *(Sr. V.P., Internal Services-Des Moines)*
Gregory A. Michel *(Sr. V.P., Acct. Grp. Dir.)*
Diane E. Stadlen *(Sr. V.P., Dir. Mktg. Analysis & Media Services)*
George F. Held *(V.P., Dir.-Caritrak)*
Allen Schoneman *(Gen. Mgr.-Raleigh, NC)*
David A. Wignall *(V.P., Database Mktg. Grp. Dir.)*
Carol A. Bodensteiner *(Pres.-CMF&Z Pub. Rels.)*
Susan A. Caley *(V.P., Dir. Admin.)*
Susan K. Neely *(Sr. V.P., Gen. Mgr.-Washington, D.C.)*

Branches:

Creswell, Munsell, Fultz & Zirbel (2)
600 E. Court Ave.
Des Moines, IA 50309-2091
Tel.: 515-246-3500
Fax: 515-246-3530
Advertising Agency
S.I.C.: 7311

Creswell, Munsell, Fultz & Zirbel (2)
1667 K St., NW, Ste. 430
Washington, DC 20006
Tel.: 202-862-4990
Fax: 202-862-5462
Advertising Agency
S.I.C.: 7311
Susan K. Neely *(Sr. V.P., Gen. Mgr., Pub. Rels.)*

Creswell, Munsell, Fultz & Zirbel (2)
3100 Smoketree Court, Ste. 803
Raleigh, NC 27604
Tel.: 919-872-1477
Fax: 919-876-0532
Advertising Agency
S.I.C.: 7311

Hutchins/Young & Rubicam (1)
400 Midtown Tower,
Rochester, NY 14604
Tel.: 716-546-6480
Fax: 716-325-0360
Approx.Billings: $65,000,000
Emp.: 125
Advertising, Promo., Pub. Rels., Yellow Pages, Employee Communications, Trade Shows & Sls. Meetings
James N. Morey *(Chm.)*
Mary Ann Sapos *(Pres. & Chief Exec. Officer)*
Charles E. Reller *(Exec. V.P., Chief Oper. Officer)*
Harvey J. Bozzi, Jr. *(Sr. V.P., Mngmt. Supvr.)*
Robert Craig *(Sr. V.P., Yellow Pages Mgr.)*
Daniel Hucko *(Sr. V.P., Mgr.-Stanton & Hucko)*
Thomas Barton *(V.P., Mgr.-Midtown Printing)*
Mark Stanton *(V.P., Pub. Rels. Mgr.)*
Robert Bell *(V.P., Adv. Div. Mgr.)*
Michael Keenahan *(Controller)*
Fran Cotterill *(Human Resources)*

Sive/Young & Rubicam (1)
36 E. Seventh St., Ste. 2500
Cincinnati, OH 45202
Tel.: 513-345-3400
Fax: 513-241-7818
Approx.Billings: $39,000,000
Emp.: 59
Advertising Agency
S.I.C.: 7311
Dale Brown *(Pres. & Chief Exec. Officer)*
Michael Kitei *(Exec. V.P., Creative Dir.)*
Michael W. Montgomery *(V.P., Fin. & Admin.)*
David Siegel *(V.P., Dir. Consumer Prods.)*
Mark Wesling *(V.P., Dir. Mktg. Services)*
Judith Bogart *(Dir., Pub. Rels.)*
Michael Blanck *(Dir., Planning & Research)*

Sudler & Hennessey (1)
1633 Broadway
New York, NY 10019
Tel.: 212-969-5800
Fax: 212-969-5991/92
Approx.Billings: $183,807,000
Emp.: 223
Advertising Agency
S.I.C.: 7311
William B. Gibson *(Chm., Pres. & Chief Exec. Officer)*
John Chervokas *(Exec. V.P., Chief Creative Officer)*
Neil Leiner *(Exec. V.P., Grp. Dir.)*
Donald Masterson *(Exec. V.P., Grp. Dir.)*
Bruce Richmond *(Exec. V.P., Grp. Dir.)*
Tim Millas *(Exec. V.P., Creative Dir.-CMC)*
Diane Cooney *(Exec. V.P., Dir. of Creative Services)*
Thomas Crotty *(Exec. V.P., Treas.)*
John Rinaldi *(Sr. V.P., Grp. Supvr.)*
Doug Burcin *(Sr. V.P., Grp. Supvr.)*
Mark Merriman *(Sr. V.P., Grp. Supvr.)*
Wayne Traub *(Sr. V.P., Acct. Supvr.)*
Wendy Mantel *(Sr. V.P., Acct. Supvr.)*
Evelyn Roces *(Sr. V.P., Acct. Supvr.)*
Barbara Morano *(Sr. V.P., Dir. Media Plng. & Dev.)*
Barry Siegel *(Sr. V.P., Dir. Mktg. Research)*
Harold Grossman *(Sr. V.P., Mktg. Research)*
Hiram Zimmerman *(Sr. V.P., Dir. Typographic Services)*
Joseph Paumi *(Sr. V.P., Creative Dir.-Art)*
Richard Russinko *(Sr. V.P., Assoc. Creative Dir.-Art)*
Arthur Kaufman *(Sr. V.P., Art Grp. Head)*
Robin Davenport *(Sr. V.P., Assoc. Creative Dir.-Copy)*
Margaret Noon *(Sr. V.P., Assoc. Creative Dir.-Art)*
Vincent Parry *(Sr. V.P., Creative Dir.-Copy)*
Jerome Ehrlich, MD *(Sr. V.P., Medical Dir.)*
Laura Byers *(V.P., Copy Supvr.)*
Maryann Hagan *(V.P., Client Acctg.)*
Thomas McGuinness *(V.P., Agency Acctg.)*
Dorothy Gallagher *(V.P., Office Mgr.)*

Group:

Sudler & Hennessey Consumer Group (2)
1180 Ave. of the Americas
New York, NY 10036
Tel.: 212-827-6500
Fax: 212-221-6073
Advertising
S.I.C.: 7311
Arthur M. Rosen *(Exec. V.P., Dir.)*
Glenn Levy *(Sr. V.P., Creative Supvr.)*
David Upright *(Sr. V.P., Creative Supvr.)*
John Draper *(Sr. V.P., Acct. Supvr.)*
Gregory Weed *(Sr. V.P., Acct. Supvr.)*
Norma Birnbaum *(Sr. V.P., Research Dir.)*
Kenneth Kopas *(Sr. V.P., Media Dir.)*
Paul Gundlach *(Sr. V.P., Acct. Supvr.)*
James Oxnam *(Sr. V.P., Dir.)*
Louisa Holland *(Sr. V.P., Program Dir.)*
Ruben Gutierrez *(Sr. V.P., Program Dir.)*
E. Hope Lang *(V.P., Program Dir.)*

Wunderman Cato Johnson (1)
675 Ave. of the Americas
New York, NY 10010
Tel.: 212-941-3000
Fax: 212-633-0957
Approx.Billings:
Advertising Agency
S.I.C.: 7311
Lester Wunderman *(Chm. Bd.)*
John Sanders *(Pres. & Chief Exec. Officer WW (New York & Detroit))*
Mitchell Kurz *(Pres./N. America)*
Richard Stollenwerck *(Pres./Latin America)*
Cindy Butchko *(V.P., Dir. Training & Resource Services)*
Fred Petito *(V.P., Fin. & Admin.)*
Steve McKenna *(Chief Fin. Officer/WW (New York))*
Rosamund Lyster *(Mgr.-Resource Services)*
Jane Beale *(Sr. V.P., Dir. Admin. & Human Resources)*
Peter Rabar *(Sr. V.P.)*
Carol A. Schautz *(Sr. V.P., Treas.)*
Mark Levine *(Sr. V.P., Strategic Plng.)*
Barbara Jack *(Sr. V.P., Bus. Devel.)*
Bernard Halligan *(V.P., Dir. Systems Devel.)*

Branches:

Wunderman Worldwide (2)
10 Munet Court, Pueblo Viejo
Guaynabo, PR 00920-1402
Tel.: 809-793-1900
Telex: 809-345-0087
Fax: 809-783-4253
Advertising Agency
S.I.C.: 7311
Janice Muniz *(Gen. Mgr.)*

Y&R/Wunderman Worldwide/Detroit (2)
200 Renaissance Ctr., Ste. 700
Detroit, MI 48243
Tel.: 313-446-8600
Direct Mktg. & Business-to-Business Communications
Wally Thursam *(Pres.)*
James Turnbull, II *(Sr. V.P., Creative Dir.)*

Young & Rubicam Chicago (1)
1 S. Wacker Dr., Ste. 1800
Chicago, IL 60606
Tel.: 312-845-4000
Twx: 9102210320
Fax: 312-845-4000
Approx.Billings: $40,000,000
Emp.: 50
Advertising Agency
S.I.C.: 7311
Patricia A. Cafferata *(Pres. & Chief Exec. Officer)*
Thomas A. Shortlidge *(Sr. V.P., Exec. Creative Dir.)*
Michael J. Faems *(Sr. V.P., Exec. Creative Dir.)*
Enid Katz *(Sr. V.P., Dir. Comml. Production)*
Steven L. Keenan *(Sr. V.P., Grp. Dir.)*

Young & Rubicam Detroit (1)
200 Renaissance Ctr., Ste. 1000
Detroit, MI 48243
Tel.: 313-446-8600
Advertising Agency
S.I.C.: 7311
Michael V. Howe *(Pres. & Chief Exec. Officer)*
Donald D. Williams *(Exec. V.P., Grp. Dir.)*
Edson K. Pool *(Sr. V.P., Grp. Dir.)*
Daniel E. Wagner *(Sr. V.P., Grp. Dir.)*
Robert A. Rosiek *(Sr. V.P., Fin. Dir.)*
Margaret M. Brophy *(Sr. V.P., Strategic Plng. Dir.)*
Catherine Coraci-McCann *(V.P., Human Resources Dir.)*

Young & Rubicam New York (1)
285 Madison Ave.
New York, NY 10017
Tel.: 212-210-3000
Twx: 710-581-3607
Fax: 212-490-9073
Advertising Agency
S.I.C.: 7311
John P. McGarry Jr. *(Pres. & Chief Exec. Officer-Y&R North America)*
Frank A. Anfield *(Pres. & Chief Exec. Officer-Y&R New York)*
Tim Pollak *(Vice Chm.-WW Dir., Client Services)*
James Hood *(Exec. V.P., Dir. Bus. Devel.)*
Paul Isacsson *(Exec. V.P., Dir. Brdcst. Programming & Pur.)*
Margaret Mark *(Exec. V.P., Dir. Brand Plng.)*
Phil Asche *(Exec. V.P., Area Dir.-Australia & New Zealand)*
Fernan Montero *(Exec. V.P., Area Dir.-Latin America)*
William Green *(Exec. V.P., Grp. Dir.)*
Larry Shapiro *(Exec. V.P., Grp. Dir.)*
John Swan *(Exec. V.P., Grp. Dir.)*
Chris Becker *(Sr. V.P., Grp. Dir.)*
Mike Feldman *(Sr. V.P., Grp. Dir.)*
Rich Kahn *(Sr. V.P., Grp. Dir.)*
Mary Ellen Kenny *(Sr. V.P., Grp. Dir.)*
Jordan Stanley *(Sr. V.P., Grp. Dir.)*
Kim Bealle *(Sr. V.P., Dir.-Com. Plng.)*
Marlene Chautin *(Sr. V.P., Assoc. Dir. Local Brdcst.)*
Scott Flood *(Sr. V.P., Dir. Bus. Devel.)*
Lori Nicholson *(Sr. V.P., Dir. Client Acctg.)*
Scott Lowe *(Sr. V.P., Assoc. Dir. Local Brdcst.)*
Thomas McQueeney *(Sr. V.P., Dir. Bus. Affairs & Admin.)*
Sandy Mitchell *(Sr. V.P., Admin. Mgr., Consumer Res.)*
Barbara Badyna *(Sr. V.P., Dir. Casting)*
Stan Stefanski *(Sr. V.P., Dir. Bus. Affairs & Admin.)*
Tom Handy *(Sr. V.P., Assoc. Dir. Bus. Affairs & Admin.)*

Young & Rubicam San Francisco (1)
100 First St.
San Francisco, CA 94105
Tel.: 415-882-0600
Twx: 910-372-7724
Fax: 415-896-0533
Approx.Billings: $140,000,000
Emp.: 130
Advertising Agency
S.I.C.: 7311
Craig W. Branigan *(Pres.)*
Peter Angelos *(Exec. V.P., Creative Dir.)*
Kathy Foley Murphy *(Sr. V.P., Dir.-Acct. Services)*
Jay Dean *(Sr. V.P., Consumer Res. Dir.)*
Sue Zeifman *(V.P., Gen. Mgr.-RPM)*
Anne Spoon *(V.P., Dir. Opers.)*

Non-U.S. Holdings:

Europe & U.K.:

Ad/Productions (1)
Ottho Heldringstraat 27 1066 XT
Amsterdam, Netherlands
Tel.: 17-28-51
Telex: 844-14170
Fax: 844-14170
Advertising
S.I.C.: 7311
Rudie Koster *(Mng. Dir.)*
Tiemen Bosma *(Pres)*

Advico Young & Rubicam AG (1)
Werbeagentur BSW, Gockhausen 8044
Zurich, Switzerland
Tel.: 1-8210222
Fax: 1-8210622
Approx.Billings: $160,200,000
Emp.: 99
Advertising
S.I.C.: 7311
Bruno Widmer *(Pres.)*
Urs Beer *(Mng. Dir.)*

Andersson Media Aktiebolag (1)
Riddargatan 17 Box 14065, 104-40
Stockholm, Sweden
Tel.: 8-7829005
Fax: 8-6650758
Advertising
S.I.C.: 7311
Ulla Andersson *(Mng. Dir.)*

Beautiful & Landor Associates (1)
19/21 Rue Valette 75005
Paris, France
Tel.: 40-469797
Telex: 842206921
Fax: 40-460806
Advertising
S.I.C.: 7311
Francis Metzler *(Mng. Dir.)*
Francois Dodet *(Deputy Gen. Mgr.)*

Cato Johnson Copenhagen (1)
Overgaden neden Vandet 17 1414
Copenhagen, K, Denmark
Tel.: (45.32) 96-01-00
Fax: (45.32) 96-04-12
S.I.C.: 7311
Kai Soborg Hansen *(Chm.)*
Claus Clausen *(Mng. Dir.)*

Cato Johnson Direct Promotion (1)
Blvd. Lambermont 368A 1030
Brussels, Belgium
Tel.: 2-2425210
Fax: 2-2429776
S.I.C.: 7311
Henry Rijsermans *(Gen. Mgr.)*

Cato Johnson Frankfurt (1)
Bleichstrasse 64 Postfach 64, D-6000
Frankfurt/Main, 1, Germany
Tel.: 69-21920
Fax: 69-219-2576
S.I.C.: 7311
Helmut Matthies *(Mng. Dir.)*

Cato Johnson Italia S.p.A. (1)
Viale Majno 21 20122
Milan, Italy
Tel.: (39.2) 7600-5200
Fax: (39.2) 7600-5233
S.I.C.: 7311
Luigi Rinaldi *(Chm. & Mng. Dir.)*

Young & Rubicam Inc.—(Continued)

Walter Cordaro *(Gen. Mgr.)*

Cato Johnson Limited **(1)**
Greater London House, Hampstead Rd.
London, NW1 7QP, United Kingdom
Tel.: 071-380-6333
Telex: 25197
Fax: 071-388-8779
S.I.C.: 7311
John Fricker *(Chm. & Mng. Dir.)*
Doug Hamilton *(Mng. Dir.)*

Cato Johnson Spain S.A. **(1)**
C/ Castello 64-1 28001
Madrid, Spain
Tel.: (34.1) 577-4974
Fax: (34.1) 577-6783
S.I.C.: 7311
Alfonso Lozano *(Mng. Dir.)*

Cato Johnson Stockholm **(1)**
Riddargatan 17 11424
Stockholm, Sweden
Tel.: (46.8) 24-24-40
Fax: (46.8) 782-9842
S.I.C.: 7311
Lars Mardell *(Mng. Dir.)*

Cato Johnson Switzerland **(1)**
8 Rue Winkelried CH-1201
Geneva, Switzerland
Tel.: (011-42-22) 31-33-20
Twx: 845-41202
Fax: (011-41-22) 36-97-53
Advertising
S.I.C.: 7311
Gabriela Ehrlich *(Dir.)*
Jorg Rindlisbacher *(Dir.)*

Cato Yasumura Behaeghel (CYB) **(1)**
32 Dock St.
London, EI8NA, United Kingdom
S.I.C.: 7311
John Fricker *(Mng. Dir.)*

G&R Pubblicita/Sudler & Hennessey **(1)**
Via Guerrazzi 20145
Milan, Italy
Tel.: (39.2) 331-3771
Telex: 843 316422
Fax: (39.2) 349-1696
Advertising
S.I.C.: 7311
Massimo Vergnano *(Pres.-Europe, Mng. Dir.)*

Geo-Young & Rubicam **(1)**
49, Vas Sofias Ave. 10676
Athens, Greece
Tel.: 01-7249211
Telex: 214704
Fax: 01-7231490
Approx.Billings: $20,600,000
Emp.: 52
Full Service Advertising
S.I.C.: 7311
Vankells Georgiades *(Mng. Dir.)*
A. Assonitis *(Vice Chm.)*
D. Haritopoulos *(Pres. & Creative Dir.)*
D. Demetrakakis *(Chief Fin. Officer)*
Y. Palaska *(Sec.)*
X. Antonopoulou *(Treas.)*

Javelin/Young & Rubicam **(1)**
18 Merrion Sq.
Dublin, 2, Ireland
Tel.: 1-767261
Fax: 1-611570
Approx.Billings: $8,000,000
Emp.: 20
Full Service Advertising & Marketing
S.I.C.: 7311
Paul Myers *(Chm.)*
Joe Dobbin *(Mng. Dir.)*
Vivienne Menzies *(Admin. Mgr.)*

Klausen & Partners A/S **(1)**
Fredericiagade 13 1310
Copenhagen, K, Denmark
Tel.: 33-937008
Fax: 33-939299
Advertising
S.I.C.: 7311
Jorgen Klausen *(Mng. Dir.)*

Moradpour, Dalsace, Langlois, Pizanti **(1)**
7/15 rue du Dome 92100
Boulogne, France
Tel.: 46-84-34-22
Fax: (011-33-1) 46-84-33-51
Advertising
S.I.C.: 7311
Edouard Moradpour *(Mng. Dir.)*

Multicontact **(1)**
12 rue Jean Renoir 21000
Dijon, France
Tel.: (011-33-80) 303-000
Advertising
S.I.C.: 7311
Emmanuel Mignot *(Mng. Dir.)*

O'T.V. & O'Space **(1)**
25/27 rue Parmentier 92800
Puteaux, La Defense France
Tel.: 42-04-03-31
Telex: 842-615866
Advertising
S.I.C.: 7311
Michel Grandjean *(Mng. Dir.)*

Paragraphe/Sudler & Hennessey **(1)**
7/15, Rue du Dome 92105
Boulogne, Cedex France
Tel.: (33.46) 84-30-79
Fax: (33.46) 84-33-80
S.I.C.: 7311
Jean-Paul Duplan *(Mng. Dir.)*

Prins, Meijer, Stamenkovits en van Walbeek/Young & Rubicam B.V. **(1)**
Frans van Mierisstraat 92 1071 RZ
Amsterdam, Netherlands
Tel.: 20-6766992
Telex: 14329 pms n1
Fax: 20-6711515
Approx.Billings: $232,700,000
Emp.: 118
S.I.C.: 7311
Tiemen Bosma *(Mng. Partner)*
Jim Prins *(Mng. Partner)*
Adrian Tiggelman *(Mng. Dir.)*
Dirk Jan Meijer *(Chm Bd)*
Hans Van Walbeek *(Exec VP)*

Rayon Vert **(1)**
45 Rue Paul Bert 92100
Boulogne, Cedex France
Tel.: 46-843388
Telex: 842 200304
Fax: 46-843096
Advertising
S.I.C.: 7311
Lefne Blanh *(Mng. Dir.)*

Riechelmann, Lopes Cardozo & Van Bercum B.V. **(1)**
Maassluisstraat 2 1062 GD
Amsterdam, Netherlands
Tel.: 20-6172851
Fax: 20-6175330
Emp.: 17
Full Service Advertising
S.I.C.: 7311
Thijs Riechelmann *(Mng. Dir.)*

Scanelo, Young & Rubicam AS **(1)**
Waldemar THR Anesgate 84b 0175
Oslo, 1, Norway
Tel.: 37-9918
Fax: 37-3289
Approx.Billings: $96,000,000
Emp.: 50
S.I.C.: 7311
Arild Langaas *(Chm. & Mng. Dir.)*

Sigma **(1)**
Muhlebachstrasse 20 8034
Zurich, Switzerland
Tel.: 1-2527150
Fax: 1-2512927
Advertising
S.I.C.: 7311
Marius Krugel *(Chm.)*
Urs Jaermann *(Gen. Mgr.)*

Strategic Identity Consultants **(1)**
7/15 Rue du Dome 92100
Boulogne, Cedex France
Tel.: 46-843498
Fax: 46-843458
Advertising
S.I.C.: 7311
Alain de Mareilhac *(Mng. Dir.)*

Sudler & Hennessey GmbH **(1)**
Lersnerstrasse 23 6000
Frankfurt/Main, 1, Germany
Tel.: (49.69) 153010
Fax: (49.69) 1530-1177
S.I.C.: 7311
William McEwen *(Gen. Mgr.)*

Sudler & Hennessey Limited **(1)**
24-28 Bloomsbury Way
London, WC1A 2PX, United Kingdom
Tel.: 071-831-9140
Fax: 071-831-5510
S.I.C.: 7311
Robin Wright *(Mng. Dir.)*

Taucher, Young & Rubicam **(1)**
Salomonkatu 17 A 00100
Helsinki, Finland
Tel.: 990-0-1920236
Fax: 90-1920236
Approx.Billings: $76,200,000
Emp.: 30
Full Service Advertising
S.I.C.: 7311
Tom Ginman *(Mng. Dir.)*
Jukka Riikonen *(Pres. & Chief Exec. Officer-Taucher Grp.)*
Pekka Salmi *(Mng. Dir.)*

Vinizius/Young & Rubicam, S.A. **(1)**
Diagonal 652-656, Edificio A-Planta 2A 08034
Barcelona, Spain
Tel.: 3-2800301
Fax: 3-2805570
Emp.: 24
S.I.C.: 7311
Francisco Segarra *(Founder & Partner)*
Juan Asensio *(Founder & Partner)*
Rafael Esteve *(Gen. Mgr.)*

Wunderman **(1)**
12 Cours Louis Lumiere 94300
Vincennes, CEDEX, France
Tel.: 49-573535
Approx.Billings: $320,000,000
Emp.: 50
Direct Marketing
S.I.C.: 7311
Jean-Yves Granger *(Mng. Dir.)*

Wunderman Cato Johnson France **(1)**
35-3 Rue de Paris 92100
Boulogne, France
Tel.: 1-46843407
Fax: 1-46843465
Approx.Billings: $52,000,000
Emp.: 80
Computer Systems/Hardware:
Apple Macintosh
S.I.C.: 7311
Gilles Colomb *(Chm.)*
Pierre De Roualle *(Mng. Dir.)*
Marc Ballu *(Mng. Dir.)*
Guillaume Barraut *(Chief Fin. Officer)*

Wunderman Taucher Turku Oy **(1)**
Eerikinkatim 15 P.O. Box 48, 20101
Turku, Finland
Direct Marketing
S.I.C.: 7331

Wunderman Tender **(1)**
Via Lazzaroni 4 20124
Milan, Italy
Tel.: 2-66711081
Telex: 323527 TENDER 1
Fax: 2-66711071
Advertising
S.I.C.: 7311
Italo de Mas *(Mng. Dir.)*

Wunderman Worldwide **(1)**
Chaussee de Wavre 59 1050
Brussels, Belgium
Tel.: 2-513-8193
Telex: 846 20205 WUNDI B
Fax: 2-513-0210
Advertising
S.I.C.: 7311
David Stokes *(Mng. Dir.)*

Wunderman Worldwide **(1)**
Sterngasse 13 A-1010
Vienna, Austria
Tel.: 222-533-5858
Fax: 222-533-5858 ext. 81
Advertising
S.I.C.: 7311
Thomas Holzhuber *(Mng. Dir.)*

Wunderman Worldwide AB **(1)**
Riddargatan 19 10441
Stockholm, Sweden
Tel.: 8-6604270
Telex: 854 10342 RINCAD S
Fax: 8-6671434
Advertising
S.I.C.: 7311
Leena Bergerus *(Mng. Dir.)*

Wunderman Worldwide A/S **(1)**
Blegdamsvej 104 DK-2100
Copenhagen, O, Denmark
Tel.: 31-420707
Fax: 35-430804
Emp.: 26
Direct Marketing
S.I.C.: 7311
John Kahler *(Mng. Dir.)*
Peter Svendsen *(Mng. Dir.)*
Susanne Louw *(Mng. Dir., Pub. Rels., Client Service/Acct. Dir.)*
Torben Jacobsen *(Controller)*
Claus Pedersen *(Print Production Mgr. & Data Services)*

Wunderman Worldwide Limited **(1)**
Greater London House, Hampstead Rd.
London, NW1 7QP, United Kingdom
Tel.: 071-3806333
Fax: 071-3888779
Advertising
S.I.C.: 7311
Tim Godden *(Chm.-UK, Mng. Dir.-Europe)*
Steve Eckels *(Pres.-Europe)*
Dave Butter *(Exec. V.P.-Europe)*
John Shaw *(Gen. Mgr.-UK)*

Wunderman Worldwide v.o.f. **(1)**
Herengracht 105 1015 BE
Amsterdam, Netherlands
Tel.: 20-6207161
Fax: 20-6278241
Emp.: 38
Direct Marketing (Full Service), Accountable Advertising
S.I.C.: 7311
Cas Saeys *(Mng. Dir.)*
Pieter Vyn *(Info. Services Dir. & Adv.)*
F. Havenaar Faure *(Office Mgr.)*

Y&R Capital Image **(1)**
23 Allee Maillasson BP 73 92105
Boulogne, Cedex France
Tel.: 46-843107
Advertising
S.I.C.: 7311
Nicole Hebert *(Mng. Dir.)*

Young & Rubicam AG **(1)**
Muhlebach-Strasse 20 CH-8034
Zurich, Switzerland
Tel.: 252-5855
Telex: 58620
Twx: 58620
Fax: 01/252 60 25
Approx.Billings: $33,000,000
Emp.: 49
S.I.C.: 7311
Marius Kruge *(Chm.)*
Urs Beer *(Mng. Dir.)*

Young & Rubicam Belgium S.A. **(1)**
Dieweg 3B 1180
Brussels, Belgium
Tel.: 2-3758012
Fax: 2-3758843
Approx.Billings: $65,500,000
Emp.: 53
Computer Systems/Hardware:
Apple Macintosh, IBM
Institutional Advertising, Direct Marketing, Sales Promotion
S.I.C.: 7311
Patrick Willemarck *(Gen. Mgr.)*

Young & Rubicam Czechoslovakia **(1)**
Olivova 6 110 00
Prague, 1, Czechoslovakia
Tel.: 422-264631/220344
Fax: 422-264102
Approx.Billings: $4,800,000
Emp.: 35
Advertising
S.I.C.: 7311
Jiri Kratena *(Mng. Dir.)*

Young & Rubicam Est **(1)**
6 Rue Hannong-Village Ouest 67383
Lingolsheim, Cedex France
Tel.: 88-772610
Fax: 88-771993
Advertising
S.I.C.: 7311
Alain Pfister *(Mng. Dir.)*
Philippe Lentschener *(Deputy Mng. Dir.-S.A.)*

Young & Rubicam France S.A. **(1)**
23 Allee Maillasson BP 73 92105
Boulogne, Cedex France
Tel.: 1-46843333
Telex: 842 201521
Fax: 1-46843272/46843270
Approx.Billings: $430,700,000
Emp.: 640
S.I.C.: 7311
Jean-Pierre Villaret *(Chm.-Paris)*
Jaques-Herve Roubert *(Deputy Mng. Dir.-Paris)*

Young & Rubicam GmbH **(1)**
Bleichstrasse 64 Postfach 4665, D-6000
Frankfurt/Main, 1, Germany
Tel.: 69-21920
Fax: 69-2192430
Approx.Billings: $365,800,000
Emp.: 511
S.I.C.: 7311
Ingo Krauss *(Chm. & Chief Exec. Officer-Y & R Adv.-Europe)*
Frans Mootz *(Deputy Mng. Partner)*
Bernd Misske *(Gen. Mgr.)*
Frans F. Mootz *(Gen. Mgr.)*

Young & Rubicam Holdings Ltd. **(1)**
Greater London House, Hampstead Rd.
London, NW1 7QP, United Kingdom
Tel.: 071-3879366
Telex: 25197
Fax: 071-3806570
Approx.Billings: $350,000,000
Emp.: 193
Advertising
S.I.C.: 7311
Chris Dickens *(Grp. Chm.-UK)*
Clive Holland *(Chm.)*
Jerry Judge *(Chief Exec. Officer)*

Young & Rubicam International European Hdqrs. **(1)**
Greater London House, Hampstead Rd.
London, NW1 7QP, United Kingdom
Tel.: 071-387 9366
Telex: 25197
Emp.: 21
S.I.C.: 7311
Joseph E. De Deo *(Pres., Y&R Europe)*
Marc Bromberg *(Vice Chm.)*
Peter Isdell-Carpenter *(European Mktg. Dir.)*
W. Barton Marsh *(European Mng. Supvr.)*
Jim Williams *(European Planning & Research Dir.)*
Don Sperring *(European Mktg. Dir.)*

Young & Rubicam Italia, S.p.A. **(1)**
Piazza Eleonora Duse 2 I-20122
Milan, Italy
Tel.: 2-77321
Fax: 2-781436
Approx.Billings: $457,600,000
Emp.: 154
Advertising
S.I.C.: 7311
Ugo Castellano *(Pres. & Chief Exec. Officer)*
Gavino Sanna *(Chm. & Exec. Creative Dir.)*
Luigi Rinaldi *(Vice Chm. & Chief Oper. Officer)*
Marco Lombardi *(Vice Chm. & Devel. Gen. Mgr.)*
Carlo D'Innella *(Gen. Mgr.)*

Young & Rubicam Ouest **(1)**
1 Rue Du Guesclin 44000
Nantes, France
Tel.: 40-455900
Telex: 842 701500
Fax: 40-356964
Advertising
S.I.C.: 7311
Pierre de Larminat *(Mng. Dir.)*

Young & Rubicam & Ogmios **(1)**
116 Blvd. de la Plage 06800
Cagnes-Sur-Mer, France
Tel.: 93-141820
Fax: 93-141444
Advertising
S.I.C.: 7311
Patrice Dilly *(Mng. Dir.)*

Young & Rubicam Sud Ouest **(1)**
Les Bureaux du Lac, Rue Robert Caumont 33049
Bordeaux, France
Tel.: 56-432821
Fax: 56-432791
Advertising
S.I.C.: 7311
Jerome Lefevre *(Mng. Dir.)*

Young & Rubicam Vienna Werbegesellschaft m.b.H. **(1)**
Postfach 999, Marc Aurel Strasse 4 A-1010
Vienna, Austria
Tel.: 222-5336681
Telex: 115815
Fax: 222-5334519
Approx.Billings: $68,700,000
Emp.: 42
Advertising
S.I.C.: 7311
Dr. Joseph Antos *(Mng. Dir.)*
Mag. Peter Lenhart *(Fin. Dir.)*

Young & Rubicam, S.A. **(1)**
Raimundo Fernandez Villaverde 65 10th Fl., Edificio Windsor, 28003
Madrid, Spain
Tel.: 1-5563113
Fax: 1-5560473
Approx.Billings: $200,100,000
Emp.: 81
S.I.C.: 7311
Pedro Sempere *(Chm.)*
Eduardo Benavent *(Mng. Dir.)*
Ignacio Cabezon *(Fin. Dir.)*
Jody Doran *(Info. Officer)*

Young & Rubicam Sweden AB (Holding) **(1)**
Riddargatan 19 Box 14082, S-114-57
Stockholm, Sweden
Tel.: 65-02-00
Telex: 10342
Twx: 854-10342
Telecopier: (08) 33-07-22
Approx.Billings: $2,740,740
Emp.: 20
S.I.C.: 7311
Brian Harrison *(Mng. Dir.)*
Lars Ruda *(Chm Bd)*
Lars Lundberg *(Pres)*
Anne Asplund *(Sec)*
Hakan Gustavson *(Treas)*
Ylva Lindahl *(Librarian)*

Young & Rubicam (Portugal) **(1)**
Ava. Duque d'Avila 26-30 1097
Lisbon, Portugal
Tel.: 1-3557161
Telex: 60663
Fax: 1-549077
Approx.Billings: $39,900,000
Emp.: 79
Computer Systems/Hardware:
Novell 286
Advertising
S.I.C.: 7311
Telmo Protasio *(Chm.)*
Jose Eduardo Silva *(Mng. Dir.)*

Young & Rubicam Copenhagen **(1)**
Enhjorningens Bastion, Langebrogade 6V. 1411
Copenhagen, K, Denmark
Tel.: 32-961122
Telex: 22235
Fax: 32-961014
Approx.Billings: $65,900,000
Emp.: 30
Advertising
S.I.C.: 7311
Hans-Henrik Rasmussen *(Mng. Dir.)*
Nico Schou Sorensen *(Chief Fin. Officer)*

Young & Rubicam Goteburg AB **(1)**
Tradgardsgaten 1 41108
Goteborg, Sweden
Tel.: 31-101320
Fax: 31-119088
Advertising
S.I.C.: 7311
Willard Sartre *(Mng. Dir.)*

North & South America:

Aser Publicidad **(1)**
Calle 21 Norte No. 3N-55,
Cali, Colombia
Tel.: 68-24-31
S.I.C.: 7311
Elizabeth Santafe *(Mng. Dir.)*
Margo Graham de Salom *(VP-Client Svcs)*

Aser Publicidad/Y&R **(1)**
Carrera 7 No. 74-09,
Bogota, Colombia
Tel.: 1-2554411
Telex: 39644865
Fax: 1-2555934
S.I.C.: 7311
Jorge Arenas Lamus *(Pres.)*
Ernesto Silva *(Mng. Dir.)*

Impact Comunicacoes **(1)**
15 19 Andar Av. Brig. Faria Liam 2100, 01452
Sao Paulo, S.P. Brazil
Tel.: 814-1022
Telex: 1181645
Fax: 814-4812
Advertising
S.I.C.: 7311
Maria Christina Carvalho Pinto Moy *(Pres.)*
Antonio Fadiga *(Gen. Mgr.)*

JMC Creatividad Orientada/Young & Rubicam **(1)**
Av. La Estlancia, Centro Banaven Torre C, Piso 5, Chuao,
Caracas, Venezuela
Tel.: 2-923066/7519891/923968
Telex: 395-24520
Fax: 2-914206
Approx.Billings: $28,000,000
Emp.: 135
Advertising, Promotions, Marketing, Direct Marketing, Public Relations, Events
S.I.C.: 7311
Jose Maria Costa *(Pres.)*
Regulo Guerrero *(Exec. V.P., Pub. Rels.)*
Vicente Lopez *(Controller)*

Sudler & Hennessey Canada **(1)**
60 Bloor St., West
Toronto, ON M4W 1J2, Canada
Tel.: 416-961-7733
Fax: 416-961-7890
Advertising
S.I.C.: 7311
Andrew Bouchat *(Gen. Mgr.)*

Wunderman do Brazil **(1)**
15-19 Andar, Av. Brigadeiro Faria Lima 2100-190 01451
Sao Paulo, S.P. Brazil
Tel.: 11-8136910
Telex: 1153488FIJUBR
Fax: 11-8149441
Advertising
S.I.C.: 7311
Francisco Britto *(Gen. Mgr.)*

Wunderman Worldwide **(1)**
60 Bloor St. W., 15th Fl.
Toronto, ON M4W 3B8, Canada
Tel.: 416-921-9050
Fax: 416-961-0971
Approx.Billings: $18,500,000
Computer Systems/Hardware:
Apple
Direct Marketing
S.I.C.: 7311
Mona Goldstein *(Mng. Dir.)*
Louise Swinton *(Sr. V.P., Admin.)*

Wunderman Worldwide **(1)**
345 Ave. Victoria, Ste. 603
Montreal, PQ H3Z 2N2, Canada
Tel.: 514-482-9726
Fax: 514-482-6781
Advertising
S.I.C.: 7311

Young & Rubicam **(1)**
15 19 Andar, Av. Brig. Faria Lima 2100 01452-002
Sao Paulo, S.P. Brazil
Tel.: 814-1022
Telex: 391-1181645
Fax: 814-4812
Advertising
S.I.C.: 7311
Lincoln Seragini *(Gen. Mgr.)*

Young & Rubicam Argentina **(1)**
Paseo Colon 275, Piso 13 1063
Buenos Aires, Argentina
Tel.: 1-3318491/8492/8493/8495
Fax: 1-3343973
Approx.Billings: $29,337,000
Emp.: 100
S.I.C.: 7311
Dario Straschnoy *(Pres.)*
Jorge Funes *(Dir.)*
Roberto Jacoby *(Mktg. Dir.)*
Jorge Lesende *(Acctg. Dir.)*

Young & Rubicam Brasil **(1)**
17-19 Andar, Av. Brigadeiro Faria Lima 2100 01451
Sao Paulo, Brazil
Tel.: 11-8141022
Telex: 1181645
Fax: 11-8144812
Approx.Billings: $45,000,000
Emp.: 120
Computer Systems/Hardware:
Aquarius
S.I.C.: 7311
Fernan Montero *(Area Dir.-Latin America (NY))*
M. Christina Carvalho Pinto *(Pres. & Creative Dir.)*
Antonio Fadiga *(Gen. Mgr.)*
Amador Camargo *(V.P., Fin.)*
Rosa Grandisky *(V.P., Consumer Insights)*

Young & Rubicam de Chile Ltda. **(1)**
Las Orquideas 979 Casilla 131, Corres 35, Santiago, Chile
Tel.: 2-2330360/0740
Telex: 645218
Fax: 2-2317564
Approx.Billings: $495,766,000
Emp.: 25
S.I.C.: 7311
Mauricio Vives *(Gen. Mgr.)*
Lutz Fuentes *(Controller)*

Young & Rubicam, Ltd. **(1)**
60 Bloor St. West
Toronto, ON M4W 1J2, Canada
Tel.: 416-961-5111
Twx: 369-06-218847
Fax: 416-961-7890
S.I.C.: 7311
William Power *(Chm., Pres. & Chief Exec. Officer-Canada)*

Young & Rubicam, Ltee. **(1)**
1600 Rene Levesque Blvd. W. Ste. 1200,
Montreal, PQ H3H 1P9, Canada
Tel.: 514-935-6375
Fax: 514-935-9479
Approx.Billings: $43,000,000
Emp.: 52
Integrated Communications
S.I.C.: 7311
Madeleine Saint-Jacques *(Pres.)*
Louis-Eric Vallee *(Exec. V.P. & Mng. Dir.)*
Suzanne Bourret *(V.P.-Acct. Dir. & Dir.-Training & Devel.)*
Christian Coutu *(Admin. Dir.)*
Guy Thouin *(ACFM Quebec Dir.)*

Young & Rubicam, S.A. de C.V. **(1)**
Leibnitz #13, Colonia Polanco 5
Mexico, D.F. 11590, Mexico
Tel.: 5-2503200
Fax: 5-2500862
Emp.: 100
S.I.C.: 7311
Eduardo Vorhauer *(Pres.)*
Martha Corredor *(Chief Fin. Officer)*
Carlos Narvaez *(Exec. V.P.)*

Young & Rubicam Sydney Pty. Ltd. **(1)**
The Denison, 65 Berry St., 17th Fl.
North Sydney, N.S.W. 2060, Australia
Tel.: 2-9316000
Telex: 790-122274 RINCAD
Fax: 2-9571080
Approx.Billings: $212,000,000
Emp.: 168
Full Service Advertising
S.I.C.: 7311
Phil Asche *(Area Dir.-Australia & New Zealand)*
Gary Kearley *(Gen. Mgr.)*
Jennifer Bryant *(Natl. Pub. Rels. Dir.)*

Asia/Pacific:

Cato Johnson Adelaide **(1)**
182-184 Fullarton Rd., 2nd Fl. P.O. Box 55, Glenside,
Dulwich, S.A. 5065, Australia
Tel.: 8-3664766
Fax: 8-3641768
S.I.C.: 7311
Andrew Malzard *(Gen. Mgr.)*

Cato Johnson Sydney **(1)**
6th Floor, 213-219 Miller St.
North Sydney, N.S.W. 2060, Australia
Tel.: 957-48-00
Telex: 22274
S.I.C.: 7311
Jef Rawlinson *(Gen. Mgr.)*

Dentsu Wunderman Direct Inc. **(1)**
2-16-7, Ginza Chuo-ku,
Tokyo, 104, Japan
Tel.: 81-3-3546-0710
Telex: 26233 Dentsu J
Fax: 3-35460720
Advertising
S.I.C.: 7311
Yuichi Katsura *(Pres.)*
Koji Fujita *(Exec. V.P.)*
Alan Moore *(Sr. V.P.-No. Asian Region)*

Young & Rubicam Inc.—(Continued)

Sudler & Hennessey **(1)**
572 St. Kilda Rd.
Melbourne, Victoria 3004, Australia
Tel.: 03-529-2855
Telex: 790-32252 RINCAD
Fax: 03-529-7013
Approx.Billings: $8,000,000
Emp.: 11
Healthcare Advertising
S.I.C.: 7311
Gwen Riggs *(Mng. Dir.)*
Sharon Radwanski *(Admin. Mgr.)*

Sudler & Hennessey **(1)**
3 Whitaker Place
Auckland, New Zealand
Tel.: 9-775019
Telex: NZ 63445
Fax: 9-395753
Advertising
S.I.C.: 7311
Steve Campbell *(Gen. Mgr.)*

Sudler & Hennessey Sydney **(1)**
The Denison, Level 15, 65 Berry St.
Sydney, N.S.W. 2060, Australia
Tel.: 02-9316111
Telex: 790 1222724 RINCAD
Fax: 02-9298620
Approx.Billings: $35,000,000
Emp.: 30
S.I.C.: 7311
David L. McLean *(Mng. Dir.-Sydney & Australia)*

Wunderman Cato Johnson **(1)**
182 Fullarton Rd., 2nd Fl. P.O. Box 55, Glenside,
Dulwich, S.A. 5065, Australia
Tel.: 8-3664766
Telex: 8266 RINCADAA
Fax: 8-3641768
Advertising
S.I.C.: 7311
William Lodge *(Chm, Australia & Mng. Dir., Adelaide)*

Wunderman Cato Johnson **(1)**
The Denison, Level 4, 65 Berry St.
North Sydney, N.S.W. 2060, Australia
Tel.: 2-9316262
Telex: 190-122271 RINCADAAA
Fax: 2-9567607
Direct Marketing
S.I.C.: 7311
John Skinner *(Deputy Chm.-Australia)*

Young & Rubicam Brisbane Pty. Ltd. **(1)**
2nd Fl., 895 Ann St.
Fortitude Valley, Queensland 4006, Australia
Tel.: 07-8541566
Fax: 07-2525562
S.I.C.: 7311
Chris Wilton *(Gen. Mgr.)*

Young & Rubicam Melbourne **(1)**
572 St. Kilda Rd.
Melbourne, Victoria 3004, Australia
Tel.: 3-5292855
Telex: 790-32252 RINCAD
Fax: 3-5295552
S.I.C.: 7311
Rod Curtis *(Mng. Dir.)*
John Skinner *(Mng. Dir.)*

Young & Rubicam New Zealand Ltd. **(1)**
3 Whitaker Place P.O. Box 37229, Parnell,
Auckland, New Zealand
Tel.: 9-3775019
Fax: 9-3095753
S.I.C.: 7311
Sandy Short *(Mng. Dir.)*
Jane von Zalinski *(Fin. Dir.)*

Young & Rubicam Pty. Ltd. **(1)**
182-184 Fullarton Rd. P.O. Box 55, Glenside,
Dulwich, S.A. 5065, Australia
Tel.: 8-3664777
Fax: 8-3332276
S.I.C.: 7311
David Minear *(Mng. Dir.)*

Africa:

Cato Johnson Cape Town **(1)**
305 Main Rd. P.O. Box 26,
Kenilworth, 7745, South Africa
Tel.: 21-761-9010
Twx: 960-527593 SA
S.I.C.: 7311
Carl Wakeham *(Mng. Dir.)*

Michael Hogg-Young & Rubicam (Pvt.) Ltd. **(1)**
Satcoy House, 125 Manica Rd. P.O. Box B.E. 130,
Harare, Zimbabwe
Tel.: 263-4-703621
Telex: 987-22136 MMDMM ZW
Fax: 4-707948
Approx.Billings: $23,000,000
Emp.: 90
Advertising
S.I.C.: 7311
Michael Hogg *(Chm.)*
Terry Kinloch *(Fin. Dir.)*

Wunderman Worldwide **(1)**
Nissan House, 3rd Fl., 15 Alice Lane
Sandton, 2146, South Africa
Tel.: 883-2820
Telex: 4-24230
Advertising
S.I.C.: 7311
David East *(Mng. Dir.)*

Wunderman Worldwide **(1)**
Satcoy House, 125 Robert Mugabe Rd. P.O. Box B.E. 71, Belvedere,
Harare, Zimbabwe
Tel.: 4-70-7948
Twx: ZW2136
Fax: 4-98722136
Advertising
S.I.C.: 7311
Chris Thompson *(Mng. Dir.)*

Y&R Cape **(1)**
305 Main Rd.
Kenilworth, 7700, South Africa
Tel.: 21-7619010
Twx: 960-527593 SA
Fax: 21-7611167
S.I.C.: 7311
Johnny Johnson *(Mng. Dir.)*

Y&R Transvaal **(1)**
Nissan House, 3rd Fl., 15 Alice Lane P.O. Box 784570, Sandhurst 2146,
Johannesburg, South Africa
Tel.: 11-8819111
Telex: 4-424230
Twx: 960-424230
Fax: 11-8841994
S.I.C.: 7311
Johnny Johnson *(Mng. Dir.)*

Young & Rubicam Cape **(1)**
305 Main Rd. P.O. Box 26,
Kenilworth, 7700, South Africa
Tel.: 21-7619010
Telex: 960-527593 SA
Fax: 21-7611167
S.I.C.: 7311
Ian Farrow *(Mng. Dir.)*

Young & Rubicam Hedley Byrne Cape **(1)**
P.O. Box 26,
Kenilworth, 7700, South Africa
Tel.: 21-7619010
Twx: 960-527593 SA
Fax: 21-7611167
S.I.C.: 7311
Roland Dewey *(Mng. Dir.)*

Young & Rubicam-Hedley Byrne Transvaal **(1)**
Nissan House, 3rd Fl., 15 Alice Ln. P.O. Box 784570,
Sandton, 2146, South Africa
Tel.: 11-883-7010
S.I.C.: 7311
Derek Vosloo *(Mng. Dir.)*

Young & Rubicam South Africa **(1)**
305 Main Rd. P.O. Box 26,
Kenilworth, 7700, South Africa
Tel.: 21-7619010
Telex: 960-527593
Fax: 21-7972969
Approx.Billings: $70,000,000
Emp.: 400
S.I.C.: 7311
David McKinstry *(Chief Exec. Officer)*
David Buirski *(Chm.-Retail Divs.)*

Ronnie Board *(Fin. Dir.)*

Young & Rubicam (Zambia) Ltd. **(1)**
P.O. Box 32497, Woodgate House, Nairobi Place
Lusaka, Zambia
Tel.: 1-228489/490/491
Telex: 965-43810
Fax: 1-225173
S.I.C.: 7311
Michael Hogg *(Chm. Bd. (Zimbabwe))*
Peter Armstrong *(Mng. Dir.)*
Ed Milco *(Chief Fin. Officer)*

YOUNG STUFF APPAREL GROUP, INC.
1407 Broadway, 6th Fl.
New York, NY 10018
Tel.: 212-221-7800
Year Founded: 1905
Approx.Sls.: $65,000,000
Emp.: 60
Mfr. of Large-Size & Missy Apparel for Women
S.I.C.: 2253
Ken Miller *(Pres.)*
Wayne Rutkay *(Chief Fin. Officer & Controller)*
John Miller *(Exec. V.P.)*
Jon Dembrow *(Sr. V.P.)*
Lori Garfinkel *(Grp. V.P.)*
Phil Magerman *(Admin./Opers.)*
Ridgeley Mayer *(Dir.-Mktg.)*
Jack Melnick *(Sec. & Treas.)*

YOUNG SUPPLY COMPANY
888 W. Baltimore Ave.
Detroit, MI 48202
Tel.: 313-875-3280
Fax: 313-875-3051
Year Founded: 1962
Approx.Sls.: $26,000,000
Emp.: 125
Wholesale Refrigeration, Air Conditioning & Heating Equipment & Supplies
S.I.C.: 5075; 5078
Ronald L. Vallan *(Pres.)*
Michael J. Sarzynski *(Exec. V.P.-Sls.)*
Louis D. Vallan *(Exec. V.P.-Sls.)*
Marlin W. Redmond *(V.P.-Branch Opers.)*
Ruth Ann Stinson *(Treas. & Dir.-Personnel)*
Michael Williams *(Controller)*
Ken Maki *(Pur. Agent)*

Outside Service Firm(s):

BDO Seidman*(Auditors)*
Troy, MI

Allen, Neet, Grosse & Pointe*(Legal Firm)*
Troy, MI

Liberty Bank & Trust*(Major Banking Relationship)*
Troy, MI

YOUNG'S MARKET COMPANY
500 S. Central Avenue
Los Angeles, CA 90013
Tel.: 213-629-5571 **DE**
Fax: 213-612-1280
Year Founded: 1888
Approx.Sls.: $780,000,000
Emp.: 1,200
Fiscal Year-end: 2/28/89
Wholesaler of Wine, Distilled Spirits & Seafood
S.I.C.: 5182; 5146
Vernon Underwood, Jr. *(Chm. Bd.)*
Dennis Hammon *(V.P., Controller & Chief Fin. Officer)*

Computer Systems/Hardware:
IBM 4341; AS 400; 36

Outside Service Firm(s):

Ernst & Young*(Auditors)*
515 S. Flower St.
Los Angeles, CA 90071
Tel.: 213-621-1666

Gibson, Dunn & Crutcher*(Legal Firm)*
333 S. Grand Ave.
Los Angeles, CA 90067
Tel.: 310-552-8500
Fax: 310-277-5827

Union Bank*(Major Banking Relationship)*
445 S. Figueroa St.
Los Angeles, CA 90071
Tel.: 213-236-5076

Subsidiary:

BetterBrands, Ltd. **(1)**
94-501 Kau St.
Waipahu, HI 96797
Tel.: 808-676-6111
Whlslr. of Wines & Distilled Spirits
S.I.C.: 5182
Ronald McKee *(Pres.)*

YOUR MAN TOURS, INC.
8331 Aviation Blvd.
Inglewood, CA 90301
Tel.: 310-649-3820
Tel.: 800-992-9000 **CA**
Fax: 310-649-2118
Assets: $10,000,000
Earnings: $500,000
Liabilities: $2,000,000
Net Worth: $8,000,000
Approx.Sls.: $20,000,000
Emp.: 100
Fiscal Year-end: 12/31/90
Travel Agency
S.I.C.: 4724
Frank J. Dupuis *(Chm. Bd. & Chief Fin. Officer)*
Lenore Dupuis *(Treas.)*
Romy Dizon *(Controller)*
Joyce Holm *(Sec.)*
Frank Channel *(Gen. Sls. Mgr.)*
Owen Moran *(Adv. Mgr.)*
Bill Price *(Mktg. Dir.)*

THE YUCAIPA COMPANIES
250 W. First St., Ste. 210
Claremont, CA 91711
Tel.: 909-626-8776
Fax: 909-624-2026
Private Investment Company
S.I.C.: 6159
Ronald Burkle *(Chm. Bd. & Partner)*
Richard d'Abo *(Partner)*
Mark Resnick *(Partner)*

Subsidiaries:

Almac's Inc. **(1)**
1 Noyes St.
East Providence, RI 02916
Tel.: 401-438-2700
Approx.Sls.: $442,000,000
Emp.: 3,500
Fiscal Year-end: 12/31/90
Computer Systems/Hardware:
Honeywell NB 0082
Supermarket Chain
S.I.C.: 5411
Phillip Segal *(Vice Chm.)*
Joseph Burkle *(Chief Exec. Officer)*
Gregg Mays *(Pres.)*
Robert D'Orsi *(Exec. V.P.-Store Opers.)*
Robert A. Halben *(Controller & Sec.)*
David L. Paulhus *(Dir.-Adv.)*
Don Volino *(Dir.-Human Resources)*

Falley's Inc. **(1)**
3120 S. Kansas Ave.
Topeka, KS 66611
Tel.: 913-267-1501
Fax: 913-267-2251
Food 4 Less Retail Grocery Stores; Meat Processing
S.I.C.: 0211; 5411
Joseph Burkle *(Chm. Bd.)*
Mark Brewer *(Pres.)*
Edward G. Alberg *(Sr. V.P.)*
Kent Laughman *(V.P.)*

Food 4 Less, Inc. **(1)**
7777 S. Harbor Blvd.
La Habra, CA 90631
Tel.: 714-738-2000
Food Retailer/Wholesaler
S.I.C.: 5141; 5411
George Golleher *(Pres.)*

YUM YUM DONUT SHOP, INC.
(d/b/a Donut Equipment & Supply Co.)
18830 E. San Jose Ave.
City of Industry, CA 91748
Tel.: 818-964-1478 **CA**
Fax: 818-912-2779
Year Founded: 1971
Approx.Sls.: $100,000,000
Emp.: 600
Retail Donut Stores
S.I.C.: 5461
Frank W. Watase *(Chm. Bd.)*
Maureen Costello *(Pres.)*
Tom Halsell *(Controller)*

Outside Service Firm(s):

Wells Fargo Bank*(Major Banking Relationship)*
9000 Flair
El Monte, CA

Division:

Quality Naturally Foods **(1)**
18830 E. San Jose Ave.
City of Industry, CA 91748
Tel.: 818-964-1478
Mfr. of Doughnuts, Except Frozen, Cookies
S.I.C.: 2051
Maureen Costello *(Pres.)*

Z. CAVARICCI INC.
2535 E. 12th St., Unit A
Los Angeles, CA 90021
Tel.: 213-629-1988
Fax: 213-629-8242
Year Founded: 1976
Approx.Sls.: $86,000,000
Emp.: 150
Mfr. of Men's, Boy's, Women's & Girl's Jeans, Slacks, Shirts, Jackets, Shorts & Skirts
S.I.C.: 2325; 2311; 2331; 2337
James Cavaricci *(Pres.)*

ZBS INDUSTRIES, INC.
701 Beta Dr.
Mayfield Village, OH 44143
Tel.: 216-461-6275
Fax: 216-461-0230
Year Founded: 1979
Sales Range: $40-59 Million
Emp.: 126
Videotape Distributor
S.I.C.: 7822
Larry Beyer *(Pres.)*
Mary Crane *(V.P.-Fin. & Controller)*
Earl Stein *(V.P.)*
Jay Schultz *(Treas. & Sec.)*

Principal(s):
Larry Beyer
Jay Schultz

Computer Systems/Hardware:
Wang VS 85

Outside Service Firm(s):

KPMG Peat Marwick*(Auditors)*
1500 National City Center
Cleveland, OH 44114
Tel.: 216-696-9100

Blue Cross & Blue Shield of Northern Ohio*(Group Insurer)*
2060 E. 9th St.
Cleveland, OH 44115
Tel.: 216-687-7000

Benesch, Friedlander, Coplan & Aronoff*(Legal Firm)*
1100 Citizens Bldg.
Cleveland, OH 44114
Tel.: 216-363-4500

Society National Bank*(Major Banking Relationship)*
Cleveland, OH

Subsidiary:

IMC, Inc. **(1)**
701 Beta Dr.
Mayfield Village, OH 44143
Tel.: 216-461-6275
Videotape Distributor
S.I.C.: 7822
Larry Beyer *(Pres.)*

H.B. ZACHRY
527 Logwood
San Antonio, TX 78221-0130
Mailing Address:
P.O. Box 21130,
San Antonio, TX 78221-0130
Tel.: 210-922-1213 **DE**
Fax: 210-927-8060
Year Founded: 1924
Sales Range: $500-999 Million
Emp.: 8,500
Fiscal Year-end: 12/31/90
Holding Company
S.I.C.: 6719
H.B. Zachry, Jr. *(Chm. Bd. & Chief Exec. Officer)*
Bruce B. Cloud *(Pres. & Chief Oper. Officer)*
Paul Autry *(Chief Information Officer)*
Charles Ebrom *(Exec. V.P.-Admin. & Fin.)*
Richard Bryan *(Sr. V.P.-Industrial Group)*
Dick Bryan *(Group V.P.-Indus.)*
Luther Boyd *(V.P.-Fin.)*
Cathy O. Green *(V.P.-Pub. Affairs)*
Murray Johnson *(V.P., Gen. Counsel & Sec.)*
Robert Kalt *(V.P.-Mktg.)*
Joe Lozano *(V.P. & Controller)*
Ed Bardgett *(Dir.-Human Resources)*
Keith Byron *(Dir.-Quality Control)*
Moon Fahel *(Dir.-Tech. Services)*
Don Patrick *(Dir.-Training)*
Wade Chancellor *(Mgr.-Intl. Opers.)*
Lad Herold *(Mgr.-Pur.)*

Principal(s):
H.B. Zachry, Jr.

Computer Systems/Hardware:
IBM 4341

Outside Service Firm(s):

Ernst & Young*(Auditors)*
1900 Frost Bank Tower, 100 W. Houston St.
San Antonio, TX 78205
Tel.: 210-228-9696
Fax: 210-554-0253

Johnson, Ralph, Reed & Cone*(Legal Firm)*
San Antonio, TX

National Bank of Commerce*(Major Banking Relationship)*
San Antonio, TX

Texas Commerce Bank*(Major Banking Relationship)*
600 Travis Street, Suite 1150
Houston, TX 77002
Tel.: 713-236-4865

Texas Commerce Bank*(Pension Manager)*
717 Travis St.
Houston, TX 77002
Tel.: 713-236-4636
Fax: 713-236-5476

Subsidiary:

H. B. Zachry Company **(1)**
527 Logwood
San Antonio, TX 78221
Tel.: 210-922-1213
Fax: 210-927-8060
Sales Range: $100-499 Million
Emp.: 6,100
General Building Contractors; Heavy Construction & Industrial Contractors
S.I.C.: 1541; 1542; 1611; 1623; 1629; 3241
Bruce B. Cloud *(Pres.)*
Charles Ebrom *(Exec. V.P.)*
Luther I. Boyd *(V.P., Treas.)*
Joe J. Lozano *(Controller)*

ZACK COMPANY
4600 W. 12th Place
Chicago, IL 60650
Tel.: 312-242-3434
Fax: 312-242-3455
Approx.Sls.: $30,000,000
Emp.: 700
Sheet Metal Contractors; Dust Collectors Fume Burners; Ventilation & Air Conditioning; Stainless Steel Kitchen Equipment; Air Pollution Control; Mechanical Piping; Boiler/Turbine Modification & Repair
S.I.C.: 1711; 1541; 1761; 1796
Christine Zack *(Chm. Bd. & Pres.)*
W.J. Harrington *(Exec. V.P.)*
H.G. Jung *(V.P.-Engrng.)*

Outside Service Firm(s):

Dugan & Lopatka*(Auditors)*
Chicago, IL

Continental Bank N. A.*(Major Banking Relationship)*
231 S. LaSalle St.
Chicago, IL 60697
Tel.: 312-828-2345
Tel.: 800-426-5754
Telex: 312-828-1783

Branch:

Zack Co. **(1)**
4401 Western Rd.
Flint, MI 48506
Tel.: 313-736-2040
Sheet Metal Contractors
S.I.C.: 1711
Eugene Lipp *(V.P. & Gen. Mgr.)*

ZACKY FARMS, INC.
2000 N. Tyler Ave.
South El Monte, CA 91733
Tel.: 818-443-9351
Fax: 818-401-4229
Year Founded: 1946
Approx.Sls.: $200,000,000
Emp.: 1,600
Producer Broiler Chickens
S.I.C.: 0251; 2015
Robert Zacky *(Pres. & Sec.)*
Hank Frederick *(Exec. V.P.)*

Computer Systems/Hardware:
IBM System 38

Outside Service Firm(s):

Chemical Banking Corp.*(Major Banking Relationship)*
277 Park Ave.
New York, NY 10041
Tel.: 212-310-6407
Fax: 212-310-4526

ZALE CORPORATION
901 W. Walnut Hill Lane
Irving, TX 75038
Tel.: 214-580-4000 **TX**
Assets: $1,789,178,000
Liabilities: $1,439,176,000
Net Worth: $350,002,000
Approx.Sls.: $1,335,269,000
Emp.: 10,000
Fiscal Year-end: 3/31/91
Import
Retail Jewelry
S.I.C.: 5944
Dean Groussman *(Chm., Pres. & Chief Exec. Officer)*
Charles F. Gill *(Asst. to Pres.)*
Ed Jaben *(Asst. to Pres.)*
Thomas T.S. Kaung *(Exec. V.P.-Fin & Admin.)*
Andreas Ludwig *(Exec. V.P. & Chief Fin. Officer)*
Joseph A. Keifer III *(Sr. V.P.-Store Opers.)*
H.R. Lively, Jr. *(Sr. V.P.-Admin.)*
Leonard R. Schneider *(Sr. V.P.-Real Estate & Property Devel.)*
Merrill J. Wertheimer *(Sr. V.P. & Controller)*
E. Peter Healey *(V.P. & Treas.)*
Dolph B.H. Simon *(V.P., Gen. Counsel & Sec.)*

Divisions:

Bailey Banks & Biddle **(1)**
901 W. Walnut Hill Ln.
Irving, TX 75038
Tel.: 214-580-4849
Fax: 214-580-4623
Emp.: 3,000
Jewelry
S.I.C.: 5944
Irving Gerstein *(Chm. Bd.)*
Dennis Bookshester *(Pres. & Chief Exec. Officer)*
Ed Jaben *(Sr. V.P.-Mktg. & Mdsg.)*
Becky Higgins *(Dir.-Adv.)*

Fine Jewelers Guild Div. **(1)**
450 W. 33rd St.
New York, NY 10001
Tel.: 212-560-1100
Emp.: 400
Jewelry
S.I.C.: 5944
James Samuels *(Pres.)*

Jeweler's Financial Service, Inc. **(1)**
901 W. Walnut Hill Ln.
Irving, TX 75038
Tel.: 214-580-4000
Indemnity Insurance
S.I.C.: 6411
John Skinner *(V.P.)*

Leased Jewelry Div. **(1)**
3000 Diamond Park
Dallas, TX 75247
Tel.: 214-634-4312
Approx.Sls.: $34,400,000
Emp.: 470
Leased Jewelry Depts. in Department Stores
S.I.C.: 5944
Alan J. Katz *(Pres.)*

Zale Store Div. **(1)**
901 W. Walnut Hill Ln.
Irving, TX 75038
Tel.: 214-580-4963
Approx.Sls.: $398,300,000
Emp.: 5,500
Retail Jewelry Chain
S.I.C.: 5944

Subsidiaries:

Akard Construction Co., Inc. **(1)**
901 W. Walnut Mill Lane
Irving, TX 75038
Tel.: 214-257-4000 (100%)
Emp.: 4
Commercial Retail Construction
S.I.C.: 1542
Bruce Lipshy *(Pres. & Chief Exec. Officer)*

Gordon Jewelry Corporation **(1)**
901 W. Walnut Hill Lane
Irving, TX 75038
Tel.: 214-580-4000
Assets: $405,149,610
Earnings: ($14,476,053)
Liabilities: $144,760,976
Net Worth: $260,388,634
Approx.Sls.: $389,560,000
Emp.: 6,100
Fiscal Year-end: 3/31/91
600 Operating Units
S.I.C.: 5944
Irving Gerstein *(Pres.)*
Vincent Ambriola *(Sr. V.P.-Mngmt. Information Systems)*
Becky Higgins *(Dir.-Mktg.)*
Ellen Kulik *(Dir.-Adv.)*

Subsidiaries:

The American-World Life Insurance Co. **(2)**
820 Fannin St.
Houston, TX 77002
Tel.: 713-222-8080 (100%)
S.I.C.: 6311

Bond's Jewelers, Inc. **(2)**
820 Fannin St.
Houston, TX 77002
Tel.: 713-222-8080
Jewelry Store
S.I.C.: 5944

Zale Corporation—(Continued)

Daniel's Jewelry Co. of Arizona, Inc. **(2)**
820 Fannin St.
Houston, TX 77002
Tel.: 713-222-8080
Jewelry Store
S.I.C.: 5944

Eleven-O-One Corp. **(2)**
820 Fannin St.
Houston, TX 77002
Tel.: 713-222-8080
Jewelry Store
S.I.C.: 5944

Gulf Coast Jewelry & Specialty Co., Inc. **(2)**
820 Fannin St.
Houston, TX 77002
Tel.: 713-222-8080
Jewelry Store
S.I.C.: 5944

Hamilton Wholesale Jewelry Co., Inc. **(2)**
820 Fannin St.
Houston, TX 77002
Tel.: 713-222-8080
Jewelry Store
S.I.C.: 5944

Mermod, Jaccard & King Jewelry Co. of Iowa, Inc. **(2)**
820 Fannin St.
Houston, TX 77002
Tel.: 713-222-8080
Jewelry Store
S.I.C.: 5944

Mermod, Jaccard & King Jewelry Co. of Nebraska **(2)**
820 Fannin St.
Houston, TX 77002
Tel.: 713-222-8080
Jewelry Store
S.I.C.: 5944

National Atlas Life Insurance Co. **(2)**
820 Fannin St.
Houston, TX 77002
Tel.: 713-222-8080
Life Insurance
S.I.C.: 6311

Oskamp Nolting Co., Inc. **(2)**
820 Fannin St.
Houston, TX 77002
Tel.: 713-222-8080
Jewelry Store
S.I.C.: 5944

Robanne Corp. **(2)**
820 Fannin St.
Houston, TX 77002
Tel.: 713-222-8080
Jewelry Store
S.I.C.: 5944

Smith Jewelers & Distributors, Inc. **(2)**
820 Fannin St.
Houston, TX 77002
Tel.: 713-222-8080
Jewelry Store
S.I.C.: 5944

Southern Realty Co. **(2)**
820 Fannin St.
Houston, TX 77002
Tel.: 713-222-8080
Jewelry Store
S.I.C.: 5944

Southwestern Wholesale Jewelry Co. **(2)**
820 Fannin St.
Houston, TX 77002
Tel.: 713-222-8080
Jewelry Store
S.I.C.: 5944

Star Engraving Co. **(2)**
820 Fannin St.
Houston, TX 77002
Tel.: 713-222-8080
S.I.C.: 5944

G. A. Stowers Furniture Co. **(2)**
820 Fannin St.
Houston, TX 77002
Tel.: 713-222-8080
Hardwood & Flooring Mills
S.I.C.: 2426

United-General Products of Knoxville, Inc. **(2)**
820 Fannin St.
Houston, TX 77002
Tel.: 713-222-8080
Jewelry Store
S.I.C.: 5944

United-Hamilton, Inc. **(2)**
820 Fannin St.
Houston, TX 77002
Tel.: 713-222-8080
Jewelry Store
S.I.C.: 5944

United Jewelers & Distributors of Texas, Inc. **(2)**
820 Fannin St.
Houston, TX 77002
Tel.: 713-222-8080
Jewelry Store
S.I.C.: 5944

United Jewelers & Distributors of Louisiana, Inc. **(2)**
820 Fannin St.
Houston, TX 77002
Tel.: 713-222-8080
Jewelry Store
S.I.C.: 5944

United Jewelers & Distributors of Arkansas, Inc. **(2)**
820 Fannin St.
Houston, TX 77002
Tel.: 713-222-8080
Jewelry Store
S.I.C.: 5944

United Jewelers & Distributors of Arizona, Inc. **(2)**
820 Fannin St.
Houston, TX 77002
Tel.: 713-222-8080
Jewelry Store
S.I.C.: 5944

Universal Service Bureau, Inc. **(2)**
820 Fannin St.
Houston, TX 77002
Tel.: 713-222-8080
Jewelry Store
S.I.C.: 5944

THE ZAMOISKI CO.
3000 Waterview Ave.
Baltimore, MD 21230
Tel.: 410-539-3000
Fax: 410-576-8472
Emp.: 435
Distribute Home Products, Major Appliances, Computer Systems, Resilient Floor Coverings
S.I.C.: 5064; 5023; 5099; 5065; 5043; 5181
C. J. Zamoiski, Jr. *(Chm. Bd., Pres. & Chief Exec. Officer)*
William Kitchell *(Chief Fin. Officer)*
Kenneth Janssen *(V.P.)*
John Mulkey *(Treas.)*

Computer Systems/Hardware:
DEC

Outside Service Firm(s):

Ellin & Tucker*(Auditors)*
Baltimore, MD

Connecticut General Life Insurance Co.*(Group Insurer)*
Baltimore, MD

Weinberg & Green*(Legal Firm)*
100 S. Charles St.
Baltimore, MD 21202
Tel.: 410-332-8795

Maryland National Bank*(Major Banking Relationship)*
Baltimore, MD 21202

Subsidiaries:

Paradies & Co. Atlanta **(1)**
1101 DeSoto Rd.
Baltimore, MD 21223
Tel.: 410-644-2900

Peerless Inc. **(1)**
1101 DeSoto Rd.
Baltimore, MD 21223
Tel.: 410-644-2900

ZANDER'S CREAMERY INC.
1300 Main St.
Cross Plains, WI 53528
Tel.: 608-798-3261
Year Founded: 1955
Approx.Sls.: $32,000,000
Emp.: 52
Mfr. of Butter
S.I.C.: 2021
Paul H. Zander *(Pres.)*
Tim Zander *(Coord.-Adv. & Mktg.)*

ZANTOP INTERNATIONAL AIRLINES, INC.
840 Willow Run Airport
Ypsilanti, MI 48198-0840
Tel.: 313-485-8900 **MI**
Fax: 313-485-8900, Ext. 722
Year Founded: 1972
Approx.Sls.: $107,600,000
Emp.: 1,450
Air Cargo Carrier
S.I.C.: 4522
Duane A. Zantop *(Chm. Bd., Pres. & Chief Exec. Officer)*
James M. Zantop *(Exec. V.P.)*
Edward Bahn *(V.P.-Maintenance)*
Robert C. Dillon *(V.P. & Treas.)*
Edwin W. Freitag *(V.P.-Personnel)*
Peter Howarth *(V.P.-Admin.)*
Neil H. Reichard *(V.P.-Cargo Sls. & Service)*
Robert Weir *(V.P.-Opers.)*
Duane G. Zantop *(V.P.-Pur.)*
James H. Loree *(Sec. & Legal Counsel)*
Gerald Karasinski *(Dir.-Data Processing)*

No. of Mfg. Plants/Facilities: 1

Outside Service Firm(s):

Drake, Watters & Co.*(Auditors)*
Jackson, MI

Butzel Long*(Legal Firm)*
Madden Bldg., 150 W. Jefferson, Ste. 900
Detroit, MI 48226-4430
Tel.: 313-225-7000
Fax: 313-225-7080

N.B.D. Bank, N.A.*(Major Banking Relationship)*
611 Woodward Ave.
Detroit, MI 48226
Tel.: 313-225-1122
Fax: 313-225-3420

Division:

Zantop International Airlines, Inc. **(1)**
P.O. Box 10136,
Macon, GA 31297
Tel.: 912-784-9900
Repair, Overhaul & Transport Aircraft, Avionics & Airframe Conversions
S.I.C.: 4581
Timothy Alman *(Mgr.-Maintenance)*
William Felton *(Dir.-Materials)*

Plant:

Zantop Aircraft Maintenance Facility **(1)**
Macon Airport,
Macon, GA 31297
Repair, Service & Overhaul Transport Aircraft, Avionics & Airframe Conversions
S.I.C.: 4581

ZAPIECKI & PARTNERS INC.
4 Sea Gate, 5th Fl.
Toledo, OH 43604
Tel.: 419-249-7000
Fax: 419-249-7010
Year Founded: 1964
Approx.Billings: $17,000,000
Emp.: 34
Automotive Aftermarket, Bldg. Products, Financial Services, Consumer Packaged Goods, Healthcare, Tourism & Travel
Michael Zapiecki *(Chm. & Chief Exec. Officer)*
Mary Jo Abrahamson *(Sr. V.P., Chief Fin. Officer & Treas.)*
Dale Leeds *(Sr. V.P.)*
Marianne McClusky *(Dir., Pub. Rels.)*

ZAPPA PLASTICS
165 Howard St.
Phillipsburg, NJ 08865
Tel.: 908-454-4500
Fax: 908-454-4507
Year Founded: 1959
Approx.Sls.: $10,000,000
Emp.: 160
Import Export
Mfr. of Plastic Injection Molded Parts & Molds
S.I.C.: 3089
R. Zappa *(Chief Exec. Officer)*
Wolfram Huschke *(Dir.-Purchasing)*
Larry Maher *(Mgr.-Sls. & Mkg.)*
Joanne Zappa *(Personnel Mgr.)*

Computer Systems/Hardware:
Compaq Desk Pro 386/20 & 486/20

ZAREMBA CORPORATION
14600 Detroit Ave., Ste. 1500
Lakewood, OH 44107
Tel.: 216-221-6600
Fax: 216-221-9742
Year Founded: 1920
Emp.: 50
Real Estate Developer
S.I.C.: 6552
Walter Zaremba *(Pres. & Chief Exec. Officer)*
Joseph J. Urbancic *(V.P.-Opers.)*

Outside Service Firm(s):

Deloitte & Touche*(Auditors)*
1717 East Ninth St.
Cleveland, OH 44114
Tel.: 216-589-1300

AmeriTrust Company, N.A.*(Major Banking Relationship)*
P.O. Box 5937, 900 Euclid Ave.
Cleveland, OH 44101-0937

ZECHMAN & ASSOCIATES ADV. INC.
333 N. Michigan Ave., Ste. 3300
Chicago, IL 60601
Tel.: 312-346-0551
Fax: 312-346-9894
Year Founded: 1972
Approx.Billings: $12,400,000
Emp.: 20
Advertising Agency
S.I.C.: 7311
Jan E. Zechman *(Pres. & Dir.-Creative)*
Richard Bach *(Dir.-Mktg. Services)*

ZELLER CORP.
1307 Baltimore St.
Defiance, OH 43512
Mailing Address:
P. O. Box 278
Defiance, OH 43512
Tel.: 419-784-2244
Fax: 419-784-0297
Approx.Sls.: $24,000,000
Emp.: 350

Fiscal Year-end: 12/31/90
Screw Machine Prods. Mfg., Universal Joints, Steel Forgings, Automotive Parts
S.I.C.: 3714; 3694
M.C. Zeller *(Pres.)*
K.W. Zeller *(Exec. V.P.)*
Jack Ehlinger *(V.P.-Opers.)*
E.A. Westmeyer *(V.P.-Treas. & Sec.)*
R.C. Leiby *(V.P.-Intl.)*

Divisions:

Allied Eastern Co. **(1)**
1611 Integrity Dr.
Columbus, OH 43209
Tel.: 614-444-0778

Motor Master Products **(1)**
815 Greenler St.
Defiance, OH 43512
Tel.: 419-782-7131

Zeller World Trade Corporation **(1)**
P.O. Box 278
Defiance, OH 43512
Tel.: 419-784-2244

ZEMCO INDUSTRIES, INC.
665 Perry St.
Buffalo, NY 14210
Tel.: 716-826-6400
Fax: 716-826-9186
Approx.Sls.: $50,000,000
Emp.: 250
Meat Provisions & Related Products
S.I.C.: 2011; 2013; 5147
Howard Zemsky *(Pres.)*
Irwin Margulis *(Exec. V.P. & Sec.)*
Toby Kinerk *(V.P.-Fin.)*
Thomas Gervasio *(Controller)*
Chuck Chilcott *(Dir.-Mngmt. Information Systems)*

Outside Service Firm(s):

Grant Thornton*(Auditors)*
Stamford, CT

Kavinoky & Cook*(Legal Firm)*
120 Delaware Ave.
Buffalo, NY 14202
Tel.: 716-856-9234

Fleet Bank*(Major Banking Relationship)*
Deer Park, NY 14202

Division:

Russett Foods **(1)**
665 Perry St.
Buffalo, NY 14210
Tel.: 716-826-6400
S.I.C.: 2011; 2013; 5147
Howard Zemsky *(Pres.)*

ZENA JEANS
1407 Broadway
New York, NY 10018
Mailing Address:
P.O. Box 684,
Cartersville, GA 30120
Tel.: 212-730-0404
Fax: 212-730-2289
Approx.Sls.: $50,000,000
Emp.: 400
Mfr. Denim Sportswear
S.I.C.: 2325; 2339; 2337; 2329
Richard Gilbert *(Pres. & Sls. Promo. Mgr.)*
George Fontini *(Exec. V.P.-Sls.)*
Marty Weisfeld *(Exec. V.P.)*
William Beck *(V.P.-Fin. & Controller)*
Kevin Boyle *(V.P.-Pub. Rels.)*
Bob Jaffe *(Natl. Sls. Mgr., Missy Zena II)*

Computer Systems/Hardware:
Adds Mentor 4000

Outside Service Firm(s):

Georgia International*(Group Insurer)*
Atlanta, GA

National Westminster Bank plc*(Major Banking Relationship)*
Astor Plaza, 1515 Broadway
New York, NY 10036

ZENITH LABORATORIES, INC.
140 Le Grand Ave.
Northvale, NJ 07647
Tel.: 201-767-1700
Fax: 201-767-7865
Approx.Sls.: $50,390,000
Emp.: 307
Mfr. Generic Pharmaceuticals
S.I.C.: 2834
John H. Klein *(Pres. & Chief Exec. Officer)*
Richard M. Shepperd *(Chief Fin. Officer)*
Ruth Wallestad *(Asst. V.P. & Treas.)*
Leonora Gavallis *(Dir.-Mktg.)*

ZENITH PRODUCTS CORP.
(Formerly Zenith Metal Prods. Corp.)
200 Commerce Dr.
Aston, PA 19014
Tel.: 215-485-4700
Fax: 215-485-0187
Approx.Sls.: $26,000,000
Emp.: 300
Sheet Metal Fabrication, Medicine Cabinets, Space Savers, Hampers & Access., Life Style Furniture
S.I.C.: 2514; 3641; 3231; 2499; 2519
A. James Aruffo *(Pres.)*
Robert S. Roggio *(Exec. V.P.)*
Kim Day *(V.P.-Sls. & Adv.)*
Thomas Della Franco *(V.P.-Fin.)*
Bert Sands *(Natl. Sls. Mgr.)*
A. Joseph McElwee *(Pur. Agent)*
Carol Aruffo *(Personnel Dir.)*

Subsidiaries:

ATZ Plastic Molders, Inc. **(1)**
200 Commerce Dr.
Aston, PA 19014
Tel.: 215-485-0187
Fax: 215-485-0187

Zenith West Corp. **(1)**
2675 Pomona Blvd.
Pomona, CA 91768
Tel.: 909-595-9550

ZEPHYR BASKETS & BALLOONS
121 Chanlon Rd.
New Providence, NJ 07974
Tel.: 908-464-6800 **NJ**
Fax: 908-771-7704
Year Founded: 1977
Approx.Rev.: $125,000,000
Emp.: 250
Fiscal Year-end: 12/31/91
Import
Personalized Gifts, Party Favors & Stationery
S.I.C.: 5112; 2754
Brian Proffitt *(Pres.)*
Beth Tanis *(Exec. V.P. & Chief Oper. Officer)*
Nancy Bernhaut *(Exec. V.P. & Chief Fin. Officer)*
John Smith *(Dir.-Mktg.)*
Vince Black *(Mgr.-Imports)*
J.M. Opheim *(Mgr.-Sls. & Mktg.)*
Principal(s):
Brian Proffitt
Beth Tanis

No. of Mfg. Plants/Facilities: 2
No. of U.S. Offices: 2

Outside Service Firm(s):

Ernst & Young*(Auditors)*
233 S. Wacker Dr.
Chicago, IL 60606
Tel.: 312-368-1800
Fax: 312-645-3095

First Union National Bank*(Major Banking Relationship)*
Chicago, IL

Bell, Boyd & Lloyd*(Legal Firm)*
Three First National Plaza
Chicago, IL 60602
Tel.: 312-372-1121

ZEPHYR INC.
P.O. Box 5069
North Muskegon, MI 49445
Tel.: 616-744-1631
Fax: 616-744-8657
Approx.Sls.: $180,000,000
Emp.: 300
Fiscal Year-end: 3/31/90
Marine Terminal Operators
S.I.C.: 4491
Allan C. Hanna *(Pres. & Chief Exec. Officer)*
Therese M. Seberry *(Corp. Sec.)*

A. ZEREGAS SONS, INC.
20-01 Broadway
Fair Lawn, NJ 07410
Mailing Address:
P.O. Box 241
Fair Lawn, NJ 07410
Tel.: 201-797-1400 **NJ**
Fax: 201-797-0148
Year Founded: 1848
Sales Range: $20-39 Million
Emp.: 150
Macaroni Products; Spaghetti & Egg Noodle Products
S.I.C.: 2098
Paul A. Vermylen *(Pres.)*
Mark E. Vermylen *(V.P. & Sec.)*
Robert A. Vermylen *(V.P.-Sls.)*
Richard Epperlein *(Treas. & Comptroller)*

No. of Mfg. Plants/Facilities: 1
No. of U.S. Offices: 1

Outside Service Firm(s):

Stephen P. Radics & Company*(Auditors)*
Haledon, NJ

Jones, Day, Reavis & Pogue*(Legal Firm)*
New York, NY

National Community Bank*(Major Banking Relationship)*
Fair Lawn, NJ

ZETEC, INC.
1370 N.W. Mall
Issaquah, WA 98027
Mailing Address:
P.O. Box 140,
Issaquah, WA 98027-0140
Tel.: 206-392-5316
Fax: 206-392-2086
Approx.Sls.: $21,000,000
Emp.: 175
Eddy Current Measuring Equipment
S.I.C.: 3825; 7389
Clyde Denton *(Pres.)*

Outside Service Firm(s):

Seattle First National Bank*(Major Banking Relationship)*
P.O. Box 24186
Seattle, WA 98124

ZIEBART INTERNATIONAL CORPORATION
1290 E. Maple Rd.
Troy, MI 48084
Mailing Address:
P.O. Box 1290
Troy, MI 48007
Tel.: 313-588-4100
Tel.: 800-877-1312 **MI**
Fax: 313-588-0718
Year Founded: 1963
Assets: $22,000,000
Net Worth: $22,000,000
Approx.Sls.: $120,000,000
Emp.: 250
Fiscal Year-end: 10/31/91
Auto Body Rustproofing & Franchising; Automotive Products & Services
S.I.C.: 7549; 6794; 5531
E.J. Hartmann *(Chm. Bd. & Pres.)*
Dan W. Janssen *(Chm. & Sr. V.P., Canada)*
W. Douglas Johnston *(Pres. & Chief Oper. Officer, Canada)*
James T. Bender *(Exec. V.P.-Ziebart Corp.)*
T.E. Wolfe *(Sr. V.P. & Treas.)*
William E. Beaver *(V.P.-Mktg.)*
Thomas R. Cunningham *(V.P.-Intl. Opers. & Pres., Ziebart Japan)*
Joseph F. DeSantis *(V.P.-Personnel)*
R. Dean Presau *(V.P.-Product Mngmt. & Tech. Services)*
David C. Vegh *(V.P. & Gen. Mgr., Ziebart Products Grp.)*
Michael Dowell *(Mgr.-National Fleet Sls.)*
Greg Long *(Mgr.-Franchise Devel.)*
R.H. May *(Sec.)*
Karen L. Newton *(Mgr.-Public Rels. & Communications)*
Principal(s):
E.J. Hartmann

No. of Mfg. Plants/Facilities: 1
No. of U.S. Offices: 2
No. of Foreign Offices: 3

Computer Systems/Hardware:
IBM System 36 & IBM PC Network

Outside Service Firm(s):

Arthur Andersen & Co.*(Auditors)*
400 Renaissance Center
Detroit, MI 48243
Tel.: 313-259-8100

May & Simpson*(Legal Firm)*
Detroit, MI

N.B.D. Bank, N.A.*(Major Banking Relationship)*
611 Woodward Ave.
Detroit, MI 48226
Tel.: 313-225-1122
Fax: 313-225-3420

Division:

Ziebart Products Group **(1)**
26500 Capital Ave.
Redford, MI 48239
Tel.: 233-937-0710
Manufacturing & Warehousing of Ziebart Products
S.I.C.: 2899; 5169; 4225
David C. Vegh *(V.P. & Gen. Mgr.)*

Subsidiaries:

Tidy Car International, Inc. **(1)**
1290 E. Maple
Troy, MI 48084
Tel.: 313-583-0170
Cable: 07
Fax: 313-588-0718
Emp.: 8
Marketing of Automobile Detailing Services
S.I.C.: 7549; 5169
Michael Remstad *(Mgr.-Mktg.)*

Tuff-Kote Dinol, Inc. **(1)**
1290 E. Maple Rd.
Troy, MI 48007
Tel.: 313-585-7995
Fax: 313-588-0718
Approx.Sls.: $10,000,000
Emp.: 10
Fiscal Year-end: 10/31/89
Marketing of Rustproofing Material for the Automotive & Industrial Markets
S.I.C.: 5169; 7549; 5531
Michael Remstad *(Mgr.-Mktg.)*
Ann Marie Roy *(Mgr.-Adv.)*

Ziebart Corp. **(1)**
1290 E. Maple Rd.
Troy, MI 48084
E.J. Hartmann *(Pres.)*

Ziebart International Corporation—(Continued)
James T. Bender *(Exec. V.P.)*

Non-U.S. Subsidiaries:

Ziebart Canada, Inc. **(1)**
150 Oakdale Rd.
Downsview, M3N 1W1, Canada
Tel.: 416-742-6613
Fax: 416-742-0558
Sales & Marketing of Ziebart Products; Franchising
S.I.C.: 5013; 7549; 6794
Dan W. Janssen *(Sr. V.P. & Chm.)*
Doug Johnston *(Chief Oper. Officer & Pres.)*
Randy Strachan *(Chief Fin. Officer, V.P. & Controller)*

Ziebart (E.C.) Limited **(1)**
P.O. Box 377,
Eastbourne, East Sussex BN22 9QF, United Kingdom
Tel.: 323 642844
Fax: 323 416063
Sales & Marketing of Ziebart Products; Franchising
S.I.C.: 5013; 7549; 6794
Lou Smith *(Mgr.-Intl. Mkt.-Europe)*
Hugh Weir *(Mgr.-Intl. Mkt.-Mid East Asia)*

Ziebart Japan Limited **(1)**
c/o Kojimachi Annex, 4-5-10, Kojimachi, Chiyoda-ku
Tokyo, 102, Japan
Tel.: 03 3263 6518
Telex: 781 27541 ziebart j
Sales & Marketing of Ziebart Products; Franchising
S.I.C.: 5013; 7549; 6794
Thomas R. Cunningham *(Pres.)*

ZIEGLER CHEMICAL & MINERAL CORP.
100 Jericho Quad, Ste. 140
Jericho, NY 11753
Tel.: 516-681-9600 **NY**
Telex: 96-1387
Fax: 516-681-9604
Year Founded: 1940
Sales Range: $20-39 Million
Emp.: 130
Gilsonite Mining; Petroleum Refining; Asphalt
S.I.C.: 2952; 2911; 1499
Gordon S. Ziegler, Sr. *(Chm. Bd.)*
Gordon S. Ziegler, Jr. *(Pres. & Chief Oper. Officer)*
Thomas DiBartolomeo *(Exec. V.P.)*
William Hyland *(V.P.-Fin.)*
Nancy Chiesa *(Controller)*
Hugh Casey *(Dir.-Pur.)*
Steve Illes *(Dir.-Research & Devel.)*
Principal(s):
Gordon S. Ziegler, Jr.

No. of Mfg. Plants/Facilities: 3

Computer Systems/Hardware:
Data General and Tandy Corp.

Outside Service Firm(s):

Tiger, Krell, Carney, Denerstein & Weber*(Auditors)*
Great Neck, NY

Chubb Group*(Group Insurer)*
P.O. Box 1615,
Warren, NJ 07061
Tel.: 201-580-2000

Kreutzer & Tashlick*(Legal Firm)*
Great Neck, NY

National Westminster Bank Plc*(Major Banking Relationship)*
Great Neck, NY

R.L. ZIEGLER CO. INC.
3201 Kauloosa Ave.
Tuscaloosa, AL 35401
Mailing Address:
P.O. Box 1640,
Tuscaloosa, AL 35403
Tel.: 205-758-3621
Fax: 205-758-0185
Approx.Sls.: $80,000,000
Emp.: 325
Fiscal Year-end: 12/31/90
Meat Packer & Processor
S.I.C.: 5147
James Hinton *(Chm. Bd.)*
W. Lackey Stephens *(Pres.)*
Ken Fitzgerald *(Chief Fin. Officer & Sec.)*
Bill Herchede *(Exec. V.P.)*

Outside Service Firm(s):

Jamison, Money, Farmer & Co.*(Auditors)*
Tuscaloosa, AL

Home Life Insurance Co.*(Group Insurer)*
New York, NY

Rosen, Harwood, Cook & Sledge*(Legal Firm)*
Tuscaloosa, AL

AmSouth Bank N.A.*(Major Banking Relationship)*
P.O. Box 11426
Birmingham, AL 35202
Tel.: 205-326-5321

AmSouth Bank N.A.*(Pension Manager)*
P.O. Box 11426
Birmingham, AL 35202
Tel.: 205-326-5321

ZIEGLER COAL HOLDING CO.
50 Jerome Lane
Fairview Heights, IL 62208
Tel.: 618-394-2400
Fax: 618-397-2473
Approx.Sls.: $100,000,000
Bituminaus Coal
S.I.C.: 1222
Michael K. Reilly *(Pres. & Chief Exec. Officer)*
C.B. Vyas *(Exec. V.P.)*
Marcel Chammess *(Sr. V.P.-Engrng.)*
William Kuzma *(V.P.-Human Resources)*
Brent Matchan *(V.P. & Gen. Counsel)*
James O'Neil *(V.P.-Sls.)*

Outside Service Firm(s):

First Chicago Trust Co. of New York*(Major Banking Relationship)*
One First Natl. Plaza, Ste. 123
Chicago, IL 60670
Tel.: 312-407-4660

Subsidiaries:

Franklin Coal **(1)**
50 Jerome Lane
Fairview Heights, IL 62208
Tel.: 618-394-2400
Bituminous Coal
S.I.C.: 1222
Michael Reilly *(Pres.)*

Old Ben Coal Co. **(1)**
50 Jerome Lane
Fairview Heights, IL 62208
Tel.: 618-394-2400
Bituminous Coal
S.I.C.: 1222
Michael K. Reilly *(Pres.)*

Ziegler Coal Co. **(1)**
50 Jerome Lane
Fairview Heights, IL 62208
Tel.: 618-394-2400
Bituminous Coal
S.I.C.: 1222
Michael Reilly *(Pres.)*

ZIEGLER INC.
901 W. 94th St.
Minneapolis, MN 55420
Tel.: 612-888-4121
Fax: 612-887-5822
Year Founded: 1914
Approx.Sls.: $125,000,000
Emp.: 475
Distributor Road Machinery & Attachments, Tractors, Trailers, Engines, Generators & Asphalt & Aggregate Equipment
S.I.C.: 5083; 5012; 5084; 5082
Corporate Giving Program: Annual Employee Pledges to the United Way Fund
Employee Matching Gifts Program: Contributions to Major Area of Education
Leonard C. Hoeft *(Chm. Bd.)*
William L. Hoeft *(Pres.)*
S.K. Erickson *(Exec. V.P. & Treas.)*
R.M. Lervick *(V.P.-Sls.)*
H.M. Mullinix *(V.P.-Admin. & Sec.)*
A.E. Pearson *(V.P.-Prod. Support)*
D.R. Shellenberger *(V.P. & Gen Mgr.-Ziegler Power Systems)*

Outside Service Firm(s):

Virchow, Krause, Helgeson & Company*(Auditors)*
Minneapolis, MN

Gray, Plant, Mooty, Mooty & Bennett*(Legal Firm)*
3400 City Center, 33 So. 6th St.
Minneapolis, MN 55402
Tel.: 612-343-2800
Fax: 612-830-0270

First Bank, N.A.*(Major Banking Relationship)*
First Bank Place
Minneapolis, MN 55480

ZIEGLER TIRE & SUPPLY COMPANY, INC.
4900 Navarre Rd., S.W.
Canton, OH 44706
Tel.: 216-477-2747 **OH**
Fax: 216-477-4318
Approx.Sls.: $16,000,000
Emp.: 60
Automotive Tires; Truck Tires & Tubes; Truck Equipment & Parts
S.I.C.: 5531; 5014
Harold Ziegler, Jr. *(Pres.)*
Harold Ziegler, Sr. *(V.P.)*
Herbert C. Ziegler *(V.P.)*
John Ziegler, Jr. *(V.P.)*
John H. Ziegler *(V.P.)*
Norman J. Ziegler *(V.P.)*
William C. Ziegler *(Treas. & Sec.)*

Outside Service Firm(s):

AmeriTrust Company, N.A.*(Major Banking Relationship)*
Canton, OH

Division:

Youngstown Tire & Supply Company **(1)**
4900 Navarre Rd., S.W.
Canton, OH 44707
Tel.: 216-277-2747
Gasoline Filling Stations; Automotive Tires
S.I.C.: 5541; 5014
Harold Ziegler, Jr. *(Pres.)*

ZIEMAN MANUFACTURING COMPANY, INC.
7909 S. Painter Ave.
Whittier, CA 90602
Tel.: 310-693-8211
Fax: 310-698-4137
Emp.: 200
Fabricates Steel Mobile Homes & Travel Trailer Chassis; Manufacture Equipment; Hauling, Trailer & Boat & Recreational Trailers
S.I.C.: 3792; 3537
Richard R. Percival *(Chm. Bd.)*
John Pollara *(Pres.)*
Eric Day *(V.P.-Opers.)*
Curt Strong *(Controller)*

Outside Service Firm(s):

Davy & Hasbach*(Auditors)*
West Covina, CA

Bank of America NT&SA*(Major Banking Relationship)*
Long Beach, CA

ZIFF COMMUNICATIONS COMPANY
One Park Ave.
New York, NY 10016
Tel.: 212-503-3500 **DE**
Fax: 212-503-3599
Year Founded: 1957
Sales Range: $40-59 Million
Emp.: 2,960
Publishers
S.I.C.: 2741; 2731; 2721
Employee Matching Gifts Program: Every December Company Chooses One Charity & Matches Employee Gifts
William B. Ziff, Jr. *(Chm. Bd.)*
Philip B. Korsant *(Pres.)*
Philip Sine *(Exec. V.P.)*
E.C. Mick Prokopis *(Exec. V.P.)*
Hugh Tietjen *(Sr. V.P.)*
Patrick Burke *(V.P., Controller & Treas.)*
J. Malcolm Morris *(V.P., Gen. Counsel & Sec.)*
Steven C. Feinman *(V.P.-Tax & Audit)*
Frederick Staudmyer *(V.P.-Human Resources)*
John Helliwell *(Exec. Dir.-Mngmt. Information Systems)*
Dorothy Boston *(Dir.-Community Affairs)*
Edward Handren *(Dir.-Facilities Mngmt.)*
Nancy Woods *(Dir.-Employee Benefits)*
Anne Tatlow *(Mgr.-Real Estate)*
Principal(s):
William B. Ziff, Jr.

Outside Service Firm(s):

Deloitte & Touche*(Auditors)*
1 World Trade Center
New York, NY 10048
Tel.: 212-669-5000

Proskauer, Rose, Goetz & Mendelsohn*(Legal Firm)*
1585 Broadway
New York, NY 10036
Tel.: 212-969-3000

The Bank of New York*(Major Banking Relationship)*
One Wall Street
New York, NY 10286
Tel.: 212-635-6805
Fax: 212-635-3201

The Bank of New York*(Pension Manager)*
One Wall Street
New York, NY 10286
Tel.: 212-635-6805
Fax: 212-635-3201

Divisions:

The Cobb Group **(1)**
9420 Bunsen Pkwy. #300
Louisville, KY 40220
Tel.: 502-491-1900
Newsletters for Users of Various P.C. Software
S.I.C.: 2721

Divisions:

Data Sources **(2)**
20 Brace Rd.
Cherry Hill, NJ 08034
Tel.: 609-354-5000
Directory of PC Hardware & Software Manufacturers, Prices & Related Data
S.I.C.: 2741
Seth Alpert *(Publr.)*

MacUser **(2)**
110 Marsh Dr.
Foster City, CA 94404
Tel.: 415-570-5110
Fax: 415-341-7242
Magazine for Users/Buyers of MacIntosh PC's
S.I.C.: 2721

Janet Ryan *(Publisher)*

PC Computing **(2)**
950 Tower Lane
Foster City, CA 94404
Tel.: 415-578-7000
Fax: 415-578-7119
Magazine for Users of IBM/MS DOS Standard PCs
S.I.C.: 2721
Michael Edelhart *(Publ.)*

PC Magazine **(2)**
1 Park Ave.
New York, NY 10016
Tel.: 212-503-5255
Magazine for Buyers of IBM/MS DOS Standard PC's
S.I.C.: 2721
Jeff Ballowe *(Publ.)*

PC Week **(2)**
800 Boylston St.
Boston, MA 02199
Tel.: 617-375-4000
Newspaper of IBM Computers to Provide Buyers in Medium and Large Corporations with News, Buyers Guides & Product Reviews
S.I.C.: 2711
Donald Byrnes *(Publ.)*

Computer Intelligence **(1)**
3344 N. Torrey Pines Ct.
La Jolla, CA 92037
Tel.: 619-450-1667
Emp.: 1,500
Marketing Research for Marketers of Computers & Related Products
S.I.C.: 2741; 8732
Hugh Tietjen *(Pres.)*

Computer Library **(1)**
One Park Avenue
New York, NY 10016
Tel.: 212-503-3500
Database Services
S.I.C.: 7375
Seth Alpert *(V.P.)*
Nancy Van Natta *(Dir.-Mktg.)*

InfoCorp **(1)**
2880 Lakeside Dr., Ste. 300
Santa Clara, CA 95056
Tel.: 408-980-4300
Market Research for Computer Industry
S.I.C.: 2741; 8732
Richard Matlack *(Pres.)*

Information Access Co. **(1)**
362 Lakeside Dr.
Foster City, CA 94404
Tel.: 415-378-5000
Fax: 415-378-5499
Electronic Database Publisher, Periodical Reference Systems
S.I.C.: 2741; 7375
Morris Goldstein *(Pres.)*

Interop, Inc. **(1)**
480 San Antonio Rd., Ste. 100
Mountain View, CA 94040
Tel.: 415-941-3399
Fax: 415-949-1779
Emp.: 52
Computer Trade Shows
S.I.C.: 7389
Daniel Lynch *(Pres.)*

Predicasts **(1)**
11001 Cedar Ave.
Cleveland, OH 44106
Tel.: 216-795-3000
Business Information & Market Research in Hard Copy & Electronic Form
S.I.C.: 7375; 2741
Richard M. Harris *(Pres.)*

Seybold Publications **(1)**
P.O. Box 644, 428 Baltimore Pike
Media, PA 19063
Tel.: 215-565-2480
Steve Edwards *(Editor)*

Seybold Publications **(1)**
428 E. Baltimore Pike
Media, PA 19063
Tel.: 215-565-2480
Publishes 3 Industry Newsletters for Multimedia Technology, Computers & High End Computer Systems
S.I.C.: 2741
Stephen Edwards *(Mgr.)*

Seybold Seminars **(1)**
6922 Wildlife Rd.
Malibu, CA 90265
Tel.: 310-457-5850
Fax: 310-457-4704
Emp.: 30
Organizer of Computer Trade Shows & Seminars; Publisher of Newsletters; Consulting Services for Computer Users & Vendors
S.I.C.: 2741; 7389
Jonathan Seybold *(Pres.)*

Ziff-Davis Press **(1)**
5903 Christie Ave.
Emeryville, CA 94608
Tel.: 510-601-2000
Fax: 510-528-5959
Books on Computers-Related Subjects
S.I.C.: 2731
Harry Blake *(Pres.)*
Larry Fox *(V.P.-Natl. Accts.)*
Robert Ryan *(V.P.-Mktg.)*

Ziff-Davis Publishing Company **(1)**
One Park Ave.
New York, NY 10016
Tel.: 212-503-3500
Fax: 212-503-3599
Emp.: 950
Publishers
S.I.C.: 2721; 2731; 2741
Eric Hippeau *(Chm. Bd.)*
J. Scott Briggs *(Pres.)*
Ronnie Sonnenberg *(Exec. V.P.)*
Rachel Greenfield *(Sr. V.P.)*
Ann Pollock Adelman *(V.P.-Mktg. Services)*
Frank Kelcz *(V.P.-Europe)*
Bert Lacy *(V.P.-Circulation)*
William Machrone *(V.P.-Technology)*
Alan Power *(V.P.-Asia/Pacific)*
James Ramaley *(V.P.-Circulation Services)*
Paul Stafford *(V.P.-Classified Adv.)*
Susan Delman *(Dir.-Mktg.)*

Ziff Information Services **(1)**
10 Presidents Landing
Medford, MA 02155
Tel.: 617-393-3200
Fax: 617-393-3211
Technical Information Services
S.I.C.: 2741
Thor Olson *(Pres.)*

Ziff Technologies **(1)**
10 Presidents Landing
Medford, MA 02155
Tel.: 617-393-3200
Emp.: 10
Computer Systems/Hardware:
VAX
Data Base Information Services, Timesharing
S.I.C.: 7374; 7375; 7379
Steven J. Caldwell *(Pres.)*

Divisions:

Logical Operations **(2)**
595 Blossom Rd.
Rochester, NY 14610
Tel.: 716-482-7700
Fax: 716-288-7411
Computer Training& Publishing
S.I.C.: 8243; 2721
Barry Keesan *(Pres.)*

PC Concepts **(2)**
3 Glenhardie Corp. Center, 1265 Drummers Lane
Wayne, PA 19087
Tel.: 215-687-5554
Fax: 215-687-3098
Computer Training
S.I.C.: 8243
Jim Pickens *(Pres.)*

Non-U.S. Holdings:

Seybold Limited **(1)**
26A Seaside
Eastbourne, BN22 7QI, United Kingdom
Tel.: 323-410621

Ziff-Davis France SARL **(1)**
Immeuble Omega, 10, Rue Thierry Le Luron 92593
Levallois-Perret, Cedex France
Tel.: 14-6395500

Ziff-Davis Germany **(1)**
Ziff Verlag GmbH, Hanover Str. 85 8000 Munich, 50, Germany
Tel.: 49 89-143120
Division of Ziff-Davis Publishing Company; Magazine for Buyers of IBM/MS DOS Standard PC's
S.I.C.: 2721
Helmut Kunkel *(Publ.)*

Ziff-Davis Taiwan **(1)**
12 F-7, No.1 Futtsin North Road
Taipei, Taiwan R.O.C.

Ziff-Davis U.K. **(1)**
Cottons Centre, Hay's Lane
London, SEI 5QT, United Kingdom
Tel.: 71-378-6800

ZILBER, LTD.
710 N. Plankington Ave.
Milwaukee, WI 53203
Tel.: 414-274-2400 **DE**
Fax: 414-274-2710
Year Founded: 1983
Assets: $173,494,000
Liabilities: $152,424,000
Net Worth: $21,070,000
Approx.Rev.: $213,304,000
Emp.: 9,680
Figure Salons; Wholesale & Retail Toys; Prescription Centers & Real Estate
S.I.C.: 5092; 5945; 5912; 6531; 7991
Joseph J. Zilber *(Chm. Bd.)*
Gerald Stein *(Pres.)*
Ronald E. Skelton *(Chief Fin. Officer & V.P.-Fin.)*
James F. Janz *(Sr. V.P.)*
Russell T. Cramer *(V.P.)*
Arthur W. Wigchers, Jr. *(V.P. & Treas.)*
James B. Young *(V.P. & Sec.)*

Outside Service Firm(s):

Arthur Andersen & Co.*(Auditors)*
One Intl. Place, 100 Oliver St.
Boston, MA 02110
Tel.: 617-330-4000
Fax: 617-439-9731

Bank of New England*(Major Banking Relationship)*
28 State Street
Boston, MA 02109
Tel.: 617-742-4000

Subsidiary:

Towne Realty, Inc. **(1)**
710 No. Plankington
Milwaukee, WI 53203
Tel.: 414-274-2400
Land Subdividers And Developers
S.I.C.: 6552
Arthur W. Wigchers *(Pres.)*

AVEDIS ZILDJIAN COMPANY
22 Longwater Dr.
Norwell, MA 02061
Tel.: 617-871-2200
Fax: 617-871-3984
Year Founded: 1623
Approx.Sls.: $20,000,000
Emp.: 95
Fiscal Year-end: 12/31/90
Export
Cymbals
S.I.C.: 3931
Armand Zildjian *(Pres.)*
James E. Roberts *(Exec. V.P. & Chief Oper. Officer)*
Jerry Donegan *(Dir.-Natl. Sls.)*
Colin Schofield *(Dir.-Mktg.)*

ZILKHA ENERGY COMPANY
1201 Louisiana, Ste. 3200
Houston, TX 77002
Tel.: 713-655-5900 **DE**
Fax: 713-655-5961
Assets: $34,400,000
Net Worth: $34,400,000
Sales Range: $10-19 Million
Emp.: 50
Fiscal Year-end: 12/31/90
Oil & Gas Exploration
S.I.C.: 1311; 1382
Selim K. Zilkha *(Chm. Bd. & Chief Exec. Officer)*
John B. Holmes, Jr. *(Pres. & Chief Oper. Officer)*
Michael E. S. Zilkha *(Exec. V.P.)*
Joseph J. Romano *(V.P. & Chief Fin. Officer)*
J. Bradley Juneau *(V.P.-Exploration)*
Glennon M. Dillon *(Controller)*
Tracy P. Mevs *(Treas. & Corp. Sec.)*

No. of Mfg. Plants/Facilities: 3
No. of U.S. Offices: 3

Computer Systems/Hardware:
IBM System 4241

Outside Service Firm(s):

KPMG Peat Marwick*(Auditors)*
3000 Republic Bank Center
Houston, TX 77002
Tel.: 713-224-4262
Fax: 713-224-4566

First Chicago Shareholder Services Trust Co.*(Major Banking Relationship)*
153 West 51st St.
New York, NY 10019
Tel.: 212-791-6422
Fax: 212-385-9798

Adams & Porter*(Commercial Insurance Carrier)*
New York, NY

Massachusetts Mutual Life Insurance Co.*(Group Insurer)*
1295 State St.
Springfield, MA 01111
Tel.: 413-788-8411
Fax: 413-730-6144

Arter & Hadden*(Legal Firm)*
1144 Union Commerce Bldg.,
Cleveland, OH 44115
Tel.: 216-696-1144

ZIM-AMERICAN ISRAELI SHIPPING CO.
(Affil. of Zim Israel Navigation Co., Ltd)
One World Trade Center
New York, NY 10048
Tel.: 212-524-1600
Tel.: 800-444-2000
Telex: ITT 427152
Fax: 212-524-1802
Approx.Sls.: $300,000,000
Emp.: 300
Break-Bulk & Container Cargo Carrier
S.I.C.: 4412
U. Adar *(Pres.-North America)*
E. Gruenhut *(Exec. V.P.)*
Joseph Merante *(Sr. V.P.-Mktg. & Sls.-No. America)*
J. Millard *(Sr. V.P.-Opers./Traffic-No. America)*
Jesse Seligson *(V.P.-Sls.)*
J. DePalma *(V.P.-Sls.)*
Walter Bergman *(Personnel Dir)*

Division:

Zim Container Service **(1)**
One World Trade Center
New York, NY 10048
Tel.: 212-432-0300

ZIMA CORP.
I-85 at Zima Park
Spartanburg, SC 29301
Mailing Address:
P.O. Box 6010
Spartanburg, SC 29304
Tel.: 803-576-5810 **SC**
Telex: 809459
Fax: 803-591-1985
Year Founded: 1969
Sales Range: $20-39 Million
Emp.: 40

Zima Corp.—(Continued)

Wholesale & Service Textile & Printing Machinery
S.I.C.: 5084; 7699
Kurt Zimmerli *(Chm. Bd., Pres., Chief Exec. Officer & Chief Oper. Officer)*
Charles Palmer *(Exec. V.P.)*
Rudy Mikelonis *(Controller)*
Conrad Schliske *(Mgr.-Tech. Services)*
Horace Bomar *(Legal Officer)*

Principal(s):
Kurt Zimmerli

No. of Mfg. Plants/Facilities: 1
No. of U.S. Offices: 1

Outside Service Firm(s):

Ernst & Young*(Auditors)*
905 E. Main St., Ste. G
Spartanburg, SC 29302
Tel.: 803-573-7801

Alexander & Alexander*(Commercial Insurance Carrier)*
Charlotte, NC

Jefferson Pilot*(Group Insurer)*
Atlanta, GA

Sparkasse*(International Bank Affiliate)*
Krefeld, Germany

Horace Bomar*(Legal Firm)*
Spartanburg, SC

South Carolina National Bank*(Major Banking Relationship)*
P.O. Box 3128,
Spartanburg, SC 29304
Tel.: 803-596-4200

Massachusetts Mutual Life Insurance Co.*(Pension Manager)*
1295 State St.
Springfield, MA 01111
Tel.: 413-788-8411
Fax: 413-730-6144

ZIMDAR ENTERPRISES
3343 Lousma Drive S.E.
Wyoming, MI 49548
Tel.: 616-452-8737 **MI**
Fax: 616-452-6981
Year Founded: 1970
Sales Range: $10-19 Million
Emp.: 200
Fiscal Year-end: 6/31/91
Manufacturer & Retailer of Picture Frames
S.I.C.: 2499; 5999
W.H. Lee *(Chm. Bd. & Chief Exec. Officer)*
Dorothy L. Zimdar *(Pres.)*
William L. Zimdar *(V.P. & Chief Fin. Officer)*
Gerry M. Reeves *(V.P.)*
William H. Lee *(Treas., Controller & Sec.)*

Principal(s):
Dorothy L. Zimdar
William L. Zimdar

Computer Systems/Hardware:
Cado

Outside Service Firm(s):

Lane & Reed*(Commercial Insurance Carrier)*
Sparta, MI

Blue Cross & Blue Shield Association*(Group Insurer)*
Grand Rapids, MI

Borre & Peterson*(Legal Firm)*
Grand Rapids, MI

Michigan National Bank*(Major Banking Relationship)*
77 Monroe Center
Grand Rapids, MI 49501
Tel.: 616-451-7600

Subsidiary:

Frames Unlimited Inc. **(1)**
3343 Lousma Drive S.E.
Wyoming, MI 49548
Tel.: 616-452-8737
S.I.C.: 5999

ZIMMER PAPER PRODUCTS INC.
1450 E. 20th St.
Indianapolis, IN 46218
Tel.: 317-636-3333
Tel.: 800-631-7845
Telex: 27489
Fax: 317-263-3427
Year Founded: 1930
Assets: $7,000,000
Liabilities: $5,000,000
Net Worth: $2,000,000
Approx.Sls.: $25,000,000
Emp.: 135
Fiscal Year-end: 12/31/91
Import Export
Manufacturer of Coated Papers for Food Packaging & Industry Applications
S.I.C.: 2679; 2672; 2671
Corporate Giving Program: Sponsor Contributor to Indianapolis Museum of Art, Symphony Orchestra & Various Cultural & Educational Organizations
Karl R. Zimmer *(Chm. Bd. & Chief Exec. Officer)*
Karl Zimmer, III *(Pres. & Chief Oper. Officer)*
Thomas Terry *(Treas. & Sec.)*
Miriam Frankovitz *(Dir.-Personnel)*
Michael Rice *(Dir.-Data Processing)*
William Camic *(Mgr.-Pur.)*
Tim Schoolman *(Sls. Coord.)*

Principal(s):
Zimmer Family

No. of Mfg. Plants/Facilities: 1

Computer Systems/Hardware:
AS 400

Outside Service Firm(s):

KPMG Peat Marwick*(Auditors)*
135 N. Pennsylvania St.
Indianapolis, IN 46204
Tel.: 317-636-5592
Fax: 317-635-3314

Ice, Miller, Donadio & Ryan*(Legal Firm)*
One American Square, Box 82001
Indianapolis, IN 46282
Tel.: 317-236-2219

INB National Bank*(Major Banking Relationship)*
One Indiana Sq.
Indianapolis, IN 46266
Tel.: 317-266-6000

ZIMMERMAN HOLDINGS, INC.
2600 Mission St., Ste. 100
San Marino, CA 91108
Tel.: 818-441-0444 **CA**
Fax: 818-441-6946
Year Founded: 1978
Approx.Sls.: $225,000,000
Emp.: 2,000
Fiscal Year-end: 2/28/91
Holding Co.; Construction, Mining, Oil Field Equipment; Flexible Metal Products; Ducting Equipment
S.I.C.: 6719; 3444; 3531; 3532
William R. Zimmerman *(Chm. Bd., Pres. & Chief Exec. Officer)*
Larry S. Dodson *(Chief Fin. Officer & Sr. V.P.)*
M. Glenn Gilbert *(Exec. V.P. & Gen. Counsel)*
Rodney Woodworth *(Sr. V.P.-Opers.)*

Principal(s):
William R. Zimmerman

No. of Mfg. Plants/Facilities: 14
No. of U.S. Offices: 20
No. of Foreign Offices: 2

Outside Service Firm(s):

Ernst & Young*(Auditors)*
515 S. Flower St.
Los Angeles, CA 90071
Tel.: 213-621-1666

Johnson & Higgins*(Commercial Insurance Carrier)*
125 Broad St.
New York, NY 10004-2424
Tel.: 212-574-7000
Fax: 212-574-8988

Metropolitan Life Insurance Co.*(Group Insurer)*
One Madison Ave.
New York, NY 10010-3690
Tel.: 215-578-9292

Wells Fargo Bank*(International Bank Affiliate)*
420 Montgomery St.
San Francisco, CA 94104

Rodi, Pollock, Pettker, Galbraith & Philips*(Legal Firm)*
801 S. Grand, Suite 400
Los Angeles, CA 90017
Tel.: 213-895-4900

Wells Fargo Bank*(Major Banking Relationship)*
420 Montgomery St.
San Francisco, CA 94104

Subsidiaries:

A & A Associates **(1)**
12118 Bloomfield
Santa Fe Springs, CA 90670
Tel.: 310-864-7431
Mfr. of Industrial Equipment
S.I.C.: 3532
Barney Kroeger *(Pres.)*

Eaton Leonard Technologies, Inc. **(1)**
6305 El Camino Real
Carlsbad, CA 92009
Tel.: 619-438-5322

Flexonics, Inc. **(1)**
6300 W. Devon
Bartlett, IL 60103
Tel.: 708-837-1811
Mfr. of Flexible Metal
S.I.C.: 3444

Mobile Drilling Company, Inc. **(1)**
3807 Madison
Indianapolis, IN 46227
Tel.: 317-787-6371

Reedrill Inc. **(1)**
1417 North
Denison, TX 75090
Tel.: 214-786-2981
Mfr. of Heavy Equipment
S.I.C.: 3531

Stainless Steel Products, Inc. **(1)**
2980 San Fernando
Burbank, CA 91504
Tel.: 818-841-9190
Ducting; Metal Plate
S.I.C.: 3443

WesTech Gear Group **(1)**
2600 Imperial
Lynwood, CA 90262
Tel.: 310-605-2600
Gears for Power Transmissions
S.I.C.: 3566

ZINIZ INC.
100 High Rise Dr., Ste. 200
Louisville, KY 40213
Tel.: 502-955-6573 **KY**
Fax: 502-966-0519
Year Founded: 1967
Approx.Sls.: $15,000,000
Emp.: 130
Manufacture Conveyor Systems
S.I.C.: 3535
Ronald Grant *(Pres.)*
Robert L. Young *(V.P. & Gen. Mgr.)*
Ralph Coomer *(Treas. & Sec.)*

Principal(s):
Ralph Coomer

THE ZIPPERTUBING CO.
13000 S. Broadway
Los Angeles, CA 90061
Mailing Address:
P.O. Box 61129
Los Angeles, CA 90061
Tel.: 310-527-0488
Fax: 310-767-1714
Year Founded: 1957
Sales Range: $10-19 Million
Emp.: 75
Export
Manufactures Zip-On Jacketing for All Applications; Zippertubing, Thermazip, Acoustizip, Ziptape, Cable Splice Kits, Pile Jacketing, Etc.
S.I.C.: 3083; 3089; 3479
Walter A. Plummer *(Chm. Bd.)*
Terry Plummer *(Pres.)*
Bruce Hoffine *(Exec. V.P.)*
David Kenyon *(Mgr.-Opers.)*
Michael Sullivan *(Mgr.-Natl. Sls.)*
Carole Orpe *(Pur. Agent)*

Outside Service Firm(s):

Deloitte & Touche*(Auditors)*
1000 Wilshire Blvd.
Los Angeles, CA 90017-2472
Tel.: 213-688-0800
Fax: 213-688-0100

First Business Bank*(Major Banking Relationship)*
Los Angeles, CA

ZIPPO MANUFACTURING COMPANY
33 Barbour St.
Bradford, PA 16701
Tel.: 814-362-4541
Fax: 814-362-3598
Emp.: 1,000
Export
Zippo Cigarette Lighters & Accessories, Contempo Lighter, Rules, Knives, Golfballs, Greenskeepers, Magnifiers & Letter Openers, Pill Boxes, Writing Instruments
S.I.C.: 3999; 3421; 3423; 3949; 3827; 3951
Michael Schuler *(Pres.)*
Robert R. Jackson *(Chief Fin. Officer)*
Jim Baldo *(V.P.-Sls. & Mktg.)*
S.B. Dorn *(V.P. & Treas.)*
Don Hazlett *(V.P.-Mfg.)*
Harriett B. Wick *(V.P. & Sec.)*
Bob Kaczmarek *(Dir.-Human Resources)*
J. Patrick Grandy *(Mgr.-Adv.)*
Dick Young *(Mgr.-Materials)*

Computer Systems/Hardware:
NCR-Series 10,000

Non-U.S. Holding:

Zippo Manufacturing Company of Canada Limited **(1)**
6158 Allandale Ave.
Niagara Falls, ON L2G 3Z5, Canada
Tel.: 416-358-3674 (100%)
Wyona Pedersen *(Gen. Mgr.)*

ZOELLER CO.
3280 Old Millers Lane
Louisville, KY 40216
Mailing Address:
P.O. Box 16347
Louisville, KY 40216
Tel.: 502-778-2731 **KY**
Fax: 502-774-3624
Year Founded: 1939
Approx.Sls.: $30,000,000
Emp.: 160
Export
Mfr. Sump & Sewage Pumps & Related Prods.
S.I.C.: 3561
Robert F. Zoeller *(Chm. Bd. & Chief Exec. Officer)*

NATIONAL REGISTER PUBLISHING

A Reed Reference Publishing Company

Directory of CORPORATE AFFILIATIONS/ U.S. PUBLIC

ACCESS ALL THE KEY ANSWERS —

WHO OWNS WHOM, WHO'S WHO

AT AMERICA'S MOST

POWERFUL PUBLIC

COMPANIES AND CORPORATIONS.

121 Chanlon Road • New Providence, New Jersey 07974
1-800-521-8110

The "Family Tree" of Every Major Public Company in America.

Now Available on Database!

Delve into the corporate structure and hierarchy of more than 45,000 publicly held U.S. business organizations with the Directory of Corporate Affiliations/U.S. Public database. Formatted to deliver a comprehensive overview, as well as specific business and financial data, it concisely profiles each parent company and its offspring, complete with key personnel and corporate linkage. With this important database, you can immediately retrieve the facts you need to:

- Track and compare vital statistics for the 5,000 leading U.S. parent companies, along with their 45,000 subsidiaries, divisions and affiliates.
- Extract basic data on sales, assets, liabilities, S.I.C. code, stock exchange, ownership percentage, personnel and much more.
- Develop contacts with 80,000 key executives and determine their corporate responsibilities.
- Insure the accuracy of your research with data on new companies, as well as mergers, acquisitions and name changes as far back as 1976.

Whether you want to research investment, acquisition or employment opportunities, evaluate the competition, discover new areas for expansion or simply track the rapidly changing business environment, the Directory of Corporate Affiliations/ U.S. Public database is *the* essential electronic resource.

Unravel the maze of today's corporate relationships and develop business strategies with greater control and accuracy. Lease the Directory of Corporate Affiliations/U.S. Public database — the superior source for detailed, in-depth organizational information on America's most influential public businesses.

National Register Publishing

A Reed Reference Publishing Company

Directory of CORPORATE AFFILIATIONS/ INTERNATIONAL

*F*IND THE ENTIRE WORLD

OF BUSINESS AND FINANCE AT

YOUR FINGERTIPS — WITH

THE **ONLY** COMPREHENSIVE

DATABASE RESOURCE

OF INTERNATIONAL COMPANIES

AND CORPORATIONS.

121 Chanlon Road • New Providence, New Jersey 07974
1-800-521-8110

The Comprehensive International Perspective on Business.

Now Available on Database!

Gain a keen and comprehensive perspective on *the 33,000 most influential multinational companies in the world* wit the Directory of Corporate Affiliations/International — no available as an efficient, economical database. Carefully drawn like a corporate "family tree," each complete profil focuses on the total business and financial picture of both parent company and offspring. With the Directory of Corporate Affiliations/International database, you can instantly and efficiently:

- Access key details about 33,000 multinational companies with 1,600 foreign parent corporations.
- Research the interrelationships between 14,000 affiliate outside the country and their 1,600 U.S. corporations.
- Extract essential facts on sales, assets, liabilities, net worth, personnel, corporate structure and much more.

Plus, critical information is reported without an American slant or bias — an especially significant feature when researching global companies with complex, even overlapping, structure or multinational subsidiaries.

Important world events, with far-reaching busines and financial consequences, are taking place every day. Control the quality, accuracy and integrity of your business intelligence even in this volatile international marketplace. Lease the Directory of Corporate Affiliations/International — the only reliable database for current information on today rapidly changing global economy.

GEOGRAPHIC INDEX TO U.S. PRIVATE COMPANIES

ALABAMA

Andalusia

ALABAMA ELECTRIC COOPERATIVE, INC., Hwy. 29 N.(36420), pg. 28
CARQUEST, 715 Bypass North(36420), pg. 224
Lakeside Coal Company, P.O. Box 550, (36420), pg. 28
United Energy Corporation, P.O. Box 550, (36420), pg. 28
Waters Coal Company, P.O. Box 550, (36420), pg. 28

Anniston

CONSOLIDATED PUBLISHING COMPANY, 216 W. 10th St.(36201), pg. 277
Gold Bond Building Products, Birmingham Hwy.(36201), pg. 790
Sentinel Consumer Products, Inc., Greenbriar Ind. Park, 100 Sentinel Dr.(36201), pg. 990
U.S. Castings Div., P.O. Box 788, (36201), pg. 1162

Athens

Steelcase, Inc./Athens Plant, 214 Durham Dr.(35611), pg. 1044

Bay Minette

Southern Electric Supply Co., Inc., 17 Hand Ave.(36507), pg. 1021
Uniroyal Chemical Co., Inc., P.O. Box 147, Highway 225(36507), pg. 1129

Bayou La Batre

QF, Inc., Shell Belt Rd.(36509), pg. 415

Bessemer

Jorgensen Steel & Aluminum/Birmingham, 200 Kilsby Circle(35023), pg. 605
Kilsby-Roberts/Birmingham, 200 Kilsby Circle(35023), pg. 606

Birmingham

ABI Food Services, Inc., 4600 East Lake Blvd.(35217), pg. 258
Accu-Cast, Inc., 4000 10th Ave. North(35202), pg. 1050
ALABAMA METAL INDUSTRIES CORPORATION, 3245 Fayette Ave.(35208), pg. 28
Aliceville Casting Co., 4000 10th Ave. North(35202), pg. 1050
Allright Birmingham, Inc., 1919 Morris Ave., Suite 555(35203), pg. 41
ALTEC INDUSTRIES, INC., 210 Inverness Center Dr.(35242), pg. 45
AMERICAN CAST IRON PIPE CO., 1501 31st Ave., N.(35207), pg. 50
Aratex Services, 2315 25th St., N.(35234), pg. 6
ASSOCIATED GROCERS OF ALABAMA, INC., 3600 Vanderbilt Rd.(35217), pg. 90
Atlas Pattern Works, 4000 10th Ave. North(35202), pg. 1050
BE & K, INC., 2000 International Park Dr.(35243), pg. 106
BARBER DAIRIES, INC., 36 Barber Court(35209), pg. 119
Barber Ice Cream Company, 36 Barber Court(35209), pg. 119
Birmingham Hill Restaurant Corp., 2033 Golden Crest Dr.(35209), pg. 1028
BUFFALO ROCK COMPANY, 111 Oxmoor Rd.(35209), pg. 187
Cain & Bultman, 501 S. 12th St.(35233), pg. 207
CITATION COMPANIES, INC., 175 Citation Ct.(35209), pg. 250
Clow Corporation, 23 Inverness Center Pkwy.(35243), pg. 733
COCA COLA BOTTLING CO. UNITED, INC., 4600 East Lake Blvd.(35217), pg. 257
CONSOLIDATED PIPE & SUPPLY COMPANY, 1205 Hilltop Pkwy.(35204), pg. 277
COWIN & COMPANY, INC., 301 Industrial Dr.(35211), pg. 291
Denver Thomas, Inc., P.O. Box 96(35201), pg. 331
Dixie Insurance Company, 2204 Lakeshore Dr.(35209), pg. 53
EBSCO INDUSTRIES, INC., P.O. Box 1943(35201), pg. 365
Ebsco Investment Services, Inc., P.O. Box 1943(35201), pg. 365
Fontaine International, Inc., 125 Cleage Dr.(35217), pg. 711
GILLIS ADVERTISING & PUBLIC RELATIONS, 3620 8th Ave. South(35222), pg. 459
Gillis Public Relations, Inc., 3620 8th Ave. South(35222), pg. 459
GRIMMER REALTY CO. INC., 2000 SouthBridge Pkwy., Ste. 100(35209), pg. 488
HARBERT CORPORATION, 1 Riverchase Parkway S.(35244), pg. 506
BARRY HUEY, BULLOCK & COOK ADVERTISING, INC., 3800 Colonnade Pkwy., Ste. 400(35243), pg. 551
A.C. LEGG PACKING COMPANY, INC., 2319 First Ave., N.(35203), pg. 666
Marks-Fitzgerald Furniture Co., 1849 Crestwood Blvd.(35210), pg. 931
Marian Valves Co., 4000 10th Ave. North(35202), pg. 1050
McWane Cast Iron Pipe Co., P.O. Box 607, (35201), pg. 733
MCWANE, INC., 23 Inverness Center Pkwy.(35242), pg. 733
MEADOWCRAFT, INC., 1401 Meadowcraft Rd.(35215), pg. 733
NATIONAL COMPUTER PRINT, INC., 5200 E. Lake Blvd.(35217), pg. 786
O'NEAL STEEL INC., 744 N. 41 St.(35222), pg. 827
Papertronics, Incorporated, 3636D 7th Ave. N(35222), pg. 63
PARISIAN, INC., 750 Lakeshore Pkwy.(35211), pg. 848
RESTAURANT COMPANY, INC., 3500 Water Oak Dr.(35243), pg. 929
Rockingham Stainless Steel, 4000 10th Ave. North(35202), pg. 1050
St. Clair Manufacturing Co., 4000 10th Ave. North(35202), pg. 1050
SAUNDERS INCORPORATED, 2801 Hwy. 280, Bldg. 1, 3rd Fl.(35223-2407), pg. 972
Southern Electric Supply Co., Inc., 3000 5th Ave. South(35233), pg. 1020
Southern Life and Health Insurance Company, 2101 Highland Ave.(35205), pg. 452
Southern Precision Div., 1500 Georgia Rd.(35210), pg. 1162
Southwestern Foundries, 4000 10th Ave. North(35202), pg. 1050
STEINER/BRESSLER ADVERTISING, 100 Brookwood Place, Ste. 400(35209), pg. 1045
STOCKHAM VALVES & FITTINGS, INC., 4000 10th Ave. N.(35212), pg. 1050
Stonewall Insurance Co., P.O. Box 1688, 2204 Lakeshore Dr.(35201-1688), pg. 54
SULLIVAN LONG & HAGERTY, INC., 801 5th Ave., N.(35203), pg. 1057
Sunnyland Refining Co., Inc., 3330 10th Ave.(35234), pg. 616
THOMPSON TRACTOR COMPANY, 2401 Pinson Hwy.(35202), pg. 1095
TUCKER WAYNE/LUCKIE & COMPANY, 600 Luckie Dr.(35223), pg. 1118
Tucker Wayne/Luckie & Company, 600 Luckie Dr.(35223), pg. 1118
United States Pipe & Foundry Company, 3300 First Ave. N.(35222), pg. 1162
UNIVERSAL SECURITIES CORPORATION, 1050 Financial Center, 505 20th Street N.(35203), pg. 1139
Wedlo, Inc., 3200 2nd Ave.(35202), pg. 1012

Boaz

Oak Products, Inc., Sand Mountain Industrial Park(35957), pg. 908
River Oaks Double-Wide Plant, Sand Mountain Industrial Park(35957), pg. 908
River Oaks Homes, Inc., Sand Mountain Industrial Park(35957), pg. 908
River Oaks Vans, Inc., Sand Mountain Industrial Park.(35957), pg. 908

Cordova

Vulcan Asphalt Refining Company, P.O. Box 388(35550), pg. 1130

Cottondale

Reliance Grating, Inc., P.O. Box 20(35453), pg. 136

Cullman

CULLMAN PRODUCTS CORPORATION, 1909 Beach Ave. S.E.(35055), pg. 304

Dadeville

Shape South, Inc., 100 Rice Ave., P.O. Box 186(36853), pg. 995

Daleville

VMC FIBERGLASS PRODUCTS INC., Industrial Park, 3 Barnes St.(36322), pg. 1142

Decatur

ALABAMA FARMERS CO-OP, 121 Somerville Rd. N.E.(35609-2227), pg. 28
Mutual Savings Fire Insurance Company, P.O. Box 2222(35602), pg. 1150
Mutual Savings Life Insurance Company, 2801 Hwy. 31 S.(35601), pg. 1150
Southern Electric Supply Co., Inc., 1420 Church St., NE(35601), pg. 1020
Southern United Fire Insurance Company, P.O. Box 2222(35602), pg. 1150
Southern United Life Insurance Company, P.O. Box 2222(35602), pg. 1150

Dothan

FLAVOR HOUSE PRODUCTS, INC., 2700 Horace Shepherd Dr.(36303), pg. 417
Showell Farms, Inc., 808 Ross Circle S.E.(36303), pg. 1000
Wiregrass Container, Inc., 2603 Cottonwood Rd.(36301), pg. 941

Elba

Dorsey Trailers, Inc., 1409 Hickman St.(36323), pg. 347

Eufaula

ABC Transportation Co., State Docks Rd.(36027), pg. 50
AMERICAN BUILDINGS CO., State Docks Rd.(36027), pg. 49

Fairfield

MidSouth Oil Co., P.O. Box 583(35064), pg. 1030

Florence

MARTIN INDUSTRIES (AL), 301 E. Tennessee(35630), pg. 715

Fort Deposit

BENCO INDUSTRIES, INC., One Benco Industrial Dr.(36032), pg. 138

Fort Payne

GAME TIME, INC., 150 Gametime Dr.(35967), pg. 442
Heil Refuse & Dump Body Co., P.O. Box 27, (35967), pg. 525

Frisco City

FARMERS CO-OP MARKET INC., Bowden & Co-op Road(36445), pg. 401

Gadsden

Southern Electric Supply Co., Inc., 433 Locust(35902), pg. 1020

Geneva

Clinton Mills, P.O. Box 699, (36340), pg. 202

Greensboro

DAIRY FRESH CORP., 903 Tuscaloosa St.(36744), pg. 310
Dairy Fresh Ice Cream, P.O. Box 159(36744), pg. 311
Hale Motors, P.O. Box 159(36744), pg. 311

Guntersville

KSG INC., 115 Grimes Dr.(35976), pg. 613
Kappler, Inc., 70 Grimes St.(35976), pg. 613

Hamilton

North River Homes, Inc., 406 Airport Rd.(35570), pg. 908

Hartselle

Cerro Wire & Cable Co., Inc., P.O. Box 1049(35640), pg. 711

Huntsville

Alabama Oil Company, 120 Woodson St. N.W.(35801), pg. 1030
Alabama Wholesale Drug Co., 822 James Record Rd.(35824), pg. 1088
American Bread Co. of Alabama Inc., 7200 Governors West(35807), pg. 49
AVEX Electronics, Inc., 4807 Bradford Dr.(35805), pg. 550
Keystone Automotive Industries, Inc.-Huntsville, 617 Meridian(35801), pg. 628
Mason & Hanger National Inc., 2227 Drake Ave., Ste. 10D(35805), pg. 718
MidSouth Ice Co., 120 Woodson St. N.W.(35801), pg. 1030
SPENCER COMPANIES INC., 120 Woodson St. N.W.(35801), pg. 1030
Spencer Oil Company, 120 Woodson St. N.W.(35801), pg. 1030

Irondale

Southern Beauty Enterprises, 2904 Commerce Sq. South(35210), pg. 130

Jasper

DRUMMOND COMPANY, INC., 3000 Hwy. 78 East(35501), pg. 349

Lanett

SKINNER CORP., 1009 N. Lanier Ave.(36863), pg. 1009

Mobile

Allright Birmingham Inc., 101 N. Royal St.(36602), pg. 41
ALTUS FEDERAL SAVINGS BANK, 851 S. Beltline Hwy.(36606), pg. 46
ASSOCIATED EQUIPMENT COMPANY, INC., 1230 N. Beltline Hwy.(36607), pg. 89
BENDER SHIPBUILDING & REPAIR COMPANY, 265 S. Water St.(36603), pg. 138
FOLMAR & ASSOCIATES, 3472 Springhill Ave.(36608), pg. 422
GULF LUMBER COMPANY, INC., 1850 Conception St.(36610), pg. 493
LEWIS COMMUNICATIONS, INC., 1668 Government St.(36604), pg. 673
MCCONNELL AUTOMOTIVE, 3150 Dauphin St.(36606), pg. 727
Southern Electric Supply Co., Inc., 3307 Moffat Rd.(36607), pg. 1020
The Triad Group, Inc., 851 S. Beltline Hwy.(36606), pg. 46
TURNER SUPPLY COMPANY, 250 N. Royal St.(36602), pg. 1119
United Financial Services, 851 S. Beltline Hwy.(36606), pg. 46
WALA-TV, 210 Government St.(36602), pg. 194
Wabash Fibre Box Co.-South, 1571 16th St. Circle(36615), pg. 1183

Monroeville

Soalco, 1699 Sheffield Dr.(36460), pg. 14

Montevallo

SEAMAN TIMBER COMPANY, INC., P.O. BOx 372(35115), pg. 986

Montgomery

B.A.S.S., INC., 5845 Carmichael Rd.(36117), pg. 105
Bassmaster Magazine, P.O. Box 17116(36141), pg. 105
ALGERNON BLAIR INTERNATIONAL, One Algernon Blair Pl.(36116), pg. 155
THE ENSTAR GROUP, INC., 172 Commerce St., 3rd Fl.(36104), pg. 382
Fishing Tackle Retailer, P.O. Box 17151(36141), pg. 105
PIKNIK PRODUCTS COMPANY, INC., 3806 Day St.(36108), pg. 870
REID & O'DONAHUE ADVERTISING, INC., 419 S. Perry St.(31604), pg. 923
RUSSELL PETROLEUM CORPORATION, 3378 Tankview Ct.(36108), pg. 957
SMITH INDUSTRIES, INC., 2781 Gunter Park Dr. E.(36109), pg. 1013
Southern Electric Supply Co., Inc., 1141 Holloway Park(36117), pg. 1021
Southern Outdoors Magazine, P.O. Box 17915(36141), pg. 105
Southern Saltwater Magazine, P.O. Box 17055(36141), pg. 106
Thermal Components, Inc., 2760 Gunter Park, West, P.O. Box 3253(36193), pg. 571
WEIL BROTHERS COTTON INC., 4444 Park Blvd.(36116), pg. 1173
WHITFIELD FOODS, INC., 1101 N. Court St.(36104), pg. 1187
JIM WILSON & ASSOCIATES, 4121 Carmichael Rd., Ste. 501(36106), pg. 1193

Muscle Shoals

Interstate Jitney Jungle Stores, Inc., 1306 Woodward Ave. (Shoals Plaza)(35660), pg. 594

Oneonta

Acorn South, 500 Acorn Dr.(35121), pg. 14

Pelham

Reliable/Bethea Power Products Inc., 3098 Highway 31, S.(35124), pg. 698

Piedmont

BOSTROM SEATING, INC., Vigo Rd., P.O. Box 566(36272), pg. 168
Garcy Corporation, , pg. 907

Prattville

CONTINENTAL EAGLE CORPORATION, Gin Shop Hill Rd.(36067), pg. 278
Wabash Fibre Box Co.-South, 947 Washington Ferry Rd., Route 5, Box 852A(36067), pg. 1183

Prichard

AUTRY GREER & SONS, INC., 2850 W. Main St.(36612), pg. 486

Red Bay

TIFFIN MOTOR HOMES, INC., 502 4th St., N.W.(35582), pg. 1097

Selma

Assurance Glass Co. of Alabama, Selfield Industrial Park(36701), pg. 463
MILLER & CO., 500 Hooper Dr.(36701), pg. 753

Sheffield

Doehler-Jarvis Plant, 2019 Ford Rd.(35660), pg. 559

South Lafayette

TALLAPOOSA RIVER ELECTRIC CO-OP, Hwy. 431(36862), pg. 1077

Sylacauga

Avondale Foreign Sales Corporation, 900 Avondale Ave.(35150), pg. 103
AVONDALE MILLS, INC., 900 Avondale Ave.(35150), pg. 103
PARKER FERTILIZER CO., INC., 201 W. Fourth St.(35150), pg. 849

Tallassee

Mount Vernon Mills, Inc., Tallassee, AL, (36078), pg. 844

Theodore

BARNETT MILLWORKS, INC., 4915 Hamilton Blvd.(36590), pg. 120

Tuscaloosa

GULF STATES PAPER CORPORATION, 1400 River Rd., N.E.(35404), pg. 494
HARCO DRUG, INC., 3925 Rice Mine Rd., N.E.(35406), pg. 507
Southern Electric Supply Co., Inc., 2006 Tenth Ave.(35402), pg. 1021
Westervelt Land Co., 1400 River Rd.(35404), pg. 494
R.L. ZIEGLER CO. INC., 3201 Kauloosa Ave.(35401), pg. 1218

Tuscumbia

Elixir Industries, Hwy. 20, Alt. 72 East(35674), pg. 376

Union Springs

DIXIE ELECTRIC COOPERATIVE, 402 E. Blackman St.(36089), pg. 341

Wetumpka

Dan River Inc.-Wetumpka Plant, 1305 Parker(36092), pg. 313

Winfield

Continental Conveyor & Equipment Company, 4th Ave. S., Industrial Pk. Rd.(35594), pg. 798

ALASKA

Anchorage

ALASKA INDUSTRIAL HARDWARE INC., 2192 Viking Dr.(99501), pg. 30
Alaska Publishing Properties, Inc., 808 E. St., Ste. 200(99501), pg. 1207
Alaska Tool & Equipment Service, 3207 Arctic Blvd.(99503), pg. 30
Alaska-West Express, Inc., 660 Ocean Dock Rd.(9950l), pg. 689
Arctic Alaska Drilling, P.O. Box 6769(99502), pg. 708
Benefit Service Corporation of Alaska, 4300 B St., Ste. 104(99503), pg. 1166
BRADLEY COMMUNICATIONS, INC., 1840 S. Bragaw, Ste. 200(99508), pg. 170
CARR GOTTSTEIN FOODS, 6411 A Street(99518), pg. 225
General Hardware Distributors, 2192 Viking Dr.(99501), pg. 30
Hoffman Construction Company of Alaska, 3201 C St., Ste. 610(99503), pg. 537
Mall Entertainment USA, Northway Mall, Ste. J-10, Penland Parkway(99504), pg. 1028
MARKAIR, INC., P.O. Box 196769(99519-6769), pg. 708
NANA REGIONAL CORPORATION, INC., 1001 E. Benson(99508), pg. 783
THE NERLAND AGENCY, INC., 808 "E" St.(99501), pg. 798
Northland Alaska, Inc., 125 W. 5th Ave.(99501), pg. 484
PORCARO BLANKENSHIP ADVERTISING, 433 West 9th Ave.(99501), pg. 881
REEVE ALEUTIAN AIRWAYS, INC., 4700 W. International Airport Rd.(99502), pg. 921

Fairbanks

Arctic Alaska Testing Laboratories, 2055 Hill Rd., P.O. Box 70843(99707), pg. 995

Healy

USIBELLI COAL MINE, INC., 3 Miles Nenana River Rd.(99743), pg. 1140

Juneau

SEALASKA CORPORATION, One Sealaska Plaza, Ste. 400(99801-1276), pg. 984

Katzebue

Nana Development Corporation, P.O. Box 49(99752), pg. 783

Ketchikan

Sealaska Timber Corporation, 2030 Sea Level Drive(99901), pg. 984

ARIZONA

Buckeye

Golden Eagle Distributor, Inc., P.O. Box 697(85326), pg. 466

Casa Grande

ARIZONA GRAINS INC., 601 E. Main Ave(85222), pg. 82
Golden Eagle Distributors, Inc., 100 N. Jefferson(85222), pg. 466
Southwide, Inc.-Western Div., P.O. Box 1006, Casa Grande Indus. Park(85222), pg. 1024
Valley Seed Co., 601 E. Main Ave.(85222), pg. 82

Chandler

Aircraft Gear Corporation-Arizona Division, 1800 So. Price Rd.(85248), pg. 27
Arizona Auction Services, Inc., d/b/a Southwest Auto Auction, 400 No. Beck Ave.(85226), pg. 293
BASHAS, P.O. Box 488(85244), pg. 124
Coleman Spas, Inc., 25805 So. Arizona Ave.(85248), pg. 695
Crafco, Inc., 6975 W. Crafco Way(85226), pg. 386
Oberg Arizona, , pg. 819
Snavely Forest Products, Inc., 302 S. 56th St.(85226), pg. 1015

Flagstaff

Amfac Resorts, Inc., 5200 E. Cortland Blvd., Ste. A-16(86004), pg. 585
Amfac Silverado Corp., 5200 E. Cortland Blvd.(86001), pg. 585
Golden Eagle Sales, Inc., 1850 E. Butler(86002), pg. 466
Fred Harvey Transportation Company, 5200 E. Cortland Blvd.(86001), pg. 585
Hawaiian Discovery Tours, Inc., 5200 E. Cortland Blvd.(86001), pg. 585
Island Holidays, Ltd., 5200 E. Cortland Blvd.(86004), pg. 585
Poipu Waste Water Corporation, 5200 E. Cortland Blvd.(86001), pg. 585

Gilbert

HUNTER CONTRACTING COMPANY, 701 N. Cooper Rd.(85234), pg. 554

Glendale

BIDDULPH OLDSMOBILE, 4611 W. Glendale(85301), pg. 149
K-J DISTRIBUTORS, INC., 5061 N. 51st Ave.(85301), pg. 612
SANDS MOTOR COMPANY, INC., 5418 N.W. Grand Ave.(85301), pg. 970
SCHUCK & SONS CONSTRUCTION CO., 8205 N. 67th Ave.(85302), pg. 979

Globe

Golden Eagle Distributors, Inc., 550 S. Broad St.(85501), pg. 466

Holbrook

Golden Eagle Sales, Inc., U.S. Hwy. 66 W.(86025), pg. 466

Laveen

Arnold Machinery Company of Arizona, 6024 W. Southern Ave.(85339), pg. 85

Mesa

BROWN EVANS COMPANY, 306 S. Country Club Dr.(85202), pg. 182
Cox Arizona Publications, Inc., 120 W. First Ave.(85202), pg. 292
Elixir Industries, 219 S. Mulberry(85202), pg. 376
EMPIRE SOUTHWEST CO., 1725 S. Country Club Rd.(85210), pg. 379
FARNSWORTH COMPANIES, 460 S. Greenfield Rd.(85206), pg. 403

Farnsworth Construction, 460 S. Greenfield Rd.(85206), pg. 403
Farnsworth Development Co., 6065 E. University Dr.(85205), pg. 403
MCAFEE CONSOLIDATED INC., 840 E. Southern(85204), pg. 726
MESA CITRUS GROWERS, 254 W. Broadway(85210), pg. 741
Price Woods, Inc., 63 E. Main St., Ste. 601(85201), pg. 1200
JOE E. WOODS, INC., 65 E. Main St., Ste. 401(85201), pg. 1200

Payson

Burgess & Niple, Inc., 1106 N. Beeline Hwy.(85541), pg. 190

Peoria

Bud West, Inc., 7733 West Olive Ave.(85345), pg. 186

Phoenix

A & M Associates, Inc., 2727 No. Central Ave.(85004), pg. 48
A S H, INC., 2630 W. Buckeye Rd.(85009), pg. 8
ABCO MARKETS, INC., 3001 W. Indian School Rd.(85017), pg. 10
Allied Security Inc., 3150 N. 24th St., Ste. 203(85016), pg. 39
Allright Corporation of Delaware, 3101 N. Central Ave., Ste. 970(85012), pg. 41
Amerco Leasing Company, 2727 No. Central Ave.(85004), pg. 48
American Color, 2340 E. Polk St.(85006), pg. 1056
American Fence Co. AZ, 2525 N. 27th Ave., (85005), pg. 52
American Fence Co. Ltd., 2525 N. 27th Ave., (85005), pg. 52
American Fence Co. of Midwest, 2525 N. 27th Ave., (85005), pg. 52
AMERICAN FENCE COMPANY, 2525 N. 27th Ave., (85009), pg. 52
MOSES ANSHELL, INC., 234 N. Central Ave., Ste. 900(85004), pg. 76
Arizona Auction Services, Inc. d/b/a Arizona Auto Auction, 3420 S. 48th St.(85040), pg. 293
ARIZONA LOTTERY, 4740 E. University Dr.(85034), pg. 82
Arizona Sash & Door Co., 850 W. Lincoln St.(85002), pg. 428
ARIZONA SUPERMARKETS, INC., 2452 W. Lincoln St.(85009), pg. 82
ARIZONA WHOLESALE SUPPLY COMPANY, 2020 E. University Dr.(85036), pg. 82
B-W ADVERTISING AGENCY, P.O. Box 10203(85064-0203), pg. 107
B-W Advertising Agency, P.O. Box 10203(85064), pg. 147
B-W Insurance Agency, 6201 N. 24th Pkwy.(85064), pg. 147
B-W Supply, Inc., 6201 N. 24th Pkwy.(85064), pg. 147
BAR-S FOODS CO., 4041 N. Central, Ste. 1300(85012), pg. 118
BEST WESTERN INTERNATIONAL, INC., 6201 N. 24th Pkwy.(85016-2023), pg. 146
BRYANT UNIVERSAL ROOFERS INC., 3311 N. 44th St., Ste. 100(85018), pg. 185
Burgess & Niple, Inc., 5025 E. Washington St., Ste. 212(85034), pg. 190
CAPITAL ELECTRIC GROUP, INC., P.O. Box 16248, (85011), pg. 215
Central Commissary, Inc., 610 S. 56th Ave.(85043), pg. 287
Commercial Resource Insurance Co., 234 N. Central Ave.(85004), pg. 662
CONTINENTAL CIRCUITS CORP., 3502 E. Roeser(85040), pg. 278
Continental/Murray, 1805 E. Jefferson(85036), pg. 279
Cramer-Krasselt, 1420 E. Missouri Ave., Ste. 100(85014), pg. 296
CUMMINS SOUTHWEST INC., 2239 N. Black Canyon Hwy.(85009), pg. 305
Ed Debevic's of Arizona, 2102 E. Highland(85016), pg. 669
Ed Debevic's/Short Orders Deluxe/Phoenix, 2102 E. Highland(85016), pg. 669
Desert Medical Supply Inc., 3740 E. LaSalle(85040), pg. 1081
Desert Production Services, 2235 W. Alice(85021), pg. 734
Design Center, 3040 N. 44th St., Ste. 201(85018), pg. 1171
Dolphin, Inc., 740 S. 59th Ave(85005), pg. 617
DOUBLE AA BUILDERS, LTD., 7319 N. 16th St., Ste. 200(85020), pg. 347
MICHAEL R. ELLISON INC., 4455 E. Camelback, Ste. C-240(85060), pg. 378
EvansGroup, Biltmore Financial Center, 2390 E. Camelback, Ste. 325(85016), pg. 391
Fairmount Mortgage, Inc., Black Kenyon Blvd.(85018), pg. 1171
Farm & Home Life Insurance Co., 300 W. Osborn Rd.(85013), pg. 243
FARNAM COMPANIES, INC., 301 W. Osborn Rd.(85013), pg. 403
Finishline Industries Inc. of Arizona, 2308 S. 11th Ave.(85997), pg. 433
Fletcher Cobre Tire Co. Inc., 2601 N. 32nd Ave.(85009), pg. 418
FLETCHER ENTERPRISES, 2601 N. 32nd Ave.(85009), pg. 418
FLORI CORP., 3622 S. 30th St.(85040), pg. 420
General Binding Corporation, 21039 N. 27th Ave.(85027), pg. 657
GOODMANS, INC., 1400 E. Indian School Rd.(85014), pg. 471
GOSNELL BUILDERS, 2728 N. 24th St.(85008), pg. 472
W. M. GRACE DEVELOPMENT, 7575 N. 16th St., Ste. 1(85020), pg. 474
Hei Rotomold, Inc., 108 E. Pioneer Rd.(85040), pg. 526
HENSLEY & CO., 4201 N. 45th Ave.(85031), pg. 530
HOLSUM BAKERY, INC., 408 S. 23rd Ave.(85009), pg. 541
HOMES & SON CONTRACTORS, INC., 2950 W. Durango St.(85009), pg. 542
HuntCor Inc., 426 N. 44th St., Ste. 410(85008), pg. 553
IMPERIAL LITHO/GRAPHICS, INC., 210 S. 4th Ave.(85003), pg. 564
Jorgensen Steel & Aluminum/Phoenix, 5445 W. Madison(85043), pg. 606
KEZ, 5555 N. 7th Ave., Ste. B-300(85013), pg. 734
KAIBAB INDUSTRIES, 4602 E. Thomas Rd.(85018), pg. 614
Kaibab Metals, Inc., 4602 E. Thomas Rd.(85018), pg. 614
Karsten Engineering Corp., 2201 W. Desert Cove(85029), pg. 617
KARSTEN MANUFACTURING CORPORATION, 2201 W. Desert Cove(85029), pg. 617
KITCHELL CORPORATION, 1707 East Highland, Ste. 100(85016), pg. 634
LSC-Marketing, Inc., 300 W. Osborn Rd.(85013), pg. 243
E. B. LANE & ASSOCIATES, INC., 733 W. McDowell(85007), pg. 656
Life Insurance Co. of Arizona, 300 W. Osborn Rd.(85013), pg. 243
Lifeshares Group, Inc., 300 W. Osborn Rd.(85013), pg. 243
M M Systems Corporation, 2985 West Whitton Ave.(85009), pg. 692
Madison Industries Inc. of Arizona, 2100 S. 11th Ave.(85007), pg. 433
Maximet, 5925 W. Monroe(85043), pg. 617
MEDIA AMERICA CORP., 3435 N. 16th St., (85016), pg. 734
MESSENGER CORPORATION, 110 S. 41st Ave.(85009), pg. 741
NATIONAL BRANDS, INC., 4633 W. Polk, (85043), pg. 786
Nationwide Commercial Co., 2721 No. Central Ave.(85004), pg. 48
Northern Automotive Corporation, 645 E. Missouri(85012), pg. 1118
J. R. NORTON COMPANY, 3200 E. Camelback Rd., Ste. 389(85018), pg. 816
OWENS POLLICK & ASSOCIATES, PHOENIX, INC., 2800 N. Central Ave., Ste. 1500(85004), pg. 834
Oxford Life Insurance Co., 2721 No. Central Ave.(85004), pg. 48
PSC Distributing, Inc., 702 N. 21st Ave.(85009), pg. 225
Phoenix Concrete Cutting, 3639 E. Superior Ave.(85040), pg. 857
Phoenix Data Incorporated, 3384 W. Osborn Rd.(85017), pg. 630
PHOENIX FUEL COMPANY, INC., 2343 N. 27th Ave.(85005), pg. 868
Phoenix Magazine, 5555 N. 7th Ave., Ste. B-200(85013), pg. 734
PISTOL PETE'S PIZZA, 2810 W. Camelback Rd.(85017), pg. 872
Ponderosa Insurance Agency, 2721 No. Central Ave.(85004), pg. 48
ARTHUR PORTER CONSTRUCTION, 11201 N. 23rd Ave., Suite 200(85029), pg. 881
Rapid Rail Systems, 2441 S. 40th St.(85034), pg. 526
REDBURN TIRE COMPANY, 3801 W. Clarendon(85019), pg. 919
Republic Western Insurance Co., 2721 No. Central Ave.(85004), pg. 48
Reservations Services, Inc. P.O. Box 10203, (85064), pg. 147
ROAD MACHINERY COMPANY, 716 S. 7th St.(85034), pg. 937
CHAS ROBERTS AIR CONDITIONING, INC., 9828 N. 19th Ave.(85021), pg. 938
Rocor Properties, Inc., 2929 E. Camelback(85016), pg. 942
J.B. RODGERS MECHANICAL CONTRACTORS, 2825 W. Thomas Rd.(85017), pg. 943
ROOFING WHOLESALE CO., INC., 1918 W. Grant(85009), pg. 946
S & W Fine Foods, 5201 N. 19th Ave.(85016), pg. 1111
SCHUFF STEEL CO., 420 S. 19th Ave.(85009), pg. 979
SHAMROCK FOODS CO., 2228 N. Black Canyon Hwy.(85009), pg. 994
Shea Homes Southwest, 40 40 E. Camelback Rd., Ste. 200(85060), pg. 996
SIGLER & REEVES, 3451 N. 34th Ave.(85017), pg. 1003
SIMMONS OIL CORP., 2425 E. Camelback Rd., Ste. 1025(85016), pg. 1005
SMITH PIPE & STEEL CO., 733 N. 19th Ave.(85009), pg. 1014
Sonee Heat Treating, 3900 N. 31st Ave.(85017), pg. 617
Sonic Messenger Service, 1121 East Missouri Suite 218(85014), pg. 1018
Standard Restaurant Equipment Co., 2922 E. McDowell Rd.(85008), pg. 1036
Star Container, Inc., 2525 E. Magnolia(85034), pg. 1082
Steris Laboratories, Inc., 620 N. 51st Ave.(85043), pg. 975
THE SWANSON COMPANY MANUFACTURERS, 3747 W. Buckeye Rd.(85009), pg. 1066
Sylvan Pools of Arizona, Inc., 2210 E. Indian School Rd.(85016), pg. 612
Tesco, 2441 S. 40th St.(85034), pg. 526
Time Index, Inc., 825 East University(85034), pg. 1097
TIME SYSTEMS, INC., 5353 N. 16th St., Ste. 400(85016), pg. 1097
Top-Seal Corp., 2236 E. University Dr.(85034), pg. 1083
Tuchetti, 2135 E. Camelback Rd.(85016), pg. 669
U-Haul International, Inc., 2727 No. Central Ave.(85004), pg. 48
U-Haul Real Estate Company, 2727 No. Central Ave.(85004), pg. 48
U-Haul Sales & Leasing Company, 2727 No. Central Ave.(85004), pg. 48
UGLY DUCKLING RENT-A-CAR, 2425 E. Camelback Rd., Ste. 650(85016), pg. 1125
Underwriters National Assurance Co., 300 W. Osborn Rd.(85013), pg. 243
UNITED PRODUCERS & CONSUMERS CO-OP, 1821 E. Jackson St.(85034), pg. 1134
Universal Homes, Inc., 3875 N. 44th St.(85018), pg. 1171
Universal Roofers, Inc., 1245 S. 7th St.(85036), pg. 185
WALLED LAKE DOOR COMPANY, 4527 N. 16th St.(85016), pg. 1161
DEL WEBB'S COVENTRY, 4550 N. Black Canyon Hwy.(85017), pg. 1171
Weitz-Cohen Construction Company, 2255 N. 44th St., Ste. 125(85008), pg. 1174
Westco Products/Phoenix, 5720 W. Jefferson St.(85043), pg. 1178
Western International Media Corporation, 4041 N. Central C 200(85012), pg. 1180
WESTERN LINEN CORP., 4131 N. 24th St., Ste. A200(85016), pg. 1180
WESTERN STATES PETROLEUM INC., 450 S. 15th Ave.(85007), pg. 1181
Western Storage Insurance Co., 2929 N. 44th St., Suite 120(85018), pg. 898
WINCUP, 7980 W. Buckeye Rd.(85043), pg. 1195
Woodstuff Manufacturing, Inc., 1635 S. 43rd Ave.(85005), pg. 986

Scottsdale

Mark Anderson Associates, Inc., 8700 Via De Ventura, Ste. 235(85258), pg. 73
Dairyland Insurance Co., 9501 E. Shea Blvd.(85260), pg. 990
Don and Charlie's, 7501 E. Camelback Rd.(85251), pg. 669
DRACKETT & LAVIDGE, INC., 6263 N. Scottsdale Rd., Ste. 190(85250), pg. 348
DRUG EMPORIUM OF ARIZONA, INC., 13402 N. Scottsdale Rd., Ste. B160(85254), pg. 349
FENDER MUSICAL INSTRUMENTS, 7975 N. Hayden Rd.(85258), pg. 406
FRANCHISE FINANCE CORP. OF AMERICA, 17207 N. Perimeter Dr.(85255), pg. 428
LAIDLAW CORPORATION, 6625 N. Scottsdale Rd.(85250), pg. 650
MARTZ & WADAS, 8700 E. Via de Ventura, Ste. 301(85258), pg. 716
NYLIFE Insurance Company of Arizona, 6263 Scottsdale Rd., Ste. 300(85250), pg. 803
PADDOCK POOL CONSTRUCTION CO., 6525 E. Thomas Rd.(85251), pg. 842
Retirement Living Affiliates, Inc., 6991 E. Camelback(85251), pg. 24
RURAL METRO CORPORATION, 8401 E. Indian School Rd.(85251), pg. 956
Scottsdale Publishing, Inc., 7320 E. Earll Dr.(85251), pg. 291
SONICAIR, 15150-1 N. Hayden Rd., Suite 200(85260), pg. 1018
THE TECH GROUP, 14677 N. 74th St.(85260), pg. 1082
Tech Poulson, Inc., 14677 N. 74th St.(85260), pg. 1083
United Planners' Group, Inc., 7333 E. Doubletree Rd., Ste. 120(85258), pg. 841

Sun Lakes

SUN LAKES MARKETING, 25612 E. J. Robson Blvd.(85248), pg. 1059

Tempe

CALIFORNIA MICRO DEVICES, 2000 W. 14th St.(85281), pg. 210
EARNHARDT'S AUTO CENTER, 7777 E. Baseline(85283), pg. 362
FOREVER LIVING PRODUCTS, 1200 S. Priest Rd.(85281), pg. 424
Frederic Printing, 4500 S. Lakeshore Dr., Ste. 430
Stephen Gould of Arizona, Inc., 4041 S. McClintock(85382), pg. 474
HOMES BY DAVE BROWN, 2164 E. Broadway, Ste. 300(85282), pg. 542
Idea Courier, Inc., 1515 W. 14th St.(85281), pg. 560
JACK ROSS MOTORS INC., 2700 N. Scottsdale Rd.(85271), pg. 949
SALT RIVER PROJECT AGRICULTURAL IMPROVEMENT AND POWER DISTRICT, 1521 Project Dr.(85281), pg. 967
Tech Medical Inc., 640 S. Rockford Dr.(85281), pg. 1083
Tech Mold, Inc., 1735 W. 10th St.(85281), pg. 1083
Tech Plastics, 1415 S. McClintock(85281), pg. 1083
UNITED DAIRYMEN OF ARIZONA, 2008 Hardy Dr.(85282), pg. 1131
XTEK/Arizona Division, 1710 W. Broadway, P.O. Box 27288(85282), pg. 1206

Tucson

Barone Sausage Company, 345 S. King Pkwy.(85733), pg. 251
CITY MEATS & PROVISIONS CO., P.O. Box 27243, (85726), pg. 251
DDC PERTEC, 2705 E. Medina, Ste. 161(85706), pg. 308
EMPIRE WEST COMPANIES, INC., 6700 N. Oracle, Ste. 100(85704), pg. 380
GOLDEN EAGLE DISTRIBUTORS, INC., 705 E. Ajo Way(85713), pg. 466
ED HOLDERNESS SUPPLIES, 450 E. Irvington Rd.(85714), pg. 538
HOLMES TUTTLE FORD, INC., 660 W. Auto Mall Dr.(85705), pg. 540
KOLD-TV, 115 W. Drachman(85705), pg. 805
Louv-Aire, Inc., 1655 N. 15th Ave.(85705), pg. 28
NPG of Arizona, Inc., 115 W. Drachman(85705), pg. 805
Preferred Properties, 1890 E. River Rd.(85718), pg. 1118
QUEBEDEAUX PONTIAC, INC., 3566 E. Speedway(85716), pg. 904

Shopper's Guide, Inc. (Tucson Shopper), 2915 E. Speedway(85716), pg. 513
SUNDT CORP., 4101 E. Irvington Rd.(85714), pg. 1060
Sundt Products, Inc., 4798 S. Julian Ave.(85714), pg. 1060
TAYLOR ADVERTISING, INC., 33 N. Stone Ave., Ste. 1000(85701), pg. 1080
TRICO ELECTRIC CO-OP, 5100 W. Ina Rd.(85743), pg. 1113
Triple S Plastics Southwest, 6680 S. Country Club Rd.(85706), pg. 1114
TUCSON REALTY & TRUST CO., 1890 E. River Rd.(85718), pg. 1118
Universal Roofers, Inc., 2819 W. Ruthrauff(85705), pg. 185

Yuma

Sun Printing Company, 2055 Arizona Ave.(85364), pg. 292

ARKANSAS

Bearden

BEARDEN LUMBER COMPANY, INC., 111 N. Plum St.(71720), pg. 129

Bella Vista

COOPER COMMUNITIES, INC., 1801 Forest Hills. Blvd.(72714), pg. 283
Cooper Ventures, Inc., 1801 Forest Hills Blvd.(72714), pg. 283
Ecco Services, Inc., 1801 Forest Hills Blvd.(72714), pg. 283

Blytheville

Blytheville Canning Company, Inc., P.O. Box 167(72316), pg. 196
Borg-Warner Automotive Control Systems-Blytheville, P.O. Box 1529, Blytheville Industrial Park(72315), pg. 166

Booneville

Spang & Company-Booneville Plant, Hwy. 10 E.(72927), pg. 1025
Today's Kids, Hwy. 10 E.(72927), pg. 1025

Conway

AMW Industries Inc., P.O. Box 1364, 584 Commerce Rd.(72032), pg. 507
AMTRAN CORPORATION, Hwy. 65 S.(72032), pg. 69
CONWAY CORPORATION, 1319 Prairie(72032), pg. 281
NABHOLZ CONSTRUCTION CORP., 612 Garland(72032), pg. 782

De Witt

CORMIER RICE MILLING COMPANY, INC., 501 W. 3rd Ave.(72042), pg. 286

Decatur

PETERSON INDUSTRIES INC., 250 S. Main St.(72722), pg. 864

Earle

EARLE INDUSTRIES, INC., Hwy. 64 E.(72331), pg. 362

El Dorado

ANTHONY FOREST PRODUCTS CO., INC., P.O. Box 1877(71730), pg. 77
Anthony International, P.O. Box 1877(71730), pg. 77
Engineered Wood Div., P.O. Box 1877(71730), pg. 77

Fayetteville

CONTINENTAL OZARK, INC., 280 N. College, Ste. 500(72701), pg. 280
Kearney Div., 3660 So. School St.(72701), pg. 357
NORTHWEST TOBACCO & CANDY CO., 612 W. Center(72701), pg. 815
PACE INDUSTRIES, INC., One McIlroy Plaza(72701), pg. 838

Foreman

Ash Grove Cement, P.O. Box 130, (71836), pg. 87

Forest City

WOODRUFF ELECTRICAL CO-OP, 3190 N. Washington(72335), pg. 1200

Fort Smith

CARCO INTERNATIONAL, INC., 2721 Midland Blvd.(72904), pg. 217
DONREY MEDIA GROUP, 3600 Wheeler Ave.(72901), pg. 345
Federal Savings Bank, 524 Garrison Ave.(72901), pg. 1194
FLANDERS INDUSTRIES, INC., 1901 Wheeler Ave.(72901), pg. 416
Plastics Research & Development Co., 3601 Jenny Land(72914), pg. 365
Okla Homer Smith Furniture Co., P.O. Box 1148(72902), pg. 235
Speer Hardware, 5400 N. 6th St.(72904), pg. 993
SUPERIOR FEDERAL BANK, 5000 Rogers Ave.(72903), pg. 1063
WELDON, WILLIAMS & LICK, INC., 711 N. A St.(72902), pg. 1175

Hardy

TOWN & COUNTRY SUPERMARKET, Main St.(72542), pg. 1103

Helena

MID SOUTH SALES, 520 Walnut(72342), pg. 750

Hope

Bruner-Ivory Handle Company, P.O. Box 647(71801), pg. 677
KLIPSCH & ASSOCIATES INC., Rte. 4, Oakhaven Rd.(71801), pg. 635

Hot Springs

Arkansas Aluminum Alloys, P.O. Box 1410(71902), pg. 1087
Carolina Mountain Water, c/o Mountain Valley Spring Co., P.O. Box 1610(71902), pg. 968
Lake Catherine, 190 Elmwood Rd.(71902), pg. 776
Mountain Valley Spring Company, 150 Central Ave.(71901), pg. 968
MUNRO & COMPANY, INC., 120 Elmwood Rd.(71901), pg. 775
KEITH SMITH FARMS, INC., 911 Gaines St.(71901), pg. 1012

Jacksonville

AMERICAN MILITARY ARMS CORPORATION, 2202 Redmond Rd.(72076), pg. 58
Arkansas Investment Casting, 2202 Redmond Rd.(72076), pg. 58
FIRST ELECTRIC COOPERATIVE, 901 N. First St.(72076), pg. 412

Jonesboro

E.C. BARTON & CO., 2929 Brown's Lane(72401), pg. 123
Colson Caster Corporation, 3700 Airport Rd.(72401), pg. 711
Wabash Fibre Box Co.-South, 4401 Sarah(72401), pg. 1183

Little Rock

AFFILIATED FOODS SOUTHWEST, 12103 Interstate 30(72209), pg. 24
Allright Little Rock, Inc., 209 W. 6th(72201), pg. 41
ARKANSAS ELECTRIC COOPERATIVES INC., 8000 Scott Hamilton Dr.(72209), pg. 83
ARKANSAS FARM BUREAU FEDERATION, 10720 Kanis Rd.(72211), pg. 83
ARKANSAS INDUSTRIAL DEVELOPMENT COMMISSION, One State Capitol Mall(72201), pg. 83
Cleveland Electric Company of Arkansas, 3401 West 65th St.(72209), pg. 255
The Climatic Corporation, 3700 W. 65th St.(72209), pg. 255
M. M. Cohn Co., Inc., 300 S. University Ave.(72201), pg. 353
COLEMAN DAIRY INC., 5801 Asher Ave.(72204), pg. 261
COMBS & HEATHCOTT, 3426 Old Cantrell Rd.(72202), pg. 267
CRANFORD JOHNSON ROBINSON WOODS, 303 W. Capitol Ave.(72201), pg. 296
DEMOCRAT PRINTING & LITHOGRAPH COMPANY, 114-22 E. 2nd St.(72201), pg. 328
DYKE INDUSTRY, INC., 309 Center St.(72201), pg. 356
Farm Bureau Casualty Insurance Co., 10720 Kanis Rd.(72203), pg. 83
Farm Bureau Mutual Insurance Co. of Arkansas, 10720 Kanis Road(72203), pg. 83
First Pyramid Life Insurance Company of America, 650 Shackleford Rd., Ste. 400(72211), pg. 1150
KATV Television, Inc., P.O. Box 77, (72203), pg. 862
Keystone Automotive Industries, Inc.-Little Rock, 6100 Forbing Rd.(72219), pg. 628
Kilsby-Roberts/Little Rock, 5207 Scott Hamilton Dr.(72209), pg. 606
ORBIT VALVE INTERNATIONAL, INC., 7200 Interstate 30(72209), pg. 828
Penske Truck Leasing, 6100 W. 65th St.(72209), pg. 859
QUALITY FOODS INC., 4901 Asher Ave.(72204), pg. 903
J. A. RIGGS TRACTOR CO., 9125 Interstate 30(72209), pg. 934
SD Leasing Company, 2201 Brookwood, Ste. 114(72201), pg. 1046
Stephens Holding Company, Inc., 111 Center St.(72201), pg. 1046
STEPHENS, INC., 111 Center Street(72201), pg. 1046
Stephens Overseas Services, Inc., 111 Center St.(72201), pg. 1046
THE UNION OF ARKANSAS CORP., 124 W. Capitol(72201), pg. 1127
Union National Bank of Arkansas, Capitol at Louisiana(72201), pg. 1127
Union National Bank of Austin, Capitol at Louisiana(72201), pg. 1127
Union National Bank of Oklahoma, Capitol at Louisiana(72201), pg. 1127
Walker & Associates, Inc., 10800 Financial Center Pkwy., Ste. 370(72211), pg. 1160
WEHCO MEDIA, INC., 115 E. Capitol St.(72203), pg. 1172
Wehco Video Inc., 115 E. Capitol St.(72203), pg. 1172
WINROCK ENTERPRISES, INC., 2101 Brookwood Dr.(72202), pg. 1197

Magnolia

AMERICAN FUEL CELL & COATED FABRICS CO. (AMFUEL), 601 Firestone Dr.(71753), pg. 55

Marianna

GES INC., Hwy. One Lee Shopping Center(72360), pg. 439

Marked Tree

Mid-South Mfg. Co., P.O. Box 278, (72365), pg. 1123

Mena

Sterling Machinery Co., Inc., 104 Port Arthur(71953), pg. 767

North Little Rock

BRUCE OAKLEY, INC., 3700 Lincoln(72114), pg. 819
RAND'S INC., 1200 Pike Ave.(72114), pg. 912
SF SERVICES, 824 N. Palm St.(72119), pg. 961
TARCO, P.O. Box 17875(72117), pg. 1076
A. TENENBAUM CO. INC., 4500 W. Bethany Rd.(72117), pg. 1087
WELSCO INC., 9006 Crystal Hill Rd.(72113), pg. 1175

Paragould

L. A. Darling Company, P.O. Box 970, (72450), pg. 711

Pine Bluff

ARKANSAS OAK FLOORING, 2200 W. 5th St.(71601), pg. 83
Coca-Cola/Dr. Pepper Bottling Co. Of South Arkansas, 205 E. Second Ave.(71601), pg. 831
THE MAD BUTCHER, INC., 2001 W. Fifth(71613), pg. 699
MINDGAMES, INC., 2720 W. 28th St.(71613), pg. 756

Portland

WILSON PUGH INC., Highway 165 South(71663), pg. 1194

Rogers

Clayton Mark, 1203 N. 6th St.(72756), pg. 70
RTW, ROGERS TOOL WORKS, INC., 205 N. 13th St.(72756), pg. 908
Rogers Tool Works, Inc., 205 N. 13th St.(72757-0009), pg. 507

Russellville

BIBLER BROTHERS, INC., P.O. Box 490(72801), pg. 148
Taber Metals, Inc., P.O. Drawer 1418(72801), pg. 1078

Searcy

Identification Systems, 501 Lincoln St.(72143), pg. 721

Sheridan

Sterling Faucet Co., P. O. Box 427, South Oklahoma St.(72150), pg. 640

Sherwood

RUSSELL CHEVROLET COMPANY, 6100 Landere Rd.(72117), pg. 957

Siloam Springs

ALLEN CANNING COMPANY, 305 E. Main St.(72761), pg. 35
Outreach Publications, P.O. Box 1010(72761), pg. 282

Springdale

HARP'S FOOD STORES, INC., 1004 S. Gutensohn Rd.(72764), pg. 510
Newly Weds Foods, Inc., 1111 Angell Dr.(72764), pg. 804
SCHMIEDING ENTERPRISES INC., 1411 S. Thompson(72765), pg. 976

Stuttgart

PRODUCERS RICE MILL INC., 518 E. Harrison St.(72160), pg. 892
RICELAND FOODS, INC., 2120 Park Ave.(72160), pg. 931

Texarkana

BUHRMAN-PHARR HARDWARE COMPANY, 212-222 Laurel St.(75502), pg. 187

Urbana

Anthony Forest Div., 1236 Urbana Rd.(71768), pg. 77

Van Buren

Therma-Tru Western Mfg. Opers., Industrial Park Rd.(72956), pg. 1091

West Memphis

ELITE LAMP, INC., P.O. Box 591(72301), pg. 376

Wynne

CMS Chemical Company, P. O. Box 1008, 2151 Bartlett Rd.(72396), pg. 515
Halstead Industrial Prods. Div., Hwy. 1(72396), pg. 502

CALIFORNIA

Adelanto

Molded Fiber Glass/West, 9400 Holly Rd.(92301-0370), pg. 764

Agoura

PAISANO PUBLICATIONS, INC., 28210 Dorothy Dr.(91301), pg. 843

Agoura Hills

MEADE ULLMAN ADVERTISING & PUBLIC RELATIONS, 30851 Agoura Rd., Ste. 102(91301), pg. 733
PIP Capital Inc., 27001 Agoura Rd.(91301), pg. 616
Pip Printing, 27001 Agoura Rd.(91301), pg. 616
J.D. POWER AND ASSOCIATES, 30401 Agoura Rd.(91301), pg. 883

Alameda

CORNNUTS INC., 1320 Harbor Bay Pkwy., Ste. 250(94501), pg. 286
Dispensing Systems Div., 2016 Clement Ave.(94501), pg. 220
Stephen Gould of California-North Bay, 1001 Marina Village Pkwy., 4th Fl.(94501), pg. 474
IA CORP., 1301 Harbor Bay Parkway(94501-6541), pg. 558
SYBEX GROUP, 2021 Challenger Dr.(94501), pg. 1069

Alhambra

Cencom Cable Television, 2215 Mission Rd.(91802), pg. 446
Design USA, 2200 W. Valley Blvd.(91803), pg. 587
JACMAR COMPANIES, INC., 2200 W. Valley Blvd.(91803), pg. 587
Jacmar Development Corp., 2200 W. Valley Blvd.(91803), pg. 587
ORTEL CORPORATION, 2015 W. Chestnut(91803), pg. 830

Altadena

CHARLES PANKOW BUILDERS, LTD., 2476 N. Lave Ave.(91001), pg. 846

Anaheim

Acurex Corp. Aerotherm Products Division, 1111 N. Armando St.(92806), pg. 16
Acurex Corp. Aerotherm Products Division, 111 North Armando St.(92806), pg. 15
ALEX FOODS, INC., PO Box 3129, 2125 E. Orangewood(92803), pg. 33
AMERICAN LOCK & SUPPLY INC., 4411 E. La Palma Ave.(92807), pg. 57
ANAHEIM MANUFACTURING COMPANY, 4240 E. LaPalma(92807), pg. 71
Belmont Plastics Co., 1745 S. Haster St.(92802), pg. 285
BISCO INDUSTRIES, 1620 S. Clementine Ave.(92802), pg. 153
California Angels Baseball Club, State College Blvd.(92805), pg. 467
California Auto Dealers Exchange, Inc., 1320 N. Tustin Ave.(92817), pg. 293
California School Book Fairs, Inc., 1221 N. Lakeview Ave.(92806), pg. 962
CORCORAN MFG. CO., INC., 1140 E. Howell St.(92805), pg. 285
CYBER SYSTEMS, INC., 2570 E. Cerritos Ave.(92806), pg. 307
ECONOLITE CONTROL PRODUCTS, INC., 3360 E. La Palma Ave.(92806), pg. 367
Environmental Landscape Products, 2209 E. Orangewood Ave.(92806), pg. 383
GANAHL LUMBER COMPANY, 1220 E. Ball Rd.(92805-5993), pg. 442
Hallmark Litho Co., 1230 S. Sherman St.(92805), pg. 840
H. Koch & Sons, 5410 E. La Palma Ave.(92807), pg. 262
Lear Siegler Telecommunications Div., 714 N. Brookhurst(92803), pg. 664
Martin Luther Hospital, P.O. Box 3304, 1830 W. Romneya Dr.(92801-1854), pg. 1127
MODEL GLASS, INC., 4887 E. La Palma, Ste. 704(92807), pg. 762
NDC Distributors, Inc., 530 E. Cerritos Ave.(92805), pg. 787
PBS BUILDING SYSTEMS OF AMERICA, 155 N. Riverview Dr.(92808), pg. 835
PACIFIC ENVELOPE COMPANY, 1600 E. Winston Rd.(92805), pg. 840
PENHALL INTERNATIONAL, 1801 Penhall Way(92803), pg. 857
PHOENIX VENTURES, 1890 S. Chris Lane(92805), pg. 869
Premier Publishing Co., 1600 E. Winston Rd.(92805), pg. 840
Quad/West Pre-Press, 1174 N. Grove, Ste. A.(92806-2198), pg. 902
SECHRIST INDUSTRIES, INC., 4225 E. La Palma Ave.(92807), pg. 987
SPECIALTY RESTAURANTS CORPORATION, 4155 E. LaPalma Ave., Ste. 250(92807), pg. 1027
STREECH ELECTRIC COMPANY, 3870 E. Eagle Dr.(92807), pg. 1053
Watlow Aov, Inc., 4545 E. La Palma Ave.(92807), pg. 1167
Yale Industrial Trucks, 2411 E. Winston(92806), pg. 1207

Arcata

Sierra Pacific Industries-Arcata Division, Samoa Road(95521), pg. 1003

Artesia

CALIFORNIA MILK PRODUCERS, 11709 E. Artesia Blvd.(90701), pg. 210
Twin Palms Care Center, 11900 E. Artesia Blvd.(90701), pg. 740

Auburn

AUBURN FAITH COMMUNITY HOSPITAL, 11815 Education St.(95604), pg. 97
NELLA OIL COMPANY, 2349 Rickenbacker Way(95603), pg. 797

Azusa

MONROVIA NURSERY CO., 18331 E. Foothill Blvd.(91702), pg. 766

Bakersfield

THE BAKERSFIELD CALIFORNIAN, 1707 Eye St.(93302-0440), pg. 115
CALCOT, LTD., 1601 E. Brundage(93307), pg. 208
CASEY CO., 7845 Panama Lane(93307), pg. 228
Cox Cable Bakersfield, Inc., 820 22nd St.(93301), pg. 294
GIUMARRA VINEYARDS, P.O. Bin 1969, (93303), pg. 460
Hood Industries Inc., 2459 Fruitdale Ave., Unit 3(93313), pg. 224
HOPPER INC., P.O. Box 2900(93303), pg. 543
KBAK-TV, 19th & Westwind Dr.(93303), pg. 194
Kern Livestock Supplement Co., Inc., 130 Industrial St.(93307), pg. 45
Paramount Farming Company, P.O. Box 1107(93308), pg. 60

Baldwin Park

IN-N-OUT BURGERS, 13502 E. Virginia(91706), pg. 564
RELIEF PRINTING CORPORATION, 5160 Rivergrade Rd.(91706), pg. 925
SUES, YOUNG & BROWN INC., 5151 Commerce Dr.(91706), pg. 1056

Bell Gardens

BELL GARDENS BICYCLE CLUB, 7301 Eastern Ave(90201), pg. 134

Benicia

INSTITUTIONAL FINANCING SERVICES, 5100 Park Rd.(94510), pg. 571
Keystone Northern California Warehouse - Benicia, 3919 Oregon St.(94510), pg. 628
M.G.C. Company, 5145 Industrial Way(94510), pg. 1126
Now Hear This (NHT), 537 Stone Rd., Ste. E(94510), pg. 578
UNDERGROUND CONSTRUCTION COMPANY, INC., 5145 Industrial Way(94510), pg. 1125

Berkeley

Berkeley Marina Restaurant Corp., 199 Seawall Dr.(94710), pg. 1028
DAVLIN PAINT COMPANY, INC., P.O. Box 2308, 700 Alston Way(94702), pg. 319
EXPERIENCE IN SOFTWARE, INC., 2000 Hearst Ave. Ste 202(94709), pg. 393
HAWS DRINKING FAUCET CO., 1435 Fourth St.(94710), pg. 518
PACIFIC STEEL CASTING CO., 1333 2nd St.(94710), pg. 841
PEERLESS LIGHTING CORP., 2246 Fifth St.(94710), pg. 855

Beverly Hills

Academy Entertainment Inc., 9250 Wilshire Blvd., Ste. 404(90212), pg. 86
THE BEVERLY HILLS HOTEL, 9641 Sunset Blvd.(90210), pg. 148
BRIDGEWATER RESOURCES CORPORATION, 9701 Wilshire Blvd., Ste. 1200(90212), pg. 175
CAPUCCI CREATIONS INTERNATIONAL, INC., 9565 Santa Monica Blvd.(90210), pg. 216
Dav-El West, 9641 Sunset Blvd.(90210), pg. 317
Ed Debevic's, 134 N. Lacienga(90211), pg. 669
JON DOUGLAS COMPANY, 427 N. Camden Dr.(90210), pg. 347
FIRST GRAY LINE CORPORATION, 335 N. Maple, Ste. 273(90210), pg. 413
JOHN PAUL MITCHELL SYSTEMS, P.O. Box 10597, (90213-3597), pg. 762
WALLACE MOIR CO., 9595 Wilshire Blvd., 10th Fl.(90212), pg. 763
WILLIAM MORRIS AGENCY, INC., 151 El Camino(90212), pg. 771
RNF MEDIA CORPORATION INC., 9440 Santa Monica Blvd.(90210), pg. 907
SHAPELL INDUSTRIES, INC., 8383 Wilshire Blvd., Ste. 700(90211), pg. 995
M.L. STERN & COMPANY, INC., 8350 Wilshire Blvd.(90211), pg. 1047

Brea

BRISTOL INDUSTRIES, 630 E. Lambert Rd.(92621), pg. 176
EARLE M. JORGENSEN COMPANY, 3050 E. Birch(92621), pg. 605
Jorgensen Steel & Aluminum, 3050 E. Birch St.(92621), pg. 605
Kilsby-Roberts, 3050 Birch St.(92621), pg. 606
KRAUSE'S SOFA FACTORY, INC., 200 N. Berry St.(92621), pg. 644
PennySaver (Harte-Hanks California CDM, Inc.), P.O. Box 8900(92622), pg. 513
Recold, Inc., 550 W. Mercury Ln.(92621), pg. 710
Thetford Corp., Warehouse Div., 2700-B Saturn(92621), pg. 358
UFE Cal Tec Inc., 1125 Beacon St.(92621-2937), pg. 1123
Uniroyal Chemical Co., Inc. (Leffingwell), P.O. Box 1880, 111 So. Berry St.(92622), pg. 1129

Brisbane

Pacific Fruit Express Co., 100 Valley Dr.(94005), pg. 75

Buena Park

Cal Graphics Division, 6370 Altura Blvd.(90620), pg. 521
KNOTT'S BERRY FARM, 8039 Beach Blvd.(90620), pg. 637
LEACH CORPORATION, 6900 Orangethorpe Ave.(90622-5032), pg. 663
MEDIEVAL DINNER & TOURNAMENT, INC., 7662 Beach Blvd.(90622), pg. 735
THE MEDISCUS GROUP, 6900 Aragon Circle(90620), pg. 736
NutriLite Products, Inc., 5600 Beach Blvd.(90620), pg. 70

Burbank

ASI Market Research, Inc., 2600 W. Olive Ave.(91505), pg. 560
Aratex Services, Inc., 115 N. First St.(91502), pg. 6
AVIBANK MFG., INC., 210 S. Victory Blvd.(91502), pg. 102
Compact Sound Services, 2813 W. Alameda Ave.(91505), pg. 74
Compact Video Services, Inc., 2813 W. Alameda(91505), pg. 74
Entertainment Partners, 2600 W. Olive St.(91505), pg. 560
Harrison Div., 3020 Empire Ave.(91504), pg. 1003
HASKEL, INC., 100 E. Graham Pl.(91502), pg. 516
Image Transform Lab, 3611 San Fernando Road(91506), pg. 74
DONALD D. LEWIS ADVERTISING, 405 Riverside Dr.(91506), pg. 672
J.H. MCCORMICK, INC., 2507 Empire Ave.(91504), pg. 727
OROAMERICA, INC., 443 N. Varney St.(91502), pg. 830
Production Payments, Inc., 2600 W. Olive St.(91505), pg. 560
RYAN HERCO PRODUCTS CORP., 2509 N. Naomi St.(91504), pg. 958
Shamrock Broadcasting, Inc., Shamrock Center, 4444 Lakeside Dr.(91505), pg. 994
SHAMROCK HOLDINGS, INC., Shamrock Center, 4444 Lakeside Dr.(91505), pg. 994
Stainless Steel Products, Inc., 2980 San Fernando(91504), pg. 1220
SWANER HARDWOOD COMPANY, INC., 5 W. Magnolia Blvd.(91502), pg. 1066
Talent & Residuals, Inc., 2600 W. Olive Ave.(91505), pg. 560
UNIHEALTH AMERICA, 4100 W. Alameda(91505), pg. 1126
Verdugo Restaurant Corp., 1250 Harvard Rd.(91503), pg. 1028
Western International Media Corporation, 500 S. Buena Vista Rd., 1180
WILSHIRE NEWPORT INC., 4002 W. Burbank Blvd.(91505), pg. 1193
WINSTON TIRE COMPANY, 900 W. Alameda(91506), pg. 1197
WORLD TITLE COMPANY, 7530 N. Glenoaks Blvd.(91504), pg. 1203

Burlingame

Aerolyte Systems, 1657 Rollins Rd.(94010), pg. 254
DAKIN, INC., Worldwide Headquarters, 1649 Adrian Rd.(94010), pg. 311
MAGIC PAN INTERNATIONAL INC., 818 Burlway Rd.(94010), pg. 700
PMT of the Southwest, Inc., 1766 El Camino Real(94010), pg. 75
Pacific Motor Transport Co., 1766 El Camino Real(94010), pg. 75
Pacific Motor Trucking Co., 1766 El Camino Real(94010), pg. 75
THE WORNICK COMPANY, 500 Airport Blvd., Ste. 442(94010), pg. 1203
Wornick Properties, Inc., 500 Airport Blvd., Ste. 442, P.O. Box 1700(94011), pg. 1203

Burney

Dicalite Corporation, Rte. 1, Box 600(96013), pg. 136

Calabasas

ENVIRONMENTAL INDUSTRIES, INC., 24121 Ventura Blvd.(91302), pg. 383
GRIFFIN HOMES, INC., 24005 Ventura Blvd.(91302), pg. 487
WESTERN DATA SYSTEMS, 26707 Agoura Rd.(91302), pg. 1178

Calistoga

CRYSTAL GEYSER, 501 Washington(94515), pg. 303

Camarillo

MEDICAL ANALYSIS SYSTEMS INC., 542 Flynn Rd.(93010), pg. 735
POWER-ONE, INC., 740 Calle Plano(93012), pg. 883
Tax Forms Printing, 943 Flynn Rd.(93012), pg. 1081

Cameron Park

Mavis Industries, Inc., 2976 Alhambra Dr.(95682), pg. 449

Campbell

Network Capital Group, 1999 S. Bascom, Ste. 400(95008), pg. 798

Canoga Park

CONDOR PACIFIC INDUSTRIES, INC., 8053 Deering Ave.(91304), pg. 273
FABER ENTERPRISES, INC., 6606 Variel Ave.(91303), pg. 395
MALIBU GRAND PRIX CORPORATION, 7301 Topanga Canyon Blvd.(91303), pg. 702
Redken Intl. (Pacific), Inc., 6625 Variel Ave.(91303), pg. 919
Redken Laboratories (DISC), Inc., 6625 Variel Ave.(91303), pg. 919
REDKEN LABORATORIES, INC., 6625 Variel Ave.(91303), pg. 919

Carlsbad

Artecon, Inc., 2440 Impala Dr., Dept. 5500(92008), pg. 809
Comprehensive Business Services Inc., 1925 Palomar Oaks Way 612

Geographic Index

Eaton Leonard Technologies, Inc., 6305 El Camino Real(92009), pg. 1220
JAZZERCISE, INC., 2808 Roosevelt St.(92008), pg. 591
Langert Golf Co., Inc., 2774 Loker Ave. W.(92008), pg. 890
Magnedyne Div., 2258 Rutherford Rd.(92008), pg. 1003
SEABOARD ELECTRONICS CO., 6986 El Camino Real, Ste. B-205(92009), pg. 983
STILLMAN SEAL, 6020 Avenida Encinas(92009), pg. 1049
THE UPPER DECK COMPANY, 5909 The Otter Place(92008), pg. 1140

Carson

Barton Brands of California, Inc., 2202 E. Del Amo Blvd.(90749), pg. 123
E F INDUSTRIES, 16434 Ishida Ave.(90248), pg. 359
GOOD COMPANIES, 118 E. 223rd St.(90745), pg. 470
PURITAN BAKERY, INC., 1624 E. Carson St.(90745), pg. 900
STANDARD COMMUNICATIONS CORPORATION, 108 W. Victoria(90746), pg. 1036
SUN COMPUTERS, INC., One Civic Plaza, Ste. 600(90745), pg. 1058

Castroville

ARTICHOKE INDUSTRIES, INC., 11599 Walsh St.(95012), pg. 87
CALIFORNIA ARTICHOKE & VEGETABLE GROWERS CORP., 11500 Del Monte Ave.(95012), pg. 209
Mr. Artichoke Packing Co., Inc., 11500 Blackie Rd.(95012), pg. 209

Cerritos

CALIFORNIA PANEL & VENEER COMPANY, 14055 Artesia Blvd.(90701), pg. 210
Cardis Corporation, 12950 E. Alondra Blvd.(90701), pg. 224
CERRITOS FORD, INC., 18900 Studebaker Rd.(90701), pg. 236
Sasco Electric, 12900 Alondra Blvd.(90701), pg. 972
SASCO GROUP, 12900 Alondra Blvd.(90701), pg. 971

Chatsworth

AMPERIF CORPORATION, 9232 Eton Ave.(91311), pg. 68
CHATSWORTH DATA CORPORATION, 20710 Lassen St.(91311), pg. 241
CUSTOM CONTROL SENSORS, INC., 21111 Plummer St.(91311), pg. 306
HYDRAULICS INTERNATIONAL, INC., 9000 Mason Ave.(91311), pg. 556
HYDRO-MILL CO., 9301 Mason Ave.(91311), pg. 557
LEVLAD, INC., 9183-5 Kelvin Ave.(91311), pg. 671
MCRB Fulfillment Co., 21330 Superior St.(91311), pg. 692
MERCURY DISTRIBUTING CO., INC., 9600 Lurline Ave.(91311), pg. 740
TimeMed Labeling Systems, Inc., 9566 Vassar Ave.(91311), pg. 1098
WINDSOR PUBLICATIONS, INC., 21827 Nordhoff St.(91311), pg. 1196

Chino

COWDEN METAL SPECIALTIES, INC., 4626 Eucalyptus Ave.(91708), pg. 291
L & L NURSERY SUPPLY, INC., 5350 G St.(91710), pg. 647
Modern Wood Products, Inc., 14211 Ramona Ave.(91710), pg. 291
Taylor's Hitek Product Finishing, Inc., 14450 Yorba Ave.(91710), pg. 291

Chula Vista

GENERAL TEXTILES, 1690 Brandywine(91911), pg. 451
HYSPAN PRECISION PRODUCTS, INC., 1685 Brandywine Ave.(91911), pg. 557

City of Commerce

Andrea International, 2220 Gaspar Ave.(90040), pg. 81
ARDELL INTERNATIONAL, INC., 2220 Gaspar Ave.(90040), pg. 81
Chairworld, Inc., 2638 Yates Ave.(90040), pg. 463
Chemifax, 6423 Bandini Blvd.(90040), pg. 159
Clubman, 2220 Gaspar Ave.(90040), pg. 81
Delore, 2220 Gaspar Ave.(90040), pg. 81
Double H West Shoe Wholesale, 2300 S. Garfield Ave.(90040), pg. 182
GiGi, 2220 Gaspar Ave.(90040), pg. 81
I SKI SKI GOGGLES, 1935 Tubeway(90040), pg. 557
Standard Flour Co., 2425 Saybrook Ave.(90040), pg. 1178
SuperNail, 2220 Gaspar Ave.(90040), pg. 81
WOLFER PRINTING COMPANY, 6670 E. Flotilla St.(90040), pg. 1199

City of Industry

ACORN ENGINEERING COMPANY, 15125 Proctor Ave.(91744), pg. 14
ADAMS RITE MANUFACTURING CO., 4040 S. Capital Ave.(91749), pg. 16
Allfast Facility, 15200 E. Don Julian Rd.(91745), pg. 37
ALLFAST FASTENING SYSTEMS, INC., 15200 E. Don Julian Rd.(91745), pg. 37
APPLIED SOLAR ENERGY CORPORATION, 15251 E. Don Julian Rd.(91746), pg. 79
BENTLEY MILLS, INC., 14641 E. Don Julian Rd.(91746), pg. 140
CACIQUE CHEESE CO., INC., 14940 Proctor Ave.(91744), pg. 206
California Hardware Co., 13085 East Temple(91746), pg. 340
CALIFORNIA HARDWARE CO., 13085 E. Temple Ave.(91746), pg. 209
CALIFORNIA MANUFACTURING ENTERPRISES, 19481 San Jose Ave.(91748), pg. 210
Costal Wood Products, Inc., 13110 Louden Lane, pg. 727
CROWN PRINCE, INC. (CA), 17031 Green Dr.(91745), pg. 302
Draw Co., 427 N. Baldwin Park Blvd.(91746), pg. 574
Elixir Industries, 17770 E. Rowland(91748), pg. 376
Great Vibrations Div., 427 N. Baldwin Park Blvd.(91746), pg. 574
GUARANTEED PRODUCTS, INC., 355 N. Vineland Ave.(91746), pg. 491
INGRAM PAPER COMPANY, 17411 Valley Blvd.(91744), pg. 569
INTERBATH, INC., 427 N. Baldwin Park Blvd.(91746), pg. 574
KERN INDUSTRIES, 13000 E. Temple Ave.(91749-1207), pg. 624
Kilsby-Roberts/Los Angeles, 3700 S. Capital Ave.(91749), pg. 606
LA VICTORIA FOODS, INC., 240 S. 6th Ave.(91746), pg. 649
M M M SALES, INC., 14214 Lomitas Ave(91746), pg. 692
Macklanburg-Duncan Co. of California, Inc., 15257 Proctor Ave.(91745), pg. 697
Ondine Div., 427 N. Baldwin Park Blvd(91746), pg. 574
Pen-Tab Industries Of California, Inc., 911 Bixby Dr.(91747), pg. 857
Plastron, 19555 E. Arenth Ave.(91748), pg. 15
PRESTO FOOD PRODUCTS, INC., 18275 Arenth Ave.(91748), pg. 888
Quadrastat Corp., 3860 S. Capitol Ave.(91749), pg. 17
REULAND ELECTRIC COMPANY, 17969 E. Railroad(91748), pg. 930
Richmond Screw Anchor Division, 17051 E. Green Drive(91716), pg. 1069
Roberts Consolidated Industries, 600 N. Baldwin Park Blvd.(91749), pg. 350
SMARTY PANTS N TOPS TOO, INC., 1115 John Reed Ct.(91745), pg. 1011
Smith Mailer, 19481 San Jose Ave.(91748), pg. 210
STROUDS, 780 So. Nogales St.(91748), pg. 1054
Troy/Trak Lighting, Inc., 14625 E. Clark Ave.(91746), pg. 588
UTILITY TRAILER MANUFACTURING CO., 17295 E. Railroad St.(91749), pg. 1141
VALLEY DETROIT DIESEL ALLISON, 13644 E. Nelson(91746), pg. 1143
Western Specialty Container, 17955 E. Ajax Circle(91748), pg. 565
WWF Paper Corporation - West (California), 2727 Workman Mill Rd.(91746), pg. 1157
YALE INDUSTRIAL TRUCKS OF SOUTHERN CALIFORNIA, 2615 Pellissier(91742), pg. 1207
YUM YUM DONUT SHOP, INC., 18830 E. San Jose Ave.(91748), pg. 1214

Claremont

GREEN SPOT PACKAGING INC., 100 S. Cambridge(91711-4842), pg. 485
THE YUCAIPA COMPANIES, 250 W. First St., Ste. 210(91711), pg. 1214

Clarksburg

DELTA SUGAR CORPORATION, 35265 Willow Ave., P.O. Box 58(95612), pg. 327

Coalinga

HARRIS FARMS, INC., Rte. 1, Box 420(93210), pg. 511
Harris Feeding Co., Rte. 1, Box 400(93210), pg. 512
Harris Ranch Restaurant, Rte. 1 Box 777, Interstate 5 & Hwy. 198(93210), pg. 512
Inn at Harris Ranch, Rte. 1 Box 777, Interstate 5 & Hwy. 198(93210), pg. 512

Compton

Anchorlok Corp., 2910 E. Ana(90221), pg. 664
BEAUCHAMP DISTRIBUTING COMPANY, 1911 S. Santa Fe Ave.(90221), pg. 130
BROOKHURST, INC., 107 W. Carob(90220), pg. 179
CONTINENTAL FORGE COMPANY, 512 E. Carlin St.(90222), pg. 279
Cragar Industries, 19007 S. Reyes(90221), pg. 761
HOLLYWOOD ALLOY CASTING COMPANY, 2000 S. Santa Fe Ave.(90221), pg. 540
Homestead Products, 1220 Kona Dr.(90220), pg. 986
HOUSTON FEARLESS 76 INC., 203 W. Artesia Blvd.(90220-5550), pg. 546
KRACO ENTERPRISES, INC., 505 E. Euclid Ave.(90224), pg. 643
MODULITE CORPORATION, 921 W. Artesia Blvd.(90220), pg. 763
MURDOCK, INC., 15800 S. Avalon(90220), pg. 776

Concord

CALIFORNIA & HAWAIIAN SUGAR COMPANY, 1390 Willow Pass Rd.(94520), pg. 210
Concord Division, 1221 Franquette Ave.(94520), pg. 75
J. E. HIGGINS LUMBER CO., 1485 Enea Ct., Ste. 1100(94520), pg. 533
Micropump, 1990 Olivera Rd.(94520), pg. 749
Tuthill Pump Company of California, 5143 Port Chicago Hwy.(94520), pg. 1120
Valley Manor Care, 3806 Clayton Rd.(94521), pg. 740

Corona

COX HOBBIES, INC., 350 W. Rincon St.(91720), pg. 294
FLEETWOOD ALUMINUM PRODUCTS, 2485 Railroad St.(91720), pg. 417
Hayden, Inc., P.O. Box 848, 1531 Pomona Rd.(91720), pg. 385
NATURE'S RECIPE PET FOODS, 341 Bonnie Circle(91720), pg. 796
Pacific Clay Products, P.O. Box 1149, (91720), pg. 840
Schnadig Corp., 1350 Railroad Ave.(91720), pg. 977
SILVERCREST WESTERN HOME INDUSTRIES CORPORATION, 299 North Smith Avenue(91720), pg. 1004

Corona del Mar

Five Crowns, 3801 E. Coast Hwy.(92625), pg. 663

Corte Madera

Midwest Agri-Commodities, 100 Tamal Plaza, Ste. 180, 200 Tamal Vista Blvd.(94925), pg. 1022

Costa Mesa

BASSO & ASSOCIATES INC. ADV. & PUBLIC RELATIONS, 3158 Redhill Ave., Ste. 200(92626), pg. 125
Boat Transit, Inc., 1343 Logan Ave.(92626), pg. 609
J. C. CARTER COMPANY, INC., 671 W. 17th St.(92627), pg. 226
DEL TACO, INC., 345 Baker St.(92626), pg. 325
GRISWOLD INDUSTRIES, INC., 1701 Placentia Ave.(92627), pg. 488
KNIGHT EQUIPMENT CORP., 2945 Airway Ave.(92627), pg. 636
LOVE'S ENTERPRISES, INC., 3195-C Airport Loop Dr., Ste. B(92626), pg. 685
Mary Kay Cosmetics, Inc., 3500 Hyland(92626), pg. 717
The Nadel Partnership, Inc., 3090 Bristol St., Ste. 200(92626), pg. 783
SALVATI MONTGOMERY SAKODA, INC., 535 Anton Blvd., Ste. 600(92626), pg. 967
Stacoswitch, Inc., 1139 Baker St.(92626), pg. 270
Valentec International Corp., 3190 Pullman Lane(92626), pg. 571
WARMINGTON HOMES, 3090 Pullman Ave., Ste. A(92626), pg. 1164

Covina

Grocers & Merchants Insurance Service, 874 S. Village Oak Dr.(91724), pg. 237

Cucamonga

General Latex & Chemical Corporation, P.O. Box 748(91729), pg. 449

Culver City

ELS Educational Services, 5761 Buckingham Pkwy.(90230), pg. 56
ELECTRO AD AGENCY, INC., 10950 Washington Blvd.(90230), pg. 374
THE GARY GROUP, 9046 Lindblade St.(90232), pg. 444
LANZ, INC., 8680 Hayden Pl.(90232), pg. 658
Jack Nadel, Inc. Div., 9950 W. Jefferson Blvd.(90232), pg. 734
L. POWELL CO., INC., 8631 Hayden Pl.(90232), pg. 882
WAHL INSTRUMENTS, 5750 Hannum Ave.(90231), pg. 1158

Cypress

Bioproducts, Inc., 5421 Philo St.(90630), pg. 152
Burns & Roe Pacific Company, 10805 Holder St., Ste.250(90630-5144), pg. 194
KYB Corp. of America, 6601 Darin Way(90630), pg. 613
PacifiCare Health Systems, Inc., 5995 Plaza Dr.(90630) pg. 1127
PacifiCare of California, 5796 Corporate Ave.(90630), pg. 1127

Dana Point

Kettenburg Marine/Dana Point, 34467 Golden Lantern(92629), pg. 626

Dinuba

RUIZ FOOD PRODUCTS, INC., 501 S. Alta(93618), pg. 955

Dixon

Heil West, Inc., 1450 N. First St.(95620), pg. 526

Dominguez Hills

EDUCATIONAL INSIGHTS, INC., 19560 Rancho Way(90220), pg. 369

Downey

ALL AMERICAN HOME CENTER, 7201 E. Firestone Blvd.(90241), pg. 35
DUARY/J.F. DUNCAN INDUSTRIES, INC., 9301 Steward & Gray Rds.(90241), pg. 350
THRIFTY OIL COMPANY, 10000 Lakewood Blvd.(90240), pg. 1096

Duarte

GLASTEEL INDUSTRIAL LAMINATES, 1727 Buena Vista(91010), pg. 461
TELE-COM PRODUCTS, INC., 1070 Hamilton Rd.(91010), pg. 1084
VARI TRONICS COMPANY, INC., 2745 E. Huntington Dr.(91010), pg. 1145

Dublin

STRAW HAT COOPERATIVE CORP., 6400 Village Pkwy.(94568), pg. 1053

El Cajon

Antiques & Collectibles, 1000 Pioneer Way(92022), pg. 656
BUCK KNIVES, INC., 1900 Weld Blvd.(92020), pg. 185

The Californian, P.O. Box 1565, 1000 Pioneer Way(92022), pg. 656
Grafalloy Inc., 1020 N. Marshall Ave., pg. 890
Precision Metal Prods., Inc., 850 W. Bradley Ave.(92022), pg. 869
Senior World (California), 1000 Pioneer Way(92022), pg. 656
SoniForm, Inc., 1908 Friendship Drive(92020), pg. 695

El Monte

BROOKS PRODUCTS, INC., 10141 Olney St.(91734), pg. 180
CHADWICK-HELMUTH COMPANY, INC., 4601 N. Arden Dr.(91731), pg. 237
CLAYTON INDUSTRIES CO., 4213 N. Temple City Blvd.(91731), pg. 253
DBM HATCH, INC., 2304 Troy Ave.(91733), pg. 308
M.C. GILL CORPORATION, 4056 Easy St.(91731), pg. 458
GREGG INDUSTRIES, INC., 10460 Hickson St.(91734), pg. 486
International Div., 4213 N. Temple City Blvd.(91731), pg. 254
KELLER CONSTRUCTION COMPANY LTD., 9950 E. Baldwin Pl.(91731), pg. 620
MCCONNELL CABINETS, INC., 3017 N. Rumford(91732), pg. 727
NAVCOM DEFENSE ELECTRONICS, INC., 4323 N. Arden Dr.(91731), pg. 796
SARGENT-FLETCHER CO., 9400 E. Flair Drive(91731), pg. 970

El Segundo

THE AEROSPACE CORPORATION, 2350 E. El Segundo Blvd.(90245-4691), pg. 22
Alpha United, 1301 E. El Segundo Blvd.(90245), pg. 690
Ampex Computer Products Division, 200 N. Nash St.(90245), pg. 998

El Toro

Professional Community Management, Inc., 23726 Birtcher Drive(92630), pg. 24

Elk Grove

GIBSON WINE COMPANY, 9750 Kent St.(95624-0726), pg. 457

Emeryville

ELECTRO-COATINGS, INC., 1401 Park Ave.(94608), pg. 374
FARALLON COMPUTING, INC., 2000 Powell St., Ste. 600(94608), pg. 399
NADY SYSTEMS, INC., 6701 Bay St.(94608), pg. 783
Ziff-Davis Press, 5903 Christie Ave.(94608), pg. 1219

Encinitas

PAUL ECKE RANCH, INC., 441 Saxony Rd.(92024), pg. 366

Encino

Dentsply/Implant Division, 15821 Ventura Blvd.(91436), pg. 330
FIRST FINANCIAL GROUP, INC., 16830 Ventura Blvd., Ste. 600(91436), pg. 413
General Growth of California, Inc., 15821 Ventura Blvd., Ste. 525(91436), pg. 449
Integrated Financial, 16530 Ventura Blvd., Ste. 500(91436), pg. 573
LARWIN COMPANY, 16255 Ventura Blvd., Ste. 900(91436), pg. 659
Ruder, Finn, Inc., 16027 Ventura Blvd. Ste. 500(91436-0032), pg. 954
TRIZEC PROPERTIES, INC., 15760 Ventura Blvd., Ste. 500(91436), pg. 1115

Escalon

Rich Fruit Pak Co., 19901 S. McHenry Ave.(95320), pg. 932

Escondido

ATI INDUSTRIES, 2425 Vineyard(92025), pg. 8
Robert F. Driver & Co., Inc., 613 W. Valley Pkwy., Ste. 220(92025-2550), pg. 349
HAWTHORNE LIFT SYSTEMS, 1044 W. Washington Ave.(92025), pg. 519
San Diego Wild Animal Park, 15500 San Pasqual Valley Rd.(92027), pg. 969

Eureka

Cox Cable Humboldt, Inc., 911 W. Wabash(95501), pg. 294
General Hospital, 2200 Harrison Ave.(95501), pg. 176
Utility Tree Service, 104 W. Street(95501), pg. 123

Exeter

JACK GRIGGS INC., 1149 S. Kaweah(93221), pg. 488

Fallbrook

Overly Manufacturing, 1501 S. Mission Rd.(92028), pg. 833

Folsom

Amfac Distribution Corporation, 81 Blue Ravine Rd.(95630), pg. 585
Amfac Health Care, 81 Blue Ravine Rd.(95630), pg. 585
WETSEL-OVIATT LUMBER COMPANY, P.O. Box 910(95763), pg. 1183
WHITMIRE DISTRIBUTION, 81 Blue Ravine Rd.(95630), pg. 1187

Fontana

AMICO-West Distr. Center, 11093 Beech Ave.(92335), pg. 29
Pacific Coast Brush Co., 11690 Pacific Ave.(92335), pg. 419
Pacific Forge, Inc., 10641 Etiwanda Ave.(92335), pg. 102
QPP Quality Piping Products, 10516 Commerce Way(92335), pg. 806
SCRIPTO-TOKAI, INC., 11591 Etiwanda Ave.(92335), pg. 983
Southern California Auto Auction, 10700 Beech Ave.(92335), pg. 293

Foster City

Information Access Co., 362 Lakeside Dr.(94404), pg. 1219
KAISER AEROSPACE & ELECTRONICS CORP., 950 Tower Lane, Ste. 800(94404), pg. 614
Leasametric, Inc., 1164 Triton Dr.(94404), pg. 712
LINC Quantum Analytics, 363-D Vintage Park Dr.(94404), pg. 648
Lincoln Property Co., Northern California, 101 Lincoln Center Dr.(94404), pg. 676
LYON'S RESTAURANTS, INC., 1165 Triton Dr.(94404), pg. 690
MacUser, 110 Marsh Dr.(94404), pg. 1218
Metric Realty, Inc., 950 Tower Lane(94404), pg. 745
PC Computing, 950 Tower Lane(94404), pg. 1219
LELAND A. WOLF & ASSOCIATES, 100 Foster City Blvd.(94404), pg. 1199

Fountain Valley

ASICS TIGER CORPORATION, 10540 Talbert Ave.(92708), pg. 8
ANDIAMO, INC., P.O. Box 8415, (92728), pg. 74
Employee Benefits America, 17360 Brookhurst(92708), pg. 841
MWC Lighting Systems, Inc., 10870 Kalama River Rd.(92708), pg. 588
PM Group Life Insurance Company, 17360 Brookhurst St.(92708), pg. 841

Fremont

AMERICAN MITAC CORPORATION, 48571 Milmont Dr.(94538), pg. 58
COVALENT SYSTEMS CORPORATION, 47436 Fremont Blvd.(94538-5026), pg. 290
Inkel Technology, 4181 Business Center Dr.(94538-6355), pg. 570
LASKEY ASSOCIATES, 39210 State St.(94538), pg. 660
LOGISTIX, 48021 Warm Springs Blvd.(94539), pg. 681
Parkmont Nursing Home, 2400 Parkside Dr.(94536), pg. 740
Sherwood Corporation, 4181 Business Center Dr.(94538-6355), pg. 570
Telescience Transmission Systems, Inc., 48761 Kato Rd.(94538), pg. 1085
Tri Valley Growers Container Division, Inc., 41099 Boyce Rd.(94538-2498), pg. 1111

Fresno

ATAPCO Globe-Weis/Fresno, 2851 E. Florence St.(93721), pg. 64
CAL/EMBLEM LABELS, INC., 4790 W. Jacquelyn Ave.(93722), pg. 208
Continental/Murray, 3912 S. Front(93725), pg. 279
Dunavant Enterprises, 1410 F St.(93771), pg. 352
Fresno Auto Dealers Auction, 278 North Marks(93706), pg. 293
Lundberg and Associates, 265 W. Bullard, Ste. 101(93704-1706), pg. 662
MOYER PRODUCTS, INC., 1540 E. Shaw, Ste. 101(93710), pg. 774
Peabody Floway, Inc., 2494 S. Railroad Ave., P.O. Box 164(93707), pg. 899
RANCHERS COTTON OIL, 2691 S. Cedar Ave.(93725), pg. 911
SEABROOK FOODS, INC., 4974 E. Clinton Way(93747), pg. 984
Ulbrich of California, Inc., 5455 E. Home Ave.(93727), pg. 1125
Uniroyal Chemical Co., Inc., 1530 E. Shaw, Ste. 105(93710), pg. 1129
United States Cold Storage of Calif., 2003 S. Cherry St.(93718), pg. 1135
Valley Fig Growers, 2028 S. 3rd.(93718), pg. 1058
WESTAIR HOLDING INC., 5570 Air Terminal Dr.(93727), pg. 1178

Fullerton

AEI HOLDING CO., INC., 1600 E. Valencia Dr.(92631), pg. 3
American Electronics, Inc., 1600 E. Valencia Dr.(92631), pg. 3
CAMBIO EQUITIES CORP., 310 N. Harbor Blvd.(92632), pg. 211
Carriage House Manor, 245 E. Wilshire(92632), pg. 740
D/B Cameras Microcheck Division, 1600 E. Valencia Dr.(92631), pg. 3
Dressen-Barnes Electronics Div., 1600 E. Valencia Dr.(92631), pg. 3
Electro-Mechanical Instruments Div., 1600 E. Valencia Dr.(92631), pg. 3
Harte-Hanks Direct Mail/California, 2337 W. Commonwealth Ave.(92633), pg. 513
JONATHAN MANUFACTURING CORP., 1101 S. Acacia Ave.(92631), pg. 602
LABEL-AIRE INC., 550 Burning Tree Rd.(92633), pg. 649
Microdot Aerospace Fastening Systems Group, 800 South State College Blvd.(92634-3001), pg. 749
North American Enclosures, Inc., 501 Airpark Drive(92633), pg. 811
Precision Power Div., 1600 E. Valencia Dr.(92634), pg. 3
Quadrant Engineering Div., 1600 E. Valencia Dr.(92634), pg. 3

Garden Grove

AIR INDUSTRIES CORPORATION, 12570 Knott St.(92641), pg. 27
BTD/TMP Worldwide, 13252 Garden Grove Blvd., Ste. 100(92643), pg. 1073
Data Aire, Inc., 7442 Orangewood(92675), pg. 277
New Hermes Inc.-West Coast, 11711 Monarch St.(92641), pg. 801
PTC Aerospace, 11752 Markon Dr.(92641), pg. 899
PTC Aerospace, 11752 Markon Dr.(92641), pg. 837
Tash, Inc., 12681 Pala Dr.(92641), pg. 1080
Todd Pipe & Supply Garden Grove, 13591 Harbor Blvd.(92643), pg. 1100

Gardena

AMELCO CORPORATION, 19208 S. Vermont Ave.(90248), pg. 47
AMERICAN MARKETING WORKS & INTERNATIONAL CORPORATION, 14501 S. Figueroa(90248), pg. 58
APPAREL VENTURES, INC., 204 W. Rosecrans(90248), pg. 78
BENJAMIN METALS COMPANY, 14400 S. Figueroa St.(90248), pg. 139
CHRISTIE ELECTRIC CORPORATION, 18120 S. Broadway(90248), pg. 249
Dauman Displays, Inc., 1970 W. 139th(90247), pg. 279
DIE CAST PRODUCTS, INC., 621 W. Rosecrans Ave.(90248), pg. 336
ERNST W. DORN CO., INC., 15905 S. Broadway(90248), pg. 346
Electronic Plating Service, Inc., 13021 S. Budlong Ave.(90247), pg. 612
ELIXIR INDUSTRIES, 17925 S. Broadway(90248), pg. 376
Elixir Industries/Alum-A-Form Div., 17905 S. Broadway(90248), pg. 376
Charles Leonard Western, Inc., 13617 S. St. Andrew Pl.(90249), pg. 668
LORBER INDUSTRIES OF CALIFORNIA, 17908 S. Figueroa(90248), pg. 683
NUHAHN, INC., 614 W. 184th St.(90248), pg. 817
OVERTON MOORE & ASSOCIATES, 1125 W. 190th St., Ste. 200(90248), pg. 833
Pacific Electricord Co., 747 W. Redondo Beach Blvd.(90247), pg. 671
PUTZMEISTER, INC., 18601 S. Main St.(90248), pg. 901
SWIFT-COR TOOL ENGINEERING, 344 W. 157th St.(90248), pg. 1067
WEISS SHEET METAL COMPANY, 1715 W. 135th St.(90249), pg. 1174

Gilroy

NOB HILL GENERAL STORE, INC., 200 E. 10th St.(95020), pg. 807

Glen Ellen

GLEN ELLEN WINERY, 1883 London Ranch Rd.(95442), pg. 461

Glendale

Adams Rite Products Inc., 540 W. Chevy Chase Dr.(91204), pg. 237
AIR CONDITIONING CO., INC., 6265 San Fernando Rd.(91201), pg. 26
Bekins BoxStores, 777 Flower St.(91201), pg. 133
THE BEKINS COMPANY, 777 Flower St.(91201), pg. 132
Bekins Moving & Storage Co., 777 Flower St.(91201), pg. 133
CALIFORNIA OFFSET PRINTERS, INC., 620 W. Elk Ave.(91204), pg. 210
CELLULAR SERVICE, INC., 6100 San Fernando Rd.(91201), pg. 231
Glendale Memorial Hospital and Medical Center, Central and Los Feliz(91225-7036), pg. 1127
MINARIK ELECTRIC COMPANY, 901 E. Thompson St.(91201), pg. 756
Public Storage Commercial Properties Group, Inc., 600 N. Brant Blvd., Ste. 300(91203), pg. 898
PUBLIC STORAGE, INC., 600 N. Brant Blvd., Ste. 300(91203), pg. 898
Southwest Doall Industrial Supply, 514 Riverdale Dr.(91204), pg. 342
ZMP, Inc., 540 W. Chevy Chase Dr.(91204), pg. 237

Glendora

CALTROL, INC., 2011 E. Financial Way(91740), pg. 211
RAIN BIRD SPRINKLER MFG. CORP., 145 N. Grand(91740), pg. 910
TREASURE CHEST ADVERTISING CO., INC., 511 W. Citrus Edge(91740), pg. 1108

Goleta

Cox Cable Santa Barbara, Inc., 22 S. Fairview(93117), pg. 294
SMARTSTAR CORPORATION, 120 Cremona Dr.(93117), pg. 1011
SOFTOOL CORPORATION, 340 S. Kellogg Ave.(93117), pg. 1016

Gonzales

VINTNERS INTERNATIONAL COMPANY, INC., P.O. Box 780(93926), pg. 1152

Geographic Index

Granada Hills

Mission Hills Restaurant Corp., 15600 Odyssey Dr.(91344), pg. 1028

Grand Terrace

Hood Communications, Inc., 21496 Main St.(92324), pg. 543

Harbor City

GHN, 24000 S. Vermont Rd.(90710), pg. 391

Hawthorne

ANCRA CORPORATION, 4880 W. Rosecrans Ave.(90250), pg. 72
BGW SYSTEMS, INC., 13130 Yukon Ave.(90250), pg. 106
MARCO COLOR LABS, INC., 12410 Wilkie Ave.(90250), pg. 706
TODD PIPE & SUPPLY HAWTHORNE, 4828 W. 145th St.(90251), pg. 1100
UDT SENSORS, INC., 12525 Chadron Ave.(90250), pg. 1122

Hayfork

Sierra Pacific Industries-Hayfork Division, (96041), pg. 1003

Hayward

ANNABELLE CANDY COMPANY, 27211 Industrial Blvd.(94545), pg. 75
Bay Cities Auto Auction, 29900 Auction Way(94544), pg. 293
Samuel Cabot, Inc., 23284 Eichler St.(94545), pg. 206
CHEMCENTRAL/San Francisco, 31702 Hayman(94544), pg. 242
Jetstream Systems, 3486 Investment Blvd.(94545), pg. 122
Kilsby-Roberts/Hayward, 31100 Weigman Rd.(94544), pg. 606
LAFAYETTE MANUFACTURING, INC., 3440 Enterprise Ave.(94545), pg. 650
LIFE LINE NUTRITIONALS, INC., 3317 Arden Rd.(94545), pg. 675
Majestic Pines Care Center, 1628 "B" St.(94541), pg. 740
MULTIPLE ALLIED SERVICES, INC., 3157 Corporate Pl.(94545), pg. 775
Old Stone Bank of California, 24970 Hesperian Blvd.(94545), pg. 823
Paxall Pak-Master Machinery, 31800 Hayman St.(94544), pg. 852
Paxall Parsons Machinery, 31800 Hayman St.(94544), pg. 852
SELECTONE CORPORATION, 23278 Bernhardt St.(94545), pg. 988

Healdsburg

MARTIN FOREST INDUSTRIES, P.O. Box 159(95448), pg. 715

Hollywood

BERTRAND ADVERTISING AGENCY, INC., 1680 N. Vine St., Ste. 406(90028), pg. 144
C & L Marketing Inc., 1750 No. Vine St.(90028), pg. 216
CAPITOL INDUSTRIES-EMI INC., 1750 N. Vine St.(90028), pg. 216
Capitol Records, Inc., 1750 N. Vine St.(90028), pg. 216
EMI Music Publishing North America, 6920 Sunset Blvd.(90028), pg. 216
KINGSLEY MACHINE CO., 850 Cahuenga Blvd.(90038), pg. 632
DAVID LANGER & CO., INC., 6430 Sunset Blvd., Suite 105(90028), pg. 657
Magnasync Moviola Corporation, 1135 Mansfield Ave.(90038), pg. 586
PARKS PRODUCTS, INC., 3611 Cahuenga(90068), pg. 850
TARGET ENTERPRISES LTD., 3375 Barham Blvd.(90068), pg. 1079

Huntington Beach

CAMBRO MANUFACTURING COMPANY, 7601 Clay Ave.(92648), pg. 211
Cercom Technologies, Inc., 15301 Transistor Ln.(92649), pg. 581
Comtool Technologies, 15301 Transistor Ln.(92649), pg. 581
Cost Care, Inc., 7711 Center Ave., Ste. 100(92647), pg. 596
INTERTRADE INDUSTRIES, 15301 Transistor Ln.(92649), pg. 581

Inglewood

ALAN LITHOGRAPH, INC., 550 N. Oak St.(90302), pg. 30
HOLLYWOOD PARK, INC., 1050 S. Prairie Ave.(90306), pg. 540
IBM FOODS, 506 S. Isis Ave.(90301), pg. 558
LOCUS COMPUTING CORP., 9800 La Cienega Blvd.(90301-4440), pg. 680
MARVIN ENGINEERING COMPANY, INC., 260 W. Beach Ave.(90302), pg. 716
STANDARD SHOE COMPANY, 1000 S. LaBrea(90301), pg. 1037
STORM PRODUCTS COMPANY, INC., 112 S. Glasgow Ave.(90301), pg. 1052
UNITED HEALTH PLAN, 3405 W. Imperial Hwy.(90303), pg. 1133
YOUR MAN TOURS, INC., 8331 Aviation Blvd.(90301), pg. 1214
Zephyr Mfg. Co., 201 S. Hindry Ave.(90307), pg. 1038

Ione

MASON OIL COMPANY, 117 W. Jackson St.(95640), pg. 718

Irvine

ADVANCED CONTROLS, INC., 16901 Jamboree Blvd.(92714), pg. 20
Alessi Incorporated, 35 Parker(92718), pg. 352
Backer Spielvogel Bates, Inc., 2010 Main St., Ste. 700(92714), pg. 108
BESTEEL INDUSTRIES, 15279 Alton Pkwy.(92718), pg. 147
BRETON CONSTRUCTION, INC., Two Corporate Park, Ste. 200(92714), pg. 174
Builders Emporium, 40 Parker(92718-1633), pg. 262
Carrows Restaurants, Inc., One Park Plaza, Ste. 900(92714), pg. 929
CASANOVA PENDRILL PUBLICIDAD INC., 3333 Michelson Dr., Ste. 300(92715), pg. 227
Century 21 Real Estate Corp., 2601 S.E. Main St.(92713), pg. 744
CORNUCOPIA, INC., 1722 Kettering(92714), pg. 287
DGWB, INC., 20 Executive Park, Ste. 200(92714), pg. 309
DEL MAR AVIONICS, 1601 Alton Ave.(92714), pg. 325
DOT PRINTER, INC., 2424 McGaw Ave.(92714), pg. 347
EMS-West, 22 Executive Park(92714), pg. 370
El Torito Restaurants, Inc., 2450 White Rd.(92714), pg. 929
EL TORITO RESTAURANTS, INC., 2450 White Rd.(92417), pg. 372
ENERGY & ENVIRONMENTAL RESEARCH CORP., 18 Mason Rd.(92718), pg. 381
EPOXYLITE CORPORATION, 9400 Toledo Way(92718), pg. 384
Far West Concepts, Inc., 2701 Alton Parkway(92714-5811), pg. 929
FLOJET CORPORATION, 12 Morgan St.(92718), pg. 419
4DAY TIRE STORES, 17662 Armstrong Ave.(17662), pg. 427
FREEDOM NEWSPAPERS INC., 17666 Fitch(92714), pg. 431
GRC Restaurants, Inc., 2701 Alton Parkway(92714-5811), pg. 929
IDC Irvine, 18008 Sky Park Circle, Ste. 145(92714), pg. 577
Irvine World News Newspaper Company, 2712 McGraw Ave.(92714), pg. 582
Jojos Restaurants, Inc., 2701 Alton(92714), pg. 929
Kitchell Contractors, Inc., 26 Executive Park, Suite 100(92714), pg. 634
LANSDALE, CARR & BAUM, 17662 Armstrong Ave.(92714), pg. 658
THE LUSK COMPANY, 17550 Gillette Ave.(92714), pg. 687
Lusk Interiors, Inc., 17550 Gillette Ave.(92713), pg. 688
MARUCHAN INC., 1902 Deere Ave.(92714), pg. 716
MCGAW, INC., 2525 McGaw Ave.(92714), pg. 729
Pepper West, Inc., 17941 Fitch(92714), pg. 860
RESTAURANT ENTERPRISES GROUP, INC., One Park Plaza, Ste. 900(92714), pg. 929
Rogerson ATS, 2201 Alton Ave.(92714), pg. 943
Rogerson Aircraft Controls, 2201 Alton Ave.(92714), pg. 943
ROGERSON AIRCRAFT CORPORATION, 2201 Alton Ave.(92714), pg. 943
Rogerson Aircraft Systems, 2201 Alton Ave.(92714), pg. 944
SHUGART CORPORATION, 9292 Jeronimo Rd.(92718), pg. 1001
Sterling Builders, Inc., 19762 MacArthur Blvd.(92715), pg. 1047
STERLING ELECTRIC, INC., 16752 Armstrong Ave.(92714), pg. 1046
Sterling Savings & Loan, 19752 MacArthur Blvd.(92715), pg. 1047
TH&M ADVERTISING, INC., 2600 Michelson Dr., Ste. 1500(92715), pg. 1073
Tropitone Furniture, 5 Marconi(92718), pg. 1116
WISDOM IMPORTS SALES CO. INC., 17401 Eastman(92714), pg. 1198

Irwindale

Davis Walker Corp., 5555 No. Irwindale Ave.(91706), pg. 525
DAVIS WIRE CORPORATION, 5555 N. Irwindale(91706), pg. 319
Fey Mfg. Co., Inc., 15854 Ornelas(91706), pg. 1038
HUGHES MARKETS INC., 19005 Live Oak Ave.(91706), pg. 552
Kennedy Company, 5801 Ayala Ave.(91706), pg. 1001
KIFUKI U.S.A. CO., INC., 15547 First St.(91706), pg. 629
STANDUN, INC., 15854 Ornelas St.(91706), pg. 1038
SUPERIOR FAST FREIGHT, 600 E. Live Oak Ave.(91706), pg. 1063

Jackson

PROSPECT MOTORS, INC., 645 Hwy. 49-88(95642), pg. 895

Kingsburg

Nutrius Dairy Feed Supplements Div., 39494 Clarkson Drive(93631), pg. 152

La Habra

Food 4 Less, Inc., 7777 S. Harbor Blvd.(90631), pg. 1214

La Jolla

Campus Point Realty Corporation, 10260 Campus Point Drive(92037), pg. 981
Computer Intelligence, 3344 N. Torrey Pines Ct.(92037), pg. 1219
THE COPLEY PRESS, INC., 7776 Ivanhoe Ave.(92037), pg. 284
National Health Laboratories Inc., 7590 Fay Ave.(92037), pg. 696

La Mesa

LA MESA R V CENTER, INC., 7601 Alvarado Rd.(92044), pg. 649

La Mirada

Andys Rental Inc., 16930 Valley View Ave.(90638), pg. 1206
INKEL CORP., 14830 Alondra Blvd.(90638), pg. 569
SOLID STATE DEVICES, INC., 14849 Firestone Blvd.(90638), pg. 1017
Western Operations, 16024 Phoebe Ave.(90638), pg. 268
X-A CABINET CORPORATION, 16930 Valley View Ave.(90638), pg. 1206

La Palma

Jani King of California, Inc., 1 Centerpointe Dr., Ste. 330(90623), pg. 589
La Palma Intercommunity Hospital, 7901 Walker St.(90623-1764), pg. 1127

La Puente

Sigma Plating Co., Ltd., 1040 Otterbein(91748), pg. 1033

Lafayette

BELL-CARTER FOODS, INC., 3742 Mt. Diablo Blvd.(94549), pg. 134

Laguna Beach

BERKELEY INDUSTRIES INC., 2825 Laguna Canyon Rd.(92652), pg. 141
First American Capital Bank, 310 Broadway(92651), pg. 1020
SOUTHERN CALIFORNIA BANCORP, 310 Broadway(92651), pg. 1020
Telonic Berkeley, 2825 Laguna Canyon Rd.(92652), pg. 141

Laguna Hills

Canyon Capital Inc., 24012 Calle de la Plata, Ste. 310(92653), pg. 612
Columbia General Life Insurance Co., 23282 Mill Creek Ste. 1300(92653), pg. 1127
TOWNSEND & O'LEARY, INC., 23282 Mill Creek Dr., 1104

Larkspur

Bonkers, Inc., Wood Island(94939), pg. 1150
Euston Station, Inc., Wood Island(94939), pg. 1150
Railhead Restaurants, Inc., Wood Island(94939), pg. 1150
Victoria Station of Arizona, Inc., Wood Island(94939), pg. 1150
Victoria Station of Atlanta, Inc., Wood Island(94939), pg. 1150
Victoria Station of Colorado, Inc., Wood Island(94939), pg. 1150
Victoria Station Incorporated, A California Corp., Wood Island(94939), pg. 1150
Victoria Station of Louisiana, Inc., Wood Island(94939), pg. 1150
Victoria Station of Texas, Inc., Wood Island(94939), pg. 1150
Victoria Station of Virginia, Inc., Wood Island(94939), pg. 1150
Victoria Station of Wisconsin, Inc., Wood Island(94939), pg. 1150

Lawndale

King Bear Auto Centers, 4603 Manhattan Beach Blvd.(90260), pg. 630
LA COMPUTER CENTER, 17013 Hawthorne Blvd.(90260), pg. 648

Lindsay

Lindsay Hospital Medical Center, 740 Sequoia Ave.(93247-1423), pg. 1127
LINDSAY OLIVE GROWERS, 650 W. Tulare Rd.(93247), pg. 676

Livermore

Davey Tree Surgery Co., 2617 S. Vasco Rd.(94550), pg. 317

Lockeford

Concrete Pipe & Products Co., Inc. of California, P.O. Box 103(95237), pg. 273

Lodi

California Custom Foods, P.O. Box 2695(95241), pg. 840
PACIFIC COAST PRODUCERS, P.O. Box 1600(95241-1600), pg. 839
PROFESSIONAL APARTMENT MANAGEMENT, INC., 2020 W. Kettleman Ln.(95241), pg. 893

Lompoc

GREFCO, Inc., Hwy 1 & 246(93436), pg. 137

Long Beach

Allright Long Beach Parking, Inc., 107 B W. Broadway(90802), pg. 41
BEACH CITY CHEVROLET CO., 3001 E. Pacific Coast Hwy.(90804), pg. 128
Casey Co., 180 E. Ocean Blvd., Ste. 910(90802), pg. 228
CORMIER CHEVROLET COMPANY, INC., 2201 E. 223 St.(90810), pg. 286
CROSBY & OVERTON, INC., 1610 W. 17th St.(90813), pg. 300

Crosby & Overton Transportation Co., 1610 W. 17th(90813), pg. 300
Dillingham Construction N.A., Inc., 135 West Victoria St.(90805), pg. 338
Gary Metals Co., Inc., 2400 E. Dominguez Blvd.(90810), pg. 889
Gold Bond Building Products, 1850 W. 8th(90813), pg. 790
Gulfstream Aerospace Corp., 4150 Donald Douglas Dr.(90808), pg. 494
HARBOR BANCORP, 11 Golden Shore(90802), pg. 506
Korn/Ferry International, 100 East Wardlow(90807), pg. 642
Long Beach Community Hospital, 1720 Termino Ave.(90804-2180), pg. 1127
MANESS INDUSTRIES, INC., 1101 E. Spring St.(90806), pg. 703
Payson Bronco, Inc., 6900 Cherry Ave.(90805), pg. 853
SCS ENGINEERS, 3711 Long Beach Blvd.(90807-3315), pg. 961
Scotsman Group, Inc., 2550 E. 68th St.(90805), pg. 982
SCS Analytical Laboratory, 2860 Walnut Ave.(90806-1834), pg. 961
SCS Field Services, 4014 Long Beach Blvd.(90807-3315), pg. 961
SILICON POWER CUBE CORPORATION, 6015 Obispo Ave.(90805), pg. 1004
SOUTHLAND INDUSTRIES, 1661 E. 32nd St.(90807), pg. 1023
TIDELANDS OIL PRODUCTION CO., 301 East Ocean, Ste. 300(90802), pg. 1096

Los Alamitos

TREND OFFSET PRINTING SERVICES, 3722 Catalina St.(90720), pg. 1109

Los Altos

M. Kamenstein, Inc., 4966 El Camino Real, Ste. 118(94022), pg. 615
Stuart Anderson's Black Angus/Cattle Company Restaurants, 4410 El Camino Real, Ste. 201(94022), pg. 60

Los Angeles

A A CATER TRUCK MANUFACTURING COMPANY, INC., 750 E. Slauson Ave.(90011), pg. 1
A K H COMPANY, INC., 6565 E. Washington Blvd.(90040), pg. 4
ABBOTT ELECTRONICS, INC., 2727 So. La Cienega(90034), pg. 9
ADMARKETING, INC., 1801 Century Park East, Ste. 2000(90067), pg. 18
Aeroperu, 530 W. 6th St., Ste. 1200(90014), pg. 22
Allied Security Inc., Wilshire Center Bldg., 3727 W. 6th St., Ste. 612(90020), pg. 40
Allright Cal. Inc., 631 S. Olive, Ste. 210(90014), pg. 41
AMERICAN PROTECTION INDUSTRIES, INC., 12233 W. Olympic Blvd., Ste. 380(90064), pg. 60
American Trading Real Estate Properties, Inc., Wilshire-Bixel Bldg., Ste.1504, 1055 Wilshire Blvd.(90017), pg. 65
ANDERSON LITHOGRAPH COMPANY, 3217 S. Garfield Ave.(90040), pg. 73
Antwerp Diamond Distributors Inc., 643 So. Olive, Ste. 400(90014), pg. 77
APPERSON BUSINESS FORMS, INC., 6855 E. Gage Ave.(90040), pg. 78
ARLEN ADVERTISING, 1516 S. Bundy Dr.(90025), pg. 83
ASCO Music, 610 South Ardmore Avenue(90005), pg. 292
ASHER/GOULD ADVERTISING, INC., 5900 Wilshire Blvd., 16th Fl.(90036), pg. 88
ASSOCIATED OF LOS ANGELES, 2585 E. Olympic Blvd.(90023), pg. 90
ASSOCIATED MACHINECRAFT CORPORATION, 637 E. Slauson Ave.(90011), pg. 90
BAKER COMMODITIES, INC., 4020 Bandini Blvd.(90023), pg. 115
BANDINI FERTILIZER COMPANY, 4139 Bandini Blvd.(90023), pg. 117
THEODORE BARRY & ASSOCIATES, 1520 Wilshire Blvd.(90017), pg. 122
BATEY/POINDEXTER, 3780 Wilshire Blvd., Ste. 210(90010), pg. 126
BEAUTY HANDBOOK CORPORATION, 10100 Santa Monica Blvd.(90067), pg. 130
BeePee Music, 610 South Ardmore Avenue(90005), pg. 292
BENO'S, 1620 S. Los Angeles St.(90015), pg. 139
BERGELECTRIC CORPORATION, 5650 Centinela Blvd.(90045), pg. 141
Braun/Ketchum Public Relations, 3580 Wilshire Blvd., Ste. 1520(90010), pg. 625
Brierley & Partners, 5900 Wilshire Blvd., Ste. 550(90036), pg. 175
M. J. BROCK & SONS, INC., 6767 Forest Lawn Dr.(90068), pg. 178
BRUSH RESEARCH MANUFACTURING COMPANY, 4642 E. Floral Dr.(90022), pg. 184
Bullock's, 800 S. Hope St.(90017), pg. 699
Bundy Properties, Teleflora Plaza, 12233 W. Olympic Blvd.(90064), pg. 60
Leo Burnett Company, 3801 Barham Blvd.(90068), pg. 192
CB Commercial Real Estate Group, Inc., 533 Fremont Ave., Ste. 1000(90071), pg. 222
CGRW ADVERTISING, INC., 5750 Wilshire Blvd., Ste. 480(90036), pg. 201
California-Gym Equipment Co., 3140 S. Pico Blvd.(90023), pg. 163
Calmark Asset Management Co., 10866 Wilshire Blvd.(90024), pg. 211
Calmark Communities, Inc., 11100 Santa Monica Blvd.(90025), pg. 211
Calmark Development Corp., 10866 Wilshire Blvd., 4th Fl.(90024), pg. 211
CALMARK INVESTMENT COMPANY, 10866 Wilshire Blvd., 4th Fl.(90024), pg. 211
Calmark Properties, Inc., 10866 Wilshire Blvd., 4th Fl.(90024), pg. 211
Calmark Realty Management, Inc., 10866 Wilshire Blvd., 4th Fl.(90024), pg. 211
CAMPBELL AND WAGMAN, 10960 Wilshire Blvd., Ste. 2300(90024), pg. 213
Capital Bank of California, 1875 Century Park E.(90067), pg. 214
Castor Advertising Corp., 11693 San Vicente Blvd., 229
CERTIFIED GROCERS ADVERTISING CO., 2601 S. Eastern Ave.(90040), pg. 236
CERTIFIED GROCERS OF CALIFORNIA, 2601 S. Eastern Ave.(90040), pg. 237
CINAMERICA THEATRES, L.P., 9200 Sunset Blvd.(90069), pg. 249
A.D. CLARK, INC., 12901 W. Jefferson Blvd.(90066), pg. 252
CLEVELAND WRECKING COMPANY, 2833 Leonia Blvd.(90058), pg. 255
COHEN/JOHNSON, INC., 2029 Century Park E., Ste. 1300(90067), pg. 259
Com Corp Factors, Inc., 3209 Humboldt St.(90031), pg. 623
Computer Service Company, P.O. Box 74901, (90004), pg. 1049
Continental Graphics Corporation, 4525 Wilshire Blvd., Suite 203(90010), pg. 279
CONTINENTAL GRAPHICS HOLDINGS, INC., 4525 Wilshire Blvd., Suite 203(90010), pg. 279
Bing Crosby Productions, Inc., 610 South Ardmore Avenue(90005), pg. 292
CROWELL, WEEDON & CO., One Wilshire Boulevard(90017), pg. 301
Crown Grocers, Inc., 2601 S. Eastern Ave.(90040), pg. 237
Daily Racing Form, Inc. Pacific, 170 S. Bimini Pl.(90004), pg. 611
Danzig/Rosenberg, L. A. Mart, 1933 So. Broadway(90007), pg. 100
Data Transportation Company, 2801 E. 46th St.(90058), pg. 133
DAVIS, BALL & COLOMBATTO ADVERTISING, INC., 865 S. Figueroa(90017), pg. 318
DAVIS COMPANIES, 2121 Ave. of the Stars, Ste. 2800(90067), pg. 318
DEARDEN'S, INC., 700 S. Main St.(90014), pg. 322
DESIGN 1 INTERIORS, 2049 Century Park E., Ste. 3000(90067), pg. 332
DEWEESE INC., 1825 S. Hill St.(90015), pg. 334
DIMAC DIRECT, 1236 Wellesley Ave. 338
Diversified Compounders, 5701 E. Union Pacific Blvd.(90022), pg. 329
CHARLES DUNN COMPANY-REALTORS, 1200 Wilshire Blvd.(90017), pg. 353
DUNN-EDWARDS CORPORATION, 4885 East 52nd Place(90040), pg. 353
Eemco Div., 4585 Electronics Place(90039), pg. 317
ECHEVARRIA ANGEL CO., INC., 3760 Union Pacific Ave.(90023), pg. 365
EISAMAN, JOHNS & LAWS ADVERTISING, INC., 5700 Wilshire Blvd.(90036), pg. 372
ROBERT ELEN & ASSOCIATES, 6430 Sunset Blvd., Ste. 1000(90028), pg. 376
ELKAY PLASTICS COMPANY, INC., 4380 Ayers Ave.(90023), pg. 377
Ellis & Ross Advertising & Design, Museum Square Penthouse 391
A. Epstein & Sons (California) Inc., 1440 South Sepulveda Blvd.(90025), pg. 384
ERNEST PAPER PRODUCTS, INC., 2424 E. 26th St.(90058), pg. 387
EvansGroup, Museum Square Penthouse 391
EVY OF CALIFORNIA, INC., 10755 Venice Blvd.(90034), pg. 392
Executive Car Leasing Company, 7807 Santa Monica Blvd.(90046), pg. 393
EXECUTIVE CAR LEASING, INC., 7800 Santa Monica Blvd.(90046), pg. 393
Eyewear Division, 123 E. 35th St.(90011), pg. 493
Fields & Devereaux/HEPY, Inc., 116 N. Robertson Blvd., Ste. 802(90048), pg. 509
FIRST COMPUTER CORPORATION, 1740 Westwood Blvd.(90024), pg. 412
FISHKING PROCESSORS, INC., 1320 Newton St.(90021), pg. 415
FIVE DOLLAR CLOTHING STORES, 2320 E. 49th St.(90058), pg. 416
Flair Communications Agency, Inc., 4929 Wilshire Blvd., Ste. 650(90010), pg. 416
FORTIFIBER CORPORATION, 4489 Bandini Blvd.(90023), pg. 425
FORTUNE FASHION, 1248 S. Flower St.(90015), pg. 425
FOTOUHI ALONSO INC. ADVERTISING & MARKETING, 1901 Ave. of the Stars, Ste. 950(90067), pg. 427
Four Star Holdings Corp., 1440 So. Sepulveda Blvd.(90025), pg. 74
FREEMAN COSMETIC CORP., 10474 Santa Monica Blvd., Ste. 300(90025), pg. 431
JOHN S. FREY ENTERPRISES, 1900 E. 64th St.(90001), pg. 433
GBF/Ayer, 5900 Wilshire Blvd., Ste. 2750(90036), pg. 104
GWP, INC., 9080 Santa Monica Blvd.(90069), pg. 441
Gannett Transit, 1731 Workman St.(90031), pg. 442
GANS INK & SUPPLY COMPANY, INC., 1441 Boyd St.(90033), pg. 442
GILMORE ENVELOPE CORP., 4540 Worth St.(90063), pg. 460
GOLDEN STATE MUTUAL LIFE INSURANCE COMPANY, 1999 W. Adams(90018), pg. 467
GOLDEN WEST BROADCASTERS, 5858 Sunset Blvd.(90028), pg. 467
GOOD STUFF FOOD COMPANY, INC., 1771 W. Blake Ave.(90031), pg. 470
GORE GRAPHICS, INC., 340 N. Madison Ave.(90004), pg. 472
The Great American Entertainment Company, 3330 Cahuenga Blvd(90068), pg. 53
LEONARD GREEN & PARTNERS, 333 S. Grand Ave., Suite 5400(90071), pg. 485
Grocers Capital Co., 2601 So. Eastern Ave.(90040), pg. 237
Grocers Development Center, 2601 So. Eastern Ave.(90040), pg. 237
Grocers Equipment Co., 5577 Sheila St.(90040), pg. 237
Grocers General Merchandise Company, 2601 S. Eastern Ave.(90040), pg. 237
Grocers Specialty Co., 2601 S. Eastern Ave.(90040), pg. 237
Group 3 Design, 9080 Santa Monica Blvd.(90069), pg. 441
GUESS ?, INC., 1444 S. Alameda(90021), pg. 493
HKM of California Corp., 3171 East 12th St.(90023), pg. 1123
Hanna-Barbera Productions, Inc., 3400 Cahuenga Blvd.(90068), pg. 53
HARDEN INDUSTRIES, INC., 13915 S. Main St.(90061), pg. 508
Hearst Entertainment Productions, Inc., 1640 S. Sepulveda Blvd.(90025), pg. 523
Hearst Real Estate Division, 1150 S. Olive St., Suite 2620(90015), pg. 524
HEHR INTERNATIONAL INC., 3333 Casitas Ave.(90039), pg. 525
Heil Steel Fabricating, Inc., d/b/a Euclid Body Co., 3121 Fruitland Av., pg. 526
J. HELLMAN PRODUCE, INC., 1601 E. Olympic Blvd., Ste. 200(90021), pg. 527
HOFFMAN BROTHERS PACKING CO., 2731 S. Soto St.(90023), pg. 537
Hollytex-Western Div., 6025 E. Randolph St.(90040), pg. 1121
Horizon Media Inc., 1801 Century Park East, Suite 1132(90067), pg. 544
HORLICK LEVIN ADVERTISING INC., 11300 W. Olympic Blvd.(90064), pg. 544
R. S. HUGHES CO., INC., 5303 San Fernando Rd., W.(90039), pg. 551
Hydril Company, 714 W. Olympic Blvd.(90015), pg. 556
IDEA MAN, INC., 1945 S. La Cienega Blvd.(90034), pg. 562
Interior Design Inc., 1440 South Sepulveda Blvd.(90025), pg. 384
INTERNATIONAL COMMUNICATIONS GROUP, INC., 1925 Century Park East, Ste. 1850(90067), pg. 576
International Creative Management, Inc., 8899 Beverly Blvd.(90048), pg. 607
ITALIA/GAL ADVERTISING, 5750 Wilshire Blvd., Ste. 480(90036), pg. 582
J & R FILM COMPANY, 1135 N. Masnfield(90038), pg. 586
JACOBS & GERBER, INC., 731 N. Fairfax(90046), pg. 587
JANIK & ASSOCIATES, INC., Ste. 610, 1901 Ave. of The Stars(90067), pg. 589
KFI, Inc., 610 S. Ardmore Ave.(90005), pg. 292
KAISER MCEUEN INC., 1631 Pontius Ave.(90025), pg. 615
KENNINGTON LTD., INC., 3209 Humboldt St.(90031), pg. 623
Kennington Properties, Inc., 1800 Century Park E., Ste. 1150(90067), pg. 623
Ketchum Advertising/Los Angeles, 11755 Wilshire Blvd., Ste. 1900(90025), pg. 625
Ketchum Directory Advertising/USA, 11755 Wilshire Blvd., Ste. 1900(90025), pg. 625
KIRK-MAYER, INC., 11801 Mississippi Ave.(90025), pg. 633
KLEIN ADVERTISING INC., 1888 Century Park East, Ste. 1104(90067-1725), pg. 635
KNAPP COMMUNICATIONS CORPORATION, 5900 Wilshire Blvd.(90036), pg. 636
KNAR GOLD & SILVER EXCHANGE, 640 S. Hill St., Ste. 241(90014), pg. 636
KOLD KIST BRANDS, INC., P.O. Box 91-1228, (90091), pg. 641
KORN/FERRY INTERNATIONAL, 1800 Century Park East, 642
Korn/Ferry International, 601 S. Figueroa, Ste. 1900(90017), pg. 642
Korn/Ferry International, 1800 Century Park East, Ste. 900(90067), pg. 642
LA REINA, INC., 316 N. Ford Blvd.(90022), pg. 649
LARSEN COLBY ADVERTISING, 5657 Wilshire Blvd., 5th Fl.(90036), pg. 659
LAWRY'S RESTAURANTS, INC., 2950 Los Feliz Blvd., Ste. 204(90039), pg. 663
KENNETH LEVENTHAL & COMPANY, 2049 Century Park East(90067), pg. 670
LITHOGRAPHIX, INC., 13500 S. Figueroa St.(90061), pg. 678
LLOYD PROPERTIES, 12400 Wilshire Blvd., Ste. 1180(90025), pg. 680
LORSCH CREATIVE NETWORK, 5950 Wilshire Blvd., 2nd Fl.(90036), pg. 684
Los Angeles Regional Office, 9229 Sunset Blvd.(90069), pg. 249
LOS ANGELES SMOKING CURING COMPANY, 778 Kohler St.(90021), pg. 684
Los Angeles Union Terminal, Inc., 746 S. Central Ave., Rm. 250(90021), pg. 75
MADISON GRAHAM COLORGRAPHICS, INC., 150 N. Myers St.(90033), pg. 699
Madison Industries, 1900 E. 64th St.(90001), pg. 433
MAGUIRE THOMAS PARTNERS, 355 S. Grande Ave., Ste. 4500(90071), pg. 701
MARK FABRICKS, INC., 1555 Newton St.(90021), pg. 708
ALBERT C. MARTIN & ASSOCIATES, 811 W. Seventh St.(90017), pg. 714
Martin/Universal Industries, 1561 N. Bonnie Beach(90063), pg. 716
GILDA MARX INC., 11755 Exposition Blvd.(90064), pg. 716

MAXINE OF HOLLYWOOD, INC., 2424 E. 28th St.(90058), pg. 723
MEASURED MARKETING SERVICES, 12800 Culver Blvd.(90066), pg. 734
Media Buyers, Inc., 5900 Wilshire Blvd., 16th Fl.(90036), pg. 88
MENDELSOHN/ZIEN ADVERTISING, INC., Westwood Gateway, 11111 Santa Monica Blvd., Ste. 2250(90025-3356), pg. 739
MERLE NORMAN COSMETICS, INC., 9130 Bellanca Ave.(90045), pg. 740
MISS ELLIETTE, INC., 4701 S. Santa Fe Ave(90058), pg. 760
MOBILE TECHNOLOGY INC., 9841 Airport Blvd., 12th Fl.(90045), pg. 762
MONICO ALLOYS, INC., 2301 E. 15th St.(90021-4848), pg. 765
Motivational Incentives Group, 8544 Sunset Blvd.(90069), pg. 1180
MUSE CORDERO CHEN, INC., 6100 Wilshire Blvd., Ste. 1600(90048), pg. 777
MUTUAL TRADING CO., INC., 431 Crocker St.(90013), pg. 779
BEN MYERSON CANDY COMPANY, INC., 928 Towne Ave.(90021), pg. 780
NBBJ/LPA, 3780 Wilshire Blvd., Ste. 300(90010), pg. 780
NDC Distributors, Inc., 8000 Maie St.(90001), pg. 787
NADEL PARTNERSHIP, INC., 1990 S. Bundy, Ste. 400(90025), pg. 782
NATIONAL CORSET SUPPLY HOUSE, 3240 E. 26th St.(90023), pg. 787
Networks America, 8981 Sunset Blvd.(90069), pg. 1180
New World Entertainment, Inc., 1440 S. Sepulveda Blvd.(90025), pg. 74
NORDEN FRUIT COMPANY, INC., 1601 E. Olympic Blvd.(90021), pg. 809
OSC CORPORATION D/B/A OLYMPIC SALES CO., 134 W. 131st St.(90061), pg. 819
VIC OLESEN & PARTNERS, INC., 1631 Pontius Ave.(90025), pg. 824
O'Neil Data Systems, Inc., 2005 Armacost Ave.(90025), pg. 827
WILLIAM O'NEIL & CO., INC., 12655 Beatrice St.(90066), pg. 827
ORGANICALLY GROWN CORPORATION, 12840 Sunset Blvd.(90049), pg. 829
Original Cylinder Corporation, 652 W. 18th St.(90015), pg. 134
Outdoor Media Inc., 8544 Sunset Blvd.(90069), pg. 1180
OWEN PACIFIC, 1236 S. Compton Ave.(90021), pg. 834
PHC Holdings, Inc., 10900 Wilshire Blvd., Ste. 1600(90024), pg. 840
Pacific Economy Company, 2601 S. Eastern Ave.(90040), pg. 237
PACIFIC HOLDING CORPORATION, Murdock Plaza, 10900 Wilshire Blvd.(90024), pg. 840
PACIFIC STATES CASUALTY CO., 4021 Rosewood, Ste. 300(90004), pg. 841
PARAMOUNT FITNESS EQUIPMENT CORP., 6450 E. Bandini Blvd.(90040-3185), pg. 848
Patriot Direct Dial Systems, 8544 Sunset Blvd.(90069), pg. 1180
PECK JONES CONSTRUCTION, 10866 Wilshire Blvd., 7th Fl.(90024), pg. 854
Pedus Building Services, 3500 W. First St.(90004), pg. 855
Pedus Food Services, 3500 W. First St.(90004), pg. 855
Pedus Office Services, 3500 W. First St.(90004), pg. 855
Pedus Security Services, 3500 W. First St.(90004), pg. 855
PEDUS SERVICES, INC., 3500 W. First St.(90004), pg. 854
Penn Emblem Co., 2428 E. 56th St.(90058), pg. 857
PETERSEN PUBLISHING COMPANY, 8490 Sunset Blvd.(90069), pg. 864
THE PHELPS GROUP, 11999 San Vicente Blvd., Ste. 401(90049), pg. 866
PIONEER ALUMINUM, INC., 3800 E. 26th St.(90023), pg. 871
PIONEER SUPERMARKETS, 1625 Sunset Blvd.(90026), pg. 872
Plastic Suppliers Inc., 12916 S. Broadway(90061), pg. 876
POLY PAK AMERICA, INC., 2939 E. Washington Blvd.(90023), pg. 880
POOL COMMUNICATIONS, 11828 LaGrange Ave.(90025), pg. 880
POTATO SALES COMPANY, INC., 1601 E. Olympic Blvd., Ste. 311(90021), pg. 882
Precision Specialty Metals, Inc., 3301 Medford St.(90063), pg. 350
PREPCO, 6190 E. Slauson Av.(90040), pg. 887
PROFESSIONAL HEALTHCARE SYSTEMS, INC., 12960 Coral Tree Place(90066), pg. 894
Promotional Broadcast Services, 8544 Sunset Blvd.(90069), pg. 1180
PURCELL INTERNATIONAL GROUP, INC., 1640 S. Sepulveda Blvd., Ste. 112(90025), pg. 900
RNL/Interplan, 221 So. Figueroa, Ste. 200(90012), pg. 908
RALEIGH ENTERPRISES, INC., 11444 W. Olympic Blvd.(90064), pg. 910
RED CALLIOPE & ASSOCIATES, INC., 13003 S. Figueroa(90061), pg. 918
REHRIG PACIFIC COMPANY, 4010 E. 26th St.(90023), pg. 922
RELIANCE STEEL & ALUMINUM CO., 2550 E. 25th St.(90058), pg. 925
GEORGE RICE & SONS, 2001 N. Soto St.(90032), pg. 931
ROLLED STEEL PRODUCTS CORPORATION, 2187 S. Garfield Ave.(90040), pg. 944
RONALD JAMES DIRECT, 11766 Wilshire Blvd., Ste. 310(90025), pg. 946
Runway Two Five Corporation, 11022 Aviation Blvd.(90045), pg. 1028
SMS Audio & Video Duplicating, 8544 Sunset Blvd.(90069), pg. 1180
S & W Fine Foods, 5010 Loma Vista Ave.(90058), pg. 1111
Santee Dairies, 231 E. 23rd St.(90011), pg. 552
Savogran of California, 3201 Union Pacific Ave.(90023), pg. 973
CECIL SAYDAH COMPANY, 2935 E. 12th St.(90023), pg. 973
L. M. SCOFIELD COMPANY, 6533 Bandini Blvd.(90040), pg. 982
SCOTT/LANCASTER/HERSHFIELD, 11111 Santa Monica Blvd., Ste. 1011(90025), pg. 982
SERVICE PACKING COMPANY, 3425 E. Vernon Ave.(90058), pg. 992
SHIELD SECURITY, INC., 200 N. Westmoreland Ave.(90004), pg. 999
SIMON MARKETING, INC., 1900 Ave. of The Stars, Ste. 400(90067), pg. 1006
Sinclair Paint Co., 6100 S. Garfield Ave.(90040), pg. 571
SINCLAIR PRINTING & LITHO, INC., 4005 Whiteside St.(90063), pg. 1008
SMITH-EMERY COMPANY, 781 E. Washington Blvd.(90021), pg. 1012
Spanish Communications Corp., 8544 Sunset Blvd.(90069), pg. 1180
SPEER, YOUNG & HOLLANDER, INC., 3580 Wilshire Blvd., Ste. 2020(90010), pg. 1030
Sports Call, Inc., 8544 Sunset Blvd.(90069), pg. 1180
Stanleigh International, Inc., 3209 Humboldt St.(90031), pg. 623
STARVING STUDENTS, INC., 8525 W. Pico Blvd., 2nd Floor(90035), pg. 1040
STEIN ROBAIRE HELM, INC., 11911 San Vicente Blvd., Ste. 324(90049), pg. 1045
STEINY & COMPANY, INC., 221 N. Ardmore Ave.(90004), pg. 1049
Strategic Compensation Associates, 644 S. Figueroa St., 2nd Fl.(90017), pg. 642
Stuart-Ironsides, Inc., 6715 McKinley Ave.(90001), pg. 1055
Sunkist Grower, Inc.-Western Division, 6055 E. Washington Blvd., Ste. 929(90040), pg. 1061
SUPERBA, INC., 1735 S. Santa Fe Ave.(90021), pg. 1063
SUPERSHUTTLE INTERNATIONAL, 7001 W. Imperial Hwy.(90045), pg. 1064
SWEDE SPORTSWEAR COMPANY, INC., 1675 S. Alameda St.(90021), pg. 1066
Tam O'Shanter Inn, 2980 Los Feliz Blvd.(90039), pg. 663
TAREN HOLDINGS, INC., 6040 Bandini Blvd.(90040), pg. 1078
Teleflora, 12233 W. Olympic Blvd.(90064), pg. 60
Thrifty Corporation, 3424 Wilshire Blvd., pg. 485
TICKETMASTER CORPORATION, 3701 Wilshire Blvd., 7th Fl.(90010), pg. 1096
Time Oil Co., 5150 Wilshire Blvd.(90036), pg. 1097
TOPA EQUITIES LTD, INC., 1800 Ave. of the Stars, Ste. 1400(90067), pg. 1101
TOTTEN TUBES, INC., 1555 Los Palos St.(90023), pg. 1103
TULIP CORPORATION, 3211 E. 26th St.(90023), pg. 1119
USA Network, 2049 Century Park East(90067), pg. 1124
U.S. Yellow Pages, 8544 Sunset Blvd.(90069), pg. 1180
Vitt Media International, Inc. - Los Angeles, 12400 Wilshire Blvd., Ste. 610(90025), pg. 1154
THE VOGEL COMMUNICATIONS GROUP, 11835 Olympic Blvd., Ste. 800(90064), pg. 1154
The Weather Channel, Inc.-Los Angeles Sales Office, 1925 Century Park East, Ste. 830(90067), pg. 654
Jervis B. Webb Co. of California, 4550 Seville Ave.(90058), pg. 1170
WELLER & O'SULLIVAN ADVERTISING, 5757 Wilshire Blvd., Penthouse(90036), pg. 1175
WESTERN INTERNATIONAL MEDIA CORPORATION, 8544 Sunset Blvd.(90069), pg. 1179
Western International Merchandising, 8544 Sunset Blvd.(90069), pg. 1180
Western International Premiums, 8544 Sunset Blvd.(90069), pg. 1180
WESTERN REINSURANCE BROKERS, INC., 3435 Wilshire Blvd., Ste. 123(90010), pg. 1181
Wilsey Foods, Inc., 633 S. Mission(90023), pg. 1193
WINDSOR FASHIONS, 3901 S. Broadway(90037), pg. 1195
Wood Knapp & Co., Inc., 5900 Wilshire Blvd.(90036), pg. 636
YOUNG'S MARKET COMPANY, 500 S. Central Avenue(90013), pg. 1214
Z. CAVARICCI INC., 2535 E. 12th St., Unit A(90021), pg. 1215
THE ZIPPERTUBING CO., 13000 S. Broadway(90061), pg. 1220

Los Gatos

RAUH, GOOD, DARLO & BARNES ADVERTISING ASSOCIATES, INC., 15425 Los Gatos Blvd.(95032), pg. 914
XA Systems Corporation, 983 University Av.(95030), pg. 272

Lynwood

Jorgensen Steel & Aluminum/Los Angeles, 10650 Alameda St.(90262), pg. 606
MANCHESTER TANK & EQUIPMENT COMPANY, 2880 Norton Ave.(90262), pg. 703
UNIVERSAL MOLDING COMPANY, 10807 Stanford Ave.(90262), pg. 1139
WesTech Gear Group, 2600 Imperial(90262), pg. 1220

Malibu

Full Circle Communications, 23410 Civic Center Way, Ste. E 10(90265), pg. 436
Seybold Seminars, 6922 Wildlife Rd.(90265), pg. 1219

Manhattan Beach

OLSON-TRAVELWORLD LTD., 1334 Parkview Ave., Ste. 210(90266), pg. 824

Marina Del Rey

CENTURY COMPUTER MARKETING, 4755 Alla Rd.(90292-6378), pg. 235
Del Rey Restaurant Corp., 13813 Fiji Way(90291), pg. 1028
Hill, Holliday/Los Angeles, 4640 Admiralty Way, 9th Fl.(90292), pg. 534
WESTERN FEDERAL SAVINGS & LOAN ASSOCIATION, 13160 Mindanao Way(90292), pg. 1179

Menlo Park

CARCO ELECTRONICS, 195 Constitution Dr.(94025), pg. 217
COMBUSTION POWER COMPANY, 1020 Marsh Rd.(94025), pg. 267
Ingersoll Engineers, 535 Middlefield Rd., Ste. 280(94025), pg. 568
SRI Development Corp., 333 Ravenswood Ave.(94025), pg. 964
SRI INTERNATIONAL, 333 Ravenswood Ave.(94025-3493), pg. 964

Mill Valley

S & P COMPANY, 100 Shoreline Dr.(94941), pg. 959

Milpitas

Allied Security Inc., 1900 McCarthy Blvd., Ste. 302(95035), pg. 39
ATARI GAMES CORPORATION, 675 Sycamore Dr.(95035), pg. 93
INTERNATIONAL MICROCIRCUITS, INC., 525 Los Coches St.(95035), pg. 579
B.T. MANCINI CO., INC., 876 So. Milpitas Blvd.(95035), pg. 703
Tengen, 675 Sycamore Dr.(95035), pg. 93

Mira Loma

ADVANCE BUSINESS GRAPHICS, 3810 Wabash Dr.(91752), pg. 18

Mission Hills

International Tableting, 15451 San Fernando Mission Blvd.(91345), pg. 866
Nature Made Nutritional Products Inc., 15451 San Fernando Mission Blvd.(91345), pg. 866
Paramount Citrus Association, P.O. Box 8599(91346), pg. 60
PHARMAVITE CORP., 15451 San Fernando Mission Blvd.(91345), pg. 866

Mission San Jose

WEIBEL VINEYARDS, 1250 Stanford Ave.(94539), pg. 1173

Modesto

Bell Carter Distributing, 806 Kiernan Ave.(95356), pg. 134
FERRY-MORSE SEED COMPANY, 555 Codoni St.(95354), pg. 407
FISHER GRAPHIC INDUSTRIES, 1137 Graphics Dr.(95351), pg. 415
E & J GALLO WINERY, 600 Yosemite Blvd.(95354), pg. 441
International Div., P.O. Box 4938(95352), pg. 407
SAVE MART SUPERMARKETS, 1800 Standiford Ave.(95352), pg. 973
Valley Fork Lift Co., P.O. Box 577440, 140 Riverside(95357), pg. 1111
Vegetable & Flower Div., P.O. Box 4938(95352), pg. 407

Monrovia

AEROVIRONMENT, INC., 222 E. Huntington Dr., Ste.200(91016), pg. 22
PACHMAYR GUN WORKS INC., 1875 S. Mountain(91016), pg. 839

Montebello

Penske Truck Leasing, 1500 So. Greenwood Ave.(90640), pg. 859
ROYAL PAPER BOX OF CALIFORNIA, 1105 S. Maple Ave.(90640), pg. 953
SUNCLIPSE, INC., 1610 S. Greenwood Ave.(90640), pg. 1059
Universal Glass Corp., 666 Union St.(90640), pg. 763

Monterey

AVADYNE, INC., 2801 Salinas Highway, Bldg. F(93940), pg. 101
The Herald, 8 Upper Ragsdale Dr.(93940), pg. 155
PRO-LOG CORPORATION, 2555 Garden Rd.(93940), pg. 892

Monterey Park

CAMINO REAL CHEVROLET, 2401 S. Atlantic Blvd.(91754), pg. 212
Casuda Canyon Restaurant Corp., 3500 Ramona Blvd.(91754), pg. 1028
REFRIGERATION SUPPLIES DISTRIBUTORS, 1201 Monterey Pass Rd.(91754), pg. 921
H. SALT SEAFOOD RESTAURANTS, 1255 Corp. Center Dr.(91754), pg. 967
Specialty Restaurant Corporation, 3700 Ramona Blvd.(91754), pg. 1028
Ultra Industries, Inc., 777 Monterey Pass Rd.(91754), pg. 697
VeloBind, Inc., 1255 Corporate Ctr. Dr.(91754), pg. 657

Moorpark

KDI American Products, Inc., 10951 W. Los Angeles Ave.(93021), pg. 612

Mountain View

Acurex Corp. Aerotherm Division, 555 Clyde Ave.(94039), pg. 15
Acurex Corp. Autodata Division, P.O. Box 7042, 555 Clyde Avenue(94039), pg. 16
Acurex Environmental, 555 Clyde Ave.(94043), pg. 16
ACUREX ENVIRONMENTAL CORPORATION, P.O. Box 7042, (94039), pg. 15
DIGITAL PATHWAYS INC., 201 Ravendale Drive(94043), pg. 337
IDC West, 2083 Landings Dr.(94043), pg. 577
INPUT, 1280 Villa St.(94041), pg. 571
Interop, Inc., 480 San Antonio Rd., Ste. 100(94040), pg. 1219
ParcPlace Systems, 1550 Plymouth St.(94043), pg. 448
RIGOLI COMMUNICATIONS, 2111 Landings Dr.(94043), pg. 934
Sasco/Valley Electric, 2288 Charleston Rd.(94043), pg. 972
TELESENSORY, 455 N. Bernardo Ave.(94039), pg. 1085

Napa

Basalt Precast Division, 2301 Napa Vallejo Hwy., P.O. Box 2490(94558), pg. 338
SYAR INDUSTRIES, INC., 2301 Napa Vallejo Hwy.(94558), pg. 1068

National City

Pacord, 206 W. 35th St.(92050), pg. 964
Western Lumber Company, Inc., 2745 Tidelands(92050), pg. 453

Newark

CARGILL SALT, 7200 Central Ave.(94560-4206), pg. 219
New Park Mall, 200 New Park Mall(94560), pg. 699

Newbury Park

MPO Videotronics, 2580 Turquoise Circle(91320), pg. 693
PTI Technologies, 2323 Teller Rd.(91320), pg. 388

Newport Beach

AMERICAN RESTAURANT GROUP, INC., 450 Newport Center Dr., Ste. 600(92660), pg. 60
BOYLE ENGINEERING CORP., 1501 Quail St.(92660), pg. 169
BROMAR INC., 15 Corporate Plaza(92660), pg. 179
CLAYTON, WILLIAMS & SHERWOOD, INC., 800 Newport Center Dr., Ste. 400(92660), pg. 254
FORSYTHE MARCELLI JOHNSON ADVERTISING, INC., 610 Newport Center Dr.(92660), pg. 425
G & A COMMUNICATIONS, 1401 Dove St., 5th Fl.(92660), pg. 438
GALARDI GROUP, INC., 4440 Von Karman(92660), pg. 441
GREENSTRIPE MEDIA, INC., 1300 Quail St., Ste. 209(92660), pg. 485
INTERCOMMUNICATIONS INC., 620 Newport Center Dr.(92660), pg. 574
IRVINE COMPANY, 550 Newport Center Dr.(92660), pg. 582
Kettenburg Marine/Newport Beach Retail, 2700-B West Coast Hwy.(92663), pg. 626
Kettenburg Marine/Newport Engines, 2633 W. Coast Hwy.(92663), pg. 626
KOLL CO., 4343 Von Karmen Ave.(92660), pg. 641
Korn/Ferry International, 1300 Dove St., Ste. 300(92600), pg. 642
LENAC, WARFORD, STONE, INC., 4701 Teller Ave.(92660), pg. 667
LINC Medical Imaging, 3991 MacArthur Blvd., Ste. 310(92660), pg. 648
WILLIAM LYON COMPANY, 4490 Von Karman(92660), pg. 690
MONEX INTERNATIONAL, LTD., 4910 Birch St.(92660), pg. 765
Pacific Equities Network, 700 Newport Center Dr.(92660), pg. 841
Pacific Financial Asset Management Corporation, 700 Newport Center Dr.(92660), pg. 841
Pacific Investment Management Co., 840 Newport Center Dr., Ste. 360(92660), pg. 841
PACIFIC MUTUAL LIFE INSURANCE COMPANY, 700 Newport Ctr. Dr.(92660), pg. 841
J. M. PETERS CO., 3501 Jamboree, Ste. 200(92660), pg. 864
PMRealty Advisors, Inc., 800 Newport Center Dr., Ste 300(92660), pg. 841
Robert F. Driver & Co., Inc., 3636 Birch St., Ste. 230(92660-2619), pg. 349
SRS TECHNOLOGIES, S. Tower, Ste. 402, 3501 Jamboree Rd.(92660), pg. 964
Service Assets Corp., 15 Corporate Plaza(92660), pg. 179
Sheldon Good & Co. of California, 840 Newport Center Dr., Suite 110(92660), pg. 470
TTA/Newport, Inc., 4440 Von Karman, Ste. 220(92660), pg. 1092
TEACHERS MANAGEMENT & INVESTMENT CORPORATION, 1082
Western International Media Corporation, 4000 Westerly Pl., Ste. 150(92660), pg. 1180

North Highlands

Butler Fleet Maintenance Services, 5304 Roseville Rd., Ste. B(95660), pg. 197
Butler Installation Services, Inc., 5304 Roseville Rd.(95660), pg. 197

North Hollywood

ALATEC PRODUCTS, INC., 12747 Saticoy St.(91605), pg. 30
Arrow Thompson Metals, 6880 Troost Ave.(91605), pg. 1095
Bekins Group, 12800 Riverside Dr., 2nd Floor(91607), pg. 1074
FADAL ENGINEERING COMPANY, INC., 7260 Atoll Ave.(91605), pg. 396
Image Transform, 4142 Lankershim Blvd.(91602), pg. 74
MCRB SERVICE BUREAU, INC., 11633 Victory Blvd.(91609), pg. 691
MtC Remco Tape Products Co., 5547 Vineland Ave.(91601), pg. 690
TMP Worldwide, Inc., 12800 Riverside Dr.(91607), pg. 1074
Technicolor Professional Film Div., 4050 Lankershim Blvd.(91608), pg. 695
Technicolor Videocassette Inc., 4050 Lankershim Blvd.(91608), pg. 695
Telephone Marketing Programs, Inc., 12800 Riverside Dr.(91607), pg. 1074

Northridge

EL CAMINO RESOURCES, LTD., 8550 Balboa Blvd., Ste. 140(91325), pg. 372
Yellow Pages Marketing Services, Inc.-Los Angeles, 18919 Nordhoff St., Ste. 4(91324), pg. 1074

Novato

C. R. Fedrick, Inc., P.O. Box 688, (94948), pg. 1060
JANDY INDUSTRIES, 21 Pimentel Ct.(94948-6101), pg. 589

Oakland

Allied Security Inc. (CA), 519 17th St., Ste. 410(94612), pg. 40
AMICO-West Distr. Center, 2651 Willow St.(94607), pg. 29
Aratex Services, 958 28th St.(94608), pg. 6
Bay Park, Inc., 1624 Franklin St., Rm. 722(94612), pg. 42
CALIFORNIA ELECTRIC SERVICE, 1143 East 12th St.(94606), pg. 209
Candlestick Waterfront Rest. Corp., 30 Jack London Sq.(94607), pg. 1028
Colombo Baking Co., 580 Julie Ann Way(94621), pg. 969
CORPORATE TRAVEL SERVICES, 300 Lakeside Dr., Ste. 250(94612), pg. 287
CROWLEY MARITIME CORPORATION, 155 Grand Ave.(94612), pg. 301
L.N. CURTIS & SONS, 1800 Peralta St.(94607), pg. 306
THE FLECTO CO., INC., 1000 45th St.(94608), pg. 417
GF INDUSTRIES, INC., 930 98th Ave.(94603), pg. 439
GF Properties, Inc., 930 98th Ave.(94603), pg. 439
GROVE VALVE & REGULATOR COMPANY, 6529 Hollis(94608), pg. 490
HOFFMAN/LEWIS, 1900 Embarcadero, 4th Fl.(94606), pg. 538
Jorgensen Steel & Aluminum/Oakland, 1699 W. Grand Ave.(94607), pg. 606
KAISER FOUNDATION HEALTH & HOSPITALS GROUP, 1 Kaiser Plaza(94612), pg. 614
Kaiser Permanente, Northern California Region, 1950 Franklin St.(94612), pg. 614
KTVU Inc., Two Jack London Sq.(94607), pg. 292
MONTEREY MECHANICAL COMPANY, 8275 San Leandro St.(94621), pg. 767
PORT OF OAKLAND, 530 Water St.(94607), pg. 881
SAN FRANCISCO FRENCH BREAD COMPANY, 7801 Edgewater Dr.(94621), pg. 969
Sierra Capital Realty Services, One Kaiser Plaza Ste. 305(94612), pg. 1003
Yankee Whaler Company, Berth 75(90731), pg. 1028

Oceanside

Coleman Water Recreation Operations, 4925 E. Oceanside Blvd.(92056), pg. 695

Ontario

COAST GRAIN COMPANY, INC., 5355 E. Airport Dr.(91761), pg. 256
HOLLYTEX CARPET MILLS, INC., 1251 S. Rockefeller(91761), pg. 540
HOOKER INDUSTRIES, 1024 W. Brooks St.(91762), pg. 543
INTERNATIONAL PERMALITE, INC., 300 N. Haven Ave.(91761), pg. 579
Keystone Automotive Industries, Inc. - Ontario, 610 East State St.(91761), pg. 627
KIPP GROUP, 930 Wanamaker Ave.(91761), pg. 632
Mico West, 701 E. Francis St.(91761), pg. 748
Spectrol Electronics Corp., 40-51 Grey Stone Dr.(01761), pg. 357
Wing Industries Western, 1516 S. Archibald(91761), pg. 1196

Orange

ACR MECHANICAL CORPORATION, P.O. Box 5380(92613), pg. 2
Box Innards, Inc., 749 N. Poplar(92668), pg. 941
GARVIN FIRE PROTECTION SYSTEMS, 501 W. Southern(92665), pg. 444
MONIER ROOF TILE, INC., 750 The City Dr. S., Ste. 200(92668), pg. 765
Orange Hill Restaurant Corp., PO Box 2307, 6410 E. Chapman(92669), pg. 1028
POLYMER DEVELOPMENT LABORATORIES, INC., 212 W. Taft Ave.(92665), pg. 880
SCHNEIDER COMMERCIAL REAL ESTATE, 1915 W. Orangewood, 977
SPIRES RESTAURANTS INC., 1544 W. Yale Ave.(92667), pg. 1031
Techform Laboratories, 2021 N. Glassell(92665), pg. 443

Oroville

Las Plumas Lumber North Division, 1245 Oro Dam Blvd.(95965), pg. 335
Setzer Forest Products-Oroville Plant, 1980 Kusel Rd.(95966), pg. 993

Oxnard

CONDOR D.C. POWER SUPPLIES INC., 2311 Statham Pkwy.(93033), pg. 273
DEARDORFF-JACKSON COMPANY, P.O. Box 1188, 1120 Mountain View Ave.(93032), pg. 323
Gene Jackson Farms, P.O. Box 5147(93031), pg. 351
Ransco Industries, Inc., 1400 E. Statham Pkwy.(93033), pg. 332

Pacheco

THE BRADY MARKETING COMPANY, 80 Berry Dr.(94553), pg. 171

Pacoima

LANCE CAMPER MANUFACTURING CORPORATION, 10234 Glenoaks Blvd.(91331), pg. 653

Palmdale

DIMAC DIRECT, 2632 East Ave, Q-14(93550), pg. 338

Palo Alto

LENA CHOW, INC., 627 Emerson St.(94301), pg. 248
HODSKINS SIMONE & SEARLS, INC., 225 Lytton Ave.(94301), pg. 537
Korn/Ferry International, Embarcadero Corporate Center, 2483 E. Bayshore Rd., Ste. 101(94303), pg. 642

Palos Verdes Estates

BRYAN HARDWICK ASSOCIATES, 425 Via Corta(90274), pg. 508

Paramount

MACCO CONSTRUCTORS, INC., P.O. Box 257, 14409 Paramount Blvd.(90723-3418), pg. 696
PARAMOUNT PETROLEUM CORP., 14700 Downey Ave.(90723), pg. 848
The Producto Machine Co., 15958 S. Downey Ave.(90723), pg. 893

Pasadena

CONVERSE PROFESSIONAL GROUP, INC., 3393 E. Foothill Blvd.(91107), pg. 281
CROWN FENCE CO., 939 S. Fair Oaks Ave.(91105), pg. 302
GOLDEN STATE FOODS CORP., 234 E. Colorado Blvd., 8th Flr.(91101), pg. 466
HUTCHINS MANUFACTURING COMPANY, 49 N. Lotus Ave.(91107), pg. 555
Kaiser Permanente, Southern California Division, 393 E. Walnut St.(91188), pg. 614
JACK LAWLOR ADVERTISING, INC., 777 Walnut St.(91101), pg. 661
JAMES M. MONTGOMERY CONSULTING ENGINEERS, 300 N. Lake St., Ste. 1200(91101), pg. 767
PACIFICA SERVICES, INC., 106 S. Mentor Ave., Ste. 200(91106), pg. 842
RUSS REID COMPANY, INC., Two N. Lake Ave., Ste. 600(91101), pg. 923
Rogerson Kratos, 403 S. Raymond Ave.(91109), pg. 944
Servo Products Company, 433 N. Fair Oaks Ave.(91103), pg. 1004
SYMONS CORPORATION, 251 S. Lake Ave., Ste. 606(91101), pg. 1069
SYSTEMS PARKING, INC., 918 E. Green St.(91106), pg. 1071
WELSH GRAPHICS, 2181 E. Foothill Blvd.(91107), pg. 1176
WHITEHAWK PARTNERSHIP, 155 S. El Molino Ave.(91101), pg. 1186

Patterson

PATTERSON FROZEN FOODS, INC., 100 W. Las Palmas(95363), pg. 851

Perris

Bell Grain & Milling, Inc., P.O. Box 758(92370), pg. 769
Golden West Homes Perris Div., 3100 N. Perris Blvd.(92557), pg. 467
Handsome Rewards, 3660 Brennan Ave.(92370), pg. 1040
NATIONAL R.V., INC., 3411 N. Perris Blvd.(92370), pg. 792
Signatures, 3660 Brennan Ave.(92370), pg. 1040
Starcrest of California, 3660 Brennan Ave.(92370), pg. 1040
STARCREST PRODUCTS OF CALIFORNIA, 3660 Brennan Ave.(92370), pg. 1040

Petaluma

REGAN HOLDING CORPORATION, 1179 N. McDowell Blvd. N.(94954), pg. 921
Willitts Design, 1129 Industrial Ave.(94952), pg. 502

Pico Rivera

General Felt Industries, Inc., 8320 Rex Rd.(90660), pg. 1121
Harwick Chemical Corp., 7225 Paramount Blvd.(90660), pg. 515
MCLAUGHLIN INDUSTRIAL DISTRIBUTORS, INC., 7141 Paramount Blvd.(90660), pg. 731
ROCKET INDUSTRIES, INC./EXCEL, THE EXERCISE COMPANY, 9935 Beverly Blvd.(90660), pg. 941

WESTCO PRODUCTS, INC., 7351 Crider Ave.(90660), pg. 1178
WINDART HOLDING INC., 9101 Perkins St.(90660), pg. 1195
Windsor Art Products, Inc., 9101 Perkins St.(90660), pg. 1195

Placentia

Hartwell Commercial Division, 620 S. Jefferson St., Unit A(92670-4783), pg. 514
THE HARTWELL CORPORATION, 900 S. Richfield Rd.(92670-6788), pg. 514
Instrument Specialties - Western Division, 505 Porter Way(92670), pg. 572
Microdot Inserts, 190 W. Crowther(92670), pg. 749
Tekra Corp., West Coast Div., 540 Porter Way(92670), pg. 1084

Placerville

Henningsen & Sons, Inc., 600 Placerville Dr.(95667), pg. 1084

Pleasant Hill

BAM PUBLICATIONS, INC., 3470 Buskirk Ave.(94523), pg. 117
BROWN & CALDWELL CONSULTING ENGINEERS, 3480 Buskirk Ave.(94523), pg. 181

Pleasanton

Ames Taping Tool Systems Co., 6691 Owens Dr.(94588), pg. 8
ARCADIAN POWER CORP., 5990 Stone Ridge Dr., Ste. 119(94588-3234), pg. 80
ASSOCIATED PROCESS CONTROLS, 7150 Koll Center Pkwy.(94566), pg. 92
COMPUTERLAND CORPORATION, 5964 W. La Positas(94566-8575), pg. 271
DILLINGHAM CONSTRUCTION CORPORATION, 5960 Inglewood Dr.(94588-8535), pg. 337
Dillingham Construction N.A., Inc., P.O. Box 1089, 5960 Inglewood Dr.(94588), pg. 338
Life Sciences International-California, 7031 Koll Center Pkwy.; Ste. 300(94566), pg. 320
S & W Fine Foods, 4900 Hopyard Rd., Ste. 285(94566), pg. 1111
SPRECKLES INDUSTRIES, INC., 4234 Hacienda Dr.(94566), pg. 1032
SUN DIAMOND GROWERS OF CALIFORNIA, 5568 Gibraltar Dr.(94588), pg. 1058
Sun-land Products of California, 5568 Gibraltar Dr.(94588), pg. 1058
Viacom Cable, 5924 Stoneridge Dr.(94566), pg. 785

Pomona

CUNA Western District, 2350 S. Garey Ave.(91766), pg. 206
Fundamental Management, Inc., 3880 W. Valley Blvd.(91769), pg. 567
GEMINI ALUMINUM CORPORATION, 3255 Pomona Blvd.(91768), pg. 448
Huntington Tile, Inc., 1315 E. Third St.(91766), pg. 840
Industrial Alloys, Inc., 3880 W. Valley Blvd.(91769), pg. 567
INDUSTRIAL WIRE PRODUCTS CORPORATION, 3880 W. Valley Blvd.(91769), pg. 567
KEYSTONE AUTOMOTIVE INDUSTRIES, INC., 700 E. Bonita Ave.(91767), pg. 627
Valley Hospital, 1410 N. Garey Ave.(91767-3810), pg. 1127
Zenith West Corp., 2675 Pomona Blvd.(91768), pg. 1217

Poway

Johnson Storage & Moving, San Diego, 12225 Kirkham Rd., Ste. 400(92064), pg. 601

Quincy

Nugget Motors, 116 E. Main St.(93971), pg. 719

Rancho Cordova

TIM & DIANE BLAGGE INC., 2590 Mercantile Dr., Suite K(95742), pg. 155
C. C. MYERS, INC., 3286 Fitzgerald Rd.(95742), pg. 780
Quality Medical Adjudication, Inc., 2897 Kilgore Rd.(95670), pg. 521
U.S. COMPUTER SERVICES, 11020 Sun Center Dr.(95670), pg. 1135
West Coast Correct Craft, Inc., 11371 Pyrites Way(95670), pg. 287

Rancho Cucamonga

FORECAST MORTGAGE CORPORATION, 10670 Civic Center Dr.(91730), pg. 423
Industrial Wire Products, 12459 Arrow Rd.(91730), pg. 567
Polyplastic Products, 10220 4th St.(91730), pg. 180
Russell-Stanley West, Inc., 9449 Santa Anita Ave.(91730), pg. 957
SCHLOSSER FORGE COMPANY, 11711 Arrow Rd.(91730), pg. 976

Rancho Dominguez

ASC Protocraft, 19335 S. Laurel Park(90220), pg. 7
ELECTRONICS STAMPING CORP., 19920 S. Alameda St.(90220), pg. 375
Great American Breaded Vegetable Co., 2910 E. Harcourt St.(90221-5502), pg. 1183
SOUTHWESTERN INDUSTRIES, INC., 2605 Homestead Pl.(90220), pg. 1023

Rancho Mirage

ED WALPERT & ASSOCIATES, 69-930 Hwy. 111, Ste. 209 & 210(02270), pg. 1161

Rancho Santa Fe

WARREN PROPERTIES, 6134 La Granada(92067), pg. 1165

Rancho Santa Margarita

NOEL-JOANNA, INC., 22942 Arroyo Vista(92688), pg. 808

Raymond

Raymond Granite Co., 36772 Rd. 606(93653), pg. 260

Redding

McColls Dairy, 2500 Angelo Ave.(96001), pg. 303
SIERRA PACIFIC INDUSTRIES, P.O. Box 496028(96049), pg. 1003

Redlands

Climet Instruments Co., 1320 W. Colton Ave.(92374), pg. 1148
RICHMOND TECHNOLOGY INC., 1897 Colton Ave.(92374), pg. 933

Redondo Beach

BOBIT PUBLISHING COMPANY, 2512 Artesia Blvd.(90278), pg. 161
TIERNAY METALS, INC., 2600 Marine Ave.(90278), pg. 1096

Redwood City

Ampex Corporation Marketing, Sales & Service, 401 Broadway(94063), pg. 998
Ampex Corporation, Video Systems Div., 401 Broadway(94063), pg. 998
Ampex Magnetic Tape Division, 401 Broadway(94063), pg. 998
Ampex Recording Systems Division, 401 Broadway(94063), pg. 998
DHL Airways, Inc., 333 Twin Dolphin Dr.(94065), pg. 309
DHL CORPORATION, 333 Twin Dolphin Dr.(94065), pg. 309
GamePro, 2421 Broadway, Ste. 200(94063), pg. 576
George S. May Intl. Co., 230 Twin Dolphin Dr., Ste. A(94065), pg. 724
NEXT, INC., 900 Chesapeake Dr.(94063), pg. 805

Reedley

SALWASSER MANUFACTURING COMPANY, INC., 20075 E. Manning(93654), pg. 968

Richmond

Gold Bond Building Products, P.O. Box 308, (94806), pg. 790

Ripon

NULAID FOODS, 200 W. 5th St.(95366), pg. 817

Riverside

BOURNS, INC., 1200 Columbia Ave.(92507-2114), pg. 168
Bourns Instruments Inc., 1200 Columbia Ave.(92507), pg. 168
CADDOCK ELECTRONICS, INC., 1717 Chicago Ave.(92507), pg. 207
Caddock Network Division, 1717 Chicago Ave.(92507), pg. 207
California Auto Dealers Exchange, Inc., 6446 Fremont Street(92504), pg. 293
J.D. DIFFENBAUGH, INC., 2375 Chicago Ave.(92507), pg. 337
HUNTER ENGINEERING CO., INC., 1455 Columbia(92507), pg. 554
Las Plumas Lumber South Division, 6464 33rd St.(92509), pg. 335
PRESS ENTERPRISE COMPANY, 3512 14th St.(92501), pg. 887
Resistor Division, 1717 Chicago Ave.(92507), pg. 207

Rosemead

HCC INDUSTRIES, 4232 TempleCity Blvd.(91770), pg. 496
Hermetic Seal Corp., 4232 Temple City Blvd.(91770), pg. 496
Los Angeles Dealers Auto Auctions, 8001 Garvey Ave.(92770-1053), pg. 293

Roseville

FUTURE FORD/HUGO INC., 650 Auto Mall Dr.(95661), pg. 437

Rosewell

ABI National Accounts, 70 Mausell Ct., Suite 100(30076), pg. 50

Sacramento

AIRCO MECHANICAL INC., 5720 Alder Ave.(95828), pg. 27
Allright Sacramento, 708 10th St., Ste. 140(95814), pg. 42
Anchor Fence Company, 8451 Rovana Cir., Ste. 1(95828), pg. 836
Bel Air, , pg. 910
BEL AIR MARKETS, 1901 Royal Oaks Dr.(95815), pg. 133
BEUTLER HEATING & AIR CONDITIONING INC., 9605 Oates Dr.(95827), pg. 148
BLUE ANCHOR, INC., 730 Howe Ave.(95825), pg. 158
BLUE DIAMOND GROWERS, 1802 C St.(95814), pg. 160
Braun/Ketchum Public Relations, 915 L. St., Ste. 1435(95814), pg. 625
CALIFORNIA STATE LOTTERY, 600 N. 10th St.(95814), pg. 210
CAMPBELL CONSTRUCTION CO., 2120 20th St.(95818), pg. 213
Concrete Pipe & Products Co., Inc. of California, P.O. Box 28758(95828), pg. 273
CRYSTAL CREAM & BUTTER COMPANY, 1013 D St.(95814), pg. 303
DE VONS JEWELERS, 1910 29th St.(95816), pg. 321
THE DORRIS LUMBER & MOULDING CO., 2601 Redding Ave.(95820), pg. 347
Elixir Industries, 3443 Airport Rd.(95834), pg. 376
FARMERS RICE COOPERATIVE, 2525 Natomas Park Dr.(95833), pg. 401
FILCO, INC., 1433 Fulton Ave., Suite D(95825), pg. 409
BOB FRINK CHEVROLET G.E.O. MANAGEMENT, 4811 Madison Ave.(95841), pg. 433
Golden State Flooring Company, 1015 N. Market Blvd.(95834), pg. 533
Golden West Homes, Sacramento Div., 9998 Old Placerville Rd.(95827), pg. 467
Hoffman Construction Company of California, 555 University Ave., Ste. 200(95825), pg. 537
HUBACHER CADILLAC INC., 548
MIKE DAUGHERTY'S HURLING CHEVROLET, INC., 2449 Fulton Ave.(95825), pg. 555
LAWSON MECHANICAL CONTRACTORS, 6090 S. Watt Ave.(95829), pg. 663
A. LEVY & J. ZENTNER CO., P.O. Box 292307(95829), pg. 671
Logistics Systems Architects, 3800 Watt Ave., Ste. 210(95821), pg. 982
LUCKY FRUIT & PRODUCE, INC., 2630 5th St.(95818), pg. 686
Master Skiis, 4590 Pell Dr.(95838), pg. 694
The Nadel Partnership, Inc., 1760 Creekside Oaks Dr., Ste. 140(95833), pg. 783
THE NIKKEL CORPORATION, 3091 Fair Oaks Blvd.(95824), pg. 807
PACIFIC COAST BUILDING PRODUCTS INC., 3001 I St.(95816), pg. 839
PALM IRON & BRIDGE WORKS, INC., 8845 Elder Creek Rd.(95828), pg. 843
ROBERT C. POWELL DEVELOPMENTS, INCORPORATED, 3610 American River Dr., 882
RGA Byproducts, P.O. Box 958(95804), pg. 931
RAPTON HONDA-GMC, 2820 Fulton Ave.(95821), pg. 913
REYNEN, BARDIS & WINN, 9985 Folsom Blvd.(95827), pg. 930
Sacramento Industrial Supply, 330 Commerce Circle(95815), pg. 341
SACRAMENTO KINGS, 1 Sports Pkwy.(95834), pg. 965
SACRAMENTO MUNICIPAL UTILITY DISTRICT, 6201 "S" St.(95817), pg. 965
SENATOR FORD, 3801 Florin Rd.(95823), pg. 989
SETZER FOREST PRODUCTS, 2555 Third St.(95818), pg. 993
SWIFT DODGE ROLLS ROYCE INC., 6250 Florin Rd.(95823), pg. 1067
TECON PACIFIC, 1980 S. River Rd. W.(95691), pg. 1084
Teichert Land Co., 3500 American River Dr.(95864), pg. 1084
A. TEICHERT & SON, INC., 3500 American River Dr.(95864), pg. 1084
U.S. Yellow Pages, 455 University Ave., Ste. 270(95825), pg. 1180
VIDEO PRODUCTS DISTRIBUTORS, INC., 6051 S. Watt Ave.(95829), pg. 1150
Vitafreze Frozen Confections, P.O. Box 1313(95806), pg. 303
Von Housen Auto Parts, 11057 Mills Station Rd.(95827), pg. 1155
VON HOUSEN MOTORS, 1810 Howe Ave.(95825), pg. 1155
Westco Products/Sacramento, 521 N. 10th St.(95814), pg. 1178
Western Farm Credit Bank, 3636 American River Dr.(95864), pg. 405
Western International Media Corporation, 455 University Ave., Ste. 270(95825), pg. 1180
WICKLAND CORPORATION, 1765 Challenge Way(95815), pg. 1188
Wickland Oil Company, Inc., 1765 Challenge Way(95815), pg. 1188
WINTER VOLVO & LINCOLN MERCURY, 3805 Florin Rd.(95823), pg. 1197

Saint Helena

SUTTER HOME WINERY, INC., 277 St. Helena Hwy. S.(94574), pg. 1065

Salinas

DICK BRUHN INC., 300 Main St.(93901), pg. 184
First National Bank of Central California, P.O. Box 1786, (93902-1786), pg. 839
KSBW, Inc., 238 John St.(93901), pg. 459
PACIFIC CAPITAL BANCORP, 1001 S. Main St.(9390[illegible]), pg. 839
RADIONICS, INC., 1800 Abbott St.(93901), pg. 909

San Bernardino

Franklin Press, 1001 S. Arrowhead Ave.(92412), pg. 279
GATE CITY BEVERAGE DISTRIBUTORS, 2505 Steele St.(92408), pg. 444
Scotfoam Corp., 1400 A East Victoria Ave.(92406), pg. 1121

San Bruno

AETNA HEALTH PLANS, 1111 Bayhill Dr., Ste. 300(94066), pg. 23
First DataBank, 1111 Bayhill Dr.(94066), pg. 522
Krames Communications, 1100 Grundy Lane(94066), pg. 611

San Carlos

Air Conditioning Co., Inc., 1700 Industrial Rd.(94070), pg. 27
KELLY-MOORE PAINT COMPANY, INC., 987 Commercial St.(94070), pg. 621
QUANTIC INDUSTRIES, INC., 990 Commercial St.(94070), pg. 904

San Clemente

HEIL-BRICE RETAIL ADVERTISING, 101 S. El Camino Real, Ste. 101(92672), pg. 525

San Diego

ACTION INSTRUMENTS, INC., 8601 Aero Dr.(92123), pg. 14
Air Conditioning Co., Inc., 7179 Construction Ct., Ste. A(92121), pg. 27
Allied Security Inc., 6151 Fairmont Ave., Ste. 207(92120), pg. 39
Allright San Diego Parking, Inc., 3740 Fifth Ave(92103), pg. 42
ARNOLDS INTERIORS, INC., 9740 Scranton, Ste. 300(92121), pg. 85
Arts & Crafts Press, 3590 Kettner Blvd.(92101), pg. 279
ATLAS HOTELS, INC., 500 Hotel Circle(92186), pg. 96
BIG BEAR SUPERMARKETS NO. 3, 5075 Federal Blvd.(92102), pg. 149
Bull, Inc., 10260 Campus Point Dr.(92121), pg. 981
JOHN BURNHAM & CO., 610 W. Ash(92101), pg. 194
Calmark Hospitality Systems, 5405 Morehouse Dr., 211
Campbell Industries, Inc., P.O. Box 1870, Harbor Dr. & 8th Ave.(92112), pg. 707
CAPENER, MATTHEWS & WALCHER, 620 C St., 6th Fl.(92101), pg. 214
Cox Cable San Diego, Inc., 5159 Federal Blvd.(92105), pg. 294
Datacomm, 438 Camino del Rio So., Ste. 201(92198), pg. 150
DEANS PHOTO SERVICE, INC., 4575 Mission George Pl.(92120), pg. 322
ROBERT F. DRIVER CO., INC., 1620 Fifth Ave.(92101-2703), pg. 349
Ektelon Corp., 8929 Aero Dr.(92123), pg. 890
EXPO INDUSTRIES, INC., 7465 Carroll Rd.(92121), pg. 393
H.G. FENTON MATERIAL COMPANY, 7220 Trade St., Ste. 300(92121), pg. 406
Fuji TruColor Foto, 4686 Mission Gorge Pl.(92120), pg. 322
GORDON & SMITH, INC., 7081 Consolidated Way(92121), pg. 472
GREEN LEAF VENTURES, INC., 6610 Convoy Ct.(92111), pg. 484
The Hahn Co., 4350 La Jolla Villiage Dr., Ste. 700(92122), pg. 1115
HAWTHORNE MACHINERY COMPANY, P.O. Box 708(92112), pg. 519
Hawthorne Power Systems, P.O. Box 708, (92112), pg. 519
RONI HICKS & ASSOCIATES, INC., 1875 Third Ave.(92101), pg. 533
HOPE DESIGN GROUP, 4520 Executive Dr., Ste. 300(92121), pg. 543
Kettenburg Marine, 3010 Carleton St.(92106), pg. 626
Kettenburg Marine, 2810 Carleton St.(92106), pg. 626
KETTENBURG MARINE CORPORATION, 2810 Carleton St.(92106), pg. 626
Keystone Automotive Industries, Inc. - San Diego, 11 30th Street(92102), pg. 627
KNOTH & MEADS COMPANY, 401 West A St., 11th Fl.(92101), pg. 637
KROMMENHOEK MCKEOWN ASSOCIATES, 1515 Morena Blvd.(92110), pg. 645
LAMBESIS COMMUNICATIONS, 11770 Bernardo Plaza Ct., Ste. 308(92128), pg. 652
LASER POWER CORPORATION, 12777 High Bluff Dr.(92130), pg. 660
Lear Siegler Accurate Corp., 4370 Jutland Dr.(92117), pg. 664
Marco Marine San Diego, P.O. Box 1870, (92112), pg. 707
MCKELLAR DEVELOPERS OF LA JOLLA, 5151 Shoreham, Suite 200(92122), pg. 730
NATIONAL STEEL & SHIPBUILDING COMPANY, Harbor Dr. at 28th(92113), pg. 794
NELSON PHOTO SUPPLIES, 722 33rd St.(92102), pg. 797
NIELSEN CONSTRUCTION COMPANY, 3127 Jefferson St.(92110), pg. 807
Ninteman Construction Company, Inc., 4375 Jutland Dr., 1060
NuEar Electronics, 10070 Mesa Rim Rd.(92121), pg. 1040
OCTUS, 9940 Barnes Canyon Rd.(92121), pg. 818
OLD STONE OF CALIFORNIA, INC., 9449 Balboa Ave., Ste.300(92133), pg. 823
PACIFIC SCENE INC., 3900 Harney St.(92110), pg. 841
Point Builders, 3130 Bonita Rd., pg. 473
Premium Advance Company, 1620 5th Ave., P.O. Box 670(92101), pg. 349
Pre-Mix Concrete Co., 7220 Trade St., Ste.300(92121), pg. 406
PROXIMA CORPORATION, 6610 Nancy Ridge Dr.(92121), pg. 896
RED CARPET REAL ESTATE SERVICES, INC., P.O. Box 85660, (92138), pg. 918
ROBINHOOD HOMES, INC., 6335 Ferris Sq., Suite G(92121), pg. 939
Robson, Cavignac & Associates, 1230 Columbia St., Ste. 400(92101-3528), pg. 662
Rubin Postaer and Associates, 625 Broadway, Ste. 1025(92101), pg. 954
Rush Press, 8835 Complex Dr.(92123), pg. 279
SAIC Commercial Enterprises, Inc., 10260 Campus Point Dr.(92121), pg. 982
SAN DIEGO CHARGERS, 9449 Friars Rd.(92108), pg. 969
SAN DIEGO ZOO, 2920 Zoo Dr.(92112), pg. 969
SCIENCE APPLICATIONS INTERNATIONAL CORPORATION, 10260 Campus Point Drive(92121-1522), pg. 981
Shea Homes San Diego, 10721 Treena St., Ste. 200(92131-1039), pg. 996
SITHE ENERGIES, U.S.A., INC., 401 "B" St., Suite 1000(92101), pg. 1009
SOUTHWEST FLOOR COVERING INC., 6965 Consolidated Way(92121), pg. 1023
SOUTHWEST MARINE, INC., P.O. Box 13308(92170), pg. 1023
Specialty Restaurants Corp, 8885 Balboa Ave.(92123), pg. 1028
SYSTECH COMPUTER CORPORATION, 6465 Nancy Ridge Dr.(92121), pg. 1071
TYLAN GENERAL, INC., 9577 Chesapeake Drive(92123), pg. 1122
Ultra Drug, 8330 Arjons Dr.(92126), pg. 384
Union-Tribune Publishing Company, 350 Camino de la Reina(92108-4106), pg. 284
THE VAGABOND INNS, 5405 Moorehouse Dr., Ste. 200(92121), pg. 1142
The Vagabond Inns, 5405 Morehouse Dr., Ste. 200(92121), pg. 1142
WAVETEK CORPORATION, 9045 Balboa Ave.(92123), pg. 1168
Wavetek San Diego Inc., P.O. Box 85265, 9045 Balboa Ave.(92123), pg. 1168
Western International Media Corporation, 610 W. Ash, Ste. 810(92101), pg. 1180
WESTERN PACIFIC DATA SYSTEMS, 7373 Engineer Rd.(92111), pg. 1180
WOODFIN HOLDING CORPORATION, 9255 Towne Center Dr., Ste. 900(92121), pg. 1200
Woodfin Hotel Management, Inc., 9255 Towne Center Dr., Ste. 900(92121), pg. 1200
Woodfin Suites, Inc., 9255 Towne Center Dr., Ste. 900(92121), pg. 1200

San Fernando

BERNARDS BROTHERS, INC., 610 Ilex St.(91340), pg. 143
Cordova Laboratories, 13177 Foothill Blvd.(91342), pg. 286
Cordova Laboratories-I.A.F. Div., 13177 Foothill Blvd.(91342), pg. 286
OH BOY CORPORATION, 1516 First St.(91340), pg. 822

San Francisco

ABI Management, Inc., 160 Spear St., Ste. 1540(94105), pg. 53
ADLAND ADVERTISING, INC., 3000 Steiner-on-Union(94123), pg. 17
Air Fresh Trucking, 2351 Powell St.(94133), pg. 1193
Allied Security Inc., 50 First Street Bldg., Ste. 511(94105), pg. 39
Allright San Francisco Parking, Inc., 655 Fourth St.(94107), pg. 42
Amfac Nurseries Cole, Inc., 44 Montgomery St.(94120), pg. 585
Anderson & Lembke, Inc., 77 Maiden Lane(94108), pg. 244
ANDERSON, ROTHSTEIN & FIQUA, 28 Geary St., 7th Fl.(94108), pg. 73
ARCATA CORPORATION, 601 California St., Ste. 1800(94108), pg. 80
The Architects Collaborative, Inc., 649 Front St.(94111), pg. 81
Arkansas & Memphis Railway Bridge and Terminal Co., Southern Pacific Bldg., One Market Plaza(94105), pg. 76
ATLAS CITRON HALIGMAN & BEDECARRE, 855 Front St.(94111), pg. 96
Backer Spielvogel Bates, Inc., 100 Spear St., Ste. 940(94105), pg. 109
BASIC AMERICAN FOODS, 550 Kearny, Ste. 1000(94108), pg. 124
Bechtel Civil, Inc., 50 Beale St.(94105), pg. 131
BECHTEL GROUP, INC., 50 Beale St.(94105), pg. 130
Bechtel, Inc. Mining & Metals Special Operation, 50 Beale St.(94105), pg. 131
Bechtel National, Inc., 50 Beale St.(94105), pg. 131
Bechtel Power Corporation, 50 Beale St.(94105), pg. 131
BLUE SHIELD OF CALIFORNIA, Blue Shield Plaza, 2 N. Point(94133), pg. 161
BYER CALIFORNIA, 66 Potrero Avenue(94103), pg. 197
CKS PARTNERS, 345 Spear St., Ste. 500(94105), pg. 202
CSE CORPORATION, 989 Market St.(94103), pg. 204
CSE Services Insurance Brokerage, 989 Market St.(94103), pg. 205
California Physicians Insurance Corp., Two North Point(94133), pg. 161
CARPENTER RIGGING, 222 Napolean St.(94124), pg. 224
Central California Traction Co., One Market Plaza(94105), pg. 76
CHEMOIL, 750 Battery St., 6th Fl.(94111), pg. 242
Chiat/Day/Mojo Inc. Advertising, 77 Maiden(94108), pg. 244
Chiat/Day/Mojo/San Francisco, 77 Maiden Lane(94108), pg. 245
Civil Service Employees Insurance Co., 989 Market St.(94103), pg. 205
Civil Service Employees Life Insurance Co., 989 Market St.(94103), pg. 205
COLSKY MEDIA, INC., 2740 Van Ness Ave., Ste. 220(94109), pg. 265
Curtis Swann, 50 Dorman St.(94124-1845), pg. 190
Dallas Terminal Railway and Union Depot Co., One Market Plaza, Southern Pacific Bldg.(94105), pg. 76
DEL MONTE FOODS, One Market Plaza(94105), pg. 325
Dimac Direct, 1400 Evans Ave.(94124-0527), pg. 338
DINWIDDIE CONSTRUCTION CO., 275 Battery St. 338
DONALDSON GROUP, 27 Maiden Lane, 7th Floor(94108), pg. 344
ELS Educational Services, 3661 Buchanan St.(34123), pg. 56
Esprit Accessories, 900 Minnesota St.(94107), pg. 388
ESPRIT DE CORP., 900 Minnesota St.(94107), pg. 388
Esprit Department, 900 Minnesota St.(94107), pg. 388
Esprit Kids, 900 Minnesota St.(94107), pg. 388
Esprit Sport, 900 Minnesota St.(94107), pg. 388
EvansGroup, 690 Fifth St.(94107), pg. 391
Execu-Fit Health Programs, Inc., One Lombard St.(94111), pg. 1127
FABIANAC, STROPES & ARMSTRONG, INC., 120 Broadway(94111), pg. 395
THE FAIRMONT HOTELS, Atop Nob Hill(94108), pg. 397
FREEMAN BLANSHEI PARTNERS, 1714 Stockton St., 4th Fl.(94133), pg. 431
FRITZ COMPANIES, INC., 706 Mission St.(94103), pg. 434
GARDNER COMMUNICATIONS, INC., 77 Geary St., Ste. 500(94108), pg. 443
GEORGE LITHOGRAPH, 650 Second St.(94107), pg. 452
The Getz Corporation, 150 Post St.(94108), pg. 712
GOLDBERG MOSER O'NEILL, 77 Maiden Lane(94108), pg. 465
GOLDEN GATE UNIVERSITY, 536 Mission St.(94105), pg. 466
GUMP'S, INC., 250 Post St.(94108), pg. 494
HAAS BROTHERS, 2200 Jerrold Ave.(94124), pg. 498
Harwick Chemical Corp., 1485 Bayshore Blvd.(94124), pg. 515
HIPPOCRATES PARTNERS, 301 Howard St., 18th Fl.(94105), pg. 535
I. Magnin & Co., 135 Stockton St.(94108), pg. 699
Integrated Media, Inc., 501 2nd St.(94107), pg. 576
JAMISON, CAWDREY, BENJAMIN, 130 Sutter St.(94104), pg. 589
The Jeans Company, Levi's Plz., 1155 Battery St.(94111), pg. 670
John Hancock Capital Growth Management, Inc., 1140 Taylor St.(94108), pg. 596
KATSIN/LOEB ADVERTISING, 1050 Battery St., 1st Fl.(94111), pg. 618
Keller & Gannon, 1453 Mission St.(94103), pg. 637
Ketchum Advertising/San Francisco, 55 Union St.(94111), pg. 625
Ketchum Advertising/USA, 55 Union St.(94111), pg. 625
Ketchum Public Relations/San Francisco, 55 Union St.(94111), pg. 625
KORET OF CALIFORNIA, 611 Mission St.(94105), pg. 642
Koret of California, 595 Market St., 15th Fl.(94105), pg. 642
Korn/Ferry International, The Transamerica Pyramid, 600 Montgomery St., 31st Fl.(94111), pg. 642
KRANSCO, 160 Pacific Ave., Ste. 200(94111), pg. 644
LEVI STRAUSS & CO., 1155 Battery St.(94111), pg. 670
Levi Strauss International, 1155 Battery St.(94111), pg. 670
Levi Strauss Sportswear, 1155 Battery St.(94111), pg. 670
Lexmark International, Inc., 425 Market St., 6th Fl.(94105), pg. 674
Livingston & Company, 250 Sutter St.(94108), pg. 679
MBT ASSOCIATES, INC., 539 Bryant St.(94107), pg. 691
MPC World, 524 2nd St.(94107), pg. 576
MACDANIELS, HENRY & SPROUL, INC., 930 Montgomery St.(94133), pg. 696
Macworld, 501 2nd St.(94107), pg. 576
MANDELBAUM MOONEY ASHLEY, 111 Maiden Lane(94108), pg. 703
Menswear Div., Levi's Plz., 1155 Battery St.(94111), pg. 670
MUHLHAUSER & YOUNG, 544 Pacific Ave., Ste. 300(94133), pg. 774
National Yellow Pages Monitor (NYPM), 785 Market St.(94103), pg. 781
Nationwide Funding Inc., 1275 Market St.(94119), pg. 795
Northwestern Pacific Railroad Co., One Market Plaza, Southern Pacific Bldg.(94105), pg. 75
O'KEEFFE'S, INC., 75 Williams Ave.(94124), pg. 823
OMEGA PERFORMANCE GROUP, 71 Stevenson St., Ste. 1450(94105), pg. 826
PC World, 501 2nd St.(94107), pg. 576
Pacific Shipper, Inc., 562 Mission St.(94105), pg. 611
PALLAS ADVERTISING, INC., 1160 Battery St., Ste. 200(94111), pg. 843
PINNE/HERBERS ADVERTISING INC., 200 Vallejo St.(94111), pg. 871
PUBLIC MEDIA CENTER, 466 Green St.(94133), pg. 898
REFERENCE SOFTWARE INTERNATIONAL, 330 Townsend St., Ste. 119(94107), pg. 921
F/S REILLY, MEDIA +, 3717 Buchanan St.(94123), pg. 923
HAL RINEY & PARTNERS, INC., 735 Battery St.(94111), pg. 935
ROYAL CRUISE LINE INC., 1 Maritime Plaza, Ste. 1400(94111), pg. 953
SP Telcom Corporation, One Market Plaza(94105), pg. 75
Safety And Fire Technology, Inc., 1240 Fitzgerald St.(94124), pg. 823
St. Louis Southwestern Railway Co., One Market Plaza, Southern Pacific Bldg.(94105), pg. 75
San Francisco Examiner, 110 5th St.(94103), pg. 524
SAN FRANCISCO GIANTS BASEBALL CLUB, Candlestick Park(94124), pg. 969
San Francisco Knitting Mills, 4610 Mission St., Ste. 300(94112), pg. 978
San Francisco Realties, 200 Hearst Bldg.(94103), pg. 524
SCHOOL APPAREL, INC., 4610 Mission St., Ste. 300(94112), pg. 978
THE SHIDLER GROUP, 4 Embarcadero Ctr., Ste. 3150(94111), pg. 999
THE SIERRA CAPITAL COMPANIES, 455 Market St., Ste. 1690(941-5), pg. 1002
Simpson Paper Co., One Post St.(94104), pg. 1007
SOUTHERN PACIFIC LINES, One Market Plaza, Southern Pacific Bldg.(94105), pg. 1022
Southern Pacific Transportation Co., One Market Plaza, Southern Pacific Bldg.(94105), pg. 75
Southern Pacific Warehouse Co., One Market Plaza, Southern Pacific Bldg.(94105), pg. 76

Sunical Land & Livestock Division, 200 Hearst Building(94103), pg. 524
Sunset Railway Co., One Market Plaza, Southern Pacific Bldg.(94105), pg. 76
SWINERTON & WALBERG CO., 580 California St.(94104), pg. 1068
TALLANT LAPOINTE & PARTNERS, INC., 825 Battery St.(94111), pg. 1077
Bob Thomas & Associates, 77 Maiden Ln., 2nd Fl.(94108), pg. 244
THE TODD-AO CORPORATION, 172 Golden Gate Ave.(94102), pg. 1099
TRI VALLEY GROWERS INC., 1255 Battery St.(94120), pg. 1111
U.S. Yellow Pages, 440 Pacific Ave.(94133), pg. 1180
Visalia Electric Railroad Co., One Market Plaza, Southern Pacific Bldg.(94105), pg. 76
West Coast Life Insurance Co., 343 Sansome St.(94104), pg. 795
Western International Media Corporation, 440 Pacific Ave.(94133), pg. 1180
Western Video Images, Inc., 600 Townsend Street, Suite 300W(94103), pg. 1182
WILBUR-ELLIS COMPANY & CONNELL BROTHERS COMPANY, 320 California St.(94104), pg. 1189
WILSEY BENNETT CO., 2351 Powell St., Ste. 500(94133), pg. 1193
Wilsey Bennett Real Estate Division, 2351 Powell St.(94133), pg. 1193
WINDMILL HOLDINGS CORP., 801 Montgomery St.(94133), pg. 1195
WINKLER MCMANUS, 150 Spear St., 16th Fl.(94105), pg. 1196
Young & Rubicam San Francisco, 100 First St.(94105), pg. 1211

San Gabriel

HOWARDS APPLIANCES, INC., 300 E. Valley Blvd.(91776), pg. 547
San Gabriel Valley Medical Center, 218 S. Santa Anita Ave.(91776-1137), pg. 1127
UVP, INC., 5100 Walnut Grove(91776), pg. 1124
Wham-O Div. of Kransco, 835 E. Elmonte Blvd.(91778), pg. 644

San Jose

ADEPT TECHNOLOGY, INC., 150 Rose Orchard Way(95134), pg. 17
Airco Commercial Services, Inc., 324 Commercial St.(95112), pg. 27
AUSTIN ASSOCIATES, INC., 2055 Gateway Place, Ste. 600(95110), pg. 98
BATTENBERG, FILLHARDT & WRIGHT, INC., 70 N. Second St.(95113), pg. 126
BORCHERS BROS., 550 Sunol St.(95126), pg. 165
Burke Flooring Products Div., 2250 S. 10th St.(95112), pg. 191
BURKE INDUSTRIES, INC., 2250 So. 10th(95112), pg. 191
BURKE INDUSTRIES INC., 2250 S. 10th St., (95112), pg. 190
Burke Rubber Co., 2250 S. 10th St.(95112), pg. 191
Certronics, Inc., 775 Commercial St.(95112), pg. 1070
THE COAKLEY HEAGERTY COMPANIES, LTD., 1155 N. First St., Ste. 201(95112), pg. 256
Commercial Parts, Ltd., 862 N . 10th St.(95112), pg. 942
CONTINENTAL NATIONAL AMERICAN REAL ESTATE INC., 830-5 Jury Ct., (95112), pg. 280
Conway Import Co. Inc., 2242 Quimby Rd.(95122), pg. 281
DARIEN & KILBURG, INC., 2099 Gateway Pl.(95110), pg. 315
KEYSTONE COFFEE, 3870 Charter Park Dr.(95136), pg. 628
94th Aero Squadron of San Jose, Inc., 1160 Coleman Ave.(95110), pg. 1028
NUTECH Engineers, Inc., 145 Martinvale Ln.(95119), pg. 818
NUTECH, INC., 145 Martinvale Ln.(95119), pg. 817
NUTECH International, Inc, 145 Martinvale Lane(95119), pg. 818
ORCHARD SUPPLY HARDWARE, 6450 Via Del Oro(95119), pg. 828
ROSENDIN ELECTRIC, INC., 880 Mabury Rd.(95133), pg. 948
Shea Homes Northern California, 25 Metro Dr., Ste. 300(95110), pg. 996
Sunshine Shippers, Inc., 2296 Senter Rd., pg. 533
TRACE PRODUCTS, 1040 E. Brokaw Ave.(95131), pg. 1104
UNIPHASE CORPORATION, 163 Baypointe Pkwy.(95134), pg. 1129
Valley Fair Shopping Ctr., 2801 Stevens Creek Rd.(95128), pg. 699
VELCON FILTERS, INC., 1750 Rogers Ave.(95112), pg. 1146

San Juan Bautista

Amfac Amycel, Inc., P.O. Box 1260, (95045), pg. 585

San Leandro

Bay Fair Shopping Ctr., 15555 E. 14th St.(94578), pg. 699
Kallista, Inc., 1658, 2701 Merced St.(94577), pg. 640
PETERSON TRACTOR COMPANY, 955 Marina Blvd.(94577), pg. 865
Standard Process & Engraving Co., 2763 Teagarden St.(94577), pg. 296

San Luis Obispo

KSBY, Inc., 467 Hill St.(93401), pg. 459

San Marcos

POLARIS POOL SYSTEMS, INC., 1709 LaCosta Meadows Dr.(92069-5194), pg. 878

San Marino

FLOWERS OF HAWAII, 2304 Huntington Drive(91108), pg. 421
ZIMMERMAN HOLDINGS, INC., 2600 Mission St., Ste. 100(91108), pg. 1220

San Mateo

J.H. BAXTER & COMPANY, 1700 S. El Camino Real(94402), pg. 127
C B R CEMENT CORPORATION, 1875 S. Grant, Ste. 1000(94402), pg. 199
Coyote Restaurant Corp., Coyote Point Dr.(94401), pg. 1028
Data Preference, Inc., 1950 Elkhorn Court(94403), pg. 712
IDG Books Worldwide, 155 Bovet Rd., Ste. 730(94402), pg. 576
Infoworld Publishing, Inc., 155 Bovet Rd., Ste. 800(94402), pg. 576
La Prensa Asociada, Inc., 207 Second Ave.(94401), pg. 92
SAN MIGUEL (U.S.A.) INC., 1400 Fashion Island Blvd., Ste. 111(94404), pg. 969
VISA U.S.A. INC., 3155 Clearview Way(94402), pg. 1153

San Pedro

The News-Pilot, 362 W. Seventh St.(90731), pg. 284
Ports O'Call Restaurant Corp., Berth 76(90731), pg. 1028

San Rafael

Phoenix American Alarm Affiliates, Inc., 2401 Kerner Blvd.(94901-5527), pg. 868
PHOENIX AMERICAN INCORPORATED, 2401 Kerner Blvd.(94901), pg. 868
Phoenix Cable Incorporated, 2401 Kerner Blvd.(94901), pg. 868
Phoenix Fiber Link Inc., 2401 Kerner Blvd.(94901), pg. 868
Phoenix Growth Capital Corp., 2401 Kerner Blvd.(94901), pg. 868
Phoenix Leasing Incorporated, 2401 Kerner Blvd.(94901), pg. 868
Phoenix Securities, Inc., 2401 Kerner Blvd.(94901), pg. 868
Phoenix Systems Exchange, Inc., 2401 Kerner Blvd.(94901), pg. 868
Reliable Graphics, , pg. 1165

San Ramon

THE ALAMO LEARNING SYSTEMS, INC., 3160 Crow Canyon Rd., Ste. 250(94583), pg. 29
Lindenmeyr Paper, 2694 Bishop Drive(94583), pg. 233
S & W Fine Foods, Inc., 3160 Crow Canyon Rd.(64583-0587), pg. 1111
Tracor Aerospace, Inc. Expendables Division, Bollinger Canyon Rd.(94583), pg. 1105

Santa Ana

ACL TECHNOLOGIES, INC., 1505 E. Warner Ave.(92705), pg. 2
Aluminum Forge Company, 502 E. Alton St.(92707), pg. 711
BELGRAVE INDUSTRIES, 3320 W. MacArthur(92704), pg. 133
Benmar, 3320 W. MacArthur Blvd.(92704), pg. 133
CALIFORNIA AVOCADO COMMISSION, 1251 E. Dyer Rd., Ste. 200(92705), pg. 209
CASE-SWAYNE CO. INC., 1632 E. 4th St.(92702), pg. 228
GOLDEN WEST HOMES, 1308 E. Wakeham Ave.(92705), pg. 467
INFOTEC DEVELOPMENT, INC., 3611 S. Harbor Blvd., Ste. 260(92704), pg. 567
Kimglass Division, 2200 S. Yale St.(92704), pg. 630
KIMSTOCK, INC., 2200 S. Yale St.(92704), pg. 630
NATIONAL MEDIA MAIL, INC., 1820 E. First St., Ste. 500(92705), pg. 792
NOVA POWER, INC., 1231 E. Dyer Rd., Ste. 110(92705), pg. 816
OLD QUAKER PAINT CO., 2209 S. Main St.(92707), pg. 823
The Orange County Register, 625 N. Grand Ave.(92701), pg. 431
PACKAGING PRODUCTS & DESIGN, 2120 S. Susan St.(92704-4494), pg. 842
RHOADES DEVELOPMENT, 1801 C Parkcourt Place(92701), pg. 931
South Coast Lighting Systems, 2200 S. Anne St.(92704), pg. 588
Standard Concrete, 117 W. Fourth St.(92701), pg. 199
U.S. DIVERS CO., INC., 3323 W. Warner Ave.(92799), pg. 1135

Santa Ana Heights

S.W. JR. ENTERPRISES, INC., 2031 Orchard Dr., Ste. 201(92707), pg. 965

Santa Barbara

Beaver Free Corp., 200 E. Carrillo St., Ste. 200(93101), pg. 842
Channel Industries, Inc., 839 Ward Dr.(93111), pg. 239
CHANNEL TECHNOLOGIES, INC., 839 Ward Dr.(93111), pg. 239
Electro Optical Ind., 839 Ward Dr.(93111), pg. 239
EVANS, HARDY & YOUNG, INC., 829 De la Vina St.(93101), pg. 390
International Transducer Corporation, 869 Ward Dr.(93111), pg. 239
Invest West Financial Corporation, Ste. 302, 200 E. Carrillo St.(93101), pg. 842
MISSION INDUSTRIES, 2936 De La Vina St.(93105), pg. 760
PACIFICA REAL ESTATE GROUP, 200 E. Carrillo St., Ste. 200(93101), pg. 842
Sloan Technology, 602 E. Montecito St.(93103), pg. 1146
Sonatech, Inc., 879 Ward Dr.(93111), pg. 239
JACOB STERN & SONS, INC., 1464 E. Valley Rd.(93108), pg. 1047

Santa Clara

A.D. Controls, 791 Nuttman St.(95054), pg. 1070
COMMERCIAL & INDUSTRIAL ADMINISTRATION CO INC, 1265 El Camino Real(95052), pg. 268
Stephen Gould of California, 4633 Old Ironsides Dr.(95050), pg. 474
Hearst Cablevision of California, Inc., 2700 Scott Blvd.(95050), pg. 523
Idylwild Corporation, 2620 Augustine Dr., Ste. 120(95054), pg. 1004
InfoCorp, 2880 Lakeside Dr., Ste. 300(95056), pg. 1219
INTECH ADVANCED ANALOG, 2270 Martin Ave.(95050), pg. 572
Potpourri (Harte-Hanks California CDM, Inc.), 1350 Duane Ave.(95054), pg. 513
PRECISION ECHO, INC., 3105 Patrick Henry Dr.(95054), pg. 885
ROGERS & ASSOCIATES ADVERTISING, INC., 3032 Bunker Hill Lane, Ste. 207(95054), pg. 943
SAE ENGINEERING, INC., 340 Martin Ave.(95050), pg. 959
SILICON VALLEY DEVELOPMENT, 2620 Augustine Dr., Ste. 101(95054), pg. 1004
Tri-Data Systems, 3270 Scott Blvd.(95054), pg. 102
ZYCON CORPORATION, 445 El Camino Real(95050), pg. 1221

Santa Cruz

GLICO HARMONY FOODS CORPORATION, 719 Swift St.(95060), pg. 462
Monterey Mushrooms, Inc., P.O. Box 1990, (95061), pg. 585
SALZ LEATHERS, INC., P.O. Box 1840(95061-1840), pg. 968

Santa Fe Springs

A & A Associates, 12118 Bloomfield(90670), pg. 1220
Alimak Elevator Company, 11912 Rivera Rd.(90670), pg. 34
American Envelope of Los Angeles, 13341 Cambridge St.(90670), pg. 199
CHEMCENTRAL/Los Angeles, 13900 S. Carmenita Rd.(90670-4997), pg. 242
Jon Donaire Pastries, Inc., 942 Sorensen Ave.(90670), pg. 888
FEDCO, INC., 9300 Santa Fe Springs Rd.(90670), pg. 404
Golden West Refining Company, 13539 E. Foster Rd.(90670), pg. 1096
MARTRADE LTD., 13705 Milroy Place(90670), pg. 716
METALCENTER, INC., 12034 Greenstone Avenue(90670), pg. 742
National Computer Supplies, 13827 Carmenita Rd.(90670), pg. 931
Nuarc Western Div., 12130 Mora Dr., Unit 817
PIPE FABRICATING & SUPPLY COMPANY, 9703 S. Norwalk Blvd.(90670), pg. 872
Powerine Oil Company, 12354 E. Lakeland Rd.(90670), pg. 883
POWERINE OIL COMPANY HOLDINGS, 12354 E. Lakeland Rd.(90670), pg. 883
RHS, 15180 Spring Ave.(90670), pg. 907
RICCOBON & COMPANY, INC., 13827 Carmenita Rd.(90670), pg. 931
Transilwrap Company, Inc., 11875 Burke St.(90670), pg. 1107
TRIANGLE DISTRIBUTING COMPANY, 12065 Pike St.(90670), pg. 1111
Votaw Precision Technologies, 13153 Lakeland Rd.(90670), pg. 614
Yellowstone Transportation Service, Inc., 13705 Milroy Pl.(90670), pg. 716

Santa Maria

DEN-MAT CORPORATION, 2727 Skyway Dr.(93455), pg. 328
KCOY-TV, 1211 McCoy Lane(93455), pg. 1043
QUINTRON SYSTEMS, INC., 2105 S. Blosser(93454), pg. 905

Santa Monica

A-MARK FINANCIAL, 100 Wilshire Blvd., 3rd Fl.(90401), pg. 1
CBM AMERICA CORP., 2020 Santa Monica Blvd., Ste. 410(90404), pg. 199
CANDLE CORPORATION, 2425 Olympic Blvd.(90404), pg. 214
CARLSBERG FINANCIAL CORP., 2800 28th St., Ste. 200(90405), pg. 220
COLLINS & AIKMAN GROUP INC., 3340 Ocean Park Blvd. Ste. 2000(90405), pg. 262
THE DEUTSCH COMPANY, 2444 Wilshire Blvd., Rm. 600(90403), pg. 333
Ellerbe Becket-Los Angeles, Colorado Place, 2501 Colorado Ave.(90404-3585), pg. 378
JOEL GOLDSTEIN MARKETING COMMUNICATIONS, 2701 Ocean Park Blvd., Ste. 201(90405), pg. 469
Gumps, 2800 Olympic Blvd., Ste. 203(90404), pg. 494
KRESSER/CRAIG, 2501 Colorado Ave., 2nd Fl.(90404-3585), pg. 644
THE MACERICH CO., 233 Wilshire Blvd., Ste. 700(90401), pg. 696
MARTIN & BENEDICT INC., 1250 6th St., Ste. 200(90401), pg. 714

Morley Construction Co., Inc., 2901 28th St.(90405), pg. 770
MORLEY GROUP, 2901 28th St.(90409), pg. 770
The Outlook, 1920 Colorado Ave.(90406), pg. 284
PSOMAS & ASSOCIATES, 3420 Ocean Park Blvd.(90405), pg. 898
RAND, 1700 Main St.(90407-2138), pg. 911
RUBIN POSTAER & ASSOCIATES, 1333 2nd St.(90401), pg. 954
SANTA MONICA FORD COMPANY, 1230 Santa Monica Blvd.(90404), pg. 970
Santa Monica Hospital Medical Center, 1250 16th St.(90404-1200), pg. 1127
SNYDER-DIAMOND, 1399 Olympic Blvd.(90404), pg. 1015
SUISSA/MILLER, 3015 Main St., Ste. 300(90405), pg. 1056
TECHNOLOGY TRANSFER INSTITUTE, 741 10th St.(90402), pg. 1084
USA PETROLEUM CORPORATION, 2701 Ocean Park Blvd., Ste. 210(90405), pg. 1124
WATT INDUSTRIES, 2716 Ocean Park Blvd.(90405), pg. 1168
WILLIAMS TELEVISION TIME, INC., 1630 21st St.(90404), pg. 1191

Santa Rosa

BIW Cable Systems-Connector Systems Div., 500 Tesconi Circle(95401), pg. 107
SANTA ROSA STEEL FORMING, INC., 1219 Briggs Ave.(95401), pg. 970

Santee

County Tool & Abrasive, 9263 Abraham Way(92071), pg. 185

Saticoy

Petoseed Co., 1905 Lirio(93003), pg. 116

Saugus

BLUE CROSS LABORATORIES, 26411 N. Golden Valley Rd.(91350), pg. 160
KEYSOR CENTURY CORPORATION, 26000 Springbrook Ave.(91350), pg. 627

Sausalito

JOHN WILLIAMS & ASSOCIATES, LTD., 180 Harbor Dr., Ste. 228(94965), pg. 1190
Yellow Pages Marketing Services, Inc.-San Francisco, 232 Bay Vista Circle, Ste. 100(94965), pg. 1074

Seal Beach

MULTI-MEDIA MARKETING COMMUNICATIONS, INC. (M.M.M.C., INC.), 3030 Old Ranch Pkwy., Ste. 210(90740-2752), pg. 775

Sebastopol

HearthSong, Inc., 400 Morris St.(95473), pg. 426
M M S Design, 7775 Healdsburg Ave.(95472), pg. 734

Selma

Harris Ranch Beef Co., P.O. Box 220, (93662), pg. 512
UP-RIGHT, INC., 1775 Park St.(93662), pg. 1139
WEST COAST GROWERS & PACKERS, INC., 1445 Nebraska(93662), pg. 1177

Sherman Oaks

Hamburger Hamlets Inc., 14156 Magnolia Blvd.(91423-1119), pg. 1169
MRS. GOOCHS NATURAL FOOD MARKETS, 15315 Magnolia Blvd., Ste. 320(91403), pg. 761
Outdoor Services, Inc., 15315 Magnolia Blvd.(91403), pg. 1180
SUNKIST GROWERS, INC., 14130 Riverside Dr.(91423-2392), pg. 1060

Simi Valley

BEMCO INC., 2255 Union Pl.(93065), pg. 138
BUGLE BOY INDUSTRIES, INC., 2900 Madera Rd.(93065), pg. 187
CERWIN VEGA, INC., 555 E. Easy St.(93065), pg. 237
Dragon International, 2900 Madera Rd.(93065), pg. 187
MICOM COMMUNICATIONS CORP., 4100 Los Angeles Ave.(93063), pg. 748

Sonoma

SONOMA MISSION INN & SPA, 18140 Sonoma Hwy.(95476), pg. 1018

Soquel

Network Home Services, Inc., 2425 Porter St., Ste 16(95073), pg. 798
NETWORK REAL ESTATE OF CALIFORNIA, INC., 2425 Porter St., Ste. 16(95073), pg. 798
Network Real Estate of Central California, Inc., 2425 Porter St., Ste. 16(95073), pg. 798
Network Real Estate, Inc., 2425 Porter St., Ste. 16(95073), pg. 798
Network Real Estate of Los Angeles, Inc., 2425 Porter St., Ste. 16(95073), pg. 798
Network Real Estate of Northern California, Inc., 2425 Porter St., Ste. 16(95073), pg. 798
Network Real Estate of Southern California, Inc., 2425 Porter St., Ste. 16(95073), pg. 798

South El Monte

BURKE ENGINEERING COMPANY, 9700 Factorial Way(91733), pg. 190
Los Angeles Die Mold, 1942 N. Rosemead Blvd.(91733), pg. 875
Rolock of California, 1475 Potrero Ave.(91733), pg. 945
ZACKY FARMS, INC., 2000 N. Tyler Ave.(91733), pg. 1215

South Gate

Flewelling Div., 12411 Industrial Ave., Box 2247(90280), pg. 359
SCHULTZ STEEL COMPANY, 5321 Firestone Blvd.(90280), pg. 979
WEATHERBY, INC., 2781 Firestone Blvd.(90280), pg. 1169
Western Metal Finishing Division, P.O. Box 1399, 10647 S. Garfield Ave.(90280), pg. 1073
WORLD OIL COMPANY, 9302 Garfield(90280), pg. 1203

South Pasadena

TACT HOLDING, 538 Mission St.(91030), pg. 1076
Trader Joes Co., 538 Mission St.(91030), pg. 1076

South San Francisco

DEUTSCH, SHEA & EVANS, INC., 601 Gateway Blvd., Ste. 950(94080), pg. 333
Golden State Flooring Company, 449 Littlefield Ave.(94080), pg. 533
LITHOTYPE COMPANY, INC., 333 Pt. San Bruno Blvd.(94080), pg. 678
Lucca Packing Div., Nalley's Fine Foods, 360 Harbor Way(94080), pg. 25
Metropolitan Furniture Corporation, 245 E. Harris Ave.(94080), pg. 1044
Nason Automotive, 450 Grand Avenue(94080), pg. 820
NuArc Co., 130 Produce Ave., Ste. E(94080), pg. 817
THE O'BRIEN CORPORATION, 450 E. Grand Ave.(94080), pg. 820
SHAKEY'S INCORPORATED, 651 Gateway Blvd., Ste. 1200(94080-7015), pg. 994
WGM/HYDRO, 270 Lawrence Ave.(94080), pg. 1156
WARRENS WALLER PRESS, 339 Harbor Way(94080), pg. 1165
West Coast Div., 660 Forbes Blvd.(94080), pg. 361

Stanton

ORCO BLOCK COMPANY, 8042 Katella Ave.(90680), pg. 828
VSI FASTENERS, INC., 12362 Beach Blvd.(90680), pg. 1142

Stockton

APACHE PLASTICS, L.P., 2050 E. Fremont(95205), pg. 77
Bioproducts, Inc., 4221 E. Mariposa Rd., P.O. Box 30416(95213-0416), pg. 152
Brooks Products, Stockton, 2441 Charter Way(95206), pg. 180
CALIFORNIA CEDAR PRODUCTS, INC., 400 Fresno Ave.(95203), pg. 209
CHASE CHEVROLET CO., Miner & Hunter(95201), pg. 240
Chase Chrysler/Plymouth, 2979 Auto Center(95212), pg. 240
Diamond Walnut Growers, Inc., 1050 S. Diamond St.(95205), pg. 1058
Express Steel and Plastics, 809 So. Aurora St.(95203), pg. 532
F. R. MANUFACTURING CORPORATION, 2807 South Hwy. 99(95205), pg. 395
HICKINBOTHAM BROS., LTD, 635 S. Aurora St.(95203), pg. 532
GEO. F. SCHULER, INC., 1705 N. Broadway(95205), pg. 979
A. G. SPANOS DEVELOPMENT, INC., 1341 W. Robinhood Dr.(95207), pg. 1025
Stockton Chili Pepper, Inc., 235 N. Center Rd.(95203), pg. 1028
Stockton Restaurant Corp., 321 W. Weber St.(95203), pg. 1028

Studio City

PROTIMEX CORPORATION, 11846 Venture Blvd., Ste. 301(91604), pg. 895

Sun City

Identification Systems, P.O. Box N, (92586), pg. 721

Sun Valley

W. Braun Co., 9455 Chivers Ave., Shadow Mountain Industrial Pk.(91352), pg. 172
PMC, INC., 12243 Branford St.(91353), pg. 836
R & G SLOANE MFG. CO., INC., 7600 N. Clybourn Ave.(91352), pg. 1010

Sunland

Cherokee Apparel Corp., 9545 Wentworth St.(91040), pg. 243
THE CHEROKEE GROUP, 9545 Wentworth St.(91040), pg. 243

Sunnyvale

ALACON, 158 Commercial St.(94086), pg. 29
Cascade Controls, Inc., 712 E. Evelyn Ave.(94086), pg. 1070
Cupertino Electric, Inc., 714 E. Evelyn Ave.(94086), pg. 1070
D.M.A. Associates, 712 E. Evelyn Ave.(94086), pg. 1070
Fuzere Manufacturing Company Inc., 1237 Birchwood Dr.(94089), pg. 975
Integral Systems, Inc., 1279 Oakmead Pkwy.(94086), pg. 573
THE LEVOLOR CORPORATION, 595 Lawrence Expwy.(94086), pg. 671
PATSON'S PRESS, 508 Tasman Dr.(94089), pg. 851
QUALITY TECHNOLOGIES CORPORATION, 610 N. Mary Ave.(94086-2906), pg. 904
READY SYSTEMS, 470 Potrero Ave.(94086), pg. 916
RESONEX, INC., 720 Palomar Ave.(94086), pg. 929
Sunnyvale Towncenter, 200 W. Washington Ave.(94086), pg. 699
SYNERGISM, INC., 712 E. Evelyn Ave.(94086), pg. 1069
Tracor ELSIN, 540 Oakmead Pkwy.(94086), pg. 1105
Tracor Ultron, 540 Oakmead Pkwy.(94086), pg. 1105
Wavetek Microwave, Inc., 488 Tosman Dr.(94089), pg. 1168

Sutter Creek

Amador Motors, P.O. Box 278, (95685), pg. 895

Sylmar

CORDOVA ENTERPRISE, P.O. Box 922079, (91391-2079), pg. 285
SIERRACIN CORPORATION, 12780 San Fernando Rd.(91342-3796), pg. 1003
Sierracin/Sylmar Corporation, 12780 San Fernando Rd.(91342), pg. 1003
TUTOR-SALIBA CORPORATION, 15901 Olden St.(91342), pg. 1120

Temecula

The Roll Seal Valve Co., Inc., 42024 Avenida Alvarado Unit B(92593), pg. 3

Terminal Island

AL LARSON BOAT SHOP, INC., 1046 S. Seaside Ave.(90731), pg. 659

Thousand Oaks

VIDICOM, L.D. BEVAN COMPANY, INC., 1125 Business Center Circle(91320), pg. 1151

Thousand Palms

Tri-Palm Estate, 32700 Desert Moon Dr.(92276), pg. 441

Tiburon

NATIONAL EMERGENCY SERVICES, INC., P.O. Box 156, 39 Main St.(94920), pg. 788

Toluca Lake

MULLE/BREEN ADVERTISING, 10137 Riverside Dr.(91602), pg. 775

Torrance

CAPITOL METALS PROCESSING, INC., 20000 S. Western Ave.(90501), pg. 216
CREATIVE DIRECT MARKETING GROUP, INC., 1815 West 213th St., Ste. 210(90501), pg. 297
The Daily Breeze, 5215 Torrance Blvd.(90509), pg. 284
Ed Debevic's/Short Orders Deluxe/Torrance, 23705 Hawthorne Blvd.(90505), pg. 669
DEXOL INDUSTRIES, INC., 1450 W. 228th(90501), pg. 334
EDELBROCK CORP., 2700 California St.(90503), pg. 367
FERRO UNION, INC., 1000 W. Francisco St.(90502), pg. 407
FINANCIAL NETWORK INVESTMENT, 2780 Skypark Dr.(90505), pg. 410
GREFCO, Inc., 3435 W. Lomita Blvd.(90509), pg. 136
The C.P. Hall Company, 444 Alaska Ave.(90503), pg. 501
Javelin Electronics, 19831 Magellan Dr.(90502-1188), pg. 64
M K DIAMOND PRODUCTS, INC., 1315 Storm Parkway(90501-2803), pg. 692
Masterite Industries, Inc., 2841 Lomita Blvd.(90505), pg. 612
94th Aero Squadron of Torrance, Inc., 2780 Skypark(90505), pg. 1028
Pacific Optical Division, 2660 Columbia St.(90503), pg. 917
PELICAN PRODUCTS, 2255 Jefferson St.(90501), pg. 856
PHONEMATE, INC., 20665 Manhattan Pl.(90501), pg. 869
PLASMA TECHNOLOGY, INC., 1754 Crenshaw Blvd.(90501), pg. 874
ROBINSON HELICOPTER COMPANY, INC., 24747 Crenshaw Blvd.(90505), pg. 940
Samsteel, Inc., 1000 W. Francisco St.(90502), pg. 407
TORRANCE NISSAN, INC., 20710 Hawthorne Blvd.(90503), pg. 1102
Tylan General, Inc.-Flow Division, 359 Van Ness Way(90501), pg. 1122
United Resources Insurance Services, Inc., 23879 Madison St.(90505), pg. 573

Trabuco Canyon

Metrologic Instruments-Western Region, 19171 Red Bluff Dr.(92679), pg. 743

Tulare

HOUCK INDUSTRIES, INC., 437 N. M St.(93274), pg. 545

Turlock

Yosemite Express Co., 4150 N. Golden St. Blvd.(95380), pg. 973

Tustin

C B J ENTERPRISES, INC., 2802 Dow Ave.(92680), pg. 199
Calavo Foods, Inc., 15661 Red Hill Ave.(92680), pg. 208
CALAVO GROWERS OF CALIFORNIA, 15661 Red Hill Ave.(92680), pg. 208
LAMP POST FRANCHISE CORPORATION, 3002 Dow, Ste. 320(92680), pg. 652

VITATECH INTERNATIONAL, INC., 2832 Dow Ave.(92680), pg. 1153

Union City

Rapid Mounting & Finishing, 33195 Lewis Ave.(94587-2201), pg. 913
Sandtex, 32980 Alvarado-Niles Rd., Ste. 820(94587), pg. 283
Shade Foods, Inc., 33063 Western Ave.(94587), pg. 810
TapeTech Tool Co., Inc., 30009 Ahern Ave.(94587), pg. 8
Westco Products/Bay Area, 32621 Central Ave.(94587), pg. 1178

Universal City

Viacom Productions Inc., 10 Universal City Plaza(91608), pg. 785

Upland

Lewis Construction Co., Inc., 1156 N. Mountain Ave.(91786), pg. 673
Lewis Development Co., 1156 N. Mountain Ave.(91786), pg. 673
LEWIS HOMES MANAGEMENT CORP., 1156 North Mountain Avenue(91786), pg. 673
Lewis Homes Of California, 1156 N. Mountain Ave.(91786), pg. 673
NEW BEDFORD PANORAMEX CORPORATION, 1037 W. 9th St.(91786), pg. 799
Republic Sales Co., Inc., 1156 N. Mountain Ave.(91786), pg. 673
Western Land Properties, 1156 N. Mountain Ave.(91786), pg. 673
Western Supply Corp., 1156 N. Mountain Ave.(91786), pg. 673

Vacaville

Baker-Hamilton, 721 Eubanks Dr.(95688), pg. 340
SERTA MATTRESS COMPANY, 3777 Vaca Valley Pkwy.(95688), pg. 991
SIMPSON DURA-VENT CO., INC., 902 Aldridge Rd.(95688), pg. 1007

Valencia

CARPETERIA, INC., 28159 Ave. Stanford(91355), pg. 224
Micro-Aire Surgical Instruments, Inc., 24971 Ave. Stanford(91355), pg. 711
Plasti-Kote Co., Pactra Hobby, 27201 Tourney Rd., Ste. 200(91355), pg. 875

Vallejo

MARINE WORLD AFRICA USA, Marine World Pkwy.(94589), pg. 707
TIMEC COMPANY, 155 Corporate Pl.(94590), pg. 1097

Van Nuys

Burton Medical Products Corporation, 7922 Haskell Ave.(91406), pg. 588
CAMERON-NEWELL ADVERTISING, INC., 15025 Oxnard St., Ste. 200(91411-2623), pg. 212
CONTINENTAL COIN CORPORATION, 5627 Sepulveda Blvd.(91411), pg. 278
Federal Stampings of California, 13630 Saticoy St.(91402), pg. 321
H W ELECTRONICS, INC., 6840 Hayvenhurst(91406), pg. 497
INDUSTRIAL ELECTRONIC ENGINEERS, INC., 7740 Lemone Ave.(91405), pg. 566
KEYES MOTORS, INC., 5855 Van Nuys Blvd.(91401), pg. 627
KINGSBRIDGE MEDIA & MARKETING, INC., 6835 Valjean Ave.(91406), pg. 631
SHAPCO, INC., 16340 Roscoe Blvd., Ste. 220(91406), pg. 995
STYLE AUTO, 7100 Sophia Ave.(91406), pg. 1055
Sun-Litho, 7950 Haskell Ave.(91406), pg. 771
Van Nuys Airport Restaurant Corp., 16320 Raymer Ave.(91406), pg. 1028
WHITE STAG MANUFACTURING COMPANY, 7915 Haskell Ave.(91409), pg. 1186

Venice

CHIAT/DAY/MOJO INC. ADVERTISING, 340 Hampton Dr.(90291), pg. 244
Livingston + Keye, 901 Abbot Kinney Blvd.(90291), pg. 679
RICE/SPECTOR INC., 217 S. Hampton Dr.(90291), pg. 931
Bob Thomas & Associates, Inc. Public Relations, 340 Main St.(90291), pg. 244

Ventura

KINKO'S CORPORATION, 225 W. Stanley Ave.(93001), pg. 632
LOST ARROW CORPORATION, 259 W. Santa Clara(93001), pg. 684
PEMKO MANUFACTURING COMPANY, 4226 Transport St.(93006), pg. 856
Valex Corp., 6080 Leland St.(93003), pg. 925
VENTURA COASTAL CORPORATION, 2325 Vista Del Mar(93002), pg. 1147

Vernon

Chorus Line, Inc., 4505 Bandini Blvd.(90040), pg. 591
COAST PACKING COMPANY, 3275 E. Vernon Ave.(90058), pg. 257
Finkel Outdoor Products of California, 3155 Bandini Blvd.(90023), pg. 200
JAZZ HOLDING CORPORATION, 4505 Bandini Blvd.(90040), pg. 591
Kal Kan Foods, Inc., 3250 E. 44th St.(90058), pg. 713
Pacific Papers Unlimited, 4550 Maywood Ave.(90058), pg. 171
TOMCO AUTO PRODUCTS, INC., 4330 E. 26th St.(90023), pg. 1100

Visalia

Ivex Packaging Corporation-Visalia, 7101 Avenue 304(93291), pg. 583
Visalia Oaks Baseball Club, 440 N. Giddings(93279), pg. 758

Walnut

LIGHTS OF AMERICA, INC., 611 Reyes Dr.(91789), pg. 675
SHEA HOMES, 655 Brea Canyon Rd.(91789), pg. 996
Shea Homes Southern California, 655 Brea Canyon Rd.(91789), pg. 996

Walnut Creek

Calaveras Cement Corporation, 2033 N. Main St., Ste. 500(94596), pg. 199
CALIFORNIA APRICOT ADVISORY BOARD, 1280 Boulevard Way(94595), pg. 209
ERM-West, Inc., 1777 Botelho Dr., Ste. 260(94596), pg. 361
INTEGRAL SYSTEMS, Tishman Bldg., 2185 N. California Blvd.(94596), pg. 572
Walnut Creek Restaurant Corp., 3800 Valle Vista(94598), pg. 1028
Western Medical Services Div., 301 Lennon Lane(94598-2404), pg. 1182
Western Permanent Services Agency, Inc., 301 Lennon Lane(94598-2404), pg. 1182
WESTERN TEMPORARY SERVICES, INC., 301 Lennon Lane(94598-2404), pg. 1181
Western Temporary Services Office Div., 301 Lennon Lane(94598-2404), pg. 1182
Western Temporary Services (USA), Inc., 301 Lennon Lane(94598-2404), pg. 1182

Watsonville

CALIFORNIA STRAWBERRY ADVISORY BOARD, 41 Hangar Way(95076), pg. 210
SKYWAY FREIGHT SYSTEMS, INC., 225 Westridge Dr.(95076), pg. 1009
Skyway Systems, Inc., 225 Westbridge Dr.(95076), pg. 1009

West Hollywood

L'ERMITAGE HOTELS, 8440 Sunset Blvd.(90069), pg. 668

West Sacramento

MTS, INC., 2500 Del Monte St., Bldg. C(95611), pg. 694
REX MOORE ELECTRICAL CONTRACTORS & ENGINEERS, P.O. Box 915(95691), pg. 768
NOR-CAL BEVERAGE CO., INC., 2286 Stone Blvd.(95691), pg. 808
Pulse Magazine, 2500 DelMonte St.(95691), pg. 694
RALEY'S, 500 W. Capital Ave.(95605), pg. 910
RICE GROWERS ASSOCIATION OF CALIFORNIA, 1550 Harbor Blvd.(95691), pg. 931
Tower Records, 2500 Del Monte Ave.(95691), pg. 694

Westlake Village

Backer Spielvogel Bates, Inc., 650 Hampshire Rd., Ste. 210(91361), pg. 109
Cherokee Shoe Company, Inc., 2985 E. Hillcrest Dr.(91362), pg. 243
Communications Planning Corporation/TMP Worldwide, 2801 Townsgate Rd., Ste. 215(91361), pg. 1073
Pallmark International, Inc., 2985 E. Hillcrest Dr.(91362), pg. 243
Practical Peripherals, 31245 La Baya Dr.(91362), pg. 519

Westminster

Spirol West, 15121 Golden West Circle(92683), pg. 1031

Whittier

CAL-AIR INC., 12484 E. Whittier Blvd.(90602), pg. 208
CALCOR SPACE FACILITY, INC., 12031 E. Philadelphia St.(90601), pg. 208
FREMONT FOREST PRODUCTS, 7200 Greenleaf Ave., Suite 310(90602), pg. 432
HOOD CORPORATION, 8201 S. Sorensen Ave.(90606), pg. 542
OLTMANS CONSTRUCTION COMPANY, 10005 Mission Mill Rd.(90608), pg. 824
PECK ROAD FORD TRUCK SALES, 2450 Kella Ave.(90601), pg. 854
Snugl Mfg. Co. Inc., 12468 E. Lambert Rd.(90608), pg. 145
ZIEMAN MANUFACTURING COMPANY, INC., 7909 S. Painter Ave.(90602), pg. 1218

Willits

ADVANCED MANUFACTURING & DEVELOPMENT, 300 E. Hill Rd.(95490), pg. 20

Wilmington

ASSOCIATED DIESEL SERVICE & EQUIPMENT COMPANY, 1741 Colon St.(90744), pg. 89

Woodland

Silvercrest Western Home Corporation, 109 County Rd. 101(95695), pg. 1004

Woodland Hills

CATALINA YACHTS, INC., 21200 Victory Blvd.(91367), pg. 229
Cooke Media Group, Inc., P.O. Box 4200(91365), pg. 282
MAKERS OF KAL, INC., 6415 DeSoto Ave.(91367), pg. 702
WEIDER HEALTH & FITNESS, 21100 Erwin St.(91367), pg. 1173

Yuba City

Sunsweet Growers Inc., 901 Walton Ave.(95991), pg. 1058

Yucaipa

MCANALLY ENTERPRISES, INC., 12215 7th St.(92399), pg. 726

COLORADO

Antonito

GREFCO, Inc., P.O. Box 308(81120), pg. 137

Arvada

Jetstream Systems, 6105 W. 55th Ave.(80002), pg. 122
SIGMAN MEAT CO. INC., 6000 W. 54th Ave.(80002), pg. 1003

Aurora

Brown-Strauss Steel, Inc., 20400 E. 26th Ave.(80011), pg. 161
Colorado Air Restaurant Corp., 10081 E. 25th Ave.(80010), pg. 1028
Denver Auto Auction, 17400 E. 31st Ave.(80011), pg. 293
Elkay Plastics Co., Inc., Stock Service Center, 14600 E. 35th Pl., Unit H(80011), pg. 377
Fashion Bar Inc., 401 S. Buckley Rd.(80017), pg. 1029
FREDERIC PRINTING COMPANY, 14701 E. 38th Ave.(80011), pg. 430
Johnson Storage & Moving, Aurora, 5050 Havana(80239), pg. 601
Niagara Envelope Co. of Colorado, 14101 E. 33rd. Place(80011), pg. 806

Boulder

Battery St. Enterprises, Running Gear Div., 2400 Central Ave., Ste. L(80301), pg. 670
Boulder Enterprise, Inc., 3550 Frontier Ave.(80301), pg. 803
CAREERTRACK INC., 3080 Center Green Dr.(80301), pg. 218
CELESTIAL SEASONINGS, 4600 Sleepytime Dr.(80301-3292), pg. 231
Denver Autometrics, 6235 Lookout Rd.(80301), pg. 331
GRAY-PRO, INC., 2741 Mapleton(80304), pg. 479
HEAD SPORTS, INC., 4801 N. 63rd St.(80301), pg. 520
Jones Optical Company, P.O. Box 3096(80307), pg. 1103
Lexmark International, Inc., 6300 Diagonal Highway(80301), pg. 674
RELA, INC., 6175 Longbow Dr.(80301), pg. 924
RELA Manufacturing Division, 6175 Longbow Dr.(80301), pg. 924
RELA Model And Machine Shop, 6175 Longbow Dr.(80301), pg. 924
RELA Product Development Div. (PDD), 6175 Longbow Dr.(80301), pg. 924
REPUBLIC TELCOM SYSTEMS CORPORATION, 6150 Lookout Rd.(80301), pg. 928
Westpeak Investment Advisors, Inc., 1050 Walnut St., Ste. 300(80302), pg. 799

Brighton

Kuner-Empson Company, 221 No. Kuner Rd.(80601), pg. 399

Broomfield

BESTOP, INC., 2100 W. Midway Blvd.(80038), pg. 147
Down Products Div., P.O. Box 343, (80020), pg. 1201
HOMESTEAD HOUSE INC., 9410 Wadsworth Pkwy.(80020), pg. 542
Marshall Erdman & Assoc., Inc., 891 Interlocken Pkwy.(80020), pg. 385

Colorado Springs

AMI INDUSTRIES, INC., 1275 North Newport Rd.(80916-2779), pg. 5
BROADMOOR HOTEL, INC., One Lake Ave. at Lake Circle(80906), pg. 177
Brown Disc Products Company, 1120-B Elkton Dr.(80907), pg. 451
Coventry Homes of Colorado, 6915 Ashely Dr.(80922), pg. 1171
CRADDOCK DEVELOPMENT CO., INC., 228 N. Cascade, Ste. 301(80903), pg. 295
DENVER EQUIPMENT COMPANY, 621 S. Sierra Madre(80903), pg. 331
El Paso Restaurant Corp., 230 Point of the Pines Dr.(80907), pg. 1028
Gates Land Co., 202 E. Cheyenne Mountain Blvd., Ste. I(80906), pg. 445
GENEVAR ENTERPRISES, 1120-B Elkton Dr.(80907), pg. 451
G. E. JOHNSON CONSTRUCTION CO., INC., 310 S. 14th St.(80904), pg. 597
Johnson Storage & Moving, Colorado Springs, 4226 N. Sinton Rd.(80907), pg. 601
MAXCOR MANUFACTURING, INC., 4230 N. Nevada St.(80907), pg. 722
MOUNTAIN STATES PIPE & SUPPLY COMPANY, 111 W. Las Vegas(80903), pg. 773
NATIONAL SYSTEMS & RESEARCH CO., 5475 Mark Dabling(80918), pg. 794
The Ohio Mattress Company Licensing And Components Group, 6275 Lake Shore Ct.(80915), pg. 985
WIGAND CORPORATION, 850 Elkton Dr.(80907), pg. 1189

Woolrich Store Co., 4432 Austin Bluffs Pkwy.(80918), pg. 1201

Commerce City

Colorado Auction Services Corporation, 6955 E. 50th Ave.(80022), pg. 293
N.W. TRANSPORT SERVICE, INC., 5601 Holly St.(80022), pg. 781
STEEL, INC., 6245 Clermont St.(80022), pg. 1044
United Foods Service, Inc., 5199 Ivy St.(80022), pg. 994

Cortez

EMPIRE ELECTRIC ASSOCIATION, Drawer K(81321), pg. 379

Denver

A Bar A Ranch, 900 S. Broadway(80209), pg. 445
APG SECURITY, INC., 12000 E. 47th Ave., Ste. 105(80239), pg. 5
Allright Colorado, Inc., 1616 Glenarm Pl., Suite 1910(80202), pg. 41
American Envelope of Denver, 5000 Kingston St.(80239), pg. 199
AMERICAN WATER WORKS ASSOCIATION, 6666 W. Quincy Ave.(80235), pg. 65
ANSCHUTZ CORPORATION, 2400 Anaconda Tower, 555 17th St.(80202), pg. 75
BMR Corporation, 999 Eighteenth St., 381
BARNHART ADVERTISING, MARKETING & PUBLIC RELATIONS, INC., 455 Sherman, Ste. 500(80203), pg. 120
Bentonite Corporation, 1999 Broadway(80202), pg. 1109
Bloomfield Refining Co., 370 17th St., Ste. 5300(80202), pg. 444
CHAMPION BOXED BEEF, 5850 York St.(80216), pg. 238
Coast to Coast, 501 S. Cherry St.(80222), pg. 993
COAST TO COAST STORES, INC., 501 S. Cherry St.(80222), pg. 257
COLORADO LOTTERY, 720 S. Colorado Blvd., Ste. 110(80222), pg. 265
C.C. Conley & Sons, Inc., 8055 E. Tufts Ave., Ste. 700(80237), pg. 484
Curtice Burns Meat Snacks, Inc., 208 So. Kalamath St.(80223), pg. 26
D & D Bean Company, P.O. Box 22139(80222), pg. 1114
Denver Baby Doe's Rest. Corp., 2530 23rd Ave.(80211), pg. 1028
Denver Freeway Restaurant Corp., 2150 Bryant St.(80211), pg. 1028
Denver & Rio Grande Western Railroad Co., P.O. Box 5482(80217), pg. 75
Denver Service Center/INTEC, 1805 East 58th Ave., Unit J(80216), pg. 1192
DENVER WHOLESALE FLORISTS COMPANY, 4800 Dahlia St.(80216), pg. 331
Design-Build West, 1225 17th St., Suite 1700(80205), pg. 907
DRIVE TRAIN INDUSTRIES, 3301 Brighton Blvd.(80217), pg. 349
J.D. EDWARDS & COMPANY, 8055 E. Tufts Ave., Ste. 1331(80237), pg. 370
ENERGY MINERALS CORPORATION, 999 Eighteenth St., Ste. 3100(80202), pg. 381
EQUITABLE BANKSHARES OF COLORADO, INC., P.O. Box 8779, (80201), pg. 385
EvansGroup, Prudential Plaza, 1050 17th St., Ste. 700(80202), pg. 391
Farmers Marketing Association, 4545 Madison St.(80216), pg. 704
Frank Paxton Lumber Company, 4837 Jackson St., Box 16343(80216), pg. 592
The Fuller Brush Company, 3065 Center Green Dr.(80301), pg. 436
GCC, Inc., 555 17th Street, Suite 3300(80202), pg. 459
GNG-1, Inc., 555 17th St., Ste. 3300(80202), pg. 459
GNG-3, Inc., 555 17th St.(80202), pg. 459
GARRISON-LONTINE ADVERTISING, 1444 Wazee(80202), pg. 443
THE GARY-WILLIAMS COMPANY, 370 17th St., Ste. 5300(80202), pg. 444
Gary-Williams Energy Corporation, 370 17th St., Ste. 5300(80202), pg. 444
THE GATES CORPORATION, 900 S. Broadway(80209), pg. 445
The Gates Rubber Company, 900 S. Broadway(80209), pg. 445
Green International, Inc., 8055 E. Tufts Ave., Ste. 700(80237), pg. 484
Gillett Broadcasting, Inc., 555 17th St., Ste. 3300(80202), pg. 459
Gillett Broadcasting of Tennessee, Inc., 555 17th St., Ste. 3300(80202), pg. 459
Gillett Corporation, 555 17th St., Ste. 3300(80202), pg. 459
Gillett-GP Corporation, 555 17th St., Ste. 3300(80202), pg. 459
Gillett Group, Inc., 555 17th St., Ste. 3300(80202), pg. 459
Gillett Group Management, Inc., 555 17th St., Ste. 3300(80202), pg. 459
GILLETT HOLDINGS, INC., 555 17th St., Ste. 3300(80202), pg. 458
Gillett Productions, Inc., 555 17th St., Ste. 3300(80202), pg. 459
Sheldon Good & Company of Colorado, Inc., 4600 S. Ulster St., Suite 700(80737), pg. 470
GORDON SIGN COMPANY, 2930 W. 9th Ave.(80204), pg. 472
Stephen Gould of Colorado, Inc., Unit 3, 4860 Ironton St.(80239), pg. 474
GREELEY GAS CO., 1301 Pennsylvania St., Ste. 800(80203), pg. 483
GREEN HOLDINGS, INC., 8055 E. Tufts Ave., Ste. 700(80237-2898), pg. 484
Green International-Guyana, Inc., 8055 E. Tufts Ave., Ste. 700(80237), pg. 484
Green Mining, Inc., 8055 E. Tufts Ave., Ste. 700(80237-2898), pg. 484
Group Insurance of Colorado, 9101 E. Kenyon Ave., Ste. 3200(80237), pg. 490
HAMILTON SWEENEY ADVERTISING, INC., 707 Sherman St.(80203), pg. 503
Hatch Grinding Company, 320 S. Lipan St.(80223), pg. 225
HENRY GILL SILVERMAN ADVERTISING, 1225 17th St., Ste. 2500(80202), pg. 530
Interplan, 1225 17th St., Suite 1700(80205), pg. 907
JOHNSON STORAGE & MOVING COMPANY, 221 Broadway(80203), pg. 600
Johnson Storage & Moving, Denver, P.O. Box 9188, (80209-0188), pg. 601
Jorgensen Steel & Aluminum/Denver, 6050 Downing St.(80216), pg. 605
KDA/HEPY, P.C., 1201 18th St., Ste. 200(80202), pg. 509
Kaiser Permanente, Colorado Division, 10350 E. Dakota Ave.(80231-1314), pg. 614
Kilsby-Roberts/Denver, 3737 Troy St.(80239), pg. 606
Lark Luggage Company, Inc., 11200 E. 45th Ave.(80239-0094), pg. 359
Ed J. Lyng Company, P.O. Box 22139(80222), pg. 1114
Manna Pro Partner L.P. (Limited Partnership), 4545 Madison St.(80216), pg. 704
MANNA PRO PARTNERS, 4545 Madison St.(80216), pg. 704
MCCLAIN FINLON ADVERTISING, 1331 17th St., Ste. 200(80202), pg. 727
Mile High Enterprises, Inc., 2800 W. 20th Ave.(80211), pg. 6
National Distributing Co., Inc., 10700 E. 40th Ave.(80239), pg. 787
OMNI Industry, 1801 Broadway, Ste. 1700(80202), pg. 463
Oppenheimer Asset Management Corp., 3410 S. Galena St.(80231), pg. 719
PEPSI-COLA BOTTLING CO., 3801 Brighton Blvd.(80216), pg. 860
Phoenix Industries, P.O. Box 22139(80222), pg. 1114
Ports of Call, Inc., 2121 Valencia St.(80220), pg. 70
QDI, Inc., 11585 E. 53rd Ave., Unit G(80239), pg. 82
RCR Publications, 1728 Downing St.(80218), pg. 295
RNL Design, 1225 17th St., Suite 1700(80205), pg. 907
RNL FACILITIES CORPORATION, 1225 17th St., Suite 1700(80202), pg. 907
RNL Technical Services, 1225 17th St., Ste. 1700(80202), pg. 908
Raynor Distribution Center, 10625 E. 51st Ave.(80239), pg. 915
The Rio Grande Industries Inc., P.O. Box 5482(80217), pg. 75
Rio Grande Land Co., 1515 Arapahoe St.(80202), pg. 75
Rocky Mountain Concepts, 451 E. 58th Ave., Ste. 1025(80216), pg. 100
RUSTCO PRODUCTS COMPANY, 1485 E. 61st Ave.(80216), pg. 957
Sabine Trucking, Inc., P.O. Box 22139(80222), pg. 1114
Samsonite Corporation, 11200 E. 45th Ave.(80239), pg. 358
SHAFER COMMERCIAL SEATING INC., 4101 E. 48th Ave.(80216-3298), pg. 994
Snavely Forest Products, Inc., P.O. Box 16107, (80216), pg. 1015
SOUTHEASTERN CAPITAL CORPORATION, 1873 S. Bellaire St., Ste. 1700(80222), pg. 1019
Space Management Systems, 1225 17th St., Ste. 1700(80202), pg. 908
STERLING LUMBER & INVESTMENT CO., 7000 N. Broadway(80221), pg. 1047
THOMAS & PERKINS, 1451 Larimer Square, Ste. 300(80202), pg. 1093
TIMPTE INDUSTRIES, INC., 1290 Broadway, Ste. 500(80203), pg. 1098
Titanium Metals Corporation, 1999 Broadway(80202), pg. 1109
TOOL KING, 2492 W. 2nd Ave.(80223), pg. 1101
TREMONT CORPORATION, 1999 Broadway(80202), pg. 1109
Trinidad Bean & Elevator Co., P.O. Box 22139(80222), pg. 1114
TRINIDAD/BENHAM CORPORATION, P.O. Box 22139(80222), pg. 1113
VENTA INC., 1055 Aurora Pkwy., Ste. 100(80204), pg. 1147
WLUC, Inc., 555 17th Street, Suite 3300(80202), pg. 459
Weitz-Cohen Construction Company, 899 Logan St., Ste. 600(80203), pg. 1174
Western International Media Corporation, 1200 17th St., Ste. 2620(80202), pg. 1180
Western Slope Refining Co., 370 17th. St., Ste. 5300(80202), pg. 444
Westlam Foods, P.O. Box 22139(80222), pg. 1114
Winnebago Color Press, Inc., 555 17th Street(80202), pg. 459
The Women's Bank, N.A., 821 17th St.(80202), pg. 385
WOODWARD-CLYDE GROUP, INC., 4582 S. Ulster St., Ste. 600(80237), pg. 1200
Woodward-Clyde Consultants, 4582 S. Ulster St., Ste. 600(80237), pg. 1201
Woodward-Clyde Federal Services, 4584 S. Ulster St., Ste. 600(80237), pg. 1201
Woodward-Clyde International, 4584 S. Ulster St., Ste. 600(80237), pg. 1201
Young Electric Sign Denver Div., 3660 E. 40th Ave.(80205), pg. 1209

Englewood

BNZ Materials, Inc., 2501 South Raritan St.(80110), pg. 732
Backer Spielvogel Bates, Inc., 384 Inverness Dr., South, Ste. 202(80112), pg. 109
Binswanger West, First Bank Bldg., Ste. 200, 5105 DTC Pkwy.(80111), pg. 152
BROYLES, ALLEBAUGH & DAVIS, INC., Denver Technological Center, 8231 E. Prentice Ave.(80111), pg. 183
CH2M HILL COMPANIES, LTD., 6060 So. Willow Dr.(80111), pg. 202
CoBank, 5500 S. Quebec St.(80111), pg. 405
Denver Metals Co., 2100 W. Oxford Ave.(80110), pg. 201
Don Massey Cadillac, Inc., 9400 E. Arapahoe Rd.(80112), pg. 719
ERM-Rocky Mountain, Inc., 5950 South Willow Dr., Ste. 310(80111), pg. 360
Full Service Beverage Company of Colorado, 2840 S. Zuni(80110), pg. 436
THE HOTSY CORPORATION, 21 Inverness Way E.(80112), pg. 545
Johnson Storage & Moving, Englewood, 6989 S. Jordan Rd.(80112), pg. 601
Jones Information Management, Inc., 9697 E. Mineral Ave.(80112), pg. 603
Jones Intercable, Inc., 9697 E. Mineral Ave.(80112), pg. 604
JONES INTERNATIONAL LTD., 9697 E. Mineral Ave.(80112), pg. 603
Jones Properties, Inc., 9697 E. Mineral Ave.(80112), pg. 603
Jones Spacelink, Ltd., 9697 E. Mineral Ave.(80112), pg. 603
KARSH & HAGAN, INC., 5500 Greenwood Plaza Blvd.(80111-2106), pg. 617
Lear Siegler Measurement Controls Corp., 74 Inverness Dr. E.(80112), pg. 664
Don Massey Buick, Inc., 9701 E. Arapahoe Rd.(80112), pg. 719
PRO HARDWARE, INC., Intl. Mktg. Hdqtrs.-Suite 360, 9137 E. Mineral Cir.-Box 6585(80155-6585), pg. 891
ROC PROPERTIES INC., 6430 South Quebec St.(80111), pg. 908
RE/MAX Insurance Div., 5445 DTC Pkwy., Ste. 1200(80111), pg. 915
RE/MAX INTERNATIONAL, INC., 5445 DTC Pkwy., Ste. 1200(80111), pg. 915
River Oaks Communities, Inc., 7395 E. Orchard Rd.(80111), pg. 908
ROBINS ENGINEERS & CONSTRUCTORS, INC., 7730 E. Belleview Ave.(80111), pg. 939
UNITED ARTISTS THEATRE CIRCUIT, INC., 9110 E. Nichols Ave, Ste. 200(80112), pg. 1130
WINDSOR INDUSTRIES, INC., 1351 W. Stanford Ave.(80110), pg. 1195

Fort Collins

ADVANCED ENERGY INDUSTRY, 1600 Prospect Pkwy.(80525), pg. 20
BALDWIN CONSTRUCTION, INC., 301 E. Lincoln Ave.(80524), pg. 115
COMLINEAR CORPORATION, 4800 Wheaton Dr.(80525), pg. 268
RANCH-WAY, INC., 416 Linden St.(80521), pg. 911

Fort Morgan

Fort Morgan Community Hospital, 1000 Lincoln St.(80701), pg. 176

Glenwood Springs

Glenwood Post, P.O. Box 550, 2014 Grand Ave.(81602), pg. 1042
HOLY CROSS ELECTRIC ASSOCIATION, 3799 Hwy. 82(81601), pg. 541

Golden

Children's World Learning Centers, Inc., 573 Park Point Dr.(80401), pg. 7
COLUMBINE SYSTEMS INC., 1707 Cole Blvd.(80401-3296), pg. 266
SPECTRUM COLOR CENTER, 6275 Joyce Dr.(80403), pg. 1029

Grand Junction

DIXSON, INC., 287 27 Rd.(81503), pg. 341
GAY JOHNSON'S INC., 1154 N. 4th St.(81501), pg. 446
Grand Junction Newspapers, Inc., 734 S. Seventh St.(81501), pg. 292

Greeley

HENSEL PHELPS CONSTRUCTION CO., 420 Sixth Ave.(80632), pg. 530
PHELPS TOINTON INC., 822 7th St., Ste. 700(80631), pg. 866
ROCHE CONSTRUCTORS, INC., 361 71st. Ave.(80634), pg. 940

Greenwood Village

CH2M Hill, Inc., 6060 S. Willow Dr.(80111), pg. 202
CH2M Hill International, Ltd., 6060 S. Willow Dr.(80111), pg. 202

Henderson

Sturgeon Electric Company, 12150 E. 112th Ave.(80640), pg. 509

Lakewood

Allied Security Inc., 1675 Carr St., Ste. 210N(80215), pg. 39
RK MECHANICAL, INC., 6701 Alameda(80226), pg. 907
ROCKY MOUNTAIN BANK NOTE COMPANY, 10455 W. 6th Ave.(80215), pg. 942

Lamar

CARDER, INC., E. Crystal St.(81052), pg. 217
Ranchers Supply Company, P.O. Box 721(81052), pg. 217

Littleton

CF & I Fabricators of Colorado, 9002 N. Moore Rd.(80120), pg. 201
THE ELECTRON CORP., 5101 S. Rio Grande St.(80120), pg. 375
Equitable Bank of Littleton, N.A., 101 W. Mineral Ave.(80120), pg. 385
Mall Entertainment USA, Southwest Plaza 2-B-735, 8501 W. Bowles Ave.(80123), pg. 1028

Lohewood

Kinning & Reil of Wyoming, 6701 West Alameda(80226), pg. 907

Longmont

Johnson Storage & Moving, Boulder/Longmont, 900 S. Sunset St.(80501), pg. 601

Loveland

U.S. Engineering Co., 729 S.E. 8th Street(80539), pg. 1135

Monte Vista

MONTE VISTA CO-OP ASSOCIATION, INC., 1901 E. Hwy. 160(81144), pg. 766

Mount Crested Butte

CRESTED BUTTE MOUNTAIN RESORT, INC., 500 Gothic Rd.(81225), pg. 299

Penrose

Estes Industries, Inc., 1295 H St.(81240), pg. 1011

Pueblo

CF&I STEEL CORPORATION, 225 Canal St.(81004), pg. 201
C & W Railway Co., 225 Canal St.(81004), pg. 201
Fountain Sand & Gravel Co., P.O. Box 535(81002), pg. 201
Kansas Metals Co., 225 Canal St.(81002), pg. 201
Pueblo Metals Co., 728 Harlem(81004), pg. 201
Pueblo Railroad Service Company, P.O. Box 5104, 2621 Line Rd.(81002), pg. 201

Sterling

KTVS-TV, P.O. Box 432, 224 N. Third(80751), pg. 1043

Thornton

North Denver Hill Corp., 9350 Grant St.(80229), pg. 1028
WESTERN DAIRYMEN COOPERATIVE, INC., 12450 N. Washington St.(80241), pg. 1178

Vail

Vail Associates, Inc., P.O. Box 7(81658), pg. 459

Walsenburg

Navajo Western Land Co., 502 W. 7th(81089), pg. 1167

CONNECTICUT

Avon

EASTERN COLOR PRINTING COMPANY, 60 Security Dr.(06001), pg. 363
MINTZ & HOKE INC., 40 Tower Lane(06001), pg. 759
M. H. RHODES, INC., 99 Thompson Rd.(06001), pg. 931

Baltic

M.S. Chambers & Son, Inc., 132 W. Main St.(06330), pg. 357

Bantam

PTC Aerospace, Rte. 202(06750), pg. 899

Berlin

ARBURG, INC., 154 Woodlawn Rd.(06037), pg. 79
BERLIN STEEL CONSTRUCTION CO., 76 Depot Rd.(06037), pg. 142
Granulator Div., 168 Woodlawn Rd.(06037), pg. 80

Bloomfield

BARTLETT BRAINARD & EACOTT, INC., 30 Tobey Rd.(06002), pg. 122
BEACON GROUP, 85 Granby St.(06002), pg. 128
Beacon Industries, Inc., 85 Granby St.(06002), pg. 128
Beacon Winch Company, 85 Granby St.(06002), pg. 129
GRAPHIC CENTER, INC., 26 Tobey Rd.(06002), pg. 478
Metal Stamping Equip. Div., 522 Cottage Grove Rd.(06002), pg. 835
THE J. M. NEY COMPANY, Ney Industrial Park(06002), pg. 805
P/A INDUSTRIES, INC., 522 Cottage Grove Rd.(06002), pg. 835
Smyth Manufacturing Company, 85 Granby St.(06002), pg. 129
Web Processing Equip. Div., 522 Cottage Grove Rd.(06002), pg. 835

Bolton

SYNDET PRODUCTS, INC., 201 Boston Turnpike(06040), pg. 1069

Branford

ARCOLA WIRE COMPANY, 13 Beaver Rd.(06405), pg. 81
Dryden & Palmer Company, 16 Business Park Dr.(06405), pg. 479
ENVIRONETICS, 21 Business Park Dr.(06405), pg. 383
GRAVYMASTER INC., 16 Business Park Dr.(06405), pg. 478
WYATT INC., Wyatt Executive Bldg., 322 E. Main St.(06405), pg. 1205

Bridgeport

ALIMAK ELEVATOR COMPANY, 1100 Boston Ave.(06610), pg. 34
American Fabrics Co., 1069 Connecticut Ave.(06609), pg. 51
BEAD INDUSTRIES INC., 110 Mountain Grove(06605), pg. 129
THE BODINE CORP., 317 Mountain Grove(06605), pg. 161
BRIDGEPORT MACHINES, INC., 500 Lindley St.(06606), pg. 175
The Cornwall & Patterson Co., 1155 Railroad Ave.(06605), pg. 884
COUNTRY HOME BAKERY, INC., 1700-1722 Barnum Ave.(06610), pg. 290
EMSON RESEARCH, INC., 1100 Boston Ave.(06610), pg. 380
FIRST CONNECTICUT SBIC, 1000 Lafayette Blvd.(06604), pg. 412
MOORE SPECIAL TOOL CO., INC., 800 Union Ave.(06607-0088), pg. 768
PRATT-READ CORPORATION, 1155 Railroad Av.(06605), pg. 884
Precision Arc Co., 60 Radel St.(06607), pg. 1013
THE PRODUCTO MACHINE CO., 990 Housatonic Ave.(06606), pg. 893
REMINGTON PRODUCTS INC., 60 Main St.(06604), pg. 926

Brookfield

RAPID POWER TECHNOLOGIES, INC., 18 Graysbridge Rd.(06804), pg. 913

Cheshire

CONSOLIDATED INDUSTRIES, INC., 677 Mixville Rd.(06410), pg. 276
Jones & Lamson Waterbury Farrel Corp., 181 W. Johnson Ave.(06410), pg. 468

Colchester

AQHI, INC., 87 Upton Rd.(06415), pg. 5
Alpha Q, Inc., 87 Upton Rd.(06415), pg. 5

Danbury

DANBURY PRINTING & LITHOGRAPH, INC., One Prindle Lane(06811), pg. 313
Ethan Allen, Inc., Ethan Allen Dr.(06811), pg. 485
GREEN MOUNTAIN HOLDING CORPORATION, Ethan Allen Drive(06811), pg. 485
KIRK & MATZ LTD., 95 Golden Hill Rd.(06811), pg. 633
TENAX CORPORATION, 4 Old Newtown Rd.(06810), pg. 1086

Danielson

C.E.M. Div. Spirol Intl. Corp., 99 Rock Ave.(06239), pg. 1031
DELTA RUBBER COMPANY, Rte. 12(06239), pg. 327
SPIROL INTERNATIONAL CORP., 965 N. Main St.(06239), pg. 1031

Dayville

Wilson Machine Knife Co., Inc., Louisa Viens Dr.(06241), pg. 556

East Berlin

Albi Manufacturing Division, 401 Berlin St.(06023), pg. 1035
Polymer & Specialty Coatings Division, 401 Berlin St.(06023), pg. 1035
STANCHEM INC., 401 Berlin St.(06023), pg. 1035

East Granby

DELTA INDUSTRIES, Bradley Park Rd.(06026), pg. 327

East Hartford

BKM ENTERPRISES, INC., 222 Pitkin St.(06108), pg. 107
BKM Total Office Today, Inc., 222 Pitkin St.(06108), pg. 107
STAVELEY SENSORS, INC., 91 Prestige Park Circle(06108), pg. 1043
WWF Paper Corporation - N.E., 45 Belden St.(06108), pg. 1157

East Norwalk

International Microwave Corporation, 25 Van Zant St.(06855), pg. 269

East Windsor

Hedberg Data Systems, Inc., Hartford Executive Pk., One Hartfield Blvd.(06088), pg. 1044
Marshall Erdman & Assoc., Inc., 7 Thompson Rd.(06088), pg. 386

Ellington

Accu-Sort Time System, P.O. Box 630(06029), pg. 11

Enfield

DELLA CONSTRUCTION CO. INC., 1 Depot Hill Rd.(06082), pg. 326
Phoenix Equity Planning Corp., 100 Bright Meadow Blvd.(06082), pg. 868
SPRINGBORN LABORATORIES, INC., One Springborn Center(06082), pg. 1033
Springborn Laboratories-Materials Science Division, Ten Springborn Center(06082), pg. 1033
Springborn Laboratories-Testing & QA Division, One Springborn Center(06082), pg. 1033

Essex

MCC, INC., P.O. Box 651, 45 Main St.(06426), pg. 691

Fairfield

BARRY BLAU & PARTNERS, INC., 1960 Bronson Rd.(06430), pg. 156
THE FAIRFIELD LUMBER & SUPPLY COMPANY, 185 Thorpe St.(06430), pg. 397
ROLOCK, INC., 1350 Kings Hwy. E.(06430), pg. 944
STG MARKETING COMMUNICATIONS, INC., 883 Black Rock Turnpike(06430), pg. 964

Farmington

CONNECTICUT SPRING & STAMPING CORPORATION, 5 Spring Lane(06032), pg. 275
Gulfstream Aerospace Corp., Northeast Farmington Ave.(06032), pg. 494
Kaiser Permanente, Northeast Division, 76 Batterson Park Rd.(06034-4011), pg. 614
KEILER & COMPANY, 304 Main St.(06032-2957), pg. 620
THE ROBERT E. MORRIS COMPANY, 17 Talcott Notch Rd.(06032), pg. 771
THE MOTORLEASE CORP., 1506 New Britain Ave.(06032), pg. 773
TRUMPF INC., Hyde Rd., Farmington Industrial Park(06032), pg. 1118

Georgetown

GILBERT & BENNETT, North Main St.(06829), pg. 457

Gilman

MARTY GILMAN, INC., 30 Gilman Rd.(06336), pg. 459

Glastonbury

CSA, INC., 107 Oakwood Dr.(06033), pg. 204
CRONIN & COMPANY, INC., 50 Nye Rd.(06033), pg. 300
DECKER RICKARD, 99 Citizens Dr.(06033), pg. 324

Greenwich

R.L. ALBERT & SON, INC., 19 W. Elm St.(06830), pg. 31
AMERICAN INSTITUTE FOR FOREIGN STUDY, 102 Greenwich Ave.(06830), pg. 56
AMERICAN OPTICAL CORP., 80 Field Point Rd.(06830), pg. 59
Au Pair in America, 102 Greenwich Ave.(06830), pg. 56
BRANT ALLEN INDUSTRIES, INC., 80 Field Point(06830), pg. 172
H.H. BROWN SHOE COMPANY, INC., 124 W. Putnam Ave.(06830), pg. 182
Camp America, 102 Greenwich Ave.(06830), pg. 56
CLIGGOT PUBLISHING, 55 Holly Hill Lane(06830), pg. 255
College Division, 102 Greenwich Ave.(06830), pg. 56
DECORATIVE CRAFTS, INC., 50 Chestnut St.(06830), pg. 324
Douglas Elliman Pickering Assoc., Inc., 30 Milbank Ave.(06830), pg. 347
DRIBECK IMPORTERS, INC., 57 Old Post Road No. 2(06830), pg. 349
DUBIN-CLARK & COMPANY, 289 Greenwich Ave.(06830), pg. 350
GENOVA HARTWICK JULIANO, INC., 15 Valley Dr.(06831), pg. 452
GRAND BANKS YACHTS, LTD., 563 Steamboat Rd.(06830), pg. 475
Greystone Realty Corporation, 2 Pickwick Plaza, 3rd Floor(06830), pg. 802
JOS. M. HERMAN SHOE CO., One Sound Shore Dr.(06830), pg. 531
INTERLAKEN CAPITAL, INC., 165 Mason St.(06830), pg. 574
JAC JACOBSEN INDUSTRIES, INC., 67 Holly Hill Ln.(06830), pg. 587
LEXMARK INTERNATIONAL, INC., 55 Railroad Ave.(06836), pg. 673
Lexmark International, Inc., P.O. Box 2868(06835-2868), pg. 674
MORAN TOWING & TRANSPORTATION CO. INC, Two Greenwich Plaza(06830), pg. 769
NFO RESEARCH, INC., 2 Pickwick Plaza(06830), pg. 780
NTC GROUP, Three Pickwick Plaza(06830), pg. 781
QUALITY BAKERS OF AMERICA COOPERATIVE, INC., 70 Riverdale Ave.(06830), pg. 903
STRATEGIC DISTRIBUTION INC., 165 Mason St.(06830), pg. 1053
UNION PEN COMPANY, 777 W. Putnam Ave.(06836), pg. 1128
WWF International Limited, 71 Arch St.(06830), pg. 1157

Guilford

THE CLINIPAD CORPORATION, 66 High St.(06437), pg. 255

Hamden

CRN INTERNATIONAL, INC., One Circular Ave.(06514), pg. 203
CONDERE CORPORATION, 2750 Dixwell Ave.(06518), pg. 273
NEW ENGLAND CORPORATION, P.O. Box 5427(06518), pg. 800
New England Log Homes, Inc., 2301 State St.(06518), pg. 800

Hartford

Adapt, Inc., Hartford Plaza(06105), pg. 662

American Brokerage Corporation, One American Row(06115), pg. 868
Arnold Fortuna Lawner & Cabot, 241 Main St.(06106), pg. 84
Aspenrise Properties, Inc., 31 Pratt St.(06103), pg. 1016
BEAUTY ENTERPRISES INC., 150 Meadow St.(06114), pg. 130
Bristol Recreation Systems, Inc., 140 Garden St.(06154), pg. 275
CM Life Insurance Company, 140 Garden St.(06154), pg. 275
Cleary Lane Associates, Inc., 31 Pratt St.(06103), pg. 1016
Connecticut Mutual Financial Services, 140 Garden St.(06154), pg. 275
CONNECTICUT MUTUAL LIFE INSURANCE COMPANY, 140 Garden St.(06154), pg. 274
Cranston Properties, Inc., 31 Pratt St.(06103), pg. 1016
Diversified Insurance Services of America, 140 Garden St.(06154), pg. 275
DONAHUE, INC., ADVERTISING, 227 Lawrence St.(06106), pg. 344
Fair Harbor Properties, Inc., 31 Pratt St.(06103), pg. 1016
Grinnell Street Associates, Inc., 31 Pratt St.(06103), pg. 1016
Groton Run Properties, Inc., 311 Pratt St.(06103), pg. 1016
GroupAmerica Insurance Co., 140 Garden St.(06105), pg. 275
High Point Equities, Inc., 31 Pratt St.(06103), pg. 1016
Kenosia Properties, Inc., 31 Pratt St.(06103), pg. 1016
Korn/Ferry International, 81 Wethersfield Ave.(06114), pg. 642
Master Plans Corporation, 31 Pratt St.(06103), pg. 1016
NEW ENGLAND DAIRIES, INC., 255 Homestead Ave.(06112), pg. 800
O'NEAL & PRELLE, 95 Elm St., P.O. Box 1139(06143-1139), pg. 827
PM Holdings, Inc., One American Row(06115), pg. 868
Pennington Corporation, 31 Pratt St.(06103), pg. 1016
Phoenix American Life Ins. Co., One American Row(06115), pg. 868
Phoenix Founders, Inc, One American Row(06115), pg. 868
PHOENIX HOME LIFE MUTUAL INSURANCE COMPANY, One American Row(06115), pg. 868
Phoenix Investment Counsel Inc., One American Row(06115), pg. 868
SAGE-ALLEN & CO., INC., 900 Main St.(06103), pg. 966
Society Commercial Properties, Inc., 31 Pratt St.(06103), pg. 1016
Society Mortgage Corporation, 31 Pratt St.(06103), pg. 1016
SOCIETY FOR SAVINGS BANCORP, INC., 31 Pratt St.(06145), pg. 1016
Solar Services, Inc., 31 Pratt St.(06103), pg. 1016
State Stamp Works, 226 South St.(06110), pg. 58
M. SWIFT & SONS INC., 10 Love Lane(06141), pg. 1068
Urbco, Inc., 140 Garden St.(06105), pg. 275
Walker Glen Properties, Inc., 31 Pratt St.(06103), pg. 1016
WINDSOR SHADE TOBACCO COMPANY, INC., 158-166 Woodland St.(06105), pg. 1196

Litchfield

PTC AEROSPACE, INC., P.O. Box 140, (06759), pg. 837

Manchester

ALLIED PRINTING SERVICES, INC., 579 Middle Turnpike W.(06040), pg. 38
Cepco, 280 Adams St.(06040), pg. 263
Cox Cable Greater Hartford, Inc., 801 Parker Street(06040), pg. 294
DYNAMIC METAL PRODUCTS COMPANY, 967 Parker St.(06040), pg. 356
HARTFORD DISTRIBUTORS INC., 131 Chapel Rd.(06040), pg. 514
HERBAL ENTERPRISES INC., 316 Hartford Rd.(06040), pg. 530
Klock Co., 1366 Tolland Turnpike(06040), pg. 263
Mal Tool & Engineering Co., 273 Adams St.(06040), pg. 263
Wickes Engineering Group, 280 Adams St.(06040), pg. 263
Wing Industries Northeastern, 60 Progress Dr., Bldg. 4(06040), pg. 1196

Meriden

CANBERRA INDUSTRIES, INC., One State St.(06450), pg. 213
THE LANE CONSTRUCTION CORP., 965 E. Main St.(06450), pg. 656
Mildrum Manufacturing Co., Napier Park(06450), pg. 783
MILLER COMPANY, 99 Center St.(06450), pg. 754
THE NAPIER COMPANY, 74 Cambridge St.(06450), pg. 783
Packard Instrument Co., Inc., One State St.(06450), pg. 213
Radiomatic Instruments, One State St.(06450), pg. 214
THE RECORD-JOURNAL PUBLISHING COMPANY, 11 Crown St.(06450), pg. 917
RLJC, Inc., 74 Cambridge St.(06450), pg. 783

Middlebury

TIMEX CORPORATION, Park Rd. Extension(06762), pg. 1098
UNIROYAL CHEMICAL COMPANY, INC., World Headquarters(06749), pg. 1129

Middlefield

COOPER INSTRUMENT CORP., Reeds Gap Rd.(06455), pg. 283

Middletown

Field Publications, 245 Long Hill Rd.(06457), pg. 611
Newfield Publications, 245 Long Hill Rd.(06457), pg. 611
NORTH & JUDD, 699 Middle St.(06457), pg. 812
Weekly Reader Corp., 245 Long Hill Rd.(06457), pg. 611

Milford

ALINABAL, INC., 28 Woodmont Rd.(06460), pg. 34
Allied Security Inc., 228 New Haven Ave.(06460), pg. 39
CONNECTICUT DRIVE SHAFT, INC., 470 Naugatuck Ave.(06460), pg. 274
DORR-OLIVER INCORPORATED, 612 Wheeler's Farms Rd.(06460), pg. 346
Eastern Steel & Metal Company, 1 Eastern Steel Rd.(06460), pg. 825
Franchise World Headquarters, 325 Bic Drive(06460), pg. 1055
Keystone Automotive Industries, Inc. - Milford, 125 Furniture Row(06460), pg. 628
Lindenmeyr Munroe, P.O. Box 3046, 249 Research Drive(06460), pg. 233
SUBWAY FRANCHISEE ADVERTISING FUND TRUST, 325 Bic Drive(06460), pg. 1055

Milldale

Firoillo A. Co. Inc., 396 Clark St.(06467), pg. 984

Naugatuck

KOMBI, LTD., 102 Great Hill Rd.(06770), pg. 641
NAUGATUCK GLASS COMPANY, Church & Bridge Sts.(06770), pg. 796
Uniroyal Chemical Co., Inc., Elm St.(06770), pg. 1129

New Britain

D&L VENTURE CORP., 227 Main St.(06051), pg. 307
MACRISTY INDUSTRIES, INC., 206 Newington Ave.(06051), pg. 698
Maguire Group Architects, Inc., One Court St.(06051), pg. 701
TILCON, INC., Black Rock Ave.(06052), pg. 1097

New Haven

Acme Chemicals & Insulation Co., 166 Chapel St.(06505), pg. 572
Amstar Corporation, 555 Long Wharf Dr.(06511), pg. 361
Amstar Technical Products Co., Inc., 555 Long Wharf Dr.(06511), pg. 361
APPAREL AMERICA, INC., 1175 State St.(06511), pg. 78
ESSTAR INCORPORATED, 555 Long Wharf Dr.(06511), pg. 361
THE EQUION CORPORATION, 555 Long Wharf Dr., 12th Fl.(06511), pg. 385
Essex Industries, Long Wharf Maritime Center, 555 Long Wharf Dr.(06511), pg. 361
THE FUSCO CORPORATION, 555 Long Wharf Dr.(06511), pg. 437
MASON & MADISON, INC., 23 Amity Rd.(06524), pg. 718
NEW HAVEN MFG. CORP., 446 Blake St.(06515), pg. 801
NEW HAVEN SAVINGS BANK, 195 Church St.(06510), pg. 801
Perri Sausage, Inc., P.O. Box 8327(06530), pg. 601
The Rockbestos Company, 285 Nicolle St.(06511), pg. 711
Sargent Manufacturing Company, 100 Sargent Dr.(06511), pg. 361
SIMKINS INDUSTRIES, INC., 260 East St.(06511), pg. 1005
Simkins New Haven Board, 259 East St.(06511), pg. 1005
Simkins New Haven Carton, 259 East St.(06508), pg. 1005
THE STROUSE, ADLER COMPANY, 78 Olive(06507), pg. 1054
U.S. REPEATING ARMS COMPANY, 275 Winchester Ave.(06511), pg. 1137
YALE UNIVERSITY PRESS, 302 Temple St.(06511), pg. 1207

New London

Electric Specialty & Supply, 389 N. Frontage Rd., I 95(06320), pg. 374

New Milford

QUALITY FOOD OILS, INC., 87 Pickett District Rd.(06776), pg. 903
Sunola Food Corp., 87 Pickett District Rd.(06776), pg. 903

Newington

AUDIO SPECIALIST, INC., 2230 Berlin Turnpike(06111), pg. 98
CONNECTICUT STATE LOTTERY, Russell Rd.(06111), pg. 275
KEENEY MANUFACTURING CO., 1170 Main St.(06111), pg. 620

North Grosvenordale

Kenyon Oil Company, Inc., P.O. Box 866, 221 Quinebaug Rd.(06255), pg. 1165

North Haven

CABLEWAVE SYSTEMS, INC., 60 Dodge Ave.(06473), pg. 206
CONNECTICUT CONTAINER CORPORATION, 455 Sackett Point Rd.(06473), pg. 274
GAMMA ONE, INC., 12 Corporate Dr.(06473), pg. 442
O. F. MOSSBERG & SONS, INC., 7 Grasso Ave.(06473), pg. 773
Primary Steel Inc., 200 McDermott Rd.(06473), pg. 889
ULBRICH STAINLESS STEELS & SPECIAL METALS, INC., 57 Dodge Ave.(06473), pg. 1125
Ulbrich Wire, Inc., 55 Defco Park Ave.(06473), pg. 1125
UNITED ALUMINUM CORPORATION, 100 United Dr.(06473), pg. 1130

North Stonington

SHIP ANALYTICS, INC., Rte. 2 & 184, North Stonington Professional Center(06359), pg. 999

Norwalk

W. Braun Co., 50 Washington St.(06854), pg. 172
Easton Press Books, 677 Connecticut Ave.(06854), pg. 691
Easton Press Videos, 677 Connecticut Ave.(06854), pg. 691
Fibreweb International, Ltd., 22 1/2 Lowndes Ave.(06854), pg. 473
FULL CIRCLE MEDIA CORP., 200 Connecticut Ave.(06856-4990), pg. 436
Hamilton Collection, 677 Connecticut Ave.(06854), pg. 691
KING INDUSTRIES, INC., Science Rd.(06852), pg. 630
MBI INC., 47 Richards Ave.(06856), pg. 691
MICROPHASE CORPORATION, 587 Connecticut Ave.(06854), pg. 749
THE NASH ENGINEERING COMPANY, 310 Wilson Ave.(06856), pg. 783
NEW HERMES INCORPORATED, 535 Connecticut Ave.(06854), pg. 801
NORWALK POWDERED METALS, INC., Muller Park(06852), pg. 816
Postal Commemorative Society Collection, 47 Richards Avenue(06856), pg. 691
RAYMOND AUTOMATION CO., INC., P.O. Box 5838(06856), pg. 915
RECORDING & STATISTICAL CORPORATION, 40 Richards Ave.(06854), pg. 917
REX MARINE CENTER, INC., 144-146 Water St.(06854), pg. 930
Thimble Collectors Club Collections, 677 Connecticut Ave.(06854), pg. 691
TRAFALGAR/GHURKA, 349 Connecticut Ave.(06854), pg. 1105
VALLERIE'S TRANSPORT SERVICE, INC., 465 Connecticut Ave.(06851), pg. 1143
R. T. VANDERBILT COMPANY, INC., 30 Winfield St.(06855), pg. 1144

Norwich

COMMERCIAL PRINTERS OF CONNECTICUT, 3 Hilltop Rd.(06360), pg. 268

Oakville

Hoboken Floors-Connecticut Div., 290 Sylvan Lake Rd.(06779), pg. 537
Sealy Connecticut, Inc., P.O. 151, 25 Hillside Ave.(06779), pg. 985

Old Greenwich

DOMECQ IMPORTERS INC., 143 Sound Beach Ave.(06870), pg. 343

Old Lyme

Nuemann (USA), 6 Visto Dr.(00371), pg. 990
SENNHEISER ELECTRONIC CORP., 6 Vista Dr.(06371), pg. 989

Old Mystic

Sirtex Printing Company, East Main St.(06372), pg. 333

Old Saybrook

CRAMER COMPANY, 139 Mill Rock Rd. E.(06475-1261), pg. 296

Orange

Stephen Gould of Connecticut Corp., 291 Lambert Rd.(06477), pg. 474
MUELHENS, INC., 15 Executive Blvd.(06477), pg. 774
SetloWear, Inc., Indian River Rd.(06477), pg. 1192

Oxford

PTA CORPORATION, 178 Christian St.(06483), pg. 837

Pawcatuck

ORTRONICS, INC., 595 Greenhaven Shores(06379), pg. 830
YARDNEY TECHNICAL PRODUCTS, INC., 82 Mechanic St.(06379-2154), pg. 1207

Plainville

PECK SPRING COMPANY, 89 Whiting St.(06062), pg. 854

Pomfret

LOOS & CO., INC., Rte. 101 & 169(06258), pg. 683

Pomfret Center

Red L Foods, 150 Searles Rd.(06259), pg. 1128

Portland

STANDARD-KNAPP, INC., 127 Main St.(06480), pg. 1036

Ridgefield

TMP Worldwide, Inc., 38C Grove St.(06877), pg. 1074

Riverside

Grand Union Capital Corporation, 26 Meadow Rd., pg. 476
GRAND UNION HOLDINGS CORPORATION, 26 Meadow Road(06878), pg. 475

Riverton

HITCHCOCK CHAIR COMPANY LTD, 13 Riverton Rd.(06065), pg. 536

Rockville

AMERBELLE CORPORATION, 104 E. Main St.(06066), pg. 47
ANO-COIL CORPORATION, 60 E. Main St.(06066), pg. 75

Rowayton

COLDWATER SEAFOOD CORPORATION, 133 Rowayton Ave.(06853), pg. 260

Shelton

AUTOSWAGE PRODUCTS, INC., 726 River Rd.(06484), pg. 101
THE W.E. BASSETT COMPANY, 100 Trap Falls Rd. Ext.(06484), pg. 125
Practical Automation, Inc., 2 Research Dr.(06484), pg. 34
RUDEL MACHINERY COMPANY, INC., P.O. Box 887, 4 Armstrong Rd.(06484), pg. 954

Simsbury

MCKINLAY & PARTNERS, INC., The Grist Mill, 75 West St.(06070), pg. 730

South Glastonbury

J.T. SLOCOMB COMPANY, 68 Matson Hill Rd.(06073), pg. 1010

South Norwalk

NORWALK CO., INC., 20 N. Water St.(06854), pg. 816
VISIRECORD SYSTEMS, INC., 345 Wilson Ave.(06854), pg. 1153

South Windsor

DYNAMIC CONTROLS CORP., 8 Nutmeg Rd. S.(06074), pg. 356
ELECTRO METHODS INC., 330 Governors Hwy.(06074), pg. 375
Waldo Bros. Company, 595 Nutmeg Rd., N.(06074-2461), pg. 1159

Southington

GIBBS WIRE & STEEL COMPANY, INC., Metals Dr.(06489), pg. 456
IDEAL FORGING CORPORATION, 167 Center St.(06489), pg. 562

Southport

THE HIGHLAND GROUP, INC., 105 Woodrow Ave.(06490), pg. 534
Strategic Events Group, 105 Woodrow Ave.(06490), pg. 534

Stamford

ADV MARKETING GROUP, INC., 408 Elm St.(06902), pg. 2
ASTON MARTIN LAGONDA OF NORTH AMERICA, INC., 1290 E. Main St.(06902), pg. 92
THE ATLAS CONSTRUCTION CO., 110 Lenox Ave.(06906), pg. 96
THE F.A. BARTLETT TREE EXPERT CO., 1290 E. Main St.(06902), pg. 123
BLOCK & NARDIZZI, One Stamford Landing(06902), pg. 157
Blue Cross and Blue Shield Northeast Marketing Region, 1055 Washington Blvd.(06901), pg. 159
BOLLIGER, INC., One Bolliger Place(06907), pg. 163
CB Commercial Real Estate Group Eastern Division, 1600 Summer St.(06905), pg. 222
CARLSON, DELGALDO, HOAG, MATTHEI ADVERTISING, INC., One Main Place, 750 E. Main St.(06902), pg. 222
CONAIR CORPORATION, 1 Cummings Point Rd.(06904), pg. 272
CONESTOGA HOLDINGS, INC., 72 Cummings Point Rd.(06902), pg. 273
Cowles Business Media, Inc., 6 River Bend(06907), pg. 291
Crown Lance, Inc., 370 W. Main St.(06902), pg. 163
Cuisinarts Inc., 1 Cummings Point Rd.(06904), pg. 272
Donnelley Marketing Data Processing Operations, 70 Seaview Ave(06902), pg. 1011
Donnelley Marketing, Inc., 70 Seaview Ave.(06902), pg. 1011
Donnelley Marketing Information Services, 70 Seaview Ave., P.O. Box 10250(06904), pg. 1011
FRASER PAPER, LTD., 9 W. Broad St.(06904), pg. 430
GARTNER GROUP, INC., 56 Top Gallant Rd.(06902), pg. 443
GENERAL ELECTRIC MASTER RETIREMENT TRUST, 3003 Summer St.(06905), pg. 449
GENEVE CORPORATION, 96 Cummings Point Rd.(06902), pg. 451
GOODWAY TOOL CORPORATION, 420 West Ave.(06902), pg. 471
GREGORY & CLYBURNE, INC., 45 Church St.(06906), pg. 486
HARGRO ENTERPRISES, INC., One Landmark Square(06901), pg. 509
Independence Holding Company, 96 Cummings Point Rd.(06902), pg. 451
INTERNATIONAL MARINE HOLDINGS, INC., 48 Signal Rd.(06902), pg. 579
Korn/Ferry International, One Landmark Square(06901), pg. 642
MARQUARDT & ROCHE INC., 600 Summer St.(06901), pg. 713
MetLife Capital Credit Corp., P.O. Box 601, 10 Stamford Forum(06904), pg. 744
MORMAC MARINE TRANSPORT, INC., 3 Landmark Sq.(06901), pg. 770
NER Holdings, Inc., One Landmark Square(06901), pg. 509
NINE WEST GROUP, INC., 9 W Broad St.(06902), pg. 807
PANCOM INTERNATIONAL CORP., 2015 W. Main St.(06902), pg. 845
Peabody Engineering Corp., 39 Maple St., P.O. Box 2331(06906), pg. 899
PLAYTEX APPAREL INC., 700 Fairfield Ave.(06904), pg. 876
Playtex Beauty Care, Inc., 700 Fairfield Ave.(06904), pg. 877
Playtex Family Products Corp., 700 Fairfield Ave.(06904), pg. 877
PLAYTEX FP GROUP INCORPORATED, 700 Fairfield Ave.(06904), pg. 877
Playtex Investment Corp., 700 Fairfield Ave.(06904), pg. 877
Playtex Marketing Corporation, 700 Fairfield Ave.(06904), pg. 877
ROTANDO LERCH & IAFELIECE ADVERTISING, 300 First Stamford Place(06902), pg. 950
SERVICE AMERICA CORPORATION, 88 Gate House Rd.(06904), pg. 992
SILGAN CORPORATION, 4 Landmark Sq., Ste. 301(06901), pg. 1004
SUN HILL INDUSTRIES, 48 Union St.(06906), pg. 1059
VICTORIA STATION INCORPORATED, 200 Broad St.(06901), pg. 1149
Carol Wright Sales, Inc., 70 Seaview Ave.(06904), pg. 1011

Stratford

AMERICAN FROZEN FOODS, INC., 355 Benton St.(06497), pg. 55
THE U.S. BAIRD CORPORATION, 1700 Stratford Ave.(06497), pg. 114
BRIDGEPORT FITTINGS, INC., 705 Lordship Blvd.(06497), pg. 175
ORIEL CORPORATION, 250 Long Beach Blvd.(06497), pg. 829
SILVERSTONE, ADKINS & BREIT, INC., 1128 Stratford Ave.(06497), pg. 1005
Space Control Corp., 1255 W. Broad St.(06497), pg. 1053

Suffield

SWEETLIFE FOODS, INC., 1120 Harvey Lane(06078), pg. 1067

Taftville

HELIKON FURNITURE CO., INC., 607 Norich Ave.(06380), pg. 526

Thomaston

SUMMIT CORPORATION OF AMERICA, 1430 Waterbury Rd.(06787), pg. 1058
Tech Systems Corp., 401 Watertown Rd.(06787), pg. 317
TREADWELL CORPORATION, 341 Railroad St.(06787), pg. 1108

Torrington

THE TURNER & SEYMOUR MFG. COMPANY, 100 Lawton St.(06790), pg. 1119

Trumbull

American Trading Real Estate Properties, Inc., Trefoil Park, 35 Corporate Dr.(06611), pg. 65
Hometown Publications, P.O. Box 298, (06611), pg. 607
HOWE FURNITURE CORPORATION, 12 Cambridge Dr.(06611), pg. 547

Unionville

SANFORD & HAWLEY, INC., 1790 Farmington Ave.(06085), pg. 970

Vernon

ITS: Intertrade Scientific, Inc., 176 Bolton Rd.(06066), pg. 748

Wallingford

Amphenol Corporation, 358 Hall Ave.(06492), pg. 648
H. B. IVES, 62 Barnes Park North(06492), pg. 583
LPL TECHNOLOGIES, INC., 358 Hall Ave.(06492-0384), pg. 648
NOVAMETRIX MEDICAL SYSTEMS INC., 1 Barnes Industrial Park Rd.(06492), pg. 817
Times Fiber Communications, Inc., 358 Hall Ave.(06492), pg. 648

Waterbury

ABRAMS PUBLISHING INC., 61 Mattatuck Heights(06705), pg. 10
M.J. DALY & SONS, INC., P.O. Box 2797, 541 Bank St.(06720), pg. 313
Electric Specialty & Supply, 2100 Thomaston Ave.(06704), pg. 374
Graphic Learning, 61 Mattatuck Heights(06705), pg. 10
High-Lites, Inc., 2142 Thomaston Ave.(06704), pg. 588
HUBBARD HALL INC., 563 S. Leonard St.(06708), pg. 549
Mitchell-Bradford International, 563 S. Leonard St.(06708), pg. 549
New Dimensions in Education, 61 Mattatuck Heights(06705), pg. 10
J.T. Slocomb Co., 235 Interstate Lane(06705), pg. 1010

Wauregan

C & M CORPORATION, 51 S. Walnut St.(06387), pg. 198

West Hartford

ABBOTT BALL COMPANY, Railroad Place(06110), pg. 9
DH Medical Supply Inc., 203 Sedgwick Rd.(06107), pg. 1081
MUNIGLE CORPORATION, 28 N. Main St.(06107), pg. 775
Underwriters Service Agency, Inc., P.O. Box 100, (06107), pg. 573
THE WIREMOLD COMPANY, 60 Woodlawn St.(06133), pg. 1197

West Haven

DEITSCH PLASTICS COMPANY, 14 Farwell St.(06516), pg. 325
HERLIN PRESS, 475 Heffernan Dr.(06516), pg. 531

Westbrook

LEE COMPANY, 2 Pettipaug Rd.(06498), pg. 665

Westport

Chessco Capital Corp., 1300 Post Rd. East(06880), pg. 244
CHESSCO INDUSTRIES, INC., 1300 Post Rd. East(06880), pg. 243
Corporate Health Strategies, Inc., 276 Post Rd., West(06880), pg. 744
GENERAL MEDIA SERVICES, INC., 23 Meeker Rd.(06880), pg. 450
MARKETING CORP. OF AMERICA, 285 Riverside Ave.(06880), pg. 709
MILLMASTER ONYX GROUP, INC., 500 Post Rd. E.(06880), pg. 755
New England Collectors Society, 512 Riverside Ave.(06880), pg. 920
NEWMAN'S OWN, INC., 246 Post Road E.(06880), pg. 804
PMC PARTNERSHIP, LTD., 90 Post Rd., West(06880), pg. 836
THE SAUGATUCK MARKETING GROUP, 18 Kings Hwy. North(06880), pg. 972

Wethersfield

Jorgensen Steel & Aluminum/Hartford, 1060 Silas Deane Hwy.(06109), pg. 606

Wilton

DELOITTE & TOUCHE, Ten Westport Rd.(06897-0820), pg. 326
LOUIS DREYFUS CORPORATION, 10 Westport Rd.(06897), pg. 348
O'HALLORAN ADVERTISING, INC., 116 Danbury Rd.(06897), pg. 822

Windsor

BLUE BELL/KING KOIL, INC., 770 Bloomfield Ave.(06095), pg. 158
REDCO FOODS, INC., 100 Northfield Dr.(06095), pg. 919
SPENCER TURBINE CO., 600 Day Hill Rd.(06095), pg. 1030
THE SPENCER TURBINE CO., 600 Day Hill Rd.(06095), pg. 1030
C.F. THOMPSON GROUP, INC., 752 Bloomfield Ave.(06095), pg. 1094

Windsor Locks

Springfield Sugar & Prod. Co., P.O. Box 385, (06096), pg. 1067

Winsted

Black Angus, Inc., 41 Meadow St.(06098), pg. 1018
Magic Maid Division, 41 Meadow St.(06098), pg. 1018
SON CHIEF ELECTRICS, INC., 41 Meadow St.(06098), pg. 1018

DELAWARE

Bridgeville

Ralph & Paul Adams, Inc., Market St. & Railroad Ave.(19933), pg. 603
DELAGRA CORPORATION, P.O. Box 126(19933), pg. 325
O. A. NEWTON & SON CO., P.O. Box 397, (19933), pg. 805

Clayton

Hanover Foods Corp., Rt. 6 & Duck Creek Rd.(19938), pg. 506

Dover

CUSTOM DECOR, INC., 1196 South Little Creek Rd.(19901), pg. 306
DELAWARE LOTTERY, Bluehen Mall, Ste. 202(19901), pg. 326
GENERAL METALCRAFT, INC., Mckee Rd.(19903), pg. 450
Rapid Distribution Service, Inc., 2392 North Du Pont Hwy.(19901), pg. 934

Frederica

ILC Dover, Inc., Harrington-Frederica Rd.(19946), pg. 560

Greenwood

DELAWARE ELECTRIC CO-OP, Rte. 13(19950), pg. 325

Middletown

QUAKER CITY MOTOR PARTS COMPANY, 680 North Broad(19709), pg. 903

Milford

BURRIS FOODS, INC., 5th & McColley Sts.(19963), pg. 195
L. D. Caulk Div., Lakeview & Clarke Ave.(19963), pg. 330
Kent Sussex Tire Service, 5th & McColley St.(19963), pg. 195
STEINER & COMPANY, 715 S. Washington St.(19963), pg. 1045

New Castle

ATLANTIC AVIATION CORP., 153 N. DuPont Hwy.(19720-5000), pg. 94
Keen Propane Division, 4061 New Castle Ave.(19720-1492), pg. 619
Keen Welding Division, 4063 New Castle Ave.(19720-1492), pg. 619
Specialty Restaurants Corp, 143 N. DuPont Hwy.(19720), pg. 1028
TECOT ELECTRIC SUPPLY COMPANY, 55 Lukens Dr.(19720), pg. 1084

Newark

ARA Healthcare Nutrition Services, Inc., 2911 Ogletown Rd.(19713), pg. 6
All American Engineering Co., 725 Dawson Dr.(19711), pg. 316
Aramont Properties, Inc.-Delaware, 2911 Ogletown Rd.(19713), pg. 6
ARAserve, Inc., 2911 Ogletown Rd.(19713), pg. 6
Aratex Services, 2911 Ogletown Rd.(19711), pg. 6
Artesian Development Corporation, 664 Churchmans Rd.(19702), pg. 86
Artesian Laboratories, Inc., 630 Churchmans Rd.(19702), pg. 86
ARTESIAN RESOURCES CORPORATION, 664 Churchmans Rd.(19702), pg. 86
Artesian Water Company, Inc., 664 Churchmans Rd.(19702), pg. 86
Barry Services Company, 222 Continental Dr., Ste. 200(19713), pg. 320
Churchmans Road Associates, L.P., 664 Churchmans Rd.(19702), pg. 87
Continental American Life Insurance Co., 300 Continental Dr.(19713), pg. 896
East Coast Service Ctr., 250 Corporate Blvd., Suite D(19702), pg. 1192
W. L. GORE & ASSOCIATES, INC., 555 Paper Mill Rd.(19714), pg. 472
The Southwood Company, 664 Churchmans Rd.(19702), pg. 87

Rehoboth Beach

Outlook, Incorporated, 28 Tidewaters Rd., Henlopen Acres(19971), pg. 632

Smyrna

METAL MASTERS FOODSERVICE EQUIPMENT, 655 Glenwood Ave., W.(19977), pg. 741

Wilmington

Allied Security Inc., 2713 Lancaster Ave., Ste. B2(19805), pg. 40
Brandywine Raceway Assn., Inc., 2200 Concord Pike(19803), pg. 172
Brandywine Realty & Development, Inc., 2200 Concord Pike(19803), pg. 172
BRANDYWINE SPORTS, INC., 2200 Concord Pike(19803), pg. 172
BUSINESS INFORMATION TECHNOLOGY, 1011 Centre Rd., 7th Fl., Ste. 400(19805), pg. 196
CONSTRUCTION MANAGEMENT SERVICE, 3600 Silverside Rd.(19810), pg. 277
Delaware Charter Guarantee & Trust Co., 1013 Center Rd.(19805), pg. 890
First State Paper, Inc., P.O. Box 10007(18950), pg. 234
Hatzel & Buehler, Inc., 3600 Silverside Rd.(19810), pg. 277
International Specialty Products, Inc., 818 Washington St.(19801), pg. 438
John Rich & Sons, 900 Market St.(19801), pg. 1201
Jones Holding Corporation, 300 Delaware Ave.(19801), pg. 602
Jones Investment Co., Inc., 300 Delaware Ave., Ste. 534(19801), pg. 602
KEEN COMPRESSED GAS CO., INC., 101 Rogers Rd.(19801), pg. 619
Keystone Crash Parts Mart - Wilmington, 214 East Lea Blvd.(19802), pg. 628
Modern Equipment Rentals Inc., 24 Brookside Dr.(19804), pg. 763
New York Life & Health Insurance Company, 300 Delaware Ave.(19801), pg. 802
NYLIFE Funding Inc., Ste. 780, 1100 N. Market St.(19801-1281), pg. 803
PML Securities Co., Christiana Executive Campus, 220 Continental Dr.(19713), pg. 896
Pepper, Hamilton & Scheetz, 1201 Markey St., Ste. 1401(19801), pg. 860
QSC, Inc., Foulkstone Plaza, 1105 N. Market St.(19899), pg. 229
Sauer Holdings, 715 Kings St., Suite 310(19801), pg. 972
Sigma Group, Christiana Executive Campus, 220 Continental Dr.(19713), pg. 896
SPEAKMAN COMPANY, 301 E. 30th(19802), pg. 1027
TDW Delaware, Inc., 1100 N. Market St., Ste. 780(19809), pg. 1192
TDW Trading, Inc., 1100 N. Market St., Ste.780(19801), pg. 1192

DISTRICT OF COLUMBIA

Washington

ABRAMSON EHRLICH MANES, INC., 1275 K St., N.W.(20005), pg. 10
Acacia Financial Corporation, 51 Louisiana Ave., N.W.(20001), pg. 10
THE ACACIA GROUP, 51 Louisiana Ave. N.W.(20001), pg. 10
Acacia Insurance Sales Corporation, 51 Louisiana Ave., N.W.(20001), pg. 10
Acacia National Life Ins. Co., 51 Louisiana Ave., N.W.(20001), pg. 11
ADWORKS, INC., 1025 Thomas Jefferson St., NW(20007), pg. 21
Allbritton Communications Company, 800 17th St., N.W., Ste. 301(20006), pg. 862
Allbritton News Bureau, Inc., 800 17th St. N.W., Ste. 301(20006), pg. 862
Allbritton Television Productions, Inc., Ste. 301, 800 17th St., N.W.(20006), pg. 862
Allright Parking Washington, Inc., 104 Irving St., N.W.(20010), pg. 42
THE AMERICAN BANKERS ASSOCIATION, 1120 Connecticut Ave., N.W.(20036), pg. 49
AMERICAN CHEMICAL SOCIETY, 1155 16th St. N.W.(20036), pg. 50
AMERICAN ENTERPRISE INSTITUTE FOR PUBLIC POLICY RESEARCH, 1150 17th St. N.W.(20036), pg. 51
AMTRAK-NATIONAL RAILROAD PASSENGER CORP., 60 Massachusetts Ave, N.E.(20002), pg. 69
ATLANTIC PLUMBING SUPPLY COMPANY, 807 V St., N.W.(20001), pg. 95
BNA Books Div., 1250 23rd St., N.W., 3rd Fl.(20037), pg. 189
BNA Business & Human Resources Div., 1231 25th St., N.W.(20037), pg. 189
BNA Editorial Support Div., 1231 25th St., N.W.(20037), pg. 189
BNA Electronic Media Div., 1231 25th St., N.W.(20037), pg. 189
BNA Environment & Safety Services Div., 1231 25th St., N.W.(20037), pg. 189
BNA Legal Services Div., 1231 25th St., N.W.(20037), pg. 189
BNA PLUS, 1231 25th St. N.W.(20037), pg. 189
BNA Software, 1231 25th St. N.W.(20037), pg. 189
Barnes, Morris, Pardoe & Foster Management Services, 1150 18th St., N.W., Ste. 1000(20036), pg. 613
Beber Silverstein & Partners, Inc., 1211 Connecticut Ave.(20036), pg. 130
Big Boy Restaurant System, Marriott Dr.(20058), pg. 376
Billcom Exposition & Conference, P.O. Box 17413, Dulles International Airport(20041), pg. 150
BillCom Exposition & Conference Group, P.O. Box 17413, Washington-Dulles Intl. Airport(20041), pg. 150
Blue Cross and Blue Shield Assn. Government Relations, Metropolitan Square Building, 655 Fifteenth St., N.W., Ste. 350(20005), pg. 159
THE BOMSTEIN AGENCY, 2201 Wisconsin Ave., NW, Ste. C-150(20007), pg. 164
THE BUREAU OF NATIONAL AFFAIRS, INC., 1231 25th St., N.W.(20037), pg. 189
Burns & Roe Enterprises, Inc., 1400 'K' St., N.W.(20005), pg. 194
Calvert Securities Corporation, 51 Louisiana Ave, NW(20001), pg. 11
Canterbury Hotel, 1733 N Street N.W.(20036), pg. 1076
Capital Bank, N.A., 815 Connecticut Ave., N.W.(20006), pg. 214
The Carlyle Group, 1001 Pennsylvania Ave. N.W.(20004), pg. 222
CARLYLE HOLDING CORPORATION, 1001 Pennsylvania Ave. N.W.(20004), pg. 222
Carpark, 1700 Pennsylvania Ave.(20006), pg. 225
THE OLIVER CARR CO., 1700 Pennsylvania Ave. N.W., Ste. 900(20006), pg. 225
Chicago Union Station Company, 400 N. Capitol St., N.W.(20001), pg. 69
GEORGE W. COCHRAN CO., INC., 2951 V St., N.E.(20018), pg. 258
Creswell, Munsell, Fultz & Zirbel, 1667 K St., NW, Ste. 430(20006), pg. 1211
CUNA Foundation, 805 15th N.W., Ste. 300(20005), pg. 298
D.C. LOTTERY & CHARITABLE GAMES CONTROL BOARD, 2101 Martin Luther King, Jr. Ave. S.E.(20020), pg. 308
Dav-El Washington D.C., Inc., 318 "I" Street, N.E.(20002), pg. 317
Defense Credit Union Council, 805 15th St. N.W.(20005), pg. 298
THE DONOHOE COMPANIES, INC., 2101 Wisconsin Ave. N.W.(20007), pg. 345
DOOR STORE, INC., 3140 M St. N.W.(20007), pg. 346
Ellerbe Becket-Washington, 1875 Connecticut Ave. N.W., Ste. 600(20009), pg. 378
Fairview Properties, Inc., 1729 H St., N.W.(20006), pg. 632
First American Bank, N.A., Washington, D.C., 740 15th St. N.W.(20005), pg. 412
FIRST AMERICAN BANKSHARES, INC., 15th & H Sts. N.W.(20005), pg. 412
FOLGER NOLAN FLEMING DOUGLAS, 725 15th St., N.W.(20005), pg. 422
FORMAN BROTHERS, INC., 4235 Sheriff Rd., N.E.(20019), pg. 424
Georgetown Marbury Hotel, 3000 'M' Street N.W.(20007), pg. 1076
GOLDBERG MARCHESANO KOHLMAN INC., 1700 Wisconsin Ave. N.W.(20007), pg. 465
Hampshire Hotel, 1310 New Hampshire Ave.(20036), pg. 1076
Higher Education Loan Program of Washington, D.C., 1800 K. St. N.W.(20005), pg. 528
ERNEST S. JOHNSTON ADVERTISING, INC., 1156 15th St., NW(20005), pg. 601
JOHNSTON, LEMON & CO. INC., 1101 Vermont Ave., N.W.(20005), pg. 601
JUDD'S INCORPORATED, 1500 Eckington Pl. N.E.(20002), pg. 608
THE KAEMPFER COMPANY, INVESTMENT BUILDERS, 1150 18th St., N.W., Ste. 1000(20036), pg. 613
Kaiser Permanente, Mid-Atlantic States Division, 4200 Wisconsin Ave., NW, Ste. 300(20016), pg. 614
Ketchum Public Relations/Washington, DC, 1201 Connecticut Ave., N.W., Ste. 300(20036), pg. 625
THE KIPLINGER WASHINGTON EDITORS, INC., 1729 H St., N.W(20006), pg. 632
WILLIAM J. KIRCHER & ASSOCIATES, 1101 14th St., NW, Ste. 900(20005), pg. 633
Korn/Ferry International, Presidential Plaza, 900 19th St., N.W.(20006), pg. 642
MSI SERVICES, INC., 1015 18th St., N.W., Ste. 800(20036), pg. 693
MARKET DEVELOPMENT GROUP INC., 1200 Potomac St., N.W.(20007), pg. 709
MAURICE ELECTRIC SUPPLY COMPANY, 500 Penn St., N.E.(20002), pg. 722
NATIONAL ACADEMY SCIENCES USA, 2101 Constitution Ave., N.W.(20418), pg. 784
NATIONAL GEOGRAPHIC SOCIETY, 17th & M Sts. N.W.(20036), pg. 789
NATION'S BUSINESS, 1615 H St., N. W.(20062), pg. 794
The News Printing Company, c/o Allbritton Communications, 800 17th St., N.W., Suite 301(20006), pg. 862
Pepper, Hamilton & Scheetz, 1300 Nineteenth St., N.W.(20036), pg. 860
PERPETUAL CORPORATION, 800 17th St. NW, Ste. 301(20006), pg. 862
QUADRANGLE DEVELOPMENT CORPORATION, 1001 G St., N.W., Ste. 700 W(20001), pg. 902
Quadrangle Management Company, 1001 G. St., N.W., Ste. 700 W(20036), pg. 902
Quality Hotel Downtown, 1315 16th St. N.W.(20036), pg. 1076
Quik Park Inc., 1001 G. St., N.W., Ste. 700 W(20036), pg. 902
Ramada Inn Downtown, 1430 Rhode Island Ave. N.W.(20036), pg. 1076
Ruder Finn/Washington, 1516 M St., N.W.(20036), pg. 954
SIGAL CONSTRUCTION, 3299 K Street N.W.(20007), pg. 1003
STEUART INVESTMENT CO., 4646 40th St. NW(20016), pg. 1048
Steuart Petroleum Company, 4646 40th St. N.W.(20016), pg. 1048
STEUART PETROLEUM COMPANY, 4646 40th St. NW(20016), pg. 1048
Steuart Seafoods, 4646 40th St. N.W.(20016), pg. 1048
TAJ INTERNATIONAL HOTELS, 1315 16th St., N.W.(20036), pg. 1076
Tax Management, Inc., 1250 23rd St., N.W., 2nd Fl.(20037), pg. 190
TEMPS & COMPANY, 3325 M. St., N.W.(20007), pg. 1086
Trenton Times Corp., Ste. 301, 800 17th St., N.W.(20006), pg. 862
ULLICO INC., 111 Massachusetts Ave., N.W.(20001), pg. 1124
The Union Labor Life Insurance Co., 111 Massachusetts Ave., N.W.(20001), pg. 1124
UNITED STATES SAVINGS BONDS DIVISION, TREASURY DEPARTMENT, 800 K St. NW(20001), pg. 1137
WJLA-TV, 3307 Tilden Street, N.W.(20008), pg. 862
Washington Terminal Company, 400 N. Capitol St., N.W.(20001), pg. 69
WESTERN DEVELOPMENT CORPORATION, 3000 K St. N.W., Suite 200(20007), pg. 1179
WOODWARD & LOTHROP/JOHN WANAMAKER, 1025 F St. N.W.(20013), pg. 1201
Zenith Administrators, Inc., 111 Massachusetts Ave., N.W.(20001), pg. 1124

FLORIDA

Alachua

Gates Energy Products, Inc., Hwy. 441 No.(32615), pg. 445
HUNTER MARINE CORPORATION, Rte. 441(32615), pg. 555

Altamonte Springs

COMPLETE INTERIORS INC., 435 Douglas Ave.(32714), pg. 270
Gould Central Florida, 825 Sunshine Ln.(32701), pg. 473
GREATER CONSTRUCTION CORP., 1105 Kensington Park Dr.(32714), pg. 483
TRI-CITY ELECTRICAL CONTRACTORS INC., 430 West Dr.(32714), pg. 1110

Apopka

VJ GROWERS, INC., 500 W. Orange Blossom Trail(32712), pg. 1141

Arcadia

The Orchid Center, P.O. Box 1116(33821), pg. 1058
SUN BULB COMPANY, INC., Hwy. 17, S.(33821), pg. 1058
Sun Chemical Company, Inc., P.O. Box 309(33821), pg. 1058

Auburndale

Auburndale Star, 213 E. Lake Ave., Box 126(33823), pg. 1042

COLORADO BOXED BEEF CO., 302 Progress Rd.(33823), pg. 265

Bartow

HOMES OF MERIT INC., Bartow Air Base(33830), pg. 542

Belle Glade

ATLANTIC SUGAR ASSOCIATION, INC., 26400 State Rd. 80(33430), pg. 95
SUGAR CANE GROWERS COOPERATIVE OF FLORIDA, Airport Road, P.O. Box 666(33430), pg. 1056

Boca Raton

All American Industries, Inc., P.O. Box 3010(33431), pg. 316
Alro Group, Boca Raton, P.O. Box 3031, 6200 Park of Commerce Blvd.(33431-0931), pg. 44
Arvida, 7900 Glades Road(33434), pg. 586
THE BARBAR GROUP, INC., 150 E. Palmetto Park Rd., Ste. 645(33432), pg. 119
Barbar Realty, Inc., 150 E. Palmetto Park Rd., Ste. 101(33432), pg. 119
Boca Raton Financial Center, 150 E. Palmetto Park Rd.(33432), pg. 119
CONCORD ASSETS GROUP, INC., 5200 Town Center Circle(33486), pg. 272
Datron Systems, Inc., P.O. Box 3010, (33431), pg. 317
DENTEC CORPORATION, 1181 S. Rogers Circle, Unit 14(33487), pg. 329
LFC HOLDING CORPORATION, 6111 Broken Sound Pkwy. N.W.(33487), pg. 647
Levitz Credit Corporation, 6111 Broken Sound Parkway, N.W.(33487), pg. 648
Levitz Furniture Corporation, 6111 Broken Sound Pkwy., N.W.(33436), pg. 647
THERAPEDIC ASSOCIATES, INC., 1801 Clint Moore Rd., Ste. 103(33487), pg. 1090
Woodfield Country Club, 3600 Club Place(33431), pg. 119
WORRELL ENTERPRISES, INC., 1450 S. Dixie Hwy.(33432), pg. 1203

Boynton Beach

OCEAN PROPERTIES, LTD., 1755 N. Congress Ave.(33426), pg. 820
Tri-City Electrical Contractors Inc., 2118 Corporate Dr.(33426), pg. 1110

Bradenton

BEALL'S, INC., 1806 38th Ave. E.(31283), pg. 129
NEW ENGLAND MACHINERY, INC., 6204 29th St. E.(34203), pg. 800
Sarasota Moving Systems Inc., 4505 30th St., W.(34207), pg. 282

Bushnell

Sumter County Times, 303 E. McCollum Ave.(33513), pg. 655

Casselberry

ROYAL JEEP EAGLE CHRYSLER PLYMOUTH, INC., 485 Hwy. 436 E.(32707), pg. 953

Clearwater

Arlo Group, Clearwater, 12490 49th St.(34622), pg. 44
Baker Brothers/Micro-Plate, 12200 34th St. North(34622), pg. 1071
Barry-Wehmiller Packaging Systems, 13325 U.S. Hwy. 19N.(34624), pg. 122
BUFKOR, INC., 13100 56th Court N., Ste. 710(34620), pg. 187
Calet, Hirsch & Ferrell, Inc./Florida, 1321 US 19 South, Ste. 404(34624), pg. 949
Clearwater Phillies, 800 Phillies Dr.(33515), pg. 867
EVA-TONE INC., 4801 Ulmerton Rd.(34622), pg. 390
FKQ ADVERTISING INC., 15351 Roosevelt Blvd.(34620), pg. 394
General Hardware Co.-St. Petersburg, 4650 Ulmerton Rd.(34622), pg. 340
Hansen Plastics Division, 2050 Sunnydale Blvd.(34625), pg. 1120
Inex Vision Systems, 13327 U.S. Hwy. 19N(34624), pg. 122
94th Aero Squadron of Pinellas County, Inc., 94th Fairchild Dr.(34620), pg. 1028
Pinellas Crabcooker, Inc., 16100 Fairchild Dr.(34620), pg. 1028
Pinellas Farmhouse, Inc., 15481 49th St. N.(34622), pg. 1028
RISSER OIL CORP., 2863 Executive Center Dr.(34622), pg. 936
St. Pete Auto Auction, 14950 Roosevelt Blvd.(34622), pg. 293
Wenczel Tile Distributing Company, 2040 Weaver Park Dr.(33575), pg. 1176

Clewiston

Bryant Sugar House, 111 Ponce de Leon Ave.(33440), pg. 1137
Clewiston Sugar House, 111 Ponce de Leon Ave.(33440), pg. 1137
United States Corrulite Corporation, P. O. Box 2307, (33440), pg. 1137
UNITED STATES SUGAR CORPORATION, 111 Ponce de Leon Ave.(33440), pg. 1137

Coconut Creek

Ed Morse Dodge, Inc., 5401 W. Sample Rd.(33083), pg. 772

Coconut Grove

ROLAND INTERNATIONAL CORPORATION, 3250 Mary Street, Ste. 402(33133), pg. 944

Coral Gables

BANANA SERVICES INC., 2100 Salzedo St., Ste. 303(33134), pg. 117
Leo Burnett International, Latin American Hdqtrs., 550 Biltmore, Ste. 870(33134), pg. 192
COMMODORE CRUISE LINE, LTD., 800 Douglas Rd.(33134), pg. 269
Crown Cruise Line, 800 Douglas Rd., Ste. 700(33134), pg. 269
GS&B-LINTAS ADVERTISING, 4104 Aurora St.(33146), pg. 440
Hicks & Associates Inc., 230 Palermo(33134), pg. 982
ARTHUR MURRAY INTL., INC., 1077 Ponce De Leon Blvd.(33134), pg. 776
NORWEGIAN CRUISE LINE, 95 Merrick Way(33134), pg. 816
POWER ENGINEERING CO. INC., 4205 Salzado St.ve.(33146), pg. 883
Royal Viking Line, Two Alhambra Plaza(33134), pg. 816
STIEFEL LABORATORIES, INC., 2801 Ponce De Leon(33134), pg. 1048
WOMETCO ENTERPRISES, INC., 3195 Ponce de Leon Blvd.(33134), pg. 1199

Coral Springs

CONTINENTAL PLASTIC CARD CO., 3651 N.W. 120th Ave.(33065), pg. 280

Dade City

Multi-Line Can Co., P.O. Box 1194, (33526), pg. 688

Dania

PIC N'PAY SUPERMARKETS, INC., 130 S.W. 1st Ave.(33004), pg. 869

Davie

SECURITY ALARMS & FIRE ENGINEERING INC., 4490 S.W. 64th Ave.(33314), pg. 987

Daytona Beach

ALUMA SHIELD INDUSTRIES, INC., 405 Fentress Blvd.(32114), pg. 46
Rand McNalley & Company, d/b/a Champion Map Corp., 200 Fentress Blvd.(32014), pg. 911
Wenczel Tile Distributing Company, 1518 State Ave.(34625), pg. 1176

Deerfield Beach

Eckerd Drug Co., 824 S. Military Trail(33442), pg. 366
Stephen Gould of Florida, Inc., 652 S.W. 12th Ave.(33442), pg. 474
Harte-Hanks Transportation Services, 1701 W. Hillsboro Blvd., Ste. 400(33442), pg. 513
JM FAMILY ENTERPRISES INC., 100 NW 12th Ave.(33443), pg. 584
KITCHENS OF THE OCEAN, INC., 104 S.E. 5th Ct.(33441), pg. 634
LIST INDUSTRIES, INC., 401 N.W. 12th Ave.(33442), pg. 677
STAINLESS INCORPORATED, One Stainless Plaza(33441-4798), pg. 1035
Richard Young Office Products, Inc., 508 S. Military Trail(33442), pg. 535

Delray Beach

Aircraft Products Company, 12807 Lake Dr.(33444), pg. 899
Built Environment Services, 660 Linton Blvd., Suite 205B(33444), pg. 370

Dover

B & R Foods, 3150 N. Gallagher Rd.(33527), pg. 861

Fort Lauderdale

ADVISORS ADVERTISING, 8200 W. Sunrise Blvd., Ste. D-2(33322), pg. 21
ALAMO RENT-A-CAR INC., 110 S.E. 6th St.(33301), pg. 30
Allied Products, 5900 N. Andrews Ave., Ste. 700(33309), pg. 276
Allied Security Inc., 2880 W. Oakland Park Blvd., Ste. 111(33311), pg. 39
BASIC FOOD INTERNATIONAL INC., 1300 S.E. 17th St., Ste. 300(33335), pg. 124
BLACK FIN YACHT CORPORATION, 3391 S.E. 14th Ave.(33316), pg. 154
Capital Factors, Inc., 1799 W. Oakland Park Blvd.(33311), pg. 214
CONSOLIDATED CIGAR CORPORATION, 5900 N. Andrews Ave., Ste. 700(33309), pg. 276
Domestic Cigars, 5900 N. Andrews Ave., Ste. 700(33309), pg. 276
Global Food Corporation, 1300 S.E. 17th St., Ste. 300(33335), pg. 124
LEON SHAFFER GOLNICK ADVERTISING, INC., 2817 E. Oakland Park Blvd.(33306), pg. 469
Sheldon Good & Company of Florida, 1300 S.E. 17th St., Suite 216(33316), pg. 470
HARRIS DRURY COHEN, 6360 N.W. 5th Way, Ste. 300(33309), pg. 511
HVIDE SHIPPING, INC., 2200 Eller Dr.(33316), pg. 556
MARKETING MAGIC INC., 4801 S. University Dr., Ste. 201W(33328), pg. 709
Mercator Asset Management Co., Inc., Paragon Center, 2400 E. Commercial Blvd., Ste. 810(33308), pg. 897
Ed Morse Chevrolet Inc., 1640 N.W. 40th Ave.(33313), pg. 772
MORSE OPERATIONS INC., 1240 N. Federal Hwy.(33304), pg. 772
94th Aero Squadron Restaurant, Inc., 2500 NW 62nd St.(33309), pg. 1028
NORTH AMERICAN COMPANY, P.O. Box 14758(33302), pg. 811
OFFICE CONNECTION, INC., 5301 N.W. 9 Ave.(33310-9157), pg. 821
Premium Products Division, 5900 N. Andrews Ave., Ste. 700(33309), pg. 276
Rexall Group, 4031 N.E. 12th Terrace(33334), pg. 1060
Rexall Inc. Consumer Products Div., 4031 N.E. 12th Terrace(33334), pg. 1060
Southern Electric Supply Co., Inc., 4700 NW 15th Ave., Bay a(33309), pg. 1021
STILES CORPORATION, 6400 N. Andrews Ave.(33309), pg. 1049
SUNDOWN VITAMIN CO., INC., 4031 N.E. 12th Terrace(33334), pg. 1060
Thompson Nutritional Products, 4031 N.E. 12th Terrace(33334), pg. 1060

Fort Myers

Christmas & Things, Edison Mall, 4125 Cleveland(33901), pg. 884
Fort Myers Miracles, Lee County Stadium, 14100 Six Mile Cypress Pkwy.(33912), pg. 758
HARPER BROS., INC., 14860 Six Mile Cypress Pkwy.(33912), pg. 510
Independent Cellular Network, Inc., 2100 Electronics Lane(33912), pg. 200
Owen-Ames-Kimball Co., 11941 Fairway Lakes Dr(33913-8338), pg. 833
Tri-City Electrical Contractors Inc., Airport Woods, 12296 Matterhorn Rd., Ste. 3A(33913), pg. 1110

Fort Pierce

Scientific Corporation, 208 Rouse Rd.(34946), pg. 535

Gainesville

ATHLETIC ATTIC PROPERTIES INC., 18 NW 33rd Ct.(32607), pg. 94
Cox Cable University City, Inc., 1115 N.W. 4th Street(32601), pg. 294
Southern Electric Supply Co., Inc., 3005 SW Williston Rd.(32608), pg. 1021

Green Cove Springs

Price Brothers Composite Pipe, Inc., Hwy. 16(32043), pg. 888

Haines City

B.C. Cook & Sons Enterprises, Inc., 413 N. 12th St.(33844), pg. 282
COOK HOLDING CORPORATION, P.O. Box 1597(33845), pg. 282
HAINES CITY CITRUS GROWERS ASSOCIATION, Railroad Ave.(33844), pg. 500
Haines City Herald & Ridge Shopper, 11 C St., Box 1596(33844), pg. 1042

Heathrow

AMERICAN AUTOMOBILE ASSOCIATION, NATIONAL TRAVEL DEPARTMENT, 1000 AAA Dr.(32746), pg. 49
CENTRAL STATES ENTERPRISES, INC., 300 International Pkwy., Suite 150(32746), pg. 234

Hialeah

COULTER CORPORATION, 601 Coulter Way(33010), pg. 289
Flamingo Products, 3095 E. 11th Ave.(33013), pg. 388
GATOR INDUSTRIES INC., 1000 S.E. 8th St.(33010), pg. 446
GUS MACHADO ENTERPRISES, 1200 W. 49th St.(33012), pg. 696
MASON DISTRIBUTORS, INC., 5105 N.W. 159th St.(33014), pg. 718
New Hermes Inc-South, 5680 NW 161st St.(33014), pg. 801

Highland City

CUTLER MANUFACTURING CORPORATION, 5204 U. S. Hwy. 98 South(33846), pg. 307

Hollywood

ATLAS PEN & PENCIL CORPORATION, 3040 N. 29th Ave.(33022), pg. 96
Nuarc Southern Div., 3912 N. 29th Ave.(33020), pg. 817
Pen Sales Corporation, 3040 N. 29th Ave.(33022), pg. 96

Hudson

Wenczel Tile Distributing Company, 14516 U.S. Hwy. 19(34667), pg. 1176

Indialantic

Level Five Research Inc., 503 5th Ave.(32903), pg. 567

Inverness

Citrus County Chronicle, P.O. Box 1899, 130 Heights Ave.(32650), pg. 655

Jacksonville

Air Land Forwarders, Inc., P.O. Box 37977(32254), pg. 1056
Aircraft Products Company, 11710 Central Pkwy.(32216), pg. 899
Allied Security Inc., 1844 Atlantic Blvd.(32207), pg. 39
Allright Jacksonville, Inc., 218 W. Adams St., Suite 505(32202), pg. 41
Anthem Health Plans of Florida Inc., P.O. Box 48000(32247-8000), pg. 90
Aratex Services, 357 E. 31st St.(32206), pg. 6
Atlantic Coast Asphalt, 5154 Edwards St.(32205), pg. 549
THE AUCHTER COMPANY, 1021 Oak St.(32204), pg. 98
BEACON SALES CORPORATION, 5905 Macy Ave.(32211), pg. 129
BEAVER STREET FISHERIES, INC., 1741 W. Beaver St.(32209), pg. 130
CAIN & BULTMAN, INC., 2145 Dennis Street(32204), pg. 207
Caribbean Moving & Storage, Inc., P.O. Box 60069(32254), pg. 1056
Chemrock Corporation, (32208), pg. 137
COGGIN-O'STEEN INVESTMENT CORP., 7400 Bay Meadows Way(32256), pg. 259
Coggin Pontiac-GMC Inc., 9201 Atlantic Blvd.(32211), pg. 259
THE WILLIAM COOK AGENCY, INC., 225 Water St., Ste. 1600(32202), pg. 282
J.B. COXWELL CONTRACT, INC., 6741 Lloyd Rd. W.(32254-1249), pg. 295
Data Storage Center, P.O. Box 6367(32254), pg. 1056
Elder Moving & Storage Co., 561 Stevens St.(32205), pg. 725
ELKINS CONSTRUCTORS, INC., 4501 Beverly Ave.(32210), pg. 377
Finkel Outdoor Products of Florida, 740 King St.(32204), pg. 200
First Trust Savings Bank, 10601-36 San Jose Blvd.(32257), pg. 491
GATE PETROLEUM COMPANY, 9540 San Jose Blvd.(32257), pg. 445
General Hardware Co.-Jacksonville, 3031 Westside Blvd.(32209), pg. 340
JERRY HAMM CHEVROLET INC., 2600 Phillips Hwy.(32207), pg. 503
HANDLING SYSTEMS ENGINEERING, 3000 W. 45th St.(32209), pg. 505
Jacksonville Crawdaddy Corp., 1643 Prudential Dr.(32207), pg. 1028
John Wieland Homes of Jacksonville, Inc., 5151 Sunbeam Rd., Ste. 19(32257), pg. 1189
Keystone Automotive Industries, Inc-Jacksonville, 4227 Clinton Ave.(32207), pg. 628
MAC PAPERS, INC., 3300 Phillips Hwy.(32207), pg. 694
MILLER ELECTRIC COMPANY, 2251 Rosselle St.(32204), pg. 754
M. D. MOODY & SONS INC., 4652 Phillips Hwy.(32207), pg. 768
Moran Towing of Florida, 9485 Regency Blvd., Ste. 460(32225), pg 769
National Distributing Co., Inc., 9423 No. Main St.(32218), pg. 787
NATIONAL MERCHANDISE CO., INC., 2321 Liberty St.(32206), pg. 792
New England Petroleum Corporation, 4655 Salisbury Rd., Ste. 220(32256), pg. 54
Niagara Envelope Co. of Florida, 5560 Shawland Rd.(32205), pg. 806
NIMNICHT CHEVROLET COMPANY, 1550 Cassat Ave.(32210), pg. 807
HARRY PEPPER & ASSOCIATES, 119 W. 8th St.(32206), pg. 859
PLOOF TRUCK LINES, INC., 1414 Lindrose St.(32206), pg. 877
PROGRESSIVE DRIVER SERVICES, INC., 2000 Corporate Square Blvd.(32216), pg. 894
Publix Super Markets, Inc., P.O. Box 2226-F, (32220), pg. 899
REGENCY DODGE INC., 9875 Atlantic Blvd.(32225), pg. 922
REGENCY GROUP INC., 121 W. Forsyth St.(32202), pg. 922
ROBINSON & ST. JOHN ADVERTISING & PUBLIC RELATIONS, INC., 6650 Southpoint Pkwy., Ste. 200(32216), pg. 940
Roux Laboratories, Inc., 3733 University Blvd. W.(32217), pg. 696
SMITH & GILLESPIE ENGINEERS, INC., 1100 Cesery Blvd.(32211), pg. 1012
THE STELLAR GROUP INC., 2900 Hartley Rd.(32257), pg. 1046
Storage Systems Engineering, 3000 W. 45 St.(32209), pg. 505
Sudco Development Co., Inc., P.O. Box 60069(32254), pg. 1056
THE SUDDATH COMPANIES, 5266 Highway Ave.(32205), pg. 1055
Suddath Moving Systems, Inc., P.O. Box 61802(32254), pg. 1056
Suddath Transportation Service, P.O. Box 60069(32254), pg. 1056
Suddath Van Lines, P.O. Box 60069(32254), pg. 1056
Summit Commercial Property, Inc., 6622 Southpoint Dr., S., Ste. 400(32216), pg. 1056
Treco Communities, Inc., 1325 San Marco Blvd.(32207), pg. 1062
Treco Property Services, Inc., 1325 San Marco Blvd.(32207), pg. 1062
Treco Realty Group, Inc., 1325 San Marco Blvd.(32207), pg. 1062
UNISON INDUSTRIES, 7575 Baymeadows Way(32256), pg. 1130
Unison Industries, 7575 Baymeadows Way(32256), pg. 1130
VOGUE & BODY SHOPS, INC., 6225 Powers Ave.(32217), pg. 1154
WOOLVERTON OLDSMOBILE-G.M.C. TRUCK, INC., 1325 Cassat Ave.(32205), pg. 1201

Jacksonville Beach

SOUTHEASTERN MEDEQUIP, INC., 905 N. 3rd St.(32250), pg. 1019

Jasper

Jasper Textile, Rte. 2, Box 35(32052), pg. 546

Jupiter

Ellison Graphics, 1400 Indiantown Rd.(33468), pg. 531

Kissimmee

General Commercial Packaging, Inc., P.O. Box 420572(34742-0572), pg. 1056
KISSIMMEE TOYOTA INC., 2535 N. Orange Blossom Trail(34744), pg. 633
REAL ESTATE CORP. OF FLORIDA, 2533 Boggy Creek Rd.(34744), pg. 917
Southern Electric Supply Co., Inc., 500 E. Donegan Ave.(34744), pg. 1021

Lake Buena Vista

Tri-City Electrical Contractors Inc., P.O. Box 22927, (32830), pg. 1110

Lake Mary

STRANG COMMUNICATIONS COMPANY, 600 Rinehart Rd.(32746), pg. 1052

Lake Park

Art Moran Auto Plaza, Inc., 3720 N. Lake Blvd.(33404), pg. 769

Lake Wales

CITRUS WORLD INC., Hwy. 27 North(33853), pg. 251
EAGER BEAVER, 4425 Hwy 27 S.(33853), pg. 362
General Engines Co., Inc., 4425 Hwy. 27 South(33853), pg. 362
Lake Wales Daily Highlander, 33 W. Orange Ave., Box 872(33859-0872), pg. 1042
Wales Industries, Inc., Hwy. 27 No.(33853), pg. 251

Lakeland

AMICO-Lakeland, 1033 Pine Chase Ave.(33801), pg. 29
Florida Auction Services Corporation, 310 County Line Rd.(33805), pg. 293
Lakeland Auto Auction, P.O. Box 90007, Interstate 4 & Hwy. 33(33804), pg. 293
PUBLIX SUPERMARKETS INC., 1936 George Jenkins Blvd.(33802), pg. 898
QUALITY PETROLEUM CORP., P.O. Box 3889, (33802-3889), pg. 903
Shopper Publishing Group, 2901 W. Memorial Blvd., Drawer 1110(33802), pg. 1042

Lantana

THE NATIONAL ENQUIRER, 600 S. East Coast Ave.(33464), pg. 788

Largo

C&D/Hit Inc., 7150 Bryan Dairy Rd.(34647), pg. 288
JACK ECKERD CORPORATION, 8333 Bryan Dairy Rd.(34647), pg. 366
Eckerd Drug Co., 8333 Bryan Dairy Rd.(34647), pg. 366
NBS Southern, Inc., 11451 S. Belcher Rd.(34643), pg. 960
OVERSTREET PAVING COMPANY, 1390 Donegan Rd.(34641), pg. 833
SOUTHERN APPAREL CORPORATION, 12420 73rd Court(34643), pg. 1020

Leesburg

CEM South, 31800 Progress Rd.(34748), pg. 1013
FLORIDA CRUSHED STONE COMPANY, 1616 S. 14th St.(34748), pg. 420

Longwood

BAIRD RAY NISSAN, INC., 2724 N. Hwy. 1792(32750), pg. 114
S. I. GOLDMAN CO., 799 Bennett Dr.(32750), pg. 467
BRUCE ROSSMEYER'S TOYOTALAND, 2925 N. Hwy. 17-92(32750), pg. 950
Scholastic Book Fairs, Inc., P.O. Box 178, (32750), pg. 962
Southeast Fire Sprinkler Company, 799 Bennett Dr.(32750), pg. 468

Madison

JIMMY DAVIS ENTERPRISES, INC., 420 Lake Shore Dr.(32340), pg. 318

Maitland

AUTOMATION INTELLIGENCE, INC., 850 Trafalgar Ct.(32751-4153), pg. 101
DEL AMERICAN PROPERTIES, INC., 1101 N. Lake Destiny Dr., Ste. 400(32751), pg. 325
MARKET DEVELOPMENT GROUP, INC., 1053 Maitland Center Common(32751), pg. 709

Medley

Miami Paper Company, 9771 NW 91st. Ct.(33178), pg. 1157

Melbourne

The Viera Company, 7380 Murrell Rd., Ste. 201(32900), pg. 351

Merritt Island

ISLAND LINCOLN-MERCURY, 1850 E. Merritt Island Causeway(32952), pg. 582

Miami

Adams International, 8948 N.W. 24th Terrace(33172), pg. 1073
AERO PERU CORPORATION, 8181 N.W. 36th St., Ste. 5(33166), pg. 22
AIR JAMAICA LTD., 444 Brickell Ave.(33131), pg. 27
Aircraft Support Group, Inc., 8095 N.W. 64th St.(33166), pg. 575
Alba Forwarding Co., Inc., 1801 N.W. 82nd Ave.(33126), pg. 30
Alcosa/Sunwise, 7925 N.W. 12th St., Suite 318(33126), pg. 506
JOHN ALDEN FINANCIAL CORPORATION, 7300 Corporate Center Dr.(33126), pg. 32
John Alden Life Insurance Company, 7300 Corporate Center Dr.(33126), pg. 33
Allied Steel Products, 3201 N.W. 167th St.(33169), pg. 480
Allright Miami, Inc., 150 S.E. Second Ave., Ste. 900(33131), pg. 41
AMERICAN INTERNATIONAL CONTAINER, INC., 3724 N.W. 73rd St.(33147), pg. 56
ATLANTIC GULF COMMUNITIES CORPORATION, 2601 S. Bayshore Dr.(33133), pg. 95
BACARDI IMPORTS, INC., 2100 Biscayne Blvd.(33137), pg. 108
BACKUS TURNER & PARTNERS, INC., 1001 S. Bayshore Dr., Ste. 2506(33131), pg. 112
Barnstorm Aviation, 6915 N.W. 43rd St.(33166), pg. 575
BEBER SILVERSTEIN & PARTNERS, INC., 3361 SW Third Ave.(33145), pg. 130
THE BERNUTH CORPORATION, 1405 S.W. 107th Ave.(33176), pg. 144
Beverage Canners Div., 3550 N.W. 110th St.(33167), pg. 148
BEVERAGE CANNERS INTERNATIONAL CORP., 3550 N.W. 110th St.(33167), pg. 148
BRAMAN WORLD CAR CENTER, 2044 Biscayne Blvd.(33137), pg. 171
BUSINESS MENS INSURANCE CORPORATION, 2620 SW 27th Ave.(33133), pg. 196
CAPITAL BANCORP, 1221 Brickell Ave.(33131), pg. 214
Capital Bank, 1221 Brickell Ave(33131), pg. 214
Caribe Express Latin American Div., 6704 N.W. 82nd. Ave.(33144), pg. 220
The William Cook Agency, Inc., 1110 Brickell Ave., Ste. 430(33131), pg. 282
COSTA CRUISE LINES, N.V., World Trade Center, 80 SW 8th St.(33130-3097), pg. 288
CRISPIN & PORTER ADVERTISING INC., 2699 S. Bayshore Dr.(33133), pg. 299
E & G FOODS, 7007 N.W. 37th Ave.(33147), pg. 358
ECUATORIANA AIRLINES, 7270 N.W. 12th St., Ste. 400(33126), pg. 367
FARM STORES, INC., 5800 N.W. 74th Ave.(33166), pg. 401
Filbert Corp. (Main Office), 7218 N.W. 56th St.(33166), pg. 1152
First American International Bank, Brickell Bay Tower, 28th Fl., 1001 S. Bayshore Dr.(33131), pg. 412
FIRST FLORIDA EQUITIES, LTD., 7740 5 W. 104th St., Ste. 200(33156), pg. 413
Five Star Homes, 1111 S. Bayshore Dr.(33131), pg. 95
Florida Home Finders, 1111 S. Bayshore Dr.(33131), pg. 95
The Flyer Publishing Corp., P.O. Box 161900, (33116), pg. 513
GARBER, GOODMAN ADVERTISING, INC., 4500 Biscayne Blvd.(33137), pg. 443
GOLD COAST ADVERTISING, 3625 N.W. 82nd Ave., Ste. 404(33166), pg. 465
Goya Foods of Florida, 1900 N.W. 92nd Ave.(33172), pg. 474
GRAPHIC PRODUCTIONS COMPANY, 5600 N.W. 32nd Ave.(33142), pg. 478
GREENWICH AIR SERVICES, Miami Intl. Airport, Bldg. 2146(33122), pg. 485
GULF DISTRIBUTION INC., 5959 N.W. 37th Ave.(33142), pg. 493
Gulfstream Aerospace Corp., 7200 Corporate Center Dr., Ste. 314(33126), pg. 494
HARRISON CONSTRUCTION CORP., 1000 N.W. 54th St.(33127), pg. 512
EDD HELMS ELECTRICAL CONTRACTING, 17830 N.E. 5th Ave.(33162), pg. 527
Edd Helms Electrical Service, Inc., 17830 N.E. 5th Ave.(33162), pg. 527
INJECTION FOOTWEAR CORP., 8730 N.W. 36th Ave.(33147), pg. 569
INTERNATIONAL AIRLINE SUPPORT GROUP, INC., 8095 N.W. 64th St.(33166), pg. 575
KEYES COMPANY, 100 N. Biscayne Blvd., 19th Fl.(33132), pg. 627
Keyes Investments, 100 No. Biscayne Blvd., 19th Fl.(33132), pg. 627
Keyes Management, 100 No. Biscayne Blvd.(33132), pg. 627
LAN-CHILE AIRLINES, 9700 So. Dixie Highway(33156), pg. 653
LUMAS REALTY, INC., 11035 S.W. 156th Pl.(33189), pg. 687
MARGO NURSERY FARMS, INC., 19995 S.W. 194th Ave.(33187), pg. 706
MCFARLAND & DRIER, INC., Rivergate West, 99 S.E. 5th St.(33131), pg. 729

MED-LAB SUPPLY COMPANY, INC., 923 N.W. 27th Ave.(33125), pg. 734
MEDIA PRINTING CORPORATION, 8050 N.W. 74th Ave.(33166), pg. 734
METRO FORD INC., 9000 N.W. 7th Ave.(33150), pg. 743
National Distributing Co., Inc., 16601 N.W. 8th Ave.(33169), pg. 787
94th Aero Squadron of Miami, Inc., 1395 NW 57th Ave., pg. 1028
NORTHWESTERN MEATS INC., 2100 N.W. 23rd St.(33142), pg. 815
PEREZ TRADING CO. INC., 3490 N.W. 125th St.(33167), pg. 860
POST BUCKLEY SCHUH & JERNIGAN, 8600 NW 36th St.(33166), pg. 881
POTAMKIN TOYOTA, INC., 19200 N.W. Second Ave.(33169), pg. 882
Prism Integrated Sanitation Management, Inc., 8300 Executive Center Dr., 4th Fl.(33166-4680), pg. 599
Publix Super Markets, Inc., P.O. Box 699030(33269), pg. 899
PURITY, INC., 1800 N.W. 70th Ave.(33126), pg. 901
REAL HOLDING MANAGEMENT CORP., 9688 S.W. 24th St.(33165), pg. 917
RealCold Storage, 8020 N.W. 60th St.(33166), pg. 1031
REPUBLIC NATIONAL BANK OF MIAMI, 10 N.W. 42nd Ave.(33126), pg. 928
ROYAL CARIBBEAN CRUISES LTD., 1050 Caribbean Way(33132), pg. 953
LILLIE RUBIN AFFILIATES INC., 15705 N.W. 13th Ave.(33169), pg. 954
RYDER & SCHILD, INC., 2100 Coral Way, 958
SANCHEZ & LEVITAN, INC., 1800 S.W. 27th Ave., Ste. 504(33145), pg. 970
SIMMONS OUTDOOR CORP., 14530 S.W. 119th Ave.(33186), pg. 1005
SPIEGEL MEATS, INC., 8020A N.W. 60th St.(33166), pg. 1030
SUNGLASS HUT CORPORATION, 120 SW 8th St.(33130), pg. 1060
TCC, 3250 Mary St.(33133), pg. 1072
TMP Worldwide, Inc., 3785 N.W. 82nd Ave., Ste. 408(33166), pg. 1074
Taca International Airlines, S. A., 4299 N. W. 36th St.(33166), pg. 1076
TASCO, 7600 N.W. 26th St.(33122), pg. 1079
Tech-Aerofoam Products, Inc., 3551 N.W. 116th St.(33167), pg. 480
TINSLEY ADVERTISING, 2660 Brickell(33129), pg. 1099
WIOD, Inc., 1401 N. Bay Causeway(33141), pg. 292
Withers/Suddath Van Lines, Inc., 6900 N.W. 74th Ave.(33152), pg. 1056
WOLFBERG, ALVAREZ & ASSOCIATES INC., 5960 S.W. 57th Ave.(33143), pg. 1199
Wollard Airport Equipment Co., 6950 N.W. 77th Ct.(33122), pg. 537
WORLD JAI-ALAI, 3500 N.W. 37th Ave.(33142), pg. 1202
World Jai-Alai Players, 3500 N.W. 37th Ave.(33142), pg. 1203
ZUBI ADVERTISING SERVICES, INC., 2600 SW Third Ave., 9th Fl.(33129), pg. 1221

Miami Beach

CHESAPEAKE FINANCIAL CORP., 6917 Collins Ave.(33141), pg. 243
Pan American Ocean Resort Hotel, 17875 Collins Ave.(33154), pg. 549
Specialty Restaurants Corp., South Point Pk., 1028

Miami Lakes

AD-TECH COMMUNICATIONS, 14361 Commerce Way(33016), pg. 16
CAPELETTI BROS., INC., 16401 NW 58 Ave.(33014), pg. 214
FREESON ADVERTISING AGENCY, 5980 Miami Lakes Dr.(33014), pg. 431
General Wig Manufacturers, Inc., 13982 N.W. 58th Ct.(33014), pg. 695
J. I. Mortgage Service Corporation, 7900 Miami Lakes Dr.(33102), pg. 633
J. I. KISLAK INC., 7900 Miami Lakes Dr.(33016), pg. 633
J. I. Kislak Mortgage Corporation, 7900 Miami Lakes Dr.(33016), pg. 633
SECURITY PLASTICS, INC., 14427 N.W. 60th Ave.(33014), pg. 987

Milton

Armstrong-Hunt, Inc., 1 Armstrong Rd.(32583), pg. 83

Mulberry

W.S. BADCOCK CORPORATION, 200 Phosphate Boulevard N.W.(33860), pg. 113

Naples

Brown Brothers Harriman Trust Co. of Florida, Collier Financial Center, 4501 Tamiami Trail North(33940), pg. 181
Cableware Technology Div., 900 Industrial Blvd.(33942), pg. 683
Christmas & Things, Inc., Coastland Ctr., 1832 N. Tamiami Trail(33940), pg. 884

North Miami

THE AD TEAM OF FLORIDA INC., 15251 NE 18th Ave.(33162), pg. 16
MOHAWK DISTILLED PRODUCTS, 11900 Biscayne Blvd.(33181-2726), pg. 763

North Miami Beach

FMS MANAGEMENT SYSTEMS, INC., 2655 N.E. 189th St.(33180), pg. 394

North Palm Beach

Mutual Service Corporation, 701 N. Federal Hwy.(33408), pg. 841

Ocala

CERTIFIED GROCERS OF FLORIDA, INC., 8305 SE 58th Ave.(32671), pg. 237
Cox Cable Greater Ocala, Inc., 2410 S.W. 27th Street(32674), pg. 294
MARK III INDUSTRIES, 5401 N.W. 44th Ave.(32675), pg. 708
Quality Computer Forms, Inc., 402 S.W. 33rd Ave.(32674), pg. 951
Southern Electric Supply Co., Inc., 111 S.E. 8th St.(32671), pg. 1021

Ocoee

Cookin' Good Distribution Ctr., 210 E. Story Rd., Drawer 847(34761), pg. 1000
Florida Auto Auction of Orlando, Inc., 600 West Hwy. 50(32761), pg. 293
SILVER SPRINGS CITRUS CO-OP, 15 S. Kissimmee Ave.(34761), pg. 1004

Okahumpka

LESTER COGGINS TRUCKING, Hwy. 33 S.(34762), pg. 259

Opa Locka

ALTERMAN TRANSPORT LINES, INC., 12805 N.W. 42nd Ave.(33054), pg. 45
W. Braun International, 13165 N.W. 45th Ave.(33054), pg. 172

Orange Park

SUNRISE NISSAN OF ORANGE PARK, 1565 Wells Rd.(32073), pg. 1062

Orlando

ACOUSTI ENGINEERING CO. OF FLORIDA, 4656 34th St. S.W.(32811), pg. 14
ADDISON STEEL INC., 7351 Overland Rd.(32810-3403), pg. 17
Advanced Technology Systems, Inc., 7641 Currency Dr.(32819), pg. 268
Allied Security Inc., 5151 Adanson St., Ste. 98(32804), pg. 39
ALLIED TIRE SALES, 3320 Maggie Blvd., Ste. A(32811), pg. 40
AMICK CONSTRUCTION LTD., 401 N. Ferguson Dr.(32805), pg. 67
Aratex Services, 379 W. Michigan St., Ste. 208(32806), pg. 6
Arlo Group, Orlando, 2505 Forsyth Rd.(32807), pg. 44
ATTORNEY'S TITLE INSURANCE FUND, 5955 T. G. Lee Blvd., Ste. 500(32822), pg. 97
Broder Bros. Co. Of Florida, Inc., 1255 LaQuinta Dr., Bldg. 130(32809), pg. 178
Brooks Products, Orlando, 690 Taft-Vineland Rd.(32824), pg. 180
Burke, Bales & Mills/HEPY, Inc., 111 N. Orange Ave., Ste. 650(32801), pg. 509
Burns & Roe Southeast, Southland Executive Park, 7800 Southland Blvd., Ste. 260(32809), pg. 194
CARSE OIL CO. INC., 1700 S. Bumby Ave.(32806), pg. 225
CHEMCENTRAL/Orlando, 8120 S. Orange Ave.(32809), pg. 242
CHIP SUPPLY INC., 7725 N. Orange Blossom Trail(32810), pg. 248
CORRECT CRAFT, INC., 6100 So. Orange Ave.(32809), pg. 287
Cramer-Krasselt, 225 E. Robinson St., Ste. 490(32802), pg. 296
DANIELS MANUFACTURING CORPORATION, 526 Thorpe Rd.(32824), pg. 314
Deco Purchasing Co., 151 E. Washington(32801), pg. 527
Eckerd Drug Co., 2100 Directors Row(32809), pg. 366
FRY/HAMMOND/BARR INCORPORATED, 600 E. Washington St.(32801), pg. 435
Furman Wholesale Lumber Div., 2021 S. Division St.(32805), pg. 437
GAI Consultants-Southeast, Inc., 1833 Edgewater Dr.(32804), pg. 439
GOUCHENOUR ADV., INC., 455 South Orange Ave., 6th Fl.(32801-3356), pg. 473
GRANTHAM COMPANY, 2685 Hansrob Rd.(32804), pg. 477
GREATER ORLANDO AUTO AUCTION, 9800 Bachman Rd.(32824), pg. 483
HEINTZELMAN'S TRUCK CENTER INC., 2424 John Young Pkwy.(32804), pg. 526
KELSEY CONSTRUCTION, INC., 306 E. Princeton St.(32804), pg. 621
Kelsey Development, 306 E. Princeton St.(32804), pg. 622
Keystone Automotive Industries, Inc.-Orlando, Suite D2, 3320 Vineland Rd.(32811), pg. 628
M.A.B. Paints, 720 Central Florida Hwy.(32824), pg. 184
Massey Cadillac, Inc., 4241 N. John Young Pkwy.(32804), pg. 719
MCNAMARA PONTIAC INC., 1010 W. Colonial Dr.(32804), pg. 732
DON MEALEY CHEVROLET INC., 3707 W. Colonial Dr.(32808), pg. 733
MEARS TRANSPORTATION GROUP, 324 W. Gore St.(32806), pg. 734
National Distributing Co., Inc., 3785 Bryn Mawr St.(32808), pg. 787
NATIONAL HEALTH PRODUCTS, 731 Kirkman Rd.(32811), pg. 791
94th Aero Squadron of Orlando, Inc., 494 Rickenbacker Dr.(32803), pg. 1028
NORMAN BROTHERS NISSAN INC., 1983 N. Semoran Blvd.(32807), pg. 810
Orlando Sun Rays, 287 S. Tampa Ave.(32805), pg. 758
Popeye's Famous Fried Chicken, 5864-66 Semoran Blvd., S.(32812), pg. 284
REED MOTORS, INC., 3776 W. Colonial Dr.(32808), pg. 920
REGAL MARINE INDUSTRIES INC., 2300 Jetport Dr.(32809), pg. 921
REPCO INCORPORATED, 2421 N. Orange Blossom Trail(32804), pg. 927
ROBINSON, YESAWICH & PEPPERDINE, 1900 Summit Tower Blvd., Ste. 600(32810), pg. 940
Southeast Correct Craft, Inc., P.O. Box 13117(32859), pg. 287
SOUTHEASTERN INVESTMENT PROPERTIES INC., 933 Lee Rd., Ste. 400A(32810), pg. 1019
Spiralkote, 1200 Central Florida Pkwy.(32837), pg. 418
Sverdrup Southern Constructors, Inc., 1900 Summit Tower Blvd., Ste. 300(32810), pg. 1066
TRANSPO ELECTRONICS, INC., 2150 Bringle Ave.(32808), pg. 1108
TRAYLOR CHEMICAL & SUPPLY CO., 1911 Traylor Blvd.(32804), pg. 1108
WFTV, Inc., 639 W. Central Blvd.(32801), pg. 292
Wenczel Tile Distributing Company, 2016 Alden Rd.(32803), pg. 1176
WILLIAMS COMPANY OF ORLANDO, INC., 2301 Silver Star Rd.(32804), pg. 1190

Ormond Beach

Ellis Pharmaceuticals, 355 Tomoka Ave.(32174), pg. 384
TANNING RESEARCH LABS., INC., 1190 U.S. 1 North(32174), pg. 1078

Oviedo

A. DUDA & SONS INC., 1975 W. State Rd. 426(32765), pg. 351

Palm Beach

Wally Findlay Galleries, Inc , 165 Worth Ave.(33480), pg. 410

Palm Harbor

CLEANERS HANGER CO., 3055 Reun Rd.(34682), pg. 254
GOLF HOSTS, INC., 36750 U.S. Hwy. 19 N.(34684), pg. 469

Palmetto

SOUTHERN AGRICULTURAL INSECTICIDES, 7600 Bayshore Rd.(34221), pg. 1020

Panama City

Century Boats By General Marine Industries, 6725 Bay Line Dr.(32404), pg. 450
GMI, Inc.-Glasstream, 6725 Bay Line Dr.(32404), pg. 450
GENERAL MARINE INDUSTRIES, INC., 6725 Bay Line Dr.(32404), pg. 449

Pensacola

Allright Pensacola Parking, 134 W. Government St.(32501), pg. 42
THE LEWIS BEAR COMPANY, 4150 W. Blount St.(32505), pg. 129
Cox Cable Pensacola, Inc., 2205 LaVista Ave.(32504), pg. 294
National Distributing Co., Inc., P.O. Box 17168, 3333 Palafox St.(32522), pg. 787
THE WINDHAM COMPANY, 627 E. Government St.(32501), pg. 1195

Perry

Florida Service Center, P.O. Box 559(32347-9998), pg. 1192
Martin Electronics, Inc., Rte. 1, P.O. Box 500(32347), pg. 612

Plant City

Dad's Cookies, 2615 Hwy. 92 East(33566), pg. 760
PARADISE FRUIT COMPANY, INC., 1200 W. Haines St.(33566), pg. 847
PRESTO FOOD STORES, INC., 607 S. Alexander St.(33566), pg. 888

Pompano Beach

Dahlstrom Manufacturing Co., Inc.-Safeway Division, 110 S.W. 16th Ave.(33069), pg. 310
Florida Supermarket, Inc., 605 S.W. 16th Terrace(33069), pg. 918
Marine Air Systems, Inc., 2000 N. Andrews Ave. Ext.(33069), pg. 1081
PUEBLO INTERNATIONAL, INC., 1300 N.W. 22nd St.(33069), pg. 899
STANDARD BRANDS OF AMERICA, INC., 2199 W. Atlantic Blvd.(33069), pg. 1035
Xtra Super Food Centers, Inc., 1300 N.W. 22nd St.(33069), pg. 899

Port St. Lucie

Southern Electric Supply Co., Inc., 600 NW Peacock Blvd., Ste. 8(34986), pg. 1021

Quincy

PRINTING HOUSE, INC., P.O. Box 310(32353), pg. 891

Riverview

Cargill Fertilizer, Inc., 8813 Highway 41 South(33569), pg. 219

Riviera Beach

Acorn of Florida, 8305 Garden Rd.(33404), pg. 14

Safety Harbor

JACOBSEN MANUFACTURING, INC., 901 Fourth St., N.(34695), pg. 588

Saint Petersburg

BARGER BUILDER & DEVELOPERS, 300 First Ave. South(33701), pg. 119
HARRY H. BELL & SONS, INC., 756 28th St., South(33712), pg. 134
COX LUMBER CO., 3300 Fairfield Ave. S.(33712), pg. 294
JABIL CIRCUIT INC., 10800 Roosevelt Blvd.(33716), pg. 587
Modern Talking Picture Service, Inc., 5000 Park St. N.(33709), pg. 612
PAYLESS CAR RENTAL SYSTEM, INC., 2350 34th Street North(33713), pg. 853
PRECISIONAIRE, INC., 2399 26th Ave. N.(33713), pg. 886
Tape & Label Engineering, 2950 47th Ave. N.(33714), pg. 1171
WWRM, Inc., 877 Executive Center Drive, W., Ste. 300(33702), pg. 293

Sanford

CODISCO INC., 601 Codisco Way(32771), pg. 258
General Felt Industries, Inc., 2772 Depot St.(32771), pg. 1121
J.F.P. & ASSOCIATES OF FLORIDA, INC., 201 W. First St.(32771), pg. 584
Jetstream Systems, 3795 S. Sanford Ave.(32773), pg. 122
Southern Electric Supply Co., Inc., 3501 S. Sanford Ave.(32773), pg. 1021
SUNNILAND CORPORATION, P.O. Box 1697(32771), pg. 1061

Sarasota

Elkins Constructors, 747 N. Washington Blvd.(34236), pg. 377
Gulf Constructors International, Inc., P.O. Drawer 4256(34230), pg. 1159
KALIN ENTERPRISES, INC., 5252 S. Tamiami Trail(34231), pg. 615
W.G. MILLS, INC., 3301 Whitfield Ave.(34243), pg. 756
94th Aero Squadron of Sarasota, Inc., 8301 N. Tamiami Trail(34243), pg. 1028
TROPITONE FURNITURE CO. INC., 1401 Commerce Blvd.(34243), pg. 1116
Veneman, P.O. Box 3197(34230), pg. 1116
Wellcraft Marine, 1651 Whitfield Ave., P.O. Box 13011(34234), pg. 759
Wenczel Tile Distributing Company, 1931 13th Ave.(34236), pg. 1176

South Bay

South Bay Growers, Inc., P.O. Box 56, (33493), pg. 1137

St. Petersburg

Anderson-Parrish Associates, Inc., Paragon Crossing Bldg., 11300 4th St., North, Suite 100(33716), pg. 661
F & F Productions, Inc., 9675 Fourth St. N.(33702), pg. 549
Federal Stampings of Florida, 7205 30th Ave. No.(33710), pg. 321
Hubbard Communications, 9675 Fourth St. N.(33702), pg. 549
WTOG-TV, Inc., 365 105th Terrace N.E.(33716), pg. 549
Weatherly Frozen Foods Group, Inc., 1000 118th Ave., N.(33702), pg. 1169

Stuart

Dickerson Realty Florida, Inc., P.O. Box 719, (33494), pg. 336
ENABLING TECHNOLOGIES COMPANY, 3102 S.E. Jay St.(34997), pg. 380
MYERS & ASSOCIATES, INC., 3727 S.E. Ocean Blvd., Ste. 203(34996), pg. 780

Sun City

SPEEDLING INCORPORATED, 4300 Old U.S. Hwy 41(33586), pg. 1029

Tallahassee

THE FLORIDA LOTTERY, 250 Marriott Dr.(32399-4000), pg. 420
MCKENZIE TANK LINES, INC., 122 Apple Yard Dr.(32304), pg. 730
ROSE PRINTING COMPANY, INC., 2503 Jackson Bluff Rd.(32314), pg. 948
Watkins Engineers & Constructors, Inc., P.O. Box 2194, 1238 Airport Ave.(32316), pg. 338

Tampa

ARA Leisure Services Group, Florida, 600 Ashley Drive(33602), pg. 6
AFFILIATED OF FLORIDA INC., 1102 N. 28th St.(33605), pg. 23
Allied Security Inc., Horizen Bldg., 4511 N. Himes Ave., Ste. 191(33614), pg. 39
Allright Florida, Inc., P.O. Box 1404(83601), pg. 41
Automation Resources, One Urban Center, 4830 W. Kennedy Blvd., Suite 665(33609), pg. 370
B & B CASH GROCERY STORE, 9330 Adamo Dr.(33619), pg. 105
Barry-Wehmiller Packaging Systems, 11316 N. 46th St., Suite 2(33617), pg. 122
Best Insurors, Inc., 1500 N. Dale Mabry Hwy.(33607), pg. 1162
BLEVINS CONCESSION SUPPLY CO., P.O. Box 79136(33619), pg. 156
BRIGGS INDUSTRIES, INC., 4350 W. Cypress St., Ste. 800(33607), pg. 175
Business Guides Inc., 3922 Coconut Palm Dr.(33619), pg. 665
Cardem Insurance Co., Ltd., 1500 N. Dale Mabry(33607), pg. 1162
Chili Pepper of Rocky Point, Inc., 2425 Rocky Point Dr.(33607), pg. 1028
Conductors Unlimited, 4934 Distribution Dr.(33605), pg. 374
Cookin' Good Distribution Ctr., 4712 W. Ohio Ave.(33614), pg. 1000
Diamond Products Company, 3901 Riga Blvd.(33619), pg. 517
Dixie Building Supplies, Inc., 1500 N. Dale Mabry Hwy.(33607), pg. 1162
Duro Paper Bag Mfg. Co., P.O. Box 5004(33675), pg. 355
ERM-South, Inc., 9501 Princess Palm Ave., Ste. 100(33619), pg. 360
Envirocon International Corp., Lincoln Center, 5401 West Kennedy Blvd., Ste. 751(33609), pg. 732
FERMAN OLDSMOBILE, 1307 W. Kennedy Blvd.(33606), pg. 406
Stephen Gould of Florida, Inc., 5723 Benjamin Center Dr.(33613), pg. 474
Greater Tampa Bay Auto Auction, 401 S. 50th St.(33619), pg. 293
GULF COAST LEAD COMPANY, INC., 1901 N. 66th St.(33619), pg. 493
Gulf Foundation Inc., 5440 W. Tyson Ave.(33611), pg. 760
H.A.T. Holding Company, 3901 Riga Blvd.(33619), pg. 517
Hamer Properties, Inc., 1500 N. Dale Mabry Hwy.(33607), pg. 1162
HAVATAMPA INCORPORATED, 3901 Riga Blvd.(33619), pg. 517
J.W. Window Components, Inc., 1500 N. Dale Mabry Hwy.(33607), pg. 1162
KASH N KARRY FOOD STORES, INC., 6422 Harney Rd.(33610), pg. 617
LAZY DAYS R V CENTER, INC., 11028 N. Florida Ave.(33612), pg. 663
LYKES BROTHERS INC. OF FLORIDA, 211 Madison St.(33602), pg. 688
LYKES ENERGY, INC., 111 Madison St.(33602), pg. 689
MCNEEL INTERNATIONAL CORP., 5401 West Kennedy Blvd., Ste. 751(33609), pg. 732
Mid-State Homes, Inc., 1500 N. Dale Mabry Hwy.(33607), pg. 1162
MISENER MARINE CONSTRUCTION, 5440 W. Tyson Ave.(33611), pg. 759
Misener Marine P.R., 5440 W. Tyson Ave.(33611), pg. 760
MOORE, EPSTEIN, MOORE, 3102 N. Habana Ave.(33607), pg. 768
National Distributing Co., Inc., 4109 Savarese Circle N.(33614), pg. 787
Normandale Properties, 4350 W. Cypress, Ste. 701(33622), pg. 828
NuArc Co., 13540 N. Florida Ave., Ste. 103(33613), pg. 817
OPUS SOUTH CORPORATION, SUITE 444, 4200 W. Cypress(33607), pg. 828
PARADIGM COMMUNICATIONS, 5301 W. Cypress St., Ste. 314(33607), pg. 847
PENNINSULAR MEAT COMPANY, INC., 4401 N. Westshore Blvd.(33614), pg. 858
Peoples Gas System, Inc., 111 Madison St.(33602), pg. 689
Phillies Cigar Company, 3901 Riga Blvd.(33619), pg. 517
REEVES SOUTHEASTERN CORPORATION, P.O. Box 1968(33601), pg. 921
RESOURCE, INC., 3825 Henderson Blvd.(33629), pg. 929
ROBBINS MANUFACTURING COMPANY, Nebraska & 131st. Ave.(33612), pg. 938
Rocky Point Village Corp., 2500 Rocky Point Dr.(33607), pg. 1028
SPALDING & EVENFLO COMPANIES, INC., 5730A N. Hoover Blvd.(33634), pg. 1024
Store Development, Inc., 1102 N. 28th St.(33605), pg. 23
SUN FINANCIAL GROUP, INC., 2502 Rocky Pt. Dr., Ste. 375(33607), pg. 1058
Tampa Bay Moving Systems Inc., 5105 W. Clifton Ave(33634), pg. 282
THEOCHEM LABS., INC., 7373 Rowlett Park Dr.(33610), pg. 1090
Tri-City Electrical Contractors Inc., 9942 Currie Davis Dr., Ste. D-7(33619), pg. 1110
TROPICAL GARMENT MANUFACTURING COMPANY, 2508 Ivy St.(33607), pg. 1116
VILLAZON COMPANY INC., 3104 N. Armenia Ave.(33607), pg. 1152
Jim Walter Computer Services, Inc., 1500 N. Dale Mabry Hwy.(33607), pg. 1162
Jim Walter Homes, Inc., 1500 N. Dale Mabry Hwy.(33607), pg. 1162
J. W. Walter, Inc., 1500 N. Dale Mabry Hwy.(33607), pg. 1162
WALTER INDUSTRIES, INC., 1500 N. Dale Mabry Hwy.(33607), pg. 1161
Walter Land Co., 1500 N. Dale Mabry Hwy.(33607), pg. 1162
Wenczel Tile Company, 6608 S. Westshore Blvd.(33616), pg. 1176
Wenczel Tile Distributing Company, 1410 N. Himes Ave.(33607), pg. 1176
WEST & COMPANY MARKETING & ADVERTISING, 401 E. Jackson St., Ste. 3600(33602), pg. 1177
WHITE MOP WRINGER COMPANY, 10702 N. 46th St.(33617), pg. 1186

Tarpon Springs

Golf Host Resorts, Inc., P.O. Box 1088(34688), pg. 469

Titusville

DAVID BOLAND, INC., 3050 S. Hopkins Ave.(32871), pg. 162
PATCH COMMUNICATIONS, 5211 S. Washington Ave.(32780), pg. 851

Umatilla

GOLDEN GEM GROWERS INC., 39017 Golden Gem Dr.(32784), pg. 466

Vero Beach

PIPER AIRCRAFT CORPORATION, 2926 Piper Dr.(32960), pg. 872
REDGATE COMMUNICATIONS CORP., 660 Beachland Blvd.(32963), pg. 919
SEALD-SWEET GROWERS, INC., 1991 74th Ave.(32966), pg. 984
Southern Electric Supply Co., Inc., 672 Old Dixie Hwy.(32965), pg. 1021
GEORGE E. WARREN CORP., 605 17th St.(32960), pg. 1164

West Melbourne

Southern Electric Supply Co., Inc., 7401 W. Ellis Rd.(32904), pg. 1021

West Palm Beach

Allright West Palm Beach, Inc., 335 Clematis St.(33402), pg. 42
Bencart, Inc., North Haverhill Road(33417), pg. 236
Boca Hamptons Management, Inc., North Haverhill Rd.(33417), pg. 236
C. V. Investments, Inc., North Haverhill Rd.(33417), pg. 236
C.V.W. Ltd. Partnership, North Haverhill Road(33409), pg. 236
Century Financial Services, North Haverhill Road(33417), pg. 236
Century Golf Courses, Inc., North Haverhill Road(33417), pg. 236
Century Real Estate, Inc., North Haverhill Road(33417), pg. 236
Century Utilities, Inc., North Haverhill Road(33417), pg. 236
CENVILL DEVELOPMENT CORP., 2601-21 S. Militar Trail(33415), pg. 235
Cenvill Management, Inc., North Haverhill Road(33417), pg. 236
Cenvill Recreation, Inc., North Haverhill Road(33417), pg. 236
Cenvill Services, North Haverhill Road(33417), pg. 236
Comark, Inc., North Haverhill Road(33417), pg. 236
F.W.D.C., Inc., North Haverhill Road(33417), pg. 236
G.D.C. Business Systems, Inc., North Haverhill Road(33417), pg. 236
Keystone Automotive Industries, Inc. - W. Palm, 940 West 13th St.(33404), pg. 628
National Distributing Co., Inc., 4268 Westroads Dr.(33407), pg. 787
94th AS of West Palm Beach, Inc., 3989 Southern Blvd.(33406), pg. 1028
OVERSEAS SERVICE CORPORATION, 1100 Northpoint Parkway(33407), pg. 833
OXBOW CORPORATION, 1601 Forum Pl.(33401), pg. 834
Palm Beach Newspapers, Inc., 2751 So. Dixie Hwy.(33416), pg. 292
Prestcon, Inc., North Haverhill Road(33417), pg. 236
THOMPSON MEDICAL COMPANY, INC., 222 Lakeview Ave., 17th Fl.(33401-6112), pg. 1094
Trump Plaza of the Palm Beaches, 525 S. Flagler Dr.(33401), pg. 1118
Weitz-Cohen Construction Company, 560 Village Blvd., Ste. 120(33409), pg. 1174
Wynmoor Homes, Inc., North Haverhill Road(33417), pg. 236
Wynmoor Ltd. Partnership, North Haverhill Rd.(33417), pg. 236
Wynmoor Management & Co., Inc., North Haverhill Road(33417), pg. 236
Wynville Realty, North Haverhill Road(33417), pg. 236

Wildwood

J.T. Slocomb Company, Wildwood Industrial Park, 901 Industrial Dr.(34785), pg. 1010

Winter Garden

HELLER BROS. PACKING CORP., 306 9th St.(34787), pg. 526

Winter Haven

BOWEN BROTHERS FRUIT CO., INC., 305 Ave. E, SW(33880), pg. 169
Winter Haven News Chief, 650 Sixth St., S.W.(33880), pg. 1042

Winter Park

ANSON-STONER, INC., 111 E. Fairbanks Ave.(32789), pg. 76
ROGER HOLLER CHEVROLET CO., 860 W. Fairbanks Ave.(32789), pg. 539
HUBBARD CONSTRUCTION CO., 1936 Lee Rd.(32789), pg. 549

PALMER ELECTRIC CO., 875 Jackson Ave.(32789), pg. 843
LUKE POTTER DODGE INC., 1050 N. Orlando Ave.(32789), pg. 882
Winter Park Leasing, Inc., 1050 N. Orlando Ave.(32789), pg. 882

Zephyrhills

Lykes Dispenser Div., 40047 Hwy. 45 E.(33540), pg. 688

GEORGIA

Acworth

AMERICO MANUFACTURING CO., INC., 6224 No. Main St.(30101), pg. 66

Albany

J & J Furniture Co., Inc., 703 Oglethorpe Ave.(31021), pg. 1163
National Distributing Co., Inc., 109 Booker Ave.(31701), pg. 787
Wingate/Taylor Maid Transportation Inc., P.O. Box 1268, (31703), pg. 191

Alpharetta

Fulfillment Unlimited, 1650 Bluegrass Lakes Pky.(30201), pg. 894
HOOVER GROUP, INC., 2001 Westside Pkwy., Ste. 155(30201), pg. 543
PROFESSIONAL BOOK DISTRIBUTORS, INC., 1650 Bluegrass Lakes Pky.(30201), pg. 894
PROTO SYSTEMS OF ATLANTA, 625 Simms Industrial Blvd.(30201), pg. 895
Southeastern Regional Office, 5895 Windward Pkwy.(30201), pg. 233

Alto

Mount Vernon Mills, Inc., Riegel Textile Div. (Alto), P.O. Box 649(30510), pg. 844

Americus

SHEFFIELD HARDWARE COMPANY, 314 N. Dudley(31709), pg. 996
THE TOG SHOP, Lester Square(31710), pg. 1100

Andoraville

Payson Georgia, Inc., 3480 Oakcliff Rd.(30340), pg. 853

Athens

Holiday Inn, P.O. Box 1666, Broad & Lumpkin Sts.(30602), pg. 140

Atlanta

AJC INTERNATIONAL, INC., 5188 Roswell Rd., N.W.(30342), pg. 4
AVA-AUTOMATIC VENDORS OF AMERICA, 2175 Parklake Dr., N.E., Ste. 200(30345), pg. 8
ACADEMY INSURANCE GROUP, INC., 6600 Peachtree Dunwoody Rd.(30328), pg. 11
Academy Life Insurance Co., 600 Embassy Row, 6600 Peachtree-Dunwoody Rd.(30328), pg. 11
ADAIR GREENE ADVERTISING, 2126 De Foors Ferry Rd., NW(30318), pg. 16
ADAMS WINE CO., 451 Sawtell Ave., S. E.(30315), pg. 17
Agra Tech Seeds, Inc., 244 Perimeter Center Pkwy. N.E.(30346), pg. 465
AgraTrade Financing, Inc., 244 Perimeter Center Pkwy.(30346), pg. 465
Agri International, Inc., 244 Perimeter Center Pkwy.(30346), pg. 465
Agvestments, Inc., 244 Perimeter Center Pkwy. N.E.(30346), pg. 465
IVAN ALLEN COMPANY, INC., 221 Peachtree Center Ave. N.E.(30303), pg. 36
ALLIED FOODS, INC., 1450 Hills Place NW(30318), pg. 38
Allright Parking of Georgia, 100 Luckie NW(30301), pg. 42
AMARLITE ARCHITECTURAL PRODUCTS, 3765 Atlanta Industrial Dr.(30331), pg. 47
AMERICAN TARA CORPORATION, Bldg. 6, 750 Hammond Dr., Ste. 200(30328), pg. 63
ANDERSON, DUSENBURY & ALBAN, 3343 Peachtree Rd., N.E., Ste. M-50(30326), pg. 72
APEX SUPPLY CO. INC., 2500 Button Gwinnett Dr.(30340), pg. 78
Aratex Services, 401 Glen Iris Dr.(30308), pg. 6
Asbury Ferst, Inc., 3550 Zip Industrial Blvd.(30354), pg. 87
ATLANTA BEVERAGE CO., 5000 Fulton Industrial Blvd. SW(30336), pg. 94
ATLANTA MARKET CENTER, 240 Peachtree St. N.W., Ste. 2200(30303), pg. 94
Atlanta Newspapers, 72 Marietta St., N.W(30303), pg. 292
Atlanta Southeastern Development Corp., 3955 No. Peachtree Rd.(30341), pg. 562
ATLANTIC STEEL COMPANY, 1300 Mecaslin St., N. W.(30318), pg. 95
ATLAS SUPPLY COMPANY, 2625 Cumberland Pkwy., Ste. 300(30339), pg. 96
AUSTIN KELLEY ADVERTISING, INC., The Palisades, 5901 Peachtree Dunwoody Rd., NE(30328), pg. 99
Automobile Auction Division, 1400 Lake Hearn Drive, N.E.(30319), pg. 293
Aviation Constructors, Inc., 2690 Cumberland Pkwy., Suite 200(30339), pg. 255
AYDLOTTE & CARTWRIGHT, INC., 6 Concourse Pkwy., Ste. 2800(30339), pg. 103
Backer Spielvogel Bates, Inc., Eight Piedmont Ctr., Ste. 420(30305), pg. 108
BANKHEAD ENTERPRISES INC., 1080 Bankhead Ave.(30318), pg. 117
BARGE-WAGENER, INC., 1815 The Exchange(30339), pg. 119
Barton Brands of Georgia, Inc., 650 Fairburn Rd., S.W.(30331), pg. 123
BEAUDRY FORD, INC., 141 Piedmont Ave., N.E.(30303), pg. 130
BEERS CONSTRUCTION COMPANY, 70 Ellis St., N.E.(30303), pg. 132
Bell South Advertising & Publishing Division, 1100 Peak St.(30309), pg. 136
Bell South Business Product Division, 880 Great S.W. Pky.(30336), pg. 136
BELL SOUTH ENTERPRISES, 713 Ralph David Abernathy St. S.W.(30310), pg. 136
BENNETT KUHN VARNER, INC., 3490 Piedmont Rd., Ste. 1450(30305), pg. 139
BETTER BRANDS OF ATLANTA, INC., 755 Jefferson St. NW(30377), pg. 148
Binswanger, 1175 Peachtree St., N.E., Ste. 408(30361), pg. 152
R.F. BROADUS & ASSOCIATES, INC., 3400 Peachtree Rd. NE, Ste. 1239(30326), pg. 177
BROCK CONTROL SYSTEMS, INC., 2859 Paces Ferry Rd., Ste. 1000(30339), pg. 178
Butler Telecommunications Group, 3836 Dekalb Technology Pkwy.(30340), pg. 197
CSI ADVERTISING INC., 3925 Peachtree Road N.E.(30317), pg. 205
CUNA South East District, 2945 Flowers Rd. So., Ste. 101(30341), pg. 205
CableRep, Inc., 1400 Lake Hearn Drive, N.E.(30319), pg. 294
CARTER, 1275 Peachtree St. N.E., Suite 100(30367-1801), pg. 226
CASCINO PURCELL FREEBAIRN, East Tower, 3343 Peachtree Rd., Ste. 1220(30326), pg. 227
W.C. CAYE & COMPANY, INC., 787 Windsor St., S.W.(30315), pg. 230
Charter Investment Co., 600 Embassy Row, 6600 Peachtree Dunwoody Rd.(30328), pg. 11
Chiat/Day/Mojo/Atlanta, 200 Galleria Pkwy.(30339), pg. 244
CHICK-FIL-A, INC., 5200 Buffington Rd.(30349), pg. 247
CITY BEVERAGE CO., 566 Wells St., S.W.(30312), pg. 251
Cleveland Consolidated Inc., 1281 Fulton Industrial Blvd. NW(30336), pg. 255
Cleveland Electric Co., 3980 Martin Luther King Dr.(30336), pg. 255
CLEVELAND GROUP, INC., 2690 Cumberland Pkwy., Ste. 200(30339), pg. 255
COLE HENDERSON DRAKE, INC., 400 Colony Square, 1201 Peachtree St. NE, Ste. 500(30361), pg. 260
COLONIAL PIPELINE COMPANY, 945 E. Paces Ferry Rd., N.E.(30326-0855), pg. 264
COLOR GRAPHICS, INC., 4540 Frederick Dr., S.W.(30336), pg. 264
COMMUNICATION TRENDS, INC., Bldg. 30, 3715 Northside Pkwy., Ste. 550(30327), pg. 269
Consultec, Inc., 6065 Roswell Rd., N.E.(30328), pg. 448
Al Copeland Enterprises, Inc., Bldg. 700, 3980 DeKalb Technology Pkwy., Ste. 775(30340), pg. 283
COVINGTON INDUSTRIES, 2625 Cumberland Pkwy.(30339), pg. 290
Cox Communications, Inc., 1400 Lake Hearn Dr. N.E.(30319), pg. 292
COX ENTERPRISES, INC., 1400 Lake Hearn Dr.(30319), pg. 292
Cox Texas Publications, Inc., 1400 Lake Hearn Dr.(30319), pg. 292
THE CRITERION GROUP, INC., 12 Piedmont Center, Ste. 100(30305), pg. 299
Days Inns of America, Inc., 2751 Bufford Hgwy., N.E.(30324), pg. 1100
Diameter Paper Co., 6200-B Purdue Dr., P.O. Box 43509(30336), pg. 171
DONINO & PARTNERS, INC., 3350 Cumberland Circle, Ste. 1950(30339), pg. 344
DORSEY TRAILERS, INC., One Paces W. 347
DYATRON/BONDO CORPORATION, 3700 Atlanta Industrial Pkwy. N.W.(30331), pg. 356
EDWARDS BAKING CO., 1 Lemon Lane N.E.(30307), pg. 369
The Enterprise Group, 1200 Ashwood Pky., Ste. 290(30338), pg. 778
57th Fighter Group of Atlanta, Inc., 3829 Clairmont Rd.(30341), pg. 1028
First American Bank of Georgia, N.A., 34 Peachtree St., N.W.(30303), pg. 412
FISCHBACH & DOUGHERTY, INC., 6065 Barfield Rd., Ste. 210(30328), pg. 414
FITZGERALD & CO., One Buckhead Plaza, 3060 Peachtree Rd. N.W., Ste. 500(30305), pg. 416
FLEXEL, INC., 115 Perimeter Center Pl., Ste. 1100(30346), pg. 418
FOOTE & DAVIES INC., 3101 McCall Dr.(30340), pg. 423
FRICKS & ASSOCIATES/ADVERTISING INC., Bldg. 500, 1100 Abernathy Rd. N.E., Ste. 1725(30328), pg. 433
Furman Wholesale Lumber Div., 1800 D Montreal Cir.(30084), pg. 436
General Hardware Co.-Atlanta, 217 Luckie St.(30301), pg. 340
General Hardware Co.-Div. Hdqtrs., 217 Luckie St.(30301), pg. 340
GENERAL WHOLESALE COMPANY, INC., 1271 A Tacoma Dr.(30318), pg. 451
Georgia Auction Services, Inc., 2244 Stewart Avenue(30315), pg. 293
Georgia Dealers Auto Auction, 7205 Campbellton Rd.(30331), pg. 293
Georgia Television Company, 1601 W. Peachtree St. N.E.(30309), pg. 292
GOLD KIST, INC., 244 Perimeter Center Pkwy., N.E.(30346), pg. 465
Golden Peanut Company, 244 Perimeter Center Pkwy. N.E.(30346), pg. 465
Golden Poultry Co., Inc., 244 Perimeter Center Pkwy. N.E.(30346), pg. 465
Graphic Systems, 1303 Logan Circle, N.W.(30318), pg. 721
GRIZZARD ADVERTISING, INC., 1144 Mailing Ave., SE(30315), pg. 488
HARDIN CONSTRUCTION GROUP, INC., 1380 W. Paces Ferry Rd.(30327), pg. 508
HEERY INTERNATIONAL, INC., 999 Peachtree St., NE(30367), pg. 525
HOLDER CORPORATION, 333 Cumberland Cir., Ste. 400(30339), pg. 538
IDEAL POOL CORP., 3955 N. Peachtree Rd.(30341), pg. 562
Insignia Mortgage & Investment Corp., 100 Ashford Center North, Ste. 440(30338), pg. 571
INTEGRATEC, 3003 Chamblee Tucker Rd.(30341), pg. 573
Tom James Of Atlanta, Inc., 2800 N. Druid Hills Rd.(30329), pg. 589
W.B. JOHNSON PROPERTY, INC., 3414 Peachtree Rd., Ste. 300(30326), pg. 598
Kaiser Permanente, Georgia Division, 3355 Lenox Rd., NE, Ste. 1000(30326), pg. 614
Kennesaw Life & Accident Insurance Company, 1447 Peachtree St. N.E., Ste. 714(30309), pg. 921
H. KESSLER & COMPANY, 87 Peachtree St., S.W.(30303), pg. 624
H. Kessler & Company, 2044 Campbellton Rd. S.W.(30303), pg. 624
Ketchum Public Relations/Atlanta, First Union Plaza, 999 Peachtree St., N.E., Ste. 1850(30309), pg. 625
Keystone Southern Warehouse - Atlanta, 777 A Wharton Dr.(30336), pg. 628
Korn/Ferry International, 303 Peachtree St., N.E., Ste. 1600(30303), pg. 642
Larkin, Inc., P.O. Box 1699(30371), pg. 667
LAROCHE HOLDINGS, INC., 1100 Johnson Ferry Rd.(30342), pg. 659
LaRoche Industries Inc., 1100 Johnson Ferry Rd.(30342), pg. 659
Law Co. Scroop Inc., 1000 Abernathy Rd., N.E.(30328), pg. 661
LAW ENGINEERING, INC., 1000 Abernathy Rd., N.E.(30328), pg. 661
LEWIS, CLARK & GRAHAM, 230 Peachtree St. N.W., Ste. 400(30303), pg. 673
Lexmark International, Inc., 1201 W. Peachtree St. N.E., 24th Fl.(30367), pg. 674
LifeSurance Corporation, 1447 Peachtree St., N.E.(30309), pg. 1150
LifeSurance Corporation, 1447 Peachtree St.(30309), pg. 921
Luker Engineering & Fabrication Group, 244 Perimeter Center Pkwy. N.E.(30346), pg. 465
Marshall Erdman & Assoc., Inc., 3097 Presidential Dr.(30340), pg. 385
MASTER COLLECTORS INC., 5883 Glenridge Dr., Ste. 260(30328), pg. 719
Metro Atlanta Properties, 6065 Barfield Rd., Ste. 210(30328), pg. 414
MRS. WINNER'S CHICKEN & BISCUIT RESTAURANTS, 5995 Barfield Rd.(30328), pg. 761
THE MONARCH COMPANY, INC., 16 Perimeter Park Dr., Ste. 110(30341), pg. 765
THE MORRISON AGENCY, 950 E. Paces Ferry Rd., Ste. 1575(30326), pg. 771
NATIONAL DISTRIBUTING CO., INC., 1 National Dr. S.W.(30336), pg. 787
National Distributing Co., Inc., 1 National Dr. S.W.(30336), pg. 787
National Media Services, Inc., One Premier Plaza, 600 Morgan Falls Rd., Suite 125(30350), pg. 1074
NATIONAL MEDIA SERVICES, INC., 600 Morgan Falls Rd., Ste. 125(30350), pg. 792
NORRELL CORPORATION, Bldg. 810
Norrell Health Care Inc., 3535 Piedmont Rd., N.E.(30305), pg. 811
Nuarc Southeastern Div., 555 Armour Circle N.E.(30324), pg. 817
OPTIWORLD, 1820 The Exchange, Ste. 450(30339), pg. 828
POLLAK LEVITT CHAIET, ADVERTISING, One Piedmont Ctr., Ste. 505(30305), pg. 879
Pool World, Inc., 3955 N. Peachtree Rd(30341), pg. 562
PURITAN/CHURCHILL CHEMICAL COMPANY, 916 Ashby St., N. W.(30318), pg. 900
R.T.M. WINNERS, 5995 Barfield Rd.(30328), pg. 908
THE REGINA COMPANY, 300 Galleria Pkwy., Ste. 1400(30339), pg. 922
THE JOEY REIMAN AGENCY, 3060 Peachtree Rd.(30305), pg. 923
Residential Support Services, Inc., 19450 Sullivan Rd.(30337), pg. 1188
RHODES, INC., 4370 Peachtree Rd., N.E.(30319), pg. 931
Ritz-Carlton Hotel Company, 3414 Peachtree Rd., Ste. 300(30326), pg. 598
ROSSER FABRAP INTERNATIONAL, 524 W. Peachtree St.(30308), pg. 950
ROYAL OAK ENTERPRISES, INC., 900 Ashwood Pkwy., Ste. 800(30338), pg. 953
H. J. RUSSELL CORP., 504 Fair St. SW(30313), pg. 957
SAE-PINKERTON & LAWS INC., 875 Douglas Rd. N.E.(30342-1410), pg. 966
SAWYER RILEY COMPTON INC., 1100 Abernathy Rd., Ste. 800(30328), pg. 973
SCHERER SCIENTIFIC, LTD., 2859 Paces Ferry Rd., Ste. 300(30339), pg. 976
SHEPHERD CONSTRUCTION CO., INC., 1800 Briarcliff Rd., NE(30329), pg. 998
Southeast Operations, 1721 Marietta Blvd.(30318), pg. 268
SPACE MASTER INTERNATIONAL, 1040 Crown Pointe Pkwy., Ste. 900(30338), pg. 1024

Specialty Restaurants Corp., 3300 Northlake Parkway(30345), pg. 1028
STANDARD GRAVURE CORP./SHEA COMMUNICATIONS, 2849 Paces Ferry Rd., Ste. 100(30339), pg. 1036
Stevens Graphics, Inc., 713 Ralph David Abernathy S.W.(30310), pg. 136
SULLIVAN HAAS COYLE, One Capital City Plaza, 3350 Peachtree Rd., Ste. 950(30326), pg. 1056
SUMMIT COMMUNICATIONS, INC., 115 Perimeter Center Pl., Suite 1057
TDA, 8399 Dunwoody Place(30350), pg. 1072
Taracorp Evans, Inc., 740 Lambert Dr.(30324), pg. 1078
TARACORP, INC., 3490 Piedmont Rd., Ste. 1311(30305), pg. 1078
TAUSCHE MARTIN LONSDORF, 1315 Peachtree St., N.E.(30309), pg. 1080
Techsteel, Inc., 2145 Plaster Bridge Rd.(30324), pg. 230
Thermo Electric (Southeast Region), 3440 Oakcliff Rd.(30340), pg. 1091
Time Products, Inc., 3780 Browns Mill Rd. S.E.(30354), pg. 1090
Transilwrap Co., Inc., 3616 McCall Pl.(30340), pg. 1107
TRANSUS INC., 2090 Jonesboro Rd., SE(30315), pg. 1108
The Travel Channel, 2690 Cumberland Pkwy.(30339), pg. 654
UNITED PARCEL SERVICE OF AMERICA, INC., 400 Perimeter Center, Terraces North(30346), pg. 1133
UNITED PARKING, INC., 100 Peachtree St., Ste. 335(30303), pg. 1134
UNITED REFRIGERATED SERVICES, 2964 Peachtree Rd., NW, Ste. 700(30305), pg. 1134
VAN WINKLE & ASSOCIATES, INC., 1819 Peachtree St. N.W., Ste. 315(30309), pg. 1144
Video Service Company, 1400 Lake Hearn Dr. N.E.(30319), pg. 294
Viking Color Corporation, 742 Ponce De Leon Place, N.E.(30306), pg. 1151
WSB, Inc., 1601 W. Peachtree St., N.E.(30309), pg. 292
Watkins Associated Developers, 1958 Monroe Dr. NE(30301), pg. 1167
WATKINS ASSOCIATED INDUSTRIES INC., 1958 Monroe Dr. NE(30324), pg. 1167
The Weather Channel, 2600 Cumberland Pkwy.(30339), pg. 654
The Weather Channel, Inc.-Atlanta Sales Office, 2600 Cumberland Pkwy.(30339), pg. 654
Weinstock's Florist Inc., 5290 Roswell Rd.(30342), pg. 638
Weinstock's Flowers & Gifts, 5290 Roswell Rd., NW(30342), pg. 638
Wells Fargo Armored Service Corp., 6165 Barfield Rd.(30328), pg. 166
WEST LUMBER CO., 280 Westminster Dr., NE(30309), pg. 1177
Western International Media Corporation, 7 Piedmont Center, Ste. 300(30305), pg. 1180
WHITE ELECTRICAL CONSTRUCTION CO., 1730 Chattahoochee Ave.(30318), pg. 1185
Wieland Financial Services, Inc., 1950 Sullivan Rd.(30337), pg. 1188
JOHN WIELAND HOMES INC., 1950 Sullivan Rd.(30337), pg. 1188
Wieland Realty Associates, Inc., 124 Johnson Ferry Road(30328), pg. 1189
Wilcox-Walter-Furlong Paper Co., P.O. Box 44105, 5255 Fulton Industrial Blvd.(30336), pg. 1157
WILEN MANUFACTURING COMPANY, INC., 3760 Southside Industrial Pkwy.(30354), pg. 1189
WILKINS OUTDOOR NETWORK, INC., 600 Morgan Falls Rd., Ste. 205(30350), pg. 1189
Robert Williams, 115 Perimeter Center Pl., Suite 1100(30346), pg. 418
WILSON, HORNE, MCCLELLAND & GRAY, INC., 400 Interstate North Pkwy., Ste. 900(30339), pg. 1193

Augusta

CASTLEBERRY'S FOOD COMPANY, 1621 15th Street(30901), pg. 229
W.C. Caye & Co., 1468 Gordon Hwy.(30901), pg. 230
Hydreco, 1885 Tobacco Rd.(30906), pg. 559
Morris Corporation, P.O. Box 936(30913), pg. 999
National Distributing Co., Inc., 3316 Perkins Rd.(30906), pg. 787
SHIVERS TRADING & OPERATING CO., 725 Broad St.(30901), pg. 999
SOUTHEASTERN EQUIPMENT COMPANY, INC., 3000 Old Savannah Rd.(30906), pg. 1019
SOUTHERN BEVERAGE PACKERS, INC., 1891 Old Savannah Rd.(30914), pg. 1020

Austell

CARAUSTAR INDUSTRIES, INC., 3100 Washington St.(30001), pg. 217

Bainbridge

ELBERTA CRATE & BOX COMPANY, P.O. Box 795, 606 Dorthan Hwy.(31717), pg. 372
FLINT RIVER MILLS, 1100 Dothan Rd.(31717), pg. 419
STONES, INC., 524 Webster St.(31717), pg. 1051

Baldwin

FIELDALE CORPORATION, P.O. Box 558(30511-0558), pg. 409

Bogart

BENSON'S, INC., Elder St.(30622), pg. 140
Benson's Old Home Kitchens, P.O. Box 429(30622), pg. 140
Seaboard Farms Division, 160 Ben Burton Rd.(30622), pg. 984

Brunswick

KING & PRINCE SEAFOOD CORPORATION, 100 Lanier Blvd.(31520), pg. 631
Standard Distributing Co. Inc., 1725 T St.(31520), pg. 787

Cairo

Bolton-Emerson-Southern, Inc., P.O. Box 769-Alton Hall Rd., (31728), pg. 163
IRA HIGDON GROCERY, INC., Alton Hall Rd.(31728), pg. 533
W. B. RODDENBERY COMPANY, INC., 17 First Ave., NE(31728), pg. 942

Calhoun

Mannington Carpet Corp., P.O. Box 281, (30701), pg. 704
Professional Travel Inc., 1015 B South Wall St.(30701), pg. 894
Wellco Carpet Corp., Box 281(30701), pg. 704

Canton

O'Dell Products, Inc., Univeter Road(30114), pg. 3

Carrollton

SOUTHWIRE COMPANY, INC., 1 S. Wire Dr.(30119), pg. 1024

Clarkston

Edward Don & Company of Georgia-Clarkston Branch, 696 Park N. Blvd.(30021), pg. 344

Cleveland

Seals Division, P.O. Box 1879(30528), pg. 433

College Park

Wenczel Tile Distributing Company, 1288 S. Perimeter Hwy.(30349), pg. 1176

Columbus

ANS Insurance Agency, 233 12th St.(31901), pg. 61
American Health & Security Insurance Co., Inc., 233 12th St.(31901), pg. 61
AMERICAN SELFCARE CORPORATION, 233 12th St., Ste. 910(31901), pg. 60
W. C. BRADLEY CO., 1017 Front Ave.(31901), pg. 170
Bradley Specialty Retailing, Inc., 1017 Front Ave.(31993), pg. 170
COLUMBUS MILLS, INC., 4600 River Rd.(31904), pg. 267
Delimatic Refreshment Services, 900 8th St.(31902), pg. 1101
Developers Investors, Inc., 1017 Front Ave.(31993), pg. 170
GEORGIA CROWN DISTRIBUTING, 7 Crown Circle(31907), pg. 453
GOOLSBY FOODS, INC., 2219 Laurel Dr.(31907), pg. 471
THE HARDAWAY COMPANY, P.O. Box 1360(31993), pg. 507
BILL HEARD ENTERPRISES, INC., 2600 Cross Country Dr., Ste. 321(31906), pg. 521
Litho-Krome Company, 1039 13th Street(31994), pg. 502
Lotus Carpet Division, 4500 River Rd.(31904), pg. 267
National Distributing Co., Inc., 513 14th St.(31904), pg. 787
PASCOE BUILDING SYSTEMS, INC., P.O. Box 7186, (31908), pg. 851
Tom's Distributing Inc., 900 8th St.(31902), pg. 1101
TOM'S FOODS, 900 8th St.(31994), pg. 1101
Tom's Snax Co., 900 8th St.(31902), pg. 1101
W.C. Caye & Co., 1016 Virginia St.(31904), pg. 230

Commerce

Mount Vernon Mills, Inc., 689 S. Elm St.(30529), pg. 844

Conley

ATLANTA MOTOR LINES, INC., 1622 Cedar Grove Rd., S.E.(30027), pg. 94

Conyers

Finishline Industries Inc. of Georgia, 1275 S. Main St.(30207), pg. 433
Gibson-Homans Conyers Div., 1721 Old Covington Hwy.(30208), pg. 457
Hano Business Forms, Inc., P.O. Box 1159, (30207), pg. 506
Madison Industries Inc. of Georgia, 1035 S. Access Rd., S.W.(30207), pg. 433
Scotfoam Corp., 1705 A Rockdale Industrial Blvd.(30207), pg. 1121

Cornelia

Schnadig Corp., P.O. Box 2000, Clarksville Highway, Rte. 2(30531), pg. 977

Dalton

ALADDIN MILLS INC., 2001 Antioch Rd.(30721), pg. 29
C&A Floor Coverings, 311 Smith Industrial Blvd.(30720), pg. 262
CONQUEST CARPET MILLS, 950 Riverbend Dr.(30720), pg. 276
Focus Carpet Co., 1627 Abutment Rd.(30720), pg. 1121
General Latex & Chemical Corporation (Georgia), P.O. Box 709(30720), pg. 449
Lewallyn Engineering, 1803 Abuttmew Rd.(30722), pg. 1090
Plastron Dalton, 207 Brookhollow Industrial Blvd.(30720), pg. 15
PROFESSIONAL TRAVEL, INC., 302 S. Thornton Ave.(30722), pg. 894
TEXTILE RUBBER & CHEMICAL COMPANY, 1400 Tiarco Dr.(30720), pg. 1090
WORLD CARPETS, INC., One World Plaza(30722), pg. 1202

Darien

ALTAMA DELTA CORP., Hwy. 251(31305), pg. 45

Dawsonville

TATUM FARMS, Rte. 3 & Hwy. 136 N.(30534), pg. 1080

Decatur

ALLIED SYSTEMS, LTD., 160 Clairmont Ave., Ste. 600(30030), pg. 40
Columbia Mall, 3604 Memorial Dr.(30032), pg. 699
DECATUR NEWS PUBLISHING COMPANY, INC., 739 Dekalb Industrial Way(30033), pg. 323
FOOD & GAS, INC., 4151 Memorial Dr., Ste. 206C(30032), pg. 423
H. Kessler & Company, 2014 Candler Rd.(30034), pg. 624
New Hermes Inc.-Southeast, 2620 Park Central Blvd.(30035), pg. 801
Sunkist Growers, Inc.-Southern Division, North Center Office, Room 217, 4319 Covington Hwy.(30035), pg. 1061
TRONCALLI MOTORS, INC., 1625 Church St.(30033), pg. 1115

Doraville

CHEMCENTRAL/Atlanta, 1 Alchemy Pl.(30340), pg. 241
TRITON INC., 4267 Winters Chapel Rd.(30360), pg. 1114

Douglas

Bioproducts, Inc., P.O. Box 2425, 1246 Loyce Lane(31533), pg. 152
Elixir Industries, Southside Industrial Park(31533), pg. 376

Douglasville

Atlanta Mfg. Facility, 4155 Scofield Rd.(30134), pg. 982
YOUNG REFINING CORP., 7982 Huey Road(30134), pg. 1210

Dublin

WAREHOUSE HOME FURNISHINGS DISTRIBUTOR, 711 Bellevue Ave.(31021), pg. 1163

East Point

South Eastern Brush Co., 1120 Oakleigh Dr.(30344), pg. 419

Eatonton

HORTON HOMES, INC., 101 Industrial Blvd.(31024), pg. 545

Elberton

Georgia Stone Industries, Inc., Hwy. 72 W.(30635), pg. 800

Ellenwood

Bellamy Brothers Constructing Company, 16 Fairview Rd.(30049), pg. 136
BELLAMY BROTHERS, INC., Fairview Rd. at Panola Rd.(30049), pg. 136

Evans

Greenfield Industries Inc., 470 Old Evans Rd.(30809), pg. 507

Fitzgerald

Elixir Industries, (31750), pg. 376
LOWELL PACKING COMPANY, P.O. Box 220(31750), pg. 685

Fort Oglethorpe

Gaston County Carpet Div., P.O. Box 5409, (30742), pg. 444

Fort Valley

BLUE BIRD CORPORATION, N. Camellia Blvd.(31030), pg. 158

Gainesville

JERRY C. CARTER, INC., 1325 S. Bradford(30503), pg. 226
GRESS FOODS INC., 950 Industrial Blvd.(30501), pg. 486
MANSFIELD OIL COMPANY, 1025 Airport Pkwy. SW(30505-0198), pg. 704
MAR-JAC INC., P.O. Box 1017(30503), pg. 705
Mar-Jac Processing, Inc., Airport Circle, Aviation Blvd.(30501), pg. 705
National Auto Research, P.O. Box 758, Hwy. 129 S. at Barrett Rd.(30501), pg. 522

Garden City

CARVER, INC., P.O. Box 7849(31418), pg. 227
Gold Bond Building Products, P.O. Box 7016, (31408), pg. 790
Oceanic Shipping Co., 6002 Commerce Blvd.(31408), pg. 1052
STRACHAN SHIPPING CO., 6002 Commerce Blvd.(31408), pg. 1052

Griffin

DUNDEE MILLS, INC., Railroad Ave.(30224), pg. 352
Southeastern Textile Co. Div., 222 E. Solomon St.(30223), pg. 146
Southeastern Textiles Hotel Co. Div., 222 E. Solomon St.(30223), pg. 146

Grovetown

GEORGIA IRON WORKS CO., 5000 Wrightsboro Rd.(30813), pg. 453

Hazlehurst

FUEL SOUTH, INC., P.O. Box 572(31539), pg. 435

Jonesboro

ATLANTA WIRE WORKS, INC., 1117 Battle Creek Rd.(30236), pg. 94

Kennesaw

THE ATHLETE'S FOOT GROUP, INC., 1950 Vaughn Rd.(30144), pg. 94
THE GEORGIA MARBLE COMPANY, 1201 Roberts Blvd.(30144), pg. 453
S & J Industries, 2130 Barrett Park Dr., Ste. 103(30144), pg. 811

La Grange

Piedmont Mechanical, Inc., 103 Cooley Industrial Way, P.O. Box 308(30241), pg. 870
Seals Division, 1618 Lukken Industrial Dr. W.(30240), pg. 433
WOODBURY BUSINESS FORMS, INC., 101 Lukken Industrial Dr. E.(30240), pg. 1200

Lavonia

Garcy Specialty Fixtures, , pg. 907

Lawrenceville

Aratex Services, 625B Old Norcross Rd.(30245), pg. 6
Crown Prince Divisional Office, 1675 Lakes Pkwy., Ste. 115(30243), pg. 302

Loganville

Action Commodities Corporation, P.O. Box 1384(30249), pg. 1087

Lula

Mar-Jac Farms, Inc., Hwy. 52(30501), pg. 705

Macon

Bibb-Disc, Inc., 237 Coliseum Dr.(31201), pg. 781
CHEROKEE BRICK & TILE CO., 3250 Waterville Rd.(31206), pg. 243
Cox Cable Middle Georgia, Inc., 252 Holt Ave.(31201), pg. 294
J.M. Huber, Clay Div., One Huber Rd.(31298), pg. 550
Keystone Automotive Industries, Inc.-Macon, 895 Third Street(31201), pg. 628
NTC Apparel Fabrics Division, 237 Coliseum Drive(31208), pg. 781
NTC Consumer Products Div., 237 Coliseum Drive(31208), pg. 781
NTC Engineered Products Div., 237 Coliseum Drive(31208), pg. 781
National Distributing Co., Inc., Two Servitex Dr.(31297), pg. 787
S & S Cafeterias, 2124 Riverside Dr.(31208), pg. 1014
S & S Diversified Food Service, Inc., 2124 Riverside Dr.(31208), pg. 1014
S & S Food Administrators, 2124 Riverside Dr.(31208), pg. 1014
Servitex, Inc., One Servitex Dr.(31297), pg. 787
Smith & Sons Catering Co., 2124 Riverside Dr.(31208), pg. 1014
SMITH & SONS FOODS, INC., 2124 Riverside Dr.(31208), pg. 1014
Zantop Aircraft Maintenance Facility, Macon Airport, (31297), pg. 1216
Zantop International Airlines, Inc., P.O. Box 10136, (31297), pg. 1216

Madison

Ivex Packaging Corporation-Madison, P.O. Box 508, (30650), pg. 583

Marietta

Alimak Elevator Company, 157 Fairground St. S.E.(30060), pg. 34
Atlanta Hill Restaurant Corp., 2239 Powers Ferry Rd.(30067), pg. 1028
Bulk Systems, 560 Webb Industrial Dr. N.E.(30062), pg. 1170
FLEXIBLE PRODUCTS COMPANY, 1007 Industrial Park Dr.(30061), pg. 418
THOMAS R. HOPSON BROKER, INC., P.O. Box 7295(30065), pg. 544
IFS Systems, Inc., 1130 N. Chase Pkwy., Ste. 200(30067), pg. 1181
N.B. Jackets Division, 1899 Powers Ferry Rd., Ste. 400(30067), pg. 135
PACESETTER STEEL SERVICE, INC., 1100 Shallowford Rd.(30066), pg. 839
Plastic Suppliers, Inc., 1174 Hayes Industrial Dr.(30062), pg. 876
Simkins Carton Div.-Marietta, 1069 Atlanta Industrial Dr.(30066), pg. 1005
SOLVAY PHARMACEUTICALS, INC., 901 Sawyer Rd.(30062-2224), pg. 1017
Southern Wholesale, 3200 Austell Road(30060), pg. 4
SUPER CLUB MUSIC CORP., 2151 Northwest Pkwy.(30067), pg. 1062
Jervis B. Webb Co. of Georgia, 560 Webb Industrial Dr., N.E.(30062), pg. 1170
Webb-Materials Handling Equip., 560 Webb Industrial Dr., N.E.(30062), pg. 1170
Wenczel Tile Distributing Company, 1691 B-Enterprise Way(30067), pg. 1176

McRae

Roydon Wear, Inc., 1409 E. Oak St.(31055), pg. 283

Millen

Bellcrest Holding Co., Inc., 206 Magnolia St.(30442), pg. 1056

Monroe

Flambeau Southeast Co., 1533 S. Broad St.(30655), pg. 809
WALTON MONROE MILLS, INC., 119 First St.(30655), pg. 1162

Montezuma

Calypso Foods, P.O. Box 306(31063), pg. 26
Southern Frozen Foods, P.O. Box 306(31063), pg. 26
Tropic Isle, P.O. Box 306(31063), pg. 26

Morrow

E.J. Brach, Inc., 1260 Southern Rd.(30260), pg. 169
Bucyrus Blades of Georgia, 7134 Hwy. 54(30260), pg. 388

Moultrie

BEADLES LUMBER COMPANY, INC., 900 6th St., N.E.(31768), pg. 129
DESTINY INDUSTRY INC., Industrial Park(31768), pg. 332
Premium Pork Processors, P.O. Box 729(31768), pg. 1061
RIVERSIDE MANUFACTURING CO., 301 Riverside Dr.(31768), pg. 937

Nashville

J.H. HARVEY COMPANY, 727 S. Davis St.(31639), pg. 515
Nashville Textile Corp., 202 Industrial Park(31639), pg. 546

Newnan

CPI Plastics, Inc., P.O. Box 639, 434 Corinth Rd.(30264), pg. 278
Eckerd Drug Co., 36 Herring Rd.(30265), pg. 366

Norcross

AGCO Corporation, 5295 Triangle Pkwy.(30092), pg. 4
AGCO INC., 2782 Simpson Circle(30071), pg. 4
ALLIANCE AMERICA, 4888 S. Old Peachtree Rd.(30071), pg. 37
Allied Security Inc., 6825 Jimmy Carter Blvd., Ste. 1860(30071), pg. 39
AMERICAN TECHNICAL SERVICES GROUP, INC., 5680 Oakbrook Pkwy, Ste. 165(30093-1841), pg. 63
Atlanta Casualty Company, 3169 Holcomb Ridge Rd.(30071), pg. 53
CLASSIC MARKETS CORP., 6689-L Peachtree Industrial Blvd.(30092), pg. 253
COMMUNICATIONS INTERNATIONAL, 6020 Unity Dr., Ste. G(30071), pg. 269
GPD LIMITED, 6753 Jones Mill Ct.(30092), pg. 440
GENERAL TIME CORP., 520 Guthridge Ct.(30092), pg. 451
Georgia Auction Services, Inc. d/b/a Community Aution Resale Services, 5900 Brook Hollow Parkway(30071), pg. 293
Georgia Div., 5855-P Oakbrook Pky.(30093), pg. 361
Gould Southern, 1826 A. Doan Way(30093), pg. 474
Harwick Chemical Corp., 5380 Peachtree Ind., Blvd., Ste. 210(30071), pg. 515
HAYES MICROCOMPUTER PRODUCTS, INC., 5835 Peachtree Corners East(30092), pg. 519
Hesston, 5295 Triangle Pkwy.(30092), pg. 4
Holmatic, Inc., 1750 Corporate Dr.(30093), pg. 122
J.M. Huber, Solem Div., 4940 Peachtree Industrial Blvd., Ste. 340(30071), pg. 550
INTERSTATE DISTRIBUTORS INC., 4101 Blue Ridge Industrial Pkwy.(30071), pg. 580
Land Span Inc., 6270 McDonough Dr.(30093), pg. 1167
MIGHTY DISTRIBUTING SYSTEM, 50 Technology Park,/ Atlanta(30092), pg. 752
National Technical Services, 5680 Oakbrook Pkwy., Ste. 165(30093-1841), pg. 64
Plaid Enterprises Inc., P.O. Box 7600, 1649 International Blvd.(30091), pg. 357
ROCK-TENN COMPANY, 504 Thrasher St.(30091), pg. 941
Rock-Tenn Company, Mill Division, Inc., P.O. Box 4098(30091), pg. 941
Rock-Tenn Converting Co., P.O. Box 4098(30091), pg. 941
Rohrer Corporation, 3150 Clinton Court(30071), pg. 944
SAUL BROS. & COMPANY, INC., 6500 Peachtree Indus. Blvd.(30071), pg. 972
SUN DATA INC., 1300 Oakbrook Drive(30093), pg. 1058
Ulbrich of Georgia, Inc., 1465 Beaver Ruin Rd.(30093), pg. 1125
WAFFLE HOUSE, INC., 5986 Financial Dr.(30071), pg. 1157
Wenczel Tile Distributing Company, 5870-A Oakbrook Pkwy.(30093), pg. 1176
Winchester Carton Corp., P.O. Box 4098(30091), pg. 941
WINKO-MATIC SIGNAL CO./MULTISONICS CORP., 6301 Best Friend Rd.(30071), pg. 1196

Perry

TOLLESON LUMBER COMPANY, INC., 903 Jernigan St.(31069), pg. 1100

Powder Springs

Atlanta Structural Concrete Div., P.O. Box 5, (30073), pg. 177

Quitman

Brooks County Packing Co., North Hyland(31643), pg. 1061

Red Oak

Atlanta Auto Auction, Inc., 4900 Buffington Rd.(30272), pg. 293

Riceboro

Interstate Paper Corporation, One Interstate Rd.(31323), pg. 580
Marsh Lumber Company, 2 Interstate Rd.(31323), pg. 580

Rincon

Fort Howard Paper Corporation, Rte. 1 Baker Hill Rd.(31326), pg. 425

Rockmart

J.L. LESTER & SON, INC., 326 S. Marble St.(30153), pg. 668

Rome

BATTEY MACHINERY COMPANY, 2960 New Calhoun Hwy., N.E.(30161), pg. 127
H. Kessler & Company, 228 Broad St.(30161), pg. 624
ROME MANUFACTURING CO., 208 E. 2nd Ave.(30161), pg. 945
J. L. TODD AUCTION CO., 531 Broad St.(30161), pg. 1099

Roswell

CIVES CORP., 411 Rouse Ln.(30076), pg. 251

Saint Marys

GILMAN PAPER CO., 1000 Osborne St.(31558), pg. 459
Saint Marys Railroad Co., 110 Osborne St., P.O. Box 520(31558), pg. 459

Saint Simons Island

Booth Seafood Sales Corp., P.O. Box 667(31522), pg. 932

Sandersville

BURGESS PIGMENT CO., Box 349(31082), pg. 190
Piedmont Minerals, P.O. Box 1056(31082), pg. 1092
THIELE KAOLIN CO., Kaolin Rd.(31082), pg. 1092
Villa South Inc., South Harris St.(31082), pg. 1092

Savannah

Allright Parking of Georgia, Inc., 401 W. Bay St.(31401), pg. 42
AMINCO, INC., 64 Ross Rd.(31405), pg. 67
Carson Products Company, 64 Ross Rd.(31405), pg. 67
Chatham Towing Company, Inc., P.O. Box 576(31402), pg. 264
Colonial Drilling & Exploration Corporation, P.O. Box 576(31402), pg. 264
Colonial Marine Industries, Inc., 26 E. Byron St.(31401), pg. 264
COLONIAL OIL INDUSTRIES, N. Lathrop Ave.(31402), pg. 263
Colonial Terminals, Inc., P.O. Box 576(31402), pg. 264
DERST BAKING COMPANY, INC., 1311 W. 52nd St. Extn.(31405), pg. 331
Enmark Stations, Inc., P.O. Box 576(31402), pg. 264
GULFSTREAM HOLDINGS CORPORATION, 500 Gulfstream Rd.(31402), pg. 494
MORRIS NEWSPAPER CORPORATION, 27 Abercorn St.(31401), pg. 771
Standard Distributing Co., Inc., 1414 Mills B. Lane Blvd.(31405), pg. 787

Scottdale

GEORGIA DUCK & CORDAGE MILLS, 21 Laredo Dr.(30079), pg. 453
Summit-Beers Construction Company, P.O. Box 866, (30079), pg. 132

Sea Island

The Cloister, (31561), pg. 983
SEA ISLAND COMPANY, 100 First St.(31561), pg. 983
Sea Island Services, Inc., 100 First St.(31561), pg. 983
Sea Island Properties, Inc., 100 First St.(31561), pg. 983

Smyrna

Apollo Industries, 1850 S. Cobb Industrial Blvd.(30082), pg. 1090
RACETRAC PETROLEUM, INC., 300 Technology Ct.(30082), pg. 909

Statesboro

T.J. MORRIS COMPANY, INC., Highway 301 S.(30458), pg. 771

Stone Mountain

GORDON BAILEY & ASSOCIATES, INC., 675 Village Square Dr.(30083), pg. 114

Sugar Valley

AMERICAN RUG CRAFTSMEN INC., 3090 Sugar Valley Rd. N.W.(30746), pg. 60

Thomasville

Aratex Services, 202 Cassidy Rd.(31792), pg. 6
SUNNYLAND FOODS, INC., 603 Cassidy Rd.(31792), pg. 1061

Tifton

DIXIE OIL COMPANY, U.S. Hwy. 82 E.(31793-1007), pg. 341

Toccoa

DEMPSTER, INC., P.O. Box 1338(30577), pg. 328
First Franklin Financial Corp., 213 E. Tugalo St.(30577), pg. 413
1ST FRANKLIN CORPORATION, 213 E. Tugalo St.(30577), pg. 413
Frandisco Life Insurance Co., 213 E. Tugalo St.(30577), pg. 413
Frandisco Property & Casualty Insurance, 213 E. Tugalo St.(30577), pg. 413
Franklin Securities, Inc., 213 E. Tugalo St.(30577), pg. 413
GEM INDUSTRIES FINANCE CORPORATION, Highway 123 N.(30577), pg. 447
Gem Southeast, Inc., Hwy. 123 N.(30577), pg. 447
Gilbert & Bennett, P.O. Box 1205(30577), pg. 458

Trion

Mount Vernon Mills, Inc., Riegel Textile Div. (Trion), P.O. Box 7(30753), pg. 844

Tucker

COLLEGIATE CONCEPTS INC., 1751 Montreal Circle(30084), pg. 262
HUB INC., 2146 Flintstone Dr.(30084), pg. 548
Kearney, 1928 Montreal Rd.(30084), pg. 357
LANE LIMITED, 2280 Mountain Industrial Blvd.(30084), pg. 657
M M SYSTEMS CORPORATION, 4520 Elmdale Dr.(30085), pg. 692
Mary Kay Cosmetics, Inc., 1651 Montreal Circle(30084), pg. 717
OGLETHORPE POWER CORP., 2100 E. Exchange Pl.(30085), pg. 822
ED TAYLOR CONSTRUCTION CO., 5175 S. Royal Atlanta Dr.(30084), pg. 1081

Union City

SOUTHERN MILLS, INC., 6501 Mall Blvd.(30291), pg. 1021

Union Point

CHIPMAN-UNION, INC., 500 Sibley Ave.(30669), pg. 248

Valdosta

Alco Health Services Corporation-Valdosta Div., 311 W. Central Ave.(31601), pg. 32
Drumheller Bag & Supply, 1105 E. Hill Ave.(31603), pg. 810
Griffin Ag Products Inc., P.O. Box 1847(31603), pg. 487
GRIFFIN CORPORATION, P.O. Box 1847(31603), pg. 487
Griffin International, P.O. Box 1848(31603), pg. 487
Griffin Mining Co., P.O. Box 1848(31603), pg. 487
Kocide Chemical Co., P.O. Box 1847(31603), pg. 487

Vidalia

Standard Distributing Co., Inc., P.O. Box 1305(30474), pg. 787

Washington

Georgia Woodlands Railroad Co., P.O. Box 549, One Harris Rd.(30673-0549), pg. 246

Waycross

Bacon Grocery Co., Inc., 102 Lee Ave.(31501), pg. 603
BIG J Super Stores, Inc., 102 Lee Ave.(31501), pg. 603
Fuel South Inc., 102 Lee Ave.(31501), pg. 603
JONES COMPANY, INC., 102 Lee Ave.(31501), pg. 603
Kwickie/Flash Foods, Inc., 102 Lee Ave.(31501), pg. 603
Standard Distributing Co., Inc., 1003 "M" St.(31501), pg. 787
Walter-Jones Cheverolet-Buick-Oldsmobile, 102 Lee Ave.(31501), pg. 603

Waynesboro

PERFECTION-SCHWANK INC., Hwy. 56, P.O. Box 749(30830-0749), pg. 861

West Point

BATSON-COOK COMPANY, 817 Fourth Ave.(31833), pg. 126
Chattahoochee Valley Railway Company, 400 W. 10th St.(31833), pg. 400
West Point-Pepperell, Inc., 400 West 10th St.(31833), pg. 400

White

Wunda Weve Carpet Yarn Plant, (30184), pg. 1205

HAWAII

Aiea

Superior Coffee & Foods/Hawaii, 99-910 Iwaena St.(96701), pg. 174

Ewa Beach

Jorgensen Steel & Aluminum/Honolulu, 91-104 Kalaeloa Blvd.(96707), pg. 606

Hilo

HT&T Company, Inc., P.O. Box 4190(96720), pg. 174
ISEMOTO CONTRACTING CO. LTD., 648 Piilani St.(96720), pg. 582
Mauna Loa Macadamia Nut Corporation, HC/01 Box 3(96720), pg. 174
Mauna Loa Orchids, Ltd., P.O. Box 4007(96720), pg. 421
Mauna Loa Orchids, Ltd., D/B/A Hawaiian Exotic Flowers, P.O. Box 4007, (96722), pg. 421
PACIFIC HAWAIIAN LTD., 1990 Kinoole St.(96720), pg. 840
PUNA PLANTATION HAWAII LTD., 50 E. Puainako St.(96720), pg. 900

Honolulu

API, Inc., 700 Bishop St.(96813), pg. 585
ASA Properties Hawaii Inc., 605 Kapiolani Blvd.(96813), pg. 863
Air Engineering Co., Inc., 2308 Pahounui Dr.(96819), pg. 47
ALOHA AIRGROUP, INC., 371 Aokea Place(96819), pg. 43
Aloha Airlines, Inc., Honolulu Intl. Airport(96820), pg. 43
Aloha IslandAir, Intl. Airport, 99 Kapalulu Place(96819), pg. 43
Amelco, Inc., 2308 Pahounui Dr.(96819), pg. 47
American Electric Co., Ltd., 2308 Pahounui Dr.(96819), pg. 47
American Factors Assoc. Australia Pty., Ltd., 700 Bishop St.(96813), pg. 585
Amfac Agribusiness, Inc., 700 Bishop St.(96813), pg. 585
Amfac Development Corp., 700 Bishop St.(96813), pg. 585
Amfac Energy, Inc., 700 Bishop St.(96813), pg. 585
Amfac Financial Inc., 700 Bishop St.(96813), pg. 585
Amfac/JMB Hawaii, Inc., 700 Bishop Street(96813), pg. 585
Amfac Property Development Corp., 700 Bishop St.(96802), pg. 585
Amfac Retail Corp., Ala Moana Pacific Center, 1585 Kapiolani Blvd.(96815), pg. 585
Amfac Sugar and Agribusiness, Inc., P.O. Box 3230(96801), pg. 585
ARMSTRONG PRODUCE LTD., 651 Ilalo St.(96813), pg. 84
Automotive Warehouse, Inc., 2760 Waiwai Loop(96819), pg. 224
Baydale, Inc., Ala Moana Pacific Center, 1585 Kapiolani Blvd.(96815), pg. 585
C. BREWER & COMPANY, LIMITED, 827 Fort St. Mall(96813), pg. 174
Brewer Environmental Industries, Inc., P.O. Box 48(96810), pg. 174
C. Brewer Properties, Inc., 827 Fort St.(96813), pg. 174
Casa Grande West Water Company, Inc., 700 Bishop St.(96813), pg. 585
Dillingham Construction Pacific, Ltd., 614 Kapahulu Ave.(96812), pg. 338
1ST FAMILY TRAVELERS HAWAII, 2155 Kalakaua Ave., Ste. 716(96815), pg. 412
Galaxy Business Products, 875 Waimanu St., Ste.102(96813), pg. 742
Hawaiian Bitumuls & Paving Company, P.O. Box 2240, 110 Puuhole St.(96804), pg. 338
Hawaiian Dredging & Construction Company, 614 Kapahulu Ave.(96812), pg. 338
Honolulu Advertiser, Inc., 605 KapiolaniBlvd.(808-525-8000), pg. 863
KHON-TV, 1116 Auahi St.(96814), pg. 194
Kaiser Permanente, Hawaii Division, 711 Kapiolani Blvd.(96813), pg. 614
Lear Siegler Hawaiian Properties Div., Amfac Bldg., 700 Bishop St., Ste. 1112(96813), pg. 664
Liberty House, Ala Moana Shopping Center(96803), pg. 585
Liberty House, Inc., Ala Moana Pacific Center, P.O. Box 2690(96845), pg. 585
MAUI DIVERS OF HAWAII, LTD., 1520 Liona St.(96814), pg. 721
MAUI VARIETIES, LTD., 7192 Kalanianaole Hwy.(96825), pg. 721
Mauna Loa Macadamia Nut Co., 827 Fort St.(96813), pg. 426
Mauna Loa Resources Inc., P.O. Box 1826, 827 Fort Street(96813), pg. 174
METPAC, LTD., 875 Waimanu St., Suite 102(96813), pg. 742
Metropolitan Arizona Corporation, 700 Bishop St.(96813), pg. 585
MUTUAL DISTRIBUTORS LTD., 320 C Waiakamilo Rd.(96817), pg. 778
MUTUAL WELDING CO., LTD, 739 Ahua(96819), pg. 779
Oahu Waste Energy Recovery, Inc., 700 Bishop Street(96801), pg. 585
PECK SIMS MUELLER, INC., 1170 Waimanu St.(96814), pg. 854
PERSIS CORPORATION, 605 Kapiolani Blvd.(96813), pg. 863
REMark Advertising, 733 Bishop St., Ste. 2165(96813), pg. 999
SERVCO PACIFIC INC., 900 Fort St. Mall Suite 500(96813), pg. 991
STARR SEIGLE MCCOMBS, INC., Pacific Tower, 19th Fl., 1001 Bishop St.(96813), pg. 1040
SunMac Hawaii, Ltd., P.O. Box 2720, 972 So. Queen St.(96803), pg. 1061
TERUYA BROS., LTD., 1276 Young St.(96814), pg. 1089
Times Super Market Ltd., 2153 N. King St.(96819), pg. 1089
Trade Wind Tours, 150 Kaiulani Ave.(96805), pg. 413
G. VON HAMM TEXTILES, INC., 916 Kaaahi Place(96817), pg. 1155

Kahului

VALLEY ISLE PRODUCE, INC., 90 Amala Pl.(96732), pg. 1143

Kaumakani

Olokele Sugar Co., Limited, P.O. Box 156, (96747), pg. 174

Keaau

Amfac Tropical Products, P.O. Box 210, (96749), pg. 585
Puna Sugar Co., Ltd., P. O. Box 210(96749), pg. 585

Kekaha

Kekaha Sugar Company, Limited, P. O. Box AA(96752), pg. 585

Kilauea

Kilauea Agronomics, Inc., P.O. Box 80, (96754), pg. 174

Lahaina

Amfac Property Investment Corp., 2530 Kekaa Dr.(96761), pg. 585
Kaanapali Water Corporation, 2530 Kekaa Dr.(96761), pg. 585
Pioneer Mill Company, Ltd., P. O. Box 727(96761), pg. 585

Lihue

H. Hackfeld & Co. Ltd., P.O. Box 751(96766), pg. 585
Kauai Sugar Storage Co., P.O. Box 1743, (96766), pg. 585
The Lihue Plantation Company, Limited, P.O. Box 751, (96766), pg. 585

Pahala

Ka'u Agribusiness Co., Inc., P.O. Box 130(96777), pg. 174

Papaikou

Mauna Kea Agribusiness Co., Inc., P.O. Box 68(96781), pg. 174

Princeville

PRINCEVILLE CORPORATION, Princeville Center, 5-4280 Kuhio Hwy.(96722), pg. 890
Princeville Hotel Corporation, Princeville Center, 5-4280 Kuhio Hwy.(96722), pg. 890
Princeville Management Corporation, Princeville Center, 5-4280 Kuhio Hwy.(96722), pg. 890
Princeville Realty Corporation, Princeville Center, 5-4280 Kuhio Hwy.(96722), pg. 890
Princeville Utilities Company, Inc., Princeville Center, 5-4280 Kuhio Hwy.(96722), pg. 890
Princeville Water Systems, Inc., Princeville Center, 5-4280 Kuhio Hwy.(96722), pg. 890

Wailuku

Wailuku Agribusiness Co., Inc., P.O. Box 520, (96793), pg. 175

Waipahu

Amfac Garden Hawaii, P.O. Box 537, (96797), pg. 585
BetterBrands, Ltd., 94-501 Kau St.(96797), pg. 1214
Oahu Sugar Company, Limited, P. O. Box O(96797), pg. 585
Waiahole Irrigation Co., Ltd., P. O. Box O(96797), pg. 585

IDAHO

Boise

Elixir Industries, 501 N. Eagle Rd.(83707), pg. 376
Farm Store No. 1, 1414 Grove St., P.O. Box 9076(83707), pg. 1045
IGI Resources, Inc., 300 Mallard Dr., Ste. 350(83706), pg. 575
IDAHO LOTTERY, 1199 Shoreline Lane(83702), pg. 561
Intermountain Gas Co., 555 S. Cole Rd.(83709), pg. 575
INTERMOUNTAIN INDUSTRIES, INC., 555 S. Cole Rd.(83709), pg. 575
J.R. Simplot Co.-Food Group, 6360 S. Federal Way(83706-9617), pg. 1007
LB INDUSTRIES INC., 1401 Shoreline Dr.(83701), pg. 647
Mac's Machinery & Supply, 7755 Mossy Cup(83709-2846), pg. 341
NASHUA HOMES OF IDAHO INC., 5200 Federal Way(83707), pg. 784
PETERSON MOTOR COMPANY, 9101 W. Fairview(83704), pg. 865
J.R. Simplot Co. Food Group, P.O. Box 9386(83707), pg. 1007
J.R. SIMPLOT COMPANY, 999 Main St.(83702), pg. 1007
WAREMART INC., 8590 Fairview Ave.(83704), pg. 1163

Buhl

CLEAR SPRINGS FOODS, INC., P.O. Box 712(83316), pg. 254
Rangen Aquaculture Research, 115 13th Ave., S.(83316), pg. 912
RANGEN, INC., 115 13th Ave., S.(83316), pg. 912
REED GRAIN & BEAN COMPANY, 9th & Elm(83316), pg. 920

Caldwell

THE CAXTON PRINTERS LTD., 312 Main St.(83605), pg. 230
Dairygold, Inc., Fifth & Albany(83605), pg. 311
J.R. Simplot Co.-Diversified Products Group, 223 Rodeo Ave.(83605), pg. 1007

Coeur D'Alene

ADVANCED INPUT DEVICES, INC., W. 250 A I D Dr.(83814), pg. 20
Brix Maritime Towing, Inc., Blackwell Island(83814), pg. 177
IDAHO FOREST INDUSTRY, INC., 2850 Seltice Way(83816), pg. 561

Firth

IDAHO SUPREME COMPANY, 614 E. 800 N. St.(83236), pg. 561

Grand View

J.R. Simplot Co.-Agriculture Group, HC85, Box 275, (83624), pg. 1007

Hayden Lake

EMPIRE AIRLINES, 11101 Airport Dr.(83835), pg. 379

Idaho Falls

ELECTRICAL WHOLESALE SUPPLY COMPANY, INC., P.O. Box 1835, 1990 Rollandet Ave.(83403), pg. 374
INDUSTRIAL CONTRACTORS, INC., 1330 W. Broadway(83402), pg. 566

Inkom

Inkom, Idaho Plant, 230 Cement Rd.(83245), pg. 87

Kendrick

GEORGE F. BROCKE & SONS, INC., Second St. & Brown(83537), pg. 178

Ketchum

SCOTT U.S.A., 110 Lewis St.(83340), pg. 983

Laclede

RILEY CREEK LUMBER COMPANY, Riley Creek Rd.(83841), pg. 935

Lewisville

IDAHOAN FOODS, One Potato Place(83431), pg. 561

Meridian

Computrol, Inc., 499 E. Corporate Dr.(83642), pg. 83
S&K Products, Inc., 4999 E. Corporate Dr.(83642), pg. 83

Nampa

Union Seed Co., 4 9th Ave. South(83651), pg. 654

Payette

American Fine Foods, Inc., 25 N. 6th St., P.O. Box 460(83661), pg. 1045

Pocatello

COWBOY OIL COMPANY, 2700 S. 5th Ave.(83204), pg. 290
J.R. Simplot Co.-Minerals & Chemical Group, 4122 Yellowstone Ave.(83202), pg. 1007
Muffler Warehouse, Inc., 1161 Wilson St.(83201), pg. 225

Rupert

MAGIC VALLEY FOODS, INC., Hwy. 24 & Hwy. 25(83350), pg. 700

ILLINOIS

Addison

American Inks & Coatings Corp., Ink Division, 1540 Wrightwood Ct.(60101), pg. 56
Claire Manufacturing Co., 500 Vista Ave.(60101), pg. 222
Detroit Diesel Allison Co., 500 S. Lombard(60101), pg. 1179
Enduro Industries, Inc., 136 Commercial Rd.(60101), pg. 939
FENTON PRESS, INC., 1544 Wrightwood(60101), pg. 406
Lane Film Products Division, 712 Winthrop(60101), pg. 657
MPO Videotronics, 131 Mitchell Ct., Ste. C-10(60101), pg. 693
MAGNECO/METREL, INC., 223 Interstate Rd.(60101), pg. 700
PETCARE PLUS, INC., 2300 Windson Ct.(60101), pg. 863
THE PROTECTOR CORPORATION, 240 E. Lake St., Ste. 306(60101), pg. 895
Rand McNally Map Services Company, 210 S. Fairbanks(60101), pg. 911
Sprayway, Inc., 600 Vista Ave.(60101), pg. 222
Wing Industries North Central, 775 Belden Ave. 1196

Albion

Champion Laboratories, Inc., 4th & Walnut Sts.(62806), pg. 1123
Luber-Finer, Inc., P.O. Box 8, (62806), pg. 1123

Alsip

Anderson Copper & Brass Company, 3800 W. 127th St.(60658), pg. 711
ARDCO, INC., 12400 S. Laramie Ave.(60658), pg. 81
Chisholm, Boyd & White Co., 4101 W. 126th St.(60658), pg. 1148
GRIFFITH LABORATORIES WORLDWIDE, INC., 1 Griffith Center(60658), pg. 487
Illinois Limited Partnership, 4501 W. 127th Street(60658), pg. 715
LOMBARD COMPANY, 4245 W. 123rd. St.(60658), pg. 681
MARTIN EXPLORATION MANAGEMENT COMPANY, 4501 W. 127th St(60658), pg. 715
New Hermes Inc-Midwest, 3642 W. 128th Pl.(60658), pg. 801
Tuthill Pump, 12500 S. Pulaski Rd.(60658), pg. 1120
Ulbrich of Illinois, Inc., 12340 S. Laramie(60658), pg. 1125

Alton

Millers' General Insurance Company, 111 E. Fourth St.(62002), pg. 755
MILLERS' MUTUAL INSURANCE ASSN. OF ILLINOIS, 111 E. Fourth St.(62001), pg. 755
MISSISSIPPI LIME CO., 7 Alby St.(62002), pg. 760

Anna

Lewis Bros. Bakeries, RR 1(62906), pg. 673

Antioch

QUAKER INDUSTRIES LIMITED, 90 McMillen Rd.(60002), pg. 903

Arlington Heights

ABI National Accounts, 657 E. Golf Rd., Suite 312(60005), pg. 50
AETNA PLYWOOD, INC., 3233 N. Arlington Heights(60004), pg. 23
Alexander Marketing Services/Chicago, 1700 W. Central Rd.(60005), pg. 33
MARK ANDERSON ASSOCIATES, INC., 9 N. Vail(60005), pg. 73
F.H. BONN COMPANY, 111 N. Hickory(60004), pg. 164
Ink Specialties Co., 1436 E. Davis St.(60005), pg. 1171
MARKETING ALTERNATIVES, INC., 3721 Ventura Dr., Ste. 180(60004), pg. 709
MERCHANDISING EQUIPMENT GROUP, 3025 W. Salt Creek Ln.(60005), pg. 739
Merchandising Equipment Group, National Marketing, 3025 W. Salt Creek Lane(60005), pg. 739
HENRY NEWGARD & COMPANY, 77 W. Seegers Rd.(60005), pg. 804
Pace, 550 W. Algonquin Rd.(60005), pg. 922
PADDOCK PUBLICATIONS, INC., 217 W. Campbell St.(60005), pg. 842
WEBER MARKING SYSTEMS, INC., 711 W. Algonquin Rd.(60005), pg. 1171

Arthur

ARTHUR CHEESE COMPANY, 320 E. Second St.(61911), pg. 87

Aurora

Aurora National Bank, 2 So. Broadway(60505), pg. 483
The Beacon-News, 101 S. River St.(60506), pg. 284
Change-O-Matic/Wesco, 1266 S. Orchard Rd.(60507), pg. 1045
EMS-Illinois, 600 N. Commons Dr.(60504), pg. 370
EBY BROWN CO., 1001 Sullivan Rd.(60506), pg. 365
GREATBANC, INC., 105 East Galena Blvd.(60505), pg. 482
MCKEE DOOR, INC., 85 Hankes Ave.(60505), pg. 730
OBERWEIS DAIRY, INC., 945 N. Lake St.(60506), pg. 820
WIL-FREDS CONSTRUCTION, INC., 274 E. Indian Trail(60505), pg. 1189

Bannockburn

OTTENHEIMER & COMPANY, INC., 2275 Half-Day Rd.(60015), pg. 831

Barrington

CAI, 550 W. Northwest Hwy.(60010), pg. 917
CLARK GUM COMPANY, 1300 S. Grove Ave.(60010), pg. 252
Knight PMD, Inc., P.O. Box 187, (60011), pg. 637
PARK CORPORATION, 511 Lake Zurich Rd.(60010), pg. 849
RECON/OPTICAL, INC., 550 W. Northwest Hwy.(60010), pg. 917

Bartlett

FLEXONICS INC., 300 E. Devon Ave.(60103), pg. 419
Flexonics, Inc., 6300 W. Devon(60103), pg. 1220

Batavia

ALDI INC., 1200 N. Kirk(60510), pg. 33
FURNAS ELECTRIC COMPANY, 1000 McKee St.(60510), pg. 437
Nordic Controls Co., 155 N. Van Nortwick(60510), pg. 437
Sealy Mattress Company of Illinois, 1030 Fabyan Pkwy.(60510), pg. 985
Watlow Batavia, Inc., 1310 Kingsland Dr.(60510), pg. 1167

Bedford Park

American National Can Co., , pg. 880
Argo Terminal Co., 8800 W. 71st St.(60638), pg. 482
Beaut-Ease Corporation, 5401 W. 65th St.(60638), pg. 556
CHEMCENTRAL/Chicago, 7050 W. 71st St.(60638), pg. 241
CHEMCENTRAL CORPORATION, 7050 W. 71st St.(60638), pg. 241
Dial Tube Company, 5133 W. 70th Pl.(60638), pg. 939
GOODMAN EQUIPMENT CORP., 5430 W. 70th Pl.(60638), pg. 470
HELLER SEASONINGS & INGREDIENTS, INC., 6363 W. 73rd St.(60638), pg. 526
TRIPLE A SPECIALTY COMPANY, 4953 W. 66th St.(60638), pg. 1114
Viskase Corporation, 6855 W. 65th St.(60638), pg. 383

Belleville

FKG Oil Company, 721 Main(62220), pg. 773
MOTO, INC., 721 Main(62220), pg. 773

Bellwood

Borg-Warner-Spring/Brummer Division, 700 So. 25th Ave.(60104), pg. 166
Dixonweb Printing Company, 815 S. 25th Ave.(60104), pg. 1010
Handschy Industries, 120 25th St.(60104), pg. 409
SLEEPECK PRINTING COMPANY, 815 S. 25th Ave.(60104), pg. 1010

Belvidere

BELVEDERE COMPANY, One Belvedere Blvd.(61008), pg. 138
Central Beauty Equipment, One Belvedere Blvd.(61008), pg. 138
SPECIALTY EQUIPMENT COMPANIES INC., 6581 Revlon Dr.(61008), pg. 1027

Bensenville

Advance Thermal Corp., 544 York Rd., pg. 1107
CALUMET PHOTOGRAPHIC, INC., 890 Supreme Dr.(60106), pg. 211
CHICAGO WHITE METAL CASTING, INC., Rt. 246
MILLER FLUID POWER CORP., 800 N. York Rd.(60106), pg. 754
National Metal Products Co., 100 Leland Ct., P.O. Box 827(60106), pg. 1078

Benton

Celebrity Boats, Inc., 451 Illinois St., pg. 609

Big Rock

EXECUTIVE CAPITAL CORP., Rte. 30(60511), pg. 392

Bloomingdale

COMARK, 471 Brighton Dr.(60108), pg. 267

Bloomington

BEER NUTS, INC., 103 N. Robinson St.(61702), pg. 132
CC Services, 1701 Towanda Ave.(61702-2020), pg. 289
Central Illinois Periodicals, Inc., PO BOX 3757, (61702), pg. 672
Country Casualty Insurance Company, P.O. Box 2100, 1701 Towanda Ave.(61702-2000), pg. 289
COUNTRY COMPANIES INSURANCE GROUP, 1711 GE Rd.(61704), pg. 289
Country Investors Life Assurance Company, 1701 Towanda Ave.(61702-2040), pg. 289
Country Life Insurance Company, 1701 Towanda Ave.(61702-2040), pg. 289
Country Mutual Insurance Company, 1700 Towanda Ave.(61702-2100), pg. 289
Country Preferred Insurance Company, P.O. Box 2100, 1701 Towanda Ave.(61702-2100), pg. 289
GROWMARK, INC., 1701 Towanda Ave.(61702), pg. 490
Northwest Farm Bureau Insurance Company, P.O. Box 2100, 1701 Towanda Ave.(61702-2100), pg. 289
State Farm Fire and Casualty Co., 112 E. Washington St.(61701), pg. 1041
State Farm General Insurance Co., 112 E. Washington St.(61701), pg. 1041
State Farm Life and Accident Assurance Co., One State Farm Plaza(61710), pg. 1041
State Farm Life Insurance Co., One State Farm Plaza(61710), pg. 1041
STATE FARM MUTUAL AUTOMOBILE INSURANCE COMPANY, One State Farm Plaza(61710), pg. 1041

Blue Island

Clark Oil & Refining Corporation--Blue Island Refinery, 131st & Kedzie Ave.(60406), pg. 253
First National Bank of Blue Island, 13057 S. Western Ave.(60406), pg. 481
G & W ELECTRIC CO., 3500 W. 127th St.(60406), pg. 438
Gilbert & Bennett, P.O. Box 56(60406), pg. 458
Kilsby-Roberts Honing/Blue Island, 2850 W. 139th St.(60406), pg. 606
MODERN DROP FORGE CO., 13810 S. Western Ave.(60406), pg. 762

Bridgeview

Ivex Packaging Corporation-Bridgeview, 8100 S. 77th Ave.(60455), pg. 583

Broadview

American Fasteners, 1919 W. 19th St.(60153), pg. 609
Arrow Fluid Power, 2111 W. 21st. St.(60153), pg. 85
Elkay Manufacturing, 2700 S. 17th Ave.(60153), pg. 377
HEADCO INDUSTRIES, INC., 2601 W. 16th St.(60153), pg. 520
Industrial Information Headquarters Co., 2601 W. 16th St.(60153), pg. 520
NATIONAL VAN LINES, INC., 2800 W. Roosevelt Rd.(60153), pg. 794
Pro-Select, 2151 Cermak Rd.(60153), pg. 815
REPLOGLE GLOBES, INC., 2801 S. 25th Ave.(60153), pg. 927
TEMPLETON, KENLY & CO., INC., 2525 Gardner Rd.(60153), pg. 1086
Woodland Molded Plastics, 3110 SA. Twenty-Sixth Ave.(60153-4575), pg. 433

Buffalo Grove

ANGUS CHEMICAL COMPANY, 1500 East Lake Cook Rd.(60089), pg. 75
COLFAX ENVELOPE CORPORATION, 951 Commerce Ct.(60089), pg. 261
GLORIA JEAN'S COFFEE BEAN CORP., 1001 Asbury(60089), pg. 464

Indeck Energy Services, Inc., 1130 Lake Cook Rd.(60089), pg. 564
MID-WEST AUTOMATION SYSTEMS, 1400 Busch Pkwy.(60089), pg. 750
SUTTER/MARTIN, INC., 165 Arlington Heights Rd.(60089), pg. 1065

Burr Ridge

Dove International, Inc., 660 W. 79th St.(60521), pg. 713
Griffith Micro Science International Inc., 200 S. Frontage Rd., Ste. 120(60521), pg. 487
IMPO GLAZTILE, 7600 County Line Rd., Unit 1(60521), pg. 564
Mid-West Company, 100 Tower Dr.(60521), pg. 939
TIMEMED LABELING SYSTEMS, INC., 144 Tower Dr.(60521), pg. 1098

Carbondale

VOGLER MOTOR COMPANY, INC., 1170 E. Main(62901), pg. 1154

Carlinville

CENTRAL ILLINOIS STEEL COMPANY, P.O. Box 78(62626), pg. 232
Ice Cream Specialties, Inc., 1100 N. Broadway(62626), pg. 884
P.F.D. Supply Corp., 1100 N. Broadway(62626), pg. 884
PRAIRIE FARMS DAIRY, INC., 1100 N. Broadway(62626), pg. 884

Carmi

MARTIN & BAYLEY INC., Hwy. 1 S., P.O. Box 385(62821), pg. 714

Carol Stream

CHRISTIANITY TODAY, INC., 465 Gundersen Dr.(60188), pg. 249
Davis Molding Co., 350 Kehoe Blvd.(60187), pg. 525
THE MEYERCORD COMPANY, 365 E. North Ave.(60188), pg. 746
TYNDALE HOUSE PUBLISHERS, INC., 351 Executive Drive(60188), pg. 1122

Carpentersville

REVCOR, INC., 251 Edwards Ave.(60110), pg. 930

Cary

Accutronics, Inc., 225 N. First St.(60013), pg. 711
COILCRAFT, INC., 1102 Silver Lake Rd.(60013), pg. 259
Tru-Test Mfg. Co., 201 Jandus Rd.(60013), pg. 288

Champaign

CENTRAL DATA CORPORATION, 1602 Newton Dr.(61821), pg. 232
I. H. FRENCH & CO. INC., 505 E. University(61820), pg. 432
C. S. JOHNSON CO., 502 S. Kenwood(61821), pg. 597

Chester

Duff Mix Div., P.O. Box 227(62233), pg. 460
GILSTER MARY LEE CORP., 1037 State St.(62233), pg. 460
Party Pac Div., P.O. Box 227, (62233), pg. 460
Py-O-My Div., P.O. Box 227(62233), pg. 460

Chicago

AAA Plumbing Pottery Corp., 4656 W. Touhy Ave.(60646), pg. 454
ARA Leisure Services, Soldier Field, 425 E. McFetridge Dr.(60605), pg. 6
ARA Leisure Services, Wrigley Field, 1060 W. Addison(60613), pg. 6
ARA Services, John Hancock Center, 875 N. Michigan Ave.(60611), pg. 6
ARA Services, Loyola University, 47 E. Pearson(60611), pg. 6
ABBELL ASSOCIATES, 332 S. Michigan Ave., Ste. 1260(60604), pg. 9
ABBOTT GROUP LTD., 3129 W. 36th St.(60632), pg. 9
Abbott Industrial Supply, 3159 W. 36th St.(60632), pg. 9
Abbott Products Inc., 3129 W. 36th St.(60632), pg. 9
ABELSON-TAYLOR, INC., 35 E. Wacker Drive(60601), pg. 10
ACCURATE PERFORATING CO., 3636 S. Kedzie Ave.(60632), pg. 11
ACME CONTINENTAL FOODS, INC., 1255 W. Oakdale(60657), pg. 13
ACTIVE ELECTRICAL SUPPLY COMPANY, 4240 W. Lawrence Ave.(60630), pg. 15
Advertising Age, 740 N. Rush St.(60611), pg. 295
AETNA BEARING COMPANY, 4600 W. Schubert(60639), pg. 23
AGENCIAS USA, 980 N. Michigan Ave.(60611), pg. 24
AIRCRAFT GEAR CORPORATION, 6633 W. 65th(60638), pg. 27
Allright Parking Chicago, Inc., 216 N. Jefferson, 2nd Fl.(60661), pg. 42
Alpha Resin Supply, 1750 N. Kingsbury St.(60614), pg. 482
THE HARRY ALTER COMPANY, 5940 N. Northwest Highway(60631), pg. 45
The Harry Alter Company, 5940 N. Northwest Hwy.(60631), pg. 1086
ALVA/AMCO PHARMACAL COMPANIES, INC., 6625 N. Avondale Ave.(60631), pg. 46
Ambria, 2300 Lincoln Park W.(60614), pg. 669
AMERICAN DECAL & MFG. CO., 4100 W. Fullerton Ave.(60639), pg. 51
AMERICAN EAGLE AIRLINES, 900 N. Franklin, Ste. 800(60610), pg. 51
American Envelope Company, 222 North LaSalle St.(60601), pg. 199
American Envelope of Chicago-Die Cut Div., 4400 W. Ohio St.(60624), pg. 199
American Envelope of Chicago-Web Div., 3001 N. Rockwell St., pg. 199
American Learning Corp., 310 S. Michigan Ave.(60604), pg. 381
AMERICAN LIBRARY ASSOCIATION, 50 E. Huron St.(60611), pg. 57
The American Meat Packing Corp., 3946 S. Normal Ave.(60609), pg. 616
AMERICAN PRINTERS & LITHOGRAPHERS, 6701 W. Oakton St.(60714), pg. 59
American Specialty Distributing, 2501 N. Elston Ave.(60647), pg. 881
American Specialty Distributing, 3231 W. 37th Place(60632), pg. 881
American Steel Foundries, 10 S. Riverside Plaza(60606), pg. 69
Amfac, Inc., 900 N. Michigan Ave., 585
AMSTED INDUSTRIES INCORPORATED, 205 N. Michigan Ave.(60601), pg. 68
AMSTED Industries International, 200 W. Monroe St.(60606), pg. 69
Arthur Andersen, 69 W. Washington(60602), pg. 72
Andersen Consulting, 69 W. Washington St.(60602), pg. 72
Andy Frain Aviation Services, Inc., 310 W. Chicago Ave.(60610), pg. 428
Archibald Candy Company, 1137 W. Jackson(60607), pg. 604
Architectural Interiors, Inc., 600 W. Fulton(60606), pg. 384
ARIAN, LOWE, TRAVIS & GUSICK, INC., 343 W. Erie St., Ste. 520(60610), pg. 82
Arocom Marketing Group, Inc., 935 West Chestnut St.(60622), pg. 737
ARRINGTON TRAVEL CENTER INC., 55 W. Monroe St.(60603), pg. 85
AUTO DRIVEAWAY CO., 310 S. Michigan Ave.(60604), pg. 100
AUTOMATED MARKETING SYSTEMS, INC., 225 W. Wacker Dr., Ste. 2275(60606), pg. 100
Avanzare, 161 E. Huron(60611), pg. 669
Ayer Chicago, 515 N. State St., Ste. 2100(60610), pg. 104
Azcon Corp., 224 S. Michigan Ave., Ste. 425(60604), pg. 161
AZTECA FOODS, INCORPORATED, 5005 So. Nagle(60638), pg. 105
BEC ADVERTISING, 5701 N. Tripp(60646), pg. 106
Backer Spielvogel Bates, Inc., 500 N. Michigan Ave., Ste. 2010(60611), pg. 108
BAIRD & WARNER INC., 200 W. Madison St.(60606), pg. 114
BAKER & MCKENZIE INTERNATIONAL, 130 E. Randolph Dr., Ste. 3900(60601), pg. 115
Bank Marketing Association, 309 W. Washington St.(60606), pg. 49
BANNER WHOLESALE GROCERS, INC., 115 S. Water Market(60608), pg. 118
Barton Beers, Ltd., 55 E. Monroe St., Ste. 1710(60603), pg. 123
BARTON BRANDS, LTD., 55 E. Monroe St., Ste. 1700(60603), pg. 123
BAYER BESS VANDERWARKER INC., 225 N. Michigan Ave., Ste. 1900(60601), pg. 128
BEECH HOLDINGS CORP., 200 N. Michigan Ave.(60601), pg. 131
Beef Industry Council, 444 N. Michigan Ave.(60611), pg. 792
BELL CHEMICAL COMPANY, 411-415 N. Wolcott Ave.(60622), pg. 134
BELTONE ELECTRONICS CORPORATION, 4201 W. Victoria(60646), pg. 137
BENNETT BROTHERS, INC., 30 E. Adams St.(60603), pg. 139
BENTLEY, BARNES & LYNN, INC., 420 N. Wabash(60611), pg. 140
LOU BERES & ASSOCIATES, INC., 410 N. Michigan Ave.(60611), pg. 141
BESSIN CORPORATION, 207 W. South Water Market(60608), pg. 146
Big Bowl Cafe, 159.5 W. Erie St.(60610), pg. 669
BIGSBY & KRUTHERS, INC., 1750 N. Clark(60614), pg. 150
Bistro Soups, Ltd., 2501 N. Damen(60647), pg. 1151
WILLIAM BLAIR & COMPANY, 135 S. LaSalle St.(60603), pg. 155
BLOMMER CHOCOLATE CO., 600 W. Kinzie St.(60610), pg. 157
Blue Crab Lounge, 21 E. Hubbard(60611), pg. 669
BLUE CROSS AND BLUE SHIELD ASSOCIATION, 676 N. St. Clair St.(60611), pg. 159
BLUE CROSS & BLUE SHIELD OF ILLINOIS, 233 N. Michigan Ave.(60601), pg. 160
BODINE ELECTRIC COMPANY, 2500 W. Bradley Pl.(60618), pg. 162
BORG-WARNER CORPORATION, 200 S. Michigan Ave.(60604), pg. 165
E.J. Brach, Inc., 4656 W. Kinzie St.(60644), pg. 169
BRADNER CENTRAL COMPANY, 333 S. Desplaines St.(60661-5596), pg. 170
Bradner Smith & Co., 333 S. DesPlaines St.(60606), pg. 171
BRAINSTORM ADVERTISING & SALES PROMOTIONS, 228 S. Wabash Ave.(60604), pg. 171
W. BRAUN COMPANY, 300 N. Canal St.(60606), pg. 172
BREUER ELECTRIC MFG. CO., 7401 W. Lawrence Ave.(60656), pg. 174
Brierley & Partners, 8420 W. Bryn Mawr, 175
Britannica Home Library Services, 310 S. Michigan Ave.(60604), pg. 381
E.H. BROWN ADVERTISING, INC., 20 N. Wacker Dr., Ste. 1865(60606-2996), pg. 181
BRUSS COMPANY, 3548 N. Kostner Ave.(60641), pg. 184
Bub City Crabshack & Bar-B-Q, 901 W. Weed St.(60622), pg. 669
BURKE COMMUNICATION INDUSTRIES, INC., 1165 N. Clark St.(60610), pg. 190
LEO BURNETT COMPANY, INC., 35 W. Wacker Dr.(60601), pg. 191
BURNHAM BROADCASTING COMPANY, 980 N. Michigan Ave., Ste. 1200(60611), pg. 193
BURRELL COMMUNICATIONS GROUP INC., 20 N. Michigan Ave.(60602), pg. 195
Business Insurance, 740 Rush St.(60611-2590), pg. 295
Business Marketing, 740 Rush St.(60611), pg. 295
CC INDUSTRIES, INC., 222 N. LaSalle St.(60601), pg. 199
CCC Information Services, 640 N. LaSalle(60610), pg. 410
CFB INDUSTRIES, INC., 1467 N. Elston(60622), pg. 201
CPM, INC., 515 N. State St., Ste. 2200(60610-4320), pg. 203
Cabell Construction Company, 120 S. Riverside Plaza(60606), pg. 609
Cadaco, 4300 W. 47th St.(60632-4476), pg. 913
Cafe Ba-Ba-Reeba, 2024 N. Halsted(60614), pg. 669
A. J. CANFIELD CO., 50 E. 89th Place(60619), pg. 214
Carbide International Inc., 5740 Tripp Ave.(60646), pg. 507
CarComp Services, Inc., 2 N. LaSalle St., Ste 2500(60602-3876), pg. 464
Cargill Investor Services, Inc., 141 W. Jackson Blvd., Ste. 1800(60604), pg. 219
CARSTENS HEALTH INDUSTRIES, INC., 7310 W. Wilson Ave.(60656), pg. 225
CASH & CARRY GROCER INC., 2844 W. Armitage Ave.(60647), pg. 228
CEBCOR (CONSOLIDATED EMPLOYMENT BENEFITS CORP.), 332 S. Michigan Ave., Ste. 850(60604), pg. 230
CENTURY AMERICA CORPORATION, 875 No. Michigan Ave.(60611), pg. 234
CENTURY 21 AGMONT REAL ESTATE, INC., 3407 W. Lawrence Ave.(60625), pg. 235
CHERNIN'S SHOES, 1001 S. Clinton(60607), pg. 243
Chicago, 414 N. Orleans, Ste. 800(60610), pg. 656
Chicago Blasting Company, 12233 Ave. O(60633), pg. 480
Chicago Boat Yard, Inc., 1269 W. Lemoyne St.(60622), pg. 201
CHICAGO CONVENTION & TOURISM BUREAU, McCormick Place-on-the-Lake(60616), pg. 245
Chicago Corp., 208 S. La Salle St., Ste. 220(66004), pg. 247
Chicago Fire Brick Company, 1467 N. Elston Ave.(60622), pg. 201
Chicago Fire Brick of Delaware, Inc., 1467 N. Elston Ave.(60622), pg. 201
CHICAGO LOCK COMPANY, 4311 W. Belmont Ave.(60641), pg. 245
CHICAGO MECHANICAL, INC., 1400 E. 97th Pl.(60628), pg. 245
CHICAGO MERCANTILE EXCHANGE, 30 So. Wacker Dr.(60606), pg. 245
Chicago Rail Link, 2728 E. 104th St.(60617-5766), pg. 246
CHICAGO READER, INC., 11 E. Illinois, 2nd Fl.(60611), pg. 245
Chicago Steel & Wire, 10257 S. Torrence Ave.(60617), pg. 691
Chicago Sun Times, 401 N. Wabash Ave.(60611), pg. 18
Chicago Transit Authority, Merchandise Mart Plaza, (60654), pg. 922
CHICAGO TUBE & IRON CO., 2531 W. 48th St.(60632), pg. 246
Chicago West Pullman & Southern R.R. Co., 2728 E. 104th St.(60617), pg. 246
Chicago West Pullman Transportation Corporation, 2728 E. 104th St.(60617-5766), pg. 246
Chicorp Financial Services, 208 S. La Salle St., Ste. 220(60604), pg. 247
CHICORP, INC., 208 S. La Salle St., Ste. 220(60604), pg. 247
Chicorp Management Inc., 208 S. LaSalle St., Ste. 1680(60604), pg. 247
City & State, 740 Rush St.(60611), pg. 295
P. J. Clarke's, 1204 No. State Pkwy.(60610), pg. 669
Classic Residence by Hyatt, 200 W. Madison(60606), pg. 495
CLEARING INTERNATIONAL, INC., 6499 W. 65th St.(60638), pg. 254
CLOVERHILL BAKERY, 2020 N. Parkside Ave.(60639), pg. 256
CODE, HENNESSY & SIMMONS, 10 S. Wacker, Ste. 3175(60606), pg. 258
Cole Taylor Bank, 850 W. Jackson Blvd.(60607), pg. 260
The Colson Group, Inc., 225 W. Washington St.(60606), pg. 711
COLUMBIA PIPE & SUPPLY COMPANY, 1120 W. Pershing Rd.(60609), pg. 266
COLUMBIAN ADVERTISING INC., 201 E. Ohio St.(60611), pg. 266
Columbian Direct Marketing, 201 East Ohio St.(60611), pg. 266
Compton's New Media Inc., 310 S. Michigan Ave.(60604), pg. 381
Computer Technology Management Inc., 600 West Fulton St.(60606), pg. 384
Consolidated Distilled Products, 3201 S. Kedzie Ave.(60623), pg. 782
CORNELL FORGE COMPANY, 6666 W. 66th St.(60638), pg. 286
Corner Bakery, 516 N. Clark St.(60610), pg. 669
CORRUGATED METALS, INC., 4800 S. Hoyne(60609), pg. 287
Cotter Acceptance Co., Inc., 2740-52 N. Clybourn(60614), pg. 288
COTTER & COMPANY, 2740 N. Clybourn Ave.(60614-1088), pg. 288
Cotter Finance Co., Inc., 2740-52 N. Clybourn Ave.(60614), pg. 288
COUGLE COMMISSION COMPANY, INC., 345 N. Aberdeen(60607), pg. 289

Crain's Chicago Business, 740 Rush St.(60611), pg. 295
Cramer-Krasselt, 225 N. Michigan Ave.(60601), pg. 296
CREATIVE MARKETING RESOURCE, INC., 919 N. Michigan Ave., 1st Fl.(60611), pg. 297
Crown Drug, 1640 W. Fulton St.(60612), pg. 384
VINCE CULLERS ADVERTISING INC., 676 St. Clair, Ste. 2222(60611), pg. 304
Custom Food Products Inc., 730 N. Albany(60612), pg. 487
CYBORG SYSTEMS, INC., 2 N. Riverside Plaza, 12th Fl.(60606), pg. 307
D & D Newspaper Circulators, Inc., 1200 N. North Branch Street(60622), pg. 672
D & H Piping, 5051 S. Western Blvd.(60609), pg. 343
DMI THE HEALTHCARE AGENCY, 211 E. Ontario St.(60611), pg. 309
Daily Racing Form, Inc. (Midwest), 1301 N. Elston Ave.(60622), pg. 611
DANN DEE DISPLAY FIXTURES, 350 N. Orleans, Ste.1000(60654-1898), pg. 314
THE DARTNELL CORPORATION, 4660 N. Ravenswood Ave.(60640), pg. 316
Daubert Chemical Company, Inc., 4700 So. Central Ave.(60638), pg. 317
DAVIDSON MARKETING, INC., 54 W. Hubbard St.(60610), pg. 318
THE DEARBORN GROUP, 33 N. Dearborn St., Ste. 1030(60602), pg. 322
DOMBROWSKI & HOLMES, INC., 5051 S. Western Blvd.(60609), pg. 343
DONTECH, 205 N. Michigan Ave.(60601), pg. 345
DORMEYER INDUSTRIES, 3418 N. Milwaukee Ave.(60641), pg. 346
DUDEK & BOCK SPRING MANUFACTURING COMPANY, 5100 W. Roosevelt Rd.(60650), pg. 351
EB (NA), 310 S. Michigan Ave.(60604), pg. 381
Eastern Lobby Shops, 980 N. Michigan Ave., Ste. 400(60611), pg. 672
Ebony Fashions, 820 S. Michigan Ave.(60605), pg. 599
The Eccentric/Big Bowl, 159 W. Erie(60611), pg. 669
Eclipse Thermal Systems, 6117 No. Elston Ave.(60646), pg. 366
ECONOMY FOLDING BOX CORP., LaSalle & 26th Sts.(60616), pg. 367
EIRE PARTNERS, INC., 230 W. Superior St., Ste. 600(60610), pg. 372
ELECTRO BRAND, INC., 5410 W. Roosevelt Rd.(60650), pg. 374
Electronic Media, 740 Rush St.(60611), pg. 295
ELGIN-HONEY HILL CORPORATION, 3707 W. Harrison St.(60624), pg. 376
Elgin National Industries, Inc., 120 S. Riverside Plaza(60606), pg. 609
ELI'S CHICAGO'S FINEST, INC., 6510 W. Dakin Ave.(60634), pg. 376
Encyclopaedia Britannica Educational Corporation, 310 S. Michigan(60604), pg. 381
ENCYCLOPAEDIA BRITANNICA EDUCATIONAL CORPORATION, 310 S. Michigan Ave.(60604), pg. 380
ENCYCLOPAEDIA BRITANNICA, INC., 310 S. Michigan Ave.(60604), pg. 381
A. EPSTEIN AND SONS, INTL., INC., 600 W. Fulton St.(60661-1199), pg. 384
Epstein Civil Engineering, Inc., 600 W. Fulton(60606), pg. 384
Epstein Construction Inc., 600 W. Fulton(60606), pg. 384
Epstein Engineering Export, Ltd., 600 W. Fulton(60606), pg. 384
Epstein Engineering, Inc., 600 W. Fulton St.(60606-1199), pg. 384
Epstein Material Handling Engineering, Inc., 600 W. Fulton(60606), pg. 384
Epstein Process Engineering, Inc., 600 W. Fulton(60661-1199), pg. 384
A. Epstein & Sons, Inc., 600 W. Fulton(60606), pg. 384
EQUINOX ADVERTISING, INC., 980 N. Michigan Ave., Ste. 1180(60611), pg. 384
EQUITY GROUP INVESTMENTS, 2 N. Riverside Plaza, Ste. 600(60606), pg. 385
Everest, One Financial Place, 440 S. LaSalle, 40th Fl.(60605), pg. 669
F & B MANUFACTURING CO., 5480 N. Northwest Hwy.(60630), pg. 393
Faber, Coe & Gregg of Chicago, Inc., 449 E. Illinois(60611), pg. 395
Fannie May Candy Shops, Inc., 1137 W. Jackson(60607), pg. 604
FARLEY CANDY COMPANY, 2945 W. 31st St.(60623), pg. 399
Farley, Inc., 233 S. Wacker Dr., Ste. 5000(60606), pg. 400
FARLEY INDUSTRIES, 233 S. Wacker Dr., Ste. 5000(60606), pg. 399
Filko/Cobra, Inc., 5480 N. Northwest Hwy.(60630), pg. 393
WALLY FINDLAY GALLERIES INTERNATIONAL, 814 N. Michigan Ave.(60611), pg. 410
A. FINKL & SONS CO., 2011 N. Southport Ave.(60614), pg. 411
Fireline Co., 1800 N. Kingsbury St.(60614), pg. 877
L. FISH CORPORATION, 4242 W. 42nd Pl.(60632), pg. 414
FLAIR COMMUNICATIONS AGENCY, INC., Flair House, 214 W. Erie St.(60610), pg. 416
Flex-O-Film Plastic Div., 1100 N. Cicero Ave.(60651), pg. 418
FLEX-O-GLASS, INC., 1100 N. Cicero Ave.(60651), pg. 418
FLYING FOOD FARE, INC., 5945 S. Keating Ave.(60629), pg. 421
Follett College Resources, 1000 W. Washington Blvd.(60607), pg. 422
FOLLETT CORPORATION, 1000 W. Washington Blvd.(60607), pg. 422
Follett Service Corporation, 1000 W. Washington Blvd.(60607), pg. 422
ANDY FRAIN SERVICES, INC., 310 W. Chicago Ave.(60610), pg. 428
Frank Paxton Lumber Company, 5701 W. 66th St.(60638), pg. 592
FRANKEL & COMPANY, 111 E. Wacker Dr.(60601), pg. 429
FRIEDMAN, EISENSTEIN, RAEMER & SCHWARTZ, 401 N. Michigan Ave., Ste. 2600(60611), pg. 433
G L Sub Company, 39 S. La Salle St.(60603), pg. 712
GSC ENTERPRISES, INC., 737 N. Michigan Ave., Ste. 1200(60611), pg. 440
GSP MARKETING SERVICES, INC., 320 W. Ohio(60606), pg. 441
GARDINER METAL COMPANY, 4820 S. Campbell Ave.(60632), pg. 443
Gardiner Solder Company, 4820 S. Campbell Ave.(60632), pg. 443
GENERAL DRUG CO., 200 N. Fairfield Ave.(60612), pg. 449
GERBER PLUMBING FIXTURES CORPORATION, 4656 W. Touhy Ave.(60646), pg. 454
GINGISS INTERNATIONAL, 180 N. LaSalle St., Ste. 1111(60601), pg. 460
GLOBE GLASS & MIRROR CO., 2 N. LaSalle, Ste. 2500(60602-3876), pg. 463
GLOBE INDUSTRIES, INC., 2638 E. 126th St.(60632), pg. 464
Globe Valve Corporation, 4656 W. Touhy Ave.(60646), pg. 454
GOLUB & CO., 625 N. Michigan Ave. Ste.2000(60611), pg. 469
GONNELLA BAKING CO., 2002-14 W. Erie St.(60612), pg. 469
SHELDON GOOD & CO., INC., 333 W. Wacker Dr., Ste. 450(60606), pg. 470
GRAHAM PAINT AND VARNISH COMPANY, 4800 S. Richmond Ave.(60632), pg. 475
GRANT/JACOBY, INC., 737 N. Michigan Ave.(60611), pg. 477
GRANT THORNTON, Prudential Plaza, Ste. 800(60601), pg. 477
Graphic Systems, 3435 N. Kimball Ave.(60618), pg. 721
GRAYMILLS CORP., 3705 N. Lincoln Ave.(60613), pg. 480
Great Books of the Western World, 310 S. Michigan Ave.(60604), pg. 381
GREAT LAKES TERMINAL & TRANSPORT CORP., 1750 N. Kingsbury St.(60614), pg. 482
Greater Chicago Auto Auction, 12000 S. Cicero Ave.(60658), pg. 293
Green Garde, 500 N. Michigan Ave.(60611), pg. 551
Griffin Wheel Co., 200 W. Monroe St.(60606), pg. 69
R.J. Grunts/Chicago, 2056 Lincoln Park West(60614), pg. 669
H. GROUP HOLDING INC., 200W. Madison St., 39th fl.(60606), pg. 495
HLB COMMUNICATIONS, INC., 875 N. Michigan Ave., Ste. 1330(60611), pg. 496
HOH Architects, Inc., 180 N. Wabash Ave.(60601), pg. 497
HOH Engineers, Inc., 180 N. Wabash Ave.(60601), pg. 497
THE HOH ORGANIZATIONS, 180 N. Wabash Ave.(60601), pg. 497
HRR Enterprises, Inc., 2129 W. Pershing Rd.(60609), pg. 616
THE C. P. HALL COMPANY, 7300 S. Central Ave.(60638), pg. 501
HAMILTON, CARVER & LEE, INC., 429 W. Superior St.(60614), pg. 503
HAMMACHER, SCHLEMMER & CO., INC., 212 W. Superior(60610), pg. 503
HANNA CORPORATION, 1765 N. Elston Ave.(60622), pg. 505
HARRINGTON & KING, 5655 Fillmore St.(60644), pg. 511
HARRIS STEEL CO., 1223 S. 55th Ct.(60650), pg. 512
HART SERVICES, INC., 101 N. Wacker Dr.(60606), pg. 513
HARZA ENGINEERING CO., Sears Tower, 233 S. Wacker Dr.(60606-6392), pg. 516
Harza Environmental Services, Inc., 233 S. Wacker Dr.(60606-6392), pg. 516
Hat Dance, 325 W. Huron(60610), pg. 669
Harry O. Hefter-Associates, Inc., 180 N. Wabash Ave.(60601), pg. 497
HELLER INTERNATIONAL, 500 W. Monroe(60661), pg. 526
Hollytex-Central Div., 13-150 Merchandise Mart(60654), pg. 1121
HOOF PRODUCTS COMPANY, 4051 W. 51st St.(60632), pg. 543
HOUSTON FOODS COMPANY, 4245 N. Knox Ave.(60641), pg. 547
H.D. HUDSON MANUFACTURING COMPANY, 500 N. Michigan Ave.(60611), pg. 551
HUMISTON-KEELING, INC., 233 E. Erie St.(60611), pg. 552
Hyatt Air, Inc., 200 W. Madison(60606), pg. 495
Hyatt Corporation, 200 W. Madison(60606), pg. 495
Hyatt Hotels Corporation, 200 W. Madison St.(60606), pg. 495
Hyatt International Corporation, 200 W. Madison(60606), pg. 495
I B DIFFUSION, LP, 350 N. Orleans, Ste. 170(60654), pg. 558
ICM Investment Co., 122 So. Michigan Ave., Ste. 1700(60603), pg. 559
ICM INDUSTRIES, INC., 122 S. Michigan Ave., Ste. 1700(60603), pg. 559
IDC SERVICES, INC., 303 East Ohio Street(60611), pg. 559
IGA, INC. (INDEPENDENT GROCERS ALLIANCE), 8725 W. Higgins(60631), pg. 560
Illinois Auto Central Div., 4750 S. Central(60638), pg. 562
Illinois State Lottery, 676 N. St. Clair(60611), pg. 563
JOHN ILTIS ASSOCIATES, 680 N. Lake Shore Dr.(60611), pg. 563
Indiana Financial Investors, Inc., 737 N. Michigan Ave., Ste. 1200(60611), pg. 674
INDUSTRIAL COATINGS GROUP, INC., 2141 S. Jefferson St.(60616), pg. 566
INDUSTRIAL STEEL & WIRE COMPANY, 1901 N. Narragansett Ave.(60639), pg. 567
INTERCOUNTY TITLE CO. OF ILLINOIS, 120 W. Madison(60602), pg. 574
Interior Space Design Inc., (ISD), 600 W. Fulton St.(60606), pg. 384
INTERNATIONAL BUSINESS INTERIORS INC., 770 N. Halstead St.(60622), pg. 575
International Furniture Div., 4820 W. Belmont Ave.(60641), pg. 977
International Tables Div., 4820 W. Belmont(60641), pg. 977
JMB REALTY CORPORATION, 900 N. Michigan Ave.(60611), pg. 584
JERNBERG INDUSTRIES, INC., 328 W. 40th Place(60609), pg. 593
JOHNSON PUBLISHING COMPANY, INC., 820 S. Michigan Ave.(60605), pg. 598
JORDAN TAMRAZ CARUSO ADVERTISING, INC., 1419 N. Wells St.(60610-1395), pg. 605
JUPITER INDUSTRIES, INC., 919 N. Michigan Ave., Ste. 1500(60611), pg. 609
The Jupiter Corporation, 919 N. Michigan Ave.(60611), pg. 609
Jupiter Energy Corp., 919 N. Michigan Ave.(60611), pg. 609
JUST PANTS, 3525 W. Peterson Ave., Ste. 10(60659-3312), pg. 610
Karpen Furniture Div., 4820 W. Belmont Ave.(60641), pg. 977
KASSEL & ZOLL PROVISIONS, INC., 1455 Willow St.(60622), pg. 618
KELLY, SCOTT AND MADISON, INC., 35 E. Wacker Dr., Ste. 1150(60601), pg. 621
KEROFF & ROSENBERG ADVERTISING INC., 444 N. Wabash(60611), pg. 624
Ketchum Advertising/Chicago, 111 N. Canal St., Ste. 1150(60606-7272), pg. 625
Ketchum Public Relations/Chicago, 142 E. Ontario St.(60611), pg. 625
Keystone Automotive Industries, Inc. - Chicago, 3301 West 47th Place(60632), pg. 627
Keystone Master Warehouse - Chicago, 3327 West 47th Place(60632), pg. 628
Keystone Recycling Center - Chicago, 3327 West 47th Place(60632), pg. 628
Samuel G. Keywell Co., 11900 S. Cottage Grove Ave.(60628), pg. 629
Knight Architects Engineers Planners, Inc., 549 W. Randolph St.(60661), pg. 637
Knight/Emerson Consulting, Inc., 549 W. Randolph St.(60661), pg. 637
LESTER B. KNIGHT & ASSOCIATES, INC., 549 W. Randolph St.(60661), pg. 637
Knight Management Consulting, Inc., 549 w. Randolph St.(60661), pg. 637
KNIGHTBRIDGE PARTNERS, 225 W. Washington, Ste. 2150(60606), pg. 637
Kobs & Draft Advertising, Inc., 142 E. Ontario(60611), pg. 109
KOKOMO SANITARY POTTERY CORP., 4656 West Touhy Avenue(60646), pg. 640
Korn/Ferry International, 120 South Riverside Plaza, Ste. 918(60606), pg. 642
KROCH'S & BRENTANO'S, INC., 29 S. Wabash Ave.(60603), pg. 645
Kropp Forge Co., 5301 W. Roosevelt Rd.(60650), pg. 1073
THE LINC GROUP, INC., 303 E. Wacker Dr., Ste. 1000(60601), pg. 648
LINC Scientific Leasing Inc., 303 E. Wacker Dr.(60601), pg. 648
LA-CO INDUSTRIES, INC., 250 N. Washtenaw Ave.(60612), pg. 648
LA PREFERIDA, INC., 3400 W. 35th St.(60632), pg. 649
Lake Michigan Construction, Inc., 100 N. Riverside Plaza(60606), pg. 829
Lake Michigan Construction III, Inc., 100 N. Riverside Plaza(60606), pg. 829
Lake Michigan Construction II, Inc., 100 N. Riverside Plaza(60606), pg. 829
Lake Michigan Properties IV, Inc., 100 N. Riverside Plaza(60606), pg. 829
Lake Michigan Properties, Inc., 100 N. Riverside Plaza(60606), pg. 829
Lake Michigan Properties III, Inc., 100 N. Riverside Plaza(60606), pg. 829
Lake Michigan Properties II, Inc., 100 N. Riverside Plaza(60606), pg. 829
LAKEWOOD ENGINEERING & MANUFACTURING CO., 501 N. Sacramento Blvd.(60612), pg. 652
LAKIN GENERAL CORPORATION, 2044 N. Dominick St.(60614), pg. 652
LANDAU & HEYMAN INC., 180 N. LaSalle, Suite 3000(60601), pg. 654
LAPHAM-HICKEY STEEL CORP., 5500 W. 73rd St.(60638), pg. 658
LASALLE PARTNERS, 11 S. LaSalle St.(60603), pg. 660
Lester B. Knight Cast Metals, Inc., 549 W. Randolph St.(60661), pg. 637
LETTUCE ENTERTAIN YOU ENTERPRISES, INC., 5419 N. Sheridan Rd.(60640), pg. 668
JACK LEVY ASSOCIATES, 1 E. Erie(60611), pg. 672
Charles Levy Transportation Co., 1200 N. North Branch Street(60162), pg. 672
THE CHARLES LEVY COMPANY, 1200 N. North Branch St.(60622), pg. 672
THE LEVY ORGANIZATION, 980 N. Michigan Ave.(60611), pg. 672
Levy Real Estate Partners, 980 N. Michigan Ave., Ste. 400(60611), pg. 672
Levy Restaurants, 980 N. Michigan Ave., Ste. 400(60611), pg. 672

LEVY SECURITY CONSULTANTS, LIMITED, 55 W. Superior St.(60610), pg. 672
LIBCO CORPORATION, 737 N. Michigan Ave., Ste. 1200(60611), pg. 674
LINC Capital Corporation, 303 E. Wacker Dr.(60601), pg. 648
LINC Capital Management, 303 E. Wacker Dr.(60601), pg. 648
LINC Management Services, 303 E. Wacker Dr.(60601), pg. 648
LINCOLN PROVISION COMPANY, INC., 824 W. 38th Place(60609), pg. 676
Lindenmeyr Paper, 541 North Fairbanks(60611), pg. 233
LOEBER MOTORS, INC., 1111 N. Clark St.(60610), pg. 680
W. E. LONG COMPANY, 300 W. Washington St.(60606), pg. 682
MAECORP INC., 155 N. Wacker Dr., Ste. 400(60606), pg. 699
Maggiano's Little Italy, 516 N. Clark St.(60610), pg. 669
MAMA TISH'S ITALIAN SPECIALTIES, 4800 S. Central Ave.(60638), pg. 703
MARKETING SUPPORT, INCORPORATED, 303 E. Wacker Dr., Ste. 711(60601), pg. 709
Marmon Corporation, 225 W. Washington St.(60606), pg. 711
THE MARMON GROUP, INC., 225 W. Washington St.(60606), pg. 710
The Marmon Group, Inc., 225 W. Washington St.(60606), pg. 711
Marmon Industrial Corporation, 225 W. Washington St.(60606), pg. 712
MARSTRAT, INC., 125 S. Franklin St.(60606), pg. 714
MAUREY MANUFACTURING CORP., 2907 S. Wabash Ave.(60616), pg. 722
MCCAIN CITRUS INC., 1821 S. Kilbourn(60623), pg. 726
MCCAIN MANUFACTURING CORP., 6200 W. 60th St.(60638), pg. 726
MCCONNAUGHY STEIN SCHMIDT BROWN, North Pier, 401 E. Illinois St., Ste. 500(60611), pg. 727
JAMES MCHUGH CONSTRUCTION CO., 2222 S. Indiana Ave.(60616), pg. 729
Media Graphics, 427 S. LaSalle St.(60605), pg. 1029
MERCHANT CAPITAL GROUP LTD, 135 S. LaSalle Street Ste. 1030(60603), pg. 739
MESIROW FINANCIAL, 350 N. Clark St.(60610), pg. 741
Metra, Commuter Rail Service Board, 547 W. Jackson(60606), pg. 922
METRON STEEL CORP., 12900 S. Metron Dr.(60633), pg. 744
GERHARDT F. MEYNE CO., 345 N. Canal St.(60606), pg. 746
MICRODOT, INC., 10 S. LaSalle St.(60603), pg. 749
MIDCO INTERNATIONAL INC., 4140 W. Victoria(60646), pg. 751
MIDLAND PAPER CO., 5860 N. Pulaski Rd.(60646), pg. 751
Midwest Division, 121 West Wacker Drive, Ste. 2016(60601), pg. 536
Midwest Equipment Co., 4242 W. 42nd Pl.(60632), pg. 414
MARILYN MIGLIN, INC., 112 E. Oak St.(60611), pg. 752
MILEX OF AMERICA, INC., 4914 N. Lincoln(60625), pg. 753
MILTON INDUSTRIES, INC., 4500 W. Cortland St.(60639), pg. 756
ED MINIAT, INC., 945 W. 38th St.(60609), pg. 757
Modern Healthcare, 740 Rush St.(60611), pg. 295
MONTGOMERY WARD & CO., INC., Montgomery Ward Plaza, 619 W. Chicago Ave.(60671), pg. 767
E. R. MOORE CO., 1810 W. Grace St.(60613), pg. 768
NWS, INC., 3247 S. Kedzie Ave.(60623), pg. 782
FRANK C. NAHSER INC., 10 S. Riverside Plaza(60606), pg. 783
NATIONAL LIVE STOCK & MEAT BOARD, 444 N. Michigan Ave.(60611), pg. 792
National Thermal Insulation, 55 E. Jackson Blvd.(60604), pg. 1107
NATIONWIDE BEEF, INC., 219 N. Green St.(60607), pg. 795
NAYLOR PIPE COMPANY, 1230 E. 92nd St.(60619), pg. 796
Naz-Dar Company, 1087 N. North Branch St.(60622), pg. 1095
NELSON BROTHERS FURNITURE CO., 2750 W. Grand Ave.(60612), pg. 797
JEFFREY NEMETZ & ASSOCIATES, INC., 750 N. Orleans, Ste. 401(60610), pg. 798
New Century Freight Traffic Association, Inc., 600 W. Jackson Blvd.(60606), pg. 712
GUST K. NEWBERG CONSTRUCTION CO., 2040 N. Ashland Ave.(60614), pg. 803
NEWLY WEDS FOODS INC., 4140 W. Fullerton Ave.(60639), pg. 804
NEWSPAPER ADVERTISING SPECIALISTS, INC. (N.A.S.), 333 N. Michigan Ave.(60601), pg. 805
NOBART, INC., 1133 S. Wabash Ave.(60605), pg. 808
Norbran Leasing, 1200 N. North Branch Street(60622), pg. 672
NORTHWESTERN GOLF COMPANY, 4701 N. Ravenswood Ave.(60640), pg. 815
NORTON ASSOCIATES, INC., 203 N. Wabash Ave., Ste. 1220(60601), pg. 815
O'BRYAN BROTHERS INC., 4220 W. Belmont Ave.(60641), pg. 820
OFFICE EQUIPMENT COMPANY OF CHICAGO, 223 W. Lake St.(60606), pg. 821
OLSON RUG COMPANY, 832 S. Central Ave.(60644), pg. 824
ON-COR FROZEN FOODS INC., 1227 W. Fulton(60607), pg. 826
O'NEIL INDUSTRIES INC., 2751 N. Clybourn Ave.(60614), pg. 827
W. E. O'Neil Construction Company, 2751 N. Clybourn Ave.(60614), pg. 827
Open Court Publishing Company, 407 S. Dearborn, Ste. 1300(60605), pg. 227
Options Clearing Corp., 440 S. LaSalle St.(60605), pg. 63
The Original A-1, 401 E. Illinois(60611), pg. 669
ORIX REAL ESTATE EQUITIES, INC., 100 N. Riverside Plaza(60606), pg. 829
OSTARR CORPORATION, 5240 So. Archer Ave.(60632), pg. 831
Oto-Sonic, Inc., 4200 W. Bryn Mawr(60646), pg. 138
R.S. OWENS, 5535 N. Lynch Ave.(60630), pg. 834
PCI Investments Inc., 2739 N. Elston Ave.(60647), pg. 851
PVS Chemicals, Inc., 12260 S. Carondolet(60633), pg. 838
Pacific Wine Co., 2701 S. Western Ave.(60608), pg. 851
PAKULA & COMPANY, 350 N. Orleans, Ste. 1001(60654-1588), pg. 843
Papoulis Greek Taverna, 620 N. State(60610), pg. 669
Paragus, 620 N. State St.(60610), pg. 669
PASCHEN CONTRACTORS, INC., 2739 N. Elston Ave.(60647), pg. 851
PATERNO IMPORTS LIMITED, 2701 S. Western Ave.(60608), pg. 851
PEERLESS CONFECTION COMPANY, 1250 W. Schubert Ave.(60614), pg. 855
Pensions & Investments, 740 Rush St.(60611), pg. 295
THE PEPPER COMPANIES, INC., 643 N. Orleans St.(60610), pg. 859
Peter Straaton, Merchandise Mart(60654), pg. 100
Pie Piper Products, Ltd., 2501 N. Damen(60647), pg. 1151
PLIBRICO CO., 1800 N. Kingsbury St.(60614), pg. 877
Plibrico Sales & Service, Inc., 1800 N. Kingsbury(60614), pg. 877
POLLENEX CORPORATION, 165 N. Canal St., Ste. 1460(60606), pg. 879
Pollenex Corporation, 165 N. Canal(60606), pg. 821
Pool Communications - Chicago, 320 N. Michigan Ave.(60610), pg. 880
PowerForce Company, Inc., 303 E. Ohio St., 25th Fl.(60611), pg. 560
Practice Development Institute, 401 N. Michigan Ave., 433
Process Color Plate, 1200 W. Monroe(60607), pg. 975
PROCTOR & GARDNER ADVERTISING, INC., 111 E. Wacker Dr., Ste. 321(60601), pg. 892
The Pump Room, The Ambassador East, 1301 N. State Parkway(60610), pg. 669
PUTMAN PUBLISHING CO., 301 E. Erie St.(60611), pg. 901
Pyle Inc., 1334 N. Kostner Ave.(60651), pg. 648
QST INDUSTRIES, INC., 231 S. Jefferson(60661), pg. 902
Rand McNally Publishing Group, 444 N. Michigan Ave.(60611), pg. 911
Rand McNally Publishing Group, 150 S. Wacker Dr.(60606), pg. 911
Rand McNally-TDM, Inc., P.O. Box 7600, (60680), pg. 911
RAPID MOUNTING & FINISHING CO., 4300 W. 47th St.(60632-4476), pg. 913
READY METAL MANUFACTURING COMPANY, 4500 W. 47th St.(60632), pg. 916
Real Estate Auctions, Inc., 333 W. Wacker Dr., Ste. 450(60606), pg. 470
REFCO GROUP LTD., 111 W. Jackson(60604), pg. 921
Refco Inc., 111 W. Jackson(60604), pg. 921
REGIONAL TRANSPORTATION AUTHORITY (RTA), One N. Dearborn St., Ste. 1100(60602), pg. 922
THE RELIABLE CORP., 1001 W. Van Buren St.(60607), pg. 924
RELIANCE ELEVATOR COMPANY, 1101 W. Adams St.(60607), pg. 925
Renaissance Center Management Co., 100 N. Riverside Plaza(60606), pg. 829
RESTONIC CORPORATION, 101 N. Wacker(60606), pg. 929
REVERE ELECTRIC SUPPLY CO., 2501 W. Washington Blvd.(60612), pg. 930
RICHCO PLASTICS COMPANY, 5825 N. Tripp Ave.(60646), pg. 933
Hal Riney & Partners, Inc., 54 W. Hubbard(60611), pg. 935
Roberts & Schaefer Co., 120 S. Riverside Plaza(60606), pg. 609
ROBINSON & MAITES, INC., 35 E. Wacker Dr., Ste. 200(60601), pg. 940
Arthur Rubloff & Co. of Florida, 100 N. Riverside Plaza(60606), pg. 829
Rubloff Capital Inc., 100 N. Riverside Plaza(60606), pg. 829
Rubloff Capital Investments Inc., 100 N. Riverside Plaza(60606), pg. 829
Rubloff-Colonial Oaks, Inc., 100 N. Riverside Plaza(60606), pg. 829
Rubloff Corporate Services, Inc., 100 N. Riverside Plaza(60606), pg. 829
Ruder, Finn, Inc., 444 N. Michigan Ave.(60611), pg. 954
Ruxton Group, 11 E. Illinois(60611), pg. 246
RYSER BROTHERS INC., 3525 W. Potomac(60651), pg. 958
S & C ELECTRIC COMPANY, 6601 N. Ridge Blvd.(60626-3997), pg. 958
SAS Institute, Inc., Two Prudential Plaza, 180 N. Stetson Ave., 52nd Fl.(60601), pg. 959
SK HAND TOOL CORP., 3535 W. 47th St.(60632), pg. 963
SPSS INC., 444 N. Michigan Ave.(60611), pg. 964
SAHARA COAL CO., 3 First National Plaza, Ste. 2000(60602), pg. 966
SAN JOSE & ASSOCIATES, 625 N. Michigan Ave., Ste. 1601(60611-3109), pg. 969
SARGENT & LUNDY, 55 E. Monroe St.(60603), pg. 971
Savoy Bar and Grill, One Financial Plaza, 44 So. LaSalle, 2nd Fl.(60605), pg. 669
SAXON PAINT & HOME CARE CENTERS INC., 3840 W. Fullerton Ave., (60647), pg. 973
SCHNADIG CORPORATION, 4820 W. Belmont Ave.(60641), pg. 977
SCHULZE & BURCH BISCUIT COMPANY, 1133 W. 35th St.(60609), pg. 979
SCHUMACHER ELECTRIC CORPORATION, 7474 N. Rogers Ave.(60626), pg. 979
SCHWINN BICYCLE COMPANY, 217 N. Jefferson St.(60661), pg. 981
Scoozi, 410 W. Huron(60610), pg. 669
Sealtron Corporation, 2615 N. Paulina St.(60614), pg. 1107
SERVICE WEB OFFSET CORPORATION, 2500 S. Dearborn St.(60616), pg. 992
Shaw's Crab House/Chicago, 21 E. Hubbard(60610), pg. 669
Shoemart Express, 1001 S. Clinton(60607), pg. 243
Siegle's Home & Building Centers, 900 W. North Ave.(60622), pg. 987
SILVESTRI CORP., 2720 N. Paulina St.(60614), pg. 1005
SMITH, BADOFSKY & RAFFEL, INC. ADVERTISING, 325 W. Huron St.(60610), pg. 1011
PETER W. SMITH & COMPANY, INC., 400 N. Michigan Ave., Ste. 520(60611), pg. 1011
SOFT SHEEN PRODUCTS, INC., 1000 E. 87th St.(60619), pg. 1016
SOMMER & MACA INDUSTRIES, INC., 5501 W. Ogden Ave.(60650), pg. 1017
SOUTHSIDE FORD TRUCK SALES INC., 810 W. Pershing Rd.(60609), pg. 1023
Special Instruments, 4201 W. Victoria(60646), pg. 138
SPURGEON MERCANTILE COMPANY, 822 W. Washington Blvd.(60607), pg. 1034
STANDARD MANIFOLD COMPANY, INC., 4020 N. Tripp Ave.(60641), pg. 1037
THE STIFFEL COMPANY, 700 N. Kingsbury(60610), pg. 1049
STOCK YARDS PACKING CO., INC., 340 N. Oakley Blvd.(60612), pg. 1049
Strombecker Chemtoy Division, 600 North Pulaski Rd.(60624), pg. 1054
STROMBECKER CORPORATION, 600 N. Pulaski Rd.(60624), pg. 1054
THE STURM COMMUNICATIONS GROUP, INC., 737 N. Michigan Ave., Ste. 1400(60611), pg. 1055
Sula Supply, 837 N. California(60622), pg. 1151
SUPERIOR GRAPHITE COMPANY, 120 S. Riverside Plaza(60606), pg. 1063
Supreme Beauty Products, 820 S. Michigan Ave.(60605), pg. 599
SWEETHEART CUP CO., INC., 7575 S. Kostner Ave.(60652), pg. 1067
TTX CO., 101 N. Wacker Dr.(60606), pg. 1075
TAB CHEMICALS, INC., 4801 S. Austin(60638), pg. 1075
TALK-A-PHONE CO., 5013 N. Kedzie Ave.(60625), pg. 1077
TARGETCOM, INC., The North Pier Terminal, 401 E. Illinois, Ste. 525(60611), pg. 1079
TASSANI COMMUNICATIONS, 515 N. State St.(60610-4320), pg. 1080
Telco Capital Corp., 737 N. Michigan, Ste. 1200(60611), pg. 674
Thompson-Starrett Construction Company, Inc., 120 S. Riverside Plaza(60606), pg. 609
THRALL ENTERPRISES, INC., 181 W. Madison St., Fl. 47(60602), pg. 1095
THYBONY WALL COVERINGS CO., 3720 N. Kedzie Ave.(60618), pg. 1096
Tool & Engineering Co., 900 W. 18th St.(60608), pg. 400
Tootsietoy Division, 600 No. Pulaski Rd.(60624), pg. 1054
Tootsietoy Preschool Products Div., 600 N. Pulaski(60624), pg. 1054
TOPCOR FINANCIAL CORPORATION, 1555 W. 44th St.(60609), pg. 1101
TORCO OIL, 111 E. Wacker Dr., Ste. 1300, (60601), pg. 1102
Torino Baking Co., 318 E. Kensington Ave.(60628), pg. 470
Toulin Inc., 625 N. Michigan(60611), pg. 441
Trailmobile, 200 E. Randolph(60601), pg. 900
Trans Union Corp., 111 W. Jackson(60604), pg. 712
TRANSCO INC., 55 E. Jackson Blvd.(60604), pg. 1106
Transco Products Inc., 55 E. Jackson Blvd.(60604), pg. 1107
Transco Realty Inc., 55 E. Jackson Blvd.(60604), pg. 1107
TRANSILWRAP COMPANY, INC., 2828 N. Paulina St., Ste. 100(60657-4098), pg. 1107
TREASURE ISLAND FOODMARTS INC., 3460 N. Broadway(60657), pg. 1109
Tri-State Dies, Inc., 913 W. 119th St.(60643), pg. 762
TRITON INDUSTRIES, INC., 1020 N. Kolmar Ave.(60651), pg. 1114
Tucci Benucch, 900 Michigan N.(60611), pg. 669
Tucci Milan, 6 W. Hubbard(60610), pg. 669
TURTLE WAX, INC., 5655 W. 73rd St.(60638), pg. 1120
USA-GLAS, Inc., 1880 W. Fullerton Ave.(60614), pg. 464
USA Network, 401 No. Michigan Ave.(60611), pg. 1124
ULTIMO LTD., 114 E. Oak St.(60611), pg. 1125
Un Grand Cafe', 2300 Lincoln Park West(60614), pg. 669
Union Tank Car Company, 111 W. Jackson(60604), pg. 712
United Exposition Service Company, 1555 W. 44th St.(60609), pg. 1102
U.S. Auto Glass Centers, Inc., 2 N. LaSalle St., Ste. 2500(60602-3876), pg. 464
U.S. FOOD PRODUCTS, INC., 1200 N. Ashland, Rm. 610(60622), pg. 1136
U.S. Yellow Pages, 401 E. Illinois St., Ste. 430(60611), pg. 1180
UNIVERSAL OVERALL COMPANY, 1060 W. Van Buren St.(60607), pg. 1139
UPPCO, INC., 5610 W. Bloomingdale(60639), pg. 1139
VIP Engineered Products, Inc., 5501 W. Grand Ave.(60639), pg. 525
VANCE INDUSTRIES, INC., 7401 W. Wilson Ave.(60656), pg. 1144
VeloBind, Inc., One E. Erie St.(60611), pg. 657
Vienna Beef, Ltd., 2501 N. Damen(60647), pg. 1151
VIENNA SAUSAGE MFG. CO., 2501 N. Damen(60647), pg. 1151
VIKING GRAPHICS, 4027 N. Kedzie Ave.(60618), pg. 1151
VINCENT FOOD INDUSTRIES, INC., 135 S. LaSalle St.(60603), pg. 1152

VITA FOOD PRODUCTS, INC., 2222 W. Lake St.(60612), pg. 1153
C.J. VITNER & CO., INC., 4202 W. 45th St.(60632), pg. 1153
THE JOHN VOLK COMPANY, 676 St. Clair(60611), pg. 1154
WCKG, Inc., 150 N. Michigan Ave., Ste. 1040(60601), pg. 292
WCTU Railway Company, 111 W. Jackson Blvd.(60604), pg. 712
WEN PRODUCTS, INC., 5810 Northwest Hwy.(60631), pg. 1156
WJPC Radio Station, 820 S. Michigan Ave(60605), pg. 599
WLNR Radio Station, 820 S. Michigan Ave.(60605), pg. 599
WTTW (CHANNEL 11), 5400 N. St. Louis(60625), pg. 1156
Wabash Fibre Box Co.-Chicago Plant, 6850 W. 62nd St.(60638), pg. 1183
WALSH CONSTRUCTION CO. OF ILLINOIS, 292 W. Adam(60607), pg. 1161
WARDROP MURTAUGH TEMPLE, 333 N. Michigan Ave.(60601), pg. 1163
WARNER CANDY COMPANY, INC., 2954 W. Lawrence Ave.(60625), pg. 1164
The Weather Channel, Inc.-Chicago Sales Office, 435 N. Michigan Ave.(60611), pg. 654
WEBER COHN & RILEY, INC., 444 N. Michigan Ave.(60611), pg. 1171
WEISER MINKUS WALEK COMMUNICATIONS, INC., 160 N. Wacker Dr.(60606), pg. 1174
Western International Media Corporation, 401 E. Illinois St., Ste. 430(60611), pg. 1180
WICKER PARK L.P., 2300 Wabansia Ave.(60647), pg. 1188
Wilcox & Follett Co., 1000 W. Washington Blvd.(60607), pg. 422
Williams Drugs Distributors, 233 E. Erie St.(60611), pg. 553
Wilson Steel & Wire, 4840 S. Western Ave.(60609), pg. 691
Woodbridge Sanitary Pottery Corp., 4656 W. Touhy Ave.(60646), pg. 454
WOODWORK CORPORATION OF AMERICA, 1432 W. 21st St.(60608), pg. 1201
WORLD'S FINEST CHOCOLATE, INC., 4801 S. Lawndale Ave.(60632), pg. 1203
Young & Rubicam Chicago, 1 S. Wacker Dr., Ste. 1800(60606), pg. 1211
ZACK COMPANY, 4600 W. 12th Place(60650), pg. 1215
ZECHMAN & ASSOCIATES ADV. INC., 333 N. Michigan Ave., Ste. 3300(60601), pg. 1216

Chicago Heights

CHICAGO HEIGHTS STEEL, 211 E. Main(60411), pg. 245
First National Bank in Chicago Heights, 100 First National Plaza(60411), pg. 483
Personal Finance Co., Box 708, First Natl. Plaza, (60411), pg. 758
Plastic Suppliers Inc., 3330 Holman Ave.(60411), pg. 876
Star Publications, 1526 Otto Blvd.(60411), pg. 18
Thrall Car Mfg. Co., 2541 State St.(60411-0218), pg. 350
Vacudyne Inc., 375 E. Joe Orr Rd.(60411), pg. 45

Cicero

AMD INDUSTRIES INC., 4620 W. 19th St.(60650), pg. 5
ARA Leisure Services, Hawthorne Race Course, 3501 Laramie(60650), pg. 6
BRAD FOOTE GEAR WORKS, INC., 1309 S. Cicero Ave.(60650), pg. 169
CHICAGO EXTRUDED METALS CO., 1601 S. 54th Ave.(60650), pg. 245
Danly Die Set Division, 2115 S. 54th Ave.(60650), pg. 275
Let Them Eat Cake, 4900 W. 25th(60650), pg. 1195
Manufacturers' Junction Railroad Company, 2335 S. Cicero Ave.(60650-2451), pg. 246
Simkins Carton Div.-Chicago, 5701 W. Ogden Ave.(60650), pg. 1005

Clinton

Action Clinton, Route 10 E., P.O. Box 111(61727), pg. 15

Collinsville

BRIDAL ORIGINALS, INC., 1700 St. Louis Rd.(62234), pg. 175

Colusa

COLUSA ELEVATOR CO., P.O. Box 26, (62329), pg. 267

Countryside

FLEETWOOD SYSTEMS, INC., 621 E. Plainfield Rd.(60525), pg. 417
HOLLYMATIC CORPORATION, 600 E. Plainfield Rd.(60525), pg. 539
SOKOL & COMPANY, 5315 Dansher Rd.(60525), pg. 1016

Crystal Lake

CURRAN CONTRACTING CO., 7502 S. Main St.(60014), pg. 305
Follett Library Book Co., 4506 Northwest Hwy.(60014), pg. 422
Mohawk Tools, P.O. Box 9000, One Precision Plaza(60039-9000), pg. 885
PRECISION TWIST DRILL CO., One Precision Plaza(60039-9000), pg. 885
TSC Carbide Co., P.O. Box 9000, One Precision Plaza(60014), pg. 885
Triumph Twist Drill Co., One Precision Plaza, Box 9000(60039-9000), pg. 885

Danville

CURT BULLOCK BUILDERS, INC., 720 S. Gilbert St.(61832), pg. 188
DSI/TMP Worldwide, P.O. Box 1067(61834-1067), pg. 1074
Dan River Cotton Co., Inc., P.O. Box 1568, 2291 Memorial Dr.(61834), pg. 313
Golden Sun Feeds, Inc., (61832), pg. 467
Hurletron Inc., 1938 E. Fairchild St.(61834), pg. 45

De Kalb

Del Monte Corp., 2009 Maplewood Ave., P.O. Box 747(60115), pg. 325
Nehring Electrical Works Company, 813 E. Locust St.(60115), pg. 261

Decatur

BLACK & CO., 1717 E. Garfield Ave.(62526), pg. 154
Burks Prosser/Enpo Industries, Inc., 1434 N. 22nd St.(62526), pg. 507
JONES & THOMAS, INC., 300 W. Main St.(62522), pg. 604
Telecommunication Products Div., 800 E. Garfield(62521), pg. 389

Deerfield

APPLIED INDUSTRIAL MATERIALS CORPORATION, 1 Parkway North, Ste. 400(60015), pg. 79
Ed Debevic's, 660 Lake Cook Rd.(60015), pg. 669
DONLEN CORP., 500 Lake Cook Rd.(60015), pg. 345
ERM-North Central, Inc., 102 Wilmot Rd., Ste. 300(60015), pg. 360
EDELMANN DIV. OF STANT, INC., 111 Deer Lake Rd., Ste. 110(60015), pg. 368
Ed's Deerfield, 660 Lake Cook Rd.(60015), pg. 669
FLODSTROM CONSTRUCTION CO., 707 Lake Cook Rd.(60015), pg. 419
INGRID-SEVKO, INC., 1419 Lake Cook Rd., Ste. 210(60015), pg. 569
J & M Advertising, 400 Lake Cook Road(60015), pg. 780
JORDAN INDUSTRIES, INC., 1751 Lake Cook Rd., Ste. 550(60015), pg. 604
KLEINSCHMIDT INC., 450 Lake-Cook Rd.(60015-4973), pg. 635
M M I COMPANIES, INC., 540 Lake Cook Rd.(60015), pg. 692
MERIDIAN TECHNOLOGY LEASING SERVICES, 570 Lake Cook Rd.(60015), pg. 740
MY OWN MEALS, INC., 400 Lake Cook Rd.(60015), pg. 779
Shaw's Deerfield, 660 Lake Cook Rd.(60015), pg. 669

Des Plaines

BAKE-LINE PRODUCTS, INC., One Bake-Line Plaza(60016), pg. 114
Bradley Printing Company, 2170 S. Mannheim Rd.(60018), pg. 478
BRESLER'S INDUSTRIES, INC., 999 E. Touhy Ave., Ste. 333(60018), pg. 174
C-LINE PRODUCTS, INC., 1530 Birchwood Ave.(60018), pg. 198
CRL, INC., 2200 E. Devon Ave.(60018), pg. 203
THE CHICAGO FAUCET CO., 2100 S. Clearwater Dr.(60018-5999), pg. 245
CLOUD CORPORATION, 424 Howard Ave.(60018), pg. 256
DIETZGEN CORPORATION, 250 Wille Rd.(60018), pg. 337
DISTRIBUTION AMERICA, 2700 River Rd.(60018), pg. 340
DOALL COMPANY, 254 N. Laurel(60016), pg. 341
DRY STORAGE CORPORATION, 1750 So. Wolf Rd.(60018), pg. 350
FAMTEC INTERNATIONAL, INC., 509 N. Third Ave.(60016), pg. 398
FRANK CONSOLIDATED ENTERPRISES INC., 666 Garland Place(60016), pg. 428
GERRARD AND COMPANY, 400 E. Touhy Ave.(60018-2684), pg. 454
GRAPHISPHERE HOLDING COMPANY, 2170 So. Mannheim Rd.(60018), pg. 478
International Metals & Machines, Inc., 2200 E. Devon Ave.(60018), pg. 203
JUSTRITE MANUFACTURING COMPANY, 2454 Dempster St.(60016), pg. 610
LA MARCHE MFG. CO., 106 Bradrock Dr.(60018), pg. 649
Larry's Industries, Inc., 999 E. Touhy Ave.(60018), pg. 174
LITTELFUSE, INC., 800 E. Northwest Hwy.(60016), pg. 678
Stan Merritt Inc./Advertising, 2400 E. Devon Ave.(60018), pg. 741
Meyer Material Company, 580 Wolf Rd.(60017), pg. 711
Midwest Litho Arts, 125 E. Oakton(60018), pg. 478
National Lamination Co., 555 Santa Rosa Dr.(60010), pg. 1078
NUTRITION WORLD, 155 W. Old Higgins Rd.(60018), pg. 818
Paper Express, 1605 Winthrop Ave.(60018), pg. 478
Pro*Portion Industries, Inc., 999 E. Touhy Ave.(60018), pg. 174
J. H. ROBERTS INDUSTRIES INC., 3158 Des Plaines Ave., Ste. 223(60018), pg. 938
SCHAWK, INC., 1695 River Rd.(60018), pg. 974
Schawkgraphics, 1600 E. Sherwin Ave.(60018), pg. 975
SERTA, INC., 2800 River Rd.(60018), pg. 991
SpeedFam Corporation, 509 N. 3rd Ave.(60016), pg. 398
THE SPRING AIR COMPANY, 2980 River Rd.(60018), pg. 1032
Symons Corporation, 200 E. Touhy Ave.(60018), pg. 1069
TASH, INC., 450 E. Jarvis Ave.(60018), pg. 1080

Dixon

Borg-Warner Automotive Control Systems-Dixon, 1700 Franklin Grove Rd.(61021), pg. 166
RAYNOR GARAGE DOOR COMPANY, E. River Rd.(61021), pg. 915

Downers Grove

THE FLEETWOOD COMPANY, 1500 Brook Dr.(60515), pg. 417
GNWC WIRE, CABLE & NETWORK PRODUCERS, 1401 Brook Drive(60515), pg. 440
Griffin Pipe Products Co., 1400 Opus Pl., Ste. 700(60515), pg. 69
LOVEJOY INC., 2655 Wisconsin Ave.(60515-4299), pg. 685
MAGNETROL INTERNATIONAL, 5300 Belmont Rd.(60515), pg. 701
May & Speh Direct, 1501 Opus Place(60515), pg. 724
MAY & SPEH, INC., 1501 Opus Place(60515), pg. 724
JOHN M. SMYTH CO., 1013 Butterfield Rd.(60515), pg. 1014
Trade Wind Tours, 1100 31st St.(60515), pg. 413
Tricon Electromechanical Plant, 5402 Janes Ave.(60515), pg. 1113
TRICON INDUSTRIES, INC., 2325 Wisconsin Ave.(60515), pg. 1113

Dundee

HAEGER INDUSTRIES, INC., 7 Maiden Lane(60118), pg. 499
Haeger Potteries, Inc., 7 Maiden Lane(60118), pg. 499
MILK SPECIALTIES COMPANY, P.O. Box 278(60118), pg. 753

DuQuoin

CHARMGLOW INDUSTRIES, INC., 500 South Madison(62832), pg. 240

East Dubuque

CRESCENT ELECTRIC SUPPLY CO., Dunleith Drive(61025), pg. 298

East Moline

EAST MOLINE METAL PRODUCTS COMPANY, 1201 7th St.(61244), pg. 363

East Peoria

fp CameoColor, Inc., 700 Pinecrest Dr.(61611), pg. 417

East Saint Louis

Aratex Services, 2010 Martin Luther King Dr.(62205), pg. 6

Edwardsville

CASSENS TRANSPORT COMPANY, 145 N. Kansas(62025), pg. 228
Edwardsville Intelligencer, 117 N. Second St.(62025), pg. 524
FLORISTS' MUTUAL INSURANCE CO., 500 St. Louis St.(62025), pg. 421

Effingham

JOHN BOOS & COMPANY, 315 S. 1st St.(62401), pg. 165
EFFINGHAM-CLAY SERVICE CO., 410 S. Willow(62401), pg. 371
LWMCK CORPORATION, 2301 S. Banker St.(62401), pg. 648
National Building Systems, 2301 S. Banker(62401), pg. 648
PETTY COMPANY, INC., P.O. Box 250, (62401), pg. 866

Elgin

American Antenna Corp, 1500 Executive Dr.(60120), pg. 216
ARTISTIC CARTON COMPANY, 1975 Big Timber Rd.(60123), pg. 87
BUTERA FINER FOODS INC., 1 Clock Tower Plaza(60120), pg. 196
CAPSONIC GROUP, INC., 460 S. Second St.(60123), pg. 216
DAVID C. COOK PUBLISHING CO., 850 N. Grove Ave.(60120), pg. 282
Daily Courier-News, 300 Lake St.(60120), pg. 284
W.J. DENNIS CO., 1111 Davis Rd.(60123-1388), pg. 329
DISPLAY TECHNOLOGIES, INC., 1355 Holmes Rd.(60123), pg. 339
GRAYLINE HOUSEWARES, 1616 Berkley St.(60123), pg. 480
GROMER SUPER MARKETS, INC., 585 N. McLean Blvd.(60123), pg. 489
Harig Grinders, 1875 Big Timber Rd.(60123), pg. 175
LEEWARDS CREATIVE CRAFTS, INC., 1200 St. Charles St.(60120), pg. 666
MASTER MOLDED PRODUCTS CORPORATION, 1000 Davis Rd.(60123), pg. 720
Pet Ag Inc., 30 W. 432 Route 20(60120), pg. 753
SEIGLE'S HOME & BUILDING CENTERS, 1331 Davis Rd.(60123), pg. 987
SIMPSON ELECTRIC CO., 853 Dundee Ave.(60120), pg. 1007

Elk Grove Village

ADVANCE MECHANICAL SYSTEMS, INC., 2001 Estes(60007), pg. 19
ANSCO PHOTO-OPTICAL PRODUCTS CORP., 1801 Touhy Ave.(60007), pg. 76
APPLE VACATIONS WEST INC., 25 Northwest Point Blvd.(60007), pg. 79
CLARK FOODSERVICE, INC., 950 Arthur Ave.(60007), pg. 252
DENA CORPORATION, 850 Nicholas Blvd.(60007), pg. 329
DRAFTING GRAPHICS, INC., 1250 Pratt Blvd.(60007), pg. 348
F J M CORPORATION, 2150 Touhy Ave.(60007), pg. 394
FIELD CONTAINER COMPANY, L.P., 1500 Nicholas Blvd.(60007), pg. 409
Forest Atwood Paper Company, 1150 Lively Blvd.(60007), pg. 1157
GLOBE-AMERADA GLASS COMPANY, 2001 Greenleaf Ave.(60007), pg. 463

Harwick Chemical Corp., 800 Estes Ave.(60007), pg. 515
Iroquois Popcorn, 1370 Lively Blvd.(6007), pg. 156
L. KARP & SONS, INC., 1301 Estes Ave.(60007), pg. 617
KUKLA PRESS, INC., 855 Morse Ave.(60007), pg. 646
LITTLE LADY FOODS, INC., 2323 Pratt Blvd.(60007), pg. 679
Maxum Exterior Coatings, 2250 Arthur Ave.(60007), pg. 886
A. W. MENDENHALL CO., INC., 2301 Lunt Ave.(60007), pg. 739
National Material Limited Partnership, 1965 Pratt Blvd.(60007), pg. 1078
Niagara Envelope Co. of Illinois, 2001 W. Arthur St.(60007), pg. 806
PETERSEN ALUMINUM CORPORATION, 955 Estes Ave.(60007), pg. 864
Portage Tool Company, 2045 Pratt Blvd.(60007), pg. 1086
PREMIER COATINGS, INC., 2250 Arthur Ave.(60007), pg. 886
RAINSOFT WATER CONDITIONING CO., 2080 E. Lunt Ave.(60007), pg. 910
ROLLEX CORPORATION, 2001 Lunt Ave.(60007), pg. 944
Roundy's Wayco Foods, 1925 Busse Rd.(60007), pg. 952
Scrap Corporation of America, 1965 Pratt Blvd.(60007), pg. 1078
SEKO-AIR FREIGHT, 790 Busse Road(60007), pg. 988
STEINER ELECTRIC CO., 1250 Touhy Ave.(60007), pg. 1045
SUN PROCESS CONVERTING COMPANY, 505 Bonnie Lane(60007), pg. 1059
TANG INDUSTRIES INC., 1965 Pratt Blvd.(60007), pg. 1078
J.J. Tourek Co., 1800 Touhy Ave.(60007), pg. 1120
NELSON WESTERBERG, INC., 1500 Arthur Ave., Ste. 200 W(60007), pg. 1178

Elmhurst

The Chamberlain Group, Inc., 845 Larch Ave.(60126), pg. 350
Chamberlain Manufacturing Corp., 845 Larch Ave.(60126), pg. 350
DUCHOSSOIS INDUSTRIES, INC., 845 Larch Ave.(60126), pg. 350
Follett College Stores Corp., 400 W. Grand(60126), pg. 422
Illinios Auto Electric Midwest Engine Warehouse Div., 515 Roman Rd.(60126), pg. 562
ILLINOIS AUTO ELECTRIC CO., 656 County Line Rd.(60126), pg. 562
MCMASTER CARR SUPPLY CO. INC., 600 County Line(60126), pg. 731
SEMBLEX CORPORATION, 199 W. Diversey(60126), pg. 989
WHITE HEN PANTRY, INC., 660 Industrial Dr.(60126), pg. 1185

Evanston

Bell & Howell Information Systems Division, 2231 W. Howard(60202), pg. 135
CENTURY PUBLISHING COMPANY, 990 Grove St.(60201), pg. 235
DocuMail Systems Division, 2300 Brummel Pl.(60202), pg. 135
Evanston Bank, 603 Main St.(60202), pg. 483
Industrial Bookstore, 1633 Central St.(60201), pg. 705
Inside Sports, Inc., 990 Grove St.(60201), pg. 235
MANUFACTURERS' NEWS, INC., 1633 Central St.(60201), pg. 705
MCDOUGAL, LITTELL & COMPANY, 1560 Sherman Ave.(60201), pg. 728
PELOUZE SCALE CO., 2120 Greenwood(60201), pg. 856
ROBINSON BUS SERVICE, 1528 Emerson St.(60201), pg. 939
SHURE BROTHERS INCORPORATED, 222 Hartrey Ave.(60202-3696), pg. 1001
T C MANUFACTURING COMPANY, INC., 1527 Lyons St.(60204), pg. 1072
Tape Coat Division, 1527 Lyon St.(60204), pg. 1072
World Publishing Company, 990 Grove St.(60201), pg. 235

Fairfield

Airtex Products, 407 W. Main St.(62837), pg. 1123

Fairview Heights

Franklin Coal, 50 Jerome Lane(62208), pg. 1218
Old Ben Coal Co., 50 Jerome Lane(62208), pg. 1218
ZIEGLER COAL HOLDING CO., 50 Jerome Lane(62208), pg. 1218

Forest Park

Arrow Sintered Products, 7650 Industrial Dr.(60130), pg. 85
NOMA-INTERNATIONAL, INC., 7400 W. Industrial Dr.(60130), pg. 808

Frankfort

Moulton Cutting Co., 965 So. Lambrecht Rd.(60423), pg. 939

Franklin Park

AAllied Die Casting Mfg., Inc., 3021 Cullerton Dr.(60131), pg. 906
Alkco Lighting Company, 11500 W. Melrose Ave.(60131), pg. 588
BADGER AIR BRUSH COMPANY, 9128 W. Belmont Ave.(60131), pg. 113
BRUNNER & LAY, INC., 9300 King(60131), pg. 184
CENTRAL GROCERS CO-OP, 3701 N. Centrella St.(60131), pg. 232
Conway Import Co. Inc., 11051 W. Addison St.(60131), pg. 281
DIVANE BROS. ELECTRIC CO., 2424 N. 25th Ave.(60131), pg. 340
DUO-FAST CORPORATION, 3702 River Rd.(60131), pg. 354
EVERFRESH BEVERAGES INC., 3333 N. Mt. Prospect Rd.(60131), pg. 391
FISHER PEN COMPANY, 9240 W. Belmont(60131), pg. 415
THE GREAT FRAME UP SYSTEMS, INC., 9335 Belmont Ave.(60131), pg. 480
IFP Hydraulics Inc., 3412 No. River Road(60131), pg. 559
Kilsby-Roberts/Chicago, 2401 25th Ave.(60131), pg. 606
Magna-Pow'r Inc., 3412 N. River Road(60131), pg. 559
NELSEN STEEL & WIRE CO., 9400 W. Belmont Ave.(60131), pg. 797
The Producto Machine Co., 2950 Hart Dr., P.O. Box 366(60131), pg. 893
Quality Lighting, Inc., 11530 Melrose Ave.(60131), pg. 588
RCM INDUSTRIES, 3021 Cullerton Dr.(60131), pg. 906
Reliable Power Products, 11411 Addison St.(60131), pg. 697
SLOAN VALVE COMPANY, 10500 Seymour Ave.(60131), pg. 1010
Water Control International Inc., 10500 Seymour Ave.(60131), pg. 1010

Freeburg

E.M. WIEGMANN & COMPANY, INC., 501 Douglas(62243), pg. 1188

Geneva

Burgess-Norton Mfg. Co., 737 Peyton St.(60134), pg. 69
MINER ENTERPRISES INC., 1200 E. State St.(60134), pg. 756

Gibson City

M&W GEAR COMPANY, 1020 S. Sangamon Ave.(60936), pg. 690

Glen Ellyn

American Selfcare Corporation, 800 Roosevelt Rd., Blag. E., Ste. 200(60137), pg. 61
Western Technical Div., 800 Roosevelt Rd., Ste. 310, Bldg. B(60137), pg. 1182

Glendale Heights

CHAMPION BUSINESS FORMS, 1966 Quincy(60139), pg. 238
REMCOR PRODUCTS CO., 500 Regency Dr.(60139), pg. 926

Glenview

Alimak Elevator Company, 2101 John's Court(60025), pg. 34
Glenview State Bank, 800 Waukegan Rd.(60025), pg. 305
MARCH MANUFACTURING INC., 1819 Pickwick Ave.(60025), pg. 706

Glenwood

RIVERDALE CHEMICAL CO., 425 W. 194th St.(60425-1584), pg. 937

Goodfield

DMI, INC., Rte. 150 E.(61742), pg. 309

Granite City

National Steel, Granite City Div., 20th & State Sts.(62040), pg. 794
Taracorp Industries, Inc., 16th & Cleveland Blvd.(62040), pg. 1078
Terminal Railroad Association of St. Louis, 2016 Madison Ave.(62040), pg. 76

Grant Park

Ivex Packaging Corporation-Engineering Group, P.O. Box 399, 221 E. Greenwood(60940), pg. 583
Ivex Packaging Corporation-Floral and Nursery Products, P.O. Box 518, 221 E. Greenwood(60940), pg. 583
Ivex Packaging Corporation-Grant Park, P.O. Box G, 304 North E. Main St.(60940), pg. 583

Gurnee

ALRA LABORATORIES, INC., 3850 Clearview Ct.(60031), pg. 44
JOSEPH J. HENDERSON & SON, INC., 4288 Grand Ave.(60031), pg. 529
PARIS PRESENTS, 3800 Swanson Ct.(60031), pg. 848
PAYSON CASTERS, INC., 2323 Delaney Rd.(60031), pg. 853

Hartford

Clark Oil & Refining Corporation--Wood River Refinery, P.O. Box 87, (62048), pg. 253
Hartford-Wood River Terminal, Piasa Lane & Hwy. 3(62048), pg. 869
PIASA MOTOR FUELS INC., Piasa Lane & Hwy. 3(62048), pg. 869
Piasa Oil Transport Inc., Piasa Lane at Hwy. 3(62048), pg. 869

Harvard

ATLAS POWER EQUIPMENT COMPANY, 201 E. Brink(60033), pg. 96
Big Foot Cattle Co., 11511 Rte. 14(60033), pg. 1151
General Power Equipment Co., 201 E. Brink St.(60033), pg. 288
Wheeler Manufacturing Co., 201 E. Brink(60033), pg. 288

Harvey

WHITING CORPORATION, 15700 Lathrop Ave.(60426), pg. 1187

Harwood Heights

F C L GRAPHICS, 4600 N. Olcott(60656), pg. 394
QUALITY CONTROL CORPORATION, 7315 W. Wilson Ave.(60656), pg. 903
REPUBLIC INDUSTRIES, INC., 7350 W. Wilson Ave.(60656), pg. 928

Hazel Crest

MI-JACK PRODUCTS, INC., 3111 W. 167th St.(60429), pg. 746

Highland

BASLER ELECTRIC COMPANY, Rte. 143(62249), pg. 125

Highland Park

SCC HOLDING CO., 1700 Old Deerfield Rd.(60035), pg. 961
Solo Cup Company, 1700 Old Deerfield Road(60035), pg. 961
P.R. Solo Cup, Inc., 1700 Old Deerfield Rd.(60035), pg. 961

Hillsboro

Eagle Zinc Co., P.O. Box 340, Rural Rte. 1(62049), pg. 335

Hillside

Bekins Van Lines Co., 330 S. Mannheim Rd.(60162), pg. 133
COMMERCIAL LIGHT COMPANY, 245 Fence Lane(60162-6006), pg. 268
ELECTRICAL INSULATION SUPPLIERS, 300 N. Mannheim Rd.(60162), pg. 374
Ivex Packaging Corporation-Hillside, 50 S. Mannheim Rd.(60172), pg. 583
Levy Home Entertainment, 4201 N. Raymond Dr.(60102), pg. 672

Hinsdale

AMLINGS FLOWERLAND, 540 W. Ogden Ave.(60521), pg. 67
Amlings Landscape Co., 540 W. Ogden Ave.(60521), pg. 67
K & R DELIVERY, INC., 15 W. 460 Frontrage Rd.(60521), pg. 610
K & R Rentals, Inc., 15 W. 460 Frontrage Rd.(60521), pg. 610
MUNSEN'S DISCOVERY ENTERPRISES, 120 E. Ogden Ave.(60521), pg. 776
Munsen's Discovery Travel, 120 E. Ogden Ave.(60521), pg. 776
TUTHILL CORPORATION, 908 N. Elm St.(60521), pg. 1120

Hodgkins

CERTIFIED GROCERS MIDWEST, INC., One Certified Dr.(60525-4894), pg. 236

Hoffman Estates

DATRON INCORPORATED, a, 2300 N. Barrington Rd., Ste. 600(60195), pg. 316
Teko Realty Corporation, 575 W. Central Rd.(60195), pg. 1093
THOMAS ENGINEERING INC., 575 W. Central Rd.(60195), pg. 1093

Homewood

AMERICAN TECHNICAL PUBLISHERS, INC., 1155 W. 175th St.(60430), pg. 63
Bank of Homewood, 2034 Ridge Rd.(60430), pg. 481
CARL BUDDIG & COMPANY, 950 W. 175th St.(60430), pg. 186
Community Bank of Homewood-Flossmoor, 18600 Dixie Hwy.(60430), pg. 481
The Edward Gray Corp., 1 Graycor Dr.(60430), pg. 480
Gray International, 1 Graycor Dr.(60430), pg. 480
GRAYCOR, INC., One Graycor Dr.(60430), pg. 479
GREAT LAKES FINANCIAL RESOURCES, INC., 18600 S. Dixie Hwy.(60430), pg. 481
Inland Construction Company, 1 Graycor Dr.(60430), pg. 480

Huntley

Robinson Industries, 11320 E. Main St., P.O. Box 68(60142), pg. 975

Ipava

BADER & CO., P.O. Box 19(61441), pg. 113

Itasca

Bankers Box/Records Storage Systems, 1789 Norwood Ave.(60143), pg. 406
CORS, One Pierce Place, Ste. 300 E.(60143), pg. 203
CIMLINC INC., 1222 Hamilton Parkway(60143), pg. 249
CONTINENTAL WEB PRESS, INC., 1430 Industrial Dr.(60143), pg. 280
Copyholder Division, 1789 Norwood Ave.(60143), pg. 406
EMKAY, INC., 805 W. Thorndale(60143), pg. 379
EXCELSIOR MANUFACTURING & SUPPLY CORP., 1465 E. Industrial Dr.(60143), pg. 392
FELLOWES MANUFACTURING CO., 1789 Norwood Ave.(60143-1095), pg. 405
THE HASSINGER COMPANIES, 300 Park Blvd., Ste. 515(60143), pg. 516

Hoffman Homes, Inc., 300 Park Blvd., Ste. 515(60143), pg. 516
Illinois Home Mortgage Corp., 300 Park Blvd.(60143), pg. 516
Information Processing Products, 1789 Norwood Ave.(60143), pg. 406
KNOWLES ELECTRONICS, INC., 1151 Maplewood Dr.(60143), pg. 637
Mary Kay Cosmetics, Inc., 800 W. Thorndale(60143), pg. 717
Nuclear Data Systems, 150 Spring Lake Dr.(60143-2096), pg. 213
OFFICE ELECTRONICS, INC., 865 W. Irving Park Rd.(60143), pg. 821
Portfolio Homes, 300 Park Blvd.(60143), pg. 516
Power Shred Division, 1789 Norwood Ave.(60143), pg. 406
RDI, INC., 1025 W. Thorndale Ave.(60143), pg. 906
Reichel & Drews Inc., 1025 W. Thorndale Ave.(60143), pg. 906
TENNESSEE RESTAURANT CORP., One Pierce Pl., Ste. 100E(60143), pg. 1087
UNITED LABORATORIES, INC., 955 Hawthorn(60143), pg. 1133

Ivesdale

Grand Prairie Co-op, Inc., Sloan Station, R.R. 1(61851), pg. 475

Jacksonville

LUNDIA DIV. OF MII, INC., 600 Capitol Way(62650), pg. 687

Jerseyville

CP Illinois, Inc., P.O. Box 70, County Road(62052), pg. 278

Joliet

Belmont Industries, U.S. Refractories Div., (60436), pg. 136
Herald-News, 300 Caterpillar Dr.(60436), pg. 284
Insta-Foam Products, Inc., 1500 Cedarwood Dr.(60435), pg. 419
Ivex Packaging Corporation-Joliet, P.O. Box 685, 292 Logan Ave.(60434), pg. 583
Ivex Packaging Corporation-Mill Division, P.O. Box 685, 292 Logan Ave.(60434), pg. 583
KEMMERER BOTTLING GROUP INC., 777 Joyce Rd.(60436), pg. 622
SHEFFIELD STEEL CORPORATION-JOLIET, 1 Industry Ave.(60434), pg. 996

Kankakee

UNITED COATINGS, INC., 2850 Festival Dr.(60901), pg. 1131

Kewanee

Empire Clothing, 1700 Burlington(61443), pg. 392

La Grange

Alamo Group, Inc., 500 Shawnut(60525), pg. 29
AMERICAN OFFICE EQUIPMENT, 405 E. Shawmut(60525), pg. 58
Funding Services Inc., 405 E. Shawmut(60525), pg. 59

Ladd

Phillips-Joanna, Inc., P.O. Box 425(61329), pg. 566

Lake Bluff

ELE INTERNATIONAL, INC., 86 Albrecht Dr.(60044), pg. 359
LIQUID CONTROLS CORPORATION, 105 Albrecht Dr.(60064), pg. 677

Lake Forest

EON LABS, INC., 207 Westminister(60045), pg. 383
H.P.H. INDUSTRIES LTD., 717 Forest Ave.(60045), pg. 497
The Popcorn Factory, 13970 W. Laurel Dr.(60045), pg. 426

Lake Zurich

ARROW PNEUMATICS CO. INC., 500 N. Oakwood Rd.(60047), pg. 85
R.A. Briggs & Co., 650 N. Church St.(60047), pg. 541
J.R. Technical, 500 Oakwood Rd.(60047), pg. 85

Lansing

Bryant Mungo Division, 17725 Volbrecht Rd.(60438), pg. 1086

Lemont

CLIPPER EXXPRESS CO., 15700 W. 103rd St.(60439), pg. 256
FOLGER ADAM COMPANY, 16300 W. 103rd St.(60439), pg. 422
The Folger Adam Company, 16300 W. 103rd St.(60439), pg. 18

Libertyville

FOULDS INC., 520 E. Church St.(60048), pg. 427
LIBERTYVILLE LINCOLN-MERCURY SALES, INC., 941 S. Milwaukee Ave.(60048), pg. 674

Lile

VOLVO SALES & SERVICE CENTER, 4375 Lincoln Ave.(60532), pg. 1155

Lincoln

Lincoln Courier, 601 Pulaski St.(62656), pg. 284

Lincolnshire

Advent Loudspeakers, 25 Tri-State International Office Center(60069), pg. 578
ALTAIR CORPORATION, 350 Barclay Blvd.(60069), pg. 45
GalenPharma, Inc., 600 Knightsbridge(60069), pg. 448
GENDERM CORPORATION, 600 Knightsbridge Pkwy.(60069), pg. 448
Harvest Industries, Inc., 350 Barclay Blvd.(60069), pg. 45
INTERNATIONAL JENSEN INC., 25 Tri-state Intl. Office Center(60069), pg. 578
IVEX PACKAGING CORPORATION, 100 Tri-State Dr., Suite 200(60069), pg. 583
Ivex Packaging Corporation-Food Packaging Division, 100 Tri-State Drive, Suite 200(60069), pg. 583
Komatsu Dresser Company, 200 Tri-State International(60069), pg. 565
LINC Equipment Services, 550 Bond St.(60069), pg. 648
Phase Linear, 25 Tri-State Intl. Office Center(60069), pg. 578
QUILL CORP., 100 Schelter Rd.(60069), pg. 905
VANCE PUBLISHING CORPORATION, 400 Knightsbridge Parkway(60069), pg. 1144

Lincolnwood

Abacus Packaging Corp., 3701 W. Lunt(60645), pg. 750
ACCURATE THREADED FASTENERS, INC., 3550 W. Pratt Ave.(60645), pg. 11
ADMIRAL MAINTENANCE SERVICE L.P., 4343 W. Touhy Ave.(60646), pg. 18
Bank of Lincolnwood, 4433 W. Touhy Ave.(60646), pg. 441
BIG JOE MANUFACTURING CO., 7225 N. Kostner(60646), pg. 149
Bones/Lincolnwood, 7110 N. Lincoln Ave.(60646), pg. 669
JELMAR COMPANY, 6600 N. Lincoln Ave.(60645), pg. 592
LONDON LITHO ALUMINUM CO., INC., 7100 N. Lawndale(60645), pg. 681
MID-CONTINENT SCREW PRODUCTS CO., 3701 W. Lunt(60645), pg. 750
Total Reproductions, Inc., 6901 Hamlin Ave.(60645), pg. 975

Lisle

Budget Rent A Car Corporation, 4225 Naperville Rd.(60532), pg. 131
HEICO INC., 4225 Naperville Rd., Ste. 200(60532), pg. 525
STERLING SUPPLY COMPANY, INC., 4900 Lincoln Ave.(60536), pg. 1047

Litchfield

ROLLER DERBY SKATE COMPANY, 311 W. Edwards St.(62056), pg. 944

Lockport

KINETIC SYSTEMS CORPORATION, 11 Maryknoll Dr.(60441), pg. 630

Lombard

Britcom Telemarketing Division, 2200 S. Main(60148), pg. 381
Cole Taylor/Yorktown, One Yorktown Center(60148), pg. 260
KYB CORPORATION OF AMERICA, 901 Oak Creek Drive(60148), pg. 613
LOMBARD LINCOLN-MERCURY & LEASING, INC., 500 E. Roosevelt Rd.(60148), pg. 681

Long Grove

CF INDUSTRIES, INC., One Salem Lake Dr.(60047), pg. 200
Communications Planning Corporation/TMP Worldwide, 3880 RFD(60047-7676), pg. 1074
TMP Worldwide, Inc., 3880 RFD(60047), pg. 1074

Lyons

BERRY BEARING CO., 4242 S. 1st Ave.(60534), pg. 144

Macomb

Haeger Potteries of Macomb, Inc., 411 Calhoun(61455), pg. 499

Madison

SPECTRULITE CONSORTIUM, INC., 1001 College Ave.(62060-0258), pg. 1029

Manteno

Ivex Packaging Corporation-Manteno, 1050 Sycamore Rd.(60950), pg. 583

Mattoon

Central Communications Company, 121 S. 17th St.(61938), pg. 563
Consolidated Communications Directories, Inc., 121 S. 17th St.(61938), pg. 563
Consolidated Communications Mobile Services, Inc., 121 S. 17th St.(61938), pg. 563
Consolidated Communications Operator Services, Inc., 121 S. 17th St.(61938), pg. 563
Consolidated Communications Public Services, Inc., 121 S. 17 St.(61938), pg. 563
Consolidated Network, Inc., 121 S. 17th St.(61938), pg. 563
Consolidated Telemarketing America, Inc., 121 S. 17th St.(61938), pg. 563
ILLINOIS CONSOLIDATED TELEPHONE CO., 121 S. 17th St.(61938), pg. 563
Justrite Mfg. Co., W. Rte. 121(61938), pg. 610

McHenry

CHROMA CORPORATION, 3900 Dayton St.(60050), pg. 249
Follett Software Company, 809 N. Front St.(60050-5589), pg. 422

Melrose Park

AGI INC., 1950 N. Ruby St.(60160), pg. 4
Anning-Johnson Company, 1959 Anson Dr.(60160), pg. 76
ANSON INDUSTRIES, INC., 1959 Anson Dr.(60160), pg. 76
Benjamin Moore & Co., North & 25th Aves.(60160), pg. 139
Dale Foods, 1501 N. 31st Ave.(65801), pg. 1152
DRAPER DANIELS MEDIA SERVICES, INC., 2525 Armitage Ave.(60160), pg. 348
Gage Food Products Company, 1501 N. 31st Ave.(60160), pg. 1152
Home Juice Co. of Florida, 2000 N. 15th Ave.(60160), pg. 542
HOME JUICE COMPANY, 2000 N. 15th Ave.(60160-1473), pg. 541
KREHER STEEL COMPANY, INC., 1550 N. 25th Ave.(60160), pg. 644
RHC/SPACEMASTER CORPORATION, 1400 N. 25th Ave.(60160), pg. 906
RAM GOLF CORPORATION, 2020 Indian Boundary Dr.(60160), pg. 910
TEMPERATURE EQUIPMENT CORPORATION, 2000 N. Ruby St.(60160), pg. 1086
Tree Fresh Foods Corp., 2000 N. 15th Ave.(60160), pg. 542
Tropar Mfg. Co., Inc., 3306 Bloomingdale(60160), pg. 1116

Mendota

O'Brien Division, P.O. Box 191(61342), pg. 525

Midlothian

ARROW CHEVROLET, INC., 14640 Cicero Ave.(60445), pg. 85
MORAN INDUSTRIES, INC., 4444 W. 147th St.(60445), pg. 769
U.S. Transparts, 4444 W. 147th St.(60445), pg. 769

Milford

Fremont Canning Co., P. O. Box 27(60953), pg. 432
HOWARD INDUSTRIES, INC., One North Dixie Hwy.(60953), pg. 547

Moline

Cox Cable Quad Cities, Inc., 3900 26th Ave.(61265), pg. 294
Moline Accessories Company, 325 19th St.(61265), pg. 767
MONTGOMERY ELEVATOR COMPANY, One Montgomery Court(61265), pg. 767
Montgomery Elevator Export Corporation, One Montgomery Court(61265), pg. 767
WILLIAMS-WHITE & CO., 600 Third Ave.(61265), pg. 1191
WILLIAMS, WHITE & COMPANY, 600 Third Ave.(61265), pg. 1191

Momence

Gilster Mary Lee Corp., 305 E. Washington(60954), pg. 460
Sevco, Inc., 100 Mechanic St.(60954), pg. 569

Montgomery

General American Door Company, 5050 Base Line Rd.(60538), pg. 739
LYON METAL PRODUCTS, INC., 420 N. Main(60538), pg. 690
PROCESSED PLASTIC COMPANY, 1001 Aucutt Rd.(60538), pg. 892

Morrison

Climco Coils Co., 400 Oakwood(61270), pg. 437

Morton Grove

CHICAGO SHOW PRINTING CO., 8330 No. Austin Ave.(60053), pg. 246
DIEBEL MANUFACTURING CO., 6505 Oakton St.(60053), pg. 336
L&J TECHNOLOGIES, 6511 Oakton(60053), pg. 647
LAWNWARE PRODUCTS, INC., 8220 N. Austin(60053), pg. 661
SCHWARZ PAPER COMPANY, 8338 N. Austin Ave.(60053), pg. 980

Mount Carmel

CAC MICROCIRCUITS, INC., 2 Southgate Drive(62863), pg. 198
Thordarson Meissner, Inc., 628 Belmont St.(62863), pg. 270

Mount Olive

Hano Business Forms, Inc., P.O. Box 278, (62069), pg. 506

Mount Prospect

ARA/Cory Refreshment Services, Inc., 431 Lakeview Ct.(60056), pg. 6
BINGHAM, 479 Business Center Dr., Ste. 109(60056), pg. 151
Cummins-Allison Corp., 891 Feehanville Dr.(60056), pg. 305
CUMMINS-AMERICAN CORP., 891 Feehanville Dr.(60056), pg. 304
ILLINOIS RANGE COMPANY, 708 W. Central Rd.(60056), pg. 563

NETWORK SERVICES COMPANY OF CHICAGO, 1550 Bishop Court(60056), pg. 798
PC DISTRIBUTING INC., 2080 Carboy Rd.(60056), pg. 835

Mount Vernon

Mount Vernon Neon, 391

Mundelein

Accucare Div., One Medline Place(60060), pg. 736
Disposamed Div., One Medline Place(60060), pg. 736
Dynacor Div., One Medline Place(60060), pg. 736
MACLEAN-FOGG CO., 1000 Allanson Rd.(60060), pg. 697
Medcrest Div., One Medline Place(60060), pg. 736
Medecore Div., One Medline Place(60060), pg. 736
MEDLINE INDUSTRIES, INC., One Medline Place(60060), pg. 736
Medline Skin Care Div., One Medline Place(60060), pg. 736
PRINT-O-TAPE, 755 Tower Rd.(60060), pg. 891

Murphysboro

Penn Aluminum International, P.O. Box 531, (62966), pg. 711

Naperville

BOSTON CHICKEN, INC., 1804 Center Point Dr.(60563), pg. 167
CATHOLIC ORDER OF FORESTERS, P.O. Box 3012, (60566), pg. 229
CENTRAL DUPAGE HEALTH SYSTEM, 1151 E. Warrenville Rd.(60563), pg. 232
HARBOUR CONTRACTORS, INC., 22 E. Chicago Ave., Ste. 200(60540), pg. 506
QUALITY CHEKD DAIRY PRODUCTS ASSOCIATION, 1733 Park Place(60563), pg. 903
RHEA & KAISER ADVERTISING, INC., Naperville Financial Ctr., 400 E. Diehl Rd.(60563), pg. 930
SOLAR PRESS, INC., 1120 Frontenac Rd.(60563-1799), pg. 1016
Varlen Corp., 305 East Shuman Blvd.(60566), pg. 358

Niles

American Specialty Foods, 5990 W. Touhy Ave.(60648), pg. 881
BRADFORD EXCHANGE LTD., 9333 Milwaukee Ave. N.(60714), pg. 170
COCA-COLA BOTTLING CO. OF CHICAGO, 7400 N. Oak Park Ave.(60714), pg. 257
FORT DEARBORN LITHOGRAPH COMPANY, 6035 Gross Point Rd.(60714), pg. 425
HEYMAN CORPORATION, 6045 W. Howard St.(60648), pg. 532
Imperial Division, 6300 W. Howard St.(60648), pg. 899
JOHNSON & QUIN, INC., 7460 N. Lehigh(60648), pg. 599
Mid Res Service Div., 7720 Lehigh Ave.(60648), pg. 751
Midwesco Energy Systems Div., 7720 Lehigh Ave.(60648), pg. 751
MIDWESCO INC., 7720 Lehigh Ave.(60648), pg. 751
Midwesco Mechanical, 7720 Lehigh Ave.(60648), pg. 751
NIGHTINGALE-CONANT CORP., 7300 N. Lehigh Ave.(60714), pg. 807
NORTHWESTERN INDUSTRIAL PIPING, 7475 Oak Park Ave.(60714), pg. 815
NUARC COMPANY, INC., 6200 W. Howard St.(60714), pg. 817
Oshkosh B'Gosh Hosiery Co., 6045 W. Howard St.(60648), pg. 532
Perma-Pipe Div., 7720 Lehigh Ave.(60648), pg. 751
PRECISION CARBIDE TOOL COMPANY, INC., 7450 N. Natchez Ave.(60714), pg. 885
GEORGE T. SCHMIDT, 6151 W. Howard St.(60648), pg. 976
Sterling Hosiery Co., 6045 W. Howard St.(60648), pg. 532
Sunshine/Salerno (IL), 7777 N. Caldwell Ave.(60648), pg. 439
Synchro-Start Products, Inc., 6250 Howard St.(60714), pg. 638
Thermal-Care Div., 7720 Lehigh Ave.(60648), pg. 751
Tru-Fit Glove & Headwear Div., 6045 W. Howard St.(60648), pg. 532
WICO CORPORATION, 6400 W. Gross Point Rd.(60714-4508), pg. 1156
Wells Lamont, 6640 W. Touhy Ave.(60174), pg. 712

North Aurora

AURORA PACKING CO., INC., 125 Grant St.(60542), pg. 98

North Chicago

COLEMAN CABLE SYSTEMS, INC., 2500 Commonwealth Ave.(60064), pg. 260
Electrical Conductors, Inc., 2500 Commonwealth Ave.(60064), pg. 261
FEDERAL CHICAGO CORPORATION, 925 22nd St.(60064), pg. 404

North Riverside

EDWARD DON & COMPANY OF ILLINOIS, 2500 S. Harlem Ave.(60546), pg. 344

Northbrook

Aeros Instruments, Inc., 3411 Commercial Ave.(60062), pg. 1034
APOLLO COLORS, INC., 3000 Dundee Rd. , Suite 415(60062), pg. 78
BELL FLAVORS & FRAGRANCES, 500 Academy Dr.(60062), pg. 134
Colony Press Inc., 707 Skokie Blvd.(60062), pg. 609
CRANE CONSTRUCTION CO., 343 Wainwright Dr.(60062), pg. 296
Culligan International Company, One Culligan Pkwy.(60062), pg. 358
EUROMARKET DESIGNS, INC., 725 Landwehr Rd.(60062), pg. 390
FLINN & DREFFEIN ENGINEERING CO., 3520 Commercial Ave.(60062), pg. 419
STEVE FOLEY CADILLAC, 100 Skokie Blvd.(60062), pg. 422
FULLERTON METALS CO., 3000 Shermer Rd.(60065-3002), pg. 436
General Binding Corporation, One GBC Plaza(60062), pg. 656
HANDGARDS INC., 950 Skokie Blvd.(60062), pg. 504
IVI Travel, 400 Skokie Blvd.(60062-2887), pg. 428
JAMES BUILDING CORPORATION, 1535 Lake Cook Rd., Ste. 302(60062), pg. 588
Lane Broadcasting, Inc., One Lane Center, 1200 Shermer Rd.(60062), pg. 657
Lane Hotels, Inc., 1200 Shermer Rd.(60062), pg. 657
LANE INDUSTRIES, INC., One Lane Center, 1200 Shermer Rd.(60062), pg. 656
Lane Properties, Inc., , pg. 657
NORTH SHORE MOVERS, 600 Waukegan Rd., (60062), pg. 813
Old World Automotive Products, 4065 Commercial Ave.(60062), pg. 824
OLD WORLD INDUSTRIES, INC., 4065 Commercial Ave.(60062), pg. 823
River Bend, Inc., 3175 Commercial Ave., Ste. 203(60062), pg. 1026
S & C Maintenance Corp., 3175 Commercial Ave., Ste. 203(60062), pg. 1026
STS Consultants, Ltd., 111 Pfingsten Rd.(60062), pg. 965
STS HOLDINGS, INC., 111 Pfingsten Rd.(60062), pg. 964
SERFILCO, LTD., 1777 Shermer Rd.(60062), pg. 990
Spatz Centers, Inc., 3175 Commercial Ave., Ste. 203(60062), pg. 1026
SPATZ & CO., 3175 Commercial Ave., Ste. 203(60062), pg. 1026
Spatz & Co. Development, 3175 Commercial Ave., Ste. 203(60062), pg. 1026
Splitfire, Inc., 4065 Commercial Ave.(60062), pg. 824
SQUIRE-COGSWELL COMPANY, 3411 Commercial Ave.(60062), pg. 1034
TEMKIN & TEMKIN, Bldg. 800, 450 Skokie Blvd.(60062), pg. 1086
VeloBind, Inc., 1135 Skokie Blvd.(60062-4100), pg. 657
ZYLKE & ASSOCIATES, 215 Revere Dr.(60062), pg. 1221

Northfield

DACOR CORPORATION, 161 Northfield Rd.(60093), pg. 310
KURTZMAN/SLAVIN/LINDA, INC., One Northfield Plaza(60093), pg. 646

Northlake

DOMINICK'S FINER FOODS, 505 Railroad Ave.(60164), pg. 343
OMNI Superstores, 505 Railroad Ave.(60164), pg. 344
SHURFINE-CENTRAL CORP., 2100 N. Mannheim Rd.(60164), pg. 1001
Transilwrap Company, Inc., One West Lake St.(60164), pg. 1107

Oak Brook

AXIA INCORPORATED, 2001 Spring Rd., Ste. 300(60521), pg. 8
ACE HARDWARE CORPORATION, 2200 Kensington Ct.(60521), pg. 12
DONALD L. ARENDS INC., 1000 Jorie Blvd.(60521), pg. 81
BUZZ BARTON & ASSOCIATES, INC., 900 Jorie Blvd.(60521), pg. 123
Binswanger Chicago, 1111 W. 22nd St., Ste. 520(60521), pg. 151
BLISTEX, INC., 1800 Swift Dr.(60521), pg. 157
Chiat/Day/Mojo/Chicago, AT&T Plaza, 1111 West 22nd St.(60521), pg. 244
Clow Water Systems Corp., 2021 Midwest Rd., Ste. 301(60521), pg. 733
Cordley Temprite, 2222 Camden St.(60521), pg. 377
ELKAY MANUFACTURING COMPANY, 2222 Camden Ct.(60521), pg. 377
ENVIRODYNE INDUSTRIES, INC., 701 Harger Rd., Ste. 121(60521), pg. 383
GREAT LAKES DREDGE & DOCK, 2122 York Rd.(60521), pg. 481
Gulfstream Marketing Midwest Region, 2001 Spring Rd.(60521), pg. 494
THE INLAND GROUP, INC., 2901 Butterfield Rd.(60521), pg. 570
MTI VACATIONS, INC., 1220 Kensington(60521), pg. 694
Salem Technical Services, 1200 Jorie Blvd.(60521-9981), pg. 320
SENTINEL COMPUTER SERVICES INC., 1010 Jorie Blvd., Ste. 150(60521), pg. 990
Sunbeam Appliance Company, 2001 S. York Rd.(60521), pg. 1059
Trase-Miller, 1220 Kensington(60521), pg. 694
U.S. CAN COMPANY, 900 Commerce Dr., Ste. 302(60521), pg. 1134

Oak Lawn

Creative Publications, 11000 S. LaVergne Ave.(60453), pg. 369
EDUCATIONAL PUBLISHING CORPORATION, 11000 S. Lavergne Ave.(60453), pg. 369
Ideal School Supply Company, 11000 S. LaVergne Ave.(60453), pg. 369
Ideal School Supply Corporation, 11000 S. Lavergne Ave.(60453), pg. 369
Whitehall Educational Toys, 11000 S. Lavergne Ave.(60453), pg. 369

Oak Park

SHAKER ADVERTISING AGENCY, The Shaker Bldg., 1100 Lake St.(60301), pg. 994
Vegetarian Times, P.O. Box 570(60303), pg. 291

Oakbrook Terrace

E.J. BRACH CORPORATION, One Tower Lane(60181), pg. 169
NATIONAL TRUCK LEASING SYSTEM, One S. 450 Summit Ave., Ste. 300(60181), pg. 794
WOZNIAK INDUSTRIES, INC., Two Mid America Plaza, Ste. 706(60181), pg. 1204

Olympia Fields

DEDERT CORPORATION, 20000 Governors Dr.(60461), pg. 324
Gateway Safety Systems Co., 1990 Governors Dr.(60461), pg. 1077
TAKATTA INC., 19900 Governors Dr.(60461), pg. 1076

Orland Park

ESROCK ADVERTISING, 14550 South 94th Ave.(60462), pg. 388

Ottawa

Carus Chemical Company, Chemical Div., 1001 Boyce Meml. Dr.(61350), pg. 227
LA SALLE COUNTY FARM SUPPLY, 3107 N. Illinois Rte. 23(61350), pg. 649

Palatine

SELLSTROM MANUFACTURING CO., One Sellstrom Dr.(60067), pg. 988
WEBER-STEPHEN PRODUCTS, 200 E. Daniels Rd.(60067), pg. 1171
WILTON CORPORATION, 300 S. Hicks(60067), pg. 1194
Wilton Engineered Products Div., 300 S. Hicks Rd.(60067), pg. 1194
Wilton Machinery Div., 300 S. Hicks Rd.(60067), pg. 1194
Wilton Packaging Div., 300 S. Hicks Rd.(60067), pg. 1194
Wilton Tool Div., 300 S. Hicks Rd.(60067), pg. 1194

Paris

Anthony Division, 2109 S. Central Ave.(61944), pg. 752
ILLINOIS CEREAL MILLS, INC., P.O. Box 550, 616 S. Jefferson Ave.(61944), pg. 562
MIDWEST BODY CORPORATION, 2109 S. Central Ave.(61944), pg. 752
Morgan Food Products, 1808 S. Main(61944), pg. 770
MORGAN MANUFACTURING COMPANY, INC., 1900 S. Marshall St.(61944), pg. 770

Park Forest

CONTINENTAL/MIDLAND, INC., 25000 S. Western Ave.(60466), pg. 279

Park Ridge

GEORGE S. MAY INTERNATIONAL COMPANY, 303 S. Northwest Hwy.(60068-4265), pg. 723
RITTENHOUSE INC., 250 S. Northwest Hwy., (60068), pg. 936
Rittenhouse Paper Co., 250 S. Northwest Hwy.(60068), pg. 936

Peoria

Brecks, 6523 N. Galena Rd.(61632), pg. 426
Custom Ad-Planner, 1720 W. Detweiller Dr.(61615), pg. 775
FLEMING PACKAGING CORP., 1028 S.W. Adams St.(61602), pg. 417
Fleming-Potter Co., 1028 S.W. Adams St.(61602), pg. 417
Fleming-Potter Fast Printing, 1114 S.W. Jefferson St.(61602), pg. 417
Fleming-Potter Webkote, 1016 S.W. Adams(61602), pg. 417
FOSTER & GALLAGHER INC., 6523 N. Galena Rd.(61632), pg. 426
HALL, HAERR, PETERSON & HARNEY, INC., Knoxville Executive Plaza, 6907 N. Knoxville(61614), pg. 501
Haulpak Division, Komatsu Dresser Company, 2300 N.E. Adams St.(61639), pg. 565
HULT FRITZ MATUSZAK & ASSOCIATES, INC., 245 N. E. Perry Ave.(61603), pg. 552
INTERSTATE PRODUCERS LIVESTOCK ASSOCIATION, 1705 W. Luthy(61615), pg. 580
Ivex Packaging Corporation-Peoria, P.O. Box 1820, Foot of Sloan St.(61656), pg. 583
KRBS Radio, 1720 W. Detweiller Dr.(61615), pg. 775
KLAUS RADIO INC., 8400 N. Allen Rd.(61615), pg. 634
Kwikee Systems, 1720 W. Detweiller Dr.(61615), pg. 775
Magazine Market Place, Inc., 6523 N. Galena Rd.(61632), pg. 426
MULTI-AD SERVICES, INC., 1720 W. Detweiller Dr.(61615), pg. 775
L. R. NELSON CORPORATION, 7719 N. Pioneer Lane(61615), pg. 797
Re Cas, 1720 W. Detweiller Dr.(61615), pg. 775
RUPPMAN NATIONAL YELLOW PAGES SERVICE (RNYPS), 2001 Ruppman Plaza(61614), pg. 956
BEN SCHWARTZ MARKET, INC., 209 W. McClure(61604), pg. 980

Peru

CARUS CORPORATION, 315 Fifth St.(61354-2857), pg. 227
Carus Publishing Company, 315 5th St.(61354), pg. 227

Cricket Magazine, 315 Fifth St.(61354), pg. 227
Ladybug Magazine, 315 Fifth St.(61354), pg. 227
MAZE NAILS, 100 Church St.(61354), pg. 725
Open Court Publishing Co.-General Books, 315 5th St.(61354), pg. 227

Petersburg

MENARD ELECTRIC COOPERATIVE, 122 S. 6th St.(62675), pg. 738

Philo

Grand Prairie Co-op, Inc., N. Harrison St.(61864), pg. 475

Plainfield

SPRING-GREEN LAWN CARE CORPORATION, 11927 Spaulding School Dr.(60544), pg. 1033

Plano

PLANO MOLDING CO., 431 E. South St.(60545), pg. 874

Posen

R.J. CORR NATURALS, INC., 14828 McKinley(60469), pg. 287

Princeton

CHAMPION PNEUMATIC MACHINERY CO., INC., 1301 N. Euclid Ave.(61356), pg. 238

Princeville

Princeville Canning Co., (61559), pg. 833

Quincy

BROADCAST ELECTRONICS, INC., 4100 N. 24th St.(62301), pg. 177
J.M. Huber, Calcium Carbonate Div., 3150 Gardner Expwy.(62301), pg. 550
THE KNAPHEIDE MFG. CO., 436 S. 6th(62301), pg. 636
MOORMAN MFG. COMPANY, 1000 N. 30th St.(62305-3115), pg. 769
PENN-DANIELS, INC., 505 N. 24th St.(62301), pg. 857
Quincy Soybean Co., 1900 Gardner Expressway(62301), pg. 769

Richmond

Claud S. Gordon Company, 5710 Kenosha St.(60071), pg. 1167
Stamptech, 5600 Wilson Rd.(60071), pg. 697
JOHN STERLING CORPORATION, 11600 Sterling Pkwy.(60071), pg. 1046

River Forest

MADIGAN BROTHERS, INC., 7440 W. Central Ave.(60305), pg. 699

Roberts

HICKS OIL-HICKS GAS, INC., U.S. 54 & 115(60962), pg. 533
Rocket Supply Corp., U.S. 54 & 115(60962), pg. 533

Rock Island

JAYDON INCORPORATED, 7800 14th St. West(61201), pg. 590
MODERN WOODMEN OF AMERICA, 1701 1st Ave.(61201), pg. 763
SERVUS FOOTWEAR COMPANY, 1136 Second(61201), pg. 993
DON E. WILLIAMS CO., 7920 14th St. W.(61201), pg. 1190

Rockford

ANDERSON INDUSTRIES INC., 803 N. Church St.(61103), pg. 73
ATWOOD INDUSTRIES, INC., 1400 Eddy Ave.(61103), pg. 97
JOHN S. BARNES CORP., 2222 15th St.(61104), pg. 120
JOSEPH BEHR & SONS INC., 1100-1200 Seminary St.(61104), pg. 132
DEVLIEG BULLARD SERVICES GROUP, 10100 Forest Hills Rd.(61115), pg. 333
Eclipse-Combustion, 1665 Elmwood Rd(61103), pg. 366
Eclipse-Controls, 1665 Elmwood Rd.(61103), pg. 366
ECLIPSE, INC., 1665 Elmwood Rd.(61103), pg. 366
Freeway Rockford, 4701 Boeing Dr.(61109), pg. 432
Ingersoll Bohle Ingersoll GmbH Inc., 1303 Eddy Ave.(61103), pg. 568
Ingersoll Cutting Tool Co., 505 Fulton Ave.(61103), pg. 568
INGERSOLL ENGINEERS INC., 1021 N. Mulford Rd.(61107), pg. 568
Ingersoll GmbH Inc., 1303 Eddy Ave.(61103), pg. 568
INGERSOLL INTERNATIONAL INC., 707 Fulton Ave.(61103), pg. 568
The Ingersoll Milling Machine Co., 707 Fulton Ave.(61103), pg. 568
MATTISON MACHINE WORKS, 545 Blackhawk Park Ave.(61101), pg. 721
Metal Cutting Tools Corp., 21 Airport Dr.(61109), pg. 507
Mid-States Forging Die & Tool Co., P.O. Box5025(61125), pg. 762
ROCKFORD ACROMATIC PRODUCT CO., 611 Beacon St.(61130), pg. 941
Rockford-Eclipse, 1665 Elmwood Rd.(61103), pg. 366
Rockford International Group, 612 Harrison Avenue(61104), pg. 942
ROCKFORD PRODUCTS CORP., 707 Harrison Ave.(61104), pg. 941
Sall-Eclipse, 2320 Kishwaukee St.(61108), pg. 366
Sieg Rockford Co., 716 N. Madison St.(61107), pg. 1002
Slick Aircraft Products, 530 Blackhawk Park Ave.(61104), pg. 1130
SMITH-SHAFER OIL CO., 1639 N. Alpine Rd., Ste. 310(61107), pg. 1014
SUNTEC INDUSTRIES INC., 2210 Harrison Ave.(61125), pg. 1062
G.C. Thorsen, Inc., 1801 Morgan St.(61102), pg. 609
Triangle Metals, Inc., 2500 Harrison Ave.(61108), pg. 1093
Waldrich Coburg Ingersoll GmbH Inc., 1302 Eddy Ave.(61103), pg. 568
Waldrich Siegen Ingersoll GmbH Inc., 1303 Eddy Ave.(61103), pg. 568

Rockton

Ice Craft, 750 N. Blackhawk Blvd.(61072), pg. 1027
Taylor Company, 750 N. Blackhawk Blvd.(61072), pg. 1027

Rolling Meadows

ACE OFFICE PRODUCTS, 1100 Hicks Rd.(60008), pg. 12
EDWARD G. DORN & ASSOCIATES, INC., 1801-H S. Hicks Rd.(60008), pg. 346
Gino's East/Rolling Meadows, Paddock Shopping Center, 1321 W. Golf Rd.(60008), pg. 669
KELSO-BURNETT COMPANY, 5200 Newport Dr.(60008), pg. 622
Lexmark International, Inc., 1701 Golf Rd., Tower Two, 2nd Fl.(60008), pg. 674
MOLON MOTOR & COIL CORP., 3737 Industrial Ave.(60008), pg. 764
POWER CONTRACTING & ENGINEERING CORP., 1895 Rohlwing Rd.(60008), pg. 883
SPOTNAILS INC., 1100 Hicks Rd.(60008), pg. 1032

Roselle

FYRNETICS, INC., 1055 Stevenson Ct. Ste. 102W(60172), pg. 438
ROMAN, INC., 555 Lawrence Ave.(60172), pg. 945

Rosemont

ARA Services, Rosemont Horizon, 6920 Mannheim Rd.(60018), pg. 6
Austin Consulting, 9801 W. Higgins Road(60018), pg. 790
DONAHOE & PUROHIT, INC., One O'Hare Centre, Ste. 5060, 6250 N. River Rd.(60018), pg. 344
G.I.C. Financial Services Corporation, 9701 Higgins Rd.(60018), pg. 492
Popeye's Famous Fried Chicken, 10600 W. Higgins Rd., Ste. 512(60018), pg. 284
THE TOWNSEND AGENCY, LTD., 9700 Higgins Rd., Ste. 600(60018), pg. 1104
VELSICOL CHEMICAL CORPORATION, 10400 W. Higgins Rd.(60018), pg. 1147

Round Lake

THE GRIEVE CORPORATION, 500 Hart Rd.(60073), pg. 486

Rowing Meadows

HOSTMARK MANAGEMENT GROUP, 1600 Golf Rd.(60008), pg. 545

Russell

CAMOSY, INC., Rt. 41 & Stateline Rd.(60075), pg. 212

Saint Charles

DANFOSS DUKES FLUID POWER INC., 950 State Ave.(60174), pg. 314
Dukane Audio Visual Div., 2900 Dukane Dr.(60174), pg. 352
Dukane Communications Systems Div., 2900 Dukane Dr.(60174), pg. 352
DUKANE CORPORATION, 2900 Dukane Dr.(60174), pg. 351
Dukane Microrobotics Division, 2900 Dukane Dr.(60174), pg. 352
Dukane SeaCom Division, 2900 Dukane Dr.(60174), pg. 352
Dukane Ultrasonics Div., 2900 Dukane Dr.(60174), pg. 352
MOLINE CORPORATION, Dean St.(60174), pg. 764
SAMPLER PUBLICATIONS INC., 707 Kautz Rd.(60174), pg. 968
Trilan Systems Corporation, 2900 Dukane Dr.(60174), pg. 352

Saint Joseph

Grand Prairie Co-op, Inc., 108 N. Main St.(61873), pg. 475
Grand Prarie Co-op, Inc., Box 330, Fulls Siding, R.R. 1(61873), pg. 475

Sauget

Cerro Copper Products Co., Hwy. 3, Mississippi Ave.(62201), pg. 711

Savanna

Metform, Inc., 2551 Wacker Rd.(61074), pg. 698

Savoy

Grand Prairie Co-op, Inc., P.O. Box 68, (61874), pg. 475

Schaumburg

Aratex Services, Inc., 1834 Walden Office Sq.(60173), pg. 7
Aratex Textile Services, Inc., 1834 Walden Office Sq., Ste. 45(60195), pg. 7
CONVENIENT FOOD MART, INC., 929 N. Plum Grove Rd.(60173), pg. 281
Jorgensen Steel & Aluminum/Chicago, 1900 Mitchell Blvd.(60193), pg. 605
RESPONSIVE MARKETING COMMUNICATIONS, INC., 1515 Woodfield Rd., Ste. 360(60173), pg. 929
RUBIN RESPONSE SERVICES, INC., 1111 Plaza Dr.(60173), pg. 954
S & W Fine Foods, 1827 Walden Office Sq.(60195), pg. 1111
The Signature Group, 200 N. Martingale(60173-2096), pg. 768
The Sterling Group, 1730 Remington Rd.(60195), pg. 640
Sunbeam-Oster Household Products, 1501 Woodfield Rd., Ste. 400N(60173), pg. 1059

Schawnburg

Stephen Gould of Illinois, Inc., 1051 Perimeter Dr.(60173-5055), pg. 474

Schiller Park

Airways Rent A Car, 4025 N. Mannheim Rd.(60176), pg. 934
American Gasket & Rubber, 9509 Winona Ave.(60176), pg. 15
ATLAS LIFT TRUCK RENTALS & SALES, INC., 5050 N. River Rd.(60176), pg. 96
ATLAS WIRE CORPORATION, 9525 W. River St.(60176), pg. 97
ATOLS TOOL AND MOLD CORP., 3828 N. River Rd.(60176), pg. 97
RIDGEVIEW MOTORS, INC., 4025 Mannheim Rd.(60176), pg. 934
Rotary Paper Manifold Co., 4250 United Pkwy.(60176), pg. 171
Vectron Datagraphics, 9815 W. Foster Ave.(60176), pg. 1151

Shelbyville

Warner-Ishi Corporation, P.O. Box 583, Rt. 166

Shorewood

Woodhaven Foods-Midwest, 1007 Geneva(60436), pg. 7

Sidney

Grand Prairie Co-op, Inc., Block, R.R. 1(61877), pg. 475

Skokie

AMERICAN LOUVER CO., 7700 Austin Ave.(60077), pg. 57
BELL & HOWELL COMPANY, 5215 Old Orchard Rd.(60077-1076), pg. 134
CASTCRAFT INDUSTRIES, INC., 3649 W. Chase Ave.(60076), pg. 228
Castcraft Software Optifont, 3649 W. Chase Ave.(60076), pg. 228
Cloud Corporation, 7455 N. St. Louis Ave.(60076), pg. 256
CRAFTY BEAVER HOME CENTER, 4811 Oakton(60076), pg. 295
ELEK-TEK, INC., 7350 N. Linder Ave.(60077), pg. 375
FEL-PRO INCORPORATED, 7450 N. McCormick Blvd.(60076), pg. 405
Florasynth Inc., 3720 Touhy Ave.(60076), pg. 420
GENERAL AUTOMATION, INC., 3300 W. Oakton(60076), pg. 448
Hirsh Company, 8051 Central Park Ave.(60076), pg. 258
The Robert Irsay Company, 8130 N. St. Louis Ave.(60076), pg. 609
Kingston Marketing Co., 7711 Gross Point Rd.(60076), pg. 1101
KLEIN TOOLS INC., 7200 McCormick Blvd.(60076), pg. 635
NORTOWN OLDSMOBILE INC., 7601 N. Skokie Blvd.(60077), pg. 816
OHMITE MANUFACTURING COMPANY, 3601 Howard St.(60076), pg. 823
Paxall Circle Machinery, 7515 N. Linder Ave.(60077), pg. 852
Paxall Clybourn Machinery, 7515 N. Linder Ave.(60077), pg. 852
THE PAXALL GROUP, INC., 7515 N. Linder Ave.(60077), pg. 852
Rand McNally Book Manufacturing Co., 8255 N. Central Park(60076), pg. 911
RAND MCNALLY & COMPANY, 8255 N. Central Park(60076), pg. 911
Rand McNally DocuSystems Group, 8255 N. Central Park(60076), pg. 911
Rand McNally International, 8255 N. Central Park(60076), pg. 911
Rand McNally Map Services Co., 8255 N. Central Park(60076), pg. 911
Rand McNally Publishing Group, 8255 N. Central Park(60076), pg. 911
RAULAND-BORG CORPORATION, 3450 W. Oakton St.(60076-2951), pg. 914
TEMPEL STEEL COMPANY, 5215 Old Orchard Rd.(60077-1076), pg. 1086
TOPCO ASSOCIATES, INC., 7711 Gross Point Rd.(60077-2697), pg. 1101
Transfertech, Inc., 3649 W. Chase Ave.(60076), pg. 228
Type Films of Chicago Co., 3649 W. Chase Ave.(60076), pg. 228
Type Founders of Chicago, 3649 W. Chase Ave.(60076), pg. 228
WOODWARD DIRECT, INC., 8001 Lincoln Ave.(60077), pg. 1201

South Barrington

ROSE PACKING COMPANY, 65 S. Barrington Rd.(60010), pg. 947

South Elgin

HOFFER PLASTICS CORPORATION, 500 N. Collins St.(60177), pg. 537

ILLINOIS HYDRAULIC CONSTRUCTION COMPANY, 1797 La Fox St.(60177), pg. 563

South Holland

GOODHEART-WILLCOX CO., INC., 123 W. Taft Drive(60473), pg. 470

Spring Grove

Forms Corporation Of America, 3106 N. Rte. 12(60081), pg. 1187
INTERMATIC INC., Intermatic Plaza(60081), pg. 575
WHITESTAR GRAPHICS, INC., P.O. Box 278, (60018), pg. 1186

Springfield

BUNN-O-MATIC CORPORATION, 1400 Stevenson Dr.(62703), pg. 188
CAPITOL GROUP, 1900 S. 8th St.(62703), pg. 215
EGIZII ELECTRIC, INC., 700 N. MacArthur Blvd.(62702), pg. 371
ILLINOIS STATE LOTTERY, 201 E. Madison(62702), pg. 563
ROBERTS FOODS, INC., 1615 W. Jefferson St.(62702), pg. 938
The State Journal-Register, One Copley Plaza(62705), pg. 284
WJCS-TV, 2680 East Cook St.(62703), pg. 442

Sterling

Frantz Bearing Div., 3201 W. LeFevre Rd.(61081), pg. 430
Frantz Export Corp., 301 W. 3rd St.(61081), pg. 430
FRANTZ MANUFACTURING CO., 301 W. 3rd St.(61081), pg. 429
NORTHWESTERN STEEL & WIRE CO., 121 Wallace St.(61081), pg. 815
Sterling Steel Ball Div., 3201 W. LeFevre Rd.(61081), pg. 430
WAHL CLIPPER CORP., 2900 N. Locust(61081), pg. 1158

Streamwood

DURACO PRODUCTS, INC., 1109 E. Lake St.(60107), pg. 354

Streator

Peabody Myers Corp., 1621 S. Illinois St.(61364), pg. 900

Sullivan

E.J. Brach, Inc., 811 S. Hamilton(61951), pg. 169

Summit

W. Braun Distribution Center, 7224 W. 60th St.(60501), pg. 172

Sycamore

IDEAL INDUSTRIES, INC., 1000 Park Ave.(60178), pg. 562
SEYMOUR OF SYCAMORE, INC., 917 Crosby Ave.(60178), pg. 994
Sycamore Systems, Inc., 449 N. California St.(60178), pg. 690

Teutopolis

SIEMER MILLING COMPANY, 111 W. Main St.(62467), pg. 1002

Tinley Park

PANDUIT COMPANY, 17301 Ridgeland Ave.(60477), pg. 845

Tolono

GRAND PRAIRIE CO-OP, INC., 1 S. Calhoun(61880), pg. 475
Grand Prairie Co-op, Inc., Apex, R.R. 1(61880), pg. 475

Troy Grove

Manley Bros., P.O. Box C(61372), pg. 887

Urbana

Grand Prairie Co-op, Inc., Deers, R.R. 3(61801), pg. 475

Vandalia

Vandalia Leader-Union, 229 So. Fifth St.(62471), pg. 655

Vernon Hills

COSMETIQUE, INC., 200 Corporate Woods Pkwy.(60061), pg. 288
INLANDER-STEINDLER PAPER, 850 Forest Edge Dr.(60061-3105), pg. 570
TIGER ELECTRONICS, INC., 980 Woodlands Pkwy.(60061), pg. 1097
WICKES LUMBER CO., 706 Deerpath Dr.(60061), pg. 1188

Villa Park

Alro Specialty Metals, Villa Park, 236 E. Sidney Ct.(60181-1198), pg. 44

Warrenville

PLYMOUTH TUBE COMPANY, 29 W. 150 Warrenville Rd.(60555), pg. 877

Waukegan

AMERICAN FLUORESCENT CORPORATION, 3821 Hawthorne Ct.(60087), pg. 54
Classic Chevrolet, 425 N. Green Bay Rd.(60085), pg. 674
Gold Bond Building Products, 515 Sea Horse Dr.(60085), pg. 790
A. L. HANSEN MFG. CO., 701 Pershing Rd.(60085), pg. 506
LAKE COUNTY PRESS, 98 Noll St.(60085), pg. 651
Luxor Corporation, 2245 Delany Rd.(60087), pg. 365
The News-Sun, 100 W. Madison Ave.(60085), pg. 284

West Chicago

GEO. J. BALL, INC., 622 Town Rd.(60185-2698), pg. 115
Ball Seed Co., 622 Town Rd.(60185-2698), pg. 116
CREATIVE MARKETING INTERNATIONAL CORP., 31W001 North Ave.(60185), pg. 297
THE JEL SERT CO., Rt. 59 & Conde St.(60185), pg. 591
Pan-American Seed Co., 728 Town Rd.(60185), pg. 116
Preferred Millwork, Inc., 980 Hawthorne Lane(60185), pg. 710
Structural Foam Plastics, 1400 Northwest Ave.(60185), pg. 1054

Westchester

Aeropak, 5 Westbrook Corp. Center Suite 900(60154), pg. 328
Allied Security Inc., 10001 W. Roosevelt Rd., Ste. 300(60154), pg. 39
Beauty-Professional, 5 West Brook Corp. Center(60159), pg. 328
Beauty Retail Products, 5 Westbrook Corp. Center,Ste. 900(60154), pg. 328
Cirrus System, Inc., One Westbrook Corp. Center, Ste. 700(60154), pg. 720
CREAM PRODUCTS CO., INC., 3 Westbrook Corp. Ctr.(60154), pg. 297
Daubert Coated Products, Inc., One Westbrook Corp. Center, Suite 900(60154), pg. 317
DAUBERT INDUSTRIES, INC., One Westbrook Corp. Center, Ste. 1000(60154), pg. 317
DEMERT & DOUGHERTY, INC., Five Westbrook Corp. Center, Ste. 900(60154), pg. 328
ECP Incorporated, One Westbrook Corp. Center, Suite 1000(60154), pg. 317
Teepak, Inc., 3 Westbrook Corporate Center(60154), pg. 535

Westmont

Everpure Inc., 660 N. Blackhawk Dr.(60559), pg. 358

Wheaton

The Daily Journal (IL), 362 Schmale Rd.(60187), pg. 284
SPRAYING SYSTEMS CO., North Ave. at Schmale Rd.(60188), pg. 1032
Torco Oil Automotive Division, 800 E. Roosevelt Rd.(60187), pg. 1102

Wheeling

J.W. ALLEN & COMPANY, 555 Allendale Dr.(60090), pg. 36
ANDERSON DIE CASTINGS, INC., 1720 S. Wolf Rd.(60090), pg. 72
BARR ELECTRIC CORPORATION, 300 W. Holbrook Dr.(60090), pg. 122
CAPITOL CONSTRUCTION GROUP, INC., 1000 Capitol Dr., Ste. 200(60090), pg. 215
Clear Shield National, Inc., 1175 Wheeling Rd.(60090), pg. 383
COLE TAYLOR FINANCIAL GROUP, 350 E. Dundee Rd., Ste. 200(60090), pg. 260
Economy Mechanical Industries, Inc., 77 S. Wheeling(60090), pg. 609
INDECK POWER EQUIPMENT COMPANY, 1111 S. Willis(60090), pg. 564
Inland Die Casting, 161 Carpenter Ave.(60090), pg. 906
Love Controls Corporation, 1475 S. Wheeling Rd.(60090), pg. 356
94th Aero Squadron of Palwaukee, Inc., 1070 S. Milwaukee Ave.(60090), pg. 1028
THE SEGERDAHL CORP., 1351 S. Wheeling Rd.(60090), pg. 987
SKOKIE VALLEY BEVERAGE CO., 199 Shepard Ave.(60090), pg. 1009

Willowbrook

Acorn of Illinois, 7630 So. Madison(60521), pg. 14
PET LIFE FOODS, INC., 7628 Plaza Ct.(60521), pg. 863
MARK SHALE, 500 Joliet Road(60521), pg. 994
STUART-IRONSIDES, INC., 7575 Plaza Court(60521), pg. 1054

Wilmette

Pioneer Press Newspapers Inc., 1232 Central Ave.(60091), pg. 18

Winfield

Alcohoplism Treatment Center, 27 W. 350 High Lake Rd.(60190), pg. 232
Central DuPage Hospital Association, 25 N. Winfield Rd.(60190), pg. 232

Wood Dale

AEC, Inc., 801 AEC Drive(60191), pg. 1047
Application Automation, Inc., 801 AEC Drive(60191), pg. 1047
Application Engineering Corporation, 801 AEC Drive(60191), pg. 1047
GEORGE SOLLITT CONSTRUCTION, 790 North Central Ave.(60191), pg. 1017
Whitlock, Inc., 801 AEC Dr.(60191), pg. 1047

Woodridge

Copco, 2240 W. 75th St.(60517), pg. 1195
Rowoco, 2240 W. 75th St.(60517), pg. 1195
Weston Gallery, 2240 W. 75th St.(60517), pg. 1195
WILTON INDUSTRIES, INC., 2240 W. 75th St.(60517), pg. 1194

Woodstock

AUTOMATIC LIQUID PACKAGING, INC., 2200 W. Lake Shore Dr.(60098), pg. 100

Zion

Kelso-Burnett Zion Branch, 3063 Sheridan(60099), pg. 622

INDIANA

Addinburg

Star Container, Inc., , pg. 1082

Albion

Albion Wire, Inc., State Rd. 8 E(46701), pg. 489
Auto Jectors, Inc., 1563 E. State Rd. 8(46701), pg. 489
Lyall Assemblies, Inc., St Rd. 9 & Cr 400 S.(46701), pg. 490

Alexandria

RAM GRAPHICS, INC., State Rd., 9 S.(46001), pg. 910

Anderson

Commercial Service Printing, 1200 E. 5th St.(46018), pg. 1164
PAY LESS SUPER MARKETS, INC., First Savings Tower, 33 W. 10th St.(46015), pg. 852
Stoops Express, Inc., P.O. Box 287, (46015), pg. 191
WARNER PRESS, INC., 1200 E. 5th St.(46018), pg. 1164
Warner Press Publishers, 1200 E. 5th St.(46018), pg. 1164

Angola

Mid West Correct Craft, Inc., P.O. Box 216(46703), pg. 287

Auburn

KRUSE INTERNATIONAL, 5400 CR 11-A at 69(46706), pg. 645
RENAISSANCE PUBLISHING CO., INC., E. 7th(46706), pg. 926

Aurora

AURORA CASKET COMPANY, U.S. 50 West(47001), pg. 98

Austin

MORGAN FOODS, INC., 90 W. Morgan St.(47102), pg. 770

Avilla

Hoosier Wire, Inc., Progress Dr.(46710), pg. 489
Pent Plastics, Inc., 303 E. 4th St.(46710), pg. 490
Wire Tech, Inc., Progress Way(46710), pg. 490

Berne

E.P. GRAPHICS, INC., 169 S. Jefferson(46711), pg. 360

Bloomington

HALL SIGN, INC., 3000 W. 3rd St.(47402), pg. 501
PTS ELECTRONICS CORPORATION, 5233 S. Hwy. 37(47401), pg. 837
SARKES TARZIAN, INCORPORATED, 205 N. College Ave.(47401), pg. 1079

Bluffton

Fremont Co., P.O. Box 532(46714), pg. 432

Boonville

Boonville Mining Services, Inc., 110 W. Division St.(47601), pg. 186
Lincoln Industries, Inc., 702 South 7th St.(47601), pg. 1221

Bremen

DLS Div., 222 E. 2nd St.(46506), pg. 1077

Bristol

BPC Division, State Rd. 15 South(46507), pg. 176
BRISTOL PRODUCTS, L.P., P.O. Box 1900, (46507), pg. 176
Bristolipe Division, 503 Vistula St.(46507), pg. 176
ESI Meats, Inc., 605 Kesco Dr., P.O. Box 157(46507), pg. 744

Butler

Therma-Tru Indiana Mfg. Opers., 108 Mutzfield Rd.(46721), pg. 1091

Carmel

Advantage Moving & Storage Co., Inc., 9998 N. Michigan Rd.(46032), pg. 724
Crest-Mayflower International, Inc., 9998 N. Michigan Rd.(46032), pg. 725
Dobson Moving & Storage, Inc., 9998 N. Michigan Rd.(46032), pg. 725

EVERGREEN HEALTHCARE LTD., 11350 North Meridian, Ste. 200(46032), pg. 391
Gentry Insurance Agency, Inc., 9998 N. Michigan Rd.(46032), pg. 725
KAUFFMAN PRODUCTS, INC., 1092 Third Ave., S.W.(46032), pg. 618
Mayflower Motor Coach, Inc., 9998 N. Michigan Rd.(46032), pg. 725
MAYFLOWER TRANSIT, INC., 9998 N. Michigan Rd.(46032), pg. 724
Mayflower Transit, Inc., 9998 N. Michigan Rd.(46032), pg. 724
NORTH AMERICAN ROOFING COMPANY, INC., 9700 N. Michigan Rd.(46032), pg. 811
QUINLAN ADVERTISING, Two Penn Mark Plaza, 11555 N. Meridian(46032), pg. 905
STANDARD LOCKNUT & LOCKWASHER, 1212 S. Rangeline Rd.(46032), pg. 1037
Stone & Simons Advertising, Inc., 701 Congressional Blvd., Ste. 120(46032), pg. 1051
Transport Service of Indiana, Inc., 9998 N. Michigan Rd.(46032), pg. 725

Clarksville

GOHMANN ASPHALT & CONSTRUCTION INC., 1630 Broadway(47129), pg. 465
Mariana Corporation, P.O. Box 2602(47131), pg. 465
Riverton Truckers, Inc., P.O. Box 2602(47131), pg. 465

Columbia City

PRECISION PLASTICS INC., 722 Sw(46725), pg. 885

Columbus

COSCO, INC., 2525 State St.(47201), pg. 287
DUNLAP & CO. INC., P.O. Box 328(47202), pg. 353
Flambeau Products-Columbus, 4325 Middle Rd.(47202), pg. 810

Corydon

THE KELLER MANUFACTURING CO., INC., Cedar & Water St.(47112), pg. 621

Covington

COVINGTON FOODS, INC., 316 Second St.(47932), pg. 290

Crawfordsville

Crawford Industries, 1414 Crawford Dr.(47933), pg. 64
GREFCO, Inc., 1489 Concord Rd.(47933), pg. 137
MCM ENTERPRISES, INC., 510 S. Oak St.(47933), pg. 691
Mid-State Wire Company, 510 S. Oak(47933), pg. 691
Precision Plastics, 1001 E. College St.(47933), pg. 885
SOMMER METALCRAFT CORPORATION, 315 Poston Dr.(47933), pg. 1018

Cromwell

Flex-Ohm, Inc., 9455 W. Gilbert Lake Rd.(46732), pg. 489

Daleville

BURLINGTON MOTOR CARRIERS INC., 14611 W. Commerce Rd.(47334), pg. 191

Elkhart

ACCRA PAC GROUP, 2730 Middlebury St.(46516), pg. 11
CARLTON MANUFACTURING, INC., 317 W. Franklin St.(46516), pg. 222
CREATION WINDOWS OF INDIANA, INC., 53061 Ada Dr.(46514), pg. 297
CROWN INTERNATIONAL, INC., P.O. Box 1000(46514), pg. 302
Elixir Industries, 2040 Industrial Parkway(46516), pg. 376
Elixir Industries, 640 Collins Rd.(46516), pg. 376
FABWEL INC., 1838 Middlebury St.(46516), pg. 396
PETE FALL FORD INC., 2525 By Pass Rd.(46514), pg. 398
FASTEC INDUSTRIAL, 23348 County Rd. 6(46515), pg. 403
Fastec SW Corporation, 23348 County Rd. 6, P.O. Box 1048(46515), pg. 403
Fie Trading Corporation, 23348 County Rd. 6, P.O. Box 1048(46515), pg. 403
General Generic Trucking Div., 2020 Toledo Rd.(46516), pg. 11
Health Care, Inc., 2835 Middlebury St.(46516), pg. 11
HOMAN LUMBER MART, INC., 1650 W. Lusher(46517), pg. 541
Kem Krest Corp., 2020 Toledo Rd.(46516), pg. 11
LASALLE-DEITCH CO., INC., 640 Industrial Pkwy.(46515), pg. 660
LaSalle Lighting, 2111 E. Industrial Pkwy.(46514), pg. 660
NIBCO, INC., 500 Simpson Ave.(46516), pg. 806
Nickles Bakery Inc., Elkhart, 600 Harrison St.(46516), pg. 807
The Selmer Co., P.O. Box 310, (46515), pg. 573
Sturgis Metals Division, Elkhart, P.O. Box 4537, 1514 W. Lusher Ave.(46515), pg. 1055
Thetford Corp., Warehouse Div., 55712-B County Rd. 15(46514), pg. 358
YODER OIL COMPANY INC., 2204 California Rd.(46514), pg. 1208

Evansville

ATL Terminal Corp., 1212 St. George Rd.(47711), pg. 97
ADPLAN ASSOCIATES, P.O. Box 59(47701), pg. 18
ANCHOR INDUSTRIES INC., 1100 Burch Dr.(47711), pg. 71
Atlas Specialized Transportation, 1212 St. George Rd.(47711), pg. 97
ATLAS VAN LINES, INC., 1212 St. George Rd.(47711), pg. 96
Atlas Van Lines Intl., 1212 St. George Rd.(47711), pg. 97
Atlas World-Class Travel, 1212 St. George Rd.(47711), pg. 97
Brake Supply Co., 4001 Vogel Rd.(47715), pg. 639
CITIZENS REALTY & INSURANCE INC., 111 S.E. 3rd St.(47708), pg. 251
EVANA AUTOMATION, 5825 Old Boonville Hwy.(47715), pg. 390
EVANSVILLE BREWING COMPANY, 1301 W. Pennsylvania Ave.(47710), pg. 391
KARGES FURNITURE COMPANY, 1501 W. Maryland(47710), pg. 616
KELLER CRESCENT CO., 1100 E. Louisiana St.(47711), pg. 620
Kentucky Indiana Lumber Co., 1700 N. Kentucky(47711), pg. 624
GEORGE KOCH SONS, INC., 10 S. 11th Ave.(47744), pg. 639
LEWIS BROTHERS BAKERIES, INC., 500 North Fulton Avenue(47710), pg. 673
RED SPOT PAINT & VARNISH CO., 1016 Columbia(47711), pg. 918
REGENCY ASSOCIATES LIMITED PARTNERSHIP, 5005 Washington Ave.(47715), pg. 922
Shelf Stable Foods, Inc., 1201 N. Stockwell Rd.(47715), pg. 1203
TRAYLOR BROTHERS, INC., 835 N. Congress Ave.(47715), pg. 1108
Uniseal, Inc., 1800 W. Maryland St.(47712), pg. 639
Windsor Plastics, Inc., 601 No. Congress Ave.(47715), pg. 492

Fort Branch

Emge Packing Co., Inc., Red Bank Rd.(47648), pg. 219

Fort Wayne

Alro Group, Fort Wayne, P.O. Box 10360, 2211 Freeman St.(46851-0360), pg. 44
Applied Holographics, Inc., 1530 Progress Rd.(46898), pg. 960
BONSIB INC., The Bonsib Building, 927 S. Harrison St.(46802), pg. 164
CHEMCENTRAL/Fort Wayne, 7415 Nelson Rd. E.(46803), pg. 241
DSI/TMP Worldwide, Pointe Inverness Office Park, 7030 Pointe Inverness Way, Ste. 200(46804), pg. 1074
ESSEX GROUP, INC., 1601 Wall St.(46802), pg. 389
Fill-Rite Division, 4204 Ferguson Rd.(46809), pg. 1120
Fort Wayne Wizards, 927 S. Harrison(46802), pg. 758
GAI Consultants, Inc., 117 Airports N. Office Park(46825), pg. 439
HWI Building Corp., 6502 Nelson Rd.(46803), pg. 508
HARDWARE WHOLESALERS, INC., 6502 Nelson Rd.(46803), pg. 508
HARRIS-KAYOT, INC., 2801 W. State Blvd.(46808), pg. 512
Holsum of Fort Wayne, Inc., 156 E. Murray(46858), pg. 673
Imaging Systems Division, 1530 Progress Rd.(46808), pg. 960
THE MEDICAL PROTECTIVE COMPANY, 5814 Reed Rd.(46835), pg. 735
NBS Imaging Systems, Inc., P.O. Box 8490, 1530 Progress Rd.(46898-8490), pg. 960
OMNI SOURCE CORPORATION, 1610 N. Calhoun St.(46808), pg. 826
PERFECTION BAKERIES INC., 350 Pearl St.(46802), pg. 861
PETROLEUM TRADERS CORPORATION, 1122 Thomas Rd.(46804), pg. 865
Power Wheels, Inc., 3405 Meyer Rd.(46896), pg. 644
REA MAGNET WIRE COMPANY, INC., 3600 E. Pontiac St.(46803), pg. 915
ROGERS MARKETS INC., 528 W. Washington Blvd.(46802), pg. 943
SBN SYSTEM INC., 1530 Progress Rd.(46808), pg. 960
Scotfoam Corp., 3005 Commercial Rd.(46809), pg. 1121
Wabash Fibre Box Co.-Fort Wayne Plant, Baer Field, Baer Field - Box 1183
ZOLLNER CORPORATION, 2425 Coliseum Blvd. S.(46803), pg. 1221

Fowler

DEMETER, INC., 98 South & East, Ste. A(47944), pg. 328

Frankfort

HARMESON MANUFACTURING COMPANY, INC., 509 W. Barner St.(46041), pg. 510

Franklin

JOHNSON COUNTY FARM BUREAU CO-OP, 755 Hamilton Ave.(46131), pg. 598
KYB Industries Inc., 1860 Northwood Plaza(46131), pg. 613

Garrett

Mossberg Industries, Hubbard Division, 2047 Second St.(46738), pg. 773

Gary

Belmont Industries, U.S. Refractories Div., 1000 N. Clark Rd.(46406), pg. 136
DIXIE DAIRY COMPANY, 1200 W. 15th Ave.(46407), pg. 341
EBSC CORPORATION, 5045 Broadway(46409), pg. 359
JACK GRAY TRANSPORT, INC., 4600 E. 15th Ave.(46403), pg. 479

Goshen

GOSHEN RUBBER CO., INC., 1525 S. 10th St.(46526), pg. 472
RIETH-RILEY CONSTRUCTION CO. INC., 3626 Eckhart Road(46526), pg. 934
STARCRAFT AUTOMOTIVE CORP., 2703 College Ave.(46526), pg. 1040

Greensburg

KOVA FERTILIZER INC., 1330 North Anderson St.(47240), pg. 643

Greenwood

Prime Technology, Inc., 56 So. Park Blvd.(46142), pg. 889

Griffith

Thermojet, 1950 N. Griffith Blvd., Ste. A(46319), pg. 283

Hammond

CALUMET CONSTRUCTION CORPORATION, 1247 169th St.(46324), pg. 211
HAMMOND LEAD PRODUCTS, INC., 5231 Hohman Ave.(46325), pg. 504
MORRISON, INC., 1834 Summer St.(46320), pg. 771
SCREW CONVEYOR CORP., 700 Hoffman St.(46327), pg. 983
SMITH MOTORS, INC., 6405 Indianapolis Blvd.(46320), pg. 1014

Hobart

SAVE MORE FOOD MART, INC., Rtes. 6 & 51(46342), pg. 973

Howe

Multi-Plex, Inc., State Rd. 9 N.(46746), pg. 318

Huntington

Noll Printing Corporation, 100 Noll Plaza(46750), pg. 832
OUR SUNDAY VISITOR, INC., 100 Noll Plaza(46750), pg. 832

Indianapolis

AM General Corporation, 1428 W. Henry St.(46221), pg. 926
The Acordia, Inc., 120 Monument Circle(46204), pg. 90
Allied Security Inc., 3901 N. Meridian St., Ste. 15(46208), pg. 39
Allison Payment Systems Div., 2200 Production Dr.(46241), pg. 305
Allright Parking of Indianapolis, Inc., 312 Massachusetts Ave.(46204), pg. 42
Alro Group, Indianapolis, 5620 Churchman Ave.(46203), pg. 44
Ambassadair Travel Club, Inc., 7337 W. Washington St.(46231), pg. 69
Amber Tours, Inc., 7337 W. Washington St.(46231), pg. 69
Amber Travel, Inc., 7337 W. Washington St.(46231), pg. 70
American Red Ball World Wide Movers, 1335 Sadlier Circle, E. Dr.(46239), pg. 918
American Trans Air Execujet, Inc., 7337 W. Washington St.(46231), pg. 70
American Trans Air, Inc., 7337 W. Washington St.(46231), pg. 70
American Trans Air Training Corp., 7337 W. Washington St.(46231), pg. 70
AMERICAN UNITED LIFE INSURANCE COMPANY, One American Square(46204), pg. 65
AMTRAN, INC., 7337 W. Washington St.(46231), pg. 69
Mark Anderson Associates, Inc., 8335 Allison Pointe Trail, Ste. 340(46250), pg. 73
Anthem Companies, Inc., 5451 Lakeview Parkway South Dr.(46268), pg. 90
APEX CORPORATION, 2060 Yandes(46202), pg. 78
Associated Group Inc., 120 Monument Circle(46204), pg. 90
THE ASSOCIATED GROUP, 120 Monument Circle(46204), pg. 90
BENJAMIN FRANKLIN LITERARY & MEDICAL SOCIETY, INC., 1100 Waterway Blvd.(46202), pg. 139
Beveridge Paper Co., 717 W. Washington St.(46204), pg. 1005
BLOOMHORST STORY O'HARA INC., 200 S. Meridian St., Ste. 510(46225), pg. 158
Brougher Agency, Inc., 525 S. Meridian St.(46225), pg. 1146
THE BRULIN CORPORATION, 2920 Dr. Andrew J. Brown Ave.(46205), pg. 184
CRE, INC., 400 Victoria Centre, 22 E. Washington(46204-3529), pg. 203
CUNA Lake Central District, 5670 Caito Drive, Suite 172(46226), pg. 205
CALDWELL VANRIPER INC., 1314 N. Meridian(46202), pg. 209
Calumet Contruction Corporation-Indianapolis Division, 5827 W. 74th St.(46278-1757), pg. 211
Car Brite Distributing, Inc., 1855 S. Draper St.(46203), pg. 358
Car Brite, Inc., 1910 S. State St.(46203), pg. 358
Caribe Express Pace Air Freight, 330 W. Wall Street Pike(46234), pg. 220
CENTRAL SUPPLY CO., INC., 8900 E. 30th St.(46219), pg. 234
Challenger Construction, Inc., 2021 N. Meridan St.(46202), pg. 328
CHEMCENTRAL/Indianapolis, 5850 W. 82nd St.(46278), pg. 242
Children's Better Health Institute, 1100 Waterway Blvd.(46202), pg. 139

CITIZENS GAS & COKE UTILITY, 2020 N. Meridian St.(46202), pg. 250
COLLINS OLDSMOBILE INC., P.O. Box 24009, 4080 Lafayette Rd.(46254), pg. 263
COMMUNICO, 1101 Southeastern Ave.(46202), pg. 270
COUNTRYMARK COOPERATIVE, INC., 950 N. Meridian St., Ste. 0700(46204-3909), pg. 290
Creative Marketing Group, Inc., 1000 Waterway Blvd.(46202), pg. 306
CRYSTAL FLASH PETROLEUM CORP., 5221 Ivy Tech Dr.(46268), pg. 303
Curtis Intl. Ltd., 1000 Waterway Blvd.(46202), pg. 306
THE CURTIS PUBLISHING COMPANY, 1000 Waterway Blvd.(46202), pg. 306
THE DEMARS CORP., 1919 N. Meridian St.(46202), pg. 327
DeMars Haka Development, Inc., 1919 N. Meridan St.(46202), pg. 328
DeMars Program Management, Inc., 1919 N. Meridan St.(46202), pg. 328
Diamond Chain Company, 402 Kentucky Ave.(46207), pg. 69
DOWNEY DESIGNS INTERNATIONAL, INC., 2265 Executive Dr.(46241), pg. 348
E & A INDUSTRIES, INC., 101 W. Ohio, Ste. 1840(46204), pg. 358
EV Services Inc., P.O. Box 80073(46280), pg. 929
Eby Brown Co., 5820 Fortune Circle(46251), pg. 365
Endless Vacation Publishing, P.O. Box 80073(46280), pg. 929
ERMCO, INC., 151 S. East St.(46202), pg. 387
Executive Telecom Systems, Inc., College Park North, 9585 Valpariso Ct.(46268), pg. 189
Farbest Inc., 950 N. Meridian(46204), pg. 290
Frontier Transport Corporation, 1560 E. Raymond St.(46203), pg. 833
Geupel DeMars, Inc., 1919 N. Meridan St.(46202), pg. 328
Ghafari Associates, Inc., 6330 E. 75th St., Ste. 118(46250), pg. 455
GLENROY CONSTRUCTION CO. INC., 450 S. Ritter Ave.(46219), pg. 462
GENE B. GLICK COMPANY, INC., 8330 Woodfield Crossing Blvd., Ste. 200(46240), pg. 462
Stephen Gould of Indiana, Inc., 8604 Allisonville Rd., Ste. 101(46250), pg. 474
THOMAS L. GREEN & CO., INC., 202 N. Miley Ave.(46222), pg. 484
GREGG APPLIANCES INC., 4151 E. 96th St.(46240), pg. 486
H & K Realty Co. Inc., 101 West Ohio, Ste. 1840(46204), pg. 358
HP DIRECT, 5561 West 74th St.(46268-4184), pg. 497
HPS, INC., 8020 Zionsville Rd.(46268), pg. 497
J.R. HAHN CO., INC., 2401 Production Dr.(46241), pg. 500
HANDLEY & MILLER, INC., 1712 N. Meridian St.(46202), pg. 505
Hebrew National Kosher Foods Div., 602 W. Ray St.(46225), pg. 788
HERFF JONES INC., 4625 W. 62nd St.(46268), pg. 531
HIGH POINT OIL CO., 3520 East 96th St., Ste. 10(46240), pg. 534
Hogan Transfer & Storage Corporation, Inc., 825 E. St. Clair(46202), pg. 724
HOLCOMB & HOKE MFG. COMPANY, INC., 1545 Van Buren(46203), pg. 538
Huber, Hunt & Nichols, Inc., P.O. Box 128, (46206), pg. 553
HUBLER CHEVROLET INC., 8220 S. U.S. 31(46227), pg. 550
THE HUNT CORPORATION, 2450 S. Tibbs Ave.(46241), pg. 553
The Hunt Paving Company, Inc., P.O. Box 128, (46206), pg. 553
INDIANA RECORDS MANAGERS, 6971 Hillsdale Ct.(46250), pg. 565
Jorgensen Steel & Aluminum/Indianapolis, 8604 Allisonville Rd., Ste. 105(46250), pg. 606
KENWORTH OF INDIANAPOLIS INC., 2929 S. Holt Rd.(46241), pg. 624
Key Health Plan, 333 N. Alabama(46204), pg. 90
Keystone Crash Parts Mart - Indianapolis, 4145 N. Keystone Ave.(46205), pg. 628
Keystone Group Inc., 8900 Keystone Crossing, Ste. 1150(46240), pg. 1024
Kilsby-Roberts Cutting Center/Indianapolis, 2233 S.W. St.(46225), pg. 606
Kilsby-Roberts/Indianapolis, 2300 S. Tibbs Ave.(46241), pg. 606
LDI, LTD., 251 N. Illinois St., Ste. 1800(46204), pg. 647
LABSCO, 7721 Records St.(46226), pg. 650
LOCKHART CADILLAC INC., 5550 N. Keystone Ave.(46220), pg. 680
Major Video Concepts, Inc., 8399 Zionsville Rd.(46268), pg. 647
MAPLEHURST FARMS, INC., 3745 Farnsworth St.(46241), pg. 705
MAYS CHEMICAL COMPANY, 7760 E. 89th St.(46256), pg. 725
MCFARLING FOODS, INC., 333 W. 14th St.(46208), pg. 729
MICRO-MET L CORP., 3419 Roosevelt Ave.(46218), pg. 748
MITCHEL & SCOT MACHINE CO., INC., 1841 Ludlow Ave.(46201), pg. 761
Mobile Drilling Company, Inc., 3807 Madison(46227), pg. 1220
MONTGOMERY, ZUKERMAN, DAVIS, INC., 1800 N. Meridian St.(46202), pg. 768
NATIONAL RETAIL HARDWARE ASSN., 5822 W. 74th St.(46278), pg. 793
OVERLAND TRANSPORTATION SYSTEM, INC., 6500 E. 30th St.(46219), pg. 832
P.M. Paper Products Div., 8525 E. 33rd St.(46226), pg. 835
P. S. INTERNATIONAL INC., 8910 Purdue Rd., Ste. 260(46268), pg. 837
Pentek Corporation, 8502 Brookville Rd.(46239-9427), pg. 357
Pioneer Express Inc., 1560 West Raymond St.(46206), pg. 833
Productive Business Interiors, 6971 Hillsdale Ct.(46250), pg. 565
Queens Group Indiana, Inc., 620 S. Belmont Ave.(46221), pg. 904
RCI Quality Services, Inc., P.O. Box 80073(46280), pg. 929
RCI Travel, P.O. Box 80073(46280), pg. 929
Radio Indianapolis, Inc., 8120 Knue Rd.(46250), pg. 1065
Red Ball Forwarders, Inc., 1335 Sadlier Circle, E. Dr.(46239), pg. 918
Red Ball Leasing, Inc., 1347 Sadlier Circle, E. Dr.(46239), pg. 918
Red Ball Van & Storage, Inc., 1347 Sadlier Circle, E. Dr.(46239), pg. 918
Reilly Chemicals S.A., 151 N. Delaware(46204), pg. 923
REILLY INDUSTRIES, INC., 1510 Market Square Center(46204), pg. 923
Reilly Industries Inc., 1500 S. Tibbs(46241), pg. 923
RESORT CONDOMINIUMS INTERNATIONAL, 3502 Woodview Trace(46268), pg. 929
Resort Quality Services, Inc., P.O. Box 80073(46280), pg. 929
Response Communications, Inc., 933 Western Dr.(46241), pg. 339
ROWTRONICS COMPANY INC., 3334 Founders Rd.(46268), pg. 953
SANISERV, 2020 Production Dr.(46241), pg. 970
The Saturday Evening Post Society, 1100 Waterway Blvd.(46202), pg. 139
Saturn of Indianapolis, 5333 Pike Plaza Rd.(46254), pg. 680
SERVAAS, INC., 1000 Waterway Blvd.(46202), pg. 991
Servaas Investments, Inc., 1000 Waterway Blvd.(46202), pg. 991
Servaas Laboratories Inc., 1200 Waterway Blvd.(46202), pg. 991
SERVICE SUPPLY CO. INC. OF INDIANA, 603 E. Washington St.(46204), pg. 992
MELVIN SIMON & ASSOCIATES, P.O. Box 7033, (46207), pg. 1006
SOVEREIGN GROUP INC., 8900 Keystone Crossing, Ste. 1150(46240), pg. 1024
SUPERIOR OIL CO. INC., 400 W. Regent St.(46225), pg. 1064
SYNDICATE SYSTEMS, INC., 250 E. 96th St., Ste. 415(46240), pg. 1069
TMP Worldwide, Inc., 7400 N. Shadeland Ave., Ste. 125(46250), pg. 1074
Technicare Cleaning Systems Inc., 2720 N. College(46204), pg. 359
THOMAS & SKINNER, INC., 1120 E. 23rd St.(46206), pg. 1093
United Chemical Products, 1650 Luett St.(46222), pg. 725
UNITED FARM BUREAU FAMILY LIFE INSURANCE CO., 130 E. Washington(46204), pg. 1131
United Farm Bureau Life Insurance Co., 130 E. Washington St.(46204), pg. 1131
VASA Brougher, Inc., 525 S. Meridian St.(46225), pg. 1146
VASA INSURANCE GROUP, INC., 525 S. Meridian St.(46225), pg. 1146
VASA Life Insurance Co., 525 S. Meridian St.(46206), pg. 1146
VASA North Atlantic Insurance Company, 525 S. Meridian St.(46225), pg. 1146
J.W. Welsch & Associates, 6435 Castleway W. Dr.(46250-1940), pg. 1058
WHEATON VAN LINES, INC., 8010 Castleton Rd.(46250), pg. 1184
F.A. WILHELM CONSTRUCTION CO., INC., 3914 Prospect St.(46203), pg. 1189
YOUNG AUTOMOTIVE GROUP, 3210 E. 96th St.(46240), pg. 1209
YOUNG & LARAMORE, 310 E. Vermont St.(46204), pg. 1209
ZIMMER PAPER PRODUCTS INC., 1450 E. 20th St.(46218), pg. 1220

Jasper

JOFCO INC., 13th & Vine St.(47547-0071), pg. 595
NORTH AMERICAN PRODUCTS CORP., 1180 Wernsing Rd.(47546), pg. 811
WHARFSIDE RESTAURANTS, INC., Der Buro Komplex, 4201-A Mannheim Road(47546-9618), pg. 1184

Jeffersonville

KITCHEN KOMPACT, INC., KK Plaza(47130), pg. 634
Wayandot, Inc., 125 Peacely St.(47130), pg. 1205

Kendallville

Dekko Wire Div., Kendallville, 811 Commerce Dr.(46755), pg. 489
GROUP DEKKO INTERNATIONAL INC., Hwy. 6 & County Rd. 400 E.(46755), pg. 489
Pent Assemblies, Inc., US 6 & Cr 400 E(46755), pg. 490
Pent Products, Inc., US 6 & Cr 400 E(46755), pg. 490
PVC Compounders, 6928 N - 400 E(46755), pg. 490
Reclaimers, Inc., 6928 N - 400 E(46755), pg. 490
Silicones, Inc., US 6 & Cr 400 E(46755), pg. 490
Taylor Made, Indiana, P.O. Box 157(46755), pg. 1080

Kokomo

KOKOMO GRAIN CO., INC., 1002 W. Morgan St.(46901), pg. 640
KOKOMO SPRING COMPANY, INC., 329 E. Firmin St.(46902), pg. 640

La Porte

Bonnie Baking Co., 800 Boyd Blvd.(46350), pg. 673

Lafayette

Chemrock Corporation, (47902), pg. 137
EGYPTIAN LACQUER MANUFACTURING COMPANY, INC., 555 Sagamore Pkwy., S.(47905), pg. 371
FAUBER CONSTRUCTION COMPANY, INC., 2200 N. 9th St.(47902), pg. 403
ROSTONE CORPORATION, 2450 Sagamore Pkwy., S.(47905), pg. 950
SCHWAB CORP., 3000 Main St.(47904), pg. 980

Logansport

SMALL PARTS, INC., 600 Humphrey St.(46947), pg. 1010

Marion

Bell Fibre Products, 3102 So. Boots St.(46953), pg. 135
BELL PACKAGING CORPORATION, 3102 S. Boots St.(46953), pg. 135
Property-Owners Insurance Co., 3950 W. Delphi Pike(46952), pg. 100

Michigan City

W.E. Anderson Div., P.O. Box 358, (46360), pg. 356
DWYER INSTRUMENTS INC., 102 Highway 212(46360), pg. 356
Erb Lumber Co. of Indiana, 910 State Hwy. 212(46360), pg. 360
First Citizens Bank, N.A., 515 Franklin Square(46360-3369), pg. 544
HORIZON BANCORP, 515 Franklin Square(46360-3369), pg. 544
JOSAM COMPANY, P.O. Box T-525 W. U.S. 20(46360), pg. 607
Mercoid Div., P.O. Box 258(46360), pg. 356
Paltier Div., 1701 Kentucky St.(46360), pg. 690
Weil-McLain, Blaine St.(46360), pg. 710

Middlebury

Harter Systems Div., 11451 Harter Dr.(46540), pg. 514
JAYCO INC., 58075 State Rd. 13 S.(46540), pg. 590
JET, Inc., P.O. Box 460(46540), pg. 590
Kenco, P.O. Box 726(46540), pg. 1025

Milford

Brock Manufacturing, P.O. Box 2000, (46542), pg. 205
CTB INC., P.O. Box 2000, (46542), pg. 205
Chore-Time/Brock International, P.O. Box 2000, (46542), pg. 205
Chore-Time Cage Systems, P.O. Box 2000, (46542), pg. 205
Chore-Time Equipment, P.O. Box 2000, (46542), pg. 205

Mishawaka

AM General Corporation, 13200 McInley Hwy.(46545), pg. 926
AM General Corporation, P.O. Box 728, (46546), pg. 926
Alco Health Services Corporation-Mishawaka Div., 1655 E. 12th St.(46544), pg. 32
JORDAN MOTORS, INC., 609 E. Jefferson(46545), pg. 605
JUHL MARKETING COMMUNICATIONS, 3930 Edison Lakes Pkwy.(46545), pg. 608
NATIONAL STEEL CORPORATION, 4100 Edison Lakes Pky.(46545), pg. 793
SOUTH BEND PLASTICS, INC., 1810 Clover Rd.(46545), pg. 1019

Mitchell

Carpenter Manufacturing, Inc., 1500 W. Main St.(47446), pg. 991

Monticello

Monticello Tank, Inc., 806 N. First St.(47960), pg. 246
WHITE COUNTY FARM BUREAU CO-OP ASSOCIATION, 210 W. Harrison St.(47960), pg. 1185

Morristown

Rubber Products Division, P.O. Box 245, U.S. 52 W.(46161-0245), pg. 433

Mount Summit

Brooks Foods, P.O. Box 157, (47361), pg. 26

Mount Vernon

Mount Vernon Democrat, 430 Main St.(47620), pg. 655

Muncie

Alro Group, Muncie, 2301 S. Walnut St.(47302), pg. 44
Borg-Warner Automotive, Inc., Transmission Systems, P.O. Box 2688, 47302, (47302), pg. 166
Broderick Company, Inc., , pg. 468
CITY MACHINE TOOL & DIE COMPANY, 1302 E. Washington St.(47305), pg. 251
N. G. GILBERT CORPORATION, 700 S. Council St.(47305), pg. 458
MAXON CORPORATION, 201 E. 18th St.(47302-4124), pg. 723
Muncie Division, 2415 S. Walnut St.(47302), pg. 1198

Munster

U.S. REDUCTION COMPANY, 9200 Calumet Ave.(46321), pg. 1137

Nappanee

FAIRMONT HOMES, INC., 502 S. Oakland(46550), pg. 397

New Albany

BEACH MOLD & TOOL INC., 999 Progress Blvd.(47150), pg. 128
KAISER TOBACCO COMPANY, INC., 415 E. Oak St.(47150), pg. 615
Keystone Automotive Industries, Inc.-Louisville, 1214 Spring Street(47150), pg. 628
SAMTEC INC., 810 Progress Blvd.(47150), pg. 968

New Haven

Superior Linkage Division, 2110 Summit St.(46774), pg. 1120

Noblesville

Indiana Seed Co., Inc., P.O. Box 440, (46060), pg. 654
INDUSTRIAL DIELECTRICS, INC., 407 S. 7th St.(46060), pg. 566
O'MALIA FOOD MARKETS INC., 1555 Westfield Rd.(46060), pg. 825

North Webster

Heaters Engineering, Inc., Rte. 1 Backwater Rd,. Box 337(46555), pg. 489

Oaktown

GREEN CONSTRUCTION OF INDIANA, INC., Hwy. 484

Paoli

PAOLI, INC., 524 N.E. Third St.(47454), pg. 846

Peru

W. C. REDMON CO., 200 Harrison Ave.(46970), pg. 919

Plymouth

Twin Y Corporation, 2526 N. Western(46563), pg. 592

Portage

HUNTER CORP., 6000 Southport Rd.(46368), pg. 554
SUMMERFIELD TRUCK CO. INC., 5900 Southport Rd.(46368), pg. 1057

Rensselaer

JASPER COUNTY FARM BUREAU CO-OP ASSOCIATION, INC., Hwy. 231, P.O. Box 238(47978), pg. 590
The Ohio Mattress Company Licensing And Componets Group, P.O. Box 258, 1132 N. Cullen(47978), pg. 985

Richmond

HOFFCO, INC., 358 N.W. F St.(47374), pg. 537
Plastic Products of Indiana, 300 Industrial Park(47374), pg. 1107
SWAYNE ROBINSON & COMPANY, 214 Main St.(47375), pg. 939
RODEFELD CO., INC., 96 W. Main St.(47374), pg. 942
TEC Fab Div., 1805 Sheridan St.(47374), pg. 873
WAYNE CORPORATION, Industries Rd.(47374-8447), pg. 1169

Rockport

The Journal-Democrat, P.O. Box 6(47635), pg. 655
PEERLESS POTTERY, INC., No. Lincoln Ave.(47635), pg. 855

Rushville

RUSH COUNTY FARM BUREAU CO-OP, 627 West 3rd St.(46173), pg. 956

Salem

Ferralloy, Becks Mill Rd.(47167), pg. 559
O.P. LINK HANDLE COMPANY, P.O. Box 350(47167-0350), pg. 676

Scottsburg

Plastic Products Division, 100 W. Country Rd., P.O. Box 4452(47170-0452), pg. 432
Rubber Products Division, P.O. Box 4452, Country Rd. 100 W.(47170-0452), pg. 433

Sellersburg

Sellersburg Stone Company, Inc., P.O. Box D, 1019 Utica St.(47172), pg. 465

Seymour

CENTRAL PHARMACEUTICALS, INC., 120 E. Third St.(47274), pg. 234
THE JOHN C. GROUB COMPANY INC., 900 A Ave. E., Freeman Field(47274), pg. 489
KOCOLENE OIL CORP., 1725 E. Tipton St.(47274), pg. 639
Lear Siegler Seymour Corp., 885 N. Chestnut St., P.O. Box 408(47274), pg. 664
ROSE ACRE FARMS, R.R. 5(47274), pg. 947
SEYMOUR MANUFACTURING COMPANY, 5th & Broadway(47274), pg. 994

Shelbyville

KCL CORPORATION, Hodell & Prospect Sts.(46176), pg. 611
Rubber Products Division, P.O. Box 38, State Rd. 44 W.(46176-0038), pg. 433

Sheridan

UNITED FEEDS, INC., 4310 W. State Rd. 38(46069), pg. 1132

Shoals

Gold Bond Building Products, P.O. Box 250, (47581), pg. 790

South Bend

AM General Corporation, 105 N. Niles Ave.(46617-2705), pg. 926
Alro Group, South Bend, P.O. Box 2319, 2025 S. Main St.(46680-2319), pg. 44
BATTEAST CONSTRUCTION COMPANY, INC., 430 E. LaSalle Ave.(46617), pg. 126
Biggs Gilmore Communications, 501 Monroe, Ste. 200(46601), pg. 150
Clark-Simon, Inc., 1901 Bendix Dr.(46628), pg. 252
Golden Cat Corporation, 348 S. Columbia St.(46601), pg. 637
HEALTH CARE DISTRIBUTORS OF INDIANA, INC., 4100 N. Technology Dr.(46628), pg. 520
Indiana Service Center/Satellite Location, 4325 N. Mayflower Rd., South Lake Center, Ste. 105(46628), pg. 1192
Interplastic Molding Products Div., 1545 S. Olive St.(46619), pg. 580
J & B Products, 461 N. Niles Ave.(46617), pg. 176
Overhill Mfg., Inc., 2502 W. Lawton St.(46628), pg. 554
PETERSEN GRAPHICS GROUP, 2920 W. Sample(46619), pg. 864
SCHURZ COMMUNICATIONS, INC., 225 W. Colfax Ave.(46626), pg. 979
South Bend Scrap & Processing, 1305 Prairie Ave.(46680), pg. 1055
South Bend Stamping Div., 601 W. Broadway(46624), pg. 361
WELLS ALUMINUM CORP., 300 S. St. Louis Blvd.(46601), pg. 1175

South Milford

Indiana Insulated Wire, State Rd 3, RR 700 S.(46786), pg. 489

Tell City

Maxon Marine, Inc., South Boundary St.(47586), pg. 246
The News, 537 Main St.(47586), pg. 655
TELL CITY CHAIR CO., 417 Seventh St.(47586), pg. 1085

Terre Haute

HULMAN & COMPANY, 900 Wabash Ave.(47808), pg. 552
KC Foods, 900 Wabash Ave.(47808), pg. 552
Wabash Fibre Box Co.-Terre Haute Plant, 2000 N. 19th St.(47804), pg. 1183
WESTON PAPER & MANUFACTURING CO., 2001 No. 19th St.(47804), pg. 1183

Tipton

Steel Parts Corp., Berryman Pike(46072), pg. 571

Union City

UNION CITY BODY COMPANY, INC., 350 W. Deerfield Rd.(47390), pg. 1128

Upland

AVIS INDUSTRIAL CORPORATION, 1909 So. Main St.(46989), pg. 102
The Pierce Co., Inc., 201 N. 8th St.(46989), pg. 102

Valparaiso

URSCHEL LABS INC., 2503 Calumet Ave.(46383), pg. 1140

Van Buren

WEAVER POPCORN COMPANY, INC., 130 E. Main St.(46991), pg. 1170

Versailles

Ohio Rod Products Company, Inc., P.O. Box 416, (47042), pg. 609

Vincennes

Hamilton, Inc., 2000 Chestnut St.(47591), pg. 3
Lewis Vincennes, Inc., 3114 Old Decker Rd.(47591), pg. 673
VINCENNES STEEL CORP., 2007 Oliphant Dr.(47591), pg. 1152

Wabash

FORD METER BOX COMPANY, 775 Manchester Ave.(46992-0443), pg. 423
Markhon Industries, Inc, 200 Bond St.(46992), pg. 623
Wabash Alloys Division, P.O. Box 466, (46992), pg. 275
Wabash Magnetics, First & Webster St.(46992), pg. 357
Wabash Magnetics, 810 N. Cass St.(46992), pg. 357

Warsaw

Stephen Gould IN, P.O. Box 44, Rte. 7, Aztec & Bell Rds.(46580), pg. 474

West Lafayette

Mid Pacific Air, P.O. Box 2835(47906), pg. 613

Winchester

LEON HENDRICKSON, RR 529
OMCO MOULD, INC., One OMCO Square(47394), pg. 819
OMCO Cast Metals, Inc., 900 N. Main St.(47394), pg. 819
OMCO Machining Concepts, Inc., 828 N. Main St.(47394), pg. 819

Wolcott

Double D Fertilizer, R.R.I. Box 2(47995), pg. 590

Yorktown

YORKTOWN TOOL & DIE CORPORATION, 104 E. Smith(47396), pg. 1208

IOWA

Adair

ADAIR FEED & GRAIN COMPANY, 110 Audubon(50002-3855), pg. 16

Afton

Heat Tech, Inc., 100 Industrial Park East(50830), pg. 489

Albia

A.Y.M. Inc., So. Clinton & 17th Ave. W.(52531), pg. 728

Amana

Amana Farms, Inc., P.O. Box 189(52203), pg. 46
Amana-Nordstrom Motel Co., P.O. Box 189(52203), pg. 46
AMANA SOCIETY, P.O. Box 189(52203), pg. 46
Amana Society Service Co., Second St.(52203), pg. 46

Ames

PMI, 620 Arrasmith Trail(50010), pg. 1100
TODD & SARGENT, INC., 620 Arrasmith Trail(50010-9022), pg. 1100

Atlantic

Walnut Grove-Nutrena Feed Div., Cargill, Inc., Second & Linn Sts.(50022), pg. 219

Bettendorf

Clarion Enterprises, Inc., 300 NW Bank Tower(52722), pg. 767
Indeco, Inc., 630 E. River Dr.(52722), pg. 597
Riverside Products Div., 225 33rd St.(52722), pg. 1013
Sivyer Steel Corporation, 225 33rd. St.(52722), pg. 1013

Boone

FAREWAY STORES, INC., 2600 E. Eighth St.(50036), pg. 399

Burlington

BURLINGTON BASKET CO., 922 Bluff Rd.(52601), pg. 191
CHITTENDEN & EASTMAN CO., 401 S. Roosevelt(52601), pg. 248
Lehigh-Leopold, 2825 Mt. Pleasant St.(52601), pg. 608
Murray Turbomachinery Corporation, 1106 Washington St.(52601), pg. 285
National Research Bureau, 424 No. Third St.(52601), pg. 100

Carter Lake

OWEN INDUSTRIES, INC., 5th & Ave. H(51510), pg. 834

Cedar Rapids

APACHE HOSE & BELTING COMPANY, 2515 18th St., S.W.(52404), pg. 77
Blevins Popcorn, 1515 H Ave. N.E.(52402), pg. 26
Cox Cable Cedar Rapids, Inc., 1939 Blairs Ferry Road, N.E.(52402), pg. 294
Creswell, Munsell, Fultz & Zirbel, 4211 Signal Ridge Rd., N.E.(52402), pg. 1211
GAZETTE COMPANY, INC., 500 Third Ave., S.E.(52401), pg. 447
HENRY RUSSELL BRUCE, INC., 1957 Blairs Ferry Rd. NE(52402), pg. 530
KGAN-TV, 600-602 Old Marion Rd., N.E.(52406), pg. 442
LARKEN INC., 3330 Southgate Ct. S.W.(52404), pg. 659
LOOMIS BROTHERS, INC., 1619 F. Ave., N.E.(52406), pg. 683
MIDCOAST INDUSTRIAL SERVICES CORPORATION, 1620 E Ave., N.E.(52402), pg. 751
Midland Forge Division, 101 S. Ave., S.W.(52406), pg. 266
National Oats Co., 1515 H Ave. N.E.(52402), pg. 25
Roush Products Co., Inc., 1000 Wenig Rd., NE(52406), pg. 1195
Taylor Associates, 1620 E. Ave. N.E.(52402), pg. 751
Taylor Associates, 701 Center Point Rd., N.E.(52402), pg. 751
D. C. Taylor Co., 1620 E Ave., N.E.(52402), pg. 751
Williams Fastener & Supply Co., P.O. Box 74678(52407), pg. 1191

Chariton

HY-VEE FOOD STORES INCORPORATED, 1801 Oceola Ave.(50049), pg. 556

Charles City

G & L Products, 1200 Fisher Rd.(50616), pg. 438

Clarinda

The Clarinda Company, 220 No. 1st St.(51632), pg. 1187

Clarion

Dodgen Feed Bodies, 721 Central Ave. West(50525), pg. 499
HAGIE MANUFACTURING CO., 721 Central Ave. West(50525), pg. 499

Clinton

CARSTENSEN FREIGHT LINE, INC., 3008 Lincoln Way(52732), pg. 226
CUSTOM PAK, INC., P.O. Box 3083(52732), pg. 306
Midwest Poly, PO Box 3023, (52732), pg. 306

Conrad

RITCHIE INDUSTRIES, INC., 120 S. Main(50621), pg. 936
Trojan Specialized Livestock Equip., 120 South Main, Box 730(50621), pg. 936

Council Bluffs

Alco Health Services Corporation-Council Bluffs Div., 3319 Nebraska Ave.(51501), pg. 31
FUTURE FOAM, INC., 25 Main Place, Ste. 500(51503), pg. 437
Timpte, Inc., 2801 23rd Ave.(51501), pg. 1098

Davenport

Bawden, Torrey & Associates, 400 Executive Sq., 400 Main St.(52801), pg. 127
E.J. Brach, Inc., 4371 Boies Ave.(52808), pg. 169
BRAMMER MANUFACTURING COMPANY, 1701 Rockingham Rd.(52802), pg. 171
THE KARTRIDG PAK CO., 807 W. Kimberly Rd.(52806), pg. 617
Kartridg Pak Co., 807 W. Kimberly Road(52806), pg. 122
Kilsby-Roberts/Davenport, 3116 W. 73rd St.(52806), pg. 606
Milltech-HOH, Inc., 4711 No. Brady St.(52806), pg. 497
SIEG COMPANY, 400 Main St., Ste.300(52801), pg. 1002
Solar Plastics-Quad Cities, 1924 Comenitz Dr.(52802), pg. 1140

Decorah

DECO PRODUCTS CO., 506 Sanford(52101), pg. 324
Watlow Infrared Company, Freeport Industrial Pk.(52101), pg. 1168

Des Moines

ADVENTURE LANDS OF AMERICA, INC., Interstate 80 & Hwy. 65(50316), pg. 21
Allied Group Inc., 701 Fifth Ave.(50304), pg. 38
ALLIED MUTUAL INSURANCE COMPANY, 701 Fifth Ave.(50304), pg. 38
AMERICAN MUTUAL LIFE INSURANCE COMPANY, 418 Sixth Ave.(50309), pg. 58
AMERICAN REPUBLIC INSURANCE CO., 601 Sixth Ave.(50309), pg. 60
Aratex Services, 2500 Delaware Ave.(50317), pg. 6
Bell Investment Acquisition Corporation, 418 6th Ave., Ste. 240(50309), pg. 778
BUDGET MARKETING, INC., 1171 W. 7th St.(50306), pg. 186
CENTRAL LIFE ASSURANCE CO., 611 5th Ave.(50309), pg. 232
CHAMBERLAIN HEALTH & BEAUTY AIDS COMPANY, 4000 N. W. 100th(50322), pg. 238
Commtron Corporation, 7900 Hickman Rd.(50322), pg. 569
Communications Data Services, Inc., 112 10th St.(50309), pg. 523
CORN STATES HYBRID SERVICE, INCORPORATED, 2505 McKinley Ave.(50321), pg. 286
Creswell, Munsell, Fultz & Zirbel, 600 E. Court Ave.(50309-2091), pg. 1211
Des Moines Tire, 120 S.W. 5th St.(50309), pg. 951
FARMERS MUTUAL HAIL INSURANCE CO., 2323 Grand Ave.(50312), pg. 401
Frank Paxton Lumber Company, 1400 Market Street(50303), pg. 592
GENERAL GROWTH COMPANIES, INC., 215 Keo(50309), pg. 449
GRAHAM GROUP, INC., 910 Grand Ave.(50309), pg. 475
HMO Iowa, Inc., 1002 1st Interstate Bank Bldg., Locust at Sixth(50309), pg. 890
Health Care Preferred, 1002 1st Interstate Bldg., Locust at 6th(50309), pg. 890
Insta-Pro International, Ltd., 10301 Dennis Dr.(50322), pg. 1114
Integrated Business Systems, 3001 McInley Ave.(50321), pg. 370
Invista Capital Management Corp., Hub Tower, 699 Walnut St.(50309), pg. 891
IOWA LOTTERY, 2015 Grand Ave.(50312), pg. 582
IOWA PAINT MFG. COMPANY, INC., 17th St. & Grand Ave.(50309), pg. 582
KRAGIE/NEWELL, 2633 Fleur Drive(50321), pg. 643
Laboratory Supply Company, 6390 N.E. 14th St.(50313), pg. 650
Life Care Services Corporation, 800 Second Ave.(50309), pg. 1174
MacMillan Oil Co., Inc., P.O. Box 4968(50306), pg. 475
Meta Farm, 10215 Dennis Dr.(50322), pg. 1114
MEYOCKS BENKSTEIN ASSOCIATES, 100 Court Ave., Ste. 303(50309), pg. 746
Mothers Back Issues, Inc., P.O. Box 10941(50340), pg. 773
Mother's Bookshelf, P. O. Box 10941(50340), pg. 773
NATIONAL TRAVELERS LIFE CO., 820 Keo Way(50309), pg. 794
Patrician Associates, Inc., 711 High St.(50309), pg. 891
Petula Associates, Ltd., 711 High St.(50309), pg. 891
Principal Casualty Insurance Company, 711 High St.(50309), pg. 891
Principal Development Associates, Inc., 711 High St.(50309), pg. 891
THE PRINCIPAL FINANCIAL GROUP, 711 High St.(50392-0150), pg. 890
Principal Life Insurance Company, 711 High St.(50309), pg. 891
Principal Management Inc., 711 High St.(50309), pg. 891
Principal Marketing Services, Inc., 711 High St.(50309), pg. 891
Principal Mutual Life Insurance Co., 711 High St.(50309-0001), pg. 891
Principal National Life Insurance Company, 711 High St.(50309), pg. 891
Princor Financial Services Corporation, 711 High St.(50309), pg. 891
T Shirt Graphics, 111 11th St.(50309-4214), pg. 1148
TOWNSEND ENGINEERING CO., 2425 Hubbell Ave.(50317), pg. 1104
TRIPLE F, INC., 10104 Douglas Ave.(50322), pg. 1114
Uniroyal Chemical Co., Inc., 1701 48th St., Ste. 102(50265), pg. 1129
THE WEITZ-COHEN CONSTRUCTION CO., 800 Second Ave.(50309), pg. 1174
The Weitz Company, Inc., 800 2nd Ave.(50309), pg. 1174
THE WEITZ CORPORATION, 800 2nd Ave.(50309), pg. 1174

Dubuque

FDL FOODS, INC., 701 E. 16th St.(52001), pg. 394
A. Y. MCDONALD INDUSTRIES, INC., 4800 Chavenelle Rd.(52002), pg. 728
A. Y. McDonald Mfg. Co., 4800 Chavenelle Rd., P.O. Box 508(52004-0508), pg. 728
A. Y. McDonald Supply Co. Inc., 4800 Chavenelle Rd.(52002), pg. 728
VALLET FOOD SERV INC., 1230 E. 12th St.(52001), pg. 1143

Eldridge

BAWDEN CORPORATION, 400 S. 14th Ave.(52748), pg. 127
Bawden Printing, Inc., 400 S. 14th Ave.(52748), pg. 127

Estherville

GOLDEN SUN FEEDS, INC., Hwy. 4 South(51334-0517), pg. 467
Shuttlecraft, 2803 Murray Rd.(51334), pg. 1008

Fairfield

DEXTER COMPANY, 501 N. 8th St.(52556), pg. 334
HAWTHORNE COMMUNICATIONS, INC., 300 North 16th St.(52556), pg. 518

Fort Dodge

Gold Bond Building Products, 1584 S. 22nd St., P.O. Box 977(50501), pg. 790
Land O'Lakes Seed Division, 2827 8th Ave. S.(50501), pg. 653
NEW COOPERATIVE INC., 2626 1st Ave., S.(50501), pg. 799

Glenwood

Opinion-Tribune, 116 So. Walnut St.(51534), pg. 655

Gowrie

CONSOLIDATED CO-OP, R.F.D., P.O. Box 48(50543), pg. 276

Grimes

Mrs. Grimes Foods, 512 N. Main St.(55435), pg. 399

Grinnell

Golden Sun Feeds, Inc., (50112), pg. 467

Grundy Center

Norwesco Contract Manufacturing Div., 311 B Avenue(50638), pg. 816

Harlan

Wilson Seeds Inc., P.O. Box 391, (51537), pg. 654

Houghton

HAWKEYE STEEL PRODUCTS, INC., P.O. Box 2000, (52631), pg. 518

Huff

FOREIGN CANDY CO., INC., 451 Black Forest Rd.(51239), pg. 424

Ida Grove

MIDWEST INDUSTRIES, INC., Hwy. 59 & 175(51445), pg. 752

Keokuk

Headco Machine Works, Inc., Box 969, Main Street Rd.(52632), pg. 520
THE HUBINGER COMPANY, P.O. Box 6647, (52632), pg. 550

Laurens

Positech Corporation, Rush Lake Rd.(50554), pg. 267

Le Mars

HARKER'S INC., 521 Eighth Ave. S.W.(51031), pg. 509

Manchester

Henderson Mfg., P.O. Box 40(52057), pg. 1193

Manson

Bioproducts, Inc., 152

Maquoketa

Golden Sun Feeds, Inc., (50260), pg. 467

Mason City

American Crystal Sugar Co., Box 1098, (50401), pg. 51
Curries Company, 525 9th St. S.E.(50401), pg. 361

Muscatine

Grain Processing Corp., 1600 Oregon St.(52761), pg. 1145
Kent Feeds Inc., 1600 Oregon St.(52761), pg. 1146
Middle West Service Company, 225 Iowa Ave.(52761), pg. 961
SC COMPANIES, INC., Stanley Bldg., 225 Iowa Ave.(52761), pg. 960
Stanley Consultants, Inc., Stanley Bldg., 225 Iowa Ave.(52761), pg. 961
VARIED INVESTMENTS, INC., 1600 Oregon St.(52761), pg. 1145

Nashua

BC Hydrotile Machinery Co., (50658), pg. 154

Newton

THE VERNON COMPANY, 604 W. 4th N.(50208), pg. 1148

Oelwein

United Farm Tools, Inc., Oelwein, Speedy City Park Rd., P.O. Box 311(50662), pg. 1132

Osceola

Iowa Assemblies, Inc., Hwy. 34 W.(50213), pg. 490

Oskaloosa

Clow Valve Div., So. 2nd St.(52577), pg. 733

Pella

PELLA CORPORATION, 102 Main St.(50219), pg. 856
VERMEER MANUFACTURING COMPANY, New Sharon Rd.(50219), pg. 1148

Pocahontas

Iowa Industrial Hydraulics, Inc., Industrial Park Rd.(50574), pg. 559

Princeton

Johnson Manufacturing Co., 114 Lost Grove Rd.(52768), pg. 443

Ralston

Redeco Industries, P.O. Box 68(51459), pg. 1177
W.C. Commodities, P.O. Box 68(51459), pg. 1177
WEST CENTRAL CO-OP, P.O. Box 68(51459), pg. 1176

Red Oak

Red Oak Express, P.O. Box 377, 2012 Commerce Dr.(51566), pg. 655

Shenandoah

EARL MAY SEED & NURSERY L.P., 208 N. Elm St.(51603), pg. 724

Sioux City

Central-United Life Insurance Co., 4301 Sergeant Rd.(51102), pg. 233
IRVING F. JENSEN CO., INC., 2220 Hawkeye Dr.(51102), pg. 593
L & R COMMUNICATIONS, LIMITED, 2301 Bridgeport Dr.(51111), pg. 647
SIOUX HONEY ASSOCIATION, 301 Lewis Blvd.(51101), pg. 1008
Solar Plastics-Sioux City Division, 1658 riverside Blvd.(55109), pg. 1140
TERMINAL GRAIN CORP., 518 8th St.(51101), pg. 1088

Spirit Lake

BERKLEY, INC., One Berkley Dr.(51360), pg. 141

Storm Lake

Vigorena Feeds, Inc., P.O. Box 1205, West Hwy. 550

Story City

American Packaging Corporation, P.O. Box 240, 125 W. Broad St.(50248), pg. 59

Waterloo

CONSTRUCTION MACHINERY COMPANY, Glenwood & Vinton(50704), pg. 277
LOCKARD CONSTRUCTION, INC., 901 Black Hawk Rd.(50701), pg. 680
WATERLOO SERVICE COMPANY, 1402 Logan(50703), pg. 1167

Waukee

DOWNEY PRINTING, 400 Deming Ave.(50263), pg. 348

West Des Moines

AMERICAN GRAIN & RELATED INDUSTRIES, 2829 Westown Pkwy. Ste. 100(50265), pg. 55
ITA GROUP, 4800 Westown Pkwy., Suite 300(50265), pg. 560
Integrated Resources Life Insurance Co., P.O. Box 65180, 2337 Westown Pkwy.(50265), pg. 573
Midwest Mutual Insurance Co., 1111 Ashworth Rd.(50265), pg. 886
Preferred Risk Life Insurance Co., 1111 Ashworth Rd.(50265), pg. 886
PREFERRED RISK MUTUAL INSURANCE, 1111 Ashworth Rd.(50265), pg. 886

West Union

H & H DISTRIBUTING COMPANY, INC., 304 S. Vine(52175), pg. 495

Wilton

STUHR ENTERPRISES INC., 403 W. First St.(52778), pg. 1055

Winnsboro

Mastercraft Corporation, Rt. 3, Box 333(71295), pg. 759

KANSAS

Abilene

DUCKWALL-ALCO STORES, INC., 401 Cottage St.(67410), pg. 351

Andover

INTERNATIONAL COLD STORAGE CO., INC., P.O. Box 425, (67002), pg. 576

Arkansas City

The Arkansas City Daily Traveler, P.O. Box 988, 5th Ave. & A St.(67005), pg. 1042
Montgomery Elevator Architectural Products Division, Strother Field Industrial Park, P.O. Box 987(67005), pg. 767

Assaria

GREAT PLAINS MANUFACTURING, INC., Second & Center(67416), pg. 482

Atchison

ATCHISON COUNTY CO-OP ASSOCIATION, 812 Main St.(66002), pg. 93
Blish-Mize Co., 223 So. 5th St.(66002), pg. 340

Beloit

FARMWAY CO-OP INC., 204 East Court Street(67420), pg. 402

Chanute

Ash Grove Cement, P.O. Box 519, (66720), pg. 87

Cimarron

Cimarron American Fidelity, 101 No. Main(67835), pg. 52

Coffeyville

ACME FOUNDRY, INC., 1502 Spruce(67337), pg. 13
HEALTH CARE LODGES, 201 W. 8th St.(67337), pg. 520
Magic Circle Manufacturing Div., 1209 Buckey(67337), pg. 13
Medicalodges, Inc., P.O. Box 509, 201 W. 8th St.(67337-0509), pg. 520

Dodge City

CRUSTBUSTER, INC., 4 Dodge Rd.(67801), pg. 303
Dodge City Daily Globe, 705 Second St., Box 820(67801), pg. 1042
Dodge City Shopper's Weekly, 316 W. Wyatt Earp(67801), pg. 1042
HYPLAINS DRESSED BEEF, INC., 2000 E. Trail(67801), pg. 557

Edwardsville

ANN RASKAS GOURMET CONFECTIONERS, 207 S. 9th St.(66113), pg. 913

Ellsworth

CASHCO, INC., Hwy. 140 W.(67439), pg. 228

Emporia

DIDDE WEB PRESS, 1200 Graphic Arts Rd.(66801), pg. 336

Fort Scott

KEY INDUSTRIES, INC., 523 E. Wall(66701), pg. 627
WARD KRAFT, INC., 2401 S. Cooper St.(66701), pg. 643
Tower Metal Products, 301 N. Hill(66701), pg. 1078

Garden City

Garden City Complex, P.O. BOx 1649(67846), pg. 1060
KSNG, P.O. Box 1076(67846), pg. 963

Girard

PRODUCERS CO-OP ASSOCIATION, INC., 300 Buffalo St.(66743), pg. 892

Great Bend

DOONAN & SONS, INC., Jct. Hwy. 56 & 156(67530), pg. 346
THE FULLER BRUSH COMPANY, Westport Addition, P.O. Box 729(67530), pg. 436
KSNC, N. Hwy. 281, P.O. Box 689(67530), pg. 963

Hays

SUNFLOWER ELECTRIC POWER CORPORATION, 301 W. 13th St.(67601), pg. 1060

Hesston

EXCEL INDUSTRIES, INC., 200 S. Ridge Rd.(67062), pg. 392
Hay & Forage Industries, 420 W. Lincoln Blvd.(67062), pg. 4

Holcomb

Holcomb Station, 1060

Holton

BMB Company, N. Vermont at 9th(66436), pg. 29

Hutchinson

GARVEY ELEVATORS INC., P.O. Box 1948(67504), pg. 443
HARRIS ENTERPRISES INC., 300 W. 2nd(67501), pg. 511
KRAUSE PLOW CORP., 305 S. Monroe St.(67501), pg. 644

Industrial Airport

DAZEY CORPORATION, One Dazey Circle(66031), pg. 321

Kansas City

ASSOCIATED WHOLESALE GROCERS, INC., 5000 Kansas Ave.(66106), pg. 92
Century Concrete, Inc., 8858 Woodend Rd.(66113), pg. 88
CRAMER INC., 625 Adams St.(66105), pg. 296
EARP MEAT COMPANY, 6550 Kansas Ave.(66111), pg. 362
FAIRBANKS MORSE PUMP CORPORATON, P.O. Box 999, 3601 Fairbanks Ave.(66106-0999), pg. 397
Garney Companies, Inc., 1331 N.W. Vivion Rd.(64118-4554), pg. 443
GARSITE/TSR, INC., 539 So. 10th(66105), pg. 443
Gear Headquarters Inc., 3012 S. 24th St.(66101), pg. 520
S-G METALS INDUSTRIES, INC., 2nd & Riverview(66118), pg. 962
Sealy Mattress Company of Kansas City, Inc., 3100 Fairfax Traffic Way(66115), pg. 985
SPANGLER, INC., 2930 S. 44th St.(66106), pg. 1025
STRONGHEART PRODUCTS, INC., 300 S. 55th St.(66106), pg. 1054
UNIVERSAL CONSTRUCTION COMPANY, 29 Greystone Ave.(66103), pg. 1138
VILE-GOLLER, FINE ART PRINTING & LITHOGRAPHY, 101 Greystone(66103), pg. 1151

Lake Quivera

Professional Securities Corp., 575 Hillcrest E.(66106), pg. 554

Lawrence

LAWRENCE PAPER COMPANY, 2801 Lakeview Rd.(66044), pg. 662

Lecompton

BARANCORP, Northern Cross Ranch, Rte. 1(66050), pg. 118
Baranski & Associates, Northern Cross Ranch, Rte. 1(66050), pg. 118
D. A. Baranski & Co., Northern Cross Ranch(66050), pg. 118
Baranski Energy Company, Northern Cross Ranch(66050), pg. 118
Joseph A. Baranski Literary Agency, Northern Cross Ranch, Rte. 1(66050), pg. 118
Baranski Publishing Company, Northern Cross Ranch, Rte. 1(66050), pg. 118
Northern Cross, Ltd., Northern Cross Ranch, Rte. 1(66050), pg. 118

Lenexa

MARKETING COMMUNICATIONS, 10605 W. 84th Terrace(66214), pg. 709
SOR INC., 14685 W. 105th St.(66215), pg. 963
WILLIAMS FOODS INC., 13301 W. 99th St.(66215), pg. 1191

Liberal

Central Realty Corp., P.O. Box 1358, (67901), pg. 1128
Cimaron Grain Co., P.O. Box 708, (67901), pg. 1128
LISC Management Services, P.O. Box 978, (67901), pg. 1128
Liberal By-Products, P.O. Box 978, (67901), pg. 1128
Liberal International Sales Corp., P.O. Box 978, (67901), pg. 1128
Liberal International Sales V.I. Inc., P.O. Box 978, (67901), pg. 1128
National Beef Packing Company, P.O. Box 978, (67901), pg. 1128
National Carriers, Inc., P.O. Box 1358(67901), pg. 1128
Southwestern Equipment Co., P.O. Box 978, (67901), pg. 1128
Supreme Cattle Co., P.O. Box 708, (67901), pg. 1128
Supreme Feeders, Inc., P.O. Box 708, (67901), pg. 1128

McPherson

Clear Creek, Inc., 2000 S. Main(67460), pg. 787
NATIONAL COOPERATIVE REFINERY ASSOCIATION, 2000 S. Main St.(67460), pg. 787
VANGUARD PLASTICS, INC., 831 N. Vanguard(67460), pg. 1145

Merriam

V.T. INC., 8500 Shawnee Mission Pkwy.(66202), pg. 1142

Minneapolis

HONORBUILT INDUSTRIES, INC., P.O. Box 266, (67467), pg. 542

Mission

The Marley Cooling Tower Co., 5800 Foxridge Dr.(66202), pg. 710
Marley Pump Co., 5800 Foxridge Dr.(66202), pg. 710
Mission Shopping Ctr., Roe Blvd. & Johnson Dr.(66222), pg. 699
Word-Tech Business Systems, 5625 Foxridge Dr.(66202), pg. 370

Mission Woods

Layne-Western Co., Inc., 1900 Shawnee Mission Pkwy.(66205), pg. 710
THE MARLEY COMPANY, 1900 Shawnee Mission Pkwy.(66205), pg. 710

Moundridge

BRADBURY COMPANY, INC., Air Industrial Pk.(67107), pg. 169
MID-KANSAS CO-OP ASSOCIATION, 307 W. Cole(67107), pg. 750

Newton

The Newton Kansan, P.O. Box 268, 121 W. 6th St.(67114), pg. 1042
Norcraft Companies, 900 S. Meridian Ave.(67114), pg. 809

Oberlin

KSNK, P.O. Box 238, (67749), pg. 963

Olathe

Abrasive Engineering & Manufacturing Div., 540 E. Hwy. 56(66061), pg. 14
INLAND ASSOCIATES, 15021 W. 117th St.(66061), pg. 570
INLAND ASSOCIATES, INC., 15021 W. 117th Street(66062), pg. 570
Olathe Daily News, 514 S. Canvas Ave.(66061), pg. 511

Ottawa

FRANKLIN FEDERAL SAVINGS ASSOCIATION, One Franklin Plaza(66067), pg. 429

Overland Park

ASH GROVE CEMENT COMPANY, 8900 Indian Creek Pkwy.(66210), pg. 87
CHRISTENSON, BARCLAY & SHAW, INC., 9300 Metcalf, Ste. 900(66212), pg. 248
ERA REAL ESTATE, 4900 College Blvd.(66211), pg. 360
ELECTRO DYNAMICS CRYSTAL CORPORATION, 9075 Cody(66214), pg. 374
FINANCIAL ASSOCIATES, 10977 Granada Lane(66211), pg. 410
Garnac Grain Co., Inc., 8000 W. 110th St., Ste. 300(66210-2315), pg. 810
HELP MANAGEMENT CORPORATION, 6800 College Blvd., Suite 600(66211), pg. 527
Help Service Corporation, 6800 College Blvd.(66211), pg. 528
Higher Education Assistance Foundation, 6800 College Blvd., Suite 600(66211), pg. 528
Higher Education Loan Program of Kansas, 6800 College Blvd., Suite 600(66211), pg. 528
Intertec Publishing, 9221 Quivira Rd.(66215), pg. 611
Kaiser Permanente, Kansas/Missouri Division, 10561 Barkley(66212), pg. 614
KROH OPERATING L.P., 4550 W. 109th St., Ste. 220(66211), pg. 645
MARKETING RESOURCES OF AMERICA, INC., 10551 Barkley(66212), pg. 709
Mayflower Contract Services, Inc., 5360 College Blvd.(66211), pg. 725
Metmor Financial, Inc., 9225 Indian Creek Parkway(66210), pg. 745
NORFOODS, INC., 7101 College Ave, Ste. 8000(66210), pg. 810
NORTH AMERICAN SALT COMPANY, 8300 College Blvd.(66210), pg. 812
Pathmark Development Group, 4550 W. 109th St, Ste. 220(66211), pg. 645
The Pritchard Corporation, 10950 Grandview Dr.(66210), pg. 155
THE SUNFLOWER GROUP, 10895 Lowell, Ste. 300(66210), pg. 1060
TALLGRASS TECHNOLOGIES CORP., 11100 W. 82nd St.(66214), pg. 1077
United States Central Credit Union, 7300 College Boulevard,Ste.600(66210), pg. 298

Parsons

Day & Zimmerman Kansas Division, Hwy. 160 E.(67357-9106), pg. 320
Peabody TecTank, Inc., P.O. Box 996, (67357), pg. 900

Pittsburg

Agri-Graphics, Inc., Box 46(66762), pg. 45
Harvest Brands, Inc., Box 46(66762), pg. 45
McNally Wellman Kansas Div., P. O. Drawer D(66762), pg. 732
Pittsburg Morning Sun, P.O. Box H, 701 N. Locust(66762), pg. 1042

Prairie Village

Yellow Pages Marketing Services, Inc.-Kansas City, 7301 Mission Rd., Ste. 107(66208), pg. 1074

Russell

King of the Road Div., P.O. Box 553(67665), pg. 247

Shawnee Mission

BARKLEY & EVERGREEN ADVERTISING, INC., 4350 Shawnee Mission Pkwy.(66205), pg. 120
Cedar Creek Properties Inc., 8900 Indian Creek Pkwy.(66225), pg. 88
Cedar Creek Realty Co., Inc., 8900 Indian Creek Pkwy.(66225), pg. 88
DARLING ENVELOPE CORPORATION, 5400 Antioch Dr.(66202), pg. 315
ERA General Agency Corp., P.O. Box 2983(66201), pg. 360
EN-COM Properties, Inc., 5453 W. 61st Pl.(66205), pg. 548
Fordyce Concrete Co., Inc., 8900 Indian Creek Pkwy.(66225), pg. 88
THE HOYT GROUP, 5453 W. 61st Pl.(66205), pg. 548
Hoyt Securities, Inc., 5453 W. 61st Pl.(66205), pg. 548
HUDSON & AFFILIATED CO., 4720 Rainbow Blvd.(66205), pg. 551
IBT, INC., P.O. Box 2982(66201), pg. 558
Material Transport Co., 8900 Indian Creek Pkwy.(66225), pg. 88
Seaboard Corporation, Grain Division, 9000 W. 67th St.(66202), pg. 984
Sunrise Industrial Automation & Design, P.O. Box 2982(66201), pg. 558
Thermo Dynamics, Inc., Fox Ridge Dr.(66202), pg. 341
Union Quarries, Inc., P.O. Box 25348, (66225), pg. 88
WESTLAKE HARDWARE, INC., 15501 W. 99th St.(66219), pg. 1183

Topeka

ADAMS BUSINESS FORMS, 200 SW Jackson(66603), pg. 16
ADMARK, INC., 3630 S.W. Burlingame Rd.(66611), pg. 18
American Bindry-Midwest, 914 Jefferson(66607), pg. 51
THE AMERICAN COMPANIES, INC., 2101 N. Topeka(66608), pg. 50
CGF INDUSTRIES, 800 Bank IV Tower(66603), pg. 201
Capper's, 616 Jefferson St.(66607), pg. 1043
Capper's Insurance Service, Inc., 616 Jefferson St.(66607), pg. 1043
Communications & Signaling, Inc., Bank IV Tower, 6th & Kansas(66603), pg. 1043
Econo-Clad Books, P.O. Box 1777(66601), pg. 51
Falley's Inc., 3120 S. Kansas Ave.(66611), pg. 1214
KSNT, 6835 N.W. U.S. Hwy. 24(66618), pg. 963
Kansas Agriculture Network, 5600 W. 6th St.(66606), pg. 1043
Kansas Information Network, 5600 W. 6th St.(66606), pg. 1043
LANDMARK HOTEL CORPORATION, 1200 Executive Dr.(60615), pg. 656
ED MARLING STORES, INC., 2950 McClure Rd.(66614), pg. 710
Prebound Periodicals, Inc., 914 Jefferson(66607), pg. 51
STAUFFER COMMUNICATIONS, INC., 616 Jefferson St.(66607), pg. 1042
The Topeka Capital-Journal, 616 Jefferson St.(66607), pg. 1042
Topeka Television, Corp., 6835 N.W. U.S. Hwy. 24(66618), pg. 963
Victory Life Insurance Company, 300 W. 8th Ave.(66603), pg. 1150
WIBW-TV AM & FM, 5600 W. 6th St.(66606), pg. 1043
Wildcat Sports Network, 5600 W. 6th St.(66606), pg. 1043

Wakeeney

WESTERN CO-OP ELECTRIC UTILITY ASSOCIATION, P.O. Box 278(67672), pg. 1178

Westwood

FISCA OIL CO., INC., 4830 Rainbow Blvd.(66205), pg. 414
Meta Plant Food, 4830 Rainbow Blvd.(66205), pg. 414

Wichita

ALADDIN PETROLEUM CORPORATION, 221 S. Broadway, Ste. 809(67202), pg. 29
Allen's Concrete, Inc., 2020 N. Amidon(67203), pg. 936
Allright Corporation, 603 N. Main(67203), pg. 41
ASSOCIATED ADVERTISING AGENCY, INC., 4601 E. Douglas(67218), pg. 89
ASSOCIATED COMPANY, INC., 1441 S. McLean Blvd.(67213), pg. 89
Associated Druggists, 3131 W. Pawnee(67213), pg. 304
Associated Group, P.O. Box 1762(67201), pg. 694
BERRY COMPANIES, INC., 3223 N. Hydraulic(67219), pg. 144
Big Cheese Pizza Corporation, 1130 Haskell(67213), pg. 464
M. BRUENGER & CO., INC., 6250 N. Broadway(67219), pg. 184
Builders Development Inc., 301 N. Main, Ste. 800(67202), pg. 444
Builders Inc., 301 N. Main, Ste. 800(67202), pg. 444
CHANCE INDUSTRIES, INC., 4219 Irving(67209), pg. 238
The Coleman Company, Inc., 250 N. St. Francis St.(67202), pg. 695
Coleman International Operation, 2111 E. 37th St. No.(67219), pg. 695
Coleman Outdoor Products, 250 N. St. Francis Ave.(67202), pg. 695
Concrete Accessories Company, Inc., 2020 N. Amidon(67204), pg. 936
CONTINENTAL AMERICAN CORP. D/B/A PIONEER BALLOON COMPANY, 555 N. Woodlawn(67208), pg. 278
DAVIS-MOORE OLDSMOBILE, INC., 6215 E. Kellogg(67218), pg. 319
Davis-Moore Recreational Vehicle Center, 6215 E. Kellogg(67218), pg. 319
Martin K. Eby Construction Company, Inc., 610 Main St.(67201), pg. 365
EBY CORPORATION, 610 N. Main St.(67201), pg. 365
EVCON HOLDINGS, 3110 N. Mead(67219), pg. 391
Excel Corp., 151 N. Main(67202), pg. 219
Farm Credit Bank of Wichita, Farm Credit Bank Bldg., 245 No. Waco(67202), pg. 405
FOLEY HOLDING COMPANY, INC., 1550 S. West St.(67213), pg. 422
Foley Tractor Company, Inc., 1550 S. West St.(67213), pg. 422
FULL SERVICE BEVERAGE COMPANY, 2901 S. Kansas(67216), pg. 436
Garvey Grain, 5255 S. Hoover(67202), pg. 444
GARVEY INDUSTRIES, INC., 301 N. Main, Ste. 860(67202), pg. 443
GOLDSMITHS, INC., 151 N. Main St.(67202), pg. 469
HENRYS, INC., 7700 E. Kellogg, Ste. 1201(67207), pg. 530
Home Heating & Air Conditioning, 250 N. St. Francis Ave.(67202), pg. 391
INSURANCE MANAGEMENT ASSOCIATES, 250 N. Water, Suite 600(67202), pg. 572
Koch Engineering Co., Inc., 4111 E. 37th St., N.(67204), pg. 639
KOCH INDUSTRIES, INCORPORATED, 411 E. 37th St. No.(67220), pg. 639
Koch Refining Company, P.O. Box 2302(67201), pg. 639
KREONITE, INC., 715 E. 10th St.(67214), pg. 644
Lario Enterprises, Inc., 301 S. Market(67202), pg. 659
LARIO OIL & GAS COMPANY, 301 S. Market(67202), pg. 658
THE LAW COMPANY, INC., 345 Riverview(67203), pg. 661
LIDA ADVERTISING COMPANY, 393 N. McLean Blvd.(67203), pg. 674
LINDER & ASSOCIATES, INC., 840 N. Main(67203), pg. 676
LOVE BOX COMPANY, INC., 700 E. 37th St. N.(67219), pg. 685
MISCO INDUSTRIES, 257 N. Broadway, Ste. 200(67202), pg. 759
PAWNEE INDUSTRIES, INC., 2024 No. Woodlawn St.(67208), pg. 852
Pawnee Specialty Products, 2024 No. Woodlawn(67208), pg. 852
PETROLEUM INC., 301 N. Main , Ste. 900(67202), pg. 865
Petroleum, Inc., 301 N. Main, Ste. 860(67202), pg. 444
QUIK PRINT INC., 3445 N. Webb Rd.(67226), pg. 905
Rich-Mix Products, 2020 N. Amidon(67204), pg. 936
RITCHIE CORPORATION, 2020 N. Amidon(67203), pg. 936
Ritchie Paving, Inc., 2020 N. Amidon(67203), pg. 936
Ritchie Sand Company, Inc., 2020 N. Amidon(67203), pg. 936
SJL OF KANSAS CORP., 833 N. Main(67203), pg. 962
Safelite Autoglass, 245 N. Waco(67201), pg. 664
SHEPLERS, INC., 6501 W. Kellogg(67209), pg. 998
STAR LUMBER & SUPPLY COMPANY, INC., 325 S. West St.(67213), pg. 1039
Steffen Dairy Foods Co., Inc., 700 E. Central(67201), pg. 884
SULLIVAN HIGDON & SINK INCORPORATED, 801 E. Douglas(67202), pg. 1056
TOWN & COUNTRY FOOD MARKETS, INC., 1522 S. Florence St.(67209), pg. 1103
WESTERN GRAIN, INC., Colorado Derby Bldg., 202 W. 1st St., Ste. 403(67202), pg. 1179

KENTUCKY

Ashland

Columbus Showcase, Ashland Division, P.O. Box 1387, (41105), pg. 267

Bardstown

Kentucky Standard, P.O. Box 639(40004), pg. 655

Bedford

The Trimble Banner-Democrat, P.O. Box 68(40006), pg. 656

Bowling Green

BVD Licensing Corporation, P.O. Box 780, (42101), pg. 400
CAMPING WORLD HOLDINGS, INC., 3 Springs Rd.(42102), pg. 213
DESA INTERNATIONAL, INC., 2701 Industrial Dr.(42101), pg. 331
Fruit of the Loom, 400
HOUCHENS INDUSTRIES INC., 900 Church St.(42101), pg. 545
Scott Tobacco, 939 Adams, P.O. Box 658(42101), pg. 282
Union Underwear Co., Inc., 1 Fruit of the Loom Dr.(42103), pg. 400

Burgin

Keystone Brush & Contact Co., 440 Burgin Danville Rd., P.O. Box 478(40310), pg. 633

Calvert City

North Star Steel Kentucky, Inc., Old Coke Plant Rd.(42029), pg. 219

Campbellsville

Central Kentucky News-Journal, P.O. Box 279, 428 Woodlawn(42718), pg. 655

Carrollton

The News-Democrat, 422 Main St.(41008), pg. 655

Cave City

Cave City Chevrolet, I-65 & Highway 90 East, pg. 719

Cold Spring

GRIFFIN INDUSTRIES, INC., 4221 Alexandria Pike(41076), pg. 487

Covington

THE BASES GROUP, 50 E. River Center Blvd., Ste. 1000(41011), pg. 124
The Bases Group, 50 E. River Center Blvd., Suite 1000(41011), pg. 124
Bases International, 50 E. River Center Blvd., Suite 1000(41011), pg. 124
The Burke Institute, 50 E. River Center Blvd., Suite 1000(41011), pg. 124
CORPOREX COMPANIES, INC., 50 E. River Center Blvd.(41011), pg. 287
Duro Paper Bag Mfg. Co., 1301 Madison Ave.(41011), pg. 355
R. A. JONES & CO. INC., 2701 Crescent Springs Rd.(41017), pg. 604
Matrix Building Co., Inc., 1650 Russell St.(41011), pg. 700

Crescent Springs

BLUE GRASS FOODS, INC., 2645 Commerce Dr.(41017), pg. 160

Cynthiana

E. D. BULLARD COMPANY, Rt. 7, Box 596(41031), pg. 188
Cynthiana Democrat, P.O. Box 160, Webster at Springdale(41031), pg. 655

Dry Ridge

Gusher Pumps Inc., Ruthman Dr.(41035), pg. 957

Elizabethtown

COCA-COLA BOTTLING COMPANY OF ELIZABETHTOWN, 1201 N. Dixie(42701), pg. 258
News-Enterprise, P.O. Box 430, 408 W. Dixie Dr.(42701), pg. 655

Erlanger

Ancra Cincinatti, 3300 Turfway Rd., Suite 110(41018), pg. 72
Stewart Decatur Security Systems, Inc., P.O. BOx 18700(41018), pg. 422
TRESSA, INC., 2711 Circleport Dr.(41018), pg. 1110

Florence

AMERICAN SIGN & MARKETING SERVICES, INC., 7430 Industrial Rd.(41042), pg. 61
HOPPLE PLASTICS, INC., 7430 Empire Dr.(41042), pg. 544
Keco Aerospace Ground Equipment Div., 7375 Industrial Rd.(41042), pg. 619
KECO INDUSTRY, INC., 7375 Industrial Rd.(41042), pg. 619
LITTLEFORD DAY, TAYLOR-STILES DIVISION, 7451 Empire Dr.(41042), pg. 679

Fort Mitchell

COLUMBIA SUSSEX CORPORATION, 207 Grandview(41017), pg. 266
PAUL HEMMER CONSTRUCTION COMPANY, 250 Grandview Dr.(41017), pg. 528

Frankfort

KENTUCKY DEPARTMENT OF TRAVEL DEVELOPMENT, 500 Mero St., Room 2200(40601-1974), pg. 623

Georgetown

Blue Ribbon Pen & Pencil Co., Bourbon & Chambers St.(40324), pg. 856
Mallard Pen & Pencil Co., Bourbon & Chambers St.(40324), pg. 856

Glasgow

UNITED FARM TOOLS, INC., 113 W. Public Sq., 4th Fl.(42141), pg. 1131

Harlan

Langley & Morgan Corp., P.O. Box 777, (40831), pg. 609

Harrodsburg

Signet Systems, Inc., Tapp Road(40330), pg. 385

Hebron

Wagstaff Eastern, 4657 Northbend(41048), pg. 1158

Henderson

Gibbs Diecasting Aluminum Corp., 369 Community Dr.(42420), pg. 639
International Tables Corp., U.S. 60 W., Industrial Park, Community D(42420), pg. 977
THE THOMPSON GROUP COMPANIES, 5840 Airline Rd.(42420), pg. 1094

Hitchins

Belmont Industries, U.S. Refractories Div., Denton Rd.(41146), pg. 136

Hopkinsville

HOPKINSVILLE ELEVATOR COMPANY, INC., Skyline Dr.(42240), pg. 543
HOPKINSVILLE MILLING CO., 2001 S. Walnut St.(42240), pg. 543

Horse Cave

BALE OF KENTUCKY, INC., 1288 E. Main St.(42749), pg. 115
Farmers Investment Company, Inc., 1288 E. Main St.(42749), pg. 115

Irvine

SOUTH EAST COAL CO., State Rt. 1840(40336), pg. 1019
South-East Coal Sales Co., P.O. Box 332, (40336), pg. 1019
South-East Ohio Coal Co., P.O. Box 332, (40336), pg. 1019

Kimper

Jesse Branch Coal Co., 8259 Upper Johns Creek Rd.(41539), pg. 145
Kyber Coal Co., 8259 Upper Johns Creek Rd.(41539), pg. 145

La Grange

The Oldham Era, 204 S. First St.(40031), pg. 655

Lawrenceburg

The Anderson News, 133 So. Main St.(40342), pg. 655

Lebanon

The Lebanon Enterprise, 119 So. Proctor·Knott Ave.(40033), pg. 655

Lexington

Benchmark Security Inc., 2355 Harrodsburg Rd.(40504), pg. 718
BIZZACK INC., 2265 Executive Dr.(40505), pg. 153
BLUE GRASS CHRYSLER-PLYMOUTH, 1651 N. Broadway(40505), pg. 156
Carolina Steel Service Center Plant, 360 Thompson Rd.(40510), pg. 223
DWC Computer Solutions Inc., 2355 Harrodsburg Rd.(40504), pg. 718
DAWAHARES, INC., 1845 Alexandria Dr.(40504), pg. 319
JAMES N. GRAY CONSTRUCTION CO., INC., 250 W. Main St., Ste. 2500(40507-1760), pg. 479
Jerrico, Inc., 101 Jerrico Dr.(40509), pg. 229
KEENELAND ASSOC., INC., 4201 Versailles Rd.(40510), pg. 620
Kentucky Indiana Lumber Co., P.O. Box 5506, (40555), pg. 624
Lexington Equipment Co., 101 Jerrico Dr.(40509), pg. 229
Lexmark International, Inc., 740 New Circle Rd.(40511), pg. 674
Long John Silver's, Inc., 101 Jerrico Dr.(40509), pg. 229
MASON COMPANY, 2355 Harrodsburg Rd.(40504), pg. 718
Mason & Hanger Engineering Inc., 2355 Harrodsburg Rd.(40504-3363), pg. 718
Mason Hanger-Silas Mason Co., 2355 Harrodsburg Rd.(40504), pg. 718
MERIDIAN COMMUNICATIONS, 444 E. Main, Ste. 200(40507), pg. 740
National Mines Corp., 101 E. Vine St.(40507), pg. 794
STEARNS ENTERPRISES, INC., 410 W. Vine St.(40507), pg. 1043
Versatech Engineering, 835 Porter Pl.(40504), pg. 718
Wabash Fibre Box Co.-Lexington Plant, 2575 Palumbo Dr.(40509), pg. 1183
Weatherly Consumer Products, Inc., 101 Prosperous Place, Ste. 200(40509), pg. 1169

Liberty

The Casey County News, P.O. Box 40, (42539), pg. 655

Louisville

AIRGUARD INDUSTRIES INC., 3807 Bishop Lane(40218), pg. 27
Alco Health Services Corporation-Louisville Div., 244 E. Woodlawn Ave.(40214), pg. 32
ALGOOD FOOD COMPANY, 2440 S. Floyd St.(40217), pg. 34
All-State Ford Truck Sales, 1357 Gardiner Lane(40232), pg. 532
ALLIED SPORTING GOODS INC., 3030 Northwestern Pkwy.(40212), pg. 40
Allright Louisville Co., Inc., 321 W. Chestnut St.(40202), pg. 41
Alro Group, Louisville, P.O. Box 17349, 310 Baxley Ave.(40217-0349), pg. 44
Aratex Services, 11200 Decimal Dr.(40299), pg. 6
BANDY CARROLL HELLIGE ADVERTISING, 239 S. Fifth St., Ste. 18(40202), pg. 117
BEHR STORES INC., 1713 Cobalt Dr.(40299), pg. 132
Bioproducts, Inc., 4820 Jennings Lane(40218), pg. 152
BLUE BOAR CAFETERIA CO., 1725 Dixie Hwy.(40256-9001), pg. 158
Boiler & Heat Exchange Div., P.O. Box 1918(40201), pg. 1154
BROWN WOOD PRESERVING COMPANY, 5200 Crittenden Dr.(40213), pg. 183
BUNTON COMPANY, 4601 E. Indian Trail(40213), pg. 188
BYERLY FORD-NISSAN INC., 4041 Dixie Hwy.(40216), pg. 198
CALDWELL TANKS, INC., 4000 Tower Rd.(40219), pg. 209
Carbide Products, P.O. Box 3727(40201), pg. 217
CARDINAL ALUMINUM CO., 6910 Preston Hwy.(40219), pg. 217
Carlisle Equipment Company, 3800 Crittenden Dr.(40217), pg. 220
CARRIER VIBRATING EQUIPMENT, INC., 3400 Fern Valley Rd.(40213), pg. 225
CHARING CROSS GROUP, 1330 S. Third St.(40208), pg. 239
CHEMCENTRAL/Louisville, 1825 Appleton Ln.(40256), pg. 242
Cissell Manufacturing Company, 831 First St.(40203), pg. 357
The Cobb Group, 9420 Bunsen Pkwy. 1218
COLLINS CHEVROLET, GEO, 717 W. Broadway(40202), pg. 263
BILL COLLINS FORD INC., 3610 Bargetown Rd.(40218), pg. 263
CREATIVE ALLIANCE, INC., 222 S. First St., Ste. 400(40202), pg. 297
CROSS MOTORS CORP., Watterson Expwy. at Newburg Rd.(40232), pg. 300
CUMMINS CUMBERLAND INC., 9822 Bluegrass Pkwy.(40299), pg. 305
D & K OPTICAL, INC., 4415 Poplar Level Rd.(40213), pg. 307
DAHLEM COMPANY, INC., 6200 Dutchman Lane(40205), pg. 310
DAIRYMEN, INC., 10140 Linn Station Rd.(40223), pg. 311
DOE-ANDERSON ADVERTISING AGENCY, INC., 223 E. Broadway(40202), pg. 342
DRUTHER'S INTERNATIONAL, INC., 1 Oxmoor Pl.(40222), pg. 350
DULING OPTICAL CORPORATION, 4415 Poplar Level Rd.(40213), pg. 352
The Enro Shirt Company, Inc., 4300 Leghorn Dr.(40218), pg. 78
Farm Credit Bank of Louisville, Farm Credit Bank Bldg., 201 W. Main St.(40202), pg. 405
FASHION SHOP OF KENTUCKY INC., 11008 Decimal Dr.(40299), pg. 403
FESSEL, SIEGFRIEDT & MOELLER, INC., 981 S. Third St.(40203), pg. 407
First Kentucky Trust Company, 101 S. Fifth St.(40202), pg. 413
FIRST NATIONAL BANK OF LOUISVILLE, 101 S. Fifth St.(40202), pg. 413
Flav-O-Rich, Inc., 10140 Linn Station Rd.(40223), pg. 311
Fontaine Modification/Components Company, P.O. Box 24475(40224), pg. 711
Frank Paxton Lumber Company, 4990 South Crittenden Drive(40233), pg. 592
GATEWAY PRESS, INC., 4500 Robards Lane(40218), pg. 446
Gohmann Asphalt & Construction of KY., Inc., P.O. Box 19257, 2001 Outer Loop(40219), pg. 465
GRINDMASTER CORPORATION, 1733 Research Dr.(40299), pg. 488
GRISANTI, INC., 9300 Shelbyville Rd., Ste. 1006(40222), pg. 488
HALL CONTRACTING CORP., 3800 Crittenden Dr.(40209), pg. 501
HENDERSON ELECTRIC CO., INC., 4502 Poplar Level Rd.(40213), pg. 529
HESCO PARTS CORPORATION, 10 Station Park(40210), pg. 531
HILLERICH & BRADSBY CO., INC., 200 W. Broadway(40202), pg. 535
Neil Huffman Chrysler Plymouth Dodge, 4126 Shelbyville Rd.(40207), pg. 551
Neil Huffman Volkswagon Mazda Suburu, 4926 Dixi Highway(40216), pg. 551
NEIL HUFFMAN NISSAN INC., 3922 Dutchmans Lane(40207), pg. 551
E.H. HUGHES COMPANY, INC., 340 Byrne Ave.(40217), pg. 552
INTERLOCK INDUSTRIES, INC., 10300 Linn Station Rd., Ste. 200(40223), pg. 574
KENTUCKY INDIANA LUMBER CO. INC., 227 E. Lee St.(40208), pg. 623
KENTUCKY MANUFACTURING CO., 2601 S. 3rd St.(40208), pg. 624
Kentucky Optical, 640 Fourth Ave.(40201), pg. 828
Kindy Optical, 4415 Poplar Level Rd.(40233), pg. 352
KURFEES COATINGS, INC., 201 E. Market St.(40202), pg. 646
LABORATORY SUPPLY COMPANY, INC., 4444 Park Blvd.(40209), pg. 649
LANTECH INC., 11000 Bluegrass Pkwy.(40299), pg. 658
JACOB LEVY & BROS., INC., 1126 W. Breckenridge St.(40210), pg. 672
LOUISVILLE BEDDING COMPANY, 10400 Bunsen Way(40299), pg. 684
LOUISVILLE SCRAP MATERIAL CO., INC., 301 E. Main St.(40202), pg. 684
The Louisville Transportation Company, 10300 Lynn Station Rd., Ste. 200(40223), pg. 574
Lugene Opticians, 640 Fourth Ave.(40201), pg. 828
MANNING EQUIPMENT, INC., 12000 Westport Rd.(40223), pg. 704
Marmon-Herrington Company, 2000 Plantside Dr.(40299), pg. 711
MERCER TRANSPORTATION CO., 1128 W. Main St.(40203), pg. 739
Metal Sales Manufacturing Corporation, 4001 Produce Rd.(40218), pg. 575
Monfried Optical, 4415 Poplar Level Rd.(40233), pg. 352
BOB MONTGOMERY CHEVROLET/HONDA, 5340 Dixie Hwy.(40216), pg. 767
NTS CORPORATION, 10172 Linn Station Rd.(40223), pg. 781
NEILL-LAVIELLE SUPPLY CO., 1711 S. Floyd St.(40217), pg. 797
NORCROSS INDUSTRIES, INC., 11405 Park Rd.(40223), pg. 809
OPTICAL CORP. OF AMERICA, 640 Fourth Ave.(40202), pg. 827
ORR SAFETY EQUIPMENT COMPANY, 2360 Millers Lane(40216), pg. 830
OTT COMMUNICATIONS, INC., 3321 Ruckreigel Pkwy.(40299), pg. 831
PARAMOUNT FOODS INC., 2800 Fern Valley Rd.(40213), pg. 848
PORCELAIN METALS CORP., 1400 S. 13th St.(40210), pg. 881
PRICE WEBER MARKETING COMMUNICATIONS, INC., 2101 Production Dr.(40299), pg. 889
PROGRESS PAINT MFG. CO., 826 W. Main St.(40202), pg. 894
Promotion Services, Inc., 10140 Linn Station Rd.(40223), pg. 311
RAPID INDUSTRIES, INC., 4003 Oaklawn Dr.(40259-0259), pg. 913
REV-A-SHELF, 2409 Plantside Dr.(40299), pg. 930
SHEEHY, KNOPF & SHAVER, INC., 101 Bullitt Lane, Ste. 107(40222), pg. 996
Southern Optical, 640 Fourth Ave.(40201), pg. 828
SOUTHLAND FLOORING SUPPLIES OF LOUISVILLE, INC., 1010 Industrial Blvd.(40219), pg. 1023
SULLIVAN & COZART INC., 822 W. Kentucky St.(40203), pg. 1056
SWOPE AUTOMOTIVE GROUP, INC., 10 Louisville Auto Center(40299), pg. 1068
TARRANT SERVICE AGENCY, INC., 1830 Cargo Ct.(40299), pg. 1079
TAYLOR DRUG STORES, INC., 4010 Crittenden Dr.(40209), pg. 1081
THERMAL AMERICAN FUSED QUARTZ CO., 1600 W. Lee St.(40201), pg. 1091
THORNTON OIL CORP., 10101 Linn Station Rd., Ste. 200(40223), pg. 1095
Thorobred Containers Incorporated, 1400 Southwestern Pkwy.(40201), pg. 575
TOWN & COUNTRY FORD INC., 6015 Preston Hwy.(40219), pg. 1103
TRI-CITY OLDSMOBILE INC., 3920 Dutchmans Lane(40207), pg. 1110
Tube-Ice Div., P.O. Box 1918(40201), pg. 1154
R.C. TWAY COAL COMPANY, 2601 S. Third St.(40208), pg. 1120
UMI Data Courier, 620 S. Third St.(40202), pg. 135
VALU DISCOUNT, INC., 3916 Dupont Square S.(40207), pg. 1143
Valve & Fitting Div., P.O. Box 1918(40201), pg. 1154
HENRY VOGT MACHINE CO., 1000 W. Ormsby Ave.(40210), pg. 1154
WLOU Radio Station, 2549 So. 3rd St.(40208), pg. 599
WEHR CONSTRUCTORS INC., 2517 Plantside Dr.(40299), pg. 1172
WHITTENBERG CONSTRUCTION CO., 4774 Allmond Ave.(40209), pg. 1187
WINE & SCHULZ INC., 3939 Produce Rd.(40218), pg. 1196
ZINIZ INC., 100 High Rise Dr., Ste. 200(40213), pg. 1220
ZOELLER CO., 3280 Old Millers Lane(40216), pg. 1220

Ludlow

DURO PAPER BAG MANUFACTURING CO., Davies & Oak Sts.(41016), pg. 355

Madisonville

Triple F Limousin Cattle, 295 S. Main St.(42431), pg. 1141
V.F. ENERGIES, INC., 295 S. Main St.(42431), pg. 1141

Millersburg

STAMLER CORPORATION, Main & Stamler Sts.(40348), pg. 1035

Murray

Murray Drug, 415 S. Fourth St.(42071), pg. 384

New Castle

Henry County Local, P.O. Box 209(40050), pg. 655

Newport

NATIONAL BAND & TAG CO., 721 York(41071), pg. 786
SENCORP, One Riverfront Place(41071), pg. 989
TRAUTH DAIRY INC., 16 E. 11th St.(41071), pg. 1108

Nicholasville

SARGENT & GREENLEAF, INC., 1 Security Dr.(40356), pg. 971
Sargent & Greenleaf International, 1 Security Dr.(40356), pg. 971

Owensboro

FIELD PACKING COMPANY, P.O. Box 766(42302), pg. 409
MPD, INC., 316 E. 9th St.(42303), pg. 693
MPH & CMI, 316 E. 9th St.(42301), pg. 693
MODERN WELDING CO., INC., 2880 New Hartford Rd.(42303), pg. 763

OWENSBORO GRAIN CO., INC., 719 E. 2nd St.(42301), pg. 834

Paducah

Alco Health Services Corp.-Paducah Div., 322 N. Third St.(42001-0028), pg. 31
Pressure Pak Container, Inc., 3200 Bullard St.(42001), pg. 70

Paris

Triple F Limousin Cattle, (40361), pg. 1141

Richmond

MADISON GROCERY CO., INC., U.S. Hwy. 25 S.(40475), pg. 699

Shelbyville

Electro-Wire, Inc., 421 Haven Hill Rd.(40065), pg. 375
Landmark Community Newspapers, Inc., P.O. Box 549, (40065), pg. 655
Ohio Valley Aluminum Company, 1100 Industrial Park(40065), pg. 575
ROLL FORMING CORPORATION, Industrial Park, P.O. Box 369(40065), pg. 944
The Sentinel-News, P.O. Box 399, 702 Washington St.(40066), pg. 655

Shepherdsville

Pioneer News, P.O. Box 98(40165), pg. 655

Somerset

SOMERSET REFINERY INC., 600 Monticello St.(42501), pg. 1017
SOUTHERN BELLE DAIRY COMPANY, INC., 607 E. Bourne Ave.(42501), pg. 1020

Springfield

The Springfield Sun, P.O. Box 31, (40069), pg. 655

Stearns

OUTDOOR VENTURE CORP., Hwy. 92(42647), pg. 832

Taylorsville

Spencer Magnet, P.O. Box 219(40071), pg. 655

Vanceburg

THE SANYMETAL PRODUCTS CO., INC., PO Box 490, Black Oak Industrial Park(41179), pg. 970

Walton

Duro Paper Bag Mfg. Co., Richwood Industrial Pk., Shoreland Dr.(41094), pg. 355

Wilder

CARLISLE EQUIPMENT COMPANY, 840 Licking Pike(41076), pg. 220

Williamstown

Grant County News, P.O. Box 247(41097), pg. 655

Winchester

EAST KENTUCKY POWER CO-OP, 4758 Lexington Rd.(40392), pg. 362

LOUISIANA

Alexandria

Southern Electric Supply Co., Inc., 3012 Broadway(71301), pg. 1021
TUDOR INC., P.O. Box 7917(71306), pg. 1118

Avery Island

MCILHENNY COMPANY, (70513), pg. 729
McIlhenny Resources, (70513), pg. 729

Baton Rouge

ACME REFRIGERATION OF BATON ROUGE INC., 11844 South Choctaw Dr.(70815), pg. 13
AIRTROL, INC., 3960 North St.(70806), pg. 28
Allright Baton Rouge, Inc., 218 Laurel(70801), pg. 41
AMERICAN LIBERTY FINANCIAL CORP., 4962 Florida Blvd.(70806), pg. 57
ANCO INSULATIONS, INC., 15981 Airline Hwy.(70817), pg. 72
ASSOCIATED GROCERS, INC., 8686 Anselmo Ln.(70810), pg. 89
BARBER BROTHERS CONTRACTING COMPANY, 2636 Dougherty Dr.(70805), pg. 119
BATON ROUGE WATER WORKS COMPANY, 8755 Goodwood(70806), pg. 126
BERNHARD MECHANICAL CONTRACTOR, INC., 10321 Airline Hwy.(70816), pg. 143
BUQUET & LE BLANC INC., 18145 Petroleum Dr.(70809), pg. 189
CAJUN ELECTRIC POWER CO-OP, 10719 Airline Hwy.(70816), pg. 207
CARTER CHAMBERS SUPPLY, INC., 6819 S. Choctaw Dr.(70806), pg. 226
COLMAN TOYOTA, 9292 Airline Hwy.(70895), pg. 263
DIAMOND MOTORS INC., 12422 Florida Blvd.(70815), pg. 335
DISTRIBUTORS OIL COMPANY, INC., 4085 Florida Blvd.(70806), pg. 340
A. K. DURNIN CHRYSLER PLYMOUTH, INC., 6815 Florida Blvd.(70806), pg. 355
EVANGELINE MEDICAL & X-RAY DISTRIBUTORS, 6781 Cezanne Ave.(70806), pg. 390
Evans Electric Supply, Inc., 1060 Nicholson Dr.(70802), pg. 923
Express 1 Stop, 2773 N. Flannery Rd.(70814), pg. 1057
FRAENKEL COMPANY, 10600 S. Choctaw Dr.(70815), pg. 428
GROUP INSURANCE INC., 10932 Cloverland Ave.(70809), pg. 490
GUARANTY CORPORATION, 929 Government St.(70802), pg. 491
HECK ENTERPRISES, INC., 5415 S. Choctaw(70805), pg. 524
HI NABOR SUPERMARKET INC., 7201 Winbourne Ave.(70805), pg. 532
LAMAR CORPORATION, 5551 Corporate Blvd.(70808), pg. 652
LaRoche Chemicals Inc., Airline Hwy.(70805), pg. 659
LOUISIANA UTILITIES SUPPLY COMPANY, 2056 Sorrel(70802), pg. 684
NEWTRON GROUP INC., 8183 W. El Cajon Dr.(70815), pg. 805
B. OLINDE & SONS COMPANY, INC., 9536 Airline Hwy.(70815), pg. 824
PALA GROUP, INC., 16347 Old Hammond Hwy.(70816), pg. 843
Pala Interstate, 16347 Old Hammond Hwy.(70816), pg. 843
Parish Water Company, Inc., 9232 Joor Rd.(70816), pg. 126
PERFORMANCE CONTRACTORS INC., 9865 Pecue Lane(70810), pg. 861
Southern Electric Supply Co., Inc., 8536 S. Choctaw Dr.(70815), pg. 1021
SULLIVAN OIL COMPANY, 2773 N. Flannery(70814), pg. 1057
THOMAS PIPE & STEEL, INC., P.O. Box 53187(70805), pg. 1093
WOODFIN-SMITH PONTIAC, INC., 300 Wooddale Blvd.(70806), pg. 1200

Bossier City

Louisiana Downs, 8000 E. Texas(71111), pg. 323

Cotton Valley

Hunt Oil Cotton Valley District, P.O. Box 38, (71018-0038), pg. 554

Donaldsonville

OURSO INVESTMENT CORPORATION, 110 Railroad Ave.(70346), pg. 832
Security Industrial Insurance Co., Inc., P.O. Box 609(70346), pg. 832

Eunice

Guillory Tank Truck Service, Rte. 2 Box 710(70535), pg. 541

Fort Myers

Gulf Coast League Twins, Lee County Stadium, 14200 Six Mile Cypress Pkwy.(33912), pg. 758

Geismar

Rubicon Inc., P.O. Box 517, (70734), pg. 1129
Uniroyal Chemical Co., Inc., P.O. Box 397, Highway 30(70734), pg. 1129

Gonzales

East Ascension Telephone Company, 913 S. Burnside Ave.(70737), pg. 364
EATEL CORPORATION, 913 S. Burnside Ave.(70737), pg. 364
PICOU BROTHERS CONSTRUCTION COMPANY, 12608 Airline Hwy.(70737), pg. 870
Picou Brothers Tractor & Rental Company of Gonzales, 12608 Airline Hwy.(70737), pg. 870

Gretna

BCP TECHNICAL SERVICE, INC., 401 Whitney Ave., Ste. 314(70056), pg. 106
REAGAN EQUIPMENT COMPANY, INC., 2550 Belle Chase Hwy.(70053), pg. 917

Hammond

CITIZENS NATIONAL BANCSHARES INC., 201 N.W. Railroad Ave.(70401), pg. 250
Citizens National Bank, 201 N.W. Railroad Ave.(70401), pg. 251
Eckerd Drug Co., 825 Pride Blvd.(70401), pg. 366

Harahan

Cox Cable Jefferson Parish, Inc., 338 Edwards Ave.(70123), pg. 294
Digicourse, Inc., 5200 Toler St.(70123), pg. 651
DIVERSIFIED GROUP, INC., 5801 Citrus Blvd.(70123), pg. 340
Intralox, Inc., 201 Laitram Lane(70123), pg. 651
THE LAITRAM CORPORATION, 220 Laitram Lane(70123), pg. 650
Laitram Machinery Inc., 220 Laitram Lane(70123), pg. 651
Lapeyre Stair, Inc., 220 Laitram Lane(70123), pg. 651
GEO. H. LEHLEITNER & CO., INC., 301 Plantation Rd.(70123), pg. 666
Southern Electric Supply Co., Inc., 5712 Jarvis St.(70123), pg. 1021

Harvey

ACME TRUCK LINE, INC., 1105 Peters Rd.(70059), pg. 13
EVANS FABRICATION, INC., 1255 Peters Rd.(70058), pg. 390
INTREPID ENTERPRISES, INC., 1848 Industrial Blvd.(70058), pg. 581
LESON CHEVROLET COMPANY, INC., 1501 Westbank Expwy.(70058), pg. 668
PRODUCTION MANAGEMENT COMPANIES, INC., 2439 Manhattan Blvd., Ste. 400(70058), pg. 893
Production Management Control Systems, Inc., 1865 Industrial Hwy.(70058), pg. 893
Production Management Industries, Inc., 2804 Peters Rd.(70058), pg. 893

Houma

Caro Produce & Institutional Foods, 2324 Bayou Blue Rd.(70364), pg. 861
Triumph-LOR, Inc., 606 Glendale Ave.(70360), pg. 1115

Jefferson

CHEMCENTRAL/New Orleans, 333 River Rd.(70121), pg. 242
Church's Fried Chicken, Inc., 1333 S. Clearview Pkwy.(70121), pg. 284
AL COPELAND ENTERPRISES, INC., 1333 S. Clearview Pkwy.(70121), pg. 283
WALLE CORPORATION, 600 Elmwood Park Blvd.(70123), pg. 1161

Jena

JUSTISS OIL CO., INC., Hwy. 84 E.(71342), pg. 610

Jennings

CHARLES HOLSTON, INC., P.O. Box 1014(70546), pg. 541

Kenner

Backer Spielvogel Bates, Inc., 2400 Veterans Memorial Blvd., Ste. 430(70062), pg. 109
Johnson Moving & Storage, New Orleans, 100 W. Airline Hwy.(70062), pg. 601
Security Van Line, Inc., 100 W. Airline Hwy.(70062), pg. 600
SECURITY VAN LINES, INC., 100 W. Airline Hwy.(70062), pg. 987
Universal Match Corp., 3740 Florida Ave., Ste. 1(70065), pg. 335

Lafayette

ABDALLA'S LAFAYETTE, INC., 900 E. St. Mary(70503), pg. 10
AMERICAN MANUFACTURING COMPANY, INC. (LA), 200 Southpark Rd.(70508), pg. 58
Hunt Oil Lafayette Land Office, Bldg. 14, 106 Oil Center Dr., Ste. 103(70508), pg. 554
SCHAD INDUSTRIES, INC., 201 Rue Iberville(70508), pg. 974
Triumph-LOR, Inc., 212 Southpark Rd.(70508), pg. 1115
Triumph-LOR, Inc., P.O. Box 51246, 212 Southpark Rd.(70505), pg. 1115

Lake Charles

SHEARMAN CORPORATION, 4900 Hwy. 90 E.(70602), pg. 996

Lake Providence

TERRAL-NORRIS SEED CO., INC., 604 Ninth St.(71254), pg. 1088

Leesville

Southern Electric Supply Co., Inc., Hyw. 171 S.(71446), pg. 1021

Livingston

HENDERSON AUCTIONEERS, Highway 190(70754), pg. 528

Lockport

BOLLINGER MACHINE SHOP AND SHIPYARD, INC., P.O. Box 250, Highway 308(70374), pg. 163

Metaire

New Orleans Pelicans, 321 Veterans Blvd.(70005), pg. 758

Metairie

CONSOLIDATED COMPANIES INC. (CONCO), 3000 34th St.(70001), pg. 276
CROWN BUICK, INC., 2121 Clearview Pkwy.(70001), pg. 302
DRUMM & ASSOCIATES, INC., 110 Veterans Blvd., Ste. 350(70005), pg. 349
L & L OIL COMPANY, INC., 3421 N. Causway Blvd., Ste. 502(70002), pg. 647
MCC GROUP, INC., 3001 17th St.(70002), pg. 691
Popeye's Famous Fried Chicken, 1405 Airline Hwy.(70001), pg. 283
REILY ELECTRIC SUPPLY, INC., 3011 Lausat(70001), pg. 923
ROYAL OLDSMOBILE MAZDA, INC., 3400 Veterans Memorial Blvd.(70002), pg. 953
VICTORY FINANCIAL GROUP, INC., 3115 6th St.(70002), pg. 1150

Minden

FIBREBOND CORPORATION, 1300 Davenport(71055), pg. 408
Mister Twister, Drawer 996(71055), pg. 997

Monroe

OUACHITA COCA-COLA BOTTLING COMPANY, P.O. Box 1571(71210), pg. 831

Morgan City

BERWICK BAY OIL CO. INC., 1020 David Dr.(70380), pg. 144

New Orleans

ARA Leisure Services, New Orleans Convention Center, 900 Convention Center Blvd.(70130), pg. 6
ARA Leisure Services, Rivergate, 4 Canal St.(70130), pg. 6
Algiers Iron Works & Dry Dock, Inc., 434 Powder St.(70114), pg. 163
Allright New Orleans, Inc., 150 Barrone St., Ste. 301(70112), pg. 42
THE BABCOCK & WILCOX COMPANY, 1010 Common St.(70161), pg. 107
BARQ'S, INC., 601 Poydras St., Ste. 1925(70130), pg. 121
BAUERLEIN INC., Poydras Center, 650 Poydras St., Ste. 1100(70130), pg. 127
BELLWETHER TECHNOLOGY CORPORATION, 203 Carondelet St., Ste. 250(70130), pg. 136
BLUMENTHAL PRINT WORKS, INC., 905 S. Broad Ave.(70125), pg. 161
Boh Brothers Construction Company, Inc., 730 S. Tonti St.(70119), pg. 162
BOH CORPORATION, 730 S. Tonti St.(70153), pg. 162
Bultman Funeral Home, 3338 St. Charles Ave.(70115), pg. 832
Container Products Inc., P.O. Box 23250, 6000 Jefferson Hwy.(70123), pg. 278
Cox Cable New Orleans, Inc., 2120 Canal Street(70112), pg. 294
Delta Queen Steamboat Company, Robin St. Wharf(70130-1890), pg. 385
DIXIE BREWING CO., INC., 2537 Tulane Ave.(70119), pg. 341
Family Inns of New Orleans, Inc., 6303 Chef Menteur(70126), pg. 398
FITZGERALD ADVERTISING INC., 1055 St. Charles Ave.(70130), pg. 416
C.B. FOX COMPANY, 220 Camp St.(70130), pg. 427
KENNETH GORDON NEW ORLEANS, LTD., 1209 Distributors Row(70123), pg. 472
Guaranty Savings Insurance Company, 1501 American Bank Bldg.(70130), pg. 1150
INDUSTRIAL METALS OF THE SOUTH, 401 N. Roman St.(70112), pg. 566
K & B, INC., 1055 St. Charles Pl.(71030), pg. 611
MORRIS KIRSCHMAN & COMPANY, INC., 5050 Almonaster(70177), pg. 633
Louisiana National Life Insurance Company, 1501 American Bank Bldg.(70130), pg. 1150
Luzianne Blue Plate Foods, 640 Magazine St.(70130), pg. 923
LYKES BROS. STEAMSHIP CO., INC., Lykes Center, 300 Poydras St.(70130), pg. 688
Lykes Lines Agency, Inc., 300 Poydras St.(70130), pg. 689
THE MAURIN-ODGEN COMPANIES, 460 Broadway St.(70118), pg. 722
Maurin-Ogden Management Corporation, 615 Baronne St., Ste. 100(70113), pg. 722
PETER A. MAYER ADVERTISING, INC., 324 Camp St.(70130), pg. 724
MetLife Security Insurance Company of Louisiana, 650 Poydras St.(70130-6101), pg. 745
National Marine, Inc., 400 Poydras St.(70130), pg. 1146
New Orleans Waterfront Rest. Corp., Bermuda St. Wharf, 2 Bermuda St.(70114), pg. 1028
ORLEANS MATERIALS & EQUIPMENT CO., INC., 5501 France Rd.(70216), pg. 829
PAN-AMERICAN LIFE INSURANCE COMPANY, 601 Poydras St.(70130), pg. 845
Paxton Beautiful Woods, 14200 Chef Menteur Hwy.(70189), pg. 592
PLYWOOD PANELS, INC., 100 Napoleon Ave.(70115), pg. 878
Production Management Structural Systems, Inc., 15160 Intracoastal Dr.(70189), pg. 893
WILLIAM B. REILY & CO., INC., 640 Magazine St.(70130), pg. 923
Robinson Lumber Company, 4000 Tchoupitoulas St.(70115), pg. 940
ROBINSON LUMBER & EXPORT COMPANY, 4000 Tchoupitoulas St.(70115), pg. 940
SUL Corporation, 1500 American Bank Bldg.(70130), pg. 1150
SCHWEGMANN GIANT SUPER MARKETS, 5300 Gentilly Rd.(70126), pg. 980
Southern United Corporation, 1500 American Bank Bldg.(70130), pg. 1150
SPERLING, 1001 Loyola Ave.(70113), pg. 1030
Standard Coffee Service, 640 Magazine St.(70130), pg. 923
STANDARD SUPPLY & HARDWARE, 832 Tchoupitoulas St.(70130), pg. 1037
Stirling Properties, Inc., 615 Baronne St., Ste. 100(70113), pg. 722
Taca International Airlines, P.O. Box 20047(70141), pg. 1076
TACA INTERNATIONAL AIRLINES, S. A., P.O. Box 20047(70141), pg. 1076
THE TIMES-PICAYUNE PUBLISHING CORP., 3800 Howard Ave.(70140), pg. 1098
Triumph-Lor, Inc., 305 Baronne, Suite 500(70112), pg. 1115
WVUE-TV, 1025 S. Jefferson Davis Pkwy.(70125), pg. 194
WALK, HAYDEL & ASSOCIATES, INC., 600 Carondelet St.(70130), pg. 1159
WEMCO, INC., 966 S. White St.(70125), pg. 1176

New Sarpy

TransAmerican Refining Corp., 2992 River Rd.(70078), pg. 1106

Oak Grove

RUFFIN BUILDING SYSTEMS, INC., 6914 Hwy. 2(71263-8930), pg. 955

Opelousas

Lou Ana Foods, Inc., 731 N. Railroad Ave.(70570), pg. 974

Plain Dealing

Laminated Beam Div., High Way 3 North(71604), pg. 77

Port Allen

WESTGATE INC., 1355 Beaulieu Ln.(70767), pg. 1182

Rayville

Continental/Murray, Hwy. 80 E.(71269), pg. 279

Ruston

T.L. JAMES & COMPANY, 106 West Mississippi Ave.(71270), pg. 588

Saint Martinville

BRUCE FOODS CORP., 1653 Old Spanishtrail(70582), pg. 183

Scott

Hunt Oil Gulf Coast District, P.O. Box 727(70583), pg. 554

Shreveport

Allright Shreveport, Inc., 729 Travis St.(71162), pg. 42
BAYOU STATE OIL CORPORATION, 1115 Hawn Ave.(71107), pg. 128
Hunt Oil Shreveport Land Office, Ste. 502, 400 Travis St.(71101-3113), pg. 554
ROUNDTREE AUTOMOTIVE GROUP, 8660 Fern Ave.(71105), pg. 952
South States Inc., P.O. Box 3945, Woolworth Rd.(71133), pg. 340

Thibodaux

Stark Candy Company, 100 Candy Lane(70301), pg. 1123

Ville Platte

Valley Canning Co., Inc., P.O. Box D, (70586), pg. 196

West Monroe

Burlington Motor Carriers, P.O.Box 1919, (71291), pg. 191

Westlake

PUMPELLY OIL, INC., Old Spanish Trail(70669), pg. 900

Westwego

Gold Bond Building Products, 10 Louisiana St.(70094), pg. 790

White Castle

CORA TEXAS MANUFACTURING CO., Texas Rd.(70788), pg. 285

MAINE

Auburn

Gates Formed-Fibre Products, P.O. Box 1300(04210-9156), pg. 445
PIONEER PLASTICS HOLDING, INC., One Pionite Rd.(04210), pg. 872

Augusta

Central Maine Morning Newspapers, 274 Western Ave.(04330), pg. 442
Joseph Kirschner Co., Riverside Dr., pg. 605
MAINE STATE LOTTERY COMMISSION, State House Station 702
Pine State Beverage, 8 Ellis Ave.(04330), pg. 871
PINE STATE TOBACCO & CANDY COMPANY, 8 Ellis Ave.(04330), pg. 871
Pine State Vending, 8 Ellis Ave.(04330), pg. 871

Bangor

COLES EXPRESS, 444 Perry Rd.(04401), pg. 261
DARLING'S, 153 Perry Rd.(04401), pg. 315
Dead River Forest Products, 55 Broadway(04401), pg. 322
Dead River Petroleum Co., 55 Broadway(04401), pg. 322
THE ERIN COMPANY, 500 Main St.(04401), pg. 387
Jordan's Foods-Bangor Division, 216 Thatcher St.(04401), pg. 605
Parts Wholesalers, Inc., 155 Perry Rd.(04401), pg. 225
Scott Motor Transport, 55 Broadway(04401), pg. 322
VILLAGE CAR COMPANY, 40-44 Summer St.(04401), pg. 1151
Westco Industrial, 160 Target Circle(04401), pg. 441

Bath

BATH IRON WORKS, 700 Washington St.(04530), pg. 126

Belfast

PENOBSCOT FROZEN FOODS, INC., One Pierce St.(04915), pg. 858

Berwick

PRIME TANNING CO., INC., Sullivan St.(03901), pg. 889

Bethel

SUNDAY RIVER SKIWAY CORPORATION, Sunday River Rd.(04217), pg. 1059

Biddeford

FIBER MATERIALS, INC., Biddeford Industrial Park, 5 Morin St.(04005), pg. 408
SHAPE INC., Biddeford Industrial Park(04005), pg. 995

Brewer

EASTERN FINE PAPER, INCORPORATED, 517 S. Main St.(04412), pg. 363

Bridgton

HOWELL LABORATORIES, INC., 124 Harrison St.(04009), pg. 548

Brunswick

Casco Cable Television Inc., Fort Andross, 14 Main St., Ste. 111(04011), pg. 1065

Caribou

Jordan's Foods-Caribou Division, Bennett Dr.(04736), pg. 605

Casco

HANCOCK LUMBER, INC., Rt. 121(04015), pg. 504

Dexter

DEXTER SHOE COMPANY, Railroad Ave.(04930), pg. 334

Fairfield

Jordan's Foods-Fairfield Division, 14 Davis St.(04937), pg. 605

Fort Kent

DAIGLE OIL CO., 44 Main St.(04743), pg. 310

Freeport

EASTLAND SHOE MANUFACTURING CORPORATION, 5 Park St.(04032), pg. 364
L.L. BEAN, INC., Casco St.(04033), pg. 648

Fryeburg

Forest Industries, Inc., 18 Fair St.(04037), pg. 972

Gardener

Yorktowne Paper Mills of Maine, 721 Water St.(04345), pg. 1209

Gorham

Hill-Loma, Inc., , pg. 468

Lewiston

AMERICAN STABILIS, INC., 60 Lexington St.(04240), pg. 61
BATES FABRICS, INC., 33 Canal St.(04243), pg. 125
Fairview Wine Co., 21 Saratoga St.(04240), pg. 1186
Federal Distillers, 21 Saratoga St.(04240), pg. 1186
GEIGER BROTHERS, Mt. Hope Ave.(04240), pg. 447
H. E. Sargent Constructor Inc., 145 River Rd.(04241), pg. 971
Hall & Knight Hardware Co., 20 Chapel St.(04240), pg. 340
Lawrence & Company, 21 Saratoga St.(04240), pg. 1186
Maine Bottlers, 21 Saratoga St.(04240), pg. 1186
WHITE ROCK DISTILLERIES INC., 21 Saratoga St.(04240), pg. 1186

Locke Mills

GILBERT MFG. CORP., P.O. Box 165, Route 26(04255), pg. 458

Machias

Down East Timberlands Division, 23 1/2 E. Main St.(04654), pg. 524

North Berwick

HUSSEY CORPORATION, Dyer St.(03906), pg. 555

Oxford

National Wood Products, Co., RFD 1 Box 1575(04270), pg. 972

Portland

Arnold Fortuna Lawner & Cabot, 600 Southborough Dr.(04106), pg. 84
DEAD RIVER COMPANY, 1 Dana St.(04112), pg. 321
DIVERSIFIED COMMUNICATIONS, 5 Milk St.(04101), pg. 340
EMERY WATERHOUSE COMPANY, Rand Road(04104), pg. 379
GUY GANNETT PUBLISHING COMPANY, 1 City Center(04101), pg. 442
THE GUTHRIE GROUP, 477 Congress St.(04101-3406), pg. 495
JORDAN'S MEATS, 38 India(04112), pg. 605
MAINE PRINTING & BUSINESS FORMS CO., P.O. Box 3878, (04104), pg. 702
Metro Medical Resources, Inc., 264 St. John St.(04102), pg. 1070
Moran Towing of Maine, 72 Commercial St., Ste. 04111(04112), pg. 769
NELSON & SMALL INC., 212 Canco Rd.(04103), pg. 798

NORTHEASTERN GRAPHIC SUPPLY, INC., 14 Industrial Way(04102), pg. 814
OAKHURST DAIRY, 364 Forest Ave.(04101), pg. 819
Portland Newspapers, 390 Congress St.(04104), pg. 442
S.P.C. TRANSPORT, 150 Read St(04104), pg. 963
WGME-TV, 1335 Washington Ave.(04104), pg. 442
Westco Industrial Corporation, 145 Presumpscott(04013), pg. 441

Presque Isle

MAINE POTATO GROWERS, INC., 56 Parsons St.(04769), pg. 702

Prospect Harbor

STINSON SEAFOOD COMPANY, Route 186(04669), pg. 1049

Sanford

WASCO PRODUCTS, INC., Pioneer Ave.(04073), pg. 1165

Scarborough

POLLACK CORPORATION, 600 Roundwood Dr.(04074), pg. 879

Solon

SOLON MANUFACTURING COMPANY, Ferry St.(04979), pg. 1017

South Gardener

Mercer Paper Tube Co., River Rd.(04345), pg. 1209

South Portland

CONNORS BRUNSWICK, INC., 778 Main St.(04106), pg. 275
Dead River Properties, 13 Atlantic Place(04106), pg. 322
Port Clyde Foods Co., 778 Main St.(04106), pg. 276
Porteous, 500 Main Mall(04106-3293), pg. 353

Stillwater

H. E. SARGENT, INC., 101 Bennoch Rd.(04489), pg. 971

Thomaston

Chemrock Corporation, (04861), pg. 137

Warren

CROWE ROPE COMPANY, P.O. Box 479(04864), pg. 301

Wells

SPENCER PRESS, INC., 90 Spencer Dr.(04090), pg. 1030

Westbrook

AMERICAN MANAGEMENT GROUP, 865 Spring St.(04092), pg. 57
Jordan's Foods-Westbrook Division, Thomas Dr.(04092), pg. 605
Lindenmeyr Munroe, 510 County Road(04092), pg. 233
Portland Glass/American Management Group, 865 Spring St.(04098), pg. 58
Proglass, 865 Spring St.(04092), pg. 58
SAUNDERS BROTHERS, 170 Forest St.(04098), pg. 972
H. A. Stiles Co., 170 Forest St.(04092), pg. 972

Wilton

Forster Mfg. Co., Inc., Depot St.(04294), pg. 21

Winslow

LAVERDIERE'S ENTERPRISES, Benton Ave.(04901), pg. 661

Yarmouth

Reed & Barton Giftsources, P. O. Box 505, (04096), pg. 920

MARYLAND

Aberdeen

Harford Systems, Inc., P.O. Box 700(21001), pg. 152

Abingdon

TABS ASSOCIATES, 2904 Emmorton Rd.(21009), pg. 1076

Annapolis

Aeronautical Radio, Inc., 2551 Riva Rd.(21401), pg. 82
ARINC INC., 2551 Riva Rd.(21401), pg. 82
ARINC Research Corp., 2551 Riva Rd.(21401), pg. 82
Capital-Gazette Communications, Inc., 213 West St.(21401), pg. 656
SASS & ASSOCIATES, 275 West St., Ste. 300(21401), pg. 972

Annapolis Junction

CRAY COMMUNICATIONS INC., 9020 Junction Dr.(20701), pg. 297

Baltimore

Advertising Distributors of Maryland, Inc., Lansdowne Industrial Pk., 100 Alco Pl.(21227), pg. 513
ALBAN TRACTOR CO. INC., 8531 Pulaski Hwy.(21237), pg. 30
Alford Packaging, 2631 Merchant Dr.(21230), pg. 34
Allied Container Corp., 901 N. Newkirk St.(21205), pg. 1027
Allied Security Inc., 1825 Woodlawn Dr., Ste. 105(21207), pg. 39
Allright Baltimore, Inc., 5 No. Liberty St.(21201), pg. 41
AMERICAN TRADING AND PRODUCTION CORPORATION, 1 N. Charles St.(21201), pg. 64
American Trading Real Estate Properties, Inc., P.O. Box 238(21203), pg. 65
Aratex Services, 2928 Washington Blvd.(21230), pg. 6
Arcata Graphics Company, 201 N. Charles St., Ste. 2100(21201), pg. 80
ATLANTIC BUILDERS GROUP INC., 23 Fontana Lane(21237), pg. 94
The Avalon Hill Game Company, 4517 Harford(21214), pg. 765
Avalon Hill/Sports Illustrated Games, 4517 Harford Rd.(21214), pg. 765
BAC-Pritchard, Inc., P.O. Box 7322(21227), pg. 69
BALTIMORE LUGGAGE COMPANY, 1919 Anapolis Rd.(21230), pg. 116
BALTIMORE ORIOLES, INC., Memorial Stadium(21218), pg. 116
BALTIMORE STATIONERY CO., 2524 Kirk Ave.(21218), pg. 116
Baumgarten Stamp Co., 342 N. Charles St.(21203), pg. 58
BRUNING PAINT COMPANY, 601 South Haven St.(21224), pg. 184
WM. T. BURNETT & CO., INC., 1500 Bush St.(21230), pg. 191
THE CAMPBELL GROUP, 326 N. Charles St., 2nd Floor(21201), pg. 213
CAREY MACHINERY & SUPPLY COMPANY, 3501 Brehms Lane(21213), pg. 218
CENTURY AUTOLINE, 1700 S. Caton Ave.(21227), pg. 235
Civic Food Center, Inc., 4701 Odnonnel St.(21224), pg. 1016
COLLMAN GRAPHICS, INC., 1820 Portal St.(21224), pg. 263
CORNERSTONE, 519 W. Pratt(21201), pg. 286
DARDA INC. (USA), 1600 Union Ave.(21211), pg. 315
EISNER & ASSOCIATES, INC., 12 W. Madison St.(21201), pg. 372
ELLICOTT MACHINE CORP., 1611 Bush St.(21230), pg. 378
Fair Lane Bowling Div., 1112 N. Rolling Rd.(21228), pg. 396
FREED & ASSOCIATES, 3600 Clipper Mill Rd.(21211), pg. 430
FUTURES PERSONNEL SERVICES, Maryland Exec. Park, Oxford Bldg., 8600 LaSalle Rd.(21286), pg. 438
Gillett Broadcasting of Maryland, Inc. WMAR-TV, 6400 York Rd.(21212), pg. 459
Gold Bond Building Products, 2301 S. Newkirk St.(21224), pg. 790
GRAY KIRK/VANSANT ADVERTISING, INC., The World Trade Center(21202), pg. 479
B. GREEN & CO., 3601 Washington Blvd.(21227), pg. 484
JOHN GROSS & CO., 1521 Edgewood St.(21227), pg. 489
G. Heileman Brewing Company, Inc., 4501 Hollins Ferry Rd.(21227), pg. 526
Hinkle Easter Products, 1600 Union Ave.(21211), pg. 315
HOTTMAN EDWARDS, 1003 N. Calvert St.(21202), pg. 545
IMAGE DYNAMICS, INCORPORATED, 1101 N. Calvert Street(21202), pg. 563
Incor, Inc., 4601 N. Point Blvd.(21219), pg. 312
Insect Control & Research Corp., 1330 Dillon Heights Ave.(21228), pg. 731
Interstate Steel Supply Co. of Maryland, 1600 Cherry Hill Rd.(21230-0165), pg. 581
Krafcor Unlimited, 6301 B. Seaforth(21224), pg. 1027
C.J. LANGENFELDER & SON, INC., 8427 Pulaski Hwy.(21237), pg. 657
Leisure Time Games, 4517 Harford(21214), pg. 765
John D. Lucas Printing Company, 1820 Portal St.(21224), pg. 263
LYON CONKLIN & COMPANY, Race & McComas Sts.(21230), pg. 690
Maintain, 1611 Sulphur Spring Rd., Stes. 111 & 118(21227), pg. 723
MARS SUPER MARKETS, INC., 7183 Holabird Ave.(21222), pg. 714
MARYLAND PAPER BOX COMPANY, 4545 Annapolis Rd.(21227), pg. 717
MARYLAND STATE LOTTERY, 6776 Reistertown Rd., Ste. 204(21215), pg. 717
Microcomputer Games, 4517 Harford Rd.(21214), pg. 765
Moldcraft Plastics Inc., 4211 Shannon Dr.(21213), pg. 880
MONARCH AVALON, INC., 4517 Harford(21214), pg. 765
Monarch Toy Co., Ltd., 4517 Harford(21214), pg. 765
MONTEBELLO BRANDS INC., 1919 Willow Spring Rd.(21222), pg. 767
Moran Towing of Maryland, World Trade Center, 401 E. Pratt St., Ste. 800(21202), pg. 769
92 Q WERQ AM/FM, 111 Park Ave.(21201), pg. 1131
Paradies & Co. Atlanta, 1101 DeSoto Rd.(21223), pg. 1216
THE PARK CIRCLE MOTOR CO., 1829 Reisterstown Rd.(21208), pg. 848
PARKS SAUSAGE COMPANY, 3330 Henry G. Parks Jr. Circle(21215), pg. 850
Peerless Inc., 1101 DeSoto Rd.(21223), pg. 1216
POLY-SEAL CORPORATION, 1810 Portal St.(21224), pg. 880
POMPEIAN, INC., 4201 Pulaski Hwy.(21224), pg. 880
RTKL ASSOCIATES INC., 400 E. Pratt St.(21202), pg. 908
THE REEVES AGENCY, INC., 2219 Maryland Ave.(21218), pg. 921
RICHARDSON, MYERS & DONOFRIO, INC., 120 W. Fayette St.(21201), pg. 933
Rita-Ann Distributors, 901 Curtain Ave.(21218), pg. 32
SCHMIDT BAKING CO., INC., 7801 Fitch Lane(21236), pg. 976
THE SCOTSMAN GROUP, INC., 8211 Town Center Dr.(21236), pg. 982
SHILLCRAFT, INC., 8899 Kelso Drive(21221), pg. 999
Simkins Maryland Board, P.O. Box 3249, (21228), pg. 1005
Snavely Forest Products, Inc., 2901 Chalbs St.(21226), pg. 1015
SO-LO-FOOD, INC., 4701 Odonnell St.(21224), pg. 1016
STOP SHOP SAVE, 770 W. North Ave.(21217), pg. 1052
Strategy Games, 4517 Harford(21214), pg. 765
Tencarva Machinery Co., P.O. Box 16312, (21210), pg. 1087
TRAHAN, BURDEN & CHARLES, INC., 1030 N. Charles St.(21201), pg. 1105
TURNBULL ENTERPRISES, INC., 3635 Benson Ave.(21227), pg. 1119
Valu Foods Inc., 4701 Odonnell St.(21224), pg. 1016
Victory Games, Inc., 4517 Harford(21214), pg. 765
WBAL-AM, 3800 Hooper Ave.(21211), pg. 522
WBAL Division, 3800 Hooper Ave.(21211), pg. 522
WBAL-TV, 3800 Hooper Ave.(21211), pg. 522
WIYY-FM, 3800 Hooper Ave.(21211), pg. 522
Westreet Industries, 8901 Kelso Dr.(21221), pg. 1027
Westreet Industries, 6301 B. Seaforth(21224), pg. 1027
WHITING-TURNER CONTRACTING CO., 300 E. Joppa Rd.(21286), pg. 1187
THE ZAMOISKI CO., 3000 Waterview Ave.(21230), pg. 1216

Bel Air

Backer Spielvogel Bates, Inc., 112 W. Pennsylvania Ave., Ste. 101(21014), pg. 109

Belcamp

Bata Shoe Co., Inc., Route 40(21017), pg. 201
CHB CORP., 1250 Brass Mill(21017), pg. 201
INDEPENDENT CAN COMPANY, 1300 Brass Mill Rd.(21017), pg. 564

Beltsville

DURON, INC., 10406 Tucker St.(20705), pg. 355
TEXTILEASE CORPORATION, 10733 Tucker St(20705), pg. 1090

Bethesda

ADS/TMP Worldwide, 4719 Hampden Lane(20814), pg. 1073
THE ASCII GROUP, INC., 7475 Wisconsin Ave.(20814), pg. 8
EARLE PALMER BROWN, 6935 Arlington St.(20814), pg. 182
Earle Palmer Brown/Bethesda, 6935 Arlington Rd.(20814), pg. 182
CEI CONSTRUCTION, INC., 7500 Old Georgetown Road(20814), pg. 200
Calvert Group, Ltd., 4550 Montgomery Ave., Ste. 1000 N(20814), pg. 11
CHEVY CHASE CARS & GEO, 7725 Wisconsin Ave.(20814), pg. 244
CLARK CONSTRUCTION GROUP, 7500 Old Georgetown Rd.(20814), pg. 252
Clark Enterprises, Inc., 7500 Old Georgetown Rd.(20814), pg. 252
COLEMAN CADILLAC INC., 10400A Auto Park Ave.(20817), pg. 261
FEDERAL DATA CORPORATION, 4800 Hampton Lane(20814), pg. 404
GOODWILL INDUSTRIES OF AMERICA, INC., 9200 Wisconsin Ave.(20814), pg. 471
INFORMATION SYSTEMS & NETWORK CORPORATION, 10411 Motor City Dr.(20817), pg. 567
MILLER & LONG CO. INC., 4824 Rugby Ave.(20814), pg. 754
MITCHELL & ASSOC., INC., 7830 Old Georgetown Rd.(20814), pg. 761
OXFORD REALTY SERVICES CORP., 7316 Wisconsin Ave.(20814), pg. 835
Pike & Fischer, 4550 Montgomery Ave.(20814), pg. 190
UNITED BROADCASTING INC., 4733 Bethesda Ave., Ste. 808(20814), pg. 1131
WEITZMAN//LIVINGSTON, INC., 4709 Montgomery Ln.(20814), pg. 1174

California

Tracor Applied Sciences, Electronic Systems Div., 402 Cottonwood Pkwy.(20619), pg. 1105
Veda Systems, Incorporated, 6 Pecan Ct., Ste A.(20619), pg. 1146

Cambridge

Coldwater Seafood Corp., Woods Rd.(21613), pg. 260

Capitol Heights

DAYCON PRODUCTS COMPANY, INC., 9001 E. Hampton Dr.(20791), pg. 321
E. C. Ernst, P.O. Box 4040(20791), pg. 866
RONALD HSU CONSTRUCTION, 207 W. Hampton Ave.(20743), pg. 548

Chestertown

DAVID A. BRAMBLE, INC., 705 Morgnel Rd.(21620), pg. 171
DIXON VALVE & COUPLING COMPANY, 800 High St.(21620), pg. 341

Cheverly

ALLECO INC., Allegheny Circle(20781), pg. 35
PEAKE PRINTERS, INC., 2500 Schuster Dr.(20781), pg. 853

Chevy Chase

SIGAL/ZUCKERMAN CO., 2 Wisconsin Circle, 1003

Geographic Index

Cockeysville

THE WARD MACHINERY COMPANY, 10615 Beaver Dam Rd.(21030), pg. 1162

College Park

Lane Honda/Hyundai, 9400 Baltimore Blvd.(20740), pg. 949
94th of College Park, Inc., 5240 Calvert Rd.(20740), pg. 1028

Columbia

Arnold Fortuna Lawner & Cabot, 9881 Broken Land Pkwy., pg. 84
B&L Jewelry Co., 6301 Stevens Forest Rd.(21045), pg. 925
Barclay & Sons, 6301 Stevens Forest Rd.(21045), pg. 925
Barlow & Eaton, 6301 Stevens Forest Rd.(21045), pg. 925
Castleberg's, 6301 Stevens Forest Rd.(21045), pg. 925
First Advantage Mortgage Corporation, 8910 Rte. 108(21045), pg. 412
GENERAL BUSINESS SERVICES, INC., 7134 Columbia Gateway Dr.(21046), pg. 449
Henebrys, 6301 Stevens Forest Rd.(21046), pg. 925
Hub Furniture Co., 6301 Stevens Forest Rd.(21045), pg. 925
The Kline Furniture Co., 6301 Stevens Forest Rd.(21045), pg. 925
MARRINER MARKETING COMMUNICATIONS, INC., 10221 Wincopin Circle, Ste. 300(21044), pg. 713
Morton's Jewelry Co., 6301 Stevens Forest Rd.(21045), pg. 925
North Atlantic Industries Systems Division, 7125 Riverwood Dr.(21046), pg. 812
Relco, 6301 Stevens Forest Rd.(21045), pg. 925
RELIABLE STORES, INC., 6301 Stevens Forest Rd.(21046), pg. 925
S&N Katz Jewelers, 6301 Stevens Forest Rd.(21045), pg. 925
Scott Jewelers, 6301 Stevens Forest Rd.(21045), pg. 925
STANDARD MEDICAL IMAGING, INC., 9002 Red Branch Rd.(21045), pg. 1037
Weiss Jewelers, 6301 Stevens Forest Rd.(21045), pg. 925

Cumberland

S. SCHWAB COMPANY, Upper Potomac Industrial Park(21502), pg. 980

Eldersburg

Londontown Corporation, 1332 Londontown Blvd.(21784), pg. 682
LONDONTOWN HOLDINGS CORPORATION, Londontown Blvd.(21784), pg. 681
Star Sportswear Manufacturing, Londontown Blvd.(21784), pg. 682

Ellicott City

C.R. DANIELS, INC., 3451 Ellicott Center Dr.(21043), pg. 314
WILKINS-ROGERS INCORPORATED, 27 Frederick Rd.(21043), pg. 1190

Federalsburg

MARYLAND PLASTICS, INC., 251 E. Central Ave.(21632), pg. 717
Maryland Plastics, Inc., 251 E. Central Ave.(21632), pg. 152

Forestville

MURRY'S, INC., 8300 Pennsylvania Ave.(20747), pg. 777
MURRY'S, INC., 8300 Pennsylvania Ave.(20747), pg. 777

Frederick

AUSHERMAN CONSTRUCTION COMPANY, 8031 Reichs Ford Rd.(21701), pg. 98
FREDERICK TRADING COMPANY, 7901 Trading Lane(21701), pg. 430

Gaithersburg

Bechtel Eastern Power Corporation, 15740 Shady Grove Rd.(20877), pg. 131
Bechtel Power Corporation, 15740 Shady Grove Rd.(20877), pg. 131
ELECTRO MECHANICAL DESIGN SERVICES, INC., 16618 Oakmont Ave.(20877), pg. 375
MASTERS INC., 7891 Beechcraft Ave.(20879), pg. 720

Germantown

Energy and Technology Management Corporation, 2021 Century Blvd., 2nd Flr.(20874), pg. 981

Glen Burnie

OPTIC GRAPHICS, INC., 101 Dover Rd.(21060), pg. 827

Greenbelt

COAKLEY & WILLIAMS INC., 7500 Greenway Center Dr.(20770), pg. 256
EBM SYSTEMS, INC., 7701 Greenbelt Rd.(20770), pg. 359
GREENHORNE & O'MARA, INC., 9001 Edmonston Rd.(20770), pg. 485

Hagerstown

JAMISON DOOR COMPANY, P.O. Box 70(21741-0070), pg. 589
Maryland Ribbon Company, 857 Willow Circle(21740), pg. 822
STATTON FURNITURE MANUFACTURING COMPANY, 504 E. First St.(21740), pg. 1042
TRISTATE ELECTRICAL SUPPLY CO., INC., 1741 Dual Hwy.(21740), pg. 1114

Hanover

J P FOODSERVICE, INC., 7250 Parkway Dr.(21076), pg. 586
Jorgensen Steel & Aluminum/Baltimore, 7463 New Ridge Rd.(21076), pg. 605
Kilsby-Roberts/Baltimore, 7463 New Ridge Rd.(21076), pg. 606
MCRB Fulfillment Co., 7447 Candlewood Rd.(21076), pg. 692

Havre de Grace

J.M. Huber, Chemicals Division, 907 Revolution St.(21078), pg. 550

Hunt Valley

FAIR LANES INC., 10944 Beaver Dam Rd.(21030-2252), pg. 396
FAWN INDUSTRIES, INC., 311 Intl. Circle, Ste. 140(21030), pg. 404

Hyattsville

Editors Press, Inc., 3401 East West Hwy.(20782), pg. 632
Kiplinger Editors, 3401 East West Hwy.(20782), pg. 632
LUSTINE OLDSMOBILE & BUICK, INC., 5323 Baltimore Ave.(20781), pg. 688

Jessup

Baltimore Aircoil Company, 7595 Montevideo Rd.(20794), pg. 69
Monroe Foods/Dessert Masters, 6855 Rappahannock Dr.(20785), pg. 484
TATE ACCESS FLOORS, INC., 7510 Montevideo Rd.(20794), pg. 1080

Kensington

SAVOY CONSTRUCTION CO. INC., 3004 McComas Ave.(20895), pg. 973
Ventilating Systems Management, 3004 McComas Ave.(20895), pg. 973

La Plata

WILLS GROUP, INC., U.S. Rte. 301(20646), pg. 1193

Landover

CEILING & PARTITIONS, INC., 8812 Spectrum Dr.(20785), pg. 230
S. FREEDMAN & SONS, INC., 3322 Pennsy Dr.(20785), pg. 430
SFA, INC., 1401 McCormick Dr.(20785), pg. 961
TSI INDUSTRIES, INC., 8507 Rainswood Dr.(20785), pg. 1075
Washington Area Distribution Center, 3400 Pennsy Dr.(20785), pg. 925
WASHINGTON BEEF COMPANY, 1300 Mercantile Lane, Ste. 100 J(20785), pg. 1165
WASHINGTON HOMES, INC., 1802 Brightseat Rd., 6th Fl.(20785-4235), pg. 1166

Lanham

ENCORE MARKETING INTERNATIONAL, 4501 Forbes Blvd.(20706), pg. 380
THE MAXIMA CORPORATION, 4200 Parliament Place, Ste. 300(20706), pg. 723
Mitchell Business Equipment, 4855 Walden Lane(20706), pg. 866
THE PHILADELPHIA BOURSE, INC., 9602 A George Palmer Hwy.(20706), pg. 866
RJO ENTERPRISES, INC., 4500 Forbes Blvd.(20706), pg. 907
ROWMAN & LITTLEFIELD PUBLISHERS, INC., 4720 Boston Way(20706), pg. 952
University Press of America, Inc., 4720 Boston Way(20706), pg. 953

Largo

All-Seasons, Inc., 1802 Brightseat Rd.(20785-4235), pg. 1166
Citadel Land, Inc., 1802 Brightseat Rd.(20785-4235), pg. 1166
Consultants Corp., 1802 Brightseat Rd.(20785-4235), pg. 1166
Designed Contracts, Inc., 1802 Brightseat Rd.(20785-4235), pg. 1166
Housing-Home Sales, Inc., 1802 Brightseat Rd.(20785-4235), pg. 1166
The Southampton Corp., 1802 Brightseat Rd.(20785-4235), pg. 1166
Washington Homes Financial Corporation, 1802 Brightseat Rd.(20785-4235), pg. 1166
Washington Homes Financial Corporation, III, 1802 Brightseat Rd.(20785-4235), pg. 1166
Washington Homes Financial Corporation, II, 1802 Brightseat Rd.(20785-4235), pg. 1166
Washington Homes, Inc. of Virginia, 1802 Brightseat Rd.(20785-4235), pg. 1166

Laurel

General Sciences Corp., 6100 Chevy Chase Dr.(20707-2929), pg. 981
Maurexco Exporters, 13 C St., Ste. D(20707), pg. 722
Nuarc Mid-Atlantic Div., 14254 Cherry Lane(20707), pg. 817
S & S GRAPHICS, INC., 14880 Sweitzer Lane(20707), pg. 959

Linthicum Heights

Keystone Automotive Industries, Inc. - Linthicum, 822 Central Ave.(21090), pg. 628
TREMONT FOODS, 703 Nursery Rd.(21090), pg. 1109

Lutherville

Stephen Gould MD, 9480 Deereco Rd.(21093), pg. 474

Montgomery Village

KETTLER BROTHERS, INC., 9426 Stewartown Rd.(20879), pg. 626

Owings Mills

LION BROTHERS COMPANY, INC., 10246 Registertown Rd.(21117), pg. 677
MALESON NAYLOR, 10220 S. Dolfield Rd.(21117), pg. 702
Sweetheart Cup Co., Inc., 10100 Reisterstown(21117), pg. 1067

Parkton

GEORGE TRANSFER, INC., I-83 at Rte. 439(21120), pg. 453

Pikesville

Port City Press, Inc., 1323 Greenwood Rd.(21208), pg. 608

Pine Point

Steuart Transportation Co., Lighthouse Rd.(20674), pg. 1048

Potomac

CATERAIR HOLDINGS CORP., 7811 Montrose Rd.(20854), pg. 229
Caterair International, 7811 Montrose Rd.(20854), pg. 229
CARL M. FREEMAN ASSOCIATES, INC., 11325 Seven Locks Rd.(20854), pg. 431
PHILLIPS PUBLISHING INC., 7811 Montrose Rd.(20854), pg. 868

Reisterstown

Community Times Extra, 11502 Reisterstown Rd.(21136), pg. 656

Rockville

American Trading Real Estate Properties, Inc., Research Blvd. Ctr., Ste. 304, 1803 Research Blvd.(20850), pg. 65
BNA Communications, Inc., 9439 Key West Ave.(20850), pg. 189
CHARTWAY TECHNOLOGIES, 20 W. Gude Dr.(20850), pg. 240
DEVLIN LUMBER & SUPPLY CORP., 1540 Rockville Pike(20852), pg. 334
Maryland Wood Preserving Corp., 1540 Rockville Pike(20852), pg. 334
Maxima Business Systems, 2101 E. Jefferson St.(20872), pg. 723
Maxima Data Systems, 2101 E. Jefferson St.(20852), pg. 723
MCCORMICK PAINT WORKS COMPANY, 2355 Lewis Ave.(20851), pg. 727
Principal Health Care, Inc., 1801 Rockville Pike, Ste. 601(20852), pg. 891
SAS Consulting Services, Inc., 1700 Rockville Pike, Ste. 330(20852), pg. 959
Taylor Lumber & Supply Corp., 1540 Rockville Pike(20852), pg. 334
Tracor Applied Sciences, Systems Technology Div., 1601 Research Blvd.(20850), pg. 1105
Tracor Technology Resources, Inc., 1601 Research Blvd.(20850), pg. 1105
WESTAT INC., 1650 Research Blvd.(20850), pg. 1178

Salisbury

CASE FOODS, INC., 1325 Mt. Herman Rd.(21801), pg. 227
PERDUE FARMS INC., Old Ocean City Rd.(21802), pg. 860
Perdue Foods Incorporated, P.O. Box 1537(21801), pg. 860
Perdue Incorporated, P.O. Box 1537(21801), pg. 860
Perdue Transportation Inc., P.O. Box 1537(21802-1537), pg. 860
Shenandoah Products, P.O. Box 1537(21801), pg. 860
Shenandoah Valley Farms, P.O. Box 1537(21801), pg. 860

Savage

Biblio Distribution Ctr., 8705 Bollman Place(20763), pg. 953
Wilcox-Walter-Furlong Paper Co. of Washington, 8750 Larkin Rd.(20763), pg. 1157

Showell

SHOWELL FARMS, INC., Pitts Rd.(21862), pg. 1000

Silver Spring

First American Bank of Maryland, 8401 Colesville Rd.(20910), pg. 412
HARKINS BUILDERS, INC., 12301 Old Columbia Pike(20904), pg. 509
Harkins Carpentry, 12301 Old Columbia Pike(20904), pg. 509
RII (RICARDS INTERNATIONAL INC.), 1010 Wayne Ave., Ste. 300(20910), pg. 907

Sparks

Farm Credit Bank of Baltimore, Farm Credit Bank Bldg., 14114 York Rd.(21152), pg. 405

Sparrows Point

Automatic Metal Blanking, Inc., 1440 Grays Rd.(21219), pg. 70

Taneytown

THE TANEY CORPORATION, 5130 Allendale Lane(21787), pg. 1077

Temple Hills

Allied Security Inc., 4467 Old Branch Ave., Ste. 104(20748), pg. 39

Towson

AMERICAN STONE-MIX, INC., 8320 Bellona Ave.(21204), pg. 63
CUNA East Central District, 8501 LaSalle Road, Suite 104(21204), pg. 205
RAIL COMPANY, 515 E. Joppa Rd., Ste. 300(21286), pg. 906

Upper Marlboro

Maxima Computer Systems Corp., 14741 Governor Oden Bowie Dr., Rm. L128(20772), pg. 723
McArdle Printing Co., Inc., 800 Commerce Dr.(20772), pg. 189

Waldorf

BESCHE OIL COMPANY, INC., Old Washington Rd.(20604), pg. 145
The Washington Savings Bank, FSB, P.O. Box 220, Charles County Plaza(20604), pg. 1166

Westminster

Baltimore Book, P.O. Box 346, (21157), pg. 655
Carroll County Times, P.O. Box 346, 201 Railroad Ave.(21157), pg. 655
Central Maryland Homes, P.O. Box 346(21157), pg. 655
Century 21 Homes Magazine-York, PA, P.O. Box 346(21157), pg. 655
Commercial Real Estate, P.O. Box 346(21157), pg. 655
Homes of York-Adams County, P.O. Box 346, (21157), pg. 655
MONUMENTAL MILLWORK, INC., 344 Manchester Rd.(21157), pg. 768

White Marsh

J. GIBSON MCILVAIN CO., P.O. Box 222(21162), pg. 729

Williamsport

Sealy of Maryland & Virginia, Inc., 70-81 Industrial Park(21795), pg. 985

MASSACHUSETTS

Acton

DATA INSTRUMENTS, INC., 100 Discovery Way(01720), pg. 316
DECK HOUSE INC., 930 Main St.(01720), pg. 324
REX LUMBER COMPANY, 840 Main St.(01720-5804), pg. 930

Agawam

Farm Credit Bank of Springfield, Farm Credit Bank Bldg., 67 Hunt St.(01001), pg. 405
Springfield Bank for Cooperatives, 67 Hunt St.(01001), pg. 405

Allston

CAMBRIDGE STREET METAL CO., INC., 500 Lincoln St.(02134), pg. 211

Amesbury

AES, 10 Industrial Way(01913), pg. 364
CARGOCAIRE ENGINEERING CORPORATION, 79 Monroe St.(01913), pg. 220
Craig Systems, 10 Industrial Way(01913), pg. 364
EASTERN TECHNOLOGIES LTD, 10 Industrial Way(01913), pg. 364
RES-Q-TECH Inc., 10 Industrial Way(01913), pg. 364
Techweld Ltd., 10 Industrial Way(01913), pg. 364
Transit Systems Inc., 10 Industrial Way(01913), pg. 364

Andover

FROST COMPANY, 224 Andover St.(01810), pg. 435
THE FRYE COMPANY, 1 Elm Sq.(01810), pg. 435
IMT, 155 River Rd.(01810), pg. 789
Industrial Materials Technology, 155 River St., (01810), pg. 789
National Forge Engineered Systems Div., 155 River Rd.(01810), pg. 789
R.W. ELECTRONICS, 206 Andover St.(01810), pg. 908
STANDARD DUPLICATING MACHINES CORP., 10 Connector Rd.(01810), pg. 1036
Standard Roneo, 10 Connector Rd.(01810), pg. 1036

Arlington

Advertiming Inc., 85 Thorndike St.(02174), pg. 1154

Ashland

A.L E. Systems, Inc., 150 Homer Ave.(01721), pg. 145
Nyacol Products, Inc., Megunco Rd., P.O. Box 349(01721), pg. 837
TELECHRON, INC., 101 Union St.(01721), pg. 1085

Assonet

MEDIA CONCEPTS CORPORATION, 25 N. Main St.(02702), pg. 734

Athol

WHIPPS, 38 S. Main(01331), pg. 1185

Attleboro

AUTOMATIC MACHINE PRODUCTS COMPANY, 17 Wall St.(02703), pg. 100
GLINES & RHODES, INC., 189 East St.(02703), pg. 463

Auburn

CONSOLIDATED BEVERAGES, INC., 12 St. Mark St.(01501), pg. 276

Ayer

HORN PACKAGING CORPORATION, 11 Westford Rd.(01432), pg. 544

Bedford

AMRAY, INC., 160 Middlesex Turnpike(01730), pg. 68
KAYE INSTRUMENTS, INC., 15 De Angelo Dr.(01730), pg. 619
MEGAPULSE, INC., 8 Preston Ct.(01730), pg. 737
MITRE CORPORATION, Burlington Rd.(01730), pg. 762

Bernardston

MOHAWK PLASTICS, INC., Northfield Rd.(01337), pg. 763

Beverly

JOHNNY APPLESEED'S, INC., 30 Tozer Road(01915), pg. 597
STOCKER & YALE, INC., 133 Brimbol Ave.(01915), pg. 1050

Billerica

FURMAN LUMBER COMPANY, 32 Manning Rd.(01821), pg. 436
Harte-Hanks Data Technologies, 25 Linnell Circle(01821), pg. 513
I D E CORPORATION, 29 Dumham Rd.(01821), pg. 560
SIPEX CORPORATION, 22 Linnell Circle(01821), pg. 1009

Boston

ADVENT INTERNATIONAL, 101 Federal St.(02110), pg. 21
ALLIED ADVERTISING AGENCY, 141 Tremont St., 12th Fl.(02111), pg. 37
Allright Boston Parking, Inc., 31 Milk Street, Ste. 402(02111), pg. 41
American Council for International Studies, 19 Bay State Rd.(02215), pg. 56
AMERICAN FINANCE GROUP, Exchange Place(02109), pg. 52
American Financial Security, Exchange Place(02109), pg. 52
ARNOLD FORTUNA LAWNER & CABOT, 101 Arch St.(02110), pg. 84
THE ATLANTIC MONTHLY MAGAZINE, 745 Boylston St.(02116), pg. 95
Back Bay Advisors, Inc., 399 Boylston St.(02116), pg. 799
BALCO, INC. (MA), 306 Northern Ave., Bldg. 53(02205), pg. 115
BECKWITH ELEVATOR CO., 274 Southampton St.(02118), pg. 131
BERENSON, ISHAM & PARTNERS, INC., 31 Milk St.(02109), pg. 141
BLAUER MANUFACTURING CO., INC., 20 Aberdeen St.(02215), pg. 156
BLUE CROSS AND BLUE SHIELD OF MASSACHUSETTS, 100 Summer St.(02110), pg. 159
Boylston Capital Advisors, 501 Boylston St.(02117), pg. 799
BRONNER SLOSBERG HUMPHREY, 695 Atlantic Ave.(02111), pg. 179
BURTMAN IRON WORKS, INC., 31 Industrial Dr.(02137), pg. 195
Cadence Capital Management, 10 Liberty Sq., 4th Fl.(02109), pg. 841
Cambridge Associates, 164 Canal St.(02116), pg. 316
CHARLES RIVER FOODS, INC., 1 Widett Circle(02118), pg. 240
Cipriani Kremer Design, 2 Copley Place(02116), pg. 84
CLARKE GOWARD FITTS MATTESON, INC., 535 Boylston St.(02116), pg. 253
COLE HERSEE COMPANY, 20 Old Colony Ave.(02127-2467), pg. 260
CONNELL LIMITED PARTNERSHIP, Fort Hill Square, One International Pl., 275
CONTINENTAL CABLEVISION, The Pilot House, Lewis Wharf(02110), pg. 278
Continental Mortgage Investors, 111 Devonshire St.(02109), pg. 492
Copley Real Estate Advisors, Inc., 399 Boylston St.(02116), pg. 799
COSMOPULOS CROWLEY DALY/CKG, 250 Boylston St.(02116), pg. 288
DRK INC., 101 Summer St., Church Green(02110), pg. 309
Digital News Publishing Company, Inc., 33 West St.(02111), pg. 576
DUVAL & PARTNERS, 585 Commercial St.(02109), pg. 356
Dynabilt Products, 31 Industrial Dr.(02136), pg. 196
ERM-New England, Inc., 205 Portland St.(02114), pg. 360
ELECTRIC SPECIALTY & SUPPLY CORP., 817 Albany St.(02119), pg. 374
FMR Corp., 82 Devonshire St.(02109), pg. 408
FIDELITY INVESTMENTS (FMR CORP.), 82 Devonshire St.(02109), pg. 408
THE FORUM CORPORATION, One Exchange Place(02109), pg. 425
GENERAL SHIP CORPORATION, 300 Northern Ave.(02210), pg. 450
THE GOLDHIRSH GROUP INC., 38 Commercial Warf(02110), pg. 467
GOLDMAN FINANCIAL GROUP, 1 Post Office Sq. 468
GORDON BROTHERS, 40 Broad St.(02109), pg. 471
Gordon Brothers Corporation, 40 Broad St.(02109), pg. 471
GUEST QUARTERS SUITE HOTELS, 30 Rowes Wharf(02110), pg. 493
Hancock Realty Investors, Inc., 200 Berkely St., 19th Fl.(02117), pg. 596
THE HAUGHEY GROUP, INC., 313 Congress St.(02210), pg. 517
Helmsman Management Services, Inc., 175 Berkeley St.(02117), pg. 674
High School Division, 19Bay State Rd.(02215), pg. 56
HILL, HOLLIDAY, CONNORS, COSMOPULOS, INC., John Hancock Tower, 200 Clarendon St.(02116), pg. 534
H. P. Hood Inc., 500 Rutherford Ave.(02129), pg. 25
HOUSE OF BIANCHI, 293 A St.(02210), pg. 546
HOUSTON EFFLER & PARTNERS, 360 Newbury St.(02115), pg. 546
IDG Communications, One Exeter Plaza(02116), pg. 576
IDG International News Group, 41 West St., 8th Fl.(02111), pg. 576
The Impex Group Limited, , pg. 468
Independence Investment Associates, Inc., One Liberty Square(02109), pg. 596
INGALLS, QUINN & JOHNSON, 855 Boylston St.(02116), pg. 567
INTERNATIONAL DATA GROUP, One Exeter Plaza(02116-2851), pg. 576
John Hancock Advisers, Inc., 101 Huntington Ave.(02199), pg. 596
John Hancock Capital Corporation, John Hancock Place(02117), pg. 596
John Hancock Leasing Corporation, John Hancock Pl.(02117), pg. 596
John Hancock Mutual Funds, 101 Huntington Ave.(0219907603), pg. 596
JOHN HANCOCK MUTUAL LIFE INSURANCE COMPANY, John Hancock Place, 200 Clarendon St.(02117), pg. 595
John Hancock Subsidiaries, Inc., John Hancock Pl.(02117), pg. 596
KELLEY & WALLWORK INC., The Milk Exchange, 177 Milk St.(02109-3410), pg. 621
Korn/Ferry International, 101 Federal St., 24th Fl.(02110), pg. 642
Korn/Ferry Organizational Consulting, 75 Federal St.(02110), pg. 642
Liberty Distributors Inc., 600 Atlantic Ave.(02210), pg. 674
Liberty Financial Companies, 600 Atlantic Ave.(02210), pg. 674
Liberty Life Assurance Company of Boston, 175 Berkeley St.(02117), pg. 674
Liberty Mutual Fire Insurance Co., 175 Berkeley St.(02117), pg. 674
LIBERTY MUTUAL INSURANCE CO., 175 Berkeley St.(02117), pg. 674
Lindenmeyr Paper, 990 Washington Street(02026), pg. 233
Loomis, Sayles & Co., One Financial Center(02111), pg. 799
Marlborough Capital Advisors, Inc., 399 Boylston St.(02116), pg. 799
MetLife-State Street Investment Services, Inc., One Financial Center(02111-2690), pg. 744
MOORGATE ADVERTISING AGENCY, Prudential Tower Bldg.(02199), pg. 768
NEW BALANCE ATHLETIC SHOE, INC., 38 Everett St.(02134), pg. 798
THE NEW ENGLAND, 501 Boylston St.(02117), pg. 799
The New England Companies, Inc., 501 Boylston St.(02117), pg. 799
New England Investment Companies, Inc., 501 Boylston St.(02117), pg. 799
New England Investment Marketing, Inc., 339 Boylston St.(02116), pg. 799
New England Life Mortgage Funding Corp., 501 Boylston St.(02117), pg. 799
New England Pension & Annuity Co., 501 Boylston St.(02117), pg. 800
New England Portfolio Advisors, Inc., 501 Boylston Street(02117), pg. 799
New England Securities Corp., 399 Boylston St.(02116), pg. 799
New England Variable Life Insurance Co, 501 Boylston St.(02117), pg. 800
Norman Levy Associates, Inc., Ten Post Office Sq., Ste. 600 S(02109), pg. 672
PC Week, 800 Boylston St.(02199), pg. 1219
PEABODY OFFICE FURNITURE CORPORATION, 234 Congress St.(02110), pg. 853
Profesco Corporation, John Hancock Place(02117), pg. 596
Professional Economic Services, Inc., John Hancock Place(02117), pg. 596
RCM Cabot, 40 Broad St.(02109), pg. 84
REED EXHIBITION COMPANIES, 221 Columbus Ave.(02116), pg. 920
ROSSIN GREENBERG SERONICK, 181 Newbury St.(02116), pg. 950
SPORTO CORP., 2 Midway St.(02210), pg. 1032
THE STACKPOLE CORPORATION, 133 Federal St., 9th Fl.(02110), pg. 1034
State Street Research & Management Company, One Financial Ctr.,30th Fl.(02111), pg. 744
Sturtevant Div., One Westinghouse Plaza(02136), pg. 547
TNE Funding Corporation, 501 Boylston St.(02117), pg. 799
TNE Investment Services Corp., 399 Boylston St.(02116), pg. 799
TRANS NATIONAL TRAVEL, 2 Charlesgate West(02215-3552), pg. 1106
WCVB Division, 5 TV Place, Needham Br.(02192), pg. 522
WCVB-TV, 5 TV Place, Needham Br.(02192), pg. 522
WWF National, 529 Main St.(02129), pg. 1157

WALDO BROS. COMPANY, 202 Southampton St.(02118), pg. 1159
WINTHROP PRINTING COMPANY, INC., 235 Old Colony Ave.(02127), pg. 1197

Braintree

ALL SEASONS SERVICES, INC., 100 Grandview Rd.(02184-2624), pg. 35
WARREN E. COLLINS, INC., 220 Wood Rd.(02184), pg. 263
THE FLATLEY COMPANY, 50 Braintree Hill Office Park(02184), pg. 416
Graphic Systems, 3 Brooks Dr.(02184), pg. 721
J. L. HAMMETT COMPANY, Hammett Place(02184), pg. 504
MASSACHUSETTS STATE LOTTERY, 15 Rockdale St.(02184), pg. 719
SYMMONS INDUSTRIES INC., 31 Brooks Dr.(02184), pg. 1069

Bridgewater

Fibertec Inc., 35 Scotland St.(02324), pg. 356
Independent Nail Company, 106 Hale St.(02324), pg. 725
GEO. E. KEITH COMPANY, 31 Perkins St.(02324), pg. 620
Walk-Over Shoes, 31 Perkins St.(02324), pg. 620

Brockton

CERTIFIED CORP., 170 Oak Hill Way(02401), pg. 236
CHRISTY'S MARKETS, INC., 22 Christy's Drive(02401), pg. 249
Jordan Dennis Company, Inc., 1010 W. Chestnut(02401), pg. 513
KNAPP SHOES INC., One Knapp Centre(02401), pg. 636

Burlington

Allied Security Inc., 41 Third Ave.(01803), pg. 39
HOLLAND MARK MARTIN, 174 Middlesex Tpke.(01803), pg. 539
ODI, 25 Mall Rd.(01803), pg. 818
ODI, 25 Mall Rd.n Woods Dr.(01803), pg. 819
SPAULDING & SLYE COMPANY, 25 Burlington Mall Rd.(01803), pg. 1026

Cambridge

ADL Management Education Institute, Inc., Acorn Park(02140), pg. 678
THE ARCHITECTS COLLABORATIVE, INC. (TAC), 46 Brattle St.(02138), pg. 80
California Paint Div., 169 Waverly(02139), pg. 210
CALIFORNIA PRODUCTS CORP., 169 Waverly(02139), pg. 210
CAMP DRESSER & MCKEE INC., One Cambridge Center(02142), pg. 212
Camp Dresser & McKee International Inc., One Cambridge Center(02142), pg. 212
Colorizer Paint Div., 169 Waverly(02139), pg. 210
Computer Corporation of America, Four Cambridge Center(02142-1489), pg. 884
GENERAL LATEX & CHEMICAL CORPORATION, 675 Massachusetts Ave.(02139), pg. 449
Arthur D. Little Enterprises, Inc., Acorn Park(02140), pg. 679
ARTHUR D. LITTLE, INC., 25 Acorn Park(02140-2390), pg. 678
Arthur D. Little Program Systems Management Co., Acorn Park(02140), pg. 678
Lotus Publishing Corporation, 55 Cambridge Pkwy.(02142), pg. 576
MarketPulse, Four Cambridge Center(02142-1489), pg. 884
New England Confectionery Co., 254 Massachusetts Ave.(02139), pg. 1123
Ox-Line Paint Div., 169 Waverly(02139), pg. 210
PRAXIS INTERNATIONAL INC., 4 Cambridge Center(02142-1489), pg. 884
Recreational Products Div., 169 Waverly(02139), pg. 210
Segue Partners, Four Cambridge Center(02142-1489), pg. 885
SEXTON CAN CO., INC., 125 Cambridge Park Dr.(02140), pg. 993
SPINNAKER SOFTWARE CORPORATION, 201 Broadway St.(02139), pg. 1031
Stark Candy Company, 254 Massachusetts Ave.(02139), pg. 1123
TAD TECHNICAL SERVICES CORP., 639 Massachusetts Ave.(02139), pg. 1071
THINKING MACHINES CORPORATION, 245 First St.(02142), pg. 1092
The H.W. Wilson Co., 955 Massachusetts Ave.(02139), pg. 1193

Canton

Acoustic Research, 330 Turnpike St.(02021), pg. 578
BLH ELECTRONICS, 75 Shawmut(02021), pg. 107
BOSTON MUTUAL LIFE INSURANCE CO., 120 Royall St.(02021), pg. 167
BUTLER AUTOMATIC, INC., 480 Neponset St.(02021), pg. 197
CHADWICK-MILLER INC., 10 Pequot Way(02021), pg. 237
CUMBERLAND FARMS, INC., 777 Dedham St.(02021), pg. 304
DeWolfe & Fiske Inc., P. O. Box 510, Pequot Industrial Pk(02021), pg. 237
Fayva, 555 Turnpike St.(02021), pg. 772
JAMES FERRERA & SONS, INC., 135 Will Dr.(02021), pg. 407
First United Small Business Investment Co., 135 Will Dr.(02021), pg. 407
Great Scott Food Markets, Inc., 135 Will Dr.(02021), pg. 407
Lauriat Inc., Pequot Industrial Pk(02021), pg. 237
MORSE SHOE, INC., 555 Turnpike St.(02021), pg. 772
Morse Shoe Leased Div., 555 Turnpike St.(02021), pg. 772
S.W.B. & Company, P.O. Box 264, 28 Cedar St.(02021), pg. 944
THOMPSON STEEL CO., INC., 120 Royall St.(02021), pg. 1094
Value King, Inc., 135 Will Dr.(02021), pg. 407

Chelsea

AMERICAN SNACKS, INC., 400 Eastern Ave.(02150), pg. 61
Cargill Petroleum, Inc., 295 Eastern Ave.(02150), pg. 219
KAYEM FOODS, INC., 75 Arlington St.(02150), pg. 619

Cherry Valley

Atlantic Health Care Resources, Inc., P.O. Box 58, 69 Main St.(01611), pg. 1070

Chestnut Hill

HMK ADVERTISING, INC., 210 Boylston St.(02167), pg. 497

Chicopee

BUXTON COMPANY, 45 Plainfield(01013), pg. 197
COLLINS ELECTRIC COMPANY, INC., 53 Second Ave(01020), pg. 263
Dudley Sports Co. Division, P.O. Box 7053, 521 Meadow St.(01021-7053), pg. 1025
FACEMATE CORPORATION, 5 W. Main St.(01020), pg. 396
Lym-Tech Scientific, P.O. Box 157, (01014), pg. 689
JOHN R. LYMAN COMPANY, 60 Depot St.(01013), pg. 689
Spalding, P.O. Box 901, 425 Meadow St.(01021), pg. 1024

Clinton

DELTA SURPRENANT WIRE & CABLE, INC., 172 Sterling St.(01510), pg. 327

Cohasset

Webb-Norfolk Conveyor, 155 King St. (Rte. 3A)(02025), pg. 1170

Concord

Middlesex Insurance Co., 34 Monument Sq.(01742), pg. 990
Middlesex Insurance Co., Route 2(01742), pg. 751
MIDDLESEX/PATRIOT GENERAL INSURANCE COMPANIES, Route 2(01742), pg. 751
Patriot General Insurance Co., Route 2(01742), pg. 751
Welch's, 100 Main St.(01742), pg. 789

Dalton

CRANE & CO., INC., 30 South St.(01226), pg. 296

Dedham

ALIMED, INC., 297 High St.(02026), pg. 34
NATIONAL AMUSEMENTS, INC., 200 Elm St.(02026), pg. 784

Dorchester

SWIFT INSTRUMENTS, INC., 952 Dorchester Ave.(02125), pg. 1068

Dracut

Keating Materials Corporation, 2140 Bridge St.(01826), pg. 619

East Boston

GODDESS BRA COMPANY, 156 Porter St.(02128), pg. 464
SYRATECH CORPORATION, 175 McClellan Hwy.(02128), pg. 1070
Wallace Silversmiths, 175 McClellan Hwy.(02128), pg. 1070

East Bridgewater

MURRAY-CARVER, 15 Witman St.(02333), pg. 776

East Dedham

PRUDENTIAL METAL SUPPLY CORP., 171 Milton St.(02026), pg. 898

East Longmeadow

AMERICAN SAW & MANUFACTURING CO., 301 Chestnut St.(01028), pg. 60

East Taunton

Aratex Services, 103 Old Colony Ave.(02718), pg. 6

East Walpole

HOLLINGSWORTH & VOSE CO., 112 Washington St.(02032), pg. 539

East Weymouth

BRADY ENTERPRISES, INC., 167 Moore Rd.(02189), pg. 171

Easton

DAVID BRETT, INC., 35 Eastman St.(02334), pg. 174

Erving

ERVING PAPER MILLS, Arch St.(01344), pg. 388

Everett

Coldwater Seafood Corp., 60 Commercial St.(02149), pg. 260
DANIELS PRINTING COMPANY, 40 Commercial St.(02149), pg. 314
HELPERN JOAN & DAVID, INC., 1935 Revere Beach Pkwy.(02149), pg. 528
Joan & David, Inc., 1935 Revere Beach Pkwy.(02149), pg. 528

Fall River

Aberdeen Mfg. Corp. Louis Hand Plant, 847 Pleasant St.(02722), pg. 200
ASHWORTH BROS., INC., 89 Globe Mills Ave.(02724), pg. 88
Priority Finishing Corp., One Middle St.(02724), pg. 243
QUAKER FABRIC CORPORATION, 941 Grinnell St.(02722), pg. 903
TRINA, INC., Ace St.(02722), pg. 1113
WHALING INDUSTRIES, INC., 387 Quarry St.(02723), pg. 1183
Whaling Manufacturing Company, Inc., 387 Quarry St.(02732), pg. 1183

Fitchburg

THE ASHER WINER COMPANY, 307 Airport Rd.(01420), pg. 88
SIMONDS INDUSTRIES INC., 135 Intervale Rd.(01420-0500), pg. 1006

Florence

THE PRO CORPORATION, 296 Nonotuck St.(01060), pg. 891

Foxboro

F. H. CHASE, INC., 69 Elm St.(02035), pg. 240
EMS Eastern Regional Office, 100 Foxboro Blvd.(02035), pg. 370
MAGUIRE GROUP INC., 225 Foxborough Blvd.(02035), pg. 701
New England Tap Corporation (NETCO), 15 Perry Dr.(02035), pg. 183

Framingham

BOSE CORPORATION, The Mountain(01701-9168), pg. 167
CIO Publishing Corp., 492 Old Connecticut Path(01701), pg. 576
CW Publishing, Inc., 375 Cochituate Rd.(01701), pg. 576
CHARLES RIVER DATA SYSTEMS, INC., 983 Concord St.(01701), pg. 240
CREATIVE PLAYTHINGS LTD., 33 Loring Dr.(01701), pg. 297
International Data Corp., 5 Speen St.(01701), pg. 577
International Marketing Services, 187 Oaks Rd.(01701), pg. 576
The Middlesex News, 33 New York Ave.(01701), pg. 513
Network World, Inc., 161 Worcester Rd., 5th Fl.(01701), pg. 576
Stereo Advertising Corp., The Mountain(01701), pg. 167
Technology Investment Strategies Corp., Five Speen St.(01701), pg. 578
World Expo Corporation, P.O. Box 9107, 111 Speen St.(01701-9107), pg. 578

Franklin

GARELICK FARMS, INC., 1199 W. Central St.(02038), pg. 443
WWF Paper Corp.-New England, 290 Beaver St.(02038), pg. 1157

Gardner

S. BENT & BROTHERS, INC., 85 Winter St.(01440), pg. 140
Gem Industries, Inc., 525 Parker St.(01440), pg. 447
SIMPLEX TIME RECORDER CO., Simplex Plaza(01441), pg. 1006

Georgetown

UNITED FOAM PLASTICS CORPORATION, 172 E. Main St.(01833), pg. 1132

Gloucester

BATTENFELD GLOUCESTER ENGINEERING CO. INC., P.O. Box 900, Blackburn Industrial Park(01930), pg. 126

Greenfield

ROGERS, LUNT & BOWLEN CO., 298 Federal St.(01302), pg. 943
RUGG MANUFACTURING COMPANY, 105 Newton St.(01301), pg. 955

Hanson

LITECONTROL CORPORATION, 100 Hawks Ave.(02341), pg. 677

Hingham

TJ CLARK ADVERTISING/PR, 99 Derby St.(02043), pg. 251
D. M. MANAGEMENT COMPANY, 25 Recreation Pk. Dr., Ste. 200(02043), pg. 309

Holliston

EASY DAY MANUFACTURING COMPANY, INC., P.O. Box 8000(01746), pg. 364

ST. JOHNSBURY TRUCKING CO., INC., 119 Jeffrey Ave.(01746), pg. 966
TMP Worldwide, Inc., The TMP Bldg., 125 Hopping Brook Rd.(01746), pg. 1074

Holyoke

Dual Manufacturing & Engineering, Inc., 80 Bigelow St.(01040), pg. 285
HAZEN PAPER COMPANY, Third Level Canal(01040), pg. 520
TOTSY MANUFACTURING COMPANY, INC., 1 Bigelow St.(01040), pg. 1103

Hopkinton

AVATAR CORPORATION, 65 South St.(01748), pg. 101
CLEARPOINT RESEARCH CORPORATION, 35 Parkwood Dr.(01748), pg. 254
INTERFACE ELECTRONICS CORPORATION, 228 South St.(01748), pg. 574
Jorgensen Steel & Aluminum/Boston, 59 South St.(01748), pg. 605
Kilsby-Roberts/Boston, 59 South St.(01748), pg. 606
SCHEDULING TECHNOLOGY CORPORATION, 42 South St.(01748), pg. 975
ZYMARK CORPORATION, Zymark Center(01748), pg. 1221

Housatonic

Rising Paper Company, 295 Park St.(01236), pg. 428

Hudson

THE ENTWISTLE COMPANY, Bigelow St.(01749), pg. 383
The Entwistle Export Co., Inc., Bigelow St.(01749), pg. 383
HYPERTRONICS CORPORATION, 16 Brent Dr.(01749), pg. 557

Hyde Park

HOWDEN SIROCCO INC., One Westinghouse Plaza(02136), pg. 547

Indian Orchard

HEAT BATH PARK METALLURGICAL, INC., 107 Front St.(01151), pg. 524
JANLYNN CORPORATION, 34 Front St.(01151), pg. 589

Lakeville

OCEAN SPRAY CRANBERRIES, INC., One Ocean Spray Dr.(02349), pg. 820
SAIC Engineering, Inc., 10 Riverside Dr.(02347), pg. 982

Lawrence

AGRI-MARK, INC., P.O. Box 5800, (01842), pg. 25
Aratex Services, 110 Glenn St.(01843), pg. 6
BOLTON-EMERSON, INC., 9 Osgood St.(01843), pg. 163
Bolton-Emerson Paper Machinery Div., 9 Osgood St.(01843), pg. 163
GREECO BROTHERS, INC., 50 Island St.(01840), pg. 483
LAWRENCE PUMPS, INC., 371 Market St.(01843), pg. 662
MALDEN MILLS INDUSTRIES, INC., 46 Stafford St.(01841), pg. 702
Mercer Paper Tube Co., 91 Glenn St.(01843), pg. 1209
OOMPHIES, INC., 5 Franklin St.(01840), pg. 827

Leominster

E. B. KINGMAN COMPANY, 96 Exchange St.(01453), pg. 631
Vertipile, Scott Dr.(01453), pg. 251

Lexington

Thomas K. Dyer, Inc., 1762 Massachusetts Ave.(02173), pg. 547
FAY, SPOFFORD & THORNDIKE, INC., 191 Spring St.(02173), pg. 404
Underwriters Service Agency, Inc., 420 Bedford St., Ste.150(02173), pg. 573

Lowell

ADRA SYSTEMS, INC., 59 Technology Dr.(01851), pg. 18
Interstate Container Corporation, Industrial Ave. E.(01853), pg. 580
MERCURY COMPUTER SYSTEMS, INC., 600 Suffolk St.(01854), pg. 740

Ludlow

LUDLOW TEXTILES CO., INC., State Street(01056), pg. 686
Mercer Paper Tube Co., State St., P.O. Box 391(01056), pg. 1209

Lunenburg

P.J. KEATING COMPANY, Reservoir Rd.(01462), pg. 619
MAKI CORPORATION, 160 Mass Ave.(01462), pg. 702
Maki Home Center, Inc., 160 Mass Ave.(01462), pg. 702

Lynn

BOSTON TRADING LTD. INC., 315 Washington St.(01902), pg. 168
EASTERN SMELTING & REFINING CORPORATION, 37-39 Bubier St.(01901), pg. 363
Richdale Dairy Stores, Inc., 626 Lynnway(01905), pg. 974
SCANGAS BROTHERS HOLDINGS, INC., 326 Lynway(01905), pg. 974
West Lynn Creamery, Inc., 626 Lynnway(01905), pg. 974

Lynnfield

CUNA North East District, Lynnfield Office Park, 40 Salem St.(01940), pg. 205

CARNEY/MOHLIN & COMPANY, 7 Kimball Lane(01940), pg. 222

Malden

ACME CANVAS CO., INC., 171 Medford St.(02148), pg. 13
ASAHI/AMERICA, INC., 19 Green St., P.O. Box 653(02148), pg. 87
Century Products Inc., 171 Medford St.(02148), pg. 13
NEW ENGLAND COFFEE COMPANY, 100 Charles St.(02148), pg. 800
PALMER MANUFACTURING COMPANY, 243 Medford St.(02148), pg. 844

Mansfield

HOECHST CERAMTEC NORTH AMERICA, INC., 171 Forbes Blvd.(02048-1148), pg. 537
KENDALL HEALTHCARE PRODUCTS CO., 15 Hampshire St.(02048), pg. 622
Kendall Healthcare Products Company, One Mansfield Corp. Center, 15 Hampshire St.(02048), pg. 622
Lindenmeyr Munroe, 240 Forbes Blvd.(02048), pg. 233

Marlborough

THE BUTCHER CO., 120 Bartlett St.(01752-3013), pg. 196
KOEHLER MANUFACTURING COMPANY, 123 Felton St.(01752), pg. 639
Massachusetts Container Corporation, 300 Cedar Hill St.(01752), pg. 274

Medford

BARON-ABRAMSON, INC., 4000 Mystic Valley Pkwy.(02155), pg. 121
Doeskin Co., 300 Middlesex Ave.(02155), pg. 1042
STATLER INDUSTRIES, 300 Middlesex Ave.(02155), pg. 1041
Ziff Information Services, 10 Presidents Landing(02155), pg. 1219
Ziff Technologies, 10 Presidents Landing(02155), pg. 1219

Merrimac

WOLVERINE MASSACHUSETTS CORPORATION, 51 E. Main St.(01860), pg. 1199

Middleboro

ALDEN SHOE CO., INC., Taunton St.(02346), pg. 33
THE READ CORPORATION, 25 Wareham St.(02346), pg. 916

Middleton

AUTOROLL MACHINE CORP., 11 River St.(01949), pg. 101

Millbury

COPPUS ENGINEERING CORP., Millbury Industrial Park, Rte. 20(01527), pg. 285
THE FELTERS COMPANY, 22 West St.(01527), pg. 406
NEW ENGLAND NEWSPAPER SUPPLY COMPANY, INC., 49 Railroad Ave.(01527), pg. 800
TBV, Inc., P.O. Box 72, 103 Worcester-Providence Road(01527), pg. 1149

Millers Falls

Aristera, Renovator's Old Mill(01349), pg. 927
Country Notebook, Renovator's Old Mill(01349), pg. 927
THE RENOVATOR'S SUPPLY, INC., Renovator's Old Mill(01349), pg. 927

Natick

IDG Communications List Services, P.O. Box 9151, 4 Chrysler Rd.(01760), pg. 576
IDG Communications Research, 4 Chrysler Rd.(01760), pg. 576

Needham

PRO MEDIA, INC., 160 Gould St.(02194), pg. 892

Needham Heights

ADVANCED INSTRUMENTS, INC., 1000 Highland Ave.(02194), pg. 20

New Bedford

BRITTANY DYEING & PRINTING CORPORATION, 1357 E. Rodney French Blvd.(02744), pg. 177
EPEC, INC., New Bedford Industrial Park(02747), pg. 384
SHARON-JAY TOGS, INC., 127 W. Rodney French Blvd.(02744), pg. 995
SHEPARD CLOTHING COMPANY, 800 Acushnet Ave.(02740), pg. 997
U.S. Ring Binder Corp., 429 Church St.(02745), pg. 657

Newburyport

BIXBY INTERNATIONAL CORP., One Preble Rd.(01950), pg. 153
SAMUEL CABOT, INC., 100 Hale St.(01950), pg. 206
Flametech Corporation, 104 Parker St.(01950), pg. 1012
Henschel Corp., 9 Hoyt Drive(01950), pg. 964

Newton

BUYER ADVERTISING, INC., 85 Wells Ave.(02159), pg. 197
FIRE CONTROL INSTRUMENTS, INC., 269 Grove St.(02166), pg. 411
FRED V. FOWLER COMPANY, INC., 66 Rowe St.(02166), pg. 427
GERRITY CO., INC., 90 Oak St.(02164), pg. 454
Ivex Packaging Corporation-Industrial Products Division, 55 Tower Rd.(02164), pg. 583

Seaboard Corporation, 200 Boylston St.(02167), pg. 984
SEABOARD FLOUR CORPORATION, 200 Boylston St.(02167), pg. 984

Newton Center

GEO-CENTERS, INC., 7 Wells Ave.(02159), pg. 452
THE ALLAN R. HACKEL ORGANIZATION, 1330 Center St.(02159), pg. 498

Newton Upper Falls

Computer Enterprises, Inc., 109 Oak St.(02164), pg. 1083
EDP/TEMPS Inc., 109 Oak St.(02164), pg. 1083
Home Care p.r.n., Inc., 109 Oak St.(02164), pg. 1083
MicroTemps Systems & Programming, 109 Oak St.(02164), pg. 1083
Mt. Waldo Operations, 90 Oak St., Box 9111(02164), pg. 454
Systems Management & Development, 109 Oak St.(02164), pg. 1083
TAC/Medical Services Inc., 109 Oak St.(02164), pg. 1083
TAC/TEMPS Inc., 109 Oak St.(02164), pg. 1083
Tech/Aid, 109 Oak St.(02164), pg. 1083
TECHNICAL AID CORPORATION, 109 Oak St.(02164), pg. 1083

North Adams

Excelsior Printing Co., 60 Roberts Dr.(01247), pg. 296
Excelsior Process & Engraving Co., Curan Hwy., Rte. 8(02147), pg. 296

North Attleboro

LEACH & GARNER COMPANY, 57 John L. Dietsch Sq.(02760), pg. 663

North Billerica

General Latex & Chemical Corporation, 67 High St.(01862), pg. 449
PURITY SUPREME, INC., 2 Billerica Pk., 101 Billerica Ave.(01862), pg. 901

North Dighton

BIW CABLE SYSTEMS, INC., 22 Joseph E. Warner Blvd.(02764), pg. 106
THE HARODITE FINISHING COMPANY INC., 66 South St.(02764), pg. 510
New England Auto Auction, Inc., 123 Williams St.(02764), pg. 293

North Easton

Peabody N.E., Inc., P.O. Box 419, 117 Eastman Street(02356), pg. 900

North Uxbridge

Nelmor Co., Inc., Rivulet St.(01538), pg. 1047

Northampton

JPS Elastomerics Corp., 395 Pleasant St.(01060), pg. 586

Northborough

ELECTRO FIBEROPTICS CORPORATION, 56 Hudson St.(01532), pg. 374

Norton

Eureka Manufacturing Co., Inc., 47 Elm St.(02766), pg. 920

Norwell

AVEDIS ZILDJIAN COMPANY, 22 Longwater Dr.(02061), pg. 1219

Norwood

GAGGENAU USA CORPORATION, 425 University Ave.(02062), pg. 441
JET SPRAY CORP., 825 University Ave.(02062), pg. 593
Jet Spray International, 825 University Ave.(02062), pg. 593
Keystone New England Warehouse - Norwood, 117 Lenox St.(02062), pg. 628
PAINE FURNITURE CO., 160 Lenox St.(02062), pg. 843
THE SAVOGRAN COMPANY, 259 Lenox St.(02062), pg. 973

Orange

RODNEY HUNT COMPANY, 46 Mill St.(01364-1251), pg. 553

Orleans

NICKERSON LUMBER COMPANY, 15 Main St.(02653), pg. 806

Oxford

Worrad Services Inc., 40 Federal Hill Rd.(01540), pg. 529

Peabody

Lindenmeyr Munroe, Corporate Headquarters, One Second St., Box 3637(01961-3637), pg. 233
MCDOUGALL ASSOCIATES, INC., 17 Centennial Dr.(01960), pg. 728

Pembroke

HYER INDUSTRIES INC./THAYER SCALE, Route 139(02359), pg. 557

Pittsfield

THE BERKSHIRE LIFE INSURANCE COMPANY, 700 South St.(01201), pg. 142

PETRICCA INDUSTRIES, INC., 444 Merrill Rd.(01202), pg. 865

Plainville

Eyecessories, 33 W. Bacon St.(02762), pg. 535
THE HILSINGER CORP., 33 W. Bacon St.(02762), pg. 535
PLAINVILLE STOCK COMPANY, INC., 104 South St.(02762), pg. 874

Quincy

BAY STATE MILLING CO., 100 Congress St.(02169), pg. 127
DEVINE & PEARSON, INC., Crown Colony Office Park, 300 Congress St.(02169), pg. 333
HOWES LEATHER COMPANY, INC., 1 Batterymarch(02169), pg. 548
NATIONAL FIRE PROTECTION ASSOCIATION, One Batterymarch Park(02269), pg. 788
Pneumatic Scale Corporation, 65 Newport Ave.(02171), pg. 122
GEORGE W. PRESCOTT PUBLISHING CO., 400 Crown Colony Dr.(02169), pg. 887
QUINCY MUTUAL FIRE INSURANCE COMPANY, 57 Washington(02169), pg. 905

Randolph

Ohio-Sealy Mattress Mfg. Co., Inc., One Posturepedic Dr.(02368), pg. 985

Raynham

TRUCCHIS MARKETS, 1062 Broadway(02767), pg. 1117

Russell

Saint Joseph

NEWS-PRESS & GAZETTE COMPANY, P.O. Box 29, (64502), pg. 804

Westfield River Paper Co., Station Rd.(01071), pg. 1005

Sharon

Dynisco, Inc., Four Commercial St.(02067), pg. 145

Shelburne Falls

Lamson and Goodnow Mfg. Co., 45 Conway St.(01370), pg. 943

Shrewsbury

ELKAY PRODUCTS, INC., 800 Boston Turnpike(01545), pg. 377

Somerset

ALDEN AUTO PARTS WHOLESALE, INC., 535 Grand Army Hwy.(02725), pg. 32
PARKS CORPORATION, 1083 County St.(02726), pg. 849

Somerville

AMES SAFETY ENVELOPE COMPANY, INC., 21 Properzi Way(02143), pg. 66
Electric Specialty & Supply, 20 Sturtevant St.(02143), pg. 374
MASSACHUSETTS ENVELOPE CO., 30 Cobble Hill Rd.(02143), pg. 718
Somerville Lumber & Supply Co., 779 McGrath Hwy.(02145), pg. 853
M.S. WALKER, INC./SEACOAST, 20 Third Ave.(02143), pg. 1160

South Attleboro

CWT Specialty Stores, Inc., 505 Collin St.(02703), pg. 1011

South Dartmouth

Concordia Custom Yachts, 300 Gulf Rd.(02748), pg. 972

South Deerfield

CHANNING L. BETE CO., INC., 200 State Rd.(01373), pg. 147

Southborough

NEW ENGLAND FROZEN FOODS, 1 Harvest Lane(01772), pg. 800

Southbridge

American Optical Corp., 14 Mechanic St.(01550), pg. 59
HYDE MANUFACTURING CO., 54 Eastford Rd.(01550), pg. 556
Precision Products Business, 14 Mechanic(01550), pg. 59

Springfield

Allright Springfield, 4 Columbus Tower, 150 Bridge St.(01103), pg. 42
BIG Y FOODS INC., 280 Chestnut St.(01102-7840), pg. 149
Brennan College Service, Inc., 45 Island Pine Rd.(01118), pg. 422
Broadstreet Plaza, 511 E. Columbus Ave.(01101), pg. 938
Chemical Specialties Corp., 54 Waltham Ave.(01109), pg. 1069
HANO BUSINESS FORMS, INC., 99 Guion St.(01104), pg. 505
MML Bay State Life Insurance Company, 1295 State St.(01111), pg. 718
MML Investors Services, Inc., One Financial Plaza, 1350 Main St.(01103), pg. 718
MML Real Estate Corporation, 1295 State Street(01111), pg. 719
MML Realty Management Corp., 1295 State St.(01111), pg. 719

MML Series Investment Fund, 1295 State St.(01111), pg. 718
MASSACHUSETTS MUTUAL LIFE INSURANCE CO., 1295 State St.(01111), pg. 718
MassMutual Holding Company, 1295 State St.(01111), pg. 719
Merriam-Webster, Inc., 47 Federal St.(01102), pg. 381
PETER PAN BUS LINES, INC., 1776 Main St.(01102), pg. 864
F. L. ROBERTS & CO. INC., 93 W. Broad St.(01105), pg. 938
Royal Greenfield Inc., 511 E. Columbus Ave.(01101), pg. 938
TECHNICARBON COMPANY, INC., 89 Guian St.(01104), pg. 1083
WGGB-TV, 1300 Liberty St.(01102-0040), pg. 442

Stoneham

A.W. CHESTERTON COMPANY, Middlesex Industrial Park, 225 Fallon Rd.(02180), pg. 244

Stoughton

BROOKFIELD ENGINEERING LABORATORIES, INC., 240 Cushing St.(02072), pg. 179
FABREEKA INTERNATIONAL, INC., 1023 Turnpike St.(02072), pg. 396
FRANKLIN SPORTS INDUSTRIES, 17 Campanelli Pkwy.(02072), pg. 429
Gould Paper Corporation, 532 Page St.(02072), pg. 473
HEATH CONSULTANTS INCORPORATED, 100 Tosca Dr.(02072), pg. 524
Hoboken Floors-New England Division, 181 Campanelli Pkwy.(07072-3703), pg. 537
New England Co. Div., 150 Maple St.(02062), pg. 146
SEMCO INDUSTRIES, 90 Hawes Way(02072), pg. 989
Spaulding Company, Inc., 90 Hawes Way(02072), pg. 989
SYSTEMS ENGINEERING & MANUFACTURING CORP., 44 Campanelli Pkwy.(02072), pg. 1071

Sudbury

CHISWICK TRADING INC., 33 Union Ave.(01776), pg. 248

Sutton

POLYVINYL FILMS, INC., Depot St.(01590), pg. 880

Taunton

ARLEY MERCHANDISE CORPORATION, 540 Miles Standish Blvd.(02780), pg. 83
REED & BARTON CORPORATION, 144 W. Britannia(02780), pg. 920
Reed & Barton Housewares, 144 W. Britannia(02780), pg. 920
Reed & Barton Silversmiths, 144 W. Britannia(02780), pg. 920
ROBERTSON FACTORIES, INC., 33 Chandler Ave.(02780), pg. 939
Rops Textiles Inc., 540 Myles Standish Blvd.(02780), pg. 83

Tewksbury

DEMOULAS SUPER MARKETS, 875 East St.(01876), pg. 328
ECRM, 554 Clark Rd.(01876), pg. 359
Stephen Gould of New England, Inc., 30 Commerce Way(01876), pg. 474
MURO PHARMACEUTICAL, INC., 890 East St.(01876), pg. 776

Townsend

STERLITE CORPORATION, 198 Main St.(01469), pg. 1047

Tyngsboro

Hussey Plastics Co., 65 Middlesex Rd.(01879), pg. 555
JOAN FABRICS CORP., 100 Vesper Executive Pk.(01879), pg. 594

Wakefield

Computer Buying Publishing, Inc., 401 Edgewate Pl., 6th Fl.(01880), pg. 576

Walpole

WALPOLE WOODWORKERS, INC., 767 East Street(02081), pg. 1161

Waltham

THE BILTRITE CORPORATION, 51 Sawyer Rd.(02254-9045), pg. 151
FOSTER MEDICAL SUPPLY, INC., 275 Wyman St.(02154), pg. 426
FOSTER-MILLER, INC., 350 2nd Ave.(02154), pg. 426
GLOBAL PETROLEUM CORP., 800 South St.(02154), pg. 463
H M K ENTERPRISES, INC., 800 South St.(02154), pg. 497
HARVEY INDUSTRIES, INC., 43 Emerson Rd.(02154), pg. 515
INTEGRA TECHNOLOGIES CORP., 132 Calvary St.(02154), pg. 572
Northeastern Regional Office, P.O. Box 9124, 404 Wyman Street(02254-9124), pg. 233
SEILER CORPORATION, 153 Second Ave.(02254), pg. 987
Service Supply Corp., 153 Second Ave.(02254), pg. 988
STANDARD-THOMSON CORPORATION, 152 Grove St.(02254), pg. 1037
STEINWAY MUSICAL PROPERTIES, INC., 800 South St.(02154), pg. 1045
VeloBind, Inc., 275 Wyman St.(02154), pg. 657
WILDER MANAGEMENT ASSOCIATES, 950 Winter St., Ste. 4300(02154), pg. 1189

Ward Hill

EASTERN CANVAS PRODUCTS, INC., 50 Rogers Rd.(01830), pg. 363

Wareham

Robertsons Auto Body, P.O. Box 231(02571), pg. 939
ROBERTSON'S AUTO SALVAGE, 2680 Cranberry Hwy.(02571), pg. 939
Springborn Environmental Sciences Division, 790 Main St.(02571), pg. 1033

Watertown

AMCELL CORPORATION, 1 Galen St.(02172), pg. 47
ARK-LES CORPORATION, 51 Water St.(02172), pg. 82
BOSTON SCIENTIFIC CORP., 480 Pleasant St.(02172), pg. 167
THE GIARDINI/RUSSELL GROUP, 100 Galen St.(02172), pg. 456
Newly Weds Foods, Inc., 70-80 Grove St.(02172), pg. 804

Wellesley

JWG ASSOCIATES, 888 Worcester Rd.(02181), pg. 586

Wenham

MULLEN ADVERTISING, INC., 36 Essex St.(01984), pg. 775

West Boylston

FALLON COMMUNITY HEALTH PLAN, 100 Hartwell St.(01583), pg. 398

West Hanover

Arcata Graphics Halliday, Circuit St.(02339), pg. 80

West Springfield

Douglas Bewick Associates/TMP Worldwide, 117 Park Ave.(01089), pg. 1074
Keystone Crash Parts Mart - West Springfield, 93 Craig Drive(01089), pg. 628
MANUFACTURERS TECHNOLOGIES, INC., 59 Interstate Dr.(01089), pg. 705
Newhouse Brake Division, 59 Kelso Ave.(01089), pg. 274
SULLIVAN PAPER COMPANY, P.O. Box 88, 61 Progress Ave.(01090), pg. 1057

West Wareham

OUIMET INDUSTRIES, 22D Patterson Brook Rd.(02576), pg. 831

West Warren

WM. E. WRIGHT LIMITED PARTNERSHIP, South St.(01092), pg. 1205

Westboro

Tekra Corp., East Coast Div., 23 Bridle Ln.(05181), pg. 1084

Westborough

W.L.M. BENSDORP COMPANY, 1800 W. Park Dr.(01581), pg. 139
DANAFILMS, INC., 5 Otis St.(01581), pg. 313
Gulf Oil, 165 Flanders Road(01581), pg. 304
MICRON SEPARATIONS, INC., 135 Flanders Rd.(01581), pg. 749

Westfield

BERKSHIRE INDUSTRIES, INC., 109 Apremont Way(01085), pg. 142
THE COLUMBIA MFG. COMPANY, INC., Cycle St.(01085), pg. 265
SAVAGE ARMS INC., Springdale Rd.(01085), pg. 973
H. B. SMITH CO., INC., 57 Main St.(01085), pg. 1013

Westford

VERYFINE PRODUCTS, INC., 210 Littleton Rd.(01886), pg. 1148

Westminster

W.E. AUBUCHON CO., INC., 95 Aubuchon Dr.(01473), pg. 97

Westport

HOYT CORPORATION, 251 Forge Rd.(02790), pg. 548

Westwood

Dimac Direct, 690 Canton St.(02090-2322), pg. 338
THE FAXON COMPANY, INC., 15 Southwest Park(02090), pg. 404
Polyken Technologies, 690 Canton St.(02090), pg. 622
Seabeam Ind., Inc., 33 S.W. Industrial Park(02090), pg. 239

Whitinsville

SMITH VALVE CORPORATION, One Main St.(01588), pg. 1014

Wilbraham

Friendly Ice Cream Corp., 1855 Boston Rd.(01095), pg. 1087

Wilmington

DIAMOND CRYSTAL SPECIALTY FOODS, INC., 10 Burlington Ave.(01887), pg. 335
Harwick Chemical Corp., 8 Jewel Dr.(01887), pg. 515
Koch Membrane Systems, 850 Main St.(01887), pg. 639
RAFFI & SWANSON, INC., 100 Eames St.(01887), pg. 909
Sweetheart Cup Corporation, 1 Burlington Ave.(01887), pg. 1067

Winchester

Century Publications, Inc., Three Church St.(01890), pg. 513

Woburn

LECHMERE, INC., 275 Wildwood St.(01801), pg. 665
LYTRON INCORPORATED, Dragon Court(01801), pg. 690
PRINTED CIRCUIT CORPORATION, 10 Micro Dr.(01801), pg. 891

Worcester

AMGRO, Inc., 472 Lincoln St.(01605), pg. 34
ALL AMERICA FINANCIAL, 440 Lincoln St.(01605), pg. 34
All American Financial, 440 Lincoln St.(01605), pg. 34
ASTRO WIRE & CABLE CORPORATION, 50 Gardner St.(01613), pg. 92
DAVID CLARK COMPANY, INC., 360 Franklin St.(01604), pg. 252
The Hanover Insurance Company, 100 N. Parkway(01605), pg. 34
Idle Wild Foods, 72 Cambridge St.(01603), pg. 1128
Idle Wild Management Corporation, 256 Franklyn St.(01604), pg. 1128
KERVICK ENTERPRISES, INC., 40 Rockdale St.(01606), pg. 624
Massachusetts Steel Treating, 112 Harding St.(01604), pg. 887
MORGAN CONSTRUCTION COMPANY, 15 Belmont St.(01605), pg. 769
N E D CORP., 18 Grafton St.(01604), pg. 780
New England Research, Inc., 100 Grove St.(01605), pg. 731
POLAR CORPORATION, 40 Walcott St.(01603), pg. 878
THE PRESMET CORP., 112 Harding St.(01604), pg. 887
STANLEY FASTENING SYSTEMS, 149 Washington(01610), pg. 1038
State Mutual Life Assurance Company of America, 440 Lincoln St.(01605), pg. 35
WALKER MAGNETICS GROUP, INC., 17 Rockdale St.(01606), pg. 1160
O. S. WALKER CO. INC., Rockdale St.(01606), pg. 1160
G.F. WRIGHT STEEL & WIRE COMPANY, 243 Stafford(01603), pg. 1205

MICHIGAN

Ada

ADA BEEF, INC., 1010 Grand River Dr.(49301), pg. 16
AMWAY CORPORATION, 7575 Fulton St. E.(49355-0001), pg. 70

Adrian

Dura Convertible Systems Div., 1365 E. Beecher St.(49221), pg. 262
Ervin Amasteel Div., 915 Tabor(49221), pg. 387
Michigan Milk Products Div., 1336 E. Maumee St.(49221), pg. 747
VENCHURS PACKAGING, INC., 800 Liberty St.(49221), pg. 1147

Albion

Guardian Industries Corp., 1000 E. North St.(49224), pg. 492
UNION STEEL PRODUCTS, INCORPORATED, 509 N. Albion St.(49224), pg. 1129

Allen Park

BELLE TIRE DISTRIBUTOR INC., 3500 Enterprise Dr.(48101), pg. 136

Alma

LOBDELL-EMERY MANUFACTURING COMPANY, P.O. Box 129, 1325 E. Superior St.(48801-0129), pg. 680

Alpena

Alro Group, Alpena, 815 W. Miller St.(49707), pg. 44
BESSER COMPANY, 801 Johnson St.(49707), pg. 146
PANEL PROCESSING, INC., 120 N. Industrial Hwy.(49707), pg. 846

Anchorville

ISI Robotics II, 6100 Titan Dr.(48004), pg. 560

Ann Arbor

Ann Arbor Computer, 1201 E. Ellsworth(48104), pg. 1170
Automobile Magazine, 120 E. Liberty(48104), pg. 611
BAILEY, KLEPINGER & MEDRICH, INC., 130 S. First St.(48104), pg. 114
Braun-Brumfield, Inc., 100 N. Staebler Rd.(48103), pg. 998
CHI SYSTEMS, INC., 130 S. First St.(48104), pg. 244
Distributor Concepts, 2460 S. Industrial Highway(48104), pg. 630
Domino's Pizza Distribution Corp., P.O. Box 990(48106), pg. 344
DOMINO'S PIZZA INC., 30 Frank Lloyd Wright Dr.(48106), pg. 344
Domino's Pizza International, Inc., P.O. Box 997(48106), pg. 344
EDWARDS BROTHERS, INC., 2500 S. State St.(48106), pg. 369
ERVIN INDUSTRIES, INC., 3893 Research Park Dr.(48108), pg. 387
FINGERLE LUMBER CO., 617 S. Fifth Ave.(48106), pg. 411
GENERAL AUTOMOTIVE CORPORATION, 2015 Washtenaw(48104), pg. 448
GREAT LAKES BANCORP, 401 East Liberty St.(48107), pg. 480
HARRIS ADVERTISING, INC., 617 E. Huron(48104), pg. 511
MALLOY LITHOGRAPHING INC., 5411 Jackson Rd.(48106), pg. 703
Mathematical Reviews, 416 4th St.(48107), pg. 58
REINALT-THOMAS CORP., 903 Airport Dr.(48108), pg. 923
SYMPLEX COMMUNICATIONS CORP., 5 Research Dr.(48103), pg. 1069
Thetford Corporation, 7101 Jackson Rd.(48103), pg. 357
TOWNSEND & BOTTUM, INC., 2245 S. State St.(48104), pg. 1104
UNISTRUT CORPORATION, 3971 South Research Park Dr.(48108), pg. 1130
University Microfilms Inc., 300 N. Zeeb Rd.(48106), pg. 135

Auburn Hills

Alexander Marketing Services/Detroit, 3271 Five Points Dr.(48326), pg. 33
FAIRVIEW CONSTRUCTION, INC, 1100 N. Opdyke Rd.(48326), pg. 397
HEIGHTS HEATING & COOLING, 2005 Pontiac Rd.(48326), pg. 525
Major Pharmaceuticals Corp., 3720 Lapeer Rd.(48326), pg. 384
MARONTATE & CO., 2701 University Dr., 5th Fl.(48326), pg. 713
Michigan Pharmacal, 3720 Lapeer Rd.(48326), pg. 384
NORTH ELECTRIC SUPPLY, INC., 1290 N. Opdyke Rd.(48326), pg. 813
WORLD COMPUTER CORP., 985 W. Entrance Dr.(48326), pg. 1202

Bad Axe

Huron Daily Tribune, 211 N. Heisterman St.(48413), pg. 524
NEEB CORPORATION, 136 W. Huron(48413), pg. 797

Bangor

GETMAN CORPORATION, 6998 34th Ave.(49013), pg. 455

Battle Creek

ARCHWAY COOKIES, INC., 5451 W. Dickman Rd.(49015), pg. 81
Arlo Group, Battle Creek, P.O. Box 20, 801 N. 20th St.(49016-0020), pg. 44
Atwood Automotive Inc., 5701 W. Dickman Rd.(49015), pg. 97
Biggs Gilmore Communications, 100 Country Pine Lane, Ste. 5(49015), pg. 150
UNION PUMP COMPANY, 4600 Dickman Rd.(49015), pg. 1128
UNITED STEEL & WIRE CO., 4909 Wayne Rd.(49015), pg. 1137

Bay City

UNITED STORES, P.O. Box 903(48707-0903), pg. 1137

Belleville

HURON VALLEY STEEL CORP., 41000 Huron River Dr.(48111), pg. 555
REPUBLIC DIE & TOOL COMPANY, 45000 Van Born Rd.(48111), pg. 928
SPRING ARBOR DISTRIBUTORS, 10885 Textile Rd.(48111), pg. 1033
Thompson-McCully Asphalt Paving Co., 5905 Belleville Rd.(48111), pg. 1094
THOMPSON-MCCULLY CO., 5905 Belleville Rd.(48111), pg. 1094
THUNDERLINE CORPORATION, 8707 Samuel Barton Dr.(48111), pg. 1096

Benton Harbor

ALL-PHASE ELECTRIC SUPPLY CO. INC., 875 Riverview Dr.(49022), pg. 35
Alro Group, Benton Harbor, 1860 Yore Ave.(49022-9610), pg. 44
CC Industries, Kaywood Div., P.O. Box 307, (49022), pg. 200
GAST MFG. CORP., 2300 M-139(49022), pg. 444
QUALITY PACKAGING PRODUCTS, INC., 352 W. Britain Ave.(49022), pg. 903
Wilderness Foods, P.O. Box 68(49022), pg. 26

Berrien Springs

TRADERS SUPERMARKETS, INC., P.O. Box 158(49103), pg. 1105

Big Rapids

Mitchell Corporation, Hanchett Manufacturing Co., 906 N. State(49307), pg. 762

Bingham Farms

THE BERLINE GROUP INC., 31600 Telegraph, Ste. 100(48025), pg. 142
PARLIAMENT CO., 30200 Telegraph Rd., Ste. 251(48025), pg. 850
TRERICE TOSTO INTERNATIONAL, 32100 Telegraph Road, Ste. 100(48010), pg. 1110

Birmingham

CONSOLIDATED INDUSTRIAL CORPORATION, 430 N. Woodward Ave.(48009), pg. 276
County Mortgage Corporation, 180 Oakland Ave.(48009-3475), pg. 414
ERB LUMBER COMPANY, 375 S. Eton Rd.(48009), pg. 360
McClelland & Duff, Inc., 375 S. Eton Rd.(48009), pg. 360
Power Base, 32100 Telegraph Rd.(48010), pg. 272
Trerice Development Co., 32100 Telegraph Road, Ste. 100(48010), pg. 1110
Trerice Management Co., 32100 Telegraph Road, Ste. 100(48010), pg. 1110
Trerice/Tosto Investment Services Co., 32100 Telegraph Road, Ste. 100(48010), pg. 1110

Blissfield

BLISSFIELD MANUFACTURING COMPANY, 626 Depot St.(49228), pg. 157

Bloomfield Hills

AMERICAN SPEEDY PRINTING CENTERS, INC., 2555 S. Telegraph Rd.(48302), pg. 61
Gates Power Drive Products, Inc., 1133 W. Long Lake Rd., Ste. 201(48013), pg. 445
Mid-States Mortgage Corp., 1760 S. Telegraph 988
Vic Olesen & Partners, Inc., 2350 Franklin, Ste. 230(48302), pg. 824
ORLEANS INTERNATIONAL, INC., 6441 Inkster, Suite 140(48301), pg. 829
Ross Roy Communications, 100 Bloomfield Hills Pkwy.(48304), pg. 950
Ross Roy Direct, 100 Bloomfield Hills Pkwy.(48304), pg. 950
Ross Roy Franchise, 100 Bloomfield Hills Pkwy.(48304), pg. 950
ROSS ROY GROUP, INC., 100 Bloomfield Hills Pkwy.(48304), pg. 949
Ross Roy Inc., 100 Bloomfield Hills Pkwy.(48304), pg. 950
Ross Roy Retail, 100 Bloomfield Hills Pkwy.(48304), pg. 950
SELIGMAN & ASSOCIATES, INC., 1760 S. Telegraph, Ste.100(48302), pg. 988
Seligman & Assocs. of Michigan, 1760 S. Telegraph 988
ROBERT SOLOMON & ASSOCIATES ADV. INC., 505 N. Woodward Ave.(48304), pg. 1017

Breckenridge

B&W CO-OP, INC., 216 Eastman(48615), pg. 107
B & W Farm Center, 7581 E. Monroe(48615), pg. 107

Bridgman

Manley Bros., Livingston Rd., P.O. Box 456(49106), pg. 887
PEMCO DIE CASTING CORPORATION, 9864 Church St.(49106), pg. 856

Brown City

FRANK INDUSTRIES, INC., 3950 Burnsline Rd.(48416), pg. 429
Xplorer Motor Home Div., 3950 Burnsline Rd.(48416), pg. 429

Burr Oak

Bleyco Paper Co. of Michigan, 951 Front St.(49030), pg. 739

Burton

FLINT MANUFACTURING CO., 3084 E. Hemphill Rd.(48529), pg. 419

Cadillac

Cadillac Pipe, 5305 Hwy. M-115(49601), pg. 886

Caledonia

Sterling Color Process, 8184 Broadmoor Ave. S.E.(49316), pg. 615

Carney

Gilbert & Bennett, P.O. Box 38(49812), pg. 458

Center Line

AETNA INDUSTRIES, INC., 24331 Sherwood(48015), pg. 23

Charlotte

LINN PRODUCTS, INC., 1700 E. Packard Hwy.(48813), pg. 677

Chelsea

CHELSEA MILLING CO., 201 North St.(48118), pg. 241
CHELSEA STATE BANK, 305 S. Main St.(48118), pg. 241

Chesaning

PEET PACKING CO. INC., P.O. Box 187(48616), pg. 855

Chesterfield

LIONEL TRAINS, INC., 50625 Richard W. Blvd.(48051-2493), pg. 677

Clare

Mitchell Corporation, Clare Div., 528 Holly St.(48617), pg. 761

Clarkston

Metrologic Instruments-Midwest, 8745 Waumegah Lake Rd.(48348), pg. 743
Precision Pipe & Supply Co., 4950 White Lake Rd.(48346), pg. 886

Clawson

CARGILL DETROIT CORP., 1250 N. Crooks Rd.(48017), pg. 219
DSIC/TMP Worldwide, 1250 Fourteen Mile Rd.(48017), pg. 1074
KEIPER RECARO, INC., 905 W. Maple Rd.(48017), pg. 620

Clinton

HARDWOODS OF MICHIGAN, INC., 430 Division St.(49236), pg. 509

Comstock Park

RAPID ENGINEERING INC., 1100 Seven Mile Rd.(49321), pg. 913

Davison

GENOVA PRODUCTS, INC., 7034 E. Court St.(48423), pg. 452
Wiltic Chemical Manufacturing, 422 Rising St.(48423), pg. 452

Dearborn

ADRAY APPLIANCE & PHOTO CENTER, INC., 20219 Carlysle(48124), pg. 18
AMERICAN AIRCRAFT PARTS MANUFACTURING CO., 25331 Trowbridge(48124), pg. 48
CARHARTT, INC., 1 Parklane Blvd.(48126), pg. 220
DALE INDUSTRIES INC., 6455 Kingsley Ave.(48126), pg. 312
ELECTRO-WIRE PRODUCTS, INC., 17000 Executive Plaza Dr.(48126), pg. 375
FREEDLAND INDUSTRIES CORPORATION, 4200 Miller Rd.(48126), pg. 430
GHAFARI ASSOCIATES, INC., 17101 Michigan Ave.(48128), pg. 455
KASLE STEEL CORPORATION, 4343 Wyoming(48126), pg. 617
LIVERNOIS ENGINEERING COMPANY, 25315 Keen(48124), pg. 679
Livernois Vehicle Co., 25241 Trowbridge St.(48124), pg. 679
VILLAGE FORD INC., 23535 Michigan Ave.(48124), pg. 1151
BILL WINK CHEVROLET & GEO, 10700 Ford Rd.(48126), pg. 1196
F.B. WRIGHT CO., 9999 Mercier Ave.(48121), pg. 1204

Detroit

A J M PACKAGING CORPORATION, 6910 Dix(48209), pg. 4
ACME MILLS CO. INC., 5151 Loraine St.(48208), pg. 13
ACORN BUILDING COMPONENTS INC., 12620 Westwood Ave.(48223), pg. 13
Acorn Distributing Co., 12612 Westwood(48223), pg. 14
Active Homes Corp., 888 Clairpoint(48215), pg. 15
Active Industries, Inc., 888 Clairpoint(48215), pg. 15
ADVANCE STEEL CO., 9635 French Rd.(48213), pg. 20
Alro Group, Detroit, 18695 Sherwood Ave.(48234), pg. 44
AMBASSADOR STEEL CO., 1469 E. Atwater(48207), pg. 47
American Bearing & Power, 1400 Howard St.(48216), pg. 582
American Steel Corp., 717 E. McNichols(48212), pg. 794
American Tire Reclamation, 6031 Joy Rd.(48204), pg. 913
AMERISURE COMPANIES, 28 W. Adams Ave.(48226), pg. 66
APEX BROACH & MACHINE CO., 6401 E. Seven Mile Rd.(48234), pg. 77
ARROW METAL PRODUCTS CORPORATION, 1200 Mt. Elliott Ave.(48207), pg. 85
Automotive Marketing Group, 1155 Brewery Park Blvd.(48207-2697), pg. 879
AUTOMOTIVE NEWS, 1400 Woodbridge Ave.(48207-3187), pg. 101
Automotive News, 1400 Woodbridge Ave.(48207), pg. 295
N W Ayer Inc., 2000 Fisher Bldg.(48202), pg. 104
Barton-Malow Company, P.O. Box 5200(48235), pg. 123
BING STEEL INC., 1130 W. Grand Blvd.(48208), pg. 151
BOOTH AMERICAN, 333 W. Fort St.(48226), pg. 165
Bowlerama Lanes, Inc., 21630 W. Seven Mile Rd.(48225), pg. 482
Brencal Contractors Inc., 6686 E. McNichols Rd.(48212), pg. 106
BRIAN UNLIMITED DISTRIBUTION COMPANY, INC., 13131 Lyndon(48227), pg. 175
BROGAN & PARTNERS ADVERTISING/PUBLIC RELATIONS INC., 2000 Fisher Bldg.(48202), pg. 178
C.F. BURGER CREAMERY COMPANY, 8101 Greenfield(48228), pg. 190
CABANA FOODS, INC., 14245 Birwood St.(48238), pg. 206
COLD HEADING CO., 4600 Bellevue Ave.(48207), pg. 259
Computer Printing Div., 433 E. Larned(48226), pg. 793
CONTINENTAL PAPER & SUPPLY CO., 6400 E. Eight Mile Rd.(48234), pg. 280
CRAIN COMMUNICATIONS, INC., 1400 Woodbridge Ave.(48207), pg. 295
Crain's Detroit Business, 1400 Woodbridge Ave.(48207-3187), pg. 295
DAVIS INDUSTRIES INC., 19250 Plymouth Rd.(48228), pg. 318
Davis Tool & Engineering Co., 19250 Plymouth Rd.(48228), pg. 318
Detroit Diesel Corp., 13400 W. Outer Dr.(48239), pg. 859
DOMESTIC LINEN SUPPLY & LAUNDRY CO., 3800 18th St.(48208), pg. 343
DREISBACH & SONS CADILLAC COMPANY, 24600 Grand River Ave.(48219), pg. 348
Dynecol, Inc., 6520 Georgia(48211), pg. 838
En-Pak, Inc., 1400 Howard St.(48216), pg. 582
EVANS INDUSTRIES, INC., 200 Renaissance Center(48243), pg. 390
FERROUS PROCESSING & TRADING CO., 9100 John Kronk Ave.(48210), pg. 407
First Federal of Michigan, 1001 Woodward Ave.(48226-1904), pg. 414
FIRSTFED MICHIGAN CORPORATION, 1001 Woodward Ave.(48226-1904), pg. 414
Fitzsimons Manufacturing Co., 3775 E. Outer Dr.(48234), pg. 284
FLINT INK CORP., 25111 Glendale Ave.(48239), pg. 419
Anthony M. Franco Inc., 400 Renaissance Center, Ste. 600(48243), pg. 950
Frankel Metal Company, 19300 Filer Ave.(48234), pg. 742
FRIGID FOOD PRODUCTS, INC., 1599 E. Warren Ave.(48207), pg. 433
GALLAGHER-KAISER CORP., 13710 Mt. Elliot(48212), pg. 441
Gaylord Lithograph Div.-Detroit, 1555 Woodrow Wilson(49238), pg. 447
GAYLORD PRINTING, INC., 15555 Woodrow Wilson(48238), pg. 446
Great Lakes Bowling Centre, Inc., 6366 Woodward Ave.(48202), pg. 482
Great Lakes Filter, 5151 Loraine St.(48208), pg. 13
GREAT LAKES SPORTSWEAR MANUFACTURING INDUSTRIES, 11371 E. State Fair(48234), pg. 482
Heat Bath Park Metallurgical Products, 8074 Military Ave.(48204), pg. 524
HERMES AUTOMOTIVE MANUFACTURING CORP., 2703 23rd St.(48216), pg. 531
Highwood Service, Inc., 400 Renaissance Court(48243), pg. 1194
IDEA ENGINEERING & FABRICATING, 13881 Elmira Rd.(48227), pg. 562
Inland Tool & Manufacturing, Inc., 20263 HooverRd.(48205), pg. 1194
INVETECH CO., 1400 Howard St.(48216), pg. 581
IPMC, Inc.-Detroit, 9125 W. Jefferson(48209), pg. 583
JEFFERSON CHEVROLET CO., 2130 E. Jefferson(48207), pg. 591
THE JOHN JOHNSON CO., 1481 14th St.(48216), pg. 597
Jorgensen Steel & Aluminum/Detroit, 13200 W. Eight Mile Rd.(48237), pg. 605
ALBERT KAHN ASSOCIATES, INC., Albert Kahn Bldg., 7430 Second Ave.(48202-2798), pg. 613
KENWAL PRODUCTS CORP., 9301 Central Ave.(48204), pg. 624
KEYWELL CORPORATION, 3075 Lonyo St.(48209), pg. 629
RAY LAETHEM PONTIAC GMC TRUCK CO., 17677 Mack Ave.(48224), pg. 650
LAFAYETTE STEEL CO., 3600 N. Military St.(48210), pg. 650
League General Insurance Co., P.O. Box 33430, (48232-5430), pg. 205
LETTS INDUSTRIES, INC., 1111 Bellevue Ave.(48207), pg. 668
EDWARD C. LEVY CO., INC., 8800 Dix Ave.(48209), pg. 672
LITTLE CAESAR ENTERPRISES, INC., 2211 Woodward Ave.(48201-3400), pg. 678
LUDINGTON NEWS CO. INC., 1600 E. Grand Blvd.(48211-3195), pg. 686
MADISON ELECTRIC CO., 6000 Woodward Ave.(48202), pg. 699
MCINERNEY-MILLER BROTHERS INC., 2001 Brewster St.(48207), pg. 729
MEADE GROUP, INC., 130 Kercheval(48236), pg. 733
Metro Cell, Inc., 6031 Joy Rd.(48204), pg. 913
Metro 25 Tire Centers, Inc., 6031 Joy Rd.(48204), pg. 913
MEXICAN INDUSTRIES IN MICHIGAN, 1616 Howard(48216), pg. 745
Michigan Bakery Supply Co., 32680 Capital St.(48207), pg. 146
Moore Bearing Co., 1400 Howard St.(48216), pg. 582
C. A. MUER CORP., 1548 Porter St.(48216), pg. 774
NTH Consultants, Ltd., 65 Cadillac Square, Ste. 2223(48226), pg. 781
OLSONITE CORPORATION, 8801 Conant Ave.(48211-1403), pg. 824
OMNICARE HEALTH PLAN, 1155 Brewery Park Blvd., Ste. 250(48207-2602), pg. 826
PVS CHEMICALS, INC., 10900 Harper Ave.(48213), pg. 837
PVS-Nolwood Chemicals, Inc., 10900 Harper Ave.(48213), pg. 838
PVS Technologies, Inc., 10900 Harper Ave.(48213), pg. 838
PARK MOTOR SALES COMPANY, 18100 Woodward Ave.(48203), pg. 849
PATTERSON LABORATORIES, INC., 11930 Pleasant Ave.(48217), pg. 852
PENSKE CORPORATION, 13400 Outer Dr. W.(48239), pg. 859
Pepper, Hamilton & Scheetz, 100 Renaissance Center, 36th Fl.(48243), pg. 860
Polk City Directory Div., 1155 Brewery Park Blvd.(48207-2697), pg. 879
R. L. POLK & CO., 1155 Brewery Park Blvd.(48207-2697), pg. 879
Polk Motor Vehicle Registrations Div., 1155 Brewery Park Blvd.(48207-2697), pg. 879
QUAEL CORP., 1927 Rosa Parks Blvd.(48216), pg. 902
RAO WHOLESALE TIRE CENTERS, INC., 6031 Joy Rd.(48204), pg. 912
RONEY & CO., One Griswold St.(48226), pg. 946
ROTARY MULTIFORMS, INC., 3900 Beaufait(48207), pg. 951
SEAMAN-PATRICK PAPER COMPANY, 2000 Howard St.(48216), pg. 986
Seven-Up Bottling Co. of Detroit, 12201 Beech Daly Rd.(48239), pg. 179
Shapero Stores, 1927 Rosa Parks Blvd.(48216), pg. 903
Sherwood Co., 6331 E. Jefferson Ave.(48207), pg. 557
SHERWOOD FOOD DISTRIBUTORS, 18615 Sherwood(48234), pg. 998
SILVER'S INC., 151 W. Fort St.(48226), pg. 1005
THE SMITH GROUP, INC., 150 W. Jefferson, Ste. 100(48226), pg. 1012
Smith Hinchman Grylls Associates, Inc., 150 W. Jefferson Ave., Ste. 100(48226), pg. 1013
Specialty Restaurants Corp, 201 W. Atwater St.(48226), pg. 1028
THE STROH BREWERY COMPANY, 100 River Place(48207), pg. 1053
TRI-MARK METAL CORP., 10106 Grinnell(48213-1192), pg. 1110
Tri-State Development Co., 1400 Howard St.(48216), pg. 582
United American Healthcare Corp., 1155 Brewery Park Blvd., Ste. 200(48207-2602), pg. 826
VAN PELT CORPORATION, 13700 Sherwood(48212), pg. 1144
VULCAN IRON WORKS, INC., 12700 Lyndon(48227), pg. 1155
WALBRIDGE ALDINGER COMPANY, 613 Abbott St.(48226-2521), pg. 1158
WALLICH LUMBER CO., 10701 Lyndon(48238), pg. 1161
Ward's Communications, Inc., 28 W. Adams(48226), pg. 611
RALPH C. WILSON ENTERPRISES, 400 Renaissance Center, Ste. 2140(48243), pg. 1194
WINSTON STEEL PRODUCTS CO., 2700 W. Warren Ave.(48208), pg. 1197
WOLVERINE PACKING CO., 1340 Winder(48207), pg. 1199
Y&R/Wunderman Worldwide/Detroit, 200 Renaissance Ctr., Ste. 700(48243), pg. 1211
Young & Rubicam Detroit, 200 Renaissance Ctr., Ste. 1000(48243), pg. 1211
YOUNG SUPPLY COMPANY, 888 W. Baltimore Ave.(48202), pg. 1214

Dexter

Thetford Corp. Mfg. Facility, 800 Baker Rd.(48130), pg. 358

Durand

Marsh Products Co., 7505 E. M-71(48429), pg. 886
PREMARC CORPORATION, 7505 Hwy. M-71(48429), pg. 886

East Detroit

COLONIAL DODGE INC., 24200 Gratiot(48021), pg. 263
COPPER & BRASS SALES, INC., 17401 Ten Mile Rd.(48021), pg. 284

East Jordan

EAST JORDAN IRON WORKS, 301 Spring St.(49727), pg. 362

Eastpointe

EDWARD V. MONAHAN INC., 21321 Kelly Rd.(48021), pg. 765

Ecorse

National Steel Great Lakes Div., 1 Quality Dr.(48229), pg. 794

Edwardsburg

GEORGIE BOY MANUFACTURING, INC., 69950 M 62(49112), pg. 453

Farmington

FARMINGTON HILLS HOLDING COMPANY, 35300 Grand River(48335), pg. 402
J. LEE HACKETT CO., 23550 Haggerty Rd.(48335), pg. 498
Kilsby-Roberts/Detroit, 23680 Research Dr.(48335), pg. 606
MECHANICAL HEAT & COLD, INC., 24535 Hallwood Ct.(48335), pg. 734
Bob Saks Jeep-Eagle, 35200 Grand River(48335), pg. 402
Bob Saks Oldsmobile Inc., 35200 Grand River(48335), pg. 402
Bob Saks Toyota, 35200 Grand River(48335), pg. 402
Selastomer Div., 23800 Research Dr.(48024), pg. 749

Farmington Hills

ACO INC., 23333 Commerce Dr.(48335-2764), pg. 2
Blue Line Distributing, 24120 Haggerty Rd.(48024), pg. 678
COMPUWARE CORPORATION, 31440 Northwestern Hwy.(48334-2564), pg. 271
ELECTRO-MATIC PRODUCTS INC., 23409 Industrial Park Ct.(48335), pg. 374
A.J. Etkin Construction Co., P.O. Box 9061, 31440 Northwestern Hwy., Ste. 150(48018), pg. 390
ALEX J. ETKIN, INC., 31440 Northwestern Hwy., Ste. 150(48334-2533), pg. 389
Stephen Gould MI, 37678 Enterprise Ct.(48331), pg. 474
HLC INDUSTRIES, 38880 Grand River(48335), pg. 496
HDS SERVICES, 33469 W. 14 Mile Rd.(48331), pg. 496
PAUL INMAN ASSOCIATES INC., 30095 Northwestern Hwy.(48334), pg. 570
LIFETIME DOORS INC., 30700 Northwestern Hwy.(48334), pg. 675
MARKETING DISPLAYS INTERNATIONAL, INC., 38271 W. 12 Mile Rd.(48331), pg. 709
MELODY FOODS, INC., 30777 Northwestern Hwy.(48334), pg. 738

NTH CONSULTANTS, LTD., 38955 Hills Tech Dr.(48331), pg. 781
PARADATA COMPUTER NETWORKS, INC., 37695 Interchange Dr.(48335), pg. 847
Prestolite Wire Corporation, 32871 Middlebelt Rd.(48334), pg. 801
BOB SELLERS PONTIAC GMC TRUCK INC., 38000 Grand River(48333-2070), pg. 988
STAR CUTTER CO., 23461 Industrial Park Dr.(48335), pg. 1039
THOMPSON ADVERTISING PRODUCTIONS, INC., 31690 W. 12 Mile Rd.(48334), pg. 1094
Unibilt, 34375 W. Twelve Mile Rd.(48331), pg. 1170
JERVIS B. WEBB COMPANY, 34375 West 12 Mile Rd.(48331), pg. 1170
Webb Electric Co., 24420 Indoplex Circle(48335), pg. 1170

Fenton

KING GROUP, INC., 1139 Pennway Circle(48430), pg. 630
King Michigan Sundries Div., 1139 Fenway Circle(48430), pg. 630

Ferndale

DETROIT COIL COMPANY, 2435 Hilton Rd.(48220), pg. 333
HENNELLS, INC., 1200 Woodward Hts.(48220), pg. 530
OVERHEAD CONVEYOR CO., 1330 Hilton Rd.(48220), pg. 832
WALKER WIRE & STEEL COMPANY, 660 E. Ten Mile Rd.(48220), pg. 1160

Flemington Hills

Automotive Chemical Corporation, 38855 Hills Tech Dr.(48212-1199), pg. 410

Flint

Alro Group, Flint, P.O. Box 496, 3501 Western Rd.(48501-0496), pg. 44
J. AUSTIN OIL CO., 2300 Austin Pky.(48507), pg. 99
DWF of Flint, Inc., 5100 Exchange Dr.(48507), pg. 331
Gaylord Central Printing & Publishing Div., 129 N. Grand Traverse(48503), pg. 447
HOUGEN MANUFACTURING INC., G5072 Corunna Rd.(48532), pg. 546
MacKenzie, Kuth & Klein Div., 209 Avon St.(48503), pg. 455
R.S. Young Environmental Clean Up, G 5305 N. Dort Hwy.(48505), pg. 1209
R.S. YOUNG EXCAVATING, INC., G-5305 N. Dort Hwy.(48505), pg. 1209
Zack Co., 4401 Western Rd.(48506), pg. 1215

Fowlerville

BENT TUBE, INC., 9649 W. Van Buren Rd.(48836), pg. 140

Fraser

ISI FLuid Power, Inc., P.O. BOx 400(48026), pg. 560
THE ISI MANUFACTURING, INC., 31915 Groesbeck Hwy.(48026), pg. 560
ISI Robotics I, 31915 Groesbeck Hwy.(48026), pg. 560
LOGGHE STAMPING COMPANY, 16711 13 Mile Rd.(48026), pg. 681
OAKLAND TOOL & MANUFACTURING COMPANY, 34700 Commerce(48026), pg. 819
SIGNET INDUSTRIES, 17085 Masonic(48026), pg. 1003

Fremont

LUBECON SYSTEMS, INC., 6735 W. 64th St.(49412-0589), pg. 686

Garden City

DEARBORN GAGE COMPANY, 32330 Ford Rd.(48135), pg. 322

Gladstone

NORTHERN MICHIGAN VENEERS, INC., Gladstone Industrial Park(49837), pg. 814

Grand Haven

CHALLENGE GRAPHICS EQUIPMENT CO., 1810 E. Industrial Park Dr.(49417), pg. 238
Challenge Technologies, 1433 Fulton St.(49417), pg. 238
Eagle-Ottawa Leather Co., 200 N. Beechtree St.(49417), pg. 1116
STANCO METAL PRODUCTS, INC., 2101 168th Ave.(49417-0307), pg. 1035

Grand Junction

MICHIGAN BLUEBERRY GROWERS ASSN., P.O. Box B, (49056), pg. 747

Grand Rapids

Abrasives, Inc., 4936 Kendrick St.(49512), pg. 889
ADVANCE PACKAGING CORPORATION, 4450 36th St., S.E.(49512), pg. 19
ALEXANDER MARKETING SERVICES, INC., 277 Crahen Ave., NE(49516), pg. 33
Alro Group, Grand Rapids, P.O. Box 1846, 1033 Freeman S.W.(49501-1846), pg. 44
AMERICAN METAL & PLASTICS, 450 32nd St. SW(49518), pg. 58
AMERICAN SEATING COMPANY, 901 Broadway NW(49504), pg. 60
Amway Hotel Corporation, Pearl Northwest at Monroe(49503), pg. 70
April Hill, Inc., 190 28th St., SE(49508), pg. 488
Arnold Fortuna Lawner & Cabot, 280051 Charlesvoix Drive, S.E.(49546), pg. 84
AVES ADVERTISING, INC., 800 Exhibitors Plaza(49503), pg. 102
Biggs Gilmore Communications, 111 Pearl St.(49503), pg. 149
BISSELL INC., 2345 Walker N.W.(49504), pg. 153
BOOTH NEWSPAPERS, INC., 155 Michigan N.W.(49503), pg. 165
COUNTRY FRESH, INC., 2555 Buchanan Ave., S.W.(49518), pg. 289
Crown Coat, Inc., 700 Wealthy St., S.W.(49501), pg. 609
H.H. CUTLER COMPANY, 120 Ionia Ave., S. W.(49501), pg. 306
Cutler Manufacturing Corp., 2455 Oak Industrial Dr. N.E.(49505), pg. 307
D & W FOOD CENTERS, INC., 3001 Orchard Vista Dr., SE(49546), pg. 308
DICKINSON PRESS, INC., 5100 33rd St. S.E.(49512), pg. 336
Fare Development Corp., 255 Colrain St., S.W.(49509), pg. 540
FROST INC., 2020 Bristol NW(49504), pg. 435
GORDON FOOD SERVICE INC., P.O. Box 1787, 333 50th St.(49501), pg. 472
GROCERS BAKING CO., 210 28th St. S.E.(49508), pg. 488
H S DIE & ENGINEERING, INC., 0-215 Lake Michigan Dr., NW(49504), pg. 497
HAVILAND ENTERPRISES, 421 Ann St., N.W.(49504), pg. 517
HOLLY'S INC., 3033 Orchard Vista Dr. S.E., Ste. 306(49546), pg. 540
Instructional Fair, Inc., 2400 Turner Ave.(49501), pg. 369
KINDEL FURNITURE COMPANY, 100 Garden S.E.(49507), pg. 630
L & L/Jiroch Distributing Co., 5075 Clay Ave., S.W.(49548), pg. 1026
Lamar Corp., 2696 Chicago Dr., S.W.(45909), pg. 886
MAGHIELSE TOOL CORPORATION, 731 Broadway, N.W.(49504), pg. 700
MEIJER, INC., 2929 Walker Ave. N.W.(49504), pg. 737
MENDENHALL & LEISTRA, 60 Monroe Center N.W., Ste. 1100(49503), pg. 739
MICHIGAN WHEEL CORPORATION, 1501 Buchanan, S.W.(49507), pg. 747
Midwest Fashions, Inc., 4550 Clyde Park S.W.(49509), pg. 307
MOSS TELECOMMUNICATIONS SERVICES, 561 Century Ave.(49503), pg. 772
Mueller, A Haworth Portfolio Co., 514 Fifth St., N.W.(49504), pg. 518
OLIVER PRODUCTS COMPANY, 445 6th St., N.W.(49504), pg. 824
OWEN-AMES-KIMBALL CO., 300 Ionia Ave. N.W.(49503), pg. 833
Owen-Ames-Kimball Engineering, Inc., 300 Ionia Ave. N.W.(49503), pg. 833
PRIDGEON & CLAY, INC., 50 Cottage Grove SW(49507), pg. 889
PRIME TECHNOLOGY, INC., 4936 Kendrick St., SE(49512), pg. 889
RANIR CORPORATION, 4617 E. Paris(49508), pg. 912
SEFTON ASSOCIATES INC., 3351 Claystone, S.E.(49546), pg. 987
Shield Insurance, 3900 Sparks Dr., S.E.(49518), pg. 1026
Nancy Skinner & Associates, 111 Pearl St.(49503), pg. 149
Slip-X Safety Treads, Inc., P. O. Box 1888(49501), pg. 153
SONNEVELDT COMPANY, 435 Ionia Ave. S.W.(49503), pg. 1018
SPARTAN STORES INC., 850 76th St., SW(49518), pg. 1026
Steelcase Financial Services, Inc., 901 44th St. S.E.(49508), pg. 1044
STEELCASE INC., 901 44th St. SE(49508), pg. 1044
Steelcase Inc./International Div., 901 44th St. S.E.(49508), pg. 1044
Steketee Paul & Sons Company, Inc., 86 Monroe Center(49503-3215), pg. 353
TCH INDUSTRIES INC., 3040 Charlevoix Dr. S.E.(49546), pg. 1072
TRANSNATIONAL MOTORS INC., 618 Kenmoor(49546), pg. 1107
United Wholesale Inc., 850 76th St., S.W.(49501), pg. 1026
UNIVERSAL COMPANIES, INC., 2801 E. Beltline N.E.(49505), pg. 1138
Universal Forest Products, Inc., 2801 East Beltline, N.E.(49505), pg. 1138
Universal Restaurants, Inc., 2801 E. Beltline N.E.(49505), pg. 1138
THE WBDC GROUP, 50 Monroe Pl. N.W.(49503), pg. 1155
WW Engineering & Science Inc., 5555 Glenwood Hills Pkwy. S.E.(49512), pg. 1058
Wickes Bumper Division, 1860 Alpine N.W.(49504), pg. 262
WILLIAMS DISTRIBUTING COMPANY, 658 Richmond N.W.(49504), pg. 1190

Grandville

GRANDVILLE PRINTING COMPANY, P.O. Box 247, (49468), pg. 476
WINDEMULLER ELECTRIC INC., 4685 Spartan Industrial Dr.(49418), pg. 1195

Greenville

PRINTCO, INC., 1321 Van Deinse(48838), pg. 891

Grosse Point Park

Jefferson Chevrolet, 15175 E. Jefferson(48230), pg. 591

Grosse Pointe

DENTON ENTERPRISES INC., 20415 Mack Ave.(48236), pg. 329

Hamtramck

KOWALSKI SAUSAGE CO., INC., 2270 Holbrook Ave.(48212), pg. 643

Harbor Springs

Control Engineering Co., 8212 Harbor Springs Rd.(49740), pg. 1170

Hastings

FLEXFAB, INC., 1843 Gun Lake Rd.(49058), pg. 418
Pro Line, 1675 Gun Lake Rd.(49058), pg. 418

Hazel Park

MEIER METAL SERVICE CENTERS, INC., 1471 E. Nine Mile Rd.(48030), pg. 737

Highland Park

DETROIT CITY DAIRY, INC., 15004 Third Ave.(48203), pg. 333
JOHN E. GREEN CO., 220 Victor Ave.(48203), pg. 484
HELM, INC., 14310 Hamilton(48203), pg. 527

Hillsdale

Hillsdale Daily News, P.O. Box 287, 33 McCollum(49242), pg. 1042
THE SHANE GROUP INC., 250 Industrial Dr.(49242), pg. 995

Holland

Beverage Management, Inc., 777 Brooks Ave.(49423), pg. 179
BRADFORD COMPANY, 13500 Quincy St.(49424), pg. 170
BROOKS BEVERAGE MANAGEMENT, INC., 777 Brooks Ave.(49423), pg. 179
CASTEX INDUSTRIES INC., 4240 Blue Star Hwy.(49423), pg. 228
Charter House Incorporated, 4660 136th Ave.(49424), pg. 1035
HAWORTH, INC., One Haworth Center(49423), pg. 518
The Holland Sentinel, 54-56 W. 8th St.(49423), pg. 1042
J B LABS, INC., 130 Central(49423), pg. 584
LOUIS PADNOS IRON & METAL CO., 120 S. River Ave.(49423), pg. 842
PRINCE CORPORATION, One Prince Center(49423), pg. 890
Thermotron Industries, Inc., Kollen Park Dr.(49423), pg. 1148
TRENDWAY CORPORATION, 13467 Quincy St.(49424), pg. 1109

Holly

CMI Schneible Co., P.O. BOx 100(48442), pg. 202

Holt

Capistar, Inc., 4147 Keller Rd.(48842), pg. 1026
SPARTAN INTERNATIONAL, 1845 S. Cedar(48842), pg. 1026

Howell

Citizens Insurance Company of America, 645 W. Grand River(48843), pg. 35
Pinckney Molded Plastics, 3970 Parsons(48843), pg. 560

Hudson

Day Industries, 3991 Munson Hwy.(49247), pg. 914
METALLOY CORPORATION, 103 W. Main St.(49247), pg. 742

Iron Mountain

BACCO CONSTRUCTION CO., P.O. Box 458(49801), pg. 108
CHAMPION, INC., 105 East A St.(49801), pg. 238

Jackson

ALLIED CHUCKER & ENGINEERING COMPANY, 3529 Scheele Dr.(49202), pg. 37
ALRO GROUP, 3100 E. High St.(49204), pg. 44
Alro Group, Jackson, P.O. Box 927, 3100 E. High St.(49204-0927), pg. 44
Alro Group, Jackson Plastics, 903 Baldan Rd.(49203), pg. 44
Alro Group, Jackson Tool-Pac, 1410 W. Ganson St.(49202), pg. 44
Central Michigan Container Corporation, 2400 E. High St.(49204), pg. 19
Crankshaft Machine Company, 314 N. Jackson St., P.O. Box 1127(49204), pg. 102
DAWN FOOD PRODUCTS, INC., 2021 Micor Dr.(49203), pg. 319
Gordon Plastics Div., P.O. Box 1107, (49204), pg. 876
HEAT CONTROLLER, INC., 1900 Wellworth Ave.(49203), pg. 524
PLASTIGAGE CORPORATION, 2917 Wildwood Ave.(49202), pg. 876
Way Bakeries, Inc., 2100 Enterprise Dr.(49203), pg. 861

Jonesville

Mark I Molded Plastics, Inc., P.O. Box 35, U.S. 12 East(49250), pg. 97

Kalamazoo

Arlo Group, Kalamazoo, 5139 Wynn Rd.(49003-3537), pg. 44
BIGGS GILMORE COMMUNICATIONS, 100 W. Michigan Ave., Suite 300(49007), pg. 149

William R. Biggs/Gilmore Associates, Inc., 100 W. Michigan Ave.(49007), pg. 149
Earle Palmer Brown/Kalamazoo, 259 E. Michigan Ave.(49007), pg. 182
GILMORE BROS., INC., 143 S. Kalamazoo Mall(49007), pg. 459
GREAT LAKES TECHNOLOGIES CORP., 300 S. Kalamazoo Mall, Ste. 210(49007), pg. 482
Harrington Market Research, 100 W. Michigan Ave.(49007), pg. 149
Haviland-Kalamazoo, 2722 N. Burdick(49007), pg. 517
HUMPHREY PRODUCTS COMPANY, 5070 E. N Ave.(49001), pg. 553
KALAMAZOO HOLDINGS, INC., 3713 W. Main St.(49007), pg. 615
KALAMAZOO LABEL CO., 321 W. Ransom St.(49007), pg. 615
Kalamazoo Scrap & Processing, 2900 Miller Rd.(49001), pg. 1055
Kalsec, Inc., 3713 W. Main St.(49007), pg. 615
LSI/KALA, 2325 Burdick St.(49007), pg. 975
Liberty Auto Parts, 2900 Miller Rd.(49001), pg. 1055
MERCHANTS PUBLISHING CO., 3500 Sprinkle Rd.(49002), pg. 739
MIDWEST FASTENERS CORPORATION, 9031 Shaver Rd.(49002), pg. 752
Mol-Bee, Inc., 1811 Vanderbilt Ave.(49002), pg. 875
Pan-O-Grav, Inc., 1807 Vanderbilt Road(49002), pg. 875
Plastic Engineering, Inc., 1825 Vanderbilt Road(49002), pg. 875
A.M. TODD COMPANY, 1717 Douglas Ave.(49007), pg. 1100

Kalkaska

WAYNE WIRE CLOTH PRODUCTS, INC., 10 Dresden St.(49646), pg. 1169

Kentwood

Bananza Air Management Systems, Inc., 5353 52nd St., S.E.(49508), pg. 913
DIELINE CORPORATION, 3755 36th St. S.E.(49512), pg. 336
Market Development Co., 5296 Eastern Ave.(49508), pg. 1026
Stow & Davis Furniture Co., 4300 44th St., S.E.(49508), pg. 1044

Kingsford

Lake Shore, Inc., 900 W. Breitung Ave.(49801), pg. 824
LODAL, INC., East Blvd.(49802), pg. 680

Lansing

Alro Group, Lansing, 1800 W. Willow St.(48915), pg. 44
AUTO-OWNERS INSURANCE, 6101 Anacapri Blvd.(48917), pg. 100
Auto-Owners Life Insurance Co., 6101 Anacapri Blvd.(48917), pg. 100
Capitol Cadillac, Corp., 5901 S. Pennsylvania Ave.(48911), pg. 719
Charitable Gaming Div., 6545 Mercantile Way(48909), pg. 747
THE DELPHI GLASS CORP. DELPHI STAINED GLASS CENTERS, 2116 E. Michigan Ave.(48912), pg. 326
DOUGLAS STEEL FABRICATING CORPORATION, 1312 S. Waverly Rd.(48917), pg. 347
Functions, 6267 Aurelius Rd.(48909), pg. 476
GRANGER CONSTRUCTION CO., 6267 Aurelius Rd.(48909), pg. 476
Home-Owners Insurance Co., 6101 Anacapri Blvd.(48917), pg. 100
JEPSON-MURRAY ADVERTISING, 1116 N. Washington Ave.(48906), pg. 593
Lansing Dairy, Inc., 2224 W. Willow(48917), pg. 738
Melling Forging Company, 1709 Thompson St.(48906), pg. 102
MICHIGAN STATE LOTTERY BUREAU, 101 E. Hillsdale(48913), pg. 747
MOTOR WHEEL CORPORATION, 4000 Collins Rd.(48910), pg. 773
Padnos-Summit, P.O. Box 13070(48901), pg. 843
Schafer Bakeries, Inc., 2701 S. Logan Central Garage(48910), pg. 861
SPARTAN OIL CORP., 419 Spring St.(48912), pg. 1026
WSYM-TV, 600 W. St. Joseph St.(48933), pg. 608
WOHLERT CORP., 708-12 E. Grand River Ave.(48906), pg. 1198

Livonia

A & W RESTAURANTS, INC., 17197 Laurel Park Dr., Ste. 500(48152), pg. 1
AM General Corporation, 11900 Hubbard Dr.(48150), pg. 926
AIR GAGE COMPANY, 12170 Globe(48150), pg. 27
American Hospital Equipment Corp., 31742 Enterprise Dr.(48150), pg. 912
AWREY BAKERIES, INC., 12301 Farmington Rd.(48150), pg. 103
PETER A. BASILE SONS INC., 13000 Newburgh Rd.(48151), pg. 124
Benjamin Woodhouse & Guenther, 14147 Farmington Rd.(48154), pg. 455
Borg-Warner Automotive, Inc., 12000 Tech Center Dr.(48150), pg. 166
Borg-Warner Automotive-Michigan Powdered Metal Products, Inc., 32059 Schoolcraft(48150), pg. 166
BILL BROWN FORD INC., 32222 Plymouth Rd.(48150), pg. 182
Cloverlanes, Inc., 28900 Schoolcraft(48150), pg. 482
COMPUTER METHODS CORPORATION, 13740 Merriman St.(48150), pg. 271
CONTRACTORS STEEL COMPANY, 36555 Amrhein Rd.(48150), pg. 280
Darin & Armstrong, Inc., 38099 Schoolcraft(48150), pg. 1159
DIGITAL ELECTRONIC AUTOMATION, 37000 Plymouth Rd.(48150), pg. 337
GREAT LAKES RECREATION CO., 28900 Schoolcraft Rd.(48150), pg. 481
KEY PLASTICS, INC., 39325 Plymouth Rd., Ste. 201(48150), pg. 627
Metropolitan Asphalt, Inc., 13000 Newburgh Rd.(48151), pg. 124
THE MILLGARD CORP., 12822 Stark Rd.(48150), pg. 755
PALMER MOVING & STORAGE CO., 31751 Enterprise Dr.(48150), pg. 844
PERFECTION AUTOMOTIVE PRODUCTS CORPORATION, 12445 Levan Rd.(48150), pg. 861
Pioneer Snacks, 3111 Industrial Rd.(48150), pg. 738
PLASTOMER CORP., 37819 Schoolcraft(48150), pg. 876
RS ELECTRONICS, 34443 Schoolcraft Rd.(48150), pg. 908
Rancare Inc., 31742 Enterprise Dr.(48150), pg. 912
RANDOLPH MEDICAL INC., 31742 Enterprise Dr.(48150), pg. 912
Shmina Construction, Inc., 13000 Newburgh Rd.(48151), pg. 124
Eberle M. Smith Associates, Inc., 14147 Farmington Rd.(48154), pg. 455
SUBURBAN COMMUNICATIONS CORP., 36251 Schoolcraft Rd.(48150), pg. 1055
WASHERS, INC., 33375 Glendale Ave.(48150), pg. 1165

Lowell

KING MILLING COMPANY, 115 Broadway(49331), pg. 631

Madison Heights

AJAX PAVING INDUSTRIES INC., One Ajax Dr.(48071), pg. 28
Alpha Bolt Company, 1524 E. Fourteen Mile Rd.(48071), pg. 1165
Fairlanes Bowl, Inc., 29600 Stephenson Hwy.(48071), pg. 482
Haden Equity, Ltd., 32200 N. Avis Dr.(48071), pg. 499
HADEN, INC., 32200 N. Avis Dr.(48071), pg. 499
Haden Investment, Ltd., 32200 N. Avis Dr.(48071), pg. 499
Haden Schweitzer Corporation, 32200 N. Avis Dr.(48071), pg. 499
James Steel & Tube Company, 29774 Stephenson Hwy., P.O. Box 545(48071), pg. 102
KASPER MACHINE COMPANY, 29275 Stephenson Hwy.(48071), pg. 618
MCNAUGHTON-MCKAY ELECTRIC CO., 1357 E. Lincoln Ave.(48071), pg. 732
NATIONAL REPRODUCTIONS CORPORATION, 29400 Stephenson Hwy.(48071), pg. 793
PULLMAN INDUSTRIES, INC., 25359 Dequindre Rd.(48071), pg. 900
RING SCREW WORKS, 31550 Stephenson Hwy.(48071), pg. 935
TRIANGLE ELECTRIC COMPANY, 29787 Stephenson Hwy.(48071), pg. 1112
WALL COLMONOY CORP., 30261 Stephenson Hwy.(48071), pg. 1160

Mason

DART CONTAINER CORP., 500 Hogsback Rd.(48854), pg. 316

Mendon

Lear Siegler Plastics Corp., 236 W. Clark St.(49072), pg. 664

Menominee

Menominee Paper Co., P.O. Box 300(49858), pg. 135

Michigan Center

AIRMASTER FAN CO., 1300 Falahee Rd.(49203), pg. 28

Midland

Ingersoll CM Systems Inc., 3505 Centennial Dr.(48640), pg. 568
Midland Daily News, 124 S. McDonald St.(48640), pg. 524

Milan

Cresive Milan Division, 555 Platt(48160), pg. 298

Monroe

MIDWAY PRODUCTS CORPORATION, 523 Detroit Ave.(48161), pg. 751
Modern Packaging Corp., 506 Huber Dr.(48161), pg. 1063

Mount Clemens

ACR INDUSTRIES INC., 15375 23 Mile Rd.(48042-4000), pg. 2
Automation Products Group, 44831 Groesbeck(48043), pg. 560
JOHN CARLO INC., 21570 Hall Rd.(48046), pg. 220
JAMES CHEVROLET INC., 35500 S. Gratiot(48043), pg. 588
JIM CAUSLEY PONTIAC GMC INC., 38111 Gratiot Ave.(48043), pg. 229

Muskegon

AMSTORE CORPORATION, 1221 E. Keating(49442), pg. 69
FLEET ENGINEERS, INC., 1800 E. Keating(49442), pg. 417
Hasper Equipment Co., 3662 Airline Rd.(49444), pg. 256
Johnson Technology, 2034 Latimer Dr.(49442), pg. 431
KURDZIEL INDUSTRIES, INC., Co-America Bank Building, 801 W. Norton Ave., Ste. 300(49441), pg. 646
LSI Truck Products Corp.-Neway/Anchor Lock, 1950 Industrial Blvd.(49442), pg. 664
Lee Industries, 1800 E. Keating Ave.(49442), pg. 417
Muskegon Construction Company, 425 Catawba Ave.(49443), pg. 833

National City

Gold Bond Gypsum Products, P.O. Box 14, (48748), pg. 790

New Troy

STANLEY KNIGHT CORPORATION, 3604 Glendora Rd.(49119), pg. 1038

Niles

HESS ENGINEERING INC., 191 Fir Road(49120-9766), pg. 532

North Muskegon

QUALITY STORES INC., 1460 Whitehall Rd.(49445), pg. 904
ZEPHYR INC., P.O. Box 5069(49445), pg. 1217

Northville

Consulting Services, Inc., 43043 W. 9 Mile Rd.(48167), pg. 492
GUARDIAN INDUSTRIES CORP., 43043 W. Nine Mile Rd.(48167), pg. 491
Photo Central Office, 43043 W. Nine Mile Rd.(48167), pg. 492

Norway

Perry/Norway, 512 9th Ave.(49870), pg. 607

Novi

DEMARIA BUILDING CO. INC., 45500 Grand River Ave.(48376), pg. 327
FABEX INC., 42400 Grand River, Ste. 201(48375), pg. 395
Integral Systems, 39555 Orchard Hill Pl., Ste. 160(48375), pg. 573
MICHIGAN MILK PRODUCERS ASSOCIATION, 41310 Bridge St.(48375), pg. 747
MICHIGAN TRACTOR AND MACHINERY CO., 24800 Novi Rd.(48375), pg. 747

Oak Park

Barton-Malow Rigging Co., 21090 Fern Ave.(48237), pg. 123
CLOVERDALE EQUIPMENT CO., 13133 Cloverdale(48237), pg. 256
MEL FARR FORD, INC., 24750 Greenfield Rd.(48237), pg. 403
MCINERNEY INC., 14100 W. Eight Mile Rd.(48237), pg. 729
The Producto Machine Co., 10200 Capital Ave.(48237), pg. 893
H.O. TRERICE COMPANY, 12950 W. Eight Mile Rd.(48237), pg. 1110

Orion

SENSOR DEVELOPMENTS INC., 1050 W. Silverbell Rd.(48359), pg. 990

Otsego

BERNEA FOOD SERVICE, INC., 557 Lincoln Rd.(49078), pg. 143

Owosso

Crown Leisure Products, 317 S. Elm St.(48867), pg. 200
MITCHELL CORPORATION OF OWOSSO, 123 N. Chipman St.(48867), pg. 761

Parma

Universal Vise & Tool Co., 8500 E. Michigan Ave.(49269), pg. 103

Paw Paw

WARNER VINEYARDS, 706 S. Kalamazoo St.(49079), pg. 1164

Pinconning

MAGLINE, INC., 503 S. Mercer St.(48650), pg. 700

Plainwell

Simpson Plainwell Paper Co., Inc., 200 Allegan St.(49080), pg. 1007

Plymouth

BRODER BROS. CO., 45555 Port St.(48170), pg. 178
FREUDENBERG-NOK (MI), 47690 E. Anchor Ct.(48170), pg. 432
LOU LARICHE CHEVROLET-SUBARU INC., 40875 Plymouth Rd.(48170), pg. 658
DON MASSEY CADILLAC INC., 40475 Ann Arbor Rd.(48170), pg. 719
NATIONAL CONCRETE PRODUCTS COMPANY, 939 S. Mill St.(48170), pg. 787
NORTHLAND CONTAINER CORP., 9070 General Dr.(48170), pg. 814
PLASTIPAK PACKAGING INC., 9135 General Ct.(48170), pg. 876
POWER PROCESS PIPING, INC., 45780 Port St.(48170), pg. 883
Saturn of Plymouth, 4301 Massey Dr.(48170), pg. 719

TAPCO PRODUCTS COMPANY, 45657 Port St.(48170-6010), pg. 1078

Pontiac

A B C APPLIANCE INC., One Silverdome Industrial Park(48343), pg. 2
GEORGE W. AUCH CO., 735 S. Paddock(48341), pg. 97
GenCon Services, Inc., 735 South Paddock St.(48341), pg. 98

Port Huron

Acheson Colloids Company, 1600 Washington Ave.(48060), pg. 12
ACHESON INDUSTRIES, INC., 511 Fort St., Rm. 315(48061-0489), pg. 12
Bindicator Company, 1915 Dove St., P.O. Box 9(48060), pg. 145
MARY MAXIM, INC., 2001 Holland Ave.(48060), pg. 722

Redford

Ziebart Products Group, 26500 Capital Ave.(48239), pg. 1217

Redford Township

Alro Specialty Metals, Redford, 24800 Plymouth Rd.(48239), pg. 44

Richmond

BEC INC., 37601 Logg Rd.(48062), pg. 106

River Rouge

BROAD VOGT & CONANT INC., 195 Campbell St.(48218), pg. 177

Rochester Hills

CHRISTIAN MEMORIAL CULTURAL CENTER, 521 E. Hamlin Rd.(48307), pg. 249
Electro-Wire Products, Inc., 1900 S. Livernois(48309), pg. 375
LETICA CORPORATION, 1700 W. Hamlin Rd.(48309), pg. 668
MACRO COMPUTER PRODUCTS INC., 2523 Product Court(48309), pg. 698
THE VIRTUAL GROUP, 2950 Waterview Dr.(48309), pg. 1153

Romulus

CHEMCENTRAL/Detroit, 13395 Huron River Dr.(48174-0906), pg. 241
EDGEWOOD TOOL & MANUFACTURING COMPANY, 8900 Inkster Rd.(48174), pg. 368
HEADER PRODUCTS INC., 11850 S. Wayne Rd.(48174), pg. 520

Roseville

ACTIVE TOOL & MANUFACTURING CO., INC., 32901 Gratiot Ave.(48066), pg. 15
ATLAS TOOL INC., 29880 Groesbeck Hwy.(48066), pg. 96
JEFFREY BUICK-NISSAN INC., 30800 Gratiot(48066), pg. 591
ROSEVILLE CHRYSLER PLYMOUTH INC., 25800 Gratiot(48066), pg. 949
U.S. MANUFACTURING CORP., 30855 Little Mack Ave.(48066), pg. 1136
The Weather Channel, Inc.-Detroit Sales Office, 25689 Kelly Road, Ste. D(48066), pg. 654

Rothbury

Kurdziel Iron of Rothbury, 2625 Winston Rd.(49452), pg. 646

Royal Oak

THE COON-DE VISSER CO., 1500 N. Stephenson Hwy.(48068), pg. 282
JIM FRESARD PONTIAC BUICK, INC., 400 N. Main St.(48067), pg. 432
Industrial & Automotive Fasteners, 3200 W. 14 Mile Rd.(48073), pg. 627
KEY MANUFACTURING GROUP, INC., 3200 W. 14 Mile Rd.(48073), pg. 627
ROYAL OAK FORD INC., 550 N. Woodward(48067), pg. 953
Warrick Controls, Inc., 4237 Normandy Ct.(48073), pg. 84

Saginaw

Cox Cable Saginaw, Inc., 720 North Bates St.(48602), pg. 294
DEB HOLDINGS, INC., 302 Waller St.(48605), pg. 323
DURO-LAST ROOFING, INC., 525 Morley Dr.(48601), pg. 355
Gase Bakery Co., 404 W. Genessee(48602), pg. 861
SBS Products, Inc., 302 Waller(48602), pg. 323
Saginaw Meat & Produce Company, P.O. Box 3304(48605), pg. 1137
U.S. GRAPHITE, INC., 1621 E. Holland Ave.(48601), pg. 1136

Saint Clair Shores

GENERAL SAFETY CORPORATION, 23001 Industrial Dr. W.(48080), pg. 450
JOHN M. OLSON COMPANY, 26210 Harper(48081), pg. 824
ROY O'BRIEN INC., 22201 E. Nine Mile Rd.(48080), pg. 820

Saline

CRESCIVE DIE & TOOL, INC., 905 Woodland Dr.(48176), pg. 298
MCNAUGHTON & GUNN, INC., 960 Woodland Dr.(48176), pg. 732
R & B MACHINE TOOL CO., 118 E. Michigan Ave.(48176), pg. 906
RENOSOL CORP., 1512 Woodland Dr.(48176), pg. 927
Saline Investment Co., P.O. Box 100(48176), pg. 906

Shelby

Oceana Foods, PO Box 156, 97 W. 2nd Street(49455), pg. 651

Sheridan

HAPPY HOLIDAY TREE FARMS, 3819 E. Sidney Rd.(48884), pg. 506

South Haven

South Haven Coil Inc., P.O. Box 409, (49090), pg. 553

Southfield

Allied Security Inc., Crossroads Centre, 16250 Northland Dr., Ste. 315(48075), pg. 39
Allsafe Security Inc., Crossroads Centre, 16250 Northland Dr., Ste. 317(48075), pg. 40
AMURCON CORPORATION, 26555 Evergreen, Ste. 1300(48076), pg. 70
Amurcon Equities, 26555 Evergreen, Ste. 1118(48076), pg. 70
Amurcon Management, 26555 Evergreen, Ste. 1118(48076), pg. 70
Amurcon Securities Corp., 26555 Evergreen, Ste. 1118(48076), pg. 70
The ARGOS Group, American Center Bldg., Ste 675, 27777 Franklin Rd.(48034), pg. 123
Automated Marketing Systems, Inc., Travellers Tower II, 26533 Evergreen(48076), pg. 100
AVIS FORD INC., 29200 Telegraph Rd.(48034), pg. 102
Backer Spielvogel Bates, Inc., Vanguard Ctr., 23800 Ten Mile Rd., Ste. 228(48034), pg. 109
BARTON-MALOW ENTERPRISES, INC., American Center Bldg., 27777 Franklin Rd., Ste. 800(48034), pg. 123
Leo Burnett Company, 26555 Evergreen Rd.(48076), pg. 192
CMI INTERNATIONAL INC., 30333 Southfield Rd.(48076), pg. 202
CUNA Central District, 15600 Providence Drive(48075), pg. 205
Clayton Manufacturing Div., Dynamic Equipment, 24750 Swanson Rd.(48034), pg. 254
CONTAINER PRODUCTS INC., 20245 W. 12 Mile Rd., Ste. 200(48076), pg. 278
CONTRACT INTERIORS INC., 10 Oak Hollow, Suite 200(48034), pg. 280
Crystal Refining, 21700 Northwest Hwy.(48075), pg. 651
DG Trim Products Div., 26899 Northwestern Hwy., Ste. 400(48034), pg. 565
W.B. DONER & COMPANY, 25900 Northwestern Hwy.(48075), pg. 344
ENGINEERING SERVICE, INC., 21556 Telegraph Rd.(48034), pg. 382
FTD/FLORISTS' TRANSWORLD DELIVERY ASSOCIATION, 29200 Northwestern Hwy.(48034), pg. 395
GIFFELS ASSOCIATES, INC., 25200 Telegraph Rd.(48034-2599), pg. 457
GOLDFARB & COMPANY ADVERTISING, 26250 Northwestern Hwy.(48076), pg. 467
GUARDIAN ALARM CO., 20800 Southfield Rd.(48075), pg. 491
HARLAN ELECTRIC CO., 24000 Telegraph Rd.(48034), pg. 509
HARLEY ELLINGTON PIERCE YEE ASSOCIATES, INC., 26913 Northwestern Hwy., Ste. 200(48034), pg. 509
Harman Automotive, 27365 W. Eleven Mile Rd.(48034), pg. 514
HOMEMAKER SHOPS, INC., 25899 W. 12 Mile Rd.(48034), pg. 542
Indian Head Gasket Div.-Detroit, 26899 Northwestern Hwy., Ste. 400(48034), pg. 565
INDIAN HEAD INDUSTRIES INC., 26899 Northwestern Hwy., Ste. 400(48034), pg. 565
Joy Service, 21700 Northwest Hwy.(48075), pg. 651
LAKESIDE REFINING CO. INC., 21700 Northwestern Hwy., Ste. 1160(48075), pg. 651
League Life Insurance Co., P.O. Box 430, (48232), pg. 205
Lear Siegler Seating Corp., 21557 Telegraph Rd.(48034), pg. 664
NORMAN LEVY ASSOCIATES, INC., 21415 Civic Center Dr.(48076), pg. 672
Linens & More, 25889 W. 12 Mile Rd.(48034), pg. 542
MGM Brakes Div., 26899 Northwestern Hwy., Ste. 400(48034), pg. 565
MACCABEES MUTUAL LIFE INSURANCE, 25800 Northwestern Hwy.(48037), pg. 696
MARS ADVERTISING CO., 24209 Northwestern Hwy.(48075), pg. 713
R. J. MARSHALL CO., 26776 W. 12 Mile Rd.(48034), pg. 714
MAXITROL CO., 23555 Telegraph Rd.(48037), pg. 723
ART MORAN PONTIAC-GMC INC., 29300 Telegraph Rd.(48034), pg. 769
NEW YORK CARPET WORLD INC., 23840 W. Eight Mile Rd.(48034), pg. 802
Peerless Distributing Co., 21700 Northwest Hwy.(48075), pg. 652
PETERSON AMERICAN CORP., 21200 Telegraph Rd.(48034), pg. 864
Petroleum Specialties, 21700 Northwest Hwy.(48075), pg. 652
Prime Technology Inc., 21665 Melrose Ave., Bldg. 7(48075), pg. 889
Professional Information Managment, 24901 Northwestern Hwy., Ste. 400(48034), pg. 988
PROGRESSIVE TOOL & INDUSTRIES CO., 21000 Telegraph Rd.(48034), pg. 894
Sterling Savings & Loan, 28400 Northwestern Hwy., 988
STONE & SIMONS ADVERTISING, INC., 24245 Northwestern Hwy.(48075), pg. 1051
TAMAROFF BUICK INC., 28585 Telegraph Rd.(48034), pg. 1077
Tamaroff Leasing Co., 28585 Telegraph Rd.(48034), pg. 1077
USA Network, 2000 Town Center, Ste. 2460(48075), pg. 1124
VESCO OIL CORP., 16055 W. 12 Mile Rd.(48076), pg. 1149
WKBD, Inc., 26905 W. 11 Mile Rd.(48034), pg. 292
Western International Media Corporation, Maccabees Center, 25800 Northwestern Hwy., Ste. 882(48075), pg. 1180
Wickes Mfg. Co., P.O. Box 999(48037-0999), pg. 262
YAFFE & CO., First Center Office Plaza, 26913 Northwestern Hwy., Ste. 500(48034), pg. 1207

Southgate

ASC INCORPORATED, One Sunroof Center(48195), pg. 7
Aeromotive Systems Co., One Sunroof Center(48195), pg. 7
American Sunroof Company, One Sunroof Center(48195), pg. 7
Automobile Specialty Co., One Sunroof Center(48195), pg. 7
STU EVANS LINCOLN-MERCURY INC., 16800 Fort St.(48195), pg. 390
SOUTHGATE FORD INC., 16501 Fort St.(48195), pg. 1023

Sparta

HANDY WACKS CORPORATION, 100 E. Averill, P.O. Box 26(49345), pg. 505
HAVILAND/WILBUR-ELLIS AGRICULTURAL, 4160 Ten Mile N. W.(49345), pg. 517
SPEEDRACK PRODUCTS GROUP, LTD., 1015 Nine Mile Rd., N.W.(49345), pg. 1029

Spring Lake

SINTEL, INC., 18437 171st Ave.(49456), pg. 1008

Springport

Specialty Castings, 211 Mill St., P.O. Box 129(49284), pg. 598

Sterling Heights

AUTOMOTIVE PLASTIC TECHNOLOGIES, INC., 6600 E. Fifteen Mile Rd.(48312), pg. 101
Borg Warner Automotive, inc., P.O Box 8002, 6700 18 1/2 Mile Rd.(48311), pg. 166
Borg-Warner Automotive, Inc., Control Systems, 6700 18 1/2 Mile Rd.(48314), pg. 166
CHIVAS PRODUCTS LTD., 42555 Merrill Rd.(48314-3266), pg. 248
Ghafari Associates, Inc., 41150 Technology Pky. Dr., Ste. 106(48314), pg. 455
JEROME-DUNCAN FORD, 8000 Ford Country Ln.(48314), pg. 593
STERLING HEIGHTS DODGE, INC., 40111 Van Dyke(48313), pg. 1046
Transilwrap Co., Inc., 6635 Nineteen Mile Rd.(48078), pg. 1107
BUFF WHELAN CHEVROLET & GEO, INC., 40445 Van Dyke Ave.(48313), pg. 1185

Stevensville

ENERGY BROKERS GUILD, 2961 W. Glenlord Rd.(49127), pg. 381
WOLLIN PRODUCTS, INC., 4295 N. Rooisevelt(49127), pg. 1199

Sturgis

THE HARTER GROUP, 400 Prairie Ave.(49091), pg. 513
Sturgis Foundry Corp., 1000 W. West(49091), pg. 83
STURGIS IRON & METAL COMPANY, INC., 70675 S. Centerville Rd.(49091), pg. 1055

Taylor

F.X. COUGHLIN CO., 27050 Wick Rd.(48180), pg. 289
Direct Marketing Group, 6400 Monroe Blvd.(48180-1884), pg. 879
MEYER JEWELERS, 20500 Eureka Rd., Ste. 200(48180), pg. 746
MURRAY'S DISCOUNT AUTO STORES, 21500 Trolley Industrial Dr.(48180), pg. 777
Sealy Mattress Company of Michigan, Inc., 21450 Trolley Industrial Dr.(48180), pg. 985

Tecumseh

FARADAY, INC., 805 S. Maumee(49286), pg. 399

Three Rivers

ARMSTRONG INTERNATIONAL, INC., 900 Maple(49093), pg. 83
Armstrong Machine Works, 816 Maple(49093), pg. 83
Armstrong-Yoshitake, Inc., 816 Maple St.(49093), pg. 84

DOCK FOUNDRY COMPANY, 428 Fourth St.(49093), pg. 342
THE JOHNSON CORPORATION, 805 Wood St(49093), pg. 597
Three Rivers Iron & Metal, 206 E. Broadway(49093), pg. 1055

Traverse City

CHERRY CENTRAL COOPERATIVE, 1771 N. US 31 South(49685), pg. 243
EMPIRE NATIONAL BANK, 1227 E. Front St.(49684), pg. 379

Trenton

MCLOUTH STEEL, 1650 W. Jefferson Ave.(48183), pg. 731

Troy

ROBERT B. AIKENS & ASSOCIATES INC., 2690 Crooks Rd.(48084), pg. 26
ALARON INC., 185 Park St.(48083), pg. 30
R. J. Baker Advertising, Inc., 1301 W. Long Lake Rd.(48098), pg. 1051
CADILLAC PRODUCTS, INC., 530 Stephenson Hwy.(48083), pg. 207
Cunningham Engineers, Inc., 5800 Crooks Rd.(48098), pg. 305
CUNNINGHAM-LIMP DEVELOPMENT CO., 5800 Crooks, Ste. 100(48098), pg. 305
G.B. DUPONT CO., INC., 500 W. Long Lake Rd.(48098), pg. 354
EFFICIENT ENGINEERING CO., 130 Town Center Dr.(48084), pg. 371
EL DORADO TIRE CO., 1120 E. Long Lake Rd.(48098), pg. 372
ENGINEERING TECHNOLOGY LTD. (E.T.), 777 Chicago Rd.(48083), pg. 382
EWI, Inc.-Stamping & Die Div., 500 Stephenson Hwy., Ste. 203(48084), pg. 361
Fastcut Tool Corporation, 1830 Stephenson Hgwy.(48083), pg. 183
Giffels Hoyem Basso, Inc., 3150 Livernois, Ste. 300(48083), pg. 457
Gray & Kilgore, Inc., 100 W. Big Beaver Rd., Ste. 300(48084), pg. 950
H. G. Productions, 1301 W. Long Lake Rd.(48098), pg. 1051
HARMONY HOUSE RECORDS & TAPES, 1755 E. Maple(48083-4287), pg. 510
Industrial Fastening Systems Group, 433 Stephenson Hwy.(48084), pg. 749
Ingersoll Milling Machine Co., Timberland Office Park, 5455 Corporate Dr., Ste. 200(48098), pg. 568
KOLON, BITTKER & DESMOND, INC., Ameritech Publishing Bldg., 100 E. Big Beaver, Ste. 1000(48083), pg. 641
MID-STATES PETROLEUM INC., 2146 Livernois(48099), pg. 750
Motor Consumer Books, 5600 Crooks Rd.(48098), pg. 522
Motor Crash Estimating Guide, 5600 Crooks Rd.(48098), pg. 522
NORTHERN WIRE & CABLE, INC., 1902 Northwood(48084), pg. 814
O/E AUTOMATION, INC., 3290 W. Big Beaver, Ste. 132(48084), pg. 819
MIKE SAVOIE CHEVROLET INC., 1900 W. Maple Rd.(48099), pg. 973
DEAN SELLERS FORD INC., 2600 W. Maple(48084), pg. 988
SIMONS MICHELSON ZIEVE, INC., 900 Wilshire Dr.(48084), pg. 1006
SOMERSET PONTIAC GMC INC., 1850 W. Maple Rd.(48084), pg. 1017
STONE, AUGUST, BAKER COMMUNICATIONS COMPANIES, 1301 W. Long Lake Rd.(48098), pg. 1050
Stone August Baker Public Relations, 1301 W. Long Lake Rd., Ste. 350(48098), pg. 1051
The Strategy Company, 1301 W. Long Lake Rd.(48098), pg. 1051
Tidy Car International, Inc., 1290 E. Maple(48084), pg. 1217
WAGGONER CORP., 1400 Rochester Rd.(48083), pg. 1158
Ziebart Corp., 1290 E. Maple Rd.(48084), pg. 1217
ZIEBART INTERNATIONAL CORPORATION, 1290 E. Maple Rd.(48084), pg. 1217

Utica

CHURCH & CHURCH INC., 7669 Auburn Rd.(48317), pg. 249
DE NOVO CORPORATION, 48380 Van Dyke(48317), pg. 321
JL Tool & Processing, Inc., 14080 23 Mile Rd.(48315), pg. 935
LOMBARDI FOODSERVICE, INC., 2465 23 Mile Rd.(48316), pg. 681
MNP CORP., 44225 Utica Rd.(48317), pg. 693
Tastee Freez Intl. Inc., 48380 Van Dyke(48317), pg. 321

Vanderbilt

H & H TUBE & MANUFACTURING CO., 108 Garfield St.(49795), pg. 495

Vicksburg

Triple S Plastics, Inc., 14320 S. Portage Rd.(49097), pg. 1114
TRIPLE S TECHNOLOGIES, INC., 14320 S. Portage Rd.(49097), pg. 1114

Wakefield

Connor Forest Industries, Inc., 601 Sunday Lake St.(49968), pg. 175

Walled Lake

AMERICAN PLASTIC TOYS INC., 799 Ladd Rd.(48390), pg. 59
Ingersoll Engineers, 39500 14 Mile Rd., Ste. 207(48390), pg. 568
WILLIAMS INTERNATIONAL, 2280 W. Maple Rd.(48390), pg. 1191

Warren

Acme Trim, 5501 Enterprise Dr.(48092), pg. 13
ART VAN FURNITURE INC., 6500 E. Fourteen Mile Rd.(48092), pg. 86
AUTOMOTIVE MOULDING COMPANY, 23751 Amber(48089), pg. 101
COLOR CUSTOM, INC., 24060 Hoover Rd.(48089), pg. 264
Electro-Spray Enameling, 22534 Groesbeck Hwy.(48089-2644), pg. 538
ELIAS BROTHERS RESTAURANTS, INC., 4199 Marcy Rd.(48091), pg. 376
EQUIPMENT MANUFACTURING, INC., 21550 Hoover Rd.(48089), pg. 385
F & M DISTRIBUTORS INC., 25800 Sherwood(48091), pg. 393
FOLAND'S JEWELRY BROKERS, 4100 E. 14 Mile(48092), pg. 421
Gentz Industries Inc., 23600 Schoenherr(48090), pg. 431
GROESBECK LUMBER & SUPPLY, INC., 23155 Groesbeck Hwy.(48089), pg. 489
HOFLEY MANUFACTURING COMPANY, 22534 Groesbeck Hwy.(48089), pg. 538
IROQUOIS DIE & MFG. CO., 24400 Hoover(48089), pg. 582
Knurlet Tool Co., 24807 Romano(48091), pg. 618
MACHINING ENTERPRISES INC., 11400 Toepfer(48089), pg. 696
MANUFACTURERS PRODUCTS COMPANY, 26020 Sherwood Ave.(48091), pg. 705
MID-WEST PAPER PRODUCTS COMPANY, 12350 E. Nine Mile Rd.(48089), pg. 750
NATIONAL LUMBER CO., 24595 Groesbeck Hwy.(48089), pg. 792
PIONEER ENGINEERING & MANUFACTURING CO., 2500 E. Nine Mile Rd.(48091), pg. 871
Pioneer Manufacturing Engineering Div., 2500 E. Nine Mile Rd.(48091), pg. 871
Pioneer Research & Development Div., 2500 E. Nine Mile Rd.(48091), pg. 871
Precise Technology & Electronics, Inc., 24727 Gibson(48089), pg. 27
PRESTIGE STAMPING, INC., 23513 Groesbeck Hwy.(48089), pg. 888
PRODUCTION TOOL SUPPLY CO., 8655 E. 8 Mile Rd.(48089), pg. 893
RING TECHNOLOGIES, INC., 12901 Stephens Dr.(48089), pg. 935
RINKE PONTIAC-GMC CO., 27100 Van Dyke(48093), pg. 935

Waterford

DUNHAM'S ATHLEISURE CORPORATION, 5000 Dixie Hwy.(48329), pg. 353

Wayne

JACK DEMMER FORD, INC., 37300 Michigan Ave.(48184), pg. 328
MARK CHEVROLET INC., 33200 Michigan Ave.(48184), pg. 708
TRANSCO INC., 35005 Michigan Ave.(48184), pg. 1107

Westland

MARTIN UNIVERSAL DESIGN, INC., 4444 Lawton Ave.(48208), pg. 715
Red Spot Westland Inc., 555 S. Edwin(48185), pg. 919

White Pigeon

The Andersons White Pigeon Terminal, 13600 Anderson Rd.(49099), pg. 74
White Pigeon Paper Company, River St.(49099), pg. 87

Wixom

Shelly Data Systems, 48733 West Rd.(48393), pg. 793

Wyoming

CHEMCENTRAL/Grand Rapids, 2940 Stafford Ave., S.W.(49548), pg. 241
Frames Unlimited Inc., 3343 Lousma Drive S.E.(49548), pg. 1220
ZIMDAR ENTERPRISES, 3343 Lousma Drive S.E.(49548), pg. 1220

Ypsilanti

Ann Arbor Assembly Corporation, 251 Airport Industrial Dr.(48198), pg. 368
Ypsi-Arbor Lanes, 2985 Washtenaw(48197), pg. 482
ZANTOP INTERNATIONAL AIRLINES, INC., 840 Willow Run Airport(48198-0840), pg. 1216

Zeeland

Bell & Howell Mailmobile Co., 411 E. Roosevelt St.(49464), pg. 135
HOWARD MILLER CLOCK COMPANY, 860 East Main Ave.(49464), pg. 754
ODL INCORPORATED, 215 E. Roosevelt Rd.(49464), pg. 819

MINNESOTA

Albert Lea

FARMSTEAD FOODS, INC., E. Main St., Box 1059(56007), pg. 402
Streater Store Fixtures Div., 411 S. 1st Ave.(56007), pg. 608
DAVE SYVERSON LINCOLN MERCURY, 2310 E. Main St.(56007), pg. 1071

Alexandria

First American Bank, 720 Broadway(56308), pg. 173

Anoka

AEC, 2022 N. Ferry St.(55303), pg. 3

Arden Hills

LAND O'LAKES, INC., 4001 Lexington Ave. N.(55126), pg. 653
Land O'Lakes Farm Centers, 4001 Lexington Ave.(55126), pg. 654
MSI INSURANCE COMPANIES, Two Pine Tree Dr.(55112-3793), pg. 693
Procor Technologies, 4001 Lexington Ave.(55126), pg. 654

Austin

ASTRUP DRUGS, INC., 1417 S.W. First Ave.(55912), pg. 93
Catalogue Marketing, Inc., 501 16th Ave., N.E.(55912), pg. 533
HUNTTING ELEVATOR CO., 109 N. Main St.(55912), pg. 555

Avon

D.H. BLATTNER & SONS, INC., P.O. Box 37(56310), pg. 156

Bayport

ANDERSEN WINDOWS INC., 100 Fourth Ave. No.(55003-1096), pg. 72

Benson

TYLER LIMITED PARTNERSHIP, P.O. Box 249, East Highway 12(56215), pg. 1122

Blaine

Jorgensen Steel & Aluminum/Minneapolis, 1775 101st Ave. N.E.(55434), pg. 606

Bloomington

ABI National Accounts, 8120 Penn Ave., South50
CUNA North Central District, 2780 East 82nd St.(55420), pg. 205
CLARKLIFT OF MINNESOTA, INC., 501 W. 78th St.(55420), pg. 253
HITCHCOCK INDUSTRIES, INC., 8701 Harriet Ave. S.(55420), pg. 536
LIFETOUCH, INC., 7831 Glenroy Rd.(55439), pg. 675
Lifetouch Portrait Studios Inc., 7831 Glenroy Rd.(55437), pg. 675
Lifetouch Senior Portraits Inc., 7831 Glenroy Rd.(55439), pg. 675
Lifetouch Video Creations, Inc., 7831 Glenroy Rd.(55439), pg. 675
Minnesota Sun Publications, 7831 East Bush Lake Rd.(55435), pg. 442
VINYL THERM, INC., 321 W. 83rd St.(55420), pg. 1152

Brainerd

ACROMETAL COMPANIES, INC., 210 N.E. 10th Ave.(56401), pg. 14
ANDERSON BROTHERS CONSTRUCTION BRAINERD, 1500 Highway 210 E.(56401), pg. 72
Brainerd Daily Dispatch, 506 James St. Box D(56401), pg. 1042
First American Bank, 321 S. Seventh St.(56401), pg. 173

Breckenridge

First American Bank, 225 N. Fifth St.(56520), pg. 173

Brooklyn Center

APG Division, 1601 67th Ave. No.(55430), pg. 1140

Burnsville

OUR OWN HARDWARE COMPANY, 2300 W. Hwy. 13(55337), pg. 832

Byron

ARGILAND COMPANY, 302 Byron Ave. N.(55920), pg. 81

Cambridge

Blue Fox Tackle Co., 645 N. Emerson(55008), pg. 810
MOTEK ENGINEERING & MANUFACTURING COMPANY, 625 Second Ave., S.E.(55008), pg. 773
Vibrax/MCA Inc., 645 N. Emerson(55008), pg. 810

Chanhassen

THE INSTANT WEB COMPANIES, 7951 Powers Blvd.(55317), pg. 571
REDMOND PRODUCTS, INC., 18930 W. 78th St.(55317), pg. 920
United Mailing, Inc., 1001 Park Rd.(55317), pg. 571
Victory Envelope, Inc., 1000 Park Rd.(55317), pg. 571

Chaska

American Crystal Sugar Co., P.O. Box 65, (55318), pg. 51
LAKE REGION MANUFACTURING COMPANY, INC., 340 Lake Hazeltine Dr.(55318), pg. 651

Circle Pines

BERMO, INC., 4501 Ball Rd., N.E.(55014), pg. 143

Cloquet

DIAMOND BRANDS, INC., 1800 Cloquet Ave.(55720), pg. 335

Cold Spring

Granit-Bronz, Inc., 202 S. 3rd Ave.(56320), pg. 260
Royal Melrose Granites, 202 S. 3rd Ave.(56320), pg. 260

Coon Rapids

GOEBEL ART, INC., 3401 Coon Rapids Blvd.(55433), pg. 464

Crookston

First American National Bank, P.O. Box 613, (56716), pg. 173

Detroit Lakes

First American Bank, P.O. Box 827, (56502), pg. 173

Dodge Center

MCNEILUS COMPANIES, Hwy. 732

Duluth

A & E Business Products, 4424 Haines Rd.(55811), pg. 1081
Davidson Printing Company, 4920 Ramsey St.(55807), pg. 21
NORTHERN DRUG COMPANY, 4444 Haines Rd.(55811), pg. 814
WDIO-TV, 10 Observation Rd.(55811), pg. 549

Eagan

BROWN-MINNEAPOLIS TANK & FABRICATING CO., 2875 Highway 182
DART TRANSIT COMPANY, INC., 800 Lone Oak Rd.(55121), pg. 316
Kilsby-Roberts/Twin Cities, 1034 Gemini Rd.(55121), pg. 606
THE SPORTSMAN'S GUIDE, INC., 900 Apollo Rd.(55121), pg. 1032
Transilwrap Co., Inc., 1299 Eagan Industrial Rd.(55121), pg. 1107
WEST PUBLISHING CO., 610 Opperman Dr.(55123), pg. 1177
West Services, Inc., 610 Opperman Dr.(55123), pg. 1177

Eden Prairie

Alco Health Services Corp.-Minneapolis, 6810 Shady Oak Rd.(55344), pg. 31
ARGOSY ELECTRONICS, INC., 10300 W. 70th St.(55344), pg. 82
E.F. JOHNSON COMPANY, 11095 Viking Dr., Ste. 220(55344), pg. 598
MAGNETIC DATA, INC., 6754 Shady Oak Rd.(55344), pg. 700
C. H. ROBINSON CO. INC., 8100 Mitchell Rd., Ste. 200(55344), pg. 939
STARKEY LABORATORIES, INC., 6700 Washington Ave. S.(55344), pg. 1040
E.A. SWEEN COMPANY, 16101 W. 78th St.(55344), pg. 1066
WESTERN PETROLEUM COMPANY, 9531 W. 78th St.(55344), pg. 1181
ZYTEC CORP., 7575 Market Place Dr.(55344), pg. 1221

Edina

Animal Fair, 5215 Edina Industrial Blvd.(55439), pg. 978
BYERLY'S INC., 7171 France Ave. So.(55435), pg. 198
KEY CADILLAC, INC., 6825 York Ave. S.(55435), pg. 626
TMP Worldwide, Inc., 6800 France Ave. South, Ste. 500(55435), pg. 1074

Elk River

THE CRETEX COMPANIES, 311 Lowell Ave.(55330), pg. 299
UNITED POWER ASSOCIATION, P.O. Box 800(55330), pg. 1134

Excelsior

FARMHAND, INC., 23610 Highway 7(55331), pg. 402
LYMAN LUMBER COMPANY, P.O. Box 40, 300 Morse Ave.(55331), pg. 689

Fairfax

SOUTH CENTRAL CO-OP, Hwy. 4, S.(55332), pg. 1019

Fairmont

ROSENS DIVERSIFIED, INC., 1120 Lake Ave.(56031), pg. 948
Rosens, Inc., 1120 Lake Ave.(56031), pg. 948

Faribault

FARIBAULT WOOLEN MILL CO., 1500 Second Ave., N. W.(55021), pg. 399

Farmington

DAKOTA ELECTRIC ASSOCIATION, 4300 220th St. W.(55024), pg. 312

Fergus Falls

Proximity Controls Corp., P.O. Box 386, Route 6(56537), pg. 356

Forest Lake

Century Fence Co., P. O. Box 100(55025), pg. 235
PLASTECH CORPORATION, 20 N. Lake St.(55025), pg. 874

Fridley

Hardwood Visuals, 5900 Main St. N.E.(55432), pg. 547
KURT MANUFACTURING CO. INC., 5280 Main St. N.E.(55421), pg. 646
Strite-Anderson Die Castings, 7585 Hwy. 65 N.E.(55432), pg. 646

Golden Valley

J.H. LARSON ELECTRICAL COMPANY, 700 Colorado Ave., S.(55416), pg. 659
JIM LUPIENT ENTERPRISES, 7100 Wayzata Blvd.(55426), pg. 687

Hastings

HASTINGS CO-OP CREAMERY COMPANY, 1701 Vermillion St.(55033), pg. 516
POLKA DOT DAIRY, 110 E. 17th St.(55033), pg. 879
SMEAD MANUFACTURING COMPANY, 600 E. Smead Blvd.(55033), pg. 1011
Thom Thumb Food Market Inc., 110 E. 17th St.(55033), pg. 879

Hibbing

Ryan Construction Company Of Minnesota, Ryan Building(55746), pg. 958

Hopkins

Powell's Inc., 1707 E. Excelsior Blvd.(55343), pg. 972
Spantek Division, 1520 So. 5th St.(55343), pg. 1140
Walser Leasing Inc., 317 Main St.(55343), pg. 1161

Hutchinson

FIRST STATE FEDERAL SAVINGS & LOAN, 201 Main St., S.(55350-2573), pg. 413
Firstate Services, Inc., 201 Main St., S.(55350-2573), pg. 414

International Falls

First American Bank, P.O. Box 511, (56649), pg. 173

Inver Grove Heights

CENEX (FARMERS UNION CENTRAL EXCHANGE, INC.), 5500 Cenex Dr.(55075), pg. 231

Lakeville

CHEMCENTRAL/Minnesota, 21675 Hamburg Ave.(55044), pg. 242
Theradyne Corporation, 21730 Hanover Ave.(55044), pg. 1065

Litchfield

FIRST DISTRICT ASSOCIATION, 216 W. Commercial St.(55355), pg. 412
JOHNSON BROS. CORP., Hwy. 22 So.(55355), pg. 597

Little Falls

Crestliner, Inc., 609 13th Ave. NE(55345), pg. 758
Glastron Boats, 700 West River Rd.(56345), pg. 759
Larson Boats, Paul Larson Memorial Dr.(56345), pg. 758

Long Prairie

Long Prairie Packing Co., Old Hwy. 71, N.W.(56347), pg. 948

Mankato

HINIKER COMPANY, Rt. 5, Box 3407(56001), pg. 535
HONEYMEAD PRODUCTS CO., 2020 S. Riverfront Drive(56001), pg. 542
HUBBARD MILLING COMPANY, 424 N. Riverfront Dr.(56002), pg. 549
TAYLOR CORPORATION, 1725 Roe Crest Dr.(56001), pg. 1081

Maple Grove

Minneapolis Auto Auction, 8001 Jefferson Hwy.(55369), pg. 293
WORLD AEROSPACE CORPORATION, 8625 Monticello Lane, N.(55369), pg. 1202

Maplewood

KSTP-AM, Inc., 2792 Maplewood Dr.(55109), pg. 549

Marcell

Valley Forest Resources Co., P.O. Box 27, (56657), pg. 1152

Marshall

First American Bank Southwest, 208 College Dr.(56258), pg. 173
LYON COUNTY CO-OP OIL CO., 1100 East Main(56258), pg. 690
SCHWAN'S SALES ENTERPRISES, 115 W. College Dr.(56258), pg. 980

Minneapolis

A. E. Development Corp., 8810 10th Ave. North(55427), pg. 731
ADOLFSON & PETERSON, INC., 6701 W. 23rd St.(55426), pg. 18
Allright Parking Minnesota, Inc., 320 Young-Quinlan Bldg., 81 S. Ninth St.(55402), pg. 42
AMERICAN FOODS GROUP, INC., 5738 Olson Memorial Hwy.(55422), pg. 54
AMERICAN LINEN SUPPLY COMPANY, 47 S. 9th St.(55402), pg. 57
AMERIDATA, INC., 10200-51st Ave. North(55442), pg. 66
ARROW TANK & ENGINEERING CO., 8950 Evergreen Blvd.(55433), pg. 85
Atlas Manufacturing Division, 732 30th Ave. S.E.(55414), pg. 1140
AUGSBURG FORTRESS, PUBLISHERS, 426 S. 5th St.(55415), pg. 98
BACHMAN'S, INC., 6010 Lyndale Ave. S.(55419), pg. 108
BANK M F & COMPANY, INC., 615 First Ave., N.E.(55413), pg. 117
BANK SHARES, INC., P.O. Box 1467(55480), pg. 117
BANNER ENGINEERING CORP., 9714 10th Ave. N.(55441), pg. 118
BAXTER ADVERTISING, INC., Interchange Tower, 600 S. Highway 169, Ste. 1950(55426), pg. 127
BENNETT RINGROSE WOLSFELD JARVIS, INC., 700 Third St., S.(55415), pg. 139
BERGQUIST COMPANY, INC., 5300 Edina Industrial Blvd.(55439), pg. 141
BITUMINOUS ROADWAYS, INC., 2825 Cedar Ave. S.(55407), pg. 153
M. R. BOLIN INC., 2318 Park Ave. S.(55404), pg. 162
BRAUNS FASHIONS, INC., 10000 Valley View Rd.(55344), pg. 172
BRIDGEMAN'S RESTAURANTS INC., 6009 Wayzata Blvd.(55416), pg. 175
Browne Medical Systems, Inc., 8990 Springbrook Dr., Ste. 120(55433), pg. 867
BUHLER INC., 1100 Xenium Ln.(55441), pg. 187
BUREAU OF ENGRAVING, 500 S. Fourth St.(55415), pg. 189
Butter Kernel Products, 706 2nd Ave., So.(55402), pg. 399
CBM INDUSTRIES, INC., 13220 Co. Rd. 199
CME-KHBB ADVERTISING, 222 S. Ninth St.(55402), pg. 202
Cargill Citro-America, Inc., P.O. Box 9300(55440), pg. 219
Cargill Financial Markets Div., P.O. Box 9300(55440), pg. 219
Cargill Flour Milling Div., P.O. Box 9300(55440), pg. 219
Cargill Nutrena Feed, P.O. Box 9300(55440), pg. 219
Cargill Salt Division, P.O. Box 9300, (55440), pg. 219
Cargill Seed Div., P.O. Box 9300(55440), pg. 219
CARLSON COMPANIES, INC., Carlson Parkway(55459), pg. 220
Carlson International Division, P.O. Box 59159, Carlson Parkway(55459), pg. 221
Carlson Learning Company, Carlson Parkway(55459), pg. 221
Carlson Leasing, Inc., P.O Box 59159, Carlson Parkway(55459-8215), pg. 221
Carlson Marketing Group, Inc., P.O. Box 59159, Carlson Parkway(55459), pg. 221
Carlson Promotion Division, P.O. Box 59159, Carlson Parkway(55459), pg. 221
Carlson Real Estate Company, 45 S. 7th St., Ste. 2222(55402), pg. 221
Carlson Retail Marketing, Carlson Parkway(55459-8207), pg. 221
Carlson Travel Group, Inc., P.O. Box 59159, Carlson Parkway(55459), pg. 221
Carlson Travel Network International, P.O. Box 59159, Carlson Pkwy.(55459), pg. 221
Carlson Travel Network Retail, P.O. Box 59159, Carlson Pkwy.(55459), pg. 221
Carlson Travel Network-Commercial, Carlson Parkway(55459), pg. 221
Carlson Travel Network-Retail, P.O. Box 59159, Carlson Parkway(55459), pg. 221
CARMICHAEL LYNCH, INC., 800 Hennepin Ave.(55403), pg. 222
CAROUSEL SNACK BARS OF MINNESOTA, 9549 Penn Ave., S.(55431), pg. 224
Carter Day Co., 500 73rd Ave., N.E.(55432), pg. 226
CARTER DAY INDUSTRIES, INC., 500 73rd Ave., N.E.(55432), pg. 226
Carter Day International, Inc., 500 73rd Ave., N.E.(55432), pg. 226
CASE FOLEY SACKETT, INC., 708 North 1st St., Ste. 110(55401), pg. 227
CASH PLUS, INC., 222 S. Ninth St., Ste. 2200(55402), pg. 228
Cat Pumps Corporation, 1681 94th Lane N.E.(55434), pg. 340
CLARITY COVERDALE RUEFF ADVERTISING, 415 First Ave. N.(55401), pg. 251
COLLE & MCVOY, INC., 7900 International Dr.(55425), pg. 261
Colony Hotels & Resorts, Inc., Carlson Parkway(55459), pg. 221
COLWELL INDUSTRIES, INC., 123 N. 3rd St.(55401), pg. 267
COWLES MEDIA COMPANY, 329 Portland Ave.(55415), pg. 291
Dakota Pork Industries, 5738 Olson Memorial Hwy.(55422), pg. 54
Damart/TMP Worldwide, 7700 France Ave., South(55435), pg. 1074

DAYTON ROGERS MFG. CO., 2824 13th Ave., S.(55407), pg. 321
DEALERS MANUFACTURING COMPANY, 5130 Main St. N.E.(55421), pg. 322
DESPATCH INDUSTRIES, 63 St. Anthony Pkwy.(55418), pg. 332
DIVERSIFIED DYNAMICS INC., 1681 94th Lane N.E.(55434), pg. 340
EGAN COS., 7100 Medicine Lake Rd.(55427), pg. 371
Egan McKay Electrical Contractors, 7100 Medicine Lake Rd.(55427), pg. 371
Egan & Sons Air Conditioning Co., 7100 Medicine Lake Rd.(55427), pg. 371
Egan & Sons Co., 7100 Medicine Lake Rd.(55427), pg. 371
Egan & Sons Insulation, 7100 Medicine Lake Rd.(55427), pg. 371
Ellerbe Becket Construction Services, 800 LaSalle Ave.(55425), pg. 378
ELLERBE BECKET, INC., 800 LaSalle Av.(55402), pg. 378
Ellerbe Becket-Minneapolis, 800 LaSalle Ave.(55425), pg. 378
Fairway Foods, Inc., 4567 W. 80th St.(55437), pg. 539
FARIBAULT FOODS INC., 1050 Baker Bldg., 706 2nd Ave. S.(55402), pg. 399
Fidelity Acceptance Corporation, 79 Towle Bldg., 330 2nd Ave. S.(55401), pg. 1016
Dave Fischbein Co., 2700 30th Ave. S.(55406), pg. 8
Flexmedics Corporation, 620 Ford Center, 420 N. 5th St.(55401-1332), pg. 867
FLO-PAC CORPORATION, 700 N. Washington Ave., Ste. 400(55401), pg. 419
Flour City Brush Co., 918 N. 3rd St.(55401), pg. 419
FOLEY-BELSAW COMPANY, 3300 E. Fifth St.(55418), pg. 422
Foley Martens Company, 3300 E. Fifth St.(55418), pg. 422
Food Ingredients, P.O. Box 116(55440), pg. 653
FORMAC CORPORATION, 4701 Humboldt Ave. N.(55430), pg. 424
GABBERT'S, INC., 3501 Galleria(55435), pg. 441
GAGE MARKETING GROUP, 10000 Highway 55(55441-6365), pg. 441
General Growth Center Companies, Inc., 400 South Hwy. 169, Ste. 800(55426), pg. 449
S. J. GROVES & SONS COMPANY, 10000 Hwy. 55 West(55441), pg. 490
C.F. HAGLIN & SONS, 4005 W. 65th St.(55435), pg. 499
HAMMEL, GREEN & ABRAHAMSON, INC., 1201 Harmon Place(55403), pg. 504
HARMONY ENGINEERING CORPORATION, 460 Hoover St., N.E.(55413), pg. 510
Hart-Carter Co., 500 73rd Ave., N.E.(55432), pg. 226
HAUENSTEIN & BURMEISTER, INC., 2629 30th Ave., S.(55406), pg. 517
HOLIDAY COMPANIES, 4567 W. 80th St.(55437), pg. 539
Holiday Stations, Inc., 4567 W. 80th St.(55437), pg. 539
Hospitality Procurement Division, Carlson Pkwy, P.O. Box 59159, (55459-8202), pg. 221
Imparts, 1620 Central Ave. NE(55413-2556), pg. 1149
INTEGRATED ENERGY CONTROLS CORP., 5150 W. 76th St.(55439), pg. 573
Interplastic Commercial Resins Division, 2015 N.E. Broadway(55413), pg. 579
JAPS-OLSON COMPANY, 30 N. 31st Ave.(55411-1694), pg. 590
JESCO, INC., 7175 Cahill Rd.(55439), pg. 593
JEWELMONT CORPORATION, 800 Boone Ave., N.(55427), pg. 594
AL JOHNSON CONSTRUCTION CO., 3209 W. 76th St.(55435), pg. 597
KAUFFMAN STEWART ADVERTISING, 890 Butler Square West, 100 North 6th St.(55403), pg. 618
KNUTSON CONSTRUCTION CO., 5500 Wayzata Blvd., Ste. 300(55416-1216), pg. 638
KOLESAR & HARTWELL INC., 1201 Marquette Ave.(55403), pg. 641
Korn/Ferry International, 2508 IDS Center, 80 S. Eigth St.(55402), pg. 642
Kraus-Anderson Construction, 523 S. 8th St.(55404), pg. 644
KRAUS-ANDERSON, INC., 523 S. 8th St.(55404), pg. 644
Kraus-Anderson Mortgage Co., 523 S. 8th St.(55404), pg. 644
Kraus-Anderson Realty Co., 523 S. 8th St.(55404), pg. 644
LAMASTER FARMER, ET AL, 430 First Ave. North, Ste. 500(55401), pg. 652
Land O'Lakes International Div., P.O. Box 116(55440), pg. 653
Land O'Lakes International Development Corp., P.O. Box 116, (55112), pg. 654
LAWSON ASSOCIATES INC., 1300 Godward St.(55413), pg. 663
LEE & RILEY, INC., 1221 Nicollet Mall(55403), pg. 666
Lifetouch National School Studios Inc., 7800 Picture Dr.(55439), pg. 675
Lifetouch Publishing Inc., 400 Paramount Plaza, 7831 Glenroy Rd.(55435), pg. 675
Litho Colorplate, 2626 2nd St. N.E., Ste. 100(55418), pg. 975
LUTHERAN BROTHERHOOD, 625 4th Ave. S.(55415), pg. 688
Lutheran Brotherhood Family for Mutual Funds, 625 4th Ave. S.(55415), pg. 688
Lutheran Brotherhood Financial Corporation, 625 4th Ave. S.(55415), pg. 688
Lutheran Brotherhood Foundation, 625 4th Ave. S.(55415), pg. 688
Lutheran Brotherhood Real Estate Products Company, 625 4th Ave. S.(55415), pg. 688
Lutheran Brotherhood Research Corp., 625 4th Ave. S.(55145), pg. 688
Lutheran Brotherhood Securities Corp., 625 4th Ave. S.(55415), pg. 688
Lutheran Brotherhood Variable Insurance Products Company, 625 4th Ave. S.(55415), pg. 688
M&H ADVERTISING, 1128 Harmon Place, Ste. 200(55403), pg. 690
E. F. MacDonald Motivation Div., P.O. Box 59159(55459), pg. 221
MALT-O-MEAL COMPANY, 80 S. 8th St., Ste. 2600(55402-2297), pg. 703
Marquette Bank Minneapolis, National Association, Sixth & Marquette(55480), pg. 117
MCCRACKEN BROOKS COMMUNICATIONS, INC., 8400 Normandale Lake Blvd., Ste. 375(55437), pg. 728
MCLAUGHLIN GORMLEY KING COMPANY, 8810 10th Ave. N.(55427), pg. 731
MICHAEL FOODS, INC., 5353 Wayzata Blvd.(55416), pg. 747
MILLER MEESTER ADVERTISING INC., 17 N. Washington(55401), pg. 754
MINCO PRODUCTS, INC., 7300 Commerce Lane(55432), pg. 756
MINISTERS LIFE INSURANCE COMPANY, 3100 W. Lake St.(55416), pg. 757
MINNESOTA TWINS BASEBALL CLUB, 501 Chicago Ave. S.(55415), pg. 758
MINSTAR, INC., 100 S. Fifth St., Ste. 2400(55402), pg. 758
M. A. MORTENSON COMPANY, 700 Meadow Ln. N.(55422), pg. 772
MUELLER MACK, 510 1st Ave. N., Ste. 200(55403), pg. 774
NATIONAL CAR RENTAL SYSTEM, INC., 7700 France Ave., S.(55435), pg. 786
National Hotel Corp., P.O. Box 59159, Carlson Parkway(55459), pg. 221
NORCOSTCO, INC., 3203 N. Hwy. 100(55422), pg. 809
NORMARK CORPORATION, 1710 E. 78th St.(55423), pg. 810
North American Financial Corp., Carlson Parkway(55459), pg. 221
North Star Steel Co., P.O. Box 9300, Dept. 51(55440), pg. 219
NORTHLAND ALUMINUM PRODUCTS, INC., Hwy. 7 at 100(55416), pg. 814
NORTHLAND ELECTRIC SUPPLY COMPANY, 521 S. 10th St.(55440), pg. 814
Northwestern Drug Company, 2001 N.E. Kennedy(55413), pg. 343
NORWESCO, INC., 1650 W. 82nd. St., Ste. 1000(55431), pg. 816
PADILLA SPEER BEARDSLEY INC., 224 Franklin Ave., W.(55404), pg. 842
PALM BEACH BEAUTY PRODUCTS CO., 950 Xenia Ave., S.(55416), pg. 843
Para Natal Care Services, Inc., 1401 West 76th St., Ste. 245(55423), pg. 867
PARK CONSTRUCTION COMPANY, 7900 Beech St., N.E.(55432), pg. 848
PATTERSON DENTAL COMPANY, 1100 E. 80th St.(55420), pg. 851
PROSPECT FOUNDRY, INC., 1225 Winter St., N.E.(55413), pg. 895
QUADION CORPORATION, 3630 Wooddale Ave.(55416), pg. 902
RTS Systems, 9600 Aldrich Ave., S.(55420), pg. 1085
Radisson Hotel Corporation, Carlwon Pkwy.(55459-8204), pg. 221
Radisson Hotels International Inc., P.O. Box 59159, Carlson Pkwy.(55459), pg. 221
Rice & Rice Inc., Thresher Square, Ste. 100, 700 South Third St.(55415), pg. 1143
JOHN ROBERTS COMPANY, 9687 E. River Rd.(55433), pg. 938
CHUCK RUHR ADVERTISING, 1221 Nicollet Mall, Ste. 600(55403), pg. 955
Ryan Construction Company, 700 International Center, 900 2nd Ave. S.(55402), pg. 958
RYAN PROPERTIES INC., 700 International Center, 900 2nd Ave. S.(55402), pg. 958
SCHERER BROS. LUMBER COMPANY, 9 Ninth Ave., N.E.(55413), pg. 976
PAUL A. SCHMITT MUSIC COMPANY, 88 S. 10th St.(55403), pg. 976
GUY SCHOENECKER, INC., 7630 Bush Lake Rd.(55439), pg. 977
SCOVILLE PRESS, INC., 14505 27th Ave., N.(55447), pg. 983
Security Products Company, 7801 Metro Pkwy.(55425), pg. 1138
Security Products Company of Delaware, Inc., 7801 Metro Pkwy.(55425), pg. 1138
Sharpe Endosurgical Corporation, 8990 Springbrook Dr., Ste. 202(55433), pg. 867
SICO INC., 7525 Cahill Rd.(55435), pg. 1001
SNYDER BROTHERS, INC., 7251 Ohms Lane(55439), pg. 1015
Solar Plastics-Minneapolis, 732 30th Ave. S.E.(55414), pg. 1140
L.H. SOWLES COMPANY, INC., 2813 Bryant Ave. S.(55408), pg. 1024
Star Tribune, Minneapolis-St. Paul, 425 Portland Ave.(55488), pg. 291
STEVENS-LEE COMPANY, 1600 Xenium Lane N.(55441), pg. 1048
T O PLASTICS, INC., 2901 E. 78th St.(55425), pg. 1074
TELEX COMMUNICATIONS, INC., 9600 Aldrich Ave. S.(55420), pg. 1085
THRIFTY DRUG STORES, INC., 8441 Wayzata Blvd.(55426), pg. 1096
TIMESAVERS INC., 5270 Hanson Ct.(55429-3161), pg. 1098
TWIN CITY DIE CASTINGS CO., 1070 33rd Ave. S.E.(55414), pg. 1121
U.S. COMMUNICATIONS CORPORATION, 901 Marquette Ave. S. 17th Fl.(55402), pg. 1135
UNIVERSAL COOPERATIVES, INC., 7801 Metro Pkwy.(55425), pg. 1138
UPPER MIDWEST INDUSTRIES, INC., 732 30th Ave., S.E.(55414), pg. 1140
Ventures Group, P.O. Box 116(55440), pg. 654
VIC MANUFACTURING, 1620 Central Ave., N.E.(55413), pg. 1149
WAGNER SPRAY TECH CORP., 1770 Fernbrook Lane(55447), pg. 1158
WALMAN OPTICAL COMPANY, 801 12th Ave. N.(55411), pg. 1161
Weinstein International Seafood, 5738 Olson Memorial Hwy.(55422), pg. 54
WELLENS & CO., INC., 6600 France Ave., S.(55435), pg. 1175
Western International Media Corporation, 10 S. Fifth St., Ste. 315(55402), pg. 1180
Weston Engraving, 2626 2nd St. N.E.(55418), pg. 975
White Drug Enterprises, Inc., 8441 Wayzata Blvd.(55426), pg. 1096
MARTIN WILLIAMS ADVERTISING INC., 10 S. Fifth St.(55402), pg. 1191
WILLIAMS STEEL & HARDWARE COMPANY, 60 28th Ave., N.(55440-0540), pg. 1191
WITCHER CONSTRUCTION COMPANY, 3601 Minnesota Dr., Ste. 650(55435), pg. 1198
XERXES CORPORATION, 7901 Xerxes Ave. S.(55431), pg. 1206
ZIEGLER INC., 901 W. 94th St.(55420), pg. 1218

Minnetonka

ACI FINANCIAL CORP., 10159 Wayzata Blvd.(55305), pg. 2
AMERICAN HARDWARE MUTUAL INSURANCE CO., 5995 Opus Pkwy.(55343), pg. 55
American Merchants Life Insurance Co., 5995 Opus Pkwy.(55343), pg. 55
Dick Carlson Associates, Upper Midwest Trade Ctr., Space 229(55343), pg. 100
COLD SPRING GRANITE COMPANY, 601 Lakeshore Pkwy.(55305), pg. 259
HAWORTH GROUP INC., 6117 Blue Circle Dr.(55343), pg. 518
Juno Tool & Plastic Corporation, 1809 S. Plymouth Rd.(55343), pg. 299
MLT Vacations, Inc., 5130 Highway 101(55345), pg. 782
OPUS CORP., 800 OPUS Center, 9900 Bren Road E.(55343), pg. 828
ROLLERBLADE, INC., 5101 Shady Oak Rd.(55343), pg. 944
SCICOM DATA SERVICES, LTD., 10101 Bren Road East(55343), pg. 981
SNYDER'S DRUG STORES, INC., 14525 Hwy. 7(55345), pg. 1015
THOMPSON ENTERPRISES INC., 12201 Minnetonka Blvd.(55343), pg. 1094

Moorhead

American Crystal Sugar Co., Box 1227, (56560), pg. 51
AMERICAN CRYSTAL SUGAR COMPANY, 101 N. Third St.(56560), pg. 51

Mora

Arcon Bridge Div., 903 E. Forest(55051), pg. 81
ARCON CONSTRUCTION CO., INC., 903 E. Forest(55051), pg. 81
Arcon Municipal Div., 903 E. Forest(55051), pg. 81
Arcon Street Construction Div., 903 E. Forest(55051), pg. 81
Bluewater, 811 E. Maple(55051), pg. 161
BLUEWATER MARINE, 811 E. Maple(55051), pg. 161
Bluewater Marine Inc., 811 E. Maple(55051), pg. 634
Engineered Polymers Corporation, 1020 E. Maple Ave.(55051), pg. 507
KLAPMEIER MANAGEMENT COMPANY, 811 E. Maple(55051), pg. 634

Moundsview

HYMAN FREIGHTWAYS INC., 5267 Program Ave.(55112), pg. 557

New Brighton

Basic Industries, 1275 Old Hwy. 8(55112), pg. 571
HYPRO CORPORATION, 375 Fifth Ave. N.W.(55112), pg. 557
JOHN RISDALL ADVERTISING, 2475 15th St., NW(55112), pg. 935

New Hope

Independent Metals, 5701 International Pkwy.(55426-3097), pg. 565

New York Mills

Lund Boats, W. Front St.(56567), pg. 759

Newport

FRITZ CO. INC., 1912 Hastings Ave.(55055), pg. 434

North Mankato

MICO INC., 1911 Lee Blvd.(56003), pg. 748

Northfield

Malt-O-Meal Co., 701 W. Fifth St.(55057), pg. 703

Norwood

BONGARDS CREAMERIES INC., 13-200 County Rd. 51(55368), pg. 164

Owatonna

FEDERATED MUTUAL INSURANCE COMPANY, 121 E. Park Square(55060), pg. 405
THE KING COMPANY, 1001 21st Ave., N. W(55060), pg. 630
MUSTANG MANUFACTURING COMPANY, INC., Country Rd. 45 N(55060), pg. 777
OWATONNA CANNING COMPANY, 900 N. Cedar Ave.(55060), pg. 833
WENGER CORPORATION, 555 Park Dr.(55060), pg. 1176

Pelican Rapids

West Central Turkeys, P.O.B. Turkey(56572), pg. 809

Perham

BARREL O'FUN SNACK FOODS CO., 800 4th St. N.W.(56573), pg. 122

Plymouth

ADVANCE MACHINE COMPANY, 14600 21st Ave. North(55447), pg. 18
Farwell, Ozmun, Kirk & Co., 5005 Nathan Lane(55442), pg. 1133
GORDON & FERGUSON OF DELAWARE, INC., 2915 Niagara Lane(55447), pg. 471
PROGRESS CASTING GROUP, INC., 2600 N. Niagara Ln.(55447), pg. 894
UNITED HARDWARE DISTRIBUTING CO., 5005 Nathan Lane(55442), pg. 1132

Princeton

CRYSTAL CABINET WORKS, INC., 1100 Crystal Dr.(55371), pg. 303

Red Wing

RED WING PUBLISHING COMPANY, 433 W. 3rd St.(55066), pg. 919
RED WING SHOE CO., INC., 314 Main St.(55066), pg. 919
Red Wing Shoe Vasque Div., 314 Main St., Riverfront Center(55066), pg. 919
S.B. Foot Tanning Co., P.O. Box 73(55066), pg. 919

Redwood Falls

FARMERS UNION MARKETING & PROCESSING ASSOCIATION, Box 319(56283), pg. 402

Renville

SOUTHERN MINNESOTA BEET SUGAR COOPERATIVE, E. Hwy 212(56284), pg. 1022

Richfield

WALSER AUTOMOTIVE CORPORATION, 2100 W. 78th St.(55423), pg. 1161

Rochester

CRENLO, INC., 1600 Fourth Ave., NW(55901), pg. 298
GREENWAY CO-OP SERVICE, 3520 Third Ave., N.E.(55903), pg. 485
Marquette Bank Rochester, P.O. BOx 4800(55903), pg. 117
Dave Syverson Truck Center, Inc., 6300 S. 63 Highway(55904), pg. 1071

Rogers

Custom Distributors, Inc., 21150 Rogers Dr.(55374), pg. 79

Rosemount

REESE ENTERPRISES, INC., 16350 Asher Ave.(55068), pg. 920

Roseville

CROWN HOLDINGS, INC., 2500 W. County Rd. C(55113), pg. 302
Crown Iron Works Company, 2500 W. County Rd. C(55113), pg. 302
Keystone Automotive Industries, Inc. - Roseville, 2980 N. Cleveland Ave.(55113), pg. 627

Round Lake

SATHERS INC., Sather Plaza(56167-0028), pg. 972

Saint Bonifacius

Norwesco Fluid Systems Div., 4365 Steiner St.(55375), pg. 816

Saint Cloud

ANDERSON TRUCKING SERVICE INC., 203 Cooper Ave. N.(56302), pg. 73
BANKERS SYSTEMS INC., 6815 Sauk View Dr.(56303), pg. 117
BRUTGER EQUITIES, INC., One Sunwood Plaza(56301), pg. 185
D.C.I., INC., 600 5th Ave., N.(56301), pg. 308
First American National Bank, 1100 W. St. Germain St.(56301), pg. 173
First American Trust Company of Minnesota, Cold Spring Ctr., 4150 Second St. S.(56302), pg. 173
Jack Frost, Inc., 309 Lincoln Ave., S.E.(56304), pg. 584
Gold'n Plump, Inc., 309 Lincoln Ave., S.E.(56302), pg. 584
G. R. HERBERGER'S, INC., 600 Mall Germain(56301), pg. 530
JFC INC., 309 Lincoln Ave. S.E.(56304), pg. 584
K & W Transportation, P.O. Box 1377, (56302), pg. 73
WOODCRAFT INDUSTRIES, INC., 525 Lincoln Ave., SE(56304), pg. 1200

Saint James

TONY DOWNS FOODS COMPANY, 400 Armstrong Blvd. N.(56081), pg. 348
S-T INDUSTRIES, INC., 301 Armstrong Blvd. N.(56081), pg. 964

Saint Louis Park

North Central Sugar Marketing Co-Op, 400 S. Cty Rd. 18, Ste. 250(55426), pg. 1022
Walser Ford Inc., 3555 S. Hwy. 100(55416), pg. 1161

Saint Paul

AP Technology Management Inc., 600 W. County Rd. D(55112), pg. 18
API GROUP INC., 2366 Rose Pl.(55113), pg. 5
Adjustable Life Insurance Company, 400 N. Robert St.(55101), pg. 758
ALL NATION INSURANCE CO., 155 Aurora Ave.(55164), pg. 35
Allied Security Inc., 2147 University Ave., Ste. 206(55114), pg. 39
AMCLYDE ENGINEERED PRODUCTS, INC., 240 E. Plato Blvd.(55107), pg. 47
Artist Graphics, 2675 Patton Rd.(55113), pg. 281
BERGER TRANSFER & STORAGE, INC., 2950 Long Lake Rd.(55113), pg. 141
BEST BRANDS, 1765 Yankee Doodle Rd.(55121), pg. 146
W. Braun Co., 1 W. Water St.(55107), pg. 172
BREMER FINANCIAL CORPORATION, 455 Minnesota St., Ste. 2000(55101), pg. 173
BROWN & BIGELOW, INC., 345 Plato Blvd. E.(55107), pg. 181
BUERKLE BUICK-HONDA CO., 3350 Hwy. 186
Cenex/Land O'Lakes, Inc., P.O. Box 64089(55164), pg. 231
Chicago Tube & Iron Company of Minnesota, 2940 Eagandale Blvd.(55121), pg. 246
The Clarinda Company Color Division, 1780 W. 7th St.(55116), pg. 1187
COLEMAN & CHRISTISON, INC., 506 Fort Rd.(55102), pg. 261
CONTROL SYSTEMS INC., 2675 Patton Rd.(55113), pg. 281
Darwin Data Systems, 1380 Energy Lane, Suite 202(55108), pg. 370
ECO WATER SYSTEMS, P.O. Box 64420(55125), pg. 367
Eco Water Systems, Inc., P.O. Box 64420, (55164), pg. 712
Ecodyne Water Systems, Inc., P.O. Box 64420, (55164), pg. 712
EDUSERV, 85 E. 7th Pl., Ste. 400(55101), pg. 369
Farm Credit Bank of St. Paul, 375 Jackson St.(55101), pg. 405
Financial Life Companies, Inc., 445 Minnesota St.(55101), pg. 813
Full Circle, P.O. Box 64089(55164), pg. 231
HARRIS MECHANICAL CONTRACTING CO., 2300 Territorial Rd.(55114), pg. 512
Harris Waldinger, Inc., 2300 Territorial Rd.(55114), pg. 512
HARTZELL CORPORATION, 2515 Wabash Ave.(55114), pg. 514
HARVEST STATES COOPERATIVES, 1667 N. Snelling Ave.(55108), pg. 514
Hoyle Products, 345 Plato Blvd., E.(55107), pg. 181
HUBBARD BROADCASTING, INC., 3415 University Ave.(55114), pg. 548
INTERPLASTIC CORP., 1225 Wolters Blvd.(55110-5145), pg. 579
KSTP-FM, Inc., 3415 University Ave.(55114), pg. 549
KSTP-TV, 3415 University Ave.(55114), pg. 549
KAMSTRA COMMUNICATIONS, INC., 370 Selby Ave., Ste. 300(55102-1880), pg. 615
KEHNE ELECTRIC COMPANY, INC., 670 Vandelia St.(55114), pg. 620
KING KOIL LICENSING COMPANY INC., 770 Transfer Rd., Ste. 13(55114), pg. 630
Knox Lumber Co., 573 N. Prior(55114), pg. 853
LAMPERT YARDS, INC., 1850 Como Ave.(55108), pg. 653
LAN-O-SHEEN, INC., 289 5th St. E., Ste. 210(55101), pg. 653
MIMLIC Corp., 400 N. Robert St.(55101), pg. 758
MICRO COMPONENT TECHNOLOGY INC., 3850 N. Victoria St.(55126), pg. 748
MIDWEST AUTO PARTS DISTRIBUTORS, INC., 2565 Kasota Ave.(55108), pg. 751
MIMLIC Asset Management Company, 400 N. Robert St.(55101), pg. 758
MIMLIC Sales Corporation, 400 N. Robert St.(55101), pg. 758
MINNESOTA BREWING COMPANY, 882 W. 7th St.(55102), pg. 757
THE MINNESOTA MUTUAL LIFE INSURANCE COMPANY, 400 N. Robert St.(55101), pg. 757
MUSKA ELECTRIC COMPANY, 1985 Oakcrest Ave.(55113), pg. 777
NWA, INC., Minneapolis-St. Paul Intl. Airport(55111), pg. 782
Nesotà Co., 400 N. Robert St.(55101), pg. 758
NEW MECH COMPANIES, INC., 1633 Eustis St.(55108), pg. 802
NOBLES INDUSTRIES, INC., 645 E. 7th St.(55106), pg. 808
NORCRAFT COMPANIES, INC., 30 E. Plato Blvd.(55107), pg. 809
NORTH CENTRAL LIFE INSURANCE COMPANIES, 445 Minnesota St.(55101), pg. 813
Northwest Aerospace Training Corporation, Minneapolis-St. Paul Intl. Airport(55111), pg. 782
Northwest Aircraft Inc., Minneapolis-St. Paul Intl. Airport(55111), pg. 782
Northwest Airlines, Inc., 5101 Northwest Dr.(55111-3034), pg. 782
OLD DUTCH FOODS, INC., 2375 Terminal Rd.(55113), pg. 823
OLD HOME FOODS, INC., 370 University Ave.(55103), pg. 823
PAPER CALMENSON & CO., P.O. Box 64432(55164), pg. 847
PEOPLES ELECTRIC COMPANY, INC., 277 E. Fillmore Ave.(55107), pg. 859
REMMELE ENGINEERING, INC., 1211 Pierce Butler Rd.(55104), pg. 926
RIHM MOTOR COMPANY, 2108 University Ave.(55114), pg. 934
Rockwood Research, 1751 West County Rd. B(55113), pg. 401
Saint Paul Bank for Cooperatives, 375 Jackson St.(55101), pg. 405
ST. PAUL METALCRAFT, INC., 3737 N. Lexington Ave.(55126), pg. 967
RON SAXON FORD, INC., 225 University Ave.(55103), pg. 973
Sealy of Minnesota, Inc., 825 Transfer Rd.(55114), pg. 985
H.M. SMYTH CO., 1085 Snelling Ave., N.(55108), pg. 1014
SPECIALTY MANUFACTURING COMPANY, 5858 Centerville Rd.(55127), pg. 1027
TRADEHOME SHOE STORES, INC., 429 Prior Ave. N.(55104), pg. 1105
United States Satellite Broadcasting, Inc., 3415 University Ave.(55114), pg. 549
VILLAUME INDUSTRIES, INC., 2926 Lone Oak Circle(55121), pg. 1151
WALDORF CORPORATION, 2250 Wabash Ave.(55114), pg. 1159

Sauk Rapids

MIDWEST VISION CENTERS, 2672 Hwy. 23 N.E.(56379), pg. 752

Savage

CONTINENTAL MACHINES, INC., 5505 W. 123rd St.(55378), pg. 279
ROAD MACHINERY & SUPPLIES CO., 5633 W. Hwy. 13(55378), pg. 937

Shakopee

CONKLIN CO. INC., 551 Valley Park Dr.(55379), pg. 274
Shakopee Valley Printing Co., 5101 Valley Industrial Blvd. South(55379), pg. 442

Shoreview

SMITH SYSTEM MANUFACTURING COMPANY, 4184 N. Lexington Ave.(55126), pg. 1014

South Saint Paul

CENTRAL LIVESTOCK ASSOCIATION, INC., Exchange Bldg.(55075), pg. 233
Central Livestock Order Buying Company, Exchange Bldg.(55075), pg. 233
First American Bank Metro, 633 S. Concord St.(55075), pg. 173
First American Information Services, Inc., 633 S. Concord, Ste. 210(55075), pg. 173
First American Insurance Agencies, Inc., 633 S. Concord, Ste. 225(55075), pg. 173
Waterous Company, 300 John E. Carroll Ave. E(55075), pg. 50

Springfield

SANBORN MANUFACTURING COMPANY, 118 W. Rock St.(56087), pg. 969
Springfield Milling Corp., 101 So. Cass St.(56087), pg. 549

Stillwater

Arrow Building Centers, 808 N. 4th St.(55082), pg. 276
CONSOLIDATED LUMBER CO., 808 N. 4th St.(55082), pg. 276
Micropure Medical, Inc., 177 Neal Ave.N.(55082), pg. 867
F.H. STOLTZE LAND & LUMBER COMPANY, 219 N. Main St.(55082), pg. 1050
UFE INCORPORATED, 1850 S. Greeley St.(55082-0007), pg. 1123

Vadnais Heights

I.C. SYSTEM, INC., 444 E. Hwy. 96(55127), pg. 558
Microvena Corporation, 3600 Labore Rd., Ste. 1(55110), pg. 867

Warren

First American Bank, 202 W. Johnson Ave.(56762), pg. 173

Warroad

MARVIN LUMBER & CEDAR COMPANY, Hwy. 716

Watertown

First American Bank, 301 Territorial St. E.(55388), pg. 173

Wayzata

CARGILL INC., 15407 McGinty Rd. W.(55391-2399), pg. 219
Cargill Marine & Terminal, 15407 McGinty Rd.(55391), pg. 219

Minnetonka Boat Works, P.O. Box 549(55391), pg. 758
SCHOTT CORPORATION, 1000 Parkers Lake Rd.(55391), pg. 978

West St. Paul

TAPEMARK, 150 E. Marie Ave.(55118), pg. 1078

Willmar

First American Bank & Trust, 302 S.W. Fifth St.(56201), pg. 173
MINNESOTA ELECTRIC SUPPLY COMPANY, 1209 E. Hwy. 12(56201), pg. 757
WILLMAR MANUFACTURING, Industrial Park(56201), pg. 1193

Winona

BADGER CONSTRUCTION EQUIPMENT CO., INSLEY DIV., Airport Industrial Park(55987), pg. 113
Badger Equipment Company, Airport Industrial Park, P.O. Box 798(55987), pg. 102
Burro Crane Co., Airport Industrial Park(55987), pg. 113
PEERLESS CHAIN CO., 1416 E. Sanborn St.(55987), pg. 855
Peerless Chain Company, 1416 E. Sanborn St.(55987), pg. 175
WATKINS INCORPORATED, P.O. Box 5570, (55987-0570), pg. 1167
Watlow Winona, Inc., 1241 Bundy Blvd.(55987), pg. 1167
WINONA KNITS, 1200 Storr's Pond Rd.(55987), pg. 1196
WINONA KNITTING MILLS, INC., 902 E. Second St.(55987), pg. 1196

Winsted

LITTFIN LUMBER COMPANY, 555 Baker Ave.(55395), pg. 678

Worthington

BEDFORD INDUSTRIES, INC., 1659 Rowe Ave.(56187), pg. 131
GORDY'S, INC., 1131 Oxford St.(56187), pg. 472

MISSISSIPPI

Bay Saint Louis

PURCELL CO., INC., 4402 E. Aloha Dr., Ste. 3(39520), pg. 900

Byhalia

GEM, INCORPORATED, 1 Gem Blvd.(38611), pg. 447

Charleston

Charleston Industries, One Industrial Park, pg. 864

Cleveland

Duo-Fast Corporation, 800 N. Pearman(38732), pg. 354

Columbus

AIRLINE MANUFACTURING COMPANY, INC., 104 Williamson Rd.(39704), pg. 27
Beneke, Tuffy Lane(39701), pg. 970
Magnolia Division, Tuffy Lane(39701), pg. 970
SANDERSON PLUMBING PRODUCTS INC., Tuffy Lane(39701), pg. 970
SEMINOLE MANUFACTURING COMPANY, 605 17th St. S.(39701), pg. 989
Southern Electric Supply Co., Inc., 1121 Gardner Blvd.(39704), pg. 1021

Europa

Foodway, Inc., 210 Highway N. (Europa Shopping Center)(39744), pg. 594

Greenville

Southern Electric Supply Co., Inc., 610 Kentucky St.(38701), pg. 1021

Greenwood

Henderson & Baird Hardware Co., Inc., 1100 Sycamore St(38930), pg. 340
Southern Electric Supply Co., Inc., 1407 Main St.(38930), pg. 1021
STAPLE COTTON COOPERATIVE ASSOCIATION, 214 W. Market St.(38930), pg. 1038
Staple Cotton Cooperative Association/Itta Bena, P.O. Box 547(38930), pg. 1039
Staple Cotton Discount Corporation, P.O. Box 547(38930), pg. 1039
VIKING RANGE CORP., 111 Front St.(38930), pg. 1151

Grenada

HANKINS LUMBER COMPANY, INC., P.O. Box 1397(38901-1397), pg. 505
Heatcraft Inc., Hwy. 51 South(38901), pg. 667
Heatcraft Inc., Hwy. 51 S.(38901), pg. 667
Southern Electric Supply Co., Inc., 361 Thomas St.(38901), pg. 1021

Gulfport

BUTCH OUSTALET FORD SAAB, INC., 9274 Hwy. 49(39503), pg. 832
Southern Electric Supply Co., Inc., 1270 28th St.(39501), pg. 1021

Guntown

COLUMBIAN ROPE COMPANY, 145 Towery St.(38849-0270), pg. 266

Hattiesburg

WHLT, 990 Hardy St., Box 232(39403), pg. 804

Horn Lake

Flavorite Laboratories, 5980 Hurt Rd.(38671), pg. 1100

Indianola

DELTA PRIDE CATFISH, INC., Industrial Park(38751), pg. 327

Jackson

Allen & Hoshall, 612 N. State St.(39201), pg. 36
BILL'S DOLLAR STORES, INC., 3800 I-55 North(39211), pg. 150
Broadcasters of Mississippi, Inc., 1820 TV Road, P.O. Box 8887(39204), pg. 804
CUNA South Central District, 5140 Galaxie Dr., Rm. 206(39206), pg. 205
Cal-Maine Egg Products Inc., 3330 Woodrow Wilson Blvd.(39209), pg. 208
Cal-Maine Farms, 3320 Woodrow Wilson Blvd.(39209), pg. 208
CAL-MAINE FOODS, INC., 3320 Woodrow Wilson Blvd.(39209), pg. 208
CAPITOL STREET CORP., 711 W. Capitol St.(39203), pg. 216
DEWEY CORPORATION, 5500 U.S. Hwy. 80 W.(39209), pg. 334
ERGON, INC., 202 E. Pearl Rd.(39201), pg. 386
Florida Jitney Jungle Stores, Inc., 453 N. Mill St.(39207), pg. 594
FORESTRY SUPPLIERS, INC., 205 W. Rankin St.(39201), pg. 424
GODWIN ADVERTISING AGENCY, INC., One Jackson Place, 188 E. Capitol, Ste. 800(39201), pg. 464
JACKSON PACKING CO. INC., P.O. Box 113(39205), pg. 587
JACKSON PAPER COMPANY, 197 N. Gallatin St.(39207), pg. 587
JITNEY-JUNGLE STORES OF AMERICA, INC., 453 N. Mill St.(39202), pg. 594
Jitney Jungle Wholesale Co., Inc., 453 N. Mill St.(39202), pg. 594
Keystone Automotive Industries, Inc.- Jackson, 325 S. Farish St.(39201), pg. 628
Lamar Financial Services Insurance Company, P.O. Box 880, 317 E. Capitol St.(39205), pg. 216
Lamar Investment Management Company, P.O. Box 880, 317 E. Capitol St.(39205), pg. 216
Lamar Leasing Co., Inc., P. O. Box 880, 317 E. Capitol St.(39205), pg. 216
Lamar Life Investors, P.O. Box 880, 317 E. Capitol St.(39205), pg. 216
MARIS, WEST & BAKER, INC., 5120 Galaxie Dr.(39206), pg. 707
McCarty Foods, Inc., P.O. Box 2718, I-55 South(39207), pg. 727
McCarty Processors, Inc., 238 Wilmington St.(39207), pg. 727
MCRAE'S, INC., McRae's Executive Plaza(39209), pg. 733
Miller Transporters, Inc., 5500 U.S. Hwy. 80 W.(39209), pg. 334
Mississippi Energies, Inc., 711 W. Capitol St., P.O. Box 3348(39203), pg. 1208
Mississippi Valley Gas Co., 711 W. Capitol St.(39203), pg. 1208
Tower Loan of Mississippi, Inc., P.O. Box 6482, 131 Channel 16 Way(39212), pg. 216
TREND LINE CORPORATION, 4400 River Oaks Dr.(39208), pg. 1109
V.G.S. CORP. D/B/A SOUTHLAND OIL COMPANY, 5170 Galaxie Dr(39206), pg. 1141
Valley Innovative Management Service, 4400 River Oaks Dr.(39208), pg. 1109
WJTV, 1820 TV Road, Box 8887, pg. 804
YAZOO INVESTMENT CORPORATION, 711 W. Capital St.(39203), pg. 1207

Kosciusko

ATAPCO Globe-Weis/Kosciusko, No. 1 Superior Dr.(39090), pg. 64

Laurel

Southern Electric Supply Co., Inc., 215 S. Magnolia St.(39440), pg. 1021
Triumph/LOR, Inc., P.O. Box 2161, (39440), pg. 1115

Long Beach

The Regina Company, 21180 Johnson Road(39560), pg. 922

Louisville

TAYLOR MACHINE WORKS, INC., 650 North Church Ave.(39339), pg. 1081

Magee

MCCARTY FARMS, P.O. Box 366(39111), pg. 727

McComb

CROFT METAL INC., 124 24th St.(39648), pg. 300

Meridian

AMR (Audio Media Research), 711 A St.(39301), pg. 854
Meridian Mfg. Co., Inc., 901 D St.(39301), pg. 953
Newell Paper Co. of Meridian, 2502 Front St.(39302), pg. 587
PEAVEY ELECTRONIC CORP., 711 A St.(39301), pg. 854
SOUTHERN ELECTRIC SUPPLY CO., INC., 301 46th Court(39301), pg. 1020
Southern Electric Supply Co., Inc., 912 13th St.(39301), pg. 1021
SOUTHERN PIPE & SUPPLY CO., INC., 4330 Hwy. 39 North(39301), pg. 1022
Webster-Portalloy Chains, Inc., 3800 Second St., P.O. Box 1747(39302), pg. 1172

Natchez

RIVERSIDE CENTRAL SERVICES, INC., 521 Main St.(39120), pg. 937

New Albany

MERCHANTS TRUCK LINE, INC., 125 Snyder St.(38652), pg. 740
New Albany Gazette, P.O. Box 300, 713 Carter Ave.(38652), pg. 655

Olive Branch

BOZOF DINETTES, INC., 6235 S. Cockrum St.(38654), pg. 169
Fraenkel Company, 8300 Industrial Dr.(38654), pg. 428

Oxford

Binswanger, 904 N. Lamar Ave.(38655), pg. 152
Southern Electric Supply Co., Inc., 607 S. 16th St.(38655), pg. 1021

Pascagoula

Mississippi Phosphates Corp., P.O. Box 848, (39568-0804), pg. 760

Pontotoc

Stearns & Foster Upholstery Furniture Co., 279 Pontotoc Indus. Pk.(38863), pg. 985

Richland

Wabash Fibre Box Co.-South, 127 Interstate Dr.(39218), pg. 1183

Ridgeland

Federal Intermediate Credit Bank of Jackson, 713 S. Pear Orchard Rd.(39157), pg. 405
SOUTHERN FARM BUREAU CASUALTY INSURANCE COMPANY, P.O. Box 1800, (39158-1800), pg. 1021

Scott

Delta & Pine Land Company, P.O. Box 157(38772), pg. 1024

Shubuta

Sunbeam Home Comfort, Hwy. 45 North, Box 38(39360), pg. 1059

Starkville

GULF STATES MANUFACTURERS, INC., Airport Rd.(39759), pg. 494

Stinnis Space Center

Mason Technologies Inc., (39529-7099), pg. 718

Tishomingo

Heil Refuse & Dump Body Co., Hwy. 25 No.(38873), pg. 525
Truck Equipment Div., Hwy. 25 N.(38873), pg. 525

Verona

Aircap Industries Corp., Hwy. 45 S.(38879), pg. 694
Gibson Continer Divison, Industrial Park South(38879), pg. 1183

Vicksburg

Southern Electric Supply Co., Inc., 520 Depot St.(39180), pg. 1021

Yazoo City

MISSISSIPPI CHEMICAL CORPORATION, U.S. Hwy. 49 E.(39194), pg. 760
Newsprint South, Inc., P.O. Box 1499(39194), pg. 760

MISSOURI

Antonia

Cue Industries, Inc., 3135 Highway M(63012), pg. 492

Aurora

Bioproducts, Inc., 117 N. Morgan St.(65605), pg. 152

Ballwin

FRU-CON CONSTRUCTION CORPORATION, 15933 Clayton Rd.(63011), pg. 435
Fru-Con Engineering Inc., 15933 Clayton Rd.(63011), pg. 435

Belton

Allied Bus Sales, Inc., 17327 So. Hwy. 71(64012), pg. 725
Quik N Tasty Foods, 822 Quiktrip Way(64012), pg. 905

Berkeley

ReCon Services, Inc., 6647 Romiss Ct.(63134), pg. 271

Blue Springs

Blue Springs Examiner, P.O. Box 1057, 500 W. R.D. Mize Rd.(64013), pg. 1042
FIKE CORPORATION, 704 S. 10th St.(64015), pg. 409

Branson

SILVER DOLLAR CITY, INC., Hwy. 76(65616), pg. 1004

Bridgeton

DIMAC CORPORATION, One Corporate Woods Dr.(63044-3838), pg. 338
DIMAC DIRECT, One Corporate Woods Dr.(63044-3838), pg. 338
GRAMEX CORPORATION, 11966 St. Charles Rock Rd.(63044), pg. 475
St. Louis Auto Auction, 13813 St. Charles Rock Rd.(63045), pg. 293

Buffalo

Batesco Quarries Div., (65622), pg. 88

Butler

Batesco Quarries Div., Hwy. 52(64730), pg. 88

Carthage

OTT FOOD PRODUCTS, 705 W. Fairview(64836), pg. 831
STEADLY COMPANY, 200 River St.(64836), pg. 1043

Caruthersville

Colson Equipment, Inc., P. O. Box 1000, (63830), pg. 711

Chesterfield

DIERBERGS MARKETS INC., 1422 Elbridge Payne Rd.(63006), pg. 337
Huntco Acquisitions Holdings, Inc., 14323 S. Outer Forty Dr.(63017), pg. 554
Huntco Health Care Co., 14323 S. Outer Forty Dr.(63017), pg. 554
HUNTCO INC., 14323 S. Outer Forty Dr.(63017), pg. 554
KANGAROOS, USA INC., 1809 Clarkson Rd.(63017), pg. 616
MARK ANDY, INC., 18081 Chesterfield Airport Rd.(63005), pg. 708
MITEK, INC., 14515 N. Outer Forty Rd.(63017), pg. 762
Penske Truck Leasing, 14528 South Outer 40(63017), pg. 859
SABRELINER CORP., 18118 Chesterfield Airport Rd.(63005-1121), pg. 965
Sachs Energy Management Systems, 16120 Chesterfield Pkwy. S., Ste. 100(63017), pg. 965
SACHS HOLDING COMPANY, 400 Chesterfield Ctr., Ste. 600(63017), pg. 965
Sachs Properties, 400 Chesterfield Ctr., Ste. 600(63017), pg. 965

Clayton

GRAYBAR ELECTRIC COMPANY, INC., 34 N. Meramec Ave.(63105), pg. 479
Graybar International, Inc., 34 N. Meramec Ave.(63103), pg. 479
HARBOUR GROUP LTD., 7701 Forsyth Blvd.(63105), pg. 506
OSBORN & BARR COMMUNICATIONS, 7800 Forsyth Blvd., 7th Fl.(63105), pg. 830
Paragon Life Insurance Co., 7701 Forsyth(63105), pg. 448
SITE OIL CO. OF MISSOURI, 50 S. Bemiston Ave.(63105), pg. 1009

Columbia

KMIZ-TV, 501 Business Loop, 70 East(65201), pg. 1043
MFA OIL COMPANY, Ray Young Dr.(65201), pg. 692
MFA INCORPORATED, 615 Locust(65201), pg. 692
SHELTER MUTUAL INSURANCE COMPANY, 1817 W. Broadway(65218), pg. 997
Watlow Columbia, Inc., 2101 Pennsylvania Dr.(65202), pg. 1167

Creve Coeur

ELDER MANUFACTURING COMPANY, 12747 Olive St.(63166), pg. 373

De Soto

NORWOOD SHOE CORPORATION, One Penaljo Dr.(63020), pg. 816

Earth City

ACF Industries, Inc., 3301 Rider Trail So.(63045), pg. 561
DIAGRAPH CORPORATION, 3401 Rider Trail S.(63045-1110), pg. 335
Jorgensen Steel & Aluminum/St. Louis, 3701 Rider Trail S.(63045), pg. 606

Ellisville

Stephen Gould Midwest, 1302 Clarkson/Clayton Center(63011), pg. 474

Excelsior Springs

Electro-Wire, Inc., 200 N. Industrial Pk. Rd.(64024), pg. 375

Fenton

Atlas/Soundolier, 1859 Intertech Dr.(63026), pg. 64
CLAYTON CORPORATION, 866 Horan Dr.(63026-2416), pg. 253
Clayton Metals Corp., 866 Horan Dr.(63026-2416), pg. 253
Clayton Plastics Corp., 866 Horan Dr.(63026-2416), pg. 253
Container Products Inc., 2391 Cassens Dr.(63026), pg. 278
Convenience Products, Inc., 866 Horan Dr.(63026-2416), pg. 253
Fabick Brothers Equipment, 1 Fabick Dr.(63026), pg. 396
Fabick & Company, 1 Fabick Dr.(63026), pg. 396
Fabick Machinery, 1 Fabick Dr.(63026), pg. 396
Fabick Tractor, 1 Fabick Dr.(63026), pg. 396
JOHN FABICK TRACTOR COMPANY, 1 Fabick Dr.(63026), pg. 396
KOLLER ENTERPRISES, INC., 1400 S. Hwy. 141(63026), pg. 641
Maritz Communications Co., 1315 N. Highway Dr.(63099), pg. 707
MARITZ INC., 1375 N. Highway Dr.(63099), pg. 707
Maritz Marketing Research, Inc., 1385 N. Highway Dr.(63026), pg. 707
Maritz Performance Improvement Company, 1400 S. Highway Dr.(63026), pg. 708
Maritz Travel Co., 1395 N. Highway Dr.(63026), pg. 708
TACONY CORPORATION, 1760 Gilsinn Lane(63026), pg. 1076
UNIGROUP, INC., One United Dr.(63026), pg. 1126
United Capital Services, Inc., One United Dr.(63026), pg. 1126
United Leasing, Inc., One United Dr.(63026), pg. 1126
United Van Lines, Inc., One United Dr.(63026), pg. 1126
Vanliner Group, Inc., One United Dr.(63026), pg. 1126

Fulton

DANUSER MACHINE CO., 500 East Third(65251), pg. 315

Gainesville

Hodgson Mill, Inc., Industrial Park(65655), pg. 1002

Gerald

Newly Weds Foods, Inc., , pg. 804

Grandview

KING LOUIE INTERNATIONAL, INC., 13500 15th St.(64030), pg. 631

Grant City

Gee Cee Cap Company, Old Hwy. 169 N.(64456), pg. 1148

Hannibal

The Hannibal Courier-Post, P.O. Box A, 200 N. 3rd St.(63401), pg. 1042
Watlow Industries, Inc., 6 Industrial Loop Dr.(63401), pg. 1168

Independence

AGCO Manufacturing Group, 627 So. Cottage St.(64051), pg. 4
The Independence Examiner, P.O. Box 458, 410 S. Liberty(64051), pg. 1042

Jefferson City

MISSOURI LOTTERY, 1823 Southridge Dr.(65109), pg. 760
Scholastic Inc. National Distribution Center, P.O. Box 1068, (65101), pg. 962

Joplin

Aero Body & Truck Equipment, Inc., E. 7th St. Rd. Bus. I-44(64801), pg. 1111
Alco Health Services Corp.-Joplin Div., 5th St. & Grand Ave.(64801), pg. 31
The Computer Patch of Joplin, 3316 E. 32nd, Box 1330(64802), pg. 1043
CONTRACT FREIGHTERS, INC., 2900 Davis Blvd.(64804), pg. 280
DOANE PRODUCTS CO., W. 20th & State Line Rd.(64802), pg. 342
Farmers Chemical Co., P.O. Box 225(64802), pg. 402
Monkem Company, Inc., P.O.Box 1196, (64802), pg. 191
Stauffer Media Systems, Inc., 3316 East 32nd Street(64802), pg. 1043
TRI-STATE MOTOR TRANSIT CO., E. 7th Street Rd. & Business I-44(64802), pg. 1111

Kansas City

ADI Warehouse Division, Carquest Corp., 3155 Terrace St.(64111), pg. 224
AMF Bowling Centers Inc., 4555 E. Red Bridge Rd.(64131), pg. 471
Allied Security Inc., 3515 Broadway, Ste. 203(64111), pg. 39
Allright Carpark, Inc., 1221 Baltimore-Suite 300(64105), pg. 41
Ambassador Cards, 2501 McGee(64108), pg. 502
AMERICAN MARKETING INDUSTRIES, INC., 10450 Holmes Rd., Ste. 501(64131), pg. 58
B & V Waste Science & Technology Corp., 4717 Grand(64112), pg. 154
BARTLETT AND COMPANY, 4800 Main St., Ste. 600(64112), pg. 122
BERNSTEIN-REIN ADVERTISING, INC., 4600 Madison(64112), pg. 144
BLACK & VEATCH, 8400 Ward Pkwy.(64114), pg. 154
Black & Veatch Architects, Inc., 4717 Grand(64112), pg. 154
Boasberg Valentine-Radford, Inc., 4600 Madison Ave., Ste. 1300(64112), pg. 1143
BURD & FLETCHER COMPANY, 321 W. 7th St.(64105), pg. 189
BURNS & MCDONNELL ENGINEERS-ARCHITECTS-CONSULTANTS, 4800 E. 63rd St.(64141), pg. 194
Burns & McDonnell Waste Consultants, Inc., 4800 E. 63rd St.(64141), pg. 194
CARTER COMPANIES, 100 Northwest Pkwy.(64068), pg. 226
CHEMCENTRAL/Kansas City, 910 No. Prospect Ave.(64120-1685), pg. 242
CLARKSON CONSTRUCTION COMPANIES, 4133 Gardner Ave.(64120), pg. 253
CONTRACTORS SUPPLY COMPANY, INC., 800 E. 18th St.(64108), pg. 281
The Cooperative Finance Assn., Inc., P.O. Box 7305, 3315 N. Oak Traffic Way(64116), pg. 402
Crown Center Redevelopment Corp., 2440 Pershing Road, Ste. 500(64108), pg. 502
DAVIS PAINT COMPANY, 1311 Iron St.(64116), pg. 319
DEAN OPERATIONS INC., 1201 W. 31st St.(64108), pg. 322
DODSON GROUP, 9201 State Line Rd.(64114), pg. 342
J.E. Dunn Construction Co., 929 Holmes(64106), pg. 354
DUNN INDUSTRIES INC., 929 Holmes(64106), pg. 354
LEO EISENBERG & CO., INC., 1101 Walnut, Ste. 800(64106), pg. 372
Ellerbe Becket-Kansas City, 605 West 47th(64112), pg. 378
FARMLAND INDUSTRIES, INC., 3315 N. Oak Trafficway(64116), pg. 402
Farmland Industries, Inc., , pg. 402
Farmland Industries U.K. Ltd., 3315 N. Oak Trafficway(64116), pg. 402
FLETCHER HUNT WIRTH ASSOCIATES, INC., 2405 Grand, Ste. 400(64108), pg. 418
Frank Paxton Lumber Company, 6311 St. John Ave.(64123), pg. 592
Funeral Security Plans, Inc., 1331 Brush Creek Blvd.(64110), pg. 804
GARNEY HOLDING COMPANY, INC., 1331 N.W. Vivion Rd.(64118-4554), pg. 443
GILBERT/ROBINSON, INC., 47th & Main(64112), pg. 458
Graphics International Inc., P.O. Box 419566, 2501 McGee(64141-6566), pg. 502
HALLMARK CARDS, INC., 2501 McGee(64108), pg. 501
Halls Merchandising Inc., 200 E. 25th St.(64108), pg. 502
HARMON SMITH INC., 801 West 47th St., Ste. 100(64112-1298), pg. 510
HAVENS STEEL CO., 7219 E. 17th St.(64126), pg. 517
HICKERSON PHELPS KIRTLEY & ASSOCIATES, Two Pershing Square, 2300 Main St.(64108), pg. 532
HOWARD NEEDLES TAMMEN & BERGENDOFF, 1201 Walnut, Ste. 700(64106), pg. 547
Jorgensen Steel & Aluminum/Kansas City, 1701 W. 25th(64108), pg. 606
KMBC Division, 1049 Central St.(64105), pg. 522
KMBC-TV, 1049 Central St.(64105), pg. 522
Kansas City Auto Auction, 3901 No. Great Midwest Dr.(64161), pg. 293
KANSAS CITY CHIEFS FOOTBALL CLUB, One Arrowhead Drive(64129), pg. 616
Kansas City Royals Radio Network, P.O. Box 419969, (64141), pg. 1043
Kansas City Terminal Railway Co., 3435 Broadway(64111), pg. 76
Kilsby-Roberts/Kansas City, 1800 N. Universal Ave.(64120), pg. 606
KOCH SUPPLIES INC., 1411 W. 29th St.(64108), pg. 639
KUHN & WITTENBORN, INC., 2405 Grand Ave., Ste. 600(64108), pg. 646
Market Directions, Inc., 300 Commerce Tower(64105), pg. 1143
MASSMAN CONSTRUCTION COMPANY, 8901 State Line Rd.(64114), pg. 719
MIDWAY FORD TRUCK CENTER INC., 7601 N.E. 38th St.(64161), pg. 751
MIDWEST MECHANICAL CONTRACTORS INC., 2720 E. 88th Terrace(64132), pg. 752
Moline Accessories Corporation, 430 W. Seventh St.(64105), pg. 767
MONARK EGG CORPORATION, 601 E. Third St.(64106), pg. 765
NKH&W, INC., 600 Broadway(64015), pg. 781
D. W. NEWCOMER'S SONS, INC., 1331 Brush Creek Blvd.(64110), pg. 804
The C. W. Nofsinger Company, 4700 E. 63rd St.(64141), pg. 194
NuArc Co., 301 W. Armour Blvd.(64111), pg. 817
PACKAGE SERVICE COMPANY, INC., 10525 N.W. Ambassador, Ste. 208(64153), pg. 842
Frank Paxton Company, 6311 St. John Ave.(64123), pg. 592
Paxton Properties, Inc., 6311 St. John Ave.(64123), pg. 592
PAYLESS CASHWAYS, INC., 2300 Main St.(64108), pg. 853
RUSSELL STOVER CANDIES, INC., 1000 Walnut(64106), pg. 957
SCHUTTE LUMBER COMPANY, 3001 Southwest Blvd.(64108), pg. 980
Signboard Hill Productions, 2501 McGee(64108), pg. 502
SIMONDS-SHIELDS-THEIS GRAIN CO., 4800 Main St., Ste. 401(64112), pg. 1006
Swingster Company, 10450 Holmes Rd.(64131), pg. 58
T. J. CINNAMONS LTD., 1010 W. 39th St.(64111), pg. 1073
TENSION ENVELOPE CORP., 819 E. 19th St.(64108-1781), pg. 1088
TOPSY'S INTERNATIONAL INC., 221 W. 74th Terrace(64114), pg. 1102
Transilwrap Co., Inc., 4231 E. 75th Terrace(64132), pg. 1107
TWENTIETH CENTURY COMPANIES, 4500 Main St., Ste. 1500(64111), pg. 1121
Twentieth Century Investors, 4500 Main St., Ste. 1500(64111), pg. 1121
Twentieth Century Investors, Inc., 4500 Main St.(64111), pg. 1121

Twentieth Century Services, 4500 Main(64111), pg. 1121
THE UHLMANN CO., 1009 Central(64105), pg. 1125
Uneco Investor Services Inc., 4800 Main St.(64112), pg. 402
U.S. ENGINEERING COMPANY, 3433 Roanoke Rd.(64111), pg. 1135
VALENTINE-RADFORD, INC., 1100 Commerce Towers(64105), pg. 1142
Value Assemblers & Manufactureres, Inc., , pg. 356
WOLCOTT & LINCOLN, INC., 4800 Main St., Ste. 565(64112), pg. 1198
XEBEC CORPORATION, 5612 Brighton Terrace(64130), pg. 1206

Kirkwood

METALTECH, INC., 206 Prospect Ave.(63122), pg. 742

Lees Summit

Laboratory Supply Company, 1009A N.E. Jib Ct.(64064), pg. 650

Liberty

FERRELL COMPANIES INC./FERRELLGAS, One Liberty Plaza(64068), pg. 407
Ferrellgas, Inc., One Liberty Plaza(64068), pg. 407

Mansfield

Mans-Steel Div., P.O. Box 137(65704), pg. 555
Mans-Steel Foundry, P.O. Box 137(65704), pg. 555

Marceline

WALSWORTH PUBLISHING COMPANY, INC., 306 N. Kansas(64658), pg. 1161

Maryland Heights

CHEMCENTRAL/St. Louis, 2646 Metro Blvd.(63043), pg. 242
CLARK DOOR CO., INC., 2564 Metro Blvd.(63043), pg. 252
FORD STEEL CO., INC., 2475 Rock Island Blvd.(63043), pg. 423
General Installation Co., 2500 Drilling Dr.(63043), pg. 31
GREY EAGLE DISTRIBUTORS INC., 2340 Millpark Dr.(63043), pg. 486
EDWARD D. JONES & CO., 201 Progress Pkwy.(63043), pg. 603
Olive Electronics, 2555 Metro Blvd.(63043), pg. 908
ROYAL WATERBEDS, 2440 Adie Rd.(63043), pg. 953
SCHNUCK MARKETS, INC., 11420 Lackland Rd.(63043), pg. 977
J. D. STREETT & CO., INC., 144 Weldon Pkwy.(63043), pg. 1053
SVERDRUP CORPORATION, 13723 Riverport Dr.(63043), pg. 1065
Sverdrup Investments, Inc., 13723 Riverport Dr.(63043), pg. 1066
VESS BEVERAGES, INC., 2525 Schuetz Rd.(63043), pg. 1149
FRED WEBER INC., 2320 Creve Coeur Mill Rd.(63043), pg. 1171

Moberly

MID-AM BUILDING SUPPLY, INC., 100 W. Sparks(65270), pg. 749

Monett

EFCO CORPORATION, County Rd. & Bridle Ln.(65708), pg. 359

Monroe City

DIEMAKERS, INC., 801 Secont St.(63456), pg. 336

Mountain Grove

RICHARDS BROTHERS OF MOUNTAIN GROVE, P.O. Box 866(65711), pg. 932

Neosho

Sunbeam Outdoor Products Co., 4101 Howard Bush Dr.(64850), pg. 1059

North Kansas City

DWF of North Kansas City, 21 W. 13th Ave.(64116), pg. 331
DEBRUCE GRAIN INC., 2702 Rockcreek Pkwy., Ste. 400(64117), pg. 323
HELZBERG'S DIAMOND SHOPS, INC., 1825 Swift Ave.(64116-3606), pg. 528
THERMAL TECHNOLOGY INDUSTRIES, 1321 Burlington(64116), pg. 1091
WESTFALL GMC TRUCK INC., 811 Atlantic(64116), pg. 1182

O'Fallon

American Envelope of St. Louis, 601 Cannonball Lane(63366), pg. 199
Hitchiner Mfg. Co., Inc., E. Terra & Cannonball Lane, P.O. Box 220(63366), pg. 536

Overland Park

Black & Veatch International, 6601 College Blvd.(66211), pg. 154

Pacific

Pacific Heater Corporation, 115 Flier Dr.(63069), pg. 1167

Perryville

Solar Press, Inc., 1205 Corporation Lane(63775), pg. 1017

Poplar Bluff

Moark Mold, Inc., "PP" Highway & Miller Road(63901), pg. 875

Richmond

RAY-CARROLL COUNTY GRAIN CO-OP, Hwy. 10 West(64085), pg. 914

Riverside

AMICO-Riverside, 601 NW Business Park Lane(64150), pg. 29

Saint Charles

Penn Emblem Co., P.O. Box 1157(63302), pg. 857

Saint Joseph

B&E Grain Company, 310 S. Third St.(64501), pg. 654
Leschen Wire Rope, 609 N. 2nd(64501), pg. 1197
Research Seeds, Inc., 310 S. Third St.(64501), pg. 654
Schreiber Milling Co., 8th & Mitchell Sts.(64503), pg. 549
WIRE ROPE CORP. OF AMERICA, INC., 609 N. 2nd St.(64501), pg. 1197

Saint Louis

Adam's Mark Hotels, 11330 Olive St. Rd.(63141), pg. 496
ADAMSON ADVERTISING, INC., 222 S. Central(63105), pg. 17
J. S. ALBERICI CONSTRUCTION CO., INC., 2150 Kienlen Ave.(63121-5592), pg. 31
ALLEN FOODS, INC., 8543 Page(63114), pg. 36
Allied Security Inc., 4232 Forest Park Blvd.(63108), pg. 39
Allright Missouri, Inc., 915 Olive St., Ste. 953C(63101), pg. 41
The Alton & Southern Railway Co., 210 N. 13th St.(63103), pg. 76
ALVEY INC., 9301 Olive Blvd.(63132), pg. 46
BENJAMIN ANSEHL COMPANY, 1555 Page Industrial Blvd.(63132), pg. 76
APEX OIL COMPANY, INC., 8182 Maryland Ave.(63105), pg. 78
ATAPCO Office Products Group, 12312 Olive Blvd., Ste. 400(63141), pg. 64
Backer Spielvogel Bates, Inc., 701 Emerson Rd., Ste. 290(63141), pg. 109
BARRY-WEHMILLER COMPANY, 8020 Forsyth Blvd.(63105), pg. 122
BEKINS DISTRIBUTION SERVICES CO., 111 West Port Plaza, Ste. 800(63146), pg. 133
BRECKENRIDGE MATERIAL COMPANY, 2829 Breckenridge Industrial Ct.(63144), pg. 173
CENTERMARK PROPERTIES, INC., 611 Olive St.(63101), pg. 231
CENTRAL STATES DIVERSIFIED, INC., 9322 Manchester Rd.(63119), pg. 234
Centrifugal & Mechanical Industries, 146 President St.(63118), pg. 609
Centrifugal & Mechanical Industries, Inc., 146 President St.(63118), pg. 609
CHEMTECH INDUSTRIES, INC., 1655 Des Peres Rd.(63131), pg. 242
Chesterfield Industrial Park, Inc., 12001 Lackland Rd.(63146), pg. 1167
CLARK OIL & REFINING CORPORATION, 8182 Maryland Ave.(63105), pg. 252
CLAYTON-DAVIS & ASSOCIATES, INCORPORATED, 8229 Maryland(63105), pg. 253
COMPUTER SALES INTERNATIONAL INC., 10845 Olive St., 3rd Fl.(63141), pg. 271
CONCORDIA PUBLISHING HOUSE, 3558 S. Jefferson(63118), pg. 272
CONTICO INTERNATIONAL, INC., 1101 N. Warson(63132), pg. 278
CONTINENTAL WATER COMPANY, 535 N. New Ballas Rd.(63141), pg. 280
CORRIGAN BROS., INC., 3545 Gratiot(63103), pg. 287
Corrigan Company Mechanical Contractors, 3545 Gratiot(63103), pg. 287
CROWN FOODS INC., 5243 Manchester(63110), pg. 302
CURTIS-TOLEDO, INC., 1905 Kienlen Ave.(63133), pg. 306
DENNIS CHEMICAL COMPANY, INC., 2700 Papin St.(63103), pg. 329
DIRECTORY DISTRIBUTING ASSOCIATES, INC., 4363 Woodson Rd.(63134), pg. 339
DUKE MANUFACTURING CO., INC., 2305 No. Broadway(63102), pg. 352
DWF of Saint Louis, Inc., 2715 LaSalle St.(63104), pg. 331
EAC CORPORATION, 347 N. Lindbergh Blvd.(63141), pg. 359
E-Z Clor/Kratz, 1920 Belt Way Dr.(63114), pg. 79
ENTERPRISE RENT-A-CAR COMPANY, 8850 Ladue Rd.(63124), pg. 382
Farm Credit Bank of St. Louis, 1415 Olive St.(63103), pg. 405
FLEISHMAN HILLARD INC., 200 N. Broadway Ave.(63102), pg. 417
LOU FUSZ AUTOMOTIVE NETWORK, 925 N. Lindbergh(63141), pg. 437
Lou Fusz Motor Company, 925 N. Lindbergh(63141), pg. 437
Gared Sports Inc., 1107 Mullanphy(63106), pg. 807
GATEWAY APPAREL, INC., 8500 Valcour(63123), pg. 445
Genelco, Inc., 1600 S. Brentwood., Ste. 500(63144), pg. 448
GENERAL AMERICAN LIFE INSURANCE CO., 700 Market St.(63101), pg. 448
Gismo Inc., 3445 Bent Ave.(63116), pg. 491
THE GLENNON COMPANIES, One City Centre(63101), pg. 462
Graphic Systems, 10866 Indian Head Ind. Blvd.(63106), pg. 721
GROSSMAN IRON & STEEL COMPANY, 5 N. Market(63102), pg. 489
GUARANTEE ELECTRICAL COMPANY, 3405 Bent Ave.(63116), pg. 490
Guarantee Interiors, 3415 Bent Ave.(63116), pg. 491
Gunther Nash Mining Constr., 2150 Kienlen(63121), pg. 31
Guth Lighting Company, 2615 Washington Blvd.(63103), pg. 588
HBE Adam's Rib, 11330 Olive St. Rd.(63141), pg. 496
HBE Bank Facilities, 11330 Olive St. Rd.(63141), pg. 496
HBE CORPORATION, 11330 Olive St.(63141), pg. 495
HBE Medical Buildings, 11330 Olive St. Rd.(63141), pg. 496
HBE Retirement Communities, 11330 Olive St. Rd.(63141), pg. 496
Harvard Interiors Manufacturing Co., 4321 Semple Ave.(63120), pg. 514
Hickey-Mitchell Company, One City Centre, 515 N. Sixth St., Suite 1800(63101-1877), pg. 795
HILL-BEHAN LUMBER COMPANY, 6515 Page Blvd.(63133), pg. 534
Hospital Building & Equipment Co., 11330 Olive St. Rd.(63141), pg. 496
HUGHES ADVERTISING INC., 130 S. Bemiston(63105), pg. 551
JACKES-EVANS MFG. CO., 4427 Geraldine Ave.(63115), pg. 587
Keystone Automotive Industries, Inc. - St. Louis, 3615 Forest Park Blvd.(63108), pg. 628
Kilsby-Roberts/St. Louis, 4735 LeBourget Dr.(63134), pg. 606
KREPS-WISE ASSOCIATES, 1608 Menard(63104), pg. 644
KUPPER PARKER COMMUNICATIONS INC., 6900 Delmar Blvd.(63130), pg. 646
LABARGE PIPE & STEEL COMPANY, 901 N. 10th St.(63101), pg. 649
Lapham-Hickey Steel Corp. (MO), 500 S. Spring Ave.(63110), pg. 658
Loose Leaf Metals Company Inc., 6800 Arsenal(63139), pg. 657
THE LORVIC CORP., 8810 Frost Ave.(63134), pg. 684
A.E. Lottes Company, 800 N. 17th(63106), pg. 225
LOUIS LONDON ADVERTISING & SALES PROMOTION, 408 N. Euclid Ave.(63108), pg. 684
LOVE MORTGAGE COMPANY, Exec. Office Bldg., 515 Olive Street, Ste. 1400(63101), pg. 685
MANNA PRO CORPORATION, 7711 Carondelet, Ste. 800(63105), pg. 704
MasterCard International, Inc., 12115 Lackland Rd.(63146), pg. 720
McCarthy Brothers Co., 1341 N. Rock Hill Rd.(63124), pg. 727
MCCARTHY BUILDING COMPANIES, 1341 N. Rock Hill Rd.(63124), pg. 727
McClelland Consultants Midwest, Inc., 1601 Dielman Rd.(63141), pg. 436
McGrath & Associates, 1920 S. Kings Hwy.(63110), pg. 808
MetLife HealthCare Management Corp., 14500 S. Forty Rd.(63017-5736), pg. 745
MIDWEST PETROLEUM CO., 3940 S. 1st St.(63118), pg. 752
THE MILNOT COMPANY, 100 S. Fourth St.(63102), pg. 756
MISS ELAINE INC., 1717 Olive St.(63103), pg. 760
Missouri Boiler & Tank Co., 2300 Papin St.(63103), pg. 808
MRS. ALISON'S COOKIE COMPANY, 1780 Burns(63132), pg. 760
Mitek Industries, 4203 Shoreline Dr.(63045), pg. 762
Moss & Lowenhaupt Cigar Co., 723 Olive St.(63101), pg. 395
National Casualty Co., One City Centre, 515 N. Sixth St., Suite 1800(63101-1877), pg. 795
Ninety-Fourth of St. Louis, Inc., 5933 McDonnel Blvd.(63134), pg. 1028
NIXDORFF KREIN INDUSTRIES INC., 760 Office Pkwy., Ste. 48(63141), pg. 807
Nooter Construction Co., 1400 So. Third St.(63104), pg. 808
NOOTER CORPORATION, 1400 S. Third St.(63104), pg. 808
Nooter/Eriksen Cogeneration Systems, Inc., 3630 S. Geyer Rd.,Ste. 310(63127), pg. 808
Pevely Dairy Company, 1001 S. Grand Blvd.(63104), pg. 884
PRINCE GARDNER INCORPORATED, 6245 Lemay Ferry Rd.(63129), pg. 890
THE PUCKETT GROUP, 4818 Washington Ave.(63108), pg. 899
ROSS ADVERTISING, INC., 311 N. Lindbergh(63141), pg. 949
SLM Electronics, 11880 Borman Dr.(63146), pg. 967
St. Louis Metallizing Co., 4123 Sarpy Ave.(63110), pg. 808
ST. LOUIS MUSIC, INC., 1400 Ferguson(63133), pg. 967
SIMMONS, DURHAM & ASSOCIATES, 906 Olive St.(63101), pg. 1005
SIMMONS UPHOLSTERED FURNITURE, INC., 1314 Hanley Industrial Ct.(63144), pg. 1005
Southern Illinois and Missouri Bridge Co., 210 N. 13th St.(63103), pg. 76
Specialty Engineered Doors-Clark Door Co., 2366 Center Line Industrial Dr.(63146), pg. 252
SPORLAN VALVE COMPANY, 7525 Sussex Ave.(63143), pg. 1032
SUNNEN PRODUCTS COMPANY, 7910 Manchester Ave.(63143), pg. 1061
Sverdrup Building Corporation, 1836 Lackland Hill Pkwy.(63146), pg. 1066

Sverdrup Environmental Inc., 801 N. Eleventh St.(63101), pg. 1066
TBWA Kerlick Switzer, TBWA House, 1000 St. Louis Union Station(63103), pg. 1071
TMP Worldwide, Inc., 12825 Flushing Meadow Dr.(63131), pg. 1074
TARLTON CORPORATION, 5500 W. Park Ave.(63110-1898), pg. 1079
TAYLOR-MORLEY, INC., 1227 Fern Ridge Pkwy., Ste. 1224, 3rd fl(63141), pg. 1081
TIFFANY INDUSTRIES, INC., 1015 Corporate Sq. Dr., Ste. 105(63132), pg. 1097
Tiffany Industries Americas Corp., 9666 Olive Blvd., Ste. 750(63132), pg. 1097
Tiffany Stand & Furniture Company, 1015 Corporate Sq., Ste. 105(63132), pg. 1097
TOBER INDUSTRIES, INC., 1520 Washington Ave.(63103), pg. 1099
TOBERMAN, 5100 Oakland Ave.(63110), pg. 1099
TUBULAR STEEL INC., 1031 Executive Pkwy.(63141), pg. 1118
Watlow Electric Company of California, 12001 Lackland Rd.(63146), pg. 1168
Watlow Electric Foreign Sales Corporation, 12001 Lackland Rd.(63146), pg. 1168
WATLOW ELECTRIC MANUFACTURING COMPANY, 12001 Lackland Rd.(63146), pg. 1167
Watlow St. Louis, Inc., 12001 Lackland Rd.(63146), pg. 1168
WEINTRAUB AND ASSOCIATES, INC., 11756 Borman Dr., Ste. 150(63146), pg. 1174
WELSH COMPANY, 1535 S. 8th(63104), pg. 1175
WESTERN DIESEL SERVICES INC., 1424 Ashby Rd.(63132), pg. 1179
THE WESTERN GROUP, 1637 N. Warson Rd.(63132), pg. 1179
Western Waterproofing Company, Inc., 1637 N. Warson(63132), pg. 1179
Western Waterproofing Company of America, Inc., 1637 N. Warson(63132), pg. 1179
WILLERT HOME PRODUCTS, INC., 4044 Park Ave.(63110), pg. 1190
WILLIAMS PATENT CRUSHER AND PULVERIZER CO., 2701 N. Broadway(63102), pg. 1191
WILSON SCULLEY ASSOCIATES, 12400 Olive Blvd., Ste. 545(63141), pg. 1194
Witte Hardware Corp., 4600 Goodfellow(63120), pg. 340
World Import Co., 1520 Washington Ave.(63103), pg. 1099

Seymour

Steel Processors Div., P.O. Box 496(65746), pg. 555

Sikeston

Lewis Bros. Bakeries (MO), 504 Kendall(63801), pg. 673

Springfield

Ash Grove Cement, P.O. Box 323, Rte. 3(65803), pg. 87
ASSOCIATED ELECTRIC CO-OP INC., 2814 S. Golden(65801), pg. 89
BASS PRO SHOPS, INC., 1935 S. Campbell(65898), pg. 125
BRADSHAW ASSOCIATES IN ADVERTISING, INC., 550 St. Louis St.(65806), pg. 171
CONSUMERS MARKETS INC., 639 W. Chestnut Expwy(65802), pg. 277
THE DANIEL CO. OF SPRINGFIELD, 3725 W. Division(65803), pg. 314
J.L. DeGraffenreid & Sons, Inc., 1301 W. Webster(65801), pg. 1152
ERICKSON TRANSPORT CORPORATION, 2255 N. Packer Rd.(65803), pg. 386
Hiland Dairy Company, 1133 E. Kearney(65803), pg. 884
Huntco Steel Co., 1200 E. Woodhurst, Bldg. J(65804), pg. 554
HUTCHENS INDUSTRIES INC., 215 N. Patterson(65802-2206), pg. 555
MD Pneumatics, Inc., 4840 W. Kearney(65803), pg. 1120
THE MARLIN COMPANY, 1200 E. Woodhurst Dr., Bldg. V(65804), pg. 710
MCLEAN ENTERPRISES, INC., 2610 N. Glenstone(65803), pg. 731
MID-AMERICA DAIRYMEN, INC., 3253 E. Chestnut Expwy.(65802), pg. 750
Missouri Auction Services Corp. d/b/a 166 Auto Action, 2944 West Sunshine(65807), pg. 293
NOBLE & ASSOCIATES, 1949 E. Sunshine(65804), pg. 808
O'REILLY AUTO INC., 233 S. Patterson(65802), pg. 829
POSITRONIC INDUSTRIES, INC., 423 N. Campbell(65806), pg. 881
REYCO INDUSTRIES, INC., 600 N. Prospect St.(65805), pg. 930
Universal Flowers, Inc., 1300 W. Poplar(65808), pg. 554
Western International Media Corporation, 1949 E. Sunshine, Corp. Center Two, Ste. 1-112(65804), pg. 1180

Stover

Fajen & Blair Division, 400 So. Walnut(65078), pg. 300

Strafford

Midwest Products, Inc., R.R.554

Sullivan

Paramount Metalizing Div., 1008 W. North Service Rd.(63080), pg. 641

Troy

Watlow Process Systems, Inc., 300-A Industrial Dr.(63379), pg. 1168

Union

Gould Packaging, Inc., 800 N. Oak St.(63084), pg. 473

Unionville

Dunlop Manufacturing Co., P.O. Box 248, (63665), pg. 1148

Volumnud

Newell Paper Co. of Columbus, 1616 7th Ave., S.(39708), pg. 587

Warrenton

BINKLEY COMPANY, Main & Elm Sts.(63383), pg. 151
Prest Rack Inc., Main & Elm Sts.(63383), pg. 151

Washington

Aerolyte Systems, One Cable Car Dr.(63090), pg. 254
CLEMCO INDUSTRIES, One Cable Car Dr.(63090), pg. 254

Webb City

DETECTO SCALE COMPANY, 203 E. Daugherty(64870), pg. 332

Wellsville

Wellsville Fire Brick Company, P.O. Box 71, West Hwy. 19(63384), pg. 201

Wright City

Amedco Health Care, Inc., 401 S. Outer Service Rd.(63390), pg. 554

MONTANA

Belgrade

BRUCE-ANDERSEN COMPANY, INC., 642 Gallatin Field Rd.(59714), pg. 183

Billings

CNJ Distributing, 1445 Broadwater(59102), pg. 286
Coluson Technologies, 12 Garden Ave.(59107), pg. 1053
CORCORAN TRUCKING COMPANY, 221 Lomond Lane(59101), pg. 285
CORNER POCKETS OF AMERICA, 1445 Broadwater(59102), pg. 286
Frontier Chevrolet Co., 1617 First Ave., N.(59101), pg. 952
NORTHWEST PIPE FITTINGS, INC., 33 S. 8th St. W.(59103), pg. 815
RYAN OLDSMOBILE, 324 S. 24th St., W.(59102), pg. 958
SafetyMaster Corporation, 12 Garden Ave.(59101), pg. 1053
SELOVER BUICK, INC., 523 N. 29th St.(59101), pg. 988
WYO-BEN, INC., 3044 Hesper Rd.(59102), pg. 1157
West Advertising/Public Relations, Inc., Transwestern 3 Bldg., 4th Fl., (59103), pg. 613

Bozeman

COUNTRY CLASSIC DAIRIES, INC., P.O. Box 968(59715), pg. 289

Butte

TOWN PUMP, INC., 600 S. Main St.(59701), pg. 1104

Clancy

Montana City Plant, 100 Montana Hwy. 518(59634), pg. 88

Columbia Falls

COLUMBIA FALLS ALUMINUM COMPANY, 2000 Aluminum Dr.(59912), pg. 265

Darby

Stoltze-Conner Lumber Co., P.O. Box 410(59289), pg. 1050

Glendive

F.T. REYNOLDS COMPANY, 1014 W. Towne St.(59330), pg. 930

Great Falls

D.A. DAVIDSON & CO., Davidson Building(59401), pg. 318
Financial Aims Corporation, Davidson Building(59401), pg. 318
National-General Supply, Inc., 410 14th St., S.W., P.O. Box 2288(59403), pg. 1174
Northwest Fence Products Co., P.O. Box 1204, 226 2nd Ave., So.(59403), pg. 1174
PACIFIC HIDE & FUR DEPOT, P.O. Box 1549(59403), pg. 840
TrustCorp., Davidson Building(59401), pg. 318
CARL WEISSMAN & SONS, INC., P.O. Box 1609(59403), pg. 1174
WENDT ADVERTISING, INC., P.O. Box 2129, (59403), pg. 1176

Helena

MONTANA LOTTERY, 2525 N. Montana Ave.(59601), pg. 766

Kalispell

EQUITY SUPPLY COMPANY, P.O. Box 579(59901), pg. 385

Missoula

WASHINGTON CORPORATION, 101 International Way(59801), pg. 1165

Poplar

A & S TRIBAL INDUSTRIES, P.O. Box 308(59255), pg. 1

Seeley Lake

PYRAMID MOUNTAIN LUMBER, Boy Scout Rd.(59868), pg. 901

West Yellowstone

HAMILTON STORES, INC., One Hamilton St.(59758), pg. 503

NEBRASKA

Alliance

Woolrich Store Co., P.O. Box 680, (69301), pg. 1201

Aurora

Chief Industries - Housing Div., P.O. Box 127(68818), pg. 247

Beatrice

Chesco Products, Inc., P.O. Box 686, (68310), pg. 64

Blair

NEBRASKA-IOWA SUPPLY COMPANY, 1160 Lincoln(68008), pg. 796

Clay Center

DAHLSTEN TRUCK LINE, INC., 101 W. Edgar St.(68933), pg. 310

Columbus

BEHLEN MFG. CO., 4025 E. 23rd St.(68601), pg. 132
Farmaster/Big Valley Div., P.O. Box 569, (68602-0569), pg. 132
NEBRASKA PUBLIC POWER DISTRICT, 1414 15th St.(68602-0499), pg. 796

Crete

FEED SERVICE CORP., R.R. 1 Box 244A(68333), pg. 405

De Witt

Cobra Tool, Inc., P.O. Box 356, (68341), pg. 64
Petersen Development Corp., P.O. Box 337, (68341), pg. 64
Petersen Manufacturing Co., Inc., P.O. Box 337(68341), pg. 64
Prosnip Corporation, P.O. Box 337, (68341), pg. 64
Unibit Corp., P.O. Box 337, (68341), pg. 64

Deshler

REINKE MANUFACTURING CO., INC., 101 Reinke Rd.(68340), pg. 924

Fremont

Golden Sun Feeds, Inc., (68025), pg. 467
Magnus Metals, S. Bell & Viaduct(68025), pg. 400
Shade Pasta, Inc., 805 S. Union(68025), pg. 810

Gering

LOCKWOOD CORPORATION, E. Hwy. 92(69341), pg. 680
MASEK DISTRIBUTING INC., 1100 Rundell Rd.(69341), pg. 717

Gibbon

Nebraska Turkey Growers, Railroad & Lawn Ave.(68840), pg. 809

Gothenburg

GRN Corp., 1000 12th Street(69138), pg. 472

Grand Island

Chief Construction, P.O. Box 2078, (68802-2078), pg. 247
Chief E-Z Breaker, Inc., 2809 E. Hwy. 30(68801), pg. 247
Chief Financial Services, 1811 W. 2nd St., Ste. 425(68803), pg. 247
Chief Industries - Agri Products Div., P.O. Box 2078(68802), pg. 247
Chief Industries - Buildings Div., P.O. Box 2078(68802), pg. 247
CHIEF INDUSTRIES, INC., 3942 W. Old Hwy. 30(68803), pg. 247
Custom Product Div., P.O. Box 2078, (68802), pg. 247
Custom Products Division, P.O. Box 2078, (68802-2078), pg. 247
Ecology System Dept., P.O. Box 2078(68802), pg. 247
Electronic Display Systems (Kallego), 2813 E. Hwy. 30(68801), pg. 247
Grand Island Contract Carriers & Brokerage, Inc., P.O. Box 2078, (68802-2078), pg. 247
The Grand Island Daily Independent, P.O. Box 1208, 1st & Cedar Sts.(68801), pg. 1042
Hornady Ammunition, (68801), pg. 544
HORNADY MANUFACTURING COMPANY, Box 1848, (68802), pg. 544
Indianhead Golf Club, 4100 Husker Hwy.(68803), pg. 247

Hastings

ALLENS OF HASTINGS, INC., 1115 W. Second St.(68901), pg. 36
Chief Ethanol Fuels, Inc., P.O. Box 488, (68902-0488), pg. 247
DUTTON-LAINSON CO., 451 W. 2nd(68902), pg. 356

Sanitas Healthcare Div., 451 W. 2nd(68904), pg. 356

Kearney

Caldwell Manufacturing, P.O. Box 338(68847), pg. 247

Lexington

LEXINGTON CO-OP OIL CO., P.O. Box A(68850), pg. 673

Lincoln

ATC Air, Inc., 301 S. 13th St., Ste. 600(68508), pg. 64
AMERICAN TOOL COMPANIES, INC., 301 S. 13th St., Ste. 600(68508), pg. 64
AMERITAS LIFE INSURANCE CORP., 5900 O St.(68510), pg. 66
BAILEY LAUERMAN & ASSOCIATES, INC., 900 NBC Center(68508), pg. 114
THE CHESAPEAKE LIFE INSURANCE CO., Gold's Galleria, 1033 O St., Ste. 5(65808), pg. 243
Cooperative Service Co., Culvert St.(68506), pg. 402
CRETE CARRIER CORP., 400 N.W. 56th(68528), pg. 299
Harvest Equity Inc., 4535 Normal Blvd., Ste. 222(68506), pg. 402
Health America/CapitalCare, Inc., 220 S. 17th St.(68508), pg. 779
Lifeshares Services Co., Gold's Galleria, 1033 "O" St., Ste. 5(68508), pg. 243
LINCOLN ELECTRIC SYSTEMS, 1040 O St.(68508), pg. 675
LINCOLN INDUSTRIES, 4700 S. 19th St.(68512), pg. 676
Nebraska Book Co., 4700 S. 19th(68512), pg. 676
NEBRASKA DEPT. OF ECONOMIC DEVELOPMENT, P.O. Box 94666, 301 Centennial Mall South(68509-4666), pg. 796
SCHNIEBER FINE FOODS, INC., 2500 State Fair Park Dr.(68504), pg. 977
SNYDER INDUSTRIES, INC., 4700 Fremont St.(68504), pg. 1015
SWANSON RUSSELL ASSOCIATES, 1222 P. St.(68508), pg. 1066
Telex Hy-gain Div., 8601 E. Cornhusker Hwy.(68505), pg. 1085
25 Corporation, 4700 S. 19th(68512), pg. 676
WOODMEN ACCIDENT & LIFE CO., 1526 K St(68508), pg. 1200

Louisville

Ash Grove Cement, P.O. Box 609, (68037), pg. 87

Minden

Royal Plastic, P.O. Box 380, (68959), pg. 458

Morrill

KELLEY BEAN CO., INC., Bean Blvd.(69358), pg. 621

Norfolk

AFFILIATED FOODS COOPERATIVE INC., 13th St. & Omaha Ave.(68701), pg. 23
BeefAmerica, 1500 S. Logan(68701), pg. 132

Oakland

HOLMQUIST GRAIN & LUMBER CO., 200 N. Logan Ave.(68045-0127), pg. 540

Omaha

AG PROCESSING INC A COOPERATIVE, P.O. Box 2047, (68103-2047), pg. 24
ALLIED OIL & SUPPLY, INC., 2209 S. 24th(68108), pg. 38
Allied Tire Co., 2209 S. 24th St.(68108), pg. 38
Allright Corporation, 202 N. 19th St.(68102), pg. 41
American Business Directories, 5707 S. 86th Circle(68127), pg. 50
AMERICAN BUSINESS INFORMATION, INC., 5711 S. 86th Circle(68127), pg. 50
American Directory Publishing, 5707 S. 86th Circle(68127), pg. 50
American Envelope of Omaha, 915 N. 43rd Ave.(68131), pg. 199
BEEFAMERICA OPERATING CO., INC., 5600 Harry Andersen Ave.(68137), pg. 131
Continental General Corporation, 8901 Indian Hills Dr.(68114), pg. 1181
Cox Cable Omaha, Inc., 11505 W. Dodge Rd.(68154), pg. 294
CULVER & ASSOCIATES, INC., 533 North 86th St.(68114), pg. 304
DWF of Omaha, 9312 G Street(68127), pg. 331
LEO A. DALY COMPANY, 8600 Indian Hills Dr.(68114), pg. 313
DATA DOCUMENTS HOLDINGS, INC., 4205 S. 96th St.(68127), pg. 316
Data Documents, Inc., 4205 S. 96th St.(68127), pg. 316
Farm Credit Bank of Omaha, Farm Credit Bank Bldg., 206 S. 19th St.(68102), pg. 405
Farmers National Company, 11516 Nichols St.(68154-4427), pg. 744
Fund Management Co., 10235 Regency Ct.(68114), pg. 779
GODFATHER'S PIZZA, INC., 9140 W. Dodge Rd.(68114), pg. 464
Guarantee American Life Company, 8801 Indian Hills Dr.(68114), pg. 491
GUARANTEE MUTUAL LIFE CO., 8801 Indian Hills Dr.(68114), pg. 491
VINOD GUPTA COMPANY, INC., 5707 South 86th Circle(68127), pg. 494
Henningsen Foods, Inc., 14334 Industrial Rd.(68137), pg. 629
ITI MARKETING SERVICES, INC., 7415 Dodge St.(68114), pg. 561
Industrial Chemical Laboratories, 1015 North 14th St.(68102), pg. 941
KAHLER FRIENDT & PARTNERS, INC., 2405 South 130th Circle(68144-5908), pg. 613
Kiewit Construction Group, Inc., 1000 Kiewit Plaza(68131), pg. 629
Kiewit Mining Group, Inc., 1000 Kiewit Plaza(68131), pg. 629
PETER KIEWIT SONS INC., 1000 Kiewit Plaza(68131), pg. 629
Kirkpatrick Pettis, 10250 Regency Cir., Ste. 200(68114), pg. 779
LORTZ DIRECT MARKETING INC., 11316 "P" St.(68137), pg. 684
LOZIER CORPORATION, 6336 Pershing Dr.(68110), pg. 686
Lozier Store Fixtures, Inc., 6336 Pershing Dr.(68110), pg. 686
Marketing Research Group, 5711 S. 86th Circle(68127), pg. 50
MASTERCRAFT FURNITURE CORP., 1111 N. 13th St.(68102), pg. 720
Mutual of Omaha, Mutual of Omaha Plaza(68175), pg. 779
Mutual of Omaha Fund Management Co., 10235 Regency Cir.(68114), pg. 779
MUTUAL OF OMAHA INSURANCE COMPANY, Mutual of Omaha Plaza(68175), pg. 779
Nebraska Engineering Co., P.O. Box 12277, (68112), pg. 1073
OMAHA CREATIVE GROUP, P.O. Box 3300, 10909 John Galt Blvd.(68103), pg. 825
Omaha Property & Casualty, 3102 Farnam St.(68131), pg. 779
Omaha Property & Casualty Co., 3102 Farnam St.(68131), pg. 779
OMAHA PUBLIC POWER DISTRICT, Energy Plaza, 444 S. 16th St. Mall(68102-2247), pg. 825
OMAHA STEAKS INTERNATIONAL, 10909 John Galt Blvd.(68103), pg. 825
Online Information Network, 5707 S. 86th Circle(68127), pg. 50
PACESETTER CORPORATION, 4343 S. 96th St.(68127), pg. 839
Paxton & Vierling, P.O. Box 1085(68101), pg. 834
PRECISION INDUSTRIES, 4611 S. 96th St.(68127), pg. 885
PROGRESS WEST, 10180 L Street(68127), pg. 894
Railway Educational Bureau, 1809 Capitol Ave.(68102), pg. 1005
THE SCOULAR COMPANY, The Scoular Building, 2027 Dodge Street(68102), pg. 983
Scoular Grain Company, 2027 Dodge(68102), pg. 983
SMITH, KAPLAN, ALLEN & REYNOLDS, INC., 111 South 108th Ave.(68154), pg. 1013
SUPERIOR INDUSTRIES OF NEBRASKA, INC., 5217 S. 132nd St.(68137), pg. 1063
Tele-Trip Co., Mutual Of Omaha Plaza(68175), pg. 779
UNITED A G CO-OP, INC., 7401 "F" St.(68127-1874), pg. 1130
United Financial Resources, 6211 "L" St.(68117), pg. 1130
United Retailers Insurance Corp., 6211 "L" St.(68117), pg. 1130
United World Life Insurance Company, Dodge at 33rd(68175), pg. 779
WARREN DISTRIBUTION, INC., 727 S. 13th St.(68102), pg. 1164
WESTIN, INC., 4727 Center St.(68106), pg. 1183
Wright & Wilhelmy Co., 10th & Jackson St.(68102), pg. 340

Schuyler

WAGNER MILLS INC., P.O. Box 545(68661), pg. 1158

Scottsbluff

KSTF-TV, P.O. Box 1619, 1402 First Ave.(69361), pg. 1043

York

Sunflower Carriers, P.O. Box 9(68467), pg. 299
The York News-Times, P.O. Box 279, 327 Platte Ave.(68467), pg. 1042

NEVADA

Boulder City

Fisher Pen Co. of Nevada, 711 Yucca St.(89005), pg. 415

Carson City

CUBIX CORPORATION, 2800 Lockheed Way(89706), pg. 303
HARDIE IRRIGATION-LANDSCAPE DIV., 788 Fairview Dr.(89701), pg. 508
MALLORY, INC., 550 Mallory Way(89701), pg. 703
UNITED ENGINE & MACHINE COMPANY, 4909 Goni Rd.(89706), pg. 1131

Dayton

BRUCE INDUSTRIES, INC., P.O. Box 1700(89403), pg. 183

Hawthorne

Day & Zimmermann, Inc., P.O. Box 15, (89415-0015), pg. 321

Las Vegas

Allied Security Inc., The Nolon Bldg., 320 E. Charleston, Ste. E(89104), pg. 39
Allright Sierra Parking Inc., 222 East Carson Av.(89101), pg. 42
DINE OUT ADVERTISING CORP., 2000 Las Vegas Blvd. South(89104), pg. 338
Disposal Urban Maintenance Procession Co., Inc., 7900 Vegas Valley Rd.(89122), pg. 1004
DUNES HOTELS AND CASINOS INC., 3650 Las Vegas Blvd., S.(89109), pg. 352
JS&A ADVERTISING, 3350 Palms Centre Dr.(89113), pg. 586
JS&A GROUP, INC., 3350 Palms Ctr. Dr.(89103), pg. 586
KLAS-TV, P.O. Box 15047, 3228 Channel 8 Dr.(89114), pg. 654
LAS VEGAS SUN, INC., 800 S. Valley View(89107), pg. 659
Lewis Building Co., Inc., 5420 S. Polaris, P.O. Box 19297(89132), pg. 673
Lewis Homes Of Nevada, 3325 Ali Baba Lane(89132), pg. 673
Northridge Industries, Inc., 202 E. Fremont St.(89101), pg. 495
R & R ADVERTISING, 8076 W. Sahara Ave.(89117), pg. 906
SILVER STATE DISPOSAL SERVICE, INC., 770 E. Sahara Blvd.(89104), pg. 1004
Standard Restaurant Equipment Co., 5675 S. Valley View Dr.(89118-2411), pg. 1036
SUMMA CORPORATION, 3800 Howard Hughes Pkwy.(89109), pg. 1057
Universal Roofers, Inc., 3430 S. Valley View Blvd.(89102), pg. 185
Vegas Electric Supply, P.O. Box 27108(89126), pg. 215
Westco Food Service, 827 N. Main St.(89101), pg. 1178
Western International Media Corporation, 1601 E. Flamingo Rd., 1180
Young Electric Sign Las Vegas Div., 5119 S. Cameron St.(89118), pg. 1209

Minden

BENTLY NEVADA CORPORATION, P.O. Box 157(89423), pg. 140
Bently Rotor Dynamics Research Corp., P.O. Box 2529(89423), pg. 140

North Las Vegas

FREHNER CONSTRUCTION COMPANY, INC., 124 W. Brooks(89030), pg. 432

Reno

Allright Sierra Parking, Inc., 220 S. Center(89501), pg. 42
AMERCO, A NEVADA CORPORATION, 1325 Airmotive Way, Ste. 100(89502), pg. 47
CALIFORNIA PACIFIC RESEARCH, INC., 1055 W. Moana(89509), pg. 210
D & D Wholesale Liquors, 550 Evans Ave.(89512), pg. 498
DOYLE MCKENNA BAYER BROWN, 1175 Harvard Way(89502), pg. 348
DUNN REBER GLENN MARZ, 50 Washington St.(89503), pg. 354
HAMILTON CO., INC., P.O. Box 10030, (89520-0012), pg. 503
JENSEN ELECTRIC COMPANY, 140 Jensen St.(89502), pg. 592
Western International Media Corporation, 1325 Airmotive Way, Ste. 175-T(89502), pg. 1180
Wooster Magikoter West Division, 1960 Joule St.(89703), pg. 1202

Sparks

Direct Dental Supply Co., 879 Deming Way(89431), pg. 851
MOUNTAIN AIR DELIVERY, 728 Spice Island Dr.(89431), pg. 773
STERLING HOMES CORP., 871 East Glendale Ave.(89431), pg. 1046
VeloBind-Reno Division, 850 Spice Island(89431), pg. 657
Westco Products/North Nevada, 475 Nugget Ave.(89431), pg. 1178

NEW HAMPSHIRE

Ashland

Tool Shop, P.O. Box 756, Main St.(03217), pg. 433

Bedford

ECKMAN CONSTRUCTION COMPANY, 84 Palomino Lane(03110), pg. 366
HARVEY CONSTRUCTION COMPANY, INC., 10 Harvey Rd.(03110), pg. 515
Keystone Crash Parts Mart - Bedford, 548 Donald St., Unit 7(03102), pg. 628

Bristol

Seals Division, Ragged Mountain Hwy., P.O. Box B(03222-0501), pg. 433

Claremont

CLAREMONT FLOCK CORPORATION, 169 Main St.(03743), pg. 251

Concord

AUTOMOTIVE SUPPLY ASSOC., INC., 129 Manchester St.(03301), pg. 101
CONCORD LITHO CO., INC., P.O. Box 464(03301-0464), pg. 272
Hobart Tafa Technologies, Inc., 146 Pembroke Rd.(03301), pg. 537
NEW HAMPSHIRE SWEEPSTAKES COMMISSION, 75 Fort Eddy Rd.(03301), pg. 801
PATSY'S, INC., 24 Hall St.(03301), pg. 851
Pitco Mastermatic Inc., P.O. Box 2272(03301), pg. 157
Sanel Auto Parts, Inc., 219 S. Main St.(03301), pg. 101

Dover

EASTERN AIR DEVICES, INC., One Progress Dr.(03820), pg. 363
ROBBINS AUTO PARTS, INC., 110-116 Washington St.(03820), pg. 938

Dublin

YANKEE PUBLISHING INCORPORATED, Main St.(03444), pg. 1207

Hampton

FOSS MANUFACTURING COMPANY INCORPORATED, 380 Lafayette Rd.(03842), pg. 426
THE HENLEY GROUP, INC., Liberty Lane(03842), pg. 529
NEW HAMPSHIRE OAK, Liberty Lane(03842), pg. 800
OMNI HOTELS, 500 Lafayette Rd.(03842), pg. 826

Hooksett

MERCHANTS RENT A CAR, INC., 1278 Hooksett Rd.(03106), pg. 739

Hudson

DELTA EDUCATION, INC., 5 Hudson Park Dr.(03051), pg. 326
Improved Blow Molding Equipment Company, Inc., 11 Sagamore Park Dr.(03051), pg. 471
Lowell Shoe, Inc., 8 Hampshire Dr.(03501), pg. 772

Jaffrey

D. D. BEAN & SONS CO., Peterborough Rd.(03452), pg. 129
W.W. Cross, Inc., 77 Webster St.(03452), pg. 129
Curtis Manufacturing Company, Inc., 30 Fitzgerald Dr.(03452), pg. 571
Jaffrey Fire Protection Co., Peterborough Rd., P.O. Box 348(03452), pg. 129

Keene

Kingsbury Assembly Machine Div., 80 Laurel St.(03431-2059), pg. 632
KINGSBURY CORPORATION, 80 Laurel St.(03431), pg. 631
Kingsbury Machining Center, Div., 80 Laurel St.(03431-2059), pg. 632
Kingsbury Service Corp., 80 Laurel St., P.O. Box 2020(03431), pg. 632
Kingsbury World Sales, 80 Laurel St., P.O. Box 2020(03431), pg. 632
Kingtool Division, 80 Laurel St.(03431-2059), pg. 632
MARKEM CORPORATION, 150 Congress St.(03431), pg. 708

Laconia

Allen-Rogers Co., P.O. Box 637, (03246), pg. 319
M & E Manufacturing Co., 19 Durkee St.(03246), pg. 875
Wilcom Products, Inc., Rt. 3 Daniel Webster Hwy.(03248), pg. 812

Littleton

LITTLETON COIN CO., INC., 253 Union St(03561), pg. 679

Londonderry

AC Leasing Corporation, 134 W. Broadway(03053), pg. 14
ACTION EQUIPMENT, 134 W. Broadway(03053), pg. 14
Action Supply, 134 W. Broadway(03053), pg. 14
Action Tire, 134 W. Broadway(03053), pg. 14
JJJ Realty Trust, 134 W. Broadway(03053), pg. 14
JENKINS SPIRITS CORP. LTD., 21 S. Perimeter Rd.(03053), pg. 592

Manchester

Allied Security Inc., 363 Lincoln St.(03103), pg. 39
Associated Foods Inc., P.O. Box 5200(03108), pg. 90
ASSOCIATED GROCERS OF NEW ENGLAND, INC., 725 Gold St.(03108), pg. 90
Associated Lease Corp., P.O. Box 5200(03108), pg. 90
Certified Wholesalers Inc., P.O. Box 5200(03108), pg. 90
COLONIAL SUPPLY CORPORATION, 25 Union St.(03103), pg. 264
DOBLES CHEVROLET, INC., 1250 S. Willow St.(03103), pg. 342
FELTON BRUSH INC., 315 Wilson St.(03103), pg. 406
French & Bean, P.O. Box 5200(03108), pg. 90
GRANITE STATE MANUFACTURING CO., 124 Joliette St.(03105), pg. 476
GRANITE STATE PACKING CO., 163 Hancock St.(03101), pg. 476
ITRAN CORPORATION, 670 N. Commercial St.(03101-1147), pg. 583
JEWELL INSTRUMENTS, INC., Grenier Industrial Air Park, 850 Perimeter Rd.(03103), pg. 594
Lindenmeyr Munroe, 468 Pepsi Road(03103), pg. 233
NYLON CORPORATION OF AMERICA, 333 Sundial Ave.(03103), pg. 818
O'NEIL GRIFFIN & ASSOCIATES, INC., 324 Commercial St.(03101), pg. 827
Plastic Products Division, Grenier Industrial Park(03103), pg. 432
SUMMA FOUR, INC., 25 Sundail Aee.(03103-7251), pg. 1057
Sweetheart Cup Corporation, 400 Gay St.(03103), pg. 1067

Meredith

Gerrity Lumber Co., Railroad Ave., Box 669(03253), pg. 454

Merrimack

GUILFORD TRANSPORTATION INDUSTRIES INC., 7 Executive Park Dr.(03054), pg. 493
Metrologic Instruments-Northeast, 301 Daniel Webster Hwy.(03054), pg. 743

Milford

HITCHINER MANUFACTURING COMPANY, INC., Elm St.(03055), pg. 536

Nashua

ADVANCED CIRCUIT TECHNOLOGY, 118 N. Eastern Blvd.(03061), pg. 20
Beebe Rubber Company, 25 Marshall St.(03060), pg. 239
CHAGNON LUMBER COMPANY, INC., 145 Temple St.(03060), pg. 238
DATAMEDIA CORPORATION, 20 Trafalgar Sq.(03063), pg. 316
Fasfax Corporation, Simon & Ledge Sts.(03060), pg. 579
INTERNATIONAL SHOE MACHINE CORP., Simon & Ledge Sts.(03060), pg. 579
TULLEY BUICK-PONTIAC COMPANY, INC., 147 Daniel Webster Hwy. S(03061), pg. 1119

New Ipswich

SEPPALA & AHO CONSTRUCTION COMPANY, Peterboro Road(03071), pg. 990

Newington

NESLAB INSTRUMENTS, INC., 25 Nimble Hill Rd.(03801), pg. 798

Panacook

RIVERSIDE MILLWORK COMPANY, INC., 77 Merrimack St.(03303), pg. 937

Peterborough

A+ Publishing, 80 Elm St.(03458), pg. 576
B C Publishing, 80 Elm St.(03458), pg. 576
BROOKSTONE COMPANY, INC., Vose Farm Rd.(03458), pg. 180
Techmedia, 80 Elm St.(03458), pg. 577

Portsmouth

First Signature Bank & Trust Co., 190 Commerce Way(03801), pg. 596

Rochester

ENCORE SHOE CORPORATION, 51 Wakefield St.(03867), pg. 380
New England Correct Craft, Inc., 142 Flagg Rd.(03867), pg. 287

Salem

Electric Specialty & Supply, 71 Lowell Rd.(03079), pg. 374
UNIVEX CORPORATION, 3 Old Rockingham Rd.(03079), pg. 1139

Somersworth

FaceMate Pond Lilt Great Falls, 200 Main St.(03878), pg. 396

Troy

TROY MILLS, INC., 18 Monadnock St.(03465), pg. 1116

NEW JERSEY

Allendale

BLACK MILLWORK CO., INC., 230 W. Crescent Ave.(07401), pg. 154

Asbury

ASBURY CARBONS, INC., Main St. & RD 87
Asbury Graphite Mills, Inc., Main St. & RD 87

Atlantic City

Ireland Gourmet Shop, P.O. Box 45, (08401), pg. 582
Trump's Castle Casino Resort, Huron Ave. & Brigantine Blvd.(08401), pg. 1118

Avenel

Ivex Packaging Corporation-Avenel, 30 Production Way(07001), pg. 583

Barrington

Anchor Optical Co., Inc., 97 E. Gloucester Pike(08007), pg. 369
EDMUND SCIENTIFIC COMPANY, 101 E. Gloucester Pike(08007-1380), pg. 369

Bayonne

BOOKAZINE COMPANY, INC., 75 Hook Dr.(07002), pg. 164
CASCHEM INC., 40 Ave. A(07002), pg. 227
JERSEY PRINTING COMPANY, INC., 111 Linnet St.(07002), pg. 593
MURALO CO., INC., 148 E. Fifth St.(07002), pg. 776

Belleville

Kimball Baggage Tag Division, 151 Cortland St.(07109), pg. 911
Metro Label Corp., 357 Cortlandt St.(07109), pg. 743

Bellmawr

Puritan Oil Company, Inc., 1 S. Black Horse Pike(08030), pg. 1165

Bergenfield

GENERAL SPORTCRAFT COMPANY LTD., 140 Woodbine St.(07621), pg. 450

Berkeley Heights

Daylux, Inc., 310 Snyder Ave.(07922), pg. 1004
SILLCOCKS PLASTICS INTERNATIONAL, INC., 310 Snyder Ave.(07922), pg. 1004

Bernardsville

Douglas Elliman-Gibbons & Ives, Inc., 30 Morristown Rd.(07924), pg. 347

Beverly

PHOENIX INTERNATIONAL, INC., 450 Broad St.(08010), pg. 868
Tactair Fluid Controls Corp., 450 Broad St., P.O. Box 158(08010), pg. 869

Blackwood

METROLOGIC INSTRUMENTS, INC., Coles Rd., Rte. 42(08012), pg. 743
Plastic Suppliers, Inc., 207 Lakeview Ave.(08012), pg. 876

Bloomfield

MINOR RUBBER CO., INC., 49 Ackerman St.(07003), pg. 758
REESE FINER FOODS, INC., 300 Broad Acres Dr.(07003), pg. 921

Bloomingdale

CENTRAL/SHIPPEE, INC., 46 Star Lake Rd.(07403), pg. 234

Bloomsbury

KOH-I-NOOR, INC., 100 North St.(08804), pg. 639
Mid-Atlantic Correct Craft, Inc., P.O. Box 403, Rt. 173(08804), pg. 287

Boonton

JOHANSON MANUFACTURING CORPORATION, 400 Rockaway Valley Rd.(07005), pg. 595
Pyro Chem, Inc., 301 Division St., P.O. Box 37(07005), pg. 166

Bordentown

National Auto Dealers Exchange, P.O. Box 188, Route 206 S.(08505), pg. 293

Bound Brook

LOFT'S SEEDS, INC., Chimney Rock Rd.(08805), pg. 681

Branchburg

FALCON SAFETY PRODUCTS INC., 25 Chubb Way(08876-1299), pg. 398

Branchville

HIGH POINT FINANCIAL CORP., Three Broad St.(07826), pg. 533
High Point Investment Advisory Services, Three Broad St.(07826), pg. 534
NBSC Investment Co., Three Broad St.(07826), pg. 534
The National Bank of Sussex County, 3 Broad St.(07826), pg. 534

Bridgeport

Day Products, 540 Pedricktown Rd.(08014), pg. 320

Bridgewater

Ground Water Associates, Inc., 1011 Rte. 22 W.(08807), pg. 556
HAMAMATSU CORP., 360 Foothill Rd.(08807-0910), pg. 502
HYDRO GROUP, INC., 1011 Rte. 22 W(08807), pg. 556

Burlington

Ceramco, 6 Terri Lane(08016), pg. 330
Macrodyne Engineering Services, Columbus Rd., P.O. Box 188(08016), pg. 869
Tactair Advanced Technology, Inc., Columbus Road, Box 188(08016), pg. 869

Butler

CARELLI, GLYNN & WARD, 1250 Route 23(07405), pg. 218

Camden

Boam Chemicals Co., Inc., 3rd St. & Jefferson Ave.(08104), pg. 694
Boam Produce (Overseas) Ltd., 3rd St. & Jefferson Ave.(08104), pg. 694
Maf Cote Specialties Co., Inc., 3rd St. & Jefferson Ave.(08104), pg. 694

MacAndrews & Forbes Co., 3rd St. & Jefferson Ave.(08104), pg. 694
MacAndrews & Forbes Ltd., 3rd St. & Jefferson Ave.(08104), pg. 694

Carlstadt

ALDINE TECHNOLOGIES, 585 Industrial Rd.(07072-1611), pg. 33
Applied Graphics Technology, 463 Barrell Ave.(07072), pg. 1136
DATABILITY, INC., One Palmer Terrace(07072), pg. 316
DEERSKIN TRADING POST, INC., 725 Dell Rd.(07072), pg. 324
EAGLE BUTTON CO., INC., 415 Fourteenth St.(07072), pg. 362
Food Oils Corporation, 145 Grant St.(07072), pg. 1114
Lensclean, Inc., 585 Industrial Rd.(07072-1611), pg. 33
PIONEER PAPER CORPORATION, 50 Triangle Blvd.(07072), pg. 872
Polo/Ralph Lauren Factory Store, 590 Commerce Blvd.(07072), pg. 880
STANBEE COMPANY, INC., 70 Broad St.(07072), pg. 1035

Carteret

TAWIL ASSOCIATES INC., 100 Wesley White Dr.(07008), pg. 1080

Cedar Knolls

CARNRICK LABS., INC., 65 Horsehill Rd.(07927), pg. 222
SINGH INDUSTRIES, 6 Saddle Rd.(07927), pg. 1008
TRANSISTOR DEVICES, INC., 85 Horsehill Rd.(07927), pg. 1107

Chatham

MAGLA PRODUCTS, 700 Shunpike Rd.(07928-2199), pg. 700

Cherry Hill

Aratex Services, Inc., 1178 Marlkress(08003), pg. 7
CCW Stamp Co., 2324 W. Rt. 70(08002), pg. 58
Data Sources, 20 Brace Rd.(08034), pg. 1218
PAOLIN & SWEENEY, 375 N. Kings Hwy.(08034), pg. 847
PENNY PLATE, INC., 603 Kressan Rd.(08034), pg. 858
ROSANIO, BAILETS & TALAMO, INC., 12 Executive Campus, Rte. 38(08002), pg. 947
TRINKLE SALES, INC., 1010 Haddonfield-Berlin Rd.(08034), pg. 1114
UNITED STATES COLD STORAGE, INC., 100 Dobbs Ln., Ste. 102(08034), pg. 1135
VeloBind, Inc., 1960 Old Cuthbert Rd.(08034), pg. 657
Western International Media Corporation, 1930 E. Marlton Pike(08003), pg. 1180

Chester

Christy Halsey Oil Co., 65 Maple Ave.(07930), pg. 736
C.M. OFFRAY & SON INC., P.O. Box 601, Rte. 24(07930), pg. 822

Cinnaminson

New Jersey Float Glass, Inc., 2600 River Road(08077), pg. 3

Clark

KARNAK CORPORATION, 330 Central Ave.(07066), pg. 617

Clifton

ALLSTATE CAN CORPORATION, 40 Isabella St.(07012), pg. 43
AMERICAN MARKING SYSTEMS, 1015 Paulson Ave.(07015), pg. 58
CAIRNS & BROTHER, INC., 60 Webro Rd.(07012), pg. 207
Equity Construction Co., Inc., 1030 Clifton Ave.(07013), pg. 889
FEDERAL BUSINESS PRODUCTS, INC., 95 Main Ave.(07014), pg. 404
GREATER NEW YORK BOX CO., 149 Entin Rd.(07014), pg. 483
PANORAMA PRESS, INC., 1 Entin Rd.(07014), pg. 846
Paterson Stamp Works, 1015 Paulson Ave.(07015), pg. 58
SWEPCO TUBE CORPORATION, One Clifton Blvd.(07015), pg. 1067
WALCO-LINCK COMPANY, 1234 Route 46(07015), pg. 1159

Clinton

Meenan Oil Div., 108 W. Main St.(08809), pg. 736

Collingswood

WHEATLAND TUBE COMPANY, 900 Haddon Ave.(08108), pg. 1184

Cranford

CONSTRUCTION SPECIALTIES, INC., 55 Winans Ave.(07016), pg. 277
Construction Specialties of California, 55 Winans Ave.(07016), pg. 277
Datasphere, Inc., 49 Meeker Ave.(07016), pg. 277
Macy Credit Corp., 61 Myrtle St.(07016), pg. 699
Special Erection Services, Inc., 55 Winans Ave.(07016), pg. 277
TECKNIT, 129 Dermody St.(07016), pg. 1084

Cresskill

GFA BRANDS, INC., 211 Knickerbocker Rd.(07626), pg. 440

Delair

ALUMINUM SHAPES, INC., 9000 River Rd.(08110), pg. 46
Delair Group, Inc., 8600 River Rd.(08110), pg. 46
ESTHER WILLIAMS SWIMMING POOL CO., 8600 River Rd.(08110), pg. 389

Delran

JCI DATA PROCESSING, INC., 501 Delran Pkwy.(08075), pg. 584

Dumont

G.L. ADVERTISING, 25 Aladin Ave.(07628), pg. 440

East Brunswick

Brunswick Square, Rte. 18(08816), pg. 699

East Hanover

TROY CORPORATION, 72 Eagle Rock Ave.(07936), pg. 1116
VARITYPER, INC., 11 Mt. Pleasant Ave.(07936), pg. 1146

East Orange

Allied Security Inc., Essex Towers, 55 Washington St., Ste. 308(07017), pg. 39

East Rutherford

ALLIED BUILDING PRODUCTS CORPORATION, 15 E. Union Ave.(07073), pg. 37
B.T.F. CORPORATION, 450 Murray Hill Pkwy.(07073), pg. 107
LEATHER WAREHOUSE, INC., 33 Rte. 17th S.(07073), pg. 664
MEEHAN TOOKER, 55 Madison Circle Dr.(07073), pg. 736
Metromedia Communication Corp., 1 Meadowlands Place(07073), pg. 744
METROMEDIA COMPANY, 1 Meadowlands Plaza(07073), pg. 743
Miller Harness, Inc., 235 Murray Hill Pkwy.(07070), pg. 693

Edgewater

OCTAGON PROCESS INC., 725 River Rd.(07020), pg. 821

Edison

CASWELL/MASSEY CO. LTD., 121 Fieldcrest Ave.(08837), pg. 229
Holmes Protection of New Jersey, Inc., , pg. 540
J.M. HUBER CORPORATION, 333 Thornall St.(08818), pg. 550
J.M. Huber, Printing Ink Div., 333 Thornall St.(08818), pg. 550
KCS ENERGY INC., 379 Thornall St.(08837), pg. 612
Modern Handling Equipment of N.J., Inc., 75 New St.(08837), pg. 763
NATIONAL FOOD STORES, INC. T/A KRAUSZER'S, 76 National Rd.(08818-3031), pg. 788
Northeast Operations, 80 Newfield Center(08837), pg. 268
Principal Residential Advisors, 379 Thornall St.(08837), pg. 891
Revlon Research Center, Inc., Rt. 696
MICHAEL STEVENS LTD., One Nixon Lane(08837), pg. 1048
TWIN COUNTY GROCERS, INC., 145 Talmadge Rd.(08818), pg. 1122
Twinco Services, Inc., 145 Talmadge Rd.(08818), pg. 1122
Twinco Trucking Co., Inc., 145 Talmadge Rd.(08818), pg. 1122

Egg Harbor City

EGG HARBOR YACHT CO., INC., 801 Philadelphia Ave.(08215), pg. 371

Elizabeth

ALPHA ELECTRONIC SIGNAL TECHNOLOGIES, INC., 711 Lidgerwood Ave.(07207), pg. 43
Apex Mfg. Co., Inc., 107 Trumbull St.(07206), pg. 1018
Food Haulers, Inc., 600 York St.(07207), pg. 1158
LEONARD WHOLESALE, INC., 1050 Sherman Ave.(07208-6008), pg. 668
MAYFAIR SUPER MARKETS, INC., 681 Newark Ave.(07208), pg. 724
MILTON CAN CO., INC., 580 Division St.(07201), pg. 756
National Transport Services Co., 600 York St.(07207), pg. 1158
PHARMACAPS INC., P.O. Box 547, 1111 Jefferson Ave.(07201), pg. 866
PRIDE PRODUCTS, INC., 5 Slater Dr.(07206), pg. 889
RSI, 600 York St.(07207), pg. 1158
Shop-Rite Beverages, Inc., 600 York St.(07207), pg. 1158
Shop-Rite Cigarettes (CT), 600 York St.(07207), pg. 1158
Shop-Rite of Bensalem Inc., 600 York St.(07207), pg. 1158
Shop-Rite Supermarkets, Inc., 600 York St.(07207), pg. 1158
TRR Carriers, Inc., 600 York St.(07207), pg. 1158
The Toy Factory, 5 Slater Dr.(07206), pg. 889
Wakefern Finance Co., 600 York St.(07207), pg. 1158
WAKEFERN FOOD CORPORATION, 600 York St.(07207), pg. 1158

Elmwood Park

MARCAL PAPER MILLS, INC., One Market St.(07407), pg. 706
NPS CORPORATION, 25 Chobot Lane(07407), pg. 781

Emerson

HUBBS IMPORTING CORP., 436 Old Hook Rd.(07630), pg. 550
RMI MARKETING & ADVERTISING, 436 Old Hook Rd.(07630), pg. 907
TRI-K INDUSTRIES, INC., 27 Bland St.(07630), pg. 1110
Vienna Biscuit Co., 436 Old Hook Rd.(07630), pg. 550

Englewood

FundsNet, Inc., 385 Nordhoff Pl.(07631), pg. 960
SPIRITE INDUSTRIES, INC., 150 S. Dean St.(07631), pg. 1031
STILLMAN & HOAG, INC., 386 Grand Ave.(07631), pg. 1049
WILD'S BAKING COMPANY, 214 S. Dean St.(07631), pg. 1189

Englewood Cliffs

E.T. BROWNE DRUG CO., INC., 140 Sylvan Ave.(07632), pg. 183
HAZEL BISHOP CORPORATION, 910 Sylvan Ave.(07632), pg. 520
KETTERING ADVERTISING DISPLAY CO., 570 Sylvan Ave.(07632), pg. 626

Englishtown

MORGAN REALTY ASSOCIATES, P.O. Box 655(07726), pg. 770

Fair Lawn

INVERNESS CORP., 17-10 Willow St.(07410), pg. 581
MACNAUGHTON EINSON GRAPHICS, 20-10 Maple Ave.(07410), pg. 698
NBO STORES INC., 33-00 Broadway(07410), pg. 780
A. ZEREGAS SONS, INC., 20-01 Broadway(07410), pg. 1217

Fairfield

Cobar Machine & Tool Co., 9 Commerce Rd.(07006), pg. 928
Duro Lite Lamps, Inc., 9 Law Dr.(07004), pg. 355
DURO-TEST CORPORATION, 9 Law Dr.(07004), pg. 355
Duro-Test Intl. Corp., 9 Law Dr.(07004), pg. 355
THE ECONOMICS PRESS, INC., 12 Daniel Rd.(07004), pg. 367
Fairfield Foods, P.O. Box 4000, 12 Commerce Rd.(07006), pg. 761
JASON INDUSTRIAL, INC., 340 Kaplan Dr.(07004), pg. 590
MICROBAND COMPANIES, INC., 286 Eldridge Rd.(07004), pg. 748
Nu-Merics Inc., 9 Commerce Rd.(07006), pg. 928
Prime Construction Co., P.O. Box 2700, 700 Rte. 46 E.(07007), pg. 889
Prime-Florida, Inc., P.O. Box 2700, 700 Rte. 46 E.(07007), pg. 889
PRIME HOSPITALITY CORP., P.O. Box 2700, (07007-2700), pg. 889
Prime Hospitality Corp Limited Partnership, 700 Route 48 East(07006), pg. 889
Prime Management Co., Inc., P.O. Box 2700, 700 Rte. 46 E.(07007), pg. 889
The RAL Corporation, P.O. Box 1405, 131 Rte. 46 West(07006), pg. 357
Specialty Restaurants Corp., 195 Passaic Ave.(07006), pg. 1029
Wilmor Warehouse & Shipping Co., Inc., 39 Plymouth St.(07006), pg. 522

Farmingdale

BEL-RAY COMPANY, INC., Bowman Ave.(07727), pg. 133
FEL CORPORATION, Route 547 & Central Ave.(07727), pg. 394
FEL CORPORATION, Rte. 547 & Central Ave.(07727), pg. 405
HARVARD INDUSTRIES, INC., Central Avenue(07727), pg. 514

Flemington

UNITED STATES BRONZE POWDERS, INC., Route 202(08822), pg. 1134

Florham Park

OHAUS CORPORATION, 29 Hanover Rd.(07932), pg. 822
The Prudential Asset Management Co., Inc., 71 Hanover Road(07932), pg. 897
STRAHMAN VALVES, INC., 3 Vreeland Rd.(07932-1590), pg. 1052
TROPAR MFG. CO., INC., 5 Vreeland Rd.(07932), pg. 1115

Fort Lee

COURISTAN INC., 2 Executive Dr.(07024), pg. 290
In-Office Coffee Company, 2143 Rt. 4(07024), pg. 1172
LEWIS & GACE, INC., 1 Bridge Plaza(07024), pg. 673
MEDIA MANAGEMENT ASSOCIATES, 1 Parker Plaza(07024), pg. 734
PHILIPP BROTHERS CHEMICALS, INC., One Parker Plaza(07024), pg. 867
Resources Life Insurance Co., One Bridge Plaza(07024), pg. 573
Sanus Corp. Health Systems, One Parker Plaza, 400 Kelby St.(07024), pg. 803
SHIFFMAN/FERGUSSON/STONE ADVERTISING INC., 1 Parker Plaza(07024), pg. 999

Franklin

Morley Shirt Company, Rte. 23(07416), pg. 306

Freehold

PAUL A. DE JESSE, INC. ADVERTISING, Professional Plaza, Broad St.(07728), pg. 321

Snavely Forest Products, Inc., P.O. Box 310, (07728), pg. 1015

Garden City

AMERICAN FUNDS ADVISOR INC., 1415 Kellum Pl.(11530), pg. 55

Garfield

ARCINCO, INC., 22 Lincoln Place(07026), pg. 81
Finkel Outdoor Products, Inc., 141 Lanza Ave.(07026), pg. 200
PRESTO LOCK, INC., 100 Outwater Lane(07026), pg. 888
Primex Plastics Corp., 65 River Drive(07026), pg. 558

Garwood

ACCURATE BUSHING CO., INC., 443 North Ave.(07027), pg. 11

Gloucester City

AMSPEC CHEMICAL CORPORATION, Water St.(08030), pg. 5

Hackensack

Bergen Record Corp., 150 River St.(07601), pg. 698
Financial Resources Group, Two University Plaza(07602), pg. 464
HANK FORSSBERG, INC., Two University Plaza, Ste. 208(07601), pg. 424
Gateway Communications, 150 River St.(07601), pg. 698
Global Financial Services, Inc., Two University Plaza(07602), pg. 464
GLOBE MORTGAGE COMPANY, Two University Plaza(07602), pg. 464
Gremac Inc., 150 River St.(07601), pg. 698
Health Waters, Inc., 282 Hudson St.(07601), pg. 968
KEY HANDLING SYSTEMS, INC., 210 S. Newman St.(07601), pg. 627
LOSURDO FOODS, INC., 20 Owens Rd.(07601), pg. 684
MACROMEDIA INC., 150 River Street(07601), pg. 698
Macromedia Leasing, 150 River St.(07601), pg. 698
Macromedia Publishing Inc., 150 River St.(07601), pg. 698
Magna Media Advertising, 150 River St.(07601), pg. 698
SUPERIOR LINEN & DRAPERY COMPANY, 385 Prospect St.(07601), pg. 1064

Hackettstown

THE BATES MFG. CO., 36 Newburgh Rd.(07840), pg. 125
Buchanan Construction Products, Inc., Hackettstown Commerce Park, 101 Bilby Rd.(07840), pg. 562
M&M/Mars, High St.(07840), pg. 713
Triumph Machine Co., P.O. Box 610(07840), pg. 29

Hainesport

PERRY GROUP, INC., 25 Mt. Laurel Rd.(08036), pg. 863

Hamburg

PLASTOID CORPORATION, 45 Gingerbread Castle Rd.(07419), pg. 876

Harrison

THE HARTZ MOUNTAIN CORP., 700 Frank E. Rodgers Blvd., S.(07029), pg. 514
Hartz Mountain Group, 700 Frank E. Roger Blvd.S.(07029), pg. 514
PEERLESS UMBRELLA CO., INC., 600 7th St.(07029), pg. 855
TRI-CHEM, INC., 1 Cape May St.(07029), pg. 1110

Hasbrouck Heights

PARKLANE HOSIERY CO., INC., 621 State Route 46(07604), pg. 849

Hawthorne

C-J Extruders Inc., One Loretto Ave.(07506), pg. 805
NEXUS PLASTICS, INC., One Loretto Ave.(07506), pg. 805

Hightstown

Daily Racing Form, Inc., 10 Lake Dr.(08520), pg. 611

Hillsborough

AJAX MANUFACTURING COMPANY, INC., 321 Valley Rd.(08876), pg. 28

Hillside

E.C.D., INC., Bldg. 798, 171 Central Ave.(07205), pg. 359

Hoboken

INNER SECRETS, INC., 1500 Hudson St.(07030), pg. 570
LEON-FERENBACH COMPANY, 95 River St.(07030), pg. 667
UNIVERSAL FOLDING BOX COMPANY, INC., Madison & 13th Sts.(07030), pg. 1138

Holmdel

Prudential Commercial Insurance Co., 23 Main St.(07733), pg. 897
Prudential General Insurance Co., 23 Main St.(07733), pg. 897
Prudential Property & Casualty Insurance Company, 23 Main St.(07733), pg. 897

Hopewell

DANA COMMUNICATIONS, INC., 2 E. Broad St.(08525), pg. 313

Iselin

IDC New Jersey, 120 Wood Ave. S., Ste. 300(08830), pg. 577

Jackson

UNEX CONVEYING SYSTEMS, INC., 10 Progress Rd.(08527), pg. 1126

Jersey City

ALBA FORWARDING CO., INC., One Exchange Place, Ste. 501(07302), pg. 30
DIFEO AUTOMOTIVE NETWORK, 947 Communipaw Ave.(07304), pg. 337
DUREX INDUSTRIES INC., 1183 W. Side Ave.(07306), pg. 354
FEDERAL FARM CREDIT BANKS FUNDING CORPORATION, 10 Exchange Place(07302), pg. 404
PAVEY ENVELOPE & TAG CORP., 25 Linden Ave. E.(07305), pg. 852
POLAROME MFG. CO. INC., 200 Theodore Conrad Dr.(07305), pg. 878
RAPID INDUSTRIAL PLASTICS COMPANY, 13 Linden Ave., E.(07305), pg. 913
REPUBLIC CONTAINER CORP., 1561 Kennedy Blvd.(07305), pg. 927
ROSENFIELD/DENTINO, INC., 239 Washington St.(03702), pg. 948
FRANK B. ROSS CO. INC., P.O. Box 4085(07304), pg. 949
SCOTT PRINTING CORPORATION, 190 Baldwin Ave.(07306), pg. 983
SOUNDESIGN CORPORATION, Harborside Financial Ctr., 400 Plaza 2(07311), pg. 1018
Standard Tag Mfg. Co., 25 Linden Ave. E.(07305), pg. 852
STAR VIDEO ENTERTAINMENT, L.P., 550 Grand St.(07302), pg. 1040

Kearny

AMERICAN STRIP STEEL INC., 55 Passaic Ave.(07032), pg. 63
L&R MANUFACTURING CO., 577 Elm St.(07032), pg. 647
STANDARD CHLORINE CHEMICAL COMPANY, 1015-25 Belleville Tpke.(07032), pg. 1035
White Rose Dairy, 1200 Harrison(07032), pg. 335
WILKATA PACKAGING CORPORATION, 300 Hoyt St.(07032), pg. 1189

Kenilworth

NATIONAL TOOL & MANUFACTURING COMPANY, 100-124 N. 12th St.(07033), pg. 794
WHITE STORAGE & RETRIEVAL SYSTEMS, INC., 30 Boright Ave.(07033), pg. 1186

Keyport

FRAGRANCE RESOURCES, INC., 275 Clark St.(07735), pg. 428

Lakewood

ARNOLD STEEL COMPANY, INC., P.O. Box 739(08701), pg. 85
BEL PAESE SALES COMPANY, INC., 1935 Swarthmore Ave.(08701), pg. 133
Glasseal Products, Inc., P.O. Box 978, 485 Oberlin(08701), pg. 496
Hermetite Corp., 485 Oberlin(08701), pg. 496

Lawrenceville

DKM Building Enterprises, L.P., Princeton Pike Park Corp. Ctr., 1009 Lenox Dr.(08648-2316), pg. 357
DKM Properties Corporation, 1009 Lenox Dr.(08648), pg. 357
S. P. DUNHAM & CO., Rte. 1, Texas Ave.(08648), pg. 353
Magazine Marketing, Inc., 191 Clarksville Rd.(08648), pg. 458
PRINCE MANUFACTURING, INC., 3 Princess Rd.(08648-2398), pg. 890
Quaker Bridge Mall, 400 Quaker Bridge Mall(08648), pg. 699

Leesburg

WHIBCO, INC., River Rd.(08327), pg. 1185

Leonia

KULITE SEMICONDUCTOR PRODUCTS, INC., One Willow Tree Rd.(07605), pg. 646
VCA TELETRONICS INC., 500 Willow Tree Rd.(07605), pg. 1141
Video Program Duplicating Div., 500 Willow Tree Rd.(07605), pg. 1141

Liberty Corner

SCHERING-PLOUGH HEALTHCARE PRODUCTS ADVERTISING CORP., 110 Allen Rd.(07938), pg. 976

Lincoln Park

Raynor Distribution Center, 550 Ryerson Rd.(07035), pg. 915

Linden

Drucker Printing, 325 Cantor Ave.(07036), pg. 736
GOMAR MANUFACTURING CO., INC., 1501 W. Blancke St.(07036), pg. 469
TURTLE & HUGHES, INC., 1900 Lower Rd.(07036), pg. 1119

Little Falls

Rystan Company, Inc., 47 Center Ave.(07424-0214), pg. 222

Little Ferry

NOREL PAPER CORPORATION, 223 Gates Rd.(07643), pg. 810

Livingston

ALLISON CORPORATION, 630 W. Mt. Pleasant Ave.(07039), pg. 40
THE CHERENSON GROUP, 3 Regent St.(07039), pg. 243
LEAR SIEGLER DIVERSIFIED HOLDINGS CORP., 220 S. Orange Ave.(07039), pg. 664
Lear Siegler Diversified Holdings Corp., 220 S. Orange Ave.(07039), pg. 424
THE PULLMAN COMPANY, 220 S. Orange Ave.(07039), pg. 899
Success Advertising, Inc., 3 Regent St.(07039), pg. 243

Lodi

FINE ORGANICS CORP., 205 Main St.(07644), pg. 411
INTERPLAST UNIVERSAL INDUSTRIES, INC., 199 Garibaldi Ave.(07644), pg. 579
STANLEY ROBERTS, INC., 65 Industrial Rd.(07644), pg. 939

Long Branch

WHEELOCK INC., 273 Branchport Ave.(07740), pg. 1185

Long Valley

WELSH FARMS, INC., 55 Fairview Ave.(07853), pg. 1175

Lyndhurst

W. Braun Co., 1050 Wall St., W.(07071), pg. 172
DIAMOND CHEMICAL CO., INC., Page & Schulyer(07071), pg. 335
NORTH AMERICAN WATCH CORPORATION, 125 Chubb Ave.(07071), pg. 812
PRC of America Corp., Brisbin Ave.(07071), pg. 875
PRC of America Supply Corp., Brisbin Ave.(07071), pg. 875
PLASTIC REEL CORP. OF AMERICA, Brisbin Ave.(07071), pg. 875
Scholastic Inc. Information Center, 1290 Wall St. West(07071), pg. 962
STANDARD TOOL & MANUFACTURING COMPANY, 738 Schuyler Ave.(07071), pg. 1037
HARRY VIOLA ADVERTISING, 125 Chubb Ave.(07071), pg. 1152

Mahwah

Funk & Wagnalls Corp., One Intl. Blvd., Ste. 444(07430), pg. 611

Maple Shade

STONHARD, INC., One Park Ave.(08052), pg. 1051

Maplewood

NJ Transit Bus Operations, 180 Boyden Ave.(07040), pg. 802

Marlton

Stephen Gould of Pennsylvania Corp., 6 Eves Dr.(08053), pg. 474
MICHAEL'S DEVELOPMENT COMPANY, 1 Stow Rd.(08053), pg. 747
RMS TECHS, INC., 5 Eves Dr.(08053), pg. 907

Mays Landing

Wheaton Coated Products, Rte. 40(08330), pg. 1184
Wheaton Safety Container Co., Rte. 40(08330), pg. 1184

Maywood

BIO MEDIC CORPORATION, 255 W. Spring Valley Ave.(07607), pg. 152
Lab Products, Inc., 255 W. Spring Valley Ave.(07607), pg. 152
LEE MYLES ASSOCIATES CORPORATION, 25 E. Spring Valley Ave.(07607), pg. 666
MYRON MANUFACTURING CORPORATION, 205 Maywood Ave.(07607), pg. 780

Mendham

Ingersoll Engineers, 88 E. Main St., Ste. 334(07945), pg. 568

Mercerville

CONGOLEUM CORPORATION, 3705 Quakerbridge Rd.(08619), pg. 274

Merchantville

CLOVER FINANCIAL CORPORATION, 23 W. Park Ave.(08109), pg. 256

Middlesex

THE BETHAM CORPORATION, Lincoln Blvd. & River Rd.(08846), pg. 147
DAQ ELECTRONICS INC., 252 Lackland Dr. East(08846), pg. 308

Midland Park

F.G. MONTABERT, 175 Paterson Ave.(07432), pg. 766

Millburn

THE JAYDOR CORPORATION, 16 Bleeker St.(07041), pg. 591
LASKY COMPANY, 67 E. Willow St.(07041), pg. 660
LINETT & HARRISON, 306 Main St.(07041), pg. 676

Millville

General Machinery Co., N. Tenth St.(08332), pg. 1184
Wheaton Cartage, 1101 Wheaton Ave.(08332), pg. 1184
Wheaton Glass Co., 3rd & "G" Sts.(08332), pg. 1184
WHEATON INC., 1101 Wheaton Ave.(08332), pg. 1184
Wheaton Injection Molding, Sharp St.(08332), pg. 1184
Wheaton Instruments, No. Tenth St.(08332), pg. 1184
Wheaton Scientific, N. Tenth St.(08332), pg. 1184

Montclair

Budde & Westermann, P.O. Box 177(07042), pg. 417
TRUNK & ASSOCIATES, INC., 98 Park St.(07042), pg. 1118

Montvale

BENJAMIN MOORE & CO., 51 Chestnut Ridge Rd.(07645), pg. 139
Butler Design Services, Inc., 110 Summit Ave.(07458), pg. 197
BUTLER INTERNATIONAL, 110 Summit Ave.(07645), pg. 197
Butler Quality Services, Inc., 110 Summit Ave.(07645), pg. 197
Butler Service Group, Inc., 110 Summit Ave.(07645), pg. 197
Butler Telecommunications Services, 110 Summit Ave.(07645), pg. 197
DATABASE AMERICA COMPANIES, 100 Paragon Dr.(07645-0419), pg. 316
Information Systems, 100 Paragon Dr.(07645), pg. 316

Montville

MAROTTA SCIENTIFIC CONTROLS, INC., 78 Boonton Ave.(07045), pg. 713
SSD&W INTEGRATED MARKETING COMMUNICATIONS, 350 Main Rd.(07045), pg. 964

Moonachie

ACRISON, INC., 20 Empire Blvd.(07074), pg. 14
DORMAN-ROTH FOODS, INC., 14 Empire Blvd.(07074), pg. 346
Elometa Corporation, 85 Oxford Dr.(07074), pg. 1108
LEONARD KREUSCH, INC., 1 Caesar Place(07074), pg. 645
MARK LIGHTING FIXTURE CO., INC., 25 Knickerbocker Rd.(07074), pg. 708
Richheimer Food, 10 Empire Blvd.(07074), pg. 1172
WECHSLER COFFEE CORP., 10 Empire Blvd.(07074), pg. 1172

Moorestown

FORMATION, INC., 121 Whittendale Dr.(08057), pg. 424
THE ROYAL CHINA & PORCELAIN COMPANIES INC., 1265 Glen Ave.(08057-0912), pg. 953
TELESCIENCES CO. SYSTEMS INC., 351 New Albany Rd.(08057), pg. 1085

Morris Plains

MONROE SYSTEMS FOR BUSINESS, INC., 1000 The American Rd.(07950), pg. 766
WEICHERT COMPANY, 1625 State Hwy. 10(07950), pg. 1173

Morristown

DUGAN, VALVA ASSOCIATES, 10 Park Ave.(07960), pg. 351
GEMINI CONSULTING, 25 Airport Road(07960), pg. 448
LOHMEYER SIMPSON COMMUNICATIONS, INC., 14 Pine St.(07960), pg. 681

Mount Laurel

AUTOMOTIVE RENTALS, INC., 9000 Midlantic Dr.(08054), pg. 101
Fleer Corporation, Executive Plaza, Ste. 300, 1120 Rte. 73(08054), pg. 695
GAI Construction Services, Inc., 300 Birchfield Dr., Ste. 301(08054), pg. 439
GAI Consultants, Inc., 300 Birchfield Dr., Ste. 301(08054), pg. 439
JOHNSON & TOWERS, INC., 2021 Briggs Rd.(08054), pg. 601
Main Line Management Services, Inc., Ste. 200, 533 Fellowship Rd.(08054), pg. 246
SEACOR Services, Inc. (SSI), 200 East Park Drive, Suite 600(08054), pg. 321
Systems Engineering Associates Co. (SEACOR), 200 East Park Dr.(08054), pg. 320

Mount Olive

TMP Worldwide, Inc., International Trade Center, 600 International Dr.(07828), pg. 1074
Yellow Pages Marketing Services, Inc.-New York, 600 International Dr.(07828), pg. 1074

Mountainside

REICHENSTEIN ADVERTISING AGENCY, 187 Mill Lane(07092), pg. 922

Neptune

Addresses Unlimited, 3601 Highway 66(07754), pg. 801
Asbury Park Press, Inc., 3601 Highway 66(07754), pg. 801
Electronic Measurements, Inc., 405 Essex Rd.(07753), pg. 145
NEW JERSEY PRESS, INC., 3601 Highway 66(07754), pg. 801

New Brunswick

SPENCER INDUSTRIES, INC., 120 Albany St. Plaza, 6th Fl.(08903-2629), pg. 1030
Triangle PWC, Inc., P.O. Box 711, (08903), pg. 1111
WARD PRODUCTS CORPORATION, 633 Nassau St.(08903), pg. 1163

New Gretna

VIKING YACHT CO., Rte. 1151

New Providence

ALPHA ONE EXCHANGE, 121 Chanlon Rd.(07974), pg. 43
CALICO CAT PRESS, INC., 121 Chanlon Rd.(07974), pg. 209
Chanlon Video Arts, 121 Chanlon Rd.(07974), pg. 960
HOLLISTER ADVERTISING, 121 Chanlon Rd.(07974), pg. 539
MANAGEMENT DYNAMICS, 121 Chanlon Rd.(07974), pg. 703
SB ENTERTAINMENT INC., 121 Chanlon Rd.(07974), pg. 960
SIMON & ASSOCIATES, 121 Chanlon Rd.(07974), pg. 1006
THE W.B. WOOD COMPANY, 150 Floral Ave.(07974), pg. 1199
ZEPHYR BASKETS & BALLOONS, 121 Chanlon Rd.(07974), pg. 1217

Newark

Aratex Services, 740 Frelinghuisen Ave.(07114), pg. 6
Arrow Typographers, Inc., 2-14 Liberty St.(07102), pg. 326
ASTER NUT PRODUCTS INC., 1455 McCarter Hwy.(07104), pg. 92
ATLAS REFINERY, 142 Lockwood St.(07105), pg. 96
BEST PROVISION CO., INC., 144 Avon Ave.(07108), pg. 146
E. J. BROOKS COMPANY, 164-192 N. 13th St.(07107), pg. 179
CENTRAL PAPER COMPANY, 60 McClellan St.(07114), pg. 233
Chatham Eight Corporation, Prudential Plaza(07102), pg. 896
Comstock Foods, 1000 S. Main St.(07105), pg. 25
DAIDONE ELECTRICAL INC., 200 Raymond Blvd.(07105), pg. 310
Dryden & Co., Inc., 100 Mulberry St.(07102), pg. 897
FISKE BROTHERS REFINING COMPANY, 129 Lockwood St.(07105), pg. 415
Gibraltar Casualty Co., 100 Mulberry St.(07102), pg. 897
HANDY MANUFACTURING CO., INC., 337 Sherman Ave.(07114), pg. 505
Handy Store Fixtures, Inc., 337 Sherman Ave.(07114), pg. 505
JARCHEM INDUSTRIES, INC., 40 Ball St.(07105), pg. 590
Jarchem Specialty Chemical Division, 40 Ball St.(07105), pg. 590
Keystone Automotive Industries, Inc. - Newark, 24 Legal Street(07114), pg. 628
Lehman Associates, Inc., 909 Broad St.(07102), pg. 1137
LEWIS ADVERTISING AGENCY, 17 Academy(07102), pg. 672
MBL Holding Corporation, 520 Broad St.(07102), pg. 778
MBL Life Assurance Corp., 520 Broad St.(07102), pg. 778
Muben Realty Co., 520 Broad St.(07101), pg. 778
MUTUAL BENEFIT LIFE INSURANCE COMPANY, 520 Broad St.(07102-3184), pg. 778
NJ TRANSIT, One El Plaza E.(07105), pg. 801
NJ Transit Corporation, Market St. & McCarter Hwy.(07101), pg. 802
NJ Transit Rail Operations, 1160 Raymond Blvd.(07101), pg. 802
Newark Rehabilitation, Inc., Prudential Plaza(07102), pg. 896
PIC Realty Corp., P.O. Box 1539, (07102), pg. 896
PRUCO Life Insurance Company, 213 Washington St.(07102), pg. 896
PRUCO, Inc., 751 Broad St.(07102), pg. 896
Pick Quick Papers, Inc., 60 McClellan St.(07114), pg. 234
PruCapital, Inc., 100 Mulberry St.(07102), pg. 897
PruCapital Management, Inc., 100 Mulberry St.(07102), pg. 897
PruCapital Securities Co., Inc., 100 Mulberry St.(07102), pg. 897
Pruco Life Insurance Company of New Jersey, 213 Washington St.(07102), pg. 896
Pruco Securities Corp., Prudential Plaza, (07102), pg. 896
Pruco Services, Inc., Prudential Plaza, (07102), pg. 896
Prudential Agricultural Credit, Inc., Prudential Plaza, (07102), pg. 897
Prudential Development & Retail Div., 751 Broad St.(07102-3777), pg. 897
Prudential Equity Investment Div., 751 Broad St.(07102-3777), pg. 897
Prudential Funding Corp., 2 Gateway Center 4, 100 Mulberry St.(07102), pg. 897
Prudential Institutional Investment Management Div., 751 Broad St.(07102-3777), pg. 897
THE PRUDENTIAL INSURANCE COMPANY OF AMERICA, Prudential Plaza(07102), pg. 896
Prudential Interfunding Corp., 100 Mulberry St.(07102), pg. 897
The Prudential Investment Corp., Prudential Plaza(07102), pg. 897
Prudential Mortgage Capital, 751 Broad St.(07102-3777), pg. 897
The Prudential Realty Group, 751 Broad St.(07102-3777), pg. 897
Prudential Reinsurance Co., 100 Mulberry St.(07102), pg. 897
Prudential Support Operations, Inc., Prudential Plaza(07101), pg. 897
PruLease, Inc., 100 Mulberry St.(07102), pg. 897
PruSupply, Inc., 100 Mulberry St.(07102), pg. 897
Seton Co., 349 Oraton St.(07104), pg. 993
SHOFAR KOSHER FOODS, INC., 124 Malvern St.(07105), pg. 1000
UNITED STATES REALTY & INVESTMENT CO., 1160 Raymond Blvd.(07102), pg. 1137

Newfield

Shieldalloy Metallurgical Corportation, P.O. Box 768(08344), pg. 742

North Bergen

A-P-A TRANSPORT CORP., 2100 88th St.(07047), pg. 5
AMERICAN TAPE CORPORATION, 1511 Tonnelle Ave.(07047), pg. 63
COLONNA BROS., INC., 4102 Bergen Tpke.(07047), pg. 264
Masback Hardware Co., 2400 83rd St.(07047), pg. 340
MEER CORPORATION, 9500 Railroad Ave.(07047), pg. 736
JOSHUA MEIER CORP., 7401 West Side Ave.(07047), pg. 737
MILLER PRODUCTS COMPANY, INC., 2220 91st St.(07047), pg. 755
NOVILLE ESSENTIAL OIL CO., INC., 1312 Fifth St.(07047), pg. 817
THE ORMOND SHOPS, INC., 7300 West Side Ave.(07047), pg. 830
SINGERS SUPERMARKETS, INC., 7801 Tonnelle Ave.(07047), pg. 1008
WESTCHESTER LACE, INC., 3901 Liberty Ave.(07047), pg. 1178

North Branch

STRUCTURAL FOAM PLASTICS, INC., P.O. box 5208, (08876), pg. 1054

North Brunswick

E.C.D. Inc., 1201 Jersey Ave.(08902), pg. 359
GENERAL AUTOMOTIVE SPECIALTY CO., INC., Rtes. 1 & 130(08902), pg. 449
MILLER PERSONNEL, INC., 720 Rte. 1 North(08902), pg. 755
Webcraft Games, Inc., 205 N. Center Dr.(08902), pg. 1171
WEBCRAFT TECHNOLOGIES, INC., Route 1 & Adams Station Rd.(08902), pg. 1171

North Plainfield

Universal Dynamics Inc., 46 Pearl St.(07076), pg. 1138

Northvale

AERCO INTERNATIONAL INC., 159 Paris Ave.(07647), pg. 21
G. JOANNOU CYCLE CO. INC., 151 Ludlow Ave.(07647), pg. 595
MULTIMATIC CORPORATION, 162 Veteran Drive(07647), pg. 775
ZENITH LABORATORIES, INC., 140 Le Grand Ave.(07647), pg. 1217

Norwood

Northfield Cheese Co., 375 Chestnut St.(07648), pg. 574
OPTYL EYEWEAR FASHION INTERNATIONAL CORP., 35 Maple St.(07648), pg. 828

Nutley

Technical Coatings Co., 57 E. Centre St(07110), pg. 139

Oakland

MULHERN BELTING, INC., 148 Bauer Dr.(07436), pg. 775

Old Bridge

BLONDER-TONGUE LABORATORIES, INC., One Jake Brown Rd.(08857), pg. 157

Oradell

BURNS & ROE ENTERPRISES, INC., 800 Kinderkamack Rd.(07649), pg. 194
JOHN H. GRAHAM & CO., INC., 617 Oradell Ave.(07649), pg. 475
KOHM ASSOCIATES, INC., 496 Kinderkamack Rd.(07649), pg. 640

Orange

ROSE ART INDUSTRIES, 555 Main St.(07050), pg. 947

Palmyra

Keystone Automotive Industries, Inc. - Palmyra, P.O. Box 52, Market at Jefferson Street(08065), pg. 628
PHILADELPHIA SIGN COMPANY, 707 W. Spring Garden St.(08065), pg. 867

Paramus

CAMPMOR INC., 810 St. Hwy. Route 213
Card Technology Corporation, 70 Eisenhower Drive(07652), pg. 960
The Garden State Plaza Corp., Rte. 4 & State Hwy. No. 17(07652), pg. 699
JENNIFER CONVERTIBLES INC., 331 Rt. 4(07652), pg. 592
I. ROKEACH & SONS, INC., South 61 Road(07652), pg. 944

SISTI, ZINBARG & HOWARD, INC., One Kalisa Way(07652), pg. 1009
GEORGE UHE CO., INC., 12 Rte. 17 N.(07652), pg. 1125

Park Ridge

CONSTRUCTION COUNSELLORS, INC., 118 Mill Rd.(07656), pg. 277
The Hertz Corporation, 225 Brae Blvd.(07656), pg. 849
Hertz Equipment Rental Corp., 225 Brae Blvd.(07656), pg. 849
NATIONAL UTILITY SERVICE, INC., 1 Maynard Dr.(07656), pg. 794
PARK RIDGE CORPORATION, 225 Brae Blvd.(07656), pg. 849

Parsippany

ATERON CORP., 5 Century Dr.(07054), pg. 93
Baker Industries, Inc., 1633 Littleton Rd.(07054), pg. 166
BUFFALO COLOR CORPORATION, 959 Rt. 46 E., Ste. 403(07054), pg. 187
Burns International Security Services, Inc., 2 Campus Dr.(07054), pg. 166
Days Inns of America, Inc., 339 Jefferson Rd.(07054), pg. 1100
ELECTRONIC DRIVES AND CONTROLS, 17 Eastmans Rd.(07054), pg. 375
THE ESTEE CORPORATION, 169 Lackawanna Ave.(07054), pg. 389
FABER/CASTELL CORPORATION, 4 Century Dr.(07054), pg. 395
General Chemical Corporation, 90 E. Halsey Rd.(07054), pg. 801
GIGANTE VAZ & PARTNERS ADVERTISING, INC., 169 Johnson Rd.(07054), pg. 457
M. H. GREENEBAUM, INC., 7 Century Dr.(07054), pg. 485
LINEAR DYNAMICS INC., 400 Lanidex Plaza(07054), pg. 676
Potters Industries, Inc., Waterview Corporate Centre, 20 Waterview Blvd.(07054), pg. 837
SEBASTIAN & COOKE, 110 Lanidex Plaza(07054), pg. 986
UC INDUSTRIES, INC., 3 Century Dr.(07054), pg. 1122
Wells Fargo Guard Services, 2 Campus Dr.(07054), pg. 166

Passaic

M. GROSSMAN SON, INC., 245 4th St.(07055), pg. 489
MELARD MANUFACTURING CORPORATION, 153 Linden St.(07055), pg. 737
Melard Plastics Inc., 153 Linden St.(07055), pg. 737
UNIFOIL CORPORATION, 217 Brook Ave.(07055), pg. 1126

Paterson

ACCURATE BOX CO., INC., 86 Fifth Ave.(07509), pg. 11
BOGUE ELECTRIC MANUFACTURING CO., 100 Pennsylvania Ave.(07509-3027), pg. 162
DOUGLAS STEPHEN PLASTICS, INC., 22-36 Green St.(07501), pg. 347
Filmco Industries Inc., 100 5th Ave.(07524), pg. 1092
THE HABAND CO., 265 N. 9th St.(07530), pg. 498
Kaysam Corporation Of America, 27 Kentucky Ave.(07053), pg. 809
MONA INDUSTRIES, INC., 76 E. 24th St.(07544-0425), pg. 764
Power Plastics Inc., 155 Sherman Ave.(07502), pg. 1097
THERMWELL PRODUCTS CO., INC., 150 E. Seventh St.(07524), pg. 1092
TIFFANY EXTRUDERS, INC., 155 Sherman Ave.(07502), pg. 1096
WELLINGTON INDUSTRIES INC., 52 Courtland St.(07503), pg. 1175

Peapack

KOMLINE-SANDERSON ENGINEERING CORP., 12 Holland Ave.(07977), pg. 641

Pennington

PEGASUS INTERNATIONAL CORPORATION, Straube Center, 114 W. Franklin Ave.(08534), pg. 855

Pennsauken

HANDEL & COMPANY, INC., 6900 Westfield Ave.(08110), pg. 504
HOLMAN ENTERPRISES, 7411 Maple Ave.(08109), pg. 540
MENU FOODS, INC., 9130 Griffith Morgan Lane(08110), pg. 739
PHOTOTYPE COLOR GRAPHICS, INC., 7890 Airport Hwy.(08109), pg. 869
Predco, Inc., P.O. Box 520(08110), pg. 341
SUZANNAH FARMS, 9105 Burrough Dover Lane(08110), pg. 1065

Pequannock

BEL-ART PRODUCTS, 6 Industrial Rd.(07440-1992), pg. 133
D & S Marketing, 6 Industrial Rd.(07440-1992), pg. 133
Maddak Inc., 6 Industrial Rd.(07440), pg. 133

Perth Amboy

SCHOTT BROTHERS, INC., 358 Lehigh St.(08861), pg. 978

Phillipsburg

OPT INDUSTRIES, INC., 300 Red School Lane(08865), pg. 819
ORBEL CORPORATION, 150 Anderson St.(08865), pg. 828
ZAPPA PLASTICS, 165 Howard St.(08865), pg. 1216

Pine Brook

THE CHILDREN'S PLACE RETAIL STORES, INC., 25 Riverside Dr.(07058), pg. 247
EINSTEIN MOOMJY INC., 20 Hook Mountain Rd.(07058), pg. 371

Piscataway

Allied Security Inc., 501 Hose Lane, Ste. 105(08854), pg. 39
Blessings Corp., 45 Knightsbridge Rd.(08854), pg. 1192
CAPTIVE PLASTICS, 251 Circle Dr., N.(08854), pg. 216
COOPERHEAT, INC., 1021 Centennial Ave.(08854), pg. 283

Plainfield

INJECTRON CORPORATION, 1000 S. Second St.(07063), pg. 569

Pleasantville

IRELAND COFFEE TEA, INC., 582
PETER LUMBER COMPANY, Washington & Lyons Court(08232), pg. 864

Pompton Lakes

ROYLE SYSTEMS GROUP, 1000 Cannonball Rd.(07442), pg. 953

Pompton Plains

EDWARDS ENGINEERING CORPORATION, 101 Alexander(07444), pg. 370

Port Reading

ALLIED OLD ENGLISH, INC., 100 Markley St.(07064-1897), pg. 38
CARDINAL INC., 400 Markley St.(07064), pg. 217
Concord Miniatures, P.O. Box 99(07064), pg. 218
Dynasty Dolls, P.O. Box 99(07064), pg. 218
Our Own Import Inc., P.O. Box 99(07064), pg. 218

Princeton

BERLITZ INTERNATIONAL, INC., 293 Wall St.(08540-1555), pg. 142
ERS ADVERTISING, INC., P.O. Box 4500, 500 College Rd., E.(08543), pg. 361
Gillespie Advertising, Inc., International Corporate Center, P.O. Box 3333(08543), pg. 458
THE GILLESPIE ORGANIZATION, INC., International Corporate Center, P.O. Box 3333(08543), pg. 458
Gillespie Public Relations, Inc., P.O. Box 3333, (08543), pg. 458
PRINCETON PARTNERS, INC., 2 Research Way, Princeton Forrestal Center(08540), pg. 890
Princeton Partners, Inc., 2 Research Way, Princeton Forrestal Center(08540), pg. 1177
QLM ASSOCIATES, INC., 470 Wall St.(08540), pg. 902
David Sarnoff Research Center, 201 Washington Rd., P.O. Box 5300(08543), pg. 964
SHENANGO FURNACE COMPANY, 101 Carnegie Center(08540), pg. 997
WECHCO, INC., 1000 Herrontown Rd.(08540), pg. 1172
West Chemical Products, Inc., 1000 Herrontown Rd.(08540), pg. 1172

Princeton Junction

CREATIVE MARKETING ALLIANCE INC., 34-c Washington Rd.(08550), pg. 297
UNITED PIECE DYE WORKS, LP, 14 Washington Rd., Bldg. 1 Rear Entrance(08550), pg. 1134

Rahway

DRI-PRINT FOILS, 329 New Brunswick Ave.(07065), pg. 349
ISFEL COMPANY, INC., 900 Hart(07065), pg. 582
LAMINAIRE CORPORATION, 960 E. Hazelwood Ave.(07065), pg. 652

Ramsey

COLORFORMS, 133 Williams Dr.(07446), pg. 265
THE OKONITE COMPANY, 102 Hilltop Rd.(07446), pg. 823

Randolph

JOHN DUSENBERY CO., INC., 220 Franklin Rd.(07869), pg. 355

Red Bank

RUSSELL-STANLEY CORPORATION, 230 Half Mile Rd.(07701), pg. 957

Ridgefield

A & E STORES, INC., 1125 Pleasantview Terrace(07657), pg. 1
Brisk Waterproofing, 720 Grand Ave.(07657), pg. 1179
Lowe Paper Co., (07657), pg. 1005

Ridgefield Park

ALFORD INDUSTRIES, INC., Industrial Ave.(07660), pg. 33
CRYSTAL CLEAR INDUSTRIES COMPANY, 2 Bergen Turnpike(07660), pg. 303

River Edge

HALOCARBON PRODUCTS CORP., 887 Kinderkamack Rd.(07661), pg. 502
Harte-Hanks Marketing Services, 65 Rte. 4(07661), pg. 513
HUFFMAN KOOS CO., Route 4 & Main St.(07661), pg. 551

Riverdale

MATHIEU CORPORATION, Five Mathews Ave.(07457), pg. 720

Rochelle Park

LOUIS SCOTT ASSOCIATES, INC., 201 W. Passaic St.(07662), pg. 982

Rockaway

Action Rockaway, 18-32 Green Pond Rd.(07866), pg. 15
ACTION TECHNOLOGY COMPANY, 18 Green Pond Rd.(07866), pg. 15
Keuffel & Esser, P.O. Box 800(07866), pg. 105
MCWILLIAMS FORGE CO., Franklin Ave.(07866), pg. 733

Roseland

ANNIN & COMPANY, One Annin Dr.(07068), pg. 75
BOBST GROUP INC., 146 Harrison Ave.(07068), pg. 161
FRANK BRISCOE CO. INC., Briscoe Building(07068), pg. 176

Roselle

ROSELLE PAPER CO., INC., 615 E. First Ave.(07203), pg. 948

Rutherford

Geographic Marketing Group (GMG), 301 Rte. 17 North, Ste. 204(07070), pg. 452
Goodkind & O'Dea, Inc., 60 Feronia Way(07070), pg. 334
Language Institute for English (L.I.F.E.), C/O FDU, Kingsland House(07070), pg. 142
Lindenmeyr Munroe, 301 Veterans Blvd.(07070-2706), pg. 233
SIMUNICO, INC., 301 Rte. 17 N.(07070), pg. 1007

Saddle Brook

AMLOID CORPORATION, 81 5th St.(07662), pg. 67
ARROW FASTENER CO., INC., 271 Mayhill St.(07662), pg. 85
COVENTRY HOTELS ASSOCIATION, 50 Kenney Pl.(07662), pg. 290
Hollytex, Park 80 Plaza West One(07662), pg. 1121
Lamston, 45 Mayhill St.(07662), pg. 877
Plymouth, 45 Mayhill St.(07662), pg. 877
PLYMOUTH LAMSTON STORES, CORP., 45 Mayhill St.(07662), pg. 877
POWER CONVERSION, INC., 280 Midland Ave.(07662), pg. 883
RITE-WAY, INC., 280 Midland Ave.(07662), pg. 936
THERMO ELECTRIC CO., INC., 109 N. Fifth St.(07662), pg. 1091

Salem

MANNINGTON MILLS, INC., Mannington Mills Rd.(08079), pg. 704

Sayreville

Sunshine/Salerno, Inc. (NJ), P.O. Box 7(08872), pg. 439

Scobeyville

LAIRD & COMPANY, 1 Laird Rd.(07724), pg. 650

Seabrook

SEABROOK BROTHERS & SONS, INC., Finley Road(08302), pg. 984

Secaucus

AGEMA INFRARED SYSTEMS, INC., 550 County Ave.(07094), pg. 24
Command Web Offset Co., 100 Castle R.(07094), pg. 698
DRUG GUILD DISTRIBUTORS, INC., 350 Meadowland Pkwy.(07094), pg. 349
FABER, COE & GREGG, INC., 10 Enterprise Av. N.(07094), pg. 395
GOYA FOODS, INC., 100 Seaview Dr.(07096), pg. 474
Hartz Mountain Industries, 400 Plaza Dr.(07094-3688), pg. 514
HARVE BENARD LTD. MANUFACTURING, 225 Meadowland Pkwy.(07096), pg. 514
HOOGOVENS ALUMINUM CORP., 101 Venture Way(07094), pg. 543
INTERNATIONAL DESIGNER ACCESSORIES, INC., 375 County Ave.(07096), pg. 578
Lion Ribbon Company, 100 Metro Way(07094), pg. 822
MARINE TRANSPORT LINES, INC., 150 Meadowland Pkwy.(07096-1550), pg. 707
Meadowlands Hospital Medical Center, Meadowlands Parkway(07094-2912), pg. 1127
METPON, 1 Harmon Plaza(07096), pg. 743
METSA, Inc., 1 Harmon Plaza(07096), pg. 744
RIBBON NARROW FABRIC COMPANY, 565 Winsor Dr.(07094), pg. 931
Rolodex Corp., 245 Secaucus Rd.(07094), pg. 571
SCHIAVONE CONSTRUCTION CO., 1600 Patterson Plank Rd.(07096), pg. 976
Sports Travel, 500 Plaza Drive(07096), pg. 611
White Rose Corporation, 2 Frozen Food Plaza(07096), pg. 335

Sewell

Electric Mobility Co., 591 Mantua Blvd.(08080), pg. 362

Short Hills

GIANETTINO & MEREDITH ADVERTISING, 788 Morris Turnpike(07078), pg. 455

THE JASON GROUP, INC., 788 Morris-Essex Turnpike(07078), pg. 590

Somerset

DI GIORGIO CORPORATION, 2 Executive Dr., Ste. 400(08873), pg. 334
Mary Kay Cosmetics, Inc., 313 Pierce St., CN6702(08873), pg. 717
SOMERSET TECHNOLOGIES, INC., Weston Canal Rd.(08873), pg. 1017
THOROUGHBRED SOFTWARE INTERNATIONAL, INC., 19 School House Rd.(08875), pg. 1095
WALDES TRUARC, INC., 500 Memorial Dr.(08875), pg. 1159

Somerville

William B. Bliss Div., 25 Chubb Way(08876-1299), pg. 398
Edwal Scientific Products Div., 25 Chubb Way(08876-1299), pg. 398
SIMMS & MCIVOR MARKETING COMMUNICATIONS, Branch Estates, 3121 Rte. 22 East(08876-3500), pg. 1005
Synergetics, Inc., 3121 Rte. 22, East(08876), pg. 1006
Tekni-Plex, Inc., 201 Industrial Pkwy.(08876), pg. 1084

South Amboy

Carriage House Manor, 901 Ernston Rd.(08879), pg. 740
Parkway Fabricators, Inc., 241 Raritan St.(08879), pg. 480

South Hackensack

J. JOSEPHSON, INC., 20 Horizon Blvd.(07606), pg. 607
SPINNERIN YARN CO., INC., 30 Wesley St.(07606), pg. 1031

South Orange

SCHEER ADVERTISING AGENCY, 76 S. Orange Ave.(07079), pg. 975

South Plainfield

Everlasting Valve Co., 108 Somogyi Court(07080), pg. 83
KENTILE FLOORS INC., Kentile Rd.(07080), pg. 623
NBS Card Services, Inc., 800 Montrose Ave.(07080), pg. 960
Rickel Home Centers, 200 Helen St.(07080), pg. 1064
TINGLEY RUBBER CORPORATION, 200 South Ave.(07080), pg. 1098
WHITTAKER, CLARK & DANIELS, INC., 1000 Coolidge St.(07080), pg. 1187

South River

R & S STRAUSS, INC., 9A Brick Plant Rd.(08882-1098), pg. 1053

Springfield

Beckley Perforating Co., 60 Brown Ave.(07081), pg. 660
WM. BLANCHARD CO., 199 Mountain Ave.(07081), pg. 155
Electroid Corp., 45 Fadem Rd.(07081), pg. 1142
GLENAYRE TURNKEY TECHNOLOGIES, INC., One Cornell Pkwy.(07081), pg. 462
KEYES MARTIN, 841 Mountain Ave.(07081), pg. 627
Laubeck Corporation, Beckley Division, 60 Brown Ave.(07081), pg. 660
QEI, INC., 60 Fadem Rd.(07081), pg. 902
VALCOR ENGINEERING CORP., 2 Lawrence Rd(07081), pg. 1142

Stewartsville

Apex Galvanizing Corp., New Village, Edison Rd., RD1149

Summit

PANARCO, INC., 480 Morris Ave.(07901), pg. 845

Teaneck

MONY Credit Corporation, West Bldg., 500 Frank W. Burr Blvd.(07666-6888), pg. 778
MONY Life Insurance Co. of America, 500 Frank W. Burr Blvd.(07666), pg. 778
MONY Realty Partners, Inc., Frank W. Burr Blvd.(07666), pg. 778
MONY Securities Corp., MONY Glenpointe Centre West, 500 Frank W. Burr Blvd., MD 75-26(07666), pg. 778

Tenafly

Penetone Corp., 74 Hudson Ave.(07670), pg. 1172

Teterboro

Florasynth Inc., 300 North St.(07608), pg. 420

Thorofare

Alco Health Services Northeast-Thorofare, 100 Friars Ln.(08086), pg. 32
C M P Printing Company, 551 Mid Atlantic Pkwy.(08086), pg. 203

Toms River

OCEAN CHEVROLET, INC., Rte. 37 & Peter Ave.(08753), pg. 820
Paeco Industries, Inc., One Executive Way(08753), pg. 480

Totowa

BALLET MAKERS, INC., One Campus Rd.(07512), pg. 116
Barnes & Noble, 81 Adams Dr.(07512), pg. 953
CARAVAN PRODUCTS COMPANY, INC., 100 Adams Dr.(07511), pg. 217
Carpro, Inc., 100 Adams Dr.(07512), pg. 217
HAROLD M. PITMAN CO., INC., 721 Union Blvd.(07512), pg. 872
SHOE-TOWN, INC., 994 Riverview Dr.(07512), pg. 999
VIBRA SCREW INC., 755 Union Blvd.(07511), pg. 1149

Towaco

AMCO FOLDING CARTONS, INC., 2 Como Ct.(07082), pg. 47

Trenton

Capitol City Publishing Co., Inc., 600 Perry St.(08638), pg. 608
Central Paper Co., 1004 Wayhead Rd. Ext.(08638), pg. 234
Chessco Process Research Products Div., 1013 Whitehead Rd. Ext.(08638), pg. 244
General Felt Industries, Inc., 1936 East St.(08619), pg. 1121
Harwick Chemical Corp., Box 5083, 88 Lakedale Dr.(08638), pg. 515
HIBBERT GROUP, P.O. Box 8116, 400 Pennington Ave.(08650-0116), pg. 532
JOURNAL REGISTER COMPANY, 50 W. State St., 12th Fl.(08608), pg. 608
Mercer Paper Tube Co., 1700 Calhoun St.(00638), pg. 1209
NEW JERSEY STATE LOTTERY, One Lawrence Park Complex, Brunswick Ave. Circle(08648), pg. 801
The Trentonian, 600 Perry St.(08602), pg. 608
WENCZEL TILE CO., 200 Enterprise Ave.(08638), pg. 1176

Turnersville

WATSON'S QUALITY TURKEY PRODUCTS, INC., Black Horse Pike(08012), pg. 1168

Union

Ardell Industries inc., 555 Lehigh Ave.(07083), pg. 604
CE DE CANDY, INC., 1091 Lousons Rd.(07083), pg. 230
Elastic Stop Nut, 2330 Vauxhall Rd.(07083), pg. 514
ELECTROCATALYTIC, INC., 2 Milltown Ct.(07083), pg. 375
The Graver Chemical Div., 2720 U.S. Hwy 20(07083), pg. 712
The Graver Company, 2720 U.S. Hwy 22(07083), pg. 712
Graver Water Division, 2720 U.S. Hwy 22(07083), pg. 712
HAROLD LEONARD & COMPANY, INC., 600 Green Lane(07083), pg. 667
MANNING & LEWIS ENGINEERING CO., 675 Rahway Ave.(07083), pg. 704
Medtech Laboratories, Inc., 2444 Morris Ave.(07083), pg. 736
MULBERRY METAL PRODUCTS, INC., 2199 Stanley Terrace(07083), pg. 775
RED DEVIL INC., 2400 Vauxhall Rd.(07083), pg. 918
SHARON CONCEPTS, INC., 1831 Burnet Ave.(07083), pg. 995
STONCO, 2345 Vauxhall Rd.(07083), pg. 1050
Unitech Division, 2720 U.S. Hwy 22(07083), pg. 712
THE VENET COMPANIES, INC., 465 Chestnut St.(07083), pg. 1147

Upper Saddle River

PIONEER COMMUNICATIONS OF AMERICA, 600 E. Crescent Ave.(07458), pg. 871
THE TEXWIPE CO., INC., 650 E. Crescent Ave.(07458), pg. 1090

Verona

CELENTANO BROTHERS, 225 Bloomfield Ave.(07044), pg. 231

Vineland

ACE GLASS INCORPORATED, 1430 N.W. Blvd.(08360), pg. 11
Casa Di Bertacchi, 1910 Gallagher Dr.(08360), pg. 932
Mrs. Schlorer's, Inc., 270 N. Mill Rd.(08360), pg. 275
RENNOC CORPORATION, 3501 Southeast Blvd.(08360-7789), pg. 927
Venice Maid Co., Inc., 270 N. Mill Rd.(08360), pg. 275

Voorhees

MOYER MITCHELL COMPANY, INC., 1014 Rural Ave.(08043), pg. 774

Waldwick

GLOBAL TURNKEY SYSTEMS INC., Four North St.(07463), pg. 463

Wall

Seely Equipment & Supply Co., Inc., 1325 Hwy. 34(07719), pg. 763

Warren

PONY SPORTS & LEISURE INC., 15 Independent Blvd.(07059), pg. 880

Wayne

Applied Coatings, 661 Rt. 23(07470), pg. 133
Arrow Group Industries, Inc., P.O. Box 928, (07474-0928), pg. 357
BONLAND INDUSTRIES, INC., 50 Newark Pompton Turnpike(07470), pg. 164
COLDWELL BANKERS/SCHLOTT REALTORS, 1550 Rte. 23 North(07470), pg. 260
CORBER CORPORATION, 400 Newark Pompton Turnpike(07470), pg. 285
Cornell Dubilier Electronics, 1700 Rt. 23 N.(07470), pg. 616
GAF Building Materials Corporation, 1361 Alps Rd.(07470), pg. 438
GAF CORPORATION, 1361 Alps Rd.(07470), pg. 438
GAF Export Corp., 1361 Alps Rd.(07470), pg. 438
GAF International Corp., 1361 Alps Road(07470), pg. 438
The Grand Union Company, 201 Willowbrook Blvd.(07470), pg. 476
HOBOKEN WOOD FLOORING CORPORATION, 70 Demarest Dr.(07470), pg. 537
KAPLAN ELECTRONICS, 1700 RT. 23 N(07470), pg. 616
Kearfott Guidance & Navigation Corp., 150 Totowa Road(07474-0595), pg. 93
MAYER BERKSHIRE CORPORATION, 25 Edison Dr.(07470), pg. 724
Mosler Electronic Systems Div., 415 Paterson-Hamburg Turnpike(07470), pg. 772

Weehawken

THE IN-HOUSE AGENCY, 331 Park Ave.(07087), pg. 564
North Pier Associates, Pier D-T, Lincoln Harbour(07087), pg. 1028

West Caldwell

HEWITT-ROBINS CORP., 40 Fairfield Place(07006), pg. 532
REITMAN INDUSTRIES, 10 Patton Dr.(07006), pg. 924

West New York

CULVER TEXTILE CORPORATION, 525 52nd St.(07093), pg. 304

West Orange

BARTON PRESS, INC., 55 Lakeside Ave.(07052), pg. 123
Douglas Elliman Knight Frank Inc., 10 Rooney Circle(07052), pg. 347
PATIENT CARE, INC., 59 Main St.(07052), pg. 851
SELECTO-FLASH, INC., 18 Central Ave.(07052), pg. 988

Westfield

CONNELL RICE & SUGAR CO., 45 Cardinal Dr.(07090), pg. 275
CROLL-REYNOLDS COMPANY, 751 Central Ave.(07090), pg. 300
TORCON, INC., 214 E. Grove St.(07090-1608), pg. 1102

Westmont

Pepper, Hamilton & Scheetz, Sentry Office Plaza, 216 Haddon Ave., Ste. 321(08108), pg. 860

Westville

J.E. BERKOWITZ, LP, Delsea Dr. & Harvard Ave.(08093), pg. 142

Westwood

LANMAN & KEMP-BARCLAY CO. INC., 25 Woodland Ave.(07675), pg. 657

Whippany

CHANNEL HOME CENTERS INC., 945 Route 10(07981), pg. 238
PHILIP FRITZE & SONS, INC., 10 School St.(07981), pg. 434
GILBERT, WHITNEY & JOHNS, INC., Jefferson Plaza, 110 S. Jefferson Rd.(07981), pg. 458
STEPHEN GOULD PAPER CO., INC., 35 S. Jefferson Rd.(07981), pg. 473
KDI Electronics, 60 S. Jefferson Rd.(07981), pg. 612
RI HOLDINGS, 75 Troy Hills Rd.(07891), pg. 907
Rowe International, Inc., 75 Troy Hill Road(07981), pg. 907

Whitehouse

FIMBEL DOOR CORPORATION, Coddington Rd.(08888), pg. 409

Willingboro

HILL INTERNATIONAL INC., 1 Leavitt Pkwy(08046), pg. 534

Wood-Ridge

Springfield Instrument Company, 76 Passaic St.(07075), pg. 1059

Woodbridge

ALPHA ASSOCIATES, INC., 2 Amboy Ave.(07095), pg. 43
CHC ADVERTISING, 1480 Rt. 9 N.(07095), pg. 201
The Kislak Company, Inc., 1000 Rt. 9(07095), pg. 633
J. I. Kislak Agency, Inc., 1000 Rt. 9(07095), pg. 633
M.E.D. COMMUNICATIONS, Aspen Corporate Park Two, 1460 Rte. 9 North(07095), pg. 692
Pathmark, 301 Blair Rd.(07095), pg. 1064
Sunshine Biscuits, Inc., 100 Woodbridge Center Dr.(07095-1196), pg. 439
SUPERMARKETS GENERAL CORPORATION, 301 Blair Rd.(07095), pg. 1064

Woodbury

E.D. Collier & Son, Reid & Namoni Sts.(08096), pg. 125
E.P. HENRY CORPORATION, 201 Park Ave.(08096), pg. 530
MediaNews Group, Eastern Operations, 309 So. Broad St.(08096), pg. 735
Paving Stone Div., 201 Park Ave.(08096), pg. 530

NEW MEXICO

Albuquerque

Albuquerque Metals Co., 3339 Second St.(87103), pg. 201
AMERICAN FURNITURE COMPANY, P.O. BOx 3685(87190), pg. 55

CUTTER FLYING SERVICE, INC., 2502 Clark Carr, Loop S.E.(87106), pg. 307
Frank Paxton Lumber Company, 1909 Bellamah N.W., P.O. Box. 25152(87125), pg. 592
FRANKS SUPPLY COMPANY, INC., 3311 Stanford, N.E.(87107), pg. 429
FURR'S SUPERMARKETS, 1730 Montano Rd. NW(87184), pg. 437
RICK JOHNSON & COMPANY, INC., 6100 Indian School Rd., NE(87110), pg. 597
KOB-TV, Inc., 4 Broadcast Plaza S.W.(87103), pg. 549
KARLER PACKING COMPANY, INC., 9111 Broadway, S.E.(87103), pg. 617
J. KORBER & COMPANY, 2311 Vassar N.E.(87107), pg. 641
MELLOY BROS. ENTERPRISES, 7707 Lomas N.E.(87110), pg. 738
Melloy Nissan, 7707 Lomas N.E.(87110), pg. 738
MOUNTAIN STATES CONSTRUCTORS, INC., West Frontage Rd. N.E.(87197), pg. 773
PLAINS ELECTRIC GENERATION TRANSMISSION CO-OP, INC., 2401 Aztec, N.E.(87107), pg. 873
QUALITY PONTIAC, INC., 1300 Lomas NE(87125), pg. 904
SCIENCE & ENGINEERING ASSOCIATES, 6100 Uptown Blvd., N.E., Ste. 700(87110), pg. 982
THUNDERBIRD STEEL CORPORATION, 4300 2nd, N.W.(87107), pg. 1096
Wellborn - DE Corp., 215 Rossmoor Rd., S.W.(87125), pg. 354

Anthony

SHARP OIL COMPANY, 217 N. Main(88021), pg. 995

Clovis

ALLSUPS CONVENIENCE STORES INC., 2112 Thornton(88101), pg. 43

Farmington

U.S. ENERTEK, INC., 4901 E. Main St.(87402), pg. 1135

Gallup

GURLEY MOTOR COMPANY, 701 W. Coal Ave.(87301), pg. 494
RICO MOTOR COMPANY, 501-23 W. Coal(87301), pg. 933

Las Cruces

STAHMANN FARMS, INC., P.O. Box 550(88005), pg. 1034

Los Alamos

Los Alamos Monitor, P.O. Box 1268, (87544), pg. 655
LOS ALAMOS TECHNICAL ASSOCIATES, INC., 1650 Trinity Dr.(87544), pg. 684

Navajo

NAVAJO FOREST PRODUCTS INDUSTRIES, P.O. Box 1280(87328), pg. 796

Roswell

BELL GAS, INC., 1811 S.E. Main(88201), pg. 134

Santa Fe

Johnson Storage & Moving, Santa Fe, Rte. 20, Box 2911, (Corner of Airport Rd. & Colony Dr.)(87501), pg. 601

Socorro

GREFCO, Inc., P.O. Box 1436(87801), pg. 137

NEW YORK

Adams

Great Lakes Cheese Of New York, Inc., 23 Phelps Rd.(13605), pg. 481

Akron

PERRY'S ICE CREAM CO., INC., 1 Ice Cream Plaza(14001), pg. 863

Albany

Albany Times Union, News Plaza, Box 15000(12212), pg. 523
Arnold Fortuna Lawner & Cabot, One Columbia Circle(12203), pg. 84
CUNA Mid East District, Two Wall Street(12205), pg. 205
Capital Newspapers, News Plaza, Box 15000(12212), pg. 523
DE NOOYER CHEVROLET INC., 127 Wolf Rd.(12205), pg. 329
HOLBROOK LUMBER COMPANY, 70 Fuller Rd.(12205), pg. 538
HUDSON VALLEY PAPER COMPANY, 981 Broadway(12201), pg. 551
Keystone Automotive Industries, Inc. - Albany, 1 Selina Drive(12205), pg. 628
Lawrence Management Group, Inc., 33 Elk St.(12207-2199), pg. 662
MAIN BROTHERS OIL COMPANY, INC., P.O. Box 11029(12211), pg. 702
MEDIA LOGIC, INC., 1520 Central Ave.(12205), pg. 734
ORANGE MOTOR COMPANY INC., 799 Central Ave.(12206), pg. 828
PARTNERS MEANY, INC., 382 Broadway(12207), pg. 850
Sealy Mattress Company of Albany, Inc., P.O. Box 5288, 99 Railroad Ave. & Brown Rd.(12205), pg. 985
Southtec, Inc., 1750 N. Broadway(12204), pg. 1019
TAGSONS PAPERS, INC., 99 Broadway(12201), pg. 1076
TRADING PORT, INC., North Manning Blvd. & Prospect Ave.(12206), pg. 1105
J. TREFFILETTI & SONS, INC., 4 N. Ferry St.(12207), pg. 1109
United Community Insurance Co., 33 Elk Street(12207-2199), pg. 662
UNITED FOOD SERVICE DISTRIBUTORS, INC., 875 Broadway(12207), pg. 1132

Amherst

BUFFALO HOSPITAL SUPPLY CO., INC., 130 Pineview Dr.(14228), pg. 187
CM Hoist Division, Audubon & Sylvan Pkwys.(14228), pg. 266
CM Mechanical Handling Systems, 140 J.J. Audubon Pkwy(14228-1187), pg. 266
CM Shredder Div., 140 J.J. Audubon Pkwy.(14228-1197), pg. 266
COLUMBUS MCKINNON CORP., 140 J.J. Audubon Pkwy.(14228-1197), pg. 266
COWPER & SIEGFRIED, 201 Ganson St.(14226), pg. 291
EATON OFFICE SUPPLY CO., INC., 180 John Glenn Dr.(14226-9500), pg. 364
STANDARD ELECTRONICS, INC., 215 John Glenn Dr.(14228), pg. 1036
ULTRA TOOL & PLASTICS, INC., 155 Pineview Dr.(14228), pg. 1125
Watson Bowman Acme Corp., 95 Pineview Drive(14228), pg. 145

Amityville

INTERSTATE DRUG EXCHANGE, INC., 1500 New Horizons Blvd.(11701), pg. 580
MONITOR AEROSPACE CORPORATION, 1000 New Horizons Blvd.(11701), pg. 765
PHILLIPS, MILLER, SPEYER & FROST, INC., 121 W. Oak St.(11701), pg. 867

Amsterdam

Esquire Novelty Co., Forest Ave.(12010), pg. 1054
THE NOTEWORTHY COMPANY, 100 Church St.(12010), pg. 816

Angola

Bison Canning Co., Inc., South Main St.(14006), pg. 474

Armonk

Color Data East, 5 N. Greenwich Rd.(10504), pg. 975
H.O. PENN MACHINERY CO. INC., 100 Business Park Dr.(10504), pg. 857

Astoria

Lifetime Television, 36-12 35th Ave.(11106), pg. 523

Au Sable Forks

Lake Placid Granite Co., P.O. Box l(12912), pg. 260

Auburn

Monorail, Inc., 23 N. Division St.(13021), pg. 266

Ballston Spa

CURTIS LUMBER COMPANY, 885 Rte. 67(12020), pg. 305

Batavia

P.W. MINOR & SON, INC., 3 Treadeasy Ave.(14020), pg. 758
WESTERN REGIONAL OFF TRACK BETTING, 700 Ellicott St.(14020), pg. 1181

Bay Shore

DVC INDUSTRIES, 1440 Fifth Ave.(11706), pg. 310
LAWRENCE METAL PRODUCTS, INC., 260 Spur Dr., S.(11706), pg. 662
RFI Corp., 100 Pine Aire Dr.(11706), pg. 612
South Shore Mall, 1653B Sunrise Hwy.(11706), pg. 699

Bayport

EDWIN B. STIMPSON COMPANY, INC., 900 Sylvan Ave.(11705), pg. 1049

Binghamton

BEN ARNOLD CO., INC., 300 Plaza Dr.(13903), pg. 84
Columbian Life Insurance Company, P.O. Box 1381, (13902), pg. 266
COLUMBIAN MUTUAL LIFE INSURANCE CO., P.O. Box 1381, (13902), pg. 266
DORON PRECISION SYSTEMS, INC., 174 Court St.(13902), pg. 346
Foron International Sales Corp., P.O. Box 400, (13902), pg. 346
Multiple Parking Services, Inc., Collier Street Ramp Garage, P.O. Box 1569(13902), pg. 42
Security Equity Life Insurance Co., 100 Court St.(13901), pg. 987
SECURITY MUTUAL LIFE INSURANCE CO. OF NEW YORK, 100 Court St.(13901), pg. 987
E. H. TITCHENER & COMPANY, 1 Titchener Place(13905), pg. 1099

Blasdell

EATON EQUIPMENT CORP., 250 Lake Ave.(14219), pg. 364

Bohemia

AERO DATA METAL CRAFTERS, 220 Knickerbocker Ave.(11716), pg. 22
Computer Systems of Long Island, Atrium Executive Center, 80 Orville Dr.(11716), pg. 370
ILC Data Device, 105 Wilbur Pl.(11716), pg. 560
ILC INDUSTRIES, INC., 105 Wilbur Pl.(11716), pg. 560
PERIPHONICS CORP., 4000 Veterans Memorial Hwy.(11716), pg. 862

Bolivar

Heritage Cutlery, Inc., Refinery Rd.(14715), pg. 943

Brewster

Dunmore Corporation/Brewster, Rte. 6(10509), pg. 353

Briarcliff Manor

Great Lakes Carbon Corp., 320 Old Briarcliff Rd.(10510), pg. 545
TETKO, INC., 333 S. Highland Ave.(10510), pg. 1089

Broadalbin

Mohawk Furniture, Inc., Five Mill St.(12025), pg. 447

Bronx

ATLANTIC TO PACIFIC BEDDING CORP., 700 Havemeyer Ave.(10473), pg. 95
BWP Distributors, Inc., 1055 Bronx River Ave.(10472), pg. 224
CLAY-PARK LABS, INC., Bathgate Industrial Park, 1700 Bathgate Ave.(10457), pg. 253
COAT, APRON & LINEN SUPPLY, 40 W. 170th St.(10452), pg. 257
DEXTER CHEMICAL CORP., 845 Edgewater Rd.(10474), pg. 334
EVERLAST SPORTS MANUFACTURING CORP., 750 E. 132nd St.(10454), pg. 392
INDUSTRIAL ACOUSTICS COMPANY, INC., 1160 Commerce Ave.(10462), pg. 565
KRASDALE FOODS INC., 400 Food Ctr. Dr.(10474), pg. 644
LOEHMANN'S, INC., 2500 Halsey St.(10461), pg. 681
NATIONAL FOODS INC., 600 Food Center Dr.(10474), pg. 788
PAPER ENTERPRISES, INC., 850 E. 140th St.(10454), pg. 847
SAVEMART INC., 332 E. 149th St.(10451), pg. 973
THE H. W. WILSON CO., 950 University Ave.(10452), pg. 1193

Bronxville

DIRECT COMMUNICATIONS CORPORATION, 45 Kraft Ave.(10708), pg. 339

Brooklyn

BAROUM EATON ALLEN CORPORATION, 67 Kent Ave.(11211), pg. 121
Bayside Fuel Oil Corp., 1810 Shore Pkwy.(11214), pg. 128
BAYSIDE FUEL OIL DEPOT CORP., 1776 Shore Pkwy.(11214), pg. 128
BELMONT METALS, INC., 314-30 Belmont Ave.(11207), pg. 137
Butler Utilities Services, Inc., 7201 20th Avenue(11214), pg. 197
CHEM-TAINER CORPORATION, 361 Neptune Ave., N.(11704), pg. 241
Commons Metro Inc., 16 Rewe St.(11211), pg. 269
CREATIVE SALON FURNITURE INC., 1768 E. 49th St.(11234), pg. 297
CUMBERLAND PACKING CORP., 2 Cumberland St.(11205), pg. 304
4C FOODS CORPORATION, 580 Fountain Ave.(11208), pg. 427
GOLDBERGER DOLL MFG. COMPANY, INC., 538 Johnson Ave.(11237), pg. 466
GUSSO MANUFACTURING, INC., 5112 Second Ave.(11232), pg. 495
HALSEY DRUG CO., INC., 1827 Pacific St.(11233), pg. 502
HAYWIN TEXTILE PRODUCTS, INC., 106 Bayard St.(11222), pg. 520
J.M.P. BAKERY CO., INC., 508 Junius St.(11212), pg. 586
KEY FOOD STORES CO-OPERATIVE, INC., 8925 Ave. D(11236), pg. 626
Kings Plaza Shopping Ctr. & Marina, 5400 Ave. U(11234), pg. 699
Ko-Rec-Type, 67 Kent Ave.(11211), pg. 121
Lafayette Precision Products Inc., 292 No. Henry St.(11222), pg. 906
Lee Spring Company, 1462 62nd St.(11219), pg. 1127
Manhattan and Bronx Surface Transit Operating Authority, 370 Jay St.(11201), pg. 745
MANHATTAN STORE INTERIORS, INC., 17 Moultrie St.(11222), pg. 704
MATECO ELECTRONICS CORP., 2375 Flatbush Ave.(11234), pg. 720
MONARCH LUGGAGE CO. INC., 5 Delavan St.(11231), pg. 765
New York City Transit Authority, 370 Jay St.(11201), pg. 745
PCM Construction, Inc., c/o Brooklyn Navy Yard, Flushing Ave. & Cumberland St., Bldg. 27(11205), pg. 529
PEERLESS IMPORTERS, INC., 16 Bridgewater St.(11222), pg. 855
RAINBOW APPAREL DISTRIBUTION CENTER, 1000 Pennsylvania Ave.(11207), pg. 910
Rose Fuel Corporation, 8301 Third Ave.(11209), pg. 128
Stereo Corp. of America, 2375 Flatbush Ave.(11234), pg. 720
Stereo Warehouse Inc., 2375 Flatbush Ave.(11234), pg. 720
TEKNI-PLEX, INC., 68 35th St.(11232), pg. 1084
VICTORIA PACKING CORPORATION, 443 E. 100th St.(11236), pg. 1149

Buffalo

ADAM MELDRUM & ANDERSON CO., INC., 389 Main St.(14203), pg. 16
BENDERSON DEVELOPMENT CO., INC., 570 Delaware Ave.(14202), pg. 138
Bergman Tool Mfg. Co., Inc., 1573 Niagara(14213), pg. 64
Bison Baseball Inc., 275 Washington St.(14203), pg. 932
Blaw Knox Food & Chemical Equipment Company, 750 E. Ferry St.(14211), pg. 156
J. C. BROCK CORP., 25 Hardwood Pl.(14210), pg. 178
Buffalo Color Corporation, 100 Lee St.(14210), pg. 187
Buffalo Waterfront Restaurant Corp., 2 Templeton Terrace(14202), pg. 1029
BUFFALO WHITE GMC, INC., 271 Dingens St.(14206), pg. 187
F.N. BURT COMPANY, INC., 2345 Walden Ave.(14225), pg. 195
CARTON-CRAFT CORPORATION, 115-121 Ash St.(14204), pg. 226
COLAD GROUP INC., 701 Seneca St.(14210), pg. 259
Concession Air Corporation, One Delaware North Place, 438 Main St.(14202), pg. 326
COOK MOVING SYSTEMS, INC., 1845 Dale Rd.(14225), pg. 282
CROWLEY WEBB & ASSOCIATES, 268 Main St., Ste. 400(14202), pg. 301
CURTIS SCREW CO., INC., 1130 Niagara St.(14213), pg. 306
JOHN W. DANFORTH CO., 1940 Fillmore Ave.(14214), pg. 314
JOSEPH DAVIS, INC., 120 W. Tupper St.(14201), pg. 318
DELAWARE NORTH COMPANIES, INC., 438 Main St.(14202), pg. 326
DINAIRE CORP., 145 Gruner Rd.(14227), pg. 338
EASTMAN MACHINE CO., 779 Washington St.(14203), pg. 364
ELAN FOODS, 28 Church Street, Ste. 206(14202), pg. 372
FERGUSON ELECTRIC CONSTRUCTION CO., INC., 333 Ellicott St.(14203), pg. 406
Frank L. Ciminelli Construction Co., 369 Franklin St.(14202), pg. 249
FRONTIER LUMBER COMPANY, INC., 1941 Elmwood Ave.(14207), pg. 434
GIBRALTAR STEEL CORP., 635 S. Park Ave.(14240), pg. 456
GLOBE INTERNATIONAL INC., 1400 Clinton St.(14206), pg. 464
GRAPHIC CONTROLS, CORP., 189 Van Rensselaer(14210), pg. 478
Graphic Controls Industrial Products Div., P.O. Box 1271(14240), pg. 478
Graphic Controls Medical Products Div., P.O. Box 1271(14240), pg. 478
ROBERT JAMES SALES INC., 269 Hinman Ave.(14216), pg. 589
The Jewett Refrigerator Co., Inc., 2 Letchworth St.(14213-1098), pg. 957
Keystone Buffalo Warehouse - Buffalo, 485 Ludwig Ave.(14227), pg. 628
McDonald Products Company, 2685 Walden Ave.(14225), pg. 1014
MCLEAN-THOMAS INC., 266 Broadway(14204), pg. 731
D. J. Mead-Hubbs & Howe, 2200 Harlem Rd.(14225), pg. 1016
MOLIN AUTO PARTS INC., 3896 Union Rd.(14225), pg. 764
MOLLENBERG-BETZ INC., 300 Scott St.(14204), pg. 764
Mosler Counter Systems Div., 200 Race St.(14027), pg. 772
Eric Mower and Associates/Buffalo, Inc., 360 Delaware Ave.(14202), pg. 774
Multiple Parking Services, Inc., 335 Statler Tower, 107 Delaware Ave.(14202), pg. 42
NATIONAL HEALTH CARE AFFILIATES, INC., 651 Delaware Ave.(14202), pg. 791
NIAGARA BLOWER COMPANY, 673 Ontario(14207), pg. 805
Niagara Envelope Co., Inc., 701 Seneca St.(14210), pg. 806
NIAGARA ENVELOPE COMPANY, INC., 693 Seneca St., 5th Fl.(14210), pg. 805
NIAGARA FRONTIER TRANSPORATION METRO SYSTEM, INC., 181 Ellicott St.(14203), pg. 806
NIAGARA TRANSFORMER CORP., 1747 Dale Rd.(14225), pg. 806
OSMOSE WOOD PRESERVING CO., 980 Ellicott St.(14209), pg. 830
PVS Chemicals, Inc., 55 Lee St.(14210), pg. 838
PLYWOOD PLASTICS INC., 111 Tonawanda St.(14207), pg. 878
QUACKENBUSH CO. INC., 505 Franklin St.(14202), pg. 902
RICH PRODUCTS CORP., 1150 Niagara St.(14213), pg. 932
RUSLANDER & SONS, INC., 18 Letchworth St.(14213), pg. 956
Russett Foods, 665 Perry St.(14210), pg. 1217
SCHUTTE & COMPANY, 1207 Delaware Ave.(14209), pg. 979
SCIPAR, 26 W. Spring St.(14221), pg. 982
SMITH METAL ARTS COMPANY, INC., 2685 Walden Ave.(14225), pg. 1013
SNYDER TANK CORP., S-3774 Lakeshore Rd.(14219), pg. 1015
Sportservice Corporation, One Delaware North Place, 438 Main St.(14202), pg. 326
Sportsystems Corporation, One Delaware North Place, 438 Main St.(14202), pg. 326
TUNMORE OLDSMOBILE INC., 2677 Delaware Ave.(14216), pg. 1119
W&F MANUFACTURING CORPORATION, INC., 2299 Kenmore Ave.(14207-1311), pg. 1155
Wood Treaters of Buffalo Co., Inc., 100 Botsford Place(14216), pg. 435
ZEMCO INDUSTRIES, INC., 665 Perry St.(14210), pg. 1217

Caledonia

Jones Chemicals, Inc., 100 Sunny Sol Blvd.(14423), pg. 603

Camden

Mystic Stamp Company, 24 Mill St.(13316), pg. 679

Camillus

CAMILLUS CUTLERY CO., 54 Main St.(13031), pg. 212

Canandaigua

LABELON CORPORATION, 10 Chapin St.(14424), pg. 649

Canastota

DIEMOLDING CORP., 125 Rasbach St.(13032), pg. 336

Carmel

Danbury Pharmacal Inc., 12 Stoneleigh Ave.(10512), pg. 975
GUIDEPOSTS ASSOCIATES, INC., 39 Seminary Hill Rd.(10512), pg. 493

Centerpoint

VENGROFF WILLIAMS & ASSOCIATES, INC., 93 Centershore Rd.(11721), pg. 1147
Vengroff Williams Realty Management, 109 Centerline Rd.(11721), pg. 1147

Central Islip

NORTH AMERICAN ENCLOSURES, INC., 85 Jetson Lane(11722), pg. 811

Chappaqua

TV Preview, Inc., 201 King St.(10514), pg. 1075

Chatham

The Columbia Corporation, Rte. 295(12037), pg. 1209

Cheektowaga

MIKEN COMPANIES, INC., 75 Boxwood Lane(14227), pg. 752
RAMA GROUP OF COMPANIES, 25 Boxwood Lane(14227), pg. 910
Specialty Restaurants Corp., 100 Amherst Villa Rd.(14229), pg. 1029

Clarence

MENNEN MEDICAL INC., 10123 Main St.(14031), pg. 739

Clarence Center

Gold Bond Building Products, Roll Rd.(14032), pg. 790

Clifton Park

Jack Byrne Minuteman Lube, 1768 Rte. 9(12065), pg. 198
Troy Savings Bank-Clifton Park, Rtes. 9 & 146(12065), pg. 1117

Cohoes

MOHAWK PAPER MILLS, INC., 465 S. Saratoga St.(12047), pg. 763
Worlite Corporation, 628 Saratoga St.(12047), pg. 619

Copiague

W. A. BAUM COMPANY, INC., 620 Oak St.(11726), pg. 127

Corning

Dutch Parking Inc., Centerway Parking Facility, 1 Centerway Square(14830), pg. 42

Cortland

CORTLAND LINE CO., INC., 3736 Kellogg Rd.(13045), pg. 287
ETL TESTING LABORATORIES, INC, Rt. 11 Industrial Park(13045), pg. 361

De Witt

Agway Data Services, Inc., 333 Butternut Dr.(13214), pg. 25
Agway Financial Corporation, 333 Butternut Dr.(13214), pg. 25
AGWAY, INC., 333 Butternut Dr.(13214), pg. 25
Agway Petroleum Corp., 333 Butternut Dr.(13214), pg. 25
Arnold Fortuna Lawner & Cabot, 5788 Widewaters Parkway(13214), pg. 84

Deer Park

D & R ADVERTISING, 100 Jeffryn Blvd.(11729), pg. 307
Diversified Wood Products, 55 N. Industry Ct.(11729), pg. 965
Garsite/TSR, Inc., 172 E. Industry Court(11729), pg. 443
GLOBAL STEEL PRODUCTS CORPORATION, 95 Marcus Blvd.(11729), pg. 463
SABBETH INDUSTRIES LTD, 55 N. Industry Court(11729), pg. 965
Sabbeth International Forest Products, 55 N. Industry Ct.(11729), pg. 965
ANTON SMIT & CO., INC., 6 Connor Lane(11729), pg. 1011
Tebbas Sales Corp., 55 N. Industry Ct.(11729), pg. 965

Depew

Arcata Graphics Buffalo, Inc., TC Indus. Pk.(14043), pg. 80

Dolgeville

DANIEL GREEN CO., 1 Main St.(13329), pg. 484

Dunkirk

DUNKIRK ICE CREAM CO., INC., One Ice Cream Dr., Rte. 60 N.(14048), pg. 353

East Bloomfield

Crosman Corporation, Rts. 5 & 20(14443), pg. 695
CROSSMAN CORP., Routes 5 & 20(14443), pg. 300
Ranging, Routes 5 & 20(14443), pg. 300

East Farmingdale

56th Fighter Group of Long Island, Inc., Republic Airport-Gate 1, Route 110(11735), pg. 1029

East Greenbush

Gold Bond Building Products, P.O. Box 566, (12061), pg. 790
Troy Savings Bank-East Greenbush, 615 Columbia Tpke.(12061), pg. 1117

East Northport

LOCKS ADVERTISING AGENCY, 222 S. Second St.(11731), pg. 680

East Rochester

ROBERTS COMMUNICATIONS INC., The Piano Works, Ste. 3500, 333 W. Commercial St.(14445), pg. 938

East Syracuse

DAIRYLEA COOPERATIVE INC., 5001 Brittonfield Pkwy.(13057), pg. 311

Edgewood

ALLMETAL SCREW PRODUCTS CORP., 200 Executive Dr.(11717), pg. 40

Ellenville

Imperial Schrade Corp., Route 209 North(12428), pg. 564

Ellicottville

FITZPATRICK & WELLER, INC., 12 Mill St.(14731), pg. 416

Elma

MADER CONSTRUCTION GROUP INC., 970 Bullis Rd.(14059), pg. 699

Elmira

CHEMUNG FORD, INC., Rte. 14(14902), pg. 242
Dutch Parking Inc., Clemens Square, 1 West Gray St.(14901), pg. 42
Elmira Litho, C St., Bldg. J, Center At Horsehead(14903), pg. 736
HARDINGE BROTHERS, INC., P.O. Box 1507(14902-1507), pg. 508
HILLIARD CORPORATION, 100 W. 4th St.(14901), pg. 535
KENNEDY VALVE, 1021 E. Water St.(14901), pg. 623
SCHWEIZER AIRCRAFT CORPORATION, P.O. Box 147(14902), pg. 981
TRAYER PRODUCTS, INC., 541 E. Clinton St.(14902), pg. 1108

Elmsford

COMMONS BROS., INC., 55 Hunter Lane(10523), pg. 269
CONWAY IMPORT CO. INC., 5 Warehouse Lane(10523), pg. 281
NEW ZEALAND LAMB CO., INC., 555 Paxter Rd.(10523), pg. 803

Endicott

Union Forging Co., 506 North St.(13760), pg. 1123

Fairport

VOIT CORP., 1451 Pittsford-Victor Rd.(14450), pg. 1154
VOIT SPORTS, INC., 100 Willowbrook Office Park, 1451 Pittsford-Victor Rd.(14450), pg. 1154

Falconer

Falconer Glass Industries, Inc., 500 S. Work St.(14733), pg. 492

Farmingdale

AMERICAN LAUBSCHER CORP., 80 Finn Court(11735), pg. 57
B. H. AIRCRAFT CO., INC., 441 Eastern Parkway(11735), pg. 106
Creative Technical Services, 40 Daniel St.(11735), pg. 339
DURO DYNE CORPORATION, P.O. Box 117(11735), pg. 355
HYGRADE METAL MOULDING MFG. CORP., 540 Smith St.(11735), pg. 557
Lindenmeyr Munroe, 1845 New Highway(11735), pg. 233
MINUTEMAN PRESS INTERNATIONAL, 1640 New Hwy.(11735), pg. 759
PLASCAL CORPORATION, 361 Eastern Pkwy.(11735), pg. 874
ROSS BICYCLES USA LTD., 51 Executive Blvd.(11735), pg. 949
D. WALDNER COMPANY, INC., 125 Rte. 110(11735), pg. 1159

Fishkill

Stephen Gould/Midhudson, 1123 Rte. 52(12524), pg. 474

Floral Park

PRENTISS INCORPORATED, 21 Vernon St.(11001), pg. 887

Florida

BIG V SUPERMARKETS, INC., 176 N. Main St.(10921), pg. 149
ShopRite Supermarkets, 176 No. Main St.(10921), pg. 149

Flushing

ANGLERS ROSLYN GROUP LTD., 45-25 162nd St.(11358), pg. 75
LINZER PRODUCTS CORP., 13330 37th Ave.(11354), pg. 677

Fonda

Kasson & Keller, Rte 334, Cayadutta St.(12068), pg. 627
KEYMARK CORPORATION, Rte. 334, Cayadutta St.(12068), pg. 627

Freeport

WEKSLER INSTRUMENTS CORP., 80 Mill Rd.(11520), pg. 1174

Fulton

The Black Clawson Company, (13069), pg. 154

Garden City

AVIS, INC., 900 Old Country Rd.(11530), pg. 102
Bowling Corp. of America, 370 Old Country Rd.(11530), pg. 239
CHARAN INDUSTRIES, INC., 370 Old Country Rd.(11530), pg. 239
Charan Realty Group, 370 Old Country Rd.(11530), pg. 239
CHRISTOPHER THOMAS ASSOCIATES INC., 1101 Stewart Ave.(11530), pg. 249
Electronic Engineers Master, 645 Stewart Ave.(11530), pg. 522
GEARON HOFFMAN CONLON & NYE ADVERTISING, INC., 1051 Franklin Ave.(11530), pg. 447
Hearst Business Communications, Inc., 645 Stewart Ave(11530), pg. 522
HUGHES-TREITLER MANUFACTURING CORPORATION, 300 Endo Blvd.(11530), pg. 552
Integrated Circuits Master Catalog, 645 Stewart Ave.(11530), pg. 522
Metropolitan Suburban Bus Authority, 700 Commercial Ave.(11530), pg. 745
Motor Magazine, 645 Stewart Ave.(11530), pg. 522
Motor Publications, 645 Stewart Ave.(11530), pg. 522
Seaway Shopping Centers, Inc., 370 Old Country Rd.(11530), pg. 239
UTP (United Technical Publications) Division, 645 Stewart Ave.(11530), pg. 522

Gardenville

Supreme Machine Div., 101-5 Industrial Pkwy.(10923), pg. 434

Geneva

Finger Lakes Printing Company, 218 Genesce St.(14456), pg. 565

Getsville

J. M. JAYSON & CO., INC., 2350 North Forest(14068), pg. 591

Glendale

ENTRON INDUSTRIES LIMITED PARTNERSHIP, 70-31 84th St.(11385), pg. 383
GEORGE KOVACS LIGHTING, INC., 67-25 Otto Rd.(11385), pg. 643
CHARLES LEONARD, INC., 79-11 Cooper Ave.(11385), pg. 668
PEN-TAB INDUSTRIES, INC., 63-15 Traffic St.(11385), pg. 856

Glenmont

FARM FAMILY MUTUAL INSURANCE CO., Rte. 9 West(12077), pg. 401

Glens Falls

CB NORTH AMERICA, INC., One Apollo Dr.(12801), pg. 199
FINCH, PRUYN & CO., INC., 1 Glen St.(12801), pg. 410
Troy Savings Bank-Glens Falls, Aviation Mall(12801), pg. 1117

Gloversville

THE GRANDOE CORPORATION, 70-82 Bleecker St.(12078), pg. 476
SLM, INC., P.O. Box 1070, RDI Patch Rd.(12078), pg. 963
NELSON A. TAYLOR CO., INC., 10 W. 9th Ave.(12078), pg. 1080

Goshen

AMALLOY, 202 Route 207 (10924), pg. 46

Grand Island

CANNON, 2170 Whitehaven Rd.(14072), pg. 214

Granville

Mettowee Lumber & Plastic Co., Inc., 85 Church St.(12832), pg. 1085
Telegraphics Printing, 85 Church St.(12832), pg. 1085
TELESCOPE CASUAL FURNITURE, INC., 85 Church St.(12832), pg. 1085

Great Neck

Georgetown Partners, Inc., 60 Cutter Mill Rd.(11021), pg. 473
GOULD INVESTORS, L.P., 60 Cutter Mill Rd.(11021), pg. 473
JIMLAR CORPORATION, 160 Great Neck Rd.(11021), pg. 594
R.G. MEADOWS, INC., 310 East Shore Rd.(11023), pg. 733
SCHARER ASSOCIATES, INC., 230 Middle Neck Rd.(11021), pg. 974
SCHUMACHER & FORELLE, INC., 277 Northern Blvd.(11021), pg. 979
SHOGYO INTERNATIONAL CORPORATION, 287 Northern Blvd.(11021), pg. 1000

Greenvale

SLANT/FIN CORPORATION, 100 Forest Drive(11548), pg. 1010

Guilderland Center

Corporate, EDP, P.O. Box 98, (12085), pg. 951
Distribution Unlimited, Inc., P.O. Box 98, (12085), pg. 951
Flint River, P.O. Box 98, (12085), pg. 951
Galesi Enterprises, P.O. Box 98, (12085), pg. 951
High Point Ventures, Inc., P.O. Box 98, (12085), pg. 951
Jacksonville Ventures, Inc., P.O. Box 98, (12085), pg. 951
Lake George Ventures, Inc., P.O. Box 98, (12085), pg. 951
Mercer Forge, Inc., P.O. Box 98, (12085), pg. 952
Plaza Investment Associates, P.O. Box 98, (12085), pg. 952
Remington Hill Ventures, P.O. Box 98, (12085), pg. 952
Rotterdam Industrial Park, P.O. Box 98, (12085), pg. 951
ROTTERDAM VENTURES INC., P.O. Box 98(12085), pg. 951
Scotia Industrial Park, Inc., P.O. Box 98, (12085), pg. 952
Tampa Ventures, Inc., P.O. Box 98, (12085), pg. 952
TOW Water Co., Inc., P.O. Box 98, (12085), pg. 952
Voorheesville Ventures, Inc., P.O. Box 98, (12085), pg. 952
Washington Avenue Ventures, Inc., P.O. Box 98, (12085), pg. 952
Winridge Aurora Ventures, Inc., P.O. Box 98, (12085), pg. 952

Hancock

Mallery Lumber Corp.-NY, 36 Labarr(13783), pg. 703

Hauppauge

ARKAY PACKAGING CORPORATION, 22 Arkay Dr.(11788), pg. 83
BREGG DATA FORMS, INC., 75 Adams Ave.(11788), pg. 173
Dunston Leathers, Inc., 400 Wireless Blvd.(11788), pg. 1136
Fairmont Electronics, 295 Oser Ave.(11788), pg. 908
FLORAL GLASS & MIRROR, INC., 895 Motor Parkway(11788), pg. 420
GENERATION METALS CORP., 300 Oser Ave.(11788), pg. 451
LNR COMMUNICATIONS, 180 Marcus Blvd.(11788), pg. 648
LEADER INSTRUMENTS CORPORATION, 380 Oser Ave.(11788), pg. 664
LINOTYPE-HELL COMPANY, 425 Oser Ave.(11788), pg. 677
MAHARAM FABRIC CORPORATION, 45 Rasons Ct.(11788), pg. 701
NORTH ATLANTIC INDUSTRIES, INC., 60 Plant Ave.(11788-3890), pg. 812
POLYMER PLASTICS CORPORATION, 65 Davids Dr.(11788), pg. 880
QUOIZEL INC., 325 Kennedy Dr.(11788), pg. 905
SOUTHERN CONTAINER CORPORATION, 115 Engineers Rd.(11788), pg. 1020
SUPPORT SYSTEMS ASSOCIATES, INC., 1300 Veterans Memorial Hwy.(11788), pg. 1064
USA Network Control Center, 300 New Highway(11788), pg. 1124
UNITED STATES LUGGAGE COMPANY, 400 Wireless Blvd.(11788), pg. 1136

Hawthorne

Burke Fuel & Heating Co., 475 Commerce St.(10532), pg. 736
FEUER LEATHER CORPORATION, 8 Skyline Dr.(10352), pg. 407
METRIC & MULTISTANDARD COMPONENTS, 120 Old Saw Mill River Rd.(10532), pg. 743
WOLFF & MUNIER, INC., 50 Broadway(10532), pg. 1199

Hempstead

DAN'S SUPREME SUPER MARKETS INC., 474 Fulton Ave.(11550), pg. 314

Hicksville

EGC MEDIA GROUP, INC., 15 Bay Ave.(11801), pg. 359
Holmes Protection of Long Island, Inc., , pg. 540
SERVO CORPORATION OF AMERICA, 111 New South Road(11801-5259), pg. 993
STRUCTURAL INDUSTRIES, INC., 96 New South Rd.(11801), pg. 1054
UNIFLEX, INC., 383 W. John St.(11802), pg. 1126
UNIVERSAL PHOTONICS, INC., 495 W. John St.(11801), pg. 1139

Hillburn

TRIUMPH PET INDUSTRIES, INC., 4th St. & Rt. 59(10931), pg. 1115

Holbrook

AUSTIN SCULPTURE, 815 Grundy Ave.(11741), pg. 99
FOUR SEASONS SOLAR PRODUCTS CORP., 5005 Veterans Memorial Hwy.(11741), pg. 427
MAJESTIC MOLDED PRODUCTS, INC., 4333 Veterans Memorial Hwy.(11741), pg. 702

Hudson

FOSTER REFRIGERATOR CORPORATION, Mill & No. Second(12534), pg. 426
GINSBERG'S INSTITUTIONAL FOODS, INC., P.O. Box 17, Rte. 66(12534), pg. 460

Hudson Falls

POLYCOAT SYSTEMS, INC., 5 Depot St.(12839), pg. 880

Huntington

FLORENCE CORPORATION, 1647 E. Jericho Turnpike(11743), pg. 420

Huntington Station

DIRECT PRESS MODERN LITHO CORPORATION, 386 Oakwood Rd.(11746), pg. 339

Inwood

APEX MILLS CORPORATION, 168 Doughty Blvd.(11696), pg. 78
MGR EQUIPMENT CORP., 22 Gates Ave.(11696), pg. 692
Signal Transformer Co., Inc., 500 Bayview Ave.(11696), pg. 571
Signal Transformer Co., Inc., 500 Bayview Ave.(11696), pg. 571

Irvington

CARRAFIELLO, DIEHL & ASSOCIATES, INC., 90 N. Broadway(10533), pg. 225

Irvington-on-Hudson

CDA/TURK GROUP, 90 North Broadway(10533), pg. 200

Islandia

SHERWOOD LUMBER CORPORATION, 300 Corporate Plaza(11722), pg. 999

Islip

Allforms Packaging Corp., 120 Allwood Ave.(11751), pg. 941

Ithaca

COURTESY CHEVROLET & IMPORTS INC., 370 Elmira Rd.(14850), pg. 290
Morse Automotive Products, 800 Warren Rd.(14850), pg. 166
THERM, INC., P.O. Box 310(14850), pg. 1090

Jackson Heights

The USAir Shuttle, 75-20 Astoria Blvd.(11370), pg. 1118

Jamaica

Alba Forwarding Co., Inc., 147-39 175th St.(11434), pg. 30
GREEN BUS LINES, INC., 16525 147th Ave.(11434), pg. 483
KING WIRE & CABLE CORPORATION, 179-45 110th Ave.(11433), pg. 631
The Long Island Rail Road Co., Jamaica Station(11435), pg. 745
MARTIN PAINT STORES, 182-20 Liberty Ave.(11432), pg. 715
NEW YORK RACING ASSOCIATION, P.O. Box 90(11417), pg. 803
WEB FOOD PRODUCTS CORP., 144-06 94th Ave.(11435), pg. 1170

Jamestown

THE AARQUE COMPANIES, 111 W. 2nd St.(14701), pg. 9
Aarque Management Corp., 111 W. 2nd St.(14701), pg. 9
Aarque Steel Corporation, 111 W. 2nd St.(14701), pg. 9
DAHLSTROM MANUFACTURING COMPANY, INC., 443 Buffalo St.(14702-0640), pg. 310
HOPE'S ARCHITECTURAL PRODUCTS INC., 84 Hopkins Ave.(14701), pg. 543
Producto Machine Co. Ring Division, Turner Rd.(14701), pg. 893

Jericho

ROSEN ASSOCIATES MANAGEMENT CORP., 333 Jericho Turnpike(11753), pg. 948
ZIEGLER CHEMICAL & MINERAL CORP., 100 Jericho Quad, Ste. 140(11753), pg. 1218

Johnson City

AZON CORPORATION, 720 Azon Rd.(13790), pg. 105

Johnstown

JOHNSTOWN KNITTING MILL CO., 309 W. Montgomery St.(12095), pg. 602

Kingston

COLONY LIQUOR DISTRIBUTORS, INC., 132 Flatbush Ave.(12401), pg. 264

Lacona

BLOUNT LUMBER COMPANY, P.O. Box 220(13083), pg. 158

Lake Success

COOPER LEDER MARCOMM, 3000 Marcus Ave.(11042), pg. 283
FRIENDLY HOLIDAYS INC., 1983 Marcus Ave.(11042), pg. 433
Jamaica Water Properties, 410 Lakeville Rd.(11042), pg. 1175
MARDEN-KANE, INC., 410 Lakeville Rd.(11042), pg. 706
Mastercard International, Inc., Four Ohio Dr.(11042), pg. 720

Lancaster

DEPEW DEVELOPMENT INC., 4429 Walden Ave.(14086), pg. 331
Industrial Lift Trucks, 4381 Walden Ave.(14086), pg. 1070
SEALING DEVICES INC., 4400 Walden Ave.(14086), pg. 984
Tetko Inc., Depew Operations, P.O. Box 346(14086), pg. 1089

Larchmont

D'AGOSTINO SUPERMARKETS INC., 1385 Boston Post Rd.(10538), pg. 310

Latham

COMMUNICATION & DESIGN AGENCY INC., 4 Avis Dr.(12110), pg. 269
IMPERIAL POOLS, INC., 33 Wade Rd.(12110), pg. 564
KELLER MOTOR CAR COMPANY, INC., 1111 Troy-Schenectady Rd.(12110), pg. 621
MICHAELS GROUP INC., 6 Century Hill Dr.(12110), pg. 747
NORTHWAY MOTORCAR CORPORATION, 727 New Loudon Rd.(12110), pg. 814
PEPSI-COLA ALBANY BOTTLING CO., INC., One Pepsi-Cola Dr.(12110), pg. 860
Troy Savings Bank-Latham, Troy-Schenectady Rd. & Sunset Dr.(12110), pg. 1117

Le Roy

JONES CHEMICALS, INC., 80 Munson St.(14482), pg. 603
UPSTATE MILK COOPERATIVES INC., 7115 W. Main St.(14482), pg. 1140

Liberty

CABLEVISION INDUSTRIES CORP., Cablevision Center(12754), pg. 206

Lindenhurst

Modern Handling Equipment Co. of NY, 1176 Farmingdale Rd., Rte. 109(11757), pg. 763

Little Falls

BURROWS PAPER CORPORATION, 501 W. Main St.(13365), pg. 195
Little Falls Color Print, Riverside Industrial Park, (13365), pg. 1057

Little Neck

LEVITON MFG. CO., INC., 59-25 Little Neck Pkwy.(11362), pg. 671

Liverpool

American Granby, Inc., 1111 Vine St.(13088), pg. 70
JOS. J. PIETRAFESA CO., INC., 7400 Morgan Rd.(13090), pg. 870
WILL & BAUMER INCORPORATED, Old Liverpool & Buckley Rd.(13088), pg. 1190
YOUNG & FRANKLIN, INC., 942 Old Liverpool Rd.(13088), pg. 1209

Locust Valley

Douglas Elliman-Jane Hayes, Inc., 71 Forest Ave.(11560), pg. 347

Long Island City

The Alan & Gray Co., 27-17 Jackson Ave.(11101), pg. 40
B & B MOTOR & CONTROL CORPORATION, 39-40 Crescent St.(11101), pg. 105
BESTFORM FOUNDATIONS, INC., 38-01 47th Ave.(11101), pg. 147
CGS INDUSTRIES, INC., 34-09 Queens Blvd.(11101), pg. 201
COSMOS COMMUNICATIONS, INC., 11-05 44th Dr.(11101), pg. 288
DUANE READE, 49-29 30th Place(11101), pg. 350
DURLACHER & CO., INC., 47-11 Van Dam St.(11101), pg. 354
EAGLE ELECTRIC MFG. CO., INC., 45-31 Court Square(11101), pg. 362
ELGIN WATCH INTERNATIONAL, INC., 33-00 Northern Blvd.(11101), pg. 376
EQUITABLE BAG COMPANY, 37-11 35th Ave.(11101), pg. 385
Greenpoint Division, 25-39 Borden Ave.(11101), pg. 428
HENRY MODELL & COMPANY, INC., 34-24 Vernon Blvd.(11106), pg. 762
PACE COLLECTION, INC., 11-11 34th Ave.(11106), pg. 838
PARAGON PAINT & VARNISH CORP., 5-49 46th Ave.(11101), pg. 848
PROPPER MANUFACTURING CO., INC., 36-04 Skillman Ave.(11101), pg. 895
QUEENS GROUP, INC., 52-35 Barnett Ave.(11104-1017), pg. 904
RIS PAPER COMPANY, 45-11 33rd St.(11101), pg. 935
SCALAMANDRE, INC., 37-24 24th St.(11101), pg. 974
Splendor Form Brassiere, Inc., 29-10 Thomson Ave.(11101), pg. 1032
SPLENDOR FORM INTERNATIONAL INC., 29-10 Thomson(11101), pg. 1031
Steinway & Sons, Steinway Place(11105), pg. 1046
VENTURA TRAVELWARE, INC., 32-33 47th Ave.(11101), pg. 1147
Ventura Travelware, Inc.-International Div., 32-33 47th Ave.(11101), pg. 1148
WELSBACH ELECTRIC CORP., 19-49 42nd St.(11105), pg. 1175
White Rose Food, 150 Price Pkwy.(11735), pg. 335

Lynbrook

LONG ISLAND WATER CORPORATION, 733 Sunrise Hwy.(11563), pg. 682

Mamaroneck

CINE MAGNETICS, INC., 606 Halstead Ave.(10543), pg. 250
MARVAL INDUSTRIES, INC., 315 Hoyt Ave.(10543), pg. 716
DON STONE ASSOCIATES INC., P.O. Box 198, (10543), pg. 1050

Manhasset

C M P PUBLICATIONS, INC., 600 Community Dr.(11030), pg. 202

Manorville

NEWPORT/CAPE DORY YACHTS, INC., 308 Line Rd.(11949), pg. 804

Maspeth

ABBOTT GLASS CO., INC., 59-30 54th St.(11378), pg. 9
ATLITE LIGHTING EQUIP, INC., 5747 47th St.(11378), pg. 97
FEDERAL DISTRIBUTING CORPORATION, 57-01 49th St.(11378), pg. 404
RICHTER & RATNER CONTRACTING CORPORATION, 55-05 Flushing Ave.(11378), pg. 933

McConnellsville

HARDEN FURNITURE COMPANY, 1 Mill Pond Way(13401), pg. 508

Mechanicville

JACK BYRNE FORD & MERCURY, INC., S. Main St.(12118), pg. 198

Melville

WALTER F. CAMERON ADVERTISING INC., 275 Broad Hollow Rd.(11747), pg. 212
GREENSTONE ROBERTS ADVERTISING, 1 Huntington Quadrangle(11747), pg. 485
A.D. Herman Construction Co., 532 Broad Hallow Rd.(11747), pg. 96
INTERNATIONAL COMPONENTS CORPORATION, 105 Maxess Rd.(11747), pg. 576
DON JAGODA ASSOCIATES, INC., 100 Marcus Dr.(11747), pg. 588
LEATHERS BEST, 30 Hub Dr.(11747), pg. 664
Len Ron Mfg. Co. Inc., 350 S. Service Rd.(11747-3233), pg. 389
MIDCOAST MORTGAGE CORPORATION, 275 Broad Hollow Road(11747), pg. 751
New York Systems Exchange Corp., 150 Broad Hollow Rd.(11747), pg. 1070
NORTHVILLE INDUSTRIES CORP., P.O. Box 2937, 25 Melville Pk. Rd.(11747), pg. 814
PERGAMENT HOME CENTERS, INC., 101 Marcus Dr.(11747), pg. 862
RECKSON ASSOCIATES, 225 Broadhollow Rd.(11747), pg. 917
J. RICHARD SMITH, LTD., 225 Broad Hollow Rd.(11747), pg. 1013

Middle Village

WALLY FRANK, LTD., 63-25 69th St.(11379), pg. 429

Middleport

BARDEN & ROBESON CORPORATION, 103 Kelly Ave.(14105), pg. 119

Milton

BROOKLYN BOTTLING CO., P.O. Box 808(12547), pg. 179

Mineola

GREAT NECK SAW MANUFACTURERS, INC., 165 E. Second St.(11501), pg. 482
VAN SON HOLLAND INK CORP. OF AMERICA, 92 Union St.(11501), pg. 1144

Montgomery

MATHIEU, DONOVAN & ASSOCIATES, INC., 77 Ward St.(12549), pg. 721

Monticello

Bell Flavors & Fragrances, 33 Lake Ave.(12701), pg. 134

Montour Falls

SHEPARD NILES, INC., 250 N. Genesee St.(14865), pg. 997

Mount Kisco

CURTIS INSTRUMENTS, INC., 200 Kisco Ave.(10549), pg. 305
ICAHN & CO., INC., 100 S. Bedford Rd.(10549), pg. 561
Trans World Airlines, Inc., 100 S. Bedford Rd.(10549), pg. 561

Mount Vernon

AIN PLASTICS, INC., 249 E. Sandford Blvd.(10550), pg. 26
SIGMUND COHN CORP., 121 S. Columbus Ave.(10553), pg. 259
Gutmann Cutlery, Inc., 120 S. Columbus Ave.(10553), pg. 556
MAGNETIC ANALYSIS CORP., 535 S. 4th Ave.(10550), pg. 700
RELIABLE AUTOMATIC SPRINKLER CO., INC., 525 N. MacQuesten Pkwy.(10552), pg. 924
TORK, INC., One Grove St.(10550), pg. 1102
UNIVERSAL BUILDERS SUPPLY, INC., 216 S. Terrace Ave.(10550), pg. 1137
Ward Leonard Electric Company, Inc., 31 South St.(10550), pg. 1127

Mountainville

STAR EXPANSION COMPANY, Pleasant Hill Rd.(10953), pg. 1039

Nanuet

Point Electric, 33 Route 304(10954), pg. 1068
SWIVELIER CO., INC., 33 Route 304(10954), pg. 1068

New Hartford

UTICA MUTUAL INSURANCE COMPANY, 180 Genesee St.(13413), pg. 1140
Utica National Insurance Group, 180 Genesee St.(13413), pg. 1141

New Hyde Park

Asher Candy Company, 1815 Gilford Ave.(11040), pg. 695
ASSOCIATED AIR FREIGHT, INC., 3333 New Hyde Park Rd.(11042), pg. 89
CASTRO CONVERTIBLE CORPORATION, 1990 Jericho Turnpike(11040), pg. 229

New Rochelle

ABI National Accounts, 466 Main St.(10801), pg. 50
AMERICAN WHITE CROSS LABORATORIES, INC., 40 Nardozzi Pl.(10801), pg. 65
THE P.J. CARLIN CONSTRUCTION COMPANY, 140 Huguenot St.(10801), pg. 220
Compilers Plus, 466 Main St.(10801), pg. 50
PLUNKETT-WEBSTER, INC., 2 Clinton Pl.(10802-0251), pg. 877
THE RAWLPLUG COMPANY, INC., Two F.B. Powers Square(10802), pg. 914
ROSENSHEIN ASSOCIATES, 77 Quaker Ridge Road(10804), pg. 948
S. SCHAFFER GROCERY CORPORATION, 27 Weyman Ave.(10805), pg. 974
Seaboard Electronics-East Coast Branch, 70 Church St.(10805), pg. 984
TUPMAN THURLOW CO. INC., Cedar Plaza, 20 Cedar St.(10801), pg. 1119

New Windsor

Mid-Valley Oil Company, Inc., 1 S. Water St.(12550), pg. 1165

New York

ABI National Accounts, 1 World Trade Center, 50
AM Entertainment, 1500 Broadway, Ste. 1915(10036), pg. 37
ASI Market Research, Inc., 79 Fifth Avenue(10003), pg. 560
Aberdeen Mfg. Corporation, 16 E. 34th St.(10016), pg. 200
Accelerated Claims Processing, Inc., 401 Park Ave. South(10016), pg. 521
Active Quilting Div., 225 W. 34th St.(10122), pg. 942
ADLER BOSCHETTO PEEBLES & PARTNERS, INC., 136 Madison Ave., 12th Fl.(10016), pg. 17
ADLER & SHAYKIN, 375 Park Ave.(10152), pg. 17
ADVERTISING CHECKING BUREAU INCORPORATED, 500 Fifth Avenue(10110), pg. 21
ADVERTISING TO WOMEN, INC., 226 E. 54th St., Ste. 501(10022), pg. 21
ADVISERS CAPITAL MANAGEMENT INC., 58 Pine St.(10005), pg. 21
AHERN NEW YORK, 322 Eighth Ave.(10001), pg. 26
Alberoy Division, 1411 Broadway(10018), pg. 133
THE ALDEN GROUP LTD., 52 Vanderbilt Ave.(10017), pg. 32
J.S. Alden Public Relations, Inc., 52 Vanderbilt Ave.(10017), pg. 32
ALEXANDER DOLL CO., INC., 615 W. 131st St.(10027), pg. 33
Alexandra De Markoff, Ltd., 625 Madison Ave.(10022), pg. 695
ALLEN & COMPANY INCORPORATED, 711 Fifth Ave.(10022), pg. 35
Allied Security Inc., 221 W. 41st St., 23rd Fl.(10036), pg. 39
Allure, 350 Madison Ave.(10017), pg. 19

Almay, Inc., 625 Madison Ave.(10022), pg. 695
AMERICAN ARBRITRATION ASSOCIATION, 140 W. 51st St.(10020), pg. 49
American Argo Corp., 350 Fifth Ave.(10118), pg. 283
AMERICAN BIBLE SOCIETY, 1865 Broadway(10023), pg. 49
AMERICAN BUREAU OF SHIPPING, Two World Trade Center-106th Fl.(10048), pg. 50
American Druggist, 60 E. 42nd St.(10165), pg. 522
American Envelope Company-Kruysman Div., 160 Varick St.(10013), pg. 199
American Export Register, One Penn Plaza(10119), pg. 1093
AMERICAN FABRICS COMPANY, 29th St. & 36th(10018), pg. 51
AMERICAN INSTITUTE OF C.P.A.'S INC., 1211 Ave. of the Americas(10036), pg. 56
AMERICAN JOURNAL OF NURSING COMPANY, 555 W. 57th St.(10019-2961), pg. 57
AMERICAN KENNEL CLUB, INC., 51 Madison Ave.(10010), pg. 57
American Life Insurance Company of New York, 666 Fifth Ave.(10103), pg. 778
American Literature Review, One Penn Plaza(10119), pg. 1093
American Standard Air Conditioning Products, 1114 Ave. of the Americas(10036), pg. 61
AMERICAN STANDARD INC., 1114 Ave. of the Americas(10036), pg. 61
American Standard Transportation Products, 1114 Ave. of the Americas(10036), pg. 61
THE AMERICAN STOCK EXCHANGE, 86 Trinity Place(10006), pg. 62
American Stock Exchange Clearing Corp., 86 Trinity Place(10006), pg. 63
American Stock Exchange Realty Associates Inc., 86 Trinity Place(10006), pg. 63
American Stock Transfer & Trust Co., 40 Wall St.(10005), pg. 812
American Trading Transportation Co., Inc., 555 Fifth Ave.(10017), pg. 65
AMERICAN VISION CENTERS, INC., 90 John St.(10038), pg. 65
Amex Commodities Corporation, 86 Trinity Place(10006), pg. 63
AMICALE INDUSTRIES, INC., 1375 Broadway(10018), pg. 66
AMMIRATI & PURIS INC., 100 Fifth Ave.(10011), pg. 67
AMSCO SCHOOL PUBLICATIONS, INC., 315 Hudson St.(10013), pg. 68
ARTHUR ANDERSEN & CO., S.C., 1345 Avenue of the Americas(10019), pg. 72
Anderson & Lembke Inc., 79 Fifth Ave., 7th Fl.(10003), pg. 244
ANDERSON & LEMBKE INC., 79 5th Ave., 17th Fl.(10003), pg. 73
ANDREWS GROUP, INCORPORATED, 21 E. 63rd St.(10021), pg. 74
ANGLO FABRICS COMPANY, INC., 561 Seventh Ave., 16th Fl.(10018), pg. 75
ANTWERP DIAMOND DISTRIBUTORS INC., 587 Fifth Ave.(10017), pg. 77
THE APPAREL GROUP, LTD., 1370 Ave. of the Americas(10019), pg. 78
APPAREL INDUSTRIES, INC., 1407 Broadway(10018), pg. 78
I. APPEL CORPORATION, 136 Madison Ave., 11th Flr.(10016), pg. 78
Aramis, Inc., 767 Fifth Ave.(10153), pg. 389
Arbor House, 1350 Ave. of the Americas(10019), pg. 522
Argo International, 140 Franklin St.(10013), pg. 323
ARGO INTERNATIONAL CORP., 140 Franklin St.(10013), pg. 81
ARNAV INDUSTRIES, INC., 31 W. 27th St.(10001), pg. 84
ARNHOLD AND S. BLEICHROEDER, INC., 45 Broadway(10006), pg. 84
Art Publishing Co., 437 Madison Ave.(10022), pg. 468
Arts & Communications Counselors, Inc., NY, 301 East 57th St.(10022), pg. 954
Arts & Entertainment Network, 235 E. 45th St.(10019), pg. 523
ASSOCIATED MERCHANDISING CORP., 1440 Broadway(10018), pg. 91
Associated Music Publishers, 24 E. 22nd St.(10010), pg. 777
THE ASSOCIATED PRESS, 50 Rockefeller Plaza(10020), pg. 91
ATLANTIC MUTUAL COMPANIES, 45 Wall St.(10005), pg. 94
Atlantic Mutual Insurance Co., 45 Wall St.(10005), pg. 94
Austin-New York, 225 Fifth Ave.(10010), pg. 99
Avon Books, 1350 Ave. of the Americas(10019), pg. 522
AVRETT, FREE & GINSBERG, INC., 800 Third Ave.(10022), pg. 103
N W AYER INCORPORATED, Worldwide Plaza, 825 Eighth Ave.(10019-7498), pg. 103
Ayer Public Relations, Worldwide Plaza, 825 Eighth Ave.(10019), pg. 104
AyerDirect, Direct Response, Worldwide Plaza, 825 Eighth Ave.(10019), pg. 104
B. Dalton Bookseller, Inc., 122 5th Ave.(10011), pg. 120
BCI Talent Payments, 79 Fifth Avenue(10003), pg. 560
BSA ADVERTISING, INC., 360 Lexington Ave.(10017), pg. 107
BAAR & BEARDS, 15 W. 37th(10018-6201), pg. 107
BABY TOGS, INC., 460 W. 34th St.(10001), pg. 107
Backer Spielvogel Bates, Inc., The Chrysler Bldg., 405 Lexington Ave.(10174), pg. 108
BACKER SPIELVOGEL BATES WORLDWIDE, INC., The Chrysler Bldg., 405 Lexington Ave.(10174), pg. 108
BAIRD, PATRICK & CO., INC., 20 Exchange Pl.(10005), pg. 114
H.J. BAKER & BRO., INC., 100 E. 42nd St.(10017), pg. 114
BALDI, BLOOM & WHELAN ADVERTISING, 41 Madison Ave.(10010), pg. 115
Ballantine Books, 201 E. 50th St.(10022), pg. 19
Bambinaggine, 100 W. 33rd St.(10001), pg. 343
Banner Radio, One Dag Hammarskjold Plaza(10017), pg. 618
BARIS SHOE COMPANY, INC., 47 W. 34th St.(10001), pg. 119
BARNES & NOBLE BOOKSTORES, INC., 122 5th Ave.(10011), pg. 120
BARNEYS NEW YORK, 106 Seventh Ave.(10011), pg. 120
BARON & ZARETSKY ADVERTISING, INC., 928 Broadway(10010), pg. 121
BARR & BARR, INC., 330 W. 42nd St.(10036), pg. 121
BARR BROTHERS & CO., INC., 90 Washington St.(10006), pg. 121
Beber Silverstein & Partners, Inc., 1500 Broadway, Ste. 902(10036), pg. 130
Beech Tree Books, 1350 Ave. of the Americas(10019), pg. 521
Beisler & Associates, Inc., 292 Madison Ave.(10017), pg. 1071
Beldoch Popper Division, 1411 Broadway(10018), pg. 133
BENTEX KIDDIE CORPORATION, 112 W. 34th St.(10120), pg. 140
BERENTER GREENHOUSE & WEBSTER, INC., 233 Park Ave., South(10003), pg. 141
The Bergman Group, 250 Park Ave., South(10003), pg. 949
BERKLIFF CORPORATION, 180 Madison Ave.(10016), pg. 142
Berlitz Publishing Company Inc., 257 Park Ave. So.(10010), pg. 142
Berlitz Translation Services, Inc., 257 Park Ave. So.(10010), pg. 142
SANFORD C. BERNSTEIN & CO., INC., 767 Fifth Ave.(10153), pg. 144
Best Hospital Supply Div., 1633 Broadway(10019), pg. 146
BEST MANUFACTURING, INC., 1633 Broadway, 18th Fl.(10019), pg. 146
Best Textile Co. Div., 1633 Broadway(10019), pg. 146
BIDDLE SAWYER CORPORATION, 2 Penn Plaza(10121), pg. 148
BIEDERMAN, KELLY & SHAFFER, INC., 475 Park Ave. South, 15th Fl.(10016), pg. 149
BILL COMMUNICATIONS, INC., 355 Park Avenue South(10010), pg. 150
DAMIAN BISCH & PARTNERS, INC. ADVERTISING, 841 Broadway(10003), pg. 153
Bishopsgate Corp., 54 E. 64th St.(10021), pg. 998
THE BLACK CLAWSON CO., 405 Lexington Ave(10174), pg. 154
BLACKSTONE PARTNERSHIP (NYC), 345 Park Ave.(10154), pg. 155
JOHN BLAIR COMMUNICATIONS, INC., 1290 Ave. of the Americas(10104), pg. 155
Bill Blass, Inc., 625 Madison Ave.(10022), pg. 695
BLOOMSBURG MILLS INC., 1460 Broadway(10036), pg. 158
BLUE TEE CORPORATION, 250 Park Avenue So.(10003), pg. 161
BOHBOT COMMUNICATIONS, INC., 41 Madison Ave., 26th Fl.(10010), pg. 162
BON JOUR INTERNATIONAL LTD., 1411 Broadway(10018), pg. 164
BONHOMME SHIRTMAKERS, LTD., 350 Fifth Ave.(10118), pg. 164
BOOZ ALLEN & HAMILTON INC., 101 Park Ave.(10178), pg. 165
Botto, Roessner, Horne & Messinger, Inc., 1133 Ave. of the Americas, 44th Fl.(10036), pg. 625
The Bravo Group, 11 West 42nd St., 2nd Fl.(10036), pg. 1210
Bride's, 350 Madison Ave.(10017), pg. 19
British Knights, 155 Ave. of the Americas, 9th Fl.(10013), pg. 980
BROWN BROTHERS, HARRIMAN & CO., 59 Wall St.(10005), pg. 181
Brown Brothers Harriman Trust Co. of New York, 63 Wall St.(10005), pg. 181
Earle Palmer Brown/New York, 345 Hudson St.(10014), pg. 182
Brown, Harris, Stevens, Inc., 14 E. 47th St.(10017), pg. 527
BURKHARDT & CHRISTY ADVERTISING, INC., Penthouse Terrace, 304 East 45th St.(10017), pg. 191
Leo Burnett Company, 950 Third Ave.(10022), pg. 192
Burson-Marsteller, 230 Park Ave. South(10003-1566), pg. 1210
LAWRENCE BUTNER ADVERTISING, INC., 228 East 45th St.(10017), pg. 197
BUTTERICK COMPANY, INC., 161 6th Ave.(10013), pg. 197
CB Commercial Real Estate Group, New York, 437 Madison Ave.(10022), pg. 222
C&C Associates, 919 Third Ave.(10022), pg. 290
CHF Industries, Inc., 1 Park Ave., 9th Fl.(10016), pg. 200
CRK ADVERTISING, 205 West 39th St., 14th Fl.(10018), pg. 203
CS First Boston Financiere, Inc., Park Avenue Plaza(10055), pg. 204
CS FIRST BOSTON GROUP, INC., Park Avenue Plaza(10055), pg. 203
CS First Boston Pacific, Inc., Park Aveune Plaza(10055), pg. 204
CS First Boston USA, Inc., Park Avenue Plaza(10055), pg. 204
CSI INTERNATIONAL CORPORATION, 800 Second Ave.(10017), pg. 205
CYB Yasumura Design, 11 West 42nd St.(10036), pg. 1210
Calabash Ltd., 100 West 33rd St.(10001), pg. 343
Calet, Hirsch & Ferrell, Inc., 250 Park Ave., South(10003), pg. 949
Calvin Klein Sport, Inc., 205 W. 39th St.(10018), pg. 635
Cameo Curtains, One Park Ave.(10016), pg. 200
Camp Hosiery, 350 Fifth Ave.(10118), pg. 400
Cancer Industries, 126 E. 56th St.(10022), pg. 607
Capezio Ballet Makers, Inc., 1411 Broadway(10018), pg. 116
Career Blazers Agency, Inc., 590 Fifth Ave.(10036), pg. 218
CAREER BLAZERS INC., 590 Fifth Ave., 7th Fl.(10036), pg. 218
Career Blazers Learning Center, 230 Park Ave.(10169), pg. 218
Career Blazers Service Company, Inc., 590 Fifth Ave.(10036), pg. 218
Career Blazers Temporary Personnel, 590 Fifth Ave.(10036), pg. 218
W. P. CAREY & CO., INC., 620 Fifth Ave., Fourth Floor(10020), pg. 218
CARLES INC., 130 E. 59th St.(10022), pg. 220
CARLSON & PARTNERS, INC., 950 Third Ave.(10022), pg. 222
CARNIVAL CREATIONS, 180 Madison Ave., Suite 901(10016), pg. 222
DANIEL CARON LTD., 205 W. 39th St.(10018), pg. 224
Carrington Parfums Ltd., 767 Fifth Ave.(10153), pg. 695
THE WILLIAM CARTER COMPANY, 112 W. 34th St.(10120), pg. 226
CASTLE-HARLAN, INC., 150 E. 58th St.(10155), pg. 229
CASTOR ADVERTISING CORP., 122 East 25th St.(10010), pg. 229
Catalyst Energy Corporation, 560 Lexington, 9th Fl.(10022), pg. 1137
Cato Johnson-New York, 675 6th Ave., 3rd Fl.(10010-5104), pg. 1210
Cato Johnson Worldwide, 675 6th Ave., 3rd Fl.(10010), pg. 1210
Centennial Capital Corporation, One New York Plaza(10004), pg. 719
Centennial Insurance Co., 45 Wall St.(10005), pg. 94
CENTURY BUSINESS CREDIT CORPORATION, 119 W. 40th St.(10018), pg. 235
Century Data Services, Inc., 119 W. 40th St.(10018), pg. 235
Cerro Sales Corporation, 540 Madison Ave.(10022), pg. 711
CHALEK & CHALEK, INC., 380 Lexington Ave.(10017), pg. 238
CHALK & PARTNERS, LTD., 79 Fifth Ave.(10003), pg. 238
Chapman Direct Advertising, 230 Park Ave., South(10003), pg. 1210
Charles of the Ritz Group Ltd., 625 Madison Ave.(10022), pg. 695
CHARRON, SCHWARTZ & PARTNERS, INC., 405 Lexington Ave., 63rd Fl.(10174), pg. 240
CHARTER HOUSE GROUP, 535 Madison Ave., 28th Fl.(10022), pg. 240
Chatham Importers, 666 3rd Ave., 10th Fl.(10017), pg. 855
Chiat/Day/Mojo/New York, 79 5th Ave.(10003), pg. 244
China Travel Bureau Ltd., Orbitair International Bldg., 225 E. 44th St.(10017), pg. 828
Christal Radio, One Dag Hammarskjold Plaza(10017), pg. 618
Christiansburg Garment Co. Inc., 1411 Broadway(10018), pg. 345
CIOCIOLA & COMPANY ADVERTISING, INC., 475 Park Ave. South(10016), pg. 250
CITY POSTAL, INC., 421 7th Ave.(10001), pg. 251
CLARK & POPE, INC., 41 East 42nd St.(10017), pg. 253
CYRUS CLARK CO., INC., 267 Fifth Ave.(10016), pg. 253
A.T. CLAYTON & COMPANY, INC., 10 E. 40th St.(10016), pg. 253
CLINE, DAVIS & MANN, INC., 450 Lexington Ave.(10022), pg. 255
Clinton Mills Sales Co., 111 W. 40th St., 22nd Fl.(10018), pg. 202
Cofinco, Inc., 99 Park Ave., 11th Fl.(10016), pg. 810
The Colligan Group, 250 Park Ave., South(10003), pg. 949
Colonial Homes, 1790 Broadway(10019), pg. 523
Colonial Sand & Stone Co., 54 E. 64th St.(10021), pg. 998
COMMONWEALTH TOY & NOVELTY COMPANY, 45 W. 25th St., 5th Fl.(10010), pg. 269
COMMUNICATIONS DIVERSIFIED, 440 Park Ave., South(10016), pg. 269
COMMUNICATIONS INTERNATIONAL, 488 Madison Ave.(10022), pg. 269
COMMUNICATIONS PLUS, INC., 102 Madison Ave.(10016), pg. 269
COMPENDIUM SYSTEMS, 535 5th Ave.(10017), pg. 270
COMPLEX INDUSTRY CORPORATION, 37 W. 37th St.(10018), pg. 270
Computer Library, One Park Avenue(10016), pg. 1219
Concord Watch Co., 650 Fifth Ave.(10019), pg. 812
The Conde Nast Publications Inc., 350 Madison Ave.(10017), pg. 19
Conde Nast Traveler, 360 Madison Ave.(10017), pg. 19
CONILL ADVERTISING, INC., 100 Ave. of the Americas(10013), pg. 274
CONTINENTAL GRAIN COMPANY, 277 Park Ave.(10172), pg. 279
CONTRACT FURNISHINGS & SYSTEMS, LTD., 20 W. 22nd St.(10010-5804), pg. 280
COOPERS & LYBRAND, 1301 Ave. of the Americas(10019), pg. 283
COORDINATED APPAREL, INC., 350 Fifth Ave., Room 1400(10118), pg. 283
CORINTHIAN MEDIA, INC., 845 Third Ave.(10022), pg. 286
Corporate Finance Magazine, 1328 Broadway(10001), pg. 410
Corporate•Technology•Public Affairs, 301 East 57th St.(10022), pg. 954
CORTEC GROUP, 200 Park Ave.(10166), pg. 287
Corum Watch Corporation, 650 Fifth Ave.(10019), pg. 812
Cosmopolitan, 224 W. 57th St.(10019), pg. 523
H. COTLER COMPANY, 10 W. 33rd St.(10001), pg. 288
Country Living, 224 W. 57th St.(10019), pg. 523
Countryside, 1700 Broadway(10019), pg. 523
Couri Carpet Co., 919 Third Ave.(10022), pg. 290
Couri-Murad & Co., 919 Third Ave.(10022), pg. 290

COWEN & COMPANY, Financial Square(10005-3597), pg. 291
Cowles Syndicate, Inc., 235 E. 45th St.(10017), pg. 524
COX ADVERTISING, 379 W. Broadway(10012), pg. 292
COX & COMPANY, INC., 200 Varick St., 4th Fl.(10014), pg. 292
COX LANDEY AND PARTNERS, INC., 501 Madison Ave.(10022), pg. 294
Crain's New York Business, 220 E. 42nd St.(10017), pg. 295
CRESMER, WOODWARD, O'MARA & ORMSBEE, 866 Third Ave.(10022), pg. 298
CROSCILL, INC., 261 Fifth Ave.(10016), pg. 300
Cross & Brown Company, 522 Fifth Ave.(10036), pg. 744
CROTON WATCH COMPANY, 15 W. 37th St.(10018), pg. 300
Crown Publishers, Inc., 201 E. 50th St.(10003), pg. 20
CULLMAN VENTURES, INC., 767 Third Ave.(10017), pg. 304
Custom Event Marketing, Inc., 633 Third Ave., 20th Fl.(10017), pg. 109
CUSTOM SHOP SHIRTMAKERS INC., 18 E. 50th St., 10th fl.(10022), pg. 306
Cutlery World, 515 W. 24th St.(10011), pg. 538
D.F.A. ADVERTISING, 161 W. 53rd St., Ste. 802(10019), pg. 309
DKM, Ltd., 230 Park Ave.(10169), pg. 357
D.V.F. Inc., 625 Madison Ave.(10022), pg. 695
Dan River Apparel Fabrics Marketing Div., 111 W. 40th St.(10018), pg. 313
DANA PERFUMES CORP., 635 Madison Ave.(10022), pg. 313
DANCKER, SELLEW & DOUGLAS, INC., 53 Park Pl., Ste. 602(10007), pg. 314
Danville Marketing, 111 W. 40th St.(10018), pg. 313
Dascit/White & Winston, Inc., 136 Madison Ave., 12th Flr.(10016), pg. 573
DAV-EL SERVICES, INC., North River, Pier 62(10011), pg. 317
DAWN JOY FASHIONS, INC., 501 7th Ave.(10018), pg. 319
DEARE MARKETING INC./MATTHEW-LAWRENCE ADVERTISING & SALES PROMOTION INC., 322 8th Ave.(10001), pg. 323
DECAL ENTERPRISES, INC., 140 Franklin St.(10013), pg. 323
Jessica Dee Communications Public Relations, 733 Third Ave., 7th Floor(10017), pg. 244
Deitsch Plastic Export Co., 535 Broadway(10012), pg. 325
MARCEL DEKKER, INC., 270 Madison Ave.(10016), pg. 325
DENTSU, YOUNG & RUBICAM PARTNERSHIPS, 810 Seventh Ave.(10019), pg. 330
Details, 379 W. Broadway(10012), pg. 1044
Details Magazine, 632 Broadway, Penthouse(10012), pg. 19
DEUTSCH/DWORIN, INC., 215 Park Ave. South(10003), pg. 333
DEWITT MEDIA, INC., 460 Park Ave. South(10016), pg. 334
T.L. DIAMOND COMPANY, 30 Rockefeller Plaza(10112), pg. 335
DiFranza Williamson, Inc., 16 West 22nd St.(10010), pg. 625
THE DIRECT MARKETING GROUP INC., 757 Third Ave., Third Fl.(10017), pg. 339
Diversion, 60 E. 42nd St.(10165), pg. 522
DOE SPUN, INC., 100 W. 33rd St.(10001), pg. 343
DOMINICK & DOMINICK, INCORPORATED, 90 Broad St.(10004), pg. 343
Dominick Futures Corporation, 90 Broad St.(10004), pg. 343
DONNKENNY, INC., 1411 Broadway(10018), pg. 345
DORRITIE LYONS & NICKEL, INC., 655 Third Ave.(10017), pg. 347
Dothan Underwear, 1359 Broadway(10118), pg. 545
Doubleday Book Shops, Inc., 673 Fifth Ave.(10022), pg. 120
DOUGLAS ELLIMAN-GIBBONS & IVES, INC., 575 Madison Ave.(10022), pg. 347
Douglas Elliman-Haldenstein, 2112 Broadway(10023), pg. 347
Dover Handbag Co., Inc., 20 W. 33rd St., Eighth Flr.(10001), pg. 1048
Dunavant Commodity Corp., 114 Liberty St.(10006), pg. 352
DWECK & CAMPBELL, INC., 536 Broadway(10012), pg. 356
THE DYSON-KISSNER-MORAN CORPORATION, 230 Park Ave., Ste. 659(10169), pg. 357
E-II HOLDINGS, INC., 600 Madison Ave.(10022), pg. 358
EMI-Manhattan Records, 810 Seventh Ave.(10019), pg. 216
Eastern News Distributors, Inc., 250 W. 55th St.(10019), pg. 523
Eastman Radio, Inc., 1 Dag Hammarskjold Plaza(10017), pg. 618
ECHO DESIGN GROUP, INC., 10 E. 40th St.(10016), pg. 365
EDELSON & SONS CORPORATION, 44 E. 32nd St.(10016), pg. 368
EDWARDSTONE & COMPANY, INC., 600 Madison Ave., 26th Fl.(10022), pg. 370
Electronic News Publishing, 488 Madison Ave., 6th Fl.(10022), pg. 576
Electronic Products Magazine, 645 Stewart Ave.(11530), pg. 522
Ellerbe Becket-New York, 200 Madison Ave.(10016), pg. 378
ELSER & AUCONE, INC., 420 Lexington Ave.(10170), pg. 378
EMIGRANT SAVINGS BANK, 5 E. 42nd St.(10017), pg. 379
JOHN EMMERLING INC., 135 East 55th St.(10022), pg. 379
EMPIRE BLUE CROSS & BLUE SHIELD, 622 Third Ave.(10017), pg. 379
EMPIRE DIAMOND CORPORATION, 350 Fifth Ave.(10001), pg. 379
EMPIRE STEEL TRADING COMPANY, 80 Wall St.(10005), pg. 380
ENTERPRISE PRESS, INC., 627-631 Greenwich St.(10014), pg. 382
N. ERLANGER, BLUMGART & COMPANY, INC., 1450 Broadway(10018), pg. 387
ERNST & YOUNG, 277 Park Ave.(10172), pg. 387
Esquire, 1790 Broadway(10019), pg. 523
ESTEE LAUDER, INC., 767 Fifth Ave.(10153), pg. 389
Estee Lauder, Intl., 767 Fifth Ave.(10153), pg. 389
European Travel & Life, 122 E. 42nd St.(10168), pg. 611
EXCELLED SHEEPSKIN & LEATHER COAT CORPORATION, 350 5th Ave.(10018), pg. 392
EXECUTIVE ENTERPRISES, INC., 22 W. 21st St.(10010), pg. 393
Executive Enterprises Publications Co., Inc., 22 W. 21st St.(10010), pg. 393
NEIL FABER MEDIA INC., 157 West 57th St.(10019), pg. 395
M. FABRIKANT & SONS, INC., 600 5th Ave.(10020), pg. 396
Faddaley Enterprises Inc., 241 W. 37th St.(10018), pg. 224
Fairfield International Corporation, 277 Park Ave.(10172), pg. 397
FAIRFIELD MAXWELL LTD., 277 Park Ave.(10172), pg. 397
FARAGO ADVERTISING, 101 Fifth Ave.(10003), pg. 399
FARRAR, STRAUS & GIROUX, INC., 19 Union Sq. W.(10003), pg. 403
FARRELL CMA, 420 Lexington Ave., Ste. 1656(10170), pg. 403
FARRELL LINES INCORPORATED, 1 Whitehall(10004), pg. 403
Fawcett Books, 1515 Broadway(10030), pg. 19
FERRARA FOODS & CONFECTIONS, INC., 195 Grand St.(10013), pg. 407
FIDUCIARY TRUST CO. INTERNATIONAL, Two World Trade Center(10048-0772), pg. 408
FIDUCIARY TRUST COMPANY INTERNATIONAL, Two World Trade Center(10048), pg. 408
Fielding Travel Books, 1350 Ave. of the Americas(10019), pg. 521
Fila Fitness Ltd., 767 Fifth Ave.(10153), pg. 695
FINANCIAL WORLD PARTNERS, 1328 Broadway(10001), pg. 410
Wally Findlay Galleries, Inc., 17 E. 57th St.(10022), pg. 410
M. FINE & SONS MANUFACTURING CO., INC., 350 Fifth Ave.(10118), pg. 411
FINLAY ENTERPRISES, INC., 521 5th Ave.(10175), pg. 411
Finlay Fine Jewelry, 521 5th Ave.(10175), pg. 411
Finora Company, Inc., 99 Park Ave., 11th Fl.(10016), pg. 810
First American Bank of New York, 350 Park Ave.(10022), pg. 412
First Boston Asset Management Corporation, 12 E. 49th St.(10017), pg. 204
The First Boston Corporation, 55 E. 52nd St.(10055), pg. 203
First Boston International Limited, Park Ave. Plaza(10055), pg. 204
First Boston Securities Corporation, Park Ave. Plaza(10055), pg. 204
First International Reinsurance Company, 485 Madison Ave.(10022), pg. 451
Flair Communications Agency, Inc., 246 East 62nd St.(10021), pg. 416
Floor Covering Weekly, 555 W. 57th St.(10019), pg. 522
FLORASYNTH INC., 410 E. 62nd St.(10021), pg. 420
Fodor's Travel Publications, Inc., 201 E. 50th St.(10022), pg. 19
FONES & MANN INC., 152 Madison Ave., 20th Fl.(10016), pg. 422
THE FOOD GROUP, 292 Madison Ave., 7th Fl.(10017), pg. 423
Foodservice Director, 633 Third Ave.(10017), pg. 150
FORBES, INC., 60 Fifth Ave.(10011), pg. 423
Forbes Magazine Division, 60 Fifth Ave.(10011), pg. 423
Forest Atwood Paper Company-New York, 185 Madison Ave.(10016), pg. 1157
FORSTMANN & COMPANY, INC., 1185 Avenue of the Americas(10128), pg. 424
Forstmann & Company, Inc., 1185 Ave. of the Americas(10036), pg. 424
FORSTMANN LITTLE & CO., 767 Fifth Ave., 44th Fl.(10153), pg. 424
Foster & Higgins, Inc., 125 Broad St.(10004), pg. 598
FOWNES BROTHERS & CO., INC., 411 5th Ave.(10016), pg. 427
FOX-KNAPP INC., 362 Fifth Ave., Ste. 601(10010), pg. 427
FRANKFURT GIPS BALKIND, ADVERTISING, 244 East 58th St.(10022), pg. 429
FRIEDMAN BENJAMIN INC. ADV., 22 W. 23rd St.(10010), pg. 433
FRIERSON MEE & HERMAN, 215 Park Ave. South(10003), pg. 433
FUGAZY INTERNATIONAL CORPORATION, 555 Madison Ave., 12 Fl.(10022), pg. 435
Fugazy Limousines, 2220 E. 40 st.(10022), pg. 435
Fugazy Travel, 555 Madison Ave., 12th Fl.(10022), pg. 435
GEORGE A. FULLER COMPANY, 919 Third Ave.(10022), pg. 436
FURMAN, ROTH ADV., 801 Second Ave.(10017), pg. 437
FURNITURE CONSULTANTS, 11 W. 19th St.(10011), pg. 437
GAF Broadcasting Co., Inc., 1180 Ave. of the Americas(10036), pg. 438
GANNETT TRANSIT, 666 Third Ave.(10017), pg. 442
Garden State Converters, 32 Bleecker St.(10012), pg. 1112
GEER, DUBOIS INC., 114 Fifth Ave.(10011), pg. 447
STEPHEN L. GELLER INC., 800 Second Ave.(10017), pg. 447
General Instrument Corporation, 767 Fifth Ave.(10153), pg. 425
GENERAL MEDIA PUBLISHING GROUP, 1965 Broadway(10023), pg. 450
GENERAL TOOLS MFG., 80 White St.(10013), pg. 451
Geneve Capital Group Inc., 485 Madison Ave.(10022), pg. 451
Gentlemen's Quarterly, 350 Madison Ave.(10017), pg. 19
GEORGIAN PRESS, INC., 175 Varick St.(10014), pg. 453
Gerber Agri-Export Inc., 855 Ave. of Americas(10001), pg. 454
J. GERBER & CO. INC., 855 Ave. of Americas(10001), pg. 453
GERSON & GERSON, INC., 462 7th Ave.(10018), pg. 454
GEYER-MCALLISTER PUBLICATIONS, INC., 51 Madison Ave.(10010), pg. 455
Gibbs & Hill, Inc., 11 Penn Plaza(10001), pg. 535
GIRGENTI, HUGHES, BUTLER & MCDOWELL, 100 6th Ave., 8th Fl.(10013-1687), pg. 460
Gitano Boy's & Men's Division, 20 W. 33rd St.(10001), pg. 460
Gitano Girl's Division, 112 W. 34th Street(10120), pg. 460
GITANO GROUP INC., 1411 Broadway(10018), pg. 460
GLAMORISE FOUNDATIONS, INC., 135 Madison Ave.(10016), pg. 460
Glamour, 350 Madison Ave.(10017), pg. 19
GLEN OAKS INDUSTRIES, INC., 16 E. 34th St.,20th Fl.(10016), pg. 461
Glen Raven Marketing Corp., 1350 Broadway(10018), pg. 461
Glen Raven Marketing Corporation, 1350 Broadway(10018), pg. 461
GLENCRAFT LINGERIE, INC., 38 E. 32nd St.(10016), pg. 462
GLOBAL MARKETING RESOURCES, 551 Fifth Ave.(10176), pg. 463
Gloria Vanderbilt Division, 1411 Broadway(10018), pg. 460
MORTON GOLDBERG ASSOCIATES, INC., 350 Park Ave.(10022), pg. 465
GOLDBERG FOSSA SEID ADVERTISING, INC., 156 Fifth Ave.(10010), pg. 465
Golden Fleece Outerwear Co., 505 8th Ave.(10018), pg. 1031
Golding Industries, One Park Ave.(10016), pg. 607
GOLDMAN, SACHS & CO., 85 Broad St.(10004), pg. 468
Goldman Sachs Money Markets Inc., 85 Broad St.(10004), pg. 468
GOLDMARK INDUSTRIES, LTD., 437 Madison Ave.(10022), pg. 468
Goldmark Partners, 437 Madison Ave.(10022), pg. 469
GOLDSMITH/JEFFREY, INC., 31 West 21st St.(10010), pg. 469
GOLODETZ CORPORATION, 666 Fifth Ave.(10103), pg. 469
M. Golodetz Export Corp., 666 Fifth Ave.(10103), pg. 469
Good Housekeeping, 959 Eighth Ave.(10019), pg. 523
CHESTER GORE COMPANY INC., 780 Third Ave.(10017), pg. 472
GOULD PAPER CORPORATION, 315 Park Ave. S.(10010), pg. 473
Gourmet, 560 Lexington Ave.(10022), pg. 19
GRACE & ROTHSCHILD, 114 Fifth Ave.(10011), pg. 474
GRAF BERTEL, 292 Madison Ave.(10017), pg. 474
EARL G. GRAVES, LTD., 130 Fifth Ave.(10011), pg. 478
Earl G. Graves Publishing Co., Inc., 130 Fifth Ave.(10011), pg. 478
GREAT SCOTT ADVERTISING CO. INC., 1185 Ave. of the Americas(10036), pg. 482
GREATER NEW YORK MUTUAL INSURANCE COMPANY, 215 Lexington Ave.(10016), pg. 483
GREENGAGE ASSOCIATES, INC., Graybar Bldg., 420 Lexington Ave., Ste. 1830(10170), pg. 485
Greenwillow Books, 1350 Ave. of the Americas(10019), pg. 521
GRIFFIN BACAL INC., 130 Fifth Ave.(10011), pg. 486
GRYBAUSKAS & PARTNERS, 24 East 21st St.(10010), pg. 490
Guardian Asset Management Corp. (GAMCORP), 201 Park Ave. S.(10003), pg. 492
The Guardian Insurance & Annuity Co. (GIAC), 201 Park Ave., S.(10003), pg. 492
Guardian Investor Services Corp., 201 Park Ave. S.(10003), pg. 492
THE GUARDIAN LIFE INSURANCE COMPANY OF AMERICA, 201 Park Ave. S.(10003), pg. 492
HKM of Delaware Corp., 600 Fifth Ave.(10020), pg. 1123
Habits, Inc., 1350 Broadway(10018), pg. 972
HAINES LUNDBERG WAEHLER, 115 Fifth Ave.(10003), pg. 500
HAMMOND FARRELL INC., 257 Park Ave. South(10010), pg. 504
Louis Hand Div., 16 E. 34th St.(10016), pg. 200
Harbour Casuals, Ltd., 1411 Broadway(10018), pg. 753
HARPER INDUSTRIES, INC., 350 Fifth Ave.(10118), pg. 510
Harper Shirt Company, 350 Fifth Ave.(10118), pg. 510
Harper's Bazaar, 1700 Broadway(10019), pg. 523
HARRISON, STAR, WIENER & BEITLER, INC., 16 W. 22nd St., 12th Fl.(10010), pg. 512
HARTZ GROUP, 667 Madison Ave.(10021), pg. 514
THE HARWOOD COMPANIES, INC., 1350 Ave. of the Americas(10019), pg. 515
HAZEN & SAWYER, 730 Broadway(10003), pg. 520
HEALTH MANAGEMENT SYSTEMS, INC., 401 Park Ave. S.(10016), pg. 521
Healthcare Group, 60 E. 42nd St.(10165), pg. 522
Hearst Book Group, 1350 Ave. of the Americas(10019), pg. 522
Hearst Books/Business Publishing Group, 959 Eighth Ave.(10019), pg. 521
Hearst Broadcasting Division, 959 Eighth Ave.(10019), pg. 522
THE HEARST CORPORATION, 959 Eighth Ave.(10019), pg. 521

Hearst Enterprises Division, 224 W. 57th St.(10019), pg. 523
Hearst Entertainment, 235 E. 45th St.(10017), pg. 523
Hearst Entertainment & Syndication, 959 Eighth Ave.(10019), pg. 523
Hearst Magazines Division, 959 Eighth Ave.(10019), pg. 523
Hearst Magazines Special Publications, 1700 Broadway(10019), pg. 523
Hearst Marine Books, 1350 Ave. of the Americas(10019), pg. 521
Hearst Newspapers Division, 959 Eighth Ave.(10019), pg. 523
Hearst Professional Magazines, Inc., 60 E. 42nd St.(10165), pg. 522
HELMSLEY ENTERPRISES, INC., 60 E. 42nd St.(10165), pg. 527
Helmsley Hotels Inc., 455 Madison Ave.(10022), pg. 527
Helmsley-Noyes Co., Inc., 60 E. 42nd St.(10022), pg. 527
The Helmsley Palace Hotel, 455 Madison Ave.(10022), pg. 527
Helmsley-Spear Conversion Sales Corp., 140 E. 56th St.(10022), pg. 527
Helmsley-Spear Inc., 60 E. 42nd St.(10165), pg. 527
HERMAN ASSOCIATES, INC., 488 Madison Ave.(10022), pg. 531
Hesco Supply Co., Inc., 959 Eighth Ave.(10019), pg. 524
Hill, Holliday/New York, 885 Third Ave.(10022), pg. 534
Hill & Wang, 19 Union Sq. W.(10003), pg. 403
HILLSIDE CAPITAL, INC., 405 Park Ave.(10022), pg. 535
Hillside Industries, Inc., 405 Park Ave.(10022), pg. 535
Hoboken Floors-Capitol Division, c/o D&D Bldg., 979 3rd Ave.(10022), pg. 537
Hoboken Floors-Eastern Flooring Division, c/o D&D Bldg., 979 3rd Ave.(10022), pg. 537
HOFFRITZ FOR CUTLERY, 515 W. 24th St.(10011), pg. 538
Hoffritz International, 515 W. 24th St.(10011), pg. 538
RON HOLLAND ADVERTISING INC., 39 E. 72nd St.(10021), pg. 539
A. J. HOLLANDER CO., INC., 257 Park Ave. S.(10010), pg. 539
HOLMES PROTECTION GROUP, INC., 440 Ninth Ave.(10001), pg. 540
Holmes Protection of New York, Incorporated, , pg. 540
HOLZER WATCH CO., INC., 501 Madison Ave.(10022), pg. 541
Home Curtain Corporation, 295 Fifth Ave.(10016), pg. 541
Home Innovations Bed Fashions, 295 Fifth Ave.(10016), pg. 541
HOME INNOVATIONS, INC., 295 Fifth Ave.(10016), pg. 541
Horizon Media Entertainment, 630 Third Ave.(10017), pg. 544
HORIZON MEDIA, INC., 630 Third Ave.(10017), pg. 544
HORIZON PAPER CO., INC., 230 Park Ave., Ste. 840(10169), pg. 544
HORSEHEAD INDUSTRIES, INC., 110 E. 59th St.(10022), pg. 545
HOST APPAREL, INC., 1359 Broadway(10018), pg. 545
Host for Her, 183 Madison Ave.(10016), pg. 545
House Beautiful, 1700 Broadway(10019), pg. 523
House & Garden, 350 Madison Ave.(10017), pg. 19
HOUSE OF PERFECTION, INC., 131 W. 33rd St.(10001), pg. 546
HOUSE OF RONNIE, INC., 1333 Broadway, 2nd Fl.(10018), pg. 546
Hyde Point Fashions, 485 Seventh Ave., 5th Fl.(10018), pg. 1079
ICC INDUSTRIES, INC., 720 Fifth Ave.(10019), pg. 558
I.C.C. Trading, Inc., 720 5th Ave.(10019), pg. 558
ICM Artists, Ltd., 40 W. 57th St.(10019), pg. 607
ICELANDAIR, 21 Penn Plaza(10001), pg. 561
IMPERIAL SCHRADE CORP., 99 Madison Ave., Ste.1500(10016), pg. 564
Incentive, 633 Third Ave.(10017), pg. 150
Industrial Equipment News, One Penn Plaza(10199), pg. 1093
INFINITY BROADCASTING CORPORATION, 600 Madison Ave.(10022), pg. 567
INFORMATION BUILDERS, 1250 Broadway(10001), pg. 567
Integrated Acquisition, Inc., 666 Third Ave.(10017), pg. 573
Integrated Funding, Inc., 10 Union Square East(10003), pg. 573
Integrated Resources Asset Management Corp., 666 Third Ave.(10017), pg. 573
Integrated Resources Capital Services, Inc., 10 Union Square East(10003), pg. 573
Integrated Resources Equipment Group, Inc., 733 Third Ave.(10017), pg. 573
Integrated Resources Equity Corp., 10 Union Square East(10003), pg. 573
INTEGRATED RESOURCES, INC., 10 Union Square East(10003), pg. 573
Integrated Resources International, Ltd., 733 Third Ave.(10017), pg. 573
Integrated Resources Marketing, Inc., 10 Union Square East(10003), pg. 573
International Circulation Distributors, 250 W. 55th St.(10019), pg. 523
International Editions, 1775 Broadway(10019), pg. 523
International Management Group (IMG), 22 East 71st St.(10021), pg. 579
FRANK IX & SONS, INC., 469 7th Ave., 11th Fl.(10018), pg. 584
J. CREW GROUP, INC., 625 6th Ave.(10011), pg. 584
J. & W. SELIGMAN & COMPANY, 130 Liberty St.(10006), pg. 584
JMCT/Direct, 445 Park Ave.(10022), pg. 604
JMCT Health, 445 Park Ave.(10022), pg. 604
JMCT Publicidad, 445 Park Ave.(10022), pg. 604
JACQUES MORET, INC., 1350 Broadway(10018), pg. 588
Jakson-A CHF Company, One Park Ave.(10016), pg. 200
JAPAN TRAVEL BUREAU INTERNATIONAL, INC., One Rockefeller Plaza, Ste. 1250(10020), pg. 590
JENNIFER DALE, INC., 180 Madison Ave., 19th Fl.(10016), pg. 592
John Peel Ltd., 1290 Ave. of the Americas(10104), pg. 1079
JOHNSON & HIGGINS, 125 Broad St.(10004), pg. 598
CAROLINE JONES ADVERTISING, INC., 1290 Ave. of the Americas(10104), pg. 603
JORDACHE ADVERTISING, 226 West 37th St.(10018), pg. 604
JORDACHE ENTERPRISES, INC., 226 W. 37th St.(10018), pg. 604
JORDAN COMPANY, 315 Park Ave., S.(10010), pg. 604
JORDAN, MCGRATH, CASE & TAYLOR INC., 445 Park Ave.(10022), pg. 604
JOSEPH, LITTLEJOHN & LEVY, 126 E. 56th St.(10022), pg. 607
JOSEPHSON INTERNATIONAL INC., 40 W. 57th St(10019), pg. 607
Joy Toy, Co., 200 5th Ave.(10010), pg. 1054
JOYCE INTERNATIONAL, INC., 114 5th Ave., 4th Fl.(10011), pg. 608
JUDY BOND, INC., 330 W. 34th St.(10001), pg. 608
JACQUES JUGEAT, INC., 225 5th Ave.(10010), pg. 608
JUNIOR GALLERY LTD., 512 7th Ave.(10018), pg. 609
K-III COMMUNICATIONS CORPORATION, 717 5th Ave., 22nd Fl.(10022), pg. 610
K-III Information, 424 W. 33rd St.(10001), pg. 611
K-III Magazines Corporation, 755 Second Ave.(10022), pg. 611
KIKK-FM Tower Corp., 1515 Broadway(10036), pg. 785
KOA HOLDINGS, 100 Park Ave.(10017), pg. 612
KPMG PEAT MARWICK, 345 Park Ave.(10154), pg. 613
KALB VOORHIS & CO., 27 William St., 3rd Fl.(10005), pg. 615
KAPRIELIAN/O'LEARY, 99 Madison Ave.(10016), pg. 616
Katz American Television, One Dag Hammarskjold Plaza(10017), pg. 618
KATZ COMMUNICATIONS, INC., One Dag Hammarskjold Plaza(10017), pg. 618
Katz Continental Television, One Dag Hammarskjold Plaza(10017), pg. 618
Katz Hispanic Radio Sales, One Dag Hammarskjold Plaza(10017), pg. 618
Katz Independent Television, One Dag Hammarskjold Plaza(10017), pg. 618
Katz Radio, One Dag Hammarskjold Plaza(10017), pg. 618
Kayser-Roth Corporation, 210 Madison Ave.(10016), pg. 263
KAZ, INC., 10 Columbus Circle, Ste. 1620(10019), pg. 619
Robert Keeshan Associates, Inc., 40 W. 57th St.(10019), pg. 607
Ketchum Advertising/New York, 220 East 42nd St.(10017), pg. 625
Ketchum Advertising/USA, 220 E. 42nd St.(10017), pg. 625
Ketchum Directory Advertising/Executive, 1133 Ave. of the Americas(10036), pg. 625
Ketchum Public Relations/New York, 1133 Ave. of the Americas(10036), pg. 625
KIDVERTISER, 270 Lafayette St.(10012), pg. 629
King Features Syndicate Division, 235 E. 45th St.(10017), pg. 524
KINNEY SYSTEM, INC., 60 Madison Ave., 7th Fl.(10010), pg. 632
KIRSHENBAUM & BOND, 145 Ave. of the Americas(10013), pg. 633
CALVIN KLEIN, INC., 205 W. 39th St.(10018), pg. 635
Calvin Klein Sport, 205 W. 39th St.(10018), pg. 635
KLEMTNER ADVERTISING INC., 375 Hudson St.(10014-3620), pg. 635
GEORGETTE KLINGER, INC., 501 Madison Ave.(10022), pg. 635
Knitmaker Division, 1411 Broadway(10018), pg. 133
Knoll International, Inc., 655 Madison Ave.(10021), pg. 1121
Alfred A. Knopf, Inc., 201 E. 50th St.(10022), pg. 20
KOBRA INTERNATIONAL LTD, 525 7th Ave., 20th Fl.(10018), pg. 638
CHARLES KOMAR & SONS, INC., 16 E. 34th St., 10th Fl.(10016), pg. 641
PERRY H. KOPLIK & SONS, 505 Park Ave.(10022), pg. 641
KORET GIVENCHY, 136 Madison Ave.(10016), pg. 642
KOREY, KAY & PARTNERS, 130 Fifth Ave.(10011), pg. 642
Korn/Ferry International, 237 Park Ave.(10017), pg. 642
KRAFT HARDWARE, INC., 306 E. 61st St.(10021), pg. 643
Krengel Mfg. Co., 545 8th Ave.(10018), pg. 58
KUONI TRAVEL, INC., 11 E. 44th St.(10017), pg. 646
LADDIN & COMPANY, INC., 2 Park Ave.(10016), pg. 650
LADY MARLENE SALES CORP., 183 Madison Ave.(10016), pg. 650
LaMarca Direct Marketing, 640 Fifth Ave.(10019), pg. 652
LAMARCA GROUP INC., 640 Fifth Ave.(10019), pg. 652
TONY LAMBERT COMPANY, 1407 Broadway(10018), pg. 652
LAND N SEA, INC., 1370 Broadway, 9th Fl.(10018), pg. 653
JACK LENOR LARSEN, INC., 41 E. 11th St.(10003), pg. 659
LAUNEY, HACHMANN & HARRIS, INC., 866 3rd Ave.(10022), pg. 661
Lautier S.A., 410 E. 62nd St.(10021), pg. 420
Lawrence Insurance Group, Inc., 500 5th Ave.(10110-0002), pg. 662
LEBHAR-FRIEDMAN, INC., 425 Park Ave.(10022), pg. 665
LEDONNE, WILNER & WEINER, INC., 1500 Broadway, Ste. 902(10036), pg. 665
LEE NATIONAL CORPORATION, 645 Fifth Ave., 8th Fl.(10022), pg. 666
LEVEL EXPORT SALES CORP., 1460 Broadway(10036), pg. 670
Licensing Div., 1411 Broadway(10018), pg. 164
Lindenmeyr Paper, 100 Park Ave.(10017), pg. 233
LINK Resources, 79 Fifth Ave.(10003), pg. 578
LIPMAN, RICHMOND, GREENE, 470 Park Ave. South(10016), pg. 677
The Lipsitt Design Group, 250 Park Ave., South(10003), pg. 950
RONALD LITOFF, LTD., 49 W. 45th St.(10036), pg. 678
Liveright Publishing Corp., 500 Fifth Ave.(10110), pg. 816
LOCKHART & PETTUS, INC., 79 Fifth Ave.(10003), pg. 680
LOIS/USA, 40 West 57th St.(10019), pg. 681
Loralyn Fashion, 463 7th Ave(10010), pg. 78
LOTAS MINARD PATTON MCIVER, 152 West 57th St.(10019), pg. 684
Lothrop, Lee & Shepard Books, 1350 Ave. of the Americas(10019), pg. 521
THE LOWE GROUP, 1345 Ave. of the Americas(10105), pg. 685
Lucedale Sportswear Company, 350 Fifth Ave., pg. 510
LUCKY WINNER, INC., 525 Seventh Ave.(10018), pg. 686
MI FUND INCORPORATED, 1384 Broadway(10018), pg. 692
MPO VIDEOTRONICS, INC., 619 W. 54th St.(10019), pg. 693
MTV Networks, 1515 Broadway(10036), pg. 785
M.W.O.S. Trade Show, 505 8th Ave.(10018), pg. 1031
MacAndrews & Forbes Group, Inc., 36 E. 63rd St.(10021), pg. 695
MACANDREWS & FORBES HOLDINGS INC., 36 E. 63rd St.(10021), pg. 694
MACHADO & CO. INC., 20 Exchange Pl., 52nd fl.(10005), pg. 696
MacKay-Shields Financial Corp., 9 West 57th St.(10019), pg. 803
MACNAMARA, KLEIN & SOLIN INC., 150 Fifth Ave.(10011), pg. 698
R. H. MACY & CO., INC., 151 W. 34th St.(10001), pg. 698
Mademoiselle, 350 Madison Ave.(10017), pg. 19
Magazine Services Inc., 15 W. 44th St.(10036), pg. 632
MAIDENFORM, INC., 90 Park Ave., 38th Fl.(10016), pg. 701
Managing Automation, One Penn Plaza(10119), pg. 1093
MANOSTAT CORPORATION, 519 Eighth Ave.(10018), pg. 704
Marboro Books Inc., 120 Fifth Ave., 4th Floor(10011), pg. 120
MARCUS BROTHERS TEXTILES, INC., 1460 Broadway(10036), pg. 706
MARGEOTES FERTITTA & WEISS, INC., 411 Lafayette St.(10003), pg. 706
MARISA CHRISTINA INC., 1410 Broadway(10018), pg. 707
Market Statistics, 355 Park Avenue South(10010), pg. 150
Marquardt & Co., 161 6th Ave.(10013), pg. 234
MARSHALL JACCOMA MITCHELL ADVERTISING, 41 Madison Ave.(10010), pg. 714
J.B. MARTIN COMPANY, 10 E. 53rd St., Ste. 3100(10022), pg. 715
Sherri Martin, 501 7th Ave.(10018), pg. 319
Marvel Entertainment Group, 387 Park Ave. S.(10016), pg. 695
MASTER INDUSTRIES CORP., 350 Fifth Ave.(10118), pg. 719
Master Trouser/ Master Apparel/ Botany 500 Slacks Ltd., 350 Fifth Ave.(10118), pg. 720
MASTERCARD INTERNATIONAL, INC., 888 Seventh Ave.(10106), pg. 720
MASTERSON ROTHBERG ADVERTISING, 342 Madison Ave.(10173), pg. 720
Mayfair Industries, Inc., 1407 Broadway(10018), pg. 78
WILLIAM DOUGLAS MCADAMS INC., 1740 Broadway(10019), pg. 726
MCCAFFERY & RATNER, INC., 370 Lexington Ave.(10017), pg. 726
MCCAFFREY AND MCCALL, 575 Lexington Ave.(10022), pg. 726
McCrory Corporation, 667 Madison Ave.(10021), pg. 934
MCKINSEY & COMPANY, INC., 55 E. 52nd St.(10022), pg. 731
MEDIA BUYING SERVICES INTL. INC., 104 Fifth Ave.(10111), pg. 734
MEDIA STORE INC., 220 East 42nd St.(10017), pg. 735
MELLON CORPORATION, 351 W. 35th St.(10001), pg. 738
MEMBERS ONLY BY EUROPE CRAFT, 441 Fifth Ave., 7th Fl.(10016), pg. 738
Men's Journal, 745 Fifth Ave.(10151), pg. 1052
MERLING, MARX & SEIDMAN, INC., 440 Park Ave. South(10016), pg. 741
STAN MERRITT INC./ADVERTISING, 369 Lexington Ave.(10017), pg. 741
METALLURG, INC., 25 E. 39th St.(10016), pg. 742
MetLife Securities, Inc., One Madison Ave.(10010), pg. 745
Metro-North Commuter Railroad Company, 347 Madison Ave.(10017), pg. 745
Metropolitan Insurance & Annuity Co., One Madison Ave.(10010), pg. 744
METROPOLITAN LIFE INSURANCE CO., 1 Madison Ave.(10010-3690), pg. 744
METROPOLITAN SUNDAY NEWSPAPERS, INC., 260 Madison Ave.(10016), pg. 745
Metropolitan Tower Life Insurance Co., One Madison Ave.(10010), pg. 744
METROPOLITAN TRANSPORTATION AUTHORITY, 347 Madison Ave.(10017), pg. 745
Mia Bambini, 100 W. 33rd St.(10001), pg. 343
Mickey & Company, 1411 Broadway(10018), pg. 345
Mid Pacific Air Corporation, 100 Park Ave.(10017), pg. 613
Midland Shirt Company, 350 Fifth Ave.(10118), pg. 510
MILADY BRASSIERE & CORSET CO., INC., 6 E. 32nd St.(10016), pg. 753
Miles Metal Company, 540 Madison Ave.(10022), pg. 712
THE MILFORD AGENCY, 30 Rockefeller Plaza, Ste. 3021(10020), pg. 753

George W. Millar Co., 161 6th Ave.(10013), pg. 234
MILLER ADVERTISING AGENCY INC., 71 Fifth Ave.(10003), pg. 753
THE MINGO GROUP, INC., 228 East 45th St.(10017), pg. 757
MR. CHRISTMAS INC., 41 Madison Ave.(10010), pg. 761
MOLESPHINI & TOBIN, INC., 301 East 45th St.(10017), pg. 764
MONARCH IMPORT CO., INC., 845 3rd Ave.(10022), pg. 765
Monitor Capital Advisors Inc., 51 Madison Ave.(10010), pg. 803
MONY Advisers, Inc., 1740 Broadway(10019), pg. 778
MONY Funding, Inc., 1740 Broadway(10019), pg. 778
MONY Securities Corp., 1740 Broadway(10019), pg. 778
MONY TAX Consulting Services, Inc., 1740 Broadway(10019), pg. 778
William Morrow & Co., Inc., 1350 Ave. of the Americas(10016), pg. 521
Morrow Junior Books, 1350 Ave. of the Americas(10019), pg. 522
MORSE DIESEL INTERNATIONAL, 1515 Broadway(10036), pg. 771
MOSS AND COMPANY, INC., 49 W. 38th St.(10018), pg. 772
MOTHER EARTH NEWS, 24 E. 23rd St., 5th Fl.(10010), pg. 773
Motor Boating & Sailing, 250 W. 55th St.(10019), pg. 523
Movado Museum Designs International Ltd., 650 Fifth Ave.(10019), pg. 812
MTV: Music Television, 1515 Broadway(10036), pg. 785
JOHN F. MURRAY ADVERTISING AGENCY INC., 685 Third Ave.(10017), pg. 776
MUSCUM BOUTIQUE INTERCONTINENTAL, LTD., 26 E. 64th St.(10021), pg. 777
MUSIC SALES CORPORATION, 225 Park Ave. S.(10003), pg. 777
MUTUAL OF AMERICA, 666 Fifth Ave.(10103), pg. 777
Mutual of America Financial Services Corp., 666 Fifth Ave.(10103), pg. 778
THE MUTUAL LIFE INSURANCE COMPANY OF NEW YORK (MONY), 1740 Broadway(10019), pg. 778
Myonne Panties, 180 Madison Ave.(10016), pg. 78
NBBJ-Rosenfield, 58 W. 40th St.(10018), pg. 780
The Nation, 72 5th Ave.(10011), pg. 998
National Attorneys Title Insurance Company--National Div., 32 Broadway(10004), pg. 786
NATIONAL BASKETBALL ASSOCIATION, Olympic Tower, 645 Fifth Ave.(10022), pg. 786
NATIONAL BULK CARRIERS, INC., 1345 Ave. of the Americas(10105), pg. 786
NATIONAL CLEANING CONTRACTORS, INC., 375 Hudson St.(10014-3658), pg. 786
The National Enquirer, Graybar Building, 420 Lexington Avenue, Ste. 440(10170), pg. 788
National Federation of Community Development Credit Unions, 59 John St., 8th Fl.(10038), pg. 298
NATIONAL FOOTBALL LEAGUE PROPERTIES, INC., 410 Park Ave.(10022), pg. 788
NATIONAL OUT-OF-HOME MEDIA/METRO 8, 51 East 42nd St., Ste. 1208(10017), pg. 792
National Pension Life Insurance Company, 666 Fifth Ave.(10103), pg. 778
National Realty Corp., 305 W. 22nd St.(10011), pg. 527
National Securities Clearing Corp., 55 Water St.(10041), pg. 63
NATIONAL SPINNING CO., INC., 183 Madison Ave.(10016), pg. 793
National Yarn Crafts, 183 Madison Ave(10016), pg. 793
NELSON COMMUNICATIONS, INC., 41 Madison Ave., 27th Fl.(10010), pg. 797
NEW HAMPTON, INC., 235 E. 45th St.(10017), pg. 801
New Hermes Inc. Northeast, 20 Cooper Sq.(10003), pg. 801
New Woman Magazine, 215 Lexington Ave.(10016), pg. 611
NEW YORK CITY DEPT. OF GENERAL SERVICES, 2 Lafayette St., Rm. 2200(10007), pg. 802
NEW YORK CITY OFF TRACK BETTING CORP., 1501 Broadway(10036), pg. 802
New York Financial Corp., 54 E. 64th St.(10021), pg. 998
New York Life Acceptance Corp., 51 Madison Ave.(10010), pg. 803
NYLIFE Advisers, Inc., 51 Madison Ave.(10010), pg. 803
NYLIFE Depositary Corporation, 51 Madison Ave.(10010), pg. 803
NYLIFE Equity Inc., 51 Madison Ave.(10010), pg. 803
New York Life Foundation, 51 Madison Ave.(10010), pg. 803
New York Life Insurance and Annuity Corporation, 51 Madison Ave.(10010), pg. 802
NEW YORK LIFE INSURANCE COMPANY, 51 Madison Ave.(10010), pg. 802
New York Life International Investment, 51 Madison Ave.(10010), pg. 803
NYLIFE Leasing Inc., 51 Madison Ave.(10010), pg. 803
NYLIFE Realty Inc., 51 Madison Ave.(10010), pg. 803
NYLIFE Securities Inc., 51 Madison Ave.(10010), pg. 803
New York Life Worldwide Holding, Inc., 51 Madison Ave.(10010), pg. 803
New York Magazine Company, 755 Second Ave.(10017), pg. 611
The New York Observer, 54 E. 64th St.(10021), pg. 998
THE NEW YORKER MAGAZINE, 20 W. 43rd St.(10036), pg. 803
J. J. Newberry Co., 667 Madison Ave.(10021), pg. 934
Newbridge Communications, 333 E. 38th St., 10 Fl.(10016), pg. 611
Newbrook Paper, 32 Bleecker St.(10012), pg. 1112
Newhouse Newspapers Metro-Suburbia, Inc., 485 Lexington Ave.(10017), pg. 19
NEWMARK, POSNER & MITCHELL, INC., 300 East 42nd St.(10017), pg. 804
Nickelodeon/Nick At Nite, 1515 Broadway(10036), pg. 785
Norell Perfumes, Inc., 767 Fifth Ave.(10153), pg. 696
Northern Pacific Corporation, 767 Fifth Ave.(10153), pg. 1118
W.W. NORTON & COMPANY, INC., 500 Fifth Ave.(10110), pg. 815
NYLIFE Inc., 372 Park Ave., So.(10010), pg. 802
OLT-I Corp., 725 Fifth Ave.(10022), pg. 934
OCTOBER FILMS, INC., 45 Rockefeller Plaza, Ste. 3014(10111), pg. 821
ODYSSEY PARTNERS, 31 W. 52nd St., 17th Fl.(10019), pg. 821
Omni Publications International Ltd., 1965 Broadway(10023), pg. 450
OMON, NEW YORK LTD., 23 Watts St.(10013), pg. 826
Oppenheimer Management Corp., 2 World Trade Center, 34th Fl.(10048), pg. 719
ORBITAIR INTERNATIONAL LTD., 225 E. 44th St.(10017-4302), pg. 828
Origins Natural Resources Inc., 767 Fifth Ave.(10153), pg. 389
OUT OF HOME MEDIA SERVICES, INC., 42 W. 38th St.(10018), pg. 832
OVERSEAS PARTNERS, INC., 375 Park Ave.(10152), pg. 833
Owners Maintenance Corp., 420 Lexington Ave.(10170), pg. 527
PC Magazine, 1 Park Ave.(10016), pg. 1219
P.D. FASHIONS, 512 Seventh Ave.(10018), pg. 836
PACE PRESS, INC., 636 11th Ave.(10036), pg. 838
PACO RABANNE PARFUMS, 70 E. 55th St.(10022), pg. 842
Pajama Craft, Inc., 1359 Broadway(10018), pg. 545
R.J. PALMER, INC., 1350 Ave. of the Americas(10019), pg. 844
Palmer Water Co., 204 E. 39th St.(10016), pg. 545
PAN AMERICAN TRADE DEVELOPMENT CORP., 310 Madison Ave.(10017), pg. 845
PARADE PUBLICATIONS INC., 750 Third Ave.(10017), pg. 847
Parsons Brinckerhoff Development Corp., One Penn Plaza, 5th Fl.(10119), pg. 850
PARSONS BRINCKERHOFF INC., 1 Penn Plaza, 5th Fl.(10119), pg. 850
Parsons Brinckerhoff International, Inc., One Penn Plaza, 5th Fl.(10119), pg. 850
Parsons Brinckerhoff Quade & Douglas, Inc., One Penn Plaza(10119), pg. 850
PARTNERS & SHEVACK, INC., 1350 Ave. of the Americas(10019-4701), pg. 850
SID PATERSON ASSOC., INC., 22 East 29th St.(10016), pg. 851
THE PATRICIAN GROUP, 502 Park Ave.(10022), pg. 851
Pearloom Fabrics, 261 5th Ave.(10016), pg. 387
PEDONE & PARTNERS INC., 100 Fifth Ave.(10011), pg. 854
DAVID L. PEISTER CO., INC., 29 W. 38th St.(10018), pg. 856
Pepper, Hamilton & Scheetz, 10 E. 53rd St., 32nd Fl.(10022), pg. 860
PERFECT PEARL COMPANY, INC., 104 W. 29th St., 3rd Fl.(10001), pg. 861
Perkins/Butler Direct Marketing, 79 Fifth Ave., 6th Fl.(10003), pg. 244
PETRO CHEM DEVELOPMENT COMPANY, 122 E. 42nd St.(10017), pg. 865
Pharmacists Public Relations Bureau, 1515 Broadway(10036), pg. 304
PHILLIPS FINE ART AUCTIONEERS, 406 E. 79th St.(10021), pg. 867
Piaget Watch Corporation, 650 Fifth Ave.(10019), pg. 812
Pierre Cardin Knits, 1411 Broadway(10018), pg. 133
Plastics Technology, 633 Third Ave.(10017), pg. 150
The Plummer Group, 866 United Nations Plaza(10017), pg. 1164
POLO/RALPH LAUREN CORPORATION, 650 Madison Ave.(10019), pg. 879
POPOFSKY ADVERTISING, INC., 60 Madison Ave.(10010-1600), pg. 880
POPPE TYSON, 40 W. 23rd St.(10010), pg. 880
Popular Mechanics, 224 W. 57th St.(10019), pg. 523
POTAMKIN MANHATTAN, 787 11th Ave. at 54th St.(10019), pg. 882
PowerForce Company, Inc., 79 Fifth Ave.(10003), pg. 560
PREMIER MILL CORP., 30 West 21st St.(10010), pg. 887
Premiere Magazine, 2 Park Ave., 4th Fl.(10016), pg. 611
Press Association, Inc., 50 Rockefeller Plaza(10020), pg. 92
PRESSMAN TOY CORP., 200 Fifth Ave., Suite 1052(10010), pg. 887
Prestige Fragrance & Cosmetics, Inc., 767 Fifth Ave.(10153), pg. 696
Prestige Fragrances, Ltd., 625 Madison Ave., 4th Fl.(10022), pg. 696
Prestige Perfumes Ltd., 767 Fifth Ave.(10153), pg. 696
PRICE WATERHOUSE - U.S., 1251 Ave. of the Americas(10020), pg. 888
Primary Coal Inc., 666 Fifth Ave.(10103), pg. 889
PRIMARY INDUSTRIES CORPORATION, 666 Fifth Ave.(10103), pg. 889
PRO CLINICA INC., 51 E. 42nd St.(10017), pg. 891
Process Materials, 100 Park Avenue(10017), pg. 233
Prudential Capital & Investment Services, Inc., 1 Seaport Plaza(10292), pg. 897
Prudential Securities Group Inc., One Seaport Plaza(10292), pg. 897
Prudential Securities Inc., 199 Gold St.(10292), pg. 897
Public Relations Productions Co., Inc., 301 East 57th St.(10022), pg. 954
PUBLIX GROUP, 350 Fifth Ave.(10118), pg. 898
PUERTO RICO TOURISM COMPANY, 575 Fifth Ave.(10017), pg. 899
PYRAMID HANDBAGS INC., 100 W. 33rd St., Ste. 800(10001), pg. 901
Qismet Ltd., 6 E. 32nd St.(10016), pg. 753
Quantum Sportswear, Ltd., 1411 Broadway(10018), pg. 753
Queens Group Design, 120 Wooster St.(10012), pg. 904
Quill Trade Paperbacks, 105 Madison Ave.(10016), pg. 522
RF Design Inc., 301 East 57th St.(10022), pg. 954
RABCO HEALTH SERVICE, 444 Madison Ave., Ste. 601(10022), pg. 908
Rabson's, 119 W. 57th St.(10019), pg. 720
The Radio Group, 640 Fifth Ave.(10019), pg. 652
RADO WATCH COMPANY, INC., 35 E. 21st St.(10010), pg. 909
Random House, 201 E. 50th St.(10022), pg. 19
Random House, Inc., 201 E. 50th St.(10022), pg. 19
RED APPLE COMPANIES, 823 11th Ave.(10019), pg. 917
Red Apple Companies Food Group, 823 11th Ave.(10019), pg. 918
Redbook, 224 West 57th(10019), pg. 523
Remco Baby, 1107 Broadway, Ste. 808(10010), pg. 926
REMCO TOYS, 1107 Broadway, Ste. 808(10010), pg. 926
RENCO GROUP, 45 Rockefeller Plaza(10111), pg. 926
Research & Forecasts, Inc., 301 East 57th St.(10022), pg. 954
Resources Funding Corp., 666 Third Ave.(10029), pg. 573
Resources Property Management Corp., 800 Second Ave., 9th Fl.(10017), pg. 573
Resources Real Estate Finance Group, Inc., 666 Third Ave.(10017), pg. 573
Restaurant Business, 633 Third Ave.(10017), pg. 150
Restaurant/Hotel Design International, 633 Third Ave.(10017), pg. 150
Retirement Advisors, Inc., 105 Madison Ave.(10016), pg. 522
Revlon Group Inc., 21 E. 63rd St.(10021), pg. 695
Revlon, Inc., 625 Madison Ave.(10022), pg. 696
Revlon International Corporation, 767 Fifth Ave.(10153), pg. 696
Revlon-Realistic Professional Products, Inc., 625 Madison Ave.(10022), pg. 696
Revlon Service, Inc., 767 Fifth Ave.(10153), pg. 696
Charles Revson, Inc., 767 Fifth Ave.(10153), pg. 696
John J. Reynolds, Inc., 685 5th Ave.(10022), pg. 527
RIKLIS FAMILY CORPORATION, 667 Madison Ave., 12th Flr.(10021), pg. 934
Hal Riney & Partners, Inc., 100 East 42nd St.(10017), pg. 935
Ritz Corporation, 767 Fifth Ave.(10153), pg. 696
Robby Len Fashions, 1411 Broadway(10018), pg. 78
Robinson, Yesawich & Pepperdine, 104 East 40th St., Ste. 707(10016), pg. 940
ROCKVILLE FABRICS CORPORATION, 225 W. 34th St.(10122), pg. 942
Rolling Stone Magazine, 1290 Ave. of the Americas(10104), pg. 1052
ROMANN & TANNENHOLZ ADVERTISING, INC., 420 Lexington Ave.(10017), pg. 945
ROSENFELD, SIROWITZ, HUMPHREY & STRAUSS, INC., 111 Fifth Ave.(10002), pg. 948
Ross Roy Communications/N.Y., 250 Park Ave., S.(10003), pg. 950
Rothchild Asset Management Inc., One Rockefeller Plaza(10020), pg. 951
Rothchild Realty Inc., One Rockefeller Plaza(10020), pg. 951
S. ROTHCHILD & CO., INC., 225 W. 37th St.(10018), pg. 951
Rothschild Inc., One Rockefeller Plaza(10020), pg. 951
ROTHSCHILD NORTH AMERICA INC., One Rockefeller Plaza(10020), pg. 951
Roxanne Swim Suits Co., Inc., 1411 Broadway(10018), pg. 753
Roydon Wear, Inc., 350 Fifth Ave.(10118), pg. 283
ROYTEX, INC., 16 E. 34th St., 17th Floor(10016), pg. 953
RUBIN EHRENTHAL & ASSOCIATES, 100 Ave. of the Americas(10013), pg. 953
M. RUBIN & SONS INC., 34-01 38th Ave.(11101), pg. 954
Ruder Finn Health Care, 301 East 57th St.(10022), pg. 954
RUDER, FINN, INC., 301 East 57th St.(10022), pg. 954
Ruder Finn Japan Desk, 301 East 57th St.(10022), pg. 954
RUMS OF PUERTO RICO, 1290 Ave. of the Americas(10104), pg. 956
Russian Travel Bureau, Inc., Orbitair International Bldg., 225 E. 44th St.(10017), pg. 828
SAS Institute, Inc., 34th Floor, 520 Madison Ave.(10022), pg. 959
SCH Holding Corp., 725 Fifth Ave.(10022), pg. 934
SFM MEDIA CORPORATION, 1180 Ave. of the Americas(10036), pg. 962
SGD INTERNATIONAL CORP., 888 Seventh Ave., Ste. 603(10019), pg. 962
SI HOLDINGS INC., 730 Broadway(10003), pg. 962
SKR RESOURCES, INC., 307 Fifth Ave.(10016), pg. 963
SACKS & ROSEN, INC. ADVERTISING, 305 East 46th St.(10017), pg. 965
Sadlier, 9 Pine St.(10005), pg. 966
WILLIAM H. SADLIER, INC., 9 Pine St.(10005), pg. 966
W.H. Sadlier Oxford, 11 Park Pl.(10007), pg. 966
Sales and Marketing Management, 633 Third Ave.(10017), pg. 150
SALLY LOU FASHIONS CORPORATION, 1400 Broadway(10018), pg. 967
MILTON SAMUELS ADVERTISING AGENCY, INC., 31 East 32nd St.(10016), pg. 968
SANDLER COMMUNICATIONS INC., 130 Fifth Ave.(10010), pg. 970
Sangre de Cristos Ranches Inc., 60 Fifth Ave.(10011), pg. 423
SANTEE PRINT WORKS, INC., 71 W. 35th St.(10001), pg. 970
SASSON JEANS FOR MEN, 350 5th Ave.(10018), pg. 972
SaTellite Data Broadcast Networks, Inc. (SATNET), 50 Rockefeller Plaza(10020), pg. 92
Saturday Review Magazine, 1965 Broadway(10023), pg. 450
Savoy Drapery Div., 16 E. 34th St.(10016), pg. 200
SCHEIN/BLATTSTEIN ADVERTISING, INC., 420 Madison Ave.(10017), pg. 975

SCHELL/MULLANEY, 79 Fifth Ave.(10005), pg. 975
G. Schirmer, Inc., 24 E. 22nd St.(10010), pg. 777
SCHNEIDER MILLS, INC., 462 7th Ave.(10018), pg. 977
Scholastic Inc., 730 Broadway(10003), pg. 962
Scholastic Productions Inc., 730 Broadway(10003), pg. 962
F. SCHUMACHER & CO., 79 Madison Ave.(10016-7878), pg. 979
SCHWARTZ & BENJAMIN, INC., 1370 Ave. of Americas(10019), pg. 980
JACK SCHWARTZ SHOES, INC., 155 Ave. of the Americas, 9th Fl.(10013), pg. 980
F.J. SCIAME CONSTRUCTION, 247 Water St.(10038), pg. 981
SCUDDER, STEVENS & CLARK, INC., 345 Park Ave.(10154), pg. 983
Security Title & Guaranty Co., 300 E. 40th(10016), pg. 527
SEIBEL & STERN CORP., 112 W. 34th St.(10120), pg. 987
Self, 350 Madison Ave.(10017), pg. 19
SERINO COYNE INC., 1515 Broadway, 36th Fl.(10036), pg. 991
1740 Ventures, Inc., 1740 Broadway(10019), pg. 778
Seventeen Magazine, 850 Third Ave.(10022), pg. 611
SHAW CREATIONS, INC., 28 W. 20th St.(10011), pg. 996
SHEPAUG CORPORATION, 54 E. 64th St.(10021), pg. 997
SHERBORNE GROUP, INC., Park Ave. Tower, 65 E. 55th St.(10022), pg. 998
SHERWOOD & SCHNEIDER ADVERTISING, 350 Hudson St.(10014), pg. 999
Showtime Satellite Networks, Inc., 1633 Broadway(10019), pg. 785
Showtime/The Movie Channel Inc. (U.K.), 1633 Broadway(10019), pg. 785
SIEBEL/MOHR, INC., 800 Third Ave.(10022), pg. 1002
SIEGEL & GALE, 1185 Ave. of the Americas(10036), pg. 1002
HENRY I. SIEGEL COMPANY, INC., 1372 Broadway(10018), pg. 1002
THE SIESEL COMPANY, 381 Park Ave. South, 5th Fl.(10016), pg. 1003
SIGALLO, LTD., 14 W. 33rd St.(10001), pg. 1003
SILVERMAN PRODUCTS & TEXTILES, 205 W. 39th St.(10018), pg. 1004
SIMMONS-BOARDMAN PUBLISHING CORP., 345 Hudson St.(10014), pg. 1005
SLATER HANFT MARTIN, INC., 111 Fifth Ave.(10003), pg. 1010
SLOANS SUPERMARKETS, INC., 2 Bennett Ave.(10033), pg. 1010
SMITH/GREENLAND, INCORPORATED, 555 West 57th St.(10019), pg. 1012
SMITH'S PERSONNEL SERVICE, INC., 41 E. 42nd St.(10017), pg. 1014
Soap Opera Digest, 888 7th Ave., 38th Fl.(10106), pg. 611
SOUTHWIDE, INC., 60 E. 42nd St.(10165), pg. 1024
FRANKLIN SPIER, INC., 650 First Ave.(10016), pg. 1031
I. SPIEWAK & SONS, INC., 505 Eighth Ave.(10018), pg. 1031
Sponsored Publications, 60 E. 42nd St.(10165), pg. 522
Sports Afield, 250 W. 55th St.(10019), pg. 523
Sportswear International, 438 West 37th St.(10018), pg. 611
SPRING, O'BRIEN & CO. INC., 220 Fifth Ave.(10001), pg. 1033
Staflex Co., 57 W. 38th St..(10018), pg. 510
STANDARD GARMENT COMPANY, INC., 48 W. 37th St.(10018), pg. 1036
Standard Research Consultants, 26 Broadway(10004), pg. 48
Standard Security Life Insurance Company of New York, 485 Madison Ave.(10022), pg. 452
STAR CHILDREN'S DRESS COMPANY, INC., 112 W. 34th St.(10120), pg. 1039
Stawasz Public Relations, 445 Park Ave.(10022), pg. 605
STEIN, KILLPATRICK & ROGAN ADVERTISING, 15 West 26th St.(10010), pg. 1045
STEINERT & ASSOCIATES, INC., 260 Madison Ave. 20th. Floor(10016), pg. 1045
STEPHEN ASSOCIATES, INC., 60 East 42nd St.(10165), pg. 1046
STERN & STERN INDUSTRIES INC., 708 Third Ave.(10017), pg. 1048
DAVID G. STEVEN, INC., 663 Fifth Ave.(10022), pg. 1048
Stevens Home Fashions, 1185 Ave. of the Americas(10036), pg. 400
THE STOGEL COMPANIES INC., 19 W. 44th St.(10036), pg. 1050
STONE ADVERTISING, 821 Broadway(10003), pg. 1050
STRAIGHT ARROW PUBLISHERS, INC., 1290 Ave. of the Americas(10104), pg. 1052
PAUL STUART, INC., Madison Ave. & 45th St.(10017), pg. 1054
Successful Meetings, 633 Third Ave.(10017), pg. 150
Sudler & Hennessey, 1633 Broadway(10019), pg. 1211
Sudler & Hennessey Consumer Group, 1180 Ave. of the Americas(10036), pg. 1211
Sunburst, 19 Union Sq. W.(10003), pg. 403
Sunday Magazine Network, 260 Madison Ave.(10016), pg. 745
Sunrise Mall Assocs., 635 Madison Ave.(10022), pg. 998
SUNWEAVE LINEN CORPORATION, 1040 Sixth Ave.(10018), pg. 1062
THE SUSSMAN/ZICCARDI GROUP, 221 West 41st St.(10036), pg. 1065
SWELL-WEAR, INC., 350 Fifth Ave.(10118), pg. 1067
SWIRL, INC., 8 W. 38th St.(10018), pg. 1068
Swirl Sales, Inc., 8 West 38th St.(10018), pg. 1068
TBWA ADVERTISING, INC., TBWA House, 292 Madison Ave.(10017), pg. 1071
TFI (Tape Films Inc.), 619 West 54th St.(10019), pg. 693
TLC BEATRICE INTERNATIONAL HOLDINGS INC., 9 West 57th St., 48th Fl.(10019), pg. 1073
TMP WORLDWIDE, INC., 1633 Broadway, 33rd Fl.(10019), pg. 1073
TSE Leasing Co., 505 8th Ave.(10018), pg. 1031
Talent & Residuals, Inc., 79 Fifth Ave.(10003), pg. 560
Tambourine Books, 105 Madison Ave.(10016), pg. 522
TARGET SPORTSWEAR, INC., 1290 Ave. of the Americas, Ste. 1800(10104), pg. 1079
TARLOW ADVERTISING, 950 Third Ave.(10022), pg. 1079
TAYLOR-GORDON/WIDMANN & CO., INC., 292 Madison Ave.(10017), pg. 1081
TEACHERS INSURANCE AND ANNUITY ASSOCIATION-COLLEGE RETIREMENT EQUITIES FUND, 730 Third Ave.(10017), pg. 1082
TeleRep, Incorporated, 875 Third Ave.(10022), pg. 293
Terry, Bath & Kitchen Products Div., 1185 Ave. of the Americas(10036), pg. 400
THOMAS PUBLISHING CO., One Penn Plaza(10119), pg. 1093
Thomas Register, One Penn Plaza(10119), pg. 1093
TICOR TITLE GUARANTEE CO., 39 Broadway(10006), pg. 1096
Times Books, 201 E. 50th St.(10022), pg. 19
TISHMAN REALTY & CONSTRUCTION CO., 666 5th Ave.(10103), pg. 1099
TITAN INDUSTRIAL CORP., 555 Madison Ave.(10022), pg. 1099
Todd-AO/East, 254 W. 54th St.(10019), pg. 1099
TORINO FASHIONS, INC., 462 7th Ave.(10018), pg. 1102
TOTAL COMMUNICATIONS GROUP, 122 East 42nd St.(10168), pg. 1102
TOURNEAU INC., 500 Madison Ave.(10022), pg. 1103
TOWERS, PERRIN, FORSTER & CROSBY, INC., 245 Park Ave.(10167), pg. 1103
ROBERT TOWERS ADVERTISING, INC., 345 Park Ave S., 8th Fl.(10010), pg. 1103
Town & Country, 1700 Broadway(10019), pg. 523
TOWNE, SILVERSTEIN, ROTTER INC., 411 Lafayette St.(10003), pg. 1104
TOY BIZ, INC., 333 E. 38th St.(10016), pg. 1104
Trade Show Enterprises, 505 8th Ave.(10018), pg. 1031
TRAINER WORTHAM & COMPANY INCORPORATED, 845 Third Ave., 6th Fl.(10022), pg. 1106
TRANSAMMONIA INC., 350 Park Ave.(10022), pg. 1106
Trappings Co., 505 8th Ave.(10018), pg. 1031
TRIAN GROUP, 900 3rd Ave., 31st Fl.(10022), pg. 1111
TRIANGLE MARKETING CORP., 32 Bleecker St.(10012), pg. 1112
Triborough Bridge & Tunnel Authority, Randall's Island(10035), pg. 745
THE TRUMP GROUP, 767 Fifth Ave., 50th Fl.(10153), pg. 1117
TRUMP ORGANIZATION, 725 Fifth Ave.(10022), pg. 1118
Trump Towers, 725 Fifth Ave.(10022), pg. 1118
The Tucker Group, 800 Third Ave.(10022), pg. 103
Turner Subscription Agency, 116 E. 16th St.(10003), pg. 404
The "21" Club, Inc., 21 W. 52nd St.(10019), pg. 1121
21 INTERNATIONAL HOLDINGS, INC., 153 E. 53 St., Ste. 5900(10022), pg. 1121
UIS Export Corporation, 600 5th Ave.(10020), pg. 1123
UIS, INC., 600 5th Ave.(10020), pg. 1123
USA NETWORK, 1230 Ave. of the Americas(10020), pg. 1124
THE UNIMAX CORPORATION, 54 E. 64th St.(10021), pg. 1127
Unimax Holding Corp., 54 E. 64th St.(10021), pg. 998
UNION HOLDINGS, INC., 30 Rockefeller Plaza, Ste. 4314(10112), pg. 1128
UNISYSTEMS, INC., 155 E. 55th St.(10022), pg. 1130
UNITED ACQUISITION CORPORATION, 823 11th Ave.(10019), pg. 1130
UNITED ENVELOPE COMPANY, INC., 525 W. 52nd St., 2nd Fl.(10019), pg. 1131
U.S. Carpet Co., 919 Third Ave.(10022), pg. 290
U.S. NEWS & WORLD REPORT, 1290 Avenue of the Americas(10104), pg. 1136
UNITED THERMAL CORPORATION, 560 Lexington Ave., 9th Fl.(10022), pg. 1137
Univision Holdings, Inc., 605 Third Ave., 12th Floor(10158-0180), pg. 502
UNIWORLD GROUP, INC., 100 Ave. of the Americas(10013), pg. 1139
Us Magazine, 1290 Ave. of the Americas(10104), pg. 1052
Utilities & Industries Management Corp., 54 E. 64th St.(10021), pg. 998
VH-1/Video Hits One, 1515 Broadway(10036), pg. 785
VV PUBLISHING CORP., 36 Cooper Square(10003), pg. 1142
VAN CLEEF & ARPELS, INC., 744 Fifth Ave., 2nd Fl.(10019), pg. 1144
Vanity Fair, 350 Madison Ave.(10017), pg. 19
Vector Realty Corp., 666 Fifth Ave.(10103), pg. 469
VeloBind, Inc., 6 East 43rd St.(10017), pg. 657
VENTURA ASSOCIATES, INC., 1211 Ave. of the Americas, 26th Floor(10036), pg. 1147
VERNON SASSOS MCGILL, INC., 156 Fifth Ave.(10010), pg. 1148
Viacom Broadcasting Inc., 1515 Broadway(10036), pg. 785
Viacom Enterprises, 1515 Broadway(10036), pg. 785
Viacom Inc., 1515 Broadway(10036), pg. 785
Viacom International Inc., 1515 Broadway(10036), pg. 785
Viacom Networks Inc., 1515 Broadway(10036), pg. 785
Viacom Satellite Networks Inc., 1515 Broadway(10036), pg. 785
Victoria, 224 W. 57th St.(10019), pg. 523
Vid America, Inc., 231 E. 55 St.(10022), pg. 74
Video Production/Post Production Div., 231 E. 55th St.(10022), pg. 1141
Villard Books, 201 E. 50th St.(10022), pg. 19
Visual Technologies, 301 East 57th St.(10022), pg. 954
VITT MEDIA INTERNATIONAL, INC., 1114 Ave. of the Americas(10036), pg. 1153
Vogue Magazine, 350 Madison Ave.(10017), pg. 19
WDP, INC., 211 E. 43rd St., Ste. 1005(10017), pg. 1156
WWF/Royal Paper Company, 185 Madison Ave., 12th Fl.(10016), pg. 1157
WALKER-PIONEER MOSS, 460 W. 34th St.(10001), pg. 1160
WARING & LAROSA, INC., 909 Third Ave.(10022), pg. 1163
WARNER, BICKING, MORRIS & PARTNERS, INC., 866 United Nations Plaza(10017), pg. 1164
WARREN EQUITIES INC., 10 E. 53rd St.(10022), pg. 1164
WARREN/KREMER/CMP/ADVERTISING/INC., 2 Park Ave.(10016), pg. 1165
WARWICK BAKER & FIORE INC., 100 Ave. of the Americas(10013), pg. 1165
Washington National Life Insurance Co. of New York, 120 W. 45th St.(10036), pg. 266
Waverly Fabrics, 79 Madison Ave.(10016-7878), pg. 979
The Weather Channel, Inc.-New York Sales Office, 780 Third Ave.(10017), pg. 654
Weatherly Capital Corp., 20 Exchange Place, 23rd Fl.(10005), pg. 1169
WEATHERLY FINANCIAL GROUP, 20 Exchange Place, 23rd Fl.(10005), pg. 1169
Weatherly Private Capital, Inc., 20 Exchange Place, 23rd Fl.(1005), pg. 1170
Weatherly Securities Corp., 20 Exchange Place, 23rd Fl.(10005), pg. 1170
Weilwood Industries, Inc., 119 W. 40th St.(10018), pg. 970
SJ WEINSTEIN ASSOCIATES INC., 100 Fifth Ave.(10011), pg. 1173
WEINSTEIN OTTERMAN & ASSOCIATES, 137 Fifth Ave.(10010), pg. 1173
WEISS, WHITTEN, CARROLL, STAGLIANO INC., 96 Morton St.(10014), pg. 1174
WELLMADE INDUSTRIES, INC., 131 West 33rd Street(10001), pg. 1175
Western International Media Corporation, 1270 Ave. of the Americas(10020), pg. 1180
WHISPER SOFT MILLS INC., 111 W. 40th St.(10018), pg. 1185
Wide World Photos, Inc., 50 Rockefeller Plaza(10020), pg. 92
David R. Williams, Inc., 1114 Ave. of the Americas(10036), pg. 1154
WILLOUGHBY'S, 110 W. 32nd St., 6th & 7th Aves.(10001), pg. 1193
WILLS AND EVANS, 280 Madison Ave.(10016), pg. 1193
WINNER COMMUNICATIONS, INC., 37 Union Square West(10003), pg. 1196
HARRY WINSTON, INC., 718 5th Ave.(10019), pg. 1197
CAROLE WREN, INC., 75 Ninth Ave., 3rd Fl.(10011), pg. 1204
Wunderman Cato Johnson, 675 Ave. of the Americas(10010), pg. 1211
Wyse Advertising/New York, 79 Fifth Ave., 11th Fl.(10003), pg. 1206
DANIEL F. YOUNG, INC., 17 Battery Pl. 8th Fl.(10004), pg. 1209
YOUNG & RUBICAM INC., 285 Madison Ave.(10017), pg. 1210
Young & Rubicam New York, 285 Madison Ave.(10017), pg. 1211
YOUNG STUFF APPAREL GROUP, INC., 1407 Broadway, 6th Fl.(10018), pg. 1214
ZENA JEANS, 1407 Broadway(10018), pg. 1217
ZIFF COMMUNICATIONS COMPANY, One Park Ave.(10016), pg. 1218
Ziff-Davis Publishing Company, One Park Ave.(10016), pg. 1219
ZIM-AMERICAN ISRAELI SHIPPING CO., One World Trade Center(10048), pg. 1219
Zim Container Service, One World Trade Center(10048), pg. 1219

New York Mills

C. WEAVER CHEVROLET, INC., Commercial Dr.(13417), pg. 1170

Newburgh

AMERICAN FELT & FILTER, 311 First St.(12550), pg. 52
HUDSON VALLEY TREE, INC., 840 Broadway(12550), pg. 551
Keystone Automotive Industries, Inc. - Newburgh, 5 Jeanne Dr.(12550), pg. 628
Mid-Valley Petroleum Corporation, 1 S. Water St.(12550), pg. 1165
Newburgh Auto Auction, Route 17K, P.O. Box 2426(12550), pg. 293

Niagara Falls

HIROSS INC., 2107 Liberty Dr.(14304), pg. 536
NUTTALL GEAR CORPORATION, 2221 Niagara Falls Blvd.(14302), pg. 818
SCRUFARI CONSTRUCTION CO. INC., 3925 Hyde Park Blvd.(14305), pg. 983
Tulip Corp., Niagara Falls Div., 3125 Highland Ave.(14305), pg. 1119

North Merrick

KING BEAR ENTERPRISES, INC., 1390 Jerusalem Ave.(11566), pg. 630

North Tonawanda

NIAGARA CUTTER, INC., Niagara Cutter Plaza, 889 Erie Ave.(14120), pg. 805
THRUWAY FASTENERS INC., 2910 Niagara Falls Blvd.(14120), pg. 1096

Norwich

Dunco Realty & Equip. Corp., 54 E. Main St.(13815), pg. 1150
Food King, Inc., 54 E. Main St.(13815), pg. 1150
Food King Independent Supermarkets, 54 E. Main St.(13815), pg. 1150

Great American Food Stores, Inc., 54 E. Main St.(13815), pg. 1150
Norwich Recycling Corp., Woods Corners(13815), pg. 1150
U Pump 'Em, 54 E. Main St.(13815), pg. 1150
Victory Discount Beverage Center, 54 E. Main St.(13815), pg. 1150
VICTORY MARKETS INC., 54 E. Main St.(13815), pg. 1150
Victory Video Inc., 54 E. Main St.(13815), pg. 1150
Village Markets, 54 E. Main St.(13815), pg. 1150

Nyack on Hudson

PAVION LTD., 60 Cedar Hill Avenue(10960), pg. 852

Oceanside

Applied Graphics Technologies, 15 Neil Court(11572), pg. 1136

Ogdensburg

Standard Shade Roller Div., P.O. Box 578, (13669), pg. 200

Olean

BLUE BIRD COACH LINES INC., One Blue Bird Sq.(14760), pg. 158

Oneida

SMITH-LEE CO., INC., 537 Fitch(13421), pg. 1013

Orangeburg

Cornell Manufacturing Company, 25 Ramland Rd.(10962), pg. 609
INNOVATIVE PLASTICS CORPORATION, 400 Rte. 303(10962), pg. 570
PENTAX PRECISION INSTRUMENTS CORP., 30 Ramland Rd.(10962-2699), pg. 859

Orchard Park

American Envelope of Buffalo, 100 Centre Dr.(14127), pg. 199
Clinicare Systems, Inc., 10 Center Dr.(14127), pg. 447
ENIDINE INCORPORATED, Seven Centre Dr.(14127), pg. 382
GAYMAR INDUSTRIES, INC., 10 Centre Drive(14127), pg. 447
NITRAM ENERGY INC., 227 Thorn Ave.(14127), pg. 807
Retec USA, Inc., 10 Centre Dr.(14127), pg. 447

Ossining

JOHN F. KOLODY INC., Central Westchester Bus. Pk., 100 Exec. Blvd.(10562), pg. 641

Owego

STAKMORE INC., Elm St.(13827), pg. 1035

Oyster Bay

COMMANDER OIL CORPORATION, One Commander Sq.(11771), pg. 268
S. R. LEON COMPANY, INC., 29 W. Main St.(11771), pg. 667

Pawling

PAWLING CORPORATION, 157 Charles Colman Blvd.(12564), pg. 852
Presray Corp., 159 Charles Colman Blvd.(12564), pg. 852

Pearl River

Glen Raven Marketing Corporation, One Blue Hill Plaza, 4th Fl.(10965), pg. 461
Glen Raven Mills Marketing Corp., 4th Floor, One Blue Hill Plaza(10965), pg. 461
Lawler, Matusky & Skelly Engineers, One Blue Hill Plaza(10965), pg. 661

Peekskill

S. M. FRANK & CO., INC., P.O. Box 789, (10566), pg. 429
Kaywoodie, 1000 N. Division St.(10566), pg. 429
Medico, Inc., 1000 N. Division St.(10566), pg. 429
SHOKAI FAR EAST LTD., 9 Elena Ct.(10566), pg. 1000
Yello-Bole, 1000 N. Division St.(10566), pg. 429

Pelham Manor

IMPERIA BROS., INC., 57 Canal Rd.(10803), pg. 563

Picasantville

Technology for Medicine, Inc., 270 Marble Ave.(10570), pg. 735

Plainview

GENERAL AEROSPACE MATERIALS CORPORATION, 95 E. Bathpage Rd.(11803), pg. 448
Stephen Gould Corporation (Plainview, NY), 151 Fairchild Ave.(11803), pg. 474
MSC INDUSTRIAL SUPPLY CO., 151 Sunnyside Blvd.(11803), pg. 693
RED WING PRODUCTS, INC., 190 Express St.(11803), pg. 919
SID TOOL CO. INC., 151 Sunnyside Blvd.(11803), pg. 1002
VEECO INSTRUMENTATIONS, INC., Terminal Dr.(11803), pg. 1146

Pleasant Valley

CONKLIN INSTRUMENT CORPORATION, West Road(12569), pg. 274

Pleasantville

KDI Paragon, Inc., 12 Paulding St.(10570), pg. 612
MEDICAL LABORATORY AUTOMATION, INC., 270 Marble Ave.(10570), pg. 735
TECA CORPORATION, Three Campus Dr.(10570), pg. 1082

Port Chester

Greeff Fabrics, 150 Midland Ave.(10573), pg. 262
Nessen Lamps, 36 Midland Ave.(10573), pg. 588
ROSCO LABORATORIES, INC., 36 Bush Ave.(10573), pg. 947
STRATMAR SYSTEMS, INC., 109 Willett Ave.(10573), pg. 1053

Port Jervis

ANDMORE SPORTSWEAR CORPORATION, 21 Minisink Ave.(12771), pg. 74
The Finals, Ltd., 21 Minisink Ave.(12771), pg. 74

Port Washington

WALTER J. BLACK, INC., 99 Seaview Blvd.(11050), pg. 154
Walter J. Black, Inc. Fulfillment Services, 99 Seaview Blvd.(11050), pg. 154
Black's Readers Service, 99 Seaview Blvd.(11050), pg. 154
BRUCKNER MACHINE & TOOL CORP., 36 Harbor Park Dr.(11050), pg. 183
The Classics Club, 99 Seaview Blvd.(11050), pg. 154
The Detective Book Club, 99 Seaview Blvd.(11050), pg. 154
DRI MARK PRODUCTS, INC., 15 Harbor Park Dr.(11050), pg. 349
The (Erle Stanley) Gardner Mystery Library, 99 Seaview Blvd.(11050), pg. 154
The Giants of Literature Series, 99 Seaview Blvd.(11050), pg. 154
The Golden Giants Series, 99 Seaview Blvd.(11050), pg. 154
E. W. HOWELL COMPANY, INC., 2 Seaview Blvd.(11050), pg. 547
The Power Line, 382 Channel Dr.(11050), pg. 898
PUBLISHERS CLEARING HOUSE, 382 Channel Dr.(11050), pg. 898
HENRY SCHEIN, INC., 5 Harbor Park Dr.(11050), pg. 975
Schein Pharmaceutical, Inc., 26 Harbor Park Dr.(11050), pg. 975
SLEEPY'S THE MATTRESS PROFESSIONALS, 2 Tri-Harbour Ct.(11050), pg. 1010
STERN'S MIRACLE-GRO PRODUCTS, INC., 800 Port Washington Blvd.(11050), pg. 1048
The Zane Grey Library, 99 Seaview Blvd.(11050), pg. 154

Poughkeepsie

Effron Fuel Oil Co., Inc., 154 Garden Street(12682), pg. 736

Purchase

CENTRAL NATIONAL-GOTTESMAN INC., 3 Manhattanville Rd.(10577-2110), pg. 233
Collins & Aikman Inc., The Centre at Purchase, Two Manhattanville Rd.(10577), pg. 263
Lindenmeyr Central, 3 Manhattanville Rd.(10577-2100), pg. 233

Queens Village

BELLACICCO & SONS, 217-44 98th Ave.(11429), pg. 136

Rego Park

GLOBUS-GATEWAY/COSMOS TOURAMA, 95-25 Queens Blvd.(11374), pg. 464
LEFRAK ORGANIZATION INC., 97-77 Queens Blvd.(11374), pg. 666

Rensselaer

Allied Security Inc. (NY), 63 Washington St., Ste. 9(12144), pg. 40

Richmond Hill

COMMERCIAL PLASTICS & SUPPLIES CORP., 98-31 Jamaica Ave.(11418), pg. 268

Ridgewood

DE FRANCISCI MACHINE CORP.(DEMACO), 46-25 Metropolitan Ave.(11385), pg. 321

Riverhead

Riverhead Savings Bank, 7 W. Main Street(11901), pg. 60

Rochester

ALP/FREDDY'S, 90 Commerce Dr.(14623), pg. 4
ADAMS COLWAY & ASSOCIATES, Corbett's Glenn, 412 Linden Ave.(14625), pg. 16
Alcor Envelope Co., 25 Verona St.(14608), pg. 40
ALLESON OF ROCHESTER, INC., 2921 Brighton-Henrietta T.L. Rd.(14623), pg. 37
ALLIANCE AUTOMATION SYSTEMS, 400 Trabold Rd.(14624), pg. 37
ALLING & CORY COMPANY, 25 Verona St.(14608), pg. 40
Allright New York Parking, Inc., P.O. Box 40310 Midtown, Lincoln First Tower(14604), pg. 42
ALTIER & SONS SHOES INC., 164 Mushroom Blvd.(14623), pg. 45
Arnold Fortuna Lawner & Cabot, Southview Commons, 100 Whitespruce Blvd.(14623), pg. 84
BUCK & PULLEYN, INC., 500 Helendale Rd.(14609), pg. 185
CVC PRODUCTS, INC., 525 Lee Rd.(14606), pg. 206
CALDWELL MANUFACTURING COMPANY, 2605 Manitou Rd.(14624), pg. 208
Comstock Michigan Fruit, 90 Linden Place(14603), pg. 25
HEATHER CROLIE, INC., 87 N. Clinton Ave.(14604), pg. 300
Curtice-Burns Foods, Inc., 90 Linden Place(14603), pg. 25
ENI, 100 Highpower Rd.(14623), pg. 360
ERDLE PERFORATING CO., 100 Pixley Indus. Pkwy.(14624), pg. 385
Eric Mower and Associates/Rochester, Inc., 96 College Ave.(14607), pg. 774
Federal Stampings of New York, 1455 Emerson St.(14606), pg. 321
FIRST FEDERAL SAVINGS AND LOAN ASSN. OF ROCHESTER, 1 First Federal Plaza(14614), pg. 413
Foley-PLP Company, 1920 Lyell Ave.(14604), pg. 422
Gannett Transit, 1029 Sibley Tower Bldg.(14604), pg. 442
Stephen Gould Corporation (Rochester, NY), 1200-C Scottsville Rd.(14624), pg. 474
Hutchins/Young & Rubicam, 400 Midtown Tower, (14604), pg. 1211
ICE COMMUNICATIONS, INC., 2290 East Ave.(14610), pg. 559
JAY INCORPORATED, 170 Linden Oaks(14625), pg. 590
THE JOLT COMPANY, 130 Linden Oakes Dr., Ste. C(14625), pg. 602
Keystone Crash Parts Mart - Rochester, 961 Lyell Ave.(14606), pg. 628
LIBERTY TOOL CORPORATION, 350 Buell Rd.(14624), pg. 674
Logical Operations, 595 Blossom Rd.(14610), pg. 1219
MAGNETIC TECHNOLOGIES CORPORATION, 770 Linden Ave.(14625), pg. 701
MATHEWS & BOUCHER, 1950 Brighton-Henrietta Town Line Rd.(14623), pg. 720
MCCURDY & CO., INC., Midtown Plaza, 285 Main St., E.(14645), pg. 728
National Brands Beverage Div., 882 Linden Ave.(14625), pg. 25
NuArc Co., 478 Thurston Rd., Suite S-22(14619), pg. 817
PFAUDLER-U.S., INC., 1000 West Ave.(14611), pg. 866
Plywood Plastics, Inc., 299 Burrows St.(14606), pg. 878
Rochester Instruments Systems, Inc., 255 N. Union St.(14605), pg. 712
ROCHESTER MIDLAND CORPORATION, 333 Hollenbeck St.(14621), pg. 940
RUMRILL-HOYT, INC., 60 Corporate Woods(14623), pg. 955
SENTRY GROUP, 900 Linden Ave.(14625), pg. 990
SIGNIFICS, INC., 28 Prince St.(14607), pg. 1004
WEGMANS FOOD MARKETS, INC., 1500 Brooks Ave.(14692-0844), pg. 1172
WILMORITE INC., 1265 Scottsville Rd.(14624), pg. 1193
WINTERKORN LILLIS INC., 400 Euclid Bldg., Midtown Plaza(14604), pg. 1197
WOLFF ASSOCIATES, INC., The Wolff Bldg., 500 East Ave.(14607), pg. 1199

Rockville Centre

FUTTER LUMBER CORPORATION, 100 Merrick Rd.(11570), pg. 437
IMPRINT PRODUCTS, L.P., 70 Randall Ave.(11570), pg. 564
RUGBY-DARBY GROUP OF COS., 100 Banks Ave.(11570), pg. 955

Rome

Carl's Drug Company, Inc., P.O. Box 203, Success Drive(13440), pg. 1150
ROME CABLE CORPORATION, 421 Ridge St.(13440), pg. 945
ROME SENTINEL CO., 333 W. Dominick St.(13440), pg. 946
ROME STRIP STEEL CO., INC., 530 Henry St.(13440), pg. 946

Ronkonkoma

QUALITY KING DISTRIBUTORS, 2060 9th Ave.(11779), pg. 903
TOPLINE ADVERTISING, 111 Gary Way(11779), pg. 1102

Roosevelt

Jay Dee Tomfor Transportation Co., 43 Debevoise Ave., P.O. Box E(11575), pg. 60

Roslyn

BROADCAST TIME, INC., 1044 Northern Blvd.(11576), pg. 177

Rouses Point

F.W. Myers & Co., Myers Bldg., 72 Lake St.(12979), pg. 780
THE MYERS GROUP (U.S) INC., Myers Bldg., 72 Lake St.(12979-1091), pg. 780
Myers Group U.S., Inc., Myers Bldg., 72 Lake St.(12979), pg. 780

Rush

GENIE MANUFACTURING CORP., 999 Rush-Henrietta, Townline Rd.(14543), pg. 452

Rye

Companion Life Insurance Co., 401 Theodore Fremd Ave.(10580-1493), pg. 779
Manhattan Electric Cable Corporation, Station Plaza(10580), pg. 370
Seacoast Electric Company, Station Plaza(10580), pg. 370

Rye Brook

PARSONS & WHITTEMORE ENTERPRISES, 4 International Dr.(10573), pg. 850
Stratmar Research Corp., Woodland Dr.(10573), pg. 1053
Stratmar Resources, Inc., Woodland Dr.(10573), pg. 1053
STROMBERG-CONNORS COMMUNICATIONS, 62 Bowman Ave.(10573), pg. 1054

Saint Albans

WALLACE & WALLACE FUEL OIL, 200-33 Linden Blvd.(11412), pg. 1160

Sanborn

VOYAGER EMBLEMS, INC., 3707 Lockport Rd.(14132-9705), pg. 1155

Saratoga Springs

SARATOGA HARNESS RACING, INC., Nelson Ave.(12866), pg. 970
STEWART'S ICE CREAM CO., INC., P.O. Box 435(12866), pg. 1048

Scarsdale

THE CURRY CORPORATION, 727 Central Ave.(10583), pg. 305
POLERA BUILDING CORP., 180 Brook St.(10583), pg. 878
J. A. Sexauer, 531 Central Park Ave.(10583), pg. 357
Valley Cottage Machine Corp., 180 Brook St.(10583), pg. 879

Schenectady

A.W. Lawrence & Company, Inc., 108 Union St.(12305-1788), pg. 662
CONTEC INTERNATIONAL, 1023 State St.(12307), pg. 278
Fitts-Lawrence, Inc., 106 Erie Blvd.(12305-2203), pg. 662
GOLUB CORPORATION, 501 Duanesburg Rd.(12306), pg. 469
INSULATING MATERIALS, INC., One Campbell Rd.(12306), pg. 572
LAWRENCE GROUP, INC., 108 Union St.(12305-1788), pg. 662
Lawrence Agency Corporation, 108 Union St.(12305-1788), pg. 662
Lawrence General Corporation, 108 Union St.(12305-1788), pg. 662
Lawrence Healthcare Administrative Services, 3000 Troy-Schenectady Rd.(12309-1614), pg. 662
Lawrence Risk Services Corporation, 106A Erie Blvd.(12305-2203), pg. 662
Lawrence United Corp., 1222 Troy-Schnectady Rd.(12309-1719), pg. 662
Logic World, Inc., 2716 Albany St.(12304-1891), pg. 662
METRO FORD SALES, INC., 3601 State St.(12304), pg. 743
North American Safety Program Administrators, 1222 Troy Rd.(12309-1719), pg. 662
Price Chopper, 501 Duanesburg Rd.(12306), pg. 469
SCHENECTADY CHEMICALS, INC., 10th & Congress St.(12303), pg. 975
Senate Insurance Company, 108 Union St.(12305-1788), pg. 662
Troy Savings Bank-Schenectady, 1626 Union St.(12309), pg. 1117

Scotia

SOFCO-MEAD, INC., 702 Potential Pkwy. 4(12302), pg. 1016
White/Mipro Receptables, Corporation Park(12302), pg. 1186

Seaford

BAST CHEVROLET INC., 3660 Sunrise Hwy.(11783), pg. 125

Seneca Falls

Identification Systems, 25 Chestnut St.(13148), pg. 721

Sherman

NUTTALL EQUIPMENT CO. INC., 128 E. Main St.(14781), pg. 818

Sidney

Keith Clark, 101 O'Neil Rd.(13838), pg. 304

Southampton

Douglas Elliman, Inc., 41 Meeting House Lane(11968), pg. 347

Spring Valley

COSCO INDUSTRIES, 56 Church St.(10977), pg. 288

Springfield Gardens

Vitarine Pharmaceuticals, Inc., 227-15 N. Conduit Ave.(11413), pg. 383

Springville

T. L. SMITH MACHINE, 7020 Henrietta Rd.(14141), pg. 1013

Staten Island

ADVANCE PUBLICATIONS INC., 950 Fingerboard Rd.(10305), pg. 19
Cox Cable Staten Island (Partnership), 100 Cable Way(10303), pg. 294

Syosset

CHAMPION ALUMINUM CORPORATION, 140 Eileen Way(11791), pg. 238
MEENAN OIL CO. LIMITED PARTNERSHIP, 6800 Jericho Turnpike(11791), pg. 736
Nuyens Liquor Importing, Inc., 40 Underhill Blvd.(11791), pg. 1186
STAR LIQUOR DEALERS, 345 Underhill Blvd.(11791), pg. 1039
Veeco UPA Technology Inc., 60 Oak Dr.(11791), pg. 1146

Syracuse

Agri-Service Agencies, Inc., P.O. Box 4910, (13221), pg. 311
Agway General Agency, P.O. Box 4851(13221), pg. 25
Agway Indemnity Insurance Company, P.O. Box 4851(13221), pg. 25
Agway Insurance Co., P.O. Box 4851(13221), pg. 25
Allied Advertising Agency, 6311 Fly Rd., Ste. E(13057), pg. 37
CARROLS CORPORATION, 968 James St.(13203), pg. 225
CRUCIBLE MATERIALS CORP., State Fair Blvd.(13209), pg. 302
Dutch Parking, Inc., 345 So. Warren St.(13202), pg. 42
EASTERN MILK PRODUCERS COOPERATIVE ASSN., INC., 2401 Burnet Ave.(13206), pg. 363
FARMERS AND TRADERS LIFE INSURANCE CO., 960 James St.(13201), pg. 401
Keystone Crash Parts Mart - North Syracuse, 731 W. Genessee St.(13204), pg. 628
ERIC MOWER AND ASSOCIATES, INC., 500 Plum St.(13204), pg. 774
MUENCH-KREUZER CANDLE COMPANY, 617 E. Hiawatha Blvd.(13208), pg. 774
OBERDORFER INDUSTRIES, INC., P.O. Box 4811(13221), pg. 819
Primacare Health Resources, Inc., 5921 Court St. Rd.(13221), pg. 1070
THE PYRAMID COMPANIES, The Clinton Exchange, 4 Clinton Sq.(13202), pg. 901
Quanta Advertising Corporation, 968 James St.(13203), pg. 225
Syracuse China Corp., 2900 Court St.(13221), pg. 1065
SYRACUSE SUPPLY COMPANY, 5921 Court St. Rd.(13221), pg. 1070
Syracuse Supply Construction & Equipment Division, Colvin Station 294, P.O. Box 37(13205), pg. 1070
Syracuse Supply Industrial Products Division, 5921 Court St. Rd.(13201), pg. 1070
Syracuse Supply Leasing Co., Inc., 5921 Court St. Rd., P.O. Box 4945(13221), pg. 1070
Telmark, Inc., P.O. Box 4943(13221), pg. 25
VENTRE PACKING COMPANY, INC., 6050 Court St. Rd.(13206-1730), pg. 1147

Tarrytown

AMPACET CORPORATION, 660 White Plains Rd.(10591), pg. 67
CARQUEST CORPORATION, 580 White Plains Rd.(10591), pg. 224
KANE-MILLER CORP., 555 White Plains Rd.(10591), pg. 616
Star Magazine, 660 White Plains Rd.(10591), pg. 611

Tonawanda

R. P. ADAMS COMPANY, INC., 225 E. Park Dr.(14150), pg. 16
Alro Specialty Metals, Tonawanda, 50 Ensminger Rd.(14150-6793), pg. 44
BRIMMS INC., 425 Fillmore Ave.(14150), pg. 176
CHEMCENTRAL/Buffalo, 3709 River Rd.(14150), pg. 241
Jorgensen Steel & Aluminum/Buffalo, 1275 Sheridan Dr.(14150), pg. 605
RONCO COMMUNICATIONS & ELECTRONICS INC., 595 Sheridan Dr.(14150), pg. 946
WSF INDUSTRIES, INC., 7 Hackett Dr.(14150), pg. 1156

Troy

At Home Respiratory and Medical, Inc., 6-102nd St.(12180), pg. 1070
The Family Insurance Agency, Inc., Second & State(12180), pg. 1117
The Family Investment Services Co., Inc., Second & State(12180), pg. 1117
The Family Mortgage Banking Co., Inc., Second & State(12180), pg. 1117
GARDEN WAY, INC., 102nd St. & 9th Ave.(12180), pg. 443
INTERSTATE COMMODITIES INC., 7 Madison St.(12181), pg. 580
KING FUELS INC., Foot Of Main St.(12181), pg. 630
LEVONIAN BROTHERS INC., 27 River St.(12180), pg. 671
Specialty Restaurants Corp., 377 River St.(12180), pg. 1029
STANDARD MANUFACTURING COMPANY, 750 Second Ave.(12182), pg. 1037
TS Capital Corp., Second & State(12180), pg. 1117
Troy Savings Bank-Hudson Valley Plaza, Vandenburgh Ave.(12180), pg. 1117
THE TROY SAVINGS BANK, Second & State(12180), pg. 1116
Troy SB Real Estate Co., Inc., Second & State(12180), pg. 1117

Uniondale

STATE-WIDE CAPITAL CORP., 152 EAB Plaza, W. Tower 7th Fl.(11556-0152), pg. 1041

Utica

COMMERCIAL TRAVELERS MUTUAL INSURANCE COMPANY, 70 Genesee(13502), pg. 269
LASER PRECISION CORP., 109 N. Genesee St.(13502), pg. 660
THE F. X. MATT BREWING CO., 811 Edward(13502), pg. 721
MELE MANUFACTURING CO., INC., 1712 Erie St.(13503), pg. 737
Monitor Life Insurance Company of New York, 70 Genesee St.(13502), pg. 269
Stetson-Harza, 181 Genesee St.(13501-2168), pg. 516
UNI-Service Operations Corporation, P.O. Box 530(13503), pg. 1141
UTICA BOILERS INC., 2201 Dwyer Ave.(13501), pg. 1140
Utica National Life Insurance Company, P.O. Box 530(13503), pg. 1141

Valhalla

Farrand Controls, 99 Wall St.(10595), pg. 955
RUHL COMPANIES, INC., 99 Wall St.(10595), pg. 955
TOLLMAN/HUNDLEY HOTELS, 100 Summit Lake Dr., 3rd. Fl.(10595), pg. 1100

Valley Cottage

FORD PRODUCTS CORPORATION, Ford Products Rd.(10989), pg. 423

Valley Stream

BALTIC LINEN COMPANY, INC., 260 W. Sunrise Hwy.(11582), pg. 116
SID HARVEY INC., 100 E. Mineola Ave.(11580), pg. 515
TRIANGLE MAINTENANCE CORPORATION, 71 S. Central Ave.(11580), pg. 1112

Vestal

CHEF ITALIA, INC., 2317 Vestal Pkwy., E.(13850), pg. 241
GREAT AMERICAN INDUSTRIES, INC., 300 Plaza Dr.(13850-3646), pg. 480

Wantagh

Meenan LI Div., 3020 Burns Ave.(11793), pg. 736

Waterford

Monsey Products Co., Inc., P.O. Box 340(12188), pg. 766

Watertown

JOHNSON NEWSPAPER CORPORATION, 260 Washington St.(13601), pg. 598
STEBBINS ENGINEERING & MFG. CO., 363 Eastern Blvd.(13601), pg. 1043

Watervliet

Hoboken Floors-Adirondack Division, 1397 Broadway(12189-3324), pg. 537
Hoboken Floors-A.S.T. Division, 1397 Broadway(12189-3324), pg. 537
Troy Savings Bank, Broadway & 16th St.(12189), pg. 1117

Waverly

Atlantic Lumber Company, P.O. Box 503(14892), pg. 965

West Hempstead

BELDOCH INDUSTRIES CORPORATION, 44 Cherry Valley Ave.(11552), pg. 133

West Henrietta

GENESEE METAL STAMPINGS, INC., 975 John St.(14586), pg. 451

West Nyack

ALLOY TECHNOLOGY INTERNATIONAL INC., 169 Western Hwy.(10994), pg. 41
Douglaston Electric, P.O. Box 348, Rte. 303(10994), pg. 1120
FISHER SKYLIGHTS, INC., 50 Snake Hill Rd.(10994), pg. 415
Scafa Tornabene, 100 Snakehill Rd.(10994), pg. 468

West Seneca

GILLOGLY CHEVROLET INC., 1777 Union Rd.(14224), pg. 459
Peter J. Schmitt Co., Inc., 355 Harlem Rd.(14224), pg. 977
PETER J. SCHMITT HOLDINGS, 355 Harlem Rd.(14224), pg. 976

Westbury

AID AUTO STORES, INC., 275 Grand Blvd.(11590-0281), pg. 26
Ames Automotive Warehouse, 275 Grand Blvd.(11590), pg. 26
Central Textile Div., 725 Summa Ave.(11590), pg. 720
COMPUTER INSTRUMENTS CORPORATION, 1000 Shames Dr.(11590), pg. 271
800-FLOWERS, 1600 Stewart Ave.(11590), pg. 371
FORTUNOFF, 1300 Old Country Rd.(11590), pg. 425
GENERAL WELDING SUPPLY CORPORATION, 400 Shames Dr.(11590), pg. 451
JOHN HASSALL, INC., P.O. Box 698, Cantiague Rock Rd.(11590), pg. 516
KING KULLEN GROCERY CO., INC., 1194 Prospect Ave.(11590), pg. 630
Lady Rose Div., 725 Summa Ave.(11590), pg. 720
Lord Bibb Div., 725 Summa Ave.(11590), pg. 720
MASTERS, INC., 725 Summa Ave.(11590), pg. 720
METPAR CORPORATION, 95 State St.(11590), pg. 742

NATHAN'S FAMOUS INC., 1400 Old Country Rd., Ste. 400(11590), pg. 784
SPECTRONICS CORPORATION, 956 Brush Hollow Rd.(11590), pg. 1029
Susan Terry Div., 725 Summa Ave.(11590), pg. 720

Westerlo

CLIFFORD B. HANNAY & SON INC., 600 E. Main St.(12193), pg. 505

Westfield

NATIONAL GRAPE CO-OP ASSOCIATION, INC., Two S. Portage St.(14787), pg. 789

Whippany

Stephen Gould Paper Co., Inc., 35 S. Jefferson Rd.(07981), pg. 474

White Plains

Allied Security Inc. (Westchester Operation), 110-122 Mamaroneck Ave., Ste. 6(10601), pg. 40
AMERICAN SAVINGS BANK, 99 Church St.(10601), pg. 60
ASSOCIATED METALS & MINERALS CORP., 3 N. Corporate Park Dr.(10604), pg. 91
BROWNING CHEMICAL CORPORATION, 707 Westchester Ave.(10604), pg. 183
BRUNSCHWIG & FILS, INC., 75 Virginia Rd. N.(10603), pg. 184
Career Blazers of White Plains, Inc., 202 Mamaroneck Ave.(10605), pg. 218
CHILEWICH PARTNERS, 12 Water St.(10601), pg. 248
COLIN SERVICE SYSTEMS, INC., 1 Brockway Place(10601), pg. 261
COMBE INCORPORATED, 1101 Westchester Ave.(10604), pg. 267
CORHAM, INC., 300 Central Ave.(10106), pg. 286
Henningsen Foods, Inc., 2 Corporate Park Dr.(10604), pg. 629
M. KAMENSTEIN, INC., 190 E. Post Rd.(10601), pg. 615
Kearney-National, Inc., 5 Corporate Park Dr.,Ste.114(10604-3805), pg. 357
NATIONAL ATTORNEYS TITLE INSURANCE COMPANY, 111 Church St.(10601), pg. 786
PECKHAM INDUSTRIES, INC., 20 Haarlem Ave.(10603), pg. 854
Petals, 300 Central Ave.(10606), pg. 286
MALCOLM PIRNIE, INC., 2 Corporate Park Dr.(10602), pg. 872
RAIL EUROPE INC., 226-230 Westchester Ave.(10604), pg. 910
STEINBACH, 535 Old Tarrytown Rd.(10603), pg. 1045

White Stone

AUSTRIAN AIRLINES, 17-20 White Stone Expy.(11357), pg. 100
WHITE ROCK PRODUCTS CORP., 16-16 White Stone Expwy.(11357), pg. 1186

Whitehall

Troy Savings Bank-Whitehall, 184 Broadway(12887), pg. 1117

Williamsville

CIMINELLI DEVELOPMENT COMPANY, INC., 350 Effjay Rd., Ste. 101(142221), pg. 249

Woodbury

ERM-Northeast, Inc., 175 Froehlich Farm Blvd.(11797), pg. 360
LACKMAN FOOD SERVICE, 303 Crossways Park Dr.(11797), pg. 650
OVERSEAS MILITARY SALES CORPORATION, 100 Crossways Park W.(11797), pg. 833
SEAMAN FURNITURE CO., INC., 300 Crossways Park Dr.(11797), pg. 986

Woodside

Pierre Cardin Formal Wear, 57-07 31st Ave.(11377), pg. 1177
West Mill Clothes, H.M.C. Div., 57-07 31st Ave.(11377), pg. 1177
WEST MILL CLOTHES, INC., 57-07 31st Ave.(11377), pg. 1177

Wyandanch

JAMECO INDUSTRIES, INC., 248 Wyandanch Ave.(11798), pg. 588

Wyoming

MARKIN TUBING, INC., Pearl Creek Rd.(14591), pg. 709

Yonkers

Aeroclo Metal Products, 700 Nepperham Ave.(10703), pg. 886
AMERICAN SPECIALTIES INC., 441 Saw Mill River Rd.(10701), pg. 61
COAST MANUFACTURING COMPANY, 200 Corporate Blvd.(10701), pg. 257
HEALTH VITAMIN COMPANY, INC., 1060 Nepperhan Ave.(10703), pg. 521
LKI, 495 S. Broadway(10705), pg. 645
PRECISION VALVE CORPORATION, 700 Nepperham Ave.(10703), pg. 885
Stewart Stamping Corp., 630 Central Park Ave.(10704), pg. 571

NORTH CAROLINA

Aberdeen

JPS Carpet Corp., P.O. Box A, Hwy. 5(28315), pg. 586

Albemarle

C&A Automotive Group, P.O. Box 580(28001), pg. 262

Altamahaw

Glen Raven Mills, Inc.-Consumer Products Division, P.O. Box 8, 3730 Altamahaw-Union Ridge Rd.(27202), pg. 461
Glen Raven Mills, Inc.-Consumer Products Division, 3730 Altamahaw-Union Ridge Rd., P.O. Box 8(27202), pg. 461
Glen Raven Mills, Inc.-Glen Touch Plant, P.O. Box 278, 3726 Altamahaw-Union Ridge Rd.(27202), pg. 461
Glen Raven Mills, Inc.-Glen Touch Plant, 3726 Altamahaw-Union Ridge Rd., P.O. Box 278(27202), pg. 462

Anderson

Glen Raven Mills, Inc.-Custom Fabrics Division-Equinox Finishing Plant, 107 Service Rd.(29621), pg. 461

Asheboro

KLAUSSNER CORPORATION, Lewallen St.(27203), pg. 634
Klaussner Furniture Industry, Lewallen St.(27203), pg. 634

Asheville

INGLES MARKETS, INC., Hwy. 70, P.O. Box 6676(28816), pg. 568
MCGUFFEY'S RESTAURANTS, INC., 13 Kenilworth Knoll(28805), pg. 729
PRICE/MCNABB, INC., One N. Pack Square(28801), pg. 888
REVCO SCIENTIFIC INC., 275 Aiken Rd.(28804), pg. 930

Belmont

Belmont Dyers Company, 10 Linestowe Dr.(28012), pg. 740
Delmont Div., 100 E. Woodrow Ave.(28012), pg. 849

Beulaville

National Spinning Co., P.O. Box 49, (28518), pg. 793

Biscoe

MYRICK CONSTRUCTION INC., Shady Oak Dr.(27209), pg. 780

Burlington

CAROLINA BIOLOGICAL SUPPLY CO., 2700 York Rd.(27215), pg. 222
COPLAND FABRICS, INC., P.O. Box 1208(27216), pg. 284
HOLT HOSIERY MILLS, INC., 2119 W. Webb Ave.(27216), pg. 541
STAR FOOD PRODUCTS, INC., 727 S. Spring St.(27215), pg. 1039
WBBB, Box 1119, 1109 Tower Dr.(27216), pg. 306
WPCM, Box 1119, 1109 Tower Dr.(27216), pg. 306

Burnsville

Glen Raven Mills, Inc.-Filament Fabrics Div., Hwy. 19 E., Drawer 100(28714), pg. 462
Glen Raven Mills, Inc.-Filament Fabrics Division, Drawer 100, Highway 19 East(28714), pg. 461

Cary

AEROGLIDE CORPORATION, 100 Aeroglide Dr.(27511), pg. 22
BAHLSEN INC., One Quality Lane(27513), pg. 114
Borg-Warner Automotive Electronic Sensors-Cary, P.O. Box 580, 406 Gregson Drive(27511), pg. 166
Lord Research Corporation, 407-T Gregson Dr.(27511), pg. 683
SAS INSTITUTE INC., SAS Campus Dr.(27513-2414), pg. 959
C.G. Sargents Sons, 100 Aeroglide Dr.(27511), pg. 22

Chapel Hill

FGI, 700 Eastowne Dr.(27514), pg. 394
RTMX-UNIFLEX INC., 800 Eastowne Dr., Ste. 111(27514), pg. 908

Charlotte

AEA, INC., 700 W. 28th St.(28206), pg. 3
AEA Inc./Auto Parts, 700 W. 28th St.(28206), pg. 3
Admiration Hosiery Mills, Inc., 4210 Yancey Rd.(28217), pg. 534
Allied Security Inc., One Idlewild Office Park, 6101 Idlewild Rd., Ste. 117(28212), pg. 39
ALLISON-ERWIN CO. INC., 2920 N. Tryon St.(28206), pg. 40
Allright Parking Charlotte, Inc., 129 W. Trade St., Suite 720(28202), pg. 42
Alro Specialty Metals, Charlotte, 2300 Distribution St.(28203), pg. 44
AMERICAN BARMAG CO., 1101 Westinghouse Blvd.(28241), pg. 49
Aratex Services, 2321 Wilkerson Blvd.(28208), pg. 6
BJ ACQUISITION CORP., 9600 H. Southern Pine Blvd.(28273), pg. 107
BARNHARDT MANUFACTURING CO., 1100 Hawthorne Ln.(28205), pg. 120
BELK STORES SERVICES INC., 2801 W. Tyvola Rd.(28217-4500), pg. 134
Binswanger Southern, 230 S. Tryon St., Ste. 930(28202), pg. 152
Broadway & Seymour, 128 S. Tryon St.(28202), pg. 370
C-B CORPORATION, 1531 Tarhill Rd.(28201), pg. 198
CRP Hose Division, 1900 Wilkinson Blvd.(28208), pg. 909
Carolina Absorbent Cotton Co., 1100 Hawthorne Ave.(28205), pg. 120
CAROLINA TRACTOR & EQUIPMENT CO., 9000 Stateville Rd.(28213), pg. 223
Central All Pro, 1323 Central Ave.(28206), pg. 3
COGENTRIX INCORPORATED, 9405 Arrowpoint Blvd.(28273), pg. 258
Collins & Aikman Textile Group, 701 McCullough Dr.(28262), pg. 262
Consolidated Engravers-East, Inc., P.O. Box 28233, (28233), pg. 357
Consolidated Group, Inc., P.O. Box 33669, (28233), pg. 357
Consolidated Screen-Makers, Inc., P.O. Box 28233, (28233), pg. 357
The William Cook Agency, Inc., Two First Union Center, 301 S. Tryon St., Ste. 310(28202), pg. 282
CROWDER CONSTRUCTION CO., 1123 E. 10th St.(28230), pg. 301
Day Engineering, 6302 Fairview Rd.(28210), pg. 320
Delmar Photographic and Printing Company, 9601 Monroe Rd.(28212), pg. 279
Delmar Studios, 9555 Monroe Rd.(28222), pg. 279
THE DOWNS GROUP, INC., 120 Greenwich Rd.(28211), pg. 348
Duff-Norton, 9415 Pioneer Ave.(28217), pg. 1032
Eckerd Drug Co., 1776 Statesville Ave.(28231), pg. 366
Erdle Perforating of Carolina, 10721 John Price Rd.(28217), pg. 385
FORMS & SUPPLY, INC., 1733 University Commercial Place(28213), pg. 424
FREDRICKSON MOTOR EXPRESS CORP., 3400 N. Graham St.(28206), pg. 430
GAS-FIRED PRODUCTS, INC., 305 Doggett St.(28203), pg. 444
General Latex & Chemical Corp (N.C.), P.O. Box 5487(28225), pg. 449
GEORGETOWN INDUSTRIES, INC., 1901 Roxborough Rd., Suite 200(28211), pg. 453
Gold Bond Building Products, 2001 Rexford Rd.(28211), pg. 790
Stephen Gould of Carolina, Inc., 9741-D Southern Pine Blvd.(28210), pg. 474
Hendrick Imports, 6950 E. Independence Blvd.(28212), pg. 529
HENDRICK MANAGEMENT CORPORATION, P.O. Box 18649, 6000 Monroe Rd., Ste. 100(28218), pg. 529
HIGHLAND MILLS INC., 340 E. 16th St.(28233), pg. 534
J.M. Huber, Wood Products Div., Mallard Creek Ctr. III-Ste.175, 8604 Cliff Cameron Dr.(28269), pg. 550
Joanna, 8701 Red Oak Blvd.(28217), pg. 200
John Wieland Homes of Charlotte, Inc., 8349-K Arrowridge Blvd.(28273), pg. 1189
Jorgensen Steel & Aluminum/Charlotte, 3731-I Woodpark Blvd.(28206), pg. 605
Kilsby-Roberts/Charlotte, 4015 Westinghouse Blvd.(28273), pg. 606
Lee Construction Co., P.O. Box 240927(28231), pg. 788
LOEFFLER KETCHUM MOUNTJOY, 7401 Carmel Exec. Park Dr.(28226), pg. 680
MAGICSILK, INC., 15150 Stateline Dr.(28273), pg. 700
MEDIA POWER, INC., 5009 Monroe Rd.(28205), pg. 734
Mid Atlantic Construction, Inc., 5701 N. Sharon Amity Rd.(28215), pg. 943
NATIONAL GYPSUM COMPANY, 2001 Rexford Rd.(28211), pg. 790
NATIONAL WELDERS SUPPLY CO. INC., 810 Gesco St.(28208), pg. 794
NuArc Co., 501 Archdale Dr., Ste. 209(28210), pg. 817
Arnold Palmer Cadillac Inc., 501 S. Caldwell St.(28202), pg. 719
PEPSI-COLA BOTTLING COMPANY OF CHARLOTTE INC., 2820 South Blvd.(28209), pg. 860
PERFORMANCE CONTRACTING GROUP, 5435 Seventy Seven Center Dr., Ste. 10(28217), pg. 861
Performance Contracting, Inc., 5435 Seventy Seven Center Dr., Ste. 10(28217), pg. 861
Pic'n Pay Stores, Inc., 10301 Old Monroe Rd.(28261), pg. 201
Piedmont Auto Exchange, 406 W. 6th St.(28206), pg. 3
Piedmont-White Mop Co., 321 Atando Ave.(28201), pg. 1186
PNEUMAFIL CORP., 4500 Chesapeake Dr.(28216), pg. 878
Pony Express Courier Corp., 5550 77 Centre Dr., Ste. 320(28217), pg. 166
LAT PURSER & ASSOCIATE, 901 S. Kings Dr., Suite 901
RADIATOR SPECIALTY COMPANY, 1900 Wilkinson Blvd.(28208), pg. 909
REPUBLIC ALLOYS, INC., 419 Atando Ave.(28206), pg. 927
ROBERTSON MARKETING INC., 803 Pressley Rd., Ste. 104(28217-0971), pg. 939
RODGERS BUILDERS, INC., 5701 N. Sharon Amity Rd.(28215), pg. 942
ROMANOFF INTERNATIONAL, INC., Ste. 100, 511111 Carmel Commons Blvd.(28226-3919), pg. 945
ROWE CORP., 1123 S. Church St.(28203), pg. 952
SOUTHERN PUMP & TANK CO. INC., 4800 N. Graham St.(28213), pg. 1022
SPECIALIZED MEDIA SERVICES, INC., 741 Kenilworth Ave., Ste. 204(28204), pg. 1027
SUNOX, INC., 4236 Statesville Rd.(28269), pg. 1062
Tekra Corp., Southeast Div., 10900-D S. Commerce Blvd.(28273), pg. 1084
Tencarva Machinery Company, 4108 Park Rd, Ste. 215(28209), pg. 1087
THERMO INDUSTRIES INC., 4300 Golf Acres Dr.(28208), pg. 1091
WSOC Radio, Inc., 1901 N. Tryon St.(28206), pg. 293
WSOC Television, Inc., 1901 N. Tryon St.(28206), pg. 293
Wing Industries Southeastern, 3353 La Salle(28216), pg. 1196

WRAY-WARD-LASETER ADVERTISING, 1100 E. Morehead St.(28204), pg. 1204

Cherryville

P/M Bearing Div., Sunbeam Indus. Park(28021), pg. 628
TRW-Keystone Powder Metal Products Co., Sunbeam Industrial Park(28021), pg. 628

Clarkton

Mount Vernon Mills, Inc., Clarkton, NC, (28433), pg. 844

Clemmons

EDGAR B. FURNITURE CO., P.O. Box 849(27012), pg. 368

Cliffside

COLONIAL PETROLEUM CO., P.O. Box 307, (28024), pg. 264
Petroleum World, Hwy. 120(28024), pg. 264

Clinton

LUNDY PACKING CO. INC., P.O. Box 49(28328), pg. 687

Concord

GESSNER INDUSTRIES, 384 Faggart Ave.(28025), pg. 455
S&D COFFEE INC., 300 U.S. Hwy. 29 S.(28025), pg. 959
Showell Farms, Inc., P.O. Box 248(28026), pg. 1001

Conover

KROEHLER FURNITURE MANUFACTURING COMPANY, INC., 1800 Conover Blvd.(28613), pg. 645

Cornelius

Curon, P.O. Box 188(28031), pg. 1121

Creedmoor

Creedmoor Manufacturing Division, , pg. 45

Dallas

First Choice Homes, Hwy. 321 North, P.O. Box 375(28034), pg. 594
Hays Flood Controls, P.O. Box 580, 114 Eason Rd.(28034-0580), pg. 945
JEWELL BUILDING SYSTEMS, P.O. Box 397(28034), pg. 594
Romac Industries, Inc., Hays Division, 114 Eason Rd.(28034-0580), pg. 945

Dover

Sid Eagle Associates, P.O. Box 308, (28526), pg. 546

Dunn

CURVCRAFT, 600 Powell Ave.(28334), pg. 306
Tomahawk Farms, Inc., 603 S. Wilson Ave.(28334), pg. 687

Durham

Integral Systems, 1000 Park Forty Plaza, Ste. 500(27713), pg. 573
NORTH CAROLINA MUTUAL LIFE INSURANCE CO., 411 W. Chapel Hill St.(27701), pg. 813
NORTH CAROLINA MUTUAL WHOLESALE DRUG CO., 816 Ellis Rd.(27703), pg. 813
Servitex, Inc., 1720 Lawson(27703), pg. 787
WEST, PAUSBACK & VAUGHAN, INC., 3101 Petty Rd., Ste. 1000(27707), pg. 1177

Elizabeth City

Agrinet Farm Radio Network, 179 Lovers Ln.(27909), pg. 914
RAY COMMUNICATIONS, INC., 179 Lovers Ln.(27909), pg. 914
Ray Satellite Network, 179 Lovers Ln.(27909), pg. 914
Ray Sports Network, 179 Lovers Ln.(27909), pg. 914

Elkin

Chatham Manufacturing Company, 304 E. Main St., (28621), pg. 202
Chatham Smith Corp., East Main St.(28621), pg. 202

Farmville

Eastern Tobacco Co., P.O. Box 166(27828), pg. 766
A.C. MONK CO., INC., P.O. Box 166(27828), pg. 766
Monk-Henderson Tobacco Co., P.O. Box 166(27828), pg. 766
Wendel Tobacco Co., P.O. Box 166(27828), pg. 766

Fayetteville

PUTT PUTT GOLF COURSES OF AMERICA, INC., Putt Putt Bldg., 3007 Ft. Bragg Rd.(28303), pg. 901
Southern Golf Distributors, Inc., 2913 Ft. Bragg Rd.(28303), pg. 901

Fletcher

Tencarva Machinery Co.-Asheville, 230-6 Rutledge Road(28732-9325), pg. 1087

Forest City

Henson Timber Products Corp., Duke Street(28043), pg. 1051

Gastonia

BRYANT SUPPLY COMPANY, INC., 605 E. Franklin Blvd.(28054), pg. 185
GURNEY INDUSTRIES INC., 619 E. Price Ave.(28054), pg. 495
Norwesco Components Div., Box 3876, (28052), pg. 816
PARKDALE MILLS, 1630 W. Garrison Blvd.(28053), pg. 849
Uniroyal Chemical Co., Inc., 214 West Ruby St.(28054), pg. 1129

Glade Valley

Topaka Scientific Safety Co., P.O. Box 486(28627), pg. 871

Glen Raven

GLEN RAVEN MILLS, INC., 1831 N. Park Ave.(27217), pg. 461
Glen Raven Mills, Inc., 1821 North Park Ave., P.O. Box 4268(27217), pg. 461
Glen Raven Mills, Inc.-Custom Fabrics Div., 1831 North Park Ave.(27217-1100), pg. 462
Glen Raven Mills, Inc.-Custom Fabrics Division, .831 North Park Ave(27217-1100), pg. 461
Glen Raven Mills, Inc.-Glenspun Div., 142 Glen Raven Rd.(27217-1100), pg. 462
Glen Raven Mills, Inc.-Glenspun Division, 142 Raven Rd.(27217-1100), pg. 461
Glen Raven Mills, Inc.-Park Ave. Finishing Division, PO Box 4268, 1821 North Park Ave.(27215), pg. 461
Glen Raven Mills, Inc.-Textured Mills Group, Glen Touch Div., 1831 North Park Ave.(27217-1100), pg. 462
Glen Raven Mills, Inc.-Textured Yarn Group, Norlina Div., 1831 North Park Ave.(27217-1100), pg. 462
Glen Raven Mills, Inc.-Textured Yarn Group-Glen Touch Division, 1831 North Park Ave.(27217-1100), pg. 461
Glen Raven Mills, Inc.-Textured Yarn Group-Norlina Division, 1831 North Park Ave.(27217-1100), pg. 461
Glen Raven Mills, Inc.-Transportation Div., (Hwy. 87 North at Ossipee), 1831 Nroth Park Ave.(27217-1100), pg. 462
Glen Raven Mills, Inc.-Transportation Division, (Highway 87 N. at Ossipee), 1831 North Park Ave.(27217-1100), pg. 462
Glen Raven Mills, Inc.-Ultraspun Plant, 232 Glen Raven Rd.(27217-1100), pg. 461
Glen Raven Mills, Inc.-Ultraspun Plant, 232 Glen Raven Rd.(27217-1100), pg. 462

Godwin

MARTINS ABBATOIR & WHOLESALE MEATS INC., Hwy. 13(28344), pg. 716

Goldsboro

FRANKLIN BAKING CO., INC., 500 W. Grantham St.(27530), pg. 429
Kemp Furniture Co., 700 W. Elm St.(27530), pg. 257
T. A. LOVING COMPANY, 400 Patetown Rd.(27530), pg. 685
SOUTHCO DISTRIBUTING COMPANY, 701 Patetown Rd.(27530), pg. 1019
WGBR, 914 W. Grantham St.(27530), pg. 306
WKTC, 914 W. Grantham St.(27530), pg. 306

Graham

Perfection-Hy-Test Rebuilding Div., 426 Maple St.(27253), pg. 711

Greensboro

Allright Carolina, Inc., 102 N. Elm St., Ste. 626(27402), pg. 41
Aratex Services, 509 Teague St.(27406), pg. 6
Arnold Concrete Products-Greensboro, P.O. Box 3346, (27402), pg. 223
Binswanger, 1 Triad Center, Ste. 110, 7736 McCloud Rd.(27409), pg. 152
BLACK CADILLAC OLDS, INC., 601 E. Bessemer Ave.(27405), pg. 153
CBP RESOURCES, INC., 2410 Randolph Ave.(27406), pg. 199
CSC Erectors, Inc., Sandy Ridge Road(27402), pg. 223
Caribe Express, 6901 L. Downwind Rd.(27409), pg. 220
CARLYLE & CO. JEWELERS, 4615 Dundas Dr.(27407), pg. 222
Carolina By-Products Co., 2410 Randolph Ave.(27420), pg. 199
CAROLINA STEEL CORPORATION, 1451 S. Elm St.(27406), pg. 223
COMPEL MARKETING, INC., P.O. Box 35565, (27425), pg. 270
THE DISSTON CO., 7345 G. West Friendly Ave.(27410), pg. 339
DRAPER CORPORATION, 5644 Hornaday Rd.(27409), pg. 348
Elastic Fabrics of America, P.O. Box 21986, (27406), pg. 202
General Hardware Co.-Greensboro, 1010 Scott Ave.(27403), pg. 340
GENEVA CORPORATION, 300 N. Greene St.(27401), pg. 451
Greensboro News & Record, 200 E. Market St., P.O. Box 20848(27420), pg. 655
HALSTEAD INDUSTRIES, INC., 300 N. Green St., Ste. 400(27401), pg. 502
HENLEY PAPER COMPANY, 8400 Triad Dr.(27409), pg. 529
Kayser-Roth Hosiery, Inc., 4905 Koger Blvd.(27407), pg. 262
THE J.W. MOORE GROUP, 7025 Albert Pick Rd.(27409), pg. 768
Morflex, Inc., 2110 Highpoint Rd.(27403), pg. 923
Pyramid Chemical Company, Inc., 1008 N. Raleigh St.(27405), pg. 1090
REPLACEMENTS, LTD., P.O. Box 26029, (27420-6029), pg. 927
Rolane Corporation, P.O. Box 5407, (27403), pg. 263
Servitex, Inc., 123 W. Lewis St.(27406), pg. 787
Sheer Hosiery Div., 4905 Koger Blvd.(27407), pg. 263
Socks Division, 4905 Koger Blvd.(27407), pg. 263
SOUTHERN FOODS, INC., 3500 Old Battleground Rd.(27410), pg. 1021
Tencarva Machinery Co., 3409 W. Wendover Ave., Ste. 101(27407), pg. 1087
TENCARVA MACHINERY CO., INC., 3409 W. Wendover Ave.(27407), pg. 1086
TRONE ADVERTISING, INC., P.O. Box 35565, (27425), pg. 1115
W.H. WEAVER CONSTRUCTION CO., P.O. Box 26040-604(27420), pg. 1170

Greenville

EMPIRE BRUSHES, INC., U. S. Hwy. 13 North(27835), pg. 379
J. H. Hudson Construction Co., P.O. Box 1983(27834), pg. 31
FRED WEBB INC., N. Green St.(27834), pg. 1170

Harrisburg

Hendrick Motorsports, 5315 Stowe Lane(28075), pg. 529

Henderson

H&H International, Box 789(27536), pg. 511
Harriet & Henderson Cotton Co., 1724 Graham Ave.(27536), pg. 511
HARRIET & HENDERSON YARNS, INC., 1724 Graham Ave.(27536), pg. 511

Hickory

ALEX LEE, INC., 120 4th St., S.W.(28601), pg. 33
BRIAN CENTER MANAGEMENT CORPORATION, 1331 4th St. Dr., N.W.(28601), pg. 175
Capital Resources, 120 4th St., S.E.(28602), pg. 33
Carolina Steel-Hickory Plant, 1115 3rd Ave. N.W.(28601), pg. 223
CENTURY FURNITURE INDUSTRIES, 401 11th St., N.W.(28601), pg. 235
HICKORY CONSTRUCTION COMPANY, 1728 9th Ave., N.W.(28601), pg. 532
HICKORY PRINTING GROUP, INC., 542 Main Ave., S.E.(28602), pg. 533
Institution Food House, Inc., 700 12th St., N.W.(28601), pg. 33
Merchants Distributors, Inc., 120 4th St., S.W.(28601), pg. 33
Merchants Transport of Hickory, 543 12th St., N.W.(28601), pg. 33
Normag Corporation, P.O. Box 6010, Bethlehem Station(28603), pg. 145
PLASTIC PACKAGING, INC., 1246 Main Ave. S.E.(28601), pg. 875
SHUFORD MILLS, INC., P.O. Box 2228(28603), pg. 1001

High Point

AIR POWER, INC., 1430 Trinity Ave.(27260), pg. 27
ALMA INDUSTRIES, 1300 Prospect St.(27260), pg. 43
Austin Productions, Hamilton Wing, Space 99
Brayton International Inc., 255 Swathmore Ave.(27264), pg. 1044
BRYANT ELECTRIC COMPANY, INC., 1901 English Rd.(27262), pg. 185
THE BURRIS AGENCY, INC., 1208 Eastchester Dr., Ste. 130(27265), pg. 195
CENTRAL TRANSPORT INC., Uwharrie Rd.(27264), pg. 234
ELECTRONIC DATA MAGNETICS, INC., 210 Old Thomasville Rd.(27264), pg. 375
Harden Galleries, 1008 Baker Rd.(27263), pg. 508
HARRISS & COVINGTON HOSIERY MILLS, 2525 E. Green Dr.(27260), pg. 512
Hatteras Yachts, 2100 Kivett Dr.(27260), pg. 758
MARKWOOD INC., 667 W. Ward Ave.(27261), pg. 710
MARSH FURNITURE COMPANY, 1001 S. Centennial St.(27260), pg. 714
SLANE HOSIERY MILLS, INC., 313-315 S. Centennmial St.(27260), pg. 1010
Stanton Cooper, 667 W. Ward Ave.(27261), pg. 710
TATUM TOOMEY & WHICKER, 1820 Eastchester Dr.(27265), pg. 1080
THOMAS BUILT BUSES, INC., 1408 Courtesy Rd.(27260), pg. 1092
U.S. FURNITURE INDUSTRIES, INC., 1200 Surrett Dr.(27260), pg. 1136
Woodmark Originals, 1920 Jarrell Ave.(27261), pg. 710

Hope Mills

Automatic Service Co., P.O. Box 114D, Hwy. 301 So.(28348), pg. 8

Jacksonville

Automatic Service Co., 1596 Catherine Lake Rd.(28540), pg. 8

Jamestown

CHEMCENTRAL/Greensboro, 108 Oakdale Rd.(27282-0100), pg. 241

King

NEW FORTIS CORP., 151 Jefferson Church Rd.(27021), pg. 800

Kings Mountain

MAUNEY HOSIERY MILLS, INC., 20 Pine St.(28086), pg. 722

Kinston

COASTAL WHOLESALE, INC., 500 E. Grainger(28503), pg. 257
The Field Controls Company, 2308 Airport Rd.(28501), pg. 525
Glen Raven Mills, Inc.-Kinston Plant, P.O. Box 3485, 800 Manning St.(28502-3485), pg. 461
Leco Feed Mills, Inc., 609 Brite St.(28501), pg. 1170
RAYOVAC Corporation, 4300 Rouse Rd.(28501), pg. 915
Servitex, Inc., 717 Summit Ave.(28501), pg. 787

Laurinburg

WEWO, Box 529, Hwy. 74(28352), pg. 306
WMXF AM/FM, Box 529, Hwy. 74(28352), pg. 306

Lenoir

BERNHARDT FURNITURE CO., 1839 Morganton Blvd., S.W.(28645), pg. 144

Lexington

BINNING'S BUILDING PRODUCTS, INC., Walser Rd.(27292), pg. 151
COBLE DAIRY PRODUCTS CO-OP, 707 N. Main St., pg. 257
Computer Technologies, Inc., 317 Ridgecrest Dr.(27292), pg. 370
Mannington Ceramic Tile, Victor St.(27293), pg. 704

Lillington

Edwards Brothers - Carolina, 800 Edwards Dr.(27546), pg. 370

Lincolnton

COCHRANE FURNITURE CO., INC., Hwy. 321 N., Box 220(28092), pg. 258
J. H. HEAFNER CO. INC., 814 E. Main St.(28092), pg. 520

Lumber Bridge

Croft Metals, Inc. of NC, Hwy. 71(28357), pg. 300

Lumberton

THE OSTERNECK CO. INC., Hwy. 72 E.(28358), pg. 831

Madison

GEM-DANDY, INC., P.O. Box 657(27025), pg. 447

Maiden

CM Furniture, Inc., Hwy. 321 N.(28650), pg. 223
Carolina Maiden Corp., (28650), pg. 223
CAROLINA MILLS, INC., 618 Carolina Ave.(28650), pg. 223

Marion

Marion Machine Company Division, P.O. Box 1169(28752), pg. 1064

Matthews

CONBRACO INDUSTRIES INC., 701 Matthews-Mint Hill Rd.(28105), pg. 272
TMP Worldwide, Inc., 3425 Tatting Rd.(28105), pg. 1074

Maxton

COX FURNITURE, Highway 74 W.(28364), pg. 294

McAdenville

STOWE-PHARR MILLS, INC., 100 Main St.(28101), pg. 1052

Mebane

KINGSDOWN, INC., 126 West Holt St.(27302), pg. 632
THE MAY APPAREL GROUP, INC., Interstate 85(27302), pg. 723

Monroe

CTB, Inc., P.O. Box 5011(28111), pg. 336
Commercial Products, Inc., P.O. Box 400, (28110), pg. 336
Dickerson Carolina, Inc., P.O. Box 400, (28110), pg. 336
THE DICKERSON GROUP, INC., 1501 Charlotte Ave.(28111), pg. 335
Dickerson, Inc., P.O. Box 400, (28110), pg. 336
Dickerson Realty Corp., P.O. Box 400, (28110), pg. 336
PERFECT FIT INDUSTRIES, INC., 201 Cuthbertson St.(28110), pg. 861
RP & C, 701 Industrial Dr., pg. 272
South Atlantic Equipment, Inc., P.O. Box 5011(28111), pg. 336

Morganton

Carolina Shoe Company, P.O. Box 1079(28655), pg. 182
Case Farms, Inc., P.O. Box 308(28655), pg. 228

Morrisville

Computer Circuitry Group, Riverbiran Bldg., Ste. 307, 4709 Creekstone Dr.(27560), pg. 571
Stephen Gould of Carolina, Inc., 2500 Gateway Centre Blvd.(27560), pg. 474

Mount Airy

North Carolina Foam Industries, Inc., P.O. Box 1528, (27030), pg. 120
RENFRO CORP., 661 Linville Rd.(27030), pg. 926
SPENCER'S INC., 238 Willow St.(27030), pg. 1030

Mount Pleasant

TUSCARORA YARNS INC., 8760 E. Franklin St.(28124), pg. 1120

Newton

CAROLINA GLOVE CO., Drawer 820(28658), pg. 223

Norlina

Glen Raven Mills, Inc.-Norlina Plant, P.O. Box 518, Highway U.S. 1 South(27563), pg. 461

North Wilkesboro

CAROLINA MIRROR COMPANY, Hwy. 268 East(28659), pg. 223

Norwood

C&A Yarn Division, Hwy. 52(28128), pg. 262

Oxford

Arnold Concrete Products-Raleigh Div., P.O. Box 1604, (27565), pg. 223

Pine Hall

Halstead Metal Prods. Div., Hwy. 311(27042), pg. 502

Raeford

HOUSE OF RAEFORD FARMS, INC., 520 E. Central Ave.(28376), pg. 546

Raleigh

AEA of Raleigh, 1115 New Hope Rd.(27610), pg. 3
Aeroglide Americas International, Inc., P.O. Box 29505(27626), pg. 22
AEROTRON, INC., 4901 Capital Blvd.(27611), pg. 22
Allied Security Inc., 3948 Browning Pl., Ste. 200(27609), pg. 39
Binswanger, One Exchange Plaza, Ste. 708(27601), pg. 152
CAPITOL BROADCASTING CO., INC., 711 Hillsborough St.(27605), pg. 215
CAROLINA BUILDERS CORPORATION, 3227 Wellington Ct.(27615), pg. 223
CENTURY DATA SYSTEMS, 506 N. Harrington St.(27603), pg. 235
Creswell, Munsell, Fultz & Zirbel, 3100 Smoketree Court, Ste. 803(27604), pg. 1211
CURTIS MEDIA GROUP INC., 3012 Highwoods Blvd.(27604), pg. 305
ELECTRICAL EQUIPMENT COMPANY, 1440 Diggs Dr.(27603-2755), pg. 374
GAI Consultants-NC, Inc., 401 Glenwood Ave.(27603), pg. 439
General Parts, Inc., 2635 Millbrook Rd.(27604), pg. 224
GOLDEN CORRAL CORPORATION, 5151 Glenwood Ave.(27612), pg. 466
HOWARD, MERRELL & PARTNERS, INC., 8521 Six Forks Rd.(27615), pg. 547
INVESTOR'S MANAGEMENT CORP., 5151 Glenwood Ave.(27612), pg. 581
Kaiser Permanente, North Carolina Division, 3120 Highwoods Blvd.(27604-1018), pg. 614
MCKINNEY & SILVER, 333 Fayetteville Mall(27601), pg. 730
Montgomery-Green Co., 1200 New Hope Rd. Ext.(27620), pg. 344
NORTH CAROLINA EQUIPMENT CO., 3101 Hillsboro St.(27602), pg. 812
Oh! Brian's Rip Roarin' Ribs, P.O. Box 29511(27626), pg. 581
PINE STATE CREAMERY CO., 500 Glenwood Ave.(27628), pg. 871
ROCKETT, BURKHEAD, LEWIS & WINSLOW, 8601 Six Forks Rd.(27615), pg. 941
Ruder, Finn/Raleigh (NC), 3600 Glenwood Ave., Ste. 100(27612), pg. 954
Servitex, Inc., 3301 Hillsborough St.(27602), pg. 787
SOUTHERN CASE, INC., 2315 Laurelbrook St.(27604), pg. 1020
Sunbelt Lodging Development Co., 5151 Glenwood Ave.(27612), pg. 581
Sunstates Properties, Inc., 4600 Marriott Dr., Suite 200(27612), pg. 1062
SUNSTATES REALTY GROUP INC., 4600 Marriott Dr., Ste. 200(27612), pg. 1062
TRIDENT FINANCIAL CORPORATION, 4601 Six Forks Rd.(27609), pg. 1113
Unigard Indemnity Co., 3515 Glenwood Ave.(27612), pg. 596
Uniroyal Chemical Co., Inc., 158 Wind Chime Ct.(27609), pg. 1129
VARIETY WHOLESALERS, INC., 3401 Greshams Lake Rd.(27615), pg. 1146
WPTF, 3012 Highwoods Blvd.(27604), pg. 306
WQDR, 3012 Highwoods Blvd.(27604), pg. 306
WRAL-TV, 2619 Western Blvd.(27605), pg. 215
WARREN DISTRIBUTING CORP., 226 Glenwood Ave.(27603), pg. 1164

Reidsville

Elixir Industries, 1203 Freeway Dr.(27320), pg. 376

Research Triangle Park

ATCOM, INC., 4920 Alston Ave.(27709), pg. 93
Escod Industries, P.O. Box 12138, (27709), pg. 571

Roanoke Rapids

The Bibb Company-Roanoke Rapids Plant, Fifth & Jackson(27870), pg. 781

Rocky Mount

BNE Land & Development Co., P.O. Box 1908(27802-1908), pg. 161
BODDIE-NOELL ENTERPRISES INC., 1021 Noell Lane(27801), pg. 161
FRANCHISE ENTERPRISES INC., 1313 Hardees Blvd.(27804), pg. 428
LEWIS ADVERTISING, INC., 1050 Country Club Dr.(27804), pg. 673

Rose Hill

MURPHY FARMS INC., Hwy. 117(28458), pg. 776

Roxboro

Decorative Fabrics - Cavel, 1803 Main St.(27573), pg. 262
Triangle Parachute, 1335 Durham Rd.(27573), pg. 383

Rutherfordton

AAllied Die Casting Mfg., Inc., P.O. Box 1178(28139), pg. 906
TANNER CO. INC., Oak Springs Rd.(28139), pg. 1078

Salisbury

SAV-RITE ADVERTISING, 2110 Executive Dr.(28145), pg. 973

Sanford

J.T. DAVENPORT & SONS, INC., Hwy. 42 East(27330), pg. 317
LEE-MOORE OIL CO., INC., 1807 Douglas Dr.(27331), pg. 665
THE PANTRY, INC., 1801 Douglas Dr.(27331), pg. 846
WHITIN ROBERTS CO., 109 N. McNeil Rd.(27330), pg. 1187
Whitin Roberts Mfg. Div., (27330), pg. 1187

Scotland Neck

Gilbert & Bennett, P.O. Box 310(27874), pg. 458

Shelby

Doran Mill Co., Drawer A(28151), pg. 346
DORAN TEXTILES INC., Hwy. 226(28151), pg. 346
Specialty Lighting, Washburn Switch Rd.(28151), pg. 588

Siler City

Palm Harbor Homes, d/b/a V.P. Homes, Inc., Hwy. 421 N.(27344), pg. 843
Selig Manufacturing Company, Hwy. 421 N.(27344), pg. 294

Snow Hill

GSH Corp., 310 Kinggold Blvd.(28580), pg. 472

Sparta

PIONEER/ECLIPSE CORP., Eclipse Rd. & Hwy. 18N(28675), pg. 871

Spindale

Decorative Fabrics - Mastercraft, P.O. Box 125, (28160), pg. 262
Mitchell Co., 400 Spindale(28160), pg. 1051
Rutherford Warehouse Corp., P.O. Box 157, (28160), pg. 1051
STONECUTTER MILLS CORP., Dallas Street(28160), pg. 1051
Stonecutter Trucking Co., P.O. Box 157, (28160), pg. 1051

Stanley

GASTON COUNTY DYEING MACHINE CO., 200 S. Main St.(28164), pg. 444
NIAGARA THERAPY MFG. CORP., 1100 Hwy. 27 S.(28164), pg. 806
Showell Farms, Inc., P.O. Box 8(27355), pg. 1000

Star

CLAYSON KNITTING CO. INC., Hwy. 220 S.(27356), pg. 253

Statesville

TOTER INCORPORATED, 841 Meacham Rd.(28677), pg. 1103

Swannanoa

BEACON MFG. CO., P.O. Box 395(28778), pg. 129

Tabor City

Aberdeen Mfg. Corp. Savoy Plant, 8th & Wall St.(28463), pg. 200
WTAB, Hwy. 701 Bypass & Avon St.(28463), pg. 306
WYNA, Hwy. 701 Bypass & Avon St.(28463), pg. 306

Tarboro

BARNHILL CONTRACTING COMPANY, 2311 N. Main St.(27886), pg. 121
GLENOIT MILLS, INC., Hwy. 33 West(27886), pg. 462
Long Equipment Co., 1201 Northern Blvd.(27886), pg. 682
LONG MFG. NC, INC., 111 Fairview St.(27886), pg. 682
WCPS, Box 100, 3403 Main St.(27886), pg. 306

Valdese

Hickory Hill Furniture Corporation, 501 Hoyle St.(28690), pg. 816

Warrenton

Warrenton Division, P.O. Box 539(27589), pg. 258

Warsaw

CARROLL'S FOODS, INC., Hwy. 24 W.(28398), pg. 225
National Spinning Co., P. O. Box 545(28398), pg. 793

Washington

HACKNEY & SONS, INC., 400 Hackney Ave.(27889), pg. 498
National Spinning Co., P. O. Box 191(27889), pg. 793

Weaverville

A-B EMBLEM DIV. OF CONRAD INDUSTRIES, INC., P. O. Box 695(28787), pg. 2
Balcrank Products, 1 Balcrank Way(38787), pg. 801
Mount Vernon Mills, Inc., Mount Vernon Forming Fabrics, P.O. Box 607(28787), pg. 844

Welcome

WALKER & ASSOCIATES, INC., P.O. Box 1029(27374), pg. 1159

Weldon

COASTAL LUMBER COMPANY, Green St. Extension(27890), pg. 257

Whiteville

National Spinning Co., P.O. Box 547, (28472), pg. 793

Wilkesboro

ITHACA INDUSTRIES INC., Hwy. 268 W.(28697), pg. 582
Olympic Manufacturing Co., , pg. 209

Wilmington

BLOCK INDUSTRIES, INC., 525 N. College Rd.(28405), pg. 157
Heatcraft Refrigeration Products Division, 602 Sunnyvale Dr.(28403), pg. 667
MILLER BUILDING CORP., 1410 Commonwealth Dr.(28403), pg. 753
Remington Apparel, 1217 S. 13th St.(28401), pg. 926
REMINGTON APPAREL, INC., 1217 S. 13th St.(28401), pg. 926
Tencarva Machinery Co., 108 N. Kerr Ave., Ste.A1(28405), pg. 1087
WORSLEY COMPANIES INC., 10 Cardinal Dr.(28403), pg. 1204

Wilson

COASTAL DAIRY PRODUCTS, INC., 400 S. Douglas St.(27894), pg. 257
Dinner Bell Foods, Inc., 2401 Wilco Blvd.(27893), pg. 53
GNC Corp, 2600 Wilco Blvd.(27893), pg. 472
HACKNEY BROTHERS, INC., 301 N. Pender St.(27893), pg. 498
Wilson Service Center, 2711 Commerce Rd.(27893), pg. 223

Winston-Salem

American Inks & Coatings Corp., Ink Division, 3755 Kimwell Dr.(27103), pg. 56
D. D. Bean & Sons (N.C.) Inc., P.O. Box N93(27115), pg. 129
BEPCO, INC., 2475 S. Stratford Rd.(27103), pg. 141
Binswanger, NCNB Plaza, Ste. 300(27101), pg. 152
Carolina Steel-Salem Plant, 1725 Vargrave St.(27107), pg. 223
Flair Communications Agency, Inc., 150 Stratford Bldg., Ste. 280(20174), pg. 416
FLAKT INC., BAHNSON DIV., 3901 West Point Blvd.(27103), pg. 416
HANES COMPANIES, INC., 2000 W. First St.(27104), pg. 505
Laboratory Supply Company, 112 Griffith Plaza Dr.(27103), pg. 650
Lowe's Food Stores, Inc., 1381 Old Mill Circle, Ste. 200(27114-4908), pg. 33
PACE OIL CO., INC., 150 Stratford Court SW(27103), pg. 838
PARRISH TIRE COMPANY, INC., 8800 N. Point Blvd.(27106), pg. 850
Salem Carriers. Inc., 245 Charlois Blvd.(27103), pg. 967
Salem Leasing Corp., 245 Charlois Blvd.(27103), pg. 967
SALEM NATIONAL CORPORATION, 245 Charlois Blvd.(27103), pg. 967
Taracorp Imaco, Inc., P.O. Box S-Salem Station(27107), pg. 1078
Taylor Bros., 2415 Stratford Rd., S.W.(27103-0597), pg. 282
TAYLOR OIL CO. INC., 110 Oakwood Dr.(27103), pg. 1082
YOUNG-PHILLIPS SALES CO., 3250 Healy Dr.(27103), pg. 1210

Youngsville

CAPTIVE-AIRE SYSTEMS, INC., 120 Wheaton Dr.(27596), pg. 216

Zebulon

NCM Decoration, Inc., 501 NCM Drive(27597), pg. 781
NMC OF NORTH AMERICA, INC., 501 NMC Drive(27597), pg. 781
Wakelon Agri-Products, Inc., P.O. Box 676(27597), pg. 1170

NORTH DAKOTA

Bismarck

BANK OF NORTH DAKOTA, 700 E. Main St.(58502), pg. 117
BASIN ELECTRIC POWER CO-OP, 1717 E. Interstate Ave.(58501), pg. 125
MEYER BROADCASTING COMPANY, 200 Fourth St. N.(58501), pg. 746

Carrington

First American Bank & Trust, P.O. Box 108, (58421), pg. 173

Casselton

First American Bank, 11 Langer Ave. N.(58012), pg. 173

Dickenson

Williams Steel & Supply, 124 East 24th St.(58601), pg. 1191

Fargo

ALLOWAY MANUFACTURING, 1330 43rd. St., N.W.(58102), pg. 41
BORDER STATES INDUSTRIES, INC., 105 25th St. N.(58108), pg. 165
BORDER STATES PAVING, INC., Cass County Rd. 20(58102), pg. 165
CASS-CLAY CREAMERY, 1220 Main Ave.(58108), pg. 228
COLE PAPERS INC., 1300 38th St., N.(58108), pg. 260
FARGO CLINIC LTD., 737 Broadway(58123), pg. 399
FARGO GLASS & PAINT COMPANY, 1801 7th Ave. N.(58102), pg. 399
FORUM PUBLISHING COMPANY, P.O. Box 2020(58102), pg. 426
ROBERT GIBB & SONS, INC., 205 40th St. S.W.(58103), pg. 456
MID AMERICA STEEL, INC., 92 N. P Ave.(58102), pg. 750
G.L. NESS AGENCY, INC., 3100 13th Ave. South, Ste. 302(58103), pg. 798
Nodak Mutual Insurance Co., 1101 First Ave., N.(58102), pg. 808
NODAK MUTUAL INSURANCE COMPANY, 1101 First Ave., N.(58102), pg. 808
PIONEER MUTUAL LIFE INSURANCE COMPANY, 203 10th St., N.(58102), pg. 872
ROTT-KELLER SUPPLY CO., 65 28th St. S.(58103-0390), pg. 951
W.W. WALLWORK, INC., 4001 W. Main(58107), pg. 1161

Finley

FINLEY FARMERS GRAIN ELEVATOR COMPANY, Burlington Northern Right-of-Way(58230), pg. 411

Fort Totten

SIOUX MANUFACTURING CORP., P.O. Box 400(58335), pg. 1008

Grafton

First American Bank & Trust, P.O. Box 511, (58237), pg. 173

Grand Forks

AGSCO, INC., 2600 Mill Rd.(58206), pg. 4
MINN-DAK GROWERS, LTD., Highway 81 N.(58203), pg. 757
NODAK ELECTRIC CO-OP, 1405 First Ave., N.(58201), pg. 808
NORTH DAKOTA MILL & ELEVATOR ASSOCIATION, 1823 Mill Road(58201), pg. 813

Larimore

First American Bank, P.O. Box 599, (58251), pg. 173

Lisbon

First American Bank, P.O. Box 273, (58054), pg. 173

Minot

DAKCO DISTRIBUTORS, INC., 101 E. Central(58701), pg. 311
Dakota Drug, Inc., 28 N. Main St.(58701), pg. 311
First American Bank & Trust, 21st S.W.(58701), pg. 173
Midco Data Systems, Inc., 101 E. Central(58701), pg. 311
MINOT BUILDERS SUPPLY ASSOCIATION, 2626 Burdick Expwy., W.(58701), pg. 758
Nodak Distributor, 18 2nd St. N.E.(58701), pg. 311
Northland Sports Inc., P.O. Box 5009, 308 8th St. NE(58701), pg. 311
WESTLIE MOTOR COMPANY, 500 S. Broadway(58701), pg. 1183

Rugby

RUGBY FARMERS UNION ELEVATOR COMPANY, 105 E. Dewey St.(58368), pg. 955

Wahpeton

Blumhardt Manufacturing Company, W. Hwy 13(58075), pg. 1073
Wil-Rich Noble Company, W. Hwy 13(58075), pg. 1073

West Fargo

INTERSTATE PAYCO SEED COMPANY, 1215 Prairie Pkwy.(58078), pg. 580

OHIO

Akron

THE FRED W. ALBRECHT GROCERY CO., 2700 Gilchrist Rd.(44305), pg. 31
BASIC COMPUTER, 1585 Frederick Blvd.(44320), pg. 124
BillCom Automotive, 341 White Pond Rd.(44313), pg. 150
THE BRENLIN GROUP, 670 W. Market St.(44303), pg. 173
THE CEDARWOOD COMPANIES, 1765 Merriman Rd.(44313), pg. 230
COMMAND PLASTIC CORPORATION, 674 Carroll St.(44304), pg. 268
Contemporary Long Term Care, 341 White Pond Rd.(44313), pg. 150
The Genie Company, 2850 Gilchrist Rd.(44305), pg. 452
Gilcrest Storage, 2700 Gilcrest Rd.(44305), pg. 31
HARWICK CHEMICAL CORP., 60 S. Seiberling St., P.O. Box 9360(44305), pg. 515
HITCHCOCK-FLEMING & ASSOCIATES, INC., 500 Wolf Ledges Pkwy.(44311), pg. 536
Jobber Retailer, 341 White Pond Rd.(44313), pg. 150
KOCH ENGINEERING COMPANY, INC., 171 Kelly Ave.(44306), pg. 638
MALONE ADVERTISING, INC., 209 S. Main St.(44308), pg. 703
MCNEIL & NRM., INC., 96 E. Crosier St.(44311), pg. 732
Modern Tire Dealer, 341 White Pond Rd.(44313), pg. 150
R.C.A. RUBBER COMPANY, 1833 E. Market St.(44305), pg. 906
Republic Chemical Company, 60 So. Seiberling St.(44305), pg. 515
The Sacks Electrical Supply Co., 711 Johnston St.(44306), pg. 1123
Seven-Up Bottling Co. of Akron, 1477 Industrial Pkwy.(44310), pg. 179
THE SPRINGWALL MATTRESS CO., 1510 Bauer Blvd.(44305), pg. 1033
Uniroyal Chemical Co., Inc., 1745 Merriman Rd.(44313), pg. 1129

Alliance

THE GENIE COMPANY, 22790 Lakepark Blvd.(44601), pg. 452
RIM Development Center, 15825 Armour Rd.(44601), pg. 239
STAR BRONZE COMPANY, 803 Mahoning St.(44601), pg. 1039

Amherst

ED MULLINAX FORD, INC., P.O. Box 280(44001), pg. 775

Archbold

Allied Security Inc. (OH), 200 N. Defiance St.(43502), pg. 40
Dinner Bell Foods, Inc., (43502), pg. 53
Frozen Specialties, Inc., 601 McArthur(43502), pg. 1195
LUGBILL BROTHERS, INC., 1396 S. Defiance(43502), pg. 686
SAUDER MANUFACTURING CORPORATION, 600 Middle St.(43502), pg. 972
SAUDER WOODWORKING CO., 502 Middle St.(43502), pg. 972

Ashland

ABBOTT LABORATORIES/ASHLAND, 268 E. Fourth St.(44805), pg. 9
Atlas Bolt & Screw Company, 1628 Troy Rd.(44805), pg. 712
THE GARBER COMPANY, 600 Union St.(44805), pg. 442
General Latex & Chemical Corp (Ohio), P.O. Box 498(44805), pg. 449
THE NATIONAL LATEX PRODUCTS CO., 246 E. Fourth St.(44805), pg. 791

Ashtabula

CARLISLE RETAILERS, INC., 4509 Main Ave.(44004), pg. 220
MOLDED FIBER GLASS COMPANIES, 1601 W. 29th St.(44004), pg. 763

Aurora

Filmco Industries, Inc., 1450 S. Chillicothe Rd.(44202), pg. 383

Barberton

Leasing Services Corp., 24 Brown St.(44203), pg. 817
MALCO PRODUCTS, INC., 361 Fairview Ave.(44203), pg. 702
Novar Controls Corp., 24 Brown St.(44203), pg. 817
Novar Corp., 24 Brown St.(44203), pg. 817
NOVAR ELECTRONICS, 24 Brown St.(44203), pg. 817
Whiz Automotive Chemicals Div., 361 Fairview Ave.(44203), pg. 702

Batavia

Jeff Wyler Chevrolet Dealership, 1117 Rte. 32(45103), pg. 1206

Jeff Wyler Nissan Dealership, 1117 Rte 32(45103), pg. 1206

Beachwood

SPRINGER SCHMID GROUP, 24800 Chagrin Blvd., Ste. 300(44122), pg. 1033

Bedford

BEN VENUE LABORATORIES, INC., 270 Northfield Rd.(44146), pg. 138

Bedford Heights

IDEAL MACARONI COMPANY, 26001 Richmond Rd.(44146), pg. 562
OLYMPIC STEEL INC., 5080 Richmond Rd.(44146), pg. 825

Bellevue

American Baler Co., 200 Hickory St., P.O. Box 29(44811), pg. 102

Bellville

Armstrong Air Conditioning Inc., 421 Monroe St.(44813), pg. 667

Big Prairie

SeaLand Technology, 9030 Township Rd. 1043, 4th St.(44611), pg. 1081

Blacklick

COLUMBUS STEEL DRUM COMPANY, 1385 Blatt Blvd.(43004), pg. 267

Bluffton

TRIPLETT ELECTRICAL INSTRUMENT CORPORATION, 1 Triplett Drive(45817), pg. 1114

Bowerston

L. J. Smith, Inc., 35280 Scio-Bowerston Rd.(44695), pg. 710

Bowling Green

Marathon Special Prods., 13300 Van Camp Rd.(43402), pg. 706

Brecksville

ASHMAN ENTERPRISES, INC., 10100 Brecksville Rd.(44141), pg. 88
BIOPRODUCTS, INC., 8221 Brecksville Rd., Bldg. 152
Intergy, Inc., 10100 Brecksville Rd.(44141), pg. 88
KLECO CORP., 10147 Brecksville Rd.(44141), pg. 634

Bridgeport

SCOTT LUMBER COMPANY, 253 N. Lincoln Ave.(43912), pg. 983

Brooklyn Heights Village

Keystone Automotive Industries, Inc. - Brooklyn Hts., 1277 East Schaaf Rd.(44131), pg. 628

Brookville

BENCHMARK HOMES, INC., 630 Hay Ave.(45309), pg. 138

Bryan

BARD MFG. CO., 1914 Randolph Dr.(43506), pg. 119
OHIO GAS COMPANY, 200 W. High(43506), pg. 822
SPANGLER CANDY COMPANY, P.O. Box 71, (43506), pg. 1025

Bucyrus

Bucyrus Blades Inc., 260 E. Beal Ave.(44820), pg. 388
Transco Railway Products Inc., 820 Hopley St.(44820), pg. 1107

Cambridge

THE BENATTY CORPORATION, 61234 Southgate Rd.(43725), pg. 138
Rason Oil & Gas Corp., 61234 Southgate Pkwy.(43725), pg. 138

Canfield

RAINBOW HOME RENTALS, 5414 Youngstown-Warren Rd.(44406), pg. 910
STANDARD LAFARGE, 6715 Tippecanoe Rd.(44406), pg. 1036

Canton

A-E Division, 1243 Raff Rd., S.W.(44710), pg. 232
The Akro Corporation, 1212 7th St. S.W.(44707), pg. 262
Canton Aggregate Division, 1243 Raff Rd., S.W.(44710), pg. 232
CANTON DROP FORGE, 4575 Southway St. S.W.(44706), pg. 214
CENTRAL ALLIED ENTERPRISES, 1243 Raff Rd., S.W.(44710), pg. 232
FORMU-3 INTERNATIONAL, INC., 4790 Douglas Circle N.W.(44718), pg. 424
HOH-Ohio, 130 Dewalt N.W.(44702), pg. 497
HARRISON PAINT CORPORATION, 1329 Harrison Ave., S.W.(44706), pg. 512
HERCULES ENGINES, INC., 101 Eleventh, S.E.(44707), pg. 531
LUNTZ CORPORATION, 237 Tuscarawas St., E.(44702), pg. 687
Ohio Tar Asphalt, 1243 Raff Rd., S.W.(44710), pg. 232
REPUBLIC STORAGE SYSTEMS COMPANY INC., 1038 Belden Ave., N.E.(44705), pg. 928
Selco Trucking Co., 601 Fifth St. SE(44702), pg. 993
Sugardale Foods Inc., 1600 Harmont Ave., N.E.(44705), pg. 432
SUMMIT ENVIRONMENTAL GROUP, 115 Dewalt Ave. N.W.(44702), pg. 1058
SUPERIOR DAIRY, INC., 4719 Navarre Rd. S.W.(44706), pg. 1063
Youngstown Tire & Supply Company, 4900 Navarre Rd., S.W.(44707), pg. 1218
ZIEGLER TIRE & SUPPLY COMPANY, INC., 4900 Navarre Rd., S.W.(44706), pg. 1218

Carrollton

Wingfoot Films Corporation, P.O. Box 98, Garfield Ave., N.W.(44615), pg. 555

Celina

MERSMAN FURNITURE, 500 W. Wayne St.(45822), pg. 741

Chagrin Falls

Ivex Packaging Corporation-Chagrin Falls, P.O. Box 300, 218 Cleveland St.(44022), pg. 583
Total Management Systems, 147 Bell St.(44022), pg. 370

Chardon

THE CHARDON RUBBER CO., 373 Washington St.(44024), pg. 239
Webb-Triax Company, 215 Fifth Ave.(44024), pg. 1170

Chesterland

Channel Products, Inc., 7100-T Wilson Mills Rd.(44026), pg. 239

Cincinnati

Agricultural Insurance Company, 515 Main St.(45202), pg. 53
MIKE ALBERT LEASING, INC., 10340 Evendale Dr.(45241), pg. 31
Alex Fries, 1000 Redna Terrace(45215), pg. 654
All About Sports, 621 Wilmer Ave.(45226), pg. 1144
Allied Advertising, 9403 Kenwood Rd., Suite D-105(45242), pg. 37
Allied Security Inc., 1313 East Kemper Road, Ste. 154(45246), pg. 39
Allright Cincinnati, Inc., 435 Elm St., Room 530(45202), pg. 41
AMANO CINCINNATI, INC., 1733 Central Ave.(45214), pg. 46
American Empire Surplus Lines Insurance Company, 910 Dixie Terminal Bldg., 49 East Fourth St.(45202), pg. 53
AMERICAN FINANCIAL CORPORATION, One E. 4th St.(45202), pg. 52
American Financial Enterprises, Inc., One E. Fourth St.(45202), pg. 53
AMERICAN LAUNDRY MACHINERY INC., 5050 Section Ave.(45212), pg. 57
American Money Management Corporation, One E. Fourth St.(45202), pg. 53
American National Fire Insurance Company, 580 Walnut St.(45202), pg. 53
AMICO-Cincinnati Distr. Center, 5210 Duff Dr.(45246), pg. 29
BARDES CORP., 4730 Madison Rd.(45227), pg. 119
BAXTER HODELL DONNELLY PRESTON INC., 3500 Red Bank Rd.(45227-4188), pg. 127
Baxter Shirk Design Collaborative, 319 W. Fourth St., Ste. 200(45202), pg. 127
Baxter/Peas, 4460 Carver Woods Rd.(45242), pg. 127
BELCAN CORPORATION, 10200 Anderson Way(45242), pg. 133
BRENDAMOUR'S SPORTING GOODS CO., 4831 Spring Grove Ave.(45232), pg. 173
BUDCO GROUP INC., 1100 Gest St.(45203), pg. 186
THE BUSCHMAN CO., 10045 International Blvd.(45246), pg. 196
CARTWRIGHT COMMUNICATIONS CO., 7812 Red Sky Dr.(45249), pg. 227
Charter Oak Financial Corporation, 4445 Lake Forest Dr.(45242), pg. 491
CHELSEA MOORE COMPANY, Fifth Third Center, Ste. 2200, 511 Walnut St.(45202-3118), pg. 241
CHICAGO WEST PULLMAN CORPORATION, 2300 Star Bank Center(45202), pg. 246
Chicago West Pullman Financial Corporation, 2300 Star Bank Center(45202), pg. 246
Chicago West Pullman Heavy Industries, 2300 Star Bank Center(45202), pg. 246
Chiquita Brands, Inc., 250 East Fifth St.(45202), pg. 53
Chiquita Brands International, Inc., 250 E. Fifth St.(45202), pg. 53
THE CINCINNATI CORDAGE & PAPER COMPANY, 800 E. Ross Ave.(45217), pg. 249
CINCINNATI GEAR COMPANY, 5657 Wooster Pike(45227), pg. 250
Cincinnati Limousine Service Inc., 8639 Beechmont Ave.(45255), pg. 1198
CINCINNATI SUB-ZERO PRODUCTS, INC., 12011 Mosteller Rd.(45241-1528), pg. 250
CINCOM SYSTEMS, INC., 2300 Montana Ave.(45211), pg. 250
COGIFER INC., 5038 Beech St.(45212), pg. 259
Connector Industries of America, 10340 Julian Dr.(45246), pg. 749
CONSOLIDATED METAL PRODUCTS, INC., 1028 Depot St.(45204), pg. 276
THE CROCKER-FELS COMPANY, 1900 Stelton Rd.(45237), pg. 299
THE CROSSET COMPANY INC., 205 Central Ave.(45202), pg. 300
DWF of Cincinnati, Inc., 1220 Findley St.(45214), pg. 331
DEKTAS & EGER, INC., 30 W. Third St.(45202), pg. 325
Dempsey & Siders Insurance Agency, 7840 Montgomery Rd.(45236), pg. 53
C.S. Dent & Co., 317 E. 8th St.(45202), pg. 476
Dinner Bell Foods, Inc., 250 E. 5th St.(45202), pg. 53
ACE DORAN HAULING & RIGGING COMPANY, 1601 Blue Rock St.(45223), pg. 346
Dugan & Meyers Construction Co., 11110 Kenwood Rd.(45242), pg. 351
DUGAN & MEYERS INTERESTS, INC., 11110 Kenwood Rd.(45242), pg. 351
E & D Grain Marketing Co, 525 Carr St.(45203), pg. 359
EDI INTERNATIONAL, INC., 525 Carr St.(45203), pg. 359
The Early & Daniel Company, Inc., 525 Carr St.(45203), pg. 359
ENERFAB INC., 4955 Spring Grove Ave.(45232), pg. 381
F & W PUBLICATIONS, INC., 1507 Dana Ave.(45207), pg. 394
FMI Properties Corp., One E. 4th St.(45202), pg. 53
George E. Fern Company, 1100 Gest St.(45203), pg. 186
FIBRE GLASS-EVERCOAT COMPANY INC., 6600 Cornell Rd.(45242), pg. 408
FICKS REED COMPANY, 4900 Charlemar Dr.(45227), pg. 408
FORD DEVELOPMENT CORPORATION, 11148 Woodward Lane(45241), pg. 423
Fort Washington Investment Advisors, Inc., 550 E. Fourth St.(45202), pg. 1181
Frank Paxton Lumber Company, 7455 Dawson, Box 43334(45243), pg. 592
FREEDMAN, GIBSON & WHITE INC., 814 Plum St.(45202), pg. 430
GACC Holding Company, One E. Fourth St.(45202), pg. 53
GARDNER PUBLICATIONS, INC., 6600 Clough Pike(45244), pg. 443
THE GIBSON GROUP INC., 2727 Madison Road, Ste. 201(45209), pg. 456
GOLD MEDAL PRODUCTS CO., 2001 Dalton Ave.(45214), pg. 465
Stephen Gould of Ohio, Inc., 10227 Alliance Rd.(45242), pg. 474
GRANDPA BRANDS COMPANY, 317 E. 8th St.(45202), pg. 476
Grandpa Soap Co., 317 E. 8th St.(45202), pg. 476
Great American Broadcasting Company, One E. Fourth St.(45202), pg. 53
Great American Broadcasting Company, 1 E. 4th St., 6th Fl.(45202), pg. 52
Great American Communications Company, One E. Fourth St., 6th Fl.(45202), pg. 53
Great American Holding Corporation, 580 Walnut St.(45202), pg. 53
Great American Insurance Company, 580 Walnut St.(45202), pg. 53
Great American Management Services, Inc., One E. Fourth St.(45202), pg. 53
Great American Television & Radio Company, Inc., One E. Fourth St.(45202), pg. 53
GUARANTEE TITLE CO., INC., 4445 Lake Forest Dr., Suite 400(45242), pg. 491
Guyan Corp., 8044 Montgomery Ste. 157(45236), pg. 681
HVC/Daly Company, 4600 Dues Dr.(45246), pg. 612
THE HABEGGER CORPORATION, 4995 Winton Rd.(45232), pg. 498
HAMILTON MUTUAL INSURANCE COMPANY OF CINCINNATI, 1520 Madison Rd.(45206), pg. 503
THE HENNEGAN COMPANY, 1001 Plum St.(45202), pg. 529
Heritage Service Corporation, 65 E. Kemper Rd.(45246), pg. 491
HICKMAN WILLIAMS & CO. INC., Chiquita Center, 250 E. 5th St., Ste. 1110(45202), pg. 532
HILL & GRIFFITH COMPANY, 1262 State Ave.(45204), pg. 534
HUDEPOHL-SCHOENLING BREWING COMPANY, 1625 Central Pkwy.(45214), pg. 550
IFS Financial Services, Inc., 318 Broadway(45202), pg. 1181
Jake Sweeney Auto Leasing, Inc., 8276 Vine St.(45216), pg. 1067
Jake Sweeney Jeep Eagle, Inc., 11535 McGillard St.(45246), pg. 1067
JAY INSTRUMENT & SPECIALTY CO., 555 N. Wayne Ave.(45215), pg. 590
Jorgensen Steel & Aluminum/Cincinnati, 601 Redna Terrace(45215), pg. 605
John R. Jurgensen Co., 11641 Mosteller Rd.(45241), pg. 1143
K-D LAMP COMPANY, 1910 Elm(45210), pg. 612
KDI CORPORATION, 5721 Dragon Way(45227), pg. 612
KDI Precision Products, Inc., 3975 McMann Rd.(45245), pg. 612
Kings Island Company, One E. Fourth St.(45202), pg. 53
KINGS TOYOTA SUZUKI, 9500 Kings Automall Rd.(45249), pg. 631
THE KIRK & BLUM MFG. CO., 3120 Forrer St.(45209), pg. 633
KLOSTERMAN'S BAKING COMPANY, 4760 Paddock Rd.(45229), pg. 636
Kluener Foods Co., 113 Circle Freeway Dr.(45246), pg. 636
KLUENER PACKING COMPANY, 2842 Massachusetts Ave.(45225), pg. 636
LA ROSA'S, INC., 2334 Boudinot(45238), pg. 649
THE F. D. LAWRENCE ELECTRIC CO., 3450 Beekman St.(45223), pg. 661
A. J. Lehman Co., 317 E. 8th St.(45202), pg. 476
LOGAN & KANAWHA COAL CO., 8044 Montgomery Rd., Ste. 157(45236), pg. 681
LUKENHEIMER CO., Beekman & Waverly St.(45214), pg. 687

Lukenheimer Co.-Energo Valves, P.O. Box 14249, (45250), pg. 687
Chas. V. Maescher & Co., Inc., 2106 Florence Ave.(45206), pg. 700
Maescher Construction Co., 500 Reading Rd. .(45206), pg. 700
MAESCHER INDUSTRIES, INC., 2106 Florence Ave.(45206), pg. 699
Manhattan Life Insurance Company, 1876 Waycross Rd.(45240), pg. 1128
Manhattan National Corporation, P. O. Box 5353, (45201), pg. 1128
MARTINY & COMPANY, 8150 Corporate Park Dr.(45242), pg. 716
MCSWAIN CARPETS INC., 4730 Glendale-Milford Rd.(45242), pg. 733
MEDIA THAT WORKS, 455 Delta Ave.(45226), pg. 735
FRANK MESSER & SONS CONSTRUCTION CO., 4612 Paddock Rd.(45229), pg. 741
THE MIAMI MARGARINE CO., 5226 Vine St.(45217), pg. 746
MIAMI SYSTEMS CORPORATION, 10150 Alliance Rd.(45242), pg. 746
Mid-America CDM, Inc., 1329 Arlington St.(45225), pg. 513
MONARCH CONSTRUCTION COMPANY, 1654 Sherman Ave.(45212), pg. 765
Monitor Construction Co., P.O. Box 42337, (45242), pg. 351
John Morrell & Co., Chiquita Center, 250 E. 5th St.(45202), pg. 54
E.K. Morris & Co., Inc., 10270 Wayne Ave.(45215), pg. 86
Tom Moser Porsche Audi, Beechmont Ave.(45230), pg. 1198
R.A. MUELLER, INC., 11270 Cornell Park Dr.(45242), pg. 774
MUTUAL MANUFACTURING & SUPPLY CO., 3300 Spring Grove Ave.(45225), pg. 778
AL NEYER, INC., 3800 Red Bank Rd.(45227), pg. 805
THE NIELSEN COMPANY, 3731 Eastern Hills Lane(45209), pg. 807
NORTHLICH STOLLEY LAWARRE, 200 W. Fourth St.(45202), pg. 814
O/B Leasing Company, 1100 Gest St.(45203), pg. 186
ONE HOUR MARTINIZING DRY CLEANING FRANCHISE (SYSTEM), 2005 Ross Ave.(45212), pg. 826
Par Beverage Co., 317 E. 8th St.(45202), pg. 476
Parsec, 1100 Gest St.(45203), pg. 186
Parsec/Dotson, Inc., 1100 Gest St.(45203), pg. 186
PERRY & DERRICK CO., 2510 Highland Ave., Ste. 510(45212), pg. 863
Pets-N-Such, 621 Wilmer Ave.(45226), pg. 1144
Piggyback Services, Inc., 1100 Gest St.(45203), pg. 186
PLANES MOVING AND STORAGE, INC., 10115 Transportation Way(45246), pg. 874
PLASTIC MOLDINGS CORP., 2181 Grand Ave.(45214), pg. 875
THE WM. POWELL COMPANY, 2503 Spring Grove Ave.(45214), pg. 882
Queensgate Press, 3956 Virginia Ave.(45227), pg. 807
RANDOM CORPORATION, 581 Northland Rd.(45240), pg. 912
REECE-CAMPBELL, INC., 1718 Rafston Ave.(45223), pg. 920
RELIABLE CASTINGS CORPORATION, 3530 Spring Grove Ave.(45223), pg. 924
RIEMEIER LUMBER COMPANY, INC., 1528 Gest St.(45203), pg. 934
Riverside Development Corp., 11110 Kenwood Rd.(45242), pg. 351
ROBBINS, INC., 4777 Eastern Ave.(45226), pg. 938
ROUGH BROTHERS, INC., 5513 Vine St.(45216), pg. 952
RUTHMAN PUMP & ENGINEERING CO., 1212 Streng St.(45223), pg. 957
SABIN ROBBINS PAPER CO., 106 Circle Freeway Dr.(45246), pg. 965
SAKRETE, INC., Fischer Ave. & B&O RR(45217), pg. 967
Sealtron, Inc., 9705 Redding Rd.(45215), pg. 496
Senco Products, Inc., 8485 Broadwell Rd.(45244), pg. 989
Sentron Medical, Inc., 8485 Broadwell Rd.(45244), pg. 989
SETCO SALES COMPANY, 5880 Hillside Ave.(45233), pg. 993
Seven-Up Royal Crown-Canada Dry of Cincinnati, 5151 Fischer Ave.(45217), pg. 179
SHELBY & SHANE MARKETING COMMUNICATIONS, 300 W. Fourth St.(45202), pg. 996
Sive/Young & Rubicam, 36 E. Seventh St., Ste. 2500(45202), pg. 1211
SOUTHERN OHIO FABRICATORS, INC., 10333 Wayne Ave.(45215), pg. 1022
Specialty Underwriters, Inc., 122 Main St.(45242), pg. 54
Spelling Entertainment Group, Inc., One E. Fourth St.(45202), pg. 54
STANDARD TEXTILE CO., INC., 1 Knollcrest Dr.(45222), pg. 1037
STEGNER FOOD PRODUCTS CO., 5 Chili Hill Drive(45238), pg. 1045
STOCKTON WEST BURKHART INC., 401 E. Court St.(45202), pg. 1050
SUPERIOR LABEL SYSTEMS, INC., 11405 Grooms Rd.(45242), pg. 1063
Superior Machine Systems, 11405 Grooms Rd.(45242), pg. 1064
SURGICAL APPLIANCE INDUSTRIES, INC., 3960 Rosslyn Dr.(45209), pg. 1065
SWALLEN'S, INC., 5533 Fair Ln.(45227), pg. 1066
JAKE SWEENEY AUTO LEASING INC., 8276 Vine St.(45216), pg. 1066
JAKE SWEENEY AUTOMOTIVE INC., 33 W. Kemper Rd.(45246), pg. 1067
Telephone Directory Advertising, Inc.-Cincinnati, 2260 Park Ave.(45206-2710), pg. 1074
THOMSON MACCONNELL CADILLAC, INC., 2820 Gilbert Ave.(45206), pg. 1095
THRIFTWAY, INC., 4901 Hunt Rd.(45242), pg. 1095
Tidewater Grain Co., 525 Carr St.(45203), pg. 359
TOWNE PROPERTIES, 1055 St. Paul Pl.(45202), pg. 1104
THE UNION CENTRAL LIFE INSURANCE CO., 1876 Waycross Rd.(45240), pg. 1127
UNITED AIR SPECIALISTS, INC., 4440 Creek Rd.(45242), pg. 1130
UNITED DAIRY FARMERS, INC., 3955 Montgomery Rd.(45212), pg. 1131
THE UNITED STATES PLAYING CARD COMPANY, Beech & Park St.(45212), pg. 1136
VALLEY ASPHALT CORPORATION, 11641 Mosteller Rd.(45241), pg. 1143
VAN LEUNENS INC., 621 Wilmer Ave.(45226), pg. 1144
Vortec Corporation, 10125 Carver Rd.(45242), pg. 246
ASHLEY F. WARD, INC., 2530 Spring Grove Rd.(45214), pg. 1162
WARM BROTHERS CONSTRUCTION COMPANY, 2335 Florence Ave.(45206), pg. 1163
WESTERN & SOUTHERN LIFE INSURANCE CO., 400 Broadway(45202), pg. 1181
WHITING MANUFACTURING CO., INC., 9999 Carver Rd.(45242), pg. 1187
WITT COMPANY, 4454 Steel Pl.(45209), pg. 1198
Witt Galvanizing Division, 4454 Steel Pl.(45209), pg. 1198
Witt Products Division, 4454 Steel Pl.(45209), pg. 1198
BILL WOESTE DEALER GROUP, 8667 Beechmont Ave.(45254), pg. 1198
WOLF BLUMBERG KRODY INC., 19 Garfield Place(45202), pg. 1199
JEFF WYLER DEALER GROUP, INC., 829 Eastgate South Dr.(45245), pg. 1206
XTEK, INC., P.O. Box 415701, (45241), pg. 1206
C. W. ZUMBIEL COMPANY, 2339 Harris Ave.(45212), pg. 1221

Cleveland

A & W FOODS, INC., 4900 Crayton Ave.(44104), pg. 1
ACTRON MANUFACTURING COMPANY, 9999 Walford Ave.(44102), pg. 15
ADEC INTERNATIONAL AUTOMATION CORP., 1360 W. Ninth St., Suite 210(44113), pg. 17
ADVANSTAR COMMUNICATIONS, 7500 Old Oak Blvd.(44130), pg. 21
Allright Parking of Cleveland, Inc., 1276 W. 3rd, Suite 400(44113), pg. 42
AMERICAN TANK & FABRICATING CO., 12314 Elmwood Ave.(44111), pg. 63
ANCHOR TOOL & DIE COMPANY, 11830 Brookpark Rd.(44130), pg. 71
ANTARES GROUP INC., 4950 Harvard Ave.(44105), pg. 76
ARGO-TECH CORPORATION, 23555 Euclid Ave.(44117), pg. 82
Arocom Direct, Inc., 1350 Euclid Ave.(44115), pg. 737
Arocom Marketing Group, Inc., 1350 Euclid Ave.(44115), pg. 737
Atlas Lederer Co., P.O. Box 20190(44120), pg. 265
The Austin Company, 3650 Mayfield Rd.(44121), pg. 790
AUSTIN POWDER CO., 25800 Science Park Dr.(44122), pg. 99
AXELBAND & BROWN & ASSOCIATES INC., 24100 Chagrin Blvd.(44122), pg. 103
BARDONS & OLIVER, INC., 1133 West 9th(44113), pg. 119
BARON ADVERTISING, INC., 645 Hanna Bldg., 1422 Euclid Ave., Ste. 645(44115), pg. 121
Benjamin Moore & Co., 4400 E. 71st St.(44105), pg. 139
BETTCHER MANUFACTURING CORP., 16000 Commerce Park Dr.(44142), pg. 148
Bioproducts, Inc., 8221 Brecksville Rd., Bldg. 152
BLUE CORAL, INC., 1215 Valley Belt Rd.(44131-1451), pg. 159
BRAND, SHICK & WESLEY, 1250 Old River Rd.(44113), pg. 172
BRITTANY CORPORATION, 1770 Huntington Bldg.(44115), pg. 177
Bronze Headquarters, 1022-30 Berea Rd.(44102), pg. 520
BROWN DERBY, INC., 7850 Northfield Rd.(44146), pg. 181
C&A Wallcoverings, 23645 Mercantile Rd.(44122), pg. 262
CARNEGIE ASSOCIATES, INC., 6545 Carnegie Ave.(44103), pg. 222
Carryore, Limited, c/o Hanna Co., 100 Erieview Plaza, 36th Floor(44114), pg. 794
Catcher, 1140 Terminal Tower(44113), pg. 1206
Chandler Products, Inc., 1491 Chardon Rd.(44117), pg. 609
The Cleveland Builders Supply Co., 2100 W. 3rd St.(44113), pg. 1036
CLEVELAND MACHINE CONTROLS, 7550 Hub Pkwy.(44125), pg. 255
Cole Key Corporation, 5340 Avion Park Dr.(44143), pg. 260
COLE NATIONAL CORPORATION, 5915 Landerbrook Dr.(44124), pg. 260
Columbia Iron & Metal Co., 6600 Grant Ave.(44105), pg. 265
COLUMBIA NATIONAL GROUP, INC., 6600 Grant Ave.(44105), pg. 265
Condor Tool & Die, Inc., 4541 Industrial Pkwy.(44135), pg. 72
Container Port Group, 1340 Depot St., Ste. 103(44116), pg. 1203
Crain's Cleveland Business, 700 West St. Clair(44113), pg. 295
THE CRAWFORD GROUP, 26650 Lakeland Blvd.(44132), pg. 297
CRES-COR/CROWN-X, 12711 Taft Ave.(44108-1683), pg. 298
DRI Industries, 4944 Commerce Pkwy.(44128), pg. 666
Det. Division of National Guardian & Beechwood Security of Cleveland, , pg. 491
DIX & EATON INCORPORATED, 1010 Euclid Ave.(44115), pg. 341
DONLEY'S, INC., 5430 Warner Rd.(44125), pg. 345
THE ELWELL-PARKER ELECTRIC CO., 4205 St. Clair Ave.(44103), pg. 378
EMERALD CORPORATION, 1775 E. 45th St.(44103), pg. 378
ERICO INTERNATIONAL, 30000 Aurora Rd. 386
Euclid Crane Division, 1365 Chardon Rd.(44117), pg. 644
Excel Media Services Inc., 1350 Euclid Ave.(44115), pg. 737
THE FLORISTS ASSN. OF GREATER CLEVELAND, INC., 1070 Hanna Bldg.(44115-2001), pg. 421
FREEMAN MANUFACTURING & SUPPLY COMPANY, 1246 W. 70th St.(44102), pg. 431
FREEWAY CORPORATION, 9301 Allen Dr.(44125), pg. 432
Stephen Gould OH, 4350 Emery Industrial Pkwy.(44128), pg. 474
GREAT LAKES CONSTRUCTION CO., 6600 Schaaf Rd.(44131), pg. 481
GREAT LAKES LITHOGRAPH CO., 4005 Clark Ave.(44109-1186), pg. 481
Griswold, Inc., Landmark Office Towers, 101 Prospect Ave., West(44115), pg. 950
HWH ARCHITECTS ENGINEERS PLANNERS INC., 1150 W. Third St.(44113), pg. 498
Hansen Coupling Division, 4050 W. 150th St.(44135), pg. 1120
HASELOW & ASSOCIATES, INC., 5885 Landerbrook Dr.(44124), pg. 516
Havens & Emerson, Inc., 700 Bond Court Bldg., 1300 E. Ninth St.(44114), pg. 661
HINKLEY LIGHTING INC., 12600 Berea Rd.(44111), pg. 535
Hurst Performances, Inc., 8700 Brook Park Rd.(44129), pg. 761
INTERNATIONAL GEAR CORPORATION, 23555 Euclid Ave.(44117), pg. 578
INTERNATIONAL MANAGEMENT GROUP (IMG), One Erieview Plaza, Ste. 1300(44114), pg. 578
THE JAYME ORGANIZATION, INC., One Corporate Exchange, 25825 Science Park Dr.(44122), pg. 591
JERGENS INC., 19520 Nottingham Rd.(44110), pg. 593
JONES, DAY, REAVIS & POGUE, North Point, 901 Lakeside Ave.(44114), pg. 603
Jorgensen Steel & Aluminum Cleveland, 26400 Richmond Rd.(44146), pg. 605
Kaiser Permanente, Ohio Division, North Point Tower, Ste. 1200, 1001 Lakeside Ave.(44114), pg. 614
KANEX, 3121 Bridge Ave.(44113), pg. 616
David Kay, Inc., 4509 Taylor Ln.(44128), pg. 426
KEN-MAC METAL, INC., 17901 Englewood Dr.(44130), pg. 622
Kirkwood Carbon, 4855 W. 130th St.(44135), pg. 633
Kirkwood Commutator, 4855 W. 130th St.(44135), pg. 633
Kirkwood Foreign Sales Corp., 4855 W. 130th St.(44135), pg. 633
KIRKWOOD INDUSTRIES, INC., 4855 W. 130th St.(44135), pg. 633
JOHN KLEIN & ASSOC., INC., 20700 Miles Ave.(44128), pg. 635
Korn/Ferry International, Eaton Center, 1111 Superior Ave., Ste. 1300(44114), pg. 642
LAWLER-HAVENS INC., 700 Bond Court Bldg., 1300 E. Ninth St.(44114), pg. 661
LEICHTUNG, INC., 4944 Commerce Pkwy.(44128), pg. 666
LIGGETT-STASHOWER, INC., 1228 Euclid Ave.(44115), pg. 675
Luria Bros. Division, 20521 Chagrin Blvd.(44122), pg. 275
MAN-GILL CHEMICAL COMPANY, 23000 St. Clair Ave.(44117), pg. 703
MARCUS ADVERTISING, INC., 25700 Science Park Dr.(44122), pg. 706
Market Wyse, 1140 Terminal Tower(44113), pg. 1206
The Markey Company, 3316 W. 67th Pl.(44102), pg. 1
MCGEAN-ROHCO, INC., 2910 Harvard Avenue(44105-3010), pg. 729
MEGAS BEAUTY AIDS, INC., 15501 Industrial Pkwy.(44135), pg. 737
Meldrum & Fewsmith Advertising Inc., 1350 Euclid Ave.(44115), pg. 737
MELDRUM & FEWSMITH COMMUNICATIONS INC., 1350 Euclid Ave.(44115), pg. 737
Meldrum & Fewsmith Yellow Pages Inc., 1350 Euclid Ave.(44115), pg. 737
Mesaba-Cliffs Mining Co., Union Commerce Bldg., 14th Floor(44115), pg. 794
Metro Parking Systems, 1476 Davenport(44114), pg. 745
METROPOLITAN PROPERTIES INC., 1476 Davenport(44114), pg. 745
Midwest Mica, 4855 W. 130th St.(44135), pg. 633
MR. GASKET COMPANY, 8700 Brookpark Rd.(44129), pg. 761
MOONEY CHEMICALS, 2301 Scranton Rd.(44113), pg. 768
Nestaway Co., 9501 Granger Rd.(44125), pg. 8
Newburgh & South Shore Railroad Company, 4200 E. 71st St.(44105-5726), pg. 246
Nic Sand, 1215 Valley Belt Rd.(44131), pg. 159
THE NORTH AMERICAN MANUFACTURING CO., 4455 E. 71st St.(44105), pg. 811
NORTH AMERICAN REFRACTORIES COMPANY, 1228 Euclid(44115), pg. 811
North Coast Behavioral Research, 945 Terminal Tower(44113), pg. 1206
NuArc Co., 909 Oakland Park(43224), pg. 817
OHIO LOTTERY COMMISSION, 615 W. Superior(44113), pg. 822
OHIO MACHINERY CO., 3993 E. Royalton Rd.(44147), pg. 822
The Ohio Mattress Company Licensing And Components Group, 10th Fl., Halle Bldg., 1228 Euclid Ave.(44115), pg. 985
PBM OFFICE PRODUCTS, 7820 E. Pleasant Valley Rd.(44131), pg. 835
Pentron Products, Inc., 9999 Walford Ave.(44102), pg. 15
PERLMUTER PRINTING COMPANY, 4437 E. 49th St.(44125), pg. 862

Pinnacle Media, 1140 Terminal Tower(44113), pg. 1206
Predicasts, 11001 Cedar Ave.(44106), pg. 1219
PREFORMED LINE PRODUCTS, 660 Beta Dr.(44143), pg. 886
Presque Isle Corp., 1815 Republic Bldg.(44114), pg. 794
RADIX WIRE COMPANY, 26260 Lakeland Blvd.(44132), pg. 909
REALTY ONE, 6000 Rockside Woods Blvd.(44131-2350), pg. 917
THE ROTOR TOOL COMPANY, 26300 Lakeland Blvd.(44132), pg. 951
SEALY CORPORATION, c/o Sealy, Inc., 1228 Euclid Ave., 10th Fl.(44115), pg. 985
Sealy, Inc., 1228 Euclid Ave., 10th Fl.(44115), pg. 985
Simkins Carton Div.-Cleveland, 7275 Wentworth Ave.(44102), pg. 1005
Simoniz Canada Ltd., 1215 Valley Belt Rd.(44131-1415), pg. 159
Specialty Restaurants Corp., 20000 Brookpark Rd.(44135), pg. 1029
THE SPOHN CORPORATION, 1775 E. 45th St.(44103), pg. 1032
The Stearns & Foster Bedding Company, 1228 Euclid Ave.(44115), pg. 985
The Stearns & Foster Upholstery Furniture Company, 10th Fl., Halle Bldg., 1228 Euclid Ave.(44115), pg. 985
Sussen, Inc., 600 Carnegie Ave.(44103), pg. 225
Things Remembered, 5340 Avion Park Dr.(44143), pg. 260
TMP Worldwide, Inc., 614 Superior Ave. W., Ste. 1120(44113-1398), pg. 1074
Transilwrap Co., Inc., 4700 Manufacturing Rd.(44135), pg. 1107
U. A. Health Care Corporation, Bank One Bldg., 1255 Euclid Ave., Ste. 500(44115-1807), pg. 826
UNGER COMPANY, 12401 Berea Rd.(44111), pg. 1126
The Universal Steel Co., 6600 Grant(44105), pg. 265
VOSS INDUSTRIES, INC., 2168 W. 25th St.(44113), pg. 1155
WATT, ROOP & CO., 1100 Superior Ave., 13th Fl.(44114), pg. 1168
WYSE ADVERTISING, INC., 24 Public Square(44113), pg. 1206
Wyse Advertising/Cleveland, 24 Public Square(44113), pg. 1206
Wyse Direct, 1140 Terminal Tower(44113), pg. 1206

Columbiana

NRM CORPORATION, 400 W. Railroad St.(44408), pg. 781
Stearns & Foster Upholstery Furniture Co., 41995 W. Park Extension(44408), pg. 985

Columbus

ASC Trim, 1533 Alum Creek Dr.(43209), pg. 7
Alco Health Services Corporation-Columbus Div., 1200 E. 5th Ave.(43219), pg. 31
Allied Eastern Co., 1611 Integrity Dr.(43209), pg. 1217
ALLIED MINERAL PRODUCTS, INC., 2700 Scioto Pkwy.(43221), pg. 38
Allied Security Inc., 1550 Old Henderson Rd., Ste. N160(43220), pg. 39
Allright Columbus Parking, Inc., 145 N. High St.(43215), pg. 41
Battelle Development Corp., 505 King Ave.(43201), pg. 126
BATTELLE MEMORIAL INSTITUTE, 505 King Ave.(43201), pg. 126
Brooks Beverages Inc., 1900 E. Dublin-Granville Rd., Ste. 200-D(43229), pg. 179
BURGESS & NIPLE, LIMITED, 5085 Reed Road(43220), pg. 190
Columbus Life Insurance Co., 303 East Broad St.(43215), pg. 1181
COLUMBUS PIPE & EQUIPMENT COMPANY, 773 E. Markison Ave.(43207), pg. 267
COLUMBUS SHOW CASE COMPANY, 850 W. 5th Ave.(43212), pg. 267
CONCRETE CONSTRUCTION COMPANY, 886 McKinley Ave.(43222), pg. 273
CRANE PLASTICS COMPANY, 2141 Fairwood Ave.(43207), pg. 296
Dayton Rogers of Ohio, 2309 McGaw Rd. West(43207), pg. 321
DECOR CORPORATION, 1519 Alum Creek Dr.(43209), pg. 324
DESCO CORPORATION, 150 E. Campus View Blvd., Suite 250(43235), pg. 332
THE DISPATCH PRINTING COMPANY, 34 S. Third St.(43216-1289), pg. 339
ERM-Midwest, Inc., 450 W. Wilson Bridge Rd.(43085), pg. 360
EBCO MFG. COMPANY, 265 N. Hamilton Rd.(43213), pg. 365
ELECTRIC POWER EQUIPMENT CO., 60 E. Spring St.(43215), pg. 373
EVANS ADHESIVE CORP., 925 W. Henderson Rd.(43220), pg. 390
EXECUTIVE JET AVIATION, INC., 625 N. Hamilton Rd.(43219), pg. 393
Family Pharmacy General Office, 3220 Cleveland Ave.(43224), pg. 32
Gates, McDonald & Co., Three Nationwide Plaza, (43216), pg. 795
S. Gumpert Co., Inc., 3200 Riverside Dr.(43221), pg. 932
Gussini Shoe Stores, 6606 Tussing Rd.(43216-6751), pg. 638
HAMEROFF/MILENTHAL/SPENCE, INC., One Columbus, 10 W. Broad St.(43215), pg. 503
HARROP INDUSTRIES, INC., 3470 E. Fifth Ave.(43219), pg. 512
Health Services Plus, Inc., 5080 Sinclair Rd., Ste. 305(43229), pg. 32
HIGHLIGHTS FOR CHILDREN, INC., 2300 W. Fifth Ave.(43215), pg. 534
HOMEWOOD CORPORATION, 750 Northlawn Dr.(43214), pg. 542
Jeffrey Division, 274 E. First Ave.(43201), pg. 565
Kathe-K Shoe Stores, 6606 Tussing Rd.(43216-6751), pg. 638
Kinnear Door, P.O. Box 10823(43201), pg. 313
THE KOBACKER COMPANY & AFFILIATES, P.O. Box 16751, 6606 Tussing Rd.(43068), pg. 638
Le Cirque Optique, 649 Broad St.(43215), pg. 1118
LORD, SULLIVAN & YODER, INC. ADVERTISING, 250 Old Wilson Bridge Rd.(43085-0800), pg. 683
Meldrum & Fewsmith Advertising Inc., 37 W. Broad St., Ste. 480(43215), pg. 737
MICRO ELECTRONICS, 1555 W. Lane Ave.(43221), pg. 748
MIDLAND MUTUAL LIFE INSURANCE CO., 250 E. Broad(43215), pg. 751
MOTORISTS MUTUAL INSURANCE CO., 471 E. Broad(43215), pg. 773
NBBJ, 55 Nationwide Blvd.(43215), pg. 780
Nationwide Financial Services, Inc., One Nationwide Plaza, (43216), pg. 795
Nationwide Health Care Corp., One Nationwide Plaza(43216), pg. 795
Nationwide Life Insurance Co., One Nationwide Plaza(43216), pg. 795
NATIONWIDE MUTUAL INSURANCE COMPANY, One Nationwide Plaza(43216), pg. 795
NATIONWISE AUTOMOTIVE, INC., 3750 Courtright Ct.(43227), pg. 795
94th Aero Squadron of Columbus, Inc., Port Columbus Intl. Airport, 5030 Sawyer Rd.(43219), pg. 1029
Ohio Auto Auction, 3905 Jackson Pike(43123), pg. 293
OHIO TRANSMISSION CORPORATION, 666 Parsons Ave.(43206), pg. 822
Olen Corporation, 4755 S. High St.(43207), pg. 641
The Optical Shops, 64 E. Broad St.(43215), pg. 1118
P/M Structural Parts Div., 2100 Advance Ave.(43207), pg. 628
PSB Co., 555 W. Goodale St.(43215), pg. 1185
Patrini Shoe Stores, 6606 Tussing Rd.(43216-6751), pg. 638
Pebsco Inc., One Nationwide Plaza(43216), pg. 795
Picway Shoe Stores, 6606 Tussing Rd.(43216-6751), pg. 638
PLASKOLITE INC., 1770 Joyce Ave.(43219), pg. 874
PLASTIC SUPPLIERS, INC., 2887 Johnstown Rd.(43219), pg. 875
Plastic Suppliers, Inc. 2400 Marilyn Lane(43219), pg. 876
QUEEN OXYGEN COMPANY, 502 Schrock Rd.(43229), pg. 904
Republic Franklin Insurance Co., 2500 Corporate Exchange Drive(43229), pg. 1141
RE:SOURCE MARKETING, 515 N. Park St.(43215), pg. 929
SBC ADVERTISING, 707 Park Meadow Rd.(43081), pg. 960
SCHOTTENSTEIN STORES CORPORATION, 3241 Westerville Rd.(43224), pg. 978
Scientific Advances Inc., 601 W. 5th Ave.(43201), pg. 126
Seven-Up Royal Crown Canada Dry of Columbus, 950 Stelzer Rd.(43219), pg. 179
The Shoe Works Shoe Stores, Inc., 6606 Tussing Rd.(43216-6751), pg. 638
SHONAC CORPORATION, 1675 Watkins Rd.(43207), pg. 1000
Solidstate Controls, Inc., 875 Dearborn Dr., P.O. Box 1216(43085), pg. 712
Specialty Restaurants Corp., 2379 W. 5th St.(43204), pg. 1029
Specialty Restaurants Corporation, 679 W. Spring St.(43215), pg. 1029
Superior Die Tool And Machine Company, 2301 Fairwood Ave.(43207), pg. 455
TRANSMET CORPORATION, 4290 Perimeter Dr.(43228), pg. 1107
TUCKERMAN OPTICAL CO., 64 E. Broad St.(43215), pg. 1118
THE UNION FORK & HOE CO., 500 Dublin Ave.(43215), pg. 1128
Valley Fair & L.F. Widmann, 3241 Westerville Rd.(43224), pg. 978
Value City Furniture, 3421 Westerville Rd.(43224), pg. 978
Walker National, Inc., P.O. Box 18155(43218), pg. 1160
WASSERSTROM COMPANY, 477 S. Front St.(43215), pg. 1167
White Castle Distributing, Inc., 555 W. Goodale St.(43216), pg. 1185
WHITE CASTLE SYSTEM, INC., 555 W. Goodale(43215), pg. 1185
YENKIN-MAJESTIC PAINT CORPORATION, 1920 Leonard Ave.(43219), pg. 1208

Copley

PVS Chemicals, Inc., 3149 Copley Rd.(44321), pg. 838

Coshocton

Clow Water Systems Corp., P.O. Box 479, So. 6th St.(43812), pg. 733
JII/Sales Promotion Associates, Inc., 545 Walnut St.(43812), pg. 604

Cuyahoga Heights

American Steel & Wire Corporation, 4300 E. 49th St.(44125), pg. 246

Dayton

All World Travel Service, Inc., 111 West First St.(45402), pg. 373
ALLIED PAPER INCORPORATED, P.O. Box 125(45449), pg. 38
Allright Dayton Parking, Inc., 100 No. Jefferson(45402), pg. 41
Alro Group, Dayton, 821 Springfield St.(45403), pg. 44
Aratex Services, 1200 Webster(45404), pg. 6
Bee-Gee Shoe Div., 153 E. Helena St.(45404), pg. 373
DAVID K. BURNAP ADVERTISING AGENCY, INC., 7106 Corporate Way(45459), pg. 191
Casa Lupita Restaurants, Inc., P.O. Box 578, (45401), pg. 744
CASSANO'S INC., 1700 E. Stroop Rd.(45429), pg. 228
Cole-Layer-Trumble Company (CLT), 3199 Klepinger(45406), pg. 320
Danis Building Construction Group, 2 River Place, Ste. 100(45405), pg. 314
Danis Heavy Construction Group, 2 River Place, Ste. 200(45405), pg. 314
Danis Highway Construction Group, 1518 E. First St.(45402), pg. 314
DANIS INDUSTRIES CORPORATION, P.O. Box 1510, (45401), pg. 314
Dayton Newspapers, Inc., Fourth & Ludlow Sts.(45402), pg. 292
DIMCO-GRAY COMPANY, 8200 S. Suburban Rd.(45458), pg. 338
The El-Bee Chargit Corp., 3155 Elbee Road(45439), pg. 373
THE ELDER-BEERMAN STORES CORP., 3155 El-Bee Rd.(45439), pg. 373
GOSIGER INC., 108 McDonough St.(45402), pg. 472
Hewitt Soap Co., 333 Linden Ave.(45403), pg. 604
IAMS COMPANY, 7250 Poe Ave.(45414), pg. 561
Jorgensen Steel & Aluminum/Dayton, 2531 Needmore Rd.(45414), pg. 605
Peter Kuntz Company, Hulman Bldg., 120 W. Second, 10th Fl.(45402), pg. 360
Landisc Systems, 3199 Klepinger Rd.(45406), pg. 320
M & M Restaurant Supply, 3581 Dayton Park Dr.(45414), pg. 629
Miami Valley Broadcasting Corporation, d/b/a WHIO-TV, 1414 Wilmington Ave.(45420), pg. 292
P/O/N Product Corp., 1605 N. Main(45405), pg. 858
P/O/N Service Corp., 1605 N. Main St.(45405), pg. 858
PENNY/OHLMANN/NEIMAN, INC., 1605 N. Main St.(45405), pg. 858
PRICE BROTHERS CO., 367 W. 2nd St.(45402), pg. 888
PRIMUS INC., 3110 Kettering Blvd.(45439), pg. 890
Rich Products Dayton, 521 Kiser St.(45404), pg. 932
Seven-Up Bottling Co. of Dayton, 3131 Transportation Rd.(45404), pg. 179
Shook, Inc., 440 Hunter Ave.(45404), pg. 1000
SHOOK NATIONAL CORPORATION, 225 Lynwood St.(45405), pg. 1000
StacoEnergy Products Co., 301 Gaddis Blvd., (45403), pg. 270
UES, INC., 4401 Dayton-Xenia Rd.(45432), pg. 1122
VAN DYNE-CROTTY, INC., 903 Brandt St.(45401), pg. 1144
WDTN-TV, P.O. Box 741, 4595 S. Dixie Ave.(45401), pg. 522
WDTN Div., P.O. Box 741, 4595 S. Dixie Ave.(45401), pg. 522
WHIO, Inc., 1414 Wilmington Ave.(45420), pg. 292
WILLIS CASE HARWOOD, INC., 3411 Office Park Dr.(45439), pg. 1192
WOOLPERT CONSULTANTS, 409 E. Monument Ave.(45402), pg. 1201

Defiance

Diehl, Inc., 24 N. Clinton St.(43512), pg. 336
DIEHL SPECIALTIES INTL., 24 N. Clinton St.(43512), pg. 336
Motor Master Products, 815 Greenler St.(43512), pg. 1217
ZELLER CORP., 1307 Baltimore St.(43512), pg. 1216
Zeller World Trade Corporation, P.O. Box 278(43512), pg. 1217

Delaware

Countrymark Co-Op Inc., 4565 Columbus Pike, Rte. 23 N.(43015), pg. 290
Flexible Corp., 970 Pittsburgh Dr.(43015), pg. 449
THE FLEXIBLE CORP., 970 Pittsburgh Dr.(43015), pg. 421

Delphos

THE COMMERCIAL BANK, 230 E. Second St.(45833), pg. 268

Dover

COMMERCIAL & ARCHITECTURAL PRODUCTS INC., 202 Harger St.(44622), pg. 268
Dover Chemical Corp., P.O. Box 40, 15th & Davis Sts.(44622), pg. 558
GREER STEEL CO., 624 Blvd.(44622), pg. 486
Midwest Operations, P.O. Box 250(44622), pg. 268

Dublin

ACESS ENERGY CORPORATION, 655 Metro Place, S.(43017), pg. 12
BSB/Leff & Squicciarini, 94 N. High St., Ste. 300(43017), pg. 108
CoMed Management Inc., 525 Metro Place North(43017), pg. 802
GUNDER & ASSOCIATES, INC., 270 Bradenton Ave.(43017), pg. 494
Information Dimensions, Inc., 655 Metro Place South(43017), pg. 126
Insurance Intermediaries, Inc., 5774 Shier-Rings Rd.(43017), pg. 795
JONES, ANASTASI & BIRCHFIELD, 6065 Frantz Rd.(43017), pg. 602
REMARKS, INC., 7155 Post Rd.(43017), pg. 925
STANLEY STEEMER INTERNATIONAL, INC., 5500 Stanley Steemer Pkwy. P.O. Box 156(43017), pg. 1038

East Liverpool

THE HALL CHINA COMPANY, Anna Ave.(43920), pg. 501

East Sparta

D & H Tool and Die, 10505 Sandyville Rd. S.E.(44626), pg. 1135
Romany Ceramics Inc., (44626), pg. 1135
Sparta Mosaic, Inc., (44626), pg. 1135
UNITED STATES CERAMIC TILE CO., 10233 Sandyville Rd., SE(44626), pg. 1135

Edgerton

Edgerton Forge, Inc., 257 E. Morrison St., R.R. 2, Box 12(43517), pg. 102

Elyria

ELYRIA FOUNDRY COMPANY, 120 Filbert St.(44036), pg. 378
INDUSTRIAL GENERAL CORPORATION, Olive & Taylor Sts.(44035), pg. 566
TRIO PRODUCTS INC., 250 Warden Ave.(44035), pg. 1114

Euclid

STAMCO INDUSTRIES INC., 26650 Lakeland Blvd.(44132-2644), pg. 1035

Fairfield

AUTOMANAGE, 5449 Dixie Highway(45014), pg. 100
KRUSE HARDWARE COMPANY, 4275 Thunderbird Lane(45014), pg. 645
PEASE INDUSTRIES, INC., 7100 Dixie Hwy.(45014), pg. 854

Findlay

DIFCO, INC., 1501 N. Main St.(45840), pg. 337
FINDLAY INDUSTRIES, INC., 4000 Fostoria Rd.(45840), pg. 410
THE HERCULES TIRE & RUBBER COMPANY, 1300 Morrical Blvd.(45840), pg. 531

Fostoria

FOSTORIA INDUSTRIES, INC., 1200 N. Main St.(44830), pg. 427
GRAY PRINTING CO., 401 E. North St.(44830), pg. 479
ROPPE CORP., 1602-10 N. Union St.(44830), pg. 947
SENECA WIRE & MANUFACTURING CO., S. Vine St.(44830), pg. 989

Fredericktown

KOKOSING CONSTRUCTION COMPANY, INC., 17531 Waterford Rd.(43019), pg. 640
Kokosing Materials, Inc., P.O. Box 334, (43109), pg. 641

Fremont

THE FREMONT CO., 802 North Front(43420), pg. 432
LUDLOW COMPOSITES CORPORATION, 2100 Commerce Dr.(43420), pg. 686

Germantown

DUPPS COMPANY, 548 N. Cherry St.(45327), pg. 354

Greenfield

Computer Stock Forms, Inc., 324 S. Washington St.(45123), pg. 951
Waddell Div. of Ghent Mfg. Co., 512 S. Washington St.(45123), pg. 455

Greenville

TREATY CO., 501 Gray Ave.(45331), pg. 1109

Groveport

RICART FORD INC., 4255 S. Hamilton Rd.(43125), pg. 931
UNITED MCGILL CORP., One Mission Park(43125), pg. 1133

Hamilton

BROWERPEASE, INC., 900 Laurel Ave.(45023), pg. 181
CHEMCENTRAL/Cincinnati, 12 Standen Dr.(45015), pg. 241
LESHNER MILLS. INC., 1010 Eaton Ave.(45013), pg. 668
MOSLER INC., 1561 Grand Blvd.(45012), pg. 772
WESTERN STATES MACHINE CO., 1798 Fairgrove Ave.(45012), pg. 1181

Hannibal

OHIO RIVER ASSOCIATES, INC., State Rt. 7, 2 Miles N.(43931), pg. 822
Ormet Corporation, State Rt. 7, 2 Miles N(43931), pg. 822

Harrison

CINCINNATI INCORPORATED, 7420 Kilby Rd.(45030), pg. 250
HUBERT COMPANY, 9555 Dry Fork Rd.(45030), pg. 550

Hilliard

RED ROOF INNS, INC., 4355 Davidson Rd.(43026-2491), pg. 918

Hillsboro

ROTARY FORMS PRESS, INC., 835 S. High St.(45133), pg. 950

Hiram

WARREN TOOL GROUP, 11900 Winrock Rd.(44234), pg. 1165

Holland

GENERAL ALUM & CHEMICAL, 1145 Corporate Dr.(43528), pg. 448

Hubbard

TRUCK WORLD INC., 1610 Thomas Rd.(44425), pg. 1117
Valley Mould Div., P. O. Box 10(44425), pg. 749

Hudson

THE FLOOD COMPANY, 1212 Barlow Rd.(44236), pg. 419

Independence

Leader National Corporation, 4807 Rockside Rd.(44131), pg. 357
PBM Publishing, 7820 E. Pleasant Valley Rd.(44131), pg. 835
RESTAURANT DEVELOPERS CORP., 5755 Granger Rd., Ste. 200(44131-1410), pg. 929

Kent

CARTER-JONES LUMBER COMPANY, 601 Tallmadge Rd.(44240), pg. 226
THE DAVEY TREE EXPERT COMPANY, 1500 N. Mantua St.(44240), pg. 317
GOUGLER INDUSTRIES, INC., 705 Lake St.(44240), pg. 473
SCHNELLER, INC., 6019 Powder Mill Rd.(44240), pg. 977

Kettering

NEAL & STEPHENS ADVERTISING, INC., 417 E. Stroop Rd.(45429), pg. 796

Kinsman

TARGET STAMPED PRODUCTS CORP., 8091 State Rte. 5(44428), pg. 1079

Lakewood

WORLD SHIPPING, INC., 11740 Clifton Blvd.(44107), pg. 1203
ZAREMBA CORPORATION, 14600 Detroit Ave., Ste. 1500(44107), pg. 1216

Lancaster

DIAMOND ELECTRONICS, INC., P.O. Box 200, (43130), pg. 335

Lebanon

GHENT MANUFACTURING, INC., South Street at Cherry(45036), pg. 455

Lexington

NEER MANUFACTURING COMPANY, 265 S. Mill St.(44904), pg. 797

Liberty Center

Structural Foam Plastics, Cherry St.(43532), pg. 1054

Lima

Lima Electric Co., Inc., 200 E. Chapman Rd.(45802), pg. 706
Nickles Bakery Inc., Lima, 775 W. North St.(45801), pg. 807
Owners Insurance Co., 2325 N. Cole St.(45801), pg. 100
RUDOLPH FOODS COMPANY, 6575 Bellefontaine Rd.(45804), pg. 954

Lockland

The Stearns & Foster Bedding Company, 200 East Forrer St.(45215), pg. 985

Lorain

Gold Bond Building Products, 1901 Henderson Dr.(44052), pg. 790

Loveland

CINCINNATI UNITED CONTRACTORS, 9501 Union Cemetery Rd.(45140), pg. 250
TOTES INCORPORATED, 10078 E. Kemper Rd.(45140), pg. 1103

Macedonia

CENTURY PRODUCTS CO., 9600 Valley View Rd.(44056-9989), pg. 235
NORANDEX INC., 8450 S. Bedford Rd.(44056), pg. 809

Maineville

U.S. TURBINE CORPORATION, 7685 S. State Rte. 48(45039), pg. 1137

Malta

Taylor Woodcraft, Box 245, S. River Rd.(43750), pg. 178

Mansfield

Barnes Pumps, Inc., 1485 Lexington Ave.(44907), pg. 507
BRODHEAD-GARRETT CO., 223 S. Illinois Ave.(44905), pg. 178
Prudential-LMI Commercial Insurance Company, 900 Springmill Rd.(44906), pg. 897

Maple Heights

BOSTON DISTRIBUTORS, INC., 5700 S. Lee Rd. at Rockside Rd.(44137), pg. 167
Century 21 Kriss & Associates, 5473 Warrensville Center Rd.(44137), pg. 917
H.B.A. King Inc., Headquarters, 5700 Lee Rd.(44137), pg. 167
Seven-Up Bottling Co. of Cleveland, 14301 Industrial Ave. N.(44137), pg. 179

Marietta

THE AIROLITE COMPANY, 114 Westview Ave.(45750), pg. 28
BROUGHTON FOODS COMPANY, 210 N. 7th St.(45750), pg. 180

Marion

Acragage, 959 Cheney Ave.(43302), pg. 1069
Air-O-Matic Power Steer Co., 959 Cheney Ave.(43302), pg. 1069
Beacon Gage, 959 Cheney Ave.(43302), pg. 1069
Cyclo-Gard, 959 Cheney Ave.(43302), pg. 1069
Desco Advertising & Marketing, 959 Cheney Ave.(43302), pg. 332
Digitec, 959 Cheney Ave.(43302), pg. 1069
LevelAc, 959 Cheney Ave.(43302), pg. 1069
Marion Power Shovel Division, 617 W. Center St.(43302), pg. 565
Meco, 959 Cheney Ave.(43302), pg. 1069
NA-CHURS PLANT FOOD COMPANY, 421 Leader St.(43302), pg. 782
ServiceRecorder, 959 Cheney Ave.(43302), pg. 1069
StarMaster, 959 Cheney Ave.(43302), pg. 1069
SYCON CORPORATION, 959 Cheney Ave.(43302), pg. 1069
WestCon, 959 Cheney Ave.(43302), pg. 1069
WYANDOT INC., 135 Wyandot Ave.(43302), pg. 1205

Martins Ferry

Nickles Bakery, Inc., 1000 Broadway(43935), pg. 807

Marysville

THE SCOTT COMPANY, 14111 Scottslawn Rd.(43041), pg. 982

Mason

DEERFIELD MANUFACTURING CO., INC., 408 Fourth Ave.(45040), pg. 324
RELIANCE MEDICAL PRODUCTS, INC., 3535 Kings Mills Rd.(45040), pg. 925
STEELOX SYSTEMS, INC., 2412 Courseview, Dr., Ste. 300(45040), pg. 1044
SUGAR CREEK PACKING CO., 3476 Irwin-Simpson Rd. Ste. 119(45040), pg. 1056

Massillon

CAMPBELL OIL CO., 611 S. Erie(44646), pg. 213
E-B ADVERTISING DISPLAY INC., 2037 Wales Rd., N.E.(44646), pg. 358
Ecodyne MRM, Inc., 607 First St., SW(44646), pg. 712
FRESH MARK, INC., 1888 Southway S.E.(44646), pg. 432
Leann, Inc., Southway S.E.(44646), pg. 432
REPUBLIC ENGINEERED STEELS, INC., 410 Oberlin Rd., SW(44647), pg. 928
Superior's Brand Meats, 1888 Southway, S.E.(44646), pg. 432

Masury

Container Products Inc., 7838 Iron St.(44438), pg. 278

Materials Park

ASM INTERNATIONAL, (44073), pg. 8

Maumee

The Andersons Investment Services Corp., 1200 Dussel Dr.(43537), pg. 74
THE ANDERSONS, 1200 Dussel Dr.(43537), pg. 73
HICKORY FARMS, INC., 1505 Holland Rd.(43537), pg. 532
LAUERER MARKIN GIBBS, INC., 1725 Indian Wood Circle(43537), pg. 660
Ransom & Randolph Div., 120 W. Wayne St.(43537), pg. 330
THERMA-TRU CORP., 1684 Woodlands Dr., Ste. 150(43537), pg. 1090

Mayfield Heights

MILLS HALL WALBORN & ASSOCIATES, 5915 Landerbrook Dr.(44124), pg. 756
NESCO, INC., 6140 Parkland Blvd.(44124), pg. 798

Mayfield Village

IMC, Inc., 701 Beta Dr.(44143), pg. 1215
INTERNATIONAL SEAWAY TRADING CORPORATION, 6680 Beta Drive(44143), pg. 579
ZBS INDUSTRIES, INC., 701 Beta Dr.(44143), pg. 1215

Mechanicsburg

Champaign Landmark, 140 S. Main St.(43044), pg. 238
Scott Farm Seed Co., 50-56 Mill St.(43044), pg. 654

Medina

DISCOUNT DRUG MART INC., 211 Commerce Dr.(44256), pg. 339
HARCO TECHNOLOGIES CORPORATION, 1055 W. Smith Rd.(44256), pg. 507

NATIONAL SOLVENT CORPORATION, 955 W. Smith Rd.(44256), pg. 793
PAR INDUSTRIES, INC., 305 Lake Rd.(44258), pg. 847
PLASTI-KOTE COMPANY INC., 1000 Lake Rd.(44256), pg. 875
A.I. ROOT COMPANY, 623 W. Liberty St.(44256), pg. 946
TRU-FIT PRODUCTS CORP., 460 Lake Rd.(44256), pg. 1117

Mentor

Aviation Product Support Inc., 7600 Tyler Blvd.(44060-4853), pg. 635
CYBEREX, INC., 7171 Industrial Park Blvd.(44060), pg. 307
Mentor AGVS, Inc., 8500 Station St.(44060), pg. 893
PRODUCTION MACHINERY CORPORATION, 8500 Station St.(44060), pg. 893
SENTINEL CONSUMER PRODUCTS, INC., 7750 Tyler Blvd.(44060), pg. 990

Miamisburg

DIGITRON TOOL CO., INC., 8641 Washington Church Rd.(45342), pg. 337
FLYNN/SABATINO, 9049 Springboro Pike(45342), pg. 421

Middleburg Heights

Allied Security Inc., 7123 Pearl Rd., Ste. 309(44130), pg. 39
Reserve Motion Control Systems, 6908 Engle Rd.(44130), pg. 162

Middlefield

Duncan Toys Company, 15981 Valplast Rd.(44062), pg. 810
Flambeau Products Corp., 15981 Valpast Rd.(44062), pg. 809

Middletown

AKERS PACKAGING SERVICE INC., 2820 Lefferson Rd.(45044), pg. 28
The Black Clawson Company, 605 Clark St.(45042), pg. 154
THE CRYSTAL TISSUE CO., 3120 S. Verity Pkwy.(45042), pg. 303
EvsWater Industrial Systems, 500 N Verity Pkwy.(45042), pg. 712
McGraw/Kokosing, Inc., P.O. Box 370, (45042), pg. 641

Milan

Automotive Aftermarket Division, 11617 State Rte. 13(44846), pg. 432
Clevite Elastomers, 33 Lockwood Rd.(44846), pg. 899

Milford

BIGG'S HYPER SHOPPES, INC., 25 Whitney Dr., Ste. 122(45150), pg. 150
FRAZIER-WILLIAMS CHEVROLET GEO, 1099 Lila Ave.(45150), pg. 430

Millbury

Guardian Transportation Corp., P.O. Box 162, Moline Martin Rd.(43447-0162), pg. 492

Millersburg

SEMAC INDUSTRIES INC., County Rd. 407(44654), pg. 989

Minerva

Mapleton Development, Inc., P.O. Box 240(44657), pg. 136

Minster

THE MINSTER MACHINE COMPANY, 240 W. Fifth St.(45865), pg. 759

Monroe

BAKER CONCRETE CONSTRUCTION, INC., 900 N. Garver Rd.(45050), pg. 115

Moreland Hills

DEVELOPERS DIVERSIFIED, 34555 Chagrin Blvd.(44022), pg. 333

Mount Gilead

HPM CORPORATION, 820 Marion Rd.(43338), pg. 497

Mount Hope

WAYNE DALTON CORPORATION, 4576 County Rd., 160(44660), pg. 312

Navarre

ALFRED NICKLES BAKERY, INC., 26 Main St.(44662), pg. 806

Nelsonville

JOHN W. BROOKS INC., 294 Harper St.(45764), pg. 180

New Philadelphia

The Gradall Co., 406 Mill Ave.(44663), pg. 559

New Vienna

Packaging Resources, Inc., 5566 New Vienna Rd.(45159), pg. 497

Newark

ENGLEFIELD, INC., 447 James Parkway(43055), pg. 382

Newbury

THE GREAT LAKES CHEESE CO., 9988 Kinsman Rd.(44065), pg. 481
NEWBURY INDUSTRIES, INC., 10975 Kinsman Rd.(44065), pg. 803

Niles

Gold Bond Building Products, 504 Walnut St.(44446), pg. 790

North Canton

CAMELOT MUSIC, INC., 8000 Freedom Ave., NW(44720), pg. 212
HAINES & CO., INC., 8050 Freedom Ave., N.W., Box 500
356th Fighter Group, Akron-Canton Airport, 2787 Mt. Pleasant Rd.(44720), pg. 1029

North Ridgeville

The Tobin Corporation, 35544 Lorain Rd.(44939), pg. 102

North Royalton

H & D STEEL SERVICE, INC., 9960 York-Alpha Dr.(44133), pg. 495

Norwalk

NORWALK FURNITURE CORPORATION, 100 Furniture Pkwy.(44857), pg. 816

Old Washington

Broughton Foods Company, I-70 & S.R. 285(43768), pg. 181

Orrville

THE WILL-BURT COMPANY, 169 S. Main(44667), pg. 1190

Painesville

Aero-Finish Inc., 1815 Blaze Nemeth Rd.(44077-4715), pg. 635
THE COE MFG. CO., 609 Bank St.(44077), pg. 258
Federal Hose Manufacturing Corp., 25 Florence Ave.(44077), pg. 418
Uniroyal Chemical Co., Inc., P.O. Box 460, (44077), pg. 1129
United States Machinery, P.O. Box 520(44077), pg. 258
United States Wallboard Machinery, P.O. Box 520(44077), pg. 258

Parma

Cox Cable Cleveland Area, Inc., 12221 Plaza Dr.(44130), pg. 294

Pataskala

Mako Construction Co., 13338 E. Broad St., Rte. 16 P.O. Box A64(43062), pg. 529

Payne

Taylor Products, Inc., P.O. Box 77(45880), pg. 1080

Pepper Pike

STERN ADVERTISING, INC., 29125 Chagrin Blvd.(44122), pg. 1047

Perrysburg

ABBEY ETNA MACHINE COMPANY, 11140 Avenue Rd.(43552), pg. 9
Alro Group, Perrysburg, 361 D St.(43551), pg. 44

Piketon

Indiana Kentucky Electric Corporation, P.O. Box 468(45661), pg. 823
OHIO VALLEY ELECTRIC CORPORATION, U.S. Rte. 23(45661), pg. 822

Pioneer

Letts Industries, Pioneer Div., One Industrial Dr.(43554), pg. 668

Piqua

Burks Pumps, Inc., 420 Third St.(45356-0603), pg. 507
Evenflo Juvenile Furniture Co., 1801 Commerce Dr.(45356), pg. 1024
THE ORR FELT COMPANY, 750 S. Main St.(45356), pg. 830
Prosser/Enpo Industries, 420 Third St.(45356-0603), pg. 507
Tri-Mark Inc., 8585 Industrial Park Dr.(45356), pg. 537

Plain City

SELECT SIRES, INC., 11740 U.S. Rt. 42(43064), pg. 988

Plymouth

Autolift Industrial Lift Trucks, 607 Bell St.(44865), pg. 877
PLYMOUTH LOCOMOTIVE INTERNATIONAL, INC., Bell & High Sts.(44865), pg. 877

Portsmouth

Mid State Products Co., P.O. Box 1388(45662), pg. 830
OSCO INDUSTRIES INC., Eleventh & Chillicothe(45662), pg. 830

Ravenna

Evenflo Products Co., 771 N. Freedom St.(44266), pg. 1024
OAK RUBBER COMPANY, 219 S. Sycamore St.(44266-1203), pg. 819
Oak Technical, Inc., 219 S. Sycamore St.(44266), pg. 819

Reynoldsburg

CARDINAL REALTY SERVICES INC., 6954 Americana Pkwy.(43068), pg. 218

Rockford

Fremont Co., P. O. Box 242(45882), pg. 432

Sabina

Palm Harbor Homes, d/b/a V.P. Homes, Inc., Rte. 22 E.(45169), pg. 843

Salem

BLISS-SALEM, INC., 530 S. Ellsworth(44460), pg. 156
EWI, INC., 100 S. Broadway Ave.(44460), pg. 361
ELECTRIC FURNACE CO., 435 W. Wilson St.(44460-0150), pg. 373
Turner Machine Company, 435 W. Wilson St.(44460), pg. 373

Sandusky

DISTRICT PETROLEUM PRODUCTS, INC., 1832 Milan Rd.(44870), pg. 340
Periodical Publishers' Service Bureau, Inc., One N. Superior St.(44870), pg. 523
Sandusky Plastics, Inc., 400 Broadway(44870), pg. 383

Sharon Center

THE RUHLIN COMPANY, 6931 Ridge Rd.(44274), pg. 955

Shelby

The Shelby Insurance Group, 175 Mansfield Ave.(44875), pg. 90
Uforma Shelby Business Forms, 40 High School Ave.(44875), pg. 746

Smithville

ELASTIC MATERIALS, INC., 200 Wellar Dr.(44677), pg. 372

Solon

CRAWFORD FITTINGS & CO., 29500 Solon Rd.(44139), pg. 297
MATRIX ESSENTIALS, INC., 30601 Carter St.(44139), pg. 721

Spencerville

Mammalian Toxicology Division, 553 N. Broadway(45887), pg. 1033

Springfield

THE WILLIAM BAYLEY CO., 1200 Warder St.(45503), pg. 128
HUGO BOSCA CO., INC., 1905 W. Jefferson(45501), pg. 166
International Steel Wool Corporation, P.O. Box 1767(45501), pg. 164
Olan Mills Inc. of Ohio, 329 Mt. Vernon Ave.(45503), pg. 756
Springfield Newspapers, Inc., 202 N. Limestone St.(45503), pg. 292

Stow

The C.P. Hall Company, 4460 Hudson Dr.(44224), pg. 501
Wilkinson Company, Inc., 1530 Commerce Dr.(44224), pg. 373

Strongsville

CHEMCENTRAL/Cleveland, 21600 Drake Rd.(44136), pg. 241
MILK MARKETING INC., 8257 Dow Circle(44136), pg. 753
NATIONAL ENGINEERING & CONTRACTING CO., 12608 Alameda Dr.(44136), pg. 788
SEQUENTIA INC., 21819 Royalton Rd.(44136), pg. 990
Transbulk, Inc., 12608 Alameda Dr.(44136), pg. 788
Tri State Steel Construction, 12608 Alameda Dr.(44136), pg. 788

Swanton

R & R Plastics, P.O. Box 177, (43558), pg. 270

Tallmadge

Alro Specialty Metals, Tallmadge, 184 South Ave.(44278), pg. 44
Chemionics Corporation, 390 S. Munroe Falls Rd.(44278), pg. 244

Tiffin

Alco Health Services Corporation-Tiffin Div., Airport Industry Pk., 1780 S. County Rd. One(44883), pg. 32
NATIONAL MACHINERY ADV. SERVICES, 161 Greenville St.(44882), pg. 792
NATIONAL MACHINERY COMPANY, 161 Greenfield St.(44883), pg. 792
Stacy Equipment Co., 325 Hall St.(44883), pg. 1172
WEBSTER INDUSTRIES INC., 325 Hall St.(44883), pg. 1171
Webster Mfg. Co., 325 Hall St.(44883), pg. 1172

Tipp City

Spring Hill Nurseries Co., Elm St.(45371), pg. 426

Toledo

AP Parts Manufacturing Company, One John Goerlich Square(43697-0965), pg. 240
Abros, Inc., 860 Curtis St., P.O. Box 940(43697), pg. 86
Alco Health Services Corporation-Toledo Div., 3145 Nebraska Ave.(43607), pg. 32
Allright Toledo, Inc., 332 N. Michigan Ave.(43624), pg. 42
Arocom Marketing Group, Inc., 425 Jefferson Ave., Ste. 808(43604), pg. 737
ART IRON, INC., 860 Curtis St.(43607-0964), pg. 86
BLADE COMMUNICATIONS, INC., 541 Superior St.(43660), pg. 155
BROWN MOTORS, 5625 W. Central Ave.(43615), pg. 182
CAPITAL TIRE, INC., 1001-17 Cherry St.(43608), pg. 215
CHEMCENTRAL/Toledo, 4051 South Ave.(43615), pg. 242
COMMUNICATIONS CONCEPTS, 3131 Executive Pkwy.(43606), pg. 269
Crown Store Equipment, 8200 Central Ave., pg. 609
Doehler-Jarvis, 5400 N. Detroit Ave.(43612), pg. 559
Doehler-Jarvis Plant, 1945 Smead Ave.(43691), pg. 559
EMPIRE PETROLEUM, INC., 2959 Nebraska Ave.(43607), pg. 379
Exothermics-Eclipse, Inc., 5040 Enterprise Blvd.(43612), pg. 366
Fiske Brothers Refining, Toledo Div., 1500 Oakdale(43605), pg. 416
HEIDTMAN STEEL PRODUCTS, INC., 2401 Front St.(43605), pg. 525
THE LATHROP COMPANY, 1220 Dussel Dr.(43537), pg. 660
MACKINNON-PARKER, INC., 4750 W. Bancroft St.(43615), pg. 697
A. Mindel & Son, Inc., 4200 Creekside Ave.(43612), pg. 993
THE NATIONAL SUPER SERVICE CO., 3115 Frenchmens Rd.(43607), pg. 794
PARKER STEEL COMPANY, 4239-41 Monroe St.(43606), pg. 849
Toledo Stamping & Manufacturing Co., P.O. Box 596(43693), pg. 801
TUFFY ASSOCIATES CORP., 1414 Baronial Plaza Dr.(43615), pg. 1119
ZAPIECKI & PARTNERS INC., 4 Sea Gate, 5th Fl.(43604), pg. 1216

Troy

Dinner Bell Foods, Inc., P.O. Box 388(45373), pg. 53
HBC International Sales Corp., Hobart Square(45373), pg. 537
HOBART BROTHERS CO., Hobart Square, 600 W. Main(45373), pg. 536
Ivex Packaging Corporation-Troy, 421 S. Union St.(45373), pg. 583
Worldwide Leasing, Hobart Square(45373), pg. 537

Twinsburg

GENERAL COMPUTER CORP. INC., 2045 Midway Dr.(44087), pg. 449
THE GIBSON-HOMANS COMPANY, 1755 Enterprise Pkwy.(44087), pg. 457
Kilsby-Roberts/Cleveland, 2060 Enterprise Pkwy.(44087), pg. 606
KOOL SEAL, INC., 1499 Enterprise Pkwy.(44087), pg. 641

Urbana

CHAMPAIGN LANDMARK, 304 Bloomfield Ave.(43078), pg. 238
Howard Paper, 504 W. Church St.(43078), pg. 428
Howard Paper Mills, 504 W. Church St.(43078), pg. 428
THE JOHNSON INDUSTRIES CORP., 605 Miami St.(43078), pg. 598

Valley City

MTD PRODUCTS, INC., 5965 Grafton Rd.(44280), pg. 694

Valley View

KENDALE INDUSTRIES, INC., 7600 Hub Parkway(44215), pg. 622
Triangle Machine Product Co., 6055 Hillcrest Dr.(44125), pg. 432
TYLER ELEVATOR PRODUCTS, INC., 6161 Halle Dr.(44125), pg. 1122

Van Wert

All America Insurance Company, 800 So. Washington(45891), pg. 233
Cafco, 800 So. Washington(45891), pg. 233
CENTRAL MUTUAL INSURANCE CO., 800 S. Washington(45891), pg. 233
Central Regional Office, 800 South Washington St(45891), pg. 233
KENNEDY MANUFACTURING COMPANY, 520 E. Sycamore St.(45891), pg. 623

Vandalia

Metromedia Steakhouses, Inc., Terminal Dr.(45377), pg. 744
PON Holding Corp., P.O. Box 578(45377), pg. 743
Ponderosa Financial Corporation, Dayton International Airport, Terminal Dr.(45377), pg. 744
Ponderosa, Inc., Dayton International Airport, Terminal Drive(45377), pg. 743
Ponlupa Restaurant Financing, Inc., Dayton International Airport, Terminal Dr.(45377), pg. 744

Wadsworth

ROHRER CORPORATION, 717 Seville Rd.(44281), pg. 944

Walbridge

RUDOLPH/LIBBE, INC., 6494 Latcha Rd.(43465), pg. 955

Warren

AMERICAN WELDING & MANUFACTURING CO., 250 Dietz Rd.(44483), pg. 65
American Welding & Manufacturing Co., Dietz Rd.(44483), pg. 431
Belmont Industries, U.S. Refractories Div., 400 Refractory Dr., N.W.(44483), pg. 136
BRAINARD STRAPPING, 2250 Larchmont Ave. N.E.(44483-2893), pg. 171
COPPERWELD STEEL COMPANY, 4000 Mahoning Ave.(44482), pg. 284
THOMAS STEEL STRIP CORP., Delaware Ave. NW(44485), pg. 1094

Warrensville

SUPERIOR CONTAINER, INC., 4500 Emery Industrial Pkwy.(44128), pg. 1063

Warrensville Heights

HEINEN'S INC., 20601 Aurora Rd.(44146), pg. 526

Wauseon

Britt Industries, Inc., 525 Enterprise Dr.(43567), pg. 646
Kurdziel Iron of Wauseon, 820 W. Leggett(43567), pg. 646

Wellston

McNally Pittsburg Mfg. Corp., P. O. Box 228(45692), pg. 732

West Chester

SCHUMACHER-DUGAN CONSTRUCTION, 6355 Centre Park Dr.(45069), pg. 979

Westerville

American Select Insurance Co., 774 Park Meadow Rd.(43081), pg. 35
Beacon Insurance Co. of America, 774 Park Meadow Rd.(43081), pg. 34
Dispatch Consumer Services, 7801 N. Central, P.O. Box 206(43081), pg. 339

Westfield Center

WESTFIELD COMPANIES, 1 Park Circle(44251), pg. 1182

Westlake

W. Braun Co., 24700 Center Ridge Rd., 172
LAKE ERIE ELECTRIC, INC., 25730 First St.(44145), pg. 651
PREPLINK, 25125 Detroit Rd.(44145), pg. 481
THE RICHARD & DAVID JACOBS GROUP, 25425 Center Ridge Road(44145), pg. 932

Wickliffe

The Hall Chemical Company, , pg. 468
PMC INDUSTRIES INC., 29100 Lakeland Blvd.(44092), pg. 836

Willard

PIONEER INDUSTRIAL PRODUCTS CO., 512 E. Tiffin St.(44890), pg. 871

Williamsburg

DUALITE INC., One Dualite Lane(45176), pg. 350
Dualite Sales & Service, Inc., One Dualite Ln.(45176), pg. 350

Willoughby

BUD INDUSTRIES, INC., 4605 E. 355th(44094), pg. 186
MCDONALD EQUIPMENT CO., 37200 Vine St.(44094), pg. 728
METAL SEAL & PRODUCTS, INC., 4323 Hamann Pkwy.(44094), pg. 741

Wilmington

GATOR FREIGHTWAYS, INC., 2483 St. Rt. 3 W.(45177), pg. 446
Units Sets, Inc., 115 Skimming Dr.(45177), pg. 951

Winesbury

Case Farms of Ohio, P.O. Box 185(44690), pg. 228

Wooster

Bell & Howell Publication Systems Company, Old Mansfield Rd.(44691), pg. 135
THE GERSTENSLAGER COMPANY, 1425 E. Bowman(44691), pg. 454
HAWKINS MARKETS, INC., 2312 Akron Rd.(44691), pg. 518
Stamping Division, 1425 E. Bowman, P.O. Box 390(44691), pg. 455
WAYNE STEEL, INC., 1070 W. Liberty St. Extn.(44691), pg. 1169
THE WOOSTER BRUSH COMPANY, 604 Madison Ave.(44691), pg. 1202

Worthington

GERBIG, SNELL/WEISHEIMER & ASSOC., INC., 8000 Ravine's Edge Ct.(43085), pg. 454

Yellow Springs

VERNAY LABORATORIES, INC., 120 E. S. College St.(45387), pg. 1148
YSI INCORPORATED, 1725 Brannum Lane(45387), pg. 1207

Youngstown

AMERICAN PAPER PRODUCTS GROUP, LTD., 8401 Southern Blvd.(44512), pg. 59
ARTHUR TREACHER'S, INC., 5121 Mahoning Ave.(44515), pg. 87
Belmont Industries, U.S. Refractories Div., 1410 Albert St.(44505), pg. 137
THE CAFARO CO., 2445 Belmont Ave.(44504), pg. 207
THE EDWARD J. DEBARTOLO CORPORATION, 7620 Market St.(44513-6085), pg. 323
GF Office Furniture, 4944 Belmont Ave.(44501), pg. 439
HYNES INDUSTRIES INC., 3760 Oakwood Ave.(44509), pg. 557
PHAR-MOR, INC., 20 Federal Plaza W.(44503), pg. 866
PHOTOGENIC MACHINE COMPANY, INC., 525 McClurg Rd.(44512), pg. 869
IRA THOMAS ASSOCIATES, INC., 20 Ohltown Rd.(44515), pg. 1092
YSD INDUSTRIES, 3710 Henricks Rd.(44515), pg. 1207

Zoar

WHITEMYER ADVERTISING, INC., Fourth St.(44697), pg. 1186

OKLAHOMA

Ada

Evergreen Mills Inc., 221 N. Rennie(74820), pg. 1145

Altus

Blancett, , pg. 909
Continental/Murray, 215 S. Main(73521), pg. 279
United Supermarkets, P.O. Box 557(73521), pg. 501

Alva

Wheeler Bros. Grain Co., 420 Santa Fe(73717), pg. 1185

Anadarko

Hollytex Carpet Mills, Inc., 505 N.E. 7th St.(73005), pg. 540

Ardmore

The Ardmore Daily Ardmoreite, 117 W. Broadway(73402), pg. 1042

Bixby

AMERICAN FOUNDRY GROUP, INC., 14602 S. Grant(74008), pg. 54

Clinton

ELK SUPPLY COMPANY, 103 Choctaw Ave.(73601), pg. 376

Duncan

COOK MANUFACTURING CORPORATION, 3920 S. 13th St.(73533), pg. 282
DUNCAN EQUIPMENT COMPANY, 1005 S. Second(73533), pg. 352

Durant

Durant Electronics, Inc., 2200 Arkansas Ave.(74701), pg. 1054
Hale-Halsell Company, P.O. Box 10(74701), pg. 500

Enid

ATWOOD DISTRIBUTING, INC., 2717 N. Van Buren(73703), pg. 97
Equity Export, Oil & Gas, Inc., 2300 N. 10th(73702), pg. 402
GROENDYKE TRANSPORTS, INC., 2510 Rock Island Blvd.(73701), pg. 489
Marine Terminal Shipping Co., 2300 N. 10th(73702), pg. 402
Union Equity, 2300 N. 10th(73702), pg. 402

Hugo

CHOCTAW ELECTRIC CO-OP, Hwy. 93 N.(74743), pg. 248

Kingfisher

KINGFISHER CO-OP ELEVATOR ASSOCIATION, 1 Co-Op Way(73750), pg. 631

Lindsay

RURAL ELECTRIC CO-OP, N. Hwy. 76(73052), pg. 956

Miami

Blitz U.S.A., Inc., 404 26th Ave., N.W.(74354), pg. 157
BLITZ USA, 404 26nd Ave. N.W.(74354), pg. 157

Muskogee

ANDERSON WHOLESALE COMPANY, 2211 W. Shawnee(74401), pg. 73
Blytheville Canning Company, Inc., 1900 North St.(74402), pg. 196
Fort Howard Paper Corporation, 5600 E. Chandler(74402), pg. 425

Geographic Index

GRIFFIN MANUFACTURING CO., 111 S. Cherokee(74403), pg. 487
W-P Milling Co., Inc., 1119 So. Cherokee(74402), pg. 45

Noble

UNITED DESIGN, P.O. Box 1200(73068), pg. 1131

Oklahoma City

ARA Magazine & Book Division, Inc., P.O. Box 25489, 7000 N. Robinson(73125), pg. 6
ACKERMAN MCQUEEN, INC., 1100 Equity Tower, 1601 NW Expressway(73118), pg. 12
ALL AMERICAN BOTTLING CORP., 15 N. Robinson, Ste. 700(73102), pg. 35
AMERICAN FIDELITY CORP., 2000 Classon Blvd.(73106), pg. 52
American Trading and Production Corporation, Oil & Gas Div., 2000 Liberty Tower, (73102), pg. 64
Anco Transportation Service, Inc., 701 No. Broadway(73102), pg. 77
C. R. ANTHONY COMPANY, 701 N. Broadway(73102), pg. 77
C. R. Anthony International, Ltd., 701 No. Broadway(73103), pg. 77
Anthony's of Sandpoint, Inc., 701 No. Broadway(73102), pg. 77
Anthony's of Sleepy Eye, Inc., 701 No. Broadway(73102), pg. 77
Anthony's of Spring Valley, Inc., 701 No. Broadway(73102), pg. 77
THE BENHAM GROUP, One Benham Place, 9400 N. Broadway(73114-0400), pg. 138
BLOOM ELECTRIC SERVICES, INC., P.O. Box 271200(73137), pg. 157
BRAUM ICE CREAM STORES INC., 3000 N.E. 63rd St.(73121), pg. 172
CHEMCENTRAL/Oklahoma City, 7301 S.W. 29th(73179), pg. 242
CLEMENTS FOODS CO., 6601 N. Harvey(73116), pg. 254
Clements Vinegar Company, 1734 N.W. 6th St.(73106), pg. 255
Consolidated Wholesale Company Division, 1740 W. Main St.(73126), pg. 440
Cox Cable Oklahoma City, Inc., 2312 N.W. 10th Street(73107), pg. 294
The Daily & Sunday Oklahoman, 9000 N. Broadway(73114), pg. 446
Ebsco Graphics, 1223 Linwood(73106), pg. 365
Forest Siding Supply, Inc., 50 N. May(73107), pg. 1091
Frank Paxton Lumber Company, 1815 S. Agnew, Box 82215(73148), pg. 592
Gulfstream Aerospace Technologies Corp., Box 22500, Wiley Post Airport(73123), pg. 494
HTB, INC., 900 N. Stiles(73104-1845), pg. 497
HOMELAND STORES, INC., 400 N.E. 36th St.(73105), pg. 542
JORDAN ASSOCIATES, 1000 W. Wilshire(73116), pg. 604
KIMRAY, INC., 52 N.W. 42nd(73118), pg. 629
Laboratory Supply Company, 723 N. Ann Arbor(73127), pg. 650
Louis Dreyfus Natural Gas, 14000 Quail Springs Pkwy., Ste. 600(73134), pg. 349
MACKLANBURG-DUNCAN CO., 4041 N. Santa Fe(73118), pg. 697
Moroch, Inc., 6801 N. Broadway, Ste. 200(73116), pg. 771
Oklahoma Publishing Company, 9000 N. Broadway(73114), pg. 446
Pyramid Electric Supply Co., Inc., 2034 NW Seventh St.(73106), pg. 1020
REEL-O-MATIC SYSTEMS, INC., 6408 S. Eastern(73149), pg. 920
ROCOR TRANSPORTATION COMPANIES INC., 4350 Will Rogers Pky. Ste. 300 S.(73128), pg. 942
T. H. ROGERS LUMBER CO. INC., 4545 Lincoln Blvd., Ste. 176(73105), pg. 943
Standard Gravure d/b/a Oklahoma Graphics, 5400 N.W. 5th St.(73127), pg. 1036
Triumph/LOR, Inc., 1333 S. E. 25th St.(73129), pg. 1115
UNITED ENGINES, INC., 5555 W. Reno(73127), pg. 1131

Perry

CHARLES MACHINE WORKS, INC., 1959 W. Fir Ave.(73077), pg. 240

Ponca City

LINDSAY MANUFACTURING INC., Bldg. 3, Darr Industrial Park(74601), pg. 676

Pryor

Gold Bond Building Products, P.O. Box 428, (74361), pg. 790
Interplastic Corporation, Hunt St. Mid-America Industrial Park(74361), pg. 579
MITCHELL COACH MANUFACTURING, 4 1/2 Mile S. U.S. Hwy. 69(74361), pg. 761

Purcell

Perfection-Hy-Test Rebuilding Div., 306 Juneau(73080), pg. 711

Sapulpa

LIBERTY GLASS COMPANY, 1000 N. Mission(74066), pg. 674

Shawnee

KGFF-AM, MacArthur & Bryan Sts.(74802-0009), pg. 1043
Shawnee News-Star, P.O. Box 1688, 215 N. Bell(74801), pg. 1042

Spiro

Triumph-LOR, Inc., P.O. Box 157, Rt. 2,Box 327-A(74959), pg. 1115

Tulsa

American Econo-Therm, 8282 South Memorial(74133), pg. 865
ANCHOR GASOLINE CORPORATION, 114 E. 5th Street(74103), pg. 71
APCO ARGENTINA INC., P.O. Box 2400, (74102), pg. 77
Arkansas Valley Distributing, 9111 E. Pine(74115), pg. 500
AUTO CRANE COMPANY, 4707 N. Mingo Rd.(74117), pg. 100
BS & B Safety Systems, P.O. Box 470590(74147-0590), pg. 579
BLUE CROSS AND BLUE SHIELD OF OKLAHOMA, 1215 S. Boulder Ave.(74119), pg. 159
BlueLines HMO, 1437 S. Boulder Ave.(74119), pg. 159
BOVAIRD SUPPLY CO., 823 S. Detroit(74102), pg. 168
CCI CORPORATION, P.O. Box 582800(74158), pg. 200
Canal Refining Co., 114 E. 5th St.(74103), pg. 71
CHEMCENTRAL/Tulsa, 4500 N. Peoria Ave.(74148), pg. 242
Container Products Inc., P.O. Box 9556, 3717 W. 21st St.-Rte. 9(74107), pg. 278
Cove Petroleum, 114 E. 5th St.(74103), pg. 71
CRANE CARRIER COMPANY, 1925 N. Sheridan(74151), pg. 296
Curtis Equipment Co., Inc., 6577 E. 40th St.(74145), pg. 500
ENERGY FUELS DEVELOPMENT CORPORATION, 320 S. Boston, Ste. 1501(74103), pg. 381
Fadler, Inc., 6511 E. 44th St.(74145), pg. 500
Foodland, Inc., 9111 E. Pine(74115), pg. 500
Foodtown, Inc., 9111 E. Pine(74115), pg. 501
Frank Paxton Lumber Company, 5420 S. 99th E. Ave.(74145), pg. 592
Git N Go, Inc., 911 E. Pine(74115), pg. 501
H.H. Foods, Inc., 9111 E. Pine(74115), pg. 501
HALE-HALSELL COMPANY, 9111 E. Pine(74115), pg. 500
HARLEY INDUSTRIES, INC., 4504 E. 67th St., Suite 202(74136), pg. 509
INTERNATIONAL CHEMICAL COMPANY, 1887 E. 71st St.(74136), pg. 576
Jorgensen Steel & Aluminum/Tulsa, 7311 E. Pine St.(74115), pg. 606
KTUL Television, Inc., P.O. Box 8, (74101), pg. 862
Kilsby-Roberts Cutting Center/Honing/Tulsa, 2522 N. Columbia Pl.(74110), pg. 606
Kilsby-Roberts/Tulsa, 3116 E. 31st St. N.(74110), pg. 606
Madison, Inc., 8500 New Sapulpa Rd.(74131), pg. 433
MANHATTAN BUILDING COMPANIES, 111 W. 5th St., Ste. 1000(74103-4235), pg. 703
Manhattan Construction Company, 111 W. 5th St., Ste. 1000(74103-4235), pg. 704
Member Service Life Insurance Co., 2727 E. 21st St.(74114), pg. 159
Mid-Continent Casualty Co., 1646 So. Boulder(74101), pg. 53
Mid-Continent Casualty Co., 1646 S. Boulder(74101), pg. 53
Mid-Continent Casualty Company, 1646 S. Boulder(74101), pg. 53
Moroch, Inc., 7136 S. Yale, Ste. 300(74136), pg. 771
PacifiCare of Oklahoma Inc., 7134 S. Yale Ave., Ste. 700(74136), pg. 1127
THE PRO-QUIP CORPORATION, 8522 E. 61st St.(74133), pg. 892
QUIKTRIP CORPORATION, 901 N. Mingo Rd.(74116), pg. 905
Sipes Super Markets, 9111 E. Pine(74115), pg. 501
SOONER PIPE & SUPPLY CORP., 1000 MidContinent Tower 401 S. Boston(74103), pg. 1018
TDW Building Corporation, 8506 E. 61st St.(74133), pg. 1192
TDW Services, Inc., 6801 S. 65th West Ave.(74101), pg. 1192
TRACO ADVERTISING, INC., P. O. Box 3286, (74101), pg. 1104
Tulsa Gauge & Instrument Co., 4445 South 91st(74147), pg. 510
Urethane Products, 10727 E. 55th Place(74145), pg. 1192
Valu-Fare Foods, Inc., 9111 E. Pine(74115), pg. 501
Valu-Foods, Inc., P.O. Box 582807(74158-2807), pg. 501
Vinson Supply Co., 1323 E. 71st St.(74136), pg. 968
T.D. WILLIAMSON, INC., 8506 E. 61st St.(74133), pg. 1192
Williamson International Corp., 8506 E. 61st St.(74133), pg. 1192
WORLD PUBLISHING COMPANY, 315 S. Boulder(74103), pg. 1203
Yuba Heat Transfer Division, 2121 N. East Ave., P.O. Box 3158(74116), pg. 275
John Zink Co., 11920 E. Apache(74116), pg. 639

Walters

COTTON ELECTRIC CO-OP, 226 N. Broadway(73572), pg. 288

Watonga

AT&L Railroad, P.O. Box 29(73772), pg. 1185
WHEELER BROTHERS GRAIN CO., 501 W. Russworm(73772), pg. 1184

OREGON

Albany

Golden West Homes, Albany Div., 2445 Pacific Blvd. S.(97321), pg. 467
National Frozen Foods Corporation - Albany, 745 - 30th Ave. S.W.(97321), pg. 789
OREGON FREEZE DRY, INC., 525 25th Ave., S.W.(97321), pg. 829

Aurora

Elixir Industries, 19527 Grim Rd.(97002), pg. 376

Beaverton

CENTRAL POINT SOFTWARE, INC., 15220 N.W. Greenbriar Pkwy., No. 200(97006), pg. 234
GRANTREE CORPORATION, 9775 S.W. Gemini Dr.(97005), pg. 477
GREGORY AFFILIATES, INC., 4800 S.W. Griffith Dr., Ste. 300(97005), pg. 486
LEUPOLD & STEVENS, INC., 600 N.W. Meadow Dr.(97006), pg. 669
PLAID PANTRIES, INC., 10025 S.W. Allen Blvd.(97005), pg. 873
Westco Products/Northwest, 6555 S.W. 111th St.(97005), pg. 1178

Bend

BROOKS RESOURCES CORPORATION, 416 N.E. Greenwood(97701), pg. 180
Mount Bachelor Village Corp., 19717 Mt. Bachelor Dr.(97705), pg. 180

Boring

VANPORT MANUFACTURING, INC., 28590 S.E. Wally Rd.(97009), pg. 1145

Brookings

C & K MARKETS, INC., 615 5th St.(97415), pg. 198

Canby

S. R. Smith, Inc., P.O. Box 400, 1017 S.W. Berg Pkwy.(97013), pg. 79

Clackamas

CODE-A-PHONE CORP., 16261 S.E. 130th Ave.(97015), pg. 258
GEM TOP MFG., INC., 8811 S.E. Herbert Ct.(97015), pg. 448
S & W Fine Foods, P.O. Box 296, 10755 S. E. Jennifer St.(97015), pg. 1111

Cornelius

Hazelnut Growers of Oregon, 401 N. 26th Ave.(97113), pg. 1058

Dayton

Monrovia Nursery Co.-Oregon, 12600 S.E. Alderman(97114), pg. 766

Dillard

ROSEBURG FOREST PRODUCTS CO., Old Hwy. 99 S.(97432), pg. 948

Durkee

Ash Grove Cement Co., Durkee Plant, P.O. Box 5, (97905), pg. 87

Eugene

Federal Stampings of Oregon, 4277 West 5th(97402), pg. 321
GUARD PUBLISHING COMPANY, 975 High St.(97401), pg. 491
MURPHY COMPANY, P.O. Box 2810(97402), pg. 776
Murphy International, P.O. Box 2810(97402), pg. 776
Murphy Plywood, P.O. Box 2810(97402), pg. 776
Murphy Properties, Inc., P.O. Box 2810(97402), pg. 776
Murphy Timber, P.O. Box 2810(97402), pg. 776
PW Pipe Co., P.O. Box 10049, (97440), pg. 1007
VITUS ELECTRICAL SUPPLY COMPANY, 2358 W. 7th Place(97402), pg. 1154
William's Bakery, P.O. Box 1375, (97440), pg. 1134

Gladstone

Powell Laboratories, P.O. Box 187(97027), pg. 223

Hillsboro

ORCAD L.P., 3175 N.W. Aloclek Dr.(97124), pg. 828

Hood River

HANEL LUMBER CO., INC., 4865 Hwy. 35(97031), pg. 505
Kearney-Western Power Products, Inc., 900 Portway Ave.(97031), pg. 357

Klamath Falls

JELD-WEN, INC., 3303 Lakeport Blvd.(97601), pg. 591

Lake Oswego

PacifiCare of Oregon, Inc., Five Centerpointe Dr., Ste. 600(97035), pg. 1127
SCR, INC., 4550 SW Kruseway, Suite 215(97035), pg. 961

McMinnville

Cascade Steel Rolling Mills, Inc., 3200 No. Hwy. 99 W.(97128), pg. 977
EVERGREEN INTERNATIONAL AVIATION, INC., 3850 Three Mile Lane(97128-9496), pg. 392

Medford

SHERMS THUNDERBIRD MARKET, 2347 Jacksonville Hwy.(97501), pg. 998
Simco/Ramic Corporation, P.O. Box 1666(97501), pg. 904

Milwaukie

WARN INDUSTRIES, INC., 13270 S.E. Pheasant Court(97222), pg. 1164

Molalla

Brazier Forest Products Of Oregon, Hwy. 211(97038), pg. 173

Newberg

A-DEC, INC., 2601 Crestview Dr.(97132), pg. 1

Nyssa

American Fine Foods, Inc. (Nyssa Plant), 100 E. Locust St.(97913), pg. 1045

Ontario

RED APPLE, INC., 555 S.W. 4th Ave.(97914), pg. 918

Portland

AFI Export, Inc., 6600 S.W. Hampton Street(97223), pg. 585
ASCG, INC., 6600 Bldg., Ste. 21, 6600 SW 92nd Ave.(97223), pg. 7
Alaskan Copper Companies, P.O. Box 5067, (97208), pg. 30
AMERICAN INDUSTRIES INC., 4033 N.W. Yeon Ave.(97210), pg. 55
Amfac Foods, Inc., 6600 S.W. Hampton St.(97223), pg. 585
BENSON INDUSTRIES, INC., 1650 N.W. Front 139
Blitz-Weinhard Brewing, 1133 W. Burnside St.(97209), pg. 526
Blue Bell Potato Chip Co., 100 N.E. Farragut St.(97211), pg. 439
BLUE CROSS & BLUE SHIELD OF OREGON, 100 S.W. Market St.(97201), pg. 160
BORDERS, PERRIN & NORRANDER, INC., 222 S.W. Yamhill St., 7th Fl.(97204), pg. 165
BRIM, INC., 305 N.E. 102nd Ave.(97220), pg. 176
Brim Services Group, 305 N.E. 102nd Ave.(97220), pg. 176
Brix Maritime Barging, Inc., 9030 N.W. St. Helens Rd.(97231), pg. 177
BRIX MARITIME CO., 9030 N.W. St. Helen's Rd.(97231), pg. 177
BRONSON LEIGH WEEKS, 5331 SW Macadam, Ste. 283(97201), pg. 179
CH2M Hill Industrial Design Corp., Parkside Plaza, 2020 S.W. 4th, 3rd Fl.(97201), pg. 202
CAPPELLI MILES WILTZ & KELLY, 101 S.W. Main, Ste. 1450(97204), pg. 216
Cartall Div., 4720 S.E. 17th Ave.(97202), pg. 854
CHEMCENTRAL/Portland, 10821 N. Lombard St.(97203), pg. 242
CHRISTENSON ELECTRIC, INC., 111 S.W. Columbia, Ste. 480(97201), pg. 248
CIRCLE A.W. PRODUCTS, CO., 13885 S.W. 72nd Ave.(97223), pg. 250
THE COATES AGENCY, 320 S.W. Oak, Ste. 300(97204), pg. 257
CONSOLIDATED METCO, INC., 13940 N. Rivergate Blvd.(97203), pg. 277
COPELAND LUMBER YARD, INC., 901 NE Glisan St.(97232), pg. 284
Custom Casting, 2141 N.W. 25th Ave.(97210), pg. 388
DSU Leasing, Inc., 4810 North Basin Ave.(97217), pg. 310
D.S.U.-PETERBILT & GMC, INC., 4810 N. Basin Ave.(97208), pg. 309
Dairy Express, Inc., 6337-A N.E. 112th Ave.(97220), pg. 689
E B 5 CORPORATION, 111 S.W. 5th Ave., Suite 2650(97204), pg. 359
Earthmoving Equipment Div., 2141 N.W. 25th Ave.(97210), pg. 388
Edelweiss, 5700 S.E. Harvey Dr.(97206), pg. 1186
ESCO CORPORATION, 2141 NW 25th Ave.(97210), pg. 388
Esco International, 2141 N.W. 25th Ave.(97210), pg. 388
EvansGroup, 308 S.W. First Ave., Ste. 200(97204), pg. 391
FABRIC WHOLESALERS, INC., 2035 N.E. 181st Ave.(97230), pg. 396
Franz Bakery, P.O. Box 14769, (97214), pg. 1134
GWC Properties, Inc., 808 S.W. 15th Ave.(97205), pg. 727
GERBER ADVERTISING, 209 S.W. Oak St.(97204), pg. 453
Graphic Arts Center, 2000 N.W. Wilson St.(97209), pg. 279
HAMPTON RESOURCES INC., 9400 S.W. Barnes Rd.(97225), pg. 504
HANNA CAR WASH INTERNATIONAL, INC., 2000 Hanna Dr.(97222), pg. 505
Health Maintenance Oregon, 1800 S.W. First, Ste. 505(97201), pg. 160
Hoffman Construction Company of Oregon, 1300 S.W. Sixth Ave.(97201), pg. 537
HOFFMAN CORPORATION, 1300 S.W. Sixth Ave.(97201), pg. 537
Hoffman Mechanical Corporation, 1300 S.W. Sixth Ave.(97201), pg. 538
Hoffman Structures, Inc., 1300 S.W. Sixth Ave.(97201), pg. 538
Industrial Materials Technology, 6651 S.E. Crosswhite Way(97206), pg. 789
K.F. Jacobson Co., 4315 S.E. McLoughlin Blvd.(97202), pg. 845
JOHNSON ACOUSTICAL & SUPPLY CO., 2001 N.W. 19th Ave.(97209), pg. 597
Kaiser Permanente, Northwest Division, 3600 N. Interstate Ave.(97227-1191), pg. 614
KARAKAS, VANSICKLE OUELLETTE ADVERTISING & PUBLIC RELATIONS, 200 SW Market St., Ste. 1400(97201), pg. 616
Kilsby-Roberts/Portland, 6650 N. Ensign St.(97217), pg. 606
Liberty Northwest Insurance Corp., 825 N.E. Multnomah St.(97232), pg. 674
THE CHAS. H. LILLY CO., 7737 N. E. Killingsworth(97218), pg. 675
M & T INCORPORATED, 15115 Southwest Sequoia Pkwy., 690
MARX/KNOLL, DENIGHT & DODGE, INC., 1230 S.W. First Ave.(97204), pg. 716
MCCALL OIL & CHEMICAL CORP., 808 S.W. 15th Ave.(97205), pg. 726
McCall Oil Real Estate Corporation, 808 S.W. 15th Ave.(97205), pg. 727
McCall Properties, Inc., 808 S.W. 15th Ave.(97205), pg. 727
Ming Surveyors, Inc., 1300 S.W. Sixth Ave.(97201), pg. 538
Multiform Enterprises, Inc., 2701 N.W. Vaughn, Ste. 890(97201), pg. 478
NORTH PACIFIC LUMBER COMPANY, 1505 SE Gideon St.(97208), pg. 813
Northwest Marine, Inc., 5555 N. Channel Ave., Bldg. 2(27217), pg. 1023
Nu-Safe Reporting, 209 S.W. Oak(92704), pg. 453
Oregon Pacific States Insurance Co., P.O. Box 1271(97207), pg. 160
PACIFIC METAL COMPANY, 3400 SW Bond Ave.(97201), pg. 841
R. B. PAMPLIN CORP., 900 S.W. 5th Ave., Ste. 1800(97204), pg. 844
PECO INC., 4707 S.E. 17th Ave.(97202-0189), pg. 854
Peco Mfg. Co., 4720 S.E. 17th Ave.(97202), pg. 854
PENDLETON WOOLEN MILLS, INC., 220 N.W. Broadway(97209), pg. 857
POP TV, 4040 SE International Way, Ste. E104(97222), pg. 693
Port Center Restaurant Corp., 4575 N. Channell Ave.(97217), pg. 1029
Portland Auto Auction, 3000 N. Hayden Island Dr.(97217), pg. 293
Portland Beavers, 1844 S.W. Morrison Ave.(97207), pg. 758
PORTLAND FOOD PRODUCTS COMPANY, 5320 S.W. Macadam Ave.(97201), pg. 881
Portland Service Division, 13817 N.E. Sandy Blvd.(97220), pg. 45
Portland Terminal Railroad Co., Union Station, Rm. 209, 800 N.W. 6th(97209), pg. 76
Portland Traction Co., 1640 S.E. Water Ave.(97214), pg. 76
ARTHUR A. POZZI CO., INC., 5550 Southwest MacAdam Ave., Ste. 230(97201), pg. 883
Precision Asbestos Abatement Company, 8025 N.E. Killingsworth(97218), pg. 538
Precision Construction Compan y, 8025 N.E. Killingsworth(97218), pg. 538
Proprietory Products Group, 2141 N.W. 25th Avenue(97210), pg. 388
RICHARDSON STRANG ASSOCIATES, 1200 N.W. Front Ave., Ste. 220(97209), pg. 933
Rivergate Plant, 13939 N. Rivergate Blvd.(97203), pg. 88
Ross Island Sand & Gravel Co., Inc., 4315 S.E. McLoughlin Blvd.(97202), pg. 845
RUNDEL PRODUCTS, INC., 1100 N.E. 28th Ave.(97232), pg. 956
Ann Sacks Tile & Stone, Inc., 535 N.E. 28th Ave.(97232), pg. 640
THE SCHMIDT/WESTERDAHL GROUP LTD., 700 S.W. Taylor, Ste. 400(97201), pg. 976
SCHNITZER STEEL INDUSTRIES, INC., 3200 N.W. Yeon Ave.(97210), pg. 977
Sentrol, Inc., 10831 S.W. Cascade Blvd.(97223), pg. 145
Sunne Controls Div., 4720 S.E. 17th Ave.(97202), pg. 854
TV Host West, Inc., 529 S.W. Third Ave., Ste. 200(97204), pg. 1075
TEMP-CONTROL MECHANICAL CORP., 4800 N. Channel(97217), pg. 1086
Total Plan Alternatives, Inc., P.O. Box 2580(97208-2580), pg. 160
TUCKER ROCKY DISTRIBUTING, 2424 N.E. Riverside Way(97211), pg. 1118
TURTLEDOVE CLEMENS, INC., 111 S.W. Front Ave.(97204), pg. 1120
UNITED GROCERS INC., P.O. Box 22187, 6433 SE Lake Road(97222), pg. 1132
UNITED STATES BAKERY, 315 N.E. 10th Ave.(97232), pg. 1134
Western International Media Corporation, 6915 S.W. Macadam, Ste. 100(92701), pg. 1180
WIEDEN & KENNEDY, INC., 320 S.W. Washington(97204), pg. 1188
WILLAMETTE-WESTERN CORPORATION, 4555 N. Channel Av.(97217), pg. 1190
Willamina Lumber Co. Inc., 9400 S.W. Barnes Rd.(97225), pg. 504
YOUNG & ROEHR, INC., 28 S.W. First, Ste. 500(97204), pg. 1210

Prineville

OCHOCO LUMBER COMPANY, 416 Combs Flat Rd.(97754), pg. 821

Roseburg

Applied Sciences Division, 17271 N. Umpqua Highway(97470), pg. 207

Salem

AGRIPAC INC., 325 Patterson N.W.(97304), pg. 25
CAPITOL CHEVROLET CADILLAC GEO, INC., 2711 Mission St. S.E.(97309), pg. 215
Country Mutual Northwest Regional Office, 2150 Country Dr. S.(97302-2209), pg. 289
MICROFLECT COMPANY, INC., 3575 25th St., S.E.(97302), pg. 749
OREGON STATE LOTTERY, 2767 22nd St. SE(97302), pg. 829
Oregon Turkey Growers, 740 NW Bassett(97304), pg. 809

Springfield

TIMBER PRODUCTS COMPANY, LP, 305 S. 4th St.(97477), pg. 1097

Stayton

NORPAC FOODS, INC. COOPERATIVE, 930 W. Washington St.(97383), pg. 810

Tangent

Discovery Plastic, P.O. Box 330, (97389), pg. 907

Tigard

Waremart Inc., 8005 Humziker Rd.(97223), pg. 1163

Tillamook

TILLAMOOK COUNTY CREAMERY ASSN., 4175 Hwy. 101 N.(97141), pg. 1097

Tualatin

Portland Chain Mfg. Co., 12475 S.W. Herman Rd.(97062), pg. 1172

Warrenton

Bioproducts, Inc., 1935 N.W. Warrenton Dr., P.O. Box 429(97146), pg. 152

Weston

SMITH FROZEN FOODS, INC., P.O. Box 68(97886), pg. 1012

White City

MARK MACHINE INC., 912 Antelope Rd.(97503), pg. 708

Wilsonville

G.I. JOE'S INC., 9805 Boeckman Rd.(97070), pg. 440

Woodburn

Silvercrest Western Home Corporation, 2450 Progress Way(97071), pg. 1004
Woodburn Foods Corp., 101 Birdseye Ave.(97304), pg. 25

PENNSYLVANIA

Allentown

BONNEY FORGE CORPORATION, Cedar & Meadow Sts.(18105), pg. 164
Bostrom Distribution Center, 2201 Hangar Pl.(18103), pg. 168
EBELING & REUSS COMPANY, 333 Court(18105), pg. 365
Hess's Department Stores, Inc., Hamilton Mall at 9th(18101), pg. 302
JAMISON PLASTIC CORPORATION, 5001 Crackersport Rd.(18104), pg. 589
LIEBERMAN-APPALUCCI, 4635 Crackersport Rd.(18104), pg. 675
PRECISION ROLL GRINDERS, INC., R.D. 6(18105), pg. 885
SERONO BAKER DIAGNOSTICS, 100 Cascade Dr.(18103), pg. 991

Allison Park

MFG Systems, Gamma Building, 4068 Mount Royal Blvd.(15101), pg. 370

Altoona

BOYER BROS. INC., 821 17th St.(16602), pg. 169
JUNIATA OFFICE SUPPLIES, 1554 Valley View Blvd.(16602), pg. 608
SMALL TUBE PRODUCTS CO., INC., Spring Meadows(16603), pg. 1010
WARD TRUCKING CORP., 2nd Ave. & 7th St.(16602), pg. 1163

Ardmore

HAJOCA CORP., 127 Coulter Ave.(19003), pg. 500
KINGSWOOD ADVERTISING, INC., Cricket Terrace Center(19003), pg. 632

Ashland

Laubeck Corporation, Laubenstein Division, 418 S. Hoffman Blvd.(17921), pg. 660

Aston

ATZ Plastic Molders, Inc., 200 Commerce Dr.(19014), pg. 1217
PHONETICS, INC., 901 Tryens Rd.(19014), pg. 869
PYROMET, INC., 5 Commerce Dr.(19014), pg. 901
ZENITH PRODUCTS CORP., 200 Commerce Dr.(19014), pg. 1217

Avoca

WARM Broadcasting Co., Wilkes Barre Scranton Hwy., Box 590(18641), pg. 1065

Avondale

Edlon Products, Inc., 117 State Rd.(19311-0667), pg. 866

Bala-Cynwyd

Communications Paper Divison, 2 Bala Plaza(19004), pg. 1157

Geographic Index

CONNELLY CONTAINERS, INC., Righters Ferry Rd.(19004), pg. 275
L.F. DRISCOLL CO., P.O. Box 468, 9 Presidential Blvd.(19004), pg. 349
ELKMAN ADVERTISING & PUBLIC RELATIONS, 150 Monument Rd.(19004), pg. 377
KEYSTONE FOODS CORPORATION, 401 City Ave., Ste. 800(19004), pg. 628
LEVLANE ADVERTISING, INC., One Belmont Ave.(19004), pg. 671
MCADAMS, RICHMAN & ONG, INC., 15 N. Presidential Blvd.(19004), pg. 725
MORGAN INDUSTRIES INC., One Presidential Blvd.(19004), pg. 770
ROBERTS & RAYMOND ASSOC., INC., 401 City Line Ave., Ste. 209(19004), pg. 939
WWF PAPER CORPORATION, 2 Bala Plaza(19004), pg. 1157
WINDERMERE COMMUNICATIONS, INC., 301 City Line Ave.(19004), pg. 1195

Beaver Falls

MOLTRUP STEEL PRODUCTS COMPANY, 14th St. & 2nd Ave.(15010), pg. 764

Beaver Springs

Mattern Hatchery, Route 1, Box 240(17812), pg. 379

Belle Vernon

THE GUTTMAN GROUP, 200 Speers Rd.(15012), pg. 495

Bellefonte

Cerro Metal Products Company, P.O. Box 388, (16823), pg. 711

Bensalem

AIR MASTER CORPORATION, 1211 Ford Rd.(19020), pg. 27
AIRLINE HYDRAULICS CORPORATION, 1-95 & Street Rd.(19020), pg. 27
GILES & RANSOME, INC., 2975 Galloway Rd.(19020), pg. 458
Transilwrap Co. of Philadelphia, 320 Camer Dr.(19020), pg. 1107

Berlin

Snyder Potato Chips, 1313 Stadium Dr.(15530), pg. 26

Berwick

Berwick Freight Car Co., Third & Oak Sts.(18603), pg. 246
DELUXE HOMES OF PENNSYLVANIA, INC., 499 W. Third St.(18603), pg. 327
KLEER PAK CORPORATION, 1411 N. Vine St.(18603), pg. 635

Berwyn

BARCLAY WHITE INCORPORATED, 22 Cassatt Ave.(19312), pg. 119
DEVON DIRECT MARKETING & ADVERTISING, INC., 200 Berwyn Park(19312), pg. 334
Pepper, Hamilton & Scheetz, 1235 Westlake Dr., Ste. 400(19312), pg. 860

Bethel Park

CENTIMARK CORPORATION, 3000 Industrial Blvd.(15102), pg. 231

Bethlehem

ALCOM PRINTING GROUP, INC., 2285 Ave. A(18017), pg. 32
JUST BORN, INC., 1300 Stefko Blvd.(18017), pg. 610
Keystone Automotive Industries, Inc. - Bethlehem, R.D. 628
PIERCING PAGODA, INC., 3910 Adler Pl.(18016), pg. 870
STIEGLER, WELLS & BRUNSWICK, INC., 3865 Adler Place(18017), pg. 1049

Blassburg

WARD MANUFACTURING, INC., 115 Gulick St.(16912), pg. 1163

Bloomsburg

THE MAGEE CARPET COMPANY, 480 W. Fifth(17815), pg. 700

Blue Bell

BIDDLE INSTRUMENTS, 510 Township Line Rd.(19422), pg. 148
CRAFTEX MILLS INC. OF PENNSYLVANIA, 450 Sentry Parkway(19422-0795), pg. 295
CROWN TEXTILE COMPANY, Three Valley Sq.(19422), pg. 302
HENKELS & MCCOY, INC., 985 Jolly Rd.(19422), pg. 529
HAL LANGERMAN CO., 25 Norristown Rd.(19422), pg. 657
NUTRI/SYSTEM INC., 380 Sentry Pkwy.(19422-2332), pg. 818

Braddock

Air-Scent International, 215-225 Eighth Ave., P.O. Box 1000(15104), pg. 1065
SURCO PRODUCTS, INC., Odomaster Industrial Park, 8th & Pine Aves.(15104), pg. 1065
Unsmoke International, 1135 Braddock Ave.(15104), pg. 1065

Bradford

ZIPPO MANUFACTURING COMPANY, 33 Barbour St.(16701), pg. 1220

Bridgeville

INTERFORM CORPORATION, Mayview & Scott Rds.(15017), pg. 574
Mulach Parking Structures Corp., 100 Hickory Grade Rd.(15017), pg. 775
MULACH STEEL CORPORATION, 100 Hickory Grade Rd.(15017), pg. 775
ROKOP CORPORATION, 400 Old Pond Rd.(15017), pg. 944

Bristol

ATAPCO Globe-Weis/Bristol, P.O. Box 11, (19007), pg. 64
Christian Dior, 250 Rittenhouse Circle(19007), pg. 602
JNY, 250 Rittenhouse Circle(19007), pg. 602
JONES APPAREL GROUP, INC., 250 Rittenhouse Circle(19007), pg. 602
Joneswear, 250 Rittenhouse Circle(19007), pg. 602
Material Handling Equipment Co., 2501 Durham Rd.(19007), pg. 763
MODERN GROUP LTD., 2501 Durham Rd.(19007), pg. 762
Modern Handling Equipment Co., 2501 Durham Rd.(19007), pg. 763
Moreco Inc., 2501 Durham Rd.(19007), pg. 763
Rena Rowan for Saville, 250 Rittenhouse Circle(19007), pg. 602
Saville, 250 Rittenhouse Circle(19007), pg. 602
West Mill Clothes, Tuxacco Accessories Div., Keystone Industrial Park, 257 Rittenhouse Circle(19007), pg. 1177

Broomall

M. A. BRUDER & SONS, INC., 600 Reed Rd.(19008), pg. 184
PENNSYLVANIA CRUSHER CORP., 600 Abbott Dr.(19008), pg. 858

Bryn Mawr

INDEPENDENT PUBLICATIONS, INC., 945 Haverford Rd.(19010), pg. 565

Burnham

FREEDOM FORGE CORPORATION, 500 N. Walnut St.(17009), pg. 430
Standard Steel, 500 N. Walnut St.(17009), pg. 431

Butler

AGR INTERNATIONAL, INC., 615 Whitestown Rd.(16001), pg. 4
Advocate Services, Inc., P.O. Box 1021(16001), pg. 993
Ervin Amasteel Div., 681 E. Butler Rd.(16001), pg. 387
Magnetics, P.O. Box 391, (16003), pg. 1025
Marmon/Keystone Corp., P.O. Box 992(16001), pg. 711
SPANG & COMPANY, 100 Brugh Ave.(16001), pg. 1025
Spang Specialty Metals, P.O. Box 391, (16003), pg. 1025
Thermojet, 125 Pillow St.(16003), pg. 283

Callery

BYRNES & KIEFER COMPANY, 131 Kline Ave.(16024), pg. 198

Camp Hill

HEMPT BROTHERS, INC., 205 Creek Rd.(17011), pg. 528
ICELAND SEAFOOD CORPORATION, 1250 Sate Hill Rd.(17011), pg. 561
L. B. SMITH, INC., 2001 State Rd.(17001-8134), pg. 1013

Canonsburg

American Specialty Foods, R.D. 313

Carbondale

Glass Products, Inc., Clindo Drive(18407), pg. 3
LAUBECK CORPORATION/CROSS, 166 Dundaff St.(18407), pg. 660

Carlisle

FROG SWITCH & MANUFACTURING COMPANY, 600 East High St.(17013), pg. 434
Holly Milk Plant, 405 Park Dr.(17013), pg. 95
MASLAND INDUSTRIES, 50 Spring Rd.(17013), pg. 717

Carnegie

MALLET & CO., Arch Street Extension(15106), pg. 703
RUSSELL INDUSTRIES, INC., 555 N. Bell Ave.(15106), pg. 957

Catasauqua

ROCK HILL MATERIALS COMPANY, 339 School St.(18032), pg. 941

Chalfont

PARAMOUNT PACKAGING CORP., 202 Oak Ave.(18914), pg. 848

Chambersburg

NIBBLE WITH GIBBLE'S, INC., 6647 Molly Pitcher Hwy. S.(17201), pg. 806
OLIVER OIL COMPANY, INC., 875 S. Main St.(17201), pg. 824
T.B. WOOD'S SONS COMPANY, 440 N. Fifth Ave.(17201), pg. 1200

Chester

BALDT, INC., P.O. Box 350(19016), pg. 115
DEE PAPER COMPANY, Front & Broomall(19016-0320), pg. 324

Chinchilla

ACKER DRILL CO. INC., Shady Lane Rd.(18410), pg. 12

Clearfield

KURTZ BROS., INC., P.O. Box 392, 4th & Reeds St.(16830), pg. 646

Cleona

HAUCK MFG. CO., 100 N. Harris St.(17042), pg. 517

Coatesville

PENGUIN INDUSTRIES, INC., Airport Industrial Mall(19320), pg. 857

Collegeville

COLLEGEVILLE FLAG MFG. COMPANY, 4th Ave. & Walnut St.(19426), pg. 261
COLLEGEVILLE/IMAGINEERING L.P., 4th Ave. & Walnut Sts.(19426), pg. 262
SUPERIOR TUBE COMPANY, Germantown Pike & Cross Keys Rd.(19426), pg. 1064

Colmar

CAPITAL CONTROLS COMPANY INC., 3000 Advance Lane(18915), pg. 215

Columbia

COLONIAL METALS CO., 217 Linden St.(17512), pg. 263

Concordville

THE FIBRE-METAL PRODUCTS COMPANY, Baltimore Pike & S. Brenton Lake Rd.(19331), pg. 408
IA CONSTRUCTION CORP., Rte. 202, P.O. Box 8(19331), pg. 558
SOUTH CHESTER TUBE CO., 210 Brinton Lake Rd.(19331), pg. 1019
WATKINS SYSTEM INC., Rte. 202(19331), pg. 1167

Conestoga

SAFE HARBOR WATER POWER CORPORATION, 5093 River Rd.(17516), pg. 966

Conshohocken

FINNAREN & HALEY, INC., 901 Washington St.(19428), pg. 411
FLORIG EQUIPMENT COMPANY, INC., 906 Ridge Pike(19428), pg. 421
Reilly-Whiteman Inc., 6801 Washington St.(19428), pg. 222
RESCO PRODUCTS, INC., 1302 Conshohocken Rd.(19428), pg. 928
RAYMOND ROSEN CO., 15 Colwell Ln.(19428), pg. 948
VeloBind, Inc., 2 Elm St.(19428), pg. 657

Coraopolis

CHEMCENTRAL/Pittsburgh, Parkway West, Montour Run Exit(15108), pg. 242
FORT PITT ACQUISITIONS COMPANY, INC., 400 Chess St.(15108), pg. 425
U.S. METALSOURCE CORPORATION, 200 Corporate Center Dr., Ste. 200(15108), pg. 1136

Corry

MCINNES STEEL COMPANY, 441 E. Main St.(16407), pg. 729

Croydon

PHILADELPHIA RESERVE SUPPLY COMPANY, 400 Mack Dr.(19021), pg. 867

Crystal Springs

Atlantic Lumber Company, P.O. Box 53(15536), pg. 965
Sabbeth World Wide Wood Corp., P.O. Box 53(15536), pg. 965

Danville

Kennedy Van Saun Corp., 2 Beaver St.(17821), pg. 732

Darlington

Pittsburgh Tube Darlington Div., (16115), pg. 873

Delano

The Ohio Mattress Company, Licensing And Components Group, Majic Industrial Park(18220), pg. 985

Delaware Water Gap

INSTRUMENT SPECIALTIES COMPANY, Rt. 611 & Broad St.(18327), pg. 572
Shawnee Press, Inc., 1 Waring Dr.(18327-1099), pg. 777

Denver

KALAS MANUFACTURING, INC., 25 Main St.(17517), pg. 615
SUNLINE COACH CO., INC., 245 S. Muddy Creek Rd.(17517), pg. 1061

Derry

INDUSTRIAL CERAMICS, INC., Porcelain Park(15627), pg. 566

Devault

DEVAULT FOODS, Devault Lane(19432), pg. 333

Donora

WEISS PACKING CO., INC., Turkey Hollow Rd.(15033), pg. 1174

Douglassville

AMERICAN CRANE & EQUIPMENT CORP., 531 Old Swede Rd.(19518), pg. 51

Downingtown

O'BRIEN MACHINERY COMPANY, 100 Green St.(19335), pg. 820

Doylestown

KDI Sylvan Pools, Inc., P.O. Box 1449(18901), pg. 612

Du Bois

McDowell Mfg. Co., P.O. Box 665, (15801), pg. 32
Triangle Auto Spring Company, P.O. Box 425, Maloney Rd.(15801), pg. 711

Earl

CONESTOGA WOOD SPECIALTIES, INC., P.O. Box 158, (17519), pg. 273

East Butler

SERVISTAR CORPORATION, Servistar Way(16029), pg. 992

East Greenville

Knoll Intl., Inc., P.O. Box 157, Water St.(18041), pg. 1121

East McKeesport

Precise Metals & Plastics, Inc., 501 Mosside Blvd.(15035), pg. 612

East Stroudsburg

THE INTERNATIONAL BOILER WORKS COMPANY, 460 Birch St.(18301), pg. 575
Mack Printing Co. Inc., 34 N. Crystal St.(18301), pg. 697
Monroe Printing Company, 34 N. Crystal St.(18301), pg. 697

Easton

Binney & Smith Inc., 1100 Church Lane(18042), pg. 502
Crayola Products Div., 1100 Church Lane(18044), pg. 502
Hallmark Art Products & International Div., PO Box 431, 1100 Church Lane(18044), pg. 502
Hallmark Educational Products Div., 1100 Church Lane(18044), pg. 502
MACK PRINTING COMPANY, 1991 Northampton St.(18042), pg. 697
Mack Publishing Co., 1991 Northampton St.(18042), pg. 697
VICTAULIC COMPANY OF AMERICA, 4901 Kesslersville Rd.(18042), pg. 1149
Victaulic International, 4901 Kesslerville Rd.(18042), pg. 1149
Victaulic Tool Company, P.O. Box 31, (18042), pg. 1149

Ebensburg

L. ROBERT KIMBALL & ASSOCIATES, 615 W. Highland Ave.(15931), pg. 629

Eddystone

Foam Product Corporation, 1500 E. Secont St.(19013), pg. 1121

Edgemont

Intertec Publishing Corp., 5072 W. Chester Pike(19028), pg. 611

Eighty Four

84 LUMBER CO., St. Rte. 371

Ellwood City

ELLWOOD CITY FORGE, Commercial Ave.(16117), pg. 378

Emmaus

RODALE PRESS, INC., 33 E. Minor St.(18098), pg. 942

Emporium

MALLERY LUMBER CORP., Star Rte., Box 702

Ephrata

HAMILTON EQUIPMENT, INC., 567 S. Reading Rd.(17522), pg. 503
Science Press, 300 W. Chestnut(17522), pg. 697

Erie

Applicator Co., 2431 W. Grandview Blvd.(16506), pg. 875
Color Cosmetics, 2310 Pittsburgh Ave.(16506), pg. 875
COMPONENT TECHNOLOGY CORP., 3409 W. 14th St.(16505), pg. 270
Erie Bronze & Aluminum Co., 6300 West Ridge Rd.(16505), pg. 730
ERIE FAMILY LIFE INSURANCE COMPANY, 100 Erie Insurance Place(16530), pg. 386
Erie Indemnity Company, 100 Erie Insurance Place(16530), pg. 386
Erie Insurance Exchange, 100 Erie Insurance Place(16530), pg. 386
Erie Insurance Group, 100 Erie Insurance Place(16530), pg. 386
ERIE PRESS SYSTEMS, 1253 W. 12th(16512), pg. 386
ERIEZ MAGNETICS, Asbury Road at Airport(16506), pg. 386
Fenestra Corporation, P.O. Box 8189, (16505), pg. 711
Flagship City Insurance Company, 100 Erie Insurance Place(16530), pg. 386
Lord Corp., Industrial Adhesives & Coatings Div., 2000 W. Grandview Blvd.(16514), pg. 683
Lord Corp., Industrial Products Div., 1952 W. Grandview Blvd.(16514-10040), pg. 683
LORD CORPORATION, 2000 W. Grandview Blvd.(16514-0038), pg. 683
McInnes Rolled Rings, 1533 E. 12th St.(16511), pg. 730
MORRIS COUPLING CO., 2240 W. 15th St.(16505), pg. 771
Penn Erie Div., 2315 W. 23rd. St.(16506), pg. 875
PLASTEK GROUP, 2425 W. 23rd. St.(16506), pg. 874
Plastek Industries, Inc., 3001 W. 15th St.(16505), pg. 875
Plastek Tool, Inc., 3001 W. 15th St.(16505), pg. 875
SNAP-TITE, INCORPORATED, 3250 W. Lake Rd.(16505), pg. 1014
Spectrum Molding, 2425 W. 23rd St.(16506), pg. 875
TAL INC., 3645 W. Lake Rd.(16505), pg. 1077
Triangle Tool Co., 3230 W. 22nd St.(16506), pg. 875
UNIFLOW MANUFACTURING CO., 1525 E. Lake Rd.(16512), pg. 1126

Exton

ERM-Computer Services, Inc., 865 Springdale Dr.(19341), pg. 360
ERM-EnviroClean, 855 Springdale Dr.(19341), pg. 360
THE ERM GROUP, 855 Springdale Dr.(19341), pg. 360
NTH Consultants, Ltd., 860 Spring Lane(19341), pg. 781
NETZSCH, INC., 119 Pickering Way(19341), pg. 798
WOLFINGTON BODY COMPANY, Route 100(19341), pg. 1199

Eynon

CASKET SHELLS, INC., First St.(18403), pg. 228

Fairfield

Arcata Graphics Fairfield Inc., P. O. Drawer AN(17320), pg. 80

Fairless Hills

General Felt, Fairless Hills, 259 Canal Rd.(19030), pg. 1121

Fairview

PHB PARKER DIE CASTINGS, 7900 W. Ridge Rd.(16415), pg. 836

Felton

Superior Division of Key Plastics, Box 160, Rd. 1(17322-0160), pg. 627

Folcroft

Adec Automation, 701 Ashland Center Three(19032), pg. 17
Parade Publications, Inc., 830 Henderson Blvd.(19032), pg. 847

Fort Washington

A-1 Transmissions, 240 New York Dr.(19034), pg. 288
Accounting Forms Company, Inc., 455 Maryland Dr.(19034), pg. 966
WALTER BENNETT COMMUNICATIONS, 7111 Valley Green Rd., Ste. 220(19034), pg. 139
COTTMAN TRANSMISSION SYSTEMS, INC., 240 New York Dr.(19034), pg. 288
Prudential Eastern Home Office, P.O. Box 388, (19034), pg. 897
SAFEGUARD BUSINESS SYSTEMS, INC., 470 Maryland Dr.(19034), pg. 966
Safeguard Financial Corp., 455 Maryland Dr.(19034), pg. 966

Forty Fort

Harte-Hanks Direct Marketing/Pennsylvania, 900 Rutter Ave.(18704), pg. 513
OMNI LENS CORPORATION, One Arlington Rd.(18704), pg. 826
VIVIAN MILLWORKS, 61 Elizabeth St.(18704), pg. 1154

Franklin

FRANKLIN STEEL COMPANY, 600 Atlantic Ave.(16323), pg. 429

Franklin Center

The Franklin Mint, U.S. Rte. 1(19091), pg. 60

Frazer

ESSEX GRAIN PRODUCTS, INC., 9 Lee Blvd.(19355), pg. 389
NATIONAL LIBERTY, 20 Moores Rd.(19355), pg. 791
Norwood Industries, Inc., 57 Morehall Rd.(19355), pg. 993

Fredericksburg

FARMER'S PRIDE, INC., West Main St.(17026), pg. 401

Freeport

Independent Tool & Die, Silverville Rd.(16229), pg. 819
Oberg Carbide Punch & Die, Silverville Rd.(16229), pg. 819
OBERG INDUSTRIES CO., Silverville Rd.(16229), pg. 819
Oberg Mfg. Co., Silverville Rd.(16229), pg. 820

Garrett

Penn Pocahontas Coal Company, Rte. 219, P.O. Box 248(15542), pg. 711

Gibsonia

Pennsylvania Services Corporation, Kramer Road(15044), pg. 293

Glen Rock

Adhesive Research, Inc., P.O. Box 100(17327), pg. 1102
Stewart Connector Systems, Inc., R.D.2, P.O. Box 2020, (17327), pg. 571

Glenshaw

GLENSHAW GLASS CO. INC., William Flinn Hwy. 1101(15116), pg. 462

Goodville

RUTT CUSTOM CABINETRY, P.O. Box 129(17528), pg. 957

Greensburg

OVERLY MANUFACTURING CO., 574 W. Otterman(15601), pg. 833
TRIBUNE REVIEW PUBLISHING CO., 622 Cabin Hill Dr.(15601), pg. 1112

Greenville

Mercer Paper Tube Co., P.O. Box 29 Arlington Rd.(16125), pg. 1209

Grove City

Bestpak, Inc., P.O. Box 1128, 600 Barkeyville Rd.(16127), pg. 583
Ivex Packaging Corporation-Grove City, P.O. Box 1128, 600 Barkeyville Rd.(16127), pg. 583

Hamburg

HOOD & COMPANY, P.O. Box 485(19526), pg. 542

Hanover

HANOVER FOODS CORPORATION, P.O. Box 334(17331), pg. 506
Miller Chemical & Fertilizer Corp., Radio Road(17331), pg. 32
THE SHERIDAN GROUP, 450 Fame Ave.(17331), pg. 998
The Sheridan Press, Inc., Fame Ave.(17331), pg. 998
SNYDER'S OF HANOVER, INC., P.O. Box 917, (17331), pg. 1015

Harrisburg

Alco Health Services Northeast-Harrisburg, 600 S. 17th St.(17104), pg. 32
American Sentinel Insurance Company, P.O. Box 1651, (17105), pg. 387
CUNA Eastern District Office, 4309 N. Front St.(17110), pg. 205
CLEVELAND BROTHERS EQUIPMENT CO., 5300 Paxton St.(17105), pg. 255
Cowles Magazines, Inc., 6405 Flank Dr.(17105), pg. 291
COWLES MAGAZINES, INC., P.O. Box 8200, (17105), pg. 291
D&H DISTRIBUTING COMPANY, 2525 N. 7th St.(17110), pg. 307
GANNETT FLEMING AFFILIATES, INC., P.O. Box 67100, (17106-7100), pg. 442
Harrisburg Stamp Co., 2741 Paxton St.(17111), pg. 58
HERSHEY CREAMERY COMPANY, 301 S. Cameron(17101), pg. 531
MONY Brokerage, Inc., P.O. Box 8009, (17105), pg. 778
NORCAM Construction Company, 1611 N. Cameron St., P.O. Box 2951(17105), pg. 937
Pepper, Hamilton & Scheetz, 200 One Keystone Plaza(17108), pg. 860
RITTER BROS., INC., 1511 N. Cameron St.(17105), pg. 936
SCHAEDLER BROTHERS, INC., 1030 S. 13th St.(17104), pg. 974
STABLER COMPANIES, INC., 635 Lucknow Rd.(17110), pg. 1034
Stabler Construction Company, 635 Lucknow Rd.(17110), pg. 1034
TV HOST INC., 3935 Jonestown Rd.(17109), pg. 1075
Total Exposition Concepts, P.O. Box 4175(17111), pg. 993
UNITED TECTONIC INDUSTRY, 7201 Paxton St.(17111), pg. 1137

Hatboro

ELASTOMERIC TECHNOLOGIES, INC., 2940 Turnpike Dr.(19040), pg. 372
HULL CORPORATION, 3535 Davisville Rd.(19040), pg. 552

Hatfield

HATFIELD QUALITY MEATS, INC., 2700 Funks Rd.(19440-2834), pg. 517
ROSENBERGERS DAIRIES, INC., 847 Forty Foot Rd.(19440), pg. 948

Hazleton

A. BARLETTA & SONS, P.O. Box 40(18201), pg. 120

BUCILLA CORPORATION, 1 Oak Ridge Rd.(18201-9764), pg. 185
BARRETT HAENTJENS & COMPANY, 225-39 N. Cedar St.(18201), pg. 499
Ivex Packaging Corporation-Polymerization and Extrusion Division, P.O. Box 658, 666 Dietrich Ave.(18201), pg. 583
Legacy Gifts, 1 Oak Ridge Rd.(10201-9847), pg. 185
Pocono Knits, Inc., 100 E. Diamond(18201), pg. 1209
STAR-PARTS INC., P.O. Box 160, 125 Butler Dr.(18201), pg. 1039
Stencils USA, 1 Oak Ridge Rd.(18201-9847), pg. 185
JACK YOUNG ASSOCIATES, 100 E. Diamond Ave.(18201-0522), pg. 1209

Hidden Valley

Hidden Valley Resort, One Craighead Dr.(15502), pg. 626

Homestead

American Shear Knive Co., 501 W. 7th Ave.(15120), pg. 88
ASKO, INC, 501 W. 7th Ave.(15120), pg. 88

Honesdale

KATZ, INC., 214 6th St.(18431), pg. 618

Horsham

Decision Data, One Progress Ave.(19044), pg. 324
Decision Data Direct, One Progress Ave.(19044), pg. 324
DECISION DATA INC., One Progress Ave.(19044), pg. 323
DUDNYK ADVERTISING, Commonwealth Corp. Center, 100 Tournament Dr.(19044), pg. 351
Kasser/Laird Distilling Co., 419 Sargon Way, Unit 8(19044), pg. 650
LETVEN-DICCICCO, INC., Horsham Business Ctr., 455 Business Ctr. Dr.(19044), pg. 669
THE PHILLIPS AGENCY, 800 Business Center Dr., Ste. 100(19044), pg. 867
QUAD SYSTEMS CORPORATION, 2 Electronic Dr.(19044), pg. 902

Huntingdon Valley

PENN COLOUR GRAPHICS, INC., 99 Buck Rd.(19006), pg. 857

Indiana

Eastern American Energy Corp., 2281 Airport Prof. Bldg.(15701), pg. 363

Industry

Great Lakes Terminal & Transport of Pennsylvania, P.O. Box 281, (15052), pg. 482

Irvine

NATIONAL FORGE COMPANY, One Front St.(16329), pg. 788
National Forge Export Corp., Front St.(16329), pg. 789

Irwin

Carbidie Corporation, Arona Rd.(15642), pg. 1032
T-R Printing & Publishing, P.O. Box280, (15642), pg. 1113

Jeannette

ELLIOTT COMPANY, N. Fourth St.(15644), pg. 378
MILLSTEIN INDUSTRIES, 4th & Gaskill Ave.(15644), pg. 756
National Plastics Corporation, 4th & Gaskill Aves.(15644), pg. 756

Jenkintown

SCHARFBERG & ASSOCIATES, LTD. ADV., 911 Benjamin Fox Pavilion(19046), pg. 974

Johnstown

CROWN AMERICAN CORPORATION, Pasquerilla Plaza(15907), pg. 301
Dollar Bargain Stores, Franklin & Locust Sts.(15901), pg. 978
G B Stores, 110 Franklin Sts.(15901), pg. 978
Glosser Bros. Department Store, Franklin & Locust Sts.(15901), pg. 978
Glosser Brothers, Inc., Franklin & Locust Sts.(15901), pg. 978
JOHNSTOWN CORPORATION, 545 Central Ave.(15902), pg. 601
UNITED METAL FABRICATORS, INC., 409 Eisenhower Blvd.(15904), pg. 1133
Warehouse Outlet Stores, Franklin & Locust Sts.(15901), pg. 978
Winner's Ladies Off-Price Specialty Store, Franklin & Locust Sts.(15901), pg. 978

Kane

Stackpole Magnet Division, 700 Elk Ave.(16735), pg. 1034

Kennett Square

CALICO CORNERS, 203 Gale Ln.(19348), pg. 209

Kimberton

MONSEY PRODUCTS COMPANY, Coldstream Rd.(19442), pg. 766

King of Prussia

AMERICAN FOODSERVICE CORP., 400 Drew Ct.(19406), pg. 54
Automatic Timing & Controls, Inc., 201 S. Gulph Rd.(19406), pg. 332
Berwind Pharmaceuticals Services, Inc., 610 Freedom Bus. Center, Ste. 204(19406), pg. 145
Burns & Roe Environmental Services, 601 S. Henderson Rd., Ste. 250(19406), pg. 194
H. S. CROCKER CO., INC., Valley Forge Square, 660 American Ave., Ste. 102(19406), pg. 299
EGGLAND'S BEST, INC., 842 First Ave.(19406), pg. 371
ELECTRO-SCIENCE LABORATORIES, INC., 416 E. Church Rd.(19406-1533), pg. 375
MAACO ENTERPRISES INC., 381 Brooks Rd.(19406), pg. 694
PHILADELPHIA GEAR CORP., 181 S. Gulph Rd.(19406), pg. 866
PREMIER REFRACTORIES & CHEMICALS INC., 901 E. Eighth Ave.(19406), pg. 887
Wells Fargo Alarm Services, 780 Fifth Ave.(19406), pg. 166
ZUCKERMAN-HONICKMAN INC., 191 S. Gulph Rd.(19406), pg. 1221

Kulpsville

NIBCO Piping Products East, P.O. Box 1387, 1510 Gehman Rd.(19443), pg. 806

Lafayette Hill

Grant Design, 2001 Joshua Rd.(19444), pg. 477
GRANT MARKETING COMMUNICATIONS INC., 2001 Joshua Rd.(19444), pg. 477
Grant Promotion, 2001 Joshua Rd.(19444), pg. 477
Grant Public Relations, 2001 Joshua Rd.(19444), pg. 477
HOLTON NAMIOTKA JONES, INC., 706 Ridge Pike(19444), pg. 541
NATIONAL LABEL COMPANY, 2025 Joshua Rd.(19444), pg. 791

Lake City

Van Air Systems, Inc., 350 Mechanic St.(16423), pg. 386

Lancaster

ERIN GROUP ADMINISTRATORS, INC., 2260 Erin Ct.(17604), pg. 387
FURNIVAL/STATE MACHINERY CO., 1857 William Penn Way(17601), pg. 437
GODFREY ADVERTISING, 2890 Hempland Rd.(17601), pg. 464
Hanover Foods Corp., Plum & Liberty Streets(17604), pg. 506
Heil Bulk Trailer Co., 3249 Hempland Rd.(17604), pg. 525
HIGH INDUSTRIES INC., 1853 William Penn Way(17605), pg. 533
HYDRO/KIRBY AGRI SERVICE, INC., 500 Running Pump Rd.(17603), pg. 556
KELLY MICHENER INC., 416-418 W. Marion St.(17603), pg. 621
KUNZLER & COMPANY, INC., 640-662 Manor St.(17603), pg. 646
LANCASTER HOST RESORT, 2300 Lincoln Hwy. E.(17602), pg. 653
LANCASTER MALLEABLE CASTINGS COMPANY, 1170 Lititz Ave.(17601), pg. 653
Lindenmeyr Munroe, 3041 Industry Drive(17603-4025), pg. 233
Marine Tech, 167 Greenfield Rd.(17602), pg. 758
RAUB SUPPLY COMPANY, James & Mulberry Streets(17601), pg. 913
Sensenich Propeller Co., P.O. Box 5100, East Airport Rd.(17601), pg. 866
Sentinel Management Services, Inc., 2250 Erin Ct.(17604), pg. 387
Totes Incorporated, 260 Centerville Rd.(17603), pg. 1103

Landisville

A. H. HOFFMAN, INC., 77 Cooper Ave.(17538), pg. 538
Hoffman Seeds, Inc., 144 Main St.(17538), pg. 538

Langhorne

EXACT EQUIPMENT CORPORATION, 850 Town Center Dr.(19047), pg. 392
Jorgensen Steel & Aluminum/Philadelphia, 58 Cabot Blvd.(19047), pg. 606
Kilsby-Roberts/Philadelphia, 58 Cabot Blvd.(19047), pg. 606

Lansdale

CLEMENS MARKETS INC., 616 E. Main St.(19446), pg. 254
R.A. INDUSTRIES, INC., Welsh Rd.(19446), pg. 906

Large

DICK CORPORATION, 900 Rte. 51(15025), pg. 335

Lawrence

Black Box Corporation, P.O. Box 12800, (15055), pg. 748

Lebanon

LEBANON CHEMICAL CORP., 1600 E. Cumberland St.(17042), pg. 665
WALTER H. WEABER SONS, INC., RD 1169
WHITE, GOOD & CO., 418 Chestnut St.(17042), pg. 1185

Leesport

R.W. EAKEN, INC., P.O. Box 171(19533), pg. 362

Lehigh Valley

Bell & Howell Phillipsburg Company, P.O. Box 7950, (18001), pg. 135

Leola

A.S.M. Industries, 1 Lark Ave.(17540), pg. 991
Elixir Industries, 304 East Main, P.O. Box 312(17540), pg. 376
ROSS ENGINEERING CO., INC., 104 N. Maple Ave.(17540), pg. 949

Lewis Run

MCCOURT LABEL CO., 20 Egbert Lane(16738), pg. 727

Lewisburg

JPM COMPANY, Rte. 15(17837), pg. 586

Library

Mathies Coal Co., Dowling St.(15129), pg. 794

Lima

PILOT AIR FREIGHT CORP., 314 N. Middletown Rd.(19037), pg. 870

Linesville

Molded Fiber Glass Tray Co., E. Erie St.(16424), pg. 764

Lionville

BENTLEY-HARRIS MANUFACTURING CO., 241 Welsh Pool Rd.(19353), pg. 140

Lititz

bioproducts, Inc., 830 W. Lexington Ave., P.O. Box 316(17543), pg. 152
Wilbur Chocolate Co., Inc., 48 No. Broad St.(17543), pg. 219
YERGER BROS., INC., 520 Front St.(17543), pg. 1208

Malvern

ALCO HEALTH SERVICES CORPORATION, 300 Chester Field Pkwy.(19355), pg. 31
ENSONIQ CORPORATION, 155 Great Valley Pkwy.(19355), pg. 382
Semex, Inc., 57 Morehall Rd.(19355), pg. 993

Manheim

FENNER MANHEIM, 311 W. Stiegel St.(17545-1010), pg. 406
LIFT-ALL CO., INC., 102 S. Heintzelman St.(17545), pg. 675
Pennsylvania Services Corp., R.D. 1, Route 72(17545), pg. 293
RAYMARK FRICTION COMPANY, 123 E. Stiegel St.(17545), pg. 914

Mars

JAMES AUSTIN CO., P.O. Box 827(16046), pg. 99
ROESSING BRONZE CO., Evans City Rd.(16046), pg. 943

Martinsburg

Cove Shoe Company, 107 Highland St.(16662), pg. 182

McConnellsburg

H.B. MELLOTT ESTATE, INC., 328 N. Second St.(17233), pg. 738

McMurray

Voltec, 3075 Washington Rd.(15317), pg. 972

Meadville

CHANNELLOCK, INC., 1306 S. Main St.(16335), pg. 239
DAD'S PRODUCTS CO., INC., Mill St.(16335), pg. 310
MEADVILLE FORGING CO., P.O. Box 459-D(16335), pg. 733
SECO WARWICK CORPORATION, 180 Mercer St.(16335), pg. 987
TALON, INC., 626 Arch St.(16335), pg. 1077

Media

Alimak Elevator Company, P.O. Box 997(19063), pg. 34
Seybold Publications, P.O. Box 644, 428 Baltimore Pike(19063), pg. 1219
Seybold Publications, 428 E. Baltimore Pike(19063), pg. 1219
SUNROC CORPORATION, 300 S. Pennell Rd.(19063), pg. 1062

Middletown

PENNSYLVANIA STATE LOTTERY, 2850 Turnpike Industrial Dr., Bldg. 858
PETROLEUM PRODUCTS CORP., 900 Eisenhower Blvd.(17057), pg. 865

Mifflintown

EMPIRE KOSHER POULTRY, INC., River Road(17059), pg. 379

Milford

Altec Lansing Consumer Products, P.O. Box 277(18337-0277), pg. 1025
The Pocono Bank, P.O. Box 1049, (18337), pg. 534
SPARKOMATIC CORPORATION, Rte. 6 & 209(18337), pg. 1025

Millersburg

BRUBAKER TOOL CORP., Front & Center(17061), pg. 183

Milton

Gold Bond Building Products, P.O. Box 338, (17847), pg. 790

MILTON SHOE MANUFACTURING COMPANY, INC., 700 Hepburn St.(17847), pg. 756

Monaca

PITTSBURGH TUBE CO., 2060 Pennsylvania Ave.(15061), pg. 873
Pittsburgh Tube Monaca Div., (15061), pg. 873
Zinc Corporation of America, 300 Frankfort Rd.(15061), pg. 545

Monroeville

ENI Engineering Company, 339 Haymaker Rd.(15146), pg. 609
GAI Construction Monitoring Services, Inc., 570 Beatty Rd.(15146), pg. 439
GAI CONSULTANTS, INC., 570 Beatty Rd.(15146), pg. 439 817

Montgomeryville

Malco Microdot, 201 Progress Dr.(18936), pg. 749
PYTTRONIC INDUSTRIES, INC., 422 Stump Rd.(18936), pg. 901
Zink & Triest, 111 Commerce Dr.(18936), pg. 1100

Montoursville

Schnadig Corp., (17754), pg. 977

Morgantown

Kayeness, Inc., 115 Thousand Oaks Blvd., Ste. 101(19543), pg. 145
McNeilus Companies, Hemlock Rd.(19543), pg. 732

Mount Jewett

PTC Thermistor Div., Drawer 1(16704), pg. 628

Mount Joy

FIRST MOUNT JOY CORPORATION, P.O. Box 308, (17552), pg. 413
NEW STANDARD CORPORATION, Pinkerton Rd.(17552), pg. 802
Rollman Supply Company, 9-15 Mt. Joy St.(17552), pg. 1001
THE SICO COMPANY, 15 Mt. Joy St.(17552), pg. 1001
Sisco Company, P.O. Box 302(17552), pg. 413
Spangles' Flour Mills of Mt. Joy, (17552), pg. 1190

Mount Wolf

New York Wire Co., Textile Mill, 152 N. Main St.(17347), pg. 947
ROOT CORPORATION, 152 N. Main St.(17347), pg. 946

Mountaintop

CORNELL IRON WORKS, INC., Crestwood Industrial Park(18707), pg. 286
Cornell Storefront Systems, Inc., Crestwood Industrial Park(18707), pg. 286

Murrysville

BECKWITH MACHINERY COMPANY, U.S. Route 22 East(15668), pg. 131

Nazareth

Transilwrap Company, Inc., 615 Daniels Rd.(18064), pg. 1107

New Britain

BATEMAN BROTHERS LUMBER CO., INC., 89 Sand Rd.(18901), pg. 125

New Castle

FISHERS BIG WHEEL INC., 102 Nesbitt Rd.(16105), pg. 415
Lockley Manufacturing Division, 310 Grove St.(16103), pg. 383
Shaw-Perkins Inc., 205 W. Washington St., P.O. Box 1486(16103), pg. 916
Snark Boats Div., P.O. Box 2360, Industrial St.(16102), pg. 383

New Kensington

BURRELL GROUP, 2400 Leechburg Rd.(15068), pg. 195
Continental Development Company, 2400 Leechburg Rd.(15068), pg. 195
Omega Transworld Ltd., 2400 Leechburg Rd.(15068), pg. 195

New Kingstown

VALK MANUFACTURING COMPANY, 66 E. Main St.(17072), pg. 1143

New Oxford

ROUND HILL FOODS, INC., South Water St.(17350), pg. 952

Newtown

DUNMORE CORPORATION, 207 Penns Trail(18940), pg. 353

Norristown

GENUARDI SUPER MARKETS INC., 805 E. Germantown Pike(19401), pg. 452
H.S. Crocker Co., Inc., Valley Forge Corp. Ctr.(19403), pg. 299
LARAMIE TIRE DISTRIBUTORS INC., 700 Markley St.(19404), pg. 658
Lockwood Folding Box, Valley Forge Corp. Ctr.(19403), pg. 300
PREMIER DENTAL PRODUCTS COMPANY, 1710 Romano Dr.(19404), pg. 886
SETON COMPANY, 2500 Monroe Blvd.(19403-2325), pg. 993
STREAMLIGHT INC., 1030 W. Germantown Pike(19403), pg. 1053

North East

BETTER BAKED FOODS, INC., 56 Smedley St.(16428), pg. 148
RIDG-U-RAK, INC., South Lake St.(16428), pg. 933

North Versailles

FlexRx, 1810 Lincoln Hwy.(15137), pg. 456

North Wales

ROSKA DIRECT MARKETING, INC., 1364 Welsh Rd.(19454), pg. 949

Northumberland

FURMAN FOODS, INC., R.R. 2(17857-0502), pg. 436

Oakmont

EDGEWATER CORPORATION, 300 College Ave.(15139-2199), pg. 368
Edgewater Steel Co., 300 College Ave.(15139), pg. 368

Oaks

DETTRA FLAG COMPANY, 120 Montgomery Ave.(19456), pg. 333
PENCO PRODUCTS, Brower Ave.(19456), pg. 857

Oil City

Allied Security Inc., 214 Center St.(16301), pg. 39

Old Forge

Keystone Crash Parts Mart - Old Forge, 433 Lawrence St.(18518), pg. 628
PANEL PRINTS, INC., 1001 Moosic Rd.(18518), pg. 846

Ottsville

MODERN CONCRETE SEPTIC TANK COMPANY, Durham Rd.(18942), pg. 762
Wehrung Family Home Center, Route 611(18942), pg. 762

Palmerton

Horsehead Resource Development Company, Inc., 613 3rd St.(18071), pg. 545

Paradise

DENLINGER, INC., 3246 Lincoln Hwy. E(17562), pg. 329

Peach Glen

KNOUSE FOODS INC., 800 Peach Glen/Idaville Rd.(17375-0001), pg. 637

Perkasie

PERKASIE INDUSTRIES CORPORATION, 50 E. Spruce St.(18944), pg. 862

Philadelphia

ARA Environmental Services, Inc., 1101 Market St.(19107), pg. 6
ARA GROUP, ARA Tower, 1101 Market St.(19107), pg. 5
ARA Leisure Convention Services, Inc., 1101 Market Street(19107), pg. 6
ARA Leisure Services, Inc., 1101 Market Street(19107), pg. 6
ARA Services, Inc., ARA Tower, 1101 Market St.(19107), pg. 5
ARA Services of Texas, Inc., 1101 Market St.(19107), pg. 6
ARA Virginia Sky-Line Co., Inc., 1101 Market St.(19106), pg. 6
ACTION MANUFACTURING CO., 100 E. Erie(19134), pg. 15
ADELPHIA LAMP & SHADE INC., 5000 Paschall Ave.(19143), pg. 17
Aero Enterprises, Inc., Philadelphia International Airport(19153), pg. 6
After Six Access, 22nd & Market Sts.(19103), pg. 24
AFTER SIX, INCORPORATED, G. St. & Hunting Pk. Ave.(19124), pg. 24
Alco Health Services Northeast-Philadelphia, 1011 W. Butler St.(19140), pg. 32
ALDAN RUBBER CO., 2701 E. Tioga St.(19134-6184), pg. 32
ALL-LUMINUM PRODUCTS, INC., 10981 Decatur Rd.(19154-3297), pg. 35
Allied Advertising Agency, 2218 Race St.(19103), pg. 37
ALLIED MERCANTILE COMPANY, 1627 Meadow St.(19124), pg. 38
Allied Security Inc., 7900 Bustleton Ave.(19152), pg. 39
ALMO CORP., 9815 Roosevelt Blvd.(19114), pg. 43
ALPHA SHIRT CO., 4309 G St.(19124), pg. 44
ALSTIN ADVERTISING, INC., The Drexel Bldg., 1435 Walnut St.(19102), pg. 45
American Envelope of Philadelphia, Fifth & Bristol(19140), pg. 199
AMERICAN PACKAGING CORPORATION, Grant Ave. & Ashton Rd.(19114), pg. 59
ANGELO BROTHERS CO., 12401 McNulty Rd.(19154), pg. 74
Araclean Services, Inc., Independence Sq. W., Sixth & Walnut Sts.(19106), pg. 6
ATLANTIC METALS CORPORATION, Orthodox St. at Delaware River(19137), pg. 95
Atlas Co. of Boston, Inc., 2121 E. Huntington St.(19125), pg. 1009
BACHMANN INDUSTRIES, INC., 1400 E. Erie Ave.(19124), pg. 108
BANKCRAFTERS, INC., 12 Oregon Ave.(19148), pg. 117
BELMONT INDUSTRIES, INC., 1900 Rittenhouse Sq.(19103), pg. 136
BERWIND CORPORATION, 3000 W. Tower, Centre Square, 1500 Market St.(19102), pg. 145
Berwind Property Group, Inc., 3000 Centre Square West(19102), pg. 145
THE BINSWANGER COMPANY, Seven Penn Center, 1635 Market St.(19103), pg. 151
Binswanger Development, Seven Penn Center, 1635 Market St.(19103), pg. 152
Binswanger Industrial, Seven Penn Center, 1635 Market St.(19103), pg. 152
Binswanger Investment, Seven Penn Center, 1635 Market St.(19103), pg. 152
Binswanger Management Corp., Seven Penn Center, 1635 Market St.(19103), pg. 152
Binswanger Realty, Seven Penn Center, 1635 Market St.(19103), pg. 152
STANLEY BLACKER, INC., 1801 Courtland St.(19140), pg. 155
Bolton-Emerson-McNiece, Inc., 1215 Unity St.(19142), pg. 163
Brokay Products, Inc., 9999 Gantry Rd.(19115), pg. 217
BROOKS PROVISIONS INC., 3445 S. Front St.(19148), pg. 180
THE BROWNSTEIN GROUP, 215 S. Broad St.(19107), pg. 183
BURGOYNE, INC., 2030 E. Byberry Rd., (19116), pg. 190
E. J. Burke Security Systems, Inc., 520 N. Delaware, Ste. 201(19123), pg. 166
BUTCHER & CO., INC., 211 S. Broad St.(19107), pg. 196
M. BUTEN & SONS INC., 5000 Ridge Ave.(19128), pg. 196
BUTLER FOODS, INC., 2300 E. Butler(19137), pg. 197
CAPITAL PANTS CO., 700 E. Erie Ave.(19134), pg. 215
CAPP, INC., 6117-6135 Market St.(19139), pg. 216
CAREERS USA INC., 1825 JFK Blvd.(19103), pg. 218
CEDAR FARMS COMPANY, INC., 2609 E. York St.(19125), pg. 230
CENTURY SEAFOOD INC., 3121-25 S. Lawrence St.(19148), pg. 235
COLONIAL BEEF CO., 3333 S. Third St.(19148), pg. 263
CoMed Communications Division, 210 W. Washington Square(19106), pg. 1092
Computer Information Services, Inc., 7300 Old York Rd.(19126), pg. 834
Connelly Containers, Inc. of Philadelphia, 4368 Main St.(19127), pg. 275
D&Z, Inc., 1818 Market St.(19103), pg. 320
DAVIS ADVERTISING INC., 1700 Market St., Ste. 2626(19103), pg. 318
Day Maintenance, 1818 Market St.(19103), pg. 320
DECHERT PRICE & RHOADS, 4000 Bell Atlantic Tower, 1717 Arch St.(19103-2793), pg. 323
DELAWARE RIBBON MANUFACTURERS, INC., 2531 Trenton Ave.(19125), pg. 326
Diamond Paper Box Co., 1330-40 Unity St.(19124), pg. 324
Dilks Stamp Co., 1613 Sansom St.(19103), pg. 58
DIRECT RESPONSE BROADCASTING NETWORK, INC., 1101 Market St., Ste. 1300(19107), pg. 339
DORLAND SWEENEY JONES, 701 Market St., Ste. 2000(19106), pg. 346
Engineering & Construction Division, 1818 Market St.(19103), pg. 320
FALCON CANDY COMPANY, 2300 Carpenter St.(19146), pg. 398
Fanta Furniture, 10981 Decatur Rd.(19154-3297), pg. 35
FARM JOURNAL, INC., 230 W. Washington Sq.(19106), pg. 401
FISHMAN & TOBIN, INC., 176 W. Louden St.(19120), pg. 415
H. FREEMAN & SON, INC., 3601 Island Rd.(19153), pg. 431
General Felt Industries, Inc., 2121 E. Wheatsheaf Ln.(19137), pg. 1121
GEOGRAPHIC MARKETING GROUP (GMG), The Curtis Center, Independence Square West(19105), pg. 452
Globe Security Systems, Inc., 520 No. Delaware, Ste. 201(19123), pg. 166
JACK GREENBERG INC., 1717 N. Delaware Ave.(19125), pg. 485
Albert M. Greenfield & Company, 1880 JFK Blvd.(19103), pg. 527
GROUP TWO ADVERTISING, INC., 2002 Ludlow St.(19103), pg. 490
HARRIS, BAIO & MCCULLOUGH INC., 520 S. Front St.(19147), pg. 511
HARRIS & DRUTT INC., 1520 Locust St.(19102), pg. 511
HAWTHORNE ADV., INC., Colonial Penn Plaza, 19th & Market Sts.(19181), pg. 518
Holmes Protection of Philadelphia, Inc., , pg. 540
J. G. HOOK, INC., 1300 Belmont Ave.(19104), pg. 543
Independence Square Properties, Independence Square(19172), pg. 858
INTERSTATE STEEL SUPPLY CO., 1800 E. Byberry Rd.(19116), pg. 580
CHARLES JACQUIN ET CIE, INC., 2633 Trenton Ave.(19125), pg. 588
Janney Montgomery Scott Inc., 1801 Market St.(19103), pg. 858
JORDON COMMERCIAL REFRIGERATOR CO., 2200 Kennedy(19137), pg. 605
Ketchum Advertising/Philadelphia, Bell Atlantic Tower, 1717 Arch St., Ste. 3300(19103-2786), pg. 625
Ketchum Public Relations/Philadelphia, Bell Atlantic Tower, 1717 Arch St., Ste. 3300(19103-2786), pg. 625
KINGSBURY, INC., 10385 Drummond Rd.(19154), pg. 632

Geographic Index

A. C. KISSLING, INC., 140 E. Richmond St.(19125), pg. 634
LA FRANCE CORPORATION, 8425 Executive Dr.(19153), pg. 649
LAVELLE AIRCRAFT COMPANY, 275 Geiger Rd.(19115), pg. 661
AL PAUL LEFTON CO., INC., Rohm & Haas Bldg., Independence Mall West(19106), pg. 666
Levy United News, 850 E. Luzerne St.(19124), pg. 672
Life Sciences International, 1818 Market St.(19103), pg. 320
Lindenmeyr Munroe, 919 Wallace St.(19123), pg. 233
Lindenmeyr National, 919 Wallace St.(19123), pg. 233
LUMCO INDUSTRIES, INC., 3812 Old York Rd.(19140), pg. 687
M.A.B. Paints, 52nd & Grays Ave.(19143), pg. 184
Manufacturing Div., P.O. Box 4584, (19131), pg. 713
MARQUETTE COPPERSMITHING CO., INC., P.O. Box 4584(19131), pg. 713
MCKINNEY INC. ADVERTISING & PUBLIC RELATIONS, One Curtis Center, One Independence Square West(19106), pg. 730
DAVID MICHAEL & CO. INC., 10801 Decatur Rd.(19154), pg. 747
Moran Towing of Pennsylvania, Inc., 1101 Market St., Ste. 2601(19107), pg. 769
Moshulu, Inc., Chestnut St. at Penn's Landing(19106), pg. 1029
NAMICO, INC., 4601 Flat Rock Rd.(19127), pg. 783
NATIONAL PROPERTY ANALYSTS, INC., 230 S. Broad St., Mezzanine(19102), pg. 792
National Video, Inc., 9990 Global Rd.(19115), pg. 1177
94th Aero Squadron of Philadelphia, Inc., No. Philadelphia Airport, 2750 Red Lion Rd.(19154), pg. 1029
NORTH AMERICAN PUBLISHING COMPANY, 401 N. Broad St.(19108), pg. 811
NuArc Co., 9810 Ashton Rd.(19114), pg. 817
O'BRIEN ENERGY SYSTEMS INC., 225 S. Eighth St.(19106), pg. 820
Operating Plant Services, 1818 Market St.(19103), pg. 320
Oxford Communities, Inc., 7300 Old York Blvd.(19126), pg. 834
Oxford Finance Companies, Inc., 7300 Old York Rd.(19126), pg. 835
OXFORD FIRST CORPORATION, 7300 Old York Rd.(19126-1884), pg. 834
P M COMPANY, 9800 Bustleton Ave.(19115), pg. 835
P.M. Health Care Div., 9800 Bustleton Ave.(19115), pg. 835
PACOR, INC., 1900 N. Sixth St.(19122), pg. 842
PARISI, INC., 3031 Red Lion Rd.(19114), pg. 848
PEARL-PRESSMAN-LIBERTY COMMUNICATIONS GROUP, 5th & Poplar Sts.(19123), pg. 853
PEIRCE-PHELPS, INC., 2000 N. 59th St.(19131), pg. 855
PENN EMBLEM CO., 10909 Dutton Rd.(19154), pg. 857
Penn Insurance & Annuity Co., Independence Square(19172), pg. 858
Penn Mutual Equity Services Inc., 1801 Market St.(19103), pg. 858
THE PENN MUTUAL LIFE INSURANCE COMPANY, Independence Square, 530 Walnut St.(19172), pg. 858
PENNOCK, 3027 Stokely Av.(19129), pg. 858
Pennsylvania Parking, Inc., 1201 Walnut St., 2nd Fl.(19107), pg. 42
PEPPER, HAMILTON & SCHEETZ, 3000 Two Logan Sq., Eighteenth & Arch Sts.(19103), pg. 860
PHILADELPHIA COCA-COLA BOTTLING CO., 725 Erie Ave. & 9th St.(19134), pg. 866
THE PHILLIES-A LIMITED PARTNERSHIP, Veterans Stadium, Broad St. & Pattison Ave.(19148), pg. 867
PINCUS BROS., INC., Independence Mall East(19106), pg. 870
Piping Design Div., P.O. Box 4584, (19131), pg. 713
A. POMERANTZ & CO., 1525 Chestnut St.(19102), pg. 880
POWELL ELECTRONICS INC., S. Island Rd. & Enterprise Ave.(19153), pg. 882
Provident Mutual Life & Annutiy Company of America, 1600 Market St.(19103), pg. 896
PROVIDENT MUTUAL LIFE INSURANCE CO., 1600 Market St.(19103), pg. 896
Quaker City Stamp Co., 4234 Macalester Ave.(19124), pg. 58
THE REICH GROUP, INC., Seven Penn Center, 1635 Market St., Ste. 200(19103), pg. 922
REIMEL CARTER ADVERTISING, INC., Academy House, 1420 Locust St.(19102), pg. 923
S.D. RICHMAN SONS, INC., 2435 E. Wheatsheaf Lane(19137), pg. 933
ROOSEVELT PAPER CO., 7601 State Rd.(19136-3496), pg. 946
RUMSEY ELECTRIC CO., 301 W. Hunting Park Ave.(19140), pg. 956
SPD TECHNOLOGIES, 13500 Roosevelt Blvd.(19116), pg. 963
Saxony Distillers Et Cie, Inc., 2633 Trenton Ave.(19125), pg. 588
SHAPSON GERO & SOMMERS, INC., 260 S. Broad St.(19102), pg. 995
SMITH-EDWARDS-DUNLAP COMPANY, Allegheny Ave. at Delaware Expwy.(19134), pg. 1012
SOUTHEASTERN PENNSYLVANIA TRANSPORTATION AUTHORITY, 714 Market St.(19106), pg. 1020
SOUTHWARK METAL MANUFACTURING COMPANY, 1600 & Washington Ave.(19146), pg. 1023
STERLING PAPER CO., 2155 E. Castor Ave.(19134), pg. 1047
STROUSE GREENBERG & CO., INC., 1626 Locust St.(19103), pg. 1054
Stuart-Ironsides, Inc., 4346 Tacony St.(19124), pg. 1055
TED THOMAS ASSOCIATES INC., ADVERTISING, 210 W. Washington Square(19106-3512), pg. 1092
TRIMFIT, INC., 10450 Drummond Rd.(19154), pg. 1113
United States Name Plate, Enterprise & Executive(19153), pg. 649
Valhalla Trading Co., 1717 N. Delaware Rd.(19125), pg. 485
Van Brunt Division, 4041 Ridge Ave.(19129), pg. 428
WALLACE LEISURE PRODUCTS, INC., 31 & Jefferson Sts.(19121), pg. 1160
Martin F. Weber Company, 2727 Southampton(19154), pg. 716
Weightman Advertising, Inc., 1818 Market St.(19103), pg. 1173
THE WEIGHTMAN GROUP, 1818 Market St.(19103), pg. 1173
Weightman Public Relations, 1818 Market St.(19103), pg. 1173
Weightman Research, 1818 Market St.(19103), pg. 1173
WEST COAST NATIONAL VIDEO, 9990 Global Rd.(19115), pg. 1177
Wilcox-Walter-Furlong Paper Co., 54th & Grays Ave.(19143), pg. 1157
WINCHELL MARKETING, 1315 Cherry St.(19107), pg. 1195
FRANK W. WINNE & SON, INC., 44 N. Front St.(19106), pg. 1196
WOLF, BLOCK, SCHORR & SOLIS-COHEN, Packard Bldg., 12th Fl., 15th & Chestnut Sts.(19102), pg. 1199
Woodhaven Foods, 11151 Roosevelt Blvd.(19154), pg. 7

Phoenixville

JOHN R. HOLLINGSWORTH CO., Nutt Rd. at French Creek(19460), pg. 539

Pittsburgh

Allegheny International Credit Corp., Two Oliver Plaza, Ste. 880(15222), pg. 1059
ALLIED SECURITY, INC., 2840 Library Rd.(15234), pg. 39
AMERICAN HEALTH COMPANIES, INC., 921 Penn Ave., 9th Fl.(15222), pg. 55
American Standard Signaling Products Group, 5800 Corporate Dr.(15237), pg. 61
American-Standard, Fluid Power Group, 5800 Corporate Dr.(15237), pg. 61
BABCOCK LUMBER COMPANY, 2220 Palmer St.(15218), pg. 107
BACHARACH INC., 625 Alpha Dr.(15238), pg. 108
BEARING SERVICE COMPANY, 500 Dargan St.(15224), pg. 130
BLATTNER/BRUNNER INC., 814 Penn Ave.(15222), pg. 156
BLAW KNOX CORP., One Oliver Plaza(15222), pg. 156
BRIDGES & COMPANY, INC., 1300 Brighton(15233), pg. 175
THE CARBIDE/GRAPHITE GROUP, INC., One Gateway Center-19th Fl.(15222), pg. 217
CHICAGO HOLDINGS, INC., 1000 RIDC Plaza(15238), pg. 245
THE CONAIR GROUP, INC., 20 Stanwix St., Ste. 620(15222), pg. 272
CREATIVE PRODUCTIONS, 7500 Thomas Blvd.(15208), pg. 297
CROWN COAL & COKE CO. INC., 200 Nine Parkway Center(15220), pg. 302
DDF&M INC. DUDRECK DEPAUL FICCO & MORGAN INC., 200 First Ave.(15222), pg. 308
DDF&M Direct, 200 First Ave.(15222), pg. 308
DAXUS CORPORATION, One Oliver Plaza(15222-2603), pg. 319
Diet Center, Inc., 921 Penn Ave., 9th Fl.(15222), pg. 55
EAT N PARK RESTAURANTS, 100 Park Manor Dr.(15205), pg. 364
ENGINEERED PRODUCTS, INC., 1844 Ardmore Blvd.(15221), pg. 382
Faber, Coe & Gregg of Pennsylvania, Inc., 2627 Penn Ave(15201), pg. 395
THE GAGE COMPANY, 3000 Liberty Ave.(15201), pg. 441
General Refractories Co., U. S. Refractories Div., 600 Grant St.(15219), pg. 136
GIANT EAGLE, INC., 101 Kappa Dr.(15238), pg. 455
Giant Eagle Market Co., 101 Kappa Dr.(15238), pg. 456
Grant Steel Corp., 3rd & Oliver(15110), pg. 265
GRAY BAUMGARTEN LAYPORT, INC., 2275 Swallow Hill Rd(15220), pg. 479
HALLMARK ADVERTISING, INC., Two Chatham Center(15219), pg. 501
HAMBURG BROTHERS INC., 40 24th Street(15222), pg. 502
Harbison-Walker Refractories, One Gateway Center(15222), pg. 565
HILLMAN COMPANY, 1900 Grant Bldg.(15219), pg. 535
Identification Systems Div., 1315 W. Liberty Ave.(15226), pg. 721
International Mill Construction, Inc., 435 Butler St., P.O. Box 925(15223), pg. 1099
International Mill Construction, Inc., 435 Butler St., P.O. Box 9525(15223), pg. 1099
Ketchum Advertising/Pittsburgh, Six PPG Place(15222), pg. 625
KETCHUM COMMUNICATIONS INC., 6 PPG Place(15222), pg. 625
KETCHUM, INC., Ketchum Center, 1030 5th Ave.(15219), pg. 626
Ketchum International Inc., Six PPG Place(15222), pg. 625
Ketchum Public Relations/Pittsburgh, Six PPG Place(15222), pg. 625
KOOLVENT ALUMINUM PRODUCTS, INC., 1417 McLaughlin Rd.(15241), pg. 641
LePage's, Inc., 120 Delta Drive(15238), pg. 287
MARC ADVERTISING, Four Station Square(15219), pg. 706
MATTHEWS INTERNATIONAL CORP., 6117 Broad St.(15206), pg. 721
Matthews Intl. Corp.-Graphic Systems Div., 1910 Cochran Rd.(15220), pg. 721
Matthews International Marking Systems Div., 6515 Penn Ave.(15206), pg. 721
Matthews International Memorial Division, 1315 W. Liberty Ave.(15226), pg. 721
Matthews Intl. Trading Corp., 1050 Brinton Rd.(15221), pg. 721
MCKEAN OLDSMOBILE COMPANY, 5001 Liberty Ave.(15224), pg. 730
MCNALLY WELLMAN COMPANY, 4800 Grand Ave.(15225), pg. 732
MEDRAD, INC., 271 Kappa Dr.(15238), pg. 736
MERITCARE, INC., One PPG Place, Ste. 2260(15222), pg. 740
Morgan Technical Services, Inc, 1 Station Square Ste. 230(15219), pg. 770
MUNROE, INC., 1820 N. Franklin St.(15233), pg. 776
NFM CREATIVE COMMUNICATIONS, 1340 Three Gateway Ctr.(15222), pg. 780
NS Land Company, 20 Stanwix St.(15222), pg. 794
PANNIER CORPORATION, 207 Sandusky St.(15212), pg. 846
PITTSBURGH BREWING COMPANY, 3340 Liberty Ave.(15201), pg. 873
Pittsburgh Gear Company, Neville Island(15255), pg. 169
PITTSBURGH PIRATES PROFESSIONAL BASEBALL CLUB, 600 Stadium Circle(15212), pg. 873
Pittsburgh Stadium Concessions, Inc., 100 Stadium Circle(15212), pg. 6
Power Piping Company, 829 Beaver Ave.(15233), pg. 509
REIDBORD BROS., INC., 5000 Baum Blvd.(15213), pg. 923
THE ST. GEORGE GROUP, INC., 2600 Centre City Tower(15222), pg. 966
SAUER INDUSTRIES, INC., 4960 U.S.X. Tower, 600 Grant St.(15219), pg. 972
SNAVELY FOREST PRODUCTS, INC., P.O. Box 9808(15227), pg. 1015
STEELITE, INC., 1010 Ohio River Blvd.(15202), pg. 1044
Tamarkin Co., Inc., 101 Kappa Dr.(15238), pg. 456
TASA CORPORATION, Two Gateway Center, Ste. 990(15222), pg. 1079
TIPPINS INCORPORATED, 435 Butler St.(15223), pg. 1099
Trumbull Investments, Inc., P.O. Box 98100(15227), pg. 1117
UNION SWITCH & SIGNAL INC., 5800 Corporate Dr.(15237), pg. 1129
VANDINE, HUMPHREY, HERBERT, ALBER & MANGES, INC., 322 Blvd. of the Allies(15222), pg. 1145
VECTURA GROUP, INC., 4 PPG Place, Ste. 300(15222), pg. 1146
WHTX-FM, 400 Ardmore Blvd.(15221), pg. 522
WPXI Inc., d/b/a WPXI-TV, 11 Television Hill(15214), pg. 292
WTAE-AM, 400 Ardmore Blvd.(15221), pg. 522
WTAE Division, 400 Ardmore Blvd.(15221), pg. 522
WTAE-TV, 400 Ardmore Blvd.(15221), pg. 523
Williams & Company, Inc., 901 Pennsylvania Ave.(15233), pg. 230
Williams House of Metals, Inc., 901 Pennsylvania Ave.(15233), pg. 230

Pittston

MARKDATA INC., Markdata Plaza(18640), pg. 708
S L C GRAPHICS, INC., 50 Rock St.(18640), pg. 963

Plains

Altec Industries Eastern Division, 250 Laird St.(18705), pg. 45

Pleasant Gap

Centre Lime & Stone Co., Inc., P.O. Box 130(16823), pg. 517

Plumsteadville

SCOTT SPECIALTY GASES, INC., 6141 Easton Road(18949), pg. 983

Plymouth Meeting

BCM ENGINEERS INC., One Plymouth Meeting Mall(19462), pg. 106
STRATTON MANAGEMENT COMPANY, Plymouth Meeting Exec. Campus, 610 W. Germantown Pike, Ste. 361(19462), pg. 1053

Pottstown

Neapco, Inc., Queen & Bailey St.(19464), pg. 1123
THE POLLOCK CORP., Industrial Hwy. & Kind Rd.(19464), pg. 879

Pottsville

GPS Healthcare, 1515 Mount Hope Ave.(17901), pg. 145
READING ANTHRACITE CO., 200 Mahantongo(17901), pg. 916
Reading Anthracite Coal Co., 200 Mahantongo(17901), pg. 916

Quakertown

E.W. KNAUSS & SON, INC., 625 E. Broad St.(18951), pg. 636
Magikitch'n, Inc., P.O. Box 729(18951), pg. 157

Radnor

Day Data Systems, 280 King of Prussia Rd.(19087), pg. 320
DAY & ZIMMERMANN, INC., 280 King of Prussia Rd.(19087), pg. 320
MDC Systems, 280 King of Prussia Rd.(19087), pg. 320
Protection Technology, 280 King of Prussia Rd.(19087), pg. 320
Transportation & Distribution Associates, 280 King of Prussia Rd.(19087), pg. 320

H. L. Yoh Company, 280 King of Prussia Rd.(19087), pg. 320

Reading

Advanced DZign Systems, 201 Schuylkill Ave.(19603), pg. 320
American Refractories Co., 1250 Clarion St.(19601), pg. 136
BACHMAN COMPANY, 50 N. 4th St.(19601), pg. 108
BERKS PRODUCTS CORPORATION, 726 Spring St.(19604), pg. 142
BOSCOV'S DEPARTMENT STORES, INC., 4500 Perkiomen Ave.(19606), pg. 167
Camp Hosiery, 1801 No. 12th St.(19604), pg. 400
DIETRICH'S MILK PRODUCTS, INC., 100 McKinley Ave.(19605-2117), pg. 337
ELBECO INCORPORATED, 4207 Pottsville Pike(19603), pg. 372
EXIDE CORPORATION, P.O. Box 14205, 635 Penn St.(19612), pg. 393
Interstate Container Corporation, Grace & Meade Sts.(19611), pg. 580
Penske Transportation Inc., Rte. 10, Green Hills(19603), pg. 859
Penske Truck Leasing Corp., P.O. Box 563, Rte. 10(19603), pg. 859
Premier Mill Corp., Exeter Industrial Park, One Birchmont Dr.(19606), pg. 887
READING BODY WORKS, INC., Hancock Blvd. & Gerry St.(19611), pg. 916
READING EAGLE COMPANY, 345 Penn St.(19603), pg. 916
READING TUBE CORP., Rte. 61(19605), pg. 916
SURGICAL SPECIALTIES, 40 S. Museum Rd.(19607), pg. 1065
WGM SAFETY CORPORATION, 205 Washington St.(19603), pg. 1156
WILLSON SAFETY PRODUCTS, 2nd & Washington Sts.(19601), pg. 1193
WINDSOR SERVICE, INC., 2415 Kutztown Rd.(19605), pg. 1196

Red Lion

BLOCKHOUSE CO., INC., 121 First Ave.(17356), pg. 157
SPECIALTY INDUSTRIES, INC., 120 N. Charles St.(17356), pg. 1027
YORKTOWNE, INC., 100 Redco Ave.(17356), pg. 1208

Rheems

JOHN COPES FOOD PRODUCTS, INC., 156 W. Harrisburg Ave.(17570), pg. 284

Richland

CARLOS R. LEFFLER INC., 225 E. Main St.(17087), pg. 666

Rosemont

Anchor Darling Industries Inc., 919 Conestoga Rd., Ste. 305, Bldg. Two(19010), pg. 230

Royersford

AMERICAN MACHINE & TOOL COMPANY, 4th Ave. & Spring St.(19468), pg. 57

Saint Marys

Graphite Specialites, 800 Theresia St.(15857), pg. 217
KEYSTONE CARBON COMPANY, 1935 State St.(15857-0313), pg. 628
Pure Carbon Company, 441 Hall Ave.(15857), pg. 1034

Sandy Lake

Spang Power Control, P.O. Box 457, Lake St.(16145), pg. 1025

Sayre

RYNONE MANUFACTURING CORPORATION, No. Thomas Ave.(18840), pg. 958

Schuylkill Haven

ALPHA MILLS CORP., 122 Margaretta St.(17972), pg. 43
TAMAQUA CABLE PRODUCTS CORPORATION, Willow St.(17972), pg. 1077

Scottdale

Blaw Knox - Duraloy Division, P.O. Box 81, Bridge St.(15683), pg. 156

Scranton

AFFILIATED FOOD DISTRIBUTORS, 1000 N. South Rd.(18508), pg. 23
GIANT MARKETS INC., 501 So. Washington Ave.(18505), pg. 456
HADDON CRAFTSMEN, INC., 1001 Wyoming Ave.(18509), pg. 499
B. LEVY & SONS, 700 North-South Rd.(18504), pg. 672
National Book Company Inc., Keystone Industrial Park(18512), pg. 816
Simplex Construction Co. Inc., Simplex Dr.(18504), pg. 1006
SIMPLEX INDUSTRIES, INC., Simplex Dr.(18504), pg. 1006
UNITED GILSONITE LABORATORIES, P.O. Box 70(18501), pg. 1132

Selinsgrove

K & L Feeds, R.D. 1(17870), pg. 379

Sharon

JOHN REYER COMPANY, City Center(16146), pg. 930
SHARON TUBE COMPANY, 134 Mill St.(16146), pg. 995

Simpson

GENTEX OPTICS, INC., 324 Main St.(18407), pg. 452

Sinking Spring

F.M. BROWN SONS, INC., 205 Woodrew Ave.(19608), pg. 183
KB Alloys, Inc., 2917 Windmill Rd.(19608), pg. 507

Snow Shoe

J. H. FRANCE REFRACTORIES CO., 1944 France Rd.(16874), pg. 428

Somerset

Somerset Welding & Steel, Inc., P.O. Box 735, (15501), pg. 934

Souderton

MOYER PACKING COMPANY, 249 Allentown Rd.(18964), pg. 774
Shelly Bros., Inc., P.O. Box 115(18964), pg. 178

Southampton

ATLANTIC DAIRY COOPERATIVE, 1225 Industrial Hwy.(18966), pg. 94
M & C SPECIALTIES COMPANY, 90 James Way(18966), pg. 690
PENNSYLVANIA PETROLEUM PRODUCT COMPANY, 1330 Industrial Hwy.(18966), pg. 858
QC, Inc., 1205 Industrial Hwy.(18966), pg. 95
Schiller-Pfeiffer, Inc., Street Rd.(18966), pg. 136

Spartansburg

Spartywood Products, Inc., Fairview Rd.(16434), pg. 989

Spring City

WEST DAIRIES, INC., P.O. Box 169, W. Bridge St., Stoney Run(19475), pg. 1177

Sproul

Belmont Industries, U.S. Refractories Div., (16682), pg. 136

State College

GLENN O. HAWBAKER, INC., 325 W. Aaron Dr.(16803), pg. 517

Stowe

Doehler-Jarvis Plant, 400 Old Reading Pike(19464), pg. 559

Stoystown

RIGGS INDUSTRIES, INC., Rte. 30 W.(15563), pg. 934

Stratton

TECHNOGRAPHICS, INC., P.O. Box 1106(18501), pg. 1083

Telford

ACCU-SORT SYSTEMS, INC., 511 School House Rd.(18969), pg. 11
FARM & HOME OIL COMPANY, 420 State Rd.(18969), pg. 401

Temple

Handel & Company, Hantex Mills, 5019 Lamont Ave.(19560), pg. 504

Terre Hill

TERRE HILL CONCRETE PRODUCTS, INC., Rte. 897 S.(17581), pg. 1089

Titusville

FRONTIER FOUNDRIES, INC., 221 Perry St.(16354-0627), pg. 434
Frontier Foundries, Inc., 221 S. Perry St.(16354), pg. 434

Trafford

SPEC Group, Pleasant Valley Rd., Box 510(15085), pg. 972

Trevose

KORMAN CO., Two Neshaminy Interplex(19047), pg. 642

Troop

GERTRUDE HAWK CHOCOLATES, INC., 9 Keystone Industrial Park(18512-1544), pg. 517

Tullytown

ATLANTIC CONCRETE PRODUCTS, INC., 8900 Old Rte. 13(19007-0098), pg. 94

Union City

Molded Fiber Glass Co., 55 4th Ave.(16438), pg. 764
Snap-Tite Ponn, 217 Titusville Rd.(16438), pg. 1015

Uniontown

Penn Medical Services, Inc., 159 Morgantown(15401), pg. 1070

Upper Darby

Young Supply Co., 8301 Lansdowne Ave.(19082), pg. 736

Valley Forge

ALCO INDUSTRIES, INC., P.O. Box 937(19482), pg. 32
AMERICAN INKS & COATINGS CORP., Pawling Rd.(19482), pg. 56
E. F. HOUGHTON & CO., Madison & Van Buren(19482), pg. 546
ROBERT E. LAMB, INC., 939 Jefferson Ave., P.O. Box 821(19482), pg. 652
PQ CORPORATION, 500 E. Swedesford Rd.(19482), pg. 836
VALLEY FORGE ASSOCIATES, Liberty Park(19493), pg. 1143

Verona

PENNEX PRODUCTS CO., INC., One Pennex Dr.(15147-3998), pg. 858

Villanova

Daniel J. Keating Construction Co., 812 Lancaster Ave.(19085), pg. 619
DANIEL J. KEATING CO., 812 Lancaster Ave.(19085), pg. 619

Warminster

W. Atlee Burpee Co., 300 Park Ave.(18974), pg. 116
CRC Industries Inc., 885 Louis Dr.(18974), pg. 145
DEL-VAL MANUFACTURING COMPANY, 200 Park Ave.(18974), pg. 325
BENJAMIN OBDYKE, INC., Jacksonville Rd.(18974), pg. 819
Pressure Products Industries, 900 Louis Dr.(18974), pg. 230
TRIBORO ELECTRIC CORP., 539 Jacksonville Rd.(18974), pg. 1112

Warren

INTERROYAL CORPORATION, 151 Struthers(16365), pg. 580
Interroyal Storage Products Div., P.O. Box 428, Struthers St.(16365), pg. 580
United Refining Company, 15 Bradley St.(16365), pg. 1130
United Refining Inc., 15 Bradley St.(16365), pg. 1130

Warrendale

RETAIL VENTURES, INC., 150 Thornhill Dr.(15095), pg. 929

Warrington

JOMAC, INC., 863 Easton Rd.(18976), pg. 602

Washington

CAMALLOY, INC., 1960 N. Main St.(15301), pg. 211
INTERCOLE, INC., 2833 Chestnut St.(15301), pg. 574

Waterford

DAN DEE PRETZEL & POTATO CHIP CO., Route 97 South(16441), pg. 313

Wawa

WAWA, INC., Red Roof, Baltimore Pike(19063), pg. 1169

Wayne

BOYD, TAMNEY & CROSS ADVERTISING/MARKETING, 440 E. Swedesford Rd., St. 3040(19087), pg. 169
LUMBERMENS MERCHANDISING CORPORATION, 137 W. Wayne Ave.(19087), pg. 687
NPS Energy Services, Inc., 950 West Valley Rd., Ste. 2800(19087), pg. 321
NPS, Inc., 950 West Valley Rd., Ste. 2800(19087), pg. 321
NASON AND CULLEN, INC., Walnut Hill Plaza, 150 S. Warner Rd.(19087), pg. 784
PC Concepts, 3 Glenhardie Corp. Center, 1265 Drummers Lane(19087), pg. 1219
THE VANGUARD GROUP, INC., 1300 Morris Dr.(19087), pg. 1145
Viscom Enterprises, 656 E. Swedesford Rd., Ste. 218(19087), pg. 436

Waynesboro

Beck Manufacturing, Inc., East 9th St.(17268), pg. 153
BITREK CORPORATION, East 9th St.(17268), pg. 153

West Chester

AMKOR ELECTRONICS, INC., 1345 Enterprise Dr.(19380), pg. 67
LASKO METAL PRODUCTS, INC., 820 Lincoln Ave.(19380), pg. 660
LENAPE FORGE, INC., 1280 Lenape Rd.(19382), pg. 667
METABO CORPORATION, 1231 Wilson Dr.(19380), pg. 741

West Conshohocken

Modern Hilift Equipment Co., 1165 Matsonford Rd.(19428), pg. 763
R. M. SHOEMAKER CO., One Tower Bridge, 100 Front St.(19428), pg. 1000

West Elizabeth

Guardian Glass Inc., P.O. Box 507, (15088), pg. 492

West Middlesex

T. BRUCE SALES, INC., Carbough St.(16159), pg. 183

West Mifflin

Samuel G. Keywell Co., 890 Noble Dr.(15122), pg. 629
TRUMBULL CORPORATION, 1020 Lebanon Rd.(15122), pg. 1117

West Pittsburg

REACTIVE METALS & ALLOYS CORPORATION (REMACOR), Rt. 168(16160), pg. 916

West Point

Colorcon, Moyer Blvd.(19486), pg. 145

West Reading

NARROW FABRIC INDUSTRIES, INC., 7th & Reading Aves.(19611), pg. 783
R.M. PALMER COMPANY, 77 Second Ave.(19611), pg. 843

Wexford

LANDAU BUILDING CO., 9855 Rinaman Rd.(15090), pg. 654
TRU-WELD GRATING, INC., 2000 Corporate Dr.(15090), pg. 1117

Wilkes-Barre

Action Lift, 1500 Hwy. 315(18711), pg. 735
THE LION, INC. (GIBBONS-STEGMAIER BREWERY), 700 N. Pennsylvania Ave., Box GS(18703), pg. 677
MEDICO INDUSTRIES, INC., 1500 Hwy. 315(18711), pg. 735
MUSKIN LEISURE PRODUCTS, INC., 401 E. Thomas St.(18705-3897), pg. 777
UNIFAX, INC., 1065 Hwy. 315, Ste. 203(18702), pg. 1126

Williamsport

Anchor Darling Valve Co., P.O. Box 3428, 701 First St.(17701), pg. 230
Grit Printing Co., 1 Maynard Street(17701), pg. 1043
Grit Publishing Company, 208 W. 3rd St.(17701), pg. 1043
LUNDY CONSTRUCTION CO., INC., Arch St. & Reach Rd.(17701), pg. 687
MHB INC., 1207 Almond St.(17701), pg. 692
TRIMTEX CO. INC., 400 Park Ave.(17701), pg. 1113

Willow Grove

ASPLUNDH TREE EXPERT CO., 708 Blair Mill Rd.(19090-1784), pg. 88
NEWAGE INDUSTRIES INC., 2300 Maryland Rd.(19090-1799), pg. 803
TINIUS OLSEN TESTING MACHINE CO., INC., 1065 Easton Rd.(19090), pg. 1098

Wilmerding

American Standard Inc., Railway Brake Prods., 100 Airbrake Ave.(15148), pg. 61

Wind Gap

Protecto Plastics, Inc., 201 Alpha Rd.(18091), pg. 857

Windber

Elton Coal Co., 509 l5th St.(15963), pg. 145
Reitz Coal Company, 509 15th St.(15963), pg. 145
Wilmore Coal Company, 509 15th St.(15963), pg. 145

Womelsdorf

Richland Shoe Co., 30 N. Third St.(19567), pg. 183

Woolrich

The Chatham Water Co., Mill St.(17779), pg. 1201
WOOLRICH, INC., Mill St.(17779), pg. 1201
Woolrich Store Div., Mill St.(17779), pg. 1201

Worcester

PALMER INTERNATIONAL, INC., Rte. 73(19490), pg. 844

Wynnewood

CAWSL CORPORATION, 7 Wynnewood Rd.(19096), pg. 229

Yardley

Yardley Products Corporation, 10 W. College Ave.(19068), pg. 341

York

Ash, U.S.A., 570 W. College Ave.(17405), pg. 330
BON TON FOODS, INC., 1120 Zinns Quarry Rd.(17405), pg. 164
C P CONVERTERS, INC., 15 Grumbacher Rd.(17402), pg. 203
Cole Business Furniture, 640 Whiteford Rd.(17405), pg. 608
DENTSPLY INTERNATIONAL INC., 570 W. College Ave.(17405), pg. 329
DONLEE TECHNOLOGIES INC., 693 N. Hills Rd.(17402), pg. 344
GUNNEBO FASTENING CORP., 180 S. Hartman St.(17403), pg. 494
Keystone Automotive Industries, Inc. - York, 1000 Roosevelt Ave.(17404), pg. 628
McCrory Stores Div., 2955 E. Market St.(17402), pg. 934
New York Wire Co., Wire Drawing Mill, Loucks Mill Rd.(17403), pg. 947
New York Wire Co., Wire Weaving Mill, 441 E. Market St.(17403), pg. 947
PACE RESOURCES, INC., 40 S. Richland Ave.(17405), pg. 838
The Pfaltzgraff Co., 140 E. Market St.(17401), pg. 1065
Print-O-Stat, Inc., 1011 W. Market St.(17405), pg. 839
SHIPLEY OIL COMPANY, 550 E. King St.(17405), pg. 999
SUSQUEHANNA PFALTZGRAFF, 140 E. Market St.(17401), pg. 1065
T.G. & Y. Holdings, Inc., 2955 E. Market St.(17402), pg. 934
T.G. & Y. Stores Co., 2955 E. Market St.(17402), pg. 934
TIGHE INDUSTRIES, INC., P.O. Box 251A, E. Prospect Rd.(17406), pg. 1097
TOPFLIGHT CORP., 160 E. 9th Ave.(17404), pg. 1102
WSBA AM/FM, Box 910(17405), pg. 1065
YORK BARBELL CO., INC., 3300 Board Rd.(17402), pg. 1208
YORK BUILDING PRODUCTS CO., INC., 1020 N. Hartley St.(17405), pg. 1208
YORK WALLCOVERINGS INC., 750 Linden Ave.(17404), pg. 1208
YORKTOWNE PAPER MILLS, INC., 1001 Loucks Mill Rd.(17405), pg. 1208
Yorktowne Paper Mills of ME, 1001 Loucks Mill Rd.(17405), pg. 1209

PUERTO RICO

Aguadilla

CARIBE EXPRESS, 405 Hangar Ramey Base(00604), pg. 220

Caguas

Tech CBI, , pg. 1083

Carolina

Pueblo International, Inc.-P.R. Div., Loiza Expwy. Corner of Campo Rico Ave.(00630), pg. 899

Cayey

MICOM Caribe, Inc., Vicks Merrel Drive, Lotio(00633), pg. 748

Condado

Stephen Gould of Puerto Rico, Inc., 884 Ashford Ave.(00907), pg. 474

Dorado

Margo Farms Del Caribe, Inc., P.O. Box 706, (00646), pg. 706

Guaynabo

Wunderman Worldwide, 10 Munet Court, Pueblo Viejo(00920-1402), pg. 1211

Hato Rey

Economy International Service Inc., P.O. Box 1247, (00920), pg. 4
First Boston (Puerto Rico), Inc., 1020 Banco Popular Center(00918), pg. 204
Mantecados Payco, 113 Chardon Ave., Box 908(00919), pg. 1073

Las Piedras

Baker Bros. de Puerto Rico, P.O. Box 14(00671), pg. 1071

Mayaguez

Aratex of Puerto Rico, Free Trade Zone, P.O. Box B(00708), pg. 6
Ropa Sultana, Inc., KM 183.3 Barrio Algarroba(00709), pg. 1192

Old San Juan

D'Jesco, Inc., P.O. Box S-1653, (00903), pg. 4
Winros, Inc., 250 San Francisco St.(00902), pg. 694

Ponce

Octavio, Inc., P.O. Box 6189, State Rd. 1063

Rio Piedras

Sealy Mattress Company of Puerto Rico, El Commandante Indus. Ctr., 985

San Juan

Leo Burnett, Inc., Banco de Ponce Bldg., Ste. 2200(00918), pg. 192
CUNA Mutual Insurance Society-Puerto Rico, G.P.O. Box 2219, (00936-2219), pg. 206
Korn/Ferry International, 431 Ponce de Leon Ave., Ste. 1508(00917), pg. 642
McFarland & Drier International, One Television Plaza, Ste. 300, 171 Quisquya St.(00919), pg. 729

Santo Domingo

Caribe Freight, Edificio Caribe Freight, Aeropuerto International de las Americas, pg. 220

RHODE ISLAND

Cranston

AMF Lang's Bowlarama Inc., 225 Niantic Ave.(02907-3121), pg. 471
Bercen Inc., 1381 Cranston St.(02920), pg. 297
Cox Cable Rhode Island, Inc., 111 Comstock Parkway(02920), pg. 294
Cranston Manufacturing Facility, One Pakula Park(02910), pg. 843
CRANSTON PRINT WORKS COMPANY, 1381 Cranston St.(02920), pg. 296
FITZGERALD & COMPANY, INC., 105 Sockanossett Cross Rd.(02920), pg. 416
C. I. HAYES, INC., 800 Wellington Ave.(02910), pg. 519
JAN-CO., INC., 35 Sockanosset Cross Rd.(02920), pg. 589
RHODE ISLAND LOTTERY, 1425 Pontiac Ave.(02920), pg. 931
SGI INC., 1471 Elmwood Ave.(02910), pg. 962
TACO INC., 1160 Cranston St.(02920), pg. 1076
TECHNIC INCORPORATED, One Spectacle St(02910), pg. 1083
Unipas, Inc., 1142 Cranston St.(02920), pg. 1076

Cumberland

MOSSBERG INDUSTRIES, INC., 160 Bearhill Rd.(02864), pg. 772
J.T. Slocomb Co., One Front St.(02864), pg. 1010

East Greenwich

AQUA FAB INDUSTRIES, INC., 1485 S. County Trail(02818), pg. 79
PAUL ARPIN VANLINES, INC., Box 1302(02818), pg. 85
POTTER HAZLEHURST INCORPORATED, 800 Quaker Lane(02818), pg. 882
Weatherking Products, Inc., 1485 S. County Trail(02818), pg. 79

East Providence

A & Z HAYWARD, INC., 655 Waterman Ave.(02914), pg. 1
B.A. BALLOU & CO. INC., 800 Waterman Ave.(02914), pg. 116
Foamex L.P., 823 Waterman Ave.(02914), pg. 1121
STAUCH VETROMILE & MITCHELL ADVERTISING, INC., 55 S. Brow St.(02914), pg. 1042
WPRI-TV, 25 Catamore Blvd.(02914), pg. 783

Esmond

NEW ENGLAND STONE INDUSTRIES, INC., 15 Branch Pike(02917-1223), pg. 800

Greenville

HART ENGINEERING CORPORATION, 29 Lark Industrial Pkwy.(02828), pg. 512

Middletown

Aquidneck Data Company, 170 Enterprise Center(02840), pg. 320

Pawtucket

American Insulated Wire Corp., 36 Freeman St.(02862), pg. 671
COLFAX, INC., 38 Colfax St.(02860), pg. 261
COOLEY, INC., 50 Esten Ave.(02862), pg. 282
DARLENE JEWELRY MANUFACTURING COMPANY, 483 Main St.(02860), pg. 315
KEY CONTAINER CORPORATION, 21 Campbell St.(02862), pg. 626
PAWTUCKET FASTENERS INC., 327 Pine St.(02862), pg. 852
TEKNOR APEX COMPANY, 505 Central Ave.(02861), pg. 1084

Providence

Admiral Packaging, Inc., 10 Admiral St.(02940), pg. 1128
AMERICAN MATHEMATICAL SOCIETY, INC., 201 Charles St.(02904), pg. 58
AMICA MUTUAL INSURANCE CO., 10 Weybosset St.(02940), pg. 66
BONANZA BUS LINES, INC., 1 Bonanza Way(02904), pg. 164
CHAFFEE CASE & PARTNERS, 196 Richmond St.(02903), pg. 237
Clifford Metal, 200 Cortiss St.(02904), pg. 658
COKEN COMPANY, INC., 150 Colfax St.(02905), pg. 259
Colony Communications Inc., 75 Fountain St.(02902), pg. 896
Coto Wabash, 55 Dupont Dr.(02907), pg. 357
Curtman Division, 623 Atwells Ave.(02909-2413), pg. 1125
DIMEO CONSTRUCTION COMPANY, 75 Chapman St.(02905), pg. 338
Drake Petroleum Company, Inc., P.O. Box 2616, Elmwood Station(02907), pg. 1165
DUFFY & SHANLEY, INC., The Penthouse, 222 Richmond St.(02903), pg. 351
EXCELL MANUFACTURING COMPANY, 200 Chestnut St.(02903), pg. 392
GILBANE BUILDING COMPANY, 7 Jackson Walkway(02940), pg. 457
Gilbane Properties, Inc., 7 Jackson Walkway(02940), pg. 457
IMPERIAL PEARL COMPANY, INC., 25 Manton Ave.(02909), pg. 564
LEONARD MONAHAN LUBARS & KELLY, 127 Dorrance St.(02903), pg. 668
Mutual Benefit Financial Service Co., 290 Westminster St.(02903), pg. 778
NARRAGANSETT CAPITAL INC., 50 Kennedy Plaza(02903), pg. 783
PAGANO, SCHENCK & KAY, INC., 1 Old Stone Square(02903), pg. 843
Providence Journal Broadcasting Corp., 75 Fountain St.(02902), pg. 896
PROVIDENCE JOURNAL COMPANY, 75 Fountain St.(02902), pg. 895

Providence Journal Telecommunications, Inc., 75 Fountain St.(02902), pg. 896
RAU FASTENERS, INC., 102 Westfield St.(02907), pg. 913
Rhode Island Monthly, 60 Branch Ave.(02904), pg. 269
RIVERS TRAINOR DOYLE & WALSH, INC., One Catamore Blvd.(02914), pg. 937
SUNBEAM-OSTER COMPANY, INC., One Citizen's Plaza, 6th Fl.(02903), pg. 1059
UNCAS MANUFACTURING COMPANY, 623 Atwells Ave.(02909-2413), pg. 1125
UNION INDUSTRIES, INC., 10 Admiral St.(02908), pg. 1128
Union Paper Co., 10 Admiral St.(02908), pg. 1128
Warex Petroleum Corporation, 355 Allens Ave.(02905), pg. 1165
Warren Oil Company, 355 Allens Ave.(02905), pg. 1165

Rumford

MARSHALL CONTRACTORS INC., 75 Newman Ave.(02916), pg. 714

Smithfield

B.T. Equipment Co., Inc., P.O. Box 17071, 115 Lydia Ann Rd.(02917), pg. 457
UVEX SAFETY, INC., 10 Thurber Blvd.(02917), pg. 1141

Warwick

FERN/HANAWAY, INC. ADVERTISING/PUBLIC RELATIONS, Airport Professional Park, 2374 Post Rd.(02886), pg. 407
KENNEY MANUFACTURING COMPANY, 1000 Jefferson Blvd.(02886), pg. 623
Metropolitan Property & Casualty Insurance Co.(Met P&C), 700 Quaker Lane(02887), pg. 744
National Diecasting Machinery, , pg. 909
PLAN INTERNATIONAL U.S.A., 155 Plan Way, Dept. MO24(02886), pg. 874

West Warwick

AMTROL INC., 1400 Division Rd.(02893), pg. 70
VICTOR CORPORATION, 618 Main St.(02893), pg. 1149

Westerly

BESS EATON DONUT FLOUR CO., INC., 79 Tom Harvey Rd.(02891), pg. 146
Guild Music Corporation, 60 Industrial Dr.(02891), pg. 1136
MOORE COMPANY, 36 Beach St.(02891), pg. 768

Woonsocket

TECH INDUSTRIES, INC., 85 Fairmount St.(02895), pg. 1083

SOUTH CAROLINA

Aiken

AIKEN ELECTRIC COOPERATIVE INC., P.O. Box 417(29802), pg. 26

Anderson

Glen Raven Mills, Inc.-Custom Fabrics Div., Equinox Plant, 200 Jackson St.(29621), pg. 462
Glen Raven Mills, Inc.-Custom Fabrics Div., Equinox Finishing Plant, 107 Service Rd.(29621), pg. 462
Glen Raven Mills, Inc.-Custom Fabrics Division-Equinox Plant, 200 Jackson St.(29621), pg. 461
Independent Publishing Company, 1000 Williamston Rd.(29621), pg. 513
Seabrook Inc., 410 Shockley Rd.(29622), pg. 348

Arcadia

MAYFAIR MILLS, INC., 1885 Hayne St.(29320), pg. 724

Beaufort

Minster Automation Inc., Industrial Park, Parker Dr.(29903), pg. 759
PHB Parker Die Castings, P.O. Drawer D(29903), pg. 836

Bennettsville

Marley Electric Heating Co., 470 Beauty Spot Rd. E.(29512), pg. 710

Blacksburg

Burton-Dixie of Blacksburg Inc., P.O. Box 608, (29702), pg. 200
CC Industries Estia Div., P.O. Box 608, (29702), pg. 200

Carlisle

Webb Forging, P.O. Box 400(29031), pg. 1170

Chapin

FRED B. JOHNSTON COMPANY, INC., 300 E. Boundry Rd.(29036), pg. 601
Weisz Graphics, 300 E. Boundry Rd.(29036), pg. 601

Charleston

Aircraft Insurance Agency, 6543 Fain St.(29411), pg. 519
Atlantic National Corporation, 6543 Fain St.(29411), pg. 519
WILLIAM M. BIRD & CO., INC., 1142 Morrison Dr.(29403), pg. 152
BURRIS CHEMICAL INC., 4210 Azalea Dr.(29415), pg. 195
EVENING POST PUBLISHING CO., 134 Columbus St.(29403-4800), pg. 391
Goer Manufacturing Co., 4500 Mariott Dr., N.(29418), pg. 907
Hawthorne Airport Services, Inc., 6543 Fain St.(29411), pg. 519
Hawthorne Aviation, 6543 Fain St.(29411), pg. 519
HAWTHORNE CORP., 6543 Fain St.(29411), pg. 518
Hawthorne Properties, Inc., 6543 Fain St.(29411), pg. 519
Hawthorne Services, Inc., 6543 Fain St.(29411), pg. 519
KERRISON DRY GOODS COMPANY, INC., 260 King St.(29401), pg. 624
Line Equipment Sales Co., Inc., 551 Meeting St.(29403), pg. 1141
PEARLSTINE DISTRIBUTORS INC., 4550 Gaynor Ave.(29411), pg. 853
RENKEN BOAT MANUFACTURING CO., 1750 Signal Point Rd.(29412), pg. 927
RUSCON CORP., 149 E. Bay St.(29401), pg. 956
Unison Insurance Co., P.O. Box 31190, (29417-1190), pg. 66
UTILITIES CONSTRUCTION CO., INC. OF SOUTH CAROLINA, 1890 Milford St.(29405), pg. 1141

Charleston Heights

CAMERON & BARKLEY COMPANY, INC., 2864 Azalea Dr.(29411), pg. 212
GENE REED CHEVROLET, 4001 Dorchester Rd.(29405), pg. 920

Cheraw

CHERAW YARN MILLS, INC., U.S. Hwy. 1(29520), pg. 242

Chester

Chester News and Reporter, P.O. Box 250, 104 York St.(29706), pg. 655

Clinton

Clinton Mills Inc., 600 Academy St.(29325), pg. 202
E. L. Mansure Div., P.O. Box 502, (29325), pg. 200
STANDARD PLYWOOD, INC., Old Laurens Road(29325), pg. 1037

Clover

S. E. HUFFMAN CORP., 1050 Huffman Way(29710), pg. 551
KLEAR KNIT INC., 510 Sunset Dr.(29710), pg. 634

Columbia

AEA of Columbia, 1825 Laurel St.(29282), pg. 3
AMBAC INTERNATIONAL CORP., I-77 at Killian Rd.(29203), pg. 47
ANCHOR CONTINENTAL INCORPORATED, 2000 S. Beltline Blvd.(29205), pg. 71
Aratex Services, 919 Airport Blvd.(29205), pg. 6
Ben Arnold Co., Inc., 700 Gervais St.(29201), pg. 84
ASSOCIATED INDUSTRIAL SUPPLY, INC., 1207 Lincoln St., Suite 200(29201), pg. 90
BEARING DISTRIBUTORS, INC., 930 S. Stadium Rd.(29202), pg. 130
Binswanger, NCNB Tower, 1301 Gervais St., Ste. 908(29201), pg. 152
Burriss Building Systems, 4186 Fernandina Rd.(29212), pg. 195
B. BURRISS COMPANIES, 1011 Kinley Rd.(29212), pg. 195
CMI INDUSTRIES, INC., P.O. Box 11589, (29211), pg. 202
CHERNOFF/SILVER & ASSOCIATES, 801 Gervais St.(29201), pg. 243
THE CLIMATIC CORP., 2270 LeGrand Rd.(29223), pg. 255
COLUMBIA LUMBER & MANUFACTURING CO., P.O. Box 23289(29224), pg. 265
Colwood Co., Inc., P.O. Box 23289, (29224), pg. 265
CONGAREE CONSTRUCTION CO., INC., 1634 Pineview Rd.(29209), pg. 274
CONSOLIDATED SYSTEMS, INC., 650 Rosewood Dr.(29201), pg. 277
Crushing & Screening Div., U.S. Hwy. 1 N.(29202), pg. 532
DEFENDER SERVICES, INC., 9031 Garners Ferry Rd.(29209), pg. 324
Deluca Valve & Instrument Co., P.O. Box 11267(29211), pg. 510
Farm Credit Bank of Columbia, Farm Credit Bank Bldg., 1401 Hampton St.(29201), pg. 405
HARDAWAY CONCRETE CO., INC., 2001 Taylor St.(29204), pg. 507
V. B. HOOK & CO., INC., PO BOX 13503, (29201), pg. 543
JIM HUDSON, PONTIAC, OLDSMOBILE GMC, 7201 Sumter Hwy.(29209), pg. 551
M. B. KAHN CONSTRUCTION CO., INC., Hwy. 555, Flintlake Rd.(29202), pg. 614
KLINE IRON & STEEL CO., INC., P.O. Box 1013, (36645), pg. 635
MASHBURN CONSTRUCTION COMPANY, 1404 Laurel St.(29201), pg. 717
MCCRORY CONSTRUCTION CO., INC., 1280 Assembly St.(29201), pg. 728
MICHAEL J. MUNGO COMPANY, INC., 4400 St. Andrews Rd.(29210), pg. 775
NEWMAN, SAYLOR & GREGORY, 2817 Millwood Ave.(29205), pg. 804
Omni Savings Bank, FSB, 1940 Blossom St.(29205-2296), pg. 414
OWEN STEEL CO., INC., 801 Blossom St.(29202), pg. 834
PALMETTO WHOLESALE CO., INC., 850 Rosewood Dr.(29201), pg. 844
PULLIAM MOTOR COMPANY, 2800 Two Notch Rd.(29204), pg. 899
RPR & ASSOCIATES, INC., P.O. Box 11348(29211), pg. 908
REPUBLIC CONTRACTING CORP., 869 Pepper St.(29209), pg. 928
WILBUR SMITH ASSOCIATES, Carnation Bank Towers(29202), pg. 1011
SOUTHEASTERN FREIGHT LINES, INC., P.O. Box 1691(29202), pg. 1019
Tencarva Machinery Co., 1405 Old Dairy Road(29201), pg. 1087
TERMINIX SERVICE, INC., 3618 Fernandino Rd.(29210), pg. 1088
THOMAS & HOWARD, P.O. Box 947(29202), pg. 1093
U.S. CONSTRUCTION CO., INC., P.O. Box 211429, (29221), pg. 1135

Conway

Aberdeen Mfg. Corp. Conway Plant, 16th Ave.(29526), pg. 200

Darlington

Clanton's Auto Auction, Highway 34 West(29532), pg. 293
DARLINGTON VENEER COMPANY, 225 4th St.(29532), pg. 315
Diamond Hill Plywood Company, 600 E. Broad St.(29532), pg. 316
MSD, INC., 700 Orange St.(29532), pg. 693

Easley

Easley Textile, 508 Greenville Rd.(29640), pg. 1068
Imperial Die Casting, Griffin Mill & Brazil Rds.(29640), pg. 906
Models Coat, 508 Greenville Rd.(29640), pg. 1068

Florence

Perfection Hy-Test Company, 1943-C Hoffmeyer Rd.(29501), pg. 711
POWERS CONSTRUCTION CO., INC., 3091 S. Cashua Dr.(29501), pg. 883
Southeastern Corp., P.O. Box 1069(29503), pg. 1020
SOUTHEASTERN STEEL COMPANY, Koppers Rd.(29503), pg. 1020
SUPERIOR MACHINE COMPANY OF SOUTH CAROLINA, INC., P.O. Box 5419(29502), pg. 1064
Trayco of S.C., Inc., 1307 National Cemetary Rd.(29502), pg. 358
YOUNG PECAN SHELLING CO., INC., 1200 Pecan St.(29501), pg. 1209

Fort Lawn

MORRISON TEXTILE MACHINERY CO., Hwy. 771

Fort Mill

OWSLEY & SONS, INC., Gold Hill Rd. at I-77 S.(29716-1449), pg. 834

Gaffney

PEELERS RUG COMPANY, INC., 1224 Champion Ferry Rd.(29341), pg. 855

Graniteville

GRANITEVILLE CO., Marshall St.(29829), pg. 476
Warren Div., Marshall St.(29829), pg. 477

Great Falls

W.S. LIBBEY COMPANY, 401 Dearborn St.(29055), pg. 674
REPUBLIC FASTENER PRODUCTS CORP., 671 Waterview Dr.(29055), pg. 928

Greenville

Am Real Corp., P.O. Box 1089, (29602), pg. 571
AMICO Greenville Distr. Center, P.O. Box 26534(29616), pg. 29
Benson's of South Carolina, 1505 Buncombe Rd.(29609), pg. 140
The Bibb Company-White Horse Rd. Plant, White Horse Rd.(29611), pg. 781
Blue Ridge Finance Co., Inc., P.O. Box 17974, Station B, 355 Woodruff Rd.(29606), pg. 398
BUILDER MARTS OF AMERICA, 1 Independence Pointe(29615), pg. 187
Canal Indemnity Company, P.O. Box 7(29602), pg. 213
CANAL INSURANCE CO., 417 E. North St.(29601), pg. 213
Carolina Steel-Greenville Plant, P.O. Box 128, (29602), pg. 223
DAVIS ELECTRICAL CONSTRUCTORS, INC., 429 N. Main St.(29602), pg. 318
DAVIS MECHANICAL CONTRACTORS, INC., 7640 Pelham Rd.(29615), pg. 318
FAIRWAY FORD, INC., 2323 Laurens Rd.(29607), pg. 397
HENDERSON ADVERTISING, INC., 60 Pointe Circle(29615), pg. 528
Heritage Lincoln-Mercury, 2424 Laurens Rd.(29607), pg. 398
INSIGNIA FINANCIAL GROUP, INC., 1 Insignia Place(29602), pg. 571
Insignia Management Group, 1 Insignia Place(29602), pg. 571
JPS Automotive, 29 Stevens St.(29605), pg. 586
JPS Converter & Industrial Corp., 33 Stevens St.(29605), pg. 586
JPS TEXTILE GROUP, INC., 555 N. Pleasantburg Dr., Ste. 202(29607), pg. 586
LESLIE ADVERTISING, 874 S. Pleasantburg Dr.(29607), pg. 668
Leslie Public Relations, 874 S. Pleasantburg Dr.(29607), pg. 668
MARSHALL & WILLIAMS CO., 301 Airport Rd.(29607), pg. 714
Mauldin Mfg. Co., Inc., 2499 Rutherford Rd.(29608), pg. 1187
MCLAUGHLIN MFG. COMPANY, 2006 Perimeter Rd.(29605), pg. 731

Mount Vernon Dryer Fabrics, P.O. Box 5837(29606), pg. 845
Mount Vernon Mills, Inc., One Shelter Pl., Ste. 700(29601), pg. 844
Mount Vernon Mills, Inc., Riegel Textile Div., P.O. Box 3478(29602), pg. 844
ORDERS DISTRIBUTING CO., 501 Congaree Rd.(29607), pg. 829
C. H. Patrick & Co., Inc., P.O. Box 2526, (29602), pg. 477
PLATT SACO LOWELL CORPORATION, P.O. Drawer 2327(29602), pg. 876
POTTER-SHACKELFORD CONSTRUCTION CO., 80 Villa Rd.(29615), pg. 882
SHEALY ELECTRICAL WHOLESALERS, 25-29 River St.(29602), pg. 996
STONE MANUFACTURING COMPANY, INC., 1500 Poinsett Hwy.(29609), pg. 1051
SUITT CONSTRUCTION COMPANY, INC., 1400 Cleveland St.(29607), pg. 1056
U.S. Finishing, 3335 Old Buncombe Rd.(29602), pg. 52
WUNDA WEVE CARPET CO., 1221 Batesville Rd.(29650), pg. 1205

Greenwood

Environmental Resorts Inc., Greenwood Bldg.(29646), pg. 486
Greenwood Cotton Co., Greenwood Bldg.(29646), pg. 486
Greenwood Development Co., Greenwood Bldg.(29646), pg. 486
GREENWOOD MILLS, INC., 104 Maxwell Ave.(29646), pg. 485
GREENWOOD PACKING PLANT, Packer St.(29648), pg. 486
Greenwood Warehouse Co., Greenwood Bldg.(29646), pg. 486
GEORGE W. PARK SEED CO., INC., Hwy. 254 North(29647), pg. 849

Greer

INTEX CHEMICAL INC., High Tee Court(29650), pg. 581
Stevens Aviation, Inc., (29651), pg. 400
Tencarva Machinery Co., Pelham Industrial Pk.(29651), pg. 1087

Hollywood

METAL TRADES, INC., 4194 Hwy. 165(29449), pg. 741

Inman

INMAN MILLS, P.O. Box 207(29349), pg. 570

Joanna

CC Industries, Kaywood-Southern Div., 200 Pickens St.(29351), pg. 200

Johnston

Mount Vernon Mills, Inc., Riegel Consumer Products Div., P.O. Box E(29832), pg. 844

Kingstree

FARMERS TELEPHONE CO-OP, 1101 E. Main St.(29556), pg. 402

La France

Mount Vernon Mills, Inc., LaFrance Industries, P.O. Box 500(29656), pg. 844

Lake City

The Coleman Company, P.O. Box 1119, Hwy. 341(29560), pg. 695
T.S. RAGSDALE COMPANY, INCORPORATED, P.O. Box 937(29560), pg. 910

Lancaster

The Lancaster News, P.O. Box 640, 701 N. White St.(29720), pg. 655

Landrum

BOMMER INDUSTRIES, INC., Hwy. 176(29356), pg. 164
Simkins Carolina Folding Box Div., (29356), pg. 1005

Laurens

PALMETTO SPINNING CORP., 1100 Church St.(29360), pg. 844

Leesville

COLUMBIA FARMS INC., Hwy. 265

Lugoff

COGSDILL TOOL PRODUCTS, INC., 1001 Guion Dr.(29078), pg. 259

Manning

SPROTT OIL CO., INC., P.O. Drawer 1332(29102), pg. 1034

Marining

The Starflo Corporation, Rte. 5, Box 472(29102), pg. 883

Mauldin

HER MAJESTY, P.O. Box 9(29662), pg. 530

McBee

MAR-MAC MANUFACTURING COMPANY, INC., Highway One, N.(29101), pg. 705

McCormick

Mount Vernon Mills, Inc., Consumer Products Div. (McCormick), Augusta Hwy.(29835), pg. 844

Moncks Corner

Industrial Acoustics Company S.C. Inc., P.O. Box 579, (29461), pg. 566

Mount Pleasant

John Wieland Homes of Charleston, Inc., 443-H Longpoint Rd.(29464), pg. 1189

Myrtle Beach

ANCHOR FINANCIAL CORPORATION, 2002 Oak St.(29577-3145), pg. 71
Cox Cable South Carolina, Inc., 1907 Oak Street(29577), pg. 294
SANDS INVESTMENTS, INC., 4612 Oleander Dr.(29577), pg. 970
Waccamaw Corporation, 3200 Pottery Dr.(29577), pg. 453

Newberry

EASTERN FLAT BED SYSTEMS, 1928 Wilson Rd.(29108), pg. 363

Norlina

Glen Raven Mills, Inc.-Norlina Plant, Hwy. U.S. 1 S., P.O. Box 518(27563), pg. 462

North Charleston

AMERICAN DEVELOPMENT CORPORATION, 1930 Hanahan Rd.(29406), pg. 51
MICHAEL BUSINESS MACHINES CORPORATION, 3290 Ashley Phosphate Rd.(29418), pg. 747
Tencarva Machinery Company, 2460 Remount Rd., Suite 107(29418), pg. 1087

Orangeburg

COX WOOD PRESERVING CO., Cannon Bridge Rd.(29116), pg. 295
Mosler, Inc., P.O. Box 2165(29116), pg. 772
The Starflo Corporation, Hwy 301 N., Crosscreek Rd.(29115), pg. 883

Pickens

THE KENT MANUFACTURING CO., Hwy. 183(29671), pg. 623

Piedmont

VARAT ENTERPRISES, INC., 58 S. Burty Rd.(29673), pg. 1145

Rock Hill

OSTROW TEXTILE CO., INC., 923 Standard & High Sts.(29730), pg. 831
SMITH ENTERPRISES, 1953 Langston St.(29730), pg. 1012

Simpsonville

FTZ Industries, Inc., 515 Palmetto Dr.(29681), pg. 119

Spartanburg

AMERICAN FAST PRINT, LIMITED, I-85 & Bryant Rd.(29303), pg. 52
ASSOCIATED PETROLEUM CARRIERS, 1746 Union Rd.(29302), pg. 91
Y.C. BALLENGER ELECTRICAL CONTRACTORS, 2627 N. Pine St.(29304), pg. 116
Beverage-Air Co., P.O. Box 5932(29304), pg. 1027
COMMUNITY CASH STORES, 3001 No. Blackstock Rd.(29301), pg. 270
Kohler Co. (SC), P.O. Box 1987, (29304), pg. 640
MILLIKEN & CO., INC., P.O. Box 1926(29304), pg. 755
Milliken Fine Goods Div., P.O. Box 1926(29304), pg. 755
Milliken Finished Apparel Div., P.O. Box 1926(29304), pg. 755
Milliken Industrial Div., P.O. Box 1926(29304), pg. 755
Milliken Interior Furnishings Div., P.O. Box 1926(29304), pg. 755
PIEDMONT MECHANICAL, INC., 116 John Dodd Rd.(29303), pg. 870
J. M. SMITH CORP., 450 Wofford St.(29301), pg. 1012
Smith Wholesale Drug Div., 450 Wofford St.(29301), pg. 1012
SPARTAN MILLS, 805 Spartan Blvd.(29301), pg. 1026
ZIMA CORP., I-85 at Zima Park(29301), pg. 1219

Summerville

BAKER MATERIAL HANDLING CORP., 2450 W. 5th North St.(29484), pg. 115
KORES NORDIC USA CORP., 2745 W. 5th North St.(29483), pg. 642
O. J. STROBEL OIL & TIRE CO., INC., 1101 N. Main St.(29483), pg. 1053

Sumter

B. L. MONTAGUE CO., 303 E. Liberty St.(29150), pg. 766
U.S. Broach & Machine Company, Bypass 378 Frontage Rd., P.O. Box 1649(29150), pg. 102

Taylors

BALLENGER PAVING COMPANY, INC., 900 W. Lee Rd.(29687), pg. 116
Staflex/Harotex, P.O. Box 1106(29687), pg. 510

Travelers Rest

SWISS-M-TEX, L.P., Hwy. 25(29690), pg. 1068
T & S BRASS & BRONZE WORKS, INC., 2 Saddlebrook Ct.(29690), pg. 1074

Union

CONSO PRODUCTS COMPANY, P.O. Box 326(29379), pg. 276
Duraco Products Inc. of South Carolina, P.O. Box 867, Hwy. 9 Adamsburg(29379), pg. 354

Ware Shoals

Mount Vernon Mills, Smith & Waters, Inc., Nation Rd.(29692), pg. 845

Wellford

JACKSON MILLS, INC., One Railroad St.(29385), pg. 587

West Columbia

Capital City Manufacturing Company, P.O. Box 1130(29171), pg. 546
LOXCREEN COMPANY, 1630 Old Dunbar Rd.(29169), pg. 686

Williamston

Mount Vernon Mills, Inc., Williamston, P.O. Box 339(29697), pg. 844

Winnsboro

FAIRFIELD ELECTRIC CO-OP, Highway 321 N.(29180), pg. 397
The JPM Company of South Carolina, Inc., Route 321(29180), pg. 586

Woodruff

Mount Vernon Mills, Inc., Woodruff, P.O. Box 459(29388), pg. 845

SOUTH DAKOTA

Aberdeen

Midwest Motel Supply, 1910 8th Ave., N.E.(57401), pg. 1063
Super 8 Management, Inc., 1910 8th Ave., N.E.(57401), pg. 1063
SUPER 8 MOTELS, INC., Box 4090, 1910 8th Ave. N.E.(57401), pg. 1062

Alcester

ALKOTA CLEANING SYSTEMS, INC., 110 Iowa St.(57001), pg. 34

Brookings

DAKTRONICS, INC., 331 32nd Ave.(57006), pg. 312
LARSON MANUFACTURING COMPANY, 2333 Eastbrook Dr.(57006), pg. 659
Star Circuits, 405 Railroad St.(57006), pg. 312

Colman

SIOUX VALLEY EMPIRE ELECTRIC ASSOCIATION, 1 1/2 Miles W. Of I-29(57017), pg. 1009
Sioux Valley Rural Television, P.O. Box 20, (57017), pg. 1009
T & R ELECTRIC SUPPLY COMPANY, INC., Hwy. 34 W.(57017), pg. 1071

Huron

Prostrollo Motor Sales, Inc., 500 4th St., N.E.(57350), pg. 895

Lennox

Koyker Mfg. Co., 100 N. Cleveland(57039), pg. 1008

Madison

APPLE LINES, INC., 212 S.W. Second St.(57042), pg. 79
EAST RIVER ELECTRICAL POWER CO., 121 S.E. First St.(57042), pg. 363
PROSTROLLO MOTOR COMPANY, 1001 S. Washington St.(57042), pg. 895
ROSCO MANUFACTURING CO., 1001 S.W. 1st St.(57042), pg. 947

Mitchell

RANDALL STORES, INC., 1705 N. Main(57301), pg. 911

Philip

SCOTCHMAN INDUSTRIES, INC., 180 E. Hwy. 14(57567), pg. 982

Pierre

SOUTH DAKOTA LOTTERY, 207 E. Capitol, Suite 1019

Rapid City

BRINK ELECTRIC CONSTRUCTION COMPANY, 2950 N. Plaza Dr.(57702), pg. 176
Brink Equipment & Supply Company, 2230 Rand Rd.(57709), pg. 176
Hills Materials Co., P.O. Box 2320(57709), pg. 815
Hubbard West, 426 Omaha St.(57709), pg. 549
MIDWEST TIRE & MUFFLER, INC., P.O. Box 4510(57701), pg. 752
NORTHWESTERN ENGINEERING CO., P.O. Box 2320(57709), pg. 815

Sioux City

GATEWAY 2000, 610 Gateway Dr., N.(57049), pg. 446

Sioux Falls

Alco Health Services Corp.-Sioux Falls Div., 1414 "M" Ave.(57104), pg. 31
THE AUSTAD COMPANY, 4500 E. 10th St.(57101), pg. 98
Building Products Inc. of S.D., 2200 E. Rice St.(57103), pg. 188
L. G. EVERIST INC., 313 S. Phillips Ave.(57102), pg. 392
Golden Sun Feeds, Inc., (50112), pg. 467
KSFY-TV, 300 No. Dakota Ave.(57102), pg. 805
LAWRENCE & SCHILLER, INC., 3932 S. Willow Ave.(57105), pg. 663
LEWIS DRUG, INC., 2701 S. Minnesota, Ste. 1(57105), pg. 673
Midland National Life Insurance Co., One Midland Plaza(57101), pg. 968
MIDWEST COAST TRANSPORT L.P., 1600 E. Benson Rd.(57117), pg. 752
SDTV, Inc., 300 No. Dakota Ave.(57102), pg. 804
SCHOENEMAN BROTHERS COMPANY, 305 E. 8th St.(57102), pg. 978
SENCORE, INC., 3200 Sencore Dr.(57107), pg. 989
SIOUX FALLS CONSTRUCTION COMPANY, 800-810 S. 7th Ave.(57101), pg. 1008
SIOUX STEEL COMPANY, 196 1/2 E. 6th St.(57102), pg. 1008

Watertown

BUILDING PRODUCTS INC., 405 First Ave., N.E.(57201), pg. 188
Twin City Die Castings Co., 122 Cessna St. N.W.(57201), pg. 1122

Webster

DAKOTAH, INC., N. Park Lane(57274), pg. 312

Winner

GROSSENBURG IMPLEMENTS, INCORPORATED, P.O. Box 311(57580-0311), pg. 489

Yankton

The Yankton Press & Dakotan, P.O. Box 56, 319 Walnut(57078), pg. 1042

TENNESSEE

Alcoa

Kings Foodservice, 269 S. Center Dr.(37701), pg. 1126

Ashland City

Apcom Inc., Hwy. 49 South(37015), pg. 1041
STATE INDUSTRIES INC., 500 Bypass Rd.(37015), pg. 1041

Athens

Heil Bulk Trailer Co., P.O. Box 160, (37303), pg. 525
Heil Bulk Trailer Div., P.O. Box 160, (37303), pg. 525

Brentwood

BELL CONSTRUCTION CO. INC., 255 Wilson Pike Circle(37027), pg. 134
Berol Corporation, 105 West Park Drive(370267), pg. 856
COLUMBIA CORPORATION, Kingsport Bldg., 215 Centerview Dr., Ste. 143(37027), pg. 265
ERM-Southeast, Inc., 215 Centerview Dr., Ste. 110(37024), pg. 360
Empire Berol U.S.A., 105 Westpark Dr.(37027), pg. 856
PEN HOLDINGS, INC., 105 West Park Drive(37027), pg. 856
Pet Specialties, Inc., 109 Park Dr., Ste. 360(37027), pg. 358
QUORUM HEALTH GROUP, INC., 155 Franklin Rd., Ste. 401(37027), pg. 905
STANDARD ADVERTISING AGENCY, 7100 Service Merchandise Dr.(37027), pg. 1035
STATE VOLUNTEER MUTUAL INSURANCE CO. INC., 101 W. Park Dr.(37027), pg. 1041
Sullivan Graphics, 100 Winners Circle(37027), pg. 1057
SULLIVAN HOLDING COMPANY, 100 Winners Circle(37027), pg. 1056
Windmill Corp. d/b/a Martha White Foods, Inc., Two Maryland Farms, Ste. 340(37027), pg. 1195

Bristol

Karl M. Harrop Co., Inc., 307 9th St.(37620), pg. 80

Chattanooga

Alco Health Services Corporation-Chattanooga Div., 200 N. Holly St.(34704), pg. 31
Allright Tenn. Inc., 701 Broad St., Ste. LL2(37402), pg. 42
American Institutional Foods, P.O. Box 367, (37401), pg. 4
AMERICAN MANUFACTURING CO. (TN), 3600 N. Hawthorne St.(37406), pg. 58
ARCADE INC., 1815 E. Main St.(37404), pg. 80
BROCK CANDY COMPANY, 4120 Jersey Pike(37422), pg. 177
Burner Systems International, Inc., 700 East 10th St.(37402), pg. 357
CUNA Southern District, Eastgate Shopping Center, 6100 Bldg., Ste. 3900, P.O. Box 8397(37411), pg. 206
CASTING MATERIAL COMPANY, 1610 Charter St.(37402), pg. 229
CAVALIER CORPORATION, 1105 East 10th(37403), pg. 229
CHATTANOOGA CHOO-CHOO HOLIDAY INN, 1400 Market St.(37402), pg. 241
Dixie Industries, Inc., 3510 N. Orchard Knob Ave.(37406), pg. 267
THE DOUBLE-COLA COMPANY, 3350 Broad St.(37408), pg. 347
THE HEIL CO., Eastgate Center(37411), pg. 525
KRYSTAL COMPANY, Krystal Bldg., One Union Sq.(37402), pg. 645
OLAN MILLS, INC., 4325 Amnicola Hwy.(37406), pg. 756
NATIONAL GROUP, INC., 2464 Amnicola Hwy.(37406), pg. 789
National Posters, Inc., 1001 Latta St.(37406), pg. 790
NORTH AMERICAN ROYALTIES, INC., 200 E. Eighth St.(37402), pg. 811
SCT YARNS, INC., 1800 S. Watkins St.(37404), pg. 961
SHERMAN & REILLY, INC., 400 W. 33rd St.(37410), pg. 998
Southern Combustion & Controls, Inc., 401 N. Market St.(37405), pg. 366
Spectra National, 1401 Godson Ave.(37406), pg. 790
Spherical Products Corp., 601 Cumberland(37409), pg. 837
Tencarva Machinery Co., 153 Business Park, Warehouse 1087
TOP FLIGHT, INC., 1300-06 Central Ave.(37408), pg. 1101
ULLENBERG CORP., 420 Bell Ave.(37405), pg. 1125
The Wheland Foundry Div., 2800 Broad St.(37402), pg. 812

Clarksville

Acme Boot Co., Inc., 1002 Stafford St.(37040), pg. 400
The Trane Company, P.O. Box 1008(37040), pg. 62
Trans Unitary Products Group-Commercial, 2701 Guthrie Highway(37040), pg. 61

Cleveland

American Uniform Co., Parker St. N.E.(37311), pg. 1045
CLEVELAND CHAIR COMPANY, 370 Ninth St. S.E.(37311), pg. 255
HARDWICK CLOTHES INC., 3800 Old Tasso Rd.(37320), pg. 508
Harrington & King, South, Inc., 3939 Michigan Ave.(37311), pg. 511
Kimstock Inc., 20th & Michigan Ave.(37311), pg. 630

Collegedale

MCKEE BAKING CO., INC., P.O. Box 750(37315-0750), pg. 730
MCKEE FOODS CORPORATION, 10000 McKee Rd.(37315), pg. 730
Sovex Natural Foods, P.O. Box 310(37315), pg. 730

Collierville

THE ALPHA CORPORATION OF TENNESSEE, P.O. 670(38027-0670), pg. 43
Glasteel Tennessee, Inc., P.O. Box 521(38017), pg. 461

Columbia

JRN, INC., 201 W. 7th St.(38401), pg. 586

Como

Como Grain Co., Hwy. 54(38223), pg. 1157

Cookeville

Dixie Royal Homes, Inc., (38501), pg. 398

Covington

TURNER DAIRIES, INC., 653 Dairy Lane(38019), pg. 1119

Crossville

Turner, Day & Woolworth Handle Corp., P.O. Box 322(38555), pg. 677

Dandridge

BUSH BROTHERS & COMPANY, 3885 Hwy. 411(37725), pg. 196

Dickson

TENNSCO CORPORATION, 201 Tennsco Dr.(37055), pg. 1088

Dyer

Dyer Grain Co., Hwy. 45(38330), pg. 1157

Dyersburg

Dyer-Lauderdale Farmers Co-op, , pg. 1087
Electric Research and Manufacturing Cooperative, Inc. (ERMCO), 2225 Industrial Rd.(38024), pg. 83
HECKETHORN MFG. COMPANY, 2005 Forrest St.(38024), pg. 524

Elizabethton

Elizabethton Twins Baseball Club, Holly Ln.(37643), pg. 758

Fayetteville

HAROLD MOORE & ASSOCIATES, INC., 1798 Wilson Pkwy.(37334), pg. 768

Franklin

CPS Corporation, 1715 Columbia Hwy.(37065), pg. 428
JAMISON BEDDING, INC., Highway 31(37064), pg. 589
MCKINNON BRIDGE CO., 205 Eddy Ln.(37064), pg. 731

Gallatin

Byron's, Inc., West Main St.(37066), pg. 932
GF OFFICE FURNITURE LTD., 525 Steam Plant Rd.(37066), pg. 439

Germantown

EZON PRODUCTS, INC., 1900 Exeter Rd.(38138), pg. 393
Horizon Media Inc., 2320 Germantown Rd., S., Ste. 202(38138), pg. 544
RUSSELL STADELMAN & COMPANY, 3059 Forest Hill Rd.(38138), pg. 1034

Goodlettsville

Moeller Marine Products, 850 Springfield Hwy.(37072), pg. 768

Greeneville

Austin Carolina Co., Hall & Cutler Sts.(37743), pg. 99
AUSTIN CO., INC., Hall & Cutler Sts.(37743), pg. 98
CEC Inc., P.O. Box 638, (37744), pg. 239
Cigar Supply Co., Hall & Cutler Sts.(37743), pg. 99
Doehler-Jarvis Plant, Rufe Taylor Rd.(37743), pg. 559
Hurd Lock & Manufacturing Co., 603 Bohannon Ave., P.O. Box 1450(37744), pg. 102
MECO CORPORATION, 1500 Industrial Rd.(37743), pg. 734
Mullins Leaf Tobacco Co., Hall & Cutler Sts.(37743), pg. 99

Harriman

Harriman Record, P.O. Box 261, 510 Devonia St.(37748), pg. 655

Hartsville

GENERAL SPRING, INC., P.O. Box 176(37074-0176), pg. 450

Hendersonville

GLOBE BUSINESS FURNITURE, INC., 90 Volunteer Dr.(37075), pg. 463

Hixson

CHATTANOOGA GROUP, 4717 Adams Rd.(37343), pg. 241

Jackson

Model Mill Co., P.O. Box 609, (38302), pg. 1195

Johnson City

Alco Health Services Corporation-Johnson City Div., 410 Princeton Rd.(37602), pg. 32
Denise Lingerie, 717 Rowland Dr.(37601), pg. 546
Enco-Johnson City Division, 2704 S. Roan St.(37601), pg. 380
HAMPTON PRINT WORKS, INC., 2212 Buffalo Rd.(37604), pg. 504
Tencarva Machinery Co., 2831 E. Oakland Ave.(37602), pg. 1087

Kenton

Kenton Grain Co., 405 Maple Heights(38233), pg. 1157
TOM WADE CO., 405 Maple Heights(38233), pg. 1157
Wade Gin Co., 105 E. Taylor St.(38233), pg. 1157
Wade Land Co., 405 Maple Heights(38233), pg. 1157

Kingsport

AFG International, Inc., P.O. Box 929, (37662), pg. 3
Arcata Graphics Kingsport, P.O. Box 711(37662), pg. 80
Arcata Graphics Sherwood, P.O. Box 3948, (37664), pg. 80
Industrial Coatings Group (Sales Office), 220 Broad St.(37660), pg. 566
Lindenmeyr Paper, 544 Fleetwood Court(37662), pg. 233
Tri-State Concrete Products Co., Inc., Hwy. 11 West(37665), pg. 177
Wholesale Electric Division, 420 Press St.(37660), pg. 1020

Kingston

Profit Management Corp., I-40 at Gallaher Rd.(37763), pg. 398
Roane County News, P.O. Box 610, 204 Franklin St.(37763), pg. 655

Knoxville

ABB ENVIRONMENTAL SYSTEMS, 1400 Centerpoint Blvd.(37932-1966), pg. 2
Allen & Hoshall, 9041 Executive Park Dr.(37990), pg. 36
Appalachian Realty Co., P.O. Box 238(37901), pg. 498
BIKE ATHLETIC CO., 2801 Red Dog Dr.(37914), pg. 150
Brink's, Inc., P.O. Box 238(37901), pg. 498
DAVIS-NEWMAN-PAYNE, 4700 Coster Rd.(37912), pg. 319
Stephen Gould of Tennessee, Southern Station Bldg., 306 W. Depot Ave., Ste. 104(34917), pg. 474
Growth Management Corp., 4300 Rutledge Pike(37914), pg. 398
THE H. T. HACKNEY CO., 502 S. Gay St.(37901), pg. 498
Heil Tank Services, Inc., P.O. Box 3386, (37917), pg. 526
Innco Management Corp., 8167 Kingston Pike(37919), pg. 398
JFG Coffee Company, 3434 Mynatt Ave., NW(37919), pg. 923
KELSO OIL COMPANY, 641 Atlantic Ave.(37912), pg. 622
KERN'S BAKERIES, INCORPORATED, 2110 Chapman Hwy.(37920), pg. 624
Knox Allright, Inc., 517 W. Clinch Ave.(37901), pg. 42
KNOX INTERNATIONAL CORP., 505 Market St., Seventh Fl.(37902), pg. 638
LAVIDGE & ASSOCIATES INC., Bearden Park Circle(37919), pg. 661
LAY PACKING COMPANY INC., P.O. Box 2447(37901), pg. 663
Levi Strauss Employee Purchase Plan, Inc., 1611 Third Creek Rd.(37921), pg. 670

Precision Disc Corp., 5055 S. National Dr.(37914), pg. 811
Pride Oil Co., Inc., 5414 Clinton Hwy.(37912), pg. 622
Rentenbach Constructors Incorporated, 2400 Sutherland Ave.(37919), pg. 927
RENTENBACH ENGINEERING COMPANY, 2400 Sutherland Ave.(37919), pg. 927
STAR SALES CO., INC., 1803 N. Central(37917), pg. 1040
Tank Service, Inc., P.O. Box 3386(37917), pg. 526
TECHNOLOGY FOR ENERGY CORPORATION, 10737 Lexington Dr.(37932), pg. 1084
Tencarva Machinery Co., 3508 Overlook Circle(37919), pg. 1087
Tennessee Tubebending Inc., 5320 S. National Dr.(37914), pg. 771
TENNESSEE VALLEY AUTHORITY, 400 W. Summitt Hill Dr.(37902-1499), pg. 1088
CHARLES TOMBRAS ADVERTISING, INC., 630 Concord St.(37919), pg. 1100
WM. S. TRIMBLE COMPANY, INC., 2200 Atchley St.(37920), pg. 1113
Volunteer Fabricators, Inc., P.O. Box 238(37901), pg. 498
THE WHITE LILY FOODS CO., P.O. Box 871(37901), pg. 1186

La Vergne

Ingram Library Services, Inc., 1125 Heil Quaker Blvd.(37086), pg. 569
Ingram Merchandising Service Inc., 1125 Heil Quaker Blvd.(37086), pg. 569
Ingram Periodicals Inc., 1117 Heil Quaker Blvd.(37086-7000), pg. 569
Kex Products, Inc., 1435 Heil Quaker Blvd.(37086), pg. 145
Perfect Equipment Corp., 1435 Heil Quaker Blvd., Box 600(37086), pg. 145
Publisher Resources Inc., 1125 Heil Quaker Blvd.(37086), pg. 569
Tennessee Book Company, 1109 Heil Quaker Blvd.(37086-9962), pg. 569
TENNESSEE FARMERS CO-OP, 200 Waldron(37086), pg. 1087

Lebanon

Barry-Carter Milling Co., P.O. Box 369, (37087), pg. 1195
Kenneth O. Lester, Inc., 825 Maddox Simpson Pkwy(37087), pg. 862

Lenoir City

Camp Hosiery, P.O. Box 370, 213 Grand St.(37771), pg. 400

Lewisburg

Co-Ex Plastics, Inc., 851 Garrett Pkwy.(37091), pg. 555
Cosmolab Div., (37091), pg. 639
WALKER DIE CASTING, INC., 1125 Higgs St.(37091), pg. 1160

Lexington

CM Chain Division, State Road 22A(38351), pg. 266
JACKSON PRODUCTS CORP., 15365 Hwy. 22(38351), pg. 587

Maryville

Knoxville Journal Corporation, 307 Harper St.(37801), pg. 863
Maryville-Alcoa Newspapers, Inc., 307 Harper St.(37801), pg. 863
MasterCraft Boat Company, Route 9(37801), pg. 695

McKenzie

Keco Milling Co., Old Hwy. 22(38201), pg. 1195

Memphis

Alco Management, Inc., 35 Union Ave., Ste. 200(38103), pg. 592
Alco Properties, Inc., 35 Union Ave., Ste. 200(38103), pg. 592
ALLEN & HOSHALL, INC., 2430 Poplar Ave.(38182), pg. 36
ALLEN & OHARA, INC., 3385 Airways Blvd.(38116), pg. 36
Allright System Parking, Inc., 8 South Third St, Concourse Level(38103), pg. 42
ANDERSON-TULLY CO., 1242 N. 2nd St.(38107), pg. 73
Aratex Services, 2860 Rudder Rd.(38130), pg. 6
ARCHER/MALMO ADV., INC., 65 Union Ave., Ste. 500(38103), pg. 80
Archer/Malmo Public Relations Div., 65 Union at Front(38103), pg. 80
W. M. BARR & CO., INC., 2105 Channel Ave.(38113), pg. 121
BELZ ENTERPRISES, 530 Oak Court Dr.(38117), pg. 138
Bluff City Cigarette Service, 3910 Delp St.(38118), pg. 968
BLUFF CITY DISTRIBUTING CO., INC., 3339 Fontaine Rd.(38116), pg. 161
BRYCE CORPORATION, 4505 Old Lamar(38118), pg. 185
BUCKMAN LABORATORIES, 1256 N. McLean Blvd.(38108), pg. 185
Buckman Laboratories, Inc., 1256 N. McLean Blvd.(38108), pg. 188
BUILDING PLASTICS, INC., 3263 Sharpe Ave.(38111), pg. 188
BULAB HOLDINGS, INC., 1256 N. McLean Blvd.(38108), pg. 188
JOHN J. CAMPBELL CO., INC., 6012 Resources Dr.(38134), pg. 212
D. CANALE FOOD SERVICES, INC., 7 W. George Ave.(38101), pg. 213
CHOCTAW, INC., 1184 Tupelo St.(38108), pg. 248
CONLEY FROG & SWITCH COMPANY, 387 E. Bodley(38109), pg. 274
CONWOOD COMPANY L.P., 813 Ridge Lake Blvd.(38120), pg. 281
THE COURT COMPANY, 5389 Estate Office Dr.(38119), pg. 290
CUMMINS MID-SOUTH, INC., 666 Riverside Dr.(38103), pg. 305
BUD DAVIS CADILLAC, INC., 5433 Poplar Ave.(38119), pg. 318
DEALERS TRANSPORT COMPANY, INC., 5405 Fox Plaza Dr., Ste. 107(38115), pg. 322
DELTA FOREMOST CHEMICAL CORP., 3915 Air Park St.(38118), pg. 327
DELTA LIFE CORPORATION, 530 Oak Court, Ste. 200(38117), pg. 327
Desoto Hardwood Flooring Company, 977 Sledge Ave.(38101), pg. 786
Dixico Division (Plant), 276 So. Pkwy., W.(38109), pg. 135
DOBBS BROTHERS MANAGEMENT, 5170 Sanderlin Ave.(38117), pg. 342
DUNAVANT ENTERPRISES, INC., 3797 New Getwell Rd.(38118), pg. 352
ECONOCOM-USA INC., 4400 S. Mendehall, Ste. 8(38141), pg. 367
ELKINGTON REALTY & DEVELOPMENT, 168 Beal St.(38103), pg. 377
FANTASTIC SAM'S INTERNATIONAL, INC., 3180 Old Getwell Rd.(38118), pg. 398
FEDERAL COMPRESS & WAREHOUSE COMPANY, INC., 165 Madison Ave., Suite 1400(38103), pg. 404
FISCHER LIME & CEMENT COMPANY, 3347 Pearson Road(38118), pg. 414
Forest Hill Dairy, 2040 Maidson Ave.(38174), pg. 1119
Furman Wholesale Lumber Div., 4341 Old Lamar(38118), pg. 436
FRED P. GATTAS COMPANY, INC., 5000 Summer Ave.(38122), pg. 446
GUARDSMARK, INC., 22 S. Second St.(38103), pg. 492
The C.P. Hall Company, P.O. Box 13303(38113), pg. 501
Harwick Chemical Corp., 4515 Poplar Ave.(38117), pg. 515
HEAVY MACHINES, INC., 4087 Viscount(38118), pg. 524
HUMPHREYS PRICE/COCHRAN & SANFORD ADVERTISING, 5100 Poplar Ave., 14th Fl.(38137), pg. 553
CHUCK HUTTON CHEVROLET COMPANY, 2471 Mt. Moriah(38115), pg. 556
IDEAL CHEMICAL & SUPPLY COMPANY, 4025 Air Park St.(38118), pg. 562
Idealease of Memphis, 3340 Pearson Rd., pg. 750
IMPERIAL MANUFACTURING COMPANY, 11 W. Butler(38103), pg. 564
INMAN CONSTRUCTION CORPORATION, 5100 Poplar Ave., Ste. 1210(38137), pg. 570
JEMISON, INC., 35 Union Ave., Ste. 200(38103), pg. 592
Kilsby-Roberts/Memphis, 1340 Channel Ave.(38113), pg. 606
LANGSTON COMPANIES, 3294 Poplar Ave.(38111), pg. 657
Layne & Bowler, 1993 Chelsea Ave.(38108), pg. 710
LEADER FEDERAL BANK FOR SAVINGS, 158 Madison Ave.(38103), pg. 663
Leader Leasing, Inc., 158 Madison Ave.(38103), pg. 664
Leader Services, Inc., 158 Madison Ave.(38103), pg. 664
LINKOUS CONSTRUCTION COMPANY, INC., 6075 Poplar, Ste. 202(38119), pg. 677
Mark Lipman Div., 22 S. Second St.(38103), pg. 493
LITHOGRAPH PRINTING COMPANY, INC., 4222 Pilot Dr.(38118), pg. 678
MANUFACTURERS CONSOLIDATION SERVICE, 187 W. Industrial Ave.(38109), pg. 705
MARTIN, COLE, DANDO & ROBERTSON, 5100 Wheelis St., Ste. 200(38117), pg. 714
Massey Cadillac, Inc., 2177 Covington Pike(38128), pg. 719
MAYER MYERS PAPER COMPANY, 1769 Latham St.(38101), pg. 724
MEMPHIS GROUP, INC., 3900 Willow Lake Blvd.(38118), pg. 738
MEMPHIS LIGHT, GAS & WATER, 220 S. Main St.(38103), pg. 738
MEMPHIS PUBLISHING COMPANY, 495 Union Ave.(38101), pg. 738
METRO FOODS, INC., 3657 Old Getwell Rd.(38118), pg. 743
MID AMERICA INTERNATIONAL TRUCKS, INC., 1750 E. Brooks Rd.(38116), pg. 750
MID-SOUTH FORD TRUCK SALES, INC., 673 E. Brooks Rd.(38116), pg. 750
MID-SOUTH MILLING COMPANY, INC., 785 Crossover Ln., Ste. 116(38117), pg. 750
NATIONAL BEDDING & FURNITURE INDUSTRIES, 736 S. Dudley(38104), pg. 786
NATIONAL MORTGAGE COMPANY, 4041 Knight Arnold Rd.(38118), pg. 792
NATIONAL SAFETY ASSOCIATES, 4260 E. Raines Rd.(38118), pg. 793
94th AS of Memphis, Inc., 2561 Democrat Rd.(38118), pg. 1029
Orgill Brothers & Company, Inc., 2100 Latham St.(38103), pg. 1178
OZARK MOTOR LINES, 3934 Homewood Rd.(38181), pg. 835
PSI Fabricators, Inc., 1790 Kirby Pkwy., Ste. 300(38138), pg. 837
PSI GROUP OF COMPANIES, 1790 Kirby Pkwy., Ste. 300(38138), pg. 837
Pemko Manufacturing, 5535 Distribution Dr.(38114), pg. 856
Peoplemark, Inc., 22 S. Second St.(38103), pg. 493
Perkins Family Restaurants, 6075 Poplar Ave., Ste. 800(38119), pg. 1088
PLANT MAINTENANCE SERVICE CORPORATION, 3000 Fite Rd.(38128), pg. 874
POWER & TELEPHONE SUPPLY COMPANY, 2701 Union Extended, Ste. 300(38112-4417), pg. 883
Process Systems, Inc. Construction Co., 1790 Kirby Pkwy. Ste. 300(38138), pg. 837
River City Protective Wear, Inc., 5321 E. Shelby Dr.(38118), pg. 996
SAMELSON-LEON COMPANY, INC., 4280 Concorde(38118), pg. 968
Schilling Enterprises, 5405 Fox Plaza Dr., Ste. 107(38115), pg. 322
Schilling Motors, Inc., 963-87 Union Ave.(38104), pg. 322
SEABROOK WALLCOVERINGS, INC., 1325 Farmville Rd.(38122), pg. 984
SEALY MATTRESS COMPANY, 4120 Air Trans Rd.(38118), pg. 986
Sealy Mattress Company of Memphis, P.O. Box 181112, 4120 Air Trans Rd.(38118), pg. 985
SEESSEL HOLDINGS, INC., 1745 Union(38104), pg. 987
SHELBY GROUP INTERNATIONAL, INC., 5321 E. Shelby Dr.(38118), pg. 996
SOUTHERN LEATHER COMPANY, 274 Monroe Ave.(38103), pg. 1021
STANDARD WELDERS SUPPLY CO., 363 Walnut(38126), pg. 1038
SUPER D DRUG STORES, 4695 Outland Center Dr., Ste. 101(38118), pg. 1062
TMP Worldwide, Inc., 889 Ridge Lake Blvd., Ste. 210(38120), pg. 1074
TVESCO, INC., 296 Adams Ave.(38101), pg. 1075
Tencarva Machinery Co., 3725 Getwell Cove(38118), pg. 1087
THOMPSON & COMPANY, Cotton Exchange Bldg., 65 Union Ave., 8th Fl.(38103), pg. 1094
Three States Supply Co., Inc., 666-E. H. Crump Blvd.(38216), pg. 1123
TRI-STATE ARMATURE ELECTRIC WORKS, 330 E. Calhoun Ave.(38126), pg. 1110
TRI-STATE MACK DISTRIBUTORS, 494 E.H. Crump Blvd.(38126), pg. 1111
UNIVERSAL LIFE INSURANCE COMPANY, 480 Linden Ave., P.O. Box 241(38126), pg. 1138
University Casework Systems, Inc., 2718 Pershing Ave.(38112), pg. 612
WALKER & ASSOCIATES, INC., 1100 Morgan Keegan Tower(38103), pg. 1159
WANG'S INTERNATIONAL, INC., 4250 E. Shelby Dr.(38118), pg. 1162
WEINSTOCK, WHITE & ASSOCIATES, 7500 Capital Dr.(38138), pg. 1174
WEST UNION CORP., 35 Union(38103), pg. 1177
WEXNER & JACOBSON, INC., 117 1/2 Union Ave.(38103), pg. 1183
KEMMONS WILSON COMPANIES, 1629 Winchester Rd.(38116), pg. 1194
WURZBURG, INC., 710 S. Fourth St.(38126), pg. 1205

Morristown

The Berkline Corporation, One Berkline Dr.(37813), pg. 285
Berkline Limited, One Berkline Drive(37814), pg. 285
Hale Brothers, Inc., 530 E. Main(37816), pg. 861
PRECISION PARTS CORP., 4188 E. Andrew Johnson Hwy.(37814), pg. 885
Southern Electric Supply Co., Inc., 3415 W. Andrew Johnson Hwy.(37814), pg. 1021

Murfreesboro

Gem Top East Inc, 1124 Haley Rd.(37130), pg. 448
Lewis Bros. Bakeries (TN), 847 Scott Dr.(37133), pg. 673
National Savings Life Insurance Company, Hwy. 231 S., P.O. Box 1338(37133), pg. 1150
Paramount Packaging Corp., 106 Samsonite Blvd.(37130), pg. 848
Perfect Equipment Corp., 855 Scott St., Box 942(37130), pg. 145

Nashville

ABINGDON PRESS, 201 8th Ave. South(37202), pg. 10
AFFILIATES GROUP INC., 4219 Hillsboro Rd., Ste. 306(37215), pg. 24
ALADDIN INDUSTRIES, INCORPORATED, 703 Murfreesboro Rd.(37210), pg. 29
Aladdin Resources, Inc., 703 Murfreesboro Rd.(37210), pg. 29
Aladdin Synergetics, Inc., 555 Mariott Dr., Ste. 400(37210), pg. 29
Allen & Hoshall, 50 Century Blvd., Ste. 100(37228), pg. 36
ALLEY-CASSETTY COAL CO., N. 37
Allied Security Inc., 475 Metroplex Dr., Ste. 204(37211), pg. 39
Allright Nashville Parking, Inc., 541 Broadway(37203), pg. 41
Alro Specialty Metals, Nashville, 143 Park S. Ct.(37210), pg. 44
AMERICAN BREAD COMPANY - SUNBEAM BAKERY, 702 Murfreesboro Rd.(37210), pg. 49
American Envelope of Nashville, 820 7th Ave. N.(37219), pg. 199
Arcata Graphics Baird Ward, Inc., P.O. Box 305127(37230), pg. 80
ATHENS PAPER CO. INC., 1898 Elmtree Dr.(37210), pg. 93
Automotive Marketing Assoc., 1645 Murfreefboro Rd., Ste. A(37217), pg. 224
B & G WHOLESALERS, INC., 337 28th Ave., N.(37209), pg. 106
THE BENSON MUSIC GROUP, 365 Great Circle Rd.(37228), pg. 140
Benson Records, 365 Great Circle Rd.(37228), pg. 140
BLEVINS INC., 421 Hart Ln.(37206), pg. 156
Bouchard Fire Protection, 1024 Harrison St.(37203), pg. 168
JOHN BOUCHARD & SONS COMPANY, 1024 Harrison St.(37203), pg. 168
J. C. BRADFORD & CO., 330 Commerce St.(37201), pg. 170
BRAID ELECTRIC COMPANY, 299 Cowan St.(37202), pg. 171

BUNTIN ADVERTISING, INC., 1001 Hawkins St.(37203), pg. 188
CARDEN & CHERRY, INC., 1220 McGavock St.(37203), pg. 217
Carolina Steel Service Center Plant, 401 Driftwood St.(37210), pg. 223
CENTRAL PARKING CORP., 2401 21st St., Ste. 300(37212), pg. 234
Central Parking Corp., 937 Church St.(37203), pg. 234
Chemrock Corporation, 1101 Kermit Dr., Ste. 503(37217), pg. 136
Chemrock Corporation, Osage St.(37210), pg. 137
CREST CADILLAC COMPANY, 2121 Metro Center Blvd.(37228), pg. 298
Crest Cadillac, Inc., 2121 Metro Center Pkwy.(37228), pg. 719
CROOKS SUPERMARKET INC., P.O. Box 50028, (37205-0028), pg. 300
CUMMINGS INC., 200 12th Ave. S.(37203), pg. 304
DOBSON & JOHNSON, INC., 4522 Harding Rd.(37205), pg. 342
ENCO MATERIALS, INC., 211-214 Boscobel St.(37213), pg. 380
ERICSON MARKETING COMMUNICATIONS, 1130 Eighth Ave. South(37203), pg. 386
GAYLORD ENTERTAINMENT CO., 2802 Opryland Dr.(37214), pg. 446
GIBSON GUITAR CORPORATION, INC., 641 Massman Dr.(37210), pg. 456
GISH, SHERWOOD & FRIENDS, INC., 460 Tenth Circle No.(37203), pg. 460
GOODRUM LEONARD & ASSOCIATES, INC., 4301 Hillsboro Rd.(37215), pg. 471
Greentree Records, 365 Great Circle Rd.(37228), pg. 140
W. L. HAILEY & COMPANY, INC., 2971 Kraft Dr.(37204), pg. 500
HARDAWAY CONSTRUCTION COMPANY, INC., 615 Main St.(37206), pg. 508
HORNER RAUSCH COMPANY, 968 Main St.(37206), pg. 544
Hospital Affiliates Development Corporation, 3401 W. End Ave.(37203), pg. 24
HUMBOLDT EXPRESS, INC., 345 Hill Ave.(37210), pg. 552
Ingram Barge Company, One Belle Meade Place, 4400 Harding Rd.(37205), pg. 569
Ingram Coal Company, One Belle Meade Place, 4400 Harding Rd.(37205), pg. 569
INGRAM INDUSTRIES INC., One Belle Meade Place, 4400 Harding Rd.(37202), pg. 568
Ingram Production Company, One Belle Meade Place, 4400 Harding Rd.(37205), pg. 569
KIRBY BUILDING SYSTEMS, INC., 555 Marriott Dr., Ste. 800(37210), pg. 632
Laboratory Supply Company, 336 Wilhagen Rd.(37217), pg. 650
The Marble Company, 421 Hart Lane(37216), pg. 156
Nashville Crawdaddy, Inc., 14 Oldham St.(37213), pg. 1029
NASHVILLE MACHINE CO. INC., 530 Woodycrest Ave.(37210-4394), pg. 784
NASHVILLE STEEL CORP., 7211 Centennial Blvd.(37209), pg. 784
NASHVILLE WIRE PRODUCT CO., 199 Polk Ave.(37210), pg. 784
94th Aero Squadron of Nashville, Inc., 1362-A Murfreesboro Rd.(37217), pg. 1029
OMAN CONSTRUCTION CO. INC., 200 42nd Ave. N.(37209), pg. 825
Opryland USA, Inc., 2804 Opryland Dr.(37214), pg. 446
Ouimet Corp., 2967 Sidco Dr.(37204), pg. 831
Ouimet Stay & Leather Co., 650 Armory Dr.(37204), pg. 831
THE PARMAN CORPORATION, 7101 Cockrill Bend Blvd.(37209), pg. 850
Parman Oil Co., 5901 Cockrill Industrial Dr.(37209), pg. 850
Parmart Stores, 5901 Cockrill Industrial Dr.(37209), pg. 850
Patten-Beers Constructors, 1901 21st Ave. South(37212), pg. 132
Pearl Drum Center, 408 Harding Indus. Dr.(37211), pg. 457
PERFORMANCE FOOD GROUP, INC., 25 Century Blvd., Ste. 509(37214), pg. 861
Permanent General Companies, 633 Thompson Lane(37204), pg. 569
PHOENIX ENTERPRISES INC., 3100 W. End Ave., Ste. 910(37203), pg. 868
Polk Bank Services Div., 2001 Elm Hill Pike(37230-5100), pg. 879
Power Discs, 365 Great Circle Dr.(37228), pg. 140
PURITY DAIRIES INC., 360 Murfreesboro Rd., (37210), pg. 901
C. B. RAGLAND COMPANY, P.O. Box 40587(37204), pg. 909
Rand McNally Book & Media Services, 418 Harding Industrial Dr.(37211), pg. 911
Riversong Records, 365 Great Circle Rd.(37228), pg. 140
ROGERS GROUP INC., 421 Great Circle Road(37228), pg. 943
SOUTHWESTERN/GREAT AMERICAN INC., 2451 Atrium Way(37210), pg. 1023
STANDARD CANDY CO., INC., 715 Massman Dr.(37210-3787), pg. 1035
Star Trasnportation, Inc., P.O. Box 100906, (37224), pg. 552
TSC INDUSTRIES, INC., 320 Plus Park Blvd.(37217), pg. 1075
Tencarva Machinery Co., 321 E. Trinity Lane(37207), pg. 1087
TENNESSEE DRESSED BEEF COMPANY, 50 Van Buren St.(37208), pg. 1087
Tennessee Insurance Co., 633 Thompson Ln.(37204), pg. 569
TENNESSEE WHOLESALE DRUG COMPANY, 200 Cumberland Bend(37228), pg. 1088
I. C. THOMASSON ASSOCIATES, INC., 2120 Eighth Ave., So.(37204), pg. 1094
TOP BILLING INC., 1222 16th Ave., S., Suite 1101
Wenczel Tile Distributing Company, 925 Twin Elms Court(37210), pg. 1176
WERTHAN PACKAGING, INC., 1400 8th Ave. N.(37202), pg. 1176

Oak Ridge

The Oak Ridger, 785 Oak Ridge Turnpike(37830), pg. 1042
TENNELEC/NUCLEUS, INC., 601 Oak Ridge Turnpike(37830), pg. 1087

Paris

KESTERSON FOOD COMPANY, INC., 211 Hwy. 69 N.(38242), pg. 624

Pigeon Forge

Airport '82 Associates Ltd., P.O. Box 10, (37863), pg. 398
FAMILY INNS OF AMERICA, INC., 509 Tammy King Rd.(37863-0010), pg. 398
Lucky Inns of America, Inc., P.O. Box 10, (37863), pg. 398
Regional Development Corp., P.O. Box 10, (37863), pg. 398
Kenneth M. Seaton Enterprises, P.O. Box 10, (37863), pg. 398
Tri-Management Corp., P.O. Box 10, (37863), pg. 398

Piney Flats

Modern Forge/Tennessee, Tri County Industrial Pk.(37686), pg. 762
THE PATY COMPANY, 220 Piney Flats Rd.(37686), pg. 852

Portland

Garcy/SLP, , pg. 907
Sunbeam Casual Furniture Co., Victor Reiter Pkwy.(37148), pg. 1059

Pulaski

Pulaski Rubber Co., P.O. Drawer I(38478), pg. 906

Rockwood

Rockwood Times, P.O. Box 297, 325 N. Kingston Ave.(37854), pg. 655

Selmer

HENCO, INC., P.O. Box 547, Selmer Industrial Park(38375), pg. 528

Sequatchie

Sequatchie Handle Works, Inc., P.O. Box 140(37374), pg. 677

Smyrna

Cumberland Freight Line, Inc., 13th Ave. & D St.(37167), pg. 304
CUMBERLAND-SWAN, INC., One Swan Drive(37167), pg. 304

Springfield

HOLLINGSWORTH OIL CO. INC., 1503 Memorial Blvd.(37172), pg. 539
TOBACCO SUPPLY, 2411 Industrial Dr.(37172), pg. 1099

Sweetwater

Vestal Manufacturing, South Main St.(37847), pg. 1162

Tullahoma

Sverdrup Technology, Inc., 600 William Northern Blvd., P.O. Box 884(37388), pg. 1066

Vonore

NATIONAL SEATING CO., 200 National Dr.(37885), pg. 793

Wartburg

Morgan County News, P.O. Box 346, Cumberland St.(37887), pg. 655

TEXAS

Abilene

FIRST ABILENE BANKSHARES, INC., 400 Pine St.(79601), pg. 411
First National Bank of Abilene, 400 Pine St.(79604), pg. 412
GSC Distributing of Abilene, 841 Oak St.(79602), pg. 440
Gooch Packing Co., Inc., P.O. Box 2738, (79604), pg. 912
Reporter Publishing Company, N. First & Cypress(79604), pg. 513
West Texas Wholesale Supply Co., 4th & Plum(79604), pg. 340
WESTERN TRAILER EQUIPMENT & MANUFACTURING CO., 1110 E. Hwy. 80(79601), pg. 1182

Addison

TGI Friday's, Inc., 14665 Midway Rd.(75244), pg. 221

Amarillo

AFFILIATED FOODS, INC., 1401 W. Farmer's Ave.(79118), pg. 24
Amarillo Gear Company, P.O. Box 1789, (79105), pg. 711
ATEX OIL CO. OF TEXAS, INC., 2740 Southwest 45th(79110), pg. 93
CACTUS FEEDERS, INC., 2209 W. 7th St.(79106), pg. 207
Flo-Line Filters, Inc., 1501 S. Johnson(79105), pg. 863
Friona Agriculture Credit Corp., P.O. Box 15568(79105), pg. 434
FRIONA INDUSTRIES, L.P., 900 Amarillo Bank Bldg., 410 S. Taylor St., Ste. 900(79101), pg. 434
GILVIN-TERRILL INC., P.O. Box 9027(79105), pg. 460
KGNC-AM & FM, P.O. Box 710, (79189), pg. 1043
MAYWOOD, INC., 900 E. Second(79120), pg. 725
Randall County Feed Yard, Rte. 4, Box 99(79119), pg. 434
Team Bank/Amarillo, P.O. Box 231(79182), pg. 1082
Texas Commerce Bank-Amarillo, 2201 Civic Circle(79109), pg. 1089
United Filters, Inc., 1501 S. Johnson(79105), pg. 863

Arlington

AMERICAN EXCELSIOR COMPANY, 850 Ave. H. East(76011), pg. 51
BERRYMAN PRODUCTS, INC., 3800 E. Randol Mill Rd.(76011), pg. 144
Brooks Products, Arlington, 2001 W. Mayfield Rd.(76015), pg. 180
Computerland, 621 Six Flags Dr.(76011), pg. 271
Dayton Rogers of Texas, 1107 Commercial Blvd. No.(76017), pg. 321
TOM JAMES COMPANY, 690 E. Lamar Blvd., Ste. 350(76011), pg. 589
MBS HOLDING, INC., 3403 E. Abram(76010), pg. 691
MARTIN SPROCKET & GEAR, INC., 3100 Sprocket Dr.(76015), pg. 715
Mayfield Building Supply Co., 3403 E. Abram(76010), pg. 691
MILLER BUSINESS SYSTEMS, INC., 223 Ave. J(76006), pg. 753
MORITZ CADILLAC-SAAB INC., 2001 N. Collins(76011), pg. 770
SALADMASTER, 912 113th St.(76010), pg. 967
SHORELINE PRODUCTS, INC., 921 W. Mayfield Rd.(76015), pg. 1000
VANDERGRIFF CHEVROLET GEO, 901 E. Division(76010), pg. 1144
WBH INDUSTRIES, INC., 3016 Avenue E.(76011), pg. 1155

Athens

COLORTYME, INC., P.O. Box 1781, (75751), pg. 265
CURTIS MATHES CORPORATION, 1 Curtis Mathes Pkwy.(75751), pg. 720

Atlanta

Anthony Forest Div., South Louis St.(75551), pg. 77

Austin

ADAMS EXTRACT CO., INC., 11206 IH-35 S.(78747), pg. 16
Allright Parking of Austin, Inc., 720 Brazos T., Suite S-14(78701), pg. 42
Atlas Van Lines of Texas, 55 I.H. 35(78769), pg. 97
Bookstop, Inc., 6106 Baldwin Dr.(78724), pg. 120
CJC HOLDINGS, INC., 7211 Circle S. Rd.(78745), pg. 202
CALCASIEU LUMBER COMPANY, 4501 Burleson Rd.(78744), pg. 208
Caliente Chili, Inc., 804 Rio Grande(78701), pg. 923
COMPUADD CORPORATION, 12303 Technology Blvd.(78727), pg. 271
Consolidated Wholesale Lumber Co., 4501 Burleson Rd.(78744), pg. 208
DURHAM TRANSPORTATION, INC., Travis Bldg, Ste. 200, 9171 Capital of Texas Highway N.(78759-7252), pg. 354
Eastway Delivery Service of Austin, Inc., 1300 Smith Rd., Ste. 102(78762), pg. 364
Farm Credit Bank of Texas, La Costa Office Park, 6210 Highway 290 East(78723), pg. 405
FELLERS & COMPANY, 5918 W. Courtyard Dr., 5th Fl.(78730), pg. 405
Fogarty & Klein Yellow Pages, Inc., 1204 Lakeway Dr., 421
GSC Distributing of Austin, 2832 M.L.K. Dr.(78702), pg. 440
GSD&M, 1250 Capital of Texas Hwy., Ste. 400(78746), pg. 441
Hart Distribution Services, 3106 Longhorn Blvd.(78759), pg. 513
Hart Forms & Services, 11500 Metric Blvd., Ste. 300(78758), pg. 513
HART GRAPHICS INC., 8000 Shoal Creek Blvd.(78758), pg. 513
Hillhouse Associates Insurance, Inc., 8834 Capital of Texas Hwy. N., Ste. 300(78720), pg. 802
IDC Texas, Shepard Mountain Exec. Suites, 6043 W. Courtyard Dr., Ste. 305(78730), pg. 577
Integrated Benefit Systems, Bldg. D, 3933 Spice Wood Springs Rd.(78759), pg. 573
MEDIATEX COMMUNICATIONS CORPORATION, P. O. Box 1569(78767), pg. 735
PCI, 12416 Hymeadow Dr.(78750), pg. 836
PD News, 12416 Hymeadow Dr.(78750), pg. 836
SAS Institute, Inc., 11920 Wilson Parke Ave.(78726), pg. 959
7UP/RC of Austin, 3411 Hidalgo St.(78702), pg. 477
SICOLA MARTIN KOONS FRANK, INC., 6850 Austin Ctr. Blvd., Ste. 270(78731), pg. 1001
Software Video Production, 12416 Hymeadow Dr.(78750), pg. 836
Texas Commerce Bank-Austin, 700 Lavaca(78701), pg. 1089
TEXAS ELECTRIC COOPERATIVES, INC., 8140 Burnet Rd.(78758), pg. 1089
Texas Monthly, Inc., P.O. Box 1569(78767), pg. 735
Tracor Aerospace, Inc., 6500 Tracor Ln.(78725-2070), pg. 1105
Tracor Applied Sciences, Analysis & Applied Research Div., 6500 Tracor Ln.(78725), pg. 1105
Tracor Flight Systems, Inc., 6500 Tracor Ln.(78725), pg. 1105
TRACOR, INC., 6500 Tracor Ln.(78725-2000), pg. 1104

U.S. CREATIVE, INC., 901 S. MoPac Expwy., Barton Oaks Plaza II, Ste. 595(78746), pg. 1135
VINDICATOR CORPORATION, 3001 Beecave Rd.(78746), pg. 1152
Visible Changes of Austin, 6001 Airport(78752), pg. 1153

Bay City

STANLEY STORES INC., 1400 8th St.(77414), pg. 1038

Baytown

Advanced Aromatics, Inc., 5501 Baker Rd.(77520), pg. 242

Beaumont

Allright Beaumont Co., 227 Main(77704), pg. 41
Beaumont Enterprise, 380 Walnut Ave.(77701), pg. 523
HELENA LABORATORIES CORPORATION, 1530 Lindbergh(77707), pg. 526
North Star Steel Texas, Inc., Old Hwy. 90(77704), pg. 219
Taylor Home Health Inc., 2865 Laurel(77702), pg. 1081
TAYLOR MEDICAL INC., 2155 IH 10 E.(77704), pg. 1081
Taylor Medical of LA, 2155 IH 10 E.(77701), pg. 1081
Texas Commerce Bank-Beaumont, 510 Park(77704), pg. 1089
TEXAS METAL WORKS, INC., 937 Pine St.(77701), pg. 1089

Bedford

GRAHAM MAGNETICS, INC., 4001 Airport Frwy., Ste. 400(76021), pg. 475

Belton

Tarco of Texas, Inc., 2403 E. 6th St.(76513), pg. 1078

Borger

J.M. Huber, Engineered Carbons Div., 1110 Penn Ave.(79007), pg. 550

Bovina

SHERLEY GRAIN COMPANY, 503 Gardner Avenue(79009), pg. 998

Breckenridge

Breck Operating Corp., 300 N. Breckenridge Ave.(76424), pg. 1041
STATES, INC., 300 N. Breckenridge Ave.(76024), pg. 1041

Brenham

BLUE BELL CREAMERIES, INC., 1000 Horton Loop, 158
Ohio-Sealy Mattress Manufacturing Co.-Houston, Hwy. Loop 290, P.O. Box 593(77833), pg. 985

Brownfield

GOODPASTURE, INC., 214 S. 6th St.(79316), pg. 471

Brownsville

Duro Paper Bag Mfg. Co., P.O. Box 4380(78523), pg. 355
Mercantile Bank, 835 East Levee, P.O. Box 2219(78520), pg. 733
Texas Commerce Bank-Rio Grande Valley, 1034 E. Levee St.(78520), pg. 1089

Brownwood

Kohler Co. (TX), P.O. Box 1709, (76801), pg. 640

Burleson

THOMAS CONVEYOR COMPANY, 555 I-35 South(76028), pg. 1093

Carrollton

ALTO Papers, 2425 Camp Dr., Ste. 150(75006), pg. 171
American Ball Manufacturing, 1225 Tappan Circle(75006), pg. 890
ARROW INDUSTRIES, INC., 2625 Belt Line Rd.(75006), pg. 85
BRAC Credit Corp., 3414 Midcourt Rd., Bldg. 2(75006), pg. 131
Elkay Plastics Co., Inc., Stock Service Center, 1580 North I-35(75006), pg. 377
LEATHER CENTER, INC., 2724 Realty Rd.(75006), pg. 664
Mary Kay Cosmetics, Inc., 1421 Patton Place(75005), pg. 717
NIBCO SWM Marketing Corp., (75006), pg. 806
Para Systems Inc., 1455 Le May Dr.(75007), pg. 270
Paxton Beautiful Woods, 1105 Sixth Avenue(75006), pg. 592
WESTERN EXTRUSIONS, 1735 Sandy Lake Rd.(75006), pg. 1179

Celina

WILLARD GRAIN & FEED, INC., 104 Ash(75009), pg. 1190

Cleburne

First National Bank in Cleburne, 403 N. Main(76031), pg. 412
Johnson Storage & Moving, Cleburne, 117 E. Industrial Blvd.(76031), pg. 601
RANGAIRE & COMPANY, 501 So. Wilhite(76031), pg. 912

Commerce

Montgomery Elevator Controls Division, U.S. Hgwy. 11(75428), pg. 767

Conroe

Eckerd Drug Co., 2061 Interstate 45 S.(77302), pg. 366

Coppell

MINYARD FOOD STORES, P.O. Box 518, 777 Freeport Pkwy.(75019), pg. 759
Minyard Properties, Inc., 777 Freeport Pkwy.(75019), pg. 759
TST/IMPRESO, INC., 652 Southwestern Blvd.(75019), pg. 1075

Corpus Christi

Allright Corpus Christi, Inc., One Shoreline Plaza, 41
Corpus Christi Caller-Times, 820 N. Lower Broadway(78401), pg. 513
Corpus Christi Transfer Company, 900 N. Staples St.(78401), pg. 725
GSC Distributing of Corpus Christi, 711 Oak Park Ave.(78408), pg. 440
SAM KANE BEEF PROCESSORS, INC., P.O. Box 9254, (78469), pg. 616
7UP of Corpus Christi, 3127 Cabaniss Pkwy.(78415), pg. 477
Texas Commerce Bank-Corpus Christi, 802 N. Carancau(78403), pg. 1089
Trademark Press, Inc., 2346 Horne Rd.(78415), pg. 513
Triumph/LOR, Inc., P.O. Drawer A, 720 Cantwell(78469), pg. 1115
WHATABURGER, INC., 4600 Parkdale Dr.(78411), pg. 1184

Corsicana

COLLIN STREET BAKERY, 401 W. Seventh Ave.(75110), pg. 262

Cypress

Demand Graphics Research, P.O. Box 777(77429), pg. 647
KWIK-KOPY CORP., One Kwik-Kopy Lane(77429), pg. 647

Dallas

ARA Leisure Services of Texas, Inc., 650 So. Griffin(75202), pg. 6
AVW Audiovisual, Inc., 2241 Irving Blvd.(75207), pg. 431
ADVENTURE TOURS USA, INC., 5459 Sherry Lane, Ste. 1900(75225), pg. 21
AFFILIATED COMPUTER SERVICES, INC., 2828 N. Haskell(75204), pg. 23
ALFORD REFRIGERATED WAREHOUSE, INC., 318 Cadiz St.(75207), pg. 34
Allied Security Inc., 1515 W. Mockingbird, Ste. 105(75235), pg. 39
Allright Parking System, Inc., 1700 Commerce Pl., Ste. 732(75201), pg. 42
American Envelope of Dallas, 14001 Inwood Rd.(75240), pg. 199
American FoodService, 4721 Simonton Rd.(75244), pg. 60
AMERICAN PRODUCE & VEGETABLE CO., 4721 Simonton Rd.(75244), pg. 59
American Transfer & Storage Co., 2605 LBJ Fwy.(75234), pg. 724
AMERISERV FOOD COMPANY, 13335 Noel Rd., Ste. 2225(75240), pg. 66
AMICO-Dallas Distr. Center, 148 Fordyce(75207), pg. 29
AMRECORP REALTY INC., 16415 Addison Rd., Ste. 200-LB6(75248), pg. 68
ANDERSON INDUSTRIES, INC., 13601 Preston Rd., Ste. 307 West(75240), pg. 72
Anthem Life Insurance Companies, Inc., 3988 N. Central Expwy.(75204), pg. 90
Aratex Services, 1900 Empire Central(75235), pg. 6
ASSOCIATED AIRCRAFT SUPPLY COMPANY, 5021 W. Jefferson(75211), pg. 89
ASSOCIATED MATERIALS INC., 2200 Ross Ave., Ste. 4100 East(75201), pg. 91
Austin Bridge & Rd.-Concrete Div., 2949 Spemmons Freeway(75247), pg. 99
Austin Bridge & Rd.-Highway Div., 3535 Travis St.(75204), pg. 99
AUSTIN INDUSTRIES, INC., 3535 Travis Ste. 300(75204), pg. 99
Austin Productions, 224 World Trade Ctr.(75207), pg. 100
Avery Mays Construction Co., P.O. Box 35612, (75235), pg. 553
BA ADVERTISING, 6500 Greenville Ave., Ste. 665(75206), pg. 105
BTD/TMP Worldwide, 9708 Skillman, Ste. 101(75243), pg. 1073
Baby Doe's, Inc., 3305 Harry Hines Blvd.(75201), pg. 1029
W. O. BANKSTON ENTERPRISES INC., 4755 McEwen Rd.(75244), pg. 118
W. O. Bankston Leasing Inc., 4747 LBJ Fwy.(75234), pg. 118
W. O. Bankston Lincoln Mercury, 4747 LBJ Fwy.(75240), pg. 118
W. O. Bankston Nissan Inc., 13130 Preston Rd.(75240), pg. 118
BERRY-BROWN ADVERTISING, INC., 2602 McKinney Ave., Ste. 300(75204), pg. 144
Bonanza Restaurants, 8080 N. Central Expy., Ste. 500(75206), pg. 744
W. Braun Co., 10480 Shady Trail Ste. 102(75220), pg. 172
BRIERLEY & PARTNERS, P.O. Box 50708, (75250), pg. 175
Briggs Weaver, 5000 Harry Hines Blvd.(75235), pg. 968
Brown Brothers Harriman Trust Co. of Texas, 4900 Trammell Crow Ctr., 2001 Ross Ave.(75201), pg. 181
Bruce Hardwood Floors, 16803 Dallas Pkwy.(75248), pg. 1112
Business Travel Management, Inc., 8777 Stemmons Fwy.(75247), pg. 717
CUNA South West District, 4455 LBJ Freeway, Suite 812(75244), pg. 205
CAMELOT COMMUNICATIONS, INC., 8140 Walnut Hill, Ste. 700(75231), pg. 212
CCC Conveyors, Inc., P.O. Box 59448, 2466 Glenda Lane(75229-4511), pg. 357
CHARLES CURTAIN COMPANY, INC., 1352 Crampton St.(75207), pg. 239
CHEMCENTRAL/Dallas, 2500 Vinson St.(75212), pg. 241
Classic Bath Products, 16803 Dallas Pkwy.(75248), pg. 1112
Club Corp Realty, 3030 LBJ Freeway, Ste. 700(75234), pg. 256
CLUB CORPORATION INTERNATIONAL, 3030 LBJ Freeway, Ste. 500(75234), pg. 256
Club Corporation Of America, 3030 LBJ Freeway, Ste. 500(75234), pg. 256
Club Resorts, Inc., 3030 LBJ Freeway, Ste. 700(75234), pg. 256
COMPONENTS CORPORATION OF AMERICA, 717 N. Harwood 270
CONTRAN CORPORATION, 3 Lincoln Ctr., 5430 LBJ Freeway, Ste. 1700(75240), pg. 281
COUNTY SEAT STORES, INC., 17950 Preston Rd.(75252), pg. 290
Crown Cable Inc., 1 Galleria Tower, 13355 Noel Rd., Ste. 1500(75240), pg. 502
Crown Media Inc., One Galleria Tower, 13355 Noel Rd., Ste. 1500(75240), pg. 502
Culco, Inc., 14303 Inwood Rd.(75240), pg. 912
Cullum Development Co., 14303 Inwood Rd.(75244), pg. 912
Cullum Distribution Center, Inc., 14303 Inwood Rd.(75240), pg. 912
DAL-TILE CORP., 7834 Hawn Freeway(75217), pg. 312
DALFORT CORP., 7701 Lemmon Ave.(75209), pg. 312
Dallas Flower Market, Inc., 2636 Farrington St.(75207), pg. 331
Deco Container, 9600 Dilworth(75243), pg. 424
Dixico, Inc., 1415 So. Vernon St.(75224), pg. 135
Dr Pepper Company, 8144 Walnut Hill Lane(75231), pg. 342
DR PEPPER/SEVEN-UP COMPANIES, INC., 8144 Walnut Hill Lane(75231), pg. 342
DUGGAN INDUSTRIES, INC., 3901 S. Lamar St.(75215), pg. 351
EAGLE LINCOLN MERCURY INC., 6116 Lemmon Ave.(75209), pg. 362
EPIC HEALTHCARE GROUP, 3333 Lee Parkway(75265-0398), pg. 384
EvansGroup, 4131 N. Central Expwy., Ste. 510(75204), pg. 391
FERGUSON INDUSTRIES, 1900 W. Northwest Hwy.(75220), pg. 406
Ferguson Industries International, 1900 W. Northwest Hwy.(75220), pg. 406
FERGUSON MANUFACTURING & EQUIPMENT COMPANY, 4900 Harry Hines Blvd.(75235), pg. 406
FIRST SOUTHWEST COMPANY, 1700 Pacific Ave., Ste. 500(75201), pg. 413
FIRST WORTHING, 8144 Walnut Hill Lane, Ste. 550(75231), pg. 414
Flexible Packaging Division (Plant), 1300 So. Polk St.(75224), pg. 135
FOXWORTH-GALBRAITH LUMBER CO., 17111 Waterview Parkway(75252), pg. 428
FREEMAN DECORATING CO., 8801 Ambassador Row(75247-4622), pg. 431
FRIENDLY CHEVROLET CO. INC., 5601 Lemmon Ave.(75209), pg. 433
Furman Wholesale Lumber Div., 11050 Plano Rd.(75238), pg. 437
GSC Distributing of Dallas, 1135 So. Lamar St.(75215), pg. 440
GAS EQUIPMENT COMPANY, INC., 11616 Harry Hines(75229), pg. 444
Gaylord Broadcasting Co., 10111 N. Central Expwy.(75231), pg. 446
General Felt Industries, Inc., 10726 Doric St.(75220), pg. 1121
GLAZERS WHOLESALE DRUG CO. INC., 14860 Landmark Blvd.(75240), pg. 461
Gould Paper Corporation, 3003 Carlisle Ave.(75204), pg. 473
Stephen Gould of Texas, Inc., 15820 Midway Rd.(75244), pg. 474
HCB CONTRACTORS, 1401 Elm St., 46th Fl.(75202), pg. 496
HI Service Enterprises, Inc., 4550 Spring Valley Rd.(75234), pg. 541
HAGGAR APPAREL COMPANY, 6113 Lemmon Ave.(75209), pg. 499
Hinderliter Heat Treating, Inc., 3890 W. Northwest Hwy., Ste. 300(75220), pg. 535
HOME INTERIORS & GIFTS, INC., 4550 Spring Valley Rd.(75244-3705), pg. 541
HUITT-ZOLLARS, INC., 3131 McKinney Ave., Ste. 600(75204), pg. 552
CAROLINE HUNT TRUST ESTATE, 200 Crescent Court, Ste. 300(75201), pg. 553
Hunt Oil Central Exploration Division, Fountain Place, 1445 Ross at Field(75202-2785), pg. 554
HUNT OIL COMPANY, Fountain Place, 1445 Ross at Field(75202-2785), pg. 553
Hunt Oil International Exploration-Fountain Place, 1445 Ross at Field(75202-2785), pg. 554
Hunt Oil International Production-Fountain Place, 1445 Ross at Field(75202-2785), pg. 554
Hutchinson Wil-Rich Manufacturing Co., 4645 N. Central Expwy.(75205), pg. 1073
I.B.C. Root Beer Company, 8144 Walnut Hill Lane(75231), pg. 342
IXL Furniture, 16803 Dallas Pkwy.(75248), pg. 1112
INDRESCO, INC., 2121 San Jacinto St., Ste. 2500(75201), pg. 565
Jani King, Inc., 4950 Keller Springs(75248), pg. 589
JANI KING INTERNATIONAL, INC., 4950 Keller Springs, Ste. 190(75248), pg. 589

JERELL, INC., 1431 Regal Row(75247), pg. 593
JOINER ROWLAND SERIO KOEPPEL, 2305 Cedar Springs, Ste. 450(75201), pg. 602
JONES BLAIR COMPANY, 2728 Empire Central(75235), pg. 602
Jones Blair Energy, Inc., P.O. Box 35286(75235), pg. 603
Jorgensen Steel & Aluminum/Dallas, 2030 W. Commerce St.(75208), pg. 605
Kaiser Permanente, Texas Division, 12720 Hillcrest Rd., Ste. 600(75230), pg. 614
Keystone Automotive Industries, Inc. - Dallas, 4949 Sharp St., Suite 104(75247), pg. 628
KNAPE & KNAPE, 3131 McKinney, Ste. 800(75204), pg. 636
KNOX OIL OF TEXAS INC., 4835 LBJ Fwy., Ste. 800(75244), pg. 638
Korn/Ferry International, 3950 Lincoln Plaza, 500 North Akard St.(75201), pg. 642
KRAUSE, NADUREK & EICKMEYER, 501 Elm St., Ste. 300, LB6(75202), pg. 644
LARKIN MEEDER & SCHWEIDEL, 7800 Stemmons Frwy., Ste. 770(75247), pg. 659
LASTING PRODUCTS, INC., 2115 W. Valley View(75234), pg. 660
Lexmark International, Inc., 1603 LBJ Freeway, 3rd Fl.(75234), pg. 674
LINCOLN PROPERTY COMPANY, 500 N. Akard(75201), pg. 676
LONE STAR CADILLAC CO., 11501 E. Northwest Hwy.(75218), pg. 682
Lone Star Forge Company, 4645 NorthCentral Expressway(75205), pg. 1073
MEPC AMERICAN PROPERTIES INCORPORATED, 15303 Dallas Pkwy., Ste. 400(75248), pg. 692
MTC Corporation, 9224 King Arthur Dr.(75247), pg. 217
MAGUIRE OIL CO., 4000 Renaissance Tower, 1201 Elm St.(75270), pg. 701
Margo's La Mode, Inc., 3909 Live Oak Dr.(75204), pg. 373
THE MARKETING CONTINUUM, INC., 4311 Oak Lawn Ave., Ste. 600(75219), pg. 709
MARLOW INDUSTRIES, 10451 Vista Park Rd.(75238), pg. 710
MARY KAY CORPORATION, 8787 Stemmons Freeway(75247), pg. 716
Mary Kay Cosmetics Inc., 8787 Stemmons Freeway(75247), pg. 716
Mayflower of Texas, 2605 LBJ Freeway(75234), pg. 725
MCCOMMUNICATIONS INC., 13140 Coit Rd., Ste. 515(75240), pg. 727
MCORP, 1717 Main, Ste. 3100(75201), pg. 732
MICHAEL, BOLGER, REINSCHMIEDT, KING (MBRK), 3110 Webb Ave.(75205), pg. 746
MICRODYNAMICS, INC., 10461 Brockwood Rd.(75238), pg. 749
MOROCH & ASSOC., INC., 3625 N. Hall, Ste. 1200(75219), pg. 770
NJF Investment Group, Inc., 2121 San Jacinto, Ste. 1440(75201), pg. 841
NATIONAL BANNER COMPANY, 11938 Harry Hines Blvd.(75229), pg. 786
National Development Co., Inc., 2711 LBJ Freeway, Suite 1044(75234), pg. 1062
NATIONAL FINANCIAL INSURANCE COMPANY, 403 S. Akard(75202), pg. 788
National Heritage, Inc., 15770 N. Dallas Pkwy., 5th Fl.(75248), pg. 392
The Neogard Corporation, 2732 Empire Central(75235), pg. 603
New Hermes Inc-Southwest, 12243 E. Northwest Hwy.(75228), pg. 801
NYLIFE Mortgage Inc., 12201 Merit Dr., Ste. 1000(75251), pg. 803
Newsprint South Sales Corp., 8111 LBJ Fwy., Ste. 1265(75251-1342), pg. 760
Niagara Envelope Co. of Texas, 10231 Plano Rd.(75238), pg. 806
Nuarc Southwestern Div., 1931 Market Center Blvd., Ste. 109(75207), pg. 817
O'CONNOR MACCIOLI, INC., 2828 Routh St., Ste. 590(75201), pg. 821
Omniflight Helicopters, Inc., 4650 Airport Pkwy.(75248), pg. 826
OMNIFLIGHT, INC., 4650 Airport Pkwy.(75248), pg. 826
PPA INDUSTRIES, INC., 8222 Douglas Ave., Ste. 660(75225), pg. 836
PACIFIC ENTERPRISES OIL COMPANY (USA), 1700 Pacific Ave., Ste. 1200(75201-4697), pg. 840
PAGE BOY COMPANY, INC., 8918 Governors Row(75247), pg. 843
Pages Drugs, 14303 Inwood Rd.(75234), pg. 912
PALM HARBOR HOMES, INC., 15301 Dallas Parkway, Ste. 800(75248), pg. 843
PARAGON GROUP, INC., 7557 Rambler Rd., Ste. 1200(75231), pg. 847
PARK PLACE MOTORCARS, 4023 Oak Lawn(75219), pg. 849
Payson Texas, Inc., 2688 Freewood Dr.(75220), pg. 853
PENROD DRILLING CORPORATION, 2100 Thanksgiving Tower, 1601 Elm Street(75201), pg. 859
PETRO-HUNT CORPORATION, 3900 Thanksgiving Tower(75201), pg. 865
PILLOWTEX CORPORATION, 4111 Mint Way(75237), pg. 870
PIPER INDUSTRIES, INC., 12001 Corporate Dr.(75228), pg. 872
PLACID OIL COMPANY, 3800 Thanksgiving Tower(75201), pg. 873
Placid Refining Company, 3800 Thanksgiving Tower(75201), pg. 873
PLASTICS MANUFACTURING COMPANY, 2700 S. Westmoreland(75233), pg. 876
POINT COMMUNICATIONS, INC., 14001 Dallas Pkwy., Ste. 450(75240), pg. 878
Premier Beverages, 8144 Walnut Hill Ln.(75231), pg. 342
The Principal/EGT Financial Corporation, 2001 Bryan Tower, Ste. 2300(75201), pg. 891
PRO-LINE CORPORATION, 2121 Panoramic Circle(75212), pg. 892
PUSKAR GIBBON CHAPIN, INC., 3500 Maple Ave., Ste. 900(75219), pg. 901
QUIK WOK CORPORATION, 4099 McEwen Dr., Ste. 150(75244), pg. 905
Radio Metroplex Inc., 3500 Maple Ave., Ste. 1600(75219-3906), pg. 1065
Redman Building Products, Inc., 2550 Walnut Hill Ln., Ste. 200(75229), pg. 919
Redman Holding Corp., 2550 Walnut Hill Ln., Ste. 200(75229), pg. 919
Redman Homes, Inc., 2550 Walnut Hill Ln., Ste. 200(75229), pg. 919
REDMAN INDUSTRIES, INC., 2550 Walnut Hill Ln., Ste. 200(75229), pg. 919
REGENCY LINCOLN MERCURY, 11810 E. Northwest Hwy.(75218), pg. 922
REPUBLIC SUPPLY COMPANY, 5646 Milton, Ste. 800(75206), pg. 928
THE RICHARDS GROUP, INC., 10000 N. Central Expwy., Ste. 1200(75231), pg. 932
Richmont Corporation, , pg. 717
RIVERSIDE PRESS, INC., 4901 Woodall St.(75247), pg. 937
Rochester Gauges Inc. Of Texas, 11616 Harry Hines Blvd.(75229), pg. 444
ROMA HOLDINGS, 10000 N. Central Expwy.(75231), pg. 945
Rosewood Corporation, 100 Crescent Court, Ste. 1700(75201), pg. 553
ROSEWOOD PROPERTY COMPANY, 500 Crescent Ct., Ste. 300(75201), pg. 949
S & A RESTAURANT CORP., 12404 Park Central Dr.(75251), pg. 958
Sammons Communications, Inc., 3010 LBJ Frwy., Ste. 800(75234), pg. 968
SAMMONS ENTERPRISES, INC., 300 Crescent Court, Ste. 700(75201), pg. 968
SAUNDERS, LUBINSKI & WHITE, INC., 7610 Stemmons Frwy., Ste. 100(75247), pg. 973
THE JULIUS SCHEPPS CO., 2535 Manana St.(75220), pg. 975
The Seven-Up Company, 8144 Walnut Hill Lane(75231), pg. 342
SEWELL VILLAGE CADILLAC CO., 7310 Lemmon Ave.(75209), pg. 993
Simkins Carton Div.-Dallas, 1115 Alma St.(75215), pg. 1005
Slaughter Bros., Inc., 11050 Plano Rd.(75238), pg. 436
Snavely Forest Products, Inc., P.O. Box 59907, (75229), pg. 1015
SNYDERGENERAL CORPORATION, 3219 McKinney Ave.(75204-2418), pg. 1015
SOUND WAREHOUSE, INC., 10911 Petal Street(75238), pg. 1018
Sound Warehouse, Inc., 10911 Petal St.(75238), pg. 995
State Farm County Mutual Insurance Co. of Texas, 17301 Preston Rd.(75379), pg. 1041
State Farm Lloyds, Inc., 17301 Preston Rd.(75379), pg. 1041
Steak and Ale Restaurants, 12404 Park Central Dr.(75251), pg. 958
STEAKLEY CHEVROLET SUBARU INC., 6411 E. Northwest Hwy.(75231), pg. 1043
STERLING JEWELRY & DISTRIBUTING CO., 5801 E. Northwest Hwy.(75231), pg. 1047
Sylvan Pools of Texas, Inc., 11306 LBJ Freeway(75238), pg. 612
TD INDUSTRIES INC., 13850 Diplomat Dr.(75234), pg. 1072
TIC Investment Corp., 4645 N. Central Expwy.(75205), pg. 1073
TIC UNITED CORPORATION, 4645 North Central Expressway(75205), pg. 1073
Taylor Publishing Co., 1550 W. Mockingbird Ln.(75235), pg. 571
TEAM BANCSHARES, INC., 3300 Oak Lawn(75219), pg. 1082
Team Bank/Dallas, P.O. Box 35207(75235), pg. 1082
Texas Commerce Bank-National Association, 2200 Ross(75201), pg. 1089
Texas Resin, 2728 Empire Central(75235), pg. 603
Tileways Inc., 7834 Hawn Freeway(75217), pg. 312
TimeMed Labeling Systems, Inc., 2808 McGowan St.(75203), pg. 1098
Tom Thumb Food & Drugs, Inc., 14303 Inwood Rd.(75244), pg. 912
Tom Thumb Stores, Inc., 14303 Inwood Rd.(75234), pg. 912
TRAMMELL CROW COMPANY, 3500 Trammell Crow Center, 2001 Ross Ave.(75201), pg. 1106
Trammell Crow Interests, 3500 Trammell Crow Center, 2001 Ross Ave.(75201), pg. 1106
Trammell Crow Residential, 3500 Trammell Crow Center, 2001 Ross Ave.(75201), pg. 1106
Transilwrap Company, Inc., 1118 Quaker St.(75207), pg. 1107
Transport Insurance Co., 4100 Harry Hines Blvd.(75219), pg. 54
Tri-Pac Div., 16803 Dallas Pkwy.(75248), pg. 1112
TRIANGLE PACIFIC CORPORATION, 16803 Dallas Pkwy.(75248), pg. 1112
U.S. Slate & Marble Co., 16803 Dallas Pkwy.(75248), pg. 1112
Uniroyal Chemical Co., Inc., 1 Metro Villa Creek Dr., Ste. 285(75234-7311), pg. 1129
U.S. Yellow Pages, 2711 N. Haskell Ave., Ste. 2105(75204), pg. 1180
Utica Lloyds of Texas, Ste. M-1188, 8350 N. Central Expwy.(75206), pg. 1141
Utica National Insurance Co. of Texas, Ste. M-1188, 8350 N. Central Expwy.(75206), pg. 1141
VANTAGE COMPANIES, 2777 Stemmons Fwy.(75207), pg. 1145
VAREL MANUFACTURING CO., 9230 Denton Dr.(75235), pg. 1145
Vought Aircraft Co., 9314 W. Jefferson Blvd.(75211), pg. 222
WSB, Inc. d/b/a KLRX (FM), 3625 N. Hall St.(75219), pg. 292
WATSON ELECTRIC SUPPLY INC., 320 S. Walton(75226), pg. 1168
Watson Food Service Industries, 3712 Haggar Way(75209), pg. 1156
Welch's Carbonated Beverages, 8144 Walnut Hill Lane(75231), pg. 342
Western Homes Corporation, 2550 Walnut Hill Ln., Ste. 200(75229), pg. 919
Western International Media Corporation, 2711 N. Haskell Ave. Ste. 2150(75204), pg. 1180
WHOLESALE ELECTRONIC SUPPLY, 2809 Ross Ave.(75201), pg. 1188
WING INDUSTRIES, INC., 11999 Plano Rd.(75243), pg. 1196
Winslow Taylor Public Relations, 4131 N. Central Expwy., Ste. 510(75204), pg. 391
WYATT CAFETERIAS INC., 10726 Plano Rd.(75238), pg. 1205

Darrouzett

Equity Country Inc., P.O. Box 266, pg. 402

Denison

Reedrill Inc., 1417 North(75090), pg. 1220

Denton

Turbo Refrigerating, P.O. Box 396(76202), pg. 1154

Duncanville

Plastic Suppliers Inc., 815 Mercury Street(75137), pg. 876

Earth

Spring Lake Feed Yard, P.O. Box 718, (78031), pg. 434

Eastland

Eastland National Bank, 201 East Main St.(76448), pg. 412

Edmonson

EDMONSON WHEAT GROWERS, INC., Hwy. 194(79032), pg. 369

El Paso

Allright Parking El Paso, Inc., 601 Magoffin Ave.(79901), pg. 42
COWTOWN BOOT COMPANY, 11401 Gateway W.(79936), pg. 291
Golden Triangle Plastics, Inc., 1325 Perdale Rd.(79936), pg. 875
HUNT BUILDING CORPORATION, 4401 N. Mesa, Ste. 201(79902), pg. 553
THE LEAVELL COMPANY, 4401 N. Mesa, Ste. 200(79902), pg. 664
Leavell Mineral Resources, Inc., 4401 No. Mesa, Ste. 200(79902), pg. 665
NATIONAL RESTAURANT SUPPLY COMPANY, 320 W. San Antonio(79901), pg. 793
PASOTEX CORPORATION, 310 N. Mesa, Ste. 614(79901), pg. 851
TRI-STATE WHOLESALE ASSOCIATED GROCERS, 1000 Hawkins(79915), pg. 1111
Young Pecan Company West, Inc., 2211 E. Missouri, Ste. E 102(79903), pg. 1210

Ennis

Tropar Mfg. Co., Inc., 2313 N. Preston St.(75119), pg. 1116

Euless

Akra Tool, 1135 S. Airport Circle(76040), pg. 1122
W S HOLDING COMPANY, 400 Fuller-Wiser Rd.(76039), pg. 1156
White Swan, Inc., 400 Fuller-Wiser Rd.(76039), pg. 1156

Farmers Branch

THERMALLOY, INC., 2021 W. Valley View(75334-8993), pg. 1091

Flatonia

SMITH FARMS, INC., 403 S. Colorado(78941), pg. 1012

Fort Worth

AFG INDUSTRIES, INC., 301 Commerce St., Ste. 3300(76102), pg. 3
Allright Parking Corporation, 210 W. 6th St., Ste. 1101(76102), pg. 42
Aratex Services, 205 E. Morningside(76104), pg. 6
Austin Bridge & Rd. Co.-Asphalt Div., P.O. Box 185130, 2301 Austin Rd.(76181), pg. 99
BASS ENTERPRISES PRODUCTION COMPANY, First City Bank Tower, 201 Main St.(76102), pg. 125
CMD-Keith Co., P.O. Box 2628(76113), pg. 620
CENTRAL ADVERTISING AGENCY, One Tandy Ctr., Ste. 300(76102), pg. 231
Ceramic Cooling Tower Co., 1100 Northway Dr.(76131), pg. 69
CROUCH SUPPLY COMPANY, INC., 902 S. Jennings Ave.(76104), pg. 301
DALLY ADVERTISING, INC., University Centre II, 1320 S. University Dr., Ste. 501(76107), pg. 312
DEEN WHOLESALE MEAT COMPANY, INC., 813 E. Northside Dr.(76102), pg. 324

Dickies Industrial Ware, 509 W. Vickery Blvd.(76101), pg. 1192
Direct Delivery Sevice, 2620 Tillar Ave.(76107), pg. 496
THE DUNLAP COMPANIES, 200 Greenleaf(76107), pg. 353
Entwistle Defense Technology Div., 3909 Hulen(76107), pg. 383
ESCO ELEVATORS, INC., 4720 Esco Dr.(76140), pg. 388
FM INDUSTRIES, INC., 8600 Will Rogers Blvd.(76140), pg. 394
Fort Worth Auto Auction, 2245 Jacksboro Hwy.(76114), pg. 293
FORT WORTH LUMBER COMPANY, 9101 South Freeway(76140), pg. 425
Frank Paxton Lumber Company, 2900 Bryan Ave., Box 1225(76101), pg. 592
Ft. Dearborn Lithograph Graphic Arts Division, P.O. Box 1293(76101), pg. 425
GSC Distributing of Ft. Worth, 500 E. Rosedale(76104), pg. 440
H & H ADVERTISING, 2620 Tillar Ave.(76107), pg. 496
H & H Printing, 2620 Tillar Ave.(76107), pg. 496
Howell Exports, 3479 W. Vickery(76107), pg. 548
HOWELL INSTRUMENTS CORP., 3479 W. Vickery Blvd.(76107), pg. 547
Ben E. Keith Co. of Oklahoma, P.O. Box 2628(76102), pg. 620
BEN E. KEITH COMPANY, 600 E. 9th & Pecan Sts.(76102), pg. 620
Legis Corporation, 2901 Stanley Ave.(76109), pg. 1002
LUBRICATION ENGINEERS, INC., 3851 Airport Frwy.(76111), pg. 686
LUSKEYS WESTERN STORES, INC., 101 N. Houston(76102-2080), pg. 688
MRS. BAIRD'S BAKERIES, INC., 7301 S. Frwy.(76134), pg. 760
Pan Handle Fruit Co., P.O. Box 2628(76113), pg. 620
PIONEER OIL COMPANY INC., 3420 E. Vickery(76105), pg. 872
REGIAN ADVERTISING & PUBLIC RELATIONS, 219 S. Main St.(76104), pg. 922
RICHMOND SCREW ANCHOR COMPANY, 7214 Burns St., Richland Hills(76118), pg. 933
SAMSILL CORPORATION, 4301 Mansfield Hwy.(76119), pg. 968
SIEGEL CORP., 2901 Stanley Ave.(76110), pg. 1002
Southwest Sample & Marketing, 2620 Tillar Ave.(76107), pg. 496
Southwestern Petroleum Canada Ltd., P.O. Box 961005(76161), pg. 1024
SOUTHWESTERN PETROLEUM CORPORATION, 534 N. Main(76161), pg. 1024
TV Host Central, Inc., 3201 N.E. Loop 820, Ste. 150(76137), pg. 1075
Team Bank, P.O. Box 2050(76113), pg. 1082
TEXAS REFINERY CORP., One Refinery Place, 840 N. Main St.(76106), pg. 1089
TEXAS STEEL CO., INC., 3901 Hemphill Rd.(76110), pg. 1090
Toll Road Restaurant Corp., 1900 Ben St.(76103), pg. 1029
Universal Blueprint Paper Co., 327 Bryan Ave.(76104), pg. 1207
Williamson-Dickie Apparel Mfg. Co., 509 W. Vickery Blvd.(76101), pg. 1192
WILLIAMSON-DICKIE MFG. CO., 319 Lipscomb(76104), pg. 1192

Friona

Friona Feed Yard Div., P.O. Box 369, (79035), pg. 434
Hi-Pro Animal Health Div., P.O. Box 519(79035), pg. 434
Hi-Pro Feed Div., P.O. Box 519(79035), pg. 434

Gainesville

Donrey Inc. TX, 306 E. California(76240), pg. 345

Galveston

Farmer's Copper & Industrial Supply, 202 37th St.(77550), pg. 401
FARMERS MARINE COPPER WORKS, 1908 Strand Ave. B(77550), pg. 401
PORT OF GALVESTON, 123 Rosenberg, 8th Fl.(77550), pg. 881

Garland

Ampco Metal Inc., Dallas Div., 204 Barnes Dr.(75042), pg. 68
Bergman Manufacturing, 1200 No. Glenbrook, P.O. Box 461148(75040), pg. 316
CUPLEX, INC., 1500 E. Hwy. 66(75040), pg. 305
Eckerd Drug Co., 4409 Action St.(75042), pg. 366
Intercontinental Mfg. Co., P.O. Box 461148, (75046), pg. 316
METRO LABEL CORP., 3525 Asset(75042), pg. 743
Priss Prints, Inc., 3960 Broadway, Ste. 105(75043), pg. 369
Raynor Distribution Center, 3727 Marquis Dr.(75042), pg. 915
Royale Paint & Body, 2766 W. Kingsley(75041), pg. 922
TELSCO INDUSTRIES, 3301 W. Kingsley Rd.(75041), pg. 1085
Weather-Matic Div., 3301 W. Kingsley Rd.(75041), pg. 1086

Gonzales

Southwestern Explosives, P.O. Box 1558(78629), pg. 99

Grand Prairie

B & R Pet Supplies, Inc., 1142 Ave. South(75050), pg. 74
Dealers Auto Auction of Dallas, Inc., 2717 East Main(75050), pg. 293
Kilsby-Roberts/Dallas, 2200 W. Marshall Dr.(75051), pg. 606
Pawnee Extrusions, 2401 Dillard(75051), pg. 852
Pennysaver Publications, Inc. (The Shopper's Guide), 1302 Ave. T.(75050), pg. 513
THE SARGENT-SOWELL COMPANY, 1185 108th St.(75050), pg. 971
Southwest Operations, 1184 113th St.(75050), pg. 268
WESTGATE FABRICS, INC., 1000 Fountain Parkway(75053), pg. 1182

Grapevine

Eastway Delivery Service of Dallas, Inc., 1200 E. Northwest Hwy., Ste. 300(76051), pg. 364
Mesco Metal Buildings Corp., P.O. Box 20(76051), pg. 73

Greenville

Wing Industries South Central, 6202 Industrial Drive(75401), pg. 1196

Harlingen

Continental/Murray, 1305 E. Oklahoma(78550), pg. 279
HYGEIA DAIRY CO., INC., 720 S. "F" St.(78550), pg. 557
7UP/RC of Harlingen, 915 Ed Carey Dr.(78550), pg. 477

Hereford

ARROWHEAD MILLS, INC., 110 S. Lawton(79045), pg. 86
Hereford State Bank, 212 East 3rd St.(79045), pg. 412

Hillsboro

TOWN SQUARE FURNITURE, INC., 402 Hawkins(76645), pg. 1104

Houston

ABS Industrial Verification, Inc., 16855 N. Chase Dr.(77060-6008), pg. 50
A.P.S., INC., 3000 Pawnee St.(77054), pg. 5
A.P.S. Supply, Inc., 3000 Pawnee St.(77054), pg. 5
Allied Security Inc., 6666 Harwin, Ste. 440(77036), pg. 39
ALLRIGHT CORPORATION, 1111 Fannin, Ste. 1300(77002), pg. 41
Allright Parking of Texas, Inc., 815 Walker St., Ste. 1047(77002), pg. 42
AMERICAN CAPITAL MANAGEMENT & RESEARCH, INC., 2800 Post Oak Blvd.(77056), pg. 50
American Trading & Production Corporation, Oil & Gas Div., 1221 Lamar, Ste. 1000(77010), pg. 64
The American-World Life Insurance Co., 820 Fannin St.(77002), pg. 1215
AMICO-Houston Distr. Center, 415 A North Wayside Dr.(77020), pg. 29
APPLETREE MARKETS, 4301 Windfern(77041), pg. 79
Baby Doe's, Inc., 8505 Cypress St.(77012), pg. 1029
Bechtel, Inc., 3000 Post Oak Blvd.(77056), pg. 131
Becon Construction Company, Inc., 650 N. Belt Dr. E.(77060), pg. 131
Bently Nevada Corporation - Alignment Service, 7651 Airport Blvd.(77061), pg. 140
BLACK GILLOCK & LANGBERG, 5851 San Felipe, Ste. 100(77057), pg. 154
BLAND CADILLAC COMPANY, 2100 Bagby(77002), pg. 155
Bond's Jewelers, Inc., 820 Fannin St.(77002), pg. 1215
BOVAY, 1300 Post Oak Blvd. 169
BRANCE KRACHY COMPANY, INC., 4411 Navigation Blvd.(77011), pg. 171
CB Commercial Real Estate Group Central Division, 2500 W. Loop S., Ste. 100(77027), pg. 222
Carolina Mirror-Houston, 17015 Park Row(77084), pg. 223
CHEMCENTRAL/Houston, 8425 Market St.(77029-2419), pg. 241
CHEMICAL EXCHANGE INDUSTRIES, 3813 Buffalo Speedway(77098), pg. 242
CORAL PETROLEUM CORPORATION, 600 Travis, Ste. 6120(77002), pg. 285
Coral Petroleum Development, 908 Town & Country Blvd.(77024), pg. 285
Coral Petroleum International, Inc., 908 Town & Country Blvd.(77024), pg. 285
THE CRISPIN COMPANY, 2929 Allen Pkwy. Ste. 2222(77019), pg. 299
DKM Resources, Inc., Interfirst Plaza, 1100 Louisiana St., Ste.4550(77002), pg. 357
Daddy Did It, 10304 Interstate 10 E, Ste. 350(77029), pg. 802
Daniel's Jewelry Co. of Arizona, Inc., 820 Fannin St.(77002), pg. 1215
Dungey & Associates, 340 N. Sam Houston Pkwy. E., Ste. 100(77060), pg. 506
ERM-Southwest, Inc., 16000 Memorial Dr., Ste. 200(77079), pg. 360
E-Z SERVE CORP., 10700 North I45, Ste. 500(77037), pg. 361
Eastway Air Cartage, Inc., 757 Kenrick(77060), pg. 364
EASTWAY DELIVERY SERVICE OF HOUSTON, INC., 8211 Laporte Frwy.(77012), pg. 364
Eastway Transportation Services, Inc., 5821 Kelley St.(77026), pg. 364
Eleven-O-One Corp., 820 Fannin St.(77002), pg. 1216
Engineers & Fabricators Co., 3501 W. 11th St.(77008), pg. 710
ENTERPRISE PRODUCTS COMPANY, 2727 N. Loop W., Ste. 700(77008), pg. 382
EQUITY FUND ADVISORS INC., Ste. 500, 550 Post Oak Blvd.(77027), pg. 385
FGMC, Inc., 7322 Southwest Freeway(77074), pg. 449
Fairfield Industries, Inc., 10627 Kinghurst(77099), pg. 397
Ferrell North America, 16800 Greenspoint Park Dr.(77060), pg. 407
FIESTA MART INC., 5235 Katy Fwy.(77007), pg. 409
FINGER FURNITURE COMPANY, INC., 4001 Gulf Fwy.(77003), pg. 411
FISH ENGINEERING & CONSTRUCTION, INC., 1990 S. Post Oak Rd., Suite 200(77056), pg. 414
Fish International Co., 1990 S. Post Oak Rd., Suite 200(77056-3846), pg. 414
Fish International Engineers, 1990 S. Post Oak Rd., Suite 200(77056-3846), pg. 414
Fish Service Corporation, 1990 S. Post Oak Rd., Suite 200(77056-3846), pg. 414
Fogarty & Klein Public Relations, 7155 Old Katy Rd., Ste. 200(77024), pg. 421
Fogarty & Klein Sales Promotion, Inc., 3303 Louisiana(77006), pg. 421
FOGARTY & KLEIN/WINIUS BRANDON, 7155 Old Katy Rd., Ste. 100(77024), pg. 421
FUGRO-MCCLELLAND, INC., 6100 Hillcroft(77081), pg. 435
GSC Distributing of Houston, 801 Service Rd.(70009), pg. 440
R. J. GALLAGHER CO., P.O. Box 20710(77225), pg. 441
GENERAL HOMES CORPORATION, 7322 Southwest Freeway(77074), pg. 449
GERLAND CORP., 2541 Gessner Dr.(77080), pg. 454
Global Insurance Company, 5718 Westheimer, Ste. 1310(77057-5732), pg. 662
A. GRACE DEVELOPMENT, PO Box 670303, (77267-0303), pg. 474
THE GRANADA GROUP, 11000 Richmond(77042), pg. 475
Greater Houston Mailing Service, Inc., 650 W. 6th St.(77007), pg. 513
GROCERS SUPPLY CO. INC., 3131 E. Holcombe Blvd.(77021), pg. 488
Grocers Supply Institution, 3131 E. Holcombe Blvd.(77021), pg. 489
Grocers Supply International, 411 Brisbane(77061), pg. 489
Grocers Supply Small Business, 3131 E. Holcombe Blvd.(77021), pg. 489
GSC Distribution of Houston, 801 Service St.(77009), pg. 440
Gulf Coast Jewelry & Specialty Co., Inc., 820 Fannin St.(77002), pg. 1216
GULF EXPLORATION, 1700 West Loop South(77069), pg. 493
GULF STATES TOYOTA, 7701 Wilshire Pl.(77040), pg. 494
Gulfstream Aerospace Corp., 3663 N. Belt E., Ste. 400(77032), pg. 494
Hamilton Wholesale Jewelry Co., Inc., 820 Fannin St.(77002), pg. 1216
Harbor Financial Insurance Agency, 340 N. Sam Houston Pkwy. E., Ste. 100(77060), pg. 506
HARBOR FINANCIAL MORTGAGE CORP., 340 N. Sam Houston Pkwy. E., Ste. 100(77060), pg. 506
Harbor Financial Property Management Co., 340 N. Sam Houston Pkwy. E., Ste. 100(77060), pg. 506
Harbor Financial Title Corp., 340 N. Sam Houston Pkwy. E., Ste. 100(77060), pg. 506
THE HIVELY AGENCY INC., 520 Post Oak Blvd., Ste. 800(77027), pg. 536
HOT SHOT DELIVERY INC., 701 Shepherd Dr.(77007), pg. 545
Houston Chronicle, 801 Texas Ave.(77002), pg. 524
Houston Engineers, P.O. Box 567, 1710 Burnett St.(77026), pg. 1194
J.M. Huber, Oil & Gas Div., 1900 West Loop So., Flrs. 16 & 17(77027), pg. 550
Hunt Oil Gulf Coast Exploration Division, Brookhollow Central Three, 2950 North Loop W., Ste. 900(77092), pg. 554
HYDRIL COMPANY, 3300 N. Sam Houston Pkwy., East(77032-3411), pg. 556
Hydril Production Technology Div., P.O. Box 721560(77272), pg. 556
IDM CONTROLS, 6116 Milwee St.(77092), pg. 560
IDM Equipment Company, 11616 Galayda Rd.(77086), pg. 560
IGLOO CORPORATION, 1001 W. Sam Houston Pkwy., N.(77043), pg. 562
Industrial Tools Div., 7007 Pinemont(77040), pg. 565
Ingram Cactus Co., One Greenway Plaza, Ste. 200(77046), pg. 569
INSURANCE CORP. OF AMERICA, 4295 San Felipe(77027), pg. 572
INTERNATIONAL SYSTEMS & CONTROLS CORP., 2727 Allen Pkwy.(77019), pg. 579
Joffko Cameroon Corporation, 6815-A Lindbergh St.(77087), pg. 595
JOFFKO INTERNATIONAL, 8038 El Rio(77054), pg. 595
BERNARD JOHNSON INCORPORATED, 3000 Wilcrest, Ste. 200(77042), pg. 598
JOHNSON SUPPLY & EQUIPMENT CORP., 10151 Stella Link(77025), pg. 601
Jones Business System, 6120 West by Northwest Blvd.(77040), pg. 324
Jorgensen Steel & Aluminum/Houston, 5311 Clinton Dr.(77020), pg. 606
KIKK AM/FM, 6306 Gulfton(77081), pg. 785
K&W, A Div. of Standco Industries, Inc., 2701 Clintor Dr.(77020), pg. 1038
KETTLE RESTAURANTS, 3131 Argonne(77098), pg. 626
Kilsby-Roberts/Houston, 4404 Windfern Rd.(77041), pg. 606
Korn/Ferry International, 1100 Milam Bldg., Ste. 3400(77002), pg. 642
KRANCO, INC., 10543 Fisher Rd.(77041), pg. 643
LEWIS & COKER SUPER MARKETS, 12561 Memorial Dr.(77024), pg. 673
LIBERTY MILITARY SALES CO., 10550 Rockley Road, Ste. 120(77099), pg. 674
LINBECK CORP., 3810 W. Alabama(77027), pg. 675
Magic Market Convenience Stores, 10700 North I45, Ste. 500(77037), pg. 362
Masterbilt Fixtures, Inc., 3131 E. Holcombe Blvd.(77021), pg. 489

MEDIACOMP, INC., One West Loop S., Ste. 720(77027), pg. 735
Mediacomp Media Management Services, One West Loop S., Ste. 720(77027), pg. 735
MEDIANEWS GROUP INC., Loop Centeral One, 4888 Loop Central Dr., Ste. 525(77081), pg. 735
Mermod, Jaccard & King Jewelry Co. of Iowa, Inc., 820 Fannin St.(77002), pg. 1216
Mermod, Jaccard & King Jewelry Co. of Nebraska, 820 Fannin St.(77002), pg. 1216
MetLife Funding Co., Citicorp Center, 1200 Smith St.(77002), pg. 744
MICROWAVE NETWORKS INCORPORATED, 10795 Rockley Rd.(77099), pg. 749
MOGAS INDUSTRIES, INC., P.O. Box 11529(77293-1529), pg. 763
Moroch & Associates, Inc., 4295 San Felipe, 770
Mustang Industrial Equipment Co., 7607 Wallisville Rd.(77020), pg. 777
Mustang Power Systems, 12800 N. W. Freeway(77040), pg. 777
MUSTANG TRACTOR & EQUIP. CO., 12800 NW Freeway(77040), pg. 777
National Atlas Life Insurance Co., 820 Fannin St.(77002), pg. 1216
NEW TEXAS TUMBLEWEED, 10304 Interstate 10 E., Ste. 350(77029), pg. 802
North Star Steel Houston, 8603 Sheldon Rd.(77049), pg. 219
NuArc Co., 5855 Sovereign Dr., Ste. 135(70036), pg. 817
O'Brien Powder Products, Inc., 9800 Genard(77041), pg. 820
O'Brien Powder Products, Inc., 9800 Genard Rd., pg. 820
OIL & GAS SUPPLY COMPANY, 8601 Boone Rd.(77099), pg. 823
Oskamp Nolting Co., Inc., 820 Fannin St.(77002), pg. 1216
OWEN HEALTH CARE, 9800 Centre Pkwy.(77036), pg. 833
Paloma Production Co. Inc., 12320 S. Main St.(77235), pg. 853
Pearce Equipment Leasing, 12320 S. Main St.(77235), pg. 853
PEARCE INDUSTRIES INC., 12320 S. Main St.(77035), pg. 853
Pearce International Inc., 12320 S. Main St.(77235), pg. 853
PENNY & SPEIER INC., 1800 W. Loop South, Ste. 400(77027), pg. 858
Pipeco, Inc., 8223 Willow Place South(77070), pg. 851
Piping Resources, 8011 Blankenship(77055), pg. 169
Popeye's Famous Fried Chicken, 2918 Dupree St.(77054), pg. 283
PORT OF HOUSTON AUTHORITY, 111 East Lood North(77029), pg. 881
Production Management Corporation, 1980 Post Oak Blvd.(77056), pg. 893
Prudential Reinsurance, 4600 Post Oak Pl., Ste. 260(77027), pg. 897
THE QUEST BUSINESS AGENCY, INC., 2900 N. Loop West, Ste. 1020(77092), pg. 904
Quintana Environmental Services, Inc., 601 Jefferson, Ste. 3800(77002), pg. 905
QUINTANA PETROLEUM CORP., 601 Jefferson St.(77253), pg. 905
Quintana Petroleum Services, 601 Jefferson(77002), pg. 905
RANDALL'S FOOD MARKETS, INC., 3663 Briar Park Dr.(77042), pg. 911
Randall's Warehouse Corporation, 10700 Telge Rd.(77095), pg. 912
REMCO ENTERPRISES, INC., 10333 Richman Ave., Ste. 300(77042), pg. 926
Rex Supply Company, 3715 Harrisburg(77001), pg. 893
RICE FOOD MARKETS INC., 5333 Gulfton(77081), pg. 931
Ridgway's, Inc., 5711 Hillcroft Ave.(77036), pg. 1207
RIVES CARLBERG, 5599 San Felipe, Ste. 1111(77056), pg. 937
RIVIANA FOODS INC., 2777 Allen Pkwy.(77019), pg. 937
Robanne Corp., 820 Fannin St.(77002), pg. 1216
RUSKA INSTRUMENT CORPORATION, 3601 Dunvale(77063), pg. 956
Ruska Laboratories, 3601 Dunvale(77063), pg. 956
SACHNOWITZ & CO., 3410 W. Dallas(77019), pg. 965
SEMCO, INC., 13813 Fm 529(77041), pg. 989
Smith Jewelers & Distributors, Inc., 820 Fannin St.(77002), pg. 1216
Southern Realty Co., 820 Fannin St.(77002), pg. 1216
Southwestern Wholesale Jewelry Co., 820 Fannin St.(77002), pg. 1216
SPECIALTY RETAILERS, INC., 10201 S. Main(77025), pg. 1029
SPRING ENGINEERS, INC., 9740 Tanner Rd.(77040), pg. 1033
Stand-Cote Industrial Coatings Div., P.O. Box 87(77001), pg. 1038
STANDCO INDUSTRIES, INC., 2701 Clinton Drive(77020), pg. 1038
Standco Oilfield Products Div., 2701 Clinton Dr.(77020), pg. 1038
Star Engraving Co., 820 Fannin St.(77002), pg. 1216
Sterling Rubber & Gasket, P.O. Box 87(77001), pg. 1038
G. A. Stowers Furniture Co., 820 Fannin St.(77002), pg. 1216
TOC Retail, Inc., 10700 North I-45, Ste. 500(77037), pg. 362
TAUBER OIL COMPANY, 55 Waugh Dr., Ste. 700(77007), pg. 1080
TAYLOR-SMITH GROUP, 2000 West Loop South, 16th Fl.(77027), pg. 1082
TEMPORARIES, INCORPORATED, 400 N. Sam Houston Pkwy E., Ste. 820(77060), pg. 1086
Texas Auto Auction Services, Inc. d/b/a Big H Auto Auction, 14450 West Rd.(77041), pg. 293
TEXAS COMMERCE BANCSHARES, INC., 712 Main St.(77002), pg. 1089
Texas Commerce Bank-Houston, 712 Main St.(77002), pg. 1089
Texas Hobby Auto Auction, 800 Brisbane Rd.(77061), pg. 294
Texas Iron Works Inc., 12320 S. Main St.(77235), pg. 853
TEXAS OLEFINS CO., 8707 Katy Fwy., Ste. 300(77024), pg. 1089
CHARLIE THOMAS AUTO WORLD, 12215 Gulf Fwy.(77207), pg. 1092
TRAILER WHEEL & FRAME COMPANY, 8222 North Freeway(77037), pg. 1105
TRANSAMERICAN REFINING CORPORATION, 140 Cypress Station, Ste. 200(77090), pg. 1106
TRIBBLE & STEPHENS CO., 10610 Haddington(77043), pg. 1112
TRIUMPH*LOR, INC., 15710 John F. Kennedy Blvd., Ste. 150(77032), pg. 1115
Triumph/LOR, Inc., 6922 LaPaseo(77087), pg. 1115
Triumph-Lor, Inc., 15333 Drummet, Suite 210(77032), pg. 1115
Tubular Services, Inc., 1010 McCarty(77029), pg. 851
Uncle Ben's, Inc., 5721 Harvey Wilson Dr.(77020), pg. 713
United-General Products of Knoxville, Inc., 820 Fannin St.(77002), pg. 1216
United-Hamilton, Inc., 820 Fannin St.(77002), pg. 1216
United Jewelers & Distributors of Arizona, Inc., 820 Fannin St.(77002), pg. 1216
United Jewelers & Distributors of Arkansas, Inc., 820 Fannin St.(77002), pg. 1216
United Jewelers & Distributors of Louisiana, Inc., 820 Fannin St.(77002), pg. 1216
United Jewelers & Distributors of Texas, Inc., 820 Fannin St.(77002), pg. 1216
United Republic Reinsurance Company, 5718 Westheimer, Ste. 1310(77057-5732), pg. 662
Universal Service Bureau, Inc., 820 Fannin St.(77002), pg. 1216
VC Management Services, 1303 Campbell Rd.(77055), pg. 1153
VANGUARD ENERGY CORP., 1111 North Loop W.(77008), pg. 1145
VISIBLE CHANGES, 1303 Campbell Rd.(77055), pg. 1153
W F I, INC., 4407 Haygood(77022), pg. 1156
Wald Moving and Storage Services, Inc., 5205 S. Rice Ave.(77001), pg. 725
WALLACE CO. INC., 5757 Oates Rd.(77078), pg. 1160
WALWORTH COMPANY, 10190 Harwin Dr.(77036), pg. 1162
Warren Refrigerator Company, Inc., 5110 Glenmont(77081), pg. 480
Waukesha-Pearce Industries, 12320 S. Main St.(77235), pg. 853
WEINERS ENTERPRISES, INC., 6005 Westview(77055), pg. 1173
Weiners Stores Inc., 6005 Westview(77055), pg. 1173
White Star Steel, 2200 Harbor Blvd.(77020), pg. 784
WILSON INDUSTRIES INC., 1301 Conti St.(77002), pg. 1193
Wyatt Field Service Co., P.O. Box 3052(77253), pg. 808
YRJ CORPORATION, 5711 Hillcroft(77036), pg. 1206
Zenith Administrators of Texas, 4600 Gulf Frwy., Ste. 300(77023), pg. 1124
ZILKHA ENERGY COMPANY, 1201 Louisiana, Ste. 3200(77002), pg. 1219

Howe

OLD AMERICAN POTTERY COMPANY, 811 N. Collins Fwy. 75 N.(75459), pg. 823

Humble

Hydril Rubber Opers., 18000 E. Tex Frwy.(77347-1888), pg. 556
MONY CS, Inc., 9810 FM 1960, Bypass Ste. 270(77338), pg. 778

Huntsville

Heil Tank Service, Inc., P.O. Box 173-20, (77340), pg. 526

Hurst

Anchor Metals, Inc., P.O. Box 157, (76053), pg. 316

Irving

Akard Construction Co., Inc., 901 W. Walnut Mill Lane(75038), pg. 1215
Backer Spielvogel Bates, Inc., 4322 N. Beltline Rd., Ste. B212(75038), pg. 109
Bankston Nissan in Irving, Inc., 1580 East Airport Fwy.(75062), pg. 118
BOLLINGER INDUSTRIES INC., 222 W. Airport Fwy.(75026), pg. 163
CMI Lloyds, 1200 Walnut Hill Lane(75062), pg. 233
CALTEX PETROLEUM CORPORATION, 125 E. John Carpenter Fwy.(75062), pg. 211
Chiat/Day/Mojo/Dallas, 600 East Las Colinas Blvd.(75039), pg. 244
DALLAS PETERBILT, INC., 515 N. Loop 12(75061), pg. 312
DARLING-DELAWARE CO., INC., 251 O'Connor Ridge Blvd., Ste. 300(75038), pg. 315
DUPEY MANAGEMENT CORP., 9015 Sterling St.(75063), pg. 354
EMS Southwest Region Office, 433 E. LAS Calinas Blvd., Suite 940(75039-5611), pg. 370
F.P.A., INC., 1000 E. Airport Fwy.(75062), pg. 394
FOJTASEK COMPANIES, INC., 2100 Union Bower Rd.(75061-6957), pg. 421
Gordon Jewelry Corporation, 901 W. Walnut Hill Lane(75038), pg. 1215
Jeweler's Financial Service, Inc., 901 W. Walnut Hill Ln.(75038), pg. 1215
LEVENSON & HILL, INC., 5215 N. O'Connor, Ste. 1100(75039), pg. 670
LONE STAR CORRUGATED CONTAINER CORPORATION, P.O. Box 157357(75015), pg. 682
MADD (MOTHERS AGAINST DRUNK DRIVING), 511 E. John Carpenter Frwy., Ste. 700(75062-8187), pg. 691
MCKONE & CO., INC., 1900 Westridge Dr.(75038), pg. 731
MONTEREY'S TEX MEX CAFE, 4441 W. Airport Fwy.(75062), pg. 767
Southwestern Regional Office, P.O. Box 152010, 1200 Walnut Hill Lane(75015), pg. 233
Tucker-Rocky Distributing, 1775 Hurd Dr.(75038), pg. 647
ZALE CORPORATION, 901 W. Walnut Hill Lane(75038), pg. 1215

Jacksonville

Three Beall Brothers 3, Inc., 1237 E. Rusk St.(75766), pg. 1029

Jasper

Jasper News-Boy, P.O. Box 1419, 302 N. Wheeler(75951), pg. 524

Katy

Pepper-Lawson, 4555 Katy Hocley Cut-off Rd.(77449), pg. 860

Kaufman

Aberdeen Mfg. Corp. Kaufman Plant, P.O. Box 70, (74142), pg. 200

Keller

AFFILIATED FOOD STORES, 100 Affiliated Drive(76244), pg. 23
Affiliated General Agency, Inc., 100 Nat Gibbs Dr.(76248), pg. 23

Kerrville

MOONEY AIRCRAFT CORPORATION, Louis Schreiner Airport, Box 72(78029), pg. 768

Kilgore

MARTIN GAS CORPORATION, 101 E. Sabine(75662), pg. 715
Pak-Sher Co., 2500 N. Longview(75662), pg. 1072
Skeeter Products, Inc., 1 Skeeter Road(75662), pg. 695

Kingwood

Lou Ana Foods Of Texas, Inc., 1801 Kingwood, Ste. 200(77339), pg. 974
Operations Management International, Inc., P.O. Box 5169(77325-5169), pg. 202

La Grange

Big Red RC & 7-Up of LaGrange, TX, 189 S. Brown(78945), pg. 477

La Porte

WEBB, MURRAY & ASSOCIATES, 608 No. 14th St.(77571), pg. 1170

Laredo

Laredo Morning Times, 111 Esperanza Dr.(78041), pg. 523

Lewisville

American Nut Co., , pg. 255
Clements Nut Co., P.O. Box 247, 614 E. Main St.(75067), pg. 255
GRANDY'S, INC., 997 Grandy's Lane(75067), pg. 476

Longview

AXELSON, INC., 110 Industrial Blvd.(75602), pg. 103
Cherco Compressors, Inc., 21 FRJ Dr., P.O. Box 7516(75607), pg. 758
Texas Commerce Bank-Longview, 213 N. Fredonia(75601), pg. 1089

Lubbock

Bollinger Health Care, 1020 S.E. Loop 289(79404), pg. 163
Cox Cable Lubbock, Inc., 6710 Hartford Avenue(79413), pg. 294
Elmer's Weights, 1020 S.E. Loop 289(79404), pg. 163
HIGGINBOTHAM-BARTLETT CO., 8302 Indiana Ave.(79423), pg. 533
PLAINS CO-OP OIL MILL, 2901 Ave. A(79404), pg. 873
PLAINS COTTON CO-OP ASSOCIATION, 3301 E. 50th St.(79404), pg. 873
Texas Commerce Bank-Lubbock, 1701 W. Hwy. 83(79408), pg. 1089

Lufkin

BROOKSHIRE BROS., INC., 1201 Ellen Trout Dr.(75901), pg. 180
CONTRACTORS SUPPLIES, INC., 303 Webber(75901), pg. 280
PERRY BROTHERS, INC., 107 W. Lufkin Ave.(75901), pg. 862

Marble Falls

Capital Marble & Granite Co. Inc., P.O. Box 1239, (78054), pg. 260
Texas Granite Corp., Hwy. 1431 West(78654), pg. 260

McAllen

Right Away Foods Corporation, 200 N. First St.(78502), pg. 1203

Valley Onions, P.O. Box 2345(78502), pg. 351

McKinney

HINDERLITER INDUSTRIES, INC., 1600 Redbud Blvd., Ste. 301(75069), pg. 535
Montgomery Elevator Division, 2101 Couch Dr.(75069), pg. 767

Mesquite

THE FIGARO COMPANY, INC., 3601 Executive Blvd.(75149), pg. 409
FRITZ CHEMICAL COMPANY, 500 Sam Houston Rd.(75149), pg. 434
Scotfoam Corp., 3210 Curtis Blvd.(75149), pg. 1121

Midland

American Trading and Production Corporation, Oil & Gas Div., Attrium Center Bldg., Ste. 300, 110 West Louisiana Ave.(79701), pg. 64
EDDINS-WALCHER COMPANY, P.O. Box 1920, 2506 West Wall Ave.(79702), pg. 367
Hunt Oil Southwestern Office, 1204 Wilco Bldg., 415 W. Wall St.(79702), pg. 554
INSILCO CORPORATION, 300 N. Marienfeld, Ste. 400(79701), pg. 571
Midland Reporter-Telegram, 201 E. Illinois St.(79701), pg. 524

Mineral Wells

ANTENNA PRODUCTS CORP., 101 S.E. 25th Ave.(76067), pg. 76
PERRY EQUIPMENT CORPORATION, Wolters Industrial Park, P.O. Box 640(76067), pg. 863

Nacogdoches

NACOMA CONSOLIDATED, INC., 7516 U.S. 59 North(75961), pg. 782
Red T. Products, 5004 South St.(75961), pg. 391
Stone Fort National Bank, 300 E. Main St.(75961), pg. 1089

Nederland

Moran Towing of Texas, 2300 Hwy. 365, Ste. 570(77627), pg. 769

New Braunfels

The Coleman Company, 766 Hwy. 306(78130), pg. 695
DETEX CORPORATION, 302 Detex Dr.(78130), pg. 333
MBank New Braunfels, 451 Main Plaza(78130), pg. 733
Mission Valley Mills, Inc., P.O. Box 141, (78130), pg. 400
Texas Commerce Bank-New Braunfels, 111 W. San Antonio St.(78130), pg. 1089

North Richland Hills

BATES CONTAINER, INC., 6433 Davis Blvd.(76180), pg. 125

Odessa

CHEMCENTRAL/Odessa, 105 Pronto(79762), pg. 242
SIVALLS, INC., 2200 E. 2nd St.(79761), pg. 1009
Texas Commerce Bank-Odessa, 620 N. Grant(79760), pg. 1089

Orange

J.M. Huber, Polymer Services Div., 6522 Interstate Hwy. 10 W.(77630), pg. 550

Orange Grove

ORANGE GROVE CO-OPERATIVE, P.O. Box 310(78372), pg. 828

Pampa

W-B SUPPLY CO., 111 N. Naida(79065), pg. 1155

Pasadena

Simpson Pasadena Paper Co., P.O. Box 872(77501), pg. 1007

Perryton

PERRYTON EQUITY, 202 S. Amherst(79070), pg. 863

Plainview

GEBO DISTRIBUTING CO., INC., P.O. Box 850(79072), pg. 447
Plainview Daily Herald, 820 Broadway(79072), pg. 524

Plano

CRISA CORPORATION, 101 E. Park Blvd., Suite 805(75074), pg. 299
Gohmann Asphalt & Construction of Texas, Inc., 3609 Pinehurst Ct.(75075), pg. 465
Gustafson, Inc., 1400 Preston Rd., Ste. 40(75903), pg. 1129
Harte-Hanks Community Newspapers, Inc., c/o Plano Star Courier, P.O. Box 86248(75086), pg. 513
Harwick Chemical Corp., 1309 West 15th St., Ste. 302(75075), pg. 515
Western Pacific Data Systems, 1601 Capital Ave.(75074), pg. 1180

Port Arthur

Standard Alloys & Manufacturing, KCS & 4th Ave.(77640), pg. 161

Poynor

Fairway District, P.O. Box 138, (75782), pg. 554
Hunt Oil Fairway Gas Plant, P.O. Box 144, (75782), pg. 554

Richardson

BLUE CROSS & BLUE SHIELD OF TEXAS, INC., 901 S. Central Expwy.(75080), pg. 160
Group Life & Health Insurance Company, 901 S. Central Expwy.(75080), pg. 160
Hanover Lloyd's Insurance Company, 801 E. Campbell Rd., Ste. 500(75081), pg. 35
Lennox Industries Inc., 2100 Lake Park Blvd.(75080), pg. 667
LENNOX INTERNATIONAL INC., 2100 Lake Park Blvd.(75080), pg. 667
Marshall Erdman & Assoc., Inc., 880 Dorothy Dr., Ste. 800(75081), pg. 386
RELIABLE CHEVROLET, 800 N. Central Expwy.(75080), pg. 924
Spectradyne Inc., 1501 N. Plano Rd.(75061), pg. 318

Richland Hills

Ohio-Sealy Mattress Manufacturing Co.-Fort Worth, 6550 Wuliger Way(76180), pg. 985

Rockwall

TMP Worldwide, Inc., 500 Turtle Cove Blvd., Ste. 150(75087), pg. 1074

San Angelo

GSC Distributing of San Angelo, 1515 N. Chadbourne(76903), pg. 440
HIRSCHFELD, INC., 112 W. 29th St.(76903), pg. 536
Hirschfeld Steel Company, Inc., 112 W. 29th St.(76903), pg. 536
SAN ANGELO ELECTRIC SERVICE COMPANY, P.O. Box 1587, 926-32 Pullman St.(76902), pg. 969
San Angelo Standard, Inc., 34 W. Harris(76903), pg. 513
Texas Commerce Bank-San Angelo, 301 W. Beauregard(76901), pg. 1089

San Antonio

AMPI Investment Corp., 6609 Blanco Rd.(78216), pg. 91
AMPI Research Corp., 6609 Blanco Rd.(78284), pg. 91
AMPI Venture, Inc., 6609 Blanco Rd.(78284), pg. 91
ALAMO INDUSTRIAL GROUP, P.O. Box 231(78291-0231), pg. 29
Alamo Iron Works, P.O. Box 231(78291), pg. 29
Allied Security Inc., 8546 Broadway, Ste. 212(78217), pg. 39
Allright San Antonio Parking, Inc., 405 No. St. Marys, Suite 920(78295), pg. 42
American Envelope of San Antonio, 232 Iowa St.(78210), pg. 199
ANDERSON ADVERTISING, INC., Anderson Exec. Center, 1017 N. Main, Ste. 300(78212), pg. 72
ASSOCIATED MILK PRODUCERS, INC., 6609 Blanco Rd.(78216), pg. 91
THE ATKINS AGENCY, 1777 NE Loop 410, Ste. 1100(78217), pg. 94
BENSON MANAGEMENT COMPANY, 16414 San Pedro Ave., Ste. 9100(78216), pg. 140
Besser/APPCO, 442 N. W.W. White Rd.(78219), pg. 146
BLOCK DISTRIBUTING COMPANY, 827-829 Coliseum Rd.(78219), pg. 157
H. E. BUTT GROCERY CO., 646 S. Main St.(78204), pg. 197
Channel Home Centers, Central Region, 7909 Fredericksburg Rd., Ste. 134(78229), pg. 239
CHEMCENTRAL/San Antonio, 1107 E. Southcross Blvd.(78214), pg. 242
COCA-COLA BOTTLING CO. OF THE SOUTHWEST, 257
BARTLETT COCKE JR. CONSTRUCTION CO., 4359 Industrial Center(78217), pg. 258
ELDORADO CHEMICAL COMPANY, 14350 Lookout Rd.(78233), pg. 373
Ray Ellison Homes, 4800 Fredericksburg Rd.(78229), pg. 914
ESSKAY MANUFACTURING CO., 122 Stribling St.(78204), pg. 389
Far West Products, Inc., P.O. Box 5369, 302 Spencer Lane(78201), pg. 284
FINESILVER MANUFACTURING COMPANY, 816 Cameron St.(78296), pg. 411
Furman Wholesale Lumber Div., 8446 Vidor(78217), pg. 437
GRANT-LYDICK BEVERAGE CO., 4518 Old Sequin Rd.(78220), pg. 477
CURTIS C. GUNN, INC., 7744 Broadway, Ste. 100(78209), pg. 494
HARTE-HANKS COMMUNICATIONS, INC., Harte-Hanks Tower, 200 Concord Plaza Dr., Ste. 800(78216), pg. 513
Harte-Hanks Graphics, 403 E. Ramsey, 513
Harte-Hanks Television, Inc. (KENS-TV), 5400 Fredricksburg Rd.(78299), pg. 513
HASSLOCHER ENTERPRISES, INC., D/B/A FRONTIER ENTERPRISES, 8520 Crownhill Blvd.(78209), pg. 516
THE DEE HOWARD COMPANY, 9610 John Saunders Intl. Airport(78216), pg. 547
Interplastic Distribution Group, 10940 Laureate Dr., Ste.8250(78249), pg. 579
Joykist/GSC Distributing, 719 S. Santa Rosa(78204), pg. 440
JUDSON-ATKINSON CANDIES, INC., 831 S. Flores(78204), pg. 608
KAEPA INC., 5410 Kaepa Ct.(78218), pg. 613
Lackland City Water Co., 4800 Fredericksburg Rd.(78229), pg. 914
LEONARD & HARRAL PACKING CO., 122 Woodhull(78214), pg. 667
Lone Star Brewing, 600 Lone Star Blvd.(78204), pg. 526
Micro-Gen Equipment Corp., 10700 Sentinel Dr.(78217), pg. 599
MILLER CURTAIN CO., INC., 1734 Centennial(78211), pg. 754
Moroch & Associates, Inc., 85 NE Loop, 770
NORTH PARK LINCOLN MERCURY INC., 9207 San Pedro(78216), pg. 813
PACE FOODS, INC., 3750 N. Pan Am Expwy.(78219), pg. 838
Pearl Container Co., 245 Newell(78215), pg. 959
RAYCO, 4800 Fredericksburg Rd.(78229), pg. 914
A. I. Root Co., 529 S. Flores St.(78204), pg. 946
San Antonio Auto Auction, 1500 Ackerman Rd.(78219), pg. 293
San Antonio Light, 420 Broadway(78205), pg. 524
Southern Steel Company, P.O. Box 2021(78297), pg. 866
SOUTHWEST RESEARCH INSTITUTE, 6220 Culebra Rd.(78228-0510), pg. 1023
STAR FOOD PROCESSING, INC., 3444 E. Commerce(78220), pg. 1039
STEVES & SONS, P.O. Drawer S(78211), pg. 1048
Strafco, 1964 S. Alamo St.(78204), pg. 225
STRAFCO, INC., 1964 S. Alamo(78204), pg. 1052
SUPERIOR AUCTIONEERS & MARKETING, INC., 12002 Huebner Rd., Ste. 200(78230), pg. 1063
Sweeney & Company Division, 2330 Roosevelt(78210), pg. 440
Texas Commerce Bank-San Antonio, 1020 N.E. Loop 410(78209), pg. 1089
Texas Drug Reps, 11722 Warfield(78216), pg. 384
Texas Homestead Mortgage Co., 4800 Fredericksburg Rd.(78229), pg. 914
Texas Transportation Co., 312 Pearl Parkway(78215), pg. 959
THOMPSON/MARINCE ADVERTISING, 70 N.E. Loop, Ste. 610(78216), pg. 1094
USAA Buying Service, USSA Bldg., (78288), pg. 1134
USAA Federal Savings Bank, USAA Bldg., (78288), pg. 1134
USAA Investment Management Co., USAA Bldg., (78288), pg. 1134
USAA Life Insurance Co., USAA Bldg., (78288), pg. 1134
USAA Satellite Communications, USAA Bldg., (78288), pg. 1134
USAA Travel Agencies, USAA Bldg., (78288), pg. 1134
UNITED SERVICES AUTOMOBILE ASSOCIATION (USAA), USAA Bldg., (78288), pg. 1134
Visible Changes of Texas, 7400 San Pedro(78216), pg. 1153
H. B. Zachry Company, 527 Logwood(78221), pg. 1215
H.B. ZACHRY, 527 Logwood(78221-0130), pg. 1215

San Marcos

THERMON MANUFACTURING COMPANY, 100 Thermon Dr.(78666), pg. 1091

Sebastian

Aguilares Ranches, 1-8 Mile West(78594), pg. 987
SEBASTIAN COTTON & GRAIN CORP., 6th & David Ramirez(78594), pg. 986

Seguin

ALAMO GROUP, INC., 1502 E. Walnut(78155), pg. 29

Shiner

KASPAR WIRE WORKS, INC., Hwy. 95 N.(77984), pg. 617

South Houston

Gulf Seal Specialties, Inc., P.O. BOx 508(77587), pg. 494
GULF STATES ASPHALT COMPANY, INC., 300 Christy Place(77587), pg. 493

Stafford

Aratex Services, 10110 Cash Rd.(77477), pg. 6
Furman Wholesale Lumber Div., 13246 Murphy Rd.(77477), pg. 437

Sulphur Springs

Fidelity Express Money Order Company Division, 130 Hillcrest Dr.(75482), pg. 440
GSC Distributing Companies Division, 942 Main St.(75482), pg. 440
GSC ENTERPRISES, INC., 130 Hillcrest Dr.(75482), pg. 440
Grocery Supply Company Division, 130 Hillcrest Dr.(75482), pg. 440
NORTHEAST TEXAS FARMERS CO-OP, 428 N. Jackson(75482), pg. 813

Sweetwater

First National Bank of Sweetwater, 201 Elm Street(79556), pg. 412

Taylor

Basler Electric Circuits, Inc., P.O.Box 1165(76574), pg. 125

Temple

ARTCO-BELL CORPORATION, 1302 Industrial Blvd.(76503), pg. 86
Artco-Bell Steel Corp., 3601 Eberhardt Rd.(76503), pg. 86

Terrell

PVS Chemicals, Inc., 503 E. Grove(75160), pg. 838

Texarkana

TRUMAN ARNOLD COMPANIES, 701 S. Robison Rd.(75501), pg. 84
E-Z MART STORES, INC., 602 W. Falvey(75501), pg. 361
Lone Star Division, Hwy. 82 W.(75501-1800), pg. 320

Munitions Technology Division, 4626 Summerhill Rd.(75503), pg. 320
Picoma Industries, 3800 Picoma Dr.(75501), pg. 153
YATES ENTERPRISES INC., 602 W. Falvey(75504), pg. 1207

The Woodlands

Valve and Controls Division, 10077 Grogan's Mill Rd., Ste. 500(77380), pg. 565
WILTEL COMMUNICATIONS SYSTEMS, INC., 8665 New Trails Dr.(77381), pg. 1194

Tomball

J.M. Huber, Flow Control Div., 14011 Park Ave., Ste. 201(77375), pg. 550

Troup

Belmont Industries, U.S. Refractories Div., (75789), pg. 136

Tulia

Swisher Country Cattle Co., P.O. Box 129, (79088), pg. 434
TAYLOR-EVANS SEED CO., 505 S. Hwy. 87(79088), pg. 1081

Tuscaloosa

Hunt Refining Company, 1855 Fairlawn Rd.(25401), pg. 554

Tyler

BROOKSHIRE GROCERY, P.O. Box 1411, 1600 W.S.W. Coop 323(75701), pg. 180
GSC Distributing of Tyler, 2400 E. Gentry Pkwy.(75710), pg. 440
ONE STOP SUPPLY, P.O. Box 689, (75710), pg. 827
The Trane Company, P.O. Box 1008(75711), pg. 62
Unitary Products Group-Residential, 6200 Troup Hwy.(75711), pg. 61

Vernon

WRIGHT BRAND FOODS, INC., 2310 McGhee St.(76384), pg. 1204

Victoria

7Up of Victoria, 3704 Billy Dr.(77901), pg. 477

Waco

CENTRAL FREIGHT LINES INC., 5601 W. Waco Dr.(76710), pg. 232
DEALERS ELECTRICAL SUPPLY CO., 2320 Columbus Ave.(76703), pg. 322
Fab-Knit Manufacturing Co., 1415 N. 4th St.(76703), pg. 73
GSC Distributing of Waco, 1809 Summer Ave.(76708), pg. 440
Olan Mills Inc. of Texas, 701 W. Loop 340(76702), pg. 756
PLANTATION FOODS INC., 2510 E. Lake Shore Dr.(76705), pg. 874
ALLEN SAMUELS CHEVROLET GEO, 1625 N. Valley Mills Dr.(76710), pg. 969
Texas Life Insurance Company, Texas Center, 900 Washington Ave.(76701), pg. 745
WOLF MANUFACTURING COMPANY, 18th & Waco Dr.(76707), pg. 1199

Webster

Alimak Elevator Company, P.O. Box 57117, 16920 Texas Ave., Ste. C13(77598), pg. 34

Wichita Falls

BURK ROYALTY CO., 1000 Petroleum Bldg.(76301-2623), pg. 190
GSC Distributing of Wichita Falls, 600 Ohio St.(76301), pg. 440
Times Publishing Company of Wichita Falls, 1301 Lamar(76307), pg. 513

Winters

WINTERS WELDING WORKS, INC., Hwy. 83(79567), pg. 1197

Yoakum

YOAKUM PACKING COMPANY, P.O. Box 192(77995), pg. 1208

UTAH

Brigham City

FLYING J. INC., 50 W. 990 S.(84302), pg. 421

Cedar City

The Coleman Company, 597 N. 1500 West(84720), pg. 695

Clearfield

Sentinel Consumer Products, Inc., P. O. Box 1417, Freeport Ctr.(84016), pg. 990

Leamington

Leamington Plant, A6 West(84648), pg. 87

Lehi

Belmont Industries, U.S. Refractories Div., 2200 N. 1100 West(84043), pg. 136

Lindon

Wordperfect Manufacturing, 510 W, 510 S.(84057), pg. 1202

Logan

LEGRAND JOHNSON CONSTRUCTION CO., 1000 S. Main(84323-0248), pg. 598

Midvale

NORBEST, INC., 6875 S. 900 E.(84047), pg. 809

Moab

Southern Paving Co., 5101 E. Old Airport Rd.(84532), pg. 598

Moroni

Moroni Feed Co., P.O. Box 368(84646), pg. 809

North Salt Lake

HERMAN HUGHES & SONS, INC., 900 N. Redwood Rd.(84054), pg. 552
PRODUCERS LIVESTOCK, 170 W. Cudahy Ln.(84054), pg. 892
WESTERN CONTROLS, 526 North 400 West(84054), pg. 1178

Ogden

ANDERSON LUMBER COMPANY, 4700 S. Harrison Blvd.(84403), pg. 73
B & K STEEL & SUPPLY, INC., 2393 S. 1900 W.(84401), pg. 105
Boman & Kemp Steel & Supply Company, 2393 S. 1900 W.(84401), pg. 105
GSL Solar Consultants & Advisors, Inc., P.O. Box 1190(84401), pg. 482
GREAT SALT LAKE MINERALS & CHEMICALS CORP., P.O. Box 1190(84402), pg. 482
The Ogden Union Railway and Depot Co., 198 W. 28th St.(84401), pg. 76
STANDARD CORPORATION, 455 23rd St.(84401), pg. 1036

Orem

WORDPERFECT CORPORATION, 1555 N. Technology Way(84057), pg. 1202

Park City

La Petite Boulangerie, Inc., P.O. Box 4000, 333 Main St.(84060), pg. 761
MRS. FIELDS' INC., 333 Main St.(84060), pg. 761

Provo

CREST DISTRIBUTING COMPANY, INC., 595 S. 200 E.(84601), pg. 298
NU SKIN INTERNATIONAL, 145 E. Center St.(84606), pg. 817
Tracor GIE, Provo Research Park, 1652 W. 820 N.(84601), pg. 1105

Saint George

ROCKY MOUNTAIN COMPANY, 825 Industrial Rd.(84770), pg. 942

Salina

Utah Turkey Growers, (84654), pg. 809

Salt Lake City

AFS Insurance Services, Inc., 1812 S. Empire Rd.(84130), pg. 89
ALLEN STEEL CO., 1340 S. 200 West(84115), pg. 36
AMERICAN GILSONITE CO., 136 E. South Temple St., Ste. 1460(84111), pg. 55
American Industrial Services, 505 E.S. Temple St.(84102), pg. 1045
ARNOLD MACHINERY CO., 2975 W. 21st So.(84119), pg. 84
ASSOCIATED FOOD STORES INC., 1812 S. Empire Rd.(84104), pg. 89
Beneficial Life Insurance, 36 S. State St.,Ste. 1310(84111), pg. 332
BONNEVILLE COMMUNICATIONS, 130 Social Hall Ave.(84111), pg. 164
Bonneville International Corp., Broadcast House, No. 5 Triad Center(84180), pg. 332
CF & I Fabricators of Utah, P.O. Box 25305(84125), pg. 201
CUNA West Central District, P.O. Box 27288, (84127), pg. 206
CUMMINS INTERMOUNTAIN DIESEL, 1030 Gale St.(84101), pg. 305
DWF of Salt Lake, Inc., 1765 S. 300 W.(84115), pg. 331
DAHLIN SMITH WHITE, INC., 4 Triad Center, Ste. 400(84180), pg. 310
DAW TECHNOLOGIES, INC., 2700 South 900 West(84119), pg. 319
Deseret Book Co., P.O. Box 30178, 40 E. Temple South(84130), pg. 332
DESERET MANAGEMENT CORPORATION, 36 S. State St., Ste. 1825(84111), pg. 332
Deseret News, 157 Regent St.(84111), pg. 332
DEVOE PAINT CORPORATION, 2179 South 300 West, 334
EVANSGROUP, 110 Social Hall Ave.(84111), pg. 390
EvansGroup, 110 Social Hall Ave.(84111), pg. 391
FOTHERINGHAM & ASSOCIATES, 215 S. State St., Ste. 300(84111-2319), pg. 427
General Implement Distributors, 2955 W. 21st So.(84119), pg. 85
HARRIS AND LOVE, INC., University Club Bldg., 136 E. South Temple, Ste. 1800(84111), pg. 512
HUNTSMAN CHEMICAL CORPORATION, 2000 Eagle Gate Tower(84111), pg. 555
INTERMOUNTAIN FARMERS ASSOCIATION, 1147 W. 2100 S.(84119), pg. 575
KSL Radio, Broadcast House(84110-1160), pg. 332
KSL-TV, Broadcast House(84180-1160), pg. 332
LAMB ENGINEERING & CONSTRUCTION CO., 125 Walton Ave.(84115), pg. 652
Lamb Leasing & Lamb Brothers General, 125 Walton Ave.(84115), pg. 652
Little America Hotels, 550 E. South Temple(84102), pg. 1008
Little America Refining, 550 E. South Temple(84102), pg. 1008
LONGYEAR COMPANY, 2340 West 1700 South(84104), pg. 682
MARTIN DOOR MFG., INC., 2828 S. 900 W.(84119), pg. 714
Missile Supply Co., 1347 S. 300 West(84115), pg. 374
MONROC, INC., 1730 Beck St.(84110), pg. 766
PST VANS, INC., 1901 W. 2100 St. S.(84119), pg. 837
Pax Company, 580 W. 13th St., S.(84115), pg. 231
Poly-Seal Div., 1754 W. 500 So.(84101), pg. 749
RADIX CORPORATION, 4855 Wiley Post Way(84116), pg. 909
RHODES INTERNATIONAL, INC., 1735 S. Redwood Rd.(84105), pg. 931
Roberts & Schaeffer Company-Salt Lake City, 1405 W. 2200 S.(84119), pg. 609
ROCKY MOUNTAIN MECHANICAL, INC., 3412 S.W. Temple(84115), pg. 942
S & W Fine Foods, 1578 W. 17th South(84104), pg. 1111
SINCLAIR OIL CORP., 550 E. South Temple(84102), pg. 1008
STANDARD INDUSTRIES, INC., 3500 S. West Temple(84115), pg. 1036
STEINER CORPORATION, 505 E. S. Temple St.(84102), pg. 1045
Steiner Foreign Linen Division, 505 E. S. Temple St.(84110), pg. 1045
Steiner U.S. Linen Div., 505 E. S. Temple St.(84110), pg. 1045
Westco Products/Intermountain, 805 W. 2500 South(84119), pg. 1178
Western International Media Corporation, 215 S. State St., Ste. 550(84111), pg. 1180
R.C. WILLEY HOME FURNISHINGS, 2301 S. 300 W.(84115), pg. 1190
WILLIAMS & ROCKWOOD, 307 West 200 South, Ste. 3005(84101), pg. 1191
WILSON PRODUCTS CO., 1811 W. 1700 So.(84104), pg. 1194
YOUNG ELECTRIC SIGN COMPANY, 336 S. 400 W.(84101), pg. 1209
Zion's Securities Corp., 102 E.S. Social Hall Ave.(84111), pg. 332

West Bountiful

Utah Auto Auction, 1650 W. 500 S.(84087), pg. 294

West Jordan

Interstate Brick Company, 9780 So. 5200 West(84084), pg. 839

West Valley City

HARMON CITY, INC., 3540 S. 4000 West, Ste. 500(84120), pg. 510

Woods Cross

CHEMCENTRAL/Salt Lake City, 2465 S. 1100 W.(84087), pg. 242

VERMONT

Arlington

MACK MOLDING COMPANY, East Arlington Rd.(05250), pg. 697

Barre

VERMONT LOTTERY COMMISSION, South Barre, P.O. Box 420(05670), pg. 1148

Bellows Falls

WHITNEY BLAKE COMPANY OF VERMONT, INC., Industrial Dr.(05101), pg. 155

Bennington

BENNINGTON IRON WORKS, INC., Harmon Rd.(05201), pg. 139
BIJUR LUBRICATING CORPORATION, 50 Kocher Dr.(05201), pg. 150

Bethel

BETHEL MILLS, INC., 1 N. Main St.(05032), pg. 148

Bradford

BRADFORD OIL COMPANY, INC., Jcts. Rts. 5 & 25(05033), pg. 170

Brattleboro

C & S WHOLESALE GROCERY INC., Old Ferry Rd.(05301), pg. 198
HOLSTEIN ASSOCIATION OF AMERICA, One Holstein Place(05301), pg. 541
Holstein-Friesian Services, Inc., 1 So. Main St.(05301), pg. 541
SPECIALTY PAPERBOARD INC., Brudies Rd.(05302), pg. 1027

Geographic Index

Burlington

G.S. BLODGETT CORPORATION, 50 Lakeside Ave.(05401), pg. 157
EDLUND COMPANY, INC., 159 Industrial Pkwy.(05401), pg. 368
KELLIHER/SAMETS MARKETING COMMUNICATIONS, 130-138 S. Willard St.(05401), pg. 621
JOHN MCKENZIE PACKING CO., INC., 160 Flynn Ave.(05401), pg. 730

Cabot

Cabot Creamery Co-Operative Inc., 130 Main Hwy.(05647), pg. 25

Colchester

Jordan's Foods-Colchester Division, Hercules Dr., P.O. Box 70(05446), pg. 605
Polhemus Inc., 1 Hercules Dr.(05446), pg. 614

Hinesburg

International Cheese Company, Inc., Main Street, pg. 576
INTERNATIONAL CHEESE COMPANY LIMITED PARTNERSHIP, Main Street(05461), pg. 575

Lyndonville

Vermont Tap & Die Co., 79 Main St.(05851), pg. 507

Manchester

THE ORVIS COMPANY, INC., U.S. Rte. 830

Montpelier

Administrative Services, Inc., National Life Dr.(05604), pg. 791
CAPITAL CITY PRESS, INC., Airport Rd.(05602), pg. 214
Champlain Life Insurance Company, National Life Dr.(05604), pg. 791
Equity Services, Inc., National Life Dr.(05604), pg. 791
NATIONAL LIFE INSURANCE COMPANY, National Life Dr.(05604), pg. 791
National Life Investment Management Co., Inc., National Life Dr.(05604), pg. 791
Redstone Properties, Inc., National Life Drive(05604), pg. 791
Sentinel Administrative Service Corporation, National Life Dr.(05604), pg. 791
Sentinel Advisors, Inc., National Life Dr.(05604), pg. 791
Vermont Life Insurance Company, National Life Dr.(05604), pg. 791

North Springfield

Fellows Corporation, Precision Dr.(05150), pg. 468
Vermont USA Machine Tool Group, Precision Dr.(05150), pg. 468

Randolph

SULLIVAN & BROWNELL, INC., P.O. Box 450, 1 Kingwood, Rte. 66(05060), pg. 1056

Rutland

CARRIS REELS, INC., Depot Lane(05701), pg. 225

Saint Albans

Associated Industrial Rubber, 5 Lemnah Dr.(05478), pg. 418
A.N. DERINGER, INC., 64-66 N. Main St.(05478), pg. 331

Shelburne

Academy Entertainment, Inc., One Pine Haven Shore Rd.(05482), pg. 86
ARTEC DISTRIBUTING, INC., One Pine Haven Shore Rd.(05482), pg. 86
Dovre Ski Products, Box 339(05482), pg. 996
HARBOUR INDUSTRIES, INC., 2075 Shelburne Rd.(05482), pg. 507
THE SHELBURNE CORPORATION, Rte. 7 S.(05482), pg. 996
Shelburne Cyclebinding Division, Rte. 7, So.(05482), pg. 996
Shelburne Husky Div., P.O. Box 158, (05482), pg. 996

South Burlington

LANE PRESS, INC., 1000 Hinesburg Rd.(05403), pg. 654
PIZZAGALLI CONSTRUCTION CO., 55 Joy Drive(05403), pg. 873

South Londonderry

STRATTON CORP., Stratton Mountain(05155), pg. 1053

Springfield

Bryant Grinder Corp., 257 Clinton St.(05156), pg. 468
J & L Metrology Company, Inc., , pg. 468

Stowe

HAYES/HARWOOD, 234 Maple St., P.O. Box 179(05672), pg. 519
TRAPP FAMILY LODGE, INC., 42 Trapp Hill Rd.(05672), pg. 1108

Westminster Station

BURT EQUIPMENT COMPANY, INC., Conn River Bridge Rd.(05159), pg. 195
Burtco Metal Systems, Conn River Bridge Rd.(05159), pg. 195

Windsor

CONE-BLANCHARD MACHINE COMPANY, 7 Everett Lane(05089), pg. 273

Winooski

BIO-TEK INSTRUMENTS, INC., Highland Park, Box 998(05404), pg. 152
TWINCRAFT, INC., P.O. Box 186(05404), pg. 1122

VIRGIN ISLANDS

Christiansted

TDW Foreign Sales Corp., 1A Gallows Bay(00820), pg. 1192

Kingshill

Vitarine Pharmaceuticals of the Virgin Islands Inc., P.O. Box 3016(00824), pg. 384

Saint Thomas

Science Applications International Corporation (SAIC Virgin Islands), c/o First Guardian Trust Co., Upper Level Drake Passage(00802), pg. 982
Servo International, Inc., 69A Kronsprindsens Gade, 3rd Fl.(00803), pg. 993

VIRGINIA

Abingdon

Hapco/American Div., Hillman Hwy.(24210), pg. 357

Alexandria

ALLIED PLYWOOD CORP., 4740 Eisenhower Ave.(22304), pg. 38
ASTRE CORPORATE GROUP, 809 Princess St.(22314), pg. 92
Betac Corporation, 2001 N. Beauregard St.(22311), pg. 147
BETAC INTERNATIONAL CORPORATION, 2001 N. Beauregard St.(22311), pg. 147
CAE LINK ALLEN DIVISION, 209 Madison St.(22314), pg. 198
Chameleon Technologies Incorporated, Ste. 11, Canal Center Plaza, Ste. 300(22314), pg. 1146
HOH Associates, 1505 Prince St.(22314), pg. 882
INDEPENDENT INSURANCE AGENTS OF AMERICA, 127 S. Peyton St.(22314), pg. 565
Industrial Microgenics, 809 Princess St.(22314), pg. 92
MAZO LERCH COMPANY, INC., 4720 Eisenhower Ave.(22304), pg. 725
MULTI MEDIA SERVICES CORP., 801 N. Fairfax St., Ste. 312(22314), pg. 775
Popeye's Famous Fried Chicken, 5510 Cherokee Ave., Ste. 230(22312), pg. 283
Smith's Moving & Storage Corp., 611 S. Pickett(22304), pg. 724
STEPHENSON, INC., 5731 General Washington Dr.(22312), pg. 1046
TAI Services, Inc., 6101 Stevenson Ave.(22304), pg. 1084
TECHNOLOGY APPLICATIONS, INC., 6101 Stevenson Ave.(22304), pg. 1083
Veda Design Group, 1800 N. Beauregard St.(22311), pg. 1146
Veda Incorporated, Ste. 300, 11 Canal Center Plaza(22314), pg. 1146
VEDA INTERNATIONAL, INC., 11 Canal Center Plaza(22314), pg. 1146
Weichert Insurance Agency, Inc., 1700 Diagonal Rd.(22314), pg. 1173
Weichert Realty Career Development, 1700 Diagonal Rd.(22314), pg. 1173
Weichert Realty, Inc., Station Center, 1700 Diagonal Rd.(22314), pg. 1173
WILLIAMS WHITTLE ASSOCIATES, INC., 711 Princess St.(22314), pg. 1191

Amelia

Lane Graphics Products Div., P.O. Box 215(23007), pg. 657

Amelia Court House

Virginia Apparel Manufacturing Co., Inc., Rte. 681(23002), pg. 1039

Annandale

Acacia Mortgage Corporation, 7023 Little River Turnpike(22003), pg. 10
JWK INTERNATIONAL CORP., Ste. 1000, 7617 Little River Turnpike(22003), pg. 586

Arlington

AM General Corporation, 2345 Crystal Dr., Ste. 808(22202), pg. 926
ADVANCED MARINE ENTERPRISES, INC., 1725 Jefferson Davis Hwy., Ste. 1300(22202), pg. 20
Allied Security Inc., 901 S. Highland St.(22204), pg. 39
ANSER (ANALYTIC SERVICES INC.), 1215 Jeff Davis Hwy., Ste. 800(22202), pg. 76
Gulfstream Aerospace Corp., 1000 Wilson Blvd., Ste. 2701(22209), pg. 494
THE IDI GROUP COMPANIES, 901 N. Stuart St.(22203), pg. 560
INTEGRATED SYSTEMS ANALYSTS, INC., 2800 Shirlington Rd., Ste. 1100(22206), pg. 573
KASTLE SYSTEMS, INC., 1501 Wilson Blvd.(22209), pg. 618
ROSENTHAL AUTOMOTIVE ORGANIZATION, 1550 Wilson Blvd., Suite 700(22209), pg. 949
ROSENTHAL CHEVROLET CO., 3400 Columbia Pike(22204), pg. 949
SPC International Corp., 1500 Wilson Blvd.(22209), pg. 1070
SYSTEM PLANNING CORP., 1500 Wilson Blvd.(22209), pg. 1070
SYSTEMS RESEARCH AND APPLICATIONS CORPORATION, 2000 15th St. N.(22201), pg. 1071
TriData Inc., 1500 Wilson Blvd.(22209), pg. 1070
Valentec International Corp., 1901 N. Ft. Meyer Dr., Ste. 1016(22209), pg. 571
VeloBind, Inc., 1840 Wilson Blvd., 657

Ashland

HOHNER/HSS INC., Lakeridge Pk., Sycamore Dr.(23005), pg. 538

Baileys Crossroads

MOZEL DEVELOPMENT CORP., 6031 Leesburg Pike(22041), pg. 774

Bedford

Bedford Bulletin, P.O. Box 331(24523), pg. 655
Rubatex Corporation, 906 Adams St.(24523), pg. 480
Servitex, Inc., P.O. Box 628(24523), pg. 788

Blacksburg

KDI Electro-Tec Corp., 1600 N. Main St.(24060), pg. 612

Bristol

Bristol Concrete Prods. Corp., 111 E. Mary St.(24201), pg. 177
Bristol Lingerie, 203 Bob Morrison Blvd.(24201), pg. 546
BRISTOL STEEL & IRON WORKS, INC., 300 Piedmont St.(24201), pg. 176
THE UNITED COMPANY, P.O. Box 1280, 1005 Glenway Ave.(24203), pg. 1131
VALLEYDALE PACKERS INC., 1119 Commonwealth Ave.(24201), pg. 1143

Brucknell

The Bibb Company-Brucknell Plant, Hwy. 501 North(24528), pg. 781

Buchanan

Groendyk Mfg. Co., Inc., 278 Main St.(24066), pg. 480

Burke

THE VAN METRE COMPANIES, 5252 Lyngate Ct.(22015), pg. 1144

Chantilly

AMERICAN SYSTEMS CORPORATION, 14200 Park Meadow Dr.(22021), pg. 63
INTERSTATE ELECTRIC SUPPLY COMPANY, INC., 14110G Sullyfield Circle(22021), pg. 580

Charlottesville

Astre Consulting Corp., 1610 Quail Run(22901), pg. 92
BETTER LIVING INC., Rte. 29 N.(22906), pg. 148
Industrial Design Associates, 1610 Quail Run(22901), pg. 92

Chase City

JONBIL INC., Hwy. 785 Industrial Ave.(23924), pg. 602

Chesapeake

W. B. Goode Company, Inc., 1640 DeBaun Ave., P.O. Box 1294(23320), pg. 470
Jacobson Metal Company, P.O. Box 7596(23324), pg. 765
Max Ward-Delmar Studios, 2210 Paramont Ave.(23320), pg. 675
MONEY POINT DIAMOND CO., 4300 Buell St.(23324), pg. 765
Potrait Industries Corporation, 2210 Paramont Ave.(23320), pg. 675
Tencarva Machinery Co., 1244 B. Executive Blvd., Ste. 114(23320), pg. 1087

Clover

Clover Yarns, Inc., P.O. Box B-8(24534), pg. 1045

Colburn

DAVIS MINING & MANUFACTURING, Miners Professional Bldg., (24230), pg. 319

Colonial Hills

American Bindry-East, 801 Ivey(23834), pg. 51

Courtland

HANCOCK PEANUT COMPANY, Hwy. 58 W. Bus(23837), pg. 504

Crozet

ACME VISIBLE RECORDS, 1000 Allview Dr.(22932), pg. 13
Betterway Publications Inc., P.O. Box 219, (22932), pg. 394

Culpeper

Fairfield Building Systems, 651 Maddox Dr.(22701), pg. 397

Danville

Dan River Danville Mfg. Div., P.O. Box 261, (24543), pg. 313
DAN RIVER INC., 2291 Memorial Dr.(24541), pg. 313
Dan River Inc.-Home Furnishings & Related Prods., Div. I, P.O. Box 261, (24543), pg. 313
Dan River Inc.-Riverside Div., P.O. Box 261, (24543), pg. 313
Servitex, Inc., 270 Piney Forest Rd.(24541), pg. 787

Dayton

Rocco Turkeys, Inc., P.O. Box 158(22821), pg. 940

Dillwyn

KYANITE MINING CORPORATION, Hwy. 15 S.(23936), pg. 647

Edinburg

Automatic Service Co. of Virginia, No. Virginia Branch, P.O. Box 218, (22824), pg. 8
Rocco Farm Foods, Inc., Route 3, P.O. Box 370(22824), pg. 940

Fairfax

Burns & Roe Industrial Services Company, 2812 Old Lee Hwy., Ste. 120(22116), pg. 194
CDM Federal Programs Corporation, 13135 Lee Jackson Memorial Hwy. Ste. 200(22033), pg. 212
DEWBERRY & DAVIS, 8401 Arlington Blvd.(22031), pg. 334
GUEST SERVICES, INC., 3055 Prosperity Ave.(22031), pg. 493
THE LONG & FOSTER COMPANIES, INC., 11351 Random Hills Rd.(22030), pg. 682
The Long & Foster Real Estate, Inc., 11351 Random Hills Rd.(22030), pg. 682
The Office of Lee Kendrick, 8401 Arlington Blvd.(22031), pg. 334
Roubin & Janeiro, Inc., 8550 Lee Hwy., Ste. 700(22031), pg. 952
ROUBINCO, INC., 8550 Lee Hwy.,Ste. 700(22031), pg. 952

Falls Church

CREATIVE HAIRDRESSERS, 2815 Hartland Rd.(22043), pg. 297
FCW Publishing Corp., 3110 Fairview Park Dr., Ste. 1040(22042), pg. 576
The Hair Cuttery, 2815 Hartland Rd.(22043), pg. 297
OMEGA WORLD TRAVEL, INC., 5203 Leesburg Pike(22041), pg. 826
Western International Media Corporation, 7700 Leesburg Pike, 1180

Fredericksburg

Fredericksburg Auto Auction, 4907 Jefferson Davis Hwy.(22401), pg. 293

Galax

The Gazette, 108 W.Stuart Dr.(24333), pg. 655

Hampton

Atlantic Homes Corp., 2 Eaton St., Ste. 1100(23669), pg. 480
THE GREAT ATLANTIC COMPANIES, 2 Eaton St., Ste. 1100(23669), pg. 480
Great Atlantic Hospitality Co. Inc., 2 Eaton St., Ste. 1100(23669), pg. 480
Great Atlantic Management Co. Inc., 2 Eaton St., Ste. 1100(23669), pg. 480
IDAB INTERNATIONAL INCORPORATED, One Enterprise Pkwy., Ste. 300(23666), pg. 559
Mason & Hanger Services Inc., P.O. Box 668, Langley Air Force Base(23665), pg. 718
PRESSURE SYSTEMS, 34 Research Dr.(23666), pg. 888

Harrisonburg

Harrisonburg Auto Auction, Exit 62 & Interstate 81, 3560 Early Rd.(22801), pg. 293
Rocco Building Supplies Inc., P.O. Box 669(22801), pg. 940
Rocco Farms, 1620 So. Main St.(22801), pg. 940
Rocco Feeds, Inc., P.O. Box 549(22801), pg. 940
ROCCO INC., 1 Kratzer Rd.(22801), pg. 940
SHENANDOAH MFG. CO. INC., 1070 Virginia Ave.(22801), pg. 997
Wetsel Seed Company, P.O. Box 791(22801), pg. 1023

Herndon

Parsons Brinckerhoff Construction Services, Inc., 475 Spring Park Place, Ste. 500(22070), pg. 850
Parsons Brinckerhoff Facilities Services, Inc., 475 Spring Park Place, Ste. 500(22070), pg. 850
E. JAMES WHITE COMPANY, 151 Spring St., Ste. 300(22070), pg. 1185

Hollins

Roinoke Service Center, Botetourt Industrial Park, Industrial Park Drive(24033), pg. 223

Hot Springs

VIRGINIA HOT SPRINGS, INC., U.S. Rte. 220(24445), pg. 1152

Independence

NAUTILUS, 709 Powerhouse Rd.(24348), pg. 796
Nautilus Virginia Inc., 709 Powerhouse Rd., P.O. Box 160(24348), pg. 796

Leesburg

Empire Press, 602 S. King St., Ste. 300(22075), pg. 291
PRECISION TUNE, INC., 784 Miller Dr. S.E.(22075), pg. 885

Lorton

Stone & Hoover Contracting, Inc., 8433 Backlick Rd., Ste. 201(22079), pg. 470

Lynchburg

Alco Health Services Corporation-Lynchburg Div., 9221 Timberland Rd.(24506), pg. 32
Allright Parking Virginia, Inc., P.O. Box 742, 10th & Commerce Key Bldg.(24505), pg. 42
Automatic Service Co. of Virginia, Lynchburg Branch, P.O. Box 10278, 3224 Odd Fellow Rd.(24506), pg. 8
C.B. FLEET COMPANY, INCORPORATED, 4615 Murray Pl.(24506), pg. 417
Lynchburg Service Center, Elon Industrial Park(24501), pg. 223
PROGRESS PRINTING COMPANY, 3523 Waterlick Rd.(24502), pg. 894

Martinsville

HOOKER FURNITURE CORPORATION, Hooker St., P.O. Box 4708(24115), pg. 543
NATIONWIDE HOMES, INC., 1100 Rives Rd.(24115), pg. 795

McLean

Falcon Associates, Ltd., 6862 Elm St., Ste. 430(22101), pg. 981
First American Bank of Virginia, 1970 Chain Bridge Rd.(22102), pg. 412
First American Metro Corp., 1751 Pinnacle Dr.(22102), pg. 412
MARS, INCORPORATED, 6885 Elm St.(22101), pg. 713
MILLER & SMITH, INC., 1568 Spring Hill Rd.(22102), pg. 755
PLANNING SYSTEMS INC., 7923 Jones Branch Dr.(22102-3304), pg. 874
STACKIG, SANDERSON & WHITE, INC., 7680 Old Springhouse Rd.(22102), pg. 1034

Middleburg

JACK KENT COOKE, INC., Kent Farms, P.O. Box 2110(22117), pg. 282

Mount Crawford

RIDDLEBERGER BROTHERS, INC., P.O. Box 27(22841), pg. 933

Mount Jackson

Mount Jackson Press, Inc., 1868 Judd's Dr.(22842), pg. 608

Newington

Marshall Erdman & Assoc., Inc., 8550 Cinder Bed Rd., 386
S.T. RESEARCH, 8419 Terminal Rd.(22122), pg. 964

Newport News

Allright Parking Virginia, Inc., 2501 Washington Ave., Ste. 300(23607), pg. 42
BASIC CONSTRUCTION COMPANY, 538 Oyster Point Rd.(23602), pg. 124
Bay Savings Bank, FSB, 2712 Washington Ave.(23607-3920), pg. 414
Plymkraft Inc., P.O. Box 1577, Warwick Station(23601), pg. 266

Norfolk

Autonet, Inc., 150 West Brambleton Ave.(23510), pg. 656
Be-Lo Markets Inc., 4603 Cape Henry Ave.(23513), pg. 212
Broadcast and Video Enterprises Div., 150 W. Brambleton Ave.(23501), pg. 654
Earle Palmer Brown/Norfolk, 248 W. Bute St.(23510), pg. 182
CAMELLIA FOOD STORES CO-OP INC., 1157 Production Rd.(23502), pg. 211
Commonwealth Building Company, 150 W. Brambleton Ave.(23510), pg. 656
Commonwealth Direct Marketing, 150 W. Brambleton Ave.(23510), pg. 656
Commonwealth Printing Company, 150 W. Brambleton Ave.(23510), pg. 656
DWF of Norfolk, 5315 Henneman Dr.(23513), pg. 331
DAVIS & PHILLIPS, INC., 121 College Place(23510), pg. 319
Diesel Marine Norshipco, P.O. Box 2100(23501), pg. 810
FARM FRESH, INC., 7530 Tidewater Drive(23505), pg. 401
Hub Furniture Store, 800 Tidewater Dr.(23504), pg. 925
LANDMARK COMMUNICATIONS, INC., 150 W. Brambleton Ave.(23510), pg. 654
MILLER OIL CO., INC., 1000 E. City Hall Ave.(23504), pg. 754
Moran Towing of Virginia, Wheat Building, 109 Main St.(23514), pg. 769
NORFOLK SHIPBUILDING & DRYDOCK CORPORATION, P.O. Box 2100(23501-2100), pg. 810
Norshipco Industrial Enterprises, P.O. Box 2100(23501), pg. 810
THE POLIZOS AGENCY, 220 W. Freemason St.(23510), pg. 879
SPIRIT CRUISES, 501 Front St.(23510), pg. 1031
The Virginian-Pilot and The Ledger Star, 150 W. Brambleton Ave.(23510), pg. 656
WLTY-FM, 720 Boush St.(23510), pg. 655
WTAR-AM, 720 Boush St.(23510), pg. 655
WTKR-TV, 720 Boush St.(23510), pg. 783

Orange

VIRGINIA METAL INDUSTRIES, INC., 12314 Old Gordonsville Rd.(22960), pg. 1152

Petersburg

ROPER BROS. LUMBER CO., INC., 130 Pocahontas St.(23803), pg. 947
SEWARD LUGGAGE COMPANY, 434 High St.(23803), pg. 993

Portsmouth

PECK IRON & METAL COMPANY, INC., 3500 Elm Ave.(23704), pg. 854

Pulaski

Xaloy, Inc., State Rd. 99(24301), pg. 1012

Reston

ADVANCED TECHNOLOGY, INC., 12005 Sunrise Valley Dr.(22091), pg. 20
MARYLAND VIRGINIA MILK PRODUCERS ASSOCIATION, INC., 1985 Isaac Newton Square(22090), pg. 717
PE SYSTEMS, 1851 Alexander Bell Drive, Ste. 105(22091), pg. 836

Richmond

AMF Azalea Bowl, 1741 Dumbarton Rd.(23227-3323), pg. 471
AMF BAKERY SYSTEMS, 2115 W. Laburnum Ave.(23227), pg. 5
AMF Bowling Centers Inc., 7275 Glen Forest Dr.(23226-3755), pg. 471
APPX Software, 951 E. Byrd St., Ste. 710(23219), pg. 623
Allright Parking Virginia, Inc., 100 Virginia St.(23219), pg. 42
American Inks & Coatings Corp., Ink Division, 111 Agency Ave.(23225), pg. 56
Best Products Co., Inc., 1400 Best Plaza(23227), pg. 17
BLUE CROSS & BLUE SHIELD OF VIRGINIA, 2015 Staples Mill Rd.(23279), pg. 160
Earle Palmer Brown/Richmond, 1710 E. Franklin St.(23219), pg. 182
E. R. CARPENTER CO., 5016 Monument Ave.(23230), pg. 224
CENTRAL COCA-COLA BOTTLING COMPANY, INC., Corporate Headquarters, 1706 Roseneath Rd.(23230), pg. 232
CHRISTIAN CHILDREN'S FUND, INC., 2821 Emerywood Pkwy.(23261-6484), pg. 248
CONCRETE PIPE & PRODUCTS CO. INC., P.O. Box 1223(23209), pg. 273
Domestic Linen Supply Co., 1321 No. 17th St.(23219), pg. 343
EDELMANN SCOTT, INC., 629 E. Main St.(23219), pg. 368
Electrical Equipment Company, 1807 Blvd. W.(23230), pg. 374
EMRICK CHEVROLET SALES CORPORATION, 1801-11 Chamberlayne Ave.(23222), pg. 380
ESTES EXPRESS LINES, INC., 1100 Commerce Rd.(23224), pg. 389
First Land & Development, Inc., P.O. Box 26303, (23260), pg. 18
Formex, Inc. - Permanent Steel Forms, P.O. Box 24129, 2800 Cofer Rd.(23224), pg. 470
GES Environmental, Inc., 8040 Kimway Drive(23228), pg. 470
GENERAL SERVICES CORPORATION, 2922 Hathaway Rd.(23225), pg. 450
W. B. GOODE COMPANY, INC., 3280 Formex Rd.(23224), pg. 470
W. B. Goode Company, Inc., 2800 Cofer Road, P.O. Box 14259(23224), pg. 470
WILLIAM H. GOODWIN TRUST, 1 James Ctr.(23219), pg. 471
HAWLEY MARTIN PARTNERS, INC., 1703 N. Parham Rd.(23229-4606), pg. 518
HUNTSINGER & JEFFER, 809 Brook Hill Circle(23227), pg. 555
KENNEDY ASSOCIATES, 951 E. Byrd St., Ste.710(23219), pg. 623
LOPC, 812 Moorefield PK. Dr.(23222), pg. 608
MACTAVISH MACHINE MANUFACTURING COMPANY, 9001 Hermitage Rd.(23228), pg. 698
Magnum Building Systems, 1000 Jefferson Davis Hwy., P.O. Box 24159(23224), pg. 470
MIL-MOR MEDIA, INC., 1407 Sherwood Ave.(23220), pg. 753
MILLER BROS. INDUSTRIES, INC., 3301 Castlewood(23234), pg. 753
M.F. Neal & Co.,Inc., 1900 E. Franklin St.(23219), pg. 694
Pocahontas Foods, USA, 7420 Ranco Rd.(23228), pg. 862
Richmond Foundry and Manufacturing Co., 3514 Mayland Ct.(23233), pg. 607
RICHMOND MOTOR COMPANY, 4600 W. Broad St.(23230), pg. 933
Richmond Service Center, Seven Hills & Settlers Roads(23231), pg. 223
SIDDALL, MATUS & COUGHTER, INC. ADVERTISING & PUBLIC RELATIONS, 700 Ross Bldg., 801 E. Main St.(23219), pg. 1002
SMYTH, BAUER & LEWIS ADVERTISING INC., 201 W. Broad St. Ste. 300(23220), pg. 1014
SOUTHERN STATES COOPERATIVE, INC., 6606 W. Broad St.(23230-6234), pg. 1022
Tencarva Machinery Co., 2231 E. Belt Blvd.(23224), pg. 1087

VATEX AMERICA, INC., 2395 Hermitage Rd.(23220), pg. 1141
VIRGINIA DEPARTMENT OF ECONOMIC DEVELOPMENT TOURISM DEVELOPMENT GROUP, 1021 E. Cary St.(23219), pg. 1152
VIRGINIA STATE LOTTERY DEPARTMENT, 2201 W. Broad St.(23220), pg. 1153
WHEAT, FIRST SECURITIES INC., 901 E. Byrd St.(23219), pg. 1184
Wilcox-Walter-Furlong Paper Co., 4245 Carolina Ave.(23261), pg. 1157
Williams Crane & Rigging, Inc., 938 E. 4th St.(23208), pg. 1191
WILLIAMS INTERNATIONAL INDUSTRIES, INC., P.O. Box 1116(23208), pg. 1191
PETER WONG & ASSOCIATES, INC., 200 E. Cary St.(23219), pg. 1199

Roanoke

Allright Roanoke Parking, Inc., Shenandoah Bldg., Ste. 719, 305 1st S.W.(24011), pg. 42
BLUE RIDGE TRANSFER CO., 1814 Hollins Rd., N.E.(24012), pg. 161
Cox Cable Roanoke, Inc., 1909 Salem Ave. S.W.(24016), pg. 294
Freeway Roanoke, 1401 Coulter Dr., N.W.(24012), pg. 432
W. B. Goode Company, Inc., 622 Mohawk Avenue, N.E., P.O. Box 13826(24037), pg. 470
Graves-Humphreys Company, 5320 Peter Creek Rd.(24033), pg. 592
HAYES, SEAY, MATTERN & MATTERN, INC., 1315 Franklin Rd. S.W.(24016), pg. 519
JM Clipper Corporation d/b/a Acadia, 1420 Coulter Dr., N.W.(24014), pg. 507
Neuhoff Farms, Inc., 2149 Electric Rd. SW(24018), pg. 1143
Old Dominion Life Insurance Co., 2301 Brambleton Ave., S.W.(24015), pg. 997
PM Properties Inc., 5221 Valley Park Rd., Ste. 3(24019), pg. 865
PM Terminals, Inc., 5221 Valley Park Dr., Ste. 3(24019), pg. 865
PM Transport, Inc., 5221 Valley Park Dr., Ste. 3(24019), pg. 865
PETROLEUM MARKETERS, INC., 5221 Valley Park Drive, Ste. 3(24019), pg. 865
SHENANDOAH LIFE INSURANCE COMPANY, 2301 Brambleton Ave., S.W.(24015), pg. 997
Stop In Food Stores, 5221 Valley Park Rd., Ste. 3(24019), pg. 865
Tencarva Machinery Co., 3646 Aerial Way Dr., Suite 1(24018), pg. 1087
Times-World Corporation, P.O. Box 2491, 201 Campbell Ave. S.W.(24010), pg. 656

Rosslyn

INTERSTATE RESOURCES, INC., 1800 N. Kent St., 580

Salem

LAYMAN CANDY COMPANY, INC., 1637 E. Main St.(24153), pg. 663

Sandston

STERNHEIMER BROTHERS INC., 5501 Ferncroft Rds.(23150), pg. 1048

South Hill

PEEBLES, INC., One Peebles St.(23970), pg. 855

Springfield

Allnewsco, Inc., 7600D Boston Blvd.(22153), pg. 862
Credit Card Service Corporation, 6860 Commercial Dr.(22150), pg. 410
FAIRFAX LUMBER & MILLWORK COMPANY INC., 7622 Backlick Rd.(22150), pg. 397
FINANCIAL PROTECTION SERVICES INC., 6860 Commercial Dr.(22151-4208), pg. 410
INTERSTATE VAN LINES, INC., 5801 Rolling Rd.(22152), pg. 581
MICO, INC., 6790 Commercial Dr.(22151), pg. 748
Robinson Export-Import Corporation, 6790 Commercial Dr.(22151), pg. 748
Rudolph & West, 6728 Industrial Rd.(22151), pg. 748

Strasburg

CHEMSTONE CORP., P.O. Box 71(22657), pg. 242
Shenandoah Valley Press, Inc., P.O. Box 777, Route 55E(22657), pg. 608

Sulfolk

BIRDSONG CORPORATION, 612 Madison Ave.(23434), pg. 153

Tazewell

Clinch River Corp., Rt. 6, P.O. Box 60(24651), pg. 609

Timberville

Rocco Further Processing, Co-op Drive(22853), pg. 940

Verona

American Safety Razor Company, Razor Blade Lane(24482), pg. 604

Vienna

Andreas Galleries, Inc., 8545 Leesburg Pike(22182), pg. 658
BTG, INC., 1945 Old Gallows Rd.(22182), pg. 107
Capital Funding Co., 8545 Leesburg Pike(22182), pg. 658
COMMTEK COMMUNICATIONS, 8330 Boone Blvd., Ste. 600(22180), pg. 269
Bruce W. Eberle & Associates, Ste. 700, 8245 Boone Blvd.(22182), pg. 365
EBERLE DIRECT MARKETING GROUP, INC., Ste. 700, 8245 Boone Blvd.(22182), pg. 365
H.B.L., Inc., 8545 Leesburg Pike(22182), pg. 658
IDC Virginia, 8300 Boone Blvd., Ste. 500(22182), pg. 577
Information Strategies Group, 800 Tower Crescent Dr., Ste. 1180(22180), pg. 578
INPUT, Inc., , pg. 571
KSK COMMUNICATIONS, LTD., 8618 Westwood Center Dr., Ste. 400(22182-2280), pg. 613
LANTZSCH-ANDREAS ENTERPRISES, INC., 8545 Leesburg Pike(22182), pg. 658
Omega List Company, 8245 Boone Blvd.(22182), pg. 365
RINGLING BROS., BARNUM & BAILEY COMBINED SHOWS, INC., 8607 Westwood Center Dr.(22182), pg. 935

Virginia Beach

American Systems Engineering Corporation, 2829 Guardian Lane, Ste. 200(23452), pg. 981
BARKER CAMPBELL & FARLEY, 240 Business Park Dr.(23462), pg. 120
COMPUTER DYNAMICS, INC., 4452 Corporation Ln., Ste. 300(23462), pg. 271
Cox Cable Hampton Roads, Inc., 5200 Cleveland Street(23462), pg. 294
VICTOR KING ADVERTISING, 1000 Centerville Turnpike(23463), pg. 630
Landmark Special Publications, 149 Business Park Dr.(23462), pg. 656
METRO INFORMATION SERVICES, 607 Lynnhaven Pkwy.(23452), pg. 743
Servitex, Inc., 5616 Shell Rd.(23455), pg. 788
STIHL INC., 536 Viking Dr.(23452), pg. 1049
Stihl Parts, Inc., 520 Viking Dr.(23452), pg. 1049
Susquehanna Radio Corp., Pembroke One Bldg., 281 Independence Blvd., Ste. 101(23462), pg. 1065

Waynesboro

BAUGHER CHEVROLET-BUICK-GEO, INC., 2551 W. Main(22980), pg. 127
WAYN-TEX INC., 901 S. Belphine Ave.(22980), pg. 1169

Williamsburg

BUSH DEVELOPMENT CORP., 4029 Ironbound Rd., Ste. 200(23188), pg. 196
COLONIAL WILLIAMSBURG FOUNDATION, Henry St. & Prince George St.(23187), pg. 264

Winchester

NATIONAL FRUIT PRODUCT COMPANY, 550 Fairmont Ave.(22601-3931), pg. 789
PAC Manufacturing & Distributing Co., 1575 Lenoir Dr.(22601), pg. 885

Woodbridge

UNIVERSAL DYNAMICS INC., 13600 Dabney Rd.(22191), pg. 1138
Universal Dynamics, Inc., 13600 Dabney Rd.(22191), pg. 1138

WASHINGTON

Auburn

MILES SAND & GRAVEL COMPANY, 12th & M St., S.E.(98002), pg. 753
VALLEY PONTIAC BUICK GMC, INC., 3104 Auburn Way N.(98002), pg. 1143

Bellevue

ACE NOVELTY COMPANY, INC., 13434 N.E. 16th(98005), pg. 12
Ace Novelty Fun Service Division, 13434 N.W. 16th(98005), pg. 12
BURNSTEAD CONSTRUCTION COMPANY, 1215 120th Ave., N.E., Ste. 201(98005), pg. 194
CUNA North West District, P.O. Box 1457, (98009), pg. 206
ERM-Northwest, Inc., 2821 Northrup Way(98004), pg. 360
Harza Northwest, Inc., P.O. Box C-96900(98004), pg. 516
MetLife Capital Corporation, 10900 N. E. 8th St., Ste. 1300(98004), pg. 744
NORTH COAST ELECTRIC COMPANY, 110 110th Ave., N.E., Ste. 616(98004), pg. 813
Northwest Media, Inc., 1705 132nd Ave. N.E.(98005), pg. 863
TOPLINE IMPORTS, INC., 3625 132nd Ave. S.E., 4th Fl.(98006), pg. 1102
TRANSCOASTAL MORTGAGE COMPANY, 10900 N.E.Fourth, Ste. 2350(98004-5841), pg. 1107
Unigard Security Insurance Co., 15805 N.E. 24th St.(98008), pg. 596
VERNELL'S CANDY COMPANY, 11959 Northrup Way(98005), pg. 1148

Bellingham

ALLSOP, INC., 4201 Meridian(98226), pg. 43
ERSHIGS, INC., 742 Marine Dr.(98225), pg. 387
HAGGEN'S, INC., 401 Harris Ave.(98225), pg. 499

Bothell

TRAVELING SOFTWARE INC., 18702 N. Creek Pkwy. S.(98011), pg. 1108

Burlington

National Frozen Foods Corporation - Burlington, 200 Washington Ave.(98233), pg. 789

Chehalis

National Frozen Foods Corporation - Chehalis, 188 Sturdevant Rd.(98532), pg. 789

Chelan

TROUT INC., Chelan Falls Rd.(98816), pg. 1116

Colville

VAAGEN BROTHERS LUMBER, INC., 565 W. 5th(99114), pg. 1142

Ellensburg

SCHAAKE PACKING COMPANY, INC., P.O. Box 128(98926), pg. 974

Everett

CERTIFIED HOLDING CORP., 11410 Beverly Park Rd.(98204), pg. 237
LEE GROCERY COMPANY, 3200-3220 Hewitt Ave.(98206), pg. 665
MILLSTONE COFFEE, INC., 729 100th St., S.E.(98208), pg. 756

Federal Way

Pacific Nuclear Systems, Inc., 1010 S. 336th St., Ste. 220(98003), pg. 818

Fife

L & L Plant Soil Division, 2507 Frank Albert Rd., Ste. 130(98424), pg. 647
PRINT NORTHWEST, 4918 20th St.E.(98424), pg. 891

Gig Harbor

KEITH UDDENBERG, INC., 7520 Soundview Dr.(98335), pg. 1125

Hoquiam

ENTERPRISES INTERNATIONAL INC., Blaine & Firman(98550), pg. 382
Ovalstrapping Inc., 710-8th St.(98550), pg. 383

Issaquah

HENRY BACON BUILDING MATERIALS, INC., 5210 E. Lake Sammamish Pkwy. S.E.(98027-7012), pg. 113
ZETEC, INC., 1370 N.W. Mall(98027), pg. 1217

Kelso

TOLLYCRAFT YACHTS CORP., 2200 Clinton Ave.(98626), pg. 1100

Kennewick

AGRINORTHWEST, INC., 2810 W. Clearwater Ave.(99336), pg. 25

Kent

Air Conditioning Co., Inc., 6952 South 220th St.(98032), pg. 27
Brower Company, 7043 S. 190th St.(98032), pg. 127
CHEMCENTRAL/Seattle, 7601 So. 190th St.(98032), pg. 242
DIADORA AMERICA, INC., 21527 88th Place S.(98031), pg. 335
HOWARD MANUFACTURING, 421 6th Ave. N.(98032), pg. 547
Kilsby-Roberts/Seattle, 22011 76th Ave. S.(98032), pg. 606
Lunstead, A Haworth Portfolio Co., 8655 S. 208th St.(98031), pg. 518
Lynden Transport, Inc., 6250 S. 228th(98032), pg. 689
PACIFIC FOODS, INC., 21612 88th Ave. S.(98031), pg. 840
RECREATIONAL EQUIPMENT, INC., 6750 S. 228th(98032), pg. 917
SMITH BROTHERS FARMS, INC., 27441 68th Ave., S.(98032), pg. 1011
South Seattle Auto Auction, 19443 77th Ave. So.(98064-5189), pg. 293

Kirkland

FLOATHE JOHNSON ASSOCIATES, INC., 550 Kirkland Way, Ste. 200(98033), pg. 419
Hoffman Construction Company of Washington, Ste. 265, 135 Lake St. South(98033), pg. 537
InVireChem, 1500 7th Ave. S.(98033), pg. 838
JEFFREY MICHAEL, 533 Sixth St. South(98033), pg. 591
PACE INTERNATIONAL CORPORATION, 500 7th Ave., S.(98033), pg. 838

Lacey

CAPITAL DEVELOPMENT CO., 691 Sleater-Kinney Rd. S.E., Ste. 100(98503), pg. 215

Lynden

LTI, Inc., P.O. Box 433(98264), pg. 689

Lynnwood

Commercial Design Architects/HEPY, Inc., 4230 198th St., S.W.(98036), pg. 509
HARRIS FORD, INC., 20006 64th Ave., W.(98036), pg. 512
ID Solutions, 6825 216th St. S.W.(98036), pg. 574

INTELLIGENT CONTROLS INC., 6825 216th St. S.W.(98066), pg. 573

Marysville

WELCO LUMBER COMPANY, P.O. Box 125(98270), pg. 1175

Moses Lake

National Frozen Foods Corporation - Moses Lake, Wheeler Rd.(98837), pg. 789

Mountlake Terrace

LLOYD CONTROLS, INC., 21414 66th Ave., W.(98043), pg. 679

Port Angeles

Rogerson Hiller Corporation, 2140 W. 18th St.(98362), pg. 944

Prosser

Milne Fruit Products, 804 Bennett Ave.(99350), pg. 821

Redman

Cascadia Technology Corporation, 2877 1052 Ave. N.E.(95052), pg. 817

Redmond

APPLIED MICROSYSTEMS CORPORATION, 5020 148th Ave., N.E.(98052), pg. 79
The Cadman Companies, P.O. Box 538(98073), pg. 199
LAKESIDE INDUSTRIES, 7735 178th Place NE(98052), pg. 651
O'Brien International, Inc., 14615 N.E. 91st(98052), pg. 695
RENA-WARE DISTRIBUTORS INC., 8383 158th Ave., N.E.(98052), pg. 926
TONE COMMANDER SYSTEMS, 4370 150th NE(98073-9739), pg. 1101

Renton

E.J. BARTELLS CO., 700 Powell Ave., S.W.(98055), pg. 122
PTC Aerospace, The Plaza Bldg., 10900 N. E. 8th St., Ste.1023(98055), pg. 837
Renton Waterfront Restaurant Corp., 1011 W. Perimeter Rd.(98055), pg. 1029

Richland

Geosafe Corporation, Battelle Blvd.(99352), pg. 126

Ridgefield

PACIFIC WOOD TREATING COPORATION, 111 W. Division, P.O. Box 518(98642), pg. 842

Seattle

J.R. ABBOTT CONSTRUCTION, INC., 3512 Airport Way(98124), pg. 9
ACME POULTRY COMPANY, INC., 1024 S. King St.(98114), pg. 13
Alaska Boat Co., P.O. Box 5030 University Station(98105), pg. 1163
Alaska Marine Lines, Inc., 5615 W. Marginal Way, S.W.(98106), pg. 689
ALASKA PULP CORPORATION, 1301 Fifth Ave, Ste. 3000(98101), pg. 30
ALASKAN COPPER COMPANIES, 3223 6th Ave., S.(98134), pg. 30
ALLIANCE MANAGEMENT, INC., 701 Dexter Ave., N., Ste. 407(98109), pg. 37
American Envelope of Seattle, 401 Andover Park East(98188), pg. 200
AMERICAN LEGEND CORPORATE, 400 Strander Blvd.(98138), pg. 57
AMERICAN PASSAGE MEDIA CORPORATION, 215 W. Harrison(98119), pg. 59
American Red Ball International, Inc., 12360 Lake City Way, N.E., Ste. 500(98125), pg. 918
Arctic Packaging & Logistics Inc., P.O. Box 3757(98124), pg. 689
ASSOCIATED GROCERS, INC., 3301 S. Norfolk St.(98118), pg. 90
THE BARTELL DRUG COMPANY, 4727 Denver Ave. S.(98134), pg. 122
BAUGH CONSTRUCTION COMPANY, 900 Poplar Place So.(98114), pg. 127
ROBERT E. BAYLEY CONSTRUCTION, 205 Columbia St.(98104), pg. 128
R. W. BECK & ASSOCIATES, INC., Fourth & Blanchard Bldg., 2101 Fourth Ave., Ste. 600(98121), pg. 131
Benefit Service Corporation, 1201 Third Ave., 12th Fl.(98101), pg. 1166
Bering Marine Corporation, P.O. Box 3757(98124), pg. 689
Borders, Perrin & Norrander, 1115 First Ave. S.(98101), pg. 165
Bowhead Equipment Company, P.O. Box 3757(98124), pg. 689
BRAZIER FOREST INDUSTRIES, INC., 4500 Columbia Center, 701 5th Ave.(98104), pg. 172
BREMS EASTMAN GLADE, INC., 3131 Elliott Ave., Ste. 280(98121), pg. 173
BROWN & HADLEY & PARTNERS, 600 Market Place Tower, 2025 1st Ave.(98121), pg. 182
CAPITAL INDUSTRIES, INC., 5801 3rd Ave. S.(98108), pg. 215
CHRISTIANSEN & FRITSCH, INC., 1008 Western Ave.(98104), pg. 249
Columbia Services, Inc., 1201 Third Ave.(98101), pg. 1166
Composite Research & Management Company, 1201 Third Ave.(98101), pg. 1166
DWF of Seattle, 330 Terry Ave. No.(98109), pg. 331
Daily Racing Form, Inc. (Northwest), 12559 26th St., N.E.(98125), pg. 611
Dairy Export Co., Inc., 635 Elliott Ave.(98119), pg. 315
DAIRYGOLD INC., 635 Elliot Ave. W.(98119), pg. 311
DARIGOLD, INC., 635 Elliott Ave., W.(98119), pg. 315
Douglas Management Company, P.O. Box 3757, (98124), pg. 689
EDELSTEIN ASSOCIATES ADVERTISING INC., 2030 First Ave., 3rd Fl.(98121), pg. 368
EDERER INC., 2925 First Ave., S.(98134), pg. 368
Elkay Plastics Co., Inc., Stock Service Center, 500 S. Brandon(98108), pg. 377
Empire Life Insurance Company, 1203 Third Ave., 6th Fl.(98101), pg. 1166
ERNST HOME CENTER, INC., 1511 6th Ave.(98101), pg. 387
Evans Food Group, Evans/Kraft Bldg., 190 Queen Anne North(98109-4924), pg. 391
Evans/Public Relations, Evans/Kraft Bldg., 190 Queen Anne Ave., North(98109-4924), pg. 391
EvansGroup, Evans/Kraft Bldg., 190 Queen Anne Ave. North(98109-4924), pg. 391
Farman's Pickle Company, 5501 4th Ave. So., Ste. 207(98108), pg. 26
Fifth Avenue Hospital, 10560 5th Ave., N.E.(98125), pg. 176
First Columbia Escrow, Inc., 1201 Third Ave.(98101), pg. 1166
Fisher Broadcasting, Inc., 100 Fourth Ave.N.(98109), pg. 415
FISHER COMPANIES, INC., 1525 One Union Sq.(98101-3211), pg. 414
Fisher Mills, Inc., 3235 16th Ave., S.W.(98134), pg. 415
Fisher Properties Inc., 1525 One Union Sq.(98101), pg. 415
FISHERIES SUPPLY COMPANY, 1900 N. Northlake Way 415
FOOD SERVICES OF AMERICA, 4025 Dell Ridge Way, S.W., Ste. 400(98106), pg. 423
Fremont Electric Company, 744 N. 34th St.(98103), pg. 224
GAI'S SEATTLE FRENCH BAKING CO., INC., 2006 Weller St.(98144), pg. 441
General Travel Services, Inc., 1201 Third Ave., 18th Fl.(98101), pg. 1166
Giftreps Northwest, 6100 4th Ave. S.(98108), pg. 100
GRIFFIN ENVELOPE, INC., 4301 E. Marginal Way S.(98134), pg. 487
HALLIDIE MACHINERY COMPANY, INC., 2200 6th Ave., S.(98134), pg. 501
HART CROWSER, INC., 1910 Fairview Ave. E.(98102), pg. 512
HERRING NEWMAN, 414 Olive Way, Ste. 300(98101), pg. 531
Holiday House, Inc., 1201 Third Ave., 18th Fl.(98101), pg. 1166
ICICLE SEAFOODS, INC., 4019 21st Ave. West(98199), pg. 561
Images Woodworking, Inc., 1601 One Union Sq.(98101), pg. 128
Jorgensen Steel & Aluminum/Seattle, 5964 Sixth Ave. S.(98108), pg. 606
Kawaguchi Travel Services, Inc., 1201 Third Ave., 18th Fl.(98101), pg. 1166
KEENERS, INC., 2900 4th Ave., S.(98124), pg. 620
Knik Construction Co., Inc., P. O. Box 3757(98124), pg. 689
Korn/Ferry International, 1201 Third Ave., Ste. 2120(98101), pg. 642
Langendorf Baking Company Of Seattle, Inc., 2901 6th Ave., S.(98134), pg. 441
LIVINGSTON & COMPANY, 800 Fifth Ave.(98104), pg. 679
Lloyd Electric Apparatus Co., 7126 W. Marginal Way, S.W.(98106), pg. 680
Lynden Air Freight, Inc., 411 First Ave. S., 689
Lynden Financial Services, Inc., P.O, Box 3757(98124), pg. 689
Lynden Forwarding, Inc., 411 First Ave. S., 689
LYNDEN INCORPORATED, 18000 Pacific Hwy. So., Ste. 800(98188), pg. 689
Lynden Logistics, Inc., P.O. Box 3757(98124), pg. 689
MSR (Mountain Safety Research), 4225 2nd Ave. S.(98134), pg. 917
MAGNOLIA HI-FI, INC., 3701 7th Ave., S.(98134), pg. 701
Marco Seattle, Inc., 2300 W. Commodore Way(98199), pg. 707
MARINE CONSTRUCTION & DESIGN CO., 2300 W. Commodore Way(98199), pg. 707
MEDIA PLUS, 1818 Westlake Ave., N., Ste. 114, pg. 734
Mill Maple Properties, Inc., 1201 Third Ave.(98101), pg. 1166
Mill Plain Four, Inc., 1201 Third Ave.(98101), pg. 1166
Mill Plain One, Inc., 1201 Third Ave.(98101), pg. 1166
Mill Plain Three, Inc., 1201 Third Ave.(98101), pg. 1166
Mill Plain Two, Inc., 1201 Third Ave.(98101), pg. 1166
Murphy Favre House Managers, Inc., 1201 Third Ave., 3rd Fl.(98101), pg. 1166
Murphy Favre, Inc., 1201 Third Ave.(98101), pg. 1166
Murphy Favre Properties, Inc., 1191 2nd Ave.(98101), pg. 1166
Mutual Travel, Inc., 1201 Third Ave., 18th Fl.(98101), pg. 1166
NATIONAL FROZEN FOODS CORP., 2371 Eastlake Ave. East(98102), pg. 789
North American Acceptance Corporation, 1201 Third Ave.(98101), pg. 1166
Northwest Parking Services Inc., 721 First Ave.(98104), pg. 42
Northwest Service, Inc., 6737 Corson Ave. S.(98108), pg. 423
Nuarc Northwestern Div., 1800 Westlake Ave. North 817
THE ODOM CORPORATION, 26 S. Hanford(98134), pg. 821
PACIFIC LUMBER & SHIPPING CO., 3131 Rainier Bank Tower(98101), pg. 840
PACIFIC NORTHERN OIL CORP., 100 W. Harrison, North Tower Ste. 200(98119), pg. 841
PACIFIC SOUND RESOURCES, 2801 S.W. Florida St.(98126), pg. 841
Parametric Portfolio Associates, Inc., 7310 Columbia Center, 701 5th Ave.(98104), pg. 841
PIZZA HAVEN INC., 12860 Interurban Ave. S.(98168), pg. 873
PRESERVATIVE PAINT COMPANY, 5400 Airport Way(98108), pg. 887
Preston Properties of Arizona, Inc., 1201 Third Ave.(98101), pg. 1167
Preston Properties of California, Inc., 1201 Third Ave.(98101), pg. 1167
Preston Properties Texas, Inc., 1201 Third Ave.(98101), pg. 1167
Preston Property Management Company, 1201 Third Ave.(98101), pg. 1167
Preston Ridge Financial Services' Corporation, 1201 Third Ave.(98101), pg. 1167
Rainier Brewing Co., 3100 Airport Way S.(98124), pg. 526
Re-Union Division, 1700 Westlake Ave. North(98109), pg. 986
RED BALL CORPORATION, 9750 Third Ave. NE Suite 200(98115), pg. 918
Rep Force, Evans/Kraft Bldg., 190 Queen Anne Ave. North(98109-4924), pg. 391
RESTAURANTS UNLIMITED, 1818 N. Northlake Way(98103), pg. 929
ROFFE, INC., 808 Howell St.(98101), pg. 943
ROMAC INDUSTRIES, INC., 1064 4th Ave. S.(98134), pg. 945
SS Service Corporation, 1201 Third Ave.(98101), pg. 1166
Seafresh Inc., P.O. Box 5030 University Station(98105), pg. 1163
SEATTLE CITY LIGHT, 1015 Third Ave.(98104), pg. 986
SEATTLE LIGHTING FIXTURE CO., 222 Second Ave.(98104), pg. 986
SEATTLE PACIFIC INDUSTRIES, INC., 1700 Westlake Ave. North(98109), pg. 986
SEATTLE PACKAGING CORPORATION, 3701 S. Norfolk(98118), pg. 986
Seattle Plant, 3801 E. Marginal Way So.(98134), pg. 88
Seattle Post-Intelligencer, 101 Elliott Ave. W.(98119-4220), pg. 524
SEATTLE TIMES COMPANY, 1120 John St.(98109), pg. 986
SELLEN CONSTRUCTION COMPANY, 228 9th Ave. N.(98109), pg. 988
SHANNON & WILSON, INC., 400 N. 34th St., Ste. 100(98103-9703), pg. 995
SHARP HARTWIG, INC., 100 W. Harrison Plaza, South Tower, Ste. 500(98119), pg. 995
Signature Travel, Inc., 1201 Third Ave., 18th Fl.(98101), pg. 1166
SIMPSON INVESTMENT CO., 1201 Third Ave., Ste. 4900(98101-3009), pg. 1007
SKYWAY LUGGAGE CO., 10 Wall St.(98121), pg. 1009
STEVEDORING SERVICES OF AMERICA, 3415 11th Ave. SW(98134), pg. 1048
STUSSER ELECTRIC COMPANY, 660 S. Andover St.(98108), pg. 1055
SUPERIOR REPROGRAPHICS, 1933 5th Ave.(98101), pg. 1064
TMP Worldwide, Inc., 10700 Meridian Ave., No., Ste. 201(98133), pg. 1074
Thaw, Inc., 1212 1st Ave. So.(98134), pg. 917
TIME OIL COMPANY, 2737 W. Commodore Way(98199), pg. 1097
TOTEM RESOURCES CORPORATION, 1100 Olive Way, Ste. 1100(98101), pg. 1103
TRIDENT SEAFOOD CORPORATION, 5303 Shilshole Ave., NW(98107), pg. 1113
Unigard Insurance Co., 1215 Fourth Ave.(98161), pg. 596
Unigard Service Corp., 1215 Fourth Ave.(98161), pg. 596
Unionbay Division, 1700 Westlake Ave. North(98109), pg. 986
UNITED GRAPHICS, INC., 1401 Broadway(98122), pg. 1132
VanFed Appraisal Company, 1201 Third Ave.(98101), pg. 1166
VanFed Investment Service, Inc., 1201 Third Ave.(98101), pg. 1166
VanFed Mortgage Company, 1201 Third Ave.(98101), pg. 1166
Victoria Station of Washington, Inc., 1880 Fairview E.(98102), pg. 1150
VITA-MILK DAIRY, INC., 427 N.E. 72nd St.(98115), pg. 1153
WM Financial, Inc., 1201 Third Ave.(98101), pg. 1166
WM Life Insurance Company, 1203 Third Ave., 6th Fl.(98101), pg. 1166
WM Trust Company, 1201 Third Ave.(98101), pg. 1166
WARDS COVE PACKING COMPANY, 88 E. Hamlin St.(98109), pg. 1163
Washington Mutual Federal Savings Bank, 1201 Third Ave.(98101), pg. 1166
Washington Mutual Life Insurance Services, 1201 Third Ave.(98101), pg. 1166
WASHINGTON MUTUAL SAVINGS BANK, 1201 Third Ave.(98101), pg. 1166
WASHINGTON STATE DAIRY PRODUCTS COMMISSION, 1107 N.E. 45th, Ste. 205(98105), pg. 1167
Westco Products/Seattle, 9883 40th Ave. So.(98118), pg. 1178
Western International Media Corporation, 720 Olive Way, Ste. 1500(98101), pg. 1180
WRIGHT-SCHUCHART, INC., 425 Pontiuf Ave. North(98109), pg. 1204

Selah

TREE TOP, INC., 220 E. 2nd Ave.(98942), pg. 1109

Shelton

Simpson Timber Co., 3rd & Franklin(98584), pg. 1007

Snohomish

CENTRAL FEED MILLS, INC., 311 Maple St.(98290), pg. 232

Spokane

ALLIED SECURITY, INTERNATIONAL, W. 425 2nd Ave.(99204), pg. 40
American Sign & Indicator Corporation, N. 2310 Fancher Way(99212), pg. 1196
THE CALKINS MANUFACTURING COMPANY, Spokane Industrial Park, Building 15(99216), pg. 210
CHEMCENTRAL/Spokane, 6308 E. Sharp(99212), pg. 242
COLUMBIA PAINT CO., P.O. Box 4569(99202), pg. 265
Cox Cable Spokane, Inc., 1717 E. Buckeye(99207), pg. 294
E Z LOADER BOAT TRAILERS, INC., N. 717 Hamilton(99202), pg. 361
Farm Credit Bank of Spokane, W. 601 First Ave.(99204), pg. 405
Merchants Insurance Agency, North 7511 Freya(99220), pg. 1124
Murphy Favre Securities Services, Inc., 601 Riverside Ave., Fl. 9(99201), pg. 1166
NORWECO, INC., E. 4003 Broadway Ave.(99220), pg. 816
Peirone Produce Company, 524 Trent(99202), pg. 1124
ROSAUER'S SUPERMARKETS, INC., W. 1815 Garland(99205), pg. 947
Snyder Bakery, P.O. Box 305(99210), pg. 1134
U.R.M. Development Corp., North 7511 Freya(99220), pg. 1124
U.R.M. STORES, INC., N. 7511 Freya(99207), pg. 1124
WAGSTAFF INC., N. 3910 Flora Rd.(99216), pg. 1158

Stanwood

TWIN CITY FOODS, INC., P.O. Box 699(98292), pg. 1122

Tacoma

Adams Natural Peanut Butter, 3303 35th St.(98409), pg. 26
Almond Roca International, 1940 E. 11th St., P.O. Box 1596(98401), pg. 182
Atlas Foundry & Machine Co., 3021 S. Wikeson St.(98409), pg. 1073
BROADCAST SUPPLY WEST, 7012 27th St., W.(98466), pg. 177
BROWN & HALEY, 1940 E. 11th St.(98421), pg. 182
BUFFELEN WOODWORKING COMPANY, 1901 Taylor Way(98421), pg. 187
Cablecraft Inc., 4401 S. Orchard St.(98411), pg. 1120
CONCRETE TECHNOLOGY CORP., 1123 Port of Tacoma Rd.(98421), pg. 273
DWF of Tacoma, 5211 S. Washington(98406), pg. 331
INTERSTATE DISTRIBUTOR COMPANY, 11707 21st Ave. S.(98444), pg. 580
JAG Northwest Inc., 1616 E. St. Paul Ave.(98421), pg. 870
MANKE LUMBER COMPANY, INC., 1717 Marine View Dr.(98422), pg. 704
Nalleys Fine Foods, 3303 S. 35th St.(98411), pg. 25
PICKERING INDUSTRIES INC., 2102 D St. E.(98421), pg. 869
Pick's Cove Marina, 1930 East "D" St.(98466), pg. 870
PREMIER INDUSTRIES, INC., 1019 Pacific Ave., Ste. 1501(98402), pg. 887
PUGET SOUND PLYWOOD, INC., P.O. Box 1378(98401), pg. 899
ROMAN MEAL COMPANY, 2101 S. Tacoma Way(98409), pg. 945
JOSEPH SIMON & SONS, INC., 2202 E. River St.(98421), pg. 1006
Simpson Tacoma Kraft Co., P.O. Box 2133, (98421), pg. 1007
Smith Tractor & Equipment Co., 3607 20th S.E.(98424), pg. 1011
U.S. Oil & Refining Co., 3001 Marshall Ave.(98421), pg. 1097

Tukwila

CELLO BAG COMPANY, INC., P.O. Box 58810(98138), pg. 231
CONTINENTAL MILLS, INC., 18125 Andover Pk. W.(98188), pg. 279
GENERRA SPORTSWEAR COMPANY, INC., 18200 Segale Parkdrive B(98188), pg. 451
Monarch Foods, Inc., 1024 Andover Park E.(98188), pg. 994
S & W Fine Foods, P.O. Box 58550, 551 Strander Blvd.(98199), pg. 1111

Tumwater

Pabst Brewing Co./Tumwater, Schmidt Place & Custer Way(98502), pg. 959

Vancouver

CADET MANUFACTURING COMPANY, 2500 W. 4th Plain Blvd.(98660), pg. 207
Elixir Industries, Bldg. 376
GOULD PACKAGING, INC., P.O. Box 61506, (98666), pg. 473
LUMBER SYSTEMS, INC., 600 S.E. Maritime Way, Ste. 687
MICROPUMP CORPORATION, 1402 N.E. 136th Ave.(98684), pg. 749
NORTHWEST PAPER CONVERTING COMPANY, 6416 N.W. Whitney Rd.(98665), pg. 814
PROPERTY MANAGEMENT SERVICES, INC., 205 E. 11th St., Ste. 100(98660), pg. 894

Walla Walla

WALLA WALLA GRAIN GROWERS, INC., P.O. Box 310(99362), pg. 1160
Walla-Walla Union Bulletin, First & Poplar Sts.(99362), pg. 986

Woodinville

Anchor Post Products-Washington Div., 13202 NE 177th Pl.(98072), pg. 836
Cuizina Italia, Inc., 18744 - 142nd N.E.(98072), pg. 789

Yakima

Milky Way, Inc., 1602-A Rudkin Road(98901), pg. 689
NOEL CANNING CORPORATION, 1001 S. 1st St.(98907), pg. 808
SNOKIST GROWERS, 18 W. Mead(98902), pg. 1015
Snyder Bakery, 16 N. Third Ave.(98902), pg. 1134
STADELMAN FRUIT INC., 314 S. 2nd Ave.(98902), pg. 1034

Zillah

H & S Fruit Co., Cheyne Rd.(98953), pg. 1034

WEST VIRGINIA

Beckley

Mining Controls, Inc., P.O. Box 1141, (25801), pg. 609

Beverley

Colonial Millwork, Inc., P.O. Box 436, (25653), pg. 710

Bluefield

RISH EQUIPMENT COMPANY, Airport Rd. Near U.S. 52(24701), pg. 935
Tabor Machine Co., P.O. Box 3037, (24701), pg. 609

Bridgeport

Fourco Glass Co., P.O. Box 890, (26330), pg. 3

Charles Town

CHARLES TOWN RACES, INC., Flowing Springs Rd.(25414), pg. 240

Charleston

Broughton Foods Company, 114 Virginia(25302), pg. 181
Charleston Food Div., 114 Virginia St. W.(25302), pg. 181
EASTERN AMERICAN ENERGY CORPORATION, 501 E. 56th St.(25304-2393), pg. 363
GAI Consultants, Inc., 4715-C MacCorkle Ave., S.E.(25304), pg. 439
Higher Education Loan Program of West Virginia, 830 Charleston Natl. Plaza(25301), pg. 528
INDUSTRIAL RUBBER PRODUCTS COMPANY, 815 Court St.(25301), pg. 566
KANAWHA STEEL & EQUIPMENT CO., Edens Fork Rd. & I-77 Jct.(25312), pg. 615
Kentucky Berwind Land Company, 1150 One Valley Sq.(25301), pg. 145
MCJUNKIN CORPORATION, 835 Hillcrest Dr.(25311), pg. 730
Mountaineer Medical/Primacare I.V., 6810 MacCorkle Ave. SE(25304), pg. 1070
Stone & Thomas Advertising & Visual Offices, 208 Hale St.(25326), pg. 1051
Stone & Thomas Merchandising Offices, Lee & Dickinson Sts.(25326), pg. 1051
TROJAN STEEL CO., 1414 McCorkle Ave., S.W.(25303), pg. 1115
WEST VIRGINIA LOTTERY, 312 MacCorkle S.E.(25314), pg. 1178

Clarksburg

Broughton Foods Company, Rte. 2(26301), pg. 181

Dunbar

Allied Security Inc., 1222 Leone Lane(25064), pg. 39
Gilbert & Bennett, P.O. Box 158(25064), pg. 458

Elkins

Mongold Lumber Co., Rte. 1, Box 6, (26241), pg. 710

Fairmont

BROWNS LUMBER & SUPPLY COMPANY, P.O. Box 1589, (26554), pg. 183
HELMICK CORPORATION, 10th St. & Minor Ave.(26554), pg. 527

Harrisville

Troy Mills, Inc., 625 N. Pennsylvania Ave.(26362), pg. 1116

Hazelton

Coastal Lumber Company, P.O. Box 237(26535), pg. 257

Huntington

CHAPMAN PRINTING COMPANY, 2450 290 First Ave.(25703), pg. 239
J. H. FLETCHER & CO., 402 High St.(25702), pg. 418
Martha White Mills of W.Va., Inc., P.O. Box 346, (25708), pg. 1195
STATE ELECTRIC SUPPLY CO., 210 20th St.(25703), pg. 1040

Jane Lew

Pittsburgh Tube Jane Lew Div., (26378), pg. 873

Kingwood

PRESTON ENERGY INC., 202 E. High St.(26537), pg. 888

Mabscott

Perry & Hylton, Inc., 144 Whitestick St.(25871), pg. 1156
WRM, INC., 144 Whitestick St.(25871), pg. 1156

Morgantown

KING PRIME, INC., P.O. Box 4484(26505), pg. 631
Sterling Faucet Co., P. O. Box 798, Route 7 East(26505), pg. 640

Newell

BELLOFRAM CORP., State Rte. 2, Box 305(26050), pg. 136
THE HOMER LAUGHLIN CHINA COMPANY, Harrison St.(26050), pg. 661

Nitro

CONCORP, INC., P.O. Box 425(25143), pg. 272
Union Boiler Co., P.O. Box 425(25143), pg. 273

Oak Hill

Long-Airdox Company, 227 W. Maple Ave.(25901), pg. 711

Parkersburg

FAHLGREN MARTIN, INC., Rosemar Rd. & Seminary Dr.(26102), pg. 396
MARMAC CORPORATION, P.O. Box 1825, (26102), pg. 710
West Virginia Retail, 1513 Seventh St.(26101), pg. 492

Princeton

Norris Screen & Mfg., Inc., 614 South Wickham Avenue(24740), pg. 609

Ravenswood

RAVENSWOOD ALUMINUM CORP., Rt. 2 South(26164), pg. 914

Spelter

Meadowbrook Co., P.O. Box 184, Main St.(26438), pg. 335

Wheeling

Blaw Knox Rolls Division, 98 Peninsula St.(26003), pg. 156
BOURY INCORPORATED, 1311 Main St.(26003), pg. 168
Centre Foundry & Machine Co., 74 Warnwood Ave.(26003), pg. 357
PAR ENTERPRISES, INC., 1535 Market St.(26003), pg. 847
STONE & THOMAS, 1030 Main St.(26003), pg. 1051

WISCONSIN

Abbotsford

ABBYLAND FOODS, INC., 502 E. Linden St.(54405), pg. 10

Algoma

WISCONSIN LABEL CORPORATION, 1102 Jefferson St.(54201), pg. 1198

Antigo

SHELDONS' INC., 626 Center St.(54409-2496), pg. 996

Appleton

AAL Capital Management Corp., 4321 N. Ballard Rd.(54919), pg. 26
AAL Distributors Inc., 4321 N. Ballard Rd.(54919), pg. 26
AID ASSOCIATION FOR LUTHERANS, 4321 N. Ballard Rd.(54919), pg. 26
B & J Supply, Inc., 1117 West Washington Street(54913), pg. 63
Duralam, Inc., P.O. Box 862(54912), pg. 971
Fox River Paper Company, 200 E. Washington St., Ste. 300(54913), pg. 428
FOX VALLEY CORPORATION, 600 S. Vulcan St.(54915), pg. 427
MILLER ELECTRIC MFG. CO., 1635 W. Spencer(54914), pg. 754
PIERCE MANUFACTURING, INC., 2600 American Dr.(54915), pg. 870
RAYOVAC Corporation, 2600 North Ballard(54912), pg. 915
Sulpaco West, 600 E. Hancock St.(54912), pg. 1057

Arcadia

A-G CO-OP CREAMERY, 502 W. Main(54612), pg. 4
ARCADIA FRYERS, 502 W. Main St.(54612), pg. 80

Augusta

Bush Brothers & Company, 600 S. Highway St.(54727), pg. 196

Baraboo

Dairy Technology Ltd., Route 1198
Flambeau Corporation, 801 Lynn Ave.(53913), pg. 809
Flambeau Plastics Co., 801 Lynn Ave.(53913), pg. 809
NORDIC GROUP OF COMPANIES, LTD., 522 South Boulevard(53913), pg. 809
Perry/Baraboo, 1300 Sauk Ave.(53913), pg. 607
WISCONSIN DAIRIES COOPERATIVE, Hwy. 12 W.(53913), pg. 1197

Barron

JEROME FOODS INC., 34 N. 7th St.(54812), pg. 593

Geographic Index

Bear Creek

Flanagan Bros. Trucking Co., 400 Clark St.(54922), pg. 416
FLANAGAN BROTHERS, 400 Clark St.(54922), pg. 416

Beaver Dam

POWER KING PRODUCTS CO., 1100 Green Valley Rd.(53916), pg. 883

Beloit

ABC SUPPLY COMPANY, INC., 820 Broad St.(53511), pg. 2
FREEMAN SHOES COMPANY, 1 Freeman Lane(53511), pg. 431

Brookfield

BADER RUTTER & ASSOC., INC., Bishop's Woods Centre, 13555 Bishop's Court(53005), pg. 113
HYDRITE CHEMICAL COMPANY, 300 N. Patrick Blvd.(53045), pg. 556
Milwaukee Electric Tool Corp., 13135 W. Lisbon Rd.(53005), pg. 361
SARGENT & POTRATZ, INC., 250 N. Sunny Slope Rd.(53005), pg. 971

Brown Deer

KRIER FOODS, INC., 4555 W. Schroeder Dr., Ste. 190(53223), pg. 645

Burlington

LAVELLE INDUSTRIES INC., 665 McHenry St.(53105), pg. 661

Butler

WESTERN STATES ENVELOPE CO., 4480 N. 132nd St.(53007), pg. 1181

Caledonia

Wisconsin Services Corp., 561 S. Highway 41(53108), pg. 294

Cedarburg

Cedarburg Dairy, P.O. Box 287(53012), pg. 952
Wabash Pioneer Container Corp., N143 W6049 Pioneer Rd.(53012-0045), pg. 1183

Chilton

M-B COMPANY INC. OF WISCONSIN, 1200 So. Park St.(53014), pg. 691

Chippewa Falls

F & F Shoe Company, Palmer & Williams St.(54729), pg. 718
MASON SHOE MFG. CO., 1251 First Ave.(54729), pg. 718
SPECTRUM INDUSTRIES, INC., 1600 Johnson St.(54729), pg. 1029
Wissota Trader & B.A. Mason, 1313 First Ave.(54729), pg. 718
Wissota Trader Ltd., 1313 First Ave.(54729), pg. 718

Clintonville

FWD CORPORATION, 105 E. 12th St.(54929), pg. 395

Clyman

AUNT NELLIE'S FARM KITCHENS, INC., 640 Caughlin Rd.(53016), pg. 98

Cross Plains

ZANDER'S CREAMERY INC., 1300 Main St.(53528), pg. 1216

Curtis

Abbyland Pork Rack, 539 N. Meridan St.(54422), pg. 10

Dale

A & N Leasing, Box 132(54931), pg. 992
SERVICE MOTOR COMPANY, W. 9614 Hwy. 10(54931), pg. 992

Deerfield

Columbia ParCar Corp., P.O. Box One, One Golf Car Rd.(53531), pg. 809
LSJ Sportswear Inc., P.O. Box 528, 54 Golf Car Rd.(53531), pg. 739

Dond Du Lac

Wells Mfg. Corp., P.O. Box 70(54935), pg. 1123

Downers Grove

BURNSIDE CONSTRUCTION CO., 2400 Wisconsin Ave.(60515), pg. 194

Durand

Durand Canning Co., P.O. Box 188(54736), pg. 399

Eau Claire

PHOENIX STEEL, INC., 2800 Melby St.(54703), pg. 869

Elkhorn

Frank Holton Co., 320 N. Church St.(53121), pg. 665
Leblanc Case Co., 320 1/2 N. Church St.(53121), pg. 665

Elm Grove

Response Systems, Inc., 735 Wyenel Dr.(53122), pg. 553

Fennimore

RAYOVAC Corporation, P.O. Box 128, 100 Rayovac Court(53809), pg. 915

Fond du Lac

Service Motor Co., N 5560, Hwy. 151(54937), pg. 992
STEENBERG HOMES, INC., 300 Rolling Meadows Dr.(54936-1257), pg. 1045

Fort Atkinson

JONES DAIRY FARM, Jones Ave.(53538), pg. 603
Nasco, 901 Janesville Ave.(53538), pg. 452
J-STARR INDUSTRIES, INC., 801 Janesville Ave.(53538), pg. 1040
Redi-Serve Foods, P. O. Box 82(53538), pg. 826

Germantown

THE F. DOHMEN COMPANY, P.O. Box 9, W 194 N 11381 McCormick Dr.(53022), pg. 343
INDEPENDENT METALS, N115 W18945 Edison Dr.(53022-0247), pg. 565

Grantsburg

MCNALLY INDUSTRIES, INC., 216 S. Pine St.(54840), pg. 731

Green Bay

AMERICAN FOODS GROUP, P.O. Box 8547, 544 Acme St.(54308), pg. 54
FORT HOWARD CORPORATION, 1919 S. Broadway(54307), pg. 425
Green Bay Dressed Beef Company, 544 Acme(54308), pg. 54
GREEN BAY PACKAGING INC., 1700 N. Webster Ave.(54302), pg. 483
IMPERIAL, INC., 789 Packer Dr.(54304), pg. 564
Label Products & Design Division, 1836 Sal St.(54308), pg. 608
Packerland Packing Co., 2580 University Ave., P.O. Box 1184(54302), pg. 459
H. C. PRANGE COMPANY, 301 N. Washington St.(54301), pg. 884
Prange Specialty Stores Group, Inc., 2800 So. Ashland Ave.(54302), pg. 884
Prange Way, 301 N. Washington St.(54301), pg. 884
SCHNEIDER NATIONAL, INC., 3101 S. Packerland Dr.(54304), pg. 977
SCHREIBER FOODS, INC., 425 Pine St.(54301), pg. 978
SHADE COMPUTER FORMS CO., 333 Main St.(54301), pg. 994
SHOPKO STORES, INC., 700 Pilgrim Way(54307-9060), pg. 1000
Thimbles Specialty Stores, Inc., 2800 So. Ashland Ave.(54302), pg. 884
WLUK-TV, 787 Lombardi Ave.(54307), pg. 194

Greendale

Dewco Milwaukee Sales, 6235 Industrial Court(53129), pg. 1190

Greenfield

EVERBRITE, INC., 4949 S. 110th St.(53228), pg. 391

Hudson

Duro Paper Bag Mfg. Co., P.O. Box 247(54016), pg. 355
ERICKSON DIVERSIFIED CORP., 509 1/2 Second St.(54016), pg. 386
ERICKSON OIL PRODUCTS, INC., 1231 Industrial St.(54016), pg. 386

Hustisford

E.R. WAGNER MFG. CO. WAGNER PRODS. DIV., 331 Riverview Dr.(53034), pg. 1158

Janesville

OMNI FLIGHT HELICOPTERS, INC., Rte. 4031, Hwy. 515(53546), pg. 826
Rath Manufacturing, 2505 Foster Ave.(53545), pg. 350
Wisconsin & Calumet Railroad Company, 203 S. Pearl St.(53545-4521), pg. 246

Kaukauna

BADGER NORTHLAND INC., 1215 Hyland Ave.(54130), pg. 113

Kenosha

Dallas & Mavis Forwarding Co., Inc. (D & M), 4314 39th Ave.(53140), pg. 609
JOCKEY INTERNATIONAL, INC., 2300 60th(53140), pg. 595
Jupiter Corp. Transportation System, 4314 39th Ave.(53140), pg. 609
Jupiter Transportation Corp., 4314 39th Ave.(53140), pg. 609
Kenosha Twins Baseball Club, 7619 Sheridan Rd.(53141), pg. 758
G. LEBLANC CORPORATION, 7001 Leblanc Blvd.(53141-1415), pg. 665
Macwhyte Co., 2906 14th Ave.(53141), pg. 69
Martin Band Instrument Co., 9002 Sheridan Rd(53140), pg. 665

Kewaskum

REGAL WARE, INC., 1675 Reigle Dr.(53040), pg. 921

Kewaunee

Kewaunee Engineering Corp., 520 N. Main St.(52416), pg. 707
Leyse, 23 Kilbourn St.(54216), pg. 1155

Kiel

Lake to Lake Dairy, 1125 8th St.(53042), pg. 653

Kohler

JOHNSONVILLE FOODS, INC., 950 Woodlake Rd.(53044), pg. 601
KOHLER COMPANY, 444 Highland Dr.(53044), pg. 639

La Crosse

CONSOLIDATED MIDWEST, INC., 3600 Hwy. 157(54603), pg. 277
DAIRYLAND POWER COOPERATIVE, 3200 East Ave. S.(54602-0817), pg. 311
Everbrite LaCrosse, 3145 Airport Rd.(54601), pg. 391
Heileman Air Services, Ltd., 2709 Fanta Reed Rd.(54601), pg. 526
G. HEILEMAN BREWING CO., INC., 100 Harborview Plaza(54601), pg. 526
INLAND PRINTING CO., INC., 2009 W. Ave. S.(54601), pg. 570
Midwest Bottle Gas Company, 3600 Hwy. 157(54602), pg. 277
OVATION MARKETING, INC., 201 Main St., 6th Fl.(54601), pg. 832
W.A. ROOSEVELT CO., 2727 Commerce St.(54601), pg. 946
Trane Commercial Systems Group, 3600 Pammel Creek Rd.(54601), pg. 61

Lake Geneva

TSR, INC., 201 Sheridan Spring Rd.(53147), pg. 1075
ALBERT TROSTEL PACKINGS, LTD., 901 Maxwell St.(53147), pg. 1116
Albert Trostel Packings Ltd., 901 Maxwell St.(53147), pg. 1116

Lake Mills

HAMLIN, INC., 612 E. Lake St.(53551), pg. 503

Little Chute

KAUKAUNA CHEESE, Hwy. 00, Little Chute Indus. Park(54140), pg. 619

Lodi

DEC Alkar Div., 105 Spring St.(53555), pg. 309

Madison

A.B.P. MIDWEST, INC., 601 Atlas Ave.(53714), pg. 2
ADVERTISING, BOELTER & LINCOLN, 123 E. Doty St.(53703), pg. 21
Alpha Distributors Ltd., 1849 Wright St.(53704), pg. 66
American Family Financial Services, Inc., 3099 E. Washington Ave.(53783), pg. 52
American Family Life Insurance Co., 3099 E. Washington Ave.(53783), pg. 52
AMERICAN FAMILY MUTUAL INSURANCE CO., 3099 E. Washington Ave.(53783), pg. 51
American Family Mutual Insurance Co., 3099 E. Washington Ave.(53783), pg. 52
American Standard Insurance Company of Wisconsin, P.O. Box 7430, 3099 E. Washington Ave.(53783), pg. 52
AMERICAN TV & APPLIANCE OF MADISON, INC., 2404 W. Beltline Hwy.(53713), pg. 65
AmFam, Inc., 3099 E. Washington Ave.(53783), pg. 52
Association of Credit Union League Executives, P.O. Box 431(53701-0431), pg. 298
AUTO GLASS SPECIALISTS, 2814 Syene Rd.(53713), pg. 100
Berg Co., 1911 S. Stoughton Rd.(53716), pg. 309
CMCI Corp., 5910 Mineral Point Rd.(53701), pg. 205
CUDIS Insurance Society, Inc., 5910 Mineral Point Rd.(53701), pg. 205
CUMIS Insurance Society, Inc., 5910 Mineral Point Rd.(53701), pg. 205
CUNA Mutual Financial Services Corp., 5910 Mineral Point Rd.(53701), pg. 205
CUNA MUTUAL INSURANCE SOCIETY, 5910 Mineral Point Rd.(53705), pg. 205
CUNA Mutual Investment Corp., 5910 Mineral Point Rd.(53701), pg. 205
Credit Union Benefits Services, Inc., 5710 Mineral Point Road(53705), pg. 298
CREDIT UNION NATIONAL ASSOCIATION, 5710 Mineral Point Rd.(53705), pg. 298
CUNA Service Group, Inc., P.O. Box 431, (53705), pg. 298
DEC/Bou-Matic, 1919 S. Stoughton Rd.(53716), pg. 309
DEC INTERNATIONAL, INC., 1919 S. Stoughton Rd.(53716), pg. 308
DEMCO INC., 4810 Forest Run Rd.(53704), pg. 328
MARSHALL ERDMAN AND ASSOCIATES, INC., 5117 University Ave.(53705), pg. 385
Filène Research Institute, 5910 Mineral Point Rd.(53705), pg. 298
J.H. FINDORFF & SON, INC., 601 W. Wilson St.(53703), pg. 411
Flambeau Micro Co., 3696 Burke Rd.(53704), pg. 809
THE HIEBING GROUP, INC., 802 E. Gorham St.(53703), pg. 533
Impressions Inc., 2016 Winnebago St.(53704), pg. 370

LINDSAY, STONE & BRIGGS ADVERTISING, INC., 100 State St.(53703), pg. 676
MADISON DAIRY PRODUCE COMPANY, 1002 E. Washington Ave.(53703), pg. 699
MAUTZ PAINT COMPANY, 939 E. Washington Ave.(53703), pg. 722
Norlight, 579 D'Onofrio Dr., pg. 607
L. L. OLDS SEED COMPANY, 2901 Packers Ave.(53704), pg. 824
RAYOVAC CORPORATION, 601 Rayovac Dr.(53711-2497), pg. 915
RAYOVAC Corporation, 2317 Winnebago St.(53704), pg. 915
RESEARCH PRODUCTS CORPORATION, 1015 E. Washington Ave.(53703), pg. 928
ROCKY ROCOCO CORPORATION, 2122 Luann Lane, Ste. 15(53713), pg. 942
Sani-Matic Systems, 1915 S. Stoughton Rd.(53708), pg. 309
SCHAEPS ICE CREAM COMPANY, 5140 Division St.(53704), pg. 974
Sound Creation, 900 John Nolen Drive, 130B(53713), pg. 1148
STEPHAN & BRADY, INCORPORATED, 1850 Hoffman St.(53701), pg. 1046
UNIVERSITY BOOK STORE, 711 State St.(53703), pg. 1139
WALDBILLIG & BESTEMAN, INC., 6225 University Ave.(53705), pg. 1159
World Council of Credit Unions, 5810 Mineral Point Rd.(53705), pg. 298

Manitowoc

HERESITE PROTECTIVE COATINGS INC., P.O. Box 250, (54221), pg. 531
INVINCIBLE METAL FURNITURE CO., 842 S. 26th St.(54220), pg. 582
LAKESIDE FOODS, INC., PO Box 1327, 508 Jay St.(54220), pg. 651

Marathon

MARATHON CHEESE CORP., 304 East St.(54448), pg. 705

Marinette

MARINETTE MARINE CORPORATION, 1600 Ely St.(54143-0198), pg. 707

Marshfield

Graham Mfg. Co., 1920 E. 26th St.(54449), pg. 361
Wick Bldg. Systems Inc. Manufactured Homes Div., 2301 E. 4th St.(54449), pg. 1188

Mauston

DUMORE CORPORATION, 1030 Veteran St.(53948), pg. 352

Mayville

MAYVILLE ENGINEERING CO., INC., 715 South St.(53050), pg. 725
Mayville Metal Products Division, First & Highland, P.O. Box 28(53050), pg. 275

Mazomanie

WICK BUILDING SYSTEMS, 404 Walter Rd.(53560), pg. 1188

Medford

Hurd Millwork Company, Inc., 520 S. Whelen Ave.(54451), pg. 1123

Menomonee Falls

Alro Specialty Metals, Menomonee Falls, N49 W13545 Campbell Dr.(53051), pg. 44
ALTO SHAAM INC., W164 N9221 Water St.(53052), pg. 46
ARANDELL-SCHMIDT CORPORATION, N82 W. 13118 Leon Rd.(53051), pg. 79
BRADLEY CORPORATION, W. 142 N. 9101 Fountain Blvd.(53051), pg. 170
THE BRADY COMPANY, N80 W12878 Fond du Lac Ave.(53051), pg. 171
KUHLMAN, INC., N57 WI 3666 Reichert Ave.(53051), pg. 646

Mequon

BIRDSALL VOSS & KLOPPENBURG, INC., 1355 W. Towne Square Rd.(53092), pg. 152
DDM/TMP Worldwide, 10144 N. Port Washington Rd.(53092), pg. 1074
M.W. KASCH COMPANY, 5401 W. Donges Bay Rd.(53092), pg. 617
YPMS/TMP Worldwide, Inc., 10144 N. Port Washington Rd.(53092), pg. 1074

Merrill

WEINBRENNER SHOE COMPANY, INC., 108 So. Polk St.(54452), pg. 1173

Middleton

CUNA Mortgage Corporation, 8410 Greenbay Blvd.(53562), pg. 298
Madison National Life Insurance Co., Inc., 6120 University Ave.(53562), pg. 451

Milwaukee

A.B. DATA, LTD., 8050 N. Port Washington Rd.(53217), pg. 1
Advanced Detection Systems, 4740 W. Electric Ave.(53219), pg. 1148
ALCO/Belgium Foundries, 1930 S. Fourth St.(53204), pg. 525
Allright Parking of Milwaukee, Inc., 710 N. Plankington Ave., Ste. 726(53202), pg. 42
AMBULATORY ONE AMERICA INC., 325 E. Chicago(53202), pg. 47
AMERICAN APPRAISAL ASSOCIATES, INC., 100 E. Wisconsin Ave., Ste. 2100(53202), pg. 48
American Appraisal Capital Services, Inc., 525 E. Michigan St.(53202), pg. 48
The American Appraisal Co., 525 E. Michigan St.(53201), pg. 48
American Bio Synthetics, 710 W. National Ave.(53204), pg. 134
AMPCO METAL INCORPORATED, 1745 S. 38th St.(53215), pg. 67
ANDREWS/MAUTNER, INC., 600 N. Broadway(53202), pg. 74
ASTRONAUTICS CORP. OF AMERICA, 4115 N. Teutonia Ave.(53209), pg. 93
BADGER TRUCK CENTER, INC., 2326 W. St. Paul Ave.(53233), pg. 113
BANKMANAGERS CORP., 7540 W. Capitol Dr.(53216), pg. 118
E. H. Boeckh Co., 525 E. Michigan St.(53202), pg. 48
Bradley Washroom Accessories Div., 7020 Parkland Ct.(53223), pg. 170
BRUNER CORPORATION, 500W. Oklahoma Ave.(53207), pg. 184
CT&I Corp. of Wisconsin, 6030 North 60th St.(53218), pg. 246
Carnes Company, Inc., 10210 W. Lincoln Ave.(53227), pg. 1148
Castaways of Wisconsin, Inc., 550 N. Harbor Dr.(53202), pg. 1029
Cramer-Krasselt, 733 N. Van Buren(53202), pg. 296
CRAMER-KRASSELT, 733 N. Van Buren(53202), pg. 296
DCI MARKETING, 2727 W. Good Hope Rd.(53209), pg. 308
DWF of Milwaukee, Inc., 425 W. Walnut(53212), pg. 331
DELTA RESINS & REFRACTORIES, INC., 6263 N. Teutonia Ave.(53209), pg. 327
Dings Dynamics Co., 4740 W. Electric Ave.(53219), pg. 1148
Dings Magnetic Co., 4740 W. Electric Ave.(53219), pg. 1148
Downey, Inc., 2203 W. Michigan St.(53233), pg. 610
EMS Central Regional Office (Corporate), 12000 W. Park Pl.(53224), pg. 370
EFFECTIVE MANAGEMENT SYSTEMS, 12000 W. Park Place(53224-3026), pg. 370
WILLIAM EISNER & ASSOCIATES INC., P.O. Box 28800(53220), pg. 372
FCN ADVERTISING, 10850 W. Park Place, Ste. 1200(53224), pg. 394
FOSTER PONTIAC, INC., 3636 S. 27th St.(53221), pg. 426
FRANKENBERRY, LAUGHLIN & CONSTABLE, INC., 207 E. Michigan St.(53202), pg. 429
Gebhardt Industrial Refrigeration, Inc., 3625 W. Elm St.(53209), pg. 1152
GREDE FOUNDRIES, INC., 9898 W. Bluemound Rd.(53226), pg. 483
Grede New Castle, Inc, 9898 W. Bluemound Rd(53226), pg. 483
Grede Permcast, Inc., 9898 W. Bluemound Rd.(53226), pg. 483
Grede Transport, Inc., 9898 W. Bluemound Rd.(53226), pg. 483
Grede Vassar, Inc., 9898 W. Bluemound Rd.(53226), pg. 483
Halper Bros., 233 E. Chicago St.(53201), pg. 925
HELWIG CARBON PRODUCTS, INC., 8900 W. Tower Ave.(53224), pg. 528
HENRI'S FOOD PRODUCTS CO., INC., 2730 W. Silver Spring Dr.(53209), pg. 530
HOFFMAN YORK & COMPTON, Plaza East, 330 E. Kilbourn Ave.(53202), pg. 538
INSTRUMENTARIUM IMAGING, INC., 300 W. Edgerton Ave.(53207), pg. 572
INTREPID CORP., 11925 W. Carmen Ave.(53225), pg. 581
J H COLLECTIBLES, 200 W. Vogel(53207), pg. 584
JOURNAL COMMUNICATIONS INC., 333 W. State St.(53201), pg. 607
Journal/Sentinel Inc., 333 W. State St.(53201), pg. 607
K & G OF WISCONSIN, INC., 2203 W. Wisconsin Ave.(53233), pg. 610
K-Promotions, Inc., 3825 W. Green Tree Rd.(53209), pg. 221
KALMBACH PUBLISHING CO., 21027 Crossroads Circle(53187), pg. 615
Ladish Malting Co., P.O. Box 2044(53201), pg. 219
LAPPIN ELECTRIC COMPANY, 1300 N. 4th St.(53212), pg. 658
MGIC Investment Corporation, P.O. Box 488, (53201), pg. 815
MRC Telecommunications Inc., 918 N. 4th St.(53203), pg. 607
MAYNARD STEEL CASTING COMPANY, 2856 S. 27th St.(53234), pg. 725
McClean-Anderson, 10600 W. Glenbrook Ct.(53212), pg. 888
MCDONALD DAVIS & ASSOCIATES, INC., 250 W. Coventry Ct.(53217), pg. 728
Media Management, Ste. 1000, 111 E. Kilbourn Ave.(53202), pg. 746
MERIDIAN INDUSTRIES, INC., 100 E. Wisconsin, Ste. 2750(53202), pg. 740
MEYER & WALLIS, INC., 111 E. Kilbourn Ave., Ste. 1000(53202), pg. 746
H. C. MILLER COMPANY, 8111 N. 87th St.(53224), pg. 754
MILWAUKEE BUCKS, INC., 1001 N. 4th St.(53203), pg. 756
The Milwaukee Journal, 333 W. State St.(53203), pg. 607
Milwaukee Sentinel, 918 N. 4th St.(53203), pg. 607
NELSON & SCHMIDT, INC., 111 E. Wisconsin Ave., Ste. 1000(53202), pg. 797
Northern Computers Inc., 5007 S. Howell Ave.(53207), pg. 65
NORTHWESTERN MUTUAL LIFE INSURANCE CO., 720 E. Wisconsin Ave.(53202), pg. 815
THE OLDENBURG GROUP COMPANIES, 8600 W. Bradley(53224), pg. 824
Pabst Brewing Co./Milwaukee, 917 W. Juneau Ave.(53233), pg. 959
Park Bank, 330 E. Kilbourn Ave.(53202), pg. 118
Penthouse Knitting Mills, 233 E. Chicago St.(53201), pg. 925
Perry/Milwaukee, 5100 W. Brown Deer Rd.(53223), pg. 607
RELIABLE KNITTING WORKS, 233 E. Chicago St.(53202), pg. 924
RITE-HITE CORPORATION, 8900 No. Arbon Dr.(53223), pg. 936
Roberts Foundry Co., Inc., 9898 W. Bluemound Rd.(53226), pg. 483
ROMAN ELECTRIC COMPANY, INC., 640 S. 70th St.(53214), pg. 945
Roundy's Inc., Milwaukee Div., 11300 W. Burleigh St.(53201), pg. 952
Scientific Dust Collectors, 4740 W. Electric Ave.(53219), pg. 1148
EVERETT SMITH INVESTMENT CO. OF DELAWARE, 800 N. Marshall St.(53202), pg. 1013
STERLING, INC., 5200 W. Clinton Ave.(53223), pg. 1047
Technical Publishing, 111 E. Wisconsin Ave.(53202), pg. 797
Towne Realty, Inc., 710 No. Plankington(53203), pg. 1219
ALBERT TROSTEL & SONS COMPANY, 10201 W. Lincoln Ave., Ste. 405(53227), pg. 1116
Tulip Corp., Milwaukee Div., 714 E. Keefe Ave.(53215), pg. 1119
FRED USINGER, INC., 1030 N. Old World Third St.(53203), pg. 1140
VENTUREDYNE, LTD., 10201 W. Lincoln Ave., Ste. 400(53227), pg. 1148
Vilter Export Corp., 2217 S. First St.(53207), pg. 1152
VILTER MANUFACTURING CORPORATION, 2217 S. First St.(53207), pg. 1152
WISN-AM, 759 N. 19th St.(53233), pg. 522
WISN Division, 759 N. 19th St.(53233), pg. 522
WISN-TV, 759 N. 19th St.(53233), pg. 522
WLTQ-FM, 759 N. 19th St.(53233), pg. 522
WTMJ, Inc., 720 E. Capitol Dr.(53212), pg. 608
WESTERN INDUSTRIES, INC., 1211 N. 62nd St.(53213), pg. 1179
WROUGHT WASHER MFG., INC., 2100 S. Bay St.(53207), pg. 1205
ZILBER, LTD., 710 N. Plankington Ave.(53203), pg. 1219

Monroe

Dorman-Roth Foods Div., Inc., 105 Third St.(53566), pg. 346
THE SWISS COLONY, 1112-7th Ave.(53566), pg. 1068

Mount Horeb

Janlin Plastic Inc., 1204 E. Lincoln St.(53572), pg. 875
Ryser Bros. of Wisconsin, 105 S. 2nd St.(53572), pg. 958

Nashotah

CONTROLLED SYSTEMS OF WISCONSIN, INC., W32882 Watertown Plank Rd.(53058), pg. 281
DICKTEN & MASCH MANUFACTURING CO., N44 W. 3341 Watertown Plank Rd.(53058), pg. 336

Neenah

Atlas Tag & Label Inc., P.O. Box 638(54957), pg. 153
JEWELERS MUTUAL INSURANCE COMPANY, 24 Jewelers Park Dr.(54957-0468), pg. 593
J. J. KELLER & ASSOCIATES, INC., 3003 W. Breezewood Lane(54957-0368), pg. 620
MENASHA CORPORATION, 1645 Bergstrom Rd.(54957-0818), pg. 738
Menasha Development Corporation, P.O. Box 367(54957-0367), pg. 739
Menasha Foreign Sales Corporation, P.O. Box 367(54957-0367), pg. 739
Menasha Transport Inc., P.O. Box 367(54957-0367), pg. 739
NEENAH FOUNDRY COMPANY, 2121 Brooks Ave.(54956), pg. 797
Stratis Corporation, 159 Old Orchard Ln.(54956), pg. 867

New Berlin

A & A MANUFACTURING CO., 2300 S. Calhoun Rd.(53151), pg. 1
CHEMCENTRAL/Milwaukee, 2400 S. 170th St.(53151), pg. 242
CHENEY COMPANY, 2445 S. Calhoun Rd.(53151), pg. 242
Frankulin Tool & Mfg. Co., 16680 W. Cleveland Ave.(53151), pg. 1205
G & L PRODUCTS, INC., 16900 W. Victor Rd.(53151), pg. 438
INDUSTRIAL TOWEL & UNIFORM, 2700 S. 160th St.(53151), pg. 567
Petron Corporation, 16700 Glendale Dr.(53151), pg. 1172
PLASTIC ENGINEERING COMPONENTS INC., 2665 So. Moorland Ave., Ste. 210(53151), pg. 875
TEKRA CORPORATION, 16700 W. Lincoln Ave.(53151), pg. 1084
U.S. MUSIC CORPORATION, 2885 S. James Dr.(53151), pg. 1136

New Richmond

ST. CROIX PRESS, INC., 1185 S. Knowles Hwy. 65(54017), pg. 966

Oconomowoc

FIBERESIN INDUSTRIES INC., P.O. Box 88, 37031 E. Wisconsin Ave.(53066), pg. 408
LA BELLE INDUSTRIES, INC., 510 S. Worthington(53066), pg. 648
Quest Electronics Div., 510 S. Worthington(53066), pg. 648

Oshkosh

CANDLE CORPORATION OF AMERICA, 627 Bay Shore Dr.(54901), pg. 214
Lapham Hickey Steel (WI), 2585 W. 20th Ave.(54903), pg. 658

Pewaukee

CENTURY FENCE COMPANY, N 11 West 24711 Silvernal Rd.(53072), pg. 235
QUAD/GRAPHICS, INC., W224 N3322 Duplainville Rd.(53072-4195), pg. 902
ROUNDY'S, INC., 23000 Roundy Dr.(53072), pg. 952
Stark Candy Company, Candy Lane & Hickory(53072), pg. 1123

Phillips

PHILLIPS PLASTICS CORPORATION, P.O. Box 29, Seven Long Lake Dr.(54555), pg. 867

Platteville

BRODBECK ENTERPRISES, INC., 1035 E. Hwy. 151(53818), pg. 178
Old Wisconsin Cheese Co., Inc., 1085 E. Mineral St.(53818), pg. 186

Plover

Plover BLFC Branch, 5680 Plover Rd.(54467), pg. 946

Plymouth

Great Lakes Of Wisconsin, 801 South St.(53073), pg. 481
PLYMOUTH CREAMERIES, INC., Schwartz St. & Factory Rd.(53073), pg. 877
Sargento Cheese Co., N. Sunset Dr.(53073), pg. 971
Sargento Food Service Corp., P.O. Box 390(53073), pg. 971
SARGENTO INCORPORATED, 1 Persnickety Place(53073), pg. 971
Specialty Foods Group, P.O. Box 350, (53073), pg. 971

Port Washington

ALLEN-EDMONDS SHOE CORP., 201 E. Seven Hills Rd.(53074), pg. 36
Modern Equipment Co., Inc., P.O. Box 266(53074), pg. 32
SIMPLICITY MANUFACTURING, INC., 500 N. Spring St.(53074), pg. 1006
Tornado Products, Inc., 500 N. Spring St.(53074), pg. 1007
TRAK INTERNATIONAL, INC., 369 W. Western Ave.(53074), pg. 1106
Woodlore, 3820 Highway KW(53074), pg. 36

Portage

PENDA CORPORATION, N7660 Industrial Rd.(53901), pg. 857
RAYOVAC Corporation, 2851 Portage Rd.(53901), pg. 915

Prairie du Sac

MUELLER SPORTS MEDICINE, INC., One Quench Dr.(53578), pg. 774

Racine

ANDIS COMPANY, 1718 Layard Ave.(53404), pg. 74
Benjamin Sheridan Co., 2600 Chicory Rd.(53403), pg. 300
COLOR ARTS, INC., 1840 Oakdale Ave.(53406), pg. 264
Hedland, 2200 South St.(53404), pg. 909
S. C. JOHNSON & SON, INC., 1525 Howe St.(53403), pg. 599
Johnson Venture Capital, Inc., 1525 Howe St.(53403), pg. 599
Johnson Wax Development Corp., 4041 N. Main St.(53402), pg. 599
MASTER APPLIANCE CORP., 2420 18th St.(53403), pg. 719
Printing Developments, Inc., 2010 Indiana St.(53405), pg. 801
Pugh Marina, 200 Dodge St.(53402), pg. 899
PUGH OIL COMPANY, 200 Dodge St.(53402), pg. 899
Pugh Oil Company, 200 Dodge St.(53402), pg. 899
RACINE FEDERATED, INC., 2200 South St.(53404), pg. 909
RAINFAIR, INC., 3600 S. Memorial Dr.(53404), pg. 910
Rydelle Laboratories, 1525 Howe St.(53403), pg. 599
White Flash Oil Co., 200 Dodge St.(53402), pg. 899
The Wyco Tool Co., 2200 South St.(53404), pg. 909
YOUNG RADIATOR COMPANY, 2825 Four Mile Rd.(53404), pg. 1210

Random Lake

TIMES PRINTING COMPANY, INC., 453 5th St.(53075), pg. 1098

Reedsburg

Seats Incorporated, 1515 Industrial St.(53959), pg. 810

Rice Lake

Roosevelt Rice Lake Branch, 310 W. Coleman(54868), pg. 946

Ripon

CONDON OIL COMPANY, INC., 126 E. Jackson St.(54971), pg. 273
LYKE CORPORATION, 656 Douglas St.(54971), pg. 688
RIPON FOODS, INC., 420 E. Oshkosh(54971), pg. 935

River Falls

Vollrath Refrigeration Inc., 719 St. Croix(54022), pg. 1155

Rothschild

WAUSAU HOMES, INC., Hwy. 51 South(54474), pg. 1168

Saint Nazianz

MILLER-ST. NAZIANZ, INC., 511 E. Main St.(54232-0127), pg. 755

Sauk City

RAYOVAC Corporation, 1100 Dallas St.(53583), pg. 915

Shaboygan Falls

RICHARDSON INDUSTRIES, INC., Rte. 2 Hwy. PP(53085), pg. 932

Shawano

MORNING GLORY FARMS REGION, 116 N. Main St.(54166), pg. 770

Sheboygan

ECLIPSE MANUFACTURING COMPANY, 1828 Oakland Ave.(53082-0788), pg. 367
JACOBSON ROST, INC., 529 Ontario Ave.(53081), pg. 588
NEMSCHOFF CHAIRS, INC., 2218 W. Water(53081), pg. 798
Old Wisconsin Sausage, 2107 S. 17th St.(53081), pg. 186
POLAR WARE COMPANY, 2806 N. 15th St.(53083), pg. 878
SCHREIER MALTING CO., 704 S. 15th St.(53081), pg. 978
Smokie Products, Inc., 2107 17th St.(53037), pg. 186
TORKE COFFEE COMPANY, INC., 3455 Paine Ave.(53081), pg. 1102
THE VOLLRATH COMPANY INC., 1236 N. 18th St.(53082), pg. 1154
WIGWAM MILLS, INC., 3402 Crocker Ave.(53081), pg. 1189

Sheboygan Falls

CURT G. JOA, INC., P.O. Box 903, Crocker Ave.(53085-0903), pg. 594
Johnsonville Sausage, Inc., County Trunk J(53085), pg. 601
RICHARDSON BROTHERS CO., Hwy. PP(53085), pg. 932

Shiocton

Shiocton Kraut Co., P.O. Box 27(54170), pg. 196

South Milwaukee

B-E HOLDINGS INC., 1100 Milwaukee Ave.(53172), pg. 106
BUCYRUS-ERIE COMPANY, 1100 Milwaukee Ave.(53172), pg. 186
Minserco, Inc., 1100 Milwaukee Ave.(53172), pg. 186

Stanley

Stanley Drying Company, P.O. Box 120, (54768), pg. 309

Staughton

Zalk Joseph Fabrications, Inc., 400 Industrial Dr.(53589), pg. 525

Stevens Point

THE COPPS CORP., 2828 Wayne St.(54481), pg. 285
Sentry Insurance, A Mutual Company, 1800 No. Point Dr.(54481), pg. 990
SENTRY INSURANCE, A MUTUAL COMPANY, 1800 N. Point Dr.(54481), pg. 990
WORZALLA PUBLISHING CO., INC., 3535 Jefferson St.(54481), pg. 1204

Sturgeon Bay

MTI Leasing, Ltd., 49 E. Yew St.(54235), pg. 707
MARINE TRAVELIFT, INC., 49 E. Yew St.(54235), pg. 707
PETERSON BUILDERS, INC., 101 Pennsylvania St.(54235), pg. 864
Shuttlelift, Inc., 49 E. Yew St.(54235), pg. 707

Thiensville

AMERICA OUTDOORS LTD, 501 N. Main St.(53092), pg. 48
Rental America, 505 N. Main St.(53092), pg. 48

Tomah

BURNSTAD BROTHERS, INC., Hwy. 12 & 16 E.(54660), pg. 194

Two Rivers

Aristo Manufacturing Co., 1704 Monroe St.(54241), pg. 742
THE METAL WARE CORP., 1700 Monroe St.(54241), pg. 741

Walworth

MINIATURE PRECISION COMPONENTS, Walworth Industrial Park(53184), pg. 757

Washburn

First American Bank of Apostle Islands, P.O. Box 278, (54891), pg. 173

Waterloo

Perry Printing Corp., 575 W. Madison St.(53594), pg. 607
Trek Bicycle Corporation, 801 W. Madison St.(53594), pg. 581

Waukesha

ALLOY PRODUCTS CORPORATION, P.O. Box 529(53187), pg. 41
Classified Insurance Company, Inc., 20800 Swenson Dr., Ste. 200(53187-1407), pg. 755
EVANS BROTHERS COMPANY, INC., W. 229 N. 1492 Westwood Dr.(53187), pg. 390
HOLOUBEK INC., W238 N1800 Rockwood Dr.(53188), pg. 540
MARKETING SERVICES UNLTD., W220 N507 Springdale Rd.(53187), pg. 709
ORTHO-KINETICS, INC., W220 N507 Springdale Rd.(53186), pg. 830
PROVIMI VEAL CORPORATION, 20800 Swenson Dr., Ste. 440(53186), pg. 896
STOLPER-FABRALLOY CO., 115 N. Janecek Rd.(53186), pg. 1050
WAUKESHA FOUNDRY INC., 1300 Lincoln Ave.(53186), pg. 1168

Waupaca

ADD, Inc., P.O. Box 267, (54981), pg. 607

Waupun

ALTO DAIRY COOPERATIVE, N. 3545 County EE(53963), pg. 45
NATIONAL RIVET & MANUFACTURING COMPANY, 21 E. Jefferson St.(53963), pg. 793

Wausau

EMPLOYERS INSURANCE OF WAUSAU A MUTUAL CO., 2000 Westwood Dr.(54401), pg. 380
Employers Insurance of Wausau a Mutual Co., 2000 Westwood Dr.(54401), pg. 795
THE HAMMERBLOW CORP., 1000 First St.(54401), pg. 504
MARATHON ELECTRIC MANUFACTURING CORP., 100 E. Randolph(54401), pg. 705
WIFC-FM, 602 Jefferson St.(54401), pg. 608
WSAU-AM, 602 Jefferson St.(54401), pg. 608
Wausau Life Insurance Company, 2000 Westwood Dr.(54401), pg. 380
Wausau Underwriters Life Insurance Company, 2400 Westwood Dr.(54401), pg. 380
Wipfli, Ullrich, Bertelson, 119 Scott Street(54402), pg. 370

Wauwatosa

FINDLEY ADHESIVES, INC., 11320 Watertown Plank Rd.(53226-3413), pg. 410
Kilsby-Roberts/Milwaukee, 11610 W. North Ave.(53226), pg. 606

West Allis

Directory Data Management, 2514 So. 102nd St.(53227), pg. 1074
PRESSED STEEL TANK CO., INC., 1445 S. 66th St.(53214), pg. 887

West Bend

AG Components Div., Hwy. 45 N.(53095), pg. 1169
AMITY LEATHER PRODUCTS COMPANY, 735 S. Main St.(53095), pg. 67
ENGER-KRESS COMPANY, 151 Wisconsin St.(53095), pg. 381
Rolfs, 735 S. Main St.(53095), pg. 67
SERIGRAPH, INC., 760 Indiana Ave.(53095), pg. 991
WEASLER ENGINEERING INC., Hwy. 45 N.(53095), pg. 1169
WESBAR CORPORATION, 4201 County Hwy. P(53095), pg. 1176

West Columbus

Dakota Bake-N-Serv, Hwy. 16 West, P.O. Box 410(53925), pg. 931

Weyauwega

Benson Corp., 512 N. Mill St.(54983), pg. 447

Whitewater

Polymer Technologies, 369 N. Newcomb St.(53190), pg. 697

Wonewoc

RAYOVAC Corporation, 503 Vine St.(53968), pg. 915

WYOMING

Afton

MAVERIK COUNTRY STORES, INC., P.O. Box 457(83110), pg. 722

Geographic Index

Casper

B & B HOMES CORPORATION, 3283 N. Nine Mile Rd.(82604), pg. 105
Belle Fourche Pipeline Co., 895 W. River Cross Rd.(82602), pg. 1117
Black Hills Trucking Co., 895 W. River Cross Rd.(82602), pg. 1117
CRUM ELECTRIC SUPPLY CO., INC., 460 Circle Drive(82601), pg. 303
Double Diamond Dist. Inc., 3400 E. Yellowstone Hwy.(82609), pg. 1204
Eighty Eight Oil Co., 895 W. River Cross Rd.(82602), pg. 1117
KGWC-TV, 304 N. Center(82602), pg. 1043
MINI MART, INC., 907 N. Poplar, Ste. 260(82601), pg. 757
RISSLER & MCMURRY COMPANY, 3245 N. Salt Creek Hwy.(82601), pg. 936
TRUE COMPANIES, 895 W. River Cross Rd.(82602), pg. 1117
True Drilling Co., P.O. Box 2360(82602), pg. 1117
True Oil Co., 895 W. River Cross Rd.(82602), pg. 1117
True Ranches, 895 W. River Cross Rd.(82602), pg. 1117
WYOMING MACHINE COMPANY, 5300 W. Old Yellowstone(82604), pg. 1206

Cheyenne

AMERICAN WYOTT CORPORATION, 1938 Wyott Dr.(82007), pg. 65
CBS Signs, Inc., 1805 Pacific Ave.(82007), pg. 472
CHEYENNE OUTFITTERS, INC., P.O. Box 12013(82003), pg. 244
FLEISCHLI OIL COMPANY, INC., 2234 W. Lincoln Way(82001), pg. 417
Johnson Storage & Moving, Cheyenne, 204 N. American Rd.(82001), pg. 601
KGWN-TV, 2923 E. Lincolnway(82001), pg. 1043
TACO JOHN'S INTERNATIONAL, INC., P.O. Box 1589, (82003-1589), pg. 1076
UNICOVER CORPORATION, One Unicover Center(82008), pg. 1126

Gillette

LARRYS, INC., 2020 Schoonover Rd.(82716), pg. 659

Greybull

BIG HORN CO-OP MARKETING ASSOCIATION, 346 S. 6th(82426), pg. 149

Jackson

MEDTECH LABORATORIES, INC., 3510 N. Lake Creek Dr.(83001), pg. 736

Laramie

BANNER ASSOCIATES INC., 620 Plaza Ct.(82070), pg. 118
Inter-Mountain Rentals, P.O. Box 1026, 2458 N. 9th St.(82070), pg. 908

Mills

WOTCO INC., 415 First St.(82602), pg. 1204

Riverton

GILPATRICK CONSTRUCTION COMPANY, 714 W. Monroe(82501), pg. 460

Teton Village

JACKSON HOLE SKI RESORT, 7658 N. Teewinot, Chairlift Rd.(83025), pg. 587

ARGENTINA
Buenos Aires

Amway Argentina, Inc., Maipu 939-P.B., pg. 70
Ayer Vazquez S.A. de Publicidad, Av. Callao 1046, 3 Piso, pg. 104
Berlitz Schools of Languages of Argentina S.A., Avenida Santa Fe 1605, pg. 143
Leo Burnett Co., Inc. Sucursal Argentina, Carlos Pellegrini 1363, 12th Fl., pg. 192
CW Communicacaciones S/A, Av Belgrano 406-Piso 9, pg. 577
Cicero/BSB Publicidad S.A., Paraguay 610, Piso 23, pg. 111
Copetro, S.A., Bouchard 644, pg. 545
Dentsply Argentina S.A.C.I., 3933/35 Zabala, pg. 330
IDC Argentina, CW Communications S/A, pg. 577
S. C. Johnson & Son de Argentina S.A.I.C., Av. Marquez 2249, pg. 599
Korn/Ferry International, Avenida Quintana 585, pg. 643
Mary Kay Cosmetics, S.A., Corrientes 345, pg. 717
Young & Rubicam Argentina, Paseo Colon 275, Piso 13, pg. 1213

AUSTRALIA
Adelaide

George Patterson Pty. Limited, 82 East Terrace, pg. 112

Alexandria

GAF (Australasia) Pty. Ltd., Beaconsfield, pg. 438

Altona

Rotor Dynamics Pty. Ltd., 1 Millers Road, pg. 141

Artarmon

Denver Equipment Pty., Ltd., 1st. Fl., 40 Dickson Ave., pg. 331

Bayswater

Thermon Australia, Private Bag 32, P.O. Box Bayswater 3153, pg. 1092

Beverly

Hannaford Seedmaster Services Australia (Pty) Ltd., 52 East Avenue, pg. 1129

Braeside

E.C. DeWitt & Company (Aust.) Pty. Ltd., 25 Macbeth St., pg. 417

Brisbane

Bucyrus (Australia) Proprietary Ltd., 9th Floor G.W.A. House, 10 Market Street, pg. 186
George Patterson (Brisbane) Pty Ltd., 459/461 Adelaide St., pg. 112

Brookvale

Simplex Intl. Time Equip. Pty. Ltd., 32 Cross Street P.O. Box 561, pg. 1006

Camberwell

Spalding Australia Pty. Ltd., P.O. Box 17, 969 Burke Rd.(3124), pg. 1025

Castle Hill

Amway of Australia Pty. Ltd., 46 Carrington Rd., P.O. Box 202, pg. 71

Chatswood

Ingersoll Engineers Pty. Ltd., 47 Neridah St., Ste. 39, pg. 568

Collingwood

Dentsply (Australia) Pty. Ltd., 58 Rupert Col., pg. 330

Cremorne

Chiat/Day/Mojo, 339 Military Rd., pg. 245

Crows Nest

IDG Communications PTY Ltd., 37-43 Alexander St., pg. 577
Mattingly & Partners/Sydney, 83 Alexander St., pg. 331
World Expo Corporation, 37-43 Alexander St., pg. 578

Dandenong

PQ Australia Pty., Ltd., , pg. 837

Darlinghurst

The Campaign Palace, 20 Burton St., pg. 111

Dingley

Panduit Aust. Pty. Ltd., No. 7 Conifer Crescent, Redwood Gardens Estate, pg. 845

Dulwich

Leo Burnett/Conaghan & May S.a. Pty. Ltd., 225 Greenhill Rd., 2nd Fl., pg. 192
Cato Johnson Adelaide, 182-184 Fullarton Rd., 2nd Fl., pg. 1213
Wunderman Cato Johnson, 182 Fullarton Rd., 2nd Fl., pg. 1214
Young & Rubicam Pty. Ltd., 182-184 Fullarton Rd., pg. 1214

Edgecliff

Carlson Marketing Group (Aust.) Pty. Limited, , pg. 221

Fortitude Valley

Young & Rubicam Brisbane Pty. Ltd., 2nd Fl., 895 Ann St., pg. 1214

Glen Waverley

Eclipse Combustion & Industrial Equipment Pty., , pg. 366

Gosford

Ashton/Scholastic Pty. Ltd., P.O. Box 579, pg. 962

Hawthorn

Ingersoll Engineers Pty. Ltd., , pg. 568

Kangaroo Point

Chiat/Day/Mojo Pty. Ltd., 69 Shafston Ave., pg. 245

Knoxfield

Mary Kay Cosmetics Pty. Ltd., 551 Burwood Hwy., pg. 717
Screen Products Australian Pty Ltd, 77 Parkhurst Dr., pg. 419

Lane Cove

SAS Institute Australia Pty. Ltd., Private Bag No. 52, pg. 960

Launceston

REPCO Bearing Company, Div. of REPCO Ltd., P.O. Box 1088, E. Tamar Highway, pg. 900

Melbourne

Austin-Australia, 3 Bowen Crescent, pg. 790
Leo Burnett/Conaghan & May (Vic.) Pty. Ltd., 464 St. Kilda Rd., 5th Fl., pg. 192
CS First Boston Australia (Holdings) Limited, 367 Collins St., Level 23, pg. 204
The Campaign Palace, 409 St. Kilda Rd., pg. 111
K&D Bond Direct, 10th Fl., West Tower, 608 St. Kilda Rd., pg. 112
Korn/Ferry International, Level 42, 80 Collins St., pg. 643
Media Decisions, 409 St. Kilda Rd., pg. 112
George Patterson Pty. Limited, 394 La Trobe St., pg. 112
Remington Australia, 548 Clayton Rd.(3168), pg. 926
Sudler & Hennessey, 572 St. Kilda Rd., pg. 1213
Uniroyal Chemical Pty. Ltd., 3 Bowen Crescent, pg 1129
Young & Rubicam Melbourne, 572 St. Kilda Rd., pg. 1214

Milsons Point

S. C. Johnson & Son Pty. Ltd., P.O. Box 277, pg. 600

Milton

Leo Burnett/Conaghan & May (Qld.) Pty. Ltd., 33 Park Rd., pg. 192

Mitchell Park

Longyear (Australia) Pty. Ltd., 919-929 Marion Rd., pg. 682

Mulgrave

Action Controls Pty. Ltd., 11/12-14 Miles St., pg. 14

Nedlands

Chiat/Day/Mojo Pty. Ltd., 33 Broadway, pg. 245

North Clayton

Hallmark Cards Australia Ltd., 611 Blackburn Rd., pg. 502

North Ryde

Kendall Australia Pty. Ltd., 82 Waterloo Rd., pg. 622

North Sydney

Leo Burnett Pty. Ltd., Leo Burnett House Level 3&4, 73 Miller St., pg. 193
Cato Johnson Sydney, 6th Floor, 213-219 Miller St., pg. 1213
Consensus Research Pty., Ltd., 107 Mount St., 3rd Fl., pg. 111
Cuibs Pty. Ltd., , pg. 206
CUNA Mutual Insurance Soc., P.O. Box 1418, pg. 206
IDC Australia, 56 Berry St., pg. 577
Leo Burnett Connaghan & May Pty. Ltd., Leo Burnett House, Levels 3&4, 73 Miller St., pg. 192
Levi Strauss (Australia) Pty. Ltd., 41 McLaren St., pg. 670
Marketforce Australia, 4th Fl., 168 Walker St., pg. 112
Media Decisions, 107 Mount St., pg. 112
George Patterson Pty. Limited, 107 Mount St., pg. 112
Training Dynamics, 275 Alfred St., 1st. Fl., pg. 426
Wunderman Cato Johnson, The Denison, Level 4, 65 Berry St., pg. 1214

Northmead

Fanner-PLP, 150 Briens Rd., pg. 886
Playtex (Pty.) Ltd., 104 Briens Road, pg. 877

Padstow

Acheson A.N.Z. Pty. Ltd., 63 Davies Road, pg. 12

Port Melbourne

Luscombe and Partners Pty. Ltd., 60 Stokes St., pg. 344

Pymble

Lexmark Australia, Level 4, Bldg. 2, 20 Bridge St., pg. 674

Richmond

Mattingly & Partners Group Pty Ltd., 21-31 Goodwood St., pg. 330
Mattingly & Partners/Melbourne, 21-31 Goodwood St., pg. 331

Rydalmere

Bose Australia, 11 Muriel Ave., pg. 167

St. Leonards

Austin-Australia, 52-56 Atchinson St., pg. 790

St. Marys

Schenectady Chemicals Australia Pty. Ltd., , pg. 975

Scoresby

Griffith Laboratories Pty., Ltd., 1 Griffith St., pg. 488

Seven Hills

Uniroyal Chemical Pty. Ltd., Unit 2, 13 Stanton Rd., pg. 1129

Smithfield

Griffith Laboratories Pty., Ltd., 23 Britton St., pg. 488

South Melbourne

Chiat/Day/Mojo, 55 Southbank Blvd., pg. 245
Marketforce Australia, 125-127 Ferrars St., pg. 112
Western Personnel Services Pty. Ltd., 88 Albert Rd., pg. 1182

Stanmore

World's Finest Chocolate Australia Pty. Ltd., 8 Bridge Rd., pg. 1203

Surrey Hills

K&D Bond Direct, 3rd. Fl., 8-24 Kippax St., pg. 112

Sydney

Burmot Australia Pty., Ltd., 1 Chandos St., St. Leonards, pg. 194
Goldman Sachs (Australia) Limited, Grosvenor Place, 225 George St., pg. 468
I-E Proprietary, Ltd., , pg. 900
Korn/Ferry International, 11th Fl., Kyle House, 31 Macquarie Pl., pg. 643
Arthur D. Little Intl., Inc., Level 23 Grosvenor Place, 225 George St., pg. 679
Sudler & Hennessey Sydney, The Denison, Level 15, 65 Berry St., pg. 1214
Viacom Intl. Pty. Ltd., 16th St., St. Martin's Tower, 31 Market St., pg. 786
Wool Filters Intl., , pg. 401

Taren Point

Florasynth Australasia Pty. Ltd., Unit 6, 181-187 Taren Point Rd., pg. 420

Turramurra

Velsicol Australia Limited, 10 William St., pg. 1147

West Perth

Marketforce Australia, 1314 Hay St., pg. 112

Westgate

Aladdin Industries Pty. Ltd., P.O. Box 22, pg. 29

Wetherill Park

Australian Coleman, Inc., 5 Hallstrom Place, pg. 695
Newly Weds Foods Asia/Pacific, 32 Davis Rd., pg. 804

Willoughby

MTV Australia, TCN Channel 9, 24 Artarmon Road, pg. 785

AUSTRIA
Breitenbrunn

Master Foods Austria GmbH, Eisenstaederstr. 80, pg. 714

Graz

Dahms Electronik GMbH, Wienerstr. 287, pg. 845

Grossebersdorf

Amway Gesellschaft M.B.H., Wienerstrasse 720, pg. 70

Hochfilzen

Tiroler Magnesit, A.G., , pg. 137

Radenthein

Oesterreichisch Heraklith, A.G., , pg. 137
Radex Austria, A.G., , pg. 137

Vienna

Austria III, Daringergasse 6, pg. 1072
Berlitz Sprachschulen GmbH, Graben 13, pg. 143
Creative Communications Werbegesellshaft, m.b.H., Gymnasiumstr. 81, pg. 111

GAF (Osterreich) GmbH, Lutzowgasse 12-14, pg. 439
Hager Gesellschaft, Seilerstatte 13, pg. 685
IDC Austria, c/o Loisel, Spiel, Zach Consulting Erwin Spiel, pg. 577
IDG Communications Verlagsges.mbH, Zieglergasse 6, pg. 577
Ideal-Standard, Pasettistrasse 32-35, pg. 62
Johnson's Wax, Ges. M.B.H., P.O. Box 39, pg. 600
Panduit Corp., Erlachplatz 2-4, pg. 845
Dr. Puttner & BSB Worldwide Werbegesellschaft m.b.H., Wambachergasse 2, pg. 111
Radex-Heraklith Industriebeteiligungs, A.G., Opernring 1, pg. 137
Refractories Consulting & Engineering GmbH, c/o Opernring 1 A-1010, pg. 137
WABCO Westinghouse G.m.b.H., Hochstadtplatz 4, Postfach 49, pg. 62
Weinberger Werbehaus Ges.m.b.H & Co. KG, Kaulbachstrasse 22, pg. 105
Wunderman Worldwide, Sterngasse 13, pg. 1212
Young & Rubicam Vienna Werbegesellschaft m.b.H., Postfach 999, Marc Aurel Strasse 4, pg. 1213
Zyntec GmbH, Seybelgasse 13, pg. 1221

BAHAMAS
Freeport

Uniroyal Chemical Company Limited, West Sunrise Highway, pg. 1129

BARBADOS
Bridgetown

Acurex Export Sales, Ltd., Bay Street, pg. 16

BELGIUM
Alleur

Instrument Specialties Europe, S.A. - European Division, 3 Avenue Du Progres, pg. 572

Antwerp

Cargill NV, Muisbroeklaan, Kaai 506, pg. 219
Cat Pumps International N.V., Harmoniestr. 29, pg. 340
Luber-Finer, Europe, N.V./S.A., Waterwilgweg, 4, pg. 1124

Brussels

Leo Burnett Worldwide Inc., Chaussee de Wavre 1789, pg. 193
ARA Belgium, S.A., Ave. Louise 326, pg. 7
ARA Services, S.A., Avenue Louise 326, pg. 7
Artic N.V. S.A., G. Huysmanspin 1 Lot, pg. 1073
The Associated Press (Belgium) S.A., Boulevard Charlemagne, pg. 92
BSB Brussels SA/NV, 26 Boulevard General Jacques, pg. 109
Berlitz Schools of Languages of Benelux S.A., 306-310 Avenue Louise, pg. 143
Cato Johnson Direct Promotion, Blvd. Lambermont 368A, pg. 1211
Compagnie Fischbein, S.A., 64 Rue Previnaire, pg. 8
DHL International N.V., Rue du Moyer 211, pg. 309
Decision Data Computer (Belgium) S.A., Chausse de La Hulpe, 122, pg. 324
Dicalite Europe Nord, S.A., Av. Louise 430-Bte. 2, pg. 137
Dicalite Trading, S.A., Av. Louise, 430-BTE 2, pg. 137
European Plumbing Prods. Group, Blvd. du Souverain 348, pg. 62
Fallek Chemical S.A., Ave. Franklyn Roosevelt 81, pg. 558
Fibelco S.A./N.V., 64 bis rus Previnaire, pg. 8
S.A. Firet, N.V., Dandermondesti 51, pg. 401
Geomedia S.A., Rue de Geneve 6, pg. 111
International Agricultural Market Development Co., Avenue Louise 416, pg. 1061
John Hancock Intl. Services S.A., Avenue des Arts 44, BTE. 4, pg. 596
Kobs & Draft Belgium, Rue de Geneve 6, pg. 112
Korn/Ferry International, 523, Avenue Louise, pg. 643
Levi Strauss Belgium, S.A., Brussels Intl. Trade Mart Sq., Atomium Avignon 272, pg. 670
Levi Strauss & Co. (Europe) S.A., 489 Ave. Louise, pg. 670
Arthur D. Little Intl., Inc., 2 Blvd. de la Woluwe, pg. 679
Lowe Communication Group, 402, Av. de Tervuren, pg. 685
Lowe Troost S.A., 402 av. de Tervuren, pg. 685
Master Foods NV, 100 Boulevard Du Souverain, pg. 714
Panduit Corp., Avenue de la Liberte, 80, pg. 845
Le Rocher, Compagnie de Reassurance, S.A., 35 Square de Meeus BTE-1, pg. 898
Saproma S.A., Avenue Edouard Lacomble 21, pg. 221
TBWA, Avenue Louise 326 (BTE 123), pg. 1072
N.V. Vectur S.A., 1243 Chaussee de Haecht, pg. 1139
WABCO Westinghouse, Ave. Van Volxem 164-166, pg. 62
Wunderman Worldwide, Chaussee de Wavre 59, pg. 1212
Young & Rubicam Belgium S.A., Dieweg 3B, pg. 1212

Diegem

Stonhard, Europe, 143 Woluwelaan, pg. 1051

Erembodegem

Gates Europe N.V., Dr. Carlierlaan 30, pg. 445
Solar Press, Inc., 3 DE Industriezone, pg. 1017

Frameries

Esco, Europe S.A., Rue des Frous-Chaux, pg. 388

Groot-Bijgaarden

N.V. Johnson Wax Belgium S.A., Noordkustlaan 16 (B), pg. 600

Herentals

N.V. Griffith Laboratories S.A., Toekomstlaan, Wolfstee Industriepark, pg. 488

Heverlee

SAS Institute NV/SA, Interleuvenlaan 10, pg. 960

Houdeng-Goegnies

Ideal-Standard, Chaussee Paul Houtart, 88, pg. 62

Landerzeel

N.V. Pipeco, S.A., Ambachstraat 6, pg. 1149

Liege

Armstrong Machine Works, S.A., Parc Industrial Des Hauts-Sarts, pg. 84

Nivelles

T.D. Williamson S.A., 6 rue du Travail, pg. 1192

Ostmalle

N.V. Southwestern Petroleum Europe S.A., Industrial Zone, pg. 1024

Sint-Niklaas

GAF (Belgium) N.V., Hoogkamerstraat 42, pg. 438
National Forge Europe NV, Industrie Park 7, pg. 789

Sint-Stevens-Woluwe

Hollingsworth & Vose Europe NV, Woluwedal 12, Box 138, pg. 539

Ternat

Bose N.V., Essenestraat 15, pg. 167

Vilvoorde

N.V. Maxon International S.A., Luchthavenlaan 16, pg. 723

Zavemtem

Polyurethane International Division, Excelsiorlaan 40, pg. 419

Zaventem

Amway Belgium Co., Ikaroslaan 4, pg. 70

BERMUDA
Hamilton

Coral Energy Ltd., P.O. Box 1651, pg. 285
Coral International Ltd., Box 1651, pg. 285
GAF Insurance Ltd., Victoria Hall, P.O. Box HM 1826, pg. 438
John Hancock Insurance Company of Bermuda Ltd., Clarendon House, Church St., pg. 596
New York Life Insurance Worldwide Ltd., Cedar House, 41 Cedar Ave., pg. 803
Newbury Insurance Co., , pg. 800
Zenith Intl. Insurance Ltd., Cedar Park Center Bldg. Cedar Ave., pg. 671

BRAZIL
Belo Horizonte

Bucyrus (Brasil) Ltda., Avenida Professor Magalhaes Penido, 439, pg. 186

Bonsucesso

Patron Comercio E Representacoes Ltda., Rua Julio Ribeiro, 78, pg. 846

Campinas

Nash do Brasil Bombas Ltda., Ave. Mercedes Benz 700, pg. 784

Jundiai

Ideal-Standard Wabco Ind. E Com. Ltda, Rua Honorato Spiandorim 189, pg. 62

Petropolis

Dentsply Industria e Comercio Ltda., R Alice Herve 86-Bigen, pg. 330

Porto Alegre

Mariner Constructors Nauticas, S.A., , pg. 664

Rio de Janeiro

Artplan Publicidade, Rua Fonta de Daudade 329, pg. 1072
Ceras Johnson Ltda., Via 8, No. 505, Jacarepagua, pg. 599
Computerworld de Brazil, Praca Floriano 19/26 andar, pg. 577
Florasynth Fragancias y Aromas Ltda., Rua Frei Fabiano N. 36, pg. 420
IDC Brazil, Computerword do Brazil Ltda, Praca Floriano 19, pg. 578

Rio Claro

Uniroyal Quimica, S.A., Avenida Brasil,5333, pg. 1130

Sao Paulo

Acheson do Brasil Ind. e Com Ltda., Rua Howard A. Acheson Jr. 279, pg. 12
Amway Do Brasil LTDA., Av. Eng. Eusebio Stevaux 1257, pg. 70
Axios, Ltda., Rua Brasilio Luz, 535, pg. 900
Bangor Punta do Brazil Ltda., , pg. 664
Berlitz Escola de Idiomas Ltda., Praca Charles Miller 16, pg. 142
Bolton-Emerson Equipmentos Industrias Ltda., , pg. 163
Bolton-Emerson Talamac Maquinas e Equipamentos Ltda., , pg. 163
Leo Burnett Publicidade, Ltda., 400 40th Ave. Cidade Jardim, pg. 193
Cargill Agricola S.A., Rua Olavo Bilac 157, pg. 219
Denison/BSB, Av. Brigadeiro Luiz Antonio 2050, pg. 111
Eriez Products Magneticos e Metalurgicos, Ltda., Caixa Postall 2632 01000, pg. 1059
Fresinbra Indus. S.A., Caixa Postal 24.065, pg. 62
GAF do Brasil Industria e Commercio, Ltda., Rua Major Sertorio 212-2, pg. 438
Gates do Brasil Ind. e Com. Ltda., Rua Cesario Alvim 602/634, pg. 445
E. F. Houghton do Brazil, Cx Postal 107 Capuava Mava, pg. 546
ICC Comercio e Industria Ltds., Alameda Lorena 1304-14 Andar, pg. 558
Ideal-Standard Brazil, Al. Jauaperi 299, pg. 62
Impact Comunicacoes, 15 19 Andar Av., pg. 1213
Imperial Clevite do Brazil, Rua Brasilio Luz, 535, pg. 900
John Hancock Servicos Internacionais S/C., Ltda., Ave. Ipiranga 324 Building C Edifico Inv, pg. 596
Korn/Ferry International, Avenida Indianapolis 80, pg. 643
Arthur D. Little Limitada, Avenida Brigadeiro Faria Lima 2003, pg. 679
Lord Industrial Ltda., Caixa Postal 31, pg. 683
MTV Brazil, Avenida Prof. Alfonso Bovero 785
Metal Leve S.A., Rua Brasilio Luz, 535, pg. 900
Metallurg do Brazil Ltda., Rua Geraldo Flausino Gomes, 85-3 andar, pg. 742
Metalurgica Detroit, Rua Brasilio Luz, 535, pg. 900
PLP Produtos Para Linhas Proformados Ltda., R. Santa Elvira 465, pg. 886
PruServicos Participacoes, S.A., c/o Prudential Atlantic Companhia Brasileira de Seguros, Rua BoaVista, pg. 898
Schenectady Quimica do Brasil Limitada, Rue Campos Bicado 52, , pg. 975
Trane do Brazil, Caixa Postal 362 Diaema, pg. 62
Uniroyal Quimica, S.A., Avenida Morumbi, 7 029, pg. 1130
Viacom Video-Audio Comunicacoes, Ltda., Alameda Jau', 1742-11 Andar, pg. 786
Wheaton do Brazil, Caixa Postal 1461, pg. 1184
Wunderman do Brazil, 15-19 Andar, Av. Brigadeiro Faria Lima 2100-190, pg. 1213
Young & Rubicam, 15 19 Andar, Av. Brig. Faria Lima 2100, pg. 1213
Young & Rubicam Brasil, 17-19 Andar, Av. Brigadeiro Faria Lima 2100, pg. 1213

BULGARIA
Sofia

IDG-Technika Communications, Ltd., 1, Slaveikov Sq., pg. 577

CANADA
Armstrong

Kohler Ltd., RR3, C-1 Palisades, pg. 640
Kohler Ltd., 4150 Spallumcheed Road, pg. 640

Arnprior

Playtex, Ltd., Arnprior, Playtex Park, pg. 876

Aurora

Bunn-O-Matic Corp. of Canada Ltd., 280 Industrial Parkway S., pg. 188

Beamsville

Enduro-Niagara Ltd., 4750 Christie Dr., pg. 939

Bedford

Wilbur-Ellis Company of Canada, Ste. 310, pg. 1189

Beebe

Barry Manufacturing Company Ltd. (BEMAC), , pg. 602

Belleville

Perfect-Hoffman Co. Ltd., 39 Dussek St., pg. 145

Boucherville

Gibson-Homans of Canada Ltd., 101 De LaBarre(J4B 2X6), pg. 457
Marmon/Keystone Canada-Montreal, 290 Chemin du Tremblay, pg. 712

Bradford

J. C. Brock Canada, Ltd, HollandSt., pg. 178

Bramalea

Besser Canada, Ltd., 387 Orenda Rd., pg. 146

Brampton

ComputerLand Canada Ltd., 2000 Clark Blvd., pg. 271
Gibbs Wire & Steel Company of Canada Ltd., 120 Walker Dr., pg. 456
Goshen Rubber of Canada Ltd., 100 Stafford Drive, pg. 472
Kampgrounds of America (Canada) Ltd., 6-A Tilbury Court, pg. 613
Thermo Electric (Canada) Ltd., 12 Rutherford Rd. So., pg. 1091

Brantford

Acheson Colloids (Canada) Ltd., P.O. Box 665, , pg. 12
Evenflo Products Division, 121 Roy Blvd., pg. 1025
Gates Canada Inc., 300 Henry St., pg. 445
S. C. Johnson & Son, Limited, 1 Webster St., pg. 600
Levi Strauss & Co. (Canada), Inc., 7080 Eastern Rd., pg. 670

Burlington

Boston Insulated Wire & Cable Co. Ltd., 1800 Ironstone Dr., pg. 107
Cumis General Insurance Co., 151 North Service Rd., pg. 206
The Cumis Group Ltd., 151 North Service Rd., pg. 206
Cumis Life Insurance Co., 151 North Service Rd., pg. 206
CUNA Mutual Insurance Co., P.O. Box 5065(L7R 4C2), pg. 206
Elliott Turbomachinery Canada, Inc., 955 Maple, pg. 378
Kingsbury Canada, Inc., 3385 Mainway Dr., pg. 632
Marmon/Keystone Canada-Toronto, 1200 Heritage Road, pg. 712
Matthews Canada Ltd., 5051 North Service Rd., pg. 721
The Nash Engineering Company of Canada, Ltd., 1149 Northside Rd., pg. 784
Union Pump (Canada) Ltd., 4211 Mainway Dr., pg. 1129
Watson Bowman Acme, Inc., 4205 Fairview St., pg. 145

Burnaby

Ames Taping Tools Co. of Canada Limited, 7779 Edmonds St., pg. 8
Vancouver Tree People, 2869 Norland Ave., pg. 317

Calgary

Alberta National Gas Company Ltd., 240 Fourth Ave. S.W., pg. 75
American Trading & Production Corp., Canadian Oil & Gas Operations, 1405-500 4th Avenue, S.W., pg. 65
Hunt Oil Canadian Division Office, 1450-801 6th Ave., S.W., pg. 554
Lennox Industries (Canada) Ltd., 3916-70th Ave., S.E., P.O. Box 5460, pg. 667
Procor LPG Storage Division, 734 7th ave. S.W., pg. 712
Procor Sulphur Services Division, 310 Southport Bldg., 1033 Southport Rd. S.W., pg. 712

Cambridge

Jamesway Co., 756 Bishop St. North, pg. 712
McRobert Springs Co., 575 Conestoga Blvd., pg. 712
Preformed Line Products Canada, 36 Raglan Pl., pg. 886

Campbellford

Cook Chocolate Canada Ltd., Second St., pg. 1203
World's Finest Chocolate Canada Ltd., Second Street, pg. 1203

Cannington

The Griffith Laboratories, Ltd., , pg. 487

Concord

Quindar Products Ltd., 106 Rayette Rd., pg. 902
Spalding Canada, 250 Courtland Ave., pg. 1025

Cornwall

Cyborg Systems of Canada, 1274 Pitt St., pg. 307
Kohler Ltd., 805 Education Rd.(K6H 6C7), pg. 640
Levi Strauss & Co. (Canada), Inc., 700 Education Rd., pg. 670

Coteau du Lac

Serevco & Company Ltd., Parc Industriel, , pg. 794

Dartmouth

Jacques/McClelland Geosciences, Inc., 3 Spectacle Lake Dr., pg. 436
Major Foods Ltd., 41 Ilsley Ave.(B3B 1K9), pg. 7

Downsview

L. D. Caulk Co. of Canada Div., 1100 Lodestar Rd., Unit 8, pg. 330
Jones Apparel Group, Inc. Canada, 55 St. Regis Crescent North, pg. 602
Laurentian Technomedia Inc., 501 Oakdale Rd., pg. 577
Producto Diemakers Supplies Ltd., 620 Supertest Rd., pg. 893
Ziebart Canada, Inc., 150 Oakdale Rd., pg. 1218

Edmonton

Canadian Lynden Transport Ltd., 10004 29A Avenue(T6N 1A8), pg. 690
Levi Strauss & Co. (Canada), Inc., 10660-85th St., pg. 670
Procrane Inc., 2440 76th Ave., pg. 712
Sealy Canada, Ltd., 14550 112th Ave., pg. 986

Elmira

Uniroyal Chemical Ltd., 25 Erb St.(N3B 3A2), pg. 1129

Etobicoke

Kohler Ltd., 195 The West Mall, pg. 640
Lennox Industries (Canada) Ltd., 400 Norris Glen Rd., pg. 667
Totes Canada Ltd., 77 Brown's Line, pg. 1103
Versa Services Ltd., 811 Islington Ave., pg. 7

Fort Erie

Erdle Perforating Co. Ltd., 22 Bowden St.(L2A 5M9), pg. 385

Guelph

Kearney-National Canada Ltd., 280 Speedvale Ave. W., pg. 358
Uniroyal Chemical Ltd., , pg. 1129

Halifax

Maritime Life Assurance Co., 2701 Dutch Village Rd.(B3J 2X5), pg. 597

Hamilton

C&W Refractories, Ltd., 191 Victoria Ave. So., pg. 201
Union Drawn Steel Co., Ltd., 1350 Burlington St. East, pg. 797
Jervis B. Webb Company of Canada Ltd., 1647 Burlington St., East, pg. 1170

Hyde Park

Faxon Canada, Ten Rutledge St., pg. 404
Thermon Canada, Blue Heron Dr., pg. 1092

Islington

The Austin Co. of Canada, 304 E. Mall, Ste. 701, pg. 790
Carlson Marketing Group Ltd., 5353 Dundas Street West(M9B 6J3), pg. 221
P. Lawson Travel, Ltd., 5353 Dundas St., W., Ste. 400, pg. 221

Kitchener

Dukane Canada Ltd., 461 Manitou Dr., pg. 352
Fowler Tools of Canada, , pg. 427
Lear Siegler Industries Ltd., Gen. Seating Div., 530 Manitou Dr., pg. 664
MTD Products Limited, 97 Kent St., pg. 694
New Balance Canada Inc., 5 Manitou Dr., Unit 15-A, pg. 799
SBN Systems Inc.-Imprinter Division, 171 Webster Rd.(N2C 2E7), pg. 960

Lachine

Canadian Shade Tree Service, Ltd., 1540 Claire Crescent, pg. 317
Woolcan, 1880 32nd Ave., pg. 1201

Laval

Kilsby-Jorgensen Steel & Aluminum Inc., 1255 Ave. Laplace, pg. 606

Lindsay

Bucyrus Blades of Canada Ltd., 199 St. David St., pg. 388
Viskase Canada Inc., 150 Colborne St. E., pg. 383

London

Amway of Canada, Ltd., 3897 Exeter Rd.(N6A 4S5), pg. 71
Parnell Foods Ltd., 487 Newbold St.(N6E 1K4), pg. 7
Spartan Plastics Canada, 1015 Green Valley Rd., pg. 1026
Strike Rite Matches Ltd., , pg. 129

Longueuil

Ivex Packaging Corporation-Longueuil, 2355 Rue De La Province(J4G 1G3), pg. 584

Malton

Playtex Apparel Canada, Ltd., 6363 Northam Dr., pg. 876
Playtex, Ltd., 6363 Northam Dr., pg. 876

Markham

Bently Nevada Canada ltd., 70 Gibson Dr., Unit 4, pg. 141
W. Braun Packaging, Canada Ltd., 215 Shields Court, pg. 172
Humphrey Fluid Power Ltd., 570 Alden Road, Unit 553
Levi Strauss & Co. (Canada), Inc., 80 Allstate Pkwy., pg. 670
Panduit Canada Ltd., 140 Amber St., pg. 845

Milton

Altec Industries, Ltd., 831 Nipissing Rd., pg. 45
Robertson-Whitehouse, 97 Bronte St., pg. 713
Toronto Auto Auction, 8277 Lawson Road, pg. 294

Mississauga

ASC/Canada Incorporated, 5280 Creekbank Road, pg. 7
Ball Superior Ltd., 1155 Birchview Dr., pg. 116
Blistex Limited, 2395 Drew Rd., pg. 157
Bloomfield Industries Canada Ltd., 5850 Keaton Crescent, pg. 1027
Canadian Hardinge Brothers Machine Tools Inc., 415 Matheson Blvd. E., pg. 508
Canadian Mini-Warehouse Properties, Ltd., 1550 Meyerside Dr., Unit 7, pg. 898
Card Technology Corp., 3198 Orlando Drive(L4V 1R5), pg. 960
Coleman Evcon Supply Limited, 3115 Peppermill Court, Unit 695
Eclipse Thermal Systems, 1145 Westport Crescent, pg. 366
GAF (Canada) Inc., 1075 The Queensway East, pg. 438
Gibson-Homans of Canada Ltd., 2540 Rena Rd.(L4T 3C9), pg. 457
Kilsby-Jorgensen Steel & Aluminum Inc., 1666 Shawson Drive East, pg. 606
Mary Kay Cosmetics Ltd., 5600 Ambler Dr.(L4W 2K9), pg. 717
Metallurg (Canada) Limited, 2700 Matheson Blvd. E., pg. 742
Mosler Canada, 280 Britannia Rd. E., pg. 62
New Hermes, Ltd., 1561 Courtneypark Dr. East, pg. 801
Odomaster Canada, 994 Westport Crescent, pg. 1065
Rauland-Borg (Canada) Inc., 6535 Millcreek Dr., Unit 5, pg. 914
Remington Products (Canada) Inc., 2254 S. Sheridan Way, pg. 926
Safeguard Business Systems Limited, 420 Britannia Rd. E., Ste. 102, pg. 966
SBN Systems Inc.-Canadian Operations, 3206 Orlando Drive(L4V 1R5), pg. 960
SBN Systems Inc.-Corporate, 3220 Orlando Drive(L4V 1R5), pg. 960
Siftco Canada, Inc., 5430 Timberlan Blvd., pg. 812
Sifto Canada, Inc., 1136 Matheson Blvd., pg. 812
Simplex Intl. Time Equip. Co. Ltd. (Canada), 6300 Viscount Rd.(L4V 1H3), pg. 1006
Slant-Fin, Ltd./Ltee, 6450 Northam Dr., pg. 1010
Star Expansion Industries, Ltd., 6680 Excelsior Ct., pg. 1039
Star Expansion Shields Ltd., 6680 Excelsior Ct., pg. 1039
Thetford Sanitation Ltd., 2299 Drew Rd., pg. 358
UFL Foods, Inc., 6320 Northwest Dr., pg. 804
United Parcel Service of Canada, 3195 Airway Dr., pg. 1133
Weber Marking Systems Canada ltd., 6180 Danville Rd., pg. 1171
Wells Manufacturing Canada Ltd., 1080 Meyerside Dr., pg. 1124

Montreal

BSB/Canada Inc., 1425 Blvd. Rene-Levesque Ouest, pg. 109
W. Braun Packaging, Canada Ltd., 100 Alexis Nikon Blvd., 172
Doner Schur Peppler, 2020 University Ave., pg. 344
Eclipse Thermal Systems, 2095 Madison, pg. 366
Ideal Parking, Inc., 5 Complexe, Place Desjardins, pg. 43
Intra-Acoustics Company, Ltd., 600 Rene-Lavesgne Blvd. W., Ste 800, pg. 566
La Societe VS Limitee, 4900 Fisher Street, pg. 7
George S. May Canada, Ltd., 615 Rene Levesque Blvd. W., Ste. 1100, pg. 724
Montreal Fast Print, 9500 Blvd. St. Laurant(H2N 1P5), pg. 52
RTA Advertising, Inc., 2050 Mountain St., 3rd Fl., pg. 193
SBN Systems Inc.-Montreal, 5640 Pare Street(H4P 2M1), pg. 960
M. Swift & Sons Canada Inc., 1801 Favard, pg. 1068
Versabec Inc., 4900 Rue Fisher, pg. 7
Wunderman Worldwide, 345 Ave. Victoria, Ste. 603, pg. 1213
Young & Rubicam, Ltee., 1600 Rene Levesque Blvd. W., pg. 1213

Mount Royal

Florasynth Canada, Inc., 5800 Andover Ave., pg. 420

Nackawic

St. Anne Chemical Co., Ltd., P.O. Box 1000, pg. 850
St. Anne Industries Ltd., Main Rd., pg. 850
St. Anne - Nackawic Pulp Co., Ltd., P.O. Box 1000, pg. 850
Southampton Sawmills, Ltd., P.O. Box 1000, pg. 850

Nanaimo

High Tree Services Ltd., P.O. Box 186, Island Highway South, pg. 317

Newcastle

Manheim's Oshawa Dealers Exchange, Hwy. 401 at Exit 425, pg. 294

Niagara Falls

Bissell Ltd., Box 1003, 6934 Kinsmen Court, pg. 153
Zippo Manufacturing Company of Canada Limited, 6158 Allandale Ave., pg. 1220

Nisku

Bently Nevada Canada Ltd., 1906 4th St., pg. 141
Bucyrus-Erie Co. of Canada Ltd., 1310 8th Street, pg. 186

North Bay

Longyear Canada Inc., P.O. Box 330, pg. 682

North York

Lexmark Canada Inc., 105 Moatfield Dr., pg. 674
SAS Institute (Canada) Inc., 225 Duncan Mill Rd., pg. 960

Oakville

Fanchem, Ltd., 1141 S. Service Road, West, Unit A, pg. 838
Procor Rail Car Division, 2001 Speers Rd., pg. 712

Orillia

Otaco Seating Co., Ltd., Harvie Settlement Rd., pg. 60

Geographic Index

Ottawa

Canadian Stebbins Engineering & Mfg. Co. Ltd., 2700 Lancaster Rd., pg. 1044
Foundation Instruments Inc., 24 Colonnade Rd., pg. 886
Metropolitan Life Holdings, Ltd., 99 Bank St., pg. 745
Metropolitan Life Insurance Company of Canada, 99 Bank St., pg. 745
Modern Building Cleaning Inc., 1470 Triole St.(K1B 3S6), pg. 7
SAIC Canada, 275 Slater St., Ste. 1003, pg. 982

Paris

Mary Maxim, Ltd., , pg. 723

Peterborough

Kendall Canada Ltd., 1100 Curity Ave., pg. 622

Pointe Claire

Manufacture Leviton du Canada, 165 Hymus Blvd., pg. 671

Port Coquitlam

Esco Ltd., 1855 Kingsway(B3C 1C1), pg. 388

Port Robinson

Esquire Canada, Inc., 125 South Street North, pg. 1054

Renfrew

Playtex Apparel Canada, Ltd., Renfrew, 550 Hall St., pg. 876

Rexdale

Certified Div., 1000 Martin Grove Rd., pg. 664
Duro-Test Canada, 419 Attwell Dr., pg. 355
Kinetics, Inc., 110 Carrier Dr., pg. 518
Levi Strauss & Co. (Canada), Inc., 90 Clairiville Dr., pg. 670
Suncrest Company of Canada, 170 Attwell Drive, Ste. 603, pg. 765
Trimfit Company Limited, 375 Rexdale Blvd., pg. 1113
Victaulic Company of Canada Limited, 65 Worcester Road, pg. 1149
Xtek Canada, Ltd., 1344 Martingrove Rd., pg. 1206

Richmond

J. J. Newberry Canadian Ltd. c/o Gault Brothers Div., 3960 Jacombs Rd., pg. 935

Richmond Hill

Bose Ltd., 8-35 E. Beaver Creek Rd., pg. 167
Scholastic-Canada, Ltd., 123 Newkirk Rd., pg. 962

Rockwood

Rockwood Gardens, Ltd., 501 Harris St., pg. 638

Saint Boniface

Cargill Ltd., 627 Plinquet, pg. 219

Saint Cesaire

D. D. Bean & Sons (Canada) Ltd., P.O. Box 180, pg. 129

Saint Hyacinthe

Griffin Canada Inc., 1375 Brouillette St., pg. 69

Saint John's

Newfoundland Geosciences, Ltd., 607 Torbay Road, pg. 436

Saint Leonard

Les Appareillager Electriques Kearney-National, 9240 Langelier Blvd., pg. 358

Sainte Marie-Beauce

Bose Canada, Inc., Parc Industrial, pg. 167

Scarborough

Canefco Limited, 50 Milne Ave., pg. 373
Directory Distributing Associates, Inc., 1800 Ellesmere Ave., pg. 339
Econolite Canada, Inc., 1650 Midland Ave., pg. 367
The Griffith Laboratories Ltd., 757 Pharmacy Ave., pg. 488
Industrial Trust Company, 200 Consilium Place, pg. 897
Milwaukee Electric Tool (Canada) Ltd., 755 Progress Ave., pg. 361
Nibchem Inc., 50 Dynamic Dr. Unit 1, pg. 806
PIC Realty Canada Ltd., 200 Consilium Place, pg. 897
Prudential Fund Management Canada Ltd., 200 Consilium Place, pg. 897
Prudential of America General Insurance Co. (Canada), 200 Consilium Place, pg. 897
Schenectady Chemicals Canada Ltd., 319 Comstock Rd., pg. 975

Simcoe

Borg-Warner Automotive (Canada) Limited, 385 Second Ave., pg. 166

Smithville

General Refractories Co. of Canada, Ltd., P.O. Box 160(L0R 2A0), pg. 137

Stoney Creek

Levi Strauss & Co. (Canada), Inc., 563 Barton St. East, pg. 670

Stratford

Prestonia Office Products Ltd., , pg. 65

Tillsonburg

Mastico Industries, Ltd., , pg. 464
Rubber Products Division, 65 Spruce St., pg. 433

Toronto

AFG Glass Inc., 101 Richmond St., West, pg. 4
American Appraisal Canada, Inc., 310 Front St. W., Suite 800, pg. 48
Arts & Communications Counselors, Inc., 55 Bloor St., West, pg. 954
The Associated Press, Ltd., 36 King St., E., pg. 92
BSB/Canada Inc., 2 St. Clair Ave. W., pg. 109
Berlitz Language Centers of Canada Ltd., 130 Bloor St. W., Ste. 603, pg. 142
Leo Burnett Company Ltd., North Tower, 175 Bloor St. E., pg. 192
The Canadian Coleman Co., Ltd., 15 N. Queen St., pg. 695
Chiat/Day/Mojo Inc. Advertising, 10 Lower Spadina, pg. 245
Color Your World, Inc., 10 Carson St., pg. 1121
DHL International Express Ltd., 6390 Northwest Dr., pg. 309
Dahlstrom of Canada Ltd., 7 Copeland St., pg. 9
Daily Racing Form, Inc. (Toronto), 245 Carlaw Ave., pg. 611
Deacon Day Advertising and The McLauchlan Group, , pg. 685
Dentsply Canada Ltd., 1100 Lodestar Ave, Unit 8, pg. 330
Doner Schur Peppler, 90 Eglinton Ave. W., pg. 344
Faber/Castell Canada Ltd., 1325 The Queensway, pg. 395
First Boston Canada Limited, 121 King St., Ste. 2500, pg. 204
Forum Learning Systems of Canada, Ltd., 10 Bay St., 426
Goldman Sachs Canada, 150 King St., West, Suite 1201, pg. 468
Haworth Ltd., 33 Yonge Street, pg. 518
Hill, Holliday/Toronto, 1133 Yonge St., pg. 534
E. F. Houghton Co. of Canada Ltd., 100 Symes Rd., pg. 546
Hussey Seating Co. (Canada) Ltd., 20 Torlake Crescent, pg. 555
IDC Canada, 36 Toronto St., 9th Fl., pg. 578
Ivex Packaging Corporation-Canadian Region, 40 Butterick Rd.(M8W 3Z8), pg. 583
Ivex Packaging Corporation-Keele Street, 500 Keele St., Unit 306(M6N 3C9), pg. 583
KnollOffice, Inc., 160 Pears Ave., pg. 1121
Kobs & Draft Advertising, 2 St. Clair Ave. W., 21st Fl., pg. 112
Korn/Ferry International, Scotia Plaza, 40 King Street West, Ste. 1814, pg. 643
Arthur D. Little of Canada Ltd., 67 Yonge St., Ste. 400, pg. 679
Metropolitan Trust Company of Canada, 6 Crescent Rd., pg. 745
Morguard Investments Limited, Toronto, 6 Crescent Rd., pg. 745
NAP-Ltd., 131 Jarvis St., Ste. 202, pg. 1074
NDAP/TMP Worldwide, 184 Front St. East, Ste. 201, pg. 1074
National Silicates Ltd., 429 Kipling Ave., pg. 837
New York Life Insurance Co. of Canada, 121 Bloor Street East, pg. 803
Ross Roy Canada, Ltd., Renaissance Ct., 162 Cumberland St., Ste. 300, pg. 950
S & C Electric Canada Ltd., 90 Belfield Rd., pg. 959
St. Anne Pulp Sales Co. Ltd., 250 Bloor Street EAst, Suite 1420, pg. 850
Segway Partners, , pg. 885
Stackpole Limited, 550 Evans Ave., pg. 1034
Steelcase Canada Ltd., 7200 Woodbine Ave.(M3C 2R7), pg. 1044
Stringer Veroni Ketchum, 160 Bedford Rd., Ste. 307, pg. 626
Sudler & Hennessey Canada, 60 Bloor St., West, pg. 1213
Sunbeam Corporation (Canada) Limited, 1040 Islington Ave.(M87 4R58), pg. 1059
Bob Thomas Associates, 10 Lower Spadina Ave., pg. 244
Trane Co. of Canada, 401 Horner Ave., pg. 62
Viacom Canada Ltd., 45 Charles St. E., pg. 785
Viacom Enterprises Canada Ltd., 45 Charles St. E., pg. 785
Vitt/Reynolds Media International Limited, 26 Soho St., Ste. 380, pg. 1154
WABCO Standard Inc., 80 Ward St., pg. 62
Western International Media Corporation, 30 St. Clair Ave., Ste. 1201, pg. 1180
Wunderman Worldwide, 60 Bloor St. W., 15th Fl., pg. 1213
Young & Rubicam, Ltd., 60 Bloor St. West, pg. 1213

Vancouver

Canadian Northern Shield, 555 W. Hasting, Rm. 1900, pg. 206
Cumis Group Insurance, 1700-555 W. Hastings St., pg. 206
Diversified Steel, 1223 Dervent Way, pg. 56

Ville d'Anjou

Berkline, Inc., 8491 Ernest Cormier, pg. 285
West Pentone Inc., 10900 Secant St.(H1J 1S5), pg. 1172

Ville Vanier

Stihl Eastern Canada Ltd., 579 Ave. Godin, pg. 1049

Waterloo

Hayes Microcomputer Products (Canada), 295 Philip St., pg. 519

Welland

Premier Refractories (Canada) Ltd., Prince Charles Dr., pg. 887
Whiting Equipment Canada, Inc., 350 Alexander St., pg. 1187

Weston

Bell & Howell Ltd., 230 Barmac Drive(M9L 2X5), pg. 135

Whitby

Stonhard, Ltd., 95 Sunray St., pg. 1052
Up-Right Scaffolds Ltd., 108 Industrial Dr., pg. 1139

Whitehorse

Yukon Alaska Transport Ltd., , pg. 690

Willowdale

William E. Coutts, Co. Ltd., 2 Hallcrown Place, pg. 502
North American Watch of Canada, Ltd., 2001 Sheppard Ave., West, pg. 812

Windsor

DNN Galvanizing Corporation, 300 Sprucewood Ave., pg. 794
Pierce Yee Associates, Ltd, , pg. 509
Ross Roy Communications Canada, Inc., 1737 Walker Rd., pg. 950
Spirol Ind. Ltd., 3103 St. Etienne Blvd., pg. 1031

Winnipeg

Automotive Accessory Co., Ltd., 771 Main St., pg. 1124
Cargill Ltd., The Cargill Bldg., 300-240 Graham Ave., pg. 219
Carter Day Industries (Canada) Ltd., 1425 Whyte Ave., pg. 226
Sheldon Good & Co. of Canada, , pg. 470

Woodstock

Hobart Brothers of Canada Ltd., (N4S 7W8), pg. 536
Thomas Built Buses of Canada, Ltd., , pg. 1093

CAYMAN ISLANDS

Georgetown

Brown Brothers Harriman Trust Co. (Cayman) Ltd., Butterfield House, , pg. 181
Coral Petroleum Ltd., P.O. Box 500, pg. 285
Equipment Assurance Ltd., P.O. Box 694, pg. 186
Sunbeam Intercontinental Ltd., , pg. 1059

CHANNEL ISLANDS

Guernsey

CSFB Fund Management Limited, Level 2, Albert House, pg. 204

CHILE

Santiago

BSB Chile Publicidad, Galvarino Gallardo, pg. 109
Berlitz Escuelas de Idiomas Ltda., Padre Mariano No. 305, pg. 142
Bucyrus Chile Ltda., Casilla 16846-Providencia, Avda 11 de Septiembre 2055, pg. 186
Leo Burnett Chile, Eliodoro Yanez 2376, pg. 192
Electronica Del Pacifico, Julio Prado 2118, pg. 845
Longyear Chile Ltda., Las Dalias 2900 (Macul), pg. 683
Publicaciones en Computacion Ltda., Pedro de Valdivia, pg. 577
Young & Rubicam de Chile Ltda., Las Orquideas 979, pg. 1213

Vina del Mar

Quimica S.C. Johnson & Son Chilena S.A.C.I., Casilla 35-D, pg. 600

COLOMBIA

Bogota

Aser Publicidad/Y&R, Carrera 7, pg. 1213
BSB/Meza, Ltda., Calle 97 A, 110
Barnes de Colombia, Apartado 12098, Calle 15 No. 41-17, pg. 900
Computerworld-Columbia, Transversal 23 No. 58-28, pg. 577
CUNA Mutual Insurance Soc., Calle 19 No. 13A-12, Piso 4, pg. 206
Florasyntesis Fragrancias y Aromas Ltda., Calle 39 Bis B, pg. 420
Instituto de Idiomas Colombia, S.A., Avenida 13, No. 88-20, pg. 143
S. C. Johnson & Son Colombiana S.A., Apartado Aereo 29632, pg. 600
Korn/Ferry International, Edivicio Progapanda Sancho, Oficina 803, pg. 643
Leo Burnett Colombia, S.A., Carrera 13 No. 89-59, pg. 192
Materiales Industriales S.A., Apartado Aereo 80046, pg. 137
Tecna Ltda., Carrara 32 No. 22-B-60/66, pg. 846

Cali

Aser Publicidad, Calle 21 Norte, pg. 1213

Cartagena

Polymer, S.A., , pg. 732

Medellin

Empresa de Refractarios Colombianos S.A., Apartado Aereo 865, pg. 137
Griffith Colombia S.A., P.O. Box AA 8589, pg. 487
Industrias Metalicas Sud Americanas Ltda. (IMSA), , pg. 712

COSTA RICA

Peralta

Comunica Leo Burnett-Costa Rica, De Pollos Kentucky, en San Pedro, 100 Metros Al Este, pg. 192

San Jose

Industria Ceramica Costarricense, S.A., Apartado Postal 4120, pg. 62
S. C. Johnson de Centroamerica S.A., Apartado Postal 600
Laboratorios Griffith de Centro America S.A., Apd. 7-2820 (1000), , pg. 488
Longyear Centroamericana S.A., Apartado Postal 5235, pg. 682

CYPRUS

Nicosia

S. C. Johnson Company Limited, Margarita House, 15 Themistocles Dervis, pg. 600

CZECH REPUBLIC

Prague

Berlitz Schools of Languages Czechsolovakia Spol.sr.o, Na Porici 12, pg. 143
Credit Suisse First Boston Czechoslovakia a.s., Staromestske nam. 15, pg. 204
FCS Forum s.s.r.o., Na Porici 12, pg. 426
IDG Czechoslovakia, Luzna 2, pg. 577
Leo Burnett Prague, Rep. Office Prague CSFR, , pg. 193
Arthur D. Little Intl., Inc., Stepanska 65, pg. 679
Young & Rubicam Czechoslovakia, Olivova 6, pg. 1212

DENMARK

Brondby

Bose A/S, Industriazej 7, pg. 167

Copenhagen

The Associated Press A/S, 55 Road Rup Lad Ser, pg. 92
Ted Bates A/S, Landemaerket 29, pg. 110
Berlitz International Danmark A/S, Vimmelskaftet 42A, pg. 142
Leo Burnett Denmark, Vesterbrogade 2B, pg. 192
Cato Johnson Copenhagen, Overgaden neden Vandet 17, pg. 1211
Dicalite Scandinavia, Rysensteensgade, 1, pg. 137
Dolriis, Gorm Larsen & Partner, Hammershusgade 9, pg. 104
IDC Scandinavia A/S, Aldersrogade 3A, pg. 578
Klausen & Partners A/S, Fredericiagade 13, pg. 1212
SAS Institute A/S, Kobmagerade 9a, pg. 960
Western Service A/S, 54 Kobmagergade, pg. 1182
Wunderman Worldwide A/S, Blegdamsvej 104, pg. 1212
Young & Rubicam Copenhagen, Enhjorningens Bastion, Langebrogade 6V., pg. 1213

Glostrup

Bell & Howell Ltd. England, Dansk Filial, Fabriksparken 22, pg. 135
Hans Folsgaard, Agentur A/S, Ejby Industrivej 2, pg. 845
Johnson Wax A/S, Midtager 18, pg. 600

Havdrup

Scan Globe A/S, 23 Ulvevej, pg. 927

Hedehusene

Finopac APS, 26, Industrivej., pg. 8

Hjorring

Intralox A/S, Egholmvej 3, , pg. 651

Ishoj

Vectur Aluminumstallningar, Baldersbaekrej 33, pg. 1139

Odense

Norgard Mikkelsen Reklamebureau A/S, Vandvaerksvej 18, pg. 112

Valby

AB Sonic International Aps, Gerdasgade13-15, pg. 352
IDG Denmark A/S, Krumtappen 4, pg. 577

Virum

GAF (Danmark) A/S, Frederiksdalsvej 141, pg. 438

DOMINICAN REPUBLIC

Santiago de los Caballeros

Sanitarios Dominicanos, S.A., P.O. Box 910, pg. 62

Santo Domingo

Leo Burnett Inc., Prolongacion Arabia No. 13, pg. 192
Cariplant S.A., Av. Abraham Lincoln, pg. 707
CUNA Mutual Insurance Soc., Calle Anibal de Espinosa No. 358, pg. 206

ECUADOR

Guayaquil

Johnsonwax del Ecuador S.A., P.O. Box 874, pg. 600

Quito

Florasyntesis Fragrancias y Aromas Ltda.-Factory, Mauel Larrea 1000, pg. 420
VIP Publicidad, Whimper 777, pg. 112

EGYPT

Giza

AMA Leo Burnett, El Nahda Tower, 7th Fl., 21 Ahmed Orabi St., pg. 192

Mohamdessen

Waffai & Associates, 23 Shehab St., Ste. 402, pg. 577

ENGLAND

London

IDC United Kingdom, 2 Bath Rd., pg. 578

FINLAND

Espoo

SAS Institute Oy, Sinikalliontie 10 PL 80, pg. 960

Hamina

Zlofin Oy, , pg. 550

Helsinki

Adshop, Erottajankatu 11, pg. 109
BSB City, Lapinlahdenkatu 3A, pg. 109
BSB Dinfo, Mikonkatu 8A, pg. 109
BSB Finnad Oy, Mikonkatu 8 A, pg. 109
BSB Media & Research, Mikonkatu 8A, pg. 110
Oy Berlitz AB, Kaivokatu 10 A 8. Krs., pg. 142
Oy Etra Ab, Lampputie 2, pg. 845
Finnad Communications, Mikonkatu 8A, pg. 111
IDC Finland, John Stenbergin Ranta 2, pg. 578
J & C Advertising, Keskustatu 4B, pg. 104
K&B DBM Marketing Oy, Iso Roobertinkatu 111
Kasanen Training/BTC Forum, Heikkilantie 6, PL 100, pg. 426
Masterfoods Oy, Lonnrotinkatu 18A, pg. 714
Suomen Levi Strauss Oy, Iso Roobertinkatu 43, pg. 671
OY Talentum Ab, Ratavartjankatu 2, pg. 577
Taucher, Young & Rubicam, Salomonkatu 17 A, pg. 1212
Oy Tulenkestavaat Tiliet, A.B., Bolevardo 17C14, pg. 137

Turku

BSB Finnad West, Yliopistonkatu 33A, pg. 109
Wunderman Taucher Turku Oy, Eerikinkatim 15, pg. 1212

FRANCE

Annecy

Ingersoll Engineers S.A., Le Concorde, 2, Ave. Zanaroli, pg. 568

Antony

Amway France, 14, Avenue Francois-Sommer, pg. 70
The Kendall Co., 15 rue Marcelin Berthelot, pg. 622

Aubervilliers

A. Epstein & Sons (France) Inc., Tour Pariferic, pg. 384

Bethune

Schenectady de France, , pg. 975

Bois-Colombes

Detrey Dentsply S.A., 72, rue du General LeClex, pg. 330

Bordeaux

Young & Rubicam Sud Ouest, Les Bureaux du Lac, Rue Robert Caumont, pg. 1213

Boulogne

Lowe & Associes, 96, av. du General Leclerc, pg. 685
Moradpour, Dalsace, Langlois, Pizanti, 7/15 rue du Dome, pg. 1212
Paragraphe/Sudler & Hennessey, 7/15, Rue du Dome, pg. 1212
Rayon Vert, 45 Rue Paul Bert, pg. 1212
Strategic Identity Consultants, 7/15 Rue du Dome, pg. 1212

Wunderman Cato Johnson France, 35-3 Rue de Paris, pg. 1212
Y&R Capital Image, 23 Allee Maillasson BP 73, pg. 1212
Young & Rubicam France S.A., 23 Allee Maillasson BP 73, pg. 1212

Breteuil-sur-Iton

Graphoil S.A., La Gueroulde B.P. 36, pg. 12

Cagnes-Sur-Mer

Young & Rubicam & Ogmios, 116 Blvd. de la Plage, pg. 1213

Carrieres-sur-Seine

Establissement Mesnel, S.A., 9-11 rue de la Riviere, pg. 1121

Cergy Pontoise

La Johnson Francaise S.A., B.P. 606, pg. 599
Maxon S.A.R.L., Avenue Du Parc, pg. 723

Claye-Souilly

WABCO Freinage de Vehicules S.A., 124 Avenue Aristide Briand, pg. 62

Clermont

Queroy S.A., Breuil le Sec (Oise),Domaine de Bailly, pg. 62

Clichy

Bell & Howell France S.A., 32-34, rue Fernand-Pelloutier, pg. 135
Black Pencil S.A.R.L., Escape Clichy, 6 allee Jean Prouve, pg. 192
Bordelais, Lemeunier & Leo Burnett, Espace Clichy, 6 Allee Jean Prouve, pg. 192

Colmar

Findley France SA, 8, rue Denis Papian, pg. 411

Contes

Mepps S.A., B.P. 09, , pg. 997

Courbevoie

Kobs & Draft, 177 rue Armand Silvestre, pg. 112

Dijon

Multicontact, 12 rue Jean Renoir, pg. 1212

Epinal

Trane Europe, B. P. 127, pg. 62

Farrebourg

Steelcase-Strafor S.A., 132-57400 Zone Industrielle, pg. 1044

Fontenay-sous-Bois

Ficomet S.A.R.L., BP 100, pg. 8
Panduit S.N.C., Z.A. des Marais, 1 Ave. Louison Bobet, pg. 845

Grasse

Lautier Florasynth S.A., 4, Ave. Alphonse Morel, pg. 420

Gregy-sur-Yerres

SAS Institute S.A., Domaine de Gregy, pg. 960

Haguenau

Mars Confectionery, 33 Chemin de la Sandlach, pg. 714

Hyeres

Coast Catamaran France, Le Viet, Route de Pierrefeu, pg. 695

La Garenne-Colombes

Sentrol Europe S.A., 6 rue d'Estienne d'Arves, pg. 145

La Tour-du-Pin

Playtex France, B.P. 55, Zone Industrielle, pg. 876

La Verpilliere

Tylan SARL, 7-8 Place de L'Europe, pg. 1122

Les Herbiers

Jeanneau Constructions Nautiques S.A., Boite Postal 83, pg. 664

Les Ulis

Action Instruments, S.A., Z.A. De Courtaboeuf, 9 Avenue du Canada, Batiment Zenith, pg. 15
Levi Strauss France, S.A., 6 Avenue du Pacifique, pg. 671

Levallois-Perret

Ziff-Davis France SARL, Immeuble Omega, 10, Rue Thierry Le Luron, pg. 1219

Limiel Brevannes

Thermo Electric S.A., 26 Rue Pasteur, pg. 1091

Lingolsheim

Young & Rubicam Est, 6 Rue Hannong-Village Ouest, pg. 1212

Marly-le-Roi

Bently Nevada France S.A.R.L., 30 Ave. de L'Admiral Lemonnier, pg. 141

Meudon-la-Foret

ESL S.N.C., 7 rue de l'Avenir, pg. 375

Montpellier

Medecine et Systemes Informatiques Intergres, Parc Euromedecine, 95 Rue Pierre Flourens, pg. 982

Nantes

Young & Rubicam Ouest, 1 Rue Du Guesclin, pg. 1213

Palaiseau

Aladdin International Corp. S.A.R.L., 5 Rue de LaCroix Martre, pg. 29

Paris

American Appraisal France, 32, Rue Notre Dame des Victoires, pg. 48
Associated Merchandising Corp. (France) S.A., 14 Rue de Castiglione, pg. 91
Atal SA, 7 rue Mariott, pg. 608
Beautiful & Landor Associates, 19/21 Rue Valette, pg. 1211
Berlitz France S.A., 29 rue de la Michodiere, pg. 143
Bernard Krief Motivation, S.A., Carlson Marketing Group, 115, rue du Bac, pg. 221
Bourns-Ohmic S.A., 21/23 Rue des Ardennes, pg. 168
Brown Harriman Corporation, 12-14 Rond Point des Champs Elysees, pg. 181
CIA Ketchum, 6, Rue Deodat de Severac, pg. 625
Compagnie Internationale Des Produits Sanitaires (CIPS) Jacob Delafon, 51 Rue Du Commandant, pg. 640
Credit Suisse First Boston France S.A., 34 rue de Lisbonne, pg. 204
Decision Data Computer (S.A.), 9 Cour des Petits Ecuries, pg. 324
Dynisco Instrument Sarl., , pg. 145
Electric Furnace France S.A.R.L., 32, Place St. Geoges, pg. 373
Goldman Sachs International Limited et Cie., 8, rue Halevy, 2nd Fl., pg. 468
IDC France, 12 Avenue George V, pg. 578
IDG Communications France, Immeuble La Fayette, pg. 577
IG Conseil S.A., 55 Rue de la Federation, pg. 625
INPUT, SARL, , pg. 571
Korn/Ferry International, 30 Avenue George V, pg. 643
G. Leblanc, 403 Rue de Pyrenees, pg. 665
Arthur D. Little Intl., Inc., 230 Rue du Faubourg, Saint Honore, pg. 679
MGTB Ayer, 2 rue du Pont Neuf, pg. 104
Mobilier International, 162 Blvd. Voltarre(75011), pg. 518
Playtex France, 6 Rue de Penthievre, pg. 876
Programmes Marketing Annuaires (PMA), 91 Avenue de la Republique, pg. 1074
Radex International S.A., 109 Rue du Faubourg St. Honore, pg. 137
Science Applications International, Europe S.A., 2 Place de la Defense, pg. 982
Sunbeam Div., 103 rue La Fayette, pg. 1059
TBWA de Plas, 25 rue du Pont-Neuf, pg. 1072

Paris la Defense

Lexmark France, Tour Pascal la Defense 7, pg. 674

Pontoise

Watlow France S.A.R.L., Immeuble Somag, Z.I. Rue Ampere, pg. 1168

Puteaux

BSB Europe/The Eurocentre, 3 rue Bellini, pg. 109
BSB France, 3 rue Bellini, pg. 109
O'T.V. & O'Space, 25/27 rue Parmentier, pg. 1212
Sofedem S.A., 46 Rue Arago, pg. 1059

Roissy

Safeguard Europe S.A., ZAC Paris Nord 2, pg. 966

Roissy Charles de Gaulle

GAF (France) S.A., Z.A.C. Paris-Nord 2, pg. 438

Rosny-sous-Bois

Thermon France, 91 Boulevard d'Alsace Lorraine, pg. 1092

Rueil-Malmaison

Acheson France S.A., 4, Passage Saint-Antoine, pg. 12
Automotive Products Group, Tour Albertler 65, Av. de Colmer, pg. 62

Saint-Denis

Mars Petfoods (UNISABI), Boite Postale No. 7, pg. 714

Saint-Germain-en-Laye

Bose S.A.R.L., 6 Rue St. Vincent, pg. 167

Saint-Leu-la-Foret

Spirol S.A., 2, Rue Charles Cros -ZAE-, pg. 1031

Saint-Maur-des-Fosses

Dicalite France, S.A., Bvld. de Creteil,163, pg. 137

Saint-Priest

Esco, S.A., Boite Postal 229, pg. 388

Sevran

WABCO Westinghouse Equipements Ferroviaires S.A., 2 Blvd. Westinghouse, pg. 62

Strasbourg

Dove Europe, , pg. 713

Suresnes

Geindre Marketing Services, Tours Suresnes 2000, 9 rue Benoit Malon, pg. 111

Trappes

Longyear France, 20, Ave Vladimir Komarov, pg. 683

Velizy-Villacoublay

Ready Systems, France, 32 Aveune L'Europe B.T. 87, pg. 916

Versailles

World Expo Corporation, 5A, rue de Bailliage, pg. 578

Villefranche-sur-Saone

Produtec Houghton S.A., 259 Rue Benoit-Mulsant, pg. 546

Vincennes

Wunderman, 12 Cours Louis Lumiere, pg. 1212

GERMANY

Aachen

The Gates Rubber Company, Eisenbahnweg 50, pg. 445

Ahlen

Comforto Group, Bergstr. 1, pg. 518
H.W. Schmidt GmbH, , pg. 518

Alzey

Intex, AM Wartberg, Playtex Park, pg. 876

Bielefeld

Bohle Werkzeugmaschinen GmbH, Postfach 150141, pg. 568

Bonn

Ideal-Standard GmbH, Euskirchener Str. 80, pg. 62

Burbach

Ingersoll Maschinen und Werkzeuge GmbH, , pg. 568
Waldrich Siegen Werkzeugmaschinen GmbH, Postfach 1320, pg. 568

Celle

Longyear Deutschland GmbH, Grafftring 1, pg. 683

Coburg

Waldrich Coburg Werkzeugmaschinenfabrik GmbH, Postfach 3253, pg. 568

Cologne

Florasynth GMBH, Mittelstr. 52-54, pg. 420
Imperial Schrade (Europe) G.m.b.H., , pg. 564
The E. F. MacDonald Verkaufsforderung GmbH, Vprgeborgstrasse 1, pg. 221
Thermo Electric GmbH, Postfach 900 406, Neue Eiler Str. 36, pg. 1091
Totes Europe, Sulzburgstrasse 144, pg. 1103

Constance

Detrey Dentsply, De-Trey-Strasse 1, pg. 330

Darmstadt

Acheson International S.A.-Equipment Div., Lerchenbergstrasse 23, pg. 12
Action Industrie Computer, GmbH, 201-203 Pallaswiesenstrasse, pg. 14

Dortmund

Pohlschroder & Co. KG, Steinbrinkstrasse 61, pg. 1044

Dreieich

Dentsply GmbH, Eisenbahnstrasse 180, pg. 330

Dusseldorf

Decision Data Computer GmbH, Bergundestr. 51, pg. 324
Gesellschaft fur Elektrometallurgie m.b.H., , pg. 742
Ingersoll Engineers GmbH, Niederkasseler Lohweg 8, pg. 568
Lowe Luerzer GmbH, Heinrichstr. 85, pg. 685
Maerz Ofenbau G.m.b.H., Corneliusstrasse 36, pg. 137
TBWA Dusseldorf GmbH, Immermannstr. 40, pg. 1072
Vectur GmbH, Voelklinger Landstr. 80, pg. 1139

Eching

Tylan GmbH, Kirchhoffstrasse 8, pg. 1122

Erkrath

Intralox, Inc. GmbH, Heinrich-Hertz-Strasse 44, pg. 651

Eschweiler

Elektrowerk Weisweiler GmbH, Durener Strasse, pg. 742

Essen

ANGUS Chemie GmbH, , pg. 75
Maxon GmbH, Ruttenscheider Platz 3, pg. 723

Frankfurt

Korn/Ferry International, Lyoner Strasse 15, ATRICOM, 6000 Frankfurt am Main 71, pg. 643

Frankfurt/Main

AMC, Bleichstrasse, 2-4, pg. 91
AdPlus GmbH, Hamburger Allee 45, , pg. 685
The Associated Press GmbH, 27 Mosel Strasse, pg. 92
Ayer Frankfurt, Hedderichstr. 108-110, pg. 104
BSB Frankfurt Werbeagentur GmbH, Hanauer Landstrasse 287-289, pg. 109
Battelle-Institut E.V., Am Romerhof 35, pg. 126
Berlitz Schools of Languages GmbH, Kaiser Str. 66, pg. 143
CSFB-Effectenbank Aktiengesellschaft, Grueneburgweg 102, , pg. 204
Cerca GmbH, Bettinastrasse 53/55, pg. 111
Michael Conrad & Leo Burnett GmbH & Co. KG, Alexanderstr. 65, pg. 192
Hamlin Electronics GmbH, 6368 Bad Vilbel bei, pg. 503
Kastner & Partner GmbH Werbeagentur, Kennedyallee 94, pg. 192
Lee Hydraulische Miniaturkomponenten, Rebstocker Str. 33-39, pg. 665
Lowe Luerzer GmbH, Hamburger Allee 45, pg. 685
TBWA, Hansaallee 30/32, pg. 1072
Young & Rubicam GmbH, Bleichstrasse 64, pg. 1213

Frechen

GAF (Deutschland) GmbH, Rudolf-Diesel-Strasse 25, pg. 438

Friedberg

Bell & Howell GmbH, Gruener Weg 8, pg. 135

Friedrichsdorf

Bose GmbH, Postfach 1125, pg. 167

Haan

Johnson Wax GmbH, , pg. 600

Haibach

Firet, G.m.b.H., , pg. 401

Hamburg

Bavaria Keytronic Technologie GmbH, Boschstrasse 23, pg. 944
ICW Copartner, An der Alster 42, pg. 104
K&D Werbeagentur, Hudwalckerstrasse 11, pg. 112
Scholz & Friends Design GmbH, Steinhoft 9, pg. 112
Scholz & Friends GmbH, Steinhoft 9, pg. 112
SpeedFam GmbH, Borsteler Chasissee 287, pg. 396
Spraying Systems Deutschland GmbH, Grossmoorring 9, pg. 1032
TBWA Hamburg GmbH, Neuer Wall 50, pg. 1072
Wilkens Ayer, An der Alster 42, pg. 104

Hanover

WABCO Westinghouse Fahrzeugbremsen G.m.b.H., Postfach 91 12 80, pg. 62

Heidelberg

SAS Institute GmbH, P.O. Box 10 53 07, Neuenheimer Landstr. 28-30, pg. 960
Steiber Div. der Borg-Warner GmbH, Kurpfalzring, pg. 166

Heilbronn

Dynisco Gerate G.m.b.H., Ind. Geb. Bollinger Hofe, Postfach 1547, pg. 145
Shure, GmbH, Lohtorstr. 24, pg. 1001

Herrenberg

Thoroughbred RD-COM GmbH, Nufringer Strasse 17A, pg. 1095

Heusenstamm

Levi Strauss Germany G.m.b.H., Rembrucker Strasse 21-25, pg. 671

Hungen

Coleman (Deutschland) GmbH, Inheiden Ezetilstrasse, pg. 695

Ingolstadt

Elektro Metall Export Gmbh, Manchingerstrasse 116, pg. 317

Ismaning

Steinheil-Lear Siegler AG, Osterfeldstrasse 82, pg. 664

Kernen/Stuttgart

Maxon GmbH, Neiderlassung Stuttgart, pg. 723

Kleve

Electric Furnace Germany, GmbH, Ringstrasse 54, Postfach 306, pg. 373

Kronau

Watlow Electric Mfg. Co. GmbH, Industriegebiet Heidig, Lauchwasenstrasse 1, pg. 1168

Kronberg

IDC Deutschland GmbH, Westerbachstr. 23A, pg. 578
World Report Verlag Gmbh, , pg. 143

Mainz

Ketchum Werbeagentur GmbH, Alexander-Diehl-Str. 2a, pg. 625

Marl

GAF Huls Chemie GmbH, Postfach 1320, pg. 438

Mulheim/Ruhr

Abbey Etna Machine Co. GmbH, Bloetterweg 139, pg. 9

Munich

Bavaria Avionik Technologie GmbH, Kirschastrasse 20, pg. 944
Bavaria Cargo Technologie GmbH, Kirschastrasse 20, pg. 944
DHL International Courier Service GmbH, Karl Hammerschmidt 5, pg. 309
Electro-Science Deutschland, 5, Stock, Sendlinger-Tor-Platz 8, pg. 375
IDG Communications, Verlag AG, Rheinstrasse 26/28, pg. 577
Komplettburo GmbH, Internationale Kommunikation, Flemingstr. 15, pg. 625
Mary Kay Cosmetics, GMBH, Fraunhoferstr 10, pg. 717
Ready Systems, Germany, Arabellastrasse 21-B, pg. 916
Veeco GmbH, P.O. Box 81, pg. 1146
Wavetek Electronics GmbH, Hans-Pinsel Strasse 9-10, pg. 1169
World Expo Corporation, Karl-Theodor-Strasse 91, pg. 578
Ziff-Davis Germany, Ziff Verlag GmbH, Hanover Str. 85, pg. 1219

Neu-Isenburg

Bently Nevada GmbH, Werner-von-Braun Str. 8-10, pg. 141

Neustadt

Kendall GmbH, Raffineriestrasse 8, pg. 622

Niederkruchten

Industrial Acoustics Company GmbH, , pg. 566

Oberursel

Auto Direkt Versicherungs AG, Oberstedter Strasse 14, pg. 795
Columbus Versicherungs Vermittlungs, Oberstedter Strasse 14, pg. 795
Nekura Versicherungs AG, Oberstedter Strasse 14, pg. 795

Offenbach/Main

ARA Services, GmbH, Strahlenbergerstrasse 127, pg. 7
Sunbeam Vertriebsgesellschaft mbH, Waldstrasse 256, pg. 1059

Ottobrunn

Panduit GMbH, Rudolf-Diesel-Strasse 18, pg. 846

Puchheim

Amway GmbH, Benzstrasse 11 a-c, pg. 70

Simbach

Deutsche Heraklith A.G., , pg. 137

Sindelfingen

Kayser Coll. Technische Ubersetzer, , pg. 143

Stuttgart

Bourns, GmbH, Breite Strasse 2, pg. 168
Wolff & Partner, Birkenwald Str. 200, pg. 112

Trier

Leonard Kreusch GmbH & Co., Martinerfeld 61, pg. 645

Ulm

Deutsche Acheson GmbH, Karlstrasse 29, pg. 12

Urmitz

Radex Deutschland, A.G., , pg. 137

Weinsberg

ASC Weinsberg Karosseriewerke Weinsberg GmbH, Lindichstrasse 11, pg. 7

Wiesbaden

Arthur D. Little Intl., Inc., Gustav-Stresemann-Ring 1, pg. 679

Wiesbaden-Bierstadt

Cat Pumps Deutschland GmbH, Rostockerstr. 9, pg. 340

GHANA

Accra

Johnson's Wax Ltd., P.O. Box 5249, pg. 600

GREECE

Athens

BSB Athens Advertising S.A., 11b Konitsis St., pg. 109
Geo-Young & Rubicam, 49, Vas Sofias Ave., pg. 1212
H.A. Samouhos Pub. Ltd., 3-5, Stiron Str., pg. 577
IDC Greece, Strategic International Ltd., 8 Isiodou St., pg. 578
Ideal-Standard S.A.I., 23 Alexandroupoleos St., pg. 62
S. C. Johnson & Son (Hellas) E.P.E., 210 Messogion Ave., Holargos, pg. 600
K&D Hellas, 264 Kifisias Ave. & 1 Kodrou St., pg. 112
Leo Burnett S.A., 371 Sygrou Ave., pg. 193
J. N. Leoussis Advertising & Marketing S.A., 4, Kartalist, pg. 1072
Velsicol Overseas Corporation, 33 Multiadou St., pg. 1147

Kavala

Penrod International Drilling Company, , pg. 859

Kessariani

S.K. Tsoumanis Representations, 29 Iroon Skopeftiriou and, Solomonidou Corner, pg. 846

Melissa

HOH International, Inc., Karaiskaki 10(15127), pg. 497

Thessaloniki

Magnomin-General Mining S.A., 17 Agia Sophia St., pg. 137

GUATEMALA

Guatemala City

Amway de Guatemala, S.A., 7A Avenida 6-69, pg. 70
Comunica Leo Burnett, 5TA Avenida 6-39, Zone 14, Colonia El Campo, pg. 192
Industria Centroamericana de Sanitarios, S.A., P.O. Box 2533, pg. 62
Olefinas, S.A., , pg. 732
Publimerca S.A., 4A Av. A 7-64, Zona 10, pg. 105

HONG KONG

Causeway Bay

Florasynth (Far East) Pte. Ltd., 1304 World Trade Centre, pg. 420
ICC (Hong Kong) Ltd., 20 th Flr., Universal House, 229-230 Gloucester Rd., pg. 559
Intertec Limited, 20th. Flr., Universal House, 229-230 Gloucester Rd., pg. 559

Central

Brown Brothers, Harriman (Hong Kong) Ltd., Gloucester Tower, 22nd Fl., Landmark Centre, pg. 181
Forum Asia Pacific, 18th Fl., EIE Tower, Bond Center, 89 Queensway, pg. 426
IDC China/Hong Kong Ltd., 12/F, Seabird House, 22 Wyndham St., pg. 578

Coswaybay

Fugro-McClelland Hong Kong, Ltd., 11-F Park Commercial Centre, 2-12 Shelter St., pg. 435

Hong Kong

Action Instruments (China) Ltd., 9/F, Unit D, Gee Chang, Hog Centre, 65 Wong Chuck, pg. 14
Amway International, Inc.-Hong Kong Branch, 26/F Citicorp centre, 18 Whitfield Rd., Causeway Bay, pg. 71
BSB Hong Kong, 2/F Asian House, 1 Hennessy Rd., pg. 110
Leo Burnett Intl., Asia Hdqtrs., City Plaza 3, 6th Fl., 14 Taiko Wan Rd., pg. 192
CS First Boston (Hong Kong) Limited, 9th Fl. One Exchange Square, pg. 204
Chadwick-Miller Intl. Ltd., Hang Seng Bank Bldg., pg. 237
Connell Brothers (Hong Kong) Ltd., 601, 6/F Stanhope House, 738 Kings Rd., pg. 1189
Dentsu, Young & Rubicam/Hong Kong, 418 Mount Parker House, 1111 King's Rd., pg. 330
Goldman Sachs (Asia) Limited, Edinburgh Tower, The Landmark, 35th Flr., pg. 468
IDAB Wamac Pacific, Trinity House, Stes. 1703-1704, 165-171 Wanchai Rd., pg. 559
IDAB WAMAC Pacific Limited, Trinity House, 165-171 Wanchai Road, pg. 559
Integrated Resources Insurance & Investment Services, Ltd., Ste. 2109 Edinburgh Towers, pg. 573
Korn/Ferry International, 808 Gloucester Tower, pg. 643
Lee Davis Ayer, 8F, C.C. Wu Bldg., 302-308 Hennessy Rd., pg. 104
MTV Asia, c/o Star TV, 12th Floor, Hutchison House, pg. 785
Oriental Source, 2nd Fl., Mount Parker House, 1111 King's Rd., pg. 331
Prudential Asia Capital Limited, Alexandra House, 16-20 Chater Rd., pg. 897
Prudential Asia Investments Limited, Alexandra House, 32nd Fl., 16-20 Chater Rd., pg. 897
Rempro Trading, Ltd., , pg. 926
SAS Institute Ltd., Room 513-515 Hong Kong Plaza, pg. 960
Sunbeam Consumer Products Far East, Ltd., Room 1505 Tai Sang Commercial Bldg., 24-, pg. 1059
Sunkist (Far East) Promotion, Ltd., Swire House, 11 Chater Rd., 12th Fl., pg. 1061
Triangle Pacific, 2nd Fl., Mount Parker House, 1111 King's Rd., pg. 331
World Expo Corporation, 701-4 Kam Chung Bldg., 54 Jaffe Rd., pg. 578
Wunderman, 4th Fl., Mount Parker House, 1111 King's Rd., pg. 331

Kowloon

Alaron Electronics Far East Ltd., Hong Kong, Silvercord Tower II, 30 Canton Rd., Suite 1402, pg. 30
Continental Conair, Ltd., Rm. 604, New World Centre, pg. 272
Continental Electric Industries, Ltd., 16 Argyle St., Mongkok, pg. 272
CUNA Mutual Insurance Soc., 185-191 Sai Yee St., pg. 206
DHL International (Hong Kong) Ltd., 13 Mok Cheong St., pg. 309
Generra Sportswear (Hong Kong) Ltd., 97 How Ming St., pg. 451
S. C. Johnson, Ltd., P.O. Box 98450, pg. 600
Jones International Ltd., Unit 804-6, Tower 1, Cheung Sha Wan Plaza, 833, pg. 602
Levi Strauss Eximco (Ltd.), Fl. 13-Mandarin Plaza Tower A, 14 Science Museum Rd., pg. 670
Levi Strauss (Far East), Ltd., 9F, Hong Kong Spinners Indus. Bldg., pg. 670
Soundesign Corp. Hong Kong Ltd., 1103 E. Ocean Centre, 98 Granville Rd., pg. 1019
Strombecker (HK) Ltd., 926-7 East Wing, New World Office Bldg., pg. 1054

Kowloon Bay

Panduit Trading Pte. Ltd., Unit 15, Block A, S/F, Tonic Industrial Centre, pg. 846
Woolkong, Ltd., 907-8 Po Lung Centre, pg. 1201

Kwai Chung

Springborn Laboratories (Hong Kong) Ltd., 1004, 10th Fl. Star Centre, 443-451 Castle Peak Rd., pg. 1033

Kwai Fong

Woolkong Ltd., Tower 1 Metroplaza No. 223, Units 2513-19 Level 25, Hing Fong Road, pg. 1201

North Point

Hayes Microcomputer Products, Inc., 39/F Unit B. Manulife Tower, 169 Electric Rd., pg. 519

Quarry Bay

Leo Burnett Ltd., City Plaza 3, 6th Fl., 14 Taikoo Wan Rd., pg. 193

Queensway

American Appraisal Hong Kong Ltd., 1301 Bond Centre, East Tower, pg. 48

Shatin

Griffith Laboratories (H.K.) Ltd., 8th Flr., Unit A-B, Supreme Industrial Bldg., pg. 487

Wanchai

Asia Computerworld, 701-4-Kam Chung Bldg., 54 Jaffe Rd., pg. 577
BSB Graffix Limited, 1201 Kam Chung Bldg., 52-54 Jaffee Rd., pg. 110
Dillingham Construction (H.K.) Limited, Easey Commercial Bldg., Room 1803-1805, pg. 338
HHCC International, Inc., 13/F Hop Hing Centre, 8-12 Hennessy Rd., pg. 534
K&D Asia-Hong Kong, 2nd Fl., Asian House, 1 Hennessy Rd., pg. 112

HUNGARY

Budapest

American Appraisal Hungary Co. Ltd., Ganz U.16, 3rd Fl., 304, pg. 49
Berlitz KFT, Sommelweis Utca 2, pg. 142
Credit Suisse First Boston Budapest Rt, Ybl Miklos Ter 8, pg. 204
IDC Hungary, , pg. 578
IDG Magyaroszagi Laplado Kft., , pg. 577
Korn/Ferry International, 1-3 Rakoczi u., pg. 643
Schwinn (USA)-Csepel Ltd., Gyepson U. 1, pg. 981

ICELAND

Reykjavik

Iselco SF, Skeifan 11/D, Reykjavik Ind. Centre, pg. 845

INDIA

Ahmedabad

Amol Dicalite Ltd., , pg. 137

Bombay

Chaitra Leo Burnett Advertising Private Ltd., 9/11, N.S. Patkar Marg., Ardeshir B. Godrej Chowk, pg. 192
Rediffusion, Readymoney Terrace, 1st Fl., 167 Dr. Annie Besant Rd., pg. 331
Sista's Private Limited, Poonam Chambers, B Block, Shivsager Estate, Dr. Annie Besant Rd., pg. 112
Vulcan - Eclipse, Mahalaymi Chambers, Bhulabhai Desai Rd., pg. 367

Geographic Index

Madras

Bi-Metal Bearing, c/o Amalgamations Ltd., 861 Anna Salai, pg. 900
Srivathsa Electrical Corp., 157, Angappa Street, pg. 846

New Delhi

IDC India, D-74 Panchsheel Enclave, pg. 578
Media Transia India Ltd., 103 Anand Lok(110049), pg. 577
Modern Home Care Products Pvt. Ltd., No. 4 Community Centre, pg. 600

INDONESIA

Bandung

C.V. Sumber Sakti, 7 Jalan Dr Susilo, pg. 846

Jakarta

AIM Communications, Price Centre Bldg., 15th Fl., Jalan Jenderal Sudirman 3-4, pg. 192
Amway Indonesia, Wisma SSK - 3rd Fl., Jl. Daan Mogot Km 11, pg. 71
BSB Indonesia, 3rd Fl., Wisma Sejahtera, J1 S. Parman Kav. 75, pg. 110
Matari Advertising, J1 HR Rasuna Said Kav, H 1-2 Kuningan, pg. 104
Metro, Samudera Indonesia Bldg., 5th Fl., Jl. Jend. S. Parman Kav. 35, pg. 331
P.T. S.C. Johnson & Son (Indonesia) Ltd., P.O. Box 41/JNG, pg. 599

IRELAND

Carrickmacross

Bose Ireland, Castleblaney Rd., pg. 167

Dublin

BSB Hunter Advertising, 9/10 Upper Pembroke St., pg. 110
Dahlstrom Manufacturing B.V., Coolcock Industrial Estate, pg. 310
Griffith Laboratories Ireland Limited, Pineview Industrial Estate, Firhouse Road, pg. 487
Javelin/Young & Rubicam, 18 Merrion Sq., pg. 1212
Johnson Wax (Ireland) Limited, Robinhood Industrial Estate, pg. 600
Masterfoods Ltd., 728 Harcourt St., pg. 714
Softrans International, Ltd., 14, Carysfort Ave., pg. 143
Up-Right (Ireland) Ltd., Pottery Rd., pg. 1139

Limerick

Draper Erin Ltd., Dock Rd., Corcanree Industrial Estate, pg. 348
Wildcat Ltd., , pg. 575

Listowel

Imperial Stag Ltd., , pg. 564

Ringaskiddy

ANGUS Fine Chemicals Ltd., , pg. 75

Shannon

Befab-Safeland, Ltd., Bay 15, Industrial Estates, pg. 317
Seven Seas Leasing, , pg. 575

ISRAEL

Bnei-Brak

Astronautics C.A. Ltd., 23 Hayerarkon Street, pg. 93

Haifa

Electrochemical Industries (Frutarom) Ltd., P.O. Box 1929, pg. 558

Tel Aviv

A. Epstein & Sons (Israel) Ltd., P.O. Box 50003, The Industry House, 29 Hamered St., pg. 384
ICC (Israel) Chemicals Ltd., 135 Dizengoff St., pg. 559
People and Computers, 64 Pinkster St.(11616), pg. 577
Alexander Schneider Ltd., 44 Petach Tikva Rd., pg. 846

Yavne

M. Alkalay Agencies, Ltd., Industrial Area, , pg. 804

ITALY

Agrate Brianza

American Appraisal Italia S.r.l., Centro Direzionale Colleoni, pg. 49

Arese

Johnson Wax S.p.A., P.le M. M. Burke 1/3, pg. 600

Bagnasco

Bagnasco S.R.L., Via Molino, 87, pg. 539

Bologna

Vista Multi National, Via C. Battisti, 2, pg. 143

Corsico

Amway Italia s.r.l., Via G. di Vittorio 10, pg. 71

Gardolo

Clevite SRL, Via Bepi Todesca 12, pg. 900

Genoa

Houghton Italia S.p.A., Casella Postale 669, pg. 546

Lainate

Panduit S.A.S., Via Como 10, pg. 846

Latina Scalo

Uniroyal Chimica, S.P.A., Viale Delle Industrie, 40, pg. 1129

Milan

Acheson Italiana s.r.l., Via G. Frua 18, pg. 12
Alpine Center, s.r.l. (Berlitz), Via Mercadante, 17, pg. 142
American Appraisal Italia S.r.l., Galleria Passarella, 2, pg. 49
Austin Italia S.p.A., Via Romagnoli 6, pg. 790
Ayer Milano, Via Cerva 24, pg. 104
BSB Italia, Via Paleocapa 7, pg. 110
BSB Medical, Via Paleocapa 7, pg. 110
Leo Burnett Co., S.R.L., Via Fatebenefratelli 14, pg. 192
Camptel International SPA, Sede amm. e. stabil.:, Via G. Di Vittorio, 358, pg. 358
Cato Johnson Italia S.p.A., Viale Majno 21, pg. 1211
Credit Suisse First Boston Italia (Compagnia Mobiliare) SpA, 21 via Bigli, pg. 204
De Art S.R.L., Via Rimini 22, pg. 330
EuroForm S.r.l., Via Montebello 30, pg. 426
GAF (Italia) S.P.I., Via Lampedusa, 13, pg. 438
G&R Pubblicita/Sudler & Hennessey, Via Guerrazzi, pg. 1212
Gariboldi Parisi Verga/Interad, P. Le Biancamano 8, pg. 685
ICC Italia S.R.L., Via Cardano 8, pg. 559
IDC Italia S.r.l., ViaR. Pitteri 110, pg. 578
IDG Communications Italia srl, Via Mecenate, pg. 577
Ideal-Standard S.p.A., Via A.M. Ampere 102, pg. 62
K&D Italia, Via Ariosto 23, pg. 112
Knoll International Italia S.p.A., 11, v. M.te Napoleone, pg. 1121
Korn/Ferry International, Piazzetta M. Bossi, 1, pg. 643
Levi Strauss Italia, S.p.A., Via Serbelloni, pg. 671
Arthur D. Little Intl., Inc., Via Serbelloni 4, pg. 679
George S. May International, S.P.A., Centro Direzionale Colleoni, pg. 724
Motivation S.P.A., Corso, Italia 17, pg. 221
Multi Language Center SrL, Via Larga, 8, pg. 143
New York Language Center, Via delle Asole, 2, pg. 143
Pirella Goettsche Lowe S.p.A., P. Le Biancamano 8, pg. 685
R.P. Partners SRL, Via Lentasio 9, pg. 626
SAS Institute S.r.l., Via San Martino della Battaglia 17, pg. 960
TBWA, Via Cusani 5, pg. 1072
Telephone Marketing Programs-SMET, Via P. Coletta, 59, pg. 1074
UPS/Alimondo, Via Fantoli 15/2, pg. 1133
Watlow Italy, Via Adige 13, pg. 1168
Wunderman Tender, Via Lazzaroni 4, pg. 1212
Young & Rubicam Italia, S.p.A., Piazza Eleonora Duse 2, pg. 1213

Padova

American Appraisal Italia S.r.l., Piazza Salvemini, 4, pg. 49
Padova Ayer, Piazza Garibaldi 8, pg. 104
TBWA, Corso Garibaldi, 18, pg. 1072

Pavia

Instant S.R.L., Via Montanari 7, S. Martino Siccomario, pg. 1139

Piossasco

WABCO Westinghouse Freni Veicoli Industriali S.p.A., Via Volvera 51, pg. 62

Pomezia

Playtex Italia S.p.A., Via Laurentian, Km. 27,200, pg. 876

Premenugo di Settala

I.C.S.A.-Florasynth, Via F. LLI. Roselli, 5, pg. 420

Reggio Emilia

Intralox Italia s.r.l., Via Y Gagarin, pg. 651

Rome

Alps Institute, Via P.L. da Palestrina, 19, pg. 142
Alps Institute s.r.l. (Berlitz), Via P.L. da Palestrina 19, pg. 142
American Appraisal Italia, S.r.l., Via Flavio Domiziano, 10, pg. 49
Ayer Roma, Via Salaria 290, pg. 104
BSB Italia, Via Romagnosi, 18/A, pg. 110
Berlitz Language Centers, S.R.L., Via Cavour 256, pg. 142
Bose S.P.A., Via Luigi Capucci, 1Z, pg. 167
Crown Lance Italia Srl, Via dei Buonvisi, 61, pg. 163
Europe Language Center SrL, V. le Giulio Cesare, 207, pg. 143
Griffith Laboratories Italia S.r.l., Via Cassia 640, pg. 487
Korn/Ferry International, Via Nicolo' Tartaglia, 11, pg. 643
Pirella Goettsche Lowe S.p.A., Via Aventina 7, pg. 685
Playtex, Italia S.p.A., Piazza L. Sturzo, 31, pg. 876
Revlon S.p.A., , pg. 696
TBWA, Via Kenia 66/A, pg. 1072
Vista Multi Method, Via di Torre Argentina, 21, pg. 143
World Languages SrL, V. le Giulio Cesare, 207, pg. 143

San Donato Milanese

Princeton Language Center, Via Pascoli, 9, pg. 143

Segrate

Ingersoll Engineers, Strada Anulare-Torre 10, pg. 568

Torino

Leo Bunett Turin, Corso Vittorio Emanuele II, pg. 193
Washington Language Center, Via Lagrange, 7, pg. 143

Turin

American Appraisal Italia S.r.l., Via Cavour, 1, pg. 49
WABCO Westinghouse Compagnia Freni S.p.A., Via Pier Carlo Boggio n. 20, pg. 62

Turino

Metalchimica srl, Via San Pio V, 36, pg. 742

JAMAICA

Kingston

CUNA Mutual Insurance Soc., 2A Manhattan Rd., pg. 206
Jamtex Ltd., 51-52 Caracas Ave., pg. 460
Noel of Jamaica Ltd., J.K.D.C. Complex, pg. 460

JAPAN

Ayase City

SpeedFam Co Ltd., No. 2647 Haykawa, pg. 398

Chiba

NDC Co. Ltd., 1-687 Mimomi-Cho, pg. 900

Fukuroi

NSK-Warner K.K., 2345 Aino, pg. 166

Kobe

Acheson (Japan) Ltd., P.O. Box 538, , pg. 12

Osaka

Jitachi Zosen Systems, Inc., , pg. 371
Nisshoku Schenectady Chemicals, Inc., , pg. 975
Steelcase Kurogane Ltd., 25-8 Ishizunaka-Mashi, Neyagawa FH1, pg. 1044

Tokyo

AA Japan Co., Kabutocho Yachiyo Bldg., 20-5 Nihonbashi Kubatocho, pg. 48
Aim Services Co., Ltd., 1-15 Nishishinbashi 1-chome, pg. 7
Amway (Japan) Limited, Arco Tower, 1-8-1 Shimomeguro Meguro-Ku, pg. 71
The Austin Co., 1-9, Kanda Nishikicho., Chiyoda-ku, pg. 790
BSB Japan Ltd., Shibaura Square Bldg., 4-9-25, Shibaura, Minato-ku, pg. 110
Bell & Howell Japan Co. K.K., Ando Fukuyoshi Bldg., 8th Fl., 11-28 Akaska 1-chome, pg. 135
The Berlitz Schools of Languages (Japan) Inc., Kowa Bldg. No. 1, 5F, 1-11-41 Akasaka, pg. 143
Bose K.K., Harajuka-R, Bldg. 2F, pg. 167
Brown Brothers, Harriman & Co., Tokyo, Daimatsu Bldg., 4th Fl., 8-14 Nihonbashi, 3-chome, pg. 181
Leo Burnett-Kyodo Co. Ltd., Akasaka Twin Tower, 17-22, Akasake 2-chome, pg. 192
Carlson Marketing Group Japan Co. Ltd., Aoyama Bldg., Room 802, pg. 221
Carlson Marketing Group Japan KK, 8F Helios Bldg., 5-1-3 Nishi-Gotanda, pg. 221
Chuo Senko Advertising Co., Ltd., 2-6-1 Ginza, Chuo-ku, pg. 103
Coleman Japan Ltd., 5th Flr., Eight Bldg., 4-5-9, Hachobori, pg. 695
Dentsu, Sudler & Hennessey, Tsukiji MK Bldg., 2-11-26, Tsukiji, pg. 330
Dentsu Wunderman Direct Inc., 2-16-7, Ginza, pg. 1213
Dentsu, Young & Rubicam/Tokyo, Kyobashi K-1 Bldg., 2-7-12 Yaesu, Chuo-ku, pg. 330
Dicalite Orient Co. Ltd., Tachibana Bldg. 5, 4-Chome Kojimachi, pg. 137
Dr Pepper Japan Co., Hibiva Bldg., 1-1-1 Shinbashi, pg. 342
ESL-Nippon Co. Ltd., Sukegawa Bldg., 1-3-4 Yanagi Bashi, pg. 375
Estee Lauder K.K., Shin Aoyama Bldg., Nishi-kan 1-1, Minami Aoyama 1-chome, pg. 389
Fallek Chemical Corp., Teisen Kandabashi Bldg., 3rd Floor, pg. 558
First Boston (Japan) Limited, Asahi Seimei Hibiya Bldg.5-1, Yurakucho, pg. 204
Florasynth-Lautier K.K., Kanda Shibasaki Bldg., No. 16-7, 1-Chome Higashi Kanda, pg. 420
GAF (Japan) Ltd., Kogen Bldg. 67 No. 17-2, pg. 438
Goldman Sachs (Japan) Corp., ARK Mori Bldg., 10th Fl., 12-32, Akasaka 1-chome, pg. 468
Griffith Laboratories, K.K., NSS Building, 13-31, Kohnan 2-Chome, pg. 487
Hitachi Zosen Systems, Inc, , pg. 371
IDC Japan, 4-7, 1 Chome Kudankita, , pg. 578
IDG Communications/Japan, Kioicho TBR Bldg., 5-7, Kojimachi(102), pg. 577
IDG/World Expo Corporation, Ichibancho First Bldg., 3F, 15-1 Ichibancho, pg. 578

Integrated Resources (Japan), Inc., 710 Sunkaido Bldg., pg. 573
International Learning Systems (Japan) Ltd., 1-7-1 Nishi-Shinjuku, Shinjuku-ku, pg. 143
Japan Directory Advertising Company, Ltd. (JDAC), 303 Yotsuya Mansion, 1-22 Arakicho, Shinjuku-ku, pg. 1074
Ketchum Advertising (Japan) Ltd., Plus One Bldg., 2-16-4 Azabu Juban, pg. 626
Kohler Japan K.K., 3-19-23 Minami-Azabu, pg. 640
Kohler Japan K.K., 3-19-23 Minami Azabu, pg. 640
Korn/Ferry International, AIU Bldg. 7th Fl., 1-3 Marunounchi 1-Chrome, pg. 643
Levi Strauss Japan K.K., 1-30 Minami Aoyama 3-chome, pg. 671
Arthur D. Little (Japan), Inc., Fukide 679
Lord Far East, Inc., 2F, Yoyogi Center Bldg., pg. 683
M A C Group (Japan), Inc., JS Ichigaya Bldg., 4th Fl., 5 Goban-cho, Chiyoda-ku, pg. 448
Metallurg (Far East) Limited, P.O. Box 5221, Tokyo Int., pg. 742
MTV Japan, 6F Tango 33 Bldg. 3-25-11, , pg. 785
Nihon Faxon, 4th Fl., Kurihara Bldg., pg. 404
Nihon Ready Systems, No. 2 Shuukaen Bldg., 2-11-2 Komazawa Setagayaku, pg. 916
Nippon Flour Mills Co., Ltd., 2715 Sendagaya Shibuya-ku, pg. 804
Panduit Corp. Japan Branch, 31-5, Omori Kita 6-chome, pg. 846
The Prudential Life Insurance Company, Ltd., Sogo Hanzomon Bldg., 1-7 Kojimachi, pg. 897
Q.P. Corporation, , pg. 629
SAS Institute Japan Ltd., Nichirei Akashi-cho Bldg., 6-4 Akashi-cho, pg. 960
Soundesign Corp. Japan Ltd., 2-chome Hatchobon, Chuo-ku, pg. 1019
Spalding Japan Inc., 10F Hibiya Chunichi Bvld., pg. 1025
Spalding Japan Inc., Central P.O. Box 2067, pg. 1025
Spraying Systems Co. Far East, Dai Ichi Iwata Bldg., 8f-5-10-18, Higashi Gotanda, pg. 1032
Sunkist Pacific, Ltd., 5-19, Akasaka 4-chome, pg. 1061
Uniroyal Chemical Japan, Parkside Annex, 5th Fl., Banchi, Sanbancho, Chiyoda-ku, pg. 1129
Veeco K.K., Denpa Bldg. 1-11-15, pg. 1146
Viacom Japan, Inc., 4F, Mitsuwa Bldg., pg. 786
Weber Marking Systems (Far East) Co. Ltd., 3-6-1 chome Tsukiji Chuo-ku, pg. 1171
Ziebart Japan Limited, c/o Kojimachi Annex, 4-5-10, Kojimachi, Chiyoda-ku, pg. 1218

Yao City

Koyo-Mattison, 34, 2-Chome, pg. 721

Yokohama

Johnson Company, Ltd., Ninomiya P.O. Box 7, pg. 599
Thermon Far East, 2-17-1 Tsuruya-cho, pg. 1092

KENYA

Nairobi

Compu News Publishing, Fatima Court Ltd., Argwings Kodaheck, pg. 577
Johnson's Wax (East Africa) Ltd., Lunga Lunga Road, pg. 600

KOREA

Ansan City

Unikor Chemical, Inc., 1130

Choongbuk

Borg-Warner Automotive Korea, Inc., 65-4 Samjung-Ri, Daeso-Myun, pg. 166

Daegu

Open Systems Consulting, 79-6 Susung-3GA, pg. 371

Seoul

Acheson Korea Ltd., 1305-6 Seocho-Dong, pg. 12
Amway Korea, Ltd., Dong Sung Bldg., 12th Fl., 158-24 Samsung-dong, pg. 71
Cargill Trading Ltd., 5th Fl., Hyundai Cheil Bldg., 80 Cheokseon-Dong, Chongro-Ku, pg. 219
Dentsu, Young & Rubicam/Seoul, 5/6 Fl., Woomi Bldg., 98-6, Nonhyun-dong, Kangnam-ku, pg. 330
Diamond Ad Ltd., Hyundai Bldg., 5th Fl., 178 Sejong-ro, Chongro-ku, pg. 111
Hahn Jung Chemical, Inc., Soh Jin Building, 6th Fl., 1130
Hi Tech Information Inc., 3rd Fl., Bo-Lim Bldg., 411-16 Do Kok Dong, pg. 577
Hyosung ASC, 11-14 Yoido dong, pg. 7
IDC Korea, Inc., 3/F Shin Bong Bldg., 835-6, Yeuksam-Dong, pg. 578
Knight Korea, 7th Fl., Hanhyo Bldg., 34-2, Youido-dong, Yongdungpo-gu, pg. 637
Kolon-Met Life Insurance Company Limited, Ms. Bldg. 6-7 Fl., 53-1 Myung-Dong 1 Ga, pg. 745
Korea Johnson Co., Ltd., Sungdong P.O. Box 39, pg. 600
Leo Burnett Sonyon, Inc., 9th fl.-Youone Bldg., 75-95, Seosomun-dong, pg. 193
Lord Korea Ltd., C.P.O. Box No. 10156, pg. 683
Open Systems Consulting, 371
Panduit Trading Pte. Ltd., Rm. 1015 Jungwoo Bldg., 13-25 Yoldo Dong, pg. 846
SAS Software Korea Ltd., 960
Watlow Korea, Samsung Bldg., St. 302, 945-3 Daechi-Dong, Kangham-ku, pg. 1168

KUWAIT

Safat

Radius Advertising, Al Khaleejia Bldg., 12 Fl., Al Sharg, pg. 193

LEBANON

Beirut

H & C, Leo Burnett, Sofil Center, 5th Fl., pg. 192

LUXEMBOURG

Luxembourg

Brown Brothers Harriman (Luxembourg) S.A., 33, Blvd. Prince Henri, pg. 181
CM Transnational, 15 Blvd. Royal, pg. 275

MALAYSIA

Kuala Lumpur

BSB Malaysia Sdn. Bhd., 11th Fl., Pernas Intl., Jalan Sultan Ismail, pg. 110
Leo Burnett Sdn. Bhd., 8th Fl., Wisma Damansara, Damansara Heights, pg. 193
Dentsu, Young & Rubicam/Kuala Lumpur, 6th Fl., Wisma MBSB, 48 Jalan Dungun, pg. 330
IDG (Malaysia) Sdn Bhd, 38-3B Jalan Pandan 3/2, pg. 577
Kobs & Draft Asia-Malaysia, 270 Jalan Ampang, pg. 112
Korn/Ferry International, 6th Fl., UBN Tower, 10 Jalan P. Ramlee, pg. 643
SAS Institute Sdn. Bhd., 28th Floor Menara Maybank, 100 Jalan Tun Perak, pg. 960
Tylus SDN BHD, 3L. Ground Floor Block C, Jalan, Jubilee, pg. 846

Penang

Levi Strauss (Malaysia) Sdn. Bhd., 78/78A Lorong Selamat, pg. 671

Petaling Jaya

Fugro-McClelland, 98 Jalan SS 15/4, pg. 435

Selangor

Amway (Malaysia) Sdn. Bhd., P.O. Box 84, Jalan Sultan, pg. 71

MEXICO

Agua Prieta

Hamlin S.A. de C.V., Calle 20 & Ave. 6, pg. 503

Azcapotzalco

S. C. Johnson & Son, S.A. de C.V., Poniente 140 No. 717, pg. 600

Chicoloapan

Tube Turns de Mexico, S.A., K.M. 22.5 Carretera Federal Mex-Puebla, pg. 1059

Col. del Valle

IDG Communicaciones S.A. de C.V., Gonzalez de Cossio 577

Col. Cuauhemoc Mexicali

Electronica Condor De Mexico, Costa Rica 273

Cuautitlan

Florasynth S.A. de C.V., , pg. 420

Guadalajara

B. W. Componentes Mexicanos De Transmissiones, S.A. de C.V., Calzada Lazardo CArdenas No. 4135-201, pg. 166
Fabrica de Valvulas, Calle 5 No. 1906, pg. 400

Guadalupe

DHL Handling Mexicana, S.A. de C.V., Prol. Madero 255 Oriente, pg. 309

Lerma

Kilsby-Jorgensen Steel & Aluminum SA de CV, Parque Industrial El Cerillo, Avenida El Cerillo 606

Matamoros

Leece-Neville de Mexico S.A. de C.V., Ave. Alvara Obregon y Claveles. H, pg. 1121

Mexico

Arellano/BSB Publicidad, Goldsmith 225, pg. 109
Berlitz de Mexico, S.A. de C.V., 530 Ejercito Nacional, pg. 142
Borg-Warner de Mexico, S.A., Av. las Granjas 473-C, Col. Jardin Azpeitia, pg. 166
Bucyrus Blades de Mexico, , pg. 388
Leo Burnett S.A. de C.V., Bosque de Duraznos 65-8P, pg. 193
C.I.C.S.A., Rosas Moreno No. 60, pg. 723
Central de Industrias, S.A., Minerva 104-602 Colonia Florida, Deleg., pg. 664
Clevite de Mexico, Monte Caucaso No. 915-6 Piso, pg. 900
Dentsply Caulk de Mexico, S.A. de C.V., Calz. Vallejo 846, Col. Industrial Vallejo, pg. 330
Dicaser S.A. de C.V., Lafayette 137
Dietzgen de Mexico S.A. de C.V., Belisario Dominquez No. 151-A, pg. 337
Draper de Mexico S.A. de C.V., Norte 75, 2591 Colonia Xochimanca, pg. 348
Duro-Test de Mexico, S.A., Paseo de la Reforma 195-10O Piso 5, pg. 355
Enterprise S.A. de C.V., Rodriguez Saro 424, pg. 366
Evenflo Mexico S.A., Apartado 18939, pg. 1025
GAF Corp. de Mexico S.A. de C.V., Calle de Lopez No. 15, pg. 438
Herramientas Klein S.A. de C.V., Avenida 1 No. 3, Parque Indus. Cartagena, pg. 635
Holophane, S.A. de C.V., , pg. 732
Hovomex S.A. de C.V., Ruben Dario 539
Ideal-Standard, S.A. de C.V., Apartado Postal 291, pg. 62
Isomex, S.A., Zettina 16, ZPEM, pg. 975
Kendall de Mexico S.A. de D.V., Poniente 44, No. 3401 Col. San Salvador, pg. 622
Kohler de Mexico, S.A. de C.V., Calle Norte 45 No. 766, pg. 640
Korn/Ferry International, Montes Urales 641, Lomas De Chapultepec, pg. 643
Lebrija Rubio Publicidad S.A., Sierra Santa Rosa 99-30, Col. Lomas de Barrilaco, pg. 104
Levi Strauss de Mexico, S.A. de C.V., Horacio 1844, 4th Fl., Col. Polanco Refornia, pg. 671
Arthur D. Little Mexicana, S.A. de C.V., Av. Sinola No. 149-10 Piso, Col. Roma, pg. 679
Longyear de Mexico S.A. de C.V., Apartado Postal 325, pg. 683
Metallurg Mexico, S.A. de CV, Eucken 16-302, pg. 742
Mosler SA de C.D., Rio Lerma 69, pg. 772
Novaquim S.A. de C.V., Insurgentes Sur, 1106 Col. Nochebuena, pg. 1130
Panamericana de Avaluos, S.A., Colonia del Valle, Moras No. 850, pg. 49
Periphonics S.A. de C.V., San Francisco No.1626-301, pg. 862
Playtex Mexicana S.A. de C.V., Avenida Constitutyentes 908-C, pg. 877
Preformados De Mexico SA, Poniente 140, 526 Fracc Ind. Vallejo, pg. 886
SyC-SELMEC, S.A. de C.V., Calz, Vallejo No. 706A, pg. 959
Stonhard Latin America, Los Juarez No. 26, pg. 1051
Tork Electro Sistemas S.A., Calle Hortensia 1102
Tubetec, Calle Mayas, No. 12, Sta. Cruz Acatlan, pg. 878
Young & Rubicam, S.A. de C.V., Leibnitz 1213

Mexico City

IDC Mexico, Select, S.A. de C.V., Av. Nuevo Leon No. 54, Desp. 501, pg. 578

Monterrey

Barnes de Mexico, Apartado 1774, pg. 900
CIQYA/Bravo Foods de Mexico, Prol. Morelos 2277, pg. 804
Korn/Ferry International, Daniel Zambrano 525, pg. 643
Laboratories Griffith de Mexico, S.A. de C.V., Apartado Postal 1832, pg. 488
Manufacturera Thermon de Mexico, S.A., Edif. Santos Despacho 415, pg. 1092
Mary Kay Cosmeticos de Mexico Pty., S.A. de C.V., Zaragoza 1300 Sur, pg. 717
Mo-Car Internacional, S.A., Apartado, Postal 5259-K, pg. 1121

Morelos

Atapco Azteca, S.A. de C.V., Calle 21 Este No. 305, pg. 65

Naucalpan de Juarez

Industrias Kolmex, S.A., Calle del Rio No.u, pg. 696
Playtex Mexicana S.A. de C.V., Calle 3 No. 28, pg. 877

Piedras Negras

Littelfuse S.A. de C.V., , pg. 678

Reynosa

Wells Manufacturera de Mexico S.A. de C.V., Carretera Laredo, Km. 9, pg. 1124

San Nocolas Tlaxcoapa

Andamios Atlas, S.A., Rio Lerma No. 5, pg. 8

Sonora

Bose S.A. de C.V., Plan de Alberque San Luis, Juarez No. 728, pg. 167
Equipo Automotriz Americana S.A. de C.V., Calle 13 N625, pg. 1077

Tijuana

Elec-Trol Mexico, Prolong, Las Lomas Local 18, pg. 503

Internacional Monterey, S.A., calle Josefina M. Conteras No. 19, pg. 986
Keystone Automotive Industries, Inc.-Tijuana, Paseo Reforma 628
Levimex de Baja California S.A. de C.V., Blvd. Los Insurgentes 20004, pg. 671
Maquiladora Clamaq S.A. de C.V., Calle 7 Sur No. 108, Ciudad Industrial, pg. 254

Tlalnepantla

Gates Rubber de Mexico, Cerrada de Galeana No. 5, pg. 445
Sunbeam Mexicana S.A. de C.V., A.V. Dr. Gustavo Baz, pg. 1059

MOROCCO
Casablanca

Johnson Wax Morocco S.A., 3 rue Jabal Boubilane, Bourgogne, pg. 600

NETHERLANDS
Amsterdam

Ad/Productions, Ottho Heldringstraat 27, pg. 1211
Austin-Nederland B.V., Turfstekerstraat 63, pg. 791
BSB Amsterdam, President Kennedylaan 1, pg. 109
Berlitz Schools of Languages B.V., Robin 87-89, pg. 143
CSFB Finance B.V., Herengracht 478, pg. 204
Credit Suisse First Boston Nederland N.V., Herengracht 478, pg. 204
DHL International BV, Parnassusweg 203, pg. 309
Faxon Europe, Hogehilweg 10, pg. 404
ICC Industries, B.V., Amteldijk 166, P.O. Box 7000, pg. 559
IDC Nederland, A. Fokkerweg, pg. 578
Intralox European, Postbus 23280, Lemeterbergweg 36D, pg. 651
Kobs & Draft bv, Amsteldijk 166, pg. 112
Korn/Ferry International, Strawinskylaan 545, pg. 642
Levi Strauss Nederland B.V., Schurenbergweg 6, pg. 671
Arthur D. Little Intl., Inc., World Trade Center, Strawinskylaan 621, pg. 679
Lowe Kuiper & Schouten B.V., Koningslaan 42, pg. 685
Noordervliet & Winninghoff/Leo Burnett B.V., Drentestraat 5, pg. 193
Prins, Meijer, Stamenkovits en van Walbeek/Young & Rubicam B.V., Frans van Mierisstraat 92, pg. 1212
Riechelmann, Lopes Cardozo & Van Bercum B.V., Maassluisstraat 2, pg. 1212
De TBWA Groep B.V., Dr. Willem Dreesweg 2, pg. 1072
Wunderman Worldwide v.o.f., Herengracht 105, pg. 1212

Apeldoorn

Vectur B.V., Zwolsweg 335, pg. 1139

Arnhem

N.V. Maxon International S.A., Groningensingel 1, pg. 723

Assen

Furigas NV, J.C. van Markenstraat 19, pg. 358

Capelle aan den Ijssel

Spanjersburg, , pg. 502
WABCO Westinghouse B.V., Mient 12-16, Postbus 26, pg. 62

Denhelder

Penrod International Drilling Company, , pg. 859

Deventer

Ayer/Nederland B.V., Keulenstraat 1, pg. 104

Edam

Bose B.V., Nijuerheidstratt, pg. 167

Eindhoven

Multicom TBWA Advertising B.V., Dillenburgstraat 5A, pg. 1072

Etten-Leur

Campa Products B.V., 29 Nijverheidsweg, pg. 358
Longyear (Nederland) B.V., P.O. Box 56, Nijverheidsweg 47, pg. 683

Giesbeek

Bell & Howell Nederland B.V., Nijverheidsstraat 22, pg. 135
Pretec Precisie Techniek B.V., Kuyperlan 28, pg. 135

Gorinchem

SPSS Europe B.V., , pg. 964

Gouda

Flameco-Eclipse B.V., Zwolleweg 5, pg. 367

Haarlem

IDG Communications Nederland BV, Schipholweg 1, pg. 577
Ideal-Standard, Lange Herenstraat 45-47, pg. 62
Mulder Hardenberg B.V., Westerhoutpark 1a,2012 JL, pg. 845

Heerenveen

Systems Engineering & Mfg. Nederlands B.V., Magnesiumweg 2, pg. 1071

Hilversum

SAS Institute B.V., Koninginneweg 31, pg. 960

Industrieweg

Pantex Cissell, 9672 AP Winschoten, pg. 358

Leiden

PQ Zeolites B.V., Stationsweg 26, pg. 837

Mijdrecht

Johnson Wax Nederland B.V., P.O. Box 22, pg. 600

Naaldwijk

Margo Imports B.V., Corelli 14, pg. 707

Oevel-Westerlo

Estee Lauder N.V., 15, Nijverheidsstraat, pg. 389

Oosterhout

Houghton-Benelux B.V., Mechelaarstraat 12, pg. 546

Pijnacker

Bently Nevada Europa B.V., Weterinweg 14, pg. 141
Thermon Benelux, Korteweg 1, pg. 1092

Roosendaal

Findley Euro BV, Zeggeveld 410

Rosmalen

Panduit Nederland, , pg. 846

Rotterdam

Dicalite Holding B.V., , pg. 137

Scheemda

Acheson Colloiden B.V., Postbus 1, pg. 12

Schiedam

GAF (Nederland) N.V., Olivier van Noortstraat 7, pg. 438

Tiel

Amway Nederland Ltd., Edisonstraat 18, pg. 71

Utrecht

Littelfuse B.V., Kanonstraat 36, pg. 678

Veenendaal

Codi International B.V., Verlaat 22, pg. 400
Colson Transportwielen B.V., , pg. 711
Firet, B.V., Verlaat 22, pg. 400

Voorburg

Bourns Benelux B.V., Van Tuyl Van Serooskerkestraat 81-85, pg. 168

Waalwijk

Henningsen Nederland B.V., Slvisweg 20, pg. 629
Henningsen-Van den Burg, Slvisweg 20, pg. 629

Warmond

Thermo Electric Intl. B.V., P.O. Box 65, pg. 1091

Woerden

Ampco Metal Nederlands B.V., , pg. 68

Zoetermeer

Finelpac B.V., Edisonstraat 9A, pg. 8

NETHERLANDS ANTILLES
Curacao

Prudential Overseas Funding Corp. N.V., Labadera Plaza, Santa Rosaweg 129 E, pg. 897

Willemstad

CUNA Mutual Insurance Soc., Curacaostaat 50, pg. 206

NEW ZEALAND
Auckland

American Motivation (N.Z.) Ltd., 5 Porters Ave., pg. 221
Amway of New Zealand Limited, Private Bag 94401, Greenmount, pg. 71
BSB New Zealand, 10th Fl., 17 Albert St., pg. 110
Leo Burnett Limited, Level 4, 100 Symonds St., pg. 193
Chiat/Day/Mojo, Kenwyn St./St. Georges Bay Rd., pg. 245
Elfin Industries, Ltd., 174 Maura Rd., pg. 72
Gestro Horne, Level 7, 110 Symonds St., pg. 111
Griffith Laboratories Limited, P.O. Box 22-434, 11-13 Bell Ave., pg. 487
Johnson Wax New Zealand Ltd., Private Bag, One hunga, pg. 600
Levi Strauss (New Zealand) Ltd., 22 Heather St., pg. 671
Longyear New Zealand Ltd., P.O. Box 43-030 Mangere, pg. 683
Mattingly & Partners/Auckland, 4th Fl., Cnr. Augustus Terrace & Parnell Rise, pg. 331
Sudler & Hennessey, 3 Whitaker Place, pg. 1214
Western Staff Services (NZ) Ltd., Level 2, Quay Tower, CNR Customs & Albert Sts., pg. 1182
Young & Rubicam New Zealand Ltd., 3 Whitaker Place, pg. 1214

Christchurch

Darby & Associates, 99-101 Victoria St., pg. 111

Grey Lynn

GAF (New Zealand) Pty., Ltd., 2 Monmouth St., pg. 438

Mangere

Hallmark Cards NZ Ltd., 59 Mahunga Dr., pg. 502

Panmure

Ashton/Scholastic Pty. Ltd., 165 Marua Rd., pg. 962

Parnell

IDG Communications Ltd., 2nd Fl., 15 Augustus Ter., pg. 577

Wellington

BSB New Zealand Limited, 43 Kent Terrace, pg. 110
Leo Burnett Limited, Level 5, Barclays House, 36 Customhouse Quay, pg. 193
CS First Boston New Zealand Holdings Limited, 10th Floor, Caltex Tower, pg. 204
Chiat/Day/Mojo, Level 2, Wool Store, 262-264 Thorndon Quay, pg. 245
Gestro Horne, The Terrace, 1st Floor, Level 8, 203 Willis St., pg. 111
IDC New Zealand, 31 Ganges Rd., pg. 578
SAS Institute (NZ) Ltd., P.O. Box 10-109, The Terrace, pg. 960

NICARAGUA
Managua

Industria Ceramica Centroamericana, S.A., Apartado Postal 2551, pg. 62

NIGERIA
Festac Town

IDG Communications (W. Africa) Ltd., Mars House, Plot 43b, First Ave., pg. 577

Ikeja

Johnson Wax Nigeria Limited, Plot 5, Block H, Isolo Industrial Estate, pg. 600

Lagos

Insight Communications Ltd., Plot 58, Akanbi Onitiri Close, Off Eric Moore Rd., pg. 111

NORWAY
Bergen

Bates Bergen A/S, Hellandgarden 2, pg. 111

Gjettum

IDC Norge, Baerumsveien 385, pg. 578

Hagan

Norsk Johnson's Wax A/S, Postboks 34, pg. 600

Holmsbu

Intralox A/S, P.B. 40, pg. 651

Larvik

Ted Bates-Vestfold, Stavernsveien 15, pg. 111

Oslo

The Associated Press A/S, Fridtiof Mansens Plass 5, pg. 92
Av-Kontakt A/S, Munkedamsveien 35, pg. 109
BSB Bates-Gruppen A/S, Munkedamsveien 35, Solli, pg. 109
BSB Naess & Morch A/S, Parkveien 60, pg. 110
Bates Advertising A/S, Parkveien 60, pg. 110
Bates Backer & Spielvogel A/S, Munkedamsveien 35, pg. 111
Bates Benjamin A/S, Cort Adelersgt. 16, pg. 111
Bates Film, Munkedamsveien 35,V, pg. 111
Ted Bates Greenhouse, Cort Adelersgt. 16, pg. 111
Bates Telemarketing, Cort Adelersgt. 16, pg. 111
Berlitz A/S, Lille Grensen 5, pg. 142
IDG Communications Norge AS, Hovinveien 43, , pg. 577
Kobs & Draft, Munkedamsveien 35, pg. 112
Levi Strauss Norway, A/S, Marcus Thrangest 2, pg. 671
Media Marketing Research, Munkedamsveien 35, pg. 112
N&T Leo Burnett A/S, Drammensveien 130, pg. 193
Nordskar & Thorkildsen Leo Burnett A/S, , pg. 193
Scanelo, Young & Rubicam AS, Waldemar THR Anesgate 84b, pg. 1212

Sandvika

Kontorservice Inc., Eyvind Lyches vei 13 B, pg. 1182

Skjetten

Klockner-Moeller Norsk A/S, Hvamveien 4, pg. 845

Stavanger

Bates Stavanger A/S, Hillevagsveien 85, pg. 111

Trollasen

SAS Institute A/S, Trollasveien 4, pg. 960

PANAMA

El Dorado

Amway de Panama S.A., Apartado 6-4200, pg. 70

Panama

Comunica Leo Burnett Publicidad, Calle Venezuela No.5 Bella Vista, pg. 192
Griffith Panama S.A., via Argentina, Balmoral Building, 10th Flr., Apt. 10A, pg. 488
Kendall S.A., Calle Ricardo Arias 622

PEOPLE'S REPUBLIC OF CHINA

Beijing

China Computerworld, 74 Lu Gu Rd., pg. 577
Dentsu, Young & Rubicam/Beijing, 10th Fl., Asia-Pacific Bldg., No. 8, Ya Bao Lu, Chaoyang District, pg. 330
IDC Beijing, c/o IDG High Tech Co., 15 Fuxing Rd., Room 821, pg. 578
IDG High Tech Company, Rm. 821, 15 Fuxing Rd., pg. 577
SAS Institute Ltd., Beijing Representative Office, Rm. 322, Kunlun Hotel, pg. 960

Shanghai

Dentsu, Young & Rubicam/Shanghai, Rm. 1206, Shanghai International Trade Centre, pg. 330

PERU

Lima

Causa Publicidad, Tarata 269, Officina 210, 2nd Fl., pg. 192
Compania Minera Raura S.A., P.O. Box 876, pg. 712
CUNA Mutual Insurance Soc., Calle Camilo Carrillo 114 Jesus Maria, pg. 206
Indeco Peruana S.A., P.O. Box 785, pg. 712
Perdomo-Ted Bates/Publicidad, Prolongacion Av., Primavera 120A, Oficinas 209-210-217, pg. 112
Servicios Expeciales de Edicion, El Comercio, Jr. Miro Quesada 247-702, pg. 577
Sunbeam del Peru S.A., Casilla Postal 5673, pg. 1059

PHILIPPINES

Davao

TCG Fibers, Philippines, , pg. 266

Legaspi

Induplex, Inc., , pg. 137

Makati

Connell Brothers Co. Philippines Inc., , pg. 1189
Panduit Philippines, Rm. 301, Ambrosio Bldg., Sen. Gil J. Puyat Ave., pg. 846

Manila

Columbian Philippines Inc., P.O. Box 7501, pg. 266
Dentsu, Young & Rubicam, Alcantara/Manila, 704 Vito Cruz, pg. 330
Griffith Laboratories (Phils.) Inc., Building No. 2, Honeydew Rd., pg. 488
S. C. Johnson & Son, Inc., , pg. 600
Levi Strauss (Philippines) Inc., 2264 Pasong Tamo Extn., pg. 671
Marketforce Advertising Philippines Inc., S-341 3rd Fl., Secretariat Bldg., PICC, CCP Complex, pg. 330

Metro Manila

Evenflo, 3/F, Dome Narcisa Bldg., 8751 Paseo De Roxas, pg. 1025
Gelmart Industries Philippines, Inc., PX Division, Km. 15, South Super Hwy., pg. 876
Hemisphere-Leo Burnett, Inc., Planters Products Inc. Bldg., 2nd Fl., Esteban St., pg. 192
Longyear Diamond Prods. (Philippines) Inc., , pg. 683
SAS Institute Ltd. (Philippines), Strata 100 Emerald Ave., pg. 960
Sanitary Wares Mfg. Corp., , pg. 62
Velsicol Chemical Corporation, 4th Floor, Marsman Building, Buendia Ave. & Washington St., pg. 1147
WS Publishing Company, Inc., 7/F Sedcco 1 Bldg., Rada St., pg. 577

Rizal

Joffko Philippines, Inc., 11 Emerald Dr., pg. 595

POLAND

Warsaw

American Appraisal Poland Sp. z.o.o., ul. Filtrowa 43, pg. 49
Berlitz-Cyztelnik Language School, UL. Wiejska 12A, pg. 143
Epstein Engineering Export (Warsaw), Ltd., Biuro Nadzora w Warszawie, Al 1 Armii Wojska Polskiego, 16 M 3, pg. 384
IDC Poland, ul. Dluga 16, pg. 578
IDG Poland S.A., ut. Tytoniowa 20, pg. 577

PORTUGAL

Amway de Portugal, Inc., Av. do Forte, 10, pg. 70

Amadora

Cone, Lda., Urb. Colina do Sol, Lote 18-Alfornel, pg. 845

Codex

Cortal-Seldex, Mobiliario De Escritorio, SA, pg. 518

Lagoa

Ceras Johnson de Portugal, Lda., Rua Maestro Raul Portela, 1, pg. 599

Lisbon

American Appraisal (Portugal) Ltd., Av. Miguel Bombarda, 36-11, pg. 49
Ayer Portugal, Av da Liberdade, 229-3 Andar, pg. 104
BSB Portugal, Avenida 5 de Outubro 35, 8th Fl., pg. 110
EPG/TBWA, Rua Marques de Fronteira 4A, pg. 1072
Young & Rubicam (Portugal), Ava. Duque d'Avila 26-30, pg. 1213

Porto

American Appraisal Portugal Consultores de. Avaliacao S.A., Av. da Boavista, 1015-6.0, pg. 49

Santa Marta de Corroios

Concorco Lda., Sociedade Corticeira Concoroco Lda., pg. 1121

QATAR

Doha

N.B.K. Geosciences, Ltd., P.O. Box 318, pg. 436

ROMANIA

Bucharest

Stinta & Technica S.A., Plata Pressi Libere no. 1, pg. 577

RUSSIA

Moscow

Berlitz Sovincenter, 12, Krasnopresenskaya NAB, pg. 143
IDC Russia, Prospekt Mira, VDNH, Pav. 4, Room 105-107, pg. 578
Information Computer Enterprise, Prospekt Mira 187-98-22, VDNH, Pavillion 577
Pepper, Hamilton & Scheetz, 19-27 Grokholsky Per.(129010), pg. 860

RUSSIAN FEDERATION

Vladivostok

Pepper, Hamilton & Scheetz, International Law Center, 2 Captain Shefaer St., pg. 860

SAUDI ARABIA

Dammam

McClelland-Suhaimi, Ltd., , pg. 436

Jeddah

Targets Adv., Shinkar Commercial Center, 2nd Fl., Medina Rd., pg. 193

SINGAPORE

Bugis Village

IDC Singapore, 62 Queen St.(0718), pg. 578

Singapore

Asia Computerworld Communications, 577
Avex Electronics Pte. Ltd., 510 Thomson Rd. 550
BSB Singapore, 100 Beach Rd., 110
Bently Nevada Sales & Service Singapore Pte. Ltd., 101 Thomson Road, Ste. 07-04A, pg. 141
Leo Burnett Pte. Ltd., 193
CS First Boston (Singapore) Limited, 50 Raffles Place, pg. 204
CS First Boston Singapore Ltd., 50 Raffles Place 28-05 Shell Tower, pg. 204
Conaif Pacific Equipment Pte. Ltd., 10 Jln. Kilang Timor 272
Connell Brothers Company Ltd., 1189
Dentsu, Young & Rubicam/Singapore, 6th Fl., 20 Kallang Ave., pg. 330
DeWitt International (Singapore) Pte. Ltd., 62 Tannery Lane, pg. 417
Fugro-McClelland, Ltd., 510 Thomson Rd., pg. 435
GAF (Singapore) Pte. Ltd., 8 N03-17 Chia Ping Rd., pg. 439
Griffith Laboratories Pte. Ltd., 1, Defu Lane 10, 488
S. C. Johnson & Son Pte. Limited, 23, Playfair Road, pg. 600
Kendall Singapore, Unit 03-39, Paramount Hotel Shopping, pg. 622
Ketchum Advertising Singapore, 5 & 7 Halifax Rd., pg. 625
Korn/Ferry International, 29-05 Shell Tower, 50 Raffles Pl.(0104), pg. 643
Arthur D. Little Far East, Inc., 152 Bearch Rd., 679
M/S Fischbein Packaging (Singapore) Pte. Ltd., No. 37, Lorong 23, pg. 9
Panduit Singapore Pte. Ltd., 5 Gul Lane, pg. 846
SAS Institute Pte. Ltd., 510 Thomson Rd., 960
UFE Pte Ltd, No. 5 Joo Koon Way, pg. 1123
Uniroyal Chemical Co., Inc. (Singapore), Cathay Building, 11, Dhoby Ghaut 1129
Up-Right (Far East) Ltd., Unit 243, Ubi Ave. 4, pg. 1139
Watlow Singapore Pte. Ltd., Ayer Rajah Industrial Estate, 55 Ayer Rajah Crescent, pg. 1168

SOUTH AFRICA

Cape Town

Electronik (Pty) Ltd., Fleetway House, Martin Hammerschlag Way, pg. 845

Fairland

S. C. Johnson & Son of South Africa (Pty.) Ltd., Private Bag XOB, pg. 600

Johannesburg

Bucyrus (Africa) Proprietary Ltd., 415 Wrench Rd., pg. 186
Y&R Transvaal, Nissan House, 3rd Fl., 15 Alice Lane, pg. 1214

Kenilworth

Cato Johnson Cape Town, 305 Main Rd., pg. 1214
Y&R Cape, 305 Main Rd., pg. 1214
Young & Rubicam Cape, 305 Main Rd., pg. 1214
Young & Rubicam Hedley Byrne Cape, , pg. 1214
Young & Rubicam South Africa, 305 Main Rd., pg. 1214

Sandton

GAF South Africa (Pty.), Ltd., P.O. Box 78838, pg. 439
Wunderman Worldwide, Nissan House, 3rd Fl., 15 Alice Lane, pg. 1214
Young & Rubicam-Hedley Byrne Transvaal, Nissan House, 3rd Fl., 15 Alice Ln., pg. 1214

Sasolburg

Orchem (Pty) Ltd. (Plant), Sunsen St., pg. 1130

SPAIN

Alicante

Thoroughbred/Quark, c/o Quark Informatica, Carlet, 3, pg. 1095

Barcelona

Acheson Colloiden B.V., Sucursal en Espana, pg. 12
Alas/DPP Barcelona S.A., Avda. Diagonal 615, 4A, pg. 109
American Appraisal Espana, S.A., Diputacion, 238 -Atico 2, pg. 48
Amway de Espana, S.A., C/Industria, 101-115, Poligono Gran Via, Zona 22A, pg. 70
BSB Publicidad S.A., Avda. Diagonal, 615-4o-A, pg. 110
Central Media, S.A., Traversera de Gracia 18-20, pg. 111
Compania General de Esencias Grupo Florasynth S.A., Poligono Industrial Congost, Ave. San Julian 154, pg. 420
Delvico/Bates, S.A., Escuelas Pias 118, pg. 111
GAF Sucursal en Espana, Loreto, 42 Entlo, pg. 439
Gates Vulca Automotive Products Division, Avenida de la Riera, 3-5, pg. 445
Harrod Devitt Sociedad Anonima, Avad. Diagonal,601,5.A, pg. 897
Levi Strauss de Espana, S.A., 2Y4 Planta 20, Torre Catalvnya, pg. 670
Lowe MBAC, Paseo de los Tilos, 3-9, pg. 685
PAMCO Espana Sociedad Anonima de Seguros, Diagonal, 601, 5-D, pg. 897
Sunbeam Iberica S.A., Rambla De Cataluna No. 98, 7th Flr., pg. 1059
TBWA, Avda. Diagonal, 604, pg. 1072
TAPSA Ayer, Numancia 187, 70-A, pg. 104
Vinizius/Young & Rubicam, S.A., Diagonal 652-656, Edificio A-Planta 2A, pg. 1212
Vituvio/Leo Burnett, , pg. 193

Bilbao

American Appraisal Espana, S.A., Colon De Larreategui, 26-3H, pg. 48
BSB Publicidad S.A., Plaza Espana 4, pg. 110

Castellar del Valles

Playtex Espana S.A., Carretera de Sabadell S/N, pg. 876

Granada

BSB Publicidad S.A., Acera del Darro 72,3o, pg. 110

Guernica

Guernica Espectaculos & Turismo, S.A., Carlos Gangoiti 14, pg. 1203

La Coruna

BSB Publicidad S.A., Juan Florez, 28, pg. 110

Las Palmas

BSB Publicidad S.A., Plaza de la Feria, 40, pg. 110

Madrid

Alas/D.P.P., Orense 12, 1st Fl., Office 10, pg. 109
American Appraisal Espana, S.A., Principe de Vergara, 9, pg. 48
The Austin Co. S.A., Magallanes 3, 10 piso, pg. 790
BSB Publicidad S.A., Goya 8, 2nd Fl., pg. 110
Bose Products B.V. Sucuvsal en Espana, Avda. de Avagon 334, pg. 167
Brandau y Compania S.A., Emillo Vargas, 15, 1 C, pg. 742
Cato Johnson Spain S.A., C/ Castello 64-1, pg. 1212
Central Media, S.A., Conde de Penalver 38-4o, pg. 111
Commercial Espanola de Componentes S.A., Ofelia Nieto 43, pg. 845
Credit Suisse First Boston Espana S.A., Edificio "Alfredo Mahou", Plaza Manuel Gomez Moreno, s/n, pg. 204
Delvico/Bates, S.A., Hermosilla 30, pg. 111
Escuelas de Idiomas Berlitz de Espana, S.A., Gran Via 80-4, pg. 143
Final Art, Rosario Pino 12, pg. 111
Grupo BSB SA, Goya 8, 1st Fl., pg. 111
ICC Iberica S.A., Paseo de la Castellana 115, pg. 559
IDC Spain, Rafael Calvo 18 20B, pg. 578
IDG Communications, S.A., Rafael Calvo, pg. 577
Johnson's Wax Espanola, S.A., Calle Orense 4-6.a, pg. 600
Kobs & Draft S.A., Rosario Pino, 12, pg. 112
Korn/Ferry International, Calle Felipe IV, 643
Arthur D. Little S.R.C., General Peron 40A, pg. 679
Longyear Iberica S.A., Avda de los Metales, S-N Leganes, pg. 683
Lowe FMS, Tambre 33, pg. 685
Playtex Espana S.A., Paseo de la Castellana 93, pg. 876
SAS Institute S.A. (Madrid), Calle Pena Sirio No. 17B, pg. 960
Santander Met., S.A. Madrid, Paseo De La Castellana 95, pg. 745
Schenectady Iberica S.A., , pg. 975
Seguros Gensis, SA, , pg. 745
TBWA Espana S.A., Profesor Waksman, 14, pg. 1072
TAPSA Ayer, Jenner 3, pg. 104
Vitruvio/Leo Burnett, Planta 27, Plaza de Pablo Ruiz, Torre Picasso S/N, pg. 193
Young & Rubicam, S.A., Raimundo Fernandez Villaverde 65, pg. 1213

Malaga

BSB Publicidad S.A., San Lorenzo, 2, 2do, pg. 110

Oviedo

BSB Publicidad S.A., Santa Susana, 43, pg. 110

Pamplona

BSB Publicidad S.A., Av. Baranain 2, pg. 110

Santander

BSB Publicidad S.A., Castilla 19, Esc. B 6toC., pg. 110

Seville

American Appraisal Espana, S.A., Calle Luis de Morales, 32-1, pg. 48
BSB Publicidad S.A., Plaza Nueva 8, duplicado, pg. 110
InterOliva, Calle Las Cruces s/n, Dos Hermanos, pg. 1183

Valencia

Alas/DPP Valencia S.A., San Vicente 53-1, pg. 109
Central Media, S.A., Plaza Colegio del Patriarca 4, pg. 111
Delvico/Bates, S.A., Plaza Porta de la Mar, 6-12, pg. 111

Valls

Griffith Laboratories Iberia S.A., Apartado de Correos 78, pg. 487

SWEDEN

Djursholm

Carlson Marketing Group Scandinavia Motivation Service AB, Box 225, , pg. 221

Eksjo

IDAB Wamac AB, , pg. 559

Goteborg

BSB Goteborg AB, Jarntorget, pg. 109
Young & Rubicam Goteburg AB, Tradgardsgaten 1, pg. 1213

Helsingborg

BSB Helsingborg AB, Kullagatan 30, pg. 110
BSB September AB, Jarnvagsgatan 14, pg. 110

Hova

WABCO Westinghouse AB, Industriegatan, pg. 62

Johanneshov

Ampco Metal Nordiska AB, Mockelv, pg. 68
GAF Norden AB, Box 824, pg. 439

Kista

IDC Sweden, Torsnaegatan 4, pg. 578
SAS Institute AB, Box 1249, Farogatan 2, pg. 960

Malmo

Master Foods AB, Box 4138, pg. 714

Mellbystrand

Intralox A/S, 8, Strandvagen 29b, pg. 651

Sollentuna

DHL International AB, Lastbilsv. 6, pg. 309

Stockholm

Allhabo Aktiebolag, Alstromergatan 20, pg. 845
Andersson Media Aktiebolag, Riddargaten 17, pg. 1211
The Associated Press AB, Vattugatten 12, pg. 92
BSB/Adaptus AB, Kungsgatan 66, pg. 109
BSB Stockholm AB, Klara Norra Kyrkogata 29, pg. 110
BSB Sweden, Klara Norra Kyrkogata 29, pg. 110
Berlitz Schools of Languages AB, Vasgatan 52, pg. 143
CW/Communications AB, Sodra Hamnvagen 22, pg. 577
Cato Johnson Stockholm, Riddargatan 17, pg. 1212
AB Ferrolegeringar, Box 7163, pg. 742
Hector & Co. A.B., Drottninggatan 25, pg. 137
K&D Adaptus Direct, Kungsgatan 66, pg. 112
Leo Burnett Sweden A.B., Kunggatan 38, pg. 193
Svenska Johnson's Vax AB, Postbox 28, pg. 600
Wunderman Worldwide AB, Riddargatan 19, pg. 1212
Young & Rubicam Sweden AB (Holding), Riddargatan 19, pg. 1213

SWITZERLAND

Altendorf

Elliott Turbomachinery S.A., Zucherstrasse 4, pg. 378

Baar

Bourns AG & Bourns (Schweiz) AG, Zugerstrasse 74, pg. 168

Basel

DHL International S.A., Picassopl. 4, pg. 309

Bern

Western Service, Inc., Marketgasse 56, pg. 1182

Bienne

Concord Watch Company, S.A., 63 Rue Central, pg. 812
Houghton A.G. Switzerland, Furstenlandstrasse 7, pg. 546
Montres Movado, S.A., 63 Rue Central, pg. 812

Bonaduz

Hamilton Bonaduz AG, , pg. 503

Bottens

Vectur S.A., , pg. 1139

Busswil

FamTec AG, Manchinenbau, pg. 398

Dubendorf

Ferrolegeringar AG, Zuerichstrasse 131, pg. 742

Ecublens

Levi Strauss (Suisse) S.A., Rte. de la Pierre, pg. 671

Fribourg

Ampco Metal S.A., 9 Route de Chesalles, pg. 68
Decision Data Computer Intl. S.A., 18 Boulevard De Perolles, pg. 324
Thermon International Services SA, 14, Grand Places, pg. 1092

Gelterkinden

Bose AG, Runenbergerstrasse 13, pg. 167

Geneva

ATAG Fiduciaire Generale SA, 6, rue d'Italie, pg. 387
Bangor Punta Overseas, S.A., 5 Rue Saint-Ours, pg. 664
Berlitz Schools of Languages AG, 1, Carrefour de Rive, pg. 143
Cargill International S.A., , pg. 219
Cato Johnson Switzerland, 8 Rue Winkelried, pg. 1212
Fiduciary Trust (International) S.A., 67, rue de Saint-Jean, P.O. Box 227, pg. 409
Finagrain, Cie Commerciale Agricole et Financiere S.A., P.O. Box 327, 16, Avenue Eugen-Pittard, pg. 279
Korn/Ferry International, 61 Rue du Rhone, pg. 643
Levi Strauss (Geneva) S.A., World Trade Center, pg. 671
SAS Institute S.A. (Geneve), Ch. des Vergers 4, pg. 960
Succursale de Geneva, 1, Quari du Mont-Blane, pg. 204

Grenchen

Littelfuse AG, Rebgasse 40, pg. 678
Movado Watch Company, S.A., Bettlach Strasse 8, pg. 812
N.A. Trading Ltd., Bettlach Strasse 8, pg. 812

Horn

Springborn Laboratories (Europe) AG, Seestrasse 21, pg. 1033

Kestenholz

Amway (Schweiz) AG, IndustrieStrasse 444, pg. 71

Kusnacht

ATC AG, Weinmanngasse 24, pg. 64

Lausanne

Bolton-Emerson S.A., Case Ville 2333, pg. 163
Servo Corporation of America, 3, Chemin du Cap, pg. 993
Sunkist (Europe) S.A., Rue du Valentin 29, pg. 1061

Schaffhausen

Georg Fischer Amasteel S.A., Muhlenstrasse 105, pg. 388
IDC Switzerland, Rhypark-Rheinweg 4, pg. 578

Wabern

Rena-Ware GmbH, Seftigenstrasse 300B, pg. 926

Weiningen

Johnson Wax AG, , pg. 600

Wettingen

Lamb AG, Landstrasse 15, pg. 383

Zug

Cat Pumps AG, Loretohohe 5, pg. 340
Credit Suisse First Boston AG, Alpenstrasse 15, pg. 204
DEC AG, Poststrasse 14, pg. 309
Effems AG, Hertizentrum 6, pg. 713
Financiere Credit Suisse-First Boston, Alpenstrasse 15, pg. 204
GAF (Switzerland) AG, Gubelstrasse II, pg. 439
ICC Handels AG, Chamerstr. 12, pg. 558
Metall Und Rohstoff AG, Bahnfostrasse 10, pg. 91
Viacom S.A., Chamerstrasse 18, pg. 786

Zurich

Advico Young & Rubicam AG, Werbeagentur BSW, Gockhausen, pg. 1211
ATAG Allgemeine Treuhand AG, Bandenerstrasse 47, pg. 387
Brown Brothers Harriman Services AG, Stockerstr. 38, pg. 181
CW Publikationen AG, Witkonerstrasse no.15, pg. 577
Detrey Dentsply AG, Nordstrasee 89, pg. 330
Goldman Sachs Finanz AG, Talstrasse 82, pg. 468
Ideal-Standard, Dohlenweg 28, pg. 62
Interelectronic Oertli AG, Kirchenweg 5, pg. 845
Knight Wendling AG, Forrlibuckstrasse 66, pg. 637
Korn/Ferry International, C.F. Meyer - Strasse 14, pg. 643
Maerz Ofenbau AG, Richard Wagnerstrasse 28, pg. 137
Matter Galbucci Leo Burnett, Werbeagentur, Ausstellungs Strasse 80, pg. 193
Moore Special Tool AG, Hohlstrasse 608, pg. 768
Sigma, Muhlebachstrasse 20, pg. 1212
TBWA, Lowenstrasse 29, pg. 1072
Teepak, Inc., Zurich Branch, P.O. Box 8025, Zahringerstrasse 32, pg. 535
Transammonia AG, Bellariastrasse 51, pg. 1106
Young & Rubicam AG, Muhlebach-Strasse 20, pg. 1212
Zweiniederlassung Zurich, Eisengasse 16, pg. 204

TAIWAN

Kaohsiung

Premier Chemical Plant, 3-1 Hsing Kung Rd., pg. 1129
Watlow Taiwan, 10F-1 No. 189, pg. 1168

Taipei

Amway Taiwan, Ltd., 8/F, No. 18, Section 4, Nan-King East Road, pg. 71
BSB/Taiwan Company Limited, 6th Fl., Chant Bldg., 120 Chien Kou N. Rd., Sec. 2(R.O.C.), pg. 110
Leo Burnett Company, Ltd.-Taiwan Branch, 7th Fl., Chung Hsin Textile Bldg., pg. 192
Chadwick-Miller Inc., 4th Fl., 36 Tah Hwei St., pg. 237
Dentsu, Young & Rubicam/Taipei, 6th Fl., 146 Sung Chiang Rd.(R.O.C.), pg. 330
IDC Taiwan, 3F-5 No. 201 Fu Hsin N. Rd.(R.O.C.), pg. 578
ICC Trading (Taiwan) Ltd., 6th Fl. No. 8 Lane 22, pg. 559
IDG Communications, Inc., 11F No. 137, Fu Hsin S. Rd., Sec 1(10639), pg. 577
S. C. Johnson & Son Taiwan Ltd., P.O. Box 87-300, pg. 600
Lin & Roe Company, Taiping & First Bldg., 550 Chung Hsiao East Rd., Section 4, pg. 194
Metropolitan Insurance and Annuity Company, Taiwan Branch, 11th Floor, 85 Jen Ai Road, Sec. 4, pg. 745
Panduit Trading Pte. Ltd., Rm. 807, 246 Chang An, East Road, Sector 2, pg. 846
Premier Chemical Co., Ltd., Bank Tower, Ste. 704, 205, Tun Hwa North Rd., pg. 1129
SAS Software Taiwan Ltd., Sung Chiang Rd., 7F,960
Springborn (Taiwan) Ltd., 3F-1, No. 135, Roosevelt Rd. Sec. 3(R.O.C.), pg. 1033
Tatung/Conair Corporation, 22 Chungshan No. Rd., pg. 272
Ziff-Davis Taiwan, 12 F-7, No.1 Futtsin North Road(R.O.C.), pg. 1219

THAILAND

Bangkok

American Appraisal Thailand Ltd., 12th Fl., American Intl. Tower, pg. 49
American Standard Sanitaryware (Thailand) Ltd., 392 Piyatanee Bldg., Sukhumvit Rd., SCI 1, pg. 62

Amway (Thailand) Limited, 52/193 Ramkhamhaeng Rd., pg. 71
BSB Thailand, 164 Sukhumvit Soi 20, pg. 110
Berlitz Thailand Ltd., Cathay House, 10th Fl., 8 North Sathorn Rd., pg. 143
Leo Burnett Ltd. Thailand, 2nd Fl. USOM Bldg., 37 Soi Somprasong 3, pg. 193
Dentsu, Young & Rubicam/Bangkok, Maneeya Centre, 8th Fl., 518/5 Ploenchit Rd., pg. 330
IDC Thailand, c/o A.R. Business Consultants, CCT Building, 8th Fl., pg. 578
S. C. Johnson & Son, Ltd., P.O. Box 11-1140, pg. 600
Kendall Thailand, 19 off Suthornkosa Rd., pg. 622
Kobs & Draft Asia-Thailand, 166/1 Sukhumvit 20 Rd., pg. 112
Korn/Ferry International, 12th Fl. Rajapark Bldg., 163 Soi Asoke (21), pg. 642
Media Transia Thailand Ltd., 14th Fl. Orakaarn Bldg., 26 Chidlom Rd.(10330), pg. 577

Pomprab

Advance Power Co. Ltd., 150/49-51 Larn luang Road, pg. 845

Samutprakan

Griffith Laboratories Limited, 482 Mu 19 Soi Pookmitr, pg. 487
Newly Weds Foods Thailand, Industrial Estate, 139/11 Moo 17, Bang Plee, pg. 804

TRINIDAD & TOBAGO

Port of Spain

Cuna Caribbean Insurance Society Ltd., 2 Rust St., Cor Maraval Rd., pg. 206
CUNA Mutual Insurance Soc., 2 Rust St., Cor Maraval Rd., pg. 206
Premiums Intl. Ltd., Park & Charlotte St., pg. 221

TURKEY

Istanbul

A4 Reklamcilik, Turizm ve Seyahat Ltd.Sti, Tesvikiye Cad No 137, pg. 1072
IDG/UFT, Eski Osmanli Sk, Dilan Sitesi A Blok, pg. 577
Markom/Leo Burnett A.S., Perlhan Sokak No. 126, Sisli, pg. 193
Rota Advertising Limited, Nisantasi, Poyracik Sok, pg. 112

Sishane Istanbul

Burc Electronics & Machinery Corp., Refik Saydam cad. 89, Arsian Han Kat: 2, pg. 845

U.A.E.

Dubai

Radius Advertising, The Blue Bldg., 2nd fl., Sharjah Rd., pg. 193

UKRAINE

Kiev

S. C. Johnson Kiev Corp., , pg. 600

UNITED ARAB EMIRATES

Dubai

BSB Madco, , pg. 110
Fugro-McClelland Middle East, 1509 Dubai International Trade Center, pg. 435

UNITED KINGDOM

Aberdeen

Triumph/LOR Oilfield Services Ltd., Kirkhill Industrial Estates, Dyce, pg. 1115
Wilson Supply International (U.K.) Ltd., 40 Abbotswell Rd., pg. 1194

Ahringham

Inex Vision Systems, , pg. 122

Andover

Preformed Line Products(Great Britain) Ltd., East Portway Industrial Estate, pg. 886

Ash

Puma Manufacturing Ltd., 37 Sandwich Rd., pg. 820

Ashford

Bell & Howell Ltd., (UK) Mailhandling Div., 33-35 Woodthorpe Rd., pg. 135

Aylesbury

ICC Chemical (UK) Limited, 7, Prebendal Ct., Oxford Rd., pg. 558
Intertec Limited, 7 Premendal Ct., Oxford Rd., pg. 559

Baldock

Able Translations Limited, Meeting House Lane, pg. 142

Basingstoke

Elliott Turbomachinery Ltd., 120 Thornycroft Indus. Estate, Worting Rd., pg. 378
Profile Intl. Microcircuits, Ltd., Brooks House, Alencon Link, pg. 579
Trane Ltd., Gastons Wood Reading Rd., pg. 62
Velsicol Chemical Limited, Worting House, , pg. 1147

Bicester

Micromedia Limited, Units 7-8, Telford Rd., Launton Indust. Estate, pg. 135

Billericay

Totes U.K. Limited, Eastman House, Radford Crescent, pg. 1103

Birmingham

John Heath & Co. Limited, 230 Bradford St., pg. 65
Houghton Vaughn plc, Legge St., pg. 546
Universal Steel Tube Co. Limited, Bertha Road Greet, pg. 878

Bistol

Kamenstein Europe, Ltd., Sentinel House, 4 Queen Sq., pg. 615

Blackpool

AD Plastics Ltd., Clifton Rd., pg. 330
C.M.W. Laboratories Dentsply, Ltd., , pg. 330

Bolton

Fort Sterling Ltd., Mansell Way, Horwich, pg. 425

Bourneville

Rail Car Services Ltd., 350 Bourneville Ln., pg. 712

Brackmills

Ingersoll Milling Machines Overseas Ltd., 4 Scotia Close, pg. 568

Brentford

DHL International (U.K.) Ltd., Kings House, Great West Road, pg. 309

Bristol

Coleman U.K., Inc., Unit 2, Parish Wharf Estate, Harbour Roa, pg. 695

Camberley

Bourns Electronics, Ltd., 90 Park St., pg. 168
D. Chaklin, Dir. European Operations, 28 Tekels Ave., pg. 93
Johnson Wax Limited, Frimley Green, pg. 600
Periphonics Voice Processing Systems Ltd., Albany Court, Albany Park, pg. 862

Cambridge

Cambridge Consultants Limited, Science Park,Milton Rd., pg. 679
SAIC UK Limited, Poseidon House, Castle Park, pg. 982
Topexpress, Ltd., Poseidon House, Castle Park(CB3 0RD), pg. 982

Central Milton Keynes

Amway (Europe) Ltd., Bank House - 1st Fl., 171 Midsummer Blvd., pg. 70

Chalfont St. Peter

Florasynth Limited, Wentworth House, 2/4 High St., pg. 420

Chatham

Panduit Limited, 61-65 Revenge Road, pg. 846

Cheltenham

Hollingsworth & Vose Co. U.K. Ltd., Postlip Mills, pg. 539

Cleator

Kangol Ltd., , pg. 712

Cobham

Cargill UK Ltd., Fairmile Lane, pg. 219

Coleshill

Maxon Combustion Systems, Ltd., Chantry House High Street, pg. 723

Corby

Spirol Ind. Ltd., Princewood Rd., Carlstrees Ind. Estate, pg. 1031

Cornwall

Henningsen Foods Ltd., "Lumeah" Perranwell Station, pg. 629

Coventry

Ampco Metal Ltd., 17, Binns Cl, Torrington Av, pg. 68

Crewe

Safeguard Systems GB, Ltd., Centurion House, Gateway, pg. 966

Cross

Lee Products Ltd., Chalfont St., pg. 665

Croydon

Kartret Switchgear Ltd., Switchgear House, Mill Lane, pg. 820

Dartford

Euroflex Screen Print Supplies Ltd., , pg. 419

Diss

Hamlin Electronics Europe Ltd., Park Road, pg. 503

Droitwich

Eclipse Thermal Systems, Ltd., Wassage Way, Hampton Lovett Indus. Estate, pg. 366

Dumfries

The Gates Rubber Company Ltd., Edinburgh Rd., Heathhall, pg. 445

Dunfermline

Bourns Electronics, Ltd., Hillend Industrial Estate, pg. 168
Hillend Environmental Industry, Ltd., Hillend Industrial Estate, pg. 526

Durham

Littelfuse Ltd., 34-36 Hutton Close, pg. 678

East Kilbride

Avex Electronics Ltd., , pg. 550

Eastbourne

Seybold Limited, 26A Seaside, pg. 1219
Ziebart (E.C.) Limited, , pg. 1218

Edinburgh

The Gates Rubber Company Limited, NCR House, 5th Floor, 2, Roseburn Gardens, pg. 445
Guardian Baillie Gifford, Ltd., 1 Rutland Ct., pg. 492

Egham

Johnson Wax (Egypt), c/o J. Wax Africa & Near East, Milton Park, pg. 600

Ellesmere Port

Fabdec Ltd., Grange Road, pg. 309

Epping

Flexible Lamps Ltd., Rubbolite House, Centre Dr., , pg. 1124

Esher

GAF (Great Britain) Co. Ltd., Rythe House, 2 Littleworth Rd., pg. 438

Exeter

Hardinge Machine Tools, Ltd., (EX2 8PN), pg. 508

Fleet

Cat Pumps (UK) Ltd., 27 Station Industrial Estate, pg. 340

Gloucester

Western Staff Services (U.K.) Ltd., 46/50 Southgate St., pg. 1182

Great Yarmouth

Penrod Drilling Corporation (UK), Main Cross Road, pg. 859

Harrow

Fugro-McClelland, Ltd., McClelland House, Chantry Place off Headstone Lane, pg. 435

Hemel Hempstead

Pneumatic Scale Europe, , pg. 122

Henley-on-Thames

Hallmark Cards Ltd., European Div., Hallmark House Station Rd., , pg. 502

High Wycombe

Fallek Chemical Company (UK) Ltd., 57-61 West Wycombe Rd., pg. 558
Veeco Instruments Ltd., Abbey Barn Road, pg. 1146

Hinckley

SpeedFam Machines Co. Ltd., Brindley Rd., pg. 398

Horsham

SOR Europe, Ltd., 2 Star Rd., pg. 963

Hortonwood Telford

The Miller Group (UK) Ltd., Unit 69, pg. 754

Huddersfield

Peabody Holmes Limited, Turnbridge, pg. 900

Huntingdon

Gates Hydraulics Ltd., Station Road, pg. 445

Ilford

TMP Ltd., Palmsaa House, (IGI 2JS), pg. 1074
TMP/Telephone Marketing Programs, Ltd., Palmsaa House, Uphall Rd., pg. 1074

Ipswich

Gas-Fired Products (U.K.) Ltd., 4-6 Chapel Lane, pg. 444

Kings Lynn

Master Foods, Hansa Road, pg. 713

Kingston-upon-Hull

Ideal-Standard Ltd., P.O. Box 60, National Ave., pg. 62

Kingswinford

Intralox Ltd., Building 69, Third Ave., Pensnett Trading Estate, pg. 651

Leamington Spa

Scholastic Publications Ltd., Merlborough House, Holly Walk, pg. 962

Leatherhead

Denver Process Equipment, Ltd., Stocks House, 9 No. St., pg. 331
WWF Paper Sales U.K., Ltd., Claire House, Bridge St., pg. 1157

Lincoln

Bucyrus-Europe Ltd., Becor House, Green Lane, pg. 186

London

ARA Europe Headquarters, Glenthorne House, Glenthorne Road, pg. 7
ARA Vending Services Ltd., Glenthorne House, Glenthorne Road, pg. 7
Advertising Age International, Cowcross Court, pg. 296
American Appraisal (U.K.) Ltd., 49 Whitehall, pg. 49
American Institute for Foreign Study, 37 Queen's Gate, pg. 56
Arthur Andersen & Co., 1 Surrey St., pg. 72
J. Aron & Company (U.K.), Limited, 5 Old Bailey, pg. 468
J. Aron & Company (U.K.), Limited, 8-10 New Fetter Lane, pg. 468
Arrington-Hillgate International, Shropshire House, , pg. 85
The Associated Press, Ltd., 12 Norwich St., pg. 92
The Austin Co. of U.K. Ltd., 35 Ballards Lane, pg. 790
Ayer Europe, Metropolis House, pg. 104
Ayer Ltd., Metropolis House, 22 Percy St., pg. 104
BNA International Inc., 17 Dartmouth Street, pg. 190
BSB Dorland Limited, 121-141 Westbourne Terrace, pg. 109
BSB Europe, 121-141 Westbourne Terrace, pg. 109
Battelle Institute, Limited, 15, Hanover Square, pg. 126
Bechtel Great Britain Ltd., Bechtel House, 245 Hammersmith Rd., pg. 131
Berlitz Schools of Languages Ltd., Wells House, 79 Wells St., pg. 143
Booz, Allen & Hamilton International (UK) Ltd., 100 Piccadilly May Fair, pg. 165
Brown Brothers Harriman Limited, Garden House, 18 Finsbury Circus, pg. 181
Bungey Medical, 30 Eastbourne Terrace, pg. 111
Leo Burnett Limited, 48 St. Martin's Lane, pg. 193
Leo Burnett Ltd., Europe/Middle East Hdqtrs., 48 St. Martin's Lane, pg. 193
CS First Boston Asset Management Limited, 2A Great Titchfield St., pg. 204
CSFB (Gilts) Limited, 2A Great Titchfield St., pg. 204
CSFB Investment Management Limited, 2A Great Titchfield St., pg. 204
Cato Johnson Limited, Greater London House, Hampstead Rd., pg. 1212
Cato Yasumura Behaeghel (CYB), 32 Dock St., pg. 1212
Chiat/Day/Mojo, Berkshire House, 168-178 High Holborn, pg. 245
Credit Suisse Financial Products, 2A Great Titchfield St., pg. 204
Credit Suisse First Boston Ltd., 2A Great Titchfield St., pg. 204
Credit Suisse First Boston UK Limited, 2A Great Titchfield St., pg. 204
The Decision Shop, 106 Westbourne Terrace, pg. 111
Doner & Company Limited, Oriel Bldg., 10-13 Margaret St., pg. 344
Dorland Business Communications, 27-29 Cursitor St., pg. 111
Draycott Partners, Ltd., 12-14 Masons Ave., pg. 800
Duncan Heath Associates, 162/170 Wardour St., pg. 607
A. Epstein & Sons (U.K.) Ltd., Vincent House, pg. 384
Ernst & Young, Becket House, 1 Lambeth Palace Rd., pg. 387
Ethical Communications, 30 Eastbourne Terrace, pg. 111
Fiduciary Trust Company of New York Ltd., 30 Old Burlington St., pg. 409
Forum Europe Ltd., Orion House, 5 Upper St. Martin's Lane, pg. 426
GFM International Investors, Limited, 11th Fl., Orion House, 5 Upper, St. Martins Lane, pg. 745
Gemini Consulting-London, 11-14 Grafton St., pg. 448
Goldman Sachs Equity Securities (U.K.) Limited, 5 Old Bailey, pg. 468
Goldman Sachs Futures Limited, 5 Old Bailey, pg. 468
Goldman Sachs Government Securities (U.K.) Limited, 5 Old Bailey, pg. 468
Goldman Sachs International Finance Limited, 5 Old Bailey, pg. 468
Goldman Sachs International Limited, 5 Old Bailey, pg. 468
Goldman Sachs Limited, 5 Old Bailey, pg. 468
Haworth U.K. Ltd., 39 Charlton St., pg. 518
Hunt Oil International Exploration-London Office, William Blake House, 8 Marshall St., pg. 554
IDC European Research Center, 2 Bath Rd., pg. 578
IDG Communications Ltd., 99 Gray's Inn Rd., pg. 577
INPUT, Ltd., , pg. 571
International Creative Management Ltd., 388/396 Oxford St., pg. 607
John Hancock Advisers International, Ltd., 34 Dover St., pg. 596
The Kendall Co. (UK) Ltd., Colgate Palmolive House, 76 Oxford St., pg. 622
Ketchum Public Relations PLC, 5 Langley St., pg. 625
Knight Wendling Ltd., 13-14, Cornwall Terrace, pg. 637
Kobs & Draft, 141 Westbourne Terrace, pg. 112
Kobs & Draft Europe, 83-89 Whitfield St., pg. 112
Korn/Ferry International, Pepys House, 12 Buckingham St., pg. 643
Arthur D. Little Ltd., Berkeley Square House, Berkeley Square, pg. 679
London & Scandinavian Metallurgical Co. Limited, 45 Wimbledon Hill Road, pg. 742
The Lowe Group, Bowater House, 68-114 Knightsbridge, pg. 685
Lowe Howard-Spink Limited, Bowater House, 68-114 Knightsbridge, pg. 685
Mann Hughes Gerrish, 30 Eastbourne Terrace, pg. 112
MTV Europe, Centro House, 20-23 Mandela Street, pg. 785
MultiServ International Ltd., Piccadilly House, 33 Regent St., pg. 358
The National Magazine Company Ltd., 72 Broadwick St., pg. 524
Pepper, Hamilton & Scheetz, City Tower, 40 Basinghall St., pg. 860
Le Rocher UK, Ltd., 37-39 Lime Street, pg. 898
Simplex Management Services, Ltd., Simplex Hse., 284-288 Chase Rd., pg. 1006
Standley Burridge Collings Ltd., 121-141 Westbourne Terrace, pg. 112
Steelcase Strafor (U.K.) Ltd., 120 Moorgate(EC2), pg. 1044
Sudler & Hennessey Limited, 24-28 Bloomsbury Way, pg. 1212
TBWA Holmes Knight Ritchie, 8 Crinan St., pg. 1072
Tillbrooks Studios, Bridge House, 63-65 N. Wharf Rd., pg. 112
Viacom Intl. Ltd., 40 Conduit St., pg. 785
Wausau Insurance Company (U.K.), Ltd., 85 Greenchurch St., pg. 380
West Point-Pepperel (U.K.) Ltd., 6 Cavendish Square, pg. 401
World Expo Corporation, 99 Gray's Inn Rd., pg. 578
Wunderman Worldwide Limited, Greater London House, Hampstead Rd., pg. 1212
Young & Rubicam Holdings Ltd., Greater London House, Hampstead Rd., pg. 1213
Young & Rubicam International European Hdqrs., Greater London House, Hampstead Rd., pg. 1213
Ziff-Davis U.K., Cottons Centre, Hay's Lane, pg. 1219

Maidenhead

AAI International Ltd., Berkshire House, 3rd Flr., Queen St., pg. 317
Ready Systems, U.K., 3rd floor, 33 Queens St., pg. 916
Segway Partners, , pg. 885

Maidstone

RAYOVAC Limited, Galleon House, King St., pg. 915
Rayovac/Vidor Limited, Galleon House, pg. 915

Malton

Chief Industries UK Ltd., Bentall Industrial Estate, pg. 247

Manchester

American Appraisal (U.K.) Ltd., Ship Canal House, King Street, pg. 49
Costain/Life Sciences International, Costain House, Styal Rd., pg. 321
Mitchell Shackleton & Co. Ltd., Green Lane Patricroft, pg. 789
Pikrose & Co., Ltd., Delta Works, pg. 712

Marlow

Maritz Limited, Dean Street, pg. 708
SAS Software, Ltd., Wittington House, pg. 960

Milton Keynes

Amway (U.K.) Limited, Snowdon Dr., Winterhill, pg. 71
Jervis B. Webb Company Ltd., Dawson Road, pg. 1170

Netherfield

Kappler Europe, Ltd., Kappler Close, pg. 613

New Barnet

E.C. DeWitt & Company Limited, 62-64 East Barnet Road, pg. 417

New Malden

Remington Consumer Products, Ltd., Apex Tower, pg. 926

Newport

Access Equipment Ltd., Audley Ave., pg. 1139
Blue Coral International, High Street(CB11 3PQ), pg. 159
John Rusling Ltd., Old Hall, Station Rd., pg. 1139

Northampton

Carlson Marketing Group (U.K.) Limited, Belgrave House, 1 Grey Friars, 7th Fl., pg. 221
Levi Strauss (U.K.) Ltd., Levi's house, Moulton Park, pg. 671

Norwich

Wavetek Datron, Hurricane Way, Norwich Airport, pg. 1169

Nottingham

Watlow Limited, Thornfield Industrial Estate, Hooton St., pg. 1168

Nuneaton

Cogsdill-Nuneaton, Ltd., Tenlons Road, pg. 259
Thetford (Aqua) Products, Ltd., Centrovell Indus. Estate, Caldwell Rd., pg. 358

Orpington

Colorcon Ltd., Murray Road, pg. 145
Cyborg Systems (UK) Ltd., Central Ct., pg. 307

Ossett

New Food Ingredients, Ltd., Owl Lane, pg. 804
RHM Ingredients, Ltd., Owl Lane, pg. 804

Plymouth

Acheson Colloids Company, Prince Rock, pg. 12
Ash Instruments Division, Dentsply Ltd., Penny Cross Close, pg. 330

Port Talbot

Transmission Div. Borg-Warner Automotive GmbH, Kenfig Industrial Estate, Margam, pg. 166

Potters Bar

ACFC Corporate Finance Limited, Station House, 3 Darkes Lake, pg. 745
Albany Life Assurance Company Limited, Station House, 3 Darkes Lane, pg. 745
MetLife (UK) Limited, Metropolitan House, Drake Lane, pg. 745

Reading

ARA Services, Ltd., ARA House, Honey End Lane, pg. 7
Acheson Industries (Europe) Ltd., Sun LifeHouse, pg. 12
Agmet Ltd., 38 Bennet Road, pg. 375
Ferro Metal & Chemical Corporation Ltd., 179, Kings Rd., pg. 867
Wavetek Electronics Ltd., Kingfisher Works, Tag Lane, pg. 1169

Renfrewshire

Playtex Limited, Playtex Park, pg. 877

Romford

Thoroughbred Europe Ltd., Abacus House, 68 a North St., pg. 1095

Rotherham

Action Instruments, Ltd., Barbot Hall Industrial Estate, pg. 15
London & Scandinavian Metallurgical Co. Ltd., Fullerton Road, pg. 742

Rugby

Automation Intelligence UK Ltd., Crastlands Court, St. Peters Rd., pg. 101
Ingersoll Engineers Limited, Bourton Hall, Bourton on Dunsmore, pg. 568

Runcorn

Hussey Seating Systems (Europe) Ltd., Astmoor Industrial Estate, , pg. 555

Saint Albans

Trace U.K., Ltd., Valley House, Spring Valley Business Centre, pg. 1104

Sevenoaks

Wilson Supply International (U.K.) Ltd., Oak House, London Rd., pg. 1194

Sheffield

Crusteel Ltd., Rutland Way, pg. 303
Kilsby-Jorgensen Steel & Aluminum Ltd., Units 7-9 Provincial Park, Nether Lane, pg. 606
Longyear U.K. Ltd., Littlemoor Eckington, pg. 683

Sittingbourne

Bose U.K., Ltd., Trinity Trading Estate, pg. 167
Capital Controls Ltd., Sittingbourne Indus. Park, Crown Quay Lane, pg. 215
Thermo Electric Intl. Ltd., P.O. Box 10, pg. 1091

Skelmersdale

Turtle Wax Manufacturing Ltd., P.O. Box 102, Gillibrands Road, pg. 1120

Slough

Mars Confectionery, Dundee Rd., pg. 713
Microdot Aerospace Limited, Blackthorne Road, pg. 749
Summa Four Limited, 246 Bedford Ave., pg. 1057

Uniroyal Chemical Ltd., Kennet House, 4 Langley Quay, pg. 1129

Somercotes

Griffith Laboratories Limited, Cotes Park Estate, pg. 487

Southhampton

SadCo Ltd., , pg. 595

Staines

Decision Data Computer (GB) Ltd., Corrie House, 48-54 London Road, pg. 324
Industrial Acoustics Company, Ltd., Central Trading Estate, pg. 566

Stockton-on-Tees

Envirodyne Limited, Salters Lane, pg. 383

Stretford

Lord Corp. (U.K.) Ltd., Lyon Motorway Estate Barton Dock Rd., pg. 683

Sunderland

Haskel Energy Systems Ltd., North Hylton Rd., pg. 516

Sunningdale

Anglo-Austrian Magnesite, Ltd., Dale House, London Rd., pg. 137

Surrey

NBS Limited-Card Services Division, 104 Oyster Lane(KT14 7HJ), pg. 960
NBS Limited-Card Systems Division, 104 Oyster Lane(KT14 7HJ), pg. 960

Sutton Coldfield

The Aluminum Powder Company, Forge Lane, pg. 742

Swanley

Adams Rite (Europe) Ltd., Unit 6, Moreton Industrial Estate, pg. 17

Swansea

Viskase, Kingsway, pg. 383

Swindon

T.D. Williamson (U.K.) Ltd., Faraday Rd., Dorcan Way, pg. 1192
Tylan (UK) Ltd., Unit 19, Westmead Industrial Estate, pg. 1122

Tamworth

Weber Marking Systems Ltd., Cavendish 7, 8 & 9, Litchfield Rd. Industrial Estate, pg. 1171

Telford

Windsor Group Limited, Windsor House, Telford Centre, pg. 803

Tewkesbury

Fisax, Unit E4, Northway Trading Estate, pg. 9

Trenent

Weber Marking Systems Ltd., MacMerry Industrial Estates, pg. 1171

Uckfield

Millbank Electronics Group Ltd., Bellbrook Industrial Estate, , pg. 65
RAM Golf UK, Bell Lane, pg. 910

Uxbridge

Hayes Microcomputer Products Ltd., 10 Roundwood Ave., pg. 519

Wakefield

Procor Engineering Ltd., , pg. 712

Warley

Benjamin Priest Ltd., Priest House, Priest St., pg. 579

Warrington

Bently Nevada (UK) Ltd., 2 Kelvin Close, pg. 141

Washington

RAYOVAC UK Limited, Stephenson Estate, pg. 915
Thermon U.K. (Ltd.), 18 Tower Rd., pg. 1092

Watford

Aladdin International Corporation (UK), Unit 4, Polychrome Estate, , pg. 29

Weybridge

Dentsply Ltd., Ham Moor Lane, Addlestone, pg. 330

Wigan

Stuart Edgar Ltd., South Lancashire Industrial Estate, pg. 425

Wiltshire

Spectrol Electronics, Drakes Way Swindon, pg. 358

Windsor

Asset Marketing, Ltd., 3 Park St., pg. 109

Winsford

Nash Engineering Co. (Great Britain) Ltd., Rd. 1, Industrial Estate, , pg. 784

Woking

Playtex Limited, 36 Chertsey Road, pg. 876

Wokingham

Lee Spring Co., Ltd., , pg. 1127

Wolverhampton

Schenectady Midland, Ltd., Four Ashes, pg. 975

Yarmouth

Wilson Supply International (U.K.) Ltd., Great Yarmouth Marine Base, pg. 1194

VENEZUELA

Caracas

The Associated Press de Venezuela, S.A., Apartado A de Correo, pg. 92
BSB/Ghersy-Quintero, C.A. Publicidad, Av. La Estancia Centro, Banaven, Torre B, Piso 3, pg. 109
Leo Burnett Venezuela, C.A., Centro Plaza, Torre B, Niveles 7 y 8, pg. 193
Centro de Idiomas Berlitz de Venezuela, Av. Fca De Miranda, Piso 1, Torre Oeste, pg. 143
Daisy de Venezuela C.A., , pg. 400
Forum Compania deEntrenamiento, Gerencial C.A., Av. Universidad, Esq. Monroy, pg. 426
IDC Venezuela, Torre Maracaibo, Piso 10, Oficina H, Av. Libertador, pg. 578
IDG Communicaciones C.A., Torre Maracaibo, Piso 10 Oficina H, pg. 577
JMC Creatividad Orientada/Young & Rubicam, Av. La Estlancia, Centro Banaven, pg. 1213
S. C. Johnson & Son de Venezuela, C.A., Apartado 70.041, pg. 600
Korn/Ferry International, , pg. 643
Oster de Venezuela S.A., Edificie Principal No. 2, Pis 2 3 ra Tra, pg. 1059
Van Raalte de Venezuela C.A., , pg. 401

YUGOSLAVIA

Ljubljana

Moj Mikro, Titova 35, pg. 577

ZAMBIA

Lusaka

Young & Rubicam (Zambia) Ltd., P.O. Box 32497, Woodgate House, Nairobi Place, pg. 1214

ZIMBABWE

Harare

Michael Hogg-Young & Rubicam (Pvt.) Ltd., Satcoy House, 125 Manica Rd., pg. 1214
Wunderman Worldwide, Satcoy House, 125 Robert Mugabe Rd., pg. 1214

ALPHABETICAL COMPENDIUM OF S.I.C. CODES

Standard Industrial Classification Manual, 1987, U.S. Government Office of Management and Budget; All codes for manufacturing unless otherwise stated.

Description	SIC Code
A	
Abrasive Products	3291
Accessory & Specialty Stores, Women's	5632
Accident & Health Insurance	6321
Accounting Services	8721
Acetate, Cellulose	2821
Acetate, Synthetic	2869
Acetate Fibers	2823
Acids, Cool Tar	2865
Acids, Fatty	2899
Acids, Inorganic, Except Nitric & Phosphoric	2899
Acids, Organic	2869
Acids, Wholesale	5169
Acoustical Tile & Board	3296
Adhesive Tape, Cellophane	2672
Adhesives	2891
Advertising, NEC	7319
Advertising Agencies	7311
Advertising Representatives, Radio, Television & Publishers'	7313
Advertising Services, Outdoor	7312
Agricultural Chemicals	2879
Air Conditioners	3585
Air Conditioning Contractors	1711
Air Conditioning Equipment & Supplies, Wholesale	5075
Air Courier Services	4513
Air Purification Equipment	3564
Air Purifiers, Portable	3634
Air & Water Resource & Solid Waste Managament	9511
Aircraft	3721
Aircraft Lighting Fixtures	3647
Aircraft Parts & Equipment	3728
Aircraft Repair & Service	4581
Airplane Models, Toys & Hobby	3944
Airplane Rental & Leasing	7359
Airports	4581
Alarms, Security	3669
Alcohol, Non-Beverage	2869
Alcoholism, Residential Rehabilitation Centers	8361
Alcoholism, Residential Hospitals	8069
Alfalfa, Wholesale	5191
Alfalfa Farms	0139
Alfalfa Prepared as Feed	2048
Alkalies	2812
Alkaline Storage Batteries	3691
Alternators & Generator Testers	3825
Alternators, Motor Vehicle	3694
Alumina	2819
Aluminum Castings, Except Dye Casting	3365
Aluminum Dye Casting	3363
Aluminum Ingots, Primary Production	3334
Aluminum Ore Mining	1099
Aluminum Products Wholesale	5051
Aluminum Rolling & Drawing, NEC	3355
Aluminum Smelting & Refining, Secondary	3341
Ambulance Services, Air	4522
Ambulance Services, Road	4119
Amines	2869
Ammonia, Anhydrous	2873
Ammonium Compounds	2819
Ammonium Phosphate	2874
Ammunition & Component Parts, More Than 30mm	3483
Ammunition & Component Parts, Small Arms	3482
Amplifiers	3651
Amusement Centers & Parks	7996
Amusement Rides & Concessions Services	7999
Amusement Rides for Carnivals	3599
Analog Converters, Electronic	3825
Animal Shelters	0752
Animal Specialties	0279
Antennas, Communication	3663
Antennas, Receiving	3679
Antibiotics, Bulk	2833
Antibiotics, Packaged	2834
Apparel & Accessories, NEC	2389
Apparel & Accessory Stores, Misc.	5699
Appliance Cords	3699
Appliances, Electric Televisions & Radio Sets, Wholesale	5064
Appliances, Household, NEC	3639
Aquaculture	0273
Architectural Services	8712
Armature Rewinding Shops	7694
Armored Car Services	7381
Asbestos Products	3292
Asphalt Paving Mixtures & Blocks	2951
Associations, Civic, Social & Fraternal	8641
Atom Smashers	3699
Audio Equipment	3651
Automatic Merchandising Machine Operators	5962
Automobile & Home Supply Stores	5531
Automobile Services, Except Repair & Car Washes	7549
Automobiles, Dealers, New & Used	5511
Automobiles, Manufacturing	3711
Automotive Dealers, NEC	5599
Automotive Lighting	3447
Automotive Trimmings	2396
B	
Baby Foods, Canned	2032
Baby Formula	2023
Badminton Equipment	3949
Bag & Envelope Making Machinery	3554
Bagel Stores, Retail	5461
Bags, Plastic, Foil & Coated Paper	2673
Bags, Paper	2674
Bags, Textile	2393
Bags, Uncoated Paper & Multiwall	2674
Bakeries	5461
Bakery Products, Fresh	2051
Bakery Products, Frozen	2053
Bakery Products, Frozen, Wholesale	5142
Bakery Products, Wholesale	5149
Balances, Except Laboratory	3596
Balances, Except Laboratory, Wholesale	5046
Balances, Laboratory	3821
Balances, Wholesale	5049
Ball Bearings & Parts	3562
Ballpoint Pens	3951
Balls, Sports	3949
Banana Farms	0179
Bandages & Dressings	3842
Bandages, Wholesale	5122
Bands, Orchestras, Actors & Other Entertainers & Entertainment Groups	7929
Banjos & Parts	3931
Bank Holding Cos.	6712
Banks, National	6021
Banks, State	6022
Barbecue Sauce	2033
Barbecues, Grills	3631
Barber Shops	7231
Barite Mining	1479
Barium Compounds	2819
Barium Diagnostic Agents	2835
Barley Farms	0119
Barley, Wholesale	5153
Barometers	3829
Barrels, Stripping, Steel & Other Metal	3412
Barrels, Wood	2449
Bathing Suits, Girls', Children's & Infants'	2369
Bathing Suits, Men's & Boys'	2329
Bathing Suits, Women's, Misses' & Juniors'	2329
Bathroom Accessories, Vitreous China & Earthenware	3261
Bathroom Fixtures, Enameled Iron	3431
Bathroom Fixtures, Plastics	3088
Bathroom Scales	3596
Batteries, Primary Dry & Wet	3692
Batteries, Storage	3691
Battery Cable Wiring Sets	3694
Bauxite Mining	1099
Bauxite, Refined	2819
Beans, Grain & Field, Buying & Marketing	5153
Bearings, Ball and Roller	3562
Bearings, Motor Vehicle	3714
Beauty Shops	7231
Beauticians	7231
Beds & Springs, Retail	5712
Beds, Household, Metal	2514
Beds, Household, Wood	2511
Bedspreads	2392
Bedspreads, Wholesale	5023
Bedsprings, Assembled	2515
Bedsprings, Wholesale	5021
Beef Cattle, Except Feedlots	0212
Beef Cattle, Feedlots	0211
Beeper Communications Service	4812
Beer & Ale, Wholesale	5181
Beets (Sugar)	0133
Belting, Rubber & Plastics	3052
Belts	2387
Berry Farms	0171
Bicycles & Parts	3751
Bicycles & Parts, Retail	5941
Bicycles & Parts, Wholesale	5091
Billboard Advertising	7312
Billiard Equipment	3949
Billiards Equipment & Supplies, Wholesale	5091
Binoculars	3827
Biological Products, Except Diagnostic Substances	2836
Bird Food	2048
Biscuits	2051
Bits, Rock, Oil & Gas Fields	3533
Bituminous Coal Mining	1221
Bituminous Coal Strip Mining	1221
Blacktop Work, Contractors	1771
Blades, Knife & Razor	3421
Blades, Saw	3425
Blast Furnaces	3212
Bleaches, Hair	2844
Bleaches, Household	2842
Bleaches, Industrial	2819
Blenders, Electric	3634
Blinds, Venetian & Vertical	2591
Blood Banks	8099
Blood Pressure Apparatus	3841
Blouses, Girls', Children's & Infants'	2361
Blouses, Wholesale	5137
Blouses & Shirts, Women's, Misses' & Juniors'	2331
Blow Torches	3423
Blueprint, Paper & Equipment	3861
Blueprinting Equipment, Wholesale	5044
Blueprinting Service	7334
Boat Dealers	5551
Boats, Fiberglass	3732
Body Shops, Automotive	7532
Boilers, Industrial	3443
Boilers, Steam & Hot Water	3433
Boilers, Wholesale	5074
Bolts, Metal	3452
Bolts, Nuts, Rivets & Screws, Wholesale	5072
Bond & Mortgage Cos.	6162
Bone China	3262

Description	SIC Code
Book Clubs, Not Publishing	5961
Book Printing	2732
Book Publishing	2731
Book Stores, New Publications	5942
Book Stores, Used Publications	5932
Bookbinding	2789
Bookcases, Household, Metal	2514
Bookcases, Household, Wood	2511
Bookcases, Office, Except Wood	2522
Bookcases, Office, Wood	2521
Bookkeeping & Billing Services	8721
Books, Blank	2782
Books, Wholesale	5192
Boot & Shoe Cut Stock & Findings	3131
Boots, Dress & Casual, Men's	3143
Boots, Plastic or Rubber	3021
Boots, Women's	3144
Borax Mining	1474
Botanical Products	2833
Bottle Caps & Tops, Metal	3466
Bottle Caps & Tops, Plastic	3089
Bottle Corks and Covers	2499
Bottles, Glass	3221
Bottles, Plastic	3085
Bottles, Rubber	3069
Bottles, Vacuum	3429
Bottling Machinery	3565
Bow Ties, Men's & Boy's	2323
Bowling Alleys & Accessories	3949
Box Making Machines for Plastic Boxes	3554
Box Making Machines for Wooden Boxes	3553
Boxes, Corrugated & Solid Fiber	2653
Boxes, Folding Paperboard	2657
Boxes, Set-up Paperboard	2652
Boxes, Nailed & Lock Corner Wooden	2441
Boxes, Paperboard, Wholesale	5113
Boxes, Plastic	3089
Boxes, Wood, Wirebound	2449
Boxing Equipment	3949
Brackets, Iron & Steel	3429
Brackets, Wood	2431
Brads, Steel	3429
Brads, Wholesale	5072
Brake Drums	3714
Brake Fluid, Hydraulic	2992
Brake Lining, Pads, Asbestos	3292
Brake Lining, Rubber	3069
Brakes, Aircraft	3728
Brakes & Brake Parts, Automotive	3714
Bran, Except Rice	2041
Bran, Rice	2044
Brandy & Brandy Spirits	2084
Brandy & Spirits, Wholesale	5182
Brass Die Castings	3364
Brass Foundries	3366
Brass Goods, Plumbers	3432
Brass Goods, Plumbers, Wholesale	5074
Brass, Rolling & Drawing	3351
Brass Smelting & Refining, Secondary	3341
Brassieres, Girdles, etc.	2342
Breakfast Cereals	2043
Breakfast Cereals, Wholesale	5149
Breathing Systems	3829
Breweries	2082
Brewers Machinery	3556
Brick & Tile Dealers, Retail	5211
Brick, Common, Face	3251
Brick, Refractory	3297
Brick, Stone & Related Construction Materials, Wholesale	5032
Bricklaying Contractors	1741
Bridge Construction	1622
Briefcases	3161
Briquettes, Fuel	2999
Broadcast Equipment	3663
Broadcasting Stations, Radio	4832
Broadcasting Stations, Television	4833
Broiler, Fryer, & Roaster Chickens	0251
Brokers, Commodity	6221
Brokers, Insurance	6411
Brokers, Real Estate	6531
Brokers, Security	6211
Brokers, Shipping	4731
Bronze, Rolling & Drawing	3351
Bronze, Smelting & Refining, Secondary	3341
Brooms, Hand & Machine	3991
Broth, Except Seafood, Canned	2032
Brushes	3991
Building Equipment, Installation or Erection, NEC	1796
Business Associations	8611
Business Consulting Services, NEC	8748
Bulbs, Growing of	0181
Bulbs, Seeds, Nursery Stock, Retail	5261
Bulbs, Seeds, Nursery Stock, Wholesale	5191
Bulldozers, Construction	3531
Bulletin Boards	2499
Bullion, Precious Metals, Wholesale	5094
Buns, Bread	2051
Burglar Alarms	3669
Burlap, Jute	2299
Burlap, Wholesale	5199
Bus Charter Services, Local	4141
Bus Services, NEC	7389
Buses, Motor	3711
Buses, Wholesale	5012
Business Forms, Manifold	2761
Business Forms, Wholesale	5112
Business Management Services	8741
Butane Gas, Bottled, Retail	5984
Butane Gas, Natural, Production	1321
Butane Gas, Wholesale	5172
Butter	2021
Butter, Wholesale	5143
Buttons	3965

C

Description	SIC Code
Cabinets, Wood, for Televisions, Radios, Phonographs & Sewing Machines	2517
Cable, Fiber	2298
Cable, Steel, Insulated	3315
Cable, Uninsulated Wire	3496
Cable Television Equipment	3663
Cable Television Services	4841
Cafeterias	5812
Cake Mixes	2045
Calcium Carbide, Chloride & Hydrochloride	2819
Camera & Photographic Supply Stores	5946
Cameras, Still & Motion Picture	3861
Cameras, Television	3663
Campers, For Mounting on Trucks	3792
Campgrounds	7033
Camping Equipment, Retail	5941
Camping Equipment, Wholesale	5091
Camping Trailers	3792
Camshafts, Motor Vehicle	3714
Can Openers, Electric	3634
Can Openers, Except Electric	3423
Cane Sugar Refining	2062
Cans, Aluminum, Metal	3411
Canvas	2211
Canvas Bags	2393
Canvas Products, Except Bags	2394
Capacitors, Electronic	3675
Capacitors, Electronic, Wholesale	5065
Caps & Plugs, Attachment, Electric	3643
Capsules, Gelatin, Empty	2899
Car Leasing, Passenger	7515
Car Phones	3663
Car Washes	7542
Carbide	2819
Carbon Black	2895
Carbon Paper	3955
Carbon Products	3624
Cardboard	2631
Cardboard, Die-Cut, Coated	2675
Cardboard, Wholesale	5113
Cards, Greeting	2771
Cards, Index	2675
Carnival & Amusement Park Equipment, Wholesale	5087
Carnival Amusement Rides	3599
Carpentry Work	1751
Carpet Laying & Removal Service	1752
Carpet Stores, Retail	5713
Carpet Sweepers, Except Vacuum Cleaners	3589
Carpet & Upholstery Cleaning	7217
Carpet Yarn	2281
Carpets, Textile Fiber	2273
Carpets, Wholesale	5023
Carry-Out Restaurants	5812
Carts, Golf, Hand	3949
Carts, Grocery	3496
Carts, Restaurant	2599
Cash Grains	0119
Cash Registers	3578
Cash Registers, Wholesale	5044
Casino Hotels	7011
Caskets, Burial	3995
Caskets, Burial, Wholesale	5087
Cassette Tapes, Blank	3695
Catalog, Order Taking	5961
Catalog Showrooms	5399
Catalogs, Printing of Only	2759
Catalogs, Publishing	2741
Catfish Farms	0273
Cathode Ray Tubes	3671
Catsup	2033
Caulking Compounds	2891
Caulking Guns, Tool, Hand	3423
Caustic Soda, Potash	2812
Caustic Soda, Wholesale	5119
Ceilings, Acoustical	3296
Ceilings, Acoustical Installation	1742
Cellophane Adhesive Tape	2672
Cellos & Parts	3931
Cellular Radio Telephone	3663
Cellular Telephone Services	4812
Cellulose, Man-Made Fibers	2823
Cellulose Fibers	2821
Cement, Hydraulic, Portland	3241
Cemeteries	6553
Centrifuges, Industrial	3569
Centrifuges, Laboratory	3821
Ceramic Kilns	3567
Ceramic Tile	3253
Ceramic Tile, Wholesale	5032
Cesspool Cleaning	7699
Chainsaw Blades	3425
Chainsaws	3546
Chainsaws, Retail	5251
Chainsaws, Wholesale	5084
Chairs, Household, Not Upholstered	2511
Chairs, Office, Except Wood	2522
Chairs, Office, Wood	2521
Chairs, Upholstered	2512
Chairs, Wholesale	5021
Chamois Leather	3111
Chamois Leather, Wholesale	5199
Chandeliers, Commercial	3646
Chandeliers, Residential	3645
Change-Making Machines	3578
Charcoal, Activated	2819
Charcoal, Except Activated	2861
Charcoal, Wholesale	5199
Chart & Graph Design Services	7336
Chart & Graph Paper, Ruled	2782
Checkbooks	2782
Check-Writing Machines	3579
Cheese, Mail-Order, Retail	5961
Cheese Curls & Puffs	2096
Cheese Products	2022
Cheese Stores, Retail	5451
Cheesecloth	2211
Cheesecloth, Wholesale	5131
Cheese-Making Machines	3556
Chemical Bulk Stations & Terminals	5169
Chemicals, NEC	2899
Chewing Gum	2067
Chewing Gum, Wholesale	5145

S.I.C. Index

Description	SIC Code
Chewing Tobacco	2131
Chewing Tobacco, Wholesale	5194
Chicken Production	0251
Child Care Centers	8351
Children's & Infants' Wear Stores	5641
Chili Con Carne, Canned	2032
Chili Pepper or Powder	2099
Chili Sauce	2033
Chimes, Electric	3699
Chimney Cleaning Service	7349
Chimney Construction & Maintenance	1741
China Closets	2511
China Tableware	3262
China, Wholesale	5023
Chisels	3423
Chlorine	2812
Chlorine, Compressed or Liquefied	2812
Chlorine, Wholesale	5169
Chocolate, Sweetened or Unsweetened	2066
Chlorine Bleach	2842
Chocolate Bars	2066
Chocolate Candy, Except Bars	2064
Chocolate Syrup	2066
Chow Mein, Chop Suey, Canned	2032
Chowders, Fish & Seafood, Canned	2091
Chowders, Fish & Seafood, Frozen	2092
Christmas Tree Growing	0811
Christmas Tree Lighting Sets	3699
Christmas Trees, Artificial	3999
Christmas Trees, Natural, Retail	5261
Christmas Trees, Wholesale	5199
Chromium Compounds	2819
Chromium Ore Mining	1061
Chromium Plating of Metals	3471
Chromium Refining	3339
Cider, Nonalcoholic	2099
Cider Presses	3556
Cigar Stores & Stands	5993
Cigarettes	2111
Cigarettes, Wholesale	5194
Cigars	2121
Cigars, Wholesale	5194
Circuit Boards	3672
Citizen's Band (CB) Radios	3663
Citric Acid	2869
Citrus Fruits	0174
Citrus Groves	0724
Clay Refractories	3255
Clays, Common, Quarrying	1459
Cleaning & Dying Plants, Except Rug	7216
Cleaning Preparations	2842
Cleansing Tissues	2676
Clock Radios	3651
Clock Repair	7631
Clocks, Except Timeclocks	3873
Clocks, Wholesale	5094
Clothes Dryers, Electric, Commercial	3582
Clothes Dryers, Electric, Household	3633
Clothes Dryers, Wood	2499
Clothing, Men's, Boys' NEC	2329
Clothing & Accessories, Women's, Children's, Infants', Wholesale	5137
Clothing & Accessory Stores, Men's & Boys'	5611
Clothing & Furnishings, Men's & Boys', Wholesale	5136
Clothing Stores, Women's	5621
Coal Mining, Anthracite	1231
Coal Mining, Bituminous, Surface	1221
Coal Mining, Bituminous, Underground	1222
Coal Mining Services	1241
Coal Products, NEC	2999
Coal Tar	2865
Coal Tar Products	5169
Coal, Wholesale	5052
Coating, Engraving & Allied Services, NEC	3479
Coating of Metals	3479
Coats, Girls', Children's, Infants'	2369
Coats, Women's, Misses', Juniors'	2339
Coats, Men's, Boys'	2311
Coaxial Cable, Nonferrous	3357
Coaxial Cable, Wholesale	5063
Cobalt Ore Mining	1061
Cocktails, Alcoholic	2085
Cocktails, Alcoholic, Premixed, Retail	5182
Cocoa, Powdered & Mix	2066
Codfish, Smoked, Dried, etc.	2091
Coffee, Instant	2095
Coffee Farms	0179
Coffee Makers, Electric	3634
Coffee Roasting	2095
Coffee Roasting & Grinding Machines	3556
Coffee Shops	5812
Coffee Stores, Retail	5499
Coils, Electronics	3677
Coils, Ignition	3694
Coils for Motors & Generators	3621
Coin-Operated Game Machines, Wholesale	5099
Coin-Operated Laundries	7215
Coin-Operated Machines, Selling Merchandise	5962
Coke Ovens	3212
Coke, Petroleum	2911
Cold Storage Locker Rental	4222
Cold Storage Warehousing	4222
Collection Agencies, Accounts	7322
Colognes	2844
Combination Utilities, NEC	4939
Combs, Plastics	3089
Comic Books Publishing	2721
Commercial Art & Graphic Design	7336
Commercial Equipment, Wholesale	5046
Communication Services, NEC	4899
Communications Equipment, Mobile & Microwave	3663
Communications Equipment, NEC	3669
Communications Equipment, Telephone & Telegraph	3661
Communications Equipment, Wholesale	5065
Communications Equipment Installation	1731
Compact Disc Players	3651
Compact Discs, Prerecorded, Except Video	3652
Compasses, Except Portable	3812
Compasses, Portable	3829
Compressors, Air & Gas, Industrial	3563
Compressors, Refrigeration	3585
Computer & Computer Software Stores	5734
Computer Consultants	7379
Computer Facilities Management Services	7376
Computer Forms	2761
Computer Hardware Rental	7377
Computer Logic Modules	3674
Computer Paper, Wholesale	5112
Computer Peripherals	3577
Computer Peripherals, Rental	7377
Computer Peripherals, Wholesale	5045
Computer Repair & Maintenance	7378
Computer Software	7372
Computer Software, Stores	5734
Computer Software, Tape & Disks, Blank	3685
Computer Software, Wholesale	5045
Computer Storage Units	3572
Computer Stores, Retail	5734
Computer Terminals	3575
Computer Terminals, Wholesale	5045
Computers, Electronic	3571
Concrete Block & Brick	3271
Concrete Block Laying	1741
Concrete & Cinder Block, Retail	5211
Concrete & Cinder Block, Wholesale	5032
Concrete Curing Compounds	2899
Concrete Mixers, Plants	3531
Concrete Products, Precast, Except Block & Brick	3272
Concrete, Ready-Mix	3273
Concrete Reinforcement Mesh	3496
Concrete Reinforcement Steel Bars	3449
Concrete Work, Except Paving	1771
Concrete Work, Paving	1611
Condensed Milk	2032
Condensers, Electronic	3675
Condensers, Electronic, Wholesale	5065
Condensers, Refrigeration	3585
Condensers, Steam	3443
Condensers for Motors & Generators	3629
Condensing Units, Air-Conditioning, Wholesale	5075
Condensing Units, Refrigeration, Wholesale	5078
Condominium Developers	1531
Conduits & Fittings, Electrical	3644
Conduits, Concrete	3272
Confectionery	2064
Confectionery Stores	5441
Confectionery, Wholesale	5145
Connectors, Electric Cord	3643
Connectors, Electronic	3678
Connectors, Electronic Wholesale	5065
Construction, Bridges, Tunnels	1622
Construction, Sand & Gravel	1442
Construction, Water, Sewer, Pipeline, Power Line	1623
Construction Equipment, Heavy Rental	7353
Construction Machinery, Except Mining	3531
Construction Material, Wholesale	5039
Construction Paper	2651
Consumer Finance Companies	6141
Contact Lenses	3851
Contact Lenses, Wholesale	5048
Containers, Wood, Nec	2449
Contractors, Family Houses	1521
Contractors, Industrial Buildings & Warehouses	1541
Contractors, Non-Residential Buildings	1542
Contractors, Residential Buildings	1522
Contractors, Special Trade	1799
Control Panels	3613
Control Transformers	3612
Control Valves	3492
Controls, Industrial	3625
Controls, Industrial, Wholesale	5084
Controls & Timing Devices	3824
Convection Ovens	3631
Convenience Food Stores	5411
Conveyor Belts	3496
Conveyor Systems, Industrial	3535
Conveyor Systems, Wholesale	5084
Cookie Stores	5461
Cookies	2052
Cookies, Wholesale	5149
Cooking Appliances	3634
Cooking Oils, Vegetable	2079
Cooking Oils, Wholesale	5149
Coolers, Drinking Fountain	3431
Copiers	3579
Copper Alloy Foundries	3366
Copper Chloride, Sulfate	2819
Copper Die-Castings	3364
Copper Ingots	3331
Copper Ore, Wholesale	5052
Copper Ore Mining	1021
Copper Rolling, Drawing, Extruding	3351
Copper Smelting	3331
Cord, Braided	2298
Cord Connectors, Electric	3643
Cord for Reinforcing Rubber Tires	2296
Cord Sets, Flexible	3357
Cordage & Twine	2298
Corduroys, Cotton	2211
Core Drills	3532
Cork, Wholesale	5085
Cork Products	2499
Corn, Wholesale	5153
Corn Chips, Wholesale	5145
Corn Chips & Snacks	2096
Corn Flakes	2043
Corn Oil	2046
Corn Pickers & Shellers	3523
Corn Popping Machines	3589
Corn Production	0115
Corn Starch	2046
Correctional Facilities, Private	8744
Correspondence Schools	8249
Cosmetics	2844

Description	SIC Code
Cosmetics, Wholesale	5122
Costume Jewelry	3961
Cottage Cheese	2026
Cotton, Finishers of Broad Woven Fabrics	2261
Cotton, Raw, Wholesale	5159
Cotton & Cottonseed Production	0131
Cotton Balers & Presses	3523
Cotton Fabric	2211
Cotton Ginning	0724
Cotton Ginning Machinery	3559
Cotton Piece Goods, Wholesale	5131
Cotton Thread	2284
Cotton Yarn	2281
Cotton Yarns, Wholesale	5199
Cottonseed Oil	2074
Cough Drops	2064
Cough Medicines	2834
Couplings, Hose	3429
Couplings, Pipe	3494
Courier Services, Air	4513
Courier Services, Except Air	4215
Crackers	2052
Crackers, Wholesale	5149
Craft & Hobby Sets	3944
Craft & Hobby Shops	5945
Craft Kits, Wholesale	5092
Cranes, Construction	3531
Cranes, Wholesale	5084
Crankshaft Assemblies	3714
Crowns & Closures, Metal	3466
Crayons	3952
Cream Substitutes	2023
Credit Card Service	7389
Credit Clearinghouses	7323
Credit Institutions, Misc. Business	6159
Credit Institutions, Short-Term Business, Except Agriculture	6153
Credit Unions, Federal	6061
Credit Unions, State	6062
Crepe Paper	2679
Crop Driers	3523
Crop Dusting	0721
Crop Planting, Cultivation & Protection Services	0721
Crop Preparation Services for Market, Except Cotton Ginning	0723
Crops, Food, Grown Under Cover	0182
Crucibles, Fire Clay	3255
Crucibles, Non-Clay	3297
Crude Oil, Wholesale	5172
Crude Oil Production	1311
Crude Petroleum Pipe Lines	4612
Crystals & Crystal Assemblies	3679
Cultured Pearl Production	0919
Cups, Foamed Plastic	3086
Cups, Paper	2656
Cups, Plastic, Except Foam	3089
Cured Meats	2011
Curio Shops	5947
Curlers, Hair	3965
Curling Irons, Electrical	3634
Current-Carrying Wiring Devices	3643
Curtains & Draperies, NEC	2391
Curtains & Fabrics, Lace	2258
Curtains, Wholesale	5023
Cylinders, Pump	3561

D

Description	SIC Code
Dairy Farms	0241
Dairy Product Stores	5451
Dairy Products, Except Dried or Canned, Wholesale	5143
Dairy Products Machinery & Equipment	3556
Dairy Products Machinery, Wholesale	5084
Data Base Information Retrieval Services	7375
Data Entry Services	7374
Data Processing Services	7374
Deciduous Tree Fruits Production	0175
Decoders, Computer	3577
Deep Sea Foreign Freight Transportation	4412
Deep Sea Foreign Passenger Transportation	4481
Dehumidifiers, Not Portable, Electric	3585
Dehumidifiers, Portable, Electric	3634
Dehydrated Fruits, Vegetables, Soups	2034
Dehydrating Equipment, Food	3556
Denims	2211
Dental Equipment	3843
Dental Equipment, Wholesale	5047
Deodorants, Non Personal	2842
Deodorants, Personal	2844
Department Stores, Retail	5311
Deposit Insurance	6399
Desalination Equipment	3559
Desalter Kits, Sea Water	2899
Desserts, Frozen, Except Bakery	2024
Desserts, Ready-to-Mix	2099
Detection Systems & Instruments	3812
Detective Agencies	7381
Detergents	2841
Detergents, Wholesale	5169
Developing & Printing, Commercial Motion Picture Film	7819
Developing & Printing, Home Movies	7384
Diamond Cutting & Polishing	3915
Diamond Mining, Industrial	1499
Diamonds, Gems, Wholesale	5094
Diamonds, Industrial & Natural, Wholesale	5085
Diapers, Cotton	2399
Diapers, Disposable	2676
Diapers, Wholesale	5137
Die-Casting Machines	3542
Die-Castings, Aluminum	3363
Die-Castings, Nonferrous, Except Aluminum	3634
Dies, Metalworking, Except Threading	3544
Dies, Thread Cutting	3545
Diesel Engines & Parts	3519
Diesel Engines & Parts, Wholesale	5084
Diet Workshops	7299
Dietary Supplements	2023
Digital Encoders	3663
Digital Test Equipment	3825
Dimension Stone	1411
Dining Room Furniture, Wood	2511
Dinners, Frozen & Packaged	2038
Dinners, Frozen, Wholesale	5142
Dinnerware, Plastic	3089
Diodes, Solid-State	3674
Diodes, Wholesale	5065
Direct Mail Advertising	7331
Direct Selling Establishments	5963
Directories, Printed, Not Published	2759
Directories, Publishing	2741
Dishes, Fine & Earthenware	3263
Dishes, Paper	2656
Dishes, Paper & Plastics, Wholesale	5113
Dishwashers, Commercial, Electric	3589
Dishwashers, Electric, Wholesale	5064
Dishwashers, Household, Electric	3639
Disinfecting & Pest Control Services	7342
Disk & Diskette Conversion Services	7379
Disk Drives, Computer	3572
Disk Drives, Wholesale	5045
Diskettes, Wholesale	5065
Dog & Cat Food	2047
Dog & Cat Food, Wholesale	5149
Dogs, Rental of, Protective	7381
Dolls	3942
Dolls, Wholesale	5092
Door Frames & Sash, Metal	3442
Door Frames & Sash, Wood	2431
Door Frames, Wholesale	5031
Door Locks & Lock Sets	3429
Door Opening & Closing Devices, Electrical	3699
Doors, Metal	3442
Doors, Wood	2431
Doughnut Shops, Retail	5461
Drafting Instruments	3829
Drafting Instruments, Wholesale	5049
Drafting Service	7389
Draperies & Fabrics, Cotton	2211
Draperies, Plastic	2391
Draperies, Silk & Man-made Fibers	2221
Draperies, Wholesale	5023
Drapery Rods, Fixture	2591
Dresses, Girls', Children's & Infants'	2361
Dresses, Womens', Misses' & Juniors'	2335
Dressing Tables	2511
Dressings, Surgical	3842
Dried Fruits & Vegetables	2034
Driers, Hand, Face & Hair, Electric	3634
Drill Bits, Metalworking	3545
Drill Bits, Wholesale	5084
Drill Bits, Woodworking	3423
Drilling Mud	2899
Drilling Mud, Wholesale	5169
Drinking Places (Alcoholic Beverages)	5813
Drug Stores, Retail	5912
Drugs, Wholesale	5122
Dry Cell Batteries	3692
Dry Cleaning	7215
Dry Ice	2813
Dry Ice, Wholesale	5169
Dryers, Laboratory	3821
Dryers, Laundry	3633
Drywall	1742
Duplicating Ink	2893
Duplicating Machines	3579
Duplicating Machines, Wholesale	5044
Durable Goods, NEC, Wholesale	5099
Dyes, Hair	2844
Dyes, Household	2899
Dyes, Synthetic	2865
Dyestuffs, Natural	2861
Dyestuffs, Wholesale	5169
Dynamite	2892

E

Description	SIC Code
Earth Moving Equipment Rental & Leasing	7353
Earth Moving, Contractors	1794
Earthenware	3263
Edge Act Corporations	6082
Editing Equipment, Motion Picture	3861
Egg Production	0252
Egg Substitutes	2015
Eggs, Wholesale	5144
Elastomers	2822
Electric Lamp Bulbs & Tubes	3641
Electric & Other Services Combined	4931
Electric Services	4911
Electric Wiring, Construction Wholesale	5063
Electrical Industrial Apparatus, NEC	3629
Electrical Work Contractors	1731
Electromedical & Electrotherapeutic Apparatus	3845
Electrometallurgical Products, Except Steel	3213
Electron Tubes	3671
Electronic Parts & Equipment, Wholesale	5065
Electronic Stores, Consumer, Radio & Television	5731
Elevator Installation	1796
Elevators, Grain Storage	4221
Elevators, Passenger & Freight	3534
Elevators, Wholesale	5084
Emergency Medical Centers, Freestanding	8011
Employment Agencies, General	7361
Enamel Tile	3253
Enamels	2851
Enamels, Wholesale	5198
Energy Measuring Equipment, Electrical	3825
Engine Repair, Automotive	7538
Engine Repair, Except Automotive	7699
Engineering Services	8711
Engines & Engine Parts, Aircraft	3724
Engines & Engine Parts, Automotive	3714
Engines, Internal Combustion, Except Aircraft & Non-Diesel Automotive	3519
Enlargers, Photographic	3861
Envelopes	2677
Envelopes, Wholesale	5112

Description	SIC Code
Epoxy Adhesives	2891
Epoxy Resins	2821
Equipment Rental & Leasing, NEC	7359
Erasers, Rubber	3069
Escalators	3534
Escrow Agents	6531
Esters	2869
Ethanol Industrial	2869
Ether	2869
Ethyl Acetate	2869
Ethyl Chloride	2869
Evaporated Milk	2023
Excavation & Foundation Work	1794
Exercise Cycles	3949
Exercising Machines	3949
Exhaust Systems & Parts, Aircraft	3724
Exhaust Systems & Parts, Motor Vehicle	3714
Explosives	2892
Extruded Shapes, Aluminum	3354
Extruded Shapes, Copper	3351
Extruded Shapes, Nonferrous, Except Copper & Aluminum	3356
Eyeglass Cases	3172
Eyeglasses, Lenses & Frames	3851

F

Description	SIC Code
Fabric, Nonwoven	2297
Fabric Shops, Retail	5949
Fabric Softeners	2842
Fabricated Metal Products, NEC	3499
Fabricated Pipe & Fabricated Pipe Fittings	3498
Fabricated Wire Products, Misc.	3469
Facial Tissues	2676
Facilities Support Management Services	8744
Facsimile Equipment	3661
Facsimile Transmission Services	4822
Factors of Commercial Paper	6153
Family Clothing Stores	5651
Family Services	8322
Fans, Electric, Household	3634
Fans, Except Household	3564
Fans, Industrial, Wholesale	5084
Farm Labor Contractors	0761
Farm Machinery & Equipment	3523
Farm Machinery & Equipment, Wholesale	5083
Farm Management Services	0762
Farm Production Warehousing & Storage	4221
Farm Supplies, Wholesale	5191
Farms, Primarily Crop	0191
Farms, Primarily Livestock	0291
Fasteners	3965
Fats & Oils, Animal & Marine	2077
Feed Grinders	3523
Feed Pre-mixes & Supplements	2048
Felt Tip Markers	3951
Fencing, Wire	3496
Fencing, Wood	2499
Ferries	4482
Fertilizers, Mixing Only	2875
Fertilizers, Nitrogenous	2873
Fertilizers, Phosphatic	2874
Fiber Cans, Tubes, Drums & Similar Products	2655
Fiber Optics Cable	3357
Fiber Optics Strands	3229
Fibers, Synthetic	2284
Field Crops, Except Cash Grains, Nec	0139
Filing Boxes, Paperboard	2652
Filing Folders	2675
Film, Movie, X-Ray, Still Camera	3861
Filters, Air for Furnaces	3564
Filters, Fluid, General	3569
Finance Leasing of Automobiles, Trucks, Machinery	6159
Financial Advice	6282
Financing of Automobiles, Furniture, Appliances	6141
Finfish, Catching	0912
Fire Alarm Apparatus	3669
Fire Extinguishers, Portable	3999
Fire Extinguishers, Wholesale	5099
First Aid Kits	3842
Fish, Canned	2091
Fish, Cured, Dried, Smoked	2091
Fish, Cured, Fresh, Wholesale	5146
Fish, Fresh & Frozen, Prepared	2092
Fish Food	2048
Fish Hatcheries	0921
Fish Sticks	2092
Fishing Lines, Nets	2298
Flags, Fabric	2399
Flagstones	3281
Flannels, Wool, Mohair	2231
Flares	2899
Flashlights	3648
Flashlights, Wholesale	5063
Flatware, Table	3914
Flavoring Concentrates, Extracts	2087
Flight Simulators	3699
Float Glass	3211
Floodlights	3648
Floor Coverings, Asphalted-Feltbase	3996
Floor Laying & Other Floor Work	1752
Floor Tile, Asphalt	3292
Floor Tile, Ceramic	3253
Floor Tile Stores	5713
Floor Waxes	2842
Floor Waxes & Polishes, Electric	3639
Florists, Retail	5992
Florists, Wholesale	5193
Flour, Blended	2041
Flour, Wholesale	5149
Flowers, Artificial Except Glass	3999
Flowers, Artificial Glass	3231
Flowers, Artificial, Retail	5999
Flowers, Artificial, Wholesale	5193
Flowers, Growing of	0181
Fluid Power Motors	3593
Fluid Power Pumps	3594
Fluid Power Valves & Fittings	3492
Fluorescent Lamps	3641
Fluorescent Lighting Fixtures, Commercial	3646
Fluorescent Lighting Fixtures, Residential	3645
Flush Valves	3432
Flying Instruction	8299
Foam Rubber	3069
Foam Rubber, Wholesale	5199
Foil, Aluminum	3353
Food Brokers	5141
Food, Mail-Order Retail	5961
Food Mixers, Household, Electric	3634
Food Preparation, NEC	2099
Food Processing Machinery	3556
Food Service, Institutional	5812
Food Stores, Misc.	5499
Food Warming Equipment, Commercial	3589
Food Warming Equipment, Commercial, Wholesale	5046
Foods, Frozen, Packaged, Wholesale	5142
Footwear, Men's	3143
Footwear, Women's	3144
Foreign Banks, Branches & Agencies	6081
Foreign Trade & International Banking Institutions	6082
Forest Nurseries & Forest Products	0831
Forestry Services	0851
Forgings, Iron & Steel	3462
Forgings, Nonferrous	3463
Forklift Trucks	3537
Forks, Garden	3423
Foundries, Gray & Ductile Iron	3321
Foundries, Malleable Iron	3322
Foundries, Nonferrous, Except Aluminum & Copper	3369
Foundries, Steel	3325
Foundries, Steel Investment	3324
Fountain Pens & Sets	3951
Flour Mill Machinery	3556
Flour Mills	2041
Freezers	3632
Freezers, Ice Cream, Commercial	3556
Freezers, Ice Cream, Household	3499
Freight Cars & Equipment	3743
Freight Forwarding	4731
Freight Packing & Crating	4783
Freight Trucking Terminals	4231
Frosting, Prepared	2099
Frozen Dinners, Packaged	2038
Frozen Fish, Packaged	2092
Frozen Fruits, Juices, Vegetables	2037
Frozen Vegetables, Juices, Fruits, Wholesale	5142
Fruit Stores	5431
Fruit Tree Production	0175
Fruits, Fresh, Wholesale	5148
Fuel Oil Dealers	5983
Fuel Pumps, Automotive	3714
Funeral Homes, Parlors	7261
Fur Goods	2371
Fur-Bearing Animals	0271
Furnaces, Industrial	3567
Furnaces, Warm Air	3585
Furnaces, Warm Air, Wholesale	5075
Furniture & Fixtures	2599
Furniture Rental & Leasing	7359
Furniture, Household, Glass & Plastic	2519
Furniture, Household, Metal	2514
Furniture, Household, Rattan, Wicker	2519
Furniture, Household, Upholstered	2512
Furniture, Household, Wood	2511
Furniture, Laboratory	3821
Furniture, Office, Metal	2522
Furniture, Office, Wood	2521
Furniture, Public Building & Related	2531
Furniture, Wholesale	5021
Furniture Stores	5712
Fuses	3613
Futures Dealers & Brokers	6221

G

Description	SIC Code
Games, Coin-Operated	3999
Games, Computer Software	7372
Games, Puzzles	3944
Garage Doors, Overhead, Metal	3442
Garage Doors, Overhead, Wood	2431
Garages, Automobile Parking	7521
Garages, Automotive Repair	7538
Garages, Prefabricated, Metal	3448
Garbage Collecting, Not Disposal	4212
Garbage Collecting & Disposal	4953
Garbage Containers, Metal	3469
Garbage Containers, Plastic	3089
Garbage Disposers, Commercial	3589
Garbage Disposers, Electric, Household	3639
Garden Handtools	3423
Garden Hose	3052
Garden Supplies & Tools, Retail	5261
Gas, Natural, Compressed	1623
Gas, Natural, Distribution	4924
Gas, Natural, Production	1311
Gas, Natural, Transmission & Distribution	4923
Gas, Natural, Transmission Only	4922
Gas & Other Services Combined	4932
Gas Masks	3842
Gas Turbines	3511
Gases, Industrial	2813
Gaskets	3053
Gaskets, Wholesale	5085
Gasoline, Natural, Production	1321
Gasoline & Oil, Retail	5541
Gauges, Machine Tool	3545
Gauges, Pressure, Temperature	3824
Gear Motors	3566
Gears, Motor Vehicle	3714
Gears, Motorcycle & Bicycle	3751
Gears, Steel	3462
Gears, Wholesale	5085
Geiger Counters	3829
Gelatin Dessert Preparations	2099

Description	SIC Code
Gem Stone Mining	1499
Gems, Preparation of for Setting	3915
General Stores, Retail	5399
Generators	3621
Generators, Aircraft & Motor Vehicle	3694
Gift Shops	5947
Gift Wrap Paper	2679
Gin, Alcoholic Beverage	2085
Ginger Ale, Bottled, Canned	2086
Glass, Flat, Colored	3211
Glass & Glazing Work	1793
Glass & Glassware, Pressed & Blown	3229
Glass Products, Made of Purchased Glass	3231
Globes, Geographical	3999
Gloves, Dress & Work	2381
Gloves, Leather	3151
Gloves, Rubber	3069
Goggles, Underwater, Safety	3851
Gold Ores Mining	1041
Government, General, NEC	9199
Granite, Crushed & Broken	1423
Grape Production	0172
Graphite Products	3624
Grave Markers, Vaults, Concrete	3272
Greeting Cards	2771
Grills for Outdoor Cooking	3631
Groceries, General Line, Wholesale	5141
Groceries & Related Products, Wholesale, NEC	5149
Guided Missle Propulsion Units & Propulsion Unit Parts	3764
Gum, Chemicals	2861
Guns, 30mm or Less	3484
Guns, More Than 30mm	3489
Guns, BB and Pellet	3484
Guns, Toy	3944
Gypsum Building Board	3275

H

Description	SIC Code
Hair Goods	3999
Hammers	3423
Handbags, Retail	5632
Handbags, Wholesale	5137
Handbags, Women's	3171
Handtools	3423
Handtools, Power Driven	3546
Hang Gliders	3721
Hardboard	2493
Hardboard, Wholesale	5031
Hardware, Wholesale	5072
Hardware Stores	5251
Harness Assemblies, Electronic	3679
Harvesting Machines	3523
Hatcheries, Fish	0921
Hatcheries, Poultry	0254
Hats	2353
Hazardous Waste Disposal Sites	4953
Headlights, Vehicular	3647
Headphones, Radio	3679
Health Food Stores	5499
Health Foods, Wholesale	5149
Health Insurance	6321
Health Lamps	3641
Health Practitioners, Offices & Clinics, NEC	8049
Health Programs, Public, Administration of	9431
Hearing Aids	3842
Hearing Aids, Retail	5999
Hearing Aids, Wholesale	5047
Heat Exchangers	3443
Heat Exchangers, Wholesale	5084
Heating & Air Conditioning Units, Combined	3585
Heating Units, Electric	3634
Heavy Construction, NEC	1629
Heavy Water	2819
Helicopters	3721
Helium	2813
Helmets, Athletic	3949
Help Supply Service	7363
Herbicides	2879
High Fidelity Equipment	3651
High Fidelity Equipment, Retail	5731
High Fidelity Equipment, Wholesale	5064
Highway & Street Construction	1611
Hinges	3429
Hobby Kits	3944
Hobby Stores	5945
Hog Production	0213
Hoists	3536
Hoists, Wholesale	5084
Holding Companies, Bank	6712
Holding Companies, Except Bank	6719
Home Construction, Single-Family	1521
Home Furnishing Stores, Misc.	5719
Home Furnishings, Wholesale	5023
Home Healthcare Services	8082
Horses & Other Equines Farms	0272
Hose Fittings & Assemblies	3492
Hose, Plastic or Rubber	3052
Hosiery, Ankle-Length	2252
Hosiery, Men's & Boys' Wholesale	5136
Hosiery, Women's & Children's Wholesale	5137
Hosiery, Women's Full Length & Knee High	2251
Hospital & Medical Service Plans	6324
Hospitals, Children's	8069
Hospitals, General	8062
Hospitals, Psychiatric	8063
Hospitals, Specialty	8069
Hospitals for Mentally Retarded	8051
Hot Tubs	2449
Hot Tubs, Retail	5999
Hot Tubs, Wholesale	5091
Hotels	7011
House Furnishings, Except Curtains & Draperies	2392
House-to-House Sales	5963
Household Appliance Stores	5722
Humidifiers, Dehumidifiers, Not Portable	3585
Humidifiers, Dehumidifiers, Portable	3634
Hunting, Trapping & Game	0971
Hydraulic Hose	3492
Hydraulic Pumps, Aircraft	3594
Hydraulic Turbines	3511
Hydraulic Valves	3492
Hydrochloric Acid	2819
Hydrogen	2813

I

Description	SIC Code
IV Transfusion Equipment	3841
Ice	2097
Ice Chests or Coolers, Except Insulated Foam Plastic	3429
Ice Chests or Coolers, Foam Plastics	3086
Ice Chests or Coolers, Plastics, not Insulated or Foam Plastic	3089
Ice Cream	2024
Ice Cream Stores	5451
Ice Cream, Wholesale	5143
Ice Skates	3949
Iced Tea, Bottled or Canned	2086
Ignition Apparatus	3694
Ignition Testing Equipment	3825
In Vitro & In Vivo Diagnostics	2835
Incinerator Operation	4953
Incinerators, Metal	3567
Industrial Chemicals, Wholesale	5169
Industrial Controls	3625
Industrial Machinery & Equipment, Wholesale	5084
Industrial Molds	3544
Industrial Patterns	3543
Industrial Supplies, Wholesale	5085
Ink	2893
Inner Tubes	3011
Inorganic Chemicals, NEC	2819
Insecticides	2879
Insecticides, Wholesale	5191
Inspection & Weighing Services for Motor Vehicle Transportation	4785
Instant Coffee	2095
Instruments & Apparatus, Medical Except Electromedical	3841
Instruments, Electrical Measurement	3825
Instruments, Musical	3931
Insulated Wire & Cable, Nonferrous	3357
Insulation Asbestos	3292
Insulation Materials, Plastic Foam	3086
Insulation Siding Board	2493
Insulation Work	1742
Insulin	2834
Insurance, Accident	6321
Insurance, Casualty	6331
Insurance, Health	6321
Insurance, Life	6311
Insurance, Surety	6351
Insurance, Title	6361
Insurance Brokers, Agents	6411
Insurance Carriers, NEC	6399
Investment Counselors	6282
Investment Firm	6211
Investment Funds, Closed-End	6726
Investment Funds, Open-End	6722
Investors, NEC	6799
Iron, Pig	3312
Iron, Pig, Wholesale	5051
Iron & Steel Scrap	5093
Iron Ore Mining	1011
Iron Ore Wholesale	5052
Irons, Electric, Household	3634
Irrigation Systems	4971

J

Description	SIC Code
Jackets, Girls', Children's, Infants'	2369
Jackets, Leather	2386
Jackets, Men's & Boys' Sport	2329
Jackets, Men's & Boys' Work	2326
Jackets, Not Tailored	2339
Jacks, Hydraulic	3569
Janitorial Service	7349
Jeans, Girls, Children's, Infants'	2369
Jeans, Men's & Boys'	2325
Jeans, Women's, Misses', Juniors'	2339
Jellies, Jams, Edible	2033
Jet Engines	3724
Jewelry	3911
Jewelry Findings & Materials	3915
Jewelry Repair	7631
Jewelry Stores, Costume	5632
Jewelry Stores, Not Costume	5944
Jewelry, Wholesale	5094
Job Counseling	8331
Juices, Fruit & Vegetable	2033

K

Description	SIC Code
Kaolin, Ground Treated	3295
Kaolin Mining	1455
Karate Instruction	7999
Kennels	0752
Ketone	2869
Ketchup	2033
Keys	3429
Kilns, Cement	3559
Kilns, Except Cement	3567
Kitchen Utensils, Metal Stamped/Pressed	3469
Kitchen Woodenware	2499
Kitchenware, Cast Aluminum	3365
Kitchenware, China	3262
Kitchenware, Earthenware	3263
Kitchenware, Plastic	3089
Kitchenware Stores	5719
Knit Fabrics, Warp	2258
Knit Fabrics, Weft	2257
Knit Fabrics, Wholesale	5131
Knit Outerwear Mills	2253
Knit Underwear & Nightwear Mills	2254
Knitting Machines	3552
Knitting Mills, NEC	2259

Description	*SIC Code*
Knitting Yarn	2281
Knitting Yarn Shops	5949
Knives, Kitchen & Table	3421
Knives, Surgical	3841
Kraft Liner Board	2631
L	
LP Gas Distribution, Retail	5984
LP Gas Production	1321
Labels, Cotton, Printed	2269
Labels, Printed	2759
Labels, Woven	2241
Laboratories, Commercial	8731
Laboratories, Medical & X-Ray	8071
Laboratories, Testing	8734
Laboratory Apparatus	3821
Lacquers	2851
Lacquers, Wholesale	5198
Ladders, Metal, Portable	3499
Ladders, Wood	2499
Laminated Cardboard	2675
Laminated Glass	3211
Laminated Plastics	3083
Lamp Light Bulbs	3641
Lamp Light Bulbs, Wholesale	5063
Lamps, Residential	3645
Landfill Sanitary	4953
Landscape Counseling & Planning	0781
Language Schools	8299
Lapidary Work	3915
Laser Diodes	3674
Laser Systems, Medical	3845
Laser Welding Equipment	3699
Launderers, Industrial	7218
Launderettes, Laundromats	7215
Laundry Equipment, Commercial	3582
Laundry Equipment, Household	3633
Laundry & Garment Services, NEC	7219
Laundry Services	7211
Law Offices	8111
Lawn & Garden Services	0782
Lawnmowers	3524
Laxatives	2834
Lead Ore Mining	1031
Lead Smelting & Refining, Primary	3339
Lead Smelting & Refining, Secondary	3341
Lead, Wholesale	5051
Leather Dyes & Stains	2865
Leather Finishing Agents	2843
Leather Goods, NEC	3199
Leather Goods, Personal Except Handbags & Purses	3172
Leather Tanning & Finishing	3111
Legal Services	8111
Lemonade	2086
Lenses, Ophthalmic	3851
Lenses, Optical	3827
Leotards, Girls', Children's & Infants'	2369
Leotards, Womens', Misses' & Juniors'	2339
Lessors of Railroad Property	6517
Lessors of Real Property, NEC	6519
Lettuce Farms	0161
Levels, Carpenters	3423
Libraries & Information Centers	8231
Licensing & Inspection of Misc. Commercial Sectors	9651
Lift Trucks	3537
Lift Trucks, Wholesale	5084
Lifts, Elevator	3534
Lighting Equipment	3648
Lighting Fixtures, Commercial	3646
Lighting Fixtures, Residential	3645
Lighting Fixtures, Vehicular	3647
Lignite Mining	1221
Limbs, Artificial	3842
Lime	3274
Lime Groves	0174
Limestone, Crushed & Broken	1422
Limestone, Wholesale	5032

Description	*SIC Code*
Linen Fabrics	2299
Linoleum	3996
Liquor, Packaged, Retail	5921
Liquors, Distilled & Blended	2085
Liquors, Wholesale	5182
Lithium	2819
Lithographic Plates	2796
Lithographic Printing	2752
Livestock, Buying & Marketing	5154
Livestock Services, Except Veterinary	0751
Loan Agents, Brokers	6163
Loan Companies, Small	6141
Loan Institutions	6159
Locker Rental, Except Cold Storage	7299
Lockers, Not Refrigerated	2542
Lockers, Refrigerated	3585
Locomotives	3743
Lodging Houses on Membership Basis	7041
Log Cabins, Prefabricated	2452
Logging Camps & Contractors	2411
Logs, Fireplace, Electric	3699
Logs, Fireplace, Gas	3433
Looseleaf Binders	2782
Looseleaf Binders, Wholesale	5112
Lotteries	7999
Lubricating Oils & Leases	2992
Lubricating Oils & Leases, Wholesale	5172
Lubrication Equipment	3569
Lubrication Systems, Aircraft	3724
Lubrication Systems & Parts, Automotive	3714
Lubrication Systems, Locomotive	3743
Luggage	3161
Luggage, Wholesale	5099
Lumber & Building Material Dealers, Retail	5211
Lumber, Frying, Stacking, Rough	2421
Lumber, Retail	5211
Lumber, Wholesale	5031
Luncheon Meat, Except Poultry	2011
Luncheon Meat, Poultry	2015
Lye, Household	2842
M	
Machinery, Electrical Equipment & Supplies, NEC	3699
Machinery, Special Industry	3559
Machines & Equipment, General Industry, NEC	3569
Magazine Publishing & Printing	2721
Magazines, Wholesale	5192
Magnesium & Alloys Bars, Rods, Shapes	3356
Magnesium Compounds	2819
Magnetic Recording Tape, Blank	3695
Magnetic Recording Tape , Prerecorded	3625
Magnetic Recording Tape, Wholesale	5065
Magnetic Storage Devices, Computer	3572
Magnets, Permanent, Ceramic or Ferrite	3264
Magnets, Permanent, Metal	3499
Mail Advertising Services	7331
Mail Order Houses	5961
Mailgram Services	4822
Mainframe Computers	3571
Malt, Barley, Rye, Wheat, etc.	2083
Malt, Wholesale	5149
Management Consulting Services	8742
Manifold Business Forms	2761
Manifold Business Forms, Wholesale	5112
Manila Folders	2675
Manufacturing Industries, NEC	3999
Maps, Publishing & Printing	2741
Margarine	2079
Margarine, Wholesale	5149
Marinas	4493
Marine Cargo Handling	4491
Marine Engines	3519
Marine Paints	2851
Marine Products Production, Misc.	0919
Marketing Consultants	8742
Marking Devices	3953
Marshmallows	2064

Description	*SIC Code*
Masking Tape	2672
Masonry, Stone Work	1741
Matches & Match Books	3999
Matches, Wholesale	5199
Materials Handling Equipment	3537
Materials Handling Equipment, Wholesale	5084
Mattresses, Innerspring, Box Spring, etc.	2515
Mattresses, Wholesale	5021
Mayonnaise	2035
Meat Markets	5421
Meat & Meat Products, Wholesale	5147
Meat Packing Plants	2011
Meat Products, Cooked, Cured	2013
Meat Products, Prepared	2013
Mechanical Power Transmission Equipment, NEC	3568
Medical Equipment, Renting, Leasing	7352
Medical Services Plans	6324
Medicinal Chemicals	2833
Melon Farms	0161
Membership Organizations, Professional	8621
Mental Hospitals	8063
Merchandising Stores, Misc. General	5399
Mercury Compounds, Medical	2833
Mercury Ore Mining	1099
Mercury Oxides, Inorganic	2819
Metal, Structural, Fabricated	3441
Metal Buildings	3448
Metal Buildings, Wholesale	5039
Metal Fasteners	3429
Metal Foil & Leaf	3497
Metal Heat Treating	3398
Metal Mining Services	1081
Metal Products, Primary, NEC	3399
Metal Stampings	3469
Metal Waste & Scrap, Wholesale	5093
Metal Work, Architectural & Ornamental	3446
Metal Work, Structural, NEC	3449
Metals Service Centers & Offices	5051
Metalworking Machinery, NEC	3549
Metalworking Tools & Machinery	3545
Metalworking Tools & Machinery, Wholesale	5084
Meters, Electric	3825
Meters, Gas, Liquid	3824
Methanol, Natural	2861
Methanol, Synthetic	2869
Methyl Alcohol	2861
Methyl Chloride	2869
Mexican Foods, Canned	2032
Mica Mining	1499
Mica Products	3299
Microcircuits Integrated	3674
Microcomputers	3571
Microfiche Readers	3861
Microscopes, Electron & Proton	3826
Microscopes, Except Electron & Proton	3827
Microwave Communication Equipment	3663
Microwave Components	3679
Microwave Ovens, Household	3631
Microwave Ovens Wholesale	5064
Milk, Bottled	2026
Milk, Concentrated & Condensed, Dried, Evaporated	2023
Milking Machines	3523
Mills, Hardwood Dimension & Flooring	2426
Millwork Products	2431
Millwork, Wholesale	5031
Mineral Products, Nonmetallic, NEC	3299
Mineral Water	2086
Minerals & Earths, Ground or Otherwise Treated	3295
Minerals, Nonmetallic, Except Fuels, Misc., NEC	1499
Minerals, Nonmetallic, Except Fuels, Services	1481
Mining, Chemical & Fertilizer Mineral, NEC	1479
Mining, Gold Ores	1041
Mining Machinery & Equipment	3532
Mining Machinery & Equipment, Wholesale	5082
Mirrors	3231
Mirrors, Optical	3827

Description	SIC Code
Missile Guidance Systems	3812
Missile Warheads	3483
Mixers, Concrete	3531
Mixers, Electric, Food	3556
Mobile Communications Equipment	3663
Mobile Homes, Except Recreational	2451
Mobile Homes, Recreational	3792
Mobile Homes, Retail	5271
Mobile Homes, Wholesale	5039
Modems	3661
Modems, Wholesale	5065
Moldings & Trim, Stamped, Metal Automotive	3465
Moldings & Trim, Stamped, Metal, Except Automotive	3442
Moldings, Plastic	3089
Moldings, Wood	2431
Monorail Systems	3536
Mortgage Brokers & Companies	6162
Mortgage Guarantee Insurance	6351
Morticians	7261
Motels	7011
Motion Picture Distribution	7822
Motion Picture Equipment	3861
Motion Picture Equipment, Wholesale	5043
Motion Picture Distribution, Services Allied	7829
Motion Picture Production, Services Allied	7819
Motion Picture Production & Distribution	7812
Motor Homes, Self-Contained	3711
Motor Vehicle Dealers, Used	5521
Motor Vehicle Distribution, Wholesale	5012
Motor Vehicle Parts	3714
Motor Vehicle Parts, Used Wholesale & Retail	5015
Motor Vehicle Supplies & New Parts, Wholesale	5013
Motorcycle Dealers	5571
Motorcycles & Parts	3751
Motorcycles & Parts, Wholesale	5012
Mufflers, Exhaust, Motor Vehicle	3714
Mufflers, Installation, Repair	7533
Museums & Art Galleries	8412
Music Sheet, Publishing	2741
Music Video Production	7812
Musical Instrument Stores	5736
Musical Instruments & Accessories	3931
Musical Instruments & Accessories, Wholesale	5099
Mutual Funds	6722
Mutual Funds, Agents	6211

N

Description	SIC Code
Nails	3315
Nails, Wholesale	5051
Napkins, Fabric	2392
Napkins, Paper & Sanitary	2676
Natural Gas, Liquid Production	1321
Natural Gas, Production	1311
Natural Gas Storage & Transmission	4922
Navigation Systems & Instruments	3812
Neckwear, Men's & Boys'	2323
Needles, Hand, Machine	3965
Needles, Hypodermic, Suture	3841
Needlework	2395
Needlework Stores	5949
Neon	2813
Neon Signs	3993
Neon Signs, Wholesale	5046
News Dealers & Newsstands	5994
News Ticker Services	7383
Newspaper Publishing	2711
Newspapers, Wholesale	5192
Newsprint	2621
Nickel & Alloy Products	3356
Nickel Ore Mining	1061
Nickel Refining, Primary	3339
Nitric Acid	2873
Nitrogen	2813
Nonclassifiable Establishments	9999
Nondurable Goods, Wholesale	5199
Nuclear Reactors	3443
Nursery Schools	8351
Nursery Stock, Production	0181
Nursery Stock, Retail	5261
Nursery Stock, Wholesale	5193
Nursing Homes, Intermediate Care	8052
Nursing Homes, Skilled Care	8051
Nuts, Candy Covered	2064
Nuts, Dehydrated, Dried, Salted, Roasted	2068
Nuts, Metal	3452
Nuts, Plastic	3089
Nylon Fabrics, Resins	2221
Nylon Fibers, Bristles, Threads	2824
Nylon Yarn, Spinning	2281
Nylon Yarn, Throwing	2282

O

Description	SIC Code
Oats, Oatmeal	2043
Oats, Wholesale	5153
Off-Highway Machinery	3536
Office Equipment, Wholesale	5049
Office Supplies, Wholesale	5112
Offset Printing	2752
Oil & Gas Field Exploration Services	1382
Oil & Gas Field Machinery & Equipment	3533
Oil & Gas Field Services, NEC	1389
Oil Royalty Traders	6792
Oil, Corn	2046
Oil, Cottonseed	2074
Oil Refining Machinery, Equipment, Wholesale	5084
Oil, Vegetable, Except Corn Oil	2079
Oils, Lubricating	2911
Oils, Sulfonated	2843
Oleo	2079
On-Line Database Information Retrieval	7375
Operators of Apartment Buildings	6513
Operators of Nonresidential Buildings	6512
Ophthalmic Goods	3851
Ophthalmic Goods, Wholesale	5048
Ophthalmic Instruments & Apparatus	3841
Optical Goods, Retail	5995
Optical Lens Machinery	3559
Optical Readers & Scanners	3577
Optical Test & Inspection Equipment	3827
Optometrists, Offices & Clinics	
Ordinance & Accessories, NEC	3489
Ore Crushing Machinery	3532
Organic Chemicals	2869
Organic Fibers	2824
Organic Pigments	2865
Ornamental Shrub & Tree Services	0783
Outboard Motors, Electric	3699
Outboard Motors, Except Electric	3519
Outboard Motors, Wholesale	5091
Oxygen, Compressed & Liquefied	2813

P

Description	SIC Code
Pacemakers	3845
Packaging Machinery	3565
Packing & Scaling Devices	3053
Padlocks	3429
Painting & Paper Hanging	1721
Paints	2851
Paints, Wholesale	5198
Pallets, Wooden	2653
Paper, Coated & Laminated, NEC	2672
Paper, Industrial & Personal Service, Wholesale	5113
Paper, Printing & Writing, Wholesale	5111
Paper & Paperboard, Die-cut	2675
Paper & Paperboard Products, Converted, NEC	2679
Paper Mills	2621
Paperboard Mills	2631
Parcel Delivery, Air	4513
Parcel Delivery, Except Air	4215
Parking Lots	7521
Parquet Flooring, Wood	2426
Particleboard	2493
Particleboard, Wholesale	5031
Partitians, Wood	2541
Pasta, Dry	2098
Patent Owners & Lessors	6794
Payroll Accounting Service	8721
Peanut Butter	2099
Pencils, Mechanical	3951
Pencils, Not Mechanical	3952
Pencils & Pens Wholesale	5112
Pens & Pen Parts	3951
Pension, Health & Welfare Funds	6371
Percale	2211
Perfumes	2844
Perfumes, Wholesale	5122
Periodicals, Publishing & Printing	2721
Periodicals, Wholesale	5192
Peripheral Equipment	3577
Peripheral Equipment, Wholesale	5045
Personal Services, NEC	7299
Pesticides	2879
Pesticides, Wholesale	5191
Pet Food, Dog & Cat	2047
Pet Food, Except Dog & Cat	2048
Pet Food Stores	5999
Pet Food, Wholesale	5149
Petroleum Brokers	5172
Petroleum Bulk Stations & Terminals, Wholesale	5171
Petroleum Gas Products &/or Distribution, Mixed or Liquified	4925
Petroleum Products, NEC	2999
Petroleum Refining	2911
Pharmaceuticals	2834
Pharmaceuticals, Wholesale	5122
Phonographs	3651
Phonographs, Wholesale	5046
Phosphate Rock	1475
Phosphates	2874
Phosphoric Acid	2874
Photocopy Machine	3861
Photocopy Machines, Wholesale	5044
Photocopy Service	7334
Photofinishing Laboratories	7384
Photographers & Photographic Studios	7221
Photographic Equipments & Supplies, Wholesale	5043
Physical Fitness Centers	7991
Pianos	3931
Pickles & Relishes	2035
Pigments, Inorganic	2816
Pigments, Organic	2865
Pins	3965
Pipe, Non-Ferrous	3356
Pipe, Sewer, Clay	3259
Pipe, Stainless Steel	3317
Pipe Lines, NEC	4619
Pipeline Construction	1623
Pizza, Frozen	2038
Pizzerias	5812
Plastering	1742
Plastic Coating of Metals	3479
Plastics, Bottle	3085
Plastics, Film, Coated, Laminated for Packaging	2671
Plastics, Film & Sheet Unsupported	3081
Plastics, Foam	3086
Plastics, Laminated, Except Packaging	3083
Plastics Materials, Wholesale	5162
Plastics, Pipe	3084
Plastics, Plumbing Fixtures	3088
Plastics Products, NEC	3089
Plastics, Resins	2821
Plastics, Resins Wholesale	5162
Plate Glass	3211
Plate Glass, Wholesale	5039
Platinum Ore Mining	1099
Plumbing Contractors	1711

Description	SIC Code
Plumbing Fixture Fittings & Trim	3432
Plumbing Fixtures, Vitreous China	3261
Plywood, Hardwood	2435
Plywood, Softwood	2436
Plywood, Wholesale	5031
Pneumatic Valves	3492
Polishes	2842
Polishes, Wholesale	5169
Polyester, Polypropylene, Polyvinyl Fabrics	2221
Polyester, Polypropylene, Polyvinyl Resins	2821
Polyester, Polypropylene, Polyvinyl Yarn	2281
Polyester Fibers, Threads	2284
Popcorn Farms	0119
Popcorn, Packaged, Except Popped	2099
Popcorn, Popped	2096
Popcorn, Wholesale	5145
Porcelain Cement, Household	2891
Porcelain Parts for Electrical & Electronic Use	3264
Portland Cement	3241
Potash Mining	1474
Potassium Chloride, Chlorate	2819
Potato Farms	0134
Potatoes, Fresh, Wholesale	5148
Pottery Products	3269
Poultry Feeds & Supplements	2048
Poultry, Processed	2015
Poultry Production	0259
Poultry Products, Wholesale	5144
Pre-Mixed Concrete, Wholesale	5032
Precious Metals & Stones, Wholesale	5094
Prefabricated Buildings, Metal	3448
Prefabricated Buildings, Wholesale	5039
Prefabricated Buildings, Wood	2452
Preschool Centers	8351
Presses, Hydraulic & Pneumatic	3542
Pressure Control Valves	3492
Pressure Gauges	3823
Pressure Sensitive Tape	2672
Pressure Sensitive Tape Wholesale	5113
Printed Circuit Boards	3672
Printing, Commercial, NEC	2759
Printers, Computer	3577
Printing, Lithographic & Off-Set	2752
Printing Gravure	2754
Printing Ink	2893
Printing Presses	3555
Printing Trade Machinery & Equipment, Wholesale	5084
Propane Production	1321
Protective Service, Guard	7381
Psychiatric Hospitals	8063
Public Finance, Taxation & Monetary Policy	9311
Public Relations Services	8743
Publishing, Book	2731
Publishing, Directory	2741
Publishing & Printing, Magazines	2721
Pulp Mills	2611
Pumps	3561
Pumps, Measuring & Dispensing	3586

R

Description	SIC Code
Racing, Including Track Operation	7948
Radar Systems	3812
Radio Stations	4832
Radioactive Waste, Disposal of	4953
Radios	3651
Railroad Cars & Locomotives, Equipment	3743
Railroad Equipment & Supplies, Wholesale	5088
Railroad Switching & Terminal Establishments	4013
Railroads, Commuter, Suburban	4111
Railroads, Line-Haul	4011
Rain Coats & Waterproof Outwear	2385
Ramie Fabrics	2299
Razor Blades	3421
Razors, Non-Electric	3421
Ready-Mix Concrete	3273
Real Estate Agents	6531
Real Estate Development	6552
Real Estate Investment Trusts	6798
Record & Prerecorded Tape Stores	5735
Records, Phonograph	3652
Rectifiers, Electronic Wholesale	5065
Rectifiers, Except Solid-State	3679
Rectifiers, Solid-State	3674
Refined Petroleum Pipe Lines	4613
Refineries, Petroleum	2911
Refractories, Clay	3255
Refractories, Non-Clay	3297
Refractory Material, Wholesale	5085
Refrigerated Warehouses	4222
Refrigeration Controls	3822
Refrigeration Machinery	3585
Refrigerators, Commercial, Wholesale	5078
Refrigerators, Household	3632
Refrigerators, Household, Wholesale	5064
Refuse Systems	4953
Regulation & Administration of Communication, Electric, Gas & Other Utilities	9631
Regulation of Agricultural Marketing & Commodities	9641
Relays	3625
Relays, Wholesale	5063
Rental of Automobiles	7514
Rental of Computers	7377
Rental of Equipment	7359
Rental of Motion Picture Films	7819
Rental of Railroad Cars	4741
Repair of Equipment	7699
Repair Shops, Air Conditioning	7623
Repair Shops, Automobile, NEC	7539
Repair Shops, Automotive Exhaust System	7533
Repair Shops, Automotive Transmission	7537
Repair Shops, Electrical & Electronic, NEC	7631
Repair Shops, Radio & Television	7622
Repair Shops, Refrigeration	7623
Research, Commercial Economic, Sociological & Educational	8732
Research & Development	8731
Research Organizations, Noncommercial	8733
Residential Care	8361
Resins	2821
Resins, Custom Compounding of Purchased Plastic	3087
Resistors, Electronic	3676
Resistors, Electronic, Wholesale	5065
Restaurants	5812
Retail Stores, Misc., NEC	5999
Ribbons, Inked	3955
Ribbons, Inked, Wholesale	5112
Rice Cleaning & Polishing	2044
Rice Production	0112
Rifles	3484
Rivets, Metal	3452
Road Construction	1611
Robes & Dressing Gowns	2384
Robots	3569
Rockets, Guided Missiles	3761
Rockets, Pyrotechnic	2899
Rolling Mill Machinery	3547
Rolling Mills	3212
Roofing Contractor, Siding, Sheet Metal Work	1761
Roofing Fabrics	2952
Roofing, Siding & Installation Materials, Wholesale	5033
Rooming & Boarding Houses	7021
Rotogravure Printing	2754
Rubber & Plastic Hose	3052
Rubber Goods, Molded, Extruded	3061
Rubber Goods, NEC	3069
Rubber, Synthetic	2822
Rugs	2273
Rugs, Wholesale	5023
Rust Removers	2842

S

Description	SIC Code
Saccharin	2869
Saddles & Parts	3199
Saddles, Motorcycle, Bicycle	3751
Safes & Vaults	3499
Safes & Vaults, Wholesale	5044
Safety Glass	3231
Safety Gloves	3842
Safety Pins	3965
Sailboats	3732
Sailboats, Wholesale	5091
Salad Dressings, Dry Mixes	2099
Salad Dressings, Except Dry Mixes	2035
Salad Oils	2079
Salads, Fresh	2099
Salmon, Smoked, etc.	2091
Salt	2899
Salt Mining	1479
Salt, Wholesale	5149
Sand, Industrial	1446
Sand & Gravel Dealers	5211
Sandpaper	3291
Sanitary Napkins	2676
Sanitary Services, NEC	4959
Sanitary Paper Food Containers	2656
Satellite Home Antennas	3679
Satellites, Communications	3663
Sauces, Tomato-Based	2033
Sauces, Vegetable Meat	2035
Sauces, Wholesale	5149
Sausages	2013
Savings & Loan, Federal	6035
Savings & Loan, State	6036
Saw Blades	3425
Saw Blades, Wholesale	5072
Sawmills	2421
Sawmills, Special Product, NEC	2429
Saws, Hand	3425
Saws, Power, Metal Cutting	3541
Saws, Power Woodworking	3553
Scaffolds, Metal	3446
Scaffolds, Wholesale	5082
Scaffolds, Wood	2499
Scales, Except Laboratory	3596
Scales, Except Laboratory, Wholesale	5046
Scales, Laboratory	3821
Schiffli Machine Embroideries	2397
School Buses	4151
School Photographers	7221
Schools & Camps, Sports	7999
Schools & Educational Services, NEC	8299
Schools for Handicapped	8211
Schools, Business & Secretarial	8244
Schools, Colleges, Universities & Professional	8221
Schools, Correspondence	8249
Schools, Dance	7911
Schools, Data Processing	8243
Schools, Elementary & Secondary	8211
Schools, Junior Colleges & Technical Institutes	8222
Schools, Riding	7999
Schools, Vocational & Correspondence	8249
Scissors, Electric	3634
Scissors, Hand	3421
Scotch Whiskey	2085
Scrap & Waste Materials, Wholesale	5093
Screening, Window, Plastic	3089
Screening, Window, Wire	3496
Screens, Door & Window, Metal Frame	3442
Screw Drivers	3423
Screw Machine Products	3451
Screws, Metal	3452
Seafood Products, Canned & Cured	2091
Seafood Products, Fresh & Frozen	2092
Sealants, Wholesale	5169
Sealing Compounds	2891
Search Systems & Instruments	3812
Seasonings	2035

Description	SIC Code
Seatbelts, Automotive & Aircraft	2399
Seatbelts, Automotive, Wholesale	5013
Seats, Automobile, Aircraft	2531
Security Dealers, Brokers	6211
Security Systems Services	7382
Semiconductor Devices	3674
Semiconductor Devices, Wholesale	5065
Service Establishment Equipment & Supplies, Except Motor Vehicle, Wholesale	5087
Service Stations, Gasoline	5541
Services, NEC	8999
Services Allied With Exchange of Securities or Commodities, NEC	6289
Servomotors	3621
Sewerage Systems	4959
Sewing Machines, Household	3639
Sewing Machines, Household, Wholesale	5064
Sewing Machines, Industrial	3559
Sewing Machines, Industrial, Wholesale	5084
Sewing Thread	2284
Shampoos, Hair	2844
Sheet Metal Work	3444
Shellfish	0913
Shelving, Not Wood	2542
Shelving, Wholesale	5046
Shelving, Wood	2541
Shingles, Asphalt, Tar	2952
Shingles, Wood	2429
Ship Building & Repairing	3731
Shirts, Men's & Boys', Except Work Shirts	2321
Shirts, Women's, Misses' & Juniors'	2337
Shoe Stores	5661
Shoes, Children's & Infants'	3149
Shoes, Men's	3143
Shoes, Wholesale	5139
Shoes, Women's	3144
Siding, Plastic	3089
Siding, Sheet Metal	3444
Signs & Advertising Displays	3993
Silver Mining	1044
Ski Wear	2329
Skids, Wooden	2448
Skis & Skiing Equipment	3949
Simulators, Training	3699
Slacks, Girls' & Children's	2369
Slacks, Men's & Boys'	2325
Slacks, Women's, Misses' & Juniors'	2339
Slippers, House	3142
Slot Machines	3999
Smoke Detectors	3669
Soaps & Cleaners	2841
Soft Drinks, Bottled or Canned	2086
Soft Drinks, Wholesale	5149
Software, Prepackaged	7372
Software, Systems Analysis, Custom	7371
Software, Wholesale	5045
Soil Preparation Services	0711
Solar Cells	3674
Solar Energy Collectors, Heaters	3433
Soldering Guns & Tools, Hand, Electric	3423
Solenoid Switches	3625
Solenoid Valves	3492
Solvents, Degreasing	2842
Solvents, Organic	2869
Sonar Systems	3812
Sound Recording Equipment	3861
Soup Mixes	2034
Soups, Canned, Except Fish & Seafood	2032
Soups, Canned, Fish & Seafood	2091
Soups, Frozen, Except Seafood	2038
Soups, Frozen, Fish & Seafood	2092
Sour Cream	2026
Soy Sauce	2035
Soybean Oil Mills	2075
Soybean Production	0116
Soybeans, Wholesale	5153
Space Capsules	3769
Space Vehicle Propulsion Units & Propulsion Unit Parts	3764
Space Vehicles	3761

Description	SIC Code
Spaghetti Sauce	2033
Spaghetti, Dry	2098
Spectrometers	3829
Speed Changers, Industrial High Speed Drives	3566
Spices	2099
Spices, Wholesale	5149
Sponge Gathering	0919
Sporting Goods	3949
Sporting Goods, Retail	5941
Sporting & Recreational Goods & Supplies, Wholesale	5091
Sports Clubs & Promoters, Professional	7941
Sports & Recreation Clubs, Membership	7997
Stainless Steel	3312
Stamp Pads, Stamping Devices	3953
Staples, Steel	3315
Staples, Wire	3496
State Banks	6022
Stationery	2678
Stationery Stores	5943
Steam & Air-Conditioning Supply	4961
Steam Fittings	3494
Steam Fittings, Wholesale	5074
Steam Turbines	3511
Steel Bars, Sheet, Strip	3316
Steel Foundries	3312
Steel, Wholesale	5051
Sterilizers, Dental	3843
Sterilizers, Laboratory	3821
Sterilizers, Medical	3842
Stevedoring	4491
Stitching & Tucking, Pleating, Decorative & Novelty	2395
Stone, Crushed & Broken, NEC	1429
Stone Quarrying	3281
Storage Batteries	3691
Stoves, Commercial	3589
Stoves, Household, Cooking	3631
Stoves, Household Heating	3433
Strip Mining, Anthracite	1231
Strip Mining, Bituminous	1221
Structural Steel Erection	1791
Sugar, Granulated, Beet	2063
Sugar, Granulated, Cane	2061
Sugar, Wholesale	5149
Sugar Beet Production	0133
Sugar Cane Production	0133
Suitcases	3161
Suits & Overcoats, Men's & Boys'	2311
Sulfuric Acid	2819
Sunflower Farms	0119
Sunflower Seed Oil	2076
Sunglasses	3851
Supermarkets	5411
Surface Active Agents	2843
Surfboards	3949
Surgical Equipment, Wholesale	5047
Surgical Instruments	3841
Surveying Instruments	3829
Surveying Services	8713
Sweeteners, Synthetic	2869
Switchboard Apparatus	3613
Switches, Electric	3643
Switches, Electronic	3679
Switchgear	3613
Switchgear, Wholesale	5063
Synthesizers, Music	3931
Synthetic Fibers	2284
Systems Analysis & Design	7371
Systems Engineering	8748

T

Description	SIC Code
Tablets, Writing	2678
Tanks & Tank Components	3795
Tape, Audio Magnetic, Prerecorded	3652
Tape, Magnetic, Blank	3695
Tape, Masking	2672
Tape, Pressure Sensitive	2672
Tape, Pressure Sensitive, Wholesale	5113
Tape Distribution for Television	7822
Tape Recorders	3651
Tape Storage Units, Computer	3572
Tapes, Audio & Video Recording, Wholesale	5065
Tax Return Preparation	7291
Tea, Wholesale	5149
Tea Blending	2099
Telegraph Services	4822
Telephone Answering Machines	3661
Telephone Communication, Except Radio	4813
Telephone Equipment, Wholesale	5065
Telephones	3661
Telephones, Cellular, Radio	3663
Television Sets	3651
Television Stations	4833
Temperature Controls, Automatic	3822
Terminals, Computer	3575
Textile Goods, NEC	2299
Textile Machinery	3552
Textile Mills, Broadwoven	2211
Textile Mills, Narrow Woven	2241
Textile Products, Fabricated, NEC	2399
Textiles, Wholesale	5131
Theaters, Movie, Drive-In	7833
Theaters, Moving Picture	7832
Theatrical Producers & Services, Except Motion Picture	7922
Theme Parks	7996
Thermostats	3822
Tile, Acoustical	3296
Tile, Asphalt	3292
Tile, Ceramic & Clay	3253
Tile, Concrete	3272
Tile, Gypsum	3275
Tile, Terrazzo, Marble, Mosaic Contractors	1743
Tile, Vinyl Asbestos	3292
Timber Tracts	0811
Timeclocks, Time-stamps	3579
Timing Devices	3625
Tin Cans	3411
Tin Compounds	2819
Tin Ore Mining	1099
Tin Smelting & Refining	3341
Tire Retreading & Repair Shop	7534
Tires & Tubes, Wholesale	5014
Tires, Cushion or Solid Rubber	3011
Title Insurance	6361
Title Search Companies	6541
Tobacco Production	0132
Tobacco Stemming & Redrying	2141
Tobacco Stores & Stands	5993
Toilet Fixtures, Iron	3431
Toilet Fixtures, Plastics	3088
Toilet Fixtures, Vitreous China	3261
Toilet Tissue	2621
Toiletries	2844
Toiletries, Wholesale	5122
Tool Rental	7359
Tools, Cutting, NEC	3545
Tools, Drilling, Oil Wells, etc.	3533
Tools, Hand, Except Power Driven	3423
Tools, Hand, Power Driven	3546
Tools, Machine, Metal Cutting	3541
Tools, Machine, Metal Forming	3542
Tools, Power Driven & Hand, Wholesale	5251
Tour Operators	4725
Towing & Tugboat Services	4492
Toy Stores	5945
Toys, Except Dolls	3944
Toys, Dolls	3942
Toys, Stuffed	3942
Toys & Hobby Goods & Supplies, Wholesale	5092
Tractors, Industrial	3537
Tractors, Lawn & Garden	3524
Trading Companies	6799
Trailer & Recreational Vehicle Utility Rental	7519
Trailers, Boat	3799
Trailers, Farm	3523
Trailers, Industrial	3537

S.I.C. Index

Alphabetical S.I.C. Compendium-continued

Description	SIC Code
Trailers, Mobile Home, Recreational	3792
Trailers, Travel, Camping	3792
Trains, Toy, & Equipment	3944
Transformers, Electric	3612
Transformers, Electric, Wholesale	5063
Transformers, Electronic	3677
Transformers, Electronic, Wholesale	5065
Transistors	3674
Transistors, Wholesale	5065
Translation Service	7389
Transmission Equipment, Motor Vehicle	3714
Transportation, Air, Nonscheduled	4522
Transportation, Air, Services, NEC	4512
Transportation, Arrangement of Freight & Cargo	4731
Transportation, Arrangement of Passenger	4729
Transportation, Deep Sea Freight, Domestic	4424
Transportation, Equipment & Supplies, Except Motor Vehicle, Wholesale	5088
Transportation, Great Lakes Freight	4432
Transportation, Intercity & Rural Bus	4131
Transportation, Local Passenger, NEC	4119
Transportation Equipment, NEC	3799
Transportation Services, NEC	4789
Travel Agencies	4724
Trophies, Metal	3499
Trophies, Silver, Nickel Silver, Pewter, Plated	3914
Trophies, Wholesale	5094
Trousers, Men's & Boys'	2325
Truck Beds & Bodies	3713
Truck Leasing	7513
Truck Trailers	3715
Truck Trailers, Wholesale	5012
Trucking, Except Local	4213
Trucking, Local	4212
Trucking, Local, with Storage	4214
Trucks, Off-Highway	3531
Trucks, Wholesale	5012
Trust Facilities, Nondeposit	6091
Trusts, Personal Investment, Management	6733
Tubes, Aluminum	3353
Tubes, Plastics	3082
Tubes, Seamless Steel	3317
Tubing, Glass	3229
Tubing, Metal	3317
Tubing, Metal, Wholesale	5051
Tuna Fish, Canned	2091
Tunnel Construction	1622
Turbine Generator Sets	3511
Turbines, Aircraft	3724
Turkeys, Processed	2015
Turkeys & Turkey Egg Products	0251
Turnstiles	3829
Turtles, Catching of	0919
Typesetting	2791
Typewriter Ribbons	3955
Typewriters	3579
Typewriters, Wholesale	5044

U

Description	SIC Code
Underwear, Men's & Boys'	2322
Ultraviolet Lamps	3641
Ultraviolet Sensors	3674
Umbrellas	3999
Underwear, Men's and Boys'	2322
Underwear, Men's and Boys', Wholesale	5136
Underwear, Women's, Misses', Children's, Infants'	2341
Underwear, Women's, Misses', Children's, Infants', Wholesale	5137
Uniform Supply Service	7213
Uranium Ore Mining	1094

V

Description	SIC Code
Vacuum Bottles	3429
Vacuum Brakes, Motor Vehicle	3714
Vacuum Brakes, Railway	3743
Vacuum Cleaner Hose	3052
Vacuum Cleaners, Electric, Household	3635
Vacuum Cleaners, Electric, Household, Wholesale	5064
Vacuum Cleaners, Electric, Industrial & Commercial	3589
Vacuum Cleaning Systems, Wholesale	5087
Vacuum Pumps, Except Laboratory	3563
Vacuum Pumps, Laboratory	3821
Vacuum Tubes	3671
Vacuum Tunnels	3443
Valves, Air Ventilating	3491
Valves, Automatic Control, Fluid Power	3492
Valves, Hard Rubber	3069
Valves, Hydraulic & Pneumatic	3492
Valves, PCV	3714
Valves, Plumbing & Heating	3494
Valves, Plumbing & Heating Wholesale	5074
Van Conversions	7532
Vanadium Ore Mining	1094
Vaporizers, Electric, Household	3634
Variety Stores	5331
Varnish Removers & Stains	2851
Varnishes	2851
Varnishes, Wholesale	5198
Veal	2011
Vegetable Farms	0161
Vegetable Juices	2033
Vegetable Oil Mills, Except Corn, Cottonseed & Soybean	2076
Vegetable Oils	2899
Vegetables, Canned	2033
Vegetables, Frozen	2037
Vegetables, Wholesale	5148
Vending Machines, Coin Operated	3581
Vending Machines, Rental	7359
Vending Machines, Wholesale	5046
Veneer, Hardwood Including Plywood	2435
Veneer, Softwood, Not Including Plywood	2436
Venetian Blinds	2591
Ventilating Fans, Electric, Household	3634
Veterinary Pharmaceutical Preparations	2834
Video Cameras	3651
Video Cassette Recorders, Players	3651
Video Game Machines	3944
Video Remote Control Devices	3651
Video Tape Production	7812
Video Tape Rental	7841
Vinegar	2099
Vineyards	0172
Vinyl Acetate	2869
Vinyl Asbestos Tile	3292
Vinyl Coated Fabrics	2295
Vinyl Fibers	2824
Vinyl Resins	2821
Vinyl Sheet & Film	3081
Vitamin Preparation	2834
Vitamins, Natural	2833
Vitamins, Wholesale	5122
Vocational Schools	8249
Voltage Regulators, Motor Vehicle	3694
Voltage Regulators, Transmission, Transformers	3612
Voltmeters	3825

W

Description	SIC Code
Wallboard, Gypsum	3275
Wallboard, Wholesale	5031
Wallboard, Wood Fiber	2493
Wallpaper	2679
Wallpaper, Wholesale	5198
Warehousing, Cold Storage	4222
Warehousing, General	4225
Warehousing & Storage, Special, NEC	4226
Warm Air Heating Equipment & Supplies, Wholesale	5075
Washers, Metal	3452
Washers, Plastics	3089
Washing Machines, Household, Electric	3633
Washing Machines, Household, Electric, Wholesale	5064
Waste Treatment Plants	4953
Wastepaper, Recycling, Wholesale	5093
Watch Crystals	3231
Watch Jewels	3915
Watches & Parts	3873
Watches & Parts, Wholesale	5094
Water Coolers, Electric	3585
Water Filters & Softeners	3589
Water Heaters, Electric, Wholesale	5064
Water Heaters, Except Electric, Wholesale	5074
Water Heaters, Household	3639
Water Purification & Softening Equipment, Household	3589
Water Quality Controls	3823
Water, Sewer Construction	1623
Water Softening Service	7389
Water Supply	4941
Water Transportation, Passenger, NEC	4489
Water Transporation Services, NEC	4499
Water Well Drilling	1781
Welding & Cutting Tools	3548
Welding & Cutting Tools, Wholesale	5084
Welding Repair	7692
Well Drilling, Oil Gas	1381
Well Drilling, Water	1781
Well Servicing Oil & Gas	1389
Wet Corn Milling	2041
Wet Corn Milling Products	5149
Wheat Production	0111
Wheat Products	2041
Wheat, Wholesale	5153
Wheel Balancing Equipment	3559
Wheel Chairs	3842
Wheelbarrows	3799
Wheels, Abrasive, Dental	3843
Wheels, Aircraft	3728
Wheels, Grinding, Abrasive	3291
Wheels, Motor Vehicle	3714
Wheels, Stamped Metal	3499
Whiskey, Scotch Whiskey	2085
Wicker Furniture	2519
Wigs	3999
Wigs, Wholesale	5199
Wind Tunnels	3443
Window Frames & Sash, Metal	3442
Window Frames & Sash, Wood	3431
Window Units	2431
Window Glass	3211
Window Glass, Wholesale	5039
Window Screens, Metal Frame	3442
Window Screens, Wood Frame	2331
Window Shades	2591
Windows & Doors, Wholesale	5031
Wines	2084
Wines, Wholesale	5182
Wire, Nonferrous	3357
Wire, Steel	3315
Wood Alcohol	2861
Wood Chips	2421
Wood Chips, Wholesale	5099
Wood Kitchen Cabinets	2434
Wood Members, Structural, NEC	2439
Wood Panels, Wholesale	5031
Wood Preserving	2491
Wood Production	0214
Wood Products	0214
Wood Products, Reconstituted	2493
Wood Stains	2851
Wooden Pallets	2448
Woodworking Machinery, Wholesale	5084
Woodworking Machines	3553
Wool Fabrics, Broad Woven	2231
Wool Fabrics, Narrow Woven	2241
Wool, Mineral	3296
Wool, Raw, Wholesale	5159
Wool Yarn	2282
Work Clothing, Men's & Boys'	2326
Wrecker Service	7549

S.I.C. Index

Description	SIC Code
Wrecking of Buildings	1795
Wrenches	3423
X	
X-Ray Apparatus	3844
X-Ray Film	3861
X-Ray Machines & Parts, Wholesale	5047
Y	
Yard Goods, Stores	5949
Yard Goods, Wholesale	5131
Yarn, Spun	2281
Yarns, Wholesale	5199
Yeast	2099
Yeast, Wholesale	5149
Yogurt	2026
Yogurt, Frozen	2024
Yogurt, Wholesale	5143
Z	
Zinc Ore, Wholesale	5052
Zinc Ore Mining	1031
Zinc Pigments	2816
Zinc, Rolling, Drawing, Extruding	3341
Zippers	3965
Zippers, Wholesale	5131
Zirconium Bars, Strips, etc.	3356
Zirconium Ore Mining	1099

NUMERICAL COMPENDIUM OF S.I.C. CODES

* NEC Denotes a Business or Service Not Elsewhere Classified

Code	Title
01	**AGRICULTURAL PRODUCTION-CROPS**
0111	Wheat Production
0112	Rice Production
0115	Corn Production
0116	Soybean Production
0119	Cash Grains, NEC
0131	Cotton & Cottonseed Production
0132	Tobacco Production
0133	Sugarcane & Sugar Beet Production
0134	Irish Potato Production
0139	Field Crops, Except Cash Grains, NEC
0161	Vegetable & Melon Production
0171	Berry Farms
0172	Production of Grapes
0173	Production of Tree Nuts
0174	Citrus Fruits Production
0175	Deciduous Tree Fruits Production
0179	Production of Fruits & Tree Nuts, NEC
0181	Ornamental Floraculture & Nursery Products Production
0182	Food Crops Grown Under Cover
0191	General Farms, Primarily Crop
02	**AGRICULTURAL PRODUCTION-LIVESTOCK**
0211	Beef Cattle Feedlots
0212	Beef Cattle, Except Feedlots
0213	Hog Production
0214	Sheep & Goats Production
0219	General Livestock, Except Dairy & Poultry
0241	Dairy Farms
0251	Broiler, Fryer & Roaster Chickens
0252	Chicken Eggs Production
0253	Turkeys & Turkey Eggs Production
0254	Poultry Hatcheries Production
0259	Poultry & Eggs Production, NEC
0271	Fur-Bearing Animals & Rabbits
0272	Horses & Other Equines Farms
0273	Animal Aquaculture
0279	Animal Specialties, NEC
0291	General Farms, Primarily Livestock & Animal
07	**AGRICULTURAL SERVICES**
0711	Soil Preparation Services
0721	Crop Planting, Cultivating & Protection Services
0722	Crop Harvesting, Primarily by Machine
0723	Crop Preparation Services for Market
0724	Cotton Ginning
0751	Livestock Services, Except Veterinary
0752	Animal Specialty Services, Except Veterinary
0761	Farm Labor Contractors & Crew Leaders
0762	Farm Management Services
0781	Landscape Counseling & Planning
0782	Lawn & Garden Services
0783	Ornamental Shrub & Tree Services
08	**FORESTRY & FOREST PRODUCTS**
0811	Timber Tracts
0831	Forest Nurseries & Forest Products
0851	Forestry Services
09	**FISHING & HUNTING**
0912	Catching of Finfish
0913	Catching or Taking of Shellfish
0919	Miscellaneous Marine Products Production
0921	Fish Hatcheries & Preserves

Code	Title
0971	Hunting, Trapping & Game Propagation
10	**METAL MINING & RELATED SERVICES**
1011	Iron Ores Mining
1021	Copper Ores Mining
1031	Lead & Zinc Ores Mining
1041	Gold Ores Mining
1044	Silver Ores Mining
1061	Ferroalloy Ores Mining, Except Vanadium
1081	Metal Mining Services
1094	Uranium-Radium-Vanadium Ores
1099	Miscellaneous Metal Ores Mining, NEC
12	**COAL MINING**
1221	Surface Mining-Bituminous Coal & Lignite
1222	Underground Mining-Bituminous Coal
1231	Anthracite Mining
1241	Coal Mining Services
13	**OIL & GAS PRODUCTION**
1311	Crude Petroleum & Natural Gas
1321	Natural Gas Liquids
1381	Drilling Oil & Gas Wells
1382	Oil & Gas Field Exploration Services
1389	Oil & Gas Field Services, NEC
14	**NONMETALLIC MINERALS**
1411	Dimension Stone
1422	Crushed & Broken Limestone
1423	Crushed & Broken Granite
1429	Crushed & Broken Stone, NEC
1442	Construction Sand & Gravel
1446	Industrial Sand
1455	Kaolin & Ball Clay
1459	Clay, Ceramic & Refractory Minerals, NEC
1474	Potash, Soda & Borate Minerals
1475	Phosphate Rock
1479	Chemical & Fertilizer Mineral Mining, NEC
1481	Nonmetallic Minerals (Except Fuel) Services
1499	Miscellaneous Nonmetallic Minerals, Except Fuels
15	**BUILDING CONTRACTORS**
1521	General Contractors-Single Family Houses
1522	General Contractors, Other Than Single-Family Houses
1531	Operative Builders
1541	General Contractors-Industrial Buildings & Warehouses
1542	General Contractors-Non-Residential Buildings
16	**HEAVY CONSTRUCTION**
1611	Highway & Street Construction, Except Elevated Hwy.
1622	Bridge, Tunnel & Elevated Highway Construction
1623	Water, Sewer, Power Line, Pipeline & Communications Construction
1629	Heavy Construction, NEC
17	**SPECIAL TRADE CONTRACTORS**
1711	Plumbing, Heating & Air Conditioning Contractors
1721	Painting & Paper Hanging Contractors
1731	Electrical Work Contractors
1741	Masonry, Stone Setting & Other Stone Work
1742	Plastering, Drywall & Insulation Work Contractors
1743	Terrazzo, Tile, Marble & Mosaic Work Contractors
1751	Carpentry Work
1752	Floor Laying & Other Floor Work, NEC

Code	Title
1761	Roofing, Siding & Sheet Metal Work
1771	Concrete Work
1781	Water Well Drilling
1791	Structural Steel Erection
1793	Glass & Glazing Work
1794	Excavating & Foundation Work
1796	Installation or Erection of Building Equipment, NEC
20	**FOOD & RELATED PRODUCTS**
2011	Meat Packing Plants
2013	Sausage & Other Prepared Meats
2015	Poultry Slaughtering & Processing
2021	Creamery Butter
2022	Natural, Processed & Imitation Cheese
2023	Dry, Condensed & Evaporated Dairy Products
2024	Ice Cream & Frozen Desserts
2026	Fluid Milk
2032	Canned Specialties
2033	Canned Fruits, Vegetables, Preserves, James & Jellies
2034	Dried & Dehydrated Fruits, Vegetables & Soup Mixes
2035	Pickled Fruits & Vegetables, Salad Dressings,Vegetable Sauces & Seasonings
2037	Frozen Fruits, Fruit Juices & Vegetables
2038	Frozen Specialties, NEC
2041	Flour & Other Grain Mill Products
2043	Cereal Breakfast Foods
2044	Rice Milling
2045	Prepared Flour Mixes & Doughs
2046	Wet Corn Milling
2047	Dog & Cat Food
2048	Prepared Feeds for Livestock
2051	Bread & Bakery Products, Except Cookies & Crackers
2052	Cookies & Crackers
2053	Frozen Baking Products, Except Bread
2061	Cane Sugar, Except Refining
2062	Cane Sugar Refining
2063	Beet Sugar Manufacturing
2064	Candy & Confectionery Products
2066	Chocolate & Cocoa Products
2067	Chewing Gum
2068	Salted & Roasted Nuts & Seeds
2074	Cottonseed Oil Mills
2075	Soybean Oil Mills
2076	Vegetable Oil Mills, Except Corn, Cottonseed & Soybean
2077	Animal & Marine Fats & Oils
2079	Shortening, Margarine, Fats & Oils, NEC
2082	Malt Beverages
2083	Malt
2084	Wines, Brandy & Brandy Spirits
2085	Distilled & Blended Liquors
2086	Bottled & Canned Soft Drinks & Carbonated Waters
2087	Flavoring Extracts & Flavoring Syrups, NEC
2091	Canned & Cured Fish & Seafoods
2092	Prepared Fresh or Frozen Fish & Seafoods
2095	Roasted Coffee
2096	Potato Chips, Corn Chips & Similar Snacks
2097	Manufactured Ice
2098	Macaroni, Spaghetti, Vermicelli & Noodles
2099	Food Preparations, NEC
21	**TOBACCO PRODUCTS**
2111	Cigarettes
2121	Cigars
2131	Tobacco (Chewing & Smoking) & Snuff
2141	Tobacco Stemming & Redrying

Code	Title
22	**TEXTILES**
2211	Broad Woven Fabric Mills, Cotton
2221	Broad Woven Fabric Mills, Man-Made Fiber & Silk
2231	Broad Woven Fabric Mills, Wool
2241	Narrow Fabrics & Other Smallwares Mills
2251	Women's Full-Length & Knee-Length Hosiery
2252	Hosiery, NEC
2253	Knit Outerwear Mills
2254	Knit Underwear & Nightwear Mills
2257	Circular Knit Fabric Mills
2258	Lace & Warp Knit Fabric Mills
2259	Knitting Mills, NEC
2261	Finishers of Broad Woven Fabrics of Cotton
2262	Finishers of Broad Woven Fabrics, Man-Made Fiber & Silk
2269	Finishers of Textiles, NEC
2273	Carpets & Rugs
2281	Yarn Spinning Mills
2282	Yarn Throwing, Twisting & Winding Mills
2284	Thread Mills
2295	Coated Fabrics, Not Rubberized
2296	Tire Cord & Fabric
2297	Nonwoven Fabrics
2298	Cordage & Twine
2299	Textile Goods, NEC
23	**APPAREL & OTHER TEXTILE PRODUCTS**
2311	Men's & Boys' Suits, Coats & Overcoats
2321	Men's & Boys' Shirts, Except Work Shirts
2322	Men's & Boys' Underwear & Nightwear
2323	Men's & Boys' Neckwear
2325	Men's & Boys' Trousers & Slacks
2326	Men's & Boys' Work Clothing
2329	Men's & Boys' Clothing, NEC
2331	Women's, Misses' & Juniors' Blouses & Shirts
2335	Women's, Misses' & Juniors' Dresses
2337	Women's, Misses' & Juniors' Suits, Skirts & Coats
2339	Women's, Misses' & Juniors' Outerwear,NEC
2341	Women's, Misses', Children's & Infants' Underwear & Nightwear
2342	Brassieres, Girdles & Allied Garments
2353	Hats, Caps & Millinery
2361	Girls', Children's & Infants' Dresses, Blouses & Shirts
2369	Girls', Children's & Infants' Outerwear, NEC
2371	Fur Goods
2381	Dress & Work Gloves, Except Knit & Leather
2384	Robes & Dressing Gowns
2385	Raincoats & Waterproof Outerwear
2386	Leather & Sheep-Lined Clothing
2387	Apparel Belts
2389	Apparel & Accessories, NEC
2391	Curtains & Draperies, NEC
2392	Housefurnishings, Except Curtains & Draperies
2393	Textile Bags
2394	Canvas & Related Products
2395	Pleating, Tucking for the Trade, Decorative & Novelty Stitching
2396	Automotive Trimmings, Apparel Findings & Related Prods.
2397	Schiffli Machine Embroideries
2399	Fabricated Textile Products, NEC
24	**LUMBER & WOOD PRODUCTS**
2411	Logging Camps & Logging Contractors
2421	Sawmills & Planing Mills, General
2426	Hardwood Dimension & Flooring Mills

Code	Title
2429	Special Product Sawmills, NEC
2431	Millwork
2434	Wood Kitchen Cabinets
2435	Hardwood Veneer & Plywood
2436	Softwood Veneer & Plywood
2439	Structural Wood Members, NEC
2441	Nailed & Lock Corner Wooden Boxes & Shook
2448	Wood Pallets & Skids
2449	Wood Containers, NEC
2451	Mobile Homes
2452	Prefabricated Wood Buildings & Components
2491	Wood Preserving
2493	Reconstituted Wood Products
2499	Wood Products, NEC
25	**FURNITURE & FIXTURES**
2511	Wood Household Furniture, Except Upholstered
2512	Wood Household Furniture, Upholstered
2514	Metal Household Furniture
2515	Mattresses, Foundations & Convertible Beds
2517	Wood Television, Radio, Phonograph & Sewing Machine Cabinets
2519	Household Furniture, NEC
2521	Wood Office Furniture
2522	Metal office Furniture
2531	Public Building & Related Furniture
2541	Wood Partitions, Shelving & Fixtures
2542	Office & Store Fixtures & Shelving, Except Wood
2591	Drapery Hardward & Window Blinds & Shades
2599	Furniture & Fixtures, NEC
26	**PAPER & RELATED PRODUCTS**
2611	Pulp Mills
2621	Paper Mills
2631	Paperboard Mills
2652	Set-Up Paperboard Boxes
2653	Corrugated & Solid Fiber Boxes
2655	Fiber Cans, Tubes, Drums & Similar Products
2656	Sanitary Food Containers, Except Folding
2657	Folding Paperboard Boxes, Including Sanitary
2671	Coated & Laminated Paper & Plastic Film
2673	Plastics, Foil & Coated Paper Bags
2674	Uncoated Paper & Multiwall Bags
2675	Die-Cut Paper, Paperboard & Cardboard
2676	Sanitary Paper Products
2677	Envelopes
2678	Stationery, Tablets & Related Products
2679	Converted Paper & Paperboard Products, NEC
27	**PRINTING & PUBLISHING**
2711	Newspapers: Publishing, or Publishing & Printing
2721	Periodicals: Publishing, or Publishing & Printing
2731	Books: Publishing, or Publishing & Printing
2732	Book Printing
2741	Miscellaneous Publishing
2752	Commercial Printing, Lithographic
2754	Commercial Printing, Gravure
2759	Commercial Printing, NEC
2761	Manifold Business Forms
2771	Gréeting Card Publishing & Printing
2782	Blankbooks, Loose Leaf Binders & Devices.
2789	Bookbinding & Related Work
2791	Typesetting
2796	Platemaking & Related Services

Code	Title
28	**CHEMICALS & RELATED PRODUCTS**
2812	Alkalies & Chlorine
2813	Industrial Gases
2816	Inorganic Pigments
2819	Industrial Inorganic Chemicals, NEC
2821	Plastics Materials, Nonvulanizable Elastomers & Synthetic Resins
2822	Synthetic Rubber (Vulcanizable Elastomers)
2823	Cellulosic Man-Made Fibers
2824	Synthetic Organic Fibers Exept Cellulosic
2833	Medicinal Chemical & Botanical Products
2834	Pharmaceutical Preparations
2835	In Vitro & In Vivo Diagnostic Substances
2836	Biological Products, Except Diagnostic Substances
2841	Soap & Other Detergents, Except Specialty Cleaners
2842	Specialty Cleaning, Polishing & Sanitation Preparations
2843	Surface Active Agents, Finishing Agents & Sulfonated Oils & Assistants
2844	Perfumes, Cosmetics & Other Toilet Preparations
2851	Paints, Varnishes, Lacquers, Enamels & Allied Products
2861	Gum & Wood Chemicals
2865	Cyclic Organic Crudes & Intermediates, Organic Dyes & Pigments
2869	Industrial Organic Chemicals, NEC
2873	Nitrogenous Fertilizers
2874	Phosphatic Fertilizers
2875	Fertilizers, Mixing Only
2879	Pesticides & Agricultural Chemicals, NEC
2891	Adhesives & Sealants
2892	Explosives
2893	Printing Ink
2895	Carbon Black
2899	Chemicals & Chemical Preparations, NEC
29	**PETROLEUM & COAL PRODUCTS**
2911	Petroleum Refining
2951	Asphalt Paving Mixtures & Blocks
2952	Asphalt Felts & Coatings
2992	Lubricating Oils & Greases
2999	Products of Petroleum & Coal, NEC
30	**RUBBER & MISCELLANEOUS PLASTICS**
3011	Tires & Inner Tubes
3021	Rubber & Plastics Footwear
3052	Rubber & Plastics Hose & Belting
3053	Gaskets, Packing & Sealing Devices
3061	Molded, Extruded & Lathe-Cut Rubber Goods
3069	Fabricated Rubber Products, NEC
3081	Unsupported Plastics Film & Sheet
3082	Unsupported Plastics Profile Shapes
3083	Laminated Plastics, Plate, Sheet & Profile Shapes
3084	Plastic Pipe
3085	Plastic Bottles
3086	Plastic Foam Products
3087	Custom Compounding of Purchased Plastic Resins
3088	Plastic Plumbing Fixtures
3089	Plastic Products, NEC
31	**LEATHER & LEATHER PRODUCTS**
3111	Leather Tanning & Finishing
3131	Boot & Shoe Cut Stock & Findings
3142	House Slippers
3143	Men's Footwear, Except Athletic
3144	Women's Footwear, Except Athletic
3149	Footwear, Except Rubber, NEC

Code	Title
3151	Leather Gloves & Mittens
3161	Luggage
3171	Women's Handbags & Purses
3172	Personal Leather Goods, Except Women's Handbags & Purses
3199	Leather Goods, NEC
32	**STONE, CLAY & GLASS PRODUCTS**
3211	Flat Glass
3221	Glass Containers
3229	Pressed & Blown Glass & Glassware, NEC
3231	Glass Products, Made of Purchased Glass
3241	Cement, Hydraulic
3251	Brick & Structural Clay Tile
3253	Ceramic Wall & Floor Tile
3255	Clay Refractories
3259	Structural Clay Products, NEC
3261	Vitreous China Plumbing Fixtures, China & Earthenware Fittings & Bathroom Accessories
3262	Vitreous China Table & Kitchen Articles
3263	Fine Earthenware (Whiteware) Table & Kitchen Articles
3264	Porcelain Electrical Supplies
3269	Pottery Products, NEC
3271	Concrete Block & Brick
3272	Concrete Products, Except Block & Brick
3273	Ready-Mix Concrete
3275	Gypsum Products
3281	Cut Stone & Stone Products
3291	Abrasive Products
3292	Asbestos Products
3299	Nonmetallic Mineral Products, NEC
33	**PRIMARY METAL INDUSTRIES**
3312	Steel Works & Blast Furnaces
3313	Electrometallurgic Products, Except Steel
3315	Steel Wiredrawing, Steel Nails & Spikes
3316	Cold Rolled Steel Sheet, Strip & Bars
3317	Steel Pipe & Tubes
3321	Gray & Ductile Iron Foundries
3322	Malleable Iron Foundries
3324	Steel Investment Foundries
3325	Steel Foundries, NEC
3331	Primary Smelting & Refining of Copper
3334	Primary Production of Aluminum
3339	Primary Smelting & Refining of Nonferrous Metals, Except Copper & Aluminum
3341	Secondary Smelting & Refining of Nonferrous Metals
3351	Rolling, Drawing & Extruding of Copper
3353	Aluminum Sheet, Plate & Foil
3354	Aluminum Extruded Products
3355	Aluminum Rolling & Drawing, NEC
3356	Rolling, Drawing & Extruding of Nonferrous Metals, Except Copper & Aluminum
3357	Drawing & Insulating of Nonferrous Wire
3363	Aluminum Die-Castings
3364	Nonferrous Die-Castings, Except Aluminum
3365	Aluminum Foundries
3366	Copper Foundries
3369	Nonferrous Foundries, Except Aluminum & Copper
3398	Metal Heat Treating
3399	Primary Metal Products, NEC
34	**FABRICATED METAL PRODUCTS**
3411	Metal Cans
3412	Metal Shipping Barrels, Drums, Kegs & Pails
3421	Cutlery

Code	Title
3423	Hand & Edge Tools, Except Machine Tools & Hand Saws
3425	Hand Saws & Blades
3429	Hardware, NEC
3431	Enameled Iron & Metal Sanitary Ware
3432	Plumbing Fixture Fittings & Trim
3433	Heating Equipment, Except Electrical & Warm Air Furnaces
3441	Fabricated Structural Metal
3442	Metal Doors, Sash, Frames, Molding & Trim
3443	Fabricated Plate Work (Boiler Shops)
3444	Sheet Metal Work
3446	Architectural & Ornamental Metal Work
3448	Prefabricated Metal Buildings & Components
3449	Miscellaneous Structural Metal Work
3451	Screw Machine Products
3452	Bolts, Nuts, Screws, Rivets & Washers
3462	Iron & Steel Forgings
3463	Nonferrous Forgings
3465	Automotive Stampings
3466	Metal Crowns & Closures
3469	Metal Stampings, NEC
3471	Electroplating, Plating, Polishing, Anodizing & Coloring
3479	Coating, Engraving & Allied Services, NEC
3482	Small Arms Ammunition
3483	Ammunition, Except Small Arms, NEC
3484	Small Arms
3489	Ordnance & Accessories, NEC
3491	Industrial Valves
3492	Fluid Power Valves & Hose Fittings
3493	Steel Springs, Except Wire
3494	Valves & Pipe Fittings, NEC
3495	Wire Springs
3496	Miscellaneous Fabricated Wire Products
3497	Metal Foil & Leaf
3498	Fabricated Pipe & Fabricated Pipe Fittings
3499	Fabricated Metal Products, NEC
35	**INDUSTRIAL EQUIPMENT & MACHINERY**
3511	Steam, Gas & Hydraulic Turbines
3519	Internal Combustion Engines, NEC
3523	Farm Machinery & Equipment
3524	Lawn & Garden Tractors, Home Lawn & Garden Equipment
3531	Construction Machinery & Equipment
3532	Mining Machinery & Equipment, Except Oil & Gas Field Machinery Equipment
3533	Oil & Gas Field Machinery & Equipment
3534	Elevators & Moving Stairways
3535	Conveyors & Conveying Equipment
3536	Overhead Traveling Cranes, Hoists & Monorail Systems
3537	Industrial Trucks, Tractors, Trailers & Stackers
3541	Machine Tools, Metal Cutting Types
3542	Machine Tools, Metal Forming Types
3543	Industrial Patterns
3544	Special Dies, Tools, Die Sets, Jigs, Fixtures, Industrial Molds
3545	Cutting Tools, Machine Tool Accessories & Machinists Precision Measuring Devices
3546	Power Driven Hand Tools
3547	Rolling Mill Machinery & Equipment
3548	Electric & Gas Welding & Soldering Equipment
3549	Metalworking Machinery, NEC
3552	Textile Machinery
3553	Woodworking Machinery
3554	Paper Industries Machinery
3555	Printing Trades Machinery & Equipment
3556	Food Products Machinery
3559	Special Industry Machinery, NEC

Code	Title
3561	Pumps & Pumping Equipment
3562	Ball & Roller Bearings
3563	Air & Gas Compressors
3564	Industrial & Commercial Fans, Blowers & Air Purification Equipment
3565	Packaging Machinery
3566	Speed Changers, Industrial High Speed Drives & Gears
3567	Industrial Process Furnaces & Ovens
3568	Mechanical Power Transmission Equipment, NEC
3569	General Industrial Machinery & Equipment, NEC
3571	Electronic Computers
3572	Computer Storage Devices
3575	Computer Terminals
3577	Computer Peripheral Equipment, NEC
3578	Calculating & Accounting Machines, Except Electronic Computers
3579	Office Machines, NEC
3581	Automatic Vending Machines
3582	Commercial Laundry, Dry Cleaning & Pressing Machines
3585	Air Conditioning, Warm Air Heating Equipment & Commercial & Industrial Refrigeration Equipment
3586	Measuring & Dispensing Pumps
3589	Service Industry Machines, NEC
3592	Carburetors, Pistons, Piston Rings & Valves
3593	Fluid Power Cylinders & Actuators
3594	Fluid Power Pumps & Motors
3596	Scales & Balances, Except Laboratory
3599	Industrial & Commercial Machinery & Equipment, NEC
36	**ELECTRONIC & ELECTRIC EQUIPMENT**
3612	Power, Distribution & Specialty Transformers
3613	Switchgear & Switchboard Apparatus
3621	Motors & Generators
3624	Carbon & Graphite Products
3625	Relays & Industrial Controls
3629	Electrical Industrial Apparatus, NEC
3631	Household Cooking Equipment
3632	Household Refrigerators & Home & Farm Freezers
3633	Household Laundry Equipment
3634	Electric Housewares & Fans
3635	Household Vacuum Cleaners
3639	Household Appliances, NEC
3641	Electric Lamp Bulbs & Tubes
3643	Current-Carrying Wiring Devices
3644	Noncurrent-Carrying Wiring Devices
3645	Residential Electric Lighting Fixtures
3646	Commercial, Industrial & Institutional Electric Lighting Fixtures
3647	Vehicular Lighting Equipment
3648	Lighting Equipment, NEC
3651	Household Audio & Video Equipment
3652	Phonograph Records & Pre-Recorded Audio Tapes & Discs
3661	Telephone & Telegraph Apparatus
3663	Radio & TV Broadcasting & Communications Equipment
3669	Communications Equipment, NEC
3671	Electron Tubes
3672	Printed Circuit Boards
3674	Semiconductors & Related Devices
3675	Electronic Capacitors
3676	Electronic Resistors
3677	Electronic Coils, Transformers & Other Inductors
3678	Electronic Connectors
3679	Electronic Components, NEC
3691	Storage Batteries
3692	Primary Batteries, Dry & Wet

Code	Title
3694	Electrical Equipment for Internal Combustion Engines
3695	Magnetic & Optical Recording Media
3699	Electrical Machinery, Equipment & Supplies, NEC
37	**TRANSPORTATION EQUIPMENT**
3711	Motor Vehicles & Passenger Car Bodies
3713	Truck & Bus Bodies
3714	Motor Vehicle Parts & Accessories
3715	Truck Trailers
3716	Motor Homes
3721	Aircraft
3724	Aircraft Engines & Engine Parts
3728	Aircraft Parts & Auxiliary Equipment, NEC
3731	Ship Building & Repairing
3732	Boat Building & Repairing
3743	Railroad Equipment
3751	Motorcycles, Bicycles & Parts
3761	Guided Missiles & Space Vehicles
3764	Guided Missile & Space Vehicle Propulsion Units & Propulsion Unit Parts
3769	Guided Missile & Space Vehicle Parts & Auxiliary Equipment, NEC
3792	Travel Trailers & Campers
3795	Tanks & Tank Components
3799	Transportation Equipment, NEC
38	**INSTRUMENTS & RELATED PRODUCTS**
3812	Navigation, Guidance, Search & Detection Systems & Instruments
3821	Laboratory Apparatus & Furniture
3822	Automatic Controls for Regulating Residential & Commercial Environments & Appliances
3823	Industrial Instruments for Measurement, Display & Control of Process Variables & Related Products
3824	Totalizing Fluid Meters & Counting Devices
3825	Instruments for Measuring & Testing of Electricity & Electrical Signals
3826	Laboratory Analytical Instruments
3827	Optical Instruments & Lenses
3829	Measuring & Controlling Devices, NEC
3841	Surgical & Medical Instruments & Apparatus
3842	Orthopedic, Prosthetic & Surgical Supplies
3843	Dental Equipment & Supplies
3844	X-Ray Apparatus, Tubes & Equipment
3845	Electromedical & Electrotherapeutic Apparatus
3851	Opthalmic Goods
3861	Photographic Equipment & Supplies
3873	Watches, Clocks, & Clockwork Operated Devices & Parts
39	**MISCELLANEOUS MANUFACTURING**
3912	Jewelry, Precious Metal
3914	Silverware, Plated Ware & Stainless Steel Ware
3915	Jewelers Findings & Materials & Lapidary Work
3925	Minerals & Earths, Ground or Otherwise Treated
3926	Mineral Wool
3927	Nonclay Refractories
3931	Musical Instruments
3942	Dolls & Stuffed Toys
3944	Games, Toys & Children's Vehicles, Except Dolls & Bicycles
3951	Pens, Mechanical Pencils & Parts
3952	Lead Pencils, Crayons & Artists' Materials
3953	Marking Devices
3955	Carbon Paper & Inked Ribbons
3961	Costume Jewelry & Costume Novelties, Except Precious Metal

Code	Title
3965	Fasteners, Buttons, Needles & Pins
3991	Brooms & Brushes
3993	Signs & Advertising Displays
3995	Burial Caskets
3996	Linoleum, Asphalt-Feltbase & Other ard Surface Floor Coverings, NEC
3999	Manufacturing Industries, NEC
40	**RAILROAD TRANSPORTATION**
4011	Railroads, Line-Haul Operating
4013	Railroad Switching & Terminal Estalishments
41	**LOCAL & INTERURBAN PASENGER TRANSIT**
4111	Local & Suburban Transit
4119	Local Passenger Transportaon, NEC
4121	Taxicabs
4131	Intercity & Rural Bus Traportation
4141	Local Bus Charter Servie
4142	Bus Charter Service, cept Local
4151	School Buses
4173	Terminal & Passenr Transportation Service Facilities for Motor Vicles
42	**TRUCKING & AREHOUSING**
4212	Local Truckin Without Storage
4213	Trucking, Expt Local
4214	Local Truck With Storage
4215	Courier Seices, Except by Air
4221	Farm Prct Warehousing & Storage
4222	Refrigerd Warehousing & Storage
4225	Gener Warehousing & Storage
4226	Spec Warehousing & Storage, NEC
4231	Teral & Joint Terminal Maintenance Facilities for Motor Frit Transportation
43	**. POSTAL SERVICE**
4311	S. Postal Service
44	**WATER TRANSPORTATION**
4412	Deep Sea Freight Transportation-Foreign
4424	Deep Sea Freight Transportation-Domestic
443	Great Lakes Freight Transportation
44	Freight Transportation-Water, NEC
4	Passenger Transportation-Deep Sea
2	Ferries
89	Water Transportation-Passenger, NEC
491	Marine Cargo Handling
4492	Towing & Tugboat Services
4493	Marinas
4499	Water Transportation Services, NEC
45	**AIR TRANSPORTATION**
4512	Air Transportation, Scheduled
4513	Air Courier Services
4522	Air Transportation, Non-Scheduled
4581	Airports, Flying Fields & Airport Terminal Services
46	**PIPELINES, EXCEPT GAS**
4612	Crude Petroleum Pipe Lines
4613	Refined Petroleum Pipe Lines
4619	Pipe Lines, NEC
47	**TRANSPORTATION SERVICES**
4724	Travel Agencies
4725	Tour Operators
4729	Arrangement of Passenger Transportation, NEC
4731	Arrangement of Transportation of Freight & Cargo
4741	Rental of Railroad Cars
4783	Packing & Crating
4785	Inspection & Weighing Services for Motor Vehicle Transportation
4789	Transportation Services, NEC
48	**COMMUNICATIONS**
4812	Radio Telephone Communications
4813	Telephone Communications, Except Radio Telephone
4822	Telegraph & Other Message Communications
4832	Radio Broadcasting Stations
4833	Television Broadcasting Stations
4841	Cable & Other Pay Television Services
4899	Communication Services, NEC
49	**ELECTRIC, GAS & SANITARY SERVICES**
4911	Electric Services
4922	Natural Gas Transmission
4923	Natural Gas Transmission & Distribution
4924	Natural Gas Distribution
4925	Mixed, Manufactured or Liquefied Petroleum Gas Production and/or Distribution
4931	Electric & Other Services Combined
4932	Gas & Other Services Combined
4939	Combination Utilities, NEC
4941	Water Supply
4952	Sewerage Systems
4953	Refuse Systems
4959	Sanitary Services, NEC
4961	Steam & Air-Conditioning Supply
4971	Irrigation Systems
50	**DURABLE WHOLESALE TRADE**
5012	Distribution of Automobiles & Other Motor Vehicles
5013	Motor Vehicle Supplies & New Parts
5014	Tires & Tubes
5015	Motor Vehicle Parts, Used
5021	Furniture
5023	Home Furnishings
5031	Lumber, Plywood, Millwork & Wood Panels
5033	Roofing, Siding & Insulation Materials
5039	Construction Materials, NEC
5043	Photographic Equipment & Supplies
5044	Office Equipment
5045	Computers & Computer Peripheral Equipment & Software
5046	Commercial Equipment
5047	Medical, Dental & Hospital Equipment & Supplies
5048	Opthalmic Goods
5049	Professional Equipment & Supplies
5051	Metals Service Centers & Offices
5052	Coal & Other Minerals & Ores
5063	Electrical Apparatus & Equipment
5064	Electrical Appliances, Television & Radio Sets
5065	Electronic Parts & Equipment
5072	Hardware
5074	Plumbing & Heating Equipment & Supplies
5075	Warm Air Heating & Air Conditioning Equipment
5078	Refrigeration Equipment & Supplies
5082	Construction & Mining Machinery & Equipment, Except Petroleum, Wholesale
5083	Farm & Garden Machinery & Equipment
5084	Industrial Machinery & Equipment
5085	Industrial Supplies

Code	Title
5087	Service Establishment Equipment & Supplies
5088	Transportation Equipment & Supplies, Except Motor Vehicles
5091	Sporting & Recreational Goods & Supplies
5092	Toys & Hobby Goods & Supplies
5093	Scrap & Waste Materials
5094	Jewelry, Watches, Precious Stones & Precious Metals, Wholesale
5099	Wholesale Durable Goods, NEC
51	**NONDURABLE WHOLESALE TRADE**
5111	Printing & Writing Paper
5112	Stationery & Office Supplies
5113	Industrial & Personal Service Paper
5122	Drugs, Drug Proprietaries & Sundries
5131	Piece Goods, Notions & Other Dry Goods
5136	Men's & Boys' Clothing & Furnishings
5137	Women's, Children's & Infants' Clothing & Accessories
5139	Footwear
5141	Groceries, General Line
5142	Packaged Frozen Foods
5143	Dairy Products, Except Dried or Canned
5144	Poultry & Poultry Products
5145	Confectionery
5146	Fish & Seafoods
5147	Meats & Meat Products
5148	Fresh Fruits & Vegetables
5149	Grocers & Related Products, NEC
5153	Grains & Field Beans-Buying & Marketing
5154	Livestock Buying & Marketing
5159	Farm Product Raw Materials Buying & Marketing, NEC
5162	Plastics Materials & Basic Forms & Shapes
5169	Chemicals & Allied Products, NEC
5171	Petroleum Bulk Stations & Terminals
5172	Petroleum & Petroleum Products, NEC-Except Bulk Stations & Terminals-Wholesale
5181	Beer & Ale
5182	Wines & Distilled Alcoholic Beverages
5191	Farm Supplies
5192	Books, Periodicals & Newspapers
5193	Flowers, Nursery Stock & Florists' Supplies-Wholesale
5194	Tobacco & Tobacco Products
5198	Paints, Varnishes & Supplies
5199	Nondurable Goods, NEC
52	**RETAIL BUILDING MATERIALS & GARDEN SUPPLIES**
5211	Lumber & Other Building Materials Dealers
5231	Paint, Glass & Wallpaper Stores
5251	Hardware Stores
5261	Retail Nurseries, Lawn & Garden Supply Stores
5271	Mobile Home Dealers
53	**RETAIL GENERAL MERCHANDISE STORES**
5311	Department Stores
5331	Variety Stores
5399	Miscellaneous General Merchandise Stores
54	**RETAIL FOOD STORES**
5411	Grocery Stores
5421	Meat & Fish Markets, Including Freezer Provisions
5441	Candy, Nut & Confectionary Stores
5451	Dairy Products Stores
5461	Retail Bakeries
5499	Miscellaneous Food Stores

Code	Title
55	**RETAIL AUTOMOTIVE DEALERS & SERVICE STATIONS**
5511	Motor Vehicle Dealers (New & Used Cars)
5521	Motor Vehicle Dealers (Used Cars Only)
5531	Auto & Home Supply Stores
5541	Gasoline Service Stations
5551	Boat Dealers
5561	Recreational Vehicle Dealers
5571	Motorcycle Dealers
5599	Automotive Dealers, NEC
56	**RETAIL APPAREL STORES**
5611	Men's & Boys' Clothing & Accessory Stores
5621	Women's Clothing Stores
5632	Women's Accessory & Specialty Stores
5641	Children's & Infants' Wear Stores
5651	Family Clothing Stores
5661	Shoe Stores
5699	Miscellaneous Apparel & Accessory Stores
57	**RETAIL FURNITURE & HOME FURNISHINGS**
5712	Furniture Stores
5713	Floor Covering Stores
5714	Drapery, Curtain & Upholstery Stores
5719	Miscellaneous Homefurnishing Stores
5722	Household Appliance Stores
5731	Radio, Television & Consumer Electronic Stores
5734	Computer & Computer Software Stores
5735	Record & Prerecorded Tape Stores
5736	Musical Instrument Stores
58	**DINING & DRINKING PLACES**
5812	Eating Places
5813	Drinking Places (Alcoholic Beverages)
59	**MISCELLANEOUS RETAIL**
5912	Drug Stores & Proprietary Stores
5921	Liquor Stores
5932	Used Merchandise Stores
5941	Sporting Goods & Bicycle Shops
5942	Book Stores
5943	Stationery Stores
5944	Jewelry Stores
5945	Hobby, Toy & Game Shops
5946	Camera & Photographic Supply Stores
5947	Gift, Novelty & Souvenir Shops
5948	Luggage & Leather Goods Stores
5949	Sewing, Needlework & Piece Goods Stores
5961	Catalog & Mail Order Houses
5962	Automatic Merchandising Machine Operators
5963	Direct Selling Establishments
5983	Fuel Oil Dealers
5984	Bottled or Bulk Liquefied Petroleum (LP) Gas Dealers
5989	Fuel Dealers, NEC
5992	Tobacco Stores & Stands
5994	News Dealers & Newsstands
5995	Optical Goods Stores
5999	Miscellaneous Retail Stores, NEC
60	**BANKS & BANKING SERVICES**
6011	Federal Reserve Banks
6019	Central Reserve Depository Institutions, NEC
6021	National Commercial Banks
6022	State Commercial Banks & Trust Companies
6029	Commercial Banks, NEC

Code	Title
6035	Savings Institutions, Federally Chartered
6036	Savings Institutions, Not Federally Chartered
6061	Credit Unions, Federally Chartered
6062	Credit Unions, Not Federally Chartered
6081	Branches & Agencies of Foreign Banks
6082	Foreign Trade & International Banking Institutions
6091	Nondeposit Trust Facilities
6099	Functions Related to Depository Banking, NEC
61	**NONDEPOSITORY FINANCIAL INSTITUTIONS**
6111	Federal & Federally Sponsored Credit Agencies
6141	Personal Credit Institutions
6153	Short-Term Business Credit Institutions, Except Agricultural
6159	Miscellaneous Business Credit Institutions
6162	Mortgage Bankers & Loan Correspondents
6163	Loan Brokers
62	**SECURITY & COMMODITY BROKERS**
6211	Security Brokers, Dealers & Flotation Companies
6221	Commodity Contracts Brokers & Dealers
6231	Security & Commodity Exchanges
6282	Investment Advice
6289	Services Allied With Exchange of Securities or Commodities, NEC
63	**INSURANCE CARRIERS**
6311	Life Insurance
6321	Accident & Health Insurance
6324	Hospital & Medical Service Plans
6331	Fire, Marine & Casualty Insurance
6351	Surety Insurance
6361	Title Insurance
6371	Pension, Health & Welfare Funds
6399	Insurance Carriers, NEC
64	**INSURANCE AGENTS, BROKERS & SERVICES**
6411	Insurance Agents, Brokers & Services
65	**REAL ESTATE**
6512	Operators of Nonresidential Buildings
6513	Operators of Apartment Buildings
6514	Operators of Dwellings Other Than Apartment Buildings
6515	Operators of Residential Mobile Home Sites
6517	Lessors of Railroad Property
6519	Lessors of Real Property, NEC
6531	Real Estate Agents & Managers
6541	Title Abstract Offices
6531	Real Estate Agents & Managers
6541	Title Abstract Offices
6552	Land Subdividers & Developers, Except Cemeteries
6553	Cemetery Subdividers & Developers
67	**HOLDING & INVESTMENT OFFICES**
6712	Offices of Bank Holding Companies
6719	Offices of Holding Companies, NEC
6722	Management Investment Companies, Open-End
6726	Unit Investment Trusts, Face-Amount Certificate Offices, Closed-End Management Investment Offices
6732	Educational Religious & Charitable Trusts
6733	Trusts, Except Educational, Religious & Charitable
6792	Oil Royalty Traders
6794	Patent Owners & Lessors
6798	Real Estate Investment Trusts
6799	Investors, NEC

Code	Title
70	**HOTELS & LODGING PLACES**
7011	Hotels & Motels
7021	Rooming & Boarding Houses
7032	Sporting & Recreational Camps
7033	Recreational Vehicle Parks & Campsites
7041	Organization Hotels & Lodging Houses, Membership Basis
72	**PERSONAL SERVICES**
7211	Power Laundries, Family & Commercial
7212	Garment Pressing & Agents for Laundries & Dry Cleaners
7213	Linen Supply Services
7215	Coin-Operated Laundries & Dry Cleaning
7216	Dry Cleaning Plants, Except Rug Cleaning
7217	Carpet & Upholstery Cleaning
7218	Industrial Launderers
7219	Laundry & Garment Services, NEC
7221	Photographic Studios, Portrait
7231	Beauty Shops
7241	Barber Shops
7251	Shoe Repair Shops & Shoe Shine Parlors
7261	Funeral Service & Crematories
7291	Tax Return Preparation Services
7299	Miscellaneous Personal Services, NEC
73	**BUSINESS SERVICES**
7311	Advertising Agencies
7312	Outdoor Advertising Services
7313	Radio, Television & Publishers' Advertising Representatives
7319	Advertising, NEC
7322	Adjustment & Collection Services
7323	Credit Reporting Services
7331	Direct Mail Advertising Services
7334	Photocopy & Duplicating Service
7335	Commercial Photography
7336	Commercial Art & Graphic Design
7338	Secretarial & Court Reporting Services
7342	Disinfecting & Pest Control Services
7349	Building Cleaning & Maintenance Services, NEC
7352	Medical Equipment Rental & Leasing
7353	Heavy Construction Equipment Rental & Leasing
7359	Equipment Rental & Leasing, NEC
7361	Computer Programming Services
7372	Prepackaged Software
7373	Computer Integrated Systems Design
7374	Computer Processing & Processing & Data Preparation Services
7375	Information Retrieval Services
7376	Computer Facilities Management Services
7377	Computer Rental & Leasing
7378	Computer Maintenance & Repair
7379	Computer Related Services, NEC
7381	Detective, Guard & Armored Car Services
7382	Security Systems Services
7383	News Syndicates
7384	Photofinishing Laboratories
7389	Business Services, NEC
75	**AUTO REPAIR, SERVICES & PARKING**
7513	Truck Rental & Leasing, Without Drivers
7514	Passenger Car Rental
7515	Passenger Car Leasing
7519	Utility Trailer & Recreational Vehicle Rental
7521	Automobile Parking
7532	Top, Body, Upholstery Repair & Paint Shops

Code	Title
7533	Automotive Exhaust System Repair Shops
7534	Tire Retreading & Repair Shops
7536	Automotive Glass Replacement Shops
7537	Automotive Transmission Repair Shops
7538	General Automotive Repair Shops
7539	Automobile Repair Shops, NEC
7542	Car Washes
7549	Automobile Services, Except Repair & Washes
76	**MISCELLANEOUS REPAIR SERVICES**
7622	Radio & Television Repair Shops
7623	Refrigeration & Air Conditioning Service & Repair Shops
7629	Electrical & Electronic Repair Shops, NEC
7631	Watch, Clock & Jewelry Repair
7641	Reupholstery & Furniture Repair
7692	Welding Repair
7694	Armature Rewinding Shops
7699	Repair Shops & Related Services, NEC
78	**MOTION PICTURES**
7812	Motion Picture & Video Tape Production
7819	Services Allied to Motion Picture Production
7822	Motion Picture & Video Tape Distribution
7829	Services Allied to Motion Picture Distribution
7832	Motion Picture Theaters, Except Drive-In
7833	Drive-In Motion Picture Theaters
7841	Video Tape Rental
79	**AMUSEMENT & RECREATION**
7911	Dance Halls, Studios & Schools
7922	Theatrical Producers (Except Motion Picture) & Miscellaneous Theatrical Services
7929	Bands, Orchestras, Actors, & Other Entertainers & Entertainment Groups
7933	Bowling Alleys
7941	Professional Sports Clubs & Promoters
7948	Racing, Including Track Operation
7991	Physical Fitness Facilities
7992	Public Golf Courses
7993	Coin-Operated Amusement Devices
7996	Amusement Parks
7997	Membership Sports & Recreation Clubs
7999	Amusement & Recreation Services, NEC
80	**HEALTH SERVICES**
8011	Offices & Clinics of Doctors of Medicine
8021	Offices & Clinics of Dentists
8031	Offices & Clinics of Doctors of Osteopathy
8041	Offices & Clinics of Chiropractors
8042	Offices & Clinics of Optometrists
8043	Offices & Clinics of Podiatrists
8049	Offices & Clinics of Health Practitioners, NEC
8051	Skilled Nursing Care Facilities
8052	Intermediate Care Facilities
8059	Nursing & Personal Care Facilities, NEC
8062	General Medical & Surgical Hospitals
8063	Psychiatric Hospitals
8069	Specialty Hospitals, Except Psychiatric
8071	Medical Laboratories
8072	Dental Laboratories
8082	Home Health Care Services
8092	Kidney Dialysis Centers
8093	Specialty Outpatient Facilities, NEC
8099	Health & Allied Services, NEC
81	**LEGAL SERVICES**
8111	Legal Services
82	**EDUCATIONAL SERVICES**
8211	Elementary & Secondary Schools
8221	Colleges, Universities & Professional Schools
8222	Junior Colleges & Technical Institutes
8231	Libraries & Information Centers
8243	Data Processing Schools
8244	Business & Secretarial Schools
8249	Vocational Schools, NEC
8299	Schools & Educational Services, NEC
83	**SOCIAL SERVICES**
8322	Individual & Family Social Services
8331	Job Training & Vocational Rehabilitation Services
8351	Child Day Care Services
8361	Residential Care
8399	Social Services, NEC
84	**MUSEUMS & BOTANICAL OR ZOOLOGICAL GARDENS**
8412	Museums & Art Galleries
8422	Arboreta & Botanical Or Zoological Gardens
86	**MEMBERSHIP ORGANIZATIONS**
8611	Business Associations
8621	Professional Membership Organizations
8631	Labor Unions & Similar Labor Organizations
8641	Civic, Social & Fraternal Associations
8651	Political Organizations
8661	Religious Organizations
8699	Membership Organizations, NEC
87	**ENGINEERING & MANAGEMENT SERVICES**
8711	Engineering Services
8712	Architectural Services
8713	Surveying Services
8721	Accounting, Auditing & Bookkeeping Services
8731	Commercial, Physical & Biological Research
8732	Commercial, Economic, Sociological & Educational Research
8733	Noncommercial Research Organizations
8734	Testing Laboratories
8741	Management Services
8742	Management Consulting Services
8743	Public Relations Services
8744	Facilities Support Management Services
8748	Business Consulting Services, NEC
88	**PRIVATE HOUSEHOLDS**
8811	Private Households
89	**SERVICES, NEC**
8999	Services, NEC
91	**EXECUTIVE, LEGISLATIVE & GENERAL GOVERNMENT**
9111	Executive Offices
9121	Legislative Bodies
9131	Executive & Legislative Offices Combined
9199	General Government, NEC
92	**JUSTICE, PUBLIC ORDER & SAFETY**
9211	Courts
9221	Police Protection
9222	Legal Counsel & Prosecution
9223	Correctional Institutions

Code	Title
9224	Fire Protection
9229	Public Order & Safety, NEC
93	**PUBLIC FINANCE ADMINISTRATION**
9311	Public Finance, Taxation & Monetary Policy
94	**HUMAN RESOURCES ADMINISTRATION**
9411	Administration of Educational Programs
9431	Administration of Public Health Programs
9441	Administration of Social Manpower Programs
9451	Administration of Veterans' Affairs
95	**ENVIRONMENTAL QUALITY & HOUSING**
9511	Air & Water Resource & Solid Waste Management
9512	Land, Mineral, Wildlife & Forest Conservation
9531	Administration of Housing Programs
9532	Administration of Urban Planning & Community & Rural Development

Code	Title
96	**ECONOMIC PROGRAM ADMINISTRATION**
9611	Administration of General Economic Programs
9621	Regulation & Administration of Transportation Programs
9631	Regulation & Administration of Communication, Electric, Gas & Other Utilities
9641	Regulation of Agricultural Marketing & Commodities
9651	Regulation, Licensing & Inspection of Miscellaneous Commercial Sectors
9661	Space Research & Technology
97	**NATIONAL SECURITY & INTERNATIONAL AFFAIRS**
9711	National Security
9721	International Affairs
9999	NonClassifiable Establishments

S.I.C. INDEX

0111 — WHEAT PRODUCTION

CHICAGO WEST PULLMAN TRANSPORTATION CORPORATION—Chicago West Pullman Corporation, pg. 246
UNION EQUITY—Farmland Industries, Inc., pg. 402

0112 — RICE PRODUCTION

PRODUCERS RICE MILL INC., pg. 892

0115 — CORN PRODUCTION

CARGILL SEED DIV.—Cargill Inc., pg. 219
INTERSTATE PAYCO SEED COMPANY, pg. 580
L. L. OLDS SEED COMPANY, pg. 824

0116 — SOYBEAN PRODUCTION

SOUTHWIDE, INC., pg. 1024

0119 — CASH GRAINS, NEC

B&W CO-OP, INC., pg. 107
CALIFORNIA ARTICHOKE & VEGETABLE GROWERS CORP., pg. 209
CHICAGO WEST PULLMAN TRANSPORTATION CORPORATION—Chicago West Pullman Corporation, pg. 246
CONTINENTAL GRAIN COMPANY, pg. 279
MAINE POTATO GROWERS, INC., pg. 702
TRIPLE F, INC., pg. 1114
UNION EQUITY—Farmland Industries, Inc., pg. 402

0131 — COTTON & COTTONSEED PRODUCTION

AMFAC, INC.—JMB Realty Corporation, pg. 585
HARRIS FARMS, INC., pg. 511
SOUTHWIDE, INC., pg. 1024

0132 — TOBACCO PRODUCTION

A.C. MONK CO., INC., pg. 766

0133 — SUGARCANE & SUGAR BEET PRODUCTION

AMFAC, INC.—JMB Realty Corporation, pg. 585
C. BREWER & COMPANY, LIMITED, pg. 174
KA'U AGRIBUSINESS CO., INC.—C. Brewer & Company, Limited, pg. 174
OAHU SUGAR COMPANY, LIMITED—JMB Realty Corporation, pg. 585
OLOKELE SUGAR CO., LIMITED—C. Brewer & Company, Limited, pg. 174
PUNA SUGAR CO., LTD.—JMB Realty Corporation, pg. 585

0134 — IRISH POTATO PRODUCTION

IDAHO SUPREME COMPANY, pg. 561
MAGIC VALLEY FOODS, INC., pg. 700
MAINE POTATO GROWERS, INC., pg. 702

0161 — VEGETABLE & MELON PRODUCTION

ALABAMA FARMERS CO-OP, pg. 28
CALIFORNIA ARTICHOKE & VEGETABLE GROWERS CORP., pg. 209
DEARDORFF-JACKSON COMPANY, pg. 323
A. DUDA & SONS INC., pg. 351
SEALD-SWEET GROWERS, INC., pg. 984
SOUTH BAY GROWERS, INC.—United States Sugar Corporation, pg. 1137
SPEEDLING INCORPORATED, pg. 1029
TRI VALLEY GROWERS INC., pg. 1111

0171 — BERRY FARMS

DEARDORFF-JACKSON COMPANY, pg. 323
MICHIGAN BLUEBERRY GROWERS ASSN., pg. 747
TOM WADE CO., pg. 1157
WEST COAST GROWERS & PACKERS, INC., pg. 1177

0172 — PRODUCTION OF GRAPES

E & J GALLO WINERY, pg. 441
TRI VALLEY GROWERS INC., pg. 1111

0173 — PRODUCTION OF TREE NUTS

HANCOCK PEANUT COMPANY, pg. 504
STAHMANN FARMS, INC., pg. 1034
SUN DIAMOND GROWERS OF CALIFORNIA, pg. 1058

0174 — CITRUS FRUITS PRODUCTION

BOWEN BROTHERS FRUIT CO., INC., pg. 169
B.C. COOK & SONS ENTERPRISES, INC.—Cook Holding Corporation, pg. 282
COOK HOLDING CORPORATION, pg. 282
A. DUDA & SONS INC., pg. 351
HAINES CITY CITRUS GROWERS ASSOCIATION, pg. 500
HELLER BROS. PACKING CORP., pg. 526
IRVINE COMPANY, pg. 582
PARAMOUNT CITRUS ASSOCIATION—American Protection Industries, Inc., pg. 60
PARAMOUNT FARMING COMPANY—American Protection Industries, Inc., pg. 60
SEALD-SWEET GROWERS, INC., pg. 984
SILVER SPRINGS CITRUS CO-OP, pg. 1004
SUNKIST (EUROPE) S.A.—Sunkist Growers, Inc., pg. 1061

0175 — DECIDUOUS TREE FRUITS PRODUCTION

HARRIS FARMS, INC., pg. 511
PARAMOUNT FARMING COMPANY—American Protection Industries, Inc., pg. 60
SUN DIAMOND GROWERS OF CALIFORNIA, pg. 1058
TRI VALLEY GROWERS INC., pg. 1111
TROUT INC., pg. 1116

0179 — PRODUCTION OF FRUITS & TREE NUTS, NEC

AMFAC TROPICAL PRODUCTS—JMB Realty Corporation, pg. 585
CHIQUITA BRANDS INTERNATIONAL, INC.—American Financial Corporation, pg. 53
DIAMOND WALNUT GROWERS, INC —Sun Diamond Growers of California, pg. 1058
HAZELNUT GROWERS OF OREGON—Sun Diamond Growers of California, pg. 1058
KILAUEA AGRONOMICS, INC.—C. Brewer & Company, Limited, pg. 174
LINDSAY OLIVE GROWERS, pg. 676
MAUNA KEA AGRIBUSINESS CO., INC.—C. Brewer & Company, Limited, pg. 174
SUN DIAMOND GROWERS OF CALIFORNIA, pg. 1058
SUNSWEET GROWERS INC.—Sun Diamond Growers of California, pg. 1058
SUPERIOR COFFEE & FOODS/HAWAII—C. Brewer & Company, Limited, pg. 174
TRI VALLEY GROWERS INC., pg. 1111
VALLEY FIG GROWERS—Sun Diamond Growers of California, pg. 1058

0181 — ORNAMENTAL FLORICULTURE & NURSERY PRODUCTS PRODUCTION

AMFAC GARDEN HAWAII—JMB Realty Corporation, pg. 585
AMFAC NURSERIES COLE, INC.—JMB Realty Corporation, pg. 585
GEO. J. BALL, INC., pg. 115
BURNSTAD BROTHERS, INC., pg. 194
W. ATLEE BURPEE CO.—Geo. J. Ball, Inc., pg. 116
CARGILL LTD.—Cargill Inc., pg. 219
CARIPLANT S.A.—Margo Nursery Farms, Inc., pg. 707
CURRAN CONTRACTING CO., pg. 305
PAUL ECKE RANCH, INC., pg. 366
FERRY-MORSE SEED COMPANY, pg. 407
MARGO FARMS DEL CARIBE, INC.—Margo Nursery Farms, Inc., pg. 706
MARGO NURSERY FARMS, INC., pg. 706
MAUNA LOA ORCHIDS, LTD.—Flowers of Hawaii, pg. 421
MAUNA LOA ORCHIDS, LTD., D/B/A HAWAIIAN EXOTIC FLOWERS—Flowers of Hawaii, pg. 421
MONROVIA NURSERY CO., pg. 766
MOYER PRODUCTS, INC., pg. 774
L. L. OLDS SEED COMPANY, pg. 824
PAN-AMERICAN SEED CO.—Geo. J. Ball, Inc., pg. 116
PETOSEED CO.—Geo. J. Ball, Inc., pg. 116
ROUGH BROTHERS, INC., pg. 952
THE SCOTT COMPANY, pg. 982
SPEEDLING INCORPORATED, pg. 1029
STOWE-PHARR MILLS, INC., pg. 1052
SUN BULB COMPANY, INC., pg. 1058
WEATHERLY CONSUMER PRODUCTS, INC.—Weatherly Financial Group, pg. 1169
WETSEL SEED COMPANY—Southern States Cooperative, Inc., pg. 1023

0182 — FOOD CROPS GROWN UNDER COVER

AMFAC AMYCEL, INC.—JMB Realty Corporation, pg. 585
MONTEREY MUSHROOMS, INC.—JMB Realty Corporation, pg. 585

0191 — GENERAL FARMS, PRIMARILY CROP

AMANA FARMS, INC.—Amana Society, pg. 46
AMERICAN PROTECTION INDUSTRIES, INC., pg. 60
HARRIS FARMS, INC., pg. 511
HUNT OIL COMPANY, pg. 553
IRVINE COMPANY, pg. 582
J. R. NORTON COMPANY, pg. 816
J.R. SIMPLOT COMPANY, pg. 1007

0211 — BEEF CATTLE FEEDLOTS

BARTLETT AND COMPANY, pg. 122
CACTUS FEEDERS, INC., pg. 207
CARGILL INC., pg. 219
FALLEY'S INC.—The Yucaipa Companies, pg. 1214
FRIONA FEED YARD DIV.—Friona Industries, L.P., pg. 434
FRIONA INDUSTRIES, L.P., pg. 434
GARNEY HOLDING COMPANY, INC., pg. 443
THE GRANADA GROUP, pg. 475
HOLSTEIN ASSOCIATION OF AMERICA, pg. 541
SCHAAKE PACKING COMPANY, INC., pg. 974
SUPREME CATTLE CO.—Union Holdings, Inc., pg. 1128
SUPREME FEEDERS, INC.—Union Holdings, Inc., pg. 1128
SWISHER COUNTRY CATTLE CO.—Friona Industries, L.P., pg. 434

0212 — BEEF CATTLE, EXCEPT FEEDLOTS

A BAR A RANCH—The Gates Corporation, pg. 445
CACTUS FEEDERS, INC., pg. 207
CONTINENTAL GRAIN COMPANY, pg. 279
A. DUDA & SONS INC., pg. 351
THE GRANADA GROUP, pg. 475
HARRIS FARMS, INC., pg. 511
HUNT OIL COMPANY, pg. 553
LANE INDUSTRIES, INC., pg. 656
LINCOLN INDUSTRIES, pg. 676
PETERSON INDUSTRIES INC., pg. 864
TRIPLE F LIMOUSIN CATTLE—V.F. Energies, Inc., pg. 1141
TRIPLE F LIMOUSIN CATTLE—V.F. Energies, Inc., pg. 1141
UNITED STATES CORRULITE CORPORATION—United States Sugar Corporation, pg. 1137
UNITED STATES SUGAR CORPORATION, pg. 1137

0213 — HOG PRODUCTION

CARGILL NUTRENA FEED—Cargill Inc., pg. 219

CARROLL'S FOODS, INC., pg. 225
CENTRAL STATES ENTERPRISES, INC., pg. 234
MURPHY FARMS INC., pg. 776
UNITED FEEDS, INC., pg. 1132

0214 — SHEEP & GOATS PRODUCTION

WOOL FILTERS INTL.—Farley Industries, pg. 401

0219 — GENERAL LIVESTOCK, EXCEPT DAIRY & POULTRY

J.R. SIMPLOT COMPANY, pg. 1007

0241 — DAIRY FARMS

FOREST HILL DAIRY—Turner Dairies, Inc., pg. 1119
HOLLY MILK PLANT—Atlantic Dairy Cooperative, pg. 95

0251 — BROILER, FRYER, & ROASTER CHICKENS PRODUCTION

CASE FARMS, INC.—Case Foods, Inc., pg. 228
CASE FARMS OF OHIO—Case Foods, Inc., pg. 228
CONTINENTAL GRAIN COMPANY, pg. 279
EMPIRE KOSHER POULTRY, INC., pg. 379
GOLD'N PLUMP, INC.—JFC Inc., pg. 584
JFC INC., pg. 584
K & L FEEDS—Empire Kosher Poultry, Inc., pg. 379
MATTERN HATCHERY—Empire Kosher Poultry, Inc., pg. 379
MCCARTY FARMS, pg. 727
PERDUE FARMS INC., pg. 860
PERDUE FOODS INCORPORATED—Perdue Farms Inc., pg. 860
PERDUE INCORPORATED—Perdue Farms Inc., pg. 860
PETERSON INDUSTRIES INC., pg. 864
SHENANDOAH PRODUCTS—Perdue Farms Inc., pg. 860
SHENANDOAH VALLEY FARMS—Perdue Farms Inc., pg. 860
ZACKY FARMS, INC., pg. 1215

0252 — CHICKEN EGGS PRODUCTION

CAL-MAINE EGG PRODUCTS INC.—Cal-Maine Foods, Inc., pg. 208
CAL-MAINE FARMS—Cal-Maine Foods, Inc., pg. 208
CAL-MAINE FOODS, INC., pg. 208
CARGILL INC., pg. 219
GOLD'N PLUMP, INC.—JFC Inc., pg. 584
JFC INC., pg. 584
MCANALLY ENTERPRISES, INC., pg. 726
ROSE ACRE FARMS, pg. 947

0253 — TURKEYS & TURKEY EGGS PRODUCTION

CARROLL'S FOODS, INC., pg. 225
CASE FARMS, INC.—Case Foods, Inc., pg. 228
CASE FARMS OF OHIO—Case Foods, Inc., pg. 228
NEBRASKA TURKEY GROWERS—Norbest, Inc., pg. 809
OREGON TURKEY GROWERS—Norbest, Inc., pg. 809
PETERSON INDUSTRIES INC., pg. 864
ROCCO TURKEYS, INC.—Rocco Inc., pg. 940
WEST CENTRAL TURKEYS—Norbest, Inc., pg. 809

0254 — POULTRY HATCHERIES PRODUCTION

A-G CO-OP CREAMERY, pg. 4
CAL-MAINE FOODS, INC., pg. 208
GOLD'N PLUMP, INC.—JFC Inc., pg. 584
GRESS FOODS INC., pg. 486
JFC INC., pg. 584
MAR-JAC FARMS, INC.—Mar-Jac Inc., pg. 705
MCCARTY FARMS, pg. 727
PERDUE FARMS INC., pg. 860
TATUM FARMS, pg. 1080

0259 — POULTRY & EGGS PRODUCTION, NEC

PETERSON INDUSTRIES INC., pg. 864

0272 — HORSES & OTHER EQUINES FARMS

JACK KENT COOKE, INC., pg. 282
HARRIS FARMS, INC., pg. 511

0273 — ANIMAL AQUACULTURE

CLEAR SPRINGS FOODS, INC., pg. 254
DELTA PRIDE CATFISH, INC., pg. 327

0291 — GENERAL FARMS, PRIMARILY LIVESTOCK & ANIMAL SPECIALTIES

AMANA FARMS, INC.—Amana Society, pg. 46
FARMERS UNION MARKETING & PROCESSING ASSOCIATION, pg. 402

0721 — CROP PLANTING, CULTIVATING & PROTECTION SERVICES

LYKES BROTHERS INC. OF FLORIDA, pg. 688

0722 — CROP HARVESTING, PRIMARILY BY MACHINE

GOLDEN GEM GROWERS INC., pg. 466

0723 — CROP PREPARATION SERVICES FOR MARKET, EXCEPT COTTON GINNING

J. C. BROCK CANADA, LTD—J. C. Brock Corp., pg. 178
CITRUS WORLD INC., pg. 251
B.C. COOK & SONS ENTERPRISES, INC.—Cook Holding Corporation, pg. 282
COOK HOLDING CORPORATION, pg. 282
DAIRY EXPORT CO., INC.—Darigold, Inc., pg. 315
DEARDORFF-JACKSON COMPANY, pg. 323
DIAMOND WALNUT GROWERS, INC.—Sun Diamond Growers of California, pg. 1058
A. DUDA & SONS INC., pg. 351
GOLDEN GEM GROWERS INC., pg. 466
HAINES CITY CITRUS GROWERS ASSOCIATION, pg. 500
HAZELNUT GROWERS OF OREGON—Sun Diamond Growers of California, pg. 1058
HELLER BROS. PACKING CORP., pg. 526
MFA INCORPORATED, pg. 692
MESA CITRUS GROWERS, pg. 741
MINN-DAK GROWERS, LTD., pg. 757
MR. ARTICHOKE PACKING CO., INC.—California Artichoke & Vegetable Growers Corp., pg. 209
OCEANA FOODS—Lakeside Foods, Inc., pg. 651
PARAMOUNT CITRUS ASSOCIATION—American Protection Industries, Inc., pg. 60
PRODUCERS CO-OP ASSOCIATION, INC., pg. 892
PRODUCERS RICE MILL INC., pg. 892
RICELAND FOODS, INC., pg. 931
C. H. ROBINSON CO. INC., pg. 939
SF SERVICES, pg. 961
THE SCOULAR COMPANY, pg. 983
SEBASTIAN COTTON & GRAIN CORP., pg. 986
SHERLEY GRAIN COMPANY, pg. 998
SUN DIAMOND GROWERS OF CALIFORNIA, pg. 1058
SUN-LAND PRODUCTS OF CALIFORNIA—Sun Diamond Growers of California, pg. 1058
SUNSWEET GROWERS INC.—Sun Diamond Growers of California, pg. 1058
VALLEY FIG GROWERS—Sun Diamond Growers of California, pg. 1058
WALES INDUSTRIES, INC.—Citrus World Inc., pg. 251

0724 — COTTON GINNING

CALCOT, LTD., pg. 208
TOM WADE CO., pg. 1157
WADE GIN CO.—Tom Wade Co., pg. 1157
WILSON PUGH INC., pg. 1194

0751 — LIVESTOCK SERVICES, EXCEPT VETERINARY

BEEF INDUSTRY COUNCIL—National Live Stock & Meat Board, pg. 792
THE GRANADA GROUP, pg. 475
KARLER PACKING COMPANY, INC., pg. 617
SELECT SIRES, INC., pg. 988

0752 — ANIMAL SPECIALTY SERVICES, EXCEPT VETERINARY

DELTA & PINE LAND COMPANY—Southwide, Inc., pg. 1024
HIGHWOOD SERVICE, INC.—Ralph C. Wilson Enterprises, pg. 1194
SOUTHWIDE, INC.-WESTERN DIV.—Southwide, Inc., pg. 1024

0762 — FARM MANAGEMENT SERVICES

B.C. COOK & SONS ENTERPRISES, INC.—Cook Holding Corporation, pg. 282
COOK HOLDING CORPORATION, pg. 282
FARMERS NATIONAL COMPANY—Metropolitan Life Insurance Co., pg. 744
GOLDEN GEM GROWERS INC., pg. 466

0781 — LANDSCAPE COUNSELING & PLANNING

AMLINGS FLOWERLAND, pg. 67
AMLINGS LANDSCAPE CO.—Amlings Flowerland, pg. 67
ASPLUNDH TREE EXPERT CO., pg. 88
CHARING CROSS GROUP, pg. 239
ENVIRONMENTAL INDUSTRIES, INC., pg. 383
GOODKIND & O'DEA, INC.—Dewberry & Davis, pg. 334
HOH ASSOCIATES—Post Buckley Schuh & Jernigan, pg. 882
PETRICCA INDUSTRIES, INC., pg. 865
STILES CORPORATION, pg. 1049
WEATHERLY CONSUMER PRODUCTS, INC.—Weatherly Financial Group, pg. 1169

0782 — LAWN & GARDEN SERVICES

THE DAVEY TREE EXPERT COMPANY, pg. 317
ENVIRONMENTAL INDUSTRIES, INC., pg. 383
SPRING-GREEN LAWN CARE CORPORATION, pg. 1033
TRIANGLE MAINTENANCE CORPORATION, pg. 1112

0783 — ORNAMENTAL SHRUB & TREE SERVICES

THE F.A. BARTLETT TREE EXPERT CO., pg. 123
CANADIAN SHADE TREE SERVICE, LTD.—The Davey Tree Expert Company, pg. 317
THE DAVEY TREE EXPERT COMPANY, pg. 317
DAVEY TREE SURGERY CO.—The Davey Tree Expert Company, pg. 317
ENVIRONMENTAL INDUSTRIES, INC., pg. 383
HIGH TREE SERVICES LTD.—The Davey Tree Expert Company, pg. 317
VANCOUVER TREE PEOPLE—The Davey Tree Expert Company, pg. 317

0811 — TIMBER TRACTS

CAPITAL DEVELOPMENT CO., pg. 215
DEAD RIVER FOREST PRODUCTS—Dead River Company, pg. 322
DOWN EAST TIMBERLANDS DIVISION—The Hearst Corporation, pg. 524
MENASHA CORPORATION, pg. 738
SUNICAL LAND & LIVESTOCK DIVISION—The Hearst Corporation, pg. 524

0831 — FOREST NURSERIES & GATHERING OF FOREST PRODUCTS

HAPPY HOLIDAY TREE FARMS, pg. 506

0851 — FORESTRY SERVICES

E.D. COLLIER & SON—Bateman Brothers Lumber Co., Inc., pg. 125
T.L. JAMES & COMPANY, pg. 588
MARTIN FOREST INDUSTRIES, pg. 715
PROPRIETORY PRODUCTS GROUP—Esco Corporation, pg. 388

0912 — CATCHING OF FINFISH

MARINE CONSTRUCTION & DESIGN CO., pg. 707

0913 — CATCHING OR TAKING OF SHELLFISH

SEABOARD CORPORATION—Seaboard Flour Corporation, pg. 984

0921 — FISH HATCHERIES & PRESERVES

CGF INDUSTRIES, pg. 201

1011 — IRON ORES MINING

MESABA-CLIFFS MINING CO.—National Steel Corporation, pg. 794
STANDARD LAFARGE, pg. 1036

1021 — COPPER ORES MINING

COMPANIA MINERA RAURA S.A.—The Marmon Group, Inc., pg. 712

1041 — GOLD ORES MINING

GREEN MINING, INC.—Green Holdings, Inc., pg. 484

1044 — SILVER ORES MINING

COMPANIA MINERA RAURA S.A.—The Marmon Group, Inc., pg. 712

1061 — FERROALLOY ORES MINING, EXCEPT VANADIUM

METALLURG, INC., pg. 742
TIROLER MAGNESIT, A.G.—Belmont Industries, Inc., pg. 137

1081 — METAL MINING SERVICES

KIEWIT MINING GROUP, INC.—Peter Kiewit Sons Inc., pg. 629
PETER KIEWIT SONS INC., pg. 629

1099 — MISCELLANEOUS METAL ORES MINING, NEC

EASTERN SMELTING & REFINING CORPORATION, pg. 363
GREEN MINING, INC.—Green Holdings, Inc., pg. 484
KYANITE MINING CORPORATION, pg. 647
LYKES BROTHERS INC. OF FLORIDA, pg. 688

1221 — SURFACE MINING-BITUMINOUS COAL & LIGNITE

BALE OF KENTUCKY, INC., pg. 115
BASIN ELECTRIC POWER CO-OP, pg. 125
BERWIND CORPORATION, pg. 145
COGENTRIX INCORPORATED, pg. 258
C.C. CONLEY & SONS, INC.—Green Holdings, Inc., pg. 484

CROWN COAL & COKE CO. INC., pg. 302
CRUSHING & SCREENING DIV.—Hewitt-Robins Corp., pg. 532
DRUMMOND COMPANY, INC., pg. 349
ELTON COAL CO.—Berwind Corporation, pg. 145
GREEN CONSTRUCTION OF INDIANA, INC., pg. 484
E.H. HUGHES COMPANY, INC., pg. 552
JESSE BRANCH COAL CO.—Berwind Corporation, pg. 145
KIEWIT MINING GROUP, INC.—Peter Kiewit Sons Inc., pg. 629
PETER KIEWIT SONS INC., pg. 629
KYBER COAL CO.—Berwind Corporation, pg. 145
LOGAN & KANAWHA COAL CO., pg. 681
MATHIES COAL CO.—National Steel Corporation, pg. 794
MOTO, INC., pg. 773
NATIONAL MINES CORP.—National Steel Corporation, pg. 794
PERRY & HYLTON, INC.—WRM, Inc., pg. 1156
REITZ COAL COMPANY—Berwind Corporation, pg. 145
SAHARA COAL CO., pg. 966
USIBELLI COAL MINE, INC., pg. 1140
WRM, INC., pg. 1156

1222 — UNDERGROUND MINING-BITUMINOUS COAL

BERWIND CORPORATION, pg. 145
C.C. CONLEY & SONS, INC.—Green Holdings, Inc., pg. 484
CROWN COAL & COKE CO. INC., pg. 302
DAVIS MINING & MANUFACTURING, pg. 319
DRUMMOND COMPANY, INC., pg. 349
FRANKLIN COAL—Ziegler Coal Holding Co., pg. 1218
KIEWIT MINING GROUP, INC.—Peter Kiewit Sons Inc., pg. 629
PETER KIEWIT SONS INC., pg. 629
LOGAN & KANAWHA COAL CO., pg. 681
MARMON CORPORATION—The Marmon Group, Inc., pg. 711
OLD BEN COAL CO.—Ziegler Coal Holding Co., pg. 1218
PRESTON ENERGY INC., pg. 888
SAHARA COAL CO., pg. 966
SOUTH EAST COAL CO., pg. 1019
THE UNITED COMPANY, pg. 1131
WALTER INDUSTRIES, INC., pg. 1161
ZIEGLER COAL HOLDING CO., pg. 1218

1231 — ANTHRACITE MINING

READING ANTHRACITE CO., pg. 916
READING ANTHRACITE COAL CO.—Reading Anthracite Co., pg. 916

1241 — COAL MINING SERVICES

KIEWIT MINING GROUP, INC.—Peter Kiewit Sons Inc., pg. 629
PETER KIEWIT SONS INC., pg. 629
LOGAN & KANAWHA COAL CO., pg. 681
PENN POCAHONTAS COAL COMPANY—The Marmon Group, Inc., pg. 711

1311 — CRUDE PETROLEUM & NATURAL GAS

ALADDIN PETROLEUM CORPORATION, pg. 29
ALBERTA NATIONAL GAS COMPANY LTD.—ANGUS Chemical Company, pg. 75
AMERICAN TRADING AND PRODUCTION CORPORATION, pg. 64
AMERICAN TRADING & PRODUCTION CORP., CANADIAN OIL & GAS OPERATIONS—American Trading and Production Corporation, pg. 65
ANCHOR GASOLINE CORPORATION, pg. 71
ANSCHUTZ CORPORATION, pg. 75
APCO ARGENTINA INC., pg. 77
BMR CORPORATION—Energy Minerals Corporation, pg. 381
BASIN ELECTRIC POWER CO-OP, pg. 125
BAYOU STATE OIL CORPORATION, pg. 128
THE BENATTY CORPORATION, pg. 138
BLOOMFIELD REFINING CO.—The Gary-Williams Company, pg. 444
BURK ROYALTY CO., pg. 190
CGF INDUSTRIES, pg. 201
EASTERN AMERICAN ENERGY CORPORATION, pg. 363
FARMLAND INDUSTRIES, INTL., INC.—Farmland Industries, Inc., pg. 402
FARMLAND INDUSTRIES U.K. LTD.—Farmland Industries, Inc., pg. 402
FLYING J. INC., pg. 421
GARVEY INDUSTRIES, INC., pg. 443
THE GARY-WILLIAMS COMPANY, pg. 444
GARY-WILLIAMS ENERGY CORPORATION—The Gary-Williams Company, pg. 444
J.M. HUBER CORPORATION, pg. 550
J.M. HUBER, OIL & GAS DIV.—J.M. Huber Corporation, pg. 550
CAROLINE HUNT TRUST ESTATE, pg. 553
HUNT OIL COMPANY, pg. 553
HUNT OIL INTERNATIONAL PRODUCTION-FOUNTAIN PLACE—Hunt Oil Company, pg. 554
INTERMOUNTAIN INDUSTRIES, INC., pg. 575
JUPITER ENERGY CORP.—Jupiter Industries, Inc., pg. 609
JUSTISS OIL CO., INC., pg. 610
KCS ENERGY INC., pg. 612
KNOX OIL OF TEXAS INC., pg. 638
KOCH INDUSTRIES, INCORPORATED, pg. 639
LARIO OIL & GAS COMPANY, pg. 658
LLOYD PROPERTIES, pg. 680
LOUIS DREYFUS NATURAL GAS—Louis Dreyfus Corporation, pg. 349
MAGUIRE OIL CO., pg. 701
MARTIN EXPLORATION MANAGEMENT COMPANY, pg. 715
NORTH AMERICAN ROYALTIES, INC., pg. 811
OXBOW CORPORATION, pg. 834
PETROLEUM, INC.—Garvey Industries, Inc., pg. 444
PLACID OIL COMPANY, pg. 873
QUINTANA PETROLEUM CORP., pg. 905
RASON OIL & GAS CORP.—The Benatty Corporation, pg. 138
ROSEWOOD CORPORATION—Caroline Hunt Trust Estate, pg. 553
SHEARMAN CORPORATION, pg. 996
STATES, INC., pg. 1041
TIDELANDS OIL PRODUCTION CO., pg. 1096
TRUE COMPANIES, pg. 1117
TRUE DRILLING CO.—True Companies, pg. 1117
TRUE OIL CO.—True Companies, pg. 1117
VANGUARD ENERGY CORP., pg. 1145
WALLACE & WALLACE FUEL OIL, pg. 1160
WESTERN SLOPE REFINING CO.—The Gary-Williams Company, pg. 444
ZILKHA ENERGY COMPANY, pg. 1219

1321 — NATURAL GAS LIQUIDS

ANCHOR GASOLINE CORPORATION, pg. 71
ENTERPRISE PRODUCTS COMPANY, pg. 382
THE JUPITER CORPORATION—Jupiter Industries, Inc., pg. 609
KEEN PROPANE DIVISION—Keen Compressed Gas Co., Inc., pg. 619
MFA OIL COMPANY, pg. 692
PM TERMINALS, INC.—Petroleum Marketers, Inc., pg. 865

1381 — DRILLING OIL & GAS WELLS

ANSCHUTZ CORPORATION, pg. 75
ARCTIC ALASKA DRILLING—Markair, Inc., pg. 708
COLONIAL DRILLING & EXPLORATION CORPORATION—Colonial Oil Industries, pg. 264
JUSTISS OIL CO., INC., pg. 610
MAGUIRE OIL CO., pg. 701
MARKAIR, INC., pg. 708
PENROD DRILLING CORPORATION, pg. 859
PENROD DRILLING CORPORATION (UK)—Penrod Drilling Corporation, pg. 859
PENROD INTERNATIONAL DRILLING COMPANY—Penrod Drilling Corporation, pg. 859
PENROD INTERNATIONAL DRILLING COMPANY—Penrod Drilling Corporation, pg. 859
PETRO-HUNT CORPORATION, pg. 865
WALLACE & WALLACE FUEL OIL, pg. 1160
RALPH C. WILSON ENTERPRISES, pg. 1194

1382 — OIL & GAS FIELD EXPLORATION SERVICES

ANSCHUTZ CORPORATION, pg. 75
BARANCORP, pg. 118
BARANSKI ENERGY COMPANY—Barancorp, pg. 118
THE BENATTY CORPORATION, pg. 138
COLONIAL DRILLING & EXPLORATION CORPORATION—Colonial Oil Industries, pg. 264
ENERGY MINERALS CORPORATION, pg. 381
FAIRFIELD INDUSTRIES, INC.—Fairfield Maxwell Ltd., pg. 397
FUGRO-McCLELLAND, INC., pg. 435
GULF EXPLORATION, pg. 493
HARBERT CORPORATION, pg. 506
CHARLES HOLSTON, INC., pg. 541
HUNT OIL COMPANY, pg. 553
HUNT OIL INTERNATIONAL EXPLORATION-FOUNTAIN PLACE—Hunt Oil Company, pg. 554
KCS ENERGY INC., pg. 612
KELSO OIL COMPANY, pg. 622
MAGUIRE OIL CO., pg. 701
PACIFIC ENTERPRISES OIL COMPANY (USA), pg. 840
PETRO-HUNT CORPORATION, pg. 865
PETROLEUM INC., pg. 865
PRIDE OIL CO., INC.—Kelso Oil Company, pg. 622
PRODUCTION MANAGEMENT COMPANIES, INC., pg. 893
QUINTANA PETROLEUM CORP., pg. 905
QUINTANA PETROLEUM SERVICES—Quintana Petroleum Corp., pg. 905
RASON OIL & GAS CORP.—The Benatty Corporation, pg. 138
ZILKHA ENERGY COMPANY, pg. 1219

1389 — OIL & GAS FIELD SERVICES, NEC

D.H. BLATTNER & SONS, INC., pg. 156
CALTEX PETROLEUM CORPORATION, pg. 211
COLONIAL PETROLEUM CO., pg. 264
DENVER SERVICE CENTER/INTEC—T.D. Williamson, Inc., pg. 1192
EAST COAST SERVICE CTR.—T.D. Williamson, Inc., pg. 1192
FLORIDA SERVICE CENTER—T.D. Williamson, Inc., pg. 1192
HARBERT CORPORATION, pg. 506
HYDRIL COMPANY—Hydril Company, pg. 556
INDIANA SERVICE CENTER/SATELLITE LOCATION—T.D. Williamson, Inc., pg. 1192
NANA REGIONAL CORPORATION, INC., pg. 783
NORTH AMERICAN SALT COMPANY, pg. 812
NORTH STAR STEEL HOUSTON—Cargill Inc., pg. 219
PETROLEUM WORLD—Colonial Petroleum Co., pg. 264
PRODUCTION MANAGEMENT COMPANIES, INC., pg. 893
TDW SERVICES, INC.—T.D. Williamson, Inc., pg. 1192
T.D. WILLIAMSON (U.K.) LTD.—T.D. Williamson, Inc. pg. 1192

1411 — DIMENSION STONE

CAPITAL MARBLE & GRANITE CO. INC.—Cold Spring Granite Company, pg. 260
CHEMSTONE CORP., pg. 242
COLD SPRING GRANITE COMPANY, pg. 259
L. G. EVERIST INC., pg. 392
THE GEORGIA MARBLE COMPANY, pg. 453
GEORGIA STONE INDUSTRIES, INC.—New England Stone Industries, Inc., pg. 800
MISSISSIPPI LIME CO., pg. 760
NEW ENGLAND STONE INDUSTRIES, INC., pg. 800
PRESQUE ISLE CORP.—National Steel Corporation, pg. 794

1422 — CRUSHED & BROKEN LIMESTONE

ASH GROVE CEMENT COMPANY, pg. 87
BALE OF KENTUCKY, INC., pg. 115
BATESCO QUARRIES DIV.—Ash Grove Cement Company, pg. 88
BATESCO QUARRIES DIV.—Ash Grove Cement Company, pg. 88
H.G. FENTON MATERIAL COMPANY, pg. 406
FLORIDA CRUSHED STONE COMPANY, pg. 420
THE GEORGIA MARBLE COMPANY, pg. 453
HARPER BROS., INC., pg. 510
HEMPT BROTHERS, INC., pg. 528
J.M. HUBER, CALCIUM CARBONATE DIV.—J.M. Huber Corporation, pg. 550
LINEAR DYNAMICS INC., pg. 676
H.B. MELLOTT ESTATE, INC., pg. 738
STABLER COMPANIES, INC., pg. 1034
UNION QUARRIES, INC.—Ash Grove Cement Company, pg. 88

1442 — CONSTRUCTION SAND & GRAVEL

BERKS PRODUCTS CORPORATION, pg. 142
THE CADMAN COMPANIES—C B R Cement Corporation, pg. 199
CENTRAL ALLIED ENTERPRISES, pg. 232
DILLINGHAM CONSTRUCTION N.A., INC.—Dillingham Construction Corporation, pg. 338
DILLINGHAM CONSTRUCTION PACIFIC, LTD.—Dillingham Construction Corporation, pg. 338
HAWAIIAN BITUMULS & PAVING COMPANY—Dillingham Construction Corporation, pg. 338
HAWAIIAN DREDGING & CONSTRUCTION COMPANY—Dillingham Construction Corporation, pg. 338
HECK ENTERPRISES, INC., pg. 524
K.F. JACOBSON CO.—R. B. Pamplin Corp., pg. 845
EDWARD C. LEVY CO., INC., pg. 672
RITCHIE CORPORATION, pg. 936
ROGERS GROUP INC., pg. 943
ROSS ISLAND SAND & GRAVEL CO., INC.—R. B. Pamplin Corp., pg. 845
STANDARD LAFARGE, pg. 1036
WHIBCO, INC., pg. 1185
YORK BUILDING PRODUCTS CO., INC., pg. 1208

1446 — INDUSTRIAL SAND

WHIBCO, INC., pg. 1185

1455 — KAOLIN & BALL CLAY

COLONIAL TERMINALS, INC.—Colonial Oil Industries, pg. 264
J.M. HUBER, CLAY DIV.—J.M. Huber Corporation, pg. 550
PIEDMONT MINERALS—Thiele Kaolin Co., pg. 1092
THIELE KAOLIN CO., pg. 1092

1459 — CLAY, CERAMIC & REFRACTORY MINERALS, NEC

APPLIED INDUSTRIAL MATERIALS CORPORATION, pg. 79
BENTONITE CORPORATION—Tremont Corporation, pg. 1109
WYO-BEN, INC., pg. 1157

1475 — PHOSPHATE ROCK

CF INDUSTRIES, INC., pg. 200
CARGILL FERTILIZER, INC.—Cargill Inc., pg. 219

1479 — CHEMICAL & FERTILIZER MINERAL MINING, NEC

H.J. BAKER & BRO., INC., pg. 114
CARGILL INC., pg. 219
CARGILL SALT DIVISION—Cargill Inc., pg. 219

1481 — NONMETALLIC MINERALS (EXCEPT FUEL) SERVICES

LONGYEAR (AUSTRALIA) PTY. LTD.—Longyear Company, pg. 682
LONGYEAR COMPANY, pg. 682

1499 — MISCELLANEOUS NONMETALLIC MINERALS, EXCEPT FUELS

AMERICAN GILSONITE CO., pg. 55
L. G. EVERIST INC., pg. 392
GREFCO, INC.—Belmont Industries, Inc., pg. 136
GREFCO, INC.—Belmont Industries, Inc., pg. 137
GREFCO, INC.—Belmont Industries, Inc., pg. 137
HARPER BROS., INC., pg. 510
E.H. HUGHES COMPANY, INC., pg. 552
L. ROBERT KIMBALL & ASSOCIATES, pg. 629
STANDARD LAFARGE, pg. 1036
WILLAMETTE-WESTERN CORPORATION, pg. 1190
ZIEGLER CHEMICAL & MINERAL CORP., pg. 1218

1521 — GENERAL CONTRACTORS-SINGLE FAMILY HOUSES

ACR MECHANICAL CORPORATION, pg. 2
AP TECHNOLOGY MANAGEMENT INC.—Adolfson & Peterson, Inc., pg. 18
J.R. ABBOTT CONSTRUCTION, INC., pg. 9
ALL-SEASONS, INC.—Washington Homes, Inc., pg. 1166
ATLANTIC HOMES CORP.—The Great Atlantic Companies, pg. 480
AUSHERMAN CONSTRUCTION COMPANY, pg. 98
BOCA HAMPTONS MANAGEMENT, INC.—Cenvill Development Corp., pg. 236
M. J. BROCK & SONS, INC., pg. 178
BURNSIDE CONSTRUCTION CO., pg. 194
BURNSTEAD CONSTRUCTION COMPANY, pg. 194
CARDINAL REALTY SERVICES INC., pg. 218
CARLSBERG FINANCIAL CORP., pg. 220
CENVILL DEVELOPMENT CORP., pg. 235
CHIEF INDUSTRIES - HOUSING DIV.—Chief Industries, Inc., pg. 247
CITADEL LAND, INC.—Washington Homes, Inc., pg. 1166
BARTLETT COCKE JR. CONSTRUCTION CO., pg. 258
COMPLETE INTERIORS INC., pg. 270
CONSULTANTS CORP.—Washington Homes, Inc., pg. 1166
COOPER COMMUNITIES, INC., pg. 283
COVENTRY HOMES OF COLORADO—Del Webb's Coventry, pg. 1171
DESIGNED CONTRACTS, INC.—Washington Homes, Inc., pg. 1166
DILLINGHAM CONSTRUCTION PACIFIC, LTD.—Dillingham Construction Corporation, pg. 338
FARNSWORTH CONSTRUCTION—Farnsworth Companies, pg. 403
FIRST CHOICE HOMES—Jewell Building Systems, pg. 594
FIRST FINANCIAL GROUP, INC., pg. 413
GENERAL HOMES CORPORATION, pg. 449
GOSNELL BUILDERS, pg. 472
HARDAWAY CONSTRUCTION COMPANY, INC., pg. 508
HAWAIIAN DREDGING & CONSTRUCTION COMPANY—Dillingham Construction Corporation, pg. 338
HOMES BY DAVE BROWN, pg. 542
HOUSING-HOME SALES, INC.—Washington Homes, Inc., pg. 1166
HUNT BUILDING CORPORATION, pg. 553
IRVINE COMPANY, pg. 582
THE JUPITER CORPORATION—Jupiter Industries, Inc., pg. 609
LARWIN COMPANY, pg. 659
LINKOUS CONSTRUCTION COMPANY, INC., pg. 677
LOMBARD COMPANY, pg. 681
MCAFEE CONSOLIDATED INC., pg. 726
MICHAELS GROUP INC., pg. 747
HAROLD MOORE & ASSOCIATES, INC., pg. 768
NEWARK REHABILITATION, INC.—The Prudential Insurance Company of America, pg. 896
PACIFIC SCENE INC., pg. 841
ARTHUR PORTER CONSTRUCTION, pg. 881
ROBINHOOD HOMES, INC., pg. 939
SAVOY CONSTRUCTION CO. INC., pg. 973
F.J. SCIAME CONSTRUCTION, pg. 981
SIMPLEX CONSTRUCTION CO. INC.—Simplex Industries, Inc., pg. 1006
THE SOUTHAMPTON CORP.—Washington Homes, Inc., pg. 1166
STERLING BUILDERS, INC.—Sterling Homes Corp., pg. 1047
SULLIVAN LONG & HAGERTY, INC., pg. 1057
TAYLOR-MORLEY, INC., pg. 1081
THOMPSON ENTERPRISES INC., pg. 1094
UNIVERSAL HOMES, INC.—Del Webb's Coventry, pg. 1171
JIM WALTER HOMES, INC.—Walter Industries, Inc., pg. 1162
WALTER INDUSTRIES, INC., pg. 1161
WASHINGTON HOMES, INC., pg. 1166
WASHINGTON HOMES, INC. OF VIRGINIA—Washington Homes, Inc., pg. 1166
WATKINS ENGINEERS & CONSTRUCTORS, INC.—Dillingham Construction Corporation, pg. 338
DEL WEBB'S COVENTRY, pg. 1171
WHITEHAWK PARTNERSHIP, pg. 1186
WICK BUILDING SYSTEMS, pg. 1188

1522 — GENERAL CONTRACTORS-RESIDENTIAL BUILDINGS, OTHER THAN SINGLE-FAMILY

ADOLFSON & PETERSON, INC., pg. 18
AFFILIATES GROUP INC., pg. 24
AMANA SOCIETY, pg. 46
BARCLAY WHITE INCORPORATED, pg. 119
BARTON-MALOW ENTERPRISES, INC., pg. 123
BAUGH CONSTRUCTION COMPANY, pg. 127
ROBERT E. BAYLEY CONSTRUCTION, pg. 128
BECHTEL CIVIL, INC.—Bechtel Group, Inc., pg. 131
BECHTEL GROUP, INC., pg. 130
BECON CONSTRUCTION COMPANY, INC.—Bechtel Group, Inc., pg. 131
BELL CONSTRUCTION CO. INC., pg. 134
DAVID BOLAND, INC., pg. 162
BURNSIDE CONSTRUCTION CO., pg. 194
BURRISS BUILDING SYSTEMS—B. Burriss Companies, pg. 195
B. BURRISS COMPANIES, pg. 195
BUSH DEVELOPMENT CORP., pg. 196
CARDINAL REALTY SERVICES INC., pg. 218
THE P.J. CARLIN CONSTRUCTION COMPANY, pg. 220
THE CEDARWOOD COMPANIES, pg. 230
CHIEF CONSTRUCTION—Chief Industries, Inc., pg. 247
COWPER & SIEGFRIED, pg. 291
CRANE CONSTRUCTION CO., pg. 296
CUNNINGHAM-LIMP DEVELOPMENT CO., pg. 305
DILLINGHAM CONSTRUCTION CORPORATION, pg. 337
DILLINGHAM CONSTRUCTION (H.K.) LIMITED—Dillingham Construction Corporation, pg. 338
DILLINGHAM CONSTRUCTION N.A., INC.—Dillingham Construction Corporation, pg. 338
DILLINGHAM CONSTRUCTION PACIFIC, LTD.—Dillingham Construction Corporation, pg. 338
ELKINGTON REALTY & DEVELOPMENT, pg. 377
EPSTEIN CONSTRUCTION INC.—A. Epstein and Sons, Intl., Inc., pg. 384
FARNSWORTH CONSTRUCTION—Farnsworth Companies, pg. 403
FIRST CHOICE HOMES—Jewell Building Systems, pg. 594
FRANK L. CIMINELLI CONSTRUCTION CO.—Ciminelli Development Company, Inc., pg. 249
GEORGE A. FULLER COMPANY, pg. 436
GULF CONSTRUCTORS INTERNATIONAL, INC.—Walbridge Aldinger Company, pg. 1159
HARBOUR CONTRACTORS, INC., pg. 506
HARDAWAY CONSTRUCTION COMPANY, INC., pg. 508
HARKINS BUILDERS, INC., pg. 509
THE HASSINGER COMPANIES, pg. 516
HAWAIIAN DREDGING & CONSTRUCTION COMPANY—Dillingham Construction Corporation, pg. 338
HOFFMAN HOMES, INC.—The Hassinger Companies, pg. 516
HOMEWOOD CORPORATION, pg. 542
RONALD HSU CONSTRUCTION, pg. 548
HUNT BUILDING CORPORATION, pg. 553
M. B. KAHN CONSTRUCTION CO., INC., pg. 614
KETTLER BROTHERS, INC., pg. 626
KRAUS-ANDERSON CONSTRUCTION—Kraus-Anderson, Inc., pg. 644
KRAUS-ANDERSON, INC., pg. 644
THE LAW COMPANY, INC., pg. 661
LINCOLN PROPERTY CO., NORTHERN CALIFORNIA—Lincoln Property Company, pg. 676
LOMBARD COMPANY, pg. 681
MACCO CONSTRUCTORS, INC., pg. 696
JAMES MCHUGH CONSTRUCTION CO., pg. 729
MID ATLANTIC CONSTRUCTION, INC.—Rodgers Builders, Inc., pg. 943
W.G. MILLS, INC., pg. 756
HAROLD MOORE & ASSOCIATES, INC., pg. 768
MORLEY GROUP, pg. 770
MOZEL DEVELOPMENT CORP., pg. 774
NEWARK REHABILITATION, INC.—The Prudential Insurance Company of America, pg. 896
O'NEIL INDUSTRIES INC., pg. 827
W. E. O'NEIL CONSTRUCTION COMPANY—O'Neil Industries Inc., pg. 827
OXFORD REALTY SERVICES CORP., pg. 835
PACIFIC SCENE INC., pg. 841
CHARLES PANKOW BUILDERS, LTD., pg. 846
PORTFOLIO HOMES—The Hassinger Companies, pg. 516
PRESTCON, INC.—Cenvill Development Corp., pg. 236
PRINCEVILLE CORPORATION, pg. 890
PRINCEVILLE HOTEL CORPORATION—Princeville Corporation, pg. 890
REECE-CAMPBELL, INC., pg. 920
RENTENBACH CONSTRUCTORS INCORPORATED—Rentenbach Engineering Company, pg. 927
RENTENBACH ENGINEERING COMPANY, pg. 927
RITTER BROS., INC., pg. 936
RODGERS BUILDERS, INC., pg. 942
RUSCON CORP., pg. 956
SAVOY CONSTRUCTION CO. INC., pg. 973
F.J. SCIAME CONSTRUCTION, pg. 981
SCRUFARI CONSTRUCTION CO. INC., pg. 983
KENNETH M. SEATON ENTERPRISES—Family Inns of America, Inc., pg. 398
SHAPELL INDUSTRIES, INC., pg. 995
R. M. SHOEMAKER CO., pg. 1000
GEORGE SOLLITT CONSTRUCTION, pg. 1017
A. G. SPANOS DEVELOPMENT, INC., pg. 1025
SULLIVAN & COZART INC., pg. 1056
SULLIVAN LONG & HAGERTY, INC., pg. 1057
SUNDT CORP., pg. 1060
SVERDRUP BUILDING CORPORATION—Sverdrup Corporation, pg. 1066
SVERDRUP CORPORATION, pg. 1065
TCC, pg. 1072
TAYLOR-MORLEY, INC., pg. 1081
TISHMAN REALTY & CONSTRUCTION CO., pg. 1099
WARREN PROPERTIES, pg. 1165
WATKINS ENGINEERS & CONSTRUCTORS, INC.—Dillingham Construction Corporation, pg. 338
WAUSAU HOMES, INC., pg. 1168
WHITEHAWK PARTNERSHIP, pg. 1186
WICK BUILDING SYSTEMS, pg. 1188
WIL-FREDS CONSTRUCTION, INC., pg. 1189
WILLIAMS COMPANY OF ORLANDO, INC., pg. 1190
WITCHER CONSTRUCTION COMPANY, pg. 1198

1531 — OPERATIVE BUILDERS

ATLANTIC HOMES CORP.—The Great Atlantic Companies, pg. 480
BUILDERS DEVELOPMENT INC.—Garvey Industries, Inc., pg. 444
BURNSIDE CONSTRUCTION CO., pg. 194
BURNSTEAD CONSTRUCTION COMPANY, pg. 194
BUSH DEVELOPMENT CORP., pg. 196
THE DONOHOE COMPANIES, INC., pg. 345
DUGAN & MEYERS CONSTRUCTION CO.—Dugan & Meyers Interests, Inc., pg. 351
F.W.D.C., INC.—Cenvill Development Corp., pg. 236
THE FLATLEY COMPANY, pg. 416
GOSNELL BUILDERS, pg. 472
THE GREAT ATLANTIC COMPANIES, pg. 480
GREATER CONSTRUCTION CORP., pg. 483
GRIFFIN HOMES, INC., pg. 487
HOMEWOOD CORPORATION, pg. 542
JOHN WIELAND HOMES OF CHARLESTON, INC.—John Wieland Homes Inc., pg. 1189
KETTLER BROTHERS, INC., pg. 626
KORMAN CO., pg. 642
LAKE GEORGE VENTURES, INC.—Rotterdam Ventures Inc., pg. 951
LEADER FEDERAL BANK FOR SAVINGS, pg. 663
LEWIS HOMES MANAGEMENT CORP., pg. 673
WILLIAM LYON COMPANY, pg. 690
MILLER & SMITH, INC., pg. 755
MONITOR CONSTRUCTION CO.—Dugan & Meyers Interests, Inc., pg. 351
NEW FORTIS CORP., pg. 800
OVERTON MOORE & ASSOCIATES, pg. 833
OXFORD REALTY SERVICES CORP., pg. 835
ARTHUR PORTER CONSTRUCTION, pg. 881
ROBERT C. POWELL DEVELOPMENTS, INCORPORATED, pg. 882
PURCELL CO., INC., pg. 900
RAYCO, pg. 914
REAL ESTATE CORP. OF FLORIDA, pg. 917
RHOADES DEVELOPMENT, pg. 931
F.J. SCIAME CONSTRUCTION, pg. 981
SELIGMAN & ASSOCIATES, INC., pg. 988
SELIGMAN & ASSOCS. OF MICHIGAN—Seligman & Associates, Inc., pg. 988
SHAPELL INDUSTRIES, INC., pg. 995
SHEA HOMES, pg. 996
THE VAN METRE COMPANIES, pg. 1144
WARMINGTON HOMES, pg. 1164
WYNMOOR LTD. PARTNERSHIP—Cenvill Development Corp., pg. 236

1541 — GENERAL CONTRACTORS-INDUSTRIAL BUILDINGS & WAREHOUSES

ACR MECHANICAL CORPORATION, pg. 2
ADOLFSON & PETERSON, INC., pg. 18
ALACON, pg. 29
J. S. ALBERICI CONSTRUCTION CO., INC., pg. 31
ATLANTIC BUILDERS GROUP INC., pg. 94
THE ATLAS CONSTRUCTION CO., pg. 96
THE AUCHTER COMPANY, pg. 98
AUSTIN-AUSTRALIA—National Gypsum Company, pg. 790
THE AUSTIN CO.—National Gypsum Company, pg. 790
THE AUSTIN CO. S.A.—National Gypsum Company, pg. 790
THE AUSTIN CO. OF U.K. LTD.—National Gypsum Company, pg. 790
THE AUSTIN COMPANY—National Gypsum Company, pg. 790
AUSTIN ITALIA S.P.A.—National Gypsum Company, pg. 790
AUSTIN-NEDERLAND B.V.—National Gypsum Company, pg. 791
AVERY MAYS CONSTRUCTION CO.—The Hunt Corporation, pg. 553
BEC INC., pg. 106
BE & K, INC., pg. 106
BARCLAY WHITE INCORPORATED, pg. 119
BARNHILL CONTRACTING COMPANY, pg. 121
BARTLETT BRAINARD & EACOTT, INC., pg. 122
BARTON-MALOW ENTERPRISES, INC., pg. 123
BATTEAST CONSTRUCTION COMPANY, INC., pg. 126
BAUGH CONSTRUCTION COMPANY, pg. 127
BECHTEL CIVIL, INC.—Bechtel Group, Inc., pg. 131
BECHTEL GREAT BRITAIN LTD.—Bechtel Group, Inc., pg. 131
BECHTEL GROUP, INC., pg. 130
BECHTEL, INC.—Bechtel Group, Inc., pg. 131
BECHTEL, INC. MINING & METALS SPECIAL OPERATION—Bechtel Group, Inc., pg. 131
BECHTEL NATIONAL, INC.—Bechtel Group, Inc., pg. 131
BECON CONSTRUCTION COMPANY, INC.—Bechtel Group, Inc., pg. 131
BELL CONSTRUCTION CO. INC., pg. 134
BERNARDS BROTHERS, INC., pg. 143
WM. BLANCHARD CO., pg. 155
BOH BROTHERS CONSTRUCTION COMPANY, INC.—Boh Corporation, pg. 162
BRENCAL CONTRACTORS INC.—BEC Inc., pg. 106
BRETON CONSTRUCTION, INC., pg. 174
FRANK BRISCOE CO. INC., pg. 176
M. J. BROCK & SONS, INC., pg. 178
BROWER COMPANY—Bay Industries Inc., pg. 127
BROWNS LUMBER & SUPPLY COMPANY, pg. 183
BURMOT AUSTRALIA PTY., LTD.—Burns & Roe Enterprises, Inc., pg. 194
BURNS & ROE ENTERPRISES, INC.—Burns & Roe Enterprises, Inc., pg. 194
BURNS & ROE ENVIRONMENTAL SERVICES—Burns & Roe Enterprises, Inc., pg. 194
BURNS & ROE INDUSTRIAL SERVICES COMPANY—Burns & Roe Enterprises, Inc., pg. 194

S.I.C. Index

BURNS & ROE PACIFIC COMPANY—Burns & Roe Enterprises, Inc., pg. 194
BURNS & ROE SOUTHEAST—Burns & Roe Enterprises, Inc., pg. 194
CEI CONSTRUCTION, INC., pg. 200
CALUMET CONTRUCTION CORPORATION-INDIANAPOLIS DIVISION—Calumet Construction Corporation, pg. 211
CANADIAN MINI-WAREHOUSE PROPERTIES, LTD.—Public Storage, Inc., pg. 898
CAPITAL DEVELOPMENT CO., pg. 215
CAPITAL FACTORS, INC.—Capital Bancorp, pg. 214
CAPITOL CONSTRUCTION GROUP, INC., pg. 215
CENVILL MANAGEMENT, INC.—Cenvill Development Corp., pg. 236
CINCINNATI UNITED CONTRACTORS, pg. 250
CLARK CONSTRUCTION GROUP, pg. 252
CONSTRUCTION COUNSELLORS, INC., pg. 277
CORPOREX COMPANIES, INC., pg. 287
COWPER & SIEGFRIED, pg. 291
CRADDOCK DEVELOPMENT CO., INC., pg. 295
CUNNINGHAM-LIMP DEVELOPMENT CO., pg. 305
DAHLEM COMPANY, INC., pg. 310
DANIS BUILDING CONSTRUCTION GROUP—Danis Industries Corporation, pg. 314
DANIS INDUSTRIES CORPORATION, pg. 314
DARIN & ARMSTRONG, INC.—Walbridge Aldinger Company, pg. 1159
DEMARIA BUILDING CO. INC., pg. 327
THE DEMARS CORP., pg. 327
DICK CORPORATION, pg. 335
DILLINGHAM CONSTRUCTION CORPORATION, pg. 337
DILLINGHAM CONSTRUCTION (H.K.) LIMITED—Dillingham Construction Corporation, pg. 338
DILLINGHAM CONSTRUCTION N.A., INC.—Dillingham Construction Corporation, pg. 338
DILLINGHAM CONSTRUCTION PACIFIC, LTD.—Dillingham Construction Corporation, pg. 338
DONLEY'S, INC., pg. 345
L.F. DRISCOLL CO., pg. 349
DUGAN & MEYERS CONSTRUCTION CO.—Dugan & Meyers Interests, Inc., pg. 351
MARTIN K. EBY CONSTRUCTION COMPANY, INC.—Eby Corporation, pg. 365
ELKINGTON REALTY & DEVELOPMENT, pg. 377
ELKINS CONSTRUCTORS, INC., pg. 377
A. EPSTEIN AND SONS, INTL., INC., pg. 384
EPSTEIN CONSTRUCTION INC.—A. Epstein and Sons, Intl., Inc., pg. 384
EPSTEIN ENGINEERING EXPORT, LTD.—A. Epstein and Sons, Intl., Inc., pg. 384
EPSTEIN ENGINEERING EXPORT (WARSAW), LTD.—A. Epstein and Sons, Intl., Inc., pg. 384
A. EPSTEIN & SONS (ISRAEL) LTD.—A. Epstein and Sons, Intl., Inc., pg. 384
A.J. ETKIN CONSTRUCTION CO.—Alex J. Etkin, Inc., pg. 390
J.H. FINDORFF & SON, INC., pg. 411
THE FLATLEY COMPANY, pg. 416
FLODSTROM CONSTRUCTION CO., pg. 419
FRU-CON CONSTRUCTION CORPORATION, pg. 435
THE FUSCO CORPORATION, pg. 437
GILBANE BUILDING COMPANY, pg. 457
GLENROY CONSTRUCTION CO. INC., pg. 462
JAMES N. GRAY CONSTRUCTION CO., INC., pg. 479
THE EDWARD GRAY CORP.—Graycor, Inc., pg. 480
GRAY INTERNATIONAL—Graycor, Inc., pg. 480
GRAYCOR, INC., pg. 479
HCB CONTRACTORS, pg. 496
C.F. HAGLIN & SONS, pg. 499
HARBERT CORPORATION, pg. 506
HARBOUR CONTRACTORS, INC., pg. 506
HARDAWAY CONSTRUCTION COMPANY, INC., pg. 508
HARFORD SYSTEMS, INC.—Bio Medic Corporation, pg. 152
HARKINS BUILDERS, INC., pg. 509
HARRISON CONSTRUCTION CORP., pg. 512
HARVEY CONSTRUCTION COMPANY, INC., pg. 515
HAWAIIAN DREDGING & CONSTRUCTION COMPANY—Dillingham Construction Corporation, pg. 338
PAUL HEMMER CONSTRUCTION COMPANY, pg. 528
HENSEL PHELPS CONSTRUCTION CO., pg. 530
A.D. HERMAN CONSTRUCTION CO.—The Atlas Construction Co., pg. 96
HICKORY CONSTRUCTION COMPANY, pg. 532
HOMES & SON CONTRACTORS, INC., pg. 542
E. W. HOWELL COMPANY, INC., pg. 547
HUBER, HUNT & NICHOLS, INC.—The Hunt Corporation, pg. 553
THE HUNT CORPORATION, pg. 553
HUNTCOR INC.—The Hunt Corporation, pg. 553
ILLINOIS HYDRAULIC CONSTRUCTION COMPANY, pg. 563
INMAN CONSTRUCTION CORPORATION, pg. 570
THE ROBERT IRSAY COMPANY—Jupiter Industries, Inc., pg. 609
ISEMOTO CONTRACTING CO. LTD., pg. 582
JOFFKO INTERNATIONAL, pg. 595
AL JOHNSON CONSTRUCTION CO., pg. 597
M. B. KAHN CONSTRUCTION CO., INC., pg. 614
DANIEL J. KEATING CONSTRUCTION CO.—Daniel J. Keating Co., pg. 619
DANIEL J. KEATING CO., pg. 619
KELLER CONSTRUCTION COMPANY LTD., pg. 620
KELSEY CONSTRUCTION, INC., pg. 621
KIEWIT CONSTRUCTION GROUP, INC.—Peter Kiewit Sons Inc., pg. 629
PETER KIEWIT SONS INC., pg. 629
KITCHELL CORPORATION, pg. 634
KOKOSING CONSTRUCTION COMPANY, INC., pg. 640
LAMB ENGINEERING & CONSTRUCTION CO., pg. 652
ROBERT E. LAMB, INC., pg. 652
LANDAU BUILDING CO., pg. 654
THE LATHROP COMPANY, pg. 660
LAWSON MECHANICAL CONTRACTORS, pg. 663
LIN & ROE COMPANY—Burns & Roe Enterprises, Inc., pg. 194
LINBECK CORP., pg. 675
LINKOUS CONSTRUCTION COMPANY, INC., pg. 677
LOCKARD CONSTRUCTION, INC., pg. 680
LOMBARD COMPANY, pg. 681
M.G.C. COMPANY—Underground Construction Company, Inc., pg. 1126
MACCO CONSTRUCTORS, INC., pg. 696
MACKINNON-PARKER, INC., pg. 697
MAESCHER INDUSTRIES, INC., pg. 699
MANHATTAN BUILDING COMPANIES, pg. 703
MANHATTAN CONSTRUCTION COMPANY—Manhattan Building Companies, pg. 704
MARSHALL CONTRACTORS INC., pg. 714
MARTIN, COLE, DANDO & ROBERTSON, pg. 714
MCAFEE CONSOLIDATED INC., pg. 726
MCCARTHY BROTHERS CO.—McCarthy Building Companies, pg. 727
MCCARTHY BUILDING COMPANIES, pg. 727
J.H. MCCORMICK, INC., pg. 727
MCCRORY CONSTRUCTION CO., INC., pg. 728
FRANK MESSER & SONS CONSTRUCTION CO., pg. 741
MID ATLANTIC CONSTRUCTION, INC.—Rodgers Builders, Inc., pg. 943
MILLER BUILDING CORP., pg. 753
W.G. MILLS, INC., pg. 756
MONARCH CONSTRUCTION COMPANY, pg. 765
MONITOR CONSTRUCTION CO.—Dugan & Meyers Interests, Inc., pg. 351
M. A. MORTENSON COMPANY, pg. 772
MUNIGLE CORPORATION, pg. 775
MUSKEGON CONSTRUCTION COMPANY—Owen-Ames-Kimball Co., pg. 833
MYRICK CONSTRUCTION INC., pg. 780
NPS CORPORATION, pg. 781
NABHOLZ CONSTRUCTION CORP., pg. 782
NASON AND CULLEN, INC., pg. 784
NATIONAL GYPSUM COMPANY, pg. 790
GUST K. NEWBERG CONSTRUCTION CO., pg. 803
AL NEYER, INC., pg. 805
NIELSEN CONSTRUCTION COMPANY, pg. 807
NINTEMAN CONSTRUCTION COMPANY, INC.—Sundt Corp., pg. 1060
NORCAM CONSTRUCTION COMPANY—Ritter Bros., Inc., pg. 937
NUHAHN, INC., pg. 817
JOHN M. OLSON COMPANY, pg. 824
OMAN CONSTRUCTION CO. INC., pg. 825
O'NEIL INDUSTRIES INC., pg. 827
OPUS CORP., pg. 828
OPUS SOUTH CORPORATION, pg. 828
OWEN-AMES-KIMBALL CO., pg. 833
OWEN-AMES-KIMBALL CO.—Owen-Ames-Kimball Co., pg. 833
OWEN-AMES-KIMBALL ENGINEERING, INC.—Owen-Ames-Kimball Co., pg. 833
PMI—Todd & Sargent, Inc., pg. 1100
PACIFIC SCENE INC., pg. 841
PALA GROUP, INC., pg. 843
PALA INTERSTATE—Pala Group, Inc., pg. 843
PECK JONES CONSTRUCTION, pg. 854
HARRY PEPPER & ASSOCIATES, pg. 859
THE PEPPER COMPANIES, INC., pg. 859
PEPPER-LAWSON—The Pepper Companies, Inc., pg. 860
PEPPER WEST, INC.—The Pepper Companies, Inc., pg. 860
PERFORMANCE CONTRACTORS INC., pg. 861
PIZZAGALLI CONSTRUCTION CO., pg. 873
PORTLAND SERVICE DIVISION—Altec Industries, Inc., pg. 45
POTTER-SHACKELFORD CONSTRUCTION CO., pg. 882
POWER CONTRACTING & ENGINEERING CORP., pg. 883
POWERS CONSTRUCTION CO., INC., pg. 883
PRICE WOODS, INC.—Joe E. Woods, Inc., pg. 1200
PUBLIC STORAGE, INC., pg. 898
RENTENBACH CONSTRUCTORS INCORPORATED—Rentenbach Engineering Company, pg. 927
RENTENBACH ENGINEERING COMPANY, pg. 927
RICHTER & RATNER CONTRACTING CORPORATION, pg. 933
RITTER BROS., INC., pg. 936
RODGERS BUILDERS, INC., pg. 942
ROUBINCO, INC., pg. 952
RUDOLPH/LIBBE, INC., pg. 955
RUFFIN BUILDING SYSTEMS, INC., pg. 955
THE RUHLIN COMPANY, pg. 955
RUSCON CORP., pg. 956
RYAN CONSTRUCTION COMPANY—Ryan Properties Inc., pg. 958
RYAN CONSTRUCTION COMPANY OF MINNESOTA—Ryan Properties Inc., pg. 958
SADCO LTD.—Joffko International, pg. 595
SAE-PINKERTON & LAWS INC., pg. 966
SAVOY CONSTRUCTION CO. INC., pg. 973
F.J. SCIAME CONSTRUCTION, pg. 981
SCRUFARI CONSTRUCTION CO. INC., pg. 983
SELLEN CONSTRUCTION COMPANY, pg. 988
SEPPALA & AHO CONSTRUCTION COMPANY, pg. 990
R. M. SHOEMAKER CO., pg. 1000
SHOOK, INC.—Shook National Corporation, pg. 1000
SHOOK NATIONAL CORPORATION, pg. 1000
GEORGE SOLLITT CONSTRUCTION, pg. 1017
THE STELLAR GROUP INC., pg. 1046
STILES CORPORATION, pg. 1049
SUITT CONSTRUCTION COMPANY, INC., pg. 1056
SUNDT CORP., pg. 1060
SUPERIOR INDUSTRIES OF NEBRASKA, INC., pg. 1063
SVERDRUP BUILDING CORPORATION—Sverdrup Corporation, pg. 1066
SVERDRUP CORPORATION, pg. 1065
SVERDRUP ENVIRONMENTAL INC.—Sverdrup Corporation, pg. 1066
SWINERTON & WALBERG CO., pg. 1068
TARLTON CORPORATION, pg. 1079
ED TAYLOR CONSTRUCTION CO., pg. 1081
THOMPSON-STARRETT CONSTRUCTION COMPANY, INC.—Jupiter Industries, Inc., pg. 609
TISHMAN REALTY & CONSTRUCTION CO., pg. 1099
TODD & SARGENT, INC., pg. 1100
TORCON, INC., pg. 1102
TOWNSEND & BOTTUM, INC., pg. 1104
TRIBBLE & STEPHENS CO., pg. 1112
TUDOR INC., pg. 1118
UNDERGROUND CONSTRUCTION COMPANY, INC., pg. 1125
UNIVERSAL CONSTRUCTION COMPANY, pg. 1138
WALBRIDGE ALDINGER COMPANY, pg. 1158
WARM BROTHERS CONSTRUCTION COMPANY, pg. 1163
WATKINS ENGINEERS & CONSTRUCTORS, INC.—Dillingham Construction Corporation, pg. 338
W.H. WEAVER CONSTRUCTION CO., pg. 1170
WEHR CONSTRUCTORS INC., pg. 1172
THE WEITZ-COHEN CONSTRUCTION CO., pg. 1174
WEITZ-COHEN CONSTRUCTION COMPANY—The Weitz-Cohen Construction Co., pg. 1174
THE WEITZ COMPANY, INC.—The Weitz Corporation, pg. 1174
THE WEITZ CORPORATION, pg. 1174
WEITZ-COHEN CONSTRUCTION COMPANY—The Weitz-Cohen Construction Co., pg. 1174
WEITZ-COHEN CONSTRUCTION COMPANY—The Weitz-Cohen Construction Co., pg. 1174
WHITTENBERG CONSTRUCTION CO., pg. 1187
WIL-FREDS CONSTRUCTION, INC., pg. 1189
F.A. WILHELM CONSTRUCTION CO., INC., pg. 1189
KEMMONS WILSON COMPANIES, pg. 1194
JOE E. WOODS, INC., pg. 1200
WRIGHT-SCHUCHART, INC., pg. 1204
H. B. ZACHRY COMPANY—H.B. Zachry, pg. 1215
ZACK COMPANY, pg. 1215

1542 — GENERAL CONTRACTORS-NONRESIDENTIAL BUILDINGS, OTHER THAN INDUSTRIAL BUILDINGS & WAREHOUSES

J.R. ABBOTT CONSTRUCTION, INC., pg. 9
ACOUSTI ENGINEERING CO. OF FLORIDA, pg. 14
ADOLFSON & PETERSON, INC., pg. 18
AKARD CONSTRUCTION CO., INC.—Zale Corporation, pg. 1215
ALACON, pg. 29
J. S. ALBERICI CONSTRUCTION CO., INC., pg. 31
AMBULATORY ONE AMERICA INC., pg. 47
ATLANTIC BUILDERS GROUP INC., pg. 94
GEORGE W. AUCH CO., pg. 97
THE AUCHTER COMPANY, pg. 98
AUSHERMAN CONSTRUCTION COMPANY, pg. 98
THE AUSTIN COMPANY—National Gypsum Company, pg. 790
AUSTIN INDUSTRIES, INC., pg. 99
BEC INC., pg. 106
BALDWIN CONSTRUCTION, INC., pg. 115
BARCLAY WHITE INCORPORATED, pg. 119
BARGER BUILDER & DEVELOPERS, pg. 119
BARNHILL CONTRACTING COMPANY, pg. 121
BARR & BARR, INC., pg. 121
BARTLETT BRAINARD & EACOTT, INC., pg. 122
BARTON-MALOW ENTERPRISES, INC., pg. 123
BATSON-COOK COMPANY, pg. 126
BATTEAST CONSTRUCTION COMPANY, INC., pg. 126
BAUGH CONSTRUCTION COMPANY, pg. 127
BECHTEL CIVIL, INC.—Bechtel Group, Inc., pg. 131
BECHTEL GROUP, INC., pg. 130
BECON CONSTRUCTION COMPANY, INC.—Bechtel Group, Inc., pg. 131
BEERS CONSTRUCTION COMPANY, pg. 132
BELL CONSTRUCTION CO. INC., pg. 134
BERNARDS BROTHERS, INC., pg. 143
BIG BEAR SUPERMARKETS NO. 3, pg. 149
WM. BLANCHARD CO., pg. 155
BRENCAL CONTRACTORS INC.—BEC Inc., pg. 106
BRIDGES & COMPANY, INC., pg. 175
FRANK BRISCOE CO. INC., pg. 176
BROWER COMPANY—Bay Industries Inc., pg. 127
BRUCE-ANDERSEN COMPANY, INC., pg. 183
BUQUET & LE BLANC INC., pg. 189
BURMOT AUSTRALIA PTY., LTD.—Burns & Roe Enterprises, Inc., pg. 194
BURNS & ROE ENTERPRISES, INC., pg. 194
BURNS & ROE ENTERPRISES, INC.—Burns & Roe Enterprises, Inc., pg. 194
BURNS & ROE ENVIRONMENTAL SERVICES—Burns & Roe Enterprises, Inc., pg. 194
BURNS & ROE INDUSTRIAL SERVICES COMPANY—Burns & Roe Enterprises, Inc., pg. 194
BURNS & ROE PACIFIC COMPANY—Burns & Roe Enterprises, Inc., pg. 194
BURNS & ROE SOUTHEAST—Burns & Roe Enterprises, Inc., pg. 194
BURNSIDE CONSTRUCTION CO., pg. 194
BURRISS BUILDING SYSTEMS—B. Burriss Companies, pg. 195
B. BURRISS COMPANIES, pg. 195
BUSH DEVELOPMENT CORP., pg. 196
CEI CONSTRUCTION, INC., pg. 200
CALUMET CONSTRUCTION CORPORATION, pg. 211
CAMOSY, INC., pg. 212
CAMPBELL CONSTRUCTION CO., pg. 213
CAPITAL DEVELOPMENT CO., pg. 215
CAPITOL CONSTRUCTION GROUP, INC., pg. 215
THE P.J. CARLIN CONSTRUCTION COMPANY, pg. 220

THE CEDARWOOD COMPANIES, pg. 230
CENVILL DEVELOPMENT CORP., pg. 235
CHAMPION, INC., pg. 238
CHIEF CONSTRUCTION—Chief Industries, Inc., pg. 247
CINCINNATI UNITED CONTRACTORS, pg. 250
CLARK CONSTRUCTION GROUP, pg. 252
COAKLEY & WILLIAMS INC., pg. 256
BARTLETT COCKE JR. CONSTRUCTION CO., pg. 258
COMPLETE INTERIORS INC., pg. 270
CONGAREE CONSTRUCTION CO., INC., pg. 274
CONSTRUCTION COUNSELLORS, INC., pg. 277
CORPOREX COMPANIES, INC., pg. 287
THE COURT COMPANY, pg. 290
COWPER & SIEGFRIED, pg. 291
CRADDOCK DEVELOPMENT CO., INC., pg. 295
CRANE CONSTRUCTION CO., pg. 296
CUNNINGHAM-LIMP DEVELOPMENT CO., pg. 305
DAHLEM COMPANY, INC., pg. 310
DARIN & ARMSTRONG, INC.—Walbridge Aldinger Company, pg. 1159
DAW TECHNOLOGIES, INC., pg. 319
DEMARIA BUILDING CO. INC., pg. 327
THE DEMARS CORP., pg. 327
DICK CORPORATION, pg. 335
J.D. DIFFENBAUGH, INC., pg. 337
DILLINGHAM CONSTRUCTION CORPORATION, pg. 337
DILLINGHAM CONSTRUCTION (H.K.) LIMITED—Dillingham Construction Corporation, pg. 338
DILLINGHAM CONSTRUCTION N.A., INC.—Dillingham Construction Corporation, pg. 338
DILLINGHAM CONSTRUCTION PACIFIC, LTD.—Dillingham Construction Corporation, pg. 338
DIMEO CONSTRUCTION COMPANY, pg. 338
DINWIDDIE CONSTRUCTION CO., pg. 338
DONLEY'S, INC., pg. 345
THE DONOHOE COMPANIES, INC., pg. 345
DOUBLE AA BUILDERS, LTD., pg. 347
L.F. DRISCOLL CO., pg. 349
DUGAN & MEYERS CONSTRUCTION CO.—Dugan & Meyers Interests, Inc., pg. 351
DUNLAP & CO. INC., pg. 353
J.E. DUNN CONSTRUCTION CO.—Dunn Industries Inc., pg. 354
MARTIN K. EBY CONSTRUCTION COMPANY, INC.—Eby Corporation, pg. 365
ECKMAN CONSTRUCTION COMPANY, pg. 366
EGIZII ELECTRIC, INC., pg. 371
ELKINS CONSTRUCTORS, INC., pg. 377
EPSTEIN CONSTRUCTION INC.—A. Epstein and Sons, Intl., Inc., pg. 384
EPSTEIN ENGINEERING EXPORT, LTD.—A. Epstein and Sons, Intl., Inc., pg. 384
EPSTEIN ENGINEERING EXPORT (WARSAW), LTD.—A. Epstein and Sons, Intl., Inc., pg. 384
A.J. ETKIN CONSTRUCTION CO.—Alex J. Etkin, Inc., pg. 390
ALEX J. ETKIN, INC., pg. 389
FAIRVIEW CONSTRUCTION, INC, pg. 397
FARNSWORTH CONSTRUCTION—Farnsworth Companies, pg. 403
J.H. FINDORFF & SON, INC., pg. 411
THE FLATLEY COMPANY, pg. 416
FLODSTROM CONSTRUCTION CO., pg. 419
FORD DEVELOPMENT CORPORATION, pg. 423
FRANK L. CIMINELLI CONSTRUCTION CO.—Ciminelli Development Company, Inc., pg. 249
FRU-CON CONSTRUCTION CORPORATION, pg. 435
GEORGE A. FULLER COMPANY, pg. 436
FUNCTIONS—Granger Construction Co., pg. 476
THE FUSCO CORPORATION, pg. 437
GARNEY HOLDING COMPANY, INC., pg. 443
GILBANE BUILDING COMPANY, pg. 457
GLENROY CONSTRUCTION CO. INC., pg. 462
GOSNELL BUILDERS, pg. 472
GRANGER CONSTRUCTION CO., pg. 476
THE EDWARD GRAY CORP.—Graycor, Inc., pg. 480
GRAY INTERNATIONAL—Graycor, Inc., pg. 480
GRAYCOR, INC., pg. 479
GULF CONSTRUCTORS INTERNATIONAL, INC.—Walbridge Aldinger Company, pg. 1159
HBE CORPORATION, pg. 495
HCB CONTRACTORS, pg. 496
C.F. HAGLIN & SONS, pg. 499
THE HAHN CO.—Trizec Properties, Inc., pg. 1115
HARBOUR CONTRACTORS, INC., pg. 506
HARDIN CONSTRUCTION GROUP, INC., pg. 508
HARKINS BUILDERS, INC., pg. 509
HARRISON CONSTRUCTION CORP., pg. 512
HARVEY CONSTRUCTION COMPANY, INC., pg. 515
HAWAIIAN DREDGING & CONSTRUCTION COMPANY—Dillingham Construction Corporation, pg. 338
PAUL HEMMER CONSTRUCTION COMPANY, pg. 528
JOSEPH J. HENDERSON & SON, INC., pg. 529
HENSEL PHELPS CONSTRUCTION CO., pg. 530
HICKORY CONSTRUCTION COMPANY, pg. 532
HOFFMAN CONSTRUCTION COMPANY OF ALASKA—Hoffman Corporation, pg. 537
HOFFMAN CONSTRUCTION COMPANY OF CALIFORNIA—Hoffman Corporation, pg. 537
HOFFMAN CONSTRUCTION COMPANY OF OREGON—Hoffman Corporation, pg. 537
HOFFMAN CONSTRUCTION COMPANY OF WASHINGTON—Hoffman Corporation, pg. 537
HOFFMAN CORPORATION, pg. 537
HOFFMAN MECHANICAL CORPORATION—Hoffman Corporation, pg. 538
HOFFMAN STRUCTURES, INC.—Hoffman Corporation, pg. 538
HOLDER CORPORATION, pg. 538
HOMES & SON CONTRACTORS, INC., pg. 542
E. W. HOWELL COMPANY, INC., pg. 547
HERMAN HUGHES & SONS, INC., pg. 552
HUNTCO HEALTH CARE CO.—Huntco Inc., pg. 554
ILLINOIS HYDRAULIC CONSTRUCTION COMPANY, pg. 563
IMAGES WOODWORKING, INC.—Robert E. Bayley Construction, pg. 128
INLAND CONSTRUCTION COMPANY—Graycor, Inc., pg. 480
INMAN CONSTRUCTION CORPORATION, pg. 570
ISEMOTO CONTRACTING CO. LTD., pg. 582
G. E. JOHNSON CONSTRUCTION CO., INC., pg. 597
M. B. KAHN CONSTRUCTION CO., INC., pg. 614
DANIEL J. KEATING CONSTRUCTION CO.—Daniel J. Keating Co., pg. 619
DANIEL J. KEATING CO., pg. 619
KELLER CONSTRUCTION COMPANY LTD., pg. 620
KELSEY CONSTRUCTION, INC., pg. 621
KIEWIT CONSTRUCTION GROUP, INC.—Peter Kiewit Sons Inc., pg. 629
PETER KIEWIT SONS INC., pg. 629
KITCHELL CORPORATION, pg. 634
KNUTSON CONSTRUCTION CO., pg. 638
KOKOSING CONSTRUCTION COMPANY, INC., pg. 640
KOLL CO., pg. 641
ROBERT E. LAMB, INC., pg. 652
LANGLEY & MORGAN CORP.—Jupiter Industries, Inc., pg. 609
THE LATHROP COMPANY, pg. 660
THE LAW COMPANY, INC., pg. 661
LIN & ROE COMPANY—Burns & Roe Enterprises, Inc., pg. 194
LINBECK CORP., pg. 675
LINCOLN PROPERTY CO., NORTHERN CALIFORNIA—Lincoln Property Company, pg. 676
LINKOUS CONSTRUCTION COMPANY, INC., pg. 677
LOMBARD COMPANY, pg. 681
LOOMIS BROTHERS, INC., pg. 683
T. A. LOVING COMPANY, pg. 685
MCC GROUP, INC., pg. 691
M.G.C. COMPANY—Underground Construction Company, Inc., pg. 1126
MACCO CONSTRUCTORS, INC., pg. 696
MACKINNON-PARKER, INC., pg. 697
MAESCHER INDUSTRIES, INC., pg. 699
MANHATTAN BUILDING COMPANIES, pg. 703
MANHATTAN CONSTRUCTION COMPANY—Manhattan Building Companies, pg. 704
MARSHALL CONTRACTORS INC., pg. 714
MARTIN, COLE, DANDO & ROBERTSON, pg. 714
MASHBURN CONSTRUCTION COMPANY, pg. 717
MASSMAN CONSTRUCTION COMPANY, pg. 719
MCAFEE CONSOLIDATED INC., pg. 726
MCCARTHY BROTHERS CO.—McCarthy Building Companies, pg. 727
MCCARTHY BUILDING COMPANIES, pg. 727
J.H. MCCORMICK, INC., pg. 727
MCCRORY CONSTRUCTION CO., INC., pg. 728
JAMES MCHUGH CONSTRUCTION CO., pg. 729
FRANK MESSER & SONS CONSTRUCTION CO., pg. 741
MID ATLANTIC CONSTRUCTION, INC.—Rodgers Builders, Inc., pg. 943
MILLER BUILDING CORP., pg. 753
W.G. MILLS, INC., pg. 756
MING SURVEYORS, INC.—Hoffman Corporation, pg. 538
EDWARD V. MONAHAN INC., pg. 765
MONARCH CONSTRUCTION COMPANY, pg. 765
MONITOR CONSTRUCTION CO.—Dugan & Meyers Interests, Inc., pg. 351
MORLEY GROUP, pg. 770
MORSE DIESEL INTERNATIONAL, pg. 771
M. A. MORTENSON COMPANY, pg. 772
MOZEL DEVELOPMENT CORP., pg. 774
MULACH PARKING STRUCTURES CORP.—Mulach Steel Corporation, pg. 775
MULACH STEEL CORPORATION, pg. 775
MUNIGLE CORPORATION, pg. 775
MUSKEGON CONSTRUCTION COMPANY—Owen-Ames-Kimball Co., pg. 833
MYRICK CONSTRUCTION INC., pg. 780
NPS CORPORATION, pg. 781
NABHOLZ CONSTRUCTION CORP., pg. 782
NASON AND CULLEN, INC., pg. 784
NATIONAL GYPSUM COMPANY, pg. 790
GUST K. NEWBERG CONSTRUCTION CO., pg. 803
AL NEYER, INC., pg. 805
NIELSEN CONSTRUCTION COMPANY, pg. 807
NINTEMAN CONSTRUCTION COMPANY, INC.—Sundt Corp., pg. 1060
THE C. W. NOFSINGER COMPANY—Burns & McDonnell Engineers-Architects-Consultants, pg. 194
NUHAHN, INC., pg. 817
JOHN M. OLSON COMPANY, pg. 824
OLTMANS CONSTRUCTION COMPANY, pg. 824
O'NEIL INDUSTRIES INC., pg. 827
OPUS CORP., pg. 828
OPUS SOUTH CORPORATION, pg. 828
OWEN-AMES-KIMBALL CO., pg. 833
OWEN-AMES-KIMBALL CO.—Owen-Ames-Kimball Co., pg. 833
OWEN-AMES-KIMBALL ENGINEERING, INC.—Owen-Ames-Kimball Co., pg. 833
CHARLES PANKOW BUILDERS, LTD., pg. 846
PARLIAMENT CO., pg. 850
PASCHEN CONTRACTORS, INC., pg. 851
PATTEN-BEERS CONSTRUCTORS—Beers Construction Company, pg. 132
PECK JONES CONSTRUCTION, pg. 854
THE PEPPER COMPANIES, INC., pg. 859
PEPPER-LAWSON—The Pepper Companies, Inc., pg. 860
PEPPER WEST, INC.—The Pepper Companies, Inc., pg. 860
PICOU BROTHERS CONSTRUCTION COMPANY, pg. 870
PIZZAGALLI CONSTRUCTION CO., pg. 873
POLERA BUILDING CORP., pg. 878
POWER CONTRACTING & ENGINEERING CORP., pg. 883
POWERS CONSTRUCTION CO., INC., pg. 883
PRECISION ASBESTOS ABATEMENT COMPANY—Hoffman Corporation, pg. 538
PRECISION CONSTRUCTION COMPAN Y—Hoffman Corporation, pg. 538
REECE-CAMPBELL, INC., pg. 920
RENTENBACH CONSTRUCTORS INCORPORATED—Rentenbach Engineering Company, pg. 927
RENTENBACH ENGINEERING COMPANY, pg. 927
RICHTER & RATNER CONTRACTING CORPORATION, pg. 933
RODGERS BUILDERS, INC., pg. 942
RUDOLPH/LIBBE, INC., pg. 955
THE RUHLIN COMPANY, pg. 955
RUSCON CORP., pg. 956
H. J. RUSSELL CORP., pg. 957
RYAN CONSTRUCTION COMPANY—Ryan Properties Inc., pg. 958
SAE-PINKERTON & LAWS INC., pg. 966
SAVOY CONSTRUCTION CO. INC., pg. 973
GEO. F. SCHULER, INC., pg. 979
SCHUMACHER-DUGAN CONSTRUCTION, pg. 979
SCHUMACHER & FORELLE, INC., pg. 979
F.J. SCIAME CONSTRUCTION, pg. 981
SELLEN CONSTRUCTION COMPANY, pg. 988
SEPPALA & AHO CONSTRUCTION COMPANY, pg. 990
R. M. SHOEMAKER CO., pg. 1000
SHOOK, INC.—Shook National Corporation, pg. 1000
SHOOK NATIONAL CORPORATION, pg. 1000
MELVIN SIMON & ASSOCIATES, pg. 1006
SIOUX FALLS CONSTRUCTION COMPANY, pg. 1008
THE SMITH GROUP, INC., pg. 1012
GEORGE SOLLITT CONSTRUCTION, pg. 1017
A. G. SPANOS DEVELOPMENT, INC., pg. 1025
THE STELLAR GROUP INC., pg. 1046
STILES CORPORATION, pg. 1049
STONE & HOOVER CONTRACTING, INC.—W. B. Goode Company, Inc., pg. 470
SUITT CONSTRUCTION COMPANY, INC., pg. 1056
SULLIVAN & COZART INC., pg. 1056
SUNDT CORP., pg. 1060
SVERDRUP BUILDING CORPORATION—Sverdrup Corporation, pg. 1066
SVERDRUP CORPORATION, pg. 1065
SVERDRUP ENVIRONMENTAL INC.—Sverdrup Corporation, pg. 1066
SWINERTON & WALBERG CO., pg. 1068
ED TAYLOR CONSTRUCTION CO., pg. 1081
TORCON, INC., pg. 1102
TOWNSEND & BOTTUM, INC., pg. 1104
TRAYLOR BROTHERS, INC., pg. 1108
TRIBBLE & STEPHENS CO., pg. 1112
TRIZEC PROPERTIES, INC., pg. 1115
TUDOR INC., pg. 1118
TUTOR-SALIBA CORPORATION, pg. 1120
UNDERGROUND CONSTRUCTION COMPANY, INC., pg. 1125
UNIVERSAL CONSTRUCTION COMPANY, pg. 1138
WALBRIDGE ALDINGER COMPANY, pg. 1158
WALSH CONSTRUCTION CO. OF ILLINOIS, pg. 1161
WARM BROTHERS CONSTRUCTION COMPANY, pg. 1163
WARMINGTON HOMES, pg. 1164
WATKINS ENGINEERS & CONSTRUCTORS, INC.—Dillingham Construction Corporation, pg. 338
W.H. WEAVER CONSTRUCTION CO., pg. 1170
WEHR CONSTRUCTORS INC., pg. 1172
THE WEITZ-COHEN CONSTRUCTION CO., pg. 1174
WHITTENBERG CONSTRUCTION CO., pg. 1187
WIL-FREDS CONSTRUCTION, INC., pg. 1189
F.A. WILHELM CONSTRUCTION CO., INC., pg. 1189
WILLIAMS COMPANY OF ORLANDO, INC., pg. 1190
JOE E. WOODS, INC., pg. 1200
WRIGHT-SCHUCHART, INC., pg. 1204
H. B. ZACHRY COMPANY—H.B. Zachry, pg. 1215

1611 — HIGHWAY & STREET CONSTRUCTION, EXCEPT ELEVATED HIGHWAYS

A-E DIVISION—Central Allied Enterprises, pg. 232
AJAX PAVING INDUSTRIES INC., pg. 28
AMICK CONSTRUCTION LTD., pg. 67
ANDERSON BROTHERS CONSTRUCTION BRAINERD, pg. 72
ARCON CONSTRUCTION CO., INC., pg. 81
ARCON STREET CONSTRUCTION DIV.—Arcon Construction Co., Inc., pg. 81
BACCO CONSTRUCTION CO., pg. 108
BALLENGER PAVING COMPANY, INC., pg. 116
BARBER BROTHERS CONTRACTING COMPANY, pg. 119
BARNHILL CONTRACTING COMPANY, pg. 121
BASIC CONSTRUCTION COMPANY, pg. 124
BECHTEL CIVIL, INC.—Bechtel Group, Inc., pg. 131
BECHTEL GROUP, INC., pg. 130
BECON CONSTRUCTION COMPANY, INC.—Bechtel Group, Inc., pg. 131
BITUMINOUS ROADWAYS, INC., pg. 153
BIZZACK INC., pg. 153
D.H. BLATTNER & SONS, INC., pg. 156
BOH BROTHERS CONSTRUCTION COMPANY, INC.—Boh Corporation, pg. 162
BORDER STATES PAVING, INC., pg. 165
DAVID A. BRAMBLE, INC., pg. 171
CEI CONSTRUCTION, INC., pg. 200
CARDER, INC., pg. 217
JOHN CARLO INC., pg. 220
CENTRAL ALLIED ENTERPRISES, pg. 232
CONCRETE CONSTRUCTION COMPANY, pg. 273
J.B. COXWELL CONTRACT, INC., pg. 295
CROWDER CONSTRUCTION CO., pg. 301
CURRAN CONTRACTING CO., pg. 305

DANIS HIGHWAY CONSTRUCTION GROUP—Danis Industries Corporation, pg. 314
DANIS INDUSTRIES CORPORATION, pg. 314
DELLA CONSTRUCTION CO. INC., pg. 326
DENTON ENTERPRISES INC., pg. 329
DEPEW DEVELOPMENT INC., pg. 331
DICKERSON CAROLINA, INC.—The Dickerson Group, Inc., pg. 336
THE DICKERSON GROUP, INC., pg. 335
DICKERSON, INC.—The Dickerson Group, Inc., pg. 336
DILLINGHAM CONSTRUCTION CORPORATION, pg. 337
DILLINGHAM CONSTRUCTION (H.K.) LIMITED—Dillingham Construction Corporation, pg. 338
DILLINGHAM CONSTRUCTION N.A., INC.—Dillingham Construction Corporation, pg. 338
DILLINGHAM CONSTRUCTION PACIFIC, LTD.—Dillingham Construction Corporation, pg. 338
FAUBER CONSTRUCTION COMPANY, INC., pg. 403
FREHNER CONSTRUCTION COMPANY, INC., pg. 432
GREEN INTERNATIONAL, INC.—Green Holdings, Inc., pg. 484
GILPATRICK CONSTRUCTION COMPANY, pg. 460
GILVIN-TERRILL INC., pg. 460
GOHMANN ASPHALT & CONSTRUCTION INC., pg. 465
GREAT LAKES CONSTRUCTION CO., pg. 481
GREEN HOLDINGS, INC., pg. 484
S. J. GROVES & SONS COMPANY, pg. 490
HALL CONTRACTING CORP., pg. 501
HARBERT CORPORATION, pg. 506
HARPER BROS., INC., pg. 510
HAWAIIAN BITUMULS & PAVING COMPANY—Dillingham Construction Corporation, pg. 338
HAWAIIAN DREDGING & CONSTRUCTION COMPANY—Dillingham Construction Corporation, pg. 338
HEMPT BROTHERS, INC., pg. 528
HENSEL PHELPS CONSTRUCTION CO., pg. 530
HILLS MATERIALS CO.—Northwestern Engineering Co., pg. 815
HUBBARD CONSTRUCTION CO., pg. 549
THE HUNT CORPORATION, pg. 553
THE HUNT PAVING COMPANY, INC.—The Hunt Corporation, pg. 553
HUNTER CONTRACTING COMPANY, pg. 554
IA CONSTRUCTION CORP., pg. 558
AL JOHNSON CONSTRUCTION CO., pg. 597
LEGRAND JOHNSON CONSTRUCTION CO., pg. 598
JOHN R. JURGENSEN CO.—Valley Asphalt Corporation, pg. 1143
P.J. KEATING COMPANY, pg. 619
KIEWIT CONSTRUCTION GROUP, INC.—Peter Kiewit Sons Inc., pg. 629
PETER KIEWIT SONS INC., pg. 629
KOKOSING CONSTRUCTION COMPANY, INC., pg. 640
KORMAN CO., pg. 642
LAKESIDE INDUSTRIES, pg. 651
THE LANE CONSTRUCTION CORP., pg. 656
C.J. LANGENFELDER & SON, INC., pg. 657
EDWARD C. LEVY CO., INC., pg. 672
LINEAR DYNAMICS INC., pg. 676
T. A. LOVING COMPANY, pg. 685
METROPOLITAN ASPHALT, INC.—Peter A. Basile Sons Inc., pg. 124
MOUNTAIN STATES CONSTRUCTORS, INC., pg. 773
NORTHWESTERN ENGINEERING CO., pg. 815
OMAN CONSTRUCTION CO. INC., pg. 825
OVERSTREET PAVING COMPANY, pg. 833
PARK CONSTRUCTION COMPANY, pg. 848
PECKHAM INDUSTRIES, INC., pg. 854
PETRICCA INDUSTRIES, INC., pg. 865
RIETH-RILEY CONSTRUCTION CO. INC., pg. 934
RISSLER & MCMURRY COMPANY, pg. 936
RITCHIE CORPORATION, pg. 936
ROGERS GROUP INC., pg. 943
ROUBIN & JANEIRO, INC.—Roubinco, Inc., pg. 952
THE RUHLIN COMPANY, pg. 955
RUSSELL INDUSTRIES, INC., pg. 957
H. E. SARGENT, INC., pg. 971
SCHUMACHER-DUGAN CONSTRUCTION, pg. 979
SHEPHERD CONSTRUCTION CO., INC., pg. 998
SIOUX FALLS CONSTRUCTION COMPANY, pg. 1008
SOUTHERN PAVING CO.—LeGrand Johnson Construction Co., pg. 598
STABLER COMPANIES, INC., pg. 1034
STABLER CONSTRUCTION COMPANY—Stabler Companies, Inc., pg. 1034
SUNDT CORP., pg. 1060
SVERDRUP CORPORATION, pg. 1065
SVERDRUP SOUTHERN CONSTRUCTORS, INC.—Sverdrup Corporation, pg. 1066
A. TEICHERT & SON, INC., pg. 1084
THOMPSON-MCCULLY ASPHALT PAVING CO.—Thompson-McCully Co., pg. 1094
THOMPSON-MCCULLY CO., pg. 1094
TILCON, INC., pg. 1097
U.S. CONSTRUCTION CO., INC., pg. 1135
VALLEY ASPHALT CORPORATION, pg. 1143
RALPH C. WILSON ENTERPRISES, pg. 1194
WINDSOR SERVICE, INC., pg. 1196
H. B. ZACHRY COMPANY—H.B. Zachry, pg. 1215

1622 — BRIDGE, TUNNEL & ELEVATED HIGHWAY CONSTRUCTION

ARCON BRIDGE DIV.—Arcon Construction Co., Inc., pg. 81
AUSTIN INDUSTRIES, INC., pg. 99
BECHTEL GROUP, INC., pg. 130
BECON CONSTRUCTION COMPANY, INC.—Bechtel Group, Inc., pg. 131
BELL CONSTRUCTION CO. INC., pg. 134
BELLAMY BROTHERS, INC., pg. 136
D.H. BLATTNER & SONS, INC., pg. 156
BOH BROTHERS CONSTRUCTION COMPANY, INC.—Boh Corporation, pg. 162
CALUMET CONSTRUCTION CORPORATION, pg. 211
CALUMET CONTRUCTION CORPORATION-INDIANAPOLIS DIVISION—Calumet Construction Corporation, pg. 211
CAPELETTI BROS., INC., pg. 214
CONGAREE CONSTRUCTION CO., INC., pg. 274
CROWDER CONSTRUCTION CO., pg. 301
DEPEW DEVELOPMENT INC., pg. 331
DICKERSON, INC.—The Dickerson Group, Inc., pg. 336
DILLINGHAM CONSTRUCTION CORPORATION, pg. 337
DILLINGHAM CONSTRUCTION (H.K.) LIMITED—Dillingham Construction Corporation, pg. 338
DILLINGHAM CONSTRUCTION N.A., INC.—Dillingham Construction Corporation, pg. 338
DILLINGHAM CONSTRUCTION PACIFIC, LTD.—Dillingham Construction Corporation, pg. 338
MARTIN K. EBY CONSTRUCTION COMPANY, INC.—Eby Corporation, pg. 365
ENGINEERED PRODUCTS, INC., pg. 382
FRU-CON CONSTRUCTION CORPORATION, pg. 435
GAI CONSTRUCTION MONITORING SERVICES, INC.—GAI Consultants, Inc., pg. 439
GAI CONSTRUCTION SERVICES, INC.—GAI Consultants, Inc., pg. 439
GAI CONSULTANTS, INC.—GAI Consultants, Inc., pg. 439
GAI CONSULTANTS, INC.—GAI Consultants, Inc., pg. 439
GAI CONSULTANTS-NC, INC.—GAI Consultants, Inc., pg. 439
GREEN INTERNATIONAL, INC.—Green Holdings, Inc., pg. 484
GILVIN-TERRILL INC., pg. 460
GREEN HOLDINGS, INC., pg. 484
S. J. GROVES & SONS COMPANY, pg. 490
W. L. HAILEY & COMPANY, INC., pg. 500
HARBERT CORPORATION, pg. 506
HAWAIIAN DREDGING & CONSTRUCTION COMPANY—Dillingham Construction Corporation, pg. 338
E.H. HUGHES COMPANY, INC., pg. 552
IRVING F. JENSEN CO., INC., pg. 593
AL JOHNSON CONSTRUCTION CO., pg. 597
JOHNSON BROS. CORP., pg. 597
KIEWIT CONSTRUCTION GROUP, INC.—Peter Kiewit Sons Inc., pg. 629
PETER KIEWIT SONS INC., pg. 629
KOKOSING CONSTRUCTION COMPANY, INC., pg. 640
KRAUS-ANDERSON CONSTRUCTION—Kraus-Anderson, Inc., pg. 644
THE LANE CONSTRUCTION CORP., pg. 656
C.J. LANGENFELDER & SON, INC., pg. 657
LARRYS, INC., pg. 659
LEE CONSTRUCTION CO.—National Engineering & Contracting Co., pg. 788
T. A. LOVING COMPANY, pg. 685
JAMES MCHUGH CONSTRUCTION CO., pg. 729
MCKINNON BRIDGE CO., pg. 731
MISENER MARINE CONSTRUCTION, pg. 759
C. C. MYERS, INC., pg. 780
NATIONAL ENGINEERING & CONTRACTING CO., pg. 788
OMAN CONSTRUCTION CO. INC., pg. 825
PARK CONSTRUCTION COMPANY, pg. 848
PROCOR SULPHUR SERVICES DIVISION—The Marmon Group, Inc., pg. 712
REPUBLIC CONTRACTING CORP., pg. 928
SCHIAVONE CONSTRUCTION CO., pg. 976
SIOUX FALLS CONSTRUCTION COMPANY, pg. 1008
GEORGE SOLLITT CONSTRUCTION, pg. 1017
SUNDT CORP., pg. 1060
SVERDRUP CORPORATION, pg. 1065
SVERDRUP SOUTHERN CONSTRUCTORS, INC.—Sverdrup Corporation, pg. 1066
TILCON, INC., pg. 1097
TRAYLOR BROTHERS, INC., pg. 1108
UNDERGROUND CONSTRUCTION COMPANY, INC., pg. 1125
WHITING-TURNER CONTRACTING CO., pg. 1187

1623 — WATER, SEWER, PIPELINE, COMMUNICATIONS & POWER LINE CONSTRUCTION

ADVANCE MECHANICAL SYSTEMS, INC., pg. 19
ARCON CONSTRUCTION CO., INC., pg. 81
ARCON MUNICIPAL DIV.—Arcon Construction Co., Inc., pg. 81
Y.C. BALLENGER ELECTRICAL CONTRACTORS, pg. 116
BASIC CONSTRUCTION COMPANY, pg. 124
BECHTEL CIVIL, INC.—Bechtel Group, Inc., pg. 131
BECHTEL EASTERN POWER CORPORATION—Bechtel Group, Inc., pg. 131
BECHTEL GREAT BRITAIN LTD.—Bechtel Group, Inc., pg. 131
BECHTEL GROUP, INC., pg. 130
BECHTEL, INC.—Bechtel Group, Inc., pg. 131
BECHTEL POWER CORPORATION—Bechtel Group, Inc., pg. 131
BECON CONSTRUCTION COMPANY, INC.—Bechtel Group, Inc., pg. 131
BOH BROTHERS CONSTRUCTION COMPANY, INC.—Boh Corporation, pg. 162
BRINK ELECTRIC CONSTRUCTION COMPANY, pg. 176
FRANK BRISCOE CO. INC., pg. 176
CALUMET CONSTRUCTION CORPORATION, pg. 211
CALUMET CONTRUCTION CORPORATION-INDIANAPOLIS DIVISION—Calumet Construction Corporation, pg. 211
CLARK CONSTRUCTION GROUP, pg. 252
COMMUNICATIONS INTERNATIONAL, pg. 269
CONCRETE CONSTRUCTION COMPANY, pg. 273
CONGAREE CONSTRUCTION CO., INC., pg. 274
JOSEPH DAVIS, INC., pg. 318
DELLA CONSTRUCTION CO. INC., pg. 326
DEPEW DEVELOPMENT INC., pg. 331
DILLINGHAM CONSTRUCTION CORPORATION, pg. 337
DILLINGHAM CONSTRUCTION (H.K.) LIMITED—Dillingham Construction Corporation, pg. 338
DILLINGHAM CONSTRUCTION N.A., INC.—Dillingham Construction Corporation, pg. 338
DILLINGHAM CONSTRUCTION PACIFIC, LTD.—Dillingham Construction Corporation, pg. 338
DIVERSIFIED GROUP, INC., pg. 340
MARTIN K. EBY CONSTRUCTION COMPANY, INC.—Eby Corporation, pg. 365
EMERALD CORPORATION, pg. 378
EQUITY CONSTRUCTION CO., INC.—Prime Hospitality Corp., pg. 889
C. R. FEDRICK, INC.—Sundt Corp., pg. 1060
FRU-CON CONSTRUCTION CORPORATION, pg. 435
GARNEY HOLDING COMPANY, INC., pg. 443
GREEN INTERNATIONAL, INC.—Green Holdings, Inc., pg. 484
ROBERT GIBB & SONS, INC., pg. 456
N. G. GILBERT CORPORATION, pg. 458
GREEN HOLDINGS, INC., pg. 484
S. J. GROVES & SONS COMPANY, pg. 490
W. L. HAILEY & COMPANY, INC., pg. 500
HALL CONTRACTING CORP., pg. 501
HARBERT CORPORATION, pg. 506
HARRIS MECHANICAL CONTRACTING CO., pg. 512
HAWAIIAN DREDGING & CONSTRUCTION COMPANY—Dillingham Construction Corporation, pg. 338
HENKELS & MCCOY, INC., pg. 529
HICKORY CONSTRUCTION COMPANY, pg. 532
HOOD COMMUNICATIONS, INC.—Hood Corporation, pg. 543
HOOD CORPORATION, pg. 542
HUBBARD CONSTRUCTION CO., pg. 549
ILLINOIS HYDRAULIC CONSTRUCTION COMPANY, pg. 563
JENSEN ELECTRIC COMPANY, pg. 592
JOHNSON BROS. CORP., pg. 597
KIEWIT CONSTRUCTION GROUP, INC.—Peter Kiewit Sons Inc., pg. 629
PETER KIEWIT SONS INC., pg. 629
KOKOSING CONSTRUCTION COMPANY, INC., pg. 640
L & R COMMUNICATIONS, LIMITED, pg. 647
LAMB ENGINEERING & CONSTRUCTION CO., pg. 652
THE LANE CONSTRUCTION CORP., pg. 656
LARRYS, INC., pg. 659
LEE CONSTRUCTION CO.—National Engineering & Contracting Co., pg. 788
MACCO CONSTRUCTORS, INC., pg. 696
MAKO CONSTRUCTION CO.—Henkels & McCoy, Inc., pg. 529
MCAFEE CONSOLIDATED INC., pg. 726
NATIONAL ENGINEERING & CONTRACTING CO., pg. 788
NORTHLAND ALASKA, INC.—Green Holdings, Inc., pg. 484
OMAN CONSTRUCTION CO. INC., pg. 825
OVERSTREET PAVING COMPANY, pg. 833
PCM CONSTRUCTION, INC.—Henkels & McCoy, Inc., pg. 529
PRIME CONSTRUCTION CO.—Prime Hospitality Corp., pg. 889
PRIME-FLORIDA, INC.—Prime Hospitality Corp., pg. 889
PRIME MANAGEMENT CO., INC.—Prime Hospitality Corp., pg. 889
REPUBLIC CONTRACTING CORP., pg. 928
ROUBIN & JANEIRO, INC.—Roubinco, Inc., pg. 952
ROUBINCO, INC., pg. 952
H. E. SARGENT, INC., pg. 971
SCHIAVONE CONSTRUCTION CO., pg. 976
THE SPOHN CORPORATION, pg. 1032
SUNDT CORP., pg. 1060
SVERDRUP CORPORATION, pg. 1065
SVERDRUP ENVIRONMENTAL INC.—Sverdrup Corporation, pg. 1066
SVERDRUP SOUTHERN CONSTRUCTORS, INC.—Sverdrup Corporation, pg. 1066
SWINERTON & WALBERG CO., pg. 1068
TARLTON CORPORATION, pg. 1079
UNDERGROUND CONSTRUCTION COMPANY, INC., pg. 1125
UTILITIES CONSTRUCTION CO., INC. OF SOUTH CAROLINA, pg. 1141
WASHINGTON CORPORATION, pg. 1165
WINTERS WELDING WORKS, INC., pg. 1197
WORRAD SERVICES INC.—Henkels & McCoy, Inc., pg. 529
H. B. ZACHRY COMPANY—H.B. Zachry, pg. 1215

1629 — HEAVY CONSTRUCTION, NEC

ACOUSTI ENGINEERING CO. OF FLORIDA, pg. 14
AMERICAN REFRACTORIES CO.—Belmont Industries, Inc., pg. 136
AMICK CONSTRUCTION LTD., pg. 67
AVIATION CONSTRUCTORS, INC.—Cleveland Group, Inc., pg. 255
THE BABCOCK & WILCOX COMPANY, pg. 107
THE BARBAR GROUP, INC., pg. 119
BECHTEL CIVIL, INC.—Bechtel Group, Inc., pg. 131
BECHTEL EASTERN POWER CORPORATION—Bechtel Group, Inc., pg. 131
BECHTEL GREAT BRITAIN LTD.—Bechtel Group, Inc., pg. 131
BECHTEL GROUP, INC., pg. 130
BECHTEL, INC.—Bechtel Group, Inc., pg. 131
BECHTEL, INC. MINING & METALS SPECIAL OPERATION—Bechtel Group, Inc., pg. 131
BECHTEL NATIONAL, INC.—Bechtel Group, Inc., pg. 131

BECHTEL POWER CORPORATION—Bechtel Group, Inc., pg. 131
BECON CONSTRUCTION COMPANY, INC.—Bechtel Group, Inc., pg. 131
BELLAMY BROTHERS, INC., pg. 136
ALGERNON BLAIR INTERNATIONAL, pg. 155
BOH BROTHERS CONSTRUCTION COMPANY, INC.—Boh Corporation, pg. 162
BOH CORPORATION, pg. 162
BRINK ELECTRIC CONSTRUCTION COMPANY, pg. 176
FRANK BRISCOE CO. INC., pg. 176
BROWN & CALDWELL CONSULTING ENGINEERS, pg. 181
BURMOT AUSTRALIA PTY., LTD.—Burns & Roe Enterprises, Inc., pg. 194
BURNS & ROE ENTERPRISES, INC.—Burns & Roe Enterprises, Inc., pg. 194
BURNS & ROE ENVIRONMENTAL SERVICES—Burns & Roe Enterprises, Inc., pg. 194
BURNS & ROE INDUSTRIAL SERVICES COMPANY—Burns & Roe Enterprises, Inc., pg. 194
BURNS & ROE PACIFIC COMPANY—Burns & Roe Enterprises, Inc., pg. 194
BURNS & ROE SOUTHEAST—Burns & Roe Enterprises, Inc., pg. 194
CEI CONSTRUCTION, INC., pg. 200
CALUMET CONSTRUCTION CORPORATION, pg. 211
CALUMET CONTRUCTION CORPORATION-INDIANAPOLIS DIVISION—Calumet Construction Corporation, pg. 211
CAPITAL DEVELOPMENT CO., pg. 215
CENTURY FENCE COMPANY, pg. 235
CLARK CONSTRUCTION GROUP, pg. 252
CLARK ENTERPRISES, INC.—Clark Construction Group, pg. 252
CLARKSON CONSTRUCTION COMPANIES, pg. 253
CLEVELAND GROUP, INC., pg. 255
CONCRETE CONSTRUCTION COMPANY, pg. 273
CONGAREE CONSTRUCTION CO., INC., pg. 274
COWIN & COMPANY, INC., pg. 291
CROWDER CONSTRUCTION CO., pg. 301
CROWLEY MARITIME CORPORATION, pg. 301
CUNNINGHAM-LIMP DEVELOPMENT CO., pg. 305
DANIS HEAVY CONSTRUCTION GROUP—Danis Industries Corporation, pg. 314
DANIS INDUSTRIES CORPORATION, pg. 314
DILLINGHAM CONSTRUCTION CORPORATION, pg. 337
DILLINGHAM CONSTRUCTION (H.K.) LIMITED—Dillingham Construction Corporation, pg. 338
DILLINGHAM CONSTRUCTION N.A., INC.—Dillingham Construction Corporation, pg. 338
DILLINGHAM CONSTRUCTION PACIFIC, LTD.—Dillingham Construction Corporation, pg. 338
DIVERSIFIED GROUP, INC., pg. 340
MARTIN K. EBY CONSTRUCTION COMPANY, INC.—Eby Corporation, pg. 365
ECCO SERVICES, INC.—Cooper Communities, Inc., pg. 283
EPSTEIN CONSTRUCTION INC.—A. Epstein and Sons, Intl., Inc., pg. 384
EPSTEIN ENGINEERING EXPORT, LTD.—A. Epstein and Sons, Intl., Inc., pg. 384
EPSTEIN ENGINEERING EXPORT (WARSAW), LTD.—A. Epstein and Sons, Intl., Inc., pg. 384
MARSHALL ERDMAN AND ASSOCIATES, INC., pg. 385
L. G. EVERIST INC., pg. 392
C. R. FEDRICK, INC.—Sundt Corp., pg. 1060
J.H. FINDORFF & SON, INC., pg. 411
FISH ENGINEERING & CONSTRUCTION, INC., pg. 414
FISH INTERNATIONAL CO.—Fish Engineering & Construction, Inc., pg. 414
FISH INTERNATIONAL ENGINEERS—Fish Engineering & Construction, Inc., pg. 414
FISH SERVICE CORPORATION—Fish Engineering & Construction, Inc., pg. 414
FRU-CON CONSTRUCTION CORPORATION, pg. 435
FUGRO-MCCLELLAND, INC., pg. 435
GEORGE A. FULLER COMPANY, pg. 436
GREEN INTERNATIONAL, INC.—Green Holdings, Inc., pg. 484
GILVIN-TERRILL INC., pg. 460
GOHMANN ASPHALT & CONSTRUCTION INC., pg. 465
GOODKIND & O'DEA, INC.—Dewberry & Davis, pg. 334
THE EDWARD GRAY CORP.—Graycor, Inc., pg. 480
GRAYCOR, INC., pg. 479
GREAT LAKES DREDGE & DOCK, pg. 481
GREEN HOLDINGS, INC., pg. 484
GREEN MINING, INC.—Green Holdings, Inc., pg. 484
S. J. GROVES & SONS COMPANY, pg. 490
HCB CONTRACTORS, pg. 496
W. L. HAILEY & COMPANY, INC., pg. 500
HALL CONTRACTING CORP., pg. 501
HARBERT CORPORATION, pg. 506
THE HARDAWAY COMPANY, pg. 507
HARPER BROS., INC., pg. 510
HAWAIIAN DREDGING & CONSTRUCTION COMPANY—Dillingham Construction Corporation, pg. 338
JOSEPH J. HENDERSON & SON, INC., pg. 529
HENSEL PHELPS CONSTRUCTION CO., pg. 530
HUBBARD CONSTRUCTION CO., pg. 549
HUNTER CORP., pg. 554
IA CONSTRUCTION CORP., pg. 558
ILLINOIS HYDRAULIC CONSTRUCTION COMPANY, pg. 563
INGRAM PRODUCTION COMPANY—Ingram Industries Inc., pg. 569
INTERNATIONAL MILL CONSTRUCTION, INC.—Tippins Incorporated, pg. 1099
ISEMOTO CONTRACTING CO. LTD., pg. 582
T.L. JAMES & COMPANY, pg. 588
AL JOHNSON CONSTRUCTION CO., pg. 597
JOHNSON BROS. CORP., pg. 597
JUSTISS OIL CO., INC., pg. 610
M. B. KAHN CONSTRUCTION CO., INC., pg. 614
KIEWIT CONSTRUCTION GROUP, INC.—Peter Kiewit Sons Inc., pg. 629
PETER KIEWIT SONS INC., pg. 629
KNIK CONSTRUCTION CO., INC.—Lynden Incorporated, pg. 689
KNUTSON CONSTRUCTION CO., pg. 638
LAMB ENGINEERING & CONSTRUCTION CO., pg. 652
THE LANE CONSTRUCTION CORP., pg. 656
C.J. LANGENFELDER & SON, INC., pg. 657
LEE CONSTRUCTION CO.—National Engineering & Contracting Co., pg. 788
LIN & ROE COMPANY—Burns & Roe Enterprises, Inc., pg. 194
T. A. LOVING COMPANY, pg. 685
MACCO CONSTRUCTORS, INC., pg. 696
MACKINNON-PARKER, INC., pg. 697
MAESCHER INDUSTRIES, INC., pg. 699
MARSHALL ERDMAN & ASSOC., INC.—Marshall Erdman and Associates, Inc., pg. 386
MASSMAN CONSTRUCTION COMPANY, pg. 719
JAMES MCHUGH CONSTRUCTION CO., pg. 729
GERHARDT F. MEYNE CO., pg. 746
MISENER MARINE CONSTRUCTION, pg. 759
MONTEREY MECHANICAL COMPANY, pg. 767
M. A. MORTENSON COMPANY, pg. 772
MOUNTAIN STATES CONSTRUCTORS, INC., pg. 773
NATIONAL ENGINEERING & CONTRACTING CO., pg. 788
NORTHLAND ALASKA, INC.—Green Holdings, Inc., pg. 484
OMAN CONSTRUCTION CO. INC., pg. 825
PEABODY N.E., INC.—The Pullman Company, pg. 900
PECK JONES CONSTRUCTION, pg. 854
HARRY PEPPER & ASSOCIATES, pg. 859
PETRO CHEM DEVELOPMENT COMPANY, pg. 865
PIZZAGALLI CONSTRUCTION CO., pg. 873
THE PRO-QUIP CORPORATION, pg. 892
REPUBLIC CONTRACTING CORP., pg. 928
RIETH-RILEY CONSTRUCTION CO. INC., pg. 934
RIGGS INDUSTRIES, INC., pg. 934
RITTER BROS., INC., pg. 936
ROWE CORP., pg. 952
H. E. SARGENT, INC., pg. 971
SCHIAVONE CONSTRUCTION CO., pg. 976
SHOOK, INC.—Shook National Corporation, pg. 1000
SHOOK NATIONAL CORPORATION, pg. 1000
SIGAL CONSTRUCTION, pg. 1003
GEORGE SOLLITT CONSTRUCTION, pg. 1017
SOUTHERN OHIO FABRICATORS, INC., pg. 1022
SUMMIT-BEERS CONSTRUCTION COMPANY—Beers Construction Company, pg. 132
SUNDT CORP., pg. 1060
SWINERTON & WALBERG CO., pg. 1068
TARLTON CORPORATION, pg. 1079
TORCON, INC., pg. 1102
TOWNSEND & BOTTUM, INC., pg. 1104
TRAYLOR BROTHERS, INC., pg. 1108
TRUMBULL CORPORATION, pg. 1117
TUTOR-SALIBA CORPORATION, pg. 1120
FRED WEBER INC., pg. 1171
WHITING-TURNER CONTRACTING CO., pg. 1187
WILLAMETTE-WESTERN CORPORATION, pg. 1190
WILLIAMS CRANE & RIGGING, INC.—Williams International Industries, Inc., pg. 1191
WILLIAMS INTERNATIONAL INDUSTRIES, INC., pg. 1191
WRIGHT-SCHUCHART, INC., pg. 1204
H. B. ZACHRY COMPANY—H.B. Zachry, pg. 1215

1711 — PLUMBING, HEATING & AIR CONDITIONING CONTRACTORS

ACR MECHANICAL CORPORATION, pg. 2
API GROUP INC., pg. 5
ADVANCE MECHANICAL SYSTEMS, INC., pg. 19
AIR CONDITIONING CO., INC., pg. 26
AIR ENGINEERING CO., INC.—Amelco Corporation, pg. 47
AIRCO COMMERCIAL SERVICES, INC.—Airco Mechanical Inc., pg. 27
AIRCO MECHANICAL INC., pg. 27
AIRTROL, INC., pg. 28
AMELCO CORPORATION, pg. 47
BALCO, INC. (MA), pg. 115
BARR ELECTRIC CORPORATION, pg. 122
BAYSIDE FUEL OIL CORP.—Bayside Fuel Oil Depot Corp., pg. 128
BERKS PRODUCTS CORPORATION, pg. 142
BERNHARD MECHANICAL CONTRACTOR, INC., pg. 143
BEUTLER HEATING & AIR CONDITIONING INC., pg. 148
BOH CORPORATION, pg. 162
JOHN BOUCHARD & SONS COMPANY, pg. 168
CAL-AIR INC., pg. 208
CHICAGO MECHANICAL, INC., pg. 245
CLEVELAND CONSOLIDATED INC.—Cleveland Group, Inc., pg. 255
CLEVELAND GROUP, INC., pg. 255
CONCORP, INC., pg. 272
CONDON OIL COMPANY, INC., pg. 273
CONTROLLED SYSTEMS OF WISCONSIN, INC., pg. 281
CORRIGAN BROS., INC., pg. 287
M.J. DALY & SONS, INC., pg. 313
JOHN W. DANFORTH CO., pg. 314
JOSEPH DAVIS, INC., pg. 318
DAVIS MECHANICAL CONTRACTORS, INC., pg. 318
DIMEO CONSTRUCTION COMPANY, pg. 338
DOWNEY, INC.—K & G Of Wisconsin, Inc., pg. 610
DUNLAP & CO. INC., pg. 353
ECONOMY MECHANICAL INDUSTRIES, INC.—Jupiter Industries, Inc., pg. 609
EGAN COS., pg. 371
EGAN & SONS AIR CONDITIONING CO.—Egan Cos., pg. 371
EGAN & SONS CO.—Egan Cos., pg. 371
EGIZII ELECTRIC, INC., pg. 371
EMERALD CORPORATION, pg. 378
FIBREBOND CORPORATION, pg. 408
GARVIN FIRE PROTECTION SYSTEMS, pg. 444
ROBERT GIBB & SONS, INC., pg. 456
S. I. GOLDMAN CO., pg. 467
JOHN E. GREEN CO., pg. 484
HARLAN ELECTRIC CO., pg. 509
HARRIS MECHANICAL CONTRACTING CO., pg. 512
HART ENGINEERING CORPORATION, pg. 512
HEIGHTS HEATING & COOLING, pg. 525
INDUSTRIAL CONTRACTORS, INC., pg. 566
THE ROBERT IRSAY COMPANY—Jupiter Industries, Inc., pg. 609
THE JUPITER CORPORATION—Jupiter Industries, Inc., pg. 609
K & G OF WISCONSIN, INC., pg. 610
KEHNE ELECTRIC COMPANY, INC., pg. 620
KUHLMAN, INC., pg. 646
LARRYS, INC., pg. 659
LAWSON MECHANICAL CONTRACTORS, pg. 663
MASTERS INC., pg. 720
MECHANICAL HEAT & COLD, INC., pg. 734
MIDWESCO INC., pg. 751
MIDWEST MECHANICAL CONTRACTORS INC., pg. 752
MOLLENBERG-BETZ INC., pg. 764
MONTEREY MECHANICAL COMPANY, pg. 767
MORRISON, INC., pg. 771
NPS CORPORATION, pg. 781
NASHVILLE MACHINE CO. INC., pg. 784
NEW MECH COMPANIES, INC., pg. 802
NORTHWESTERN INDUSTRIAL PIPING, pg. 815
PIEDMONT MECHANICAL, INC., pg. 870
PIEDMONT MECHANICAL, INC.—Piedmont Mechanical, Inc., pg. 870
POWER PROCESS PIPING, INC., pg. 883
QUACKENBUSH CO. INC., pg. 902
RK MECHANICAL, INC., pg. 907
RIDDLEBERGER BROTHERS, INC., pg. 933
CHAS ROBERTS AIR CONDITIONING, INC., pg. 938
ROCKY MOUNTAIN MECHANICAL, INC., pg. 942
J.B. RODGERS MECHANICAL CONTRACTORS, pg. 943
SOUTHEAST FIRE SPRINKLER COMPANY—S. I. Goldman Co., pg. 468
SOUTHLAND INDUSTRIES, pg. 1023
SPARTAN OIL CORP., pg. 1026
THE SPOHN CORPORATION, pg. 1032
TD INDUSTRIES INC., pg. 1072
TEMP-CONTROL MECHANICAL CORP., pg. 1086
THOMPSON ENTERPRISES INC., pg. 1094
TRIANGLE MAINTENANCE CORPORATION, pg. 1112
UNION BOILER CO.—Concorp, Inc., pg. 273
U.S. ENGINEERING COMPANY, pg. 1135
WOLFF & MUNIER, INC., pg. 1199
WRIGHT-SCHUCHART, INC., pg. 1204
ZACK CO.—Zack Company, pg. 1215
ZACK COMPANY, pg. 1215

1721 — PAINTING & PAPER HANGING CONTRACTORS

COLUMBIA PAINT CO., pg. 265
TRIANGLE MAINTENANCE CORPORATION, pg. 1112

1731 — ELECTRICAL WORK CONTRACTORS

API GROUP INC., pg. 5
ADVANCED TECHNOLOGY SYSTEMS, INC.—Commercial Light Company, pg. 268
AMELCO CORPORATION, pg. 47
AMERICAN ELECTRIC CO., LTD.—Amelco Corporation, pg. 47
AMERICAN SYSTEMS CORPORATION, pg. 63
AMERICAN TECHNICAL SERVICES GROUP, INC., pg. 63
ARKANSAS ELECTRIC COOPERATIVES INC., pg. 83
Y.C. BALLENGER ELECTRICAL CONTRACTORS, pg. 116
BARR ELECTRIC CORPORATION, pg. 122
BERGELECTRIC CORPORATION, pg. 141
BLOOM ELECTRIC SERVICES, INC., pg. 157
BRYANT ELECTRIC COMPANY, INC., pg. 185
CENTRAL COMMUNICATIONS COMPANY—Illinois Consolidated Telephone Co., pg. 563
CHRISTENSON ELECTRIC, INC., pg. 248
CLEVELAND CONSOLIDATED INC.—Cleveland Group, Inc., pg. 255
CLEVELAND GROUP, INC., pg. 255
COKEN COMPANY, INC., pg. 259
COLLINS ELECTRIC COMPANY, INC., pg. 263
COMMERCIAL LIGHT COMPANY, pg. 268
COMMUNICATIONS INTERNATIONAL, pg. 269
CONSTRUCTION MANAGEMENT SERVICE, pg. 277
CUMMINGS INC., pg. 304
CUPERTINO ELECTRIC, INC.—Synergism, Inc., pg. 1070
DAIDONE ELECTRICAL INC., pg. 310
DAVIS ELECTRICAL CONSTRUCTORS, INC., pg. 318
JOSEPH DAVIS, INC., pg. 318
DIVANE BROS. ELECTRIC CO., pg. 340
EGIZII ELECTRIC, INC., pg. 371
ELECTRIC POWER EQUIPMENT CO., pg. 373
ERMCO, INC., pg. 387
E. C. ERNST—The Philadelphia Bourse, Inc., pg. 866
FARNSWORTH CONSTRUCTION—Farnsworth Companies, pg. 403
FERGUSON ELECTRIC CONSTRUCTION CO., INC., pg. 406
N. G. GILBERT CORPORATION, pg. 458
GUARANTEE ELECTRICAL COMPANY, pg. 490
HARLAN ELECTRIC CO., pg. 509
HATZEL & BUEHLER, INC.—Construction Management Service, pg. 277
HAUENSTEIN & BURMEISTER, INC., pg. 517
EDD HELMS ELECTRICAL CONTRACTING, pg. 527

EDD HELMS ELECTRICAL SERVICE, INC.—Edd Helms Electrical Contracting, pg. 527
HENDERSON ELECTRIC CO., INC., pg. 529
HUNTER CORP., pg. 554
JENSEN ELECTRIC COMPANY, pg. 592
KEHNE ELECTRIC COMPANY, INC., pg. 620
KELSO-BURNETT COMPANY, pg. 622
KELSO-BURNETT ZION BRANCH—Kelso-Burnett Company, pg. 622
LAKE ERIE ELECTRIC, INC., pg. 651
LAMINAIRE CORPORATION, pg. 652
LINDER & ASSOCIATES, INC., pg. 676
MILLER ELECTRIC COMPANY, pg. 754
MOSS TELECOMMUNICATIONS SERVICES, pg. 772
MUSKA ELECTRIC COMPANY, pg. 777
HENRY NEWGARD & COMPANY, pg. 804
NEWTRON GROUP INC., pg. 805
NOVA POWER, INC., pg. 816
PALMER ELECTRIC CO., pg. 843
PEIRCE-PHELPS, INC., pg. 855
PEOPLES ELECTRIC COMPANY, INC., pg. 859
QUINTRON SYSTEMS, INC., pg. 905
ROCKY MOUNTAIN MECHANICAL, INC., pg. 942
ROMAN ELECTRIC COMPANY, INC., pg. 945
RONCO COMMUNICATIONS & ELECTRONICS INC., pg. 946
ROSENDIN ELECTRIC, INC., pg. 948
ROWE CORP., pg. 952
SASCO ELECTRIC—Sasco Group, pg. 972
SASCO GROUP, pg. 971
SASCO/VALLEY ELECTRIC—Sasco Group, pg. 972
STEINY & COMPANY, INC., pg. 1049
STILES CORPORATION, pg. 1049
STREECH ELECTRIC COMPANY, pg. 1053
STURGEON ELECTRIC COMPANY—Harlan Electric Co., pg. 509
THOMPSON ENTERPRISES INC., pg. 1094
TRI-CITY ELECTRICAL CONTRACTORS INC., pg. 1110
TRI-CITY ELECTRICAL CONTRACTORS INC.—Tri-City Electrical Contractors Inc., pg. 1110
TRI-CITY ELECTRICAL CONTRACTORS INC.—Tri-City Electrical Contractors Inc., pg. 1110
TRI-STATE ARMATURE ELECTRIC WORKS, pg. 1110
TRIANGLE ELECTRIC COMPANY, pg. 1112
TRIANGLE MAINTENANCE CORPORATION, pg. 1112
TRI-CITY ELECTRICAL CONTRACTORS INC.—Tri-City Electrical Contractors Inc., pg. 1110
TRI-CITY ELECTRICAL CONTRACTORS INC.—Tri-City Electrical Contractors Inc., pg. 1110
UNION BOILER CO.—Concorp, Inc., pg. 273
UTILITIES CONSTRUCTION CO., INC. OF SOUTH CAROLINA, pg. 1141
JERVIS B. WEBB COMPANY, pg. 1170
WEBB ELECTRIC CO.—Jervis B. Webb Company, pg. 1170
WEBB, MURRAY & ASSOCIATES, pg. 1170
WELSBACH ELECTRIC CORP., pg. 1175
WESTGATE INC., pg. 1182
WINDEMULLER ELECTRIC INC., pg. 1195
WRIGHT-SCHUCHART, INC., pg. 1204

1741 — MASONRY, STONE SETTING & OTHER STONE WORK CONTRACTORS

CSC ERECTORS, INC.—Carolina Steel Corporation, pg. 223
DBM HATCH, INC., pg. 308
DELLA CONSTRUCTION CO. INC., pg. 326
DILLINGHAM CONSTRUCTION N.A., INC.—Dillingham Construction Corporation, pg. 338
E.P. HENRY CORPORATION, pg. 530
JESCO, INC., pg. 593
ROUBIN & JANEIRO, INC.—Roubinco, Inc., pg. 952
ROUBINCO, INC., pg. 952

1742 — PLASTERING, DRYWALL, ACOUSTICAL & INSULATION WORK CONTRACTORS

ACOUSTI ENGINEERING CO. OF FLORIDA, pg. 14
ANCO INSULATIONS, INC., pg. 72
ANNING-JOHNSON COMPANY—Anson Industries, Inc., pg. 76
ANSON INDUSTRIES, INC., pg. 76
CEILING & PARTITIONS, INC., pg. 230
F. H. CHASE, INC., pg. 240
DILLINGHAM CONSTRUCTION N.A., INC.—Dillingham Construction Corporation, pg. 338
GUARANTEE INTERIORS—Guarantee Electrical Company, pg. 491
HAUENSTEIN & BURMEISTER, INC., pg. 517
JOHNSON ACOUSTICAL & SUPPLY CO., pg. 597
MADER CONSTRUCTION GROUP INC., pg. 699
NATIONAL THERMAL INSULATION—Transco Inc., pg. 1107
PERFORMANCE CONTRACTING GROUP, pg. 861
PERFORMANCE CONTRACTING, INC.—Performance Contracting Group, pg. 861
SUPERIOR INDUSTRIES OF NEBRASKA, INC., pg. 1063
TRANSCO PRODUCTS INC.—Transco Inc., pg. 1107

1743 — TERRAZZO, TILE, MARBLE & MOSAIC WORK CONTRACTORS

NEW ENGLAND STONE INDUSTRIES, INC., pg. 800

1751 — CARPENTRY WORK

FRANTZ EXPORT CORP.—Frantz Manufacturing Co., pg. 430
HARKINS CARPENTRY—Harkins Builders, Inc., pg. 509
B.T. MANCINI CO., INC., pg. 703
NACOMA CONSOLIDATED, INC., pg. 782
SCHUCK & SONS CONSTRUCTION CO., pg. 979
TRIANGLE MAINTENANCE CORPORATION, pg. 1112

1752 — FLOOR LAYING & OTHER FLOOR WORK, NEC

CENTIMARK CORPORATION, pg. 231
GUARANTEE INTERIORS—Guarantee Electrical Company, pg. 491
HOBOKEN WOOD FLOORING CORPORATION, pg. 537
RAYMOND ROSEN CO., pg. 948
SOUTHWEST FLOOR COVERING INC., pg. 1023
STONHARD, EUROPE—Stonhard, Inc., pg. 1051
STONHARD, INC., pg. 1051
STONHARD LATIN AMERICA—Stonhard, Inc., pg. 1051
STONHARD, LTD.—Stonhard, Inc., pg. 1052

1761 — ROOFING, SIDING & SHEET METAL WORK

ANNING-JOHNSON COMPANY—Anson Industries, Inc., pg. 76
ANSON INDUSTRIES, INC., pg. 76
ATLAS MANUFACTURING DIVISION—Upper Midwest Industries, Inc., pg. 1140
BEACON SALES CORPORATION, pg. 129
BRYANT UNIVERSAL ROOFERS INC., pg. 185
JOHN J. CAMPBELL CO., INC., pg. 212
CENTIMARK CORPORATION, pg. 231
CORRIGAN BROS., INC., pg. 287
M.J. DALY & SONS, INC., pg. 313
KOOLVENT ALUMINUM PRODUCTS, INC., pg. 641
B.T. MANCINI CO., INC., pg. 703
MIDCOAST INDUSTRIAL SERVICES CORPORATION, pg. 751
NORTH AMERICAN ROOFING COMPANY, INC., pg. 811
OWEN PACIFIC, pg. 834
PACIFIC COAST BUILDING PRODUCTS INC., pg. 839
TAYLOR ASSOCIATES—Midcoast Industrial Services Corporation, pg. 751
D. C. TAYLOR CO.—Midcoast Industrial Services Corporation, pg. 751
U.S. ENGINEERING COMPANY, pg. 1135
UNIVERSAL ROOFERS, INC.—Bryant Universal Roofers Inc., pg. 185
UNIVERSAL ROOFERS, INC.—Bryant Universal Roofers Inc., pg. 185
UNIVERSAL ROOFERS, INC.—Bryant Universal Roofers Inc., pg. 185
WEISS SHEET METAL COMPANY, pg. 1174
ZACK COMPANY, pg. 1215

1771 — CONCRETE WORK

BACCO CONSTRUCTION CO., pg. 108
BAKER CONCRETE CONSTRUCTION, INC., pg. 115
BANKHEAD ENTERPRISES INC., pg. 117
CALUMET CONSTRUCTION CORPORATION, pg. 211
CALUMET CONTRUCTION CORPORATION-INDIANAPOLIS DIVISION—Calumet Construction Corporation, pg. 211
CLARK ENTERPRISES, INC.—Clark Construction Group, pg. 252
DILLINGHAM CONSTRUCTION CORPORATION, pg. 337
DONLEY'S, INC., pg. 345
FORD DEVELOPMENT CORPORATION, pg. 423
HAWAIIAN BITUMULS & PAVING COMPANY—Dillingham Construction Corporation, pg. 338
INTREPID ENTERPRISES, INC., pg. 581
JESCO, INC., pg. 593
LINBECK CORP., pg. 675
MACCO CONSTRUCTORS, INC., pg. 696
MAESCHER INDUSTRIES, INC., pg. 699
MILLER & LONG CO. INC., pg. 754
THE MILLGARD CORP., pg. 755
MORLEY GROUP, pg. 770
RITCHIE CORPORATION, pg. 936
ROUBINCO, INC., pg. 952
TOWNSEND & BOTTUM, INC., pg. 1104

1781 — WATER WELL DRILLING

HYDRO GROUP, INC., pg. 556
LAYNE-WESTERN CO., INC.—The Marley Company, pg. 710
THE MARLEY COMPANY, pg. 710

1791 — STRUCTURAL STEEL ERECTION

ADDISON STEEL INC., pg. 17
ALLEN STEEL CO., pg. 36
BELMONT INDUSTRIES, INC., pg. 136
BERLIN STEEL CONSTRUCTION CO., pg. 142
BRISTOL STEEL & IRON WORKS, INC., pg. 176
BROAD VOGT & CONANT INC., pg. 177
BROWN-MINNEAPOLIS TANK & FABRICATING CO., pg. 182
CALUMET CONSTRUCTION CORPORATION, pg. 211
CALUMET CONTRUCTION CORPORATION-INDIANAPOLIS DIVISION—Calumet Construction Corporation, pg. 211
CINCINNATI UNITED CONTRACTORS, pg. 250
ELASTIC MATERIALS, INC., pg. 372
HAVENS STEEL CO., pg. 517
HIGH INDUSTRIES INC., pg. 533
HUNTER CORP., pg. 554
IDEA ENGINEERING & FABRICATING, pg. 562
NATIONAL ENGINEERING & CONTRACTING CO., pg. 788
OVERHEAD CONVEYOR CO., pg. 832
PALM IRON & BRIDGE WORKS, INC., pg. 843
PASCOE BUILDING SYSTEMS, INC., pg. 851
RAPID INDUSTRIES, INC., pg. 913
RIGGS INDUSTRIES, INC., pg. 934
SCHUFF STEEL CO., pg. 979
SOUTHERN OHIO FABRICATORS, INC., pg. 1022
L.H. SOWLES COMPANY, INC., pg. 1024
THOMAS PIPE & STEEL, INC., pg. 1093
TOWNSEND & BOTTUM, INC., pg. 1104
VULCAN IRON WORKS, INC., pg. 1155

1793 — GLASS & GLAZING WORK

ABBOTT GLASS CO., INC., pg. 9
BENSON INDUSTRIES, INC., pg. 139
CARCOMP SERVICES, INC.—Globe Glass & Mirror Co., pg. 464
DILLINGHAM CONSTRUCTION N.A., INC.—Dillingham Construction Corporation, pg. 338
FALCONER GLASS INDUSTRIES, INC.—Guardian Industries Corp., pg. 492
GLOBE GLASS & MIRROR CO., pg. 463
MODEL GLASS, INC., pg. 762
PORTLAND GLASS/AMERICAN MANAGEMENT GROUP—American Management Group, pg. 58
SAFELITE AUTOGLASS—Lear Siegler Diversified Holdings Corp., pg. 664
TSI INDUSTRIES, INC., pg. 1075
USA-GLAS, INC.—Globe Glass & Mirror Co., pg. 464
U.S. AUTO GLASS CENTERS, INC.—Globe Glass & Mirror Co., pg. 464

1794 — EXCAVATING & FOUNDATION WORK

BOH BROTHERS CONSTRUCTION COMPANY, INC.—Boh Corporation, pg. 162
DAVID A. BRAMBLE, INC., pg. 171
CALUMET CONSTRUCTION CORPORATION, pg. 211
CALUMET CONTRUCTION CORPORATION-INDIANAPOLIS DIVISION—Calumet Construction Corporation, pg. 211
CARDER, INC., pg. 217
DELLA CONSTRUCTION CO. INC., pg. 326
FORD DEVELOPMENT CORPORATION, pg. 423
LEE CONSTRUCTION CO.—National Engineering & Contracting Co., pg. 788
MAESCHER INDUSTRIES, INC., pg. 699
MANESS INDUSTRIES, INC., pg. 703
THE MILLGARD CORP., pg. 755
MISENER MARINE CONSTRUCTION, pg. 759
NATIONAL ENGINEERING & CONTRACTING CO., pg. 788
TOWNSEND & BOTTUM, INC., pg. 1104
TRUMBULL CORPORATION, pg. 1117
R.S. YOUNG EXCAVATING, INC., pg. 1209

1795 — WRECKING & DEMOLITION WORK

CHICAGO BLASTING COMPANY—Graycor, Inc., pg. 480
CLEVELAND WRECKING COMPANY, pg. 255
THE EDWARD GRAY CORP.—Graycor, Inc., pg. 480
GRAYCOR, INC., pg. 479
PENHALL INTERNATIONAL, pg. 857
PHOENIX CONCRETE CUTTING—Penhall International, pg. 857
THE POLLOCK CORP., pg. 879

1796 — INSTALLATION OR ERECTION OF BUILDING EQUIPMENT, NEC

BALCO, INC. (MA), pg. 115
BARTON-MALOW ENTERPRISES, INC., pg. 123
CALUMET CONSTRUCTION CORPORATION, pg. 211
CALUMET CONTRUCTION CORPORATION-INDIANAPOLIS DIVISION—Calumet Construction Corporation, pg. 211
F. H. CHASE, INC., pg. 240
DILLINGHAM CONSTRUCTION N.A., INC.—Dillingham Construction Corporation, pg. 338
HADEN INVESTMENT, LTD.—Haden, Inc., pg. 499
HAWAIIAN DREDGING & CONSTRUCTION COMPANY—Dillingham Construction Corporation, pg. 338
HENKELS & MCCOY, INC., pg. 529
HUNTER CORP., pg. 554
MAKO CONSTRUCTION CO.—Henkels & McCoy, Inc., pg. 529
MONTGOMERY ELEVATOR COMPANY, pg. 767
NASHVILLE MACHINE CO. INC., pg. 784
PASCHEN CONTRACTORS, INC., pg. 851
PIEDMONT MECHANICAL, INC., pg. 870
POWER PROCESS PIPING, INC., pg. 883
RELIANCE ELEVATOR COMPANY, pg. 925
TODD & SARGENT, INC., pg. 1100
TOWNSEND & BOTTUM, INC., pg. 1104
ZACK COMPANY, pg. 1215

1799 — SPECIAL TRADE CONTRACTORS, NEC

API GROUP INC., pg. 5
ABBOTT GLASS CO., INC., pg. 9
AMERICAN FENCE CO. AZ—American Fence Company, pg. 52
AMERICAN FENCE CO. LTD.—American Fence Company, pg. 52
AMERICAN FENCE CO. OF MIDWEST—American Fence Company, pg. 52
AMERICAN FENCE COMPANY, pg. 52
AMERICAN TECHNICAL SERVICES GROUP, INC., pg. 63
ANCHOR FENCE COMPANY—PPA Industries, Inc., pg. 836

ANNING-JOHNSON COMPANY—Anson Industries, Inc., pg. 76
ANSON INDUSTRIES, INC., pg. 76
BALCO, INC. (MA), pg. 115
BARTON-MALOW RIGGING CO.—Barton-Malow Enterprises, Inc., pg. 123
BLISS-SALEM, INC., pg. 156
BRISK WATERPROOFING—The Western Group, pg. 1179
CANADIAN STEBBINS ENGINEERING & MFG. CO. LTD.—Stebbins Engineering & Mfg. Co., pg. 1044
CERAMIC COOLING TOWER CO.—Amsted Industries Incorporated, pg. 69
CONSTRUCTION SPECIALTIES, INC., pg. 277
JACK KENT COOKE, INC., pg. 282
CROWN FENCE CO., pg. 302
JOHN W. DANFORTH CO., pg. 314
DILLINGHAM CONSTRUCTION N.A., INC.—Dillingham Construction Corporation, pg. 338
EVANS FABRICATION, INC., pg. 390
W. B. GOODE COMPANY, INC., pg. 470
JOHN E. GREEN CO., pg. 484
HAUENSTEIN & BURMEISTER, INC., pg. 517
HAWAIIAN BITUMULS & PAVING COMPANY—Dillingham Construction Corporation, pg. 338
IDEAL POOL CORP., pg. 562
JOHNSON ACOUSTICAL & SUPPLY CO., pg. 597
KDI CORPORATION, pg. 612
KDI SYLVAN POOLS, INC.—KDI Corporation, pg. 612
LONGYEAR CANADA INC.—Longyear Company, pg. 682
MACCO CONSTRUCTORS, INC., pg. 696
MAIN BROTHERS OIL COMPANY, INC., pg. 702
MANESS INDUSTRIES, INC., pg. 703
NORTHWEST FENCE PRODUCTS CO.—Carl Weissman & Sons, Inc., pg. 1174
PPA INDUSTRIES, INC., pg. 836
PSI FABRICATORS, INC.—PSI Group of Companies, pg. 837
PSI GROUP OF COMPANIES, pg. 837
PADDOCK POOL CONSTRUCTION CO., pg. 842
PLIBRICO SALES & SERVICE, INC.—Plibrico Co., pg. 877
POWER PROCESS PIPING, INC., pg. 883
PROCESS SYSTEMS, INC. CONSTRUCTION CO.—PSI Group of Companies, pg. 837
RK MECHANICAL, INC., pg. 907
ROCHE CONSTRUCTORS, INC., pg. 940
SCS FIELD SERVICES—SCS Engineers, pg. 961
SIMPLEX CONSTRUCTION CO. INC.—Simplex Industries, Inc., pg. 1006
SOUTHWEST FLOOR COVERING INC., pg. 1023
SPECIAL ERECTION SERVICES, INC.—Construction Specialties, Inc., pg. 277
STEBBINS ENGINEERING & MFG. CO., pg. 1043
STONE & HOOVER CONTRACTING, INC.—W. B. Goode Company, Inc., pg. 470
SUPERIOR INDUSTRIES OF NEBRASKA, INC., pg. 1063
SYLVAN POOLS OF ARIZONA, INC.—KDI Corporation, pg. 612
SYLVAN POOLS OF TEXAS, INC.—KDI Corporation, pg. 612
TOWNSEND & BOTTUM, INC., pg. 1104
U.S. ENGINEERING COMPANY, pg. 1135
UNIVERSITY CASEWORK SYSTEMS, INC.—KDI Corporation, pg. 612
WEBB, MURRAY & ASSOCIATES, pg. 1170
WELSBACH ELECTRIC CORP., pg. 1175
WENGER CORPORATION, pg. 1176
THE WESTERN GROUP, pg. 1179
WESTERN WATERPROOFING COMPANY OF AMERICA, INC.—The Western Group, pg. 1179
WINTERS WELDING WORKS, INC., pg. 1197
YOUNG ELECTRIC SIGN COMPANY, pg. 1209

2011 — MEAT PACKING PLANTS

ABBYLAND FOODS, INC., pg. 10
ABBYLAND PORK RACK—Abbyland Foods, Inc., pg. 10
ADA BEEF, INC., pg. 16
AMERICAN FOODS GROUP, pg. 54
AMERICAN FOODS GROUP, INC., pg. 54
THE AMERICAN MEAT PACKING CORP.—Kane-Miller Corp., pg. 616
AURORA PACKING CO., INC., pg. 98
BAKER COMMODITIES, INC., pg. 115
BAR-S FOODS CO., pg. 118
BEEFAMERICA—BeefAmerica Operating Co., Inc., pg. 132
BEEFAMERICA OPERATING CO., INC., pg. 131
BESSIN CORPORATION, pg. 146
BIG FOOT CATTLE CO.—Vienna Sausage Mfg. Co., pg. 1151
BROOKS COUNTY PACKING CO.—Sunnyland Foods, Inc., pg. 1061
BUTLER FOODS, INC., pg. 197
CARGILL INC., pg. 219
CHAMPION BOXED BEEF, pg. 238
DAKOTA PORK INDUSTRIES—American Foods Group, pg. 54
DEVAULT FOODS, pg. 333
DINNER BELL FOODS, INC.—American Financial Corporation, pg. 53
EMGE PACKING CO., INC.—Cargill Inc., pg. 219
EXCEL CORP.—Cargill Inc., pg. 219
FARMERS UNION MARKETING & PROCESSING ASSOCIATION, pg. 402
FARMSTEAD FOODS, INC., pg. 402
FIELD PACKING COMPANY, pg. 409
FRESH MARK, INC., pg. 432
GILLETT HOLDINGS, INC., pg. 458
GOOCH PACKING CO., INC.—Randall's Food Markets, Inc., pg. 912
GRANITE STATE PACKING CO., pg. 476
GREEN BAY DRESSED BEEF COMPANY—American Foods Group, pg. 54
GREENWOOD PACKING PLANT, pg. 486
HARRIS FARMS, INC., pg. 511
HARRIS RANCH BEEF CO.—Harris Farms, Inc., pg. 512
HATFIELD QUALITY MEATS, INC., pg. 517
HOFFMAN BROTHERS PACKING CO., pg. 537
HYPLAINS DRESSED BEEF, INC., pg. 557
IDLE WILD FOODS—Union Holdings, Inc., pg. 1128
JACKSON PACKING CO. INC., pg. 587
JONES DAIRY FARM, pg. 603
JORDAN'S FOODS-WESTBROOK DIVISION—Jordan's Meats, pg. 605
JORDAN'S FOODS-CARIBOU DIVISION—Jordan's Meats, pg. 605
KANE-MILLER CORP., pg. 616
KOWALSKI SAUSAGE CO., INC., pg. 643
LAY PACKING COMPANY INC., pg. 663
LEONARD & HARRAL PACKING CO., pg. 667
LONG PRAIRIE PACKING CO.—Rosens Diversified, Inc., pg. 948
LOWELL PACKING COMPANY, pg. 685
LUNDY PACKING CO. INC., pg. 687
MARTINS ABBATOIR & WHOLESALE MEATS INC., pg. 716
MCLEAN ENTERPRISES, INC., pg. 731
JOHN MORRELL & CO.—American Financial Corporation, pg. 54
MOYER PACKING COMPANY, pg. 774
PACKERLAND PACKING CO.—Gillett Holdings, Inc., pg. 459
PARKS SAUSAGE COMPANY, pg. 850
PEET PACKING CO. INC., pg. 855
PREMIUM PORK PROCESSORS—Sunnyland Foods, Inc., pg. 1061
PROVIMI VEAL CORPORATION, pg. 896
ROCCO FARMS—Rocco Inc., pg. 940
ROCCO FURTHER PROCESSING—Rocco Inc., pg. 940
ROSENS DIVERSIFIED, INC., pg. 948
RUSSETT FOODS—Zemco Industries, Inc., pg. 1217
SIGMAN MEAT CO. INC., pg. 1003
STOCK YARDS PACKING CO., INC., pg. 1049
SUNNYLAND FOODS, INC., pg. 1061
THE SWISS COLONY, pg. 1068
TENNESSEE DRESSED BEEF COMPANY, pg. 1087
TOM THUMB FOOD & DRUGS, INC.—Randall's Food Markets, Inc., pg. 912
TOMAHAWK FARMS, INC.—Lundy Packing Co. Inc., pg. 687
UNION HOLDINGS, INC., pg. 1128
VALLEYDALE PACKERS INC., pg. 1143
WEB FOOD PRODUCTS CORP., pg. 1170
WEINSTEIN INTERNATIONAL SEAFOOD—American Foods Group, pg. 54
WEISS PACKING CO., INC., pg. 1174
ZEMCO INDUSTRIES, INC., pg. 1217

2013 — SAUSAGES & OTHER PREPARED MEAT PRODUCTS

RALPH & PAUL ADAMS, INC.—Jones Dairy Farm, pg. 603
AMERICAN FOODS GROUP, INC., pg. 54
AMERICAN FOODSERVICE CORP., pg. 54
BAR-S FOODS CO., pg. 118
BARONE SAUSAGE COMPANY—City Meats & Provisions Co., pg. 251
BEEFAMERICA OPERATING CO., INC., pg. 131
BEL PAESE SALES COMPANY, INC., pg. 133
BESSIN CORPORATION, pg. 146
BEST PROVISION CO., INC., pg. 146
BLUE GRASS FOODS, INC., pg. 160
CARL BUDDIG & COMPANY, pg. 186
CASTLEBERRY'S FOOD COMPANY, pg. 229
CHEF ITALIA, INC., pg. 241
CHIPICO PICKLES—Vienna Sausage Mfg. Co., pg. 1151
CURTICE BURNS MEAT SNACKS, INC.—Agway, Inc., pg. 26
DI GIORGIO CORPORATION, pg. 334
DINNER BELL FOODS, INC.—American Financial Corporation, pg. 53
TONY DOWNS FOODS COMPANY, pg. 348
ESI MEATS, INC.—Metromedia Company, pg. 744
EXCEL CORP.—Cargill Inc., pg. 219
FIELD PACKING COMPANY, pg. 409
GILLETT HOLDINGS, INC., pg. 458
M. H. GREENEBAUM, INC., pg. 485
HEBREW NATIONAL KOSHER FOODS DIV.—National Foods Inc., pg. 788
HENNINGSEN NEDERLAND B.V.—Kifuki U.S.A. Co., Inc., pg. 629
JOHNSONVILLE FOODS, INC., pg. 601
JOHNSONVILLE SAUSAGE, INC.—Johnsonville Foods, Inc., pg. 601
JONES DAIRY FARM, pg. 603
JORDAN'S MEATS, pg. 605
JORDAN'S FOODS-BANGOR DIVISION—Jordan's Meats, pg. 605
JORDAN'S FOODS-WESTBROOK DIVISION—Jordan's Meats, pg. 605
JORDAN'S FOODS-CARIBOU DIVISION—Jordan's Meats, pg. 605
JOSEPH KIRSCHNER CO.—Jordan's Meats, pg. 605
SAM KANE BEEF PROCESSORS, INC., pg. 616
KAYEM FOODS, INC., pg. 619
KEYSTONE FOODS CORPORATION, pg. 628
A. C. KISSLING, INC., pg. 634
E.W. KNAUSS & SON, INC., pg. 636
KOWALSKI SAUSAGE CO., INC., pg. 643
KUNZLER & COMPANY, INC., pg. 646
LAKESIDE FOODS, INC., pg. 651
LEVONIAN BROTHERS INC., pg. 671
MHB INC., pg. 692
JOHN MCKENZIE PACKING CO., INC., pg. 730
THE MILNOT COMPANY, pg. 756
MURRY'S, INC., pg. 777
NATIONAL FOODS INC., pg. 788
NATIONWIDE BEEF, INC., pg. 795
OLD WISCONSIN SAUSAGE—Carl Buddig & Company, pg. 186
PACKERLAND PACKING CO.—Gillett Holdings, Inc., pg. 459
PARKS SAUSAGE COMPANY, pg. 850
PERRI SAUSAGE, INC.—Johnsonville Foods, Inc., pg. 601
ROCCO FURTHER PROCESSING—Rocco Inc., pg. 940
ROSE PACKING COMPANY, pg. 947
RUSSETT FOODS—Zemco Industries, Inc., pg. 1217
SHOFAR KOSHER FOODS, INC., pg. 1000
SIGMAN MEAT CO. INC., pg. 1003
SMOKIE PRODUCTS, INC.—Carl Buddig & Company, pg. 186
STAR FOOD PRODUCTS, INC., pg. 1039
SUGAR CREEK PACKING CO., pg. 1056
SUPERIOR'S BRAND MEATS—Fresh Mark, Inc., pg. 432
SUZANNAH FARMS, pg. 1065
THE SWISS COLONY, pg. 1068
TEEPAK, INC.—Hillside Capital, Inc., pg. 535
FRED USINGER, INC., pg. 1140
VIENNA SAUSAGE MFG. CO., pg. 1151
WEB FOOD PRODUCTS CORP., pg. 1170
WEINSTEIN INTERNATIONAL SEAFOOD—American Foods Group, pg. 54
WEISS PACKING CO., INC., pg. 1174
WRIGHT BRAND FOODS, INC., pg. 1204
YOAKUM PACKING COMPANY, pg. 1208
ZEMCO INDUSTRIES, INC., pg. 1217

2015 — POULTRY SLAUGHTERING & PROCESSING

A-G CO-OP CREAMERY, pg. 4
ACME CONTINENTAL FOODS, INC., pg. 13
ACME POULTRY COMPANY, INC., pg. 13
ARCADIA FRYERS, pg. 80
BAR-S FOODS CO., pg. 118
CAL-MAINE FOODS, INC., pg. 208
CARGILL INC., pg. 219
CHARLES RIVER FOODS, INC., pg. 240
COLUMBIA FARMS INC., pg. 265
EMPIRE KOSHER POULTRY, INC., pg. 379
FARMER'S PRIDE, INC., pg. 401
FIELDALE CORPORATION, pg. 409
JACK FROST, INC.—JFC Inc., pg. 584
GOLD KIST, INC., pg. 465
GRESS FOODS INC., pg. 486
HENNINGSEN FOODS, INC.—Kifuki U.S.A. Co., Inc., pg. 629
HENNINGSEN-VAN DEN BURG—Kifuki U.S.A. Co., Inc., pg. 629
HOUSE OF RAEFORD FARMS, INC., pg. 546
IBM FOODS, pg. 558
JEROME FOODS INC., pg. 593
JORDAN'S FOODS-BANGOR DIVISION—Jordan's Meats, pg. 605
JORDAN'S FOODS-WESTBROOK DIVISION—Jordan's Meats, pg. 605
MAR-JAC INC., pg. 705
MAR-JAC PROCESSING, INC.—Mar-Jac Inc., pg. 705
MCCARTY FARMS, pg. 727
MONARK EGG CORPORATION, pg. 765
NATIONAL FOODS INC., pg. 788
PERDUE FARMS INC., pg. 860
PERDUE FOODS INCORPORATED—Perdue Farms Inc., pg. 860
PERDUE INCORPORATED—Perdue Farms Inc., pg. 860
ROCCO FARMS—Rocco Inc., pg. 940
ROCCO FURTHER PROCESSING—Rocco Inc., pg. 940
ROCCO INC., pg. 940
ROCCO TURKEYS, INC.—Rocco Inc., pg. 940
ROUND HILL FOODS, INC., pg. 952
SEABOARD CORPORATION—Seaboard Flour Corporation, pg. 984
SHENANDOAH PRODUCTS—Perdue Farms Inc., pg. 860
SHENANDOAH VALLEY FARMS—Perdue Farms Inc., pg. 860
SHOWELL FARMS, INC., pg. 1000
WATSON'S QUALITY TURKEY PRODUCTS, INC., pg. 1168
WEISS PACKING CO., INC., pg. 1174
ZACKY FARMS, INC., pg. 1215

2021 — CREAMERY BUTTER

BONGARDS CREAMERIES INC., pg. 164
BROUGHTON FOODS COMPANY, pg. 180
CABOT CREAMERY CO-OPERATIVE INC.—Agri-Mark, Inc., pg. 25
CASS-CLAY CREAMERY, pg. 228
CHARLESTON FOOD DIV.—Broughton Foods Company, pg. 181
COUNTRY CLASSIC DAIRIES, INC., pg. 289
CRYSTAL CREAM & BUTTER COMPANY, pg. 303
DAIRYGOLD INC., pg. 311
DAIRYGOLD, INC.—Dairygold Inc., pg. 311
DAIRYMEN, INC., pg. 311
DIETRICH'S MILK PRODUCTS, INC., pg. 337
HYGEIA DAIRY CO., INC., pg. 557
LAND O'LAKES, INC., pg. 653
MADISON DAIRY PRODUCE COMPANY, pg. 699
MARYLAND VIRGINIA MILK PRODUCERS ASSOCIATION, INC., pg. 717
MICHAEL FOODS, INC., pg. 747
MID-AMERICA DAIRYMEN, INC., pg. 750
NEW ENGLAND DAIRIES, INC., pg. 800
OLD HOME FOODS, INC., pg. 823
PRAIRIE FARMS DAIRY, INC., pg. 884
SHAMROCK FOODS CO., pg. 994
SUPERIOR DAIRY, INC., pg. 1063
WISCONSIN DAIRIES COOPERATIVE, pg. 1197
ZANDER'S CREAMERY INC., pg. 1216

2022 — NATURAL, PROCESSED & IMITATION CHEESE

A-G CO-OP CREAMERY, pg. 4
AGWAY, INC., pg. 25
ALTO DAIRY COOPERATIVE, pg. 45
ARCADIA FRYERS, pg. 80
ARTHUR CHEESE COMPANY, pg. 87
BEL PAESE SALES COMPANY, INC., pg. 133
BONGARDS CREAMERIES INC., pg. 164
CABOT CREAMERY CO-OPERATIVE INC.—Agri-Mark, Inc., pg. 25
CACIQUE CHEESE CO., INC., pg. 206
COASTAL WHOLESALE, INC., pg. 257
COLEMAN DAIRY INC., pg. 261
COUNTRY CLASSIC DAIRIES, INC., pg. 289
DAIRYGOLD INC., pg. 311
DAIRYGOLD, INC.—Dairygold Inc., pg. 311
DAIRYMEN, INC., pg. 311
DIETRICH'S MILK PRODUCTS, INC., pg. 337
DORMAN-ROTH FOODS, INC., pg. 346
FIRST DISTRICT ASSOCIATION, pg. 412
THE GREAT LAKES CHEESE CO., pg. 481
GREAT LAKES CHEESE OF NEW YORK, INC.—The Great Lakes Cheese Co., pg. 481
GREAT LAKES OF WISCONSIN—The Great Lakes Cheese Co., pg. 481
INTERNATIONAL CHEESE COMPANY LIMITED PARTNERSHIP, pg. 575
KAUKAUNA CHEESE, pg. 619
LAND O'LAKES, INC., pg. 653
LOSURDO FOODS, INC., pg. 684
MAPLEHURST FARMS, INC., pg. 705
MARATHON CHEESE CORP., pg. 705
MICHAEL FOODS, INC., pg. 747
MID-AMERICA DAIRYMEN, INC., pg. 750
MORNING GLORY FARMS REGION, pg. 770
NEW ENGLAND DAIRIES, INC., pg. 800
NORTHFIELD CHEESE CO.—Interlaken Capital, Inc., pg. 574
OLD WISCONSIN CHEESE CO., INC.—Carl Buddig & Company, pg. 186
RYSER BROS. OF WISCONSIN—Ryser Brothers Inc., pg. 958
RYSER BROTHERS INC., pg. 958
SARGENTO CHEESE CO.—Sargento Incorporated, pg. 971
SARGENTO FOOD SERVICE CORP.—Sargento Incorporated, pg. 971
SARGENTO INCORPORATED, pg. 971
SCHREIBER FOODS, INC., pg. 978
SMITH ENTERPRISES, pg. 1012
SUPERIOR DAIRY, INC., pg. 1063
THE SWISS COLONY, pg. 1068
TILLAMOOK COUNTY CREAMERY ASSN., pg. 1097
WISCONSIN DAIRIES COOPERATIVE, pg. 1197

2023 — DRY, CONDENSED & EVAPORATED DAIRY PRODUCTS

ALTO DAIRY COOPERATIVE, pg. 45
AMWAY CORPORATION, pg. 70
AVADYNE, INC., pg. 101
BONGARDS CREAMERIES INC., pg. 164
DAIRYGOLD INC., pg. 311
DAIRYGOLD, INC.—Dairygold Inc., pg. 311
DIEHL, INC.—Diehl Specialties Intl., pg. 336
DIEHL SPECIALTIES INTL., pg. 336
DIETRICH'S MILK PRODUCTS, INC., pg. 337
GAGE FOOD PRODUCTS COMPANY—Vincent Food Industries, Inc., pg. 1152
MARYLAND VIRGINIA MILK PRODUCERS ASSOCIATION, INC., pg. 717
MICHAEL FOODS, INC., pg. 747
MID-AMERICA DAIRYMEN, INC., pg. 750
THE MILNOT COMPANY, pg. 756
MORNING GLORY FARMS REGION, pg. 770
OLD HOME FOODS, INC., pg. 823
STEFFEN DAIRY FOODS CO., INC.—Prairie Farms Dairy, Inc., pg. 884
SUPERIOR DAIRY, INC., pg. 1063
UPSTATE MILK COOPERATIVES INC., pg. 1140
WISCONSIN DAIRIES COOPERATIVE, pg. 1197

2024 — ICE CREAM & FROZEN DESSERTS

ARTIC N.V. S.A.—TLC Beatrice International Holdings Inc., pg. 1073
BARBER ICE CREAM COMPANY—Barber Dairies, Inc., pg. 119
BLUE BELL CREAMERIES, INC., pg. 158
BRAUM ICE CREAM STORES INC., pg. 172
BROUGHTON FOODS COMPANY, pg. 180
CHARLESTON FOOD DIV.—Broughton Foods Company, pg. 181
COASTAL DAIRY PRODUCTS, INC., pg. 257
COASTAL WHOLESALE, INC., pg. 257
COBLE DAIRY PRODUCTS CO-OP, pg. 257
COLEMAN DAIRY INC., pg. 261
COUNTRY CLASSIC DAIRIES, INC., pg. 289
COUNTRY FRESH, INC., pg. 289
CRYSTAL CREAM & BUTTER COMPANY, pg. 303
DAIRY FRESH CORP., pg. 310
DAIRY FRESH ICE CREAM—Dairy Fresh Corp., pg. 311
DAIRYMEN, INC., pg. 311
DOVE EUROPE—Mars, Incorporated, pg. 713
DOVE INTERNATIONAL, INC.—Mars, Incorporated, pg. 713
DUNKIRK ICE CREAM CO., INC., pg. 353
ELGIN-HONEY HILL CORPORATION, pg. 376
FRIENDLY ICE CREAM CORP.—Tennessee Restaurant Corp., pg. 1087
HERSHEY CREAMERY COMPANY, pg. 531
HYGEIA DAIRY CO., INC., pg. 557
LAND O'LAKES, INC., pg. 653
LARRY'S INDUSTRIES, INC.—Bresler's Industries, Inc., pg. 174
MAPLEHURST FARMS, INC., pg. 705
MARYLAND VIRGINIA MILK PRODUCERS ASSOCIATION, INC., pg. 717
MELODY FOODS, INC., pg. 738
MICHAEL FOODS, INC., pg. 747
MORNING GLORY FARMS REGION, pg. 770
NEW ENGLAND FROZEN FOODS, pg. 800
NEWLY WEDS FOODS INC., pg. 804
OBERWEIS DAIRY, INC., pg. 820
PERRY'S ICE CREAM CO., INC., pg. 863
SCANGAS BROTHERS HOLDINGS, INC., pg. 974
SCHAEPS ICE CREAM COMPANY, pg. 974
SCHWAN'S SALES ENTERPRISES, pg. 980
SHAMROCK FOODS CO., pg. 994
SOKOL & COMPANY, pg. 1016
STEWART'S ICE CREAM CO., INC., pg. 1048
SUPERIOR DAIRY, INC., pg. 1063
TILLAMOOK COUNTY CREAMERY ASSN., pg. 1097
TURNER DAIRIES, INC., pg. 1119
VITAFREZE FROZEN CONFECTIONS—Crystal Cream & Butter Company, pg. 303
WEATHERLY FROZEN FOODS GROUP, INC.—Weatherly Financial Group, pg. 1169
WELSH FARMS, INC., pg. 1175
WEST LYNN CREAMERY, INC.—Scangas Brothers Holdings, Inc., pg. 974

2026 — FLUID MILK

ALTO DAIRY COOPERATIVE, pg. 45
BARBER DAIRIES, INC., pg. 119
BROUGHTON FOODS COMPANY, pg. 180
C.F. BURGER CREAMERY COMPANY, pg. 190
CABOT CREAMERY CO-OPERATIVE INC.—Agri-Mark, Inc., pg. 25
CASS-CLAY CREAMERY, pg. 228
CHARLESTON FOOD DIV.—Broughton Foods Company, pg. 181
COASTAL WHOLESALE, INC., pg. 257
COBLE DAIRY PRODUCTS CO-OP, pg. 257
COLEMAN DAIRY INC., pg. 261
COUNTRY CLASSIC DAIRIES, INC., pg. 289
COUNTRY FRESH, INC., pg. 289
CRYSTAL CREAM & BUTTER COMPANY, pg. 303
DAIRY FRESH CORP., pg. 310
DAIRYMEN, INC., pg. 311
DARIGOLD, INC., pg. 315
DIEHL SPECIALTIES INTL., pg. 336
EASTERN MILK PRODUCERS COOPERATIVE ASSN., INC., pg. 363
ELGIN-HONEY HILL CORPORATION, pg. 376
EQUITY SUPPLY COMPANY, pg. 385
GARELICK FARMS, INC., pg. 443
HASTINGS CO-OP CREAMERY COMPANY, pg. 516
HYGEIA DAIRY CO., INC., pg. 557
LAND O'LAKES, INC., pg. 653
MAPLEHURST FARMS, INC., pg. 705
MARYLAND & VIRGINIA MILK PRODUCERS ASSOCIATION, pg. 717
MARYLAND VIRGINIA MILK PRODUCERS ASSOCIATION, INC., pg. 717
MCCOLLS DAIRY—Crystal Cream & Butter Company, pg. 303
MELODY FOODS, INC., pg. 738
MICHAEL FOODS, INC., pg. 747
MICHIGAN MILK PRODUCERS ASSOCIATION, pg. 747
MID-AMERICA DAIRYMEN, INC., pg. 750
MORNING GLORY FARMS REGION, pg. 770
NEW ENGLAND DAIRIES, INC., pg. 800
OAKHURST DAIRY, pg. 819
OLD HOME FOODS, INC., pg. 823
PEVELY DAIRY COMPANY—Prairie Farms Dairy, Inc., pg. 884
PRAIRIE FARMS DAIRY, INC., pg. 884
PURITY DAIRIES INC., pg. 901
ROSENBERGERS DAIRIES, INC., pg. 948
SANTEE DAIRIES—Hughes Markets Inc., pg. 552
SCANGAS BROTHERS HOLDINGS, INC., pg. 974
SHAMROCK FOODS CO., pg. 994
SMITH BROTHERS FARMS, INC., pg. 1011
SOUTHERN BELLE DAIRY COMPANY, INC., pg. 1020
SUPERIOR DAIRY, INC., pg. 1063
TILLAMOOK COUNTY CREAMERY ASSN., pg. 1097
TURNER DAIRIES, INC., pg. 1119
UNITED DAIRY FARMERS, INC., pg. 1131
VITA-MILK DAIRY, INC., pg. 1153
WELSH FARMS, INC., pg. 1175
WEST LYNN CREAMERY, INC.—Scangas Brothers Holdings, Inc., pg. 974
WISCONSIN DAIRIES COOPERATIVE, pg. 1197

2032 — CANNED SPECIALTIES

ALLIED OLD ENGLISH, INC., pg. 38
H.J. BAKER & BRO., INC., pg. 114
BISON CANNING CO., INC.—Goya Foods, Inc., pg. 474
BISTRO SOUPS, LTD.—Vienna Sausage Mfg. Co., pg. 1151
CALAVO FOODS, INC.—Calavo Growers of California, pg. 208
CASTLEBERRY'S FOOD COMPANY, pg. 229
CENTRAL COMMISSARY, INC.—Cornucopia, Inc., pg. 287
CONNELLY CONTAINERS, INC., pg. 275
CORNUCOPIA, INC., pg. 287
DEL MONTE FOODS, pg. 325
GOYA FOODS OF FLORIDA—Goya Foods, Inc., pg. 474
LA PREFERIDA, INC., pg. 649
MCILHENNY COMPANY, pg. 729
MORGAN FOODS, INC., pg. 770
SCHWAN'S SALES ENTERPRISES, pg. 980
STEGNER FOOD PRODUCTS CO., pg. 1045
VENICE MAID CO., INC.—Connelly Containers, Inc., pg. 275
WILSON PRODUCTS CO., pg. 1194
THE WORNICK COMPANY, pg. 1203

2033 — CANNED FRUITS, VEGETABLES, PRESERVES, JAMS & JELLIES

AGRIPAC INC., pg. 25
AGWAY, INC., pg. 25
ALGOOD FOOD COMPANY, pg. 34
ALLEN CANNING COMPANY, pg. 35
AMERICAN FINE FOODS, INC.—Steiner Corporation, pg. 1045
AMERICAN FINE FOODS, INC. (NYSSA PLANT)—Steiner Corporation, pg. 1045
ARTICHOKE INDUSTRIES, INC., pg. 87
AUNT NELLIE'S FARM KITCHENS, INC., pg. 98
H.J. BAKER & BRO., INC., pg. 114
BELL-CARTER FOODS, INC., pg. 134
BLYTHEVILLE CANNING COMPANY, INC.—Bush Brothers & Company, pg. 196
BROOKS FOODS—Agway, Inc., pg. 26
BUSH BROTHERS & COMPANY, pg. 196
BUTTER KERNEL PRODUCTS—Faribault Foods Inc., pg. 399
CALIFORNIA CUSTOM FOODS—Pacific Coast Producers, pg. 840
CARAVAN PRODUCTS COMPANY, INC., pg. 217
CARGILL CITRO-AMERICA, INC.—Cargill Inc., pg. 219
CASE-SWAYNE CO. INC., pg. 228
CHERRY CENTRAL COOPERATIVE, pg. 243
CLEMENTS FOODS CO., pg. 254
COMSTOCK FOODS—Agway, Inc., pg. 25
COMSTOCK MICHIGAN FRUIT—Agway, Inc., pg. 25
CURTICE-BURNS FOODS, INC.—Agway, Inc., pg. 25
DEL MONTE CORP.—Del Monte Foods, pg. 325
DEL MONTE FOODS, pg. 325
THE ESTEE CORPORATION, pg. 389
EVERFRESH BEVERAGES INC., pg. 391
FARIBAULT FOODS INC., pg. 399
THE FIGARO COMPANY, INC., pg. 409
THE FREMONT CO., pg. 432
FURMAN FOODS, INC., pg. 436
GAGE FOOD PRODUCTS COMPANY—Vincent Food Industries, Inc., pg. 1152
GRAVYMASTER INC., pg. 478
HOME JUICE COMPANY, pg. 541
INTERNATIONAL CHEESE COMPANY, INC.—International Cheese Company Limited Partnership, pg. 576
INTEROLIVA—Westin, Inc., pg. 1183
A. C. KISSLING, INC., pg. 634
KNOTT'S BERRY FARM, pg. 637
KNOUSE FOODS INC., pg. 637
KUNER-EMPSON COMPANY—Faribault Foods Inc., pg. 399
LA VICTORIA FOODS, INC., pg. 649
LAKESIDE FOODS, INC., pg. 651
MCILHENNY COMPANY, pg. 729
MORGAN FOODS, INC., pg. 770
NALLEYS FINE FOODS—Agway, Inc., pg. 25
NATIONAL GRAPE CO-OP ASSOCIATION, INC., pg. 789
NEWMAN'S OWN, INC., pg. 804
NORPAC FOODS, INC. COOPERATIVE, pg. 810
OCEAN SPRAY CRANBERRIES, INC., pg. 820
OWATONNA CANNING COMPANY, pg. 833
PACIFIC COAST PRODUCERS, pg. 839
PARAMOUNT CITRUS ASSOCIATION—American Protection Industries, Inc., pg. 60
PORTLAND FOOD PRODUCTS COMPANY, pg. 881
PREPCO, pg. 887
PRESTO FOOD PRODUCTS, INC., pg. 888
PRINCEVILLE CANNING CO.—Owatonna Canning Company, pg. 833
ROMANOFF INTERNATIONAL, INC., pg. 945
RUSTCO PRODUCTS COMPANY, pg. 957
SAN MIGUEL (U.S.A.) INC., pg. 969
SCHWAN'S SALES ENTERPRISES, pg. 980
SHIOCTON KRAUT CO.—Bush Brothers & Company, pg. 196
SILVER SPRINGS CITRUS CO-OP, pg. 1004
SNOKIST GROWERS, pg. 1015
STEINER CORPORATION, pg. 1045
THE SWISS COLONY, pg. 1068
TREE TOP, INC., pg. 1109
TRI VALLEY GROWERS INC., pg. 1111
VALLEY CANNING CO., INC.—Bush Brothers & Company, pg. 196
VENTURA COASTAL CORPORATION, pg. 1147
VERYFINE PRODUCTS, INC., pg. 1148
WARNER VINEYARDS, pg. 1164
WELCH'S—National Grape Co-Op Association, Inc., pg. 789
WESTIN, INC., pg. 1183
WILDERNESS FOODS—Agway, Inc., pg. 26
WILLIAMS FOODS INC., pg. 1191

2034 — DRIED & DEHYDRATED FRUITS & VEGETABLES & SOUP MIXES

ARROW INDUSTRIES, INC., pg. 85
BASIC AMERICAN FOODS, pg. 124
GEORGE F. BROCKE & SONS, INC., pg. 178
JOHN COPES FOOD PRODUCTS, INC., pg. 284
DALE FOODS—Vincent Food Industries, Inc., pg. 1152
DEL MONTE FOODS, pg. 325
FARLEY CANDY COMPANY, pg. 399
4C FOODS CORPORATION, pg. 427
GAGE FOOD PRODUCTS COMPANY—Vincent Food Industries, Inc., pg. 1152

HENNINGSEN FOODS, INC.—Kifuki U.S.A. Co., Inc., pg. 629
IDAHOAN FOODS, pg. 561
IDAHO SUPREME COMPANY, pg. 561
MAGIC VALLEY FOODS, INC., pg. 700
MARUCHAN INC., pg. 716
WILLIAM B. REILY & CO., INC., pg. 923
SUN DIAMOND GROWERS OF CALIFORNIA, pg. 1058
SUNSWEET GROWERS INC.—Sun Diamond Growers of California, pg. 1058
TREE TOP, INC., pg. 1109
VALLEY FIG GROWERS—Sun Diamond Growers of California, pg. 1058
VINCENT FOOD INDUSTRIES, INC., pg. 1152
WEST COAST GROWERS & PACKERS, INC., pg. 1177

2035 — PICKLED FRUITS & VEGETABLES, VEGETABLE SAUCES & SEASONINGS & SALAD DRESSINGS

M. ALKALAY AGENCIES, LTD.—Newly Weds Foods Inc., pg. 804
ALLEN FOODS, INC., pg. 36
BRUCE FOODS CORP., pg. 183
CALIENTE CHILI, INC.—William B. Reily & Co., Inc., pg. 923
CENTRAL COMMISSARY, INC.—Cornucopia, Inc., pg. 287
CLEMENTS FOODS CO., pg. 254
CONNELLY CONTAINERS, INC., pg. 275
CONWAY IMPORT CO. INC., pg. 281
CORNUCOPIA, INC., pg. 287
DALE FOODS—Vincent Food Industries, Inc., pg. 1152
J.L. DEGRAFFENREID & SONS, INC.—Vincent Food Industries, Inc., pg. 1152
DEL MONTE FOODS, pg. 325
FARIBAULT FOODS INC., pg. 399
FARMAN'S PICKLE COMPANY—Agway, Inc., pg. 26
FLANAGAN BROTHERS, pg. 416
GRIFFIN MANUFACTURING CO., pg. 487
HENRI'S FOOD PRODUCTS CO., INC., pg. 530
A. C. KISSLING, INC., pg. 634
LOSURDO FOODS, INC., pg. 684
LUZIANNE BLUE PLATE FOODS—William B. Reily & Co., Inc., pg. 923
MRS. SCHLORER'S, INC.—Connelly Containers, Inc., pg. 275
NATIONAL FOODS INC., pg. 788
NEWLY WEDS FOODS ASIA/PACIFIC—Newly Weds Foods Inc., pg. 804
NEWMAN'S OWN, INC., pg. 804
OTT FOOD PRODUCTS, pg. 831
PACE FOODS, INC., pg. 838
PIKNIK PRODUCTS COMPANY, INC., pg. 870
PURITY, INC., pg. 901
RHM INGREDIENTS, LTD.—Newly Weds Foods Inc., pg. 804
WILLIAM B. REILY & CO., INC., pg. 923
W. B. RODDENBERY COMPANY, INC., pg. 942
ROMANOFF INTERNATIONAL, INC., pg. 945
RYSER BROS. OF WISCONSIN—Ryser Brothers Inc., pg. 958
RYSER BROTHERS INC., pg. 958
THE SWISS COLONY, pg. 1068
TRI VALLEY GROWERS INC., pg. 1111
VENTRE PACKING COMPANY, INC., pg. 1147
VERYFINE PRODUCTS, INC., pg. 1148
VICTORIA PACKING CORPORATION, pg. 1149
VIENNA SAUSAGE MFG. CO., pg. 1151
VINCENT FOOD INDUSTRIES, INC., pg. 1152
WILLIAMS FOODS INC., pg. 1191

2037 — FROZEN FRUITS, FRUIT JUICES & VEGETABLES

ADAMS WINE CO., pg. 17
AGRIPAC INC., pg. 25
AGWAY, INC., pg. 25
AMFAC FOODS, INC.—JMB Realty Corporation, pg. 585
ARTICHOKE INDUSTRIES, INC., pg. 87
CARGILL AGRICOLA S.A.—Cargill Inc., pg. 219
CHESAPEAKE FINANCIAL CORP., pg. 243
CITRUS WORLD INC., pg. 251
JOHN COPES FOOD PRODUCTS, INC., pg. 284
CUIZINA ITALIA, INC.—National Frozen Foods Corp., pg. 789
DELAGRA CORPORATION, pg. 325
EVERFRESH BEVERAGES INC., pg. 391
FRIGID FOOD PRODUCTS, INC., pg. 433
GOLDEN GEM GROWERS INC., pg. 466
GREAT AMERICAN BREADED VEGETABLE CO.—Westin, Inc., pg. 1183
INTERNATIONAL AGRICULTURAL MARKET DEVELOPMENT CO.—Sunkist Growers, Inc., pg. 1061
LAKESIDE FOODS, INC., pg. 651
MAGIC VALLEY FOODS, INC., pg. 700
MCCAIN CITRUS INC., pg. 726
MILNE FRUIT PRODUCTS—Ocean Spray Cranberries, Inc., pg. 821
NATIONAL FROZEN FOODS CORP., pg. 789
NATIONAL FROZEN FOODS CORPORATION - ALBANY—National Frozen Foods Corp., pg. 789
NATIONAL FROZEN FOODS CORPORATION - BURLINGTON—National Frozen Foods Corp., pg. 789
NATIONAL FROZEN FOODS CORPORATION - CHEHALIS—National Frozen Foods Corp., pg. 789
NATIONAL FROZEN FOODS CORPORATION - MOSES LAKE—National Frozen Foods Corp., pg. 789
NATIONAL GRAPE CO-OP ASSOCIATION, INC., pg. 789
NORPAC FOODS, INC. COOPERATIVE, pg. 810
OCEAN SPRAY CRANBERRIES, INC., pg. 820
OH BOY CORPORATION, pg. 822
PATTERSON FROZEN FOODS, INC., pg. 851
PENOBSCOT FROZEN FOODS, INC., pg. 858
SCANGAS BROTHERS HOLDINGS, INC., pg. 974
SEABROOK BROTHERS & SONS, INC., pg. 984
SEABROOK FOODS, INC., pg. 984
J.R. SIMPLOT CO. FOOD GROUP—J.R. Simplot Company, pg. 1007
J.R. SIMPLOT COMPANY, pg. 1007
SMITH FROZEN FOODS, INC., pg. 1012
SUNKIST (EUROPE) S.A.—Sunkist Growers, Inc., pg. 1061
SUNKIST GROWERS, INC., pg. 1060
TWIN CITY FOODS, INC., pg. 1122
VERYFINE PRODUCTS, INC., pg. 1148
WALES INDUSTRIES, INC.—Citrus World Inc., pg. 251
WARNER VINEYARDS, pg. 1164
WELCH'S—National Grape Co-Op Association, Inc., pg. 789
WESTIN, INC., pg. 1183
WHITE ROCK PRODUCTS CORP., pg. 1186

2038 — FROZEN SPECIALTIES, NEC

AZTECA FOODS, INCORPORATED, pg. 105
CASA DI BERTACCHI—Rich Products Corp., pg. 932
CELENTANO BROTHERS, pg. 231
TONY DOWNS FOODS COMPANY, pg. 348
FROZEN SPECIALTIES, INC.—Windmill Holdings Corp., pg. 1195
IBM FOODS, pg. 558
THE JEL SERT CO., pg. 591
KEYSTONE FOODS CORPORATION, pg. 628
KOLD KIST BRANDS, INC., pg. 641
LITTLE LADY FOODS, INC., pg. 679
LUZIANNE BLUE PLATE FOODS—William B. Reily & Co., Inc., pg. 923
MICHAEL FOODS, INC., pg. 747
OH BOY CORPORATION, pg. 822
ON-COR FROZEN FOODS INC., pg. 826
PENOBSCOT FROZEN FOODS, INC., pg. 858
RED L FOODS—Union Holdings, Inc., pg. 1128
REDI-SERVE FOODS—On-Cor Frozen Foods Inc., pg. 826
RICH FRUIT PAK CO.—Rich Products Corp., pg. 932
RICH PRODUCTS CORP., pg. 932
ROMAN MEAL COMPANY, pg. 945
WOODBURN FOODS CORP.—Agripac Inc., pg. 25

2041 — FLOUR & OTHER GRAIN MILL PRODUCTS

ARROWHEAD MILLS, INC., pg. 86
BARRY-CARTER MILLING CO.—Windmill Holdings Corp., pg. 1195
BARTLETT AND COMPANY, pg. 122
BAY STATE MILLING CO., pg. 127
F.M. BROWN SONS, INC., pg. 183
CARGILL FLOUR MILLING DIV.—Cargill Inc., pg. 219
CARGILL INC., pg. 219
E & D GRAIN MARKETING CO—EDI International, Inc., pg. 359
EDI INTERNATIONAL, INC., pg. 359
FIROILLO A. CO. INC.—Seaboard Flour Corporation, pg. 984
FISHER COMPANIES, INC., pg. 414
FISHER MILLS, INC.—Fisher Companies, Inc., pg. 415
HODGSON MILL, INC.—Siemer Milling Company, pg. 1002
HOPKINSVILLE MILLING CO., pg. 543
ILLINOIS CEREAL MILLS, INC., pg. 562
KING MILLING COMPANY, pg. 631
LOSURDO FOODS, INC., pg. 684
MARTHA WHITE MILLS OF W.VA., INC.—Windmill Holdings Corp., pg. 1195
MODEL MILL CO.—Windmill Holdings Corp., pg. 1195
NEWLY WEDS FOODS THAILAND—Newly Weds Foods Inc., pg. 804
NORTH DAKOTA MILL & ELEVATOR ASSOCIATION, pg. 813
ROMAN MEAL COMPANY, pg. 945
ROUSH PRODUCTS CO., INC.—Windmill Holdings Corp., pg. 1195
SEABOARD CORPORATION—Seaboard Flour Corporation, pg. 984
SEABOARD FLOUR CORPORATION, pg. 984
SIEMER MILLING COMPANY, pg. 1002
SOVEX NATURAL FOODS—McKee Foods Corporation, pg. 730
SPANGLES' FLOUR MILLS OF MT. JOY—Wilkins-Rogers Incorporated, pg. 1190
THE UHLMANN CO., pg. 1125
THE WHITE LILY FOODS CO., pg. 1186
WILKINS-ROGERS INCORPORATED, pg. 1190
WINDMILL CORP. D/B/A MARTHA WHITE FOODS, INC.—Windmill Holdings Corp., pg. 1195
WINDMILL HOLDINGS CORP., pg. 1195

2043 — CEREAL BREAKFAST FOODS

GAGE FOOD PRODUCTS COMPANY—Vincent Food Industries, Inc., pg. 1152
MALT-O-MEAL COMPANY, pg. 703
NATIONAL OATS CO.—Agway, Inc., pg. 25

2044 — RICE MILLING

CORMIER RICE MILLING COMPANY, INC., pg. 286
FARMERS RICE COOPERATIVE, pg. 401
MARS, INCORPORATED, pg. 713
PRODUCERS RICE MILL INC., pg. 892
RICE GROWERS ASSOCIATION OF CALIFORNIA, pg. 931
RICELAND FOODS, INC., pg. 931
RIVIANA FOODS INC., pg. 937
UNCLE BEN'S, INC.—Mars, Incorporated, pg. 713

2045 — PREPARED FLOUR MIXES & DOUGHS

M. ALKALAY AGENCIES, LTD.—Newly Weds Foods Inc., pg. 804
J.W. ALLEN & COMPANY, pg. 36
BROKAY PRODUCTS, INC.—Caravan Products Company, Inc., pg. 217
CARAVAN PRODUCTS COMPANY, INC., pg. 217
CHELSEA MILLING CO., pg. 241
CONTINENTAL MILLS, INC., pg. 279
DAWN FOOD PRODUCTS, INC., pg. 319
DUFF MIX DIV.—Gilster Mary Lee Corp., pg. 460
4C FOODS CORPORATION, pg. 427
GILSTER MARY LEE CORP., pg. 460
HUBBARD MILLING COMPANY, pg. 549
LUZIANNE BLUE PLATE FOODS—William B. Reily & Co., Inc., pg. 923
NEWLY WEDS FOODS ASIA/PACIFIC—Newly Weds Foods Inc., pg. 804
NEWLY WEDS FOODS THAILAND—Newly Weds Foods Inc., pg. 804
NIPPON FLOUR MILLS CO., LTD.—Newly Weds Foods Inc., pg. 804
PARK CORPORATION, pg. 849
PARTY PAC DIV.—Gilster Mary Lee Corp., pg. 460
PY-O-MY DIV.—Gilster Mary Lee Corp., pg. 460
RHM INGREDIENTS, LTD.—Newly Weds Foods Inc., pg. 804
RUSTCO PRODUCTS COMPANY, pg. 957
WESTCO PRODUCTS, INC., pg. 1178
WINDMILL CORP. D/B/A MARTHA WHITE FOODS, INC.—Windmill Holdings Corp., pg. 1195

2046 — WET CORN MILLING

CARGILL INC., pg. 219
FOOD OILS CORPORATION—Trinidad/Benham Corporation, pg. 1114
GRAIN PROCESSING CORP.—Varied Investments, Inc., pg. 1145
THE HUBINGER COMPANY, pg. 550
LOU ANA FOODS, INC.—Schad Industries, Inc., pg. 974
LOU ANA FOODS OF TEXAS, INC.—Schad Industries, Inc., pg. 974
SCHAD INDUSTRIES, INC., pg. 974

2047 — DOG & CAT FOOD

ALLIED FOODS, INC., pg. 38
ALTAIR CORPORATION, pg. 45
BIOPRODUCTS, INC., pg. 152
BUSH BROTHERS & COMPANY, pg. 196
CARGILL INC., pg. 219
DAD'S PRODUCTS CO., INC., pg. 310
DOANE PRODUCTS CO., pg. 342
E-II HOLDINGS, INC., pg. 358
HARTZ GROUP, pg. 514
HARTZ MOUNTAIN GROUP—Hartz Group, pg. 514
HARVEST INDUSTRIES, INC.—Altair Corporation, pg. 45
HUBBARD MILLING COMPANY, pg. 549
IAMS COMPANY, pg. 561
KAL KAN FOODS, INC.—Mars, Incorporated, pg. 713
KENT FEEDS INC.—Varied Investments, Inc., pg. 1146
KERN LIVESTOCK SUPPLEMENT CO., INC.—Altair Corporation, pg. 45
MFA INCORPORATED, pg. 692
MANNA PRO CORPORATION, pg. 704
MANNA PRO PARTNER L.P. (LIMITED PARTNERSHIP)—Manna Pro Corporation, pg. 704
MARS, INCORPORATED, pg. 713
MARS PETFOODS (UNISABI)—Mars, Incorporated, pg. 714
MENU FOODS, INC., pg. 739
META FARM—Triple F, Inc., pg. 1114
MORGAN FOOD PRODUCTS—Morgan Manufacturing Company, Inc., pg. 770
MORGAN MANUFACTURING COMPANY, INC., pg. 770
NATURE'S RECIPE PET FOODS, pg. 796
NULAID FOODS, pg. 817
PET LIFE FOODS, INC., pg. 863
PET SPECIALTIES, INC.—E-II Holdings, Inc., pg. 358
SCHREIBER MILLING CO.—Hubbard Milling Company, pg. 549
STRONGHEART PRODUCTS, INC., pg. 1054
TENNESSEE FARMERS CO-OP, pg. 1087
TRIUMPH PET INDUSTRIES, INC., pg. 1115
W-P MILLING CO., INC.—Altair Corporation, pg. 45

2048 — PREPARED FEEDS & FEED INGREDIENTS FOR ANIMALS & FOWLS, EXCEPT DOGS & CATS

AG PROCESSING INC A COOPERATIVE, pg. 24
ALTAIR CORPORATION, pg. 45
ARGILAND COMPANY, pg. 81
H.J. BAKER & BRO., INC., pg. 114
BAKER COMMODITIES, INC., pg. 115
BELL GRAIN & MILLING, INC.—Moorman Mfg. Company, pg. 769
BIOPRODUCTS, INC., pg. 152
F.M. BROWN SONS, INC., pg. 183
CARGILL INC., pg. 219
CARGILL LTD.—Cargill Inc., pg. 219
CARGILL NUTRENA FEED—Cargill Inc., pg. 219
CENTRAL FEED MILLS, INC., pg. 232
CHAMPAIGN LANDMARK, pg. 238
CHAMPAIGN LANDMARK—Champaign Landmark, pg. 238
CONTINENTAL GRAIN COMPANY, pg. 279
COUNTRYMARK CO-OP INC.—Countrymark Cooperative, Inc., pg. 290
DAD'S PRODUCTS CO., INC., pg. 310
DARLING-DELAWARE CO., INC., pg. 315
E-II HOLDINGS, INC., pg. 358

EVERGREEN MILLS INC.—Varied Investments, Inc., pg. 1145
FARMERS MARKETING ASSOCIATION—Manna Pro Partners, pg. 704
FARMERS UNION MARKETING & PROCESSING ASSOCIATION, pg. 402
FARMLAND INDUSTRIES, INC., pg. 402
FEED SERVICE CORP., pg. 405
FLINT RIVER MILLS, pg. 419
GOLD KIST, INC., pg. 465
GOLDEN GEM GROWERS INC., pg. 466
GOLDEN SUN FEEDS, INC., pg. 467
GOLDEN SUN FEEDS, INC.—Golden Sun Feeds, Inc., pg. 467
GROWMARK, INC., pg. 490
HARVEST BRANDS, INC.—Altair Corporation, pg. 45
HARVEST INDUSTRIES, INC.—Altair Corporation, pg. 45
A. H. HOFFMAN, INC., pg. 538
HOLMQUIST GRAIN & LUMBER CO., pg. 540
HUBBARD MILLING COMPANY, pg. 549
KECO MILLING CO.—Windmill Holdings Corp., pg. 1195
KENT FEEDS INC.—Varied Investments, Inc., pg. 1146
KERN LIVESTOCK SUPPLEMENT CO., INC.—Altair Corporation, pg. 45
MFA INCORPORATED, pg. 692
MANNA PRO CORPORATION, pg. 704
MANNA PRO PARTNER L.P. (LIMITED PARTNERSHIP)—Manna Pro Corporation, pg. 704
MANNA PRO PARTNERS, pg. 704
MARTRADE LTD., pg. 716
META FARM—Triple F, Inc., pg. 1114
MID-KANSAS CO-OP ASSOCIATION, pg. 750
MID-SOUTH MILLING COMPANY, INC., pg. 750
MILK SPECIALTIES COMPANY, pg. 753
MOORMAN MFG. COMPANY, pg. 769
MORONI FEED CO.—Norbest, Inc., pg. 809
NULAID FOODS, pg. 817
NUTRIUS DAIRY FEED SUPPLEMENTS DIV.—Bioproducts, Inc., pg. 152
PET AG INC.—Milk Specialties Company, pg. 753
PET SPECIALTIES, INC.—E-II Holdings, Inc., pg. 358
PRODUCERS CO-OP ASSOCIATION, INC., pg. 892
QUINCY SOYBEAN CO.—Moorman Mfg. Company, pg. 769
RANCH-WAY, INC., pg. 911
RANGEN, INC., pg. 912
ROCCO FARM FOODS, INC.—Rocco Inc., pg. 940
ROCCO INC., pg. 940
SF SERVICES, pg. 961
SCHREIBER MILLING CO.—Hubbard Milling Company, pg. 549
SCHREIER MALTING CO., pg. 978
SEABOARD CORPORATION—Seaboard Flour Corporation, pg. 984
SPRINGFIELD MILLING CORP.—Hubbard Milling Company, pg. 549
JACOB STERN & SONS, INC., pg. 1047
TENNESSEE FARMERS CO-OP, pg. 1087
A.M. TODD COMPANY, pg. 1100
UNITED FEEDS, INC., pg. 1132
W-P MILLING CO., INC.—Altair Corporation, pg. 45
WALNUT GROVE-NUTRENA FEED DIV., CARGILL, INC.—Cargill Inc., pg. 219
WEST CENTRAL CO-OP, pg. 1176

2051 — BREAD & OTHER BAKERY PRODUCTS, EXCEPT COOKIES & CRACKERS

AMANA SOCIETY, pg. 46
AMERICAN BREAD COMPANY - SUNBEAM BAKERY, pg. 49
APRIL HILL, INC.—Grocers Baking Co., pg. 488
BELLACICCO & SONS, pg. 136
BENSON'S, INC., pg. 140
BEST BRANDS, pg. 146
BETTER BAKED FOODS, INC., pg. 148
BYRNES & KIEFER COMPANY, pg. 198
CERTIFIED GROCERS OF CALIFORNIA, pg. 237
CLOVERHILL BAKERY, pg. 256
COLOMBO BAKING CO.—San Francisco French Bread Company, pg. 969
DAKOTA BAKE-N-SERV—Rhodes International, Inc., pg. 931
DERST BAKING COMPANY, INC., pg. 331
JON DONAIRE PASTRIES, INC.—Presto Food Products, Inc., pg. 888
EDWARDS BAKING CO., pg. 369
ELI'S CHICAGO'S FINEST, INC., pg. 376
FRANKLIN BAKING CO., INC., pg. 429
GAI'S SEATTLE FRENCH BAKING CO., INC., pg. 441
GASE BAKERY CO.—Perfection Bakeries Inc., pg. 861
GONNELLA BAKING CO., pg. 469
GOOD STUFF FOOD COMPANY, INC., pg. 470
HOLSUM BAKERY, INC., pg. 541
HOLSUM OF FORT WAYNE, INC.—Lewis Brothers Bakeries, Inc., pg. 673
J.M.P. BAKERY CO., INC., pg. 586
KLOSTERMAN'S BAKING COMPANY, pg. 636
LANGENDORF BAKING COMPANY OF SEATTLE, INC.—Gai's Seattle French Baking Co., Inc., pg. 441
LET THEM EAT CAKE—Wilton Industries, Inc., pg. 1195
LEWIS BROS. BAKERIES—Lewis Brothers Bakeries, Inc., pg. 673
LEWIS BROS. BAKERIES (MO)—Lewis Brothers Bakeries, Inc., pg. 673
LEWIS BROS. BAKERIES (TN)—Lewis Brothers Bakeries, Inc., pg. 673
LEWIS BROTHERS BAKERIES, INC., pg. 673
W. E. LONG COMPANY, pg. 682
MCKEE BAKING CO., INC., pg. 730
MCKEE FOODS CORPORATION, pg. 730
MRS. BAIRD'S BAKERIES, INC., pg. 760
NEWLY WEDS FOODS INC., pg. 804
ALFRED NICKLES BAKERY, INC., pg. 806
NICKLES BAKERY INC., ELKHART—Alfred Nickles Bakery, Inc., pg. 807
NICKLES BAKERY INC., LIMA—Alfred Nickles Bakery, Inc., pg. 807
PIE PIPER PRODUCTS, LTD.—Vienna Sausage Mfg. Co., pg. 1151
PURITAN BAKERY, INC., pg. 900
QUALITY BAKERS OF AMERICA COOPERATIVE, INC., pg. 903
RHODES INTERNATIONAL, INC., pg. 931
RICH PRODUCTS DAYTON—Rich Products Corp., pg. 932
RIPON FOODS, INC., pg. 935
SAN FRANCISCO FRENCH BREAD COMPANY, pg. 969
SCHAFER BAKERIES, INC.—Perfection Bakeries Inc., pg. 861
SCHMIDT BAKING CO., INC., pg. 976
SEILER CORPORATION, pg. 987
THE SWISS COLONY, pg. 1068
VICTORY MARKETS INC., pg. 1150
WAY BAKERIES, INC.—Perfection Bakeries Inc., pg. 861
WILD'S BAKING COMPANY, pg. 1189
WILTON INDUSTRIES, INC., pg. 1194

2052 — COOKIES & CRACKERS

ARCHWAY COOKIES, INC., pg. 81
BAHLSEN INC., pg. 114
BAKE-LINE PRODUCTS, INC., pg. 114
BELLACICCO & SONS, pg. 136
DAD'S COOKIES—Mrs. Alison's Cookie Company, pg. 760
DAN DEE PRETZEL & POTATO CHIP CO., pg. 313
GF INDUSTRIES, INC., pg. 439
GAI'S SEATTLE FRENCH BAKING CO., INC., pg. 441
LANGENDORF BAKING COMPANY OF SEATTLE, INC.—Gai's Seattle French Baking Co., Inc., pg. 441
MCKEE BAKING CO., INC., pg. 730
MCKEE FOODS CORPORATION, pg. 730
MRS. ALISON'S COOKIE COMPANY, pg. 760
MRS. FIELDS' INC., pg. 761
SCHULZE & BURCH BISCUIT COMPANY, pg. 979
SUNSHINE BISCUITS, INC.—GF Industries, Inc., pg. 439
SUNSHINE/SALERNO (IL)—GF Industries, Inc., pg. 439
SUNSHINE/SALERNO, INC (NJ)—GF Industries, Inc., pg. 439
SWEETHEART CUP CO., INC., pg. 1067
SWEETHEART CUP CO., INC.—Sweetheart Cup Co., Inc., pg. 1067
WILD'S BAKING COMPANY, pg. 1189

2053 — FROZEN BAKING PRODUCTS, EXCEPT BREAD

APRIL HILL, INC.—Grocers Baking Co., pg. 488
CLOVERHILL BAKERY, pg. 256
COUNTRY HOME BAKERY, INC., pg. 290
EDWARDS BAKING CO., pg. 369
ELI'S CHICAGO'S FINEST, INC., pg. 376
PERFECTION BAKERIES INC., pg. 861
SEILER CORPORATION, pg. 987

2061 — CANE SUGAR, EXCEPT REFINING

AMFAC, INC.—JMB Realty Corporation, pg. 585
ATLANTIC SUGAR ASSOCIATION, INC., pg. 95
C. BREWER & COMPANY, LIMITED, pg. 174
BRYANT SUGAR HOUSE—United States Sugar Corporation, pg. 1137
CALIFORNIA & HAWAIIAN SUGAR COMPANY, pg. 210
CLEWISTON SUGAR HOUSE—United States Sugar Corporation, pg. 1137
CORA TEXAS MANUFACTURING CO., pg. 285
KA'U AGRIBUSINESS CO., INC.—C. Brewer & Company, Limited, pg. 174
KAUAI SUGAR STORAGE CO.—JMB Realty Corporation, pg. 585
KEKAHA SUGAR COMPANY, LIMITED—JMB Realty Corporation, pg. 585
THE LIHUE PLANTATION COMPANY, LIMITED—JMB Realty Corporation, pg. 585
PIONEER MILL COMPANY, LTD.—JMB Realty Corporation, pg. 585
SOUTHERN MINNESOTA BEET SUGAR COOPERATIVE, pg. 1022
SUGAR CANE GROWERS COOPERATIVE OF FLORIDA, pg. 1056
UNITED STATES SUGAR CORPORATION, pg. 1137
WHITFIELD FOODS, INC., pg. 1187

2062 — CANE SUGAR REFINING

AMERICAN CRYSTAL SUGAR COMPANY, pg. 51
CALIFORNIA & HAWAIIAN SUGAR COMPANY, pg. 210
CORA TEXAS MANUFACTURING CO., pg. 285
GRIFFIN MANUFACTURING CO., pg. 487
L. KARP & SONS, INC., pg. 617

2063 — BEET SUGAR MANUFACTURING

AMERICAN CRYSTAL SUGAR COMPANY, pg. 51
DELTA SUGAR CORPORATION, pg. 327
SOUTHERN MINNESOTA BEET SUGAR COOPERATIVE, pg. 1022
SPRECKLES INDUSTRIES, INC., pg. 1032

2064 — CANDY & OTHER CONFECTIONERY PRODUCTS

ANNABELLE CANDY COMPANY, pg. 75
ARCHIBALD CANDY COMPANY—Jordan Company, pg. 604
ASHER CANDY COMPANY—MacAndrews & Forbes Holdings Inc., pg. 695
BOYER BROS. INC., pg. 169
E.J. BRACH CORPORATION, pg. 169
E.J. BRACH, INC.—E.J. Brach Corporation, pg. 169
E.J. BRACH, INC.—E.J. Brach Corporation, pg. 169
BROCK CANDY COMPANY, pg. 177
BROWN & HALEY, pg. 182
CE DE CANDY, INC., pg. 230
CONCORD DIVISION—Annabelle Candy Company, pg. 75
FALCON CANDY COMPANY, pg. 398
FANNIE MAY CANDY SHOPS, INC.—Jordan Company, pg. 604
FARLEY CANDY COMPANY, pg. 399
FLEER CORPORATION—MacAndrews & Forbes Holdings Inc., pg. 695
GLICO HARMONY FOODS CORPORATION, pg. 462
GRAVYMASTER INC., pg. 478
GERTRUDE HAWK CHOCOLATES, INC., pg. 517
JUDSON-ATKINSON CANDIES, INC., pg. 608
JUST BORN, INC., pg. 610
M&M/MARS—Mars, Incorporated, pg. 713
MARS CONFECTIONERY—Mars, Incorporated, pg. 713
MARS, INCORPORATED, pg. 713
MASTER FOODS—Mars, Incorporated, pg. 713
MASTER FOODS NV—Mars, Incorporated, pg. 714
MASTERFOODS LTD.—Mars, Incorporated, pg. 714
MASTERFOODS OY—Mars, Incorporated, pg. 714
MAUNA LOA MACADAMIA NUT CORPORATION—C. Brewer & Company, Limited, pg. 174
BEN MYERSON CANDY COMPANY, INC., pg. 780
NATIONAL FOOD STORES, INC. T/A KRAUSZER'S, pg. 788
NEW ENGLAND CONFECTIONERY CO.—UIS, Inc., pg. 1123
NORFOODS, INC., pg. 810
OLD DUTCH FOODS, INC., pg. 823
R.M. PALMER COMPANY, pg. 843
PEERLESS CONFECTION COMPANY, pg. 855
PORTLAND FOOD PRODUCTS COMPANY, pg. 881
POWELL'S INC.—Sathers Inc., pg. 972
ANN RASKAS GOURMET CONFECTIONERS, pg. 913
REDCO FOODS, INC., pg. 919
RUSSELL STOVER CANDIES, INC., pg. 957
SHADE FOODS, INC.—Norfoods, Inc., pg. 810
SHELLY BROS., INC.—Brock Candy Company, pg. 178
SPANGLER CANDY COMPANY, pg. 1025
STANDARD CANDY CO., INC., pg. 1035
STARK CANDY COMPANY—UIS, Inc., pg. 1123
STARK CANDY COMPANY—UIS, Inc., pg. 1123
STARK CANDY COMPANY—UIS, Inc., pg. 1123
THE SWISS COLONY, pg. 1068
VERNELL'S CANDY COMPANY, pg. 1148

2066 — CHOCOLATE & COCOA PRODUCTS

ANNABELLE CANDY COMPANY, pg. 75
W.L.M. BENSDORP COMPANY, pg. 139
BLOMMER CHOCOLATE CO., pg. 157
E.J. BRACH CORPORATION, pg. 169
E.J. BRACH, INC.—E.J. Brach Corporation, pg. 169
E.J. BRACH, INC.—E.J. Brach Corporation, pg. 169
BROCK CANDY COMPANY, pg. 177
BROWN & HALEY, pg. 182
CARGILL AGRICOLA S.A.—Cargill Inc., pg. 219
CONCORD DIVISION—Annabelle Candy Company, pg. 75
COOK CHOCOLATE CANADA LTD.—World's Finest Chocolate, Inc., pg. 1203
FARLEY CANDY COMPANY, pg. 399
GILSTER MARY LEE CORP.—Gilster Mary Lee Corp., pg. 460
S. GUMPERT CO., INC.—Rich Products Corp., pg. 932
M&M/MARS—Mars, Incorporated, pg. 713
MARS, INCORPORATED, pg. 713
MASTER FOODS—Mars, Incorporated, pg. 713
NORFOODS, INC., pg. 810
PY-O-MY DIV.—Gilster Mary Lee Corp., pg. 460
RUSSELL STOVER CANDIES, INC., pg. 957
SHADE FOODS, INC.—Norfoods, Inc., pg. 810
THE SWISS COLONY, pg. 1068
VERNELL'S CANDY COMPANY, pg. 1148
WILBUR CHOCOLATE CO., INC.—Cargill Inc., pg. 219
WORLD'S FINEST CHOCOLATE AUSTRALIA PTY. LTD.—World's Finest Chocolate, Inc., pg. 1203
WORLD'S FINEST CHOCOLATE CANADA LTD.—World's Finest Chocolate, Inc., pg. 1203
WORLD'S FINEST CHOCOLATE, INC., pg. 1203

2067 — CHEWING GUM

CLARK GUM COMPANY, pg. 252
FLEER CORPORATION—MacAndrews & Forbes Holdings Inc., pg. 695

2068 — SALTED & ROASTED NUTS & SEEDS

ASTER NUT PRODUCTS INC., pg. 92
C. BREWER & COMPANY, LIMITED, pg. 174
DELIMATIC REFRESHMENT SERVICES—Tom's Foods, pg. 1101
FLAVOR HOUSE PRODUCTS, INC., pg. 417
MAUNA KEA AGRIBUSINESS CO., INC.—C. Brewer & Company, Limited, pg. 174
MAUNA LOA MACADAMIA NUT CORPORATION—C. Brewer & Company, Limited, pg. 174
SUN DIAMOND GROWERS OF CALIFORNIA, pg. 1058
THE SWISS COLONY, pg. 1068
TOM'S DISTRIBUTING INC.—Tom's Foods, pg. 1101
TOM'S FOODS, pg. 1101
TOM'S SNAX CO.—Tom's Foods, pg. 1101

WAILUKU AGRIBUSINESS CO., INC.—C. Brewer & Company, Limited, pg. 175

2074 — COTTONSEED OIL MILLS

MALLET & CO., pg. 703
PLAINS CO-OP OIL MILL, pg. 873
RANCHERS COTTON OIL, pg. 911

2075 — SOYBEAN OIL MILLS

AG PROCESSING INC A COOPERATIVE, pg. 24
CARGILL AGRICOLA S.A.—Cargill Inc., pg. 219
CARGILL INC., pg. 219
CONTINENTAL GRAIN COMPANY, pg. 279
MALLET & CO., pg. 703
MOORMAN MFG. COMPANY, pg. 769
OWENSBORO GRAIN CO., INC., pg. 834
RICELAND FOODS, INC., pg. 931
WEST CENTRAL CO-OP, pg. 1176

2076 — VEGETABLE OIL MILLS, EXCEPT CORN, COTTONSEED, & SOYBEAN

H.J. BAKER & BRO., INC., pg. 114
CARGILL INC., pg. 219
CASCHEM INC., pg. 227
COAST PACKING COMPANY, pg. 257
COLFAX, INC., pg. 261
FARMERS UNION MARKETING & PROCESSING ASSOCIATION, pg. 402
LOU ANA FOODS OF TEXAS, INC.—Schad Industries, Inc., pg. 974
MALLET & CO., pg. 703
SCHAD INDUSTRIES, INC., pg. 974

2077 — ANIMAL & MARINE FATS & OILS

H.J. BAKER & BRO., INC., pg. 114
BAKER COMMODITIES, INC., pg. 115
CBP RESOURCES, INC., pg. 199
COAST PACKING COMPANY, pg. 257
COLFAX, INC., pg. 261
DARLING-DELAWARE CO., INC., pg. 315
FARMERS UNION MARKETING & PROCESSING ASSOCIATION, pg. 402
GRIFFIN INDUSTRIES, INC., pg. 487
HRR ENTERPRISES, INC.—Kane-Miller Corp., pg. 616
JONES DAIRY FARM, pg. 603
KANE-MILLER CORP., pg. 616
MOYER PACKING COMPANY, pg. 774
JACOB STERN & SONS, INC., pg. 1047

2079 — SHORTENING, TABLE OILS, MARGARINE & OTHER EDIBLE FATS & OILS, NEC

ARROWHEAD MILLS, INC., pg. 86
COAST PACKING COMPANY, pg. 257
COLFAX, INC., pg. 261
FOOD OILS CORPORATION—Trinidad/Benham Corporation, pg. 1114
INTEROLIVA—Westin, Inc., pg. 1183
KANE-MILLER CORP., pg. 616
LOU ANA FOODS, INC.—Schad Industries, Inc., pg. 974
LOU ANA FOODS OF TEXAS, INC.—Schad Industries, Inc., pg. 974
MADISON DAIRY PRODUCE COMPANY, pg. 699
MALLET & CO., pg. 703
THE MIAMI MARGARINE CO., pg. 746
OTT FOOD PRODUCTS, pg. 831
POMPEIAN, INC., pg. 880
RICELAND FOODS, INC., pg. 931
RUSTCO PRODUCTS COMPANY, pg. 957
SCHAD INDUSTRIES, INC., pg. 974
SUNNYLAND REFINING CO., INC.—Kane-Miller Corp., pg. 616
WILSEY FOODS, INC.—Wilsey Bennett Co., pg. 1193

2082 — MALT BEVERAGES

BLITZ-WEINHARD BREWING—G. Heileman Brewing Co., Inc., pg. 526
DIXIE BREWING CO., INC., pg. 341
EVANSVILLE BREWING COMPANY, pg. 391
G. HEILEMAN BREWING CO., INC., pg. 526
G. HEILEMAN BREWING COMPANY, INC.—G. Heileman Brewing Co., Inc., pg. 526
HUDEPOHL-SCHOENLING BREWING COMPANY, pg. 550
LADISH MALTING CO.—Cargill Inc., pg. 219
A. J. LEHMAN CO.—Grandpa Brands Company, pg. 476
THE LION, INC. (GIBBONS-STEGMAIER BREWERY), pg. 677
THE F. X. MATT BREWING CO., pg. 721
MINNESOTA BREWING COMPANY, pg. 757
NOR-CAL BEVERAGE CO., INC., pg. 808
PABST BREWING CO./MILWAUKEE—S & P Company, pg. 959
PABST BREWING CO./TUMWATER—S & P Company, pg. 959
PITTSBURGH BREWING COMPANY, pg. 873
RAINIER BREWING CO.—G. Heileman Brewing Co., Inc., pg. 526
S & P COMPANY, pg. 959
SAN MIGUEL (U.S.A.) INC., pg. 969
THE STROH BREWERY COMPANY, pg. 1053
WATKINS INCORPORATED, pg. 1167
WHITE ROCK PRODUCTS CORP., pg. 1186

2083 — MALT

CARGILL INC., pg. 219
PABST BREWING CO./MILWAUKEE—S & P Company, pg. 959
SCHREIER MALTING CO., pg. 978
WINDMILL HOLDINGS CORP., pg. 1195

2084 — WINES, BRANDY & BRANDY SPIRITS

ADAMS WINE CO., pg. 17
E & J GALLO WINERY, pg. 441
GIBSON WINE COMPANY, pg. 457
GIUMARRA VINEYARDS, pg. 460
GLEN ELLEN WINERY, pg. 461
CHARLES JACQUIN ET CIE, INC., pg. 588
LAIRD & COMPANY, pg. 650
MOHAWK DISTILLED PRODUCTS, pg. 763
NWS, INC., pg. 782
PINE STATE BEVERAGE—Pine State Tobacco & Candy Company, pg. 871
SAXONY DISTILLERS ET CIE, INC.—Charles Jacquin et Cie, Inc., pg. 588
SUN DIAMOND GROWERS OF CALIFORNIA, pg. 1058
SUTTER HOME WINERY, INC., pg. 1065
WARNER VINEYARDS, pg. 1164
WEIBEL VINEYARDS, pg. 1173
WHITE ROCK DISTILLERIES INC., pg. 1186

2085 — DISTILLED & BLENDED LIQUORS

BARTON BRANDS, LTD., pg. 123
FAIRVIEW WINE CO.—White Rock Distilleries Inc., pg. 1186
FEDERAL DISTILLERS—White Rock Distilleries Inc., pg. 1186
GRAIN PROCESSING CORP.—Varied Investments, Inc., pg. 1145
JOHN GROSS & CO., pg. 489
CHARLES JACQUIN ET CIE, INC., pg. 588
JENKINS SPIRITS CORP. LTD., pg. 592
KASSER/LAIRD DISTILLING CO.—Laird & Company, pg. 650
LAIRD & COMPANY, pg. 650
LAWRENCE & COMPANY—White Rock Distilleries Inc., pg. 1186
MAINE DISTILLERS—White Rock Distilleries Inc., pg. 1186
MONTEBELLO BRANDS INC., pg. 767
NWS, INC., pg. 782
SAXONY DISTILLERS ET CIE, INC.—Charles Jacquin et Cie, Inc., pg. 588
M.S. WALKER, INC./SEACOAST, pg. 1160
WHITE ROCK DISTILLERIES INC., pg. 1186

2086 — BOTTLED & CANNED SOFT DRINKS & CARBONATED WATERS

ALL AMERICAN BOTTLING CORP., pg. 35
BARQ'S, INC., pg. 121
BEVERAGE CANNERS DIV.—Beverage Canners International Corp., pg. 148
BEVERAGE CANNERS INTERNATIONAL CORP., pg. 148
BEVERAGE MANAGEMENT, INC.—Brooks Beverage Management, Inc., pg. 179
BIG RED RC & 7-UP OF LAGRANGE, TX—Grant-Lydick Beverage Co., pg. 477
BROOKS BEVERAGE MANAGEMENT, INC., pg. 179
BROOKS BEVERAGES INC.—Brooks Beverage Management, Inc., pg. 179
BUFFALO ROCK COMPANY, pg. 187
A. J. CANFIELD CO., pg. 214
CENTRAL COCA-COLA BOTTLING COMPANY, INC., pg. 232
CHESAPEAKE FINANCIAL CORP., pg. 243
COCA-COLA BOTTLING CO. OF CHICAGO, pg. 257
COCA-COLA BOTTLING CO. OF THE SOUTHWEST, pg. 257
COCA-COLA BOTTLING COMPANY OF ELIZABETHTOWN, pg. 258
COCA-COLA/DR. PEPPER BOTTLING CO. OF SOUTH ARKANSAS—Ouachita Coca-Cola Bottling Company, pg. 831
R.J. CORR NATURALS, INC., pg. 287
CRYSTAL GEYSER, pg. 303
DR PEPPER COMPANY—Dr Pepper/Seven-Up Companies, Inc., pg. 342
DR PEPPER JAPAN CO.—Dr Pepper/Seven-Up Companies, Inc., pg. 342
THE DOUBLE-COLA COMPANY, pg. 347
FULL SERVICE BEVERAGE COMPANY, pg. 436
FULL SERVICE BEVERAGE COMPANY OF COLORADO—Full Service Beverage Company, pg. 436
GRANT-LYDICK BEVERAGE CO., pg. 477
GREEN SPOT PACKAGING INC., pg. 485
HOME JUICE COMPANY, pg. 541
I.B.C. ROOT BEER COMPANY—Dr Pepper/Seven-Up Companies, Inc., pg. 342
THE JOLT COMPANY, pg. 602
KEMMERER BOTTLING GROUP INC., pg. 622
KRIER FOODS, INC., pg. 645
A. J. LEHMAN CO.—Grandpa Brands Company, pg. 476
THE MONARCH COMPANY, INC., pg. 765
MOUNTAIN VALLEY SPRING COMPANY—Sammons Enterprises, Inc., pg. 968
NATIONAL BRANDS BEVERAGE DIV.—Agway, Inc., pg. 25
NEWMAN'S OWN, INC., pg. 804
NOEL CANNING CORPORATION, pg. 808
NOR-CAL BEVERAGE CO., INC., pg. 808
OUACHITA COCA-COLA BOTTLING COMPANY, pg. 831
PEPSI-COLA ALBANY BOTTLING CO., INC., pg. 860
PEPSI-COLA BOTTLING CO., pg. 860
PEPSI-COLA BOTTLING COMPANY OF CHARLOTTE INC., pg. 860
PHILADELPHIA COCA-COLA BOTTLING CO., pg. 866
POLAR CORPORATION, pg. 878
PREMIER BEVERAGES—Dr Pepper/Seven-Up Companies, Inc., pg. 342
SEVEN-UP BOTTLING CO. OF AKRON—Brooks Beverage Management, Inc., pg. 179
SEVEN-UP BOTTLING CO. OF CLEVELAND—Brooks Beverage Management, Inc., pg. 179
SEVEN-UP BOTTLING CO. OF DAYTON—Brooks Beverage Management, Inc., pg. 179
SEVEN-UP BOTTLING CO. OF DETROIT—Brooks Beverage Management, Inc., pg. 179
THE SEVEN-UP COMPANY—Dr Pepper/Seven-Up Companies, Inc., pg. 342
7UP OF CORPUS CHRISTI—Grant-Lydick Beverage Co., pg. 477
7UP OF VICTORIA—Grant-Lydick Beverage Co., pg. 477
7UP/RC OF AUSTIN—Grant-Lydick Beverage Co., pg. 477
7UP/RC OF HARLINGEN—Grant-Lydick Beverage Co., pg. 477
SEVEN-UP ROYAL CROWN-CANADA DRY OF CINCINNATI—Brooks Beverage Management, Inc., pg. 179
SEVEN-UP ROYAL CROWN CANADA DRY OF COLUMBUS—Brooks Beverage Management, Inc., pg. 179
SOUTHERN BEVERAGE PACKERS, INC., pg. 1020
STEWART'S ICE CREAM CO., INC., pg. 1048
SUNCREST COMPANY OF CANADA—The Monarch Company, Inc., pg. 765
TLC BEATRICE INTERNATIONAL HOLDINGS INC., pg. 1073
VESS BEVERAGES, INC., pg. 1149
WELCH'S CARBONATED BEVERAGES—Dr Pepper/Seven-Up Companies, Inc., pg. 342
WHITE ROCK PRODUCTS CORP., pg. 1186

2087 — FLAVORING EXTRACTS & FLAVORING SYRUPS, NEC

ALLEN FOODS, INC., pg. 36
BOAM PRODUCE (OVERSEAS) LTD.—MacAndrews & Forbes Holdings Inc., pg. 694
BRADY ENTERPRISES, INC., pg. 171
BROKAY PRODUCTS, INC.—Caravan Products Company, Inc., pg. 217
BYRNES & KIEFER COMPANY, pg. 198
CARAVAN PRODUCTS COMPANY, INC., pg. 217
CHESAPEAKE FINANCIAL CORP., pg. 243
DALE FOODS—Vincent Food Industries, Inc., pg. 1152
DAWN FOOD PRODUCTS, INC., pg. 319
DR PEPPER COMPANY—Dr Pepper/Seven-Up Companies, Inc., pg. 342
THE DOUBLE-COLA COMPANY, pg. 347
ELECTROCHEMICAL INDUSTRIES (FRUTAROM) LTD.—ICC Industries, Inc., pg. 558
FLORASYNTH AUSTRALASIA PTY. LTD.—Florasynth Inc., pg. 420
FLORASYNTH (FAR EAST) PTE. LTD.—Florasynth Inc., pg. 420
FLORASYNTH GMBH—Florasynth Inc., pg. 420
FLORASYNTH INC., pg. 420
FLORASYNTH S.A. DE C.V.—Florasynth Inc., pg. 420
HOME JUICE COMPANY, pg. 541
I.C.S.A.-FLORASYNTH—Florasynth Inc., pg. 420
THE JEL SERT CO., pg. 591
KALSEC, INC.—Kalamazoo Holdings, Inc., pg. 615
L. KARP & SONS, INC., pg. 617
A. J. LEHMAN CO.—Grandpa Brands Company, pg. 476
MACANDREWS & FORBES CO.—MacAndrews & Forbes Holdings Inc., pg. 694
MACANDREWS & FORBES HOLDINGS INC., pg. 694
MACANDREWS & FORBES LTD.—MacAndrews & Forbes Holdings Inc., pg. 694
MARTRADE LTD., pg. 716
MEER CORPORATION, pg. 736
DAVID MICHAEL & CO. INC., pg. 747
MILNE FRUIT PRODUCTS—Ocean Spray Cranberries, Inc., pg. 821
M.F. NEAL & CO.,INC.—MacAndrews & Forbes Holdings Inc., pg. 694
PREMIER BEVERAGES—Dr Pepper/Seven-Up Companies, Inc., pg. 342
PURITY, INC., pg. 901
THE SWISS COLONY, pg. 1068
VINCENT FOOD INDUSTRIES, INC., pg. 1152

2091 — CANNED & CURED FISH & SEAFOODS

H.J. BAKER & BRO., INC., pg. 114
BRUCE FOODS CORP., pg. 183
CONNORS BRUNSWICK, INC., pg. 275
ICICLE SEAFOODS, INC., pg. 561
LOS ANGELES SMOKING CURING COMPANY, pg. 684
PORT CLYDE FOODS CO.—Connors Brunswick, Inc., pg. 276
ROMANOFF INTERNATIONAL, INC., pg. 945
STINSON SEAFOOD COMPANY, pg. 1049
VITA FOOD PRODUCTS, INC., pg. 1153

2092 — PREPARED FRESH OR FROZEN FISH & SEAFOODS

AMERICAN FOODS GROUP, pg. 54
AMFAC FOODS, INC.—JMB Realty Corporation, pg. 585
HARRY H. BELL & SONS, INC., pg. 134
CGF INDUSTRIES, pg. 201
COLDWATER SEAFOOD CORPORATION, pg. 260
CONNORS BRUNSWICK, INC., pg. 275
DELTA PRIDE CATFISH, INC., pg. 327

FISHKING PROCESSORS, INC., pg. 415
ICELAND SEAFOOD CORPORATION, pg. 561
KITCHENS OF THE OCEAN, INC., pg. 634
PORT CLYDE FOODS CO.—Connors Brunswick, Inc., pg. 276
QF, INC.—Fishking Processors, Inc., pg. 415
RICH PRODUCTS CORP., pg. 932
STINSON SEAFOOD COMPANY, pg. 1049
TRIDENT SEAFOOD CORPORATION, pg. 1113

2095 — ROASTED COFFEE

CARGILL AGRICOLA S.A.—Cargill Inc., pg. 219
IRELAND COFFEE TEA, INC., pg. 582
JFG COFFEE COMPANY—William B. Reily & Co., Inc., pg. 923
LUZIANNE BLUE PLATE FOODS—William B. Reily & Co., Inc., pg. 923
MILLSTONE COFFEE, INC., pg. 756
PARK CORPORATION, pg. 849
WILLIAM B. REILY & CO., INC., pg. 923
S&D COFFEE INC., pg. 959
SUPERIOR COFFEE & FOODS/HAWAII—C. Brewer & Company, Limited, pg. 174
TORKE COFFEE COMPANY, INC., pg. 1102
WECHSLER COFFEE CORP., pg. 1172

2096 — POTATO CHIPS, CORN CHIPS & SIMILAR SNACKS

AGWAY, INC., pg. 25
ASTER NUT PRODUCTS INC., pg. 92
AZTECA FOODS, INCORPORATED, pg. 105
BACHMAN COMPANY, pg. 108
BARREL O'FUN SNACK FOODS CO., pg. 122
BLUE BELL POTATO CHIP CO.—GF Industries, Inc., pg. 439
BON TON FOODS, INC., pg. 164
CABANA FOODS, INC., pg. 206
CORNNUTS INC., pg. 286
DAN DEE PRETZEL & POTATO CHIP CO., pg. 313
NIBBLE WITH GIBBLE'S, INC., pg. 806
OLD DUTCH FOODS, INC., pg. 823
THE POPCORN FACTORY—Foster & Gallagher Inc., pg. 426
PREPCO, pg. 887
RUDOLPH FOODS COMPANY, pg. 954
SNYDER POTATO CHIPS—Agway, Inc., pg. 26
C.J. VITNER & CO., INC., pg. 1153
WEAVER POPCORN COMPANY, INC., pg. 1170

2097 — MANUFACTURED ICE

MIDSOUTH ICE CO.—Spencer Companies Inc., pg. 1030
SPENCER COMPANIES INC., pg. 1030
UNITED STATES COLD STORAGE, INC., pg. 1135

2098 — MACARONI, SPAGHETTI, VERMICELLI & NOODLES

FOULDS INC., pg. 427
GILSTER MARY LEE CORP., pg. 460
A. ZEREGAS SONS, INC., pg. 1217

2099 — FOOD PREPARATIONS, NEC

ADAMS EXTRACT CO., INC., pg. 16
ADAMS NATURAL PEANUT BUTTER—Agway, Inc., pg. 26
ALEX FOODS, INC., pg. 33
ALGOOD FOOD COMPANY, pg. 34
M. ALKALAY AGENCIES, LTD.—Newly Weds Foods Inc., pg. 804
J.W. ALLEN & COMPANY, pg. 36
ALLIED OLD ENGLISH, INC., pg. 38
AMERICAN NUT CO.—Clements Foods Co., pg. 255
ARROW INDUSTRIES, INC., pg. 85
AZTECA FOODS, INCORPORATED, pg. 105
BACHMAN COMPANY, pg. 108
BLEVINS CONCESSION SUPPLY CO., pg. 156
BLEVINS POPCORN—Agway, Inc., pg. 26
CALIENTE CHILI, INC.—William B. Reily & Co., Inc., pg. 923
CALYPSO FOODS—Agway, Inc., pg. 26
CASE-SWAYNE CO. INC., pg. 228
CELESTIAL SEASONINGS, pg. 231
CHIQUITA BRANDS INTERNATIONAL, INC.—American Financial Corporation, pg. 53
CLEMENTS FOODS CO., pg. 254
CLEMENTS NUT CO.—Clements Foods Co., pg. 255
CLEMENTS VINEGAR COMPANY—Clements Foods Co., pg. 255
JOHN COPES FOOD PRODUCTS, INC., pg. 284
CUMBERLAND PACKING CORP., pg. 304
CURTICE-BURNS FOODS, INC.—Agway, Inc., pg. 25
CUSTOM FOOD PRODUCTS INC.—Griffith Laboratories Worldwide, Inc., pg. 487
DEL MONTE FOODS, pg. 325
DELIMATIC REFRESHMENT SERVICES—Tom's Foods, pg. 1101
DIAMOND CRYSTAL SPECIALTY FOODS, INC., pg. 335
EMPIRE KOSHER POULTRY, INC., pg. 379
FLAVORITE LABORATORIES—A.M. Todd Company, pg. 1100
GAGE FOOD PRODUCTS COMPANY—Vincent Food Industries, Inc., pg. 1152
GEM, INCORPORATED, pg. 447
GLICO HARMONY FOODS CORPORATION, pg. 462
GRAVYMASTER INC., pg. 478
GRIFFITH COLOMBIA S.A.—Griffith Laboratories Worldwide, Inc., pg. 487
GRIFFITH LABORATORIES (H.K.) LTD.—Griffith Laboratories Worldwide, Inc., pg. 487
GRIFFITH LABORATORIES IBERIA S.A.—Griffith Laboratories Worldwide, Inc., pg. 487
GRIFFITH LABORATORIES IRELAND LIMITED—Griffith Laboratories Worldwide, Inc., pg. 487
GRIFFITH LABORATORIES ITALIA S.R.L.—Griffith Laboratories Worldwide, Inc., pg. 487
GRIFFITH LABORATORIES, K.K.—Griffith Laboratories Worldwide, Inc., pg. 487
GRIFFITH LABORATORIES LIMITED—Griffith Laboratories Worldwide, Inc., pg. 487
THE GRIFFITH LABORATORIES, LTD.—Griffith Laboratories Worldwide, Inc., pg. 487
GRIFFITH LABORATORIES (PHILS.) INC.—Griffith Laboratories Worldwide, Inc., pg. 488
GRIFFITH LABORATORIES PTY., LTD.—Griffith Laboratories Worldwide, Inc., pg. 488
N.V. GRIFFITH LABORATORIES S.A.—Griffith Laboratories Worldwide, Inc., pg. 488
GRIFFITH LABORATORIES WORLDWIDE, INC., pg. 487
GRIFFITH PANAMA S.A.—Griffith Laboratories Worldwide, Inc., pg. 488
S. GUMPERT CO., INC.—Rich Products Corp., pg. 932
HANOVER FOODS CORP.—Hanover Foods Corporation, pg. 506
HANOVER FOODS CORPORATION, pg. 506
HELLER SEASONINGS & INGREDIENTS, INC., pg. 526
HELMSLEY ENTERPRISES, INC., pg. 527
HELMSLEY-SPEAR INC.—Helmsley Enterprises, Inc., pg. 527
HULMAN & COMPANY, pg. 552
IROQUOIS POPCORN—Blevins Concession Supply Co., pg. 156
JFG COFFEE COMPANY—William B. Reily & Co., Inc., pg. 923
KANE-MILLER CORP., pg. 616
L. KARP & SONS, INC., pg. 617
KNOUSE FOODS INC., pg. 637
LA REINA, INC., pg. 649
LABORATORIES GRIFFITH DE MEXICO, S.A. DE C.V.—Griffith Laboratories Worldwide, Inc., pg. 488
LABORATORIOS GRIFFITH DE CENTRO AMERICA S.A.—Griffith Laboratories Worldwide, Inc., pg. 488
A.C. LEGG PACKING COMPANY, INC., pg. 666
LUCCA PACKING DIV., NALLEY'S FINE FOODS—Agway, Inc., pg. 25
LUZIANNE BLUE PLATE FOODS—William B. Reily & Co., Inc., pg. 923
MAKERS OF KAL, INC., pg. 702
MEER CORPORATION, pg. 736
DAVID MICHAEL & CO. INC., pg. 747
MICHAEL FOODS, INC., pg. 747
MORGAN FOOD PRODUCTS—Morgan Manufacturing Company, Inc., pg. 770
MORGAN MANUFACTURING COMPANY, INC., pg. 770
MY OWN MEALS, INC., pg. 779
NATIONAL FRUIT PRODUCT COMPANY, pg. 789
NATIONAL OATS CO.—Agway, Inc., pg. 25
NEWLY WEDS FOODS ASIA/PACIFIC—Newly Weds Foods Inc., pg. 804
NEWLY WEDS FOODS INC., pg. 804
NEWLY WEDS FOODS, INC.—Newly Weds Foods Inc., pg. 804
NEWLY WEDS FOODS, INC.—Newly Weds Foods Inc., pg. 804
NEWMAN'S OWN, INC., pg. 804
NORFOODS, INC., pg. 810
NUTRILITE PRODUCTS, INC.—Amway Corporation, pg. 70
OH BOY CORPORATION, pg. 822
OLD DUTCH FOODS, INC., pg. 823
OREGON FREEZE DRY, INC., pg. 829
PARADISE FRUIT COMPANY, INC., pg. 847
PHARMACAPS INC., pg. 866
PORTLAND FOOD PRODUCTS COMPANY, pg. 881
PREPCO, pg. 887
PRESTO FOOD PRODUCTS, INC., pg. 888
RHM INGREDIENTS, LTD.—Newly Weds Foods Inc., pg. 804
REDCO FOODS, INC., pg. 919
WILLIAM B. REILY & CO., INC., pg. 923
RICH PRODUCTS CORP., pg. 932
W. B. RODDENBERY COMPANY, INC., pg. 942
I. ROKEACH & SONS, INC., pg. 944
RUIZ FOOD PRODUCTS, INC., pg. 955
S&D COFFEE INC., pg. 959
SCHWAN'S SALES ENTERPRISES, pg. 980
SHADE PASTA, INC.—Norfoods, Inc., pg. 810
SNYDER'S OF HANOVER, INC., pg. 1015
SOKOL & COMPANY, pg. 1016
STAR FOOD PROCESSING, INC., pg. 1039
STEGNER FOOD PRODUCTS CO., pg. 1045
SUNDOWN VITAMIN CO., INC., pg. 1060
SUNNYLAND REFINING CO., INC.—Kane-Miller Corp., pg. 616
TLC BEATRICE INTERNATIONAL HOLDINGS INC., pg. 1073
TEEPAK, INC.—Hillside Capital, Inc., pg. 535
THOMPSON MEDICAL COMPANY, INC., pg. 1094
TOM'S DISTRIBUTING INC.—Tom's Foods, pg. 1101
TOM'S FOODS, pg. 1101
TOM'S SNAX CO.—Tom's Foods, pg. 1101
TROPIC ISLE—Agway, Inc., pg. 26
VENTRE PACKING COMPANY, INC., pg. 1147
VICTORIA PACKING CORPORATION, pg. 1149
WATKINS INCORPORATED, pg. 1167
WEST LYNN CREAMERY, INC.—Scangas Brothers Holdings, Inc., pg. 974
WHITFIELD FOODS, INC., pg. 1187
WILBUR CHOCOLATE CO., INC.—Cargill Inc., pg. 219
WILLIAMS FOODS INC., pg. 1191
THE WORNICK COMPANY, pg. 1203
WYANDOT INC., pg. 1205

2111 — CIGARETTES

NATIONAL FOOD STORES, INC. T/A KRAUSZER'S, pg. 788

2121 — CIGARS

CONSOLIDATED CIGAR CORPORATION, pg. 276
WALLY FRANK, LTD., pg. 429
HAVATAMPA INCORPORATED, pg. 517
LANE LIMITED, pg. 657
VILLAZON COMPANY INC., pg. 1152

2131 — TOBACCO (CHEWING & SMOKING) & SNUFF

ALLIED PRODUCTS—Consolidated Cigar Corporation, pg. 276
AUSTIN CAROLINA CO.—Austin Co., Inc., pg. 99
AUSTIN CO., INC., pg. 98
CIGAR SUPPLY CO.—Austin Co., Inc., pg. 99
CONSOLIDATED CIGAR CORPORATION, pg. 276
CONWOOD COMPANY L.P., pg. 281
WALLY FRANK, LTD., pg. 429
S. M. FRANK & CO., INC., pg. 429
LANE LIMITED, pg. 657
MULLINS LEAF TOBACCO CO.—Austin Co., Inc., pg. 99
SCOTT TOBACCO—Conwood Company L.P., pg. 282
TAYLOR BROS.—Conwood Company L.P., pg. 282

2141 — TOBACCO STEMMING & REDRYING

FENNER MANHEIM, pg. 406
T.S. RAGSDALE COMPANY, INCORPORATED, pg. 910

2211 — BROAD WOVEN FABRIC MILLS, COTTON

ABERDEEN MFG. CORPORATION—CC Industries, Inc., pg. 200
ADVENT INTERNATIONAL, pg. 21
AVONDALE FOREIGN SALES CORPORATION—Avondale Mills, Inc., pg. 103
AVONDALE MILLS FABRIC DIV.—Avondale Mills, Inc., pg. 103
AVONDALE MILLS, INC., pg. 103
BEACON MFG. CO., pg. 129
BLOOMSBURG MILLS INC., pg. 158
F.H. BONN COMPANY, pg. 164
CC INDUSTRIES, INC., pg. 199
CMI INDUSTRIES, INC., pg. 202
CAROLINA ABSORBENT COTTON CO.—Barnhardt Manufacturing Co., pg. 120
CAROLINA MILLS, INC., pg. 223
CYRUS CLARK CO., INC., pg. 253
CLINTON MILLS—CMI Industries, Inc., pg. 202
CLINTON MILLS INC.—CMI Industries, Inc., pg. 202
CLINTON MILLS SALES CO.—CMI Industries, Inc., pg. 202
COLLINS & AIKMAN GROUP INC., pg. 262
COLLINS & AIKMAN TEXTILE GROUP—Collins & Aikman Group Inc., pg. 262
CRAFTEX MILLS INC. OF PENNSYLVANIA, pg. 295
CROWN TEXTILE COMPANY, pg. 302
DAN RIVER DANVILLE MFG. DIV.—Dan River Inc., pg. 313
DAN RIVER INC., pg. 313
DORAN MILL CO.—Doran Textiles Inc., pg. 346
DORAN TEXTILES INC., pg. 346
DUNDEE MILLS, INC., pg. 352
EASTERN CANVAS PRODUCTS, INC., pg. 363
ELASTIC FABRICS OF AMERICA—CMI Industries, Inc., pg. 202
N. ERLANGER, BLUMGART & COMPANY, INC., pg. 387
FARLEY INDUSTRIES, pg. 399
GLEN RAVEN MILLS, INC., pg. 461
GLEN RAVEN MILLS, INC.-CUSTOM FABRICS DIVISION-EQUINOX PLANT—Glen Raven Mills, Inc., pg. 461
GLEN RAVEN MILLS, INC.-FILAMENT FABRICS DIVISION—Glen Raven Mills, Inc., pg. 461
GLENOIT MILLS, INC., pg. 462
GOLDING INDUSTRIES—Joseph, Littlejohn & Levy, pg. 607
GRANITEVILLE CO., pg. 476
GREENWOOD MILLS, INC., pg. 485
HOME INNOVATIONS BED FASHIONS—Home Innovations, Inc., pg. 541
INMAN MILLS, pg. 570
FRANK IX & SONS, INC., pg. 584
JPS TEXTILE GROUP, INC., pg. 586
JACKSON MILLS, INC., pg. 587
JOANNA—CC Industries, Inc., pg. 200
LESHNER MILLS, INC., pg. 668
W.S. LIBBEY COMPANY, pg. 674
MAYFAIR MILLS, INC., pg. 724
MISSION VALLEY MILLS, INC.—Farley Industries, pg. 400
MITCHELL CO.—Stonecutter Mills Corp., pg. 1051
MOUNT VERNON MILLS, INC.—R. B. Pamplin Corp., pg. 844
MOUNT VERNON MILLS, INC.—R. B. Pamplin Corp., pg. 844
MOUNT VERNON MILLS, INC., RIEGEL CONSUMER PRODUCTS DIV.—R. B. Pamplin Corp., pg. 844
MOUNT VERNON MILLS, INC., RIEGEL TEXTILE DIV.—R. B. Pamplin Corp., pg. 844
MOUNT VERNON MILLS, INC., RIEGEL TEXTILE DIV. (TRION)—R. B. Pamplin Corp., pg. 844
MOUNT VERNON MILLS, INC., WILLIAMSTON—R. B. Pamplin Corp., pg. 844
NTC APPAREL FABRICS DIVISION—NTC Group, pg. 781
NTC GROUP, pg. 781
NOEL-JOANNA, INC., pg. 808

PLAINS COTTON CO-OP ASSOCIATION, pg. 873
QST INDUSTRIES, INC., pg. 902
SAVOY DRAPERY DIV.—CC Industries, Inc., pg. 200
F. SCHUMACHER & CO., pg. 979
SPARTAN MILLS, pg. 1026
SPINNERIN YARN CO., INC., pg. 1031
STANDARD TEXTILE CO., INC., pg. 1037
STERN & STERN INDUSTRIES INC., pg. 1048
STEVENS HOME FASHIONS—Farley Industries, pg. 400
STONECUTTER MILLS CORP., pg. 1051
WALTON MONROE MILLS, INC., pg. 1162
WEST POINT-PEPPERELL, INC.—Farley Industries, pg. 400
FRANK W. WINNE & SON, INC., pg. 1196

2221 — BROAD WOVEN FABRIC MILLS, MAN-MADE FIBER & SILK

ACME MILLS CO. INC., pg. 13
APEX MILLS CORPORATION, pg. 78
ASHWORTH BROS., INC., pg. 88
BEACON MFG. CO., pg. 129
BLOOMSBURG MILLS INC., pg. 158
BLUMENTHAL PRINT WORKS, INC., pg. 161
COLLINS & AIKMAN GROUP INC., pg. 262
COPLAND FABRICS, INC., pg. 284
CRAFTEX MILLS INC. OF PENNSYLVANIA, pg. 295
DAN RIVER DANVILLE MFG. DIV.—Dan River Inc., pg. 313
DAN RIVER INC., pg. 313
DECORATIVE FABRICS - MASTERCRAFT—Collins & Aikman Group Inc., pg. 262
DORAN TEXTILES INC., pg. 346
FARLEY INDUSTRIES, pg. 399
GLEN RAVEN MILLS, INC., pg. 461
GLEN RAVEN MILLS, INC.-FILAMENT FABRICS DIVISION—Glen Raven Mills, Inc., pg. 461
GREENWOOD MILLS, INC., pg. 485
HOME INNOVATIONS BED FASHIONS—Home Innovations, Inc., pg. 541
JPS AUTOMOTIVE—JPS Textile Group, Inc., pg. 586
JPS CONVERTER & INDUSTRIAL CORP.—JPS Textile Group, Inc., pg. 586
JPS TEXTILE GROUP, INC., pg. 586
JACKSON MILLS, INC., pg. 587
KEARNEY-WESTERN POWER PRODUCTS, INC.—The Dyson-Kissner-Moran Corporation, pg. 357
LOUISVILLE BEDDING COMPANY, pg. 684
MALDEN MILLS INDUSTRIES, INC., pg. 702
J.B. MARTIN COMPANY, pg. 715
MAYFAIR MILLS, INC., pg. 724
MILLIKEN & CO., INC., pg. 755
MISSION VALLEY MILLS, INC.—Farley Industries, pg. 400
MITCHELL CO.—Stonecutter Mills Corp., pg. 1051
MOUNT VERNON MILLS, INC., LAFRANCE INDUSTRIES—R. B. Pamplin Corp., pg. 844
MOUNT VERNON MILLS, INC., TALLASSEE, AL—R. B. Pamplin Corp., pg. 844
NTC APPAREL FABRICS DIVISION—NTC Group, pg. 781
NTC GROUP, pg. 781
QUAKER FABRIC CORPORATION, pg. 903
ROOT CORPORATION, pg. 946
SCALAMANDRE, INC., pg. 974
SCHNEIDER MILLS, INC., pg. 977
STEVENS HOME FASHIONS—Farley Industries, pg. 400
STONECUTTER MILLS CORP., pg. 1051
TETKO, INC., pg. 1089
WEST POINT-PEPPERELL, INC.—Farley Industries, pg. 400

2231 — BROAD WOVEN FABRIC MILLS, WOOL (INCLUDING DYEING & FINISHING)

AMANA SOCIETY, pg. 46
AMERBELLE CORPORATION, pg. 47
BEACON MFG. CO., pg. 129
BELMONT DYERS COMPANY—Meridian Industries, Inc., pg. 740
CAROLINA MILLS, INC., pg. 223
CENTRAL/SHIPPEE, INC., pg. 234
CHATHAM MANUFACTURING COMPANY—CMI Industries, Inc., pg. 202
CHATHAM SMITH CORP.—CMI Industries, Inc., pg. 202
COLLINS & AIKMAN TEXTILE GROUP—Collins & Aikman Group Inc., pg. 262
CRAFTEX MILLS INC. OF PENNSYLVANIA, pg. 295
DECORATIVE FABRICS - CAVEL—Collins & Aikman Group Inc., pg. 262
DOWN PRODUCTS DIV.—Woolrich, Inc., pg. 1201
FARIBAULT WOOLEN MILL CO., pg. 399
THE FELTERS COMPANY, pg. 406
FORSTMANN & COMPANY, INC., pg. 424
GLEN RAVEN MILLS, INC.-CUSTOM FABRICS DIVISION-EQUINOX PLANT—Glen Raven Mills, Inc., pg. 461
GLEN RAVEN MILLS, INC.-CUSTOM FABRICS DIVISION-EQUINOX FINISHING PLANT—Glen Raven Mills, Inc., pg. 461
GLEN RAVEN MILLS, INC.-GLENSPUN DIVISION—Glen Raven Mills, Inc., pg. 461
GLEN RAVEN MILLS, INC.-PARK AVE. FINISHING DIVISION—Glen Raven Mills, Inc., pg. 461
GLENOIT MILLS, INC., pg. 462
GREEFF FABRICS—Collins & Aikman Group Inc., pg. 262
GREENWOOD MILLS, INC., pg. 485
JOAN FABRICS CORP., pg. 594
MERIDIAN INDUSTRIES, INC., pg. 740
MILLIKEN & CO., INC., pg. 755
MILLIKEN FINE GOODS DIV.—Milliken & Co., Inc., pg. 755
MILLIKEN FINISHED APPAREL DIV.—Milliken & Co., Inc., pg. 755
MILLIKEN INDUSTRIAL DIV.—Milliken & Co., Inc., pg. 755
NTC APPAREL FABRICS DIVISION—NTC Group, pg. 781
PENDLETON WOOLEN MILLS, INC., pg. 857
SCALAMANDRE, INC., pg. 974
UNITED PIECE DYE WORKS, LP, pg. 1134
WOOL FILTERS INTL.—Farley Industries, pg. 401
WOOLCAN—Woolrich, Inc., pg. 1201
WOOLKONG LTD.—Woolrich, Inc., pg. 1201
WOOLRICH, INC., pg. 1201

2241 — NARROW FABRICS & OTHER SMALLWARES MILLS: COTTON, WOOL, SILK, & MAN-MADE FIBER

AMERICAN FABRICS COMPANY, pg. 51
BENTLEY-HARRIS MANUFACTURING CO., pg. 140
DELAWARE RIBBON MANUFACTURERS, INC., pg. 326
EAGLE BUTTON CO., INC., pg. 362
EASTERN CANVAS PRODUCTS, INC., pg. 363
FARLEY INDUSTRIES, pg. 399
GLENOIT MILLS, INC., pg. 462
GLOBE INTERNATIONAL INC., pg. 464
JPS ELASTOMERICS CORP.—JPS Textile Group, Inc., pg. 586
LESHNER MILLS. INC., pg. 668
F.G. MONTABERT, pg. 766
MOORE COMPANY, pg. 768
MOUNT VERNON MILLS, INC.—R. B. Pamplin Corp., pg. 844
MOUNT VERNON MILLS, INC., RIEGEL TEXTILE DIV. (ALTO)—R. B. Pamplin Corp., pg. 844
NARROW FABRIC INDUSTRIES, INC., pg. 783
DAVID L. PEISTER CO., INC., pg. 856
RIBBON NARROW FABRIC COMPANY, pg. 931
TRIMTEX CO. INC., pg. 1113
WEST POINT-PEPPERELL, INC.—Farley Industries, pg. 400
WM. E. WRIGHT LIMITED PARTNERSHIP, pg. 1205

2251 — WOMEN'S FULL-LENGTH & KNEE-LENGTH HOSIERY, EXCEPT SOCKS

ADMIRATION HOSIERY MILLS, INC.—Highland Mills Inc., pg. 534
CAMP HOSIERY—Farley Industries, pg. 400
GLEN RAVEN MILLS, INC., pg. 461
GLEN RAVEN MILLS, INC.-CONSUMER PRODUCTS DIVISION—Glen Raven Mills, Inc., pg. 461
GLEN RAVEN MILLS, INC.-NORLINA PLANT—Glen Raven Mills, Inc., pg. 461
GLEN RAVEN MILLS, INC.-TEXTURED YARN GROUP-NORLINA DIVISION—Glen Raven Mills, Inc., pg. 461
HIGHLAND MILLS INC., pg. 534
HOLT HOSIERY MILLS, INC., pg. 541
ITHACA INDUSTRIES INC., pg. 582
KAYSER-ROTH CORPORATION—Collins & Aikman Group Inc., pg. 263
KAYSER-ROTH HOSIERY, INC.—Collins & Aikman Group Inc., pg. 262
MAYER BERKSHIRE CORPORATION, pg. 724
SHEER HOSIERY DIV.—Collins & Aikman Group Inc., pg. 263
SLANE HOSIERY MILLS, INC., pg. 1010
STERLING HOSIERY CO.—Heyman Corporation, pg. 532
TRIMFIT COMPANY LIMITED—Trimfit, Inc., pg. 1113
TRIMFIT, INC., pg. 1113
UNION UNDERWEAR CO., INC.—Farley Industries, pg. 400

2252 — HOSIERY, NEC

ADMIRATION HOSIERY MILLS, INC.—Highland Mills Inc., pg. 534
CAMP HOSIERY—Farley Industries, pg. 400
CAMP HOSIERY—Farley Industries, pg. 400
CHIPMAN-UNION, INC., pg. 248
CLAYSON KNITTING CO. INC., pg. 253
FARLEY INDUSTRIES, pg. 399
HIGHLAND MILLS INC., pg. 534
ITHACA INDUSTRIES INC., pg. 582
KAYSER-ROTH CORPORATION—Collins & Aikman Group Inc., pg. 263
KAYSER-ROTH HOSIERY, INC.—Collins & Aikman Group Inc., pg. 262
MAUNEY HOSIERY MILLS, INC., pg. 722
MAYER BERKSHIRE CORPORATION, pg. 724
RELIABLE KNITTING WORKS, pg. 924
RENFRO CORP., pg. 926
SLANE HOSIERY MILLS, INC., pg. 1010
TRIMFIT COMPANY LIMITED—Trimfit, Inc., pg. 1113
TRIMFIT, INC., pg. 1113
UNION UNDERWEAR CO., INC.—Farley Industries, pg. 400
WIGWAM MILLS, INC., pg. 1189

2253 — KNIT OUTERWEAR MILLS

AMERICAN ARGO CORP.—Coordinated Apparel, Inc., pg. 283
ANDMORE SPORTSWEAR CORPORATION, pg. 74
APPAREL INDUSTRIES, INC., pg. 78
BONHOMME SHIRTMAKERS, LTD., pg. 164
DAVID BRETT, INC., pg. 174
CALABASH LTD.—Doe Spun, Inc., pg. 343
THE WILLIAM CARTER COMPANY, pg. 226
COVINGTON INDUSTRIES, pg. 290
DOE SPUN, INC., pg. 343
ECHO DESIGN GROUP, INC., pg. 365
THE FINALS, LTD.—Andmore Sportswear Corporation, pg. 74
FOX-KNAPP INC., pg. 427
THE GRANDOE CORPORATION, pg. 476
GURNEY INDUSTRIES INC., pg. 495
HALPER BROS.—Reliable Knitting Works, pg. 925
HARPER SHIRT COMPANY—Harper Industries, Inc., pg. 510
JOHNSTOWN KNITTING MILL CO., pg. 602
KAYSER-ROTH CORPORATION—Collins & Aikman Group Inc., pg. 263
CHARLES KOMAR & SONS, INC., pg. 641
TONY LAMBERT COMPANY, pg. 652
LONDONTOWN CORPORATION—Londontown Holdings Corporation, pg. 682
LONDONTOWN HOLDINGS CORPORATION, pg. 681
MALDEN MILLS INDUSTRIES, INC., pg. 702
PENTHOUSE KNITTING MILLS—Reliable Knitting Works, pg. 925
POCONO KNITS, INC.—Jack Young Associates, pg. 1209
RELIABLE KNITTING WORKS, pg. 924
ROFFE, INC., pg. 943
SCHOOL APPAREL, INC., pg. 978
WHALING INDUSTRIES, INC., pg. 1183
WHALING MANUFACTURING COMPANY, INC.—Whaling Industries, Inc., pg. 1183
WIGWAM MILLS, INC., pg. 1189
WINONA KNITTING MILLS, INC., pg. 1196
JACK YOUNG ASSOCIATES, pg. 1209
YOUNG STUFF APPAREL GROUP, INC., pg. 1214

2254 — KNIT UNDERWEAR & NIGHTWEAR MILLS

JENNIFER DALE, INC., pg. 592
JOCKEY INTERNATIONAL, INC., pg. 595
JOHNSTOWN KNITTING MILL CO., pg. 602
CHARLES KOMAR & SONS, INC., pg. 641
MAYER BERKSHIRE CORPORATION, pg. 724
SPARTAN MILLS, pg. 1026

2257 — CIRCULAR KNIT FABRIC MILLS

AMERICAN FABRICS COMPANY, pg. 51
BRITTANY DYEING & PRINTING CORPORATION, pg. 177
COLLINS & AIKMAN GROUP INC., pg. 262
COLLINS & AIKMAN TEXTILE GROUP—Collins & Aikman Group Inc., pg. 262
GLENOIT MILLS, INC., pg. 462
GURNEY INDUSTRIES INC., pg. 495
LORBER INDUSTRIES OF CALIFORNIA, pg. 683

2258 — LACE & WARP KNIT FABRIC MILLS

AMERICAN FABRICS COMPANY, pg. 51
APEX MILLS CORPORATION, pg. 78
CMI INDUSTRIES, INC., pg. 202
CLINTON MILLS—CMI Industries, Inc., pg. 202
CLINTON MILLS INC.—CMI Industries, Inc., pg. 202
CLINTON MILLS SALES CO.—CMI Industries, Inc., pg. 202
COLLINS & AIKMAN GROUP INC., pg. 262
COLLINS & AIKMAN TEXTILE GROUP—Collins & Aikman Group Inc., pg. 262
ELASTIC FABRICS OF AMERICA—CMI Industries, Inc., pg. 202
MOORE COMPANY, pg. 768
SPARTAN MILLS, pg. 1026
WESTCHESTER LACE, INC., pg. 1178

2259 — KNITTING MILLS, NEC

B.T.F. CORPORATION, pg. 107
CAROLINA GLOVE CO., pg. 223
JOMAC, INC., pg. 602

2261 — FINISHERS OF BROAD WOVEN FABRICS OF COTTON

AMERBELLE CORPORATION, pg. 47
AMERICAN FAST PRINT, LIMITED, pg. 52
AMERICAN MARKETING WORKS & INTERNATIONAL CORPORATION, pg. 58
R.A. BRIGGS & CO.—Home Innovations, Inc., pg. 541
BRITTANY DYEING & PRINTING CORPORATION, pg. 177
CLAREMONT FLOCK CORPORATION, pg. 251
CRANSTON PRINT WORKS COMPANY, pg. 296
DEITSCH PLASTICS COMPANY, pg. 325
FACEMATE CORPORATION, pg. 396
FACEMATE POND LILT GREAT FALLS—Facemate Corporation, pg. 396
HANES COMPANIES, INC., pg. 505
THE HARODITE FINISHING COMPANY INC., pg. 510
HOLOUBEK INC., pg. 540
LORBER INDUSTRIES OF CALIFORNIA, pg. 683
MERIDIAN INDUSTRIES, INC., pg. 740
MITCHELL CO.—Stonecutter Mills Corp., pg. 1051
PEELERS RUG COMPANY, INC., pg. 855
PRIORITY FINISHING CORP.—The Cherokee Group, pg. 243
SANTEE PRINT WORKS, INC., pg. 970
SCALAMANDRE, INC., pg. 974
STONECUTTER MILLS CORP., pg. 1051
UNITED PIECE DYE WORKS, LP, pg. 1134
VERTIPILE—Claremont Flock Corporation, pg. 251
WESTGATE FABRICS, INC., pg. 1182

2262 — FINISHERS OF BROAD WOVEN FABRICS OF MAN-MADE FIBER & SILK

AMERBELLE CORPORATION, pg. 47
BLUMENTHAL PRINT WORKS, INC., pg. 161
CLAREMONT FLOCK CORPORATION, pg. 251
COLLINS & AIKMAN GROUP INC., pg. 262
CRANSTON PRINT WORKS COMPANY, pg. 296

FACEMATE CORPORATION, pg. 396
FACEMATE POND LILT GREAT FALLS—Facemate Corporation, pg. 396
GLEN RAVEN MILLS, INC., pg. 461
HAMPTON PRINT WORKS, INC., pg. 504
HANES COMPANIES, INC., pg. 505
THE HARODITE FINISHING COMPANY INC., pg. 510
LORBER INDUSTRIES OF CALIFORNIA, pg. 683
MITCHELL CO.—Stonecutter Mills Corp., pg. 1051
PRIORITY FINISHING CORP.—The Cherokee Group, pg. 243
STEVENS HOME FASHIONS—Farley Industries, pg. 400
STONECUTTER MILLS CORP., pg. 1051
UNITED PIECE DYE WORKS, LP, pg. 1134
VERTIPILE—Claremont Flock Corporation, pg. 251

2269 — FINISHERS OF TEXTILES, NEC

BEACON MFG. CO., pg. 129
COLLINS & AIKMAN GROUP INC., pg. 262
GENERRA SPORTSWEAR (HONG KONG) LTD.—Generra Sportswear Company, Inc., pg. 451
GLEN RAVEN MILLS, INC., pg. 461
MOUNT VERNON MILLS, INC.—R. B. Pamplin Corp., pg. 844
MOUNT VERNON MILLS, INC., RIEGEL TEXTILE DIV.—R. B. Pamplin Corp., pg. 844
MOUNT VERNON MILLS, INC., WOODRUFF—R. B. Pamplin Corp., pg. 845
SCALAMANDRE, INC., pg. 974
SPARTAN MILLS, pg. 1026
STOWE-PHARR MILLS, INC., pg. 1052

2273 — CARPETS & RUGS

THE AKRO CORPORATION—Collins & Aikman Group Inc., pg. 262
ALADDIN MILLS INC., pg. 29
AMERICAN RUG CRAFTSMEN INC., pg. 60
BENTLEY MILLS, INC., pg. 140
C&A FLOOR COVERINGS—Collins & Aikman Group Inc., pg. 262
C&C ASSOCIATES—Couristan Inc., pg. 290
COLLINS & AIKMAN GROUP INC., pg. 262
COLLINS & AIKMAN TEXTILE GROUP—Collins & Aikman Group Inc., pg. 262
CONQUEST CARPET MILLS, pg. 276
COURI CARPET CO.—Couristan Inc., pg. 290
COURI-MURAD & CO.—Couristan Inc., pg. 290
COURISTAN INC., pg. 290
DAN RIVER INC., pg. 313
DECORATIVE FABRICS - CAVEL—Collins & Aikman Group Inc., pg. 262
FOCUS CARPET CO.—21 International Holdings, Inc., pg. 1121
GENERAL FELT INDUSTRIES, INC.—21 International Holdings, Inc., pg. 1121
HOLLYTEX CARPET MILLS, INC., pg. 540
HOLLYTEX CARPET MILLS, INC.—Hollytex Carpet Mills, Inc., pg. 540
THE MAGEE CARPET COMPANY, pg. 700
MASLAND INDUSTRIES, pg. 717
MILLIKEN & CO., INC., pg. 755
MITCHELL CORPORATION OF OWOSSO, pg. 761
PEELERS RUG COMPANY, INC., pg. 855
RHS, pg. 907
SCALAMANDRE, INC., pg. 974
STEVENS HOME FASHIONS—Farley Industries, pg. 400
U.S. CARPET CO.—Couristan Inc., pg. 290
WORLD CARPETS, INC., pg. 1202
WUNDA WEVE CARPET CO., pg. 1205
WUNDA WEVE CARPET YARN PLANT—Wunda Weve Carpet Co., pg. 1205

2281 — YARN SPINNING MILLS: COTTON, MAN-MADE FIBERS, SILK, WOOL, MOHAIR & ANIMAL FIBERS

AMICALE INDUSTRIES, INC., pg. 66
AVONDALE FOREIGN SALES CORPORATION—Avondale Mills, Inc., pg. 103
AVONDALE MILLS, INC., pg. 103
AVONDALE MILLS YARN DIV.—Avondale Mills, Inc., pg. 103
BEACON MFG. CO., pg. 129
THE BIBB COMPANY-BRUCKNELL PLANT—NTC Group, pg. 781
THE BIBB COMPANY-ROANOKE RAPIDS PLANT—NTC Group, pg. 781
THE BIBB COMPANY-WHITE HORSE RD. PLANT—NTC Group, pg. 781
CMI INDUSTRIES, INC., pg. 202
CAROLINA MILLS, INC., pg. 223
CHERAW YARN MILLS, INC., pg. 242
CLINTON MILLS—CMI Industries, Inc., pg. 202
CLINTON MILLS INC.—CMI Industries, Inc., pg. 202
CLINTON MILLS SALES CO.—CMI Industries, Inc., pg. 202
COLLINS & AIKMAN GROUP INC., pg. 262
COLLINS & AIKMAN TEXTILE GROUP—Collins & Aikman Group Inc., pg. 262
DAN RIVER DANVILLE MFG. DIV.—Dan River Inc., pg. 313
DELMONT DIV.—Parkdale Mills, pg. 849
ELASTIC FABRICS OF AMERICA—CMI Industries, Inc., pg. 202
GLEN RAVEN MILLS, INC., pg. 461
GLEN RAVEN MILLS, INC.-KINSTON PLANT—Glen Raven Mills, Inc., pg. 461
GLEN RAVEN MILLS, INC.-GLEN TOUCH PLANT—Glen Raven Mills, Inc., pg. 461
GLEN RAVEN MILLS, INC.-TEXTURED YARN GROUP-GLEN TOUCH DIVISION—Glen Raven Mills, Inc., pg. 461
GLEN RAVEN MILLS, INC.-ULTRASPUN PLANT—Glen Raven Mills, Inc., pg. 461
JOHN H. GRAHAM & CO., INC., pg. 475
HARRIET & HENDERSON YARNS, INC., pg. 511
JPS CONVERTER & INDUSTRIAL CORP.—JPS Textile Group, Inc., pg. 586
JPS CARPET CORP.—JPS Textile Group, Inc., pg. 586
THE KENT MANUFACTURING CO., pg. 623
W.S. LIBBEY COMPANY, pg. 674
LORBER INDUSTRIES OF CALIFORNIA, pg. 683
MITCHELL CO.—Stonecutter Mills Corp., pg. 1051
MOUNT VERNON MILLS, INC., CLARKTON, NC—R. B. Pamplin Corp., pg. 844
MOUNT VERNON MILLS, INC., RIEGEL TEXTILE DIV. (TRION)—R. B. Pamplin Corp., pg. 844
MOUNT VERNON MILLS, INC., WOODRUFF—R. B. Pamplin Corp., pg. 845
NTC CONSUMER PRODUCTS DIV.—NTC Group, pg. 781
NTC ENGINEERED PRODUCTS DIV.—NTC Group, pg. 781
NTC GROUP, pg. 781
NATIONAL SPINNING CO., INC., pg. 793
NATIONAL SPINNING CO.—National Spinning Co., Inc., pg. 793
NATIONAL SPINNING CO.—National Spinning Co., Inc., pg. 793
NATIONAL SPINNING CO.—National Spinning Co., Inc., pg. 793
NATIONAL SPINNING CO.—National Spinning Co., Inc., pg. 793
NATIONAL YARN CRAFTS—National Spinning Co., Inc., pg. 793
THE OSTERNECK CO. INC., pg. 831
PALMETTO SPINNING CORP., pg. 844
PARKDALE MILLS, pg. 849
SCT YARNS, INC., pg. 961
SHUFORD MILLS, INC., pg. 1001
STEVENS HOME FASHIONS—Farley Industries, pg. 400
STONECUTTER MILLS CORP., pg. 1051
STOWE-PHARR MILLS, INC., pg. 1052
TUSCARORA YARNS INC., pg. 1120
WALTON MONROE MILLS, INC., pg. 1162

2282 — YARN TEXTURIZING, THROWING, TWISTING & WINDING MILLS

C&A YARN DIVISION—Collins & Aikman Group Inc., pg. 262
COLLINS & AIKMAN GROUP INC., pg. 262
COLLINS & AIKMAN TEXTILE GROUP—Collins & Aikman Group Inc., pg. 262
CULVER TEXTILE CORPORATION, pg. 304
THE KENT MANUFACTURING CO., pg. 623
LEON-FERENBACH COMPANY, pg. 667
MOUNT VERNON MILLS, INC., MOUNT VERNON FORMING FABRICS—R. B. Pamplin Corp., pg. 844
PALMETTO SPINNING CORP., pg. 844

2284 — THREAD MILLS

CAROLINA MAIDEN CORP.—Carolina Mills, Inc., pg. 223
LUDLOW TEXTILES CO., INC., pg. 686
SCT YARNS, INC., pg. 961

2295 — COATED FABRICS, NOT RUBBERIZED

ACME CHEMICALS & INSULATION CO.—Insulating Materials, Inc., pg. 572
ALDAN RUBBER CO., pg. 32
ALPHA ASSOCIATES, INC., pg. 43
AMERBELLE CORPORATION, pg. 47
CC INDUSTRIES, INC., pg. 199
COLLINS & AIKMAN GROUP INC., pg. 262
COOLEY, INC., pg. 282
DURO-LAST ROOFING, INC., pg. 355
FINDLAY INDUSTRIES, INC., pg. 410
GOULD PACKAGING, INC., pg. 473
THE GRAVER CHEMICAL DIV.—The Marmon Group, Inc., pg. 712
INDUSTRIAL COATINGS GROUP, INC., pg. 566
INTERPLAST UNIVERSAL INDUSTRIES, INC., pg. 579
JOANNA—CC Industries, Inc., pg. 200
J. JOSEPHSON, INC., pg. 607
W.S. LIBBEY COMPANY, pg. 674
LUDLOW COMPOSITES CORPORATION, pg. 686
MERIDIAN INDUSTRIES, INC., pg. 740
NORWOOD INDUSTRIES, INC.—Seton Company, pg. 993
THE OSTERNECK CO. INC., pg. 831
RAINFAIR, INC., pg. 910
SCHNELLER, INC., pg. 977
SETON COMPANY, pg. 993
THE STIFFEL COMPANY, pg. 1049
TEKRA CORPORATION, pg. 1084

2296 — TIRE CORD & FABRIC

STERN & STERN INDUSTRIES INC., pg. 1048

2297 — NONWOVEN FABRICS

ALDINE TECHNOLOGIES, pg. 33
BEACON MFG. CO., pg. 129
FARLEY INDUSTRIES, pg. 399
FIRET, B.V.—Farley Industries, pg. 400
FORT HOWARD CORPORATION, pg. 425
FORT HOWARD PAPER CORPORATION—Fort Howard Corporation, pg. 425
FORT HOWARD PAPER CORPORATION—Fort Howard Corporation, pg. 425
FOSS MANUFACTURING COMPANY INCORPORATED, pg. 426
GLENOIT MILLS, INC., pg. 462
W.S. LIBBEY COMPANY, pg. 674
R. B. PAMPLIN CORP., pg. 844
RIBBON NARROW FABRIC COMPANY, pg. 931
TRI-CHEM, INC., pg. 1110
TROY MILLS, INC., pg. 1116
WEST POINT-PEPPERELL, INC.—Farley Industries, pg. 400

2298 — CORDAGE & TWINE

ANCRA CORPORATION, pg. 72
COLUMBIAN ROPE COMPANY, pg. 266
COLUMBUS MILLS, INC., pg. 267
CORTLAND LINE CO., INC., pg. 287
CROWE ROPE COMPANY, pg. 301
ELFIN INDUSTRIES, LTD.—Ancra Corporation, pg. 72
LOTUS CARPET DIVISION—Columbus Mills, Inc., pg. 267
LUDLOW TEXTILES CO., INC., pg. 686
SHUFORD MILLS, INC., pg. 1001
TCG FIBERS, PHILIPPINES—Columbian Rope Company, pg. 266
UNIVERSAL COOPERATIVES, INC., pg. 1138

2299 — TEXTILE GOODS, NEC

ACME MILLS CO. INC., pg. 13
ANGLO FABRICS COMPANY, INC., pg. 75
BARNHARDT MANUFACTURING CO., pg. 120
F.H. BONN COMPANY, pg. 164
BUCILLA CORPORATION, pg. 185
WM. T. BURNETT & CO., INC., pg. 191
BURTON-DIXIE OF BLACKSBURG INC.—CC Industries, Inc., pg. 200
CAROLINA MILLS, INC., pg. 223
E. R. CARPENTER CO., pg. 224
COLLINS & AIKMAN TEXTILE GROUP—Collins & Aikman Group Inc., pg. 262
DAN RIVER DANVILLE MFG. DIV.—Dan River Inc., pg. 313
DAN RIVER INC.-HOME FURNISHINGS & RELATED PRODS., DIV. I—Dan River Inc., pg. 313
C.R. DANIELS, INC., pg. 314
EUREKA MANUFACTURING CO., INC.—Reed & Barton Corporation, pg. 920
FACEMATE CORPORATION, pg. 396
FINDLAY INDUSTRIES, INC., pg. 410
GLENOIT MILLS, INC., pg. 462
HOLLYTEX—21 International Holdings, Inc., pg. 1121
LESHNER MILLS. INC., pg. 668
MELLON CORPORATION, pg. 738
MILLIKEN & CO., INC., pg. 755
MOUNT VERNON DRYER FABRICS—R. B. Pamplin Corp., pg. 845
NASHVILLE TEXTILE CORP.—House of Ronnie, Inc., pg. 546
THE ORR FELT COMPANY, pg. 830
OUIMET CORP.—Ouimet Industries, pg. 831
OUIMET INDUSTRIES, pg. 831
SOUTHERN MILLS, INC., pg. 1021
TROY MILLS, INC., pg. 1116
WAYN-TEX INC., pg. 1169

2311 — MEN'S & BOYS' SUITS, COATS & OVERCOATS

AFTER SIX ACCESS—After Six, Incorporated, pg. 24
AFTER SIX, INCORPORATED, pg. 24
AMERICAN UNIFORM CO.—Steiner Corporation, pg. 1045
ARNAV INDUSTRIES, INC., pg. 84
STANLEY BLACKER, INC., pg. 155
BROOKHURST, INC., pg. 179
ELDER MANUFACTURING COMPANY, pg. 373
THE ENRO SHIRT COMPANY, INC.—The Apparel Group, Ltd., pg. 78
ESSKAY MANUFACTURING CO., pg. 389
GORDON & FERGUSON OF DELAWARE, INC., pg. 471
HAGGAR APPAREL COMPANY, pg. 499
HARDWICK CLOTHES INC., pg. 508
HARVE BENARD LTD. MANUFACTURING, pg. 514
TOM JAMES COMPANY, pg. 589
LONDONTOWN CORPORATION—Londontown Holdings Corporation, pg. 682
LONDONTOWN HOLDINGS CORPORATION, pg. 681
PIERRE CARDIN FORMAL WEAR—West Mill Clothes, Inc., pg. 1177
JOS. J. PIETRAFESA CO., INC., pg. 870
PINCUS BROS., INC., pg. 870
POLO/RALPH LAUREN CORPORATION, pg. 879
REIDBORD BROS., INC., pg. 923
REMINGTON APPAREL, INC., pg. 926
RIVERSIDE MANUFACTURING CO., pg. 937
SCHOTT BROTHERS, INC., pg. 978
SEMINOLE MANUFACTURING COMPANY, pg. 989
SHEPARD CLOTHING COMPANY, pg. 997
STANDARD TEXTILE CO., INC., pg. 1037
TARGET SPORTSWEAR, INC., pg. 1079
WEST MILL CLOTHES, H.M.C. DIV.—West Mill Clothes, Inc., pg. 1177
WEST MILL CLOTHES, INC., pg. 1177
Z. CAVARICCI INC., pg. 1215

2321 — MEN'S & BOYS' SHIRTS, EXCEPT WORK SHIRTS

AMERICAN MARKETING INDUSTRIES, INC., pg. 58
THE APPAREL GROUP, LTD., pg. 78
BLOCK INDUSTRIES, INC., pg. 157
BON JOUR INTERNATIONAL LTD., pg. 164

BONHOMME SHIRTMAKERS, LTD., pg. 164
CHEROKEE APPAREL CORP.—The Cherokee Group, pg. 243
THE CHEROKEE GROUP, pg. 243
CODI INTERNATIONAL B.V.—Farley Industries, pg. 400
COM CORP FACTORS, INC.—Kennington Ltd., Inc., pg. 623
H. COTLER COMPANY, pg. 288
COVINGTON INDUSTRIES, pg. 290
CUSTOM SHOP SHIRTMAKERS INC., pg. 306
DOTHAN UNDERWEAR—Host Apparel, Inc., pg. 545
ELBECO INCORPORATED, pg. 372
ELDER MANUFACTURING COMPANY, pg. 373
THE ENRO SHIRT COMPANY, INC.—The Apparel Group, Ltd., pg. 78
M. FINE & SONS MANUFACTURING CO., INC., pg. 411
FOX-KNAPP INC., pg. 427
GREECO BROTHERS, INC., pg. 483
HARDWICK CLOTHES INC., pg. 508
HARPER INDUSTRIES, INC., pg. 510
THE HARWOOD COMPANIES, INC., pg. 515
HOLOUBEK INC., pg. 540
KARSTEN MANUFACTURING CORPORATION, pg. 617
KENNINGTON LTD., INC., pg. 623
KING LOUIE INTERNATIONAL, INC., pg. 631
KLEAR KNIT INC., pg. 634
CALVIN KLEIN, INC., pg. 635
CALVIN KLEIN SPORT—Calvin Klein, Inc., pg. 635
KNAPP SHOES INC., pg. 636
KOBRA INTERNATIONAL LTD, pg. 638
LSJ SPORTSWEAR INC.—Merchant Capital Group Ltd, pg. 739
MENSWEAR DIV.—Levi Strauss & Co., pg. 670
MERCHANT CAPITAL GROUP LTD, pg. 739
MORLEY SHIRT COMPANY—Custom Shop Shirtmakers Inc., pg. 306
PUBLIX GROUP, pg. 898
RAM GOLF CORPORATION, pg. 910
REMINGTON APPAREL, INC., pg. 926
RIKLIS FAMILY CORPORATION, pg. 934
RIVERSIDE MANUFACTURING CO., pg. 937
SEATTLE PACIFIC INDUSTRIES, INC., pg. 986
STANLEIGH INTERNATIONAL, INC.—Kennington Ltd., Inc., pg. 623
SWELL-WEAR, INC., pg. 1067
WEMCO, INC., pg. 1176
WEST MILL CLOTHES, TUXACCO ACCESSORIES DIV.—West Mill Clothes, Inc., pg. 1177

2322 — MEN'S & BOYS' UNDERWEAR & NIGHTWEAR

AMERICAN MARKETING INDUSTRIES, INC., pg. 58
ANIMAL FAIR—Guy Schoenecker, Inc., pg. 978
BVD LICENSING CORPORATION—Farley Industries, pg. 400
THE WILLIAM CARTER COMPANY, pg. 226
THE CHEROKEE GROUP, pg. 243
DOTHAN UNDERWEAR—Host Apparel, Inc., pg. 545
ELDER MANUFACTURING COMPANY, pg. 373
FARLEY INDUSTRIES, pg. 399
FRUIT OF THE LOOM—Farley Industries, pg. 400
HANDEL & COMPANY, HANTEX MILLS—Handel & Company, Inc., pg. 504
HANDEL & COMPANY, INC., pg. 504
THE HARWOOD COMPANIES, INC., pg. 515
HOST APPAREL, INC., pg. 545
JOCKEY INTERNATIONAL, INC., pg. 595
CALVIN KLEIN SPORT—Calvin Klein, Inc., pg. 635
KOMBI, LTD., pg. 641
MERIDIAN MFG. CO., INC.—Roytex, Inc., pg. 953
PAJAMA CRAFT, INC.—Host Apparel, Inc., pg. 545
REMINGTON APPAREL, INC., pg. 926
GUY SCHOENECKER, INC., pg. 977
STONE MANUFACTURING COMPANY, INC., pg. 1051
UNION UNDERWEAR CO., INC.—Farley Industries, pg. 400

2323 — MEN'S & BOYS' NECKWEAR

THE APPAREL GROUP, LTD., pg. 78
REMINGTON APPAREL—Remington Apparel, Inc., pg. 926
REMINGTON APPAREL, INC., pg. 926
SUPERBA, INC., pg. 1063
WEMCO, INC., pg. 1176

2325 — MEN'S & BOYS' TROUSERS & SLACKS

THE ASHER WINER COMPANY, pg. 88
STANLEY BLACKER, INC., pg. 155
BON JOUR INTERNATIONAL LTD., pg. 164
CARHARTT, INC., pg. 220
CODI INTERNATIONAL B.V.—Farley Industries, pg. 400
H. COTLER COMPANY, pg. 288
COVINGTON INDUSTRIES, pg. 290
ELBECO INCORPORATED, pg. 372
ELDER MANUFACTURING COMPANY, pg. 373
M. FINE & SONS MANUFACTURING CO., INC., pg. 411
FISHMAN & TOBIN, INC., pg. 415
H. FREEMAN & SON, INC., pg. 431
GLEN OAKS INDUSTRIES, INC., pg. 461
GREECO BROTHERS, INC., pg. 483
HAGGAR APPAREL COMPANY, pg. 499
HARDWICK CLOTHES INC., pg. 508
JAMTEX LTD.—Gitano Group Inc., pg. 460
THE JEANS COMPANY—Levi Strauss & Co., pg. 670
JONBIL INC., pg. 602
JORDACHE ENTERPRISES, INC., pg. 604
CALVIN KLEIN, INC., pg. 635
CALVIN KLEIN SPORT—Calvin Klein, Inc., pg. 635
KNAPP SHOES INC., pg. 636
KOBRA INTERNATIONAL LTD, pg. 638
LEVI STRAUSS (AUSTRALIA) PTY. LTD.—Levi Strauss & Co., pg. 670
LEVI STRAUSS BELGIUM, S.A.—Levi Strauss & Co., pg. 670
LEVI STRAUSS & CO., pg. 670
LEVI STRAUSS & CO. (CANADA), INC.—Levi Strauss & Co., pg. 670
LEVI STRAUSS & CO. (EUROPE) S.A.—Levi Strauss & Co., pg. 670
LEVI STRAUSS DE ESPANA, S.A.—Levi Strauss & Co., pg. 670
LEVI STRAUSS DE MEXICO, S.A. DE C.V.—Levi Strauss & Co., pg. 671
LEVI STRAUSS EXIMCO (LTD.)—Levi Strauss & Co., pg. 670
LEVI STRAUSS (FAR EAST), LTD.—Levi Strauss & Co., pg. 670
LEVI STRAUSS FRANCE, S.A.—Levi Strauss & Co., pg. 671
LEVI STRAUSS (GENEVA) S.A.—Levi Strauss & Co., pg. 671
LEVI STRAUSS GERMANY G.M.B.H.—Levi Strauss & Co., pg. 671
LEVI STRAUSS ITALIA, S.P.A.—Levi Strauss & Co., pg. 671
LEVI STRAUSS JAPAN K.K.—Levi Strauss & Co., pg. 671
LEVI STRAUSS (MALAYSIA) SDN. BHD.—Levi Strauss & Co., pg. 671
LEVI STRAUSS NEDERLAND B.V.—Levi Strauss & Co., pg. 671
LEVI STRAUSS (NEW ZEALAND) LTD.—Levi Strauss & Co., pg. 671
LEVI STRAUSS NORWAY, A/S—Levi Strauss & Co., pg. 671
LEVI STRAUSS (PHILIPPINES) INC.—Levi Strauss & Co., pg. 671
LEVI STRAUSS SPORTSWEAR—Levi Strauss & Co., pg. 670
LEVI STRAUSS (U.K.) LTD.—Levi Strauss & Co., pg. 671
LSJ SPORTSWEAR INC.—Merchant Capital Group Ltd, pg. 739
MASTER INDUSTRIES CORP., pg. 719
MASTER TROUSER/ MASTER APPAREL/ BOTANY 500 SLACKS LTD.—Master Industries Corp., pg. 720
MENSWEAR DIV.—Levi Strauss & Co., pg. 670
MERCHANT CAPITAL GROUP LTD, pg. 739
NOEL OF JAMAICA LTD.—Gitano Group Inc., pg. 460
PINCUS BROS., INC., pg. 870
RAM GOLF CORPORATION, pg. 910
REIDBORD BROS., INC., pg. 923
REMINGTON APPAREL, INC., pg. 926
ROME MANUFACTURING CO., pg. 945
SASSON JEANS FOR MEN, pg. 972
SCHOOL APPAREL, INC., pg. 978
SEATTLE PACIFIC INDUSTRIES, INC., pg. 986
SEMINOLE MANUFACTURING COMPANY, pg. 989
SPENCER INDUSTRIES, INC., pg. 1030
SUOMEN LEVI STRAUSS OY—Levi Strauss & Co., pg. 671
TROPICAL GARMENT MANUFACTURING COMPANY, pg. 1116
WEMCO, INC., pg. 1176
Z. CAVARICCI INC., pg. 1215
ZENA JEANS, pg. 1217

2326 — MEN'S & BOYS' WORK CLOTHING

ARATEX OF PUERTO RICO—ARA Group, pg. 6
BLAUER MANUFACTURING CO., INC., pg. 156
CARHARTT, INC., pg. 220
DESIGN USA—Jacmar Companies, Inc., pg. 587
ELDER MANUFACTURING COMPANY, pg. 373
M. FINE & SONS MANUFACTURING CO., INC., pg. 411
FINESILVER MANUFACTURING COMPANY, pg. 411
FISHMAN & TOBIN, INC., pg. 415
GREECO BROTHERS, INC., pg. 483
JACMAR COMPANIES, INC., pg. 587
KEY INDUSTRIES, INC., pg. 627
LEVI STRAUSS (AUSTRALIA) PTY. LTD.—Levi Strauss & Co., pg. 670
LEVI STRAUSS BELGIUM, S.A.—Levi Strauss & Co., pg. 670
LEVI STRAUSS & CO., pg. 670
LEVI STRAUSS & CO. (CANADA), INC.—Levi Strauss & Co., pg. 670
LEVI STRAUSS & CO. (EUROPE) S.A.—Levi Strauss & Co., pg. 670
LEVI STRAUSS DE ESPANA, S.A.—Levi Strauss & Co., pg. 670
LEVI STRAUSS DE MEXICO, S.A. DE C.V.—Levi Strauss & Co., pg. 671
LEVI STRAUSS EXIMCO (LTD.)—Levi Strauss & Co., pg. 670
LEVI STRAUSS (FAR EAST), LTD.—Levi Strauss & Co., pg. 670
LEVI STRAUSS FRANCE, S.A.—Levi Strauss & Co., pg. 671
LEVI STRAUSS (GENEVA) S.A.—Levi Strauss & Co., pg. 671
LEVI STRAUSS GERMANY G.M.B.H.—Levi Strauss & Co., pg. 671
LEVI STRAUSS ITALIA, S.P.A.—Levi Strauss & Co., pg. 671
LEVI STRAUSS JAPAN K.K.—Levi Strauss & Co., pg. 671
LEVI STRAUSS (MALAYSIA) SDN. BHD.—Levi Strauss & Co., pg. 671
LEVI STRAUSS NEDERLAND B.V.—Levi Strauss & Co., pg. 671
LEVI STRAUSS (NEW ZEALAND) LTD.—Levi Strauss & Co., pg. 671
LEVI STRAUSS NORWAY, A/S—Levi Strauss & Co., pg. 671
LEVI STRAUSS (PHILIPPINES) INC.—Levi Strauss & Co., pg. 671
LEVI STRAUSS (U.K.) LTD.—Levi Strauss & Co., pg. 671
OTTENHEIMER & COMPANY, INC., pg. 831
RIVERSIDE MANUFACTURING CO., pg. 937
M. RUBIN & SONS INC., pg. 954
I. SPIEWAK & SONS, INC., pg. 1031
SUOMEN LEVI STRAUSS OY—Levi Strauss & Co., pg. 671
UNIVERSAL OVERALL COMPANY, pg. 1139
THE VERNON COMPANY, pg. 1148
WILLIAMSON-DICKIE APPAREL MFG. CO.—Williamson-Dickie Mfg. Co., pg. 1192
WILLIAMSON-DICKIE MFG. CO., pg. 1192

2329 — MEN'S & BOYS' CLOTHING, NEC

ASICS TIGER CORPORATION, pg. 8
ALLESON OF ROCHESTER, INC., pg. 37
ALPHA MILLS CORP., pg. 43
AMERICAN MARKETING INDUSTRIES, INC., pg. 58
ANDERSON INDUSTRIES, INC., pg. 72
ANDMORE SPORTSWEAR CORPORATION, pg. 74
THE APPAREL GROUP, LTD., pg. 78
APPAREL INDUSTRIES, INC., pg. 78
BATTERY ST. ENTERPRISES, RUNNING GEAR DIV.—Levi Strauss & Co., pg. 670
STANLEY BLACKER, INC., pg. 155
BLOCK INDUSTRIES, INC., pg. 157
BON JOUR INTERNATIONAL LTD., pg. 164
CB NORTH AMERICA, INC., pg. 199
CGS INDUSTRIES, INC., pg. 201
CAPUCCI CREATIONS INTERNATIONAL, INC., pg. 216
CARHARTT, INC., pg. 220
COVINGTON INDUSTRIES, pg. 290
DOTHAN UNDERWEAR—Host Apparel, Inc., pg. 545
DOWN PRODUCTS DIV.—Woolrich, Inc., pg. 1201
ELDER MANUFACTURING COMPANY, pg. 373
FAB-KNIT MANUFACTURING CO.—Anderson Industries, Inc., pg. 73
THE FINALS, LTD.—Andmore Sportswear Corporation, pg. 74
FISHMAN & TOBIN, INC., pg. 415
FOX-KNAPP INC., pg. 427
GENERRA SPORTSWEAR COMPANY, INC., pg. 451
GOLDEN FLEECE OUTERWEAR CO.—I. Spiewak & Sons, Inc., pg. 1031
GORDON & FERGUSON OF DELAWARE, INC., pg. 471
GORDON & SMITH, INC., pg. 472
GREAT LAKES SPORTSWEAR MANUFACTURING INDUSTRIES, pg. 482
GREECO BROTHERS, INC., pg. 483
GUESS ?, INC., pg. 493
HAGGAR APPAREL COMPANY, pg. 499
HARDWICK CLOTHES INC., pg. 508
HARPER INDUSTRIES, INC., pg. 510
THE HARWOOD COMPANIES, INC., pg. 515
HOLOUBEK INC., pg. 540
JORDACHE ENTERPRISES, INC., pg. 604
KSG INC., pg. 613
KAPPLER, INC.—KSG Inc., pg. 613
KARSTEN MANUFACTURING CORPORATION, pg. 617
KING LOUIE INTERNATIONAL, INC., pg. 631
KNAPP SHOES INC., pg. 636
TONY LAMBERT COMPANY, pg. 652
LEVI STRAUSS (AUSTRALIA) PTY. LTD.—Levi Strauss & Co., pg. 670
LEVI STRAUSS BELGIUM, S.A.—Levi Strauss & Co., pg. 670
LEVI STRAUSS & CO., pg. 670
LEVI STRAUSS & CO. (CANADA), INC.—Levi Strauss & Co., pg. 670
LEVI STRAUSS & CO. (EUROPE) S.A.—Levi Strauss & Co., pg. 670
LEVI STRAUSS DE ESPANA, S.A.—Levi Strauss & Co., pg. 670
LEVI STRAUSS DE MEXICO, S.A. DE C.V.—Levi Strauss & Co., pg. 671
LEVI STRAUSS EXIMCO (LTD.)—Levi Strauss & Co., pg. 670
LEVI STRAUSS (FAR EAST), LTD.—Levi Strauss & Co., pg. 670
LEVI STRAUSS FRANCE, S.A.—Levi Strauss & Co., pg. 671
LEVI STRAUSS (GENEVA) S.A.—Levi Strauss & Co., pg. 671
LEVI STRAUSS GERMANY G.M.B.H.—Levi Strauss & Co., pg. 671
LEVI STRAUSS ITALIA, S.P.A.—Levi Strauss & Co., pg. 671
LEVI STRAUSS JAPAN K.K.—Levi Strauss & Co., pg. 671
LEVI STRAUSS (MALAYSIA) SDN. BHD.—Levi Strauss & Co., pg. 671
LEVI STRAUSS NEDERLAND B.V.—Levi Strauss & Co., pg. 671
LEVI STRAUSS (NEW ZEALAND) LTD.—Levi Strauss & Co., pg. 671
LEVI STRAUSS NORWAY, A/S—Levi Strauss & Co., pg. 671
LEVI STRAUSS (PHILIPPINES) INC.—Levi Strauss & Co., pg. 671
LEVI STRAUSS SPORTSWEAR—Levi Strauss & Co., pg. 670
LEVI STRAUSS (U.K.) LTD.—Levi Strauss & Co., pg. 671
LOST ARROW CORPORATION, pg. 684
MEMBERS ONLY BY EUROPE CRAFT, pg. 738
MENSWEAR DIV.—Levi Strauss & Co., pg. 670
MERIDIAN MFG. CO., INC.—Roytex, Inc., pg. 953
MIDLAND SHIRT COMPANY—Harper Industries, Inc., pg. 510
NEW BALANCE ATHLETIC SHOE, INC., pg. 798
PENDLETON WOOLEN MILLS, INC., pg. 857
POCONO KNITS, INC.—Jack Young Associates, pg. 1209
POLO/RALPH LAUREN CORPORATION, pg. 879
RENNOC CORPORATION, pg. 927
RIKLIS FAMILY CORPORATION, pg. 934

ROFFE, INC., pg. 943
S. ROTHCHILD & CO., INC., pg. 951
ROYDON WEAR, INC.—Coordinated Apparel, Inc., pg. 283
ROYDON WEAR, INC.—Coordinated Apparel, Inc., pg. 283
M. RUBIN & SONS INC., pg. 954
SCHOTT BROTHERS, INC., pg. 978
SEATTLE PACIFIC INDUSTRIES, INC., pg. 986
SPENCER INDUSTRIES, INC., pg. 1030
I. SPIEWAK & SONS, INC., pg. 1031
STANDARD MANUFACTURING COMPANY, pg. 1037
STONE MANUFACTURING COMPANY, INC., pg. 1051
SUOMEN LEVI STRAUSS OY—Levi Strauss & Co., pg. 671
SWELL-WEAR, INC., pg. 1067
THAW, INC.—Recreational Equipment, Inc., pg. 917
TRAPPINGS CO.—I. Spiewak & Sons, Inc., pg. 1031
WHITE STAG MANUFACTURING COMPANY, pg. 1186
WOLF MANUFACTURING COMPANY, pg. 1199
WOOLCAN—Woolrich, Inc., pg. 1201
WOOLKONG LTD.—Woolrich, Inc., pg. 1201
WOOLRICH, INC., pg. 1201
JACK YOUNG ASSOCIATES, pg. 1209
ZENA JEANS, pg. 1217

2331 — WOMEN'S, MISSES' & JUNIORS' BLOUSES & SHIRTS

THE APPAREL GROUP, LTD., pg. 78
STANLEY BLACKER, INC., pg. 155
BYER CALIFORNIA, pg. 197
CHEROKEE APPAREL CORP.—The Cherokee Group, pg. 243
THE CHEROKEE GROUP, pg. 243
CHRISTIAN DIOR—Jones Apparel Group, Inc., pg. 602
DONNKENNY, INC., pg. 345
SID EAGLE ASSOCIATES—House of Ronnie, Inc., pg. 546
ELDER MANUFACTURING COMPANY, pg. 373
ESPRIT DE CORP., pg. 388
FADDALEY ENTERPRISES INC.—Daniel Caron Ltd., pg. 224
FARLEY INDUSTRIES, pg. 399
HARDWICK CLOTHES INC., pg. 508
HARVE BENARD LTD. MANUFACTURING, pg. 514
HOUSE OF PERFECTION, INC., pg. 546
J H COLLECTIBLES, pg. 584
JNY—Jones Apparel Group, Inc., pg. 602
JACQUES MORET, INC., pg. 588
JERELL, INC., pg. 593
JONES APPAREL GROUP, INC., pg. 602
JONESWEAR—Jones Apparel Group, Inc., pg. 602
JUDY BOND, INC., pg. 608
KING LOUIE INTERNATIONAL, INC., pg. 631
CALVIN KLEIN SPORT—Calvin Klein, Inc., pg. 635
KOBRA INTERNATIONAL LTD, pg. 638
LAND N SEA, INC., pg. 653
LSJ SPORTSWEAR INC.—Merchant Capital Group Ltd, pg. 739
LUCKY WINNER, INC., pg. 686
MAYFAIR INDUSTRIES, INC.—Apparel America, Inc., pg. 78
MERCHANT CAPITAL GROUP LTD, pg. 739
MICKEY & COMPANY—Donnkenny, Inc., pg. 345
REMINGTON APPAREL, INC., pg. 926
RENA ROWAN FOR SAVILLE—Jones Apparel Group, Inc., pg. 602
SEATTLE PACIFIC INDUSTRIES, INC., pg. 986
HENRY I. SIEGEL COMPANY, INC., pg. 1002
STANDARD GARMENT COMPANY, INC., pg. 1036
SWELL-WEAR, INC., pg. 1067
TANNER CO. INC., pg. 1078
TAREN HOLDINGS, INC., pg. 1078
VAN RAALTE DE VENEZUELA C.A.—Farley Industries, pg. 401
Z. CAVARICCI INC., pg. 1215

2335 — WOMEN'S, MISSES' & JUNIORS' DRESSES

BRIDAL ORIGINALS, INC., pg. 175
BYER CALIFORNIA, pg. 197
CHORUS LINE, INC.—Jazz Holding Corporation, pg. 591
DAWN JOY FASHIONS, INC., pg. 319
DONNKENNY, INC., pg. 345
ELDER MANUFACTURING COMPANY, pg. 373
ESPRIT DE CORP., pg. 388
HARDWICK CLOTHES INC., pg. 508
HARVE BENARD LTD. MANUFACTURING, pg. 514
HOUSE OF BIANCHI, pg. 546
JNY—Jones Apparel Group, Inc., pg. 602
JAZZ HOLDING CORPORATION, pg. 591
JERELL, INC., pg. 593
JONES APPAREL GROUP, INC., pg. 602
JONESWEAR—Jones Apparel Group, Inc., pg. 602
KOBRA INTERNATIONAL LTD, pg. 638
LANZ, INC., pg. 658
SHERRI MARTIN—Dawn Joy Fashions, Inc., pg. 319
MISS ELLIETTE, INC., pg. 760
REMINGTON APPAREL, INC., pg. 926
RENA ROWAN FOR SAVILLE—Jones Apparel Group, Inc., pg. 602
SALLY LOU FASHIONS CORPORATION, pg. 967
HENRY I. SIEGEL COMPANY, INC., pg. 1002
STANDARD GARMENT COMPANY, INC., pg. 1036
TANNER CO. INC., pg. 1078
TORINO FASHIONS, INC., pg. 1102
VAN RAALTE DE VENEZUELA C.A.—Farley Industries, pg. 401
VARAT ENTERPRISES, INC., pg. 1145
WICKER PARK L.P., pg. 1188

2337 — WOMEN'S, MISSES' & JUNIORS' SUITS, SKIRTS & COATS

AMERICAN UNIFORM CO.—Steiner Corporation, pg. 1045
ARATEX OF PUERTO RICO—ARA Group, pg. 6
ARNAV INDUSTRIES, INC., pg. 84
STANLEY BLACKER, INC., pg. 155
BROOKHURST, INC., pg. 179
DESIGN USA—Jacmar Companies, Inc., pg. 587
DOWN PRODUCTS DIV.—Woolrich, Inc., pg. 1201
EDELWEISS—White Stag Manufacturing Company, pg. 1186
ELDER MANUFACTURING COMPANY, pg. 373
KENNETH GORDON NEW ORLEANS, LTD., pg. 472
HARDWICK CLOTHES INC., pg. 508
HARVE BENARD LTD. MANUFACTURING, pg. 514
JNY—Jones Apparel Group, Inc., pg. 602
JACMAR COMPANIES, INC., pg. 587
JONES APPAREL GROUP, INC., pg. 602
JONESWEAR—Jones Apparel Group, Inc., pg. 602
KING LOUIE INTERNATIONAL, INC., pg. 631
CALVIN KLEIN, INC., pg. 635
KOBRA INTERNATIONAL LTD, pg. 638
LANZ, INC., pg. 658
P.D. FASHIONS, pg. 836
PINCUS BROS., INC., pg. 870
REMINGTON APPAREL, INC., pg. 926
SAVILLE—Jones Apparel Group, Inc., pg. 602
HENRY I. SIEGEL COMPANY, INC., pg. 1002
TANNER CO. INC., pg. 1078
TAREN HOLDINGS, INC., pg. 1078
VARAT ENTERPRISES, INC., pg. 1145
WOOLCAN—Woolrich, Inc., pg. 1201
WOOLKONG LTD.—Woolrich, Inc., pg. 1201
WOOLRICH, INC., pg. 1201
Z. CAVARICCI INC., pg. 1215
ZENA JEANS, pg. 1217

2339 — WOMEN'S, MISSES' & JUNIORS' OUTERWEAR, NEC

ASICS TIGER CORPORATION, pg. 8
ALPHA MILLS CORP., pg. 43
ANDERSON INDUSTRIES, INC., pg. 72
ANDMORE SPORTSWEAR CORPORATION, pg. 74
APPAREL AMERICA, INC., pg. 78
APPAREL INDUSTRIES, INC., pg. 78
APPAREL VENTURES, INC., pg. 78
BAAR & BEARDS, pg. 107
BALLET MAKERS, INC., pg. 116
BATTERY ST. ENTERPRISES, RUNNING GEAR DIV.—Levi Strauss & Co., pg. 670
BLAUER MANUFACTURING CO., INC., pg. 156
DAVID BRETT, INC., pg. 174
BYER CALIFORNIA, pg. 197
CAPITAL PANTS CO., pg. 215
CHRISTIAN DIOR—Jones Apparel Group, Inc., pg. 602
CHRISTIANSBURG GARMENT CO. INC.—Donnkenny, Inc., pg. 345
COMPLEX INDUSTRY CORPORATION, pg. 270
COVINGTON INDUSTRIES, pg. 290
DEWEESE INC., pg. 334
DOWN PRODUCTS DIV.—Woolrich, Inc., pg. 1201
DURLACHER & CO., INC., pg. 354
SID EAGLE ASSOCIATES—House of Ronnie, Inc., pg. 546
ECHO DESIGN GROUP, INC., pg. 365
ELDER MANUFACTURING COMPANY, pg. 373
FAB-KNIT MANUFACTURING CO.—Anderson Industries, Inc., pg. 73
FARLEY INDUSTRIES, pg. 399
THE FINALS, LTD.—Andmore Sportswear Corporation, pg. 74
GENERRA SPORTSWEAR COMPANY, INC., pg. 451
GUESS ?, INC., pg. 493
HABITS, INC.—Saul Bros. & Company, Inc., pg. 972
HARDWICK CLOTHES INC., pg. 508
J H COLLECTIBLES, pg. 584
JNY—Jones Apparel Group, Inc., pg. 602
JACQUES MORET, INC., pg. 588
JONBIL INC., pg. 602
JONES APPAREL GROUP, INC., pg. 602
JORDACHE ENTERPRISES, INC., pg. 604
JUNIOR GALLERY LTD., pg. 609
KSG INC., pg. 613
KAPPLER, INC.—KSG Inc., pg. 613
KARSTEN MANUFACTURING CORPORATION, pg. 617
KING LOUIE INTERNATIONAL, INC., pg. 631
CALVIN KLEIN SPORT—Calvin Klein, Inc., pg. 635
KOBRA INTERNATIONAL LTD, pg. 638
LANZ, INC., pg. 658
LEVI STRAUSS (AUSTRALIA) PTY. LTD.—Levi Strauss & Co., pg. 670
LEVI STRAUSS BELGIUM, S.A.—Levi Strauss & Co., pg. 670
LEVI STRAUSS & CO., pg. 670
LEVI STRAUSS & CO. (CANADA), INC.—Levi Strauss & Co., pg. 670
LEVI STRAUSS & CO. (EUROPE) S.A.—Levi Strauss & Co., pg. 670
LEVI STRAUSS DE ESPANA, S.A.—Levi Strauss & Co., pg. 670
LEVI STRAUSS DE MEXICO, S.A. DE C.V.—Levi Strauss & Co., pg. 671
LEVI STRAUSS EXIMCO (LTD.)—Levi Strauss & Co., pg. 670
LEVI STRAUSS (FAR EAST), LTD.—Levi Strauss & Co., pg. 670
LEVI STRAUSS FRANCE, S.A.—Levi Strauss & Co., pg. 671
LEVI STRAUSS (GENEVA) S.A.—Levi Strauss & Co., pg. 671
LEVI STRAUSS GERMANY G.M.B.H.—Levi Strauss & Co., pg. 671
LEVI STRAUSS ITALIA, S.P.A.—Levi Strauss & Co., pg. 671
LEVI STRAUSS JAPAN K.K.—Levi Strauss & Co., pg. 671
LEVI STRAUSS (MALAYSIA) SDN. BHD.—Levi Strauss & Co., pg. 671
LEVI STRAUSS NEDERLAND B.V.—Levi Strauss & Co., pg. 671
LEVI STRAUSS (NEW ZEALAND) LTD.—Levi Strauss & Co., pg. 671
LEVI STRAUSS NORWAY, A/S—Levi Strauss & Co., pg. 671
LEVI STRAUSS (PHILIPPINES) INC.—Levi Strauss & Co., pg. 671
LEVI STRAUSS SPORTSWEAR—Levi Strauss & Co., pg. 670
LEVI STRAUSS (U.K.) LTD.—Levi Strauss & Co., pg. 671
LONDONTOWN CORPORATION—Londontown Holdings Corporation, pg. 682
LSJ SPORTSWEAR INC.—Merchant Capital Group Ltd, pg. 739
LUCKY WINNER, INC., pg. 686
MARISA CHRISTINA INC., pg. 707
GILDA MARX INC., pg. 716
MASTER INDUSTRIES CORP., pg. 719
MAXINE OF HOLLYWOOD, INC., pg. 723
MERCHANT CAPITAL GROUP LTD, pg. 739
MILADY BRASSIERE & CORSET CO., INC., pg. 753
OTTENHEIMER & COMPANY, INC., pg. 831
PAGE BOY COMPANY, INC., pg. 843
PENDLETON WOOLEN MILLS, INC., pg. 857
JOS. J. PIETRAFESA CO., INC., pg. 870
RENA ROWAN FOR SAVILLE—Jones Apparel Group, Inc., pg. 602
RENNOC CORPORATION, pg. 927
RIVERSIDE MANUFACTURING CO., pg. 937
ROBBY LEN FASHIONS—Apparel America, Inc., pg. 78
ROFFE, INC., pg. 943
S. ROTHCHILD & CO., INC., pg. 951
ROXANNE SWIM SUITS CO., INC.—Milady Brassiere & Corset Co., Inc., pg. 753
SAUL BROS. & COMPANY, INC., pg. 972
SEATTLE PACIFIC INDUSTRIES, INC., pg. 986
SHARON-JAY TOGS, INC., pg. 995
HENRY I. SIEGEL COMPANY, INC., pg. 1002
I. SPIEWAK & SONS, INC., pg. 1031
STANDARD GARMENT COMPANY, INC., pg. 1036
SUOMEN LEVI STRAUSS OY—Levi Strauss & Co., pg. 671
SWEDE SPORTSWEAR COMPANY, INC., pg. 1066
SWELL-WEAR, INC., pg. 1067
SWIRL, INC., pg. 1068
TAREN HOLDINGS, INC., pg. 1078
TARGET SPORTSWEAR, INC., pg. 1079
TIGHE INDUSTRIES, INC., pg. 1097
THE TOG SHOP, pg. 1100
TRU-FIT GLOVE & HEADWEAR DIV.—Heyman Corporation, pg. 532
UNION UNDERWEAR CO., INC.—Farley Industries, pg. 400
VAN RAALTE DE VENEZUELA C.A.—Farley Industries, pg. 401
VARAT ENTERPRISES, INC., pg. 1145
THE VERNON COMPANY, pg. 1148
WHITE STAG MANUFACTURING COMPANY, pg. 1186
WICKER PARK L.P., pg. 1188
WOOLCAN—Woolrich, Inc., pg. 1201
WOOLKONG LTD.—Woolrich, Inc., pg. 1201
WOOLRICH, INC., pg. 1201
CAROLE WREN, INC., pg. 1204
ZENA JEANS, pg. 1217

2341 — WOMEN'S, MISSES', CHILDREN'S & INFANTS' UNDERWEAR & NIGHTWEAR

ALPHA MILLS CORP., pg. 43
ANIMAL FAIR—Guy Schoenecker, Inc., pg. 978
I. APPEL CORPORATION, pg. 78
BVD LICENSING CORPORATION—Farley Industries, pg. 400
BERKLIFF CORPORATION, pg. 142
BESTFORM FOUNDATIONS, INC., pg. 147
BRISTOL LINGERIE—House of Ronnie, Inc., pg. 546
THE WILLIAM CARTER COMPANY, pg. 226
THE CHEROKEE GROUP, pg. 243
DONNKENNY, INC., pg. 345
EDELSON & SONS CORPORATION, pg. 368
FARLEY INDUSTRIES, pg. 399
FRUIT OF THE LOOM—Farley Industries, pg. 400
GLENCRAFT LINGERIE, INC., pg. 462
HOST APPAREL, INC., pg. 545
HOST FOR HER—Host Apparel, Inc., pg. 545
HOUSE OF RONNIE, INC., pg. 546
JASPER TEXTILE—House of Ronnie, Inc., pg. 546
JOCKEY INTERNATIONAL, INC., pg. 595
KATZ, INC., pg. 618
CHARLES KOMAR & SONS, INC., pg. 641
MAIDENFORM, INC., pg. 701
MISS ELAINE INC., pg. 760
MOUNT VERNON MILLS, INC.—R. B. Pamplin Corp., pg. 844
MOUNT VERNON MILLS, INC., CONSUMER PRODUCTS DIV. (MCCORMICK)—R. B. Pamplin Corp., pg. 844
NATIONAL CORSET SUPPLY HOUSE, pg. 787
O'BRYAN BROTHERS INC., pg. 820
PAJAMA CRAFT, INC.—Host Apparel, Inc., pg. 545
RIKLIS FAMILY CORPORATION, pg. 934
S. SCHWAB COMPANY, pg. 980
SPENCER'S INC., pg. 1030
SPLENDOR FORM INTERNATIONAL INC., pg. 1031
UNION UNDERWEAR CO., INC.—Farley Industries, pg. 400
VAN RAALTE DE VENEZUELA C.A.—Farley Industries, pg. 401
VARAT ENTERPRISES, INC., pg. 1145

2342 — BRASSIERES, GIRDLES & ALLIED GARMENTS

BESTFORM FOUNDATIONS, INC., pg. 147
CARNIVAL CREATIONS, pg. 222
GELMART INDUSTRIES PHILIPPINES, INC.—Playtex Apparel Inc., pg. 876
GLAMORISE FOUNDATIONS, INC., pg. 460
GODDESS BRA COMPANY, pg. 464
HARBOUR CASUALS, LTD.—Milady Brassiere & Corset Co., Inc., pg. 753
INNER SECRETS, INC., pg. 570
INTEX—Playtex Apparel Inc., pg. 876
LADY MARLENE SALES CORP., pg. 650
MAIDENFORM, INC., pg. 701
MILADY BRASSIERE & CORSET CO., INC., pg. 753
PLAYTEX APPAREL CANADA, LTD.—Playtex Apparel Inc., pg. 876
PLAYTEX APPAREL CANADA, LTD., RENFREW—Playtex Apparel Inc., pg. 876
PLAYTEX APPAREL INC., pg. 876
PLAYTEX FRANCE—Playtex Apparel Inc., pg. 876
PLAYTEX ITALIA S.P.A.—Playtex Apparel Inc., pg. 876
PLAYTEX, LTD.—Playtex Apparel Inc., pg. 876
PLAYTEX, LTD., ARNPRIOR—Playtex Apparel Inc., pg. 876
PLAYTEX MEXICANA S.A. DE C.V.—Playtex Apparel Inc., pg. 877
QISMET LTD.—Milady Brassiere & Corset Co., Inc., pg. 753
QUANTUM SPORTSWEAR, LTD.—Milady Brassiere & Corset Co., Inc., pg. 753
REMINGTON APPAREL, INC., pg. 926
SPIRITE INDUSTRIES, INC., pg. 1031
SPLENDOR FORM BRASSIERE, INC.—Splendor Form International Inc., pg. 1032
SPLENDOR FORM INTERNATIONAL INC., pg. 1031
THE STROUSE, ADLER COMPANY, pg. 1054

2353 — HATS, CAPS & MILLINERY

DURLACHER & CO., INC., pg. 354
GEE CEE CAP COMPANY—The Vernon Company, pg. 1148
M. GROSSMAN SON, INC., pg. 489
KANGOL LTD.—The Marmon Group, Inc., pg. 712
KING LOUIE INTERNATIONAL, INC., pg. 631
MILLER BROS. INDUSTRIES, INC., pg. 753
REMINGTON APPAREL, INC., pg. 926
THE VERNON COMPANY, pg. 1148
VOYAGER EMBLEMS, INC., pg. 1155

2361 — GIRLS', CHILDREN'S, & INFANTS' DRESSES, BLOUSES & SHIRTS

BABY TOGS, INC., pg. 107
BENTEX KIDDIE CORPORATION, pg. 140
CAPITAL CITY MANUFACTURING COMPANY—House of Perfection, Inc., pg. 546
THE CHEROKEE GROUP, pg. 243
COVINGTON INDUSTRIES, pg. 290
EVY OF CALIFORNIA, INC., pg. 392
GERSON & GERSON, INC., pg. 454
HOUSE OF PERFECTION, INC., pg. 546
ISFEL COMPANY, INC., pg. 582
LAND N SEA, INC., pg. 653
CHARLES LEONARD WESTERN, INC.—Charles Leonard, Inc., pg. 668
THE MAY APPAREL GROUP, INC., pg. 723
MAYFAIR INDUSTRIES, INC.—Apparel America, Inc., pg. 78
ROYDON WEAR, INC.—Coordinated Apparel, Inc., pg. 283
ROYDON WEAR, INC.—Coordinated Apparel, Inc., pg. 283
STAR CHILDREN'S DRESS COMPANY, INC., pg. 1039
TAREN HOLDINGS, INC., pg. 1078
VIRGINIA APPAREL MANUFACTURING CO., INC.—Star Children's Dress Company, Inc., pg. 1039

2369 — GIRLS', CHILDREN'S & INFANTS' OUTERWEAR, NEC

BABY TOGS, INC., pg. 107
BALLET MAKERS, INC., pg. 116
BENTEX KIDDIE CORPORATION, pg. 140
COVINGTON INDUSTRIES, pg. 290
H.H. CUTLER COMPANY, pg. 306
DOE SPUN, INC., pg. 343
EVY OF CALIFORNIA, INC., pg. 392
HOUSE OF PERFECTION, INC., pg. 546
ISFEL COMPANY, INC., pg. 582
JACQUES MORET, INC., pg. 588
ROFFE, INC., pg. 943
S. ROTHCHILD & CO., INC., pg. 951
S. SCHWAB COMPANY, pg. 980
TAREN HOLDINGS, INC., pg. 1078
TAWIL ASSOCIATES INC., pg. 1080
TRU-FIT GLOVE & HEADWEAR DIV.—Heyman Corporation, pg. 532
WELLMADE INDUSTRIES, INC., pg. 1175
WHITE STAG MANUFACTURING COMPANY, pg. 1186
CAROLE WREN, INC., pg. 1204

2381 — DRESS & WORK GLOVES, EXCEPT KNIT & ALL LEATHER

CAROLINA GLOVE CO., pg. 223
FOWNES BROTHERS & CO., INC., pg. 427
THE GRANDOE CORPORATION, pg. 476
JOMAC, INC., pg. 602
THE MARMON GROUP, INC., pg. 710
WELLS LAMONT—The Marmon Group, Inc., pg. 712

2384 — ROBES & DRESSING GOWNS

I. APPEL CORPORATION, pg. 78
EDELSON & SONS CORPORATION, pg. 368
THE HARWOOD COMPANIES, INC., pg. 515
SWIRL, INC., pg. 1068

2385 — RAINCOATS & WATERPROOF OUTERWEAR

KAPPLER EUROPE, LTD.—KSG Inc., pg. 613
LONDONTOWN CORPORATION—Londontown Holdings Corporation, pg. 682
LONDONTOWN HOLDINGS CORPORATION, pg. 681
PYRAMID HANDBAGS INC., pg. 901
RAINFAIR, INC., pg. 910
STAR SPORTSWEAR MANUFACTURING—Londontown Holdings Corporation, pg. 682
SWELL-WEAR, INC., pg. 1067
TOTES INCORPORATED, pg. 1103
WHALING INDUSTRIES, INC., pg. 1183
WHALING MANUFACTURING COMPANY, INC.—Whaling Industries, Inc., pg. 1183

2386 — LEATHER & SHEEP-LINED CLOTHING

CAPUCCI CREATIONS INTERNATIONAL, INC., pg. 216
EMPIRE CLOTHING—Excelled Sheepskin & Leather Coat Corporation, pg. 392
EXCELLED SHEEPSKIN & LEATHER COAT CORPORATION, pg. 392
LEATHER WAREHOUSE, INC., pg. 664
LONDONTOWN CORPORATION—Londontown Holdings Corporation, pg. 682
LONDONTOWN HOLDINGS CORPORATION, pg. 681
SCHOTT BROTHERS, INC., pg. 978

2387 — APPAREL BELTS

THE CHEROKEE GROUP, pg. 243
ECHO DESIGN GROUP, INC., pg. 365

2389 — APPAREL & ACCESSORIES, NEC

AUGSBURG FORTRESS, PUBLISHERS, pg. 98
BAAR & BEARDS, pg. 107
BALLET MAKERS, INC., pg. 116
BON JOUR INTERNATIONAL LTD., pg. 164
COUNTY SEAT STORES, INC., pg. 290
GEM-DANDY, INC., pg. 447
HER MAJESTY, pg. 530
HEYMAN CORPORATION, pg. 532
KAYSER-ROTH HOSIERY, INC.—Collins & Aikman Group Inc., pg. 262
MAR-MAC MANUFACTURING COMPANY, INC., pg. 705
E. R. MOORE CO., pg. 768
SOCKS DIVISION—Collins & Aikman Group Inc., pg. 263
TALON, INC., pg. 1077
TIGHE INDUSTRIES, INC., pg. 1097

2391 — CURTAINS & DRAPERIES

ABERDEEN MFG. CORP. CONWAY PLANT—CC Industries, Inc., pg. 200
ABERDEEN MFG. CORP. SAVOY PLANT—CC Industries, Inc., pg. 200
ABERDEEN MFG. CORPORATION—CC Industries, Inc., pg. 200
ARLEY MERCHANDISE CORPORATION, pg. 83
BATES FABRICS, INC., pg. 125
CC INDUSTRIES, INC., pg. 199
CAMEO CURTAINS—CC Industries, Inc., pg. 200
CHARLES CURTAIN COMPANY, INC., pg. 239
CROSCILL, INC., pg. 300
EASTERN CANVAS PRODUCTS, INC., pg. 363
HOME CURTAIN CORPORATION—Home Innovations, Inc., pg. 541
HOME INNOVATIONS, INC., pg. 541
MILLER CURTAIN CO., INC., pg. 754
PERFECT FIT INDUSTRIES, INC., pg. 861
ROBERTSON FACTORIES, INC., pg. 939
WEST POINT-PEPPERELL, INC.—Farley Industries, pg. 400
WHITING MANUFACTURING CO., INC., pg. 1187

2392 — HOUSEFURNISHINGS, EXCEPT CURTAINS & DRAPERIES

ABERDEEN MFG. CORP. CONWAY PLANT—CC Industries, Inc., pg. 200
ABERDEEN MFG. CORP. KAUFMAN PLANT—CC Industries, Inc., pg. 200
ABERDEEN MFG. CORP. LOUIS HAND PLANT—CC Industries, Inc., pg. 200
ABERDEEN MFG. CORP. SAVOY PLANT—CC Industries, Inc., pg. 200
ABERDEEN MFG. CORPORATION—CC Industries, Inc., pg. 200
ARLEY MERCHANDISE CORPORATION, pg. 83
BATES FABRICS, INC., pg. 125
BURLINGTON BASKET CO., pg. 191
CC INDUSTRIES, INC., pg. 199
CAMEO CURTAINS—CC Industries, Inc., pg. 200
CHARLES CURTAIN COMPANY, INC., pg. 239
CROSCILL, INC., pg. 300
DAKOTAH, INC., pg. 312
EARLE INDUSTRIES, INC., pg. 362
EASY DAY MANUFACTURING COMPANY, INC., pg. 364
N. ERLANGER, BLUMGART & COMPANY, INC., pg. 387
FARLEY INDUSTRIES, pg. 399
GEM, INCORPORATED, pg. 447
LOUIS HAND DIV.—CC Industries, Inc., pg. 200
HOME CURTAIN CORPORATION—Home Innovations, Inc., pg. 541
HOME INNOVATIONS, INC., pg. 541
JAKSON-A CHF COMPANY—CC Industries, Inc., pg. 200
LESHNER MILLS, INC., pg. 668
LOUISVILLE BEDDING COMPANY, pg. 684
JOHN R. LYMAN COMPANY, pg. 689
MAGLA PRODUCTS, pg. 700
MILLER CURTAIN CO., INC., pg. 754
MILLIKEN & CO., INC., pg. 755
MOUNT VERNON MILLS, INC.—R. B. Pamplin Corp., pg. 844
MOUNT VERNON MILLS, INC., RIEGEL CONSUMER PRODUCTS DIV.—R. B. Pamplin Corp., pg. 844
NOEL-JOANNA, INC., pg. 808
PERFECT FIT INDUSTRIES, INC., pg. 861
PILLOWTEX CORPORATION, pg. 870
RESTONIC CORPORATION, pg. 929
ROPS TEXTILES INC.—Arley Merchandise Corporation, pg. 83
CECIL SAYDAH COMPANY, pg. 973
SUNBEAM-OSTER HOUSEHOLD PRODUCTS—Sunbeam-Oster Company, Inc., pg. 1059
SUNWEAVE LINEN CORPORATION, pg. 1062
TERRY, BATH & KITCHEN PRODUCTS DIV.—Farley Industries, pg. 400
TRINA, INC., pg. 1113
WELLINGTON INDUSTRIES INC., pg. 1175
WEST POINT-PEPPEREL (U.K.) LTD.—Farley Industries, pg. 401
WHISPER SOFT MILLS INC., pg. 1185
WHITE MOP WRINGER COMPANY, pg. 1186
WHITING MANUFACTURING CO., INC., pg. 1187
WILEN MANUFACTURING COMPANY, INC., pg. 1189
WORLD CARPETS, INC., pg. 1202

2393 — TEXTILE BAGS

DRUMHELLER BAG & SUPPLY—Norfoods, Inc., pg. 810
LANGSTON COMPANIES, pg. 657
MAINE POTATO GROWERS, INC., pg. 702
NORFOODS, INC., pg. 810
WILLIAM B. REILY & CO., INC., pg. 923
WERTHAN PACKAGING, INC., pg. 1176

2394 — CANVAS & RELATED PRODUCTS

ACME CANVAS CO., INC., pg. 13
ANCHOR INDUSTRIES INC., pg. 71
F.H. BONN COMPANY, pg. 164
CENTURY PRODUCTS INC.—Acme Canvas Co., Inc., pg. 13
THE COLEMAN COMPANY—MacAndrews & Forbes Holdings Inc., pg. 695
THE COLEMAN COMPANY—MacAndrews & Forbes Holdings Inc., pg. 695
COLEMAN (DEUTSCHLAND) GMBH—MacAndrews & Forbes Holdings Inc., pg. 695
COLEMAN OUTDOOR PRODUCTS—MacAndrews & Forbes Holdings Inc., pg. 695
COOLEY, INC., pg. 282
C.R. DANIELS, INC., pg. 314
MARTY GILMAN, INC., pg. 459
GLEN RAVEN MILLS, INC.-CUSTOM FABRICS DIVISION—Glen Raven Mills, Inc., pg. 461
INDUSTRIAS KOLMEX, S.A.—MacAndrews & Forbes Holdings Inc., pg. 696
THE JOHN JOHNSON CO., pg. 597
KLEIN TOOLS INC., pg. 635
OUTDOOR VENTURE CORP., pg. 832

2395 — PLEATING, DECORATIVE & NOVELTY STITCHING & TUCKING FOR THE TRADE

A-B EMBLEM DIV. OF CONRAD INDUSTRIES, INC., pg. 2
ACTIVE QUILTING DIV.—Rockville Fabrics Corporation, pg. 942
BUCILLA CORPORATION, pg. 185
HOUSE OF BIANCHI, pg. 546
LION BROTHERS COMPANY, INC., pg. 677
DAVID L. PEISTER CO., INC., pg. 856
PENN EMBLEM CO., pg. 857
PENN EMBLEM CO.—Penn Emblem Co., pg. 857
PENN EMBLEM CO.—Penn Emblem Co., pg. 857
STENCILS USA—Bucilla Corporation, pg. 185
VOYAGER EMBLEMS, INC., pg. 1155

2396 — AUTOMOTIVE TRIMMINGS, APPAREL FINDINGS & RELATED PRODUCTS

AMERICAN FAST PRINT, LIMITED, pg. 52
CADILLAC PRODUCTS, INC., pg. 207
CONSO PRODUCTS COMPANY, pg. 276
CROWN TEXTILE COMPANY, pg. 302
FACEMATE CORPORATION, pg. 396
FINDLAY INDUSTRIES, INC., pg. 410
HOLOUBEK INC., pg. 540
HOME CURTAIN CORPORATION—Home Innovations, Inc., pg. 541
LSJ SPORTSWEAR INC.—Merchant Capital Group Ltd, pg. 739
MASLAND INDUSTRIES, pg. 717
MERCHANT CAPITAL GROUP LTD, pg. 739
MEXICAN INDUSTRIES IN MICHIGAN, pg. 745
OUIMET STAY & LEATHER CO.—Ouimet Industries, pg. 831
PERFECT-HOFFMAN CO. LTD.—Berwind Corporation, pg. 145
QST INDUSTRIES, INC., pg. 902

SCALAMANDRE, INC., pg. 974
STAFLEX CO.—The Harodite Finishing Company Inc., pg. 510
STAFLEX/HAROTEX—The Harodite Finishing Company Inc., pg. 510
TROY MILLS, INC.—Troy Mills, Inc., pg. 1116
WM. E. WRIGHT LIMITED PARTNERSHIP, pg. 1205

2397 — SCHIFFLI MACHINE EMBROIDERIES

SWISS-M-TEX, L.P., pg. 1068

2399 — FABRICATED TEXTILE PRODUCTS, NEC

A & S TRIBAL INDUSTRIES, pg. 1
AMFAC, INC.—JMB Realty Corporation, pg. 585
ANNIN & COMPANY, pg. 75
BESTOP, INC., pg. 147
C&A AUTOMOTIVE GROUP—Collins & Aikman Group Inc., pg. 262
THE COLEMAN COMPANY—MacAndrews & Forbes Holdings Inc., pg. 695
THE COLEMAN COMPANY—MacAndrews & Forbes Holdings Inc., pg. 695
COLLEGEVILLE FLAG MFG. COMPANY, pg. 261
COLLEGEVILLE/IMAGINEERING L.P., pg. 262
C.R. DANIELS, INC., pg. 314
DESIGN USA—Jacmar Companies, Inc., pg. 587
DETTRA FLAG COMPANY, pg. 333
EQUIPO AUTOMOTRIZ AMERICANA S.A. DE C.V.—Takatta Inc., pg. 1077
GENERAL SAFETY CORPORATION, pg. 450
GLEN RAVEN MILLS, INC.-CUSTOM FABRICS DIVISION—Glen Raven Mills, Inc., pg. 461
JACMAR COMPANIES, INC., pg. 587
NSK-WARNER K.K.—Borg-Warner Corporation, pg. 166
NATIONAL BANNER COMPANY, pg. 786
OUTDOOR VENTURE CORP., pg. 832
PENN EMBLEM CO., pg. 857
SIRTEX PRINTING COMPANY—Dettra Flag Company, pg. 333
TAKATTA INC., pg. 1076
TALON, INC., pg. 1077
NELSON A. TAYLOR CO., INC., pg. 1080
VOYAGER EMBLEMS, INC., pg. 1155

2411 — LOGGING CAMPS & LOGGING CONTRACTORS

BRIDGEWATER RESOURCES CORPORATION, pg. 175
CALIFORNIA CEDAR PRODUCTS, INC., pg. 209
CONNOR FOREST INDUSTRIES, INC.—Bridgewater Resources Corporation, pg. 175
GREGORY AFFILIATES, INC., pg. 486
MANKE LUMBER COMPANY, INC., pg. 704
MENASHA CORPORATION, pg. 738
SIMPSON INVESTMENT CO., pg. 1007

2421 — SAWMILLS & PLANING MILLS, GENERAL

ALLEN-ROGERS CO.—Davis Mining & Manufacturing, pg. 319
ANTHONY FOREST PRODUCTS CO., INC., pg. 77
ATLANTIC LUMBER COMPANY—Sabbeth Industries Ltd, pg. 965
BEADLES LUMBER COMPANY, INC., pg. 129
BEARDEN LUMBER COMPANY, INC., pg. 129
BIBLER BROTHERS, INC., pg. 148
BRAZIER FOREST INDUSTRIES, INC., pg. 172
BRAZIER FOREST PRODUCTS OF OREGON—Brazier Forest Industries, Inc., pg. 173
WILLIAM BROJACK LUMBER COMPANY, pg. 179
COASTAL LUMBER COMPANY, pg. 257
THE COE MFG. CO., pg. 258
CONNOR FOREST INDUSTRIES, INC.—Bridgewater Resources Corporation, pg. 175
CURTIS LUMBER COMPANY, pg. 305
DESOTO HARDWOOD FLOORING COMPANY—National Bedding & Furniture Industries, pg. 786
FRANK PAXTON LUMBER COMPANY—Jeld-Wen, Inc., pg. 592
GERRITY LUMBER CO.—Gerrity Co., Inc., pg. 454
GREGORY AFFILIATES, INC., pg. 486
GULF LUMBER COMPANY, INC., pg. 493
GULF STATES PAPER CORPORATION, pg. 494
HAMPTON RESOURCES INC., pg. 504
HANEL LUMBER CO., INC., pg. 505
HARDWOODS OF MICHIGAN, INC., pg. 509
IDAHO FOREST INDUSTRY, INC., pg. 561
JELD-WEN, INC., pg. 591
KAIBAB INDUSTRIES, pg. 614
LAMINATED BEAM DIV.—Anthony Forest Products Co., Inc., pg. 77
MALLERY LUMBER CORP., pg. 702
MALLERY LUMBER CORP.-NY—Mallery Lumber Corp., pg. 703
J. GIBSON MCILVAIN CO., pg. 729
METTOWEE LUMBER & PLASTIC CO., INC.—Telescope Casual Furniture, Inc., pg. 1085
NICKERSON LUMBER COMPANY, pg. 806
OCHOCO LUMBER COMPANY, pg. 821
PACIFIC LUMBER & SHIPPING CO., pg. 840
PLUNKETT-WEBSTER, INC., pg. 877
PRATT-READ CORPORATION, pg. 884
PYRAMID MOUNTAIN LUMBER, pg. 901
RILEY CREEK LUMBER COMPANY, pg. 935
ROBBINS MANUFACTURING COMPANY, pg. 938
ROSEBURG FOREST PRODUCTS CO., pg. 948
SIERRA PACIFIC INDUSTRIES, pg. 1003
SIMPSON INVESTMENT CO., pg. 1007
SIMPSON TIMBER CO.—Simpson Investment Co., pg. 1007
SIMUNICO, INC., pg. 1007
SOUTHAMPTON SAWMILLS, LTD.—Parsons & Whittemore Enterprises, pg. 850
SPARTYWOOD PRODUCTS, INC.—Semac Industries Inc., pg. 989
STANDARD PLYWOOD, INC., pg. 1037
STOLTZE-CONNER LUMBER CO.—F.H. Stoltze Land & Lumber Company, pg. 1050
F.H. STOLTZE LAND & LUMBER COMPANY, pg. 1050
TOLLESON LUMBER COMPANY, INC., pg. 1100
VAAGEN BROTHERS LUMBER, INC., pg. 1142
VANPORT MANUFACTURING, INC., pg. 1145
WALTER H. WEABER SONS, INC., pg. 1169
WELCO LUMBER COMPANY, pg. 1175
WEST LUMBER CO., pg. 1177
WETSEL-OVIATT LUMBER COMPANY, pg. 1183
WILLAMINA LUMBER CO. INC.—Hampton Resources Inc., pg. 504
WOODWORK CORPORATION OF AMERICA, pg. 1201

2426 — HARDWOOD DIMENSION & FLOORING MILLS

AIRLINE MANUFACTURING COMPANY, INC., pg. 27
ANDERSON-TULLY CO., pg. 73
ARKANSAS OAK FLOORING, pg. 83
BABCOCK LUMBER COMPANY, pg. 107
BRIDGEWATER RESOURCES CORPORATION, pg. 175
WILLIAM BROJACK LUMBER COMPANY, pg. 179
BRUCE HARDWOOD FLOORS—Triangle Pacific Corporation, pg. 1112
DAVIS MINING & MANUFACTURING, pg. 319
DESOTO HARDWOOD FLOORING COMPANY—National Bedding & Furniture Industries, pg. 786
FITZPATRICK & WELLER, INC., pg. 416
HANCOCK LUMBER, INC., pg. 504
HARDWOODS OF MICHIGAN, INC., pg. 509
MILLER & CO., pg. 753
NAVAJO FOREST PRODUCTS INDUSTRIES, pg. 796
NORWALK FURNITURE CORPORATION, pg. 816
PRATT-READ CORPORATION, pg. 884
ROBBINS, INC., pg. 938
G. A. STOWERS FURNITURE CO.—Zale Corporation, pg. 1216
TATE ACCESS FLOORS, INC., pg. 1080
TRIANGLE PACIFIC CORPORATION, pg. 1112
WOODCRAFT INDUSTRIES, INC., pg. 1200

2429 — SPECIAL PRODUCT SAWMILLS, NEC

THE COE MFG. CO., pg. 258

2431 — MILLWORK

ANDERSEN WINDOWS INC., pg. 72
ANTHONY FOREST PRODUCTS CO., INC., pg. 77
ARIZONA SASH & DOOR CO.—Foxworth-Galbraith Lumber Co., pg. 428
BARNETT MILLWORKS, INC., pg. 120
BAY INDUSTRIES INC., pg. 127
BLACK MILLWORK CO., INC., pg. 154
BLOUNT LUMBER COMPANY, pg. 158
BUFFELEN WOODWORKING COMPANY, pg. 187
CURT BULLOCK BUILDERS, INC., pg. 188
CAROLINA BUILDERS CORPORATION, pg. 223
COMMERCIAL & ARCHITECTURAL PRODUCTS INC., pg. 268
CONESTOGA WOOD SPECIALTIES, INC., pg. 273
WAYNE DALTON CORPORATION, pg. 312
DI GIORGIO CORPORATION, pg. 334
THE DORRIS LUMBER & MOULDING CO., pg. 347
ERB LUMBER COMPANY, pg. 360
FIMBEL DOOR CORPORATION, pg. 409
FOJTASEK COMPANIES, INC., pg. 421
FRANTZ BEARING DIV.—Frantz Manufacturing Co., pg. 430
FRANTZ MANUFACTURING CO., pg. 429
GANAHL LUMBER COMPANY, pg. 442
GERRITY CO., INC., pg. 454
GRAHAM MFG. CO.—ESSTAR Incorporated, pg. 361
HARVEY INDUSTRIES, INC., pg. 515
THOMAS R. HOPSON BROKER, INC., pg. 544
HURD MILLWORK COMPANY, INC.—UIS, Inc., pg. 1123
J.W. WINDOW COMPONENTS, INC.—Walter Industries, Inc., pg. 1162
JELD-WEN, INC., pg. 591
JOANNA—CC Industries, Inc., pg. 200
PETER KUNTZ COMPANY—Erb Lumber Company, pg. 360
LDI, LTD., pg. 647
LIFETIME DOORS INC., pg. 675
MANHATTAN BUILDING COMPANIES, pg. 703
MARVIN LUMBER & CEDAR COMPANY, pg. 716
MAYWOOD, INC., pg. 725
MCCLELLAND & DUFF, INC.—Erb Lumber Company, pg. 360
MIDWEST OPERATIONS—Commercial & Architectural Products Inc., pg. 268
NATIONAL WOOD PRODUCTS, CO.—Saunders Brothers, pg. 972
NAVAJO FOREST PRODUCTS INDUSTRIES, pg. 796
THE NIKKEL CORPORATION, pg. 807
NORANDEX INC., pg. 809
NORTHEAST OPERATIONS—Commercial & Architectural Products Inc., pg. 268
ODL INCORPORATED, pg. 819
PEASE INDUSTRIES, INC., pg. 854
PELLA CORPORATION, pg. 856
PLYWOOD PANELS, INC., pg. 878
RICHARDSON INDUSTRIES, INC., pg. 932
RIVERSIDE MILLWORK COMPANY, INC., pg. 937
SAUNDERS BROTHERS, pg. 972
SCHUCK & SONS CONSTRUCTION CO., pg. 979
SETZER FOREST PRODUCTS, pg. 993
SETZER FOREST PRODUCTS-OROVILLE PLANT—Setzer Forest Products, pg. 993
SIERRA PACIFIC INDUSTRIES, pg. 1003
SIMPSON INVESTMENT CO., pg. 1007
SIMPSON TIMBER CO.—Simpson Investment Co., pg. 1007
L. J. SMITH, INC.—Marmac Corporation, pg. 710
SOUTHEAST OPERATIONS—Commercial & Architectural Products Inc., pg. 268
SOUTHWEST OPERATIONS—Commercial & Architectural Products Inc., pg. 268
STANDARD SHADE ROLLER DIV.—CC Industries, Inc., pg. 200
STEVES & SONS, pg. 1048
THE TANEY CORPORATION, pg. 1077
THERMA-TRU CORP., pg. 1090
THERMWELL PRODUCTS CO., INC., pg. 1092
WM. S. TRIMBLE COMPANY, INC., pg. 1113
TWIN Y CORPORATION—Jeld-Wen, Inc., pg. 592
VINYL THERM, INC., pg. 1152
VIVIAN MILLWORKS, pg. 1154
WALLED LAKE DOOR COMPANY, pg. 1161
WESTERN OPERATIONS—Commercial & Architectural Products Inc., pg. 268
WIGAND CORPORATION, pg. 1189
WING INDUSTRIES, INC., pg. 1196
WING INDUSTRIES SOUTH CENTRAL—Wing Industries, Inc., pg. 1196
WOODWORK CORPORATION OF AMERICA, pg. 1201

2434 — WOOD KITCHEN CABINETS

BLOUNT LUMBER COMPANY, pg. 158
BRAMMER MANUFACTURING COMPANY, pg. 171
CLASSIC BATH PRODUCTS—Triangle Pacific Corporation, pg. 1112
CRYSTAL CABINET WORKS, INC., pg. 303
IXL FURNITURE—Triangle Pacific Corporation, pg. 1112
LEGIS CORPORATION—Siegel Corp., pg. 1002
MARSH FURNITURE COMPANY, pg. 714
MCCONNELL CABINETS, INC., pg. 727
NORCRAFT COMPANIES—Norcraft Companies, Inc., pg. 809
NORCRAFT COMPANIES, INC., pg. 809
RIVERSIDE MILLWORK COMPANY, INC., pg. 937
SIEGEL CORP., pg. 1002
TRI-PAC DIV.—Triangle Pacific Corporation, pg. 1112
TRIANGLE PACIFIC CORPORATION, pg. 1112
U.S. SLATE & MARBLE CO.—Triangle Pacific Corporation, pg. 1112
WOODWORK CORPORATION OF AMERICA, pg. 1201
YORKTOWNE, INC., pg. 1208

2435 — HARDWOOD VENEER & PLYWOOD

BRIDGEWATER RESOURCES CORPORATION, pg. 175
WILLIAM BROJACK LUMBER COMPANY, pg. 179
DARLINGTON VENEER COMPANY, pg. 315
GREGORY AFFILIATES, INC., pg. 486
MALLERY LUMBER CORP., pg. 702
MALLERY LUMBER CORP.-NY—Mallery Lumber Corp., pg. 703
MILLER & CO., pg. 753
NORTHERN MICHIGAN VENEERS, INC., pg. 814
PICKERING INDUSTRIES INC., pg. 869
PLYWOOD PANELS, INC., pg. 878
SIMPSON TIMBER CO.—Simpson Investment Co., pg. 1007
TIMBER PRODUCTS COMPANY, LP, pg. 1097

2436 — SOFTWOOD VENEER & PLYWOOD

PACIFIC LUMBER & SHIPPING CO., pg. 840
PUGET SOUND PLYWOOD, INC., pg. 899
ROSEBURG FOREST PRODUCTS CO., pg. 948
SIMPSON INVESTMENT CO., pg. 1007
SIMPSON TIMBER CO.—Simpson Investment Co., pg. 1007
TIMBER PRODUCTS COMPANY, LP, pg. 1097
VIVIAN MILLWORKS, pg. 1154

2439 — STRUCTURAL WOOD MEMBERS, NEC

CALCASIEU LUMBER COMPANY, pg. 208
CAROLINA BUILDERS CORPORATION, pg. 223
CHAGNON LUMBER COMPANY, INC., pg. 238
GERRITY CO., INC., pg. 454
LITTFIN LUMBER COMPANY, pg. 678
NATIONAL LUMBER CO., pg. 792
NICKERSON LUMBER COMPANY, pg. 806
RICHARDSON INDUSTRIES, INC., pg. 932
RIEMEIER LUMBER COMPANY, INC., pg. 934
SCHUCK & SONS CONSTRUCTION CO., pg. 979
SEAMAN TIMBER COMPANY, INC., pg. 986
VILLAUME INDUSTRIES, INC., pg. 1151

2441 — NAILED & LOCK CORNER WOODEN BOXES & SHOOK

SEATTLE PACKAGING CORPORATION, pg. 986
VILLAUME INDUSTRIES, INC., pg. 1151

2448 — WOOD PALLETS & SKIDS

ELBERTA CRATE & BOX COMPANY, pg. 372

STEPHEN GOULD PAPER CO., INC., pg. 473
JELD-WEN, INC., pg. 591
LOVE BOX COMPANY, INC., pg. 685
SEAMAN TIMBER COMPANY, INC., pg. 986
SEMAC INDUSTRIES INC., pg. 989
SPARTYWOOD PRODUCTS, INC.—Semac Industries Inc., pg. 989
VILLAUME INDUSTRIES, INC., pg. 1151

2449 — WOOD CONTAINERS, NEC

ELBERTA CRATE & BOX COMPANY, pg. 372
HORN PACKAGING CORPORATION, pg. 544
L & L NURSERY SUPPLY, INC., pg. 647
SEMAC INDUSTRIES INC., pg. 989
VILLAUME INDUSTRIES, INC., pg. 1151
WETSEL-OVIATT LUMBER COMPANY, pg. 1183

2451 — MOBILE HOMES

B & B HOMES CORPORATION, pg. 105
CHIEF INDUSTRIES - HOUSING DIV.—Chief Industries, Inc., pg. 247
CHIEF INDUSTRIES, INC., pg. 247
DESTINY INDUSTRY INC., pg. 332
FAIRMONT HOMES, INC., pg. 397
GOLDEN WEST HOMES, pg. 467
GOLDEN WEST HOMES PERRIS DIV.—Golden West Homes, pg. 467
HOMES OF MERIT INC., pg. 542
HORTON HOMES, INC., pg. 545
JACOBSEN MANUFACTURING, INC., pg. 588
LB INDUSTRIES INC., pg. 647
NASHUA HOMES OF IDAHO INC., pg. 784
PALM HARBOR HOMES, INC., pg. 843
ROC PROPERTIES INC., pg. 908
REDMAN HOMES, INC.—Redman Industries, Inc., pg. 919
REDMAN INDUSTRIES, INC., pg. 919
RIVER OAKS DOUBLE-WIDE PLANT—ROC Properties Inc., pg. 908
RIVER OAKS HOMES, INC.—ROC Properties Inc., pg. 908
SCIENTIFIC CORPORATION—Hinderliter Industries, Inc., pg. 535
SCOTSMAN GROUP, INC.—The Scotsman Group, Inc., pg. 982
SILVERCREST WESTERN HOME INDUSTRIES CORPORATION, pg. 1004
WALPOLE WOODWORKERS, INC., pg. 1161
WESTERN HOMES CORPORATION—Redman Industries, Inc., pg. 919
WICK BLDG. SYSTEMS INC. MANUFACTURED HOMES DIV.—Wick Building Systems, pg. 1188
WICK BUILDING SYSTEMS, pg. 1188

2452 — PREFABRICATED WOOD BUILDINGS & COMPONENTS

ACTIVE HOMES CORP.—Active Tool & Manufacturing Co., Inc., pg. 15
ACTIVE TOOL & MANUFACTURING CO., INC., pg. 15
BARDEN & ROBESON CORPORATION, pg. 119
BERKS PRODUCTS CORPORATION, pg. 142
CALCASIEU LUMBER COMPANY, pg. 208
CARLSBERG FINANCIAL CORP., pg. 220
CAROLINA BUILDERS CORPORATION, pg. 223
COLEMAN SPAS, INC.—MacAndrews & Forbes Holdings Inc., pg. 695
COLUMBIA LUMBER & MANUFACTURING CO., pg. 265
DECK HOUSE INC., pg. 324
DELUXE HOMES OF PENNSYLVANIA, INC., pg. 327
DIXIE ROYAL HOMES, INC.—Family Inns of America, Inc., pg. 398
ESTHER WILLIAMS SWIMMING POOL CO., pg. 389
THE FAIRFIELD LUMBER & SUPPLY COMPANY, pg. 397
FAR WEST PRODUCTS, INC.—Al Copeland Enterprises, Inc., pg. 284
GAME TIME, INC., pg. 442
INSILCO CORPORATION, pg. 571
LWMCK CORPORATION, pg. 648
LAS PLUMAS LUMBER NORTH DIVISION—Di Giorgio Corporation, pg. 335
LAS PLUMAS LUMBER SOUTH DIVISION—Di Giorgio Corporation, pg. 335
NATIONAL BUILDING SYSTEMS—LWMCK Corporation, pg. 648
NATIONWIDE HOMES, INC., pg. 795
NEW ENGLAND LOG HOMES, INC.—New England Corporation, pg. 800
NICKERSON LUMBER COMPANY, pg. 806
PBS BUILDING SYSTEMS OF AMERICA, pg. 835
PHILADELPHIA SIGN COMPANY, pg. 867
RIDG-U-RAK, INC., pg. 933
RIEMEIER LUMBER COMPANY, INC., pg. 934
SCOTSMAN GROUP, INC.—The Scotsman Group, Inc., pg. 982
SIMPLEX INDUSTRIES, INC., pg. 1006
VILLAUME INDUSTRIES, INC., pg. 1151
WALPOLE WOODWORKERS, INC., pg. 1161
WICK BUILDING SYSTEMS, pg. 1188

2491 — WOOD PRESERVING

J.H. BAXTER & COMPANY, pg. 127
BROWN WOOD PRESERVING COMPANY, pg. 183
CHARTER HOUSE INCORPORATED—Stainless Incorporated, pg. 1035
COX WOOD PRESERVING CO., pg. 295
ENGINEERED WOOD DIV.—Anthony Forest Products Co., Inc., pg. 77
FRONTIER LUMBER COMPANY, INC., pg. 434
MANKE LUMBER COMPANY, INC., pg. 704
NAVAJO FOREST PRODUCTS INDUSTRIES, pg. 796
OSMOSE WOOD PRESERVING CO., pg. 830
PACIFIC SOUND RESOURCES, pg. 841
PACIFIC WOOD TREATING COPORATION, pg. 842
RICHARDSON INDUSTRIES, INC., pg. 932
ROBBINS MANUFACTURING COMPANY, pg. 938
SEAMAN TIMBER COMPANY, INC., pg. 986
SWANER HARDWOOD COMPANY, INC., pg. 1066
TEXAS ELECTRIC COOPERATIVES, INC., pg. 1089
TOLLESON LUMBER COMPANY, INC., pg. 1100
WIGAND CORPORATION, pg. 1189

2493 — RECONSTITUTED WOOD PRODUCTS

ANTHONY FOREST PRODUCTS CO., INC., pg. 77
HARMESON MANUFACTURING COMPANY, INC., pg. 510
J.M. HUBER, WOOD PRODUCTS DIV.—J.M. Huber Corporation, pg. 550
INTERNATIONAL PERMALITE, INC., pg. 579
NAVAJO FOREST PRODUCTS INDUSTRIES, pg. 796
PACIFIC LUMBER & SHIPPING CO., pg. 840
PANEL PROCESSING, INC., pg. 846
ROSEBURG FOREST PRODUCTS CO., pg. 948
TIMBER PRODUCTS COMPANY, LP, pg. 1097

2499 — WOOD PRODUCTS, NEC

ALLEN-ROGERS CO.—Davis Mining & Manufacturing, pg. 319
ANNIN & COMPANY, pg. 75
APPLICATOR CO.—Plastek Group, pg. 875
JOHN BOOS & COMPANY, pg. 165
BRIDGEWATER RESOURCES CORPORATION, pg. 175
BRUNER-IVORY HANDLE COMPANY—O.P. Link Handle Company, pg. 677
BURLINGTON BASKET CO., pg. 191
CALIFORNIA CEDAR PRODUCTS, INC., pg. 209
CARLSON COMPANIES, INC., pg. 220
CARRIS REELS, INC., pg. 225
CHESAPEAKE FINANCIAL CORP., pg. 243
COASTAL LUMBER COMPANY, pg. 257
CONCORCO LDA.—21 International Holdings, Inc., pg. 1121
DAKIN, INC., pg. 311
DEAD RIVER COMPANY, pg. 321
DIAMOND BRANDS, INC., pg. 335
EUREKA MANUFACTURING CO., INC.—Reed & Barton Corporation, pg. 920
FOREST INDUSTRIES, INC.—Saunders Brothers, pg. 972
FORSTER MFG. CO., INC.—Advent International, pg. 21
GEM, INCORPORATED, pg. 447
GERRITY CO., INC., pg. 454
GILBERT MFG. CORP., pg. 458
GOLDEN WEST HOMES, pg. 467
HOWARD MANUFACTURING, pg. 547
LASTING PRODUCTS, INC., pg. 660
O.P. LINK HANDLE COMPANY, pg. 676
MALLERY LUMBER CORP., pg. 702
MALLERY LUMBER CORP.-NY—Mallery Lumber Corp., pg. 703
MOORE COMPANY, pg. 768
MURPHY COMPANY, pg. 776
NORTH AMERICAN ENCLOSURES, INC., pg. 811
PRATT-READ CORPORATION, pg. 884
PRECISION PLASTICS—Precision Plastics Inc., pg. 885
REED & BARTON CORPORATION, pg. 920
A. I. ROOT CO.—A.I. Root Company, pg. 946
ROYAL OAK ENTERPRISES, INC., pg. 953
SAUNDERS BROTHERS, pg. 972
SEQUATCHIE HANDLE WORKS, INC.—O.P. Link Handle Company, pg. 677
SHARON CONCEPTS, INC., pg. 995
SIERRA PACIFIC INDUSTRIES, pg. 1003
SIERRA PACIFIC INDUSTRIES-ARCATA DIVISION—Sierra Pacific Industries, pg. 1003
SIERRA PACIFIC INDUSTRIES-HAYFORK DIVISION—Sierra Pacific Industries, pg. 1003
SIMPSON TIMBER CO.—Simpson Investment Co., pg. 1007
SOLON MANUFACTURING COMPANY, pg. 1017
H. A. STILES CO.—Saunders Brothers, pg. 972
STRUCTURAL INDUSTRIES, INC., pg. 1054
STUHR ENTERPRISES INC., pg. 1055
TURNER, DAY & WOOLWORTH HANDLE CORP.—O.P. Link Handle Company, pg. 677
VILLAUME INDUSTRIES, INC., pg. 1151
WALPOLE WOODWORKERS, INC., pg. 1161
WESTON GALLERY—Wilton Industries, Inc., pg. 1195
YERGER BROS., INC., pg. 1208
ZENITH PRODUCTS CORP., pg. 1217
ZIMDAR ENTERPRISES, pg. 1220

2511 — WOOD HOUSEHOLD FURNITURE, EXCEPT UPHOLSTERED

AMANA SOCIETY, pg. 46
S. BENT & BROTHERS, INC., pg. 140
BERNHARDT FURNITURE CO., pg. 144
BRITTANY CORPORATION, pg. 177
CENTURY FURNITURE INDUSTRIES, pg. 235
CENTURY PRODUCTS CO., pg. 235
CHESAPEAKE FINANCIAL CORP., pg. 243
CLEVELAND CHAIR COMPANY, pg. 255
COCHRANE FURNITURE CO., INC., pg. 258
COSCO, INC., pg. 287
DINAIRE CORP., pg. 338
ETHAN ALLEN, INC.—Green Mountain Holding Corporation, pg. 485
EVENFLO JUVENILE FURNITURE CO.—Spalding & Evenflo Companies, Inc., pg. 1024
FINKEL OUTDOOR PRODUCTS OF FLORIDA—CC Industries, Inc., pg. 200
FOLEY MARTENS COMPANY—Foley-Belsaw Company, pg. 422
GOOD COMPANIES, pg. 470
GREEN MOUNTAIN HOLDING CORPORATION, pg. 485
HARDEN FURNITURE COMPANY, pg. 508
HARDEN GALLERIES—Harden Furniture Company, pg. 508
HELIKON FURNITURE CO., INC., pg. 526
HOOKER FURNITURE CORPORATION, pg. 543
IMPERIAL MANUFACTURING COMPANY, pg. 564
KARGES FURNITURE COMPANY, pg. 616
THE KELLER MANUFACTURING CO., INC., pg. 621
KINDEL FURNITURE COMPANY, pg. 630
KITCHEN KOMPACT, INC., pg. 634
MERSMAN FURNITURE, pg. 741
NATIONAL BEDDING & FURNITURE INDUSTRIES, pg. 786
NORWALK FURNITURE CORPORATION, pg. 816
PACE COLLECTION, INC., pg. 838
PAOLI, INC., pg. 846
QUAKER INDUSTRIES LIMITED, pg. 903
RED CALLIOPE & ASSOCIATES, INC., pg. 918
RESTONIC CORPORATION, pg. 929
RICHARDSON BROTHERS CO., pg. 932
RICHARDSON INDUSTRIES, INC., pg. 932
SAUDER WOODWORKING CO., pg. 972
SAUNDERS BROTHERS, pg. 972
SCHNADIG CORPORATION, pg. 977
SEALY CORPORATION, pg. 985
SIMUNICO, INC., pg. 1007
OKLA HOMER SMITH FURNITURE CO.—Century Products Co., pg. 235
SPALDING & EVENFLO COMPANIES, INC., pg. 1024
SPECTRUM INDUSTRIES, INC., pg. 1029
STATTON FURNITURE MANUFACTURING COMPANY, pg. 1042
SWANER HARDWOOD COMPANY, INC., pg. 1066
TELESCOPE CASUAL FURNITURE, INC., pg. 1085
TELL CITY CHAIR CO., pg. 1085
TOWN SQUARE FURNITURE, INC., pg. 1104
U.S. FURNITURE INDUSTRIES, INC., pg. 1136
WARRENTON DIVISION—Cochrane Furniture Co., Inc., pg. 258
WELSH COMPANY, pg. 1175
WOODLORE—Allen-Edmonds Shoe Corp., pg. 36
WOODSTUFF MANUFACTURING, INC.—Sealy Corporation, pg. 986
WOODWORK CORPORATION OF AMERICA, pg. 1201
X-A CABINET CORPORATION, pg. 1206
YERGER BROS., INC., pg. 1208

2512 — WOOD HOUSEHOLD FURNITURE, UPHOLSTERED

THE BERKLINE CORPORATION—Corber Corporation, pg. 285
BERKLINE, INC.—Corber Corporation, pg. 285
BERKLINE LIMITED—Corber Corporation, pg. 285
BERNHARDT FURNITURE CO., pg. 144
CM FURNITURE, INC.—Carolina Mills, Inc., pg. 223
CARLTON MANUFACTURING, INC., pg. 222
CENTURY FURNITURE INDUSTRIES, pg. 235
COCHRANE FURNITURE CO., INC., pg. 258
CORBER CORPORATION, pg. 285
COX FURNITURE, pg. 294
ETHAN ALLEN, INC.—Green Mountain Holding Corporation, pg. 485
FICKS REED COMPANY, pg. 408
FRAENKEL COMPANY, pg. 428
GREEN MOUNTAIN HOLDING CORPORATION, pg. 485
HICKORY HILL FURNITURE CORPORATION—Norwalk Furniture Corporation, pg. 816
HITCHCOCK CHAIR COMPANY LTD, pg. 536
INTERNATIONAL FURNITURE DIV.—Schnadig Corporation, pg. 977
JAMISON BEDDING, INC., pg. 589
KARPEN FURNITURE DIV.—Schnadig Corporation, pg. 977
KINDEL FURNITURE COMPANY, pg. 630
KLAUSSNER CORPORATION, pg. 634
KLAUSSNER FURNITURE INDUSTRY—Klaussner Corporation, pg. 634
KROEHLER FURNITURE MANUFACTURING COMPANY, INC., pg. 645
LEATHER CENTER, INC., pg. 664
MARKWOOD INC., pg. 710
NORWALK FURNITURE CORPORATION, pg. 816
SCHNADIG CORPORATION, pg. 977
SELIG MANUFACTURING COMPANY—Cox Furniture, pg. 294
SIMMONS UPHOLSTERED FURNITURE, INC., pg. 1005
STAKMORE INC., pg. 1035
STANTON COOPER—Markwood Inc., pg. 710
STATTON FURNITURE MANUFACTURING COMPANY, pg. 1042
TELESCOPE CASUAL FURNITURE, INC., pg. 1085
U.S. FURNITURE INDUSTRIES, INC., pg. 1136
WELSH COMPANY, pg. 1175
WOODMARK ORIGINALS—Markwood Inc., pg. 710

2514 — METAL HOUSEHOLD FURNITURE

ALL-LUMINUM PRODUCTS, INC., pg. 35
BENSON CORP.—Gem Industries Finance Corporation, pg. 447
BOZOF DINETTES, INC., pg. 169
CC INDUSTRIES, INC., pg. 199
CLEVELAND CHAIR COMPANY, pg. 255
COSCO, INC., pg. 287
CROWN LEISURE PRODUCTS—CC Industries, Inc., pg. 200
CUSTOM PRODUCTS DIVISION—Chief Industries, Inc., pg. 247
ENERGY BROKERS GUILD, pg. 381

FANTA FURNITURE—All-Luminum Products, Inc., pg. 35
FINKEL OUTDOOR PRODUCTS OF CALIFORNIA—CC Industries, Inc., pg. 200
FINKEL OUTDOOR PRODUCTS, INC.—CC Industries, Inc., pg. 200
FLANDERS INDUSTRIES, INC., pg. 416
GEM INDUSTRIES, INC.—Gem Industries Finance Corporation, pg. 447
GEM SOUTHEAST, INC.—Gem Industries Finance Corporation, pg. 447
IXL FURNITURE—Triangle Pacific Corporation, pg. 1112
IMPERIAL MANUFACTURING COMPANY, pg. 564
LEAR SIEGLER SEYMOUR CORP.—Lear Siegler Diversified Holdings Corp., pg. 664
MASTERCRAFT FURNITURE CORP., pg. 720
MEADOWCRAFT, INC., pg. 733
MECO CORPORATION, pg. 734
MOHAWK FURNITURE, INC.—Gem Industries Finance Corporation, pg. 447
RENCO GROUP, pg. 926
RESTONIC CORPORATION, pg. 929
RYNONE MANUFACTURING CORPORATION, pg. 958
TELESCOPE CASUAL FURNITURE, INC., pg. 1085
THE TURNER & SEYMOUR MFG. COMPANY, pg. 1119
U.S. FURNITURE INDUSTRIES, INC., pg. 1136
WALLACE LEISURE PRODUCTS, INC., pg. 1160
WELLINGTON INDUSTRIES INC., pg. 1175
WELSH COMPANY, pg. 1175
ZENITH PRODUCTS CORP., pg. 1217

2515 — MATTRESSES, FOUNDATIONS & CONVERTIBLE BEDS

W.S. BADCOCK CORPORATION, pg. 113
BLUE BELL/KING KOIL, INC., pg. 158
CASTRO CONVERTIBLE CORPORATION, pg. 229
CENTRAL DE INDUSTRIAS, S.A.—Lear Siegler Diversified Holdings Corp., pg. 664
CHITTENDEN & EASTMAN CO., pg. 248
COSCO, INC., pg. 287
ECHEVARRIA ANGEL CO., INC., pg. 365
FRAENKEL COMPANY, pg. 428
INTERNACIONAL MONTEREY, S.A.—Sealy Corporation, pg. 986
JAMISON BEDDING, INC., pg. 589
KING KOIL LICENSING COMPANY INC., pg. 630
NATIONAL BEDDING & FURNITURE INDUSTRIES, pg. 786
NOEL-JOANNA, INC., pg. 808
THE OHIO MATTRESS COMPANY LICENSING AND COMPONENTS GROUP—Sealy Corporation, pg. 985
THE OHIO MATTRESS COMPANY LICENSING AND COMPONENTS GROUP—Sealy Corporation, pg. 985
THE OHIO MATTRESS COMPANY, LICENSING AND COMPONENTS GROUP—Sealy Corporation, pg. 985
OHIO-SEALY MATTRESS MANUFACTURING CO.-FORT WORTH—Sealy Corporation, pg. 985
OHIO-SEALY MATTRESS MANUFACTURING CO.-HOUSTON—Sealy Corporation, pg. 985
RED CALLIOPE & ASSOCIATES, INC., pg. 918
RESTONIC CORPORATION, pg. 929
SEALY CANADA, LTD.—Sealy Corporation, pg. 986
SEALY CONNECTICUT, INC.—Sealy Corporation, pg. 985
SEALY CORPORATION, pg. 985
SEALY, INC.—Sealy Corporation, pg. 985
SEALY MATTRESS COMPANY, pg. 986
SEALY MATTRESS COMPANY OF ALBANY, INC.—Sealy Corporation, pg. 985
SEALY MATTRESS COMPANY OF ILLINOIS—Sealy Corporation, pg. 985
SEALY MATTRESS COMPANY OF KANSAS CITY, INC.—Sealy Corporation, pg. 985
SEALY MATTRESS COMPANY OF MEMPHIS—Sealy Corporation, pg. 985
SEALY MATTRESS COMPANY OF MICHIGAN, INC.—Sealy Corporation, pg. 985
SEALY MATTRESS COMPANY OF PUERTO RICO—Sealy Corporation, pg. 985
SEALY OF MARYLAND & VIRGINIA, INC.—Sealy Corporation, pg. 985
SEALY OF MINNESOTA, INC.—Sealy Corporation, pg. 985
SERTA, INC., pg. 991
SERTA MATTRESS COMPANY, pg. 991
THE SPRING AIR COMPANY, pg. 1032
THE SPRINGWALL MATTRESS CO., pg. 1033
THE STEARNS & FOSTER BEDDING COMPANY—Sealy Corporation, pg. 985
THE STEARNS & FOSTER BEDDING COMPANY—Sealy Corporation, pg. 985
STEARNS & FOSTER UPHOLSTERY FURNITURE CO.—Sealy Corporation, pg. 985
STEARNS & FOSTER UPHOLSTERY FURNITURE CO.—Sealy Corporation, pg. 985
THE STEARNS & FOSTER UPHOLSTERY FURNITURE COMPANY—Sealy Corporation, pg. 985
THE OHIO MATTRESS COMPANY LICENSING AND COMPONETS GROUP—Sealy Corporation, pg. 985
THERAPEDIC ASSOCIATES, INC., pg. 1090
TRINA, INC., pg. 1113

2517 — WOOD TELEVISION, RADIO, PHONOGRAPH & SEWING MACHINE CABINETS

BOSE CANADA, INC.—Bose Corporation, pg. 167
PACE COLLECTION, INC., pg. 838

2519 — HOUSEHOLD FURNITURE, NEC

ALL-LUMINUM PRODUCTS, INC., pg. 35
BURLINGTON BASKET CO., pg. 191
BURTON-DIXIE OF BLACKSBURG INC.—CC Industries, Inc., pg. 200
COSCO, INC., pg. 287
FANTA FURNITURE—All-Luminum Products, Inc., pg. 35
FICKS REED COMPANY, pg. 408
HOOKER FURNITURE CORPORATION, pg. 543
M. KAMENSTEIN, INC., pg. 615
LAWNWARE PRODUCTS, INC., pg. 661
LEATHER CENTER, INC., pg. 664
OAK PRODUCTS, INC.—ROC Properties Inc., pg. 908
PRECISION PLASTICS—Precision Plastics Inc., pg. 885
W. C. REDMON CO., pg. 919
SUNBEAM CASUAL FURNITURE CO.—Sunbeam-Oster Company, Inc., pg. 1059
TROPITONE FURNITURE CO. INC., pg. 1116
WELSH COMPANY, pg. 1175
ZENITH PRODUCTS CORP., pg. 1217

2521 — WOOD OFFICE FURNITURE

ALMA INDUSTRIES, pg. 43
ARTCO-BELL CORPORATION, pg. 86
BELVEDERE COMPANY, pg. 138
BRAYTON INTERNATIONAL INC.—Steelcase Inc., pg. 1044
CRAMER INC., pg. 296
CURVCRAFT, pg. 306
EAC CORPORATION, pg. 359
FLEWELLING DIV.—EAC Corporation, pg. 359
GF OFFICE FURNITURE LTD., pg. 439
GLOBE BUSINESS FURNITURE, INC., pg. 463
HARDWOOD VISUALS—Howe Furniture Corporation, pg. 547
THE HARTER GROUP, pg. 513
HAWORTH, INC., pg. 518
HOWE FURNITURE CORPORATION, pg. 547
JOFCO INC., pg. 595
KINETICS, INC.—Haworth, Inc., pg. 518
KLAUSSNER FURNITURE INDUSTRY—Klaussner Corporation, pg. 634
KNOLL INTL., INC.—21 International Holdings, Inc., pg. 1121
LUNSTEAD, A HAWORTH PORTFOLIO CO.—Haworth, Inc., pg. 518
METROPOLITAN FURNITURE CORPORATION—Steelcase Inc., pg. 1044
MUELLER, A HAWORTH PORTFOLIO CO.—Haworth, Inc., pg. 518
NACOMA CONSOLIDATED, INC., pg. 782
OSCEOLA DIV.—EAC Corporation, pg. 359
PACE COLLECTION, INC., pg. 838
PAOLI, INC., pg. 846
POHLSCHRODER & CO. KG—Steelcase Inc., pg. 1044
SAUDER MANUFACTURING CORPORATION, pg. 972
SPECTRUM INDUSTRIES, INC., pg. 1029
STANDARD MANIFOLD COMPANY, INC., pg. 1037
STEELCASE CANADA LTD.—Steelcase Inc., pg. 1044
STEELCASE INC., pg. 1044
STEELCASE INC./INTERNATIONAL DIV.—Steelcase Inc., pg. 1044
STEELCASE KUROGANE LTD.—Steelcase Inc., pg. 1044
STEELCASE-STRAFOR S.A.—Steelcase Inc., pg. 1044
STEELCASE STRAFOR (U.K.) LTD.—Steelcase Inc., pg. 1044
STOW & DAVIS FURNITURE CO.—Steelcase Inc., pg. 1044
TIFFANY INDUSTRIES, INC., pg. 1097
U.S. FURNITURE INDUSTRIES, INC., pg. 1136
WOODWORK CORPORATION OF AMERICA, pg. 1201
YERGER BROS., INC., pg. 1208

2522 — METAL OFFICE FURNITURE

ACME VISIBLE RECORDS, pg. 13
AMES COLOR FILE DIVISION—Ames Safety Envelope Company, Inc., pg. 66
AMES SAFETY ENVELOPE COMPANY, INC., pg. 66
ARTCO-BELL CORPORATION, pg. 86
ATAL SA—Joyce International, Inc., pg. 608
BALTIMORE STATIONERY CO., pg. 116
BELVEDERE COMPANY, pg. 138
CHAIRWORLD, INC.—Globe Business Furniture, Inc., pg. 463
COMFORTO GROUP—Haworth, Inc., pg. 518
CRAMER INC., pg. 296
CURVCRAFT, pg. 306
EAC CORPORATION, pg. 359
FLEWELLING DIV.—EAC Corporation, pg. 359
GF OFFICE FURNITURE—GF Office Furniture Ltd., pg. 439
GF OFFICE FURNITURE LTD., pg. 439
GENERAL METALCRAFT, INC., pg. 450
GLOBE BUSINESS FURNITURE, INC., pg. 463
THE HARTER GROUP, pg. 513
HARVARD INDUSTRIES, INC., pg. 514
HARVARD INTERIORS MANUFACTURING CO.—Harvard Industries, Inc., pg. 514
HAWORTH, INC., pg. 518
HOOKER FURNITURE CORPORATION, pg. 543
HOWE FURNITURE CORPORATION, pg. 547
INVINCIBLE METAL FURNITURE CO., pg. 582
JOYCE INTERNATIONAL, INC., pg. 608
KINETICS, INC.—Haworth, Inc., pg. 518
KNOLL INTL., INC.—21 International Holdings, Inc., pg. 1121
LEHIGH-LEOPOLD—Joyce International, Inc., pg. 608
LUXOR CORPORATION—Ebsco Industries, Inc., pg. 365
MUELLER, A HAWORTH PORTFOLIO CO.—Haworth, Inc., pg. 518
OSCEOLA DIV.—EAC Corporation, pg. 359
PHOENIX ENTERPRISES INC., pg. 868
POHLSCHRODER & CO. KG—Steelcase Inc., pg. 1044
H.W. SCHMIDT GMBH—Haworth, Inc., pg. 518
SCHWAB CORP., pg. 980
SMITH SYSTEM MANUFACTURING COMPANY, pg. 1014
STEELCASE CANADA LTD.—Steelcase Inc., pg. 1044
STEELCASE INC., pg. 1044
STEELCASE, INC./ATHENS PLANT—Steelcase Inc., pg. 1044
STEELCASE INC./INTERNATIONAL DIV.—Steelcase Inc., pg. 1044
STEELCASE KUROGANE LTD.—Steelcase Inc., pg. 1044
STEELCASE-STRAFOR S.A.—Steelcase Inc., pg. 1044
STEELCASE STRAFOR (U.K.) LTD.—Steelcase Inc., pg. 1044
TENNSCO CORPORATION, pg. 1088
TIFFANY INDUSTRIES, INC., pg. 1097
TIFFANY STAND & FURNITURE COMPANY—Tiffany Industries, Inc., pg. 1097
TRENDWAY CORPORATION, pg. 1109
U.S. FURNITURE INDUSTRIES, INC., pg. 1136
VISIRECORD SYSTEMS, INC., pg. 1153

2531 — PUBLIC BUILDING & RELATED FURNITURE

ALMA INDUSTRIES, pg. 43
AMERICAN SEATING COMPANY, pg. 60
ARTCO-BELL CORPORATION, pg. 86
BALTIMORE STATIONERY CO., pg. 116
BLOCKHOUSE CO., INC., pg. 157
BOSTROM SEATING, INC., pg. 168
CENTRAL DE INDUSTRIAS, S.A.—Lear Siegler Diversified Holdings Corp., pg. 664
THE COLUMBIA MFG. COMPANY, INC., pg. 265
CUTLER MANUFACTURING CORPORATION, pg. 307
EAC CORPORATION, pg. 359
GAME TIME, INC., pg. 442
J. L. HAMMETT COMPANY, pg. 504
HUSSEY CORPORATION, pg. 555
HUSSEY SEATING COMPANY—Hussey Corporation, pg. 555
KEIPER RECARO, INC., pg. 620
LEAR SIEGLER DIVERSIFIED HOLDINGS CORP.—Forstmann Little & Co., pg. 424
LEAR SIEGLER INDUSTRIES LTD., GEN. SEATING DIV.—Lear Siegler Diversified Holdings Corp., pg. 664
NATIONAL SEATING CO., pg. 793
NEMSCHOFF CHAIRS, INC., pg. 798
PTC AEROSPACE—The Pullman Company, pg. 899
PTC AEROSPACE—The Pullman Company, pg. 899
THE PULLMAN COMPANY, pg. 899
SAUDER MANUFACTURING CORPORATION, pg. 972
SEATS INCORPORATED—Nordic Group of Companies, Ltd., pg. 810
SMITH SYSTEM MANUFACTURING COMPANY, pg. 1014

2541 — WOOD PARTITIONS, SHELVING, LOCKERS & OFFICE & STORE FIXTURES

ALLSOP, INC., pg. 43
ALMA INDUSTRIES, pg. 43
AMSTORE CORPORATION, pg. 69
BANKCRAFTERS, INC., pg. 117
BERG CO.—DEC International, Inc., pg. 309
BURKE COMMUNICATION INDUSTRIES, INC., pg. 190
CAPITOL CONSTRUCTION GROUP, INC., pg. 215
COLUMBUS SHOW CASE COMPANY, pg. 267
COLUMBUS SHOWCASE, ASHLAND DIVISION—Columbus Show Case Company, pg. 267
COMMERCIAL & ARCHITECTURAL PRODUCTS INC., pg. 268
CREATIVE SALON FURNITURE INC., pg. 297
DANN DEE DISPLAY FIXTURES, pg. 314
GARCY SPECIALTY FIXTURES—RHC/Spacemaster Corporation, pg. 907
GLOBE BUSINESS FURNITURE, INC., pg. 463
GOER MANUFACTURING CO.—RHC/Spacemaster Corporation, pg. 907
THE H. T. HACKNEY CO., pg. 498
HANDY MANUFACTURING CO., INC., pg. 505
THE HARTER GROUP, pg. 513
HARTER SYSTEMS DIV.—The Harter Group, pg. 514
HOLCOMB & HOKE MFG. COMPANY, INC., pg. 538
HOOKER FURNITURE CORPORATION, pg. 543
M. KAMENSTEIN, INC., pg. 615
LOZIER CORPORATION, pg. 686
LOZIER STORE FIXTURES, INC.—Lozier Corporation, pg. 686
LUNDIA DIV. OF MII, INC., pg. 687
LYON METAL PRODUCTS, INC., pg. 690
MANHATTAN STORE INTERIORS, INC., pg. 704
MERCHANDISING EQUIPMENT GROUP, pg. 739
PARISI, INC., pg. 848
PHILADELPHIA SIGN COMPANY, pg. 867
RHC/SPACEMASTER CORPORATION, pg. 906
SAUNDERS BROTHERS, pg. 972
SPEEDRACK PRODUCTS GROUP, LTD., pg. 1029
WM. S. TRIMBLE COMPANY, INC., pg. 1113
VOLUNTEER FABRICATORS, INC.—The H. T. Hackney Co., pg. 498
WADDELL DIV. OF GHENT MFG. CO.—Ghent Manufacturing, Inc., pg. 455
WOODWORK CORPORATION OF AMERICA, pg. 1201
YERGER BROS., INC., pg. 1208

2542 — OFFICE & STORE FIXTURES, PARTITIONS, SHELVING & LOCKERS, EXCEPT WOOD

ALLSOP, INC., pg. 43
AMERICAN SPECIALTIES INC., pg. 61
ATAPCO OFFICE PRODUCTS GROUP—American Trading and Production Corporation, pg. 64
BANKCRAFTERS, INC., pg. 117
BURKE COMMUNICATION INDUSTRIES, INC., pg. 190

BURTMAN IRON WORKS, INC., pg. 195
COLUMBUS SHOW CASE COMPANY, pg. 267
COLUMBUS SHOWCASE, ASHLAND DIVISION—Columbus Show Case Company, pg. 267
CRAMER INC., pg. 296
CREATIVE SALON FURNITURE INC., pg. 297
DANN DEE DISPLAY FIXTURES, pg. 314
L. A. DARLING COMPANY—The Marmon Group, Inc., pg. 711
DYNABILT PRODUCTS—Burtman Iron Works, Inc., pg. 196
EBSCO INDUSTRIES, INC., pg. 365
GLOBAL STEEL PRODUCTS CORPORATION, pg. 463
GLOBE BUSINESS FURNITURE, INC., pg. 463
HANDY MANUFACTURING CO., INC., pg. 505
THE HARTER GROUP, pg. 513
HARVARD INTERIORS MANUFACTURING CO.—Harvard Industries, Inc., pg. 514
HIRSH COMPANY—Code, Hennessy & Simmons, pg. 258
HOLCOMB & HOKE MFG. COMPANY, INC., pg. 538
INTERROYAL CORPORATION, pg. 580
LIST INDUSTRIES, INC., pg. 677
LOZIER CORPORATION, pg. 686
LOZIER STORE FIXTURES, INC.—Lozier Corporation, pg. 686
LUNDIA DIV. OF MII, INC., pg. 687
LUXOR CORPORATION—Ebsco Industries, Inc., pg. 365
LYON METAL PRODUCTS, INC., pg. 690
MANHATTAN STORE INTERIORS, INC., pg. 704
MARKETING DISPLAYS INTERNATIONAL, INC., pg. 709
MERCHANDISING EQUIPMENT GROUP, pg. 739
METPAR CORPORATION, pg. 742
MOSLER COUNTER SYSTEMS DIV.—Mosler Inc., pg. 772
MOSLER INC., pg. 772
MOSLER SA DE C.D.—Mosler Inc., pg. 772
PALTIER DIV.—Lyon Metal Products, Inc., pg. 690
PENCO PRODUCTS, pg. 857
POLYMER PLASTICS CORPORATION, pg. 880
RHC/SPACEMASTER CORPORATION, pg. 906
READY METAL MANUFACTURING COMPANY, pg. 916
REPUBLIC STORAGE SYSTEMS COMPANY INC., pg. 928
SPEEDRACK PRODUCTS GROUP, LTD., pg. 1029
SYCAMORE SYSTEMS, INC.—Lyon Metal Products, Inc., pg. 690
TRENDWAY CORPORATION, pg. 1109
VIRGINIA METAL INDUSTRIES, INC., pg. 1152
WADDELL DIV. OF GHENT MFG. CO.—Ghent Manufacturing, Inc., pg. 455
WELSH COMPANY, pg. 1175

2591 — DRAPERY HARDWARE & WINDOW BLINDS & SHADES

CC INDUSTRIES, INC., pg. 199
CC INDUSTRIES, KAYWOOD DIV.—CC Industries, Inc., pg. 200
CC INDUSTRIES, KAYWOOD-SOUTHERN DIV.—CC Industries, Inc., pg. 200
JOANNA—CC Industries, Inc., pg. 200
KENNEY MANUFACTURING COMPANY, pg. 623
THE LEVOLOR CORPORATION, pg. 671
W.S. LIBBEY COMPANY, pg. 674
E. L. MANSURE DIV.—CC Industries, Inc., pg. 200
STANDARD SHADE ROLLER DIV.—CC Industries, Inc., pg. 200

2599 — FURNITURE & FIXTURES, NEC

BELVEDERE COMPANY, pg. 138
COSCO, INC., pg. 287
CRAMER INC., pg. 296
CREATIVE SALON FURNITURE INC., pg. 297
CUSTOM PRODUCTS DIVISION—Chief Industries, Inc., pg. 247
GEM SOUTHEAST, INC.—Gem Industries Finance Corporation, pg. 447
HACKNEY BROTHERS, INC., pg. 498
HARVARD INTERIORS MANUFACTURING CO.—Harvard Industries, Inc., pg. 514
HIRSH COMPANY—Code, Hennessy & Simmons, pg. 258
HOUSTON FOODS COMPANY, pg. 547
HUNTCO STEEL CO.—Huntco Inc., pg. 554
KENNEDY MANUFACTURING COMPANY, pg. 623
LYON METAL PRODUCTS, INC., pg. 690
MOHAWK FURNITURE, INC.—Gem Industries Finance Corporation, pg. 447
PARISI, INC., pg. 848
THE SANYMETAL PRODUCTS CO., INC., pg. 970
SHAFER COMMERCIAL SEATING INC., pg. 994
SICO INC., pg. 1001
SIMUNICO, INC., pg. 1007
STAINLESS INCORPORATED, pg. 1035
THERADYNE CORPORATION—Surgical Appliance Industries, Inc., pg. 1065
TURNBULL ENTERPRISES, INC., pg. 1119
UNITED METAL FABRICATORS, INC., pg. 1133

2611 — PULP MILLS

ALASKA PULP CORPORATION, pg. 30
BRANT ALLEN INDUSTRIES, INC., pg. 172
CHICAGO WEST PULLMAN TRANSPORTATION CORPORATION—Chicago West Pullman Corporation, pg. 246
CLEANERS HANGER CO., pg. 254
PARSONS & WHITTEMORE ENTERPRISES, pg. 850
ST. ANNE - NACKAWIC PULP CO., LTD.—Parsons & Whittemore Enterprises, pg. 850
SIMPSON INVESTMENT CO., pg. 1007
SIMPSON PAPER CO.—Simpson Investment Co., pg. 1007
SIMPSON PASADENA PAPER CO.—Simpson Investment Co., pg. 1007
SIMPSON TACOMA KRAFT CO.—Simpson Investment Co., pg. 1007

2621 — PAPER MILLS

BELL FIBRE PRODUCTS—Bell Packaging Corporation, pg. 135
BRANT ALLEN INDUSTRIES, INC., pg. 172
BURROWS PAPER CORPORATION, pg. 195
C&A WALLCOVERINGS—Collins & Aikman Group Inc., pg. 262
COLLINS & AIKMAN TEXTILE GROUP—Collins & Aikman Group Inc., pg. 262
CONNELLY CONTAINERS, INC., pg. 275
CONNELLY CONTAINERS, INC. OF PHILADELPHIA—Connelly Containers, Inc., pg. 275
CRANE & CO., INC., pg. 296
THE CRYSTAL TISSUE CO., pg. 303
DOESKIN CO.—Statler Industries, pg. 1042
EASTERN FINE PAPER, INCORPORATED, pg. 363
ERVING PAPER MILLS, pg. 388
FINCH, PRUYN & CO., INC., pg. 410
FORT HOWARD CORPORATION, pg. 425
FORT HOWARD PAPER CORPORATION—Fort Howard Corporation, pg. 425
FORT HOWARD PAPER CORPORATION—Fort Howard Corporation, pg. 425
FOX RIVER PAPER COMPANY—Fox Valley Corporation, pg. 428
FRASER PAPER, LTD., pg. 430
GOULD PAPER CORPORATION, pg. 473
HOLLINGSWORTH & VOSE CO., pg. 539
HOVOMEX S.A. DE C.V.—Hollingsworth & Vose Co., pg. 539
HOWARD PAPER—Fox Valley Corporation, pg. 428
HOWARD PAPER MILLS—Fox Valley Corporation, pg. 428
KURTZ BROS., INC., pg. 646
LANGSTON COMPANIES, pg. 657
LIVERIGHT PUBLISHING CORP.—W.W. Norton & Company, Inc., pg. 816
MARCAL PAPER MILLS, INC., pg. 706
MISSISSIPPI CHEMICAL CORPORATION, pg. 760
MOHAWK PAPER MILLS, INC., pg. 763
NEWSPRINT SOUTH, INC.—Mississippi Chemical Corporation, pg. 760
RISING PAPER COMPANY—Fox Valley Corporation, pg. 428
RITTENHOUSE PAPER CO.—Rittenhouse Inc., pg. 936
ROSELLE PAPER CO., INC., pg. 948
SABIN ROBBINS PAPER CO., pg. 965
SIMPSON INVESTMENT CO., pg. 1007
SIMPSON PAPER CO.—Simpson Investment Co., pg. 1007
SIMPSON PASADENA PAPER CO.—Simpson Investment Co., pg. 1007
SIMPSON TACOMA KRAFT CO.—Simpson Investment Co., pg. 1007
STATLER INDUSTRIES, pg. 1041
STUART EDGAR LTD.—Fort Howard Corporation, pg. 425
TAGSONS PAPERS, INC., pg. 1076
TIME INDEX, INC.—Time Systems, Inc., pg. 1097
YORK WALLCOVERINGS INC., pg. 1208

2631 — PAPERBOARD MILLS

BELL FIBRE PRODUCTS—Bell Packaging Corporation, pg. 135
BEVERIDGE PAPER CO.—Simkins Industries, Inc., pg. 1005
THE COLUMBIA CORPORATION—Yorktowne Paper Mills, Inc., pg. 1209
DURALAM, INC.—Sargento Incorporated, pg. 971
GOULD PAPER CORPORATION, pg. 473
GREEN BAY PACKAGING INC., pg. 483
GULF STATES PAPER CORPORATION, pg. 494
INTERSTATE PAPER CORPORATION—Interstate Resources, Inc., pg. 580
INTERSTATE RESOURCES, INC., pg. 580
KEY CONTAINER CORPORATION, pg. 626
LOWE PAPER CO.—Simkins Industries, Inc., pg. 1005
MENASHA CORPORATION, pg. 738
MERCER PAPER TUBE CO.—Yorktowne Paper Mills, Inc., pg. 1209
QUEENS GROUP, INC., pg. 904
RISING PAPER COMPANY—Fox Valley Corporation, pg. 428
ROCK-TENN COMPANY, pg. 941
ROCK-TENN COMPANY, MILL DIVISION, INC.—Rock-Tenn Company, pg. 941
SIMKINS INDUSTRIES, INC., pg. 1005
SIMKINS MARYLAND BOARD—Simkins Industries, Inc., pg. 1005
SIMKINS NEW HAVEN BOARD—Simkins Industries, Inc., pg. 1005
SIMPSON INVESTMENT CO., pg. 1007
SIMPSON PAPER CO.—Simpson Investment Co., pg. 1007
SIMPSON TACOMA KRAFT CO.—Simpson Investment Co., pg. 1007
SPECIALTY PAPERBOARD INC., pg. 1027
WESTFIELD RIVER PAPER CO.—Simkins Industries, Inc., pg. 1005
WESTON PAPER & MANUFACTURING CO., pg. 1183
WHITE PIGEON PAPER COMPANY—Artistic Carton Company, pg. 87
YORKTOWNE PAPER MILLS OF MAINE—Yorktowne Paper Mills, Inc., pg. 1209
YORKTOWNE PAPER MILLS OF ME—Yorktowne Paper Mills, Inc., pg. 1209

2652 — SET-UP PAPERBOARD BOXES

ARTISTIC CARTON COMPANY, pg. 87
BANKERS BOX/RECORDS STORAGE SYSTEMS—Fellowes Manufacturing Co., pg. 406
F.N. BURT COMPANY, INC., pg. 195
COPYHOLDER DIVISION—Fellowes Manufacturing Co., pg. 406
FELLOWES MANUFACTURING CO., pg. 405
SCHWARZ PAPER COMPANY, pg. 980
SMEAD MANUFACTURING COMPANY, pg. 1011
SPENCER'S INC., pg. 1030
UNIVERSAL FOLDING BOX COMPANY, INC., pg. 1138
WILKATA PACKAGING CORPORATION, pg. 1189
C. W. ZUMBIEL COMPANY, pg. 1221

2653 — CORRUGATED & SOLID FIBER BOXES

ACCURATE BOX CO., INC., pg. 11
ADVANCE PACKAGING CORPORATION, pg. 19
AKERS PACKAGING SERVICE INC., pg. 28
BATES CONTAINER, INC., pg. 125
BELL FIBRE PRODUCTS—Bell Packaging Corporation, pg. 135
BELL PACKAGING CORPORATION, pg. 135
BRADFORD COMPANY, pg. 170
CENTRAL MICHIGAN CONTAINER CORPORATION—Advance Packaging Corporation, pg. 19
CONNECTICUT CONTAINER CORPORATION, pg. 274
CONNELLY CONTAINERS, INC., pg. 275
STEPHEN GOULD PAPER CO., INC., pg. 473
GREATER NEW YORK BOX CO., pg. 483
GREEN BAY PACKAGING INC., pg. 483
HORN PACKAGING CORPORATION, pg. 544
INTERSTATE CONTAINER CORPORATION—Interstate Resources, Inc., pg. 580
INTERSTATE RESOURCES, INC., pg. 580
KEY CONTAINER CORPORATION, pg. 626
LAWRENCE PAPER COMPANY, pg. 662
LONE STAR CORRUGATED CONTAINER CORPORATION, pg. 682
LOVE BOX COMPANY, INC., pg. 685
MASSACHUSETTS CONTAINER CORPORATION—Connecticut Container Corporation, pg. 274
MENASHA CORPORATION, pg. 738
MENOMINEE PAPER CO.—Bell Packaging Corporation, pg. 135
MODERN PACKAGING CORP.—Superior Container, Inc., pg. 1063
PRECISION PLASTICS—Precision Plastics Inc., pg. 885
QUALITY PACKAGING PRODUCTS, INC., pg. 903
W. C. REDMON CO., pg. 919
REPUBLIC CONTAINER CORP., pg. 927
ROCK-TENN COMPANY, pg. 941
ROCK-TENN CONVERTING CO.—Rock-Tenn Company, pg. 941
SEATTLE PACKAGING CORPORATION, pg. 986
SPECIALTY INDUSTRIES, INC., pg. 1027
SUNCLIPSE, INC., pg. 1059
SUPERIOR CONTAINER, INC., pg. 1063
THOROBRED CONTAINERS INCORPORATED—Interlock Industries, Inc., pg. 575
WABASH FIBRE BOX CO.-CHICAGO PLANT—Weston Paper & Manufacturing Co., pg. 1183
WABASH FIBRE BOX CO.-FORT WAYNE PLANT—Weston Paper & Manufacturing Co., pg. 1183
WABASH FIBRE BOX CO.-LEXINGTON PLANT—Weston Paper & Manufacturing Co., pg. 1183
WABASH FIBRE BOX CO.-SOUTH—Weston Paper & Manufacturing Co., pg. 1183
WABASH FIBRE BOX CO.-SOUTH—Weston Paper & Manufacturing Co., pg. 1183
WABASH FIBRE BOX CO.-TERRE HAUTE PLANT—Weston Paper & Manufacturing Co., pg. 1183
WABASH PIONEER CONTAINER CORP.—Weston Paper & Manufacturing Co., pg. 1183
WESTON PAPER & MANUFACTURING CO., pg. 1183
WILKATA PACKAGING CORPORATION, pg. 1189
WURZBURG, INC., pg. 1205

2655 — FIBER CANS, TUBES, DRUMS & SIMILAR PRODUCTS

MERCER PAPER TUBE CO.—Yorktowne Paper Mills, Inc., pg. 1209
MILTON CAN CO., INC., pg. 756
PIONEER PAPER CORPORATION, pg. 872
REPUBLIC CONTAINER CORP., pg. 927
YORKTOWNE PAPER MILLS, INC., pg. 1208
YORKTOWNE PAPER MILLS OF MAINE—Yorktowne Paper Mills, Inc., pg. 1209
YORKTOWNE PAPER MILLS OF ME—Yorktowne Paper Mills, Inc., pg. 1209

2656 — SANITARY FOOD CONTAINERS, EXCEPT FOLDING

A J M PACKAGING CORPORATION, pg. 4
ACCURATE BOX CO., INC., pg. 11
CAMBRO MANUFACTURING COMPANY, pg. 211
CENTRAL STATES DIVERSIFIED, INC., pg. 234
INGRID-SEVKO, INC., pg. 569
SCC HOLDING CO., pg. 961
SOLO CUP COMPANY—SCC Holding Co., pg. 961

2657 — FOLDING PAPERBOARD BOXES, INCLUDING SANITARY

ACCURATE BOX CO., INC., pg. 11
AMCO FOLDING CARTONS, INC., pg. 47
AMERICAN PACKAGING CORPORATION, pg. 59
ARKAY PACKAGING CORPORATION, pg. 83

BELL PACKAGING CORPORATION, pg. 135
BUFKOR, INC., pg. 187
BURD & FLETCHER COMPANY, pg. 189
F.N. BURT COMPANY, INC., pg. 195
CARTON-CRAFT CORPORATION, pg. 226
DEE PAPER COMPANY, pg. 324
DIAMOND PAPER BOX CO.—Dee Paper Company, pg. 324
DURALAM, INC.—Sargento Incorporated, pg. 971
ECONOMY FOLDING BOX CORP., pg. 367
FIELD CONTAINER COMPANY, L.P., pg. 409
GREATER NEW YORK BOX CO., pg. 483
GREEN BAY PACKAGING INC., pg. 483
GULF STATES PAPER CORPORATION, pg. 494
HICKORY PRINTING GROUP, INC., pg. 533
ICE CREAM SPECIALTIES, INC.—Prairie Farms Dairy, Inc., pg. 884
MARYLAND PAPER BOX COMPANY, pg. 717
MENOMINEE PAPER CO.—Bell Packaging Corporation, pg. 135
QUEENS GROUP INDIANA, INC.—Queens Group, Inc., pg. 904
ROCK-TENN COMPANY, pg. 941
ROYAL PAPER BOX OF CALIFORNIA, pg. 953
SCHWARZ PAPER COMPANY, pg. 980
SIMKINS CAROLINA FOLDING BOX DIV.—Simkins Industries, Inc., pg. 1005
SIMKINS CARTON DIV.-CHICAGO—Simkins Industries, Inc., pg. 1005
SIMKINS CARTON DIV.-CLEVELAND—Simkins Industries, Inc., pg. 1005
SIMKINS CARTON DIV.-DALLAS—Simkins Industries, Inc., pg. 1005
SIMKINS CARTON DIV.-MARIETTA—Simkins Industries, Inc., pg. 1005
SIMKINS INDUSTRIES, INC., pg. 1005
SIMKINS NEW HAVEN CARTON—Simkins Industries, Inc., pg. 1005
STERLING PAPER CO., pg. 1047
SWEETHEART CUP CO., INC., pg. 1067
SWEETHEART CUP CORPORATION—Sweetheart Cup Co., Inc., pg. 1067
SWEETHEART CUP CORPORATION—Sweetheart Cup Co., Inc., pg. 1067
UNIVERSAL FOLDING BOX COMPANY, INC., pg. 1138
WALDORF CORPORATION, pg. 1159
WILKATA PACKAGING CORPORATION, pg. 1189
WINCHESTER CARTON CORP.—Rock-Tenn Company, pg. 941

2671 — COATED & LAMINATED PAPER & PLASTICS FILM

THE BETHAM CORPORATION, pg. 147
BRYCE CORPORATION, pg. 185
C P CONVERTERS, INC., pg. 203
CPS CORPORATION—Fox Valley Corporation, pg. 428
CADILLAC PRODUCTS, INC., pg. 207
CENTRAL NATIONAL-GOTTESMAN INC., pg. 233
CONTINENTAL PLASTIC CARD CO., pg. 280
DIXICO, INC.—Bell Packaging Corporation, pg. 135
DUNMORE CORPORATION/BREWSTER—Dunmore Corporation, pg. 353
ECP INCORPORATED—Daubert Industries, Inc., pg. 317
ERVING PAPER MILLS, pg. 388
FORTIFIBER CORPORATION, pg. 425
FOX VALLEY CORPORATION, pg. 427
FUZERE MANUFACTURING COMPANY INC.—Schawk, Inc., pg. 975
HANDY WACKS CORPORATION, pg. 505
KCL CORPORATION, pg. 611
MAF COTE SPECIALTIES CO., INC.—MacAndrews & Forbes Holdings Inc., pg. 694
NOREL PAPER CORPORATION, pg. 810
PARAMOUNT PACKAGING CORP., pg. 848
PARAMOUNT PACKAGING CORP.—Paramount Packaging Corp., pg. 848
ROHRER CORPORATION, pg. 944
UNICOVER CORPORATION, pg. 1126
UNIFOIL CORPORATION, pg. 1126
YERGER BROS., INC., pg. 1208
ZIMMER PAPER PRODUCTS INC., pg. 1220

2672 — COATED & LAMINATED PAPER, NEC

ALFORD INDUSTRIES, INC., pg. 33
AMERICAN TAPE CORPORATION, pg. 63
AMES TAPING TOOL SYSTEMS CO.—AXIA Incorporated, pg. 8
ANCHOR CONTINENTAL INCORPORATED, pg. 71
BELL PACKAGING CORPORATION, pg. 135
THE BETHAM CORPORATION, pg. 147
CADILLAC PRODUCTS, INC., pg. 207
CAL/EMBLEM LABELS, INC., pg. 208
CENTRAL NATIONAL-GOTTESMAN INC., pg. 233
EASTERN FINE PAPER, INCORPORATED, pg. 363
FORTIFIBER CORPORATION, pg. 425
GOULD PACKAGING, INC., pg. 473
GOULD PACKAGING, INC.—Gould Packaging, Inc., pg. 473
KALAMAZOO LABEL CO., pg. 615
LABELON CORPORATION, pg. 649
LEPAGE'S, INC.—Cortec Group, pg. 287
LORBER INDUSTRIES OF CALIFORNIA, pg. 683
MCCOURT LABEL CO., pg. 727
MENOMINEE PAPER CO.—Bell Packaging Corporation, pg. 135
METRO LABEL CORP.—Metro Label Corp., pg. 743
THE MEYERCORD COMPANY, pg. 746
P M COMPANY, pg. 835
PACKAGE SERVICE COMPANY, INC., pg. 842
PARAMOUNT PACKAGING CORP., pg. 848
PARAMOUNT PACKAGING CORP.—Paramount Packaging Corp., pg. 848
POLYKEN TECHNOLOGIES—Kendall Healthcare Products Co., pg. 622
PRINT-O-TAPE, pg. 891
SHUFORD MILLS, INC., pg. 1001
SIMPSON PASADENA PAPER CO.—Simpson Investment Co., pg. 1007
SIMPSON PLAINWELL PAPER CO., INC.—Simpson Investment Co., pg. 1007
TAPE COAT DIVISION—T C Manufacturing Company, Inc., pg. 1072
TAPEMARK, pg. 1078
TECHNICARBON COMPANY, INC., pg. 1083
TIMEMED LABELING SYSTEMS, INC., pg. 1098
UNIVERSAL BLUEPRINT PAPER CO.—YRJ Corporation, pg. 1207
WILTON CORPORATION, pg. 1194
WURZBURG, INC., pg. 1205
ZIMMER PAPER PRODUCTS INC., pg. 1220

2673 — PLASTICS, FOIL & COATED PAPER BAGS

AMCELL CORPORATION, pg. 47
ARROW INDUSTRIES, INC., pg. 85
CADILLAC PRODUCTS, INC., pg. 207
DIXICO, INC.—Bell Packaging Corporation, pg. 135
EQUITABLE BAG COMPANY, pg. 385
FORTIFIBER CORPORATION, pg. 425
IVEX PACKAGING CORPORATION, pg. 583
THE NOTEWORTHY COMPANY, pg. 816
PACKAGING PRODUCTS & DESIGN, pg. 842
PARAMOUNT PACKAGING CORP., pg. 848
PARAMOUNT PACKAGING CORP.—Paramount Packaging Corp., pg. 848
POLY PAK AMERICA, INC., pg. 880
SOUTHERN CONTAINER CORPORATION, pg. 1020
TIFFANY EXTRUDERS, INC., pg. 1096
UNION INDUSTRIES, INC., pg. 1128
UNION PAPER CO.—Union Industries, Inc., pg. 1128

2674 — UNCOATED PAPER & MULTIWALL BAGS

A J M PACKAGING CORPORATION, pg. 4
CADILLAC PRODUCTS, INC., pg. 207
CENTRAL STATES DIVERSIFIED, INC., pg. 234
EASTERN FINE PAPER, INCORPORATED, pg. 363
EASY DAY MANUFACTURING COMPANY, INC., pg. 364
EQUITABLE BAG COMPANY, pg. 385
IVEX PACKAGING CORPORATION, pg. 583
MAINE POTATO GROWERS, INC., pg. 702
MARYLAND PAPER BOX COMPANY, pg. 717
THE NOTEWORTHY COMPANY, pg. 816
SIMPSON PASADENA PAPER CO.—Simpson Investment Co., pg. 1007
SIMPSON PLAINWELL PAPER CO., INC.—Simpson Investment Co., pg. 1007
SOUTHERN CONTAINER CORPORATION, pg. 1020
WERTHAN PACKAGING, INC., pg. 1176

2675 — DIE-CUT PAPER, PAPERBOARD & CARDBOARD

AMERICAN TRADING AND PRODUCTION CORPORATION, pg. 64
ATAPCO OFFICE PRODUCTS GROUP—American Trading and Production Corporation, pg. 64
CHICAGO WEST PULLMAN TRANSPORTATION CORPORATION—Chicago West Pullman Corporation, pg. 246
COLAD GROUP INC., pg. 259
THE COLUMBIA CORPORATION—Yorktowne Paper Mills, Inc., pg. 1209
ELECTRONIC DATA MAGNETICS, INC., pg. 375
GUSSO MANUFACTURING, INC., pg. 495
RAPID MOUNTING & FINISHING CO., pg. 913
ROHRER CORPORATION, pg. 944
SIMPSON PAPER CO.—Simpson Investment Co., pg. 1007
SIMPSON TACOMA KRAFT CO.—Simpson Investment Co., pg. 1007
SMEAD MANUFACTURING COMPANY, pg. 1011
SULA SUPPLY—Vienna Sausage Mfg. Co., pg. 1151
TAPEMARK, pg. 1078
WEBER MARKING SYSTEMS, INC., pg. 1171
WURZBURG, INC., pg. 1205

2676 — SANITARY PAPER PRODUCTS

CENTRAL STATES DIVERSIFIED, INC., pg. 234
THE CLINIPAD CORPORATION, pg. 255
ERVING PAPER MILLS, pg. 388
FORT HOWARD CORPORATION, pg. 425
FORT HOWARD PAPER CORPORATION—Fort Howard Corporation, pg. 425
FORT HOWARD PAPER CORPORATION—Fort Howard Corporation, pg. 425
IVEX PACKAGING CORPORATION, pg. 583
LENSCLEAN, INC.—Aldine Technologies, pg. 33
MEGAS BEAUTY AIDS, INC., pg. 737
PLAYTEX FAMILY PRODUCTS CORP.—Playtex FP Group Incorporated, pg. 877
ROCHESTER MIDLAND CORPORATION, pg. 940
STATLER INDUSTRIES, pg. 1041
TAGSONS PAPERS, INC., pg. 1076
TRINA, INC., pg. 1113
WINCUP, pg. 1195

2677 — ENVELOPES

AMERICAN ENVELOPE COMPANY—CC Industries, Inc., pg. 199
AMERICAN ENVELOPE COMPANY-KRUYSMAN DIV.—CC Industries, Inc., pg. 199
AMERICAN ENVELOPE OF BUFFALO—CC Industries, Inc., pg. 199
AMERICAN ENVELOPE OF CHICAGO-DIE CUT DIV.—CC Industries, Inc., pg. 199
AMERICAN ENVELOPE OF CHICAGO-WEB DIV.—CC Industries, Inc., pg. 199
AMERICAN ENVELOPE OF DALLAS—CC Industries, Inc., pg. 199
AMERICAN ENVELOPE OF DENVER—CC Industries, Inc., pg. 199
AMERICAN ENVELOPE OF LOS ANGELES—CC Industries, Inc., pg. 199
AMERICAN ENVELOPE OF NASHVILLE—CC Industries, Inc., pg. 199
AMERICAN ENVELOPE OF OMAHA—CC Industries, Inc., pg. 199
AMERICAN ENVELOPE OF PHILADELPHIA—CC Industries, Inc., pg. 199
AMERICAN ENVELOPE OF SAN ANTONIO—CC Industries, Inc., pg. 199
AMERICAN ENVELOPE OF SEATTLE—CC Industries, Inc., pg. 200
AMERICAN ENVELOPE OF ST. LOUIS—CC Industries, Inc., pg. 199
AMERICAN PAPER PRODUCTS GROUP, LTD., pg. 59
CC INDUSTRIES, INC., pg. 199
DARLING ENVELOPE CORPORATION, pg. 315
GILMORE ENVELOPE CORP., pg. 460
GRIFFIN ENVELOPE, INC., pg. 487
THE INSTANT WEB COMPANIES, pg. 571
IVEX PACKAGING CORPORATION, pg. 583
MASSACHUSETTS ENVELOPE CO., pg. 718
NIAGARA ENVELOPE CO., INC.—Niagara Envelope Company, Inc., pg. 806
NIAGARA ENVELOPE CO. OF FLORIDA—Niagara Envelope Company, Inc., pg. 806
NIAGARA ENVELOPE COMPANY, INC., pg. 805
THE NOTEWORTHY COMPANY, pg. 816
PACIFIC ENVELOPE COMPANY, pg. 840
PAVEY ENVELOPE & TAG CORP., pg. 852
TENSION ENVELOPE CORP., pg. 1088
UNITED ENVELOPE COMPANY, INC., pg. 1131
WESTERN STATES ENVELOPE CO., pg. 1181

2678 — STATIONERY, TABLETS & RELATED PRODUCTS

AMERICAN TARA CORPORATION, pg. 63
AMERICAN TRADING AND PRODUCTION CORPORATION, pg. 64
ATAPCO OFFICE PRODUCTS GROUP—American Trading and Production Corporation, pg. 64
B & J SUPPLY, INC.—American Tara Corporation, pg. 63
CRAWFORD INDUSTRIES—American Trading and Production Corporation, pg. 64
THE CRYSTAL TISSUE CO., pg. 303
CULLMAN VENTURES, INC., pg. 304
FOX VALLEY CORPORATION, pg. 427
HALLMARK CARDS, INC., pg. 501
IMPRINT PRODUCTS, L.P., pg. 564
IVEX PACKAGING CORPORATION, pg. 583
KORES NORDIC USA CORP., pg. 642
KURTZ BROS., INC., pg. 646
MASSACHUSETTS ENVELOPE CO., pg. 718
P M COMPANY, pg. 835
PEN-TAB INDUSTRIES, INC., pg. 856
PEN-TAB INDUSTRIES OF CALIFORNIA, INC.—Pen-Tab Industries, Inc., pg. 857
RITTENHOUSE INC., pg. 936
RUNDEL PRODUCTS, INC., pg. 956
SCHWARZ PAPER COMPANY, pg. 980
SULA SUPPLY—Vienna Sausage Mfg. Co., pg. 1151

2679 — CONVERTED PAPER & PAPERBOARD PRODUCTS, NEC

AMERICAN EXCELSIOR COMPANY, pg. 51
AMERICAN TARA CORPORATION, pg. 63
ATLAS TAG & LABEL INC.—Bissell Inc., pg. 153
BRADFORD COMPANY, pg. 170
C&A WALLCOVERINGS—Collins & Aikman Group Inc., pg. 262
CPS CORPORATION—Fox Valley Corporation, pg. 428
CENTRAL STATES DIVERSIFIED, INC., pg. 234
COLAD GROUP INC., pg. 259
COLLINS & AIKMAN GROUP INC., pg. 262
COLUMBIAN ROPE COMPANY, pg. 266
DIETZGEN CORPORATION, pg. 337
FORT HOWARD CORPORATION, pg. 425
FORT HOWARD PAPER CORPORATION—Fort Howard Corporation, pg. 425
FORT HOWARD PAPER CORPORATION—Fort Howard Corporation, pg. 425
FORTIFIBER CORPORATION, pg. 425
FOX VALLEY CORPORATION, pg. 427
GILMAN PAPER CO., pg. 459
GREEFF FABRICS—Collins & Aikman Group Inc., pg. 262
GULF STATES PAPER CORPORATION, pg. 494
HALLMARK CARDS, INC., pg. 501
HOLLYMATIC CORPORATION, pg. 539
IVEX PACKAGING CORPORATION, pg. 583
PERRY H. KOPLIK & SONS, pg. 641
MARCAL PAPER MILLS, INC., pg. 706
MASSACHUSETTS ENVELOPE CO., pg. 718
MELLON CORPORATION, pg. 738
MENASHA CORPORATION, pg. 738

S.I.C. Index

THE NOTEWORTHY COMPANY, pg. 816
PACKAGE SERVICE COMPANY, INC., pg. 842
PAPERTRONICS, INCORPORATED—American Tara Corporation, pg. 63
PARAMOUNT PACKAGING CORP., pg. 848
PARAMOUNT PACKAGING CORP.—Paramount Packaging Corp., pg. 848
PEN-TAB INDUSTRIES, INC., pg. 856
PEN-TAB INDUSTRIES OF CALIFORNIA, INC.—Pen-Tab Industries, Inc., pg. 857
PLYMKRAFT INC.—Columbian Rope Company, pg. 266
ROOSEVELT PAPER CO., pg. 946
ROSELLE PAPER CO., INC., pg. 948
SCHWARZ PAPER COMPANY, pg. 980
SMITH-LEE CO., INC., pg. 1013
SOLO CUP COMPANY—SCC Holding Co., pg. 961
SULLIVAN PAPER COMPANY, pg. 1057
SUNCLIPSE, INC., pg. 1059
UVP, INC., pg. 1124
WEBER MARKING SYSTEMS CANADA LTD.—Weber Marking Systems, Inc., pg. 1171
WEBER MARKING SYSTEMS (FAR EAST) CO. LTD.—Weber Marking Systems, Inc., pg. 1171
WISCONSIN LABEL CORPORATION, pg. 1198
YORK WALLCOVERINGS INC., pg. 1208
ZIMMER PAPER PRODUCTS INC., pg. 1220

2711 — NEWSPAPERS: PUBLISHING, OR PUBLISHING & PRINTING

ADVANCE PUBLICATIONS INC., pg. 19
ALBANY TIMES UNION—The Hearst Corporation, pg. 523
THE ANDERSON NEWS—Landmark Communications, Inc., pg. 655
ANTIQUES & COLLECTIBLES—Landmark Communications, Inc., pg. 656
THE ARDMORE DAILY ARDMOREITE—Stauffer Communications, Inc., pg. 1042
THE ARKANSAS CITY DAILY TRAVELER—Stauffer Communications, Inc., pg. 1042
ASBURY PARK PRESS, INC.—New Jersey Press, Inc., pg. 801
ATLANTA NEWSPAPERS—Cox Enterprises, Inc., pg. 292
AUBURNDALE STAR—Stauffer Communications, Inc., pg. 1042
AUTOMOTIVE NEWS, pg. 101
THE BAKERSFIELD CALIFORNIAN, pg. 115
BALTIMORE BOOK—Landmark Communications, Inc., pg. 655
THE BEACON-NEWS—The Copley Press, Inc., pg. 284
BEAUMONT ENTERPRISE—The Hearst Corporation, pg. 523
BEDFORD BULLETIN—Landmark Communications, Inc., pg. 655
BLADE COMMUNICATIONS, INC., pg. 155
BLUE SPRINGS EXAMINER—Stauffer Communications, Inc., pg. 1042
BOOTH NEWSPAPERS, INC., pg. 165
BRAINERD DAILY DISPATCH—Stauffer Communications, Inc., pg. 1042
THE CALIFORNIAN—Landmark Communications, Inc., pg. 656
CAPITAL-GAZETTE COMMUNICATIONS, INC.—Landmark Communications, Inc., pg. 656
CAPITAL NEWSPAPERS—The Hearst Corporation, pg. 523
CAPITOL CITY PUBLISHING CO., INC.—Journal Register Company, pg. 608
CARROLL COUNTY TIMES—Landmark Communications, Inc., pg. 655
THE CASEY COUNTY NEWS—Landmark Communications, Inc., pg. 655
CENTRAL KENTUCKY NEWS-JOURNAL—Landmark Communications, Inc., pg. 655
CENTRAL MARYLAND HOMES—Landmark Communications, Inc., pg. 655
CENTURY PUBLICATIONS, INC.—Harte-Hanks Communications, Inc., pg. 513
CENTURY 21 HOMES MAGAZINE-YORK, PA—Landmark Communications, Inc., pg. 655
CHESTER NEWS AND REPORTER—Landmark Communications, Inc., pg. 655
CHICAGO READER, INC., pg. 245
CHICAGO SUN TIMES—Adler & Shaykin, pg. 18
CITRUS COUNTY CHRONICLE—Landmark Communications, Inc., pg. 655
CITY & STATE—Crain Communications, Inc., pg. 295
COMMERCIAL REAL ESTATE—Landmark Communications, Inc., pg. 655
COMMUNITY TIMES EXTRA—Landmark Communications, Inc., pg. 656
CONSOLIDATED PUBLISHING COMPANY, pg. 277
JACK KENT COOKE, INC., pg. 282
COOKE MEDIA GROUP, INC.—Jack Kent Cooke, Inc., pg. 282
THE COPLEY PRESS, INC., pg. 284
CORPUS CHRISTI CALLER-TIMES—Harte-Hanks Communications, Inc., pg. 513
COWLES MEDIA COMPANY, pg. 291
COX ARIZONA PUBLICATIONS, INC.—Cox Enterprises, Inc., pg. 292
COX ENTERPRISES, INC., pg. 292
COX ENTERPRISES NEWSPAPER DIVISION—Cox Enterprises, Inc., pg. 292
COX TEXAS PUBLICATIONS, INC.—Cox Enterprises, Inc., pg. 292
CRAIN COMMUNICATIONS, INC., pg. 295
CROWN PUBLISHERS, INC.—Advance Publications Inc., pg. 20
CYNTHIANA DEMOCRAT—Landmark Communications, Inc., pg. 655
THE DAILY BREEZE—The Copley Press, Inc., pg. 284
DAILY COURIER-NEWS—The Copley Press, Inc., pg. 284
THE DAILY JOURNAL (IL)—The Copley Press, Inc., pg. 284
DAILY RACING FORM, INC.—K-III Communications Corporation, pg. 611
DAILY RACING FORM, INC. PACIFIC—K-III Communications Corporation, pg. 611
THE DAILY & SUNDAY OKLAHOMAN—Gaylord Entertainment Co., pg. 446
DAYTON NEWSPAPERS, INC.—Cox Enterprises, Inc., pg. 292
DECATUR NEWS PUBLISHING COMPANY, INC., pg. 323
DESERET NEWS—Deseret Management Corporation, pg. 332
THE DISPATCH PRINTING COMPANY, pg. 339
DODGE CITY DAILY GLOBE—Stauffer Communications, Inc., pg. 1042
DODGE CITY SHOPPER'S WEEKLY—Stauffer Communications, Inc., pg. 1042
DONREY INC. TX—Donrey Media Group, pg. 345
DONREY MEDIA GROUP, pg. 345
EDWARDSVILLE INTELLIGENCER—The Hearst Corporation, pg. 524
EVENING POST PUBLISHING CO., pg. 391
FINGER LAKES PRINTING COMPANY—Independent Publications, Inc., pg. 565
THE FLYER PUBLISHING CORP.—Harte-Hanks Communications, Inc., pg. 513
FORUM PUBLISHING COMPANY, pg. 426
FREEDOM NEWSPAPERS INC., pg. 431
GUY GANNETT PUBLISHING COMPANY, pg. 442
GAZETTE COMPANY, INC., pg. 447
THE GAZETTE—Landmark Communications, Inc., pg. 655
GLENWOOD POST—Stauffer Communications, Inc., pg. 1042
THE GRAND ISLAND DAILY INDEPENDENT—Stauffer Communications, Inc., pg. 1042
GRAND JUNCTION NEWSPAPERS, INC.—Cox Enterprises, Inc., pg. 292
GRANT COUNTY NEWS—Landmark Communications, Inc., pg. 655
GREENSBORO NEWS & RECORD—Landmark Communications, Inc., pg. 655
GUARD PUBLISHING COMPANY, pg. 491
HAINES CITY HERALD & RIDGE SHOPPER—Stauffer Communications, Inc., pg. 1042
THE HANNIBAL COURIER-POST—Stauffer Communications, Inc., pg. 1042
HARRIMAN RECORD—Landmark Communications, Inc., pg. 655
HARRIS ENTERPRISES INC., pg. 511
HARTE-HANKS COMMUNICATIONS, INC., pg. 513
HARTE-HANKS COMMUNITY NEWSPAPERS, INC.—Harte-Hanks Communications, Inc., pg. 513
THE HEARST CORPORATION, pg. 521
HEARST ENTERPRISES DIVISION—The Hearst Corporation, pg. 523
HEARST NEWSPAPERS DIVISION—The Hearst Corporation, pg. 523
HENRY COUNTY LOCAL—Landmark Communications, Inc., pg. 655
HERALD-NEWS—The Copley Press, Inc., pg. 284
THE HERALD—Blade Communications, Inc., pg. 155
HILLSDALE DAILY NEWS—Stauffer Communications, Inc., pg. 1042
THE HOLLAND SENTINEL—Stauffer Communications, Inc., pg. 1042
HOMES OF YORK-ADAMS COUNTY—Landmark Communications, Inc., pg. 655
HOMETOWN PUBLICATIONS—Journal Communications Inc., pg. 607
HONOLULU ADVERTISER, INC.—Persis Corporation, pg. 863
HOUSTON CHRONICLE—The Hearst Corporation, pg. 524
HURON DAILY TRIBUNE—The Hearst Corporation, pg. 524
THE INDEPENDENCE EXAMINER—Stauffer Communications, Inc., pg. 1042
INDEPENDENT PUBLICATIONS, INC., pg. 565
INDEPENDENT PUBLISHING COMPANY—Harte-Hanks Communications, Inc., pg. 513
JASPER NEWS-BOY—The Hearst Corporation, pg. 524
JOHNSON NEWSPAPER CORPORATION, pg. 598
JOURNAL COMMUNICATIONS INC., pg. 607
THE JOURNAL-DEMOCRAT—Landmark Communications, Inc., pg. 655
JOURNAL REGISTER COMPANY, pg. 608
JOURNAL/SENTINEL INC.—Journal Communications Inc., pg. 607
K-III COMMUNICATIONS CORPORATION, pg. 610
KENTUCKY STANDARD—Landmark Communications, Inc., pg. 655
KNOXVILLE JOURNAL CORPORATION—Persis Corporation, pg. 863
LA PRENSA ASOCIADA, INC.—The Associated Press, pg. 92
LAKE WALES DAILY HIGHLANDER—Stauffer Communications, Inc., pg. 1042
THE LANCASTER NEWS—Landmark Communications, Inc., pg. 655
LANDMARK COMMUNICATIONS, INC., pg. 654
LANDMARK COMMUNITY NEWSPAPERS, INC.—Landmark Communications, Inc., pg. 655
LAREDO MORNING TIMES—The Hearst Corporation, pg. 523
LAS VEGAS SUN, INC., pg. 659
THE LEBANON ENTERPRISE—Landmark Communications, Inc., pg. 655
LEBHAR-FRIEDMAN, INC., pg. 665
LINCOLN COURIER—The Copley Press, Inc., pg. 284
LOS ALAMOS MONITOR—Landmark Communications, Inc., pg. 655
LYKE CORPORATION, pg. 688
MACROMEDIA INC., pg. 698
MARYVILLE-ALCOA NEWSPAPERS, INC.—Persis Corporation, pg. 863
MEDIANEWS GROUP, EASTERN OPERATIONS—MediaNews Group Inc., pg. 735
MEDIANEWS GROUP INC., pg. 735
MEMPHIS PUBLISHING COMPANY, pg. 738
METROPOLITAN SUNDAY NEWSPAPERS, INC., pg. 745
THE MIDDLESEX NEWS—Harte-Hanks Communications, Inc., pg. 513
MIDLAND DAILY NEWS—The Hearst Corporation, pg. 524
MIDLAND REPORTER-TELEGRAM—The Hearst Corporation, pg. 524
THE MILWAUKEE JOURNAL—Journal Communications Inc., pg. 607
MILWAUKEE SENTINEL—Journal Communications Inc., pg. 607
MORGAN COUNTY NEWS—Landmark Communications, Inc., pg. 655
MORRIS CORPORATION—Shivers Trading & Operating Co., pg. 999
MORRIS NEWSPAPER CORPORATION, pg. 771
MOUNT VERNON DEMOCRAT—Landmark Communications, Inc., pg. 655
THE NATIONAL ENQUIRER, pg. 788
NEW ALBANY GAZETTE—Landmark Communications, Inc., pg. 655
NEW JERSEY PRESS, INC., pg. 801
THE NEW YORK OBSERVER—Shepaug Corporation, pg. 998
THE NEWS—Landmark Communications, Inc., pg. 655
THE NEWS-DEMOCRAT—Landmark Communications, Inc., pg. 655
NEWS-ENTERPRISE—Landmark Communications, Inc., pg. 655
THE NEWS-PILOT—The Copley Press, Inc., pg. 284
NEWS-PRESS & GAZETTE COMPANY, pg. 804
THE NEWS PRINTING COMPANY—Perpetual Corporation, pg. 862
THE NEWS-SUN—The Copley Press, Inc., pg. 284
THE NEWTON KANSAN—Stauffer Communications, Inc., pg. 1042
NORTH AMERICAN PUBLISHING COMPANY, pg. 811
NORTHWEST MEDIA, INC.—Persis Corporation, pg. 863
THE OAK RIDGER—Stauffer Communications, Inc., pg. 1042
OKLAHOMA PUBLISHING COMPANY—Gaylord Entertainment Co., pg. 446
OLATHE DAILY NEWS—Harris Enterprises Inc., pg. 511
THE OLDHAM ERA—Landmark Communications, Inc., pg. 655
OPINION-TRIBUNE—Landmark Communications, Inc., pg. 655
THE ORANGE COUNTY REGISTER—Freedom Newspapers Inc., pg. 431
THE OUTLOOK—The Copley Press, Inc., pg. 284
PC WEEK—Ziff Communications Company, pg. 1219
PACIFIC SHIPPER, INC.—K-III Communications Corporation, pg. 611
PADDOCK PUBLICATIONS, INC., pg. 842
PALM BEACH NEWSPAPERS, INC.—Cox Enterprises, Inc., pg. 292
PENNYSAVER (HARTE-HANKS CALIFORNIA CDM, INC.)—Harte-Hanks Communications, Inc., pg. 513
PENNYSAVER PUBLICATIONS, INC. (THE SHOPPER'S GUIDE)—Harte-Hanks Communications, Inc., pg. 513
PERSIS CORPORATION, pg. 863
PIONEER NEWS—Landmark Communications, Inc., pg. 655
PIONEER PRESS NEWSPAPERS INC.—Adler & Shaykin, pg. 18
PITTSBURG MORNING SUN—Stauffer Communications, Inc., pg. 1042
PLAINVIEW DAILY HERALD—The Hearst Corporation, pg. 524
POTPOURRI (HARTE-HANKS CALIFORNIA CDM, INC.)—Harte-Hanks Communications, Inc., pg. 513
GEORGE W. PRESCOTT PUBLISHING CO., pg. 887
PRESS ENTERPRISE COMPANY, pg. 887
PROVIDENCE JOURNAL COMPANY, pg. 895
RAMA GROUP OF COMPANIES, pg. 910
READING EAGLE COMPANY, pg. 916
THE RECORD-JOURNAL PUBLISHING COMPANY, pg. 917
RED OAK EXPRESS—Landmark Communications, Inc., pg. 655
RED WING PUBLISHING COMPANY, pg. 919
REPORTER PUBLISHING COMPANY—Harte-Hanks Communications, Inc., pg. 513
ROANE COUNTY NEWS—Landmark Communications, Inc., pg. 655
ROCKWOOD TIMES—Landmark Communications, Inc., pg. 655
ROME SENTINEL CO., pg. 946
SAN ANGELO STANDARD, INC.—Harte-Hanks Communications, Inc., pg. 513
SAN ANTONIO LIGHT—The Hearst Corporation, pg. 524
SAN FRANCISCO EXAMINER—The Hearst Corporation, pg. 524
SCHURZ COMMUNICATIONS, INC., pg. 979
SCOTTSDALE PUBLISHING, INC.—Cowles Media Company, pg. 291
SEATTLE POST-INTELLIGENCER—The Hearst Corporation, pg. 524
SEATTLE TIMES COMPANY, pg. 986
SENIOR WORLD (CALIFORNIA)—Landmark Communications, Inc., pg. 656
THE SENTINEL-NEWS—Landmark Communications, Inc., pg. 655
SHAWNEE NEWS-STAR—Stauffer Communications, Inc., pg. 1042
SHEARMAN CORPORATION, pg. 996
SHIVERS TRADING & OPERATING CO., pg. 999
SHOPPER PUBLISHING GROUP—Stauffer Communications, Inc., pg. 1042

SHOPPER'S GUIDE, INC. (TUCSON SHOPPER)—Harte-Hanks Communications, Inc., pg. 513
SPENCER MAGNET—Landmark Communications, Inc., pg. 655
SPRINGFIELD NEWSPAPERS, INC.—Cox Enterprises, Inc., pg. 292
THE SPRINGFIELD SUN—Landmark Communications, Inc., pg. 655
STANDARD CORPORATION, pg. 1036
STAR PUBLICATIONS—Adler & Shaykin, pg. 18
STAR TRIBUNE, MINNEAPOLIS-ST. PAUL—Cowles Media Company, pg. 291
THE STATE JOURNAL-REGISTER—The Copley Press, Inc., pg. 284
STAUFFER COMMUNICATIONS, INC., pg. 1042
SUBURBAN COMMUNICATIONS CORP., pg. 1055
SUMTER COUNTY TIMES—Landmark Communications, Inc., pg. 655
SUN-LITHO—Morris Newspaper Corporation, pg. 771
SUN PRINTING COMPANY—Cox Enterprises, Inc., pg. 292
T-R PRINTING & PUBLISHING—Tribune Review Publishing Co., pg. 1113
THE TIMES-PICAYUNE PUBLISHING CORP., pg. 1098
TIMES PUBLISHING COMPANY OF WICHITA FALLS—Harte-Hanks Communications, Inc., pg. 513
TIMES-WORLD CORPORATION—Landmark Communications, Inc., pg. 656
THE TOPEKA CAPITAL-JOURNAL—Stauffer Communications, Inc., pg. 1042
TRENTON TIMES CORP.—Perpetual Corporation, pg. 862
THE TRENTONIAN—Journal Register Company, pg. 608
TRIBUNE REVIEW PUBLISHING CO., pg. 1112
THE TRIMBLE BANNER-DEMOCRAT—Landmark Communications, Inc., pg. 656
UNION-TRIBUNE PUBLISHING COMPANY—The Copley Press, Inc., pg. 284
VV PUBLISHING CORP., pg. 1142
VANDALIA LEADER-UNION—Landmark Communications, Inc., pg. 655
THE VIRGINIAN-PILOT AND THE LEDGER STAR—Landmark Communications, Inc., pg. 656
WALLA-WALLA UNION BULLETIN—Seattle Times Company, pg. 986
WEHCO MEDIA, INC., pg. 1172
WINTER HAVEN NEWS CHIEF—Stauffer Communications, Inc., pg. 1042
WORLD PUBLISHING COMPANY, pg. 1203
WORRELL ENTERPRISES, INC., pg. 1203
THE YANKTON PRESS & DAKOTAN—Stauffer Communications, Inc., pg. 1042
THE YORK NEWS-TIMES—Stauffer Communications, Inc., pg. 1042

2721 — PERIODICALS: PUBLISHING, OR PUBLISHING & PRINTING

A+ PUBLISHING—International Data Group, pg. 576
ADD, INC.—Journal Communications Inc., pg. 607
ADVANCE PUBLICATIONS INC., pg. 19
ADVANSTAR COMMUNICATIONS, pg. 21
ADVERTISING AGE—Crain Communications, Inc., pg. 295
ALASKA PUBLISHING PROPERTIES, INC.—Yankee Publishing Incorporated, pg. 1207
ALLURE—Advance Publications Inc., pg. 19
AMERICAN ARBRITRATION ASSOCIATION, pg. 49
AMERICAN CHEMICAL SOCIETY, pg. 50
AMERICAN DRUGGIST—The Hearst Corporation, pg. 522
AMERICAN EXPORT REGISTER—Thomas Publishing Co., pg. 1093
AMERICAN JOURNAL OF NURSING COMPANY, pg. 57
AMERICAN LITERATURE REVIEW—Thomas Publishing Co., pg. 1093
APPLIED GRAPHICS TECHNOLOGY—U.S. News & World Report, pg. 1136
THE ATLANTIC MONTHLY MAGAZINE, pg. 95
AUTOMOBILE MAGAZINE—K-III Communications Corporation, pg. 611
AUTOMOTIVE NEWS, pg. 101
AUTOMOTIVE NEWS—Crain Communications, Inc., pg. 295
B.A.S.S., INC., pg. 105
B C PUBLISHING—International Data Group, pg. 576
BNA BUSINESS & HUMAN RESOURCES DIV.—The Bureau of National Affairs, Inc., pg. 189
BNA ENVIRONMENT & SAFETY SERVICES DIV.—The Bureau of National Affairs, Inc., pg. 189
BNA INTERNATIONAL INC.—The Bureau of National Affairs, Inc., pg. 190
BNA LEGAL SERVICES DIV.—The Bureau of National Affairs, Inc., pg. 189
BAM PUBLICATIONS, INC., pg. 117
BASSMASTER MAGAZINE—B.A.S.S., Inc., pg. 105
BENJAMIN FRANKLIN LITERARY & MEDICAL SOCIETY, INC., pg. 139
CHANNING L. BETE CO., INC., pg. 147
BILL COMMUNICATIONS, INC., pg. 150
BILLCOM AUTOMOTIVE—Bill Communications, Inc., pg. 150
BILLCOM EXPOSITION & CONFERENCE GROUP—Bill Communications, Inc., pg. 150
BOBIT PUBLISHING COMPANY, pg. 161
BOULDER ENTERPRISE, INC.—The New Yorker Magazine, pg. 803
BRIDE'S—Advance Publications Inc., pg. 19
THE BUREAU OF NATIONAL AFFAIRS, INC., pg. 189
BUSINESS GUIDES INC.—Lebhar-Friedman, Inc., pg. 665
BUSINESS INSURANCE—Crain Communications, Inc., pg. 295
BUSINESS MARKETING—Crain Communications, Inc., pg. 295
BUTTERICK COMPANY, INC., pg. 197
CIO PUBLISHING CORP.—International Data Group, pg. 576
C M P PRINTING COMPANY—C M P Publications, Inc., pg. 203
C M P PUBLICATIONS, INC., pg. 202
CW PUBLISHING, INC.—International Data Group, pg. 576
CALIFORNIA OFFSET PRINTERS, INC., pg. 210
CAPPER'S—Stauffer Communications, Inc., pg. 1043
CARUS CORPORATION, pg. 227
CENTURY PUBLISHING COMPANY, pg. 235
CHICAGO—Landmark Communications, Inc., pg. 656
CHRISTIANITY TODAY, INC., pg. 249
CLIGGOT PUBLISHING, pg. 255
THE COBB GROUP—Ziff Communications Company, pg. 1218
COLONIAL HOMES—The Hearst Corporation, pg. 523
COMMTEK COMMUNICATIONS, pg. 269
COMPENDIUM SYSTEMS, pg. 270
COMPUTER BUYING PUBLISHING, INC.—International Data Group, pg. 576
THE CONDE NAST PUBLICATIONS INC.—Advance Publications Inc., pg. 19
CONDE NAST TRAVELER—Advance Publications Inc., pg. 19
CONTEMPORARY LONG TERM CARE—Bill Communications, Inc., pg. 150
CORPORATE FINANCE MAGAZINE—Financial World Partners, pg. 410
COSMOPOLITAN—The Hearst Corporation, pg. 523
COUNTRY LIVING—The Hearst Corporation, pg. 523
COUNTRYSIDE—The Hearst Corporation, pg. 523
COWLES BUSINESS MEDIA, INC.—Cowles Media Company, pg. 291
COWLES MAGAZINES, INC.—Cowles Media Company, pg. 291
COWLES MAGAZINES, INC., pg. 291
CRAIN COMMUNICATIONS, INC., pg. 295
CRAIN'S CHICAGO BUSINESS—Crain Communications, Inc., pg. 295
CRAIN'S CLEVELAND BUSINESS—Crain Communications, Inc., pg. 295
CRAIN'S DETROIT BUSINESS—Crain Communications, Inc., pg. 295
CRAIN'S NEW YORK BUSINESS—Crain Communications, Inc., pg. 295
CRICKET MAGAZINE—Carus Corporation, pg. 227
CROWN PUBLISHERS, INC.—Advance Publications Inc., pg. 20
MARCEL DEKKER, INC., pg. 325
DETAILS MAGAZINE—Advance Publications Inc., pg. 19
DIGITAL NEWS PUBLISHING COMPANY, INC.—International Data Group, pg. 576
DIVERSION—The Hearst Corporation, pg. 522
E.P. GRAPHICS, INC., pg. 360
EDWARDS BROTHERS - CAROLINA—Edwards Brothers, Inc., pg. 370
EDWARDS BROTHERS, INC., pg. 369
ELECTRONIC MEDIA—Crain Communications, Inc., pg. 295
ELECTRONIC NEWS PUBLISHING—International Data Group, pg. 576
ELECTRONIC PRODUCTS MAGAZINE—The Hearst Corporation, pg. 522
EMPIRE PRESS—Cowles Magazines, Inc., pg. 291
ENDLESS VACATION PUBLISHING—Resort Condominiums International, pg. 929
ESQUIRE—The Hearst Corporation, pg. 523
EUROPEAN TRAVEL & LIFE—K-III Communications Corporation, pg. 611
EXECUTIVE ENTERPRISES, INC., pg. 393
EXECUTIVE ENTERPRISES PUBLICATIONS CO., INC.—Executive Enterprises, Inc., pg. 393
F & W PUBLICATIONS, INC., pg. 394
FCW PUBLISHING CORP.—International Data Group, pg. 576
FARM JOURNAL, INC., pg. 401
FIELD PUBLICATIONS—K-III Communications Corporation, pg. 611
FIRST DATABANK—The Hearst Corporation, pg. 522
FISHING TACKLE RETAILER—B.A.S.S., Inc., pg. 105
FLOOR COVERING WEEKLY—The Hearst Corporation, pg. 522
FOODSERVICE DIRECTOR—Bill Communications, Inc., pg. 150
FORBES, INC., pg. 423
FORBES MAGAZINE DIVISION—Forbes, Inc., pg. 423
GAMEPRO—International Data Group, pg. 576
GARDNER PUBLICATIONS, INC., pg. 443
GENERAL MEDIA PUBLISHING GROUP, pg. 450
GENTLEMEN'S QUARTERLY—Advance Publications Inc., pg. 19
GEYER-MCALLISTER PUBLICATIONS, INC., pg. 455
GLAMOUR—Advance Publications Inc., pg. 19
THE GOLDHIRSH GROUP INC., pg. 467
GOOD HOUSEKEEPING—The Hearst Corporation, pg. 523
GOURMET—Advance Publications Inc., pg. 19
EARL G. GRAVES, LTD., pg. 478
EARL G. GRAVES PUBLISHING CO., INC.—Earl G. Graves, Ltd., pg. 478
GRIT PUBLISHING COMPANY—Stauffer Communications, Inc., pg. 1043
GUIDEPOSTS ASSOCIATES, INC., pg. 493
HARPER'S BAZAAR—The Hearst Corporation, pg. 523
HEALTHCARE GROUP—The Hearst Corporation, pg. 522
HEARST BOOKS/BUSINESS PUBLISHING GROUP—The Hearst Corporation, pg. 521
HEARST BUSINESS COMMUNICATIONS, INC.—The Hearst Corporation, pg. 522
THE HEARST CORPORATION, pg. 521
HEARST MAGAZINES DIVISION—The Hearst Corporation, pg. 523
HEARST MAGAZINES SPECIAL PUBLICATIONS—The Hearst Corporation, pg. 523
HEARST PROFESSIONAL MAGAZINES, INC.—The Hearst Corporation, pg. 522
HIGHLIGHTS FOR CHILDREN, INC., pg. 534
HIPPOCRATES PARTNERS, pg. 535
HOUSE BEAUTIFUL—The Hearst Corporation, pg. 523
HOUSE & GARDEN—Advance Publications Inc., pg. 19
IDC IRVINE—International Data Group, pg. 577
IMPRESSIONS INC.—Edwards Brothers, Inc., pg. 370
INCENTIVE—Bill Communications, Inc., pg. 150
INDUSTRIAL EQUIPMENT NEWS—Thomas Publishing Co., pg. 1093
INFOWORLD PUBLISHING, INC.—International Data Group, pg. 576
INSIDE SPORTS, INC.—Century Publishing Company, pg. 235
INSTITUTIONAL DISTRIBUTION—Bill Communications, Inc., pg. 150
INTEGRATED MEDIA, INC.—International Data Group, pg. 576
INTERNATIONAL DATA CORP.—International Data Group, pg. 577
INTERNATIONAL DATA GROUP, pg. 576
INTERNATIONAL EDITIONS—The Hearst Corporation, pg. 523
INTERTEC PUBLISHING—K-III Communications Corporation, pg. 611
INTERTEC PUBLISHING CORP.—K-III Communications Corporation, pg. 611
JOBBER RETAILER—Bill Communications, Inc., pg. 150
JOHNSON PUBLISHING COMPANY, INC., pg. 598
K-III COMMUNICATIONS CORPORATION, pg. 610
K-III INFORMATION—K-III Communications Corporation, pg. 611
K-III MAGAZINES CORPORATION—K-III Communications Corporation, pg. 611
KALMBACH PUBLISHING CO., pg. 615
KIPLINGER EDITORS—The Kiplinger Washington Editors, Inc., pg. 632
THE KIPLINGER WASHINGTON EDITORS, INC., pg. 632
KNAPP COMMUNICATIONS CORPORATION, pg. 636
LADYBUG MAGAZINE—Carus Corporation, pg. 227
LANDMARK COMMUNICATIONS, INC., pg. 654
LANDMARK SPECIAL PUBLICATIONS—Landmark Communications, Inc., pg. 656
LEBHAR-FRIEDMAN, INC., pg. 665
LOGICAL OPERATIONS—Ziff Communications Company, pg. 1219
LOTUS PUBLISHING CORPORATION—International Data Group, pg. 576
MPC WORLD—International Data Group, pg. 576
MACUSER—Ziff Communications Company, pg. 1218
MACWORLD—International Data Group, pg. 576
MADEMOISELLE—Advance Publications Inc., pg. 19
MANAGING AUTOMATION—Thomas Publishing Co., pg. 1093
MARKET STATISTICS—Bill Communications, Inc., pg. 150
MARVEL ENTERTAINMENT GROUP—MacAndrews & Forbes Holdings Inc., pg. 695
MEDIATEX COMMUNICATIONS CORPORATION, pg. 735
MEN'S JOURNAL—Straight Arrow Publishers, Inc., pg. 1052
METROPOLITAN SUNDAY NEWSPAPERS, INC., pg. 745
MIDWEST DIVISION—Hippocrates Partners, pg. 536
MODERN HEALTHCARE—Crain Communications, Inc., pg. 295
MODERN TIRE DEALER—Bill Communications, Inc., pg. 150
MONROE PRINTING COMPANY—Mack Printing Company, pg. 697
MORROW JUNIOR BOOKS—The Hearst Corporation, pg. 522
MOTHER EARTH NEWS, pg. 773
MOTOR BOATING & SAILING—The Hearst Corporation, pg. 523
MOTOR MAGAZINE—The Hearst Corporation, pg. 522
MOTOR PUBLICATIONS—The Hearst Corporation, pg. 522
THE NATION—Shepaug Corporation, pg. 998
NATIONAL AUTO RESEARCH—The Hearst Corporation, pg. 522
NATIONAL GEOGRAPHIC SOCIETY, pg. 789
THE NATIONAL MAGAZINE COMPANY LTD.—The Hearst Corporation, pg. 524
NETWORK WORLD, INC.—International Data Group, pg. 576
NEW WOMAN MAGAZINE—K-III Communications Corporation, pg. 611
NEW YORK MAGAZINE COMPANY—K-III Communications Corporation, pg. 611
THE NEW YORKER MAGAZINE, pg. 803
NEWFIELD PUBLICATIONS—K-III Communications Corporation, pg. 611
NORTH AMERICAN PUBLISHING COMPANY, pg. 811
OMNI PUBLICATIONS INTERNATIONAL LTD.—General Media Publishing Group, pg. 450
PC COMPUTING—Ziff Communications Company, pg. 1219
PC MAGAZINE—Ziff Communications Company, pg. 1219
PC WORLD—International Data Group, pg. 576
PCI, pg. 836
PAISANO PUBLICATIONS, INC., pg. 843
PARADE PUBLICATIONS INC., pg. 847
PARADE PUBLICATIONS, INC.—Parade Publications Inc., pg. 847
PENSIONS & INVESTMENTS—Crain Communications, Inc., pg. 295
PERSIS CORPORATION, pg. 863
PETERSEN PUBLISHING COMPANY, pg. 864
PHILLIPS PUBLISHING INC., pg. 868
PLASTICS TECHNOLOGY—Bill Communications, Inc., pg. 150
POPULAR MECHANICS—The Hearst Corporation, pg. 523
PREMIERE MAGAZINE—K-III Communications Corporation, pg. 611
PULSE MAGAZINE—MTS, Inc., pg. 694
PUTMAN PUBLISHING CO., pg. 901
RCR PUBLICATIONS—Crain Communications, Inc., pg. 295
REDBOOK—The Hearst Corporation, pg. 523

S.I.C. Index

RESTAURANT BUSINESS—Bill Communications, Inc., pg. 150
RESTAURANT/HOTEL DESIGN INTERNATIONAL—Bill Communications, Inc., pg. 150
RETIREMENT ADVISORS, INC.—The Hearst Corporation, pg. 522
RODALE PRESS, INC., pg. 942
A. I. ROOT CO.—A.I. Root Company, pg. 946
A.I. ROOT COMPANY, pg. 946
SI HOLDINGS INC., pg. 962
ST. CROIX PRESS, INC., pg. 966
SALES AND MARKETING MANAGEMENT—Bill Communications, Inc., pg. 150
THE SATURDAY EVENING POST SOCIETY—Benjamin Franklin Literary & Medical Society, Inc., pg. 139
SATURDAY REVIEW MAGAZINE—General Media Publishing Group, pg. 450
SCHOLASTIC INC.—SI Holdings Inc., pg. 962
SCHOLASTIC INC. NATIONAL DISTRIBUTION CENTER—SI Holdings Inc., pg. 962
SCHOLASTIC PUBLICATIONS LTD.—SI Holdings Inc., pg. 962
SELF—Advance Publications Inc., pg. 19
SEVENTEEN MAGAZINE—K-III Communications Corporation, pg. 611
THE SHERIDAN GROUP, pg. 998
THE SHERIDAN PRESS, INC.—The Sheridan Group, pg. 998
SIMMONS-BOARDMAN PUBLISHING CORP., pg. 1005
SOAP OPERA DIGEST—K-III Communications Corporation, pg. 611
SOFTWARE VIDEO PRODUCTION—PCI, pg. 836
SOUTHERN OUTDOORS MAGAZINE—B.A.S.S., Inc., pg. 105
SOUTHERN SALTWATER MAGAZINE—B.A.S.S., Inc., pg. 106
SOUTHWESTERN/GREAT AMERICAN INC., pg. 1023
SPANGLER, INC., pg. 1025
SPORTS AFIELD—The Hearst Corporation, pg. 523
SPORTSWEAR INTERNATIONAL—K-III Communications Corporation, pg. 611
STAR MAGAZINE—K-III Communications Corporation, pg. 611
STRAIGHT ARROW PUBLISHERS, INC., pg. 1052
STRANG COMMUNICATIONS COMPANY, pg. 1052
SUCCESSFUL MEETINGS—Bill Communications, Inc., pg. 150
TSR, INC., pg. 1075
TV HOST INC., pg. 1075
TAX MANAGEMENT, INC.—The Bureau of National Affairs, Inc., pg. 190
TECHNICAL PUBLISHING—Nelson & Schmidt, Inc., pg. 797
TEXAS MONTHLY, INC.—Mediatex Communications Corporation, pg. 735
THOMAS PUBLISHING CO., pg. 1093
THOMAS REGISTER—Thomas Publishing Co., pg. 1093
TOWN & COUNTRY—The Hearst Corporation, pg. 523
TYNDALE HOUSE PUBLISHERS, INC., pg. 1122
U.S. NEWS & WORLD REPORT, pg. 1136
US MAGAZINE—Straight Arrow Publishers, Inc., pg. 1052
VANCE PUBLISHING CORPORATION, pg. 1144
VANITY FAIR—Advance Publications Inc., pg. 19
VEGETARIAN TIMES—Cowles Magazines, Inc., pg. 291
VICTORIA—The Hearst Corporation, pg. 523
VOGUE MAGAZINE—Advance Publications Inc., pg. 19
WARD'S COMMUNICATIONS, INC.—K-III Communications Corporation, pg. 611
WEEKLY READER CORP.—K-III Communications Corporation, pg. 611
WEIDER HEALTH & FITNESS, pg. 1173
WINDSOR PUBLICATIONS, INC., pg. 1196
WOOD KNAPP & CO., INC.—Knapp Communications Corporation, pg. 636
WORLD PUBLISHING COMPANY—Century Publishing Company, pg. 235
YANKEE PUBLISHING INCORPORATED, pg. 1207
ZIFF COMMUNICATIONS COMPANY, pg. 1218
ZIFF-DAVIS GERMANY—Ziff Communications Company, pg. 1219
ZIFF-DAVIS PUBLISHING COMPANY—Ziff Communications Company, pg. 1219

2731 — BOOKS: PUBLISHING, OR PUBLISHING & PRINTING

ABINGDON PRESS, pg. 10
ABRAMS PUBLISHING INC., pg. 10
ADVANCE PUBLICATIONS INC., pg. 19
ADVERTISING AGE INTERNATIONAL—Crain Communications, Inc., pg. 296
AMERICAN ARBRITRATION ASSOCIATION, pg. 49
AMERICAN BIBLE SOCIETY, pg. 49
AMERICAN KENNEL CLUB, INC., pg. 57
AMERICAN LIBRARY ASSOCIATION, pg. 57
AMERICAN MATHEMATICAL SOCIETY, INC., pg. 58
AMERICAN TECHNICAL PUBLISHERS, INC., pg. 63
AMSCO SCHOOL PUBLICATIONS, INC., pg. 68
AMWAY CORPORATION, pg. 70
ARBOR HOUSE—The Hearst Corporation, pg. 522
ARCATA CORPORATION, pg. 80
ARCATA GRAPHICS HALLIDAY—Arcata Corporation, pg. 80
ART PUBLISHING CO.—Goldmark Industries, Ltd., pg. 468
ASHTON/SCHOLASTIC PTY. LTD.—SI Holdings Inc., pg. 962
AUTOMOTIVE NEWS, pg. 101
AVON BOOKS—The Hearst Corporation, pg. 522
BNA BOOKS DIV.—The Bureau of National Affairs, Inc., pg. 189
BNA EDITORIAL SUPPORT DIV.—The Bureau of National Affairs, Inc., pg. 189
BNA INTERNATIONAL INC.—The Bureau of National Affairs, Inc., pg. 190
BNA PLUS—The Bureau of National Affairs, Inc., pg. 189
BALLANTINE BOOKS—Advance Publications Inc., pg. 19
BARANSKI PUBLISHING COMPANY—Barancorp, pg. 118
BARNES & NOBLE—Rowman & Littlefield Publishers, Inc., pg. 953
BEAUTY HANDBOOK CORPORATION, pg. 130
BEECH TREE BOOKS—The Hearst Corporation, pg. 521
BELL & HOWELL COMPANY, pg. 134
BERLITZ PUBLISHING COMPANY INC.—Berlitz International, Inc., pg. 142
CHANNING L. BETE CO., INC., pg. 147
WALTER J. BLACK, INC., pg. 154
BLACK'S READERS SERVICE—Walter J. Black, Inc., pg. 154
BRAUN-BRUMFIELD, INC.—The Sheridan Group, pg. 998
BRITANNICA HOME LIBRARY SERVICES—Encyclopaedia Britannica, Inc., pg. 381
THE BUREAU OF NATIONAL AFFAIRS, INC., pg. 189
CALICO CAT PRESS, INC., pg. 209
CAMBRIDGE ASSOCIATES—The Dartnell Corporation, pg. 316
CARUS CORPORATION, pg. 227
THE CAXTON PRINTERS LTD., pg. 230
THE CLASSICS CLUB—Walter J. Black, Inc., pg. 154
COLWELL INDUSTRIES, INC., pg. 267
COMMUNICATIONS INTERNATIONAL, pg. 269
DAVID C. COOK PUBLISHING CO., pg. 282
CROWN PUBLISHERS, INC.—Advance Publications Inc., pg. 20
THE DARTNELL CORPORATION, pg. 316
MARCEL DEKKER, INC., pg. 325
DELTA EDUCATION, INC., pg. 326
DESERET BOOK CO.—Deseret Management Corporation, pg. 332
THE DETECTIVE BOOK CLUB—Walter J. Black, Inc., pg. 154
EB (NA)—Encyclopaedia Britannica, Inc., pg. 381
E.P. GRAPHICS, INC., pg. 360
EDWARDS BROTHERS - CAROLINA—Edwards Brothers, Inc., pg. 370
EDWARDS BROTHERS, INC., pg. 369
ENCYCLOPAEDIA BRITANNICA EDUCATIONAL CORPORATION—Encyclopaedia Britannica, Inc., pg. 381
ENCYCLOPAEDIA BRITANNICA, INC., pg. 381
THE (ERLE STANLEY) GARDNER MYSTERY LIBRARY—Walter J. Black, Inc., pg. 154
EXECUTIVE ENTERPRISES, INC., pg. 393
EXECUTIVE ENTERPRISES PUBLICATIONS CO., INC.—Executive Enterprises, Inc., pg. 393
FARRAR, STRAUS & GIROUX, INC., pg. 403
FAWCETT BOOKS—Advance Publications Inc., pg. 19
FIELD PUBLICATIONS—K-III Communications Corporation, pg. 611
FIELDING TRAVEL BOOKS—The Hearst Corporation, pg. 521
FODOR'S TRAVEL PUBLICATIONS, INC.—Advance Publications Inc., pg. 19
FUNK & WAGNALLS CORP.—K-III Communications Corporation, pg. 611
GARDNER PUBLICATIONS, INC., pg. 443
GENERAL MEDIA PUBLISHING GROUP, pg. 450
THE GIANTS OF LITERATURE SERIES—Walter J. Black, Inc., pg. 154
THE GOLDEN GIANTS SERIES—Walter J. Black, Inc., pg. 154
GOODHEART-WILLCOX CO., INC., pg. 470
GRAPHIC LEARNING—Abrams Publishing Inc., pg. 10
GRAY PRINTING CO., pg. 479
GREAT BOOKS OF THE WESTERN WORLD—Encyclopaedia Britannica, Inc., pg. 381
GREENWILLOW BOOKS—The Hearst Corporation, pg. 521
GUIDEPOSTS ASSOCIATES, INC., pg. 493
HADDON CRAFTSMEN, INC., pg. 499
HEARST BOOK GROUP—The Hearst Corporation, pg. 522
HEARST BOOKS/BUSINESS PUBLISHING GROUP—The Hearst Corporation, pg. 521
THE HEARST CORPORATION, pg. 521
HEARST MAGAZINES DIVISION—The Hearst Corporation, pg. 523
HEARST MARINE BOOKS—The Hearst Corporation, pg. 521
IDG BOOKS WORLDWIDE—International Data Group, pg. 576
IMPRESSIONS INC.—Edwards Brothers, Inc., pg. 370
INDUSTRIAL INFORMATION HEADQUARTERS CO.—Headco Industries, Inc., pg. 520
K-III COMMUNICATIONS CORPORATION, pg. 610
ALFRED A. KNOPF, INC.—Advance Publications Inc., pg. 20
LOTHROP, LEE & SHEPARD BOOKS—The Hearst Corporation, pg. 521
MCDOUGAL, LITTELL & COMPANY, pg. 728
MEDIA AMERICA CORP., pg. 734
MERRIAM-WEBSTER, INC.—Encyclopaedia Britannica, Inc., pg. 381
WILLIAM MORROW & CO., INC.—The Hearst Corporation, pg. 521
MOTOR CONSUMER BOOKS—The Hearst Corporation, pg. 522
MOTOR PUBLICATIONS—The Hearst Corporation, pg. 522
NATIONAL GEOGRAPHIC SOCIETY, pg. 789
NEW DIMENSIONS IN EDUCATION—Abrams Publishing Inc., pg. 10
NEWBRIDGE COMMUNICATIONS—K-III Communications Corporation, pg. 611
NEWFIELD PUBLICATIONS—K-III Communications Corporation, pg. 611
NORTH AMERICAN PUBLISHING COMPANY, pg. 811
W.W. NORTON & COMPANY, INC., pg. 815
OPEN COURT PUBLISHING COMPANY—Carus Corporation, pg. 227
OUR SUNDAY VISITOR, INC., pg. 832
PBM PUBLISHING—PBM Office Products, pg. 835
PHOENIX MAGAZINE—Media America Corp., pg. 734
PIKE & FISCHER—The Bureau of National Affairs, Inc., pg. 190
PREMIER PUBLISHING CO.—Pacific Envelope Company, pg. 840
QUILL TRADE PAPERBACKS—The Hearst Corporation, pg. 522
RAND MCNALLY & COMPANY, pg. 911
RAND MCNALLY PUBLISHING GROUP—Rand McNally & Company, pg. 911
RANDOM HOUSE, INC.—Advance Publications Inc., pg. 19
READING EAGLE COMPANY, pg. 916
RODALE PRESS, INC., pg. 942
ROLLING STONE MAGAZINE—Straight Arrow Publishers, Inc., pg. 1052
ROWMAN & LITTLEFIELD PUBLISHERS, INC., pg. 952
WILLIAM H. SADLIER, INC., pg. 966
SCHOLASTIC-CANADA, LTD.—SI Holdings Inc., pg. 962
SCHOLASTIC INC.—SI Holdings Inc., pg. 962
SCHOLASTIC PUBLICATIONS LTD.—SI Holdings Inc., pg. 962
SCIENCE PRESS—Mack Printing Company, pg. 697
THE SHERIDAN GROUP, pg. 998
THE SHERIDAN PRESS, INC.—The Sheridan Group, pg. 998
SMITH-EDWARDS-DUNLAP COMPANY, pg. 1012
SOUTHWESTERN/GREAT AMERICAN INC., pg. 1023
SYBEX GROUP, pg. 1069
TAMBOURINE BOOKS—The Hearst Corporation, pg. 522
TAX MANAGEMENT, INC.—The Bureau of National Affairs, Inc., pg. 190
TIMES BOOKS—Advance Publications Inc., pg. 19
TYNDALE HOUSE PUBLISHERS, INC., pg. 1122
UTP (UNITED TECHNICAL PUBLICATIONS) DIVISION—The Hearst Corporation, pg. 522
UNIVERSITY PRESS OF AMERICA, INC.—Rowman & Littlefield Publishers, Inc., pg. 953
VILLARD BOOKS—Advance Publications Inc., pg. 19
WALSWORTH PUBLISHING COMPANY, INC., pg. 1161
WARNER PRESS, INC., pg. 1164
WEST PUBLISHING CO., pg. 1177
THE H. W. WILSON CO., pg. 1193
WINDSOR PUBLICATIONS, INC., pg. 1196
WORLD REPORT VERLAG GMBH—Berlitz International, Inc., pg. 143
YALE UNIVERSITY PRESS, pg. 1207
THE ZANE GREY LIBRARY—Walter J. Black, Inc., pg. 154
ZIFF COMMUNICATIONS COMPANY, pg. 1218
ZIFF-DAVIS PRESS—Ziff Communications Company, pg. 1219
ZIFF-DAVIS PUBLISHING COMPANY—Ziff Communications Company, pg. 1219

2732 — BOOK PRINTING

ARCATA CORPORATION, pg. 80
ARCATA GRAPHICS COMPANY—Arcata Corporation, pg. 80
ARCATA GRAPHICS KINGSPORT—Arcata Corporation, pg. 80
DELMAR PHOTOGRAPHIC AND PRINTING COMPANY—Continental Graphics Holdings, Inc., pg. 279
GRAPHIC CENTER, INC., pg. 478
JUDD'S INCORPORATED, pg. 608
MALLOY LITHOGRAPHING INC., pg. 703
MCNAUGHTON & GUNN, INC., pg. 732
RAND MCNALLY & COMPANY, pg. 911
ROSE PRINTING COMPANY, INC., pg. 948
THE SEGERDAHL CORP., pg. 987
WEST PUBLISHING CO., pg. 1177
WORZALLA PUBLISHING CO., INC., pg. 1204

2741 — MISCELLANEOUS PUBLISHING

AMERICAN AUTOMOBILE ASSOCIATION, NATIONAL TRAVEL DEPARTMENT, pg. 49
AMERICAN BUSINESS INFORMATION, INC., pg. 50
AMWAY CORPORATION, pg. 70
ARANDELL-SCHMIDT CORPORATION, pg. 79
ARKANSAS ELECTRIC COOPERATIVES INC., pg. 83
ASSOCIATED MUSIC PUBLISHERS—Music Sales Corporation, pg. 777
AUGSBURG FORTRESS, PUBLISHERS, pg. 98
AUTOMATED MARKETING SYSTEMS, INC., pg. 100
AUTONET, INC.—Landmark Communications, Inc., pg. 656
BARANCORP, pg. 118
BASSMASTER MAGAZINE—B.A.S.S., Inc., pg. 105
BELL & HOWELL COMPANY, pg. 134
BELL SOUTH ENTERPRISES, pg. 136
CHANNING L. BETE CO., INC., pg. 147
BOOKAZINE COMPANY, INC., pg. 164
BUTTERICK COMPANY, INC., pg. 197
C M P PUBLICATIONS, INC., pg. 202
CAL GRAPHICS DIVISION—The Hearst Corporation, pg. 521
CAPITOL INDUSTRIES-EMI INC., pg. 216
CAREERTRACK INC., pg. 218
COMMUNICATIONS INTERNATIONAL, pg. 269
COMPILERS PLUS—American Business Information, Inc., pg. 50
COMPUTER INTELLIGENCE—Ziff Communications Company, pg. 1219
CONCORDIA PUBLISHING HOUSE, pg. 272
COWLES SYNDICATE, INC.—The Hearst Corporation, pg. 524
COX ENTERPRISES, INC., pg. 292
CROWN PUBLISHERS, INC.—Advance Publications Inc., pg. 20
THE CURTIS PUBLISHING COMPANY, pg. 306
THE DARTNELL CORPORATION, pg. 316

S.I.C. Index

DATA SOURCES—Ziff Communications Company, pg. 1218
DISPATCH CONSUMER SERVICES—The Dispatch Printing Company, pg. 339
DIVERSIFIED COMMUNICATIONS, pg. 340
DONTECH, pg. 345
EMI MUSIC PUBLISHING NORTH AMERICA—Capitol Industries-EMI Inc., pg. 216
THE ECONOMICS PRESS, INC., pg. 367
EDUCATIONAL PUBLISHING CORPORATION, pg. 369
ELECTRONIC ENGINEERS MASTER—The Hearst Corporation, pg. 522
ENCYCLOPAEDIA BRITANNICA, INC., pg. 381
FIELD PUBLICATIONS—K-III Communications Corporation, pg. 611
FINANCIAL WORLD PARTNERS, pg. 410
FISHING TACKLE RETAILER—B.A.S.S., Inc., pg. 105
GENERAL MEDIA PUBLISHING GROUP, pg. 450
GEYER-MCALLISTER PUBLICATIONS, INC., pg. 455
GOLDMARK INDUSTRIES—Goldmark Industries, Ltd., pg. 468
HAINES & CO., INC., pg. 500
INFOCORP—Ziff Communications Company, pg. 1219
INFORMATION ACCESS CO.—Ziff Communications Company, pg. 1219
INSTITUTIONAL DISTRIBUTION—Bill Communications, Inc., pg. 150
INTEGRATED CIRCUITS MASTER CATALOG—The Hearst Corporation, pg. 522
JII/SALES PROMOTION ASSOCIATES, INC.—Jordan Industries, Inc., pg. 604
J. J. KELLER & ASSOCIATES, INC., pg. 620
LIFETOUCH PUBLISHING INC.—Lifetouch, Inc., pg. 675
MACK PRINTING COMPANY, pg. 697
MANUFACTURERS' NEWS, INC., pg. 705
MCARDLE PRINTING CO., INC.—The Bureau of National Affairs, Inc., pg. 189
METROPOLITAN SUNDAY NEWSPAPERS, INC., pg. 745
MOTHER EARTH NEWS, pg. 773
MOTOR CRASH ESTIMATING GUIDE—The Hearst Corporation, pg. 522
MUSCUM BOUTIQUE INTERCONTINENTAL, LTD., pg. 777
MUSIC SALES CORPORATION, pg. 777
NATIONAL RESEARCH BUREAU—Automated Marketing Systems, Inc., pg. 100
O'NEIL DATA SYSTEMS, INC.—William O'Neil & Co., Inc., pg. 827
P/O/N PRODUCT CORP.—Penny/Ohlmann/Neiman, Inc., pg. 858
PATCH COMMUNICATIONS, pg. 851
PHILLIPS PUBLISHING INC., pg. 868
R. L. POLK & CO., pg. 879
PREDICASTS—Ziff Communications Company, pg. 1219
PRINTING HOUSE, INC., pg. 891
RAND MCNALLEY & COMPANY, D/B/A CHAMPION MAP CORP.—Rand McNally & Company, pg. 911
RAND MCNALLY & COMPANY, pg. 911
RAND MCNALLY PUBLISHING GROUP—Rand McNally & Company, pg. 911
RAND MCNALLY PUBLISHING GROUP—Rand McNally & Company, pg. 911
RENAISSANCE PUBLISHING CO., INC., pg. 926
RHODE ISLAND MONTHLY—Communications International, pg. 269
WILLIAM H. SADLIER, INC., pg. 966
SAMPLER PUBLICATIONS INC., pg. 968
SCAFA TORNABENE—Goldmark Industries, Ltd., pg. 468
G. SCHIRMER, INC.—Music Sales Corporation, pg. 777
SCHOLASTIC INC.—SI Holdings Inc., pg. 962
SCICOM DATA SERVICES, LTD., pg. 981
SEYBOLD PUBLICATIONS—Ziff Communications Company, pg. 1219
SEYBOLD SEMINARS—Ziff Communications Company, pg. 1219
SHAWNEE PRESS, INC.—Music Sales Corporation, pg. 777
SOUTHERN OUTDOORS MAGAZINE—B.A.S.S., Inc., pg. 105
SOUTHERN SALTWATER MAGAZINE—B.A.S.S., Inc., pg. 106
SPONSORED PUBLICATIONS—The Hearst Corporation, pg. 522
STRAIGHT ARROW PUBLISHERS, INC., pg. 1052
SUNDAY MAGAZINE NETWORK—Metropolitan Sunday Newspapers, Inc., pg. 745
TAYLOR PUBLISHING CO.—Insilco Corporation, pg. 571
TEXAS ELECTRIC COOPERATIVES, INC., pg. 1089
THOMAS PUBLISHING CO., pg. 1093
WEST PUBLISHING CO., pg. 1177
THE H. W. WILSON CO., pg. 1193
WINDSOR PUBLICATIONS, INC., pg. 1196
WOLFER PRINTING COMPANY, pg. 1199
YANKEE PUBLISHING INCORPORATED, pg. 1207
ZIFF COMMUNICATIONS COMPANY, pg. 1218
ZIFF-DAVIS PUBLISHING COMPANY—Ziff Communications Company, pg. 1219
ZIFF INFORMATION SERVICES—Ziff Communications Company, pg. 1219

2752 — COMMERCIAL PRINTING, LITHOGRAPHIC

ADAMS BUSINESS FORMS, pg. 16
ADVANCE BUSINESS GRAPHICS, pg. 18
ALAN LITHOGRAPH, INC., pg. 30
ALBERTS COPYING DIV.—National Reproductions Corporation, pg. 793
ALCOM PRINTING GROUP, INC., pg. 32
IVAN ALLEN COMPANY, INC., pg. 36
AMERICAN DECAL & MFG. CO., pg. 51
AMERICAN PRINTERS & LITHOGRAPHERS, pg. 59
ANDERSON LITHOGRAPH COMPANY, pg. 73
APPLIED GRAPHICS TECHNOLOGIES—U.S. News & World Report, pg. 1136
ARANDELL-SCHMIDT CORPORATION, pg. 79
ARCADE INC., pg. 80
ARCATA CORPORATION, pg. 80
ARTS & CRAFTS PRESS—Continental Graphics Holdings, Inc., pg. 279
AUTOMATIC LIQUID PACKAGING, INC., pg. 100
BANKERS SYSTEMS INC., pg. 117
BARTON PRESS, INC., pg. 123
BAWDEN CORPORATION, pg. 127
BAWDEN PRINTING, INC.—Bawden Corporation, pg. 127
BELL SOUTH ENTERPRISES, pg. 136
CHANNING L. BETE CO., INC., pg. 147
BRAUN-BRUMFIELD, INC.—The Sheridan Group, pg. 998
BRIAN UNLIMITED DISTRIBUTION COMPANY, INC., pg. 175
BUREAU OF ENGRAVING, pg. 189
BURKE COMMUNICATION INDUSTRIES, INC., pg. 190
CGF INDUSTRIES, pg. 201
C M P PRINTING COMPANY—C M P Publications, Inc., pg. 203
CAPITAL CITY PRESS, INC., pg. 214
THE CAXTON PRINTERS LTD., pg. 230
CHAMPION BUSINESS FORMS, pg. 238
KEITH CLARK—Cullman Ventures, Inc., pg. 304
COLFAX ENVELOPE CORPORATION, pg. 261
COLLMAN GRAPHICS, INC., pg. 263
COLOR DATA EAST—Schawk, Inc., pg. 975
COLOR GRAPHICS, INC., pg. 264
COLWELL INDUSTRIES, INC., pg. 267
COMMAND WEB OFFSET CO.—MacNaughton Einson Graphics, pg. 698
COMMERCIAL PRINTERS OF CONNECTICUT, pg. 268
COMMONWEALTH PRINTING COMPANY—Landmark Communications, Inc., pg. 656
COMPUTER PRINTING DIV.—National Reproductions Corporation, pg. 793
CONCORD LITHO CO., INC., pg. 272
CONTINENTAL GRAPHICS CORPORATION—Continental Graphics Holdings, Inc., pg. 279
CONTINENTAL WEB PRESS, INC., pg. 280
COSCO INDUSTRIES, pg. 288
COSMOS COMMUNICATIONS, INC., pg. 288
CUMMINS-AMERICAN CORP., pg. 304
DANBURY PRINTING & LITHOGRAPH, INC., pg. 313
DANIELS PRINTING COMPANY, pg. 314
DEMOCRAT PRINTING & LITHOGRAPH COMPANY, pg. 328
DICKINSON PRESS, INC., pg. 336
DIRECT PRESS MODERN LITHO CORPORATION, pg. 339
DIXONWEB PRINTING COMPANY—Sleepeck Printing Company, pg. 1010
DOT PRINTER, INC., pg. 347
EASTERN COLOR PRINTING COMPANY, pg. 363
EDITORS PRESS, INC.—The Kiplinger Washington Editors, Inc., pg. 632
ELLISON GRAPHICS—Herlin Press, pg. 531
ENTERPRISE PRESS, INC., pg. 382
F C L GRAPHICS, pg. 394
FENTON PRESS, INC., pg. 406
FLEMING PACKAGING CORP., pg. 417
FOOTE & DAVIES INC., pg. 423
FORT DEARBORN LITHOGRAPH COMPANY, pg. 425
FORUM PUBLISHING COMPANY, pg. 426
THE FRANKLIN MINT—American Protection Industries, Inc., pg. 60
FREDERIC PRINTING—Frederic Printing Company, pg. 430
FREDERIC PRINTING COMPANY, pg. 430
FT. DEARBORN LITHOGRAPH GRAPHIC ARTS DIVISION—Fort Dearborn Lithograph Company, pg. 425
THE GARBER COMPANY, pg. 442
GATEWAY PRESS, INC., pg. 446
GAYLORD CENTRAL PRINTING & PUBLISHING DIV.—Gaylord Printing, Inc., pg. 447
GAYLORD LITHOGRAPH DIV.-DETROIT—Gaylord Printing, Inc., pg. 447
GAYLORD PRINTING, INC., pg. 446
GEORGE LITHOGRAPH, pg. 452
GORE GRAPHICS, INC., pg. 472
GRANDVILLE PRINTING COMPANY, pg. 476
GRAPHIC ARTS CENTER—Continental Graphics Holdings, Inc., pg. 279
GRAPHIC CENTER, INC., pg. 478
GRAPHIC PRODUCTIONS COMPANY, pg. 478
GREAT LAKES LITHOGRAPH CO., pg. 481
GREENSBORO NEWS & RECORD—Landmark Communications, Inc., pg. 655
GRIT PRINTING CO.—Stauffer Communications, Inc., pg. 1043
GUARD PUBLISHING COMPANY, pg. 491
H & H ADVERTISING, pg. 496
HART GRAPHICS INC., pg. 513
THE HENNEGAN COMPANY, pg. 529
HERLIN PRESS, pg. 531
HICKORY PRINTING GROUP, INC., pg. 533
HOLOUBEK INC., pg. 540
IMPERIAL LITHO/GRAPHICS, INC., pg. 564
INLAND PRINTING CO., INC., pg. 570
THE INSTANT WEB COMPANIES, pg. 571
INTERFORM CORPORATION, pg. 574
JAPS-OLSON COMPANY, pg. 590
JERSEY PRINTING COMPANY, INC., pg. 593
JOHNSON & QUIN, INC., pg. 599
JOURNAL COMMUNICATIONS INC., pg. 607
JUDD'S INCORPORATED, pg. 608
KOA HOLDINGS, pg. 612
KERVICK ENTERPRISES, INC., pg. 624
KIMBALL BAGGAGE TAG DIVISION—Rand McNally & Company, pg. 911
THE KIPLINGER WASHINGTON EDITORS, INC., pg. 632
KUKLA PRESS, INC., pg. 646
KURTZ BROS., INC., pg. 646
KWIK-KOPY CORP., pg. 647
LSI/KALA—Schawk, Inc., pg. 975
LABEL PRODUCTS & DESIGN DIVISION—Journal Communications Inc., pg. 608
LAKE COUNTY PRESS, pg. 651
LANE PRESS, INC., pg. 654
LASKY COMPANY, pg. 660
LITHO COLORPLATE—Schawk, Inc., pg. 975
LITHO-KROME COMPANY—Hallmark Cards, Inc., pg. 502
LITHOGRAPH PRINTING COMPANY, INC., pg. 678
LITHOGRAPHIX, INC., pg. 678
LITHOTYPE COMPANY, INC., pg. 678
JOHN D. LUCAS PRINTING COMPANY—Collman Graphics, Inc., pg. 263
LYKE CORPORATION, pg. 688
MACK PRINTING CO. INC.—Mack Printing Company, pg. 697
MACK PRINTING COMPANY, pg. 697
MACNAUGHTON EINSON GRAPHICS, pg. 698
MADISON GRAHAM COLORGRAPHICS, INC., pg. 699
MAINE PRINTING & BUSINESS FORMS CO., pg. 702
MEDIA PRINTING CORPORATION, pg. 734
MENASHA CORPORATION, pg. 738
MERCHANTS PUBLISHING CO., pg. 739
MESSENGER CORPORATION, pg. 741
THE MEYERCORD COMPANY, pg. 746
MIDWEST LITHO ARTS—Graphisphere Holding Company, pg. 478
MIKEN COMPANIES, INC., pg. 752
H. C. MILLER COMPANY, pg. 754
MONROE PRINTING COMPANY—Mack Printing Company, pg. 697
MOUNT JACKSON PRESS, INC.—Judd's Incorporated, pg. 608
NATIONAL BANNER COMPANY, pg. 786
NATIONAL COMPUTER SUPPLIES—Riccobon & Company, Inc., pg. 931
NATIONAL GROUP, INC., pg. 789
NATIONAL POSTERS, INC.—National Group, Inc., pg. 790
NATIONAL REPRODUCTIONS CORPORATION, pg. 793
THE NIELSEN COMPANY, pg. 807
OFFICE ELECTRONICS, INC., pg. 821
OLIVER PRODUCTS COMPANY, pg. 824
OPTIC GRAPHICS, INC., pg. 827
PIP CAPITAL INC.—Kane-Miller Corp., pg. 616
PACE PRESS, INC., pg. 838
PACE RESOURCES, INC., pg. 838
PANEL PRINTS, INC., pg. 846
PANORAMA PRESS, INC., pg. 846
PATSON'S PRESS, pg. 851
PEAKE PRINTERS, INC., pg. 853
PEARL-PRESSMAN-LIBERTY COMMUNICATIONS GROUP, pg. 853
DAVID L. PEISTER CO., INC., pg. 856
PERLMUTER PRINTING COMPANY, pg. 862
PERRY/BARABOO—Journal Communications Inc., pg. 607
PERRY/MILWAUKEE—Journal Communications Inc., pg. 607
PERRY/NORWAY—Journal Communications Inc., pg. 607
PERRY PRINTING CORP.—Journal Communications Inc., pg. 607
PETERSEN GRAPHICS GROUP, pg. 864
PETTY COMPANY, INC., pg. 866
PHOTOTYPE COLOR GRAPHICS, INC., pg. 869
PIONEER PAPER CORPORATION, pg. 872
PORT CITY PRESS, INC.—Judd's Incorporated, pg. 608
PRINT NORTHWEST, pg. 891
PRINT-O-STAT, INC.—Pace Resources, Inc., pg. 839
PRINTCO, INC., pg. 891
PRINTING HOUSE, INC., pg. 891
PROCESS COLOR PLATE—Schawk, Inc., pg. 975
PROGRESS PRINTING COMPANY, pg. 894
QUAD/GRAPHICS, INC., pg. 902
QUAD/WEST PRE-PRESS—Quad/Graphics, Inc., pg. 902
QUEENSGATE PRESS—The Nielsen Company, pg. 807
QUIK PRINT INC., pg. 905
RAMA GROUP OF COMPANIES, pg. 910
RAND MCNALLY & COMPANY, pg. 911
READING EAGLE COMPANY, pg. 916
RECORDING & STATISTICAL CORPORATION, pg. 917
REGENCY GROUP INC., pg. 922
RELIABLE GRAPHICS—Warrens Waller Press, pg. 1165
RICCOBON & COMPANY, INC., pg. 931
GEORGE RICE & SONS, pg. 931
RIVERSIDE PRESS, INC., pg. 937
JOHN ROBERTS COMPANY, pg. 938
ROCKY MOUNTAIN BANK NOTE COMPANY, pg. 942
RUSH PRESS—Continental Graphics Holdings, Inc., pg. 279
S & S GRAPHICS, INC., pg. 959
S L C GRAPHICS, INC., pg. 963
SCHAWK, INC., pg. 974
SCHAWKGRAPHICS—Schawk, Inc., pg. 975
SCOTT PRINTING CORPORATION, pg. 983
SCOVILLE PRESS, INC., pg. 983
THE SEGERDAHL CORP., pg. 987
SELECTO-FLASH, INC., pg. 988
SEMCO INDUSTRIES, pg. 989
SERIGRAPH, INC., pg. 991
SHENANDOAH VALLEY PRESS, INC.—Judd's Incorporated, pg. 608
THE SHERIDAN GROUP, pg. 998
THE SHERIDAN PRESS, INC.—The Sheridan Group, pg. 998
SINCLAIR PRINTING & LITHO, INC., pg. 1008
SLEEPECK PRINTING COMPANY, pg. 1010
SMITH-EDWARDS-DUNLAP COMPANY, pg. 1012
H.M. SMYTH CO., pg. 1014
SOLAR PRESS, INC., pg. 1016
SOLAR PRESS, INC.—Solar Press, Inc., pg. 1017
SPANGLER, INC., pg. 1025
SPAULDING COMPANY, INC.—Semco Industries, pg. 989
SPENCER PRESS, INC., pg. 1030

STANDARD GRAVURE CORP./SHEA COMMUNICATIONS, pg. 1036
STANDARD GRAVURE D/B/A OKLAHOMA GRAPHICS—Standard Gravure Corp./Shea Communications, pg. 1036
STEPHENSON, INC., pg. 1046
STERLING COLOR PROCESS—Kalamazoo Label Co., pg. 615
STEVENS GRAPHICS, INC.—Bell South Enterprises, pg. 136
TAYLOR CORPORATION, pg. 1081
TELEGRAPHICS PRINTING—Telescope Casual Furniture, Inc., pg. 1085
TIMES PRINTING COMPANY, INC., pg. 1098
TOTAL REPRODUCTIONS, INC.—Schawk, Inc., pg. 975
TREASURE CHEST ADVERTISING CO., INC., pg. 1108
TREND OFFSET PRINTING SERVICES, pg. 1109
TWEDDLE LITHO COMPANY, pg. 1120
UNIMAX HOLDING CORP.—Shepaug Corporation, pg. 998
UNITED ENVELOPE COMPANY, INC., pg. 1131
UNITED GRAPHICS, INC., pg. 1132
THE VERNON COMPANY, pg. 1148
VILE-GOLLER, FINE ART PRINTING & LITHOGRAPHY, pg. 1151
WALLE CORPORATION, pg. 1161
WARRENS WALLER PRESS, pg. 1165
WEBCRAFT GAMES, INC.—Webcraft Technologies, Inc., pg. 1171
WEBCRAFT TECHNOLOGIES, INC., pg. 1171
WELSH GRAPHICS, pg. 1176
WESTON ENGRAVING—Schawk, Inc., pg. 975
WINTHROP PRINTING COMPANY, INC., pg. 1197
WOLFER PRINTING COMPANY, pg. 1199

2754 — COMMERCIAL PRINTING, GRAVURE

ALLFORMS PACKAGING CORP.—Rock-Tenn Company, pg. 941
BARTON PRESS, INC., pg. 123
BUREAU OF ENGRAVING, pg. 189
BURGOYNE, INC., pg. 190
M.S. CHAMBERS & SON, INC.—The Dyson-Kissner-Moran Corporation, pg. 357
COLWELL INDUSTRIES, INC., pg. 267
CONSOLIDATED ENGRAVERS-EAST, INC.—The Dyson-Kissner-Moran Corporation, pg. 357
CONSOLIDATED GROUP, INC.—The Dyson-Kissner-Moran Corporation, pg. 357
H & H ADVERTISING, pg. 496
INLAND PRINTING CO., INC., pg. 570
KWIK-KOPY CORP., pg. 647
MENASHA CORPORATION, pg. 738
OFFICE ELECTRONICS, INC., pg. 821
O'NEIL DATA SYSTEMS, INC.—William O'Neil & Co., Inc., pg. 827
PHOTOTYPE COLOR GRAPHICS, INC., pg. 869
QUAD/GRAPHICS, INC., pg. 902
RELIEF PRINTING CORPORATION, pg. 925
THE SEGERDAHL CORP., pg. 987
STANDARD GRAVURE CORP./SHEA COMMUNICATIONS, pg. 1036
TOP FLIGHT, INC., pg. 1101
UNIMAX HOLDING CORP.—Shepaug Corporation, pg. 998
THE VERNON COMPANY, pg. 1148
ZEPHYR BASKETS & BALLOONS, pg. 1217

2759 — COMMERCIAL PRINTING, NEC

AGI INC., pg. 4
ALLECO INC., pg. 35
IVAN ALLEN COMPANY, INC., pg. 36
ALLIED PRINTING SERVICES, INC., pg. 38
AMERICAN DECAL & MFG. CO., pg. 51
AMERICAN SPEEDY PRINTING CENTERS, INC., pg. 61
ARCATA CORPORATION, pg. 80
ARCATA GRAPHICS BAIRD WARD, INC.—Arcata Corporation, pg. 80
ARCATA GRAPHICS BUFFALO, INC.—Arcata Corporation, pg. 80
ARCATA GRAPHICS COMPANY—Arcata Corporation, pg. 80
ARCATA GRAPHICS FAIRFIELD INC.—Arcata Corporation, pg. 80
ASHER CANDY COMPANY—MacAndrews & Forbes Holdings Inc., pg. 695
BALTIMORE STATIONERY CO., pg. 116
BRADLEY PRINTING COMPANY—Graphisphere Holding Company, pg. 478
BROWN & BIGELOW, INC., pg. 181
BUREAU OF ENGRAVING, pg. 189
BURKE COMMUNICATION INDUSTRIES, INC., pg. 190
CALIFORNIA OFFSET PRINTERS, INC., pg. 210
CARSTENS HEALTH INDUSTRIES, INC., pg. 225
CENTRAL STATES DIVERSIFIED, INC., pg. 234
M.S. CHAMBERS & SON, INC.—The Dyson-Kissner-Moran Corporation, pg. 357
CINE MAGNETICS, INC., pg. 250
COLOR ARTS, INC., pg. 264
COLOR DATA EAST—Schawk, Inc., pg. 975
COMMONWEALTH PRINTING COMPANY—Landmark Communications, Inc., pg. 656
CONSOLIDATED COMMUNICATIONS DIRECTORIES, INC.—Illinois Consolidated Telephone Co., pg. 563
CONSOLIDATED ENGRAVERS-EAST, INC.—The Dyson-Kissner-Moran Corporation, pg. 357
CONSOLIDATED GROUP, INC.—The Dyson-Kissner-Moran Corporation, pg. 357
H. S. CROCKER CO., INC., pg. 299
CULLMAN VENTURES, INC., pg. 304
DAILY RACING FORM, INC. (MIDWEST)—K-III Communications Corporation, pg. 611
DAILY RACING FORM, INC. (NORTHWEST)—K-III Communications Corporation, pg. 611
DAILY RACING FORM, INC. (TORONTO)—K-III Communications Corporation, pg. 611
DOWNEY PRINTING, pg. 348
DRAFTING GRAPHICS, INC., pg. 348
DRUCKER PRINTING—Meehan Tooker, pg. 736
EASTERN COLOR PRINTING COMPANY, pg. 363
ELMIRA LITHO—Meehan Tooker, pg. 736
FITTS-LAWRENCE, INC.—Lawrence Group, Inc., pg. 662
FLEER CORPORATION—MacAndrews & Forbes Holdings Inc., pg. 695
FLEMING PACKAGING CORP., pg. 417
GEIGER BROTHERS, pg. 447
GORE GRAPHICS, INC., pg. 472
GRAPHIC CONTROLS, CORP., pg. 478
GRAPHIC PRODUCTIONS COMPANY, pg. 478
GRAPHISPHERE HOLDING COMPANY, pg. 478
GRAY PRINTING CO., pg. 479
HALLMARK LITHO CO.—Pacific Envelope Company, pg. 840
HERFF JONES INC., pg. 531
HOYLE PRODUCTS—Brown & Bigelow, Inc., pg. 181
THE INSTANT WEB COMPANIES, pg. 571
JAPS-OLSON COMPANY, pg. 590
KWIK-KOPY CORP., pg. 647
LSI/KALA—Schawk, Inc., pg. 975
LITHO COLORPLATE—Schawk, Inc., pg. 975
LOCKWOOD FOLDING BOX—H. S. Crocker Co., Inc., pg. 300
MACK PRINTING COMPANY, pg. 697
MEEHAN TOOKER, pg. 736
MENASHA CORPORATION, pg. 738
METRO LABEL CORP., pg. 743
METRO LABEL CORP.—Metro Label Corp., pg. 743
H. C. MILLER COMPANY, pg. 754
MINUTEMAN PRESS INTERNATIONAL, pg. 759
MORRIS NEWSPAPER CORPORATION, pg. 771
MULTI-AD SERVICES, INC., pg. 775
NATIONAL GROUP, INC., pg. 789
NOLL PRINTING CORPORATION—Our Sunday Visitor, Inc., pg. 832
OFFICE ELECTRONICS, INC., pg. 821
PIP CAPITAL INC.—Kane-Miller Corp., pg. 616
PATSON'S PRESS, pg. 851
PIP PRINTING—Kane-Miller Corp., pg. 616
POWER PLASTICS INC.—Tiffany Extruders, Inc., pg. 1097
PROCESS COLOR PLATE—Schawk, Inc., pg. 975
QUEENS GROUP, INC., pg. 904
QUEENS GROUP INDIANA, INC.—Queens Group, Inc., pg. 904
RAND MCNALLY BOOK & MEDIA SERVICES—Rand McNally & Company, pg. 911
RELIEF PRINTING CORPORATION, pg. 925
SCHAWK, INC., pg. 974
SCHAWKGRAPHICS—Schawk, Inc., pg. 975
SCIENCE PRESS—Mack Printing Company, pg. 697
THE SEGERDAHL CORP., pg. 987
SERIGRAPH, INC., pg. 991
SERVICE WEB OFFSET CORPORATION, pg. 992
SMITH-EDWARDS-DUNLAP COMPANY, pg. 1012
H.M. SMYTH CO., pg. 1014
STANDARD GRAVURE CORP./SHEA COMMUNICATIONS, pg. 1036
STANDARD GRAVURE D/B/A OKLAHOMA GRAPHICS—Standard Gravure Corp./Shea Communications, pg. 1036
SULLIVAN GRAPHICS—Sullivan Holding Company, pg. 1057
SULLIVAN HOLDING COMPANY, pg. 1056
SUN-LITHO—Morris Newspaper Corporation, pg. 771
SUPERIOR LABEL SYSTEMS, INC., pg. 1063
TAPE & LABEL ENGINEERING—Weber Marking Systems, Inc., pg. 1171
TAYLOR CORPORATION, pg. 1081
TOPFLIGHT CORP., pg. 1102
TRADEMARK PRESS, INC.—Harte-Hanks Communications, Inc., pg. 513
THE UPPER DECK COMPANY, pg. 1140
VATEX AMERICA, INC., pg. 1141
WEBER MARKING SYSTEMS, INC., pg. 1171
WELDON, WILLIAMS & LICK, INC., pg. 1175
WERTHAN PACKAGING, INC., pg. 1176
WESTON ENGRAVING—Schawk, Inc., pg. 975
WINTHROP PRINTING COMPANY, INC., pg. 1197
WORLD PUBLISHING COMPANY, pg. 1203

2761 — MANIFOLD BUSINESS FORMS

ADAMS BUSINESS FORMS, pg. 16
ALLIED PAPER INCORPORATED, pg. 38
AMERICAN TRADING AND PRODUCTION CORPORATION, pg. 64
APPERSON BUSINESS FORMS, INC., pg. 78
BREGG DATA FORMS, INC., pg. 173
COMPUTER STOCK FORMS, INC.—Rotary Forms Press, Inc., pg. 951
CRANE & CO., INC., pg. 296
CULLMAN VENTURES, INC., pg. 304
DATA DOCUMENTS, INC.—Data Documents Holdings, Inc., pg. 316
FEDERAL BUSINESS PRODUCTS, INC., pg. 404
FORMS CORPORATION OF AMERICA—Whitestar Graphics, Inc., pg. 1187
HANO BUSINESS FORMS, INC., pg. 505
HANO BUSINESS FORMS, INC.—Hano Business Forms, Inc., pg. 506
HICKORY PRINTING GROUP, INC., pg. 533
INTERFORM CORPORATION, pg. 574
JOHNSON & QUIN, INC., pg. 599
WARD KRAFT, INC., pg. 643
MIAMI SYSTEMS CORPORATION, pg. 746
OFFICE CONNECTION, INC., pg. 821
OFFICE ELECTRONICS, INC., pg. 821
PIP CAPITAL INC.—Kane-Miller Corp., pg. 616
QUALITY COMPUTER FORMS, INC.—Rotary Forms Press, Inc., pg. 951
ROTARY FORMS PRESS, INC., pg. 950
ROTARY MULTIFORMS, INC., pg. 951
SHADE COMPUTER FORMS CO., pg. 994
TST/IMPRESO, INC., pg. 1075
TAX FORMS PRINTING—Taylor Corporation, pg. 1081
TECHNICARBON COMPANY, INC., pg. 1083
UFORMA SHELBY BUSINESS FORMS—Miami Systems Corporation, pg. 746
UNITS SETS, INC.—Rotary Forms Press, Inc., pg. 951
WEBER MARKING SYSTEMS, INC., pg. 1171
WHITESTAR GRAPHICS, INC., pg. 1186
WOODBURY BUSINESS FORMS, INC., pg. 1200
WURZBURG, INC., pg. 1205

2771 — GREETING CARD PUBLISHING & PRINTING

AMBASSADOR CARDS—Hallmark Cards, Inc., pg. 502
BURGOYNE, INC., pg. 190
DAVID C. COOK PUBLISHING CO., pg. 282
WILLIAM E. COUTTS, CO. LTD.—Hallmark Cards, Inc., pg. 502
HALLMARK CARDS AUSTRALIA LTD.—Hallmark Cards, Inc., pg. 502
HALLMARK CARDS, INC., pg. 501
HALLMARK CARDS LTD., EUROPEAN DIV.—Hallmark Cards, Inc., pg. 502
HALLMARK CARDS NZ LTD.—Hallmark Cards, Inc., pg. 502
OUTREACH PUBLICATIONS—David C. Cook Publishing Co., pg. 282
THE VERNON COMPANY, pg. 1148

2782 — BLANKBOOKS, LOOSE LEAF BINDERS & DEVICES

AMERICAN TRADING AND PRODUCTION CORPORATION, pg. 64
ARCATA GRAPHICS KINGSPORT—Arcata Corporation, pg. 80
ATAPCO OFFICE PRODUCTS GROUP—American Trading and Production Corporation, pg. 64
KEITH CLARK—Cullman Ventures, Inc., pg. 304
COLAD GROUP INC., pg. 259
DVC INDUSTRIES, pg. 310
EBSCO INDUSTRIES, INC., pg. 365
GEIGER BROTHERS, pg. 447
GENERAL BINDING CORPORATION—Lane Industries, Inc., pg. 656
GENERAL BINDING CORPORATION—Lane Industries, Inc., pg. 657
GRAPHIC CONTROLS, CORP., pg. 478
CHARLES LEONARD, INC., pg. 668
LOOSE LEAF METALS COMPANY INC.—Lane Industries, Inc., pg. 657
JOSHUA MEIER CORP., pg. 737
H. C. MILLER COMPANY, pg. 754
MYRON MANUFACTURING CORPORATION, pg. 780
OPTIC GRAPHICS, INC., pg. 827
U.S. RING BINDER CORP.—Lane Industries, Inc., pg. 657

2789 — BOOKBINDING & RELATED WORK

THE AMERICAN COMPANIES, INC., pg. 50
ARCATA GRAPHICS SHERWOOD—Arcata Corporation, pg. 80
BRADLEY PRINTING COMPANY—Graphisphere Holding Company, pg. 478
CONCORD LITHO CO., INC., pg. 272
DVC INDUSTRIES, pg. 310
E.P. GRAPHICS, INC., pg. 360
ECONO-CLAD BOOKS—The American Companies, Inc., pg. 51
EDITORS PRESS, INC.—The Kiplinger Washington Editors, Inc., pg. 632
GEIGER BROTHERS, pg. 447
GRAPHISPHERE HOLDING COMPANY, pg. 478
LANE GRAPHICS PRODUCTS DIV.—Lane Industries, Inc., pg. 657
MIKEN COMPANIES, INC., pg. 752
PREBOUND PERIODICALS, INC.—The American Companies, Inc., pg. 51
RAND MCNALLY & COMPANY, pg. 911
ROSE PRINTING COMPANY, INC., pg. 948
THE SEGERDAHL CORP., pg. 987
SMITH-EDWARDS-DUNLAP COMPANY, pg. 1012
TREND OFFSET PRINTING SERVICES, pg. 1109
WORZALLA PUBLISHING CO., INC., pg. 1204

2791 — TYPESETTING

ALCOM PRINTING GROUP, INC., pg. 32
ARROW TYPOGRAPHERS, INC.—Delaware North Companies, Inc., pg. 326
CASTCRAFT INDUSTRIES, INC., pg. 228
CASTCRAFT SOFTWARE OPTIFONT—Castcraft Industries, Inc., pg. 228
THE CLARINDA COMPANY—Whitestar Graphics, Inc., pg. 1187
COSMOS COMMUNICATIONS, INC., pg. 288
GEORGE LITHOGRAPH, pg. 452
GRAPHIC CENTER, INC., pg. 478
IMPERIAL LITHO/GRAPHICS, INC., pg. 564
MAY & SPEH, INC., pg. 724
MEDIA GRAPHICS—Spectrum Industries, Inc., pg. 1029
O'NEIL DATA SYSTEMS, INC.—William O'Neil & Co., Inc., pg. 827
PEARL-PRESSMAN-LIBERTY COMMUNICATIONS GROUP, pg. 853

RECORDING & STATISTICAL CORPORATION, pg. 917
ST. CROIX PRESS, INC., pg. 966
SMITH-EDWARDS-DUNLAP COMPANY, pg. 1012
SPECTRUM INDUSTRIES, INC., pg. 1029
TWEDDLE LITHO COMPANY, pg. 1120
UNIMAX HOLDING CORP.—Shepaug Corporation, pg. 998
WHITESTAR GRAPHICS, INC., pg. 1186

2796 — PLATEMAKING AND RELATED SERVICES

AMERICAN COLOR—Sullivan Holding Company, pg. 1056
ATLAS PEN & PENCIL CORPORATION, pg. 96
BUREAU OF ENGRAVING, pg. 189
THE CLARINDA COMPANY COLOR DIVISION—Whitestar Graphics, Inc., pg. 1187
COLOR DATA EAST—Schawk, Inc., pg. 975
COLWELL INDUSTRIES, INC., pg. 267
CONSOLIDATED ENGRAVERS-EAST, INC.—The Dyson-Kissner-Moran Corporation, pg. 357
GAMMA ONE, INC., pg. 442
LSI/KALA—Schawk, Inc., pg. 975
LITHO COLORPLATE—Schawk, Inc., pg. 975
PENN COLOUR GRAPHICS, INC., pg. 857
PREPLINK—Great Lakes Lithograph Co., pg. 481
PRINTING DEVELOPMENTS, INC.—New Hampshire Oak, pg. 801
PROCESS COLOR PLATE—Schawk, Inc., pg. 975
SCHAWK, INC., pg. 974
SCHAWKGRAPHICS—Schawk, Inc., pg. 975
SULLIVAN HOLDING COMPANY, pg. 1056
UNIMAX HOLDING CORP.—Shepaug Corporation, pg. 998
VECTRON DATAGRAPHICS—Viking Graphics, pg. 1151
VIKING GRAPHICS, pg. 1151
WESTON ENGRAVING—Schawk, Inc., pg. 975

2812 — ALKALIES & CHLORINE

ELECTROCHEMICAL INDUSTRIES (FRUTAROM) LTD.—ICC Industries, Inc., pg. 558
GENERAL CHEMICAL CORPORATION—New Hampshire Oak, pg. 801
HAVILAND ENTERPRISES, pg. 517
HUBBARD HALL INC., pg. 549
HYDRITE CHEMICAL COMPANY, pg. 556
JONES CHEMICALS, INC., pg. 603
JONES CHEMICALS, INC.—Jones Chemicals, Inc., pg. 603

2813 — INDUSTRIAL GASES

CARBIDE PRODUCTS—The Carbide/Graphite Group, Inc., pg. 217
LAROCHE INDUSTRIES INC.—Laroche Holdings, Inc., pg. 659
NATIONAL WELDERS SUPPLY CO. INC., pg. 794
SCOTT SPECIALTY GASES, INC., pg. 983
WELSCO INC., pg. 1175

2816 — INORGANIC PIGMENTS

W. M. BARR & CO., INC., pg. 121
DEXTER CHEMICAL CORP., pg. 334
FLINT INK CORP., pg. 419
HAMMOND LEAD PRODUCTS, INC., pg. 504
J.M. HUBER CORPORATION, pg. 550
J.M. HUBER, CHEMICALS DIVISION—J.M. Huber Corporation, pg. 550
MOONEY CHEMICALS, pg. 768
PAWNEE SPECIALTY PRODUCTS—Pawnee Industries, Inc., pg. 852
SPECTRUM COLOR CENTER, pg. 1029
WELLBORN - DE CORP.—Dunn-Edwards Corporation, pg. 354
WHITTAKER, CLARK & DANIELS, INC., pg. 1187
ZINC CORPORATION OF AMERICA—Horsehead Industries, Inc., pg. 545

2819 — INDUSTRIAL INORGANIC CHEMICALS, NEC

ALRO GROUP, pg. 44
ALRO SPECIALTY METALS, CHARLOTTE—Alro Group, pg. 44
ALRO SPECIALTY METALS, MENOMONEE FALLS—Alro Group, pg. 44
ALRO SPECIALTY METALS, NASHVILLE—Alro Group, pg. 44
ALRO SPECIALTY METALS, REDFORD—Alro Group, pg. 44
ALRO SPECIALTY METALS, TALLMADGE—Alro Group, pg. 44
ALRO SPECIALTY METALS, TONAWANDA—Alro Group, pg. 44
ALRO SPECIALTY METALS, VILLA PARK—Alro Group, pg. 44
ATLANTIC METALS CORPORATION, pg. 95
H.J. BAKER & BRO., INC., pg. 114
BERWIND CORPORATION, pg. 145
BUCKMAN LABORATORIES, INC.—Bulab Holdings, Inc., pg. 188
BULAB HOLDINGS, INC., pg. 188
CARBIDE PRODUCTS—The Carbide/Graphite Group, Inc., pg. 217
CARGILL INC., pg. 219
CARGILL NV—Cargill Inc., pg. 219
CARUS CHEMICAL COMPANY, CHEMICAL DIV.—Carus Corporation, pg. 227
CARUS CORPORATION, pg. 227
CHEMICAL EXCHANGE INDUSTRIES, pg. 242
CHEMTECH INDUSTRIES, INC., pg. 242
CHESSCO INDUSTRIES, INC., pg. 243
DELTA FOREMOST CHEMICAL CORP., pg. 327
DEXTER CHEMICAL CORP., pg. 334
DOVER CHEMICAL CORP.—ICC Industries, Inc., pg. 558
ECP INCORPORATED—Daubert Industries, Inc., pg. 317
ELECTROCHEMICAL INDUSTRIES (FRUTAROM) LTD.—ICC Industries, Inc., pg. 558
FARMLAND INDUSTRIES, INC., pg. 402
FARNAM COMPANIES, INC., pg. 403
FRITZ CHEMICAL COMPANY, pg. 434
GAF (BELGIUM) N.V.—GAF Corporation, pg. 438
GAF (CANADA) INC.—GAF Corporation, pg. 438
GAF CORP. DE MEXICO S.A. DE C.V.—GAF Corporation, pg. 438
GAF (DANMARK) A/S—GAF Corporation, pg. 438
GAF (GREAT BRITAIN) CO. LTD.—GAF Corporation, pg. 438
GAF HULS CHEMIE GMBH—GAF Corporation, pg. 438
GAF (NEDERLAND) N.V.—GAF Corporation, pg. 438
GAF (NEW ZEALAND) PTY., LTD.—GAF Corporation, pg. 438
GENERAL ALUM & CHEMICAL, pg. 448
GRAIN PROCESSING CORP.—Varied Investments, Inc., pg. 1145
GREAT SALT LAKE MINERALS & CHEMICALS CORP., pg. 482
HAMMOND LEAD PRODUCTS, INC., pg. 504
HEAT BATH PARK METALLURGICAL, INC., pg. 524
HEAT BATH PARK METALLURGICAL PRODUCTS—Heat Bath Park Metallurgical, Inc., pg. 524
HUBBARD HALL INC., pg. 549
J.M. HUBER, SOLEM DIV.—J.M. Huber Corporation, pg. 550
HYDRITE CHEMICAL COMPANY, pg. 556
JONES CHEMICALS, INC., pg. 603
JONES CHEMICALS, INC.—Jones Chemicals, Inc., pg. 603
MATHIEU CORPORATION, pg. 720
MCGEAN-ROHCO, INC., pg. 729
MILLMASTER ONYX GROUP, INC., pg. 755
MITCHELL-BRADFORD INTERNATIONAL—Hubbard Hall Inc., pg. 549
MOONEY CHEMICALS, pg. 768
NTC GROUP, pg. 781
NATIONAL SILICATES LTD.—PQ Corporation, pg. 837
NYACOL PRODUCTS, INC.—PQ Corporation, pg. 837
OLD WORLD INDUSTRIES, INC., pg. 823
PMC, INC., pg. 836
PQ AUSTRALIA PTY., LTD.—PQ Corporation, pg. 837
PQ ZEOLITES B.V.—PQ Corporation, pg. 837
PQ CORPORATION, pg. 836
PVS CHEMICALS, INC., pg. 837
PVS CHEMICALS, INC.—PVS Chemicals, Inc., pg. 838
PVS TECHNOLOGIES, INC.—PVS Chemicals, Inc., pg. 838
C. H. PATRICK & CO., INC.—Graniteville Co., pg. 477
PENETONE CORP.—Wechco, Inc., pg. 1172
PORTAGE TOOL COMPANY—Tempel Steel Company, pg. 1086
POWER CONVERSION, INC., pg. 883
PREMIER INDUSTRIES, INC., pg. 887
RADIATOR SPECIALTY COMPANY, pg. 909
REILLY CHEMICALS S.A.—Reilly Industries, Inc., pg. 923
REILLY INDUSTRIES, INC., pg. 923
ROYAL OAK ENTERPRISES, INC., pg. 953
ST. ANNE CHEMICAL CO., LTD.—Parsons & Whittemore Enterprises, pg. 850
SPHERICAL PRODUCTS CORP.—PQ Corporation, pg. 837
TECHFORM LABORATORIES—Gardiner Metal Company, pg. 443
TECHNIC INCORPORATED, pg. 1083
UNIROYAL CHEMICAL LTD.—Uniroyal Chemical Company, Inc., pg. 1129
VELSICOL CHEMICAL CORPORATION, pg. 1147
WEST CHEMICAL PRODUCTS, INC.—Wechco, Inc., pg. 1172
WHITTAKER, CLARK & DANIELS, INC., pg. 1187

2821 — PLASTICS MATERIALS, SYNTHETIC RESINS & NONVULCANIZABLE ELASTOMERS

ACME CHEMICALS & INSULATION CO.—Insulating Materials, Inc., pg. 572
THE ALPHA CORPORATION OF TENNESSEE, pg. 43
AMPACET CORPORATION, pg. 67
BORG-WARNER CORPORATION, pg. 165
WM. T. BURNETT & CO., INC., pg. 191
CARGILL INC., pg. 219
CHROMA CORPORATION, pg. 249
CO-EX PLASTICS, INC.—Huntsman Chemical Corporation, pg. 555
DAUBERT INDUSTRIES, INC., pg. 317
DELTA RESINS & REFRACTORIES, INC., pg. 327
DENNIS CHEMICAL COMPANY, INC., pg. 329
DIVERSIFIED COMPOUNDERS—Dennis Chemical Company, Inc., pg. 329
ENGINEERED POLYMERS CORPORATION—Harbour Group Ltd., pg. 507
ENVIRODYNE LIMITED—Envirodyne Industries, Inc., pg. 383
EPOXYLITE CORPORATION, pg. 384
FINDLAY INDUSTRIES, INC., pg. 410
THE FLECTO CO., INC., pg. 417
FLEXIBLE PRODUCTS COMPANY, pg. 418
FOAMEX L.P.—21 International Holdings, Inc., pg. 1121
GATOR INDUSTRIES INC., pg. 446
GENERAL FELT INDUSTRIES, INC.—21 International Holdings, Inc., pg. 1121
GENEVE CORPORATION, pg. 451
GEORGIA DUCK & CORDAGE MILLS, pg. 453
M.C. GILL CORPORATION, pg. 458
HEWITT-ROBINS CORP., pg. 532
HUNTSMAN CHEMICAL CORPORATION, pg. 555
ICC INDUSTRIES, INC., pg. 558
IGLOO CORPORATION, pg. 562
INTERPLASTIC CORP., pg. 579
INTERPLASTIC CORPORATION—Interplastic Corp., pg. 579
INTERPLASTIC DISTRIBUTION GROUP—Interplastic Corp., pg. 579
INTERPLASTIC MOLDING PRODUCTS DIV.—Interplastic Corp., pg. 580
JONES BLAIR COMPANY, pg. 602
KEYSOR CENTURY CORPORATION, pg. 627
LAUBECK CORPORATION/CROSS, pg. 660
MARVAL INDUSTRIES, INC., pg. 716
METPAR CORPORATION, pg. 742
NYLON CORPORATION OF AMERICA, pg. 818
THE O'BRIEN CORPORATION, pg. 820
PMC, INC., pg. 836
PALMER INTERNATIONAL, INC., pg. 844
PLASCAL CORPORATION, pg. 874
POLYMER DEVELOPMENT LABORATORIES, INC., pg. 880
PRIMEX PLASTICS CORP.—ICC Industries, Inc., pg. 558
PVC COMPOUNDERS—Group Dekko International Inc., pg. 490
SCHENECTADY CHEMICALS CANADA LTD.—Schenectady Chemicals, Inc., pg. 975
SCHENECTADY CHEMICALS, INC., pg. 975
SOLAR PLASTICS-MINNEAPOLIS—Upper Midwest Industries, Inc., pg. 1140
SOLAR PLASTICS-QUAD CITIES—Upper Midwest Industries, Inc., pg. 1140
SOLAR PLASTICS-SIOUX CITY DIVISION—Upper Midwest Industries, Inc., pg. 1140
SOUTHERN PRECISION DIV.—Walter Industries, Inc., pg. 1162
TEKNOR APEX COMPANY, pg. 1084
TEXAS RESIN—Jones Blair Company, pg. 603
TRANSILWRAP COMPANY, INC., pg. 1107
UPPER MIDWEST INDUSTRIES, INC., pg. 1140
URETHANE PRODUCTS—T.D. Williamson, Inc., pg. 1192

2822 — SYNTHETIC RUBBER (VULCANIZABLE ELASTOMERS)

ALDAN RUBBER CO., pg. 32
BINGHAM, pg. 151
CASCHEM INC., pg. 227
CLEVITE ELASTOMERS—The Pullman Company, pg. 899
FINDLAY INDUSTRIES, INC., pg. 410
THE FLECTO CO., INC., pg. 417
GATOR INDUSTRIES INC., pg. 446
GENERAL LATEX & CHEMICAL CORPORATION—General Latex & Chemical Corporation, pg. 449
GENERAL LATEX & CHEMICAL CORPORATION (GEORGIA)—General Latex & Chemical Corporation, pg. 449
GENERAL LATEX & CHEMICAL CORP (OHIO)—General Latex & Chemical Corporation, pg. 449
GENERAL LATEX & CHEMICAL CORPORATION, pg. 449
HEAT BATH PARK METALLURGICAL, INC., pg. 524
HEAT BATH PARK METALLURGICAL PRODUCTS—Heat Bath Park Metallurgical, Inc., pg. 524
INSTA-FOAM PRODUCTS, INC.—Flexible Products Company, pg. 419
MILLMASTER ONYX GROUP, INC., pg. 755
MINOR RUBBER CO., INC., pg. 758
MOELLER MARINE PRODUCTS—Moore Company, pg. 768
PALMER INTERNATIONAL, INC., pg. 844
ALBERT TROSTEL PACKINGS LTD.—Albert Trostel & Sons Company, pg. 1116

2823 — CELLULOSIC MAN-MADE FIBERS

LESHNER MILLS. INC., pg. 668
MILLIKEN & CO., INC., pg. 755

2824 — SYNTHETIC ORGANIC FIBERS EXCEPT CELLULOSIC

CLEVITE ELASTOMERS—The Pullman Company, pg. 899
FINDLAY INDUSTRIES, INC., pg. 410
J.M. HUBER, POLYMER SERVICES DIV.—J.M. Huber Corporation, pg. 550
MILLIKEN & CO., INC., pg. 755

2833 — MEDICINAL CHEMICAL & BOTANICAL PRODUCTS

ALRA LABORATORIES, INC., pg. 44
THE BRULIN CORPORATION, pg. 184
CUMBERLAND-SWAN, INC., pg. 304
HALSEY DRUG CO., INC., pg. 502
J B LABS, INC., pg. 584
R. J. MARSHALL CO., pg. 714
NATIONAL HEALTH PRODUCTS, pg. 791
SETON COMPANY, pg. 993
THOMPSON NUTRITIONAL PRODUCTS—Sundown Vitamin Co., Inc., pg. 1060

2834 — PHARMACEUTICAL PREPARATIONS

ACCRA PAC GROUP, pg. 11
ALRA LABORATORIES, INC., pg. 44
ALVA/AMCO PHARMACAL COMPANIES, INC., pg. 46
ASTRE CORPORATE GROUP, pg. 92
BEN VENUE LABORATORIES, INC., pg. 138
BERWIND PHARMACEUTICALS SERVICES, INC.—Berwind Corporation, pg. 145
BLISTEX, INC., pg. 157
BRIMMS INC., pg. 176
CBP RESOURCES, INC., pg. 199

CARNRICK LABS., INC., pg. 222
CENTRAL PHARMACEUTICALS, INC., pg. 234
CLAY-PARK LABS, INC., pg. 253
THE CLINIPAD CORPORATION, pg. 255
COMBE INCORPORATED, pg. 267
CONKLIN CO. INC., pg. 274
CROWN DRUG—Eon Labs, Inc., pg. 384
CUMBERLAND-SWAN, INC., pg. 304
DANBURY PHARMACAL INC.—Henry Schein, Inc., pg. 975
C.S. DENT & CO.—Grandpa Brands Company, pg. 476
E.C. DEWITT & COMPANY LIMITED—C.B. Fleet Company, Incorporated, pg. 417
ELLIS PHARMACEUTICALS—Eon Labs, Inc., pg. 384
EON LABS, INC., pg. 383
FARNAM COMPANIES, INC., pg. 403
C.B. FLEET COMPANY, INCORPORATED, pg. 417
GALENPHARMA, INC.—GenDerm Corporation, pg. 448
GENDERM CORPORATION, pg. 448
GRANDPA BRANDS COMPANY, pg. 476
HALSEY DRUG CO., INC., pg. 502
HAVILAND ENTERPRISES, pg. 517
ICC COMERCIO E INDUSTRIA LTDS.—ICC Industries, Inc., pg. 558
ICC HANDELS AG—ICC Industries, Inc., pg. 558
ICC INDUSTRIES, INC., pg. 558
J B LABS, INC., pg. 584
KAZ, INC., pg. 619
LANMAN & KEMP-BARCLAY CO. INC., pg. 657
LENSCLEAN, INC.—Aldine Technologies, pg. 33
LIFE LINE NUTRITIONALS, INC., pg. 675
MACANDREWS & FORBES HOLDINGS INC., pg. 694
MAJOR PHARMACEUTICALS CORP.—Eon Labs, Inc., pg. 384
MCGAW, INC., pg. 729
MEDTECH LABORATORIES, INC., pg. 736
MEER CORPORATION, pg. 736
MERIDIAN INDUSTRIES, INC., pg. 740
MICHIGAN PHARMACAL—Eon Labs, Inc., pg. 384
MOORMAN MFG. COMPANY, pg. 769
MURO PHARMACEUTICAL, INC., pg. 776
MURRAY DRUG—Eon Labs, Inc., pg. 384
PALM BEACH BEAUTY PRODUCTS CO., pg. 843
PENNEX PRODUCTS CO., INC., pg. 858
PHARMACAPS INC., pg. 866
PHARMAVITE CORP., pg. 866
REVLON, INC.—MacAndrews & Forbes Holdings Inc., pg. 696
REXALL GROUP—Sundown Vitamin Co., Inc., pg. 1060
REXALL INC. CONSUMER PRODUCTS DIV.—Sundown Vitamin Co., Inc., pg. 1060
RYSTAN COMPANY, INC.—Carnrick Labs., Inc., pg. 222
SCHEIN PHARMACEUTICAL, INC.—Henry Schein, Inc., pg. 975
SEMEX, INC.—Seton Company, pg. 993
SENTINEL CONSUMER PRODUCTS, INC., pg. 990
SENTINEL CONSUMER PRODUCTS, INC.—Sentinel Consumer Products, Inc., pg. 990
SETON COMPANY, pg. 993
SOLVAY PHARMACEUTICALS, INC., pg. 1017
STERIS LABORATORIES, INC.—Henry Schein, Inc., pg. 975
STIEFEL LABORATORIES, INC., pg. 1048
SUNDOWN VITAMIN CO., INC., pg. 1060
T C MANUFACTURING COMPANY, INC., pg. 1072
TEXAS DRUG REPS—Eon Labs, Inc., pg. 384
THOMPSON MEDICAL COMPANY, INC., pg. 1094
TRIPLE F, INC., pg. 1114
ULTRA DRUG—Eon Labs, Inc., pg. 384
VITARINE PHARMACEUTICALS, INC.—Eon Labs, Inc., pg. 383
VITATECH INTERNATIONAL, INC., pg. 1153
WEIDER HEALTH & FITNESS, pg. 1173
WHITMIRE DISTRIBUTION, pg. 1187
YORK BARBELL CO., INC., pg. 1208
ZENITH LABORATORIES, INC., pg. 1217

2835 — IN VITRO & IN VIVO DIAGNOSTIC SUBSTANCES

ENVIRONETICS, pg. 383
MEDICAL ANALYSIS SYSTEMS INC., pg. 735
SERONO BAKER DIAGNOSTICS, pg. 991

2836 — BIOLOGICAL PRODUCTS, EXCEPT DIAGNOSTIC SUBSTANCES

BUCKMAN LABORATORIES, pg. 185
CAROLINA BIOLOGICAL SUPPLY CO., pg. 222

2841 — SOAP & OTHER DETERGENTS, EXCEPT SPECIALTY CLEANERS

AMWAY CORPORATION, pg. 70
JAMES AUSTIN CO., pg. 99
BLUE CROSS LABORATORIES, pg. 160
BREWER ENVIRONMENTAL INDUSTRIES, INC.—C. Brewer & Company, Limited, pg. 174
THE BRULIN CORPORATION, pg. 184
CERAS JOHNSON DE PORTUGAL, LDA.—S. C. Johnson & Son, Inc., pg. 599
CERAS JOHNSON LTDA.—S. C. Johnson & Son, Inc., pg. 599
DARLING-DELAWARE CO., INC., pg. 315
DEB HOLDINGS, INC., pg. 323
C.S. DENT & CO.—Grandpa Brands Company, pg. 476
DIAMOND CHEMICAL CO., INC., pg. 335
GRANDPA BRANDS COMPANY, pg. 476
GRANDPA SOAP CO.—Grandpa Brands Company, pg. 476
HAVILAND ENTERPRISES, pg. 517
JOHNSON COMPANY, LTD.—S. C. Johnson & Son, Inc., pg. 599
LA JOHNSON FRANCAISE S.A.—S. C. Johnson & Son, Inc., pg. 599
S. C. JOHNSON DE CENTROAMERICA S.A.—S. C. Johnson & Son, Inc., pg. 600
S. C. JOHNSON, LTD.—S. C. Johnson & Son, Inc., pg. 600
S. C. JOHNSON & SON COLOMBIANA S.A.—S. C. Johnson & Son, Inc., pg. 600
S. C. JOHNSON & SON DE ARGENTINA S.A.I.C.—S. C. Johnson & Son, Inc., pg. 599
S. C. JOHNSON & SON DE VENEZUELA, C.A.—S. C. Johnson & Son, Inc., pg. 600
S. C. JOHNSON & SON (HELLAS) E.P.E.—S. C. Johnson & Son, Inc., pg. 600
S. C. JOHNSON & SON, INC., pg. 599
S. C. JOHNSON & SON, INC.—S. C. Johnson & Son, Inc., pg. 600
S. C. JOHNSON & SON, LIMITED—S. C. Johnson & Son, Inc., pg. 600
S. C. JOHNSON & SON, LTD.—S. C. Johnson & Son, Inc., pg. 600
S. C. JOHNSON & SON OF SOUTH AFRICA (PTY.) LTD.—S. C. Johnson & Son, Inc., pg. 600
S. C. JOHNSON & SON PTE. LIMITED—S. C. Johnson & Son, Inc., pg. 600
S. C. JOHNSON & SON PTY. LTD.—S. C. Johnson & Son, Inc., pg. 600
S. C. JOHNSON & SON, S.A. DE C.V.—S. C. Johnson & Son, Inc., pg. 600
S. C. JOHNSON & SON TAIWAN LTD.—S. C. Johnson & Son, Inc., pg. 600
S. C. JOHNSON KIEV CORP.—S. C. Johnson & Son, Inc., pg. 600
JOHNSON WAX AG—S. C. Johnson & Son, Inc., pg. 600
JOHNSON WAX A/S—S. C. Johnson & Son, Inc., pg. 600
JOHNSON WAX (EGYPT)—S. C. Johnson & Son, Inc., pg. 600
JOHNSON WAX GMBH—S. C. Johnson & Son, Inc., pg. 600
JOHNSON WAX (IRELAND) LIMITED—S. C. Johnson & Son, Inc., pg. 600
JOHNSON WAX LIMITED—S. C. Johnson & Son, Inc., pg. 600
JOHNSON WAX MOROCCO S.A.—S. C. Johnson & Son, Inc., pg. 600
JOHNSON WAX NEDERLAND B.V.—S. C. Johnson & Son, Inc., pg. 600
JOHNSON WAX NEW ZEALAND LTD.—S. C. Johnson & Son, Inc., pg. 600
JOHNSON WAX NIGERIA LIMITED—S. C. Johnson & Son, Inc., pg. 600
N.V. JOHNSON WAX BELGIUM S.A.—S. C. Johnson & Son, Inc., pg. 600
JOHNSON WAX S.P.A.—S. C. Johnson & Son, Inc., pg. 600
JOHNSON'S WAX ESPANOLA, S.A.—S. C. Johnson & Son, Inc., pg. 600
JOHNSON'S WAX, GES. M.B.H.—S. C. Johnson & Son, Inc., pg. 600
JOHNSON'S WAX LTD.—S. C. Johnson & Son, Inc., pg. 600
JOHNSONWAX DEL ECUADOR S.A.—S. C. Johnson & Son, Inc., pg. 600
KOREA JOHNSON CO., LTD.—S. C. Johnson & Son, Inc., pg. 600
MALCO PRODUCTS, INC., pg. 702
MILLMASTER ONYX GROUP, INC., pg. 755
MODERN HOME CARE PRODUCTS PVT. LTD.—S. C. Johnson & Son, Inc., pg. 600
MONA INDUSTRIES, INC., pg. 764
NAMICO, INC., pg. 783
NORSK JOHNSON'S WAX A/S—S. C. Johnson & Son, Inc., pg. 600
PARK CORPORATION, pg. 849
PRISM INTEGRATED SANITATION MANAGEMENT, INC.—S. C. Johnson & Son, Inc., pg. 599
P.T. S.C. JOHNSON & SON (INDONESIA) LTD.—S. C. Johnson & Son, Inc., pg. 599
PURITAN/CHURCHILL CHEMICAL COMPANY, pg. 900
PYRAMID CHEMICAL COMPANY, INC.—Theochem Labs., Inc., pg. 1090
QUIMICA S.C. JOHNSON & SON CHILENA S.A.C.I.—S. C. Johnson & Son, Inc., pg. 600
ROCHESTER MIDLAND CORPORATION, pg. 940
SBS PRODUCTS, INC.—Deb Holdings, Inc., pg. 323
SVENSKA JOHNSON'S VAX AB—S. C. Johnson & Son, Inc., pg. 600
THEOCHEM LABS., INC., pg. 1090
TIME PRODUCTS, INC.—Theochem Labs., Inc., pg. 1090
TWINCRAFT, INC., pg. 1122
WEST CHEMICAL PRODUCTS, INC.—Wechco, Inc., pg. 1172
WEST PENTONE INC.—Wechco, Inc., pg. 1172

2842 — SPECIALTY CLEANING, POLISHING & SANITATION PREPARATIONS

ADVANCE MACHINE COMPANY, pg. 18
AIR-SCENT INTERNATIONAL—Surco Products, Inc., pg. 1065
AMERICO MANUFACTURING CO., INC., pg. 66
AMWAY CORPORATION, pg. 70
APOLLO INDUSTRIES—Theochem Labs., Inc., pg. 1090
JAMES AUSTIN CO., pg. 99
BERRYMAN PRODUCTS, INC., pg. 144
BISSELL INC., pg. 153
BLUE CORAL, INC., pg. 159
BLUE CORAL INTERNATIONAL—Blue Coral, Inc., pg. 159
BLUE CROSS LABORATORIES, pg. 160
THE BRULIN CORPORATION, pg. 184
THE BUTCHER CO., pg. 196
CRC INDUSTRIES INC.—Berwind Corporation, pg. 145
CAMPA PRODUCTS B.V.—The Dyson-Kissner-Moran Corporation, pg. 358
CAR BRITE, INC.—E & A Industries, Inc., pg. 358
CERAS JOHNSON DE PORTUGAL, LDA.—S. C. Johnson & Son, Inc., pg. 599
CERAS JOHNSON LTDA.—S. C. Johnson & Son, Inc., pg. 599
CHEMIFAX—Blue Coral, Inc., pg. 159
A.W. CHESTERTON COMPANY, pg. 244
CLAIRE MANUFACTURING CO.—Carlyle Holding Corporation, pg. 222
CLAYTON INDUSTRIES CO., pg. 253
CONKLIN CO. INC., pg. 274
C.S. DENT & CO.—Grandpa Brands Company, pg. 476
DENTEC CORPORATION, pg. 329
DIAMOND CHEMICAL CO., INC., pg. 335
E & A INDUSTRIES, INC., pg. 358
ELDORADO CHEMICAL COMPANY, pg. 373
FINE ORGANICS CORP., pg. 411
FREEMAN MANUFACTURING & SUPPLY COMPANY, pg. 431
THE FULLER BRUSH COMPANY, pg. 436
GAF CORPORATION, pg. 438
GEM, INCORPORATED, pg. 447
THE HARTZ MOUNTAIN CORP., pg. 514
HAVILAND ENTERPRISES, pg. 517
INDUSTRIAL CHEMICAL LABORATORIES—Rochester Midland Corporation, pg. 941
INTEX CHEMICAL INC., pg. 581
JELMAR COMPANY, pg. 592
JOHNSON COMPANY, LTD.—S. C. Johnson & Son, Inc., pg. 599
LA JOHNSON FRANCAISE S.A.—S. C. Johnson & Son, Inc., pg. 599
S. C. JOHNSON DE CENTROAMERICA S.A.—S. C. Johnson & Son, Inc., pg. 600
S. C. JOHNSON, LTD.—S. C. Johnson & Son, Inc., pg. 600
S. C. JOHNSON & SON COLOMBIANA S.A.—S. C. Johnson & Son, Inc., pg. 600
S. C. JOHNSON & SON DE ARGENTINA S.A.I.C.—S. C. Johnson & Son, Inc., pg. 599
S. C. JOHNSON & SON DE VENEZUELA, C.A.—S. C. Johnson & Son, Inc., pg. 600
S. C. JOHNSON & SON (HELLAS) E.P.E.—S. C. Johnson & Son, Inc., pg. 600
S. C. JOHNSON & SON, INC., pg. 599
S. C. JOHNSON & SON, INC.—S. C. Johnson & Son, Inc., pg. 600
S. C. JOHNSON & SON, LIMITED—S. C. Johnson & Son, Inc., pg. 600
S. C. JOHNSON & SON, LTD.—S. C. Johnson & Son, Inc., pg. 600
S. C. JOHNSON & SON OF SOUTH AFRICA (PTY.) LTD.—S. C. Johnson & Son, Inc., pg. 600
S. C. JOHNSON & SON PTE. LIMITED—S. C. Johnson & Son, Inc., pg. 600
S. C. JOHNSON & SON PTY. LTD.—S. C. Johnson & Son, Inc., pg. 600
S. C. JOHNSON & SON, S.A. DE C.V.—S. C. Johnson & Son, Inc., pg. 600
S. C. JOHNSON & SON TAIWAN LTD.—S. C. Johnson & Son, Inc., pg. 600
JOHNSON WAX AG—S. C. Johnson & Son, Inc., pg. 600
JOHNSON WAX A/S—S. C. Johnson & Son, Inc., pg. 600
JOHNSON WAX (EGYPT)—S. C. Johnson & Son, Inc., pg. 600
JOHNSON WAX GMBH—S. C. Johnson & Son, Inc., pg. 600
JOHNSON WAX (IRELAND) LIMITED—S. C. Johnson & Son, Inc., pg. 600
JOHNSON WAX LIMITED—S. C. Johnson & Son, Inc., pg. 600
JOHNSON WAX MOROCCO S.A.—S. C. Johnson & Son, Inc., pg. 600
JOHNSON WAX NEDERLAND B.V.—S. C. Johnson & Son, Inc., pg. 600
JOHNSON WAX NEW ZEALAND LTD.—S. C. Johnson & Son, Inc., pg. 600
JOHNSON WAX NIGERIA LIMITED—S. C. Johnson & Son, Inc., pg. 600
N.V. JOHNSON WAX BELGIUM S.A.—S. C. Johnson & Son, Inc., pg. 600
JOHNSON WAX S.P.A.—S. C. Johnson & Son, Inc., pg. 600
JOHNSON'S WAX ESPANOLA, S.A.—S. C. Johnson & Son, Inc., pg. 600
JOHNSON'S WAX, GES. M.B.H.—S. C. Johnson & Son, Inc., pg. 600
JOHNSON'S WAX LTD.—S. C. Johnson & Son, Inc., pg. 600
JOHNSONWAX DEL ECUADOR S.A.—S. C. Johnson & Son, Inc., pg. 600
KOREA JOHNSON CO., LTD.—S. C. Johnson & Son, Inc., pg. 600
L&R MANUFACTURING CO., pg. 647
LAMINAIRE CORPORATION, pg. 652
MALCO PRODUCTS, INC., pg. 702
MAN-GILL CHEMICAL COMPANY, pg. 703
MODERN HOME CARE PRODUCTS PVT. LTD.—S. C. Johnson & Son, Inc., pg. 600
NEW HAMPSHIRE OAK, pg. 800
NORSK JOHNSON'S WAX A/S—S. C. Johnson & Son, Inc., pg. 600
OCTAGON PROCESS INC., pg. 821
PACE INTERNATIONAL CORPORATION, pg. 838
PATTERSON LABORATORIES, INC., pg. 852
PENETONE CORP.—Wechco, Inc., pg. 1172
PIONEER/ECLIPSE CORP., pg. 871
PRISM INTEGRATED SANITATION MANAGEMENT, INC.—S. C. Johnson & Son, Inc., pg. 599
P.T. S.C. JOHNSON & SON (INDONESIA) LTD.—S. C. Johnson & Son, Inc., pg. 599
PURITAN/CHURCHILL CHEMICAL COMPANY, pg. 900
PYRAMID CHEMICAL COMPANY, INC.—Theochem Labs., Inc., pg. 1090

QUIMICA S.C. JOHNSON & SON CHILENA S.A.C.I.—S. C. Johnson & Son, Inc., pg. 600
RADIATOR SPECIALTY COMPANY, pg. 909
REILLY-WHITEMAN INC.—Carlyle Holding Corporation, pg. 222
ROCHESTER MIDLAND CORPORATION, pg. 940
FRANK B. ROSS CO. INC., pg. 949
SERVAAS, INC., pg. 991
SERVAAS LABORATORIES INC.—Servaas, Inc., pg. 991
SIMONIZ CANADA LTD.—Blue Coral, Inc., pg. 159
SURCO PRODUCTS, INC., pg. 1065
SVENSKA JOHNSON'S VAX AB—S. C. Johnson & Son, Inc., pg. 600
TECHNICARE CLEANING SYSTEMS INC.—EBSC Corporation, pg. 359
TEXAS REFINERY CORP., pg. 1089
THE TEXWIPE CO., INC., pg. 1090
THEOCHEM LABS., INC., pg. 1090
THETFORD (AQUA) PRODUCTS, LTD.—The Dyson-Kissner-Moran Corporation, pg. 358
THETFORD CORPORATION—The Dyson-Kissner-Moran Corporation, pg. 357
THETFORD SANITATION LTD.—The Dyson-Kissner-Moran Corporation, pg. 358
TIME PRODUCTS, INC.—Theochem Labs., Inc., pg. 1090
TOPAKA SCIENTIFIC SAFETY CO.—Pioneer/Eclipse Corp., pg. 871
TRINA, INC., pg. 1113
TURTLE WAX, INC., pg. 1120
TURTLE WAX MANUFACTURING LTD.—Turtle Wax, Inc., pg. 1120
UNITED LABORATORIES, INC., pg. 1133
UNIVERSAL PHOTONICS, INC., pg. 1139
UNSMOKE INTERNATIONAL—Surco Products, Inc., pg. 1065
WALCO-LINCK COMPANY, pg. 1159
WEST CHEMICAL PRODUCTS, INC.—Wechco, Inc., pg. 1172
WEST PENTONE INC.—Wechco, Inc., pg. 1172
WILLERT HOME PRODUCTS, INC., pg. 1190

2843 — SURFACE ACTIVE AGENTS, FINISHING AGENTS, SULFONATED OILS & ASSISTANTS

ATLAS REFINERY, pg. 96
BLUE CROSS LABORATORIES, pg. 160
CBP RESOURCES, INC., pg. 199
CHEMTECH INDUSTRIES, INC., pg. 242
CONKLIN CO. INC., pg. 274
THE C. P. HALL COMPANY, pg. 501
KENDALL HEALTHCARE PRODUCTS CO., pg. 622
MILLIKEN & CO., INC., pg. 755
MILLMASTER ONYX GROUP, INC., pg. 755
MONA INDUSTRIES, INC., pg. 764
PACE INTERNATIONAL CORPORATION, pg. 838
PATTERSON LABORATORIES, INC., pg. 852
JACOB STERN & SONS, INC., pg. 1047

2844 — PERFUMES, COSMETICS & OTHER TOILET PREPARATIONS

AIR-SCENT INTERNATIONAL—Surco Products, Inc., pg. 1065
ALEXANDRA DE MARKOFF, LTD.—MacAndrews & Forbes Holdings Inc., pg. 695
ALMAY, INC.—MacAndrews & Forbes Holdings Inc., pg. 695
AMERICAN SAFETY RAZOR COMPANY—Jordan Company, pg. 604
AMINCO, INC., pg. 67
AMWAY CORPORATION, pg. 70
ANDREA INTERNATIONAL—Ardell International, Inc., pg. 81
BENJAMIN ANSEHL COMPANY, pg. 76
ARAMIS, INC.—Estee Lauder, Inc., pg. 389
ARDELL INTERNATIONAL, INC., pg. 81
BEAUTY-PROFESSIONAL—DeMert & Dougherty, Inc., pg. 328
BILL BLASS, INC.—MacAndrews & Forbes Holdings Inc., pg. 695
BRIMMS INC., pg. 176
E.T. BROWNE DRUG CO., INC., pg. 183
CARRINGTON PARFUMS LTD.—MacAndrews & Forbes Holdings Inc., pg. 695
CARSON PRODUCTS COMPANY—Aminco, Inc., pg. 67
CHAMBERLAIN HEALTH & BEAUTY AIDS COMPANY, pg. 238
CHARLES OF THE RITZ GROUP LTD.—MacAndrews & Forbes Holdings Inc., pg. 695
CLUBMAN—Ardell International, Inc., pg. 81
COMBE INCORPORATED, pg. 267
CONAIR CORPORATION, pg. 272
COSMOLAB DIV.—Koh-I-Noor, Inc., pg. 639
DANA PERFUMES CORP., pg. 313
DELORE—Ardell International, Inc., pg. 81
DEMERT & DOUGHERTY, INC., pg. 328
DENA CORPORATION, pg. 329
C.S. DENT & CO.—Grandpa Brands Company, pg. 476
E.C. DEWITT & COMPANY LIMITED—C.B. Fleet Company, Incorporated, pg. 417
DIAMOND PRODUCTS COMPANY—Havatampa Incorporated, pg. 517
ESTEE LAUDER, INC., pg. 389
ESTEE LAUDER K.K.—Estee Lauder, Inc., pg. 389
ESTEE LAUDER N.V.—Estee Lauder, Inc., pg. 389
FINLAY ENTERPRISES, INC., pg. 411
C.B. FLEET COMPANY, INCORPORATED, pg. 417
THE FLEETWOOD COMPANY, pg. 417
FLORASYNTH AUSTRALASIA PTY. LTD.—Florasynth Inc., pg. 420
FLORASYNTH (FAR EAST) PTE. LTD.—Florasynth Inc., pg. 420
FLORASYNTH GMBH—Florasynth Inc., pg. 420
FLORASYNTH INC., pg. 420
FLORASYNTH S.A. DE C.V.—Florasynth Inc., pg. 420
FORT PITT ACQUISITIONS COMPANY, INC., pg. 425
FREEMAN COSMETIC CORP., pg. 431
GIGI—Ardell International, Inc., pg. 81
GRANDPA BRANDS COMPANY, pg. 476
HAZEL BISHOP CORPORATION, pg. 520
HEWITT SOAP CO.—Jordan Company, pg. 604
ICC INDUSTRIES, INC., pg. 558
INVERNESS CORP., pg. 581
JOHNSON PUBLISHING COMPANY, INC., pg. 598
S. C. JOHNSON & SON, INC., pg. 599
S. C. JOHNSON KIEV CORP.—S. C. Johnson & Son, Inc., pg. 600
GEORGETTE KLINGER, INC., pg. 635
LEN RON MFG. CO. INC.—Estee Lauder, Inc., pg. 389
LENSCLEAN, INC.—Aldine Technologies, pg. 33
LEVLAD, INC., pg. 671
M & E MANUFACTURING CO.—Plastek Group, pg. 875
MACANDREWS & FORBES HOLDINGS INC., pg. 694
MARY KAY CORPORATION, pg. 716
MARY KAY COSMETICOS DE MEXICO PTY., S.A. DE C.V.—Mary Kay Corporation, pg. 717
MARY KAY COSMETICS, INC.—Mary Kay Corporation, pg. 716
MARY KAY COSMETICS, INC.—Mary Kay Corporation, pg. 717
MATRIX ESSENTIALS, INC., pg. 721
MEDLINE SKIN CARE DIV.—Medline Industries, Inc., pg. 736
MEGAS BEAUTY AIDS, INC., pg. 737
MERLE NORMAN COSMETICS, INC., pg. 740
NORELL PERFUMES, INC.—MacAndrews & Forbes Holdings Inc., pg. 696
NOVILLE ESSENTIAL OIL CO., INC., pg. 817
ODOMASTER CANADA—Surco Products, Inc., pg. 1065
ORIGINS NATURAL RESOURCES INC.—Estee Lauder, Inc., pg. 389
PALM BEACH BEAUTY PRODUCTS CO., pg. 843
PARKS PRODUCTS, INC., pg. 850
PENNEX PRODUCTS CO., INC., pg. 858
PLAYTEX BEAUTY CARE, INC.—Playtex FP Group Incorporated, pg. 877
POLAROME MFG. CO. INC., pg. 878
POLO/RALPH LAUREN CORPORATION, pg. 879
PORTLAND FOOD PRODUCTS COMPANY, pg. 881
RANIR CORPORATION, pg. 912
REDKEN INTL. (PACIFIC), INC.—Redken Laboratories, Inc., pg. 919
REDKEN LABORATORIES, INC., pg. 919
REDMOND PRODUCTS, INC., pg. 920
REVLON, INC.—MacAndrews & Forbes Holdings Inc., pg. 696
REVLON-REALISTIC PROFESSIONAL PRODUCTS, INC.—MacAndrews & Forbes Holdings Inc., pg. 696
REVLON SERVICE, INC.—MacAndrews & Forbes Holdings Inc., pg. 696
CHARLES REVSON, INC.—MacAndrews & Forbes Holdings Inc., pg. 696
ROUX LABORATORIES, INC.—MacAndrews & Forbes Holdings Inc., pg. 696
SBS PRODUCTS, INC.—Deb Holdings, Inc., pg. 323
SENTINEL CONSUMER PRODUCTS, INC., pg. 990
SENTINEL CONSUMER PRODUCTS, INC.—Sentinel Consumer Products, Inc., pg. 990
SETON COMPANY, pg. 993
SOFT SHEEN PRODUCTS, INC., pg. 1016
SUPERNAIL—Ardell International, Inc., pg. 81
SURCO PRODUCTS, INC., pg. 1065
TANNING RESEARCH LABS., INC., pg. 1078
THOMPSON NUTRITIONAL PRODUCTS—Sundown Vitamin Co., Inc., pg. 1060
TRESSA, INC., pg. 1110
TRI-K INDUSTRIES, INC., pg. 1110
TRINA, INC., pg. 1113
UNSMOKE INTERNATIONAL—Surco Products, Inc., pg. 1065

2851 — PAINTS, VARNISHES, LACQUERS, ENAMELS & ALLIED PRODUCTS

ACHESON INDUSTRIES, INC., pg. 12
BENJAMIN MOORE & CO., pg. 139
M. A. BRUDER & SONS, INC., pg. 184
THE BRULIN CORPORATION, pg. 184
BRUNING PAINT COMPANY, pg. 184
SAMUEL CABOT, INC., pg. 206
CALIFORNIA PAINT DIV.—California Products Corp., pg. 210
CALIFORNIA PRODUCTS CORP., pg. 210
CHEMICAL SPECIALTIES CORP.—Syndet Products, Inc., pg. 1069
COLORIZER PAINT DIV.--California Products Corp., pg. 210
CROFT METAL INC., pg. 300
DAVIS PAINT COMPANY, pg. 319
DAVLIN PAINT COMPANY, INC., pg. 319
DENNIS CHEMICAL COMPANY, INC., pg. 329
DEVOE PAINT CORPORATION, pg. 334
DUNN-EDWARDS CORPORATION, pg. 353
DUREX INDUSTRIES INC., pg. 354
DURON, INC., pg. 355
EGYPTIAN LACQUER MANUFACTURING COMPANY, INC., pg. 371
ELECTRO-SPRAY ENAMELING—Hofley Manufacturing Company, pg. 538
ELIXIR INDUSTRIES, pg. 376
FARMLAND INDUSTRIES, INC., pg. 402
FINGERLE LUMBER CO., pg. 411
THE FLECTO CO., INC., pg. 417
THE FLOOD COMPANY, pg. 419
GRAHAM PAINT AND VARNISH COMPANY, pg. 475
GULF STATES ASPHALT COMPANY, INC., pg. 493
HARRISON PAINT CORPORATION, pg. 512
HERESITE PROTECTIVE COATINGS INC., pg. 531
IOWA PAINT MFG. COMPANY, INC., pg. 582
ISOMEX, S.A.—Schenectady Chemicals, Inc., pg. 975
JONES BLAIR COMPANY, pg. 602
JONES BLAIR ENERGY, INC.—Jones Blair Company, pg. 603
KELLY-MOORE PAINT COMPANY, INC., pg. 621
KING INDUSTRIES, INC., pg. 630
KOOL SEAL, INC., pg. 641
KURFEES COATINGS, INC., pg. 646
LINEAR DYNAMICS INC., pg. 676
LORD CORP. (U.K.) LTD.—Lord Corporation, pg. 683
LORD CORPORATION, pg. 683
LORD FAR EAST, INC.—Lord Corporation, pg. 683
LORD INDUSTRIAL LTDA.—Lord Corporation, pg. 683
LORD KOREA LTD.—Lord Corporation, pg. 683
M.A.B. PAINTS—M. A. Bruder & Sons, Inc., pg. 184
M.A.B. PAINTS—M. A. Bruder & Sons, Inc., pg. 184
MARTIN PAINT STORES, pg. 715
MAUTZ PAINT COMPANY, pg. 722
MCCORMICK PAINT WORKS COMPANY, pg. 727
MILLMASTER ONYX GROUP, INC., pg. 755
MURALO CO., INC., pg. 776
NATIONAL LABEL COMPANY, pg. 791
NATIONAL SOLVENT CORPORATION, pg. 793
THE NEOGARD CORPORATION—Jones Blair Company, pg. 603
NISSHOKU SCHENECTADY CHEMICALS, INC.—Schenectady Chemicals, Inc., pg. 975
THE O'BRIEN CORPORATION, pg. 820
O'BRIEN POWDER PRODUCTS, INC.—The O'Brien Corporation, pg. 820
O'BRIEN POWDER PRODUCTS, INC.—The O'Brien Corporation, pg. 820
OLD QUAKER PAINT CO., pg. 823
OX-LINE PAINT DIV.—California Products Corp., pg. 210
PARAGON PAINT & VARNISH CORP., pg. 848
PARKS CORPORATION, pg. 849
PERRY & DERRICK CO., pg. 863
PLASTI-KOTE CO., PACTRA HOBBY—Plasti-Kote Company Inc., pg. 875
PLASTI-KOTE COMPANY INC., pg. 875
POLYMER PLASTICS CORPORATION, pg. 880
PREMIER COATINGS, INC., pg. 886
PRESERVATIVE PAINT COMPANY, pg. 887
PROGRESS PAINT MFG. CO., pg. 894
RAFFI & SWANSON, INC., pg. 909
RECREATIONAL PRODUCTS DIV.—California Products Corp., pg. 210
RED SPOT PAINT & VARNISH CO., pg. 918
RED SPOT WESTLAND INC.—Red Spot Paint & Varnish Co., pg. 919
SAVOGRAN OF CALIFORNIA—The Savogran Company, pg. 973
THE SAVOGRAN COMPANY, pg. 973
SCHENECTADY CHEMICALS AUSTRALIA PTY. LTD.—Schenectady Chemicals, Inc., pg. 975
SCHENECTADY CHEMICALS, INC., pg. 975
SCHENECTADY DE FRANCE—Schenectady Chemicals, Inc., pg. 975
SCHENECTADY IBERICA S.A.—Schenectady Chemicals, Inc., pg. 975
SCHENECTADY MIDLAND, LTD.—Schenectady Chemicals, Inc., pg. 975
SCHENECTADY QUIMICA DO BRASIL LIMITADA—Schenectady Chemicals, Inc., pg. 975
SEYMOUR OF SYCAMORE, INC., pg. 994
SINCLAIR PAINT CO.—Insilco Corporation, pg. 571
SOUTHWESTERN PETROLEUM CORPORATION, pg. 1024
STANCHEM INC., pg. 1035
STAR BRONZE COMPANY, pg. 1039
STONHARD, INC., pg. 1051
STONHARD LATIN AMERICA—Stonhard, Inc., pg. 1051
SYNDET PRODUCTS, INC., pg. 1069
TEXAS RESIN—Jones Blair Company, pg. 603
TROY CORPORATION, pg. 1116
UNITED COATINGS, INC., pg. 1131
UNITED GILSONITE LABORATORIES, pg. 1132
WELLBORN - DE CORP.—Dunn-Edwards Corporation, pg. 354
YENKIN-MAJESTIC PAINT CORPORATION, pg. 1208

2861 — GUM & WOOD CHEMICALS

AMSPEC CHEMICAL CORPORATION, pg. 5
ARROW INDUSTRIES, INC., pg. 85

2865 — CYCLIC ORGANIC CRUDES & INTERMEDIATES, ORGANIC DYES AND PIGMENTS

APOLLO COLORS, INC., pg. 78
BERWIND CORPORATION, pg. 145
BUFFALO COLOR CORPORATION, pg. 187
COLORCON—Berwind Corporation, pg. 145
DEXTER CHEMICAL CORP., pg. 334
FLINT INK CORP., pg. 419
HARWICK CHEMICAL CORP., pg. 515
HINKLE EASTER PRODUCTS—Darda Inc. (USA), pg. 315
MARVAL INDUSTRIES, INC., pg. 716
PMC, INC., pg. 836
REILLY CHEMICALS S.A.—Reilly Industries, Inc., pg. 923
REILLY INDUSTRIES, INC., pg. 923
SCHENECTADY CHEMICALS CANADA LTD.—Schenectady Chemicals, Inc., pg. 975
SCHENECTADY CHEMICALS, INC., pg. 975
STANDARD CHLORINE CHEMICAL COMPANY, pg. 1035
VELSICOL CHEMICAL CORPORATION, pg. 1147
WHITTAKER, CLARK & DANIELS, INC., pg. 1187

2869 — INDUSTRIAL ORGANIC CHEMICALS, NEC

AMSPEC CHEMICAL CORPORATION, pg. 5
ADVANCED AROMATICS, INC.—Chemical Exchange Industries, pg. 242
AMERICAN BIO SYNTHETICS—Bell Flavors & Fragrances, pg. 134
ANGUS CHEMICAL COMPANY, pg. 75
ANGUS CHEMIE GMBH—ANGUS Chemical Company, pg. 75
ANGUS FINE CHEMICALS LTD.—ANGUS Chemical Company, pg. 75
ATLANTIC METALS CORPORATION, pg. 95
BELL CHEMICAL COMPANY, pg. 134
BORG-WARNER CORPORATION, pg. 165
BUCKMAN LABORATORIES, INC.—Bulab Holdings, Inc., pg. 188
BULAB HOLDINGS, INC., pg. 188
CENTRE LIME & STONE CO., INC.—Glenn O. Hawbaker, Inc., pg. 517
CHEMICAL EXCHANGE INDUSTRIES, pg. 242
CHIEF ETHANOL FUELS, INC.—Chief Industries, Inc., pg. 247
CRANSTON PRINT WORKS COMPANY, pg. 296
DOVER CHEMICAL CORP.—ICC Industries, Inc., pg. 558
ENERGY FUELS DEVELOPMENT CORPORATION, pg. 381
FINE ORGANICS CORP., pg. 411
GAF CORPORATION, pg. 438
GENERAL CHEMICAL CORPORATION—New Hampshire Oak, pg. 801
THE C. P. HALL COMPANY, pg. 501
ICC INDUSTRIES, INC., pg. 558
INTERNATIONAL SPECIALTY PRODUCTS, INC.—GAF Corporation, pg. 438
KING INDUSTRIES, INC., pg. 630
LORD CORPORATION, pg. 683
LORD FAR EAST, INC.—Lord Corporation, pg. 683
LORD INDUSTRIAL LTDA.—Lord Corporation, pg. 683
LORD KOREA LTD.—Lord Corporation, pg. 683
MATHIEU CORPORATION, pg. 720
MILLMASTER ONYX GROUP, INC., pg. 755
MOONEY CHEMICALS, pg. 768
MORFLEX, INC.—Reilly Industries, Inc., pg. 923
NOVILLE ESSENTIAL OIL CO., INC., pg. 817
PARKS CORPORATION, pg. 849
PHILIPP BROTHERS CHEMICALS, INC., pg. 867
PREMIER CHEMICAL PLANT—Uniroyal Chemical Company, Inc., pg. 1129
REILLY-WHITEMAN INC.—Carlyle Holding Corporation, pg. 222
RUBICON INC.—Uniroyal Chemical Company, Inc., pg. 1129
TEKNOR APEX COMPANY, pg. 1084
UNIROYAL CHEMICAL CO., INC.—Uniroyal Chemical Company, Inc., pg. 1129
UNIROYAL CHEMICAL COMPANY, INC., pg. 1129
UNIROYAL CHEMICAL COMPANY LIMITED—Uniroyal Chemical Company, Inc., pg. 1129
UNIROYAL CHEMICAL LTD.—Uniroyal Chemical Company, Inc., pg. 1129
UNIROYAL CHIMICA, S.P.A.—Uniroyal Chemical Company, Inc., pg. 1129
UNIROYAL QUIMICA, S.A.—Uniroyal Chemical Company, Inc., pg. 1130
VELSICOL CHEMICAL CORPORATION, pg. 1147
WEST CHEMICAL PRODUCTS, INC.—Wechco, Inc., pg. 1172

2873 — NITROGENOUS FERTILIZERS

H.J. BAKER & BRO., INC., pg. 114
BANDINI FERTILIZER COMPANY, pg. 117
CF INDUSTRIES, INC., pg. 200
CARGILL FERTILIZER, INC.—Cargill Inc., pg. 219
CENEX/LAND O'LAKES, INC.—CENEX (Farmers Union Central Exchange, Inc.), pg. 231
CONKLIN CO. INC., pg. 274
COUNTRYMARK COOPERATIVE, INC., pg. 290
DOUBLE D FERTILIZER—Jasper County Farm Bureau Co-op Association, Inc., pg. 590
FARMLAND INDUSTRIES, INC., pg. 402
GENERAL CHEMICAL CORPORATION—New Hampshire Oak, pg. 801
LAROCHE INDUSTRIES INC.—Laroche Holdings, Inc., pg. 659
LEBANON CHEMICAL CORP., pg. 665
MFA INCORPORATED, pg. 692
MILLER CHEMICAL & FERTILIZER CORP.—Alco Industries, Inc., pg. 32
MISSISSIPPI CHEMICAL CORPORATION, pg. 760
MISSISSIPPI PHOSPHATES CORP.—Mississippi Chemical Corporation, pg. 760
PACE INTERNATIONAL CORPORATION, pg. 838
THE SCOTT COMPANY, pg. 982
SECURITY PRODUCTS COMPANY—Universal Cooperatives, Inc., pg. 1138
SECURITY PRODUCTS COMPANY OF DELAWARE, INC.—Universal Cooperatives, Inc., pg. 1138
J.R. SIMPLOT COMPANY, pg. 1007
STERN'S MIRACLE-GRO PRODUCTS, INC., pg. 1048
TENNESSEE FARMERS CO-OP, pg. 1087

2874 — PHOSPHATIC FERTILIZERS

H.J. BAKER & BRO., INC., pg. 114
BANDINI FERTILIZER COMPANY, pg. 117
CF INDUSTRIES, INC., pg. 200
CARGILL FERTILIZER, INC.—Cargill Inc., pg. 219
CARGILL INC., pg. 219
CENEX/LAND O'LAKES, INC.—CENEX (Farmers Union Central Exchange, Inc.), pg. 231
FARMERS CHEMICAL CO.—Farmland Industries, Inc., pg. 402
GOODPASTURE, INC., pg. 471
GROWMARK, INC., pg. 490
HYDRITE CHEMICAL COMPANY, pg. 556
LEBANON CHEMICAL CORP., pg. 665
THE CHAS. H. LILLY CO., pg. 675
MFA INCORPORATED, pg. 692
MILLER CHEMICAL & FERTILIZER CORP.—Alco Industries, Inc., pg. 32
THE SCOTT COMPANY, pg. 982
SECURITY PRODUCTS COMPANY—Universal Cooperatives, Inc., pg. 1138
J.R. SIMPLOT COMPANY, pg. 1007
STERN'S MIRACLE-GRO PRODUCTS, INC., pg. 1048
TENNESSEE FARMERS CO-OP, pg. 1087

2875 — FERTILIZERS, MIXING ONLY

CHAMPAIGN LANDMARK, pg. 238
CHAMPAIGN LANDMARK—Champaign Landmark, pg. 238
COUNTRYMARK CO-OP INC.—Countrymark Cooperative, Inc., pg. 290
GOLD KIST, INC., pg. 465
GREENWAY CO-OP SERVICE, pg. 485
LEBANON CHEMICAL CORP., pg. 665
LOFT'S SEEDS, INC., pg. 681
MOYER PRODUCTS, INC., pg. 774
NA-CHURS PLANT FOOD COMPANY, pg. 782
PARKER FERTILIZER CO., INC., pg. 849
ROSENS DIVERSIFIED, INC., pg. 948
J.R. SIMPLOT COMPANY, pg. 1007

2879 — PESTICIDES & AGRICULTURAL CHEMICALS, NEC

AGSCO, INC., pg. 4
BANDINI FERTILIZER COMPANY, pg. 117
THE F.A. BARTLETT TREE EXPERT CO., pg. 123
BIOPRODUCTS, INC., pg. 152
CERAS JOHNSON LTDA.—S. C. Johnson & Son, Inc., pg. 599
CLAIRE MANUFACTURING CO.—Carlyle Holding Corporation, pg. 222
DEXOL INDUSTRIES, INC., pg. 334
FARNAM COMPANIES, INC., pg. 403
GREEN GARDE—H.D. Hudson Manufacturing Company, pg. 551
GRIFFIN CORPORATION, pg. 487
GUSTAFSON, INC.—Uniroyal Chemical Company, Inc., pg. 1129
INSECT CONTROL & RESEARCH CORP.—McLaughlin Gormley King Company, pg. 731
S. C. JOHNSON & SON, INC., pg. 599
LEBANON CHEMICAL CORP., pg. 665
LOFT'S SEEDS, INC., pg. 681
MCLAUGHLIN GORMLEY KING COMPANY, pg. 731
MILLER CHEMICAL & FERTILIZER CORP.—Alco Industries, Inc., pg. 32
MORFLEX, INC.—Reilly Industries, Inc., pg. 923
MOYER PRODUCTS, INC., pg. 774
NUTRIUS DAIRY FEED SUPPLEMENTS DIV.—Bioproducts, Inc., pg. 152
OCTAGON PROCESS INC., pg. 821
PACE INTERNATIONAL CORPORATION, pg. 838
PHILIPP BROTHERS CHEMICALS, INC., pg. 867
PREMIER CHEMICAL PLANT—Uniroyal Chemical Company, Inc., pg. 1129
PRENTISS INCORPORATED, pg. 887
RIVERDALE CHEMICAL CO., pg. 937
ROCHESTER MIDLAND CORPORATION, pg. 940
RUBICON INC.—Uniroyal Chemical Company, Inc., pg. 1129
SECURITY PRODUCTS COMPANY—Universal Cooperatives, Inc., pg. 1138
SECURITY PRODUCTS COMPANY OF DELAWARE, INC.—Universal Cooperatives, Inc., pg. 1138
J.R. SIMPLOT COMPANY, pg. 1007
SOUTHERN AGRICULTURAL INSECTICIDES, pg. 1020
SPRAYWAY, INC.—Carlyle Holding Corporation, pg. 222
TENNESSEE FARMERS CO-OP, pg. 1087
TROY CORPORATION, pg. 1116
UNIROYAL CHEMICAL CO., INC.—Uniroyal Chemical Company, Inc., pg. 1129
UNIROYAL CHEMICAL CO., INC. (LEFFINGWELL)—Uniroyal Chemical Company, Inc., pg. 1129
UNIROYAL CHEMICAL COMPANY, INC., pg. 1129
UNIROYAL CHEMICAL COMPANY LIMITED—Uniroyal Chemical Company, Inc., pg. 1129
UNIROYAL CHEMICAL LTD.—Uniroyal Chemical Company, Inc., pg. 1129
UNIROYAL CHIMICA, S.P.A.—Uniroyal Chemical Company, Inc., pg. 1129
UNIROYAL QUIMICA, S.A.—Uniroyal Chemical Company, Inc., pg. 1130
UNIVERSAL COOPERATIVES, INC., pg. 1138
VELSICOL CHEMICAL CORPORATION, pg. 1147
WALCO-LINCK COMPANY, pg. 1159
WATKINS INCORPORATED, pg. 1167
WEST CHEMICAL PRODUCTS, INC.—Wechco, Inc., pg. 1172
WILLERT HOME PRODUCTS, INC., pg. 1190

2891 — ADHESIVES & SEALANTS

ADHESIVE RESEARCH, INC.—Topflight Corp., pg. 1102
AUTOMOTIVE CHEMICAL CORPORATION—Findley Adhesives, Inc., pg. 410
BINNEY & SMITH INC.—Hallmark Cards, Inc., pg. 502
BIXBY INTERNATIONAL CORP., pg. 153
BLUE CORAL, INC., pg. 159
CHEMIONICS CORPORATION—Chessco Industries, Inc., pg. 244
CHESSCO INDUSTRIES, INC., pg. 243
CLAYTON CORPORATION, pg. 253
DAUBERT CHEMICAL COMPANY, INC.—Daubert Industries, Inc., pg. 317
DAUBERT COATED PRODUCTS, INC.—Daubert Industries, Inc., pg. 317
DAUBERT INDUSTRIES, INC., pg. 317
DELTA RESINS & REFRACTORIES, INC., pg. 327
DENNIS CHEMICAL COMPANY, INC., pg. 329
DUBIN-CLARK & COMPANY, pg. 350
ELIXIR INDUSTRIES, pg. 376
EPOXYLITE CORPORATION, pg. 384
EVANS ADHESIVE CORP., pg. 390
FINDLEY ADHESIVES, INC., pg. 410
FINDLEY EURO BV—Findley Adhesives, Inc., pg. 410
FINDLEY FRANCE SA—Findley Adhesives, Inc., pg. 411
GENOVA PRODUCTS, INC., pg. 452
THE GIBSON-HOMANS COMPANY, pg. 457
GIBSON-HOMANS CONYERS DIV.—The Gibson-Homans Company, pg. 457
GIBSON-HOMANS OF CANADA LTD.—The Gibson-Homans Company, pg. 457
GULF SEAL SPECIALTIES, INC.—Gulf States Asphalt Company, Inc., pg. 494
HARBOUR GROUP LTD., pg. 506
HEAT TECH, INC.—Group Dekko International Inc., pg. 489
HEATERS ENGINEERING, INC.—Group Dekko International Inc., pg. 489
IGLOO CORPORATION, pg. 562
LAKIN GENERAL CORPORATION, pg. 652
LEPAGE'S, INC.—Cortec Group, pg. 287
LINEAR DYNAMICS INC., pg. 676
LORD CORP., INDUSTRIAL ADHESIVES & COATINGS DIV.—Lord Corporation, pg. 683
LORD CORP. (U.K.) LTD.—Lord Corporation, pg. 683
LORD CORPORATION, pg. 683
LORD FAR EAST, INC.—Lord Corporation, pg. 683
LORD INDUSTRIAL LTDA.—Lord Corporation, pg. 683
LORD KOREA LTD.—Lord Corporation, pg. 683
MACKLANBURG-DUNCAN CO. OF CALIFORNIA, INC.—Macklanburg-Duncan Co., pg. 697
PALMER INTERNATIONAL, INC., pg. 844
POLYKEN TECHNOLOGIES—Kendall Healthcare Products Co., pg. 622
POLYMER PLASTICS CORPORATION, pg. 880
RADIATOR SPECIALTY COMPANY, pg. 909
RAFFI & SWANSON, INC., pg. 909
RED DEVIL INC., pg. 918
ROBERTS CONSOLIDATED INDUSTRIES—Dubin-Clark & Company, pg. 350
SIERRACIN CORPORATION, pg. 1003
SPARTAN INTERNATIONAL, pg. 1026
STONHARD LATIN AMERICA—Stonhard, Inc., pg. 1051
TEXAS REFINERY CORP., pg. 1089
TOPFLIGHT CORP., pg. 1102
TURTLE WAX, INC., pg. 1120
UNISEAL, INC.—George Koch Sons, Inc., pg. 639
WILTIC CHEMICAL MANUFACTURING—Genova Products, Inc., pg. 452

2892 — EXPLOSIVES

AUSTIN POWDER CO., pg. 99
DAVIS MINING & MANUFACTURING, pg. 319
KDI CORPORATION, pg. 612
LAROCHE INDUSTRIES INC.—Laroche Holdings, Inc., pg. 659
MARTIN ELECTRONICS, INC.—KDI Corporation, pg. 612
SOUTHWESTERN EXPLOSIVES—Austin Powder Co., pg. 99

2893 — PRINTING INK

AMERICAN INKS & COATINGS CORP., pg. 56
DUREX INDUSTRIES INC., pg. 354
FABER/CASTELL CORPORATION, pg. 395
FIELD CONTAINER COMPANY, L.P., pg. 409
GANS INK & SUPPLY COMPANY, INC., pg. 442
HANDSCHY INDUSTRIES—Field Container Company, L.P., pg. 409
J.M. HUBER CORPORATION, pg. 550
J.M. HUBER, PRINTING INK DIV.—J.M. Huber Corporation, pg. 550
MARKEM CORPORATION, pg. 708
MATTHEWS INTERNATIONAL CORP., pg. 721
MELLON CORPORATION, pg. 738
MILLMASTER ONYX GROUP, INC., pg. 755
NAZ-DAR COMPANY—Thrall Enterprises, Inc., pg. 1095
NEW HAMPSHIRE OAK, pg. 800
RAFFI & SWANSON, INC., pg. 909
THRALL ENTERPRISES, INC., pg. 1095

2895 — CARBON BLACK

J.M. HUBER CORPORATION, pg. 550
J.M. HUBER, ENGINEERED CARBONS DIV.—J.M. Huber Corporation, pg. 550

2899 — CHEMICALS & CHEMICAL PREPARATIONS, NEC

AMSPEC CHEMICAL CORPORATION, pg. 5
ACHESON INDUSTRIES, INC., pg. 12
ALCO INDUSTRIES, INC., pg. 32
AMALLOY, pg. 46
ANGUS CHEMICAL COMPANY, pg. 75

ANGUS CHEMIE GMBH—ANGUS Chemical Company, pg. 75
ANGUS FINE CHEMICALS LTD.—ANGUS Chemical Company, pg. 75
ARROW FASTENER CO., INC., pg. 85
ARROW INDUSTRIES, INC., pg. 85
ATLANTA MFG. FACILITY—L. M. Scofield Company, pg. 982
BELL CHEMICAL COMPANY, pg. 134
BERCEN INC.—Cranston Print Works Company, pg. 297
BINGHAM, pg. 151
BUCKMAN LABORATORIES, pg. 185
CRC INDUSTRIES INC.—Berwind Corporation, pg. 145
CARBIDE PRODUCTS—The Carbide/Graphite Group, Inc., pg. 217
CARGILL SALT, pg. 219
CASTING MATERIAL COMPANY, pg. 229
CERAS JOHNSON DE PORTUGAL, LDA.—S. C. Johnson & Son, Inc., pg. 599
CHEMTECH INDUSTRIES, INC., pg. 242
CHESSCO INDUSTRIES, INC., pg. 243
CRANSTON PRINT WORKS COMPANY, pg. 296
DELTA RESINS & REFRACTORIES, INC., pg. 327
DEMERT & DOUGHERTY, INC., pg. 328
C.S. DENT & CO.—Grandpa Brands Company, pg. 476
DEUTSCHE HERAKLITH A.G.—Belmont Industries, Inc., pg. 137
DIAMOND BRANDS, INC., pg. 335
ELECTRO-COATINGS, INC., pg. 374
ESQUIRE CANADA, INC.—Strombecker Corporation, pg. 1054
EZON PRODUCTS, INC., pg. 393
FISHER PEN COMPANY, pg. 415
FLEXIBLE PRODUCTS COMPANY, pg. 418
FLORASYNTH (FAR EAST) PTE. LTD.—Florasynth Inc., pg. 420
FLORASYNTH INC., pg. 420
FLORASYNTH S.A. DE C.V.—Florasynth Inc., pg. 420
FRAGRANCE RESOURCES, INC., pg. 428
THE FULLER BRUSH COMPANY, pg. 436
GARDINER SOLDER COMPANY—Gardiner Metal Company, pg. 443
GOLDMAN FINANCIAL GROUP, pg. 468
GRANDPA BRANDS COMPANY, pg. 476
GULF STATES ASPHALT COMPANY, INC., pg. 493
HAVILAND ENTERPRISES, pg. 517
HAVILAND-KALAMAZOO—Haviland Enterprises, pg. 517
HEAT BATH PARK METALLURGICAL, INC., pg. 524
HEAT BATH PARK METALLURGICAL PRODUCTS—Heat Bath Park Metallurgical, Inc., pg. 524
HOOKER INDUSTRIES, pg. 543
HOUGHTON A.G. SWITZERLAND—E. F. Houghton & Co., pg. 546
E. F. HOUGHTON & CO., pg. 546
E. F. HOUGHTON CO. OF CANADA LTD.—E. F. Houghton & Co., pg. 546
E. F. HOUGHTON DO BRAZIL—E. F. Houghton & Co., pg. 546
HOUGHTON ITALIA S.P.A.—E. F. Houghton & Co., pg. 546
HOUGHTON VAUGHN PLC—E. F. Houghton & Co., pg. 546
HOUGHTON-BENELUX B.V.—E. F. Houghton & Co., pg. 546
J.M. HUBER CORPORATION, pg. 550
HYDRITE CHEMICAL COMPANY, pg. 556
INK SPECIALTIES CO.—Weber Marking Systems, Inc., pg. 1171
INTEX CHEMICAL INC., pg. 581
INVIRECHEM—Pace International Corporation, pg. 838
JARCHEM INDUSTRIES, INC., pg. 590
JOHNSON COMPANY, LTD.—S. C. Johnson & Son, Inc., pg. 599
LA JOHNSON FRANCAISE S.A.—S. C. Johnson & Son, Inc., pg. 599
JOHNSON MANUFACTURING CO.—Gardiner Metal Company, pg. 443
S. C. JOHNSON DE CENTROAMERICA S.A.—S. C. Johnson & Son, Inc., pg. 600
S. C. JOHNSON, LTD.—S. C. Johnson & Son, Inc., pg. 600
S. C. JOHNSON & SON COLOMBIANA S.A.—S. C. Johnson & Son, Inc., pg. 600
S. C. JOHNSON & SON DE ARGENTINA S.A.I.C.—S. C. Johnson & Son, Inc., pg. 599
S. C. JOHNSON & SON DE VENEZUELA, C.A.—S. C. Johnson & Son, Inc., pg. 600
S. C. JOHNSON & SON (HELLAS) E.P.E.—S. C. Johnson & Son, Inc., pg. 600
S. C. JOHNSON & SON, INC.—S. C. Johnson & Son, Inc., pg. 600
S. C. JOHNSON & SON, LIMITED—S. C. Johnson & Son, Inc., pg. 600
S. C. JOHNSON & SON, LTD.—S. C. Johnson & Son, Inc., pg. 600
S. C. JOHNSON & SON OF SOUTH AFRICA (PTY.) LTD.—S. C. Johnson & Son, Inc., pg. 600
S. C. JOHNSON & SON PTE. LIMITED—S. C. Johnson & Son, Inc., pg. 600
S. C. JOHNSON & SON PTY. LTD.—S. C. Johnson & Son, Inc., pg. 600
S. C. JOHNSON & SON, S.A. DE C.V.—S. C. Johnson & Son, Inc., pg. 600
S. C. JOHNSON & SON TAIWAN LTD.—S. C. Johnson & Son, Inc., pg. 600
JOHNSON WAX AG—S. C. Johnson & Son, Inc., pg. 600
JOHNSON WAX A/S—S. C. Johnson & Son, Inc., pg. 600
JOHNSON WAX (EGYPT)—S. C. Johnson & Son, Inc., pg. 600
JOHNSON WAX GMBH—S. C. Johnson & Son, Inc., pg. 600
JOHNSON WAX (IRELAND) LIMITED—S. C. Johnson & Son, Inc., pg. 600
JOHNSON WAX LIMITED—S. C. Johnson & Son, Inc., pg. 600
JOHNSON WAX MOROCCO S.A.—S. C. Johnson & Son, Inc., pg. 600
JOHNSON WAX NEDERLAND B.V.—S. C. Johnson & Son, Inc., pg. 600
JOHNSON WAX NEW ZEALAND LTD.—S. C. Johnson & Son, Inc., pg. 600
JOHNSON WAX NIGERIA LIMITED—S. C. Johnson & Son, Inc., pg. 600
N.V. JOHNSON WAX BELGIUM S.A.—S. C. Johnson & Son, Inc., pg. 600
JOHNSON WAX S.P.A.—S. C. Johnson & Son, Inc., pg. 600
JOHNSON'S WAX ESPANOLA, S.A.—S. C. Johnson & Son, Inc., pg. 600
JOHNSON'S WAX, GES. M.B.H.—S. C. Johnson & Son, Inc., pg. 600
JOHNSON'S WAX LTD.—S. C. Johnson & Son, Inc., pg. 600
JOHNSONWAX DEL ECUADOR S.A.—S. C. Johnson & Son, Inc., pg. 600
KING INDUSTRIES, INC., pg. 630
KOCH REFINING COMPANY—Koch Industries, Incorporated, pg. 639
KOREA JOHNSON CO., LTD.—S. C. Johnson & Son, Inc., pg. 600
LA-CO INDUSTRIES, INC., pg. 648
LABELON CORPORATION, pg. 649
LANE LIMITED, pg. 657
MAGNOMIN-GENERAL MINING S.A.—Belmont Industries, Inc., pg. 137
MCGEAN-ROHCO, INC., pg. 729
MODERN HOME CARE PRODUCTS PVT. LTD.—S. C. Johnson & Son, Inc., pg. 600
NORSK JOHNSON'S WAX A/S—S. C. Johnson & Son, Inc., pg. 600
NORTH AMERICAN SALT COMPANY, pg. 812
NOVILLE ESSENTIAL OIL CO., INC., pg. 817
OCTAGON PROCESS INC., pg. 821
OESTERREICHISCH HERAKLITH, A.G.—Belmont Industries, Inc., pg. 137
OLD WORLD AUTOMOTIVE PRODUCTS—Old World Industries, Inc., pg. 824
OLD WORLD INDUSTRIES, INC., pg. 823
PACE INTERNATIONAL CORPORATION, pg. 838
PENETONE CORP.—Wechco, Inc., pg. 1172
POLAROME MFG. CO. INC., pg. 878
POLYKEN TECHNOLOGIES—Kendall Healthcare Products Co., pg. 622
POLYMER PLASTICS CORPORATION, pg. 880
PRODUTEC HOUGHTON S.A.—E. F. Houghton & Co., pg. 546
THE PROTECTOR CORPORATION, pg. 895
P.T. S.C. JOHNSON & SON (INDONESIA) LTD.—S. C. Johnson & Son, Inc., pg. 599
PURITAN/CHURCHILL CHEMICAL COMPANY, pg. 900
PYRO CHEM, INC.—Borg-Warner Corporation, pg. 166
QUIMICA S.C. JOHNSON & SON CHILENA S.A.C.I.—S. C. Johnson & Son, Inc., pg. 600
RADIATOR SPECIALTY COMPANY, pg. 909
WILLIAM B. REILY & CO., INC., pg. 923
L. M. SCOFIELD COMPANY, pg. 982
SIERRACIN CORPORATION, pg. 1003
SIFTCO CANADA, INC.—North American Salt Company, pg. 812
SIFTO CANADA, INC.—North American Salt Company, pg. 812
STANCHEM INC., pg. 1035
JACOB STERN & SONS, INC., pg. 1047
SURCO PRODUCTS, INC., pg. 1065
SVENSKA JOHNSON'S VAX AB—S. C. Johnson & Son, Inc., pg. 600
T C MANUFACTURING COMPANY, INC., pg. 1072
TECHNIC INCORPORATED, pg. 1083
A.M. TODD COMPANY, pg. 1100
TRACOR AEROSPACE, INC. EXPENDABLES DIVISION—Tracor, Inc., pg. 1105
TRICON INDUSTRIES, INC., pg. 1113
TURTLE WAX, INC., pg. 1120
WYO-BEN, INC., pg. 1157
WARREN DISTRIBUTION, INC., pg. 1164
WEBER MARKING SYSTEMS, INC., pg. 1171
WEST CHEMICAL PRODUCTS, INC.—Wechco, Inc., pg. 1172
WHITTAKER, CLARK & DANIELS, INC., pg. 1187
ZIEBART PRODUCTS GROUP—Ziebart International Corporation, pg. 1217

2911 — PETROLEUM REFINING

BERRYMAN PRODUCTS, INC., pg. 144
CENEX (FARMERS UNION CENTRAL EXCHANGE, INC.), pg. 231
CLARK OIL & REFINING CORPORATION, pg. 252
CLARK OIL & REFINING CORPORATION--BLUE ISLAND REFINERY—Clark Oil & Refining Corporation, pg. 253
CLARK OIL & REFINING CORPORATION--WOOD RIVER REFINERY—Clark Oil & Refining Corporation, pg. 253
COMMANDER OIL CORPORATION, pg. 268
CONTRAN CORPORATION, pg. 281
DRAKE PETROLEUM COMPANY, INC.—Warren Equities Inc., pg. 1165
E-Z SERVE CORP., pg. 361
ERGON, INC., pg. 386
FLINT INK CORP., pg. 419
THE GARY-WILLIAMS COMPANY, pg. 444
GOLDEN WEST REFINING COMPANY—Thrifty Oil Company, pg. 1096
GREAT LAKES CARBON CORP.—Horsehead Industries, Inc., pg. 545
GROWMARK, INC., pg. 490
HARBERT CORPORATION, pg. 506
HUDSON & AFFILIATED CO., pg. 551
HUNT OIL COMPANY, pg. 553
KENYON OIL COMPANY, INC.—Warren Equities Inc., pg. 1165
KOCH INDUSTRIES, INCORPORATED, pg. 639
KOCH REFINING COMPANY—Koch Industries, Incorporated, pg. 639
LAKESIDE REFINING CO. INC., pg. 651
LITTLE AMERICA REFINING—Sinclair Oil Corp., pg. 1008
MFA OIL COMPANY, pg. 692
MID-VALLEY OIL COMPANY, INC.—Warren Equities Inc., pg. 1165
NATIONAL COOPERATIVE REFINERY ASSOCIATION, pg. 787
R. B. PAMPLIN CORP., pg. 844
PARAMOUNT PETROLEUM CORP., pg. 848
PECKHAM INDUSTRIES, INC., pg. 854
PLACID REFINING COMPANY—Placid Oil Company, pg. 873
POWERINE OIL COMPANY—Powerine Oil Company Holdings, pg. 883
POWERINE OIL COMPANY HOLDINGS, pg. 883
PURITAN OIL COMPANY, INC.—Warren Equities Inc., pg. 1165
ROSE FUEL CORPORATION—Bayside Fuel Oil Depot Corp., pg. 128
SIMMONS OIL CORP., pg. 1005
SINCLAIR OIL CORP., pg. 1008
SOMERSET REFINERY INC., pg. 1017
SOUTHWESTERN PETROLEUM CORPORATION, pg. 1024
THRIFTY OIL COMPANY, pg. 1096
TIMEC COMPANY, pg. 1097
UNITED ACQUISITION CORPORATION, pg. 1130
UNITED REFINING COMPANY—United Acquisition Corporation, pg. 1130
UNITED REFINING INC.—United Acquisition Corporation, pg. 1130
U.S. OIL & REFINING CO.—Time Oil Company, pg. 1097
V.G.S. CORP. D/B/A SOUTHLAND OIL COMPANY, pg. 1141
VULCAN ASPHALT REFINING COMPANY—United Acquisition Corporation, pg. 1130
WALLACE & WALLACE FUEL OIL, pg. 1160
WAREX PETROLEUM CORPORATION—Warren Equities Inc., pg. 1165
WARREN OIL COMPANY—Warren Equities Inc., pg. 1165
WORLD OIL COMPANY, pg. 1203
YOUNG REFINING CORP., pg. 1210
ZIEGLER CHEMICAL & MINERAL CORP., pg. 1218

2951 — ASPHALT PAVING MIXTURES & BLOCKS

AJAX PAVING INDUSTRIES INC., pg. 28
BANKHEAD ENTERPRISES INC., pg. 117
A. BARLETTA & SONS, pg. 120
BITUMINOUS ROADWAYS, INC., pg. 153
CENTRAL ALLIED ENTERPRISES, pg. 232
CRAFCO, INC.—Ergon, Inc., pg. 386
ELASTIC MATERIALS, INC., pg. 372
THE GIBSON-HOMANS COMPANY, pg. 457
GOHMANN ASPHALT & CONSTRUCTION INC., pg. 465
GOHMANN ASPHALT & CONSTRUCTION OF KY., INC.—Gohmann Asphalt & Construction Inc., pg. 465
GOHMANN ASPHALT & CONSTRUCTION OF TEXAS, INC.—Gohmann Asphalt & Construction Inc., pg. 465
GULF STATES ASPHALT COMPANY, INC., pg. 493
GLENN O. HAWBAKER, INC., pg. 517
IA CONSTRUCTION CORP., pg. 558
K.F. JACOBSON CO.—R. B. Pamplin Corp., pg. 845
P.J. KEATING COMPANY, pg. 619
KEATING MATERIALS CORPORATION—P.J. Keating Company, pg. 619
EDWARD C. LEVY CO., INC., pg. 672
OHIO TAR ASPHALT—Central Allied Enterprises, pg. 232
R. B. PAMPLIN CORP., pg. 844
PECKHAM INDUSTRIES, INC., pg. 854
RITCHIE CORPORATION, pg. 936
ROGERS GROUP INC., pg. 943
ROSS ISLAND SAND & GRAVEL CO., INC.—R. B. Pamplin Corp., pg. 845
ROUBINCO, INC., pg. 952
RUSSELL INDUSTRIES, INC., pg. 957
STABLER COMPANIES, INC., pg. 1034
STANDARD LAFARGE, pg. 1036
THOMPSON-MCCULLY ASPHALT PAVING CO.—Thompson-McCully Co., pg. 1094
THOMPSON-MCCULLY CO., pg. 1094
TILCON, INC., pg. 1097
TRUMBULL CORPORATION, pg. 1117
UNITED REFINING COMPANY—United Acquisition Corporation, pg. 1130
VALLEY ASPHALT CORPORATION, pg. 1143
WINDSOR SERVICE, INC., pg. 1196

2952 — ASPHALT FELTS & COATINGS

BENCHMARK HOMES, INC., pg. 138
CONKLIN CO. INC., pg. 274
DELTA RESINS & REFRACTORIES, INC., pg. 327
GAF BUILDING MATERIALS CORPORATION—GAF Corporation, pg. 438
GAF CORPORATION, pg. 438
GATE PETROLEUM COMPANY, pg. 445
THE GIBSON-HOMANS COMPANY, pg. 457
GIBSON-HOMANS OF CANADA LTD.—The Gibson-Homans Company, pg. 457
GULF STATES ASPHALT COMPANY, INC., pg. 493
HEMPT BROTHERS, INC., pg. 528
K.F. JACOBSON CO.—R. B. Pamplin Corp., pg. 845
KARNAK CORPORATION, pg. 617
KOOL SEAL, INC., pg. 641
MIDCOAST INDUSTRIAL SERVICES CORPORATION, pg. 751

MONSEY PRODUCTS COMPANY, pg. 766
POLYCOAT SYSTEMS, INC., pg. 880
ROSS ISLAND SAND & GRAVEL CO., INC.—R. B. Pamplin Corp., pg. 845
TARCO, pg. 1078
TEXAS REFINERY CORP., pg. 1089
TRUMBULL CORPORATION, pg. 1117
WINDSOR SERVICE, INC., pg. 1196
ZIEGLER CHEMICAL & MINERAL CORP., pg. 1218

2992 — LUBRICATING OILS & GREASES

ACHESON A.N.Z. PTY. LTD.—Acheson Industries, Inc., pg. 12
ACHESON COLLOIDEN B.V.—Acheson Industries, Inc., pg. 12
ACHESON COLLOIDS (CANADA) LTD.—Acheson Industries, Inc., pg. 12
ACHESON COLLOIDS COMPANY—Acheson Industries, Inc., pg. 12
ACHESON COLLOIDS COMPANY—Acheson Industries, Inc., pg. 12
ACHESON DO BRASIL IND. E COM LTDA.—Acheson Industries, Inc., pg. 12
ACHESON INDUSTRIES (EUROPE) LTD.—Acheson Industries, Inc., pg. 12
ACHESON INDUSTRIES, INC., pg. 12
ACHESON (JAPAN) LTD.—Acheson Industries, Inc., pg. 12
ACHESON KOREA LTD.—Acheson Industries, Inc., pg. 12
BEL-RAY COMPANY, INC., pg. 133
BELL CHEMICAL COMPANY, pg. 134
CRC INDUSTRIES INC.—Berwind Corporation, pg. 145
CENEX (FARMERS UNION CENTRAL EXCHANGE, INC.), pg. 231
CENTURY AUTOLINE, pg. 235
CONKLIN CO. INC., pg. 274
DAUBERT CHEMICAL COMPANY, INC.—Daubert Industries, Inc., pg. 317
DAUBERT COATED PRODUCTS, INC.—Daubert Industries, Inc., pg. 317
DAUBERT INDUSTRIES, INC., pg. 317
DELTA RESINS & REFRACTORIES, INC., pg. 327
DEMERT & DOUGHERTY, INC., pg. 328
DEUTSCHE ACHESON GMBH—Acheson Industries, Inc., pg. 12
ECP INCORPORATED—Daubert Industries, Inc., pg. 317
FARMLAND INDUSTRIES, INC., pg. 402
FISKE BROTHERS REFINING COMPANY, pg. 415
FISKE BROTHERS REFINING, TOLEDO DIV.—Fiske Brothers Refining Company, pg. 416
HALOCARBON PRODUCTS CORP., pg. 502
E. F. HOUGHTON & CO., pg. 546
KING INDUSTRIES, INC., pg. 630
LUBECON SYSTEMS, INC., pg. 686
LUBRICATION ENGINEERS, INC., pg. 686
MFA OIL COMPANY, pg. 692
NATIONAL SOLVENT CORPORATION, pg. 793
OCTAGON PROCESS INC., pg. 821
PACE INTERNATIONAL CORPORATION, pg. 838
PENNSYLVANIA PETROLEUM PRODUCT COMPANY, pg. 858
PETRON CORPORATION—Wechco, Inc., pg. 1172
SOUTHWESTERN PETROLEUM CORPORATION, pg. 1024
STUART-IRONSIDES, INC., pg. 1054
SUPERIOR GRAPHITE COMPANY, pg. 1063
TEXAS REFINERY CORP., pg. 1089
UNIVERSAL COOPERATIVES, INC., pg. 1138
WEST PENTONE INC.—Wechco, Inc., pg. 1172

2999 — PRODUCTS OF PETROLEUM & COAL, NEC

ASBURY CARBONS, INC., pg. 87
CENEX (FARMERS UNION CENTRAL EXCHANGE, INC.), pg. 231
COPETRO, S.A.—Horsehead Industries, Inc., pg. 545
COUNTRYMARK COOPERATIVE, INC., pg. 290
DELTA RESINS & REFRACTORIES, INC., pg. 327
FABRICA DE VALVULAS—Farley Industries, pg. 400
GREAT LAKES CARBON CORP.—Horsehead Industries, Inc., pg. 545
GULF STATES ASPHALT COMPANY, INC., pg. 493
HORSEHEAD INDUSTRIES, INC., pg. 545
T.S. RAGSDALE COMPANY, INCORPORATED, pg. 910
WALTER INDUSTRIES, INC., pg. 1161

3011 — TIRES & INNER TUBES

COMMERCIAL PLASTICS & SUPPLIES CORP., pg. 268
CONDERE CORPORATION, pg. 273
GAY JOHNSON'S INC., pg. 446
THE HERCULES TIRE & RUBBER COMPANY, pg. 531
HERCULES TIRE & RUBBER COMPANY, pg. 531
KEX PRODUCTS, INC.—Berwind Corporation, pg. 145
PERFECT EQUIPMENT CORP.—Berwind Corporation, pg. 145
UNIVERSAL COOPERATIVES, INC., pg. 1138

3021 — RUBBER & PLASTICS FOOTWEAR

COMMERCIAL PLASTICS & SUPPLIES CORP., pg. 268
DACOR CORPORATION, pg. 310
GATOR INDUSTRIES INC., pg. 446
KANGAROOS, USA INC., pg. 616
KAYSAM CORPORATION OF AMERICA—Norcross Industries, Inc., pg. 809
MASON SHOE MFG. CO., pg. 718
NORCROSS INDUSTRIES, INC., pg. 809
PARKWAY FABRICATORS, INC.—Great American Industries, Inc., pg. 480
PONY SPORTS & LEISURE INC., pg. 880
RED WING SHOE CO., INC., pg. 919
SERVUS FOOTWEAR COMPANY, pg. 993
TOTES INCORPORATED, pg. 1103

3052 — RUBBER & PLASTICS HOSE & BELTING

ACTION CLINTON—Action Technology Company, pg. 15
ACTION ROCKAWAY—Action Technology Company, pg. 15
ACTION TECHNOLOGY COMPANY, pg. 15
AMERICAN GASKET & RUBBER—Action Technology Company, pg. 15
ASSOCIATED INDUSTRIAL RUBBER—Flexfab, Inc., pg. 418
CRP HOSE DIVISION—Radiator Specialty Company, pg. 909
COMMERCIAL PLASTICS & SUPPLIES CORP., pg. 268
C.R. DANIELS, INC., pg. 314
FABEX INC., pg. 395
FEDERAL HOSE MANUFACTURING CORP.—Flexfab, Inc., pg. 418
FLEXFAB, INC., pg. 418
GATES CANADA INC.—The Gates Corporation, pg. 445
THE GATES CORPORATION, pg. 445
GATES DO BRASIL IND. E COM. LTDA.—The Gates Corporation, pg. 445
GATES EUROPE N.V.—The Gates Corporation, pg. 445
GATES HYDRAULICS LTD.—The Gates Corporation, pg. 445
THE GATES RUBBER COMPANY—The Gates Corporation, pg. 445
THE GATES RUBBER COMPANY LIMITED—The Gates Corporation, pg. 445
GATES RUBBER DE MEXICO—The Gates Corporation, pg. 445
GATES VULCA AUTOMOTIVE PRODUCTS DIVISION—The Gates Corporation, pg. 445
GLOBE INTERNATIONAL INC., pg. 464
GOODWAY TOOL CORPORATION, pg. 471
INTRALOX A/S—The Laitram Corporation, pg. 651
INTRALOX EUROPEAN—The Laitram Corporation, pg. 651
INTRALOX, INC. GMBH—The Laitram Corporation, pg. 651
INTRALOX ITALIA S.R.L.—The Laitram Corporation, pg. 651
INTRALOX LTD.—The Laitram Corporation, pg. 651
JAFFREY FIRE PROTECTION CO.—D. D. Bean & Sons Co., pg. 129
JASON INDUSTRIAL, INC., pg. 590
MULHERN BELTING, INC., pg. 775
PLASTRON—Action Technology Company, pg. 15
PLASTRON DALTON—Action Technology Company, pg. 15
RAIN BIRD SPRINKLER MFG. CORP., pg. 910
SNAP-TITE, INCORPORATED, pg. 1014
SNAP-TITE PONN—Snap-Tite, Incorporated, pg. 1015
TEKNOR APEX COMPANY, pg. 1084

3053 — GASKETS, PACKING & SEALING DEVICES

ACTION CLINTON—Action Technology Company, pg. 15
ACTION ROCKAWAY—Action Technology Company, pg. 15
ACTION TECHNOLOGY COMPANY, pg. 15
AMERICAN GASKET & RUBBER—Action Technology Company, pg. 15
BORG-WARNER-SPRING/BRUMMER DIVISION—Borg-Warner Corporation, pg. 166
A.W. CHESTERTON COMPANY, pg. 244
DELTA RUBBER COMPANY, pg. 327
FEL-PRO INCORPORATED, pg. 405
FREUDENBERG-NOK (MI), pg. 432
GNC CORP—Goshen Rubber Co., Inc., pg. 472
GRN CORP.—Goshen Rubber Co., Inc., pg. 472
GSH CORP.—Goshen Rubber Co., Inc., pg. 472
GOSHEN RUBBER OF CANADA LTD.—Goshen Rubber Co., Inc., pg. 472
HARBOUR GROUP LTD., pg. 506
INDIAN HEAD GASKET DIV.-DETROIT—Indian Head Industries Inc., pg. 565
JM CLIPPER CORPORATION D/B/A ACADIA—Harbour Group Ltd., pg. 507
K&W, A DIV. OF STANDCO INDUSTRIES, INC.—Standco Industries, Inc., pg. 1038
MARQUETTE COPPERSMITHING CO., INC., pg. 713
MR. GASKET COMPANY, pg. 761
PAWLING CORPORATION, pg. 852
PLASTIC PRODUCTS DIVISION—Freudenberg-NOK (MI), pg. 432
PLASTIC PRODUCTS DIVISION—Freudenberg-NOK (MI), pg. 432
PLASTOMER CORP., pg. 876
PLASTRON—Action Technology Company, pg. 15
PLASTRON DALTON—Action Technology Company, pg. 15
RADIATOR SPECIALTY COMPANY, pg. 909
RUBBER PRODUCTS DIVISION—Freudenberg-NOK (MI), pg. 433
RUBBER PRODUCTS DIVISION—Freudenberg-NOK (MI), pg. 433
RUBBER PRODUCTS DIVISION—Freudenberg-NOK (MI), pg. 433
RUBBER PRODUCTS DIVISION—Freudenberg-NOK (MI), pg. 433
SEALING DEVICES INC., pg. 984
SEALS DIVISION—Freudenberg-NOK (MI), pg. 433
SEALS DIVISION—Freudenberg-NOK (MI), pg. 433
SEALS DIVISION—Freudenberg-NOK (MI), pg. 433
STAND-COTE INDUSTRIAL COATINGS DIV.—Standco Industries, Inc., pg. 1038
STANDCO INDUSTRIES, INC., pg. 1038
STERLING RUBBER & GASKET—Standco Industries, Inc., pg. 1038
STILLMAN SEAL, pg. 1049
ALBERT TROSTEL PACKINGS, LTD., pg. 1116
ALBERT TROSTEL PACKINGS LTD.—Albert Trostel & Sons Company, pg. 1116
WOODLAND MOLDED PLASTICS—Freudenberg-NOK (MI), pg. 433

3061 — MOLDED, EXTRUDED & LATHE-CUT RUBBER GOODS

BEEBE RUBBER COMPANY—The Chardon Rubber Co., pg. 239
CEC INC.—The Chardon Rubber Co., pg. 239
THE CHARDON RUBBER CO., pg. 239
DELTA RUBBER COMPANY, pg. 327
EVANS INDUSTRIES, INC., pg. 390
THE GATES CORPORATION, pg. 445
THE GATES RUBBER COMPANY—The Gates Corporation, pg. 445
HYDRIL COMPANY, pg. 556
HYDRIL RUBBER OPERS.—Hydril Company, pg. 556
MOORE COMPANY, pg. 768
PAWLING CORPORATION, pg. 852
ROPPE CORP., pg. 947
STILLMAN SEAL, pg. 1049
ALBERT TROSTEL PACKINGS LTD.—Albert Trostel & Sons Company, pg. 1116
VERNAY LABORATORIES, INC., pg. 1148

3069 — FABRICATED RUBBER PRODUCTS, NEC

A & A MANUFACTURING CO., pg. 1
ABBOTT LABORATORIES/ASHLAND, pg. 9
ALCO INDUSTRIES, INC., pg. 32
ALDAN RUBBER CO., pg. 32
ALLIED PRODUCTS—Consolidated Cigar Corporation, pg. 276
AMERICAN CAST IRON PIPE CO., pg. 50
AMERICAN EXCELSIOR COMPANY, pg. 51
AMERICAN FUEL CELL & COATED FABRICS CO. (AMFUEL), pg. 55
ASBURY FERST, INC.—Asbury Carbons, Inc., pg. 87
BATA SHOE CO., INC.—CHB Corp., pg. 201
THE BILTRITE CORPORATION, pg. 151
BINGHAM, pg. 151
BURKE INDUSTRIES, INC., pg. 191
BURKE INDUSTRIES INC., pg. 190
CEC INC.—The Chardon Rubber Co., pg. 239
CHB CORP., pg. 201
CAIRNS & BROTHER, INC., pg. 207
THE CHARDON RUBBER CO., pg. 239
COLLINS & AIKMAN GROUP INC., pg. 262
COMMERCIAL PLASTICS & SUPPLIES CORP., pg. 268
CONCORCO LDA.—21 International Holdings, Inc., pg. 1121
CONSOLIDATED INDUSTRIAL CORPORATION, pg. 276
CONTINENTAL AMERICAN CORP. D/B/A PIONEER BALLOON COMPANY, pg. 278
DACOR CORPORATION, pg. 310
DELTA RUBBER COMPANY, pg. 327
EASY DAY MANUFACTURING COMPANY, INC., pg. 364
ESTABLISSEMENT MESNEL, S.A.—21 International Holdings, Inc., pg. 1121
EVENFLO PRODUCTS CO.—Spalding & Evenflo Companies, Inc., pg. 1024
FABREEKA INTERNATIONAL, INC., pg. 396
FEL-PRO INCORPORATED, pg. 405
FLEXFAB, INC., pg. 418
FOAM PRODUCT CORPORATION—21 International Holdings, Inc., pg. 1121
GAF CORPORATION, pg. 438
THE GATES CORPORATION, pg. 445
THE GATES RUBBER COMPANY—The Gates Corporation, pg. 445
GENERAL FELT, FAIRLESS HILLS—21 International Holdings, Inc., pg. 1121
GENERAL FELT INDUSTRIES, INC.—21 International Holdings, Inc., pg. 1121
GENERAL FELT INDUSTRIES, INC.—21 International Holdings, Inc., pg. 1121
GENERAL FELT INDUSTRIES, INC.—21 International Holdings, Inc., pg. 1121
GENERAL FELT INDUSTRIES, INC.—21 International Holdings, Inc., pg. 1121
GLOBE INTERNATIONAL INC., pg. 464
GOSHEN RUBBER CO., INC., pg. 472
GOULD PACKAGING, INC., pg. 473
GOULD PACKAGING, INC.—Gould Packaging, Inc., pg. 473
GREAT AMERICAN INDUSTRIES, INC., pg. 480
GROENDYK MFG. CO., INC.—Great American Industries, Inc., pg. 480
HALSTEAD INDUSTRIAL PRODS. DIV.—Halstead Industries, Inc., pg. 502
HALSTEAD INDUSTRIES, INC., pg. 502
HERCULES TIRE & RUBBER COMPANY, pg. 531
JPS ELASTOMERICS CORP.—JPS Textile Group, Inc., pg. 586
JASON INDUSTRIAL, INC., pg. 590
JOMAC, INC., pg. 602
KRACO ENTERPRISES, INC., pg. 643
LAKIN GENERAL CORPORATION, pg. 652
LAVELLE INDUSTRIES INC., pg. 661
LEAR SIEGLER ACCURATE CORP.—Lear Siegler Diversified Holdings Corp., pg. 664
LORD CORPORATION, pg. 683
LORD INDUSTRIAL LTDA.—Lord Corporation, pg. 683
M & C SPECIALTIES COMPANY, pg. 690

MTC REMCO TAPE PRODUCTS CO.—M & C Specialties Company, pg. 690
MAGLA PRODUCTS, pg. 700
MATTHEWS INTERNATIONAL CORP., pg. 721
MATTHEWS INTL. CORP.-GRAPHIC SYSTEMS DIV.—Matthews International Corp., pg. 721
MERIDIAN INDUSTRIES, INC., pg. 740
MICRODOT AEROSPACE FASTENING SYSTEMS GROUP—MICRODOT, Inc., pg. 749
MILLER PRODUCTS COMPANY, INC., pg. 755
MILTON INDUSTRIES, INC., pg. 756
MINOR RUBBER CO., INC., pg. 758
MITCHELL CORPORATION OF OWOSSO, pg. 761
MOELLER MARINE PRODUCTS—Moore Company, pg. 768
MOORE COMPANY, pg. 768
MORSE AUTOMOTIVE PRODUCTS—Borg-Warner Corporation, pg. 166
THE NATIONAL LATEX PRODUCTS CO., pg. 791
OAK RUBBER COMPANY, pg. 819
OAK TECHNICAL, INC.—Oak Rubber Company, pg. 819
OUIMET CORP.—Ouimet Industries, pg. 831
OUIMET INDUSTRIES, pg. 831
PARKWAY FABRICATORS, INC.—Great American Industries, Inc., pg. 480
PAWLING CORPORATION, pg. 852
PIONEER INDUSTRIAL PRODUCTS CO., pg. 871
PLASTIC DIVISION—Reese Enterprises, Inc., pg. 921
PLAYTEX FAMILY PRODUCTS CORP.—Playtex FP Group Incorporated, pg. 877
PLAYTEX FP GROUP INCORPORATED, pg. 877
PRIDE PRODUCTS, INC., pg. 889
QUADION CORPORATION, pg. 902
R.C.A. RUBBER COMPANY, pg. 906
RADIATOR SPECIALTY COMPANY, pg. 909
REESE ENTERPRISES, INC., pg. 920
RENOSOL CORP., pg. 927
ROPPE CORP., pg. 947
RUBATEX CORPORATION—Great American Industries, Inc., pg. 480
STAND-COTE INDUSTRIAL COATINGS DIV.—Standco Industries, Inc., pg. 1038
STANDCO INDUSTRIES, INC., pg. 1038
STEVENS HOME FASHIONS—Farley Industries, pg. 400
SUNBEAM-OSTER HOUSEHOLD PRODUCTS—Sunbeam-Oster Company, Inc., pg. 1059
TEKNOR APEX COMPANY, pg. 1084
TEXTILE RUBBER & CHEMICAL COMPANY, pg. 1090
THERAPEDIC ASSOCIATES, INC., pg. 1090
THERMWELL PRODUCTS CO., INC., pg. 1092
TINGLEY RUBBER CORPORATION, pg. 1098
THE TOY FACTORY—Pride Products, Inc., pg. 889
VERNAY LABORATORIES, INC., pg. 1148
WALWORTH COMPANY, pg. 1162
WELSH COMPANY, pg. 1175

3081 — UNSUPPORTED PLASTICS FILM & SHEET

C-J EXTRUDERS INC.—Nexus Plastics, Inc., pg. 805
CELLO BAG COMPANY, INC., pg. 231
CO-EX PLASTICS, INC.—Huntsman Chemical Corporation, pg. 555
GOMAR MANUFACTURING CO., INC., pg. 469
HOPPLE PLASTICS, INC., pg. 544
ICC INDUSTRIES, INC., pg. 558
KEY PLASTICS, INC., pg. 627
MCNEEL INTERNATIONAL CORP., pg. 732
MOHAWK PLASTICS, INC., pg. 763
NEXUS PLASTICS, INC., pg. 805
OLEFINAS, S.A.—McNeel International Corp., pg. 732
PAWNEE EXTRUSIONS—Pawnee Industries, Inc., pg. 852
PHILLIPS-JOANNA, INC.—Industrial Coatings Group, Inc., pg. 566
PLASTIC SUPPLIERS, INC., pg. 875
PLASTIC SUPPLIERS, INC.—Plastic Suppliers, Inc., pg. 876
PLASTIC SUPPLIERS, INC.—Plastic Suppliers, Inc., pg. 876
PLASTOMER CORP., pg. 876
POLY PAK AMERICA, INC., pg. 880
POLYMER, S.A.—McNeel International Corp., pg. 732
POLYVINYL FILMS, INC., pg. 880
SNYDER INDUSTRIES, INC., pg. 1015
TRANSILWRAP COMPANY, INC., pg. 1107
ROBERT WILLIAMS—Flexel, Inc., pg. 418

3082 — UNSUPPORTED PLASTICS PROFILE SHAPES

EAGLE ELECTRIC MFG. CO., INC., pg. 362
INDUSTRIAL GENERAL CORPORATION, pg. 566
KENTILE FLOORS INC., pg. 623

3083 — LAMINATED PLASTICS, PLATE, SHEET & PROFILE SHAPES

AUTOMOTIVE PLASTIC TECHNOLOGIES, INC., pg. 101
BNZ MATERIALS, INC.—McNeel International Corp., pg. 732
BIXBY INTERNATIONAL CORP., pg. 153
CAMBRO MANUFACTURING COMPANY, pg. 211
COSTAL WOOD PRODUCTS, INC.—McConnell Cabinets, Inc., pg. 727
DEITSCH PLASTICS COMPANY, pg. 325
DUNMORE CORPORATION, pg. 353
DUNMORE CORPORATION/BREWSTER—Dunmore Corporation, pg. 353
M.C. GILL CORPORATION, pg. 458
O'KEEFFE'S, INC., pg. 823
PIONEER PLASTICS HOLDING, INC., pg. 872
PLASTIC SUPPLIERS, INC., pg. 875
PLASTOMER CORP., pg. 876
SAUDER WOODWORKING CO., pg. 972
SCHNELLER, INC., pg. 977
SPARTAN INTERNATIONAL, pg. 1026
TEKNOR APEX COMPANY, pg. 1084
TRIO PRODUCTS INC., pg. 1114
UNITED FOAM PLASTICS CORPORATION, pg. 1132
THE ZIPPERTUBING CO., pg. 1220

3084 — PLASTICS PIPE

APACHE PLASTICS, L.P., pg. 77
CELLO BAG COMPANY, INC., pg. 231
ERSHIGS, INC., pg. 387
GENOVA PRODUCTS, INC., pg. 452
PAWLING CORPORATION, pg. 852
THE SWANSON COMPANY MANUFACTURERS, pg. 1066
VANGUARD PLASTICS, INC., pg. 1145
WHEATLAND TUBE COMPANY, pg. 1184
WINROCK ENTERPRISES, INC., pg. 1197

3085 — PLASTICS BOTTLES

DOUGLAS STEPHEN PLASTICS, INC., pg. 347
IGLOO CORPORATION, pg. 562
KEYSOR CENTURY CORPORATION, pg. 627
PAWNEE INDUSTRIES, INC., pg. 852
SILGAN CORPORATION, pg. 1004
UNIVERSAL COOPERATIVES, INC., pg. 1138

3086 — PLASTICS FOAM PRODUCTS

ALADDIN INDUSTRIES, INCORPORATED, pg. 29
AMERICAN EXCELSIOR COMPANY, pg. 51
BLITZ U.S.A., INC.—Blitz USA, pg. 157
BRADFORD COMPANY, pg. 170
BURTON-DIXIE OF BLACKSBURG INC.—CC Industries, Inc., pg. 200
THE COLEMAN COMPANY—MacAndrews & Forbes Holdings Inc., pg. 695
H. S. CROCKER CO., INC., pg. 299
CURON—21 International Holdings, Inc., pg. 1121
EGAN COS., pg. 371
EGAN & SONS INSULATION—Egan Cos., pg. 371
FINDLAY INDUSTRIES, INC., pg. 410
FLEXIBLE PRODUCTS COMPANY, pg. 418
FUTURE FOAM, INC., pg. 437
HP PACKAGING HOLDINGS—Hargro Enterprises, Inc., pg. 509
H.P.H. INDUSTRIES LTD., pg. 497
HILLSIDE CAPITAL, INC., pg. 535
HILLSIDE INDUSTRIES, INC.—Hillside Capital, Inc., pg. 535
IGLOO CORPORATION, pg. 562
INNOVATIVE PLASTICS CORPORATION, pg. 570
LOCKWOOD FOLDING BOX—H. S. Crocker Co., Inc., pg. 300
NMC OF NORTH AMERICA, INC., pg. 781
PLASTOMER CORP., pg. 876
POLYMER DEVELOPMENT LABORATORIES, INC., pg. 880
SCC HOLDING CO., pg. 961
H.M. SMYTH CO., pg. 1014
TECH-AEROFOAM PRODUCTS, INC.—Great American Industries, Inc., pg. 480
UC INDUSTRIES, INC., pg. 1122
UNITED FOAM PLASTICS CORPORATION, pg. 1132
WINCUP, pg. 1195

3087 — CUSTOM COMPOUNDING OF PURCHASED PLASTICS RESINS

ALPHA RESIN SUPPLY—Great Lakes Terminal & Transport Corp., pg. 482
COLOR CUSTOM, INC., pg. 264
EVANS INDUSTRIES, INC., pg. 390
FLEXIBLE PRODUCTS COMPANY, pg. 418
INTERPLASTIC MOLDING PRODUCTS DIV.—Interplastic Corp., pg. 580
KEYSOR CENTURY CORPORATION, pg. 627
PLASTEK INDUSTRIES, INC.—Plastek Group, pg. 875
PLASTIGAGE CORPORATION, pg. 876
SIOUX MANUFACTURING CORP., pg. 1008
THERMON MANUFACTURING COMPANY, pg. 1091

3088 — PLASTICS PLUMBING FIXTURES

BENEKE—Sanderson Plumbing Products Inc., pg. 970
BRIGGS INDUSTRIES, INC., pg. 175
CAMPA PRODUCTS B.V.—The Dyson-Kissner-Moran Corporation, pg. 358
COLEMAN SPAS, INC.—MacAndrews & Forbes Holdings Inc., pg. 695
COMPAGNIE INTERNATIONALE DES PRODUITS SANITAIRES (CIPS) JACOB DELAFON—Kohler Company, pg. 640
FLAMBEAU SOUTHEAST CO.—Nordic Group of Companies, Ltd., pg. 809
GENOVA PRODUCTS, INC., pg. 452
HARBOUR GROUP LTD., pg. 506
KIMGLASS DIVISION—Kimstock, Inc., pg. 630
KIMSTOCK, INC., pg. 630
KOHLER LTD.—Kohler Company, pg. 640
KOHLER LTD.—Kohler Company, pg. 640
MELARD MANUFACTURING CORPORATION, pg. 737
MELARD PLASTICS INC.—Melard Manufacturing Corporation, pg. 737
PLASKOLITE INC., pg. 874
SANDERSON PLUMBING PRODUCTS INC., pg. 970
THETFORD (AQUA) PRODUCTS, LTD.—The Dyson-Kissner-Moran Corporation, pg. 358
THETFORD CORPORATION—The Dyson-Kissner-Moran Corporation, pg. 357
THETFORD CORP. MFG. FACILITY—The Dyson-Kissner-Moran Corporation, pg. 358
THETFORD SANITATION LTD.—The Dyson-Kissner-Moran Corporation, pg. 358

3089 — PLASTICS PRODUCTS, NEC

THE AARQUE COMPANIES, pg. 9
AARQUE STEEL CORPORATION—The Aarque Companies, pg. 9
ABBOTT LABORATORIES/ASHLAND, pg. 9
ADMIRAL PACKAGING, INC.—Union Industries, Inc., pg. 1128
ALCO INDUSTRIES, INC., pg. 32
ALFORD INDUSTRIES, INC., pg. 33
ALRO GROUP, pg. 44
ALRO GROUP, JACKSON PLASTICS—Alro Group, pg. 44
AMERICAN EXCELSIOR COMPANY, pg. 51
AMERICAN INTERNATIONAL CONTAINER, INC., pg. 56
AMERICAN METAL & PLASTICS, pg. 58
AMERICAN NATIONAL CAN CO.—Poly-Seal Corporation, pg. 880
ANGLERS ROSLYN GROUP LTD., pg. 75
APACHE PLASTICS, L.P., pg. 77
ARISTO MANUFACTURING CO.—The Metal Ware Corp., pg. 742
ASSOCIATED MATERIALS INC., pg. 91
AUTOMOTIVE PLASTIC TECHNOLOGIES, INC., pg. 101
AZON CORPORATION, pg. 105
BPC DIVISION—Bristol Products, L.P., pg. 176
BANKCRAFTERS, INC., pg. 117
BEDFORD INDUSTRIES, INC., pg. 131
BELMONT PLASTICS CO.—Corcoran Mfg. Co., Inc., pg. 285
THE BILTRITE CORPORATION, pg. 151
BINGHAM, pg. 151
BINNING'S BUILDING PRODUCTS, INC., pg. 151
BIXBY INTERNATIONAL CORP., pg. 153
BRADFORD COMPANY, pg. 170
BRISTOL PRODUCTS, L.P., pg. 176
BRISTOLIPE DIVISION—Bristol Products, L.P., pg. 176
BRITTANY CORPORATION, pg. 177
BROCK MANUFACTURING—CTB Inc., pg. 205
E. J. BROOKS COMPANY, pg. 179
BROOKS PRODUCTS, ARLINGTON—Brooks Products, Inc., pg. 180
BROOKS PRODUCTS, INC., pg. 180
BROOKS PRODUCTS, ORLANDO—Brooks Products, Inc., pg. 180
BURKE COMMUNICATION INDUSTRIES, INC., pg. 190
C-LINE PRODUCTS, INC., pg. 198
CC INDUSTRIES ESTIA DIV.—CC Industries, Inc., pg. 200
CP ILLINOIS, INC.—Container Products Inc., pg. 278
CPI PLASTICS, INC.—Container Products Inc., pg. 278
CADILLAC PRODUCTS, INC., pg. 207
CAIRNS & BROTHER, INC., pg. 207
CAMBRO MANUFACTURING COMPANY, pg. 211
THE CANADIAN COLEMAN CO., LTD.—MacAndrews & Forbes Holdings Inc., pg. 695
CAPSONIC GROUP, INC., pg. 216
CAPTIVE PLASTICS, pg. 216
E. R. CARPENTER CO., pg. 224
CENTRAL STATES DIVERSIFIED, INC., pg. 234
THE CHARDON RUBBER CO., pg. 239
CHEM-TAINER CORPORATION, pg. 241
CLAYTON CORPORATION, pg. 253
CLAYTON PLASTICS CORP.—Clayton Corporation, pg. 253
CLEAR SHIELD NATIONAL, INC.—Envirodyne Industries, Inc., pg. 383
CO-EX PLASTICS, INC.—Huntsman Chemical Corporation, pg. 555
COAST CATAMARAN FRANCE—MacAndrews & Forbes Holdings Inc., pg. 695
COLEMAN OUTDOOR PRODUCTS—MacAndrews & Forbes Holdings Inc., pg. 695
COLLINS & AIKMAN GROUP INC., pg. 262
COLOR CUSTOM, INC., pg. 264
COMMAND PLASTIC CORPORATION, pg. 268
COMMERCIAL PLASTICS & SUPPLIES CORP., pg. 268
COMPONENT TECHNOLOGY CORP., pg. 270
CONAIR CORPORATION, pg. 272
CONSOLIDATED INDUSTRIAL CORPORATION, pg. 276
CONTICO INTERNATIONAL, INC., pg. 278
COSCO INDUSTRIES, pg. 288
CRANE PLASTICS COMPANY, pg. 296
CUE INDUSTRIES, INC.—Guardian Industries Corp., pg. 492
CUSTOM PAK, INC., pg. 306
CUTLER MANUFACTURING CORPORATION, pg. 307
DACOR CORPORATION, pg. 310
DANAFILMS, INC., pg. 313
C.R. DANIELS, INC., pg. 314
DART CONTAINER CORP., pg. 316
DAUBERT CHEMICAL COMPANY, INC.—Daubert Industries, Inc., pg. 317
DAUBERT COATED PRODUCTS, INC.—Daubert Industries, Inc., pg. 317
DAY PRODUCTS—Day & Zimmermann, Inc., pg. 320
DICKTEN & MASCH MANUFACTURING CO., pg. 336
DIEMOLDING CORP., pg. 336
DIMCO-GRAY COMPANY, pg. 338
DOUGLAS STEPHEN PLASTICS, INC., pg. 347
DUNMORE CORPORATION, pg. 353
DURACO PRODUCTS, INC., pg. 354
DURACO PRODUCTS INC. OF SOUTH CAROLINA—Duraco Products, Inc., pg. 354
DURANT ELECTRONICS, INC.—Strombecker Corporation, pg. 1054
DURO PAPER BAG MANUFACTURING CO., pg. 355
DURO PAPER BAG MFG. CO.—Duro Paper Bag Manufacturing Co., pg. 355
ELKAY PLASTICS COMPANY, INC., pg. 377
ELKAY PRODUCTS, INC., pg. 377

ENVIRODYNE INDUSTRIES, INC., pg. 383
ERSHIGS, INC., pg. 387
EVANS INDUSTRIES, INC., pg. 390
EVENFLO MEXICO S.A.—Spalding & Evenflo Companies, Inc., pg. 1025
EVENFLO PRODUCTS CO.—Spalding & Evenflo Companies, Inc., pg. 1024
EVENFLO PRODUCTS DIVISION—Spalding & Evenflo Companies, Inc., pg. 1025
F. R. MANUFACTURING CORPORATION, pg. 395
FAWN INDUSTRIES, INC., pg. 404
FIBERESIN INDUSTRIES INC., pg. 408
FILMCO INDUSTRIES, INC.—Envirodyne Industries, Inc., pg. 383
FINDLAY INDUSTRIES, INC., pg. 410
FLAMBEAU CORPORATION—Nordic Group of Companies, Ltd., pg. 809
FLAMBEAU MICRO CO.—Nordic Group of Companies, Ltd., pg. 809
FLAMBEAU PLASTICS CO.—Nordic Group of Companies, Ltd., pg. 809
FLAMBEAU PRODUCTS CORP.—Nordic Group of Companies, Ltd., pg. 809
FLAMBEAU SOUTHEAST CO.—Nordic Group of Companies, Ltd., pg. 809
FLEX-O-GLASS, INC., pg. 418
FLEXEL, INC., pg. 418
FORSTER MFG. CO., INC.—Advent International, pg. 21
GARELICK FARMS, INC., pg. 443
GATES FORMED-FIBRE PRODUCTS—The Gates Corporation, pg. 445
GENOVA PRODUCTS, INC., pg. 452
GERRARD AND COMPANY, pg. 454
M.C. GILL CORPORATION, pg. 458
MARTY GILMAN, INC., pg. 459
GOLDEN TRIANGLE PLASTICS, INC.—Plastic Engineering Components Inc., pg. 875
GORDON PLASTICS DIV.—Plastigage Corporation, pg. 876
GOULD PACKAGING, INC., pg. 473
GOULD PACKAGING, INC.—Gould Packaging, Inc., pg. 473
STEPHEN GOULD PAPER CO., INC., pg. 473
HANDGARDS INC., pg. 504
HANSEN PLASTICS DIVISION—Tuthill Corporation, pg. 1120
HARDIE IRRIGATION-LANDSCAPE DIV., pg. 508
HARTWELL COMMERCIAL DIVISION—The Hartwell Corporation, pg. 514
THE HARTWELL CORPORATION, pg. 514
HARTZ MOUNTAIN GROUP—Hartz Group, pg. 514
HARTZELL CORPORATION, pg. 514
THE HEIL CO., pg. 525
HEIL ROTOMOLD, INC.—The Heil Co., pg. 526
HENNELLS, INC., pg. 530
HILLSIDE CAPITAL, INC., pg. 535
HILLSIDE INDUSTRIES, INC.—Hillside Capital, Inc., pg. 535
HOFFER PLASTICS CORPORATION, pg. 537
HOLCOMB & HOKE MFG. COMPANY, INC., pg. 538
HOPPLE PLASTICS, INC., pg. 544
HUNTCO HEALTH CARE CO.—Huntco Inc., pg. 554
IDEAL-STANDARD S.A.I.—American Standard Inc., pg. 62
IGLOO CORPORATION, pg. 562
IMPROVED BLOW MOLDING EQUIPMENT COMPANY, INC.—Goodman Equipment Corp., pg. 471
INGRID-SEVKO, INC., pg. 569
INJECTRON CORPORATION, pg. 569
INTERPLASTIC CORP., pg. 579
INTERTRADE INDUSTRIES, pg. 581
IVEX PACKAGING CORPORATION, pg. 583
J & B PRODUCTS—Bristol Products, L.P., pg. 176
JAMISON PLASTIC CORPORATION, pg. 589
JANLIN PLASTIC INC.—Plastic Engineering Components Inc., pg. 875
JELD-WEN, INC., pg. 591
THE JOHNSON INDUSTRIES CORP., pg. 598
JUNO TOOL & PLASTIC CORPORATION—The Cretex Companies, pg. 299
KEENEY MANUFACTURING CO., pg. 620
KEYSOR CENTURY CORPORATION, pg. 627
KIMSTOCK, INC., pg. 630
E. B. KINGMAN COMPANY, pg. 631
KLEER PAK CORPORATION, pg. 635
KOCH INDUSTRIES, INCORPORATED, pg. 639
KOHLER COMPANY, pg. 639
KOHLER LTD.—Kohler Company, pg. 640
KOLLER ENTERPRISES, INC., pg. 641
KRACO ENTERPRISES, INC., pg. 643
LANE FILM PRODUCTS DIVISION—Lane Industries, Inc., pg. 657
LAWNWARE PRODUCTS, INC., pg. 661
LEAR SIEGLER PLASTICS CORP.—Lear Siegler Diversified Holdings Corp., pg. 664
LETICA CORPORATION, pg. 668
LINCOLN INDUSTRIES, INC.—Zoeller Co., pg. 1221
LORD CORP. (U.K.) LTD.—Lord Corporation, pg. 683
LORD CORPORATION, pg. 683
LORD FAR EAST, INC.—Lord Corporation, pg. 683
LORD INDUSTRIAL LTDA.—Lord Corporation, pg. 683
MACK MOLDING COMPANY, pg. 697
MACLEAN-FOGG CO., pg. 697
MAGLA PRODUCTS, pg. 700
MAJESTIC MOLDED PRODUCTS, INC., pg. 702
MARK I MOLDED PLASTICS, INC.—Atwood Industries, Inc., pg. 97
MARYLAND PLASTICS, INC., pg. 717
MARYLAND PLASTICS, INC.—Bio Medic Corporation, pg. 152
MASTER MOLDED PRODUCTS CORPORATION, pg. 720
MEDLINE INDUSTRIES, INC., pg. 736
JOSHUA MEIER CORP., pg. 737
MENASHA CORPORATION, pg. 738
METTOWEE LUMBER & PLASTIC CO., INC.—Telescope Casual Furniture, Inc., pg. 1085
MICRODOT AEROSPACE FASTENING SYSTEMS GROUP—MICRODOT, Inc., pg. 749
MILLER PRODUCTS COMPANY, INC., pg. 755
MILTON CAN CO., INC., pg. 756
MINIATURE PRECISION COMPONENTS, pg. 757
MOARK MOLD, INC.—Plastic Engineering Components Inc., pg. 875
MOLDCRAFT PLASTICS INC.—Poly-Seal Corporation, pg. 880
MOLDED FIBER GLASS COMPANIES, pg. 763
MOLDED FIBER GLASS TRAY CO.—Molded Fiber Glass Companies, pg. 764
MOSSBERG INDUSTRIES, HUBBARD DIVISION—Mossberg Industries, Inc., pg. 773
MOSSBERG INDUSTRIES, INC., pg. 772
MUSKIN LEISURE PRODUCTS, INC., pg. 777
NMC OF NORTH AMERICA, INC., pg. 781
THE NATIONAL LATEX PRODUCTS CO., pg. 791
NATIONAL TOOL & MANUFACTURING COMPANY, pg. 794
NIBCO, INC., pg. 806
NORDIC GROUP OF COMPANIES, LTD., pg. 809
NOREL PAPER CORPORATION, pg. 810
NORTH CAROLINA FOAM INDUSTRIES, INC.—Barnhardt Manufacturing Co., pg. 120
NORTHLAND ALUMINUM PRODUCTS, INC., pg. 814
NORWESCO, INC., pg. 816
OAK PRODUCTS, INC.—ROC Properties Inc., pg. 908
OLSONITE CORPORATION, pg. 824
OUIMET CORP.—Ouimet Industries, pg. 831
OUIMET INDUSTRIES, pg. 831
OUIMET STAY & LEATHER CO.—Ouimet Industries, pg. 831
PTA CORPORATION, pg. 837
PW PIPE CO.—Simpson Investment Co., pg. 1007
PACESETTER CORPORATION, pg. 839
PACKAGE SERVICE COMPANY, INC., pg. 842
PACKAGING PRODUCTS & DESIGN, pg. 842
PACKAGING RESOURCES, INC.—H.P.H. Industries Ltd., pg. 497
PAK-SHER CO.—T C Manufacturing Company, Inc., pg. 1072
PAN-O-GRAV, INC.—Plastic Engineering Components Inc., pg. 875
PAR INDUSTRIES, INC., pg. 847
PARAMOUNT PACKAGING CORP., pg. 848
PARKWAY FABRICATORS, INC.—Great American Industries, Inc., pg. 480
PAWLING CORPORATION, pg. 852
PAWNEE SPECIALTY PRODUCTS—Pawnee Industries, Inc., pg. 852
PENDA CORPORATION, pg. 857
PENN ERIE DIV.—Plastek Group, pg. 875
PENT PLASTICS, INC.—Group Dekko International Inc., pg. 490
PHILADELPHIA SIGN COMPANY, pg. 867
PHILLIPS PLASTICS CORPORATION, pg. 867
PIONEER PAPER CORPORATION, pg. 872
PLANO MOLDING CO., pg. 874
PLASKOLITE INC., pg. 874
PLASTECH CORPORATION, pg. 874
PLASTEK GROUP, pg. 874
PLASTEK TOOL, INC.—Plastek Group, pg. 875
PLASTIC ENGINEERING COMPONENTS INC., pg. 875
PLASTIC ENGINEERING, INC.—Plastic Engineering Components Inc., pg. 875
PLASTIC MOLDINGS CORP., pg. 875
PLASTIC PACKAGING, INC., pg. 875
PLASTIC PRODUCTS OF INDIANA—Transilwrap Company, Inc., pg. 1107
PLASTIC SUPPLIERS, INC., pg. 875
PLASTICS MANUFACTURING COMPANY, pg. 876
PLASTIPAK PACKAGING INC., pg. 876
POLY-SEAL CORPORATION, pg. 880
POLYMER PLASTICS CORPORATION, pg. 880
POLYPLASTIC PRODUCTS—Brooks Products, Inc., pg. 180
PRECISE METALS & PLASTICS, INC.—KDI Corporation, pg. 612
PRECISION PLASTICS—Precision Plastics Inc., pg. 885
PRECISION PLASTICS INC., pg. 885
PRICE BROTHERS COMPOSITE PIPE, INC.—Price Brothers Co., pg. 888
THE PRO CORPORATION, pg. 891
QUADION CORPORATION, pg. 902
R & R PLASTICS—Component Technology Corp., pg. 270
RANIR CORPORATION, pg. 912
RAPID INDUSTRIAL PLASTICS COMPANY, pg. 913
RED WING PRODUCTS, INC., pg. 919
REESE ENTERPRISES, INC., pg. 920
REHRIG PACIFIC COMPANY, pg. 922
RICHCO PLASTICS COMPANY, pg. 933
RICHMOND TECHNOLOGY INC., pg. 933
ROSTONE CORPORATION, pg. 950
ROYAL PLASTIC—M.C. Gill Corporation, pg. 458
RUSSELL-STANLEY WEST, INC.—Russell-Stanley Corporation, pg. 957
SAMSILL CORPORATION, pg. 968
SANDUSKY PLASTICS, INC.—Envirodyne Industries, Inc., pg. 383
SCRIPTO-TOKAI, INC., pg. 983
SEATTLE PACKAGING CORPORATION, pg. 986
SECURITY PLASTICS, INC., pg. 987
SEQUENTIA INC., pg. 990
SEVCO, INC.—Ingrid-Sevko, Inc., pg. 569
SIERRACIN CORPORATION, pg. 1003
SIGNET INDUSTRIES, pg. 1003
SILLCOCKS PLASTICS INTERNATIONAL, INC., pg. 1004
SIMPSON INVESTMENT CO., pg. 1007
R & G SLOANE MFG. CO., INC., pg. 1010
SMITH METAL ARTS COMPANY, INC., pg. 1013
SOLO CUP COMPANY—SCC Holding Co., pg. 961
SOUTH BEND PLASTICS, INC., pg. 1019
SOUTHERN CASE, INC., pg. 1020
SPALDING & EVENFLO COMPANIES, INC., pg. 1024
SPARTAN PLASTICS CANADA—Spartan International, pg. 1026
SPECIALTY MANUFACTURING COMPANY, pg. 1027
SPECTRUM MOLDING—Plastek Group, pg. 875
SPEEDLING INCORPORATED, pg. 1029
THE STERLING GROUP—Kohler Company, pg. 640
STERLITE CORPORATION, pg. 1047
STROMBECKER CORPORATION, pg. 1054
STROMBECKER (HK) LTD.—Strombecker Corporation, pg. 1054
STRUCTURAL FOAM PLASTICS—Structural Foam Plastics, Inc., pg. 1054
STRUCTURAL FOAM PLASTICS—Structural Foam Plastics, Inc., pg. 1054
STRUCTURAL FOAM PLASTICS, INC., pg. 1054
SWEETHEART CUP CO., INC., pg. 1067
SWEETHEART CUP CORPORATION—Sweetheart Cup Co., Inc., pg. 1067
SWEETHEART CUP CORPORATION—Sweetheart Cup Co., Inc., pg. 1067
T O PLASTICS, INC., pg. 1074
TAPCO PRODUCTS COMPANY, pg. 1078
NELSON A. TAYLOR CO., INC., pg. 1080
THE TECH GROUP, pg. 1082
TECH INDUSTRIES, INC., pg. 1083
TECH MEDICAL INC.—The Tech Group, pg. 1083
TECH PLASTICS—The Tech Group, pg. 1083
TECH POULSON, INC.—The Tech Group, pg. 1083
TEKNI-PLEX, INC., pg. 1084
TEKNI-PLEX, INC.—Tekni-Plex, Inc., pg. 1084
TENAX CORPORATION, pg. 1086
THERMAL TECHNOLOGY INDUSTRIES, pg. 1091
THETFORD CORPORATION—The Dyson-Kissner-Moran Corporation, pg. 357
TOTER INCORPORATED, pg. 1103
TRANSILWRAP CO., INC.—Transilwrap Company, Inc., pg. 1107
TRANSILWRAP CO., INC.—Transilwrap Company, Inc., pg. 1107
TRANSILWRAP CO., INC.—Transilwrap Company, Inc., pg. 1107
TRANSILWRAP CO., INC.—Transilwrap Company, Inc., pg. 1107
TRANSILWRAP CO., INC.—Transilwrap Company, Inc., pg. 1107
TRANSILWRAP COMPANY, INC., pg. 1107
TRANSILWRAP COMPANY, INC.—Transilwrap Company, Inc., pg. 1107
TRANSILWRAP COMPANY, INC.—Transilwrap Company, Inc., pg. 1107
TRANSILWRAP COMPANY, INC.—Transilwrap Company, Inc., pg. 1107
TRANSILWRAP COMPANY, INC.—Transilwrap Company, Inc., pg. 1107
TRANSILWRAP CO. OF PHILADELPHIA—Transilwrap Company, Inc., pg. 1107
TRI-CHEM, INC., pg. 1110
TRIANGLE TOOL CO.—Plastek Group, pg. 875
TRICON INDUSTRIES, INC., pg. 1113
TRIO PRODUCTS INC., pg. 1114
TRIPLE S PLASTICS, INC.—Triple S Technologies, Inc., pg. 1114
TRIPLE S TECHNOLOGIES, INC., pg. 1114
ALBERT TROSTEL PACKINGS, LTD., pg. 1116
TROY MILLS, INC., pg. 1116
TULIP CORPORATION, pg. 1119
UC INDUSTRIES, INC., pg. 1122
UFE CAL TEC INC.—UFE Incorporated, pg. 1123
UFE INCORPORATED, pg. 1123
UFE PTE LTD—UFE Incorporated, pg. 1123
ULTRA TOOL & PLASTICS, INC., pg. 1125
UNIFLEX, INC., pg. 1126
UNION PAPER CO.—Union Industries, Inc., pg. 1128
UNITED STATES CORRULITE CORPORATION—United States Sugar Corporation, pg. 1137
VISKASE—Envirodyne Industries, Inc., pg. 383
VISKASE CANADA INC.—Envirodyne Industries, Inc., pg. 383
VISKASE CORPORATION—Envirodyne Industries, Inc., pg. 383
WEATHER STRIP DIVISION—Reese Enterprises, Inc., pg. 921
WHEATLAND TUBE COMPANY, pg. 1184
WHEATON DO BRAZIL—Wheaton Inc., pg. 1184
WHEATON INC., pg. 1184
WHEATON INJECTION MOLDING—Wheaton Inc., pg. 1184
WHEATON SAFETY CONTAINER CO.—Wheaton Inc., pg. 1184
WHITE MOP WRINGER COMPANY, pg. 1186
WINDSOR PLASTICS, INC.—Guardian Industries Corp., pg. 492
WINGFOOT FILMS CORPORATION—Huntsman Chemical Corporation, pg. 555
WOLLIN PRODUCTS, INC., pg. 1199
WOZNIAK INDUSTRIES, INC., pg. 1204
XERXES CORPORATION, pg. 1206
YORK WALLCOVERINGS INC., pg. 1208
ZAPPA PLASTICS, pg. 1216
THE ZIPPERTUBING CO., pg. 1220

3111 — LEATHER TANNING & FINISHING

DARLING-DELAWARE CO., INC., pg. 315
EAGLE-OTTAWA LEATHER CO.—Albert Trostel & Sons Company, pg. 1116
HOWES LEATHER COMPANY, INC., pg. 548
LEATHERS BEST, pg. 664
OUIMET CORP.—Ouimet Industries, pg. 831
OUIMET INDUSTRIES, pg. 831
PRIME TANNING CO., INC., pg. 889
SALZ LEATHERS, INC., pg. 968

S.B. FOOT TANNING CO.—Red Wing Shoe Co., Inc., pg. 919
SETON CO.—Seton Company, pg. 993
SETON COMPANY, pg. 993
ALBERT TROSTEL & SONS COMPANY, pg. 1116
WELLS LAMONT—The Marmon Group, Inc., pg. 712

3131 — BOOT & SHOE CUT STOCK & FINDINGS

ALLEN-EDMONDS SHOE CORP., pg. 36
BATA SHOE CO., INC.—CHB Corp., pg. 201
BIXBY INTERNATIONAL CORP., pg. 153
CHB CORP., pg. 201
HOWES LEATHER COMPANY, INC., pg. 548
INJECTION FOOTWEAR CORP., pg. 569
OUIMET CORP.—Ouimet Industries, pg. 831
OUIMET INDUSTRIES, pg. 831
STANBEE COMPANY, INC., pg. 1035
EDWIN B. STIMPSON COMPANY, INC., pg. 1049

3142 — HOUSE SLIPPERS

ANIMAL FAIR—Guy Schoenecker, Inc., pg. 978
DEXTER SHOE COMPANY, pg. 334
DANIEL GREEN CO., pg. 484
MUNRO & COMPANY, INC., pg. 775
GUY SCHOENECKER, INC., pg. 977

3143 — MEN'S FOOTWEAR, EXCEPT ATHLETIC

ACME BOOT CO., INC.—Farley Industries, pg. 400
ALDEN SHOE CO., INC., pg. 33
ALLEN-EDMONDS SHOE CORP., pg. 36
ALTAMA DELTA CORP., pg. 45
JOHN W. BROOKS INC., pg. 180
H.H. BROWN SHOE COMPANY, INC., pg. 182
CAROLINA SHOE COMPANY—H.H. Brown Shoe Company, Inc., pg. 182
THE CHEROKEE GROUP, pg. 243
COVE SHOE COMPANY—H.H. Brown Shoe Company, Inc., pg. 182
COWTOWN BOOT COMPANY, pg. 291
DEXTER SHOE COMPANY, pg. 334
ENCORE SHOE CORPORATION, pg. 380
F & F SHOE COMPANY—Mason Shoe Mfg. Co., pg. 718
FARLEY INDUSTRIES, pg. 399
FREEMAN SHOES COMPANY, pg. 431
JOS. M. HERMAN SHOE CO., pg. 531
INJECTION FOOTWEAR CORP., pg. 569
KNAPP SHOES INC., pg. 636
L.L. BEAN, INC., pg. 648
MASON SHOE MFG. CO., pg. 718
P.W. MINOR & SON, INC., pg. 758
MORSE SHOE, INC., pg. 772
MUNRO & COMPANY, INC., pg. 775
RED WING SHOE CO., INC., pg. 919
RICHLAND SHOE CO.—H.H. Brown Shoe Company, Inc., pg. 183
SPORTO CORP., pg. 1032
WEINBRENNER SHOE COMPANY, INC., pg. 1173

3144 — WOMEN'S FOOTWEAR, EXCEPT ATHLETIC

JOHN W. BROOKS INC., pg. 180
THE CHEROKEE GROUP, pg. 243
DEXTER SHOE COMPANY, pg. 334
EASTLAND SHOE MANUFACTURING CORPORATION, pg. 364
ENCORE SHOE CORPORATION, pg. 380
FARLEY INDUSTRIES, pg. 399
INJECTION FOOTWEAR CORP., pg. 569
KANGAROOS, USA INC., pg. 616
KNAPP SHOES INC., pg. 636
LOWELL SHOE, INC.—Morse Shoe, Inc., pg. 772
MASON SHOE MFG. CO., pg. 718
MILTON SHOE MANUFACTURING COMPANY, INC., pg. 756
P.W. MINOR & SON, INC., pg. 758
MORSE SHOE, INC., pg. 772
NORWOOD SHOE CORPORATION, pg. 816
OOMPHIES, INC., pg. 827
RED WING SHOE CO., INC., pg. 919
SPORTO CORP., pg. 1032
WEINBRENNER SHOE COMPANY, INC., pg. 1173

3149 — FOOTWEAR, EXCEPT RUBBER, NEC

ASICS TIGER CORPORATION, pg. 8
BALLET MAKERS, INC., pg. 116
JOHN W. BROOKS INC., pg. 180
CAPEZIO BALLET MAKERS, INC.—Ballet Makers, Inc., pg. 116
THE CHEROKEE GROUP, pg. 243
DEXTER SHOE COMPANY, pg. 334
THE FRYE COMPANY, pg. 435
DANIEL GREEN CO., pg. 484
HEAD SPORTS, INC., pg. 520
KANGAROOS, USA INC., pg. 616
LOWELL SHOE, INC.—Morse Shoe, Inc., pg. 772
MILTON SHOE MANUFACTURING COMPANY, INC., pg. 756
MUNRO & COMPANY, INC., pg. 775
NEW BALANCE ATHLETIC SHOE, INC., pg. 798
SPORTO CORP., pg. 1032

3151 — LEATHER GLOVES & MITTENS

CAROLINA GLOVE CO., pg. 223
KLEIN TOOLS INC., pg. 635
SHELBY GROUP INTERNATIONAL, INC., pg. 996

3161 — LUGGAGE

ANDIAMO, INC., pg. 74
ATLAS CO. OF BOSTON, INC.—Skyway Luggage Co., pg. 1009
BALTIMORE LUGGAGE COMPANY, pg. 116
COAST MANUFACTURING COMPANY, pg. 257
DUNSTON LEATHERS, INC.—United States Luggage Company, pg. 1136
E-II HOLDINGS, INC., pg. 358
EASTERN CANVAS PRODUCTS, INC., pg. 363
FABER/CASTELL CORPORATION, pg. 395
KORET GIVENCHY, pg. 642
LARK LUGGAGE COMPANY, INC.—E-II Holdings, Inc., pg. 359
G. LEBLANC CORPORATION, pg. 665
G. LEBLANC—G. Leblanc Corporation, pg. 665
MONARCH LUGGAGE CO. INC., pg. 765
POLO/RALPH LAUREN CORPORATION, pg. 879
PONY SPORTS & LEISURE INC., pg. 880
PYRAMID HANDBAGS INC., pg. 901
SGI INC., pg. 962
SAMSONITE CORPORATION—E-II Holdings, Inc., pg. 358
SEWARD LUGGAGE COMPANY, pg. 993
SKYWAY LUGGAGE CO., pg. 1009
TRAFALGAR/GHURKA, pg. 1105
UNITED STATES LUGGAGE COMPANY, pg. 1136
VENTURA TRAVELWARE, INC., pg. 1147

3171 — WOMEN'S HANDBAGS & PURSES

CERTIFIED CORP., pg. 236
THE CHEROKEE GROUP, pg. 243
CUE INDUSTRIES, INC.—Guardian Industries Corp., pg. 492
C.R. DANIELS, INC., pg. 314
DOVER HANDBAG CO., INC.—Michael Stevens Ltd., pg. 1048
INTERNATIONAL DESIGNER ACCESSORIES, INC., pg. 578
KORET GIVENCHY, pg. 642
PRINCE GARDNER INCORPORATED, pg. 890
PYRAMID HANDBAGS INC., pg. 901
RENCO GROUP, pg. 926
TRAFALGAR/GHURKA, pg. 1105
TRINA, INC., pg. 1113

3172 — PERSONAL LEATHER GOODS, EXCEPT WOMEN'S HANDBAGS & PURSES

ALLIED PRODUCTS—Consolidated Cigar Corporation, pg. 276
AMITY LEATHER PRODUCTS COMPANY, pg. 67
HUGO BOSCA CO., INC., pg. 166
BUXTON COMPANY, pg. 197
ENGER-KRESS COMPANY, pg. 381
INTERNATIONAL DESIGNER ACCESSORIES, INC., pg. 578
KORET GIVENCHY, pg. 642
PRINCE GARDNER INCORPORATED, pg. 890
PYRAMID HANDBAGS INC., pg. 901
ROLFS—Amity Leather Products Company, pg. 67
TRAFALGAR/GHURKA, pg. 1105
TRINA, INC., pg. 1113

3199 — LEATHER GOODS, NEC

A & A MANUFACTURING CO., pg. 1
HUGO BOSCA CO., INC., pg. 166
BUXTON COMPANY, pg. 197
GEIGER BROTHERS, pg. 447
KLEIN TOOLS INC., pg. 635
KORET GIVENCHY, pg. 642
THE MARMON GROUP, INC., pg. 710
OUIMET STAY & LEATHER CO.—Ouimet Industries, pg. 831
TRAFALGAR/GHURKA, pg. 1105

3211 — FLAT GLASS

AFG GLASS INC.—AFG Industries, Inc., pg. 4
AFG INDUSTRIES, INC., pg. 3
J.E. BERKOWITZ, LP, pg. 142
FALCONER GLASS INDUSTRIES, INC.—Guardian Industries Corp., pg. 492
FLORAL GLASS & MIRROR, INC., pg. 420
FOURCO GLASS CO.—AFG Industries, Inc., pg. 3
GLOBE-AMERADA GLASS COMPANY, pg. 463
GUARDIAN GLASS INC.—Guardian Industries Corp., pg. 492
GUARDIAN INDUSTRIES CORP., pg. 491
NEW JERSEY FLOAT GLASS, INC.—AFG Industries, Inc., pg. 3
O'DELL PRODUCTS, INC.—AFG Industries, Inc., pg. 3
O'KEEFFE'S, INC., pg. 823
PELLA CORPORATION, pg. 856
SOUTHERN WHOLESALE—AFG Industries, Inc., pg. 4

3221 — GLASS CONTAINERS

COCA COLA BOTTLING CO. UNITED, INC., pg. 257
GLENSHAW GLASS CO. INC., pg. 462
WHEATON DO BRAZIL—Wheaton Inc., pg. 1184

3229 — PRESSED & BLOWN GLASS & GLASSWARE, NEC

CAMBRO MANUFACTURING COMPANY, pg. 211
CRISA CORPORATION, pg. 299
CRYSTAL CLEAR INDUSTRIES COMPANY, pg. 303
DULING OPTICAL CORPORATION, pg. 352
EVENFLO MEXICO S.A.—Spalding & Evenflo Companies, Inc., pg. 1025
EVENFLO PRODUCTS CO.—Spalding & Evenflo Companies, Inc., pg. 1024
EVENFLO PRODUCTS DIVISION—Spalding & Evenflo Companies, Inc., pg. 1025
GAF BUILDING MATERIALS CORPORATION—GAF Corporation, pg. 438
GAF CORPORATION, pg. 438
INGRID-SEVKO, INC., pg. 569
NATIONAL PLASTICS CORPORATION—Millstein Industries, pg. 756
THE PFALTZGRAFF CO.—Susquehanna Pfaltzgraff, pg. 1065
SALADMASTER, pg. 967
SIERRACIN CORPORATION, pg. 1003
WHEATON COATED PRODUCTS—Wheaton Inc., pg. 1184
WHEATON GLASS CO.—Wheaton Inc., pg. 1184
WHEATON INC., pg. 1184
WHEATON INSTRUMENTS—Wheaton Inc., pg. 1184
WHEATON SCIENTIFIC—Wheaton Inc., pg. 1184

3231 — GLASS PRODUCTS, MADE OF PURCHASED GLASS

AFG INDUSTRIES, INC., pg. 3
ACE GLASS INCORPORATED, pg. 11
ACORN BUILDING COMPONENTS INC., pg. 13
ALADDIN INDUSTRIES, INCORPORATED, pg. 29
ARDCO, INC., pg. 81
ASSURANCE GLASS CO. OF ALABAMA—Globe-Amerada Glass Company, pg. 463
J.E. BERKOWITZ, LP, pg. 142
CAROLINA MIRROR COMPANY, pg. 223
CAROLINA MIRROR-HOUSTON—Carolina Mirror Company, pg. 223
CRISA CORPORATION, pg. 299
FALCONER GLASS INDUSTRIES, INC.—Guardian Industries Corp., pg. 492
FIMBEL DOOR CORPORATION, pg. 409
FLORAL GLASS & MIRROR, INC., pg. 420
GLASS PRODUCTS, INC.—AFG Industries, Inc., pg. 3
GLOBE-AMERADA GLASS COMPANY, pg. 463
GUARDIAN INDUSTRIES CORP., pg. 491
GUARDIAN INDUSTRIES CORP.—Guardian Industries Corp., pg. 492
HAMILTON, INC.—AFG Industries, Inc., pg. 3
HARTZ MOUNTAIN GROUP—Hartz Group, pg. 514
K-D LAMP COMPANY, pg. 612
KIMSTOCK, INC., pg. 630
NAUGATUCK GLASS COMPANY, pg. 796
PQ CORPORATION, pg. 836
PELLA CORPORATION, pg. 856
POTTERS INDUSTRIES, INC.—PQ Corporation, pg. 837
NELSON A. TAYLOR CO., INC., pg. 1080
VANCE INDUSTRIES, INC., pg. 1144
ZENITH PRODUCTS CORP., pg. 1217

3241 — CEMENT, HYDRAULIC

ASH GROVE CEMENT—Ash Grove Cement Company, pg. 87
ASH GROVE CEMENT—Ash Grove Cement Company, pg. 87
ASH GROVE CEMENT—Ash Grove Cement Company, pg. 87
ASH GROVE CEMENT CO., DURKEE PLANT—Ash Grove Cement Company, pg. 87
ASH GROVE CEMENT COMPANY, pg. 87
C B R CEMENT CORPORATION, pg. 199
CALAVERAS CEMENT CORPORATION—C B R Cement Corporation, pg. 199
HILLS MATERIALS CO.—Northwestern Engineering Co., pg. 815
INKOM, IDAHO PLANT—Ash Grove Cement Company, pg. 87
LEAMINGTON PLANT—Ash Grove Cement Company, pg. 87
MONTANA CITY PLANT—Ash Grove Cement Company, pg. 88
NORTHWESTERN ENGINEERING CO., pg. 815
SEATTLE PLANT—Ash Grove Cement Company, pg. 88
STANDARD CONCRETE—C B R Cement Corporation, pg. 199
TILCON, INC., pg. 1097
H. B. ZACHRY COMPANY—H.B. Zachry, pg. 1215

3251 — BRICK & STRUCTURAL CLAY TILE

INTERSTATE BRICK COMPANY—Pacific Coast Building Products Inc., pg. 839
LINEAR DYNAMICS INC., pg. 676

3253 — CERAMIC WALL & FLOOR TILE

CURRAN CONTRACTING CO., pg. 305
DAL-TILE CORP., pg. 312
HUNTINGTON TILE, INC.—Pacific Holding Corporation, pg. 840
PACIFIC HOLDING CORPORATION, pg. 840
ROMANY CERAMICS INC.—United States Ceramic Tile Co., pg. 1135
ANN SACKS TILE & STONE, INC.—Kohler Company, pg. 640

SPARTA MOSAIC, INC.—United States Ceramic Tile Co., pg. 1135
UNITED STATES CERAMIC TILE CO., pg. 1135
WENCZEL TILE CO., pg. 1176

3255 — CLAY REFRACTORIES

THE BABCOCK & WILCOX COMPANY, pg. 107
BELMONT INDUSTRIES, U.S. REFRACTORIES DIV.—Belmont Industries, Inc., pg. 136
BELMONT INDUSTRIES, U.S. REFRACTORIES DIV.—Belmont Industries, Inc., pg. 136
BELMONT INDUSTRIES, U.S. REFRACTORIES DIV.—Belmont Industries, Inc., pg. 136
BELMONT INDUSTRIES, U.S. REFRACTORIES DIV.—Belmont Industries, Inc., pg. 136
CFB INDUSTRIES, INC., pg. 201
C&W REFRACTORIES, LTD.—CFB Industries, Inc., pg. 201
CHEROKEE BRICK & TILE CO., pg. 243
CHICAGO FIRE BRICK OF DELAWARE, INC.—CFB Industries, Inc., pg. 201
EMPRESA DE REFRACTARIOS COLOMBIANOS S.A.—Belmont Industries, Inc., pg. 137
FIRELINE CO.—Plibrico Co., pg. 877
J. H. FRANCE REFRACTORIES CO., pg. 428
GENERAL REFRACTORIES CO. OF CANADA, LTD.—Belmont Industries, Inc., pg. 137
GENERAL REFRACTORIES CO., U. S. REFRACTORIES DIV.—Belmont Industries, Inc., pg. 136
HARBISON-WALKER REFRACTORIES—INDRESCO, Inc., pg. 565
MAPLETON DEVELOPMENT, INC.—Belmont Industries, Inc., pg. 136
NORTH AMERICAN REFRACTORIES COMPANY, pg. 811
PACIFIC CLAY PRODUCTS—Pacific Holding Corporation, pg. 840
PACIFIC HOLDING CORPORATION, pg. 840
PLIBRICO CO., pg. 877
RADEX AUSTRIA, A.G.—Belmont Industries, Inc., pg. 137
RESCO PRODUCTS, INC., pg. 928
WELLSVILLE FIRE BRICK COMPANY—CFB Industries, Inc., pg. 201
WORLITE CORPORATION—P.J. Keating Company, pg. 619

3259 — STRUCTURAL CLAY PRODUCTS, NEC

CHEROKEE BRICK & TILE CO., pg. 243
PACIFIC COAST BUILDING PRODUCTS INC., pg. 839
SIMPSON DURA-VENT CO., INC., pg. 1007
TARCO, pg. 1078

3261 — VITREOUS CHINA PLUMBING FIXTURES & CHINA & EARTHENWARE FITTINGS & BATHROOM ACCESSORIES

AAA PLUMBING POTTERY CORP.—Gerber Plumbing Fixtures Corporation, pg. 454
AMERICAN STANDARD INC., pg. 61
AMERICAN STANDARD SANITARYWARE (THAILAND) LTD.—American Standard Inc., pg. 62
BRIGGS INDUSTRIES, INC., pg. 175
CC INDUSTRIES, INC., pg. 199
COMPAGNIE INTERNATIONALE DES PRODUITS SANITAIRES (CIPS) JACOB DELAFON—Kohler Company, pg. 640
GERBER PLUMBING FIXTURES CORPORATION, pg. 454
IDEAL-STANDARD BRAZIL—American Standard Inc., pg. 62
IDEAL-STANDARD GMBH—American Standard Inc., pg. 62
IDEAL-STANDARD LTD.—American Standard Inc., pg. 62
IDEAL-STANDARD, S.A. DE C.V.—American Standard Inc., pg. 62
IDEAL-STANDARD S.A.I.—American Standard Inc., pg. 62
IDEAL-STANDARD S.P.A.—American Standard Inc., pg. 62
INDUSTRIA CENTROAMERICANA DE SANITARIOS, S.A.—American Standard Inc., pg. 62
INDUSTRIA CERAMICA CENTROAMERICANA, S.A.—American Standard Inc., pg. 62
INDUSTRIA CERAMICA COSTARRICENSE, S.A.—American Standard Inc., pg. 62
KALLISTA, INC.—Kohler Company, pg. 640
KOHLER CO. (SC)—Kohler Company, pg. 640
KOHLER CO. (TX)—Kohler Company, pg. 640
KOHLER COMPANY, pg. 639
KOKOMO SANITARY POTTERY CORP., pg. 640
PEERLESS POTTERY, INC., pg. 855
QUEROY S.A.—American Standard Inc., pg. 62
SANITARIOS DOMINICANOS, S.A.—American Standard Inc., pg. 62
SANITARY WARES MFG. CORP.—American Standard Inc., pg. 62
WOODBRIDGE SANITARY POTTERY CORP.—Gerber Plumbing Fixtures Corporation, pg. 454

3262 — VITREOUS CHINA TABLE & KITCHEN ARTICLES

THE HALL CHINA COMPANY, pg. 501
THE HOMER LAUGHLIN CHINA COMPANY, pg. 661
THE PFALTZGRAFF CO.—Susquehanna Pfaltzgraff, pg. 1065
SYRACUSE CHINA CORP.—Susquehanna Pfaltzgraff, pg. 1065

3263 — FINE EARTHENWARE (WHITEWARE) TABLE & KITCHEN ARTICLES

THE PFALTZGRAFF CO.—Susquehanna Pfaltzgraff, pg. 1065
ROWOCO—Wilton Industries, Inc., pg. 1195
SUSQUEHANNA PFALTZGRAFF, pg. 1065

3264 — PORCELAIN ELECTRICAL SUPPLIES

INDUSTRIAL CERAMICS, INC., pg. 566
PORCELAIN METALS CORP., pg. 881

3269 — POTTERY PRODUCTS, NEC

BRITTANY CORPORATION, pg. 177
COPCO—Wilton Industries, Inc., pg. 1195
DAKIN, INC., pg. 311
HAEGER INDUSTRIES, INC., pg. 499
HAEGER POTTERIES, INC.—Haeger Industries, Inc., pg. 499
HAEGER POTTERIES OF MACOMB, INC.—Haeger Industries, Inc., pg. 499
LASTING PRODUCTS, INC., pg. 660
LION RIBBON COMPANY—C.M. Offray & Son Inc., pg. 822
MARYLAND RIBBON COMPANY—C.M. Offray & Son Inc., pg. 822
THE MEYERCORD COMPANY, pg. 746
NORTHLAND ALUMINUM PRODUCTS, INC., pg. 814
C.M. OFFRAY & SON INC., pg. 822
THE PFALTZGRAFF CO.—Susquehanna Pfaltzgraff, pg. 1065
PORCELAIN METALS CORP., pg. 881
ROWOCO—Wilton Industries, Inc., pg. 1195
SUSQUEHANNA PFALTZGRAFF, pg. 1065
UNITED DESIGN, pg. 1131

3271 — CONCRETE BLOCK & BRICK

BRISTOL CONCRETE PRODS. CORP.—Bristol Steel & Iron Works, Inc., pg. 177
BRISTOL STEEL & IRON WORKS, INC., pg. 176
BROOKS PRODUCTS, ARLINGTON—Brooks Products, Inc., pg. 180
BROOKS PRODUCTS, INC., pg. 180
BROOKS PRODUCTS, ORLANDO—Brooks Products, Inc., pg. 180
CHEROKEE BRICK & TILE CO., pg. 243
CONTRACTORS SUPPLIES, INC., pg. 280
DEMCO INC., pg. 328
DILLINGHAM CONSTRUCTION N.A., INC.—Dillingham Construction Corporation, pg. 338
EVANS INDUSTRIES, INC., pg. 390
FISCHER LIME & CEMENT COMPANY, pg. 414
HAWAIIAN BITUMULS & PAVING COMPANY—Dillingham Construction Corporation, pg. 338
E.P. HENRY CORPORATION, pg. 530
IMPERIA BROS., INC., pg. 563
K.F. JACOBSON CO.—R. B. Pamplin Corp., pg. 845
ORCO BLOCK COMPANY, pg. 828
POLYPLASTIC PRODUCTS—Brooks Products, Inc., pg. 180
ROSS ISLAND SAND & GRAVEL CO., INC.—R. B. Pamplin Corp., pg. 845
TERRE HILL CONCRETE PRODUCTS, INC., pg. 1089
TRI-STATE CONCRETE PRODUCTS CO., INC.—Bristol Steel & Iron Works, Inc., pg. 177
YORK BUILDING PRODUCTS CO., INC., pg. 1208

3272 — CONCRETE PRODUCTS, EXCEPT BLOCK & BRICK

ARNOLD CONCRETE PRODUCTS-GREENSBORO—Carolina Steel Corporation, pg. 223
ARNOLD CONCRETE PRODUCTS-RALEIGH DIV.—Carolina Steel Corporation, pg. 223
ATLANTA MFG. FACILITY—L. M. Scofield Company, pg. 982
ATLANTA STRUCTURAL CONCRETE DIV.—Bristol Steel & Iron Works, Inc., pg. 177
ATLANTIC CONCRETE PRODUCTS, INC., pg. 94
BASALT PRECAST DIVISION—Dillingham Construction Corporation, pg. 338
BROOKS PRODUCTS, ARLINGTON—Brooks Products, Inc., pg. 180
BROOKS PRODUCTS, INC., pg. 180
BROOKS PRODUCTS, ORLANDO—Brooks Products, Inc., pg. 180
CADILLAC PIPE—Premarc Corporation, pg. 886
CAROLINA STEEL CORPORATION, pg. 223
CHOCTAW, INC., pg. 248
THE CLEVELAND BUILDERS SUPPLY CO.—Standard Lafarge, pg. 1036
COLONIAL SAND & STONE CO.—Shepaug Corporation, pg. 998
CONCRETE PIPE & PRODUCTS CO. INC., pg. 273
CONCRETE PIPE & PRODUCTS CO., INC. OF CALIFORNIA—Concrete Pipe & Products Co. Inc., pg. 273
CONCRETE TECHNOLOGY CORP., pg. 273
THE CRETEX COMPANIES, pg. 299
DEMCO INC., pg. 328
DILLINGHAM CONSTRUCTION N.A., INC.—Dillingham Construction Corporation, pg. 338
DONLEY'S, INC., pg. 345
THE FAIRFIELD LUMBER & SUPPLY COMPANY, pg. 397
FIBREBOND CORPORATION, pg. 408
FRITZ CHEMICAL COMPANY, pg. 434
HEMPT BROTHERS, INC., pg. 528
HIGH INDUSTRIES INC., pg. 533
K.F. JACOBSON CO.—R. B. Pamplin Corp., pg. 845
LAMAR CORP.—Premarc Corporation, pg. 886
LINEAR DYNAMICS INC., pg. 676
MARSH PRODUCTS CO.—Premarc Corporation, pg. 886
MARTIN INDUSTRIES (AL), pg. 715
MILES SAND & GRAVEL COMPANY, pg. 753
MODERN CONCRETE SEPTIC TANK COMPANY, pg. 762
MONIER ROOF TILE, INC., pg. 765
NATIONAL CONCRETE PRODUCTS COMPANY, pg. 787
PHELPS TOINTON INC., pg. 866
POLYPLASTIC PRODUCTS—Brooks Products, Inc., pg. 180
PRECISION PIPE & SUPPLY CO.—Premarc Corporation, pg. 886
PREMARC CORPORATION, pg. 886
PRICE BROTHERS CO., pg. 888
RITCHIE CORPORATION, pg. 936
ROSS ISLAND SAND & GRAVEL CO., INC.—R. B. Pamplin Corp., pg. 845
L. M. SCOFIELD COMPANY, pg. 982
SIMPSON DURA-VENT CO., INC., pg. 1007
TARCO, pg. 1078
TECON PACIFIC, pg. 1084
A. TEICHERT & SON, INC., pg. 1084
TERRE HILL CONCRETE PRODUCTS, INC., pg. 1089
WEHRUNG FAMILY HOME CENTER—Modern Concrete Septic Tank Company, pg. 762

3273 — READY-MIXED CONCRETE

BACCO CONSTRUCTION CO., pg. 108
A. BARLETTA & SONS, pg. 120
BERKS PRODUCTS CORPORATION, pg. 142
BRECKENRIDGE MATERIAL COMPANY, pg. 173
CANTON AGGREGATE DIVISION—Central Allied Enterprises, pg. 232
CENTRAL ALLIED ENTERPRISES, pg. 232
CENTURY CONCRETE, INC.—Ash Grove Cement Company, pg. 88
CHAMPION, INC., pg. 238
COMMERCIAL PRODUCTS, INC.—The Dickerson Group, Inc., pg. 336
CONTRACTORS SUPPLIES, INC., pg. 280
DILLINGHAM CONSTRUCTION N.A., INC.—Dillingham Construction Corporation, pg. 338
FORDYCE CONCRETE CO., INC.—Ash Grove Cement Company, pg. 88
FOUNTAIN SAND & GRAVEL CO.—CF&I Steel Corporation, pg. 201
HARDAWAY CONCRETE CO., INC., pg. 507
HAWAIIAN BITUMULS & PAVING COMPANY—Dillingham Construction Corporation, pg. 338
HECK ENTERPRISES, INC., pg. 524
K.F. JACOBSON CO.—R. B. Pamplin Corp., pg. 845
LEGRAND JOHNSON CONSTRUCTION CO., pg. 598
P.J. KEATING COMPANY, pg. 619
EDWARD C. LEVY CO., INC., pg. 672
MCNEILUS COMPANIES, pg. 732
H.B. MELLOTT ESTATE, INC., pg. 738
MEYER MATERIAL COMPANY—The Marmon Group, Inc., pg. 711
PRE-MIX CONCRETE CO.—H.G. Fenton Material Company, pg. 406
ROCK HILL MATERIALS COMPANY, pg. 941
ROGERS GROUP INC., pg. 943
ROSS ISLAND SAND & GRAVEL CO., INC.—R. B. Pamplin Corp., pg. 845
SAKRETE, INC., pg. 967
THOMPSON-MCCULLY CO., pg. 1094

3274 — LIME

ASH GROVE CEMENT—Ash Grove Cement Company, pg. 87
ASH GROVE CEMENT CO., DURKEE PLANT—Ash Grove Cement Company, pg. 87
ASH GROVE CEMENT COMPANY, pg. 87
CARBIDE PRODUCTS—The Carbide/Graphite Group, Inc., pg. 217
EDWARD C. LEVY CO., INC., pg. 672
MISSISSIPPI LIME CO., pg. 760
RIVERGATE PLANT—Ash Grove Cement Company, pg. 88

3275 — GYPSUM PRODUCTS

THE COE MFG. CO., pg. 258
GOLD BOND BUILDING PRODUCTS—National Gypsum Company, pg. 790
GOLD BOND GYPSUM PRODUCTS—National Gypsum Company, pg. 790
INDUSTRIAL ACOUSTICS COMPANY, INC., pg. 565
NATIONAL GYPSUM COMPANY, pg. 790

3281 — CUT STONE & STONE PRODUCTS

GEORGIA STONE INDUSTRIES, INC.—New England Stone Industries, Inc., pg. 800
MATTHEWS INTERNATIONAL CORP., pg. 721
MONROC, INC., pg. 766
NEW ENGLAND STONE INDUSTRIES, INC., pg. 800
PAVING STONE DIV.—E.P. Henry Corporation, pg. 530
PECKHAM INDUSTRIES, INC., pg. 854
RYNONE MANUFACTURING CORPORATION, pg. 958
SELLERSBURG STONE COMPANY, INC.—Gohmann Asphalt & Construction Inc., pg. 465
TARCO, pg. 1078
YORK BUILDING PRODUCTS CO., INC., pg. 1208

3291 — ABRASIVE PRODUCTS

ABRASIVE ENGINEERING & MANUFACTURING DIV.—Acrometal Companies, Inc., pg. 14
CHEROKEE BRICK & TILE CO., pg. 243
CURTIS-TOLEDO, INC., pg. 306
ERVIN AMASTEEL DIV.—Ervin Industries, Inc., pg. 387
ERVIN INDUSTRIES, INC., pg. 387
FOLEY-BELSAW COMPANY, pg. 422

GOULD PACKAGING, INC., pg. 473
H.P.H. INDUSTRIES LTD., pg. 497
INTERNATIONAL STEEL WOOL CORPORATION—F.H. Bonn Company, pg. 164
METABO CORPORATION, pg. 741
NIC SAND—Blue Coral, Inc., pg. 159
ANTON SMIT & CO., INC., pg. 1011
UNIVERSAL PHOTONICS, INC., pg. 1139

3292 — ASBESTOS PRODUCTS

THE CLEVELAND BUILDERS SUPPLY CO.—Standard Lafarge, pg. 1036

3295 — MINERALS & EARTHS, GROUND OR OTHERWISE TREATED

AMOL DICALITE LTD.—Belmont Industries, Inc., pg. 137
APPLIED INDUSTRIAL MATERIALS CORPORATION, pg. 79
ASBURY GRAPHITE MILLS, INC.—Asbury Carbons, Inc., pg. 87
BELMONT INDUSTRIES, INC., pg. 136
BURGESS PIGMENT CO., pg. 190
CHEMROCK CORPORATION—Belmont Industries, Inc., pg. 136
CHEMROCK CORPORATION—Belmont Industries, Inc., pg. 137
CHEMROCK CORPORATION—Belmont Industries, Inc., pg. 137
CHEMROCK CORPORATION—Belmont Industries, Inc., pg. 137
CHEMROCK CORPORATION—Belmont Industries, Inc., pg. 137
DICALITE CORPORATION—Belmont Industries, Inc., pg. 136
DICALITE EUROPE NORD, S.A.—Belmont Industries, Inc., pg. 137
DICALITE ORIENT CO. LTD.—Belmont Industries, Inc., pg. 137
DICASER S.A. DE C.V.—Belmont Industries, Inc., pg. 137
GAF CORPORATION, pg. 438
GOLDEN CAT CORPORATION—Knightbridge Partners, pg. 637
GREAT LAKES CARBON CORP.—Horsehead Industries, Inc., pg. 545
GREFCO, INC.—Belmont Industries, Inc., pg. 136
GREFCO, INC.—Belmont Industries, Inc., pg. 137
GREFCO, INC.—Belmont Industries, Inc., pg. 137
GREFCO, INC.—Belmont Industries, Inc., pg. 137
GREFCO, INC.—Belmont Industries, Inc., pg. 137
GLENN O. HAWBAKER, INC., pg. 517
HEMPT BROTHERS, INC., pg. 528
HILL & GRIFFITH COMPANY, pg. 534
J.M. HUBER CORPORATION, pg. 550
INDUPLEX, INC.—Belmont Industries, Inc., pg. 137
INTERNATIONAL SPECIALTY PRODUCTS, INC.—GAF Corporation, pg. 438
STANDARD LAFARGE, pg. 1036
SUPERIOR GRAPHITE COMPANY, pg. 1063
THERMAL AMERICAN FUSED QUARTZ CO., pg. 1091
WHIBCO, INC., pg. 1185

3296 — MINERAL WOOL

BALDT, INC., pg. 115
E.J. BARTELLS CO., pg. 122
GALLAGHER-KAISER CORP., pg. 441
INDUSTRIAL ACOUSTICS COMPANY, INC., pg. 565
INDUSTRIAL ACOUSTICS COMPANY, LTD.—Industrial Acoustics Company, Inc., pg. 566
PACOR, INC., pg. 842
TRANSCO INC., pg. 1106

3297 — NONCLAY REFRACTORIES

ALLIED MINERAL PRODUCTS, INC., pg. 38
E.J. BARTELLS CO., pg. 122
BELMONT INDUSTRIES, U.S. REFRACTORIES DIV.—Belmont Industries, Inc., pg. 136
BELMONT INDUSTRIES, U.S. REFRACTORIES DIV.—Belmont Industries, Inc., pg. 136
BELMONT INDUSTRIES, U.S. REFRACTORIES DIV.—Belmont Industries, Inc., pg. 136
BELMONT INDUSTRIES, U.S. REFRACTORIES DIV.—Belmont Industries, Inc., pg. 136
BELMONT INDUSTRIES, U.S. REFRACTORIES DIV.—Belmont Industries, Inc., pg. 136
BELMONT INDUSTRIES, U.S. REFRACTORIES DIV.—Belmont Industries, Inc., pg. 136
BELMONT INDUSTRIES, U.S. REFRACTORIES DIV.—Belmont Industries, Inc., pg. 137
CHEROKEE BRICK & TILE CO., pg. 243
CHISHOLM, BOYD & WHITE CO.—Venturedyne, Ltd., pg. 1148
GENERAL REFRACTORIES CO., U. S. REFRACTORIES DIV.—Belmont Industries, Inc., pg. 136
MAGNECO/METREL, INC., pg. 700
NORTH AMERICAN REFRACTORIES COMPANY, pg. 811
PACIFIC HOLDING CORPORATION, pg. 840
PLIBRICO CO., pg. 877
PREMIER REFRACTORIES (CANADA) LTD.—Premier Refractories & Chemicals Inc., pg. 887
PREMIER REFRACTORIES & CHEMICALS INC., pg. 887
RADEX DEUTSCHLAND, A.G.—Belmont Industries, Inc., pg. 137
RESCO PRODUCTS, INC., pg. 928

3299 — NONMETALLIC MINERAL PRODUCTS, NEC

AMERICAN FOUNDRY GROUP, INC., pg. 54
AUSTIN SCULPTURE, pg. 99
CHEROKEE BRICK & TILE CO., pg. 243
DILLINGHAM CONSTRUCTION N.A., INC.—Dillingham Construction Corporation, pg. 338
EXPO INDUSTRIES, INC., pg. 393
KIRKWOOD INDUSTRIES, INC., pg. 633
MAGNECO/METREL, INC., pg. 700
RESCO PRODUCTS, INC., pg. 928

3312 — STEEL WORKS, BLAST FURNACES, INCLUDING COKE OVENS & ROLLING MILLS

AM GENERAL CORPORATION—Renco Group, pg. 926
AM GENERAL CORPORATION—Renco Group, pg. 926
ABBOTT BALL COMPANY, pg. 9
AMERICAN STEEL CORP.—National Steel Corporation, pg. 794
AMERICAN STEEL & WIRE CORPORATION—Chicago West Pullman Corporation, pg. 246
ARTCO-BELL STEEL CORP.—Artco-Bell Corporation, pg. 86
ATLANTIC STEEL COMPANY, pg. 95
THE BABCOCK & WILCOX COMPANY, pg. 107
BERGMAN MANUFACTURING—Datron Incorporated, pg. 316
THE BRENLIN GROUP, pg. 173
CF&I STEEL CORPORATION, pg. 201
CAPITOL METALS PROCESSING, INC., pg. 216
CARGILL INC., pg. 219
CASCADE STEEL ROLLING MILLS, INC.—Schnitzer Steel Industries, Inc., pg. 977
CAWSL CORPORATION, pg. 229
CENTURY FENCE COMPANY, pg. 235
CHICAGO HEIGHTS STEEL, pg. 245
CHICAGO WEST PULLMAN TRANSPORTATION CORPORATION—Chicago West Pullman Corporation, pg. 246
COGIFER INC., pg. 259
CONTRAN CORPORATION, pg. 281
COPPERWELD STEEL COMPANY, pg. 284
CRUCIBLE MATERIALS CORP., pg. 302
DRUMMOND COMPANY, INC., pg. 349
DUBIN-CLARK & COMPANY, pg. 350
EDGEWATER CORPORATION, pg. 368
EDGEWATER STEEL CO.—Edgewater Corporation, pg. 368
FERROUS PROCESSING & TRADING CO., pg. 407
A. FINKL & SONS CO., pg. 411
FORMEX, INC. - PERMANENT STEEL FORMS—W. B. Goode Company, Inc., pg. 470
FREEDOM FORGE CORPORATION, pg. 430
FROG SWITCH & MANUFACTURING COMPANY, pg. 434
GARY METALS CO., INC.—Primary Industries Corporation, pg. 889
GEORGETOWN INDUSTRIES, INC., pg. 453
GOLDMAN FINANCIAL GROUP, pg. 468
HURON VALLEY STEEL CORP., pg. 555
IDEAL POOL CORP., pg. 562
KEENEY MANUFACTURING CO., pg. 620
KOCH REFINING COMPANY—Koch Industries, Incorporated, pg. 639
MCLOUTH STEEL, pg. 731
MCWANE, INC., pg. 733
NATIONAL FORGE COMPANY, pg. 788
NATIONAL STEEL CORPORATION, pg. 793
NATIONAL STEEL, GRANITE CITY DIV.—National Steel Corporation, pg. 794
NATIONAL STEEL GREAT LAKES DIV.—National Steel Corporation, pg. 794
NAYLOR PIPE COMPANY, pg. 796
NORTH STAR STEEL CO.—Cargill Inc., pg. 219
NORTH STAR STEEL KENTUCKY, INC.—Cargill Inc., pg. 219
NORTH STAR STEEL TEXAS, INC.—Cargill Inc., pg. 219
NORTHWESTERN STEEL & WIRE CO., pg. 815
PHELPS TOINTON INC., pg. 866
PRECISION SPECIALTY METALS, INC.—Dubin-Clark & Company, pg. 350
PRIMARY STEEL INC.—Primary Industries Corporation, pg. 889
RENCO GROUP, pg. 926
ROCKET INDUSTRIES, INC./EXCEL, THE EXERCISE COMPANY, pg. 941
ROTTERDAM VENTURES INC., pg. 951
SCHNITZER STEEL INDUSTRIES, INC., pg. 977
SCHULTZ STEEL COMPANY, pg. 979
SCRAP CORPORATION OF AMERICA—Tang Industries Inc., pg. 1078
SHEFFIELD STEEL CORPORATION-JOLIET, pg. 996
SOUTHERN STEEL COMPANY—Phelps Tointon Inc., pg. 866
STANDARD STEEL—Freedom Forge Corporation, pg. 431
THOMAS STEEL STRIP CORP., pg. 1094
TRU-WELD GRATING, INC., pg. 1117
UNION STEEL PRODUCTS, INCORPORATED, pg. 1129
VALEX CORP.—Reliance Steel & Aluminum Co., pg. 925
THE VOLLRATH COMPANY INC., pg. 1154
WEBB FORGING—Jervis B. Webb Company, pg. 1170
XTEK CANADA, LTD.—Xtek, Inc., pg. 1206

3313 — ELECTROMETALLURGICAL PRODUCTS, EXCEPT STEEL

THE ALUMINUM POWDER COMPANY—Metallurg, Inc., pg. 742
APPLIED INDUSTRIAL MATERIALS CORPORATION, pg. 79
BRANDAU Y COMPANIA S.A.—Metallurg, Inc., pg. 742
ELEKTROWERK WEISWEILER GMBH—Metallurg, Inc., pg. 742
AB FERROLEGERINGAR—Metallurg, Inc., pg. 742
FERROUS PROCESSING & TRADING CO., pg. 407
LONDON & SCANDINAVIAN METALLURGICAL CO. LIMITED—Metallurg, Inc., pg. 742
MARKIN TUBING, INC., pg. 709
METALCHIMICA SRL—Metallurg, Inc., pg. 742
METALLURG (CANADA) LIMITED—Metallurg, Inc., pg. 742
METALLURG DO BRAZIL LTDA.—Metallurg, Inc., pg. 742
METALLURG (FAR EAST) LIMITED—Metallurg, Inc., pg. 742
METALLURG, INC., pg. 742
METALLURG MEXICO, S.A. DE CV—Metallurg, Inc., pg. 742
REACTIVE METALS & ALLOYS CORPORATION (REMACOR), pg. 916

3315 — STEEL WIREDRAWING & STEEL NAILS & SPIKES

AMERICAN INSULATED WIRE CORP.—Leviton Mfg. Co., Inc., pg. 671
AMSTED INDUSTRIES INCORPORATED, pg. 68
ARROW FASTENER CO., INC., pg. 85
ASSOCIATED MATERIALS INC., pg. 91
CF&I STEEL CORPORATION, pg. 201
CENTURY FENCE COMPANY, pg. 235
CHICAGO STEEL & WIRE—MCM Enterprises, Inc., pg. 691
CLEANERS HANGER CO., pg. 254
DUO-FAST CORPORATION, pg. 354
E.C.D., INC., pg. 359
E.C.D. INC.—E.C.D., Inc., pg. 359
ELECTRO-WIRE PRODUCTS, INC., pg. 375
GEORGETOWN INDUSTRIES, INC., pg. 453
GERRARD AND COMPANY, pg. 454
HOBART BROTHERS OF CANADA LTD.—Hobart Brothers Co., pg. 536
INDEPENDENT NAIL COMPANY—Maze Nails, pg. 725
INDUSTRIAL WIRE PRODUCTS CORPORATION, pg. 567
LESCHEN WIRE ROPE—Wire Rope Corp. of America, Inc., pg. 1197
LOOS & CO., INC., pg. 683
MACWHYTE CO.—Amsted Industries Incorporated, pg. 69
MAZE NAILS, pg. 725
MID-STATE WIRE COMPANY—MCM Enterprises, Inc., pg. 691
NASHVILLE WIRE PRODUCT CO., pg. 784
NELSEN STEEL & WIRE CO., pg. 797
NORTH STAR STEEL TEXAS, INC.—Cargill Inc., pg. 219
NORTHWESTERN STEEL & WIRE CO., pg. 815
PRICE BROTHERS CO., pg. 888
RADIX WIRE COMPANY, pg. 909
REEVES SOUTHEASTERN CORPORATION, pg. 921
ROOT CORPORATION, pg. 946
SENCORP, pg. 989
THOMAS STEEL STRIP CORP., pg. 1094
THE TURNER & SEYMOUR MFG. COMPANY, pg. 1119
ULBRICH STAINLESS STEELS & SPECIAL METALS, INC., pg. 1125
ULBRICH WIRE, INC.—Ulbrich Stainless Steels & Special Metals, Inc., pg. 1125
UNION DRAWN STEEL CO., LTD.—Nelsen Steel & Wire Co., pg. 797
VICTOR CORPORATION, pg. 1149
WALKER WIRE & STEEL COMPANY, pg. 1160
WILSON STEEL & WIRE—MCM Enterprises, Inc., pg. 691
WIRE ROPE CORP. OF AMERICA, INC., pg. 1197
WIRE TECH, INC.—Group Dekko International Inc., pg. 490

3316 — COLD ROLLED STEEL SHEET, STRIP & BARS

THE AARQUE COMPANIES, pg. 9
CHICAGO WEST PULLMAN TRANSPORTATION CORPORATION—Chicago West Pullman Corporation, pg. 246
SIGMUND COHN CORP., pg. 259
CONSOLIDATED METAL PRODUCTS, INC., pg. 276
COPPERWELD STEEL COMPANY, pg. 284
ESCO CORPORATION, pg. 388
FREEDLAND INDUSTRIES CORPORATION, pg. 430
GERRARD AND COMPANY, pg. 454
GIBRALTAR STEEL CORP., pg. 456
GREER STEEL CO., pg. 486
HYNES INDUSTRIES INC., pg. 557
MCLOUTH STEEL, pg. 731
MOLTRUP STEEL PRODUCTS COMPANY, pg. 764
NATIONAL STEEL CORPORATION, pg. 793
NELSEN STEEL & WIRE CO., pg. 797
ORBEL CORPORATION, pg. 828
PEGASUS INTERNATIONAL CORPORATION, pg. 855
RENCO GROUP, pg. 926
REPUBLIC ENGINEERED STEELS, INC., pg. 928
ROLLED STEEL PRODUCTS CORPORATION, pg. 944
ROME STRIP STEEL CO., INC., pg. 946
THOMAS STEEL STRIP CORP., pg. 1094
THOMPSON STEEL CO., INC., pg. 1094
ULBRICH STAINLESS STEELS & SPECIAL METALS, INC., pg. 1125
UNION DRAWN STEEL CO., LTD.—Nelsen Steel & Wire Co., pg. 797

3317 — STEEL PIPE & TUBES

AMERICAN CAST IRON PIPE CO., pg. 50
AVIS INDUSTRIAL CORPORATION, pg. 102
BROWN-STRAUSS STEEL, INC.—Blue Tee Corporation, pg. 161
BURT EQUIPMENT COMPANY, INC., pg. 195
CF&I STEEL CORPORATION, pg. 201
CARGILL INC., pg. 219

CAWSL CORPORATION, pg. 229
CENTRAL ILLINOIS STEEL COMPANY, pg. 232
CONSOLIDATED PIPE & SUPPLY COMPANY, pg. 277
DUBIN-CLARK & COMPANY, pg. 350
FERRO UNION, INC., pg. 407
JAMES STEEL & TUBE COMPANY—Avis Industrial Corporation, pg. 102
MARKIN TUBING, INC., pg. 709
MCWANE CAST IRON PIPE CO.—McWane, Inc., pg. 733
MID-WEST COMPANY—J. H. Roberts Industries Inc., pg. 939
MORRIS COUPLING CO., pg. 771
MOULTON CUTTING CO.—J. H. Roberts Industries Inc., pg. 939
NAYLOR PIPE COMPANY, pg. 796
PEGASUS INTERNATIONAL CORPORATION, pg. 855
PITTSBURGH TUBE CO., pg. 873
PLYMOUTH TUBE COMPANY, pg. 877
RATH MANUFACTURING—Dubin-Clark & Company, pg. 350
SAMSTEEL, INC.—Ferro Union, Inc., pg. 407
SHAPCO, INC., pg. 995
SHARON TUBE COMPANY, pg. 995
SUPERIOR TUBE COMPANY, pg. 1064
TUBETEC—Plymouth Tube Company, pg. 878
UNIVERSAL STEEL TUBE CO. LIMITED—Plymouth Tube Company, pg. 878
WHEATLAND TUBE COMPANY, pg. 1184

3321 — GRAY & DUCTILE IRON FOUNDRIES

ACME FOUNDRY, INC., pg. 13
AMERICAN CAST IRON PIPE CO., pg. 50
AMSTED INDUSTRIES INCORPORATED, pg. 68
BENNINGTON IRON WORKS, INC., pg. 139
BLAW KNOX CORP., pg. 156
JOHN BOUCHARD & SONS COMPANY, pg. 168
BRITT INDUSTRIES, INC.—Kurdziel Industries, Inc., pg. 646
BRITTANY CORPORATION, pg. 177
CMI INTERNATIONAL INC., pg. 202
CENTRE FOUNDRY & MACHINE CO.—The Dyson-Kissner-Moran Corporation, pg. 357
CLOW CORPORATION—McWane, Inc., pg. 733
CLOW WATER SYSTEMS CORP.—McWane, Inc., pg. 733
CLOW WATER SYSTEMS CORP.—McWane, Inc., pg. 733
COGIFER INC., pg. 259
DENVER THOMAS, INC.—Denver Equipment Company, pg. 331
DEXTER COMPANY, pg. 334
DIXON VALVE & COUPLING COMPANY, pg. 341
DOCK FOUNDRY COMPANY, pg. 342
EAST JORDAN IRON WORKS, pg. 362
THE ELECTRON CORP., pg. 375
ELYRIA FOUNDRY COMPANY, pg. 378
GEORGIA IRON WORKS CO., pg. 453
GOUGLER INDUSTRIES, INC., pg. 473
GREDE FOUNDRIES, INC., pg. 483
GREGG INDUSTRIES, INC., pg. 486
GRIFFIN PIPE PRODUCTS CO.—Amsted Industries Incorporated, pg. 69
HELMICK CORPORATION, pg. 527
RODNEY HUNT COMPANY, pg. 553
JOHNSTOWN CORPORATION, pg. 601
KIMRAY, INC., pg. 629
KOHLER COMPANY, pg. 639
KURDZIEL INDUSTRIES, INC., pg. 646
KURDZIEL IRON OF ROTHBURY—Kurdziel Industries, Inc., pg. 646
KURDZIEL IRON OF WAUSEON—Kurdziel Industries, Inc., pg. 646
MAGIC CIRCLE MANUFACTURING DIV.—Acme Foundry, Inc., pg. 13
MARMON CORPORATION—The Marmon Group, Inc., pg. 711
MCWANE, INC., pg. 733
MOLINE CORPORATION, pg. 764
NEENAH FOUNDRY COMPANY, pg. 797
NORTH AMERICAN ROYALTIES, INC., pg. 811
OMCO MOULD, INC., pg. 819
OMCO CAST METALS, INC.—OMCO Mould, Inc., pg. 819
OSCO INDUSTRIES INC., pg. 830
PROSPECT FOUNDRY, INC., pg. 895
SWAYNE ROBINSON & COMPANY, pg. 939
SPECIALTY CASTINGS—The Johnson Corporation, pg. 598
STURGIS FOUNDRY CORP.—Armstrong International, Inc., pg. 83
THE TURNER & SEYMOUR MFG. COMPANY, pg. 1119
U.S. CASTINGS DIV.—Walter Industries, Inc., pg. 1162
UNITED STATES PIPE & FOUNDRY COMPANY—Walter Industries, Inc., pg. 1162
WALTER INDUSTRIES, INC., pg. 1161
WARD MANUFACTURING, INC., pg. 1163
WATEROUS COMPANY—American Cast Iron Pipe Co., pg. 50
THE WHELAND FOUNDRY DIV.—North American Royalties, Inc., pg. 812
T.B. WOOD'S SONS COMPANY, pg. 1200

3322 — MALLEABLE IRON FOUNDRIES

CMI INTERNATIONAL INC., pg. 202
DENVER THOMAS, INC.—Denver Equipment Company, pg. 331
DIXON VALVE & COUPLING COMPANY, pg. 341
GAS EQUIPMENT COMPANY, INC., pg. 444
LANCASTER MALLEABLE CASTINGS COMPANY, pg. 653
MCWANE, INC., pg. 733
VICTAULIC COMPANY OF AMERICA, pg. 1149
VICTAULIC COMPANY OF CANADA LIMITED—Victaulic Company of America, pg. 1149
WARD MANUFACTURING, INC., pg. 1163
WEBSTER INDUSTRIES INC., pg. 1171

3324 — STEEL INVESTMENT FOUNDRIES

AMERICAN FOUNDRY GROUP, INC., pg. 54
BLAW KNOX CORP., pg. 156
CMI INTERNATIONAL INC., pg. 202

3325 — STEEL FOUNDRIES, NEC

ALCO/BELGIUM FOUNDRIES—Heico Inc., pg. 525
AMERICAN CAST IRON PIPE CO., pg. 50
AMERICAN FOUNDRY GROUP, INC., pg. 54
AMERICAN STEEL FOUNDRIES—Amsted Industries Incorporated, pg. 69
AMSTED INDUSTRIES INCORPORATED, pg. 68
ATLAS FOUNDRY & MACHINE CO.—TIC United Corporation, pg. 1073
BLAW KNOX CORP., pg. 156
BLAW KNOX - DURALOY DIVISION—Blaw Knox Corp., pg. 156
BLAW KNOX ROLLS DIVISION—Blaw Knox Corp., pg. 156
BRODERICK COMPANY, INC.—Goldman Financial Group, pg. 468
CMI INTERNATIONAL INC., pg. 202
DENVER THOMAS, INC.—Denver Equipment Company, pg. 331
ERIE BRONZE & ALUMINUM CO.—McInnes Steel Company, pg. 730
ESCO LTD.—Esco Corporation, pg. 388
FROG SWITCH & MANUFACTURING COMPANY, pg. 434
GREDE FOUNDRIES, INC., pg. 483
GRIFFIN CANADA INC.—Amsted Industries Incorporated, pg. 69
GRIFFIN WHEEL CO.—Amsted Industries Incorporated, pg. 69
BARRETT HAENTJENS & COMPANY, pg. 499
HILL-LOMA, INC.—Goldman Financial Group, pg. 468
HUTCHENS INDUSTRIES INC., pg. 555
JOHNSTOWN CORPORATION, pg. 601
KERVICK ENTERPRISES, INC., pg. 624
MARMON CORPORATION—The Marmon Group, Inc., pg. 711
MAYNARD STEEL CASTING COMPANY, pg. 725
MCGRAW/KOKOSING, INC.—Kokosing Construction Company, Inc., pg. 641
MONEY POINT DIAMOND CO., pg. 765
OLSONITE CORPORATION, pg. 824
OVERSEAS PARTNERS, INC., pg. 833
PACIFIC STEEL CASTING CO., pg. 841
RIVERSIDE PRODUCTS DIV.—Everett Smith Investment Co. of Delaware, pg. 1013
ROLOCK, INC., pg. 944
SHAW-PERKINS INC.—Reactive Metals & Alloys Corporation (REMACOR), pg. 916
SIVYER STEEL CORPORATION—Everett Smith Investment Co. of Delaware, pg. 1013
THOMAS STEEL STRIP CORP., pg. 1094
UNITED STATES PIPE & FOUNDRY COMPANY—Walter Industries, Inc., pg. 1162
WAUKESHA FOUNDRY INC., pg. 1168

3331 — PRIMARY SMELTING & REFINING OF COPPER

CERRO COPPER PRODUCTS CO.—The Marmon Group, Inc., pg. 711
S-G METALS INDUSTRIES, INC., pg. 962

3334 — PRIMARY PRODUCTION OF ALUMINUM

ADEC AUTOMATION—Adec International Automation Corp., pg. 17
COLUMBIA FALLS ALUMINUM COMPANY, pg. 265
CROFT METAL INC., pg. 300
HUNTER ENGINEERING CO., INC., pg. 554
LINN PRODUCTS, INC., pg. 677
ORMET CORPORATION—Ohio River Associates, Inc., pg. 822
QUADION CORPORATION, pg. 902
RAVENSWOOD ALUMINUM CORP., pg. 914
S-G METALS INDUSTRIES, INC., pg. 962
U.S. REDUCTION COMPANY, pg. 1137

3339 — PRIMARY SMELTING & REFINING OF NONFERROUS METALS, EXCEPT COPPER & ALUMINUM

CRUCIBLE MATERIALS CORP., pg. 302
T.L. DIAMOND COMPANY, pg. 335
HUNTER ENGINEERING CO., INC., pg. 554
LEACH & GARNER COMPANY, pg. 663
MCGEAN-ROHCO, INC., pg. 729
THE J. M. NEY COMPANY, pg. 805
LOUIS PADNOS IRON & METAL CO., pg. 842
PYROMET, INC., pg. 901
REACTIVE METALS & ALLOYS CORPORATION (REMACOR), pg. 916
S-G METALS INDUSTRIES, INC., pg. 962
TITANIUM METALS CORPORATION—Tremont Corporation, pg. 1109
TREMONT CORPORATION, pg. 1109

3341 — SECONDARY SMELTING & REFINING OF NONFERROUS METALS

JOSEPH BEHR & SONS INC., pg. 132
BELMONT METALS, INC., pg. 137
COLLINS & AIKMAN GROUP INC., pg. 262
COLONIAL METALS CO., pg. 263
CONNELL LIMITED PARTNERSHIP, pg. 275
DELAWARE NORTH COMPANIES, INC., pg. 326
ELIXIR INDUSTRIES, pg. 376
GLINES & RHODES, INC., pg. 463
GULF COAST LEAD COMPANY, INC., pg. 493
HURON VALLEY STEEL CORP., pg. 555
LEACH & GARNER COMPANY, pg. 663
NORTHLAND ALUMINUM PRODUCTS, INC., pg. 814
RECLAIMERS, INC.—Group Dekko International Inc., pg. 490
ROESSING BRONZE CO., pg. 943
SPANG & COMPANY, pg. 1025
SPANG SPECIALTY METALS—Spang & Company, pg. 1025
TABER METALS, INC.—Tang Industries Inc., pg. 1078
TECHNIC INCORPORATED, pg. 1083
TOWER METAL PRODUCTS—Tang Industries Inc., pg. 1078
WESTERN EXTRUSIONS, pg. 1179

3351 — ROLLING, DRAWING & EXTRUDING OF COPPER

ALBION WIRE, INC.—Group Dekko International Inc., pg. 489
AMPCO METAL INCORPORATED, pg. 67
ARCOLA WIRE COMPANY, pg. 81
CAWSL CORPORATION, pg. 229
CERRO COPPER PRODUCTS CO.—The Marmon Group, Inc., pg. 711
CERRO WIRE & CABLE CO., INC.—The Marmon Group, Inc., pg. 711
CHICAGO EXTRUDED METALS CO., pg. 245
COLEMAN CABLE SYSTEMS, INC., pg. 260
COLLINS & AIKMAN GROUP INC., pg. 262
DEKKO WIRE DIV., KENDALLVILLE—Group Dekko International Inc., pg. 489
ESSEX GROUP, INC., pg. 389
H & H TUBE & MANUFACTURING CO., pg. 495
HALSTEAD INDUSTRIES, INC., pg. 502
HALSTEAD METAL PRODS. DIV.—Halstead Industries, Inc., pg. 502
INDECO PERUANA S.A.—The Marmon Group, Inc., pg. 712
MARMON CORPORATION—The Marmon Group, Inc., pg. 711
THE MARMON GROUP, INC., pg. 710
READING TUBE CORP., pg. 916
THE ROCKBESTOS COMPANY—The Marmon Group, Inc., pg. 711
ROESSING BRONZE CO., pg. 943
ROLL FORMING CORPORATION, pg. 944
SERVAAS, INC., pg. 991
SMALL TUBE PRODUCTS CO., INC., pg. 1010
TAMAQUA CABLE PRODUCTS CORPORATION, pg. 1077

3353 — ALUMINUM SHEET, PLATE & FOIL

BRADBURY COMPANY, INC., pg. 169
ELIXIR INDUSTRIES, pg. 376
KCL CORPORATION, pg. 611
KOOLVENT ALUMINUM PRODUCTS, INC., pg. 641
ROLL FORMING CORPORATION, pg. 944
SPECTRULITE CONSORTIUM, INC., pg. 1029
UNITED ALUMINUM CORPORATION, pg. 1130

3354 — ALUMINUM EXTRUDED PRODUCTS

ADEC AUTOMATION—Adec International Automation Corp., pg. 17
ALUMINUM SHAPES, INC., pg. 46
BURT EQUIPMENT COMPANY, INC., pg. 195
CARDINAL ALUMINUM CO., pg. 217
COLLINS & AIKMAN GROUP INC., pg. 262
CONSTRUCTION SPECIALTIES OF CALIFORNIA—Construction Specialties, Inc., pg. 277
CROFT METAL INC., pg. 300
GEMINI ALUMINUM CORPORATION, pg. 448
GENERAL SHIP CORPORATION, pg. 450
INTERNATIONAL MARINE HOLDINGS, INC., pg. 579
KEYMARK CORPORATION, pg. 627
LINN PRODUCTS, INC., pg. 677
LOXCREEN COMPANY, pg. 686
MAKI CORPORATION, pg. 702
MAKI HOME CENTER, INC.—Maki Corporation, pg. 702
THE MARMON GROUP, INC., pg. 710
OHIO VALLEY ALUMINUM COMPANY—Interlock Industries, Inc., pg. 575
PENN ALUMINUM INTERNATIONAL—The Marmon Group, Inc., pg. 711
WELLS ALUMINUM CORP., pg. 1175

3355 — ALUMINUM ROLLING & DRAWING, NEC

ARCOLA WIRE COMPANY, pg. 81
COLEMAN CABLE SYSTEMS, INC., pg. 260
ESCO CORPORATION, pg. 388
ESSEX GROUP, INC., pg. 389
GUARANTEED PRODUCTS, INC., pg. 491
HARBOUR GROUP LTD., pg. 506
KB ALLOYS, INC.—Harbour Group Ltd., pg. 507
LPL TECHNOLOGIES, INC., pg. 648
ROLL FORMING CORPORATION, pg. 944
UNIVERSAL MOLDING COMPANY, pg. 1139

3356 — ROLLING, DRAWING & EXTRUDING OF NONFERROUS METALS, EXCEPT COPPER & ALUMINUM

ADEC AUTOMATION—Adec International Automation Corp., pg. 17
AMALLOY, pg. 46
AMERICAN SHEAR KNIVE CO.—Asko, Inc, pg. 88
ATLAS WIRE CORPORATION, pg. 97
E. J. BROOKS COMPANY, pg. 179
DELAWARE NORTH COMPANIES, INC., pg. 326
ESSEX GROUP, INC., pg. 389
FARMER'S COPPER & INDUSTRIAL SUPPLY—Farmers Marine Copper Works, pg. 401
FARMERS MARINE COPPER WORKS, pg. 401
GARDINER METAL COMPANY, pg. 443
GARDINER SOLDER COMPANY—Gardiner Metal Company, pg. 443
HYGRADE METAL MOULDING MFG. CORP., pg. 557
INSILCO CORPORATION, pg. 571
JOHNSON MANUFACTURING CO.—Gardiner Metal Company, pg. 443
LPL TECHNOLOGIES, INC., pg. 648
LEACH & GARNER COMPANY, pg. 663
MILLER COMPANY, pg. 754
PIPE FABRICATING & SUPPLY COMPANY, pg. 872
ROLL FORMING CORPORATION, pg. 944
SCRAP CORPORATION OF AMERICA—Tang Industries Inc., pg. 1078
SPECTRULITE CONSORTIUM, INC., pg. 1029
SUNBEAM-OSTER COMPANY, INC., pg. 1059
TARACORP, INC., pg. 1078
TITANIUM METALS CORPORATION—Tremont Corporation, pg. 1109
TREMONT CORPORATION, pg. 1109
ULBRICH WIRE, INC.—Ulbrich Stainless Steels & Special Metals, Inc., pg. 1125

3357 — DRAWING & INSULATING OF NONFERROUS WIRE

ARCOLA WIRE COMPANY, pg. 81
BIW CABLE SYSTEMS-CONNECTOR SYSTEMS DIV.—BIW Cable Systems, Inc., pg. 107
BIW CABLE SYSTEMS, INC., pg. 106
WHITNEY BLAKE COMPANY OF VERMONT, INC., pg. 155
BOSTON INSULATED WIRE & CABLE CO. LTD.—BIW Cable Systems, Inc., pg. 107
C & M CORPORATION, pg. 198
CABLEWAVE SYSTEMS, INC., pg. 206
COLEMAN CABLE SYSTEMS, INC., pg. 260
COLLINS & AIKMAN GROUP INC., pg. 262
ELECTRO-WIRE PRODUCTS, INC.—Electro-Wire Products, Inc., pg. 375
ESSEX GROUP, INC., pg. 389
FLEX-OHM, INC.—Group Dekko International Inc., pg. 489
W. L. GORE & ASSOCIATES, INC., pg. 472
HARBOUR INDUSTRIES, INC., pg. 507
HOOSIER WIRE, INC.—Group Dekko International Inc., pg. 489
INDIANA INSULATED WIRE—Group Dekko International Inc., pg. 489
INDUSTRIAL ALLOYS, INC.—Industrial Wire Products Corporation, pg. 567
INSILCO CORPORATION, pg. 571
INTERCOLE, INC., pg. 574
KALAS MANUFACTURING, INC., pg. 615
NEHRING ELECTRICAL WORKS COMPANY—Coleman Cable Systems, Inc., pg. 261
THE OKONITE COMPANY, pg. 823
ORBEL CORPORATION, pg. 828
ORTRONICS, INC., pg. 830
PLASTOID CORPORATION, pg. 876
PREFORMADOS DE MEXICO SA—Preformed Line Products, pg. 886
PRESTOLITE WIRE CORPORATION—New Hampshire Oak, pg. 801
RADIX WIRE COMPANY, pg. 909
REA MAGNET WIRE COMPANY, INC., pg. 915
ROME CABLE CORPORATION, pg. 945
ROOT CORPORATION, pg. 946
ROYLE SYSTEMS GROUP, pg. 953
SILICONES, INC.—Group Dekko International Inc., pg. 490
SOUTHWIRE COMPANY, INC., pg. 1024
STORM PRODUCTS COMPANY, INC., pg. 1052
THERMO ELECTRIC (CANADA) LTD.—Thermo Electric Co., Inc., pg. 1091
THERMO ELECTRIC CO., INC., pg. 1091
THERMO ELECTRIC GMBH—Thermo Electric Co., Inc., pg. 1091
THERMO ELECTRIC INTL. B.V.—Thermo Electric Co., Inc., pg. 1091
THERMO ELECTRIC INTL. LTD.—Thermo Electric Co., Inc., pg. 1091
THERMO ELECTRIC S.A.—Thermo Electric Co., Inc., pg. 1091
THERMO ELECTRIC (SOUTHEAST REGION)—Thermo Electric Co., Inc., pg. 1091
THERMON MANUFACTURING COMPANY, pg. 1091
TIMES FIBER COMMUNICATIONS, INC.—LPL Technologies, Inc., pg. 648
TRIBORO ELECTRIC CORP., pg. 1112

3363 — ALUMINUM DIE-CASTINGS

ANDERSON DIE CASTINGS, INC., pg. 72
BLAW KNOX CORP., pg. 156
CMI INTERNATIONAL INC., pg. 202
CHICAGO WHITE METAL CASTING, INC., pg. 246
CONSOLIDATED METCO, INC., pg. 277
CROFT METAL INC., pg. 300
DIE CAST PRODUCTS, INC., pg. 336
DIEMAKERS, INC., pg. 336
DOEHLER-JARVIS—ICM Industries, Inc., pg. 559
ERIE BRONZE & ALUMINUM CO.—McInnes Steel Company, pg. 730
EVANS INDUSTRIES, INC., pg. 390
FABWEL INC., pg. 396
FEDERAL CHICAGO CORPORATION, pg. 404
GIBBS DIECASTING ALUMINUM CORP.—George Koch Sons, Inc., pg. 639
HOLLYWOOD ALLOY CASTING COMPANY, pg. 540
MCINNES STEEL COMPANY, pg. 729
METALLOY CORPORATION, pg. 742
PHB PARKER DIE CASTINGS, pg. 836
PHB PARKER DIE CASTINGS—PHB Parker Die Castings, pg. 836
PACE INDUSTRIES, INC., pg. 838
PECO INC., pg. 854
PEMCO DIE CASTING CORPORATION, pg. 856
REULAND ELECTRIC COMPANY, pg. 930
ST. PAUL METALCRAFT, INC., pg. 967
TCH INDUSTRIES INC., pg. 1072
TWIN CITY DIE CASTINGS CO., pg. 1121
TWIN CITY DIE CASTINGS CO.—Twin City Die Castings Co., pg. 1122
WALKER DIE CASTING, INC., pg. 1160
WAUKESHA FOUNDRY INC., pg. 1168

3364 — NONFERROUS DIE-CASTINGS, EXCEPT ALUMINUM

AMERICAN FOUNDRY GROUP, INC., pg. 54
ANDERSON DIE CASTINGS, INC., pg. 72
CHICAGO WHITE METAL CASTING, INC., pg. 246
DECO PRODUCTS CO., pg. 324
DIE CAST PRODUCTS, INC., pg. 336
DIEMAKERS, INC., pg. 336
DIXON VALVE & COUPLING COMPANY, pg. 341
DOLPHIN, INC.—Karsten Manufacturing Corporation, pg. 617
ECLIPSE, INC., pg. 366
ECLIPSE THERMAL SYSTEMS—Eclipse, Inc., pg. 366
ERIE BRONZE & ALUMINUM CO.—McInnes Steel Company, pg. 730
EVANS INDUSTRIES, INC., pg. 390
FEDERAL CHICAGO CORPORATION, pg. 404
HITCHINER MANUFACTURING COMPANY, INC., pg. 536
KARSTEN MANUFACTURING CORPORATION, pg. 617
LA FRANCE CORPORATION, pg. 649
MCINNES STEEL COMPANY, pg. 729
PHB PARKER DIE CASTINGS, pg. 836
PHB PARKER DIE CASTINGS—PHB Parker Die Castings, pg. 836
PECO INC., pg. 854
THE RENOVATOR'S SUPPLY, INC., pg. 927
SALL-ECLIPSE—Eclipse, Inc., pg. 366
SERVAAS, INC., pg. 991
SERVAAS INVESTMENTS, INC.—Servaas, Inc., pg. 991
SHENANGO FURNACE COMPANY, pg. 997
TCH INDUSTRIES INC., pg. 1072
TWIN CITY DIE CASTINGS CO., pg. 1121
UNITED STATES NAME PLATE—La France Corporation, pg. 649

3365 — ALUMINUM FOUNDRIES

ADEC AUTOMATION—Adec International Automation Corp., pg. 17
ALUMINUM SHAPES, INC., pg. 46
COLLINS & AIKMAN GROUP INC., pg. 262
CONSOLIDATED INDUSTRIES, INC., pg. 276
CONSOLIDATED METCO, INC., pg. 277
CUSTOM CASTING—Esco Corporation, pg. 388
DIXON VALVE & COUPLING COMPANY, pg. 341
FRONTIER FOUNDRIES, INC., pg. 434
FRONTIER FOUNDRIES, INC.—Frontier Foundries, Inc., pg. 434
HITCHINER MANUFACTURING COMPANY, INC., pg. 536
NORTHLAND ALUMINUM PRODUCTS, INC., pg. 814
OBERDORFER INDUSTRIES, INC., pg. 819
REGAL WARE, INC., pg. 921
RELIABLE CASTINGS CORPORATION, pg. 924
SUPREME MACHINE DIV.—Frontier Foundries, Inc., pg. 434
TWIN CITY DIE CASTINGS CO., pg. 1121

3366 — COPPER FOUNDRIES

AMERICAN FOUNDRY GROUP, INC., pg. 54
AMPCO METAL INC., DALLAS DIV.—Ampco Metal Incorporated, pg. 68
AMPCO METAL INCORPORATED, pg. 67
AMPCO METAL LTD.—Ampco Metal Incorporated, pg. 68
AMPCO METAL NEDERLANDS B.V.—Ampco Metal Incorporated, pg. 68
AMPCO METAL NORDISKA AB—Ampco Metal Incorporated, pg. 68
AMPCO METAL S.A.—Ampco Metal Incorporated, pg. 68
IDENTIFICATION SYSTEMS DIV.—Matthews International Corp., pg. 721
MATTHEWS INTERNATIONAL CORP., pg. 721
MATTHEWS INTERNATIONAL MEMORIAL DIVISION—Matthews International Corp., pg. 721
MICHIGAN WHEEL CORPORATION, pg. 747
WAUKESHA FOUNDRY INC., pg. 1168

3369 — NONFERROUS FOUNDRIES, EXCEPT ALUMINUM & COPPER

ACTION MANUFACTURING CO., pg. 15
CUSTOM CASTING—Esco Corporation, pg. 388
DECO PRODUCTS CO., pg. 324
GAS EQUIPMENT COMPANY, INC., pg. 444
HARTZELL CORPORATION, pg. 514
HITCHCOCK INDUSTRIES, INC., pg. 536
HITCHINER MANUFACTURING COMPANY, INC., pg. 536
KARSTEN MANUFACTURING CORPORATION, pg. 617
KERVICK ENTERPRISES, INC., pg. 624
MAXIMET—Karsten Manufacturing Corporation, pg. 617
OMCO CAST METALS, INC.—OMCO Mould, Inc., pg. 819
PEMCO DIE CASTING CORPORATION, pg. 856
ST. PAUL METALCRAFT, INC., pg. 967
TWIN CITY DIE CASTINGS CO., pg. 1121
WALL COLMONOY CORP., pg. 1160

3398 — METAL HEAT TREATING

ALLOY TECHNOLOGY INTERNATIONAL INC., pg. 41
COOPERHEAT, INC., pg. 283
HINDERLITER HEAT TREATING, INC.—Hinderliter Industries, Inc., pg. 535
HINDERLITER INDUSTRIES, INC., pg. 535
KARSTEN MANUFACTURING CORPORATION, pg. 617
KLOCK CO.—Collins & Aikman Group Inc., pg. 263
MAXCOR MANUFACTURING, INC., pg. 722
PMC INDUSTRIES INC., pg. 836
PIPE FABRICATING & SUPPLY COMPANY, pg. 872
SONEE HEAT TREATING—Karsten Manufacturing Corporation, pg. 617
THOMPSON STEEL CO., INC., pg. 1094
WALL COLMONOY CORP., pg. 1160

3399 — PRIMARY METAL PRODUCTS, NEC

ABBOTT BALL COMPANY, pg. 9
ALINABAL, INC., pg. 34
ALLOY TECHNOLOGY INTERNATIONAL INC., pg. 41
BORG-WARNER AUTOMOTIVE-MICHIGAN POWDERED METAL PRODUCTS, INC.—Borg-Warner Corporation, pg. 166
E. J. BROOKS COMPANY, pg. 179
DUO-FAST CORPORATION, pg. 354
ENIDINE INCORPORATED, pg. 382
FRANTZ MANUFACTURING CO., pg. 429
GAF CORPORATION, pg. 438
HADEN, INC., pg. 499
HADEN SCHWEITZER CORPORATION—Haden, Inc., pg. 499
HORSEHEAD INDUSTRIES, INC., pg. 545
ICM INDUSTRIES, INC., pg. 559
INTERNATIONAL SPECIALTY PRODUCTS, INC.—GAF Corporation, pg. 438
KEYSTONE CARBON COMPANY, pg. 628
LPL TECHNOLOGIES, INC., pg. 648
NATIONAL FORGE COMPANY, pg. 788
NATIONAL LAMINATION CO.—Tang Industries Inc., pg. 1078
P/M STRUCTURAL PARTS DIV.—Keystone Carbon Company, pg. 628
PADNOS-SUMMIT—Louis Padnos Iron & Metal Co., pg. 843
TRANSMET CORPORATION, pg. 1107
UNITED STATES BRONZE POWDERS, INC., pg. 1134
WALL COLMONOY CORP., pg. 1160

3411 — METAL CANS

ALLIED FOODS, INC., pg. 38
ALLSTATE CAN CORPORATION, pg. 43
BLITZ USA, pg. 157
DEL MONTE FOODS, pg. 325
F. R. MANUFACTURING CORPORATION, pg. 395
HYDRIL COMPANY—Hydril Company, pg. 556
INDEPENDENT CAN COMPANY, pg. 564
INGRID-SEVKO, INC., pg. 569
JUSTRITE MANUFACTURING COMPANY, pg. 610
KERN INDUSTRIES, pg. 624
MILTON CAN CO., INC., pg. 756
PEARL CONTAINER CO.—S & P Company, pg. 959
S & P COMPANY, pg. 959
SEXTON CAN CO., INC., pg. 993
SILGAN CORPORATION, pg. 1004
TRI VALLEY GROWERS INC., pg. 1111
U.S. CAN COMPANY, pg. 1134
WHITE MOP WRINGER COMPANY, pg. 1186

3412 — METAL SHIPPING BARRELS, DRUMS, KEGS, PAILS

CONTAINER PRODUCTS INC., pg. 278
CONTAINER PRODUCTS INC.—Container Products Inc., pg. 278
CONTAINER PRODUCTS INC.—Container Products Inc., pg. 278
CONTAINER PRODUCTS INC.—Container Products Inc., pg. 278
CONTAINER PRODUCTS INC.—Container Products Inc., pg. 278
F.X. COUGHLIN CO., pg. 289
HOOVER GROUP, INC., pg. 543
HYDRIL COMPANY—Hydril Company, pg. 556
RUSSELL-STANLEY CORPORATION, pg. 957
SEATTLE PACKAGING CORPORATION, pg. 986
WITT COMPANY, pg. 1198

3421 — CUTLERY

ACE OFFICE PRODUCTS, pg. 12
AMERICAN SAFETY RAZOR COMPANY—Jordan Company, pg. 604
ARDELL INDUSTRIES INC.—Jordan Company, pg. 604
THE W.E. BASSETT COMPANY, pg. 125

BUCK KNIVES, INC., pg. 185
CAMILLUS CUTLERY CO., pg. 212
EDUCATIONAL PUBLISHING CORPORATION, pg. 369
GUTMANN CUTLERY, INC.—Hyde Manufacturing Co., pg. 556
HYDE MANUFACTURING CO., pg. 556
IMPERIAL SCHRADE CORP., pg. 564
IMPERIAL SCHRADE CORP.—Imperial Schrade Corp., pg. 564
IMPERIAL STAG LTD.—Imperial Schrade Corp., pg. 564
KLEIN TOOLS INC., pg. 635
LONE STAR FORGE COMPANY—TIC United Corporation, pg. 1073
PARKS PRODUCTS, INC., pg. 850
REVLON, INC.—MacAndrews & Forbes Holdings Inc., pg. 696
STANLEY ROBERTS, INC., pg. 939
STAINLESS INCORPORATED, pg. 1035
THE VERNON COMPANY, pg. 1148
WAHL CLIPPER CORP., pg. 1158
WILSON MACHINE KNIFE CO., INC.—Hyde Manufacturing Co., pg. 556
ZIPPO MANUFACTURING COMPANY, pg. 1220

3423 — HAND & EDGE TOOLS, EXCEPT MACHINE TOOLS & HAND SAWS

AXIA INCORPORATED, pg. 8
AMERICAN TOOL COMPANIES, INC., pg. 64
AMERICAN WELDING & MANUFACTURING CO.—Freedom Forge Corporation, pg. 431
AMES TAPING TOOL SYSTEMS CO.—AXIA Incorporated, pg. 8
AMES TAPING TOOLS CO. OF CANADA LIMITED—AXIA Incorporated, pg. 8
AMPCO METAL INCORPORATED, pg. 67
ARDELL INDUSTRIES INC.—Jordan Company, pg. 604
ARROW FASTENER CO., INC., pg. 85
ASKO, INC, pg. 88
BERGMAN TOOL MFG. CO., INC.—American Tool Companies, Inc., pg. 64
BOLTON-EMERSON MACHINE KNIFE DIV.—Bolton-Emerson, Inc., pg. 163
CHANNELLOCK, INC., pg. 239
COBAR MACHINE & TOOL CO.—Republic Fastener Products Corp., pg. 928
THE CORNWALL & PATTERSON CO.—Pratt-Read Corporation, pg. 884
DANIELS MANUFACTURING CORPORATION, pg. 314
DEXOL INDUSTRIES, INC., pg. 334
THE DISSTON CO., pg. 339
DUBIN-CLARK & COMPANY, pg. 350
DUFF-NORTON—Spreckles Industries, Inc., pg. 1032
DUO-FAST CORPORATION, pg. 354
DUO-FAST CORPORATION—Duo-Fast Corporation, pg. 354
ESSTAR INCORPORATED, pg. 361
EDLUND COMPANY, INC., pg. 368
GENERAL TOOLS MFG., pg. 451
GERRARD AND COMPANY, pg. 454
GREEN GARDE—H.D. Hudson Manufacturing Company, pg. 551
HARBOUR GROUP LTD., pg. 506
HECKETHORN MFG. COMPANY, pg. 524
HERRAMIENTAS KLEIN S.A. DE C.V.—Klein Tools Inc., pg. 635
HIRSH COMPANY—Code, Hennessy & Simmons, pg. 258
HYDE MANUFACTURING CO., pg. 556
KLEIN TOOLS INC., pg. 635
LOOS & CO., INC., pg. 683
MTD PRODUCTS, INC., pg. 694
MARK MACHINE INC., pg. 708
MEADVILLE FORGING CO., pg. 733
MILTON INDUSTRIES, INC., pg. 756
NORMAG CORPORATION—Berwind Corporation, pg. 145
NU-MERICS INC.—Republic Fastener Products Corp., pg. 928
PRATT-READ CORPORATION, pg. 884
PRECISION TWIST DRILL CO., pg. 885
RTW, ROGERS TOOL WORKS, INC., pg. 908
THE RAWLPLUG COMPANY, INC., pg. 914
RED DEVIL INC., pg. 918
REPUBLIC FASTENER PRODUCTS CORP., pg. 928
ROBERTS CONSOLIDATED INDUSTRIES—Dubin-Clark & Company, pg. 350
RUGG MANUFACTURING COMPANY, pg. 955
SK HAND TOOL CORP., pg. 963
S-T INDUSTRIES, INC., pg. 964
TRIUMPH TWIST DRILL CO.—Precision Twist Drill Co., pg. 885
THE UNION FORK & HOE CO., pg. 1128
WEN PRODUCTS, INC., pg. 1156
WARREN TOOL GROUP, pg. 1165
WILTON CORPORATION, pg. 1194
THE WOOSTER BRUSH COMPANY, pg. 1202
ZIPPO MANUFACTURING COMPANY, pg. 1220

3425 — HAND SAWS & SAW BLADES

AMERICAN SAW & MANUFACTURING CO., pg. 60
THE DISSTON CO., pg. 339
FOLEY-BELSAW COMPANY, pg. 422
GREAT NECK SAW MANUFACTURERS, INC., pg. 482
KLEIN TOOLS INC., pg. 635
PRECISION CARBIDE TOOL COMPANY, INC., pg. 885

3429 — HARDWARE, NEC

ADAMS RITE MANUFACTURING CO., pg. 16
AMERICAN STRIP STEEL INC., pg. 63
ANDERSON INDUSTRIES INC., pg. 73
ARMSTRONG INTERNATIONAL, INC., pg. 83
ATWOOD INDUSTRIES, INC., pg. 97
AVIBANK MFG., INC., pg. 102
AVIS INDUSTRIAL CORPORATION, pg. 102
BOMMER INDUSTRIES, INC., pg. 164
THE CANADIAN COLEMAN CO., LTD.—MacAndrews & Forbes Holdings Inc., pg. 695
CHARTER HOUSE GROUP, pg. 240
CHICAGO LOCK COMPANY, pg. 245
COLSON CASTER CORPORATION—The Marmon Group, Inc., pg. 711
THE COLSON GROUP, INC.—The Marmon Group, Inc., pg. 711
COMMERCIAL & ARCHITECTURAL PRODUCTS INC., pg. 268
DECO PRODUCTS CO., pg. 324
W.J. DENNIS CO., pg. 329
DIEBEL MANUFACTURING CO., pg. 336
DIMCO-GRAY COMPANY, pg. 338
DIXON VALVE & COUPLING COMPANY, pg. 341
ESSTAR INCORPORATED, pg. 361
ERICO INTERNATIONAL, pg. 386
ESSEX INDUSTRIES—ESSTAR Incorporated, pg. 361
EVANS INDUSTRIES, INC., pg. 390
FIBRE GLASS-EVERCOAT COMPANY INC., pg. 408
FINGERLE LUMBER CO., pg. 411
FLANDERS INDUSTRIES, INC., pg. 416
FRANKLIN STEEL COMPANY, pg. 429
FRANTZ MANUFACTURING CO., pg. 429
GATES HYDRAULICS LTD.—The Gates Corporation, pg. 445
GENERAL SAFETY CORPORATION, pg. 450
MARTY GILMAN, INC., pg. 459
A. L. HANSEN MFG. CO., pg. 506
THE HARTWELL CORPORATION, pg. 514
HARTZELL CORPORATION, pg. 514
JOHN HASSALL, INC., pg. 516
HECKETHORN MFG. COMPANY, pg. 524
HIRSH COMPANY—Code, Hennessy & Simmons, pg. 258
HOUCK INDUSTRIES, INC., pg. 545
HURD LOCK & MANUFACTURING CO.—Avis Industrial Corporation, pg. 102
HYNES INDUSTRIES INC., pg. 557
THE ISI MANUFACTURING, INC., pg. 560
INDUSTRIAS METALICAS SUD AMERICANAS LTDA. (IMSA)—The Marmon Group, Inc., pg. 712
INTERNATIONAL MARINE HOLDINGS, INC., pg. 579
H. B. IVES, pg. 583
JACKES-EVANS MFG. CO., pg. 587
JASON INDUSTRIAL, INC., pg. 590
KETTENBURG MARINE CORPORATION, pg. 626
KETTENBURG MARINE/DANA POINT—Kettenburg Marine Corporation, pg. 626
KLEIN TOOLS INC., pg. 635
KRAFT HARDWARE, INC., pg. 643
LINN PRODUCTS, INC., pg. 677
MTD PRODUCTS, INC., pg. 694
MACHINING ENTERPRISES INC., pg. 696
MACKLANBURG-DUNCAN CO., pg. 697
MAUREY MANUFACTURING CORP., pg. 722
MICRODOT AEROSPACE LIMITED—MICRODOT, Inc., pg. 749
MINER ENTERPRISES INC., pg. 756
MOELLER MARINE PRODUCTS—Moore Company, pg. 768
MORRIS COUPLING CO., pg. 771
MOSLER INC., pg. 772
MOSLER SA DE C.D.—Mosler Inc., pg. 772
MOTOR WHEEL CORPORATION, pg. 773
NORTH & JUDD, pg. 812
PAYSON BRONCO, INC.—Payson Casters, Inc., pg. 853
PAYSON CASTERS, INC., pg. 853
PAYSON GEORGIA, INC.—Payson Casters, Inc., pg. 853
PAYSON TEXAS, INC.—Payson Casters, Inc., pg. 853
PETERSON AMERICAN CORP., pg. 864
PHELPS TOINTON INC., pg. 866
PRESTO LOCK, INC., pg. 888
REPUBLIC INDUSTRIES, INC., pg. 928
REV-A-SHELF, pg. 930
ROLLEX CORPORATION, pg. 944
SARGENT & GREENLEAF, INC., pg. 971
SARGENT MANUFACTURING COMPANY—ESSTAR Incorporated, pg. 361
SERVICE SUPPLY CO. INC. OF INDIANA, pg. 992
SEYMOUR MANUFACTURING COMPANY, pg. 994
THE SHELBURNE CORPORATION, pg. 996
SHELBURNE HUSKY DIV.—The Shelburne Corporation, pg. 996
SNAP-TITE, INCORPORATED, pg. 1014
SOVEREIGN GROUP INC., pg. 1024
JOHN STERLING CORPORATION, pg. 1046
SURCO PRODUCTS, INC., pg. 1065
THERMA-TRU INDIANA MFG. OPERS.—Therma-Tru Corp., pg. 1091
THERMA-TRU WESTERN MFG. OPERS.—Therma-Tru Corp., pg. 1091
THE TOBIN CORPORATION—Avis Industrial Corporation, pg. 102
WM. S. TRIMBLE COMPANY, INC., pg. 1113
TRIPLE A SPECIALTY COMPANY, pg. 1114
TUTHILL CORPORATION, pg. 1120
UNIVERSAL BUILDERS SUPPLY, INC., pg. 1137
VOSS INDUSTRIES, INC., pg. 1155
E.R. WAGNER MFG. CO. WAGNER PRODS. DIV., pg. 1158
RALPH C. WILSON ENTERPRISES, pg. 1194
WILTON CORPORATION, pg. 1194
YARDLEY PRODUCTS CORPORATION—Dixon Valve & Coupling Company, pg. 341

3431 — ENAMELED IRON & METAL SANITARY WARE

ACORN ENGINEERING COMPANY, pg. 14
AMERICAN SPECIALTIES INC., pg. 61
AMERICAN STANDARD INC., pg. 61
BOMMER INDUSTRIES, INC., pg. 164
BRADLEY CORPORATION, pg. 170
BRADLEY WASHROOM ACCESSORIES DIV.—Bradley Corporation, pg. 170
BRIGGS INDUSTRIES, INC., pg. 175
ELKAY MANUFACTURING COMPANY, pg. 377
EXCELSIOR MANUFACTURING & SUPPLY CORP., pg. 392
GLOBAL STEEL PRODUCTS CORPORATION, pg. 463
HAWS DRINKING FAUCET CO., pg. 518
IDEAL-STANDARD—American Standard Inc., pg. 62
JOSAM COMPANY, pg. 607
KALLISTA, INC.—Kohler Company, pg. 640
MAGLA PRODUCTS, pg. 700
MELARD PLASTICS INC.—Melard Manufacturing Corporation, pg. 737
METPAR CORPORATION, pg. 742
OAK PRODUCTS, INC.—ROC Properties Inc., pg. 908
POLAR WARE COMPANY, pg. 878
SEALAND TECHNOLOGY—Nelson A. Taylor Co., Inc., pg. 1081
STANCO METAL PRODUCTS, INC., pg. 1035
THE STERLING GROUP—Kohler Company, pg. 640

3432 — PLUMBING FIXTURE FITTINGS & TRIM

A.Y.M. INC.—A. Y. McDonald Industries, Inc., pg. 728
ACORN ENGINEERING COMPANY, pg. 14
AMERICAN STANDARD INC., pg. 61
ANDERSON COPPER & BRASS COMPANY—The Marmon Group, Inc., pg. 711
BRADLEY CORPORATION, pg. 170
BRADLEY WASHROOM ACCESSORIES DIV.—Bradley Corporation, pg. 170
BRIGGS INDUSTRIES, INC., pg. 175
CERRO METAL PRODUCTS COMPANY—The Marmon Group, Inc., pg. 711
THE CHICAGO FAUCET CO., pg. 245
COMPAGNIE INTERNATIONALE DES PRODUITS SANITAIRES (CIPS) JACOB DELAFON—Kohler Company, pg. 640
GENOVA PRODUCTS, INC., pg. 452
GERBER PLUMBING FIXTURES CORPORATION, pg. 454
GLOBE VALVE CORPORATION—Gerber Plumbing Fixtures Corporation, pg. 454
HARDEN INDUSTRIES, INC., pg. 508
HAWS DRINKING FAUCET CO., pg. 518
IDEAL-STANDARD GMBH—American Standard Inc., pg. 62
IDEAL-STANDARD, S.A. DE C.V.—American Standard Inc., pg. 62
IDEAL-STANDARD S.A.I.—American Standard Inc., pg. 62
INTERBATH, INC., pg. 574
JAMECO INDUSTRIES, INC., pg. 588
JOSAM COMPANY, pg. 607
KALLISTA, INC.—Kohler Company, pg. 640
KEENEY MANUFACTURING CO., pg. 620
KOHLER COMPANY, pg. 639
MACRISTY INDUSTRIES, INC., pg. 698
THE MARMON GROUP, INC., pg. 710
A. Y. MCDONALD INDUSTRIES, INC., pg. 728
A. Y. MCDONALD MFG. CO.—A. Y. McDonald Industries, Inc., pg. 728
MELARD MANUFACTURING CORPORATION, pg. 737
L. R. NELSON CORPORATION, pg. 797
NIBCO, INC., pg. 806
QUEROY S.A.—American Standard Inc., pg. 62
R.A. INDUSTRIES, INC., pg. 906
RAIN BIRD SPRINKLER MFG. CORP., pg. 910
THE RENOVATOR'S SUPPLY, INC., pg. 927
THE SHANE GROUP INC., pg. 995
SLOAN VALVE COMPANY, pg. 1010
SMITH INDUSTRIES, INC., pg. 1013
SPEAKMAN COMPANY, pg. 1027
STANDARD ALLOYS & MANUFACTURING—Blue Tee Corporation, pg. 161
THE STERLING GROUP—Kohler Company, pg. 640
SYMMONS INDUSTRIES INC., pg. 1069
T & S BRASS & BRONZE WORKS, INC., pg. 1074
TELSCO INDUSTRIES, pg. 1085
VANCE INDUSTRIES, INC., pg. 1144

3433 — HEATING EQUIPMENT, EXCEPT ELECTRIC & WARM AIR FURNACES

AERCO INTERNATIONAL INC., pg. 21
AMERICAN STANDARD AIR CONDITIONING PRODUCTS—American Standard Inc., pg. 61
BURNER SYSTEMS INTERNATIONAL, INC.—The Dyson-Kissner-Moran Corporation, pg. 357
C.I.C.S.A.—Maxon Corporation, pg. 723
CANEFCO LIMITED—Electric Furnace Co., pg. 373
COMBUSTION POWER COMPANY, pg. 267
DESA INTERNATIONAL, INC., pg. 331
DONLEE TECHNOLOGIES INC., pg. 344
ECLIPSE, INC., pg. 366
ECLIPSE THERMAL SYSTEMS—Eclipse, Inc., pg. 366
ECLIPSE THERMAL SYSTEMS, LTD.—Eclipse, Inc., pg. 366
EDWARDS ENGINEERING CORPORATION, pg. 370
EXCELSIOR MANUFACTURING & SUPPLY CORP., pg. 392
FLAMECO-ECLIPSE B.V.—Eclipse, Inc., pg. 367
FORD PRODUCTS CORPORATION, pg. 423
GAS-FIRED PRODUCTS (U.K.) LTD.—Gas-Fired Products, Inc., pg. 444
HAUCK MFG. CO., pg. 517
THE INTERNATIONAL BOILER WORKS COMPANY, pg. 575
JACKES-EVANS MFG. CO., pg. 587
THE KING COMPANY, pg. 630
KOMLINE-SANDERSON ENGINEERING CORP., pg. 641

LENNOX INDUSTRIES (CANADA) LTD.—Lennox International Inc., pg. 667
LONG MFG. NC, INC., pg. 682
MACRISTY INDUSTRIES, INC., pg. 698
THE MARLEY COMPANY, pg. 710
MARLEY ELECTRIC HEATING CO.—The Marley Company, pg. 710
MAXON CORPORATION, pg. 723
N.V. MAXON INTERNATIONAL S.A.—Maxon Corporation, pg. 723
MIDCO INTERNATIONAL INC., pg. 751
MUNROE, INC., pg. 776
THE NORTH AMERICAN MANUFACTURING CO., pg. 811
PERFECTION-SCHWANK INC., pg. 861
PRECISION PARTS CORP., pg. 885
RESEARCH PRODUCTS CORPORATION, pg. 928
SLANT/FIN CORPORATION, pg. 1010
SLANT-FIN, LTD./LTEE—Slant/Fin Corporation, pg. 1010
H. B. SMITH CO., INC., pg. 1013
THERMON MANUFACTURING COMPANY, pg. 1091
UTICA BOILERS INC., pg. 1140
HENRY VOGT MACHINE CO., pg. 1154
VULCAN - ECLIPSE—Eclipse, Inc., pg. 367
WEIL-MCLAIN—The Marley Company, pg. 710
THE WILL-BURT COMPANY, pg. 1190
YOUNG RADIATOR COMPANY, pg. 1210
JOHN ZINK CO.—Koch Industries, Incorporated, pg. 639

3441 — FABRICATED STRUCTURAL METAL

ABROS, INC.—Art Iron, Inc., pg. 86
ADDISON STEEL INC., pg. 17
ALAMO INDUSTRIAL GROUP, pg. 29
ALAMO IRON WORKS—Alamo Industrial Group, pg. 29
ALL AMERICAN INDUSTRIES, INC.—Datron Incorporated, pg. 316
ANCHOR METALS, INC.—Datron Incorporated, pg. 316
ARNOLD STEEL COMPANY, INC., pg. 85
ART IRON, INC., pg. 86
B & K STEEL & SUPPLY, INC., pg. 105
BELMONT INDUSTRIES, INC., pg. 136
BENNINGTON IRON WORKS, INC., pg. 139
BERLIN STEEL CONSTRUCTION CO., pg. 142
BINKLEY COMPANY, pg. 151
BOMAN & KEMP STEEL & SUPPLY COMPANY—B & K Steel & Supply, Inc., pg. 105
BRISTOL STEEL & IRON WORKS, INC., pg. 176
BROWN-MINNEAPOLIS TANK & FABRICATING CO., pg. 182
T. BRUCE SALES, INC., pg. 183
BURT EQUIPMENT COMPANY, INC., pg. 195
BURTCO METAL SYSTEMS—Burt Equipment Company, Inc., pg. 195
CF & I FABRICATORS OF COLORADO—CF&I Steel Corporation, pg. 201
CF & I FABRICATORS OF UTAH—CF&I Steel Corporation, pg. 201
CAROLINA STEEL CORPORATION, pg. 223
CAROLINA STEEL-HICKORY PLANT—Carolina Steel Corporation, pg. 223
CAROLINA STEEL-SALEM PLANT—Carolina Steel Corporation, pg. 223
W.C. CAYE & COMPANY, INC., pg. 230
CENTRAL ILLINOIS STEEL COMPANY, pg. 232
DOUGLAS STEEL FABRICATING CORPORATION, pg. 347
EAST MOLINE METAL PRODUCTS COMPANY, pg. 363
EQUIPMENT MANUFACTURING, INC., pg. 385
FORMEX, INC. - PERMANENT STEEL FORMS—W. B. Goode Company, Inc., pg. 470
W. B. GOODE COMPANY, INC., pg. 470
HAVENS STEEL CO., pg. 517
HIGH INDUSTRIES INC., pg. 533
HIRSCHFELD, INC., pg. 536
HIRSCHFELD STEEL COMPANY, INC.—Hirschfeld, Inc., pg. 536
RODNEY HUNT COMPANY, pg. 553
HYSPAN PRECISION PRODUCTS, INC., pg. 557
IDEA ENGINEERING & FABRICATING, pg. 562
IMPERIAL POOLS, INC., pg. 564
KEWAUNEE ENGINEERING CORP.—Marine Travelift, Inc., pg. 707
THE KIRK & BLUM MFG. CO., pg. 633
KLINE IRON & STEEL CO., INC., pg. 635
MARINE TRAVELIFT, INC., pg. 707
MID AMERICA STEEL, INC., pg. 750
MODERN WELDING CO., INC., pg. 763
MULACH STEEL CORPORATION, pg. 775
MUTUAL WELDING CO., LTD, pg. 779
NASHVILLE MACHINE CO. INC., pg. 784
ORLEANS MATERIALS & EQUIPMENT CO., INC., pg. 829
OWEN INDUSTRIES, INC., pg. 834
OWEN STEEL CO., INC., pg. 834
PAXTON & VIERLING—Owen Industries, Inc., pg. 834
PETERSEN ALUMINUM CORPORATION, pg. 864
PHOENIX STEEL, INC., pg. 869
RIGGS INDUSTRIES, INC., pg. 934
SOUTHEASTERN STEEL COMPANY, pg. 1020
SOUTHERN OHIO FABRICATORS, INC., pg. 1022
TROJAN STEEL CO., pg. 1115
UNISTRUT CORPORATION, pg. 1130
UP-RIGHT, INC., pg. 1139
VESTAL MANUFACTURING—Walter Industries, Inc., pg. 1162
VINCENNES STEEL CORP., pg. 1152
WATSON BOWMAN ACME CORP.—Berwind Corporation, pg. 145
WATSON BOWMAN ACME, INC.—Berwind Corporation, pg. 145
WESTERN INDUSTRIES, INC., pg. 1179
WHITING CORPORATION, pg. 1187
WHITING EQUIPMENT CANADA, INC.—Whiting Corporation, pg. 1187

3442 — METAL DOORS, SASH, FRAMES, MOLDING & TRIM

ACORN BUILDING COMPONENTS INC., pg. 13
AIR MASTER CORPORATION, pg. 27
ALLIED STEEL PRODUCTS—Great American Industries, Inc., pg. 480
AMARLITE ARCHITECTURAL PRODUCTS, pg. 47
BAY INDUSTRIES INC., pg. 127
THE WILLIAM BAYLEY CO., pg. 128
BINNING'S BUILDING PRODUCTS, INC., pg. 151
BLACK MILLWORK CO., INC., pg. 154
BLOUNT LUMBER COMPANY, pg. 158
CURT BULLOCK BUILDERS, INC., pg. 188
CGF INDUSTRIES, pg. 201
CALDWELL MANUFACTURING COMPANY, pg. 208
THE CHAMBERLAIN GROUP, INC.—Duchossois Industries, Inc., pg. 350
CHAMPION ALUMINUM CORPORATION, pg. 238
CLARK DOOR CO., INC., pg. 252
CONSTRUCTION SPECIALTIES, INC., pg. 277
CORNELL IRON WORKS, INC., pg. 286
CORNELL STOREFRONT SYSTEMS, INC.—Cornell Iron Works, Inc., pg. 286
CREATION WINDOWS OF INDIANA, INC., pg. 297
CROFT METAL INC., pg. 300
CULLMAN PRODUCTS CORPORATION, pg. 304
CURRIES COMPANY—ESSTAR Incorporated, pg. 361
CUSTOM PRODUCTS DIVISION—Chief Industries, Inc., pg. 247
WAYNE DALTON CORPORATION, pg. 312
DI GIORGIO CORPORATION, pg. 334
DUCHOSSOIS INDUSTRIES, INC., pg. 350
EFCO CORPORATION, pg. 359
ELIXIR INDUSTRIES, pg. 376
FENESTRA CORPORATION—The Marmon Group, Inc., pg. 711
FILMCO INDUSTRIES INC.—Thermwell Products Co., Inc., pg. 1092
FIMBEL DOOR CORPORATION, pg. 409
FINISHLINE INDUSTRIES INC. OF ARIZONA—John S. Frey Enterprises, pg. 433
FINISHLINE INDUSTRIES INC. OF GEORGIA—John S. Frey Enterprises, pg. 433
FLEETWOOD ALUMINUM PRODUCTS, pg. 417
FLORENCE CORPORATION, pg. 420
FRANTZ MANUFACTURING CO., pg. 429
JOHN S. FREY ENTERPRISES, pg. 433
GENERAL AMERICAN DOOR COMPANY—Merchant Capital Group Ltd, pg. 739
HARVEY INDUSTRIES, INC., pg. 515
HEHR INTERNATIONAL INC., pg. 525
HOPE'S ARCHITECTURAL PRODUCTS INC., pg. 543
JAMISON DOOR COMPANY, pg. 589
JELD-WEN, INC., pg. 591
KASSON & KELLER—Keymark Corporation, pg. 627
KEYMARK CORPORATION, pg. 627
LARSON MANUFACTURING COMPANY, pg. 659
LOXCREEN COMPANY, pg. 686
MADISON, INC.—John S. Frey Enterprises, pg. 433
MADISON INDUSTRIES—John S. Frey Enterprises, pg. 433
MADISON INDUSTRIES INC. OF ARIZONA—John S. Frey Enterprises, pg. 433
MADISON INDUSTRIES INC. OF GEORGIA—John S. Frey Enterprises, pg. 433
MAKI CORPORATION, pg. 702
MAKI HOME CENTER, INC.—Maki Corporation, pg. 702
MARTIN DOOR MFG., INC., pg. 714
MCKEE DOOR, INC., pg. 730
MERCHANT CAPITAL GROUP LTD, pg. 739
O'KEEFFE'S, INC., pg. 823
OVERLY MANUFACTURING CO., pg. 833
PACESETTER CORPORATION, pg. 839
PEASE INDUSTRIES, INC., pg. 854
PEMKO MANUFACTURING—Pemko Manufacturing Company, pg. 856
PEMKO MANUFACTURING COMPANY, pg. 856
PERKASIE INDUSTRIES CORPORATION, pg. 862
PHELPS TOINTON INC., pg. 866
RAYNOR GARAGE DOOR COMPANY, pg. 915
REDMAN BUILDING PRODUCTS, INC.—Redman Industries, Inc., pg. 919
ROLL FORMING CORPORATION, pg. 944
SOALCO—Acorn Building Components Inc., pg. 14
SPECIALTY ENGINEERED DOORS-CLARK DOOR CO.—Clark Door Co., Inc., pg. 252
STEVES & SONS, pg. 1048
TSI INDUSTRIES, INC., pg. 1075
THERMA-TRU CORP., pg. 1090
THERMWELL PRODUCTS CO., INC., pg. 1092
WM. S. TRIMBLE COMPANY, INC., pg. 1113
ULTRA INDUSTRIES, INC.—Macklanburg-Duncan Co., pg. 697
WBH INDUSTRIES, INC., pg. 1155
WASCO PRODUCTS, INC., pg. 1165

3443 — FABRICATED PLATE WORK (BOILER SHOPS)

R. P. ADAMS COMPANY, INC., pg. 16
AERCO INTERNATIONAL INC., pg. 21
ALASKAN COPPER COMPANIES, pg. 30
ALL AMERICAN INDUSTRIES, INC.—Datron Incorporated, pg. 316
AMERICAN TANK & FABRICATING CO., pg. 63
ARDCO, INC., pg. 81
ARMSTRONG-HUNT, INC.—Armstrong International, Inc., pg. 83
ARMSTRONG INTERNATIONAL, INC., pg. 83
ARROW TANK & ENGINEERING CO., pg. 85
BAC-PRITCHARD, INC.—Amsted Industries Incorporated, pg. 69
THE BABCOCK & WILCOX COMPANY, pg. 107
THE WILLIAM BAYLEY CO., pg. 128
BROWN-MINNEAPOLIS TANK & FABRICATING CO., pg. 182
T. BRUCE SALES, INC., pg. 183
BURTMAN IRON WORKS, INC., pg. 195
CALDWELL TANKS, INC., pg. 209
CENTRAL ILLINOIS STEEL COMPANY, pg. 232
COMBUSTION POWER COMPANY, pg. 267
CONBRACO INDUSTRIES INC., pg. 272
CONCORP, INC., pg. 272
CONNELL LIMITED PARTNERSHIP, pg. 275
CONSOLIDATED SYSTEMS, INC., pg. 277
D.C.I., INC., pg. 308
DEDERT CORPORATION, pg. 324
DELTA INDUSTRIES, pg. 327
DENVER AUTOMETRICS—Denver Equipment Company, pg. 331
DONLEE TECHNOLOGIES INC., pg. 344
DYNABILT PRODUCTS—Burtman Iron Works, Inc., pg. 196
EASTERN TECHNOLOGIES LTD, pg. 364
ECODYNE MRM, INC.—The Marmon Group, Inc., pg. 712
ECODYNE WATER SYSTEMS, INC.—The Marmon Group, Inc., pg. 712
ENERFAB INC., pg. 381
ENGINEERS & FABRICATORS CO.—The Marley Company, pg. 710
FURIGAS NV—The Dyson-Kissner-Moran Corporation, pg. 358
G L SUB COMPANY—The Marmon Group, Inc., pg. 712
GARSITE/TSR, INC.—Garsite/TSR, Inc., pg. 443
GASTON COUNTY DYEING MACHINE CO., pg. 444
THE GERSTENSLAGER COMPANY, pg. 454
HAVENS STEEL CO., pg. 517
THE HEIL CO., pg. 525
HYDRIL COMPANY—Hydril Company, pg. 556
JUSTISS OIL CO., INC., pg. 610
KOCH ENGINEERING CO., INC.—Koch Industries, Incorporated, pg. 639
GEORGE KOCH SONS, INC., pg. 639
LAUBECK CORPORATION, LAUBENSTEIN DIVISION—Laubeck Corporation/Cross, pg. 660
LENAPE FORGE, INC., pg. 667
LIVERNOIS ENGINEERING COMPANY, pg. 679
LYTRON INCORPORATED, pg. 690
MANCHESTER TANK & EQUIPMENT COMPANY, pg. 703
MANNING & LEWIS ENGINEERING CO., pg. 704
MANUFACTURERA THERMON DE MEXICO, S.A.—Thermon Manufacturing Company, pg. 1092
MAQUILADORA CLAMAQ S.A. DE C.V.—Clayton Industries Co., pg. 254
THE MARLEY COMPANY, pg. 710
THE MARLEY COOLING TOWER CO.—The Marley Company, pg. 710
MID AMERICA STEEL, INC., pg. 750
MODERN EQUIPMENT CO., INC.—Alco Industries, Inc., pg. 32
MODERN WELDING CO., INC., pg. 763
MONTICELLO TANK, INC.—Chicago Tube & Iron Co., pg. 246
MUNROE, INC., pg. 776
MURDOCK, INC., pg. 776
MUTUAL WELDING CO., LTD, pg. 779
NIAGARA BLOWER COMPANY, pg. 805
NITRAM ENERGY INC., pg. 807
NOOTER CORPORATION, pg. 808
PAPER CALMENSON & CO., pg. 847
PEABODY TECTANK, INC.—The Pullman Company, pg. 900
PERRY EQUIPMENT CORPORATION, pg. 863
PERRY GROUP, INC., pg. 863
PIPE FABRICATING & SUPPLY COMPANY, pg. 872
PLANT MAINTENANCE SERVICE CORPORATION, pg. 874
PRECISION PARTS CORP., pg. 885
PRESSED STEEL TANK CO., INC., pg. 887
PROCOR RAIL CAR DIVISION—The Marmon Group, Inc., pg. 712
RP & C—Conbraco Industries Inc., pg. 272
RECOLD, INC.—The Marley Company, pg. 710
ROLOCK, INC., pg. 944
ROTTERDAM VENTURES INC., pg. 951
SECO WARWICK CORPORATION, pg. 987
SIVALLS, INC., pg. 1009
H. B. SMITH CO., INC., pg. 1013
EVERETT SMITH INVESTMENT CO. OF DELAWARE, pg. 1013
SNYDER INDUSTRIES, INC., pg. 1015
SOUTHERN OHIO FABRICATORS, INC., pg. 1022
STAINLESS STEEL PRODUCTS, INC.—Zimmerman Holdings, Inc., pg. 1220
SUNDT PRODUCTS, INC.—Sundt Corp., pg. 1060
TIC UNITED CORPORATION, pg. 1073
TACO INC., pg. 1076
THERMON AUSTRALIA—Thermon Manufacturing Company, pg. 1092
THERMON BENELUX—Thermon Manufacturing Company, pg. 1092
THERMON CANADA—Thermon Manufacturing Company, pg. 1092
THERMON FAR EAST—Thermon Manufacturing Company, pg. 1092
THERMON FRANCE—Thermon Manufacturing Company, pg. 1092
THERMON U.K. (LTD.)—Thermon Manufacturing Company, pg. 1092
TIMPTE, INC.—Timpte Industries, Inc., pg. 1098
TIMPTE INDUSTRIES, INC., pg. 1098
TROJAN STEEL CO., pg. 1115
UNION BOILER CO.—Concorp, Inc., pg. 273
UNITED AIR SPECIALISTS, INC., pg. 1130
UNITED MCGILL CORP., pg. 1133
UPPER MIDWEST INDUSTRIES, INC., pg. 1140
HENRY VOGT MACHINE CO., pg. 1154
VOSS INDUSTRIES, INC., pg. 1155

WSF INDUSTRIES, INC., pg. 1156
WHITING CORPORATION, pg. 1187
WHITING EQUIPMENT CANADA, INC.—Whiting Corporation, pg. 1187
WILKINSON COMPANY, INC.—Electric Furnace Co., pg. 373
WINTERS WELDING WORKS, INC., pg. 1197
XALOY, INC.—Peter W. Smith & Company, Inc., pg. 1012
JOHN ZINK CO.—Koch Industries, Incorporated, pg. 639

3444 — SHEET METAL WORK

API GROUP INC., pg. 5
THE AARQUE COMPANIES, pg. 9
AARQUE STEEL CORPORATION—The Aarque Companies, pg. 9
ADVANCED MANUFACTURING & DEVELOPMENT, pg. 20
AERO DATA METAL CRAFTERS, pg. 22
THE AIROLITE COMPANY, pg. 28
ASSOCIATED MATERIALS INC., pg. 91
BONLAND INDUSTRIES, INC., pg. 164
CALCOR SPACE FACILITY, INC., pg. 208
CHICAGO MECHANICAL, INC., pg. 245
CHIEF INDUSTRIES, INC., pg. 247
CODISCO INC., pg. 258
CONSOLIDATED PIPE & SUPPLY COMPANY, pg. 277
CORRUGATED METALS, INC., pg. 287
DALE INDUSTRIES INC., pg. 312
DELTA INDUSTRIES, pg. 327
DURO DYNE CORPORATION, pg. 355
DYNAMIC METAL PRODUCTS COMPANY, pg. 356
ELIXIR INDUSTRIES, pg. 376
ENGINEERED PRODUCTS, INC., pg. 382
FABWEL INC., pg. 396
FISHER SKYLIGHTS, INC., pg. 415
FLEXONICS INC., pg. 419
FLEXONICS, INC.—Zimmerman Holdings, Inc., pg. 1220
GENERAL AMERICAN DOOR COMPANY—Merchant Capital Group Ltd, pg. 739
HARMONY ENGINEERING CORPORATION, pg. 510
HARRIS WALDINGER, INC.—Harris Mechanical Contracting Co., pg. 512
HARTWELL COMMERCIAL DIVISION—The Hartwell Corporation, pg. 514
HEIDTMAN STEEL PRODUCTS, INC., pg. 525
HUGHES-TREITLER MANUFACTURING CORPORATION, pg. 552
INCOR, INC.—Dale Industries Inc., pg. 312
JACKES-EVANS MFG. CO., pg. 587
KDI PARAGON, INC.—KDI Corporation, pg. 612
THE KIRK & BLUM MFG. CO., pg. 633
GEORGE KOCH SONS, INC., pg. 639
LINN PRODUCTS, INC., pg. 677
LOUV-AIRE, INC.—The Airolite Company, pg. 28
M M SYSTEMS CORPORATION, pg. 692
M M SYSTEMS CORPORATION—M M Systems Corporation, pg. 692
THE MARLEY COMPANY, pg. 710
METAL SALES MANUFACTURING CORPORATION—Interlock Industries, Inc., pg. 575
METALTECH, INC., pg. 742
MONTEREY MECHANICAL COMPANY, pg. 767
BENJAMIN OBDYKE, INC., pg. 819
OVERLY MANUFACTURING CO., pg. 833
PSB CO.—White Castle System, Inc., pg. 1185
PRIMARY INDUSTRIES CORPORATION, pg. 889
ROLL FORMING CORPORATION, pg. 944
ROSS ENGINEERING CO., INC., pg. 949
SIMPSON DURA-VENT CO., INC., pg. 1007
SINTEL, INC., pg. 1008
SIOUX STEEL COMPANY, pg. 1008
EVERETT SMITH INVESTMENT CO. OF DELAWARE, pg. 1013
SMITH SYSTEM MANUFACTURING COMPANY, pg. 1014
SOUTHWARK METAL MANUFACTURING COMPANY, pg. 1023
STANCO METAL PRODUCTS, INC., pg. 1035
SUNDT PRODUCTS, INC.—Sundt Corp., pg. 1060
SWIFT-COR TOOL ENGINEERING, pg. 1067
SYMONS CORPORATION, pg. 1069
TARCO, pg. 1078
E. H. TITCHENER & COMPANY, pg. 1099
UNISTRUT CORPORATION, pg. 1130
UNITED MCGILL CORP., pg. 1133
UPPER MIDWEST INDUSTRIES, INC., pg. 1140
WASCO PRODUCTS, INC., pg. 1165
ZIMMERMAN HOLDINGS, INC., pg. 1220

3446 — ARCHITECTURAL & ORNAMENTAL METAL WORK

ABROS, INC.—Art Iron, Inc., pg. 86
ALABAMA METAL INDUSTRIES CORPORATION, pg. 28
AMARLITE ARCHITECTURAL PRODUCTS, pg. 47
ANDAMIOS ATLAS, S.A.—AXIA Incorporated, pg. 8
ANNIN & COMPANY, pg. 75
ART IRON, INC., pg. 86
HAPCO/AMERICAN DIV.—The Dyson-Kissner-Moran Corporation, pg. 357
INDUSTRIAL ACOUSTICS COMPANY, INC., pg. 565
LAPEYRE STAIR, INC.—The Laitram Corporation, pg. 651
LAWRENCE METAL PRODUCTS, INC., pg. 662
MULACH STEEL CORPORATION, pg. 775
PAWLING CORPORATION, pg. 852
REESE ENTERPRISES, INC., pg. 920
RELIANCE GRATING, INC.—Belmont Industries, Inc., pg. 136
ROLL FORMING CORPORATION, pg. 944
STAINLESS INCORPORATED, pg. 1035
JOHN STERLING CORPORATION, pg. 1046
TRU-WELD GRATING, INC., pg. 1117
UNISTRUT CORPORATION, pg. 1130
UP-RIGHT, INC., pg. 1139
VIRGINIA METAL INDUSTRIES, INC., pg. 1152
WENGER CORPORATION, pg. 1176

3448 — PREFABRICATED METAL BUILDINGS & COMPONENTS

ACORN ENGINEERING COMPANY, pg. 14
AMERICAN BUILDINGS CO., pg. 49
ANDERSON INDUSTRIES, INC., pg. 72
ARROW GROUP INDUSTRIES, INC.—The Dyson-Kissner-Moran Corporation, pg. 357
BEHLEN MFG. CO., pg. 132
BESTEEL INDUSTRIES, pg. 147
BROCK MANUFACTURING—CTB Inc., pg. 205
CURT BULLOCK BUILDERS, INC., pg. 188
CHIEF INDUSTRIES - AGRI PRODUCTS DIV.—Chief Industries, Inc., pg. 247
CHIEF INDUSTRIES - BUILDINGS DIV.—Chief Industries, Inc., pg. 247
CHIEF INDUSTRIES UK LTD.—Chief Industries, Inc., pg. 247
CUSTOM PRODUCT DIV.—Chief Industries, Inc., pg. 247
DELUXE HOMES OF PENNSYLVANIA, INC., pg. 327
FORMEX, INC. - PERMANENT STEEL FORMS—W. B. Goode Company, Inc., pg. 470
FOUR SEASONS SOLAR PRODUCTS CORP., pg. 427
W. B. GOODE COMPANY, INC., pg. 470
GULF STATES MANUFACTURERS, INC., pg. 494
JEWELL BUILDING SYSTEMS, pg. 594
KIRBY BUILDING SYSTEMS, INC., pg. 632
LUNDY CONSTRUCTION CO., INC., pg. 687
MAGLINE, INC., pg. 700
MAGNUM BUILDING SYSTEMS—W. B. Goode Company, Inc., pg. 470
MESCO METAL BUILDINGS CORP.—Anderson Industries, Inc., pg. 73
MUTUAL WELDING CO., LTD, pg. 779
PASCOE BUILDING SYSTEMS, INC., pg. 851
RUFFIN BUILDING SYSTEMS, INC., pg. 955
SCOTSMAN GROUP, INC.—The Scotsman Group, Inc., pg. 982
STEELITE, INC., pg. 1044
STEELOX SYSTEMS, INC., pg. 1044
TRI STATE STEEL CONSTRUCTION—National Engineering & Contracting Co., pg. 788
UNITED MCGILL CORP., pg. 1133
WICK BUILDING SYSTEMS, pg. 1188

3449 — MISCELLANEOUS STRUCTURAL METAL WORK

THE AARQUE COMPANIES, pg. 9
ALABAMA METAL INDUSTRIES CORPORATION, pg. 28
AMERICAN TANK & FABRICATING CO., pg. 63
CAPITAL INDUSTRIES, INC., pg. 215
CROFT METAL INC., pg. 300
DAHLSTROM MANUFACTURING COMPANY, INC., pg. 310
ELEKTRO METALL EXPORT GMBH—Datron Incorporated, pg. 317
ENCO-JOHNSON CITY DIVISION—Enco Materials, Inc., pg. 380
ENCO MATERIALS, INC., pg. 380
FRANKLIN STEEL COMPANY, pg. 429
GAME TIME, INC., pg. 442
GEM INDUSTRIES, INC.—Gem Industries Finance Corporation, pg. 447
HECKETHORN MFG. COMPANY, pg. 524
HYDRIL COMPANY—Hydril Company, pg. 556
HYDRO GROUP, INC., pg. 556
GEORGE KOCH SONS, INC., pg. 639
MACHINING ENTERPRISES INC., pg. 696
MARKHON INDUSTRIES, INC—Kennedy Manufacturing Company, pg. 623
O'KEEFFE'S, INC., pg. 823
OWEN STEEL CO., INC., pg. 834
PASCOE BUILDING SYSTEMS, INC., pg. 851
PAXTON & VIERLING—Owen Industries, Inc., pg. 834
PHELPS TOINTON INC., pg. 866
REINKE MANUFACTURING CO., INC., pg. 924
ROLL FORMING CORPORATION, pg. 944
SOUTHERN OHIO FABRICATORS, INC., pg. 1022
M. SWIFT & SONS CANADA INC.—M. Swift & Sons Inc., pg. 1068
M. SWIFT & SONS INC., pg. 1068
UNITED DESIGN, pg. 1131
UPPER MIDWEST INDUSTRIES, INC., pg. 1140

3451 — SCREW MACHINE PRODUCTS

AMERICAN LAUBSCHER CORP., pg. 57
BARDES CORP., pg. 119
COLLINS & AIKMAN GROUP INC., pg. 262
THE CRETEX COMPANIES, pg. 299
CURTIS SCREW CO., INC., pg. 306
GENERAL AUTOMATION, INC., pg. 448
HEADER PRODUCTS INC., pg. 520
KURT MANUFACTURING CO. INC., pg. 646
MACHINING ENTERPRISES INC., pg. 696
MEDICO INDUSTRIES, INC., pg. 735
METAL SEAL & PRODUCTS, INC., pg. 741
MITCHEL & SCOT MACHINE CO., INC., pg. 761
NATIONAL TOOL & MANUFACTURING COMPANY, pg. 794
PECK SPRING COMPANY, pg. 854
QUALITY CONTROL CORPORATION, pg. 903
THE RAWLPLUG COMPANY, INC., pg. 914
THE SHANE GROUP INC., pg. 995
J.J. TOUREK CO.—Tuthill Corporation, pg. 1120
TRIANGLE MACHINE PRODUCT CO.—Freeway Corporation, pg. 432
VALENTEC INTERNATIONAL CORP.—Insilco Corporation, pg. 571
ASHLEY F. WARD, INC., pg. 1162

3452 — BOLTS, NUTS, SCREWS, RIVETS & WASHERS

ACCURATE THREADED FASTENERS, INC., pg. 11
AIR INDUSTRIES CORPORATION, pg. 27
ALABAMA METAL INDUSTRIES CORPORATION, pg. 28
ALLECO INC., pg. 35
ALLFAST FASTENING SYSTEMS, INC., pg. 37
ALLMETAL SCREW PRODUCTS CORP., pg. 40
ALPHA BOLT COMPANY—Washers, Inc., pg. 1165
AMERICAN FASTENERS—Jupiter Industries, Inc., pg. 609
ARROW FASTENER CO., INC., pg. 85
ATLAS BOLT & SCREW COMPANY—The Marmon Group, Inc., pg. 712
AVIBANK MFG., INC., pg. 102
AVIS INDUSTRIAL CORPORATION, pg. 102
BRISTOL INDUSTRIES, pg. 176
C.E.M. DIV. SPIROL INTL. CORP.—Spirol International Corp., pg. 1031
CHANDLER PRODUCTS, INC.—Jupiter Industries, Inc., pg. 609
COLD HEADING CO., pg. 259
CONTINENTAL/MIDLAND, INC., pg. 279
CORNELL MANUFACTURING COMPANY—Jupiter Industries, Inc., pg. 609
DANUSER MACHINE CO., pg. 315
THE DEUTSCH COMPANY, pg. 333
G.B. DUPONT CO., INC., pg. 354
ELASTIC STOP NUT—Harvard Industries, Inc., pg. 514
FLAMETECH CORPORATION—Peter W. Smith & Company, Inc., pg. 1012
FREEWAY CORPORATION, pg. 432
FREEWAY ROANOKE—Freeway Corporation, pg. 432
FREEWAY ROCKFORD—Freeway Corporation, pg. 432
G L SUB COMPANY—The Marmon Group, Inc., pg. 712
HARVARD INDUSTRIES, INC., pg. 514
INDUSTRIAL & AUTOMOTIVE FASTENERS—Key Manufacturing Group, Inc., pg. 627
KEY MANUFACTURING GROUP, INC., pg. 627
MNP CORP., pg. 693
MACLEAN-FOGG CO., pg. 697
THE MARMON GROUP, INC., pg. 710
MARMON INDUSTRIAL CORPORATION—The Marmon Group, Inc., pg. 712
METFORM, INC.—Maclean-Fogg Co., pg. 698
MICRODOT AEROSPACE FASTENING SYSTEMS GROUP—MICRODOT, Inc., pg. 749
MICRODOT, INC., pg. 749
MID-CONTINENT SCREW PRODUCTS CO., pg. 750
MIDWEST FASTENERS CORPORATION, pg. 752
NATIONAL RIVET & MANUFACTURING COMPANY, pg. 793
O. A. NEWTON & SON CO., pg. 805
OHIO ROD PRODUCTS COMPANY, INC.—Jupiter Industries, Inc., pg. 609
PAWTUCKET FASTENERS INC., pg. 852
PRESTIGE STAMPING, INC., pg. 888
THE RAWLPLUG COMPANY, INC., pg. 914
RING SCREW WORKS, pg. 935
ROCKFORD PRODUCTS CORP., pg. 941
SEMBLEX CORPORATION, pg. 989
SERVICE SUPPLY CO. INC. OF INDIANA, pg. 992
SPIROL IND. LTD.—Spirol International Corp., pg. 1031
SPIROL INTERNATIONAL CORP., pg. 1031
SPIROL S.A.—Spirol International Corp., pg. 1031
SPIROL WEST—Spirol International Corp., pg. 1031
STAMPTECH—Maclean-Fogg Co., pg. 697
STANDCO INDUSTRIES, INC., pg. 1038
STAR EXPANSION COMPANY, pg. 1039
STAR EXPANSION INDUSTRIES, LTD.—Star Expansion Company, pg. 1039
STAR EXPANSION SHIELDS LTD.—Star Expansion Company, pg. 1039
EDWIN B. STIMPSON COMPANY, INC., pg. 1049
THE TOBIN CORPORATION—Avis Industrial Corporation, pg. 102
TRIANGLE AUTO SPRING COMPANY—The Marmon Group, Inc., pg. 711
TRU-FIT PRODUCTS CORP., pg. 1117
VOSS INDUSTRIES, INC., pg. 1155
WASHERS, INC., pg. 1165
WICKES MFG. CO.—Collins & Aikman Group Inc., pg. 262
WROUGHT WASHER MFG., INC., pg. 1205
XALOY, INC.—Peter W. Smith & Company, Inc., pg. 1012
YARDLEY PRODUCTS CORPORATION—Dixon Valve & Coupling Company, pg. 341

3462 — IRON & STEEL FORGINGS

ASHMAN ENTERPRISES, INC., pg. 88
ASSOCIATED MACHINECRAFT CORPORATION, pg. 90
AVIS INDUSTRIAL CORPORATION, pg. 102
BALDT, INC., pg. 115
CANTON DROP FORGE, pg. 214
COLUMBUS MCKINNON CORP., pg. 266
CONSOLIDATED INDUSTRIES, INC., pg. 276
CORNELL FORGE COMPANY, pg. 286
EDGERTON FORGE, INC.—Avis Industrial Corporation, pg. 102
EDGEWATER CORPORATION, pg. 368
EDGEWATER STEEL CO.—Edgewater Corporation, pg. 368
ELLWOOD CITY FORGE, pg. 378
FOLEY-PLP COMPANY—Foley-Belsaw Company, pg. 422
FROG SWITCH & MANUFACTURING COMPANY, pg. 434
GUNNEBO FASTENING CORP., pg. 494
IMT—National Forge Company, pg. 789
IDEAL FORGING CORPORATION, pg. 562
INDUSTRIAL GENERAL CORPORATION, pg. 566

INTERGY, INC.—Ashman Enterprises, Inc., pg. 88
JERNBERG INDUSTRIES, INC., pg. 593
KERVICK ENTERPRISES, INC., pg. 624
KROPP FORGE CO.—TIC United Corporation, pg. 1073
LENAPE FORGE, INC., pg. 667
LETTS INDUSTRIES, INC., pg. 668
MACLEAN-FOGG CO., pg. 697
MCINNES STEEL COMPANY, pg. 729
MCWILLIAMS FORGE CO., pg. 733
MEADVILLE FORGING CO., pg. 733
MELLING FORGING COMPANY—Avis Industrial Corporation, pg. 102
MERCER FORGE, INC.—Rotterdam Ventures Inc., pg. 952
MITCHELL SHACKLETON & CO. LTD.—National Forge Company, pg. 789
MODERN DROP FORGE CO., pg. 762
NTC GROUP, pg. 781
NATIONAL FORGE COMPANY, pg. 788
PACIFIC FORGE, INC.—Avis Industrial Corporation, pg. 102
RING SCREW WORKS, pg. 935
SCHLOSSER FORGE COMPANY, pg. 976
UIS, INC., pg. 1123
UNION FORGING CO.—UIS, Inc., pg. 1123
W F I, INC., pg. 1156
JERVIS B. WEBB COMPANY, pg. 1170
WEBB FORGING—Jervis B. Webb Company, pg. 1170
WEBSTER INDUSTRIES INC., pg. 1171
WOZNIAK INDUSTRIES, INC., pg. 1204

3463 — NONFERROUS FORGINGS

ADEC AUTOMATION—Adec International Automation Corp., pg. 17
ALUMINUM FORGE COMPANY—The Marmon Group, Inc., pg. 711
AVIS INDUSTRIAL CORPORATION, pg. 102
CANTON DROP FORGE, pg. 214
CONSOLIDATED INDUSTRIES, INC., pg. 276
CONTINENTAL FORGE COMPANY, pg. 279
INDUSTRIAL GENERAL CORPORATION, pg. 566
JERNBERG INDUSTRIES, INC., pg. 593
JONATHAN MANUFACTURING CORP., pg. 602
KERVICK ENTERPRISES, INC., pg. 624
KROPP FORGE CO.—TIC United Corporation, pg. 1073
LENAPE FORGE, INC., pg. 667
LETTS INDUSTRIES, INC., pg. 668
LETTS INDUSTRIES, PIONEER DIV.—Letts Industries, Inc., pg. 668
LONE STAR FORGE COMPANY—TIC United Corporation, pg. 1073
MARMON CORPORATION—The Marmon Group, Inc., pg. 711
MCWILLIAMS FORGE CO., pg. 733
PACIFIC FORGE, INC.—Avis Industrial Corporation, pg. 102
PHOENIX INTERNATIONAL, INC., pg. 868
PRECISION METAL PRODS., INC.—Phoenix International, Inc., pg. 869
RING SCREW WORKS, pg. 935
SCHLOSSER FORGE COMPANY, pg. 976
UIS, INC., pg. 1123
W F I, INC., pg. 1156

3465 — AUTOMOTIVE STAMPINGS

THE AARQUE COMPANIES, pg. 9
AARQUE STEEL CORPORATION—The Aarque Companies, pg. 9
ACTIVE TOOL & MANUFACTURING CO., INC., pg. 15
AETNA INDUSTRIES, INC., pg. 23
AMERICAN METAL & PLASTICS, pg. 58
ANCHOR TOOL & DIE COMPANY, pg. 71
ANDERSON INDUSTRIES INC., pg. 73
ARROW METAL PRODUCTS CORPORATION, pg. 85
BENT TUBE, INC., pg. 140
CHIVAS PRODUCTS LTD., pg. 248
CONDOR TOOL & DIE, INC.—Anchor Tool & Die Company, pg. 72
CRAGAR INDUSTRIES—Mr. Gasket Company, pg. 761
CRESCIVE DIE & TOOL, INC., pg. 298
CRESIVE MILAN DIVISION—Crescive Die & Tool, Inc., pg. 298
DAVIS INDUSTRIES INC., pg. 318
DAVIS TOOL & ENGINEERING CO.—Davis Industries Inc., pg. 318
DIELINE CORPORATION, pg. 336
EDGEWOOD TOOL & MANUFACTURING COMPANY, pg. 368
FREEDLAND INDUSTRIES CORPORATION, pg. 430
THE GERSTENSLAGER COMPANY, pg. 454
HIGHWOOD SERVICE, INC.—Ralph C. Wilson Enterprises, pg. 1194
HOFLEY MANUFACTURING COMPANY, pg. 538
INDUSTRIAL GENERAL CORPORATION, pg. 566
IROQUOIS DIE & MFG. CO., pg. 582
KAUFFMAN PRODUCTS, INC., pg. 618
LETTS INDUSTRIES, INC., pg. 668
LOBDELL-EMERY MANUFACTURING COMPANY, pg. 680
LOGGHE STAMPING COMPANY, pg. 681
MANUFACTURERS PRODUCTS COMPANY, pg. 705
MIDWAY PRODUCTS CORPORATION, pg. 751
MITCHELL CORPORATION OF OWOSSO, pg. 761
NEW STANDARD CORPORATION, pg. 802
OAKLAND TOOL & MANUFACTURING COMPANY, pg. 819
PRESTIGE STAMPING, INC., pg. 888
PRIDGEON & CLAY, INC., pg. 889
PRINCE CORPORATION, pg. 890
PULLMAN INDUSTRIES, INC., pg. 900
REPUBLIC DIE & TOOL COMPANY, pg. 928
SIGNET INDUSTRIES, pg. 1003
SOUTH BEND STAMPING DIV.—EWI, Inc., pg. 361
STAMCO INDUSTRIES INC., pg. 1035
STEEL PARTS CORP.—Insilco Corporation, pg. 571
WAGGONER CORP., pg. 1158
WICKES MFG. CO.—Collins & Aikman Group Inc., pg. 262

3466 — METAL CROWNS & CLOSURES

AMERICAN INTERNATIONAL CONTAINER, INC., pg. 56
MOELLER MARINE PRODUCTS—Moore Company, pg. 768

3469 — METAL STAMPINGS, NEC

A & S TRIBAL INDUSTRIES, pg. 1
APG DIVISION—Upper Midwest Industries, Inc., pg. 1140
THE AARQUE COMPANIES, pg. 9
AARQUE STEEL CORPORATION—The Aarque Companies, pg. 9
ACCURATE PERFORATING CO., pg. 11
ACCURATE THREADED FASTENERS, INC., pg. 11
ACTIVE TOOL & MANUFACTURING CO., INC., pg. 15
ALCO INDUSTRIES, INC., pg. 32
ALINABAL, INC., pg. 34
ALLIANCE AMERICA, pg. 37
AMERICAN DEVELOPMENT CORPORATION, pg. 51
AMERICAN MANUFACTURING CO. (TN), pg. 58
AMERICAN PROTECTION INDUSTRIES, INC., pg. 60
AMERICAN SPECIALTIES INC., pg. 61
AMTROL INC., pg. 70
ANCHOR FENCE COMPANY—PPA Industries, Inc., pg. 836
ANCHOR TOOL & DIE COMPANY, pg. 71
ASSOCIATED MACHINECRAFT CORPORATION, pg. 90
BENSON CORP.—Gem Industries Finance Corporation, pg. 447
BERMO, INC., pg. 143
BETTCHER MANUFACTURING CORP., pg. 148
BOMMER INDUSTRIES, INC., pg. 164
BRITTANY CORPORATION, pg. 177
BRONZE HEADQUARTERS—Headco Industries, Inc., pg. 520
CALIFORNIA MANUFACTURING ENTERPRISES, pg. 210
CARSTENS HEALTH INDUSTRIES, INC., pg. 225
CLAYTON METALS CORP.—Clayton Corporation, pg. 253
CONDOR TOOL & DIE, INC.—Anchor Tool & Die Company, pg. 72
CONNECTICUT SPRING & STAMPING CORPORATION, pg. 275
CONTICO INTERNATIONAL, INC., pg. 278
COPCO—Wilton Industries, Inc., pg. 1195
COSCO INDUSTRIES, pg. 288
COWDEN METAL SPECIALTIES, INC., pg. 291
CULLMAN PRODUCTS CORPORATION, pg. 304
DAHLSTROM MANUFACTURING B.V.—Dahlstrom Manufacturing Company, Inc., pg. 310
DAHLSTROM MANUFACTURING CO., INC.-SAFEWAY DIVISION—Dahlstrom Manufacturing Company, Inc., pg. 310
DAHLSTROM MANUFACTURING COMPANY, INC., pg. 310
DAVIS INDUSTRIES INC., pg. 318
DAYTON ROGERS MFG. CO., pg. 321
DAYTON ROGERS OF OHIO—Dayton Rogers Mfg. Co., pg. 321
DAYTON ROGERS OF TEXAS—Dayton Rogers Mfg. Co., pg. 321
DEERFIELD MANUFACTURING CO., INC., pg. 324
DETEX CORPORATION, pg. 333
DIEBEL MANUFACTURING CO., pg. 336
THE DISSTON CO., pg. 339
DUAL MANUFACTURING & ENGINEERING, INC.—Corber Corporation, pg. 285
DUDEK & BOCK SPRING MANUFACTURING COMPANY, pg. 351
EAST MOLINE METAL PRODUCTS COMPANY, pg. 363
ECLIPSE MANUFACTURING COMPANY, pg. 367
ERDLE PERFORATING OF CAROLINA—Erdle Perforating Co., pg. 385
ERDLE PERFORATING CO., pg. 385
ERDLE PERFORATING CO. LTD.—Erdle Perforating Co., pg. 385
FEDERAL STAMPINGS OF CALIFORNIA—Dayton Rogers Mfg. Co., pg. 321
FEDERAL STAMPINGS OF FLORIDA—Dayton Rogers Mfg. Co., pg. 321
FEDERAL STAMPINGS OF NEW YORK—Dayton Rogers Mfg. Co., pg. 321
FEDERAL STAMPINGS OF OREGON—Dayton Rogers Mfg. Co., pg. 321
FERROUS PROCESSING & TRADING CO., pg. 407
FREEWAY CORPORATION, pg. 432
GEM SOUTHEAST, INC.—Gem Industries Finance Corporation, pg. 447
GENESEE METAL STAMPINGS, INC., pg. 451
THE GERSTENSLAGER COMPANY, pg. 454
HARRINGTON & KING, pg. 511
HARRINGTON & KING, SOUTH, INC.—Harrington & King, pg. 511
HEADCO MACHINE WORKS, INC.—Headco Industries, Inc., pg. 520
HOFLEY MANUFACTURING COMPANY, pg. 538
INDUSTRIAL GENERAL CORPORATION, pg. 566
INSTRUMENT SPECIALTIES COMPANY, pg. 572
INSTRUMENT SPECIALTIES - WESTERN DIVISION—Instrument Specialties Company, pg. 572
THE JOHNSON INDUSTRIES CORP., pg. 598
KAUFFMAN PRODUCTS, INC., pg. 618
KENDALE INDUSTRIES, INC., pg. 622
KENNEDY MANUFACTURING COMPANY, pg. 623
LA BELLE INDUSTRIES, INC., pg. 648
MTD PRODUCTS LIMITED—MTD Products, Inc., pg. 694
MAXCOR MANUFACTURING, INC., pg. 722
MAYVILLE ENGINEERING CO., INC., pg. 725
MCDOWELL MFG. CO.—Alco Industries, Inc., pg. 32
MICRODOT AEROSPACE FASTENING SYSTEMS GROUP—MICRODOT, Inc., pg. 749
MIDWEST BODY CORPORATION, pg. 752
NATIONAL METAL PRODUCTS CO.—Tang Industries Inc., pg. 1078
NEW STANDARD CORPORATION, pg. 802
NORTHLAND ALUMINUM PRODUCTS, INC., pg. 814
OBERG INDUSTRIES CO., pg. 819
OBERG MFG. CO.—Oberg Industries Co., pg. 820
PPA INDUSTRIES, INC., pg. 836
PAR INDUSTRIES, INC., pg. 847
PETERSON AMERICAN CORP., pg. 864
PORCELAIN METALS CORP., pg. 881
PRIDGEON & CLAY, INC., pg. 889
PULLMAN INDUSTRIES, INC., pg. 900
RAU FASTENERS, INC., pg. 913
ROWOCO—Wilton Industries, Inc., pg. 1195
SIGNAL TRANSFORMER CO., INC.—Insilco Corporation, pg. 571
SMALL PARTS, INC., pg. 1010
SMITH MAILER—California Manufacturing Enterprises, pg. 210
SPECIALTY MANUFACTURING COMPANY, pg. 1027
SPIROL INTERNATIONAL CORP., pg. 1031
SPRING ENGINEERS, INC., pg. 1033
STAMCO INDUSTRIES INC., pg. 1035
STAMPING DIVISION—The Gerstenslager Company, pg. 455
EDWIN B. STIMPSON COMPANY, INC., pg. 1049
TARGET STAMPED PRODUCTS CORP., pg. 1079
THERM, INC., pg. 1090
TOLEDO STAMPING & MANUFACTURING CO.—New Hampshire Oak, pg. 801
TRITON INDUSTRIES, INC., pg. 1114
UNICOVER CORPORATION, pg. 1126
THE VOLLRATH COMPANY INC., pg. 1154
WAGGONER CORP., pg. 1158
WELSH COMPANY, pg. 1175
WESTERN INDUSTRIES, INC., pg. 1179
WILLERT HOME PRODUCTS, INC., pg. 1190
WITT COMPANY, pg. 1198
WOZNIAK INDUSTRIES, INC., pg. 1204
WROUGHT WASHER MFG., INC., pg. 1205

3471 — ELECTROPLATING, PLATING, POLISHING, ANODIZING & COLORING

AERO-FINISH INC.—Kleco Corp., pg. 635
ANO-COIL CORPORATION, pg. 75
CALIFORNIA MANUFACTURING ENTERPRISES, pg. 210
CEPCO—Collins & Aikman Group Inc., pg. 263
CULLMAN PRODUCTS CORPORATION, pg. 304
ELECTRONIC PLATING SERVICE, INC.—KDI Corporation, pg. 612
FELLOWES MANUFACTURING CO., pg. 405
HARRIS-KAYOT, INC., pg. 512
HYDRITE CHEMICAL COMPANY, pg. 556
KEN-MAC METAL, INC., pg. 622
KOLLER ENTERPRISES, INC., pg. 641
LINN PRODUCTS, INC., pg. 677
MARCO COLOR LABS, INC., pg. 706
MAXCOR MANUFACTURING, INC., pg. 722
OVERSEAS PARTNERS, INC., pg. 833
PARAMOUNT METALIZING DIV.—Koller Enterprises, Inc., pg. 641
PRECISION ROLL GRINDERS, INC., pg. 885
SIGMA PLATING CO., LTD.—Standun, Inc., pg. 1038
SUMMIT CORPORATION OF AMERICA, pg. 1058
TRACOR GIE—Tracor, Inc., pg. 1105
TRACOR, INC., pg. 1104
WELSH COMPANY, pg. 1175
WESTERN METAL FINISHING DIVISION—TIC United Corporation, pg. 1073
WOZNIAK INDUSTRIES, INC., pg. 1204

3479 — COATING, ENGRAVING & ALLIED SERVICES, NEC

ALLIANCE AMERICA, pg. 37
AMSTED INDUSTRIES INCORPORATED, pg. 68
APPLIED COATINGS—Bel-Art Products, pg. 133
BOLTON-EMERSON S.A.—Bolton-Emerson, Inc., pg. 163
CALIFORNIA MANUFACTURING ENTERPRISES, pg. 210
COLE KEY CORPORATION—Cole National Corporation, pg. 260
CONSOLIDATED SYSTEMS, INC., pg. 277
DNN GALVANIZING CORPORATION—National Steel Corporation, pg. 794
DAUBERT CHEMICAL COMPANY, INC.—Daubert Industries, Inc., pg. 317
DAUBERT COATED PRODUCTS, INC.—Daubert Industries, Inc., pg. 317
DAUBERT INDUSTRIES, INC., pg. 317
DONLEE TECHNOLOGIES INC., pg. 344
DUNMORE CORPORATION, pg. 353
DUNMORE CORPORATION/BREWSTER—Dunmore Corporation, pg. 353
NATIONAL FORGE COMPANY, pg. 788
NESTAWAY CO.—AXIA Incorporated, pg. 8
NORTHLAND ALUMINUM PRODUCTS, INC., pg. 814
PLASMA TECHNOLOGY, INC., pg. 874
REEVES SOUTHEASTERN CORPORATION, pg. 921
SEREVCO & COMPANY LTD.—National Steel Corporation, pg. 794
TRANSCO INC., pg. 1106
WSF INDUSTRIES, INC., pg. 1156
WELSH COMPANY, pg. 1175
WESTERN METAL FINISHING DIVISION—TIC United Corporation, pg. 1073
WITT COMPANY, pg. 1198
THE ZIPPERTUBING CO., pg. 1220

3482 — SMALL ARMS AMMUNITION

ADEC INTERNATIONAL AUTOMATION CORP., pg. 17
HORNADY MANUFACTURING COMPANY, pg. 544
MEDICO INDUSTRIES, INC., pg. 735
VALENTEC INTERNATIONAL CORP.—Insilco Corporation, pg. 571
VALLEY FOREST RESOURCES CO.—Villaume Industries, Inc., pg. 1152

3483 — AMMUNITION, EXCEPT SMALL ARMS, NEC

ADEC INTERNATIONAL AUTOMATION CORP., pg. 17
ALL AMERICAN INDUSTRIES, INC.—Datron Incorporated, pg. 316
DAY & ZIMMERMAN KANSAS DIVISION—Day & Zimmermann, Inc., pg. 320
LONE STAR DIVISION—Day & Zimmermann, Inc., pg. 320
MASON COMPANY, pg. 718
MASON HANGER-SILAS MASON CO.—Mason Company, pg. 718
MASON TECHNOLOGIES INC.—Mason Company, pg. 718
TRACOR AEROSPACE, INC. EXPENDABLES DIVISION—Tracor, Inc., pg. 1105
TRACOR, INC., pg. 1104

3484 — SMALL ARMS

ADEC INTERNATIONAL AUTOMATION CORP., pg. 17
THE CANADIAN COLEMAN CO., LTD.—MacAndrews & Forbes Holdings Inc., pg. 695
THE COLEMAN COMPANY, INC.—MacAndrews & Forbes Holdings Inc., pg. 695
CONNELL LIMITED PARTNERSHIP, pg. 275
CROSMAN CORPORATION—MacAndrews & Forbes Holdings Inc., pg. 695
O. F. MOSSBERG & SONS, INC., pg. 773
PACHMAYR GUN WORKS INC., pg. 839
SAVAGE ARMS INC., pg. 973
U.S. REPEATING ARMS COMPANY, pg. 1137
WEATHERBY, INC., pg. 1169

3489 — ORDNANCE & ACCESSORIES, NEC

ACTION MANUFACTURING CO., pg. 15
ALLIED CHUCKER & ENGINEERING COMPANY, pg. 37
CHAMBERLAIN MANUFACTURING CORP.—Duchossois Industries, Inc., pg. 350
DEMPSTER, INC., pg. 328
DUCHOSSOIS INDUSTRIES, INC., pg. 350
HARVARD INDUSTRIES, INC., pg. 514
HARVARD INTERIORS MANUFACTURING CO.—Harvard Industries, Inc., pg. 514
KDI PRECISION PRODUCTS, INC.—KDI Corporation, pg. 612
QUANTIC INDUSTRIES, INC., pg. 904

3491 — INDUSTRIAL VALVES

CASHCO, INC., pg. 228
DELUCA VALVE & INSTRUMENT CO.—Harley Industries, Inc., pg. 510
ECLIPSE, INC., pg. 366
ECLIPSE THERMAL SYSTEMS—Eclipse, Inc., pg. 366
FIKE CORPORATION, pg. 409
GROVE VALVE & REGULATOR COMPANY, pg. 490
J.M. HUBER CORPORATION, pg. 550
KENNEDY VALVE, pg. 623
LUKENHEIMER CO., pg. 687
MAROTTA SCIENTIFIC CONTROLS, INC., pg. 713
MILTON INDUSTRIES, INC., pg. 756
MOGAS INDUSTRIES, INC., pg. 763
ROCKFORD-ECLIPSE—Eclipse, Inc., pg. 366
ROMAC INDUSTRIES, INC., HAYS DIVISION—Romac Industries, Inc., pg. 945
SPECIALTY MANUFACTURING COMPANY, pg. 1027
UNION PUMP COMPANY, pg. 1128
UNITED STATES PIPE & FOUNDRY COMPANY—Walter Industries, Inc., pg. 1162
WALWORTH COMPANY, pg. 1162

3492 — FLUID POWER VALVES & HOSE FITTINGS

AMERICAN BARMAG CO., pg. 49
AMERICAN ELECTRONICS, INC.—AEI Holding Co., Inc., pg. 3
AMERICAN STANDARD INC., pg. 61
AMERICAN-STANDARD, FLUID POWER GROUP—American Standard Inc., pg. 61
THE BABCOCK & WILCOX COMPANY, pg. 107
CGF INDUSTRIES, pg. 201
CRAWFORD FITTINGS & CO., pg. 297
DIXON VALVE & COUPLING COMPANY, pg. 341
FIKE CORPORATION, pg. 409
THE GRADALL CO.—ICM Industries, Inc., pg. 559
GRAYMILLS CORP., pg. 480
GRISWOLD INDUSTRIES, INC., pg. 488
HLC INDUSTRIES, pg. 496
HANSEN COUPLING DIVISION—Tuthill Corporation, pg. 1120
HUMPHREY PRODUCTS COMPANY, pg. 553
HYDRECO—ICM Industries, Inc., pg. 559
LUKENHEIMER CO., pg. 687
NEW HAVEN MFG. CORP., pg. 801
QUADRASTAT CORP.—Adams Rite Manufacturing Co., pg. 17
THE ROLL SEAL VALVE CO., INC.—AEI Holding Co., Inc., pg. 3
SNAP-TITE, INCORPORATED, pg. 1014
TUTHILL CORPORATION, pg. 1120
VALCOR ENGINEERING CORP., pg. 1142
WALWORTH COMPANY, pg. 1162
WATEROUS COMPANY—American Cast Iron Pipe Co., pg. 50

3493 — STEEL SPRINGS, EXCEPT WIRE

AMERICAN STEEL FOUNDRIES—Amsted Industries Incorporated, pg. 69
AMSTED INDUSTRIES INCORPORATED, pg. 68
DUDEK & BOCK SPRING MANUFACTURING COMPANY, pg. 351
LEE SPRING CO., LTD.—The Unimax Corporation, pg. 1127
THE MARMON GROUP, INC., pg. 710
PETERSON AMERICAN CORP., pg. 864
SMALL PARTS, INC., pg. 1010
THE UNIMAX CORPORATION, pg. 1127
UNIMAX HOLDING CORP.—Shepaug Corporation, pg. 998

3494 — VALVES & PIPE FITTINGS, NEC

A.Y.M. INC.—A. Y. McDonald Industries, Inc., pg. 728
R. P. ADAMS COMPANY, INC., pg. 16
AERCO INTERNATIONAL INC., pg. 21
AMERICAN CAST IRON PIPE CO., pg. 50
AMTROL INC., pg. 70
ANCHOR DARLING VALVE CO.—Cawsl Corporation, pg. 230
ANDERSON COPPER & BRASS COMPANY—The Marmon Group, Inc., pg. 711
APEX GALVANIZING CORP.—Victaulic Company of America, pg. 1149
ARMSTRONG INTERNATIONAL, INC., pg. 83
ARMSTRONG MACHINE WORKS—Armstrong International, Inc., pg. 83
ARMSTRONG MACHINE WORKS, S.A.—Armstrong International, Inc., pg. 84
ARMSTRONG-YOSHITAKE, INC.—Armstrong International, Inc., pg. 84
AUTOMATIC MACHINE PRODUCTS COMPANY, pg. 100
BECK MANUFACTURING, INC.—Bitrek Corporation, pg. 153
BELLOFRAM CORP., pg. 136
BONNEY FORGE CORPORATION, pg. 164
BRIDGEPORT FITTINGS, INC., pg. 175
C.I.C.S.A.—Maxon Corporation, pg. 723
CASHCO, INC., pg. 228
CLEVITE DE MEXICO—The Pullman Company, pg. 900
CLEVITE SRL—The Pullman Company, pg. 900
CLOW CORPORATION—McWane, Inc., pg. 733
CLOW VALVE DIV.—McWane, Inc., pg. 733
CLOW WATER SYSTEMS CORP.—McWane, Inc., pg. 733
CONBRACO INDUSTRIES INC., pg. 272
CONTINENTAL MACHINES, INC., pg. 279
DATRON SYSTEMS, INC.—Datron Incorporated, pg. 317
DILLINGHAM CONSTRUCTION N.A., INC.—Dillingham Construction Corporation, pg. 338
DUFF-NORTON—Spreckles Industries, Inc., pg. 1032
ECLIPSE, INC., pg. 366
EVERLASTING VALVE CO.—Armstrong International, Inc., pg. 83
FIKE CORPORATION, pg. 409
FORD METER BOX COMPANY, pg. 423
GRISWOLD INDUSTRIES, INC., pg. 488
HARDIE IRRIGATION-LANDSCAPE DIV., pg. 508
HAWS DRINKING FAUCET CO., pg. 518
J.M. HUBER, FLOW CONTROL DIV.—J.M. Huber Corporation, pg. 550
HYDRIL COMPANY, pg. 556
I-E PROPRIETARY, LTD.—The Pullman Company, pg. 900
IDEAL FORGING CORPORATION, pg. 562
IDEAL-STANDARD WABCO IND. E COM. LTDA—American Standard Inc., pg. 62
IMPERIAL CLEVITE DO BRAZIL—The Pullman Company, pg. 900
IMPERIAL DIVISION—The Pullman Company, pg. 899
ROBERT JAMES SALES INC., pg. 589
THE JOHNSON CORPORATION, pg. 597
JOSAM COMPANY, pg. 607
KEENEY MANUFACTURING CO., pg. 620
KENNEDY VALVE, pg. 623
THE MARMON GROUP, INC., pg. 710
MAROTTA SCIENTIFIC CONTROLS, INC., pg. 713
MAXON CORPORATION, pg. 723
N.V. MAXON INTERNATIONAL S.A.—Maxon Corporation, pg. 723
A. Y. MCDONALD INDUSTRIES, INC., pg. 728
A. Y. MCDONALD MFG. CO.—A. Y. McDonald Industries, Inc., pg. 728
MORRIS COUPLING CO., pg. 771
NIBCO, INC., pg. 806
THE NORTH AMERICAN MANUFACTURING CO., pg. 811
ORBIT VALVE INTERNATIONAL, INC., pg. 828
N.V. PIPECO, S.A.—Victaulic Company of America, pg. 1149
THE WM. POWELL COMPANY, pg. 882
QUALITY CONTROL CORPORATION, pg. 903
RP & C—Conbraco Industries Inc., pg. 272
ROCKFORD-ECLIPSE—Eclipse, Inc., pg. 366
ROMAC INDUSTRIES, INC., pg. 945
ROMAC INDUSTRIES, INC., HAYS DIVISION—Romac Industries, Inc., pg. 945
THE SHANE GROUP INC., pg. 995
SMITH VALVE CORPORATION, pg. 1014
SNAP-TITE, INCORPORATED, pg. 1014
THE SPENCER TURBINE CO., pg. 1030
THE STARFLO CORPORATION—The Wm. Powell Company, pg. 883
STERLING, INC., pg. 1047
STOCKHAM VALVES & FITTINGS, INC., pg. 1050
STRAHMAN VALVES, INC., pg. 1052
SUNBEAM-OSTER COMPANY, INC., pg. 1059
SWEPCO TUBE CORPORATION, pg. 1067
SYMMONS INDUSTRIES INC., pg. 1069
TBV, INC.—Victaulic Company of America, pg. 1149
T & S BRASS & BRONZE WORKS, INC., pg. 1074
TACTAIR FLUID CONTROLS CORP.—Phoenix International, Inc., pg. 869
T.D. WILLIAMSON (U.K.) LTD.—T.D. Williamson, Inc., pg. 1192
TEXAS METAL WORKS, INC., pg. 1089
VALVE AND CONTROLS DIVISION—INDRESCO, Inc., pg. 565
VICTAULIC COMPANY OF AMERICA, pg. 1149
VICTAULIC COMPANY OF CANADA LIMITED—Victaulic Company of America, pg. 1149
HENRY VOGT MACHINE CO., pg. 1154
WALWORTH COMPANY, pg. 1162
WARD MANUFACTURING, INC., pg. 1163
T.D. WILLIAMSON, INC., pg. 1192
T.D. WILLIAMSON S.A.—T.D. Williamson, Inc., pg. 1192
WINROCK ENTERPRISES, INC., pg. 1197
YOUNG & FRANKLIN, INC., pg. 1209

3495 — WIRE SPRINGS

CALDWELL MANUFACTURING COMPANY, pg. 208
CONNECTICUT SPRING & STAMPING CORPORATION, pg. 275
GENERAL SPRING, INC., pg. 450
HOOVER GROUP, INC., pg. 543
KOKOMO SPRING COMPANY, INC., pg. 640
LEE SPRING COMPANY—The Unimax Corporation, pg. 1127
MCROBERT SPRINGS CO.—The Marmon Group, Inc., pg. 712
PECK SPRING COMPANY, pg. 854
PETERSON AMERICAN CORP., pg. 864
SMALL PARTS, INC., pg. 1010
SPRING ENGINEERS, INC., pg. 1033
STEADLY COMPANY, pg. 1043
THE TURNER & SEYMOUR MFG. COMPANY, pg. 1119

3496 — MISCELLANEOUS FABRICATED WIRE PRODUCTS

AXIA INCORPORATED, pg. 8
ANCHOR FENCE COMPANY—PPA Industries, Inc., pg. 836
APACHE HOSE & BELTING COMPANY, pg. 77
AUTOSWAGE PRODUCTS, INC., pg. 101
AVIS INDUSTRIAL CORPORATION, pg. 102
THE WILLIAM BAYLEY CO., pg. 128
BIO MEDIC CORPORATION, pg. 152
BRIDGEWATER RESOURCES CORPORATION, pg. 175
CABLECRAFT INC.—Tuthill Corporation, pg. 1120
CLEANERS HANGER CO., pg. 254
SIGMUND COHN CORP., pg. 259
COLSON EQUIPMENT, INC.—The Marmon Group, Inc., pg. 711
CONNECTICUT SPRING & STAMPING CORPORATION, pg. 275
DAVIS WALKER CORP.—Heico Inc., pg. 525
DAVIS WIRE CORPORATION, pg. 319
DELTA SURPRENANT WIRE & CABLE, INC., pg. 327
DUDEK & BOCK SPRING MANUFACTURING COMPANY, pg. 351
EAGLE BUTTON CO., INC., pg. 362
FELLOWES MANUFACTURING CO., pg. 405
GNWC WIRE, CABLE & NETWORK PRODUCERS, pg. 440
GEORGETOWN INDUSTRIES, INC., pg. 453
GERRARD AND COMPANY, pg. 454
GILBERT & BENNETT, pg. 457
GRAYLINE HOUSEWARES, pg. 480
HARFORD SYSTEMS, INC.—Bio Medic Corporation, pg. 152
HEWITT-ROBINS CORP., pg. 532
HYNES INDUSTRIES INC., pg. 557
HYSPAN PRECISION PRODUCTS, INC., pg. 557
KASPAR WIRE WORKS, INC., pg. 617
LAB PRODUCTS, INC.—Bio Medic Corporation, pg. 152
LAIDLAW CORPORATION, pg. 650
LASTING PRODUCTS, INC., pg. 660
LESCHEN WIRE ROPE—Wire Rope Corp. of America, Inc., pg. 1197
LIFT-ALL CO., INC., pg. 675
MICRO-MET L CORP., pg. 748
NASHVILLE WIRE PRODUCT CO., pg. 784
NELSEN STEEL & WIRE CO., pg. 797
ORBEL CORPORATION, pg. 828
PPA INDUSTRIES, INC., pg. 836
PEERLESS CHAIN CO., pg. 855
PETERSON AMERICAN CORP., pg. 864
THE PIERCE CO., INC.—Avis Industrial Corporation, pg. 102
PORTLAND CHAIN MFG. CO.—Webster Industries Inc., pg. 1172
PREFORMED LINE PRODUCTS CANADA—Preformed Line Products, pg. 886
PREST RACK INC.—Binkley Company, pg. 151
PRICE BROTHERS CO., pg. 888
RENCO GROUP, pg. 926
ROOT CORPORATION, pg. 946
SENCORP, pg. 989
SENECA WIRE & MANUFACTURING CO., pg. 989
SEYMOUR MANUFACTURING COMPANY, pg. 994
SOMMER METALCRAFT CORPORATION, pg. 1018
SPEEDRACK PRODUCTS GROUP, LTD., pg. 1029
TETKO, INC., pg. 1089
E. H. TITCHENER & COMPANY, pg. 1099
TUTHILL CORPORATION, pg. 1120
UNITED STEEL & WIRE CO., pg. 1137
WALPOLE WOODWORKERS, INC., pg. 1161

WEBSTER-PORTALLOY CHAINS, INC.—Webster Industries Inc., pg. 1172
WIRE ROPE CORP. OF AMERICA, INC., pg. 1197
G.F. WRIGHT STEEL & WIRE COMPANY, pg. 1205

3497 — METAL FOIL & LEAF

BRYCE CORPORATION, pg. 185
DRI-PRINT FOILS, pg. 349
GOMAR MANUFACTURING CO., INC., pg. 469
MACRISTY INDUSTRIES, INC., pg. 698
PENNY PLATE, INC., pg. 858

3498 — FABRICATED PIPE & FABRICATED PIPE FITTINGS

APEX SUPPLY CO. INC., pg. 78
ASHMAN ENTERPRISES, INC., pg. 88
BENT TUBE, INC., pg. 140
BURNER SYSTEMS INTERNATIONAL, INC.—The Dyson-Kissner-Moran Corporation, pg. 357
CONSOLIDATED PIPE & SUPPLY COMPANY, pg. 277
DILLINGHAM CONSTRUCTION N.A., INC.—Dillingham Construction Corporation, pg. 338
FABEX INC., pg. 395
H & H TUBE & MANUFACTURING CO., pg. 495
HARLAN ELECTRIC CO., pg. 509
INDUSTRIAL CONTRACTORS, INC., pg. 566
LYON CONKLIN & COMPANY, pg. 690
MACRISTY INDUSTRIES, INC., pg. 698
MANUFACTURING DIV.—Marquette Coppersmithing Co., Inc., pg. 713
MARQUETTE COPPERSMITHING CO., INC., pg. 713
MIDWESCO INC., pg. 751
NPS CORPORATION, pg. 781
PMC INDUSTRIES INC., pg. 836
PIEDMONT MECHANICAL, INC., pg. 870
PIPE FABRICATING & SUPPLY COMPANY, pg. 872
PIPECO, INC.—Pasotex Corporation, pg. 851
PIPING DESIGN DIV.—Marquette Coppersmithing Co., Inc., pg. 713
POWER PIPING COMPANY—Harlan Electric Co., pg. 509
QUACKENBUSH CO. INC., pg. 902
REPUBLIC INDUSTRIES, INC., pg. 928
ROCKET INDUSTRIES, INC./EXCEL, THE EXERCISE COMPANY, pg. 941
SPENCER TURBINE CO., pg. 1030
SPIROL INTERNATIONAL CORP., pg. 1031
STANDCO INDUSTRIES, INC., pg. 1038
TUBULAR SERVICES, INC.—Pasotex Corporation, pg. 851

3499 — FABRICATED METAL PRODUCTS, NEC

A & A MANUFACTURING CO., pg. 1
A & S TRIBAL INDUSTRIES, pg. 1
AMI INDUSTRIES, INC., pg. 5
THE AARQUE COMPANIES, pg. 9
ABBOTT GROUP LTD., pg. 9
ABBOTT PRODUCTS INC.—Abbott Group Ltd., pg. 9
ACROMETAL COMPANIES, INC., pg. 14
ACROMETAL COMPANIES, INC.—Acrometal Companies, Inc., pg. 14
AEROCLO METAL PRODUCTS—Precision Valve Corporation, pg. 886
ALADDIN INDUSTRIES, INCORPORATED, pg. 29
ALADDIN INTERNATIONAL CORP. S.A.R.L.—Aladdin Industries, Incorporated, pg. 29
ALADDIN INTERNATIONAL CORPORATION (UK)—Aladdin Industries, Incorporated, pg. 29
ALCO INDUSTRIES, INC., pg. 32
ALLIED CHUCKER & ENGINEERING COMPANY, pg. 37
ALLIED SECURITY, INTERNATIONAL, pg. 40
ALLOY TECHNOLOGY INTERNATIONAL INC., pg. 41
AMERICAN SYSTEMS CORPORATION, pg. 63
AMERICAN TANK & FABRICATING CO., pg. 63
AMSTED INDUSTRIES INCORPORATED, pg. 68
BANKCRAFTERS, INC., pg. 117
BECKLEY PERFORATING CO.—Laubeck Corporation/Cross, pg. 660
BETTCHER MANUFACTURING CORP., pg. 148
BRAINARD STRAPPING, pg. 171
BRUCE INDUSTRIES, INC., pg. 183
CHICAGO WEST PULLMAN CORPORATION, pg. 246
CHOCTAW, INC., pg. 248
CLARK DOOR CO., INC., pg. 252
COOK MANUFACTURING CORPORATION, pg. 282
CRENLO, INC., pg. 298
CRES-COR/CROWN-X, pg. 298
CRUCIBLE MATERIALS CORP., pg. 302
D.C.I., INC., pg. 308
DAHLSTROM OF CANADA LTD.—The Aarque Companies, pg. 9
DAY INDUSTRIES—The Rawlplug Company, Inc., pg. 914
DESCO CORPORATION, pg. 332
DIAMOND CHAIN COMPANY—Amsted Industries Incorporated, pg. 69
DILLINGHAM CONSTRUCTION N.A., INC.—Dillingham Construction Corporation, pg. 338
EMSON RESEARCH, INC., pg. 380
ERIEZ PRODUCTS MAGNETICOS E METALURGICOS, LTDA.—Sunbeam-Oster Company, Inc., pg. 1059
EVANS FABRICATION, INC., pg. 390
G & L PRODUCTS, INC., pg. 438
GARY METALS CO., INC.—Primary Industries Corporation, pg. 889
GENERAL MACHINERY CO.—Wheaton Inc., pg. 1184
GENERAL SHIP CORPORATION, pg. 450
GERRARD AND COMPANY, pg. 454
GIBRALTAR STEEL CORP., pg. 456
CLIFFORD B. HANNAY & SON INC., pg. 505
HARFORD SYSTEMS, INC.—Bio Medic Corporation, pg. 152
HARTZ MOUNTAIN GROUP—Hartz Group, pg. 514
HERFF JONES INC., pg. 531
HOOD & COMPANY, pg. 542
HUGHES-TREITLER MANUFACTURING CORPORATION, pg. 552
JONATHAN MANUFACTURING CORP., pg. 602
KURT MANUFACTURING CO. INC., pg. 646
LASTING PRODUCTS, INC., pg. 660
LAUBECK CORPORATION/CROSS, pg. 660
CHARLES LEONARD, INC., pg. 668
LOUISVILLE SCRAP MATERIAL CO., INC., pg. 684
MACHINING ENTERPRISES INC., pg. 696
MAXCOR MANUFACTURING, INC., pg. 722
MAXIMET—Karsten Manufacturing Corporation, pg. 617
MCNALLY INDUSTRIES, INC., pg. 731
MEDICO INDUSTRIES, INC., pg. 735
MICRODOT AEROSPACE FASTENING SYSTEMS GROUP—MICRODOT, Inc., pg. 749
MICRODOT, INC., pg. 749
MOELLER MARINE PRODUCTS—Moore Company, pg. 768
MOSLER DROPOSITORY DIV.—Mosler Inc., pg. 772
MOSLER INC., pg. 772
MOSLER, INC.—Mosler Inc., pg. 772
MOSLER SA DE C.D.—Mosler Inc., pg. 772
MOSSBERG INDUSTRIES, HUBBARD DIVISION—Mossberg Industries, Inc., pg. 773
MOSSBERG INDUSTRIES, INC., pg. 772
NORWALK POWDERED METALS, INC., pg. 816
R.S. OWENS, pg. 834
PEERLESS CHAIN COMPANY—Bridgewater Resources Corporation, pg. 175
PNEUMAFIL CORP., pg. 878
PRECISION VALVE CORPORATION, pg. 885
PREDCO, INC.—Dixon Valve & Coupling Company, pg. 341
THE PRESMET CORP., pg. 887
PRODUCTION MANAGEMENT COMPANIES, INC., pg. 893
PULLMAN INDUSTRIES, INC., pg. 900
THE RAWLPLUG COMPANY, INC., pg. 914
RAYMARK FRICTION COMPANY, pg. 914
ROLODEX CORP.—Insilco Corporation, pg. 571
ROSS ENGINEERING CO., INC., pg. 949
SARGENT & GREENLEAF, INC., pg. 971
SCHWAB CORP., pg. 980
SCHWEIZER AIRCRAFT CORPORATION, pg. 981
SENTRY GROUP, pg. 990
EVERETT SMITH INVESTMENT CO. OF DELAWARE, pg. 1013
SOVEREIGN GROUP INC., pg. 1024
SPECIALTY ENGINEERED DOORS-CLARK DOOR CO.—Clark Door Co., Inc., pg. 252
SPRAYING SYSTEMS CO., pg. 1032
SPRAYING SYSTEMS CO. FAR EAST—Spraying Systems Co., pg. 1032
SPRAYING SYSTEMS DEUTSCHLAND GMBH—Spraying Systems Co., pg. 1032
STACKPOLE MAGNET DIVISION—The Stackpole Corporation, pg. 1034
STAINLESS INCORPORATED, pg. 1035
THOMAS & SKINNER, INC., pg. 1093
THUNDERLINE CORPORATION, pg. 1096
TRANSCO INC., pg. 1106
TRANSCO PRODUCTS INC.—Transco Inc., pg. 1107
TRICON INDUSTRIES, INC., pg. 1113
TRITON INDUSTRIES, INC., pg. 1114
TROPAR MFG. CO., INC.—Tropar Mfg. Co., Inc., pg. 1116
TROPAR MFG. CO., INC., pg. 1115
TROPAR MFG. CO., INC.—Tropar Mfg. Co., Inc., pg. 1116
TUTHILL CORPORATION, pg. 1120
U.S. MANUFACTURING CORP., pg. 1136
UNITED STATES PIPE & FOUNDRY COMPANY—Walter Industries, Inc., pg. 1162
UP-RIGHT, INC., pg. 1139
VORTEC CORPORATION—Chicago West Pullman Corporation, pg. 246
O.S. WALKER CO., INC.—Walker Magnetics Group, Inc., pg. 1160
WHEATON INC., pg. 1184
WITT COMPANY, pg. 1198

3511 — STEAM, GAS, & HYDRAULIC TURBINES; & TURBINE GENERATOR SET UNITS

COPPUS ENGINEERING CORP., pg. 285
DETROIT DIESEL ALLISON CO.—Western Diesel Services Inc., pg. 1179
ELLIOTT COMPANY, pg. 378
EVANS INDUSTRIES, INC., pg. 390
JOHN R. HOLLINGSWORTH CO., pg. 539
IFP HYDRAULICS INC.—ICM Industries, Inc., pg. 559
INDUSTRIAL ACOUSTICS COMPANY S.C. INC.—Industrial Acoustics Company, Inc., pg. 566
MAGNA-POW'R INC.—ICM Industries, Inc., pg. 559
MURRAY TURBOMACHINERY CORPORATION—Coppus Engineering Corp., pg. 285
THE SPENCER TURBINE CO., pg. 1030
STOLPER-FABRALLOY CO., pg. 1050
TIC UNITED CORPORATION, pg. 1073
U.S. TURBINE CORPORATION, pg. 1137

3519 — INTERNAL COMBUSTION ENGINES, NEC

AMSTED INDUSTRIES INCORPORATED, pg. 68
BURGESS-NORTON MFG. CO.—Amsted Industries Incorporated, pg. 69
CUMMINS INTERMOUNTAIN DIESEL, pg. 305
DETROIT DIESEL CORP.—Penske Corporation, pg. 859
EVANS INDUSTRIES, INC., pg. 390
ILLINIOS AUTO ELECTRIC MIDWEST ENGINE WAREHOUSE DIV.—Illinois Auto Electric Co., pg. 562
ILLINOIS AUTO ELECTRIC CO., pg. 562
JOHNSON & TOWERS, INC., pg. 601
KOHLER COMPANY, pg. 639
KOHLER DE MEXICO, S.A. DE C.V.—Kohler Company, pg. 640
MUSTANG TRACTOR & EQUIP. CO., pg. 777
PENSKE CORPORATION, pg. 859
TRIPLE A SPECIALTY COMPANY, pg. 1114

3523 — FARM MACHINERY & EQUIPMENT

AGCO CORPORATION—AGCO Inc., pg. 4
AGCO INC., pg. 4
AGCO MANUFACTURING GROUP—AGCO Inc., pg. 4
ALAMO GROUP, INC., pg. 29
ALLOWAY MANUFACTURING, pg. 41
ANDIS COMPANY, pg. 74
BMB COMPANY—Alamo Group, Inc., pg. 29
BADGER NORTHLAND INC., pg. 113
BEHLEN MFG. CO., pg. 132
BLUMHARDT MANUFACTURING COMPANY—TIC United Corporation, pg. 1073
CTB INC., pg. 205
THE CALKINS MANUFACTURING COMPANY, pg. 210
CARTER DAY CO.—Carter Day Industries, Inc., pg. 226
CARTER DAY INDUSTRIES, INC., pg. 226
CARTER DAY INDUSTRIES (CANADA) LTD.—Carter Day Industries, Inc., pg. 226
CHORE-TIME CAGE SYSTEMS—CTB Inc., pg. 205
CHORE-TIME EQUIPMENT—CTB Inc., pg. 205
CONTINENTAL EAGLE CORPORATION, pg. 278
CORN STATES HYBRID SERVICE, INCORPORATED, pg. 286
CRENLO, INC., pg. 298
CRUSTBUSTER, INC., pg. 303
DEC AG—DEC International, Inc., pg. 309
DEC/BOU-MATIC—DEC International, Inc., pg. 309
DEC INTERNATIONAL, INC., pg. 308
DMI, INC., pg. 309
DANUSER MACHINE CO., pg. 315
DODGEN FEED BODIES—Hagie Manufacturing Co., pg. 499
DYER-LAUDERDALE FARMERS CO-OP—Tennessee Farmers Co-op, pg. 1087
FABDEC LTD.—DEC International, Inc., pg. 309
FARMHAND, INC., pg. 402
FARNAM COMPANIES, INC., pg. 403
FONTAINE INTERNATIONAL, INC.—The Marmon Group, Inc., pg. 711
GARDEN WAY, INC., pg. 443
GREAT PLAINS MANUFACTURING, INC., pg. 482
HAGIE MANUFACTURING CO., pg. 499
HART-CARTER CO.—Carter Day Industries, Inc., pg. 226
HAWKEYE STEEL PRODUCTS, INC., pg. 518
HAY & FORAGE INDUSTRIES—AGCO Inc., pg. 4
HENDERSON MFG.—Willmar Manufacturing, pg. 1193
HESSTON—AGCO Inc., pg. 4
HINIKER COMPANY, pg. 535
HOFFCO, INC., pg. 537
H.D. HUDSON MANUFACTURING COMPANY, pg. 551
HUTCHINSON WIL-RICH MANUFACTURING CO.—TIC United Corporation, pg. 1073
JAMESWAY CO.—The Marmon Group, Inc., pg. 712
KRAUSE PLOW CORP., pg. 644
LOCKWOOD CORPORATION, pg. 680
LONG MFG. NC, INC., pg. 682
M&W GEAR COMPANY, pg. 690
THE MARMON GROUP, INC., pg. 710
MID AMERICA STEEL, INC., pg. 750
MILLER-ST. NAZIANZ, INC., pg. 755
MOORMAN MFG. COMPANY, pg. 769
MUSTANG TRACTOR & EQUIP. CO., pg. 777
NEBRASKA ENGINEERING CO.—TIC United Corporation, pg. 1073
O. A. NEWTON & SON CO., pg. 805
PEABODY MYERS CORP.—The Pullman Company, pg. 900
POWER KING PRODUCTS CO., pg. 883
REINKE MANUFACTURING CO., INC., pg. 924
RITCHIE INDUSTRIES, INC., pg. 936
C.G. SARGENTS SONS—Aeroglide Corporation, pg. 22
THE SCOTT COMPANY, pg. 982
SERVICE MOTOR COMPANY, pg. 992
SEYMOUR MANUFACTURING COMPANY, pg. 994
SHENANDOAH MFG. CO. INC., pg. 997
SHORELINE PRODUCTS, INC., pg. 1000
J-STARR INDUSTRIES, INC., pg. 1040
STEVENS-LEE COMPANY, pg. 1048
THOMAS CONVEYOR COMPANY, pg. 1093
TIFFANY INDUSTRIES, INC., pg. 1097
TRIUMPH MACHINE CO.—Alamo Group, Inc., pg. 29
TROJAN SPECIALIZED LIVESTOCK EQUIP.—Ritchie Industries, Inc., pg. 936
TYLER LIMITED PARTNERSHIP, pg. 1122
THE UNION FORK & HOE CO., pg. 1128
UNITED FARM TOOLS, INC., pg. 1131
UNITED FARM TOOLS, INC., OELWEIN—United Farm Tools, Inc., pg. 1132
UNIVERSAL COOPERATIVES, INC., pg. 1138
UP-RIGHT, INC., pg. 1139
VALK MANUFACTURING COMPANY, pg. 1143
VERMEER MANUFACTURING COMPANY, pg. 1148
VIBRA SCREW INC., pg. 1149
WESBAR CORPORATION, pg. 1176
WIL-RICH NOBLE COMPANY—TIC United Corporation, pg. 1073
WILLMAR MANUFACTURING, pg. 1193
WILTON CORPORATION, pg. 1194
YELLOWSTONE TRANSPORTATION SERVICE, INC.—Martrade Ltd., pg. 716

3524 — LAWN & GARDEN TRACTORS & HOME LAWN & GARDEN EQUIPMENT

AIRCAP INDUSTRIES CORP.—MTD Products, Inc., pg. 694
ATLAS POWER EQUIPMENT COMPANY, pg. 96
BELMONT INDUSTRIES, INC., pg. 136
BUNTON COMPANY, pg. 188
CRUSTBUSTER, INC., pg. 303
THE DISSTON CO., pg. 339
EXCEL INDUSTRIES, INC., pg. 392
GARDEN WAY, INC., pg. 443
GENERAL POWER EQUIPMENT CO.—Cotter & Company, pg. 288
HOFFCO, INC., pg. 537
MTD PRODUCTS, INC., pg. 694
MTD PRODUCTS LIMITED—MTD Products, Inc., pg. 694
MARK MACHINE INC., pg. 708
POWER KING PRODUCTS CO., pg. 883
SCHILLER-PFEIFFER, INC.—Belmont Industries, Inc., pg. 136
SIMPLICITY MANUFACTURING, INC., pg. 1006
SPECIALTY MANUFACTURING COMPANY, pg. 1027
SUNBEAM-OSTER COMPANY, INC., pg. 1059
TORNADO PRODUCTS, INC.—Simplicity Manufacturing, Inc., pg. 1007
THE UNION FORK & HOE CO., pg. 1128
WHEELER MANUFACTURING CO.—Cotter & Company, pg. 288

3531 — CONSTRUCTION MACHINERY & EQUIPMENT

ACCESS EQUIPMENT LTD.—Up-Right, Inc., pg. 1139
AMCLYDE ENGINEERED PRODUCTS, INC., pg. 47
ANCRA CORPORATION, pg. 72
ARNOLD MACHINERY CO., pg. 84
ASHMAN ENTERPRISES, INC., pg. 88
AUTO CRANE COMPANY, pg. 100
AVIS INDUSTRIAL CORPORATION, pg. 102
B-E HOLDINGS INC., pg. 106
BADGER EQUIPMENT COMPANY—Avis Industrial Corporation, pg. 102
BEACON WINCH COMPANY—Beacon Group, pg. 129
BESSER COMPANY, pg. 146
BLAW KNOX CORP., pg. 156
BUCYRUS BLADES DE MEXICO—Esco Corporation, pg. 388
BUCYRUS BLADES OF CANADA LTD.—Esco Corporation, pg. 388
BUCYRUS BLADES OF GEORGIA—Esco Corporation, pg. 388
THE CADMAN COMPANIES—C B R Cement Corporation, pg. 199
CARGILL DETROIT CORP., pg. 219
CHARLES MACHINE WORKS, INC., pg. 240
CHICAGO WEST PULLMAN HEAVY INDUSTRIES—Chicago West Pullman Corporation, pg. 246
CONLEY FROG & SWITCH COMPANY, pg. 274
CRAFCO, INC.—Ergon, Inc., pg. 386
CRENLO, INC., pg. 298
CROWN HOLDINGS, INC., pg. 302
CROWN IRON WORKS COMPANY—Crown Holdings, Inc., pg. 302
CRUSHING & SCREENING DIV.—Hewitt-Robins Corp., pg. 532
DANUSER MACHINE CO., pg. 315
DUTTON-LAINSON CO., pg. 356
EAGER BEAVER, pg. 362
EARTHMOVING EQUIPMENT DIV.—Esco Corporation, pg. 388
ELFIN INDUSTRIES, LTD.—Ancra Corporation, pg. 72
EMPIRE SOUTHWEST CO., pg. 379
EQUIPMENT MANUFACTURING, INC., pg. 385
ESCO CORPORATION, pg. 388
ESCO, EUROPE S.A.—Esco Corporation, pg. 388
ESCO, S.A.—Esco Corporation, pg. 388
EVANS INDUSTRIES, INC., pg. 390
FM INDUSTRIES, INC., pg. 394
FWD CORPORATION, pg. 395
FERGUSON MANUFACTURING & EQUIPMENT COMPANY, pg. 406
FROG SWITCH & MANUFACTURING COMPANY, pg. 434
GETMAN CORPORATION, pg. 455
GOODMAN EQUIPMENT CORP., pg. 470
HAULPAK DIVISION, KOMATSU DRESSER COMPANY—INDRESCO, Inc., pg. 565
HAWTHORNE LIFT SYSTEMS, pg. 519
INDRESCO, INC., pg. 565
INDUSTRIAL GENERAL CORPORATION, pg. 566
C. S. JOHNSON CO., pg. 597
KEWAUNEE ENGINEERING CORP.—Marine Travelift, Inc., pg. 707
KLEIN TOOLS INC., pg. 635
KOKOSING MATERIALS, INC.—Kokosing Construction Company, Inc., pg. 641
KOMATSU DRESSER COMPANY—INDRESCO, Inc., pg. 565
KRAUSE PLOW CORP., pg. 644
LAFAYETTE MANUFACTURING, INC., pg. 650
LOCKWOOD CORPORATION, pg. 680
MARION POWER SHOVEL DIVISION—INDRESCO, Inc., pg. 565
MAULDIN MFG. CO., INC.—Whitin Roberts Co., pg. 1187
MCNEILUS COMPANIES, pg. 732
MI-JACK PRODUCTS, INC., pg. 746
MUSTANG MANUFACTURING COMPANY, INC., pg. 777
MUSTANG TRACTOR & EQUIP. CO., pg. 777
PAPER CALMENSON & CO., pg. 847
PIKROSE & CO., LTD.—The Marmon Group, Inc., pg. 712
R.A. INDUSTRIES, INC., pg. 906
RACINE FEDERATED, INC., pg. 909
RADIATOR SPECIALTY COMPANY, pg. 909
RAPID INDUSTRIES, INC., pg. 913
THE READ CORPORATION, pg. 916
REEDRILL INC.—Zimmerman Holdings, Inc., pg. 1220
ROSCO MANUFACTURING CO., pg. 947
T. L. SMITH MACHINE, pg. 1013
STAMLER CORPORATION, pg. 1035
STONHARD, EUROPE—Stonhard, Inc., pg. 1051
STONHARD LATIN AMERICA—Stonhard, Inc., pg. 1051
STONHARD, LTD.—Stonhard, Inc., pg. 1052
TRAK INTERNATIONAL, INC., pg. 1106
TYLER LIMITED PARTNERSHIP, pg. 1122
UNIVERSAL BUILDERS SUPPLY, INC., pg. 1137
UP-RIGHT, INC., pg. 1139
VALK MANUFACTURING COMPANY, pg. 1143
WARN INDUSTRIES, INC., pg. 1164
THE WYCO TOOL CO.—Racine Federated, Inc., pg. 909
XTEK, INC., pg. 1206
ZIMMERMAN HOLDINGS, INC., pg. 1220

3532 — MINING MACHINERY & EQUIPMENT, EXCEPT OIL & GAS FIELD MACHINERY EQUIPMENT

A & A ASSOCIATES—Zimmerman Holdings, Inc., pg. 1220
ACRISON, INC., pg. 14
ALIMAK ELEVATOR COMPANY, pg. 34
B-E HOLDINGS INC., pg. 106
BIJUR LUBRICATING CORPORATION, pg. 150
BLUE TEE CORPORATION, pg. 161
BOONVILLE MINING SERVICES, INC.—Bucyrus-Erie Company, pg. 186
BUCYRUS (AFRICA) PROPRIETARY LTD.—Bucyrus-Erie Company, pg. 186
BUCYRUS (AUSTRALIA) PROPRIETARY LTD.—Bucyrus-Erie Company, pg. 186
BUCYRUS (BRASIL) LTDA.—Bucyrus-Erie Company, pg. 186
BUCYRUS CHILE LTDA.—Bucyrus-Erie Company, pg. 186
BUCYRUS-ERIE CO. OF CANADA LTD.—Bucyrus-Erie Company, pg. 186
BUCYRUS-ERIE COMPANY, pg. 186
BUCYRUS-EUROPE LTD.—Bucyrus-Erie Company, pg. 186
BURRELL GROUP, pg. 195
CLINCH RIVER CORP.—Jupiter Industries, Inc., pg. 609
CRUSHING & SCREENING DIV.—Hewitt-Robins Corp., pg. 532
DENVER AUTOMETRICS—Denver Equipment Company, pg. 331
DENVER EQUIPMENT COMPANY, pg. 331
DENVER EQUIPMENT PTY., LTD.—Denver Equipment Company, pg. 331
DENVER PROCESS EQUIPMENT, LTD.—Denver Equipment Company, pg. 331
DIFCO, INC., pg. 337
DINGS MAGNETIC CO.—Venturedyne, Ltd., pg. 1148
DORR-OLIVER INCORPORATED, pg. 346
DOUBLE DIAMOND DIST. INC.—Wotco Inc., pg. 1204
ELGIN NATIONAL INDUSTRIES, INC.—Jupiter Industries, Inc., pg. 609
FM INDUSTRIES, INC., pg. 394
J. H. FLETCHER & CO., pg. 418
GETMAN CORPORATION, pg. 455
GOODMAN EQUIPMENT CORP., pg. 470
GREENFIELD INDUSTRIES INC.—Harbour Group Ltd., pg. 507
HARBERT CORPORATION, pg. 506
HAULPAK DIVISION, KOMATSU DRESSER COMPANY—INDRESCO, Inc., pg. 565
INDRESCO, INC., pg. 565
JEFFREY DIVISION—INDRESCO, Inc., pg. 565
LONG-AIRDOX COMPANY—The Marmon Group, Inc., pg. 711
LONGYEAR (AUSTRALIA) PTY. LTD.—Longyear Company, pg. 682
LONGYEAR CANADA INC.—Longyear Company, pg. 682
LONGYEAR CENTROAMERICANA S.A.—Longyear Company, pg. 682
LONGYEAR CHILE LTDA.—Longyear Company, pg. 683
LONGYEAR COMPANY, pg. 682
LONGYEAR DE MEXICO S.A. DE C.V.—Longyear Company, pg. 683
LONGYEAR DEUTSCHLAND GMBH—Longyear Company, pg. 683
LONGYEAR IBERICA S.A.—Longyear Company, pg. 683
MCLAUGHLIN MFG. COMPANY, pg. 731
MCNALLY WELLMAN COMPANY, pg. 732
METAL CUTTING TOOLS CORP.—Harbour Group Ltd., pg. 507
MINSERCO, INC.—Bucyrus-Erie Company, pg. 186
NORRIS SCREEN & MFG., INC.—Jupiter Industries, Inc., pg. 609
OMEGA TRANSWORLD LTD.—Burrell Group, pg. 195
PENNSYLVANIA CRUSHER CORP., pg. 858
ROGERS TOOL WORKS, INC.—Harbour Group Ltd., pg. 507
SCREW CONVEYOR CORP., pg. 983
EVERETT SMITH INVESTMENT CO. OF DELAWARE, pg. 1013
STAMLER CORPORATION, pg. 1035
TABOR MACHINE CO.—Jupiter Industries, Inc., pg. 609
VENTUREDYNE, LTD., pg. 1148
WOTCO INC., pg. 1204
XTEK/ARIZONA DIVISION—Xtek, Inc., pg. 1206
XTEK, INC., pg. 1206
ZIMMERMAN HOLDINGS, INC., pg. 1220

3533 — OIL & GAS FIELD MACHINERY & EQUIPMENT

AXELSON, INC., pg. 103
BESSER COMPANY, pg. 146
BRUNNER & LAY, INC., pg. 184
THE BUSCHMAN CO., pg. 196
FM INDUSTRIES, INC., pg. 394
HOPPER INC., pg. 543
HOUSTON ENGINEERS—Wilson Industries Inc., pg. 1194
HYDRIL COMPANY, pg. 556
HYDRIL COMPANY—Hydril Company, pg. 556
INGRAM CACTUS CO.—Ingram Industries Inc., pg. 569
KIMRAY, INC., pg. 629
MCNEILUS COMPANIES, pg. 732
MURDOCK, INC., pg. 776
STANDCO INDUSTRIES, INC., pg. 1038
STANDCO OILFIELD PRODUCTS DIV.—Standco Industries, Inc., pg. 1038
TIMEC COMPANY, pg. 1097
TRIUMPH*LOR, INC., pg. 1115
TRIUMPH-LOR, INC.—Triumph*Lor, Inc., pg. 1115
T.D. WILLIAMSON, INC., pg. 1192
WILSON INDUSTRIES INC., pg. 1193

3534 — ELEVATORS & MOVING STAIRWAYS

ALIMAK ELEVATOR COMPANY, pg. 34
ALIMAK ELEVATOR COMPANY—Alimak Elevator Company, pg. 34
BECKWITH ELEVATOR CO., pg. 131
CHENEY COMPANY, pg. 242
ESCO ELEVATORS, INC., pg. 388
HAUENSTEIN & BURMEISTER, INC., pg. 517
KLECO CORP., pg. 634
MOLINE ACCESSORIES COMPANY—Montgomery Elevator Company, pg. 767
MONTGOMERY ELEVATOR ARCHITECTURAL PRODUCTS DIVISION—Montgomery Elevator Company, pg. 767
MONTGOMERY ELEVATOR COMPANY, pg. 767
MONTGOMERY ELEVATOR CONTROLS DIVISION—Montgomery Elevator Company, pg. 767
MONTGOMERY ELEVATOR DIVISION—Montgomery Elevator Company, pg. 767
MONTGOMERY ESCALATOR DIVISION—Montgomery Elevator Company, pg. 767
STERLING MACHINERY CO., INC.—Montgomery Elevator Company, pg. 767
TYLER ELEVATOR PRODUCTS, INC., pg. 1122

3535 — CONVEYORS & CONVEYING EQUIPMENT

AEC, INC.—Sterling, Inc., pg. 1047
ALVEY INC., pg. 46
ASHWORTH BROS., INC., pg. 88
BADGER EQUIPMENT COMPANY—Avis Industrial Corporation, pg. 102
BAVARIA CARGO TECHNOLOGIE GMBH—Rogerson Aircraft Corporation, pg. 944
BLAW KNOX CORP., pg. 156
BROCK MANUFACTURING—CTB Inc., pg. 205
BUHLER INC., pg. 187
CARRIER VIBRATING EQUIPMENT, INC., pg. 225
CONTINENTAL CONVEYOR & EQUIPMENT COMPANY—NESCO, Inc., pg. 798
DAHLSTROM OF CANADA LTD.—The Aarque Companies, pg. 9
DIAMOND CHAIN COMPANY—Amsted Industries Incorporated, pg. 69
EVANA AUTOMATION, pg. 390
FLEETWOOD SYSTEMS, INC., pg. 417
FROST INC., pg. 435
GEORGIA DUCK & CORDAGE MILLS, pg. 453
GERRARD AND COMPANY, pg. 454
HEWITT-ROBINS CORP., pg. 532
IDEA ENGINEERING & FABRICATING, pg. 562
INTRALOX A/S—The Laitram Corporation, pg. 651
INTRALOX EUROPEAN—The Laitram Corporation, pg. 651
INTRALOX, INC.—The Laitram Corporation, pg. 651
INTRALOX, INC. GMBH—The Laitram Corporation, pg. 651
INTRALOX ITALIA S.R.L.—The Laitram Corporation, pg. 651
INTRALOX LTD.—The Laitram Corporation, pg. 651
JETSTREAM SYSTEMS—Barry-Wehmiller Company, pg. 122
C. S. JOHNSON CO., pg. 597
KEY HANDLING SYSTEMS, INC., pg. 627
GEORGE KOCH SONS, INC., pg. 639
THE LAITRAM CORPORATION, pg. 650
LONG-AIRDOX COMPANY—The Marmon Group, Inc., pg. 711
MARTIN SPROCKET & GEAR, INC., pg. 715
B. L. MONTAGUE CO., pg. 766
NATIONAL OATS CO.—Agway, Inc., pg. 25
OVERHEAD CONVEYOR CO., pg. 832
PENTEK CORPORATION—The Dyson-Kissner-Moran Corporation, pg. 357
PRODUCTION MACHINERY CORPORATION, pg. 893
RAPID INDUSTRIES, INC., pg. 913
SANTA ROSA STEEL FORMING, INC., pg. 970
SCREW CONVEYOR CORP., pg. 983
SEMCO, INC., pg. 989
SPENCER TURBINE CO., pg. 1030
STAMLER CORPORATION, pg. 1035
STOCKER & YALE, INC., pg. 1050
UNEX CONVEYING SYSTEMS, INC., pg. 1126
WALKER MAGNETICS GROUP, INC., pg. 1160
JERVIS B. WEBB COMPANY, pg. 1170
WEBB-TRIAX COMPANY—Jervis B. Webb Company, pg. 1170
WEBSTER INDUSTRIES INC., pg. 1171
WEBSTER MFG. CO.—Webster Industries Inc., pg. 1172
WHITE STORAGE & RETRIEVAL SYSTEMS, INC., pg. 1186
WHITING EQUIPMENT CANADA, INC.—Whiting Corporation, pg. 1187
WHITLOCK, INC.—Sterling, Inc., pg. 1047

ZINIZ INC., pg. 1220

3536 — OVERHEAD TRAVELING CRANES, HOISTS & MONORAIL SYSTEMS

AEC, INC.—Sterling, Inc., pg. 1047
AMCLYDE ENGINEERED PRODUCTS, INC., pg. 47
AMERICAN CRANE & EQUIPMENT CORP., pg. 51
AVIS INDUSTRIAL CORPORATION, pg. 102
COLUMBUS MCKINNON CORP., pg. 266
DUFF-NORTON—Spreckles Industries, Inc., pg. 1032
EAST MOLINE METAL PRODUCTS COMPANY, pg. 363
EDERER CRANES—Ederer Inc., pg. 368
EDERER INC., pg. 368
EUCLID CRANE DIVISION—Kranco, Inc., pg. 644
THE HEIL CO., pg. 525
IDEA ENGINEERING & FABRICATING, pg. 562
INDUSTRIAL LIFT TRUCKS—Syracuse Supply Company, pg. 1070
KEY HANDLING SYSTEMS, INC., pg. 627
KRANCO, INC., pg. 643
MARINE TRAVELIFT, INC., pg. 707
META SERVICES INC.—Ederer Inc., pg. 368
MI-JACK PRODUCTS, INC., pg. 746
MODERN EQUIPMENT CO., INC.—Alco Industries, Inc., pg. 32
POSITECH CORPORATION—Columbus McKinnon Corp., pg. 267
RAPID INDUSTRIES, INC., pg. 913
SHEPARD NILES, INC., pg. 997
SHUTTLELIFT, INC.—Marine Travelift, Inc., pg. 707
STAR CRANES—Ederer Inc., pg. 368
UNIVERSAL BUILDERS SUPPLY, INC., pg. 1137
O.S. WALKER CO., INC.—Walker Magnetics Group, Inc., pg. 1160
WASHINGTON CRANES—Ederer Inc., pg. 368
WHITING CORPORATION, pg. 1187
WHITING EQUIPMENT CANADA, INC.—Whiting Corporation, pg. 1187
WHITLOCK, INC.—Sterling, Inc., pg. 1047

3537 — INDUSTRIAL TRUCKS, TRACTORS, TRAILERS & STACKERS

ACCESS EQUIPMENT LTD.—Up-Right, Inc., pg. 1139
AUTOLIFT INDUSTRIAL LIFT TRUCKS—Plymouth Locomotive International, Inc., pg. 877
BAKER MATERIAL HANDLING CORP., pg. 115
BIG JOE MANUFACTURING CO., pg. 149
BLAW KNOX CORP., pg. 156
BURTMAN IRON WORKS, INC., pg. 195
CLARKLIFT OF MINNESOTA, INC., pg. 253
DYNABILT PRODUCTS—Burtman Iron Works, Inc., pg. 196
THE ELWELL-PARKER ELECTRIC CO., pg. 378
FWD CORPORATION, pg. 395
IDAB INTERNATIONAL INCORPORATED, pg. 559
INDUSTRIAS METALICAS SUD AMERICANAS LTDA. (IMSA)—The Marmon Group, Inc., pg. 712
INSTANT S.R.L.—Up-Right, Inc., pg. 1139
THE KNAPHEIDE MFG. CO., pg. 636
LEVITON MFG. CO., INC., pg. 671
MARINE TRAVELIFT, INC., pg. 707
MAYVILLE ENGINEERING CO., INC., pg. 725
MUSTANG INDUSTRIAL EQUIPMENT CO.—Mustang Tractor & Equip. Co., pg. 777
MUSTANG MANUFACTURING COMPANY, INC., pg. 777
MUSTANG TRACTOR & EQUIP. CO., pg. 777
O. A. NEWTON & SON CO., pg. 805
PLYMOUTH LOCOMOTIVE INTERNATIONAL, INC., pg. 877
R.A. INDUSTRIES, INC., pg. 906
RAPID INDUSTRIES, INC., pg. 913
ROSS ENGINEERING CO., INC., pg. 949
JOHN RUSLING LTD.—Up-Right, Inc., pg. 1139
TAYLOR MACHINE WORKS, INC., pg. 1081
UNIVERSAL BUILDERS SUPPLY, INC., pg. 1137
UP-RIGHT (FAR EAST) LTD.—Up-Right, Inc., pg. 1139
UP-RIGHT (IRELAND) LTD.—Up-Right, Inc., pg. 1139
UP-RIGHT SCAFFOLDS LTD.—Up-Right, Inc., pg. 1139
VECTUR ALUMINUMSTALLNINGAR—Up-Right, Inc., pg. 1139
VECTUR B.V.—Up-Right, Inc., pg. 1139
VECTUR GMBH—Up-Right, Inc., pg. 1139
N.V. VECTUR S.A.—Up-Right, Inc., pg. 1139
VECTUR S.A.—Up-Right, Inc., pg. 1139
WEBB-TRIAX COMPANY—Jervis B. Webb Company, pg. 1170
ZIEMAN MANUFACTURING COMPANY, INC., pg. 1218

3541 — MACHINE TOOLS, METAL CUTTING TYPES

ABBEY ETNA MACHINE COMPANY, pg. 9
ALLMETAL SCREW PRODUCTS CORP., pg. 40
APEX BROACH & MACHINE CO., pg. 77
AVIS INDUSTRIAL CORPORATION, pg. 102
THE U.S. BAIRD CORPORATION, pg. 114
BLAW KNOX CORP., pg. 156
THE BODINE CORP., pg. 161
BRIDGEPORT MACHINES, INC., pg. 175
BRYANT GRINDER CORP.—Goldman Financial Group, pg. 468
CINCINNATI INCORPORATED, pg. 250
CITY MACHINE TOOL & DIE COMPANY, pg. 251
CONTINENTAL MACHINES, INC., pg. 279
CRANKSHAFT MACHINE COMPANY—Avis Industrial Corporation, pg. 102
CURTIS-TOLEDO, INC., pg. 306
DEVLIEG BULLARD SERVICES GROUP, pg. 333
EFFICIENT ENGINEERING CO., pg. 371
ENDURO INDUSTRIES, INC.—J. H. Roberts Industries Inc., pg. 939
ENDURO-NIAGARA LTD.—J. H. Roberts Industries Inc., pg. 939
FADAL ENGINEERING COMPANY, INC., pg. 396
FAMTEC AG—FamTec International, Inc., pg. 398
FAMTEC INTERNATIONAL, INC., pg. 398
FELLOWS CORPORATION—Goldman Financial Group, pg. 468
FREEDOM FORGE CORPORATION, pg. 430
GREENFIELD INDUSTRIES INC.—Harbour Group Ltd., pg. 507
HARDINGE BROTHERS, INC., pg. 508
HARIG GRINDERS—Bridgeport Machines, Inc., pg. 175
S. E. HUFFMAN CORP., pg. 551
THE ISI MANUFACTURING, INC., pg. 560
INGERSOLL INTERNATIONAL INC., pg. 568
INGERSOLL MASCHINEN UND WERKZEUGE GMBH—Ingersoll International Inc., pg. 568
THE INGERSOLL MILLING MACHINE CO.—Ingersoll International Inc., pg. 568
JOHNSON TECHNOLOGY—Freedom Forge Corporation, pg. 431
JONES & LAMSON WATERBURY FARREL CORP.—Goldman Financial Group, pg. 468
KARSTEN ENGINEERING CORP.—Karsten Manufacturing Corporation, pg. 617
KASPER MACHINE COMPANY, pg. 618
KINGSBURY CORPORATION, pg. 631
KINGSBURY MACHINING CENTER, DIV.—Kingsbury Corporation, pg. 632
KINGTOOL DIVISION—Kingsbury Corporation, pg. 632
KNURLET TOOL CO.—Kasper Machine Company, pg. 618
KOYO-MATTISON—Mattison Machine Works, pg. 721
MATTISON MACHINE WORKS, pg. 721
METAL CUTTING TOOLS CORP.—Harbour Group Ltd., pg. 507
MOORE SPECIAL TOOL CO., INC., pg. 768
NRM CORPORATION, pg. 781
NELMOR CO., INC.—Sterling, Inc., pg. 1047
NIAGARA CUTTER, INC., pg. 805
PMC INDUSTRIES INC., pg. 836
PLASTIC ENGINEERING COMPONENTS INC., pg. 875
PRODUCTION MACHINERY CORPORATION, pg. 893
R & B MACHINE TOOL CO., pg. 906
RTW, ROGERS TOOL WORKS, INC., pg. 908
ROGERS TOOL WORKS, INC.—Harbour Group Ltd., pg. 507
SCOTCHMAN INDUSTRIES, INC., pg. 982
SETCO SALES COMPANY, pg. 993
SPEEDFAM CO LTD.—FamTec International, Inc., pg. 398
SPEEDFAM CORPORATION—FamTec International, Inc., pg. 398
SPEEDFAM GMBH—FamTec International, Inc., pg. 398
SPEEDFAM MACHINES CO. LTD.—FamTec International, Inc., pg. 398
STAR CUTTER CO., pg. 1039
SUNNEN PRODUCTS COMPANY, pg. 1061
THE THOMPSON GROUP COMPANIES, pg. 1094
U.S. BROACH & MACHINE COMPANY—Avis Industrial Corporation, pg. 102
UNIVERSAL PHOTONICS, INC., pg. 1139
UNIVERSAL VISE & TOOL CO.—Avis Industrial Corporation, pg. 103
URSCHEL LABS INC., pg. 1140
VERMONT USA MACHINE TOOL GROUP—Goldman Financial Group, pg. 468
WILTON CORPORATION, pg. 1194

3542 — MACHINE TOOLS, METAL FORMING TYPES

ATI INDUSTRIES, pg. 8
ABBEY ETNA MACHINE CO. GMBH—Abbey Etna Machine Company, pg. 9
ABBEY ETNA MACHINE COMPANY, pg. 9
AMERICAN BARMAG CO., pg. 49
ARROW FASTENER CO., INC., pg. 85
THE BABCOCK & WILCOX COMPANY, pg. 107
BLAW KNOX CORP., pg. 156
CINCINNATI INCORPORATED, pg. 250
CLEARING INTERNATIONAL, INC., pg. 254
CONNELL LIMITED PARTNERSHIP, pg. 275
EFFICIENT ENGINEERING CO., pg. 371
ERIE PRESS SYSTEMS, pg. 386
GOUGLER INDUSTRIES, INC., pg. 473
HPM CORPORATION, pg. 497
HECKETHORN MFG. COMPANY, pg. 524
HESS ENGINEERING INC., pg. 532
THE ISI MANUFACTURING, INC., pg. 560
INSTA-PRO INTERNATIONAL, LTD.—Triple F, Inc., pg. 1114
JONES & LAMSON WATERBURY FARREL CORP.—Goldman Financial Group, pg. 468
MCNEIL & NRM., INC., pg. 732
THE MINSTER MACHINE COMPANY, pg. 759
MITEK, INC., pg. 762
MITEK INDUSTRIES—Mitek, Inc., pg. 762
MURDOCK, INC., pg. 776
NRM CORPORATION, pg. 781
NATIONAL MACHINERY ADV. SERVICES, pg. 792
NATIONAL MACHINERY COMPANY, pg. 792
PROGRESSIVE TOOL & INDUSTRIES CO., pg. 894
RING SCREW WORKS, pg. 935
C.G. SARGENTS SONS—Aeroglide Corporation, pg. 22
SOMMER METALCRAFT CORPORATION, pg. 1018
SPEEDFAM CO LTD.—FamTec International, Inc., pg. 398
STERLING, INC., pg. 1047
TAPCO PRODUCTS COMPANY, pg. 1078
TULIP CORPORATION, pg. 1119
WILLIAMS-WHITE & CO., pg. 1191

3543 — INDUSTRIAL PATTERNS

NEENAH FOUNDRY COMPANY, pg. 797
RELIABLE CASTINGS CORPORATION, pg. 924
SOUTHERN PRECISION DIV.—Walter Industries, Inc., pg. 1162
STOCKER & YALE, INC., pg. 1050
WHIPPS, pg. 1185

3544 — SPECIAL DIES & TOOLS, DIE SETS, JIGS & FIXTURES & INDUSTRIAL MOLDS

ACTIVE TOOL & MANUFACTURING CO., INC., pg. 15
AETNA INDUSTRIES, INC., pg. 23
ANCHOR TOOL & DIE COMPANY, pg. 71
APEX BROACH & MACHINE CO., pg. 77
ATLAS TOOL INC., pg. 96
ATOLS TOOL AND MOLD CORP., pg. 97
BARDES CORP., pg. 119
BEACH MOLD & TOOL INC., pg. 128
BRUBAKER TOOL CORP., pg. 183
CAPTIVE PLASTICS, pg. 216
CARBIDIE CORPORATION—Spreckles Industries, Inc., pg. 1032
CITY MACHINE TOOL & DIE COMPANY, pg. 251
CONDOR TOOL & DIE, INC.—Anchor Tool & Die Company, pg. 72
CONNELL LIMITED PARTNERSHIP, pg. 275
CRESCIVE DIE & TOOL, INC., pg. 298
D & H TOOL AND DIE—United States Ceramic Tile Co., pg. 1135
DANLY DIE SET DIVISION—Connell Limited Partnership, pg. 275
DIEBEL MANUFACTURING CO., pg. 336
DIEMAKERS, INC., pg. 336
DIGITRON TOOL CO., INC., pg. 337
DYNAMIC METAL PRODUCTS COMPANY, pg. 356
EFFICIENT ENGINEERING CO., pg. 371
FLAMBEAU CORPORATION—Nordic Group of Companies, Ltd., pg. 809
FRANKULIN TOOL & MFG. CO.—Wrought Washer Mfg., Inc., pg. 1205
GOUGLER INDUSTRIES, INC., pg. 473
HPM CORPORATION, pg. 497
H S DIE & ENGINEERING, INC., pg. 497
HESS ENGINEERING INC., pg. 532
INDEPENDENT TOOL & DIE—Oberg Industries Co., pg. 819
INTERCOLE, INC., pg. 574
JL TOOL & PROCESSING, INC.—Ring Technologies, Inc., pg. 935
JERGENS INC., pg. 593
KINGSLEY MACHINE CO., pg. 632
KIPP GROUP, pg. 632
MAGHIELSE TOOL CORPORATION, pg. 700
MATTHEWS INTERNATIONAL CORP., pg. 721
MITCHELL CORPORATION, HANCHETT MANUFACTURING CO.—Mitchell Corporation of Owosso, pg. 762
MITCHELL CORPORATION OF OWOSSO, pg. 761
MOARK MOLD, INC.—Plastic Engineering Components Inc., pg. 875
MOL-BEE, INC.—Plastic Engineering Components Inc., pg. 875
MOORE SPECIAL TOOL CO., INC., pg. 768
NATIONAL FORGE COMPANY, pg. 788
NATIONAL TOOL & MANUFACTURING COMPANY, pg. 794
NORDIC GROUP OF COMPANIES, LTD., pg. 809
OMCO MOULD, INC., pg. 819
OBERG CARBIDE PUNCH & DIE—Oberg Industries Co., pg. 819
OBERG INDUSTRIES CO., pg. 819
OBERG MFG. CO.—Oberg Industries Co., pg. 820
OVERSEAS PARTNERS, INC., pg. 833
PMC INDUSTRIES INC., pg. 836
PTA CORPORATION, pg. 837
PEMCO DIE CASTING CORPORATION, pg. 856
PRIDGEON & CLAY, INC., pg. 889
PRODUCTO DIEMAKERS SUPPLIES LTD.—The Producto Machine Co., pg. 893
PRODUCTO MACHINE CO. RING DIVISION—The Producto Machine Co., pg. 893
THE PRODUCTO MACHINE CO., pg. 893
PROGRESSIVE TOOL & INDUSTRIES CO., pg. 894
REMMELE ENGINEERING, INC., pg. 926
RING TECHNOLOGIES, INC., pg. 935
STOCKER & YALE, INC., pg. 1050
STRUCTURAL FOAM PLASTICS, INC., pg. 1054
TARGET STAMPED PRODUCTS CORP., pg. 1079
TRIANGLE TOOL CO.—Plastek Group, pg. 875
TRIPLE S PLASTICS, INC.—Triple S Technologies, Inc., pg. 1114
TRIPLE S TECHNOLOGIES, INC., pg. 1114
ULTRA TOOL & PLASTICS, INC., pg. 1125
WAGSTAFF EASTERN—Wagstaff Inc., pg. 1158
WAGSTAFF INC., pg. 1158
YORKTOWN TOOL & DIE CORPORATION, pg. 1208

3545 — CUTTING TOOLS, MACHINE TOOL ACCESSORIES & MACHINISTS PRECISION MEASURING DEVICES

A & A MANUFACTURING CO., pg. 1
ATI INDUSTRIES, pg. 8
ACKER DRILL CO. INC., pg. 12
AIR GAGE COMPANY, pg. 27
APEX BROACH & MACHINE CO., pg. 77
AVIS INDUSTRIAL CORPORATION, pg. 102
THE U.S. BAIRD CORPORATION, pg. 114
BARDONS & OLIVER, INC., pg. 119
BLAW KNOX CORP., pg. 156

BRIDGEPORT MACHINES, INC., pg. 175
BRUBAKER TOOL CORP., pg. 183
CARBIDE INTERNATIONAL INC.—Harbour Group Ltd., pg. 507
CHALLENGE GRAPHICS EQUIPMENT CO., pg. 238
CHALLENGE TECHNOLOGIES—Challenge Graphics Equipment Co., pg. 238
CLEVELAND MACHINE CONTROLS, pg. 255
COGSDILL TOOL PRODUCTS, INC., pg. 259
COGSDILL-NUNEATON, LTD.—Cogsdill Tool Products, Inc., pg. 259
CONTINENTAL MACHINES, INC., pg. 279
CRANKSHAFT MACHINE COMPANY—Avis Industrial Corporation, pg. 102
DEARBORN GAGE COMPANY, pg. 322
DOALL COMPANY, pg. 341
DUMORE CORPORATION, pg. 352
EDGEWOOD TOOL & MANUFACTURING COMPANY, pg. 368
FAMTEC INTERNATIONAL, INC., pg. 398
GENERAL TOOLS MFG., pg. 451
GREENFIELD INDUSTRIES INC.—Harbour Group Ltd., pg. 507
HARBOUR GROUP LTD., pg. 506
HOUGEN MANUFACTURING INC., pg. 546
HYER INDUSTRIES INC./THAYER SCALE, pg. 557
THE ISI MANUFACTURING, INC., pg. 560
INGERSOLL CUTTING TOOL CO.—Ingersoll International Inc., pg. 568
INGERSOLL MASCHINEN UND WERKZEUGE GMBH—Ingersoll International Inc., pg. 568
KASPER MACHINE COMPANY, pg. 618
KURT MANUFACTURING CO. INC., pg. 646
M K DIAMOND PRODUCTS, INC., pg. 692
METAL CUTTING TOOLS CORP.—Harbour Group Ltd., pg. 507
METAL STAMPING EQUIP. DIV.—P/A Industries, Inc., pg. 835
MOHAWK TOOLS—Precision Twist Drill Co., pg. 885
MOORE SPECIAL TOOL CO., INC., pg. 768
N E D CORP., pg. 780
NORTH AMERICAN PRODUCTS CORP., pg. 811
P/A INDUSTRIES, INC., pg. 835
PMC INDUSTRIES INC., pg. 836
PRECISION TWIST DRILL CO., pg. 885
THE RAWLPLUG COMPANY, INC., pg. 914
ROGERS TOOL WORKS, INC.—Harbour Group Ltd., pg. 507
S & J INDUSTRIES—North American Products Corp., pg. 811
S-T INDUSTRIES, INC., pg. 964
ST. PAUL METALCRAFT, INC., pg. 967
SETCO SALES COMPANY, pg. 993
SILICON VALLEY DEVELOPMENT, pg. 1004
SIMONDS INDUSTRIES INC., pg. 1006
J.T. SLOCOMB COMPANY, pg. 1010
ANTON SMIT & CO., INC., pg. 1011
TSC CARBIDE CO.—Precision Twist Drill Co., pg. 885
THE THOMPSON GROUP COMPANIES, pg. 1094
UNIVERSAL VISE & TOOL CO.—Avis Industrial Corporation, pg. 103
VERMONT TAP & DIE CO.—Harbour Group Ltd., pg. 507
WALDES TRUARC, INC., pg. 1159
O.S. WALKER CO., INC.—Walker Magnetics Group, Inc., pg. 1160
WALKER MAGNETICS GROUP, INC., pg. 1160
O. S. WALKER CO. INC., pg. 1160
WEB PROCESSING EQUIP. DIV.—P/A Industries, Inc., pg. 835
ZEPHYR MFG. CO.—Standun, Inc., pg. 1038

3546 — POWER DRIVEN HAND TOOLS

AMERICAN MACHINE & TOOL COMPANY, pg. 57
CHESCO PRODUCTS, INC.—American Tool Companies, Inc., pg. 64
CONTINENTAL/MIDLAND, INC., pg. 279
DANIELS MANUFACTURING CORPORATION, pg. 314
DESA INTERNATIONAL, INC., pg. 331
THE DISSTON CO., pg. 339
DUMORE CORPORATION, pg. 352
HOFFCO, INC., pg. 537
HOUGEN MANUFACTURING INC., pg. 546
S. E. HUFFMAN CORP., pg. 551
HUTCHINS MANUFACTURING COMPANY, pg. 555
INDUSTRIAL TOOLS DIV.—INDRESCO, Inc., pg. 565
MATTISON MACHINE WORKS, pg. 721
METABO CORPORATION, pg. 741
MILWAUKEE ELECTRIC TOOL CORP.—ESSTAR Incorporated, pg. 361
PROSNIP CORPORATION—American Tool Companies, Inc., pg. 64
REPUBLIC FASTENER PRODUCTS CORP., pg. 928
THE ROTOR TOOL COMPANY, pg. 951
GEORGE T. SCHMIDT, pg. 976
STANDUN, INC., pg. 1038
STIHL EASTERN CANADA LTD.—Stihl Inc., pg. 1049
STIHL INC., pg. 1049
G.C. THORSEN, INC.—Jupiter Industries, Inc., pg. 609
UNIBIT CORP.—American Tool Companies, Inc., pg. 64
WEN PRODUCTS, INC., pg. 1156
WILTON CORPORATION, pg. 1194
THE WYCO TOOL CO.—Racine Federated, Inc., pg. 909

3547 — ROLLING MILL MACHINERY & EQUIPMENT

BLAW KNOX CORP., pg. 156
BLISS-SALEM, INC., pg. 156
BRADBURY COMPANY, INC., pg. 169
HEADER PRODUCTS INC., pg. 520
HEIDTMAN STEEL PRODUCTS, INC., pg. 525
HUNTER ENGINEERING CO., INC., pg. 554
MORGAN CONSTRUCTION COMPANY, pg. 769
PRODUCTION MACHINERY CORPORATION, pg. 893
TIPPINS INCORPORATED, pg. 1099
WDP, INC., pg. 1156
XTEK, INC., pg. 1206

3548 — ELECTRIC & GAS WELDING & SOLDERING EQUIPMENT

AMALLOY, pg. 46
AMPCO METAL INCORPORATED, pg. 67
COGSDILL TOOL PRODUCTS, INC., pg. 259
ELECTRO-MATIC PRODUCTS INC., pg. 374
ERICO INTERNATIONAL, pg. 386
THE FIBRE-METAL PRODUCTS COMPANY, pg. 408
HOBART BROTHERS CO., pg. 536
HOFLEY MANUFACTURING COMPANY, pg. 538
MILLER ELECTRIC MFG. CO., pg. 754
THE MILLER GROUP (UK) LTD.—Miller Electric Mfg. Co., pg. 754
MORGAN CONSTRUCTION COMPANY, pg. 769
SUPERIOR GRAPHITE COMPANY, pg. 1063
TRI-MARK INC.—Hobart Brothers Co., pg. 537
TRU-FIT PRODUCTS CORP., pg. 1117
WALL COLMONOY CORP., pg. 1160
WELSCO INC., pg. 1175

3549 — METALWORKING MACHINERY, NEC

ABBEY ETNA MACHINE CO. GMBH—Abbey Etna Machine Company, pg. 9
ABBEY ETNA MACHINE COMPANY, pg. 9
APEX BROACH & MACHINE CO., pg. 77
THE U.S. BAIRD CORPORATION, pg. 114
BALCRANK PRODUCTS—New Hampshire Oak, pg. 801
BLAW KNOX CORP., pg. 156
BLISS-SALEM, INC., pg. 156
BRIDGEPORT MACHINES, INC., pg. 175
CROWN HOLDINGS, INC., pg. 302
CROWN IRON WORKS COMPANY—Crown Holdings, Inc., pg. 302
EFFICIENT ENGINEERING CO., pg. 371
THE ENTWISTLE COMPANY, pg. 383
ENTWISTLE DEFENSE TECHNOLOGY DIV.—The Entwistle Company, pg. 383
THE ENTWISTLE EXPORT CO., INC.—The Entwistle Company, pg. 383
HESS ENGINEERING INC., pg. 532
INGERSOLL MASCHINEN UND WERKZEUGE GMBH—Ingersoll International Inc., pg. 568
KINGSBURY ASSEMBLY MACHINE DIV.—Kingsbury Corporation, pg. 632
KINGSBURY CANADA, INC.—Kingsbury Corporation, pg. 632
KINGSBURY CORPORATION, pg. 631
KINGSLEY MACHINE CO., pg. 632
KINGTOOL DIVISION—Kingsbury Corporation, pg. 632
MOORE SPECIAL TOOL CO., INC., pg. 768
MURDOCK, INC., pg. 776
PRODUCTION MACHINERY CORPORATION, pg. 893
ROKOP CORPORATION, pg. 944
SINTEL, INC., pg. 1008
STANDARD LOCKNUT & LOCKWASHER, pg. 1037
THOMAS ENGINEERING INC., pg. 1093
TIPPINS INCORPORATED, pg. 1099
U.S. MANUFACTURING CORP., pg. 1136
WALKER MAGNETICS GROUP, INC., pg. 1160
WILTON CORPORATION, pg. 1194

3552 — TEXTILE MACHINERY

AMERICAN BARMAG CO., pg. 49
AMERICAN MANUFACTURING COMPANY, INC. (LA), pg. 58
ASHWORTH BROS., INC., pg. 88
BATSON-COOK COMPANY, pg. 126
DRAPER CORPORATION, pg. 348
DRAPER DE MEXICO S.A. DE C.V.—Draper Corporation, pg. 348
DRAPER ERIN LTD.—Draper Corporation, pg. 348
EASTMAN MACHINE CO., pg. 364
GASTON COUNTY CARPET DIV.—Gaston County Dyeing Machine Co., pg. 444
GASTON COUNTY DYEING MACHINE CO., pg. 444
GESSNER INDUSTRIES, pg. 455
GLEN RAVEN MILLS, INC., pg. 461
W. L. GORE & ASSOCIATES, INC., pg. 472
FRED B. JOHNSTON COMPANY, INC., pg. 601
THE KING COMPANY, pg. 630
MARSHALL & WILLIAMS CO., pg. 714
MORRISON TEXTILE MACHINERY CO., pg. 771
PNEUMAFIL CORP., pg. 878
ROWE CORP., pg. 952
SEABROOK INC.—Draper Corporation, pg. 348
WHITIN ROBERTS CO., pg. 1187
WHITIN ROBERTS MFG. DIV.—Whitin Roberts Co., pg. 1187

3553 — WOODWORKING MACHINERY

THE COE MFG. CO., pg. 258
HIRSH COMPANY—Code, Hennessy & Simmons, pg. 258
LONDON LITHO ALUMINUM CO., INC., pg. 681
LUMBER SYSTEMS, INC., pg. 687
MATTISON MACHINE WORKS, pg. 721
TIMESAVERS INC., pg. 1098
WILLIAMS, WHITE & COMPANY, pg. 1191
WILTON CORPORATION, pg. 1194

3554 — PAPER INDUSTRIES MACHINERY

ATLANTA WIRE WORKS, INC., pg. 94
BOLTON-EMERSON, INC., pg. 163
BOLTON-EMERSON PAPER MACHINERY DIV.—Bolton-Emerson, Inc., pg. 163
BOLTON-EMERSON S.A.—Bolton-Emerson, Inc., pg. 163
BOLTON-EMERSON-SOUTHERN, INC.—Bolton-Emerson, Inc., pg. 163
BUTLER AUTOMATIC, INC., pg. 197
CHALLENGE GRAPHICS EQUIPMENT CO., pg. 238
DENVER EQUIPMENT COMPANY, pg. 331
DORR-OLIVER INCORPORATED, pg. 346
ENTERPRISES INTERNATIONAL INC., pg. 382
FORT STERLING LTD.—Fort Howard Corporation, pg. 425
GENERAL BINDING CORPORATION—Lane Industries, Inc., pg. 656
CURT G. JOA, INC., pg. 594
MARK ANDY, INC., pg. 708
OVALSTRAPPING INC.—Enterprises International Inc., pg. 383
SUPERIOR MACHINE COMPANY OF SOUTH CAROLINA, INC., pg. 1064
THE WARD MACHINERY COMPANY, pg. 1162
WHITING EQUIPMENT CANADA, INC.—Whiting Corporation, pg. 1187

3555 — PRINTING TRADES MACHINERY AND EQUIPMENT

ANO-COIL CORPORATION, pg. 75
AUTOROLL MACHINE CORP., pg. 101
BEACON GROUP, pg. 128
BELMONT INDUSTRIES, INC., pg. 136
BOBST GROUP INC., pg. 161
BUTLER AUTOMATIC, INC., pg. 197
CHALLENGE TECHNOLOGIES—Challenge Graphics Equipment Co., pg. 238
DIDDE WEB PRESS, pg. 336
DUREX INDUSTRIES INC., pg. 354
FISHER GRAPHIC INDUSTRIES, pg. 415
HESCO SUPPLY CO., INC.—The Hearst Corporation, pg. 524
KINGSLEY MACHINE CO., pg. 632
LINOTYPE-HELL COMPANY, pg. 677
MARK ANDY, INC., pg. 708
MCCAIN MANUFACTURING CORP., pg. 726
NEW HERMES INCORPORATED, pg. 801
PANARCO, INC., pg. 845
SMYTH MANUFACTURING COMPANY—Beacon Group, pg. 129

3556 — FOOD PRODUCTS MACHINERY

ACRISON, INC., pg. 14
AEROGLIDE CORPORATION, pg. 22
ALLOY PRODUCTS CORPORATION, pg. 41
BARRY-WEHMILLER COMPANY, pg. 122
BLAW KNOX CORP., pg. 156
BLAW KNOX FOOD & CHEMICAL EQUIPMENT COMPANY—Blaw Knox Corp., pg. 156
BOBST GROUP INC., pg. 161
CARTER DAY CO.—Carter Day Industries, Inc., pg. 226
CUISINARTS INC.—Conair Corporation, pg. 272
DEC AG—DEC International, Inc., pg. 309
DEC/BOU-MATIC—DEC International, Inc., pg. 309
DEC INTERNATIONAL, INC., pg. 308
DAWN FOOD PRODUCTS, INC., pg. 319
DEDERT CORPORATION, pg. 324
DUARY/J.F. DUNCAN INDUSTRIES, INC., pg. 350
DUPPS COMPANY, pg. 354
THOMAS L. GREEN & CO., INC., pg. 484
GRINDMASTER CORPORATION, pg. 488
HOLLYMATIC CORPORATION, pg. 539
HOLMATIC, INC.—Barry-Wehmiller Company, pg. 122
IDEAL MACARONI COMPANY, pg. 562
ILLINOIS RANGE COMPANY, pg. 563
JORDON COMMERCIAL REFRIGERATOR CO., pg. 605
KARTRIDG PAK CO.—Barry-Wehmiller Company, pg. 122
THE LAITRAM CORPORATION, pg. 650
MALLET & CO., pg. 703
PARAMOUNT CITRUS ASSOCIATION—American Protection Industries, Inc., pg. 60
PNEUMATIC SCALE CORPORATION—Barry-Wehmiller Company, pg. 122
STANLEY KNIGHT CORPORATION, pg. 1038
STEFFEN DAIRY FOODS CO., INC.—Prairie Farms Dairy, Inc., pg. 884
STEVENS-LEE COMPANY, pg. 1048
TAYLOR COMPANY—Specialty Equipment Companies Inc., pg. 1027
TRIPLE F, INC., pg. 1114
URSCHEL LABS INC., pg. 1140

3559 — SPECIAL INDUSTRY MACHINERY, NEC

AEC, INC.—Sterling, Inc., pg. 1047
A.S.M. INDUSTRIES—Serfilco, Ltd., pg. 991
AXIA INCORPORATED, pg. 8
ACRISON, INC., pg. 14
AEROGLIDE CORPORATION, pg. 22
AEROLYTE SYSTEMS—Clemco Industries, pg. 254
ALAMO INDUSTRIAL GROUP, pg. 29
ALAMO IRON WORKS—Alamo Industrial Group, pg. 29
ALLIANCE AUTOMATION SYSTEMS, pg. 37
ALTAIR CORPORATION, pg. 45
AMANO CINCINNATI, INC., pg. 46
AMERICAN OPTICAL CORP., pg. 59
ANCHOR CONTINENTAL INCORPORATED, pg. 71
APEX BROACH & MACHINE CO., pg. 77
APPLICATION AUTOMATION, INC.—Sterling, Inc., pg. 1047

APPLICATION ENGINEERING CORPORATION—Sterling, Inc., pg. 1047
ARMSTRONG MACHINE WORKS—Armstrong International, Inc., pg. 83
AUTO JECTORS, INC.—Group Dekko International Inc., pg. 489
AXELSON, INC., pg. 103
BAKER BROS. DE PUERTO RICO—Systems Engineering & Manufacturing Corp., pg. 1071
BAKER BROTHERS/MICRO-PLATE—Systems Engineering & Manufacturing Corp., pg. 1071
BANANZA AIR MANAGEMENT SYSTEMS, INC.—Rapid Engineering Inc., pg. 913
BARNES PUMPS, INC.—Harbour Group Ltd., pg. 507
BATTENFELD GLOUCESTER ENGINEERING CO. INC., pg. 126
BERWIND CORPORATION, pg. 145
BESSER/APPCO—Besser Company, pg. 146
BESSER CANADA, LTD.—Besser Company, pg. 146
BESSER COMPANY, pg. 146
BLAW KNOX CORP., pg. 156
BOLTON-EMERSON, INC., pg. 163
BRAKE SUPPLY CO.—George Koch Sons, Inc., pg. 639
BRUNNER & LAY, INC., pg. 184
BUHLER INC., pg. 187
BURKS PUMPS, INC.—Harbour Group Ltd., pg. 507
CARGILL DETROIT CORP., pg. 219
CARTER DAY CO.—Carter Day Industries, Inc., pg. 226
CARVER, INC., pg. 227
CENTRIFUGAL & MECHANICAL INDUSTRIES—Jupiter Industries, Inc., pg. 609
COMPAGNIE FISCHBEIN, S.A.—AXIA Incorporated, pg. 8
THE CONAIR GROUP, INC., pg. 272
CONTINENTAL EAGLE CORPORATION, pg. 278
CONVERTING MACHINERY DIV.—Bolton-Emerson, Inc., pg. 163
CROWN HOLDINGS, INC., pg. 302
CROWN IRON WORKS COMPANY—Crown Holdings, Inc., pg. 302
DEC/BOU-MATIC—DEC International, Inc., pg. 309
DORR-OLIVER INCORPORATED, pg. 346
DUPPS COMPANY, pg. 354
EDELBROCK CORP., pg. 367
EFFICIENT ENGINEERING CO., pg. 371
ELECTRONIC MEASUREMENTS, INC.—Berwind Corporation, pg. 145
ERIEZ MAGNETICS, pg. 386
DAVE FISCHBEIN CO.—AXIA Incorporated, pg. 8
FOSTER-MILLER, INC., pg. 426
GASTON COUNTY CARPET DIV.—Gaston County Dyeing Machine Co., pg. 444
GASTON COUNTY DYEING MACHINE CO., pg. 444
GOODMAN EQUIPMENT CORP., pg. 470
GOUGLER INDUSTRIES, INC., pg. 473
GRANITE STATE MANUFACTURING CO., pg. 476
HADEN, INC., pg. 499
HADEN INVESTMENT, LTD.—Haden, Inc., pg. 499
HADEN SCHWEITZER CORPORATION—Haden, Inc., pg. 499
HANDLING SYSTEMS ENGINEERING, pg. 505
HEATH CONSULTANTS INCORPORATED, pg. 524
HULL CORPORATION, pg. 552
IDAB WAMAC AB—IDAB International Incorporated, pg. 559
IDAB WAMAC PACIFIC LIMITED—IDAB International Incorporated, pg. 559
THE ISI MANUFACTURING, INC., pg. 560
INTERNATIONAL SHOE MACHINE CORP., pg. 579
JETSTREAM SYSTEMS—Barry-Wehmiller Company, pg. 122
R. A. JONES & CO. INC., pg. 604
KINGSBURY ASSEMBLY MACHINE DIV.—Kingsbury Corporation, pg. 632
KINGSBURY CORPORATION, pg. 631
KINGTOOL DIVISION—Kingsbury Corporation, pg. 632
KOCH ENGINEERING COMPANY, INC., pg. 638
GEORGE KOCH SONS, INC., pg. 639
KOMLINE-SANDERSON ENGINEERING CORP., pg. 641
THE LAITRAM CORPORATION, pg. 650
LAITRAM MACHINERY INC.—The Laitram Corporation, pg. 651
LITTLEFORD DAY, TAYLOR-STILES DIVISION, pg. 679
MACTAVISH MACHINE MANUFACTURING COMPANY, pg. 698
MANNING & LEWIS ENGINEERING CO., pg. 704
MARION MACHINE COMPANY DIVISION—Superior Machine Company Of South Carolina, Inc., pg. 1064
MARKEM CORPORATION, pg. 708
MARSHALL & WILLIAMS CO., pg. 714
MASTER APPLIANCE CORP., pg. 719
MATTHEWS INTERNATIONAL CORP., pg. 721
MATTHEWS INTERNATIONAL MARKING SYSTEMS DIV.—Matthews International Corp., pg. 721
MCCLEAN-ANDERSON—Price Brothers Co., pg. 888
MICRO-GEN EQUIPMENT CORP.—S. C. Johnson & Son, Inc., pg. 599
MID-WEST AUTOMATION SYSTEMS, pg. 750
MODERN EQUIPMENT CO., INC.—Alco Industries, Inc., pg. 32
MURRAY-CARVER, pg. 776
NRM CORPORATION, pg. 781
NELMOR CO., INC.—Sterling, Inc., pg. 1047
NETZSCH, INC., pg. 798
NEWBURY INDUSTRIES, INC., pg. 803
O. A. NEWTON & SON CO., pg. 805
PENNSYLVANIA CRUSHER CORP., pg. 858
PERFECT EQUIPMENT CORP.—Berwind Corporation, pg. 145
PLYMOUTH LOCOMOTIVE INTERNATIONAL, INC., pg. 877
PNEUMAFIL CORP., pg. 878
PREMIER MILL CORP., pg. 887
PREMIER MILL CORP.—Premier Mill Corp., pg. 887
R & B MACHINE TOOL CO., pg. 906
R.A. INDUSTRIES, INC., pg. 906
RDI, INC., pg. 906
RAPID ENGINEERING INC., pg. 913
REMMELE ENGINEERING, INC., pg. 926
RICHMOND SCREW ANCHOR COMPANY, pg. 933
SERFILCO, LTD., pg. 990
SNUGL MFG. CO. INC.—Berwind Corporation, pg. 145
SOMMER & MACA INDUSTRIES, INC., pg. 1017
STANDARD COMMUNICATIONS CORPORATION, pg. 1036
STANDARD TOOL & MANUFACTURING COMPANY, pg. 1037
STERLING, INC., pg. 1047
EDWIN B. STIMPSON COMPANY, INC., pg. 1049
SYSTEMS ENGINEERING & MANUFACTURING CORP., pg. 1071
TECHNIC INCORPORATED, pg. 1083
THOMAS ENGINEERING INC., pg. 1093
U.S. ENERTEK, INC., pg. 1135
UNIVERSAL DYNAMICS, INC.—Universal Dynamics Inc., pg. 1138
VACUDYNE INC.—Altair Corporation, pg. 45
VENTUREDYNE, LTD., pg. 1148
HENRY VOGT MACHINE CO., pg. 1154
WHIBCO, INC., pg. 1185
WHITING CORPORATION, pg. 1187
WHITING EQUIPMENT CANADA, INC.—Whiting Corporation, pg. 1187
WHITLOCK, INC.—Sterling, Inc., pg. 1047
XTEK CANADA, LTD.—Xtek, Inc., pg. 1206
XTEK, INC., pg. 1206

3561 — PUMPS, AND PUMPING EQUIPMENT

A.S.M. INDUSTRIES—Serfilco, Ltd., pg. 991
BARNES DE COLOMBIA—The Pullman Company, pg. 900
BARNES DE MEXICO—The Pullman Company, pg. 900
BARNES PUMPS, INC.—Harbour Group Ltd., pg. 507
BELLOFRAM CORP., pg. 136
BIJUR LUBRICATING CORPORATION, pg. 150
BURKS PROSSER/ENPO INDUSTRIES, INC.—Harbour Group Ltd., pg. 507
BURKS PUMPS, INC.—Harbour Group Ltd., pg. 507
CGF INDUSTRIES, pg. 201
J. C. CARTER COMPANY, INC., pg. 226
CAT PUMPS CORPORATION—Diversified Dynamics Inc., pg. 340
CAT PUMPS DEUTSCHLAND GMBH—Diversified Dynamics Inc., pg. 340
CAT PUMPS (UK) LTD.—Diversified Dynamics Inc., pg. 340
A.W. CHESTERTON COMPANY, pg. 244
CONTINENTAL MACHINES, INC., pg. 279
CROLL-REYNOLDS COMPANY, pg. 300
DENVER EQUIPMENT COMPANY, pg. 331
DENVER EQUIPMENT PTY., LTD.—Denver Equipment Company, pg. 331
DENVER THOMAS, INC.—Denver Equipment Company, pg. 331
DIVERSIFIED DYNAMICS INC., pg. 340
DORR-OLIVER INCORPORATED, pg. 346
EPOXYLITE CORPORATION, pg. 384
FM INDUSTRIES, INC., pg. 394
FAIRBANKS MORSE PUMP CORPORATON, pg. 397
FLOJET CORPORATION, pg. 419
GEORGIA IRON WORKS CO., pg. 453
BARRETT HAENTJENS & COMPANY, pg. 499
HARBOUR GROUP LTD., pg. 506
HARLEY INDUSTRIES, INC., pg. 509
HASKEL ENERGY SYSTEMS LTD.—Haskel, Inc., pg. 516
HASKEL, INC., pg. 516
HYDRECO—ICM Industries, Inc., pg. 559
HYPRO CORPORATION, pg. 557
GEORGE KOCH SONS, INC., pg. 639
KOMLINE-SANDERSON ENGINEERING CORP., pg. 641
LAWRENCE PUMPS, INC., pg. 662
LAYNE & BOWLER—The Marley Company, pg. 710
MARCH MANUFACTURING INC., pg. 706
THE MARLEY COMPANY, pg. 710
MARLEY PUMP CO.—The Marley Company, pg. 710
A. Y. MCDONALD INDUSTRIES, INC., pg. 728
A. Y. MCDONALD MFG. CO.—A. Y. McDonald Industries, Inc., pg. 728
MCNALLY INDUSTRIES, INC., pg. 731
MICROPUMP—Micropump Corporation, pg. 749
MICROPUMP CORPORATION, pg. 749
THE NASH ENGINEERING COMPANY, pg. 783
THE NASH ENGINEERING COMPANY OF CANADA, LTD.—The Nash Engineering Company, pg. 784
NETZSCH, INC., pg. 798
PEABODY FLOWAY, INC.—The Pullman Company, pg. 899
PLASTIC PRODUCTS DIVISION—Freudenberg-NOK (MI), pg. 432
PLASTIC PRODUCTS DIVISION—Freudenberg-NOK (MI), pg. 432
PNEUMAFIL CORP., pg. 878
PUTZMEISTER, INC., pg. 901
R.A. INDUSTRIES, INC., pg. 906
REAGAN EQUIPMENT COMPANY, INC., pg. 917
RUTHMAN PUMP & ENGINEERING CO., pg. 957
SERFILCO, LTD., pg. 990
SHERWOOD CO.—Hypro Corporation, pg. 557
STANDARD ALLOYS & MANUFACTURING—Blue Tee Corporation, pg. 161
STATE INDUSTRIES INC., pg. 1041
STERLING, INC., pg. 1047
SUNTEC INDUSTRIES INC., pg. 1062
SYSTEMS ENGINEERING & MFG. NEDERLANDS B.V.—Systems Engineering & Manufacturing Corp., pg. 1071
TACO INC., pg. 1076
TUTHILL CORPORATION, pg. 1120
TUTHILL PUMP—Tuthill Corporation, pg. 1120
TUTHILL PUMP COMPANY OF CALIFORNIA—Tuthill Corporation, pg. 1120
UNION PUMP (CANADA) LTD.—Union Pump Company, pg. 1129
UNION PUMP COMPANY, pg. 1128
UNIPAS, INC.—Taco Inc., pg. 1076
WATEROUS COMPANY—American Cast Iron Pipe Co., pg. 50
WAUKESHA FOUNDRY INC., pg. 1168
WILSON INDUSTRIES INC., pg. 1193
WOODLAND MOLDED PLASTICS—Freudenberg-NOK (MI), pg. 433
ZOELLER CO., pg. 1220

3562 — BALL AND ROLLER BEARINGS

ACCURATE BUSHING CO., INC., pg. 11
AETNA BEARING COMPANY, pg. 23
ALINABAL, INC., pg. 34
BEARING SERVICE COMPANY, pg. 130
FRANTZ BEARING DIV.—Frantz Manufacturing Co., pg. 430
FRANTZ MANUFACTURING CO., pg. 429
FREEWAY CORPORATION, pg. 432
HOWDEN SIROCCO INC., pg. 547
JONATHAN MANUFACTURING CORP., pg. 602
KENDALE INDUSTRIES, INC., pg. 622
MORGAN CONSTRUCTION COMPANY, pg. 769
STERLING STEEL BALL DIV.—Frantz Manufacturing Co., pg. 430
STILLMAN SEAL, pg. 1049

3563 — AIR & GAS COMPRESSORS

ACHESON INTERNATIONAL S.A.-EQUIPMENT DIV.—Acheson Industries, Inc., pg. 12
CRL, INC., pg. 203
CHAMPION PNEUMATIC MACHINERY CO., INC., pg. 238
CHERCO COMPRESSORS, INC.—Minstar, Inc., pg. 758
CROLL-REYNOLDS COMPANY, pg. 300
CURTIS-TOLEDO, INC., pg. 306
DEUTSCHE ACHESON GMBH—Acheson Industries, Inc., pg. 12
ELLIOTT COMPANY, pg. 378
FM INDUSTRIES, INC., pg. 394
HARLEY INDUSTRIES, INC., pg. 509
HOBART TAFA TECHNOLOGIES, INC.—Hobart Brothers Co., pg. 537
INTERNATIONAL METALS & MACHINES, INC.—CRL, Inc., pg. 203
MIDWEST PRODUCTS, INC.—Huntco Inc., pg. 554
NASH DO BRASIL BOMBAS LTDA.—The Nash Engineering Company, pg. 784
NASH ENGINEERING CO. (GREAT BRITAIN) LTD.—The Nash Engineering Company, pg. 784
THE NASH ENGINEERING COMPANY, pg. 783
NORWALK CO., INC., pg. 816
OIL & GAS SUPPLY COMPANY, pg. 823
OVERHILL MFG., INC.—Huntco Inc., pg. 554
SANBORN MANUFACTURING COMPANY, pg. 969
SCOTT SPECIALTY GASES, INC., pg. 983
THE SPENCER TURBINE CO., pg. 1030
SQUIRE-COGSWELL COMPANY, pg. 1034
WAGNER SPRAY TECH CORP., pg. 1158

3564 — INDUSTRIAL & COMMERCIAL FANS & BLOWERS & AIR PURIFICATION EQUIPMENT

R. P. ADAMS COMPANY, INC., pg. 16
AIRGUARD INDUSTRIES INC., pg. 27
AMERICAN STANDARD AIR CONDITIONING PRODUCTS—American Standard Inc., pg. 61
AMERICAN STANDARD INC., pg. 61
BUHLER INC., pg. 187
CAPTIVE-AIRE SYSTEMS, INC., pg. 216
CARNES COMPANY, INC.—Venturedyne, Ltd., pg. 1148
CARTER DAY INDUSTRIES (CANADA) LTD.—Carter Day Industries, Inc., pg. 226
CMI SCHNEIBLE CO.—CMI International Inc., pg. 202
COPPUS ENGINEERING CORP., pg. 285
CROLL-REYNOLDS COMPANY, pg. 300
DURO DYNE CORPORATION, pg. 355
ECLIPSE-COMBUSTION—Eclipse, Inc., pg. 366
GALLAGHER-KAISER CORP., pg. 441
GENIE MANUFACTURING CORP., pg. 452
HILLIARD CORPORATION, pg. 535
HOWDEN SIROCCO INC., pg. 547
THE KING COMPANY, pg. 630
THE KIRK & BLUM MFG. CO., pg. 633
LAKEWOOD ENGINEERING & MANUFACTURING CO., pg. 652
MD PNEUMATICS, INC.—Tuthill Corporation, pg. 1120
MAL TOOL & ENGINEERING CO.—Collins & Aikman Group Inc., pg. 263
MOLON MOTOR & COIL CORP., pg. 764
THE NORTH AMERICAN MANUFACTURING CO., pg. 811
PEABODY HOLMES LIMITED—The Pullman Company, pg. 900
PNEUMAFIL CORP., pg. 878
PRECISIONAIRE, INC., pg. 886
REGAL WARE, INC., pg. 921
REVCOR, INC., pg. 930
SPENCER TURBINE CO., pg. 1030
THE SPENCER TURBINE CO., pg. 1030
SURCO PRODUCTS, INC., pg. 1065
TUTHILL CORPORATION, pg. 1120
UNITED AIR SPECIALISTS, INC., pg. 1130
UNITED MCGILL CORP., pg. 1133
WOLVERINE MASSACHUSETTS CORPORATION, pg. 1199
XERXES CORPORATION, pg. 1206

3565 — PACKAGING MACHINERY

BOBST GROUP INC., pg. 161
CLOUD CORPORATION, pg. 256
DEC ALKAR DIV.—DEC International, Inc., pg. 309
DEC/BOU-MATIC—DEC International, Inc., pg. 309
DE FRANCISCI MACHINE CORP.(DEMACO), pg. 321
DENVER EQUIPMENT COMPANY, pg. 331
EXACT EQUIPMENT CORPORATION, pg. 392
FABDEC LTD.—DEC International, Inc., pg. 309
FLEETWOOD SYSTEMS, INC., pg. 417
HOLMATIC, INC.—Barry-Wehmiller Company, pg. 122
HOYT CORPORATION, pg. 548
HULL CORPORATION, pg. 552
INDECO PACKAGING DIV.—Thermon Manufacturing Company, pg. 1092
KCL CORPORATION, pg. 611
THE KARTRIDG PAK CO., pg. 617
KARTRIDG PAK CO.—Barry-Wehmiller Company, pg. 122
LABEL-AIRE INC., pg. 649
NEW ENGLAND MACHINERY, INC., pg. 800
PAXALL CIRCLE MACHINERY—The Paxall Group, Inc., pg. 852
PAXALL CLYBOURN MACHINERY—The Paxall Group, Inc., pg. 852
THE PAXALL GROUP, INC., pg. 852
PAXALL PAK-MASTER MACHINERY—The Paxall Group, Inc., pg. 852
PAXALL PARSONS MACHINERY—The Paxall Group, Inc., pg. 852
PNEUMATIC SCALE CORPORATION—Barry-Wehmiller Company, pg. 122
PNEUMATIC SCALE EUROPE—Barry-Wehmiller Company, pg. 122
RAYMOND AUTOMATION CO., INC., pg. 915
SALWASSER MANUFACTURING COMPANY, INC., pg. 968
SANI-MATIC SYSTEMS—DEC International, Inc., pg. 309
STANDARD-KNAPP, INC., pg. 1036
SUPERIOR MACHINE SYSTEMS—Superior Label Systems, Inc., pg. 1064
THOMAS ENGINEERING INC., pg. 1093
WSF INDUSTRIES, INC., pg. 1156

3566 — SPEED CHANGERS, INDUSTRIAL HIGH SPEED DRIVES & GEARS

AMARILLO GEAR COMPANY—The Marmon Group, Inc., pg. 711
BORG-WARNER AUTOMOTIVE (CANADA) LIMITED—Borg-Warner Corporation, pg. 166
BRAD FOOTE GEAR WORKS, INC., pg. 169
CGF INDUSTRIES, pg. 201
CINCINNATI GEAR COMPANY, pg. 250
CLEVELAND MACHINE CONTROLS, pg. 255
DUFF-NORTON—Spreckles Industries, Inc., pg. 1032
HOFFCO, INC., pg. 537
HOWARD INDUSTRIES, INC., pg. 547
HOWDEN SIROCCO INC., pg. 547
MARTIN SPROCKET & GEAR, INC., pg. 715
MOLON MOTOR & COIL CORP., pg. 764
NUTTALL GEAR CORPORATION, pg. 818
PHILADELPHIA GEAR CORP., pg. 866
PITTSBURGH GEAR COMPANY—Brad Foote Gear Works, Inc., pg. 169
REULAND ELECTRIC COMPANY, pg. 930
SUNTEC INDUSTRIES INC., pg. 1062
WESTECH GEAR GROUP—Zimmerman Holdings, Inc., pg. 1220
XTEK, INC., pg. 1206

3567 — INDUSTRIAL PROCESS FURNACES & OVENS

AMTROL INC., pg. 70
BARD MFG. CO., pg. 119
CHESTERFIELD INDUSTRIAL PARK, INC.—Watlow Electric Manufacturing Company, pg. 1167
COOPERHEAT, INC., pg. 283
DESPATCH INDUSTRIES, pg. 332
DONLEE TECHNOLOGIES INC., pg. 344
DORR-OLIVER INCORPORATED, pg. 346
ENI ENGINEERING COMPANY—Jupiter Industries, Inc., pg. 609
ECLIPSE, INC., pg. 366
ELECTRIC FURNACE CO., pg. 373
ELECTRIC FURNACE GERMANY, GMBH—Electric Furnace Co., pg. 373
FLINN & DREFFEIN ENGINEERING CO., pg. 419
FLINT MANUFACTURING CO., pg. 419
FOSTORIA INDUSTRIES, INC., pg. 427
GALLAGHER-KAISER CORP., pg. 441
GAS-FIRED PRODUCTS, INC., pg. 444
THE GRIEVE CORPORATION, pg. 486
HARROP INDUSTRIES, INC., pg. 512
HAUCK MFG. CO., pg. 517
C. I. HAYES, INC., pg. 519
THE KIRK & BLUM MFG. CO., pg. 633
GEORGE KOCH SONS, INC., pg. 639
KOMLINE-SANDERSON ENGINEERING CORP., pg. 641
MARTIN INDUSTRIES (AL), pg. 715
PACIFIC HEATER CORPORATION—Watlow Electric Manufacturing Company, pg. 1167
RAPID ENGINEERING INC., pg. 913
SECO WARWICK CORPORATION, pg. 987
SHENANDOAH MFG. CO. INC., pg. 997
J.J. TOUREK CO.—Tuthill Corporation, pg. 1120
WSF INDUSTRIES, INC., pg. 1156
WATLOW AOV, INC.—Watlow Electric Manufacturing Company, pg. 1167
WATLOW BATAVIA, INC.—Watlow Electric Manufacturing Company, pg. 1167
WATLOW COLUMBIA, INC.—Watlow Electric Manufacturing Company, pg. 1167
WATLOW ELECTRIC MANUFACTURING COMPANY, pg. 1167
WATLOW ELECTRIC MFG. CO. GMBH—Watlow Electric Manufacturing Company, pg. 1168
WATLOW INDUSTRIES, INC.—Watlow Electric Manufacturing Company, pg. 1168
WATLOW LIMITED—Watlow Electric Manufacturing Company, pg. 1168
WATLOW PROCESS SYSTEMS, INC.—Watlow Electric Manufacturing Company, pg. 1168
WATLOW ST. LOUIS, INC.—Watlow Electric Manufacturing Company, pg. 1168
WHITING CORPORATION, pg. 1187
WHITING EQUIPMENT CANADA, INC.—Whiting Corporation, pg. 1187
WOLVERINE MASSACHUSETTS CORPORATION, pg. 1199
JOHN ZINK CO.—Koch Industries, Incorporated, pg. 639

3568 — MECHANICAL POWER TRANSMISSION EQUIPMENT, NEC

ACCURATE BUSHING CO., INC., pg. 11
AMSTED INDUSTRIES INCORPORATED, pg. 68
BI-METAL BEARING—The Pullman Company, pg. 900
DIAMOND CHAIN COMPANY—Amsted Industries Incorporated, pg. 69
DINGS DYNAMICS CO.—Venturedyne, Ltd., pg. 1148
FRANTZ MANUFACTURING CO., pg. 429
GEAR HEADQUARTERS INC.—Headco Industries, Inc., pg. 520
HILLIARD CORPORATION, pg. 535
KINGSBURY, INC., pg. 632
LOVEJOY INC., pg. 685
MAGNUS METALS—Farley Industries, pg. 400
MARTIN SPROCKET & GEAR, INC., pg. 715
P/M BEARING DIV.—Keystone Carbon Company, pg. 628
REPCO BEARING COMPANY, DIV. OF REPCO LTD.—The Pullman Company, pg. 900
SUNTEC INDUSTRIES INC., pg. 1062
SUPERIOR LINKAGE DIVISION—Tuthill Corporation, pg. 1120
J.J. TOUREK CO.—Tuthill Corporation, pg. 1120
WEASLER ENGINEERING INC., pg. 1169
T.B. WOOD'S SONS COMPANY, pg. 1200

3569 — GENERAL INDUSTRIAL MACHINERY & EQUIPMENT, NEC

ACROMETAL COMPANIES, INC., pg. 14
R. P. ADAMS COMPANY, INC., pg. 16
ADEPT TECHNOLOGY, INC., pg. 17
ALAMO INDUSTRIAL GROUP, pg. 29
ALAMO IRON WORKS—Alamo Industrial Group, pg. 29
ALRO GROUP, pg. 44
ALRO GROUP, BOCA RATON—Alro Group, pg. 44
ALRO GROUP, JACKSON—Alro Group, pg. 44
AMERICAN BALER CO.—Avis Industrial Corporation, pg. 102
AMERICAN MACHINE & TOOL COMPANY, pg. 57
AMSTED INDUSTRIES INCORPORATED, pg. 68
ARLO GROUP, CLEARWATER—Alro Group, pg. 44
ARLO GROUP, KALAMAZOO—Alro Group, pg. 44
ARLO GROUP, ORLANDO—Alro Group, pg. 44
ARROW PNEUMATICS CO. INC., pg. 85
ASTRONAUTICS CORP. OF AMERICA, pg. 93
AVIS INDUSTRIAL CORPORATION, pg. 102
AXELSON, INC., pg. 103
BALTIMORE AIRCOIL COMPANY—Amsted Industries Incorporated, pg. 69
BIJUR LUBRICATING CORPORATION, pg. 150
BORG-WARNER-SPRING/BRUMMER DIVISION—Borg-Warner Corporation, pg. 166
CRL, INC., pg. 203
CAPTIVE-AIRE SYSTEMS, INC., pg. 216
CENTRIFUGAL & MECHANICAL INDUSTRIES—Jupiter Industries, Inc., pg. 609
CENTRIFUGAL & MECHANICAL INDUSTRIES, INC.—Jupiter Industries, Inc., pg. 609
CONTINENTAL CONVEYOR & EQUIPMENT COMPANY—NESCO, Inc., pg. 798
DENVER AUTOMETRICS—Denver Equipment Company, pg. 331
DENVER EQUIPMENT COMPANY, pg. 331
DESPATCH INDUSTRIES, pg. 332
DORR-OLIVER INCORPORATED, pg. 346
DUFF-NORTON—Spreckles Industries, Inc., pg. 1032
DURO DYNE CORPORATION, pg. 355
ENGINEERING SERVICE, INC., pg. 382
ERIEZ MAGNETICS, pg. 386
FWD CORPORATION, pg. 395
FIKE CORPORATION, pg. 409
GREAT LAKES FILTER—Acme Mills Co. Inc., pg. 13
THE HAMMERBLOW CORP., pg. 504
CLIFFORD B. HANNAY & SON INC., pg. 505
HARDIE IRRIGATION-LANDSCAPE DIV., pg. 508
HARLEY INDUSTRIES, INC., pg. 509
HOYT CORPORATION, pg. 548
ICM INDUSTRIES, INC., pg. 559
THE INGERSOLL MILLING MACHINE CO.—Ingersoll International Inc., pg. 568
INTERNATIONAL DIV.—Clayton Industries Co., pg. 254
INTERNATIONAL METALS & MACHINES, INC.—CRL, Inc., pg. 203
JAG NORTHWEST INC.—Pickering Industries Inc., pg. 870
THE JOHNSON CORPORATION, pg. 597
KINGSBURY ASSEMBLY MACHINE DIV.—Kingsbury Corporation, pg. 632
KINGSBURY CORPORATION, pg. 631
KINGTOOL DIVISION—Kingsbury Corporation, pg. 632
KNIGHT EQUIPMENT CORP., pg. 636
KOCH MEMBRANE SYSTEMS—Koch Industries, Incorporated, pg. 639
KOMLINE-SANDERSON ENGINEERING CORP., pg. 641
LAFAYETTE PRECISION PRODUCTS INC.—RDI, Inc., pg. 906
LANTECH INC., pg. 658
LUBECON SYSTEMS, INC., pg. 686
LUKENHEIMER CO., pg. 687
MARK ANDY, INC., pg. 708
MILTON INDUSTRIES, INC., pg. 756
MODERN EQUIPMENT CO., INC.—Alco Industries, Inc., pg. 32
MOLINE CORPORATION, pg. 764
MUNROE, INC., pg. 776
NESCO, INC., pg. 798
NETZSCH, INC., pg. 798
PRESSURE PRODUCTS INDUSTRIES—Cawsl Corporation, pg. 230
RDI, INC., pg. 906
REICHEL & DREWS INC.—RDI, Inc., pg. 906
RELIABLE AUTOMATIC SPRINKLER CO., INC., pg. 924
SCOTT SPECIALTY GASES, INC., pg. 983
SENCORP, pg. 989
SERFILCO, LTD., pg. 990
SMITH INDUSTRIES, INC., pg. 1013
SNAP-TITE, INCORPORATED, pg. 1014
SOUTH CHESTER TUBE CO., pg. 1019
SPENCER TURBINE CO., pg. 1030
STANDARD-KNAPP, INC., pg. 1036
TEMPLETON, KENLY & CO., INC., pg. 1086
TRIANGLE PARACHUTE—The Entwistle Company, pg. 383
U.S. DIVERS CO., INC., pg. 1135
VELCON FILTERS, INC., pg. 1146
WAYNE WIRE CLOTH PRODUCTS, INC., pg. 1169
WESTERN STATES MACHINE CO., pg. 1181
WHITIN ROBERTS CO., pg. 1187
WHITING CORPORATION, pg. 1187
WHITING EQUIPMENT CANADA, INC.—Whiting Corporation, pg. 1187
WICKES MFG. CO.—Collins & Aikman Group Inc., pg. 262
WILLIAMS PATENT CRUSHER AND PULVERIZER CO., pg. 1191
WILTON CORPORATION, pg. 1194
WURZBURG, INC., pg. 1205
THE WYCO TOOL CO.—Racine Federated, Inc., pg. 909

3571 — ELECTRONIC COMPUTERS

ACTION CONTROLS PTY. LTD.—Action Instruments, Inc., pg. 14
ACTION INDUSTRIE COMPUTER, GMBH—Action Instruments, Inc., pg. 14
ACTION INSTRUMENTS, INC., pg. 14
ADRA SYSTEMS, INC., pg. 18
ASTRONAUTICS C.A. LTD.—Astronautics Corp. of America, pg. 93
ASTRONAUTICS CORP. OF AMERICA, pg. 93
CANBERRA INDUSTRIES, INC., pg. 213
D. CHAKLIN, DIR. EUROPEAN OPERATIONS—Astronautics Corp. of America, pg. 93
COMMUNICATIONS INTERNATIONAL, pg. 269
COMPUTER DYNAMICS, INC., pg. 271
DAQ ELECTRONICS INC., pg. 308
DDC PERTEC, pg. 308
DATAMEDIA CORPORATION, pg. 316
FASFAX CORPORATION—International Shoe Machine Corp., pg. 579
FORMATION, INC., pg. 424
GLOBAL TURNKEY SYSTEMS INC., pg. 463
IDEA COURIER, INC.—I D E Corporation, pg. 560
INKEL TECHNOLOGY—Inkel Corp., pg. 570
INTEGRATED SYSTEMS ANALYSTS, INC., pg. 573
INTERNATIONAL SHOE MACHINE CORP., pg. 579
KLEINSCHMIDT INC., pg. 635
OCTUS, pg. 818
PRO-LOG CORPORATION, pg. 892
PROXIMA CORPORATION, pg. 896
RADIX CORPORATION, pg. 909
RANDOM CORPORATION, pg. 912
SHERWOOD CORPORATION—Inkel Corp., pg. 570
TECHNOLOGY APPLICATIONS, INC., pg. 1083
THINKING MACHINES CORPORATION, pg. 1092

3572 — COMPUTER STORAGE DEVICES

AMPEX RECORDING SYSTEMS DIVISION—Sherborne Group, Inc., pg. 998
COMMUNICATIONS INTERNATIONAL, pg. 269
DDC PERTEC, pg. 308
NORTH ATLANTIC INDUSTRIES, INC., pg. 812
SHUGART CORPORATION, pg. 1001
TALLGRASS TECHNOLOGIES CORP., pg. 1077

3575 — COMPUTER TERMINALS

ADVANCED INPUT DEVICES, INC., pg. 20
AMERIDATA, INC., pg. 66
AMPEX COMPUTER PRODUCTS DIVISION—Sherborne Group, Inc., pg. 998
ARK-LES CORPORATION, pg. 82
CHARLES RIVER DATA SYSTEMS, INC., pg. 240
COMMUNICATIONS INTERNATIONAL, pg. 269
CONTEC INTERNATIONAL, pg. 278
CUBIX CORPORATION, pg. 303
INDUSTRIAL ELECTRONIC ENGINEERS, INC., pg. 566
PROGRESS CASTING GROUP, INC., pg. 894
SHUGART CORPORATION, pg. 1001

3577 — COMPUTER PERIPHERAL EQUIPMENT, NEC

ACCU-SORT SYSTEMS, INC., pg. 11
AVATAR CORPORATION, pg. 101
BELL & HOWELL COMPANY, pg. 134
BLACK BOX CORPORATION—MICOM Communications Corp., pg. 748
BROWN DISC PRODUCTS COMPANY—Genevar Enterprises, pg. 451
CBM AMERICA CORP., pg. 199
CHATSWORTH DATA CORPORATION, pg. 241
COMMUNICATIONS INTERNATIONAL, pg. 269
COMPUTER CIRCUITRY GROUP—Insilco Corporation, pg. 571
CRAY COMMUNICATIONS INC., pg. 297
CURTIS MANUFACTURING COMPANY, INC.—Insilco Corporation, pg. 571
DDC PERTEC, pg. 308
DECISION DATA COMPUTER GMBH—Decision Data Inc., pg. 324
DECISION DATA INC., pg. 323
DISPLAY TECHNOLOGIES, INC., pg. 339
DUKANE CORPORATION, pg. 351
FARALLON COMPUTING, INC., pg. 399
GENEVAR ENTERPRISES, pg. 451
GRAHAM MAGNETICS, INC., pg. 475
ID SOLUTIONS—Intelligent Controls Inc., pg. 574
I D E CORPORATION, pg. 560
IDEA COURIER, INC.—I D E Corporation, pg. 560
INDUSTRIAL ELECTRONIC ENGINEERS, INC., pg. 566
INFOTEC DEVELOPMENT, INC., pg. 567
INTEGRA TECHNOLOGIES CORP., pg. 572
INTELLIGENT CONTROLS INC., pg. 573
ITRAN CORPORATION, pg. 583
KDI ELECTRO-TEC CORP.—KDI Corporation, pg. 612
KENNEDY COMPANY—Shugart Corporation, pg. 1001
KINETIC SYSTEMS CORPORATION, pg. 630
KLEINSCHMIDT INC., pg. 635
LEXMARK INTERNATIONAL, INC., pg. 673
LEXMARK INTERNATIONAL, INC.—Lexmark International, Inc., pg. 674
LITTLE FALLS COLOR PRINT—Sullivan Paper Company, pg. 1057
LLOYD CONTROLS, INC., pg. 679
LLOYD ELECTRIC APPARATUS CO.—Lloyd Controls, Inc., pg. 680
MAGNETIC TECHNOLOGIES CORPORATION, pg. 701
MERCURY COMPUTER SYSTEMS, INC., pg. 740
METROLOGIC INSTRUMENTS, INC., pg. 743
MICOM CARIBE, INC.—MICOM Communications Corp., pg. 748
MICOM COMMUNICATIONS CORP., pg. 748
MICOM COMMUNICATIONS CORP.—MICOM Communications Corp., pg. 748
NER HOLDINGS, INC.—Hargro Enterprises, Inc., pg. 509
NORTH ATLANTIC INDUSTRIES, INC., pg. 812
NORTH ATLANTIC INDUSTRIES SYSTEMS DIVISION—North Atlantic Industries, Inc., pg. 812
NORTHERN COMPUTERS INC.—American Trading and Production Corporation, pg. 65
PEGASUS INTERNATIONAL CORPORATION, pg. 855
PERIPHONICS CORP., pg. 862
PRACTICAL AUTOMATION, INC.—Alinabal, Inc., pg. 34
PRO-LOG CORPORATION, pg. 892
PROXIMA CORPORATION, pg. 896
QEI, INC., pg. 902
ROBERTSON MARKETING INC., pg. 939
SHUGART CORPORATION, pg. 1001
STEWART STAMPING CORP.—Insilco Corporation, pg. 571
SULLIVAN PAPER COMPANY, pg. 1057
SULPACO WEST—Sullivan Paper Company, pg. 1057
SYSTECH COMPUTER CORPORATION, pg. 1071
TRACE PRODUCTS, pg. 1104
TRI-DATA SYSTEMS—Avatar Corporation, pg. 102
WEBER MARKING SYSTEMS, INC., pg. 1171

3578 — CALCULATING & ACCOUNTING MACHINES, EXCEPT ELECTRONIC COMPUTERS

THE BATES MFG. CO., pg. 125
COMMUNICATIONS INTERNATIONAL, pg. 269
CUMMINS-ALLISON CORP.—Cummins-American Corp., pg. 305
CUMMINS-AMERICAN CORP., pg. 304
MONROE SYSTEMS FOR BUSINESS, INC., pg. 766
RI HOLDINGS, pg. 907
ROWE INTERNATIONAL, INC.—RI Holdings, pg. 907

3579 — OFFICE MACHINES, NEC

THE AARQUE COMPANIES, pg. 9
ACCU-SORT TIME SYSTEM—Accu-Sort Systems, Inc., pg. 11
ACE OFFICE PRODUCTS, pg. 12
ARROW FASTENER CO., INC., pg. 85
ARTIST GRAPHICS—Control Systems Inc., pg. 281
THE BATES MFG. CO., pg. 125
BELL & HOWELL COMPANY, pg. 134
BELL & HOWELL GMBH—Bell & Howell Company, pg. 135
BELL & HOWELL INFORMATION SYSTEMS DIVISION—Bell & Howell Company, pg. 135
BELL & HOWELL LTD., (UK) MAILHANDLING DIV.—Bell & Howell Company, pg. 135
CONTROL SYSTEMS INC., pg. 281
CUMMINS-ALLISON CORP.—Cummins-American Corp., pg. 305
CUMMINS-AMERICAN CORP., pg. 304
CUTLER MANUFACTURING CORPORATION, pg. 307
DAKTRONICS, INC., pg. 312
FELLOWES MANUFACTURING CO., pg. 405
GENERAL BINDING CORPORATION—Lane Industries, Inc., pg. 656
HARCO TECHNOLOGIES CORPORATION, pg. 507
INFORMATION PROCESSING PRODUCTS—Fellowes Manufacturing Co., pg. 406
LABELON CORPORATION, pg. 649
LANE INDUSTRIES, INC., pg. 656
LEXMARK INTERNATIONAL, INC., pg. 673
LEXMARK INTERNATIONAL, INC.—Lexmark International, Inc., pg. 674
MAGNETIC TECHNOLOGIES CORPORATION, pg. 701
MICHAEL BUSINESS MACHINES CORPORATION, pg. 747
MONROE SYSTEMS FOR BUSINESS, INC., pg. 766
NEW HAVEN MFG. CORP., pg. 801
PANARCO, INC., pg. 845
PHONEMATE, INC., pg. 869
POWER SHRED DIVISION—Fellowes Manufacturing Co., pg. 406
PRETEC PRECISIE TECHNIEK B.V.—Bell & Howell Company, pg. 135
STANDARD DUPLICATING MACHINES CORP., pg. 1036
TICKETMASTER CORPORATION, pg. 1096
VARITYPER, INC., pg. 1146
VELOBIND, INC.—Lane Industries, Inc., pg. 657
VELOBIND, INC.—Lane Industries, Inc., pg. 657
VELOBIND-RENO DIVISION—Lane Industries, Inc., pg. 657
WEBER MARKING SYSTEMS, INC., pg. 1171

3581 — AUTOMATIC VENDING MACHINES

BUCYRUS BLADES INC.—Esco Corporation, pg. 388
CAVALIER CORPORATION, pg. 229
GOLD MEDAL PRODUCTS CO., pg. 465
KASPAR WIRE WORKS, INC., pg. 617
RI HOLDINGS, pg. 907
ROWE INTERNATIONAL, INC.—RI Holdings, pg. 907
WOMETCO ENTERPRISES, INC., pg. 1199

3582 — COMMERCIAL LAUNDRY, DRY CLEANING & PRESSING MACHINES

AMERICAN LAUNDRY MACHINERY INC., pg. 57
CISSELL MANUFACTURING COMPANY—The Dyson-Kissner-Moran Corporation, pg. 357
DEXTER COMPANY, pg. 334
IMPARTS—Vic Manufacturing, pg. 1149
MULTIMATIC CORPORATION, pg. 775
VIC MANUFACTURING, pg. 1149

3585 — AIR CONDITIONING & WARM AIR HEATING EQUIPMENT & COMMERCIAL & INDUSTRIAL REFRIGERATION EQUIPMENT

ACME REFRIGERATION OF BATON ROUGE INC., pg. 13
ACUREX CORP. AEROTHERM PRODUCTS DIVISION—Acurex Environmental Corporation, pg. 16
ACUREX CORP. AEROTHERM PRODUCTS DIVISION—Acurex Environmental Corporation, pg. 15
ALADDIN INDUSTRIES PTY. LTD.—Aladdin Industries, Incorporated, pg. 29
ALUMA SHIELD INDUSTRIES, INC., pg. 46
AMERICAN STANDARD AIR CONDITIONING PRODUCTS—American Standard Inc., pg. 61
AMERICAN STANDARD INC., pg. 61
AMSTED INDUSTRIES INCORPORATED, pg. 68
AMTROL INC., pg. 70
ARDCO, INC., pg. 81
ARMSTRONG AIR CONDITIONING INC.—Lennox International Inc., pg. 667
ARMSTRONG INTERNATIONAL, INC., pg. 83
ARROW FLUID POWER—Arrow Pneumatics Co. Inc., pg. 85
ARROW PNEUMATICS CO. INC., pg. 85
BEUTLER HEATING & AIR CONDITIONING INC., pg. 148
BLISSFIELD MANUFACTURING COMPANY, pg. 157
BONLAND INDUSTRIES, INC., pg. 164
BORG-WARNER CORPORATION, pg. 165
CARGOCAIRE ENGINEERING CORPORATION, pg. 220
CARNES COMPANY, INC.—Venturedyne, Ltd., pg. 1148
CERAMIC COOLING TOWER CO.—Amsted Industries Incorporated, pg. 69
THE COLEMAN COMPANY, INC.—MacAndrews & Forbes Holdings Inc., pg. 695
CONSTRUCTION SPECIALTIES, INC., pg. 277
CORDLEY TEMPRITE—Elkay Manufacturing Company, pg. 377
DEC/BOU-MATIC—DEC International, Inc., pg. 309
DATA AIRE, INC.—Construction Specialties, Inc., pg. 277
DONLEE TECHNOLOGIES INC., pg. 344
EBCO MFG. COMPANY, pg. 365
ECLIPSE-CONTROLS—Eclipse, Inc., pg. 366
EDWARDS ENGINEERING CORPORATION, pg. 370
ELKAY MANUFACTURING COMPANY, pg. 377
THE EQUION CORPORATION, pg. 385
THE FIELD CONTROLS COMPANY—Heico Inc., pg. 525
FLAKT INC., BAHNSON DIV., pg. 416
FORD PRODUCTS CORPORATION, pg. 423
FOSTER REFRIGERATOR CORPORATION, pg. 426
FOSTORIA INDUSTRIES, INC., pg. 427
PHILIP FRITZE & SONS, INC., pg. 434
H M K ENTERPRISES, INC., pg. 497
HACKNEY BROTHERS, INC., pg. 498
HARFORD SYSTEMS, INC.—Bio Medic Corporation, pg. 152
HAYDEN, INC.—The Equion Corporation, pg. 385
HEAT CONTROLLER, INC., pg. 524
HEATCRAFT REFRIGERATION PRODUCTS DIVISION—Lennox International Inc., pg. 667
HEICO INC., pg. 525
HIROSS INC., pg. 536
HOME HEATING & AIR CONDITIONING—EVCON Holdings, pg. 391
IGLOO CORPORATION, pg. 562
INDUSTRIAS KOLMEX, S.A.—MacAndrews & Forbes Holdings Inc., pg. 696
INTERNATIONAL COLD STORAGE CO., INC., pg. 576
THE ROBERT IRSAY COMPANY—Jupiter Industries, Inc., pg. 609
JET SPRAY CORP., pg. 593
JET SPRAY INTERNATIONAL—Jet Spray Corp., pg. 593
THE JEWETT REFRIGERATOR CO., INC.—Ruslander & Sons, Inc., pg. 957
THE JOHNSON INDUSTRIES CORP., pg. 598
KECO AEROSPACE GROUND EQUIPMENT DIV.—Keco Industry, Inc., pg. 619
KECO INDUSTRY, INC., pg. 619
GEORGE KOCH SONS, INC., pg. 639
LARKIN, INC.—Lennox International Inc., pg. 667
LENNOX INDUSTRIES (CANADA) LTD.—Lennox International Inc., pg. 667
LENNOX INDUSTRIES (CANADA) LTD.—Lennox International Inc., pg. 667
LENNOX INDUSTRIES INC.—Lennox International Inc., pg. 667
LENNOX INTERNATIONAL INC., pg. 667
MGR EQUIPMENT CORP., pg. 692
MARINE AIR SYSTEMS, INC.—Nelson A. Taylor Co., Inc., pg. 1081
MARTIN INDUSTRIES (AL), pg. 715
MIDWESCO INC., pg. 751
PNEUMAFIL CORP., pg. 878
RED T. PRODUCTS—EVCON Holdings, pg. 391
REMCOR PRODUCTS CO., pg. 926
RUSLANDER & SONS, INC., pg. 956
SANISERV, pg. 970
SIGNET SYSTEMS, INC.—The Equion Corporation, pg. 385
SLANT/FIN CORPORATION, pg. 1010
SLANT-FIN, LTD./LTEE—Slant/Fin Corporation, pg. 1010
SNYDERGENERAL CORPORATION, pg. 1015
SOMERSET TECHNOLOGIES, INC., pg. 1017
STANLEY KNIGHT CORPORATION, pg. 1038
STEELITE, INC., pg. 1044
STEVENS-LEE COMPANY, pg. 1048
SUNROC CORPORATION, pg. 1062
THE TRANE COMPANY—American Standard Inc., pg. 62
TRANE DO BRAZIL—American Standard Inc., pg. 62
TRANE COMMERCIAL SYSTEMS GROUP—American Standard Inc., pg. 61
TRANE CO. OF CANADA—American Standard Inc., pg. 62
TRANE EUROPE—American Standard Inc., pg. 62
TRANE LTD.—American Standard Inc., pg. 62
TRANS UNITARY PRODUCTS GROUP-COMMERCIAL—American Standard Inc., pg. 61
TURBO REFRIGERATING—Henry Vogt Machine Co., pg. 1154
UNIFLOW MANUFACTURING CO., pg. 1126
UNITARY PRODUCTS GROUP-RESIDENTIAL—American Standard Inc., pg. 61
VENTUREDYNE, LTD., pg. 1148
VILTER EXPORT CORP.—Vilter Manufacturing Corporation, pg. 1152
VILTER MANUFACTURING CORPORATION, pg. 1152
HENRY VOGT MACHINE CO., pg. 1154
VOLLRATH REFRIGERATION INC.—The Vollrath Company Inc., pg. 1155
VORTEC CORPORATION—Chicago West Pullman Corporation, pg. 246
WARREN REFRIGERATOR COMPANY, INC.—Great American Industries, Inc., pg. 480

3586 — MEASURING & DISPENSING PUMPS

AUTOMOTIVE ACCESSORY CO., LTD.—UIS, Inc., pg. 1124
FILL-RITE DIVISION—Tuthill Corporation, pg. 1120
KOMLINE-SANDERSON ENGINEERING CORP., pg. 641
PEARCE INDUSTRIES INC., pg. 853
TUTHILL PUMP—Tuthill Corporation, pg. 1120

3589 — SERVICE INDUSTRY MACHINES, NEC

ADVANCE MACHINE COMPANY, pg. 18
ALADDIN INDUSTRIES, INCORPORATED, pg. 29
ALADDIN SYNERGETICS, INC.—Aladdin Industries, Incorporated, pg. 29
ALKOTA CLEANING SYSTEMS, INC., pg. 34
ALTO SHAAM INC., pg. 46
AMERICAN WYOTT CORPORATION, pg. 65
BARNES PUMPS, INC.—Harbour Group Ltd., pg. 507
BISSELL INC., pg. 153
G.S. BLODGETT CORPORATION, pg. 157
BREUER ELECTRIC MFG. CO., pg. 174
BRUNER CORPORATION, pg. 184
BUNN-O-MATIC CORPORATION, pg. 188
BURKS PUMPS, INC.—Harbour Group Ltd., pg. 507
CALDWELL MANUFACTURING—Chief Industries, Inc., pg. 247
CASTEX INDUSTRIES INC., pg. 228
CHARMGLOW INDUSTRIES, INC., pg. 240
CHIEF E-Z BREAKER, INC.—Chief Industries, Inc., pg. 247
CHIEF INDUSTRIES - AGRI PRODUCTS DIV.—Chief Industries, Inc., pg. 247
CHIEF INDUSTRIES, INC., pg. 247
CISSELL MANUFACTURING COMPANY—The Dyson-Kissner-Moran Corporation, pg. 357
CLEMCO INDUSTRIES, pg. 254
CLOW VALVE DIV.—McWane, Inc., pg. 733
COLUMBIAN ROPE COMPANY, pg. 266
CRES-COR/CROWN-X, pg. 298
CULLIGAN INTERNATIONAL COMPANY—E-II Holdings, Inc., pg. 358
DUARY/J.F. DUNCAN INDUSTRIES, INC., pg. 350
DUKE MANUFACTURING CO., INC., pg. 352

E-II HOLDINGS, INC., pg. 358
ECO WATER SYSTEMS, pg. 367
ECO WATER SYSTEMS, INC.—The Marmon Group, Inc., pg. 712
ECODYNE WATER SYSTEMS, INC.—The Marmon Group, Inc., pg. 712
ECOLOGY SYSTEM DEPT.—Chief Industries, Inc., pg. 247
ELECTRONIC DISPLAY SYSTEMS (KALLEGO)—Chief Industries, Inc., pg. 247
ENERFAB INC., pg. 381
EVERPURE INC.—E-II Holdings, Inc., pg. 358
EVSWATER INDUSTRIAL SYSTEMS—The Marmon Group, Inc., pg. 712
FOSTER REFRIGERATOR CORPORATION, pg. 426
THE GENIE COMPANY, pg. 452
THE GRAVER COMPANY—The Marmon Group, Inc., pg. 712
HACKNEY BROTHERS, INC., pg. 498
HANNA CAR WASH INTERNATIONAL, INC., pg. 505
HEICO INC., pg. 525
HILLEND ENVIRONMENTAL INDUSTRY, LTD.—The Heil Co., pg. 526
JACKSON PRODUCTS CORP., pg. 587
JANDY INDUSTRIES, pg. 589
KDI PARAGON, INC.—KDI Corporation, pg. 612
KNIGHT EQUIPMENT CORP., pg. 636
KRAUSE PLOW CORP., pg. 644
LINDSAY MANUFACTURING INC., pg. 676
MAN-GILL CHEMICAL COMPANY, pg. 703
THE MARLEY COMPANY, pg. 710
THE MARMON GROUP, INC.—The Marmon Group, Inc., pg. 711
MARMON INDUSTRIAL CORPORATION—The Marmon Group, Inc., pg. 712
MARTIN INDUSTRIES (AL), pg. 715
MIDCO INTERNATIONAL INC., pg. 751
MODERN CONCRETE SEPTIC TANK COMPANY, pg. 762
MONORAIL, INC.—Columbian Rope Company, pg. 266
MUSKIN LEISURE PRODUCTS, INC., pg. 777
NATIONAL SAFETY ASSOCIATES, pg. 793
THE NATIONAL SUPER SERVICE CO., pg. 794
NOBLES INDUSTRIES, INC., pg. 808
NORTHLAND ALUMINUM PRODUCTS, INC., pg. 814
O'BRIEN DIVISION—Heico Inc., pg. 525
PEABODY MYERS CORP.—The Pullman Company, pg. 900
PIONEER/ECLIPSE CORP., pg. 871
POLARIS POOL SYSTEMS, INC., pg. 878
RAINSOFT WATER CONDITIONING CO., pg. 910
THE REGINA COMPANY, pg. 922
THE REGINA COMPANY—The Regina Company, pg. 922
SCIENTIFIC DUST COLLECTORS—Venturedyne, Ltd., pg. 1148
SPECIALTY EQUIPMENT COMPANIES INC., pg. 1027
SPENCER TURBINE CO., pg. 1030
THE SPENCER TURBINE CO., pg. 1030
STANLEY KNIGHT CORPORATION, pg. 1038
STANLEY STEEMER INTERNATIONAL, INC., pg. 1038
STEVENS-LEE COMPANY, pg. 1048
SUNDT PRODUCTS, INC.—Sundt Corp., pg. 1060
THETFORD CORPORATION—The Dyson-Kissner-Moran Corporation, pg. 357
WHITE MOP WRINGER COMPANY, pg. 1186
WINDSOR INDUSTRIES, INC., pg. 1195

3592 — CARBURETORS, PISTONS, PISTON RINGS & VALVES

AMSTED INDUSTRIES INCORPORATED, pg. 68
BURGESS-NORTON MFG. CO.—Amsted Industries Incorporated, pg. 69
DANFOSS DUKES FLUID POWER INC., pg. 314
FREEDOM FORGE CORPORATION, pg. 430
HANNA CORPORATION, pg. 505
METAL LEVE S.A.—The Pullman Company, pg. 900
PLASTIC PRODUCTS DIVISION—Freudenberg-NOK (MI), pg. 432
PLASTIC PRODUCTS DIVISION—Freudenberg-NOK (MI), pg. 432
RITE-WAY, INC., pg. 936
ROCKET INDUSTRIES, INC./EXCEL, THE EXERCISE COMPANY, pg. 941
TRW-KEYSTONE POWDER METAL PRODUCTS CO.—Keystone Carbon Company, pg. 628
TOMCO AUTO PRODUCTS, INC., pg. 1100
UNITED ENGINE & MACHINE COMPANY, pg. 1131
WOODLAND MOLDED PLASTICS—Freudenberg-NOK (MI), pg. 433
ZOLLNER CORPORATION, pg. 1221

3593 — FLUID POWER CYLINDERS & ACTUATORS

AMERICAN STANDARD INC., pg. 61
AVIS INDUSTRIAL CORPORATION, pg. 102
BELLOFRAM CORP., pg. 136
CGF INDUSTRIES, pg. 201
HUMPHREY PRODUCTS COMPANY, pg. 553
ICM INDUSTRIES, INC., pg. 559
IOWA INDUSTRIAL HYDRAULICS, INC.—ICM Industries, Inc., pg. 559
MILLER FLUID POWER CORP., pg. 754
POSITECH CORPORATION—Columbus McKinnon Corp., pg. 267
SNAP-TITE, INCORPORATED, pg. 1014
UNIVERSAL VISE & TOOL CO.—Avis Industrial Corporation, pg. 103
WILLIAMS, WHITE & COMPANY, pg. 1191
WILSON INDUSTRIES INC., pg. 1193

3594 — FLUID POWER PUMPS & MOTORS

AMW INDUSTRIES INC.—Harbour Group Ltd., pg. 507
JOHN S. BARNES CORP., pg. 120
CGF INDUSTRIES, pg. 201
HYDRECO—ICM Industries, Inc., pg. 559
REULAND ELECTRIC COMPANY, pg. 930
WHIPPS, pg. 1185

3596 — SCALES & BALANCES, EXCEPT LABORATORY

DETECTO SCALE COMPANY, pg. 332
EDLUND COMPANY, INC., pg. 368
EXACT EQUIPMENT CORPORATION, pg. 392
FERGUSON INDUSTRIES, pg. 406
FERGUSON INDUSTRIES INTERNATIONAL—Ferguson Industries, pg. 406
OHAUS CORPORATION, pg. 822
PELOUZE SCALE CO., pg. 856
SUNBEAM HOME COMFORT—Sunbeam-Oster Company, Inc., pg. 1059
THOMAS ENGINEERING INC., pg. 1093

3599 — INDUSTRIAL & COMMERCIAL MACHINERY & EQUIPMENT, NEC

A & A MANUFACTURING CO., pg. 1
AMF BAKERY SYSTEMS, pg. 5
AQHI, INC., pg. 5
ALGIERS IRON WORKS & DRY DOCK, INC.—Bollinger Machine Shop And Shipyard, Inc., pg. 163
ALPHA Q, INC.—AQHI, Inc., pg. 5
ANCHOR TOOL & DIE COMPANY, pg. 71
ARBURG, INC., pg. 79
AVIS INDUSTRIAL CORPORATION, pg. 102
BC HYDROTILE MACHINERY CO.—The Black Clawson Co., pg. 154
BASIC INDUSTRIES—Insilco Corporation, pg. 571
THE BLACK CLAWSON CO., pg. 154
THE BLACK CLAWSON COMPANY—The Black Clawson Co., pg. 154
THE BLACK CLAWSON COMPANY—The Black Clawson Co., pg. 154
BLISS-SALEM, INC., pg. 156
BOLLINGER MACHINE SHOP AND SHIPYARD, INC., pg. 163
JOHN BOUCHARD & SONS COMPANY, pg. 168
BRUNNER & LAY, INC., pg. 184
J. C. CARTER COMPANY, INC., pg. 226
CHANCE INDUSTRIES, INC., pg. 238
CINCINNATI INCORPORATED, pg. 250
CLEARING INTERNATIONAL, INC., pg. 254
CLEMCO INDUSTRIES, pg. 254
DELTA RESINS & REFRACTORIES, INC., pg. 327
JOHN DUSENBERY CO., INC., pg. 355
EDLON PRODUCTS, INC.—Pfaudler-U.S., Inc., pg. 866
FABEX INC., pg. 395
FARMERS MARINE COPPER WORKS, pg. 401
FLEXONICS INC., pg. 419
FLO-LINE FILTERS, INC.—Perry Equipment Corporation, pg. 863
FLORIG EQUIPMENT COMPANY, INC., pg. 421
FORMAC CORPORATION, pg. 424
GENERAL SHIP CORPORATION, pg. 450
GOUGLER INDUSTRIES, INC., pg. 473
GRANULATOR DIV.—Arburg, Inc., pg. 80
HANNA CORPORATION, pg. 505
HARMONY ENGINEERING CORPORATION, pg. 510
HARRIS-KAYOT, INC., pg. 512
HYDRO-MILL CO., pg. 557
IDAB WAMAC AB—IDAB International Incorporated, pg. 559
JUSTRITE MFG. CO.—Justrite Manufacturing Company, pg. 610
KARTRIDG PAK CO.—Barry-Wehmiller Company, pg. 122
KOCH ENGINEERING CO., INC.—Koch Industries, Incorporated, pg. 639
LAMINAIRE CORPORATION, pg. 652
LITTLEFORD DAY, TAYLOR-STILES DIVISION, pg. 679
LODAL, INC., pg. 680
LORD CORP., INDUSTRIAL PRODUCTS DIV.—Lord Corporation, pg. 683
MAL TOOL & ENGINEERING CO.—Collins & Aikman Group Inc., pg. 263
MARION MACHINE COMPANY DIVISION—Superior Machine Company Of South Carolina, Inc., pg. 1064
MARVIN ENGINEERING COMPANY, INC., pg. 716
METAL TRADES, INC., pg. 741
MICHIGAN WHEEL CORPORATION, pg. 747
MILLER FLUID POWER CORP., pg. 754
MOLINE CORPORATION, pg. 764
MOSLER INC., pg. 772
MOTEK ENGINEERING & MANUFACTURING COMPANY, pg. 773
NASHVILLE MACHINE CO. INC., pg. 784
NESCO, INC., pg. 798
OMCO MOULD, INC., pg. 819
OMCO MACHINING CONCEPTS, INC.—OMCO Mould, Inc., pg. 819
OSTARR CORPORATION, pg. 831
PMC INDUSTRIES INC., pg. 836
PAXTON & VIERLING—Owen Industries, Inc., pg. 834
PERRY EQUIPMENT CORPORATION, pg. 863
PFAUDLER-U.S., INC., pg. 866
PLATT SACO LOWELL CORPORATION, pg. 876
POLHEMUS INC.—Kaiser Aerospace & Electronics Corp., pg. 614
PRECISION ROLL GRINDERS, INC., pg. 885
PROSSER/ENPO INDUSTRIES—Harbour Group Ltd., pg. 507
PTI TECHNOLOGIES—Esco Corporation, pg. 388
REEL-O-MATIC SYSTEMS, INC., pg. 920
RITE-HITE CORPORATION, pg. 936
ROBINS ENGINEERS & CONSTRUCTORS, INC., pg. 939
ROLOCK, INC., pg. 944
SINTEL, INC., pg. 1008
J.T. SLOCOMB COMPANY, pg. 1010
SPRING ENGINEERS, INC., pg. 1033
STANDARD-THOMSON CORPORATION, pg. 1037
STANDARD TOOL & MANUFACTURING COMPANY, pg. 1037
STAR-PARTS INC., pg. 1039
STOCKER & YALE, INC., pg. 1050
STRITE-ANDERSON DIE CASTINGS—Kurt Manufacturing Co. Inc., pg. 646
SUPERIOR MACHINE COMPANY OF SOUTH CAROLINA, INC., pg. 1064
TEXAS STEEL CO., INC., pg. 1090
TOWNSEND ENGINEERING CO., pg. 1104
TURNER MACHINE COMPANY—Electric Furnace Co., pg. 373
UNITED FILTERS, INC.—Perry Equipment Corporation, pg. 863
UNIVERSAL VISE & TOOL CO.—Avis Industrial Corporation, pg. 103
VOTAW PRECISION TECHNOLOGIES—Kaiser Aerospace & Electronics Corp., pg. 614
WICKES ENGINEERING GROUP—Collins & Aikman Group Inc., pg. 263
WILLIAMS, WHITE & COMPANY, pg. 1191
ZMP, INC.—Certified Holding Corp., pg. 237

3612 — POWER, DISTRIBUTION & SPECIALTY TRANSFORMERS

ABBOTT ELECTRONICS, INC., pg. 9
ARKANSAS ELECTRIC COOPERATIVES INC., pg. 83
BACHMANN INDUSTRIES, INC., pg. 108
BENTLY NEVADA CORPORATION, pg. 140
BOGUE ELECTRIC MANUFACTURING CO., pg. 162
BORG-WARNER AUTOMOTIVE (CANADA) LIMITED—Borg-Warner Corporation, pg. 166
CHRISTIE ELECTRIC CORPORATION, pg. 249
CIRCLE A.W. PRODUCTS, CO., pg. 250
COILCRAFT, INC., pg. 259
COMPONENTS CORPORATION OF AMERICA, pg. 270
CYBEREX, INC., pg. 307
ELECTRIC RESEARCH AND MANUFACTURING COOPERATIVE, INC. (ERMCO)—Arkansas Electric Cooperatives Inc., pg. 83
ELECTRO-MATIC PRODUCTS INC., pg. 374
KEARNEY-NATIONAL CANADA LTD.—The Dyson-Kissner-Moran Corporation, pg. 358
LES APPAREILLAGER ELECTRIQUES KEARNEY-NATIONAL—The Dyson-Kissner-Moran Corporation, pg. 358
MALLORY, INC., pg. 703
PARA SYSTEMS INC.—Components Corporation Of America, pg. 270
RAPID POWER TECHNOLOGIES, INC., pg. 913
SAE ENGINEERING, INC., pg. 959
SAN ANGELO ELECTRIC SERVICE COMPANY, pg. 969
SCHOTT CORPORATION, pg. 978
SHERMAN & REILLY, INC., pg. 998
SIGNAL TRANSFORMER CO., INC.—Insilco Corporation, pg. 571
SOLIDSTATE CONTROLS, INC.—The Marmon Group, Inc., pg. 712
SPANG & COMPANY, pg. 1025
STACOENERGY PRODUCTS CO.—Components Corporation Of America, pg. 270
TEMPEL STEEL COMPANY, pg. 1086
THORDARSON MEISSNER, INC.—Components Corporation Of America, pg. 270
TRIPLE A SPECIALTY COMPANY, pg. 1114

3613 — SWITCHGEAR & SWITCHBOARD APPARATUS

ARMSTRONG INTERNATIONAL, INC., pg. 83
CIRCLE A.W. PRODUCTS, CO., pg. 250
CORNELL DUBILIER ELECTRONICS—Kaplan Electronics, pg. 616
CYBEREX, INC., pg. 307
EAGLE ELECTRIC MFG. CO., INC., pg. 362
GENERAL AUTOMOTIVE SPECIALTY CO., INC., pg. 449
GUARANTEE ELECTRICAL COMPANY, pg. 490
JENSEN ELECTRIC COMPANY, pg. 592
KARTRET SWITCHGEAR LTD.—O'Brien Energy Systems Inc., pg. 820
KEARNEY—The Dyson-Kissner-Moran Corporation, pg. 357
KEARNEY DIV.—The Dyson-Kissner-Moran Corporation, pg. 357
KELSO-BURNETT COMPANY, pg. 622
KOHLER COMPANY, pg. 639
LITTELFUSE B.V.—Littelfuse, Inc., pg. 678
LITTELFUSE, INC., pg. 678
LITTELFUSE LTD.—Littelfuse, Inc., pg. 678
LITTELFUSE S.A. DE C.V.—Littelfuse, Inc., pg. 678
MINARIK ELECTRIC COMPANY, pg. 756
ROMAN ELECTRIC COMPANY, INC., pg. 945
S & C ELECTRIC CANADA LTD.—S & C Electric Company, pg. 959
S & C ELECTRIC COMPANY, pg. 958
SPD TECHNOLOGIES, pg. 963
SYC-SELMEC, S.A. DE C.V.—S & C Electric Company, pg. 959
SHOGYO INTERNATIONAL CORPORATION, pg. 1000
SPANG & COMPANY, pg. 1025
SYNCHRO-START PRODUCTS, INC.—Knowles Electronics, Inc., pg. 638
TRICON INDUSTRIES, INC., pg. 1113

3621 — MOTORS & GENERATORS

AMERICAN ELECTRONICS, INC.—AEI Holding Co., Inc., pg. 3
ARCADIAN POWER CORP., pg. 80
AVIS INDUSTRIAL CORPORATION, pg. 102
B & B MOTOR & CONTROL CORPORATION, pg. 105
THE BABCOCK & WILCOX COMPANY, pg. 107
BODINE ELECTRIC COMPANY, pg. 162
BOGUE ELECTRIC MANUFACTURING CO., pg. 162
BORG-WARNER AUTOMOTIVE (CANADA) LIMITED—Borg-Warner Corporation, pg. 166
CONTEC INTERNATIONAL, pg. 278
CONTINENTAL MACHINES, INC., pg. 279
CYBEREX, INC., pg. 307
DETROIT DIESEL ALLISON CO.—Western Diesel Services Inc., pg. 1179
EASTERN AIR DEVICES, INC., pg. 363
ELECTRO-MECHANICAL INSTRUMENTS DIV.—AEI Holding Co., Inc., pg. 3
ELOMETA CORPORATION—Treadwell Corporation, pg. 1108
GARDEN STATE CONVERTERS—Triangle Marketing Corp., pg. 1112
HOBART BROTHERS CO., pg. 536
INTERMATIC INC., pg. 575
KIRKWOOD INDUSTRIES, INC., pg. 633
KOHLER COMPANY, pg. 639
KOHLER DE MEXICO, S.A. DE C.V.—Kohler Company, pg. 640
LEECE-NEVILLE DE MEXICO S.A. DE C.V.—21 International Holdings, Inc., pg. 1121
LIMA ELECTRIC CO., INC.—Marathon Electric Manufacturing Corp., pg. 706
MAGNEDYNE DIV.—Sierracin Corporation, pg. 1003
MARATHON ELECTRIC MANUFACTURING CORP., pg. 705
MOLON MOTOR & COIL CORP., pg. 764
O'BRIEN MACHINERY COMPANY, pg. 820
THE PIERCE CO., INC.—Avis Industrial Corporation, pg. 102
PUMA MANUFACTURING LTD.—O'Brien Energy Systems Inc., pg. 820
RAIL CAR SERVICES LTD.—The Marmon Group, Inc., pg. 712
REAGAN EQUIPMENT COMPANY, INC., pg. 917
REULAND ELECTRIC COMPANY, pg. 930
M. H. RHODES, INC., pg. 931
SIERRACIN CORPORATION, pg. 1003
SOUTH HAVEN COIL INC.—Humphrey Products Company, pg. 553
STAFLEX/HAROTEX—The Harodite Finishing Company Inc., pg. 510
STERLING ELECTRIC, INC., pg. 1046
TECH SYSTEMS CORP.—Datron Incorporated, pg. 317
TEMPEL STEEL COMPANY, pg. 1086
TREADWELL CORPORATION, pg. 1108
UPPCO, INC., pg. 1139

3624 — CARBON & GRAPHITE PRODUCTS

CARBIDE PRODUCTS—The Carbide/Graphite Group, Inc., pg. 217
THE CARBIDE/GRAPHITE GROUP, INC., pg. 217
ELECTRODES—The Carbide/Graphite Group, Inc., pg. 217
GRAPHITE SPECIALITES—The Carbide/Graphite Group, Inc., pg. 217
HELWIG CARBON PRODUCTS, INC., pg. 528
HORSEHEAD INDUSTRIES, INC., pg. 545
KIRKWOOD INDUSTRIES, INC., pg. 633
PURE CARBON COMPANY—The Stackpole Corporation, pg. 1034
SPLITFIRE, INC.—Old World Industries, Inc., pg. 824
THE STACKPOLE CORPORATION, pg. 1034
STACKPOLE LIMITED—The Stackpole Corporation, pg. 1034
U.S. GRAPHITE, INC., pg. 1136

3625 — RELAYS & INDUSTRIAL CONTROLS

ALTAIR CORPORATION, pg. 45
AUTOMATIC TIMING & CONTROLS, INC.—Desco Corporation, pg. 332
AUTOMATION INTELLIGENCE, INC., pg. 101
AUTOMATION INTELLIGENCE UK LTD.—Automation Intelligence, Inc., pg. 101
BANNER ENGINEERING CORP., pg. 118
BASLER ELECTRIC COMPANY, pg. 125
BENMAR—Belgrave Industries, pg. 133
CLEVELAND MACHINE CONTROLS, pg. 255
CLIMCO COILS CO.—Furnas Electric Company, pg. 437
CORNELL DUBILIER ELECTRONICS—Kaplan Electronics, pg. 616
CRAMER COMPANY, pg. 296
CUSTOM CONTROL SENSORS, INC., pg. 306
CYBEREX, INC., pg. 307
DIMCO-GRAY COMPANY, pg. 338
DORMEYER INDUSTRIES, pg. 346
ELECTRO-MATIC PRODUCTS INC., pg. 374
ELECTRONIC DRIVES AND CONTROLS, pg. 375
ENTERPRISE S.A. DE C.V.—Eclipse, Inc., pg. 366
FIMBEL DOOR CORPORATION, pg. 409
FURNAS ELECTRIC COMPANY, pg. 437
GOODWAY TOOL CORPORATION, pg. 471
HARDIE IRRIGATION-LANDSCAPE DIV., pg. 508
HEAT TECH, INC.—Group Dekko International Inc., pg. 489
HEATERS ENGINEERING, INC.—Group Dekko International Inc., pg. 489
HURLETRON INC.—Altair Corporation, pg. 45
INTERMATIC INC., pg. 575
JENSEN ELECTRIC COMPANY, pg. 592
THE KNAPHEIDE MFG. CO., pg. 636
KURT MANUFACTURING CO. INC., pg. 646
L&J TECHNOLOGIES, pg. 647
MARLOW INDUSTRIES, pg. 710
MARMON INDUSTRIAL CORPORATION—The Marmon Group, Inc., pg. 712
NORDIC CONTROLS CO.—Furnas Electric Company, pg. 437
QUINDAR PRODUCTS LTD.—QEI, Inc., pg. 902
REULAND ELECTRIC COMPANY, pg. 930
M. H. RHODES, INC., pg. 931
S & C ELECTRIC COMPANY, pg. 958
SOUTHWESTERN INDUSTRIES, INC., pg. 1023
SPANG & COMPANY, pg. 1025
SPANG POWER CONTROL—Spang & Company, pg. 1025
TACO INC., pg. 1076
TELECHRON, INC., pg. 1085
TIMEX CORPORATION, pg. 1098
TORK ELECTRO SISTEMAS S.A.—Tork, Inc., pg. 1102
TRANSBULK, INC.—National Engineering & Contracting Co., pg. 788
TRIPLETT ELECTRICAL INSTRUMENT CORPORATION, pg. 1114
THE UNIMAX CORPORATION, pg. 1127
VOLTEC—Sauer Industries, Inc., pg. 972
WARD LEONARD ELECTRIC COMPANY, INC.—The Unimax Corporation, pg. 1127
WARRICK CONTROLS, INC.—Armstrong International, Inc., pg. 84
JERVIS B. WEBB COMPANY, pg. 1170

3629 — ELECTRICAL INDUSTRIAL APPARATUS, NEC

ADVANCED CONTROLS, INC., pg. 20
BOGUE ELECTRIC MANUFACTURING CO., pg. 162
CONDOR D.C. POWER SUPPLIES INC., pg. 273
DORMEYER INDUSTRIES, pg. 346
DYNISCO, INC.—Berwind Corporation, pg. 145
ELECTRONICA CONDOR DE MEXICO—Condor D.C. Power Supplies Inc., pg. 273
G & L PRODUCTS—G & L Products, Inc., pg. 438
HOBART BROTHERS CO., pg. 536
KAYENESS, INC.—Berwind Corporation, pg. 145
KEARNEY-NATIONAL, INC.—The Dyson-Kissner-Moran Corporation, pg. 357
LA MARCHE MFG. CO., pg. 649
LEACH CORPORATION, pg. 663
MATECO ELECTRONICS CORP., pg. 720
RABSON'S—Mateco Electronics Corp., pg. 720
SCHUMACHER ELECTRIC CORPORATION, pg. 979
SHERMAN & REILLY, INC., pg. 998
SOLIDSTATE CONTROLS, INC.—The Marmon Group, Inc., pg. 712
SOUTH HAVEN COIL INC.—Humphrey Products Company, pg. 553
SPANG POWER CONTROL—Spang & Company, pg. 1025
SPIROL IND. LTD.—Spirol International Corp., pg. 1031
SPIROL INTERNATIONAL CORP., pg. 1031
STEREO CORP. OF AMERICA—Mateco Electronics Corp., pg. 720
STEREO WAREHOUSE INC.—Mateco Electronics Corp., pg. 720
TRIPLE A SPECIALTY COMPANY, pg. 1114
TRIPLETT ELECTRICAL INSTRUMENT CORPORATION, pg. 1114
VICTOR CORPORATION, pg. 1149
WOLLARD AIRPORT EQUIPMENT CO.—Hobart Brothers Co., pg. 537
XEBEC CORPORATION, pg. 1206
YARDNEY TECHNICAL PRODUCTS, INC., pg. 1207

3631 — HOUSEHOLD COOKING EQUIPMENT

W. C. BRADLEY CO., pg. 170
THE CANADIAN COLEMAN CO., LTD.—MacAndrews & Forbes Holdings Inc., pg. 695
THE CLIMATIC CORP., pg. 255
DAZEY CORPORATION, pg. 321
LEYSE—The Vollrath Company Inc., pg. 1155
MECO CORPORATION, pg. 734
PRIDE PRODUCTS, INC., pg. 889
SUNBEAM OUTDOOR PRODUCTS CO.—Sunbeam-Oster Company, Inc., pg. 1059
VIKING RANGE CORP., pg. 1151
WEBER-STEPHEN PRODUCTS, pg. 1171

3632 — HOUSEHOLD REFRIGERATORS & HOME & FARM FREEZERS

DAZEY CORPORATION, pg. 321
LITTELFUSE, INC., pg. 678
PRIDE PRODUCTS, INC., pg. 889
RANGAIRE & COMPANY, pg. 912
STEVENS-LEE COMPANY, pg. 1048
UNIFLOW MANUFACTURING CO., pg. 1126

3633 — HOUSEHOLD LAUNDRY EQUIPMENT

PRIDE PRODUCTS, INC., pg. 889

3634 — ELECTRIC HOUSEWARES & FANS

AMERICAN STABILIS, INC., pg. 61
BUNN-O-MATIC CORP. OF CANADA LTD.—Bunn-O-Matic Corporation, pg. 188
CADET MANUFACTURING COMPANY, pg. 207
THE COLEMAN COMPANY, INC.—MacAndrews & Forbes Holdings Inc., pg. 695
CONAIR CORPORATION, pg. 272
EBCO MFG. COMPANY, pg. 365
HEAT TECH, INC.—Group Dekko International Inc., pg. 489
HEATERS ENGINEERING, INC.—Group Dekko International Inc., pg. 489
HOMESTEAD PRODUCTS—Seattle Lighting Fixture Co., pg. 986
HOWDEN SIROCCO INC., pg. 547
KAZ, INC., pg. 619
LASKO METAL PRODUCTS, INC., pg. 660
LITECONTROL CORPORATION, pg. 677
MARTIN INDUSTRIES (AL), pg. 715
THE METAL WARE CORP., pg. 741
POLLENEX CORPORATION, pg. 879
POLLENEX CORPORATION—Odyssey Partners, pg. 821
PRIDE PRODUCTS, INC., pg. 889
REGAL WARE, INC., pg. 921
REMINGTON PRODUCTS INC., pg. 926
RESEARCH PRODUCTS CORPORATION, pg. 928
SEATTLE LIGHTING FIXTURE CO., pg. 986
SLANT/FIN CORPORATION, pg. 1010
SUNBEAM DEL PERU S.A.—Sunbeam-Oster Company, Inc., pg. 1059
SUNBEAM MEXICANA S.A. DE C.V.—Sunbeam-Oster Company, Inc., pg. 1059
SUNBEAM-OSTER COMPANY, INC., pg. 1059
SUNBEAM-OSTER HOUSEHOLD PRODUCTS—Sunbeam-Oster Company, Inc., pg. 1059
SURCO PRODUCTS, INC., pg. 1065
TATUNG/CONAIR CORPORATION—Conair Corporation, pg. 272
WAHL CLIPPER CORP., pg. 1158

3635 — HOUSEHOLD VACUUM CLEANERS

BISSELL INC., pg. 153
CLAYTON INDUSTRIES CO., pg. 253
LINDSAY MANUFACTURING INC., pg. 676
PRIDE PRODUCTS, INC., pg. 889
THE REGINA COMPANY, pg. 922
THE REGINA COMPANY—The Regina Company, pg. 922
WHITE MOP WRINGER COMPANY, pg. 1186

3639 — HOUSEHOLD APPLIANCES, NEC

AERCO INTERNATIONAL INC., pg. 21
ANAHEIM MANUFACTURING COMPANY, pg. 71
BLACK ANGUS, INC.—Son Chief Electrics, Inc., pg. 1018
DUCHOSSOIS INDUSTRIES, INC., pg. 350
FORD PRODUCTS CORPORATION, pg. 423
THE GENIE COMPANY, pg. 452
H M K ENTERPRISES, INC., pg. 497
MAGIC MAID DIVISION—Son Chief Electrics, Inc., pg. 1018
OSTER DE VENEZUELA S.A.—Sunbeam-Oster Company, Inc., pg. 1059
PRECISION PARTS CORP., pg. 885
PRIDE PRODUCTS, INC., pg. 889
SON CHIEF ELECTRICS, INC., pg. 1018
STATE INDUSTRIES INC., pg. 1041
UNIVEX CORPORATION, pg. 1139
WHITE MOP WRINGER COMPANY, pg. 1186

3641 — ELECTRIC LAMP BULBS & TUBES

BRUCE INDUSTRIES, INC., pg. 183
CHADWICK-HELMUTH COMPANY, INC., pg. 237
DURO-TEST CORPORATION, pg. 355
JUSTRITE MANUFACTURING COMPANY, pg. 610
PHOTOGENIC MACHINE COMPANY, INC., pg. 869
SPECTRONICS CORPORATION, pg. 1029
UVP, INC., pg. 1124
ZENITH PRODUCTS CORP., pg. 1217

3643 — CURRENT-CARRYING WIRING DEVICES

ADVANCE POWER CO. LTD.—Panduit Company, pg. 845
ALLHABO AKTIEBOLAG—Panduit Company, pg. 845
ARK-LES CORPORATION, pg. 82
ASTRO WIRE & CABLE CORPORATION, pg. 92
AVIS INDUSTRIAL CORPORATION, pg. 102
BIW CABLE SYSTEMS-CONNECTOR SYSTEMS DIV.—BIW Cable Systems, Inc., pg. 107
BIW CABLE SYSTEMS, INC., pg. 106
BARDES CORP., pg. 119
BRIDGEPORT FITTINGS, INC., pg. 175
BUCHANAN CONSTRUCTION PRODUCTS, INC.—Ideal Industries, Inc., pg. 562
BURC ELECTRONICS & MACHINERY CORP.—Panduit Company, pg. 845
C.V. SUMBER SAKTI—Panduit Company, pg. 846
CIRCLE A.W. PRODUCTS, CO., pg. 250
COMMERCIAL ESPANOLA DE COMPONENTES S.A.—Panduit Company, pg. 845
COMPONENTS CORPORATION OF AMERICA, pg. 270
CONE, LDA.—Panduit Company, pg. 845
DAHMS ELECTRONIK GMBH—Panduit Company, pg. 845
EAGLE ELECTRIC MFG. CO., INC., pg. 362
ELECTRONICA DEL PACIFICO—Panduit Company, pg. 845
ELECTRONIK (PTY) LTD.—Panduit Company, pg. 845
ERICO INTERNATIONAL, pg. 386
OY ETRA AB—Panduit Company, pg. 845
FTZ INDUSTRIES, INC.—Bardes Corp., pg. 119
GROUP DEKKO INTERNATIONAL INC., pg. 489
HANS FOLSGAARD, AGENTUR A/S—Panduit Company, pg. 845
HEAT TECH, INC.—Group Dekko International Inc., pg. 489
HEATERS ENGINEERING, INC.—Group Dekko International Inc., pg. 489
IDEAL INDUSTRIES, INC., pg. 562
INTERELECTRONIC OERTLI AG—Panduit Company, pg. 845

S.I.C. Index

IOWA ASSEMBLIES, INC.—Group Dekko International Inc., pg. 490
ISELCO SF—Panduit Company, pg. 845
KEARNEY—The Dyson-Kissner-Moran Corporation, pg. 357
KEARNEY DIV.—The Dyson-Kissner-Moran Corporation, pg. 357
KLOCKNER-MOELLER NORSK A/S—Panduit Company, pg. 845
LEVIMEX DE BAJA CALIFORNIA S.A. DE C.V.—Leviton Mfg. Co., Inc., pg. 671
LEVITON MFG. CO., INC., pg. 671
MACLEAN-FOGG CO., pg. 697
MANUFACTURE LEVITON DU CANADA—Leviton Mfg. Co., Inc., pg. 671
MARATHON ELECTRIC MANUFACTURING CORP., pg. 705
MARATHON SPECIAL PRODS.—Marathon Electric Manufacturing Corp., pg. 706
MULDER HARDENBERG B.V.—Panduit Company, pg. 845
PLP PRODUTOS PARA LINHAS PROFORMADOS LTDA.—Preformed Line Products, pg. 886
PACIFIC ELECTRICORD CO.—Leviton Mfg. Co., Inc., pg. 671
PANDUIT AUST. PTY. LTD.—Panduit Company, pg. 845
PANDUIT CANADA LTD.—Panduit Company, pg. 845
PANDUIT COMPANY, pg. 845
PANDUIT CORP.—Panduit Company, pg. 845
PANDUIT CORP. JAPAN BRANCH—Panduit Company, pg. 846
PANDUIT GMBH—Panduit Company, pg. 846
PANDUIT LIMITED—Panduit Company, pg. 846
PANDUIT NEDERLAND—Panduit Company, pg. 846
PANDUIT PHILIPPINES—Panduit Company, pg. 846
PANDUIT S.A.S.—Panduit Company, pg. 846
PANDUIT SINGAPORE PTE. LTD.—Panduit Company, pg. 846
PANDUIT S.N.C.—Panduit Company, pg. 845
PANDUIT TRADING PTE. LTD.—Panduit Company, pg. 846
PANDUIT TRADING PTE. LTD.—Panduit Company, pg. 846
PATRON COMERCIO E REPRESENTACOES LTDA.—Panduit Company, pg. 846
PENT ASSEMBLIES, INC.—Group Dekko International Inc., pg. 490
PENT PRODUCTS, INC.—Group Dekko International Inc., pg. 490
PERKASIE INDUSTRIES CORPORATION, pg. 862
PREFORMED LINE PRODUCTS, pg. 886
PREFORMED LINE PRODUCTS(GREAT BRITAIN) LTD.—Preformed Line Products, pg. 886
RAPID POWER TECHNOLOGIES, INC., pg. 913
S & C ELECTRIC COMPANY, pg. 958
S.K. TSOUMANIS REPRESENTATIONS—Panduit Company, pg. 846
ALEXANDER SCHNEIDER LTD.—Panduit Company, pg. 846
SHOGYO INTERNATIONAL CORPORATION, pg. 1000
SRIVATHSA ELECTRICAL CORP.—Panduit Company, pg. 846
STACOSWITCH, INC.—Components Corporation Of America, pg. 270
EDWIN B. STIMPSON COMPANY, INC., pg. 1049
STORM PRODUCTS COMPANY, INC., pg. 1052
TECNA LTDA.—Panduit Company, pg. 846
THE TOBIN CORPORATION—Avis Industrial Corporation, pg. 102
TYLUS SDN BHD—Panduit Company, pg. 846
THE WIREMOLD COMPANY, pg. 1197

3644 — NONCURRENT-CARRYING WIRING DEVICES

ADVANCE POWER CO. LTD.—Panduit Company, pg. 845
ALLHABO AKTIEBOLAG—Panduit Company, pg. 845
THE ALPHA CORPORATION OF TENNESSEE, pg. 43
BENTLEY-HARRIS MANUFACTURING CO., pg. 140
BERGQUIST COMPANY, INC., pg. 141
BLAW KNOX CORP., pg. 156
BRIDGEPORT FITTINGS, INC., pg. 175
BURC ELECTRONICS & MACHINERY CORP.—Panduit Company, pg. 845
C.V. SUMBER SAKTI—Panduit Company, pg. 846
COMMERCIAL ESPANOLA DE COMPONENTES S.A.—Panduit Company, pg. 845
CONE, LDA.—Panduit Company, pg. 845
DAHMS ELECTRONIK GMBH—Panduit Company, pg. 845
EAGLE ELECTRIC MFG. CO., INC., pg. 362
ELECTRONICA DEL PACIFICO—Panduit Company, pg. 845
ELECTRONIK (PTY) LTD.—Panduit Company, pg. 845
OY ETRA AB—Panduit Company, pg. 845
HANS FOLSGAARD, AGENTUR A/S—Panduit Company, pg. 845
IDEAL INDUSTRIES, INC., pg. 562
INDUSTRIAL DIELECTRICS, INC., pg. 566
INSULATING MATERIALS, INC., pg. 572
INTERELECTRONIC OERTLI AG—Panduit Company, pg. 845
ISELCO SF—Panduit Company, pg. 845
KLOCKNER-MOELLER NORSK A/S—Panduit Company, pg. 845
MACLEAN-FOGG CO., pg. 697
MULBERRY METAL PRODUCTS, INC., pg. 775
MULDER HARDENBERG B.V.—Panduit Company, pg. 845
NEER MANUFACTURING COMPANY, pg. 797
PANDUIT AUST. PTY. LTD.—Panduit Company, pg. 845
PANDUIT CANADA LTD.—Panduit Company, pg. 845
PANDUIT COMPANY, pg. 845
PANDUIT CORP.—Panduit Company, pg. 845
PANDUIT CORP. JAPAN BRANCH—Panduit Company, pg. 846
PANDUIT GMBH—Panduit Company, pg. 846
PANDUIT LIMITED—Panduit Company, pg. 846
PANDUIT NEDERLAND—Panduit Company, pg. 846
PANDUIT PHILIPPINES—Panduit Company, pg. 846
PANDUIT S.A.S.—Panduit Company, pg. 846
PANDUIT SINGAPORE PTE. LTD.—Panduit Company, pg. 846
PANDUIT S.N.C.—Panduit Company, pg. 845
PANDUIT TRADING PTE. LTD.—Panduit Company, pg. 846
PANDUIT TRADING PTE. LTD.—Panduit Company, pg. 846
PATRON COMERCIO E REPRESENTACOES LTDA.—Panduit Company, pg. 846
PREFORMED LINE PRODUCTS, pg. 886
PREFORMED LINE PRODUCTS CANADA—Preformed Line Products, pg. 886
RELIABLE/BETHEA POWER PRODUCTS INC.—Maclean-Fogg Co., pg. 698
RELIABLE POWER PRODUCTS—Maclean-Fogg Co., pg. 697
S & C ELECTRIC COMPANY, pg. 958
S.K. TSOUMANIS REPRESENTATIONS—Panduit Company, pg. 846
ALEXANDER SCHNEIDER LTD.—Panduit Company, pg. 846
SRIVATHSA ELECTRICAL CORP.—Panduit Company, pg. 846
EDWIN B. STIMPSON COMPANY, INC., pg. 1049
TECNA LTDA.—Panduit Company, pg. 846
TRIANGLE PWC, INC.—Trian Group, pg. 1111
TYLUS SDN BHD—Panduit Company, pg. 846
E.M. WIEGMANN & COMPANY, INC., pg. 1188
THE WIREMOLD COMPANY, pg. 1197

3645 — RESIDENTIAL ELECTRIC LIGHTING FIXTURES

ADELPHIA LAMP & SHADE INC., pg. 17
AMERICAN FLUORESCENT CORPORATION, pg. 54
CHESAPEAKE FINANCIAL CORP., pg. 243
CRYSTAL CLEAR INDUSTRIES COMPANY, pg. 303
DEL-VAL MANUFACTURING COMPANY, pg. 325
ELITE LAMP, INC., pg. 376
FANNER-PLP—Preformed Line Products, pg. 886
HIGH-LITES, INC.—Jac Jacobsen Industries, Inc., pg. 588
HINKLEY LIGHTING INC., pg. 535
INTERMATIC INC., pg. 575
JAC JACOBSEN INDUSTRIES, INC., pg. 587
GEORGE KOVACS LIGHTING, INC., pg. 643
LAWNWARE PRODUCTS, INC., pg. 661
LIGHTS OF AMERICA, INC., pg. 675
MTD PRODUCTS, INC., pg. 694
MWC LIGHTING SYSTEMS, INC.—Jac Jacobsen Industries, Inc., pg. 588
A. Y. MCDONALD INDUSTRIES, INC., pg. 728
A. Y. MCDONALD SUPPLY CO. INC.—A. Y. McDonald Industries, Inc., pg. 728
MODULITE CORPORATION, pg. 763
NATIONAL PLASTICS CORPORATION—Millstein Industries, pg. 756
NESSEN LAMPS—Jac Jacobsen Industries, Inc., pg. 588
PHILADELPHIA SIGN COMPANY, pg. 867
POINT ELECTRIC—Swivelier Co., Inc., pg. 1068
QUALITY LIGHTING, INC.—Jac Jacobsen Industries, Inc., pg. 588
QUOIZEL INC., pg. 905
RANGAIRE & COMPANY, pg. 912
THE RENOVATOR'S SUPPLY, INC., pg. 927
SHOGYO INTERNATIONAL CORPORATION, pg. 1000
SPECIALTY LIGHTING—Jac Jacobsen Industries, Inc., pg. 588
THE STIFFEL COMPANY, pg. 1049
SWIVELIER CO., INC., pg. 1068
TRIBORO ELECTRIC CORP., pg. 1112
TROY/TRAK LIGHTING, INC.—Jac Jacobsen Industries, Inc., pg. 588

3646 — COMMERCIAL, INDUSTRIAL & INSTITUTIONAL ELECTRIC LIGHTING FIXTURES

ALKCO LIGHTING COMPANY—Jac Jacobsen Industries, Inc., pg. 588
AMERICAN FLUORESCENT CORPORATION, pg. 54
ATLITE LIGHTING EQUIP, INC., pg. 97
BURTON MEDICAL PRODUCTS CORPORATION—Jac Jacobsen Industries, Inc., pg. 588
FANNER-PLP—Preformed Line Products, pg. 886
FOSTORIA INDUSTRIES, INC., pg. 427
GARCY CORPORATION—RHC/Spacemaster Corporation, pg. 907
GUTH LIGHTING COMPANY—Jac Jacobsen Industries, Inc., pg. 588
HIGH-LITES, INC.—Jac Jacobsen Industries, Inc., pg. 588
HOLOPHANE, S.A. DE C.V.—McNeel International Corp., pg. 732
JAC JACOBSEN INDUSTRIES, INC., pg. 587
JENSEN ELECTRIC COMPANY, pg. 592
LITECONTROL CORPORATION, pg. 677
MWC LIGHTING SYSTEMS, INC.—Jac Jacobsen Industries, Inc., pg. 588
MARK LIGHTING FIXTURE CO., INC., pg. 708
A. Y. MCDONALD INDUSTRIES, INC., pg. 728
A. Y. MCDONALD SUPPLY CO. INC.—A. Y. McDonald Industries, Inc., pg. 728
PERKASIE INDUSTRIES CORPORATION, pg. 862
QUALITY LIGHTING, INC.—Jac Jacobsen Industries, Inc., pg. 588
RHC/SPACEMASTER CORPORATION, pg. 906
RANGAIRE & COMPANY, pg. 912
SOUTH COAST LIGHTING SYSTEMS—Jac Jacobsen Industries, Inc., pg. 588
SPECIALTY LIGHTING—Jac Jacobsen Industries, Inc., pg. 588
STONCO, pg. 1050
SWIVELIER CO., INC., pg. 1068
TROY/TRAK LIGHTING, INC.—Jac Jacobsen Industries, Inc., pg. 588
WENGER CORPORATION, pg. 1176
THE WIREMOLD COMPANY, pg. 1197

3647 — VEHICULAR LIGHTING EQUIPMENT

BRUCE INDUSTRIES, INC., pg. 183
FLEXIBLE LAMPS LTD.—UIS, Inc., pg. 1124
K-D LAMP COMPANY, pg. 612

3648 — LIGHTING EQUIPMENT, NEC

AMERICAN LOUVER CO., pg. 57
THE CANADIAN COLEMAN CO., LTD.—MacAndrews & Forbes Holdings Inc., pg. 695
COLEMAN OUTDOOR PRODUCTS—MacAndrews & Forbes Holdings Inc., pg. 695
HUMPHREY PRODUCTS COMPANY, pg. 553
INDUSTRIAS KOLMEX, S.A.—MacAndrews & Forbes Holdings Inc., pg. 696
JUSTRITE MANUFACTURING COMPANY, pg. 610
KOEHLER MANUFACTURING COMPANY, pg. 639
PEERLESS LIGHTING CORP., pg. 855
PLASKOLITE INC., pg. 874
RAYOVAC CORPORATION, pg. 915
THE RENOVATOR'S SUPPLY, INC., pg. 927
ROSCO LABORATORIES, INC., pg. 947
THE SHANE GROUP INC., pg. 995
SPECTRONICS CORPORATION, pg. 1029
STREAMLIGHT INC., pg. 1053
UVP, INC., pg. 1124
WENGER CORPORATION, pg. 1176
THE WIREMOLD COMPANY, pg. 1197
YARDNEY TECHNICAL PRODUCTS, INC., pg. 1207

3651 — HOUSEHOLD AUDIO & VIDEO EQUIPMENT

ACADEMY ENTERTAINMENT, INC.—Artec Distributing, Inc., pg. 86
ACADEMY ENTERTAINMENT INC.—Artec Distributing, Inc., pg. 86
ACOUSTIC RESEARCH—International Jensen Inc., pg. 578
AEROTRON, INC., pg. 22
ALTEC LANSING CONSUMER PRODUCTS—Sparkomatic Corporation, pg. 1025
AMERICAN TRADING AND PRODUCTION CORPORATION, pg. 64
AMPEX CORPORATION, VIDEO SYSTEMS DIV.—Sherborne Group, Inc., pg. 998
APEX MFG. CO., INC.—Soundesign Corporation, pg. 1018
ATLAS/SOUNDOLIER—American Trading and Production Corporation, pg. 64
BGW SYSTEMS, INC., pg. 106
BOSE CORPORATION, pg. 167
BOSE IRELAND—Bose Corporation, pg. 167
CERWIN VEGA, INC., pg. 237
CROWN INTERNATIONAL, INC., pg. 302
EMI-MANHATTAN RECORDS—Capitol Industries-EMI Inc., pg. 216
EVA-TONE INC., pg. 390
INTERNATIONAL JENSEN INC., pg. 578
KLIPSCH & ASSOCIATES INC., pg. 635
KNOWLES ELECTRONICS, INC., pg. 637
KRACO ENTERPRISES, INC., pg. 643
MAGNASYNC MOVIOLA CORPORATION—J & R Film Company, pg. 586
MATECO ELECTRONICS CORP., pg. 720
CURTIS MATHES CORPORATION, pg. 720
NADY SYSTEMS, INC., pg. 783
NOW HEAR THIS (NHT)—International Jensen Inc., pg. 578
NUEMANN (USA)—Sennheiser Electronic Corp., pg. 990
PEAVEY ELECTRONIC CORP., pg. 854
PHASE LINEAR—International Jensen Inc., pg. 578
PRECISION ECHO, INC., pg. 885
RI HOLDINGS, pg. 907
RABSON'S—Mateco Electronics Corp., pg. 720
ROWE INTERNATIONAL, INC.—RI Holdings, pg. 907
SLM ELECTRONICS—St. Louis Music, Inc., pg. 967
SENNHEISER ELECTRONIC CORP., pg. 989
SHOGYO INTERNATIONAL CORPORATION, pg. 1000
SHURE BROTHERS INCORPORATED, pg. 1001
SOUNDESIGN CORPORATION, pg. 1018
SPARKOMATIC CORPORATION, pg. 1025
STEREO CORP. OF AMERICA—Mateco Electronics Corp., pg. 720
STEREO WAREHOUSE INC.—Mateco Electronics Corp., pg. 720

3652 — PHONOGRAPH RECORDS & PRE-RECORDED AUDIO TAPES & DISCS

THE BENSON MUSIC GROUP, pg. 140
CAPITOL INDUSTRIES-EMI INC., pg. 216
CAPITOL RECORDS, INC.—Capitol Industries-EMI Inc., pg. 216
KEYSOR CENTURY CORPORATION, pg. 627
NIGHTINGALE-CONANT CORP., pg. 807
PRECISION ECHO, INC., pg. 885
SHAPE INC., pg. 995
SHAPE SOUTH, INC.—Shape Inc., pg. 995

3661 — TELEPHONE & TELEGRAPH APPARATUS

CODE-A-PHONE CORP., pg. 258
COMMUNICATIONS INTERNATIONAL, pg. 269
CONKLIN INSTRUMENT CORPORATION, pg. 274

DUKANE CANADA LTD.—Dukane Corporation, pg. 352
DUKANE CORPORATION, pg. 351
HAYES MICROCOMPUTER PRODUCTS, INC., pg. 519
INTERNATIONAL MICROWAVE CORPORATION—Communications International, pg. 269
ODYSSEY PARTNERS, pg. 821
PHONEMATE, INC., pg. 869
PRACTICAL PERIPHERALS—Hayes Microcomputer Products, Inc., pg. 519
PREFORMED LINE PRODUCTS, pg. 886
SEABOARD ELECTRONICS CO., pg. 983
SENCORE, INC., pg. 989
STANDARD COMMUNICATIONS CORPORATION, pg. 1036
SYMPLEX COMMUNICATIONS CORP., pg. 1069
TELESCIENCES CO. SYSTEMS INC., pg. 1085
TONE COMMANDER SYSTEMS, pg. 1101
TRILAN SYSTEMS CORPORATION—Dukane Corporation, pg. 352
VARI TRONICS COMPANY, INC., pg. 1145
VINDICATOR CORPORATION, pg. 1152
WHEELOCK INC., pg. 1185

3663 — RADIO & TELEVISION BROADCASTING & COMMUNICATIONS EQUIPMENT

AMERICAN TRADING AND PRODUCTION CORPORATION, pg. 64
ANTENNA PRODUCTS CORP., pg. 76
BLONDER-TONGUE LABORATORIES, INC., pg. 157
BROADCAST ELECTRONICS, INC., pg. 177
COMMUNICATIONS INTERNATIONAL, pg. 269
CONKLIN INSTRUMENT CORPORATION, pg. 274
CONSOLIDATED COMMUNICATIONS MOBILE SERVICES, INC.—Illinois Consolidated Telephone Co., pg. 563
CONTEC INTERNATIONAL, pg. 278
DIAMOND ELECTRONICS, INC., pg. 335
DORON PRECISION SYSTEMS, INC., pg. 346
ENI, pg. 360
FARADAY, INC., pg. 399
FOUNDATION INSTRUMENTS INC.—Preformed Line Products, pg. 886
GLENAYRE TURNKEY TECHNOLOGIES, INC., pg. 462
GRANITE STATE MANUFACTURING CO., pg. 476
HOWELL LABORATORIES, INC., pg. 548
E.F. JOHNSON COMPANY, pg. 598
KAISER AEROSPACE & ELECTRONICS CORP., pg. 614
KLEINSCHMIDT INC., pg. 635
KRACO ENTERPRISES, INC., pg. 643
LNR COMMUNICATIONS, pg. 648
MICROFLECT COMPANY, INC., pg. 749
MOSLER INC., pg. 772
NEW BEDFORD PANORAMEX CORPORATION, pg. 799
ORTEL CORPORATION, pg. 830
PROVIDENCE JOURNAL COMPANY, pg. 895
QEI, INC., pg. 902
QUINDAR PRODUCTS LTD.—QEI, Inc., pg. 902
RAULAND-BORG CORPORATION, pg. 914
REPUBLIC TELCOM SYSTEMS CORPORATION, pg. 928
SCIENTIFIC CORPORATION—Hinderliter Industries, Inc., pg. 535
SELECTONE CORPORATION, pg. 988
SENCORE, INC., pg. 989
SPECTRADYNE INC.—Davis Companies, pg. 318
SYSTEM PLANNING CORP., pg. 1070
TALK-A-PHONE CO., pg. 1077
TELESCIENCE TRANSMISSION SYSTEMS, INC.—Telesciences Co. Systems Inc., pg. 1085
TRACOR AEROSPACE, INC. EXPENDABLES DIVISION—Tracor, Inc., pg. 1105
WARD PRODUCTS CORPORATION, pg. 1163
WHEELOCK INC., pg. 1185

3669 — COMMUNICATIONS EQUIPMENT, NEC

ADVANCED DETECTION SYSTEMS—Venturedyne, Ltd., pg. 1148
AMERICAN TRADING AND PRODUCTION CORPORATION, pg. 64
ANTENNA PRODUCTS CORP., pg. 76
APPLIED SOLAR ENERGY CORPORATION, pg. 79
ASTRONAUTICS CORP. OF AMERICA, pg. 93
ATLAS/SOUNDOLIER—American Trading and Production Corporation, pg. 64
BS & B SAFETY SYSTEMS—International Systems & Controls Corp., pg. 579
DAVID CLARK COMPANY, INC., pg. 252
COMMUNICATIONS INTERNATIONAL, pg. 269
COMPUTER SERVICE COMPANY—Steiny & Company, Inc., pg. 1049
CRAY COMMUNICATIONS INC., pg. 297
DIGITAL PATHWAYS INC., pg. 337
DUCHOSSOIS INDUSTRIES, INC., pg. 350
DUKANE CORPORATION, pg. 351
ECONOLITE CANADA, INC.—Econolite Control Products, Inc., pg. 367
ECONOLITE CONTROL PRODUCTS, INC., pg. 367
ELECTRO FIBEROPTICS CORPORATION, pg. 374
FALCON SAFETY PRODUCTS INC., pg. 398
FARADAY, INC., pg. 399
FEL CORPORATION, pg. 405
THE FOLGER ADAM COMPANY—Adler & Shaykin, pg. 18
FYRNETICS, INC., pg. 438
GDE SYSTEMS—Carlyle Holding Corporation, pg. 222
GLENAYRE TURNKEY TECHNOLOGIES, INC., pg. 462
HENSCHEL CORP.—SPD Technologies, pg. 964
HUBBARD COMMUNICATIONS—Hubbard Broadcasting, Inc., pg. 549
JENSEN ELECTRIC COMPANY, pg. 592
KRACO ENTERPRISES, INC., pg. 643
LA BELLE INDUSTRIES, INC., pg. 648
LEAR SIEGLER TELECOMMUNICATIONS DIV.—Lear Siegler Diversified Holdings Corp., pg. 664
MPH & CMI—MPD, Inc., pg. 693
MICROWAVE NETWORKS INCORPORATED, pg. 749
MOSLER ELECTRONIC SYSTEMS DIV.—Mosler Inc., pg. 772
MOSLER INC., pg. 772
MOSLER SA DE C.D.—Mosler Inc., pg. 772
NOVAR ELECTRONICS, pg. 817
PREFORMED LINE PRODUCTS, pg. 886
RTS SYSTEMS—Telex Communications, Inc., pg. 1085
RADIONICS, INC., pg. 909
REPCO INCORPORATED, pg. 927
SENTROL, INC.—Berwind Corporation, pg. 145
SERVO CORPORATION OF AMERICA, pg. 993
SUMMA FOUR, INC., pg. 1057
SUNROC CORPORATION, pg. 1062
TALK-A-PHONE CO., pg. 1077
TORK, INC., pg. 1102
TRACOR AEROSPACE, INC.—Tracor, Inc., pg. 1105
TRACOR ELSIN—Tracor, Inc., pg. 1105
TRACOR ULTRON—Tracor, Inc., pg. 1105
TRILAN SYSTEMS CORPORATION—Dukane Corporation, pg. 352
TYLAN GENERAL, INC.-FLOW DIVISION—Tylan General, Inc., pg. 1122
VEECO INSTRUMENTATIONS, INC., pg. 1146
VIDICOM, L.D. BEVAN COMPANY, INC., pg. 1151
WELLS FARGO ALARM SERVICES—Borg-Warner Corporation, pg. 166
WHEELOCK INC., pg. 1185

3672 — PRINTED CIRCUIT BOARDS

ACCUTRONICS, INC.—The Marmon Group, Inc., pg. 711
BASLER ELECTRIC CIRCUITS, INC.—Basler Electric Company, pg. 125
BUREAU OF ENGRAVING, pg. 189
CUPLEX, INC., pg. 305
DAKTRONICS, INC., pg. 312
EPEC, INC., pg. 384
GLASTEEL INDUSTRIAL LAMINATES, pg. 461
THE MARMON GROUP, INC., pg. 710
MASON COMPANY, pg. 718
MASON HANGER-SILAS MASON CO.—Mason Company, pg. 718
NUCLEAR DATA SYSTEMS—Canberra Industries, Inc., pg. 213
PRINTED CIRCUIT CORPORATION, pg. 891
PROTO SYSTEMS OF ATLANTA, pg. 895
SPANG & COMPANY, pg. 1025
STAR CIRCUITS—Daktronics, Inc., pg. 312
ZYCON CORPORATION, pg. 1221

3674 — SEMICONDUCTORS & RELATED DEVICES

AMKOR ELECTRONICS, INC., pg. 67
AMPERIF CORPORATION, pg. 68
APPLIED SOLAR ENERGY CORPORATION, pg. 79
BLH ELECTRONICS, pg. 107
CALIFORNIA MICRO DEVICES, pg. 210
CLEARPOINT RESEARCH CORPORATION, pg. 254
EEMCO DIV.—Datron Incorporated, pg. 317
ENTRON INDUSTRIES LIMITED PARTNERSHIP, pg. 383
GREAT AMERICAN INDUSTRIES, INC., pg. 480
ILC DATA DEVICE—ILC Industries, Inc., pg. 560
ILC INDUSTRIES, INC., pg. 560
INKEL TECHNOLOGY—Inkel Corp., pg. 570
INTECH ADVANCED ANALOG, pg. 572
INTERFACE ELECTRONICS CORPORATION, pg. 574
INTERNATIONAL MICROCIRCUITS, INC., pg. 579
INTERNATIONAL MICROWAVE CORPORATION—Communications International, pg. 269
E.F. JOHNSON COMPANY, pg. 598
KULITE SEMICONDUCTOR PRODUCTS, INC., pg. 646
LEACH CORPORATION, pg. 663
ORIEL CORPORATION, pg. 829
QUALITY TECHNOLOGIES CORPORATION, pg. 904
SAMTEC INC., pg. 968
SILICON POWER CUBE CORPORATION, pg. 1004
SIPEX CORPORATION, pg. 1009
SOLID STATE DEVICES, INC., pg. 1017
SPECTRONICS CORPORATION, pg. 1029
TAYLOR CORPORATION, pg. 1081
THERMALLOY, INC., pg. 1091
TORK, INC., pg. 1102
VEECO INSTRUMENTATIONS, INC., pg. 1146

3675 — ELECTRONIC CAPACITORS

CORNELL DUBILIER ELECTRONICS—Kaplan Electronics, pg. 616
INTERFACE ELECTRONICS CORPORATION, pg. 574
JOHANSON MANUFACTURING CORPORATION, pg. 595
RFI CORP.—KDI Corporation, pg. 612
SHURE BROTHERS INCORPORATED, pg. 1001

3676 — ELECTRONIC RESISTORS

APPLIED SCIENCES DIVISION—Caddock Electronics, Inc., pg. 207
BOURNS, INC., pg. 168
ELECTRO-SCIENCE LABORATORIES, INC., pg. 375
OHMITE MANUFACTURING COMPANY, pg. 823
RESISTOR DIVISION—Caddock Electronics, Inc., pg. 207
SIPEX CORPORATION, pg. 1009

3677 — ELECTRONIC COILS, TRANSFORMERS & OTHER INDUCTORS

COILCRAFT, INC., pg. 259
COMPONENTS CORPORATION OF AMERICA, pg. 270
DETROIT COIL COMPANY, pg. 333
DORMEYER INDUSTRIES, pg. 346
FEL CORPORATION, pg. 394
LITTELFUSE, INC., pg. 678
ORTRONICS, INC., pg. 830
PPA INDUSTRIES, INC., pg. 836
SCHOTT CORPORATION, pg. 978
SCHUMACHER ELECTRIC CORPORATION, pg. 979
STACOENERGY PRODUCTS CO.—Components Corporation Of America, pg. 270
TEMPEL STEEL COMPANY, pg. 1086
THORDARSON MEISSNER, INC.—Components Corporation Of America, pg. 270
TRACOR, INC., pg. 1104
TRANSISTOR DEVICES, INC., pg. 1107

3678 — ELECTRONIC CONNECTORS

AMPHENOL CORPORATION—LPL Technologies, Inc., pg. 648
ARCOLA WIRE COMPANY, pg. 81
BEAD INDUSTRIES INC., pg. 129
CABLEWAVE SYSTEMS, INC., pg. 206
ELASTOMERIC TECHNOLOGIES, INC., pg. 372
ELECTRO-MATIC PRODUCTS INC., pg. 374
GENERAL AUTOMOTIVE SPECIALTY CO., INC., pg. 449
GLASSEAL PRODUCTS, INC.—HCC Industries, pg. 496
HCC INDUSTRIES, pg. 496
HYPERTRONICS CORPORATION, pg. 557
E.F. JOHNSON COMPANY, pg. 598
KDI CORPORATION, pg. 612
MASTERITE INDUSTRIES, INC.—KDI Corporation, pg. 612
NORTHERN WIRE & CABLE, INC., pg. 814
POSITRONIC INDUSTRIES, INC., pg. 881
PYLE INC.—LPL Technologies, Inc., pg. 648
RUBBER PRODUCTS DIVISION—Freudenberg-NOK (MI), pg. 433
RUBBER PRODUCTS DIVISION—Freudenberg-NOK (MI), pg. 433
RUBBER PRODUCTS DIVISION—Freudenberg-NOK (MI), pg. 433
RUBBER PRODUCTS DIVISION—Freudenberg-NOK (MI), pg. 433
SAMTEC INC., pg. 968
STEWART CONNECTOR SYSTEMS, INC.—Insilco Corporation, pg. 571
TRICON INDUSTRIES, INC., pg. 1113

3679 — ELECTRONIC COMPONENTS, NEC

A.L E. SYSTEMS, INC.—Berwind Corporation, pg. 145
ABBOTT ELECTRONICS, INC., pg. 9
ACTION MANUFACTURING CO., pg. 15
ADVANCED CIRCUIT TECHNOLOGY, pg. 20
ADVANCED ENERGY INDUSTRY, pg. 20
ALLMETAL SCREW PRODUCTS CORP., pg. 40
ALLSOP, INC., pg. 43
ALTAIR CORPORATION, pg. 45
AMERICAN ELECTRONICS, INC.—AEI Holding Co., Inc., pg. 3
AMERICAN SYSTEMS CORPORATION, pg. 63
ANTENNA PRODUCTS CORP., pg. 76
APPLIED SCIENCES DIVISION—Caddock Electronics, Inc., pg. 207
ATLAS/SOUNDOLIER—American Trading and Production Corporation, pg. 64
AUTOSWAGE PRODUCTS, INC., pg. 101
AVEX ELECTRONICS, INC.—J.M. Huber Corporation, pg. 550
BLH ELECTRONICS, pg. 107
BELTONE ELECTRONICS CORPORATION, pg. 137
BERGQUIST COMPANY, INC., pg. 141
BERKELEY INDUSTRIES INC., pg. 141
BUD INDUSTRIES, INC., pg. 186
BUD WEST, INC.—Bud Industries, Inc., pg. 186
C B J ENTERPRISES, INC., pg. 199
CABLEWAVE SYSTEMS, INC., pg. 206
CADDOCK ELECTRONICS, INC., pg. 207
CADDOCK NETWORK DIVISION—Caddock Electronics, Inc., pg. 207
CALCOR SPACE FACILITY, INC., pg. 208
CENTRAL DATA CORPORATION, pg. 232
THE CHAMBERLAIN GROUP, INC.—Duchossois Industries, Inc., pg. 350
CHANNEL INDUSTRIES, INC.—Channel Technologies, Inc., pg. 239
CHANNEL PRODUCTS, INC.—Channel Technologies, Inc., pg. 239
CHANNEL TECHNOLOGIES, INC., pg. 239
DAVID CLARK COMPANY, INC., pg. 252
COMMUNICATIONS INTERNATIONAL, pg. 269
COMPONENTS CORPORATION OF AMERICA, pg. 270
CONDOR D.C. POWER SUPPLIES INC., pg. 273
CONNECTOR INDUSTRIES OF AMERICA—MICRODOT, Inc., pg. 749
CONTINENTAL CIRCUITS CORP., pg. 278
CRAY COMMUNICATIONS INC., pg. 297
DLS DIV.—Takatta Inc., pg. 1077
DATA INSTRUMENTS, INC., pg. 316
DATRON SYSTEMS, INC.—Datron Incorporated, pg. 317
DETROIT COIL COMPANY, pg. 333
DRESSEN-BARNES ELECTRONICS DIV.—AEI Holding Co., Inc., pg. 3
ELECTRO DYNAMICS CRYSTAL CORPORATION, pg. 374
ELECTRO MECHANICAL DESIGN SERVICES, INC., pg. 375
ELECTRO-MECHANICAL INSTRUMENTS DIV.—AEI Holding Co., Inc., pg. 3
ELECTRO OPTICAL IND.—Channel Technologies, Inc., pg. 239
ELECTRONICS STAMPING CORP., pg. 375

S.I.C. Index

ENTRON INDUSTRIES LIMITED PARTNERSHIP, pg. 383
FARRAND CONTROLS—Ruhl Companies, Inc., pg. 955
FAWN INDUSTRIES, INC., pg. 404
GDE SYSTEMS—Carlyle Holding Corporation, pg. 222
GENERAL AUTOMOTIVE SPECIALTY CO., INC., pg. 449
W. L. GORE & ASSOCIATES, INC., pg. 472
GREAT AMERICAN INDUSTRIES, INC., pg. 480
HCC INDUSTRIES, pg. 496
HAMLIN, INC., pg. 503
HARMONY ENGINEERING CORPORATION, pg. 510
HIROSS INC., pg. 536
HOWELL LABORATORIES, INC., pg. 548
J.M. HUBER CORPORATION, pg. 550
HURLETRON INC.—Altair Corporation, pg. 45
INTECH ADVANCED ANALOG, pg. 572
JPM COMPANY, pg. 586
THE JPM COMPANY OF SOUTH CAROLINA, INC.—JPM Company, pg. 586
JABIL CIRCUIT INC., pg. 587
JOHANSON MANUFACTURING CORPORATION, pg. 595
E.F. JOHNSON COMPANY, pg. 598
KDI ELECTRO-TEC CORP.—KDI Corporation, pg. 612
KDI ELECTRONICS—KDI Corporation, pg. 612
KIRKWOOD INDUSTRIES, INC., pg. 633
LA MARCHE MFG. CO., pg. 649
LAMINAIRE CORPORATION, pg. 652
LEACH CORPORATION, pg. 663
LITTELFUSE, INC., pg. 678
LYALL ASSEMBLIES, INC.—Group Dekko International Inc., pg. 490
MPD, INC., pg. 693
MAGNETICS—Spang & Company, pg. 1025
MICRODOT AEROSPACE FASTENING SYSTEMS GROUP—MICRODOT, Inc., pg. 749
MICRODOT, INC., pg. 749
MICROPHASE CORPORATION, pg. 749
MINCO PRODUCTS, INC., pg. 756
NORTHLAND ALUMINUM PRODUCTS, INC., pg. 814
NUEMANN (USA)—Sennheiser Electronic Corp., pg. 990
OHMITE MANUFACTURING COMPANY, pg. 823
ORTRONICS, INC., pg. 830
OTO-SONIC, INC.—Beltone Electronics Corporation, pg. 138
PPA INDUSTRIES, INC., pg. 836
PEGASUS INTERNATIONAL CORPORATION, pg. 855
PENT ASSEMBLIES, INC.—Group Dekko International Inc., pg. 490
PENT PRODUCTS, INC.—Group Dekko International Inc., pg. 490
POWER-ONE, INC., pg. 883
PRECISION POWER DIV.—AEI Holding Co., Inc., pg. 3
PYTTRONIC INDUSTRIES, INC., pg. 901
QUAD SYSTEMS CORPORATION, pg. 902
QUEROY S.A.—American Standard Inc., pg. 62
RAYMOND ROSEN CO., pg. 948
RUHL COMPANIES, INC., pg. 955
SPD TECHNOLOGIES, pg. 963
SEABEAM IND., INC.—Channel Technologies, Inc., pg. 239
SENNHEISER ELECTRONIC CORP., pg. 989
SHOGYO INTERNATIONAL CORPORATION, pg. 1000
SOLID STATE DEVICES, INC., pg. 1017
SPANG & COMPANY, pg. 1025
SPANG & COMPANY-BOONEVILLE PLANT—Spang & Company, pg. 1025
SPANG POWER CONTROL—Spang & Company, pg. 1025
STAVELEY SENSORS, INC., pg. 1043
TECKNIT, pg. 1084
TELEX COMMUNICATIONS, INC., pg. 1085
TELEX HY-GAIN DIV.—Telex Communications, Inc., pg. 1085
TELONIC BERKELEY—Berkeley Industries Inc., pg. 141
TEMPEL STEEL COMPANY, pg. 1086
TENNELEC/NUCLEUS, INC., pg. 1087
THERMO DYNAMICS, INC.—Dixson, Inc., pg. 341
THOMAS & SKINNER, INC., pg. 1093
G.C. THORSEN, INC.—Jupiter Industries, Inc., pg. 609
TOPFLIGHT CORP., pg. 1102
TRACOR, INC., pg. 1104
TRANSISTOR DEVICES, INC., pg. 1107
TRICON INDUSTRIES, INC., pg. 1113
VARI TRONICS COMPANY, INC., pg. 1145
VEECO INSTRUMENTATIONS, INC., pg. 1146
WABASH MAGNETICS—The Dyson-Kissner-Moran Corporation, pg. 357
WARD PRODUCTS CORPORATION, pg. 1163
WHEELOCK INC., pg. 1185
ZYNTEC GMBH—Zytec Corp., pg. 1221
ZYTEC CORP., pg. 1221

3691 — STORAGE BATTERIES

EXIDE CORPORATION, pg. 393
GATES ENERGY PRODUCTS, INC.—The Gates Corporation, pg. 445
MO-CAR INTERNACIONAL, S.A.—21 International Holdings, Inc., pg. 1121
YARDNEY TECHNICAL PRODUCTS, INC., pg. 1207

3692 — PRIMARY BATTERIES, DRY & WET

EXIDE CORPORATION, pg. 393
THE GATES CORPORATION, pg. 445
POWER CONVERSION, INC., pg. 883
RAYOVAC CORPORATION, pg. 915
RAYOVAC CORPORATION—RAYOVAC Corporation, pg. 915
RAYOVAC UK LIMITED—RAYOVAC Corporation, pg. 915
RAYOVAC/VIDOR LIMITED—RAYOVAC Corporation, pg. 915
YARDNEY TECHNICAL PRODUCTS, INC., pg. 1207

3694 — ELECTRICAL EQUIPMENT FOR INTERNAL COMBUSTION ENGINES

BOGUE ELECTRIC MANUFACTURING CO., pg. 162
BORG-WARNER AUTOMOTIVE CONTROL SYSTEMS-BLYTHEVILLE—Borg-Warner Corporation, pg. 166
BORG-WARNER AUTOMOTIVE, INC., CONTROL SYSTEMS—Borg-Warner Corporation, pg. 166
DATRON SYSTEMS, INC.—Datron Incorporated, pg. 317
EDELBROCK CORP., pg. 367
F & B MANUFACTURING CO., pg. 393
FILKO/COBRA, INC.—F & B Manufacturing Co., pg. 393
HEATCRAFT INC.—Lennox International Inc., pg. 667
HEATCRAFT INC.—Lennox International Inc., pg. 667
HESCO PARTS CORPORATION, pg. 531
MALLORY, INC., pg. 703
MR. GASKET COMPANY, pg. 761
RITE-WAY, INC., pg. 936
TRANSPO ELECTRONICS, INC., pg. 1108
TRIPLE A SPECIALTY COMPANY, pg. 1114
WELLS MFG. CORP.—UIS, Inc., pg. 1123
ZELLER CORP., pg. 1216

3695 — MAGNETIC & OPTICAL RECORDING MEDIA

AMPEX MAGNETIC TAPE DIVISION—Sherborne Group, Inc., pg. 998
BELL & HOWELL COMPANY, pg. 134
GRAHAM MAGNETICS, INC., pg. 475
SHERBORNE GROUP, INC., pg. 998
WORDPERFECT CORPORATION, pg. 1202

3699 — ELECTRICAL MACHINERY, EQUIPMENT & SUPPLIES, NEC

AB SONIC INTERNATIONAL APS—Dukane Corporation, pg. 352
ALTEC LANSING CONSUMER PRODUCTS—Sparkomatic Corporation, pg. 1025
AMERICAN STANDARD INC., pg. 61
ATLANTIC AVIATION CORP., pg. 94
BARD MFG. CO., pg. 119
BENTLY NEVADA CORPORATION, pg. 140
CAC MICROCIRCUITS, INC., pg. 198
CARCO ELECTRONICS, pg. 217
THE CHAMBERLAIN GROUP, INC.—Duchossois Industries, Inc., pg. 350
CIRCLE A.W. PRODUCTS, CO., pg. 250
COMLINEAR CORPORATION, pg. 268
COMMUNICATIONS INTERNATIONAL, pg. 269
CRENLO, INC., pg. 298
DEL MAR AVIONICS, pg. 325
DETEX CORPORATION, pg. 333
DUCHOSSOIS INDUSTRIES, INC., pg. 350
DUKANE CORPORATION, pg. 351
DUKANE MICROROBOTICS DIVISION—Dukane Corporation, pg. 352
FM INDUSTRIES, INC., pg. 394
G & W ELECTRIC CO., pg. 438
THE GENIE COMPANY, pg. 452
HOME HEATING & AIR CONDITIONING—EVCON Holdings, pg. 391
THE HOTSY CORPORATION, pg. 545
HOWELL LABORATORIES, INC., pg. 548
L&R MANUFACTURING CO., pg. 647
MARTIN DOOR MFG., INC., pg. 714
MCKEE DOOR, INC., pg. 730
MICRO COMPONENT TECHNOLOGY INC., pg. 748
MICRODOT AEROSPACE FASTENING SYSTEMS GROUP—MICRODOT, Inc., pg. 749
MICRODOT, INC., pg. 749
MR. CHRISTMAS INC., pg. 761
NOMA-INTERNATIONAL, INC., pg. 808
NUCLEAR DATA SYSTEMS—Canberra Industries, Inc., pg. 213
OSTARR CORPORATION, pg. 831
PLP PRODUTOS PARA LINHAS PROFORMADOS LTDA.—Preformed Line Products, pg. 886
RAYNOR GARAGE DOOR COMPANY, pg. 915
REPUBLIC INDUSTRIES, INC., pg. 928
REPUBLIC STORAGE SYSTEMS COMPANY INC., pg. 928
S.T. RESEARCH, pg. 964
SARGENT & GREENLEAF, INC., pg. 971
SMITH INDUSTRIES, INC., pg. 1013
STANDARD TOOL & MANUFACTURING COMPANY, pg. 1037
STAVELEY SENSORS, INC., pg. 1043
SURCO PRODUCTS, INC., pg. 1065
THOMAS ENGINEERING INC., pg. 1093
TRIBORO ELECTRIC CORP., pg. 1112
TRIPLE A SPECIALTY COMPANY, pg. 1114
UNIPHASE CORPORATION, pg. 1129
VARI TRONICS COMPANY, INC., pg. 1145
WICO CORPORATION, pg. 1156

3711 — MOTOR VEHICLES & PASSENGER CAR BODIES

AM GENERAL CORPORATION—Renco Group, pg. 926
AM GENERAL CORPORATION—Renco Group, pg. 926
ASC PROTOCRAFT—ASC Incorporated, pg. 7
ASC TRIM—ASC Incorporated, pg. 7
ASC WEINSBERG KAROSSERIEWERKE WEINSBERG GMBH—ASC Incorporated, pg. 7
BLUE BIRD CORPORATION, pg. 158
CHANCE INDUSTRIES, INC., pg. 238
CRANE CARRIER COMPANY, pg. 296
EASTERN TECHNOLOGIES LTD, pg. 364
FWD CORPORATION, pg. 395
FLEXIBLE CORP.—General Automotive Corporation, pg. 449
THE FLEXIBLE CORP., pg. 421
FONTAINE INTERNATIONAL, INC.—The Marmon Group, Inc., pg. 711
GENERAL AUTOMOTIVE CORPORATION, pg. 448
HACKNEY BROTHERS, INC., pg. 498
HAULPAK DIVISION, KOMATSU DRESSER COMPANY—INDRESCO, Inc., pg. 565
HONORBUILT INDUSTRIES, INC., pg. 542
JAYCO INC., pg. 590
LODAL, INC., pg. 680
THE MARMON GROUP, INC., pg. 710
PICOU BROTHERS TRACTOR & RENTAL COMPANY OF GONZALES—Picou Brothers Construction Company, pg. 870
PIERCE MANUFACTURING, INC., pg. 870
TIC UNITED CORPORATION, pg. 1073
THOMAS BUILT BUSES OF CANADA, LTD.—Thomas Built Buses, Inc., pg. 1093
TOOL & ENGINEERING CO.—Farley Industries, pg. 400
WAYNE CORPORATION, pg. 1169

3713 — TRUCK & BUS BODIES

A A CATER TRUCK MANUFACTURING COMPANY, INC., pg. 1
ALTEC INDUSTRIES EASTERN DIVISION—Altec Industries, Inc., pg. 45
ALTEC INDUSTRIES, INC., pg. 45
AMTRAN CORPORATION, pg. 69
BLUE BIRD CORPORATION, pg. 158
CREEDMOOR MANUFACTURING DIVISION—Altec Industries, Inc., pg. 45
CRENLO, INC., pg. 298
FLORIG EQUIPMENT COMPANY, INC., pg. 421
THE FLEXIBLE CORP., pg. 421
GARSITE/TSR, INC.—Garsite/TSR, Inc., pg. 443
HACKNEY BROTHERS, INC., pg. 498
HACKNEY & SONS, INC., pg. 498
HEIL BULK TRAILER CO.—The Heil Co., pg. 525
HEIL BULK TRAILER DIV.—The Heil Co., pg. 525
THE HEIL CO., pg. 525
HEIL REFUSE & DUMP BODY CO.—The Heil Co., pg. 525
HEIL STEEL FABRICATING, INC.—The Heil Co., pg. 526
HEIL TANK SERVICE, INC.—The Heil Co., pg. 526
HEIL TANK SERVICES, INC.—The Heil Co., pg. 526
HEIL WEST, INC.—The Heil Co., pg. 526
KENTUCKY MANUFACTURING CO., pg. 624
LINEAR DYNAMICS INC., pg. 676
LOCKWOOD CORPORATION, pg. 680
MIDWEST BODY CORPORATION, pg. 752
PIERCE MANUFACTURING, INC., pg. 870
RAPID RAIL SYSTEMS—The Heil Co., pg. 526
READING BODY WORKS, INC., pg. 916
RIGGS INDUSTRIES, INC., pg. 934
RIVER OAKS VANS, INC.—ROC Properties Inc., pg. 908
SOMERSET WELDING & STEEL, INC.—Riggs Industries, Inc., pg. 934
TANK SERVICE, INC.—The Heil Co., pg. 526
TESCO—The Heil Co., pg. 526
THOMAS BUILT BUSES, INC., pg. 1092
THOMAS BUILT BUSES OF CANADA, LTD.—Thomas Built Buses, Inc., pg. 1093
TIMPTE, INC.—Timpte Industries, Inc., pg. 1098
TIMPTE INDUSTRIES, INC., pg. 1098
UNION CITY BODY COMPANY, INC., pg. 1128
VMC FIBERGLASS PRODUCTS INC., pg. 1142

3714 — MOTOR VEHICLE PARTS & ACCESSORIES

AP PARTS MANUFACTURING COMPANY—Charter House Group, pg. 240
ASC INCORPORATED, pg. 7
ASC TRIM—ASC Incorporated, pg. 7
ACRAGAGE—Sycon Corporation, pg. 1069
AEROMOTIVE SYSTEMS CO.—ASC Incorporated, pg. 7
AIR-O-MATIC POWER STEER CO.—Sycon Corporation, pg. 1069
AIRTEX PRODUCTS—UIS, Inc., pg. 1123
ALLISON CORPORATION, pg. 40
ALTEC INDUSTRIES, LTD.—Altec Industries, Inc., pg. 45
AMBAC INTERNATIONAL CORP., pg. 47
AMERICAN SIGN & INDICATOR CORPORATION—Winko-Matic Signal Co./Multisonics Corp., pg. 1196
AMERICAN STANDARD INC., pg. 61
AMERICAN STANDARD TRANSPORTATION PRODUCTS—American Standard Inc., pg. 61
AMERICAN SUNROOF COMPANY—ASC Incorporated, pg. 7
ANCHORLOK CORP.—Lear Siegler Diversified Holdings Corp., pg. 664
ANN ARBOR ASSEMBLY CORPORATION—Edgewood Tool & Manufacturing Company, pg. 368
ANTHONY DIVISION—MidWest Body Corporation, pg. 752
ATWOOD INDUSTRIES, INC., pg. 97
AUTOMOTIVE ACCESSORY CO., LTD.—UIS, Inc., pg. 1124
AUTOMOTIVE MOULDING COMPANY, pg. 101
AVIS INDUSTRIAL CORPORATION, pg. 102
BEACON GAGE—Sycon Corporation, pg. 1069
BEPCO, INC., pg. 141
BERWIND CORPORATION, pg. 145
BESTOP, INC., pg. 147
BINKLEY COMPANY, pg. 151
BLUE BIRD CORPORATION, pg. 158
BORG-WARNER AUTOMOTIVE (CANADA) LIMITED—Borg-Warner Corporation, pg. 166
BORG-WARNER AUTOMOTIVE CONTROL SYSTEMS-BLYTHEVILLE—Borg-Warner Corporation, pg. 166
BORG-WARNER AUTOMOTIVE, INC., CONTROL SYSTEMS—Borg-Warner Corporation, pg. 166

BORG-WARNER AUTOMOTIVE, INC., TRANSMISSION SYSTEMS—Borg-Warner Corporation, pg. 166
BORG-WARNER AUTOMOTIVE KOREA, INC.—Borg-Warner Corporation, pg. 166
BORG-WARNER AUTOMOTIVE-MICHIGAN POWDERED METAL PRODUCTS, INC.—Borg-Warner Corporation, pg. 166
BORG-WARNER CORPORATION, pg. 165
BORG-WARNER-SPRING/BRUMMER DIVISION—Borg-Warner Corporation, pg. 166
THE BRENLIN GROUP, pg. 173
CABLECRAFT INC.—Tuthill Corporation, pg. 1120
CERTIFIED DIV.—Lear Siegler Diversified Holdings Corp., pg. 664
CHAMPION LABORATORIES, INC.—UIS, Inc., pg. 1123
CHANDLER PRODUCTS, INC.—Jupiter Industries, Inc., pg. 609
CONNECTICUT DRIVE SHAFT, INC., pg. 274
CONSOLIDATED METCO, INC., pg. 277
CONTICO INTERNATIONAL, INC., pg. 278
COOK MANUFACTURING CORPORATION, pg. 282
CYCLO-GARD—Sycon Corporation, pg. 1069
DG TRIM PRODUCTS DIV.—Indian Head Industries Inc., pg. 565
DMI, INC., pg. 309
DEALERS MANUFACTURING COMPANY, pg. 322
DESCO CORPORATION, pg. 332
DIGITRON TOOL CO., INC., pg. 337
DIXSON, INC., pg. 341
DURA CONVERTIBLE SYSTEMS DIV.—Collins & Aikman Group Inc., pg. 262
DYATRON/BONDO CORPORATION, pg. 356
EDELMANN DIV. OF STANT, INC., pg. 368
EDGERTON FORGE, INC.—Avis Industrial Corporation, pg. 102
EDGEWOOD TOOL & MANUFACTURING COMPANY, pg. 368
ELECTRO-WIRE PRODUCTS, INC.—Electro-Wire Products, Inc., pg. 375
ELIXIR INDUSTRIES, pg. 376
THE EQUION CORPORATION, pg. 385
EVANS INDUSTRIES, INC., pg. 390
FEL-PRO INCORPORATED, pg. 405
FENNER MANHEIM, pg. 406
FEY MFG. CO., INC.—Standun, Inc., pg. 1038
FIBRE GLASS-EVERCOAT COMPANY INC., pg. 408
FINDLAY INDUSTRIES, INC., pg. 410
FLEET ENGINEERS, INC., pg. 417
FLEXIBLE LAMPS LTD.—UIS, Inc., pg. 1124
THE FLEXIBLE CORP., pg. 421
FRESINBRA INDUS. S.A.—American Standard Inc., pg. 62
THE GATES CORPORATION, pg. 445
GATES POWER DRIVE PRODUCTS, INC.—The Gates Corporation, pg. 445
GEAR HEADQUARTERS INC.—Headco Industries, Inc., pg. 520
GENERAL AUTOMOTIVE CORPORATION, pg. 448
GLOBE INDUSTRIES, INC., pg. 464
HKM OF CALIFORNIA CORP.—UIS, Inc., pg. 1123
THE HAMMERBLOW CORP., pg. 504
HARMAN AUTOMOTIVE—Harvard Industries, Inc., pg. 514
HARVARD INDUSTRIES, INC., pg. 514
HAULPAK DIVISION, KOMATSU DRESSER COMPANY—INDRESCO, Inc., pg. 565
HAYDEN, INC.—The Equion Corporation, pg. 385
HERMES AUTOMOTIVE MANUFACTURING CORP., pg. 531
HESCO PARTS CORPORATION, pg. 531
HOFFCO, INC., pg. 537
HOLMAN ENTERPRISES, pg. 540
HOOKER INDUSTRIES, pg. 543
HURD LOCK & MANUFACTURING CO.—Avis Industrial Corporation, pg. 102
HYDRECO—ICM Industries, Inc., pg. 559
HYOSUNG ASC—ASC Incorporated, pg. 7
ICM INDUSTRIES, INC., pg. 559
INDIAN HEAD INDUSTRIES INC., pg. 565
INLAND TOOL & MANUFACTURING, INC.—Ralph C. Wilson Enterprises, pg. 1194
JOSAM COMPANY, pg. 607
KYB CORPORATION OF AMERICA, pg. 613
KYB INDUSTRIES INC.—KYB Corporation of America, pg. 613
KEIPER RECARO, INC., pg. 620
KENCO—Sparkomatic Corporation, pg. 1025
KEYSTONE AUTOMOTIVE INDUSTRIES, INC., pg. 627
KLECO CORP., pg. 634
KRACO ENTERPRISES, INC., pg. 643
LSI TRUCK PRODUCTS CORP.-NEWAY/ANCHOR LOCK—Lear Siegler Diversified Holdings Corp., pg. 664
LEAR SIEGLER SEATING CORP.—Lear Siegler Diversified Holdings Corp., pg. 664
LEE INDUSTRIES—Fleet Engineers, Inc., pg. 417
LEVELAC—Sycon Corporation, pg. 1069
LITTELFUSE, INC., pg. 678
LUBER-FINER, EUROPE, N.V./S.A.—UIS, Inc., pg. 1124
LUBER-FINER, INC.—UIS, Inc., pg. 1123
M&W GEAR COMPANY, pg. 690
MGM BRAKES DIV.—Indian Head Industries Inc., pg. 565
MACLEAN-FOGG CO., pg. 697
MARMON CORPORATION—The Marmon Group, Inc., pg. 711
THE MARMON GROUP, INC., pg. 710
MASTICO INDUSTRIES, LTD.—Globe Industries, Inc., pg. 464
MECO—Sycon Corporation, pg. 1069
MICO INC., pg. 748
MICO WEST—Mico Inc., pg. 748
MID-SOUTH MFG. CO.—UIS, Inc., pg. 1123
MR. GASKET COMPANY, pg. 761
MITCHELL CORPORATION, CLARE DIV.—Mitchell Corporation of Owosso, pg. 761
MITCHELL CORPORATION OF OWOSSO, pg. 761
MORSE AUTOMOTIVE PRODUCTS—Borg-Warner Corporation, pg. 166
MOTOR WHEEL CORPORATION, pg. 773
NSK-WARNER K.K.—Borg-Warner Corporation, pg. 166
NEAPCO, INC.—UIS, Inc., pg. 1123
NEWHOUSE BRAKE DIVISION—Connecticut Drive Shaft, Inc., pg. 274
OLSONITE CORPORATION, pg. 824
ORIGINAL CYLINDER CORPORATION—Belgrave Industries, pg. 134
PERFECT EQUIPMENT CORP.—Berwind Corporation, pg. 145
PERFECTION AUTOMOTIVE PRODUCTS CORPORATION, pg. 861
PERFECTION HY-TEST COMPANY—The Marmon Group, Inc., pg. 711
THE PIERCE CO., INC.—Avis Industrial Corporation, pg. 102
QUADRASTAT CORP.—Adams Rite Manufacturing Co., pg. 17
READING BODY WORKS, INC., pg. 916
RING SCREW WORKS, pg. 935
RITE-WAY, INC., pg. 936
RUBBER PRODUCTS DIVISION—Freudenberg-NOK (MI), pg. 433
RUBBER PRODUCTS DIVISION—Freudenberg-NOK (MI), pg. 433
RUBBER PRODUCTS DIVISION—Freudenberg-NOK (MI), pg. 433
RUBBER PRODUCTS DIVISION—Freudenberg-NOK (MI), pg. 433
SERVICERECORDER—Sycon Corporation, pg. 1069
THE SHANE GROUP INC., pg. 995
SIGNET SYSTEMS, INC.—The Equion Corporation, pg. 385
SNUGL MFG. CO. INC.—Berwind Corporation, pg. 145
SNYDER TANK CORP., pg. 1015
SPARKOMATIC CORPORATION, pg. 1025
THE SPENCER TURBINE CO., pg. 1030
STANCO METAL PRODUCTS, INC., pg. 1035
STANDARD-THOMSON CORPORATION, pg. 1037
STANDUN, INC., pg. 1038
STARMASTER—Sycon Corporation, pg. 1069
STEIBER DIV. DER BORG-WARNER GMBH—Borg-Warner Corporation, pg. 166
STERLING, INC., pg. 1047
SUPERIOR LINKAGE DIVISION—Tuthill Corporation, pg. 1120
SYCON CORPORATION, pg. 1069
TAKATTA INC., pg. 1076
THERMAL COMPONENTS, INC.—Insilco Corporation, pg. 571
J.J. TOUREK CO.—Tuthill Corporation, pg. 1120
TRANSMISSION DIV. BORG-WARNER AUTOMOTIVE GMBH—Borg-Warner Corporation, pg. 166
TRAYER PRODUCTS, INC., pg. 1108
TRIANGLE AUTO SPRING COMPANY—The Marmon Group, Inc., pg. 711
UIS, INC., pg. 1123
VERNAY LABORATORIES, INC., pg. 1148
WABCO FREINAGE DE VEHICULES S.A.—American Standard Inc., pg. 62
WABCO WESTINGHOUSE—American Standard Inc., pg. 62
WABCO WESTINGHOUSE AB—American Standard Inc., pg. 62
WABCO WESTINGHOUSE B.V.—American Standard Inc., pg. 62
WABCO WESTINGHOUSE EQUIPEMENTS FERROVIAIRES S.A.—American Standard Inc., pg. 62
WABCO WESTINGHOUSE FAHRZEUGBREMSEN G.M.B.H.—American Standard Inc., pg. 62
WABCO WESTINGHOUSE FRENI VEICOLI INDUSTRIALI S.P.A.—American Standard Inc., pg. 62
WABCO WESTINGHOUSE G.M.B.H.—American Standard Inc., pg. 62
WARN INDUSTRIES, INC., pg. 1164
WARNER-ISHI CORPORATION—Borg-Warner Corporation, pg. 166
WELLS MANUFACTURERA DE MEXICO S.A. DE C.V.—UIS, Inc., pg. 1124
WELLS MANUFACTURING CANADA LTD.—UIS, Inc., pg. 1124
WELLS MFG. CORP.—UIS, Inc., pg. 1123
WESTCON—Sycon Corporation, pg. 1069
WICKES BUMPER DIVISION—Collins & Aikman Group Inc., pg. 262
WICKES MFG. CO.—Collins & Aikman Group Inc., pg. 262
WINKO-MATIC SIGNAL CO./MULTISONICS CORP., pg. 1196
YOUNG RADIATOR COMPANY, pg. 1210
ZELLER CORP., pg. 1216

3715 — TRUCK TRAILERS

AJAX MANUFACTURING COMPANY, INC., pg. 28
BANKHEAD ENTERPRISES INC., pg. 117
CRANE CARRIER COMPANY, pg. 296
DORSEY TRAILERS, INC., pg. 347
DORSEY TRAILERS, INC.—Dorsey Trailers, Inc., pg. 347
EAGER BEAVER, pg. 362
EASTERN TECHNOLOGIES LTD, pg. 364
FLORIG EQUIPMENT COMPANY, INC., pg. 421
FONTAINE INTERNATIONAL, INC.—The Marmon Group, Inc., pg. 711
GARSITE/TSR, INC.—Garsite/TSR, Inc., pg. 443
GENERAL ENGINES CO., INC.—Eager Beaver, pg. 362
HACKNEY BROTHERS, INC., pg. 498
HACKNEY & SONS, INC., pg. 498
KENTUCKY MANUFACTURING CO., pg. 624
LEAR SIEGLER DIVERSIFIED HOLDINGS CORP.—Forstmann Little & Co., pg. 424
MAGLINE, INC., pg. 700
THE MARMON GROUP, INC., pg. 710
PROCOR ENGINEERING LTD.—The Marmon Group, Inc., pg. 712
THE PULLMAN COMPANY, pg. 899
REINKE MANUFACTURING CO., INC., pg. 924
RIGGS INDUSTRIES, INC., pg. 934
SOMERSET WELDING & STEEL, INC.—Riggs Industries, Inc., pg. 934
TIMPTE, INC.—Timpte Industries, Inc., pg. 1098
TIMPTE INDUSTRIES, INC., pg. 1098
TRAILMOBILE—The Pullman Company, pg. 900
R.C. TWAY COAL COMPANY, pg. 1120
UTILITY TRAILER MANUFACTURING CO., pg. 1141
WESBAR CORPORATION, pg. 1176

3716 — MOTOR HOMES

ASC INCORPORATED, pg. 7
STARCRAFT AUTOMOTIVE CORP., pg. 1040

3721 — AIRCRAFT

ALUMINUM FORGE COMPANY—The Marmon Group, Inc., pg. 711
GULFSTREAM HOLDINGS CORPORATION, pg. 494
THE DEE HOWARD COMPANY, pg. 547
MOONEY AIRCRAFT CORPORATION, pg. 768
PIPER AIRCRAFT CORPORATION, pg. 872
ROBINSON HELICOPTER COMPANY, INC., pg. 940
ROGERSON HILLER CORPORATION—Rogerson Aircraft Corporation, pg. 944
SABRELINER CORP., pg. 965
SCHWEIZER AIRCRAFT CORPORATION, pg. 981
TRACOR, INC., pg. 1104
VOUGHT AIRCRAFT CO.—Carlyle Holding Corporation, pg. 222

3724 — AIRCRAFT ENGINES & ENGINE PARTS

ACCURATE BUSHING CO., INC., pg. 11
AMERICAN STANDARD INC., pg. 61
AMERICAN WELDING & MANUFACTURING CO., pg. 65
AMERICAN WELDING & MANUFACTURING CO.—Freedom Forge Corporation, pg. 431
B. H. AIRCRAFT CO., INC., pg. 106
BEACON INDUSTRIES, INC.—Beacon Group, pg. 128
CALIFORNIA MANUFACTURING ENTERPRISES, pg. 210
DELTA INDUSTRIES, pg. 327
ELECTRO METHODS INC., pg. 375
FREEDOM FORGE CORPORATION, pg. 430
GAST MFG. CORP., pg. 444
GENTZ INDUSTRIES INC.—Freedom Forge Corporation, pg. 431
GULFSTREAM HOLDINGS CORPORATION, pg. 494
HITCHCOCK INDUSTRIES, INC., pg. 536
HUGHES-TREITLER MANUFACTURING CORPORATION, pg. 552
INTERNATIONAL GEAR CORPORATION, pg. 578
LAVELLE AIRCRAFT COMPANY, pg. 661
LEE COMPANY, pg. 665
LEE HYDRAULISCHE MINIATURKOMPONENTEN—Lee Company, pg. 665
LEE PRODUCTS LTD.—Lee Company, pg. 665
MICRODOT INSERTS—MICRODOT, Inc., pg. 749
PALMER MANUFACTURING COMPANY, pg. 844
PHOENIX INTERNATIONAL, INC., pg. 868
PIPER AIRCRAFT CORPORATION, pg. 872
ROGERSON AIRCRAFT CORPORATION, pg. 943
SABRELINER CORP., pg. 965
SENSENICH PROPELLER CO.—The Philadelphia Bourse, Inc., pg. 866
J.T. SLOCOMB COMPANY, pg. 1010
STEIBER DIV. DER BORG-WARNER GMBH—Borg-Warner Corporation, pg. 166
TECHNOLOGY APPLICATIONS, INC., pg. 1083
UNISON INDUSTRIES, pg. 1130
UNISON INDUSTRIES—Unison Industries, pg. 1130
WALL COLMONOY CORP., pg. 1160
WILLIAMS INTERNATIONAL, pg. 1191
WORLD AEROSPACE CORPORATION, pg. 1202

3728 — AIRCRAFT PARTS & AUXILIARY EQUIPMENT, NEC

AAI INTERNATIONAL LTD.—Datron Incorporated, pg. 317
ACL TECHNOLOGIES, pg. 2
ACR INDUSTRIES INC., pg. 2
AMI INDUSTRIES, INC., pg. 5
ATI INDUSTRIES, pg. 8
ACUREX CORP. AEROTHERM PRODUCTS DIVISION—Acurex Environmental Corporation, pg. 16
AIRCRAFT GEAR CORPORATION, pg. 27
AIRCRAFT PRODUCTS COMPANY—The Pullman Company, pg. 899
AIRCRAFT PRODUCTS COMPANY—The Pullman Company, pg. 899
ALL AMERICAN ENGINEERING CO.—Datron Incorporated, pg. 316
ALUMINUM FORGE COMPANY—The Marmon Group, Inc., pg. 711
AMERICAN AIRCRAFT PARTS MANUFACTURING CO., pg. 48
AMERICAN FUEL CELL & COATED FABRICS CO. (AMFUEL), pg. 55
APEX CORPORATION, pg. 78
ARGO-TECH CORPORATION, pg. 82
ASSOCIATED COMPANY, INC., pg. 89
ASTRONAUTICS C.A. LTD.—Astronautics Corp. of America, pg. 93
ASTRONAUTICS CORP. OF AMERICA, pg. 93
ATLANTIC AVIATION CORP., pg. 94

BAVARIA AVIONIK TECHNOLOGIE GMBH—Rogerson Aircraft Corporation, pg. 944
BAVARIA CARGO TECHNOLOGIE GMBH—Rogerson Aircraft Corporation, pg. 944
BAVARIA KEYTRONIC TECHNOLOGIE GMBH—Rogerson Aircraft Corporation, pg. 944
BEFAB-SAFELAND, LTD.—Datron Incorporated, pg. 317
BERKSHIRE INDUSTRIES, INC., pg. 142
BORG-WARNER-SPRING/BRUMMER DIVISION—Borg-Warner Corporation, pg. 166
CABLECRAFT INC.—Tuthill Corporation, pg. 1120
CABLEWARE TECHNOLOGY DIV.—Loos & Co., Inc., pg. 683
CALCOR SPACE FACILITY, INC., pg. 208
CALIFORNIA MANUFACTURING ENTERPRISES, pg. 210
J. C. CARTER COMPANY, INC., pg. 226
CERTIFIED HOLDING CORP., pg. 237
D. CHAKLIN, DIR. EUROPEAN OPERATIONS—Astronautics Corp. of America, pg. 93
COX & COMPANY, INC., pg. 292
THE DEUTSCH COMPANY, pg. 333
DIGITRON TOOL CO., INC., pg. 337
DYNAMIC CONTROLS CORP., pg. 356
EASTERN TECHNOLOGIES LTD, pg. 364
FABER ENTERPRISES, INC., pg. 395
FREEDOM FORGE CORPORATION, pg. 430
GARSITE/TSR, INC., pg. 443
M.C. GILL CORPORATION, pg. 458
GULFSTREAM HOLDINGS CORPORATION, pg. 494
HARMONY ENGINEERING CORPORATION, pg. 510
HARRISON DIV.—Sierracin Corporation, pg. 1003
THE DEE HOWARD COMPANY, pg. 547
HUGHES-TREITLER MANUFACTURING CORPORATION, pg. 552
HYDRAULICS INTERNATIONAL, INC., pg. 556
HYDRO-MILL CO., pg. 557
INTERNATIONAL GEAR CORPORATION, pg. 578
JOHNSON TECHNOLOGY—Freedom Forge Corporation, pg. 431
KAISER AEROSPACE & ELECTRONICS CORP., pg. 614
KLECO CORP., pg. 634
H. KOCH & SONS—Collins & Aikman Group Inc., pg. 262
KROPP FORGE CO.—TIC United Corporation, pg. 1073
LEE COMPANY, pg. 665
LEE HYDRAULISCHE MINIATURKOMPONENTEN—Lee Company, pg. 665
LEE PRODUCTS LTD.—Lee Company, pg. 665
LONE STAR FORGE COMPANY—TIC United Corporation, pg. 1073
MAL TOOL & ENGINEERING CO.—Collins & Aikman Group Inc., pg. 263
MANHATTAN BUILDING COMPANIES, pg. 703
MCWILLIAMS FORGE CO., pg. 733
MICRODOT AEROSPACE LIMITED—MICRODOT, Inc., pg. 749
MONITOR AEROSPACE CORPORATION, pg. 765
MOONEY AIRCRAFT CORPORATION, pg. 768
MURDOCK, INC., pg. 776
NOBLES INDUSTRIES, INC., pg. 808
PTC AEROSPACE, INC., pg. 837
PIPER AIRCRAFT CORPORATION, pg. 872
ROCKFORD ACROMATIC PRODUCT CO., pg. 941
ROGERSON ATS—Rogerson Aircraft Corporation, pg. 943
ROGERSON AIRCRAFT CONTROLS—Rogerson Aircraft Corporation, pg. 943
ROGERSON AIRCRAFT CORPORATION, pg. 943
ROGERSON AIRCRAFT SYSTEMS—Rogerson Aircraft Corporation, pg. 944
ROGERSON KRATOS—Rogerson Aircraft Corporation, pg. 944
ROLL FORMING CORPORATION, pg. 944
SABRELINER CORP., pg. 965
SARGENT-FLETCHER CO., pg. 970
SCHWEIZER AIRCRAFT CORPORATION, pg. 981
SIERRACIN CORPORATION, pg. 1003
SIERRACIN/SYLMAR CORPORATION—Sierracin Corporation, pg. 1003
SWIFT-COR TOOL ENGINEERING, pg. 1067
TECHNOLOGY APPLICATIONS, INC., pg. 1083
TRACOR AEROSPACE, INC.—Tracor, Inc., pg. 1105
TRACOR AEROSPACE, INC. EXPENDABLES DIVISION—Tracor, Inc., pg. 1105
TRACOR, INC., pg. 1104
TUTHILL CORPORATION, pg. 1120
WALL COLMONOY CORP., pg. 1160
WESTERN METAL FINISHING DIVISION—TIC United Corporation, pg. 1073
WOHLERT CORP., pg. 1198
ZMP, INC.—Certified Holding Corp., pg. 237

3731 — SHIP BUILDING & REPAIRING

ALGIERS IRON WORKS & DRY DOCK, INC.—Bollinger Machine Shop And Shipyard, Inc., pg. 163
BATH IRON WORKS, pg. 126
BENDER SHIPBUILDING & REPAIR COMPANY, pg. 138
BOLLINGER MACHINE SHOP AND SHIPYARD, INC., pg. 163
CAMPBELL INDUSTRIES, INC.—Marine Construction & Design Co., pg. 707
CROWLEY MARITIME CORPORATION, pg. 301
DIESEL MARINE NORSHIPCO—Norfolk Shipbuilding & Drydock Corporation, pg. 810
FIBRE GLASS-EVERCOAT COMPANY INC., pg. 408
GENERAL SHIP CORPORATION, pg. 450
WILLIAM H. GOODWIN TRUST, pg. 471
GRAND BANKS YACHTS, LTD., pg. 475
INTERTRADE INDUSTRIES, pg. 581
KETTENBURG MARINE CORPORATION, pg. 626
THE KNAPHEIDE MFG. CO., pg. 636
AL LARSON BOAT SHOP, INC., pg. 659
MARCO SEATTLE, INC.—Marine Construction & Design Co., pg. 707
MARINE CONSTRUCTION & DESIGN CO., pg. 707
MARINETTE MARINE CORPORATION, pg. 707
MAXON MARINE, INC.—Chicago West Pullman Corporation, pg. 246
METAL TRADES, INC., pg. 741
MINSTAR, INC., pg. 758
NATIONAL STEEL & SHIPBUILDING COMPANY, pg. 794
NORFOLK SHIPBUILDING & DRYDOCK CORPORATION, pg. 810
PACORD—SPD Technologies, pg. 964
PETERSON BUILDERS, INC., pg. 864
PRODUCTION MANAGEMENT COMPANIES, INC., pg. 893
SOUTHWEST MARINE, INC., pg. 1023
TECHNOLOGY APPLICATIONS, INC., pg. 1083

3732 — BOAT BUILDING & REPAIRING

ALGIERS IRON WORKS & DRY DOCK, INC.—Bollinger Machine Shop And Shipyard, Inc., pg. 163
BANGOR PUNTA DO BRAZIL LTDA.—Lear Siegler Diversified Holdings Corp., pg. 664
BLACK FIN YACHT CORPORATION, pg. 154
BLUEWATER MARINE, pg. 161
BLUEWATER MARINE INC.—Klapmeier Management Company, pg. 634
BOLLINGER MACHINE SHOP AND SHIPYARD, INC., pg. 163
CATALINA YACHTS, INC., pg. 229
CENTURY BOATS BY GENERAL MARINE INDUSTRIES—General Marine Industries, Inc., pg. 450
COAST CATAMARAN FRANCE—MacAndrews & Forbes Holdings Inc., pg. 695
THE COLEMAN COMPANY—MacAndrews & Forbes Holdings Inc., pg. 695
COLEMAN WATER RECREATION OPERATIONS—MacAndrews & Forbes Holdings Inc., pg. 695
CORRECT CRAFT, INC., pg. 287
CRESTLINER, INC.—Minstar, Inc., pg. 758
EGG HARBOR YACHT CO., INC., pg. 371
GMI, INC.-GLASSTREAM—General Marine Industries, Inc., pg. 450
GENERAL MARINE INDUSTRIES, INC., pg. 449
GLASTRON BOATS—Minstar, Inc., pg. 759
HARRIS-KAYOT, INC., pg. 512
HATTERAS YACHTS—Minstar, Inc., pg. 758
HUNTER MARINE CORPORATION, pg. 555
INTERTRADE INDUSTRIES, pg. 581
JEANNEAU CONSTRUCTIONS NAUTIQUES S.A.—Lear Siegler Diversified Holdings Corp., pg. 664
KETTENBURG MARINE—Kettenburg Marine Corporation, pg. 626
KETTENBURG MARINE CORPORATION, pg. 626
KLAPMEIER MANAGEMENT COMPANY, pg. 634
LARSON BOATS—Minstar, Inc., pg. 758
LUND BOATS—Minstar, Inc., pg. 759
MARINER CONSTRUCTORS NAUTICAS, S.A.—Lear Siegler Diversified Holdings Corp., pg. 664
MARINETTE MARINE CORPORATION, pg. 707
MASTERCRAFT CORPORATION—Minstar, Inc., pg. 759
MID-ATLANTIC CORRECT CRAFT, INC.—Correct Craft, Inc., pg. 287
MID WEST CORRECT CRAFT, INC.—Correct Craft, Inc., pg. 287
MINSTAR, INC., pg. 758
NEW ENGLAND CORRECT CRAFT, INC.—Correct Craft, Inc., pg. 287
NEWPORT/CAPE DORY YACHTS, INC., pg. 804
PETERSON BUILDERS, INC., pg. 864
REGAL MARINE INDUSTRIES INC., pg. 921
RENKEN BOAT MANUFACTURING CO., pg. 927
SNARK BOATS DIV.—The Entwistle Company, pg. 383
SOUTHEAST CORRECT CRAFT, INC.—Correct Craft, Inc., pg. 287
TIMPTE INDUSTRIES, INC., pg. 1098
VIKING YACHT CO., pg. 1151
WELLCRAFT MARINE—Minstar, Inc., pg. 759
WEST COAST CORRECT CRAFT, INC.—Correct Craft, Inc., pg. 287

3743 — RAILROAD EQUIPMENT

ACF INDUSTRIES, INC.—Icahn & Co., Inc., pg. 561
AMERICAN STANDARD INC., pg. 61
AMERICAN STANDARD INC., RAILWAY BRAKE PRODS.—American Standard Inc., pg. 61
AMERICAN STANDARD SIGNALING PRODUCTS GROUP—American Standard Inc., pg. 61
AMWAY CORPORATION, pg. 70
BERWICK FREIGHT CAR CO.—Chicago West Pullman Corporation, pg. 246
BINKLEY COMPANY, pg. 151
CHICAGO WEST PULLMAN CORPORATION, pg. 246
COGIFER INC., pg. 259
DUCHOSSOIS INDUSTRIES, INC., pg. 350
ELLICOTT MACHINE CORP., pg. 378
FM INDUSTRIES, INC., pg. 394
H M K ENTERPRISES, INC., pg. 497
MARMON INDUSTRIAL CORPORATION—The Marmon Group, Inc., pg. 712
MINER ENTERPRISES INC., pg. 756
PLYMOUTH LOCOMOTIVE INTERNATIONAL, INC., pg. 877
PROCOR ENGINEERING LTD.—The Marmon Group, Inc., pg. 712
PROCOR RAIL CAR DIVISION—The Marmon Group, Inc., pg. 712
RAIL CAR SERVICES LTD.—The Marmon Group, Inc., pg. 712
SLOAN VALVE COMPANY, pg. 1010
THRALL CAR MFG. CO.—Duchossois Industries, Inc., pg. 350
TRANSCO INC., pg. 1106
TRANSCO RAILWAY PRODUCTS INC.—Transco Inc., pg. 1107
UNION SWITCH & SIGNAL INC., pg. 1129
UNION TANK CAR COMPANY—The Marmon Group, Inc., pg. 712
WABCO WESTINGHOUSE COMPAGNIA FRENI S.P.A.—American Standard Inc., pg. 62
WHITING CORPORATION, pg. 1187
WHITING EQUIPMENT CANADA, INC.—Whiting Corporation, pg. 1187
YSD INDUSTRIES, pg. 1207

3751 — MOTORCYCLES, BICYCLES & PARTS

THE COLUMBIA MFG. COMPANY, INC., pg. 265
HOOKER INDUSTRIES, pg. 543
INTREPID CORP., pg. 581
G. JOANNOU CYCLE CO. INC., pg. 595
LDI, LTD., pg. 647
ROSS BICYCLES USA LTD., pg. 949
SCHWINN BICYCLE COMPANY, pg. 981
SCHWINN (USA)-CSEPEL LTD.—Schwinn Bicycle Company, pg. 981
TREK BICYCLE CORPORATION—Intrepid Corp., pg. 581
TUCKER ROCKY DISTRIBUTING, pg. 1118
TUCKER-ROCKY DISTRIBUTING—LDI, Ltd., pg. 647

3761 — GUIDED MISSILES & SPACE VEHICLES

THE AEROSPACE CORPORATION, pg. 22
ALUMINUM FORGE COMPANY—The Marmon Group, Inc., pg. 711
INFOTEC DEVELOPMENT, INC., pg. 567
INTEGRATED SYSTEMS ANALYSTS, INC., pg. 573
SRS TECHNOLOGIES, pg. 964
TECHNOLOGY APPLICATIONS, INC., pg. 1083
TRACOR APPLIED SCIENCES, ANALYSIS & APPLIED RESEARCH DIV.—Tracor, Inc., pg. 1105

3764 — GUIDED MISSILE & SPACE VEHICLE PROPULSION UNITS & PROPULSION UNIT PARTS

THE AEROSPACE CORPORATION, pg. 22
ALUMINUM FORGE COMPANY—The Marmon Group, Inc., pg. 711
AMERICAN FUEL CELL & COATED FABRICS CO. (AMFUEL), pg. 55
LAVELLE AIRCRAFT COMPANY, pg. 661
QUADRANT ENGINEERING DIV.—AEI Holding Co., Inc., pg. 3
TECHNOLOGY APPLICATIONS, INC., pg. 1083

3769 — GUIDED MISSILE & SPACE VEHICLE PARTS & AUXILIARY EQUIPMENT, NEC

ATI INDUSTRIES, pg. 8
ACUREX CORP. AEROTHERM DIVISION—Acurex Environmental Corporation, pg. 15
THE AEROSPACE CORPORATION, pg. 22
AIRCRAFT GEAR CORPORATION, pg. 27
ALUMINUM FORGE COMPANY—The Marmon Group, Inc., pg. 711
THE DEUTSCH COMPANY, pg. 333
HUGHES-TREITLER MANUFACTURING CORPORATION, pg. 552
INTERCONTINENTAL MFG. CO.—Datron Incorporated, pg. 316
KAISER AEROSPACE & ELECTRONICS CORP., pg. 614
MURDOCK, INC., pg. 776
TECHNOLOGY APPLICATIONS, INC., pg. 1083
TRACOR APPLIED SCIENCES, ELECTRONIC SYSTEMS DIV.—Tracor, Inc., pg. 1105
TRACOR, INC., pg. 1104

3792 — TRAVEL TRAILERS & CAMPERS

ANDERSON INDUSTRIES, INC., pg. 72
B & B HOMES CORPORATION, pg. 105
BLUE BIRD CORPORATION, pg. 158
THE COLEMAN COMPANY, INC.—MacAndrews & Forbes Holdings Inc., pg. 695
E Z LOADER BOAT TRAILERS, INC., pg. 361
FRANK INDUSTRIES, INC., pg. 429
GEM TOP MFG., INC., pg. 448
GEORGIE BOY MANUFACTURING, INC., pg. 453
HONORBUILT INDUSTRIES, INC., pg. 542
KING OF THE ROAD DIV.—Chief Industries, Inc., pg. 247
LANCE CAMPER MANUFACTURING CORPORATION, pg. 653
MARK III INDUSTRIES, pg. 708
MITCHELL COACH MANUFACTURING, pg. 761
NATIONAL R.V., INC., pg. 792
SUNLINE COACH CO., INC., pg. 1061
TIFFIN MOTOR HOMES, INC., pg. 1097
XPLORER MOTOR HOME DIV.—Frank Industries, Inc., pg. 429
ZIEMAN MANUFACTURING COMPANY, INC., pg. 1218

3795 — TANKS & TANK COMPONENTS

ROTTERDAM VENTURES INC., pg. 951
SIOUX MANUFACTURING CORP., pg. 1008

3799 — TRANSPORTATION EQUIPMENT, NEC

AMERICAN SYSTEMS CORPORATION, pg. 63
THE CALKINS MANUFACTURING COMPANY, pg. 210

THE COLEMAN COMPANY, INC.—MacAndrews & Forbes Holdings Inc., pg. 695
COLUMBIA PARCAR CORP.—Nordic Group of Companies, Ltd., pg. 809
FWD CORPORATION, pg. 395
FLAMBEAU CORPORATION—Nordic Group of Companies, Ltd., pg. 809
MARMON-HERRINGTON COMPANY—The Marmon Group, Inc., pg. 711
MINER ENTERPRISES INC., pg. 756
NORDIC GROUP OF COMPANIES, LTD., pg. 809
SHORELINE PRODUCTS, INC., pg. 1000
SPECIALTY EQUIPMENT COMPANIES INC., pg. 1027

3812 — NAVIGATION, GUIDANCE, SEARCH & DETECTION SYSTEMS & INSTRUMENTS

AGEMA INFRARED SYSTEMS, INC., pg. 24
ASTRONAUTICS C.A. LTD.—Astronautics Corp. of America, pg. 93
ASTRONAUTICS CORP. OF AMERICA, pg. 93
BAVARIA AVIONIK TECHNOLOGIE GMBH—Rogerson Aircraft Corporation, pg. 944
D. CHAKLIN, DIR. EUROPEAN OPERATIONS—Astronautics Corp. of America, pg. 93
CHANNEL TECHNOLOGIES, INC., pg. 239
CLIMET INSTRUMENTS CO.—Venturedyne, Ltd., pg. 1148
COMMUNICATIONS INTERNATIONAL, pg. 269
COMPUTER INSTRUMENTS CORPORATION, pg. 271
CONDOR PACIFIC INDUSTRIES, INC., pg. 273
DIGICOURSE, INC.—The Laitram Corporation, pg. 651
DUKANE CORPORATION, pg. 351
DWYER INSTRUMENTS INC., pg. 356
GRANITE STATE MANUFACTURING CO., pg. 476
HEATH CONSULTANTS INCORPORATED, pg. 524
INFOTEC DEVELOPMENT, INC., pg. 567
INTERNATIONAL MARINE HOLDINGS, INC., pg. 579
INTERNATIONAL TRANSDUCER CORPORATION—Channel Technologies, Inc., pg. 239
JEWELL INSTRUMENTS, INC., pg. 594
KEARFOTT GUIDANCE & NAVIGATION CORP.—Astronautics Corp. of America, pg. 93
THE LAITRAM CORPORATION, pg. 650
LOCKLEY MANUFACTURING DIVISION—The Entwistle Company, pg. 383
MEGAPULSE, INC., pg. 737
NAVCOM DEFENSE ELECTRONICS, INC., pg. 796
NORTH ATLANTIC INDUSTRIES, INC., pg. 812
BENJAMIN PRIEST LTD.—International Marine Holdings, Inc., pg. 579
QUANTIC INDUSTRIES, INC., pg. 904
RECON/OPTICAL, INC., pg. 917
ROGERSON AIRCRAFT CORPORATION, pg. 943
ROGERSON KRATOS—Rogerson Aircraft Corporation, pg. 944
SONATECH, INC.—Channel Technologies, Inc., pg. 239
STEINHEIL-LEAR SIEGLER AG—Lear Siegler Diversified Holdings Corp., pg. 664
STOCKER & YALE, INC., pg. 1050
SYSTEM PLANNING CORP., pg. 1070
THERMOTRON INDUSTRIES, INC.—Venturedyne, Ltd., pg. 1148
TRACOR FLIGHT SYSTEMS, INC.—Tracor, Inc., pg. 1105
VEECO INSTRUMENTATIONS, INC., pg. 1146

3821 — LABORATORY APPARATUS & FURNITURE

BROOKFIELD ENGINEERING LABORATORIES, INC., pg. 179
CVC PRODUCTS, INC., pg. 206
CAROLINA BIOLOGICAL SUPPLY CO., pg. 222
DESPATCH INDUSTRIES, pg. 332
DETECTO SCALE COMPANY, pg. 332
ELKAY PRODUCTS, INC., pg. 377
HAMILTON BONADUZ AG—Hamilton Co., Inc., pg. 503
HAMILTON CO., INC., pg. 503
HARROP INDUSTRIES, INC., pg. 512
HAVILAND ENTERPRISES, pg. 517
THE JEWETT REFRIGERATOR CO., INC.—Ruslander & Sons, Inc., pg. 957
MEDICAL LABORATORY AUTOMATION, INC., pg. 735
NESLAB INSTRUMENTS, INC., pg. 798
NOBLES INDUSTRIES, INC., pg. 808
OHAUS CORPORATION, pg. 822
SPECIALTY EQUIPMENT COMPANIES INC., pg. 1027
SQUIRE-COGSWELL COMPANY, pg. 1034
WALKER MAGNETICS GROUP, INC., pg. 1160

3822 — AUTOMATIC CONTROLS FOR REGULATING RESIDENTIAL & COMMERCIAL ENVIRONMENTS & APPLIANCES

AERCO INTERNATIONAL INC., pg. 21
AIRMASTER FAN CO., pg. 28
AMERICAN STABILIS, INC., pg. 61
AMERICAN STANDARD INC., pg. 61
W.E. ANDERSON DIV.—Dwyer Instruments Inc., pg. 356
BERWIND CORPORATION, pg. 145
BONLAND INDUSTRIES, INC., pg. 164
CUSTOM CONTROL SENSORS, INC., pg. 306
DWYER INSTRUMENTS INC., pg. 356
ELECTROCATALYTIC, INC., pg. 375
FOSTER-MILLER, INC., pg. 426
JAY INSTRUMENT & SPECIALTY CO., pg. 590
LOVE CONTROLS CORPORATION—Dwyer Instruments Inc., pg. 356
MALLORY, INC., pg. 703
MAXITROL CO., pg. 723
MERCOID DIV.—Dwyer Instruments Inc., pg. 356
NESLAB INSTRUMENTS, INC., pg. 798
PRODUCTION MANAGEMENT COMPANIES, INC., pg. 893
PROXIMITY CONTROLS CORP.—Dwyer Instruments Inc., pg. 356
REMINGTON PRODUCTS INC., pg. 926
ROLOCK, INC., pg. 944
SOR INC., pg. 963
SLANT/FIN CORPORATION, pg. 1010
SPORLAN VALVE COMPANY, pg. 1032
STERLING, INC., pg. 1047
SUNBEAM-OSTER COMPANY, INC., pg. 1059
TECHNOLOGY FOR ENERGY CORPORATION, pg. 1084
TORK, INC., pg. 1102
WATLOW ELECTRIC MANUFACTURING COMPANY, pg. 1167

3823 — INDUSTRIAL INSTRUMENTS FOR MEASUREMENT, DISPLAY & CONTROL OF PROCESS VARIABLES & RELATED PRODUCTS

AEC, INC.—Sterling, Inc., pg. 1047
ACTION CONTROLS PTY. LTD.—Action Instruments, Inc., pg. 14
ACTION INSTRUMENTS, INC., pg. 14
AMERICAN STABILIS, INC., pg. 61
W.E. ANDERSON DIV.—Dwyer Instruments Inc., pg. 356
APPLICATION ENGINEERING CORPORATION—Sterling, Inc., pg. 1047
BENTLY NEVADA CORPORATION, pg. 140
BINDICATOR COMPANY—Berwind Corporation, pg. 145
BLISS-SALEM, INC., pg. 156
BOURNS INSTRUMENTS INC.—Bourns, Inc., pg. 168
CRL, INC., pg. 203
CAPP, INC., pg. 216
CLAUD S. GORDON COMPANY—Watlow Electric Manufacturing Company, pg. 1167
COMPUTER INSTRUMENTS CORPORATION, pg. 271
COOK MANUFACTURING CORPORATION, pg. 282
COOPER INSTRUMENT CORP., pg. 283
CUSTOM CONTROL SENSORS, INC., pg. 306
DESCO CORPORATION, pg. 332
DESPATCH INDUSTRIES, pg. 332
DIGITAL ELECTRONIC AUTOMATION, pg. 337
DUKANE CORPORATION, pg. 351
DWYER INSTRUMENTS INC., pg. 356
ECLIPSE COMBUSTION & INDUSTRIAL EQUIPMENT PTY.—Eclipse, Inc., pg. 366
ERIEZ MAGNETICS, pg. 386
THE FIELD CONTROLS COMPANY—Heico Inc., pg. 525
FIRE CONTROL INSTRUMENTS, INC., pg. 411
FLINN & DREFFEIN ENGINEERING CO., pg. 419
FORD METER BOX COMPANY, pg. 423
GASTON COUNTY DYEING MACHINE CO., pg. 444
GENERAL TOOLS MFG., pg. 451
HAUCK MFG. CO., pg. 517
HEATH CONSULTANTS INCORPORATED, pg. 524
J.M. HUBER CORPORATION, pg. 550
INTEGRATED ENERGY CONTROLS CORP., pg. 573
INTERMATIC INC., pg. 575
INTERNATIONAL METALS & MACHINES, INC.—CRL, Inc., pg. 203
JAY INSTRUMENT & SPECIALTY CO., pg. 590
JEWELL INSTRUMENTS, INC., pg. 594
THE KARTRIDG PAK CO., pg. 617
KARTRIDG PAK CO.—Barry-Wehmiller Company, pg. 122
KAYE INSTRUMENTS, INC., pg. 619
KEYSTONE CARBON COMPANY, pg. 628
KINETIC SYSTEMS CORPORATION, pg. 630
KURT MANUFACTURING CO. INC., pg. 646
LEAR SIEGLER MEASUREMENT CONTROLS CORP.—Lear Siegler Diversified Holdings Corp., pg. 664
LIQUID CONTROLS CORPORATION, pg. 677
LLOYD CONTROLS, INC., pg. 679
LOVE CONTROLS CORPORATION—Dwyer Instruments Inc., pg. 356
MPH & CMI—MPD, Inc., pg. 693
MAGNETIC DATA, INC., pg. 700
MAGNETROL INTERNATIONAL, pg. 701
MAROTTA SCIENTIFIC CONTROLS, INC., pg. 713
MERCOID DIV.—Dwyer Instruments Inc., pg. 356
MIDWESCO INC., pg. 751
MINCO PRODUCTS, INC., pg. 756
NRM CORPORATION, pg. 781
NATIONAL FORGE ENGINEERED SYSTEMS DIV.—National Forge Company, pg. 789
NATIONAL FORGE EUROPE NV—National Forge Company, pg. 789
NOVAR CONTROLS CORP.—Novar Electronics, pg. 817
PTC THERMISTOR DIV.—Keystone Carbon Company, pg. 628
PHOENIX DATA INCORPORATED—Kinetic Systems Corporation, pg. 630
PROXIMITY CONTROLS CORP.—Dwyer Instruments Inc., pg. 356
QEI, INC., pg. 902
QUAD/GRAPHICS, INC., pg. 902
QUANTIC INDUSTRIES, INC., pg. 904
RACINE FEDERATED, INC., pg. 909
RELA, INC., pg. 924
ROLOCK, INC., pg. 944
SECHRIST INDUSTRIES, INC., pg. 987
SHAPE SOUTH, INC.—Shape Inc., pg. 995
SHOGYO INTERNATIONAL CORPORATION, pg. 1000
SNAP-TITE, INCORPORATED, pg. 1014
SPOTNAILS INC., pg. 1032
STANDARD-THOMSON CORPORATION, pg. 1037
STRAHMAN VALVES, INC., pg. 1052
SYMPLEX COMMUNICATIONS CORP., pg. 1069
TECHNOLOGY FOR ENERGY CORPORATION, pg. 1084
THERMO ELECTRIC (CANADA) LTD.—Thermo Electric Co., Inc., pg. 1091
THERMO ELECTRIC CO., INC., pg. 1091
THERMO ELECTRIC GMBH—Thermo Electric Co., Inc., pg. 1091
THERMO ELECTRIC INTL. B.V.—Thermo Electric Co., Inc., pg. 1091
THERMO ELECTRIC INTL. LTD.—Thermo Electric Co., Inc., pg. 1091
THERMO ELECTRIC S.A.—Thermo Electric Co., Inc., pg. 1091
THERMO ELECTRIC (SOUTHEAST REGION)—Thermo Electric Co., Inc., pg. 1091
THERMON MANUFACTURING COMPANY, pg. 1091
TRACOR, INC., pg. 1104
H.O. TRERICE COMPANY, pg. 1110
TRIPLETT ELECTRICAL INSTRUMENT CORPORATION, pg. 1114
VARI TRONICS COMPANY, INC., pg. 1145
VEDA SYSTEMS, INCORPORATED—Veda International, Inc., pg. 1146
WAHL INSTRUMENTS, pg. 1158
WALKER MAGNETICS GROUP, INC., pg. 1160
WATLOW ELECTRIC MANUFACTURING COMPANY, pg. 1167
WATLOW INFRARED COMPANY—Watlow Electric Manufacturing Company, pg. 1168
WATLOW WINONA, INC.—Watlow Electric Manufacturing Company, pg. 1167
JERVIS B. WEBB COMPANY OF CANADA LTD.—Jervis B. Webb Company, pg. 1170
WEKSLER INSTRUMENTS CORP., pg. 1174
YSI INCORPORATED, pg. 1207
JOHN ZINK CO.—Koch Industries, Incorporated, pg. 639

3824 — TOTALIZING FLUID METERS & COUNTING DEVICES

AUTOMATIC TIMING & CONTROLS, INC.—Desco Corporation, pg. 332
CAPITAL CONTROLS COMPANY INC., pg. 215
CAPITAL CONTROLS LTD.—Capital Controls Company Inc., pg. 215
CURTIS INSTRUMENTS, INC., pg. 305
DESCO CORPORATION, pg. 332
DIXSON, INC., pg. 341
DWYER INSTRUMENTS INC., pg. 356
GARSITE/TSR, INC.—Garsite/TSR, Inc., pg. 443
GREAT AMERICAN INDUSTRIES, INC., pg. 480
INTERMATIC INC., pg. 575
KEX PRODUCTS, INC.—Berwind Corporation, pg. 145
LEUPOLD & STEVENS, INC., pg. 669
PERFECT EQUIPMENT CORP.—Berwind Corporation, pg. 145
M. H. RHODES, INC., pg. 931
ROMAC INDUSTRIES, INC., HAYS DIVISION—Romac Industries, Inc., pg. 945

3825 — INSTRUMENTS FOR MEASURING & TESTING OF ELECTRICITY & ELECTRICAL SIGNALS

ACL TECHNOLOGIES, pg. 2
ACTION INSTRUMENTS, INC., pg. 14
ACTRON MANUFACTURING COMPANY, pg. 15
ACUREX CORP. AUTODATA DIVISION—Acurex Environmental Corporation, pg. 16
ALESSI INCORPORATED—Dukane Corporation, pg. 352
AMERICAN ELECTRONICS, INC.—AEI Holding Co., Inc., pg. 3
APPLIED MICROSYSTEMS CORPORATION, pg. 79
ATERON CORP., pg. 93
BACHARACH INC., pg. 108
BIDDLE INSTRUMENTS, pg. 148
CHRISTIE ELECTRIC CORPORATION, pg. 249
COMPUTER INSTRUMENTS CORPORATION, pg. 271
CURTIS INSTRUMENTS, INC., pg. 305
CYBER SYSTEMS, INC., pg. 307
DETEX CORPORATION, pg. 333
DIGITEC—Sycon Corporation, pg. 1069
DIXSON, INC., pg. 341
DOALL COMPANY, pg. 341
DYNISCO GERATE G.M.B.H.—Berwind Corporation, pg. 145
DYNISCO INSTRUMENT SARL.—Berwind Corporation, pg. 145
DYNISCO (U.K.) LIMITED—Berwind Corporation, pg. 145
ELE INTERNATIONAL, INC., pg. 359
ELEC-TROL MEXICO—Hamlin, Inc., pg. 503
ELECTRO-SCIENCE LABORATORIES, INC., pg. 375
ERIEZ MAGNETICS, pg. 386
HAMLIN, INC., pg. 503
HOWELL INSTRUMENTS CORP., pg. 547
HYDRIL COMPANY, pg. 556
JEWELL INSTRUMENTS, INC., pg. 594
LA BELLE INDUSTRIES, INC., pg. 648
MAGNETIC ANALYSIS CORP., pg. 700
MALLORY, INC., pg. 703
MAROTTA SCIENTIFIC CONTROLS, INC., pg. 713
MICRO COMPONENT TECHNOLOGY INC., pg. 748
MILTON INDUSTRIES, INC., pg. 756
MINING CONTROLS, INC.—Jupiter Industries, Inc., pg. 609
PHONETICS, INC., pg. 869
PRECISE TECHNOLOGY & ELECTRONICS, INC.—Air Gage Company, pg. 27
PRESSURE SYSTEMS, pg. 888
QUEST ELECTRONICS DIV.—La Belle Industries, Inc., pg. 648
RECON/OPTICAL, INC., pg. 917
ROCHESTER INSTRUMENTS SYSTEMS, INC.—The Marmon Group, Inc., pg. 712
RUSKA INSTRUMENT CORPORATION, pg. 956
SENSOR DEVELOPMENTS INC., pg. 990
SENTROL EUROPE S.A.—Berwind Corporation, pg. 145
SERVO CORPORATION OF AMERICA, pg. 993

SHUGART CORPORATION, pg. 1001
SIMPSON ELECTRIC CO., pg. 1007
SUNBEAM-OSTER COMPANY, INC., pg. 1059
TELESCIENCES CO. SYSTEMS INC., pg. 1085
TINIUS OLSEN TESTING MACHINE CO., INC., pg. 1098
TRANSISTOR DEVICES, INC., pg. 1107
TRIPLE A SPECIALTY COMPANY, pg. 1114
TRIPLETT ELECTRICAL INSTRUMENT CORPORATION, pg. 1114
TYLAN GENERAL, INC., pg. 1122
TYLAN GENERAL, INC.-FLOW DIVISION—Tylan General, Inc., pg. 1122
TYLAN GMBH—Tylan General, Inc., pg. 1122
TYLAN SARL—Tylan General, Inc., pg. 1122
VEECO INSTRUMENTATIONS, INC., pg. 1146
VEECO UPA TECHNOLOGY INC.—Veeco Instrumentations, Inc., pg. 1146
O.S. WALKER CO., INC.—Walker Magnetics Group, Inc., pg. 1160
WALKER NATIONAL, INC.—Walker Magnetics Group, Inc., pg. 1160
WALKER SCIENTIFIC—Walker Magnetics Group, Inc., pg. 1160
WAVETEK CORPORATION, pg. 1168
WAVETEK DATRON—Wavetek Corporation, pg. 1169
WAVETEK ELECTRONICS GMBH—Wavetek Corporation, pg. 1169
WAVETEK ELECTRONICS LTD.—Wavetek Corporation, pg. 1169
WAVETEK MICROWAVE, INC.—Wavetek Corporation, pg. 1168
WAVETEK SAN DIEGO INC.—Wavetek Corporation, pg. 1168
WILCOM PRODUCTS, INC.—North Atlantic Industries, Inc., pg. 812
YSI INCORPORATED, pg. 1207
ZETEC, INC., pg. 1217

3826 — LABORATORY ANALYTICAL INSTRUMENTS

ADVANCED INSTRUMENTS, INC., pg. 20
AMRAY, INC., pg. 68
COULTER CORPORATION, pg. 289
HAMILTON BONADUZ AG—Hamilton Co., Inc., pg. 503
HAMILTON CO., INC., pg. 503
HARROP INDUSTRIES, INC., pg. 512
HAVILAND ENTERPRISES, pg. 517
KEUFFEL & ESSER—Azon Corporation, pg. 105
MICRON SEPARATIONS, INC., pg. 749
ORIEL CORPORATION, pg. 829
RESONEX, INC., pg. 929
SPECTRONICS CORPORATION, pg. 1029
YSI INCORPORATED, pg. 1207

3827 — OPTICAL INSTRUMENTS & LENSES

CALUMET PHOTOGRAPHIC, INC., pg. 211
CHRISTIE ELECTRIC CORPORATION, pg. 249
D & K OPTICAL, INC., pg. 307
EDMUND SCIENTIFIC COMPANY, pg. 369
FELLOWS CORPORATION—Goldman Financial Group, pg. 468
J & L METROLOGY COMPANY, INC.—Goldman Financial Group, pg. 468
LASER POWER CORPORATION, pg. 660
LEUPOLD & STEVENS, INC., pg. 669
LINEAR DYNAMICS INC., pg. 676
ORIEL CORPORATION, pg. 829
RANGING—Crossman Corp., pg. 300
RECON/OPTICAL, INC., pg. 917
RELIANCE MEDICAL PRODUCTS, INC., pg. 925
SERVO CORPORATION OF AMERICA, pg. 993
SLANT/FIN CORPORATION, pg. 1010
STOCKER & YALE, INC., pg. 1050
SWIFT INSTRUMENTS, INC., pg. 1068
TASCO, pg. 1079
VERMONT USA MACHINE TOOL GROUP—Goldman Financial Group, pg. 468
ZIPPO MANUFACTURING COMPANY, pg. 1220

3829 — MEASURING & CONTROLLING DEVICES, NEC

ACL TECHNOLOGIES, pg. 2
AGR INTERNATIONAL, INC., pg. 4
AKRA TOOL—UDT Sensors, Inc., pg. 1122
ASSOCIATED PROCESS CONTROLS, pg. 92
ASTRONAUTICS CORP. OF AMERICA, pg. 93
BENTLY NEVADA GMBH—Bently Nevada Corporation, pg. 141
BENTLY NEVADA (UK) LTD.—Bently Nevada Corporation, pg. 141
BIDDLE INSTRUMENTS, pg. 148
BROOKFIELD ENGINEERING LABORATORIES, INC., pg. 179
CAPP, INC., pg. 216
CARGILL DETROIT CORP., pg. 219
CHADWICK-HELMUTH COMPANY, INC., pg. 237
COMMUNICATIONS INTERNATIONAL, pg. 269
COMPUTER INSTRUMENTS CORPORATION, pg. 271
COOPER INSTRUMENT CORP., pg. 283
DATA INSTRUMENTS, INC., pg. 316
DEL MAR AVIONICS, pg. 325
DESPATCH INDUSTRIES, pg. 332
DIETZGEN CORPORATION, pg. 337
DWYER INSTRUMENTS INC., pg. 356
ECRM, pg. 359
ELECTRO FIBEROPTICS CORPORATION, pg. 374
FALCON SAFETY PRODUCTS INC., pg. 398
FILL-RITE DIVISION—Tuthill Corporation, pg. 1120
FORD METER BOX COMPANY, pg. 423
GAS EQUIPMENT COMPANY, INC., pg. 444
GENERAL SCIENCES CORP.—Science Applications International Corporation, pg. 981
HEATH CONSULTANTS INCORPORATED, pg. 524
HYDRIL COMPANY, pg. 556
INEX VISION SYSTEMS—Barry-Wehmiller Company, pg. 122
KULITE SEMICONDUCTOR PRODUCTS, INC., pg. 646
LA BELLE INDUSTRIES, INC., pg. 648
THE LAITRAM CORPORATION, pg. 650
LEUPOLD & STEVENS, INC., pg. 669
LIBERTY TOOL CORPORATION, pg. 674
M&W GEAR COMPANY, pg. 690
MAGNETIC ANALYSIS CORP., pg. 700
MARTIN UNIVERSAL DESIGN, INC., pg. 715
MAXITROL CO., pg. 723
METROLOGIC INSTRUMENTS-MIDWEST—Metrologic Instruments, Inc., pg. 743
METROLOGIC INSTRUMENTS-NORTHEAST—Metrologic Instruments, Inc., pg. 743
METROLOGIC INSTRUMENTS-WESTERN REGION—Metrologic Instruments, Inc., pg. 743
MILTON INDUSTRIES, INC., pg. 756
MINIATURE PRECISION COMPONENTS, pg. 757
NUCLEAR DATA SYSTEMS—Canberra Industries, Inc., pg. 213
ORTHO-KINETICS, INC., pg. 830
PACKARD INSTRUMENT CO., INC.—Canberra Industries, Inc., pg. 213
PLASTIC ENGINEERING COMPONENTS INC., pg. 875
PRESSURE SYSTEMS, pg. 888
QUEST ELECTRONICS DIV.—La Belle Industries, Inc., pg. 648
RANDOM CORPORATION, pg. 912
RELA, INC., pg. 924
ROCHESTER GAUGES INC. OF TEXAS—Gas Equipment Company, Inc., pg. 444
ROTOR DYNAMICS PTY. LTD.—Bently Nevada Corporation, pg. 141
SHIP ANALYTICS, INC., pg. 999
SLANT/FIN CORPORATION, pg. 1010
SPRINGFIELD INSTRUMENT COMPANY—Sunbeam-Oster Company, Inc., pg. 1059
STEINHEIL-LEAR SIEGLER AG—Lear Siegler Diversified Holdings Corp., pg. 664
STOCKER & YALE, INC., pg. 1050
STRAHMAN VALVES, INC., pg. 1052
SUNBEAM HOME COMFORT—Sunbeam-Oster Company, Inc., pg. 1059
SWIFT INSTRUMENTS, INC., pg. 1068
TECHNOLOGY FOR ENERGY CORPORATION, pg. 1084
TENNELEC/NUCLEUS, INC., pg. 1087
TIMEX CORPORATION, pg. 1098
TORK, INC., pg. 1102
TRIPLETT ELECTRICAL INSTRUMENT CORPORATION, pg. 1114
UDT SENSORS, INC., pg. 1122
VENTUREDYNE, LTD., pg. 1148
WABASH MAGNETICS—The Dyson-Kissner-Moran Corporation, pg. 357
WAVETEK CORPORATION, pg. 1168
WHIPPS, pg. 1185
YSI INCORPORATED, pg. 1207
ZYMARK CORPORATION, pg. 1221

3841 — SURGICAL & MEDICAL INSTRUMENTS & APPARATUS

AEROS INSTRUMENTS, INC.—Squire-Cogswell Company, pg. 1034
AMERICAN SAFETY RAZOR COMPANY—Jordan Company, pg. 604
ASTRE CORPORATE GROUP, pg. 92
W. A. BAUM COMPANY, INC., pg. 127
BIO-TEK INSTRUMENTS, INC., pg. 152
BOSTON SCIENTIFIC CORP., pg. 167
CARSTENS HEALTH INDUSTRIES, INC., pg. 225
CINCINNATI SUB-ZERO PRODUCTS, INC., pg. 250
WARREN E. COLLINS, INC., pg. 263
DEL MAR AVIONICS, pg. 325
DEN-MAT CORPORATION, pg. 328
GAYMAR INDUSTRIES, INC., pg. 447
W. L. GORE & ASSOCIATES, INC., pg. 472
HELENA LABORATORIES CORPORATION, pg. 526
THE JEWETT REFRIGERATOR CO., INC.—Ruslander & Sons, Inc., pg. 957
KENDALL CANADA LTD.—Kendall Healthcare Products Co., pg. 622
KENDALL HEALTHCARE PRODUCTS CO., pg. 622
KENDALL HEALTHCARE PRODUCTS COMPANY—Kendall Healthcare Products Co., pg. 622
KIPP GROUP, pg. 632
LAKE REGION MANUFACTURING COMPANY, INC., pg. 651
MANOSTAT CORPORATION, pg. 704
THE MARMON GROUP, INC., pg. 710
MEDRAD, INC., pg. 736
MENNEN MEDICAL INC., pg. 739
MICRO-AIRE SURGICAL INSTRUMENTS, INC.—The Marmon Group, Inc., pg. 711
NOVAMETRIX MEDICAL SYSTEMS INC., pg. 817
PENTAX PRECISION INSTRUMENTS CORP., pg. 859
PROPPER MANUFACTURING CO., INC., pg. 895
RELIANCE MEDICAL PRODUCTS, INC., pg. 925
SURGICAL SPECIALTIES, pg. 1065
TECA CORPORATION, pg. 1082
UVEX SAFETY, INC., pg. 1141

3842 — ORTHOPEDIC, PROSTHETIC & SURGICAL APPLIANCES & SUPPLIES

ACORN ENGINEERING COMPANY, pg. 14
ALIMED, INC., pg. 34
AMERICAN OPTICAL CORP., pg. 59
AMERICAN WHITE CROSS LABORATORIES, INC., pg. 65
APPLICATOR CO.—Plastek Group, pg. 875
ARGOSY ELECTRONICS, INC., pg. 82
BELTONE ELECTRONICS CORPORATION, pg. 137
THE BETHAM CORPORATION, pg. 147
E. D. BULLARD COMPANY, pg. 188
CAIRNS & BROTHER, INC., pg. 207
CHATTANOOGA GROUP, pg. 241
DAVID CLARK COMPANY, INC., pg. 252
THE CLINIPAD CORPORATION, pg. 255
WARREN E. COLLINS, INC., pg. 263
ELECTRIC MOBILITY CO.—Eager Beaver, pg. 362
THE FIBRE-METAL PRODUCTS COMPANY, pg. 408
GOULD PACKAGING, INC., pg. 473
KALLISTA, INC.—Kohler Company, pg. 640
KAZ, INC., pg. 619
KENDALL CANADA LTD.—Kendall Healthcare Products Co., pg. 622
THE KENDALL CO. (UK) LTD.—Kendall Healthcare Products Co., pg. 622
KENDALL HEALTHCARE PRODUCTS CO., pg. 622
KENDALL HEALTHCARE PRODUCTS COMPANY—Kendall Healthcare Products Co., pg. 622
MADDAK INC.—Bel-Art Products, pg. 133
MEDLINE INDUSTRIES, INC., pg. 736
MEGAS BEAUTY AIDS, INC., pg. 737
MERIDIAN INDUSTRIES, INC., pg. 740
NUEAR ELECTRONICS—Starkey Laboratories, Inc., pg. 1040
ORTHO-KINETICS, INC., pg. 830
OTO-SONIC, INC.—Beltone Electronics Corporation, pg. 138
POLLENEX CORPORATION, pg. 879
POLLENEX CORPORATION—Odyssey Partners, pg. 821
POLYMER TECHNOLOGIES—Maclean-Fogg Co., pg. 697
PROPPER MANUFACTURING CO., INC., pg. 895
RABCO HEALTH SERVICE, pg. 908
RETEC USA, INC.—Gaymar Industries, Inc., pg. 447
SANITAS HEALTHCARE DIV.—Dutton-Lainson Co., pg. 356
SECHRIST INDUSTRIES, INC., pg. 987
SELLSTROM MANUFACTURING CO., pg. 988
SIMUNICO, INC., pg. 1007
SIOUX MANUFACTURING CORP., pg. 1008
SOLON MANUFACTURING COMPANY, pg. 1017
STARKEY LABORATORIES, INC., pg. 1040
SUNBEAM HOME COMFORT—Sunbeam-Oster Company, Inc., pg. 1059
SURGICAL APPLIANCE INDUSTRIES, INC., pg. 1065
THERADYNE CORPORATION—Surgical Appliance Industries, Inc., pg. 1065
WILLSON SAFETY PRODUCTS, pg. 1193

3843 — DENTAL EQUIPMENT & SUPPLIES

A-DEC, INC., pg. 1
AD PLASTICS LTD.—Dentsply International Inc., pg. 330
ASH INSTRUMENTS DIVISION, DENTSPLY LTD.—Dentsply International Inc., pg. 330
BARNHARDT MANUFACTURING CO., pg. 120
BELMONT INDUSTRIES, INC., pg. 136
C.M.W. LABORATORIES DENTSPLY, LTD.—Dentsply International Inc., pg. 330
L. D. CAULK DIV.—Dentsply International Inc., pg. 330
CERAMCO—Dentsply International Inc., pg. 330
DE ART S.R.L.—Dentsply International Inc., pg. 330
DENTSPLY CAULK DE MEXICO, S.A. DE C.V.—Dentsply International Inc., pg. 330
DENTSPLY GMBH—Dentsply International Inc., pg. 330
DENTSPLY/IMPLANT DIVISION—Dentsply International Inc., pg. 330
DENTSPLY INDUSTRIA E COMERCIO LTDA.—Dentsply International Inc., pg. 330
DENTSPLY INTERNATIONAL INC., pg. 329
DENTSPLY LTD.—Dentsply International Inc., pg. 330
DETREY DENTSPLY—Dentsply International Inc., pg. 330
HAWS DRINKING FAUCET CO., pg. 518
L&R MANUFACTURING CO., pg. 647
THE LORVIC CORP., pg. 684
THE J. M. NEY COMPANY, pg. 805
PATTERSON DENTAL COMPANY, pg. 851
PHOENIX INTERNATIONAL, INC., pg. 868
RANIR CORPORATION, pg. 912
RANSOM & RANDOLPH DIV.—Dentsply International Inc., pg. 330

3844 — X-RAY APPARATUS, TUBES & EQUIPMENT

AMRAY, INC., pg. 68
SPECTRONICS CORPORATION, pg. 1029

3845 — ELECTROMEDICAL & ELECTROTHERAPEUTIC APPARATUS

AUTOMATIC LIQUID PACKAGING, INC., pg. 100
DEL MAR AVIONICS, pg. 325
MENNEN MEDICAL INC., pg. 739
MICRO-AIRE SURGICAL INSTRUMENTS, INC.—The Marmon Group, Inc., pg. 711
NUCLEAR DATA SYSTEMS—Canberra Industries, Inc., pg. 213
TELESENSORY, pg. 1085
VERNAY LABORATORIES, INC., pg. 1148
WALKER MAGNETICS GROUP, INC., pg. 1160

3851 — OPHTHALMIC GOODS

AMERICAN OPTICAL CORP., pg. 59
DULING OPTICAL CORPORATION, pg. 352
EYEWEAR DIVISION—Guess ?, Inc., pg. 493
GENTEX OPTICS, INC., pg. 452
THE HILSINGER CORP., pg. 535
I SKI SKI GOGGLES, pg. 557
JONES OPTICAL COMPANY—Totes Incorporated, pg. 1103
NORTH AMERICAN WATCH CORPORATION, pg. 812
OMNI LENS CORPORATION, pg. 826
OPTYL EYEWEAR FASHION INTERNATIONAL CORP., pg. 828
SELLSTROM MANUFACTURING CO., pg. 988
SHELBY GROUP INTERNATIONAL, INC., pg. 996
SIMMONS OUTDOOR CORP., pg. 1005
SWIFT INSTRUMENTS, INC., pg. 1068
UVEX SAFETY, INC., pg. 1141
WGM SAFETY CORPORATION, pg. 1156
WALMAN OPTICAL COMPANY, pg. 1161
WILLSON SAFETY PRODUCTS, pg. 1193

3861 — PHOTOGRAPHIC EQUIPMENT & SUPPLIES

AZON CORPORATION, pg. 105
BELL & HOWELL COMPANY, pg. 134
CASTCRAFT INDUSTRIES, INC., pg. 228
CINE MAGNETICS, INC., pg. 250
D/B CAMERAS MICROCHECK DIVISION—AEI Holding Co., Inc., pg. 3
DIETZGEN CORPORATION, pg. 337
DUKANE CORPORATION, pg. 351
GENERAL CHEMICAL CORPORATION—New Hampshire Oak, pg. 801
HPS, INC., pg. 497
HAMAMATSU CORP., pg. 502
HARGRO ENTERPRISES, INC., pg. 509
HOUSTON FEARLESS 76 INC., pg. 546
J & R FILM COMPANY, pg. 586
KENDALL HEALTHCARE PRODUCTS CO., pg. 622
KEUFFEL & ESSER—Azon Corporation, pg. 105
KREONITE, INC., pg. 644
LEXMARK FRANCE—Lexmark International, Inc., pg. 674
LEXMARK INTERNATIONAL, INC.—Lexmark International, Inc., pg. 674
LONDON LITHO ALUMINUM CO., INC., pg. 681
MPO VIDEOTRONICS—MPO Videotronics, Inc., pg. 693
MPO VIDEOTRONICS, INC., pg. 693
MAGNASYNC MOVIOLA CORPORATION—J & R Film Company, pg. 586
MICROMEDIA LIMITED—Bell & Howell Company, pg. 135
N.B. JACKETS DIVISION—Bell & Howell Company, pg. 135
NUARC COMPANY, INC., pg. 817
PRC OF AMERICA CORP.—Plastic Reel Corp. of America, pg. 875
PRC OF AMERICA SUPPLY CORP.—Plastic Reel Corp. of America, pg. 875
PHOTOGENIC MACHINE COMPANY, INC., pg. 869
PLASTIC REEL CORP. OF AMERICA, pg. 875
PRETEC PRECISIE TECHNIEK B.V.—Bell & Howell Company, pg. 135
RANGING—Crossman Corp., pg. 300
RECON/OPTICAL, INC., pg. 917
RIDGWAY'S, INC.—YRJ Corporation, pg. 1207
STAR-PARTS INC., pg. 1039
UNIVERSAL BLUEPRINT PAPER CO.—YRJ Corporation, pg. 1207
YRJ CORPORATION, pg. 1206

3873 — WATCHES, CLOCKS, CLOCKWORK OPERATED DEVICES & PARTS

AMERICAN SIGN & MARKETING SERVICES, INC., pg. 61
CONCORD WATCH COMPANY, S.A.—North American Watch Corporation, pg. 812
CROTON WATCH COMPANY, pg. 300
DETEX CORPORATION, pg. 333
ELGIN WATCH INTERNATIONAL, INC., pg. 376
GENERAL TIME CORP., pg. 451
MOVADO WATCH COMPANY, S.A.—North American Watch Corporation, pg. 812
NORTH AMERICAN WATCH CORPORATION, pg. 812
RADO WATCH COMPANY, INC., pg. 909
M. H. RHODES, INC., pg. 931
DAVID G. STEVEN, INC., pg. 1048
STOCKER & YALE, INC., pg. 1050
TELECHRON, INC., pg. 1085
TIMEX CORPORATION, pg. 1098
TOURNEAU INC., pg. 1103
TROPAR MFG. CO., INC., pg. 1115

3911 — JEWELRY, PRECIOUS METAL

A & Z HAYWARD, INC., pg. 1
AMERICAN PROTECTION INDUSTRIES, INC., pg. 60
B.A. BALLOU & CO. INC., pg. 116
CJC HOLDINGS, INC., pg. 202
DOWNEY DESIGNS INTERNATIONAL, INC., pg. 348
EXCELL MANUFACTURING COMPANY, pg. 392
THE FRANKLIN MINT—American Protection Industries, Inc., pg. 60
IMPERIAL PEARL COMPANY, INC., pg. 564
JEWELMONT CORPORATION, pg. 594
RONALD LITOFF, LTD., pg. 678
THE NAPIER COMPANY, pg. 783
OROAMERICA, INC., pg. 830
PLAINVILLE STOCK COMPANY, INC., pg. 874
REED & BARTON CORPORATION, pg. 920
RLJC, INC.—The Napier Company, pg. 783
UNCAS MANUFACTURING COMPANY, pg. 1125

3914 — SILVERWARE, PLATED WARE & STAINLESS STEEL WARE

AMERICAN SHEAR KNIVE CO.—Asko, Inc, pg. 88
ASKO, INC, pg. 88
IMPERIAL SCHRADE CORP., pg. 564
KIRK & MATZ LTD., pg. 633
LEACH & GARNER COMPANY, pg. 663
METAL MASTERS FOODSERVICE EQUIPMENT, pg. 741
R.S. OWENS, pg. 834
REED & BARTON CORPORATION, pg. 920
REED & BARTON SILVERSMITHS—Reed & Barton Corporation, pg. 920
STANLEY ROBERTS, INC., pg. 939
ROGERS, LUNT & BOWLEN CO., pg. 943
SALADMASTER, pg. 967
WALLACE SILVERSMITHS—Syratech Corporation, pg. 1070

3915 — JEWELERS FINDINGS & MATERIALS & LAPIDARY WORK

B.A. BALLOU & CO. INC., pg. 116
L&R MANUFACTURING CO., pg. 647
LEACH & GARNER COMPANY, pg. 663

3931 — MUSICAL INSTRUMENTS

BRIMMS INC., pg. 176
THE CORNWALL & PATTERSON CO.—Pratt-Read Corporation, pg. 884
ENSONIQ CORPORATION, pg. 382
FENDER MUSICAL INSTRUMENTS, pg. 406
GIBSON GUITAR CORPORATION, INC., pg. 456
GUILD MUSIC CORPORATION—U.S. Music Corporation, pg. 1136
HOHNER/HSS INC., pg. 538
FRANK HOLTON CO.—G. Leblanc Corporation, pg. 665
LEBLANC CASE CO.—G. Leblanc Corporation, pg. 665
G. LEBLANC CORPORATION, pg. 665
G. LEBLANC—G. Leblanc Corporation, pg. 665
MARTIN BAND INSTRUMENT CO.—G. Leblanc Corporation, pg. 665
THE SELMER CO.—Integrated Resources, Inc., pg. 573
STEINWAY MUSICAL PROPERTIES, INC., pg. 1045
STEINWAY & SONS—Steinway Musical Properties, Inc., pg. 1046
U.S. MUSIC CORPORATION, pg. 1136
AVEDIS ZILDJIAN COMPANY, pg. 1219

3942 — DOLLS & STUFFED TOYS

ACE NOVELTY COMPANY, INC., pg. 12
ACE NOVELTY FUN SERVICE DIVISION—Ace Novelty Company, Inc., pg. 12
ALEXANDER DOLL CO., INC., pg. 33
ANIMAL FAIR—Guy Schoenecker, Inc., pg. 978
CENTURY PRODUCTS CO., pg. 235
COMMONWEALTH TOY & NOVELTY COMPANY, pg. 269
DAKIN, INC., pg. 311
GOLDBERGER DOLL MFG. COMPANY, INC., pg. 466
PRIDE PRODUCTS, INC., pg. 889
REMCO BABY—Remco Toys, pg. 926
REMCO TOYS, pg. 926
TOTSY MANUFACTURING COMPANY, INC., pg. 1103
TOY BIZ, INC., pg. 1104
THE TOY FACTORY—Pride Products, Inc., pg. 889
WELSH COMPANY, pg. 1175

3944 — GAMES, TOYS & CHILDREN'S VEHICLES; EXCEPT DOLLS & BICYCLES

AMERICAN PLASTIC TOYS INC., pg. 59
AMLOID CORPORATION, pg. 67
BENJAMIN SHERIDAN CO.—Crossman Corp., pg. 300
BINNEY & SMITH INC.—Hallmark Cards, Inc., pg. 502
CENTURY PRODUCTS CO., pg. 235
COLORFORMS, pg. 265
COX HOBBIES, INC., pg. 294
CROSSMAN CORP., pg. 300
DARDA INC. (USA), pg. 315
DUNCAN TOYS COMPANY—Nordic Group of Companies, Ltd., pg. 810
DURANT ELECTRONICS, INC.—Strombecker Corporation, pg. 1054
ESQUIRE NOVELTY CO.—Strombecker Corporation, pg. 1054
ESTES INDUSTRIES, INC.—Peter W. Smith & Company, Inc., pg. 1011
FLAMBEAU CORPORATION—Nordic Group of Companies, Ltd., pg. 809
GENERAL SPORTCRAFT COMPANY LTD., pg. 450
GOLDBERGER DOLL MFG. COMPANY, INC., pg. 466
JANLYNN CORPORATION, pg. 589
JOY TOY, CO.—Strombecker Corporation, pg. 1054
LIONEL TRAINS, INC., pg. 677
MINDGAMES, INC., pg. 756
NORDIC GROUP OF COMPANIES, LTD., pg. 809
ODYSSEY PARTNERS, pg. 821
PLAID ENTERPRISES INC.—The Dyson-Kissner-Moran Corporation, pg. 357
PRESSMAN TOY CORP., pg. 887
PRIDE PRODUCTS, INC., pg. 889
PROCESSED PLASTIC COMPANY, pg. 892
RAPID MOUNTING & FINISHING CO., pg. 913
W. C. REDMON CO., pg. 919
ROSE ART INDUSTRIES, pg. 947
SLM, INC., pg. 963
SPALDING & EVENFLO COMPANIES, INC., pg. 1024
SPANG & COMPANY, pg. 1025
STROMBECKER CHEMTOY DIVISION—Strombecker Corporation, pg. 1054
STROMBECKER CORPORATION, pg. 1054
STROMBECKER (HK) LTD.—Strombecker Corporation, pg. 1054
STUHR ENTERPRISES INC., pg. 1055
TSR, INC., pg. 1075
TODAY'S KIDS—Spang & Company, pg. 1025
TOOTSIETOY DIVISION—Strombecker Corporation, pg. 1054
TOOTSIETOY PRESCHOOL PRODUCTS DIV.—Strombecker Corporation, pg. 1054
TOY BIZ, INC., pg. 1104
THE TOY FACTORY—Pride Products, Inc., pg. 889
UNISYSTEMS, INC., pg. 1130
THE UNITED STATES PLAYING CARD COMPANY, pg. 1136

3949 — SPORTING & ATHLETIC GOODS, NEC

ALLSOP, INC., pg. 43
AMERICAN BALL MANUFACTURING—Prince Manufacturing, Inc., pg. 890
ARMSTRONG INTERNATIONAL, INC., pg. 83
BALTIMORE ORIOLES, INC., pg. 116
BEAD INDUSTRIES INC., pg. 129
BERKLEY, INC., pg. 141
BIKE ATHLETIC CO., pg. 150
BLUE FOX TACKLE CO.—Normark Corporation, pg. 810
BOLLINGER INDUSTRIES INC., pg. 163
BRIMMS INC., pg. 176
CADACO—Rapid Mounting & Finishing Co., pg. 913
CALIFORNIA-GYM EQUIPMENT CO.—Bollinger Industries Inc., pg. 163
CENTURY FENCE COMPANY, pg. 235
CHATTANOOGA GROUP, pg. 241
THE COLEMAN COMPANY, INC.—MacAndrews & Forbes Holdings Inc., pg. 695
COLEMAN INTERNATIONAL OPERATION—MacAndrews & Forbes Holdings Inc., pg. 695
COLEMAN WATER RECREATION OPERATIONS—MacAndrews & Forbes Holdings Inc., pg. 695
COMPUTROL, INC.—Armstrong International, Inc., pg. 83
CREATIVE PLAYTHINGS LTD., pg. 297
CROSMAN CORPORATION—MacAndrews & Forbes Holdings Inc., pg. 695
DACOR CORPORATION, pg. 310
DELAIR GROUP, INC.—Aluminum Shapes, Inc., pg. 46
DOVRE SKI PRODUCTS—The Shelburne Corporation, pg. 996
DUDLEY SPORTS CO. DIVISION—Spalding & Evenflo Companies, Inc., pg. 1025
EKTELON CORP.—Prince Manufacturing, Inc., pg. 890
ELMER'S WEIGHTS—Bollinger Industries Inc., pg. 163
ESTHER WILLIAMS SWIMMING POOL CO., pg. 389
EVERLAST SPORTS MANUFACTURING CORP., pg. 392
FIBRE GLASS-EVERCOAT COMPANY INC., pg. 408
FLAMBEAU CORPORATION—Nordic Group of Companies, Ltd., pg. 809
FLAMBEAU PRODUCTS CORP.—Nordic Group of Companies, Ltd., pg. 809
FRANKLIN SPORTS INDUSTRIES, pg. 429
GAME TIME, INC., pg. 442
GARED SPORTS INC.—Nixdorff Krein Industries Inc., pg. 807
GENERAL SPORTCRAFT COMPANY LTD., pg. 450
MARTY GILMAN, INC., pg. 459
GORDON & SMITH, INC., pg. 472
GRAFALLOY INC.—Prince Manufacturing, Inc., pg. 890
THE GRANDOE CORPORATION, pg. 476
GUTMANN CUTLERY, INC.—Hyde Manufacturing Co., pg. 556
HEAD SPORTS, INC., pg. 520
HILLERICH & BRADSBY CO., INC., pg. 535
HUSSEY CORPORATION, pg. 555
KDI AMERICAN PRODUCTS, INC.—KDI Corporation, pg. 612
KARSTEN MANUFACTURING CORPORATION, pg. 617
KOMBI, LTD., pg. 641
KRANSCO, pg. 644
LANGERT GOLF CO., INC.—Prince Manufacturing, Inc., pg. 890
MSR (MOUNTAIN SAFETY RESEARCH)—Recreational Equipment, Inc., pg. 917
MASTER SKIS—MacAndrews & Forbes Holdings Inc., pg. 694
MASTERCRAFT BOAT COMPANY—MacAndrews & Forbes Holdings Inc., pg. 695
MEPPS S.A.—Sheldons' Inc., pg. 997
MISTER TWISTER—Sheldons' Inc., pg. 997
MUSKIN LEISURE PRODUCTS, INC., pg. 777
NAUTILUS, pg. 796
NIXDORFF KREIN INDUSTRIES INC., pg. 807
NORDIC GROUP OF COMPANIES, LTD., pg. 809
NORMARK CORPORATION, pg. 810
NORTHWESTERN GOLF COMPANY, pg. 815
O'BRIEN INTERNATIONAL, INC.—MacAndrews & Forbes Holdings Inc., pg. 695
THE ORVIS COMPANY, INC., pg. 830
PARAMOUNT FITNESS EQUIPMENT CORP., pg. 848
PARKWAY FABRICATORS, INC.—Great American Industries, Inc., pg. 480
PENGUIN INDUSTRIES, INC., pg. 857
PONY SPORTS & LEISURE INC., pg. 880
PRINCE MANUFACTURING, INC., pg. 890
PRO LINE—Flexfab, Inc., pg. 418
PRO-SELECT—Northwestern Golf Company, pg. 815
PROTECTO PLASTICS, INC.—Penguin Industries, Inc., pg. 857
RAM GOLF CORPORATION, pg. 910
ROCKET INDUSTRIES, INC./EXCEL, THE EXERCISE COMPANY, pg. 941

ROLLER DERBY SKATE COMPANY, pg. 944
ROLLERBLADE, INC., pg. 944
S&K PRODUCTS, INC.—Armstrong International, Inc., pg. 83
THE SHANE GROUP INC., pg. 995
THE SHELBURNE CORPORATION, pg. 996
SHELDONS' INC., pg. 996
SKEETER PRODUCTS, INC.—MacAndrews & Forbes Holdings Inc., pg. 695
S. R. SMITH, INC.—Aqua Fab Industries, Inc., pg. 79
SONIFORM, INC.—MacAndrews & Forbes Holdings Inc., pg. 695
SPALDING—Spalding & Evenflo Companies, Inc., pg. 1024
SPALDING AUSTRALIA PTY. LTD.—Spalding & Evenflo Companies, Inc., pg. 1025
SPALDING CANADA—Spalding & Evenflo Companies, Inc., pg. 1025
SPALDING & EVENFLO COMPANIES, INC., pg. 1024
SPALDING JAPAN INC.—Spalding & Evenflo Companies, Inc., pg. 1025
SPALDING JAPAN INC.—Spalding & Evenflo Companies, Inc., pg. 1025
SUNBEAM OUTDOOR PRODUCTS CO.—Sunbeam-Oster Company, Inc., pg. 1059
U.S. DIVERS CO., INC., pg. 1135
VIBRAX/MCA INC.—Normark Corporation, pg. 810
VOIT CORP., pg. 1154
VOIT SPORTS, INC., pg. 1154
WEATHERKING PRODUCTS, INC.—Aqua Fab Industries, Inc., pg. 79
WEIDER HEALTH & FITNESS, pg. 1173
WELLINGTON INDUSTRIES INC., pg. 1175
YORK BARBELL CO., INC., pg. 1208
ZIPPO MANUFACTURING COMPANY, pg. 1220

3951 — PENS, MECHANICAL PENCILS & PARTS

BEROL CORPORATION—Pen Holdings, Inc., pg. 856
BLUE RIBBON PEN & PENCIL CO.—Pen Holdings, Inc., pg. 856
DRI MARK PRODUCTS, INC., pg. 349
EMPIRE BEROL U.S.A.—Pen Holdings, Inc., pg. 856
FABER/CASTELL CORPORATION, pg. 395
FISHER PEN CO. OF NEVADA—Fisher Pen Company, pg. 415
FISHER PEN COMPANY, pg. 415
KOH-I-NOOR, INC., pg. 639
MALLARD PEN & PENCIL CO.—Pen Holdings, Inc., pg. 856
PEN HOLDINGS, INC., pg. 856
SCRIPTO-TOKAI, INC., pg. 983
UNION PEN COMPANY, pg. 1128
ZIPPO MANUFACTURING COMPANY, pg. 1220

3952 — LEAD PENCILS, CRAYONS, & ARTISTS' MATERIALS

ASBURY FERST, INC.—Asbury Carbons, Inc., pg. 87
BADGER AIR BRUSH COMPANY, pg. 113
BEROL CORPORATION—Pen Holdings, Inc., pg. 856
BINNEY & SMITH INC.—Hallmark Cards, Inc., pg. 502
BLUE RIBBON PEN & PENCIL CO.—Pen Holdings, Inc., pg. 856
COLWELL INDUSTRIES, INC., pg. 267
CRAYOLA PRODUCTS DIV.—Hallmark Cards, Inc., pg. 502
DUREX INDUSTRIES INC., pg. 354
EMPIRE BEROL U.S.A.—Pen Holdings, Inc., pg. 856
FABER/CASTELL CANADA LTD.—Faber/Castell Corporation, pg. 395
FABER/CASTELL CORPORATION, pg. 395
FLAMBEAU CORPORATION—Nordic Group of Companies, Ltd., pg. 809
HALLMARK ART PRODUCTS & INTERNATIONAL DIV.—Hallmark Cards, Inc., pg. 502
HALLMARK CARDS, INC., pg. 501
HALLMARK EDUCATIONAL PRODUCTS DIV.—Hallmark Cards, Inc., pg. 502
KEUFFEL & ESSER—Azon Corporation, pg. 105
KOH-I-NOOR, INC., pg. 639
MALLARD PEN & PENCIL CO.—Pen Holdings, Inc., pg. 856
NORTHEASTERN GRAPHIC SUPPLY, INC., pg. 814
ROSE ART INDUSTRIES, pg. 947
SCRIPTO-TOKAI, INC., pg. 983
TRANSILWRAP COMPANY, INC., pg. 1107
TRI-CHEM, INC., pg. 1110
UNION PEN COMPANY, pg. 1128

3953 — MARKING DEVICES

AMERICAN MARKING SYSTEMS, pg. 58
BEROL CORPORATION—Pen Holdings, Inc., pg. 856
CONSOLIDATED SCREEN-MAKERS, INC.—The Dyson-Kissner-Moran Corporation, pg. 357
COSCO INDUSTRIES, pg. 288
DIAGRAPH CORPORATION, pg. 335
GRAPHIC CONTROLS, CORP., pg. 478
MATTHEWS CANADA LTD.—Matthews International Corp., pg. 721
THE MEYERCORD COMPANY, pg. 746
PANNIER CORPORATION, pg. 846
WEBER MARKING SYSTEMS CANADA LTD.—Weber Marking Systems, Inc., pg. 1171
WEBER MARKING SYSTEMS (FAR EAST) CO. LTD.—Weber Marking Systems, Inc., pg. 1171
WEBER MARKING SYSTEMS, INC., pg. 1171
WEBER MARKING SYSTEMS LTD.—Weber Marking Systems, Inc., pg. 1171

3955 — CARBON PAPER & INKED RIBBONS

BAROUM EATON ALLEN CORPORATION, pg. 121
CRANE & CO., INC., pg. 296
HARGRO ENTERPRISES, INC., pg. 509
KO-REC-TYPE—Baroum Eaton Allen Corporation, pg. 121
KORES NORDIC USA CORP., pg. 642
LEXMARK CANADA INC.—Lexmark International, Inc., pg. 674
LEXMARK FRANCE—Lexmark International, Inc., pg. 674
LEXMARK INTERNATIONAL, INC.—Lexmark International, Inc., pg. 674
MELLON CORPORATION, pg. 738
RITTENHOUSE INC., pg. 936
TECHNICARBON COMPANY, INC., pg. 1083
WEBER MARKING SYSTEMS, INC., pg. 1171

3961 — COSTUME JEWELRY & COSTUME NOVELTIES, EXCEPT PRECIOUS METAL

CRANSTON MANUFACTURING FACILITY—Pakula & Company, pg. 843
DARLENE JEWELRY MANUFACTURING COMPANY, pg. 315
HERFF JONES INC., pg. 531
INVERNESS CORP., pg. 581
THE NAPIER COMPANY, pg. 783
PAKULA & COMPANY, pg. 843
PERFECT PEARL COMPANY, INC., pg. 861
REED & BARTON CORPORATION, pg. 920

3965 — FASTENERS, BUTTONS, NEEDLES & PINS

ANCRA CORPORATION, pg. 72
EAGLE BUTTON CO., INC., pg. 362
ELFIN INDUSTRIES, LTD.—Ancra Corporation, pg. 72
NORTH & JUDD, pg. 812
RAU FASTENERS, INC., pg. 913
REPUBLIC FASTENER PRODUCTS CORP., pg. 928
ROBERTSON-WHITEHOUSE—The Marmon Group, Inc., pg. 713
EDWIN B. STIMPSON COMPANY, INC., pg. 1049
TALON, INC., pg. 1077
WM. E. WRIGHT LIMITED PARTNERSHIP, pg. 1205

3991 — BROOMS & BRUSHES

BINNEY & SMITH INC.—Hallmark Cards, Inc., pg. 502
BRUSH RESEARCH MANUFACTURING COMPANY, pg. 184
CORCORAN MFG. CO., INC., pg. 285
EASY DAY MANUFACTURING COMPANY, INC., pg. 364
EMPIRE BRUSHES, INC., pg. 379
FELTON BRUSH INC., pg. 406
FLO-PAC CORPORATION, pg. 419
FLOUR CITY BRUSH CO.—Flo-Pac Corporation, pg. 419
THE FULLER BRUSH COMPANY, pg. 436
LINZER PRODUCTS CORP., pg. 677
M & E MANUFACTURING CO.—Plastek Group, pg. 875
MURALO CO., INC., pg. 776
PACIFIC COAST BRUSH CO.—Flo-Pac Corporation, pg. 419
PARKS PRODUCTS, INC., pg. 850
PLASTI-KOTE COMPANY INC., pg. 875
PLAYTEX FAMILY PRODUCTS CORP.—Playtex FP Group Incorporated, pg. 877
PLAYTEX FP GROUP INCORPORATED, pg. 877
RANIR CORPORATION, pg. 912
SOUTH EASTERN BRUSH CO.—Flo-Pac Corporation, pg. 419
THE WOOSTER BRUSH COMPANY, pg. 1202
WOOSTER MAGIKOTER WEST DIVISION—The Wooster Brush Company, pg. 1202

3993 — SIGNS & ADVERTISING DISPLAYS

AMD INDUSTRIES INC., pg. 5
AMCO FOLDING CARTONS, INC., pg. 47
AMERICAN SIGN & MARKETING SERVICES, INC., pg. 61
ATLITE LIGHTING EQUIP, INC., pg. 97
BENCO INDUSTRIES, INC., pg. 138
BUFKOR, INC., pg. 187
BURKE COMMUNICATION INDUSTRIES, INC., pg. 190
CGF INDUSTRIES, pg. 201
CHICAGO SHOW PRINTING CO., pg. 246
COMMONS BROS., INC., pg. 269
COSCO INDUSTRIES, pg. 288
CUMMINGS INC., pg. 304
DAKTRONICS, INC., pg. 312
DAUMAN DISPLAYS, INC.—Continental Graphics Holdings, Inc., pg. 279
DUALITE INC., pg. 350
DUALITE SALES & SERVICE, INC.—Dualite Inc., pg. 350
DUNLOP MANUFACTURING CO.—The Vernon Company, pg. 1148
EVERBRITE, INC., pg. 391
EVERBRITE LACROSSE—Everbrite, Inc., pg. 391
GHN—Everbrite, Inc., pg. 391
GEIGER BROTHERS, pg. 447
GERRARD AND COMPANY, pg. 454
GORDON SIGN COMPANY, pg. 472
HALL SIGN, INC., pg. 501
KETTERING ADVERTISING DISPLAY CO., pg. 626
LA FRANCE CORPORATION, pg. 649
MARKETING DISPLAYS INTERNATIONAL, INC., pg. 709
MEASURED MARKETING SERVICES, pg. 734
METRO LABEL CORP.—Metro Label Corp., pg. 743
MOUNT VERNON NEON—Everbrite, Inc., pg. 391
PANNIER CORPORATION, pg. 846
PHILADELPHIA SIGN COMPANY, pg. 867
RAPID MOUNTING & FINISHING CO., pg. 913
RENAISSANCE PUBLISHING CO., INC., pg. 926
THE SARGENT-SOWELL COMPANY, pg. 971
SELECTO-FLASH, INC., pg. 988
TOPFLIGHT CORP., pg. 1102
UNION PEN COMPANY, pg. 1128
UNITED STATES NAME PLATE—La France Corporation, pg. 649
THE VERNON COMPANY, pg. 1148
YERGER BROS., INC., pg. 1208
YOUNG ELECTRIC SIGN COMPANY, pg. 1209
YOUNG ELECTRIC SIGN DENVER DIV.—Young Electric Sign Company, pg. 1209
YOUNG ELECTRIC SIGN LAS VEGAS DIV.—Young Electric Sign Company, pg. 1209

3995 — BURIAL CASKETS

AURORA CASKET COMPANY, pg. 98
CASKET SHELLS, INC., pg. 228

3996 — LINOLEUM, ASPHALTED-FELT-BASE, & OTHER HARD SURFACE FLOOR COVERINGS, NEC

BURKE INDUSTRIES INC., pg. 190
CONGOLEUM CORPORATION, pg. 274
HILLSIDE CAPITAL, INC., pg. 535
HILLSIDE INDUSTRIES, INC.—Hillside Capital, Inc., pg. 535
KENTILE FLOORS INC., pg. 623
MANNINGTON MILLS, INC., pg. 704
STONHARD LATIN AMERICA—Stonhard, Inc., pg. 1051

3999 — MANUFACTURING INDUSTRIES, NEC

ALLIED PRODUCTS—Consolidated Cigar Corporation, pg. 276
AMERICAN SPECIALTIES INC., pg. 61
ANDIS COMPANY, pg. 74
ATARI GAMES CORPORATION, pg. 93
ATWOOD INDUSTRIES, INC., pg. 97
AUTOSWAGE PRODUCTS, INC., pg. 101
THE W.E. BASSETT COMPANY, pg. 125
BEAD INDUSTRIES INC., pg. 129
D. D. BEAN & SONS (CANADA) LTD.—D. D. Bean & Sons Co., pg. 129
D. D. BEAN & SONS CO., pg. 129
D. D. BEAN & SONS (N.C.) INC.—D. D. Bean & Sons Co., pg. 129
BELVEDERE COMPANY, pg. 138
BRIMMS INC., pg. 176
CC INDUSTRIES, INC., pg. 199
CANDLE CORPORATION OF AMERICA, pg. 214
CARSON PRODUCTS COMPANY—Aminco, Inc., pg. 67
CENTRAL BEAUTY EQUIPMENT—Belvedere Company, pg. 138
THE CHEROKEE GROUP, pg. 243
CONSOLIDATED CIGAR CORPORATION, pg. 276
COSCO INDUSTRIES, pg. 288
CREATIVE PRODUCTIONS, pg. 297
CREATIVE SALON FURNITURE INC., pg. 297
W.W. CROSS, INC.—D. D. Bean & Sons Co., pg. 129
DAZEY CORPORATION, pg. 321
DELAIR GROUP, INC.—Aluminum Shapes, Inc., pg. 46
DETAILS—Steelcase Inc., pg. 1044
DIAMOND BRANDS, INC., pg. 335
EDUCATIONAL INSIGHTS, INC., pg. 369
EMERY WATERHOUSE COMPANY, pg. 379
FARNAM COMPANIES, INC., pg. 403
FIBER MATERIALS, INC., pg. 408
FINKEL OUTDOOR PRODUCTS OF CALIFORNIA—CC Industries, Inc., pg. 200
FINKEL OUTDOOR PRODUCTS, INC.—CC Industries, Inc., pg. 200
WALLY FRANK, LTD., pg. 429
THE FRANKLIN MINT—American Protection Industries, Inc., pg. 60
GENERAL WIG MANUFACTURERS, INC.—MacAndrews & Forbes Holdings Inc., pg. 695
GHENT MANUFACTURING, INC., pg. 455
GRANDPA BRANDS COMPANY, pg. 476
HALLMARK CARDS, INC., pg. 501
HARTZ GROUP, pg. 514
THE HARTZ MOUNTAIN CORP., pg. 514
HARTZ MOUNTAIN GROUP—Hartz Group, pg. 514
HAZEN PAPER COMPANY, pg. 520
THE HILSINGER CORP., pg. 535
HOECHST CERAMTEC NORTH AMERICA, INC., pg. 537
HOPPER INC., pg. 543
HUDSON VALLEY TREE, INC., pg. 551
HURST PERFORMANCES, INC.—Mr. Gasket Company, pg. 761
ILC DOVER, INC.—ILC Industries, Inc., pg. 560
LAIDLAW CORPORATION, pg. 650
TONY LAMBERT COMPANY, pg. 652
LANE LIMITED, pg. 657
M & C SPECIALTIES COMPANY, pg. 690
MAGICSILK, INC., pg. 700
MELE MANUFACTURING CO., INC., pg. 737
MR. CHRISTMAS INC., pg. 761
NATIONAL BAND & TAG CO., pg. 786
NIAG. RA THERAPY MFG. CORP., pg. 806
NORTHERN CROSS, LTD.—Barancorp, pg. 118
PACKAGE SERVICE COMPANY, INC., pg. 842
PANNIER CORPORATION, pg. 846
PEERLESS UMBRELLA CO., INC., pg. 855
PHILLIES CIGAR COMPANY—Havatampa Incorporated, pg. 517
PRO-LINE CORPORATION, pg. 892
RENAISSANCE PUBLISHING CO., INC., pg. 926
RENNOC CORPORATION, pg. 927
REPLOGLE GLOBES, INC., pg. 927

4226 — SPECIAL WAREHOUSING & STORAGE, NEC

AMERICAN TRANSFER & STORAGE CO.—Mayflower Transit, Inc., pg. 724
BEKINS MOVING & STORAGE CO.—The Bekins Company, pg. 133
CENEX (FARMERS UNION CENTRAL EXCHANGE, INC.), pg. 231
CROWLEY MARITIME CORPORATION, pg. 301
FEDERAL COMPRESS & WAREHOUSE COMPANY, INC., pg. 404
THE IMPEX GROUP LIMITED—Goldman Financial Group, pg. 468
INGRAM PERIODICALS INC.—Ingram Industries Inc., pg. 569
MACRISTY INDUSTRIES, INC., pg. 698
MARTRADE LTD., pg. 716
F.W. MYERS & CO.—The Myers Group (U.S) Inc., pg. 780
THE MYERS GROUP (U.S) INC., pg. 780
MYERS GROUP U.S., INC.—The Myers Group (U.S) Inc., pg. 780
NORTHLAND CONTAINER CORP., pg. 814
PROCOR LPG STORAGE DIVISION—The Marmon Group, Inc., pg. 712
RIVERSIDE CENTRAL SERVICES, INC., pg. 937
SECURITY VAN LINES, INC., pg. 987
TRUE COMPANIES, pg. 1117
NELSON WESTERBERG, INC., pg. 1178

4231 — TERMINAL & JOINT TERMINAL MAINTENANCE FACILITIES FOR MOTOR FREIGHT TRANSPORTATION

ARGO TERMINAL CO.—Great Lakes Terminal & Transport Corp., pg. 482
GREAT LAKES TERMINAL & TRANSPORT OF PENNSYLVANIA—Great Lakes Terminal & Transport Corp., pg. 482
THE JUPITER CORPORATION—Jupiter Industries, Inc., pg. 609
MILLER TRANSPORTERS, INC.—Dewey Corporation, pg. 334

4412 — DEEP SEA FREIGHT TRANSPORTATION-FOREIGN

AMERICAN TRADING TRANSPORTATION CO., INC.—American Trading and Production Corporation, pg. 65
FAIRFIELD MAXWELL LTD., pg. 397
FARRELL LINES INCORPORATED, pg. 403
LYKES BROS. STEAMSHIP CO., INC., pg. 688
LYKES LINES AGENCY, INC.—Lykes Bros. Steamship Co., Inc., pg. 689
MARINE TRANSPORT LINES, INC., pg. 707
MORMAC MARINE TRANSPORT, INC., pg. 770
F.W. MYERS & CO.—The Myers Group (U.S) Inc., pg. 780
THE MYERS GROUP (U.S) INC., pg. 780
MYERS GROUP U.S., INC.—The Myers Group (U.S) Inc., pg. 780
ZIM-AMERICAN ISRAELI SHIPPING CO., pg. 1219

4424 — DEEP SEA FREIGHT TRANSPORTATION-DOMESTIC

ALASKA MARINE LINES, INC.—Lynden Incorporated, pg. 689
AMERICAN TRADING TRANSPORTATION CO., INC.—American Trading and Production Corporation, pg. 65
CARGILL INC., pg. 219
CARGILL MARINE & TERMINAL—Cargill Inc., pg. 219
GUARDIAN TRANSPORTATION CORP.—Guardian Industries Corp., pg. 492
LYNDEN INCORPORATED, pg. 689
MARINE TRANSPORT LINES, INC., pg. 707
NATIONAL MARINE, INC.—Vectura Group, Inc., pg. 1146
TOTEM RESOURCES CORPORATION, pg. 1103

4449 — FREIGHT TRANSPORTATION-WATER, NEC

AMERICAN TRADING TRANSPORTATION CO., INC.—American Trading and Production Corporation, pg. 65
BRIX MARITIME BARGING, INC.—Brix Maritime Co., pg. 177
BRIX MARITIME CO., pg. 177
CARGILL INC., pg. 219
CARGILL MARINE & TERMINAL—Cargill Inc., pg. 219
CONTAINER PORT GROUP—World Shipping, Inc., pg. 1203
ERGON, INC., pg. 386
GARNAC GRAIN CO., INC.—Norfoods, Inc., pg. 810
INGRAM INDUSTRIES INC., pg. 568
TRANSAMMONIA INC., pg. 1106

4481 — PASSENGER TRANSPORTATION-DEEP SEA

COMMODORE CRUISE LINE, LTD., pg. 269
COSTA CRUISE LINES, N.V., pg. 288
NORWEGIAN CRUISE LINE, pg. 816
ROYAL CRUISE LINE INC., pg. 953
SPIRIT CRUISES, pg. 1031

4489 — WATER TRANSPORTATION-PASSENGER, NEC

DELTA QUEEN STEAMBOAT COMPANY—Equity Group Investments, pg. 385
INGRAM MATERIALS CO.—Ingram Industries Inc., pg. 569
WILLAMETTE-WESTERN CORPORATION, pg. 1190

4491 — MARINE CARGO HANDLING

BRIX MARITIME BARGING, INC.—Brix Maritime Co., pg. 177
BRIX MARITIME CO., pg. 177
CARGILL MARINE & TERMINAL—Cargill Inc., pg. 219
CHICAGO BOAT YARD, INC.—CFB Industries, Inc., pg. 201
CROWLEY MARITIME CORPORATION, pg. 301
FARRELL LINES INCORPORATED, pg. 403
LAN-CHILE AIRLINES, pg. 653
F.W. MYERS & CO.—The Myers Group (U.S) Inc., pg. 780
THE MYERS GROUP (U.S) INC., pg. 780
MYERS GROUP U.S., INC.—The Myers Group (U.S) Inc., pg. 780
PORT OF GALVESTON, pg. 881
STEVEDORING SERVICES OF AMERICA, pg. 1048
STRACHAN SHIPPING CO., pg. 1052
VECTURA GROUP, INC., pg. 1146
ZEPHYR INC., pg. 1217

4492 — TOWING & TUGBOAT SERVICES

BERING MARINE CORPORATION—Lynden Incorporated, pg. 689
BRIX MARITIME BARGING, INC.—Brix Maritime Co., pg. 177
BRIX MARITIME CO., pg. 177
BRIX MARITIME TOWING, INC.—Brix Maritime Co., pg. 177
CROWLEY MARITIME CORPORATION, pg. 301
THE GUTTMAN GROUP, pg. 495
HVIDE SHIPPING, INC., pg. 556
INGRAM BARGE COMPANY—Ingram Industries Inc., pg. 569
MORAN TOWING & TRANSPORATION CO. INC, pg. 769
VECTURA GROUP, INC., pg. 1146

4493 — MARINAS

AMERICAN BUREAU OF SHIPPING, pg. 50
AL LARSON BOAT SHOP, INC., pg. 659
PICK'S COVE MARINA—Pickering Industries Inc., pg. 870

4499 — WATER TRANSPORTATION SERVICES, NEC

AMERICAN BUREAU OF SHIPPING, pg. 50
BERWICK BAY OIL CO. INC., pg. 144
CROSBY & OVERTON, INC., pg. 300
FUGRO-MCCLELLAND, INC., pg. 435
MTI LEASING, LTD.—Marine Travelift, Inc., pg. 707
MORAN TOWING & TRANSPORATION CO. INC, pg. 769

4512 — AIR TRANSPORTATION, SCHEDULED

ATC AIR, INC.—American Tool Companies, Inc., pg. 64
AERO PERU CORPORATION, pg. 22
AEROPERU—Aero Peru Corporation, pg. 22
AIR JAMAICA LTD., pg. 27
ALOHA AIRGROUP, INC., pg. 43
ALOHA AIRLINES, INC.—Aloha Airgroup, Inc., pg. 43
ALOHA ISLANDAIR—Aloha Airgroup, Inc., pg. 43
AMERICAN EAGLE AIRLINES, pg. 51
AMERICAN TRANS AIR EXECUJET, INC.—Amtran, Inc., pg. 70
AMERICAN TRANS AIR, INC.—Amtran, Inc., pg. 70
AMTRAN, INC., pg. 69
AUSTRIAN AIRLINES, pg. 100
EMPIRE AIRLINES, pg. 379
EVERGREEN INTERNATIONAL AVIATION, INC., pg. 392
HEILEMAN AIR SERVICES, LTD.—G. Heileman Brewing Co., Inc., pg. 526
G. HEILEMAN BREWING CO., INC., pg. 526
HYATT AIR, INC.—H. Group Holding Inc., pg. 495
ICELANDAIR, pg. 561
LAN-CHILE AIRLINES, pg. 653
MARKAIR EXPRESS—Markair, Inc., pg. 708
MARKAIR, INC., pg. 708
MICHAEL, BOLGER, REINSCHMIEDT, KING (MBRK), pg. 746
F.W. MYERS & CO.—The Myers Group (U.S) Inc., pg. 780
THE MYERS GROUP (U.S) INC., pg. 780
MYERS GROUP U.S., INC.—The Myers Group (U.S) Inc., pg. 780
NWA, INC., pg. 782
NORTHWEST AIRLINES, INC.—NWA, Inc., pg. 782
PORTS OF CALL, INC.—Amtran, Inc., pg. 70
REEVE ALEUTIAN AIRWAYS, INC., pg. 921
ROYAL CRUISE LINE INC., pg. 953
SEKO-AIR FREIGHT, pg. 988
TACA INTERNATIONAL AIRLINES, S. A., pg. 1076
TRANS WORLD AIRLINES, INC.—Icahn & Co., Inc., pg. 561
UPS/ALIMONDO—United Parcel Service of America, Inc., pg. 1133
THE USAIR SHUTTLE—Trump Organization, pg. 1118
WESTAIR HOLDING INC., pg. 1178

4513 — AIR COURIER SERVICES

CITY POSTAL, INC., pg. 251
DHL AIRWAYS, INC.—DHL Corporation, pg. 309
DHL CORPORATION, pg. 309
DHL HANDLING MEXICANA, S.A. DE C.V.—DHL Corporation, pg. 309
DHL INTERNATIONAL AB—DHL Corporation, pg. 309
DHL INTERNATIONAL BV—DHL Corporation, pg. 309
DHL INTERNATIONAL COURIER SERVICE GMBH—DHL Corporation, pg. 309
DHL INTERNATIONAL EXPRESS LTD.—DHL Corporation, pg. 309
DHL INTERNATIONAL (HONG KONG) LTD.—DHL Corporation, pg. 309
DHL INTERNATIONAL N.V.—DHL Corporation, pg. 309
DHL INTERNATIONAL S.A.—DHL Corporation, pg. 309
DHL INTERNATIONAL (U.K.) LTD.—DHL Corporation, pg. 309
HEILEMAN AIR SERVICES, LTD.—G. Heileman Brewing Co., Inc., pg. 526
KOA HOLDINGS, pg. 612
MID PACIFIC AIR—KOA Holdings, pg. 613
MID PACIFIC AIR CORPORATION—KOA Holdings, pg. 613
PILOT AIR FREIGHT CORP., pg. 870
PONY EXPRESS COURIER CORP.—Borg-Warner Corporation, pg. 166
SEKO-AIR FREIGHT, pg. 988
SKYWAY FREIGHT SYSTEMS, INC., pg. 1009
SONICAIR, pg. 1018
UPS/ALIMONDO—United Parcel Service of America, Inc., pg. 1133
UNITED PARCEL SERVICE OF AMERICA, INC., pg. 1133
UNITED PARCEL SERVICE OF CANADA—United Parcel Service of America, Inc., pg. 1133

4522 — AIR TRANSPORTATION, NON-SCHEDULED

ATLANTIC AVIATION CORP., pg. 94
CARIBE EXPRESS, pg. 220
CUTTER FLYING SERVICE, INC., pg. 307
EVERGREEN INTERNATIONAL AVIATION, INC., pg. 392
EXECUTIVE JET AVIATION, INC., pg. 393
ICELANDAIR, pg. 561
OMNI FLIGHT HELICOPTERS, INC., pg. 826
OMNIFLIGHT HELICOPTERS, INC.—Omniflight, Inc., pg. 826
OMNIFLIGHT, INC., pg. 826
PORTS OF CALL, INC.—Amtran, Inc., pg. 70
RALEIGH ENTERPRISES, INC., pg. 910
ZANTOP INTERNATIONAL AIRLINES, INC., pg. 1216

4581 — AIRPORTS, FLYING FIELDS & AIRPORT TERMINAL SERVICES

ALOHA AIRLINES, INC.—Aloha Airgroup, Inc., pg. 43
AVIATION PRODUCT SUPPORT INC.—Kleco Corp., pg. 635
CUTTER FLYING SERVICE, INC., pg. 307
DALFORT CORP., pg. 312
EVERGREEN INTERNATIONAL AVIATION, INC., pg. 392
GREENWICH AIR SERVICES, pg. 485
HAWTHORNE AIRPORT SERVICES, INC.—Hawthorne Corp., pg. 519
HAWTHORNE AVIATION—Hawthorne Corp., pg. 519
HAWTHORNE CORP., pg. 518
HAWTHORNE SERVICES, INC.—Hawthorne Corp., pg. 519
NORTHWEST AEROSPACE TRAINING CORPORATION—NWA, Inc., pg. 782
NORTHWEST AIRCRAFT INC.—NWA, Inc., pg. 782
PORT OF OAKLAND, pg. 881
PRINCEVILLE CORPORATION, pg. 890
STEVENS AVIATION, INC.—Farley Industries, pg. 400
ZANTOP AIRCRAFT MAINTENANCE FACILITY—Zantop International Airlines, Inc., pg. 1216
ZANTOP INTERNATIONAL AIRLINES, INC.—Zantop International Airlines, Inc., pg. 1216

4612 — CRUDE PETROLEUM PIPE LINES

BELLE FOURCHE PIPELINE CO.—True Companies, pg. 1117
CLEAR CREEK, INC.—National Cooperative Refinery Association, pg. 787
KOCH INDUSTRIES, INCORPORATED, pg. 639
TRUE COMPANIES, pg. 1117
VANGUARD ENERGY CORP., pg. 1145

4613 — REFINED PETROLEUM PIPE LINES

BELLE FOURCHE PIPELINE CO.—True Companies, pg. 1117
COLONIAL PIPELINE COMPANY, pg. 264
KOCH INDUSTRIES, INCORPORATED, pg. 639
TRUE COMPANIES, pg. 1117

4724 — TRAVEL AGENCIES

ADVENTURE TOURS USA, INC., pg. 21
ALL WORLD TRAVEL SERVICE, INC.—The Elder-Beerman Stores Corp., pg. 373
AMBASSADAIR TRAVEL CLUB, INC.—Amtran, Inc., pg. 69
AMBER TRAVEL, INC.—Amtran, Inc., pg. 70
APPLE VACATIONS WEST INC., pg. 79
ARRINGTON TRAVEL CENTER INC., pg. 85
ASBURY PARK PRESS, INC.—New Jersey Press, Inc., pg. 801
CARLSON COMPANIES, INC., pg. 220
CARLSON TRAVEL GROUP, INC.—Carlson Companies, Inc., pg. 221
CARLSON TRAVEL NETWORK INTERNATIONAL—Carlson Companies, Inc., pg. 221

CARLSON TRAVEL NETWORK RETAIL—Carlson Companies, Inc., pg. 221
CARLSON TRAVEL NETWORK-COMMERCIAL—Carlson Companies, Inc., pg. 221
CARLSON TRAVEL NETWORK-RETAIL—Carlson Companies, Inc., pg. 221
COLUMBIAN PHILIPPINES INC.—Columbian Rope Company, pg. 266
CORPORATE TRAVEL SERVICES, pg. 287
ENCORE MARKETING INTERNATIONAL, pg. 380
FRANK CONSOLIDATED ENTERPRISES INC., pg. 428
FRIENDLY HOLIDAYS INC., pg. 433
FUGAZY INTERNATIONAL CORPORATION, pg. 435
FUGAZY TRAVEL—Fugazy International Corporation, pg. 435
GENERAL TRAVEL SERVICES, INC.—Washington Mutual Savings Bank, pg. 1166
THE GETZ CORPORATION—The Marmon Group, Inc., pg. 712
HAWAIIAN DISCOVERY TOURS, INC.—JMB Realty Corporation, pg. 585
HOLIDAY HOUSE, INC.—Washington Mutual Savings Bank, pg. 1166
IVI TRAVEL—Frank Consolidated Enterprises Inc., pg. 428
KAWAGUCHI TRAVEL SERVICES, INC.—Washington Mutual Savings Bank, pg. 1166
KUONI TRAVEL, INC., pg. 646
P. LAWSON TRAVEL, LTD.—Carlson Companies, Inc., pg. 221
MARITZ TRAVEL CO.—Maritz Inc., pg. 708
MUTUAL TRAVEL, INC.—Washington Mutual Savings Bank, pg. 1166
NEW JERSEY PRESS, INC., pg. 801
OLSON-TRAVELWORLD LTD., pg. 824
OMEGA WORLD TRAVEL, INC., pg. 826
PROFESSIONAL TRAVEL, INC., pg. 894
PROFESSIONAL TRAVEL INC.—Professional Travel, Inc., pg. 894
RCI TRAVEL—Resort Condominiums International, pg. 929
ROYAL CRUISE LINE INC., pg. 953
SIGNATURE TRAVEL, INC.—Washington Mutual Savings Bank, pg. 1166
TRANS NATIONAL TRAVEL, pg. 1106
YOUR MAN TOURS, INC., pg. 1214

4725 — TOUR OPERATORS

AMBER TOURS, INC.—Amtran, Inc., pg. 69
CARLSON COMPANIES, INC., pg. 220
1ST FAMILY TRAVELERS HAWAII, pg. 412
GLOBUS-GATEWAY/COSMOS TOURAMA, pg. 464
JAPAN TRAVEL BUREAU INTERNATIONAL, INC., pg. 590
KENTUCKY DEPARTMENT OF TRAVEL DEVELOPMENT, pg. 623
MTI VACATIONS, INC., pg. 694
MARITZ TRAVEL CO.—Maritz Inc., pg. 708
MUNSEN'S DISCOVERY ENTERPRISES, pg. 776
ROYAL CARIBBEAN CRUISES LTD., pg. 953
TRADE WIND TOURS—1st Family Travelers Hawaii, pg. 413
TRASE-MILLER—MTI Vacations, Inc., pg. 694

4729 — ARRANGEMENT OF PASSENGER TRANSPORTATION, NEC

BOLLIGER, INC., pg. 163
BUSINESS TRAVEL MANAGEMENT, INC.—Mary Kay Corporation, pg. 717
CENTRAL PARKING CORP., pg. 234
CENTRAL PARKING CORP.—Central Parking Corp., pg. 234
ECUATORIANA AIRLINES, pg. 367
FORT MORGAN COMMUNITY HOSPITAL—Brim, Inc., pg. 176
GENERAL HOSPITAL—Brim, Inc., pg. 176
MARITZ INC., pg. 707
SPIRIT CRUISES, pg. 1031
WORLD SHIPPING, INC., pg. 1203

4731 — ARRANGEMENT OF TRANSPORTATION OF FREIGHT & CARGO

AJC INTERNATIONAL, INC., pg. 4
ALBA FORWARDING CO., INC., pg. 30
ALBA FORWARDING CO., INC.—Alba Forwarding Co., Inc., pg. 30
ALBA FORWARDING CO., INC.—Alba Forwarding Co., Inc., pg. 30
AMERICAN RED BALL INTERNATIONAL, INC.—Red Ball Corporation, pg. 918
ASSOCIATED AIR FREIGHT, INC., pg. 89
THE BEKINS COMPANY, pg. 132
BOAT TRANSIT, INC.—Jupiter Industries, Inc., pg. 609
BOLLIGER, INC., pg. 163
CHATHAM TOWING COMPANY, INC.—Colonial Oil Industries, pg. 264
CLIPPER EXXPRESS CO., pg. 256
COLONIAL MARINE INDUSTRIES, INC.—Colonial Oil Industries, pg. 264
CONTRAN CORPORATION, pg. 281
CREST-MAYFLOWER INTERNATIONAL, INC.—Mayflower Transit, Inc., pg. 725
A.N. DERINGER, INC., pg. 331
FAIRFIELD MAXWELL LTD., pg. 397
FARRELL LINES INCORPORATED, pg. 403
FRITZ COMPANIES, INC., pg. 434
GATOR FREIGHTWAYS, INC., pg. 446
LYNDEN AIR FREIGHT, INC.—Lynden Incorporated, pg. 689
LYNDEN FORWARDING, INC.—Lynden Incorporated, pg. 689
MANUFACTURERS CONSOLIDATION SERVICE, pg. 705
MARTRADE LTD., pg. 716
MOUNTAIN AIR DELIVERY, pg. 773
F.W. MYERS & CO.—The Myers Group (U.S) Inc., pg. 780
THE MYERS GROUP (U.S) INC., pg. 780
MYERS GROUP U.S., INC.—The Myers Group (U.S) Inc., pg. 780
PERDUE TRANSPORTATION INC.—Perdue Farms Inc., pg. 860
RED BALL FORWARDERS, INC.—Red Ball Corporation, pg. 918
C. H. ROBINSON CO. INC., pg. 939
SAINT MARYS RAILROAD CO.—Gilman Paper Co., pg. 459
SECURITY VAN LINES, INC., pg. 987
STEUART INVESTMENT CO., pg. 1048
STEUART TRANSPORTATION CO.—Steuart Investment Co., pg. 1048
SUPERIOR FAST FREIGHT, pg. 1063
WORLD SHIPPING, INC., pg. 1203
YOSEMITE EXPRESS CO.—Save Mart Supermarkets, pg. 973
DANIEL F. YOUNG, INC., pg. 1209

4741 — RENTAL OF RAILROAD CARS

ACF INDUSTRIES, INC.—Icahn & Co., Inc., pg. 561
DUCHOSSOIS INDUSTRIES, INC., pg. 350
G L SUB COMPANY—The Marmon Group, Inc., pg. 712
LINCOLN INDUSTRIES, pg. 676
THE MARMON GROUP, INC., pg. 710
MARMON INDUSTRIAL CORPORATION—The Marmon Group, Inc., pg. 712
PACIFIC FRUIT EXPRESS CO.—Anschutz Corporation, pg. 75
SP TELCOM CORPORATION—Anschutz Corporation, pg. 75
TTX CO., pg. 1075
UNION TANK CAR COMPANY—The Marmon Group, Inc., pg. 712

4783 — PACKING & CRATING

CALAVO GROWERS OF CALIFORNIA, pg. 208
SUNMAC HAWAII, LTD.—Sunkist Growers, Inc., pg. 1061

4785 — INSPECTION & WEIGHING SERVICES FOR MOTOR VEHICLE TRANSPORTATION

GOODKIND & O'DEA, INC.—Dewberry & Davis, pg. 334
TRIBOROUGH BRIDGE & TUNNEL AUTHORITY—Metropolitan Transportation Authority, pg. 745

4789 — TRANSPORTATION SERVICES, NEC

ARKANSAS & MEMPHIS RAILWAY BRIDGE AND TERMINAL CO.—Anschutz Corporation, pg. 76
LOUISVILLE SCRAP MATERIAL CO., INC., pg. 684
MLT VACATIONS, INC.—NWA, Inc., pg. 782
MARIANA CORPORATION—Gohmann Asphalt & Construction Inc., pg. 465
THE OGDEN UNION RAILWAY AND DEPOT CO.—Anschutz Corporation, pg. 76
RIVERTON TRUCKERS, INC.—Gohmann Asphalt & Construction Inc., pg. 465
SAUNDERS INCORPORATED, pg. 972
SOUTHERN ILLINOIS AND MISSOURI BRIDGE CO.—Anschutz Corporation, pg. 76
TRANSCO INC., pg. 1106

4812 — RADIO TELEPHONE COMMUNICATIONS

CELLULAR SERVICE, INC., pg. 231
COMMUNICATIONS INTERNATIONAL, pg. 269
EATEL CORPORATION, pg. 364

4813 — TELEPHONE COMMUNICATIONS, EXCEPT RADIO TELEPHONE

AERONAUTICAL RADIO, INC.—Arinc Inc., pg. 82
AMANA SOCIETY SERVICE CO.—Amana Society, pg. 46
AMWAY CORPORATION, pg. 70
ATCOM, INC., pg. 93
BTG, INC., pg. 107
COMARK, INC.—Cenvill Development Corp., pg. 236
FARMERS TELEPHONE CO-OP, pg. 402
ILLINOIS CONSOLIDATED TELEPHONE CO., pg. 563
METROMEDIA COMMUNICATION CORP.—Metromedia Company, pg. 744
ROTTERDAM VENTURES INC., pg. 951

4822 — TELEGRAPH & OTHER MESSAGE COMMUNICATIONS

BELL & HOWELL GMBH—Bell & Howell Company, pg. 135
BELL & HOWELL LTD., (UK) MAILHANDLING DIV.—Bell & Howell Company, pg. 135
COMMUNICATIONS INTERNATIONAL, pg. 269
SOVEREIGN GROUP INC., pg. 1024

4832 — RADIO BROADCASTING STATIONS

AGRINET FARM RADIO NETWORK—Ray Communications, Inc., pg. 914
BONNEVILLE INTERNATIONAL CORP.—Deseret Management Corporation, pg. 332
BOOTH AMERICAN, pg. 165
BROADCAST DIVISION—Cox Enterprises, Inc., pg. 292
CALIFORNIA ANGELS BASEBALL CLUB—Golden West Broadcasters, pg. 467
CAPITOL BROADCASTING CO., INC., pg. 215
COX ENTERPRISES, INC., pg. 292
CROWN MEDIA INC.—Hallmark Cards, Inc., pg. 502
CURTIS MEDIA GROUP INC., pg. 305
DONREY MEDIA GROUP, pg. 345
FISHER BROADCASTING, INC.—Fisher Companies, Inc., pg. 415
FORUM PUBLISHING COMPANY, pg. 426
FREEDOM NEWSPAPERS INC., pg. 431
GACC HOLDING COMPANY—American Financial Corporation, pg. 53
GAF BROADCASTING CO., INC.—GAF Corporation, pg. 438
GAF CORPORATION, pg. 438
GAYLORD BROADCASTING CO.—Gaylord Entertainment Co., pg. 446
GOLDEN WEST BROADCASTERS, pg. 467
GREAT AMERICAN BROADCASTING COMPANY—American Financial Corporation, pg. 53
GREAT AMERICAN BROADCASTING COMPANY—American Financial Corporation, pg. 52
GREAT AMERICAN TELEVISION & RADIO COMPANY, INC.—American Financial Corporation, pg. 53
GREEN CONSTRUCTION OF INDIANA, INC., pg. 484
GUARANTY CORPORATION, pg. 491
HARRIS ENTERPRISES INC., pg. 511
HEARST BROADCASTING DIVISION—The Hearst Corporation, pg. 522
THE HEARST CORPORATION, pg. 521
HUBBARD BROADCASTING, INC., pg. 548
INFINITY BROADCASTING CORPORATION, pg. 567
JOHNSON PUBLISHING COMPANY, INC., pg. 598
JOURNAL COMMUNICATIONS INC., pg. 607
KEZ—Media America Corp., pg. 734
KFI, INC.—Cox Enterprises, Inc., pg. 292
KGFF-AM—Stauffer Communications, Inc., pg. 1043
KGNC-AM & FM—Stauffer Communications, Inc., pg. 1043
KIKK AM/FM—National Amusements, Inc., pg. 785
KIKK-FM TOWER CORP.—National Amusements, Inc., pg. 785
KSL RADIO—Deseret Management Corporation, pg. 332
KSTP-AM, INC.—Hubbard Broadcasting, Inc., pg. 549
KSTP-FM, INC.—Hubbard Broadcasting, Inc., pg. 549
KANSAS AGRICULTURE NETWORK—Stauffer Communications, Inc., pg. 1043
KANSAS CITY ROYALS RADIO NETWORK—Stauffer Communications, Inc., pg. 1043
KANSAS INFORMATION NETWORK—Stauffer Communications, Inc., pg. 1043
LANDMARK COMMUNICATIONS, INC., pg. 654
LANE INDUSTRIES, INC., pg. 656
MEDIA AMERICA CORP., pg. 734
MEYER BROADCASTING COMPANY, pg. 746
MORRIS NEWSPAPER CORPORATION, pg. 771
NATIONAL AMUSEMENTS, INC., pg. 784
92 Q WERQ AM/FM—United Broadcasting Inc., pg. 1131
OKLAHOMA PUBLISHING COMPANY—Gaylord Entertainment Co., pg. 446
RADIO INDIANAPOLIS, INC.—Susquehanna Pfaltzgraff, pg. 1065
RADIO METROPLEX INC.—Susquehanna Pfaltzgraff, pg. 1065
RAY COMMUNICATIONS, INC., pg. 914
RAY SPORTS NETWORK—Ray Communications, Inc., pg. 914
READING EAGLE COMPANY, pg. 916
RICH PRODUCTS CORP., pg. 932
SCHURZ COMMUNICATIONS, INC., pg. 979
SHAMROCK BROADCASTING, INC.—Shamrock Holdings, Inc., pg. 994
STAUFFER COMMUNICATIONS, INC., pg. 1042
SUMMIT COMMUNICATIONS, INC., pg. 1057
SUSQUEHANNA PFALTZGRAFF, pg. 1065
SUSQUEHANNA RADIO CORP.—Susquehanna Pfaltzgraff, pg. 1065
SARKES TARZIAN, INCORPORATED, pg. 1079
UNITED BROADCASTING INC., pg. 1131
VIACOM BROADCASTING INC.—National Amusements, Inc., pg. 785
VIACOM ENTERPRISES CANADA LTD.—National Amusements, Inc., pg. 785
VIACOM INC.—National Amusements, Inc., pg. 785
VIACOM INTERNATIONAL INC.—National Amusements, Inc., pg. 785
VIACOM INTL. LTD.—National Amusements, Inc., pg. 785
VIACOM INTL. PTY. LTD.—National Amusements, Inc., pg. 786
VIACOM JAPAN, INC.—National Amusements, Inc., pg. 786
VIACOM S.A.—National Amusements, Inc., pg. 786
VIACOM VIDEO-AUDIO COMUNICACOES, LTDA.—National Amusements, Inc., pg. 786
WARM BROADCASTING CO.—Susquehanna Pfaltzgraff, pg. 1065
WBAL-AM—The Hearst Corporation, pg. 522
WBAL DIVISION—The Hearst Corporation, pg. 522
WBBB—Curtis Media Group Inc., pg. 306
WCKG, INC.—Cox Enterprises, Inc., pg. 292
WCPS—Curtis Media Group Inc., pg. 306
WEWO—Curtis Media Group Inc., pg. 306
WGBR—Curtis Media Group Inc., pg. 306
WHIO, INC.—Cox Enterprises, Inc., pg. 292
WHTX-FM—The Hearst Corporation, pg. 522
WIBW-TV AM & FM—Stauffer Communications, Inc., pg. 1043
WIFC-FM—Journal Communications Inc., pg. 608
WIOD, INC.—Cox Enterprises, Inc., pg. 292
WISN-AM—The Hearst Corporation, pg. 522
WISN DIVISION—The Hearst Corporation, pg. 522
WIYY-FM—The Hearst Corporation, pg. 522
WKTC—Curtis Media Group Inc., pg. 306

S.I.C. Index

WLTQ-FM—The Hearst Corporation, pg. 522
WLTY-FM—Landmark Communications, Inc., pg. 655
WMXF AM/FM—Curtis Media Group Inc., pg. 306
WPCM—Curtis Media Group Inc., pg. 306
WPTF—Curtis Media Group Inc., pg. 306
WQDR—Curtis Media Group Inc., pg. 306
WSAU-AM—Journal Communications Inc., pg. 608
WSB, INC.—Cox Enterprises, Inc., pg. 292
WSB, INC. D/B/A KLRX (FM)—Cox Enterprises, Inc., pg. 292
WSBA AM/FM—Susquehanna Pfaltzgraff, pg. 1065
WSOC RADIO, INC.—Cox Enterprises, Inc., pg. 293
WTAB—Curtis Media Group Inc., pg. 306
WTAE-AM—The Hearst Corporation, pg. 522
WTAE DIVISION—The Hearst Corporation, pg. 522
WTAR-AM—Landmark Communications, Inc., pg. 655
WTMJ, INC.—Journal Communications Inc., pg. 608
WWRM, INC.—Cox Enterprises, Inc., pg. 293
WYNA—Curtis Media Group Inc., pg. 306
WEHCO MEDIA, INC., pg. 1172
WILDCAT SPORTS NETWORK—Stauffer Communications, Inc., pg. 1043

4833 — TELEVISION BROADCASTING STATIONS

ALLBRITTON COMMUNICATIONS COMPANY—Perpetual Corporation, pg. 862
BLADE COMMUNICATIONS, INC., pg. 155
BONNEVILLE INTERNATIONAL CORP.—Deseret Management Corporation, pg. 332
BROADCAST DIVISION—Cox Enterprises, Inc., pg. 292
BROADCASTERS OF MISSISSIPPI, INC.—News-Press & Gazette Company, pg. 804
BURNHAM BROADCASTING COMPANY, pg. 193
CAPITOL BROADCASTING CO., INC., pg. 215
COX ENTERPRISES, INC., pg. 292
DIVERSIFIED COMMUNICATIONS, pg. 340
DONREY MEDIA GROUP, pg. 345
F & F PRODUCTIONS, INC.—Hubbard Broadcasting, Inc., pg. 549
FISHER BROADCASTING, INC.—Fisher Companies, Inc., pg. 415
FISHER COMPANIES, INC., pg. 414
FORUM PUBLISHING COMPANY, pg. 426
FREEDOM NEWSPAPERS INC., pg. 431
GACC HOLDING COMPANY—American Financial Corporation, pg. 53
GAYLORD BROADCASTING CO.—Gaylord Entertainment Co., pg. 446
GAYLORD ENTERTAINMENT CO., pg. 446
GAZETTE COMPANY, INC., pg. 447
GEORGIA TELEVISION COMPANY—Cox Enterprises, Inc., pg. 292
GILLETT BROADCASTING OF MARYLAND, INC. WMAR-TV—Gillett Holdings, Inc., pg. 459
GILLETT HOLDINGS, INC., pg. 458
GREAT AMERICAN BROADCASTING COMPANY—American Financial Corporation, pg. 53
GREAT AMERICAN BROADCASTING COMPANY—American Financial Corporation, pg. 52
GREAT AMERICAN TELEVISION & RADIO COMPANY, INC.—American Financial Corporation, pg. 53
HARTE-HANKS COMMUNICATIONS, INC., pg. 513
HARTE-HANKS TELEVISION, INC. (KENS-TV)—Harte-Hanks Communications, Inc., pg. 513
HEARST BROADCASTING DIVISION—The Hearst Corporation, pg. 522
THE HEARST CORPORATION, pg. 521
HIGHWOOD SERVICE, INC.—Ralph C. Wilson Enterprises, pg. 1194
HUBBARD BROADCASTING, INC., pg. 548
JOHNSON PUBLISHING COMPANY, INC., pg. 598
JOURNAL COMMUNICATIONS INC., pg. 607
KATV TELEVISION, INC.—Perpetual Corporation, pg. 862
KBAK-TV—Burnham Broadcasting Company, pg. 194
KCOY-TV—Stauffer Communications, Inc., pg. 1043
KGWC-TV—Stauffer Communications, Inc., pg. 1043
KGWN-TV—Stauffer Communications, Inc., pg. 1043
KHON-TV—Burnham Broadcasting Company, pg. 194
KLAS-TV—Landmark Communications, Inc., pg. 654
KMBC DIVISION—The Hearst Corporation, pg. 522
KMBC-TV—The Hearst Corporation, pg. 522
KMIZ-TV—Stauffer Communications, Inc., pg. 1043
KOB-TV, INC.—Hubbard Broadcasting, Inc., pg. 549
KSBW, INC.—Gillett Holdings, Inc., pg. 459
KSBY, INC.—Gillett Holdings, Inc., pg. 459
KSFY-TV—News-Press & Gazette Company, pg. 805
KSL-TV—Deseret Management Corporation, pg. 332
KSNC—SJL of Kansas Corp., pg. 963
KSNG—SJL of Kansas Corp., pg. 963
KSNK—SJL of Kansas Corp., pg. 963
KSNT—SJL of Kansas Corp., pg. 963
KSTF-TV—Stauffer Communications, Inc., pg. 1043
KSTP-TV—Hubbard Broadcasting, Inc., pg. 549
KTUL TELEVISION, INC.—Perpetual Corporation, pg. 862
KTVS-TV—Stauffer Communications, Inc., pg. 1043
KOLD-TV—News-Press & Gazette Company, pg. 805
KTVU INC.—Cox Enterprises, Inc., pg. 292
LANDMARK COMMUNICATIONS, INC., pg. 654
MTV NETWORKS—National Amusements, Inc., pg. 785
MACROMEDIA INC., pg. 698
MEDIA AMERICA CORP., pg. 734
MEYER BROADCASTING COMPANY, pg. 746
MIAMI VALLEY BROADCASTING CORPORATION, D/B/A WHIO-TV—Cox Enterprises, Inc., pg. 292
MORRIS NEWSPAPER CORPORATION, pg. 771
NPG OF ARIZONA, INC.—News-Press & Gazette Company, pg. 805
NARRAGANSETT CAPITAL INC., pg. 783
NATIONAL AMUSEMENTS, INC., pg. 784
NEWS-PRESS & GAZETTE COMPANY, pg. 804
OKLAHOMA PUBLISHING COMPANY—Gaylord Entertainment Co., pg. 446
PERPETUAL CORPORATION, pg. 862
PROVIDENCE JOURNAL COMPANY, pg. 895
SDTV, INC.—News-Press & Gazette Company, pg. 804
SJL OF KANSAS CORP., pg. 962
SCHURZ COMMUNICATIONS, INC., pg. 979
SHAMROCK BROADCASTING, INC.—Shamrock Holdings, Inc., pg. 994
SIOUX VALLEY RURAL TELEVISION—Sioux Valley Empire Electric Association, pg. 1009
SPECTRADYNE INC.—Davis Companies, pg. 318
STANDARD CORPORATION, pg. 1036
STAUFFER COMMUNICATIONS, INC., pg. 1042
SARKES TARZIAN, INCORPORATED, pg. 1079
TOPEKA TELEVISION, CORP.—SJL of Kansas Corp., pg. 963
USA NETWORK CONTROL CENTER—USA Network, pg. 1124
USA NETWORK, pg. 1124
UNIVISION HOLDINGS, INC.—Hallmark Cards, Inc., pg. 502
VIACOM ENTERPRISES CANADA LTD.—National Amusements, Inc., pg. 785
VIACOM INC.—National Amusements, Inc., pg. 785
VIACOM INTERNATIONAL INC.—National Amusements, Inc., pg. 785
VIACOM INTL. LTD.—National Amusements, Inc., pg. 785
VIACOM INTL. PTY. LTD.—National Amusements, Inc., pg. 786
VIACOM JAPAN, INC.—National Amusements, Inc., pg. 786
VIACOM S.A.—National Amusements, Inc., pg. 786
VIACOM VIDEO-AUDIO COMUNICACOES, LTDA.—National Amusements, Inc., pg. 786
WALA-TV—Burnham Broadcasting Company, pg. 194
WBAL DIVISION—The Hearst Corporation, pg. 522
WBAL-TV—The Hearst Corporation, pg. 522
WCVB DIVISION—The Hearst Corporation, pg. 522
WCVB-TV—The Hearst Corporation, pg. 522
WDIO-TV—Hubbard Broadcasting, Inc., pg. 549
WDTN-TV—The Hearst Corporation, pg. 522
WDTN DIV.—The Hearst Corporation, pg. 522
WFTV, INC.—Cox Enterprises, Inc., pg. 292
WHLT—News-Press & Gazette Company, pg. 804
WIBW-TV AM & FM—Stauffer Communications, Inc., pg. 1043
WISN-AM—The Hearst Corporation, pg. 522
WISN DIVISION—The Hearst Corporation, pg. 522
WISN-TV—The Hearst Corporation, pg. 522
WJLA-TV—Perpetual Corporation, pg. 862
WJTV—News-Press & Gazette Company, pg. 804
WKBD, INC.—Cox Enterprises, Inc., pg. 292
WLUC, INC.—Gillett Holdings, Inc., pg. 459
WLUK-TV—Burnham Broadcasting Company, pg. 194
WPRI-TV—Narragansett Capital Inc., pg. 783
WPXI INC., D/B/A WPXI-TV—Cox Enterprises, Inc., pg. 292
WSOC TELEVISION, INC.—Cox Enterprises, Inc., pg. 293
WSYM-TV—Journal Communications Inc., pg. 608
WTAE DIVISION—The Hearst Corporation, pg. 522
WTAE-TV—The Hearst Corporation, pg. 523
WTKR-TV—Narragansett Capital Inc., pg. 783
WTMJ, INC.—Journal Communications Inc., pg. 608
WTOG-TV, INC.—Hubbard Broadcasting, Inc., pg. 549
WTTW (CHANNEL 11), pg. 1156
WVUE-TV—Burnham Broadcasting Company, pg. 194
WEHCO MEDIA, INC., pg. 1172
RALPH C. WILSON ENTERPRISES, pg. 1194

4841 — CABLE & OTHER PAY TELEVISION SERVICES

BLADE COMMUNICATIONS, INC., pg. 155
CABLEVISION INDUSTRIES CORP., pg. 206
CAPITOL BROADCASTING CO., INC., pg. 215
CASCO CABLE TELEVISION INC.—Susquehanna Pfaltzgraff, pg. 1065
CENCOM CABLE TELEVISION—Gaylord Entertainment Co., pg. 446
CONTINENTAL CABLEVISION, pg. 278
CONWAY CORPORATION, pg. 281
COX CABLE BAKERSFIELD, INC.—Cox Enterprises, Inc., pg. 294
COX CABLE CEDAR RAPIDS, INC.—Cox Enterprises, Inc., pg. 294
COX CABLE CLEVELAND AREA, INC.—Cox Enterprises, Inc., pg. 294
COX CABLE GREATER HARTFORD, INC.—Cox Enterprises, Inc., pg. 294
COX CABLE GREATER OCALA, INC.—Cox Enterprises, Inc., pg. 294
COX CABLE HAMPTON ROADS, INC.—Cox Enterprises, Inc., pg. 294
COX CABLE HUMBOLDT, INC.—Cox Enterprises, Inc., pg. 294
COX CABLE JEFFERSON PARISH, INC.—Cox Enterprises, Inc., pg. 294
COX CABLE LUBBOCK, INC.—Cox Enterprises, Inc., pg. 294
COX CABLE MIDDLE GEORGIA, INC.—Cox Enterprises, Inc., pg. 294
COX CABLE NEW ORLEANS, INC.—Cox Enterprises, Inc., pg. 294
COX CABLE OKLAHOMA CITY, INC.—Cox Enterprises, Inc., pg. 294
COX CABLE OMAHA, INC.—Cox Enterprises, Inc., pg. 294
COX CABLE PENSACOLA, INC.—Cox Enterprises, Inc., pg. 294
COX CABLE QUAD CITIES, INC.—Cox Enterprises, Inc., pg. 294
COX CABLE RHODE ISLAND, INC.—Cox Enterprises, Inc., pg. 294
COX CABLE ROANOKE, INC.—Cox Enterprises, Inc., pg. 294
COX CABLE SAGINAW, INC.—Cox Enterprises, Inc., pg. 294
COX CABLE SAN DIEGO, INC.—Cox Enterprises, Inc., pg. 294
COX CABLE SANTA BARBARA, INC.—Cox Enterprises, Inc., pg. 294
COX CABLE SOUTH CAROLINA, INC.—Cox Enterprises, Inc., pg. 294
COX CABLE SPOKANE, INC.—Cox Enterprises, Inc., pg. 294
COX CABLE UNIVERSITY CITY, INC.—Cox Enterprises, Inc., pg. 294
COX ENTERPRISES, INC., pg. 292
CROWN CABLE INC.—Hallmark Cards, Inc., pg. 502
CROWN CRUISE LINE—Commodore Cruise Line, Ltd., pg. 269
CROWN MEDIA INC.—Hallmark Cards, Inc., pg. 502
DIVERSIFIED COMMUNICATIONS, pg. 340
GAYLORD ENTERTAINMENT CO., pg. 446
HEARST CABLEVISION OF CALIFORNIA, INC.—The Hearst Corporation, pg. 523
THE HEARST CORPORATION, pg. 521
HIGH INDUSTRIES INC., pg. 533
JONES INTERCABLE, INC.—Jones International Ltd., pg. 604
JONES INTERNATIONAL LTD., pg. 603
JONES SPACELINK, LTD.—Jones International Ltd., pg. 603
LANDMARK COMMUNICATIONS, INC., pg. 654
LIFETIME TELEVISION—The Hearst Corporation, pg. 523
MICROBAND COMPANIES, INC., pg. 748
NATIONAL AMUSEMENTS, INC., pg. 784
NICKELODEON/NICK AT NITE—National Amusements, Inc., pg. 785
PHOENIX CABLE INCORPORATED—Phoenix American Incorporated, pg. 868
SAMMONS COMMUNICATIONS, INC.—Sammons Enterprises, Inc., pg. 968
SCHURZ COMMUNICATIONS, INC., pg. 979
SPECTRADYNE INC.—Davis Companies, pg. 318
SUMMIT COMMUNICATIONS, INC., pg. 1057
SUSQUEHANNA PFALTZGRAFF, pg. 1065
THE TRAVEL CHANNEL—Landmark Communications, Inc., pg. 654
VH-1/VIDEO HITS ONE—National Amusements, Inc., pg. 785
VIACOM CABLE—National Amusements, Inc., pg. 785
VIACOM CANADA LTD.—National Amusements, Inc., pg. 785
VIACOM ENTERPRISES CANADA LTD.—National Amusements, Inc., pg. 785
VIACOM INTERNATIONAL INC.—National Amusements, Inc., pg. 785
VIACOM INTL. LTD.—National Amusements, Inc., pg. 785
VIACOM INTL. PTY. LTD.—National Amusements, Inc., pg. 786
VIACOM JAPAN, INC.—National Amusements, Inc., pg. 786
VIACOM S.A.—National Amusements, Inc., pg. 786
VIACOM VIDEO-AUDIO COMUNICACOES, LTDA.—National Amusements, Inc., pg. 786
VIDEO SERVICE COMPANY—Cox Enterprises, Inc., pg. 294
THE WEATHER CHANNEL—Landmark Communications, Inc., pg. 654
WEHCO MEDIA, INC., pg. 1172
WEHCO VIDEO INC.—Wehco Media, Inc., pg. 1172

4899 — COMMUNICATION SERVICES, NEC

ALLNEWSCO, INC.—Perpetual Corporation, pg. 862
BOOTH AMERICAN, pg. 165
BOOZ ALLEN & HAMILTON INC., pg. 165
BROADCAST AND VIDEO ENTERPRISES DIV.—Landmark Communications, Inc., pg. 654
BUTLER FLEET MAINTENANCE SERVICES—Butler International, pg. 197
BUTLER INSTALLATION SERVICES, INC.—Butler International, pg. 197
BUTLER QUALITY SERVICES, INC.—Butler International, pg. 197
BUTLER TELECOMMUNICATIONS GROUP—Butler International, pg. 197
BUTLER TELECOMMUNICATIONS SERVICES—Butler International, pg. 197
BUTLER UTILITIES SERVICES, INC.—Butler International, pg. 197
CONUS COMMUNICATION COMPANY LIMITED PARTNERSHIP—Hubbard Broadcasting, Inc., pg. 549
COX CABLE STATEN ISLAND (PARTNERSHIP)—Cox Enterprises, Inc., pg. 294
HEARST ENTERTAINMENT & SYNDICATION—The Hearst Corporation, pg. 523
HENKELS & MCCOY, INC., pg. 529
IRVINE COMPANY, pg. 582
JOURNAL COMMUNICATIONS INC., pg. 607
MRC TELECOMMUNICATIONS INC.—Journal Communications Inc., pg. 607
NEWS-PRESS & GAZETTE COMPANY, pg. 804
NORLIGHT—Journal Communications Inc., pg. 607
QUINTRON SYSTEMS, INC., pg. 905
RAY SATELLITE NETWORK—Ray Communications, Inc., pg. 914
SJL OF KANSAS CORP., pg. 962
SAMMONS ENTERPRISES, INC., pg. 968
SHOWTIME SATELLITE NETWORKS, INC.—National Amusements, Inc., pg. 785
SHOWTIME/THE MOVIE CHANNEL INC. (U.K.)—National Amusements, Inc., pg. 785
SUMMIT COMMUNICATIONS, INC., pg. 1057
UNITED STATES SATELLITE BROADCASTING, INC.—Hubbard Broadcasting, Inc., pg. 549

VIACOM INC.—National Amusements, Inc., pg. 785
VIACOM NETWORKS INC.—National Amusements, Inc., pg. 785
VIACOM SATELLITE NETWORKS INC.—National Amusements, Inc., pg. 785

4911 — ELECTRIC SERVICES

AEC, pg. 3
AIKEN ELECTRIC COOPERATIVE INC., pg. 26
ALABAMA ELECTRIC COOPERATIVE, INC., pg. 28
AMANA SOCIETY SERVICE CO.—Amana Society, pg. 46
ASSOCIATED ELECTRIC CO-OP INC., pg. 89
BASIN ELECTRIC POWER CO-OP, pg. 125
BURNS & MCDONNELL ENGINEERS-ARCHITECTS-CONSULTANTS, pg. 194
CAJUN ELECTRIC POWER CO-OP, pg. 207
CATALYST ENERGY CORPORATION—United Thermal Corporation, pg. 1137
CHOCTAW ELECTRIC CO-OP, pg. 248
CONWAY CORPORATION, pg. 281
COTTON ELECTRIC CO-OP, pg. 288
DAIRYLAND POWER COOPERATIVE, pg. 311
DAKOTA ELECTRIC ASSOCIATION, pg. 312
DELAWARE ELECTRIC CO-OP, pg. 325
DIXIE ELECTRIC COOPERATIVE, pg. 341
EAST KENTUCKY POWER CO-OP, pg. 362
EAST RIVER ELECTRICAL POWER CO., pg. 363
EGAN COS., pg. 371
EGAN MCKAY ELECTRICAL CONTRACTORS—Egan Cos., pg. 371
EMPIRE ELECTRIC ASSOCIATION, pg. 379
FAIRFIELD ELECTRIC CO-OP, pg. 397
FIRST ELECTRIC COOPERATIVE, pg. 412
GARDEN CITY COMPLEX—Sunflower Electric Power Corporation, pg. 1060
HOLCOMB STATION—Sunflower Electric Power Corporation, pg. 1060
HOLY CROSS ELECTRIC ASSOCIATION, pg. 541
INDIANA KENTUCKY ELECTRIC CORPORATION—Ohio Valley Electric Corporation, pg. 823
LINCOLN ELECTRIC SYSTEMS, pg. 675
MENARD ELECTRIC COOPERATIVE, pg. 738
NANA REGIONAL CORPORATION, INC., pg. 783
NEBRASKA PUBLIC POWER DISTRICT, pg. 796
NODAK ELECTRIC CO-OP, pg. 808
O'BRIEN ENERGY SYSTEMS INC., pg. 820
OGLETHORPE POWER CORP., pg. 822
OHIO VALLEY ELECTRIC CORPORATION, pg. 822
OMAHA PUBLIC POWER DISTRICT, pg. 825
PLAINS ELECTRIC GENERATION TRANSMISSION CO-OP, INC., pg. 873
POWER ENGINEERING CO. INC., pg. 883
RURAL ELECTRIC CO-OP, pg. 956
SACRAMENTO MUNICIPAL UTILITY DISTRICT, pg. 965
SAFE HARBOR WATER POWER CORPORATION, pg. 966
SEATTLE CITY LIGHT, pg. 986
SIOUX VALLEY EMPIRE ELECTRIC ASSOCIATION, pg. 1009
SUNFLOWER ELECTRIC POWER CORPORATION, pg. 1060
TALLAPOOSA RIVER ELECTRIC CO-OP, pg. 1077
TENNESSEE VALLEY AUTHORITY, pg. 1088
TRICO ELECTRIC CO-OP, pg. 1113
UNITED POWER ASSOCIATION, pg. 1134
WESTERN CO-OP ELECTRIC UTILITY ASSOCIATION, pg. 1178
WOODRUFF ELECTRICAL CO-OP, pg. 1200

4922 — NATURAL GAS TRANSMISSION

ENTERPRISE PRODUCTS COMPANY, pg. 382
HARBERT CORPORATION, pg. 506
HINDERLITER INDUSTRIES, INC., pg. 535
PROCOR LPG STORAGE DIVISION—The Marmon Group, Inc., pg. 712
STEUART INVESTMENT CO., pg. 1048

4923 — NATURAL GAS TRANSMISSION & DISTRIBUTION

ACESS ENERGY CORPORATION, pg. 12
UNION HOLDINGS, INC., pg. 1128
YAZOO INVESTMENT CORPORATION, pg. 1207

4924 — NATURAL GAS DISTRIBUTION

GREELEY GAS CO., pg. 483
IGI RESOURCES, INC.—Intermountain Industries, Inc., pg. 575
INTERMOUNTAIN GAS CO.—Intermountain Industries, Inc., pg. 575
INTERMOUNTAIN INDUSTRIES, INC., pg. 575
KCS ENERGY INC., pg. 612
LYKES ENERGY, INC., pg. 689
MISSISSIPPI ENERGIES, INC.—Yazoo Investment Corporation, pg. 1208
MISSISSIPPI VALLEY GAS CO.—Yazoo Investment Corporation, pg. 1208
OHIO GAS COMPANY, pg. 822
PEOPLES GAS SYSTEM, INC.—Lykes Energy, Inc., pg. 689
TORCO OIL, pg. 1102
UNION HOLDINGS, INC., pg. 1128
VANGUARD ENERGY CORP., pg. 1145

4925 — MIXED, MANUFACTURED OR LIQUEFIED PETROLEUM GAS PRODUCTION AND/OR DISTRIBUTION

CITIZENS GAS & COKE UTILITY, pg. 250
CLARK OIL & REFINING CORPORATION, pg. 252
PRODUCTION MANAGEMENT COMPANIES, INC., pg. 893
VANGUARD ENERGY CORP., pg. 1145

4931 — ELECTRIC & OTHER SERVICES COMBINED

SALT RIVER PROJECT AGRICULTURAL IMPROVEMENT AND POWER DISTRICT, pg. 967
SITHE ENERGIES, U.S.A., INC., pg. 1009

4932 — GAS & OTHER SERVICES COMBINED

CITIZENS GAS & COKE UTILITY, pg. 250

4939 — COMBINATION UTILITIES, NEC

PETER A. BASILE SONS INC., pg. 124
SHMINA CONSTRUCTION, INC.—Peter A. Basile Sons Inc., pg. 124

4941 — WATER SUPPLY

AMANA SOCIETY SERVICE CO.—Amana Society, pg. 46
ARTESIAN RESOURCES CORPORATION, pg. 86
ARTESIAN WATER COMPANY, INC.—Artesian Resources Corporation, pg. 86
BATON ROUGE WATER WORKS COMPANY, pg. 126
BURNS & MCDONNELL ENGINEERS-ARCHITECTS-CONSULTANTS, pg. 194
CASA GRANDE WEST WATER COMPANY, INC.—JMB Realty Corporation, pg. 585
THE CHATHAM WATER CO.—Woolrich, Inc., pg. 1201
CONTINENTAL WATER COMPANY, pg. 280
GOODKIND & O'DEA, INC.—Dewberry & Davis, pg. 334
H. HACKFELD & CO. LTD.—JMB Realty Corporation, pg. 585
HAVENS & EMERSON, INC.—Lawler-Havens Inc., pg. 661
KAANAPALI WATER CORPORATION—JMB Realty Corporation, pg. 585
LAWLER-HAVENS INC., pg. 661
LONG ISLAND WATER CORPORATION, pg. 682
PARISH WATER COMPANY, INC.—Baton Rouge Water Works Company, pg. 126
PRINCEVILLE UTILITIES COMPANY, INC.—Princeville Corporation, pg. 890
PRINCEVILLE WATER SYSTEMS, INC.—Princeville Corporation, pg. 890
RAYCO, pg. 914
STS CONSULTANTS, LTD.—STS Holdings, Inc., pg. 965
THE SOUTHWOOD COMPANY—Artesian Resources Corporation, pg. 87
WOOLRICH, INC., pg. 1201

4952 — SEWERAGE SYSTEMS

BURNS & MCDONNELL ENGINEERS-ARCHITECTS-CONSULTANTS, pg. 194
CENTURY UTILITIES, INC.—Cenvill Development Corp., pg. 236
RAYCO, pg. 914

4953 — REFUSE SYSTEMS

ABB ENVIRONMENTAL SYSTEMS, pg. 2
ARA ENVIRONMENTAL SERVICES, INC.—ARA Group, pg. 6
BROWN & CALDWELL CONSULTING ENGINEERS, pg. 181
BURNS & MCDONNELL ENGINEERS-ARCHITECTS-CONSULTANTS, pg. 194
BURNS & MCDONNELL WASTE CONSULTANTS, INC.—Burns & McDonnell Engineers-Architects-Consultants, pg. 194
DISPOSAL URBAN MAINTENANCE PROCESSION CO., INC.—Silver State Disposal Service, Inc., pg. 1004
DOMBROWSKI & HOLMES, INC., pg. 343
FUGRO-MCCLELLAND, INC., pg. 435
FUNCTIONS—Granger Construction Co., pg. 476
GRANGER CONSTRUCTION CO., pg. 476
GUILLORY TANK TRUCK SERVICE—Charles Holston, Inc., pg. 541
HARZA ENVIRONMENTAL SERVICES, INC.—Harza Engineering Co., pg. 516
HAVENS & EMERSON, INC.—Lawler-Havens Inc., pg. 661
HORSEHEAD INDUSTRIES, INC., pg. 545
HORSEHEAD RESOURCE DEVELOPMENT COMPANY, INC.—Horsehead Industries, Inc., pg. 545
LAWLER-HAVENS INC., pg. 661
MAECORP INC., pg. 699
OMNI SOURCE CORPORATION, pg. 826
SEACOR SERVICES, INC. (SSI)—Day & Zimmermann, Inc., pg. 321
SILVER STATE DISPOSAL SERVICE, INC., pg. 1004
R.S. YOUNG ENVIRONMENTAL CLEAN UP—R.S. Young Excavating, Inc., pg. 1209
JOHN ZINK CO.—Koch Industries, Incorporated, pg. 639

4959 — SANITARY SERVICES, NEC

CORDOVA LABORATORIES—Cordova Enterprise, pg. 286

4961 — STEAM & AIR-CONDITIONING SUPPLY

COGENTRIX INCORPORATED, pg. 258
UNITED THERMAL CORPORATION, pg. 1137

4971 — IRRIGATION SYSTEMS

ECODYNE WATER SYSTEMS, INC.—The Marmon Group, Inc., pg. 712
EVSWATER INDUSTRIAL SYSTEMS—The Marmon Group, Inc., pg. 712
THE GRAVER COMPANY—The Marmon Group, Inc., pg. 712
GRAVER WATER DIVISION—The Marmon Group, Inc., pg. 712
SALT RIVER PROJECT AGRICULTURAL IMPROVEMENT AND POWER DISTRICT, pg. 967
UNITECH DIVISION—The Marmon Group, Inc., pg. 712
WAIAHOLE IRRIGATION CO., LTD.—JMB Realty Corporation, pg. 585

5012 — WHOLESALE DISTRIBUTION OF AUTOMOBILES & OTHER MOTOR VEHICLES

AM GENERAL CORPORATION—Renco Group, pg. 926
AM GENERAL CORPORATION—Renco Group, pg. 926
ACME TRIM—Acme Mills Co. Inc., pg. 13
ALLIED BUS SALES, INC.—Mayflower Transit, Inc., pg. 725
ARIZONA AUCTION SERVICES, INC. D/B/A ARIZONA AUTO AUCTION—Cox Enterprises, Inc., pg. 293
ARIZONA AUCTION SERVICES, INC., D/B/A SOUTHWEST AUTO AUCTION—Cox Enterprises, Inc., pg. 293
ASTON MARTIN LAGONDA OF NORTH AMERICA, INC., pg. 92
ATLANTA AUTO AUCTION, INC.—Cox Enterprises, Inc., pg. 293
AUTOMOBILE AUCTION DIVISION—Cox Enterprises, Inc., pg. 293
BADGER TRUCK CENTER, INC., pg. 113
BAY CITIES AUTO AUCTION—Cox Enterprises, Inc., pg. 293
BIDDULPH OLDSMOBILE, pg. 149
CALIFORNIA AUTO DEALERS EXCHANGE, INC.—Cox Enterprises, Inc., pg. 293
CALIFORNIA AUTO DEALERS EXCHANGE, INC.—Cox Enterprises, Inc., pg. 293
CARCO INTERNATIONAL, INC., pg. 217
CLANTON'S AUTO AUCTION—Cox Enterprises, Inc., pg. 293
CLEVELAND BROTHERS EQUIPMENT CO., pg. 255
COLORADO AUCTION SERVICES CORPORATION—Cox Enterprises, Inc., pg. 293
COX ENTERPRISES, INC., pg. 292
DEALERS AUTO AUCTION OF DALLAS, INC.—Cox Enterprises, Inc., pg. 293
DENVER AUTO AUCTION—Cox Enterprises, Inc., pg. 293
DOONAN & SONS, INC., pg. 346
FLORIDA AUCTION SERVICES CORPORATION—Cox Enterprises, Inc., pg. 293
FLORIDA AUTO AUCTION OF ORLANDO, INC.—Cox Enterprises, Inc., pg. 293
FONTAINE MODIFICATION/COMPONENTS COMPANY—The Marmon Group, Inc., pg. 711
FORT WORTH AUTO AUCTION—Cox Enterprises, Inc., pg. 293
FREDERICKSBURG AUTO AUCTION—Cox Enterprises, Inc., pg. 293
FRESNO AUTO DEALERS AUCTION—Cox Enterprises, Inc., pg. 293
GEORGIA AUCTION SERVICES, INC.—Cox Enterprises, Inc., pg. 293
GEORGIA AUCTION SERVICES, INC. D/B/A COMMUNITY AUTION RESALE SERVICES—Cox Enterprises, Inc., pg. 293
GEORGIA DEALERS AUTO AUCTION—Cox Enterprises, Inc., pg. 293
GREATER CHICAGO AUTO AUCTION—Cox Enterprises, Inc., pg. 293
GREATER ORLANDO AUTO AUCTION, pg. 483
GREATER TAMPA BAY AUTO AUCTION—Cox Enterprises, Inc., pg. 293
GULF STATES TOYOTA, pg. 494
HARRIS FORD, INC., pg. 512
HARRISONBURG AUTO AUCTION—Cox Enterprises, Inc., pg. 293
JM FAMILY ENTERPRISES INC., pg. 584
KANSAS CITY AUTO AUCTION—Cox Enterprises, Inc., pg. 293
LB INDUSTRIES INC., pg. 647
LAKELAND AUTO AUCTION—Cox Enterprises, Inc., pg. 293
LOS ANGELES DEALERS AUTO AUCTIONS—Cox Enterprises, Inc., pg. 293
MANHEIM'S OSHAWA DEALERS EXCHANGE—Cox Enterprises, Inc., pg. 294
MASEK DISTRIBUTING INC., pg. 717
MAYFLOWER CONTRACT SERVICES, INC.—Mayflower Transit, Inc., pg. 725
MID AMERICA INTERNATIONAL TRUCKS, INC., pg. 750
MIDWAY FORD TRUCK CENTER INC., pg. 751
MINNEAPOLIS AUTO AUCTION—Cox Enterprises, Inc., pg. 293
MISSOURI AUCTION SERVICES CORP. D/B/A 166 AUTO ACTION—Cox Enterprises, Inc., pg. 293
NATIONAL AUTO DEALERS EXCHANGE—Cox Enterprises, Inc., pg. 293
NEW ENGLAND AUTO AUCTION, INC.—Cox Enterprises, Inc., pg. 293
NEWBURGH AUTO AUCTION—Cox Enterprises, Inc., pg. 293
NUTTALL EQUIPMENT CO. INC., pg. 818

S.I.C. Index

OHIO AUTO AUCTION—Cox Enterprises, Inc., pg. 293
PECK ROAD FORD TRUCK SALES, pg. 854
PENNSYLVANIA SERVICES CORP.—Cox Enterprises, Inc., pg. 293
PENNSYLVANIA SERVICES CORPORATION—Cox Enterprises, Inc., pg. 293
PORTLAND AUTO AUCTION—Cox Enterprises, Inc., pg. 293
PULLIAM MOTOR COMPANY, pg. 899
RENCO GROUP, pg. 926
RIHM MOTOR COMPANY, pg. 934
ROUNDTREE AUTOMOTIVE GROUP, pg. 952
ST. LOUIS AUTO AUCTION—Cox Enterprises, Inc., pg. 293
ST. PETE AUTO AUCTION—Cox Enterprises, Inc., pg. 293
SAN ANTONIO AUTO AUCTION—Cox Enterprises, Inc., pg. 293
SERVCO PACIFIC INC., pg. 991
SHORELINE PRODUCTS, INC., pg. 1000
SOUTH SEATTLE AUTO AUCTION—Cox Enterprises, Inc., pg. 293
SOUTHEASTERN EQUIPMENT COMPANY, INC., pg. 1019
SOUTHERN CALIFORNIA AUTO AUCTION—Cox Enterprises, Inc., pg. 293
SUMMERFIELD TRUCK CO. INC., pg. 1057
DAVE SYVERSON LINCOLN MERCURY, pg. 1071
TEXAS AUTO AUCTION SERVICES, INC. D/B/A BIG H AUTO AUCTION—Cox Enterprises, Inc., pg. 293
TEXAS HOBBY AUTO AUCTION—Cox Enterprises, Inc., pg. 294
TORONTO AUTO AUCTION—Cox Enterprises, Inc., pg. 294
TRANSNATIONAL MOTORS INC., pg. 1107
TRI-STATE MACK DISTRIBUTORS, pg. 1111
TRONCALLI MOTORS, INC., pg. 1115
U-HAUL SALES & LEASING COMPANY—Amerco, A Nevada Corporation, pg. 48
UTAH AUTO AUCTION—Cox Enterprises, Inc., pg. 294
W.W. WALLWORK, INC., pg. 1161
WISCONSIN SERVICES CORP.—Cox Enterprises, Inc., pg. 294
WOLFINGTON BODY COMPANY, pg. 1199
ZIEGLER INC., pg. 1218

5013 — MOTOR VEHICLE SUPPLIES & NEW PARTS-WHOLESALE

ADI WAREHOUSE DIVISION, CARQUEST CORP.—Carquest Corporation, pg. 224
AEA, INC., pg. 3
AEA INC./AUTO PARTS—AEA, Inc., pg. 3
AEA OF COLUMBIA—AEA, Inc., pg. 3
AEA OF RALEIGH—AEA, Inc., pg. 3
A.P.S., INC., pg. 5
ASC/CANADA INCORPORATED—ASC Incorporated, pg. 7
ASC INCORPORATED, pg. 7
A S H, INC., pg. 8
AID AUTO STORES, INC., pg. 26
ALDEN AUTO PARTS WHOLESALE, INC., pg. 32
AMERICAN SUNROOF COMPANY—ASC Incorporated, pg. 7
ANDERSON WHOLESALE COMPANY, pg. 73
ATLAS SUPPLY COMPANY, pg. 96
ATWOOD DISTRIBUTING, INC., pg. 97
J. AUSTIN OIL CO., pg. 99
AUTOMOBILE SPECIALTY CO.—ASC Incorporated, pg. 7
AUTOMOTIVE SUPPLY ASSOC., INC., pg. 101
AUTOMOTIVE WAREHOUSE, INC.—Carquest Corporation, pg. 224
BWP DISTRIBUTORS, INC.—Carquest Corporation, pg. 224
BADGER TRUCK CENTER, INC., pg. 113
BALE OF KENTUCKY, INC., pg. 115
BORG-WARNER AUTOMOTIVE, INC.—Borg-Warner Corporation, pg. 166
BORG WARNER AUTOMOTIVE, INC.—Borg-Warner Corporation, pg. 166
BORG-WARNER DE MEXICO, S.A.—Borg-Warner Corporation, pg. 166
BOSTROM DISTRIBUTION CENTER—Bostrom Seating, Inc., pg. 168
THE BRENLIN GROUP, pg. 173
CCI CORPORATION, pg. 200
CARDIS CORPORATION—Carquest Corporation, pg. 224
CARQUEST CORPORATION, pg. 224
CENEX (FARMERS UNION CENTRAL EXCHANGE, INC.), pg. 231
CENTRAL ALL PRO—AEA, Inc., pg. 3
CHIVAS PRODUCTS LTD., pg. 248
COLE HERSEE COMPANY, pg. 260
COMMERCIAL PARTS, LTD.—Rocor Transportation Companies Inc., pg. 942
DARLING'S, pg. 315
DRIVE TRAIN INDUSTRIES, pg. 349
DYATRON/BONDO CORPORATION, pg. 356
EBY BROWN CO.—Eby Brown Co., pg. 365
ELIXIR INDUSTRIES, pg. 376
EZON PRODUCTS, INC., pg. 393
FEL-PRO INCORPORATED, pg. 405
FISHERIES SUPPLY COMPANY, pg. 415
FLORIG EQUIPMENT COMPANY, INC., pg. 421
FREDERICK TRADING COMPANY, pg. 430
FREMONT ELECTRIC COMPANY—Carquest Corporation, pg. 224
GATE PETROLEUM COMPANY, pg. 445
GENERAL PARTS, INC.—Carquest Corporation, pg. 224
J. GERBER & CO. INC., pg. 453
GLOBE-AMERADA GLASS COMPANY, pg. 463
W. B. GOODE COMPANY, INC., pg. 470
HKM OF DELAWARE CORP.—UIS, Inc., pg. 1123
HATCH GRINDING COMPANY—Carquest Corporation, pg. 225
HERCULES TIRE & RUBBER COMPANY, pg. 531
HESCO PARTS CORPORATION, pg. 531
ILLINOIS AUTO ELECTRIC CO., pg. 562
J. KORBER & COMPANY, pg. 641
LARAMIE TIRE DISTRIBUTORS INC., pg. 658
LIBERTY AUTO PARTS—Sturgis Iron & Metal Company, Inc., pg. 1055
A.E. LOTTES COMPANY—Carquest Corporation, pg. 225
MANNING EQUIPMENT, INC., pg. 704
MASEK DISTRIBUTING INC., pg. 717
MIDWAY FORD TRUCK CENTER INC., pg. 751
MIDWEST AUTO PARTS DISTRIBUTORS, INC., pg. 751
MIDWEST TIRE & MUFFLER, INC., pg. 752
MIGHTY DISTRIBUTING SYSTEM, pg. 752
MOLIN AUTO PARTS INC., pg. 764
MORGAN INDUSTRIES INC., pg. 770
MUFFLER WAREHOUSE, INC.—Carquest Corporation, pg. 225
MUTUAL DISTRIBUTORS LTD., pg. 778
NORTHERN AUTOMOTIVE CORPORATION—The Trump Group, pg. 1118
O'REILLY AUTO INC., pg. 829
PSC DISTRIBUTING, INC.—Carquest Corporation, pg. 225
PARTS WHOLESALERS, INC.—Carquest Corporation, pg. 225
PEARCE INDUSTRIES INC., pg. 853
PETER PAN BUS LINES, INC., pg. 864
THE PROTECTOR CORPORATION, pg. 895
QUAKER CITY MOTOR PARTS COMPANY, pg. 903
RAO WHOLESALE TIRE CENTERS, INC., pg. 912
ROBBINS AUTO PARTS, INC., pg. 938
RODEFELD CO., INC., pg. 942
ROUNDTREE AUTOMOTIVE GROUP, pg. 952
SF SERVICES, pg. 961
SANEL AUTO PARTS, INC.—Automotive Supply Assoc., Inc., pg. 101
SIEG COMPANY, pg. 1002
SOMERSET WELDING & STEEL, INC.—Riggs Industries, Inc., pg. 934
SOUTHEASTERN EQUIPMENT COMPANY, INC., pg. 1019
SPARTAN OIL CORP., pg. 1026
STAR SALES CO., INC., pg. 1040
STRAFCO—Carquest Corporation, pg. 225
STRAFCO, INC., pg. 1052
STURGIS IRON & METAL COMPANY, INC., pg. 1055
SUSSEN, INC.—Carquest Corporation, pg. 225
TRAILER WHEEL & FRAME COMPANY, pg. 1105
TRANSNATIONAL MOTORS INC., pg. 1107
TRANSPO ELECTRONICS, INC., pg. 1108
TRONCALLI MOTORS, INC., pg. 1115
UIS EXPORT CORPORATION—UIS, Inc., pg. 1123
VON HOUSEN AUTO PARTS—Von Housen Motors, pg. 1155
VON HOUSEN MOTORS, pg. 1155
W.W. WALLWORK, INC., pg. 1161
CARL WEISSMAN & SONS, INC., pg. 1174
WELLS MANUFACTURING CANADA LTD.—UIS, Inc., pg. 1124
WESTLIE MOTOR COMPANY, pg. 1183
BUFF WHELAN CHEVROLET & GEO, INC., pg. 1185
ZIEBART CANADA, INC.—Ziebart International Corporation, pg. 1218
ZIEBART (E.C.) LIMITED—Ziebart International Corporation, pg. 1218
ZIEBART JAPAN LIMITED—Ziebart International Corporation, pg. 1218

5014 — TIRES & TUBES-WHOLESALE

A K H COMPANY, INC., pg. 4
ALLIED OIL & SUPPLY, INC., pg. 38
ATLAS SUPPLY COMPANY, pg. 96
J. AUSTIN OIL CO., pg. 99
BALE OF KENTUCKY, INC., pg. 115
BELL GAS, INC., pg. 134
BELLE TIRE DISTRIBUTOR INC., pg. 136
BURRIS FOODS, INC., pg. 195
CAMPBELL OIL CO., pg. 213
CAPITAL TIRE, INC., pg. 215
DES MOINES TIRE—Rott-Keller Supply Co., pg. 951
EL DORADO TIRE CO., pg. 372
GROSSENBURG IMPLEMENTS, INCORPORATED, pg. 489
J. H. HEAFNER CO. INC., pg. 520
KENT SUSSEX TIRE SERVICE—Burris Foods, Inc., pg. 195
LARAMIE TIRE DISTRIBUTORS INC., pg. 658
CARLOS R. LEFFLER INC., pg. 666
MIDWEST TIRE & MUFFLER, INC., pg. 752
PARRISH TIRE COMPANY, INC., pg. 850
RAO WHOLESALE TIRE CENTERS, INC., pg. 912
REDBURN TIRE COMPANY, pg. 919
ROTT-KELLER SUPPLY CO., pg. 951
SF SERVICES, pg. 961
SPARTAN OIL CORP., pg. 1026
STRAFCO, INC., pg. 1052
O. J. STROBEL OIL & TIRE CO., INC., pg. 1053
YOUNGSTOWN TIRE & SUPPLY COMPANY—Ziegler Tire & Supply Company, Inc., pg. 1218
ZIEGLER TIRE & SUPPLY COMPANY, INC., pg. 1218

5015 — MOTOR VEHICLE PARTS, USED-WHOLESALE & RETAIL

AEA, INC., pg. 3
ASTON MARTIN LAGONDA OF NORTH AMERICA, INC., pg. 92
COLE HERSEE COMPANY, pg. 260
FREDERICK TRADING COMPANY, pg. 430
NATIONWISE AUTOMOTIVE, INC., pg. 795
ROBERTSON'S AUTO SALVAGE, pg. 939
SPROTT OIL CO., INC., pg. 1034

5021 — FURNITURE-WHOLESALE

IVAN ALLEN COMPANY, INC., pg. 36
AMERICAN FURNITURE COMPANY, pg. 55
BKM ENTERPRISES, INC., pg. 107
BKM TOTAL OFFICE TODAY, INC.—BKM Enterprises, Inc., pg. 107
W.S. BADCOCK CORPORATION, pg. 113
BLUE RIDGE TRANSFER CO., pg. 161
BRODHEAD-GARRETT CO., pg. 178
BRUNSCHWIG & FILS, INC., pg. 184
CM FURNITURE, INC.—Carolina Mills, Inc., pg. 223
CARLSON COMPANIES, INC., pg. 220
CAROLINA MILLS, INC., pg. 223
CHITTENDEN & EASTMAN CO., pg. 248
COLE BUSINESS FURNITURE—Joyce International, Inc., pg. 608
CONTRACT FURNISHINGS & SYSTEMS, LTD., pg. 280
CONTRACT INTERIORS INC., pg. 280
DANCKER, SELLEW & DOUGLAS, INC., pg. 314
DECORATIVE CRAFTS, INC., pg. 324
EDWARD DON & COMPANY OF ILLINOIS, pg. 344
EATON OFFICE SUPPLY CO., INC., pg. 364
EBSCO INDUSTRIES, INC., pg. 365
FICKS REED COMPANY, pg. 408
FRAENKEL COMPANY, pg. 428
FURNITURE CONSULTANTS, pg. 437
GALAXY BUSINESS PRODUCTS—Metpac, Ltd., pg. 742
GENEVA CORPORATION, pg. 451
GOLDSMITHS, INC., pg. 469
GOODMANS, INC., pg. 471
HAUENSTEIN & BURMEISTER, INC., pg. 517
HAWORTH LTD.—Haworth, Inc., pg. 518
HAWORTH U.K. LTD.—Haworth, Inc., pg. 518
INTERNATIONAL BUSINESS INTERIORS INC., pg. 575
J & J FURNITURE CO, INC.—Warehouse Home Furnishings Distributor, pg. 1163
JOYCE INTERNATIONAL, INC., pg. 608
KINGSDOWN, INC., pg. 632
KNOLLOFFICE, INC.—21 International Holdings, Inc., pg. 1121
KRAUSE'S SOFA FACTORY, INC., pg. 644
LOPC—Joyce International, Inc., pg. 608
JACK LENOR LARSEN, INC., pg. 659
LASALLE-DEITCH CO., INC., pg. 660
MID-WEST PAPER PRODUCTS COMPANY, pg. 750
MIDWEST MOTEL SUPPLY—Super 8 Motels, Inc., pg. 1063
MILLER BUSINESS SYSTEMS, INC., pg. 753
OFFICE EQUIPMENT COMPANY OF CHICAGO, pg. 821
ONE STOP SUPPLY, pg. 827
PEABODY OFFICE FURNITURE CORPORATION, pg. 853
PHOENIX ENTERPRISES INC., pg. 868
A. POMERANTZ & CO., pg. 880
L. POWELL CO., INC., pg. 882
PRINT-O-STAT, INC.—Pace Resources, Inc., pg. 839
GUY SCHOENECKER, INC., pg. 977
SERVCO PACIFIC INC., pg. 991
SILVER'S INC., pg. 1005
SKINNER CORP., pg. 1009
TAYLOR WOODCRAFT—Brodhead-Garrett Co., pg. 178
WALLACE LEISURE PRODUCTS, INC., pg. 1160
WANG'S INTERNATIONAL, INC., pg. 1162
WAREHOUSE HOME FURNISHINGS DISTRIBUTOR, pg. 1163
WASSERSTROM COMPANY, pg. 1167

5023 — HOME FURNISHINGS-WHOLESALE

ALLISON-ERWIN CO. INC., pg. 40
AMERICAN FURNITURE COMPANY, pg. 55
ANDERSON WHOLESALE COMPANY, pg. 73
ARIZONA WHOLESALE SUPPLY COMPANY, pg. 82
BKM ENTERPRISES, INC., pg. 107
BKM TOTAL OFFICE TODAY, INC.—BKM Enterprises, Inc., pg. 107
BALTIC LINEN COMPANY, INC., pg. 116
BENNETT BROTHERS, INC., pg. 139
WILLIAM M. BIRD & CO., INC., pg. 152
C&C ASSOCIATES—Couristan Inc., pg. 290
CAIN & BULTMAN, INC., pg. 207
CAIN & BULTMAN—Cain & Bultman, Inc., pg. 207
CARLSON COMPANIES, INC., pg. 220
COLE PAPERS INC., pg. 260
COTTER & COMPANY, pg. 288
COURI CARPET CO.—Couristan Inc., pg. 290
COURI-MURAD & CO.—Couristan Inc., pg. 290
COURISTAN INC., pg. 290
CRISA CORPORATION, pg. 299
EBELING & REUSS COMPANY, pg. 365
FARGO GLASS & PAINT COMPANY, pg. 399
GRAPHICS INTERNATIONAL INC.—Hallmark Cards, Inc., pg. 502
HAMBURG BROTHERS INC., pg. 502
HAYWIN TEXTILE PRODUCTS, INC., pg. 520
HERBAL ENTERPRISES INC., pg. 530
HOLLYTEX—21 International Holdings, Inc., pg. 1121
HOME INTERIORS & GIFTS, INC., pg. 541
JACQUES JUGEAT, INC., pg. 608
KRUSE HARDWARE COMPANY, pg. 645
JACK LENOR LARSEN, INC., pg. 659
LASALLE-DEITCH CO., INC., pg. 660
GEO. H. LEHLEITNER & CO., INC., pg. 666
MCSWAIN CARPETS INC., pg. 733
NATIONAL BRANDS, INC., pg. 786
NATIONAL MERCHANDISE CO., INC., pg. 792
NELSON & SMALL INC., pg. 798
NEW YORK CARPET WORLD INC., pg. 802
ORDERS DISTRIBUTING CO., pg. 829
OSTROW TEXTILE CO., INC., pg. 831
PERFECT FIT INDUSTRIES, INC., pg. 861
RAUB SUPPLY COMPANY, pg. 913
RENA-WARE DISTRIBUTORS INC., pg. 926

RENA-WARE GMBH—Rena-Ware Distributors Inc., pg. 926
ROBERTSON FACTORIES, INC., pg. 939
RAYMOND ROSEN CO., pg. 948
THE ROYAL CHINA & PORCELAIN COMPANIES INC., pg. 953
ROYAL WATERBEDS, pg. 953
RUGBY-DARBY GROUP OF COS., pg. 955
GUY SCHOENECKER, INC., pg. 977
F. SCHUMACHER & CO., pg. 979
SUPERIOR LINEN & DRAPERY COMPANY, pg. 1064
THUNDERBIRD STEEL CORPORATION, pg. 1096
U.S. CARPET CO.—Couristan Inc., pg. 290
WAVERLY FABRICS—F. Schumacher & Co., pg. 979
WEST UNION CORP., pg. 1177
WESTGATE FABRICS, INC., pg. 1182
WILLITTS DESIGN—Hallmark Cards, Inc., pg. 502
WILTON INDUSTRIES, INC., pg. 1194
THE ZAMOISKI CO., pg. 1216

5031 — LUMBER, PLYWOOD, MILLWORK, WOOD PANELS-WHOLESALE

AETNA PLYWOOD, INC., pg. 23
ALLIED PLYWOOD CORP., pg. 38
AMES TAPING TOOL SYSTEMS CO.—AXIA Incorporated, pg. 8
ANDERSON LUMBER COMPANY, pg. 73
ANTHONY FOREST DIV.—Anthony Forest Products Co., Inc., pg. 77
ANTHONY FOREST DIV.—Anthony Forest Products Co., Inc., pg. 77
ANTHONY FOREST PRODUCTS CO., INC., pg. 77
ANTHONY INTERNATIONAL—Anthony Forest Products Co., Inc., pg. 77
ARIZONA SASH & DOOR CO.—Foxworth-Galbraith Lumber Co., pg. 428
ATLANTIC LUMBER COMPANY—Sabbeth Industries Ltd, pg. 965
BABCOCK LUMBER COMPANY, pg. 107
HENRY BACON BUILDING MATERIALS, INC., pg. 113
E.C. BARTON & CO., pg. 123
BATEMAN BROTHERS LUMBER CO., INC., pg. 125
BAY INDUSTRIES INC., pg. 127
THE BERNUTH CORPORATION, pg. 144
BLOUNT LUMBER COMPANY, pg. 158
BORCHERS BROS., pg. 165
BRAZIER FOREST INDUSTRIES, INC., pg. 172
BRIDGEWATER RESOURCES CORPORATION, pg. 175
BROWER COMPANY—Bay Industries Inc., pg. 127
BUILDER MARTS OF AMERICA, pg. 187
CALCASIEU LUMBER COMPANY, pg. 208
CALIFORNIA PANEL & VENEER COMPANY, pg. 210
CAROLINA BUILDERS CORPORATION, pg. 223
CARTER-JONES LUMBER COMPANY, pg. 226
CENTRAL NATIONAL-GOTTESMAN INC., pg. 233
COLUMBIA LUMBER & MANUFACTURING CO., pg. 265
CONSOLIDATED WHOLESALE LUMBER CO.—Calcasieu Lumber Company, pg. 208
COPELAND LUMBER YARD, INC., pg. 284
COUNTRYMARK COOPERATIVE, INC., pg. 290
COX WOOD PRESERVING CO., pg. 295
DAVIS MOLDING CO.—Heico Inc., pg. 525
DESOTO HARDWOOD FLOORING COMPANY—National Bedding & Furniture Industries, pg. 786
DI GIORGIO CORPORATION, pg. 334
DIAMOND HILL PLYWOOD COMPANY—Darlington Veneer Company, pg. 316
DIVERSIFIED WOOD PRODUCTS—Sabbeth Industries Ltd, pg. 965
DIXIE BUILDING SUPPLIES, INC.—Walter Industries, Inc., pg. 1162
DYKE INDUSTRY, INC., pg. 356
ERB LUMBER COMPANY, pg. 360
EXPO INDUSTRIES, INC., pg. 393
THE FAIRFIELD LUMBER & SUPPLY COMPANY, pg. 397
FINGERLE LUMBER CO., pg. 411
FLORENCE CORPORATION, pg. 420
FORT WORTH LUMBER COMPANY, pg. 425
FOXWORTH-GALBRAITH LUMBER CO., pg. 428
FRANK PAXTON LUMBER COMPANY—Jeld-Wen, Inc., pg. 592
FRANK PAXTON LUMBER COMPANY—Jeld-Wen, Inc., pg. 592
FRANK PAXTON LUMBER COMPANY—Jeld-Wen, Inc., pg. 592
FRANK PAXTON LUMBER COMPANY—Jeld-Wen, Inc., pg. 592
FRANK PAXTON LUMBER COMPANY—Jeld-Wen, Inc., pg. 592
FRANK PAXTON LUMBER COMPANY—Jeld-Wen, Inc., pg. 592
FRANK PAXTON LUMBER COMPANY—Jeld-Wen, Inc., pg. 592
FRANK PAXTON LUMBER COMPANY—Jeld-Wen, Inc., pg. 592
FRANK PAXTON LUMBER COMPANY—Jeld-Wen, Inc., pg. 592
FREMONT FOREST PRODUCTS, pg. 432
FRONTIER LUMBER COMPANY, INC., pg. 434
FUTTER LUMBER CORPORATION, pg. 437
GANAHL LUMBER COMPANY, pg. 442
GENEVA CORPORATION, pg. 451
GEORGETOWN INDUSTRIES, INC., pg. 453
GERRITY CO., INC., pg. 454
GOLDEN STATE FLOORING COMPANY—J. E. Higgins Lumber Co., pg. 533
GREGORY AFFILIATES, INC., pg. 486
HANCOCK LUMBER, INC., pg. 504
HANKINS LUMBER COMPANY, INC., pg. 505
J. E. HIGGINS LUMBER CO., pg. 533
HILL-BEHAN LUMBER COMPANY, pg. 534
HOBOKEN WOOD FLOORING CORPORATION, pg. 537
HOLBROOK LUMBER COMPANY, pg. 538
ED HOLDERNESS SUPPLIES, pg. 538
THOMAS R. HOPSON BROKER, INC., pg. 544
HURD MILLWORK COMPANY, INC.—UIS, Inc., pg. 1123
KAIBAB INDUSTRIES, pg. 614
KENTUCKY INDIANA LUMBER CO.—Kentucky Indiana Lumber Co. Inc., pg. 624
KENTUCKY INDIANA LUMBER CO.—Kentucky Indiana Lumber Co. Inc., pg. 624
KENTUCKY INDIANA LUMBER CO. INC., pg. 623
LUMBERMENS MERCHANDISING CORPORATION, pg. 687
LUMCO INDUSTRIES, INC., pg. 687
MBS HOLDING, INC., pg. 691
MAINE POTATO GROWERS, INC., pg. 702
MAKI CORPORATION, pg. 702
MAKI HOME CENTER, INC.—Maki Corporation, pg. 702
MAYFIELD BUILDING SUPPLY CO.—MBS Holding, Inc., pg. 691
J. GIBSON MCILVAIN CO., pg. 729
MCLEAN-THOMAS INC., pg. 731
MICO, INC., pg. 748
MID-AM BUILDING SUPPLY, INC., pg. 749
MINOT BUILDERS SUPPLY ASSOCIATION, pg. 758
MOLDED FIBER GLASS/WEST—Molded Fiber Glass Companies, pg. 764
MONUMENTAL MILLWORK, INC., pg. 768
NATIONAL LUMBER CO., pg. 792
THE NIKKEL CORPORATION, pg. 807
NORANDEX INC., pg. 809
NORTH PACIFIC LUMBER COMPANY, pg. 813
OUR OWN HARDWARE COMPANY, pg. 832
P. S. INTERNATIONAL INC., pg. 837
PACESETTER CORPORATION, pg. 839
PACIFIC LUMBER & SHIPPING CO., pg. 840
PAN AMERICAN TRADE DEVELOPMENT CORP., pg. 845
PAXTON BEAUTIFUL WOODS—Jeld-Wen, Inc., pg. 592
PAXTON BEAUTIFUL WOODS—Jeld-Wen, Inc., pg. 592
FRANK PAXTON COMPANY—Jeld-Wen, Inc., pg. 592
PHILADELPHIA RESERVE SUPPLY COMPANY, pg. 867
PICKERING INDUSTRIES INC., pg. 869
PIONEER PLASTICS HOLDING, INC., pg. 872
PLYWOOD PANELS, INC., pg. 878
PLYWOOD PLASTICS INC., pg. 878
ARTHUR A. POZZI CO., INC., pg. 883
PUGET SOUND PLYWOOD, INC., pg. 899
RAYCO, pg. 914
REX LUMBER COMPANY, pg. 930
RICHARDSON INDUSTRIES, INC., pg. 932
RIEMEIER LUMBER COMPANY, INC., pg. 934
RIVERSIDE MILLWORK COMPANY, INC., pg. 937
ROBBINS MANUFACTURING COMPANY, pg. 938
ROBINSON EXPORT-IMPORT CORPORATION—Mico Inc., pg. 748
ROBINSON LUMBER COMPANY—Robinson Lumber & Export Company, pg. 940
T. H. ROGERS LUMBER CO. INC., pg. 943
ROSEBURG FOREST PRODUCTS CO., pg. 948
SCR, INC., pg. 961
SABBETH INDUSTRIES LTD, pg. 965
SABBETH INTERNATIONAL FOREST PRODUCTS—Sabbeth Industries Ltd, pg. 965
SABBETH WORLD WIDE WOOD CORP.—Sabbeth Industries Ltd, pg. 965
SANFORD & HAWLEY, INC., pg. 970
SCHERER BROS. LUMBER COMPANY, pg. 976
SCHUCK & SONS CONSTRUCTION CO., pg. 979
SCHUTTE LUMBER COMPANY, pg. 980
SEMAC INDUSTRIES INC., pg. 989
SERVISTAR CORPORATION, pg. 992
SHERWOOD LUMBER CORPORATION, pg. 999
SIMPSON INVESTMENT CO., pg. 1007
SIMPSON TIMBER CO.—Simpson Investment Co., pg. 1007
SLAUGHTER BROS., INC.—Furman Lumber Company, pg. 436
SNAVELY FOREST PRODUCTS, INC., pg. 1015
RUSSELL STADELMAN & COMPANY, pg. 1034
H. A. STILES CO.—Saunders Brothers, pg. 972
STONES, INC., pg. 1051
SWANER HARDWOOD COMPANY, INC., pg. 1066
TEBBAS SALES CORP.—Sabbeth Industries Ltd, pg. 965
TIMBER PRODUCTS COMPANY, LP, pg. 1097
UNIVERSAL COMPANIES, INC., pg. 1138
UNIVERSAL FOREST PRODUCTS, INC.—Universal Companies, Inc., pg. 1138
VAAGEN BROTHERS LUMBER, INC., pg. 1142
W B H INTERNATIONAL, INC.—WBH Industries, Inc., pg. 1156
WBH INDUSTRIES, INC., pg. 1155
WALLICH LUMBER CO., pg. 1161
WEST LUMBER CO., pg. 1177
WESTERN LUMBER COMPANY, INC.—Georgetown Industries, Inc., pg. 453
WING INDUSTRIES NORTH CENTRAL—Wing Industries, Inc., pg. 1196
WING INDUSTRIES NORTHEASTERN—Wing Industries, Inc., pg. 1196
WING INDUSTRIES SOUTHEASTERN—Wing Industries, Inc., pg. 1196
WING INDUSTRIES WESTERN—Wing Industries, Inc., pg. 1196
WOOD TREATERS OF BUFFALO CO., INC.—Frontier Lumber Company, Inc., pg. 435

5032 — BRICK, STONE & RELATED CONSTRUCTION MATERIALS-WHOLESALE

AMERICAN STONE-MIX, INC., pg. 63
BORCHERS BROS., pg. 165
CAPITAL MARBLE & GRANITE CO. INC.—Cold Spring Granite Company, pg. 260
COLD SPRING GRANITE COMPANY, pg. 259
DAL-TILE CORP., pg. 312
H.G. FENTON MATERIAL COMPANY, pg. 406
FLORIDA CRUSHED STONE COMPANY, pg. 420
GEORGETOWN INDUSTRIES, INC., pg. 453
GILPATRICK CONSTRUCTION COMPANY, pg. 460
HENNINGSEN & SONS, INC.—A. Teichert & Son, Inc., pg. 1084
E.P. HENRY CORPORATION, pg. 530
HILLS MATERIALS CO.—Northwestern Engineering Co., pg. 815
INGRAM MATERIALS CO.—Ingram Industries Inc., pg. 569
INTERSTATE BRICK COMPANY—Pacific Coast Building Products Inc., pg. 839
MBS HOLDING, INC., pg. 691
MARIANA CORPORATION—Gohmann Asphalt & Construction Inc., pg. 465
MCLEAN-THOMAS INC., pg. 731
MILES SAND & GRAVEL COMPANY, pg. 753
MONROC, INC., pg. 766
OLEN CORPORATION—Kokosing Construction Company, Inc., pg. 641
PETRICCA INDUSTRIES, INC., pg. 865
RIVERTON TRUCKERS, INC.—Gohmann Asphalt & Construction Inc., pg. 465
ANN SACKS TILE & STONE, INC.—Kohler Company, pg. 640
SYAR INDUSTRIES, INC., pg. 1068
THUNDERBIRD STEEL CORPORATION, pg. 1096
WHIBCO, INC., pg. 1185

5033 — ROOFING, SIDING & INSULATION MATERIALS-WHOLESALE

ALLIED BUILDING PRODUCTS CORPORATION, pg. 37
BORCHERS BROS., pg. 165
EASTERN STEEL & METAL COMPANY—Olympic Steel Inc., pg. 825
FOREST SIDING SUPPLY, INC.—Thermal Technology Industries, pg. 1091
HARVEY INDUSTRIES, INC., pg. 515
INDUSTRIAL ACOUSTICS COMPANY GMBH—Industrial Acoustics Company, Inc., pg. 566
INTRA-ACOUSTICS COMPANY, LTD.—Industrial Acoustics Company, Inc., pg. 566
LYON CONKLIN & COMPANY, pg. 690
M M SYSTEMS CORPORATION, pg. 692
M M SYSTEMS CORPORATION—M M Systems Corporation, pg. 692
MCLEAN-THOMAS INC., pg. 731
MOLDED FIBER GLASS/WEST—Molded Fiber Glass Companies, pg. 764
PERFORMANCE CONTRACTING GROUP, pg. 861
PERFORMANCE CONTRACTING, INC.—Performance Contracting Group, pg. 861
SANFORD & HAWLEY, INC., pg. 970

5039 — WHOLESALE CONSTRUCTION MATERIALS, NEC

ABC SUPPLY COMPANY, INC., pg. 2
AFG INTERNATIONAL, INC.—AFG Industries, Inc., pg. 3
API GROUP INC., pg. 5
ABBOTT GLASS CO., INC., pg. 9
ACORN BUILDING COMPONENTS INC., pg. 13
ACORN DISTRIBUTING CO.—Acorn Building Components Inc., pg. 14
ACORN OF ILLINOIS—Acorn Building Components Inc., pg. 14
ACORN OF FLORIDA—Acorn Building Components Inc., pg. 14
ACORN SOUTH—Acorn Building Components Inc., pg. 14
ALASKAN COPPER COMPANIES, pg. 30
AMERICAN FENCE COMPANY, pg. 52
ANCHOR INDUSTRIES INC., pg. 71
ANCO INSULATIONS, INC., pg. 72
THE AUSTIN CO. OF CANADA—National Gypsum Company, pg. 790
HENRY BACON BUILDING MATERIALS, INC., pg. 113
E.C. BARTON & CO., pg. 123
BENSON INDUSTRIES, INC., pg. 139
BERKS PRODUCTS CORPORATION, pg. 142
WILLIAM M. BIRD & CO., INC., pg. 152
BLACK & CO., pg. 154
BORCHERS BROS., pg. 165
BRECKENRIDGE MATERIAL COMPANY, pg. 173
BUILDER MARTS OF AMERICA, pg. 187
BUILDING PLASTICS, INC., pg. 188
BUILDING PRODUCTS INC., pg. 188
BUILDING PRODUCTS INC. OF S.D.—Building Products Inc., pg. 188
CAMALLOY, INC., pg. 211
THE CLEVELAND BUILDERS SUPPLY CO.—Standard Lafarge, pg. 1036
EASTERN STEEL & METAL COMPANY—Olympic Steel Inc., pg. 825
EMERY WATERHOUSE COMPANY, pg. 379
ENGINEERED PRODUCTS, INC., pg. 382
FALCONER GLASS INDUSTRIES, INC.—Guardian Industries Corp., pg. 492
FARGO GLASS & PAINT COMPANY, pg. 399
FINGERLE LUMBER CO., pg. 411
FISCHER LIME & CEMENT COMPANY, pg. 414
FLORENCE CORPORATION, pg. 420
FOURCO GLASS CO.—AFG Industries, Inc., pg. 3
FOXWORTH-GALBRAITH LUMBER CO., pg. 428
FREDERICK TRADING COMPANY, pg. 430
GAF BUILDING MATERIALS CORPORATION—GAF Corporation, pg. 438
GAF CORPORATION, pg. 438
GANAHL LUMBER COMPANY, pg. 442
GOLD BOND BUILDING PRODUCTS—National Gypsum Company, pg. 790
J.R. HAHN CO., INC., pg. 500

HARDWARE WHOLESALERS, INC., pg. 508
HILL-BEHAN LUMBER COMPANY, pg. 534
ED HOLDERNESS SUPPLIES, pg. 538
IMPO GLAZTILE, pg. 564
INKOM, IDAHO PLANT—Ash Grove Cement Company, pg. 87
INTREPID ENTERPRISES, INC., pg. 581
JEWELL BUILDING SYSTEMS, pg. 594
JOHNSON ACOUSTICAL & SUPPLY CO., pg. 597
P.J. KEATING COMPANY, pg. 619
LUMBERMENS MERCHANDISING CORPORATION, pg. 687
MAINE POTATO GROWERS, INC., pg. 702
J. GIBSON MCILVAIN CO., pg. 729
MCLEAN-THOMAS INC., pg. 731
METALL UND ROHSTOFF AG—Associated Metals & Minerals Corp., pg. 91
MODEL GLASS, INC., pg. 762
NATIONAL GYPSUM COMPANY, pg. 790
O'KEEFFE'S, INC., pg. 823
PPA INDUSTRIES, INC., pg. 836
P. S. INTERNATIONAL INC., pg. 837
PACESETTER CORPORATION, pg. 839
PACIFIC COAST BUILDING PRODUCTS INC., pg. 839
PALMETTO WHOLESALE CO., INC., pg. 844
R. B. PAMPLIN CORP., pg. 844
PHILADELPHIA RESERVE SUPPLY COMPANY, pg. 867
PLYWOOD PLASTICS INC., pg. 878
PROGLASS—American Management Group, pg. 58
PRUDENTIAL METAL SUPPLY CORP., pg. 898
REEVES SOUTHEASTERN CORPORATION, pg. 921
ROCCO BUILDING SUPPLIES INC.—Rocco Inc., pg. 940
ROCCO INC., pg. 940
ROGERS GROUP INC., pg. 943
T. H. ROGERS LUMBER CO. INC., pg. 943
ROOFING WHOLESALE CO., INC., pg. 946
S-G METALS INDUSTRIES, INC., pg. 962
SANFORD & HAWLEY, INC., pg. 970
SCHERER BROS. LUMBER COMPANY, pg. 976
SCHUTTE LUMBER COMPANY, pg. 980
THE SCOTSMAN GROUP, INC., pg. 982
SHEFFIELD HARDWARE COMPANY, pg. 996
SIOUX STEEL COMPANY, pg. 1008
SPACE MASTER INTERNATIONAL, pg. 1024
SUNNILAND CORPORATION, pg. 1061
TAPCO PRODUCTS COMPANY, pg. 1078
TECH-AEROFOAM PRODUCTS, INC.—Great American Industries, Inc., pg. 480
THOMPSON ENTERPRISES INC., pg. 1094
TILCON, INC., pg. 1097
U.S. METALSOURCE CORPORATION, pg. 1136
W B H INTERNATIONAL, INC.—WBH Industries, Inc., pg. 1156
WILLIAMS COMPANY OF ORLANDO, INC., pg. 1190

5043 — PHOTOGRAPHIC EQUIPMENT & SUPPLIES-WHOLESALE

ANSCO PHOTO-OPTICAL PRODUCTS CORP., pg. 76
BELL & HOWELL FRANCE S.A.—Bell & Howell Company, pg. 135
BELL & HOWELL LTD.—Bell & Howell Company, pg. 135
BENNETT BROTHERS, INC., pg. 139
DEANS PHOTO SERVICE, INC., pg. 322
LEXMARK AUSTRALIA—Lexmark International, Inc., pg. 674
LEXMARK INTERNATIONAL, INC.—Lexmark International, Inc., pg. 674
LEXMARK INTERNATIONAL, INC.—Lexmark International, Inc., pg. 674
LEXMARK INTERNATIONAL, INC.—Lexmark International, Inc., pg. 674
LEXMARK INTERNATIONAL, INC.—Lexmark International, Inc., pg. 674
LEXMARK INTERNATIONAL, INC.—Lexmark International, Inc., pg. 674
LONDON LITHO ALUMINUM CO., INC., pg. 681
MPO VIDEOTRONICS—MPO Videotronics, Inc., pg. 693
THE MARBLE COMPANY—Blevins Inc., pg. 156
NELSON PHOTO SUPPLIES, pg. 797
WILLOUGHBY'S, pg. 1193
YOUNG-PHILLIPS SALES CO., pg. 1210
THE ZAMOISKI CO., pg. 1216

5044 — OFFICE EQUIPMENT-WHOLESALE

AVA-AUTOMATIC VENDORS OF AMERICA, pg. 8
AEROGLIDE AMERICAS INTERNATIONAL, INC.—Aeroglide Corporation, pg. 22
AMERICAN OFFICE EQUIPMENT, pg. 58
AMERICAN OFFICE EQUIPMENT DISTRIBUTING, INC.—American Office Equipment, pg. 59
AMFAC DISTRIBUTION CORPORATION—JMB Realty Corporation, pg. 585
BALTIMORE STATIONERY CO., pg. 116
CENTURY DATA SYSTEMS, pg. 235
FUNDING SERVICES INC.—American Office Equipment, pg. 59
INVINCIBLE METAL FURNITURE CO., pg. 582
LEXINGTON EQUIPMENT CO.—Castle-Harlan, Inc., pg. 229
LEXMARK AUSTRALIA—Lexmark International, Inc., pg. 674
LEXMARK INTERNATIONAL, INC.—Lexmark International, Inc., pg. 674
LEXMARK INTERNATIONAL, INC.—Lexmark International, Inc., pg. 674
LEXMARK INTERNATIONAL, INC.—Lexmark International, Inc., pg. 674
LEXMARK INTERNATIONAL, INC.—Lexmark International, Inc., pg. 674
LINOTYPE-HELL COMPANY, pg. 677
MID-WEST PAPER PRODUCTS COMPANY, pg. 750
MILLER BUSINESS SYSTEMS, INC., pg. 753
MITCHELL BUSINESS EQUIPMENT—The Philadelphia Bourse, Inc., pg. 866
OFFICE CONNECTION, INC., pg. 821
PBM OFFICE PRODUCTS, pg. 835
PROCOR LPG STORAGE DIVISION—The Marmon Group, Inc., pg. 712
SUN DATA INC., pg. 1058
VELOBIND, INC.—Lane Industries, Inc., pg. 657
VELOBIND, INC.—Lane Industries, Inc., pg. 657
VELOBIND, INC.—Lane Industries, Inc., pg. 657
VELOBIND, INC.—Lane Industries, Inc., pg. 657
VELOBIND, INC.—Lane Industries, Inc., pg. 657
VELOBIND, INC.—Lane Industries, Inc., pg. 657
VELOBIND, INC.—Lane Industries, Inc., pg. 657
VELOBIND-RENO DIVISION—Lane Industries, Inc., pg. 657
YOUNG-PHILLIPS SALES CO., pg. 1210

5045 — COMPUTERS & COMPUTER PERIPHERAL EQUIPMENT & SOFTWARE-WHOLESALE

ALLISON-ERWIN CO. INC., pg. 40
CENTURY DATA SYSTEMS, pg. 235
CERTIFIED GROCERS ADVERTISING CO., pg. 236
CIMLINC INC., pg. 249
COMARK, pg. 267
COMMTRON CORPORATION—Ingram Industries Inc., pg. 569
COMPUTER SALES INTERNATIONAL INC., pg. 271
COMPUTERLAND—ComputerLand Corporation, pg. 271
D&H DISTRIBUTING COMPANY, pg. 307
DAKCO DISTRIBUTORS, INC., pg. 311
DECISION DATA COMPUTER (BELGIUM) S.A.—Decision Data Inc., pg. 324
DECISION DATA COMPUTER (GB) LTD.—Decision Data Inc., pg. 324
DECISION DATA COMPUTER INTL. S.A.—Decision Data Inc., pg. 324
DECISION DATA COMPUTER (S.A.)—Decision Data Inc., pg. 324
EBM SYSTEMS, INC., pg. 359
ECONOCOM-USA INC., pg. 367
ELEK-TEK, INC., pg. 375
FOLLETT SERVICE CORPORATION—Follett Corporation, pg. 422
FOLLETT SOFTWARE COMPANY—Follett Corporation, pg. 422
GALAXY BUSINESS PRODUCTS—Metpac, Ltd., pg. 742
GATEWAY 2000, pg. 446
GRAHAM MAGNETICS, INC., pg. 475
H W ELECTRONICS, INC., pg. 497
INDIANA RECORDS MANAGERS, pg. 565
INGRAM DISTRIBUTION GROUP INC.—Ingram Industries Inc., pg. 569
INGRAM ENTERTAINMENT INC.—Ingram Industries Inc., pg. 569
INGRAM MICRO INC.—Ingram Industries Inc., pg. 569
INLAND ASSOCIATES, pg. 570
INLAND ASSOCIATES, INC., pg. 570
INTEGRAL SYSTEMS—Integral Systems, pg. 573
INTEGRAL SYSTEMS, INC.—Integral Systems, pg. 573
LA COMPUTER CENTER, pg. 648
DAVID LANGER & CO., INC., pg. 657
LEXMARK AUSTRALIA—Lexmark International, Inc., pg. 674
LEXMARK INTERNATIONAL, INC.—Lexmark International, Inc., pg. 674
LEXMARK INTERNATIONAL, INC.—Lexmark International, Inc., pg. 674
LEXMARK INTERNATIONAL, INC.—Lexmark International, Inc., pg. 674
LEXMARK INTERNATIONAL, INC.—Lexmark International, Inc., pg. 674
MACRO COMPUTER PRODUCTS INC., pg. 698
NATIONAL BRANDS, INC., pg. 786
NIHON READY SYSTEMS—Ready Systems, pg. 916
PC DISTRIBUTING INC., pg. 835
PEGASUS INTERNATIONAL CORPORATION, pg. 855
PEIRCE-PHELPS, INC., pg. 855
PERIPHONICS VOICE PROCESSING SYSTEMS LTD.—Periphonics Corp., pg. 862
ROBERTSON MARKETING INC., pg. 939
STANDARD MANIFOLD COMPANY, INC., pg. 1037
SUN COMPUTERS, INC., pg. 1058
SYMPLEX COMMUNICATIONS CORP., pg. 1069
SYRACUSE SUPPLY COMPANY, pg. 1070
SYRACUSE SUPPLY INDUSTRIAL PRODUCTS DIVISION—Syracuse Supply Company, pg. 1070
THOROUGHBRED EUROPE LTD.—Thoroughbred Software International, Inc., pg. 1095
THOROUGHBRED/QUARK—Thoroughbred Software International, Inc., pg. 1095
THE VIRTUAL GROUP, pg. 1153
VITUS ELECTRICAL SUPPLY COMPANY, pg. 1154
WESTERN PACIFIC DATA SYSTEMS, pg. 1180
WESTERN PACIFIC DATA SYSTEMS—Western Pacific Data Systems, pg. 1180
RICHARD YOUNG OFFICE PRODUCTS, INC.—Hillman Company, pg. 535

5046 — COMMERCIAL EQUIPMENT-WHOLESALE, NEC

AVA-AUTOMATIC VENDORS OF AMERICA, pg. 8
J.W. ALLEN & COMPANY, pg. 36
ALLISON-ERWIN CO. INC., pg. 40
ALLSUPS CONVENIENCE STORES INC., pg. 43
AMERIDATA, INC., pg. 66
BLEVINS CONCESSION SUPPLY CO., pg. 156
BLOOMFIELD INDUSTRIES CANADA LTD.—Specialty Equipment Companies Inc., pg. 1027
BLUFF CITY CIGARETTE SERVICE—Samelson-Leon Company, Inc., pg. 968
CARTER DAY CO.—Carter Day Industries, Inc., pg. 226
CAVALIER CORPORATION, pg. 229
CERTIFIED GROCERS OF CALIFORNIA, pg. 237
CROUCH SUPPLY COMPANY, INC., pg. 301
CUISINARTS INC.—Conair Corporation, pg. 272
CURTIS EQUIPMENT CO., INC.—Hale-Halsell Company, pg. 500
EDWARD DON & COMPANY OF ILLINOIS, pg. 344
H & H DISTRIBUTING COMPANY, INC., pg. 495
HUBERT COMPANY, pg. 550
J P FOODSERVICE, INC., pg. 586
HAROLD LEONARD & COMPANY, INC., pg. 667
LITTLE CAESAR ENTERPRISES, INC., pg. 678
LOMBARDI FOODSERVICE, INC., pg. 681
LOZIER STORE FIXTURES, INC.—Lozier Corporation, pg. 686
MICHIGAN BAKERY SUPPLY CO.—Best Brands, pg. 146
MONTGOMERY-GREEN CO.—Edward Don & Company of Illinois, pg. 344
NATIONAL RESTAURANT SUPPLY COMPANY, pg. 793
A. POMERANTZ & CO., pg. 880
REPUBLIC STORAGE SYSTEMS COMPANY INC., pg. 928
STANDARD INDUSTRIES, INC., pg. 1036
STANDARD RESTAURANT EQUIPMENT CO.—Standard Industries, Inc., pg. 1036
STANDARD RESTAURANT EQUIPMENT CO.—Standard Industries, Inc., pg. 1036
H. A. STILES CO.—Saunders Brothers, pg. 972
SUNBEAM CORPORATION (CANADA) LIMITED—Sunbeam-Oster Company, Inc., pg. 1059
UNION STEEL PRODUCTS, INCORPORATED, pg. 1129
WASSERSTROM COMPANY, pg. 1167

5047 — MEDICAL, DENTAL & HOSPITAL EQUIPMENT & SUPPLIES-WHOLESALE

AMEDCO HEALTH CARE, INC.—Huntco Inc., pg. 554
AMERICAN HOSPITAL EQUIPMENT CORP.—Randolph Medical Inc., pg. 912
AT HOME RESPIRATORY AND MEDICAL, INC.—Syracuse Supply Company, pg. 1070
ATLANTIC HEALTH CARE RESOURCES, INC.—Syracuse Supply Company, pg. 1070
AUTOMATIC LIQUID PACKAGING, INC., pg. 100
BUFFALO HOSPITAL SUPPLY CO., INC., pg. 187
C.M.W. LABORATORIES DENTSPLY, LTD.—Dentsply International Inc., pg. 330
L. D. CAULK CO. OF CANADA DIV.—Dentsply International Inc., pg. 330
L. D. CAULK DIV.—Dentsply International Inc., pg. 330
THE CROCKER-FELS COMPANY, pg. 299
DH MEDICAL SUPPLY INC.—Taylor Medical Inc., pg. 1081
DE ART S.R.L.—Dentsply International Inc., pg. 330
DENTSPLY ARGENTINA S.A.C.I.—Dentsply International Inc., pg. 330
DENTSPLY (AUSTRALIA) PTY. LTD.—Dentsply International Inc., pg. 330
DENTSPLY CANADA LTD.—Dentsply International Inc., pg. 330
DENTSPLY GMBH—Dentsply International Inc., pg. 330
DENTSPLY INDUSTRIA E COMERCIO LTDA.—Dentsply International Inc., pg. 330
DENTSPLY INTERNATIONAL INC., pg. 329
DENTSPLY LTD.—Dentsply International Inc., pg. 330
DESERT MEDICAL SUPPLY INC.—Taylor Medical Inc., pg. 1081
DETREY DENTSPLY—Dentsply International Inc., pg. 330
DETREY DENTSPLY AG—Dentsply International Inc., pg. 330
DETREY DENTSPLY S.A.—Dentsply International Inc., pg. 330
DIRECT DENTAL SUPPLY CO.—Patterson Dental Company, pg. 851
ENVIRONETICS, pg. 383
EVANGELINE MEDICAL & X-RAY DISTRIBUTORS, pg. 390
FOSTER MEDICAL SUPPLY, INC., pg. 426
GPS HEALTHCARE—Berwind Corporation, pg. 145
HUNTCO HEALTH CARE CO.—Huntco Inc., pg. 554
INSTRUMENTARIUM IMAGING, INC., pg. 572
LABORATORY SUPPLY COMPANY, INC., pg. 649
MED-LAB SUPPLY COMPANY, INC., pg. 734
MEDCREST DIV.—Medline Industries, Inc., pg. 736
MEDECORE DIV.—Medline Industries, Inc., pg. 736
METPAC, LTD., pg. 742
METRO MEDICAL RESOURCES, INC.—Syracuse Supply Company, pg. 1070
MOUNTAINEER MEDICAL/PRIMACARE I.V.—Syracuse Supply Company, pg. 1070
PATTERSON DENTAL COMPANY, pg. 851
PENN MEDICAL SERVICES, INC.—Syracuse Supply Company, pg. 1070
PREMIER DENTAL PRODUCTS COMPANY, pg. 886
PRIMACARE HEALTH RESOURCES, INC.—Syracuse Supply Company, pg. 1070
PROPPER MANUFACTURING CO., INC., pg. 895
RANCARE INC.—Randolph Medical Inc., pg. 912
RANDOLPH MEDICAL INC., pg. 912
RANSOM & RANDOLPH DIV.—Dentsply International Inc., pg. 330
RUGBY-DARBY GROUP OF COS., pg. 955
HENRY SCHEIN, INC., pg. 975
STANDARD MEDICAL IMAGING, INC., pg. 1037
STANDARD WELDERS SUPPLY CO., pg. 1038
TAYLOR HOME HEALTH INC.—Taylor Medical Inc., pg. 1081
TAYLOR MEDICAL INC., pg. 1081
TAYLOR MEDICAL OF LA—Taylor Medical Inc., pg. 1081

5048 — OPTHALMIC GOODS-WHOLESALE

AMERICAN OPTICAL CORP.—American Optical Corp., pg. 59
TASCO, pg. 1079

5049 — PROFESSIONAL EQUIPMENT & SUPPLIES-WHOLESALE, NEC

ACCUCARE DIV.—Medline Industries, Inc., pg. 736
IVAN ALLEN COMPANY, INC., pg. 36
ASH, U.S.A.—Dentsply International Inc., pg. 330
BALTIMORE STATIONERY CO., pg. 116
BEL-ART PRODUCTS, pg. 133
DENTSPLY INTERNATIONAL INC., pg. 329
DIETZGEN CORPORATION, pg. 337
DIETZGEN DE MEXICO S.A. DE C.V.—Dietzgen Corporation, pg. 337
DISPOSAMED DIV.—Medline Industries, Inc., pg. 736
DYNACOR DIV.—Medline Industries, Inc., pg. 736
EDMUND SCIENTIFIC COMPANY, pg. 369
FORESTRY SUPPLIERS, INC., pg. 424
GRAVES-HUMPHREYS COMPANY—Jeld-Wen, Inc., pg. 592
KEUFFEL & ESSER—Azon Corporation, pg. 105
NOVAMETRIX MEDICAL SYSTEMS INC., pg. 817
TAPETECH TOOL CO., INC.—AXIA Incorporated, pg. 8
TASCO, pg. 1079
TASH, INC., pg. 1080
VAN SON HOLLAND INK CORP. OF AMERICA, pg. 1144
WAVETEK CORPORATION, pg. 1168
JERVIS B. WEBB COMPANY LTD.—Jervis B. Webb Company, pg. 1170

5051 — METALS SERVICE CENTERS & OFFICES

ABBOTT GROUP LTD., pg. 9
ABBOTT INDUSTRIAL SUPPLY—Abbott Group Ltd., pg. 9
ADVANCE STEEL CO., pg. 20
ALAMO INDUSTRIAL GROUP, pg. 29
ALAMO IRON WORKS—Alamo Industrial Group, pg. 29
ALASKAN COPPER COMPANIES, pg. 30
ALLIED BUILDING PRODUCTS CORPORATION, pg. 37
ALRO GROUP, pg. 44
ALRO GROUP, ALPENA—Alro Group, pg. 44
ALRO GROUP, BENTON HARBOR—Alro Group, pg. 44
ALRO GROUP, BOCA RATON—Alro Group, pg. 44
ALRO GROUP, DAYTON—Alro Group, pg. 44
ALRO GROUP, DETROIT—Alro Group, pg. 44
ALRO GROUP, FLINT—Alro Group, pg. 44
ALRO GROUP, FORT WAYNE—Alro Group, pg. 44
ALRO GROUP, GRAND RAPIDS—Alro Group, pg. 44
ALRO GROUP, INDIANAPOLIS—Alro Group, pg. 44
ALRO GROUP, JACKSON—Alro Group, pg. 44
ALRO GROUP, LANSING—Alro Group, pg. 44
ALRO GROUP, LOUISVILLE—Alro Group, pg. 44
ALRO GROUP, MUNCIE—Alro Group, pg. 44
ALRO GROUP, PERRYSBURG—Alro Group, pg. 44
ALRO GROUP, SOUTH BEND—Alro Group, pg. 44
AMBASSADOR STEEL CO., pg. 47
AMERICAN INDUSTRIES INC., pg. 55
AMERICAN STRIP STEEL INC., pg. 63
AMERICAN TANK & FABRICATING CO., pg. 63
ARLO GROUP, BATTLE CREEK—Alro Group, pg. 44
ARLO GROUP, CLEARWATER—Alro Group, pg. 44
ARLO GROUP, ORLANDO—Alro Group, pg. 44
ARROW THOMPSON METALS—Thompson Steel Co., Inc., pg. 1095
ART IRON, INC., pg. 86
ASBURY CARBONS, INC., pg. 87
ASSOCIATED METALS & MINERALS CORP., pg. 91
B & K STEEL & SUPPLY, INC., pg. 105
BENJAMIN METALS COMPANY, pg. 139
BING STEEL INC., pg. 151
BOMAN & KEMP STEEL & SUPPLY COMPANY—B & K Steel & Supply, Inc., pg. 105
CT&I CORP. OF WISCONSIN—Chicago Tube & Iron Co., pg. 246
CAMALLOY, INC., pg. 211
CAMBRIDGE STREET METAL CO., INC., pg. 211
CARGILL INC., pg. 219
CAROLINA STEEL CORPORATION, pg. 223
CAROLINA STEEL-GREENVILLE PLANT—Carolina Steel Corporation, pg. 223
CAROLINA STEEL SERVICE CENTER PLANT—Carolina Steel Corporation, pg. 223
CASTING MATERIAL COMPANY, pg. 229
CENTURY AMERICA CORPORATION, pg. 234
CERRO SALES CORPORATION—The Marmon Group, Inc., pg. 711
CHICAGO TUBE & IRON CO., pg. 246
CHICAGO TUBE & IRON COMPANY OF MINNESOTA—Chicago Tube & Iron Co., pg. 246
CHICAGO WEST PULLMAN CORPORATION, pg. 246
CLIFFORD METAL—Lapham-Hickey Steel Corp., pg. 658
COLUMBIA IRON & METAL CO.—Columbia National Group, Inc., pg. 265
COLUMBIA NATIONAL GROUP, INC., pg. 265
COLUMBUS PIPE & EQUIPMENT COMPANY, pg. 267
CONSOLIDATED PIPE & SUPPLY COMPANY, pg. 277
CONTRACTORS STEEL COMPANY, pg. 280
COPPER & BRASS SALES, INC., pg. 284
THE CRISPIN COMPANY, pg. 299
CRUSTEEL LTD.—Crucible Materials Corp., pg. 303
DIAL TUBE COMPANY—J. H. Roberts Industries Inc., pg. 939
DIVERSIFIED STEEL—American Industries Inc., pg. 56
DUBIN-CLARK & COMPANY, pg. 350
DUGGAN INDUSTRIES, INC., pg. 351
EASTERN STEEL & METAL COMPANY—Olympic Steel Inc., pg. 825
EMPIRE STEEL TRADING COMPANY, pg. 380
ENCO MATERIALS, INC., pg. 380
ESCO INTERNATIONAL—Esco Corporation, pg. 388
EXPRESS STEEL AND PLASTICS—Hickinbotham Bros., Ltd, pg. 532
FERROLEGERINGAR AG—Metallurg, Inc., pg. 742
FORD STEEL CO., INC., pg. 423
FRITZ CHEMICAL COMPANY, pg. 434
FULLERTON METALS CO., pg. 436
R. J. GALLAGHER CO., pg. 441
GARY METALS CO., INC.—Primary Industries Corporation, pg. 889
GENERAL AEROSPACE MATERIALS CORPORATION, pg. 448
J. GERBER & CO. INC., pg. 453
GIBBS WIRE & STEEL COMPANY, INC., pg. 456
GIBBS WIRE & STEEL COMPANY OF CANADA LTD.—Gibbs Wire & Steel Company, Inc., pg. 456
GIBRALTAR STEEL CORP., pg. 456
GRANT STEEL CORP.—Columbia National Group, Inc., pg. 265
H & D STEEL SERVICE, INC., pg. 495
HARRIS STEEL CO., pg. 512
HICKINBOTHAM BROS., LTD, pg. 532
HICKMAN WILLIAMS & CO. INC., pg. 532
HIRSCHFELD, INC., pg. 536
HIRSCHFELD STEEL COMPANY, INC.—Hirschfeld, Inc., pg. 536
HOOGOVENS ALUMINUM CORP., pg. 543
HOPPER INC., pg. 543
HUB INC., pg. 548
INDEPENDENT METALS, pg. 565
INDEPENDENT METALS—Independent Metals, pg. 565
INDUSTRIAL METALS OF THE SOUTH, pg. 566
INDUSTRIAL STEEL & WIRE COMPANY, pg. 567
INTERSTATE STEEL SUPPLY CO., pg. 580
INTERSTATE STEEL SUPPLY CO. OF MARYLAND—Interstate Steel Supply Co., pg. 581
ROBERT JAMES SALES INC., pg. 589
EARLE M. JORGENSEN COMPANY, pg. 605
JORGENSEN STEEL & ALUMINUM—Earle M. Jorgensen Company, pg. 605
JORGENSEN STEEL & ALUMINUM/BIRMINGHAM—Earle M. Jorgensen Company, pg. 605
JORGENSEN STEEL & ALUMINUM/CHARLOTTE—Earle M. Jorgensen Company, pg. 605
JORGENSEN STEEL & ALUMINUM/INDIANAPOLIS—Earle M. Jorgensen Company, pg. 606
JORGENSEN STEEL & ALUMINUM/LOS ANGELES—Earle M. Jorgensen Company, pg. 606
KAIBAB INDUSTRIES, pg. 614
KAIBAB METALS, INC.—Kaibab Industries, pg. 614
KASLE STEEL CORPORATION, pg. 617
KEN-MAC METAL, INC., pg. 622
KENWAL PRODUCTS CORP., pg. 624
KILSBY-ROBERTS—Earle M. Jorgensen Company, pg. 606
KILSBY-ROBERTS/BALTIMORE—Earle M. Jorgensen Company, pg. 606
KILSBY-ROBERTS/BIRMINGHAM—Earle M. Jorgensen Company, pg. 606
KILSBY-ROBERTS/BOSTON—Earle M. Jorgensen Company, pg. 606
KILSBY-ROBERTS/CHARLOTTE—Earle M. Jorgensen Company, pg. 606
KILSBY-ROBERTS/CHICAGO—Earle M. Jorgensen Company, pg. 606
KILSBY-ROBERTS/CLEVELAND—Earle M. Jorgensen Company, pg. 606
KILSBY-ROBERTS CUTTING CENTER/HONING/TULSA—Earle M. Jorgensen Company, pg. 606
KILSBY-ROBERTS CUTTING CENTER/INDIANAPOLIS—Earle M. Jorgensen Company, pg. 606
KILSBY-ROBERTS/DALLAS—Earle M. Jorgensen Company, pg. 606
KILSBY-ROBERTS/DAVENPORT—Earle M. Jorgensen Company, pg. 606
KILSBY-ROBERTS/DENVER—Earle M. Jorgensen Company, pg. 606
KILSBY-ROBERTS/DETROIT—Earle M. Jorgensen Company, pg. 606
KILSBY-ROBERTS/HAYWARD—Earle M. Jorgensen Company, pg. 606
KILSBY-ROBERTS HONING/BLUE ISLAND—Earle M. Jorgensen Company, pg. 606
KILSBY-ROBERTS/HOUSTON—Earle M. Jorgensen Company, pg. 606
KILSBY-ROBERTS/INDIANAPOLIS—Earle M. Jorgensen Company, pg. 606
KILSBY-ROBERTS/KANSAS CITY—Earle M. Jorgensen Company, pg. 606
KILSBY-ROBERTS/LITTLE ROCK—Earle M. Jorgensen Company, pg. 606
KILSBY-ROBERTS/LOS ANGELES—Earle M. Jorgensen Company, pg. 606
KILSBY-ROBERTS/MEMPHIS—Earle M. Jorgensen Company, pg. 606
KILSBY-ROBERTS/MILWAUKEE—Earle M. Jorgensen Company, pg. 606
KILSBY-ROBERTS/PHILADELPHIA—Earle M. Jorgensen Company, pg. 606
KILSBY-ROBERTS/PORTLAND—Earle M. Jorgensen Company, pg. 606
KILSBY-ROBERTS/ST. LOUIS—Earle M. Jorgensen Company, pg. 606
KILSBY-ROBERTS/SEATTLE—Earle M. Jorgensen Company, pg. 606
KILSBY-ROBERTS/TULSA—Earle M. Jorgensen Company, pg. 606
KILSBY-ROBERTS/TWIN CITIES—Earle M. Jorgensen Company, pg. 606
KLINE IRON & STEEL CO., INC., pg. 635
KREHER STEEL COMPANY, INC., pg. 644
LABARGE PIPE & STEEL COMPANY, pg. 649
LAFAYETTE STEEL CO., pg. 650
LAPHAM-HICKEY STEEL CORP., pg. 658
LAUBECK CORPORATION, BECKLEY DIVISION—Laubeck Corporation/Cross, pg. 660
LONDON LITHO ALUMINUM CO., INC., pg. 681
LOUISIANA UTILITIES SUPPLY COMPANY, pg. 684
LYNCHBURG SERVICE CENTER—Carolina Steel Corporation, pg. 223
LYON CONKLIN & COMPANY, pg. 690
M M SYSTEMS CORPORATION, pg. 692
M M SYSTEMS CORPORATION—M M Systems Corporation, pg. 692
MNP CORP., pg. 693
THE MARMON GROUP, INC., pg. 710
MARMON/KEYSTONE CANADA-MONTREAL—The Marmon Group, Inc., pg. 712
MARMON/KEYSTONE CANADA-TORONTO—The Marmon Group, Inc., pg. 712
MARMON/KEYSTONE CORP.—The Marmon Group, Inc., pg. 711
MCJUNKIN CORPORATION, pg. 730
MEIER METAL SERVICE CENTERS, INC., pg. 737
A. W. MENDENHALL CO., INC., pg. 739
METRON STEEL CORP., pg. 744
MILES METAL COMPANY—The Marmon Group, Inc., pg. 712
MITCHEL & SCOT MACHINE CO., INC., pg. 761
MONICO ALLOYS, INC., pg. 765
E.K. MORRIS & CO., INC.—Art Iron, Inc., pg. 86
MULACH STEEL CORPORATION, pg. 775
NASHVILLE STEEL CORP., pg. 784
NATIONAL FORGE EXPORT CORP.—National Forge Company, pg. 789
NATIONAL MATERIAL LIMITED PARTNERSHIP—Tang Industries Inc., pg. 1078
NEILL-LAVIELLE SUPPLY CO., pg. 797
NORTH STAR STEEL CO.—Cargill Inc., pg. 219
NORTHWEST PIPE FITTINGS, INC., pg. 815
OLYMPIC STEEL INC., pg. 825
O'NEAL STEEL INC., pg. 827
ORLEANS MATERIALS & EQUIPMENT CO., INC., pg. 829
ORTRONICS, INC., pg. 830
OWEN INDUSTRIES, INC., pg. 834
PACESETTER STEEL SERVICE, INC., pg. 839
PACIFIC HIDE & FUR DEPOT, pg. 840
PACIFIC METAL COMPANY, pg. 841
PAN AMERICAN TRADE DEVELOPMENT CORP., pg. 845
PARKER STEEL COMPANY, pg. 849
PAXTON & VIERLING—Owen Industries, Inc., pg. 834
PEGASUS INTERNATIONAL CORPORATION, pg. 855
PHOENIX STEEL, INC., pg. 869
PIONEER ALUMINUM, INC., pg. 871
PLYMOUTH TUBE COMPANY, pg. 877
PRECISION SPECIALTY METALS, INC.—Dubin-Clark & Company, pg. 350
PRIMARY INDUSTRIES CORPORATION, pg. 889
PRIMARY STEEL INC.—Primary Industries Corporation, pg. 889
RELIANCE STEEL & ALUMINUM CO., pg. 925
RICHMOND SERVICE CENTER—Carolina Steel Corporation, pg. 223
RIDG-U-RAK, INC., pg. 933
ROINOKE SERVICE CENTER—Carolina Steel Corporation, pg. 223
ROLLED STEEL PRODUCTS CORPORATION, pg. 944
SAMSTEEL, INC.—Ferro Union, Inc., pg. 407
SMITH PIPE & STEEL CO., pg. 1014
SOUTHEASTERN STEEL COMPANY, pg. 1020
SPANG & COMPANY, pg. 1025
STANDARD ALLOYS & MANUFACTURING—Blue Tee Corporation, pg. 161
STEEL, INC., pg. 1044
M. SWIFT & SONS INC., pg. 1068
TDW FOREIGN SALES CORP.—T.D. Williamson, Inc., pg. 1192
A. TENENBAUM CO. INC., pg. 1087
THOMPSON STEEL CO., INC., pg. 1094
THUNDERBIRD STEEL CORPORATION, pg. 1096
TIERNAY METALS, INC., pg. 1096
TITAN INDUSTRIAL CORP., pg. 1099
TOTTEN TUBES, INC., pg. 1103
TROJAN STEEL CO., pg. 1115
TUBETEC—Plymouth Tube Company, pg. 878
TUBULAR STEEL INC., pg. 1118
ULBRICH OF CALIFORNIA, INC.—Ulbrich Stainless Steels & Special Metals, Inc., pg. 1125
ULBRICH OF GEORGIA, INC.—Ulbrich Stainless Steels & Special Metals, Inc., pg. 1125
ULBRICH OF ILLINOIS, INC.—Ulbrich Stainless Steels & Special Metals, Inc., pg. 1125
U.S. METALSOURCE CORPORATION, pg. 1136
THE UNIVERSAL STEEL CO.—Columbia National Group, Inc., pg. 265
VAN PELT CORPORATION, pg. 1144
WATSON BOWMAN ACME, INC.—Berwind Corporation, pg. 145
WAYNE STEEL, INC., pg. 1169
CARL WEISSMAN & SONS, INC., pg. 1174
WESTERN SPECIALTY CONTAINER—Independent Can Company, pg. 565
WHITE STAR STEEL—Nashville Steel Corp., pg. 784
WILLIAMS & COMPANY, INC.—Cawsl Corporation, pg. 230
WILLIAMS STEEL & HARDWARE COMPANY, pg. 1191
WILSON SERVICE CENTER—Carolina Steel Corporation, pg. 223
WINSTON STEEL PRODUCTS CO., pg. 1197
WIRE TECH, INC.—Group Dekko International Inc., pg. 490

5052 — COAL & OTHER MINERALS & ORES-WHOLESALE

ALLEY-CASSETTY COAL CO., pg. 37
APPLIED INDUSTRIAL MATERIALS CORPORATION, pg. 79

SID HARVEY INC., pg. 515
HICKMAN WILLIAMS & CO. INC., pg. 532
INTERNATIONAL CHEMICAL COMPANY, pg. 576
LOGAN & KANAWHA COAL CO., pg. 681
MONROC, INC., pg. 766
PRIMARY COAL INC.—Primary Industries Corporation, pg. 889
PRIMARY INDUSTRIES CORPORATION, pg. 889
TASA CORPORATION, pg. 1079
THE UNITED COMPANY, pg. 1131
V.F. ENERGIES, INC., pg. 1141
R. T. VANDERBILT COMPANY, INC., pg. 1144
WGM/HYDRO, pg. 1156

5063 — ELECTRICAL APPARATUS & EQUIPMENT, WIRING SUPPLIES & CONSTRUCTION MATERIALS-WHOLESALE

ACTIVE ELECTRICAL SUPPLY COMPANY, pg. 15
ADVANCE POWER CO. LTD.—Panduit Company, pg. 845
ALL-PHASE ELECTRIC SUPPLY CO. INC., pg. 35
ALLHABO AKTIEBOLAG—Panduit Company, pg. 845
ALPHA ELECTRONIC SIGNAL TECHNOLOGIES, INC., pg. 43
ANDERSON WHOLESALE COMPANY, pg. 73
ANGELO BROTHERS CO., pg. 74
ARGO INTERNATIONAL—Decal Enterprises, Inc., pg. 323
ARGO INTERNATIONAL CORP., pg. 81
ARKANSAS ELECTRIC COOPERATIVES INC., pg. 83
ASSOCIATED OF LOS ANGELES, pg. 90
BATTEY MACHINERY COMPANY, pg. 127
BENTLY NEVADA CANADA LTD.—Bently Nevada Corporation, pg. 141
BENTLY NEVADA EUROPA B.V.—Bently Nevada Corporation, pg. 141
BENTLY NEVADA FRANCE S.A.R.L.—Bently Nevada Corporation, pg. 141
BENTLY NEVADA SALES & SERVICE SINGAPORE PTE. LTD.—Bently Nevada Corporation, pg. 141
BORDER STATES INDUSTRIES, INC., pg. 165
BRAID ELECTRIC COMPANY, pg. 171
BRANCE KRACHY COMPANY, INC., pg. 171
BRINK EQUIPMENT & SUPPLY COMPANY—Brink Electric Construction Company, pg. 176
BRYANT SUPPLY COMPANY, INC., pg. 185
BUHRMAN-PHARR HARDWARE COMPANY, pg. 187
BUILDER MARTS OF AMERICA, pg. 187
BURC ELECTRONICS & MACHINERY CORP.—Panduit Company, pg. 845
C.V. SUMBER SAKTI—Panduit Company, pg. 846
CAMERON & BARKLEY COMPANY, INC., pg. 212
CAPITAL ELECTRIC GROUP, INC., pg. 215
CARTWRIGHT COMMUNICATIONS CO., pg. 227
CENTRAL SUPPLY CO., INC., pg. 234
CHAMPION, INC., pg. 238
CLEVELAND ELECTRIC CO.—Cleveland Group, Inc., pg. 255
CLEVELAND GROUP, INC., pg. 255
COMMERCIAL ESPANOLA DE COMPONENTES S.A.—Panduit Company, pg. 845
CONDUCTORS UNLIMITED—Electrical Insulation Suppliers, pg. 374
CONE, LDA.—Panduit Company, pg. 845
CRESCENT ELECTRIC SUPPLY CO., pg. 298
CRUM ELECTRIC SUPPLY CO., INC., pg. 303
CUMMINS MID-SOUTH, INC., pg. 305
DAHMS ELECTRONIK GMBH—Panduit Company, pg. 845
DEALERS ELECTRICAL SUPPLY CO., pg. 322
DOUGLASTON ELECTRIC—Turtle & Hughes, Inc., pg. 1120
DURO LITE LAMPS, INC.—Duro-Test Corporation, pg. 355
DURO-TEST CANADA—Duro-Test Corporation, pg. 355
DURO-TEST INTL. CORP.—Duro-Test Corporation, pg. 355
DURO-TEST DE MEXICO, S.A.—Duro-Test Corporation, pg. 355
ELECTRIC SPECIALTY & SUPPLY—Electric Specialty & Supply Corp., pg. 374
ELECTRIC SPECIALTY & SUPPLY CORP., pg. 374
ELECTRICAL EQUIPMENT COMPANY, pg. 374
ELECTRICAL EQUIPMENT COMPANY—Electrical Equipment Company, pg. 374
ELECTRICAL INSULATION SUPPLIERS, pg. 374
ELECTRICAL WHOLESALE SUPPLY COMPANY, INC., pg. 374
ELECTRO-MATIC PRODUCTS INC., pg. 374
ELECTRONICA DEL PACIFICO—Panduit Company, pg. 845
ELECTRONIK (PTY) LTD.—Panduit Company, pg. 845
OY ETRA AB—Panduit Company, pg. 845
EVANS ELECTRIC SUPPLY, INC.—Reily Electric Supply, Inc., pg. 923
FERGUSON ELECTRIC CONSTRUCTION CO., INC., pg. 406
FREDERICK TRADING COMPANY, pg. 430
GRAYBAR ELECTRIC COMPANY, INC., pg. 479
GRAYBAR INTERNATIONAL, INC.—Graybar Electric Company, Inc., pg. 479
HANS FOLSGAARD, AGENTUR A/S—Panduit Company, pg. 845
HEADCO INDUSTRIES, INC., pg. 520
INDUSTRIAL ELECTRONIC ENGINEERS, INC., pg. 566
INTERELECTRONIC OERTLI AG—Panduit Company, pg. 845
INTERSTATE ELECTRIC SUPPLY COMPANY, INC., pg. 580
ISELCO SF—Panduit Company, pg. 845
KING WIRE & CABLE CORPORATION, pg. 631
KLOCKNER-MOELLER NORSK A/S—Panduit Company, pg. 845
LAPPIN ELECTRIC COMPANY, pg. 658
J.H. LARSON ELECTRICAL COMPANY, pg. 659
THE F. D. LAWRENCE ELECTRIC CO., pg. 661
LEADER INSTRUMENTS CORPORATION, pg. 664
LINE EQUIPMENT SALES CO., INC.—Utilities Construction Co., Inc. Of South Carolina, pg. 1141
LITTELFUSE AG—Littelfuse, Inc., pg. 678
MADISON ELECTRIC CO., pg. 699
MANHATTAN ELECTRIC CABLE CORPORATION—Edwardstone & Company, Inc., pg. 370
MAURICE ELECTRIC SUPPLY COMPANY, pg. 722
MCDONALD EQUIPMENT CO., pg. 728
MCJUNKIN CORPORATION, pg. 730
MCNAUGHTON-MCKAY ELECTRIC CO., pg. 732
MINARIK ELECTRIC COMPANY, pg. 756
MINNESOTA ELECTRIC SUPPLY COMPANY, pg. 757
MISSILE SUPPLY CO.—Electrical Insulation Suppliers, pg. 374
REX MOORE ELECTRICAL CONTRACTORS & ENGINEERS, pg. 768
MOSLER CANADA—American Standard Inc., pg. 62
MULDER HARDENBERG B.V.—Panduit Company, pg. 845
NORTH ELECTRIC SUPPLY, INC., pg. 813
NORTHERN WIRE & CABLE, INC., pg. 814
NORTHLAND ELECTRIC SUPPLY COMPANY, pg. 814
PALMER ELECTRIC CO., pg. 843
PANDUIT AUST. PTY. LTD.—Panduit Company, pg. 845
PANDUIT CANADA LTD.—Panduit Company, pg. 845
PANDUIT CORP.—Panduit Company, pg. 845
PANDUIT CORP. JAPAN BRANCH—Panduit Company, pg. 846
PANDUIT GMBH—Panduit Company, pg. 846
PANDUIT LIMITED—Panduit Company, pg. 846
PANDUIT NEDERLAND—Panduit Company, pg. 846
PANDUIT PHILIPPINES—Panduit Company, pg. 846
PANDUIT S.A.S.—Panduit Company, pg. 846
PANDUIT SINGAPORE PTE. LTD.—Panduit Company, pg. 846
PANDUIT S.N.C.—Panduit Company, pg. 845
PANDUIT TRADING PTE. LTD.—Panduit Company, pg. 846
PANDUIT TRADING PTE. LTD.—Panduit Company, pg. 846
PLOVER BLFC BRANCH—W.A. Roosevelt Co., pg. 946
PLYWOOD PLASTICS, INC.—Plywood Plastics Inc., pg. 878
POWELL ELECTRONICS INC., pg. 882
POWER ENGINEERING CO. INC., pg. 883
PYRAMID ELECTRIC SUPPLY CO., INC.—Southern Electric Supply Co., Inc., pg. 1020
RAUB SUPPLY COMPANY, pg. 913
RAYOVAC LIMITED—RAYOVAC Corporation, pg. 915
REILY ELECTRIC SUPPLY, INC., pg. 923
REVERE ELECTRIC SUPPLY CO., pg. 930
W.A. ROOSEVELT CO., pg. 946
RUMSEY ELECTRIC CO., pg. 956
S.K. TSOUMANIS REPRESENTATIONS—Panduit Company, pg. 846
THE SACKS ELECTRICAL SUPPLY CO.—UIS, Inc., pg. 1123
SCHAEDLER BROTHERS, INC., pg. 974
ALEXANDER SCHNEIDER LTD.—Panduit Company, pg. 846
SEACOAST ELECTRIC COMPANY—Edwardstone & Company, Inc., pg. 370
SHEALY ELECTRICAL WHOLESALERS, pg. 996
SIMPLEX INTL. TIME EQUIP. CO. LTD. (CANADA)—Simplex Time Recorder Co., pg. 1006
SIMPLEX INTL. TIME EQUIP. PTY. LTD.—Simplex Time Recorder Co., pg. 1006
SIMPLEX MANAGEMENT SERVICES, LTD.—Simplex Time Recorder Co., pg. 1006
SOUTH STATES INC.—Distribution America, pg. 340
SOUTHERN ELECTRIC SUPPLY CO., INC., pg. 1020
SOUTHERN ELECTRIC SUPPLY CO., INC.—Southern Electric Supply Co., Inc., pg. 1021
SOUTHERN ELECTRIC SUPPLY CO., INC.—Southern Electric Supply Co., Inc., pg. 1021
SRIVATHSA ELECTRICAL CORP.—Panduit Company, pg. 846
STACY EQUIPMENT CO.—Webster Industries Inc., pg. 1172
STATE ELECTRIC SUPPLY CO., pg. 1040
STEINER ELECTRIC CO., pg. 1045
STREECH ELECTRIC COMPANY, pg. 1053
STUSSER ELECTRIC COMPANY, pg. 1055
SUMMA FOUR LIMITED—Summa Four, Inc., pg. 1057
T & R ELECTRIC SUPPLY COMPANY, INC., pg. 1071
TVESCO, INC., pg. 1075
TECNA LTDA.—Panduit Company, pg. 846
TECOT ELECTRIC SUPPLY COMPANY, pg. 1084
TRI-STATE ARMATURE ELECTRIC WORKS, pg. 1110
TRISTATE ELECTRICAL SUPPLY CO., INC., pg. 1114
TURNER SUPPLY COMPANY, pg. 1119
TURTLE & HUGHES, INC., pg. 1119
TYLUS SDN BHD—Panduit Company, pg. 846
UTILITIES CONSTRUCTION CO., INC. OF SOUTH CAROLINA, pg. 1141
VEGAS ELECTRIC SUPPLY—Capital Electric Group, Inc., pg. 215
VITUS ELECTRICAL SUPPLY COMPANY, pg. 1154
WATLOW TAIWAN—Watlow Electric Manufacturing Company, pg. 1168
WATSON ELECTRIC SUPPLY INC., pg. 1168
CARL WEISSMAN & SONS, INC., pg. 1174
WESTERN CONTROLS, pg. 1178
WHITE ELECTRICAL CONSTRUCTION CO., pg. 1185
WHOLESALE ELECTRIC DIVISION—Southern Electric Supply Co., Inc., pg. 1020

5064 — ELECTRICAL APPLIANCES, TELEVISION & RADIO SETS-WHOLESALE

ADVENT LOUDSPEAKERS—International Jensen Inc., pg. 578
ALARON ELECTRONICS FAR EAST LTD., HONG KONG—Alaron Inc., pg. 30
ALARON INC., pg. 30
ALLISON-ERWIN CO. INC., pg. 40
ARIZONA WHOLESALE SUPPLY COMPANY, pg. 82
BENNETT BROTHERS, INC., pg. 139
BISSELL LTD.—Bissell Inc., pg. 153
TIM & DIANE BLAGGE INC., pg. 155
BLUFF CITY DISTRIBUTING CO., INC., pg. 161
BOSE AG—Bose Corporation, pg. 167
BOSE LTD.—Bose Corporation, pg. 167
BOSE U.K., LTD.—Bose Corporation, pg. 167
CAIN & BULTMAN, INC., pg. 207
CALIFORNIA ELECTRIC SERVICE, pg. 209
THE CLIMATIC CORP., pg. 255
THE COLEMAN COMPANY, INC.—MacAndrews & Forbes Holdings Inc., pg. 695
CONTINENTAL CONAIR, LTD.—Conair Corporation, pg. 272
CONTINENTAL ELECTRIC INDUSTRIES, LTD.—Conair Corporation, pg. 272
CRESCENT ELECTRIC SUPPLY CO., pg. 298
D&H DISTRIBUTING COMPANY, pg. 307
ELECTRO BRAND, INC., pg. 374
FARGO GLASS & PAINT COMPANY, pg. 399
GAGGENAU USA CORPORATION, pg. 441
GROSSENBURG IMPLEMENTS, INCORPORATED, pg. 489
HARDWARE WHOLESALERS, INC., pg. 508
HARTZELL CORPORATION, pg. 514
HERBAL ENTERPRISES INC., pg. 530
INKEL CORP., pg. 569
INTREPID CORP., pg. 581
JOHNSON SUPPLY & EQUIPMENT CORP., pg. 601
KLAUS RADIO INC., pg. 634
GEO. H. LEHLEITNER & CO., INC., pg. 666
MPO VIDEOTRONICS—MPO Videotronics, Inc., pg. 693
MPO VIDEOTRONICS, INC., pg. 693
MOORE SPECIAL TOOL CO., INC., pg. 768
MUTUAL DISTRIBUTORS LTD., pg. 778
NATIONAL BRANDS, INC., pg. 786
NELSON & SMALL INC., pg. 798
OUR OWN HARDWARE COMPANY, pg. 832
PALMER ELECTRIC CO., pg. 843
PEIRCE-PHELPS, INC., pg. 855
POLLENEX CORPORATION, pg. 879
RAUB SUPPLY COMPANY, pg. 913
ROMAN ELECTRIC COMPANY, INC., pg. 945
RAYMOND ROSEN CO., pg. 948
ROTT-KELLER SUPPLY CO., pg. 951
GUY SCHOENECKER, INC., pg. 977
SEBASTIAN & COOKE, pg. 986
SERVCO PACIFIC INC., pg. 991
SKINNER CORP., pg. 1009
SOUNDESIGN CORPORATION, pg. 1018
SOUTHERN RADIO CORPORATION, pg. 1022
SUES, YOUNG & BROWN INC., pg. 1056
SUNBEAM APPLIANCE COMPANY—Sunbeam-Oster Company, Inc., pg. 1059
TACONY CORPORATION, pg. 1076
TELE-COM PRODUCTS, INC., pg. 1084
TRANE EUROPE—American Standard Inc., pg. 62
TRANE LTD.—American Standard Inc., pg. 62
WARREN DISTRIBUTING CORP., pg. 1164
WATLOW FRANCE S.A.R.L.—Watlow Electric Manufacturing Company, pg. 1168
WATSON ELECTRIC SUPPLY INC., pg. 1168
WHOLESALE ELECTRONIC SUPPLY, pg. 1188
WILLIAMS DISTRIBUTING COMPANY, pg. 1190
THE ZAMOISKI CO., pg. 1216

5065 — ELECTRONIC PARTS & EQUIPMENT-WHOLESALE

ACTION INDUSTRIE COMPUTER, GMBH—Action Instruments, Inc., pg. 14
ACTION INSTRUMENTS (CHINA) LTD.—Action Instruments, Inc., pg. 14
ACTION INSTRUMENTS, LTD.—Action Instruments, Inc., pg. 15
ACTIVE ELECTRICAL SUPPLY COMPANY, pg. 15
ALLISON-ERWIN CO. INC., pg. 40
ALMO CORP., pg. 43
AMERICAN MITAC CORPORATION, pg. 58
AMPEX CORPORATION MARKETING, SALES & SERVICE—Sherborne Group, Inc., pg. 998
ASSOCIATED AIRCRAFT SUPPLY COMPANY, pg. 89
ATLAS/SOUNDOLIER—American Trading and Production Corporation, pg. 64
BELL & HOWELL LTD.—Bell & Howell Company, pg. 135
BERGQUIST COMPANY, INC., pg. 141
BERKELEY INDUSTRIES INC., pg. 141
BISCO INDUSTRIES, pg. 153
TIM & DIANE BLAGGE INC., pg. 155
BORDER STATES INDUSTRIES, INC., pg. 165
BOURNS AG & BOURNS (SCHWEIZ) AG—Bourns, Inc., pg. 168
BOURNS BENELUX B.V.—Bourns, Inc., pg. 168
BOURNS ELECTRONICS, LTD.—Bourns, Inc., pg. 168
BOURNS, GMBH—Bourns, Inc., pg. 168
BOURNS-OHMIC S.A.—Bourns, Inc., pg. 168
BROADCAST SUPPLY WEST, pg. 177
BRYANT SUPPLY COMPANY, INC., pg. 185
CAPP, INC., pg. 216
CENTURY COMPUTER MARKETING, pg. 235
CHIP SUPPLY INC., pg. 248
CIMLINC INC., pg. 249
ECONOCOM-USA INC., pg. 367
ELECTRONIC DRIVES AND CONTROLS, pg. 375
FAIRMONT ELECTRONICS—RS Electronics, pg. 908
FOLLETT COLLEGE RESOURCES—Follett Corporation, pg. 422
FRED V. FOWLER COMPANY, INC., pg. 427
FREDERICK TRADING COMPANY, pg. 430
THE GENIE COMPANY—The Genie Company, pg. 452
SID HARVEY INC., pg. 515

HAUENSTEIN & BURMEISTER, INC., pg. 517
HAYES MICROCOMPUTER PRODUCTS, INC.—Hayes Microcomputer Products, Inc., pg. 519
HAYES MICROCOMPUTER PRODUCTS LTD.—Hayes Microcomputer Products, Inc., pg. 519
INTERNATIONAL COMPONENTS CORPORATION, pg. 576
JOHNSON SUPPLY & EQUIPMENT CORP., pg. 601
KLAUS RADIO INC., pg. 634
DAVID LANGER & CO., INC., pg. 657
LEASAMETRIC, INC.—The Marmon Group, Inc., pg. 712
LONDON LITHO ALUMINUM CO., INC., pg. 681
MSD, INC., pg. 693
MANHATTAN ELECTRIC CABLE CORPORATION—Edwardstone & Company, Inc., pg. 370
NATIONAL BRANDS, INC., pg. 786
OLIVE ELECTRONICS—RS Electronics, pg. 908
PPA INDUSTRIES, INC., pg. 836
PEGASUS INTERNATIONAL CORPORATION, pg. 855
PEIRCE-PHELPS, INC., pg. 855
PIONEER COMMUNICATIONS OF AMERICA, pg. 871
POWELL ELECTRONICS INC., pg. 882
POWER & TELEPHONE SUPPLY COMPANY, pg. 883
RS ELECTRONICS, pg. 908
R.W. ELECTRONICS, pg. 908
RAO WHOLESALE TIRE CENTERS, INC., pg. 912
RAULAND-BORG (CANADA) INC.—Rauland-Borg Corporation, pg. 914
RESERVE MOTION CONTROL SYSTEMS—Bodine Electric Company, pg. 162
RONCO COMMUNICATIONS & ELECTRONICS INC., pg. 946
SEBASTIAN & COOKE, pg. 986
SENNHEISER ELECTRONIC CORP., pg. 989
SERVO INTERNATIONAL, INC.—Servo Corporation of America, pg. 993
SHOKAI FAR EAST LTD., pg. 1000
NANCY SKINNER & ASSOCIATES—Biggs Gilmore Communications, pg. 149
SLOAN TECHNOLOGY—Veeco Instrumentations, Inc., pg. 1146
SOUNDESIGN CORP. HONG KONG LTD.—Soundesign Corporation, pg. 1019
SOUNDESIGN CORP. JAPAN LTD.—Soundesign Corporation, pg. 1019
STANDARD ELECTRONICS, INC., pg. 1036
STEINER ELECTRIC CO., pg. 1045
SUMMA FOUR LIMITED—Summa Four, Inc., pg. 1057
TELONIC BERKELEY—Berkeley Industries Inc., pg. 141
TRINKLE SALES, INC., pg. 1114
TYLAN (UK) LTD.—Tylan General, Inc., pg. 1122
VEECO GMBH—Veeco Instrumentations, Inc., pg. 1146
VEECO INSTRUMENTS LTD.—Veeco Instrumentations, Inc., pg. 1146
VEECO K.K.—Veeco Instrumentations, Inc., pg. 1146
WALKER & ASSOCIATES, INC., pg. 1159
WATSON ELECTRIC SUPPLY INC., pg. 1168
WAVETEK ELECTRONICS GMBH—Wavetek Corporation, pg. 1169
WAVETEK ELECTRONICS LTD.—Wavetek Corporation, pg. 1169
WESTERN CONTROLS, pg. 1178
WHOLESALE ELECTRONIC SUPPLY, pg. 1188
WILTEL COMMUNICATIONS SYSTEMS, INC., pg. 1194
THE ZAMOISKI CO., pg. 1216

5072 — HARDWARE-WHOLESALE

ATC AG—American Tool Companies, Inc., pg. 64
ACE HARDWARE CORPORATION, pg. 12
ADAMS RITE (EUROPE) LTD.—Adams Rite Manufacturing Co., pg. 17
ALASKA INDUSTRIAL HARDWARE INC., pg. 30
ALLMETAL SCREW PRODUCTS CORP., pg. 40
AMERICAN FASTENERS—Jupiter Industries, Inc., pg. 609
AMERICAN LOCK & SUPPLY INC., pg. 57
AMFAC DISTRIBUTION CORPORATION—JMB Realty Corporation, pg. 585
ARIZONA SASH & DOOR CO.—Foxworth-Galbraith Lumber Co., pg. 428
ATWOOD DISTRIBUTING, INC., pg. 97
BENSON INDUSTRIES, INC., pg. 139
BLACK & CO., pg. 154
BORCHERS BROS., pg. 165
BUHRMAN-PHARR HARDWARE COMPANY, pg. 187
CALIFORNIA HARDWARE CO., pg. 209
CARDER, INC., pg. 217
CENEX (FARMERS UNION CENTRAL EXCHANGE, INC.), pg. 231
COAST TO COAST—Servistar Corporation, pg. 993
COBRA TOOL, INC.—American Tool Companies, Inc., pg. 64
COTTER & COMPANY, pg. 288
DAVIS PAINT COMPANY, pg. 319
DECO PRODUCTS CO., pg. 324
EMERY WATERHOUSE COMPANY, pg. 379
EXCELSIOR MANUFACTURING & SUPPLY CORP., pg. 392
FARWELL, OZMUN, KIRK & CO.—United Hardware Distributing Co., pg. 1133
FINGERLE LUMBER CO., pg. 411
FRANTZ EXPORT CORP.—Frantz Manufacturing Co., pg. 430
FREDERICK TRADING COMPANY, pg. 430
R. J. GALLAGHER CO., pg. 441
GENERAL HARDWARE DISTRIBUTORS—Alaska Industrial Hardware Inc., pg. 30
GROCERS SUPPLY CO. INC., pg. 488
GUTMANN CUTLERY, INC.—Hyde Manufacturing Co., pg. 556
HARDWARE WHOLESALERS, INC., pg. 508
THE HARTWELL CORPORATION, pg. 514
HERBAL ENTERPRISES INC., pg. 530
HILL-BEHAN LUMBER COMPANY, pg. 534
IMPERIAL SCHRADE (EUROPE) G.M.B.H.—Imperial Schrade Corp., pg. 564
KRUSE HARDWARE COMPANY, pg. 645
LUGBILL BROTHERS, INC., pg. 686
MADISON GROCERY CO., INC., pg. 699
MCLAUGHLIN INDUSTRIAL DISTRIBUTORS, INC., pg. 731
METRIC & MULTISTANDARD COMPONENTS, pg. 743
MICO, INC., pg. 748
MID-CONTINENT SCREW PRODUCTS CO., pg. 750
MUTUAL DISTRIBUTORS LTD., pg. 778
NATIONAL-GENERAL SUPPLY, INC.—Carl Weissman & Sons, Inc., pg. 1174
OUR OWN HARDWARE COMPANY, pg. 832
PACIFIC HIDE & FUR DEPOT, pg. 840
PALMETTO WHOLESALE CO., INC., pg. 844
PRO HARDWARE, INC., pg. 891
RADIATOR SPECIALTY COMPANY, pg. 909
RANCHERS SUPPLY COMPANY—Carder, Inc., pg. 217
RICHMOND SCREW ANCHOR DIVISION—Symons Corporation, pg. 1069
ROCKFORD INTERNATIONAL GROUP—Rockford Products Corp., pg. 942
RUDOLPH & WEST—Mico Inc., pg. 748
RUSH COUNTY FARM BUREAU CO-OP, pg. 956
SERVICE SUPPLY CO. INC. OF INDIANA, pg. 992
SERVISTAR CORPORATION, pg. 992
SHEFFIELD HARDWARE COMPANY, pg. 996
SNYDER-DIAMOND, pg. 1015
SOMMER & MACA INDUSTRIES, INC., pg. 1017
SOUTH STATES INC.—Distribution America, pg. 340
SOUTHTEC, INC.—South Chester Tube Co., pg. 1019
SOVEREIGN GROUP INC., pg. 1024
STANDARD SUPPLY & HARDWARE, pg. 1037
TENNESSEE FARMERS CO-OP, pg. 1087
THREE STATES SUPPLY CO., INC.—UIS, Inc., pg. 1123
THRUWAY FASTENERS INC., pg. 1096
UNITED HARDWARE DISTRIBUTING CO., pg. 1132
UNIVERSAL COOPERATIVES, INC., pg. 1138
VSI FASTENERS, INC., pg. 1142
WBH INDUSTRIES, INC., pg. 1155
CARL WEISSMAN & SONS, INC., pg. 1174
WEST UNION CORP., pg. 1177
WILLIAMS FASTENER & SUPPLY CO.—Williams Steel & Hardware Company, pg. 1191
WILTON CORPORATION, pg. 1194

5074 — PLUMBING & HEATING EQUIPMENT & SUPPLIES-WHOLESALE

AMFAC DISTRIBUTION CORPORATION—JMB Realty Corporation, pg. 585
APEX SUPPLY CO. INC., pg. 78
ASSOCIATED EQUIPMENT COMPANY, INC., pg. 89
ATLANTIC PLUMBING SUPPLY COMPANY, pg. 95
BPC DIVISION—Bristol Products, L.P., pg. 176
BATTEY MACHINERY COMPANY, pg. 127
BORCHERS BROS., pg. 165
BRISTOL PRODUCTS, L.P., pg. 176
BUHRMAN-PHARR HARDWARE COMPANY, pg. 187
BUILDER MARTS OF AMERICA, pg. 187
CALCASIEU LUMBER COMPANY, pg. 208
CAPITOL GROUP, pg. 215
CENTRAL SUPPLY CO., INC., pg. 234
COLONIAL SUPPLY CORPORATION, pg. 264
COLUMBIA PIPE & SUPPLY COMPANY, pg. 266
COLUMBUS PIPE & EQUIPMENT COMPANY, pg. 267
CONSOLIDATED PIPE & SUPPLY COMPANY, pg. 277
ELECTRIC FURNACE FRANCE S.A.R.L.—Electric Furnace Co., pg. 373
EXCELSIOR MANUFACTURING & SUPPLY CORP., pg. 392
FREDERICK TRADING COMPANY, pg. 430
GAGGENAU USA CORPORATION, pg. 441
HAJOCA CORP., pg. 500
HARDWARE WHOLESALERS, INC., pg. 508
HUMPHREY FLUID POWER LTD.—Humphrey Products Company, pg. 553
IDEAL-STANDARD—American Standard Inc., pg. 62
IDEAL-STANDARD—American Standard Inc., pg. 62
IDEAL-STANDARD—American Standard Inc., pg. 62
INDECK POWER EQUIPMENT COMPANY, pg. 564
JAMECO INDUSTRIES, INC., pg. 588
KOHLER JAPAN K.K.—Kohler Company, pg. 640
KOHLER JAPAN K.K.—Kohler Company, pg. 640
KOHLER LTD.—Kohler Company, pg. 640
J.H. LARSON ELECTRICAL COMPANY, pg. 659
MAXON COMBUSTION SYSTEMS, LTD.—Maxon Corporation, pg. 723
MAXON GMBH—Maxon Corporation, pg. 723
MAXON GMBH—Maxon Corporation, pg. 723
N.V. MAXON INTERNATIONAL S.A.—Maxon Corporation, pg. 723
MAXON S.A.R.L.—Maxon Corporation, pg. 723
A. Y. MCDONALD INDUSTRIES, INC., pg. 728
A. Y. MCDONALD SUPPLY CO. INC.—A. Y. McDonald Industries, Inc., pg. 728
MEENAN LI DIV.—Meenan Oil Co. Limited Partnership, pg. 736
MODERN CONCRETE SEPTIC TANK COMPANY, pg. 762
MOLLENBERG-BETZ INC., pg. 764
MOUNTAIN STATES PIPE & SUPPLY COMPANY, pg. 773
MUNROE, INC., pg. 776
MUTUAL MANUFACTURING & SUPPLY CO., pg. 778
NIBCHEM INC.—Nibco, Inc., pg. 806
NIBCO PIPING PRODUCTS EAST—Nibco, Inc., pg. 806
NIBCO SWM MARKETING CORP.—Nibco, Inc., pg. 806
NORTHLAND ELECTRIC SUPPLY COMPANY, pg. 814
NORTHWEST PIPE FITTINGS, INC., pg. 815
PEIRCE-PHELPS, INC., pg. 855
PRIMUS INC., pg. 890
QPP QUALITY PIPING PRODUCTS—Nibco, Inc., pg. 806
THE RAL CORPORATION—The Dyson-Kissner-Moran Corporation, pg. 357
RAUB SUPPLY COMPANY, pg. 913
ROBINSON EXPORT-IMPORT CORPORATION—Mico Inc., pg. 748
ROMAC INDUSTRIES, INC., pg. 945
W.A. ROOSEVELT CO., pg. 946
J. A. SEXAUER—The Dyson-Kissner-Moran Corporation, pg. 357
SHEFFIELD HARDWARE COMPANY, pg. 996
SISCO COMPANY—First Mount Joy Corporation, pg. 413
SLOAN VALVE COMPANY, pg. 1010
SNYDER-DIAMOND, pg. 1015
SOUTH STATES INC.—Distribution America, pg. 340
SOUTHERN PIPE & SUPPLY CO., INC., pg. 1022
SPRAYING SYSTEMS CO. FAR EAST—Spraying Systems Co., pg. 1032
SPRAYING SYSTEMS DEUTSCHLAND GMBH—Spraying Systems Co., pg. 1032
STERLING SUPPLY COMPANY, INC., pg. 1047
TD INDUSTRIES INC., pg. 1072
THERMO INDUSTRIES INC., pg. 1091
TODD PIPE & SUPPLY GARDEN GROVE—Todd Pipe & Supply Hawthorne, pg. 1100
TODD PIPE & SUPPLY HAWTHORNE, pg. 1100
TREATY CO., pg. 1109
VICTAULIC INTERNATIONAL—Victaulic Company of America, pg. 1149
VICTAULIC TOOL COMPANY—Victaulic Company of America, pg. 1149
WATER CONTROL INTERNATIONAL INC.—Sloan Valve Company, pg. 1010
CARL WEISSMAN & SONS, INC., pg. 1174
WESTCO INDUSTRIAL CORPORATION—The Gage Company, pg. 441

5075 — WARM AIR HEATING & AIR CONDITIONING EQUIPMENT & SUPPLIES-WHOLESALE

ALLISON-ERWIN CO. INC., pg. 40
THE HARRY ALTER COMPANY, pg. 45
THE HARRY ALTER COMPANY—Temperature Equipment Corporation, pg. 1086
APEX SUPPLY CO. INC., pg. 78
ARIZONA WHOLESALE SUPPLY COMPANY, pg. 82
ASAHI/AMERICA, INC., pg. 87
ASSOCIATED EQUIPMENT COMPANY, INC., pg. 89
BRYANT MUNGO DIVISION—Temperature Equipment Corporation, pg. 1086
BURKE ENGINEERING COMPANY, pg. 190
CADET MANUFACTURING COMPANY, pg. 207
CAPITOL GROUP, pg. 215
CENTRAL SUPPLY CO., INC., pg. 234
THE CLIMATIC CORP., pg. 255
CODISCO INC., pg. 258
COLONIAL SUPPLY CORPORATION, pg. 264
EXCELSIOR MANUFACTURING & SUPPLY CORP., pg. 392
FASTEC INDUSTRIAL, pg. 403
FREDERICK TRADING COMPANY, pg. 430
THE HABEGGER CORPORATION, pg. 498
SID HARVEY INC., pg. 515
HEATCRAFT INC.—Lennox International Inc., pg. 667
HEIGHTS HEATING & COOLING, pg. 525
INTREPID CORP., pg. 581
JOHNSON SUPPLY & EQUIPMENT CORP., pg. 601
GEORGE KOCH SONS, INC., pg. 639
LYON CONKLIN & COMPANY, pg. 690
A. Y. MCDONALD INDUSTRIES, INC., pg. 728
A. Y. MCDONALD SUPPLY CO. INC.—A. Y. McDonald Industries, Inc., pg. 728
MICRO-MET L CORP., pg. 748
MOLLENBERG-BETZ INC., pg. 764
MUTUAL MANUFACTURING & SUPPLY CO., pg. 778
PEIRCE-PHELPS, INC., pg. 855
W.A. ROOSEVELT CO., pg. 946
SIGLER & REEVES, pg. 1003
SOUTHERN PIPE & SUPPLY CO., INC., pg. 1022
SQUIRE-COGSWELL COMPANY, pg. 1034
TD INDUSTRIES INC., pg. 1072
TARRANT SERVICE AGENCY, INC., pg. 1079
TEMPERATURE EQUIPMENT CORPORATION, pg. 1086
THERMO INDUSTRIES INC., pg. 1091
WATLOW LIMITED—Watlow Electric Manufacturing Company, pg. 1168
WATLOW SINGAPORE PTE. LTD.—Watlow Electric Manufacturing Company, pg. 1168
YOUNG SUPPLY COMPANY, pg. 1214

5078 — REFRIGERATION EQUIPMENT & SUPPLIES-WHOLESALE

ACME REFRIGERATION OF BATON ROUGE INC., pg. 13
THE HARRY ALTER COMPANY, pg. 45
THE HARRY ALTER COMPANY—Temperature Equipment Corporation, pg. 1086
AMERICAN EXCELSIOR COMPANY, pg. 51
ARDCO, INC., pg. 81
AUSTRALIAN COLEMAN, INC.—MacAndrews & Forbes Holdings Inc., pg. 695
BRYANT MUNGO DIVISION—Temperature Equipment Corporation, pg. 1086
BURKE ENGINEERING COMPANY, pg. 190
CALCASIEU LUMBER COMPANY, pg. 208
COLEMAN JAPAN LTD.—MacAndrews & Forbes Holdings Inc., pg. 695
COLEMAN U.K., INC.—MacAndrews & Forbes Holdings Inc., pg. 695
CUMMINS INTERMOUNTAIN DIESEL, pg. 305
D&H DISTRIBUTING COMPANY, pg. 307

FASTEC INDUSTRIAL, pg. 403
FILBERT CORP. (MAIN OFFICE)—Vilter Manufacturing Corporation, pg. 1152
GEBHARDT INDUSTRIAL REFRIGERATION, INC.—Vilter Manufacturing Corporation, pg. 1152
J. GERBER & CO. INC., pg. 453
INTREPID CORP., pg. 581
JOHNSON SUPPLY & EQUIPMENT CORP., pg. 601
JORDON COMMERCIAL REFRIGERATOR CO., pg. 605
MASEK DISTRIBUTING INC., pg. 717
MOLLENBERG-BETZ INC., pg. 764
REFRIGERATION SUPPLIES DISTRIBUTORS, pg. 921
REVCO SCIENTIFIC INC., pg. 930
W.A. ROOSEVELT CO., pg. 946
TD INDUSTRIES INC., pg. 1072
TEMPERATURE EQUIPMENT CORPORATION, pg. 1086
VILTER MANUFACTURING CORPORATION, pg. 1152
WILLIAMS & COMPANY, INC.—Cawsl Corporation, pg. 230
YOUNG SUPPLY COMPANY, pg. 1214

5082 — CONSTRUCTION & MINING MACHINERY & EQUIPMENT, EXCEPT PETROLEUM-WHOLESALE

ACTION LIFT—Medico Industries, Inc., pg. 735
ALBAN TRACTOR CO. INC., pg. 30
ASSOCIATED DIESEL SERVICE & EQUIPMENT COMPANY, pg. 89
AUSTIN POWDER CO., pg. 99
B.T. EQUIPMENT CO., INC.—Gilbane Building Company, pg. 457
BADGER CONSTRUCTION EQUIPMENT CO., INSLEY DIV., pg. 113
BERRY COMPANIES, INC., pg. 144
BRINK'S, INC.—The H. T. Hackney Co., pg. 498
CARLISLE EQUIPMENT COMPANY, pg. 220
CARLISLE EQUIPMENT COMPANY—Carlisle Equipment Company, pg. 220
CAROLINA TRACTOR & EQUIPMENT CO., pg. 223
W.C. CAYE & COMPANY, INC., pg. 230
CHAMPION, INC., pg. 238
CHOCTAW, INC., pg. 248
CLOVERDALE EQUIPMENT CO., pg. 256
CONSTRUCTION MACHINERY COMPANY, pg. 277
CONTRACTORS SUPPLY COMPANY, INC., pg. 281
DAVIS MINING & MANUFACTURING, pg. 319
DEAN OPERATIONS INC., pg. 322
EMPIRE SOUTHWEST CO., pg. 379
FABICK BROTHERS EQUIPMENT—John Fabick Tractor Company, pg. 396
FABICK & COMPANY—John Fabick Tractor Company, pg. 396
FABICK MACHINERY—John Fabick Tractor Company, pg. 396
JOHN FABICK TRACTOR COMPANY, pg. 396
FOLEY HOLDING COMPANY, INC., pg. 422
FOLEY TRACTOR COMPANY, INC.—Foley Holding Company, Inc., pg. 422
FORESTRY SUPPLIERS, INC., pg. 424
FRANKS SUPPLY COMPANY, INC., pg. 429
FURNIVAL/STATE MACHINERY CO., pg. 437
GILES & RANSOME, INC., pg. 458
GOODMAN EQUIPMENT CORP., pg. 470
THE H. T. HACKNEY CO., pg. 498
HASPER EQUIPMENT CO.—Cloverdale Equipment Co., pg. 256
KOMATSU DRESSER COMPANY—INDRESCO, Inc., pg. 565
LETTS INDUSTRIES, INC., pg. 668
LONGYEAR DIAMOND PRODS. (PHILIPPINES) INC.—Longyear Company, pg. 683
LONGYEAR FRANCE—Longyear Company, pg. 683
LONGYEAR (NEDERLAND) B.V.—Longyear Company, pg. 683
LONGYEAR NEW ZEALAND LTD.—Longyear Company, pg. 683
LONGYEAR U.K. LTD.—Longyear Company, pg. 683
MEDICO INDUSTRIES, INC., pg. 735
MI-JACK PRODUCTS, INC., pg. 746
MICHIGAN TRACTOR AND MACHINERY CO., pg. 747
M. D. MOODY & SONS INC., pg. 768
MUSTANG TRACTOR & EQUIP. CO., pg. 777
NORTH CAROLINA EQUIPMENT CO., pg. 812
NUTTALL EQUIPMENT CO. INC., pg. 818
OHIO MACHINERY CO., pg. 822
OWSLEY & SONS, INC., pg. 834
PEARCE INDUSTRIES INC., pg. 853
H.O. PENN MACHINERY CO. INC., pg. 857
PETERSON TRACTOR COMPANY, pg. 865
RICHMOND SCREW ANCHOR DIVISION—Symons Corporation, pg. 1069
J. A. RIGGS TRACTOR CO., pg. 934
RISH EQUIPMENT COMPANY, pg. 935
ROAD MACHINERY COMPANY, pg. 937
ROAD MACHINERY & SUPPLIES CO., pg. 937
RUSCON CORP., pg. 956
L. B. SMITH, INC., pg. 1013
SOMERSET WELDING & STEEL, INC.—Riggs Industries, Inc., pg. 934
SYRACUSE SUPPLY COMPANY, pg. 1070
SYRACUSE SUPPLY CONSTRUCTION & EQUIPMENT DIVISION—Syracuse Supply Company, pg. 1070
THOMPSON TRACTOR COMPANY, pg. 1095
UNITED TECTONIC INDUSTRY, pg. 1137
UP-RIGHT, INC., pg. 1139
WYOMING MACHINE COMPANY, pg. 1206
ZIEGLER INC., pg. 1218

5083 — FARM & GARDEN MACHINERY & EQUIPMENT-WHOLESALE

AMERICA OUTDOORS LTD, pg. 48
B & W FARM CENTER—B&W Co-op, Inc., pg. 107
CARCO INTERNATIONAL, INC., pg. 217
CENEX (FARMERS UNION CENTRAL EXCHANGE, INC.), pg. 231
CLEVELAND BROTHERS EQUIPMENT CO., pg. 255
COTTER & COMPANY, pg. 288
A. DUDA & SONS INC., pg. 351
EATON EQUIPMENT CORP., pg. 364
EFFINGHAM-CLAY SERVICE CO., pg. 371
EMPIRE SOUTHWEST CO., pg. 379
FROST COMPANY, pg. 435
GILES & RANSOME, INC., pg. 458
GROSSENBURG IMPLEMENTS, INCORPORATED, pg. 489
HAMILTON EQUIPMENT, INC., pg. 503
ILLINOIS AUTO ELECTRIC CO., pg. 562
INTREPID CORP., pg. 581
KRUSE HARDWARE COMPANY, pg. 645
LONG EQUIPMENT CO.—Long MFG. NC, Inc., pg. 682
LONG MFG. NC, INC., pg. 682
MASEK DISTRIBUTING INC., pg. 717
MILLER-ST. NAZIANZ, INC., pg. 755
MONTE VISTA CO-OP ASSOCIATION, INC., pg. 766
PETERSON TRACTOR COMPANY, pg. 865
ROTT-KELLER SUPPLY CO., pg. 951
ROWE CORP., pg. 952
RUSH COUNTY FARM BUREAU CO-OP, pg. 956
SF SERVICES, pg. 961
SERVICE MOTOR CO.—Service Motor Company, pg. 992
SEYMOUR MANUFACTURING COMPANY, pg. 994
SHEFFIELD HARDWARE COMPANY, pg. 996
STIHL INC., pg. 1049
THOMPSON TRACTOR COMPANY, pg. 1095
TIFFANY INDUSTRIES AMERICAS CORP.—Tiffany Industries, Inc., pg. 1097
UNIVERSAL COOPERATIVES, INC., pg. 1138
UP-RIGHT, INC., pg. 1139
ZIEGLER INC., pg. 1218

5084 — INDUSTRIAL MACHINERY & EQUIPMENT-WHOLESALE

ACTION INSTRUMENTS (CHINA) LTD.—Action Instruments, Inc., pg. 14
ACTION INSTRUMENTS, LTD.—Action Instruments, Inc., pg. 15
ADAMS INTERNATIONAL—TLC Beatrice International Holdings Inc., pg. 1073
AEROGLIDE AMERICAS INTERNATIONAL, INC.—Aeroglide Corporation, pg. 22
AIR POWER, INC., pg. 27
ALAMO INDUSTRIAL GROUP, pg. 29
ALAMO IRON WORKS—Alamo Industrial Group, pg. 29
ALBAN TRACTOR CO. INC., pg. 30
AMALLOY, pg. 46
APEX SUPPLY CO. INC., pg. 78
ARGO INTERNATIONAL—Decal Enterprises, Inc., pg. 323
ARGO INTERNATIONAL CORP., pg. 81
ASAHI/AMERICA, INC., pg. 87
ASSOCIATED DIESEL SERVICE & EQUIPMENT COMPANY, pg. 89
ASSOCIATED INDUSTRIAL SUPPLY, INC., pg. 90
ATLAS LIFT TRUCK RENTALS & SALES, INC., pg. 96
AUTOMATIC LIQUID PACKAGING, INC., pg. 100
BECKWITH MACHINERY COMPANY, pg. 131
JOSEPH BEHR & SONS INC., pg. 132
BERRY COMPANIES, INC., pg. 144
BLACK & CO., pg. 154
BOBST GROUP INC., pg. 161
BOVAIRD SUPPLY CO., pg. 168
BRIGGS WEAVER—Sammons Enterprises, Inc., pg. 968
BRUCKNER MACHINE & TOOL CORP., pg. 183
BRUNNER & LAY, INC., pg. 184
BUFFALO WHITE GMC, INC., pg. 187
BUHLER INC., pg. 187
CALTROL, INC., pg. 211
CANADIAN HARDINGE BROTHERS MACHINE TOOLS INC.—Hardinge Brothers, Inc., pg. 508
CAREY MACHINERY & SUPPLY COMPANY, pg. 218
CAROLINA TRACTOR & EQUIPMENT CO., pg. 223
CARTER CHAMBERS SUPPLY, INC., pg. 226
CARTER DAY CO.—Carter Day Industries, Inc., pg. 226
CARTER DAY INTERNATIONAL, INC.—Carter Day Industries, Inc., pg. 226
CAT PUMPS AG—Diversified Dynamics Inc., pg. 340
CAT PUMPS INTERNATIONAL N.V.—Diversified Dynamics Inc., pg. 340
CERAMIC COOLING TOWER CO.—Amsted Industries Incorporated, pg. 69
CHALLENGE GRAPHICS EQUIPMENT CO., pg. 238
CONE-BLANCHARD MACHINE COMPANY, pg. 273
CONNELL BROTHERS (HONG KONG) LTD.—Wilbur-Ellis Company & Connell Brothers Company, pg. 1189
THE COON-DE VISSER CO., pg. 282
CROWN IRON WORKS COMPANY—Crown Holdings, Inc., pg. 302
CUMMINS CUMBERLAND INC., pg. 305
CUMMINS INTERMOUNTAIN DIESEL, pg. 305
CUMMINS MID-SOUTH, INC., pg. 305
CUMMINS SOUTHWEST INC., pg. 305
DEALERS TRANSPORT COMPANY, INC., pg. 322
DECAL ENTERPRISES, INC., pg. 323
DETROIT DIESEL ALLISON CO.—Western Diesel Services Inc., pg. 1179
ERNST W. DORN CO., INC., pg. 346
DUNCAN EQUIPMENT COMPANY, pg. 352
DUTTON-LAINSON CO., pg. 356
DYNISCO GERATE G.M.B.H.—Berwind Corporation, pg. 145
EATON EQUIPMENT CORP., pg. 364
ECLIPSE-COMBUSTION—Eclipse, Inc., pg. 366
ECLIPSE THERMAL SYSTEMS—Eclipse, Inc., pg. 366
ELLIOTT TURBOMACHINERY CANADA, INC.—Elliott Company, pg. 378
ELLIOTT TURBOMACHINERY S.A.—Elliott Company, pg. 378
EWI, INC.-STAMPING & DIE DIV.—EWI, Inc., pg. 361
EXOTHERMICS-ECLIPSE, INC.—Eclipse, Inc., pg. 366
F J M CORPORATION, pg. 394
FASTCUT TOOL CORPORATION—Brubaker Tool Corp., pg. 183
FIBELCO S.A./N.V.—AXIA Incorporated, pg. 8
FICOMET S.A.R.L.—AXIA Incorporated, pg. 8
FINELPAC B.V.—AXIA Incorporated, pg. 8
FINOPAC APS—AXIA Incorporated, pg. 8
FISAX—AXIA Incorporated, pg. 9
DAVE FISCHBEIN CO.—AXIA Incorporated, pg. 8
FLORI CORP., pg. 420
FOLEY HOLDING COMPANY, INC., pg. 422
FOLEY TRACTOR COMPANY, INC.—Foley Holding Company, Inc., pg. 422
FRED V. FOWLER COMPANY, INC., pg. 427
FOWLER TOOLS OF CANADA—Fred V. Fowler Company, Inc., pg. 427
FREEMAN MANUFACTURING & SUPPLY COMPANY, pg. 431
FURNIVAL/STATE MACHINERY CO., pg. 437
GPD LIMITED, pg. 440
GAS EQUIPMENT COMPANY, INC., pg. 444
GENERAL WELDING SUPPLY CORPORATION, pg. 451
GESSNER INDUSTRIES, pg. 455
GILES & RANSOME, INC., pg. 458
GOODMAN EQUIPMENT CORP., pg. 470
GOSIGER INC., pg. 472
GRAVES-HUMPHREYS COMPANY—Jeld-Wen, Inc., pg. 592
HBC INTERNATIONAL SALES CORP.—Hobart Brothers Co., pg. 537
HCC INDUSTRIES, pg. 496
J. LEE HACKETT CO., pg. 498
HALLIDIE MACHINERY COMPANY, INC., pg. 501
HAMILTON EQUIPMENT, INC., pg. 503
HARDINGE MACHINE TOOLS, LTD.—Hardinge Brothers, Inc., pg. 508
HARLEY INDUSTRIES, INC., pg. 509
HAVILAND ENTERPRISES, pg. 517
HAWTHORNE LIFT SYSTEMS, pg. 519
HAWTHORNE MACHINERY COMPANY, pg. 519
HEAVY MACHINES, INC., pg. 524
HERCULES ENGINES, INC., pg. 531
HOWDEN SIROCCO INC., pg. 547
IDM CONTROLS, pg. 560
IGA, INC. (INDEPENDENT GROCERS ALLIANCE), pg. 560
ILLINOIS AUTO ELECTRIC CO., pg. 562
IMPERIAL, INC., pg. 564
INDECK POWER EQUIPMENT COMPANY, pg. 564
JAY INSTRUMENT & SPECIALTY CO., pg. 590
KANAWHA STEEL & EQUIPMENT CO., pg. 615
KEEN WELDING DIVISION—Keen Compressed Gas Co., Inc., pg. 619
KINGSBURY WORLD SALES—Kingsbury Corporation, pg. 632
THE KNAPHEIDE MFG. CO., pg. 636
KOCH SUPPLIES INC., pg. 639
KOMATSU DRESSER COMPANY—INDRESCO, Inc., pg. 565
LAMB AG—Enterprises International Inc., pg. 383
LANTECH INC., pg. 658
LETTS INDUSTRIES, INC., pg. 668
LIBERTY TOOL CORPORATION, pg. 674
M/S FISCHBEIN PACKAGING (SINGAPORE) PTE. LTD.—AXIA Incorporated, pg. 9
MASEK DISTRIBUTING INC., pg. 717
MATERIAL HANDLING EQUIPMENT CO.—Modern Group Ltd., pg. 763
MATTHEWS INTERNATIONAL CORP., pg. 721
MATTHEWS INTL. TRADING CORP.—Matthews International Corp., pg. 721
MCJUNKIN CORPORATION, pg. 730
MCMASTER CARR SUPPLY CO. INC., pg. 731
MEDICO INDUSTRIES, INC., pg. 735
METRIC & MULTISTANDARD COMPONENTS, pg. 743
MI-JACK PRODUCTS, INC., pg. 746
MODERN GROUP LTD., pg. 762
MODERN HANDLING EQUIPMENT CO. OF NY—Modern Group Ltd., pg. 763
MODERN HANDLING EQUIPMENT CO.—Modern Group Ltd., pg. 763
MODERN HANDLING EQUIPMENT OF N.J., INC.—Modern Group Ltd., pg. 763
MODERN HILIFT EQUIPMENT CO.—Modern Group Ltd., pg. 763
MONTGOMERY ELEVATOR COMPANY, pg. 767
MONTGOMERY ELEVATOR EXPORT CORPORATION—Montgomery Elevator Company, pg. 767
MOORE SPECIAL TOOL AG—Moore Special Tool Co., Inc., pg. 768
THE ROBERT E. MORRIS COMPANY, pg. 771
R.A. MUELLER, INC., pg. 774
MUNROE, INC., pg. 776
MUSTANG POWER SYSTEMS—Mustang Tractor & Equip. Co., pg. 777
NASHVILLE MACHINE CO. INC., pg. 784
NATIONAL WELDERS SUPPLY CO. INC., pg. 794
NEW ENGLAND NEWSPAPER SUPPLY COMPANY, INC., pg. 800
NEW ENGLAND TAP CORPORATION (NETCO)—Brubaker Tool Corp., pg. 183
NORTH CAROLINA EQUIPMENT CO., pg. 812
NORTHWEST PIPE FITTINGS, INC., pg. 815
NORWECO, INC., pg. 816
NOVAR CORP.—Novar Electronics, pg. 817
O'BRIEN ENERGY SYSTEMS INC., pg. 820
OHIO TRANSMISSION CORPORATION, pg. 822

LOUIS PADNOS IRON & METAL CO., pg. 842
PAN AMERICAN TRADE DEVELOPMENT CORP., pg. 845
FRANK PAXTON COMPANY—Jeld-Wen, Inc., pg. 592
PEARCE INDUSTRIES INC., pg. 853
PECO INC., pg. 854
H.O. PENN MACHINERY CO. INC., pg. 857
PEREZ TRADING CO. INC., pg. 860
PERRY GROUP, INC., pg. 863
PETERSON TRACTOR COMPANY, pg. 865
PRECISION ARC CO.—Smith Industries, Inc., pg. 1013
PRECISION INDUSTRIES, pg. 885
PRIME TECHNOLOGY, INC., pg. 889
PRIME TECHNOLOGY, INC.—Prime Technology, Inc., pg. 889
QUEEN OXYGEN COMPANY, pg. 904
REPUBLIC SUPPLY COMPANY, pg. 928
J. A. RIGGS TRACTOR CO., pg. 934
RUDEL MACHINERY COMPANY, INC., pg. 954
SAMMONS ENTERPRISES, INC., pg. 968
SEELY EQUIPMENT & SUPPLY CO., INC.—Modern Group Ltd., pg. 763
SERVICE MOTOR COMPANY, pg. 992
SHORELINE PRODUCTS, INC., pg. 1000
SID TOOL CO. INC., pg. 1002
SMITH TRACTOR & EQUIPMENT CO.—Smith Brothers Farms, Inc., pg. 1011
SOONER PIPE & SUPPLY CORP., pg. 1018
SOUTHERN COMBUSTION & CONTROLS, INC.—Eclipse, Inc., pg. 366
SOUTHERN PUMP & TANK CO. INC., pg. 1022
SPANTEK DIVISION—Upper Midwest Industries, Inc., pg. 1140
SQUIRE-COGSWELL COMPANY, pg. 1034
STANDARD ALLOYS & MANUFACTURING—Blue Tee Corporation, pg. 161
STANDARD SUPPLY & HARDWARE, pg. 1037
STANDARD WELDERS SUPPLY CO., pg. 1038
STIHL INC., pg. 1049
STIHL PARTS, INC.—Stihl Inc., pg. 1049
SUNOX, INC., pg. 1062
SYRACUSE SUPPLY COMPANY, pg. 1070
SYRACUSE SUPPLY INDUSTRIAL PRODUCTS DIVISION—Syracuse Supply Company, pg. 1070
TLC BEATRICE INTERNATIONAL HOLDINGS INC., pg. 1073
TENCARVA MACHINERY CO., INC., pg. 1086
TENCARVA MACHINERY CO.-ASHEVILLE—Tencarva Machinery Co., Inc., pg. 1087
TENCARVA MACHINERY COMPANY—Tencarva Machinery Co., Inc., pg. 1087
TENCARVA MACHINERY COMPANY—Tencarva Machinery Co., Inc., pg. 1087
THERMON AUSTRALIA—Thermon Manufacturing Company, pg. 1092
THERMON FAR EAST—Thermon Manufacturing Company, pg. 1092
THERMON INTERNATIONAL SERVICES SA—Thermon Manufacturing Company, pg. 1092
THERMON U.K. (LTD.)—Thermon Manufacturing Company, pg. 1092
THOMPSON TRACTOR COMPANY, pg. 1095
TRIUMPH*LOR, INC., pg. 1115
TRIUMPH-LOR, INC.—Triumph*Lor, Inc., pg. 1115
TRIUMPH-LOR, INC.—Triumph*Lor, Inc., pg. 1115
TRIUMPH-LOR, INC.—Triumph*Lor, Inc., pg. 1115
TRIUMPH-LOR, INC.—Triumph*Lor, Inc., pg. 1115
TRIUMPH-LOR, INC.—Triumph*Lor, Inc., pg. 1115
TRIUMPH/LOR OILFIELD SERVICES LTD.—Triumph*Lor, Inc., pg. 1115
TRUMPF INC., pg. 1118
TURNER SUPPLY COMPANY, pg. 1119
UNION STEEL PRODUCTS, INCORPORATED, pg. 1129
UNITED ENGINES, INC., pg. 1131
UNIVERSAL DYNAMICS INC.—Universal Dynamics Inc., pg. 1138
VALLEY DETROIT DIESEL ALLISON, pg. 1143
VAREL MANUFACTURING CO., pg. 1145
VEECO GMBH—Veeco Instrumentations, Inc., pg. 1146
VEECO INSTRUMENTS LTD.—Veeco Instrumentations, Inc., pg. 1146
VEECO K.K.—Veeco Instrumentations, Inc., pg. 1146
VINSON SUPPLY CO.—Sammons Enterprises, Inc., pg. 968
W-B SUPPLY CO., pg. 1155
WAGNER SPRAY TECH CORP., pg. 1158
WATLOW ELECTRIC FOREIGN SALES CORPORATION—Watlow Electric Manufacturing Company, pg. 1168
WATLOW ITALY—Watlow Electric Manufacturing Company, pg. 1168
WATLOW KOREA—Watlow Electric Manufacturing Company, pg. 1168
WATLOW LIMITED—Watlow Electric Manufacturing Company, pg. 1168
WATLOW SINGAPORE PTE. LTD.—Watlow Electric Manufacturing Company, pg. 1168
WATLOW TAIWAN—Watlow Electric Manufacturing Company, pg. 1168
WATSON ELECTRIC SUPPLY INC., pg. 1168
WELSCO INC., pg. 1175
WESTERN DIESEL SERVICES INC., pg. 1179
WILSON INDUSTRIES INC., pg. 1193
WILTON CORPORATION, pg. 1194
ZIEGLER INC., pg. 1218
ZIMA CORP., pg. 1219

5085 — INDUSTRIAL SUPPLIES-WHOLESALE

ABRASIVES, INC.—Prime Technology, Inc., pg. 889
AIRLINE HYDRAULICS CORPORATION, pg. 27
ALAMO INDUSTRIAL GROUP, pg. 29
ALAMO IRON WORKS—Alamo Industrial Group, pg. 29
ALATEC PRODUCTS, INC., pg. 30
AMERICAN INTERNATIONAL CONTAINER, INC., pg. 56
ANGLO-AUSTRIAN MAGNESITE, LTD.—Belmont Industries, Inc., pg. 137
APACHE HOSE & BELTING COMPANY, pg. 77
ASSOCIATED INDUSTRIAL SUPPLY, INC., pg. 90
BATTEY MACHINERY COMPANY, pg. 127
BEARING DISTRIBUTORS, INC., pg. 130
BECKWITH MACHINERY COMPANY, pg. 131
THE BERNUTH CORPORATION, pg. 144
BERRY BEARING CO., pg. 144
BLACK & CO., pg. 154
JOHN BOUCHARD & SONS COMPANY, pg. 168
W. BRAUN COMPANY, pg. 172
W. BRAUN INTERNATIONAL—W. Braun Company, pg. 172
W. BRAUN DISTRIBUTION CENTER—W. Braun Company, pg. 172
BRIGGS WEAVER—Sammons Enterprises, Inc., pg. 968
BRINK'S, INC.—The H. T. Hackney Co., pg. 498
BRUCKNER MACHINE & TOOL CORP., pg. 183
BRYANT SUPPLY COMPANY, INC., pg. 185
C&W REFRACTORIES, LTD.—CFB Industries, Inc., pg. 201
CALIFORNIA HARDWARE CO., pg. 209
THE CALKINS MANUFACTURING COMPANY, pg. 210
CAMERON & BARKLEY COMPANY, INC., pg. 212
CAREY MACHINERY & SUPPLY COMPANY, pg. 218
CARPENTER RIGGING, pg. 224
CARTER CHAMBERS SUPPLY, INC., pg. 226
CENTRAL SUPPLY CO., INC., pg. 234
COLUMBIA PIPE & SUPPLY COMPANY, pg. 266
COLUMBUS STEEL DRUM COMPANY, pg. 267
THE COON-DE VISSER CO., pg. 282
COUNTY TOOL & ABRASIVE—Buck Knives, Inc., pg. 185
DECAL ENTERPRISES, INC., pg. 323
DEWCO MILWAUKEE SALES—Don E. Williams Co., pg. 1190
DICALITE FRANCE, S.A.—Belmont Industries, Inc., pg. 137
DICALITE SCANDINAVIA—Belmont Industries, Inc., pg. 137
DICALITE TRADING, S.A.—Belmont Industries, Inc., pg. 137
DUNCAN EQUIPMENT COMPANY, pg. 352
EMERY WATERHOUSE COMPANY, pg. 379
ERVIN INDUSTRIES, INC., pg. 387
FABREEKA INTERNATIONAL, INC., pg. 396
FEL-PRO INCORPORATED, pg. 405
GEORG FISCHER AMASTEEL S.A.—Ervin Industries, Inc., pg. 388
FRED V. FOWLER COMPANY, INC., pg. 427
FRANTZ EXPORT CORP.—Frantz Manufacturing Co., pg. 430
FREEMAN MANUFACTURING & SUPPLY COMPANY, pg. 431
THE GAGE COMPANY, pg. 441
R. J. GALLAGHER CO., pg. 441
GLOBE INTERNATIONAL INC., pg. 464
THE H. T. HACKNEY CO., pg. 498
J.R. HAHN CO., INC., pg. 500
HAJOCA CORP., pg. 500
HAVILAND ENTERPRISES, pg. 517
HEADCO INDUSTRIES, INC., pg. 520
HECTOR & CO. A.B.—Belmont Industries, Inc., pg. 137
HICKMAN WILLIAMS & CO. INC., pg. 532
HILL-BEHAN LUMBER COMPANY, pg. 534
HUB INC., pg. 548
IBT, INC., pg. 558
INDUSTRIAL RUBBER PRODUCTS COMPANY, pg. 566
INGRAM PAPER COMPANY, pg. 569
INLANDER-STEINDLER PAPER, pg. 570
INTERNATIONAL SHOE MACHINE CORP., pg. 579
INVETECH CO., pg. 581
JOHNSON ACOUSTICAL & SUPPLY CO., pg. 597
JOHNSON SUPPLY & EQUIPMENT CORP., pg. 601
KEEN COMPRESSED GAS CO., INC., pg. 619
KRUSE HARDWARE COMPANY, pg. 645
LANTECH INC., pg. 658
LIBERTY GLASS COMPANY, pg. 674
MSC INDUSTRIAL SUPPLY CO., pg. 693
MATERIALES INDUSTRIALES S.A.—Belmont Industries, Inc., pg. 137
MCJUNKIN CORPORATION, pg. 730
MCMASTER CARR SUPPLY CO. INC., pg. 731
METRIC & MULTISTANDARD COMPONENTS, pg. 743
MICROFLECT COMPANY, INC., pg. 749
B. L. MONTAGUE CO., pg. 766
NPS CORPORATION, pg. 781
NEILL-LAVIELLE SUPPLY CO., pg. 797
NORTHWEST PIPE FITTINGS, INC., pg. 815
PHOENIX VENTURES, pg. 869
PIPING RESOURCES—Bovaird Supply Co., pg. 169
PRECISION INDUSTRIES, pg. 885
PRODUCTION TOOL SUPPLY CO., pg. 893
RADEX INTERNATIONAL S.A.—Belmont Industries, Inc., pg. 137
RADEX-HERAKLITH INDUSTRIEBETEILIGUNGS, A.G.—Belmont Industries, Inc., pg. 137
REX SUPPLY COMPANY—Production Tool Supply Co., pg. 893
ROMAC INDUSTRIES, INC., pg. 945
SACRAMENTO INDUSTRIAL SUPPLY—DoAll Company, pg. 341
SEALING DEVICES INC., pg. 984
SERVICE SUPPLY CO. INC. OF INDIANA, pg. 992
SID TOOL CO. INC., pg. 1002
SINGH INDUSTRIES, pg. 1008
SOMERSET WELDING & STEEL, INC.—Riggs Industries, Inc., pg. 934
SOUTH STATES INC.—Distribution America, pg. 340
SOUTHERN PUMP & TANK CO. INC., pg. 1022
SOUTHWEST DOALL INDUSTRIAL SUPPLY—DoAll Company, pg. 342
STANDARD SUPPLY & HARDWARE, pg. 1037
SUNRISE INDUSTRIAL AUTOMATION & DESIGN—IBT, Inc., pg. 558
SYRACUSE SUPPLY COMPANY, pg. 1070
THRALL ENTERPRISES, INC., pg. 1095
TRICON INDUSTRIES, INC., pg. 1113
OY TULENKESTAVAAT TILIET, A.B.—Belmont Industries, Inc., pg. 137
TULSA GAUGE & INSTRUMENT CO.—Harley Industries, Inc., pg. 510
VAN SON HOLLAND INK CORP. OF AMERICA, pg. 1144
VINSON SUPPLY CO.—Sammons Enterprises, Inc., pg. 968
CARL WEISSMAN & SONS, INC., pg. 1174
WESTCO INDUSTRIAL CORPORATION—The Gage Company, pg. 441
WHITE/MIPRO RECEPTABLES—White Mop Wringer Company, pg. 1186
DON E. WILLIAMS CO., pg. 1190
WILLIAMS STEEL & HARDWARE COMPANY, pg. 1191
F.B. WRIGHT CO., pg. 1204
ZUCKERMAN-HONICKMAN INC., pg. 1221

5087 — SERVICE ESTABLISHMENT EQUIPMENT & SUPPLIES-WHOLESALE

B-W SUPPLY, INC.—Best Western International, Inc., pg. 147
BLEVINS CONCESSION SUPPLY CO., pg. 156
BRUNER CORPORATION, pg. 184
THE BUTCHER CO., pg. 196
CONESTOGA HOLDINGS, INC., pg. 273
CONTINENTAL PAPER & SUPPLY CO., pg. 280
L.N. CURTIS & SONS, pg. 306
CUTLER MANUFACTURING CORPORATION, pg. 307
DAYCON PRODUCTS COMPANY, INC., pg. 321
DEFENDER SERVICES, INC., pg. 324
EDWARD DON & COMPANY OF ILLINOIS, pg. 344
E-Z MART STORES, INC., pg. 361
FORT PITT ACQUISITIONS COMPANY, INC., pg. 425
S. FREEDMAN & SONS, INC., pg. 430
INDUSTRIAL TOWEL & UNIFORM, pg. 567
J P FOODSERVICE, INC., pg. 586
JACKSON PAPER COMPANY, pg. 587
KESTERSON FOOD COMPANY, INC., pg. 624
KINNING & REIL OF WYOMING—RK Mechanical, Inc., pg. 907
D. J. MEAD-HUBBS & HOWE—Sofco-Mead, Inc., pg. 1016
MERCURY DISTRIBUTING CO., INC., pg. 740
MONTGOMERY-GREEN CO.—Edward Don & Company of Illinois, pg. 344
NATIONAL RESTAURANT SUPPLY COMPANY, pg. 793
NEWELL PAPER CO. OF COLUMBUS—Jackson Paper Company, pg. 587
NEWELL PAPER CO. OF MERIDIAN—Jackson Paper Company, pg. 587
PAPER ENTERPRISES, INC., pg. 847
SAFETYMASTER CORPORATION—Strategic Distribution Inc., pg. 1053
SCHNIEBER FINE FOODS, INC., pg. 977
SOFCO-MEAD, INC., pg. 1016
SOUTHERN LEATHER COMPANY, pg. 1021
SOUTHLAND FLOORING SUPPLIES OF LOUISVILLE, INC., pg. 1023
SYNDICATE SYSTEMS, INC., pg. 1069
WASSERSTROM COMPANY, pg. 1167

5088 — TRANSPORTATION EQUIPMENT & SUPPLIES, EXCEPT MOTOR VEHICLES-WHOLESALE

ADAMS RITE PRODUCTS INC.—Certified Holding Corp., pg. 237
AIRCRAFT SUPPORT GROUP, INC.—International Airline Support Group, Inc., pg. 575
AMSTED INDUSTRIES INTERNATIONAL—Amsted Industries Incorporated, pg. 69
ATLANTIC AVIATION CORP., pg. 94
CRL, INC., pg. 203
CARRYORE, LIMITED—National Steel Corporation, pg. 794
CURRAN CONTRACTING CO., pg. 305
DECAL ENTERPRISES, INC., pg. 323
FISHERIES SUPPLY COMPANY, pg. 415
GENERATION METALS CORP., pg. 451
GULFSTREAM AEROSPACE CORP.—Gulfstream Holdings Corporation, pg. 494
GULFSTREAM AEROSPACE CORP.—Gulfstream Holdings Corporation, pg. 494
GULFSTREAM AEROSPACE CORP.—Gulfstream Holdings Corporation, pg. 494
GULFSTREAM AEROSPACE CORP.—Gulfstream Holdings Corporation, pg. 494
GULFSTREAM MARKETING MIDWEST REGION—Gulfstream Holdings Corporation, pg. 494
HAWTHORNE CORP., pg. 518
INTERNATIONAL AIRLINE SUPPORT GROUP, INC., pg. 575
INTERNATIONAL MARINE HOLDINGS, INC., pg. 579
INTERNATIONAL METALS & MACHINES, INC.—CRL, Inc., pg. 203
JOHNSON & TOWERS, INC., pg. 601
KETTENBURG MARINE—Kettenburg Marine Corporation, pg. 626
KETTENBURG MARINE CORPORATION, pg. 626
KETTENBURG MARINE/NEWPORT BEACH RETAIL—Kettenburg Marine Corporation, pg. 626
KETTENBURG MARINE/NEWPORT ENGINES—Kettenburg Marine Corporation, pg. 626
MARCO MARINE SAN DIEGO—Marine Construction & Design Co., pg. 707
MASEK DISTRIBUTING INC., pg. 717
MEMPHIS GROUP, INC., pg. 738
MICRODOT AEROSPACE LIMITED—MICRODOT, Inc., pg. 749
MOONEY AIRCRAFT CORPORATION, pg. 768
REAGAN EQUIPMENT COMPANY, INC., pg. 917

SABRELINER CORP., pg. 965
SENSENICH PROPELLER CO.—The Philadelphia Bourse, Inc., pg. 866
SOUTHEASTERN EQUIPMENT COMPANY, INC., pg. 1019

5091 — SPORTING & RECREATIONAL GOODS & SUPPLIES-WHOLESALE

ANDERSON WHOLESALE COMPANY, pg. 73
AQUA FAB INDUSTRIES, INC., pg. 79
THE AUSTAD COMPANY, pg. 98
AUSTRALIAN COLEMAN, INC.—MacAndrews & Forbes Holdings Inc., pg. 695
BANGOR PUNTA OVERSEAS, S.A.—Lear Siegler Diversified Holdings Corp., pg. 664
BASS PRO SHOPS, INC., pg. 125
BENNETT BROTHERS, INC., pg. 139
BOAT TRANSIT, INC.—Jupiter Industries, Inc., pg. 609
CAMPING WORLD HOLDINGS, INC., pg. 213
COLEMAN EVCON SUPPLY LIMITED—MacAndrews & Forbes Holdings Inc., pg. 695
COLEMAN JAPAN LTD.—MacAndrews & Forbes Holdings Inc., pg. 695
COLEMAN SPAS, INC.—MacAndrews & Forbes Holdings Inc., pg. 695
COLEMAN U.K., INC.—MacAndrews & Forbes Holdings Inc., pg. 695
CORDOVA LABORATORIES—Cordova Enterprise, pg. 286
CORTLAND LINE CO., INC., pg. 287
CUSTOM DISTRIBUTORS, INC.—Aqua Fab Industries, Inc., pg. 79
DAKCO DISTRIBUTORS, INC., pg. 311
EATON EQUIPMENT CORP., pg. 364
EBSCO INDUSTRIES, INC., pg. 365
HUNTER MARINE CORPORATION, pg. 555
M.W. KASCH COMPANY, pg. 617
KRANSCO, pg. 644
KRUSE HARDWARE COMPANY, pg. 645
MPO VIDEOTRONICS, INC., pg. 693
MILLER HARNESS, INC.—MPO Videotronics, Inc., pg. 693
NELSON & SMALL INC., pg. 798
NORTHLAND SPORTS INC.—Dakco Distributors, Inc., pg. 311
OUR OWN HARDWARE COMPANY, pg. 832
PELICAN PRODUCTS, pg. 856
ROLLERBLADE, INC., pg. 944
SCOTT U.S.A., pg. 983
SPALDING—Spalding & Evenflo Companies, Inc., pg. 1024
SPALDING AUSTRALIA PTY. LTD.—Spalding & Evenflo Companies, Inc., pg. 1025
SPALDING CANADA—Spalding & Evenflo Companies, Inc., pg. 1025
SPALDING JAPAN INC.—Spalding & Evenflo Companies, Inc., pg. 1025
SPALDING JAPAN INC.—Spalding & Evenflo Companies, Inc., pg. 1025
TASCO, pg. 1079
TREK BICYCLE CORPORATION—Intrepid Corp., pg. 581
VIKING YACHT CO., pg. 1151

5092 — TOYS & HOBBY GOODS & SUPPLIES-WHOLESALE

ACE NOVELTY COMPANY, INC., pg. 12
ACE NOVELTY FUN SERVICE DIVISION—Ace Novelty Company, Inc., pg. 12
ANDERSON WHOLESALE COMPANY, pg. 73
CARDINAL INC., pg. 217
COMMONWEALTH TOY & NOVELTY COMPANY, pg. 269
DAKIN, INC., pg. 311
DARDA INC. (USA), pg. 315
JAYDON INCORPORATED, pg. 590
M.W. KASCH COMPANY, pg. 617
MONARCH AVALON, INC., pg. 765
RI HOLDINGS, pg. 907
REMCO BABY—Remco Toys, pg. 926
REMCO TOYS, pg. 926
ROSE ART INDUSTRIES, pg. 947
STAR SALES CO., INC., pg. 1040
TSR, INC., pg. 1075
TASH, INC., pg. 1080
TIGER ELECTRONICS, INC., pg. 1097
UNICOVER CORPORATION, pg. 1126
THE UNITED STATES PLAYING CARD COMPANY, pg. 1136
ZILBER, LTD., pg. 1219

5093 — SCRAP AND WASTE MATERIALS

ALBUQUERQUE METALS CO.—CF&I Steel Corporation, pg. 201
ARKANSAS ALUMINUM ALLOYS—A. Tenenbaum Co. Inc., pg. 1087
JOSEPH BEHR & SONS INC., pg. 132
CLOVER YARNS, INC.—Steiner & Company, pg. 1045
COLONIAL METALS CO., pg. 263
COLUMBIA IRON & METAL CO.—Columbia National Group, Inc., pg. 265
COLUMBIA NATIONAL GROUP, INC., pg. 265
CONNELL LIMITED PARTNERSHIP, pg. 275
DENVER METALS CO.—CF&I Steel Corporation, pg. 201
DUGGAN INDUSTRIES, INC., pg. 351
GROSSMAN IRON & STEEL COMPANY, pg. 489
KALAMAZOO SCRAP & PROCESSING—Sturgis Iron & Metal Company, Inc., pg. 1055
KANSAS METALS CO.—CF&I Steel Corporation, pg. 201
SAMUEL G. KEYWELL CO.—Keywell Corporation, pg. 629
SAMUEL G. KEYWELL CO.—Keywell Corporation, pg. 629
LUNTZ CORPORATION, pg. 687
NORTH PACIFIC LUMBER COMPANY, pg. 813
NORWICH RECYCLING CORP.—Victory Markets Inc., pg. 1150
OAHU WASTE ENERGY RECOVERY, INC.—JMB Realty Corporation, pg. 585
OHIO VALLEY ALUMINUM COMPANY—Interlock Industries, Inc., pg. 575
OMNI SOURCE CORPORATION, pg. 826
LOUIS PADNOS IRON & METAL CO., pg. 842
PADNOS-SUMMIT—Louis Padnos Iron & Metal Co., pg. 843
PECK IRON & METAL COMPANY, INC., pg. 854
THE POLLOCK CORP., pg. 879
PUEBLO METALS CO.—CF&I Steel Corporation, pg. 201
RECLAIMERS, INC.—Group Dekko International Inc., pg. 490
REPUBLIC ALLOYS, INC., pg. 927
S.D. RICHMAN SONS, INC., pg. 933
ROCK-TENN COMPANY, pg. 941
ROCK-TENN COMPANY, MILL DIVISION, INC.—Rock-Tenn Company, pg. 941
JOSEPH SIMON & SONS, INC., pg. 1006
SOUTH BEND SCRAP & PROCESSING—Sturgis Iron & Metal Company, Inc., pg. 1055
STEINER & COMPANY, pg. 1045
STURGIS IRON & METAL COMPANY, INC., pg. 1055
STURGIS METALS DIVISION, ELKHART—Sturgis Iron & Metal Company, Inc., pg. 1055
A. TENENBAUM CO. INC., pg. 1087
THREE RIVERS IRON & METAL—Sturgis Iron & Metal Company, Inc., pg. 1055
CARL WEISSMAN & SONS, INC., pg. 1174

5094 — JEWELRY, WATCHES, PRECIOUS STONES & PRECIOUS METALS-WHOLESALE

A-MARK FINANCIAL, pg. 1
ANTWERP DIAMOND DISTRIBUTORS INC., pg. 77
ANTWERP DIAMOND DISTRIBUTORS INC.—Antwerp Diamond Distributors Inc., pg. 77
BENNETT BROTHERS, INC., pg. 139
CONCORD WATCH CO.—North American Watch Corporation, pg. 812
CONTINENTAL COIN CORPORATION, pg. 278
CORUM WATCH CORPORATION—North American Watch Corporation, pg. 812
DOWNEY DESIGNS INTERNATIONAL, INC., pg. 348
EMPIRE DIAMOND CORPORATION, pg. 379
M. FABRIKANT & SONS, INC., pg. 396
LEON HENDRICKSON, pg. 529
HERBAL ENTERPRISES INC., pg. 530
HOLZER WATCH CO., INC., pg. 541
INVERNESS CORP., pg. 581
JEWELMONT CORPORATION, pg. 594
KNAR GOLD & SILVER EXCHANGE, pg. 636
HOWARD MILLER CLOCK COMPANY, pg. 754
MONEX INTERNATIONAL, LTD., pg. 765
N.A. TRADING LTD.—North American Watch Corporation, pg. 812
NORTH AMERICAN WATCH CORPORATION, pg. 812
NORTH AMERICAN WATCH OF CANADA, LTD.—North American Watch Corporation, pg. 812
PAKULA & COMPANY, pg. 843
PIAGET WATCH CORPORATION—North American Watch Corporation, pg. 812
RAM GRAPHICS, INC., pg. 910
REED & BARTON HOUSEWARES—Reed & Barton Corporation, pg. 920
ULLENBERG CORP., pg. 1125
VAN CLEEF & ARPELS, INC., pg. 1144
WEDLO, INC.—Peter W. Smith & Company, Inc., pg. 1012
HARRY WINSTON, INC., pg. 1197

5099 — WHOLESALE DURABLE GOODS, NEC

AMERICAN MILITARY ARMS CORPORATION, pg. 58
AMPEX CORPORATION MARKETING, SALES & SERVICE—Sherborne Group, Inc., pg. 998
ARTEC DISTRIBUTING, INC., pg. 86
AUSTIN POWDER CO., pg. 99
BEADLES LUMBER COMPANY, INC., pg. 129
THE BENSON MUSIC GROUP, pg. 140
BLEVINS INC., pg. 156
CAMELOT MUSIC, INC., pg. 212
CAPITOL INDUSTRIES-EMI INC., pg. 216
CARLSON COMPANIES, INC., pg. 220
D&H DISTRIBUTING COMPANY, pg. 307
DANVILLE MARKETING—Dan River Inc., pg. 313
THE DELPHI GLASS CORP. DELPHI STAINED GLASS CENTERS, pg. 326
DIAMOND HILL PLYWOOD COMPANY—Darlington Veneer Company, pg. 316
EVA-TONE INC., pg. 390
HARDWARE WHOLESALERS, INC., pg. 508
HENSON TIMBER PRODUCTS CORP.—Stonecutter Mills Corp., pg. 1051
HERBAL ENTERPRISES INC., pg. 530
A. J. HOLLANDER CO., INC., pg. 539
INGRAM LIBRARY SERVICES, INC.—Ingram Industries Inc., pg. 569
INTERNATIONAL LEARNING SYSTEMS (JAPAN) LTD.—Berlitz International, Inc., pg. 143
JAYDON INCORPORATED, pg. 590
G. LEBLANC CORPORATION, pg. 665
G. LEBLANC—G. Leblanc Corporation, pg. 665
NATIONAL WELDERS SUPPLY CO. INC., pg. 794
NEW ENGLAND CORPORATION, pg. 800
ORR SAFETY EQUIPMENT COMPANY, pg. 830
PACIFIC LUMBER & SHIPPING CO., pg. 840
SGI INC., pg. 962
ST. ANNE INDUSTRIES LTD.—Parsons & Whittemore Enterprises, pg. 850
ST. ANNE PULP SALES CO. LTD.—Parsons & Whittemore Enterprises, pg. 850
ST. LOUIS MUSIC, INC., pg. 967
THE SARGENT-SOWELL COMPANY, pg. 971
SERVCO PACIFIC INC., pg. 991
STAR VIDEO ENTERTAINMENT, L.P., pg. 1040
VJ GROWERS, INC., pg. 1141
VANPORT MANUFACTURING, INC., pg. 1145
WEATHERKING PRODUCTS, INC.—Aqua Fab Industries, Inc., pg. 79
THE ZAMOISKI CO., pg. 1216

5111 — PRINTING & WRITING PAPER-WHOLESALE

THE ALAN & GRAY CO.—Alling & Cory Company, pg. 40
ALCOR ENVELOPE CO.—Alling & Cory Company, pg. 40
ALLING & CORY COMPANY, pg. 40
ALTO PAPERS—Bradner Central Company, pg. 171
AMERICAN OFFICE EQUIPMENT, pg. 58
ATHENS PAPER CO. INC., pg. 93
BLEYCO PAPER CO. OF MICHIGAN—A. W. Mendenhall Co., Inc., pg. 739
BRADNER CENTRAL COMPANY, pg. 170
BRADNER SMITH & CO.—Bradner Central Company, pg. 171
CENTRAL NATIONAL-GOTTESMAN INC., pg. 233
CENTRAL PAPER CO.—Central Paper Company, pg. 234
CENTRAL PAPER COMPANY, pg. 233
THE CINCINNATI CORDAGE & PAPER COMPANY, pg. 249
A.T. CLAYTON & COMPANY, INC., pg. 253
COLE PAPERS INC., pg. 260
DIAMETER PAPER CO.—Bradner Central Company, pg. 171
FIRST STATE PAPER, INC.—Central Paper Company, pg. 234
FOREST ATWOOD PAPER COMPANY—WWF Paper Corporation, pg. 1157
FUNDING SERVICES INC.—American Office Equipment, pg. 59
THE GIBSON GROUP INC., pg. 456
GOULD CENTRAL FLORIDA—Stephen Gould Paper Co., Inc., pg. 473
GOULD SOUTHERN—Stephen Gould Paper Co., Inc., pg. 474
STEPHEN GOULD OF ARIZONA, INC.—Stephen Gould Paper Co., Inc., pg. 474
STEPHEN GOULD OF CALIFORNIA—Stephen Gould Paper Co., Inc., pg. 474
STEPHEN GOULD OF CALIFORNIA-NORTH BAY—Stephen Gould Paper Co., Inc., pg. 474
STEPHEN GOULD OF CAROLINA, INC.—Stephen Gould Paper Co., Inc., pg. 474
STEPHEN GOULD OF CAROLINA, INC.—Stephen Gould Paper Co., Inc., pg. 474
STEPHEN GOULD OF COLORADO, INC.—Stephen Gould Paper Co., Inc., pg. 474
STEPHEN GOULD OF CONNECTICUT CORP.—Stephen Gould Paper Co., Inc., pg. 474
STEPHEN GOULD CORPORATION (PLAINVIEW, NY)—Stephen Gould Paper Co., Inc., pg. 474
STEPHEN GOULD CORPORATION (ROCHESTER, NY)—Stephen Gould Paper Co., Inc., pg. 474
STEPHEN GOULD OF FLORIDA, INC.—Stephen Gould Paper Co., Inc., pg. 474
STEPHEN GOULD OF FLORIDA, INC.—Stephen Gould Paper Co., Inc., pg. 474
STEPHEN GOULD OF ILLINOIS, INC.—Stephen Gould Paper Co., Inc., pg. 474
STEPHEN GOULD IN—Stephen Gould Paper Co., Inc., pg. 474
STEPHEN GOULD OF INDIANA, INC.—Stephen Gould Paper Co., Inc., pg. 474
STEPHEN GOULD MD—Stephen Gould Paper Co., Inc., pg. 474
STEPHEN GOULD MI—Stephen Gould Paper Co., Inc., pg. 474
STEPHEN GOULD/MIDHUDSON—Stephen Gould Paper Co., Inc., pg. 474
STEPHEN GOULD MIDWEST—Stephen Gould Paper Co., Inc., pg. 474
STEPHEN GOULD OF NEW ENGLAND, INC.—Stephen Gould Paper Co., Inc., pg. 474
STEPHEN GOULD OH—Stephen Gould Paper Co., Inc., pg. 474
STEPHEN GOULD OF OHIO, INC.—Stephen Gould Paper Co., Inc., pg. 474
STEPHEN GOULD PAPER CO., INC.—Stephen Gould Paper Co., Inc., pg. 474
STEPHEN GOULD OF PENNSYLVANIA CORP.—Stephen Gould Paper Co., Inc., pg. 474
STEPHEN GOULD OF PUERTO RICO, INC.—Stephen Gould Paper Co., Inc., pg. 474
STEPHEN GOULD OF TENNESSEE—Stephen Gould Paper Co., Inc., pg. 474
STEPHEN GOULD OF TEXAS, INC.—Stephen Gould Paper Co., Inc., pg. 474
KARL M. HARROP CO., INC.—Arcata Corporation, pg. 80
HENLEY PAPER COMPANY, pg. 529
HORIZON PAPER CO., INC., pg. 544
HUDSON VALLEY PAPER COMPANY, pg. 551
INGRAM PAPER COMPANY, pg. 569
INLANDER-STEINDLER PAPER, pg. 570
JACKSON PAPER COMPANY, pg. 587
KURTZ BROS., INC., pg. 646
LINDENMEYR MUNROE—Central National-Gottesman Inc., pg. 233
LINDENMEYR MUNROE—Central National-Gottesman Inc., pg. 233
MAC PAPERS, INC., pg. 694
MARQUARDT & CO.—Central Paper Company, pg. 234
D. J. MEAD-HUBBS & HOWE—Sofco-Mead, Inc., pg. 1016
A. W. MENDENHALL CO., INC., pg. 739
MIAMI PAPER COMPANY—WWF Paper Corporation, pg. 1157
MIDLAND PAPER CO., pg. 751

GEORGE W. MILLAR CO.—Central Paper Company, pg. 234
MISSISSIPPI CHEMICAL CORPORATION, pg. 760
NEWBROOK PAPER—Triangle Marketing Corp., pg. 1112
NEWELL PAPER CO. OF COLUMBUS—Jackson Paper Company, pg. 587
NEWELL PAPER CO. OF MERIDIAN—Jackson Paper Company, pg. 587
NEWSPRINT SOUTH SALES CORP.—Mississippi Chemical Corporation, pg. 760
PACIFIC PAPERS UNLIMITED—Bradner Central Company, pg. 171
PAPER EXPRESS—Graphisphere Holding Company, pg. 478
RIS PAPER COMPANY, pg. 935
ROTARY PAPER MANIFOLD CO.—Bradner Central Company, pg. 171
SEAMAN-PATRICK PAPER COMPANY, pg. 986
SEATTLE PACKAGING CORPORATION, pg. 986
TRIANGLE MARKETING CORP., pg. 1112
WWF INTERNATIONAL LIMITED—WWF Paper Corporation, pg. 1157
WWF NATIONAL—WWF Paper Corporation, pg. 1157
WWF PAPER CORPORATION, pg. 1157
WWF PAPER SALES U.K., LTD.—WWF Paper Corporation, pg. 1157
WWF/ROYAL PAPER COMPANY—WWF Paper Corporation, pg. 1157
WILCOX-WALTER-FURLONG PAPER CO.—WWF Paper Corporation, pg. 1157
WILCOX-WALTER-FURLONG PAPER CO. OF WASHINGTON—WWF Paper Corporation, pg. 1157

5112 — STATIONERY & OFFICE SUPPLIES-WHOLESALE

A & E BUSINESS PRODUCTS—Taylor Corporation, pg. 1081
ABBOTT GROUP LTD., pg. 9
IVAN ALLEN COMPANY, INC., pg. 36
ALLING & CORY COMPANY, pg. 40
AMERICAN MARKING SYSTEMS, pg. 58
AMES COLOR FILE DIVISION—Ames Safety Envelope Company, Inc., pg. 66
AMES SAFETY ENVELOPE COMPANY, INC., pg. 66
ANDERSON WHOLESALE COMPANY, pg. 73
ATAPCO OFFICE PRODUCTS GROUP—American Trading and Production Corporation, pg. 64
BALTIMORE STATIONERY CO., pg. 116
THE CAXTON PRINTERS LTD., pg. 230
CENTRAL PAPER CO.—Central Paper Company, pg. 234
CENTRAL PAPER COMPANY, pg. 233
CHAPMAN PRINTING COMPANY, pg. 239
COLUMBINE SYSTEMS INC., pg. 266
CURTIS SWANN—Burgoyne, Inc., pg. 190
DAKIN, INC., pg. 311
EATON OFFICE SUPPLY CO., INC., pg. 364
FORMS & SUPPLY, INC., pg. 424
GALAXY BUSINESS PRODUCTS—Metpac, Ltd., pg. 742
GRAPHICS INTERNATIONAL INC.—Hallmark Cards, Inc., pg. 502
JOHN HEATH & CO. LIMITED—American Trading and Production Corporation, pg. 65
HUDSON VALLEY PAPER COMPANY, pg. 551
HY-VEE FOOD STORES INCORPORATED, pg. 556
INDIANA RECORDS MANAGERS, pg. 565
KURTZ BROS., INC., pg. 646
CHARLES LEONARD, INC., pg. 668
THE CHARLES LEVY COMPANY, pg. 672
MAINE PRINTING & BUSINESS FORMS CO., pg. 702
MILLBANK ELECTRONICS GROUP LTD.—American Trading and Production Corporation, pg. 65
NIAGARA ENVELOPE COMPANY, INC., pg. 805
OFFICE CONNECTION, INC., pg. 821
PBM OFFICE PRODUCTS, pg. 835
PICK QUICK PAPERS, INC.—Central Paper Company, pg. 234
PRESTONIA OFFICE PRODUCTS LTD.—American Trading and Production Corporation, pg. 65
QUILL CORP., pg. 905
THE RELIABLE CORP., pg. 924
RICCOBON & COMPANY, INC., pg. 931
SILVER'S INC., pg. 1005
STANDARD MANIFOLD COMPANY, INC., pg. 1037
WASSERSTROM COMPANY, pg. 1167
ZEPHYR BASKETS & BALLOONS, pg. 1217

5113 — INDUSTRIAL & PERSONAL SERVICE PAPER-WHOLESALE

ALLING & CORY COMPANY, pg. 40
AMERICAN PACKAGING CORPORATION, pg. 59
BAGNASCO S.R.L.—Hollingsworth & Vose Co., pg. 539
CENTRAL NATIONAL-GOTTESMAN INC., pg. 233
CHICAGO DIVISION—Clark Foodservice, Inc., pg. 252
CHISWICK TRADING INC., pg. 248
CINCINNATI DIVISION—Clark Foodservice, Inc., pg. 252
CLARK FOODSERVICE, INC., pg. 252
CLARK-SIMON, INC.—Clark Foodservice, Inc., pg. 252
CLEVELAND DIVISION—Clark Foodservice, Inc., pg. 252
COLE PAPERS INC., pg. 260
COLUMBUS DIVISION—Clark Foodservice, Inc., pg. 252
CONESTOGA HOLDINGS, INC., pg. 273
CONTINENTAL PAPER & SUPPLY CO., pg. 280
DAKCO DISTRIBUTORS, INC., pg. 311
DETROIT DIVISION—Clark Foodservice, Inc., pg. 252
EARP MEAT COMPANY, pg. 362
ERNEST PAPER PRODUCTS, INC., pg. 387
EVANS BROTHERS COMPANY, INC., pg. 390
FIBREWEB INTERNATIONAL, LTD.—Gould Paper Corporation, pg. 473
S. FREEDMAN & SONS, INC., pg. 430
THE GIBSON GROUP INC., pg. 456
GORDON FOOD SERVICE INC., pg. 472
GRAPHICS INTERNATIONAL INC.—Hallmark Cards, Inc., pg. 502
HEARST ENTERPRISES DIVISION—The Hearst Corporation, pg. 523
HENLEY PAPER COMPANY, pg. 529
HOLLINGSWORTH & VOSE CO. U.K. LTD.—Hollingsworth & Vose Co., pg. 539
HOLLINGSWORTH & VOSE EUROPE NV—Hollingsworth & Vose Co., pg. 539
HOVOMEX S.A. DE C.V.—Hollingsworth & Vose Co., pg. 539
HUDSON VALLEY PAPER COMPANY, pg. 551
INDIANAPOLIS DIVISION—Clark Foodservice, Inc., pg. 252
INLANDER-STEINDLER PAPER, pg. 570
J P FOODSERVICE, INC., pg. 586
JACKSON PAPER COMPANY, pg. 587
JORDAN'S FOODS-BANGOR DIVISION—Jordan's Meats, pg. 605
JORDAN'S FOODS-FAIRFIELD DIVISION—Jordan's Meats, pg. 605
JORDAN'S FOODS-WESTBROOK DIVISION—Jordan's Meats, pg. 605
JORDAN'S FOODS-CARIBOU DIVISION—Jordan's Meats, pg. 605
JORDAN'S FOODS-COLCHESTER DIVISION—Jordan's Meats, pg. 605
KAISER TOBACCO COMPANY, INC., pg. 615
KEYSTONE FOODS CORPORATION, pg. 628
PERRY H. KOPLIK & SONS, pg. 641
LOMBARDI FOODSERVICE, INC., pg. 681
LONE STAR CORRUGATED CONTAINER CORPORATION, pg. 682
LOUISVILLE DIVISION—Clark Foodservice, Inc., pg. 252
M & C SPECIALTIES COMPANY, pg. 690
MTC REMCO TAPE PRODUCTS CO.—M & C Specialties Company, pg. 690
MAYER MYERS PAPER COMPANY, pg. 724
D. J. MEAD-HUBBS & HOWE—Sofco-Mead, Inc., pg. 1016
MID-STATE DIVISION—Clark Foodservice, Inc., pg. 252
MILWAUKEE DIVISION—Clark Foodservice, Inc., pg. 252
MISSION INDUSTRIES, pg. 760
NATIONAL RESTAURANT SUPPLY COMPANY, pg. 793
NETWORK SERVICES COMPANY OF CHICAGO, pg. 798
NEWELL PAPER CO. OF COLUMBUS—Jackson Paper Company, pg. 587
NEWELL PAPER CO. OF MERIDIAN—Jackson Paper Company, pg. 587
ORLANDO DIVISION—Clark Foodservice, Inc., pg. 252
OZARK DIVISION—Clark Foodservice, Inc., pg. 252
PAPER ENTERPRISES, INC., pg. 847
PEORIA DIVISION—Clark Foodservice, Inc., pg. 252
PEREZ TRADING CO. INC., pg. 860
RIVIERA BEACH DIVISION—Clark Foodservice, Inc., pg. 252
ROCHESTER MIDLAND CORPORATION, pg. 940
ROSELAND DIVISION—Clark Foodservice, Inc., pg. 252
SCC HOLDING CO., pg. 961
SCHNIEBER FINE FOODS, INC., pg. 977
SOFCO-MEAD, INC., pg. 1016
P.R. SOLO CUP, INC.—SCC Holding Co., pg. 961
SONNEVELDT COMPANY, pg. 1018
SOUTH BEND DIVISION—Clark Foodservice, Inc., pg. 252
ST. LOUIS DIVISION—Clark Foodservice, Inc., pg. 252
SUNCLIPSE, INC., pg. 1059
TECHNOGRAPHICS, INC., pg. 1083
TEKRA CORPORATION, pg. 1084
TWIN CITIES DIVISION—Clark Foodservice, Inc., pg. 252
UNGER COMPANY, pg. 1126
WWF PAPER CORPORATION, pg. 1157
WINCHESTER CARTON CORP.—Rock-Tenn Company, pg. 941
WIREGRASS CONTAINER, INC.—Rock-Tenn Company, pg. 941

5122 — DRUGS, DRUG PROPRIETARIES & DRUGGISTS' SUNDRIES-WHOLESALE

AFFILIATED FOODS, INC., pg. 24
ALABAMA WHOLESALE DRUG CO.—Tennessee Wholesale Drug Company, pg. 1088
THE FRED W. ALBRECHT GROCERY CO., pg. 31
ALCO HEALTH SERVICES CORPORATION, pg. 31
ALEXANDRA DE MARKOFF, LTD.—MacAndrews & Forbes Holdings Inc., pg. 695
ALMAY, INC.—MacAndrews & Forbes Holdings Inc., pg. 695
ALVA/AMCO PHARMACAL COMPANIES, INC., pg. 46
AMFAC DISTRIBUTION CORPORATION—JMB Realty Corporation, pg. 585
AMFAC HEALTH CARE—JMB Realty Corporation, pg. 585
ANDREWS GROUP, INCORPORATED, pg. 74
AUTOMATIC LIQUID PACKAGING, INC., pg. 100
BASIC FOOD INTERNATIONAL INC., pg. 124
THE LEWIS BEAR COMPANY, pg. 129
BEAUTY ENTERPRISES INC., pg. 130
BISSELL LTD.—Bissell Inc., pg. 153
BLISTEX LIMITED—Blistex, Inc., pg. 157
BROWNING CHEMICAL CORPORATION, pg. 183
C-B CORPORATION, pg. 198
CHARLES OF THE RITZ GROUP LTD.—MacAndrews & Forbes Holdings Inc., pg. 695
COLOR COSMETICS—Plastek Group, pg. 875
COMMONS BROS., INC., pg. 269
COMMONS METRO INC.—Commons Bros., Inc., pg. 269
CONSOLIDATED COMPANIES INC. (CONCO), pg. 276
THE CROCKER-FELS COMPANY, pg. 299
CUMBERLAND-SWAN, INC., pg. 304
D.V.F. INC.—MacAndrews & Forbes Holdings Inc., pg. 695
DAKCO DISTRIBUTORS, INC., pg. 311
DAKOTA DRUG, INC.—Dakco Distributors, Inc., pg. 311
DEB HOLDINGS, INC., pg. 323
E.C. DEWITT & COMPANY (AUST.) PTY. LTD.—C.B. Fleet Company, Incorporated, pg. 417
DEWITT INTERNATIONAL (SINGAPORE) PTE. LTD.—C.B. Fleet Company, Incorporated, pg. 417
DIET CENTER, INC.—American Health Companies, Inc., pg. 55
THE F. DOHMEN COMPANY, pg. 343
DRUG GUILD DISTRIBUTORS, INC., pg. 349
ESTEE LAUDER, INTL.—Estee Lauder, Inc., pg. 389
FAMILY PHARMACY GENERAL OFFICE—Alco Health Services Corporation, pg. 32
FERRO METAL & CHEMICAL CORPORATION LTD.—Philipp Brothers Chemicals, Inc., pg. 867
FILA FITNESS LTD.—MacAndrews & Forbes Holdings Inc., pg. 695
FLORASYNTH (FAR EAST) PTE. LTD.—Florasynth Inc., pg. 420
FLORASYNTH GMBH—Florasynth Inc., pg. 420
FLORASYNTH LIMITED—Florasynth Inc., pg. 420
FLORASYNTH S.A. DE C.V.—Florasynth Inc., pg. 420
FOREVER LIVING PRODUCTS, pg. 424
GALENPHARMA, INC.—GenDerm Corporation, pg. 448
GENDERM CORPORATION, pg. 448
GENERAL DRUG CO., pg. 449
GROCERS SUPPLY CO. INC., pg. 488
GULF DISTRIBUTION INC., pg. 493
HEALTH CARE DISTRIBUTORS OF INDIANA, INC., pg. 520
HUMISTON-KEELING, INC., pg. 552
INTERSTATE DRUG EXCHANGE, INC., pg. 580
INVERNESS CORP., pg. 581
JAYDON INCORPORATED, pg. 590
S. C. JOHNSON & SON, INC., pg. 599
KENDALL AUSTRALIA PTY. LTD.—Kendall Healthcare Products Co., pg. 622
THE KENDALL CO.—Kendall Healthcare Products Co., pg. 622
THE KENDALL CO. (UK) LTD.—Kendall Healthcare Products Co., pg. 622
KENDALL DE MEXICO S.A. DE D.V.—Kendall Healthcare Products Co., pg. 622
KENDALL GMBH—Kendall Healthcare Products Co., pg. 622
KENDALL S.A.—Kendall Healthcare Products Co., pg. 622
KENDALL SINGAPORE—Kendall Healthcare Products Co., pg. 622
KENDALL THAILAND—Kendall Healthcare Products Co., pg. 622
KING GROUP, INC., pg. 630
KING MICHIGAN SUNDRIES DIV.—King Group, Inc., pg. 630
LEONARD WHOLESALE, INC., pg. 668
MASON DISTRIBUTORS, INC., pg. 718
MERCURY DISTRIBUTING CO., INC., pg. 740
MARILYN MIGLIN, INC., pg. 752
JOHN PAUL MITCHELL SYSTEMS, pg. 762
MUELHENS, INC., pg. 774
NATIONAL MERCHANDISE CO., INC., pg. 792
NORTH CAROLINA MUTUAL WHOLESALE DRUG CO., pg. 813
NORTHERN DRUG COMPANY, pg. 814
NORTHWESTERN DRUG COMPANY—The F. Dohmen Company, pg. 343
NU SKIN INTERNATIONAL, pg. 817
PACO RABANNE PARFUMS, pg. 842
PARIS PRESENTS, pg. 848
PAVION LTD., pg. 852
PHARMAVITE CORP., pg. 866
PLAYTEX BEAUTY CARE, INC.—Playtex FP Group Incorporated, pg. 877
PLAYTEX MARKETING CORPORATION—Playtex FP Group Incorporated, pg. 877
POLAROME MFG. CO. INC., pg. 878
PRESTIGE FRAGRANCE & COSMETICS, INC.—MacAndrews & Forbes Holdings Inc., pg. 696
PRESTIGE FRAGRANCES, LTD.—MacAndrews & Forbes Holdings Inc., pg. 696
PRESTIGE PERFUMES LTD.—MacAndrews & Forbes Holdings Inc., pg. 696
RANIR CORPORATION, pg. 912
REDKEN LABORATORIES (DISC), INC.—Redken Laboratories, Inc., pg. 919
REVLON INTERNATIONAL CORPORATION—MacAndrews & Forbes Holdings Inc., pg. 696
REVLON S.P.A.—MacAndrews & Forbes Holdings Inc., pg. 696
REXALL GROUP—Sundown Vitamin Co., Inc., pg. 1060
RITA-ANN DISTRIBUTORS—Alco Health Services Corporation, pg. 32
RUGBY-DARBY GROUP OF COS., pg. 955
RYDELLE LABORATORIES—S. C. Johnson & Son, Inc., pg. 599
HENRY SCHEIN, INC., pg. 975
SCHEIN PHARMACEUTICAL, INC.—Henry Schein, Inc., pg. 975
SCHERER SCIENTIFIC, LTD., pg. 976
SEMEX, INC.—Seton Company, pg. 993
SETON COMPANY, pg. 993
J. M. SMITH CORP., pg. 1012
SOUTHERN BEAUTY ENTERPRISES—Beauty Enterprises Inc., pg. 130
STAR SALES CO., INC., pg. 1040
SUNDOWN VITAMIN CO., INC., pg. 1060
TENNESSEE WHOLESALE DRUG COMPANY, pg. 1088
THOMPSON MEDICAL COMPANY, INC., pg. 1094
TRI-STATE WHOLESALE ASSOCIATED GROCERS, pg. 1111
GEORGE UHE CO., INC., pg. 1125
WILLIAMS DRUGS DISTRIBUTORS—Humiston-Keeling, Inc., pg. 553

5131 — PIECE GOODS, NOTIONS & OTHER DRY GOODS-WHOLESALE

AMANA SOCIETY, pg. 46
ANDERSON WHOLESALE COMPANY, pg. 73
AVONDALE MILLS FABRIC DIV.—Avondale Mills, Inc., pg. 103
AVONDALE MILLS, INC., pg. 103
BLUMENTHAL PRINT WORKS, INC., pg. 161
BRUNSCHWIG & FILS, INC., pg. 184
CONNELL BROTHERS (HONG KONG) LTD.—Wilbur-Ellis Company & Connell Brothers Company, pg. 1189
CONTINENTAL CONAIR, LTD.—Conair Corporation, pg. 272
FABRIC WHOLESALERS, INC., pg. 396
HAMPTON PRINT WORKS, INC., pg. 504
HARP'S FOOD STORES, INC., pg. 510
THE JOHN JOHNSON CO., pg. 597
JACK LENOR LARSEN, INC., pg. 659
LEVEL EXPORT SALES CORP., pg. 670
MAHARAM FABRIC CORPORATION, pg. 701
MALDEN MILLS INDUSTRIES, INC., pg. 702
MARCUS BROTHERS TEXTILES, INC., pg. 706
MARK FABRICKS, INC., pg. 708
MOUNT VERNON MILLS, INC.—R. B. Pamplin Corp., pg. 844
P. S. INTERNATIONAL INC., pg. 837
QST INDUSTRIES, INC., pg. 902
ROCKVILLE FABRICS CORPORATION, pg. 942
SCHOTTENSTEIN STORES CORPORATION, pg. 978
F. SCHUMACHER & CO., pg. 979
SILVERMAN PRODUCTS & TEXTILES, pg. 1004
STANLEY DRYING COMPANY—DEC International, Inc., pg. 309
STAR SALES CO., INC., pg. 1040
TASH, INC., pg. 1080
G. VON HAMM TEXTILES, INC., pg. 1155
WEILWOOD INDUSTRIES, INC.—Santee Print Works, Inc., pg. 970
FRANK W. WINNE & SON, INC., pg. 1196
WM. E. WRIGHT LIMITED PARTNERSHIP, pg. 1205

5136 — MEN'S & BOYS CLOTHING & FURNISHINGS-WHOLESALE

ALPHA SHIRT CO., pg. 44
BOSTON TRADING LTD. INC., pg. 168
BRODER BROS. CO., pg. 178
BRODER BROS. CO. OF FLORIDA, INC.—Broder Bros. Co., pg. 178
BUGLE BOY INDUSTRIES, INC., pg. 187
CALVIN KLEIN SPORT, INC.—Calvin Klein, Inc., pg. 635
DAISY DE VENEZUELA C.A.—Farley Industries, pg. 400
DRAGON INTERNATIONAL—Bugle Boy Industries, Inc., pg. 187
FINESILVER MANUFACTURING COMPANY, pg. 411
GITANO BOY'S & MEN'S DIVISION—Gitano Group Inc., pg. 460
GITANO GROUP INC., pg. 460
GORDON & FERGUSON OF DELAWARE, INC., pg. 471
HAGGAR APPAREL COMPANY, pg. 499
HARRISS & COVINGTON HOSIERY MILLS, pg. 512
SID HARVEY INC., pg. 515
HEYMAN CORPORATION, pg. 532
JOCKEY INTERNATIONAL, INC., pg. 595
JORDACHE ENTERPRISES, INC., pg. 604
KAYSER-ROTH CORPORATION—Collins & Aikman Group Inc., pg. 263
LEVI STRAUSS & CO. (CANADA), INC.—Levi Strauss & Co., pg. 670
LEVI STRAUSS INTERNATIONAL—Levi Strauss & Co., pg. 670
LEVI STRAUSS (SUISSE) S.A.—Levi Strauss & Co., pg. 671
LOST ARROW CORPORATION, pg. 684
MPO VIDEOTRONICS, INC., pg. 693
MEMBERS ONLY BY EUROPE CRAFT, pg. 738
OSHKOSH B'GOSH HOSIERY CO.—Heyman Corporation, pg. 532
POLO/RALPH LAUREN CORPORATION, pg. 879
RAM GRAPHICS, INC., pg. 910
RECREATIONAL EQUIPMENT, INC., pg. 917
RENFRO CORP., pg. 926
RIVER CITY PROTECTIVE WEAR, INC.—Shelby Group International, Inc., pg. 996
ROLANE CORPORATION—Collins & Aikman Group Inc., pg. 263
ROYTEX, INC., pg. 953
M. RUBIN & SONS INC., pg. 954
SCHOOL APPAREL, INC., pg. 978
SCHOTTENSTEIN STORES CORPORATION, pg. 978
SEATTLE PACIFIC INDUSTRIES, INC., pg. 986
SHELBY GROUP INTERNATIONAL, INC., pg. 996
SIGALLO, LTD., pg. 1003
SOUTHERN APPAREL CORPORATION, pg. 1020
STAR SPORTSWEAR MANUFACTURING—Londontown Holdings Corporation, pg. 682
STYLE AUTO, pg. 1055
SUPERBA, INC., pg. 1063
T SHIRT GRAPHICS—The Vernon Company, pg. 1148
TARGET SPORTSWEAR, INC., pg. 1079
TOTES CANADA LTD.—Totes Incorporated, pg. 1103
TOTES EUROPE—Totes Incorporated, pg. 1103
TOTES U.K. LIMITED—Totes Incorporated, pg. 1103
TRU-FIT GLOVE & HEADWEAR DIV.—Heyman Corporation, pg. 532

5137 — WOMEN'S, CHILDREN'S, & INFANTS' CLOTHING & ACCESSORIES-WHOLESALE

ALBEROY DIVISION—Beldoch Industries Corporation, pg. 133
BARON-ABRAMSON, INC., pg. 121
BELDOCH INDUSTRIES CORPORATION, pg. 133
BELDOCH POPPER DIVISION—Beldoch Industries Corporation, pg. 133
BOSTON TRADING LTD. INC., pg. 168
BRODER BROS. CO., pg. 178
BRODER BROS. CO. OF FLORIDA, INC.—Broder Bros. Co., pg. 178
CALVIN KLEIN SPORT, INC.—Calvin Klein, Inc., pg. 635
DANIEL CARON LTD., pg. 224
CERTIFIED CORP., pg. 236
DAISY DE VENEZUELA C.A.—Farley Industries, pg. 400
EDELSON & SONS CORPORATION, pg. 368
ESPRIT DE CORP., pg. 388
EVENFLO PRODUCTS CO.—Spalding & Evenflo Companies, Inc., pg. 1024
FIVE DOLLAR CLOTHING STORES, pg. 416
FORTUNE FASHION, pg. 425
GENERRA SPORTSWEAR COMPANY, INC., pg. 451
GITANO GIRL'S DIVISION—Gitano Group Inc., pg. 460
GITANO GROUP INC., pg. 460
GLORIA VANDERBILT DIVISION—Gitano Group Inc., pg. 460
KENNETH GORDON NEW ORLEANS, LTD., pg. 472
HAMPTON PRINT WORKS, INC., pg. 504
SID HARVEY INC., pg. 515
HELPERN JOAN & DAVID, INC., pg. 528
HEYMAN CORPORATION, pg. 532
I B DIFFUSION, LP, pg. 558
JACQUES MORET, INC., pg. 588
JERELL, INC., pg. 593
JOAN & DAVID, INC.—Helpern Joan & David, Inc., pg. 528
JONES APPAREL GROUP, INC. CANADA—Jones Apparel Group, Inc., pg. 602
JORDACHE ENTERPRISES, INC., pg. 604
KAYSER-ROTH CORPORATION—Collins & Aikman Group Inc., pg. 263
KNITMAKER DIVISION—Beldoch Industries Corporation, pg. 133
LEVI STRAUSS & CO. (CANADA), INC.—Levi Strauss & Co., pg. 670
LEVI STRAUSS (SUISSE) S.A.—Levi Strauss & Co., pg. 671
LOST ARROW CORPORATION, pg. 684
MPO VIDEOTRONICS, INC., pg. 693
MARISA CHRISTINA INC., pg. 707
NATIONAL CORSET SUPPLY HOUSE, pg. 787
ORGANICALLY GROWN CORPORATION, pg. 829
OSHKOSH B'GOSH HOSIERY CO.—Heyman Corporation, pg. 532
PIERRE CARDIN KNITS—Beldoch Industries Corporation, pg. 133
PLAYTEX ESPANA S.A.—Playtex Apparel Inc., pg. 876
PLAYTEX FRANCE—Playtex Apparel Inc., pg. 876
PLAYTEX, ITALIA S.P.A.—Playtex Apparel Inc., pg. 876
PLAYTEX MARKETING CORPORATION—Playtex FP Group Incorporated, pg. 877
PLAYTEX MEXICANA S.A. DE C.V.—Playtex Apparel Inc., pg. 877
RECREATIONAL EQUIPMENT, INC., pg. 917
RENFRO CORP., pg. 926
RIVER CITY PROTECTIVE WEAR, INC.—Shelby Group International, Inc., pg. 996
SCHOOL APPAREL, INC., pg. 978
SCHOTTENSTEIN STORES CORPORATION, pg. 978
SEATTLE PACIFIC INDUSTRIES, INC., pg. 986
SEIBEL & STERN CORP., pg. 987
STAR SPORTSWEAR MANUFACTURING—Londontown Holdings Corporation, pg. 682
STYLE AUTO, pg. 1055
T SHIRT GRAPHICS—The Vernon Company, pg. 1148
TARGET SPORTSWEAR, INC., pg. 1079
TOTES CANADA LTD.—Totes Incorporated, pg. 1103
TOTES EUROPE—Totes Incorporated, pg. 1103
TOTES U.K. LIMITED—Totes Incorporated, pg. 1103
TRU-FIT GLOVE & HEADWEAR DIV.—Heyman Corporation, pg. 532
VARAT ENTERPRISES, INC., pg. 1145

5139 — FOOTWEAR-WHOLESALE

ALLEN-EDMONDS SHOE CORP., pg. 36
BARIS SHOE COMPANY, INC., pg. 119
BRITISH KNIGHTS—Jack Schwartz Shoes, Inc., pg. 980
COWTOWN BOOT COMPANY, pg. 291
DIADORA AMERICA, INC., pg. 335
GATOR INDUSTRIES INC., pg. 446
HELPERN JOAN & DAVID, INC., pg. 528
INTERNATIONAL SEAWAY TRADING CORPORATION, pg. 579
JIMLAR CORPORATION, pg. 594
JOAN & DAVID, INC.—Helpern Joan & David, Inc., pg. 528
KAEPA INC., pg. 613
KANGAROOS, USA INC., pg. 616
GEO. E. KEITH COMPANY, pg. 620
B. LEVY & SONS, pg. 672
MORSE SHOE, INC., pg. 772
NEW BALANCE CANADA INC.—New Balance Athletic Shoe, Inc., pg. 799
PALLMARK INTERNATIONAL, INC.—The Cherokee Group, pg. 243
SCHOTTENSTEIN STORES CORPORATION, pg. 978
SCHWARTZ & BENJAMIN, INC., pg. 980
JACK SCHWARTZ SHOES, INC., pg. 980
SOUTHERN LEATHER COMPANY, pg. 1021
SPORTO CORP., pg. 1032
STYLE AUTO, pg. 1055
TOBER INDUSTRIES, INC., pg. 1099
TOPLINE IMPORTS, INC., pg. 1102
WALK-OVER SHOES—Geo. E. Keith Company, pg. 620

5141 — GROCERIES, GENERAL LINE-WHOLESALE

AJC INTERNATIONAL, INC., pg. 4
AFFILIATED OF FLORIDA INC., pg. 23
AFFILIATED FOOD DISTRIBUTORS, pg. 23
AFFILIATED FOOD STORES, pg. 23
AFFILIATED FOODS COOPERATIVE INC., pg. 23
AFFILIATED FOODS, INC., pg. 24
AFFILIATED FOODS SOUTHWEST, pg. 24
AFFILIATED GENERAL AGENCY, INC.—Affiliated Food Stores, pg. 23
THE FRED W. ALBRECHT GROCERY CO., pg. 31
ALEX LEE, INC., pg. 33
ALLEN FOODS, INC., pg. 36
ALPHA DISTRIBUTORS LTD.—AmeriServ Food Company, pg. 66
AMERICAN SPECIALTY DISTRIBUTING—Portland Food Products Company, pg. 881
AMERICAN SPECIALTY DISTRIBUTING—Portland Food Products Company, pg. 881
AMERICAN SPECIALTY FOODS—Portland Food Products Company, pg. 881
AMERISERV FOOD COMPANY, pg. 66
ASSOCIATED FOOD STORES INC., pg. 89
ASSOCIATED FOODS INC.—Associated Grocers of New England, Inc., pg. 90
ASSOCIATED GROCERS, INC., pg. 90
ASSOCIATED GROCERS OF ALABAMA, INC., pg. 90
ASSOCIATED GROCERS OF NEW ENGLAND, INC., pg. 90
ASSOCIATED WHOLESALE GROCERS, INC., pg. 92
B & R FOODS—Performance Food Group, Inc., pg. 861
BANNER WHOLESALE GROCERS, INC., pg. 118
BASIC AMERICAN FOODS, pg. 124
THE LEWIS BEAR COMPANY, pg. 129
BEAVER STREET FISHERIES, INC., pg. 130
BELL CARTER DISTRIBUTING—Bell-Carter Foods, Inc., pg. 134
BROOKSHIRE BROS., INC., pg. 180
C & S WHOLESALE GROCERY INC., pg. 198
CAMELLIA FOOD STORES CO-OP INC., pg. 211
CAPISTAR, INC.—Spartan Stores Inc., pg. 1026
CARLSON COMPANIES, INC., pg. 220
CENTRAL GROCERS CO-OP, pg. 232
CERTIFIED GROCERS ADVERTISING CO., pg. 236
CERTIFIED GROCERS MIDWEST, INC., pg. 236
CERTIFIED GROCERS OF CALIFORNIA, pg. 237
CERTIFIED WHOLESALERS INC.—Associated Grocers of New England, Inc., pg. 90
CIQYA/BRAVO FOODS DE MEXICO—Newly Weds Foods Inc., pg. 804
CLARK-SIMON, INC.—Clark Foodservice, Inc., pg. 252
COASTAL WHOLESALE, INC., pg. 257
CONNELL RICE & SUGAR CO., pg. 275
CONSOLIDATED COMPANIES INC. (CONCO), pg. 276
CONSOLIDATED WHOLESALE COMPANY DIVISION—GSC Enterprises, Inc., pg. 440
CULLUM DISTRIBUTION CENTER, INC.—Randall's Food Markets, Inc., pg. 912
DAHLSTEN TRUCK LINE, INC., pg. 310
DECO PURCHASING CO.—Helmsley Enterprises, Inc., pg. 527
DI GIORGIO CORPORATION, pg. 334
DOMINO'S PIZZA DISTRIBUTION CORP.—Domino's Pizza Inc., pg. 344
EBY BROWN CO.—Eby Brown Co., pg. 365
EFFEMS AG—Mars, Incorporated, pg. 713
FERRARA FOODS & CONFECTIONS, INC., pg. 407
JAMES FERRERA & SONS, INC., pg. 407
FOOD 4 LESS, INC.—The Yucaipa Companies, pg. 1214
FOOD SERVICES OF AMERICA, pg. 423
FOREVER LIVING PRODUCTS, pg. 424
4C FOODS CORPORATION, pg. 427
FRENCH & BEAN—Associated Grocers of New England, Inc., pg. 90
GSC DISTRIBUTING COMPANIES DIVISION—GSC Enterprises, Inc., pg. 440
GSC ENTERPRISES, INC., pg. 440
GENUARDI SUPER MARKETS INC., pg. 452
GINSBERG'S INSTITUTIONAL FOODS, INC., pg. 460
GOLDEN STATE FOODS CORP., pg. 466
GOYA FOODS, INC., pg. 474
B. GREEN & CO., pg. 484
AUTRY GREER & SONS, INC., pg. 486
GROCERS SPECIALTY CO.—Certified Grocers Of California, pg. 237
GROCERS SUPPLY CO. INC., pg. 488
GROCERY SUPPLY COMPANY DIVISION—GSC Enterprises, Inc., pg. 440
H & H DISTRIBUTING COMPANY, INC., pg. 495
THE H. T. HACKNEY CO., pg. 498
HALE-HALSELL COMPANY, pg. 500
IRA HIGDON GROCERY, INC., pg. 533
HOLIDAY COMPANIES, pg. 539
HOUCHENS INDUSTRIES INC., pg. 545
HUBBS IMPORTING CORP., pg. 550
HULMAN & COMPANY, pg. 552
HY-VEE FOOD STORES INCORPORATED, pg. 556
PAUL INMAN ASSOCIATES INC., pg. 570
INSTITUTION FOOD HOUSE, INC.—Alex Lee, Inc., pg. 33
INTERSTATE DISTRIBUTORS INC., pg. 580
JERRICO, INC.—Castle-Harlan, Inc., pg. 229
JITNEY JUNGLE WHOLESALE CO., INC.—Jitney-Jungle Stores of America, Inc., pg. 594
JORDAN'S MEATS, pg. 605
JORDAN'S FOODS-BANGOR DIVISION—Jordan's Meats, pg. 605
JORDAN'S FOODS-FAIRFIELD DIVISION—Jordan's Meats, pg. 605
JORDAN'S FOODS-WESTBROOK DIVISION—Jordan's Meats, pg. 605
JORDAN'S FOODS-CARIBOU DIVISION—Jordan's Meats, pg. 605

JORDAN'S FOODS-COLCHESTER DIVISION—Jordan's Meats, pg. 605
KEENERS, INC., pg. 620
KEY FOOD STORES CO-OPERATIVE, INC., pg. 626
KINGSTON MARKETING CO.—Topco Associates, Inc., pg. 1101
KLUENER FOODS CO.—Kluener Packing Company, pg. 636
KRASDALE FOODS INC., pg. 644
LACKMAN FOOD SERVICE, pg. 650
LEE GROCERY COMPANY, pg. 665
LEONARD WHOLESALE, INC., pg. 668
J.L. LESTER & SON, INC., pg. 668
KENNETH O. LESTER, INC.—Performance Food Group, Inc., pg. 862
LITTLE CAESAR ENTERPRISES, INC., pg. 678
LOMBARDI FOODSERVICE, INC., pg. 681
LOSURDO FOODS, INC., pg. 684
M & M RESTAURANT SUPPLY—Keystone Foods Corporation, pg. 629
M M M SALES, INC., pg. 692
MADISON GROCERY CO., INC., pg. 699
MAZO LERCH COMPANY, INC., pg. 725
MCFARLING FOODS, INC., pg. 729
MERCHANTS DISTRIBUTORS, INC.—Alex Lee, Inc., pg. 33
MINYARD FOOD STORES, pg. 759
T.J. MORRIS COMPANY, INC., pg. 771
MURRY'S, INC., pg. 777
NATIONAL FOOD STORES, INC. T/A KRAUSZER'S, pg. 788
NICKLES BAKERY, INC.—Alfred Nickles Bakery, Inc., pg. 807
P. S. INTERNATIONAL INC., pg. 837
PERFORMANCE FOOD GROUP, INC., pg. 861
PETER J. SCHMITT CO., INC.—Peter J. Schmitt Holdings, pg. 977
POCAHONTAS FOODS, USA—Performance Food Group, Inc., pg. 862
PREPCO, pg. 887
PUBLIX SUPER MARKETS, INC.—Publix Supermarkets Inc., pg. 899
PUEBLO INTERNATIONAL, INC., pg. 899
PUEBLO INTERNATIONAL, INC.-P.R. DIV.—Pueblo International, Inc., pg. 899
QUALITY FOODS INC., pg. 903
C. B. RAGLAND COMPANY, pg. 909
RAND'S INC., pg. 912
RICHARDS BROTHERS OF MOUNTAIN GROVE, pg. 932
ROUNDY'S, INC., pg. 952
ROUNDY'S INC., MILWAUKEE DIV.—Roundy's, Inc., pg. 952
ROUNDY'S WAYCO FOODS—Roundy's, Inc., pg. 952
S.P.C. TRANSPORT, pg. 963
SAMELSON-LEON COMPANY, INC., pg. 968
S. SCHAFFER GROCERY CORPORATION, pg. 974
PETER J. SCHMITT HOLDINGS, pg. 976
SCHNIEBER FINE FOODS, INC., pg. 977
SHOP-RITE BEVERAGES, INC.—Wakefern Food Corporation, pg. 1158
SHURFINE-CENTRAL CORP., pg. 1001
SONNEVELDT COMPANY, pg. 1018
SPARTAN STORES INC., pg. 1026
SUNSHINE/SALERNO, INC. (NJ)—GF Industries, Inc., pg. 439
SWEENEY & COMPANY DIVISION—GSC Enterprises, Inc., pg. 440
SWEETLIFE FOODS, INC., pg. 1067
TLC BEATRICE INTERNATIONAL HOLDINGS INC., pg. 1073
THOMAS & HOWARD, pg. 1093
TOPCO ASSOCIATES, INC., pg. 1101
TRADING PORT, INC., pg. 1105
J. TREFFILETTI & SONS, INC., pg. 1109
TRI-STATE WHOLESALE ASSOCIATED GROCERS, pg. 1111
TRUCCHIS MARKETS, pg. 1117
TUPMAN THURLOW CO. INC., pg. 1119
TWIN COUNTY GROCERS, INC., pg. 1122
U.R.M. STORES, INC., pg. 1124
UNITED A G CO-OP, INC., pg. 1130
UNITED DAIRY FARMERS, INC., pg. 1131
UNITED STORES, pg. 1137
VALLET FOOD SERV INC., pg. 1143
VALLEY ISLE PRODUCE, INC., pg. 1143
VALU-FOODS, INC.—Hale-Halsell Company, pg. 501
W S HOLDING COMPANY, pg. 1156
WAKEFERN FINANCE CO.—Wakefern Food Corporation, pg. 1158
WAKEFERN FOOD CORPORATION, pg. 1158
WESTIN, INC., pg. 1183
WHITE SWAN, INC.—W S Holding Company, pg. 1156

5142 — PACKAGED FROZEN FOODS-WHOLESALE

AFFILIATED FOODS COOPERATIVE INC., pg. 23
ALCOSA/SUNWISE—Hanover Foods Corporation, pg. 506
AMERICAN FOODSERVICE—American Produce & Vegetable Co., pg. 60
AMERICAN FROZEN FOODS, INC., pg. 55
AMERICAN INSTITUTIONAL FOODS—AJC International, Inc., pg. 4
AMERICAN PRODUCE & VEGETABLE CO., pg. 59
BACARDI IMPORTS, INC., pg. 108
BASIC FOOD INTERNATIONAL INC., pg. 124
THE LEWIS BEAR COMPANY, pg. 129
BEAVER STREET FISHERIES, INC., pg. 130
BROWN DERBY, INC., pg. 181
BURRIS FOODS, INC., pg. 195
C & S WHOLESALE GROCERY INC., pg. 198
CMD-KEITH CO.—Ben E. Keith Company, pg. 620
CALAVO GROWERS OF CALIFORNIA, pg. 208
CAMELLIA FOOD STORES CO-OP INC., pg. 211
D. CANALE FOOD SERVICES, INC., pg. 213
CEDAR FARMS COMPANY, INC., pg. 230
CERTIFIED GROCERS ADVERTISING CO., pg. 236
CERTIFIED GROCERS MIDWEST, INC., pg. 236
CERTIFIED GROCERS OF CALIFORNIA, pg. 237
CLARK-SIMON, INC.—Clark Foodservice, Inc., pg. 252
CONNELL RICE & SUGAR CO., pg. 275
CONSOLIDATED COMPANIES INC. (CONCO), pg. 276
CROWN FOODS INC., pg. 302
D'JESCO, INC.—AJC International, Inc., pg. 4
EARP MEAT COMPANY, pg. 362
EDWARDS BAKING CO., pg. 369
ELI'S CHICAGO'S FINEST, INC., pg. 376
EVANS BROTHERS COMPANY, INC., pg. 390
FLYING FOOD FARE, INC., pg. 421
FOOD SERVICES OF AMERICA, pg. 423
GENUARDI SUPER MARKETS INC., pg. 452
GLOBAL FOOD CORPORATION—Basic Food International Inc., pg. 124
GOLDEN GEM GROWERS INC., pg. 466
GORDON FOOD SERVICE INC., pg. 472
JACK GREENBERG INC., pg. 485
HALE-HALSELL COMPANY, pg. 500
HARKER'S INC., pg. 509
J. HELLMAN PRODUCE, INC., pg. 527
IRA HIGDON GROCERY, INC., pg. 533
JORDAN'S MEATS, pg. 605
JORDAN'S FOODS-BANGOR DIVISION—Jordan's Meats, pg. 605
JORDAN'S FOODS-FAIRFIELD DIVISION—Jordan's Meats, pg. 605
JORDAN'S FOODS-WESTBROOK DIVISION—Jordan's Meats, pg. 605
JORDAN'S FOODS-CARIBOU DIVISION—Jordan's Meats, pg. 605
JORDAN'S FOODS-COLCHESTER DIVISION—Jordan's Meats, pg. 605
KEENERS, INC., pg. 620
BEN E. KEITH CO. OF OKLAHOMA—Ben E. Keith Company, pg. 620
BEN E. KEITH COMPANY, pg. 620
KESTERSON FOOD COMPANY, INC., pg. 624
KEYSTONE FOODS CORPORATION, pg. 628
KING & PRINCE SEAFOOD CORPORATION, pg. 631
KINGS FOODSERVICE—Unifax, Inc., pg. 1126
KINGSTON MARKETING CO.—Topco Associates, Inc., pg. 1101
LEE GROCERY COMPANY, pg. 665
LOMBARDI FOODSERVICE, INC., pg. 681
MADISON GROCERY CO., INC., pg. 699
MCINERNEY-MILLER BROTHERS INC., pg. 729
MONARCH DIV.—J P Foodservice, Inc., pg. 586
MURRY'S, INC., pg. 777
PIONEER SNACKS—Melody Foods, Inc., pg. 738
RAND'S INC., pg. 912
RED L FOODS—Union Holdings, Inc., pg. 1128
REMARKS, INC., pg. 925
ROBERTS FOODS, INC., pg. 938
ROMAN MEAL COMPANY, pg. 945
RYSER BROTHERS INC., pg. 958
SCHNIEBER FINE FOODS, INC., pg. 977
SEAFRESH INC.—Wards Cove Packing Company, pg. 1163
SHAMROCK FOODS CO., pg. 994
SONNEVELDT COMPANY, pg. 1018
SOUTHERN FROZEN FOODS—Agway, Inc., pg. 26
SPARTAN STORES INC., pg. 1026
TLC BEATRICE INTERNATIONAL HOLDINGS INC., pg. 1073
TOPCO ASSOCIATES, INC., pg. 1101
TREMONT FOODS, pg. 1109
TRI-STATE WHOLESALE ASSOCIATED GROCERS, pg. 1111
TUPMAN THURLOW CO. INC., pg. 1119
TWIN COUNTY GROCERS, INC., pg. 1122
UNIFAX, INC., pg. 1126
UNITED STORES, pg. 1137
VALHALLA TRADING CO.—Jack Greenberg Inc., pg. 485
VALLEY ISLE PRODUCE, INC., pg. 1143
WHITE ROSE CORPORATION—Di Giorgio Corporation, pg. 335

5143 — DAIRY PRODUCTS, EXCEPT DRIED OR CANNED-WHOLESALE

AFFILIATED FOODS COOPERATIVE INC., pg. 23
AGWAY, INC., pg. 25
ALTO DAIRY COOPERATIVE, pg. 45
ASSOCIATED MILK PRODUCERS, INC., pg. 91
ATLANTIC DAIRY COOPERATIVE, pg. 94
BERNEA FOOD SERVICE, INC., pg. 143
BRESLER'S INDUSTRIES, INC., pg. 174
C.F. BURGER CREAMERY COMPANY, pg. 190
C & S WHOLESALE GROCERY INC., pg. 198
CABOT CREAMERY CO-OPERATIVE INC.—Agri-Mark, Inc., pg. 25
CALIFORNIA MILK PRODUCERS, pg. 210
CAMELLIA FOOD STORES CO-OP INC., pg. 211
CEDAR FARMS COMPANY, INC., pg. 230
CERTIFIED GROCERS ADVERTISING CO., pg. 236
CERTIFIED GROCERS OF CALIFORNIA, pg. 237
DAIRY FRESH CORP., pg. 310
DAIRYGOLD INC., pg. 311
DAIRYGOLD, INC.—Dairygold Inc., pg. 311
DAIRYMEN, INC., pg. 311
DETROIT CITY DAIRY, INC., pg. 333
DIXIE DAIRY COMPANY, pg. 341
EARP MEAT COMPANY, pg. 362
ELAN FOODS, pg. 372
GARELICK FARMS, INC., pg. 443
GORDON FOOD SERVICE INC., pg. 472
THE GREAT LAKES CHEESE CO., pg. 481
JACK GREENBERG INC., pg. 485
M. H. GREENEBAUM, INC., pg. 485
HALE-HALSELL COMPANY, pg. 500
IRA HIGDON GROCERY, INC., pg. 533
HILAND DAIRY COMPANY—Prairie Farms Dairy, Inc., pg. 884
H. P. HOOD INC.—Agway, Inc., pg. 25
KLUENER PACKING COMPANY, pg. 636
LAKE TO LAKE DAIRY—Land O'Lakes, Inc., pg. 653
LAND O'LAKES, INC., pg. 653
LANSING DAIRY, INC.—Melody Foods, Inc., pg. 738
MAMA TISH'S ITALIAN SPECIALTIES, pg. 703
MANTECADOS PAYCO—TLC Beatrice International Holdings Inc., pg. 1073
MAPLEHURST FARMS, INC., pg. 705
MARYLAND & VIRGINIA MILK PRODUCERS ASSOCIATION, pg. 717
MARYLAND VIRGINIA MILK PRODUCERS ASSOCIATION, INC., pg. 717
MELODY FOODS, INC., pg. 738
METRO FOODS, INC., pg. 743
MICHIGAN MILK PRODUCERS ASSOCIATION, pg. 747
MID-AMERICA DAIRYMEN, INC., pg. 750
MILK MARKETING INC., pg. 753
MONROE FOODS/DESSERT MASTERS—B. Green & Co., pg. 484
MORNING GLORY FARMS REGION, pg. 770
NEW ENGLAND FROZEN FOODS, pg. 800
OBERWEIS DAIRY, INC., pg. 820
PEVELY DAIRY COMPANY—Prairie Farms Dairy, Inc., pg. 884
PINE STATE CREAMERY CO., pg. 871
PIONEER SNACKS—Melody Foods, Inc., pg. 738
PLYMOUTH CREAMERIES, INC., pg. 877
POLKA DOT DAIRY, pg. 879
PRAIRIE FARMS DAIRY, INC., pg. 884
REMARKS, INC., pg. 925
ROCKY MOUNTAIN COMPANY, pg. 942
RYSER BROS. OF WISCONSIN—Ryser Brothers Inc., pg. 958
RYSER BROTHERS INC., pg. 958
S.P.C. TRANSPORT, pg. 963
SARGENTO CHEESE CO.—Sargento Incorporated, pg. 971
SARGENTO FOOD SERVICE CORP.—Sargento Incorporated, pg. 971
SARGENTO INCORPORATED, pg. 971
SCANGAS BROTHERS HOLDINGS, INC., pg. 974
SOUTHERN BELLE DAIRY COMPANY, INC., pg. 1020
SPARTAN STORES INC., pg. 1026
SPECIALTY FOODS GROUP—Sargento Incorporated, pg. 971
TLC BEATRICE INTERNATIONAL HOLDINGS INC., pg. 1073
TILLAMOOK COUNTY CREAMERY ASSN., pg. 1097
TRAUTH DAIRY INC., pg. 1108
TREMONT FOODS, pg. 1109
TURNER DAIRIES, INC., pg. 1119
TWIN COUNTY GROCERS, INC., pg. 1122
UNITED DAIRY FARMERS, INC., pg. 1131
UNITED DAIRYMEN OF ARIZONA, pg. 1131
UPSTATE MILK COOPERATIVES INC., pg. 1140
VALHALLA TRADING CO.—Jack Greenberg Inc., pg. 485
WEST DAIRIES, INC., pg. 1177
WEST LYNN CREAMERY, INC.—Scangas Brothers Holdings, Inc., pg. 974
WESTERN DAIRYMEN COOPERATIVE, INC., pg. 1178
WHITE ROSE CORPORATION—Di Giorgio Corporation, pg. 335
WHITE ROSE DAIRY—Di Giorgio Corporation, pg. 335

5144 — POULTRY & POULTRY PRODUCTS-WHOLESALE

A & W FOODS, INC., pg. 1
AJC INTERNATIONAL, INC., pg. 4
AFFILIATED FOODS COOPERATIVE INC., pg. 23
AMERICAN PRODUCE & VEGETABLE CO., pg. 59
CARGILL INC., pg. 219
CASE FOODS, INC., pg. 227
CEDAR FARMS COMPANY, INC., pg. 230
CITY MEATS & PROVISIONS CO., pg. 251
COUGLE COMMISSION COMPANY, INC., pg. 289
CROWN FOODS INC., pg. 302
LOUIS DREYFUS CORPORATION, pg. 348
EGGLAND'S BEST, INC., pg. 371
JORDAN'S FOODS-BANGOR DIVISION—Jordan's Meats, pg. 605
KASSEL & ZOLL PROVISIONS, INC., pg. 618
KEENERS, INC., pg. 620
KEYSTONE FOODS CORPORATION, pg. 628
KLUENER PACKING COMPANY, pg. 636
MAINE POTATO GROWERS, INC., pg. 702
THE MARKEY COMPANY—A & W Foods, Inc., pg. 1
MCCARTY FARMS, pg. 727
MCCARTY FOODS, INC.—McCarty Farms, pg. 727
MCCARTY PROCESSORS, INC.—McCarty Farms, pg. 727
MCINERNEY-MILLER BROTHERS INC., pg. 729
METRO FOODS, INC., pg. 743
MOYER MITCHELL COMPANY, INC., pg. 774
NEBRASKA TURKEY GROWERS—Norbest, Inc., pg. 809
NORBEST, INC., pg. 809
NORTHWESTERN MEATS INC., pg. 815
NULAID FOODS, pg. 817
OREGON TURKEY GROWERS—Norbest, Inc., pg. 809
ORLEANS INTERNATIONAL, INC., pg. 829
PLANTATION FOODS INC., pg. 874
PROTIMEX CORPORATION, pg. 895
ROCKY MOUNTAIN COMPANY, pg. 942
SEABOARD FARMS DIVISION—Seaboard Flour Corporation, pg. 984
SHERWOOD FOOD DISTRIBUTORS, pg. 998
SMITH FARMS, INC., pg. 1012
KEITH SMITH FARMS, INC., pg. 1012

TATUM FARMS, pg. 1080
VALLET FOOD SERV INC., pg. 1143
WEST CENTRAL TURKEYS—Norbest, Inc., pg. 809

5145 — CONFECTIONERY-WHOLESALE

R.L. ALBERT & SON, INC., pg. 31
ANDERSON WHOLESALE COMPANY, pg. 73
BEER NUTS, INC., pg. 132
BLEVINS CONCESSION SUPPLY CO., pg. 156
E.J. BRACH CORPORATION, pg. 169
E.J. BRACH, INC.—E.J. Brach Corporation, pg. 169
C & S WHOLESALE GROCERY INC., pg. 198
CAMELLIA FOOD STORES CO-OP INC., pg. 211
CERTIFIED CORP., pg. 236
DAKCO DISTRIBUTORS, INC., pg. 311
EBY BROWN CO.—Eby Brown Co., pg. 365
EVANS BROTHERS COMPANY, INC., pg. 390
FERRARA FOODS & CONFECTIONS, INC., pg. 407
FOREIGN CANDY CO., INC., pg. 424
FRITZ CO. INC., pg. 434
GLICO HARMONY FOODS CORPORATION, pg. 462
GROCERS SUPPLY CO. INC., pg. 488
H & H DISTRIBUTING COMPANY, INC., pg. 495
HENCO, INC., pg. 528
HUBBS IMPORTING CORP., pg. 550
KAISER TOBACCO COMPANY, INC., pg. 615
KING MICHIGAN SUNDRIES DIV.—King Group, Inc., pg. 630
LAYMAN CANDY COMPANY, INC., pg. 663
MASTER FOODS AB—Mars, Incorporated, pg. 714
MASTER FOODS AUSTRIA GMBH—Mars, Incorporated, pg. 714
NODAK DISTRIBUTOR—Dakco Distributors, Inc., pg. 311
NORTHWEST TOBACCO & CANDY CO., pg. 815
PINE STATE TOBACCO & CANDY COMPANY, pg. 871
S.P.C. TRANSPORT, pg. 963
SAMELSON-LEON COMPANY, INC., pg. 968
SATHERS INC., pg. 972
SOUTHCO DISTRIBUTING COMPANY, pg. 1019
TLC BEATRICE INTERNATIONAL HOLDINGS INC., pg. 1073
WARNER CANDY COMPANY, INC., pg. 1164
WEAVER POPCORN COMPANY, INC., pg. 1170
YOUNG PECAN SHELLING CO., INC., pg. 1209

5146 — FISH & SEAFOODS-WHOLESALE

AJC INTERNATIONAL, INC., pg. 4
AMERICAN FOODS GROUP, INC., pg. 54
BEAVER STREET FISHERIES, INC., pg. 130
CENTURY SEAFOOD INC., pg. 235
CITY MEATS & PROVISIONS CO., pg. 251
CONNELL RICE & SUGAR CO., pg. 275
DELTA PRIDE CATFISH, INC., pg. 327
E & G FOODS, pg. 358
KEENERS, INC., pg. 620
KESTERSON FOOD COMPANY, INC., pg. 624
LIBERAL BY-PRODUCTS—Union Holdings, Inc., pg. 1128
LIBERAL INTERNATIONAL SALES CORP.—Union Holdings, Inc., pg. 1128
LIBERAL INTERNATIONAL SALES V.I. INC.—Union Holdings, Inc., pg. 1128
MCINERNEY-MILLER BROTHERS INC., pg. 729
NATIONAL BEEF PACKING COMPANY—Union Holdings, Inc., pg. 1128
NORTHWESTERN MEATS INC., pg. 815
REMARKS, INC., pg. 925
ROCKY MOUNTAIN COMPANY, pg. 942
SEAFRESH INC.—Wards Cove Packing Company, pg. 1163
STEUART INVESTMENT CO., pg. 1048
STEUART SEAFOODS—Steuart Investment Co., pg. 1048
WILBUR-ELLIS COMPANY OF CANADA—Wilbur-Ellis Company & Connell Brothers Company, pg. 1189
YOUNG'S MARKET COMPANY, pg. 1214

5147 — MEATS & MEAT PRODUCTS-WHOLESALE

A & W FOODS, INC., pg. 1
AJC INTERNATIONAL, INC., pg. 4
ABBYLAND FOODS, INC., pg. 10
ABBYLAND PORK RACK—Abbyland Foods, Inc., pg. 10
AFFILIATED FOOD DISTRIBUTORS, pg. 23
AFFILIATED FOODS COOPERATIVE INC., pg. 23
AFFILIATED FOODS, INC., pg. 24
THE LEWIS BEAR COMPANY, pg. 129
BLUE GRASS FOODS, INC., pg. 160
BROOKS PROVISIONS INC., pg. 180
BROWN DERBY, INC., pg. 181
BRUSS COMPANY, pg. 184
BUTLER FOODS, INC., pg. 197
CEDAR FARMS COMPANY, INC., pg. 230
CERTIFIED GROCERS ADVERTISING CO., pg. 236
CERTIFIED GROCERS OF CALIFORNIA, pg. 237
CHAMPION BOXED BEEF, pg. 238
CHIPICO PICKLES—Vienna Sausage Mfg. Co., pg. 1151
CITY MEATS & PROVISIONS CO., pg. 251
COLONIAL BEEF CO., pg. 263
COLORADO BOXED BEEF CO., pg. 265
CONNELL RICE & SUGAR CO., pg. 275
CONSOLIDATED COMPANIES INC. (CONCO), pg. 276
THE COPPS CORP., pg. 285
COUGLE COMMISSION COMPANY, INC., pg. 289
CROWN FOODS INC., pg. 302
DEEN WHOLESALE MEAT COMPANY, INC., pg. 324
LOUIS DREYFUS CORPORATION, pg. 348
E & G FOODS, pg. 358
EARP MEAT COMPANY, pg. 362
FDL FOODS, INC., pg. 394
GENUARDI SUPER MARKETS INC., pg. 452
GORDON FOOD SERVICE INC., pg. 472
HALE-HALSELL COMPANY, pg. 500
IRA HIGDON GROCERY, INC., pg. 533
HOME DIVISION—Southern Foods, Inc., pg. 1021
IDLE WILD FOODS—Union Holdings, Inc., pg. 1128
INSTITUTIONAL DIVISION—Southern Foods, Inc., pg. 1021
JORDAN'S MEATS, pg. 605
JORDAN'S FOODS-BANGOR DIVISION—Jordan's Meats, pg. 605
JORDAN'S FOODS-FAIRFIELD DIVISION—Jordan's Meats, pg. 605
JORDAN'S FOODS-WESTBROOK DIVISION—Jordan's Meats, pg. 605
JORDAN'S FOODS-CARIBOU DIVISION—Jordan's Meats, pg. 605
JORDAN'S FOODS-COLCHESTER DIVISION—Jordan's Meats, pg. 605
SAM KANE BEEF PROCESSORS, INC., pg. 616
KASSEL & ZOLL PROVISIONS, INC., pg. 618
KEENERS, INC., pg. 620
KING PRIME, INC., pg. 631
A. C. KISSLING, INC., pg. 634
KLUENER PACKING COMPANY, pg. 636
LEONARD & HARRAL PACKING CO., pg. 667
LEVONIAN BROTHERS INC., pg. 671
LINCOLN PROVISION COMPANY, INC., pg. 676
MCINERNEY-MILLER BROTHERS INC., pg. 729
METRO FOODS, INC., pg. 743
ED MINIAT, INC., pg. 757
MONROE FOODS/DESSERT MASTERS—B. Green & Co., pg. 484
NATIONWIDE BEEF, INC., pg. 795
NEW ZEALAND LAMB CO., INC., pg. 803
NORTHWESTERN MEATS INC., pg. 815
OMAHA STEAKS INTERNATIONAL, pg. 825
ORLEANS INTERNATIONAL, INC., pg. 829
PENNINSULAR MEAT COMPANY, INC., pg. 858
PROTIMEX CORPORATION, pg. 895
QUALITY FOODS INC., pg. 903
REMARKS, INC., pg. 925
ROCKY MOUNTAIN COMPANY, pg. 942
RUSSETT FOODS—Zemco Industries, Inc., pg. 1217
SERVICE PACKING COMPANY, pg. 992
SHAMROCK FOODS CO., pg. 994
SHERWOOD FOOD DISTRIBUTORS, pg. 998
SIGMAN MEAT CO. INC., pg. 1003
SOUTHERN FOODS, INC., pg. 1021
SPARTAN STORES INC., pg. 1026
SPIEGEL MEATS, INC., pg. 1030
STAR FOOD PRODUCTS, INC., pg. 1039
STOCK YARDS PACKING CO., INC., pg. 1049
TENNESSEE DRESSED BEEF COMPANY, pg. 1087
TWIN COUNTY GROCERS, INC., pg. 1122
U.S. FOOD PRODUCTS, INC., pg. 1136
VALLEY ISLE PRODUCE, INC., pg. 1143
VIENNA SAUSAGE MFG. CO., pg. 1151
WASHINGTON BEEF COMPANY, pg. 1165
WOLVERINE PACKING CO., pg. 1199
ZEMCO INDUSTRIES, INC., pg. 1217
R.L. ZIEGLER CO. INC., pg. 1218

5148 — FRESH FRUITS & VEGETABLES-WHOLESALE

AJC INTERNATIONAL, INC., pg. 4
AFFILIATED FOOD DISTRIBUTORS, pg. 23
AFFILIATED FOODS COOPERATIVE INC., pg. 23
AFFILIATED FOODS, INC., pg. 24
AGRINORTHWEST, INC., pg. 25
AMERICAN PRODUCE & VEGETABLE CO., pg. 59
ARMSTRONG PRODUCE LTD., pg. 84
BANANA SERVICES INC., pg. 117
BASIC FOOD INTERNATIONAL INC., pg. 124
BEL AIR MARKETS, pg. 133
BOWEN BROTHERS FRUIT CO., INC., pg. 169
C. BREWER & COMPANY, LIMITED, pg. 174
J. C. BROCK CORP., pg. 178
BROOKLYN BOTTLING CO., pg. 179
CMD-KEITH CO.—Ben E. Keith Company, pg. 620
CALAVO GROWERS OF CALIFORNIA, pg. 208
CALIFORNIA ARTICHOKE & VEGETABLE GROWERS CORP., pg. 209
CAMELLIA FOOD STORES CO-OP INC., pg. 211
CERTIFIED GROCERS OF CALIFORNIA, pg. 237
CHERRY CENTRAL COOPERATIVE, pg. 243
CHIQUITA BRANDS, INC.—American Financial Corporation, pg. 53
CHIQUITA BRANDS INTERNATIONAL, INC.—American Financial Corporation, pg. 53
CHRISTY'S MARKETS, INC., pg. 249
CONSOLIDATED COMPANIES INC. (CONCO), pg. 276
THE CROSSET COMPANY INC., pg. 300
A. DUDA & SONS INC., pg. 351
FOOD SERVICES OF AMERICA, pg. 423
GLOBAL FOOD CORPORATION—Basic Food International Inc., pg. 124
GOLDEN GEM GROWERS INC., pg. 466
GORDON FOOD SERVICE INC., pg. 472
HAINES CITY CITRUS GROWERS ASSOCIATION, pg. 500
HALE-HALSELL COMPANY, pg. 500
J. HELLMAN PRODUCE, INC., pg. 527
V. B. HOOK & CO., INC., pg. 543
INTERNATIONAL AGRICULTURAL MARKET DEVELOPMENT CO.—Sunkist Growers, Inc., pg. 1061
JORDAN'S MEATS, pg. 605
JORDAN'S FOODS-BANGOR DIVISION—Jordan's Meats, pg. 605
JORDAN'S FOODS-FAIRFIELD DIVISION—Jordan's Meats, pg. 605
JORDAN'S FOODS-WESTBROOK DIVISION—Jordan's Meats, pg. 605
JORDAN'S FOODS-CARIBOU DIVISION—Jordan's Meats, pg. 605
JORDAN'S FOODS-COLCHESTER DIVISION—Jordan's Meats, pg. 605
BEN E. KEITH CO. OF OKLAHOMA—Ben E. Keith Company, pg. 620
BEN E. KEITH COMPANY, pg. 620
A. LEVY & J. ZENTNER CO., pg. 671
LUCKY FRUIT & PRODUCE, INC., pg. 686
MAINE POTATO GROWERS, INC., pg. 702
MARTIN & BAYLEY INC., pg. 714
MRS. GOOCHS NATURAL FOOD MARKETS, pg. 761
NORDEN FRUIT COMPANY, INC., pg. 809
POTATO SALES COMPANY, INC., pg. 882
QUALITY FOODS INC., pg. 903
C. H. ROBINSON CO. INC., pg. 939
ROCKY MOUNTAIN COMPANY, pg. 942
SCHMIEDING ENTERPRISES INC., pg. 976
SPARTAN STORES INC., pg. 1026
STADELMAN FRUIT INC., pg. 1034
SUNKIST (EUROPE) S.A.—Sunkist Growers, Inc., pg. 1061
SUNKIST (FAR EAST) PROMOTION, LTD.—Sunkist Growers, Inc., pg. 1061
SUNKIST GROWER, INC.-WESTERN DIVISION—Sunkist Growers, Inc., pg. 1061
SUNKIST GROWERS, INC., pg. 1060
SUNKIST GROWERS, INC.-SOUTHERN DIVISION—Sunkist Growers, Inc., pg. 1061
SUNKIST PACIFIC, LTD.—Sunkist Growers, Inc., pg. 1061
TROUT INC., pg. 1116
VALLET FOOD SERV INC., pg. 1143
VALLEY ISLE PRODUCE, INC., pg. 1143
WAILUKU AGRIBUSINESS CO., INC.—C. Brewer & Company, Limited, pg. 175

5149 — GROCERIES AND RELATED PRODUCTS-WHOLESALE, NEC

AJC INTERNATIONAL, INC., pg. 4
AFFILIATED FOODS, INC., pg. 24
R.L. ALBERT & SON, INC., pg. 31
ALL AMERICAN BOTTLING CORP., pg. 35
AMERICAN BREAD CO. OF ALABAMA INC.—American Bread Company - Sunbeam Bakery, pg. 49
AMERICAN PRODUCE & VEGETABLE CO., pg. 59
AMERICAN SPECIALTY FOODS—Portland Food Products Company, pg. 881
AMFAC SUGAR AND AGRIBUSINESS, INC.—JMB Realty Corporation, pg. 585
ARROW INDUSTRIES, INC., pg. 85
ASSOCIATED FOOD STORES INC., pg. 89
AWREY BAKERIES, INC., pg. 103
BACARDI IMPORTS, INC., pg. 108
BAHLSEN INC., pg. 114
BASIC FOOD INTERNATIONAL INC., pg. 124
BAY STATE MILLING CO., pg. 127
BERNEA FOOD SERVICE, INC., pg. 143
BLUE LINE DISTRIBUTING—Little Caesar Enterprises, Inc., pg. 678
BOURY INCORPORATED, pg. 168
THE BRADY MARKETING COMPANY, pg. 171
C. BREWER & COMPANY, LIMITED, pg. 174
BROOKLYN BOTTLING CO., pg. 179
BRUCE FOODS CORP., pg. 183
BYRNES & KIEFER COMPANY, pg. 198
CALAVO GROWERS OF CALIFORNIA, pg. 208
CAMELLIA FOOD STORES CO-OP INC., pg. 211
CARO PRODUCE & INSTITUTIONAL FOODS—Performance Food Group, Inc., pg. 861
CAROLINA MOUNTAIN WATER—Sammons Enterprises, Inc., pg. 968
CARROLS CORPORATION, pg. 225
CASE FOODS, INC., pg. 227
CERTIFIED GROCERS ADVERTISING CO., pg. 236
CERTIFIED GROCERS MIDWEST, INC., pg. 236
CERTIFIED GROCERS OF CALIFORNIA, pg. 237
CLARK-SIMON, INC.—Clark Foodservice, Inc., pg. 252
COCA COLA BOTTLING CO. UNITED, INC., pg. 257
COFINCO, INC.—Norfoods, Inc., pg. 810
COLOMBO BAKING CO.—San Francisco French Bread Company, pg. 969
CONNELL BROTHERS (HONG KONG) LTD.—Wilbur-Ellis Company & Connell Brothers Company, pg. 1189
R.J. CORR NATURALS, INC., pg. 287
CROWN PRINCE, INC. (CA), pg. 302
CRYSTAL GEYSER, pg. 303
DAWN FOOD PRODUCTS, INC., pg. 319
DEL MONTE FOODS, pg. 325
DIAMOND WALNUT GROWERS, INC.—Sun Diamond Growers of California, pg. 1058
DIET CENTER, INC.—American Health Companies, Inc., pg. 55
EARP MEAT COMPANY, pg. 362
EBY BROWN CO., pg. 365
EFFEMS AG—Mars, Incorporated, pg. 713
ESSEX GRAIN PRODUCTS, INC., pg. 389
FLORASYNTH (FAR EAST) PTE. LTD.—Florasynth Inc., pg. 420
FLORASYNTH LIMITED—Florasynth Inc., pg. 420
FRANZ BAKERY—United States Bakery, pg. 1134
GFA BRANDS, INC., pg. 440
GATE CITY BEVERAGE DISTRIBUTORS, pg. 444
GLICO HARMONY FOODS CORPORATION, pg. 462
GLOBAL FOOD CORPORATION—Basic Food International Inc., pg. 124
M. GOLODETZ EXPORT CORP.—Golodetz Corporation, pg. 469
GORDON FOOD SERVICE INC., pg. 472
GOYA FOODS, INC., pg. 474
GROCERS BAKING CO., pg. 488
HALE BROTHERS, INC.—Performance Food Group, Inc., pg. 861
THE HARTZ MOUNTAIN CORP., pg. 514

HAZELNUT GROWERS OF OREGON—Sun Diamond Growers of California, pg. 1058
HEALTH WATERS, INC.—Sammons Enterprises, Inc., pg. 968
HENCO, INC., pg. 528
HENRI'S FOOD PRODUCTS CO., INC., pg. 530
IN-OFFICE COFFEE COMPANY—Wechsler Coffee Corp., pg. 1172
INGLES MARKETS, INC., pg. 568
IRELAND COFFEE TEA, INC., pg. 582
IRELAND GOURMET SHOP—Ireland Coffee Tea, Inc., pg. 582
J P FOODSERVICE, INC., pg. 586
THE JOLT COMPANY, pg. 602
KERN INDUSTRIES, pg. 624
KERN'S BAKERIES, INCORPORATED, pg. 624
KESTERSON FOOD COMPANY, INC., pg. 624
KEYSTONE COFFEE, pg. 628
KINGS FOODSERVICE—Unifax, Inc., pg. 1126
KNOTT'S BERRY FARM, pg. 637
LA PREFERIDA, INC., pg. 649
LAND O'LAKES, INC., pg. 653
LEWIS BROTHERS BAKERIES, INC., pg. 673
MACHADO & CO. INC., pg. 696
THE MIAMI MARGARINE CO., pg. 746
THE MONARCH COMPANY, INC., pg. 765
MOUNTAIN VALLEY SPRING COMPANY—Sammons Enterprises, Inc., pg. 968
MUTUAL TRADING CO., INC., pg. 779
NEW ENGLAND COFFEE COMPANY, pg. 800
NEW FOOD INGREDIENTS, LTD.—Newly Weds Foods Inc., pg. 804
NORFOODS, INC., pg. 810
NORTH DAKOTA MILL & ELEVATOR ASSOCIATION, pg. 813
THE ODOM CORPORATION, pg. 821
OTT FOOD PRODUCTS, pg. 831
PACIFIC FOODS, INC., pg. 840
PARAMOUNT FOODS INC., pg. 848
PEIRONE PRODUCE COMPANY—U.R.M. Stores, Inc., pg. 1124
PEPSI-COLA BOTTLING CO., pg. 860
PERFECTION BAKERIES INC., pg. 861
PERFORMANCE FOOD GROUP, INC., pg. 861
PETER J. SCHMITT CO., INC.—Peter J. Schmitt Holdings, pg. 977
POCAHONTAS FOODS, USA—Performance Food Group, Inc., pg. 862
PRODUCERS RICE MILL INC., pg. 892
QUALITY FOOD OILS, INC., pg. 903
REDCO FOODS, INC., pg. 919
REESE FINER FOODS, INC., pg. 921
F.T. REYNOLDS COMPANY, pg. 930
RICHHEIMER FOOD—Wechsler Coffee Corp., pg. 1172
ROBERTS FOODS, INC., pg. 938
ROCKY MOUNTAIN COMPANY, pg. 942
RUSSELL STOVER CANDIES, INC., pg. 957
RYSER BROS. OF WISCONSIN—Ryser Brothers Inc., pg. 958
RYSER BROTHERS INC., pg. 958
S&D COFFEE INC., pg. 959
S.P.C. TRANSPORT, pg. 963
SAMMONS ENTERPRISES, INC., pg. 968
SAN FRANCISCO FRENCH BREAD COMPANY, pg. 969
SCHULZE & BURCH BISCUIT COMPANY, pg. 979
SEAFRESH INC.—Wards Cove Packing Company, pg. 1163
SHAMROCK FOODS CO., pg. 994
SIOUX HONEY ASSOCIATION, pg. 1008
SKOKIE VALLEY BEVERAGE CO., pg. 1009
SNYDER BAKERY—United States Bakery, pg. 1134
SNYDER BAKERY—United States Bakery, pg. 1134
SNYDER'S OF HANOVER, INC., pg. 1015
STANDARD FLOUR CO.—Westco Products, Inc., pg. 1178
SUN DIAMOND GROWERS OF CALIFORNIA, pg. 1058
SUN-LAND PRODUCTS OF CALIFORNIA—Sun Diamond Growers of California, pg. 1058
SUNCREST COMPANY OF CANADA—The Monarch Company, Inc., pg. 765
SUNOLA FOOD CORP.—Quality Food Oils, Inc., pg. 903
SUNSWEET GROWERS INC.—Sun Diamond Growers of California, pg. 1058
E.A. SWEEN COMPANY, pg. 1066
TLC BEATRICE INTERNATIONAL HOLDINGS INC., pg. 1073
TEEPAK, INC., ZURICH BRANCH—Hillside Capital, Inc., pg. 535
THOMPSON MEDICAL COMPANY, INC., pg. 1094
TREMONT FOODS, pg. 1109
TRI-STATE WHOLESALE ASSOCIATED GROCERS, pg. 1111
TWIN COUNTY GROCERS, INC., pg. 1122
UFL FOODS, INC.—Newly Weds Foods Inc., pg. 804
U.R.M. STORES, INC., pg. 1124
UNIFAX, INC., pg. 1126
UNITED STATES BAKERY, pg. 1134
VALLET FOOD SERV INC., pg. 1143
VALLEY FIG GROWERS—Sun Diamond Growers of California, pg. 1058
C.J. VITNER & CO., INC., pg. 1153
WARDS COVE PACKING COMPANY, pg. 1163
WECHSLER COFFEE CORP., pg. 1172
WESTCO FOOD SERVICE—Westco Products, Inc., pg. 1178
WESTCO PRODUCTS, INC., pg. 1178
WESTCO PRODUCTS/SEATTLE—Westco Products, Inc., pg. 1178
WILLIAM'S BAKERY—United States Bakery, pg. 1134
WILLS GROUP, INC., pg. 1193
WINE & SCHULZ INC., pg. 1196
WOODHAVEN FOODS—ARA Group, pg. 7
WOODHAVEN FOODS-MIDWEST—ARA Group, pg. 7
WYANDOT INC., pg. 1205
ZINK & TRIEST—A.M. Todd Company, pg. 1100

5153 — GRAIN & FIELD BEANS-BUYING & MARKETING

ADAIR FEED & GRAIN COMPANY, pg. 16
AGWAY, INC., pg. 25
ALABAMA FARMERS CO-OP, pg. 28
AMERICAN GRAIN & RELATED INDUSTRIES, pg. 55
THE ANDERSONS, pg. 73
ARGILAND COMPANY, pg. 81
ATCHISON COUNTY CO-OP ASSOCIATION, pg. 93
B&W CO-OP, INC., pg. 107
BADER & CO., pg. 113
BARTLETT AND COMPANY, pg. 122
BIG HORN CO-OP MARKETING ASSOCIATION, pg. 149
CARGILL INC., pg. 219
CENTRAL STATES ENTERPRISES, INC., pg. 234
CHAMPAIGN LANDMARK, pg. 238
CHAMPAIGN LANDMARK—Champaign Landmark, pg. 238
CIMARON GRAIN CO.—Union Holdings, Inc., pg. 1128
COAST GRAIN COMPANY, INC., pg. 256
COLUSA ELEVATOR CO., pg. 267
COMO GRAIN CO.—Tom Wade Co., pg. 1157
CONNELL RICE & SUGAR CO., pg. 275
CONSOLIDATED CO-OP, pg. 276
COUNTRYMARK CO-OP INC.—Countrymark Cooperative, Inc., pg. 290
COUNTRYMARK COOPERATIVE, INC., pg. 290
DEBRUCE GRAIN INC., pg. 323
DEMETER, INC., pg. 328
LOUIS DREYFUS CORPORATION, pg. 348
DYER GRAIN CO.—Tom Wade Co., pg. 1157
THE EARLY & DANIEL COMPANY, INC.—EDI International, Inc., pg. 359
EDMONSON WHEAT GROWERS, INC., pg. 369
EFFINGHAM-CLAY SERVICE CO., pg. 371
EQUITY SUPPLY COMPANY, pg. 385
ESSEX GRAIN PRODUCTS, INC., pg. 389
FARBEST INC.—Countrymark Cooperative, Inc., pg. 290
FARMERS MARKETING ASSOCIATION—Manna Pro Partners, pg. 704
FARMWAY CO-OP INC., pg. 402
FINAGRAIN, CIE COMMERCIALE AGRICOLE ET FINANCIERE S.A.—Continental Grain Company, pg. 279
FINLEY FARMERS GRAIN ELEVATOR COMPANY, pg. 411
C.B. FOX COMPANY, pg. 427
FRIONA INDUSTRIES, L.P., pg. 434
GARNAC GRAIN CO., INC.—Norfoods, Inc., pg. 810
GARVEY ELEVATORS INC., pg. 443
GARVEY INDUSTRIES, INC., pg. 443
GARVEY INTERNATIONAL, INC.—Garvey Industries, Inc., pg. 444
GOODPASTURE, INC., pg. 471
GRAND PRAIRIE CO-OP, INC., pg. 475
GRAND PRAIRIE CO-OP, INC.—Grand Prairie Co-op, Inc., pg. 475
GRAND PRAIRIE CO-OP, INC.—Grand Prairie Co-op, Inc., pg. 475
GRAND PRAIRIE CO-OP, INC.—Grand Prairie Co-op, Inc., pg. 475
GRAND PRAIRIE CO-OP, INC.—Grand Prairie Co-op, Inc., pg. 475
GRAND PRAIRIE CO-OP, INC.—Grand Prairie Co-op, Inc., pg. 475
GRAND PRAIRIE CO-OP, INC.—Grand Prairie Co-op, Inc., pg. 475
GRAND PRAIRIE CO-OP, INC.—Grand Prairie Co-op, Inc., pg. 475
GRAND PRARIE CO-OP, INC.—Grand Prairie Co-op, Inc., pg. 475
GROWMARK, INC., pg. 490
HARVEST STATES COOPERATIVES, pg. 514
HONEYMEAD PRODUCTS CO., pg. 542
HOPKINSVILLE ELEVATOR COMPANY, INC., pg. 543
HUNTTING ELEVATOR CO., pg. 555
INTERSTATE COMMODITIES INC., pg. 580
JOHNSON COUNTY FARM BUREAU CO-OP, pg. 598
KELLEY BEAN CO., INC., pg. 621
KENTON GRAIN CO.—Tom Wade Co., pg. 1157
KINGFISHER CO-OP ELEVATOR ASSOCIATION, pg. 631
KOKOMO GRAIN CO., INC., pg. 640
LA SALLE COUNTY FARM SUPPLY, pg. 649
LECO FEED MILLS, INC.—Fred Webb Inc., pg. 1170
MFA INCORPORATED, pg. 692
MAINE POTATO GROWERS, INC., pg. 702
MANNA PRO PARTNERS, pg. 704
MARTRADE LTD., pg. 716
NEW COOPERATIVE INC., pg. 799
NORFOODS, INC., pg. 810
NORTHEAST TEXAS FARMERS CO-OP, pg. 813
BRUCE OAKLEY, INC., pg. 819
ORANGE GROVE CO-OPERATIVE, pg. 828
OWENSBORO GRAIN CO., INC., pg. 834
PERRYTON EQUITY, pg. 863
PRODUCERS CO-OP ASSOCIATION, INC., pg. 892
PRODUCERS RICE MILL INC., pg. 892
RANGEN, INC., pg. 912
REED GRAIN & BEAN COMPANY, pg. 920
RICE GROWERS ASSOCIATION OF CALIFORNIA, pg. 931
RUGBY FARMERS UNION ELEVATOR COMPANY, pg. 955
RUSH COUNTY FARM BUREAU CO-OP, pg. 956
THE SCOULAR COMPANY, pg. 983
SEABOARD CORPORATION—Seaboard Flour Corporation, pg. 984
SEABOARD CORPORATION, GRAIN DIVISION—Seaboard Flour Corporation, pg. 984
SEBASTIAN COTTON & GRAIN CORP., pg. 986
SHERLEY GRAIN COMPANY, pg. 998
SIMONDS-SHIELDS-THEIS GRAIN CO., pg. 1006
SOUTH CENTRAL CO-OP, pg. 1019
TERRAL-NORRIS SEED CO., INC., pg. 1088
TERMINAL GRAIN CORP., pg. 1088
TIDEWATER GRAIN CO.—EDI International, Inc., pg. 359
TOBERMAN, pg. 1099
TRINIDAD/BENHAM CORPORATION, pg. 1113
UNION EQUITY—Farmland Industries, Inc., pg. 402
VALLEY SEED CO.—Arizona Grains Inc., pg. 82
TOM WADE CO., pg. 1157
WAGNER MILLS INC., pg. 1158
WAKELON AGRI-PRODUCTS, INC.—Fred Webb Inc., pg. 1170
WALLA WALLA GRAIN GROWERS, INC., pg. 1160
FRED WEBB INC., pg. 1170
WEST CENTRAL CO-OP, pg. 1176
WESTERN GRAIN, INC., pg. 1179
WHEELER BROTHERS GRAIN CO., pg. 1184
WHITE COUNTY FARM BUREAU CO-OP ASSOCIATION, pg. 1185
WILLARD GRAIN & FEED, INC., pg. 1190
WOLCOTT & LINCOLN, INC., pg. 1198

5154 — LIVESTOCK-BUYING & MARKETING

E.J. BRACH, INC.—E.J. Brach Corporation, pg. 169
CENTRAL LIVESTOCK ASSOCIATION, INC., pg. 233
CENTRAL LIVESTOCK ORDER BUYING COMPANY—Central Livestock Association, Inc., pg. 233
EFFINGHAM-CLAY SERVICE CO., pg. 371
INTERSTATE PRODUCERS LIVESTOCK ASSOCIATION, pg. 580
KLUENER PACKING COMPANY, pg. 636
A.C. MONK CO., INC., pg. 766
PRODUCERS LIVESTOCK, pg. 892
ROSENS DIVERSIFIED, INC., pg. 948

5159 — FARM-PRODUCT RAW MATERIALS-BUYING & MARKETING, NEC

ALABAMA FARMERS CO-OP, pg. 28
AMERICAN LEGEND CORPORATE, pg. 57
AMFAC SUGAR AND AGRIBUSINESS, INC.—JMB Realty Corporation, pg. 585
BAKER COMMODITIES, INC., pg. 115
BALE OF KENTUCKY, INC., pg. 115
BIRDSONG CORPORATION, pg. 153
BLUE DIAMOND GROWERS, pg. 160
CALCOT, LTD., pg. 208
CALIFORNIA & HAWAIIAN SUGAR COMPANY, pg. 210
CARGILL INC., pg. 219
CHILEWICH PARTNERS, pg. 248
COUNTRYMARK COOPERATIVE, INC., pg. 290
DAN RIVER COTTON CO., INC.—Dan River Inc., pg. 313
DUNAVANT ENTERPRISES—Dunavant Enterprises, Inc., pg. 352
DUNAVANT ENTERPRISES, INC., pg. 352
EQUITY SUPPLY COMPANY, pg. 385
FARBEST INC.—Countrymark Cooperative, Inc., pg. 290
FARMERS INVESTMENT COMPANY, INC.—Bale Of Kentucky, Inc., pg. 115
FARMWAY CO-OP INC., pg. 402
FEUER LEATHER CORPORATION, pg. 407
A. J. HOLLANDER CO., INC., pg. 539
MFA INCORPORATED, pg. 692
A.C. MONK CO., INC., pg. 766
PLAINS COTTON CO-OP ASSOCIATION, pg. 873
SEBASTIAN COTTON & GRAIN CORP., pg. 986
SOUTHWIDE, INC., pg. 1024
STAPLE COTTON COOPERATIVE ASSOCIATION, pg. 1038
TOBACCO SUPPLY, pg. 1099
WEIL BROTHERS COTTON INC., pg. 1173
WELLENS & CO., INC., pg. 1175
YOUNG PECAN COMPANY WEST, INC.—Young Pecan Shelling Co., Inc., pg. 1210

5162 — PLASTICS MATERIALS & BASIC FORMS & SHAPES-WHOLESALE

AIN PLASTICS, INC., pg. 26
ALPHA RESIN SUPPLY—Great Lakes Terminal & Transport Corp., pg. 482
AMERICAN EXCELSIOR COMPANY, pg. 51
BACHMANN INDUSTRIES, INC., pg. 108
CONESTOGA HOLDINGS, INC., pg. 273
DELTA RESINS & REFRACTORIES, INC., pg. 327
FOSTER-MILLER, INC., pg. 426
GENERAL LATEX & CHEMICAL CORPORATION, pg. 449
INTERPLASTIC DISTRIBUTION GROUP—Interplastic Corp., pg. 579
KLEER PAK CORPORATION, pg. 635
LANTECH INC., pg. 658
MARCO COLOR LABS, INC., pg. 706
A. W. MENDENHALL CO., INC., pg. 739
MOLDED FIBER GLASS/WEST—Molded Fiber Glass Companies, pg. 764
PENDA CORPORATION, pg. 857
PLASTIGAGE CORPORATION, pg. 876
RAPID INDUSTRIAL PLASTICS COMPANY, pg. 913
RYAN HERCO PRODUCTS CORP., pg. 958
THUNDERBIRD STEEL CORPORATION, pg. 1096

5169 — CHEMICALS & ALLIED PRODUCTS-WHOLESALE, NEC

AMERICO MANUFACTURING CO., INC., pg. 66
ARATEX SERVICES—ARA Group, pg. 6
H.J. BAKER & BRO., INC., pg. 114
BELL FLAVORS & FRAGRANCES, pg. 134
THE BERNUTH CORPORATION, pg. 144
BIDDLE SAWYER CORPORATION, pg. 148
BLUE CROSS LABORATORIES, pg. 160
BOAM CHEMICALS CO., INC.—MacAndrews & Forbes Holdings Inc., pg. 694

C. BREWER & COMPANY, LIMITED, pg. 174
BREWER ENVIRONMENTAL INDUSTRIES, INC.—C. Brewer & Company, Limited, pg. 174
BROWNING CHEMICAL CORPORATION, pg. 183
BURRIS CHEMICAL INC., pg. 195
CMS CHEMICAL COMPANY—Harwick Chemical Corp., pg. 515
CAR BRITE DISTRIBUTING, INC.—E & A Industries, Inc., pg. 358
CHEMCENTRAL CORPORATION, pg. 241
CHEMTECH INDUSTRIES, INC., pg. 242
COLORCON LTD.—Berwind Corporation, pg. 145
CONNELL BROTHERS CO. PHILIPPINES INC.—Wilbur-Ellis Company & Connell Brothers Company, pg. 1189
COUNTRYMARK CO-OP INC.—Countrymark Cooperative, Inc., pg. 290
CROUCH SUPPLY COMPANY, INC., pg. 301
DELTA RESINS & REFRACTORIES, INC., pg. 327
E.C. DEWITT & COMPANY (AUST.) PTY. LTD.—C.B. Fleet Company, Incorporated, pg. 417
DYNECOL, INC.—PVS Chemicals, Inc., pg. 838
E-Z CLOR/KRATZ—Aqua Fab Industries, Inc., pg. 79
R.W. EAKEN, INC., pg. 362
FALLEK CHEMICAL COMPANY (UK) LTD.—ICC Industries, Inc., pg. 558
FALLEK CHEMICAL S.A.—ICC Industries, Inc., pg. 558
FANCHEM, LTD.—PVS Chemicals, Inc., pg. 838
FERRO METAL & CHEMICAL CORPORATION LTD.—Philipp Brothers Chemicals, Inc., pg. 867
FOOD & GAS, INC., pg. 423
GAF (AUSTRALASIA) PTY. LTD.—GAF Corporation, pg. 438
GAF (BELGIUM) N.V.—GAF Corporation, pg. 438
GAF (CANADA) INC.—GAF Corporation, pg. 438
GAF CORP. DE MEXICO S.A. DE C.V.—GAF Corporation, pg. 438
GAF CORPORATION, pg. 438
GAF (DANMARK) A/S—GAF Corporation, pg. 438
GAF (DEUTSCHLAND) GMBH—GAF Corporation, pg. 438
GAF DO BRASIL INDUSTRIA E COMMERCIO, LTDA.—GAF Corporation, pg. 438
GAF EXPORT CORP.—GAF Corporation, pg. 438
GAF (FRANCE) S.A.—GAF Corporation, pg. 438
GAF (GREAT BRITAIN) CO. LTD.—GAF Corporation, pg. 438
GAF (ITALIA) S.P.I.—GAF Corporation, pg. 438
GAF (JAPAN) LTD.—GAF Corporation, pg. 438
GAF (NEDERLAND) N.V.—GAF Corporation, pg. 438
GAF (NEW ZEALAND) PTY., LTD.—GAF Corporation, pg. 438
GAF NORDEN AB—GAF Corporation, pg. 439
GAF (OSTERREICH) GMBH—GAF Corporation, pg. 439
GAF (SINGAPORE) PTE. LTD.—GAF Corporation, pg. 439
GAF SOUTH AFRICA (PTY.), LTD.—GAF Corporation, pg. 439
GAF SUCURSAL EN ESPANA—GAF Corporation, pg. 439
GAF (SWITZERLAND) AG—GAF Corporation, pg. 439
GENERAL LATEX & CHEMICAL CORPORATION, pg. 449
GREAT LAKES TERMINAL & TRANSPORT CORP., pg. 482
GRIFFIN CORPORATION, pg. 487
HVC/DALY COMPANY—KDI Corporation, pg. 612
THE HALL CHEMICAL COMPANY—Goldman Financial Group, pg. 468
HANNAFORD SEEDMASTER SERVICES AUSTRALIA (PTY) LTD.—Uniroyal Chemical Company, Inc., pg. 1129
HARWICK CHEMICAL CORP., pg. 515
HAVILAND ENTERPRISES, pg. 517
HAVILAND-KALAMAZOO—Haviland Enterprises, pg. 517
HUBBARD HALL INC., pg. 549
R. S. HUGHES CO., INC., pg. 551
ICC COMERCIO E INDUSTRIA LTDS.—ICC Industries, Inc., pg. 558
ICC HANDELS AG—ICC Industries, Inc., pg. 558
ICC (HONG KONG) LTD.—ICC Industries, Inc., pg. 559
ICC INDUSTRIES, B.V.—ICC Industries, Inc., pg. 559
IDEAL CHEMICAL & SUPPLY COMPANY, pg. 562
INLANDER-STEINDLER PAPER, pg. 570
JARCHEM SPECIALTY CHEMICAL DIVISION—Jarchem Industries, Inc., pg. 590
KEEN COMPRESSED GAS CO., INC., pg. 619
LAN-O-SHEEN, INC., pg. 653
LONDON LITHO ALUMINUM CO., INC., pg. 681
MFA INCORPORATED, pg. 692
MARTIN GAS CORPORATION, pg. 715
MATHIEU CORPORATION, pg. 720
MAYS CHEMICAL COMPANY, pg. 725
NORTH AMERICAN SALT COMPANY, pg. 812
NORWECO, INC., pg. 816
ORR SAFETY EQUIPMENT COMPANY, pg. 830
PVS CHEMICALS, INC., pg. 837
PVS-NOLWOOD CHEMICALS, INC.—PVS Chemicals, Inc., pg. 838
PAN AMERICAN TRADE DEVELOPMENT CORP., pg. 845
PENETONE CORP.—Wechco, Inc., pg. 1172
PREMIER CHEMICAL CO., LTD.—Uniroyal Chemical Company, Inc., pg. 1129
THE PROTECTOR CORPORATION, pg. 895
REPUBLIC CHEMICAL COMPANY—Harwick Chemical Corp., pg. 515
REPUBLIC SUPPLY COMPANY, pg. 928
STANDARD WELDERS SUPPLY CO., pg. 1038
SUPERIOR OIL CO. INC., pg. 1064
TAB CHEMICALS, INC., pg. 1075
TAUBER OIL COMPANY, pg. 1080
TEXAS OLEFINS CO., pg. 1089
TIDY CAR INTERNATIONAL, INC.—Ziebart International Corporation, pg. 1217
TRAYLOR CHEMICAL & SUPPLY CO., pg. 1108
GEORGE UHE CO., INC., pg. 1125
UNIROYAL CHEMICAL CO., INC. (SINGAPORE)—Uniroyal Chemical Company, Inc., pg. 1129
UNIROYAL CHEMICAL LTD.—Uniroyal Chemical Company, Inc., pg. 1129
UNITED CHEMICAL PRODUCTS—Mays Chemical Company, pg. 725
UNITED LABORATORIES, INC., pg. 1133
WGM/HYDRO, pg. 1156
WALTER INDUSTRIES, INC., pg. 1161
WARREN DISTRIBUTION, INC., pg. 1164
WHITTAKER, CLARK & DANIELS, INC., pg. 1187
WILBUR-ELLIS COMPANY & CONNELL BROTHERS COMPANY, pg. 1189
ZIEBART PRODUCTS GROUP—Ziebart International Corporation, pg. 1217

5171 — PETROLEUM BULK STATIONS & TERMINALS-WHOLESALE

TRUMAN ARNOLD COMPANIES, pg. 84
ATEX OIL CO. OF TEXAS, INC., pg. 93
BALE OF KENTUCKY, INC., pg. 115
BAYSIDE FUEL OIL DEPOT CORP., pg. 128
BELL GAS, INC., pg. 134
BESCHE OIL COMPANY, INC., pg. 145
BIG HORN CO-OP MARKETING ASSOCIATION, pg. 149
CAMPBELL OIL CO., pg. 213
CHEMTECH INDUSTRIES, INC., pg. 242
COLONIAL TERMINALS, INC.—Colonial Oil Industries, pg. 264
CONDON OIL COMPANY, INC., pg. 273
CONTINENTAL OZARK, INC., pg. 280
CREST DISTRIBUTING COMPANY, INC., pg. 298
DIXIE OIL COMPANY, pg. 341
EMPIRE PETROLEUM, INC., pg. 379
ENGLEFIELD, INC., pg. 382
ERGON, INC., pg. 386
FIRST MOUNT JOY CORPORATION, pg. 413
JACK GRIGGS INC., pg. 488
HARTFORD-WOOD RIVER TERMINAL—Piasa Motor Fuels Inc., pg. 869
HICKS OIL-HICKS GAS, INC., pg. 533
HIGH POINT OIL CO., pg. 534
KOCH INDUSTRIES, INCORPORATED, pg. 639
LA SALLE COUNTY FARM SUPPLY, pg. 649
CARLOS R. LEFFLER INC., pg. 666
LYON COUNTY CO-OP OIL CO., pg. 690
MAINE POTATO GROWERS, INC., pg. 702
MANSFIELD OIL COMPANY, pg. 704
MCCALL OIL & CHEMICAL CORP., pg. 726
MID-STATES PETROLEUM INC., pg. 750
NEW ENGLAND PETROLEUM CORPORATION—American Financial Corporation, pg. 54
OLIVER OIL COMPANY, INC., pg. 824
PM PROPERTIES INC.—Petroleum Marketers, Inc., pg. 865
PACIFIC NORTHERN OIL CORP., pg. 841
THE PARMAN CORPORATION, pg. 850
PARMAN OIL CO.—The Parman Corporation, pg. 850
PETROLEUM MARKETERS, INC., pg. 865
PETROLEUM PRODUCTS CORP., pg. 865
PHOENIX FUEL COMPANY, INC., pg. 868
PIASA MOTOR FUELS INC., pg. 869
PUMPELLY OIL, INC., pg. 900
F. L. ROBERTS & CO. INC., pg. 938
RUSSELL PETROLEUM CORPORATION, pg. 957
SHARP OIL COMPANY, pg. 995
SIMMONS OIL CORP., pg. 1005
SISCO COMPANY—First Mount Joy Corporation, pg. 413
SOUTHERN STATES COOPERATIVE, INC., pg. 1022
SPARTAN OIL CORP., pg. 1026
STEUART INVESTMENT CO., pg. 1048
STEUART PETROLEUM COMPANY—Steuart Investment Co., pg. 1048
STEUART PETROLEUM COMPANY, pg. 1048
TAUBER OIL COMPANY, pg. 1080
TAYLOR OIL CO. INC., pg. 1082
TRUCK WORLD INC., pg. 1117
WATERLOO SERVICE COMPANY, pg. 1167
WESTERN PETROLEUM COMPANY, pg. 1181
WESTERN STATES PETROLEUM INC., pg. 1181
WHITE COUNTY FARM BUREAU CO-OP ASSOCIATION, pg. 1185
WORSLEY COMPANIES INC., pg. 1204
WYATT INC., pg. 1205

5172 — PETROLEUM & PETROLEUM PRODUCTS WHOLESALERS, EXCEPT BULK STATIONS & TERMINALS

ACHESON COLLOIDEN B.V.—Acheson Industries, Inc., pg. 12
ACHESON FRANCE S.A.—Acheson Industries, Inc., pg. 12
ACHESON ITALIANA S.R.L.—Acheson Industries, Inc., pg. 12
AGWAY, INC., pg. 25
AGWAY PETROLEUM CORP.—Agway, Inc., pg. 25
ALABAMA OIL COMPANY—Spencer Companies Inc., pg. 1030
ALLIED OIL & SUPPLY, INC., pg. 38
APEX OIL COMPANY, INC., pg. 78
ATLANTIC AVIATION CORP., pg. 94
J. AUSTIN OIL CO., pg. 99
BERWICK BAY OIL CO. INC., pg. 144
BRADFORD OIL COMPANY, INC., pg. 170
BROWN EVANS COMPANY, pg. 182
CAMPBELL OIL CO., pg. 213
CARGILL INC., pg. 219
CARGILL PETROLEUM, INC.—Cargill Inc., pg. 219
CARSE OIL CO. INC., pg. 225
CARTER COMPANIES, pg. 226
JERRY C. CARTER, INC., pg. 226
CASEY CO., pg. 228
CASEY CO.—Casey Co., pg. 228
CENEX (FARMERS UNION CENTRAL EXCHANGE, INC.), pg. 231
CHAMPAIGN LANDMARK, pg. 238
CHEMOIL, pg. 242
COLONIAL OIL INDUSTRIES, pg. 263
COMMANDER OIL CORPORATION, pg. 268
CONDON OIL COMPANY, INC., pg. 273
CONSOLIDATED CO-OP, pg. 276
CONSOLIDATED MIDWEST, INC., pg. 277
CORAL ENERGY LTD.—Coral Petroleum Corporation, pg. 285
CORAL INTERNATIONAL LTD.—Coral Petroleum Corporation, pg. 285
CORAL PETROLEUM CORPORATION, pg. 285
CORAL PETROLEUM LTD.—Coral Petroleum Corporation, pg. 285
COUNTRYMARK CO-OP INC.—Countrymark Cooperative, Inc., pg. 290
COWBOY OIL COMPANY, pg. 290
CUMBERLAND FARMS, INC., pg. 304
DAIGLE OIL CO., pg. 310
DEAD RIVER COMPANY, pg. 321
DEAD RIVER PETROLEUM CO.—Dead River Company, pg. 322
DISTRIBUTORS OIL COMPANY, INC., pg. 340
DISTRICT PETROLEUM PRODUCTS, INC., pg. 340
E-Z MART STORES, INC., pg. 361
EDDINS-WALCHER COMPANY, pg. 367
EFFINGHAM-CLAY SERVICE CO., pg. 371
ENGLEFIELD, INC., pg. 382
FAIRFIELD MAXWELL LTD., pg. 397
FARM & HOME OIL COMPANY, pg. 401
FARMLAND INDUSTRIES, INC., pg. 402
FERRELL NORTH AMERICA—Ferrell Companies Inc./Ferrellgas, pg. 407
FERRELLGAS, INC.—Ferrell Companies Inc./Ferrellgas, pg. 407
FINLEY FARMERS GRAIN ELEVATOR COMPANY, pg. 411
FLEISCHLI OIL COMPANY, INC., pg. 417
FLYING J. INC., pg. 421
FUEL SOUTH, INC., pg. 435
THE GARY-WILLIAMS COMPANY, pg. 444
GATE PETROLEUM COMPANY, pg. 445
GAY JOHNSON'S INC., pg. 446
GLOBAL PETROLEUM CORP., pg. 463
GREAT LAKES CARBON CORP.—Horsehead Industries, Inc., pg. 545
GREENWAY CO-OP SERVICE, pg. 485
THE GUTTMAN GROUP, pg. 495
THE H. T. HACKNEY CO., pg. 498
HOLLINGSWORTH OIL CO. INC., pg. 539
HORSEHEAD INDUSTRIES, INC., pg. 545
HUDSON & AFFILIATED CO., pg. 551
ILLINOIS LIMITED PARTNERSHIP—Martin Exploration Management Company, pg. 715
JONES COMPANY, INC., pg. 603
KAIBAB INDUSTRIES, pg. 614
KING FUELS INC., pg. 630
KNOX OIL OF TEXAS INC., pg. 638
L & L OIL COMPANY, INC., pg. 647
LEE-MOORE OIL CO., INC., pg. 665
LEXINGTON CO-OP OIL CO., pg. 673
MACMILLAN OIL CO., INC.—Graham Group, Inc., pg. 475
MAIN BROTHERS OIL COMPANY, INC., pg. 702
MAINE POTATO GROWERS, INC., pg. 702
MARTIN GAS CORPORATION, pg. 715
MASON OIL COMPANY, pg. 718
MCCALL OIL & CHEMICAL CORP., pg. 726
MEENAN OIL CO. LIMITED PARTNERSHIP, pg. 736
MID SOUTH SALES, pg. 750
MIDSOUTH OIL CO.—Spencer Companies Inc., pg. 1030
MIDWEST PETROLEUM CO., pg. 752
MILLER OIL CO., INC., pg. 754
NEBRASKA-IOWA SUPPLY COMPANY, pg. 796
NEEB CORPORATION, pg. 797
NORTHVILLE INDUSTRIES CORP., pg. 814
PACE OIL CO., INC., pg. 838
PACIFIC NORTHERN OIL CORP., pg. 841
PETROLEUM TRADERS CORPORATION, pg. 865
PHOENIX VENTURES, pg. 869
PIONEER OIL COMPANY INC., pg. 872
PRESTO FOOD STORES, INC., pg. 888
PUGH OIL COMPANY, pg. 899
PUMPELLY OIL, INC., pg. 900
QUALITY PETROLEUM CORP., pg. 903
RACETRAC PETROLEUM, INC., pg. 909
RISSER OIL CORP., pg. 936
F. L. ROBERTS & CO. INC., pg. 938
SF SERVICES, pg. 961
SABRELINER CORP., pg. 965
SHIPLEY OIL COMPANY, pg. 999
THE SICO COMPANY, pg. 1001
SIMMONS OIL CORP., pg. 1005
SOMERSET REFINERY INC., pg. 1017
SOUTHERN STATES COOPERATIVE, INC., pg. 1022
SPELLING ENTERTAINMENT GROUP, INC.—American Financial Corporation, pg. 54
SPENCER COMPANIES INC., pg. 1030
SPROTT OIL CO., INC., pg. 1034
STEUART INVESTMENT CO., pg. 1048
J. D. STREETT & CO., INC., pg. 1053
O. J. STROBEL OIL & TIRE CO., INC., pg. 1053
SULLIVAN OIL COMPANY, pg. 1057
SUPERIOR OIL CO. INC., pg. 1064
TAUBER OIL COMPANY, pg. 1080
TENNESSEE FARMERS CO-OP, pg. 1087
TEXAS OLEFINS CO., pg. 1089
TIME OIL CO.—Time Oil Company, pg. 1097
TIME OIL COMPANY, pg. 1097
TORCO OIL, pg. 1102
TRANSAMERICAN REFINING CORP.—Transamerican Refining Corporation, pg. 1106
TRANSAMERICAN REFINING CORPORATION, pg. 1106
TRANSAMMONIA INC., pg. 1106
TRUCK WORLD INC., pg. 1117
TRUE COMPANIES, pg. 1117

UNIVERSAL COOPERATIVES, INC., pg. 1138
V.G.S. CORP. D/B/A SOUTHLAND OIL COMPANY, pg. 1141
VESCO OIL CORP., pg. 1149
GEORGE E. WARREN CORP., pg. 1164
WARREN DISTRIBUTION, INC., pg. 1164
WARREN EQUITIES INC., pg. 1164
WESTERN PETROLEUM COMPANY, pg. 1181
WICKLAND CORPORATION, pg. 1188
WICKLAND OIL COMPANY, INC.—Wickland Corporation, pg. 1188
WILLS GROUP, INC., pg. 1193
WORLD OIL COMPANY, pg. 1203
YODER OIL COMPANY INC., pg. 1208

5181 — BEER & ALE-WHOLESALE

ATLANTA BEVERAGE CO., pg. 94
BARTON BEERS, LTD.—Barton Brands, Ltd., pg. 123
BEAUCHAMP DISTRIBUTING COMPANY, pg. 130
BETTER BRANDS OF ATLANTA, INC., pg. 148
CMD-KEITH CO.—Ben E. Keith Company, pg. 620
CITY BEVERAGE CO., pg. 251
CONSOLIDATED BEVERAGES, INC., pg. 276
DRIBECK IMPORTERS, INC., pg. 349
GATE CITY BEVERAGE DISTRIBUTORS, pg. 444
GENERAL WHOLESALE COMPANY, INC., pg. 451
GEORGIA CROWN DISTRIBUTING, pg. 453
GLAZERS WHOLESALE DRUG CO. INC., pg. 461
GOLDEN EAGLE DISTRIBUTOR, INC.—Golden Eagle Distributors, Inc., pg. 466
GOLDEN EAGLE DISTRIBUTORS, INC., pg. 466
GOLDEN EAGLE DISTRIBUTORS, INC.—Golden Eagle Distributors, Inc., pg. 466
GOLDEN EAGLE DISTRIBUTORS, INC.—Golden Eagle Distributors, Inc., pg. 466
GOLDEN EAGLE SALES, INC.—Golden Eagle Distributors, Inc., pg. 466
GOLDEN EAGLE SALES, INC.—Golden Eagle Distributors, Inc., pg. 466
GRANTHAM COMPANY, pg. 477
GREY EAGLE DISTRIBUTORS INC., pg. 486
HARTFORD DISTRIBUTORS INC., pg. 514
G. HEILEMAN BREWING CO., INC., pg. 526
HENSLEY & CO., pg. 530
K-J DISTRIBUTORS, INC., pg. 612
BEN E. KEITH CO. OF OKLAHOMA—Ben E. Keith Company, pg. 620
BEN E. KEITH COMPANY, pg. 620
A. LEVY & J. ZENTNER CO., pg. 671
MONARCH IMPORT CO., INC., pg. 765
MONTEBELLO BRANDS INC., pg. 767
B. OLINDE & SONS COMPANY, INC., pg. 824
PATERNO IMPORTS LIMITED, pg. 851
PEARLSTINE DISTRIBUTORS INC., pg. 853
THE JULIUS SCHEPPS CO., pg. 975
TRIANGLE DISTRIBUTING COMPANY, pg. 1111
WISDOM IMPORTS SALES CO. INC., pg. 1198
THE ZAMOISKI CO., pg. 1216

5182 — WINES & DISTILLED ALCOHOLIC BEVERAGES-WHOLESALE

ADAMS WINE CO., pg. 17
AMERICAN PRODUCE & VEGETABLE CO., pg. 59
BEN ARNOLD CO., INC., pg. 84
BEN ARNOLD CO., INC.—Ben Arnold Co., Inc., pg. 84
ARTHUR TREACHER'S, INC., pg. 87
B & G WHOLESALERS, INC., pg. 106
BACARDI IMPORTS, INC., pg. 108
BARTON BRANDS, LTD., pg. 123
BARTON BRANDS OF CALIFORNIA, INC.—Barton Brands, Ltd., pg. 123
BARTON BRANDS OF GEORGIA, INC.—Barton Brands, Ltd., pg. 123
BEAUCHAMP DISTRIBUTING COMPANY, pg. 130
BETTER BRANDS OF ATLANTA, INC., pg. 148
BETTERBRANDS, LTD.—Young's Market Company, pg. 1214
BLOCK DISTRIBUTING COMPANY, pg. 157
CHATHAM IMPORTERS—Peerless Importers, Inc., pg. 855
CITY BEVERAGE CO., pg. 251
COLONY LIQUOR DISTRIBUTORS, INC., pg. 264
DAHLSTEN TRUCK LINE, INC., pg. 310
DOMECQ IMPORTERS INC., pg. 343
FORMAN BROTHERS, INC., pg. 424
E & J GALLO WINERY, pg. 441
GENERAL WHOLESALE COMPANY, INC., pg. 451
GEORGIA CROWN DISTRIBUTING, pg. 453
GLAZERS WHOLESALE DRUG CO. INC., pg. 461
GLEN ELLEN WINERY, pg. 461
GRANTHAM COMPANY, pg. 477
HAAS BROTHERS, pg. 498
CHARLES JACQUIN ET CIE, INC., pg. 588
THE JAYDOR CORPORATION, pg. 591
LEONARD KREUSCH, INC., pg. 645
LKI—Leonard Kreusch, Inc., pg. 645
LAIRD & COMPANY, pg. 650
A. LEVY & J. ZENTNER CO., pg. 671
MONARCH IMPORT CO., INC., pg. 765
MONTEBELLO BRANDS INC., pg. 767
BEN MYERSON CANDY COMPANY, INC., pg. 780
NDC DISTRIBUTORS, INC.—National Distributing Co., Inc., pg. 787
NWS, INC., pg. 782
NATIONAL DISTRIBUTING CO., INC., pg. 787
NATIONAL DISTRIBUTING CO., INC.—National Distributing Co., Inc., pg. 787
NATIONAL DISTRIBUTING CO., INC.—National Distributing Co., Inc., pg. 787
NATIONAL DISTRIBUTING CO., INC.—National Distributing Co., Inc., pg. 787
NATIONAL DISTRIBUTING CO., INC.—National Distributing Co., Inc., pg. 787
NATIONAL DISTRIBUTING CO., INC.—National Distributing Co., Inc., pg. 787
NATIONAL DISTRIBUTING CO., INC.—National Distributing Co., Inc., pg. 787
NATIONAL DISTRIBUTING CO., INC.—National Distributing Co., Inc., pg. 787
NATIONAL DISTRIBUTING CO., INC.—National Distributing Co., Inc., pg. 787
NATIONAL DISTRIBUTING CO., INC.—National Distributing Co., Inc., pg. 787
NATIONAL DISTRIBUTING CO., INC.—National Distributing Co., Inc., pg. 787
NATIONAL DISTRIBUTING CO., INC.—National Distributing Co., Inc., pg. 787
J. J. NEWBERRY CANADIAN LTD. C/O GAULT BROTHERS DIV.—Riklis Family Corporation, pg. 935
NUYENS LIQUOR IMPORTING, INC.—White Rock Distilleries Inc., pg. 1186
PACIFIC WINE CO.—Paterno Imports Limited, pg. 851
PATERNO IMPORTS LIMITED, pg. 851
PEARLSTINE DISTRIBUTORS INC., pg. 853
PEERLESS IMPORTERS, INC., pg. 855
PINE STATE TOBACCO & CANDY COMPANY, pg. 871
REITMAN INDUSTRIES, pg. 924
THE JULIUS SCHEPPS CO., pg. 975
STANDARD DISTRIBUTING CO., INC.—National Distributing Co., Inc., pg. 787
STAR LIQUOR DEALERS, pg. 1039
VINTNERS INTERNATIONAL COMPANY, INC., pg. 1152
M.S. WALKER, INC./SEACOAST, pg. 1160
WHITE ROCK DISTILLERIES INC., pg. 1186
YOUNG'S MARKET COMPANY, pg. 1214

5191 — FARM SUPPLIES-WHOLESALE

A-G CO-OP CREAMERY, pg. 4
AGSCO, INC., pg. 4
ADAIR FEED & GRAIN COMPANY, pg. 16
ALABAMA FARMERS CO-OP, pg. 28
AMERICA OUTDOORS LTD, pg. 48
ARGILAND COMPANY, pg. 81
ATCHISON COUNTY CO-OP ASSOCIATION, pg. 93
B&W CO-OP, INC., pg. 107
BAKER COMMODITIES, INC., pg. 115
GEO. J. BALL, INC., pg. 115
BALL SEED CO.—Geo. J. Ball, Inc., pg. 116
BIG HORN CO-OP MARKETING ASSOCIATION, pg. 149
C. BREWER & COMPANY, LIMITED, pg. 174
GEORGE F. BROCKE & SONS, INC., pg. 178
CARDER, INC., pg. 217
CARGILL INC., pg. 219
CARGILL LTD.—Cargill Inc., pg. 219
CARGILL SEED DIV.—Cargill Inc., pg. 219
CARGILL TRADING LTD.—Cargill Inc., pg. 219
CARGILL UK LTD.—Cargill Inc., pg. 219
CENEX (FARMERS UNION CENTRAL EXCHANGE, INC.), pg. 231
CHAMPAIGN LANDMARK, pg. 238
CONSOLIDATED CO-OP, pg. 276
COUNTRYMARK CO-OP INC.—Countrymark Cooperative, Inc., pg. 290
COUNTRYMARK COOPERATIVE, INC., pg. 290
CURRAN CONTRACTING CO., pg. 305
DEBRUCE GRAIN INC., pg. 323
EDMONSON WHEAT GROWERS, INC., pg. 369
EFFINGHAM-CLAY SERVICE CO., pg. 371
FARMERS CO-OP MARKET INC., pg. 401
FARMERS MARKETING ASSOCIATION—Manna Pro Partners, pg. 704
FARMWAY CO-OP INC., pg. 402
FINLEY FARMERS GRAIN ELEVATOR COMPANY, pg. 411
FREDERICK TRADING COMPANY, pg. 430
FRIONA INDUSTRIES, L.P., pg. 434
GSC ENTERPRISES, INC., pg. 440
GERBER AGRI-EXPORT INC.—J. Gerber & Co. Inc., pg. 454
J. GERBER & CO. INC., pg. 453
GOLD KIST, INC., pg. 465
GRAND PRAIRIE CO-OP, INC., pg. 475
GRAND PRAIRIE CO-OP, INC.—Grand Prairie Co-op, Inc., pg. 475
GRAND PRAIRIE CO-OP, INC.—Grand Prairie Co-op, Inc., pg. 475
GRAND PRAIRIE CO-OP, INC.—Grand Prairie Co-op, Inc., pg. 475
GRAND PRAIRIE CO-OP, INC.—Grand Prairie Co-op, Inc., pg. 475
GRAND PRAIRIE CO-OP, INC.—Grand Prairie Co-op, Inc., pg. 475
GRAND PRAIRIE CO-OP, INC.—Grand Prairie Co-op, Inc., pg. 475
GRAND PRAIRIE CO-OP, INC.—Grand Prairie Co-op, Inc., pg. 475
GRAND PRARIE CO-OP, INC.—Grand Prairie Co-op, Inc., pg. 475
GREENWAY CO-OP SERVICE, pg. 485
GRIFFIN CORPORATION, pg. 487
GROWMARK, INC., pg. 490
HARDIE IRRIGATION-LANDSCAPE DIV., pg. 508
HAVILAND/WILBUR-ELLIS AGRICULTURAL, pg. 517
HI-PRO ANIMAL HEALTH DIV.—Friona Industries, L.P., pg. 434
HI-PRO FEED DIV.—Friona Industries, L.P., pg. 434
HOFFMAN SEEDS, INC.—A. H. Hoffman, Inc., pg. 538
HOPKINSVILLE ELEVATOR COMPANY, INC., pg. 543
HUNTTING ELEVATOR CO., pg. 555
HYDRO/KIRBY AGRI SERVICE, INC., pg. 556
INTERMOUNTAIN FARMERS ASSOCIATION, pg. 575
INTERNATIONAL CHEMICAL COMPANY, pg. 576
INTERSTATE COMMODITIES INC., pg. 580
JOHNSON COUNTY FARM BUREAU CO-OP, pg. 598
KINGFISHER CO-OP ELEVATOR ASSOCIATION, pg. 631
KOVA FERTILIZER INC., pg. 643
L & L NURSERY SUPPLY, INC., pg. 647
LA SALLE COUNTY FARM SUPPLY, pg. 649
LAND O'LAKES, INC., pg. 653
LEXINGTON CO-OP OIL CO., pg. 673
MFA INCORPORATED, pg. 692
MAINE POTATO GROWERS, INC., pg. 702
MANNA PRO PARTNERS, pg. 704
MISSISSIPPI CHEMICAL CORPORATION, pg. 760
MONTE VISTA CO-OP ASSOCIATION, INC., pg. 766
NEW COOPERATIVE INC., pg. 799
NORTH PACIFIC LUMBER COMPANY, pg. 813
NORTHEAST TEXAS FARMERS CO-OP, pg. 813
BRUCE OAKLEY, INC., pg. 819
OWENSBORO GRAIN CO., INC., pg. 834
PAN AMERICAN TRADE DEVELOPMENT CORP., pg. 845
PRODUCERS CO-OP ASSOCIATION, INC., pg. 892
RANCHERS SUPPLY COMPANY—Carder, Inc., pg. 217
RAY-CARROLL COUNTY GRAIN CO-OP, pg. 914
ROSENS DIVERSIFIED, INC., pg. 948
ROSENS, INC.—Rosens Diversified, Inc., pg. 948
RUGBY FARMERS UNION ELEVATOR COMPANY, pg. 955
RUSH COUNTY FARM BUREAU CO-OP, pg. 956
SF SERVICES, pg. 961
THE SCOTT COMPANY, pg. 982
SEYMOUR MANUFACTURING COMPANY, pg. 994
SOUTH CENTRAL CO-OP, pg. 1019
SOUTHERN AGRICULTURAL INSECTICIDES, pg. 1020
SOUTHERN STATES COOPERATIVE, INC., pg. 1022
SPEEDLING INCORPORATED, pg. 1029
SUNNILAND CORPORATION, pg. 1061
TERRAL-NORRIS SEED CO., INC., pg. 1088
TERMINAL GRAIN CORP., pg. 1088
TOBERMAN, pg. 1099
TRANSAMMONIA AG—Transammonia Inc., pg. 1106
TRANSAMMONIA INC., pg. 1106
TRAYLOR CHEMICAL & SUPPLY CO., pg. 1108
UNIVERSAL COOPERATIVES, INC., pg. 1138
VALLEY SEED CO.—Arizona Grains Inc., pg. 82
WGM/HYDRO, pg. 1156
TOM WADE CO., pg. 1157
WATKINS INCORPORATED, pg. 1167
WESTERN STATES PETROLEUM INC., pg. 1181
WHEELER BROS. GRAIN CO.—Wheeler Brothers Grain Co., pg. 1185
WHITE COUNTY FARM BUREAU CO-OP ASSOCIATION, pg. 1185
WILLARD GRAIN & FEED, INC., pg. 1190

5192 — BOOKS, PERIODICALS & NEWSPAPERS-WHOLESALE

BELL & HOWELL LTD.—Bell & Howell Company, pg. 135
BIBLIO DISTRIBUTION CTR.—Rowman & Littlefield Publishers, Inc., pg. 953
BOOKAZINE COMPANY, INC., pg. 164
EASTERN NEWS DISTRIBUTORS, INC.—The Hearst Corporation, pg. 523
EASTON PRESS BOOKS—MBI Inc., pg. 691
FUNK & WAGNALLS CORP.—K-III Communications Corporation, pg. 611
HADDON CRAFTSMEN, INC., pg. 499
INGRAM BOOK COMPANY—Ingram Industries Inc., pg. 569
INGRAM DISTRIBUTION GROUP INC.—Ingram Industries Inc., pg. 569
INTERNATIONAL CIRCULATION DISTRIBUTORS—The Hearst Corporation, pg. 523
INTERTEC PUBLISHING CORP.—K-III Communications Corporation, pg. 611
THE CHARLES LEVY COMPANY, pg. 672
LUDINGTON NEWS CO. INC., pg. 686
MARBORO BOOKS INC.—Barnes & Noble Bookstores, Inc., pg. 120
NATIONAL BOOK COMPANY INC.—W.W. Norton & Company, Inc., pg. 816
NATION'S BUSINESS, pg. 794
NEBRASKA BOOK CO.—Lincoln Industries, pg. 676
OPEN COURT PUBLISHING CO.-GENERAL BOOKS—Carus Corporation, pg. 227
SPRING ARBOR DISTRIBUTORS, pg. 1033

5193 — FLOWERS, NURSERY STOCK & FLORISTS' SUPPLIES-WHOLESALE

GEO. J. BALL, INC., pg. 115
BALL SEED CO.—Geo. J. Ball, Inc., pg. 116
BALL SUPERIOR LTD.—Geo. J. Ball, Inc., pg. 116
CORHAM, INC., pg. 286
THE CROSSET COMPANY INC., pg. 300
DENVER WHOLESALE FLORISTS COMPANY, pg. 331
EARL MAY SEED & NURSERY L.P., pg. 724
MONROVIA NURSERY CO., pg. 766
STAR SALES CO., INC., pg. 1040
SUN BULB COMPANY, INC., pg. 1058
UNIVERSAL FLOWERS, INC.—Huntco Inc., pg. 554
WEINSTOCK'S FLOWERS & GIFTS—KNOX International Corp., pg. 638

5194 — TOBACCO & TOBACCO PRODUCTS-WHOLESALE

C & S WHOLESALE GROCERY INC., pg. 198
GEORGE W. COCHRAN CO., INC., pg. 258
DAKCO DISTRIBUTORS, INC., pg. 311
EBY BROWN CO.—Eby Brown Co., pg. 365
FABER, COE & GREGG OF CHICAGO, INC.—Faber, Coe & Gregg, Inc., pg. 395

FABER, COE & GREGG OF PENNSYLVANIA, INC.—Faber, Coe & Gregg, Inc., pg. 395
FRITZ CO. INC., pg. 434
H & H DISTRIBUTING COMPANY, INC., pg. 495
KAISER TOBACCO COMPANY, INC., pg. 615
KING MICHIGAN SUNDRIES DIV.—King Group, Inc., pg. 630
LAYMAN CANDY COMPANY, INC., pg. 663
LEE GROCERY COMPANY, pg. 665
NATIONAL FOOD STORES, INC. T/A KRAUSZER'S, pg. 788
NODAK DISTRIBUTOR—Dakco Distributors, Inc., pg. 311
NORTHWEST TOBACCO & CANDY CO., pg. 815
PINE STATE TOBACCO & CANDY COMPANY, pg. 871
SAMELSON-LEON COMPANY, INC., pg. 968
SHOP-RITE CIGARETTES (CT)—Wakefern Food Corporation, pg. 1158
SOUTHCO DISTRIBUTING COMPANY, pg. 1019
SPEEDLING INCORPORATED, pg. 1029

5198 — PAINTS, VARNISHES, & SUPPLIES-WHOLESALE

WILLIAM M. BIRD & CO., INC., pg. 152
M. A. BRUDER & SONS, INC., pg. 184
BRUNSCHWIG & FILS, INC., pg. 184
BUILDER MARTS OF AMERICA, pg. 187
CHEMICAL SPECIALTIES CORP.—Syndet Products, Inc., pg. 1069
ERNST W. DORN CO., INC., pg. 346
DUNN-EDWARDS CORPORATION, pg. 353
EMERY WATERHOUSE COMPANY, pg. 379
FARGO GLASS & PAINT COMPANY, pg. 399
FINGERLE LUMBER CO., pg. 411
FREDERICK TRADING COMPANY, pg. 430
HAMILTON EQUIPMENT, INC., pg. 503
KELLY-MOORE PAINT COMPANY, INC., pg. 621
M.A.B. PAINTS—M. A. Bruder & Sons, Inc., pg. 184
M.A.B. PAINTS—M. A. Bruder & Sons, Inc., pg. 184
MAUTZ PAINT COMPANY, pg. 722
MUTUAL DISTRIBUTORS LTD., pg. 778
OUR OWN HARDWARE COMPANY, pg. 832
PERGAMENT HOME CENTERS, INC., pg. 862
PREMIER COATINGS, INC., pg. 886
PRESERVATIVE PAINT COMPANY, pg. 887
PROGRESS PAINT MFG. CO., pg. 894
SEABROOK WALLCOVERINGS, INC., pg. 984
SERVISTAR CORPORATION, pg. 992
SHEFFIELD HARDWARE COMPANY, pg. 996
SYNDET PRODUCTS, INC., pg. 1069
THUNDERBIRD STEEL CORPORATION, pg. 1096
THYBONY WALL COVERINGS CO., pg. 1096
TRU-TEST MFG. CO.—Cotter & Company, pg. 288

5199 — NONDURABLE GOODS-WHOLESALE, NEC

ARA MAGAZINE & BOOK DIVISION, INC.—ARA Group, pg. 6
ALLIED PRODUCTS—Consolidated Cigar Corporation, pg. 276
AMERICAN FELT & FILTER, pg. 52
AMWAY CORPORATION, pg. 70
ARROW BUILDING CENTERS—Consolidated Lumber Co., pg. 276
ARROW INDUSTRIES, INC., pg. 85
B & R PET SUPPLIES, INC.—The Andersons, pg. 74
BIDDLE SAWYER CORPORATION, pg. 148
BRODHEAD-GARRETT CO., pg. 178
CASTCRAFT INDUSTRIES, INC., pg. 228
CHADWICK-MILLER INC., pg. 237
CHADWICK-MILLER INC.—Chadwick-Miller Inc., pg. 237
CHADWICK-MILLER INTL. LTD.—Chadwick-Miller Inc., pg. 237
CHICAGO DIVISION—Clark Foodservice, Inc., pg. 252
CINCINNATI DIVISION—Clark Foodservice, Inc., pg. 252
CLARK FOODSERVICE, INC., pg. 252
CLEVELAND DIVISION—Clark Foodservice, Inc., pg. 252
COLUMBUS DIVISION—Clark Foodservice, Inc., pg. 252
CONSOLIDATED LUMBER CO., pg. 276
CUSTOM DECOR, INC., pg. 306
DEITSCH PLASTIC EXPORT CO.—Deitsch Plastics Company, pg. 325
DETROIT DIVISION—Clark Foodservice, Inc., pg. 252
DEWOLFE & FISKE INC.—Chadwick-Miller Inc., pg. 237
DUPEY MANAGEMENT CORP., pg. 354
EARP MEAT COMPANY, pg. 362
EBSCO INDUSTRIES, INC., pg. 365
ELKAY PLASTICS COMPANY, INC., pg. 377
FEUER LEATHER CORPORATION, pg. 407
FOLLETT COLLEGE RESOURCES—Follett Corporation, pg. 422
FOLLETT CORPORATION, pg. 422
FOLLETT LIBRARY BOOK CO.—Follett Corporation, pg. 422
THE HARTZ MOUNTAIN CORP., pg. 514
HARTZ MOUNTAIN GROUP—Hartz Group, pg. 514
HENCO, INC., pg. 528
HICKMAN WILLIAMS & CO. INC., pg. 532
A. J. HOLLANDER CO., INC., pg. 539
HOUSTON FOODS COMPANY, pg. 547
HULMAN & COMPANY, pg. 552
IDEA MAN, INC., pg. 562
INDIANAPOLIS DIVISION—Clark Foodservice, Inc., pg. 252
INGRAM INDUSTRIES INC., pg. 568
JAYDON INCORPORATED, pg. 590
KALSEC, INC.—Kalamazoo Holdings, Inc., pg. 615
L & L NURSERY SUPPLY, INC., pg. 647
LANGSTON COMPANIES, pg. 657
LINCOLN INDUSTRIES, pg. 676
LONDON LITHO ALUMINUM CO., INC., pg. 681
LOUISVILLE DIVISION—Clark Foodservice, Inc., pg. 252
MAGICSILK, INC., pg. 700
MARGO IMPORTS B.V.—Margo Nursery Farms, Inc., pg. 707
MARGO NURSERY FARMS, INC., pg. 706
MARKETING CORP. OF AMERICA, pg. 709
MCJUNKIN CORPORATION, pg. 730
MEASURED MARKETING SERVICES, pg. 734
METALCENTER, INC., pg. 742
MIDSOUTH ICE CO.—Spencer Companies Inc., pg. 1030
MID-STATE DIVISION—Clark Foodservice, Inc., pg. 252
MILWAUKEE DIVISION—Clark Foodservice, Inc., pg. 252
A. MINDEL & SON, INC.—Seton Company, pg. 993
MUENCH-KREUZER CANDLE COMPANY, pg. 774
MUTUAL DISTRIBUTORS LTD., pg. 778
JACK NADEL, INC. DIV.—Measured Marketing Services, pg. 734
NORTHLAND CONTAINER CORP., pg. 814
B. OLINDE & SONS COMPANY, INC., pg. 824
ORLANDO DIVISION—Clark Foodservice, Inc., pg. 252
OUIMET STAY & LEATHER CO.—Ouimet Industries, pg. 831
OZARK DIVISION—Clark Foodservice, Inc., pg. 252
PAN AMERICAN TRADE DEVELOPMENT CORP., pg. 845
PAR BEVERAGE CO.—Grandpa Brands Company, pg. 476
PENNOCK, pg. 858
PEORIA DIVISION—Clark Foodservice, Inc., pg. 252
PEREZ TRADING CO. INC., pg. 860
RIVIERA BEACH DIVISION—Clark Foodservice, Inc., pg. 252
ROSELAND DIVISION—Clark Foodservice, Inc., pg. 252
SCHWAN'S SALES ENTERPRISES, pg. 980
SETON COMPANY, pg. 993
SILVESTRI CORP., pg. 1005
SMITH ENTERPRISES, pg. 1012
SOUTH BEND DIVISION—Clark Foodservice, Inc., pg. 252
SOUTHERN LEATHER COMPANY, pg. 1021
SPARTAN STORES INC., pg. 1026
SPENCER COMPANIES INC., pg. 1030
SPINNERIN YARN CO., INC., pg. 1031
ST. LOUIS DIVISION—Clark Foodservice, Inc., pg. 252
SUNGLASS HUT CORPORATION, pg. 1060
SWINGSTER COMPANY—American Marketing Industries, Inc., pg. 58
TASH, INC., pg. 1080
TEXTILE RUBBER & CHEMICAL COMPANY, pg. 1090
TWIN CITIES DIVISION—Clark Foodservice, Inc., pg. 252
GEORGE UHE CO., INC., pg. 1125
UNITED STATES COLD STORAGE, INC., pg. 1135
UNIVERSAL MATCH CORP.—Diamond Brands, Inc., pg. 335
VJ GROWERS, INC., pg. 1141
VALLEY SEED CO.—Arizona Grains Inc., pg. 82
WGM/HYDRO, pg. 1156
WANG'S INTERNATIONAL, INC., pg. 1162
WARNER CANDY COMPANY, INC., pg. 1164
MARTIN F. WEBER COMPANY—Martin Universal Design, Inc., pg. 716
WILCOX & FOLLETT CO.—Follett Corporation, pg. 422
YOUNG-PHILLIPS SALES CO., pg. 1210

5211 — LUMBER & OTHER BUILDING MATERIALS DEALERS

AMFAC, INC.—JMB Realty Corporation, pg. 585
ANDERSON LUMBER COMPANY, pg. 73
ARROW BUILDING CENTERS—Consolidated Lumber Co., pg. 276
HENRY BACON BUILDING MATERIALS, INC., pg. 113
E.C. BARTON & CO., pg. 123
BATSON-COOK COMPANY, pg. 126
BETHEL MILLS, INC., pg. 148
BETTER LIVING INC., pg. 148
BORCHERS BROS., pg. 165
BRECKENRIDGE MATERIAL COMPANY, pg. 173
BROWNS LUMBER & SUPPLY COMPANY, pg. 183
CURT BULLOCK BUILDERS, INC., pg. 188
CALCASIEU LUMBER COMPANY, pg. 208
CARDINAL REALTY SERVICES INC., pg. 218
CARTER-JONES LUMBER COMPANY, pg. 226
W.C. CAYE & COMPANY, INC., pg. 230
CHAGNON LUMBER COMPANY, INC., pg. 238
CHANNEL HOME CENTERS, CENTRAL REGION—Channel Home Centers Inc., pg. 239
CHANNEL HOME CENTERS INC., pg. 238
CHICAGO FIRE BRICK COMPANY—CFB Industries, Inc., pg. 201
CHURCH & CHURCH INC., pg. 249
COLUMBIA LUMBER & MANUFACTURING CO., pg. 265
COLWOOD CO., INC.—Columbia Lumber & Manufacturing Co., pg. 265
CONSOLIDATED LUMBER CO., pg. 276
COPELAND LUMBER YARD, INC., pg. 284
COX LUMBER CO., pg. 294
CRAFTY BEAVER HOME CENTER, pg. 295
CURTIS LUMBER COMPANY, pg. 305
DEMCO INC., pg. 328
DENLINGER, INC., pg. 329
DEVLIN LUMBER & SUPPLY CORP., pg. 334
ERB LUMBER COMPANY, pg. 360
84 LUMBER CO., pg. 371
ELK SUPPLY COMPANY, pg. 376
ERB LUMBER CO. OF INDIANA—Erb Lumber Company, pg. 360
ERNST HOME CENTER, INC., pg. 387
FAIRFAX LUMBER & MILLWORK COMPANY INC., pg. 397
THE FAIRFIELD LUMBER & SUPPLY COMPANY, pg. 397
FINGERLE LUMBER CO., pg. 411
FOXWORTH-GALBRAITH LUMBER CO., pg. 428
FURMAN LUMBER COMPANY, pg. 436
GANAHL LUMBER COMPANY, pg. 442
GEORGETOWN INDUSTRIES, INC., pg. 453
GERRITY CO., INC., pg. 454
GROESBECK LUMBER & SUPPLY, INC., pg. 489
HANCOCK LUMBER, INC., pg. 504
HIGGINBOTHAM-BARTLETT CO., pg. 533
HILL-BEHAN LUMBER COMPANY, pg. 534
HOLMQUIST GRAIN & LUMBER CO., pg. 540
HOMAN LUMBER MART, INC., pg. 541
IMPERIA BROS., INC., pg. 563
JASPER COUNTY FARM BUREAU CO-OP ASSOCIATION, INC., pg. 590
KINNEAR DOOR—Wayne Dalton Corporation, pg. 313
KNOX LUMBER CO.—Payless Cashways, Inc., pg. 853
PETER KUNTZ COMPANY—Erb Lumber Company, pg. 360
LAMPERT YARDS, INC., pg. 653
JACOB LEVY & BROS., INC., pg. 672
LUGBILL BROTHERS, INC., pg. 686
LYMAN LUMBER COMPANY, pg. 689
MAKI CORPORATION, pg. 702
MAKI HOME CENTER, INC.—Maki Corporation, pg. 702
MANHATTAN BUILDING COMPANIES, pg. 703
MARVIN LUMBER & CEDAR COMPANY, pg. 716
NATIONAL LUMBER CO., pg. 792
NICKERSON LUMBER COMPANY, pg. 806
ORCHARD SUPPLY HARDWARE, pg. 828
PACIFIC COAST BUILDING PRODUCTS INC., pg. 839
THE PATY COMPANY, pg. 852
FRANK PAXTON COMPANY—Jeld-Wen, Inc., pg. 592
PAYLESS CASHWAYS, INC., pg. 853
PETER LUMBER COMPANY, pg. 864
RESIDENTIAL SUPPORT SERVICES, INC.—John Wieland Homes Inc., pg. 1188
RICHARDSON INDUSTRIES, INC., pg. 932
RICKEL HOME CENTERS—Supermarkets General Corporation, pg. 1064
RIEMEIER LUMBER COMPANY, INC., pg. 934
RIVERSIDE MILLWORK COMPANY, INC., pg. 937
T. H. ROGERS LUMBER CO. INC., pg. 943
ROPER BROS. LUMBER CO., INC., pg. 947
RUGG MANUFACTURING COMPANY, pg. 955
RUSH COUNTY FARM BUREAU CO-OP, pg. 956
S.W. JR. ENTERPRISES, INC., pg. 965
SANFORD & HAWLEY, INC., pg. 970
SCHERER BROS. LUMBER COMPANY, pg. 976
SCHOENEMAN BROTHERS COMPANY, pg. 978
SCOTT LUMBER COMPANY, pg. 983
SEIGLE'S HOME & BUILDING CENTERS, pg. 987
SIEGLE'S HOME & BUILDING CENTERS—Seigle's Home & Building Centers, pg. 987
SOMERVILLE LUMBER & SUPPLY CO.—Payless Cashways, Inc., pg. 853
STAR LUMBER & SUPPLY COMPANY, INC., pg. 1039
STERLING LUMBER & INVESTMENT CO., pg. 1047
STONES, INC., pg. 1051
SUPERIOR INDUSTRIES OF NEBRASKA, INC., pg. 1063
SUPERMARKETS GENERAL CORPORATION, pg. 1064
THOMPSON ENTERPRISES INC., pg. 1094
WALDO BROS. COMPANY, pg. 1159
WALLICH LUMBER CO., pg. 1161
WEST LUMBER CO., pg. 1177
WESTERN LUMBER COMPANY, INC.—Georgetown Industries, Inc., pg. 453
WICKES LUMBER CO., pg. 1188

5231 — PAINT, GLASS, & WALLPAPER STORES

M. A. BRUDER & SONS, INC., pg. 184
CHANNEL HOME CENTERS, CENTRAL REGION—Channel Home Centers Inc., pg. 239
CHANNEL HOME CENTERS INC., pg. 238
COLOR YOUR WORLD, INC.—21 International Holdings, Inc., pg. 1121
DURON, INC., pg. 355
FALCONER GLASS INDUSTRIES, INC.—Guardian Industries Corp., pg. 492
FINGERLE LUMBER CO., pg. 411
FINNAREN & HALEY, INC., pg. 411
KELLY-MOORE PAINT COMPANY, INC., pg. 621
LAMPERT YARDS, INC., pg. 653
MAKI CORPORATION, pg. 702
MAKI HOME CENTER, INC.—Maki Corporation, pg. 702
MARTIN PAINT STORES, pg. 715
MAUTZ PAINT COMPANY, pg. 722
OLD QUAKER PAINT CO., pg. 823
ORCHARD SUPPLY HARDWARE, pg. 828
PRESERVATIVE PAINT COMPANY, pg. 887
SAXON PAINT & HOME CARE CENTERS INC., pg. 973
SEABROOK WALLCOVERINGS, INC., pg. 984
WELLBORN - DE CORP.—Dunn-Edwards Corporation, pg. 354

5251 — HARDWARE STORES

ACO INC., pg. 2
ACE HARDWARE CORPORATION, pg. 12
ALASKA INDUSTRIAL HARDWARE INC., pg. 30
ALL AMERICAN HOME CENTER, pg. 35
W.E. AUBUCHON CO., INC., pg. 97
BEST PRODUCTS CO., INC.—Adler & Shaykin, pg. 17
BLACK & CO., pg. 154
BUHRMAN-PHARR HARDWARE COMPANY, pg. 187
BUILDERS EMPORIUM—Collins & Aikman Group Inc., pg. 262
CARDINAL REALTY SERVICES INC., pg. 218
CHANNEL HOME CENTERS, CENTRAL REGION—Channel Home Centers Inc., pg. 239
CHANNEL HOME CENTERS INC., pg. 238
CONSOLIDATED PIPE & SUPPLY COMPANY, pg. 277
DEVLIN LUMBER & SUPPLY CORP., pg. 334
DISTRIBUTION AMERICA, pg. 340
ERNST HOME CENTER, INC., pg. 387
FINGERLE LUMBER CO., pg. 411
KRUSE HARDWARE COMPANY, pg. 645
MARVIN LUMBER & CEDAR COMPANY, pg. 716

MAURICE ELECTRIC SUPPLY COMPANY, pg. 722
ORCHARD SUPPLY HARDWARE, pg. 828
OUR OWN HARDWARE COMPANY, pg. 832
RUSH COUNTY FARM BUREAU CO-OP, pg. 956
SCHOENEMAN BROTHERS COMPANY, pg. 978
SCOTT LUMBER COMPANY, pg. 983
SEIGLE'S HOME & BUILDING CENTERS, pg. 987
SNYDER-DIAMOND, pg. 1015
SPEER HARDWARE—Servistar Corporation, pg. 993
TSC INDUSTRIES, INC., pg. 1075
TOOL KING, pg. 1101
TRANSPORT SERVICE OF INDIANA, INC.—Mayflower Transit, Inc., pg. 725
UNITED PRODUCERS & CONSUMERS CO-OP, pg. 1134
WESTLAKE HARDWARE, INC., pg. 1183

5261 — RETAIL NURSERIES, LAWN & GARDEN SUPPLY STORES

AIRCAP INDUSTRIES CORP.—MTD Products, Inc., pg. 694
ALLISON-ERWIN CO. INC., pg. 40
AMLINGS FLOWERLAND, pg. 67
W.E. AUBUCHON CO., INC., pg. 97
BACHMAN'S, INC., pg. 108
BRECKS—Foster & Gallagher Inc., pg. 426
CHANNEL HOME CENTERS, CENTRAL REGION—Channel Home Centers Inc., pg. 239
CHANNEL HOME CENTERS INC., pg. 238
COPELAND LUMBER YARD, INC., pg. 284
CORHAM, INC., pg. 286
EDMONSON WHEAT GROWERS, INC., pg. 369
FARMWAY CO-OP INC., pg. 402
H.G. FENTON MATERIAL COMPANY, pg. 406
FOSTER & GALLAGHER INC., pg. 426
GEBO DISTRIBUTING CO., INC., pg. 447
MFA INCORPORATED, pg. 692
EARL MAY SEED & NURSERY L.P., pg. 724
BRUCE OAKLEY, INC., pg. 819
GEORGE W. PARK SEED CO., INC., pg. 849
QUALITY STORES INC., pg. 904
RAY-CARROLL COUNTY GRAIN CO-OP, pg. 914
ROCKWOOD GARDENS, LTD.—KNOX International Corp., pg. 638
THE SCOTT COMPANY, pg. 982
SOUTHERN STATES COOPERATIVE, INC., pg. 1022
SPRING HILL NURSERIES CO.—Foster & Gallagher Inc., pg. 426
VALLEY SEED CO.—Arizona Grains Inc., pg. 82
WHEELER BROS. GRAIN CO.—Wheeler Brothers Grain Co., pg. 1185

5271 — MOBILE HOME DEALERS

STEENBERG HOMES, INC., pg. 1045

5311 — DEPARTMENT STORES

ADAM MELDRUM & ANDERSON CO., INC., pg. 16
ALLENS OF HASTINGS, INC., pg. 36
BEALL'S, INC., pg. 129
BELK STORES SERVICES INC., pg. 134
BENO'S, pg. 139
BIGG'S HYPER SHOPPES, INC., pg. 150
BOSCOV'S DEPARTMENT STORES, INC., pg. 167
BULLOCK'S—R. H. Macy & Co., Inc., pg. 699
CARLISLE RETAILERS, INC., pg. 220
CENTRAL TEXTILE DIV.—Masters, Inc., pg. 720
M. M. COHN CO., INC.—The Dunlap Companies, pg. 353
CROWN AMERICAN CORPORATION, pg. 301
DOLLAR BARGAIN STORES—Schottenstein Stores Corporation, pg. 978
DUCKWALL-ALCO STORES, INC., pg. 351
S. P. DUNHAM & CO., pg. 353
THE DUNLAP COMPANIES, pg. 353
THE ELDER-BEERMAN STORES CORP., pg. 373
ERNST HOME CENTER, INC., pg. 387
EUROMARKET DESIGNS, INC., pg. 390
EXPRESS 1 STOP—Sullivan Oil Company, pg. 1057
F & M DISTRIBUTORS INC., pg. 393
FEDCO, INC., pg. 404
FISHERS BIG WHEEL INC., pg. 415
G.I. JOE'S INC., pg. 440
GEE BEE DEPARTMENT STORES—Schottenstein Stores Corporation, pg. 978
GILMORE BROS., INC., pg. 459
GLOSSER BROS. DEPARTMENT STORE—Schottenstein Stores Corporation, pg. 978
GLOSSER BROTHERS, INC.—Schottenstein Stores Corporation, pg. 978
H.B.A. KING INC.—Boston Distributors, Inc., pg. 167
G. R. HERBERGER'S, INC., pg. 530
HESS'S DEPARTMENT STORES, INC.—Crown American Corporation, pg. 302
I. MAGNIN & CO.—R. H. Macy & Co., Inc., pg. 699
KERRISON DRY GOODS COMPANY, INC., pg. 624
H. KESSLER & COMPANY, pg. 624
H. KESSLER & COMPANY—H. Kessler & Company, pg. 624
H. KESSLER & COMPANY—H. Kessler & Company, pg. 624
H. KESSLER & COMPANY—H. Kessler & Company, pg. 624
LADY ROSE DIV.—Masters, Inc., pg. 720
LECHMERE, INC., pg. 665
LEWIS DRUG, INC., pg. 673
LIBERTY HOUSE—JMB Realty Corporation, pg. 585
LIBERTY HOUSE, INC.—JMB Realty Corporation, pg. 585
LOEHMANN'S, INC., pg. 681
LORD BIBB DIV.—Masters, Inc., pg. 720
R. H. MACY & CO., INC., pg. 698
MASTERS, INC., pg. 720
MCCURDY & CO., INC., pg. 728
MCRAE'S, INC., pg. 733
MONTGOMERY WARD & CO., INC., pg. 767
PARISIAN, INC., pg. 848
PEEBLES, INC., pg. 855
PLYMOUTH LAMSTON STORES, CORP., pg. 877
PORTEOUS—The Dunlap Companies, pg. 353
H. C. PRANGE COMPANY, pg. 884
QUALITY STORES INC., pg. 904
SAGE-ALLEN & CO., INC., pg. 966
SCHOTTENSTEIN STORES CORPORATION, pg. 978
SERVCO PACIFIC INC., pg. 991
SHEPLERS, INC., pg. 998
SHOPKO STORES, INC., pg. 1000
SPECIALTY RETAILERS, INC., pg. 1029
SPURGEON MERCANTILE COMPANY, pg. 1034
STEINBACH, pg. 1045
STEKETEE PAUL & SONS COMPANY, INC.—The Dunlap Companies, pg. 353
STERLING JEWELRY & DISTRIBUTING CO., pg. 1047
STONE & THOMAS, pg. 1051
STONE & THOMAS MERCHANDISING OFFICES—Stone & Thomas, pg. 1051
SWALLEN'S, INC., pg. 1066
T.G. & Y. STORES CO.—Riklis Family Corporation, pg. 934
SUSAN TERRY DIV.—Masters, Inc., pg. 720
THREE BEALL BROTHERS 3, INC.—Specialty Retailers, Inc., pg. 1029
VAN LEUNENS INC., pg. 1144
WAREHOUSE OUTLET STORES—Schottenstein Stores Corporation, pg. 978
WEINERS ENTERPRISES, INC., pg. 1173
WEINERS STORES INC.—Weiners Enterprises, Inc., pg. 1173
WINNER'S LADIES OFF-PRICE SPECIALTY STORE—Schottenstein Stores Corporation, pg. 978
WOODWARD & LOTHROP/JOHN WANAMAKER, pg. 1201

5331 — VARIETY STORES

THE FRED W. ALBRECHT GROCERY CO., pg. 31
ALLIED TIRE SALES, pg. 40
BACHMAN'S, INC., pg. 108
BILL'S DOLLAR STORES, INC., pg. 150
DUCKWALL-ALCO STORES, INC., pg. 351
LAVERDIERE'S ENTERPRISES, pg. 661
MAUI VARIETIES, LTD., pg. 721
MCCRORY CORPORATION—Riklis Family Corporation, pg. 934
MCCRORY STORES DIV.—Riklis Family Corporation, pg. 934
J. J. NEWBERRY CO.—Riklis Family Corporation, pg. 934
PERRY BROTHERS, INC., pg. 862
RIKLIS FAMILY CORPORATION, pg. 934
STERNHEIMER BROTHERS.INC., pg. 1048
VARIETY WHOLESALERS, INC., pg. 1146

5399 — MISCELLANEOUS GENERAL MERCHANDISE STORES

THE ANDERSONS, pg. 73
ASSOCIATED FOOD STORES INC., pg. 89
ASTRUP DRUGS, INC., pg. 93
ATWOOD DISTRIBUTING, INC., pg. 97
BENNETT BROTHERS, INC., pg. 139
BERWICK BAY OIL CO. INC., pg. 144
BEST PRODUCTS CO., INC.—Adler & Shaykin, pg. 17
CATALOGUE MARKETING, INC.—Hickory Farms, Inc., pg. 533
CUMBERLAND FARMS, INC., pg. 304
DAIRY EXPORT CO., INC.—Darigold, Inc., pg. 315
F & M DISTRIBUTORS INC., pg. 393
FUEL SOUTH, INC., pg. 435
FRED P. GATTAS COMPANY, INC., pg. 446
HALLS MERCHANDISING INC.—Hallmark Cards, Inc., pg. 502
HAMILTON STORES, INC., pg. 503
KNOTT'S BERRY FARM, pg. 637
LEWIS DRUG, INC., pg. 673
MFA INCORPORATED, pg. 692
MEIJER, INC., pg. 737
THE PANTRY, INC., pg. 846
PENN-DANIELS, INC., pg. 857
PERGAMENT HOME CENTERS, INC., pg. 862
PETROLEUM MARKETERS, INC., pg. 865
QUIKTRIP CORPORATION, pg. 905
RALEY'S, pg. 910
SOUTHEASTERN EQUIPMENT COMPANY, INC., pg. 1019
TSC INDUSTRIES, INC., pg. 1075
WANG'S INTERNATIONAL, INC., pg. 1162
WHITE HEN PANTRY, INC., pg. 1185
WOOLRICH, INC., pg. 1201
WOOLRICH STORE DIV.—Woolrich, Inc., pg. 1201
YODER OIL COMPANY INC., pg. 1208

5411 — GROCERY STORES

ABCO MARKETS, INC., pg. 10
THE FRED W. ALBRECHT GROCERY CO., pg. 31
ALDI INC., pg. 33
ALLENS OF HASTINGS, INC., pg. 36
ALLSUPS CONVENIENCE STORES INC., pg. 43
APPLETREE MARKETS, pg. 79
ARIZONA SUPERMARKETS, INC., pg. 82
TRUMAN ARNOLD COMPANIES, pg. 84
ASSOCIATED GROCERS, INC., pg. 89
B & B CASH GROCERY STORE, pg. 105
BASHAS, pg. 124
BE-LO MARKETS INC.—Camellia Food Stores Co-op Inc., pg. 212
BEL AIR MARKETS, pg. 133
BESCHE OIL COMPANY, INC., pg. 145
BIG BEAR SUPERMARKETS NO. 3, pg. 149
BIG V SUPERMARKETS, INC., pg. 149
BIG Y FOODS INC., pg. 149
BIGG'S HYPER SHOPPES, INC., pg. 150
BRODBECK ENTERPRISES, INC., pg. 178
BROOKSHIRE BROS., INC., pg. 180
BROOKSHIRE GROCERY, pg. 180
BURNSTAD BROTHERS, INC., pg. 194
BUTERA FINER FOODS INC., pg. 196
H. E. BUTT GROCERY CO., pg. 197
BYERLY'S INC., pg. 198
C & K MARKETS, INC., pg. 198
CARSE OIL CO. INC., pg. 225
CASH & CARRY GROCER INC., pg. 228
CIVIC FOOD CENTER, INC.—So-Lo-Food, Inc., pg. 1016
CLEMENS MARKETS INC., pg. 254
COMMUNITY CASH STORES, pg. 270
CONSUMERS MARKETS INC., pg. 277
CONVENIENT FOOD MART, INC., pg. 281
THE COPPS CORP., pg. 285
COVINGTON FOODS, INC., pg. 290
CREAM PRODUCTS CO., INC., pg. 297
CREST DISTRIBUTING COMPANY, INC., pg. 298
CROOKS SUPERMARKET INC., pg. 300
CRYSTAL FLASH PETROLEUM CORP., pg. 303
CULCO, INC.—Randall's Food Markets, Inc., pg. 912
D & W FOOD CENTERS, INC., pg. 308
D'AGOSTINO SUPERMARKETS INC., pg. 310
DAN'S SUPREME SUPER MARKETS INC., pg. 314
J.T. DAVENPORT & SONS, INC., pg. 317
JIMMY DAVIS ENTERPRISES, INC., pg. 318
DEMOULAS SUPER MARKETS, pg. 328
DIERBERGS MARKETS INC., pg. 337
DOMINICK'S FINER FOODS, pg. 343
ENGLEFIELD, INC., pg. 382
ERICKSON DIVERSIFIED CORP., pg. 386
ERICKSON OIL PRODUCTS, INC., pg. 386
FALLEY'S INC.—The Yucaipa Companies, pg. 1214
FAREWAY STORES, INC., pg. 399
FARM FRESH, INC., pg. 401
FARM STORES, INC., pg. 401
FIESTA MART INC., pg. 409
FLORIDA JITNEY JUNGLE STORES, INC.—Jitney-Jungle Stores of America, Inc., pg. 594
FOOD 4 LESS, INC.—The Yucaipa Companies, pg. 1214
FOOD KING INDEPENDENT SUPERMARKETS—Victory Markets Inc., pg. 1150
FOOD SERVICES OF AMERICA, pg. 423
FOODWAY, INC.—Jitney-Jungle Stores of America, Inc., pg. 594
FURR'S SUPERMARKETS, pg. 437
GES INC., pg. 439
GENUARDI SUPER MARKETS INC., pg. 452
GERLAND CORP., pg. 454
GIANT EAGLE, INC., pg. 455
GIANT MARKETS INC., pg. 456
GOLUB CORPORATION, pg. 469
GOOLSBY FOODS, INC., pg. 471
GORDY'S, INC., pg. 472
THE GRAND UNION COMPANY—Grand Union Holdings Corporation, pg. 476
GRAND UNION HOLDINGS CORPORATION, pg. 475
GREAT AMERICAN FOOD STORES, INC.—Victory Markets Inc., pg. 1150
GREAT SCOTT FOOD MARKETS, INC.—James Ferrera & Sons, Inc., pg. 407
AUTRY GREER & SONS, INC., pg. 486
GROMER SUPER MARKETS, INC., pg. 489
THE JOHN C. GROUB COMPANY INC., pg. 489
HAGGEN'S, INC., pg. 499
HALE-HALSELL COMPANY, pg. 500
HARMON CITY, INC., pg. 510
HARP'S FOOD STORES, INC., pg. 510
J.H. HARVEY COMPANY, pg. 515
HAWKINS MARKETS, INC., pg. 518
HEINEN'S INC., pg. 526
HI NABOR SUPERMARKET INC., pg. 532
HOLIDAY COMPANIES, pg. 539
HOMELAND STORES, INC., pg. 542
HOUCHENS INDUSTRIES INC., pg. 545
HUGHES MARKETS INC., pg. 552
HY-VEE FOOD STORES INCORPORATED, pg. 556
ILLINOIS LIMITED PARTNERSHIP—Martin Exploration Management Company, pg. 715
INGLES MARKETS, INC., pg. 568
INTERSTATE JITNEY JUNGLE STORES, INC.—Jitney-Jungle Stores of America, Inc., pg. 594
JITNEY-JUNGLE STORES OF AMERICA, INC., pg. 594
JONES COMPANY, INC., pg. 603
KASH N KARRY FOOD STORES, INC., pg. 617
KENYON OIL COMPANY, INC.—Warren Equities Inc., pg. 1165
KING FUELS INC., pg. 630
KING KULLEN GROCERY CO., INC., pg. 630
KWICKIE/FLASH FOODS, INC.—Jones Company, Inc., pg. 603
LA ROSA'S, INC., pg. 649
LEWIS & COKER SUPER MARKETS, pg. 673
LOWE'S FOOD STORES, INC.—Alex Lee, Inc., pg. 33
THE MAD BUTCHER, INC., pg. 699
MAGIC MARKET CONVENIENCE STORES—E-Z Serve Corp., pg. 362
MARS SUPER MARKETS, INC., pg. 714
MAVERIK COUNTRY STORES, INC., pg. 722
MAYFAIR SUPER MARKETS, INC., pg. 724
MEIJER, INC., pg. 737
THE MIAMI MARGARINE CO., pg. 746
MICHAEL FOODS, INC., pg. 747
MID SOUTH SALES, pg. 750
MINI MART, INC., pg. 757
MINYARD FOOD STORES, pg. 759
MOTO, INC., pg. 773
MURRY'S, INC., pg. 777

NATIONAL FOOD STORES, INC. T/A KRAUSZER'S, pg. 788
NOB HILL GENERAL STORE, INC., pg. 807
O'MALIA FOOD MARKETS INC., pg. 825
OMNI SUPERSTORES—Dominick's Finer Foods, pg. 344
PACIFIC HAWAIIAN LTD., pg. 840
THE PANTRY, INC., pg. 846
PARMART STORES—The Parman Corporation, pg. 850
PATHMARK—Supermarkets General Corporation, pg. 1064
PAY LESS SUPER MARKETS, INC., pg. 852
PIC N'PAY SUPERMARKETS, INC., pg. 869
PIONEER SUPERMARKETS, pg. 872
PLAID PANTRIES, INC., pg. 873
PRESTO FOOD STORES, INC., pg. 888
PRICE CHOPPER—Golub Corporation, pg. 469
PUBLIX SUPERMARKETS INC., pg. 898
PUEBLO INTERNATIONAL, INC.-P.R. DIV.—Pueblo International, Inc., pg. 899
PUNA PLANTATION HAWAII LTD., pg. 900
PURITY SUPREME, INC., pg. 901
RACETRAC PETROLEUM, INC., pg. 909
RALEY'S, pg. 910
RANDALL STORES, INC., pg. 911
RANDALL'S FOOD MARKETS, INC., pg. 911
REAL HOLDING MANAGEMENT CORP., pg. 917
RED APPLE COMPANIES, pg. 917
RED APPLE, INC., pg. 918
F.T. REYNOLDS COMPANY, pg. 930
RICE FOOD MARKETS INC., pg. 931
RICHDALE DAIRY STORES, INC.—Scangas Brothers Holdings, Inc., pg. 974
F. L. ROBERTS & CO. INC., pg. 938
ROGERS MARKETS INC., pg. 943
ROSAUER'S SUPERMARKETS, INC., pg. 947
RUSSELL PETROLEUM CORPORATION, pg. 957
SAVE MART SUPERMARKETS, pg. 973
SAVE MORE FOOD MART, INC., pg. 973
SCANGAS BROTHERS HOLDINGS, INC., pg. 974
SCHNUCK MARKETS, INC., pg. 977
BEN SCHWARTZ MARKET, INC., pg. 980
SCHWEGMANN GIANT SUPER MARKETS, pg. 980
SEESSEL HOLDINGS, INC., pg. 987
SERVCO PACIFIC INC., pg. 991
SHERMS THUNDERBIRD MARKET, pg. 998
SHOP-RITE OF BENSALEM INC.—Wakefern Food Corporation, pg. 1158
SHOP-RITE SUPERMARKETS, INC.—Wakefern Food Corporation, pg. 1158
SHOPRITE SUPERMARKETS—Big V Supermarkets, Inc., pg. 149
SINGERS SUPERMARKETS, INC., pg. 1008
SITE OIL CO. OF MISSOURI, pg. 1009
SLOANS SUPERMARKETS, INC., pg. 1010
SO-LO-FOOD, INC., pg. 1016
SPENCER COMPANIES INC., pg. 1030
STANLEY STORES INC., pg. 1038
STEWART'S ICE CREAM CO., INC., pg. 1048
STOP IN FOOD STORES—Petroleum Marketers, Inc., pg. 865
STOP SHOP SAVE, pg. 1052
SULLIVAN OIL COMPANY, pg. 1057
SUPERMARKETS GENERAL CORPORATION, pg. 1064
THE SWISS COLONY, pg. 1068
TOC RETAIL, INC.—E-Z Serve Corp., pg. 362
TACT HOLDING, pg. 1076
TERUYA BROS., LTD., pg. 1089
THOM THUMB FOOD MARKET INC.—Polka Dot Dairy, pg. 879
THORNTON OIL CORP., pg. 1095
THRIFTWAY, INC., pg. 1095
TIMES SUPER MARKET LTD.—Teruya Bros., Ltd., pg. 1089
TOM THUMB FOOD & DRUGS, INC.—Randall's Food Markets, Inc., pg. 912
TOM THUMB STORES, INC.—Randall's Food Markets, Inc., pg. 912
TOWN & COUNTRY FOOD MARKETS, INC., pg. 1103
TOWN & COUNTRY SUPERMARKET, pg. 1103
TOWN PUMP, INC., pg. 1104
TRADER JOES CO.—TACT Holding, pg. 1076
TRADERS SUPERMARKETS, INC., pg. 1105
TRADING PORT, INC., pg. 1105
TREASURE ISLAND FOODMARTS INC., pg. 1109
TRITON INC., pg. 1114
TRUCCHIS MARKETS, pg. 1117
U.R.M. STORES, INC., pg. 1124
KEITH UDDENBERG, INC., pg. 1125
UNITED DAIRY FARMERS, INC., pg. 1131
UNITED GROCERS INC., pg. 1132
VALU DISCOUNT, INC., pg. 1143
VALU-FARE FOODS, INC.—Hale-Halsell Company, pg. 501
VALU FOODS INC.—So-Lo-Food, Inc., pg. 1016
VALUE KING, INC.—James Ferrera & Sons, Inc., pg. 407
VENTA INC., pg. 1147
VICTORY DISCOUNT BEVERAGE CENTER—Victory Markets Inc., pg. 1150
VICTORY MARKETS INC., pg. 1150
VILLAGE MARKETS—Victory Markets Inc., pg. 1150
WAREMART INC., pg. 1163
WAREMART INC.—Waremart Inc., pg. 1163
WAWA, INC., pg. 1169
WEGMANS FOOD MARKETS, INC., pg. 1172
WORSLEY COMPANIES INC., pg. 1204
XTRA SUPER FOOD CENTERS, INC.—Pueblo International, Inc., pg. 899
YATES ENTERPRISES INC., pg. 1207

5421 — MEAT & FISH MARKETS, INCLUDING FREEZER PROVISIONS

AMERICAN FROZEN FOODS, INC., pg. 55
BEL AIR MARKETS, pg. 133
CROWN FOODS INC., pg. 302
FAREWAY STORES, INC., pg. 399
KOLD KIST BRANDS, INC., pg. 641
KOWALSKI SAUSAGE CO., INC., pg. 643
THE MAD BUTCHER, INC., pg. 699
PARMART STORES—The Parman Corporation, pg. 850
PUBLIX SUPERMARKETS INC., pg. 898
SEESSEL HOLDINGS, INC., pg. 987
STOCK YARDS PACKING CO., INC., pg. 1049
FRED USINGER, INC., pg. 1140

5431 — FRUIT STORES & VEGETABLE MARKETS

BIG BEAR SUPERMARKETS NO. 3, pg. 149
BLUE ANCHOR, INC., pg. 158
J. C. BROCK CORP., pg. 178
CROWN FOODS INC., pg. 302
TWIN COUNTY GROCERS, INC., pg. 1122

5441 — CANDY, NUT & CONFECTIONERY STORES

ARCHIBALD CANDY COMPANY—Jordan Company, pg. 604
BLEVINS CONCESSION SUPPLY CO., pg. 156
DUANE READE, pg. 350
E-Z MART STORES, INC., pg. 361
FANNIE MAY CANDY SHOPS, INC.—Jordan Company, pg. 604
HICKORY FARMS, INC., pg. 532
JOYKIST/GSC DISTRIBUTING—GSC Enterprises, Inc., pg. 440
PACIFIC FOODS, INC., pg. 840
RUSSELL STOVER CANDIES, INC., pg. 957

5451 — DAIRY PRODUCTS STORES

BRAUM ICE CREAM STORES INC., pg. 172
BROUGHTON FOODS COMPANY, pg. 180
C.F. BURGER CREAMERY COMPANY, pg. 190
COLONNA BROS., INC., pg. 264
DAIRY EXPORT CO., INC.—Darigold, Inc., pg. 315
DAIRYGOLD INC., pg. 311
DAIRYGOLD, INC.—Dairygold Inc., pg. 311
DAIRYMEN, INC., pg. 311
DIXIE DAIRY COMPANY, pg. 341
HASTINGS CO-OP CREAMERY COMPANY, pg. 516
MARYLAND VIRGINIA MILK PRODUCERS ASSOCIATION, INC., pg. 717
OBERWEIS DAIRY, INC., pg. 820
RICHDALE DAIRY STORES, INC.—Scangas Brothers Holdings, Inc., pg. 974
SCANGAS BROTHERS HOLDINGS, INC., pg. 974
TENNESSEE RESTAURANT CORP., pg. 1087
TURNER DAIRIES, INC., pg. 1119
UPSTATE MILK COOPERATIVES INC., pg. 1140
WEST DAIRIES, INC., pg. 1177
WOMETCO ENTERPRISES, INC., pg. 1199

5461 — RETAIL BAKERIES

AWREY BAKERIES, INC., pg. 103
BEL AIR MARKETS, pg. 133
BESS EATON DONUT FLOUR CO., INC., pg. 146
BRODBECK ENTERPRISES, INC., pg. 178
BYERLY'S INC., pg. 198
DERST BAKING COMPANY, INC., pg. 331
LA PETITE BOULANGERIE, INC.—Mrs. Fields' Inc., pg. 761
LET THEM EAT CAKE—Wilton Industries, Inc., pg. 1195
MRS. BAIRD'S BAKERIES, INC., pg. 760
MRS. FIELDS' INC., pg. 761
PUBLIX SUPERMARKETS INC., pg. 898
YUM YUM DONUT SHOP, INC., pg. 1214

5499 — MISCELLANEOUS FOOD STORES

CARR GOTTSTEIN FOODS, pg. 225
CRYSTAL GEYSER, pg. 303
FARMERS RICE COOPERATIVE, pg. 401
GLORIA JEAN'S COFFEE BEAN CORP., pg. 464
HICKORY FARMS, INC., pg. 532
MRS. GOOCHS NATURAL FOOD MARKETS, pg. 761
MURRY'S, INC., pg. 777
NUTRITION WORLD, pg. 818
OTT FOOD PRODUCTS, pg. 831

5511 — MOTOR VEHICLE DEALERS (NEW & USED CARS)

ALL-STATE FORD TRUCK SALES—Hesco Parts Corporation, pg. 532
AMADOR MOTORS—Prospect Motors, Inc., pg. 895
ARROW CHEVROLET, INC., pg. 85
AUTOMANAGE, pg. 100
AVIS FORD INC., pg. 102
BAIRD RAY NISSAN, INC., pg. 114
W. O. BANKSTON ENTERPRISES INC., pg. 118
W. O. BANKSTON LINCOLN MERCURY—W. O. Bankston Enterprises Inc., pg. 118
BANKSTON NISSAN IN IRVING, INC.—W. O. Bankston Enterprises Inc., pg. 118
W. O. BANKSTON NISSAN INC.—W. O. Bankston Enterprises Inc., pg. 118
BAST CHEVROLET INC., pg. 125
BAUGHER CHEVROLET-BUICK-GEO, INC., pg. 127
BEACH CITY CHEVROLET CO., pg. 128
BEAUDRY FORD, INC., pg. 130
BENSON MANAGEMENT COMPANY, pg. 140
BIDDULPH OLDSMOBILE, pg. 149
BLACK CADILLAC OLDS, INC., pg. 153
BLAND CADILLAC COMPANY, pg. 155
BLUE GRASS CHRYSLER-PLYMOUTH, pg. 156
BRAMAN WORLD CAR CENTER, pg. 171
BILL BROWN FORD INC., pg. 182
BROWN MOTORS, pg. 182
BUERKLE BUICK-HONDA CO., pg. 186
BYERLY FORD-NISSAN INC., pg. 198
JACK BYRNE FORD & MERCURY, INC., pg. 198
CAMINO REAL CHEVROLET, pg. 212
CAPITOL CADILLAC, CORP.—Don Massey Cadillac Inc., pg. 719
CAPITOL CHEVROLET CADILLAC GEO, INC., pg. 215
CASSENS TRANSPORT COMPANY, pg. 228
JIM CAUSLEY PONTIAC GMC INC., pg. 229
CERRITOS FORD, INC., pg. 236
CHASE CHEVROLET CO., pg. 240
CHASE CHRYSLER/PLYMOUTH—Chase Chevrolet Co., pg. 240
CHEMUNG FORD, INC., pg. 242
CHEVY CHASE CARS & GEO, pg. 244
CLASSIC CHEVROLET—Libertyville Lincoln-Mercury Sales, Inc., pg. 674
COGGIN-O'STEEN INVESTMENT CORP., pg. 259
COGGIN PONTIAC-GMC INC.—Coggin-O'Steen Investment Corp., pg. 259
COLEMAN CADILLAC INC., pg. 261
COLLINS CHEVROLET, GEO, pg. 263
BILL COLLINS FORD INC., pg. 263
COLLINS OLDSMOBILE INC., pg. 263
COLMAN TOYOTA, pg. 263
COLONIAL DODGE INC., pg. 263
CORMIER CHEVROLET COMPANY, INC., pg. 286
COURTESY CHEVROLET & IMPORTS INC., pg. 290
CREST CADILLAC COMPANY, pg. 298
CROSS MOTORS CORP., pg. 300
CROWN BUICK, INC., pg. 302
THE CURRY CORPORATION, pg. 305
DALLAS PETERBILT, INC., pg. 312
DARLING'S, pg. 315
BUD DAVIS CADILLAC, INC., pg. 318
DAVIS-MOORE OLDSMOBILE, INC., pg. 319
DEALERS TRANSPORT COMPANY, INC., pg. 322
JACK DEMMER FORD, INC., pg. 328
DE NOOYER CHEVROLET INC., pg. 329
DIAMOND MOTORS INC., pg. 335
DIFEO AUTOMOTIVE NETWORK, pg. 337
DOBLES CHEVROLET, INC., pg. 342
DON MASSEY CADILLAC, INC.—Don Massey Cadillac Inc., pg. 719
DREISBACH & SONS CADILLAC COMPANY, pg. 348
A. K. DURNIN CHRYSLER PLYMOUTH, INC., pg. 355
EAGLE LINCOLN MERCURY INC., pg. 362
EARNHARDT'S AUTO CENTER, pg. 362
EMRICK CHEVROLET SALES CORPORATION, pg. 380
STU EVANS LINCOLN-MERCURY INC., pg. 390
F.P.A., INC., pg. 394
FAIRWAY FORD, INC., pg. 397
PETE FALL FORD INC., pg. 398
FARMINGTON HILLS HOLDING COMPANY, pg. 402
FERMAN OLDSMOBILE, pg. 406
STEVE FOLEY CADILLAC, pg. 422
FOSTER PONTIAC, INC., pg. 426
FRANK CONSOLIDATED ENTERPRISES INC., pg. 428
FRAZIER-WILLIAMS CHEVROLET GEO, pg. 430
JIM FRESARD PONTIAC BUICK, INC., pg. 432
FRIENDLY CHEVROLET CO. INC., pg. 433
BOB FRINK CHEVROLET G.E.O. MANAGEMENT, pg. 433
FRONTIER CHEVROLET CO.—Roundtree Automotive Group, pg. 952
LOU FUSZ AUTOMOTIVE NETWORK, pg. 437
LOU FUSZ MOTOR COMPANY—Lou Fusz Automotive Network, pg. 437
FUTURE FORD/HUGO INC., pg. 437
GILLOGLY CHEVROLET INC., pg. 459
GOEBEL ART, INC., pg. 464
GULF STATES TOYOTA, pg. 494
CURTIS C. GUNN, INC., pg. 494
GURLEY MOTOR COMPANY, pg. 494
H.B.L., INC.—Lantzsch-Andreas Enterprises, Inc., pg. 658
HALE MOTORS—Dairy Fresh Corp., pg. 311
JERRY HAMM CHEVROLET INC., pg. 503
HARRIS FORD, INC., pg. 512
BILL HEARD CHEVROLET INC.—Bill Heard Enterprises, Inc., pg. 521
BILL HEARD ENTERPRISES, INC., pg. 521
HEINTZELMAN'S TRUCK CENTER INC., pg. 526
HENDRICK IMPORTS—Hendrick Management Corporation, pg. 529
ROGER HOLLER CHEVROLET CO., pg. 539
HOLMAN ENTERPRISES, pg. 540
HOLMES TUTTLE FORD, INC., pg. 540
HUBACHER CADILLAC INC., pg. 548
HUBLER CHEVROLET INC., pg. 550
JIM HUDSON, PONTIAC, OLDSMOBILE GMC, pg. 551
NEIL HUFFMAN CHRYSLER PLYMOUTH DODGE—Neil Huffman Nissan Inc., pg. 551
NEIL HUFFMAN VOLKSWAGON MAZDA SUBURU—Neil Huffman Nissan Inc., pg. 551
NEIL HUFFMAN NISSAN INC., pg. 551
MIKE DAUGHERTY'S HURLING CHEVROLET, INC., pg. 555
CHUCK HUTTON CHEVROLET COMPANY, pg. 556
ISLAND LINCOLN-MERCURY, pg. 582
JAKE SWEENEY JEEP EAGLE, INC.—Jake Sweeney Automotive Inc., pg. 1067
JAMES CHEVROLET INC., pg. 588
JEFFERSON CHEVROLET CO., pg. 591
JEFFREY BUICK-NISSAN INC., pg. 591
JEROME-DUNCAN FORD, pg. 593
JORDAN MOTORS, INC., pg. 605
KELLER MOTOR CAR COMPANY, INC., pg. 621
KENWORTH OF INDIANAPOLIS INC., pg. 624
KEY CADILLAC, INC., pg. 626

S.I.C. Index

KEYES MOTORS, INC., pg. 627
KINGS TOYOTA SUZUKI, pg. 631
KISSIMMEE TOYOTA INC., pg. 633
LB INDUSTRIES INC., pg. 647
RAY LAETHEM PONTIAC GMC TRUCK CO., pg. 650
LANE HONDA/HYUNDAI—Rosenthal Automotive Organization, pg. 949
LANTZSCH-ANDREAS ENTERPRISES, INC., pg. 658
LOU LARICHE CHEVROLET-SUBARU INC., pg. 658
LESON CHEVROLET COMPANY, INC., pg. 668
LIBERTYVILLE LINCOLN-MERCURY SALES, INC., pg. 674
LOCKHART CADILLAC INC., pg. 680
LOEBER MOTORS, INC., pg. 680
LOMBARD LINCOLN-MERCURY & LEASING, INC., pg. 681
LONE STAR CADILLAC CO., pg. 682
JIM LUPIENT ENTERPRISES, pg. 687
LUSTINE OLDSMOBILE & BUICK, INC., pg. 688
GUS MACHADO ENTERPRISES, pg. 696
MARK CHEVROLET INC., pg. 708
DON MASSEY BUICK, INC.—Don Massey Cadillac Inc., pg. 719
MASSEY CADILLAC, INC.—Don Massey Cadillac Inc., pg. 719
MASSEY CADILLAC, INC.—Don Massey Cadillac Inc., pg. 719
DON MASSEY CADILLAC INC., pg. 719
MCCONNELL AUTOMOTIVE, pg. 727
MCINERNEY INC., pg. 729
MCKEAN OLDSMOBILE COMPANY, pg. 730
MCNAMARA PONTIAC INC., pg. 732
MEADE GROUP, INC., pg. 733
DON MEALEY CHEVROLET INC., pg. 733
MELLOY BROS. ENTERPRISES, pg. 738
MELLOY NISSAN—Melloy Bros. Enterprises, pg. 738
MERCHANTS RENT A CAR, INC., pg. 739
METRO FORD INC., pg. 743
METRO FORD SALES, INC., pg. 743
MID AMERICA INTERNATIONAL TRUCKS, INC., pg. 750
MID-SOUTH FORD TRUCK SALES, INC., pg. 750
MIDWAY FORD TRUCK CENTER INC., pg. 751
BOB MONTGOMERY CHEVROLET/HONDA, pg. 767
ART MORAN PONTIAC-GMC INC., pg. 769
MORITZ CADILLAC-SAAB INC., pg. 770
ED MORSE CHEVROLET INC.—Morse Operations Inc., pg. 772
ED MORSE DODGE, INC.—Morse Operations Inc., pg. 772
MORSE OPERATIONS INC., pg. 772
ED MULLINAX FORD, INC., pg. 775
NIMNICHT CHEVROLET COMPANY, pg. 807
NORMAN BROTHERS NISSAN INC., pg. 810
NORTH PARK LINCOLN MERCURY INC., pg. 813
NORTHWAY MOTORCAR CORPORATION, pg. 814
NORTOWN OLDSMOBILE INC., pg. 816
817
ROY O'BRIEN INC., pg. 820
OCEAN CHEVROLET, INC., pg. 820
ORANGE MOTOR COMPANY INC., pg. 828
BUTCH OUSTALET FORD SAAB, INC., pg. 832
OVERSEAS MILITARY SALES CORPORATION, pg. 833
PAR ENTERPRISES, INC., pg. 847
THE PARK CIRCLE MOTOR CO., pg. 848
PARK MOTOR SALES COMPANY, pg. 849
PARK PLACE MOTORCARS, pg. 849
PATSY'S, INC., pg. 851
PENSKE CORPORATION, pg. 859
PETERSON MOTOR COMPANY, pg. 865
POTAMKIN MANHATTAN, pg. 882
POTAMKIN TOYOTA, INC., pg. 882
LUKE POTTER DODGE INC., pg. 882
POWER ENGINEERING CO. INC., pg. 883
PROSPECT MOTORS, INC., pg. 895
PROSTROLLO MOTOR COMPANY, pg. 895
PROSTROLLO MOTOR SALES, INC.—Prostrollo Motor Company, pg. 895
PULLIAM MOTOR COMPANY, pg. 899
QUALITY PONTIAC, INC., pg. 904
QUEBEDEAUX PONTIAC, INC., pg. 904
RAPTON HONDA-GMC, pg. 913
GENE REED CHEVROLET, pg. 920
REED MOTORS, INC., pg. 920
REGENCY DODGE INC., pg. 922
REGENCY LINCOLN MERCURY, pg. 922
RELIABLE CHEVROLET, pg. 924
RICART FORD INC., pg. 931
RICHMOND MOTOR COMPANY, pg. 933
RICO MOTOR COMPANY, pg. 933
RINKE PONTIAC-GMC CO., pg. 935
ROSENTHAL AUTOMOTIVE ORGANIZATION, pg. 949
ROSENTHAL CHEVROLET CO., pg. 949
ROSEVILLE CHRYSLER PLYMOUTH INC., pg. 949
JACK ROSS MOTORS INC., pg. 949
BRUCE ROSSMEYER'S TOYOTALAND, pg. 950
ROUNDTREE AUTOMOTIVE GROUP, pg. 952
ROYAL JEEP EAGLE CHRYSLER PLYMOUTH, INC., pg. 953
ROYAL OAK FORD INC., pg. 953
ROYAL OLDSMOBILE MAZDA, INC., pg. 953
RUSSELL CHEVROLET COMPANY, pg. 957
RYAN OLDSMOBILE, pg. 958
ALLEN SAMUELS CHEVROLET GEO, pg. 969
SANDS MOTOR COMPANY, INC., pg. 970
SANTA MONICA FORD COMPANY, pg. 970
SATURN OF INDIANAPOLIS—Lockhart Cadillac Inc., pg. 680
SATURN OF PLYMOUTH—Don Massey Cadillac Inc., pg. 719
MIKE SAVOIE CHEVROLET INC., pg. 973
RON SAXON FORD, INC., pg. 973
SCHILLING MOTORS, INC.—Dealers Transport Company, Inc., pg. 322
DEAN SELLERS FORD INC., pg. 988
BOB SELLERS PONTIAC GMC TRUCK INC., pg. 988
SELOVER BUICK, INC., pg. 988
SENATOR FORD, pg. 989
SERVCO PACIFIC INC., pg. 991
SEWELL VILLAGE CADILLAC CO., pg. 993
L. B. SMITH, INC., pg. 1013
SMITH MOTORS, INC., pg. 1014
SOMERSET PONTIAC GMC INC., pg. 1017
SOUTHGATE FORD INC., pg. 1023
STEAKLEY CHEVROLET SUBARU INC., pg. 1043
STERLING HEIGHTS DODGE, INC., pg. 1046
STILLMAN & HOAG, INC., pg. 1049
SUNRISE NISSAN OF ORANGE PARK, pg. 1062
JAKE SWEENEY AUTOMOTIVE INC., pg. 1067
SWIFT DODGE ROLLS ROYCE INC., pg. 1067
SWOPE AUTOMOTIVE GROUP, INC., pg. 1068
DAVE SYVERSON TRUCK CENTER, INC.—Dave Syverson Lincoln Mercury, pg. 1071
DAVE SYVERSON LINCOLN MERCURY, pg. 1071
TAMAROFF BUICK INC., pg. 1077
CHARLIE THOMAS AUTO WORLD, pg. 1092
THOMSON MACCONNELL CADILLAC, INC., pg. 1095
TORCO OIL AUTOMOTIVE DIVISION—Torco Oil, pg. 1102
TORRANCE NISSAN, INC., pg. 1102
TOWN & COUNTRY FORD INC., pg. 1103
TRI-CITY OLDSMOBILE INC., pg. 1110
TRI-STATE MACK DISTRIBUTORS, pg. 1111
TRONCALLI MOTORS, INC., pg. 1115
TULLEY BUICK-PONTIAC COMPANY, INC., pg. 1119
TUNMORE OLDSMOBILE INC., pg. 1119
V.T. INC., pg. 1142
VALLEY PONTIAC BUICK GMC, INC., pg. 1143
VANDERGRIFF CHEVROLET GEO, pg. 1144
VILLAGE CAR COMPANY, pg. 1151
VILLAGE FORD INC., pg. 1151
VOGLER MOTOR COMPANY, INC., pg. 1154
VOLVO SALES & SERVICE CENTER, pg. 1155
VON HOUSEN MOTORS, pg. 1155
W.W. WALLWORK, INC., pg. 1161
WALSER AUTOMOTIVE CORPORATION, pg. 1161
WALSER FORD INC.—Walser Automotive Corporation, pg. 1161
WATKINS SYSTEM INC., pg. 1167
C. WEAVER CHEVROLET, INC., pg. 1170
WESTFALL GMC TRUCK INC., pg. 1182
WESTLIE MOTOR COMPANY, pg. 1183
BUFF WHELAN CHEVROLET & GEO, INC., pg. 1185
BILL WINK CHEVROLET & GEO, pg. 1196
WINTER VOLVO & LINCOLN MERCURY, pg. 1197
BILL WOESTE DEALER GROUP, pg. 1198
WOODFIN-SMITH PONTIAC, INC., pg. 1200
WOOLVERTON OLDSMOBILE-G.M.C. TRUCK, INC., pg. 1201
JEFF WYLER CHEVROLET DEALERSHIP—Jeff Wyler Dealer Group, Inc., pg. 1206
JEFF WYLER DEALER GROUP, INC., pg. 1206
JEFF WYLER NISSAN DEALERSHIP—Jeff Wyler Dealer Group, Inc., pg. 1206
YOUNG AUTOMOTIVE GROUP, pg. 1209

5521 — MOTOR VEHICLE DEALERS (USED CARS ONLY)

JACK DEMMER FORD, INC., pg. 328
MARMON-HERRINGTON COMPANY—The Marmon Group, Inc., pg. 711
RUSSELL CHEVROLET COMPANY, pg. 957
SOUTHEASTERN EQUIPMENT COMPANY, INC., pg. 1019

5531 — AUTO & HOME SUPPLY STORES

ADI WAREHOUSE DIVISION, CARQUEST CORP.—Carquest Corporation, pg. 224
A K H COMPANY, INC., pg. 4
A.P.S. SUPPLY, INC.—A.P.S., Inc., pg. 5
A S H, INC., pg. 8
J. AUSTIN OIL CO., pg. 99
AUTO GLASS SPECIALISTS, pg. 100
AUTOMOTIVE MARKETING ASSOC.—Carquest, pg. 224
AUTOMOTIVE SUPPLY ASSOC., INC., pg. 101
AUTOMOTIVE WAREHOUSE, INC.—Carquest Corporation, pg. 224
BWP DISTRIBUTORS, INC.—Carquest Corporation, pg. 224
BAUGHER CHEVROLET-BUICK-GEO, INC., pg. 127
BEACH CITY CHEVROLET CO., pg. 128
BELLE TIRE DISTRIBUTOR INC., pg. 136
BURRIS FOODS, INC., pg. 195
CCI CORPORATION, pg. 200
CARDIS CORPORATION—Carquest Corporation, pg. 224
CARQUEST, pg. 224
CARQUEST CORPORATION, pg. 224
COLE HERSEE COMPANY, pg. 260
COLEMAN CADILLAC INC., pg. 261
CONDERE CORPORATION, pg. 273
EARNHARDT'S AUTO CENTER, pg. 362
FLETCHER COBRE TIRE CO. INC.—Fletcher Enterprises, pg. 418
4DAY TIRE STORES, pg. 427
FREMONT ELECTRIC COMPANY—Carquest Corporation, pg. 224
FRIENDLY CHEVROLET CO. INC., pg. 433
GAY JOHNSON'S INC., pg. 446
GEBO DISTRIBUTING CO., INC., pg. 447
GEM TOP MFG., INC., pg. 448
GENERAL PARTS, INC.—Carquest Corporation, pg. 224
GLOSSER BROTHERS, INC.—Schottenstein Stores Corporation, pg. 978
HATCH GRINDING COMPANY—Carquest Corporation, pg. 225
J. KORBER & COMPANY, pg. 641
A.E. LOTTES COMPANY—Carquest Corporation, pg. 225
LUSTINE OLDSMOBILE & BUICK, INC., pg. 688
MCKENZIE TANK LINES, INC., pg. 730
MCNEILUS COMPANIES, pg. 732
MID AMERICA INTERNATIONAL TRUCKS, INC., pg. 750
MOLIN AUTO PARTS INC., pg. 764
MUFFLER WAREHOUSE, INC.—Carquest Corporation, pg. 225
MURRAY'S DISCOUNT AUTO STORES, pg. 777
NATIONWISE AUTOMOTIVE, INC., pg. 795
NORTHERN AUTOMOTIVE CORPORATION—The Trump Group, pg. 1118
NORTHERN PACIFIC CORPORATION—The Trump Group, pg. 1118
PSC DISTRIBUTING, INC.—Carquest Corporation, pg. 225
PARRISH TIRE COMPANY, INC., pg. 850
PARTS WHOLESALERS, INC.—Carquest Corporation, pg. 225
PATSY'S, INC., pg. 851
PENTRON PRODUCTS, INC.—Actron Manufacturing Company, pg. 15
QUAKER CITY MOTOR PARTS COMPANY, pg. 903
REINALT-THOMAS CORP., pg. 923
ROBBINS AUTO PARTS, INC., pg. 938
ROUNDTREE AUTOMOTIVE GROUP, pg. 952
RUSSELL CHEVROLET COMPANY, pg. 957
SANEL AUTO PARTS, INC.—Automotive Supply Assoc., Inc., pg. 101
SOUTHEASTERN EQUIPMENT COMPANY, INC., pg. 1019
SOUTHWESTERN EQUIPMENT CO.—Union Holdings, Inc., pg. 1128
STRAFCO—Carquest Corporation, pg. 225
STRAFCO, INC., pg. 1052
R & S STRAUSS, INC., pg. 1053
SUSSEN, INC.—Carquest Corporation, pg. 225
TSC INDUSTRIES, INC., pg. 1075
THOMSON MACCONNELL CADILLAC, INC., pg. 1095
TRAILER WHEEL & FRAME COMPANY, pg. 1105
TRANSCO INC., pg. 1107
TRONCALLI MOTORS, INC., pg. 1115
VON HOUSEN MOTORS, pg. 1155
W.W. WALLWORK, INC., pg. 1161
BUFF WHELAN CHEVROLET & GEO, INC., pg. 1185
WINSTON TIRE COMPANY, pg. 1197
ZIEBART INTERNATIONAL CORPORATION, pg. 1217
ZIEGLER TIRE & SUPPLY COMPANY, INC., pg. 1218

5541 — GASOLINE SERVICE STATIONS

ALLSUPS CONVENIENCE STORES INC., pg. 43
TRUMAN ARNOLD COMPANIES, pg. 84
ATEX OIL CO. OF TEXAS, INC., pg. 93
J. AUSTIN OIL CO., pg. 99
BELL GAS, INC., pg. 134
BESCHE OIL COMPANY, INC., pg. 145
BIG HORN CO-OP MARKETING ASSOCIATION, pg. 149
BRADFORD OIL COMPANY, INC., pg. 170
CAPITOL CHEVROLET CADILLAC GEO, INC., pg. 215
CARSE OIL CO. INC., pg. 225
CARTER COMPANIES, pg. 226
CONDON OIL COMPANY, INC., pg. 273
COWBOY OIL COMPANY, pg. 290
CRYSTAL FLASH PETROLEUM CORP., pg. 303
CUMBERLAND FARMS, INC., pg. 304
DAIGLE OIL CO., pg. 310
JIMMY DAVIS ENTERPRISES, INC., pg. 318
DEAD RIVER COMPANY, pg. 321
DIXIE OIL COMPANY, pg. 341
E-Z SERVE CORP., pg. 361
EMPIRE PETROLEUM, INC., pg. 379
ENGLEFIELD, INC., pg. 382
ENMARK STATIONS, INC.—Colonial Oil Industries, pg. 264
EQUITY SUPPLY COMPANY, pg. 385
ERICKSON OIL PRODUCTS, INC., pg. 386
FKG OIL COMPANY—Moto, Inc., pg. 773
FARM & HOME OIL COMPANY, pg. 401
FARM STORES, INC., pg. 401
FARMWAY CO-OP INC., pg. 402
FIRST MOUNT JOY CORPORATION, pg. 413
FISCA OIL CO., INC., pg. 414
FLYING J. INC., pg. 421
FOOD & GAS, INC., pg. 423
GATE PETROLEUM COMPANY, pg. 445
GREENWAY CO-OP SERVICE, pg. 485
GULF OIL—Cumberland Farms, Inc., pg. 304
FRED HARVEY TRANSPORTATION COMPANY—JMB Realty Corporation, pg. 585
HICKS OIL-HICKS GAS, INC., pg. 533
HIGH POINT OIL CO., pg. 534
HOLIDAY COMPANIES, pg. 539
HOLMQUIST GRAIN & LUMBER CO., pg. 540
HUDSON & AFFILIATED CO., pg. 551
ILLINOIS LIMITED PARTNERSHIP—Martin Exploration Management Company, pg. 715
JONES COMPANY, INC., pg. 603
KELSO OIL COMPANY, pg. 622
KING FUELS INC., pg. 630
KOCOLENE OIL CORP., pg. 639
KWICKIE/FLASH FOODS, INC.—Jones Company, Inc., pg. 603
MANSFIELD OIL COMPANY, pg. 704
MAVERIK COUNTRY STORES, INC., pg. 722
META PLANT FOOD—Fisca Oil Co., Inc., pg. 414
MID-KANSAS CO-OP ASSOCIATION, pg. 750
MID-STATES PETROLEUM INC., pg. 750
MIDWEST PETROLEUM CO., pg. 752
MONTE VISTA CO-OP ASSOCIATION, INC., pg. 766
MOTO, INC., pg. 773
NELLA OIL COMPANY, pg. 797
NORTHVILLE INDUSTRIES CORP., pg. 814
OLIVER OIL COMPANY, INC., pg. 824
THE PARMAN CORPORATION, pg. 850
PARMAN OIL CO.—The Parman Corporation, pg. 850
PIASA MOTOR FUELS INC., pg. 869
PIONEER OIL COMPANY INC., pg. 872
PRESTO FOOD STORES, INC., pg. 888

PRIDE OIL CO., INC.—Kelso Oil Company, pg. 622
R.T.M. WINNERS, pg. 908
RACETRAC PETROLEUM, INC., pg. 909
RAY-CARROLL COUNTY GRAIN CO-OP, pg. 914
RICHDALE DAIRY STORES, INC.—Scangas Brothers Holdings, Inc., pg. 974
F. L. ROBERTS & CO. INC., pg. 938
RUSSELL PETROLEUM CORPORATION, pg. 957
THE SICO COMPANY, pg. 1001
SINCLAIR OIL CORP., pg. 1008
SISCO COMPANY—First Mount Joy Corporation, pg. 413
SITE OIL CO. OF MISSOURI, pg. 1009
SMITH-SHAFER OIL CO., pg. 1014
SPENCER COMPANIES INC., pg. 1030
J. D. STREETT & CO., INC., pg. 1053
TAYLOR OIL CO. INC., pg. 1082
THOM THUMB FOOD MARKET INC.—Polka Dot Dairy, pg. 879
THORNTON OIL CORP., pg. 1095
TIME OIL COMPANY, pg. 1097
TOWN & COUNTRY FOOD MARKETS, INC., pg. 1103
TOWN PUMP, INC., pg. 1104
TRANSCO INC., pg. 1107
TRANSPORT SERVICE OF INDIANA, INC.—Mayflower Transit, Inc., pg. 725
TRITON INC., pg. 1114
TRUCK WORLD INC., pg. 1117
U PUMP 'EM—Victory Markets Inc., pg. 1150
USA PETROLEUM CORPORATION, pg. 1124
UNITED ACQUISITION CORPORATION, pg. 1130
UNITED REFINING COMPANY—United Acquisition Corporation, pg. 1130
VICTORY MARKETS INC., pg. 1150
WESTERN STATES PETROLEUM INC., pg. 1181
WICKLAND CORPORATION, pg. 1188
WICKLAND OIL COMPANY, INC.—Wickland Corporation, pg. 1188
YODER OIL COMPANY INC., pg. 1208
YOUNGSTOWN TIRE & SUPPLY COMPANY—Ziegler Tire & Supply Company, Inc., pg. 1218

5551 — BOAT DEALERS

BILL COLLINS FORD INC., pg. 263
FISHERIES SUPPLY COMPANY, pg. 415
KETTENBURG MARINE CORPORATION, pg. 626
MINNETONKA BOAT WORKS—Minstar, Inc., pg. 758
MINSTAR, INC., pg. 758
REX MARINE CENTER, INC., pg. 930
TOLLYCRAFT YACHTS CORP., pg. 1100

5561 — RECREATIONAL VEHICLE DEALERS

DAVIS-MOORE OLDSMOBILE, INC., pg. 319
DAVIS-MOORE RECREATIONAL VEHICLE CENTER—Davis-Moore Oldsmobile, Inc., pg. 319
EARNHARDT'S AUTO CENTER, pg. 362
MIKE DAUGHERTY'S HURLING CHEVROLET, INC., pg. 555
LA MESA R V CENTER, INC., pg. 649
LANCE CAMPER MANUFACTURING CORPORATION, pg. 653
LAZY DAYS R V CENTER, INC., pg. 663

5571 — MOTORCYCLE DEALERS

ALLEN SAMUELS CHEVROLET GEO, pg. 969

5599 — AUTOMOTIVE DEALERS, NEC

ATHLETIC ATTIC PROPERTIES INC., pg. 94
CUTTER FLYING SERVICE, INC., pg. 307
ALLEN SAMUELS CHEVROLET GEO, pg. 969
TRAILER WHEEL & FRAME COMPANY, pg. 1105
USA PETROLEUM CORPORATION, pg. 1124

5611 — MEN'S & BOYS' CLOTHING & ACCESSORY STORES

BARNEYS NEW YORK, pg. 120
BIGSBY & KRUTHERS, INC., pg. 150
DICK BRUHN INC., pg. 184
D&L VENTURE CORP., pg. 307
FASHION BAR INC.—Specialty Retailers, Inc., pg. 1029
GINGISS INTERNATIONAL, pg. 460
GUESS ?, INC., pg. 493
TOM JAMES COMPANY, pg. 589
TOM JAMES OF ATLANTA, INC.—Tom James Company, pg. 589
JEFFREY MICHAEL, pg. 591
L.L. BEAN, INC., pg. 648
LEVI STRAUSS EMPLOYEE PURCHASE PLAN, INC.—Levi Strauss & Co., pg. 670
HENRY MODELL & COMPANY, INC., pg. 762
MORLEY SHIRT COMPANY—Custom Shop Shirtmakers Inc., pg. 306
NBO STORES INC., pg. 780
POLO/RALPH LAUREN CORPORATION, pg. 879
RETAIL VENTURES, INC., pg. 929
RIKLIS FAMILY CORPORATION, pg. 934
MARK SHALE, pg. 994
SUPERBA, INC., pg. 1063
ULTIMO LTD., pg. 1125
WINONA KNITS, pg. 1196

5621 — WOMEN'S CLOTHING STORES

A & E STORES, INC., pg. 1
BARNEYS NEW YORK, pg. 120
BRAUNS FASHIONS, INC., pg. 172
DICK BRUHN INC., pg. 184
THE CHEROKEE GROUP, pg. 243
D&L VENTURE CORP., pg. 307
FASHION BAR INC.—Specialty Retailers, Inc., pg. 1029
FASHION SHOP OF KENTUCKY INC., pg. 403
FIVE DOLLAR CLOTHING STORES, pg. 416
GUESS ?, INC., pg. 493
KALIN ENTERPRISES, INC., pg. 615
L.L. BEAN, INC., pg. 648
PRANGE SPECIALTY STORES GROUP, INC.—H. C. Prange Company, pg. 884
LILLIE RUBIN AFFILIATES INC., pg. 954
MARK SHALE, pg. 994
SMARTY PANTS N TOPS TOO, INC., pg. 1011
THIMBLES SPECIALTY STORES, INC.—H. C. Prange Company, pg. 884
THE TOG SHOP, pg. 1100
ULTIMO LTD., pg. 1125
VOGUE & BODY SHOPS, INC., pg. 1154
WINDSOR FASHIONS, pg. 1195
WINONA KNITS, pg. 1196

5632 — WOMEN'S ACCESSORY & SPECIALTY STORES

A & E STORES, INC., pg. 1
BEHR STORES INC., pg. 132
DICK BRUHN INC., pg. 184
CWT SPECIALTY STORES, INC.—Peter W. Smith & Company, Inc., pg. 1011
DEERSKIN TRADING POST, INC., pg. 324
DENISE LINGERIE—House of Ronnie, Inc., pg. 546
FIVE DOLLAR CLOTHING STORES, pg. 416
GATEWAY APPAREL, INC., pg. 445
HELPERN JOAN & DAVID, INC., pg. 528
HEYMAN CORPORATION, pg. 532
HOUSE OF RONNIE, INC., pg. 546
MARGO'S LA MODE, INC.—The Elder-Beerman Stores Corp., pg. 373
THE ORMOND SHOPS, INC., pg. 830
PACIFIC HIDE & FUR DEPOT, pg. 840
PARKLANE HOSIERY CO., INC., pg. 849
POLLACK CORPORATION, pg. 879
POLO/RALPH LAUREN CORPORATION, pg. 879
H. C. PRANGE COMPANY, pg. 884
RAINBOW APPAREL DISTRIBUTION CENTER, pg. 910
STANDARD SHOE COMPANY, pg. 1037
TAREN HOLDINGS, INC., pg. 1078
WINDSOR FASHIONS, pg. 1195

5641 — CHILDREN'S & INFANTS' WEAR STORES

BAMBINAGGINE—Doe Spun, Inc., pg. 343
THE CHILDREN'S PLACE RETAIL STORES, INC., pg. 247
MIA BAMBINI—Doe Spun, Inc., pg. 343

5651 — FAMILY CLOTHING STORES

ABDALLA'S LAFAYETTE, INC., pg. 10
C. R. ANTHONY COMPANY, pg. 77
C. R. ANTHONY INTERNATIONAL, LTD.—C. R. Anthony Company, pg. 77
ANTHONY'S OF SANDPOINT, INC.—C. R. Anthony Company, pg. 77
ANTHONY'S OF SLEEPY EYE, INC.—C. R. Anthony Company, pg. 77
ANTHONY'S OF SPRING VALLEY, INC.—C. R. Anthony Company, pg. 77
BURNSTAD BROTHERS, INC., pg. 194
DAWAHARES, INC., pg. 319
GEBO DISTRIBUTING CO., INC., pg. 447
GENERAL TEXTILES, pg. 451
GLOSSER BROTHERS, INC.—Schottenstein Stores Corporation, pg. 978
HENRYS, INC., pg. 530
JUST PANTS, pg. 610
MADIGAN BROTHERS, INC., pg. 699
SAGE-ALLEN & CO., INC., pg. 966
SOUTHERN APPAREL CORPORATION, pg. 1020
STONE MANUFACTURING COMPANY, INC., pg. 1051
WINONA KNITS, pg. 1196

5661 — SHOE STORES

ALTIER & SONS SHOES INC., pg. 45
THE ATHLETE'S FOOT GROUP, INC., pg. 94
ATHLETIC ATTIC PROPERTIES INC., pg. 94
BEE-GEE SHOE DIV.—The Elder-Beerman Stores Corp., pg. 373
CHB CORP., pg. 201
CHERNIN'S SHOES, pg. 243
CHEYENNE OUTFITTERS, INC., pg. 244
COWTOWN BOOT COMPANY, pg. 291
DEERSKIN TRADING POST, INC., pg. 324
THE ELDER-BEERMAN STORES CORP., pg. 373
FAYVA—Morse Shoe, Inc., pg. 772
GENERAL TEXTILES, pg. 451
GUSSINI SHOE STORES—The Kobacker Company & Affiliates, pg. 638
HELPERN JOAN & DAVID, INC., pg. 528
HENRYS, INC., pg. 530
KATHE-K SHOE STORES—The Kobacker Company & Affiliates, pg. 638
THE KOBACKER COMPANY & AFFILIATES, pg. 638
L.L. BEAN, INC., pg. 648
HENRY MODELL & COMPANY, INC., pg. 762
MORSE SHOE, INC., pg. 772
MORSE SHOE LEASED DIV.—Morse Shoe, Inc., pg. 772
NINE WEST GROUP, INC., pg. 807
PATRINI SHOE STORES—The Kobacker Company & Affiliates, pg. 638
PIC'N PAY STORES, INC.—CHB Corp., pg. 201
PICWAY SHOE STORES—The Kobacker Company & Affiliates, pg. 638
JOHN REYER COMPANY, pg. 930
SHOE-TOWN, INC., pg. 999
THE SHOE WORKS SHOE STORES, INC.—The Kobacker Company & Affiliates, pg. 638
SHOEMART EXPRESS—Chernin's Shoes, pg. 243
SHONAC CORPORATION, pg. 1000
STANDARD SHOE COMPANY, pg. 1037
TRADEHOME SHOE STORES, INC., pg. 1105
WEXNER & JACOBSON, INC., pg. 1183
WINDSOR FASHIONS, pg. 1195

5699 — MISCELLANEOUS APPAREL & ACCESSORY STORES

CHEYENNE OUTFITTERS, INC., pg. 244
CUSTOM SHOP SHIRTMAKERS INC., pg. 306
DUNHAM'S ATHLEISURE CORPORATION, pg. 353
GATEWAY APPAREL, INC., pg. 445
GROSSENBURG IMPLEMENTS, INCORPORATED, pg. 489
JAZZERCISE, INC., pg. 591
LUSKEYS WESTERN STORES, INC., pg. 688
NORCOSTCO, INC., pg. 809
PENDLETON WOOLEN MILLS, INC., pg. 857
RECREATIONAL EQUIPMENT, INC., pg. 917
RETAIL VENTURES, INC., pg. 929
I. SPIEWAK & SONS, INC., pg. 1031
PAUL STUART, INC., pg. 1054

5712 — FURNITURE STORES

AMERICAN FURNITURE COMPANY, pg. 55
AMERICAN TV & APPLIANCE OF MADISON, INC., pg. 65
ARNOLDS INTERIORS, INC., pg. 85
ART VAN FURNITURE INC., pg. 86
ATLANTIC TO PACIFIC BEDDING CORP., pg. 95
BKM ENTERPRISES, INC., pg. 107
BKM TOTAL OFFICE TODAY, INC.—BKM Enterprises, Inc., pg. 107
W.S. BADCOCK CORPORATION, pg. 113
DEARDEN'S, INC., pg. 322
DOOR STORE, INC., pg. 346
THE ELDER-BEERMAN STORES CORP., pg. 373
EUROMARKET DESIGNS, INC., pg. 390
FINGER FURNITURE COMPANY, INC., pg. 411
L. FISH CORPORATION, pg. 414
GABBERT'S, INC., pg. 441
GEM INDUSTRIES, INC.—Gem Industries Finance Corporation, pg. 447
GOLDSMITHS, INC., pg. 469
GRANTREE CORPORATION, pg. 477
HOMESTEAD HOUSE INC., pg. 542
HUB FURNITURE CO.—Reliable Stores, Inc., pg. 925
HUFFMAN KOOS CO., pg. 551
JENNIFER CONVERTIBLES INC., pg. 592
KALIN ENTERPRISES, INC., pg. 615
KEMP FURNITURE CO.—Coastal Lumber Company, pg. 257
MORRIS KIRSCHMAN & COMPANY, INC., pg. 633
THE KLINE FURNITURE CO.—Reliable Stores, Inc., pg. 925
KNOLLOFFICE, INC.—21 International Holdings, Inc., pg. 1121
LFC HOLDING CORPORATION, pg. 647
LEVITZ FURNITURE CORPORATION—LFC Holding Corporation, pg. 647
LUSK INTERIORS, INC.—The Lusk Company, pg. 688
MARKS-FITZGERALD FURNITURE CO.—Rhodes, Inc., pg. 931
ED MARLING STORES, INC., pg. 710
MOHAWK FURNITURE, INC.—Gem Industries Finance Corporation, pg. 447
NELSON BROTHERS FURNITURE CO., pg. 797
B. OLINDE & SONS COMPANY, INC., pg. 824
RELIABLE STORES, INC., pg. 925
RHODES, INC., pg. 931
RUTT CUSTOM CABINETRY, pg. 957
SEAMAN FURNITURE CO., INC., pg. 986
SERVCO PACIFIC INC., pg. 991
SHAPELL INDUSTRIES, INC., pg. 995
SKINNER CORP., pg. 1009
JOHN M. SMYTH CO., pg. 1014
STROUDS, pg. 1054
VENTA INC., pg. 1147
D. WALDNER COMPANY, INC., pg. 1159
WAREHOUSE HOME FURNISHINGS DISTRIBUTOR, pg. 1163
R.C. WILLEY HOME FURNISHINGS, pg. 1190

5713 — FLOOR COVERING STORES

W.S. BADCOCK CORPORATION, pg. 113
CARPETERIA, INC., pg. 224
COLOR YOUR WORLD, INC.—21 International Holdings, Inc., pg. 1121
DESIGN CENTER—Del Webb's Coventry, pg. 1171
EINSTEIN MOOMJY INC., pg. 371
L. FISH CORPORATION, pg. 414
LUSK INTERIORS, INC.—The Lusk Company, pg. 688
MAUTZ PAINT COMPANY, pg. 722
MCSWAIN CARPETS INC., pg. 733
NELSON BROTHERS FURNITURE CO., pg. 797
NEW YORK CARPET WORLD INC., pg. 802
OLSON RUG COMPANY, pg. 824
RAYMOND ROSEN CO., pg. 948

5714 — DRAPERY, CURTAIN & UPHOLSTERY STORES

CALICO CORNERS, pg. 209
CHARLES CURTAIN COMPANY, INC., pg. 239
LUSK INTERIORS, INC.—The Lusk Company, pg. 688
MAUTZ PAINT COMPANY, pg. 722
SAXON PAINT & HOME CARE CENTERS INC., pg. 973

5719 — MISCELLANEOUS HOMEFURNISHING STORES

ADRAY APPLIANCE & PHOTO CENTER, INC., pg. 18
W.E. AUBUCHON CO., INC., pg. 97
BEST PRODUCTS CO., INC.—Adler & Shaykin, pg. 17
BETTER LIVING INC., pg. 148
CHARLES CURTAIN COMPANY, INC., pg. 239
CUTLERY WORLD—Hoffritz for Cutlery, pg. 538
DUANE READE, pg. 350
EUROMARKET DESIGNS, INC., pg. 390
FINGER FURNITURE COMPANY, INC., pg. 411
FORTUNOFF, pg. 425
GEBO DISTRIBUTING CO., INC., pg. 447
GEORGETOWN INDUSTRIES, INC., pg. 453
HAMMACHER, SCHLEMMER & CO., INC., pg. 503
HOFFRITZ FOR CUTLERY, pg. 538
HOFFRITZ INTERNATIONAL—Hoffritz for Cutlery, pg. 538
HOMEMAKER SHOPS, INC., pg. 542
HOMESTEAD HOUSE INC., pg. 542
LAPPIN ELECTRIC COMPANY, pg. 658
LEEWARDS CREATIVE CRAFTS, INC., pg. 666
LINENS & MORE—Homemaker Shops, Inc., pg. 542
LUSK INTERIORS, INC.—The Lusk Company, pg. 688
MICO, INC., pg. 748
OLD AMERICAN POTTERY COMPANY, pg. 823
OSTROW TEXTILE CO., INC., pg. 831
H. C. PRANGE COMPANY, pg. 884
SAXON PAINT & HOME CARE CENTERS INC., pg. 973
SLEEPY'S THE MATTRESS PROFESSIONALS, pg. 1010
STROUDS, pg. 1054
TOC RETAIL, INC.—E-Z Serve Corp., pg. 362
THOMPSON ENTERPRISES INC., pg. 1094
WACCAMAW CORPORATION—Georgetown Industries, Inc., pg. 453
WANG'S INTERNATIONAL, INC., pg. 1162

5722 — HOUSEHOLD APPLIANCE STORES

A B C APPLIANCE INC., pg. 2
ADRAY APPLIANCE & PHOTO CENTER, INC., pg. 18
AMERICAN FURNITURE COMPANY, pg. 55
AMERICAN TV & APPLIANCE OF MADISON, INC., pg. 65
W.S. BADCOCK CORPORATION, pg. 113
BEST PRODUCTS CO., INC.—Adler & Shaykin, pg. 17
CALIFORNIA ELECTRIC SERVICE, pg. 209
DEARDEN'S, INC., pg. 322
FILCO, INC., pg. 409
GREGG APPLIANCES INC., pg. 486
GROSSENBURG IMPLEMENTS, INCORPORATED, pg. 489
HOWARDS APPLIANCES, INC., pg. 547
MORRIS KIRSCHMAN & COMPANY, INC., pg. 633
LECHMERE, INC., pg. 665
LYKES ENERGY, INC., pg. 689
ED MARLING STORES, INC., pg. 710
MASEK DISTRIBUTING INC., pg. 717
MIDWEST BOTTLE GAS COMPANY—Consolidated Midwest, Inc., pg. 277
MOLLENBERG-BETZ INC., pg. 764
NELSON BROTHERS FURNITURE CO., pg. 797
PALMER ELECTRIC CO., pg. 843
REMINGTON PRODUCTS INC., pg. 926
SISCO COMPANY—First Mount Joy Corporation, pg. 413
STANDARD BRANDS OF AMERICA, INC., pg. 1035
R.C. WILLEY HOME FURNISHINGS, pg. 1190

5731 — RADIO, TELEVISION & CONSUMER ELECTRONIC STORES

ADRAY APPLIANCE & PHOTO CENTER, INC., pg. 18
AUDIO SPECIALIST, INC., pg. 98
W.S. BADCOCK CORPORATION, pg. 113
BEST PRODUCTS CO., INC.—Adler & Shaykin, pg. 17
DEARDEN'S, INC., pg. 322
GREGG APPLIANCES INC., pg. 486
HOWARDS APPLIANCES, INC., pg. 547
LIBERTY MILITARY SALES CO., pg. 674
MAGNOLIA HI-FI, INC., pg. 701
ED MARLING STORES, INC., pg. 710
CURTIS MATHES CORPORATION, pg. 720
SAVEMART INC., pg. 973
SERVCO PACIFIC INC., pg. 991
STANDARD BRANDS OF AMERICA, INC., pg. 1035
R.C. WILLEY HOME FURNISHINGS, pg. 1190
WILLOUGHBY'S, pg. 1193

5734 — COMPUTER & COMPUTER SOFTWARE STORES

THE ASCII GROUP, INC., pg. 8
BASIC COMPUTER, pg. 124
THE COMPUTER PATCH OF JOPLIN—Stauffer Communications, Inc., pg. 1043
COMPUTERLAND CANADA LTD.—ComputerLand Corporation, pg. 271
COMPUTERLAND CORPORATION, pg. 271
EL CAMINO RESOURCES, LTD., pg. 372
ELEK-TEK, INC., pg. 375
FIRST COMPUTER CORPORATION, pg. 412
GATEWAY 2000, pg. 446
GRAMEX CORPORATION, pg. 475
H W ELECTRONICS, INC., pg. 497
LA COMPUTER CENTER, pg. 648
MICRO ELECTRONICS, pg. 748
NEW YORK SYSTEMS EXCHANGE CORP.—Syracuse Supply Company, pg. 1070
OSC CORPORATION D/B/A OLYMPIC SALES CO., pg. 819
SUN COMPUTERS, INC., pg. 1058
WILLOUGHBY'S, pg. 1193

5735 — RECORD & PRERECORDED TAPE STORES

BRODBECK ENTERPRISES, INC., pg. 178
EASTON PRESS VIDEOS—MBI Inc., pg. 691
HARMONY HOUSE RECORDS & TAPES, pg. 510
MTS, INC., pg. 694
NIGHTINGALE-CONANT CORP., pg. 807
SERVCO PACIFIC INC., pg. 991
SOUND WAREHOUSE, INC., pg. 1018
SUPER CLUB MUSIC CORP., pg. 1062
TOWER RECORDS—MTS, Inc., pg. 694

5736 — MUSICAL INSTRUMENT STORES

FILCO, INC., pg. 409
G. LEBLANC CORPORATION, pg. 665
PAUL A. SCHMITT MUSIC COMPANY, pg. 976

5812 — EATING PLACES

A & W RESTAURANTS, INC., pg. 1
A.B.P. MIDWEST, INC., pg. 2
ARA/CORY REFRESHMENT SERVICES, INC.—ARA Group, pg. 6
ARA FOOD SERVICES, LTD.—ARA Group, pg. 7
ARA GROUP, pg. 5
ARA HEALTHCARE NUTRITION SERVICES, INC.—ARA Group, pg. 6
ARA LEISURE CONVENTION SERVICES, INC.—ARA Group, pg. 6
ARA LEISURE SERVICES GROUP, FLORIDA—ARA Group, pg. 6
ARA LEISURE SERVICES, HAWTHORNE RACE COURSE—ARA Group, pg. 6
ARA LEISURE SERVICES, INC.—ARA Group, pg. 6
ARA LEISURE SERVICES, NEW ORLEANS CONVENTION CENTER—ARA Group, pg. 6
ARA LEISURE SERVICES OF TEXAS, INC.—ARA Group, pg. 6
ARA LEISURE SERVICES, RIVERGATE—ARA Group, pg. 6
ARA LEISURE SERVICES, SOLDIER FIELD—ARA Group, pg. 6
ARA LEISURE SERVICES, WRIGLEY FIELD—ARA Group, pg. 6
ARA SERVICES, INC.—ARA Group, pg. 5
ARA SERVICES, JOHN HANCOCK CENTER—ARA Group, pg. 6
ARA SERVICES, LOYOLA UNIVERSITY—ARA Group, pg. 6
ARA SERVICES, ROSEMONT HORIZON—ARA Group, pg. 6
ARA VIRGINIA SKY-LINE CO., INC.—ARA Group, pg. 6
AERO ENTERPRISES, INC.—ARA Group, pg. 6
ALL SEASONS SERVICES, INC., pg. 35
AMERICAN RESTAURANT GROUP, INC., pg. 60
AMERICAN SNACKS, INC., pg. 61
ARASERVE, INC.—ARA Group, pg. 6
ATLANTA HILL RESTAURANT CORP.—Specialty Restaurants Corporation, pg. 1028
ATLAS HOTELS, INC., pg. 96
BJ ACQUISITION CORP., pg. 107
BELL GARDENS BICYCLE CLUB, pg. 134
BERKELEY MARINA RESTAURANT CORP.—Specialty Restaurants Corporation, pg. 1028
BIG BOY RESTAURANT SYSTEM—Elias Brothers Restaurants, Inc., pg. 376
BIG CHEESE PIZZA CORPORATION—Godfather's Pizza, Inc., pg. 464
BIRMINGHAM HILL RESTAURANT CORP.—Specialty Restaurants Corporation, pg. 1028
BLUE BOAR CAFETERIA CO., pg. 158
BODDIE-NOELL ENTERPRISES INC., pg. 161
BONANZA RESTAURANTS—Metromedia Company, pg. 744
BONKERS, INC.—Victoria Station Incorporated, pg. 1150
BOSTON CHICKEN, INC., pg. 167
BOURY INCORPORATED, pg. 168
BOWLING CORP. OF AMERICA—Charan Industries, Inc., pg. 239
BRAUM ICE CREAM STORES INC., pg. 172
BRESLER'S INDUSTRIES, INC., pg. 174
BRIDGEMAN'S RESTAURANTS INC., pg. 175
BRODBECK ENTERPRISES, INC., pg. 178
BROWN DERBY, INC., pg. 181
BUB CITY CRABSHACK & BAR-B-Q—Lettuce Entertain You Enterprises, Inc., pg. 669
BUFFALO WATERFRONT RESTAURANT CORP.—Specialty Restaurants Corporation, pg. 1029
CAFE BA-BA-REEBA—Lettuce Entertain You Enterprises, Inc., pg. 669
CANDLESTICK WATERFRONT REST. CORP.—Specialty Restaurants Corporation, pg. 1028
CARLSON COMPANIES, INC., pg. 220
CAROUSEL SNACK BARS OF MINNESOTA, pg. 224
CARROLS CORPORATION, pg. 225
CARROWS RESTAURANTS, INC.—Restaurant Enterprises Group, Inc., pg. 929
CASA LUPITA RESTAURANTS, INC.—Metromedia Company, pg. 744
CASSANO'S INC., pg. 228
CASUDA CANYON RESTAURANT CORP.—Specialty Restaurants Corporation, pg. 1028
CATERAIR HOLDINGS CORP., pg. 229
CATERAIR INTERNATIONAL—Caterair Holdings Corp., pg. 229
CHATTANOOGA CHOO-CHOO HOLIDAY INN, pg. 241
CHEF ITALIA, INC., pg. 241
CHESAPEAKE FINANCIAL CORP., pg. 243
CHICK-FIL-A, INC., pg. 247
CHILI PEPPER OF ROCKY POINT, INC.—Specialty Restaurants Corporation, pg. 1028
CHURCH'S FRIED CHICKEN, INC.—Al Copeland Enterprises, Inc., pg. 284
P. J. CLARKE'S—Lettuce Entertain You Enterprises, Inc., pg. 669
COLORADO AIR RESTAURANT CORP.—Specialty Restaurants Corporation, pg. 1028
COLUMBIA SUSSEX CORPORATION, pg. 266
CONCESSION AIR CORPORATION—Delaware North Companies, Inc., pg. 326
AL COPELAND ENTERPRISES, INC., pg. 283
COYOTE RESTAURANT CORP.—Specialty Restaurants Corporation, pg. 1028
DARIGOLD, INC., pg. 315
JIMMY DAVIS ENTERPRISES, INC., pg. 318
DE NOVO CORPORATION, pg. 321
ED DEBEVIC'S OF ARIZONA—Lettuce Entertain You Enterprises, Inc., pg. 669
ED DEBEVIC'S—Lettuce Entertain You Enterprises, Inc., pg. 669
ED DEBEVIC'S—Lettuce Entertain You Enterprises, Inc., pg. 669
ED DEBEVIC'S/SHORT ORDERS DELUXE/PHOENIX—Lettuce Entertain You Enterprises, Inc., pg. 669
ED DEBEVIC'S/SHORT ORDERS DELUXE/TORRANCE—Lettuce Entertain You Enterprises, Inc., pg. 669
DEL REY RESTAURANT CORP.—Specialty Restaurants Corporation, pg. 1028
DELAWARE NORTH COMPANIES, INC., pg. 326
DENVER BABY DOE'S REST. CORP.—Specialty Restaurants Corporation, pg. 1028
DENVER FREEWAY RESTAURANT CORP.—Specialty Restaurants Corporation, pg. 1028
DOMINO'S PIZZA INC., pg. 344
DON AND CHARLIE'S—Lettuce Entertain You Enterprises, Inc., pg. 669
DRUTHER'S INTERNATIONAL, INC., pg. 350
DUNES HOTELS AND CASINOS INC., pg. 352
EAT N PARK RESTAURANTS, pg. 364
EL PASO RESTAURANT CORP.—Specialty Restaurants Corporation, pg. 1028
EL TORITO RESTAURANTS, INC.—Restaurant Enterprises Group, Inc., pg. 929
EL TORITO RESTAURANTS, INC., pg. 372
ELIAS BROTHERS RESTAURANTS, INC., pg. 376
EUSTON STATION, INC.—Victoria Station Incorporated, pg. 1150
FMS MANAGEMENT SYSTEMS, INC., pg. 394
FAIR LANES INC., pg. 396
FAMILY INNS OF AMERICA, INC., pg. 398
FAR WEST CONCEPTS, INC.—Restaurant Enterprises Group, Inc., pg. 929
57TH FIGHTER GROUP OF ATLANTA, INC.—Specialty Restaurants Corporation, pg. 1028
56TH FIGHTER GROUP OF LONG ISLAND, INC.—Specialty Restaurants Corporation, pg. 1029
FIVE CROWNS—Lawry's Restaurants, Inc., pg. 663
FRANCHISE ENTERPRISES INC., pg. 428
FRIENDLY ICE CREAM CORP.—Tennessee Restaurant Corp., pg. 1087
GRC RESTAURANTS, INC.—Restaurant Enterprises Group, Inc., pg. 929
GALARDI GROUP, INC., pg. 441
GAY JOHNSON'S INC., pg. 446
GILBERT/ROBINSON, INC., pg. 458
GINO'S EAST/ROLLING MEADOWS—Lettuce Entertain You Enterprises, Inc., pg. 669
GODFATHER'S PIZZA, INC., pg. 464
GOLDEN CORRAL CORPORATION, pg. 466
GOLF HOST RESORTS, INC.—Golf Hosts, Inc., pg. 469
A. GRACE DEVELOPMENT, pg. 474
GRANDY'S, INC., pg. 476
GREEN LEAF VENTURES, INC., pg. 484
GRISANTI, INC., pg. 488
GROWTH MANAGEMENT CORP.—Family Inns of America, Inc., pg. 398
GUEST SERVICES, INC., pg. 493
HDS SERVICES, pg. 496
HAMBURGER HAMLETS INC.—Weatherly Financial Group, pg. 1169
HARRIS FARMS, INC., pg. 511
HARRIS RANCH RESTAURANT—Harris Farms, Inc., pg. 512
HASSLOCHER ENTERPRISES, INC., D/B/A FRONTIER ENTERPRISES, pg. 516
HAT DANCE—Lettuce Entertain You Enterprises, Inc., pg. 669
HELMSLEY ENTERPRISES, INC., pg. 527
HELMSLEY-SPEAR INC.—Helmsley Enterprises, Inc., pg. 527
HIGH INDUSTRIES INC., pg. 533
HOLLY'S INC., pg. 540
IN-N-OUT BURGERS, pg. 564
INNCO MANAGEMENT CORP.—Family Inns of America, Inc., pg. 398
INVESTOR'S MANAGEMENT CORP., pg. 581
IRELAND GOURMET SHOP—Ireland Coffee Tea, Inc., pg. 582
JRN, INC., pg. 586
JACKSONVILLE CRAWDADDY CORP.—Specialty Restaurants Corporation, pg. 1028
JACMAR COMPANIES, INC., pg. 587

JERRICO, INC.—Castle-Harlan, Inc., pg. 229
W.B. JOHNSON PROPERTY, INC., pg. 598
KETTLE RESTAURANTS, pg. 626
KNOTT'S BERRY FARM, pg. 637
KRYSTAL COMPANY, pg. 645
LA ROSA'S, INC., pg. 649
LAMP POST FRANCHISE CORPORATION, pg. 652
LANDMARK HOTEL CORPORATION, pg. 656
LARKEN INC., pg. 659
LAWRY'S RESTAURANTS, INC., pg. 663
LETTUCE ENTERTAIN YOU ENTERPRISES, INC., pg. 668
THE LEVY ORGANIZATION, pg. 672
LEVY RESTAURANTS—The Levy Organization, pg. 672
LITTLE CAESAR ENTERPRISES, INC., pg. 678
LONG JOHN SILVER'S, INC.—Castle-Harlan, Inc., pg. 229
LOVE'S ENTERPRISES, INC., pg. 685
LUCKY INNS OF AMERICA, INC.—Family Inns of America, Inc., pg. 398
LYON'S RESTAURANTS, INC., pg. 690
MAGIC PAN INTERNATIONAL INC., pg. 700
MAJOR FOODS LTD.—ARA Group, pg. 7
MALL ENTERTAINMENT USA—Specialty Restaurants Corporation, pg. 1028
MALL ENTERTAINMENT USA—Specialty Restaurants Corporation, pg. 1028
MARKETING CORP. OF AMERICA, pg. 709
MCCRORY STORES DIV.—Riklis Family Corporation, pg. 934
MCGUFFEY'S RESTAURANTS, INC., pg. 729
MCLEAN ENTERPRISES, INC., pg. 731
MEDIEVAL DINNER & TOURNAMENT, INC., pg. 735
METROMEDIA STEAKHOUSES, INC.—Metromedia Company, pg. 744
MILE HIGH ENTERPRISES, INC.—ARA Group, pg. 6
MISSION HILLS RESTAURANT CORP.—Specialty Restaurants Corporation, pg. 1028
MRS. WINNER'S CHICKEN & BISCUIT RESTAURANTS, pg. 761
MONARCH FOODS, INC.—Shakey's Incorporated, pg. 994
MONTEREY'S TEX MEX CAFE, pg. 767
C. A. MUER CORP., pg. 774
NATHAN'S FAMOUS INC., pg. 784
NEW ORLEANS WATERFRONT REST. CORP.—Specialty Restaurants Corporation, pg. 1028
NEW TEXAS TUMBLEWEED, pg. 802
94TH AERO SQUADRON OF COLUMBUS, INC.—Specialty Restaurants Corporation, pg. 1029
94TH AERO SQUADRON OF MIAMI, INC.—Specialty Restaurants Corporation, pg. 1028
94TH AERO SQUADRON OF ORLANDO, INC.—Specialty Restaurants Corporation, pg. 1028
94TH AERO SQUADRON OF PALWAUKEE, INC.—Specialty Restaurants Corporation, pg. 1028
94TH AERO SQUADRON OF PINELLAS COUNTY, INC.—Specialty Restaurants Corporation, pg. 1028
94TH AERO SQUADRON RESTAURANT, INC.—Specialty Restaurants Corporation, pg. 1028
94TH AERO SQUADRON OF SAN JOSE, INC.—Specialty Restaurants Corporation, pg. 1028
94TH AERO SQUADRON OF SARASOTA, INC.—Specialty Restaurants Corporation, pg. 1028
94TH AERO SQUADRON OF TORRANCE, INC.—Specialty Restaurants Corporation, pg. 1028
94TH AS OF WEST PALM BEACH, INC.—Specialty Restaurants Corporation, pg. 1028
94TH OF COLLEGE PARK, INC.—Specialty Restaurants Corporation, pg. 1028
NINETY-FOURTH OF ST. LOUIS, INC.—Specialty Restaurants Corporation, pg. 1028
NORTH DENVER HILL CORP.—Specialty Restaurants Corporation, pg. 1028
NORTH PIER ASSOCIATES—Specialty Restaurants Corporation, pg. 1028
ORANGE HILL RESTAURANT CORP.—Specialty Restaurants Corporation, pg. 1028
P.F.D. SUPPLY CORP.—Prairie Farms Dairy, Inc., pg. 884
PAPOULIS GREEK TAVERNA—Lettuce Entertain You Enterprises, Inc., pg. 669
PARNELL FOODS LTD.—ARA Group, pg. 7
PEDUS FOOD SERVICES—Pedus Services, Inc., pg. 855
PEDUS SERVICES, INC., pg. 854
PERKINS FAMILY RESTAURANTS—Tennessee Restaurant Corp., pg. 1088
PINELLAS CRABCOOKER, INC.—Specialty Restaurants Corporation, pg. 1028
PINELLAS FARMHOUSE, INC.—Specialty Restaurants Corporation, pg. 1028
PISTOL PETE'S PIZZA, pg. 872
PITTSBURGH STADIUM CONCESSIONS, INC.—ARA Group, pg. 6
PIZZA HAVEN INC., pg. 873
PONDEROSA, INC.—Metromedia Company, pg. 743
PORTS O'CALL RESTAURANT CORP.—Specialty Restaurants Corporation, pg. 1028
PREPCO, pg. 887
PRIME HOSPITALITY CORP., pg. 889
PRIME HOSPITALITY CORP LIMITED PARTNERSHIP—Prime Hospitality Corp., pg. 889
PRO*PORTION INDUSTRIES, INC.—Bresler's Industries, Inc., pg. 174
PROFIT MANAGEMENT CORP.—Family Inns of America, Inc., pg. 398
QUIK WOK CORPORATION, pg. 905
R.T.M. WINNERS, pg. 908
RAILHEAD RESTAURANTS, INC.—Victoria Station Incorporated, pg. 1150
RESTAURANT COMPANY, INC., pg. 929
RESTAURANT DEVELOPERS CORP., pg. 929
RESTAURANT ENTERPRISES GROUP, INC., pg. 929
RESTAURANTS UNLIMITED, pg. 929
F. L. ROBERTS & CO. INC., pg. 938
ROCKY POINT VILLAGE CORP.—Specialty Restaurants Corporation, pg. 1028
ROCKY ROCOCO CORPORATION, pg. 942
ROMA HOLDINGS, pg. 945
RUNWAY TWO FIVE CORPORATION—Specialty Restaurants Corporation, pg. 1028
S & A RESTAURANT CORP., pg. 958
H. SALT SEAFOOD RESTAURANTS, pg. 967
SAVOY BAR AND GRILL—Lettuce Entertain You Enterprises, Inc., pg. 669
SCHNUCK MARKETS, INC., pg. 977
SCHWAN'S SALES ENTERPRISES, pg. 980
SCOOZI—Lettuce Entertain You Enterprises, Inc., pg. 669
SEILER CORPORATION, pg. 987
SERVICE AMERICA CORPORATION, pg. 992
SHAKEY'S INCORPORATED, pg. 994
SILVER DOLLAR CITY, INC., pg. 1004
SMITH & SONS FOODS, INC., pg. 1014
SPECIALTY RESTAURANTS CORPORATION, pg. 1027
SPIRES RESTAURANTS INC., pg. 1031
SPORTSERVICE CORPORATION—Delaware North Companies, Inc., pg. 326
STEAK AND ALE RESTAURANTS—S & A Restaurant Corp., pg. 958
STOCKTON CHILI PEPPER, INC.—Specialty Restaurants Corporation, pg. 1028
STOCKTON RESTAURANT CORP.—Specialty Restaurants Corporation, pg. 1028
STRAW HAT COOPERATIVE CORP., pg. 1053
STUART ANDERSON'S BLACK ANGUS/CATTLE COMPANY RESTAURANTS—American Restaurant Group, Inc., pg. 60
THE SWISS COLONY, pg. 1068
TGI FRIDAY'S, INC.—Carlson Companies, Inc., pg. 221
T. J. CINNAMONS LTD., pg. 1073
TACO JOHN'S INTERNATIONAL, INC., pg. 1076
TAM O'SHANTER INN—Lawry's Restaurants, Inc., pg. 663
TASTEE FREEZ INTL. INC.—De Novo Corporation, pg. 321
TENNESSEE RESTAURANT CORP., pg. 1087
TOWN PUMP, INC., pg. 1104
TRAPP FAMILY LODGE, INC., pg. 1108
TREND LINE CORPORATION, pg. 1109
TUCCI BENUCCH—Lettuce Entertain You Enterprises, Inc., pg. 669
THE "21" CLUB, INC.—21 International Holdings, Inc., pg. 1121
UNITED FOOD SERVICE DISTRIBUTORS, INC., pg. 1132
UNIVERSAL COMPANIES, INC., pg. 1138
UNIVERSAL RESTAURANTS, INC.—Universal Companies, Inc., pg. 1138
VALLEY INNOVATIVE MANAGEMENT SERVICE—Trend Line Corporation, pg. 1109
VAN NUYS AIRPORT RESTAURANT CORP.—Specialty Restaurants Corporation, pg. 1028
VERDUGO RESTAURANT CORP.—Specialty Restaurants Corporation, pg. 1028
VERSA SERVICES LTD.—ARA Group, pg. 7
VERSABEC INC.—ARA Group, pg. 7
VICTORIA STATION OF ARIZONA, INC.—Victoria Station Incorporated, pg. 1150
VICTORIA STATION OF ATLANTA, INC.—Victoria Station Incorporated, pg. 1150
VICTORIA STATION OF COLORADO, INC.—Victoria Station Incorporated, pg. 1150
VICTORIA STATION INCORPORATED, pg. 1149
VICTORIA STATION INCORPORATED, A CALIFORNIA CORP.—Victoria Station Incorporated, pg. 1150
VICTORIA STATION OF LOUISIANA, INC.—Victoria Station Incorporated, pg. 1150
VICTORIA STATION OF TEXAS, INC.—Victoria Station Incorporated, pg. 1150
VICTORIA STATION OF VIRGINIA, INC.—Victoria Station Incorporated, pg. 1150
VICTORIA STATION OF WASHINGTON, INC.—Victoria Station Incorporated, pg. 1150
VICTORIA STATION OF WISCONSIN, INC.—Victoria Station Incorporated, pg. 1150
VILLA SOUTH INC.—Thiele Kaolin Co., pg. 1092
WAFFLE HOUSE, INC., pg. 1157
WALNUT CREEK RESTAURANT CORP.—Specialty Restaurants Corporation, pg. 1028
WHARFSIDE RESTAURANTS, INC., pg. 1184
WHATABURGER, INC., pg. 1184
WHITE CASTLE DISTRIBUTING, INC.—White Castle System, Inc., pg. 1185
WHITE CASTLE SYSTEM, INC., pg. 1185
WOMETCO ENTERPRISES, INC., pg. 1199
WYATT CAFETERIAS INC., pg. 1205
YANKEE WHALER COMPANY—Specialty Restaurants Corporation, pg. 1028

5813 — DRINKING PLACES (ALCOHOLIC BEVERAGES)

CARROWS RESTAURANTS, INC.—Restaurant Enterprises Group, Inc., pg. 929
CHATTANOOGA CHOO-CHOO HOLIDAY INN, pg. 241
CORNER POCKETS OF AMERICA, pg. 286
EL TORITO RESTAURANTS, INC.—Restaurant Enterprises Group, Inc., pg. 929
FAR WEST CONCEPTS, INC.—Restaurant Enterprises Group, Inc., pg. 929
GRC RESTAURANTS, INC.—Restaurant Enterprises Group, Inc., pg. 929
GILBERT/ROBINSON, INC., pg. 458
GOLF HOST RESORTS, INC.—Golf Hosts, Inc., pg. 469
INDIANHEAD GOLF CLUB—Chief Industries, Inc., pg. 247
W.B. JOHNSON PROPERTY, INC., pg. 598
LETTUCE ENTERTAIN YOU ENTERPRISES, INC., pg. 668
PRIME HOSPITALITY CORP., pg. 889
RESTAURANT ENTERPRISES GROUP, INC., pg. 929
SPECIALTY RESTAURANTS CORPORATION, pg. 1027

5912 — DRUG STORES & PROPRIETARY STORES

ALP/FREDDY'S, pg. 4
THE FRED W. ALBRECHT GROCERY CO., pg. 31
ALLIED MERCANTILE COMPANY, pg. 38
ANDREWS GROUP, INCORPORATED, pg. 74
ASTRUP DRUGS, INC., pg. 93
THE BARTELL DRUG COMPANY, pg. 122
BEL AIR MARKETS, pg. 133
BIG V SUPERMARKETS, INC., pg. 149
A.D. CLARK, INC., pg. 252
DISCOUNT DRUG MART INC., pg. 339
DRUG EMPORIUM OF ARIZONA, INC., pg. 349
DUANE READE, pg. 350
JACK ECKERD CORPORATION, pg. 366
ECKERD DRUG CO.—Jack Eckerd Corporation, pg. 366
ERICKSON DIVERSIFIED CORP., pg. 386
F & M DISTRIBUTORS INC., pg. 393
HAGGEN'S, INC., pg. 499
HARCO DRUG, INC., pg. 507
HY-VEE FOOD STORES INCORPORATED, pg. 556
K & B, INC., pg. 611
KASH N KARRY FOOD STORES, INC., pg. 617
LAVERDIERE'S ENTERPRISES, pg. 661
LEWIS DRUG, INC., pg. 673
PAGES DRUGS—Randall's Food Markets, Inc., pg. 912
PHAR-MOR, INC., pg. 866
PUBLIX SUPERMARKETS INC., pg. 898
QUAEL CORP., pg. 902
RALEY'S, pg. 910
REAL HOLDING MANAGEMENT CORP., pg. 917
SCHNUCK MARKETS, INC., pg. 977
SHAPERO STORES—Quael Corp., pg. 903
SNYDER BROTHERS, INC., pg. 1015
SNYDER'S DRUG STORES, INC., pg. 1015
SUPER D DRUG STORES, pg. 1062
SUPERMARKETS GENERAL CORPORATION, pg. 1064
TAYLOR DRUG STORES, INC., pg. 1081
THRIFTWAY, INC., pg. 1095
THRIFTY DRUG STORES, INC., pg. 1096
TOM THUMB FOOD & DRUGS, INC.—Randall's Food Markets, Inc., pg. 912
TOM THUMB STORES, INC.—Randall's Food Markets, Inc., pg. 912
WHITE DRUG ENTERPRISES, INC.—Thrifty Drug Stores, Inc., pg. 1096
ZILBER, LTD., pg. 1219

5921 — LIQUOR STORES

BIG BEAR SUPERMARKETS NO. 3, pg. 149
BIG Y FOODS INC., pg. 149
BRODBECK ENTERPRISES, INC., pg. 178
BYERLY'S INC., pg. 198
A.D. CLARK, INC., pg. 252
KASH N KARRY FOOD STORES, INC., pg. 617
KORET OF CALIFORNIA, pg. 642
PIONEER SUPERMARKETS, pg. 872
PUBLIX SUPERMARKETS INC., pg. 898
RALEY'S, pg. 910
TACT HOLDING, pg. 1076
TRADER JOES CO.—TACT Holding, pg. 1076

5932 — USED MERCHANDISE STORES

GRANTREE CORPORATION, pg. 477
PAINE FURNITURE CO., pg. 843

5941 — SPORTING GOODS & BICYCLE SHOPS

ALL ABOUT SPORTS—Van Leunens Inc., pg. 1144
ALLIED SPORTING GOODS INC., pg. 40
THE ATHLETE'S FOOT GROUP, INC., pg. 94
BASS PRO SHOPS, INC., pg. 125
BRENDAMOUR'S SPORTING GOODS CO., pg. 173
CAMPING WORLD HOLDINGS, INC., pg. 213
CAMPMOR INC., pg. 213
CREATIVE PLAYTHINGS LTD., pg. 297
DUNHAM'S ATHLEISURE CORPORATION, pg. 353
GORDON & SMITH, INC., pg. 472
GRAMEX CORPORATION, pg. 475
L.L. BEAN, INC., pg. 648
MILLER HARNESS, INC.—MPO Videotronics, Inc., pg. 693
HENRY MODELL & COMPANY, INC., pg. 762
RAM GOLF UK—RAM Golf Corporation, pg. 910
RECREATIONAL EQUIPMENT, INC., pg. 917

5942 — BOOK STORES

B. DALTON BOOKSELLER, INC.—Barnes & Noble Bookstores, Inc., pg. 120
BARNES & NOBLE BOOKSTORES, INC., pg. 120
BOOKSTOP, INC.—Barnes & Noble Bookstores, Inc., pg. 120
BRENNAN COLLEGE SERVICE, INC.—Follett Corporation, pg. 422
BRODBECK ENTERPRISES, INC., pg. 178
CAREERTRACK INC., pg. 218
CHADWICK-MILLER INC., pg. 237
DOUBLEDAY BOOK SHOPS, INC.—Barnes & Noble Bookstores, Inc., pg. 120
FOLLETT COLLEGE STORES CORP.—Follett Corporation, pg. 422
FOLLETT CORPORATION, pg. 422
KROCH'S & BRENTANO'S, INC., pg. 645
LAURIAT INC.—Chadwick-Miller Inc., pg. 237
LINCOLN INDUSTRIES, pg. 676
MTS, INC., pg. 694
NEBRASKA BOOK CO.—Lincoln Industries, pg. 676
UNIVERSITY BOOK STORE, pg. 1139

5943 — STATIONERY STORES

S. FREEDMAN & SONS, INC., pg. 430
J. L. HAMMETT COMPANY, pg. 504
INDIANA RECORDS MANAGERS, pg. 565
JUNIATA OFFICE SUPPLIES, pg. 608
MARYLAND PAPER BOX COMPANY, pg. 717
MID-WEST PAPER PRODUCTS COMPANY, pg. 750
MILLER BUSINESS SYSTEMS, INC., pg. 753
SILVER'S INC., pg. 1005
TOP FLIGHT, INC., pg. 1101
UNIVERSITY BOOK STORE, pg. 1139

5944 — JEWELRY STORES

A & Z HAYWARD, INC., pg. 1
ADRAY APPLIANCE & PHOTO CENTER, INC., pg. 18
B&L JEWELRY CO.—Reliable Stores, Inc., pg. 925
BARCLAY & SONS—Reliable Stores, Inc., pg. 925
BARLOW & EATON—Reliable Stores, Inc., pg. 925
BEST PRODUCTS CO., INC.—Adler & Shaykin, pg. 17
BOND'S JEWELERS, INC.—Zale Corporation, pg. 1215
CARLYLE & CO. JEWELERS, pg. 222
CASTLEBERG'S—Reliable Stores, Inc., pg. 925
CONTINENTAL COIN CORPORATION, pg. 278
DANIEL'S JEWELRY CO. OF ARIZONA, INC.—Zale Corporation, pg. 1215
DE VONS JEWELERS, pg. 321
DEARDEN'S, INC., pg. 322
ELEVEN-O-ONE CORP.—Zale Corporation, pg. 1216
FOLAND'S JEWELRY BROKERS, pg. 421
FORTUNOFF, pg. 425
GORDON BROTHERS, pg. 471
GORDON BROTHERS CORPORATION—Gordon Brothers, pg. 471
GORDON JEWELRY CORPORATION—Zale Corporation, pg. 1215
GULF COAST JEWELRY & SPECIALTY CO., INC.—Zale Corporation, pg. 1216
HAMILTON WHOLESALE JEWELRY CO., INC.—Zale Corporation, pg. 1216
HELZBERG'S DIAMOND SHOPS, INC., pg. 528
HENEBRYS—Reliable Stores, Inc., pg. 925
MERMOD, JACCARD & KING JEWELRY CO. OF IOWA, INC.—Zale Corporation, pg. 1216
MERMOD, JACCARD & KING JEWELRY CO. OF NEBRASKA—Zale Corporation, pg. 1216
MEYER JEWELERS, pg. 746
MORTON'S JEWELRY CO.—Reliable Stores, Inc., pg. 925
N.A. TRADING LTD.—North American Watch Corporation, pg. 812
NORTH AMERICAN WATCH OF CANADA, LTD.—North American Watch Corporation, pg. 812
OSKAMP NOLTING CO., INC.—Zale Corporation, pg. 1216
PIERCING PAGODA, INC., pg. 870
POLLACK CORPORATION, pg. 879
RELCO—Reliable Stores, Inc., pg. 925
RELIABLE STORES, INC., pg. 925
ROBANNE CORP.—Zale Corporation, pg. 1216
S&N KATZ JEWELERS—Reliable Stores, Inc., pg. 925
SCOTT JEWELERS—Reliable Stores, Inc., pg. 925
SMITH JEWELERS & DISTRIBUTORS, INC.—Zale Corporation, pg. 1216
SOUTHERN REALTY CO.—Zale Corporation, pg. 1216
SOUTHWESTERN WHOLESALE JEWELRY CO.—Zale Corporation, pg. 1216
STAR ENGRAVING CO.—Zale Corporation, pg. 1216
TOURNEAU INC., pg. 1103
UNITED-GENERAL PRODUCTS OF KNOXVILLE, INC.—Zale Corporation, pg. 1216
UNITED-HAMILTON, INC.—Zale Corporation, pg. 1216
UNITED JEWELERS & DISTRIBUTORS OF ARIZONA, INC.—Zale Corporation, pg. 1216
UNITED JEWELERS & DISTRIBUTORS OF ARKANSAS, INC.—Zale Corporation, pg. 1216
UNITED JEWELERS & DISTRIBUTORS OF LOUISIANA, INC.—Zale Corporation, pg. 1216
UNITED JEWELERS & DISTRIBUTORS OF TEXAS, INC.—Zale Corporation, pg. 1216
UNIVERSAL SERVICE BUREAU, INC.—Zale Corporation, pg. 1216
VAN CLEEF & ARPELS, INC., pg. 1144
WEDLO, INC.—Peter W. Smith & Company, Inc., pg. 1012
WEISS JEWELERS—Reliable Stores, Inc., pg. 925
HARRY WINSTON, INC., pg. 1197
ZALE CORPORATION, pg. 1215

5945 — HOBBY, TOY & GAME SHOPS

LEEWARDS CREATIVE CRAFTS, INC., pg. 666
PLAID ENTERPRISES INC.—The Dyson-Kissner-Moran Corporation, pg. 357
WHAM-O DIV. OF KRANSCO—Kransco, pg. 644
ZILBER, LTD., pg. 1219

5946 — CAMERA & PHOTOGRAPHIC SUPPLY STORES

ADRAY APPLIANCE & PHOTO CENTER, INC., pg. 18
FILCO, INC., pg. 409
FOLAND'S JEWELRY BROKERS, pg. 421
NELSON PHOTO SUPPLIES, pg. 797
WILLOUGHBY'S, pg. 1193

5947 — GIFT, NOVELTY & SOUVENIR SHOPS

BROOKSTONE COMPANY, INC., pg. 180
CHRISTMAS & THINGS, INC.—H. C. Prange Company, pg. 884
COLE KEY CORPORATION—Cole National Corporation, pg. 260
COLE NATIONAL CORPORATION, pg. 260
CONCESSION AIR CORPORATION—Delaware North Companies, Inc., pg. 326
JIMMY DAVIS ENTERPRISES, INC., pg. 318
FABER, COE & GREGG, INC., pg. 395
FOLAND'S JEWELRY BROKERS, pg. 421
GUMPS—Gump's, Inc., pg. 494
GUMP'S, INC., pg. 494
HAMMACHER, SCHLEMMER & CO., INC., pg. 503
FRED HARVEY TRANSPORTATION COMPANY—JMB Realty Corporation, pg. 585
KING GROUP, INC., pg. 630
SILVER DOLLAR CITY, INC., pg. 1004
SILVER'S INC., pg. 1005
THINGS REMEMBERED—Cole National Corporation, pg. 260
TRAPP FAMILY LODGE, INC., pg. 1108
WACCAMAW CORPORATION—Georgetown Industries, Inc., pg. 453

5948 — LUGGAGE & LEATHER GOODS STORES

ADRAY APPLIANCE & PHOTO CENTER, INC., pg. 18
BEST PRODUCTS CO., INC.—Adler & Shaykin, pg. 17
DEERSKIN TRADING POST, INC., pg. 324

5949 — SEWING, NEEDLEWORK & PIECE GOODS STORES

DUANE READE, pg. 350
LEEWARDS CREATIVE CRAFTS, INC., pg. 666

5961 — CATALOG & MAIL ORDER HOUSES

AXIA INCORPORATED, pg. 8
ADDRESSES UNLIMITED—New Jersey Press, Inc., pg. 801
AMWAY CORPORATION, pg. 70
ANDMORE SPORTSWEAR CORPORATION, pg. 74
BASS PRO SHOPS, INC., pg. 125
WALTER J. BLACK, INC. FULFILLMENT SERVICES—Walter J. Black, Inc., pg. 154
BRECKS—Foster & Gallagher Inc., pg. 426
BROOKSTONE COMPANY, INC., pg. 180
W. ATLEE BURPEE CO.—Geo. J. Ball, Inc., pg. 116
CAMPMOR INC., pg. 213
CAREERTRACK INC., pg. 218
CHEYENNE OUTFITTERS, INC., pg. 244
COLLIN STREET BAKERY, pg. 262
COMPUADD CORPORATION, pg. 271
CORHAM, INC., pg. 286
COSMETIQUE, INC., pg. 288
COUNTRY NOTEBOOK—The Renovator's Supply, Inc., pg. 927
D. M. MANAGEMENT COMPANY, pg. 309
DRI INDUSTRIES—Leichtung, Inc., pg. 666
DEERSKIN TRADING POST, INC., pg. 324
THE DELPHI GLASS CORP. DELPHI STAINED GLASS CENTERS, pg. 326
DIRECT DENTAL SUPPLY CO.—Patterson Dental Company, pg. 851
EASTON PRESS BOOKS—MBI Inc., pg. 691
EASTON PRESS VIDEOS—MBI Inc., pg. 691
EDGAR B. FURNITURE CO., pg. 368
EDMUND SCIENTIFIC COMPANY, pg. 369
ELEK-TEK, INC., pg. 375
FLEXRX—Giant Eagle, Inc., pg. 456
FOSTER & GALLAGHER INC., pg. 426
THE FRANKLIN MINT—American Protection Industries, Inc., pg. 60
FULFILLMENT UNLIMITED—Professional Book Distributors, Inc., pg. 894
THE FULLER BRUSH COMPANY—The Fuller Brush Company, pg. 436
GENEVE CORPORATION, pg. 451
THE HABAND CO., pg. 498
HAMILTON COLLECTION—MBI Inc., pg. 691
HAMMACHER, SCHLEMMER & CO., INC., pg. 503
HANDSOME REWARDS—Starcrest Products of California, pg. 1040
HEARTHSONG, INC.—Foster & Gallagher Inc., pg. 426
LEON HENDRICKSON, pg. 529
IMPRINT PRODUCTS, L.P., pg. 564
INDUSTRIAL BOOKSTORE—Manufacturers' News, Inc., pg. 705
J. CREW GROUP, INC., pg. 584
JOHNNY APPLESEED'S, INC., pg. 597
DAVID KAY, INC.—Foster & Gallagher Inc., pg. 426
KNOX INTERNATIONAL CORP., pg. 638
L.L. BEAN, INC., pg. 648
LEICHTUNG, INC., pg. 666
LITTLETON COIN CO., INC., pg. 679
MBI INC., pg. 691
MAGAZINE MARKET PLACE, INC.—Foster & Gallagher Inc., pg. 426
MARBORO BOOKS INC.—Barnes & Noble Bookstores, Inc., pg. 120
MARKDATA INC., pg. 708
MARKETING COMMUNICATIONS, pg. 709
MARY MAXIM, INC., pg. 722
MCMASTER CARR SUPPLY CO. INC., pg. 731
MOTHERS BACK ISSUES, INC.—Mother Earth News, pg. 773
MOTHER'S BOOKSHELF—Mother Earth News, pg. 773
MYSTIC STAMP COMPANY—Littleton Coin Co., Inc., pg. 679
NASCO—Geneve Corporation, pg. 452
NEW ENGLAND COLLECTORS SOCIETY—Reed & Barton Corporation, pg. 920
NEW HAMPTON, INC., pg. 801
OMAHA STEAKS INTERNATIONAL, pg. 825
THE ORVIS COMPANY, INC., pg. 830
GEORGE W. PARK SEED CO., INC., pg. 849
PETALS—Corham, Inc., pg. 286
POSTAL COMMEMORATIVE SOCIETY COLLECTION—MBI Inc., pg. 691
POWELL LABORATORIES—Carolina Biological Supply Co., pg. 223
PROFESSIONAL BOOK DISTRIBUTORS, INC., pg. 894
PUBLISHERS CLEARING HOUSE, pg. 898
QUILL CORP., pg. 905
REPLACEMENTS, LTD., pg. 927
ROCKWOOD GARDENS, LTD.—KNOX International Corp., pg. 638
SHEPLERS, INC., pg. 998
SHILLCRAFT, INC., pg. 999
SIGNATURES—Starcrest Products of California, pg. 1040
THE SPORTSMAN'S GUIDE, INC., pg. 1032
SPRING HILL NURSERIES CO.—Foster & Gallagher Inc., pg. 426
STARCREST OF CALIFORNIA—Starcrest Products of California, pg. 1040
STARCREST PRODUCTS OF CALIFORNIA, pg. 1040
STOCK YARDS PACKING CO., INC., pg. 1049
SUNSHINE SHIPPERS, INC.—Hickory Farms, Inc., pg. 533
THIMBLE COLLECTORS CLUB COLLECTIONS—MBI Inc., pg. 691
THE TOG SHOP, pg. 1100
UNICOVER CORPORATION, pg. 1126
WILTON INDUSTRIES, INC., pg. 1194
WISSOTA TRADER LTD.—Mason Shoe Mfg. Co., pg. 718
CAROL WRIGHT SALES, INC.—Peter W. Smith & Company, Inc., pg. 1011

5962 — AUTOMATIC MERCHANDISING MACHINE OPERATORS

ARA BELGIUM, S.A.—ARA Group, pg. 7
ARA EUROPE HEADQUARTERS—ARA Group, pg. 7
ARA N.V.—ARA Group, pg. 7
ARA SERVICES, GMBH—ARA Group, pg. 7
ARA SERVICES, LTD.—ARA Group, pg. 7
ARA SERVICES, S.A.—ARA Group, pg. 7
ARA VENDING SERVICES LTD.—ARA Group, pg. 7
AVA-AUTOMATIC VENDORS OF AMERICA, pg. 8
AIM SERVICES CO., LTD.—ARA Group, pg. 7
ARASERVE, INC.—ARA Group, pg. 6
AUTOMATIC SERVICE CO.—AVA-Automatic Vendors of America, pg. 8
AUTOMATIC SERVICE CO. OF VIRGINIA, LYNCHBURG BRANCH—AVA-Automatic Vendors of America, pg. 8
AUTOMATIC SERVICE CO. OF VIRGINIA, NO. VIRGINIA BRANCH—AVA-Automatic Vendors of America, pg. 8
CENTRAL COCA-COLA BOTTLING COMPANY, INC., pg. 232
EFFECTIVE MANAGEMENT SYSTEMS, pg. 370
LA SOCIETE VS LIMITEE—ARA Group, pg. 7
MAJOR FOODS LTD.—ARA Group, pg. 7
PINE STATE VENDING—Pine State Tobacco & Candy Company, pg. 871
SEILER CORPORATION, pg. 987
SERVICE AMERICA CORPORATION, pg. 992
TREND LINE CORPORATION, pg. 1109
VALLEY INNOVATIVE MANAGEMENT SERVICE—Trend Line Corporation, pg. 1109
VERSA SERVICES LTD.—ARA Group, pg. 7
VERSABEC INC.—ARA Group, pg. 7
WEST DAIRIES, INC., pg. 1177

5963 — DIRECT SELLING ESTABLISHMENTS

ABI FOOD SERVICES, INC.—Coca Cola Bottling Co. United, Inc., pg. 258
AMWAY BELGIUM CO.—Amway Corporation, pg. 70
AMWAY DE ESPANA, S.A.—Amway Corporation, pg. 70
AMWAY DE GUATEMALA, S.A.—Amway Corporation, pg. 70
AMWAY DE MEXICO, S.A. DE C.V.—Amway Corporation, pg. 70
AMWAY DE PANAMA S.A.—Amway Corporation, pg. 70
AMWAY (EUROPE) LTD.—Amway Corporation, pg. 70
AMWAY FRANCE—Amway Corporation, pg. 70
AMWAY GESELLSCHAFT M.B.H.—Amway Corporation, pg. 70
AMWAY GMBH—Amway Corporation, pg. 70
AMWAY INTERNATIONAL, INC.-HONG KONG BRANCH—Amway Corporation, pg. 71
AMWAY ITALIA S.R.L.—Amway Corporation, pg. 71
AMWAY (JAPAN) LIMITED—Amway Corporation, pg. 71
AMWAY KOREA, LTD.—Amway Corporation, pg. 71
AMWAY (MALAYSIA) SDN. BHD.—Amway Corporation, pg. 71
AMWAY NEDERLAND LTD.—Amway Corporation, pg. 71
AMWAY OF AUSTRALIA PTY. LTD.—Amway Corporation, pg. 71
AMWAY OF CANADA, LTD.—Amway Corporation, pg. 71
AMWAY OF NEW ZEALAND LIMITED—Amway Corporation, pg. 71
AMWAY (SCHWEIZ) AG—Amway Corporation, pg. 71
AMWAY TAIWAN, LTD.—Amway Corporation, pg. 71
AMWAY (THAILAND) LIMITED—Amway Corporation, pg. 71
AMWAY (U.K.) LIMITED—Amway Corporation, pg. 71
CALIFORNIA SCHOOL BOOK FAIRS, INC.—SI Holdings Inc., pg. 962
EASTERN MILK PRODUCERS COOPERATIVE ASSN., INC., pg. 363
EFFECTIVE MANAGEMENT SYSTEMS, pg. 370
THE FULLER BRUSH COMPANY—The Fuller Brush Company, pg. 436
THE HEARST CORPORATION, pg. 521
MARY KAY CORPORATION, pg. 716
MARY KAY COSMETICS, GMBH—Mary Kay Corporation, pg. 717

MARY KAY COSMETICS INC.—Mary Kay Corporation, pg. 716
MARY KAY COSMETICS PTY. LTD.—Mary Kay Corporation, pg. 717
PERIODICAL PUBLISHERS' SERVICE BUREAU, INC.—The Hearst Corporation, pg. 523
RENA-WARE DISTRIBUTORS INC., pg. 926
RENA-WARE GMBH—Rena-Ware Distributors Inc., pg. 926
SCHOLASTIC BOOK FAIRS, INC.—SI Holdings Inc., pg. 962
SOUTHEASTERN MEDEQUIP, INC., pg. 1019
STANDARD COFFEE SERVICE—William B. Reily & Co., Inc., pg. 923
UPSTATE MILK COOPERATIVES INC., pg. 1140

5983 — FUEL OIL DEALERS

BAYSIDE FUEL OIL CORP.—Bayside Fuel Oil Depot Corp., pg. 128
BERKS PRODUCTS CORPORATION, pg. 142
BESCHE OIL COMPANY, INC., pg. 145
BRADFORD OIL COMPANY, INC., pg. 170
BURKE FUEL & HEATING CO.—Meenan Oil Co. Limited Partnership, pg. 736
CHRISTY HALSEY OIL CO.—Meenan Oil Co. Limited Partnership, pg. 736
COLONIAL OIL INDUSTRIES, pg. 263
DAIGLE OIL CO., pg. 310
DEAD RIVER COMPANY, pg. 321
DISTRICT PETROLEUM PRODUCTS, INC., pg. 340
EFFRON FUEL OIL CO., INC.—Meenan Oil Co. Limited Partnership, pg. 736
FARM & HOME OIL COMPANY, pg. 401
FIRST MOUNT JOY CORPORATION, pg. 413
GATE PETROLEUM COMPANY, pg. 445
GAY JOHNSON'S INC., pg. 446
GLOBAL PETROLEUM CORP., pg. 463
KING FUELS INC., pg. 630
CARLOS R. LEFFLER INC., pg. 666
LYON COUNTY CO-OP OIL CO., pg. 690
MACMILLAN OIL CO., INC.—Graham Group, Inc., pg. 475
MAIN BROTHERS OIL COMPANY, INC., pg. 702
MEENAN LI DIV.—Meenan Oil Co. Limited Partnership, pg. 736
MEENAN OIL CO. LIMITED PARTNERSHIP, pg. 736
MEENAN OIL DIV.—Meenan Oil Co. Limited Partnership, pg. 736
MID-STATES PETROLEUM INC., pg. 750
MID-VALLEY OIL COMPANY, INC.—Warren Equities Inc., pg. 1165
MIDWEST BOTTLE GAS COMPANY—Consolidated Midwest, Inc., pg. 277
OLIVER OIL COMPANY, INC., pg. 824
PM PROPERTIES INC.—Petroleum Marketers, Inc., pg. 865
PETROLEUM MARKETERS, INC., pg. 865
SHIPLEY OIL COMPANY, pg. 999
THE SICO COMPANY, pg. 1001
SISCO COMPANY—First Mount Joy Corporation, pg. 413
SOUTHERN STATES COOPERATIVE, INC., pg. 1022
SPARTAN OIL CORP., pg. 1026
YODER OIL COMPANY INC., pg. 1208
YOUNG SUPPLY CO.—Meenan Oil Co. Limited Partnership, pg. 736

5984 — BOTTLED OR BULK LIQUIFIED PETROLEUM (LP) GAS DEALERS

CONSOLIDATED MIDWEST, INC., pg. 277
DEAD RIVER COMPANY, pg. 321
ERGON, INC., pg. 386
FERRELL COMPANIES INC./FERRELLGAS, pg. 407
FERRELLGAS, INC.—Ferrell Companies Inc./Ferrellgas, pg. 407
GAY JOHNSON'S INC., pg. 446
HICKS OIL-HICKS GAS, INC., pg. 533
JASPER COUNTY FARM BUREAU CO-OP ASSOCIATION, INC., pg. 590
KEEN COMPRESSED GAS CO., INC., pg. 619
LA SALLE COUNTY FARM SUPPLY, pg. 649
LYKES ENERGY, INC., pg. 689
MIDWEST BOTTLE GAS COMPANY—Consolidated Midwest, Inc., pg. 277

5989 — FUEL DEALERS, NEC

ALLEY-CASSETTY COAL CO., pg. 37
INGRAM COAL COMPANY—Ingram Industries Inc., pg. 569
MCCALL OIL & CHEMICAL CORP., pg. 726
PUGH OIL COMPANY, pg. 899

5992 — FLORISTS

AMLINGS FLOWERLAND, pg. 67
BRODBECK ENTERPRISES, INC., pg. 178
DENVER WHOLESALE FLORISTS COMPANY, pg. 331
800-FLOWERS, pg. 371
TELEFLORA—American Protection Industries, Inc., pg. 60

5993 — TOBACCO STORES & STANDS

DUANE READE, pg. 350
KAISER TOBACCO COMPANY, INC., pg. 615
MOSS & LOWENHAUPT CIGAR CO.—Faber, Coe & Gregg, Inc., pg. 395

5994 — NEWS DEALERS & NEWSSTANDS

ARA SERVICES, INC.—ARA Group, pg. 5
AERO ENTERPRISES, INC.—ARA Group, pg. 6
EASTERN LOBBY SHOPS—The Levy Organization, pg. 672
FABER, COE & GREGG, INC., pg. 395
THE LEVY ORGANIZATION, pg. 672

5995 — OPTICAL GOODS STORES

AMERICAN VISION CENTERS, INC., pg. 65
D & K OPTICAL, INC., pg. 307
HORNER RAUSCH COMPANY, pg. 544
KINDY OPTICAL—Duling Optical Corporation, pg. 352
MIDWEST VISION CENTERS, pg. 752
MONFRIED OPTICAL—Duling Optical Corporation, pg. 352
OPTICAL CORP. OF AMERICA, pg. 827
OPTIWORLD, pg. 828
TUCKERMAN OPTICAL CO., pg. 1118

5999 — MISCELLANEOUS RETAIL STORES, NEC

ALLIED SECURITY, INTERNATIONAL, pg. 40
BANK M F & COMPANY, INC., pg. 117
M. BUTEN & SONS INC., pg. 196
CAREERTRACK INC., pg. 218
CASWELL/MASSEY CO. LTD., pg. 229
COLE NATIONAL CORPORATION, pg. 260
COMMUNICATIONS INTERNATIONAL, pg. 269
CUMMINS MID-SOUTH, INC., pg. 305
CUTLERY WORLD—Hoffritz for Cutlery, pg. 538
DECOR CORPORATION, pg. 324
THE DELPHI GLASS CORP. DELPHI STAINED GLASS CENTERS, pg. 326
DUANE READE, pg. 350
DUPEY MANAGEMENT CORP., pg. 354
E B 5 CORPORATION, pg. 359
FARMERS CO-OP MARKET INC., pg. 401
WALLY FINDLAY GALLERIES, INC.—Wally Findlay Galleries International, pg. 410
WALLY FINDLAY GALLERIES, INC.—Wally Findlay Galleries International, pg. 410
WALLY FINDLAY GALLERIES INTERNATIONAL, pg. 410
FORESTRY SUPPLIERS, INC., pg. 424
FRAMES UNLIMITED INC.—Zimdar Enterprises, pg. 1220
HARCO DRUG, INC., pg. 507
HOFFRITZ FOR CUTLERY, pg. 538
HOFFRITZ INTERNATIONAL—Hoffritz for Cutlery, pg. 538
IDEAL POOL CORP., pg. 562
JASPER COUNTY FARM BUREAU CO-OP ASSOCIATION, INC., pg. 590
MARVIN LUMBER & CEDAR COMPANY, pg. 716
MAUREXCO EXPORTERS—Maurice Electric Supply Company, pg. 722
OLD AMERICAN POTTERY COMPANY, pg. 823
B. OLINDE & SONS COMPANY, INC., pg. 824
PADDOCK POOL CONSTRUCTION CO., pg. 842
PETCARE PLUS, INC., pg. 863
PETS-N-SUCH—Van Leunens Inc., pg. 1144
SUNGLASS HUT CORPORATION, pg. 1060
SUPERIOR AUCTIONEERS & MARKETING, INC., pg. 1063
UNICOVER CORPORATION, pg. 1126
UNITED PRODUCERS & CONSUMERS CO-OP, pg. 1134
D. WALDNER COMPANY, INC., pg. 1159
WILLOUGHBY'S, pg. 1193
THE W.B. WOOD COMPANY, pg. 1199
ZIMDAR ENTERPRISES, pg. 1220

6011 — FEDERAL RESERVE BANKS

OLD STONE BANK OF CALIFORNIA—Old Stone of California, Inc., pg. 823

6021 — NATIONAL COMMERCIAL BANKS

AURORA NATIONAL BANK—GreatBanc, Inc., pg. 483
BANK SHARES, INC., pg. 117
BROWN BROTHERS HARRIMAN TRUST CO. OF FLORIDA—Brown Brothers, Harriman & Co., pg. 181
BROWN BROTHERS HARRIMAN TRUST CO. OF NEW YORK—Brown Brothers, Harriman & Co., pg. 181
BROWN BROTHERS HARRIMAN TRUST CO. OF TEXAS—Brown Brothers, Harriman & Co., pg. 181
CAPITAL BANK, N.A.—Capital Bancorp, pg. 214
CITIZENS NATIONAL BANK—Citizens National Bancshares Inc., pg. 251
EASTLAND NATIONAL BANK—First Abilene Bankshares, Inc., pg. 412
EMPIRE NATIONAL BANK, pg. 379
EQUITABLE BANK OF LITTLETON, N.A.—Equitable Bankshares of Colorado, Inc., pg. 385
EQUITABLE BANKSHARES OF COLORADO, INC., pg. 385
EVANSTON BANK—GreatBanc, Inc., pg. 483
FIRST AMERICAN BANK OF GEORGIA, N.A.—First American Bankshares, Inc., pg. 412
FIRST AMERICAN BANK, N.A., WASHINGTON, D.C.—First American Bankshares, Inc., pg. 412
FIRST AMERICAN CAPITAL BANK—Southern California Bancorp, pg. 1020
FIRST AMERICAN METRO CORP.—First American Bankshares, Inc., pg. 412
FIRST CITIZENS BANK, N.A.—Horizon Bancorp, pg. 544
FIRST NATIONAL BANK IN CHICAGO HEIGHTS—GreatBanc, Inc., pg. 483
FIRST NATIONAL BANK OF ABILENE—First Abilene Bankshares, Inc., pg. 412
FIRST NATIONAL BANK OF BLUE ISLAND—Great Lakes Financial Resources, Inc., pg. 481
FIRST NATIONAL BANK OF SWEETWATER—First Abilene Bankshares, Inc., pg. 412
HIGH POINT FINANCIAL CORP., pg. 533
MCORP, pg. 732
MERCANTILE BANK—MCorp, pg. 733
THE NATIONAL BANK OF SUSSEX COUNTY—High Point Financial Corp., pg. 534
THE POCONO BANK—High Point Financial Corp., pg. 534
SOUTHERN CALIFORNIA BANCORP, pg. 1020
STONE FORT NATIONAL BANK—Texas Commerce Bancshares, Inc., pg. 1089
TEAM BANK—Team Bancshares, Inc., pg. 1082
TEAM BANK/AMARILLO—Team Bancshares, Inc., pg. 1082
TEAM BANK/DALLAS—Team Bancshares, Inc., pg. 1082
TEXAS COMMERCE BANCSHARES, INC., pg. 1089
TEXAS COMMERCE BANK-AMARILLO—Texas Commerce Bancshares, Inc., pg. 1089
TEXAS COMMERCE BANK-AUSTIN—Texas Commerce Bancshares, Inc., pg. 1089
TEXAS COMMERCE BANK-BEAUMONT—Texas Commerce Bancshares, Inc., pg. 1089
TEXAS COMMERCE BANK-CORPUS CHRISTI—Texas Commerce Bancshares, Inc., pg. 1089
TEXAS COMMERCE BANK-HOUSTON—Texas Commerce Bancshares, Inc., pg. 1089
TEXAS COMMERCE BANK-LONGVIEW—Texas Commerce Bancshares, Inc., pg. 1089
TEXAS COMMERCE BANK-LUBBOCK—Texas Commerce Bancshares, Inc., pg. 1089
TEXAS COMMERCE BANK-NATIONAL ASSOCIATION—Texas Commerce Bancshares, Inc., pg. 1089
TEXAS COMMERCE BANK-NEW BRAUNFELS—Texas Commerce Bancshares, Inc., pg. 1089
TEXAS COMMERCE BANK-ODESSA—Texas Commerce Bancshares, Inc., pg. 1089
TEXAS COMMERCE BANK-RIO GRANDE VALLEY—Texas Commerce Bancshares, Inc., pg. 1089
TEXAS COMMERCE BANK-SAN ANGELO—Texas Commerce Bancshares, Inc., pg. 1089
TEXAS COMMERCE BANK-SAN ANTONIO—Texas Commerce Bancshares, Inc., pg. 1089
TRUSTCORP.—D.A. Davidson & Co., pg. 318
UNION NATIONAL BANK OF ARKANSAS—The Union of Arkansas Corp., pg. 1127
UNION NATIONAL BANK OF AUSTIN—The Union of Arkansas Corp., pg. 1127
UNION NATIONAL BANK OF OKLAHOMA—The Union of Arkansas Corp., pg. 1127
THE WOMEN'S BANK, N.A.—Equitable Bankshares of Colorado, Inc., pg. 385

6022 — STATE COMMERCIAL BANKS & TRUST COMPANIES

AMERICAN SAVINGS BANK, pg. 60
ANCHOR FINANCIAL CORPORATION, pg. 71
BANK OF HOMEWOOD—Great Lakes Financial Resources, Inc., pg. 481
BANK OF LINCOLNWOOD—GSC Enterprises, Inc., pg. 441
BANK OF NORTH DAKOTA, pg. 117
BANKMANAGERS CORP., pg. 118
BREMER FINANCIAL CORPORATION, pg. 173
CAPITAL BANK—Capital Bancorp, pg. 214
CAPITAL BANK OF CALIFORNIA—Capital Bancorp, pg. 214
CHELSEA STATE BANK, pg. 241
COLE TAYLOR BANK—Cole Taylor Financial Group, pg. 260
COLE TAYLOR FINANCIAL GROUP, pg. 260
COLE TAYLOR/YORKTOWN—Cole Taylor Financial Group, pg. 260
THE COMMERCIAL BANK, pg. 268
COMMUNITY BANK OF HOMEWOOD-FLOSSMOOR—Great Lakes Financial Resources, Inc., pg. 481
CUMMINS-AMERICAN CORP., pg. 304
FIDUCIARY TRUST COMPANY INTERNATIONAL, pg. 408
FIRST AMERICAN BANK OF MARYLAND—First American Bankshares, Inc., pg. 412
FIRST AMERICAN BANK OF NEW YORK—First American Bankshares, Inc., pg. 412
FIRST AMERICAN BANK OF VIRGINIA—First American Bankshares, Inc., pg. 412
FIRST AMERICAN BANKSHARES, INC., pg. 412
FIRST KENTUCKY TRUST COMPANY—First National Bank of Louisville, pg. 413
FIRST NATIONAL BANK OF CENTRAL CALIFORNIA—Pacific Capital Bancorp, pg. 839
FIRST NATIONAL BANK OF LOUISVILLE, pg. 413
FIRST SIGNATURE BANK & TRUST CO.—John Hancock Mutual Life Insurance Company, pg. 596
GLENVIEW STATE BANK—Cummins-American Corp., pg. 305
GREAT LAKES FINANCIAL RESOURCES, INC., pg. 481
HEREFORD STATE BANK—First Abilene Bankshares, Inc., pg. 412
MARQUETTE BANK ROCHESTER—Bank Shares, Inc., pg. 117
MBANK NEW BRAUNFELS—MCorp, pg. 733
MCORP, pg. 732
PACIFIC CAPITAL BANCORP, pg. 839
PARK BANK—Bankmanagers Corp., pg. 118
RIVERHEAD SAVINGS BANK—American Savings Bank, pg. 60
TAYLOR CORPORATION, pg. 1081

6029 — COMMERCIAL BANKS, NEC

BREMER FINANCIAL SERVICES, INC.—Bremer Financial Corporation, pg. 173
BROWN BROTHERS, HARRIMAN & CO., pg. 181
FIRST AMERICAN BANK—Bremer Financial Corporation, pg. 173

FIRST AMERICAN BANK—Bremer Financial Corporation, pg. 173
FIRST AMERICAN BANK—Bremer Financial Corporation, pg. 173
FIRST AMERICAN BANK—Bremer Financial Corporation, pg. 173
FIRST AMERICAN BANK—Bremer Financial Corporation, pg. 173
FIRST AMERICAN BANK—Bremer Financial Corporation, pg. 173
FIRST AMERICAN BANK—Bremer Financial Corporation, pg. 173
FIRST AMERICAN BANK—Bremer Financial Corporation, pg. 173
FIRST AMERICAN BANK—Bremer Financial Corporation, pg. 173
FIRST AMERICAN BANK—Bremer Financial Corporation, pg. 173
FIRST AMERICAN BANK OF APOSTLE ISLANDS—Bremer Financial Corporation, pg. 173
FIRST AMERICAN BANK METRO—Bremer Financial Corporation, pg. 173
FIRST AMERICAN BANK SOUTHWEST—Bremer Financial Corporation, pg. 173
FIRST AMERICAN BANK & TRUST—Bremer Financial Corporation, pg. 173
FIRST AMERICAN BANK & TRUST—Bremer Financial Corporation, pg. 173
FIRST AMERICAN BANK & TRUST—Bremer Financial Corporation, pg. 173
FIRST AMERICAN BANK & TRUST—Bremer Financial Corporation, pg. 173
FIRST AMERICAN NATIONAL BANK—Bremer Financial Corporation, pg. 173
FIRST AMERICAN NATIONAL BANK—Bremer Financial Corporation, pg. 173
SOCIETY FOR SAVINGS BANCORP, INC., pg. 1016

6035 — SAVINGS INSTITUTIONS, FEDERALLY CHARTERED

ALTUS FEDERAL SAVINGS BANK, pg. 46
BAY SAVINGS BANK, FSB—FirstFed Michigan Corporation, pg. 414
COUNTY MORTGAGE CORPORATION—FirstFed Michigan Corporation, pg. 414
THE ENSTAR GROUP, INC., pg. 382
FEDERAL SAVINGS BANK—Kemmons Wilson Companies, pg. 1194
FIRST FEDERAL OF MICHIGAN—FirstFed Michigan Corporation, pg. 414
FIRST FEDERAL SAVINGS AND LOAN ASSN. OF ROCHESTER, pg. 413
FIRST STATE FEDERAL SAVINGS & LOAN, pg. 413
FIRST TRUST SAVINGS BANK—Guarantee Title Co., Inc., pg. 491
FIRSTFED MICHIGAN CORPORATION, pg. 414
GREAT LAKES BANCORP, pg. 480
HERITAGE SERVICE CORPORATION—Guarantee Title Co., Inc., pg. 491
LEADER FEDERAL BANK FOR SAVINGS, pg. 663
OMNI SAVINGS BANK, FSB—FirstFed Michigan Corporation, pg. 414
SOCIETY FOR SAVINGS BANCORP, INC., pg. 1016
STERLING SAVINGS & LOAN—Seligman & Associates, Inc., pg. 988
STERLING SAVINGS & LOAN—Sterling Homes Corp., pg. 1047
SUPERIOR FEDERAL BANK, pg. 1063
TOPA SAVINGS BANK—Topa Equities Ltd, Inc., pg. 1101
THE TROY SAVINGS BANK, pg. 1116
WASHINGTON MUTUAL FEDERAL SAVINGS BANK—Washington Mutual Savings Bank, pg. 1166
THE WASHINGTON SAVINGS BANK, FSB—Washington Homes, Inc., pg. 1166
WESTERN FEDERAL SAVINGS & LOAN ASSOCIATION, pg. 1179
KEMMONS WILSON COMPANIES, pg. 1194

6036 — SAVINGS INSTITUTIONS, NOT FEDERALLY CHARTERED

EMIGRANT SAVINGS BANK, pg. 379
FRANKLIN FEDERAL SAVINGS ASSOCIATION, pg. 429
THE GUARDIAN LIFE INSURANCE COMPANY OF AMERICA, pg. 492
HELLER INTERNATIONAL, pg. 526
MACANDREWS & FORBES HOLDINGS INC., pg. 694
NEW HAVEN SAVINGS BANK, pg. 801
WASHINGTON MUTUAL SAVINGS BANK, pg. 1166

6061 — CREDIT UNIONS, FEDERALLY CHARTERED

FEDERAL FARM CREDIT BANKS FUNDING CORPORATION, pg. 404
TOWER LOAN OF MISSISSIPPI, INC.—Capitol Street Corp., pg. 216

6081 — BRANCHES & AGENCIES OF FOREIGN BANKS

BROWN BROTHERS, HARRIMAN & CO., pg. 181
BROWN BROTHERS HARRIMAN (LUXEMBOURG) S.A.—Brown Brothers, Harriman & Co., pg. 181
BROWN BROTHERS HARRIMAN TRUST CO. (CAYMAN) LTD.—Brown Brothers, Harriman & Co., pg. 181
CS FIRST BOSTON AUSTRALIA (HOLDINGS) LIMITED—CS First Boston Group, Inc., pg. 204
CS FIRST BOSTON (HONG KONG) LIMITED—CS First Boston Group, Inc., pg. 204
CS FIRST BOSTON (SINGAPORE) LIMITED—CS First Boston Group, Inc., pg. 204
CREDIT SUISSE FIRST BOSTON AG—CS First Boston Group, Inc., pg. 204
CREDIT SUISSE FIRST BOSTON UK LIMITED—CS First Boston Group, Inc., pg. 204
FINANCIERE CREDIT SUISSE-FIRST BOSTON—CS First Boston Group, Inc., pg. 204
FIRST AMERICAN INTERNATIONAL BANK—First American Bankshares, Inc., pg. 412
FIRST BOSTON CANADA LIMITED—CS First Boston Group, Inc., pg. 204
FIRST BOSTON (JAPAN) LIMITED—CS First Boston Group, Inc., pg. 204
SUCCURSALE DE GENEVA—CS First Boston Group, Inc., pg. 204

6082 — FOREIGN TRADE & INTERNATIONAL BANKING INSTITUTIONS

PRUDENTIAL ASIA CAPITAL LIMITED—The Prudential Insurance Company of America, pg. 897

6091 — NONDEPOSIT TRUST FACILITIES

FIRST AMERICAN TRUST COMPANY OF MINNESOTA—Bremer Financial Corporation, pg. 173
INDUSTRIAL TRUST COMPANY—The Prudential Insurance Company of America, pg. 897
LANE INDUSTRIES, INC., pg. 656
METROPOLITAN TRUST COMPANY OF CANADA—Metropolitan Life Insurance Co., pg. 745

6099 — FUNCTIONS RELATED TO DEPOSITORY BANKING, NEC

BROWN BROTHERS, HARRIMAN & CO., pg. 181
THE CARLYLE GROUP—Carlyle Holding Corporation, pg. 222
CARLYLE HOLDING CORPORATION, pg. 222
CIRRUS SYSTEM, INC.—Mastercard International, Inc., pg. 720
CONTINENTAL COIN CORPORATION, pg. 278
FIDELITY EXPRESS MONEY ORDER COMPANY DIVISION—GSC Enterprises, Inc., pg. 440
UNITED SERVICES AUTOMOBILE ASSOCIATION (USAA), pg. 1134

6141 — PERSONAL CREDIT INSTITUTIONS

AMGRO, INC.—All America Financial, pg. 34
AMERICAN FAMILY FINANCIAL SERVICES, INC.—American Family Mutual Insurance Co., pg. 52
AMFAC, INC.—JMB Realty Corporation, pg. 585
FAIRMOUNT MORTGAGE, INC.—Del Webb's Coventry, pg. 1171
FIDELITY ACCEPTANCE CORPORATION—Society for Savings Bancorp, Inc., pg. 1016
MID-STATE HOMES, INC.—Walter Industries, Inc., pg. 1162
NESOTA CO.—The Minnesota Mutual Life Insurance Company, pg. 758
NEW YORK FINANCIAL CORP.—Shepaug Corporation, pg. 998
PERSONAL FINANCE CO.—The Minnesota Mutual Life Insurance Company, pg. 758
PUBLIX SUPER MARKETS, INC.—Publix Supermarkets Inc., pg. 899
L. B. SMITH, INC., pg. 1013
TOPA THRIFT & LOAN ASSOCIATION—Topa Equities Ltd, Inc., pg. 1101
U-HAUL INTERNATIONAL, INC.—Amerco, A Nevada Corporation, pg. 48
U.R.M. DEVELOPMENT CORP.—U.R.M. Stores, Inc., pg. 1124
UNITED STATES REALTY & INVESTMENT CO., pg. 1137
WASHINGTON HOMES FINANCIAL CORPORATION—Washington Homes, Inc., pg. 1166
WASHINGTON HOMES FINANCIAL CORPORATION, III—Washington Homes, Inc., pg. 1166
WASHINGTON HOMES FINANCIAL CORPORATION, II—Washington Homes, Inc., pg. 1166

6153 — SHORT-TERM BUSINESS CREDIT INSTITUTIONS, EXCEPT AGRICULTURAL

ACACIA FINANCIAL CORPORATION—The Acacia Group, pg. 10
BLUE RIDGE FINANCE CO., INC.—Fairway Ford, Inc., pg. 398
BORG-WARNER CORPORATION, pg. 165
CENTURY BUSINESS CREDIT CORPORATION, pg. 235
CHICAGO HOLDINGS, INC., pg. 245
CONCORD ASSETS GROUP, INC., pg. 272
THE EL-BEE CHARGIT CORP.—The Elder-Beerman Stores Corp., pg. 373
EQUITY FUND ADVISORS INC., pg. 385
GOLDMAN SACHS MONEY MARKETS INC.—Goldman, Sachs & Co., pg. 468
GRIMMER REALTY CO. INC., pg. 488
HCB CONTRACTORS, pg. 496
HAWTHORNE CORP., pg. 518
INTEGRATEC, pg. 573
LANDAU & HEYMAN INC., pg. 654
LYNDEN FINANCIAL SERVICES, INC.—Lynden Incorporated, pg. 689
MACY CREDIT CORP.—R. H. Macy & Co., Inc., pg. 699
MASTERCARD INTERNATIONAL, INC., pg. 720
MASTERCARD INTERNATIONAL, INC.—Mastercard International, Inc., pg. 720
MASTERCARD INTERNATIONAL, INC.—Mastercard International, Inc., pg. 720
OXFORD FINANCE COMPANIES, INC.—Oxford First Corporation, pg. 835
OXFORD FIRST CORPORATION, pg. 834
SPATZ & CO., pg. 1026
STROUSE GREENBERG & CO., INC., pg. 1054
VISA U.S.A. INC., pg. 1153

6159 — MISCELLANEOUS BUSINESS CREDIT INSTITUTIONS

ACACIA FINANCIAL CORPORATION—The Acacia Group, pg. 10
AGRATRADE FINANCING, INC.—Gold Kist, Inc., pg. 465
AGWAY FINANCIAL CORPORATION—Agway, Inc., pg. 25
ALLEGHENY INTERNATIONAL CREDIT CORP.—Sunbeam-Oster Company, Inc., pg. 1059
BRAC CREDIT CORP.—Beech Holdings Corp., pg. 131
BELL & HOWELL ACCEPTANCE CORPORATION—Bell & Howell Company, pg. 135
CSFB (GILTS) LIMITED—CS First Boston Group, Inc., pg. 204
W. P. CAREY & CO., INC., pg. 218
CARGILL INC., pg. 219
CHARTER INVESTMENT CO.—Academy Insurance Group, Inc., pg. 11
CHICAGO WEST PULLMAN FINANCIAL CORPORATION—Chicago West Pullman Corporation, pg. 246
CHICORP FINANCIAL SERVICES—Chicorp, Inc., pg. 247
CHICORP, INC., pg. 247
COBANK—Federal Farm Credit Banks Funding Corporation, pg. 405
COLE TAYLOR FINANCIAL GROUP, pg. 260
THE COOPERATIVE FINANCE ASSN., INC.—Farmland Industries, Inc., pg. 402
COTTER ACCEPTANCE CO., INC.—Cotter & Company, pg. 288
THE DYSON-KISSNER-MORAN CORPORATION, pg. 357
FARM CREDIT BANK OF BALTIMORE—Federal Farm Credit Banks Funding Corporation, pg. 405
FARM CREDIT BANK OF COLUMBIA—Federal Farm Credit Banks Funding Corporation, pg. 405
FARM CREDIT BANK OF LOUISVILLE—Federal Farm Credit Banks Funding Corporation, pg. 405
FARM CREDIT BANK OF OMAHA—Federal Farm Credit Banks Funding Corporation, pg. 405
FARM CREDIT BANK OF ST. LOUIS—Federal Farm Credit Banks Funding Corporation, pg. 405
FARM CREDIT BANK OF ST. PAUL—Federal Farm Credit Banks Funding Corporation, pg. 405
FARM CREDIT BANK OF SPOKANE—Federal Farm Credit Banks Funding Corporation, pg. 405
FARM CREDIT BANK OF SPRINGFIELD—Federal Farm Credit Banks Funding Corporation, pg. 405
FARM CREDIT BANK OF TEXAS—Federal Farm Credit Banks Funding Corporation, pg. 405
FARM CREDIT BANK OF WICHITA—Federal Farm Credit Banks Funding Corporation, pg. 405
FEDERAL INTERMEDIATE CREDIT BANK OF JACKSON—Federal Farm Credit Banks Funding Corporation, pg. 405
FIRST CONNECTICUT SBIC, pg. 412
FIRST FRANKLIN FINANCIAL CORP.—1st Franklin Corporation, pg. 413
FIRST UNITED SMALL BUSINESS INVESTMENT CO.—James Ferrera & Sons, Inc., pg. 407
FRIONA AGRICULTURE CREDIT CORP.—Friona Industries, L.P., pg. 434
GOLODETZ CORPORATION, pg. 469
INDUSTRIAL TRUST COMPANY—The Prudential Insurance Company of America, pg. 897
JOHN HANCOCK LEASING CORPORATION—John Hancock Mutual Life Insurance Company, pg. 596
EDWARD D. JONES & CO., pg. 603
LEADER FEDERAL BANK FOR SAVINGS, pg. 663
LEVITZ CREDIT CORPORATION—LFC Holding Corporation, pg. 648
MGIC INVESTMENT CORPORATION—Northwestern Mutual Life Insurance Co., pg. 815
MACKAY-SHIELDS FINANCIAL CORP.—New York Life Insurance Company, pg. 803
MERIDIAN TECHNOLOGY LEASING SERVICES, pg. 740
METLIFE CAPITAL CREDIT CORP.—Metropolitan Life Insurance Co., pg. 744
METLIFE FUNDING CO.—Metropolitan Life Insurance Co., pg. 744
METLIFE SECURITIES, INC.—Metropolitan Life Insurance Co., pg. 745
METRIC REALTY, INC.—Metropolitan Life Insurance Co., pg. 745
NATIONAL COMPUTER PRINT, INC., pg. 786
NETWORK HOME SERVICES, INC.—Network Real Estate of California, Inc., pg. 798
NEW YORK CITY OFF TRACK BETTING CORP., pg. 802
NEW YORK LIFE INSURANCE COMPANY, pg. 802
O/E AUTOMATION, INC., pg. 819
OLD STONE OF CALIFORNIA, INC., pg. 823
OXFORD FINANCE COMPANIES, INC.—Oxford First Corporation, pg. 835
OXFORD FIRST CORPORATION, pg. 834
PONDEROSA FINANCIAL CORPORATION—Metromedia Company, pg. 744
PONLUPA RESTAURANT FINANCING, INC.—Metromedia Company, pg. 744
THE PRINCIPAL/EGT FINANCIAL CORPORATION—The Principal Financial Group, pg. 891
PROFESSIONAL SECURITIES CORP.—Huntco Inc., pg. 554
PRUCAPITAL, INC.—The Prudential Insurance Company of America, pg. 897

PRUDENTIAL AGRICULTURAL CREDIT, INC.—The Prudential Insurance Company of America, pg. 897
THE PRUDENTIAL ASSET MANAGEMENT CO., INC.—The Prudential Insurance Company of America, pg. 897
REGAN HOLDING CORPORATION, pg. 921
SAINT PAUL BANK FOR COOPERATIVES—Federal Farm Credit Banks Funding Corporation, pg. 405
SCOTSMAN GROUP, INC.—The Scotsman Group, Inc., pg. 982
SENCORP, pg. 989
SOVEREIGN GROUP INC., pg. 1024
SPRINGFIELD BANK FOR COOPERATIVES—Federal Farm Credit Banks Funding Corporation, pg. 405
STAPLE COTTON COOPERATIVE ASSOCIATION, pg. 1038
STAPLE COTTON DISCOUNT CORPORATION—Staple Cotton Cooperative Association, pg. 1039
SUMMERFIELD TRUCK CO. INC., pg. 1057
SUN DATA INC., pg. 1058
WESTERN FARM CREDIT BANK—Federal Farm Credit Banks Funding Corporation, pg. 405
THE YUCAIPA COMPANIES, pg. 1214

6162 — MORTGAGE BANKERS & LOAN CORRESPONDENTS

ALTUS MORTGAGE CORPORATION—Altus Federal Savings Bank, pg. 46
BLUE RIDGE FINANCE CO., INC.—Fairway Ford, Inc., pg. 398
CARDINAL REALTY SERVICES INC., pg. 218
CARLSBERG FINANCIAL CORP., pg. 220
DELTA LIFE CORPORATION, pg. 327
DUNGEY & ASSOCIATES—Harbor Financial Mortgage Corp., pg. 506
FGMC, INC.—General Homes Corporation, pg. 449
FIRST ADVANTAGE MORTGAGE CORPORATION—First American Bankshares, Inc., pg. 412
GFM INTERNATIONAL INVESTORS, LIMITED—Metropolitan Life Insurance Co., pg. 745
GARVEY INDUSTRIES, INC., pg. 443
GLOBE MORTGAGE COMPANY, pg. 464
SHELDON GOOD & CO., INC., pg. 470
GUARANTY CORPORATION, pg. 491
HARBOR FINANCIAL INSURANCE AGENCY—Harbor Financial Mortgage Corp., pg. 506
HARBOR FINANCIAL MORTGAGE CORP., pg. 506
HARBOR FINANCIAL PROPERTY MANAGEMENT CO.—Harbor Financial Mortgage Corp., pg. 506
HARBOR FINANCIAL TITLE CORP.—Harbor Financial Mortgage Corp., pg. 506
ILLINOIS HOME MORTGAGE CORP.—The Hassinger Companies, pg. 516
INTEGRATED FUNDING, INC.—Integrated Resources, Inc., pg. 573
KALIN ENTERPRISES, INC., pg. 615
J. I. KISLAK INC., pg. 633
KRAUS-ANDERSON MORTGAGE CO.—Kraus-Anderson, Inc., pg. 644
LEADER FEDERAL BANK FOR SAVINGS, pg. 663
METMOR FINANCIAL, INC.—Metropolitan Life Insurance Co., pg. 745
MID-STATES MORTGAGE CORP.—Seligman & Associates, Inc., pg. 988
MIDCOAST MORTGAGE CORPORATION, pg. 751
MORGUARD INVESTMENTS LIMITED, TORONTO—Metropolitan Life Insurance Co., pg. 745
NATIONAL MORTGAGE COMPANY, pg. 792
NETWORK CAPITAL GROUP—Network Real Estate of California, Inc., pg. 798
NETWORK HOME SERVICES, INC.—Network Real Estate of California, Inc., pg. 798
NEW ENGLAND LIFE MORTGAGE FUNDING CORP.—The New England, pg. 799
OXFORD FINANCE COMPANIES, INC.—Oxford First Corporation, pg. 835
OXFORD FIRST CORPORATION, pg. 834
PRINCIPAL RESIDENTIAL ADVISORS—The Principal Financial Group, pg. 891
PRUDENTIAL MORTGAGE CAPITAL—The Prudential Insurance Company of America, pg. 897
THE PRUDENTIAL REALTY GROUP—The Prudential Insurance Company of America, pg. 897
SCHNEIDER COMMERCIAL REAL ESTATE, pg. 977
SHAPELL INDUSTRIES, INC., pg. 995
SOCIETY MORTGAGE CORPORATION—Society for Savings Bancorp, Inc., pg. 1016
STATE-WIDE CAPITAL CORP., pg. 1041
TRANSCOASTAL MORTGAGE COMPANY, pg. 1107
TRECO REALTY GROUP, INC.—Sunstates Realty Group Inc., pg. 1062
VANFED MORTGAGE COMPANY—Washington Mutual Savings Bank, pg. 1166

6163 — LOAN BROKERS

ACACIA MORTGAGE CORPORATION—The Acacia Group, pg. 10
ACTION COMMODITIES CORPORATION—Tennessee Dressed Beef Company, pg. 1087
HELP MANAGEMENT CORPORATION, pg. 527
HIGHER EDUCATION ASSISTANCE FOUNDATION—Help Management Corporation, pg. 528
HIGHER EDUCATION LOAN PROGRAM OF KANSAS—Help Management Corporation, pg. 528
HIGHER EDUCATION LOAN PROGRAM OF WEST VIRGINIA—Help Management Corporation, pg. 528
J. I. KISLAK INC., pg. 633
REGENCY GROUP INC., pg. 922
RESOURCES FUNDING CORP.—Integrated Resources, Inc., pg. 573
RESOURCES REAL ESTATE FINANCE GROUP, INC.—Integrated Resources, Inc., pg. 573
TOPA EQUITIES LTD, INC., pg. 1101

6211 — SECURITY BROKERS, DEALERS & FLOTATION COMPANIES

AAL DISTRIBUTORS INC.—Aid Association For Lutherans, pg. 26
ALLEN & COMPANY INCORPORATED, pg. 35
ALTUS SERVICES, INC.—Altus Federal Savings Bank, pg. 46
AMERICAN FUNDS ADVISOR INC., pg. 55
AMERICAN LIBERTY FINANCIAL CORP., pg. 57
AMERITAS LIFE INSURANCE CORP., pg. 66
ARNHOLD AND S. BLEICHROEDER, INC., pg. 84
BAIRD, PATRICK & CO., INC., pg. 114
BARR BROTHERS & CO., INC., pg. 121
SANFORD C. BERNSTEIN & CO., INC., pg. 144
BISHOPSGATE CORP.—Shepaug Corporation, pg. 998
WILLIAM BLAIR & COMPANY, pg. 155
J. C. BRADFORD & CO., pg. 170
BROWN BROTHERS, HARRIMAN & CO., pg. 181
BROWN BROTHERS, HARRIMAN (HONG KONG) LTD.—Brown Brothers, Harriman & Co., pg. 181
BROWN BROTHERS HARRIMAN LIMITED—Brown Brothers, Harriman & Co., pg. 181
BROWN BROTHERS HARRIMAN SERVICES AG—Brown Brothers, Harriman & Co., pg. 181
BROWN BROTHERS, HARRIMAN & CO., TOKYO—Brown Brothers, Harriman & Co., pg. 181
BROWN HARRIMAN CORPORATION—Brown Brothers, Harriman & Co., pg. 181
BULL, INC.—Science Applications International Corporation, pg. 981
BUTCHER & CO., INC., pg. 196
CS FIRST BOSTON FINANCIERE, INC.—CS First Boston Group, Inc., pg. 204
CS FIRST BOSTON GROUP, INC., pg. 203
CS FIRST BOSTON PACIFIC, INC.—CS First Boston Group, Inc., pg. 204
CS FIRST BOSTON SINGAPORE LTD.—CS First Boston Group, Inc., pg. 204
CS FIRST BOSTON USA, INC.—CS First Boston Group, Inc., pg. 204
CSFB-EFFECTENBANK AKTIENGESELLSCHAFT—CS First Boston Group, Inc., pg. 204
CSFB INVESTMENT MANAGEMENT LIMITED—CS First Boston Group, Inc., pg. 204
CALVERT GROUP, LTD.—The Acacia Group, pg. 11
CAPITOL STREET CORP., pg. 216
CARGILL INC., pg. 219
CARGILL INVESTOR SERVICES, INC.—Cargill Inc., pg. 219
CHICAGO CORP.—Chicorp, Inc., pg. 247
CHICORP, INC., pg. 247
CODE, HENNESSY & SIMMONS, pg. 258
COLUMBIAN PHILIPPINES INC.—Columbian Rope Company, pg. 266
CONNECTICUT MUTUAL FINANCIAL SERVICES—Connecticut Mutual Life Insurance Company, pg. 275
CORDOVA LABORATORIES-I.A.F. DIV.—Cordova Enterprise, pg. 286
COWEN & COMPANY, pg. 291
CREDIT SUISSE FIRST BOSTON BUDAPEST RT—CS First Boston Group, Inc., pg. 204
CREDIT SUISSE FIRST BOSTON ESPANA S.A.—CS First Boston Group, Inc., pg. 204
CREDIT SUISSE FIRST BOSTON FRANCE S.A.—CS First Boston Group, Inc., pg. 204
CREDIT SUISSE FIRST BOSTON ITALIA (COMPAGNIA MOBILIARE) SPA—CS First Boston Group, Inc., pg. 204
CREDIT SUISSE FIRST BOSTON LTD.—CS First Boston Group, Inc., pg. 204
CROWELL, WEEDON & CO., pg. 301
D.A. DAVIDSON & CO., pg. 318
DOMINICK & DOMINICK, INCORPORATED, pg. 343
DOMINICK FUTURES CORPORATION—Dominick & Dominick, Incorporated, pg. 343
EQUITY SERVICES, INC.—National Life Insurance Company, pg. 791
FARMLAND SECURITIES CO.—Farmland Industries, Inc., pg. 402
FINANCIAL AIMS CORPORATION—D.A. Davidson & Co., pg. 318
FINANCIAL NETWORK INVESTMENT, pg. 410
THE FIRST BOSTON CORPORATION—CS First Boston Group, Inc., pg. 203
FIRST BOSTON (JAPAN) LIMITED—CS First Boston Group, Inc., pg. 204
FIRST BOSTON (PUERTO RICO), INC.—CS First Boston Group, Inc., pg. 204
FIRST BOSTON SECURITIES CORPORATION—CS First Boston Group, Inc., pg. 204
FIRST SOUTHWEST COMPANY, pg. 413
FIRSTATE SERVICES, INC.—First State Federal Savings & Loan, pg. 414
FOLGER NOLAN FLEMING DOUGLAS, pg. 422
FRANKLIN SECURITIES, INC.—1st Franklin Corporation, pg. 413
GOLDMAN SACHS (ASIA) LIMITED—Goldman, Sachs & Co., pg. 468
GOLDMAN, SACHS & CO., pg. 468
GOLDMAN SACHS FINANZ AG—Goldman, Sachs & Co., pg. 468
GOLDMAN SACHS INTERNATIONAL LIMITED—Goldman, Sachs & Co., pg. 468
GOLDMAN SACHS (JAPAN) CORP.—Goldman, Sachs & Co., pg. 468
GOLDMARK PARTNERS—Goldmark Industries, Ltd., pg. 469
GOULD INVESTORS, L.P., pg. 473
LEONARD GREEN & PARTNERS, pg. 485
GUARDIAN INVESTOR SERVICES CORP.—The Guardian Life Insurance Company of America, pg. 492
ICAHN & CO., INC., pg. 561
INDEPENDENCE HOLDING COMPANY—Geneve Corporation, pg. 451
INTEGRATED RESOURCES CAPITAL SERVICES, INC.—Integrated Resources, Inc., pg. 573
INTEGRATED RESOURCES EQUITY CORP.—Integrated Resources, Inc., pg. 573
INTEGRATED RESOURCES, INC., pg. 573
INTEGRATED RESOURCES INSURANCE & INVESTMENT SERVICES, LTD.—Integrated Resources, Inc., pg. 573
INTEGRATED RESOURCES (JAPAN), INC.—Integrated Resources, Inc., pg. 573
INTEGRATED RESOURCES MARKETING, INC.—Integrated Resources, Inc., pg. 573
J. & W. SELIGMAN & COMPANY, pg. 584
JANNEY MONTGOMERY SCOTT INC.—The Penn Mutual Life Insurance Company, pg. 858
JOHN HANCOCK MUTUAL FUNDS—John Hancock Mutual Life Insurance Company, pg. 596
JOHNSTON, LEMON & CO. INC., pg. 601
EDWARD D. JONES & CO., pg. 603
JORDAN COMPANY, pg. 604
KALB VOORHIS & CO., pg. 615
KEYSTONE GROUP INC.—Sovereign Group Inc., pg. 1024
LIBERTY DISTRIBUTORS INC.—Liberty Mutual Insurance Co., pg. 674
LIBERTY FINANCIAL COMPANIES—Liberty Mutual Insurance Co., pg. 674
MML INVESTORS SERVICES, INC.—Massachusetts Mutual Life Insurance Co., pg. 718
MML SERIES INVESTMENT FUND—Massachusetts Mutual Life Insurance Co., pg. 718
MESIROW FINANCIAL, pg. 741
MONY SECURITIES CORP.—The Mutual Life Insurance Company of New York (MONY), pg. 778
MURPHY FAVRE, INC.—Washington Mutual Savings Bank, pg. 1166
MUTUAL BENEFIT FINANCIAL SERVICE CO.—Mutual Benefit Life Insurance Company, pg. 778
NBSC INVESTMENT CO.—High Point Financial Corp., pg. 534
NATIONAL LIFE INSURANCE COMPANY, pg. 791
THE NEW ENGLAND, pg. 799
NEW ENGLAND SECURITIES CORP.—The New England, pg. 799
NYLIFE MORTGAGE INC.—New York Life Insurance Company, pg. 803
NYLIFE SECURITIES INC.—New York Life Insurance Company, pg. 803
NYLIFE FUNDING INC.—New York Life Insurance Company, pg. 803
WILLIAM O'NEIL & CO., INC., pg. 827
OXBOW CORPORATION, pg. 834
PML SECURITIES CO.—Provident Mutual Life Insurance Co., pg. 896
PACIFIC EQUITIES NETWORK—Pacific Mutual Life Insurance Company, pg. 841
PARAMETRIC PORTFOLIO ASSOCIATES, INC.—Pacific Mutual Life Insurance Company, pg. 841
PHOENIX AMERICAN ALARM AFFILIATES, INC.—Phoenix American Incorporated, pg. 868
PHOENIX ENTERPRISES INC., pg. 868
PHOENIX EQUITY PLANNING CORP.—Phoenix Home Life Mutual Insurance Company, pg. 868
PHOENIX SECURITIES, INC.—Phoenix American Incorporated, pg. 868
PROVIDENT MUTUAL LIFE INSURANCE CO., pg. 896
PRUCAPITAL SECURITIES CO., INC.—The Prudential Insurance Company of America, pg. 897
PRUCO SECURITIES CORP.—The Prudential Insurance Company of America, pg. 896
PRUDENTIAL EQUITY INVESTMENT DIV.—The Prudential Insurance Company of America, pg. 897
THE PRUDENTIAL INSURANCE COMPANY OF AMERICA, pg. 896
THE PRUDENTIAL INVESTMENT CORP.—The Prudential Insurance Company of America, pg. 897
PRUDENTIAL SECURITIES INC.—The Prudential Insurance Company of America, pg. 897
REVLON, INC.—MacAndrews & Forbes Holdings Inc., pg. 696
RONEY & CO., pg. 946
ROTHSCHILD INC.—Rothschild North America Inc., pg. 951
ROTHSCHILD NORTH AMERICA INC., pg. 951
SIGMA GROUP—Provident Mutual Life Insurance Co., pg. 896
STEPHENS, INC., pg. 1046
M.L. STERN & COMPANY, INC., pg. 1047
TNE FUNDING CORPORATION—The New England, pg. 799
TNE INVESTMENT SERVICES CORP.—The New England, pg. 799
TEACHERS MANAGEMENT & INVESTMENT CORPORATION, pg. 1082
TRERICE/TOSTO INVESTMENT SERVICES CO.—Trerice Tosto International, pg. 1110
TWENTIETH CENTURY INVESTORS—Twentieth Century Companies, pg. 1121
TWENTIETH CENTURY INVESTORS, INC.—Twentieth Century Companies, pg. 1121
UNITED SERVICES AUTOMOBILE ASSOCIATION (USAA), pg. 1134
UNIVERSAL SECURITIES CORPORATION, pg. 1139
UTILITIES & INDUSTRIES MANAGEMENT CORP.—Shepaug Corporation, pg. 998
WEATHERLY PRIVATE CAPITAL, INC.—Weatherly Financial Group, pg. 1170
WEATHERLY SECURITIES CORP.—Weatherly Financial Group, pg. 1170
WHEAT, FIRST SECURITIES INC., pg. 1184

6221 — COMMODITY CONTRACTS BROKERS & DEALERS

AMERITAS LIFE INSURANCE CORP., pg. 66
J. ARON & COMPANY (U.K.), LIMITED—Goldman, Sachs & Co., pg. 468
BROMAR INC., pg. 179
CARGILL INC., pg. 219
CARGILL INVESTOR SERVICES, INC.—Cargill Inc., pg. 219
CHICORP, INC., pg. 247
CONTINENTAL GRAIN COMPANY, pg. 279
DOMINICK & DOMINICK, INCORPORATED, pg. 343
DUNAVANT COMMODITY CORP.—Dunavant Enterprises, Inc., pg. 352
GOLDMAN SACHS (ASIA) LIMITED—Goldman, Sachs & Co., pg. 468
GOLDMAN, SACHS & CO., pg. 468
GOLDMAN SACHS (JAPAN) CORP.—Goldman, Sachs & Co., pg. 468
THE GRANADA GROUP, pg. 475
MARTRADE LTD., pg. 716
P. S. INTERNATIONAL INC., pg. 837
PRIMARY COAL INC.—Primary Industries Corporation, pg. 889
PRIMARY INDUSTRIES CORPORATION, pg. 889
REFCO GROUP LTD., pg. 921
REFCO INC.—Refco Group Ltd., pg. 921
SIMONDS-SHIELDS-THEIS GRAIN CO., pg. 1006
WOLCOTT & LINCOLN, INC., pg. 1198

6231 — SECURITY & COMMODITY EXCHANGES

THE AMERICAN STOCK EXCHANGE, pg. 62
AMERICAN STOCK EXCHANGE CLEARING CORP.—The American Stock Exchange, pg. 63
AMERICAN STOCK EXCHANGE REALTY ASSOCIATES INC.—The American Stock Exchange, pg. 63
AMEX COMMODITIES CORPORATION—The American Stock Exchange, pg. 63
CHICAGO MERCANTILE EXCHANGE, pg. 245
NATIONAL SECURITIES CLEARING CORP.—The American Stock Exchange, pg. 63
OPTIONS CLEARING CORP.—The American Stock Exchange, pg. 63

6282 — INVESTMENT ADVICE

AAL CAPITAL MANAGEMENT CORP.—Aid Association For Lutherans, pg. 26
ACFC CORPORATE FINANCE LIMITED—Metropolitan Life Insurance Co., pg. 745
BACK BAY ADVISORS, INC.—The New England, pg. 799
BAKER & MCKENZIE INTERNATIONAL, pg. 115
SANFORD C. BERNSTEIN & CO., INC., pg. 144
WILLIAM BLAIR & COMPANY, pg. 155
CALMARK INVESTMENT COMPANY, pg. 211
CALMARK PROPERTIES, INC.—Calmark Investment Company, pg. 211
CARGILL FINANCIAL MARKETS DIV.—Cargill Inc., pg. 219
CARGILL INC., pg. 219
CENTENNIAL CAPITAL CORPORATION—Massachusetts Mutual Life Insurance Co., pg. 719
CHIEF FINANCIAL SERVICES—Chief Industries, Inc., pg. 247
COMPOSITE RESEARCH & MANAGEMENT COMPANY—Washington Mutual Savings Bank, pg. 1166
CONNECTICUT MUTUAL FINANCIAL SERVICES—Connecticut Mutual Life Insurance Company, pg. 275
DRAYCOTT PARTNERS, LTD.—The New England, pg. 800
FIDUCIARY TRUST COMPANY INTERNATIONAL, pg. 408
FIDUCIARY TRUST COMPANY OF NEW YORK LTD.—Fiduciary Trust Company International, pg. 409
FIRST BOSTON ASSET MANAGEMENT CORPORATION—CS First Boston Group, Inc., pg. 204
FIRSTATE SERVICES, INC.—First State Federal Savings & Loan, pg. 414
FOLGER NOLAN FLEMING DOUGLAS, pg. 422
FORT WASHINGTON INVESTMENT ADVISORS, INC.—Western & Southern Life Insurance Co., pg. 1181
GOLODETZ CORPORATION, pg. 469
GREYSTONE REALTY CORPORATION—New York Life Insurance Company, pg. 802
LEON HENDRICKSON, pg. 529
HIGH POINT INVESTMENT ADVISORY SERVICES—High Point Financial Corp., pg. 534
IFS FINANCIAL SERVICES, INC.—Western & Southern Life Insurance Co., pg. 1181
INDEPENDENCE INVESTMENT ASSOCIATES, INC.—John Hancock Mutual Life Insurance Company, pg. 596
JOHN HANCOCK ADVISERS, INC.—John Hancock Mutual Life Insurance Company, pg. 596
JOSEPH, LITTLEJOHN & LEVY, pg. 607
LOOMIS, SAYLES & CO.—The New England, pg. 799
MANHATTAN NATIONAL CORPORATION—The Union Central Life Insurance Co., pg. 1128
MARLBOROUGH CAPITAL ADVISORS, INC.—The New England, pg. 799
MESIROW FINANCIAL, pg. 741
MIMLIC ASSET MANAGEMENT COMPANY—The Minnesota Mutual Life Insurance Company, pg. 758
MONITOR CAPITAL ADVISORS INC.—New York Life Insurance Company, pg. 803
MONY ADVISERS, INC.—The Mutual Life Insurance Company of New York (MONY), pg. 778
MURPHY FAVRE SECURITIES SERVICES, INC.—Washington Mutual Savings Bank, pg. 1166
NTC GROUP, pg. 781
NATIONAL LIFE INVESTMENT MANAGEMENT CO., INC.—National Life Insurance Company, pg. 791
NEW ENGLAND PORTFOLIO ADVISORS, INC.—The New England, pg. 799
NYLIFE ADVISERS, INC.—New York Life Insurance Company, pg. 803
OPPENHEIMER ASSET MANAGEMENT CORP.—Massachusetts Mutual Life Insurance Co., pg. 719
OPPENHEIMER MANAGEMENT CORP.—Massachusetts Mutual Life Insurance Co., pg. 719
PACIFIC INVESTMENT MANAGEMENT CO.—Pacific Mutual Life Insurance Company, pg. 841
PARAMETRIC PORTFOLIO ASSOCIATES, INC.—Pacific Mutual Life Insurance Company, pg. 841
PMREALTY ADVISORS, INC.—Pacific Mutual Life Insurance Company, pg. 841
PRESTON RIDGE FINANCIAL SERVICES CORPORATION—Washington Mutual Savings Bank, pg. 1167
PROVIDENT MUTUAL LIFE INSURANCE CO., pg. 896
RE/MAX INTERNATIONAL, INC., pg. 915
ROTHSCHILD ASSET MANAGEMENT INC.—Rothschild North America Inc., pg. 951
SENTINEL ADVISORS, INC.—National Life Insurance Company, pg. 791
SIGMA GROUP—Provident Mutual Life Insurance Co., pg. 896
STATE STREET RESEARCH & MANAGEMENT COMPANY—Metropolitan Life Insurance Co., pg. 744
STRATTON MANAGEMENT COMPANY, pg. 1053
TRAINER WORTHAM & COMPANY INCORPORATED, pg. 1106
TRIDENT FINANCIAL CORPORATION, pg. 1113
TWENTIETH CENTURY COMPANIES, pg. 1121
UNITED PLANNERS' GROUP, INC.—Pacific Mutual Life Insurance Company, pg. 841
UNITED SERVICES AUTOMOBILE ASSOCIATION (USAA), pg. 1134
VANFED INVESTMENT SERVICE, INC.—Washington Mutual Savings Bank, pg. 1166
THE VANGUARD GROUP, INC., pg. 1145
WM FINANCIAL, INC.—Washington Mutual Savings Bank, pg. 1166
WESTPEAK INVESTMENT ADVISORS, INC.—The New England, pg. 799

6289 — SERVICES ALLIED WITH EXCHANGE OF SECURITIES OR COMMODITIES, NEC

ASSOCIATED GROUP INC.—The Associated Group, pg. 90
THE ASSOCIATED GROUP, pg. 90
CARGILL INC., pg. 219
HCB CONTRACTORS, pg. 496
INTEGRATED FINANCIAL—Integrated Resources, Inc., pg. 573
MONEX INTERNATIONAL, LTD., pg. 765
THE MUTUAL LIFE INSURANCE COMPANY OF NEW YORK (MONY), pg. 778
NTC GROUP, pg. 781
OPTIONS CLEARING CORP.—The American Stock Exchange, pg. 63
PHOENIX INVESTMENT COUNSEL INC.—Phoenix Home Life Mutual Insurance Company, pg. 868
PREMIUM ADVANCE COMPANY—Robert F. Driver Co., Inc., pg. 349
SENTINEL ADMINISTRATIVE SERVICE CORPORATION—National Life Insurance Company, pg. 791
STEPHENS, INC., pg. 1046
STEPHENS OVERSEAS SERVICES, INC.—Stephens, Inc., pg. 1046

6311 — LIFE INSURANCE

THE ACACIA GROUP, pg. 10
ACACIA NATIONAL LIFE INS. CO.—The Acacia Group, pg. 11
ACADEMY INSURANCE GROUP, INC., pg. 11
ACADEMY LIFE INSURANCE CO.—Academy Insurance Group, Inc., pg. 11
ADJUSTABLE LIFE INSURANCE COMPANY—The Minnesota Mutual Life Insurance Company, pg. 758
AID ASSOCIATION FOR LUTHERANS, pg. 26
ALBANY LIFE ASSURANCE COMPANY LIMITED—Metropolitan Life Insurance Co., pg. 745
JOHN ALDEN LIFE INSURANCE COMPANY—John Alden Financial Corporation, pg. 33
ALL AMERICA FINANCIAL, pg. 34
ALLIED GROUP INC.—Allied Mutual Insurance Company, pg. 38
ALLIED MUTUAL INSURANCE COMPANY, pg. 38
ALTUS SERVICES, INC.—Altus Federal Savings Bank, pg. 46
AMERICAN FAMILY LIFE INSURANCE CO.—American Family Mutual Insurance Co., pg. 52
AMERICAN FAMILY MUTUAL INSURANCE CO., pg. 51
AMERICAN FIDELITY CORP., pg. 52
AMERICAN FINANCIAL CORPORATION, pg. 52
AMERICAN HEALTH & SECURITY INSURANCE CO., INC.—American SelfCare Corporation, pg. 61
AMERICAN LIBERTY FINANCIAL CORP., pg. 57
AMERICAN MERCHANTS LIFE INSURANCE CO.—American Hardware Mutual Insurance Co., pg. 55
AMERICAN MUTUAL LIFE INSURANCE COMPANY, pg. 58
AMERICAN REPUBLIC INSURANCE CO., pg. 60
AMERICAN UNITED LIFE INSURANCE COMPANY, pg. 65
THE AMERICAN-WORLD LIFE INSURANCE CO.—Zale Corporation, pg. 1215
AMERITAS LIFE INSURANCE CORP., pg. 66
ANTHEM LIFE INSURANCE COMPANIES, INC.—The Associated Group, pg. 90
ASSOCIATED GROUP INC.—The Associated Group, pg. 90
THE ASSOCIATED GROUP, pg. 90
AUTO-OWNERS LIFE INSURANCE CO.—Auto-Owners Insurance, pg. 100
BENEFICIAL LIFE INSURANCE—Deseret Management Corporation, pg. 332
THE BERKSHIRE LIFE INSURANCE COMPANY, pg. 142
BOSTON MUTUAL LIFE INSURANCE CO., pg. 167
BRISTOL RECREATION SYSTEMS, INC.—Connecticut Mutual Life Insurance Company, pg. 275
CM LIFE INSURANCE COMPANY—Connecticut Mutual Life Insurance Company, pg. 275
CM TRANSNATIONAL—Connecticut Mutual Life Insurance Company, pg. 275
CSE CORPORATION, pg. 204
CUNA MUTUAL INSURANCE SOCIETY, pg. 205
CATHOLIC ORDER OF FORESTERS, pg. 229
CENTRAL LIFE ASSURANCE CO., pg. 232
CHAMPLAIN LIFE INSURANCE COMPANY—National Life Insurance Company, pg. 791
THE CHESAPEAKE LIFE INSURANCE CO., pg. 243
CIVIL SERVICE EMPLOYEES LIFE INSURANCE CO.—CSE Corporation, pg. 205
COLUMBIA GENERAL LIFE INSURANCE CO.—UniHealth America, pg. 1127
COLUMBIAN LIFE INSURANCE COMPANY—Columbian Mutual Life Insurance Co., pg. 266
COLUMBIAN MUTUAL LIFE INSURANCE CO., pg. 266
COLUMBUS LIFE INSURANCE CO.—Western & Southern Life Insurance Co., pg. 1181
COMPANION LIFE INSURANCE CO.—Mutual of Omaha Insurance Company, pg. 779
CONNECTICUT MUTUAL LIFE INSURANCE COMPANY, pg. 274
CONTINENTAL AMERICAN LIFE INSURANCE CO.—Provident Mutual Life Insurance Co., pg. 896
COUNTRY COMPANIES INSURANCE GROUP, pg. 289
COUNTRY INVESTORS LIFE ASSURANCE COMPANY—Country Companies Insurance Group, pg. 289
COUNTRY LIFE INSURANCE COMPANY—Country Companies Insurance Group, pg. 289
CUMIS GROUP INSURANCE—CUNA Mutual Insurance Society, pg. 206
THE CUMIS GROUP LTD.—CUNA Mutual Insurance Society, pg. 206
CUMIS LIFE INSURANCE CO.—CUNA Mutual Insurance Society, pg. 206
DELTA LIFE CORPORATION, pg. 327
ROBERT F. DRIVER CO., INC., pg. 349
EMPIRE LIFE INSURANCE COMPANY—Washington Mutual Savings Bank, pg. 1166
ERIE FAMILY LIFE INSURANCE COMPANY, pg. 386
ERIE INSURANCE GROUP—Erie Family Life Insurance Company, pg. 386
ERIN GROUP ADMINISTRATORS, INC., pg. 387
FARM & HOME LIFE INSURANCE CO.—The Chesapeake Life Insurance Co., pg. 243
FARMERS AND TRADERS LIFE INSURANCE CO., pg. 401
FARMLAND INSURANCE AGENCY, INC.—Farmland Industries, Inc., pg. 402
FINANCIAL LIFE COMPANIES, INC.—North Central Life Insurance Companies, pg. 813
FIRST PYRAMID LIFE INSURANCE COMPANY OF AMERICA—Victory Financial Group, Inc., pg. 1150
FLORISTS' MUTUAL INSURANCE CO., pg. 421
FRANDISCO LIFE INSURANCE CO.—1st Franklin Corporation, pg. 413
GAF INSURANCE LTD.—GAF Corporation, pg. 438
GENERAL AMERICAN LIFE INSURANCE CO., pg. 448
GOLDEN STATE MUTUAL LIFE INSURANCE COMPANY, pg. 467
GREAT AMERICAN HOLDING CORPORATION—American Financial Corporation, pg. 53
GROUP LIFE & HEALTH INSURANCE COMPANY—Blue Cross & Blue Shield of Texas, Inc., pg. 160
GROUPAMERICA INSURANCE CO.—Connecticut Mutual Life Insurance Company, pg. 275
GUARANTEE AMERICAN LIFE COMPANY—Guarantee Mutual Life Co., pg. 491
GUARANTEE MUTUAL LIFE CO., pg. 491
GUARANTY CORPORATION, pg. 491
GUARANTY SAVINGS INSURANCE COMPANY—Victory Financial Group, Inc., pg. 1150
GUARDIAN BAILLIE GIFFORD, LTD.—The Guardian Life Insurance Company of America, pg. 492
THE GUARDIAN INSURANCE & ANNUITY CO. (GIAC)—The Guardian Life Insurance Company of America, pg. 492
THE GUARDIAN LIFE INSURANCE COMPANY OF AMERICA, pg. 492
INTEGRATED RESOURCES, INC., pg. 573
JOHN HANCOCK MUTUAL LIFE INSURANCE COMPANY, pg. 595
KOLON-MET LIFE INSURANCE COMPANY LIMITED—Metropolitan Life Insurance Co., pg. 745
LAMAR FINANCIAL SERVICES INSURANCE COMPANY—Capitol Street Corp., pg. 216
LEAGUE LIFE INSURANCE CO.—CUNA Mutual Insurance Society, pg. 205
LIBERTY LIFE ASSURANCE COMPANY OF BOSTON—Liberty Mutual Insurance Co., pg. 674
LIFE INSURANCE CO. OF ARIZONA—The Chesapeake Life Insurance Co., pg. 243
LIFESURANCE CORPORATION—Victory Financial Group, Inc., pg. 1150
LOUISIANA NATIONAL LIFE INSURANCE COMPANY—Victory Financial Group, Inc., pg. 1150
LUTHERAN BROTHERHOOD, pg. 688
M M I COMPANIES, INC., pg. 692

MML BAY STATE LIFE INSURANCE COMPANY—Massachusetts Mutual Life Insurance Co., pg. 718
MML PENSION INSURANCE COMPANY—Massachusetts Mutual Life Insurance Co., pg. 718
MSI INSURANCE COMPANIES, pg. 693
MADISON NATIONAL LIFE INSURANCE CO., INC.—Geneve Corporation, pg. 451
MANHATTAN LIFE INSURANCE COMPANY—The Union Central Life Insurance Co., pg. 1128
MANHATTAN NATIONAL CORPORATION—The Union Central Life Insurance Co., pg. 1128
MARITIME LIFE ASSURANCE CO.—John Hancock Mutual Life Insurance Company, pg. 597
MASSACHUSETTS MUTUAL LIFE INSURANCE CO., pg. 718
MCWANE, INC., pg. 733
MEMBER SERVICE LIFE INSURANCE CO.—Blue Cross and Blue Shield of Oklahoma, pg. 159
MERCHANTS INSURANCE AGENCY—U.R.M. Stores, Inc., pg. 1124
METLIFE SECURITY INSURANCE COMPANY OF LOUISIANA—Metropolitan Life Insurance Co., pg. 745
METROPOLITAN INSURANCE & ANNUITY CO.—Metropolitan Life Insurance Co., pg. 744
METROPOLITAN LIFE INSURANCE CO., pg. 744
METROPOLITAN LIFE INSURANCE COMPANY OF CANADA—Metropolitan Life Insurance Co., pg. 745
METROPOLITAN TOWER LIFE INSURANCE CO.—Metropolitan Life Insurance Co., pg. 744
MIDLAND MUTUAL LIFE INSURANCE CO., pg. 751
MIDLAND NATIONAL LIFE INSURANCE CO.—Sammons Enterprises, Inc., pg. 968
MIMLIC SALES CORPORATION—The Minnesota Mutual Life Insurance Company, pg. 758
MINISTERS LIFE INSURANCE COMPANY, pg. 757
THE MINNESOTA MUTUAL LIFE INSURANCE COMPANY, pg. 757
MOTORISTS MUTUAL INSURANCE CO., pg. 773
MUTUAL OF AMERICA, pg. 777
MUTUAL BENEFIT LIFE INSURANCE COMPANY, pg. 778
THE MUTUAL LIFE INSURANCE COMPANY OF NEW YORK (MONY), pg. 778
MUTUAL OF OMAHA—Mutual of Omaha Insurance Company, pg. 779
MUTUAL SAVINGS LIFE INSURANCE COMPANY—Victory Financial Group, Inc., pg. 1150
NATIONAL ATLAS LIFE INSURANCE CO.—Zale Corporation, pg. 1216
NATIONAL FINANCIAL INSURANCE COMPANY, pg. 788
NATIONAL LIBERTY, pg. 791
NATIONAL LIFE INSURANCE COMPANY, pg. 791
NATIONAL SAVINGS LIFE INSURANCE COMPANY—Victory Financial Group, Inc., pg. 1150
NATIONAL TRAVELERS LIFE CO., pg. 794
NATIONWIDE LIFE INSURANCE CO.—Nationwide Mutual Insurance Company, pg. 795
NEKURA VERSICHERUNGS AG—Nationwide Mutual Insurance Company, pg. 795
THE NEW ENGLAND, pg. 799
NEW ENGLAND PENSION & ANNUITY CO.—The New England, pg. 800
NEW ENGLAND VARIABLE LIFE INSURANCE CO—The New England, pg. 800
NEW YORK LIFE ACCEPTANCE CORP.—New York Life Insurance Company, pg. 803
NEW YORK LIFE FOUNDATION—New York Life Insurance Company, pg. 803
NEW YORK LIFE & HEALTH INSURANCE COMPANY—New York Life Insurance Company, pg. 802
NEW YORK LIFE INSURANCE AND ANNUITY CORPORATION—New York Life Insurance Company, pg. 802
NEW YORK LIFE INSURANCE COMPANY, pg. 802
NEW YORK LIFE INSURANCE CO. OF CANADA—New York Life Insurance Company, pg. 803
NEW YORK LIFE INSURANCE WORLDWIDE LTD.—New York Life Insurance Company, pg. 803
NORTH CAROLINA MUTUAL LIFE INSURANCE CO., pg. 813
NORTH CENTRAL LIFE INSURANCE COMPANIES, pg. 813
NORTHWESTERN MUTUAL LIFE INSURANCE CO., pg. 815
NYLIFE INSURANCE COMPANY OF ARIZONA—New York Life Insurance Company, pg. 803
OLD DOMINION LIFE INSURANCE CO.—Shenandoah Life Insurance Company, pg. 997
OREGON PACIFIC STATES INSURANCE CO.—Blue Cross & Blue Shield of Oregon, pg. 160
OURSO INVESTMENT CORPORATION, pg. 832
PM GROUP LIFE INSURANCE COMPANY—Pacific Mutual Life Insurance Company, pg. 841
PRUCO LIFE INSURANCE COMPANY—The Prudential Insurance Company of America, pg. 896
PACIFIC MUTUAL LIFE INSURANCE COMPANY, pg. 841
PACIFICARE HEALTH SYSTEMS, INC.—UniHealth America, pg. 1127
PAN-AMERICAN LIFE INSURANCE COMPANY, pg. 845
PARAGON LIFE INSURANCE CO.—General American Life Insurance Co., pg. 448
PENN INSURANCE & ANNUITY CO.—The Penn Mutual Life Insurance Company, pg. 858
THE PENN MUTUAL LIFE INSURANCE COMPANY, pg. 858
PHOENIX AMERICAN LIFE INS. CO.—Phoenix Home Life Mutual Insurance Company, pg. 868
PHOENIX HOME LIFE MUTUAL INSURANCE COMPANY, pg. 868
PIONEER MUTUAL LIFE INSURANCE COMPANY, pg. 872
PREFERRED RISK LIFE INSURANCE CO.—Preferred Risk Mutual Insurance, pg. 886
PREFERRED RISK MUTUAL INSURANCE, pg. 886
THE PRINCIPAL FINANCIAL GROUP, pg. 890
PRINCIPAL MUTUAL LIFE INSURANCE COMPANY—The Principal Financial Group, pg. 891
PRINCIPAL MUTUAL LIFE INSURANCE CO.—The Principal Financial Group, pg. 891
PRINCIPAL NATIONAL LIFE INSURANCE COMPANY—The Principal Financial Group, pg. 891
PROVIDENT MUTUAL LIFE & ANNUTIY COMPANY OF AMERICA—Provident Mutual Life Insurance Co., pg. 896
PROVIDENT MUTUAL LIFE INSURANCE CO., pg. 896
PRUCO LIFE INSURANCE COMPANY OF NEW JERSEY—The Prudential Insurance Company of America, pg. 896
PRUDENTIAL EASTERN HOME OFFICE—The Prudential Insurance Company of America, pg. 897
THE PRUDENTIAL INSURANCE COMPANY OF AMERICA, pg. 896
THE PRUDENTIAL LIFE INSURANCE COMPANY, LTD.—The Prudential Insurance Company of America, pg. 897
REGAN HOLDING CORPORATION, pg. 921
RESOURCES LIFE INSURANCE CO.—Integrated Resources, Inc., pg. 573
SAMMONS ENTERPRISES, INC., pg. 968
SECURITY EQUITY LIFE INSURANCE CO.—Security Mutual Life Insurance Co. of New York, pg. 987
SECURITY INDUSTRIAL INSURANCE CO., INC.—Ourso Investment Corporation, pg. 832
SECURITY MUTUAL LIFE INSURANCE CO. OF NEW YORK, pg. 987
SEGUROS GENSIS, SA—Metropolitan Life Insurance Co., pg. 745
SENTRY INSURANCE, A MUTUAL COMPANY, pg. 990
THE SHELBY INSURANCE GROUP—The Associated Group, pg. 90
SHELTER MUTUAL INSURANCE COMPANY, pg. 997
SHENANDOAH LIFE INSURANCE COMPANY, pg. 997
THE SIGNATURE GROUP—Montgomery Ward & Co., Inc., pg. 768
SOUTHERN LIFE AND HEALTH INSURANCE COMPANY—Geneve Corporation, pg. 452
SOUTHERN UNITED CORPORATION—Victory Financial Group, Inc., pg. 1150
SOUTHERN UNITED LIFE INSURANCE COMPANY—Victory Financial Group, Inc., pg. 1150
STANDARD SECURITY LIFE INSURANCE COMPANY OF NEW YORK—Geneve Corporation, pg. 452
STATE FARM LIFE AND ACCIDENT ASSURANCE CO.—State Farm Mutual Automobile Insurance Company, pg. 1041
STATE FARM LIFE INSURANCE CO.—State Farm Mutual Automobile Insurance Company, pg. 1041
STATE FARM MUTUAL AUTOMOBILE INSURANCE COMPANY, pg. 1041
TEACHERS INSURANCE AND ANNUITY ASSOCIATION-COLLEGE RETIREMENT EQUITIES FUND, pg. 1082
TEXAS LIFE INSURANCE COMPANY—Metropolitan Life Insurance Co., pg. 745
TOWERS, PERRIN, FORSTER & CROSBY, INC., pg. 1103
TWINCO SERVICES, INC.—Twin County Grocers, Inc., pg. 1122
ULLICO INC., pg. 1124
UNDERWRITERS NATIONAL ASSURANCE CO.—The Chesapeake Life Insurance Co., pg. 243
THE UNION CENTRAL LIFE INSURANCE CO., pg. 1127
THE UNION LABOR LIFE INSURANCE CO.—ULLICO Inc., pg. 1124
UNITED FARM BUREAU FAMILY LIFE INSURANCE CO., pg. 1131
UNITED SERVICES AUTOMOBILE ASSOCIATION (USAA), pg. 1134
UNIVERSAL LIFE INSURANCE COMPANY, pg. 1138
UTICA NATIONAL LIFE INSURANCE COMPANY—Utica Mutual Insurance Company, pg. 1141
VASA INSURANCE GROUP, INC., pg. 1146
VERMONT LIFE INSURANCE COMPANY—National Life Insurance Company, pg. 791
VICTORY FINANCIAL GROUP, INC., pg. 1150
VICTORY LIFE INSURANCE COMPANY—Victory Financial Group, Inc., pg. 1150
WM LIFE INSURANCE COMPANY—Washington Mutual Savings Bank, pg. 1166
WASHINGTON MUTUAL LIFE INSURANCE SERVICES—Washington Mutual Savings Bank, pg. 1166
WASHINGTON NATIONAL LIFE INSURANCE CO. OF NEW YORK—Columbian Mutual Life Insurance Co., pg. 266
WAUSAU LIFE INSURANCE COMPANY—Employers Insurance of Wausau a Mutual Co., pg. 380
WAUSAU UNDERWRITERS LIFE INSURANCE COMPANY—Employers Insurance of Wausau a Mutual Co., pg. 380
WEST COAST LIFE INSURANCE CO.—Nationwide Mutual Insurance Company, pg. 795
WESTERN & SOUTHERN LIFE INSURANCE CO., pg. 1181
WESTFIELD COMPANIES, pg. 1182
WINDSOR GROUP LIMITED—New York Life Insurance Company, pg. 803
WOODMEN ACCIDENT & LIFE CO., pg. 1200

6321 — ACCIDENT & HEALTH INSURANCE

AFS INSURANCE SERVICES, INC.—Associated Food Stores Inc., pg. 89
ACADEMY INSURANCE GROUP, INC., pg. 11
ACADEMY LIFE INSURANCE CO.—Academy Insurance Group, Inc., pg. 11
AID ASSOCIATION FOR LUTHERANS, pg. 26
JOHN ALDEN LIFE INSURANCE COMPANY—John Alden Financial Corporation, pg. 33
AMERICAN FAMILY MUTUAL INSURANCE CO., pg. 51
AMERICAN FIDELITY CORP., pg. 52
AMERICAN LIBERTY FINANCIAL CORP., pg. 57
AMERICAN REPUBLIC INSURANCE CO., pg. 60
AMERICAN SENTINEL INSURANCE COMPANY—Erin Group Administrators, Inc., pg. 387
AMERITAS LIFE INSURANCE CORP., pg. 66
ASSOCIATED GROUP INC.—The Associated Group, pg. 90
THE ASSOCIATED GROUP, pg. 90
AUTO DIREKT VERSICHERUNGS AG—Nationwide Mutual Insurance Company, pg. 795
BLUE CROSS AND BLUE SHIELD OF MASSACHUSETTS, pg. 159
BLUE CROSS & BLUE SHIELD OF ILLINOIS, pg. 160
BLUE SHIELD OF CALIFORNIA, pg. 161
CMCI CORP.—CUNA Mutual Insurance Society, pg. 205
CUDIS INSURANCE SOCIETY, INC.—CUNA Mutual Insurance Society, pg. 205
CUNA MUTUAL INSURANCE SOCIETY, pg. 205
CENTRAL LIFE ASSURANCE CO., pg. 232
CIMARRON AMERICAN FIDELITY—American Fidelity Corp., pg. 52
COLUMBIAN LIFE INSURANCE COMPANY—Columbian Mutual Life Insurance Co., pg. 266
COLUMBIAN MUTUAL LIFE INSURANCE CO., pg. 266
COMMERCIAL TRAVELERS MUTUAL INSURANCE COMPANY, pg. 269
COUNTRY COMPANIES INSURANCE GROUP, pg. 289
CUMIS GROUP INSURANCE—CUNA Mutual Insurance Society, pg. 206
THE CUMIS GROUP LTD.—CUNA Mutual Insurance Society, pg. 206
ROBERT F. DRIVER CO., INC., pg. 349
EMPIRE BLUE CROSS & BLUE SHIELD, pg. 379
ERIN GROUP ADMINISTRATORS, INC., pg. 387
FEDERATED MUTUAL INSURANCE COMPANY, pg. 405
FLORISTS' MUTUAL INSURANCE CO., pg. 421
FRANDISCO LIFE INSURANCE CO.—1st Franklin Corporation, pg. 413
GENERAL AMERICAN LIFE INSURANCE CO., pg. 448
GIBRALTAR CASUALTY CO.—The Prudential Insurance Company of America, pg. 897
GOLDEN STATE MUTUAL LIFE INSURANCE COMPANY, pg. 467
GROUP INSURANCE INC., pg. 490
GROUP INSURANCE OF COLORADO—Group Insurance Inc., pg. 490
GROUPAMERICA INSURANCE CO.—Connecticut Mutual Life Insurance Company, pg. 275
GUARANTEE MUTUAL LIFE CO., pg. 491
THE GUARDIAN LIFE INSURANCE COMPANY OF AMERICA, pg. 492
HEALTH AMERICA/CAPITALCARE, INC.—Mutual of Omaha Insurance Company, pg. 779
INSURANCE CORP. OF AMERICA, pg. 572
JOHN HANCOCK MUTUAL LIFE INSURANCE COMPANY, pg. 595
LAWRENCE INSURANCE GROUP, INC.—Lawrence Group, Inc., pg. 662
LEAGUE LIFE INSURANCE CO.—CUNA Mutual Insurance Society, pg. 205
MML BAY STATE LIFE INSURANCE COMPANY—Massachusetts Mutual Life Insurance Co., pg. 718
MML PENSION INSURANCE COMPANY—Massachusetts Mutual Life Insurance Co., pg. 718
MSI INSURANCE COMPANIES, pg. 693
MARITIME LIFE ASSURANCE CO.—John Hancock Mutual Life Insurance Company, pg. 597
MASSACHUSETTS MUTUAL LIFE INSURANCE CO., pg. 718
MCWANE, INC., pg. 733
METLIFE HEALTHCARE MANAGEMENT CORP.—Metropolitan Life Insurance Co., pg. 745
METROPOLITAN INSURANCE AND ANNUITY COMPANY, TAIWAN BRANCH—Metropolitan Life Insurance Co., pg. 745
METROPOLITAN LIFE INSURANCE CO., pg. 744
MILLERS' MUTUAL INSURANCE ASSN. OF ILLINOIS, pg. 755
MINISTERS LIFE INSURANCE COMPANY, pg. 757
MOTORISTS MUTUAL INSURANCE CO., pg. 773
THE MUTUAL LIFE INSURANCE COMPANY OF NEW YORK (MONY), pg. 778
MUTUAL OF OMAHA INSURANCE COMPANY, pg. 779
MUTUAL SAVINGS LIFE INSURANCE COMPANY—Victory Financial Group, Inc., pg. 1150
NATIONAL FINANCIAL INSURANCE COMPANY, pg. 788
NATIONAL LIFE INSURANCE COMPANY, pg. 791
NATIONAL SAVINGS LIFE INSURANCE COMPANY—Victory Financial Group, Inc., pg. 1150
NATIONAL TRAVELERS LIFE CO., pg. 794
NATIONWIDE HEALTH CARE CORP.—Nationwide Mutual Insurance Company, pg. 795
NATIONWIDE MUTUAL INSURANCE COMPANY, pg. 795
NEKURA VERSICHERUNGS AG—Nationwide Mutual Insurance Company, pg. 795
THE NEW ENGLAND, pg. 799
NEW YORK LIFE FOUNDATION—New York Life Insurance Company, pg. 803
NEW YORK LIFE & HEALTH INSURANCE COMPANY—New York Life Insurance Company, pg. 802
NEW YORK LIFE INSURANCE AND ANNUITY CORPORATION—New York Life Insurance Company, pg. 802
NEW YORK LIFE INSURANCE COMPANY, pg. 802
NORTH CENTRAL LIFE INSURANCE COMPANIES, pg. 813
NYLIFE INSURANCE COMPANY OF ARIZONA—New York Life Insurance Company, pg. 803
PACIFIC MUTUAL LIFE INSURANCE COMPANY, pg. 841
PAN-AMERICAN LIFE INSURANCE COMPANY, pg. 845
PREFERRED RISK LIFE INSURANCE CO.—Preferred Risk Mutual Insurance, pg. 886
PREFERRED RISK MUTUAL INSURANCE, pg. 886

PRUCO LIFE INSURANCE COMPANY OF NEW JERSEY—The Prudential Insurance Company of America, pg. 896
THE PRUDENTIAL INSURANCE COMPANY OF AMERICA, pg. 896
SECURITY EQUITY LIFE INSURANCE CO.—Security Mutual Life Insurance Co. of New York, pg. 987
SECURITY MUTUAL LIFE INSURANCE CO. OF NEW YORK, pg. 987
SENATE INSURANCE COMPANY—Lawrence Group, Inc., pg. 662
SENTINEL MANAGEMENT SERVICES, INC.—Erin Group Administrators, Inc., pg. 387
SENTRY INSURANCE, A MUTUAL COMPANY, pg. 990
SHELTER MUTUAL INSURANCE COMPANY, pg. 997
STATE VOLUNTEER MUTUAL INSURANCE CO. INC., pg. 1041
TENNESSEE INSURANCE CO.—Ingram Industries Inc., pg. 569
TWINCO SERVICES, INC.—Twin County Grocers, Inc., pg. 1122
ULLICO INC., pg. 1124
THE UNION CENTRAL LIFE INSURANCE CO., pg. 1127
THE UNION LABOR LIFE INSURANCE CO.—ULLICO Inc., pg. 1124
UNIVERSAL LIFE INSURANCE COMPANY, pg. 1138
VASA INSURANCE GROUP, INC., pg. 1146
WASHINGTON MUTUAL LIFE INSURANCE SERVICES—Washington Mutual Savings Bank, pg. 1166
WOODMEN ACCIDENT & LIFE CO., pg. 1200

6324 — HOSPITAL & MEDICAL SERVICE PLANS

ACCELERATED CLAIMS PROCESSING, INC.—Health Management Systems, Inc., pg. 521
THE ACORDIA, INC.—The Associated Group, pg. 90
AMERICAN SELFCARE CORPORATION, pg. 60
AMERICAN SELFCARE CORPORATION—American SelfCare Corporation, pg. 61
AMERITAS LIFE INSURANCE CORP., pg. 66
ANTHEM COMPANIES, INC.—The Associated Group, pg. 90
ANTHEM HEALTH PLANS OF FLORIDA INC.—The Associated Group, pg. 90
ASSOCIATED GROUP INC.—The Associated Group, pg. 90
THE ASSOCIATED GROUP, pg. 90
BLUE CROSS AND BLUE SHIELD OF OKLAHOMA, pg. 159
BLUE CROSS AND BLUE SHIELD ASSOCIATION, pg. 159
BLUE CROSS & BLUE SHIELD OF TEXAS, INC., pg. 160
BLUE CROSS & BLUE SHIELD OF VIRGINIA, pg. 160
BLUELINES HMO—Blue Cross and Blue Shield of Oklahoma, pg. 159
CENTRAL LIFE ASSURANCE CO., pg. 232
ERIN GROUP ADMINISTRATORS, INC., pg. 387
FALLON COMMUNITY HEALTH PLAN, pg. 398
GROUP INSURANCE OF COLORADO—Group Insurance Inc., pg. 490
GROUP LIFE & HEALTH INSURANCE COMPANY—Blue Cross & Blue Shield of Texas, Inc., pg. 160
HMO IOWA, INC.—The Principal Financial Group, pg. 890
HEALTH CARE PREFERRED—The Principal Financial Group, pg. 890
HEALTH MAINTENANCE OREGON—Blue Cross & Blue Shield of Oregon, pg. 160
HILLHOUSE ASSOCIATES INSURANCE, INC.—New York Life Insurance Company, pg. 802
KAISER FOUNDATION HEALTH & HOSPITALS GROUP, pg. 614
KAISER PERMANENTE, COLORADO DIVISION—Kaiser Foundation Health & Hospitals Group, pg. 614
KAISER PERMANENTE, GEORGIA DIVISION—Kaiser Foundation Health & Hospitals Group, pg. 614
KAISER PERMANENTE, HAWAII DIVISION—Kaiser Foundation Health & Hospitals Group, pg. 614
KAISER PERMANENTE, KANSAS/MISSOURI DIVISION—Kaiser Foundation Health & Hospitals Group, pg. 614
KAISER PERMANENTE, MID-ATLANTIC STATES DIVISION—Kaiser Foundation Health & Hospitals Group, pg. 614
KAISER PERMANENTE, NORTH CAROLINA DIVISION—Kaiser Foundation Health & Hospitals Group, pg. 614
KAISER PERMANENTE, NORTHEAST DIVISION—Kaiser Foundation Health & Hospitals Group, pg. 614
KAISER PERMANENTE, NORTHERN CALIFORNIA REGION—Kaiser Foundation Health & Hospitals Group, pg. 614
KAISER PERMANENTE, NORTHWEST DIVISION—Kaiser Foundation Health & Hospitals Group, pg. 614
KAISER PERMANENTE, OHIO DIVISION—Kaiser Foundation Health & Hospitals Group, pg. 614
KAISER PERMANENTE, SOUTHERN CALIFORNIA DIVISION—Kaiser Foundation Health & Hospitals Group, pg. 614
KAISER PERMANENTE, TEXAS DIVISION—Kaiser Foundation Health & Hospitals Group, pg. 614
KEY HEALTH PLAN—The Associated Group, pg. 90
METROPOLITAN LIFE INSURANCE CO., pg. 744
NEW YORK LIFE INSURANCE COMPANY, pg. 802
PACIFICARE HEALTH SYSTEMS, INC.—UniHealth America, pg. 1127
PACIFICARE OF CALIFORNIA—UniHealth America, pg. 1127
PACIFICARE OF OREGON, INC.—UniHealth America, pg. 1127
THE PRINCIPAL FINANCIAL GROUP, pg. 890
SANUS CORP. HEALTH SYSTEMS—New York Life Insurance Company, pg. 803
TOTAL PLAN ALTERNATIVES, INC.—Blue Cross & Blue Shield of Oregon, pg. 160
TWINCO SERVICES, INC.—Twin County Grocers, Inc., pg. 1122
LELAND A. WOLF & ASSOCIATES, pg. 1199

6331 — FIRE, MARINE & CASUALTY INSURANCE

AGRICULTURAL INSURANCE COMPANY—American Financial Corporation, pg. 53
AGWAY INDEMNITY INSURANCE COMPANY—Agway, Inc., pg. 25
ALL AMERICA FINANCIAL, pg. 34
ALL NATION INSURANCE CO., pg. 35
ALLIED GROUP INC.—Allied Mutual Insurance Company, pg. 38
ALLIED MUTUAL INSURANCE COMPANY, pg. 38
AMERICAN EMPIRE SURPLUS LINES INSURANCE COMPANY—American Financial Corporation, pg. 53
AMERICAN FAMILY MUTUAL INSURANCE CO., pg. 51
AMERICAN FAMILY MUTUAL INSURANCE CO.—American Family Mutual Insurance Co., pg. 52
AMERICAN FINANCIAL CORPORATION, pg. 52
AMERICAN HARDWARE MUTUAL INSURANCE CO., pg. 55
AMERICAN NATIONAL FIRE INSURANCE COMPANY—American Financial Corporation, pg. 53
AMERICAN SELECT INSURANCE CO.—All America Financial, pg. 35
AMERICAN STANDARD INSURANCE COMPANY OF WISCONSIN—American Family Mutual Insurance Co., pg. 52
AMERISURE COMPANIES, pg. 66
AMFAM, INC.—American Family Mutual Insurance Co., pg. 52
AMICA MUTUAL INSURANCE CO., pg. 66
ARKANSAS FARM BUREAU FEDERATION, pg. 83
ATLANTA CASUALTY COMPANY—American Financial Corporation, pg. 53
ATLANTIC MUTUAL COMPANIES, pg. 94
AUTO-OWNERS INSURANCE, pg. 100
BEACON INSURANCE CO. OF AMERICA—All America Financial, pg. 34
CSE CORPORATION, pg. 204
CUMIS INSURANCE SOCIETY, INC.—CUNA Mutual Insurance Society, pg. 205
CANADIAN NORTHERN SHIELD—CUNA Mutual Insurance Society, pg. 206
CANAL INDEMNITY COMPANY—Canal Insurance Co., pg. 213
CANAL INSURANCE CO., pg. 213
CIMARRON AMERICAN FIDELITY—American Fidelity Corp., pg. 52
CITIZENS INSURANCE COMPANY OF AMERICA—All America Financial, pg. 35
CLASSIFIED INSURANCE COMPANY, INC.—Millers' Mutual Insurance Assn. Of Illinois, pg. 755
COUNTRY CASUALTY INSURANCE COMPANY—Country Companies Insurance Group, pg. 289
COUNTRY COMPANIES INSURANCE GROUP, pg. 289
COUNTRY MUTUAL INSURANCE COMPANY—Country Companies Insurance Group, pg. 289
COUNTRY MUTUAL NORTHWEST REGIONAL OFFICE—Country Companies Insurance Group, pg. 289
COUNTRY PREFERRED INSURANCE COMPANY—Country Companies Insurance Group, pg. 289
DAIRYLAND INSURANCE CO.—Sentry Insurance, A Mutual Company, pg. 990
DIXIE INSURANCE COMPANY—American Financial Corporation, pg. 53
DODSON GROUP, pg. 342
CHARLES DUNN COMPANY-REALTORS, pg. 353
EMPLOYERS INSURANCE OF WAUSAU A MUTUAL CO., pg. 380
EMPLOYERS INSURANCE OF WAUSAU A MUTUAL CO.—Nationwide Mutual Insurance Company, pg. 795
FARM BUREAU CASUALTY INSURANCE CO.—Arkansas Farm Bureau Federation, pg. 83
FARM BUREAU MUTUAL INSURANCE CO. OF ARKANSAS—Arkansas Farm Bureau Federation, pg. 83
FARM FAMILY MUTUAL INSURANCE CO., pg. 401
FEDERATED MUTUAL INSURANCE COMPANY, pg. 405
FRANDISCO PROPERTY & CASUALTY INSURANCE—1st Franklin Corporation, pg. 413
GREAT AMERICAN HOLDING CORPORATION—American Financial Corporation, pg. 53
GREAT AMERICAN INSURANCE COMPANY—American Financial Corporation, pg. 53
GREATER NEW YORK MUTUAL INSURANCE COMPANY, pg. 483
THE HANOVER INSURANCE COMPANY—All America Financial, pg. 34
HANOVER LLOYD'S INSURANCE COMPANY—All America Financial, pg. 35
INSURANCE CORP. OF AMERICA, pg. 572
JEWELERS MUTUAL INSURANCE COMPANY, pg. 593
LAWRENCE INSURANCE GROUP, INC.—Lawrence Group, Inc., pg. 662
LEADER NATIONAL CORPORATION—The Dyson-Kissner-Moran Corporation, pg. 357
LEAGUE GENERAL INSURANCE CO.—CUNA Mutual Insurance Society, pg. 205
LIBERTY MUTUAL FIRE INSURANCE CO.—Liberty Mutual Insurance Co., pg. 674
LIBERTY MUTUAL INSURANCE CO., pg. 674
LIBERTY NORTHWEST INSURANCE CORP.—Liberty Mutual Insurance Co., pg. 674
M M I COMPANIES, INC., pg. 692
MSI INSURANCE COMPANIES, pg. 693
MCWANE, INC., pg. 733
THE MEDICAL PROTECTIVE COMPANY, pg. 735
MERCHANTS INSURANCE AGENCY—U.R.M. Stores, Inc., pg. 1124
METROPOLITAN PROPERTY & CASUALTY INSURANCE CO.(MET P&C)—Metropolitan Life Insurance Co., pg. 744
MID-CONTINENT CASUALTY CO.—American Financial Corporation, pg. 53
MID-CONTINENT CASUALTY CO.—American Financial Corporation, pg. 53
MID-CONTINENT CASUALTY COMPANY—American Financial Corporation, pg. 53
MIDDLESEX INSURANCE CO.—Sentry Insurance, A Mutual Company, pg. 990
MIDWEST MUTUAL INSURANCE CO.—Preferred Risk Mutual Insurance, pg. 886
MILLERS' MUTUAL INSURANCE ASSN. OF ILLINOIS, pg. 755
MOTORISTS MUTUAL INSURANCE CO., pg. 773
MUTUAL SAVINGS FIRE INSURANCE COMPANY—Victory Financial Group, Inc., pg. 1150
NATIONWIDE MUTUAL INSURANCE COMPANY, pg. 795
NODAK MUTUAL INSURANCE CO.—Nodak Mutual Insurance Company, pg. 808
NORTH AMERICAN SAFETY PROGRAM ADMINISTRATORS—Lawrence Group, Inc., pg. 662
NORTHWEST FARM BUREAU INSURANCE COMPANY—Country Companies Insurance Group, pg. 289
OMAHA PROPERTY & CASUALTY—Mutual of Omaha Insurance Company, pg. 779
OMAHA PROPERTY & CASUALTY CO.—Mutual of Omaha Insurance Company, pg. 779
PACIFIC STATES CASUALTY CO., pg. 841
PREFERRED RISK MUTUAL INSURANCE, pg. 886
PRINCIPAL CASUALTY INSURANCE COMPANY—The Principal Financial Group, pg. 891
THE PRINCIPAL FINANCIAL GROUP, pg. 890
THE PRUDENTIAL INSURANCE COMPANY OF AMERICA, pg. 896
PRUDENTIAL-LMI COMMERCIAL INSURANCE COMPANY—The Prudential Insurance Company of America, pg. 897
PRUDENTIAL OF AMERICA GENERAL INSURANCE CO. (CANADA)—The Prudential Insurance Company of America, pg. 897
PRUDENTIAL PROPERTY & CASUALTY INSURANCE COMPANY—The Prudential Insurance Company of America, pg. 897
QUINCY MUTUAL FIRE INSURANCE COMPANY, pg. 905
LE ROCHER, COMPAGNIE DE REASSURANCE, S.A.—The Prudential Insurance Company of America, pg. 898
LE ROCHER UK, LTD.—The Prudential Insurance Company of America, pg. 898
SECURITY INDUSTRIAL INSURANCE CO., INC.—Ourso Investment Corporation, pg. 832
SENTRY INSURANCE, A MUTUAL COMPANY—Sentry Insurance, A Mutual Company, pg. 990
SENTRY INSURANCE, A MUTUAL COMPANY, pg. 990
THE SIGNATURE GROUP—Montgomery Ward & Co., Inc., pg. 768
SOUTHERN FARM BUREAU CASUALTY INSURANCE COMPANY, pg. 1021
SOUTHERN LIFE AND HEALTH INSURANCE COMPANY—Geneve Corporation, pg. 452
SOUTHERN UNITED FIRE INSURANCE COMPANY—Victory Financial Group, Inc., pg. 1150
SPECIALTY UNDERWRITERS, INC.—American Financial Corporation, pg. 54
STATE FARM COUNTY MUTUAL INSURANCE CO. OF TEXAS—State Farm Mutual Automobile Insurance Company, pg. 1041
STATE FARM FIRE AND CASUALTY CO.—State Farm Mutual Automobile Insurance Company, pg. 1041
STATE FARM GENERAL INSURANCE CO.—State Farm Mutual Automobile Insurance Company, pg. 1041
STATE FARM LLOYDS, INC.—State Farm Mutual Automobile Insurance Company, pg. 1041
STATE FARM MUTUAL AUTOMOBILE INSURANCE COMPANY, pg. 1041
STATE VOLUNTEER MUTUAL INSURANCE CO. INC., pg. 1041
STONEWALL INSURANCE CO.—American Financial Corporation, pg. 54
TRANSPORT INSURANCE CO.—American Financial Corporation, pg. 54
UNIGARD INDEMNITY CO.—John Hancock Mutual Life Insurance Company, pg. 596
UNIGARD INSURANCE CO.—John Hancock Mutual Life Insurance Company, pg. 596
UNIGARD SECURITY INSURANCE CO.—John Hancock Mutual Life Insurance Company, pg. 596
UNISON INSURANCE CO.—Amerisure Companies, pg. 66
UNITED COMMUNITY INSURANCE CO.—Lawrence Group, Inc., pg. 662
UNITED FARM BUREAU FAMILY LIFE INSURANCE CO., pg. 1131
UNITED REPUBLIC REINSURANCE COMPANY—Lawrence Group, Inc., pg. 662
UNITED SERVICES AUTOMOBILE ASSOCIATION (USAA), pg. 1134
UTICA LLOYDS OF TEXAS—Utica Mutual Insurance Company, pg. 1141
UTICA MUTUAL INSURANCE COMPANY, pg. 1140
UTICA NATIONAL INSURANCE CO. OF TEXAS—Utica Mutual Insurance Company, pg. 1141
VASA INSURANCE GROUP, INC., pg. 1146
WAUSAU INSURANCE COMPANY (U.K.), LTD.—Employers Insurance of Wausau a Mutual Co., pg. 380
WESTFIELD COMPANIES, pg. 1182

6351 — SURETY INSURANCE

AMERICAN FIDELITY CORP., pg. 52
BUTCHER & CO., INC., pg. 196
CENTRAL MUTUAL INSURANCE CO., pg. 233
EDUSERV, pg. 369
THE HANOVER INSURANCE COMPANY—All America Financial, pg. 34
INSURANCE CORP. OF AMERICA, pg. 572
MSI INSURANCE COMPANIES, pg. 693
THE MEDICAL PROTECTIVE COMPANY, pg. 735
PRUDENTIAL REINSURANCE—The Prudential Insurance Company of America, pg. 897
RCI QUALITY SERVICES, INC.—Resort Condominiums International, pg. 929
THE SHELBY INSURANCE GROUP—The Associated Group, pg. 90
STATE VOLUNTEER MUTUAL INSURANCE CO. INC., pg. 1041
WESTFIELD COMPANIES, pg. 1182

6361 — TITLE INSURANCE

ATTORNEY'S TITLE INSURANCE FUND, pg. 97
CENTRAL MUTUAL INSURANCE CO., pg. 233
HOME-OWNERS INSURANCE CO.—Auto-Owners Insurance, pg. 100
INTERCOUNTY TITLE CO. OF ILLINOIS, pg. 574
MSI INSURANCE COMPANIES, pg. 693
NATIONAL ATTORNEYS TITLE INSURANCE COMPANY, pg. 786
NATIONAL ATTORNEYS TITLE INSURANCE COMPANY--NATIONAL DIV.—National Attorneys Title Insurance Company, pg. 786
OWNERS INSURANCE CO.—Auto-Owners Insurance, pg. 100
PROPERTY-OWNERS INSURANCE CO.—Auto-Owners Insurance, pg. 100
SECURITY TITLE & GUARANTY CO.—Helmsley Enterprises, Inc., pg. 527
TICOR TITLE GUARANTEE CO., pg. 1096
WORLD TITLE COMPANY, pg. 1203

6371 — PENSION, HEALTH & WELFARE FUNDS

AMERITAS LIFE INSURANCE CORP., pg. 66
THE ASSOCIATED GROUP, pg. 90
THE BERKSHIRE LIFE INSURANCE COMPANY, pg. 142
SANFORD C. BERNSTEIN & CO., INC., pg. 144
CONNECTICUT MUTUAL LIFE INSURANCE COMPANY, pg. 274
THE DEARBORN GROUP, pg. 322
INTEGRATED RESOURCES ASSET MANAGEMENT CORP.—Integrated Resources, Inc., pg. 573
METROPOLITAN LIFE INSURANCE CO., pg. 744
THE MUTUAL LIFE INSURANCE COMPANY OF NEW YORK (MONY), pg. 778
NATIONWIDE FUNDING INC.—Nationwide Mutual Insurance Company, pg. 795
NEW ENGLAND PORTFOLIO ADVISORS, INC.—The New England, pg. 799
NEW YORK LIFE INSURANCE COMPANY, pg. 802
PACIFIC MUTUAL LIFE INSURANCE COMPANY, pg. 841
THE PRUDENTIAL ASSET MANAGEMENT CO., INC.—The Prudential Insurance Company of America, pg. 897
PRUDENTIAL EASTERN HOME OFFICE—The Prudential Insurance Company of America, pg. 897
SANTANDER MET., S.A. MADRID—Metropolitan Life Insurance Co., pg. 745
SEGUROS GENSIS, SA—Metropolitan Life Insurance Co., pg. 745

6399 — INSURANCE CARRIERS, NEC

AGRI-SERVICE AGENCIES, INC.—Dairylea Cooperative Inc., pg. 311
AMERICAN FAMILY MUTUAL INSURANCE CO., pg. 51
BERWIND CORPORATION, pg. 145
CERTIFIED GROCERS OF CALIFORNIA, pg. 237
FARMERS UNION MARKETING & PROCESSING ASSOCIATION, pg. 402
FLINT INK CORP., pg. 419
GENEVE CAPITAL GROUP INC.—Geneve Corporation, pg. 451
GRAND ISLAND CONTRACT CARRIERS & BROKERAGE, INC.—Chief Industries, Inc., pg. 247
MID-CONTINENT CASUALTY CO.—American Financial Corporation, pg. 53
PRUDENTIAL COMMERCIAL INSURANCE CO.—The Prudential Insurance Company of America, pg. 897
THE PRUDENTIAL INSURANCE COMPANY OF AMERICA, pg. 896
TELE-TRIP CO.—Mutual of Omaha Insurance Company, pg. 779
UNITED WORLD LIFE INSURANCE COMPANY—Mutual of Omaha Insurance Company, pg. 779
VANLINER GROUP, INC.—Unigroup, Inc., pg. 1126

6411 — INSURANCE AGENTS, BROKERS & SERVICE

ABI MANAGEMENT, INC.—American Financial Corporation, pg. 53
ACI FINANCIAL CORP., pg. 2
ANS INSURANCE AGENCY—American SelfCare Corporation, pg. 61
ADAPT, INC.—Lawrence Group, Inc., pg. 662
ADMINISTRATIVE SERVICES, INC.—National Life Insurance Company, pg. 791
AGWAY GENERAL AGENCY—Agway, Inc., pg. 25
AGWAY INSURANCE CO.—Agway, Inc., pg. 25
AIRCRAFT INSURANCE AGENCY—Hawthorne Corp., pg. 519
AMERCO, A NEVADA CORPORATION, pg. 47
AMERICAN BROKERAGE CORPORATION—Phoenix Home Life Mutual Insurance Company, pg. 868
ASSOCIATED GROUP INC.—The Associated Group, pg. 90
THE ASSOCIATED GROUP, pg. 90
ATLANTIC MUTUAL COMPANIES, pg. 94
A.W. LAWRENCE & COMPANY, INC.—Lawrence Group, Inc., pg. 662
B-W INSURANCE AGENCY—Best Western International, Inc., pg. 147
BENCART, INC.—Cenvill Development Corp., pg. 236
BENEFIT SERVICE CORPORATION—Washington Mutual Savings Bank, pg. 1166
BENEFIT SERVICE CORPORATION OF ALASKA—Washington Mutual Savings Bank, pg. 1166
BEST INSURORS, INC.—Walter Industries, Inc., pg. 1162
BLUE CROSS & BLUE SHIELD OF OREGON, pg. 160
BROUGHER AGENCY, INC.—VASA Insurance Group, Inc., pg. 1146
JOHN BURNHAM & CO., pg. 194
BURRELL GROUP, pg. 195
BUSINESS MENS INSURANCE CORPORATION, pg. 196
CSE CORPORATION, pg. 204
CSE SERVICES INSURANCE BROKERAGE—CSE Corporation, pg. 205
CAPPER'S INSURANCE SERVICE, INC.—Stauffer Communications, Inc., pg. 1043
CARDEM INSURANCE CO., LTD.—Walter Industries, Inc., pg. 1162
CENTURY FINANCIAL SERVICES—Cenvill Development Corp., pg. 236
CENVILL DEVELOPMENT CORP., pg. 235
CITIZENS REALTY & INSURANCE INC., pg. 251
CIVIL SERVICE EMPLOYEES INSURANCE CO.—CSE Corporation, pg. 205
COLUMBIA SERVICES, INC.—Washington Mutual Savings Bank, pg. 1166
COLUMBUS VERSICHERUNGS VERMITTLUNGS—Nationwide Mutual Insurance Company, pg. 795
COMMERCIAL & INDUSTRIAL ADMINISTRATION CO. INC, pg. 268
COMMERCIAL RESOURCE INSURANCE CO.—Lawrence Group, Inc., pg. 662
CONSTRUCTION COUNSELLORS, INC., pg. 277
CONSULTEC, INC.—General American Life Insurance Co., pg. 448
CONTINENTAL DEVELOPMENT COMPANY—Burrell Group, pg. 195
COOPER COMMUNITIES, INC., pg. 283
CUMIS GENERAL INSURANCE CO.—CUNA Mutual Insurance Society, pg. 206
CUNA MUTUAL INSURANCE CO.—CUNA Mutual Insurance Society, pg. 206
CUNA MUTUAL INSURANCE SOC.—CUNA Mutual Insurance Society, pg. 206
DASCIT/WHITE & WINSTON, INC.—Integrated Resources, Inc., pg. 573
DEMPSEY & SIDERS INSURANCE AGENCY—American Financial Corporation, pg. 53
A.N. DERINGER, INC., pg. 331
DIVERSIFIED INSURANCE SERVICES OF AMERICA—Connecticut Mutual Life Insurance Company, pg. 275
ROBERT F. DRIVER CO., INC., pg. 349
DRYDEN & CO., INC.—The Prudential Insurance Company of America, pg. 897
EMPLOYEE BENEFITS AMERICA—Pacific Mutual Life Insurance Company, pg. 841
EQUIPMENT ASSURANCE LTD.—Bucyrus-Erie Company, pg. 186
ERIE INDEMNITY COMPANY—Erie Family Life Insurance Company, pg. 386
ERIE INSURANCE EXCHANGE—Erie Family Life Insurance Company, pg. 386
FARMERS MUTUAL HAIL INSURANCE CO., pg. 401
FINANCIAL ASSOCIATES, pg. 410
FIRST AMERICAN INSURANCE AGENCIES, INC.—Bremer Financial Corporation, pg. 173
FIRST INTERNATIONAL REINSURANCE COMPANY—Geneve Corporation, pg. 451
FIRSTATE SERVICES, INC.—First State Federal Savings & Loan, pg. 414
FLAGSHIP CITY INSURANCE COMPANY—Erie Family Life Insurance Company, pg. 386
GATES, MCDONALD & CO.—Nationwide Mutual Insurance Company, pg. 795
GENELCO, INC.—General American Life Insurance Co., pg. 448
GENEVE CORPORATION, pg. 451
GENTRY INSURANCE AGENCY, INC.—Mayflower Transit, Inc., pg. 725
HAMILTON MUTUAL INSURANCE COMPANY OF CINCINNATI, pg. 503
HELMSMAN MANAGEMENT SERVICES, INC.—Liberty Mutual Insurance Co., pg. 674
HICKEY-MITCHELL COMPANY—Nationwide Mutual Insurance Company, pg. 795
INGRAM INDUSTRIES INC., pg. 568
INSURANCE INTERMEDIARIES, INC.—Nationwide Mutual Insurance Company, pg. 795
INSURANCE MANAGEMENT ASSOCIATES, pg. 572
INTEGRATED BENEFIT SYSTEMS—Integrated Resources, Inc., pg. 573
INTEGRATED RESOURCES, INC., pg. 573
INTEGRATED RESOURCES LIFE INSURANCE CO.—Integrated Resources, Inc., pg. 573
JEWELER'S FINANCIAL SERVICE, INC.—Zale Corporation, pg. 1215
JOHN HANCOCK INSURANCE COMPANY OF BERMUDA LTD.—John Hancock Mutual Life Insurance Company, pg. 596
JOHN HANCOCK MUTUAL LIFE INSURANCE COMPANY, pg. 595
JOHN HANCOCK PROPERTY AND CASUALTY HOLDING CO.—John Hancock Mutual Life Insurance Company, pg. 596
JOHNSON & HIGGINS, pg. 598
KENNESAW LIFE & ACCIDENT INSURANCE COMPANY—Regan Holding Corporation, pg. 921
J. I. KISLAK INC., pg. 633
LSC-MARKETING, INC.—The Chesapeake Life Insurance Co., pg. 243
LAWRENCE AGENCY CORPORATION—Lawrence Group, Inc., pg. 662
LAWRENCE HEALTHCARE ADMINISTRATIVE SERVICES—Lawrence Group, Inc., pg. 662
LAWRENCE RISK SERVICES CORPORATION—Lawrence Group, Inc., pg. 662
LAWRENCE UNITED CORP.—Lawrence Group, Inc., pg. 662
LEADER SERVICES, INC.—Leader Federal Bank For Savings, pg. 664
LIFESHARES SERVICES CO.—The Chesapeake Life Insurance Co., pg. 243
LUNDBERG AND ASSOCIATES—Lawrence Group, Inc., pg. 662
LUTHERAN BROTHERHOOD, pg. 688
MBL LIFE ASSURANCE CORP.—Mutual Benefit Life Insurance Company, pg. 778
MSI INSURANCE COMPANIES, pg. 693
MACCABEES MUTUAL LIFE INSURANCE, pg. 696
METROPOLITAN LIFE INSURANCE CO., pg. 744
MIDDLESEX INSURANCE CO.—Middlesex/Patriot General Insurance Companies, pg. 751
MIDDLESEX/PATRIOT GENERAL INSURANCE COMPANIES, pg. 751
MIDLAND NATIONAL LIFE INSURANCE CO.—Sammons Enterprises, Inc., pg. 968
WALLACE MOIR CO., pg. 763
MONY LIFE INSURANCE CO. OF AMERICA—The Mutual Life Insurance Company of New York (MONY), pg. 778
MUTUAL BENEFIT LIFE INSURANCE COMPANY, pg. 778
THE MUTUAL LIFE INSURANCE COMPANY OF NEW YORK (MONY), pg. 778
MUTUAL SERVICE CORPORATION—Pacific Mutual Life Insurance Company, pg. 841
NATIONAL CASUALTY CO.—Nationwide Mutual Insurance Company, pg. 795
NATIONAL MORTGAGE COMPANY, pg. 792
NATIONWIDE COMMERCIAL CO.—Amerco, A Nevada Corporation, pg. 48
NETWORK HOME SERVICES, INC.—Network Real Estate of California, Inc., pg. 798
THE NEW ENGLAND, pg. 799
NEW ENGLAND INVESTMENT MARKETING, INC.—The New England, pg. 799
NEW YORK LIFE INSURANCE COMPANY, pg. 802
NEW YORK LIFE INSURANCE CO. OF CANADA—New York Life Insurance Company, pg. 803
NEWBURY INSURANCE CO.—The New England, pg. 800
OXFORD LIFE INSURANCE CO.—Amerco, A Nevada Corporation, pg. 48
PATRIOT GENERAL INSURANCE CO.—Middlesex/Patriot General Insurance Companies, pg. 751
PEBSCO INC.—Nationwide Mutual Insurance Company, pg. 795
PENN MUTUAL EQUITY SERVICES INC.—The Penn Mutual Life Insurance Company, pg. 858
PERMANENT GENERAL COMPANIES—Ingram Industries Inc., pg. 569
PONDEROSA INSURANCE AGENCY—Amerco, A Nevada Corporation, pg. 48
PRINCIPAL MARKETING SERVICES, INC.—The Principal Financial Group, pg. 891
THE PRUDENTIAL ASSET MANAGEMENT CO., INC.—The Prudential Insurance Company of America, pg. 897
PRUDENTIAL GENERAL INSURANCE CO.—The Prudential Insurance Company of America, pg. 897
THE PRUDENTIAL INSURANCE COMPANY OF AMERICA, pg. 896
PRUDENTIAL INTERFUNDING CORP.—The Prudential Insurance Company of America, pg. 897
PRUDENTIAL REINSURANCE CO.—The Prudential Insurance Company of America, pg. 897
PRULEASE, INC.—The Prudential Insurance Company of America, pg. 897
RE/MAX INSURANCE DIV.—RE/MAX International, Inc., pg. 915
RE/MAX INTERNATIONAL, INC., pg. 915
REPUBLIC WESTERN INSURANCE CO.—Amerco, A Nevada Corporation, pg. 48
ROBSON, CAVIGNAC & ASSOCIATES—Lawrence Group, Inc., pg. 662
SS SERVICE CORPORATION—Washington Mutual Savings Bank, pg. 1166
SANTANDER MET., S.A. MADRID—Metropolitan Life Insurance Co., pg. 745
SELIGMAN & ASSOCIATES, INC., pg. 988
TOPA INSURANCE COMPANY—Topa Equities Ltd, Inc., pg. 1101
UNDERWRITERS SERVICE AGENCY, INC.—Integrated Resources, Inc., pg. 573
UNDERWRITERS SERVICE AGENCY, INC.—Integrated Resources, Inc., pg. 573
UNIGARD SERVICE CORP.—John Hancock Mutual Life Insurance Company, pg. 596
UNITED RESOURCES INSURANCE SERVICES, INC.—Integrated Resources, Inc., pg. 573
VASA BROUGHER, INC.—VASA Insurance Group, Inc., pg. 1146
VASA LIFE INSURANCE CO.—VASA Insurance Group, Inc., pg. 1146

VASA NORTH ATLANTIC INSURANCE COMPANY—VASA Insurance Group, Inc., pg. 1146
WESTERN REINSURANCE BROKERS, INC., pg. 1181
RALPH C. WILSON ENTERPRISES, pg. 1194
ZENITH INTL. INSURANCE LTD.—Levi Strauss & Co., pg. 671

6512 — OPERATORS OF NONRESIDENTIAL BUILDINGS

AMERICAN TRADING AND PRODUCTION CORPORATION, pg. 64
BAY FAIR SHOPPING CTR.—R. H. Macy & Co., Inc., pg. 699
BIG Y FOODS INC., pg. 149
BINSWANGER MANAGEMENT CORP.—The Binswanger Company, pg. 152
BRADLEY SPECIALTY RETAILING, INC.—W. C. Bradley Co., pg. 170
BRUNSWICK SQUARE—R. H. Macy & Co., Inc., pg. 699
BUILDERS INC.—Garvey Industries, Inc., pg. 444
BUNDY PROPERTIES—American Protection Industries, Inc., pg. 60
CBM INDUSTRIES, INC., pg. 199
CALMARK INVESTMENT COMPANY, pg. 211
CALMARK PROPERTIES, INC.—Calmark Investment Company, pg. 211
CARPRO, INC.—Caravan Products Company, Inc., pg. 217
THE CEDARWOOD COMPANIES, pg. 230
CENTERMARK PROPERTIES, INC., pg. 231
CHARAN INDUSTRIES, INC., pg. 239
CHELSEA MOORE COMPANY, pg. 241
CHESTERFIELD INDUSTRIAL PARK, INC.—Watlow Electric Manufacturing Company, pg. 1167
COLFAX, INC., pg. 261
COLUMBIA MALL—R. H. Macy & Co., Inc., pg. 699
CORPOREX COMPANIES, INC., pg. 287
COWPER & SIEGFRIED, pg. 291
CRADDOCK DEVELOPMENT CO., INC., pg. 295
CRETE CARRIER CORP., pg. 299
HEATHER CROLIE, INC., pg. 300
CROWN AMERICAN CORPORATION, pg. 301
CROWN CENTER REDEVELOPMENT CORP.—Hallmark Cards, Inc., pg. 502
DAHLEM COMPANY, INC., pg. 310
DANIS INDUSTRIES CORPORATION, pg. 314
DARIGOLD, INC., pg. 315
DEAD RIVER PROPERTIES—Dead River Company, pg. 322
THE EDWARD J. DEBARTOLO CORPORATION, pg. 323
DESCO CORPORATION, pg. 332
DUNCO REALTY & EQUIP. CORP.—Victory Markets Inc., pg. 1150
FARMERS INVESTMENT COMPANY, INC.—Bale Of Kentucky, Inc., pg. 115
THE FLATLEY COMPANY, pg. 416
FOLEY HOLDING COMPANY, INC., pg. 422
FRIENDLY CHEVROLET CO. INC., pg. 433
GF INDUSTRIES, INC., pg. 439
GF PROPERTIES, INC.—GF Industries, Inc., pg. 439
GALESI ENTERPRISES—Rotterdam Ventures Inc., pg. 951
THE GARDEN STATE PLAZA CORP.—R. H. Macy & Co., Inc., pg. 699
GENERAL GROWTH CENTER COMPANIES, INC.—General Growth Companies, Inc., pg. 449
GOSNELL BUILDERS, pg. 472
CURTIS C. GUNN, INC., pg. 494
HBE CORPORATION, pg. 495
THE HAHN CO.—Trizec Properties, Inc., pg. 1115
HARTZ GROUP, pg. 514
HARTZ MOUNTAIN INDUSTRIES—Hartz Group, pg. 514
BILL HEARD ENTERPRISES, INC., pg. 521
THE HEARST CORPORATION, pg. 521
HESS'S DEPARTMENT STORES, INC.—Crown American Corporation, pg. 302
HOLDER CORPORATION, pg. 538
THE IDI GROUP COMPANIES, pg. 560
INDEPENDENCE SQUARE PROPERTIES—The Penn Mutual Life Insurance Company, pg. 858
INGLES MARKETS, INC., pg. 568
JONES PROPERTIES, INC.—Jones International Ltd., pg. 603
KERRISON DRY GOODS COMPANY, INC., pg. 624
KINGS PLAZA SHOPPING CTR. & MARINA—R. H. Macy & Co., Inc., pg. 699
LB INDUSTRIES INC., pg. 647
LINCOLN PROPERTY CO., NORTHERN CALIFORNIA—Lincoln Property Company, pg. 676
LINCOLN PROPERTY COMPANY, pg. 676
MARKETING CORP. OF AMERICA, pg. 709
MCKENZIE TANK LINES, INC., pg. 730
METROPOLITAN LIFE INSURANCE CO., pg. 744
MICO, INC., pg. 748
MISSION SHOPPING CTR.—R. H. Macy & Co., Inc., pg. 699
NATIONAL LUMBER CO., pg. 792
NEW PARK MALL—R. H. Macy & Co., Inc., pg. 699
O'REILLY AUTO INC., pg. 829
OWNERS MAINTENANCE CORP.—Helmsley Enterprises, Inc., pg. 527
THE PRUDENTIAL REALTY GROUP—The Prudential Insurance Company of America, pg. 897
QUAKER BRIDGE MALL—R. H. Macy & Co., Inc., pg. 699
RALEIGH ENTERPRISES, INC., pg. 910
RECKSON ASSOCIATES, pg. 917
THE RIO GRANDE INDUSTRIES INC.—Anschutz Corporation, pg. 75
RYAN PROPERTIES INC., pg. 958
SCHWEGMANN GIANT SUPER MARKETS, pg. 980
SEALASKA CORPORATION, pg. 984
SEAWAY SHOPPING CENTERS, INC.—Charan Industries, Inc., pg. 239
SETON COMPANY, pg. 993
SHAPELL INDUSTRIES, INC., pg. 995
SIEG COMPANY, pg. 1002
MELVIN SIMON & ASSOCIATES, pg. 1006
SOUTH SHORE MALL—R. H. Macy & Co., Inc., pg. 699
SPARTAN OIL CORP., pg. 1026
SUNNYVALE TOWNCENTER—R. H. Macy & Co., Inc., pg. 699
SUNRISE MALL ASSOCS.—Shepaug Corporation, pg. 998
SVERDRUP CORPORATION, pg. 1065
SVERDRUP INVESTMENTS, INC.—Sverdrup Corporation, pg. 1066
TDW BUILDING CORPORATION—T.D. Williamson, Inc., pg. 1192
TOWN & COUNTRY FOOD MARKETS, INC., pg. 1103
TOWN PUMP, INC., pg. 1104
TRIZEC PROPERTIES, INC., pg. 1115
THE TRUMP GROUP, pg. 1117
TRUMP ORGANIZATION, pg. 1118
TRUMP TOWERS—Trump Organization, pg. 1118
U-HAUL REAL ESTATE COMPANY—Amerco, A Nevada Corporation, pg. 48
UNITED STATES REALTY & INVESTMENT CO., pg. 1137
VALLEY FAIR SHOPPING CTR.—R. H. Macy & Co., Inc., pg. 699
VANTAGE COMPANIES, pg. 1145
VICTORY MARKETS INC., pg. 1150
WARM BROTHERS CONSTRUCTION COMPANY, pg. 1163
WASHINGTON AVENUE VENTURES, INC.—Rotterdam Ventures Inc., pg. 952
WATKINS ASSOCIATED DEVELOPERS—Watkins Associated Industries Inc., pg. 1167
WATLOW ELECTRIC COMPANY OF CALIFORNIA—Watlow Electric Manufacturing Company, pg. 1168
WESTLAKE HARDWARE, INC., pg. 1183
KEMMONS WILSON COMPANIES, pg. 1194

6513 — OPERATORS OF APARTMENT BUILDINGS

AFFILIATES GROUP INC., pg. 24
AMFAC RESORTS, INC.—JMB Realty Corporation, pg. 585
BRUTGER EQUITIES, INC., pg. 185
BUILDERS DEVELOPMENT INC.—Garvey Industries, Inc., pg. 444
BUILDERS INC.—Garvey Industries, Inc., pg. 444
CALMARK INVESTMENT COMPANY, pg. 211
CALMARK PROPERTIES, INC.—Calmark Investment Company, pg. 211
CARDINAL REALTY SERVICES INC., pg. 218
CHARING CROSS GROUP, pg. 239
CHELSEA MOORE COMPANY, pg. 241
CITIZENS REALTY & INSURANCE INC., pg. 251
CLASSIC RESIDENCE BY HYATT—H. Group Holding Inc., pg. 495
CLAYTON, WILLIAMS & SHERWOOD, INC., pg. 254
DEVELOPERS DIVERSIFIED, pg. 333
ERB LUMBER COMPANY, pg. 360
THE FLATLEY COMPANY, pg. 416
I. H. FRENCH & CO. INC., pg. 432
GARVEY INDUSTRIES, INC., pg. 443
GENERAL SERVICES CORPORATION, pg. 450
GOLF HOSTS, INC., pg. 469
GULF COAST LEAD COMPANY, INC., pg. 493
HIGH POINT VENTURES, INC.—Rotterdam Ventures Inc., pg. 951
THE INLAND GROUP, INC., pg. 570
JACKSONVILLE VENTURES, INC.—Rotterdam Ventures Inc., pg. 951
LINCOLN PROPERTY CO., NORTHERN CALIFORNIA—Lincoln Property Company, pg. 676
LITTLE AMERICA HOTELS—Sinclair Oil Corp., pg. 1008
THE MACERICH CO., pg. 696
NATIONAL LUMBER CO., pg. 792
OXFORD REALTY SERVICES CORP., pg. 835
PURCELL CO., INC., pg. 900
RAYCO, pg. 914
REALTY ONE, pg. 917
REMINGTON HILL VENTURES—Rotterdam Ventures Inc., pg. 952
ROTTERDAM VENTURES INC., pg. 951
A. G. SPANOS DEVELOPMENT, INC., pg. 1025
SPRINGER SCHMID GROUP, pg. 1033
TAMPA VENTURES, INC.—Rotterdam Ventures Inc., pg. 952
TAYLOR-MORLEY, INC., pg. 1081
THE TRUMP GROUP, pg. 1117
TRUMP PLAZA OF THE PALM BEACHES—Trump Organization, pg. 1118
TRUMP TOWERS—Trump Organization, pg. 1118
KEMMONS WILSON COMPANIES, pg. 1194
WINRIDGE AURORA VENTURES, INC.—Rotterdam Ventures Inc., pg. 952
WOODFIN SUITES, INC.—Woodfin Holding Corporation, pg. 1200

6514 — OPERATORS OF DWELLINGS OTHER THAN APARTMENT BUILDINGS

CARLSON REAL ESTATE COMPANY—Carlson Companies, Inc., pg. 221
CLAYTON, WILLIAMS & SHERWOOD, INC., pg. 254
THE IDI GROUP COMPANIES, pg. 560
LARIO ENTERPRISES, INC.—Lario Oil & Gas Company, pg. 659
MICHAEL J. MUNGO COMPANY, INC., pg. 775

6515 — OPERATORS OF RESIDENTIAL MOBILE HOME SITES

CLAYTON, WILLIAMS & SHERWOOD, INC., pg. 254
PURCELL CO., INC., pg. 900
ROC PROPERTIES INC., pg. 908

6519 — LESSORS OF REAL PROPERTY, NEC

AMERICAN TRADING AND PRODUCTION CORPORATION, pg. 64
AMFAC/JMB HAWAII, INC.—JMB Realty Corporation, pg. 585
BERWIND CORPORATION, pg. 145
BRECK OPERATING CORP.—States, Inc., pg. 1041
B.C. COOK & SONS ENTERPRISES, INC.—Cook Holding Corporation, pg. 282
COOK HOLDING CORPORATION, pg. 282
DOUGLAS MANAGEMENT COMPANY—Lynden Incorporated, pg. 689
GAY JOHNSON'S INC., pg. 446
H. GROUP HOLDING INC., pg. 495
HAMER PROPERTIES, INC.—Walter Industries, Inc., pg. 1162
JONES COMPANY, INC., pg. 603
KENTUCKY BERWIND LAND COMPANY—Berwind Corporation, pg. 145
KWICKIE/FLASH FOODS, INC.—Jones Company, Inc., pg. 603
THE LEAVELL COMPANY, pg. 664
LINCOLN INDUSTRIES, pg. 676
MCKENZIE TANK LINES, INC., pg. 730
METRO PARKING SYSTEMS—Metropolitan Properties Inc., pg. 745
MOLINE ACCESSORIES CORPORATION—Montgomery Elevator Company, pg. 767
ROTTERDAM VENTURES INC., pg. 951
J. W. WALTER, INC.—Walter Industries, Inc., pg. 1162
WILMORE COAL COMPANY—Berwind Corporation, pg. 145

6531 — REAL ESTATE AGENTS & MANAGERS

AM REAL CORP.—Insignia Financial Group, Inc., pg. 571
ROBERT B. AIKENS & ASSOCIATES INC., pg. 26
ALCO MANAGEMENT, INC.—Jemison, Inc., pg. 592
ALCO PROPERTIES, INC.—Jemison, Inc., pg. 592
ALLIANCE MANAGEMENT, INC., pg. 37
ALTUS REAL ESTATE SERVICES, INC.—Altus Federal Savings Bank, pg. 46
ALTUS SERVICES, INC.—Altus Federal Savings Bank, pg. 46
AMERICAN TRADING REAL ESTATE PROPERTIES, INC.—American Trading and Production Corporation, pg. 65
AMERICAN TRADING REAL ESTATE PROPERTIES, INC.—American Trading and Production Corporation, pg. 65
AMERICAN TRADING REAL ESTATE PROPERTIES, INC.—American Trading and Production Corporation, pg. 65
AMERISURE COMPANIES, pg. 66
AMURCON CORPORATION, pg. 70
AMWAY CORPORATION, pg. 70
ARAMONT PROPERTIES, INC.-DELAWARE—ARA Group, pg. 6
ATLANTIC GULF COMMUNITIES CORPORATION, pg. 95
BAIRD & WARNER INC., pg. 114
BARANCORP, pg. 118
D. A. BARANSKI & CO.—Barancorp, pg. 118
BEAVER FREE CORP.—Pacifica Real Estate Group, pg. 842
BENDERSON DEVELOPMENT CO., INC., pg. 138
BERWIND CORPORATION, pg. 145
BERWIND PROPERTY GROUP, INC.—Berwind Corporation, pg. 145
BINSWANGER CHICAGO—The Binswanger Company, pg. 151
THE BINSWANGER COMPANY, pg. 151
BINSWANGER INDUSTRIAL—The Binswanger Company, pg. 152
BINSWANGER INVESTMENT—The Binswanger Company, pg. 152
BINSWANGER SOUTHERN—The Binswanger Company, pg. 152
BRANDYWINE REALTY & DEVELOPMENT, INC.—Brandywine Sports, Inc., pg. 172
BRANDYWINE SPORTS, INC., pg. 172
BROWN BROTHERS, HARRIMAN & CO., pg. 181
BROWN, HARRIS, STEVENS, INC.—Helmsley Enterprises, Inc., pg. 527
JOHN BURNHAM & CO., pg. 194
CB COMMERCIAL REAL ESTATE GROUP CENTRAL DIVISION—Carlyle Holding Corporation, pg. 222
CB COMMERCIAL REAL ESTATE GROUP EASTERN DIVISION—Carlyle Holding Corporation, pg. 222
CB COMMERCIAL REAL ESTATE GROUP, INC.—Carlyle Holding Corporation, pg. 222
CB COMMERCIAL REAL ESTATE GROUP, NEW YORK—Carlyle Holding Corporation, pg. 222
CTB, INC.—The Dickerson Group, Inc., pg. 336
THE CAFARO CO., pg. 207
CAMBIO EQUITIES CORP., pg. 211
CAMPUS POINT REALTY CORPORATION—Science Applications International Corporation, pg. 981
CAPITAL DEVELOPMENT CO., pg. 215
CARDINAL REALTY SERVICES INC., pg. 218
CARLSBERG FINANCIAL CORP., pg. 220
THE CARLYLE GROUP—Carlyle Holding Corporation, pg. 222
CARLYLE HOLDING CORPORATION, pg. 222
THE OLIVER CARR CO., pg. 225
CARTER, pg. 226
CASTLE-HARLAN, INC., pg. 229
CENTRAL REALTY CORP.—Union Holdings, Inc., pg. 1128
CENTURY REAL ESTATE, INC.—Cenvill Development Corp., pg. 236

CENTURY 21 AGMONT REAL ESTATE, INC., pg. 235
CENTURY 21 REAL ESTATE CORP.—Metropolitan Life Insurance Co., pg. 744
CHARAN REALTY GROUP—Charan Industries, Inc., pg. 239
CHARING CROSS GROUP, pg. 239
CHELSEA MOORE COMPANY, pg. 241
CITIZENS REALTY & INSURANCE INC., pg. 251
CLARION ENTERPRISES, INC.—Montgomery Elevator Company, pg. 767
COAKLEY & WILLIAMS INC., pg. 256
COLDWELL BANKERS/SCHLOTT REALTORS, pg. 260
COLE-LAYER-TRUMBLE COMPANY (CLT)—Day & Zimmermann, Inc., pg. 320
COLONIAL DRILLING & EXPLORATION CORPORATION—Colonial Oil Industries, pg. 264
CONTINENTAL NATIONAL AMERICAN REAL ESTATE INC., pg. 280
COPLEY REAL ESTATE ADVISORS, INC.—The New England, pg. 799
COTTER FINANCE CO., INC.—Cotter & Company, pg. 288
CRADDOCK DEVELOPMENT CO., INC., pg. 295
CROSS & BROWN COMPANY—Metropolitan Life Insurance Co., pg. 744
DARIGOLD, INC., pg. 315
DAY & ZIMMERMANN, INC., pg. 320
DEAD RIVER COMPANY, pg. 321
DEL AMERICAN PROPERTIES, INC., pg. 325
THE DICKERSON GROUP, INC., pg. 335
DICKERSON REALTY CORP.—The Dickerson Group, Inc., pg. 336
DICKERSON REALTY FLORIDA, INC.—The Dickerson Group, Inc., pg. 336
DOBSON & JOHNSON, INC., pg. 342
DOUGLAS ELLIMAN-GIBBONS & IVES, INC., pg. 347
CHARLES DUNN COMPANY-REALTORS, pg. 353
E & A INDUSTRIES, INC., pg. 358
ERA GENERAL AGENCY CORP.—ERA Real Estate, pg. 360
ERA REAL ESTATE, pg. 360
LEO EISENBERG & CO., INC., pg. 372
EMPIRE WEST COMPANIES, INC., pg. 380
EZON PRODUCTS, INC., pg. 393
FMI PROPERTIES CORP.—American Financial Corporation, pg. 53
FARNSWORTH DEVELOPMENT CO.—Farnsworth Companies, pg. 403
FIRST COLUMBIA ESCROW, INC.—Washington Mutual Savings Bank, pg. 1166
FIRST FLORIDA EQUITIES, LTD., pg. 413
FISCHBACH & DOUGHERTY, INC., pg. 414
FISHER COMPANIES, INC., pg. 414
FISHER PROPERTIES INC.—Fisher Companies, Inc., pg. 415
FLETCHER ENTERPRISES, pg. 418
GWC PROPERTIES, INC.—McCall Oil & Chemical Corp., pg. 727
GWP, INC., pg. 441
THE GATES CORPORATION, pg. 445
GAY JOHNSON'S INC., pg. 446
GENERAL GROWTH COMPANIES, INC., pg. 449
GENERAL SERVICES CORPORATION, pg. 450
GILBANE PROPERTIES, INC.—Gilbane Building Company, pg. 457
GILLETT HOLDINGS, INC., pg. 458
GOLUB & CO., pg. 469
SHELDON GOOD & CO., INC., pg. 470
THE GREAT ATLANTIC COMPANIES, pg. 480
GREAT ATLANTIC HOSPITALITY CO. INC.—The Great Atlantic Companies, pg. 480
GREAT ATLANTIC MANAGEMENT CO. INC.—The Great Atlantic Companies, pg. 480
ALBERT M. GREENFIELD & COMPANY—Helmsley Enterprises, Inc., pg. 527
HCB CONTRACTORS, pg. 496
H & K REALTY CO. INC.—E & A Industries, Inc., pg. 358
HEARST REAL ESTATE DIVISION—The Hearst Corporation, pg. 524
HELMSLEY ENTERPRISES, INC., pg. 527
HELMSLEY-NOYES CO., INC.—Helmsley Enterprises, Inc., pg. 527
HELMSLEY-SPEAR CONVERSION SALES CORP.—Helmsley Enterprises, Inc., pg. 527
HELMSLEY-SPEAR INC.—Helmsley Enterprises, Inc., pg. 527
HOSTMARK MANAGEMENT GROUP, pg. 545
THE HOYT GROUP, pg. 548
HYATT CORPORATION—H. Group Holding Inc., pg. 495
THE INLAND GROUP, INC., pg. 570
INSIGNIA FINANCIAL GROUP, INC., pg. 571
INSIGNIA MANAGEMENT GROUP—Insignia Financial Group, Inc., pg. 571
INSIGNIA MORTGAGE & INVESTMENT CORP.—Insignia Financial Group, Inc., pg. 571
INTEGRATED ACQUISITION, INC.—Integrated Resources, Inc., pg. 573
INTEGRATED RESOURCES, INC., pg. 573
INVEST WEST FINANCIAL CORPORATION—Pacifica Real Estate Group, pg. 842
IRVINE COMPANY, pg. 582
JAMES BUILDING CORPORATION, pg. 588
J. M. JAYSON & CO., INC., pg. 591
JEMISON, INC., pg. 592
S. C. JOHNSON & SON, INC., pg. 599
JOHNSON WAX DEVELOPMENT CORP.—S. C. Johnson & Son, Inc., pg. 599
KETTLER BROTHERS, INC., pg. 626
L. ROBERT KIMBALL & ASSOCIATES, pg. 629
J. I. KISLAK INC., pg. 633
KOHLER COMPANY, pg. 639
KORMAN CO., pg. 642
KRAUS-ANDERSON, INC., pg. 644
KRAUS-ANDERSON REALTY CO.—Kraus-Anderson, Inc., pg. 644
KRUSE INTERNATIONAL, pg. 645
LAKE MICHIGAN CONSTRUCTION, INC.—Orix Real Estate Equities, Inc., pg. 829
LAMAR CORPORATION, pg. 652
LAMAR LEASING CO., INC.—Capitol Street Corp., pg. 216
LASALLE PARTNERS, pg. 660
LASKEY ASSOCIATES, pg. 660
LEADER FEDERAL BANK FOR SAVINGS, pg. 663
LEHMAN ASSOCIATES, INC.—United States Realty & Investment Co., pg. 1137
LIFE CARE SERVICES CORPORATION—The Weitz Corporation, pg. 1174
LLOYD PROPERTIES, pg. 680
THE LONG & FOSTER COMPANIES, INC., pg. 682
THE LONG & FOSTER REAL ESTATE, INC.—The Long & Foster Companies, Inc., pg. 682
LOS ANGELES UNION TERMINAL, INC.—Anschutz Corporation, pg. 75
LOVE MORTGAGE COMPANY, pg. 685
MML REAL ESTATE CORPORATION—Massachusetts Mutual Life Insurance Co., pg. 719
MML REALTY MANAGEMENT CORP.—Massachusetts Mutual Life Insurance Co., pg. 719
MACRISTY INDUSTRIES, INC., pg. 698
MAGUIRE GROUP INC., pg. 701
MAGUIRE THOMAS PARTNERS, pg. 701
MARKAIR, INC., pg. 708
MAUI VARIETIES, LTD., pg. 721
THE MAURIN-OGDEN COMPANIES, pg. 722
MAURIN-OGDEN MANAGEMENT CORPORATION—The Maurin-Ogden Companies, pg. 722
MCCALL OIL REAL ESTATE CORPORATION—McCall Oil & Chemical Corp., pg. 727
METRO ATLANTA PROPERTIES—Fischbach & Dougherty, Inc., pg. 414
METROPOLITAN LIFE INSURANCE CO., pg. 744
MICHAEL'S DEVELOPMENT COMPANY, pg. 747
MID STATE PRODUCTS CO.—Osco Industries Inc., pg. 830
MILL MAPLE PROPERTIES, INC.—Washington Mutual Savings Bank, pg. 1166
MILL PLAIN FOUR, INC.—Washington Mutual Savings Bank, pg. 1166
MILL PLAIN ONE, INC.—Washington Mutual Savings Bank, pg. 1166
MILL PLAIN THREE, INC.—Washington Mutual Savings Bank, pg. 1166
MILL PLAIN TWO, INC.—Washington Mutual Savings Bank, pg. 1166
MINYARD PROPERTIES, INC.—Minyard Food Stores, pg. 759
MISCO INDUSTRIES, pg. 759
MORECO INC.—Modern Group Ltd., pg. 763
MORGAN REALTY ASSOCIATES, pg. 770
MUBEN REALTY CO.—Mutual Benefit Life Insurance Company, pg. 778
MURPHY FAVRE HOUSE MANAGERS, INC.—Washington Mutual Savings Bank, pg. 1166
MURPHY FAVRE PROPERTIES, INC.—Washington Mutual Savings Bank, pg. 1166
NTS CORPORATION, pg. 781
NATIONAL DEVELOPMENT CO., INC.—Sunstates Realty Group Inc., pg. 1062
NATIONAL PROPERTY ANALYSTS, INC., pg. 792
NATIONAL REALTY CORP.—Helmsley Enterprises, Inc., pg. 527
NETWORK REAL ESTATE OF CALIFORNIA, INC., pg. 798
NETWORK REAL ESTATE OF CENTRAL CALIFORNIA, INC.—Network Real Estate of California, Inc., pg. 798
NETWORK REAL ESTATE, INC.—Network Real Estate of California, Inc., pg. 798
NETWORK REAL ESTATE OF LOS ANGELES, INC.—Network Real Estate of California, Inc., pg. 798
NETWORK REAL ESTATE OF NORTHERN CALIFORNIA, INC.—Network Real Estate of California, Inc., pg. 798
NETWORK REAL ESTATE OF SOUTHERN CALIFORNIA, INC.—Network Real Estate of California, Inc., pg. 798
NORMANDALE PROPERTIES—Opus South Corporation, pg. 828
NORTH AMERICAN ACCEPTANCE CORPORATION—Washington Mutual Savings Bank, pg. 1166
NORTHRIDGE INDUSTRIES, INC.—H. Group Holding Inc., pg. 495
NORTHWESTERN ENGINEERING CO., pg. 815
ORIX REAL ESTATE EQUITIES, INC., pg. 829
OXFORD REALTY SERVICES CORP., pg. 835
PIC REALTY CORP.—The Prudential Insurance Company of America, pg. 896
PACIFIC HOLDING CORPORATION, pg. 840
PACIFICA REAL ESTATE GROUP, pg. 842
PETERSEN DEVELOPMENT CORP.—American Tool Companies, Inc., pg. 64
PMREALTY ADVISORS, INC.—Pacific Mutual Life Insurance Company, pg. 841
PRESTON PROPERTIES OF ARIZONA, INC.—Washington Mutual Savings Bank, pg. 1167
PRESTON PROPERTIES OF CALIFORNIA, INC.—Washington Mutual Savings Bank, pg. 1167
PRESTON PROPERTIES TEXAS, INC.—Washington Mutual Savings Bank, pg. 1167
PRESTON PROPERTY MANAGEMENT COMPANY—Washington Mutual Savings Bank, pg. 1167
PRINCEVILLE CORPORATION, pg. 890
PRINCEVILLE MANAGEMENT CORPORATION—Princeville Corporation, pg. 890
PRINCEVILLE REALTY CORPORATION—Princeville Corporation, pg. 890
PROFESSIONAL APARTMENT MANAGEMENT, INC., pg. 893
PROGRESS WEST, pg. 894
PROPERTY MANAGEMENT SERVICES, INC., pg. 894
PRUDENTIAL DEVELOPMENT & RETAIL DIV.—The Prudential Insurance Company of America, pg. 897
THE PRUDENTIAL REALTY GROUP—The Prudential Insurance Company of America, pg. 897
PURCELL CO., INC., pg. 900
RE/MAX INTERNATIONAL, INC., pg. 915
REALTY ONE, pg. 917
RED CARPET REAL ESTATE SERVICES, INC., pg. 918
REGENCY GROUP INC., pg. 922
RESOURCES PROPERTY MANAGEMENT CORP.—Integrated Resources, Inc., pg. 573
JOHN J. REYNOLDS, INC.—Helmsley Enterprises, Inc., pg. 527
RICE FOOD MARKETS INC., pg. 931
ROLAND INTERNATIONAL CORPORATION, pg. 944
ROSEN ASSOCIATES MANAGEMENT CORP., pg. 948
ROSEWOOD CORPORATION—Caroline Hunt Trust Estate, pg. 553
ROSEWOOD PROPERTY COMPANY, pg. 949
ROTHSCHILD NORTH AMERICA INC., pg. 951
ROTTERDAM VENTURES INC., pg. 951
ARTHUR RUBLOFF & CO. OF FLORIDA—Orix Real Estate Equities, Inc., pg. 829
SAN FRANCISCO REALTIES—The Hearst Corporation, pg. 524
SANDS INVESTMENTS, INC., pg. 970
SCHNEIDER COMMERCIAL REAL ESTATE, pg. 977
SEA ISLAND COMPANY, pg. 983
SEA ISLAND PROPERTIES, INC.—Sea Island Company, pg. 983
SELIGMAN & ASSOCIATES, INC., pg. 988
SHAPELL INDUSTRIES, INC., pg. 995
SHELDON GOOD & CO. OF CALIFORNIA—Sheldon Good & Co., Inc., pg. 470
SHELDON GOOD & CO. OF CANADA—Sheldon Good & Co., Inc., pg. 470
THE SIERRA CAPITAL COMPANIES, pg. 1002
SIERRA CAPITAL REALTY SERVICES—The Sierra Capital Companies, pg. 1003
THE SMITH GROUP, INC., pg. 1012
SOUTHEASTERN INVESTMENT PROPERTIES INC., pg. 1019
SPAULDING & SLYE COMPANY, pg. 1026
STILES CORPORATION, pg. 1049
STIRLING PROPERTIES, INC.—The Maurin-Odgen Companies, pg. 722
SUMMA CORPORATION, pg. 1057
SUN LAKES MARKETING, pg. 1059
SUNSTATES PROPERTIES, INC.—Sunstates Realty Group Inc., pg. 1062
SUNSTATES REALTY GROUP INC., pg. 1062
SVERDRUP INVESTMENTS, INC.—Sverdrup Corporation, pg. 1066
SYSTEMS PARKING, INC., pg. 1071
TEACHERS MANAGEMENT & INVESTMENT CORPORATION, pg. 1082
TOWNE PROPERTIES, pg. 1104
TRAMMELL CROW COMPANY, pg. 1106
TRECO COMMUNITIES, INC.—Sunstates Realty Group Inc., pg. 1062
TRECO PROPERTY SERVICES, INC.—Sunstates Realty Group Inc., pg. 1062
TRECO REALTY GROUP, INC.—Sunstates Realty Group Inc., pg. 1062
TRERICE DEVELOPMENT CO.—Trerice Tosto International, pg. 1110
TRERICE MANAGEMENT CO.—Trerice Tosto International, pg. 1110
TRERICE TOSTO INTERNATIONAL, pg. 1110
TRI-PALM ESTATE—GWP, Inc., pg. 441
THE TRIAD GROUP, INC.—Altus Federal Savings Bank, pg. 46
TUCSON REALTY & TRUST CO., pg. 1118
UNITED PARKING, INC., pg. 1134
UNITED SERVICES AUTOMOBILE ASSOCIATION (USAA), pg. 1134
UNITED STATES REALTY & INVESTMENT CO., pg. 1137
THE VAN METRE COMPANIES, pg. 1144
VANFED APPRAISAL COMPANY—Washington Mutual Savings Bank, pg. 1166
VENGROFF WILLIAMS REALTY MANAGEMENT—Vengroff Williams & Associates, Inc., pg. 1147
THE VIERA COMPANY—A. Duda & Sons Inc., pg. 351
WATT INDUSTRIES, pg. 1168
WEICHERT COMPANY, pg. 1173
WEICHERT REALTY, INC.—Weichert Company, pg. 1173
WIELAND REALTY ASSOCIATES, INC.—John Wieland Homes Inc., pg. 1189
ZILBER, LTD., pg. 1219
ZION'S SECURITIES CORP.—Deseret Management Corporation, pg. 332

6552 — LAND SUBDIVIDERS & DEVELOPERS, EXCEPT CEMETERIES

API, INC.—JMB Realty Corporation, pg. 585
ASA PROPERTIES HAWAII INC.—Persis Corporation, pg. 863
ABBELL ASSOCIATES, pg. 9
ROBERT B. AIKENS & ASSOCIATES INC., pg. 26
ALADDIN RESOURCES, INC.—Aladdin Industries, Incorporated, pg. 29
ALCO PROPERTIES, INC.—Jemison, Inc., pg. 592
AMERICAN FACTORS ASSOC. AUSTRALIA PTY., LTD.—JMB Realty Corporation, pg. 585
AMERICAN TRADING REAL ESTATE PROPERTIES, INC.—American Trading and Production Corporation, pg. 65
AMFAC DEVELOPMENT CORP.—JMB Realty Corporation, pg. 585
AMFAC FINANCIAL INC.—JMB Realty Corporation, pg. 585
AMFAC/JMB HAWAII, INC.—JMB Realty Corporation, pg. 585

6552—LAND SUBDIVIDERS & DEVELOPERS, EXCEPT CEMETERIES

AMFAC PROPERTY DEVELOPMENT CORP.—JMB Realty Corporation, pg. 585
AMFAC SILVERADO CORP.—JMB Realty Corporation, pg. 585
AMRECORP REALTY INC., pg. 68
AMURCON CORPORATION, pg. 70
ARTESIAN DEVELOPMENT CORPORATION—Artesian Resources Corporation, pg. 86
ARTESIAN RESOURCES CORPORATION, pg. 86
ARVIDA—JMB Realty Corporation, pg. 586
ATLANTIC GULF COMMUNITIES CORPORATION, pg. 95
BE & K, INC., pg. 106
BNE LAND & DEVELOPMENT CO.—Boddie-Noell Enterprises Inc., pg. 161
BARCLAY WHITE INCORPORATED, pg. 119
BELZ ENTERPRISES, pg. 138
BENDERSON DEVELOPMENT CO., INC., pg. 138
THE BINSWANGER COMPANY, pg. 151
BINSWANGER DEVELOPMENT—The Binswanger Company, pg. 152
BODDIE-NOELL ENTERPRISES INC., pg. 161
BRANDYWINE REALTY & DEVELOPMENT, INC.—Brandywine Sports, Inc., pg. 172
BRANDYWINE SPORTS, INC., pg. 172
BRIM, INC., pg. 176
M. J. BROCK & SONS, INC., pg. 178
BROOKS RESOURCES CORPORATION, pg. 180
BUDCO GROUP INC., pg. 186
BUILDERS DEVELOPMENT INC.—Garvey Industries, Inc., pg. 444
BUILDERS INC.—Garvey Industries, Inc., pg. 444
BURRELL GROUP, pg. 195
BUSH DEVELOPMENT CORP., pg. 196
CC INDUSTRIES, INC., pg. 199
C.V.W. LTD. PARTNERSHIP—Cenvill Development Corp., pg. 236
THE CAFARO CO., pg. 207
CALMARK INVESTMENT COMPANY, pg. 211
CALMARK PROPERTIES, INC.—Calmark Investment Company, pg. 211
CAMBIO EQUITIES CORP., pg. 211
THE OLIVER CARR CO., pg. 225
CARTER, pg. 226
CEDAR CREEK PROPERTIES INC.—Ash Grove Cement Company, pg. 88
CEDAR CREEK REALTY CO., INC.—Ash Grove Cement Company, pg. 88
THE CEDARWOOD COMPANIES, pg. 230
CHARAN INDUSTRIES, INC., pg. 239
CHARING CROSS GROUP, pg. 239
CHURCHMANS ROAD ASSOCIATES, L.P.—Artesian Resources Corporation, pg. 87
CIMINELLI DEVELOPMENT COMPANY, INC., pg. 249
CLOVER FINANCIAL CORPORATION, pg. 256
COLONIAL OIL INDUSTRIES, pg. 263
COMPLETE INTERIORS INC., pg. 270
CONCORD ASSETS GROUP, INC., pg. 272
CONCRETE CONSTRUCTION COMPANY, pg. 273
CONSTRUCTION COUNSELLORS, INC., pg. 277
CONTINENTAL DEVELOPMENT COMPANY—Burrell Group, pg. 195
COOPER COMMUNITIES, INC., pg. 283
COOPER VENTURES, INC.—Cooper Communities, Inc., pg. 283
CORPOREX COMPANIES, INC., pg. 287
CRADDOCK DEVELOPMENT CO., INC., pg. 295
CROWN AMERICAN CORPORATION, pg. 301
CULLUM DEVELOPMENT CO.—Randall's Food Markets, Inc., pg. 912
DKM PROPERTIES CORPORATION—The Dyson-Kissner-Moran Corporation, pg. 357
DANIS INDUSTRIES CORPORATION, pg. 314
DEAN OPERATIONS INC., pg. 322
THE EDWARD J. DEBARTOLO CORPORATION, pg. 323
DEL AMERICAN PROPERTIES, INC., pg. 325
THE DEMARS CORP., pg. 327
DEMARS HAKA DEVELOPMENT, INC.—The DeMars Corp., pg. 328
DEVELOPERS DIVERSIFIED, pg. 333
THE DONOHOE COMPANIES, INC., pg. 345
JON DOUGLAS COMPANY, pg. 347
CHARLES DUNN COMPANY-REALTORS, pg. 353
LEO EISENBERG & CO., INC., pg. 372
ELKINGTON REALTY & DEVELOPMENT, pg. 377
EQUITY FUND ADVISORS INC., pg. 385
THE ERIN COMPANY, pg. 387
F.W.D.C., INC.—Cenvill Development Corp., pg. 236
FARNSWORTH DEVELOPMENT CO.—Farnsworth Companies, pg. 403
FIRST FINANCIAL GROUP, INC., pg. 413
FIRST FLORIDA EQUITIES, LTD., pg. 413
FIRST LAND & DEVELOPMENT, INC.—Adler & Shaykin, pg. 18
FIRST WORTHING, pg. 414
FLINT RIVER—Rotterdam Ventures Inc., pg. 951
FOLMAR & ASSOCIATES, pg. 422
FORECAST MORTGAGE CORPORATION, pg. 423
CARL M. FREEMAN ASSOCIATES, INC., pg. 431
THE FUSCO CORPORATION, pg. 437
GARNEY HOLDING COMPANY, INC., pg. 443
GARVEY INDUSTRIES, INC., pg. 443
GATES LAND CO.—The Gates Corporation, pg. 445
GENERAL GROWTH COMPANIES, INC., pg. 449
GENERAL GROWTH OF CALIFORNIA, INC.—General Growth Companies, Inc., pg. 449
GENE B. GLICK COMPANY, INC., pg. 462
GOLODETZ CORPORATION, pg. 469
GOLUB & CO., pg. 469
GOSNELL BUILDERS, pg. 472
W. M. GRACE DEVELOPMENT, pg. 474
GRAHAM GROUP, INC., pg. 475
THE GREAT ATLANTIC COMPANIES, pg. 480
GRIMMER REALTY CO. INC., pg. 488
HARBERT CORPORATION, pg. 506
THE HASSINGER COMPANIES, pg. 516
HAWTHORNE PROPERTIES, INC.—Hawthorne Corp., pg. 519
THE HEARST CORPORATION, pg. 521
HELMSLEY ENTERPRISES, INC., pg. 527
HIGH INDUSTRIES INC., pg. 533
HUNT BUILDING CORPORATION, pg. 553
CAROLINE HUNT TRUST ESTATE, pg. 553
THE IDI GROUP COMPANIES, pg. 560
IDYLWILD CORPORATION—Silicon Valley Development, pg. 1004
IRVINE COMPANY, pg. 582
JMB REALTY CORPORATION, pg. 584
JAMES BUILDING CORPORATION, pg. 588
THE JUPITER CORPORATION—Jupiter Industries, Inc., pg. 609
THE KAEMPFER COMPANY, INVESTMENT BUILDERS, pg. 613
KENNINGTON PROPERTIES, INC.—Kennington Ltd., Inc., pg. 623
KEYES COMPANY, pg. 627
KITCHELL CORPORATION, pg. 634
KOLL CO., pg. 641
KORMAN CO., pg. 642
KROH OPERATING L.P., pg. 645
LB INDUSTRIES INC., pg. 647
LAKE MICHIGAN CONSTRUCTION, INC.—Orix Real Estate Equities, Inc., pg. 829
LANDAU & HEYMAN INC., pg. 654
LEADER FEDERAL BANK FOR SAVINGS, pg. 663
LEAR SIEGLER HAWAIIAN PROPERTIES DIV.—Lear Siegler Diversified Holdings Corp., pg. 664
THE LEAVELL COMPANY, pg. 664
LEE NATIONAL CORPORATION, pg. 666
LEFRAK ORGANIZATION INC., pg. 666
THE LEVY ORGANIZATION, pg. 672
LEVY REAL ESTATE PARTNERS—The Levy Organization, pg. 672
LIFE CARE SERVICES CORPORATION—The Weitz Corporation, pg. 1174
LINCOLN PROPERTY COMPANY, pg. 676
LLOYD PROPERTIES, pg. 680
LUMAS REALTY, INC., pg. 687
THE LUSK COMPANY, pg. 687
M & T INCORPORATED, pg. 690
MEPC AMERICAN PROPERTIES INCORPORATED, pg. 692
THE MACERICH CO., pg. 696
MAGUIRE THOMAS PARTNERS, pg. 701
ALBERT C. MARTIN & ASSOCIATES, pg. 714
THE MAURIN-ODGEN COMPANIES, pg. 722
MCLEAN ENTERPRISES, INC., pg. 731
METRO PARKING SYSTEMS—Metropolitan Properties Inc., pg. 745
METROPOLITAN ARIZONA CORPORATION—JMB Realty Corporation, pg. 585
METROPOLITAN PROPERTIES INC., pg. 745
MICHAEL'S DEVELOPMENT COMPANY, pg. 747
MILLER & SMITH, INC., pg. 755
WALLACE MOIR CO., pg. 763
MOUNT BACHELOR VILLAGE CORP.—Brooks Resources Corporation, pg. 180
MT. WALDO OPERATIONS—Gerrity Co., Inc., pg. 454
MUNIGLE CORPORATION, pg. 775
THE MUTUAL LIFE INSURANCE COMPANY OF NEW YORK (MONY), pg. 778
NS LAND COMPANY—National Steel Corporation, pg. 794
NTS CORPORATION, pg. 781
NATIONAL BULK CARRIERS, INC., pg. 786
NATIONAL DEVELOPMENT CO., INC.—Sunstates Realty Group Inc., pg. 1062
NAVAJO WESTERN LAND CO.—Watkins Associated Industries Inc., pg. 1167
AL NEYER, INC., pg. 805
NORTH AMERICAN COMPANY, pg. 811
NORTH RIVER HOMES, INC.—ROC Properties Inc., pg. 908
NORTHWESTERN ENGINEERING CO., pg. 815
OCEAN PROPERTIES, LTD., pg. 820
OPUS CORP., pg. 828
ORIX REAL ESTATE EQUITIES, INC., pg. 829
OXFORD COMMUNITIES, INC.—Oxford First Corporation, pg. 834
OXFORD FIRST CORPORATION, pg. 834
OXFORD REALTY SERVICES CORP., pg. 835
PIC REALTY CANADA LTD.—The Prudential Insurance Company of America, pg. 897
PACIFIC HOLDING CORPORATION, pg. 840
PARAGON GROUP, INC., pg. 847
THE PATRICIAN GROUP, pg. 851
PAXTON PROPERTIES, INC.—Jeld-Wen, Inc., pg. 592
J. M. PETERS CO., pg. 864
PROFESSIONAL APARTMENT MANAGEMENT, INC., pg. 893
PROGRESS WEST, pg. 894
THE PRUDENTIAL REALTY GROUP—The Prudential Insurance Company of America, pg. 897
PURCELL CO., INC., pg. 900
LAT PURSER & ASSOCIATE, pg. 901
THE PYRAMID COMPANIES, pg. 901
QUADRANGLE DEVELOPMENT CORPORATION, pg. 902
ROC PROPERTIES INC., pg. 908
RAYCO, pg. 914
REGENCY ASSOCIATES LIMITED PARTNERSHIP, pg. 922
REGENCY GROUP INC., pg. 922
REGIONAL DEVELOPMENT CORP.—Family Inns of America, Inc., pg. 398
REYNEN, BARDIS & WINN, pg. 930
THE RICHARD & DAVID JACOBS GROUP, pg. 932
RIO GRANDE LAND CO.—Anschutz Corporation, pg. 75
RIVER BEND, INC.—Spatz & Co., pg. 1026
RIVER OAKS COMMUNITIES, INC.—ROC Properties Inc., pg. 908
ROCOR PROPERTIES, INC.—Rocor Transportation Companies Inc., pg. 942
ROLAND INTERNATIONAL CORPORATION, pg. 944
ROSEN ASSOCIATES MANAGEMENT CORP., pg. 948
ROSENSHEIN ASSOCIATES, pg. 948
ROSEWOOD PROPERTY COMPANY, pg. 949
JACK ROSS MOTORS INC., pg. 949
ROTHSCHILD REALTY INC.—Rothschild North America Inc., pg. 951
ROTTERDAM VENTURES INC., pg. 951
ARTHUR RUBLOFF & CO. OF FLORIDA—Orix Real Estate Equities, Inc., pg. 829
H. J. RUSSELL CORP., pg. 957
SACHS HOLDING COMPANY, pg. 965
SACHS PROPERTIES—Sachs Holding Company, pg. 965
KENNETH M. SEATON ENTERPRISES—Family Inns of America, Inc., pg. 398
1740 VENTURES, INC.—The Mutual Life Insurance Company of New York (MONY), pg. 778
SHAPCO, INC., pg. 995
SHAPELL INDUSTRIES, INC., pg. 995
SIGAL/ZUCKERMAN CO., pg. 1003
SILICON VALLEY DEVELOPMENT, pg. 1004
THE SMITH GROUP, INC., pg. 1012
SOUTHEASTERN INVESTMENT PROPERTIES INC., pg. 1019
SPATZ CENTERS, INC.—Spatz & Co., pg. 1026
SPATZ & CO., pg. 1026
SPATZ & CO. DEVELOPMENT—Spatz & Co., pg. 1026
STEARNS ENTERPRISES, INC., pg. 1043
STERLING BUILDERS, INC.—Sterling Homes Corp., pg. 1047
STROUSE GREENBERG & CO., INC., pg. 1054
SUMMA CORPORATION, pg. 1057
SUN LAKES MARKETING, pg. 1059
SUNDAY RIVER SKIWAY CORPORATION, pg. 1059
SUNSTATES PROPERTIES, INC.—Sunstates Realty Group Inc., pg. 1062
SUNSTATES REALTY GROUP INC., pg. 1062
SVERDRUP CORPORATION, pg. 1065
SVERDRUP INVESTMENTS, INC.—Sverdrup Corporation, pg. 1066
TASA CORPORATION, pg. 1079
TAYLOR-MORLEY, INC., pg. 1081
TEACHERS MANAGEMENT & INVESTMENT CORPORATION, pg. 1082
TISHMAN REALTY & CONSTRUCTION CO., pg. 1099
TOWNE PROPERTIES, pg. 1104
TOWNE REALTY, INC.—Zilber, Ltd., pg. 1219
TRAMMELL CROW COMPANY, pg. 1106
TRECO COMMUNITIES, INC.—Sunstates Realty Group Inc., pg. 1062
THE TRUMP GROUP, pg. 1117
TRUMP ORGANIZATION, pg. 1118
UNITED FINANCIAL SERVICES—Altus Federal Savings Bank, pg. 46
URBCO, INC.—Connecticut Mutual Life Insurance Company, pg. 275
URSCHEL LABS INC., pg. 1140
THE VAN METRE COMPANIES, pg. 1144
VECTOR REALTY CORP.—Golodetz Corporation, pg. 469
VOORHEESVILLE VENTURES, INC.—Rotterdam Ventures Inc., pg. 952
WALTER LAND CO.—Walter Industries, Inc., pg. 1162
THE WEITZ CORPORATION, pg. 1174
WESTERN DEVELOPMENT CORPORATION, pg. 1179
WILDER MANAGEMENT ASSOCIATES, pg. 1189
WILMORITE INC., pg. 1193
WILSEY BENNETT CO., pg. 1193
WILSEY BENNETT REAL ESTATE DIVISION—Wilsey Bennett Co., pg. 1193
JIM WILSON & ASSOCIATES, pg. 1193
KEMMONS WILSON COMPANIES, pg. 1194
WINROCK ENTERPRISES, INC., pg. 1197
WYNMOOR HOMES, INC.—Cenvill Development Corp., pg. 236
WYNMOOR LTD. PARTNERSHIP—Cenvill Development Corp., pg. 236
WYNVILLE REALTY—Cenvill Development Corp., pg. 236
ZAREMBA CORPORATION, pg. 1216

6553 — CEMETERY SUBDIVIDERS & DEVELOPERS

CHRISTIAN MEMORIAL CULTURAL CENTER, pg. 249
G L SUB COMPANY—The Marmon Group, Inc., pg. 712
D. W. NEWCOMER'S SONS, INC., pg. 804
OURSO INVESTMENT CORPORATION, pg. 832
SECURITY INDUSTRIAL INSURANCE CO., INC.—Ourso Investment Corporation, pg. 832
ASHLEY F. WARD, INC., pg. 1162

6712 — OFFICES OF BANK HOLDING COMPANIES

API GROUP INC., pg. 5
ANCHOR FINANCIAL CORPORATION, pg. 71
CS FIRST BOSTON AUSTRALIA (HOLDINGS) LIMITED—CS First Boston Group, Inc., pg. 204
CS FIRST BOSTON NEW ZEALAND HOLDINGS LIMITED—CS First Boston Group, Inc., pg. 204
CAPITAL BANCORP, pg. 214
CHARTER OAK FINANCIAL CORPORATION—Guarantee Title Co., Inc., pg. 491
CITIZENS NATIONAL BANCSHARES INC., pg. 250
COLE TAYLOR FINANCIAL GROUP, pg. 260
CUMMINS-AMERICAN CORP., pg. 304
EQUITABLE BANKSHARES OF COLORADO, INC., pg. 385
FINANCIERE CREDIT SUISSE-FIRST BOSTON—CS First Boston Group, Inc., pg. 204
FIRST ABILENE BANKSHARES, INC., pg. 411

FIRST AMERICAN BANKSHARES, INC., pg. 412
FIRST BOSTON INTERNATIONAL LIMITED—CS First Boston Group, Inc., pg. 204
1ST FRANKLIN CORPORATION, pg. 413
FIRSTFED MICHIGAN CORPORATION, pg. 414
GSC ENTERPRISES, INC., pg. 440
GREAT LAKES FINANCIAL RESOURCES, INC., pg. 481
GREATBANC, INC., pg. 482
GUARANTEE TITLE CO., INC., pg. 491
HARBOR BANCORP, pg. 506
HIGH POINT FINANCIAL CORP., pg. 533
HORIZON BANCORP, pg. 544
PACIFIC CAPITAL BANCORP, pg. 839
REPUBLIC NATIONAL BANK OF MIAMI, pg. 928
SUL CORPORATION—Victory Financial Group, Inc., pg. 1150
TEAM BANCSHARES, INC., pg. 1082
TEXAS COMMERCE BANCSHARES, INC., pg. 1089
THE UNION OF ARKANSAS CORP., pg. 1127

6719 — OFFICES OF HOLDING COMPANIES, NEC

AEI HOLDING CO., INC., pg. 3
API GROUP INC., pg. 5
AQHI, INC., pg. 5
ARA GROUP, pg. 5
ASC INCORPORATED, pg. 7
THE AARQUE COMPANIES, pg. 9
ABBOTT GROUP LTD., pg. 9
ACADEMY INSURANCE GROUP, INC., pg. 11
ACROMETAL COMPANIES, INC., pg. 14
JOHN ALDEN FINANCIAL CORPORATION, pg. 32
ALEX LEE, INC., pg. 33
ALLECO INC., pg. 35
ALOHA AIRGROUP, INC., pg. 43
AMERICAN FINANCIAL CORPORATION, pg. 52
AMERICAN FINANCIAL ENTERPRISES, INC.—American Financial Corporation, pg. 53
AMERICAN HEALTH COMPANIES, INC., pg. 55
AMERICAN MANAGEMENT GROUP, pg. 57
AMERICAN MARKETING INDUSTRIES, INC., pg. 58
AMERICAN PROTECTION INDUSTRIES, INC., pg. 60
AMFAC RETAIL CORP.—JMB Realty Corporation, pg. 585
AMTRAN, INC., pg. 69
ANCHOR DARLING INDUSTRIES INC.—Cawsl Corporation, pg. 230
ANDERSON INDUSTRIES, INC., pg. 72
ANDERSON INDUSTRIES INC., pg. 73
ANDREWS GROUP, INCORPORATED, pg. 74
ANSCHUTZ CORPORATION, pg. 75
ARINC INC., pg. 82
ARMSTRONG INTERNATIONAL, INC., pg. 83
BEN ARNOLD CO., INC., pg. 84
ASBURY CARBONS, INC., pg. 87
AUTOMOTIVE PRODUCTS GROUP—American Standard Inc., pg. 62
B & K STEEL & SUPPLY, INC., pg. 105
BEC INC., pg. 106
BANK SHARES, INC., pg. 117
BANKMANAGERS CORP., pg. 118
W. O. BANKSTON ENTERPRISES INC., pg. 118
BARANCORP, pg. 118
BARDES CORP., pg. 119
BASS ENTERPRISES PRODUCTION COMPANY, pg. 125
BAWDEN CORPORATION, pg. 127
BEACON GROUP, pg. 128
BEECH HOLDINGS CORP., pg. 131
BEERS CONSTRUCTION COMPANY, pg. 132
THE BEKINS COMPANY, pg. 132
BELGRAVE INDUSTRIES, pg. 133
BELMONT INDUSTRIES, INC., pg. 136
THE BERKLINE CORPORATION—Corber Corporation, pg. 285
BESSIN CORPORATION, pg. 146
BIG Y FOODS INC., pg. 149
BITREK CORPORATION, pg. 153
BLACKSTONE PARTNERSHIP (NYC), pg. 155
ALGERNON BLAIR INTERNATIONAL, pg. 155
BOH CORPORATION, pg. 162
BOSTON SCIENTIFIC CORP., pg. 167
BOURY INCORPORATED, pg. 168
BREMER FINANCIAL CORPORATION, pg. 173
THE BRENLIN GROUP, pg. 173
BRIDGEWATER RESOURCES CORPORATION, pg. 175
BUTCHER & CO., INC., pg. 196
BUTLER INTERNATIONAL, pg. 197
CBP RESOURCES, INC., pg. 199
CC INDUSTRIES, INC., pg. 199
CHB CORP., pg. 201
CHF INDUSTRIES, INC.—CC Industries, Inc., pg. 200
CMI INTERNATIONAL INC., pg. 202
CRL, INC., pg. 203
CS FIRST BOSTON GROUP, INC., pg. 203
CSE CORPORATION, pg. 204
CUNA MUTUAL INSURANCE SOCIETY, pg. 205
CUNA MUTUAL INVESTMENT CORP.—CUNA Mutual Insurance Society, pg. 205
C. V. INVESTMENTS, INC.—Cenvill Development Corp., pg. 236
CARAUSTAR INDUSTRIES, INC., pg. 217
CARLSON COMPANIES, INC., pg. 220
CARLYLE HOLDING CORPORATION, pg. 222
CERTIFIED HOLDING CORP., pg. 237
CHANNEL TECHNOLOGIES, INC., pg. 239
CHESTERFIELD INDUSTRIAL PARK, INC.—Watlow Electric Manufacturing Company, pg. 1167
CHI SYSTEMS, INC., pg. 244
CHICAGO HOLDINGS, INC., pg. 245
CHICAGO WEST PULLMAN CORPORATION, pg. 246
CHICORP, INC., pg. 247
CLARK ENTERPRISES, INC.—Clark Construction Group, pg. 252
CLUB CORPORATION OF AMERICA—Club Corporation International, pg. 256
COAST TO COAST STORES, INC., pg. 257
CODISCO INC., pg. 258
COLE NATIONAL CORPORATION, pg. 260
COLLINS & AIKMAN INC.—Collins & Aikman Group Inc., pg. 263
COLUMBIAN PHILIPPINES INC.—Columbian Rope Company, pg. 266
COMMONWEALTH BUILDING COMPANY—Landmark Communications, Inc., pg. 656
CONCORP, INC., pg. 272
CONESTOGA HOLDINGS, INC., pg. 273
CONTINENTAL GRAPHICS HOLDINGS, INC., pg. 279
CONTINENTAL NATIONAL AMERICAN REAL ESTATE INC., pg. 280
CONTINENTAL WATER COMPANY, pg. 280
CONTRAN CORPORATION, pg. 281
COOK HOLDING CORPORATION, pg. 282
CORDOVA ENTERPRISE, pg. 285
CORTEC GROUP, pg. 287
COUNTRY COMPANIES INSURANCE GROUP, pg. 289
COX COMMUNICATIONS, INC.—Cox Enterprises, Inc., pg. 292
THE CRAWFORD GROUP, pg. 297
CROWN HOLDINGS, INC., pg. 302
CROWN LANCE, INC.—Bolliger, Inc., pg. 163
CUE INDUSTRIES, INC.—Guardian Industries Corp., pg. 492
CULLMAN VENTURES, INC., pg. 304
CUNNINGHAM-LIMP DEVELOPMENT CO., pg. 305
D&L VENTURE CORP., pg. 307
DEC INTERNATIONAL, INC., pg. 308
DHL CORPORATION, pg. 309
DARIGOLD, INC., pg. 315
DATA DOCUMENTS HOLDINGS, INC., pg. 316
DATRON INCORPORATED, pg. 316
DAUBERT INDUSTRIES, INC., pg. 317
DAVIS COMPANIES, pg. 318
DEAN OPERATIONS INC., pg. 322
DEB HOLDINGS, INC., pg. 323
DEL TACO, INC., pg. 325
DELAWARE NORTH COMPANIES, INC., pg. 326
DENTSPLY INTERNATIONAL INC., pg. 329
DESERET MANAGEMENT CORPORATION, pg. 332
DIMAC CORPORATION, pg. 338
DIVERSIFIED DYNAMICS INC., pg. 340
DIVERSIFIED GROUP, INC., pg. 340
DR PEPPER/SEVEN-UP COMPANIES, INC., pg. 342
DUBIN-CLARK & COMPANY, pg. 350
DUGAN & MEYERS CONSTRUCTION CO.—Dugan & Meyers Interests, Inc., pg. 351
DUGAN & MEYERS INTERESTS, INC., pg. 351
DUNES HOTELS AND CASINOS INC., pg. 352
DUNN INDUSTRIES INC., pg. 354
E-II HOLDINGS, INC., pg. 358
EATEL CORPORATION, pg. 364
EBERLE DIRECT MARKETING GROUP, INC., pg. 365
EBY CORPORATION, pg. 365
EDUCATIONAL PUBLISHING CORPORATION, pg. 369
EDWARDSTONE & COMPANY, INC., pg. 370
ELOMETA CORPORATION—Treadwell Corporation, pg. 1108
ENTERPRISES INTERNATIONAL INC., pg. 382
EQUITY GROUP INVESTMENTS, pg. 385
EUROPEAN PLUMBING PRODS. GROUP—American Standard Inc., pg. 62
FMR CORP.—Fidelity Investments (FMR Corp.), pg. 408
FAIRFIELD FOODS—Mrs. Fields' Inc., pg. 761
FAMTEC INTERNATIONAL, INC., pg. 398
FARLEY, INC.—Farley Industries, pg. 400
FARNSWORTH COMPANIES, pg. 403
FINANCIAL PROTECTION SERVICES INC., pg. 410
FINANCIAL RESOURCES GROUP—Globe Mortgage Company, pg. 464
FINLAY ENTERPRISES, INC., pg. 411
FISHER COMPANIES, INC., pg. 414
FORSTMANN LITTLE & CO., pg. 424
FOX VALLEY CORPORATION, pg. 427
FREEDOM FORGE CORPORATION, pg. 430
FRU-CON CONSTRUCTION CORPORATION, pg. 435
FUNDAMENTAL MANAGEMENT, INC.—Industrial Wire Products Corporation, pg. 567
LOU FUSZ AUTOMOTIVE NETWORK, pg. 437
GACC HOLDING COMPANY—American Financial Corporation, pg. 53
G B STORES—Schottenstein Stores Corporation, pg. 978
GCC, INC.—Gillett Holdings, Inc., pg. 459
GF INDUSTRIES, INC., pg. 439
GNG-1, INC.—Gillett Holdings, Inc., pg. 459
GNG-3, INC.—Gillett Holdings, Inc., pg. 459
THE GATES CORPORATION, pg. 445
GEM INDUSTRIES FINANCE CORPORATION, pg. 447
GENERAL AUTOMOTIVE CORPORATION, pg. 448
GENEVAR ENTERPRISES, pg. 451
GEORGIAN PRESS, INC., pg. 453
GILLETT BROADCASTING, INC.—Gillett Holdings, Inc., pg. 459
GILLETT BROADCASTING OF TENNESSEE, INC.—Gillett Holdings, Inc., pg. 459
GILLETT CORPORATION—Gillett Holdings, Inc., pg. 459
GILLETT-GP CORPORATION—Gillett Holdings, Inc., pg. 459
GILLETT GROUP, INC.—Gillett Holdings, Inc., pg. 459
GILLETT GROUP MANAGEMENT, INC.—Gillett Holdings, Inc., pg. 459
GILLETT HOLDINGS, INC., pg. 458
GILLETT PRODUCTIONS, INC.—Gillett Holdings, Inc., pg. 459
GLOBAL FINANCIAL SERVICES, INC.—Globe Mortgage Company, pg. 464
GOLDMARK INDUSTRIES, LTD., pg. 468
GRAPHISPHERE HOLDING COMPANY, pg. 478
GRAYCOR, INC., pg. 479
GREAT AMERICAN COMMUNICATIONS COMPANY—American Financial Corporation, pg. 53
GREAT AMERICAN HOLDING CORPORATION—American Financial Corporation, pg. 53
GREEN HOLDINGS, INC., pg. 484
GREEN MOUNTAIN HOLDING CORPORATION, pg. 485
GREGORY AFFILIATES, INC., pg. 486
GUILFORD TRANSPORTATION INDUSTRIES INC., pg. 493
GUYAN CORP.—Logan & Kanawha Coal Co., pg. 681
H.A.T. HOLDING COMPANY—Havatampa Incorporated, pg. 517
THE HOH ORGANIZATIONS, pg. 497
H.P.H. INDUSTRIES LTD., pg. 497
THE H. T. HACKNEY CO., pg. 498
HADEN, INC., pg. 499
HAMBURGER HAMLETS INC.—Weatherly Financial Group, pg. 1169
HANES COMPANIES, INC., pg. 505
HARBERT CORPORATION, pg. 506
HARBOUR GROUP LTD., pg. 506
HARRIS ENTERPRISES INC., pg. 511
HENDRICK MANAGEMENT CORPORATION, pg. 529
THE HENLEY GROUP, INC., pg. 529
HICKS OIL-HICKS GAS, INC., pg. 533
HIGH INDUSTRIES INC., pg. 533
HLI HOLDINGS, INC.—Howell Laboratories, Inc., pg. 548
HORSEHEAD INDUSTRIES, INC., pg. 545
HOWELL EXPORTS—Howell Instruments Corp., pg. 548
CAROLINE HUNT TRUST ESTATE, pg. 553
HUNTCO ACQUISITIONS HOLDINGS, INC.—Huntco Inc., pg. 554
HUNTCO INC., pg. 554
HYATT CORPORATION—H. Group Holding Inc., pg. 495
HYMAN FREIGHTWAYS INC., pg. 557
ICM INVESTMENT CO.—ICM Industries, Inc., pg. 559
ICM INDUSTRIES, INC., pg. 559
INDEPENDENCE HOLDING COMPANY—Geneve Corporation, pg. 451
INGERSOLL INTERNATIONAL INC., pg. 568
INSILCO CORPORATION, pg. 571
INTERLAKEN CAPITAL, INC., pg. 574
INTERLOCK INDUSTRIES, INC., pg. 574
INTERMOUNTAIN INDUSTRIES, INC., pg. 575
INTERNATIONAL SYSTEMS & CONTROLS CORP., pg. 579
IVEX PACKAGING CORPORATION, pg. 583
JFC INC., pg. 584
JEMISON, INC., pg. 592
JOHN HANCOCK SUBSIDIARIES, INC.—John Hancock Mutual Life Insurance Company, pg. 596
JONES INTERNATIONAL LTD., pg. 603
JORDAN INDUSTRIES, INC., pg. 604
JOURNAL COMMUNICATIONS INC., pg. 607
JUPITER INDUSTRIES, INC., pg. 609
THE JUPITER CORPORATION—Jupiter Industries, Inc., pg. 609
K-III COMMUNICATIONS CORPORATION, pg. 610
KDI CORPORATION, pg. 612
KOA HOLDINGS, pg. 612
KSG INC., pg. 613
KALAMAZOO HOLDINGS, INC., pg. 615
KAPLAN ELECTRONICS, pg. 616
KEARNEY-NATIONAL CANADA LTD.—The Dyson-Kissner-Moran Corporation, pg. 358
KEYWELL CORPORATION, pg. 629
PETER KIEWIT SONS INC., pg. 629
J. I. KISLAK INC., pg. 633
KITCHELL CORPORATION, pg. 634
KLAPMEIER MANAGEMENT COMPANY, pg. 634
KNIGHTBRIDGE PARTNERS, pg. 637
KNOLL INTERNATIONAL, INC.—21 International Holdings, Inc., pg. 1121
LB INDUSTRIES INC., pg. 647
LFC HOLDING CORPORATION, pg. 647
LANE INDUSTRIES, INC., pg. 656
LAROCHE HOLDINGS, INC., pg. 659
LAWRENCE GROUP, INC., pg. 662
LAWRENCE INSURANCE GROUP, INC.—Lawrence Group, Inc., pg. 662
LEAR SIEGLER DIVERSIFIED HOLDINGS CORP., pg. 664
LENNOX INTERNATIONAL INC., pg. 667
LIBCO CORPORATION, pg. 674
LIFESHARES GROUP, INC.—The Chesapeake Life Insurance Co., pg. 243
LIFESURANCE CORPORATION—Regan Holding Corporation, pg. 921
LONDONTOWN HOLDINGS CORPORATION, pg. 681
LOUISIANA NATIONAL LIFE INSURANCE COMPANY—Victory Financial Group, Inc., pg. 1150
THE LUSK COMPANY, pg. 687
LYNDEN INCORPORATED, pg. 689
MBI INC., pg. 691
MBL HOLDING CORPORATION—Mutual Benefit Life Insurance Company, pg. 778
MBS HOLDING, INC., pg. 691
MCM ENTERPRISES, INC., pg. 691
MIMLIC CORP.—The Minnesota Mutual Life Insurance Company, pg. 758
MACANDREWS & FORBES GROUP, INC.—MacAndrews & Forbes Holdings Inc., pg. 695
MANHATTAN BUILDING COMPANIES, pg. 703
MARKAIR, INC., pg. 708
THE MARMON GROUP, INC., pg. 710
MARTIN PAINT STORES, pg. 715
MARY KAY CORPORATION, pg. 716
MASON COMPANY, pg. 718
MASSMUTUAL HOLDING COMPANY—Massachusetts Mutual Life Insurance Co., pg. 719
MAUI DIVERS OF HAWAII, LTD., pg. 721
MAUI VARIETIES, LTD., pg. 721
MAUNA LOA RESOURCES INC.—C. Brewer & Company, Limited, pg. 174
MCCARTHY BUILDING COMPANIES, pg. 727

MCORP, pg. 732
MELLOY BROS. ENTERPRISES, pg. 738
METPON—Metromedia Company, pg. 743
METROMEDIA COMPANY, pg. 743
METROPOLITAN LIFE HOLDINGS, LTD.—Metropolitan Life Insurance Co., pg. 745
METSA, INC.—Metromedia Company, pg. 744
MID STATE PRODUCTS CO.—Osco Industries Inc., pg. 830
MIDCOAST INDUSTRIAL SERVICES CORPORATION, pg. 751
MILLSTEIN INDUSTRIES, pg. 756
MISCO INDUSTRIES, pg. 759
MRS. FIELDS' INC., pg. 761
MOORE COMPANY, pg. 768
THE MUTUAL LIFE INSURANCE COMPANY OF NEW YORK (MONY), pg. 778
NWA, INC., pg. 782
NATIONAL AMUSEMENTS, INC., pg. 784
NATIONAL LIFE INVESTMENT MANAGEMENT CO., INC.—National Life Insurance Company, pg. 791
NATIONWIDE MUTUAL INSURANCE COMPANY, pg. 795
NESCO, INC., pg. 798
THE NEW ENGLAND COMPANIES, INC.—The New England, pg. 799
NEW ENGLAND INVESTMENT COMPANIES, INC.—The New England, pg. 799
NEW YORK LIFE INTERNATIONAL INVESTMENT—New York Life Insurance Company, pg. 803
NEW YORK LIFE WORLDWIDE HOLDING, INC.—New York Life Insurance Company, pg. 803
NEWAGE INDUSTRIES INC., pg. 803
NORCROSS INDUSTRIES, INC., pg. 809
NORDIC GROUP OF COMPANIES, LTD., pg. 809
NORFOODS, INC., pg. 810
NORTH CENTRAL LIFE INSURANCE COMPANIES, pg. 813
NORTHWEST PAPER CONVERTING COMPANY, pg. 814
NORTHWESTERN ENGINEERING CO., pg. 815
NORWESCO, INC., pg. 816
NYLIFE INC.—New York Life Insurance Company, pg. 802
OLT-I CORP.—Riklis Family Corporation, pg. 934
THE ODOM CORPORATION, pg. 821
OHIO RIVER ASSOCIATES, INC., pg. 822
THE OLDENBURG GROUP COMPANIES, pg. 824
OUIMET INDUSTRIES, pg. 831
OURSO INVESTMENT CORPORATION, pg. 832
OVERSEAS PARTNERS, INC., pg. 833
OXFORD FIRST CORPORATION, pg. 834
OXFORD REALTY SERVICES CORP., pg. 835
PHC HOLDINGS, INC.—Pacific Holding Corporation, pg. 840
PM HOLDINGS, INC.—Phoenix Home Life Mutual Insurance Company, pg. 868
PON HOLDING CORP.—Metromedia Company, pg. 743
PPA INDUSTRIES, INC., pg. 836
PRUCO, INC.—The Prudential Insurance Company of America, pg. 896
PACIFIC FINANCIAL ASSET MANAGEMENT CORPORATION—Pacific Mutual Life Insurance Company, pg. 841
PACIFIC HOLDING CORPORATION, pg. 840
PACIFICA REAL ESTATE GROUP, pg. 842
R. B. PAMPLIN CORP., pg. 844
PARK RIDGE CORPORATION, pg. 849
PARSONS BRINCKERHOFF INC., pg. 850
PARSONS & WHITTEMORE ENTERPRISES, pg. 850
PEN HOLDINGS, INC., pg. 856
PENHALL INTERNATIONAL, pg. 857
PERPETUAL CORPORATION, pg. 862
THE PHILADELPHIA BOURSE, INC., pg. 866
PHOENIX ENTERPRISES INC., pg. 868
PLAYTEX APPAREL INC., pg. 876
PLAYTEX FP GROUP INCORPORATED, pg. 877
PLAYTEX INVESTMENT CORP.—Playtex FP Group Incorporated, pg. 877
POWERINE OIL COMPANY HOLDINGS, pg. 883
PREFERRED RISK MUTUAL INSURANCE, pg. 886
PREMARC CORPORATION, pg. 886
PREMIER INDUSTRIES, INC., pg. 887
PRUDENTIAL ASIA INVESTMENTS LIMITED—The Prudential Insurance Company of America, pg. 897
PRUDENTIAL CAPITAL & INVESTMENT SERVICES, INC.—The Prudential Insurance Company of America, pg. 897
THE PRUDENTIAL INSURANCE COMPANY OF AMERICA, pg. 896
PRUDENTIAL SECURITIES GROUP INC.—The Prudential Insurance Company of America, pg. 897
PRUSERVICOS PARTICIPACOES, S.A., C/O PRUDENTIAL ATLANTIC COMPANHIA BRASILEIRA DE SEGUROS—The Prudential Insurance Company of America, pg. 898
PUBLIC STORAGE, INC., pg. 898
PUGH OIL COMPANY, pg. 899
QSC, INC.—Castle-Harlan, Inc., pg. 229
RCM INDUSTRIES, pg. 906
RNL FACILITIES CORPORATION, pg. 907
ROC PROPERTIES INC., pg. 908
RABCO HEALTH SERVICE, pg. 908
REDMAN HOLDING CORP.—Redman Industries, Inc., pg. 919
REDMAN INDUSTRIES, INC., pg. 919
REGAN HOLDING CORPORATION, pg. 921
REGENCY GROUP INC., pg. 922
REVLON GROUP INC.—MacAndrews & Forbes Holdings Inc., pg. 695
RIKLIS FAMILY CORPORATION, pg. 934
THE RIO GRANDE INDUSTRIES INC.—Anschutz Corporation, pg. 75
J. H. ROBERTS INDUSTRIES INC., pg. 938
C. H. ROBINSON CO. INC., pg. 939
ROBINSON LUMBER & EXPORT COMPANY, pg. 940
ROCOR TRANSPORTATION COMPANIES INC., pg. 942
ROLAND INTERNATIONAL CORPORATION, pg. 944
ROSS ROY GROUP, INC., pg. 949
ROWE CORP., pg. 952
RUHL COMPANIES, INC., pg. 955
S & P COMPANY, pg. 959
SC COMPANIES, INC., pg. 960
SCC HOLDING CO., pg. 961
SCH HOLDING CORP.—Riklis Family Corporation, pg. 934
SI HOLDINGS INC., pg. 962
STS HOLDINGS, INC., pg. 964
SAFEGUARD FINANCIAL CORP.—Safeguard Business Systems, Inc., pg. 966
SARGENTO INCORPORATED, pg. 971
SCANGAS BROTHERS HOLDINGS, INC., pg. 974
SCHERER SCIENTIFIC, LTD., pg. 976
PETER J. SCHMITT HOLDINGS, pg. 976
SCHURZ COMMUNICATIONS, INC., pg. 979
SCHWINN BICYCLE COMPANY, pg. 981
SEABOARD FLOUR CORPORATION, pg. 984
SEALASKA CORPORATION, pg. 984
SEMCO INDUSTRIES, pg. 989
SHAMROCK HOLDINGS, INC., pg. 994
THE SHANE GROUP INC., pg. 995
SHEPAUG CORPORATION, pg. 997
SHERBORNE GROUP, INC., pg. 998
SHOOK NATIONAL CORPORATION, pg. 1000
SHURE, GMBH—Shure Brothers Incorporated, pg. 1001
SIEGEL CORP., pg. 1002
SILGAN CORPORATION, pg. 1004
SIMMONS UPHOLSTERED FURNITURE, INC., pg. 1005
SIMPSON INVESTMENT CO., pg. 1007
SIMUNICO, INC., pg. 1007
PETER W. SMITH & COMPANY, INC., pg. 1011
EVERETT SMITH INVESTMENT CO. OF DELAWARE, pg. 1013
SOFCO-MEAD, INC., pg. 1016
SOUTHEASTERN CAPITAL CORPORATION, pg. 1019
SOUTHWESTERN/GREAT AMERICAN INC., pg. 1023
SPARTAN MILLS, pg. 1026
SPECIALTY RETAILERS, INC., pg. 1029
SPELLING ENTERTAINMENT GROUP, INC.—American Financial Corporation, pg. 54
SPORTO CORP., pg. 1032
STANDARD LAFARGE, pg. 1036
STEINWAY MUSICAL PROPERTIES, INC., pg. 1045
STEPHENS HOLDING COMPANY, INC.—Stephens, Inc., pg. 1046
STERLING HOMES CORP., pg. 1046
STERLING LUMBER & INVESTMENT CO., pg. 1047
SUBURBAN COMMUNICATIONS CORP., pg. 1055
SULLIVAN HOLDING COMPANY, pg. 1056
SYNDICATE SYSTEMS, INC., pg. 1069
SYNERGISM, INC., pg. 1069
SYRATECH CORPORATION, pg. 1070
T.G. & Y. HOLDINGS, INC.—Riklis Family Corporation, pg. 934
TVESCO, INC., pg. 1075
TACT HOLDING, pg. 1076
TANG INDUSTRIES INC., pg. 1078
TAREN HOLDINGS, INC., pg. 1078
THE TECH GROUP, pg. 1082
TENNESSEE RESTAURANT CORP., pg. 1087
TERUYA BROS., LTD., pg. 1089
TIMPTE INDUSTRIES, INC., pg. 1098
TOTEM RESOURCES CORPORATION, pg. 1103
TREMONT CORPORATION, pg. 1109
TRIAN GROUP, pg. 1111
TRIDENT SEAFOOD CORPORATION, pg. 1113
TRIPLE F, INC., pg. 1114
THE TRUMP GROUP, pg. 1117
21 INTERNATIONAL HOLDINGS, INC., pg. 1121
ULLICO INC., pg. 1124
UNIGROUP, INC., pg. 1126
UNION HOLDINGS, INC., pg. 1128
UNITED ACQUISITION CORPORATION, pg. 1130
UNIVERSAL DYNAMICS INC., pg. 1138
V.T. INC., pg. 1142
THE VANGUARD GROUP, INC., pg. 1145
VARIED INVESTMENTS, INC., pg. 1145
VEDA INTERNATIONAL, INC., pg. 1146
VIACOM INC.—National Amusements, Inc., pg. 785
VICTORY FINANCIAL GROUP, INC., pg. 1150
VINCENT FOOD INDUSTRIES, INC., pg. 1152
WALTER INDUSTRIES, INC., pg. 1161
WASHINGTON CORPORATION, pg. 1165
WATKINS ASSOCIATED INDUSTRIES INC., pg. 1167
WATLOW ELECTRIC COMPANY OF CALIFORNIA—Watlow Electric Manufacturing Company, pg. 1168
WEATHERLY FINANCIAL GROUP, pg. 1169
DEL WEBB'S COVENTRY, pg. 1171
WECHCO, INC., pg. 1172
WEHCO MEDIA, INC., pg. 1172
WEINERS ENTERPRISES, INC., pg. 1173
WESTIN, INC., pg. 1183
WHALING INDUSTRIES, INC., pg. 1183
WHITE ROCK DISTILLERIES INC., pg. 1186
WHITESTAR GRAPHICS, INC., pg. 1186
WICKLAND CORPORATION, pg. 1188
WILLIAMS INTERNATIONAL INDUSTRIES, INC., pg. 1191
WILSEY BENNETT CO., pg. 1193
JIM WILSON & ASSOCIATES, pg. 1193
WINDART HOLDING INC., pg. 1195
WINDMILL HOLDINGS CORP., pg. 1195
WINNEBAGO COLOR PRESS, INC.—Gillett Holdings, Inc., pg. 459
WOODFIN HOLDING CORPORATION, pg. 1200
WORLD PUBLISHING COMPANY, pg. 1203
YRJ CORPORATION, pg. 1206
YAZOO INVESTMENT CORPORATION, pg. 1207
H.B. ZACHRY, pg. 1215
ZIMMERMAN HOLDINGS, INC., pg. 1220

6722 — MANAGEMENT INVESTMENT COMPANIES, OPEN-END

COST CARE, INC.—John Hancock Mutual Life Insurance Company, pg. 596
THE DEARBORN GROUP, pg. 322
DRUMM & ASSOCIATES, INC., pg. 349
FMR CORP.—Fidelity Investments (FMR Corp.), pg. 408
FIDELITY INVESTMENTS (FMR CORP.), pg. 408
HILLMAN COMPANY, pg. 535
JOHN HANCOCK ADVISERS INTERNATIONAL, LTD.—John Hancock Mutual Life Insurance Company, pg. 596
S. C. JOHNSON & SON, INC., pg. 599
KEYES MANAGEMENT—Keyes Company, pg. 627
LAMAR INVESTMENT MANAGEMENT COMPANY—Capitol Street Corp., pg. 216
LAMAR LIFE INVESTORS—Capitol Street Corp., pg. 216
METLIFE-STATE STREET INVESTMENT SERVICES, INC.—Metropolitan Life Insurance Co., pg. 744
MUTUAL OF OMAHA FUND MANAGEMENT CO.—Mutual of Omaha Insurance Company, pg. 779
NATIONWIDE FINANCIAL SERVICES, INC.—Nationwide Mutual Insurance Company, pg. 795
NEW YORK LIFE INSURANCE COMPANY, pg. 802
PHOENIX EQUITY PLANNING CORP.—Phoenix Home Life Mutual Insurance Company, pg. 868
PRUDENTIAL FUND MANAGEMENT CANADA LTD.—The Prudential Insurance Company of America, pg. 897
SCUDDER, STEVENS & CLARK, INC., pg. 983
STRATTON GROWTH FUND, INC.—Stratton Management Company, pg. 1053
STRATTON MANAGEMENT COMPANY, pg. 1053
STRATTON MONTHLY DIVIDEND SHARES, INC.—Stratton Management Company, pg. 1053
TRECO REALTY GROUP, INC.—Sunstates Realty Group Inc., pg. 1062

6726 — UNIT INVESTMENT TRUSTS, FACE-AMOUNT CERTIFICATE OFFICES, CLOSED-END MANAGEMENT INVESTMENT OFFICES

ALL AMERICA FINANCIAL, pg. 34
ALL AMERICAN FINANCIAL—All America Financial, pg. 34
AMERICAN CAPITAL MANAGEMENT & RESEARCH, INC., pg. 50
COST CARE, INC.—John Hancock Mutual Life Insurance Company, pg. 596
COUNTRY COMPANIES INSURANCE GROUP, pg. 289
DRUMM & ASSOCIATES, INC., pg. 349
GUARDIAN ASSET MANAGEMENT CORP. (GAMCORP)—The Guardian Life Insurance Company of America, pg. 492
JOHNSTON, LEMON & CO. INC., pg. 601
MI FUND INCORPORATED, pg. 692
NEW YORK LIFE INSURANCE COMPANY, pg. 802
PHOENIX FOUNDERS, INC—Phoenix Home Life Mutual Insurance Company, pg. 868

6732 — EDUCATIONAL, RELIGIOUS & CHARITABLE TRUSTS

CHRISTIAN CHILDREN'S FUND, INC., pg. 248

6733 — TRUSTS, EXCEPT EDUCATIONAL, RELIGIOUS & CHARITABLE

FIDUCIARY TRUST COMPANY INTERNATIONAL, pg. 408
GENERAL ELECTRIC MASTER RETIREMENT TRUST, pg. 449
PRUDENTIAL INSTITUTIONAL INVESTMENT MANAGEMENT DIV.—The Prudential Insurance Company of America, pg. 897
ZENITH ADMINISTRATORS OF TEXAS—ULLICO Inc., pg. 1124

6792 — OIL ROYALTY TRADERS

AMERICAN LIBERTY FINANCIAL CORP., pg. 57
THE LEAVELL COMPANY, pg. 664

6794 — PATENT OWNERS & LESSORS

AMERICAN VISION CENTERS, INC., pg. 65
TRUMAN ARNOLD COMPANIES, pg. 84
ATHLETIC ATTIC PROPERTIES INC., pg. 94
BOSTON TRADING LTD. INC., pg. 168
BRESLER'S INDUSTRIES, INC., pg. 174
BROWN DERBY, INC., pg. 181
BUDGET RENT A CAR CORPORATION—Beech Holdings Corp., pg. 131
CAREER BLAZERS SERVICE COMPANY, INC.—Career Blazers Inc., pg. 218
CENTURY DATA SERVICES, INC.—Century Business Credit Corporation, pg. 235
CENTURY 21 REAL ESTATE CORP.—Metropolitan Life Insurance Co., pg. 744
THE CHEROKEE GROUP, pg. 243
COLORTYME, INC., pg. 265
COMPREHENSIVE BUSINESS SERVICES INC.—KOA Holdings, pg. 612
COMPUTERLAND CANADA LTD.—ComputerLand Corporation, pg. 271
COMPUTERLAND CORPORATION, pg. 271
THE DELPHI GLASS CORP. DELPHI STAINED GLASS CENTERS, pg. 326
DOMINO'S PIZZA INTERNATIONAL, INC.—Domino's Pizza Inc., pg. 344
DRUTHER'S INTERNATIONAL, INC., pg. 350
FOOD KING, INC.—Victory Markets Inc., pg. 1150

GILES & RANSOME, INC., pg. 458
GLORIA JEAN'S COFFEE BEAN CORP., pg. 464
HICKORY FARMS, INC., pg. 532
J. G. HOOK, INC., pg. 543
JACMAR COMPANIES, INC., pg. 587
JAN-CO., INC., pg. 589
JERRICO, INC.—Castle-Harlan, Inc., pg. 229
KOA HOLDINGS, pg. 612
KING BEAR ENTERPRISES, INC., pg. 630
LA ROSA'S, INC., pg. 649
LEE MYLES ASSOCIATES CORPORATION, pg. 666
LITTLE CAESAR ENTERPRISES, INC., pg. 678
LONDONTOWN CORPORATION—Londontown Holdings Corporation, pg. 682
LONG JOHN SILVER'S, INC.—Castle-Harlan, Inc., pg. 229
MCCRORY STORES DIV.—Riklis Family Corporation, pg. 934
MILEX OF AMERICA, INC., pg. 753
MORAN INDUSTRIES, INC., pg. 769
MORGAN INDUSTRIES INC., pg. 770
NATIONAL AMUSEMENTS, INC., pg. 784
OCEAN CHEVROLET, INC., pg. 820
THE OHIO MATTRESS COMPANY LICENSING AND COMPONENTS GROUP—Sealy Corporation, pg. 985
PAYLESS CAR RENTAL SYSTEM, INC., pg. 853
POLO/RALPH LAUREN CORPORATION, pg. 879
PONDEROSA, INC.—Metromedia Company, pg. 743
PRECISION TUNE, INC., pg. 885
RESTAURANT DEVELOPERS CORP., pg. 929
M. RUBIN & SONS INC., pg. 954
STRAW HAT COOPERATIVE CORP., pg. 1053
SUBWAY FRANCHISEE ADVERTISING FUND TRUST, pg. 1055
TASTEE FREEZ INTL. INC.—De Novo Corporation, pg. 321
TOPSY'S INTERNATIONAL INC., pg. 1102
VIACOM INTERNATIONAL INC.—National Amusements, Inc., pg. 785
VICTORY VIDEO INC.—Victory Markets Inc., pg. 1150
ZIEBART CANADA, INC.—Ziebart International Corporation, pg. 1218
ZIEBART (E.C.) LIMITED—Ziebart International Corporation, pg. 1218
ZIEBART INTERNATIONAL CORPORATION, pg. 1217
ZIEBART JAPAN LIMITED—Ziebart International Corporation, pg. 1218

6798 — REAL ESTATE INVESTMENT TRUSTS

ALLIANCE MANAGEMENT, INC., pg. 37
AMRECORP REALTY INC., pg. 68
ASPENRISE PROPERTIES, INC.—Society for Savings Bancorp, Inc., pg. 1016
CAMBIO EQUITIES CORP., pg. 211
CLAYTON, WILLIAMS & SHERWOOD, INC., pg. 254
CLEARY LANE ASSOCIATES, INC.—Society for Savings Bancorp, Inc., pg. 1016
CLOVER FINANCIAL CORPORATION, pg. 256
CONNECTICUT MUTUAL LIFE INSURANCE COMPANY, pg. 274
CRANSTON PROPERTIES, INC.—Society for Savings Bancorp, Inc., pg. 1016
THE DEARBORN GROUP, pg. 322
DEVELOPERS INVESTORS, INC.—W. C. Bradley Co., pg. 170
EXECUTIVE CAPITAL CORP., pg. 392
FAIR HARBOR PROPERTIES, INC.—Society for Savings Bancorp, Inc., pg. 1016
FORBES, INC., pg. 423
GEORGIAN PRESS, INC., pg. 453
THE GREAT ATLANTIC COMPANIES, pg. 480
GRINNELL STREET ASSOCIATES, INC.—Society for Savings Bancorp, Inc., pg. 1016
THE HEARST CORPORATION, pg. 521
HIGH POINT EQUITIES, INC.—Society for Savings Bancorp, Inc., pg. 1016
INDIANA FINANCIAL INVESTORS, INC.—Libco Corporation, pg. 674
JMB REALTY CORPORATION, pg. 584
JAMES BUILDING CORPORATION, pg. 588
THE KAEMPFER COMPANY, INVESTMENT BUILDERS, pg. 613
KENOSIA PROPERTIES, INC.—Society for Savings Bancorp, Inc., pg. 1016
KEYES INVESTMENTS—Keyes Company, pg. 627
LASKEY ASSOCIATES, pg. 660
LOVE MORTGAGE COMPANY, pg. 685
MASTER PLANS CORPORATION—Society for Savings Bancorp, Inc., pg. 1016
MCCALL PROPERTIES, INC.—McCall Oil & Chemical Corp., pg. 727
MESIROW FINANCIAL, pg. 741
NYLIFE DEPOSITARY CORPORATION—New York Life Insurance Company, pg. 803
THE PATRICIAN GROUP, pg. 851
PENNINGTON CORPORATION—Society for Savings Bancorp, Inc., pg. 1016
PLAZA INVESTMENT ASSOCIATES—Rotterdam Ventures Inc., pg. 952
PROGRESS WEST, pg. 894
REGENCY ASSOCIATES LIMITED PARTNERSHIP, pg. 922
REINALT-THOMAS CORP., pg. 923
ROSEN ASSOCIATES MANAGEMENT CORP., pg. 948
THE SHIDLER GROUP, pg. 999
SOCIETY COMMERCIAL PROPERTIES, INC.—Society for Savings Bancorp, Inc., pg. 1016
STEARNS ENTERPRISES, INC., pg. 1043
TRAMMELL CROW COMPANY, pg. 1106
VENGROFF WILLIAMS REALTY MANAGEMENT—Vengroff Williams & Associates, Inc., pg. 1147
WALKER GLEN PROPERTIES, INC.—Society for Savings Bancorp, Inc., pg. 1016

6799 — INVESTORS, NEC

AFI EXPORT, INC.—JMB Realty Corporation, pg. 585
ADLER & SHAYKIN, pg. 17
ADVENT INTERNATIONAL, pg. 21
ADVISERS CAPITAL MANAGEMENT INC., pg. 21
AMFAC PROPERTY INVESTMENT CORP.—JMB Realty Corporation, pg. 585
ANDERSON INDUSTRIES INC., pg. 73
BUTCHER & CO., INC., pg. 196
CADENCE CAPITAL MANAGEMENT—Pacific Mutual Life Insurance Company, pg. 841
CAPITAL RESOURCES—Alex Lee, Inc., pg. 33
THE CARLYLE GROUP—Carlyle Holding Corporation, pg. 222
CARLYLE HOLDING CORPORATION, pg. 222
CENTURY AMERICA CORPORATION, pg. 234
CHILEWICH PARTNERS, pg. 248
DKM RESOURCES, INC.—The Dyson-Kissner-Moran Corporation, pg. 357
THE DEARBORN GROUP, pg. 322
FORECAST MORTGAGE CORPORATION, pg. 423
I. H. FRENCH & CO. INC., pg. 432
GOLODETZ CORPORATION, pg. 469
HARBERT CORPORATION, pg. 506
HOMES OF MERIT INC., pg. 542
HUNTCO ACQUISITIONS HOLDINGS, INC.—Huntco Inc., pg. 554
ICC INDUSTRIES, INC., pg. 558
INTEGRATED RESOURCES, INC., pg. 573
INVISTA CAPITAL MANAGEMENT CORP.—The Principal Financial Group, pg. 891
JOHNSON VENTURE CAPITAL, INC.—S. C. Johnson & Son, Inc., pg. 599
JORDAN COMPANY, pg. 604
KIRKPATRICK PETTIS—Mutual of Omaha Insurance Company, pg. 779
THE LEAVELL COMPANY, pg. 664
LEE NATIONAL CORPORATION, pg. 666
MESIROW FINANCIAL, pg. 741
METROPOLITAN PROPERTIES INC., pg. 745
NJF INVESTMENT GROUP, INC.—Pacific Mutual Life Insurance Company, pg. 841
NARRAGANSETT CAPITAL INC., pg. 783
NYLIFE EQUITY INC.—New York Life Insurance Company, pg. 803
NYLIFE REALTY INC.—New York Life Insurance Company, pg. 803
NORTH AMERICAN COMPANY, pg. 811
NORTH CENTRAL LIFE INSURANCE COMPANIES, pg. 813
ODYSSEY PARTNERS, pg. 821
OXBOW CORPORATION, pg. 834
PACIFIC MUTUAL LIFE INSURANCE COMPANY, pg. 841
PATRICIAN ASSOCIATES, INC.—The Principal Financial Group, pg. 891
PETULA ASSOCIATES, LTD.—The Principal Financial Group, pg. 891
PHOENIX AMERICAN INCORPORATED, pg. 868
PHOENIX GROWTH CAPITAL CORP.—Phoenix American Incorporated, pg. 868
PHOENIX LEASING INCORPORATED—Phoenix American Incorporated, pg. 868
PRINCIPAL DEVELOPMENT ASSOCIATES, INC.—The Principal Financial Group, pg. 891
THE PRINCIPAL FINANCIAL GROUP, pg. 890
RIVERSIDE DEVELOPMENT CORP.—Dugan & Meyers Interests, Inc., pg. 351
ROTHSCHILD INC.—Rothschild North America Inc., pg. 951
ROTHSCHILD NORTH AMERICA INC., pg. 951
SCIENTIFIC ADVANCES INC.—Battelle Memorial Institute, pg. 126
TIC INVESTMENT CORP.—TIC United Corporation, pg. 1073
UNITED STATES REALTY & INVESTMENT CO., pg. 1137
WEATHERLY CAPITAL CORP.—Weatherly Financial Group, pg. 1169
WEATHERLY FINANCIAL GROUP, pg. 1169

7011 — HOTELS & MOTELS

ARA SERVICES, INC.—ARA Group, pg. 5
ADVENTURE LANDS OF AMERICA, INC., pg. 21
AMANA-NORDSTROM MOTEL CO.—Amana Society, pg. 46
AMWAY HOTEL CORPORATION—Amway Corporation, pg. 70
ATLAS HOTELS, INC., pg. 96
BENSON'S, INC., pg. 140
BEST WESTERN INTERNATIONAL, INC., pg. 146
THE BEVERLY HILLS HOTEL, pg. 148
BROADMOOR HOTEL, INC., pg. 177
BROWN DERBY, INC., pg. 181
BRUTGER EQUITIES, INC., pg. 185
CANTERBURY HOTEL—Taj International Hotels, pg. 1076
CARDINAL REALTY SERVICES INC., pg. 218
CARLSON COMPANIES, INC., pg. 220
CHATTANOOGA CHOO-CHOO HOLIDAY INN, pg. 241
CLUB RESORTS, INC.—Club Corporation International, pg. 256
COLONY HOTELS & RESORTS, INC.—Carlson Companies, Inc., pg. 221
COLUMBIA SUSSEX CORPORATION, pg. 266
COVENTRY HOTELS ASSOCIATION, pg. 290
CRADDOCK DEVELOPMENT CO., INC., pg. 295
CRESTED BUTTE MOUNTAIN RESORT, INC., pg. 299
CROWN AMERICAN CORPORATION, pg. 301
DAYS INNS OF AMERICA, INC.—Tollman/Hundley Hotels, pg. 1100
DAYS INNS OF AMERICA, INC.—Tollman/Hundley Hotels, pg. 1100
DUNES HOTELS AND CASINOS INC., pg. 352
THE FAIRMONT HOTELS, pg. 397
FAMILY INNS OF AMERICA, INC., pg. 398
FAMILY INNS OF NEW ORLEANS, INC.—Family Inns of America, Inc., pg. 398
FARMERS INVESTMENT COMPANY, INC.—Bale Of Kentucky, Inc., pg. 115
THE FLATLEY COMPANY, pg. 416
GAYLORD ENTERTAINMENT CO., pg. 446
GEORGETOWN MARBURY HOTEL—Taj International Hotels, pg. 1076
GOLF HOST RESORTS, INC.—Golf Hosts, Inc., pg. 469
GOLF HOSTS, INC., pg. 469
GOSNELL BUILDERS, pg. 472
THE GREAT ATLANTIC COMPANIES, pg. 480
GREAT ATLANTIC HOSPITALITY CO. INC.—The Great Atlantic Companies, pg. 480
GREEN CONSTRUCTION OF INDIANA, INC., pg. 484
GROWTH MANAGEMENT CORP.—Family Inns of America, Inc., pg. 398
GUEST QUARTERS SUITE HOTELS, pg. 493
GUEST SERVICES, INC., pg. 493
HBE CORPORATION, pg. 495
HAMPSHIRE HOTEL—Taj International Hotels, pg. 1076
HARRIS FARMS, INC., pg. 511
HELMSLEY ENTERPRISES, INC., pg. 527
HELMSLEY HOTELS INC.—Helmsley Enterprises, Inc., pg. 527
THE HELMSLEY PALACE HOTEL—Helmsley Enterprises, Inc., pg. 527
HELMSLEY-SPEAR INC.—Helmsley Enterprises, Inc., pg. 527
HIDDEN VALLEY RESORT—Kettler Brothers, Inc., pg. 626
HIGH INDUSTRIES INC., pg. 533
HOLIDAY INN—Benson's, Inc., pg. 140
HOLLY'S INC., pg. 540
HOSTMARK MANAGEMENT GROUP, pg. 545
HUBBARD BROADCASTING, INC., pg. 548
HYATT CORPORATION—H. Group Holding Inc., pg. 495
HYATT HOTELS CORPORATION—H. Group Holding Inc., pg. 495
INN AT HARRIS RANCH—Harris Farms, Inc., pg. 512
INNCO MANAGEMENT CORP.—Family Inns of America, Inc., pg. 398
ISLAND HOLIDAYS, LTD.—JMB Realty Corporation, pg. 585
JRN, INC., pg. 586
JACKSON HOLE SKI RESORT, pg. 587
W.B. JOHNSON PROPERTY, INC., pg. 598
KOHLER COMPANY, pg. 639
LANCASTER HOST RESORT, pg. 653
LANDMARK HOTEL CORPORATION, pg. 656
LANE HOTELS, INC.—Lane Industries, Inc., pg. 657
LANE INDUSTRIES, INC., pg. 656
LARKEN INC., pg. 659
L'ERMITAGE HOTELS, pg. 668
LUCKY INNS OF AMERICA, INC.—Family Inns of America, Inc., pg. 398
MCLEAN ENTERPRISES, INC., pg. 731
NANA DEVELOPMENT CORPORATION—Nana Regional Corporation, Inc., pg. 783
NANA REGIONAL CORPORATION, INC., pg. 783
NATIONAL HOTEL CORP.—Carlson Companies, Inc., pg. 221
OCEAN PROPERTIES, LTD., pg. 820
OMNI HOTELS, pg. 826
PAN AMERICAN OCEAN RESORT HOTEL—Hubbard Broadcasting, Inc., pg. 549
PRIME HOSPITALITY CORP., pg. 889
PRIME HOSPITALITY CORP LIMITED PARTNERSHIP—Prime Hospitality Corp., pg. 889
PRINCEVILLE CORPORATION, pg. 890
PRINCEVILLE HOTEL CORPORATION—Princeville Corporation, pg. 890
PROFIT MANAGEMENT CORP.—Family Inns of America, Inc., pg. 398
QUALITY HOTEL DOWNTOWN—Taj International Hotels, pg. 1076
RADISSON HOTEL CORPORATION—Carlson Companies, Inc., pg. 221
RADISSON HOTELS INTERNATIONAL INC.—Carlson Companies, Inc., pg. 221
RALEIGH ENTERPRISES, INC., pg. 910
RAMADA INN DOWNTOWN—Taj International Hotels, pg. 1076
RED ROOF INNS, INC., pg. 918
RITZ-CARLTON HOTEL COMPANY—W.B. Johnson Property, Inc., pg. 598
ROSEWOOD PROPERTY COMPANY, pg. 949
SEA ISLAND COMPANY, pg. 983
SEA ISLAND SERVICES, INC.—Sea Island Company, pg. 983
SONOMA MISSION INN & SPA, pg. 1018
SPRINGER SCHMID GROUP, pg. 1033
STRATTON CORP., pg. 1053
SUNBELT LODGING DEVELOPMENT CO.—Investor's Management Corp., pg. 581
SUPER 8 MOTELS, INC., pg. 1062
SVERDRUP INVESTMENTS, INC.—Sverdrup Corporation, pg. 1066
TCC, pg. 1072
TAJ INTERNATIONAL HOTELS, pg. 1076
TOLLMAN/HUNDLEY HOTELS, pg. 1100
TOWN PUMP, INC., pg. 1104
TRAPP FAMILY LODGE, INC., pg. 1108
TRUMP ORGANIZATION, pg. 1118
THE VAGABOND INNS, pg. 1142
THE VAGABOND INNS—The Vagabond Inns, pg. 1142
VAIL ASSOCIATES, INC.—Gillett Holdings, Inc., pg. 459
VILLA SOUTH INC.—Thiele Kaolin Co., pg. 1092
VIRGINIA HOT SPRINGS, INC., pg. 1152
WARREN PROPERTIES, pg. 1165
THE WINDHAM COMPANY, pg. 1195
WOODFIN HOLDING CORPORATION, pg. 1200

WOODFIN HOTEL MANAGEMENT, INC.—Woodfin Holding Corporation, pg. 1200
WOODFIN SUITES, INC.—Woodfin Holding Corporation, pg. 1200

7032 — SPORTING & RECREATIONAL CAMPS

CENVILL RECREATION, INC.—Cenvill Development Corp., pg. 236

7033 — RECREATIONAL VEHICLE PARKS & CAMPSITES

ADVENTURE LANDS OF AMERICA, INC., pg. 21
KOA HOLDINGS, pg. 612
KAMPGROUNDS OF AMERICA (CANADA) LTD.—KOA Holdings, pg. 613
SILVER DOLLAR CITY, INC., pg. 1004

7211 — POWER LAUNDRIES, FAMILY & COMMERCIAL

BTD/TMP WORLDWIDE—TMP Worldwide, Inc., pg. 1073
DOMESTIC LINEN SUPPLY & LAUNDRY CO., pg. 343

7213 — LINEN SUPPLY SERVICES

ARA SERVICES, INC.—ARA Group, pg. 5
AMERICAN LINEN SUPPLY COMPANY, pg. 57
ARATEX SERVICES—ARA Group, pg. 6
ARATEX SERVICES, INC.—ARA Group, pg. 7
BEST MANUFACTURING, INC., pg. 146
COAT, APRON & LINEN SUPPLY, pg. 257
DOMESTIC LINEN SUPPLY & LAUNDRY CO., pg. 343
MISSION INDUSTRIES, pg. 760
NATIONAL DISTRIBUTING CO., INC., pg. 787
SERVITEX, INC.—National Distributing Co., Inc., pg. 787
SERVITEX, INC.—National Distributing Co., Inc., pg. 787
SERVITEX, INC.—National Distributing Co., Inc., pg. 787
STEINER CORPORATION, pg. 1045
VERSA SERVICES LTD.—ARA Group, pg. 7
WESTERN LINEN CORP., pg. 1180

7216 — DRY CLEANING PLANTS, EXCEPT RUG CLEANING

ARACLEAN SERVICES, INC.—ARA Group, pg. 6

7217 — CARPET & UPHOLSTERY CLEANING

CASTEX INDUSTRIES INC., pg. 228
STANLEY STEEMER INTERNATIONAL, INC., pg. 1038

7218 — INDUSTRIAL LAUNDERERS

ARA SERVICES, INC.—ARA Group, pg. 5
AMERICAN LINEN SUPPLY COMPANY, pg. 57
ARACLEAN SERVICES, INC.—ARA Group, pg. 6
ARATEX SERVICES—ARA Group, pg. 6
ARATEX SERVICES, INC.—ARA Group, pg. 6
DOMESTIC LINEN SUPPLY CO.—Domestic Linen Supply & Laundry Co., pg. 343
DOMESTIC LINEN SUPPLY & LAUNDRY CO., pg. 343
INDUSTRIAL TOWEL & UNIFORM, pg. 567
MISSION INDUSTRIES, pg. 760
TEXTILEASE CORPORATION, pg. 1090
VAN DYNE-CROTTY, INC., pg. 1144
VERSA SERVICES LTD.—ARA Group, pg. 7
WESTERN LINEN CORP., pg. 1180

7219 — LAUNDRY & GARMENT SERVICES, NEC

ARATEX TEXTILE SERVICES, INC.—ARA Group, pg. 7
CHANGE-O-MATIC/WESCO—Steiner Corporation, pg. 1045

7221 — PHOTOGRAPHIC STUDIOS, PORTRAIT

AMFAC, INC.—JMB Realty Corporation, pg. 585
BELL & HOWELL LTD. ENGLAND, DANSK FILIAL—Bell & Howell Company, pg. 135
BELL & HOWELL LTD., (UK) MAILHANDLING DIV.—Bell & Howell Company, pg. 135
CINE MAGNETICS, INC., pg. 250
LIFETOUCH, INC., pg. 675
LIFETOUCH NATIONAL SCHOOL STUDIOS INC.—Lifetouch, Inc., pg. 675
LIFETOUCH PORTRAIT STUDIOS INC.—Lifetouch, Inc., pg. 675
LIFETOUCH SENIOR PORTRAITS INC.—Lifetouch, Inc., pg. 675
LIFETOUCH VIDEO CREATIONS, INC.—Lifetouch, Inc., pg. 675
MAX WARD-DELMAR STUDIOS—Lifetouch, Inc., pg. 675
OLAN MILLS, INC., pg. 756
OLAN MILLS INC. OF OHIO—Olan Mills, Inc., pg. 756
OLAN MILLS INC. OF TEXAS—Olan Mills, Inc., pg. 756
POTRAIT INDUSTRIES CORPORATION—Lifetouch, Inc., pg. 675

7231 — BEAUTY SHOPS

CREATIVE HAIRDRESSERS, pg. 297
FANTASTIC SAM'S INTERNATIONAL, INC., pg. 398
THE HAIR CUTTERY—Creative Hairdressers, pg. 297
VISIBLE CHANGES, pg. 1153
VISIBLE CHANGES OF AUSTIN—Visible Changes, pg. 1153
VISIBLE CHANGES OF TEXAS—Visible Changes, pg. 1153

7241 — BARBER SHOPS

FANTASTIC SAM'S INTERNATIONAL, INC., pg. 398

7261 — FUNERAL SERVICE & CREMATORIES

BULTMAN FUNERAL HOME—Ourso Investment Corporation, pg. 832
FUNERAL SECURITY PLANS, INC.—D. W. Newcomer's Sons, Inc., pg. 804
D. W. NEWCOMER'S SONS, INC., pg. 804
OURSO INVESTMENT CORPORATION, pg. 832
SECURITY INDUSTRIAL INSURANCE CO., INC.—Ourso Investment Corporation, pg. 832

7299 — MISCELLANEOUS PERSONAL SERVICES, NEC

DELTA LIFE CORPORATION, pg. 327
DOMESTIC LINEN SUPPLY & LAUNDRY CO., pg. 343
FORMU-3 INTERNATIONAL, INC., pg. 424
GINGISS INTERNATIONAL, pg. 460
MISSION INDUSTRIES, pg. 760
NORCOSTCO, INC., pg. 809
NUTRI/SYSTEM INC., pg. 818
REPUBLIC STORAGE SYSTEMS COMPANY INC., pg. 928
SGD INTERNATIONAL CORP., pg. 962
WILLIAMSON-DICKIE APPAREL MFG. CO.—Williamson-Dickie Mfg. Co., pg. 1192
WILLIAMSON-DICKIE MFG. CO., pg. 1192

7311 — ADVERTISING AGENCIES

LEO BURNETT WORLDWIDE INC.—Leo Burnett Company, Inc., pg. 193
ADS/TMP WORLDWIDE—TMP Worldwide, Inc., pg. 1073
A & M ASSOCIATES, INC.—Amerco, A Nevada Corporation, pg. 48
AMA LEO BURNETT—Leo Burnett Company, Inc., pg. 192
ABELSON-TAYLOR, INC., pg. 10
AD/PRODUCTIONS—Young & Rubicam Inc., pg. 1211
ADLER BOSCHETTO PEEBLES & PARTNERS, INC., pg. 17
ADMARKETING, INC., pg. 18
ADPLUS GMBH—The Lowe Group, pg. 685
ADSHOP—Backer Spielvogel Bates Worldwide, Inc., pg. 109
ADVICO YOUNG & RUBICAM AG—Young & Rubicam Inc., pg. 1211
AGRI-GRAPHICS, INC.—Altair Corporation, pg. 45
ALAS/D.P.P.—Backer Spielvogel Bates Worldwide, Inc., pg. 109
ALAS/DPP BARCELONA S.A.—Backer Spielvogel Bates Worldwide, Inc., pg. 109
ALAS/DPP VALENCIA S.A.—Backer Spielvogel Bates Worldwide, Inc., pg. 109
THE ALDEN GROUP LTD., pg. 32
ALEXANDER MARKETING SERVICES, INC., pg. 33
ALLIED ADVERTISING AGENCY, pg. 37
AMERCO, A NEVADA CORPORATION, pg. 47
AMMIRATI & PURIS INC., pg. 67
MARK ANDERSON ASSOCIATES, INC., pg. 73
ANDERSSON MEDIA AKTIEBOLAG—Young & Rubicam Inc., pg. 1211
ANSON-STONER, INC., pg. 76
ARCHER/MALMO ADV., INC., pg. 80
ARELLANO/BSB PUBLICIDAD—Backer Spielvogel Bates Worldwide, Inc., pg. 109
ARNOLD FORTUNA LAWNER & CABOT, pg. 84
ARTPLAN PUBLICIDADE—TBWA Advertising, Inc., pg. 1072
ASER PUBLICIDAD—Young & Rubicam Inc., pg. 1213
ASER PUBLICIDAD/Y&R—Young & Rubicam Inc., pg. 1213
ASHER/GOULD ADVERTISING, INC., pg. 88
ASSET MARKETING, LTD.—Backer Spielvogel Bates Worldwide, Inc., pg. 109
AUSTRIA III—TBWA Advertising, Inc., pg. 1072
AV-KONTAKT A/S—Backer Spielvogel Bates Worldwide, Inc., pg. 109
AVRETT, FREE & GINSBERG, INC., pg. 103
AYER CHICAGO—N W Ayer Incorporated, pg. 104
AYER EUROPE—N W Ayer Incorporated, pg. 104
AYER FRANKFURT—N W Ayer Incorporated, pg. 104
N W AYER INCORPORATED, pg. 103
AYER LTD.—N W Ayer Incorporated, pg. 104
AYER MILANO—N W Ayer Incorporated, pg. 104
AYER/NEDERLAND B.V.—N W Ayer Incorporated, pg. 104
AYER PORTUGAL—N W Ayer Incorporated, pg. 104
AYER ROMA—N W Ayer Incorporated, pg. 104
AYER VAZQUEZ S.A. DE PUBLICIDAD—N W Ayer Incorporated, pg. 104
BSB/ADAPTUS AB—Backer Spielvogel Bates Worldwide, Inc., pg. 109
BSB AMSTERDAM—Backer Spielvogel Bates Worldwide, Inc., pg. 109
BSB ATHENS ADVERTISING S.A.—Backer Spielvogel Bates Worldwide, Inc., pg. 109
BSB BATES-GRUPPEN A/S—Backer Spielvogel Bates Worldwide, Inc., pg. 109
BSB BRUSSELS SA/NV—Backer Spielvogel Bates Worldwide, Inc., pg. 109
BSB CHILE PUBLICIDAD—Backer Spielvogel Bates Worldwide, Inc., pg. 109
BSB CITY—Backer Spielvogel Bates Worldwide, Inc., pg. 109
BSB DINFO—Backer Spielvogel Bates Worldwide, Inc., pg. 109
BSB DORLAND LIMITED—Backer Spielvogel Bates Worldwide, Inc., pg. 109
BSB EUROPE—Backer Spielvogel Bates Worldwide, Inc., pg. 109
BSB EUROPE/THE EUROCENTRE—Backer Spielvogel Bates Worldwide, Inc., pg. 109
BSB FINNAD OY—Backer Spielvogel Bates Worldwide, Inc., pg. 109
BSB FINNAD WEST—Backer Spielvogel Bates Worldwide, Inc., pg. 109
BSB FRANCE—Backer Spielvogel Bates Worldwide, Inc., pg. 109
BSB FRANKFURT WERBEAGENTUR GMBH—Backer Spielvogel Bates Worldwide, Inc., pg. 109
BSB/GHERSY-QUINTERO, C.A. PUBLICIDAD—Backer Spielvogel Bates Worldwide, Inc., pg. 109
BSB GOTEBORG AB—Backer Spielvogel Bates Worldwide, Inc., pg. 109
BSB GRAFFIX LIMITED—Backer Spielvogel Bates Worldwide, Inc., pg. 110
BSB HELSINGBORG AB—Backer Spielvogel Bates Worldwide, Inc., pg. 110
BSB HONG KONG—Backer Spielvogel Bates Worldwide, Inc., pg. 110
BSB HUNTER ADVERTISING—Backer Spielvogel Bates Worldwide, Inc., pg. 110
BSB INDONESIA—Backer Spielvogel Bates Worldwide, Inc., pg. 110
BSB ITALIA—Backer Spielvogel Bates Worldwide, Inc., pg. 110
BSB JAPAN LTD.—Backer Spielvogel Bates Worldwide, Inc., pg. 110
BSB MADCO—Backer Spielvogel Bates Worldwide, Inc., pg. 110
BSB MALAYSIA SDN. BHD.—Backer Spielvogel Bates Worldwide, Inc., pg. 110
BSB MEDIA & RESEARCH—Backer Spielvogel Bates Worldwide, Inc., pg. 110
BSB MEDICAL—Backer Spielvogel Bates Worldwide, Inc., pg. 110
BSB/MEZA, LTDA.—Backer Spielvogel Bates Worldwide, Inc., pg. 110
BSB NAESS & MORCH A/S—Backer Spielvogel Bates Worldwide, Inc., pg. 110
BSB NEW ZEALAND—Backer Spielvogel Bates Worldwide, Inc., pg. 110
BSB PORTUGAL—Backer Spielvogel Bates Worldwide, Inc., pg. 110
BSB PUBLICIDAD S.A.—Backer Spielvogel Bates Worldwide, Inc., pg. 110
BSB SEPTEMBER AB—Backer Spielvogel Bates Worldwide, Inc., pg. 110
BSB SINGAPORE—Backer Spielvogel Bates Worldwide, Inc., pg. 110
BSB STOCKHOLM AB—Backer Spielvogel Bates Worldwide, Inc., pg. 110
BSB SWEDEN—Backer Spielvogel Bates Worldwide, Inc., pg. 110
BSB/TAIWAN COMPANY LIMITED—Backer Spielvogel Bates Worldwide, Inc., pg. 110
BSB THAILAND—Backer Spielvogel Bates Worldwide, Inc., pg. 110
BTD/TMP WORLDWIDE—TMP Worldwide, Inc., pg. 1073
BTD/TMP WORLDWIDE—TMP Worldwide, Inc., pg. 1073
B-W ADVERTISING AGENCY—Best Western International, Inc., pg. 147
BACKER SPIELVOGEL BATES, INC.—Backer Spielvogel Bates Worldwide, Inc., pg. 108
BACKER SPIELVOGEL BATES WORLDWIDE, INC., pg. 108
BADER RUTTER & ASSOC., INC., pg. 113
GORDON BAILEY & ASSOCIATES, INC., pg. 114
R. J. BAKER ADVERTISING, INC.—Stone, August, Baker Communications Companies, pg. 1051
BARANCORP, pg. 118
BARANSKI & ASSOCIATES—Barancorp, pg. 118
BARNHART ADVERTISING, MARKETING & PUBLIC RELATIONS, INC., pg. 120
BATES ADVERTISING A/S—Backer Spielvogel Bates Worldwide, Inc., pg. 110
TED BATES A/S—Backer Spielvogel Bates Worldwide, Inc., pg. 110
BATES BACKER & SPIELVOGEL A/S—Backer Spielvogel Bates Worldwide, Inc., pg. 111
BATES BENJAMIN A/S—Backer Spielvogel Bates Worldwide, Inc., pg. 111
BATES BERGEN A/S—Backer Spielvogel Bates Worldwide, Inc., pg. 111
BATES FILM—Backer Spielvogel Bates Worldwide, Inc., pg. 111
TED BATES GREENHOUSE—Backer Spielvogel Bates Worldwide, Inc., pg. 111
BATES STAVANGER A/S—Backer Spielvogel Bates Worldwide, Inc., pg. 111
BATES TELEMARKETING—Backer Spielvogel Bates Worldwide, Inc., pg. 111
TED BATES-VESTFOLD—Backer Spielvogel Bates Worldwide, Inc., pg. 111
BAYER BESS VANDERWARKER INC., pg. 128
BEAUTIFUL & LANDOR ASSOCIATES—Young & Rubicam Inc., pg. 1211
BEBER SILVERSTEIN & PARTNERS, INC., pg. 130
BENTLEY, BARNES & LYNN, INC., pg. 140
BERENSON, ISHAM & PARTNERS, INC., pg. 141
BERENTER GREENHOUSE & WEBSTER, INC., pg. 141
BERRY-BROWN ADVERTISING, INC., pg. 144
BIEDERMAN, KELLY & SHAFFER, INC., pg. 149
BIGGS GILMORE COMMUNICATIONS, pg. 149
BLACK PENCIL S.A.R.L.—Leo Burnett Company, Inc., pg. 192
BORDELAIS, LEMEUNIER & LEO BURNETT—Leo Burnett Company, Inc., pg. 192

BORDERS, PERRIN & NORRANDER, INC., pg. 165
BOTTO, ROESSNER, HORNE & MESSINGER, INC.—Ketchum Communications Inc., pg. 625
BRIERLEY & PARTNERS, pg. 175
BRIERLEY & PARTNERS—Brierley & Partners, pg. 175
BRIERLEY & PARTNERS—Brierley & Partners, pg. 175
E.H. BROWN ADVERTISING, INC., pg. 181
BUCK & PULLEYN, INC., pg. 185
BUNGEY MEDICAL—Backer Spielvogel Bates Worldwide, Inc., pg. 111
DAVID K. BURNAP ADVERTISING AGENCY, INC., pg. 191
LEO BURNETT CHILE—Leo Burnett Company, Inc., pg. 192
LEO BURNETT CO., INC. SUCURSAL ARGENTINA—Leo Burnett Company, Inc., pg. 192
LEO BURNETT CO., S.R.L.—Leo Burnett Company, Inc., pg. 192
LEO BURNETT COMPANY, INC., pg. 191
LEO BURNETT COMPANY LTD.—Leo Burnett Company, Inc., pg. 192
LEO BURNETT/CONAGHAN & MAY (QLD.) PTY. LTD.—Leo Burnett Company, Inc., pg. 192
LEO BURNETT/CONAGHAN & MAY (VIC.) PTY. LTD.—Leo Burnett Company, Inc., pg. 192
LEO BURNETT/CONAGHAN & MAY S.A. PTY. LTD.—Leo Burnett Company, Inc., pg. 192
LEO BURNETT DENMARK—Leo Burnett Company, Inc., pg. 192
LEO BURNETT INC.—Leo Burnett Company, Inc., pg. 192
LEO BURNETT, INC.—Leo Burnett Company, Inc., pg. 192
LEO BURNETT-KYODO CO. LTD.—Leo Burnett Company, Inc., pg. 192
LEO BURNETT LIMITED—Leo Burnett Company, Inc., pg. 193
LEO BURNETT LIMITED—Leo Burnett Company, Inc., pg. 193
LEO BURNETT LIMITED—Leo Burnett Company, Inc., pg. 193
LEO BURNETT LTD.—Leo Burnett Company, Inc., pg. 193
LEO BURNETT LTD. THAILAND—Leo Burnett Company, Inc., pg. 193
LEO BURNETT PTE. LTD.—Leo Burnett Company, Inc., pg. 193
LEO BURNETT PTY. LTD.—Leo Burnett Company, Inc., pg. 193
LEO BURNETT PUBLICIDADE, LTDA.—Leo Burnett Company, Inc., pg. 193
LEO BURNETT S.A. DE C.V.—Leo Burnett Company, Inc., pg. 193
LEO BURNETT SDN. BHD.—Leo Burnett Company, Inc., pg. 193
LEO BURNETT VENEZUELA, C.A.—Leo Burnett Company, Inc., pg. 193
BURRELL COMMUNICATIONS GROUP INC., pg. 195
BURSON-MARSTELLER—Young & Rubicam Inc., pg. 1210
CALET, HIRSCH & FERRELL, INC.—Ross Roy Group, Inc., pg. 949
THE CAMPAIGN PALACE—Backer Spielvogel Bates Worldwide, Inc., pg. 111
CARDEN & CHERRY, INC., pg. 217
CARLSON PROMOTION DIVISION—Carlson Companies, Inc., pg. 221
CASTOR ADVERTISING CORP., pg. 229
CASTOR ADVERTISING CORP.—Castor Advertising Corp., pg. 229
CATO JOHNSON CAPE TOWN—Young & Rubicam Inc., pg. 1214
CATO JOHNSON DIRECT PROMOTION—Young & Rubicam Inc., pg. 1211
CATO JOHNSON ITALIA S.P.A.—Young & Rubicam Inc., pg. 1211
CATO JOHNSON LIMITED—Young & Rubicam Inc., pg. 1212
CATO JOHNSON-NEW YORK—Young & Rubicam Inc., pg. 1210
CATO JOHNSON SPAIN S.A.—Young & Rubicam Inc., pg. 1212
CATO JOHNSON SWITZERLAND—Young & Rubicam Inc., pg. 1212
CATO JOHNSON WORLDWIDE—Young & Rubicam Inc., pg. 1210
CATO YASUMURA BEHAEGHEL (CYB)—Young & Rubicam Inc., pg. 1212
CAUSA PUBLICIDAD—Leo Burnett Company, Inc., pg. 192
CENTRAL MEDIA, S.A.—Backer Spielvogel Bates Worldwide, Inc., pg. 111
CERCA GMBH—Backer Spielvogel Bates Worldwide, Inc., pg. 111
CHAITRA LEO BURNETT ADVERTISING PRIVATE LTD.—Leo Burnett Company, Inc., pg. 192
THE CHERENSON GROUP, pg. 243
CHIAT/DAY/MOJO INC. ADVERTISING, pg. 244
CHUO SENKO ADVERTISING CO., LTD.—N W Ayer Incorporated, pg. 103
CICERO/BSB PUBLICIDAD S.A.—Backer Spielvogel Bates Worldwide, Inc., pg. 111
CLARITY COVERDALE RUEFF ADVERTISING, pg. 251
CLAYTON-DAVIS & ASSOCIATES, INCORPORATED, pg. 253
COLLE & MCVOY, INC., pg. 261
COLONIAL WILLIAMSBURG FOUNDATION, pg. 264
COLUMBIAN ADVERTISING INC., pg. 266
COMED COMMUNICATIONS DIVISION—Ted Thomas Associates Inc., Advertising, pg. 1092
COMMUNICATIONS PLANNING CORPORATION/TMP WORLDWIDE—TMP Worldwide, Inc., pg. 1074
COMUNICA LEO BURNETT—Leo Burnett Company, Inc., pg. 192
COMUNICA LEO BURNETT-COSTA RICA—Leo Burnett Company, Inc., pg. 192
MICHAEL CONRAD & LEO BURNETT GMBH & CO. KG—Leo Burnett Company, Inc., pg. 192
CONSENSUS RESEARCH PTY., LTD.—Backer Spielvogel Bates Worldwide, Inc., pg. 111
THE WILLIAM COOK AGENCY, INC., pg. 282
COSMOPULOS CROWLEY DALY/CKG, pg. 288
CRAMER-KRASSELT, pg. 296
CRANFORD JOHNSON ROBINSON WOODS, pg. 296
CREATIVE COMMUNICATIONS WERBEGESELLSHAFT, M.B.H.—Backer Spielvogel Bates Worldwide, Inc., pg. 111
CRESWELL, MUNSELL, FULTZ & ZIRBEL—Young & Rubicam Inc., pg. 1211
CRESWELL, MUNSELL, FULTZ & ZIRBEL—Young & Rubicam Inc., pg. 1211
CRESWELL, MUNSELL, FULTZ & ZIRBEL—Young & Rubicam Inc., pg. 1211
CRESWELL, MUNSELL, FULTZ & ZIRBEL—Young & Rubicam Inc., pg. 1211
CRISPIN & PORTER ADVERTISING INC., pg. 299
VINCE CULLERS ADVERTISING INC., pg. 304
DDF&M INC. DUDRECK DEPAUL FICCO & MORGAN INC., pg. 308
D & S MARKETING—Bel-Art Products, pg. 133
DSI/TMP WORLDWIDE—TMP Worldwide, Inc., pg. 1074
DARBY & ASSOCIATES—Backer Spielvogel Bates Worldwide, Inc., pg. 111
DAVIS ADVERTISING INC., pg. 318
DEACON DAY ADVERTISING AND THE MCLAUCHLAN GROUP—The Lowe Group, pg. 685
THE DECISION SHOP—Backer Spielvogel Bates Worldwide, Inc., pg. 111
DELVICO/BATES, S.A.—Backer Spielvogel Bates Worldwide, Inc., pg. 111
DENISON/BSB—Backer Spielvogel Bates Worldwide, Inc., pg. 111
DENTSU, SUDLER & HENNESSEY—Dentsu, Young & Rubicam Partnerships, pg. 330
DENTSU WUNDERMAN DIRECT INC.—Young & Rubicam Inc., pg. 1213
DENTSU, YOUNG & RUBICAM, ALCANTARA/ MANILA—Dentsu, Young & Rubicam Partnerships, pg. 330
DENTSU, YOUNG & RUBICAM/BANGKOK—Dentsu, Young & Rubicam Partnerships, pg. 330
DENTSU, YOUNG & RUBICAM/BEIJING—Dentsu, Young & Rubicam Partnerships, pg. 330
DENTSU, YOUNG & RUBICAM/HONG KONG—Dentsu, Young & Rubicam Partnerships, pg. 330
DENTSU, YOUNG & RUBICAM/KUALA LUMPUR—Dentsu, Young & Rubicam Partnerships, pg. 330
DENTSU, YOUNG & RUBICAM PARTNERSHIPS, pg. 330
DENTSU, YOUNG & RUBICAM/SEOUL—Dentsu, Young & Rubicam Partnerships, pg. 330
DENTSU, YOUNG & RUBICAM/SHANGHAI—Dentsu, Young & Rubicam Partnerships, pg. 330
DENTSU, YOUNG & RUBICAM/SINGAPORE—Dentsu, Young & Rubicam Partnerships, pg. 330
DENTSU, YOUNG & RUBICAM/TAIPEI—Dentsu, Young & Rubicam Partnerships, pg. 330
DENTSU, YOUNG & RUBICAM/TOKYO—Dentsu, Young & Rubicam Partnerships, pg. 330
DESCO ADVERTISING & MARKETING—Desco Corporation, pg. 332
DEUTSCH/DWORIN, INC., pg. 333
DIAMOND AD LTD.—Backer Spielvogel Bates Worldwide, Inc., pg. 111
DIFRANZA WILLIAMSON, INC.—Ketchum Communications Inc., pg. 625
DIMAC CORPORATION, pg. 338
THE DIRECT MARKETING GROUP INC., pg. 339
DIRECTORY DATA MANAGEMENT—TMP Worldwide, Inc., pg. 1074
DOE-ANDERSON ADVERTISING AGENCY, INC., pg. 342
DOLRIIS, GORM LARSEN & PARTNER—N W Ayer Incorporated, pg. 104
DONER & COMPANY LIMITED—W.B. Doner & Company, pg. 344
DONER SCHUR PEPPLER—W.B. Doner & Company, pg. 344
W.B. DONER & COMPANY, pg. 344
DORLAND BUSINESS COMMUNICATIONS—Backer Spielvogel Bates Worldwide, Inc., pg. 111
DRAPER DANIELS MEDIA SERVICES, INC., pg. 348
EPG/TBWA—TBWA Advertising, Inc., pg. 1072
BRUCE W. EBERLE & ASSOCIATES—Eberle Direct Marketing Group, Inc., pg. 365
ELKMAN ADVERTISING & PUBLIC RELATIONS, pg. 377
ERIC MOWER AND ASSOCIATES/ROCHESTER, INC.—Eric Mower and Associates, Inc., pg. 774
ETHICAL COMMUNICATIONS—Backer Spielvogel Bates Worldwide, Inc., pg. 111
EVANSGROUP, pg. 390
NEIL FABER MEDIA INC., pg. 395
FABIANAC, STROPES & ARMSTRONG, INC., pg. 395
FEDERAL DISTRIBUTING CORPORATION, pg. 404
FINAL ART—Backer Spielvogel Bates Worldwide, Inc., pg. 111
FINANCIAL LIFE COMPANIES, INC.—North Central Life Insurance Companies, pg. 813
FINNAD COMMUNICATIONS—Backer Spielvogel Bates Worldwide, Inc., pg. 111
FISHER GRAPHIC INDUSTRIES, pg. 415
FITTS-LAWRENCE, INC.—Lawrence Group, Inc., pg. 662
FLAIR COMMUNICATIONS AGENCY, INC., pg. 416
FOGARTY & KLEIN/WINIUS BRANDON, pg. 421
FOGARTY & KLEIN YELLOW PAGES, INC.—Fogarty & Klein/Winius Brandon, pg. 421
ANTHONY M. FRANCO INC.—Ross Roy Group, Inc., pg. 950
FRY/HAMMOND/BARR INCORPORATED, pg. 435
GBF/AYER—N W Ayer Incorporated, pg. 104
G&R PUBBLICITA/SUDLER & HENNESSEY—Young & Rubicam Inc., pg. 1212
GS&B-LINTAS ADVERTISING, pg. 440
GARIBOLDI PARISI VERGA/INTERAD—The Lowe Group, pg. 685
GEINDRE MARKETING SERVICES—Backer Spielvogel Bates Worldwide, Inc., pg. 111
GEOGRAPHIC MARKETING GROUP (GMG), pg. 452
GEOMEDIA S.A.—Backer Spielvogel Bates Worldwide, Inc., pg. 111
GEO-YOUNG & RUBICAM—Young & Rubicam Inc., pg. 1212
GERBER ADVERTISING, pg. 453
GESTRO HORNE—Backer Spielvogel Bates Worldwide, Inc., pg. 111
THE GILLESPIE ORGANIZATION, INC., pg. 458
GILLIS ADVERTISING & PUBLIC RELATIONS, pg. 459
CHESTER GORE COMPANY INC., pg. 472
GOUCHENOUR ADV., INC., pg. 473
GRANT MARKETING COMMUNICATIONS INC., pg. 477
GRAY & KILGORE, INC.—Ross Roy Group, Inc., pg. 950
GREENSTONE ROBERTS ADVERTISING, pg. 485
GRISWOLD, INC.—Ross Roy Group, Inc., pg. 950
GRUPO BSB SA—Backer Spielvogel Bates Worldwide, Inc., pg. 111
H & C, LEO BURNETT—Leo Burnett Company, Inc., pg. 192
HAGER GESELLSCHAFT—The Lowe Group, pg. 685
HAMEROFF/MILENTHAL/SPENCE, INC., pg. 503
HANDLEY & MILLER, INC., pg. 505
HARRIS DRURY COHEN, pg. 511
HEMISPHERE-LEO BURNETT, INC.—Leo Burnett Company, Inc., pg. 192
HENDERSON ADVERTISING, INC., pg. 528
HERLIN PRESS, pg. 531
THE HIGHLAND GROUP, INC., pg. 534
HILL, HOLLIDAY, CONNORS, COSMOPULOS, INC., pg. 534
HOFFMAN YORK & COMPTON, pg. 538
MICHAEL HOGG-YOUNG & RUBICAM (PVT.) LTD.—Young & Rubicam Inc., pg. 1214
HORIZON MEDIA, INC., pg. 544
HORLICK LEVIN ADVERTISING INC., pg. 544
ICW COPARTNER—N W Ayer Incorporated, pg. 104
IMPACT COMUNICACOES—Young & Rubicam Inc., pg. 1213
INGALLS, QUINN & JOHNSON, pg. 567
INSIGHT COMMUNICATIONS LTD.—Backer Spielvogel Bates Worldwide, Inc., pg. 111
J & C ADVERTISING—N W Ayer Incorporated, pg. 104
JMC CREATIVIDAD ORIENTADA/YOUNG & RUBICAM—Young & Rubicam Inc., pg. 1213
JAVELIN/YOUNG & RUBICAM—Young & Rubicam Inc., pg. 1212
JONES, ANASTASI & BIRCHFIELD, pg. 602
JORDAN, MCGRATH, CASE & TAYLOR INC., pg. 604
JORDAN TAMRAZ CARUSO ADVERTISING, INC., pg. 605
K&D HELLAS—Backer Spielvogel Bates Worldwide, Inc., pg. 112
K&D ITALIA—Backer Spielvogel Bates Worldwide, Inc., pg. 112
K&D WERBEAGENTUR—Backer Spielvogel Bates Worldwide, Inc., pg. 112
KAISER MCEUEN INC., pg. 615
KASTNER & PARTNER GMBH WERBEAGENTUR—Leo Burnett Company, Inc., pg. 192
KELLER CRESCENT CO., pg. 620
KEROFF & ROSENBERG ADVERTISING INC., pg. 624
KETCHUM ADVERTISING SINGAPORE—Ketchum Communications Inc., pg. 625
KETCHUM COMMUNICATIONS INC., pg. 625
KLAUSEN & PARTNERS A/S—Young & Rubicam Inc., pg. 1212
KLEMTNER ADVERTISING INC., pg. 635
KNOTH & MEADS COMPANY, pg. 637
KOBS & DRAFT—Backer Spielvogel Bates Worldwide, Inc., pg. 112
KOBS & DRAFT ADVERTISING—Backer Spielvogel Bates Worldwide, Inc., pg. 112
KOBS & DRAFT ASIA-MALAYSIA—Backer Spielvogel Bates Worldwide, Inc., pg. 112
KOBS & DRAFT ASIA-THAILAND—Backer Spielvogel Bates Worldwide, Inc., pg. 112
KOBS & DRAFT BELGIUM—Backer Spielvogel Bates Worldwide, Inc., pg. 112
KOBS & DRAFT BV—Backer Spielvogel Bates Worldwide, Inc., pg. 112
KOBS & DRAFT EUROPE—Backer Spielvogel Bates Worldwide, Inc., pg. 112
KOBS & DRAFT S.A.—Backer Spielvogel Bates Worldwide, Inc., pg. 112
KOLON, BITTKER & DESMOND, INC., pg. 641
KRESSER/CRAIG, pg. 644
LAMARCA GROUP INC., pg. 652
LAUERER MARKIN GIBBS, INC., pg. 660
LEBRIJA RUBIO PUBLICIDAD S.A.—N W Ayer Incorporated, pg. 104
LEDONNE, WILNER & WEINER, INC., pg. 665
LEE DAVIS AYER—N W Ayer Incorporated, pg. 104
AL PAUL LEFTON CO., INC., pg. 666
LEO BURNETT COLOMBIA, S.A.—Leo Burnett Company, Inc., pg. 192
LEO BURNETT S.A.—Leo Burnett Company, Inc., pg. 193
J. N. LEOUSSIS ADVERTISING & MARKETING S.A.—TBWA Advertising, Inc., pg. 1072
LESLIE ADVERTISING, pg. 668
LIVINGSTON & COMPANY, pg. 679
LOCKHART & PETTUS, INC., pg. 680
LOIS/USA, pg. 681
LORD, SULLIVAN & YODER, INC. ADVERTISING, pg. 683
LORSCH CREATIVE NETWORK, pg. 684
LOWE & ASSOCIES—The Lowe Group, pg. 685
LOWE COMMUNICATION GROUP—The Lowe Group, pg. 685
LOWE FMS—The Lowe Group, pg. 685

S.I.C. Index

THE LOWE GROUP, pg. 685
THE LOWE GROUP—The Lowe Group, pg. 685
LOWE HOWARD-SPINK LIMITED—The Lowe Group, pg. 685
LOWE KUIPER & SCHOUTEN B.V.—The Lowe Group, pg. 685
LOWE LUERZER GMBH—The Lowe Group, pg. 685
LOWE LUERZER GMBH—The Lowe Group, pg. 685
LOWE MBAC—The Lowe Group, pg. 685
LOWE TROOST S.A.—The Lowe Group, pg. 685
MGTB AYER—N W Ayer Incorporated, pg. 104
MACNAMARA, KLEIN & SOLIN INC., pg. 698
MANN HUGHES GERRISH—Backer Spielvogel Bates Worldwide, Inc., pg. 112
MARGEOTES FERTITTA & WEISS, INC., pg. 706
MARKETFORCE ADVERTISING PHILIPPINES INC.—Dentsu, Young & Rubicam Partnerships, pg. 330
MARKETFORCE AUSTRALIA—Backer Spielvogel Bates Worldwide, Inc., pg. 112
MARKETING CORP. OF AMERICA, pg. 709
MARKOM/LEO BURNETT A.S.—Leo Burnett Company, Inc., pg. 193
MARQUARDT & ROCHE INC., pg. 713
MATARI ADVERTISING—N W Ayer Incorporated, pg. 104
MATTER GALBUCCI LEO BURNETT, WERBEAGENTUR—Leo Burnett Company, Inc., pg. 193
MATTINGLY & PARTNERS/AUCKLAND—Dentsu, Young & Rubicam Partnerships, pg. 331
MATTINGLY & PARTNERS GROUP PTY LTD.—Dentsu, Young & Rubicam Partnerships, pg. 330
MATTINGLY & PARTNERS/MELBOURNE—Dentsu, Young & Rubicam Partnerships, pg. 331
MATTINGLY & PARTNERS/SYDNEY—Dentsu, Young & Rubicam Partnerships, pg. 331
MCADAMS, RICHMAN & ONG, INC., pg. 725
MCCAFFERY & RATNER, INC., pg. 726
MCFARLAND & DRIER, INC., pg. 729
MCFARLAND & DRIER INTERNATIONAL—McFarland & Drier, Inc., pg. 729
MEDIA DECISIONS—Backer Spielvogel Bates Worldwide, Inc., pg. 112
MEDIA MARKETING RESEARCH—Backer Spielvogel Bates Worldwide, Inc., pg. 112
MELDRUM & FEWSMITH COMMUNICATIONS INC., pg. 737
STAN MERRITT INC./ADVERTISING, pg. 741
MEYER & WALLIS, INC., pg. 746
MILLER MEESTER ADVERTISING INC., pg. 754
MORADPOUR, DALSACE, LANGLOIS, PIZANTI—Young & Rubicam Inc., pg. 1212
ERIC MOWER AND ASSOCIATES/BUFFALO, INC.—Eric Mower and Associates, Inc., pg. 774
ERIC MOWER AND ASSOCIATES, INC., pg. 774
MULTICONTACT—Young & Rubicam Inc., pg. 1212
N&T LEO BURNETT A/S—Leo Burnett Company, Inc., pg. 193
NATIONAL MEDIA SERVICES, INC.—TMP Worldwide, Inc., pg. 1074
NELSON & SCHMIDT, INC., pg. 797
NOORDERVLIET & WINNINGHOFF/LEO BURNETT B.V.—Leo Burnett Company, Inc., pg. 193
NORGARD MIKKELSEN REKLAMEBUREAU A/S—Backer Spielvogel Bates Worldwide, Inc., pg. 112
NU-SAFE REPORTING—Gerber Advertising, pg. 453
O'T.V. & O'SPACE—Young & Rubicam Inc., pg. 1212
VIC OLESEN & PARTNERS, INC., pg. 824
ORIENTAL SOURCE—Dentsu, Young & Rubicam Partnerships, pg. 331
P/O/N SERVICE CORP.—Penny/Ohlmann/Neiman, Inc., pg. 858
PADOVA AYER—N W Ayer Incorporated, pg. 104
PARAGRAPHE/SUDLER & HENNESSEY—Young & Rubicam Inc., pg. 1212
GEORGE PATTERSON (BRISBANE) PTY LTD.—Backer Spielvogel Bates Worldwide, Inc., pg. 112
GEORGE PATTERSON PTY. LIMITED—Backer Spielvogel Bates Worldwide, Inc., pg. 112
PENNY/OHLMANN/NEIMAN, INC., pg. 858
PERDOMO-TED BATES/PUBLICIDAD—Backer Spielvogel Bates Worldwide, Inc., pg. 112
PIRELLA GOETTSCHE LOWE S.P.A.—The Lowe Group, pg. 685
PIRELLA GOETTSCHE LOWE S.P.A.—The Lowe Group, pg. 685
THE PLUMMER GROUP—Warner, Bicking, Morris & Partners, Inc., pg. 1164
POOL COMMUNICATIONS - CHICAGO—Pool Communications, pg. 880
POOL COMMUNICATIONS, pg. 880
POPPE TYSON, pg. 880
POTTER HAZLEHURST INCORPORATED, pg. 882
PRINS, MEIJER, STAMENKOVITS EN VAN WALBEEK/ YOUNG & RUBICAM B.V.—Young & Rubicam Inc., pg. 1212
PROCTOR & GARDNER ADVERTISING, INC., pg. 892
PUBLIMERCA S.A.—N W Ayer Incorporated, pg. 105
DR. PUTTNER & BSB WORLDWIDE WERBEGESELLSCHAFT M.B.H.—Backer Spielvogel Bates Worldwide, Inc., pg. 111
QUANTA ADVERTISING CORPORATION—Carrols Corporation, pg. 225
RTA ADVERTISING, INC.—Leo Burnett Company, Inc., pg. 193
RADIUS ADVERTISING—Leo Burnett Company, Inc., pg. 193
RAYON VERT—Young & Rubicam Inc., pg. 1212
REDIFFUSION—Dentsu, Young & Rubicam Partnerships, pg. 331
RICE & RICE INC.—Valentine-Radford, Inc., pg. 1143
RIECHELMANN, LOPES CARDOZO & VAN BERCUM B.V.—Young & Rubicam Inc., pg. 1212
HAL RINEY & PARTNERS, INC.—Hal Riney & Partners, Inc., pg. 935
HAL RINEY & PARTNERS, INC.—Hal Riney & Partners, Inc., pg. 935
HAL RINEY & PARTNERS, INC., pg. 935
ROBINSON & ST. JOHN ADVERTISING & PUBLIC RELATIONS, INC., pg. 940
ROBINSON, YESAWICH & PEPPERDINE, pg. 940
ROSS ROY CANADA, LTD.—Ross Roy Group, Inc., pg. 950
ROSS ROY COMMUNICATIONS—Ross Roy Group, Inc., pg. 950
ROSS ROY COMMUNICATIONS CANADA, INC.—Ross Roy Group, Inc., pg. 950
ROSS ROY GROUP, INC., pg. 949
ROSS ROY INC.—Ross Roy Group, Inc., pg. 950
ROSS ROY RETAIL—Ross Roy Group, Inc., pg. 950
ROTA ADVERTISING LIMITED—Backer Spielvogel Bates Worldwide, Inc., pg. 112
RUBIN POSTAER & ASSOCIATES, pg. 954
RUDER, FINN, INC., pg. 954
CHUCK RUHR ADVERTISING, pg. 955
SCANELO, YOUNG & RUBICAM AS—Young & Rubicam Inc., pg. 1212
SCHOLZ & FRIENDS DESIGN GMBH—Backer Spielvogel Bates Worldwide, Inc., pg. 112
SCHOLZ & FRIENDS GMBH—Backer Spielvogel Bates Worldwide, Inc., pg. 112
SERINO COYNE INC., pg. 991
SIEGEL & GALE, pg. 1002
SIGMA—Young & Rubicam Inc., pg. 1212
SIMMS & MCIVOR MARKETING COMMUNICATIONS, pg. 1005
SIMONS MICHELSON ZIEVE, INC., pg. 1006
SISTA'S PRIVATE LIMITED—Backer Spielvogel Bates Worldwide, Inc., pg. 112
SIVE/YOUNG & RUBICAM—Young & Rubicam Inc., pg. 1211
SMITH/GREENLAND, INCORPORATED, pg. 1012
SPRING, O'BRIEN & CO. INC., pg. 1033
STANDLEY BURRIDGE COLLINGS LTD.—Backer Spielvogel Bates Worldwide, Inc., pg. 112
STEPHAN & BRADY, INCORPORATED, pg. 1046
THE STOGEL COMPANIES INC., pg. 1050
STONE, AUGUST, BAKER COMMUNICATIONS COMPANIES, pg. 1050
STONE & SIMONS ADVERTISING, INC., pg. 1051
STONE & SIMONS ADVERTISING, INC.—Stone & Simons Advertising, Inc., pg. 1051
STRATEGIC IDENTITY CONSULTANTS—Young & Rubicam Inc., pg. 1212
SUDLER & HENNESSEY—Young & Rubicam Inc., pg. 1211
SUDLER & HENNESSEY CANADA—Young & Rubicam Inc., pg. 1213
SUDLER & HENNESSEY CONSUMER GROUP—Young & Rubicam Inc., pg. 1211
SUDLER & HENNESSEY LIMITED—Young & Rubicam Inc., pg. 1212
SUDLER & HENNESSEY SYDNEY—Young & Rubicam Inc., pg. 1214
THE SUSSMAN/ZICCARDI GROUP, pg. 1065
SYNERGETICS, INC.—Simms & McIvor Marketing Communications, pg. 1006
TBWA ADVERTISING, INC., pg. 1071
TBWA DE PLAS—TBWA Advertising, Inc., pg. 1072
TBWA DUSSELDORF GMBH—TBWA Advertising, Inc., pg. 1072
TBWA ESPANA S.A.—TBWA Advertising, Inc., pg. 1072
DE TBWA GROEP B.V.—TBWA Advertising, Inc., pg. 1072
TBWA HOLMES KNIGHT RITCHIE—TBWA Advertising, Inc., pg. 1072
TBWA KERLICK SWITZER—TBWA Advertising, Inc., pg. 1071
TDA, pg. 1072
TMP WORLDWIDE, INC., pg. 1073
TMP WORLDWIDE, INC.—TMP Worldwide, Inc., pg. 1074
TMP WORLDWIDE, INC.—TMP Worldwide, Inc., pg. 1074
TMP WORLDWIDE, INC.—TMP Worldwide, Inc., pg. 1074
TMP WORLDWIDE, INC.—TMP Worldwide, Inc., pg. 1074
TTA/NEWPORT, INC.—Ted Thomas Associates Inc., Advertising, pg. 1092
TAPSA AYER—N W Ayer Incorporated, pg. 104
TAPSA AYER—N W Ayer Incorporated, pg. 104
TARGETS ADV.—Leo Burnett Company, Inc., pg. 193
TAUCHER, YOUNG & RUBICAM—Young & Rubicam Inc., pg. 1212
TELEPHONE DIRECTORY ADVERTISING, INC.-CINCINNATI—TMP Worldwide, Inc., pg. 1074
TEMKIN & TEMKIN, pg. 1086
TED THOMAS ASSOCIATES INC., ADVERTISING, pg. 1092
TILLBROOKS STUDIOS—Backer Spielvogel Bates Worldwide, Inc., pg. 112
TINSLEY ADVERTISING, pg. 1099
TOWNE, SILVERSTEIN, ROTTER INC., pg. 1104
TRIANGLE PACIFIC—Dentsu, Young & Rubicam Partnerships, pg. 331
TUCKER WAYNE/LUCKIE & COMPANY, pg. 1118
U-HAUL INTERNATIONAL, INC.—Amerco, A Nevada Corporation, pg. 48
U.R.M. STORES, INC., pg. 1124
VIP PUBLICIDAD—Backer Spielvogel Bates Worldwide, Inc., pg. 112
VALENTINE-RADFORD, INC., pg. 1142
VEDA DESIGN GROUP—Veda International, Inc., pg. 1146
VINIZIUS/YOUNG & RUBICAM, S.A.—Young & Rubicam Inc., pg. 1212
HARRY VIOLA ADVERTISING, pg. 1152
VITRUVIO/LEO BURNETT—Leo Burnett Company, Inc., pg. 193
WALKER & ASSOCIATES, INC., pg. 1159
WARING & LAROSA, INC., pg. 1163
WARNER, BICKING, MORRIS & PARTNERS, INC., pg. 1164
WARWICK BAKER & FIORE INC., pg. 1165
THE WEIGHTMAN GROUP, pg. 1173
WEIGHTMAN PUBLIC RELATIONS—The Weightman Group, pg. 1173
WEIGHTMAN RESEARCH—The Weightman Group, pg. 1173
WEINBERGER WERBEHAUS GES.M.B.H & CO. KG—N W Ayer Incorporated, pg. 105
WEST ADVERTISING/PUBLIC RELATIONS, INC.—KOA Holdings, pg. 613
WEST & COMPANY MARKETING & ADVERTISING, pg. 1177
WESTERN INTERNATIONAL MEDIA CORPORATION, pg. 1179
WILKENS AYER—N W Ayer Incorporated, pg. 104
WILLIAMS WHITTLE ASSOCIATES, INC., pg. 1191
WOLFF & PARTNER—Backer Spielvogel Bates Worldwide, Inc., pg. 112
WRAY-WARD-LASETER ADVERTISING, pg. 1204
WUNDERMAN—Young & Rubicam Inc., pg. 1212
WUNDERMAN—Dentsu, Young & Rubicam Partnerships, pg. 331
WUNDERMAN CATO JOHNSON—Young & Rubicam Inc., pg. 1211
WUNDERMAN CATO JOHNSON FRANCE—Young & Rubicam Inc., pg. 1212
WUNDERMAN DO BRAZIL—Young & Rubicam Inc., pg. 1213
WUNDERMAN TENDER—Young & Rubicam Inc., pg. 1212
WUNDERMAN WORLDWIDE—Young & Rubicam Inc., pg. 1212
WUNDERMAN WORLDWIDE—Young & Rubicam Inc., pg. 1211
WUNDERMAN WORLDWIDE AB—Young & Rubicam Inc., pg. 1212
WUNDERMAN WORLDWIDE A/S—Young & Rubicam Inc., pg. 1212
WUNDERMAN WORLDWIDE LIMITED—Young & Rubicam Inc., pg. 1212
WUNDERMAN WORLDWIDE V.O.F.—Young & Rubicam Inc., pg. 1212
WYSE ADVERTISING, INC., pg. 1206
YPMS/TMP WORLDWIDE, INC.—TMP Worldwide, Inc., pg. 1074
Y&R CAPE—Young & Rubicam Inc., pg. 1214
Y&R CAPITAL IMAGE—Young & Rubicam Inc., pg. 1212
Y&R TRANSVAAL—Young & Rubicam Inc., pg. 1214
YOUNG & RUBICAM—Young & Rubicam Inc., pg. 1213
YOUNG & RUBICAM ARGENTINA—Young & Rubicam Inc., pg. 1213
YOUNG & RUBICAM BELGIUM S.A.—Young & Rubicam Inc., pg. 1212
YOUNG & RUBICAM BRASIL—Young & Rubicam Inc., pg. 1213
YOUNG & RUBICAM CAPE—Young & Rubicam Inc., pg. 1214
YOUNG & RUBICAM CHICAGO—Young & Rubicam Inc., pg. 1211
YOUNG & RUBICAM COPENHAGEN—Young & Rubicam Inc., pg. 1213
YOUNG & RUBICAM CZECHOSLOVAKIA—Young & Rubicam Inc., pg. 1212
YOUNG & RUBICAM DE CHILE LTDA.—Young & Rubicam Inc., pg. 1213
YOUNG & RUBICAM DETROIT—Young & Rubicam Inc., pg. 1211
YOUNG & RUBICAM EST—Young & Rubicam Inc., pg. 1212
YOUNG & RUBICAM GOTEBURG AB—Young & Rubicam Inc., pg. 1213
YOUNG & RUBICAM HEDLEY BYRNE CAPE—Young & Rubicam Inc., pg. 1214
YOUNG & RUBICAM-HEDLEY BYRNE TRANSVAAL—Young & Rubicam Inc., pg. 1214
YOUNG & RUBICAM HOLDINGS LTD.—Young & Rubicam Inc., pg. 1213
YOUNG & RUBICAM INC., pg. 1210
YOUNG & RUBICAM INTERNATIONAL EUROPEAN HDQRS.—Young & Rubicam Inc., pg. 1213
YOUNG & RUBICAM ITALIA, S.P.A.—Young & Rubicam Inc., pg. 1213
YOUNG & RUBICAM NEW YORK—Young & Rubicam Inc., pg. 1211
YOUNG & RUBICAM & OGMIOS—Young & Rubicam Inc., pg. 1213
YOUNG & RUBICAM OUEST—Young & Rubicam Inc., pg. 1213
YOUNG & RUBICAM (PORTUGAL)—Young & Rubicam Inc., pg. 1213
YOUNG & RUBICAM PTY. LTD.—Young & Rubicam Inc., pg. 1214
YOUNG & RUBICAM, S.A.—Young & Rubicam Inc., pg. 1213
YOUNG & RUBICAM SAN FRANCISCO—Young & Rubicam Inc., pg. 1211
YOUNG & RUBICAM SUD OUEST—Young & Rubicam Inc., pg. 1213
YOUNG & RUBICAM (ZAMBIA) LTD.—Young & Rubicam Inc., pg. 1214
ZECHMAN & ASSOCIATES ADV. INC., pg. 1216
ZYLKE & ASSOCIATES, pg. 1221

7312 — OUTDOOR ADVERTISING SERVICES

DONREY MEDIA GROUP, pg. 345
DUALITE INC., pg. 350
DUALITE SALES & SERVICE, INC.—Dualite Inc., pg. 350
MORRIS CORPORATION—Shivers Trading & Operating Co., pg. 999
SIGNBOARD HILL PRODUCTIONS—Hallmark Cards, Inc., pg. 502

7313 — RADIO, TELEVISION & PUBLISHERS' ADVERTISING REPRESENTATIVES

BANNER RADIO—Katz Communications, Inc., pg. 618
JOHN BLAIR COMMUNICATIONS, INC., pg. 155
CABLEREP, INC.—Cox Enterprises, Inc., pg. 294
CHRISTAL RADIO—Katz Communications, Inc., pg. 618
CRESMER, WOODWARD, O'MARA & ORMSBEE, pg. 298
EASTMAN RADIO, INC.—Katz Communications, Inc., pg. 618
KATZ AMERICAN TELEVISION—Katz Communications, Inc., pg. 618
KATZ COMMUNICATIONS, INC., pg. 618
KATZ CONTINENTAL TELEVISION—Katz Communications, Inc., pg. 618
KATZ HISPANIC RADIO SALES—Katz Communications, Inc., pg. 618
KATZ INDEPENDENT TELEVISION—Katz Communications, Inc., pg. 618
KATZ RADIO—Katz Communications, Inc., pg. 618
NEWHOUSE NEWSPAPERS METRO-SUBURBIA, INC.—Advance Publications Inc., pg. 19
RUXTON GROUP—Chicago Reader, Inc., pg. 246
TELEREP, INCORPORATED—Cox Enterprises, Inc., pg. 293
THE WEATHER CHANNEL, INC.-ATLANTA SALES OFFICE—Landmark Communications, Inc., pg. 654
THE WEATHER CHANNEL, INC.-CHICAGO SALES OFFICE—Landmark Communications, Inc., pg. 654
THE WEATHER CHANNEL, INC.-DETROIT SALES OFFICE—Landmark Communications, Inc., pg. 654
THE WEATHER CHANNEL, INC.-LOS ANGELES SALES OFFICE—Landmark Communications, Inc., pg. 654
THE WEATHER CHANNEL, INC.-NEW YORK SALES OFFICE—Landmark Communications, Inc., pg. 654

7319 — ADVERTISING, NEC

ADVERTISING CHECKING BUREAU INCORPORATED, pg. 21
AMERICAN MANUFACTURING CO. (TN), pg. 58
AMERICAN PASSAGE MEDIA CORPORATION, pg. 59
ASSOCIATED DRUGGISTS—Cullman Ventures, Inc., pg. 304
ATLAS PEN & PENCIL CORPORATION, pg. 96
BURKE COMMUNICATION INDUSTRIES, INC., pg. 190
CPM, INC., pg. 203
CRN INTERNATIONAL, INC., pg. 203
CHICAGO SHOW PRINTING CO., pg. 246
CORINTHIAN MEDIA, INC., pg. 286
DRAPER DANIELS MEDIA SERVICES, INC., pg. 348
FOGARTY & KLEIN SALES PROMOTION, INC.—Fogarty & Klein/Winius Brandon, pg. 421
H & H ADVERTISING, pg. 496
HARRIS & DRUTT INC., pg. 511
IDC SERVICES, INC., pg. 559
JII/SALES PROMOTION ASSOCIATES, INC.—Jordan Industries, Inc., pg. 604
LAMARCA GROUP INC., pg. 652
MEDIA BUYERS, INC.—Asher/Gould Advertising, Inc., pg. 88
MEDIACOMP MEDIA MANAGEMENT SERVICES—Mediacomp, Inc., pg. 735
PHARMACISTS PUBLIC RELATIONS BUREAU—Cullman Ventures, Inc., pg. 304
QUAD/GRAPHICS, INC., pg. 902
RAMA GROUP OF COMPANIES, pg. 910
VITT MEDIA INTERNATIONAL, INC., pg. 1153
DAVID R. WILLIAMS, INC.—Vitt Media International, Inc., pg. 1154

7322 — ADJUSTMENT & COLLECTION SERVICES

G L SUB COMPANY—The Marmon Group, Inc., pg. 712
I.C. SYSTEM, INC., pg. 558
MASTER COLLECTORS INC., pg. 719
VENGROFF WILLIAMS & ASSOCIATES, INC., pg. 1147

7323 — CREDIT REPORTING SERVICES

TRANS UNION CORP.—The Marmon Group, Inc., pg. 712

7331 — DIRECT MAIL ADVERTISING SERVICES

ADVERTISING DISTRIBUTORS OF MARYLAND, INC.—Harte-Hanks Communications, Inc., pg. 513
AMERICAN BUSINESS INFORMATION, INC., pg. 50
ASBURY PARK PRESS, INC.—New Jersey Press, Inc., pg. 801
ATLAS PEN & PENCIL CORPORATION, pg. 96
CHANNING L. BETE CO., INC., pg. 147
BLADE COMMUNICATIONS, INC., pg. 155
BRADFORD EXCHANGE LTD., pg. 170
BRIAN UNLIMITED DISTRIBUTION COMPANY, INC., pg. 175
CGF INDUSTRIES, pg. 201
COLONY PRESS INC.—Jupiter Industries, Inc., pg. 609
COMMONWEALTH DIRECT MARKETING—Landmark Communications, Inc., pg. 656
CONTINENTAL WEB PRESS, INC., pg. 280
CORINTHIAN DIRECT—Corinthian Media, Inc., pg. 286
CREATIVE TECHNICAL SERVICES—The Direct Marketing Group Inc., pg. 339
CUSTOM EVENT MARKETING, INC.—Backer Spielvogel Bates Worldwide, Inc., pg. 109
DIMAC DIRECT—DIMAC Corporation, pg. 338
DONNELLEY MARKETING, INC.—Peter W. Smith & Company, Inc., pg. 1011
BRUCE W. EBERLE & ASSOCIATES—Eberle Direct Marketing Group, Inc., pg. 365
EVA-TONE INC., pg. 390
FITTS-LAWRENCE, INC.—Lawrence Group, Inc., pg. 662
FLEMING PACKAGING CORP., pg. 417
FOGARTY & KLEIN SALES PROMOTION, INC.—Fogarty & Klein/Winius Brandon, pg. 421
GREATER HOUSTON MAILING SERVICE, INC.—Harte-Hanks Communications, Inc., pg. 513
HAINES & CO., INC., pg. 500
HARTE-HANKS COMMUNICATIONS, INC., pg. 513
HARTE-HANKS DIRECT MAIL/CALIFORNIA—Harte-Hanks Communications, Inc., pg. 513
HARTE-HANKS DIRECT MARKETING/ PENNSYLVANIA—Harte-Hanks Communications, Inc., pg. 513
HIBBERT GROUP, pg. 532
I.C. SYSTEM, INC., pg. 558
IMPERIAL LITHO/GRAPHICS, INC., pg. 564
THE INSTANT WEB COMPANIES, pg. 571
JOHNSON & QUIN, INC., pg. 599
JORDAN DENNIS COMPANY, INC.—Harte-Hanks Communications, Inc., pg. 513
THE JUPITER CORPORATION—Jupiter Industries, Inc., pg. 609
K&B DBM MARKETING OY—Backer Spielvogel Bates Worldwide, Inc., pg. 111
K&D ADAPTUS DIRECT—Backer Spielvogel Bates Worldwide, Inc., pg. 112
K&D BOND DIRECT—Backer Spielvogel Bates Worldwide, Inc., pg. 112
KOBS & DRAFT—Backer Spielvogel Bates Worldwide, Inc., pg. 112
KOBS & DRAFT ADVERTISING, INC.—Backer Spielvogel Bates Worldwide, Inc., pg. 109
MARKETING COMMUNICATIONS, pg. 709
MAY & SPEH DIRECT—May & Speh, Inc., pg. 724
MAY & SPEH, INC., pg. 724
MEASURED MARKETING SERVICES, pg. 734
MID-AMERICA CDM, INC.—Harte-Hanks Communications, Inc., pg. 513
NEW JERSEY PRESS, INC., pg. 801
OMEGA LIST COMPANY—Eberle Direct Marketing Group, Inc., pg. 365
PENNYSAVER PUBLICATIONS, INC. (THE SHOPPER'S GUIDE)—Harte-Hanks Communications, Inc., pg. 513
R. L. POLK & CO., pg. 879
SCICOM DATA SERVICES, LTD., pg. 981
THE SEGERDAHL CORP., pg. 987
SHOPPER'S GUIDE, INC. (TUCSON SHOPPER)—Harte-Hanks Communications, Inc., pg. 513
THE SIGNATURE GROUP—Montgomery Ward & Co., Inc., pg. 768
TABS ASSOCIATES, pg. 1076
WEBCRAFT TECHNOLOGIES, INC., pg. 1171
WUNDERMAN TAUCHER TURKU OY—Young & Rubicam Inc., pg. 1212

7334 — PHOTOCOPY & DUPLICATING SERVICES

KINKO'S CORPORATION, pg. 632
PIP CAPITAL INC.—Kane-Miller Corp., pg. 616

7335 — COMMERCIAL PHOTOGRAPHY

APPLIED GRAPHICS TECHNOLOGIES—U.S. News & World Report, pg. 1136
EARLE PALMER BROWN, pg. 182
DELMAR STUDIOS—Continental Graphics Holdings, Inc., pg. 279
FRANKLIN PRESS—Continental Graphics Holdings, Inc., pg. 279
WALKER-PIONEER MOSS, pg. 1160

7336 — COMMERCIAL ART & GRAPHIC DESIGN

APPLIED GRAPHICS TECHNOLOGIES—U.S. News & World Report, pg. 1136
EARLE PALMER BROWN, pg. 182
HARTE-HANKS GRAPHICS—Harte-Hanks Communications, Inc., pg. 513
INFORMATION SYSTEMS—Database America Companies, pg. 316
M M S DESIGN—Measured Marketing Services, pg. 734
MADISON GRAHAM COLORGRAPHICS, INC., pg. 699
ALBERT C. MARTIN & ASSOCIATES, pg. 714
MARTIN UNIVERSAL DESIGN, INC., pg. 715
MESSENGER CORPORATION, pg. 741
NOBART, INC., pg. 808
HAROLD M. PITMAN CO., INC., pg. 872
RALEIGH ENTERPRISES, INC., pg. 910
RAM GRAPHICS, INC., pg. 910
RAND MCNALLY BOOK & MEDIA SERVICES—Rand McNally & Company, pg. 911
TAYLOR'S HITEK PRODUCT FINISHING, INC.—Cowden Metal Specialties, Inc., pg. 291
VIKING GRAPHICS, pg. 1151
WALKER-PIONEER MOSS, pg. 1160

7342 — DISINFECTING & PEST CONTROL SERVICES

PRISM INTEGRATED SANITATION MANAGEMENT, INC.—S. C. Johnson & Son, Inc., pg. 599
TERMINIX SERVICE, INC., pg. 1088
TRIANGLE MAINTENANCE CORPORATION, pg. 1112

7349 — BUILDING CLEANING & MAINTENANCE SERVICES, NEC

ARA FOOD SERVICES, LTD.—ARA Group, pg. 7
ARA SERVICES, INC.—ARA Group, pg. 5
ADMIRAL MAINTENANCE SERVICE L.P., pg. 18
ANTARES GROUP INC., pg. 76
ARATEX SERVICES—ARA Group, pg. 6
CBM INDUSTRIES, INC., pg. 199
CHARING CROSS GROUP, pg. 239
COLIN SERVICE SYSTEMS, INC., pg. 261
DEFENDER SERVICES, INC., pg. 324
EBSC CORPORATION, pg. 359
JANI KING, INC.—Jani King International, Inc., pg. 589
JANI KING INTERNATIONAL, INC., pg. 589
JOFFKO INTERNATIONAL, pg. 595
MASON & HANGER SERVICES INC.—Mason Company, pg. 718
MASON HANGER-SILAS MASON CO.—Mason Company, pg. 718
MIDWESCO INC., pg. 751
MODERN BUILDING CLEANING INC.—ARA Group, pg. 7
NATIONAL CLEANING CONTRACTORS, INC., pg. 786
PARSONS BRINCKERHOFF FACILITIES SERVICES, INC.—Parsons Brinckerhoff Inc., pg. 850
S & C MAINTENANCE CORP.—Spatz & Co., pg. 1026
SADCO LTD.—Joffko International, pg. 595
TRIANGLE MAINTENANCE CORPORATION, pg. 1112
VERSA SERVICES LTD.—ARA Group, pg. 7

7352 — MEDICAL EQUIPMENT RENTAL & LEASING

AT HOME RESPIRATORY AND MEDICAL, INC.—Syracuse Supply Company, pg. 1070
ATLANTIC HEALTH CARE RESOURCES, INC.—Syracuse Supply Company, pg. 1070
BERWIND PHARMACEUTICALS SERVICES, INC.—Berwind Corporation, pg. 145
CLINICARE SYSTEMS, INC.—Gaymar Industries, Inc., pg. 447
LINC SCIENTIFIC LEASING INC.—The LINC Group, Inc., pg. 648
LEADER LEASING, INC.—Leader Federal Bank For Savings, pg. 664
LINC CAPITAL CORPORATION—The LINC Group, Inc., pg. 648
LINC CAPITAL MANAGEMENT—The LINC Group, Inc., pg. 648
LINC EQUIPMENT SERVICES—The LINC Group, Inc., pg. 648
LINC MANAGEMENT SERVICES—The LINC Group, Inc., pg. 648
LINC MEDICAL IMAGING—The LINC Group, Inc., pg. 648
LINC QUANTUM ANALYTICS—The LINC Group, Inc., pg. 648
THE MEDISCUS GROUP, pg. 736
METRO MEDICAL RESOURCES, INC.—Syracuse Supply Company, pg. 1070
MOBILE TECHNOLOGY INC., pg. 762
MOUNTAINEER MEDICAL/PRIMACARE I.V.—Syracuse Supply Company, pg. 1070
PENN MEDICAL SERVICES, INC.—Syracuse Supply Company, pg. 1070
PRIMACARE HEALTH RESOURCES, INC.—Syracuse Supply Company, pg. 1070
SYRACUSE SUPPLY COMPANY, pg. 1070
TAYLOR HOME HEALTH INC.—Taylor Medical Inc., pg. 1081

7353 — HEAVY CONSTRUCTION EQUIPMENT RENTAL & LEASING

ACTION EQUIPMENT, pg. 14
BELLAMY BROTHERS CONSTRUCTING COMPANY—Bellamy Brothers, Inc., pg. 136
FOLEY HOLDING COMPANY, INC., pg. 422
HERTZ EQUIPMENT RENTAL CORP.—Park Ridge Corporation, pg. 849
MANESS INDUSTRIES, INC., pg. 703
MI-JACK PRODUCTS, INC., pg. 746
SYRACUSE SUPPLY COMPANY, pg. 1070
UNITED TECTONIC INDUSTRY, pg. 1137
UP-RIGHT, INC., pg. 1139
WILLIAMS CRANE & RIGGING, INC.—Williams International Industries, Inc., pg. 1191
WILLIAMS INTERNATIONAL INDUSTRIES, INC., pg. 1191

7359 — EQUIPMENT RENTAL & LEASING, NEC

A & N LEASING—Service Motor Company, pg. 992
ALLBRITTON NEWS BUREAU, INC.—Perpetual Corporation, pg. 862
ALOHA AIRLINES, INC.—Aloha Airgroup, Inc., pg. 43
AMERICAN FINANCE GROUP, pg. 52
AMES TAPING TOOL SYSTEMS CO.—AXIA Incorporated, pg. 8
ANDYS RENTAL INC.—X-A Cabinet Corporation, pg. 1206
ATLANTIC NATIONAL CORPORATION—Hawthorne Corp., pg. 519
BARNSTORM AVIATION—International Airline Support Group, Inc., pg. 575
BOWHEAD EQUIPMENT COMPANY—Lynden Incorporated, pg. 689
BUDCO GROUP INC., pg. 186
CANYON CAPITAL INC.—KOA Holdings, pg. 612
CARLSON LEASING, INC.—Carlson Companies, Inc., pg. 221
CHESSCO CAPITAL CORP.—Chessco Industries, Inc., pg. 244
CHICAGO HOLDINGS, INC., pg. 245

CLARKLIFT OF MINNESOTA, INC., pg. 253
CLOVERDALE EQUIPMENT CO., pg. 256
CONNELL RICE & SUGAR CO., pg. 275
THE CURRY CORPORATION, pg. 305
DATA PREFERENCE, INC.—The Marmon Group, Inc., pg. 712
ECONOCOM-USA INC., pg. 367
EMPIRE SOUTHWEST CO., pg. 379
FRANKS SUPPLY COMPANY, INC., pg. 429
FURNIVAL/STATE MACHINERY CO., pg. 437
GOODMANS, INC., pg. 471
GRANTREE CORPORATION, pg. 477
GREAT AMERICAN MANAGEMENT SERVICES, INC.—American Financial Corporation, pg. 53
HASPER EQUIPMENT CO.—Cloverdale Equipment Co., pg. 256
HERTZ EQUIPMENT RENTAL CORP.—Park Ridge Corporation, pg. 849
INDECK POWER EQUIPMENT COMPANY, pg. 564
INTEGRATED RESOURCES EQUIPMENT GROUP, INC.—Integrated Resources, Inc., pg. 573
INTERNATIONAL AIRLINE SUPPORT GROUP, INC., pg. 575
KOA HOLDINGS, pg. 612
THE LINC GROUP, INC., pg. 648
LAMAR LEASING CO., INC.—Capitol Street Corp., pg. 216
LEADER LEASING, INC.—Leader Federal Bank For Savings, pg. 664
LEASAMETRIC, INC.—The Marmon Group, Inc., pg. 712
LIBCO CORPORATION, pg. 674
MPO VIDEOTRONICS, INC., pg. 693
THE MARMON GROUP, INC., pg. 710
THE MEDISCUS GROUP, pg. 736
METLIFE CAPITAL CREDIT CORP.—Metropolitan Life Insurance Co., pg. 744
MILWAUKEE ELECTRIC TOOL (CANADA) LTD.—ESSTAR Incorporated, pg. 361
MODERN EQUIPMENT RENTALS INC.—Modern Group Ltd., pg. 763
MODERN GROUP LTD., pg. 762
MODERN HANDLING EQUIPMENT CO. OF NY—Modern Group Ltd., pg. 763
MODERN HANDLING EQUIPMENT CO.—Modern Group Ltd., pg. 763
MODERN HANDLING EQUIPMENT OF N.J., INC.—Modern Group Ltd., pg. 763
MORGAN INDUSTRIES INC., pg. 770
MULTIFORM ENTERPRISES, INC.—GranTree Corporation, pg. 478
NORTH AMERICAN FINANCIAL CORP.—Carlson Companies, Inc., pg. 221
O/B LEASING COMPANY—Budco Group Inc., pg. 186
PHOENIX FIBER LINK INC.—Phoenix American Incorporated, pg. 868
PHOENIX SYSTEMS EXCHANGE, INC.—Phoenix American Incorporated, pg. 868
POP TV—MPO Videotronics, Inc., pg. 693
PROCRANE INC.—The Marmon Group, Inc., pg. 712
PROFESSIONAL SECURITIES CORP.—Huntco Inc., pg. 554
RAINBOW HOME RENTALS, pg. 910
RAY SATELLITE NETWORK—Ray Communications, Inc., pg. 914
REMCO ENTERPRISES, INC., pg. 926
RENTAL AMERICA—America Outdoors Ltd, pg. 48
SD LEASING COMPANY—Stephens, Inc., pg. 1046
SERVICE MOTOR COMPANY, pg. 992
SEVEN SEAS LEASING—International Airline Support Group, Inc., pg. 575
SOUTH ATLANTIC EQUIPMENT, INC.—The Dickerson Group, Inc., pg. 336
STEINER CORPORATION, pg. 1045
SUN FINANCIAL GROUP, INC., pg. 1058
SYRACUSE SUPPLY COMPANY, pg. 1070
TSE LEASING CO.—I. Spiewak & Sons, Inc., pg. 1031
TELCO CAPITAL CORP.—Libco Corporation, pg. 674
TELMARK, INC.—Agway, Inc., pg. 25
TRIUMPH*LOR, INC., pg. 1115
TRIUMPH/LOR OILFIELD SERVICES LTD.—Triumph*Lor, Inc., pg. 1115
U-HAUL INTERNATIONAL, INC.—Amerco, A Nevada Corporation, pg. 48
UP-RIGHT, INC., pg. 1139
VICTAULIC TOOL COMPANY—Victaulic Company of America, pg. 1149
WILDCAT LTD.—International Airline Support Group, Inc., pg. 575
WILSON INDUSTRIES INC., pg. 1193
WORLDWIDE LEASING—Hobart Brothers Co., pg. 537
YALE INDUSTRIAL TRUCKS OF SOUTHERN CALIFORNIA, pg. 1207
YOUNG ELECTRIC SIGN COMPANY, pg. 1209

7361 — EMPLOYMENT AGENCIES

CAPITOL INDUSTRIES-EMI INC., pg. 216
CAREER BLAZERS AGENCY, INC.—Career Blazers Inc., pg. 218
CAREER BLAZERS INC., pg. 218
CAREER BLAZERS OF WHITE PLAINS, INC.—Career Blazers Inc., pg. 218
CAREERS USA INC., pg. 218
FUTURES PERSONNEL SERVICES, pg. 438
GOODWILL INDUSTRIES OF AMERICA, INC., pg. 471
GRAY-PRO, INC., pg. 479
KORN/FERRY INTERNATIONAL, pg. 642
MILLER PERSONNEL, INC., pg. 755
NATIONAL EMERGENCY SERVICES, INC., pg. 788
PROGRESSIVE DRIVER SERVICES, INC., pg. 894
PURCELL INTERNATIONAL GROUP, INC., pg. 900
SMITH'S PERSONNEL SERVICE, INC., pg. 1014
TOP BILLING INC., pg. 1101
WESTERN SERVICE A/S—Western Temporary Services, Inc., pg. 1182
WESTERN SERVICE, INC.—Western Temporary Services, Inc., pg. 1182
WESTERN STAFF SERVICES (NZ) LTD.—Western Temporary Services, Inc., pg. 1182
WESTERN STAFF SERVICES (U.K.) LTD.—Western Temporary Services, Inc., pg. 1182
WESTERN TEMPORARY SERVICES, INC., pg. 1181

7363 — HELP SUPPLY SERVICES

BARRY SERVICES COMPANY—Day & Zimmermann, Inc., pg. 320
CORS, pg. 203
CAREER BLAZERS INC., pg. 218
CAREER BLAZERS LEARNING CENTER—Career Blazers Inc., pg. 218
CAREER BLAZERS TEMPORARY PERSONNEL—Career Blazers Inc., pg. 218
COMPUTER ENTERPRISES, INC.—Technical Aid Corporation, pg. 1083
DAY DATA SYSTEMS—Day & Zimmermann, Inc., pg. 320
DAY & ZIMMERMANN, INC., pg. 320
EDP/TEMPS INC.—Technical Aid Corporation, pg. 1083
ANDY FRAIN SERVICES, INC., pg. 428
GRAY-PRO, INC., pg. 479
HOME CARE P.R.N., INC.—Technical Aid Corporation, pg. 1083
KONTORSERVICE INC.—Western Temporary Services, Inc., pg. 1182
MICROTEMPS SYSTEMS & PROGRAMMING—Technical Aid Corporation, pg. 1083
NORRELL CORPORATION, pg. 810
NORRELL HEALTH CARE INC.—Norrell Corporation, pg. 811
PEOPLEMARK, INC.—Guardsmark, Inc., pg. 493
PIONEER ENGINEERING & MANUFACTURING CO., pg. 871
SALEM TECHNICAL SERVICES—Day & Zimmermann, Inc., pg. 320
SMITH'S PERSONNEL SERVICE, INC., pg. 1014
SYSTEMS MANAGEMENT & DEVELOPMENT—Technical Aid Corporation, pg. 1083
TAC/MEDICAL SERVICES INC.—Technical Aid Corporation, pg. 1083
TAC/TEMPS INC.—Technical Aid Corporation, pg. 1083
TECH/AID—Technical Aid Corporation, pg. 1083
TECHNICAL AID CORPORATION, pg. 1083
TEMPORARIES, INCORPORATED, pg. 1086
TEMPS & COMPANY, pg. 1086
WATKINS SYSTEM INC., pg. 1167
WESTERN MEDICAL SERVICES DIV.—Western Temporary Services, Inc., pg. 1182
WESTERN PERMANENT SERVICES AGENCY, INC.—Western Temporary Services, Inc., pg. 1182
WESTERN PERSONNEL SERVICES PTY. LTD.—Western Temporary Services, Inc., pg. 1182
WESTERN SERVICE A/S—Western Temporary Services, Inc., pg. 1182
WESTERN SERVICE, INC.—Western Temporary Services, Inc., pg. 1182
WESTERN STAFF SERVICES (NZ) LTD.—Western Temporary Services, Inc., pg. 1182
WESTERN STAFF SERVICES (U.K.) LTD.—Western Temporary Services, Inc., pg. 1182
WESTERN TECHNICAL DIV.—Western Temporary Services, Inc., pg. 1182
WESTERN TEMPORARY SERVICES, INC., pg. 1181
WESTERN TEMPORARY SERVICES OFFICE DIV.—Western Temporary Services, Inc., pg. 1182
WESTERN TEMPORARY SERVICES (USA), INC.—Western Temporary Services, Inc., pg. 1182
H. L. YOH COMPANY—Day & Zimmermann, Inc., pg. 320

7371 — COMPUTER PROGRAMMING SERVICES

ADRA SYSTEMS, INC., pg. 18
AUSTIN CONSULTING—National Gypsum Company, pg. 790
CINCOM SYSTEMS, INC., pg. 250
COMPUTER CORPORATION OF AMERICA—Praxis International Inc., pg. 884
COMPUTER TECHNOLOGY MANAGEMENT INC.—A. Epstein and Sons, Intl., Inc., pg. 384
COMPUTERLAND—ComputerLand Corporation, pg. 271
DWC COMPUTER SOLUTIONS INC.—Mason Company, pg. 718
DATABILITY, INC., pg. 316
DAXUS CORPORATION, pg. 319
FALCON ASSOCIATES, LTD.—Science Applications International Corporation, pg. 981
GENERAL COMPUTER CORP. INC., pg. 449
JCI DATA PROCESSING, INC., pg. 584
KENNEDY ASSOCIATES, pg. 623
LEVEL FIVE RESEARCH INC.—Information Builders, pg. 567
MARKETPULSE—Praxis International Inc., pg. 884
MASON COMPANY, pg. 718
MAVIS INDUSTRIES, INC.—General Computer Corp. Inc., pg. 449
MAY & SPEH, INC., pg. 724
MEDIACOMP, INC., pg. 735
MILLTECH-HOH, INC.—The HOH Organizations, pg. 497
NPS, INC.—Day & Zimmermann, Inc., pg. 321
NEXT, INC., pg. 805
NORRELL CORPORATION, pg. 810
OMNI INDUSTRY—Global Turnkey Systems Inc., pg. 463
OXFORD FIRST CORPORATION, pg. 834
PARADATA COMPUTER NETWORKS, INC., pg. 847
PRAXIS INTERNATIONAL INC., pg. 884
RMS TECHS, INC., pg. 907
RNL FACILITIES CORPORATION, pg. 907
RAND MCNALLY-TDM, INC.—Rand McNally & Company, pg. 911
SCIPAR, pg. 982
SEGUE PARTNERS—Praxis International Inc., pg. 885
SEGWAY PARTNERS—Praxis International Inc., pg. 885
SEGWAY PARTNERS—Praxis International Inc., pg. 885
SOFTOOL CORPORATION, pg. 1016
SPACE MANAGEMENT SYSTEMS—RNL Facilities Corporation, pg. 908
SVERDRUP CORPORATION, pg. 1065
SVERDRUP TECHNOLOGY, INC.—Sverdrup Corporation, pg. 1066
TENGEN—Atari Games Corporation, pg. 93
VEDA INCORPORATED—Veda International, Inc., pg. 1146
WESTERN DATA SYSTEMS, pg. 1178
WORDPERFECT CORPORATION, pg. 1202

7372 — PREPACKAGED SOFTWARE

APPX SOFTWARE—Kennedy Associates, pg. 623
ACTION INDUSTRIE COMPUTER, GMBH—Action Instruments, Inc., pg. 14
ACTION INSTRUMENTS, INC., pg. 14
ACTION INSTRUMENTS, S.A.—Action Instruments, Inc., pg. 15
AGWAY DATA SERVICES, INC.—Agway, Inc., pg. 25
AMERIDATA, INC., pg. 66
APPLIED MICROSYSTEMS CORPORATION, pg. 79
AUTOMATION INTELLIGENCE, INC., pg. 101
AUTOMATION INTELLIGENCE UK LTD.—Automation Intelligence, Inc., pg. 101
BNA SOFTWARE—The Bureau of National Affairs, Inc., pg. 189
BELLWETHER TECHNOLOGY CORPORATION, pg. 136
BETAC CORPORATION—Betac International Corporation, pg. 147
BOOZ ALLEN & HAMILTON INC., pg. 165
CANDLE CORPORATION, pg. 214
CENTRAL POINT SOFTWARE, INC., pg. 234
CHARTWAY TECHNOLOGIES, pg. 240
CINCOM SYSTEMS, INC., pg. 250
COMMUNICATIONS DATA SERVICES, INC.—The Hearst Corporation, pg. 523
COMPTON'S NEW MEDIA INC.—Encyclopaedia Britannica, Inc., pg. 381
COMPUADD CORPORATION, pg. 271
COMPUTER DYNAMICS, INC., pg. 271
COMPUTER INFORMATION SERVICES, INC.—Oxford First Corporation, pg. 834
COMPUTER METHODS CORPORATION, pg. 271
COMPUTER TECHNOLOGY MANAGEMENT INC.—A. Epstein and Sons, Intl., Inc., pg. 384
COMPUWARE CORPORATION, pg. 271
COVALENT SYSTEMS CORPORATION, pg. 290
CYBORG SYSTEMS OF CANADA—Cyborg Systems, Inc., pg. 307
CYBORG SYSTEMS, INC., pg. 307
CYBORG SYSTEMS (UK) LTD.—Cyborg Systems, Inc., pg. 307
DAQ ELECTRONICS INC., pg. 308
DWC COMPUTER SOLUTIONS INC.—Mason Company, pg. 718
DAKCO DISTRIBUTORS, INC., pg. 311
DAXUS CORPORATION, pg. 319
DECISION DATA COMPUTER (BELGIUM) S.A.—Decision Data Inc., pg. 324
DECISION DATA COMPUTER (GB) LTD.—Decision Data Inc., pg. 324
DISTRIBUTOR CONCEPTS—King Group, Inc., pg. 630
DORON PRECISION SYSTEMS, INC., pg. 346
EMS-MICHIGAN—Effective Management Systems, pg. 370
ERM-COMPUTER SERVICES, INC.—The ERM Group, pg. 360
J.D. EDWARDS & COMPANY, pg. 370
EFFECTIVE MANAGEMENT SYSTEMS, pg. 370
EXPERIENCE IN SOFTWARE, INC., pg. 393
FARALLON COMPUTING, INC., pg. 399
FINANCIAL LIFE COMPANIES, INC.—North Central Life Insurance Companies, pg. 813
GENERAL COMPUTER CORP. INC., pg. 449
HEDBERG DATA SYSTEMS, INC.—Steelcase Inc., pg. 1044
IFS SYSTEMS, INC.—Western & Southern Life Insurance Co., pg. 1181
INFORMATION BUILDERS, pg. 567
INFORMATION DIMENSIONS, INC.—Battelle Memorial Institute, pg. 126
INFORMATION SYSTEMS & NETWORK CORPORATION, pg. 567
INTEGRAL SYSTEMS, pg. 572
INTEGRAL SYSTEMS—Integral Systems, pg. 573
INTEGRAL SYSTEMS, INC.—Integral Systems, pg. 573
KENNEDY ASSOCIATES, pg. 623
KLEINSCHMIDT INC., pg. 635
LAWSON ASSOCIATES INC., pg. 663
LOCUS COMPUTING CORP., pg. 680
LOGISTIX, pg. 681
MACRO COMPUTER PRODUCTS INC., pg. 698
MANUFACTURERS TECHNOLOGIES, INC., pg. 705
MASON COMPANY, pg. 718
MASON HANGER-SILAS MASON CO.—Mason Company, pg. 718
MAVIS INDUSTRIES, INC.—General Computer Corp. Inc., pg. 449
MEDIACOMP, INC., pg. 735
MICRODYNAMICS, INC., pg. 749
NEXT, INC., pg. 805
ORCAD L.P., pg. 828
PACE RESOURCES, INC., pg. 838
PEGASUS INTERNATIONAL CORPORATION, pg. 855
PRAXIS INTERNATIONAL INC., pg. 884
PROFESSIONAL HEALTHCARE SYSTEMS, INC., pg. 894
RTMX-UNIFLEX INC., pg. 908

RADIX CORPORATION, pg. 909
RAND MCNALLY BOOK & MEDIA SERVICES—Rand McNally & Company, pg. 911
RAND MCNALLY-TDM, INC.—Rand McNally & Company, pg. 911
READY SYSTEMS, pg. 916
READY SYSTEMS, FRANCE—Ready Systems, pg. 916
READY SYSTEMS, GERMANY—Ready Systems, pg. 916
READY SYSTEMS, U.K.—Ready Systems, pg. 916
REFERENCE SOFTWARE INTERNATIONAL, pg. 921
SAS CONSULTING SERVICES, INC.—SAS Institute Inc., pg. 959
SAS INSTITUTE AB—SAS Institute Inc., pg. 960
SAS INSTITUTE A/S—SAS Institute Inc., pg. 960
SAS INSTITUTE AUSTRALIA PTY. LTD.—SAS Institute Inc., pg. 960
SAS INSTITUTE (CANADA) INC.—SAS Institute Inc., pg. 960
SAS INSTITUTE GMBH—SAS Institute Inc., pg. 960
SAS INSTITUTE INC., pg. 959
SAS INSTITUTE JAPAN LTD.—SAS Institute Inc., pg. 960
SAS INSTITUTE LTD.—SAS Institute Inc., pg. 960
SAS INSTITUTE LTD. (PHILIPPINES)—SAS Institute Inc., pg. 960
SAS INSTITUTE NV/SA—SAS Institute Inc., pg. 960
SAS INSTITUTE (NZ) LTD.—SAS Institute Inc., pg. 960
SAS INSTITUTE OY—SAS Institute Inc., pg. 960
SAS INSTITUTE PTE. LTD.—SAS Institute Inc., pg. 960
SAS INSTITUTE S.A.—SAS Institute Inc., pg. 960
SAS INSTITUTE S.A. (GENEVE)—SAS Institute Inc., pg. 960
SAS INSTITUTE S.A. (MADRID)—SAS Institute Inc., pg. 960
SAS INSTITUTE SDN. BHD.—SAS Institute Inc., pg. 960
SAS INSTITUTE S.R.L.—SAS Institute Inc., pg. 960
SAS SOFTWARE KOREA LTD.—SAS Institute Inc., pg. 960
SAS SOFTWARE, LTD.—SAS Institute Inc., pg. 960
SAS SOFTWARE TAIWAN LTD.—SAS Institute Inc., pg. 960
SI HOLDINGS INC., pg. 962
SPSS EUROPE B.V.—SPSS Inc., pg. 964
SPSS INC., pg. 964
SRS TECHNOLOGIES, pg. 964
SAFEGUARD BUSINESS SYSTEMS, INC., pg. 966
SAS INSTITUTE B.V.—SAS Institute Inc., pg. 960
SCHEDULING TECHNOLOGY CORPORATION, pg. 975
SCHOLASTIC INC.—SI Holdings Inc., pg. 962
SCHOLASTIC INC. INFORMATION CENTER—SI Holdings Inc., pg. 962
SEABOARD ELECTRONICS CO., pg. 983
SHIP ANALYTICS, INC., pg. 999
SMARTSTAR CORPORATION, pg. 1011
SMITH INDUSTRIES, INC., pg. 1013
SOFTOOL CORPORATION, pg. 1016
SPINNAKER SOFTWARE CORPORATION, pg. 1031
STAUFFER MEDIA SYSTEMS, INC.—Stauffer Communications, Inc., pg. 1043
SUPPORT SYSTEMS ASSOCIATES, INC., pg. 1064
SVERDRUP CORPORATION, pg. 1065
SVERDRUP TECHNOLOGY, INC.—Sverdrup Corporation, pg. 1066
THOROUGHBRED EUROPE LTD.—Thoroughbred Software International, Inc., pg. 1095
THOROUGHBRED RD-COM GMBH—Thoroughbred Software International, Inc., pg. 1095
THOROUGHBRED SOFTWARE INTERNATIONAL, INC., pg. 1095
TRAVELING SOFTWARE INC., pg. 1108
U.S. COMPUTER SERVICES, pg. 1135
WENGER CORPORATION, pg. 1176
WESTERN DATA SYSTEMS, pg. 1178
WORDPERFECT CORPORATION, pg. 1202
WORLD COMPUTER CORP., pg. 1202
XA SYSTEMS CORPORATION—Compuware Corporation, pg. 272

7373 — COMPUTER INTEGRATED SYSTEMS DESIGN

AMERICAN DEVELOPMENT CORPORATION, pg. 51
AQUIDNECK DATA COMPANY—Day & Zimmermann, Inc., pg. 320
ARTECON, INC.—Nordic Group of Companies, Ltd., pg. 809
AUSTIN CONSULTING—National Gypsum Company, pg. 790
AUTOMATION INTELLIGENCE, INC., pg. 101
BENJAMIN WOODHOUSE & GUENTHER—Ghafari Associates, Inc., pg. 455
BETAC CORPORATION—Betac International Corporation, pg. 147
BRIDGEPORT MACHINES, INC., pg. 175
CIMLINC INC., pg. 249
COMPUTER TECHNOLOGY MANAGEMENT INC.—A. Epstein and Sons, Intl., Inc., pg. 384
CRANKSHAFT MACHINE COMPANY—Avis Industrial Corporation, pg. 102
DAXUS CORPORATION, pg. 319
DORON PRECISION SYSTEMS, INC., pg. 346
FOSTER-MILLER, INC., pg. 426
GHAFARI ASSOCIATES, INC., pg. 455
GHAFARI ASSOCIATES, INC.—Ghafari Associates, Inc., pg. 455
GHAFARI ASSOCIATES, INC.—Ghafari Associates, Inc., pg. 455
GROCERS DEVELOPMENT CENTER—Certified Grocers Of California, pg. 237
IA CORP., pg. 558
INSTRUMENT SPECIALTIES EUROPE, S.A. - EUROPEAN DIVISION—Instrument Specialties Company, pg. 572
INTERPLAN—RNL Facilities Corporation, pg. 907
MAY & SPEH, INC., pg. 724
NATIONAL SYSTEMS & RESEARCH CO., pg. 794
NEXT, INC., pg. 805
NORDIC GROUP OF COMPANIES, LTD., pg. 809
PRAXIS INTERNATIONAL INC., pg. 884
PROFESSIONAL HEALTHCARE SYSTEMS, INC., pg. 894
RNL/INTERPLAN—RNL Facilities Corporation, pg. 908
SCIPAR, pg. 982
EBERLE M. SMITH ASSOCIATES, INC.—Ghafari Associates, Inc., pg. 455
SVERDRUP CORPORATION, pg. 1065
SVERDRUP TECHNOLOGY, INC.—Sverdrup Corporation, pg. 1066
SYMPLEX COMMUNICATIONS CORP., pg. 1069
SYSTEMS RESEARCH AND APPLICATIONS CORPORATION, pg. 1071
VEDA INCORPORATED—Veda International, Inc., pg. 1146
WORLD COMPUTER CORP., pg. 1202

7374 — COMPUTER PROCESSING & DATA PREPARATION & PROCESSING SERVICES

AFFILIATED COMPUTER SERVICES, INC., pg. 23
AGWAY DATA SERVICES, INC.—Agway, Inc., pg. 25
ALPHA ONE EXCHANGE, pg. 43
BRIAN UNLIMITED DISTRIBUTION COMPANY, INC., pg. 175
COMPUTER TECHNOLOGY MANAGEMENT INC.—A. Epstein and Sons, Intl., Inc., pg. 384
COMPUWARE CORPORATION, pg. 271
CORPORATE HEALTH STRATEGIES, INC.—Metropolitan Life Insurance Co., pg. 744
DAKCO DISTRIBUTORS, INC., pg. 311
DATABASE AMERICA COMPANIES, pg. 316
DAXUS CORPORATION, pg. 319
EDUSERV, pg. 369
FEDERAL DATA CORPORATION, pg. 404
G.D.C. BUSINESS SYSTEMS, INC.—Cenvill Development Corp., pg. 236
GENERAL COMPUTER CORP. INC., pg. 449
HARTE-HANKS DATA TECHNOLOGIES—Harte-Hanks Communications, Inc., pg. 513
HEALTH MANAGEMENT SYSTEMS, INC., pg. 521
HELM, INC., pg. 527
HELP SERVICE CORPORATION—Help Management Corporation, pg. 528
INFORMATION SYSTEMS—Database America Companies, pg. 316
INPUT, pg. 571
INPUT, INC.—INPUT, pg. 571
INPUT, K.K.—INPUT, pg. 571
INPUT, LTD.—INPUT, pg. 571
INPUT, SARL—INPUT, pg. 571
JCI DATA PROCESSING, INC., pg. 584
JONES INFORMATION MANAGEMENT, INC.—Jones International Ltd., pg. 603
LOGIC WORLD, INC.—Lawrence Group, Inc., pg. 662
MAVIS INDUSTRIES, INC.—General Computer Corp. Inc., pg. 449
MAY & SPEH, INC., pg. 724
MIDCO DATA SYSTEMS, INC.—Dakco Distributors, Inc., pg. 311
O'NEIL DATA SYSTEMS, INC.—William O'Neil & Co., Inc., pg. 827
WILLIAM O'NEIL & CO., INC., pg. 827
POWER BASE—Compuware Corporation, pg. 272
QUALITY MEDICAL ADJUDICATION, INC.—Health Management Systems, Inc., pg. 521
RALEIGH ENTERPRISES, INC., pg. 910
RESPONSE SYSTEMS, INC.—Humiston-Keeling, Inc., pg. 553
SCICOM DATA SERVICES, LTD., pg. 981
J. M. SMITH CORP., pg. 1012
SVERDRUP CORPORATION, pg. 1065
SVERDRUP TECHNOLOGY, INC.—Sverdrup Corporation, pg. 1066
TWENTIETH CENTURY COMPANIES, pg. 1121
TWENTIETH CENTURY SERVICES—Twentieth Century Companies, pg. 1121
U-HAUL INTERNATIONAL, INC.—Amerco, A Nevada Corporation, pg. 48
URSCHEL LABS INC., pg. 1140
JIM WALTER COMPUTER SERVICES, INC.—Walter Industries, Inc., pg. 1162
XA SYSTEMS CORPORATION—Compuware Corporation, pg. 272
ZIFF TECHNOLOGIES—Ziff Communications Company, pg. 1219

7375 — INFORMATION RETRIEVAL SERVICES

AMERICAN BUSINESS INFORMATION, INC., pg. 50
BNA ELECTRONIC MEDIA DIV.—The Bureau of National Affairs, Inc., pg. 189
BNA PLUS—The Bureau of National Affairs, Inc., pg. 189
BATTELLE MEMORIAL INSTITUTE, pg. 126
THE BUREAU OF NATIONAL AFFAIRS, INC., pg. 189
COMPILERS PLUS—American Business Information, Inc., pg. 50
COMPTON'S NEW MEDIA INC.—Encyclopaedia Britannica, Inc., pg. 381
COMPUTER LIBRARY—Ziff Communications Company, pg. 1219
DONNELLEY MARKETING DATA PROCESSING OPERATIONS—Peter W. Smith & Company, Inc., pg. 1011
DONNELLEY MARKETING, INC.—Peter W. Smith & Company, Inc., pg. 1011
EBSCO INDUSTRIES, INC., pg. 365
EXECUTIVE TELECOM SYSTEMS, INC.—The Bureau of National Affairs, Inc., pg. 189
THE FAXON COMPANY, INC., pg. 404
INFORMATION ACCESS CO.—Ziff Communications Company, pg. 1219
JCI DATA PROCESSING, INC., pg. 584
MAY & SPEH, INC., pg. 724
PRAXIS INTERNATIONAL INC., pg. 884
PREDICASTS—Ziff Communications Company, pg. 1219
PROFESSIONAL HEALTHCARE SYSTEMS, INC., pg. 894
TECHNICAL PUBLISHING—Nelson & Schmidt, Inc., pg. 797
UMI DATA COURIER—Bell & Howell Company, pg. 135
ZIFF TECHNOLOGIES—Ziff Communications Company, pg. 1219

7376 — COMPUTER FACILITIES MANAGEMENT SERVICES

AQUIDNECK DATA COMPANY—Day & Zimmermann, Inc., pg. 320
DAXUS CORPORATION, pg. 319
MAXIMA COMPUTER SYSTEMS CORP.—The Maxima Corporation, pg. 723
THE MAXIMA CORPORATION, pg. 723
MAY & SPEH, INC., pg. 724
SVERDRUP CORPORATION, pg. 1065
SVERDRUP TECHNOLOGY, INC.—Sverdrup Corporation, pg. 1066

7377 — COMPUTER RENTAL & LEASING

COMPUTER SALES INTERNATIONAL INC., pg. 271
DDC PERTEC, pg. 308
DATA PREFERENCE, INC.—The Marmon Group, Inc., pg. 712
DECISION DATA INC., pg. 323
ECONOCOM-USA INC., pg. 367
EL CAMINO RESOURCES, LTD., pg. 372
WILLIAM H. GOODWIN TRUST, pg. 471
IDEA COURIER, INC.—I D E Corporation, pg. 560
LEADER LEASING, INC.—Leader Federal Bank For Savings, pg. 664
LEASAMETRIC, INC.—The Marmon Group, Inc., pg. 712
MACRO COMPUTER PRODUCTS INC., pg. 698
MERIDIAN TECHNOLOGY LEASING SERVICES, pg. 740
NEW YORK SYSTEMS EXCHANGE CORP.—Syracuse Supply Company, pg. 1070

7378 — COMPUTER MAINTENANCE & REPAIR

AUTOMATION INTELLIGENCE, INC., pg. 101
CENTURY COMPUTER MARKETING, pg. 235
DISPLAY TECHNOLOGIES, INC., pg. 339
ECONOCOM-USA INC., pg. 367
HAYES MICROCOMPUTER PRODUCTS (CANADA)—Hayes Microcomputer Products, Inc., pg. 519
PERIPHONICS CORP., pg. 862
RECON SERVICES, INC.—Computer Sales International Inc., pg. 271
SENTINEL COMPUTER SERVICES INC., pg. 990
THE VIRTUAL GROUP, pg. 1153
WESTERN DATA SYSTEMS, pg. 1178

7379 — COMPUTER RELATED SERVICES, NEC

AUSTIN CONSULTING—National Gypsum Company, pg. 790
AUTOMATION INTELLIGENCE, INC., pg. 101
AUTOMATION INTELLIGENCE UK LTD.—Automation Intelligence, Inc., pg. 101
BUSINESS INFORMATION TECHNOLOGY, pg. 196
COMMUNICATIONS INTERNATIONAL, pg. 269
COMPUTER DYNAMICS, INC., pg. 271
COMPUTER METHODS CORPORATION, pg. 271
COMPUTER TECHNOLOGY MANAGEMENT INC.—A. Epstein and Sons, Intl., Inc., pg. 384
COMPUWARE CORPORATION, pg. 271
DATA TRANSPORTATION COMPANY—The Bekins Company, pg. 133
DATABASE AMERICA COMPANIES, pg. 316
DATASPHERE, INC.—Construction Specialties, Inc., pg. 277
DAXUS CORPORATION, pg. 319
DECISION DATA—Decision Data Inc., pg. 324
DECISION DATA DIRECT—Decision Data Inc., pg. 324
DECISION DATA INC., pg. 323
E F INDUSTRIES, pg. 359
EMS-MICHIGAN—Effective Management Systems, pg. 370
ERM-COMPUTER SERVICES, INC.—The ERM Group, pg. 360
ECONOCOM-USA INC., pg. 367
EFFECTIVE MANAGEMENT SYSTEMS, pg. 370
FIRST AMERICAN INFORMATION SERVICES, INC.—Bremer Financial Corporation, pg. 173
GREAT AMERICAN MANAGEMENT SERVICES, INC.—American Financial Corporation, pg. 53
INFORMATION SYSTEMS—Database America Companies, pg. 316
INTEGRAL SYSTEMS, pg. 572
INTEGRAL SYSTEMS, INC.—Integral Systems, pg. 573
JCI DATA PROCESSING, INC., pg. 584
JONES BUSINESS SYSTEM—Decision Data Inc., pg. 324
KANEX, pg. 616
KAYE INSTRUMENTS, INC., pg. 619
KING GROUP, INC., pg. 630
KLEINSCHMIDT INC., pg. 635
LANDISC SYSTEMS—Day & Zimmermann, Inc., pg. 320
MCRB FULFILLMENT CO.—MCRB Service Bureau, Inc., pg. 692
MCRB FULFILLMENT CO.—MCRB Service Bureau, Inc., pg. 692
MCRB SERVICE BUREAU, INC., pg. 691
MAINTAIN—The Maxima Corporation, pg. 723
ALBERT C. MARTIN & ASSOCIATES, pg. 714

MAXIMA BUSINESS SYSTEMS—The Maxima Corporation, pg. 723
MAXIMA COMPUTER SYSTEMS CORP.—The Maxima Corporation, pg. 723
THE MAXIMA CORPORATION, pg. 723
MAXIMA DATA SYSTEMS—The Maxima Corporation, pg. 723
MAY & SPEH, INC., pg. 724
METLIFE CAPITAL CORPORATION—Metropolitan Life Insurance Co., pg. 744
O/E AUTOMATION, INC., pg. 819
PRAXIS INTERNATIONAL INC., pg. 884
PROFESSIONAL INFORMATION MANAGMENT—Seligman & Associates, Inc., pg. 988
RAND MCNALLY PUBLISHING GROUP—Rand McNally & Company, pg. 911
SRS TECHNOLOGIES, pg. 964
SEGUE PARTNERS—Praxis International Inc., pg. 885
SEGWAY PARTNERS—Praxis International Inc., pg. 885
SEGWAY PARTNERS—Praxis International Inc., pg. 885
SOLAR SERVICES, INC.—Society for Savings Bancorp, Inc., pg. 1016
SUN DATA INC., pg. 1058
SUPPORT SYSTEMS ASSOCIATES, INC., pg. 1064
TECHNOLOGY TRANSFER INSTITUTE, pg. 1084
TRACE PRODUCTS, pg. 1104
TRACE U.K., LTD.—Trace Products, pg. 1104
VEDA INCORPORATED—Veda International, Inc., pg. 1146
WW ENGINEERING & SCIENCE INC.—Summit Environmental Group, pg. 1058
XA SYSTEMS CORPORATION—Compuware Corporation, pg. 272
ZIFF TECHNOLOGIES—Ziff Communications Company, pg. 1219

7381 — DETECTIVE, GUARD & ARMORED CAR SERVICES

APG SECURITY, INC., pg. 5
ALLIED SECURITY, INC., pg. 39
AMERICAN FINANCIAL SECURITY—American Finance Group, pg. 52
BAKER INDUSTRIES, INC.—Borg-Warner Corporation, pg. 166
E. J. BURKE SECURITY SYSTEMS, INC.—Borg-Warner Corporation, pg. 166
BURNS INTERNATIONAL SECURITY SERVICES, INC.—Borg-Warner Corporation, pg. 166
COLIN SERVICE SYSTEMS, INC., pg. 261
DEFENDER SERVICES, INC., pg. 324
ANDY FRAIN SERVICES, INC., pg. 428
GLOBE SECURITY SYSTEMS, INC.—Borg-Warner Corporation, pg. 166
GUARDIAN ALARM CO., pg. 491
GUARDSMARK, INC., pg. 492
MARK LIPMAN DIV.—Guardsmark, Inc., pg. 493
RICE FOOD MARKETS INC., pg. 931
SHIELD SECURITY, INC., pg. 999
WELLS FARGO ARMORED SERVICE CORP.—Borg-Warner Corporation, pg. 166
WELLS FARGO GUARD SERVICES—Borg-Warner Corporation, pg. 166

7382 — SECURITY SYSTEMS SERVICES

ANTARES GROUP INC., pg. 76
BAKER INDUSTRIES, INC.—Borg-Warner Corporation, pg. 166
BORG-WARNER CORPORATION, pg. 165
BURNS INTERNATIONAL SECURITY SERVICES, INC.—Borg-Warner Corporation, pg. 166
COMMUNICATIONS & SIGNALING, INC.—Stauffer Communications, Inc., pg. 1043
ENABLING TECHNOLOGIES COMPANY, pg. 380
FOLGER ADAM COMPANY, pg. 422
GUARDIAN ALARM CO., pg. 491
GUARDSMARK, INC., pg. 492
HOLMES PROTECTION GROUP, INC., pg. 540
KASTLE SYSTEMS, INC., pg. 618
LEASING SERVICES CORP.—Novar Electronics, pg. 817
LEVY SECURITY CONSULTANTS, LIMITED, pg. 672
MOSLER ELECTRONIC SYSTEMS DIV.—Mosler Inc., pg. 772
MOSLER INC., pg. 772
NOVAR CORP.—Novar Electronics, pg. 817
PE SYSTEMS, pg. 836
PEDUS BUILDING SERVICES—Pedus Services, Inc., pg. 855
PEDUS SECURITY SERVICES—Pedus Services, Inc., pg. 855
PEDUS SERVICES, INC., pg. 854
PROTECTION TECHNOLOGY—Day & Zimmermann, Inc., pg. 320
RMS TECHS, INC., pg. 907
SECURITY ALARMS & FIRE ENGINEERING INC., pg. 987
SENTROL, INC.—Berwind Corporation, pg. 145
SIMPLEX TIME RECORDER CO., pg. 1006
STEWART DECATUR SECURITY SYSTEMS, INC.—Folger Adam Company, pg. 422
WELLS FARGO ALARM SERVICES—Borg-Warner Corporation, pg. 166

7383 — NEWS SYNDICATES

ADVERTISING CHECKING BUREAU INCORPORATED, pg. 21
THE ASSOCIATED PRESS A/S—The Associated Press, pg. 92
THE ASSOCIATED PRESS AB—The Associated Press, pg. 92
THE ASSOCIATED PRESS (BELGIUM) S.A.—The Associated Press, pg. 92
THE ASSOCIATED PRESS DE VENEZUELA, S.A.—The Associated Press, pg. 92
THE ASSOCIATED PRESS GMBH—The Associated Press, pg. 92
THE ASSOCIATED PRESS, LTD.—The Associated Press, pg. 92
THE ASSOCIATED PRESS, pg. 91
LEBHAR-FRIEDMAN, INC., pg. 665
PRESS ASSOCIATION, INC.—The Associated Press, pg. 92
SATELLITE DATA BROADCAST NETWORKS, INC. (SATNET)—The Associated Press, pg. 92
WIDE WORLD PHOTOS, INC.—The Associated Press, pg. 92

7384 — PHOTOFINISHING LABORATORIES

ANDREWS GROUP, INCORPORATED, pg. 74
CINE MAGNETICS, INC., pg. 250
COMPACT VIDEO SERVICES, INC.—Andrews Group, Incorporated, pg. 74
DEANS PHOTO SERVICE, INC., pg. 322
FUJI TRUCOLOR FOTO—Deans Photo Service, Inc., pg. 322
GREAT LAKES TECHNOLOGIES CORP., pg. 482
GUARDIAN INDUSTRIES CORP., pg. 491
IMAGE TRANSFORM—Andrews Group, Incorporated, pg. 74
IMAGE TRANSFORM LAB—Andrews Group, Incorporated, pg. 74
MACANDREWS & FORBES HOLDINGS INC., pg. 694
PHOTO CENTRAL OFFICE—Guardian Industries Corp., pg. 492

7389 — BUSINESS SERVICES, NEC

AVW AUDIOVISUAL, INC.—Freeman Decorating Co., pg. 431
ABLE TRANSLATIONS LIMITED—Berlitz International, Inc., pg. 142
ADVANSTAR COMMUNICATIONS, pg. 21
THE ALAMO LEARNING SYSTEMS, INC., pg. 29
AMERICAN ARBITRATION ASSOCIATION, pg. 49
AMERICAN BIBLE SOCIETY, pg. 49
AMERICAN MOTIVATION (N.Z.) LTD.—Carlson Companies, Inc., pg. 221
AMERICAN PROTECTION INDUSTRIES, INC., pg. 60
ARTHUR ANDERSEN & CO., S.C., pg. 72
ANDERSON INDUSTRIES INC., pg. 73
APPLIED HOLOGRAPHICS, INC.—SBN System Inc., pg. 960
ARKANSAS INDUSTRIAL DEVELOPMENT COMMISSION, pg. 83
ARTESIAN RESOURCES CORPORATION, pg. 86
ATLANTA MARKET CENTER, pg. 94
AUTO DRIVEAWAY CO., pg. 100
AUTOMATIC LIQUID PACKAGING, INC., pg. 100
AUTOMOTIVE MARKETING GROUP—R. L. Polk & Co., pg. 879
BALTIMORE STATIONERY CO., pg. 116
BANK M F & COMPANY, INC., pg. 117
BARANCORP, pg. 118
JOSEPH A. BARANSKI LITERARY AGENCY—Barancorp, pg. 118
W. M. BARR & CO., INC., pg. 121
BEISLER & ASSOCIATES, INC.—TBWA Advertising, Inc., pg. 1071
BEL AIR MARKETS, pg. 133
THE BENSON MUSIC GROUP, pg. 140
BERLITZ TRANSLATION SERVICES, INC.—Berlitz International, Inc., pg. 142
BERNARD KRIEF MOTIVATION, S.A., CARLSON MARKETING GROUP—Carlson Companies, Inc., pg. 221
BEST WESTERN INTERNATIONAL, INC., pg. 146
BRITCOM TELEMARKETING DIVISION—Encyclopaedia Britannica, Inc., pg. 381
BROCK CONTROL SYSTEMS, INC., pg. 178
BUDCO GROUP INC., pg. 186
BUDGET MARKETING, INC., pg. 186
CAE LINK ALLEN DIVISION, pg. 198
CARD TECHNOLOGY CORPORATION—SBN System Inc., pg. 960
CARLSON COMPANIES, INC., pg. 220
CARLSON INTERNATIONAL DIVISION—Carlson Companies, Inc., pg. 221
CARLSON MARKETING GROUP (AUST.) PTY. LIMITED—Carlson Companies, Inc., pg. 221
CARLSON MARKETING GROUP, INC.—Carlson Companies, Inc., pg. 221
CARLSON MARKETING GROUP JAPAN CO. LTD.—Carlson Companies, Inc., pg. 221
CARLSON MARKETING GROUP JAPAN KK—Carlson Companies, Inc., pg. 221
CARLSON MARKETING GROUP LTD.—Carlson Companies, Inc., pg. 221
CARLSON MARKETING GROUP SCANDINAVIA MOTIVATION SERVICE AB—Carlson Companies, Inc., pg. 221
CARLSON MARKETING GROUP (U.K.) LIMITED—Carlson Companies, Inc., pg. 221
CARLSON RETAIL MARKETING—Carlson Companies, Inc., pg. 221
CENTRAL LIVESTOCK ASSOCIATION, INC., pg. 233
CHARLESTON INDUSTRIES—Petersen Aluminum Corporation, pg. 864
CHINA TRAVEL BUREAU LTD.—Orbitair International Ltd., pg. 828
CLASSIC MARKETS CORP., pg. 253
CLOUD CORPORATION, pg. 256
CONTRACT INTERIORS INC., pg. 280
COTTER FINANCE CO., INC.—Cotter & Company, pg. 288
CREATIVE PRODUCTIONS, pg. 297
CUSTOMER SERVICES DIV.—Ingersoll International Inc., pg. 568
DALE FOODS—Vincent Food Industries, Inc., pg. 1152
DAW TECHNOLOGIES, INC., pg. 319
DELAWARE CHARTER GUARANTEE & TRUST CO.—The Principal Financial Group, pg. 890
DEMERT & DOUGHERTY, INC., pg. 328
DESIGN-BUILD WEST—RNL Facilities Corporation, pg. 907
DESIGN 1 INTERIORS, pg. 332
DIRECTORY DISTRIBUTING ASSOCIATES, INC., pg. 339
DIRECTORY DISTRIBUTING ASSOCIATES, INC.—Directory Distributing Associates, Inc., pg. 339
DUNCAN HEATH ASSOCIATES—Josephson International Inc., pg. 607
EV SERVICES INC.—Resort Condominiums International, pg. 929
BRUCE W. EBERLE & ASSOCIATES—Eberle Direct Marketing Group, Inc., pg. 365
EBSCO INDUSTRIES, INC., pg. 365
ECO WATER SYSTEMS, pg. 367
ENVIROCON INTERNATIONAL CORP.—McNeel International Corp., pg. 732
ERNST & YOUNG, pg. 387
FTD/FLORISTS' TRANSWORLD DELIVERY ASSOCIATION, pg. 395
FAMILY PHARMACY GENERAL OFFICE—Alco Health Services Corporation, pg. 32
FAXON CANADA—The Faxon Company, Inc., pg. 404
THE FAXON COMPANY, INC., pg. 404
FAXON EUROPE—The Faxon Company, Inc., pg. 404
FINORA COMPANY, INC.—Norfoods, Inc., pg. 810
FRANCHISE FINANCE CORP. OF AMERICA, pg. 428
FREEMAN DECORATING CO., pg. 431
FULL CIRCLE MEDIA CORP., pg. 436
FUNDSNET, INC.—SBN System Inc., pg. 960
GANNETT TRANSIT, pg. 442
GENERAL BINDING CORPORATION—Lane Industries, Inc., pg. 656
SHELDON GOOD & CO., INC., pg. 470
GOODKIND & O'DEA, INC.—Dewberry & Davis, pg. 334
THE GREAT ATLANTIC COMPANIES, pg. 480
JACK GRIGGS INC., pg. 488
HARRINGTON MARKET RESEARCH—Biggs Gilmore Communications, pg. 149
HARTE-HANKS MARKETING SERVICES—Harte-Hanks Communications, Inc., pg. 513
HEALTH SERVICES PLUS, INC.—Alco Health Services Corporation, pg. 32
HEATH CONSULTANTS INCORPORATED, pg. 524
HELM, INC., pg. 527
HENDERSON AUCTIONEERS, pg. 528
HENNINGSEN FOODS LTD.—Kifuki U.S.A. Co., Inc., pg. 629
HILL-LOMA, INC.—Goldman Financial Group, pg. 468
HOSPITALITY PROCUREMENT DIVISION—Carlson Companies, Inc., pg. 221
IDC SERVICES, INC., pg. 559
ITI MARKETING SERVICES, INC., pg. 561
INDEPENDENT PUBLICATIONS, INC., pg. 565
INSTITUTIONAL FINANCING SERVICES, pg. 571
INTERNATIONAL CREATIVE MANAGEMENT, INC.—Josephson International Inc., pg. 607
INTERNATIONAL CREATIVE MANAGEMENT LTD.—Josephson International Inc., pg. 607
INTERNATIONAL DATA GROUP, pg. 576
INTEROP, INC.—Ziff Communications Company, pg. 1219
INVETECH CO., pg. 581
JS&A GROUP, INC., pg. 586
JAPS-OLSON COMPANY, pg. 590
JOHN HANCOCK CAPITAL CORPORATION—John Hancock Mutual Life Insurance Company, pg. 596
JOHN HANCOCK NETWORKING INSURANCE AGENCY—John Hancock Mutual Life Insurance Company, pg. 596
K-PROMOTIONS, INC.—Carlson Companies, Inc., pg. 221
KAYSER COLL. TECHNISCHE UBERSETZER—Berlitz International, Inc., pg. 143
KETCHUM, INC., pg. 626
KRUSE INTERNATIONAL, pg. 645
NORMAN LEVY ASSOCIATES, INC., pg. 672
M.W.O.S. TRADE SHOW—I. Spiewak & Sons, Inc., pg. 1031
THE E. F. MACDONALD VERKAUFSFORDERUNG GMBH—Carlson Companies, Inc., pg. 221
E. F. MACDONALD MOTIVATION DIV.—Carlson Companies, Inc., pg. 221
MARITZ INC., pg. 707
MARITZ PERFORMANCE IMPROVEMENT COMPANY—Maritz Inc., pg. 708
ALBERT C. MARTIN & ASSOCIATES, pg. 714
MASON HANGER-SILAS MASON CO.—Mason Company, pg. 718
GEORGE S. MAY INTERNATIONAL COMPANY, pg. 723
METRO INFORMATION SERVICES, pg. 743
WILLIAM MORRIS AGENCY, INC., pg. 771
MOTIVATION S.P.A.—Carlson Companies, Inc., pg. 221
MUSCUM BOUTIQUE INTERCONTINENTAL, LTD., pg. 777
NBBJ, pg. 780
NBS IMAGING SYSTEMS, INC.—SBN System Inc., pg. 960
NBS SOUTHERN, INC.—SBN System Inc., pg. 960
NFO RESEARCH, INC., pg. 780
NATIONAL YELLOW PAGES MONITOR (NYPM)—NFO Research, Inc., pg. 781
NIHON FAXON—The Faxon Company, Inc., pg. 404
NORFOODS, INC., pg. 810
NORMAN LEVY ASSOCIATES, INC.—Norman Levy Associates, Inc., pg. 672
NORTHERN CROSS, LTD.—Barancorp, pg. 118
OMEGA LIST COMPANY—Eberle Direct Marketing Group, Inc., pg. 365
ONE HOUR MARTINIZING DRY CLEANING FRANCHISE (SYSTEM), pg. 826
ORBITAIR INTERNATIONAL LTD., pg. 828

PIONEER ENGINEERING & MANUFACTURING CO., pg. 871
R. L. POLK & CO., pg. 879
POLK MOTOR VEHICLE REGISTRATIONS DIV.—R. L. Polk & Co., pg. 879
THE POLLOCK CORP., pg. 879
THE POWER LINE—Publishers Clearing House, pg. 898
PREMIUMS INTL. LTD.—Carlson Companies, Inc., pg. 221
PRICE WATERHOUSE - U.S., pg. 888
THE PRINCIPAL FINANCIAL GROUP, pg. 890
PRINCIPAL HEALTH CARE, INC.—The Principal Financial Group, pg. 891
PRINCIPAL MANAGEMENT INC.—The Principal Financial Group, pg. 891
PRINCOR FINANCIAL SERVICES CORPORATION—The Principal Financial Group, pg. 891
PRUSUPPLY, INC.—The Prudential Insurance Company of America, pg. 897
PUBLISHERS CLEARING HOUSE, pg. 898
PUEBLO RAILROAD SERVICE COMPANY—CF&I Steel Corporation, pg. 201
PUERTO RICO TOURISM COMPANY, pg. 899
QUALITY FOOD OILS, INC., pg. 903
RNL/INTERPLAN—RNL Facilities Corporation, pg. 908
RAND MCNALLY MAP SERVICES CO.—Rand McNally & Company, pg. 911
RE/MAX INTERNATIONAL, INC., pg. 915
RELA PRODUCT DEVELOPMENT DIV. (PDD)—RELA, Inc., pg. 924
RESERVATIONS SERVICES, INC.—Best Western International, Inc., pg. 147
RESORT CONDOMINIUMS INTERNATIONAL, pg. 929
RESORT QUALITY SERVICES, INC.—Resort Condominiums International, pg. 929
RESPONSE COMMUNICATIONS, INC.—The Direct Marketing Group Inc., pg. 339
RICHARDSON INDUSTRIES, INC., pg. 932
RURAL METRO CORPORATION, pg. 956
RUSSIAN TRAVEL BUREAU, INC.—Orbitair International Ltd., pg. 828
SBN SYSTEM INC., pg. 960
SGD INTERNATIONAL CORP., pg. 962
SAPROMA S.A.—Carlson Companies, Inc., pg. 221
SCHUMACHER & FORELLE, INC., pg. 979
THE SCOTSMAN GROUP, INC., pg. 982
SEYBOLD SEMINARS—Ziff Communications Company, pg. 1219
SHELLY DATA SYSTEMS—National Reproductions Corporation, pg. 793
THE SIGNATURE GROUP—Montgomery Ward & Co., Inc., pg. 768
SOFTRANS INTERNATIONAL, LTD.—Berlitz International, Inc., pg. 143
SOUND WAREHOUSE, INC.—Shamrock Holdings, Inc., pg. 995
I. SPIEWAK & SONS, INC., pg. 1031
SPRINGBORN ENVIRONMENTAL SCIENCES DIVISION—Springborn Laboratories, Inc., pg. 1033
STRATMAR RESEARCH CORP.—Stratmar Systems, Inc., pg. 1053
STRATMAR SYSTEMS, INC., pg. 1053
SUPERIOR AUCTIONEERS & MARKETING, INC., pg. 1063
SUPERIOR REPROGRAPHICS, pg. 1064
TDW DELAWARE, INC.—T.D. Williamson, Inc., pg. 1192
TDW TRADING, INC.—T.D. Williamson, Inc., pg. 1192
TELEFLORA—American Protection Industries, Inc., pg. 60
J. L. TODD AUCTION CO., pg. 1099
TOWERS, PERRIN, FORSTER & CROSBY, INC., pg. 1103
TRADE SHOW ENTERPRISES—I. Spiewak & Sons, Inc., pg. 1031
TURNER SUBSCRIPTION AGENCY—The Faxon Company, Inc., pg. 404
VANCE PUBLISHING CORPORATION, pg. 1144
VENCHURS PACKAGING, INC., pg. 1147
THE VERNON COMPANY, pg. 1148
VINCENT FOOD INDUSTRIES, INC., pg. 1152
VIRGINIA DEPARTMENT OF ECONOMIC DEVELOPMENT TOURISM DEVELOPMENT GROUP, pg. 1152
WARMINGTON HOMES, pg. 1164
WIELAND FINANCIAL SERVICES, INC.—John Wieland Homes Inc., pg. 1188
WORDPERFECT MANUFACTURING—WordPerfect Corporation, pg. 1202
WORLD EXPO CORPORATION—International Data Group, pg. 578
ZETEC, INC., pg. 1217

7513 — TRUCK RENTAL & LEASING, WITHOUT DRIVERS

AVA-AUTOMATIC VENDORS OF AMERICA, pg. 8
AMERCO, A NEVADA CORPORATION, pg. 47
AMERICAN FINANCE GROUP, pg. 52
BEAUDRY FORD, INC., pg. 130
THE CURRY CORPORATION, pg. 305
DSU LEASING, INC.—D.S.U.-Peterbilt & GMC, Inc., pg. 310
DONLEN CORP., pg. 345
EXECUTIVE CAR LEASING COMPANY—Executive Car Leasing, Inc., pg. 393
EXECUTIVE CAR LEASING, INC., pg. 393
FRANK CONSOLIDATED ENTERPRISES INC., pg. 428
BILL HEARD LEASING, INC.—Bill Heard Enterprises, Inc., pg. 521
BILL HEARD ENTERPRISES, INC., pg. 521
THE HERTZ CORPORATION—Park Ridge Corporation, pg. 849
HOLMAN ENTERPRISES, pg. 540
JEROME-DUNCAN FORD, pg. 593
K & R DELIVERY, INC., pg. 610
KENWORTH OF INDIANAPOLIS INC., pg. 624
MCKENZIE TANK LINES, INC., pg. 730
MID-SOUTH FORD TRUCK SALES, INC., pg. 750
MODERN GROUP LTD., pg. 762
NATIONAL TRUCK LEASING SYSTEM, pg. 794
NORTHWEST SERVICE, INC.—Food Services of America, pg. 423
PST VANS, INC., pg. 837
PENSKE CORPORATION, pg. 859
PENSKE TRANSPORTATION INC.—Penske Corporation, pg. 859
PENSKE TRUCK LEASING—Penske Corporation, pg. 859
PENSKE TRUCK LEASING—Penske Corporation, pg. 859
PENSKE TRUCK LEASING—Penske Corporation, pg. 859
PENSKE TRUCK LEASING CORP.—Penske Corporation, pg. 859
RED BALL LEASING, INC.—Red Ball Corporation, pg. 918
SALEM CARRIERS. INC.—Salem National Corporation, pg. 967
SALEM LEASING CORP.—Salem National Corporation, pg. 967
SALEM NATIONAL CORPORATION, pg. 967
SOUTHSIDE FORD TRUCK SALES INC., pg. 1023
SYRACUSE SUPPLY COMPANY, pg. 1070
SYRACUSE SUPPLY LEASING CO., INC.—Syracuse Supply Company, pg. 1070
DAVE SYVERSON LINCOLN MERCURY, pg. 1071
TRANSCO INC., pg. 1107
UNITED LEASING, INC.—Unigroup, Inc., pg. 1126
VILLAGE CAR COMPANY, pg. 1151
WALSER AUTOMOTIVE CORPORATION, pg. 1161
WATKINS SYSTEM INC., pg. 1167
C. WEAVER CHEVROLET, INC., pg. 1170
WESTLIE MOTOR COMPANY, pg. 1183

7514 — PASSENGER CAR RENTAL

AIRWAYS RENT A CAR—Ridgeview Motors, Inc., pg. 934
ALAMO RENT-A-CAR INC., pg. 30
AVIS, INC., pg. 102
W. O. BANKSTON LEASING INC.—W. O. Bankston Enterprises Inc., pg. 118
BEAUDRY FORD, INC., pg. 130
BUDGET RENT A CAR CORPORATION—Beech Holdings Corp., pg. 131
BUERKLE BUICK-HONDA CO., pg. 186
EAGLE LINCOLN MERCURY INC., pg. 362
ENTERPRISE RENT-A-CAR COMPANY, pg. 382
FIRST GRAY LINE CORPORATION, pg. 413
STEVE FOLEY CADILLAC, pg. 422
FRANK CONSOLIDATED ENTERPRISES INC., pg. 428
FRAZIER-WILLIAMS CHEVROLET GEO, pg. 430
THE HERTZ CORPORATION—Park Ridge Corporation, pg. 849
HOLMAN ENTERPRISES, pg. 540
KINGS TOYOTA SUZUKI, pg. 631
LB INDUSTRIES INC., pg. 647
LIBERTYVILLE LINCOLN-MERCURY SALES, INC., pg. 674
LONE STAR CADILLAC CO., pg. 682
MERCHANTS RENT A CAR, INC., pg. 739
NATIONAL CAR RENTAL SYSTEM, INC., pg. 786
SERVICE ASSETS CORP.—Bromar Inc., pg. 179
JAKE SWEENEY AUTO LEASING INC., pg. 1066
TAMAROFF LEASING CO.—Tamaroff Buick Inc., pg. 1077
U-HAUL INTERNATIONAL, INC.—Amerco, A Nevada Corporation, pg. 48
UGLY DUCKLING RENT-A-CAR, pg. 1125
VANDERGRIFF CHEVROLET GEO, pg. 1144
WALSER AUTOMOTIVE CORPORATION, pg. 1161
WALSER LEASING INC.—Walser Automotive Corporation, pg. 1161
WESTLIE MOTOR COMPANY, pg. 1183

7515 — PASSENGER CAR LEASING

MIKE ALBERT LEASING, INC., pg. 31
BYERLY FORD-NISSAN INC., pg. 198
CAPITAL FUNDING CO.—Lantzsch-Andreas Enterprises, Inc., pg. 658
CAPITOL CHEVROLET CADILLAC GEO, INC., pg. 215
THE CURRY CORPORATION, pg. 305
EAGLE LINCOLN MERCURY INC., pg. 362
EMKAY, INC., pg. 379
ENTERPRISE RENT-A-CAR COMPANY, pg. 382
EXECUTIVE CAR LEASING COMPANY—Executive Car Leasing, Inc., pg. 393
EXECUTIVE CAR LEASING, INC., pg. 393
FRAZIER-WILLIAMS CHEVROLET GEO, pg. 430
GILLOGLY CHEVROLET INC., pg. 459
JEROME-DUNCAN FORD, pg. 593
KINGS TOYOTA SUZUKI, pg. 631
LB INDUSTRIES INC., pg. 647
LONE STAR CADILLAC CO., pg. 682
MERCHANTS RENT A CAR, INC., pg. 739
THE MOTORLEASE CORP., pg. 773
NATIONAL CAR RENTAL SYSTEM, INC., pg. 786
PROSPECT MOTORS, INC., pg. 895
RIDGEVIEW MOTORS, INC., pg. 934
SENATOR FORD, pg. 989
I. SPIEWAK & SONS, INC., pg. 1031
JAKE SWEENEY AUTO LEASING INC., pg. 1066
TSE LEASING CO.—I. Spiewak & Sons, Inc., pg. 1031
TAMAROFF LEASING CO.—Tamaroff Buick Inc., pg. 1077
THOMSON MACCONNELL CADILLAC, INC., pg. 1095
TRADE SHOW ENTERPRISES—I. Spiewak & Sons, Inc., pg. 1031
VANDERGRIFF CHEVROLET GEO, pg. 1144
WALSER LEASING INC.—Walser Automotive Corporation, pg. 1161
C. WEAVER CHEVROLET, INC., pg. 1170
BUFF WHELAN CHEVROLET & GEO, INC., pg. 1185
WINTER PARK LEASING, INC.—Luke Potter Dodge Inc., pg. 882

7519 — UTILITY TRAILER & RECREATIONAL VEHICLE RENTAL

AMERCO, A NEVADA CORPORATION, pg. 47
AMERCO LEASING COMPANY—Amerco, A Nevada Corporation, pg. 48
AUTOMOTIVE RENTALS, INC., pg. 101
INTER-MOUNTAIN RENTALS—ROC Properties Inc., pg. 908
NATIONAL TRUCK LEASING SYSTEM, pg. 794
RIVER OAKS COMMUNITIES, INC.—ROC Properties Inc., pg. 908
STILLMAN & HOAG, INC., pg. 1049
U-HAUL INTERNATIONAL, INC.—Amerco, A Nevada Corporation, pg. 48
U-HAUL SALES & LEASING COMPANY—Amerco, A Nevada Corporation, pg. 48

7521 — AUTOMOBILE PARKING

ALLRIGHT BIRMINGHAM INC.—Allright Corporation, pg. 41
ALLRIGHT CORPORATION, pg. 41
ALLRIGHT CORPORATION—Allright Corporation, pg. 41
ALLRIGHT CORPORATION OF DELAWARE—Allright Corporation, pg. 41
ALLRIGHT PARKING CORPORATION—Allright Corporation, pg. 42
ALLRIGHT PARKING EL PASO, INC.—Allright Corporation, pg. 42
ALLRIGHT PARKING SYSTEM, INC.—Allright Corporation, pg. 42
ALLRIGHT PARKING VIRGINIA, INC.—Allright Corporation, pg. 42
ALLRIGHT PENSACOLA PARKING—Allright Corporation, pg. 42
ALLRIGHT SIERRA PARKING INC.—Allright Corporation, pg. 42
ALLRIGHT WEST PALM BEACH, INC.—Allright Corporation, pg. 42
BAY PARK, INC.—Allright Corporation, pg. 42
CARPARK—The Oliver Carr Co., pg. 225
CENTRAL PARKING CORP.—Central Parking Corp., pg. 234
CONCESSION AIR CORPORATION—Delaware North Companies, Inc., pg. 326
DUTCH PARKING INC.—Allright Corporation, pg. 42
IDEAL PARKING, INC.—Allright Corporation, pg. 43
KINNEY SYSTEM, INC., pg. 632
KNOX ALLRIGHT, INC.—Allright Corporation, pg. 42
METROPOLITAN PROPERTIES INC., pg. 745
MULTIPLE PARKING SERVICES, INC.—Allright Corporation, pg. 42
MULTIPLE PARKING SERVICES, INC.—Allright Corporation, pg. 42
NORTHWEST PARKING SERVICES INC.—Allright Corporation, pg. 42
PENNSYLVANIA PARKING, INC.—Allright Corporation, pg. 42
SYSTEMS PARKING, INC., pg. 1071
UNITED PARKING, INC., pg. 1134

7532 — TOP, BODY, UPHOLSTERY REPAIR SHOPS & PAINT SHOPS

ASC/CANADA INCORPORATED—ASC Incorporated, pg. 7
BAUGHER CHEVROLET-BUICK-GEO, INC., pg. 127
BEACH CITY CHEVROLET CO., pg. 128
DALLAS PETERBILT, INC., pg. 312
EAGLE LINCOLN MERCURY INC., pg. 362
MEL FARR FORD, INC., pg. 403
MAACO ENTERPRISES INC., pg. 694
MULTIPLE ALLIED SERVICES, INC., pg. 775
ROBERTSONS AUTO BODY—Robertson's Auto Salvage, pg. 939
ROYALE PAINT & BODY—Regency Lincoln Mercury, pg. 922

7533 — AUTOMOTIVE EXHAUST SYSTEM REPAIR SHOPS

MIDWEST TIRE & MUFFLER, INC., pg. 752
TUFFY ASSOCIATES CORP., pg. 1119

7534 — TIRE RETREADING & REPAIR SHOPS

BURRIS FOODS, INC., pg. 195
CONDERE CORPORATION, pg. 273
PARRISH TIRE COMPANY, INC., pg. 850
REDBURN TIRE COMPANY, pg. 919

7536 — AUTOMOTIVE GLASS REPLACEMENT SHOPS

AUTO GLASS SPECIALISTS, pg. 100
CARCOMP SERVICES, INC.—Globe Glass & Mirror Co., pg. 464
GLOBE GLASS & MIRROR CO., pg. 463
USA-GLAS, INC.—Globe Glass & Mirror Co., pg. 464
U.S. AUTO GLASS CENTERS, INC.—Globe Glass & Mirror Co., pg. 464

7537 — AUTOMOTIVE TRANSMISSION REPAIR SHOPS

AUTOMOTIVE AFTERMARKET DIVISION—Freudenberg-NOK (MI), pg. 432
COTTMAN TRANSMISSION SYSTEMS, INC., pg. 288
LEE MYLES ASSOCIATES CORPORATION, pg. 666
U.S. TRANSPARTS—Moran Industries, Inc., pg. 769

C. WEAVER CHEVROLET, INC., pg. 1170

7538 — GENERAL AUTOMOTIVE REPAIR SHOPS

A A CATER TRUCK MANUFACTURING COMPANY, INC., pg. 1
A S H, INC., pg. 8
AERO BODY & TRUCK EQUIPMENT, INC.—Tri-State Motor Transit Co., pg. 1111
ASSOCIATED DIESEL SERVICE & EQUIPMENT COMPANY, pg. 89
BAST CHEVROLET INC., pg. 125
BEACH CITY CHEVROLET CO., pg. 128
BYERLY FORD-NISSAN INC., pg. 198
CAMPBELL OIL CO., pg. 213
CAPITOL CHEVROLET CADILLAC GEO, INC., pg. 215
CLARKLIFT OF MINNESOTA, INC., pg. 253
COLLINS CHEVROLET, GEO, pg. 263
CUMMINS CUMBERLAND INC., pg. 305
CUMMINS MID-SOUTH, INC., pg. 305
D.S.U.-PETERBILT & GMC, INC., pg. 309
DAVIS-MOORE OLDSMOBILE, INC., pg. 319
JACK DEMMER FORD, INC., pg. 328
DREISBACH & SONS CADILLAC COMPANY, pg. 348
DRIVE TRAIN INDUSTRIES, pg. 349
EAGLE LINCOLN MERCURY INC., pg. 362
EARNHARDT'S AUTO CENTER, pg. 362
FLETCHER COBRE TIRE CO. INC.—Fletcher Enterprises, pg. 418
FRIENDLY CHEVROLET CO. INC., pg. 433
ILLINOIS AUTO CENTRAL DIV.—Illinois Auto Electric Co., pg. 562
KENWORTH OF INDIANAPOLIS INC., pg. 624
LA MESA R V CENTER, INC., pg. 649
MID AMERICA INTERNATIONAL TRUCKS, INC., pg. 750
MULTIPLE ALLIED SERVICES, INC., pg. 775
NUTTALL EQUIPMENT CO. INC., pg. 818
OCEAN CHEVROLET, INC., pg. 820
OHIO MACHINERY CO., pg. 822
THE PARK CIRCLE MOTOR CO., pg. 848
PATSY'S, INC., pg. 851
RIHM MOTOR COMPANY, pg. 934
SUMMERFIELD TRUCK CO. INC., pg. 1057
DAVE SYVERSON LINCOLN MERCURY, pg. 1071
VON HOUSEN MOTORS, pg. 1155
C. WEAVER CHEVROLET, INC., pg. 1170
WESTERN DIESEL SERVICES INC., pg. 1179
WESTERN TRAILER EQUIPMENT & MANUFACTURING CO., pg. 1182
BUFF WHELAN CHEVROLET & GEO, INC., pg. 1185

7539 — AUTOMOBILE REPAIR SHOPS, NEC

A K H COMPANY, INC., pg. 4
AUTO GLASS SPECIALISTS, pg. 100
BALCRANK PRODUCTS—New Hampshire Oak, pg. 801
D.S.U.-PETERBILT & GMC, INC., pg. 309
GLOBE-AMERADA GLASS COMPANY, pg. 463
W.W. WALLWORK, INC., pg. 1161
C. WEAVER CHEVROLET, INC., pg. 1170
WESTLIE MOTOR COMPANY, pg. 1183

7542 — CAR WASHES

F. L. ROBERTS & CO. INC., pg. 938

7549 — AUTOMOBILE SERVICES, EXCEPT REPAIR & CAR WASHES

JACK BYRNE MINUTEMAN LUBE—Jack Byrne Ford & Mercury, Inc., pg. 198
COLONIAL OIL INDUSTRIES, pg. 263
CONDERE CORPORATION, pg. 273
PAC MANUFACTURING & DISTRIBUTING CO.—Precision Tune, Inc., pg. 885
PRECISION TUNE, INC., pg. 885
TIDY CAR INTERNATIONAL, INC.—Ziebart International Corporation, pg. 1217
ZIEBART CANADA, INC.—Ziebart International Corporation, pg. 1218
ZIEBART (E.C.) LIMITED—Ziebart International Corporation, pg. 1218
ZIEBART INTERNATIONAL CORPORATION, pg. 1217
ZIEBART JAPAN LIMITED—Ziebart International Corporation, pg. 1218

7622 — RADIO & TELEVISION REPAIR SHOPS

CUTTER FLYING SERVICE, INC., pg. 307
PTS ELECTRONICS CORPORATION, pg. 837
RAULAND-BORG (CANADA) INC.—Rauland-Borg Corporation, pg. 914

7623 — REFRIGERATION & AIR CONDITIONING SERVICE & REPAIR SHOPS

CAL-AIR INC., pg. 208
CUMMINS SOUTHWEST INC., pg. 305
ILLINOIS AUTO CENTRAL DIV.—Illinois Auto Electric Co., pg. 562
MIDWESCO INC., pg. 751
TD INDUSTRIES INC., pg. 1072

7629 — ELECTRICAL & ELECTRONIC REPAIR SHOPS, NEC

AMERICAN TECHNICAL SERVICES GROUP, INC., pg. 63
CALIFORNIA ELECTRIC SERVICE, pg. 209
EBM SYSTEMS, INC., pg. 359
ECO WATER SYSTEMS, pg. 367
ELECTRICAL EQUIPMENT COMPANY, pg. 374
ELECTRICAL EQUIPMENT COMPANY—Electrical Equipment Company, pg. 374
MED-LAB SUPPLY COMPANY, INC., pg. 734
MEMPHIS GROUP, INC., pg. 738
MILWAUKEE ELECTRIC TOOL (CANADA) LTD.—ESSTAR Incorporated, pg. 361
MOUNTAINEER MEDICAL/PRIMACARE I.V.—Syracuse Supply Company, pg. 1070
NATIONAL TECHNICAL SERVICES—American Technical Services Group, Inc., pg. 64
PACIFICA SERVICES, INC., pg. 842
RAYMOND ROSEN CO., pg. 948
SAN ANGELO ELECTRIC SERVICE COMPANY, pg. 969
STANDARD MEDICAL IMAGING, INC., pg. 1037
SUNBEAM CORPORATION (CANADA) LIMITED—Sunbeam-Oster Company, Inc., pg. 1059

7631 — WATCH, CLOCK & JEWELRY REPAIR

FINLAY ENTERPRISES, INC., pg. 411

7692 — WELDING REPAIR

ANCHOR TOOL & DIE COMPANY, pg. 71
MUNROE, INC., pg. 776
NORWECO, INC., pg. 816
L. B. SMITH, INC., pg. 1013

7694 — ARMATURE REWINDING SHOPS

CLEVELAND ELECTRIC CO.—Cleveland Group, Inc., pg. 255
CLEVELAND GROUP, INC., pg. 255
ELECTRICAL EQUIPMENT COMPANY, pg. 374
ELECTRICAL EQUIPMENT COMPANY—Electrical Equipment Company, pg. 374
ELECTRONIC DRIVES AND CONTROLS, pg. 375
HEAVY MACHINES, INC., pg. 524
TRI-STATE ARMATURE ELECTRIC WORKS, pg. 1110

7699 — REPAIR SHOPS & RELATED SERVICES, NEC

ALASKA TOOL & EQUIPMENT SERVICE—Alaska Industrial Hardware Inc., pg. 30
ALBAN TRACTOR CO. INC., pg. 30
ALLIED SECURITY, INTERNATIONAL, pg. 40
ATLANTIC HEALTH CARE RESOURCES, INC.—Syracuse Supply Company, pg. 1070
BOLTON-EMERSON-MCNIECE, INC.—Bolton-Emerson, Inc., pg. 163
CARTER CHAMBERS SUPPLY, INC., pg. 226
CLAYTON MANUFACTURING DIV., DYNAMIC EQUIPMENT—Clayton Industries Co., pg. 254
COLE KEY CORPORATION—Cole National Corporation, pg. 260
COLE NATIONAL CORPORATION, pg. 260
CONTAINER PORT GROUP—World Shipping, Inc., pg. 1203
CROWLEY MARITIME CORPORATION, pg. 301
CUMMINS SOUTHWEST INC., pg. 305
ELLIOTT TURBOMACHINERY LTD.—Elliott Company, pg. 378
JOHN FABICK TRACTOR COMPANY, pg. 396
W. B. GOODE COMPANY, INC., pg. 470
THE GREAT FRAME UP SYSTEMS, INC., pg. 480
HOPPER INC., pg. 543
ILLINOIS AUTO ELECTRIC CO., pg. 562
INTERNATIONAL DIV.—Clayton Industries Co., pg. 254
INTERNATIONAL MARINE HOLDINGS, INC., pg. 579
KING FUELS INC., pg. 630
KINGSBURY SERVICE CORP.—Kingsbury Corporation, pg. 632
METRO MEDICAL RESOURCES, INC.—Syracuse Supply Company, pg. 1070
MOUNTAINEER MEDICAL/PRIMACARE I.V.—Syracuse Supply Company, pg. 1070
MUNROE, INC., pg. 776
NEWTRON GROUP INC., pg. 805
PENN MEDICAL SERVICES, INC.—Syracuse Supply Company, pg. 1070
PLANT MAINTENANCE SERVICE CORPORATION, pg. 874
RELIANCE ELEVATOR COMPANY, pg. 925
ROAD MACHINERY COMPANY, pg. 937
SHIPLEY OIL COMPANY, pg. 999
SOVEREIGN GROUP INC., pg. 1024
STARKEY LABORATORIES, INC., pg. 1040
TRIANGLE MAINTENANCE CORPORATION, pg. 1112
UNITED TECTONIC INDUSTRY, pg. 1137
WALKER NATIONAL, INC.—Walker Magnetics Group, Inc., pg. 1160
YALE INDUSTRIAL TRUCKS OF SOUTHERN CALIFORNIA, pg. 1207
ZIMA CORP., pg. 1219

7812 — MOTION PICTURE & VIDEO TAPE PRODUCTION

ABINGDON PRESS, pg. 10
ARTS & ENTERTAINMENT NETWORK—The Hearst Corporation, pg. 523
BNA COMMUNICATIONS, INC.—The Bureau of National Affairs, Inc., pg. 189
THE BENSON MUSIC GROUP, pg. 140
THE BUREAU OF NATIONAL AFFAIRS, INC., pg. 189
BURNHAM BROADCASTING COMPANY, pg. 193
CHANLON VIDEO ARTS—SB Entertainment Inc., pg. 960
THE DARTNELL CORPORATION, pg. 316
ENCYCLOPAEDIA BRITANNICA EDUCATIONAL CORPORATION, pg. 380
FOUR STAR HOLDINGS CORP.—Andrews Group, Incorporated, pg. 74
GREAT AMERICAN BROADCASTING COMPANY—American Financial Corporation, pg. 52
HANNA-BARBERA PRODUCTIONS, INC.—American Financial Corporation, pg. 53
HEARST ENTERTAINMENT PRODUCTIONS, INC.—The Hearst Corporation, pg. 523
JOSEPHSON INTERNATIONAL INC., pg. 607
ROBERT KEESHAN ASSOCIATES, INC.—Josephson International Inc., pg. 607
KING FEATURES SYNDICATE DIVISION—The Hearst Corporation, pg. 524
MARITZ COMMUNICATIONS CO.—Maritz Inc., pg. 707
MARITZ INC., pg. 707
NATIONAL AMUSEMENTS, INC., pg. 784
NATIONAL FIRE PROTECTION ASSOCIATION, pg. 788
NEW WORLD ENTERTAINMENT, INC.—Andrews Group, Incorporated, pg. 74
RESOURCE, INC., pg. 929
SB ENTERTAINMENT INC., pg. 960
SI HOLDINGS INC., pg. 962
SCHOLASTIC INC.—SI Holdings Inc., pg. 962
SCHOLASTIC PRODUCTIONS INC.—SI Holdings Inc., pg. 962
SNAP-TITE, INCORPORATED, pg. 1014
SPRING, O'BRIEN & CO. INC., pg. 1033
THE TODD-AO CORPORATION, pg. 1099
TODD-AO/EAST—The Todd-AO Corporation, pg. 1099
TYNDALE HOUSE PUBLISHERS, INC., pg. 1122
VCA TELETRONICS INC., pg. 1141
VIACOM INTERNATIONAL INC.—National Amusements, Inc., pg. 785
VIACOM PRODUCTIONS INC.—National Amusements, Inc., pg. 785
WESTERN VIDEO IMAGES, INC.—Western Temporary Services, Inc., pg. 1182

7819 — SERVICES ALLIED TO MOTION PICTURE PRODUCTION

ANDREWS GROUP, INCORPORATED, pg. 74
C & L MARKETING INC.—Capitol Industries-EMI Inc., pg. 216
CINE MAGNETICS, INC., pg. 250
COMPACT VIDEO SERVICES, INC.—Andrews Group, Incorporated, pg. 74
IDC SERVICES, INC., pg. 559
IMAGE TRANSFORM—Andrews Group, Incorporated, pg. 74
IMAGE TRANSFORM LAB—Andrews Group, Incorporated, pg. 74
RALEIGH ENTERPRISES, INC., pg. 910
VCA TELETRONICS INC., pg. 1141

7822 — MOTION PICTURE & VIDEO TAPE DISTRIBUTION

AMERICAN FINANCIAL CORPORATION, pg. 52
ANDREWS GROUP, INCORPORATED, pg. 74
ASCO MUSIC—Cox Enterprises, Inc., pg. 292
BEEPEE MUSIC—Cox Enterprises, Inc., pg. 292
BING CROSBY PRODUCTIONS, INC.—Cox Enterprises, Inc., pg. 292
FOUR STAR HOLDINGS CORP.—Andrews Group, Incorporated, pg. 74
HEARST ENTERTAINMENT—The Hearst Corporation, pg. 523
IMC, INC.—ZBS Industries, Inc., pg. 1215
INGRAM DISTRIBUTION GROUP INC.—Ingram Industries Inc., pg. 569
KDI CORPORATION, pg. 612
THE CHARLES LEVY COMPANY, pg. 672
MPO VIDEOTRONICS, INC., pg. 693
MODERN TALKING PICTURE SERVICE, INC.—KDI Corporation, pg. 612
NATIONAL AMUSEMENTS, INC., pg. 784
SPELLING ENTERTAINMENT GROUP, INC.—American Financial Corporation, pg. 54
TFI (TAPE FILMS INC.)—MPO Videotronics, Inc., pg. 693
VIACOM ENTERPRISES—National Amusements, Inc., pg. 785
VIACOM INC.—National Amusements, Inc., pg. 785
VIACOM INTERNATIONAL INC.—National Amusements, Inc., pg. 785
VID AMERICA, INC.—Andrews Group, Incorporated, pg. 74
VIDEO PRODUCTS DISTRIBUTORS, INC., pg. 1150
ZBS INDUSTRIES, INC., pg. 1215

7829 — SERVICES ALLIED TO MOTION PICTURE DISTRIBUTION

OCTOBER FILMS, INC., pg. 821

7832 — MOTION PICTURE THEATERS, EXCEPT DRIVE-IN

CINAMERICA THEATRES, L.P., pg. 249
WOMETCO ENTERPRISES, INC., pg. 1199

7833 — DRIVE-IN MOTION PICTURE THEATERS

NATIONAL AMUSEMENTS, INC., pg. 784

7841 — VIDEO TAPE RENTAL

H. E. BUTT GROCERY CO., pg. 197
NATIONAL VIDEO, INC.—West Coast National Video, pg. 1177
PUEBLO INTERNATIONAL, INC., pg. 899
SOUND WAREHOUSE, INC., pg. 1018
VICTORY VIDEO INC.—Victory Markets Inc., pg. 1150
WEST COAST NATIONAL VIDEO, pg. 1177

7911 — DANCE HALLS, STUDIOS & SCHOOLS

ARTHUR MURRAY INTL., INC., pg. 776

7922 — THEATRICAL PRODUCERS, (EXCEPT MOTION PICTURE) & MISCELLANEOUS THEATRICAL SERVICES

ALLBRITTON TELEVISION PRODUCTIONS, INC.—Perpetual Corporation, pg. 862
DESERT PRODUCTION SERVICES—Media America Corp., pg. 734
DUNCAN HEATH ASSOCIATES—Josephson International Inc., pg. 607
THE GREAT AMERICAN ENTERTAINMENT COMPANY—American Financial Corporation, pg. 53
ICM ARTISTS, LTD.—Josephson International Inc., pg. 607
INTERNATIONAL CREATIVE MANAGEMENT, INC.—Josephson International Inc., pg. 607
INTERNATIONAL CREATIVE MANAGEMENT LTD.—Josephson International Inc., pg. 607
JOSEPHSON INTERNATIONAL INC., pg. 607
OPRYLAND USA, INC.—Gaylord Entertainment Co., pg. 446
TICKETMASTER CORPORATION, pg. 1096

7929 — BANDS, ORCHESTRAS, ACTORS, & OTHER ENTERTAINERS & ENTERTAINMENT GROUPS

GAYLORD ENTERTAINMENT CO., pg. 446

7933 — BOWLING ALLEYS

AMF AZALEA BOWL—William H. Goodwin Trust, pg. 471
AMF BOWLING CENTERS INC.—William H. Goodwin Trust, pg. 471
AMF BOWLING CENTERS INC.—William H. Goodwin Trust, pg. 471
AMF LANG'S BOWLARAMA INC.—William H. Goodwin Trust, pg. 471
BOWLERAMA LANES, INC.—Great Lakes Recreation Co., pg. 482
BOWLING CORP. OF AMERICA—Charan Industries, Inc., pg. 239
CHARAN INDUSTRIES, INC., pg. 239
CLOVERLANES, INC.—Great Lakes Recreation Co., pg. 482
FAIR LANE BOWLING DIV.—Fair Lanes Inc., pg. 396
FAIR LANES INC., pg. 396
FAIRLANES BOWL, INC.—Great Lakes Recreation Co., pg. 482
GREAT LAKES BOWLING CENTRE, INC.—Great Lakes Recreation Co., pg. 482
GREAT LAKES RECREATION CO., pg. 481
YPSI-ARBOR LANES—Great Lakes Recreation Co., pg. 482

7941 — PROFESSIONAL SPORTS CLUBS & PROMOTERS

CALIFORNIA ANGELS BASEBALL CLUB—Golden West Broadcasters, pg. 467
CLEARWATER PHILLIES—The Phillies-A Limited Partnership, pg. 867
JACK KENT COOKE, INC., pg. 282
THE EDWARD J. DEBARTOLO CORPORATION, pg. 323
GOLDEN WEST BROADCASTERS, pg. 467
GUERNICA ESPECTACULOS & TURISMO, S.A.—World Jai-alai, pg. 1203
MILWAUKEE BUCKS, INC., pg. 756
MINNESOTA TWINS BASEBALL CLUB, pg. 758
NATIONAL BASKETBALL ASSOCIATION, pg. 786
NATIONAL FOOTBALL LEAGUE PROPERTIES, INC., pg. 788
THE PHILLIES-A LIMITED PARTNERSHIP, pg. 867
PITTSBURGH PIRATES PROFESSIONAL BASEBALL CLUB, pg. 873
RICH PRODUCTS CORP., pg. 932
SACRAMENTO KINGS, pg. 965
SAN DIEGO CHARGERS, pg. 969
SAN FRANCISCO GIANTS BASEBALL CLUB, pg. 969
WORLD JAI-ALAI, pg. 1202
WORLD JAI-ALAI PLAYERS—World Jai-alai, pg. 1203

7948 — RACING, INCLUDING TRACK OPERATION

BRANDYWINE RACEWAY ASSN., INC.—Brandywine Sports, Inc., pg. 172
BRANDYWINE SPORTS, INC., pg. 172
CHARLES TOWN RACES, INC., pg. 240
THE EDWARD J. DEBARTOLO CORPORATION, pg. 323
DELAWARE NORTH COMPANIES, INC., pg. 326
HENDRICK MOTORSPORTS—Hendrick Management Corporation, pg. 529
HOLLYWOOD PARK, INC., pg. 540
KEENELAND ASSOC., INC., pg. 620
LOUISIANA DOWNS—The Edward J. DeBartolo Corporation, pg. 323
MALIBU GRAND PRIX CORPORATION, pg. 702
NEW YORK RACING ASSOCIATION, pg. 803
SARATOGA HARNESS RACING, INC., pg. 970
SPORTSYSTEMS CORPORATION—Delaware North Companies, Inc., pg. 326

7991 — PHYSICAL FITNESS FACILITIES

JAZZERCISE, INC., pg. 591
GEORGETTE KLINGER, INC., pg. 635
MALIBU GRAND PRIX CORPORATION, pg. 702
NUTRI/SYSTEM INC., pg. 818
ZILBER, LTD., pg. 1219

7992 — PUBLIC GOLF COURSES

CENTURY GOLF COURSES, INC.—Cenvill Development Corp., pg. 236
INDIANHEAD GOLF CLUB—Chief Industries, Inc., pg. 247
KOHLER COMPANY, pg. 639

7993 — COIN-OPERATED AMUSEMENT DEVICES

DUNES HOTELS AND CASINOS INC., pg. 352

7996 — AMUSEMENT PARKS

ADVENTURE LANDS OF AMERICA, INC., pg. 21
HBE CORPORATION, pg. 495
KINGS ISLAND COMPANY—American Financial Corporation, pg. 53
KNOTT'S BERRY FARM, pg. 637
MARINE WORLD AFRICA USA, pg. 707

7997 — MEMBERSHIP SPORTS & RECREATION CLUBS

CLUB CORPORATION INTERNATIONAL, pg. 256
GOLF HOST RESORTS, INC.—Golf Hosts, Inc., pg. 469
KANSAS CITY CHIEFS FOOTBALL CLUB, pg. 616
KOHLER COMPANY, pg. 639
MALIBU GRAND PRIX CORPORATION, pg. 702
TENNANAH LAKE GOLF & TENNIS CLUB, INC.—Construction Counsellors, Inc., pg. 277

7999 — AMUSEMENT AND RECREATION SERVICES, NEC

ALASKA BOAT CO.—Wards Cove Packing Company, pg. 1163
AMANA SOCIETY, pg. 46
ARIZONA LOTTERY, pg. 82
BELL GARDENS BICYCLE CLUB, pg. 134
BILLCOM EXPOSITION & CONFERENCE—Bill Communications, Inc., pg. 150
BOWLING CORP. OF AMERICA—Charan Industries, Inc., pg. 239
CALIFORNIA STATE LOTTERY, pg. 210
CHARITABLE GAMING DIV.—Michigan State Lottery Bureau, pg. 747
COLORADO LOTTERY, pg. 265
CONNECTICUT STATE LOTTERY, pg. 275
D.C. LOTTERY & CHARITABLE GAMES CONTROL BOARD, pg. 308
DELAWARE LOTTERY, pg. 326
DIVERSIFIED COMMUNICATIONS, pg. 340
DUNES HOTELS AND CASINOS INC., pg. 352
THE FLORIDA LOTTERY, pg. 420
GUEST SERVICES, INC., pg. 493
IDAHO LOTTERY, pg. 561
ILLINOIS STATE LOTTERY, pg. 563
ILLINOIS STATE LOTTERY—Illinois State Lottery, pg. 563
INTERNATIONAL DATA CORP.—International Data Group, pg. 577
INTERNATIONAL DATA GROUP, pg. 576
IOWA LOTTERY, pg. 582
LDI, LTD., pg. 647
MAINE STATE LOTTERY COMMISSION, pg. 702
MAJOR VIDEO CONCEPTS, INC.—LDI, Ltd., pg. 647
MASSACHUSETTS STATE LOTTERY, pg. 719
MICHIGAN STATE LOTTERY BUREAU, pg. 747
MISSOURI LOTTERY, pg. 760
MONTANA LOTTERY, pg. 766
NEW HAMPSHIRE SWEEPSTAKES COMMISSION, pg. 801
NEW JERSEY STATE LOTTERY, pg. 801
OHIO LOTTERY COMMISSION, pg. 822
OREGON STATE LOTTERY, pg. 829
PENNSYLVANIA STATE LOTTERY, pg. 858
PHILLIPS FINE ART AUCTIONEERS, pg. 867
PICK'S COVE MARINA—Pickering Industries Inc., pg. 870
PUTT PUTT GOLF COURSES OF AMERICA, INC., pg. 901
RHODE ISLAND LOTTERY, pg. 931
RINGLING BROS., BARNUM & BAILEY COMBINED SHOWS, INC., pg. 935
SILVER DOLLAR CITY, INC., pg. 1004
SOUTH DAKOTA LOTTERY, pg. 1019
TOPCOR FINANCIAL CORPORATION, pg. 1101
TOTAL EXPOSITION CONCEPTS—Servistar Corporation, pg. 993
TRUMP'S CASTLE CASINO RESORT—Trump Organization, pg. 1118
UNITED EXPOSITION SERVICE COMPANY—Topcor Financial Corporation, pg. 1102
VERMONT LOTTERY COMMISSION, pg. 1148
VIRGINIA HOT SPRINGS, INC., pg. 1152
VIRGINIA STATE LOTTERY DEPARTMENT, pg. 1153
WEATHERKING PRODUCTS, INC.—Aqua Fab Industries, Inc., pg. 79
WEST VIRGINIA LOTTERY, pg. 1178
WESTERN REGIONAL OFF TRACK BETTING, pg. 1181

8011 — OFFICES & CLINICS OF DOCTORS OF MEDICINE

FARGO CLINIC LTD., pg. 399
GPS HEALTHCARE—Berwind Corporation, pg. 145
UNITED HEALTH PLAN, pg. 1133

8042 — OFFICES & CLINICS OF OPTOMETRISTS

MIDWEST VISION CENTERS, pg. 752

8051 — SKILLED NURSING CARE FACILITIES

ARA SERVICES, INC.—ARA Group, pg. 5
COLUMBIA CORPORATION, pg. 265
EVERGREEN HEALTHCARE LTD., pg. 391
HEALTH CARE LODGES, pg. 520
MERITCARE, INC., pg. 740
NATIONAL HEALTH CARE AFFILIATES, INC., pg. 791
NATIONAL HERITAGE, INC.—Evergreen Healthcare Ltd., pg. 392

8052 — INTERMEDIATE CARE FACILITIES

EVERGREEN HEALTHCARE LTD., pg. 391
NATIONAL HERITAGE, INC.—Evergreen Healthcare Ltd., pg. 392

8059 — NURSING & PERSONAL CARE FACILITIES, NEC

CARRIAGE HOUSE MANOR—Meritcare, Inc., pg. 740
MAJESTIC PINES CARE CENTER—Meritcare, Inc., pg. 740
MERITCARE, INC., pg. 740
PARKMONT NURSING HOME—Meritcare, Inc., pg. 740
TWIN PALMS CARE CENTER—Meritcare, Inc., pg. 740
VALLEY MANOR CARE—Meritcare, Inc., pg. 740

8062 — GENERAL MEDICAL & SURGICAL HOSPITALS

AUBURN FAITH COMMUNITY HOSPITAL, pg. 97
CENTRAL DUPAGE HEALTH SYSTEM, pg. 232
CENTRAL DUPAGE HOSPITAL ASSOCIATION—Central DuPage Health System, pg. 232
HEALTH MANAGEMENT SYSTEMS, INC., pg. 521

8069 — SPECIALTY HOSPITALS, EXCEPT PSYCHIATRIC

EPIC HEALTHCARE GROUP, pg. 384

8071 — MEDICAL LABORATORIES

NATIONAL HEALTH LABORATORIES INC.—MacAndrews & Forbes Holdings Inc., pg. 696
PRUCO SERVICES, INC.—The Prudential Insurance Company of America, pg. 896
THE PRUDENTIAL INSURANCE COMPANY OF AMERICA, pg. 896
REVLON, INC.—MacAndrews & Forbes Holdings Inc., pg. 696
UNITED HEALTH PLAN, pg. 1133

8082 — HOME HEALTH CARE SERVICES

HOME CARE P.R.N., INC.—Technical Aid Corporation, pg. 1083
NORRELL HEALTH CARE INC.—Norrell Corporation, pg. 811
PATIENT CARE, INC., pg. 851
TAC/MEDICAL SERVICES INC.—Technical Aid Corporation, pg. 1083
WESTERN MEDICAL SERVICES DIV.—Western Temporary Services, Inc., pg. 1182

8093 — SPECIALTY OUTPATIENT FACILITIES, NEC

ALCOHOLISM TREATMENT CENTER—Central DuPage Health System, pg. 232
CENTRAL DUPAGE HEALTH SYSTEM, pg. 232

8099 — HEALTH & ALLIED SERVICES, NEC

AETNA HEALTH PLANS, pg. 23
DIET CENTER, INC.—American Health Companies, Inc., pg. 55
EXECU-FIT HEALTH PROGRAMS, INC.—UniHealth America, pg. 1127
NATIONAL HEALTH CARE AFFILIATES, INC., pg. 791
OMNICARE HEALTH PLAN, pg. 826
OWEN HEALTH CARE, pg. 833
UNIHEALTH AMERICA, pg. 1126
UNITED AMERICAN HEALTHCARE CORP.—OmniCare Health Plan, pg. 826

8111 — LEGAL SERVICES

AMWAY CORPORATION, pg. 70
DECHERT PRICE & RHOADS, pg. 323
JONES, DAY, REAVIS & POGUE, pg. 603
PEPPER, HAMILTON & SCHEETZ—Pepper, Hamilton & Scheetz, pg. 860
PEPPER, HAMILTON & SCHEETZ—Pepper, Hamilton & Scheetz, pg. 860
PEPPER, HAMILTON & SCHEETZ—Pepper, Hamilton & Scheetz, pg. 860
PEPPER, HAMILTON & SCHEETZ—Pepper, Hamilton & Scheetz, pg. 860
PEPPER, HAMILTON & SCHEETZ—Pepper, Hamilton & Scheetz, pg. 860
PEPPER, HAMILTON & SCHEETZ—Pepper, Hamilton & Scheetz, pg. 860
PEPPER, HAMILTON & SCHEETZ—Pepper, Hamilton & Scheetz, pg. 860
PEPPER, HAMILTON & SCHEETZ—Pepper, Hamilton & Scheetz, pg. 860
PEPPER, HAMILTON & SCHEETZ—Pepper, Hamilton & Scheetz, pg. 860
PEPPER, HAMILTON & SCHEETZ, pg. 860
U-HAUL INTERNATIONAL, INC.—Amerco, A Nevada Corporation, pg. 48
WOLF, BLOCK, SCHORR & SOLIS-COHEN, pg. 1199

8221 — COLLEGES, UNIVERSITIES & PROFESSIONAL SCHOOLS

ADL MANAGEMENT EDUCATION INSTITUTE, INC.—Arthur D. Little, Inc., pg. 678
GOLDEN GATE UNIVERSITY, pg. 466

8243 — DATA PROCESSING SCHOOLS

LOGICAL OPERATIONS—Ziff Communications Company, pg. 1219
PC CONCEPTS—Ziff Communications Company, pg. 1219
TECHNOLOGY TRANSFER INSTITUTE, pg. 1084

8249 — VOCATIONAL SCHOOLS, NEC

BUREAU OF ENGRAVING, pg. 189
FOLEY-BELSAW COMPANY, pg. 422
THE LOUISVILLE TRANSPORTATION COMPANY—Interlock Industries, Inc., pg. 574
RAILWAY EDUCATIONAL BUREAU—Simmons-Boardman Publishing Corp., pg. 1005
WEICHERT REALTY CAREER DEVELOPMENT—Weichert Company, pg. 1173

8299 — SCHOOLS AND EDUCATIONAL SERVICES, NEC

ALPINE CENTER, S.R.L. (BERLITZ)—Berlitz International, Inc., pg. 142
ALPS INSTITUTE—Berlitz International, Inc., pg. 142
ALPS INSTITUTE S.R.L. (BERLITZ)—Berlitz International, Inc., pg. 142
AMERICAN COUNCIL FOR INTERNATIONAL STUDIES—American Institute For Foreign Study, pg. 56
AMERICAN INSTITUTE FOR FOREIGN STUDY, pg. 56
AMERICAN INSTITUTE FOR FOREIGN STUDY—American Institute For Foreign Study, pg. 56
AMERICAN LEARNING CORP.—Encyclopaedia Britannica, Inc., pg. 381
AU PAIR IN AMERICA—American Institute For Foreign Study, pg. 56
AUGSBURG FORTRESS, PUBLISHERS, pg. 98
OY BERLITZ AB—Berlitz International, Inc., pg. 142
BERLITZ A/S—Berlitz International, Inc., pg. 142
BERLITZ DE MEXICO, S.A. DE C.V.—Berlitz International, Inc., pg. 142
BERLITZ ESCOLA DE IDIOMAS LTDA.—Berlitz International, Inc., pg. 142
BERLITZ ESCUELAS DE IDIOMAS LTDA.—Berlitz International, Inc., pg. 142
BERLITZ FRANCE S.A.—Berlitz International, Inc., pg. 143
BERLITZ INTERNATIONAL DANMARK A/S—Berlitz International, Inc., pg. 142
BERLITZ INTERNATIONAL, INC., pg. 142
BERLITZ KFT—Berlitz International, Inc., pg. 142
BERLITZ LANGUAGE CENTERS OF CANADA LTD.—Berlitz International, Inc., pg. 142
BERLITZ LANGUAGE CENTERS, S.R.L.—Berlitz International, Inc., pg. 142
BERLITZ SCHOOLS OF LANGUAGES AB—Berlitz International, Inc., pg. 143
BERLITZ SCHOOLS OF LANGUAGES OF ARGENTINA S.A.—Berlitz International, Inc., pg. 143
BERLITZ SCHOOLS OF LANGUAGES OF BENELUX S.A.—Berlitz International, Inc., pg. 143
BERLITZ SCHOOLS OF LANGUAGES B.V.—Berlitz International, Inc., pg. 143
BERLITZ SCHOOLS OF LANGUAGES CZECHSOLOVAKIA SPOL.SR.O—Berlitz International, Inc., pg. 143
BERLITZ SCHOOLS OF LANGUAGES GMBH—Berlitz International, Inc., pg. 143
THE BERLITZ SCHOOLS OF LANGUAGES (JAPAN) INC.—Berlitz International, Inc., pg. 143
BERLITZ SCHOOLS OF LANGUAGES LTD.—Berlitz International, Inc., pg. 143
BERLITZ SCHOOLS OF LANGUAGES AG—Berlitz International, Inc., pg. 143
BERLITZ SOVINCENTER—Berlitz International, Inc., pg. 143
BERLITZ SPRACHSCHULEN GMBH—Berlitz International, Inc., pg. 143
BERLITZ THAILAND LTD.—Berlitz International, Inc., pg. 143
BERLITZ-CYZTELNIK LANGUAGE SCHOOL—Berlitz International, Inc., pg. 143
BUREAU OF ENGRAVING, pg. 189
CAMP AMERICA—American Institute For Foreign Study, pg. 56
CENTRO DE IDIOMAS BERLITZ DE VENEZUELA—Berlitz International, Inc., pg. 143
COLLEGE DIVISION—American Institute For Foreign Study, pg. 56
ELS EDUCATIONAL SERVICES—American Institute For Foreign Study, pg. 56
ELS EDUCATIONAL SERVICES—American Institute For Foreign Study, pg. 56
ESCUELAS DE IDIOMAS BERLITZ DE ESPANA, S.A.—Berlitz International, Inc., pg. 143
EUROPE LANGUAGE CENTER SRL—Berlitz International, Inc., pg. 143
EXECUTIVE ENTERPRISES, INC., pg. 393
EXECUTIVE ENTERPRISES PUBLICATIONS CO., INC.—Executive Enterprises, Inc., pg. 393
HIGH SCHOOL DIVISION—American Institute For Foreign Study, pg. 56
INSTITUTO DE IDIOMAS COLOMBIA, S.A.—Berlitz International, Inc., pg. 143
LANGUAGE INSTITUTE FOR ENGLISH (L.I.F.E.)—Berlitz International, Inc., pg. 142
MULTI LANGUAGE CENTER SRL—Berlitz International, Inc., pg. 143
NEW YORK LANGUAGE CENTER—Berlitz International, Inc., pg. 143
PRINCETON LANGUAGE CENTER—Berlitz International, Inc., pg. 143
VISTA MULTI METHOD—Berlitz International, Inc., pg. 143
VISTA MULTI NATIONAL—Berlitz International, Inc., pg. 143
WASHINGTON LANGUAGE CENTER—Berlitz International, Inc., pg. 143
WORLD LANGUAGES SRL—Berlitz International, Inc., pg. 143

8351 — CHILD DAY CARE SERVICES

CHILDREN'S WORLD LEARNING CENTERS, INC.—ARA Group, pg. 7

8361 — RESIDENTIAL CARE

NEWARK REHABILITATION, INC.—The Prudential Insurance Company of America, pg. 896
PLAN INTERNATIONAL U.S.A., pg. 874
THE PRUDENTIAL INSURANCE COMPANY OF AMERICA, pg. 896

8412 — MUSEUMS & ART GALLERIES

ANDREAS GALLERIES, INC.—Lantzsch-Andreas Enterprises, Inc., pg. 658

8422 — ARBORETA & BOTANICAL OR ZOOLOGICAL GARDENS

SAN DIEGO WILD ANIMAL PARK—San Diego Zoo, pg. 969
SAN DIEGO ZOO, pg. 969
WOMETCO ENTERPRISES, INC., pg. 1199

8611 — BUSINESS ASSOCIATIONS

THE AMERICAN BANKERS ASSOCIATION, pg. 49
AMERICAN BUREAU OF SHIPPING, pg. 50
ARIZONA GRAINS INC., pg. 82
ASSOCIATION OF CREDIT UNION LEAGUE EXECUTIVES—Credit Union National Association, pg. 298
BANK MARKETING ASSOCIATION—The American Bankers Association, pg. 49
THE BRADY MARKETING COMPANY, pg. 171
CALIFORNIA APRICOT ADVISORY BOARD, pg. 209
CALIFORNIA AVOCADO COMMISSION, pg. 209
CALIFORNIA STRAWBERRY ADVISORY BOARD, pg. 210
COUNTRYMARK COOPERATIVE, INC., pg. 290
CREDIT UNION BENEFITS SERVICES, INC.—Credit Union National Association, pg. 298
CREDIT UNION NATIONAL ASSOCIATION, pg. 298
CUNA MORTGAGE CORPORATION—Credit Union National Association, pg. 298
CUNA SERVICE GROUP, INC.—Credit Union National Association, pg. 298
DEFENSE CREDIT UNION COUNCIL—Credit Union National Association, pg. 298
EDMONSON WHEAT GROWERS, INC., pg. 369
FILENE RESEARCH INSTITUTE—Credit Union National Association, pg. 298
THE FLORISTS ASSN. OF GREATER CLEVELAND, INC., pg. 421
GENCON SERVICES, INC.—George W. Auch Co., pg. 98
INDEPENDENT INSURANCE AGENTS OF AMERICA, pg. 565
INTERSTATE PRODUCERS LIVESTOCK ASSOCIATION, pg. 580
LINDSAY OLIVE GROWERS, pg. 676
MEMPHIS LIGHT, GAS & WATER, pg. 738
MICHIGAN MILK PRODUCERS ASSOCIATION, pg. 747
NATIONAL FEDERATION OF COMMUNITY DEVELOPMENT CREDIT UNIONS—Credit Union National Association, pg. 298
NATIONAL FIRE PROTECTION ASSOCIATION, pg. 788
QUALITY CHEKD DAIRY PRODUCTS ASSOCIATION, pg. 903
RUMS OF PUERTO RICO, pg. 956
UNITED HEALTH PLAN, pg. 1133
UNITED SERVICES AUTOMOBILE ASSOCIATION (USAA), pg. 1134
UNITED STATES CENTRAL CREDIT UNION—Credit Union National Association, pg. 298
WASHINGTON STATE DAIRY PRODUCTS COMMISSION, pg. 1167
WORLD COUNCIL OF CREDIT UNIONS—Credit Union National Association, pg. 298

8621 — PROFESSIONAL MEMBERSHIP ORGANIZATIONS

ASM INTERNATIONAL, pg. 8
AMERICAN INSTITUTE OF C.P.A.'S INC., pg. 56
AMWAY CORPORATION, pg. 70
U-HAUL INTERNATIONAL, INC.—Amerco, A Nevada Corporation, pg. 48

8631 — LABOR UNIONS & SIMILAR LABOR ORGANIZATIONS

FOSTER & HIGGINS, INC.—Johnson & Higgins, pg. 598

8641 — CIVIC, SOCIAL & FRATERNAL ASSOCIATIONS

B.A.S.S., INC., pg. 105
BASSMASTER MAGAZINE—B.A.S.S., Inc., pg. 105

8661 — RELIGIOUS ORGANIZATIONS

STRANG COMMUNICATIONS COMPANY, pg. 1052

8699 — MEMBERSHIP ORGANIZATIONS, NEC

AMERICAN WATER WORKS ASSOCIATION, pg. 65
MADD (MOTHERS AGAINST DRUNK DRIVING), pg. 691
NODAK MUTUAL INSURANCE COMPANY, pg. 808
THE SIGNATURE GROUP—Montgomery Ward & Co., Inc., pg. 768

8711 — ENGINEERING SERVICES

ABS INDUSTRIAL VERIFICATION, INC.—American Bureau of Shipping, pg. 50
AM GENERAL CORPORATION—Renco Group, pg. 926
ASC INCORPORATED, pg. 7
ASCG, INC., pg. 7
ACME TRIM—Acme Mills Co. Inc., pg. 13
ADVANCED DZIGN SYSTEMS—Day & Zimmermann, Inc., pg. 320
ADVANCED MARINE ENTERPRISES, INC., pg. 20
ADVANCED TECHNOLOGY, INC., pg. 20
THE AEROSPACE CORPORATION, pg. 22
AIRCO COMMERCIAL SERVICES, INC.—Airco Mechanical Inc., pg. 27
ALLEN & HOSHALL, INC., pg. 36
AMBULATORY ONE AMERICA INC., pg. 47
AMCLYDE ENGINEERED PRODUCTS, INC., pg. 47
AMERICAN FINANCIAL CORPORATION, pg. 52
AMERICAN SYSTEMS CORPORATION, pg. 63
AMERICAN SYSTEMS ENGINEERING CORPORATION—Science Applications International Corporation, pg. 981
ANDERSON-PARRISH ASSOCIATES, INC.—Lawler-Havens Inc., pg. 661
ARINC RESEARCH CORP.—Arinc Inc., pg. 82
AUSTIN-AUSTRALIA—National Gypsum Company, pg. 790
THE AUSTIN CO.—National Gypsum Company, pg. 790
THE AUSTIN CO. S.A.—National Gypsum Company, pg. 790
THE AUSTIN CO. OF U.K. LTD.—National Gypsum Company, pg. 790
THE AUSTIN COMPANY—National Gypsum Company, pg. 790
AUSTIN ITALIA S.P.A.—National Gypsum Company, pg. 790
AUSTIN-NEDERLAND B.V.—National Gypsum Company, pg. 791
BCM ENGINEERS INC., pg. 106
BCP TECHNICAL SERVICE, INC., pg. 106
BE & K, INC., pg. 106
B & V WASTE SCIENCE & TECHNOLOGY CORP.—Black & Veatch, pg. 154
BALCO, INC. (MA), pg. 115
BANNER ASSOCIATES INC., pg. 118
BECHTEL CIVIL, INC.—Bechtel Group, Inc., pg. 131
BECHTEL EASTERN POWER CORPORATION—Bechtel Group, Inc., pg. 131
BECHTEL GREAT BRITAIN LTD.—Bechtel Group, Inc., pg. 131
BECHTEL GROUP, INC., pg. 130
BECHTEL, INC.—Bechtel Group, Inc., pg. 131
BECHTEL, INC. MINING & METALS SPECIAL OPERATION—Bechtel Group, Inc., pg. 131
BECHTEL NATIONAL, INC.—Bechtel Group, Inc., pg. 131
BECHTEL POWER CORPORATION—Bechtel Group, Inc., pg. 131
R. W. BECK & ASSOCIATES, INC., pg. 131
BELCAN CORPORATION, pg. 133
THE BENHAM GROUP, pg. 138
BENJAMIN WOODHOUSE & GUENTHER—Ghafari Associates, Inc., pg. 455
BENNETT RINGROSE WOLSFELD JARVIS, INC., pg. 139
BLACK & VEATCH, pg. 154

BLACK & VEATCH INTERNATIONAL—Black & Veatch, pg. 154
BLAW KNOX CORP., pg. 156
BOOZ ALLEN & HAMILTON INC., pg. 165
BOVAY, pg. 169
BOYLE ENGINEERING CORP., pg. 169
BROWN & CALDWELL CONSULTING ENGINEERS, pg. 181
BURGESS & NIPLE, INC.—Burgess & Niple, Limited, pg. 190
BURGESS & NIPLE, LIMITED, pg. 190
BURMOT AUSTRALIA PTY., LTD.—Burns & Roe Enterprises, Inc., pg. 194
BURNS & MCDONNELL ENGINEERS-ARCHITECTS-CONSULTANTS, pg. 194
BURNS & ROE ENTERPRISES, INC., pg. 194
BURNS & ROE ENTERPRISES, INC.—Burns & Roe Enterprises, Inc., pg. 194
BURNS & ROE ENVIRONMENTAL SERVICES—Burns & Roe Enterprises, Inc., pg. 194
BURNS & ROE INDUSTRIAL SERVICES COMPANY—Burns & Roe Enterprises, Inc., pg. 194
BURNS & ROE PACIFIC COMPANY—Burns & Roe Enterprises, Inc., pg. 194
BURNS & ROE SOUTHEAST—Burns & Roe Enterprises, Inc., pg. 194
BUTLER DESIGN SERVICES, INC.—Butler International, pg. 197
BUTLER SERVICE GROUP, INC.—Butler International, pg. 197
CDM FEDERAL PROGRAMS CORPORATION—Camp Dresser & McKee Inc., pg. 212
CH2M HILL COMPANIES, LTD., pg. 202
CH2M HILL, INC.—CH2M Hill Companies, Ltd., pg. 202
CH2M HILL INDUSTRIAL DESIGN CORP.—CH2M Hill Companies, Ltd., pg. 202
CH2M HILL INTERNATIONAL, LTD.—CH2M Hill Companies, Ltd., pg. 202
CAMP DRESSER & MCKEE INC., pg. 212
CAMP DRESSER & MCKEE INTERNATIONAL INC.—Camp Dresser & McKee Inc., pg. 212
CANNON, pg. 214
COMBUSTION POWER COMPANY, pg. 267
COMPUTER DYNAMICS, INC., pg. 271
CONGAREE CONSTRUCTION CO., INC., pg. 274
CONVERSE PROFESSIONAL GROUP, INC., pg. 281
COOPER COMMUNITIES, INC., pg. 283
COSTAIN/LIFE SCIENCES INTERNATIONAL—Day & Zimmermann, Inc., pg. 321
COWPER & SIEGFRIED, pg. 291
CUNNINGHAM ENGINEERS, INC.—Cunningham-Limp Development Co., pg. 305
CUNNINGHAM-LIMP DEVELOPMENT CO., pg. 305
D&Z, INC.—Day & Zimmermann, Inc., pg. 320
DAHLSTROM MANUFACTURING COMPANY, INC., pg. 310
LEO A. DALY COMPANY, pg. 313
DAY ENGINEERING—Day & Zimmermann, Inc., pg. 320
DAY & ZIMMERMANN, INC., pg. 320
DEDERT CORPORATION, pg. 324
DEWBERRY & DAVIS, pg. 334
DILLINGHAM CONSTRUCTION PACIFIC, LTD.—Dillingham Construction Corporation, pg. 338
DIVANE BROS. ELECTRIC CO., pg. 340
THOMAS K. DYER, INC.—Howard Needles Tammen & Bergendoff, pg. 547
THE ERM GROUP, pg. 360
ERM-MIDWEST, INC.—The ERM Group, pg. 360
ERM-NEW ENGLAND, INC.—The ERM Group, pg. 360
ERM-NORTH CENTRAL, INC.—The ERM Group, pg. 360
ERM-NORTHEAST, INC.—The ERM Group, pg. 360
ERM-NORTHWEST, INC.—The ERM Group, pg. 360
ERM-ROCKY MOUNTAIN, INC.—The ERM Group, pg. 360
ERM-SOUTH, INC.—The ERM Group, pg. 360
ERM-SOUTHEAST, INC.—The ERM Group, pg. 360
ERM-SOUTHWEST, INC.—The ERM Group, pg. 360
ERM-WEST, INC.—The ERM Group, pg. 361
EFFICIENT ENGINEERING CO., pg. 371
ELASTOMERIC TECHNOLOGIES, INC., pg. 372
ELGIN NATIONAL INDUSTRIES, INC.—Jupiter Industries, Inc., pg. 609
ENERGY & ENVIRONMENTAL RESEARCH CORP., pg. 381
ENGINEERING & CONSTRUCTION DIVISION—Day & Zimmermann, Inc., pg. 320
ENGINEERING SERVICE, INC., pg. 382
ENGINEERING TECHNOLOGY LTD. (E.T.), pg. 382
A. EPSTEIN AND SONS, INTL., INC., pg. 384
EPSTEIN CIVIL ENGINEERING, INC.—A. Epstein and Sons, Intl., Inc., pg. 384
EPSTEIN ENGINEERING EXPORT, LTD.—A. Epstein and Sons, Intl., Inc., pg. 384
EPSTEIN ENGINEERING EXPORT (WARSAW), LTD.—A. Epstein and Sons, Intl., Inc., pg. 384
EPSTEIN ENGINEERING, INC.—A. Epstein and Sons, Intl., Inc., pg. 384
EPSTEIN MATERIAL HANDLING ENGINEERING, INC.—A. Epstein and Sons, Intl., Inc., pg. 384
EPSTEIN PROCESS ENGINEERING, INC.—A. Epstein and Sons, Intl., Inc., pg. 384
A. EPSTEIN & SONS (CALIFORNIA) INC.—A. Epstein and Sons, Intl., Inc., pg. 384
A. EPSTEIN & SONS (FRANCE) INC.—A. Epstein and Sons, Intl., Inc., pg. 384
A. EPSTEIN & SONS (ISRAEL) LTD.—A. Epstein and Sons, Intl., Inc., pg. 384
A. EPSTEIN & SONS (U.K.) LTD.—A. Epstein and Sons, Intl., Inc., pg. 384
FAY, SPOFFORD & THORNDIKE, INC., pg. 404
FISH ENGINEERING & CONSTRUCTION, INC., pg. 414
FISH INTERNATIONAL CO.—Fish Engineering & Construction, Inc., pg. 414
FISH INTERNATIONAL ENGINEERS—Fish Engineering & Construction, Inc., pg. 414
FISH SERVICE CORPORATION—Fish Engineering & Construction, Inc., pg. 414
FRU-CON CONSTRUCTION CORPORATION, pg. 435
FUGRO-MCCLELLAND, INC., pg. 435
GAI CONSULTANTS, INC., pg. 439
GAI CONSULTANTS-SOUTHEAST, INC.—GAI Consultants, Inc., pg. 439
GANNETT FLEMING AFFILIATES, INC., pg. 442
GHAFARI ASSOCIATES, INC., pg. 455
GHAFARI ASSOCIATES, INC.—Ghafari Associates, Inc., pg. 455
GHAFARI ASSOCIATES, INC.—Ghafari Associates, Inc., pg. 455
GIFFELS ASSOCIATES, INC., pg. 457
GIFFELS HOYEM BASSO, INC.—Giffels Associates, Inc., pg. 457
GOODKIND & O'DEA, INC.—Dewberry & Davis, pg. 334
JAMES N. GRAY CONSTRUCTION CO., INC., pg. 479
GREEN HOLDINGS, INC., pg. 484
GROUND WATER ASSOCIATES, INC.—Hydro Group, Inc., pg. 556
HOH ENGINEERS, INC.—The HOH Organizations, pg. 497
THE HOH ORGANIZATIONS, pg. 497
HTB, INC., pg. 497
HWH ARCHITECTS ENGINEERS PLANNERS INC., pg. 498
HAINES LUNDBERG WAEHLER, pg. 500
HAMMEL, GREEN & ABRAHAMSON, INC., pg. 504
HARLEY ELLINGTON PIERCE YEE ASSOCIATES, INC., pg. 509
HART CROWSER, INC., pg. 512
HARZA ENGINEERING CO., pg. 516
HARZA NORTHWEST, INC.—Harza Engineering Co., pg. 516
HAVENS & EMERSON, INC.—Lawler-Havens Inc., pg. 661
HAWAIIAN DREDGING & CONSTRUCTION COMPANY—Dillingham Construction Corporation, pg. 338
HAYES, SEAY, MATTERN & MATTERN, INC., pg. 519
HAZEN & SAWYER, pg. 520
HEERY INTERNATIONAL, INC., pg. 525
HARRY O. HEFTER-ASSOCIATES, INC.—The HOH Organizations, pg. 497
HENKELS & MCCOY, INC., pg. 529
HOPE DESIGN GROUP, pg. 543
HOWARD NEEDLES TAMMEN & BERGENDOFF, pg. 547
HUITT-ZOLLARS, INC., pg. 552
INDECK ENERGY SERVICES, INC.—Indeck Power Equipment Company, pg. 564
INGERSOLL ENGINEERS—Ingersoll Engineers Inc., pg. 568
INGERSOLL ENGINEERS—Ingersoll Engineers Inc., pg. 568
INGERSOLL ENGINEERS—Ingersoll Engineers Inc., pg. 568
INGERSOLL MASCHINEN UND WERKZEUGE GMBH—Ingersoll International Inc., pg. 568
INTEGRATED SYSTEMS ANALYSTS, INC., pg. 573
JOFFKO INTERNATIONAL, pg. 595
JOFFKO PHILIPPINES, INC.—Joffko International, pg. 595
BERNARD JOHNSON INCORPORATED, pg. 598
THE JUPITER CORPORATION—Jupiter Industries, Inc., pg. 609
ALBERT KAHN ASSOCIATES, INC., pg. 613
L. ROBERT KIMBALL & ASSOCIATES, pg. 629
KIRK-MAYER, INC., pg. 633
KNIGHT/EMERSON CONSULTING, INC.—Lester B. Knight & Associates, Inc., pg. 637
LESTER B. KNIGHT & ASSOCIATES, INC., pg. 637
LAKE ERIE ELECTRIC, INC., pg. 651
ROBERT E. LAMB, INC., pg. 652
LAW ENGINEERING, INC., pg. 661
LAWLER-HAVENS INC., pg. 661
LAWLER, MATUSKY & SKELLY ENGINEERS—Lawler-Havens Inc., pg. 661
LEAR SIEGLER DIVERSIFIED HOLDINGS CORP.—Forstmann Little & Co., pg. 424
LEWALLYN ENGINEERING—Textile Rubber & Chemical Company, pg. 1090
LIFE SCIENCES INTERNATIONAL—Day & Zimmermann, Inc., pg. 320
LIFE SCIENCES INTERNATIONAL-CALIFORNIA—Day & Zimmermann, Inc., pg. 320
LIN & ROE COMPANY—Burns & Roe Enterprises, Inc., pg. 194
LIVERNOIS ENGINEERING COMPANY, pg. 679
LIVERNOIS VEHICLE CO.—Livernois Engineering Company, pg. 679
LOS ALAMOS TECHNICAL ASSOCIATES, INC., pg. 684
MDC SYSTEMS—Day & Zimmermann, Inc., pg. 320
MACRODYNE ENGINEERING SERVICES—Phoenix International, Inc., pg. 869
MAERZ OFENBAU AG—Belmont Industries, Inc., pg. 137
MAERZ OFENBAU G.M.B.H.—Belmont Industries, Inc., pg. 137
MAGNETIC TECHNOLOGIES CORPORATION, pg. 701
MAKO CONSTRUCTION CO.—Henkels & McCoy, Inc., pg. 529
ALBERT C. MARTIN & ASSOCIATES, pg. 714
MASON COMPANY, pg. 718
MASON & HANGER ENGINEERING INC.—Mason Company, pg. 718
MASON & HANGER NATIONAL INC.—Mason Company, pg. 718
MASON HANGER-SILAS MASON CO.—Mason Company, pg. 718
THE MAXIMA CORPORATION, pg. 723
MEDLINE INDUSTRIES, INC., pg. 736
MI-JACK PRODUCTS, INC., pg. 746
MONA INDUSTRIES, INC., pg. 764
JAMES M. MONTGOMERY CONSULTING ENGINEERS, pg. 767
MUNITIONS TECHNOLOGY DIVISION—Day & Zimmermann, Inc., pg. 320
NPS CORPORATION, pg. 781
NPS, INC.—Day & Zimmermann, Inc., pg. 321
NTH CONSULTANTS, LTD., pg. 781
NASH ENGINEERING CO. (GREAT BRITAIN) LTD.—The Nash Engineering Company, pg. 784
NATIONAL GYPSUM COMPANY, pg. 790
NESCO, INC., pg. 798
THE C. W. NOFSINGER COMPANY—Burns & McDonnell Engineers-Architects-Consultants, pg. 194
THE NORTH AMERICAN MANUFACTURING CO., pg. 811
NUTECH ENGINEERS, INC.—Nutech, Inc., pg. 818
NUTECH, INC., pg. 817
NUTECH INTERNATIONAL, INC—Nutech, Inc., pg. 818
THE OFFICE OF LEE KENDRICK—Dewberry & Davis, pg. 334
OPERATING PLANT SERVICES—Day & Zimmermann, Inc., pg. 320
OPUS CORP., pg. 828
PSI FABRICATORS, INC.—PSI Group of Companies, pg. 837
PSI GROUP OF COMPANIES, pg. 837
PACIFICA SERVICES, INC., pg. 842
PARSONS BRINCKERHOFF CONSTRUCTION SERVICES, INC.—Parsons Brinckerhoff Inc., pg. 850
PARSONS BRINCKERHOFF INC., pg. 850
PARSONS BRINCKERHOFF INTERNATIONAL, INC.—Parsons Brinckerhoff Inc., pg. 850
PARSONS BRINCKERHOFF QUADE & DOUGLAS, INC.—Parsons Brinckerhoff Inc., pg. 850
PEABODY ENGINEERING CORP.—The Pullman Company, pg. 899
PIONEER ENGINEERING & MANUFACTURING CO., pg. 871
MALCOLM PIRNIE, INC., pg. 872
POWER ENGINEERING CO. INC., pg. 883
PRECISE TECHNOLOGY & ELECTRONICS, INC.—Air Gage Company, pg. 27
THE PRITCHARD CORPORATION—Black & Veatch, pg. 155
PROCESS SYSTEMS, INC. CONSTRUCTION CO.—PSI Group of Companies, pg. 837
PRODUCTION MANAGEMENT COMPANIES, INC., pg. 893
PSOMAS & ASSOCIATES, pg. 898
THE PULLMAN COMPANY, pg. 899
RJO ENTERPRISES, INC., pg. 907
RTKL ASSOCIATES INC., pg. 908
REFRACTORIES CONSULTING & ENGINEERING GMBH—Belmont Industries, Inc., pg. 137
RENCO GROUP, pg. 926
RENTENBACH ENGINEERING COMPANY, pg. 927
ROBERTS & SCHAEFER CO.—Jupiter Industries, Inc., pg. 609
ROBERTS & SCHAEFFER COMPANY-SALT LAKE CITY—Jupiter Industries, Inc., pg. 609
ROCKY MOUNTAIN MECHANICAL, INC., pg. 942
ROSSER FABRAP INTERNATIONAL, pg. 950
SAIC COMMERCIAL ENTERPRISES, INC.—Science Applications International Corporation, pg. 982
SAIC ENGINEERING, INC.—Science Applications International Corporation, pg. 982
SAIC UK LIMITED—Science Applications International Corporation, pg. 982
SC COMPANIES, INC., pg. 960
SCS ENGINEERS, pg. 961
SFA, INC., pg. 961
SPEC GROUP—Sauer Industries, Inc., pg. 972
SRS TECHNOLOGIES, pg. 964
STS CONSULTANTS, LTD.—STS Holdings, Inc., pg. 965
SADCO LTD.—Joffko International, pg. 595
SAIC CANADA—Science Applications International Corporation, pg. 982
SARGENT & LUNDY, pg. 971
SCHUMACHER & FORELLE, INC., pg. 979
SCIENCE & ENGINEERING ASSOCIATES, pg. 982
SERVO PRODUCTS COMPANY—Silicon Valley Development, pg. 1004
SHANNON & WILSON, INC., pg. 995
SHIP ANALYTICS, INC., pg. 999
EBERLE M. SMITH ASSOCIATES, INC.—Ghafari Associates, Inc., pg. 455
SMITH & GILLESPIE ENGINEERS, INC., pg. 1012
THE SMITH GROUP, INC., pg. 1012
SMITH HINCHMAN GRYLLS ASSOCIATES, INC.—The Smith Group, Inc., pg. 1013
SPRINGBORN LABORATORIES, INC., pg. 1033
STANLEY CONSULTANTS, INC.—SC Companies, Inc., pg. 961
STETSON-HARZA—Harza Engineering Co., pg. 516
STONE & HOOVER CONTRACTING, INC.—W. B. Goode Company, Inc., pg. 470
STREATER STORE FIXTURES DIV.—Joyce International, Inc., pg. 608
SVERDRUP BUILDING CORPORATION—Sverdrup Corporation, pg. 1066
SVERDRUP CORPORATION, pg. 1065
SVERDRUP ENVIRONMENTAL INC.—Sverdrup Corporation, pg. 1066
SVERDRUP TECHNOLOGY, INC.—Sverdrup Corporation, pg. 1066
SYSTEMS ENGINEERING ASSOCIATES CO. (SEACOR)—Day & Zimmermann, Inc., pg. 320
TAD TECHNICAL SERVICES CORP., pg. 1071
TACTAIR ADVANCED TECHNOLOGY, INC.—Phoenix International, Inc., pg. 869
TEXAS ELECTRIC COOPERATIVES, INC., pg. 1089
I. C. THOMASSON ASSOCIATES, INC., pg. 1094
THOMPSON-STARRETT CONSTRUCTION COMPANY, INC.—Jupiter Industries, Inc., pg. 609
TRACOR APPLIED SCIENCES, SYSTEMS TECHNOLOGY DIV.—Tracor, Inc., pg. 1105
VIP ENGINEERED PRODUCTS, INC.—Heico Inc., pg. 525
VEDA INCORPORATED—Veda International, Inc., pg. 1146
VERSATECH ENGINEERING—Mason Company, pg. 718

THE WBDC GROUP, pg. 1155
WW ENGINEERING & SCIENCE INC.—Summit Environmental Group, pg. 1058
WALK, HAYDEL & ASSOCIATES, INC., pg. 1159
WATKINS ENGINEERS & CONSTRUCTORS, INC.—Dillingham Construction Corporation, pg. 338
WEBB, MURRAY & ASSOCIATES, pg. 1170
THE WEITZ COMPANY, INC.—The Weitz Corporation, pg. 1174
WHITING CORPORATION, pg. 1187
WOLFBERG, ALVAREZ & ASSOCIATES INC., pg. 1199
WOLFF & MUNIER, INC., pg. 1199
WOODWARD-CLYDE GROUP, INC., pg. 1200
WOODWARD-CLYDE FEDERAL SERVICES—Woodward-Clyde Group, Inc., pg. 1201
WOODWARD-CLYDE INTERNATIONAL—Woodward-Clyde Group, Inc., pg. 1201
WOOLPERT CONSULTANTS, pg. 1201
ZALK JOSEPH FABRICATIONS, INC.—Heico Inc., pg. 525

8712 — ARCHITECTURAL SERVICES

ADVANCED DZIGN SYSTEMS—Day & Zimmermann, Inc., pg. 320
IVAN ALLEN COMPANY, INC., pg. 36
AMBULATORY ONE AMERICA INC., pg. 47
ANDERSON-PARRISH ASSOCIATES, INC.—Lawler-Havens Inc., pg. 661
THE ARCHITECTS COLLABORATIVE, INC. (TAC), pg. 80
THE ARCHITECTS COLLABORATIVE, INC.—The Architects Collaborative, Inc. (TAC), pg. 81
ARCHITECTURAL INTERIORS, INC.—A. Epstein and Sons, Intl., Inc., pg. 384
ARROW BUILDING CENTERS—Consolidated Lumber Co., pg. 276
AUSTIN-AUSTRALIA—National Gypsum Company, pg. 790
THE AUSTIN CO.—National Gypsum Company, pg. 790
THE AUSTIN CO. S.A.—National Gypsum Company, pg. 790
THE AUSTIN CO. OF U.K. LTD.—National Gypsum Company, pg. 790
THE AUSTIN COMPANY—National Gypsum Company, pg. 790
AUSTIN ITALIA S.P.A.—National Gypsum Company, pg. 790
AUSTIN-NEDERLAND B.V.—National Gypsum Company, pg. 791
BCP TECHNICAL SERVICE, INC., pg. 106
BANNER ASSOCIATES INC., pg. 118
BAXTER HODELL DONNELLY PRESTON INC., pg. 127
BAXTER SHIRK DESIGN COLLABORATIVE—Baxter Hodell Donnelly Preston Inc., pg. 127
BAXTER/PEAS—Baxter Hodell Donnelly Preston Inc., pg. 127
THE BENHAM GROUP, pg. 138
BENJAMIN WOODHOUSE & GUENTHER—Ghafari Associates, Inc., pg. 455
BLACK & VEATCH, pg. 154
BLACK & VEATCH ARCHITECTS, INC.—Black & Veatch, pg. 154
BLACK & VEATCH INTERNATIONAL—Black & Veatch, pg. 154
BOVAY, pg. 169
BOYLE ENGINEERING CORP., pg. 169
BURGESS & NIPLE, INC.—Burgess & Niple, Limited, pg. 190
BURGESS & NIPLE, LIMITED, pg. 190
BURNS & MCDONNELL ENGINEERS-ARCHITECTS-CONSULTANTS, pg. 194
CANNON, pg. 214
CONSOLIDATED LUMBER CO., pg. 276
D&Z, INC.—Day & Zimmermann, Inc., pg. 320
LEO A. DALY COMPANY, pg. 313
DAY & ZIMMERMANN, INC., pg. 320
DESIGN-BUILD WEST—RNL Facilities Corporation, pg. 907
DEWBERRY & DAVIS, pg. 334
ELLERBE BECKET, INC., pg. 378
A. EPSTEIN AND SONS, INTL., INC., pg. 384
EPSTEIN ENGINEERING EXPORT, LTD.—A. Epstein and Sons, Intl., Inc., pg. 384
EPSTEIN ENGINEERING EXPORT (WARSAW), LTD.—A. Epstein and Sons, Intl., Inc., pg. 384
A. EPSTEIN & SONS (CALIFORNIA) INC.—A. Epstein and Sons, Intl., Inc., pg. 384
A. EPSTEIN & SONS (FRANCE) INC.—A. Epstein and Sons, Intl., Inc., pg. 384
A. EPSTEIN & SONS, INC.—A. Epstein and Sons, Intl., Inc., pg. 384
A. EPSTEIN & SONS (ISRAEL) LTD.—A. Epstein and Sons, Intl., Inc., pg. 384
A. EPSTEIN & SONS (U.K.) LTD.—A. Epstein and Sons, Intl., Inc., pg. 384
FRU-CON CONSTRUCTION CORPORATION, pg. 435
FRU-CON ENGINEERING INC.—Fru-Con Construction Corporation, pg. 435
GHAFARI ASSOCIATES, INC., pg. 455
GHAFARI ASSOCIATES, INC.—Ghafari Associates, Inc., pg. 455
GHAFARI ASSOCIATES, INC.—Ghafari Associates, Inc., pg. 455
GIFFELS ASSOCIATES, INC., pg. 457
GIFFELS HOYEM BASSO, INC.—Giffels Associates, Inc., pg. 457
GREENHORNE & O'MARA, INC., pg. 485
HOH ARCHITECTS, INC.—The HOH Organizations, pg. 497
THE HOH ORGANIZATIONS, pg. 497
HTB, INC., pg. 497
HWH ARCHITECTS ENGINEERS PLANNERS INC., pg. 498
HAINES LUNDBERG WAEHLER, pg. 500
HAMMEL, GREEN & ABRAHAMSON, INC., pg. 504
HARLEY ELLINGTON PIERCE YEE ASSOCIATES, INC., pg. 509
HARZA ENGINEERING CO., pg. 516
HARZA NORTHWEST, INC.—Harza Engineering Co., pg. 516
HAYES, SEAY, MATTERN & MATTERN, INC., pg. 519
HEERY INTERNATIONAL, INC., pg. 525
HOPE DESIGN GROUP, pg. 543
HOWARD NEEDLES TAMMEN & BERGENDOFF, pg. 547
HUNTCO HEALTH CARE CO.—Huntco Inc., pg. 554
INDECO, INC.—Johnson Bros. Corp., pg. 597
JOFFKO INTERNATIONAL, pg. 595
JOFFKO PHILIPPINES, INC.—Joffko International, pg. 595
BERNARD JOHNSON INCORPORATED, pg. 598
ALBERT KAHN ASSOCIATES, INC., pg. 613
KELLER & GANNON—Lester B. Knight & Associates, Inc., pg. 637
L. ROBERT KIMBALL & ASSOCIATES, pg. 629
KIRK-MAYER, INC., pg. 633
KNIGHT ARCHITECTS ENGINEERS PLANNERS, INC.—Lester B. Knight & Associates, Inc., pg. 637
KNIGHT KOREA—Lester B. Knight & Associates, Inc., pg. 637
LESTER B. KNIGHT & ASSOCIATES, INC., pg. 637
KROMMENHOEK MCKEOWN ASSOCIATES, pg. 645
ROBERT E. LAMB, INC., pg. 652
LESTER B. KNIGHT CAST METALS, INC.—Lester B. Knight & Associates, Inc., pg. 637
LIVERNOIS ENGINEERING COMPANY, pg. 679
MBT ASSOCIATES, INC., pg. 691
MAGUIRE GROUP ARCHITECTS, INC.—Maguire Group Inc., pg. 701
MAGUIRE GROUP INC., pg. 701
ALBERT C. MARTIN & ASSOCIATES, pg. 714
MASON & HANGER ENGINEERING INC.—Mason Company, pg. 718
MI-JACK PRODUCTS, INC., pg. 746
MULACH PARKING STRUCTURES CORP.—Mulach Steel Corporation, pg. 775
NBBJ, pg. 780
NBBJ/LPA—NBBJ, pg. 780
NBBJ-ROSENFIELD—NBBJ, pg. 780
NADEL PARTNERSHIP, INC., pg. 782
THE NADEL PARTNERSHIP, INC.—Nadel Partnership, Inc., pg. 783
THE NADEL PARTNERSHIP, INC.—Nadel Partnership, Inc., pg. 783
THE C. W. NOFSINGER COMPANY—Burns & McDonnell Engineers-Architects-Consultants, pg. 194
OPUS CORP., pg. 828
OPUS SOUTH CORPORATION, pg. 828
POST BUCKLEY SCHUH & JERNIGAN, pg. 881
RNL DESIGN—RNL Facilities Corporation, pg. 907
RNL FACILITIES CORPORATION, pg. 907
RTKL ASSOCIATES INC., pg. 908
ROSSER FABRAP INTERNATIONAL, pg. 950
SC COMPANIES, INC., pg. 960
SADCO LTD.—Joffko International, pg. 595
SCHUMACHER & FORELLE, INC., pg. 979
EBERLE M. SMITH ASSOCIATES, INC.—Ghafari Associates, Inc., pg. 455
THE SMITH GROUP, INC., pg. 1012
SMITH HINCHMAN GRYLLS ASSOCIATES, INC.—The Smith Group, Inc., pg. 1013
STANLEY CONSULTANTS, INC.—SC Companies, Inc., pg. 961
STETSON-HARZA—Harza Engineering Co., pg. 516
SVERDRUP BUILDING CORPORATION—Sverdrup Corporation, pg. 1066
SVERDRUP CORPORATION, pg. 1065
SVERDRUP ENVIRONMENTAL INC.—Sverdrup Corporation, pg. 1066
TAD TECHNICAL SERVICES CORP., pg. 1071
TAYLOR ASSOCIATES—Midcoast Industrial Services Corporation, pg. 751
THE WBDC GROUP, pg. 1155
WOLFBERG, ALVAREZ & ASSOCIATES INC., pg. 1199
WOOLPERT CONSULTANTS, pg. 1201

8713 — SURVEYING SERVICES

DEWBERRY & DAVIS, pg. 334
EPSTEIN CIVIL ENGINEERING, INC.—A. Epstein and Sons, Intl., Inc., pg. 384
GOODKIND & O'DEA, INC.—Dewberry & Davis, pg. 334
GREENHORNE & O'MARA, INC., pg. 485
L. ROBERT KIMBALL & ASSOCIATES, pg. 629
ALBERT C. MARTIN & ASSOCIATES, pg. 714
PSOMAS & ASSOCIATES, pg. 898
SVERDRUP CORPORATION, pg. 1065
SVERDRUP ENVIRONMENTAL INC.—Sverdrup Corporation, pg. 1066
TAD TECHNICAL SERVICES CORP., pg. 1071
WOOLPERT CONSULTANTS, pg. 1201

8721 — ACCOUNTING, AUDITING & BOOKKEEPING SERVICES

A & M ASSOCIATES, INC.—Amerco, A Nevada Corporation, pg. 48
ALTUS SERVICES, INC.—Altus Federal Savings Bank, pg. 46
AMERCO, A NEVADA CORPORATION, pg. 47
ARTHUR ANDERSEN—Arthur Andersen & Co., S.C., pg. 72
ARTHUR ANDERSEN & CO.—Arthur Andersen & Co., S.C., pg. 72
ARTHUR ANDERSEN & CO., S.C., pg. 72
ATAG ALLGEMEINE TREUHAND AG—Ernst & Young, pg. 387
ATAG FIDUCIAIRE GENERALE SA—Ernst & Young, pg. 387
BRIAN CENTER MANAGEMENT CORPORATION, pg. 175
CARLSBERG FINANCIAL CORP., pg. 220
COMPREHENSIVE BUSINESS SERVICES INC.—KOA Holdings, pg. 612
COOPERATIVE SERVICE CO.—Farmland Industries, Inc., pg. 402
COOPERS & LYBRAND, pg. 283
DELOITTE & TOUCHE, pg. 326
ENTERTAINMENT PARTNERS—IDC Services, Inc., pg. 560
ERNST & YOUNG, pg. 387
ERNST & YOUNG—Ernst & Young, pg. 387
FRIEDMAN, EISENSTEIN, RAEMER & SCHWARTZ, pg. 433
GRANT THORNTON, pg. 477
IDC SERVICES, INC., pg. 559
INTEGRATEC, pg. 573
KPMG PEAT MARWICK, pg. 613
KENNETH LEVENTHAL & COMPANY, pg. 670
NEW CENTURY FREIGHT TRAFFIC ASSOCIATION, INC.—The Marmon Group, Inc., pg. 712
POWERFORCE COMPANY, INC.—IDC Services, Inc., pg. 560
PRICE WATERHOUSE - U.S., pg. 888
PRODUCTION PAYMENTS, INC.—IDC Services, Inc., pg. 560
TALENT & RESIDUALS, INC.—IDC Services, Inc., pg. 560
U-HAUL INTERNATIONAL, INC.—Amerco, A Nevada Corporation, pg. 48

8731 — COMMERCIAL PHYSICAL & BIOLOGICAL RESEARCH

AEROVIRONMENT, INC., pg. 22
AGMET LTD.—Electro-Science Laboratories, Inc., pg. 375
AMERICAN CRYSTAL SUGAR CO.—American Crystal Sugar Company, pg. 51
ARTESIAN LABORATORIES, INC.—Artesian Resources Corporation, pg. 86
ARTESIAN RESOURCES CORPORATION, pg. 86
ASTRE CORPORATE GROUP, pg. 92
BCM ENGINEERS INC., pg. 106
BATTELLE DEVELOPMENT CORP.—Battelle Memorial Institute, pg. 126
BATTELLE MEMORIAL INSTITUTE, pg. 126
BECHTEL GROUP, INC., pg. 130
BECHTEL NATIONAL, INC.—Bechtel Group, Inc., pg. 131
BETAC CORPORATION—Betac International Corporation, pg. 147
BETAC INTERNATIONAL CORPORATION, pg. 147
BIO-TEK INSTRUMENTS, INC., pg. 152
C. BREWER & COMPANY, LIMITED, pg. 174
BROWN & CALDWELL CONSULTING ENGINEERS, pg. 181
CAMBRIDGE CONSULTANTS LIMITED—Arthur D. Little, Inc., pg. 679
CIMLINC INC., pg. 249
COMBUSTION POWER COMPANY, pg. 267
DUCHOSSOIS INDUSTRIES, INC., pg. 350
ESL S.N.C.—Electro-Science Laboratories, Inc., pg. 375
ELECTRO-SCIENCE DEUTSCHLAND—Electro-Science Laboratories, Inc., pg. 375
ELECTRO-SCIENCE LABORATORIES, INC., pg. 375
ERIEZ MAGNETICS, pg. 386
GAI CONSULTANTS, INC., pg. 439
GENERAL SCIENCES CORP.—Science Applications International Corporation, pg. 981
GEO-CENTERS, INC., pg. 452
GEOSAFE CORPORATION—Battelle Memorial Institute, pg. 126
HART CROWSER, INC., pg. 512
HEATH CONSULTANTS INCORPORATED, pg. 524
IMT—National Forge Company, pg. 789
INDUSTRIAL MATERIALS TECHNOLOGY—National Forge Company, pg. 789
INFOTEC DEVELOPMENT, INC., pg. 567
KILAUEA AGRONOMICS, INC.—C. Brewer & Company, Limited, pg. 174
ARTHUR D. LITTLE, INC., pg. 678
THE MAXIMA CORPORATION, pg. 723
MITRE CORPORATION, pg. 762
PIONEER ENGINEERING & MANUFACTURING CO., pg. 871
PIONEER RESEARCH & DEVELOPMENT DIV.—Pioneer Engineering & Manufacturing Co., pg. 871
MALCOLM PIRNIE, INC., pg. 872
PLANNING SYSTEMS INC., pg. 874
QUINTRON SYSTEMS, INC., pg. 905
RAND, pg. 911
RANGEN AQUACULTURE RESEARCH—Rangen, Inc., pg. 912
REVLON RESEARCH CENTER, INC.—MacAndrews & Forbes Holdings Inc., pg. 696
SFA, INC., pg. 961
SRI INTERNATIONAL, pg. 964
SRS TECHNOLOGIES, pg. 964
S.T. RESEARCH, pg. 964
DAVID SARNOFF RESEARCH CENTER—SRI International, pg. 964
SCIENCE APPLICATIONS INTERNATIONAL CORPORATION, pg. 981
SCIPAR, pg. 982
SEMEX, INC.—Seton Company, pg. 993
SHIP ANALYTICS, INC., pg. 999
SOUND CREATION—Venturedyne, Ltd., pg. 1148
SOUTHWEST RESEARCH INSTITUTE, pg. 1023
SOUTHWIDE, INC., pg. 1024
SPRINGBORN LABORATORIES, INC., pg. 1033
SPRINGBORN LABORATORIES-MATERIALS SCIENCE DIVISION—Springborn Laboratories, Inc., pg. 1033
SVERDRUP CORPORATION, pg. 1065
SYSTEM PLANNING CORP., pg. 1070
TECHNOLOGY APPLICATIONS, INC., pg. 1083
UES, INC., pg. 1122

WW ENGINEERING & SCIENCE INC.—Summit Environmental Group, pg. 1058

8732 — COMMERCIAL ECONOMIC, SOCIOLOGICAL & EDUCATIONAL RESEARCH

ASI MARKET RESEARCH, INC.—IDC Services, Inc., pg. 560
ASI MARKET RESEARCH, INC.—IDC Services, Inc., pg. 560
ADVENT INTERNATIONAL, pg. 21
THE BASES GROUP, pg. 124
BOOZ ALLEN & HAMILTON INC., pg. 165
COMPUTER INTELLIGENCE—Ziff Communications Company, pg. 1219
DATACOMM—Bill Communications, Inc., pg. 150
DONNELLEY MARKETING INFORMATION SERVICES—Peter W. Smith & Company, Inc., pg. 1011
GOLDMAN FINANCIAL GROUP, pg. 468
GOUCHENOUR ADV., INC., pg. 473
HARRINGTON MARKET RESEARCH—Biggs Gilmore Communications, pg. 149
INFOCORP—Ziff Communications Company, pg. 1219
INTERNATIONAL DATA GROUP, pg. 576
RMS TECHS, INC., pg. 907
ROCKWOOD RESEARCH—Farm Journal, Inc., pg. 401
VITT MEDIA INTERNATIONAL, INC., pg. 1153
WESTAT INC., pg. 1178

8733 — NONCOMMERCIAL RESEARCH ORGANIZATIONS

AMERICAN ENTERPRISE INSTITUTE FOR PUBLIC POLICY RESEARCH, pg. 51
ANSER (ANALYTIC SERVICES INC.), pg. 76
NATIONAL ACADEMY SCIENCES USA, pg. 784
SVERDRUP CORPORATION, pg. 1065
SVERDRUP TECHNOLOGY, INC.—Sverdrup Corporation, pg. 1066

8734 — TESTING LABORATORIES

ARCTIC ALASKA TESTING LABORATORIES—Shannon & Wilson, Inc., pg. 995
BOOZ ALLEN & HAMILTON INC., pg. 165
CROSBY & OVERTON, INC., pg. 300
ETL TESTING LABORATORIES, INC, pg. 361
ERIEZ MAGNETICS, pg. 386
GEORGIA DIV.—ETL Testing Laboratories, Inc, pg. 361
N.V. GRIFFITH LABORATORIES S.A.—Griffith Laboratories Worldwide, Inc., pg. 488
GRIFFITH MICRO SCIENCE INTERNATIONAL INC.—Griffith Laboratories Worldwide, Inc., pg. 487
HART CROWSER, INC., pg. 512
IMT—National Forge Company, pg. 789
INDUSTRIAL MATERIALS TECHNOLOGY—National Forge Company, pg. 789
LAW ENGINEERING, INC., pg. 661
LORD RESEARCH CORPORATION—Lord Corporation, pg. 683
MAMMALIAN TOXICOLOGY DIVISION—Springborn Laboratories, Inc., pg. 1033
QC, INC.—Atlantic Dairy Cooperative, pg. 95
RELA MODEL AND MACHINE SHOP—RELA, Inc., pg. 924
RELA PRODUCT DEVELOPMENT DIV. (PDD)—RELA, Inc., pg. 924
RUSTCO PRODUCTS COMPANY, pg. 957
SCS ANALYTICAL LABORATORY—SCS Engineers, pg. 961
SMITH-EMERY COMPANY, pg. 1012
SPRINGBORN ENVIRONMENTAL SCIENCES DIVISION—Springborn Laboratories, Inc., pg. 1033
SPRINGBORN LABORATORIES (EUROPE) AG—Springborn Laboratories, Inc., pg. 1033
SPRINGBORN LABORATORIES (HONG KONG) LTD.—Springborn Laboratories, Inc., pg. 1033
SPRINGBORN LABORATORIES, INC., pg. 1033
SPRINGBORN LABORATORIES-MATERIALS SCIENCE DIVISION—Springborn Laboratories, Inc., pg. 1033
SPRINGBORN LABORATORIES-TESTING & QA DIVISION—Springborn Laboratories, Inc., pg. 1033
SPRINGBORN (TAIWAN) LTD.—Springborn Laboratories, Inc., pg. 1033
SVERDRUP CORPORATION, pg. 1065
SVERDRUP TECHNOLOGY, INC.—Sverdrup Corporation, pg. 1066
WEST COAST DIV.—ETL Testing Laboratories, Inc, pg. 361

8741 — MANAGEMENT SERVICES

ARA SERVICES, INC.—ARA Group, pg. 5
ADMINISTRATIVE SERVICES, INC.—National Life Insurance Company, pg. 791
ADVANCED MARINE ENTERPRISES, INC., pg. 20
ADVANCED TECHNOLOGY, INC., pg. 20
ADVENT INTERNATIONAL, pg. 21
AMERICAN APPRAISAL ASSOCIATES, INC., pg. 48
AMERICAN APPRAISAL CANADA, INC.—American Appraisal Associates, Inc., pg. 48
AMERICAN APPRAISAL CAPITAL SERVICES, INC.—American Appraisal Associates, Inc., pg. 48
AMERICAN APPRAISAL ESPANA, S.A.—American Appraisal Associates, Inc., pg. 48
AMERICAN APPRAISAL ESPANA, S.A.—American Appraisal Associates, Inc., pg. 48
AMERICAN APPRAISAL HONG KONG LTD.—American Appraisal Associates, Inc., pg. 48
AMERICAN APPRAISAL ITALIA S.R.L.—American Appraisal Associates, Inc., pg. 49
AMERICAN APPRAISAL (U.K.) LTD.—American Appraisal Associates, Inc., pg. 49
AMERICAN TRADING & PRODUCTION CORPORATION, OIL & GAS DIV.—American Trading and Production Corporation, pg. 64
ARINC RESEARCH CORP.—Arinc Inc., pg. 82
ARRINGTON-HILLGATE INTERNATIONAL—Arrington Travel Center Inc., pg. 85
ASSOCIATED MERCHANDISING CORP., pg. 91
THE ATLAS CONSTRUCTION CO., pg. 96
GEORGE W. AUCH CO., pg. 97
AUTOMATED MARKETING SYSTEMS, INC., pg. 100
AUTOMATED MARKETING SYSTEMS, INC.—Automated Marketing Systems, Inc., pg. 100
BCM ENGINEERS INC., pg. 106
BALDWIN CONSTRUCTION, INC., pg. 115
BARTON-MALOW COMPANY—Barton-Malow Enterprises, Inc., pg. 123
THE BASES GROUP—The Bases Group, pg. 124
BASES INTERNATIONAL—The Bases Group, pg. 124
BEEF INDUSTRY COUNCIL—National Live Stock & Meat Board, pg. 792
BENSON MANAGEMENT COMPANY, pg. 140
BILLCOM EXPOSITION & CONFERENCE—Bill Communications, Inc., pg. 150
BORG WARNER AUTOMOTIVE, INC.—Borg-Warner Corporation, pg. 166
BRENNAN COLLEGE SERVICE, INC.—Follett Corporation, pg. 422
BRIM, INC., pg. 176
THE BURKE INSTITUTE—The Bases Group, pg. 124
LEO BURNETT INTL., ASIA HDQTRS.—Leo Burnett Company, Inc., pg. 192
LEO BURNETT INTERNATIONAL, LATIN AMERICAN HDQTRS.—Leo Burnett Company, Inc., pg. 192
LEO BURNETT LTD., EUROPE/MIDDLE EAST HDQTRS.—Leo Burnett Company, Inc., pg. 193
BURNS & MCDONNELL ENGINEERS-ARCHITECTS-CONSULTANTS, pg. 194
CS FIRST BOSTON ASSET MANAGEMENT LIMITED—CS First Boston Group, Inc., pg. 204
CALUMET CONSTRUCTION CORPORATION, pg. 211
CALUMET CONTRUCTION CORPORATION-INDIANAPOLIS DIVISION—Calumet Construction Corporation, pg. 211
CANNON, pg. 214
W. P. CAREY & CO., INC., pg. 218
CARLSON LEARNING COMPANY—Carlson Companies, Inc., pg. 221
CEBCOR (CONSOLIDATED EMPLOYMENT BENEFITS CORP.), pg. 230
CENVILL SERVICES—Cenvill Development Corp., pg. 236
CHARING CROSS GROUP, pg. 239
CHICAGO WEST PULLMAN CORPORATION, pg. 246
CLEVELAND GROUP, INC., pg. 255
CONSTRUCTION MANAGEMENT SERVICE, pg. 277
CONSULTING SERVICES, INC.—Guardian Industries Corp., pg. 492
COOPER COMMUNITIES, INC., pg. 283
COORDINATED APPAREL, INC., pg. 283
D&Z, INC.—Day & Zimmermann, Inc., pg. 320
THE DEMARS CORP., pg. 327
DESCO ADVERTISING & MARKETING—Desco Corporation, pg. 332
ERM-ENVIROCLEAN—The ERM Group, pg. 360
ELLERBE BECKET CONSTRUCTION SERVICES—Ellerbe Becket, Inc., pg. 378
A.J. ETKIN CONSTRUCTION CO.—Alex J. Etkin, Inc., pg. 390
ALEX J. ETKIN, INC., pg. 389
FAIRFIELD INTERNATIONAL CORPORATION—Fairfield Maxwell Ltd., pg. 397
FAIRFIELD MAXWELL LTD., pg. 397
FOLLETT COLLEGE STORES CORP.—Follett Corporation, pg. 422
FORT MORGAN COMMUNITY HOSPITAL—Brim, Inc., pg. 176
FUNDAMENTAL MANAGEMENT, INC.—Industrial Wire Products Corporation, pg. 567
GSL SOLAR CONSULTANTS & ADVISORS, INC.—Great Salt Lake Minerals & Chemicals Corp., pg. 482
GENCON SERVICES, INC.—George W. Auch Co., pg. 98
GENERAL GROWTH CENTER COMPANIES, INC.—General Growth Companies, Inc., pg. 449
GENERAL HOSPITAL—Brim, Inc., pg. 176
GLENROY CONSTRUCTION CO. INC., pg. 462
GREEN HOLDINGS, INC., pg. 484
HEERY INTERNATIONAL, INC., pg. 525
HIGH INDUSTRIES INC., pg. 533
THE HUNT CORPORATION, pg. 553
IDC SERVICES, INC., pg. 559
INTERNATIONAL MANAGEMENT GROUP (IMG), pg. 578
JOFFKO INTERNATIONAL, pg. 595
JOFFKO PHILIPPINES, INC.—Joffko International, pg. 595
M. B. KAHN CONSTRUCTION CO., INC., pg. 614
DANIEL J. KEATING CO., pg. 619
KELSEY CONSTRUCTION, INC., pg. 621
KITCHELL CORPORATION, pg. 634
KNIGHT WENDLING AG—Lester B. Knight & Associates, Inc., pg. 637
KNIGHT WENDLING LTD.—Lester B. Knight & Associates, Inc., pg. 637
LISC MANAGEMENT SERVICES—Union Holdings, Inc., pg. 1128
LEO BURNETT CONNAGHAN & MAY PTY. LTD.—Leo Burnett Company, Inc., pg. 192
ARTHUR D. LITTLE ENTERPRISES, INC.—Arthur D. Little, Inc., pg. 679
ARTHUR D. LITTLE PROGRAM SYSTEMS MANAGEMENT CO.—Arthur D. Little, Inc., pg. 678
LYNDEN LOGISTICS, INC.—Lynden Incorporated, pg. 689
MACKINNON-PARKER, INC., pg. 697
MAIN LINE MANAGEMENT SERVICES, INC.—Chicago West Pullman Corporation, pg. 246
MANAGEMENT DYNAMICS, pg. 703
MARITZ INC., pg. 707
MARTRADE LTD., pg. 716
MCCARTHY BUILDING COMPANIES, pg. 727
MEDIANEWS GROUP, EASTERN OPERATIONS—MediaNews Group Inc., pg. 735
MERCATOR ASSET MANAGEMENT CO., INC.—The Prudential Insurance Company of America, pg. 897
MINYARD PROPERTIES, INC.—Minyard Food Stores, pg. 759
EDWARD V. MONAHAN INC., pg. 765
MORSE DIESEL INTERNATIONAL, pg. 771
MORSE OPERATIONS INC., pg. 772
NANA DEVELOPMENT CORPORATION—Nana Regional Corporation, Inc., pg. 783
NASON AND CULLEN, INC., pg. 784
THE C. W. NOFSINGER COMPANY—Burns & McDonnell Engineers-Architects-Consultants, pg. 194
NORTHWESTERN ENGINEERING CO., pg. 815
PSI GROUP OF COMPANIES, pg. 837
PARAGON GROUP, INC., pg. 847
PARK RIDGE CORPORATION, pg. 849
PARLIAMENT CO., pg. 850
PEDUS OFFICE SERVICES—Pedus Services, Inc., pg. 855
PEGASUS INTERNATIONAL CORPORATION, pg. 855
POWER ENGINEERING CO. INC., pg. 883
POWERFORCE COMPANY, INC.—IDC Services, Inc., pg. 560
PRUCAPITAL MANAGEMENT, INC.—The Prudential Insurance Company of America, pg. 897
PRUDENTIAL FUNDING CORP.—The Prudential Insurance Company of America, pg. 897
PRUDENTIAL SUPPORT OPERATIONS, INC.—The Prudential Insurance Company of America, pg. 897
QUORUM HEALTH GROUP, INC., pg. 905
RPR & ASSOCIATES, INC., pg. 908
REECE-CAMPBELL, INC., pg. 920
ROTHSCHILD NORTH AMERICA INC., pg. 951
THE RUHLIN COMPANY, pg. 955
STS CONSULTANTS, LTD.—STS Holdings, Inc., pg. 965
SACHS ENERGY MANAGEMENT SYSTEMS—Sachs Holding Company, pg. 965
SADCO LTD.—Joffko International, pg. 595
SCHUMACHER & FORELLE, INC., pg. 979
SEILER CORPORATION, pg. 987
THE SMITH GROUP, INC., pg. 1012
SPATZ CENTERS, INC.—Spatz & Co., pg. 1026
SUPER 8 MANAGEMENT, INC.—Super 8 Motels, Inc., pg. 1063
SVERDRUP BUILDING CORPORATION—Sverdrup Corporation, pg. 1066
SVERDRUP CORPORATION, pg. 1065
SVERDRUP ENVIRONMENTAL INC.—Sverdrup Corporation, pg. 1066
SVERDRUP INVESTMENTS, INC.—Sverdrup Corporation, pg. 1066
SVERDRUP TECHNOLOGY, INC.—Sverdrup Corporation, pg. 1066
TALENT & RESIDUALS, INC.—IDC Services, Inc., pg. 560
TIME SYSTEMS, INC., pg. 1097
TISHMAN REALTY & CONSTRUCTION CO., pg. 1099
TWENTIETH CENTURY SERVICES—Twentieth Century Companies, pg. 1121
U-HAUL INTERNATIONAL, INC.—Amerco, A Nevada Corporation, pg. 48
WW ENGINEERING & SCIENCE INC.—Summit Environmental Group, pg. 1058
WALK, HAYDEL & ASSOCIATES, INC., pg. 1159
F.A. WILHELM CONSTRUCTION CO., INC., pg. 1189
WOODFIN HOLDING CORPORATION, pg. 1200
WOODFIN HOTEL MANAGEMENT, INC.—Woodfin Holding Corporation, pg. 1200
WYNMOOR MANAGEMENT & CO., INC.—Cenvill Development Corp., pg. 236
YOUNG PECAN COMPANY WEST, INC.—Young Pecan Shelling Co., Inc., pg. 1210
ZENITH ADMINISTRATORS, INC.—ULLICO Inc., pg. 1124

8742 — MANAGEMENT CONSULTING SERVICES

AMC—Associated Merchandising Corp., pg. 91
ADVERTISING CHECKING BUREAU INCORPORATED, pg. 21
THE ALAMO LEARNING SYSTEMS, INC., pg. 29
ALLEN & OHARA, INC., pg. 36
AMERICAN APPRAISAL ESPANA, S.A.—American Appraisal Associates, Inc., pg. 48
AMERICAN APPRAISAL FRANCE—American Appraisal Associates, Inc., pg. 48
AMERICAN APPRAISAL HUNGARY CO. LTD.—American Appraisal Associates, Inc., pg. 49
AMERICAN APPRAISAL ITALIA S.R.L.—American Appraisal Associates, Inc., pg. 49
AMERICAN APPRAISAL ITALIA S.R.L.—American Appraisal Associates, Inc., pg. 49
AMERICAN APPRAISAL ITALIA S.R.L.—American Appraisal Associates, Inc., pg. 49
AMERICAN APPRAISAL POLAND SP. Z.O.O.—American Appraisal Associates, Inc., pg. 49
AMERICAN APPRAISAL (PORTUGAL) LTD.—American Appraisal Associates, Inc., pg. 49
AMERICAN APPRAISAL THAILAND LTD.—American Appraisal Associates, Inc., pg. 49
AMERICAN APPRAISAL (U.K.) LTD.—American Appraisal Associates, Inc., pg. 49
ARCHITECTURAL INTERIORS, INC.—A. Epstein and Sons, Intl., Inc., pg. 384
ASSOCIATED MERCHANDISING CORP. (FRANCE) S.A.—Associated Merchandising Corp., pg. 91
AUSTIN CONSULTING—National Gypsum Company, pg. 790

S.I.C. Index

AVERY MAYS CONSTRUCTION CO.—The Hunt Corporation, pg. 553
THEODORE BARRY & ASSOCIATES, pg. 122
BARTON-MALOW COMPANY—Barton-Malow Enterprises, Inc., pg. 123
BECHTEL CIVIL, INC.—Bechtel Group, Inc., pg. 131
BECHTEL EASTERN POWER CORPORATION—Bechtel Group, Inc., pg. 131
BECHTEL GREAT BRITAIN LTD.—Bechtel Group, Inc., pg. 131
BECHTEL GROUP, INC., pg. 130
BECHTEL, INC.—Bechtel Group, Inc., pg. 131
BECHTEL, INC. MINING & METALS SPECIAL OPERATION—Bechtel Group, Inc., pg. 131
BECHTEL NATIONAL, INC.—Bechtel Group, Inc., pg. 131
BECHTEL POWER CORPORATION—Bechtel Group, Inc., pg. 131
R. W. BECK & ASSOCIATES, INC., pg. 131
BECON CONSTRUCTION COMPANY, INC.—Bechtel Group, Inc., pg. 131
THE BENHAM GROUP, pg. 138
BOOZ ALLEN & HAMILTON INC., pg. 165
BOOZ, ALLEN & HAMILTON INTERNATIONAL (UK) LTD.—Booz Allen & Hamilton Inc., pg. 165
CBM INDUSTRIES, INC., pg. 199
CRN INTERNATIONAL, INC., pg. 203
CUNA MUTUAL FINANCIAL SERVICES CORP.—CUNA Mutual Insurance Society, pg. 205
CEBCOR (CONSOLIDATED EMPLOYMENT BENEFITS CORP.), pg. 230
CENTRAL DUPAGE HEALTH SYSTEM, pg. 232
CHORE-TIME/BROCK INTERNATIONAL—CTB Inc., pg. 205
COMED MANAGEMENT INC.—New York Life Insurance Company, pg. 802
COMPUTER TECHNOLOGY MANAGEMENT INC.—A. Epstein and Sons, Intl., Inc., pg. 384
CUNNINGHAM ENGINEERS, INC.—Cunningham-Limp Development Co., pg. 305
DAY MAINTENANCE—Day & Zimmermann, Inc., pg. 320
DAY & ZIMMERMANN, INC., pg. 320
DAY & ZIMMERMANN, INC.—Day & Zimmermann, Inc., pg. 321
DOBBS BROTHERS MANAGEMENT, pg. 342
ECP INCORPORATED—Daubert Industries, Inc., pg. 317
ERM-ENVIROCLEAN—The ERM Group, pg. 360
EGGLAND'S BEST, INC., pg. 371
ENABLING TECHNOLOGIES COMPANY, pg. 380
A. EPSTEIN AND SONS, INTL., INC., pg. 384
EPSTEIN CONSTRUCTION INC.—A. Epstein and Sons, Intl., Inc., pg. 384
EPSTEIN ENGINEERING EXPORT, LTD.—A. Epstein and Sons, Intl., Inc., pg. 384
EPSTEIN ENGINEERING EXPORT (WARSAW), LTD.—A. Epstein and Sons, Intl., Inc., pg. 384
EPSTEIN MATERIAL HANDLING ENGINEERING, INC.—A. Epstein and Sons, Intl., Inc., pg. 384
EPSTEIN PROCESS ENGINEERING, INC.—A. Epstein and Sons, Intl., Inc., pg. 384
ERNST & YOUNG, pg. 387
EUROFORM S.R.L.—The Forum Corporation, pg. 426
FCS FORUM S.S.R.O.—The Forum Corporation, pg. 426
FAMILY PHARMACY GENERAL OFFICE—Alco Health Services Corporation, pg. 32
FORT MORGAN COMMUNITY HOSPITAL—Brim, Inc., pg. 176
FORUM ASIA PACIFIC—The Forum Corporation, pg. 426
FORUM COMPANIA DEENTRENAMIENTO—The Forum Corporation, pg. 426
THE FORUM CORPORATION, pg. 425
FORUM EUROPE LTD.—The Forum Corporation, pg. 426
FORUM LEARNING SYSTEMS OF CANADA, LTD.—The Forum Corporation, pg. 426
GEORGE A. FULLER COMPANY, pg. 436
GEMINI CONSULTING, pg. 448
GEMINI CONSULTING-LONDON—Gemini Consulting, pg. 448
GENERAL BUSINESS SERVICES, INC., pg. 449
GENERAL HOSPITAL—Brim, Inc., pg. 176
GEO-CENTERS, INC., pg. 452
GLEN RAVEN MARKETING CORP.—Glen Raven Mills, Inc., pg. 461
GLEN RAVEN MILLS MARKETING CORP.—Glen Raven Mills, Inc., pg. 461
GOLDMAN FINANCIAL GROUP, pg. 468
GOODWILL INDUSTRIES OF AMERICA, INC., pg. 471
HEALTH SERVICES PLUS, INC.—Alco Health Services Corporation, pg. 32
HILL INTERNATIONAL INC., pg. 534
HUBER, HUNT & NICHOLS, INC.—The Hunt Corporation, pg. 553
HUNTCOR INC.—The Hunt Corporation, pg. 553
HYATT INTERNATIONAL CORPORATION—H. Group Holding Inc., pg. 495
INGERSOLL ENGINEERS—Ingersoll Engineers Inc., pg. 568
INGERSOLL ENGINEERS—Ingersoll Engineers Inc., pg. 568
INGERSOLL ENGINEERS—Ingersoll Engineers Inc., pg. 568
INGERSOLL ENGINEERS—Ingersoll Engineers Inc., pg. 568
INGERSOLL ENGINEERS GMBH—Ingersoll Engineers Inc., pg. 568
INGERSOLL ENGINEERS INC., pg. 568
INGERSOLL ENGINEERS LIMITED—Ingersoll Engineers Inc., pg. 568
INGERSOLL ENGINEERS PTY. LTD.—Ingersoll Engineers Inc., pg. 568
INGERSOLL ENGINEERS PTY. LTD.—Ingersoll Engineers Inc., pg. 568
INGERSOLL ENGINEERS S.A.—Ingersoll Engineers Inc., pg. 568
INPUT, pg. 571
INPUT, INC.—INPUT, pg. 571
INPUT, K.K.—INPUT, pg. 571
INPUT, LTD.—INPUT, pg. 571
INPUT, SARL—INPUT, pg. 571
INTERIOR DESIGN INC.—A. Epstein and Sons, Intl., Inc., pg. 384
INTERIOR SPACE DESIGN INC., (ISD)—A. Epstein and Sons, Intl., Inc., pg. 384
INTERNATIONAL DATA CORP.—International Data Group, pg. 577
INTERNATIONAL DATA GROUP, pg. 576
INTERNATIONAL MARKETING SERVICES—International Data Group, pg. 576
JOHN HANCOCK INTL. SERVICES S.A.—John Hancock Mutual Life Insurance Company, pg. 596
JOHN HANCOCK SERVICOS INTERNACIONAIS S/C., LTDA.—John Hancock Mutual Life Insurance Company, pg. 596
JOHNSTON, LEMON & CO. INC., pg. 601
KASANEN TRAINING/BTC FORUM—The Forum Corporation, pg. 426
KITCHELL CORPORATION, pg. 634
LESTER B. KNIGHT & ASSOCIATES, INC., pg. 637
KNIGHT MANAGEMENT CONSULTING, INC.—Lester B. Knight & Associates, Inc., pg. 637
KNIGHT PMD, INC.—Lester B. Knight & Associates, Inc., pg. 637
ROBERT E. LAMB, INC., pg. 652
ARTHUR D. LITTLE OF CANADA LTD.—Arthur D. Little, Inc., pg. 679
ARTHUR D. LITTLE FAR EAST, INC.—Arthur D. Little, Inc., pg. 679
ARTHUR D. LITTLE, INC., pg. 678
ARTHUR D. LITTLE INTL., INC.—Arthur D. Little, Inc., pg. 679
ARTHUR D. LITTLE INTL., INC.—Arthur D. Little, Inc., pg. 679
ARTHUR D. LITTLE (JAPAN), INC.—Arthur D. Little, Inc., pg. 679
ARTHUR D. LITTLE LIMITADA—Arthur D. Little, Inc., pg. 679
ARTHUR D. LITTLE LTD.—Arthur D. Little, Inc., pg. 679
ARTHUR D. LITTLE MEXICANA, S.A. DE C.V.—Arthur D. Little, Inc., pg. 679
ARTHUR D. LITTLE S.R.C.—Arthur D. Little, Inc., pg. 679
M A C GROUP (JAPAN), INC.—Gemini Consulting, pg. 448
MDC SYSTEMS—Day & Zimmermann, Inc., pg. 320
MSI SERVICES, INC., pg. 693
MANAGEMENT DYNAMICS, pg. 703
MARITZ INC., pg. 707
MARITZ LIMITED—Maritz Inc., pg. 708
MARKET STATISTICS—Bill Communications, Inc., pg. 150
MARKETING CORP. OF AMERICA, pg. 709
GEORGE S. MAY CANADA, LTD.—George S. May International Company, pg. 724
GEORGE S. MAY INTERNATIONAL COMPANY, pg. 723
GEORGE S. MAY INTERNATIONAL, S.P.A.—George S. May International Company, pg. 724
MCCARTHY BROTHERS CO.—McCarthy Building Companies, pg. 727
MCKINSEY & COMPANY, INC., pg. 731
MIDCOAST INDUSTRIAL SERVICES CORPORATION, pg. 751
MIDDLE WEST SERVICE COMPANY—SC Companies, Inc., pg. 961
NBBJ, pg. 780
NPS ENERGY SERVICES, INC.—Day & Zimmermann, Inc., pg. 321
NATIONAL LIVE STOCK & MEAT BOARD, pg. 792
NYLIFE LEASING INC.—New York Life Insurance Company, pg. 803
ODI, pg. 818
ODI—ODI, pg. 819
OMEGA PERFORMANCE GROUP, pg. 826
OPERATING PLANT SERVICES—Day & Zimmermann, Inc., pg. 320
OVERSEAS SERVICE CORPORATION, pg. 833
PACIFICA SERVICES, INC., pg. 842
PANAMERICANA DE AVALUOS, S.A.—American Appraisal Associates, Inc., pg. 49
PARCPLACE SYSTEMS—Gemini Consulting, pg. 448
PHOENIX ENTERPRISES INC., pg. 868
J.D. POWER AND ASSOCIATES, pg. 883
PRACTICE DEVELOPMENT INSTITUTE—Friedman, Eisenstein, Raemer & Schwartz, pg. 433
PRIMUS INC., pg. 890
PROFESCO CORPORATION—John Hancock Mutual Life Insurance Company, pg. 596
PRUDENTIAL OVERSEAS FUNDING CORP. N.V.—The Prudential Insurance Company of America, pg. 897
RAIL COMPANY, pg. 906
RII (RICARDS INTERNATIONAL INC.), pg. 907
RNL TECHNICAL SERVICES—RNL Facilities Corporation, pg. 908
SRI INTERNATIONAL, pg. 964
SANUS CORP. HEALTH SYSTEMS—New York Life Insurance Company, pg. 803
STEREO ADVERTISING CORP.—Bose Corporation, pg. 167
SVERDRUP BUILDING CORPORATION—Sverdrup Corporation, pg. 1066
SVERDRUP CORPORATION, pg. 1065
SYSTEMS ENGINEERING ASSOCIATES CO. (SEACOR)—Day & Zimmermann, Inc., pg. 320
I. C. THOMASSON ASSOCIATES, INC., pg. 1094
TORCON, INC., pg. 1102
TOWERS, PERRIN, FORSTER & CROSBY, INC., pg. 1103
TRACOR TECHNOLOGY RESOURCES, INC.—Tracor, Inc., pg. 1105
TRAINING DYNAMICS—The Forum Corporation, pg. 426
UNITED SERVICES AUTOMOBILE ASSOCIATION (USAA), pg. 1134
VEDA INCORPORATED—Veda International, Inc., pg. 1146
WABCO STANDARD INC.—American Standard Inc., pg. 62
WILLIAMSON INTERNATIONAL CORP.—T.D. Williamson, Inc., pg. 1192
THE W.B. WOOD COMPANY, pg. 1199
WOODWARD-CLYDE GROUP, INC., pg. 1200
WOODWARD-CLYDE CONSULTANTS—Woodward-Clyde Group, Inc., pg. 1201
WOODWARD-CLYDE FEDERAL SERVICES—Woodward-Clyde Group, Inc., pg. 1201
WOODWARD-CLYDE INTERNATIONAL—Woodward-Clyde Group, Inc., pg. 1201

8743 — PUBLIC RELATIONS SERVICES

BADER RUTTER & ASSOC., INC., pg. 113
EARLE PALMER BROWN, pg. 182
CLAYTON-DAVIS & ASSOCIATES, INCORPORATED, pg. 253
COLLEGIATE CONCEPTS INC., pg. 262
COMMONWEALTH TOY & NOVELTY COMPANY, pg. 269
EVANSGROUP, pg. 390
FOGARTY & KLEIN PUBLIC RELATIONS—Fogarty & Klein/Winius Brandon, pg. 421
GRANT PUBLIC RELATIONS—Grant Marketing Communications Inc., pg. 477
HLB COMMUNICATIONS, INC., pg. 496
IDC SERVICES, INC., pg. 559
KENTUCKY DEPARTMENT OF TRAVEL DEVELOPMENT, pg. 623
LAMARCA GROUP INC., pg. 652
PADILLA SPEER BEARDSLEY INC., pg. 842
THE RADIO GROUP—LaMarca Group Inc., pg. 652
RUDER, FINN, INC., pg. 954
RUMRILL-HOYT, INC., pg. 955
SANDS INVESTMENTS, INC., pg. 970
SPRING, O'BRIEN & CO. INC., pg. 1033

8744 — FACILITIES SUPPORT MANAGEMENT SERVICES

ANDY FRAIN AVIATION SERVICES, INC.—Andy Frain Services, Inc., pg. 428
ARCHITECTURAL INTERIORS, INC.—A. Epstein and Sons, Intl., Inc., pg. 384
THE ARGOS GROUP—Barton-Malow Enterprises, Inc., pg. 123
ATLANTA MARKET CENTER, pg. 94
BARTON-MALOW ENTERPRISES, INC., pg. 123
BRIM, INC., pg. 176
HEATH CONSULTANTS INCORPORATED, pg. 524
INTERIOR DESIGN INC.—A. Epstein and Sons, Intl., Inc., pg. 384
INTERIOR SPACE DESIGN INC., (ISD)—A. Epstein and Sons, Intl., Inc., pg. 384
MAY & SPEH, INC., pg. 724
SVERDRUP CORPORATION, pg. 1065
SVERDRUP TECHNOLOGY, INC.—Sverdrup Corporation, pg. 1066
TRANSPORTATION & DISTRIBUTION ASSOCIATES—Day & Zimmermann, Inc., pg. 320
TRIANGLE MAINTENANCE CORPORATION, pg. 1112

8748 — BUSINESS CONSULTING SERVICES, NEC

ALLEN & OHARA, INC., pg. 36
AMERICAN APPRAISAL ASSOCIATES, INC., pg. 48
ANDERSEN CONSULTING—Arthur Andersen & Co., S.C., pg. 72
BOOZ ALLEN & HAMILTON INC., pg. 165
THE DARTNELL CORPORATION, pg. 316
FRIEDMAN, EISENSTEIN, RAEMER & SCHWARTZ, pg. 433
GENERAL BUSINESS SERVICES, INC., pg. 449
GUARDSMARK, INC., pg. 492
HAINES LUNDBERG WAEHLER, pg. 500
HARROD DEVITT SOCIEDAD ANONIMA—The Prudential Insurance Company of America, pg. 897
LAW ENGINEERING, INC., pg. 661
KENNETH LEVENTHAL & COMPANY, pg. 670
MSI SERVICES, INC., pg. 693
MANAGEMENT DYNAMICS, pg. 703
MARITZ MARKETING RESEARCH, INC.—Maritz Inc., pg. 707
ALBERT C. MARTIN & ASSOCIATES, pg. 714
NATIONAL LIVE STOCK & MEAT BOARD, pg. 792
NATIONAL UTILITY SERVICE, INC., pg. 794
NEW YORK CITY DEPT. OF GENERAL SERVICES, pg. 802
OPERATIONS MANAGEMENT INTERNATIONAL, INC.—CH2M Hill Companies, Ltd., pg. 202
PEGASUS INTERNATIONAL CORPORATION, pg. 855
PROFESSIONAL ECONOMIC SERVICES, INC.—John Hancock Mutual Life Insurance Company, pg. 596
SPC INTERNATIONAL CORP.—System Planning Corp., pg. 1070
WILBUR SMITH ASSOCIATES, pg. 1011
SPRINGBORN LABORATORIES, INC., pg. 1033
TASSANI COMMUNICATIONS, pg. 1080

8999 — SERVICES, NEC

ABS INDUSTRIAL VERIFICATION, INC.—American Bureau of Shipping, pg. 50
AMERICAN HEALTH COMPANIES, INC., pg. 55
BECHTEL CIVIL, INC.—Bechtel Group, Inc., pg. 131
BECHTEL EASTERN POWER CORPORATION—Bechtel Group, Inc., pg. 131
BECHTEL GREAT BRITAIN LTD.—Bechtel Group, Inc., pg. 131
BECHTEL GROUP, INC., pg. 130
BECHTEL, INC.—Bechtel Group, Inc., pg. 131

BECHTEL, INC. MINING & METALS SPECIAL OPERATION—Bechtel Group, Inc., pg. 131
BECHTEL NATIONAL, INC.—Bechtel Group, Inc., pg. 131
BECHTEL POWER CORPORATION—Bechtel Group, Inc., pg. 131
E. H. BOECKH CO.—American Appraisal Associates, Inc., pg. 48
CROSBY & OVERTON, INC., pg. 300
DIET CENTER, INC.—American Health Companies, Inc., pg. 55
GARTNER GROUP, INC., pg. 443
JWK INTERNATIONAL CORP., pg. 586
MRC TELECOMMUNICATIONS INC.—Journal Communications Inc., pg. 607
MARITZ INC., pg. 707
MARITZ LIMITED—Maritz Inc., pg. 708
MARVIN LUMBER & CEDAR COMPANY, pg. 716
NTH CONSULTANTS, LTD., pg. 781
NORLIGHT—Journal Communications Inc., pg. 607
PE SYSTEMS, pg. 836
QUINTANA PETROLEUM CORP., pg. 905
QUINTANA PETROLEUM SERVICES—Quintana Petroleum Corp., pg. 905
ROWTRONICS COMPANY INC., pg. 953

9199 — GENERAL GOVERNMENT, NEC

THE BUREAU OF NATIONAL AFFAIRS, INC., pg. 189

9224 — FIRE PROTECTION

RURAL METRO CORPORATION, pg. 956
TRIDATA INC.—System Planning Corp., pg. 1070

9311 — PUBLIC FINANCE, TAXATION & MONETARY POLICY

MARYLAND STATE LOTTERY, pg. 717
UNITED STATES SAVINGS BONDS DIVISION, TREASURY DEPARTMENT, pg. 1137

9511 — AIR & WATER RESOURCE & SOLID WASTE MANAGEMENT

BEMCO INC., pg. 138
GENERAL SCIENCES CORP.—Science Applications International Corporation, pg. 981
POIPU WASTE WATER CORPORATION—JMB Realty Corporation, pg. 585

9532 — ADMINISTRATION OF URBAN PLANNING & COMMUNITY & RURAL DVELOPMENT

RNL FACILITIES CORPORATION, pg. 907

9611 — ADMINISTRATION OF GENERAL ECONOMIC PROGRAMS

CHICAGO CONVENTION & TOURISM BUREAU, pg. 245
NEBRASKA DEPT. OF ECONOMIC DEVELOPMENT, pg. 796

9621 — REGULATION & ADMINISTRATION OF TRANSPORTATION PROGRAMS

PORT OF HOUSTON AUTHORITY, pg. 881
SOUTHEASTERN PENNSYLVANIA TRANSPORTATION AUTHORITY, pg. 1020

9641 — REGULATION OF AGRICULTURAL MARKETING & COMMODITIES

AMFAC AGRIBUSINESS, INC.—JMB Realty Corporation, pg. 585
U-HAUL INTERNATIONAL, INC.—Amerco, A Nevada Corporation, pg. 48

9651 — REGULATION, LICENSING & INSPECTION OF MISCELLANEOUS COMMERCIAL SECTORS

HUBBS IMPORTING CORP., pg. 550

CORPORATE RESPONSIBILITIES INDEX

CHAIRMAN OF THE BOARD

Abbey, Nelson Dan, Jr., Chm. Bd. & Chief Exec. Officer--Abbey Etna Machine Company, Perrysburg, OH, pg. 9
Abbott, Helen, Chm. Bd.--Cine Magnetics, Inc., Mamaroneck, NY, pg. 250
Abelson, Marv, Chm. Bd.--Abelson-Taylor, Inc., Chicago, IL, pg. 10
Abplanalp, Robert H., Chm. Bd., Pres. & Chief Exec. Officer--Precision Valve Corporation, Yonkers, NY, pg. 885
Abraham, Lee, Chm. Bd. & Chief Exec. Officer--Associated Merchandising Corp., New York, NY, pg. 91
Abrams, Allan, Chm. Bd. & Pres.--Arrow Fastener Co., Inc., Saddle Brook, NJ, pg. 85
Ach, Roger W., II, Chm. Bd.--Chicago West Pullman Transportation Corporation, Chicago, IL, pg. 246
Acheson, James C., Chm. Bd.--Acheson Industries, Inc., Port Huron, MI, pg. 12
Acker, Stanley, Chm., Pres. & Chief Exec. Officer--Pavion Ltd., Nyack on Hudson, NY, pg. 852
Ackerman, Don E., Chm. Bd.--Decision Data Inc., Horsham, PA, pg. 323
Acklie, Duane W., Chm.--Crete Carrier Corp., Lincoln, NE, pg. 299
Adam, Robert B., Chm. Bd.--Adam Meldrum & Anderson Co., Inc., Buffalo, NY, pg. 16
Adams, Daniel, Chm. Bd.--Attorney's Title Insurance Fund, Orlando, FL, pg. 97
Adams, H. Mat, Chm. & Chief Exec. Officer--Adams Colway & Associates, Rochester, NY, pg. 16
Adams, Peter D., Chm. & Pres.--Adams Rite Manufacturing Co., City of Industry, CA, pg. 16
Adams, Thomas B., Chm.-Advisory Bd.--Brogan & Partners Advertising/Public Relations Inc, Detroit, MI, pg. 178
Addison, E. Christopher, Chm. Bd.--Addison Steel Inc., Orlando, FL, pg. 17
Adelman, Sheldon G., Chm. Bd. & Chief Exec. Officer--Blue Coral, Inc., Cleveland, OH, pg. 159
Adelman, Sheldon G., Chm. Bd. & Chief Exec. Officer--McKay Chemical Co., Los Angeles, CA, pg. 159
Adelman, Sheldon G., Chm. Bd. & Chief Exec. Officer--Simoniz Canada Ltd., Cleveland, OH, pg. 159
Adelman, Sheldon G., Chm. Bd. & Chief Exec. Officer--Nic Sand, Cleveland, OH, pg. 159
Adelman, Sheldon G., Chm. Bd. & Chief Exec. Officer--Chemifax, City of Commerce, CA, pg. 159
Ades, Alan, Chm., Pres. & Chief Exec. Officer--A & E Stores, Inc., Ridgefield, NJ, pg. 1
Adolfson, David G., Chm. Bd., Pres. & Chief Exec. Officer--Adolfson & Peterson, Inc., Minneapolis, MN, pg. 18
Agley, Randolph J., Chm. Bd.--F & M Distributors Inc., Warren, MI, pg. 393
Ahnger, Donald C., Chm. Bd.--Midway Ford Truck Center Inc., Kansas City, MO, pg. 751
Ahrens, Jay, Chm. Bd., Pres. & Chief Exec. Officer--Holly's Inc., Grand Rapids, MI, pg. 540
Aiken, William, Chm. Bd. & Chief Exec. Officer--ACO Inc., Farmington Hills, MI, pg. 2
Aikens, Robert B., Chm. Bd.--Robert B. Aikens & Associates Inc., Troy, MI, pg. 26
Ailloni-Charas, Dan, Dr., Chm. Bd.--Stratmar Systems, Inc., Port Chester, NY, pg. 1053
Akers, William C., Chm. Bd.--The Crystal Tissue Co., Middletown, OH, pg. 303
Akins, A.M., Chm. Bd.--U.R.M. Stores, Inc., Spokane, WA, pg. 1124
Alberici, Gabriel J., Chm. Bd. & Treas.--J. S. Alberici Construction Co., Inc., Saint Louis, MO, pg. 31
Albers, John R., Chm. Bd., Pres. & Chief Exec. Officer--Dr Pepper/Seven-Up Companies, Inc., Dallas, TX, pg. 342
Albers, John R., Chm. & Chief Exec. Officer--Dr Pepper Company, Dallas, TX, pg. 342
Albers, Murrey R., Chm. Bd. & Pres.--United States Bakery, Portland, OR, pg. 1134
Albert, Michael P., Chm. Bd. & Pres.--The Harodite Finishing Company Inc., North Dighton, MA, pg. 510
Albrecht, Fred I., Chm. Bd.--The Fred W. Albrecht Grocery Co., Akron, OH, pg. 31
Albrecht, Randal A., Chm. Bd.--DEC International, Inc., Madison, WI, pg. 308
Alcantara, Severo, Chm.--Dentsu, Young & Rubicam, Alcantara/Manila, Manila, Philippines, pg. 330
Alcorn, David C., Chm. Bd. & Chief Exec. Officer--Donlee Technologies Inc., York, PA, pg. 344
Alderson, N. Leonard, Chm. Bd.--Cargill International S.A., Geneva,, Switzerland, pg. 219
Alexander, Norman E., Chm. Bd.--Ampacet Corporation, Tarrytown, NY, pg. 67
Alfond, Harold, Chm. Bd.--Dexter Shoe Company, Dexter, ME, pg. 334
Alford, Olita M., Chm. Bd.--Alford Refrigerated Warehouse, Inc., Dallas, TX, pg. 34
Allan, William, Chm. Bd.--Star Food Processing, Inc., San Antonio, TX, pg. 1039
Allard, Gerald R., Chm. Bd.--Jewell Instruments, Inc., Manchester, NH, pg. 594
Allard, Gerald R., Chm. Bd.--Granite State Manufacturing Co., Manchester, NH, pg. 476
Allard, Jean Marc, Chm. Bd., Pres. & Chief Exec. Officer--Hubbard Construction Co., Winter Park, FL, pg. 549
Allbritton, Joe L., Chm. Bd. & Chief Exec. Officer--Perpetual Corporation, Washington, DC, pg. 862
Allbritton, Joe L., Chm. Bd.--Allbritton News Bureau, Inc., Washington, DC, pg. 862
Allen, Benjamin F., Chm. Bd.--Allen Foods, Inc., Saint Louis, MO, pg. 36
Allen, David, Chm., Pres. & Chief Exec. Officer--AMD Industries Inc., Cicero, IL, pg. 5
Allen, Floyd E., Chm. Bd.--Mid-West Paper Products Company, Warren, MI, pg. 750
Allen, Guy F., Chm. Bd. & Pres.--R.G. Meadows, Inc., Great Neck, NY, pg. 733
Allen, Ivan, Jr., Chm. Bd.--Ivan Allen Company, Inc., Atlanta, GA, pg. 36
Allen, John W., Chm. Bd.--J.W. Allen & Company, Wheeling, IL, pg. 36
Allen, Michael, Chm. Bd.--Simpson Electric Co., Elgin, IL, pg. 1007
Allen, Robert B., Sr., Chm. Bd.--Allen Steel Co., Salt Lake City, UT, pg. 36
Allen, Roderick, Chm. Bd. & Chief Exec. Officer--Allen Canning Company, Siloam Springs, AR, pg. 35
Allen, Terrence J., Chm. Bd. & Pres.--Pemco Die Casting Corporation, Bridgman, MI, pg. 856
Allison, James R., Sr., Chm. Bd. & Chief Exec. Officer--Allison-Erwin Co. Inc., Charlotte, NC, pg. 40
Allison, Robert S., Chm. & Chief Exec. Officer--Doe-Anderson Advertising Agency, Inc., Louisville, KY, pg. 342
Alperson, Robert, Chm. Bd. & Pres.--Rolled Steel Products Corporation, Los Angeles, CA, pg. 944
Alpert, Norman R., Chm. Bd., Pres. & Chief Exec. Officer--Bio-Tek Instruments, Inc., Winooski, VT, pg. 152
Alstadt, Donald M., Chm. Bd.--Lord Corporation, Erie, PA, pg. 683
Alter, James M., Chm. Bd. & Chief Exec. Officer--The Harry Alter Company, Chicago, IL, pg. 45
Altier, Richard L., Chm. Bd.--Altier & Sons Shoes Inc., Rochester, NY, pg. 45
Altobello, Daniel, Chm. Bd.--Caterair Holdings Corp., Potomac, MD, pg. 229
Altobello, Daniel, Chm., Pres. & Chief Exec. Officer--Caterair International, Potomac, MD, pg. 229
Alvarez, Antonio C., Chm. Bd.--Long MFG. NC, Inc., Tarboro, NC, pg. 682
Alvarez, Paul H., Chm. Bd., Pres. & Chief Exec. Officer--Ketchum Communications Inc., Pittsburgh, PA, pg. 625
Amant, Charles, Chm. Bd.--Alkota Cleaning Systems, Inc., Alcester, SD, pg. 34
Amen, Lou, Chm. Bd.--Certified Grocers Of California, Los Angeles, CA, pg. 237
Ament, Werner E., Chm. Bd., Pres., Chief Exec. Officer & Sec.--Milex of America, Inc., Chicago, IL, pg. 753
Ames, Richard S., Chm. & Chief Exec. Officer--Command Plastic Corporation, Akron, OH, pg. 268
Ammirati, Ralph, Chm. & Creative Dir.--Ammirati & Puris Inc., New York, NY, pg. 67
Amore, Joe, Chm. Bd., Pres. & Chief Exec. Officer--BeefAmerica Operating Co., Inc., Omaha, NE, pg. 131
Amos, George H., Jr., Chm. Bd.--Tucson Realty & Trust Co., Tucson, AZ, pg. 1118
Amoss, W. James, Jr., Chm. Bd. & Chief Exec. Officer--Lykes Bros. Steamship Co., Inc., New Orleans, LA, pg. 688
Amsterdam, J., Chm. Bd.--Leviton Mfg. Co., Inc., Little Neck, NY, pg. 671
Anchel, Edward, Chm. Bd. & Pres.--Sparkomatic Corporation, Milford, PA, pg. 1025
Anchel, Edward, Chm. Bd. & Pres.--Kenco, Middlebury, IN, pg. 1025
Anchel, Edward, Chm. & Pres.--Altec Lansing Consumer Products, Milford, PA, pg. 1025
Andersen, John, Exec. V.P.--Edward G. Dorn & Associates, Inc., Rolling Meadows, IL, pg. 346
Anderson, Bruce, Chm. Bd.--MSI Insurance Companies, Arden Hills, MN, pg. 693
Anderson, Clifford I., Chm. Bd. & Pres.--Crown Holdings, Inc., Roseville, MN, pg. 302
Anderson, Clifford I., Chm. Bd. & Pres.--Crown Iron Works Company, Roseville, MN, pg. 302
Anderson, E. Dean, Chm. Bd. & Chief Exec. Officer--Leslie Advertising, Greenville, SC, pg. 668
Anderson, F.E., Chm. Bd.--Pacific Coast Building Products Inc., Sacramento, CA, pg. 839
Anderson, Gordon B., Chm. Bd. & Pres.--Gordy's, Inc., Worthington, MN, pg. 472
Anderson, James, Chm. Bd. & Chief Exec. Officer--Anderson Brothers Construction Brainerd, Brainerd, MN, pg. 72
Anderson, James F., Chm. Bd.--Anderson Advertising, Inc., San Antonio, TX, pg. 72
Anderson, James T., Chm.--Anderson Wholesale Company, Muskogee, OK, pg. 73
Anderson, John R., Chm. Bd.--Atwood Industries, Inc., Rockford, IL, pg. 97
Anderson, John R., Chm. Bd. & Pres.--Anderson Industries Inc., Rockford, IL, pg. 73
Anderson, Lee R., Sr., Chm. Bd. & Chief Exec. Officer--API Group Inc., Saint Paul, MN, pg. 5
Anderson, Liz, Chm. Bd.--Washington State Dairy Products Commission, Seattle, WA, pg. 1167
Anderson, R. Quintus, Chm. Bd. & Pres.--The Aarque Companies, Jamestown, NY, pg. 9
Anderson, Ralph, Chm Bd., Pres., & Chief Exec. Officer--Belcan Corporation, Cincinnati, OH, pg. 133
Anderson, Richard E., Chm. Bd. & Pres.--Cadet Manufacturing Company, Vancouver, WA, pg. 207
Anderson, Thomas L., Chm. Bd. & Pres.--Anderson Industries, Inc., Dallas, TX, pg. 72
Anderson, Tom, Chm. Bd.--The Andersons, Maumee, OH, pg. 73
Andis, M. L., Chm. Bd. & Pres.--Andis Company, Racine, WI, pg. 74
Andrade, Jose E., Chm. Bd.--Thomas Publishing Co., New York, NY, pg. 1093
Andrasick, James, Chm. Bd.--Brewer Environmental Industries, Inc., Honolulu, HI, pg. 174
Andrasick, James S., Chm. Bd.--Ka'u Agribusiness Co., Inc., Pahala, HI, pg. 174
Andrasick, James S., Chm. Bd.--Mauna Kea Agribusiness Co., Inc., Papaikou, HI, pg. 174
Andrasick, James S., Chm. Bd.--Olokele Sugar Co., Limited, Kaumakani, HI, pg. 174
Andrasick, James S., Chm. Bd.--HT&T Company, Inc., Hilo, HI, pg. 174
Andrews, George W., Chm. Bd. & Pres.--Keco Industry, Inc., Florence, KY, pg. 619
Andrews, Mark, Jr., Chm. Bd.--Mark Andy, Inc., Chesterfield, MO, pg. 708
Angelo, Stanley, Jr., Chm. Bd.--Angelo Brothers Co., Philadelphia, PA, pg. 74
Anshell, J.G., Chm. Bd. & Chief Exec. Officer--Moses Anshell, Inc., Phoenix, AZ, pg. 76
Anthony, Beryl, Sr., Chm. Bd.--Anthony Forest Products Co., Inc., El Dorado, AR, pg. 77
Anthony, John E., Chm. Bd. & Pres.--Bearden Lumber Company, Inc., Bearden, AR, pg. 129
Appalucci, Joseph L., Chm. & Chief Exec. Officer--Lieberman-Appalucci, Allentown, PA, pg. 675
Appell, L.J., Jr., Chm. Bd.--The Pfaltzgraff Co., York, PA, pg. 1065
Appell, Louis, Jr., Chm. Bd.--Syracuse China Corp., Syracuse, NY, pg. 1065
Appelwick, Robert A., Chm. Bd. & Chief Exec. Officer--Apple Lines, Inc., Madison, SD, pg. 79
Apperson, R.P., Chm. Bd. & Pres.--Apperson Business Forms, Inc., Los Angeles, CA, pg. 78
Applegate, Leslie T., Chm. Bd. & Chief Exec. Officer--Surgical Appliance Industries, Inc., Cincinnati, OH, pg. 1065
Apthorp, James W., Chm. Bd.--Atlantic Gulf Communities Corporation, Miami, FL, pg. 95
Aquilina, Joseph, Chm. Bd.--Victoria Packing Corporation, Brooklyn, NY, pg. 1149
Arakelian, George H., Chm. Bd. & Pres.--Standard Manufacturing Company, Troy, NY, pg. 1037

Arcati, Thomas, Chm. Bd.--Champion Aluminum Corporation, Syosset, NY, pg. 238
Arch, D.C., Chm. Bd. & Chief Exec. Officer--Blistex, Inc., Oak Brook, IL, pg. 157
Archer, James P., Chm. Bd.--Jackson Paper Company, Jackson, MS, pg. 587
Archibald, Delbert M., Chm. Bd.--Printing House, Inc., Quincy, FL, pg. 891
Arenberg, Julius T., Chm. Bd.--Columbia Pipe & Supply Company, Chicago, IL, pg. 266
Arend, John R., Chm. Bd. & Chief Exec. Officer--International Chemical Company, Tulsa, OK, pg. 576
Arens, Richard P., Chm. Bd., Pres., Chief Exec. & Fin. Officer--Alacon, Sunnyvale, CA, pg. 29
Aretsky, Kenneth, Chm. & Chief Oper. Officer--The "21" Club, Inc., New York, NY, pg. 1121
Armbrecht, Edward C., Jr., Chm. Bd. & Co-Chief Exec. Officer--Stone & Thomas, Wheeling, WV, pg. 1051
Armstrong, Brad, Chm.--Earle Palmer Brown/Richmond, Richmond, VA, pg. 182
Armstrong, Frank A., Chm. Bd.--The Monarch Company, Inc., Atlanta, GA, pg. 765
Armstrong, Frank, III, Chm. & Pres.--National Fruit Product Company, Winchester, VA, pg. 789
Armstrong, L.F., Chm. Bd.--Armstrong International, Inc., Three Rivers, MI, pg. 83
Armstrong, Ronald, Chm. Bd. & Creative Dir.--Fabianac, Stropes & Armstrong, Inc., San Francisco, CA, pg. 395
Arnhold, Henry H., Chm. Bd.--Arnhold and S. Bleichroeder, Inc., New York, NY, pg. 84
Arnold, H.G., Chm. Bd. & Chief Fin. Officer--Venta Inc., Denver, CO, pg. 1147
Arnold, Isaac, Jr., Chm. Bd.--Quintana Petroleum Corp., Houston, TX, pg. 905
Arnold, John A., Chm. Bd.--Petroleum Products Corp., Middletown, PA, pg. 865
Arnold, Robert H., Chm. Bd.--Ames Safety Envelope Company, Inc., Somerville, MA, pg. 66
Arnold, Rudolph P., Chm. Bd.--Society for Savings Bancorp, Inc., Hartford, CT, pg. 1016
Aronoff, Morton, Chm. Bd.--Gate City Beverage Distributors, San Bernardino, CA, pg. 444
Aronson, Arnold, Chm. Bd. & Chief Exec. Officer--Woodward & Lothrop/John Wanamaker, Washington, DC, pg. 1201
Arquilla, George, Jr., Chm. Bd.--Burnside Construction Co., Downers Grove, WI, pg. 194
Arst, Maryon G., Chm. Bd.--Goldsmiths, Inc., Wichita, KS, pg. 469
Asch, Robert, Chm. Bd.--Twincraft, Inc., Winooski, VT, pg. 1122
Aschinger, Carl J., Jr., Chm. Bd., Pres. & Chief Exec. Officer--Columbus Show Case Company, Columbus, OH, pg. 267
Ash, Carroll L., Co-Chm., Pres. & Chief Exec. Officer--Trojan Steel Co., Charleston, WV, pg. 1115
Ashcroft, John, Chm. Bd.--Puritan/Churchill Chemical Company, Atlanta, GA, pg. 900
Asher, Harold, Chm.-Exec. Committee--Asher/Gould Advertising, Inc., Los Angeles, CA, pg. 88
Ashkenazi, Ely, Chm. Bd. & Chief Exec. Officer--Soundesign Corporation, Jersey City, NJ, pg. 1018
Asplundh, Robert, Chm. Bd.--Asplundh Tree Expert Co., Willow Grove, PA, pg. 88
Atkins, Chip, Chm. Bd.--The Atkins Agency, San Antonio, TX, pg. 94
Atlas, Jeff, Chm.--Atlas Citron Haligman & Bedecarre, San Francisco, CA, pg. 96
Atols, John M., Chm. Bd. & Chief Exec. Officer--Atols Tool and Mold Corp., Schiller Park, IL, pg. 97
Atwater, Hal B., Chm. Bd.--Davis-Newman-Payne, Knoxville, TN, pg. 319
Auch, Frederick J., Jr., Chm. Bd. & Chief Exec. Officer--George W. Auch Co., Pontiac, MI, pg. 97
Augustine, James N., Chm. Bd. & Chief Exec. Officer--Insurance Corp. of America, Houston, TX, pg. 572
Ausherman, Ernest W., Chm. Bd.--Ausherman Construction Company, Frederick, MD, pg. 98
Austad, Oscar, Chm. Bd.--The Austad Company, Sioux Falls, SD, pg. 98
Austin, Harry G., Jr., Chm. Bd.--James Austin Co., Mars, PA, pg. 99
Austin, Mike, Chm. Bd. & Pres.--Austin Associates, Inc., San Jose, CA, pg. 98
Autry, Gene, Chm. Bd., Pres. & Chief Exec. Officer--Golden West Broadcasters, Los Angeles, CA, pg. 467
Aveni, Joseph T., Chm. Bd. & Chief Exec. Officer--Realty One, Cleveland, OH, pg. 917
Aveni, Vincent T., Chm. Emeritus--Realty One, Cleveland, OH, pg. 917
Avrett, John G., Chm. & Chief Exec. Officer--Avrett, Free & Ginsberg, Inc., New York, NY, pg. 103
Awrey, Robert C., Chm. Bd.--Awrey Bakeries, Inc., Livonia, MI, pg. 103
Axelrad, Milton S., Chm. Bd.--Pakula & Company, Chicago, IL, pg. 843
Axtell, Dean R., Chm. Bd. & Dir.-Intl. Sls.--Trak International, Inc., Port Washington, WI, pg. 1106
Azzar, James D., Chm. Bd.--Hollymatic Corporation, Countryside, IL, pg. 539
Babcock, Fred C., Chm. Bd.--Babcock Lumber Company, Pittsburgh, PA, pg. 107
Bachhuber, Ted J., Chm. Bd.--Mayville Engineering Co., Inc., Mayville, WI, pg. 725
Bachman, John C., Chm. Bd., Pres., Chief Exec. & Oper. Officer--Automated Marketing Systems, Inc., Chicago, IL, pg. 100
Bachman, Stanley F., Chm. Bd.--Bachman's, Inc., Minneapolis, MN, pg. 108
Bachmann, Thomas M., Chm. Bd., Pres. & Chief Exec. Officer--Calico Cat Press, Inc., New Providence, NJ, pg. 209
Backus, Roberta, Chm. Bd., Chief Exec. Officer & New Bus. Contact--Backus Turner & Partners, Inc., Miami, FL, pg. 112
Badcock, Wogan S., Jr., Chm. Bd. & Pres.--W.S. Badcock Corporation, Mulberry, FL, pg. 113
Badtke, Donald J., Chm. Bd. & Pres.--Stanley Knight Corporation, New Troy, MI, pg. 1038
Baer, Albert, Chm. Bd. & Chief Exec. Officer--Imperial Schrade Corp., New York, NY, pg. 564
Baer, Albert M., Chm. Bd.--Imperial Schrade Corp., Ellenville, NY, pg. 564
Bagley, Paul, Chm. Bd.--Franchise Finance Corp. of America, Scottsdale, AZ, pg. 428
Bahke, Dr. T., Chm. Bd.--Robins Engineers & Constructors, Inc., Englewood, CO, pg. 939
Bailey, Coley L., Chm. Bd.--Mississippi Chemical Corporation, Yazoo City, MS, pg. 760
Bailey, Edgar H., Chm. Bd. & Pres.--Leader Federal Bank For Savings, Memphis, TN, pg. 663
Bailey, Harvey A., Chm.--Bailey, Klepinger & Medrich, Inc., Ann Arbor, MI, pg. 114
Bailey, J.H., Chm. Bd. & Chief Exec. Officer--The Cretex Companies, Elk River, MN, pg. 299
Bailey, James G., Chm.--Master Collectors Inc., Atlanta, GA, pg. 719
Bailey, John, Chm. Bd., Pres., Chief Exec. & Fin. Officer & Treas.--Cal/Emblem Labels, Inc., Fresno, CA, pg. 208
Bailey, John H., Chm. Bd., Pres., Chief Exec. & Chief Oper. Officer--The Climatic Corp., Columbia, SC, pg. 255
Bailey, Richard W., Chm. & Chief Exec. Officer--Bailey Lauerman & Associates, Inc., Lincoln, NE, pg. 114
Bain, H., Chm. Bd. & Pres.--Homewood Corporation, Columbus, OH, pg. 542
Baird, Clayton D., Chm. Bd.--Mrs. Baird's Bakeries, Inc., Fort Worth, TX, pg. 760
Baird, John W., Chm. Bd.--Baird & Warner Inc., Chicago, IL, pg. 114
Baker, Clyde N., Jr., Chm. Bd.--STS Holdings, Inc., Northbrook, IL, pg. 964
Baker, Clyde N., Jr., Chm. Bd.--STS Consultants, Ltd., Northbrook, IL, pg. 965
Baker, Daniel L., Chm. Bd. & Pres.--Baker Concrete Construction, Inc., Monroe, OH, pg. 115
Baker, Edwin M., Chm. Bd.--Guard Publishing Company, Eugene, OR, pg. 491
Baker, Newell A., Chm. Bd.--J. D. Streett & Co., Inc., Maryland Heights, MO, pg. 1053
Baker, R.E., Chm. Bd.--Newage Industries Inc., Testing Instruments Division, Willow Grove, PA, pg. 803
Baker, Raymond E., Chm. Bd.--Newage Industries Inc., Willow Grove, PA, pg. 803
Baker, Ronald, Chm. Bd., Pres. & Chief Exec. Officer--Millmaster Onyx Group, Inc., Westport, CT, pg. 755
Baker, W.G., Jr., Chm. Bd. & Chief Exec. Officer--Pachmayr Gun Works Inc., Monrovia, CA, pg. 839
Baker, Wilder D., Chm. & Chief Exec. Officer--Warwick Baker & Fiore Inc., New York, NY, pg. 1165
Balc, Alex, Jr., Chm. Bd.--C. S. Johnson Co., Champaign, IL, pg. 597
Ball, Fred, Chm. Bd.--Associated Wholesale Grocers, Inc., Kansas City, KS, pg. 92
Ball, G. Carl, Chm. Bd.--Geo. J. Ball, Inc., West Chicago, IL, pg. 115
Ball, John H., Chm. Bd. & Chief Exec. Officer--R. M. Shoemaker Co., West Conshohocken, PA, pg. 1000
Ball, Rex M., Chm. Bd. & Chief Exec. Officer--HTB, Inc., Oklahoma City, OK, pg. 497
Ballard, Larry C., Chm. Bd., Pres. & Chief Exec. Officer--Sentry Insurance, A Mutual Company, Stevens Point, WI, pg. 990
Ballenger, Thomas C., Chm. Bd.--Plastic Packaging, Inc., Hickory, NC, pg. 875
Balsamo, Salvatore, Chm. Bd., Pres. & Chief Exec. Officer--Technical Aid Corporation, Newton Upper Falls, MA, pg. 1083
Bancroft, Joseph C., Chm. Bd.--Croft Metal Inc., McComb, MS, pg. 300
Bank, Marvin F., Chm. Bd.--Bank M F & Company, Inc., Minneapolis, MN, pg. 117
Bankston, William O., Chm. Bd.--W. O. Bankston Enterprises Inc., Dallas, TX, pg. 118
Bankuty, Geza E., Chm. Bd., Pres. & Chief Exec. Officer--New England Machinery, Inc., Bradenton, FL, pg. 800
Barancik, C.L., Chm. Bd.--Justrite Manufacturing Company, Des Plaines, IL, pg. 610
Baranski, Dennis A., Chm. Bd., Pres. & Chief Exec. Officer--Barancorp, Lecompton, KS, pg. 118
Barbar, George E., Chm. Bd. & Pres.--The Barbar Group, Inc., Boca Raton, FL, pg. 119
Barbee, Robert P., Chm. Bd. & Chief Exec. Officer--Pneumafil Corp., Charlotte, NC, pg. 878
Barber, George W., Jr., Chm. Bd., Chief Fin. Officer & Treas.--Barber Dairies, Inc., Birmingham, AL, pg. 119
Barber, Miles H., Chm. Bd. & Chief Exec. Officer--Commercial & Industrial Administration Co. inc, Santa Clara, CA, pg. 268
Barclay, H. Douglas, Chm. Bd.--Syracuse Supply Company, Syracuse, NY, pg. 1070
Bard, Richard O., Chm. Bd.--Bard Mfg. Co., Bryan, OH, pg. 119
Barden, G. Richard, Chm. Bd.--Barden & Robeson Corporation, Middleport, NY, pg. 119
Barensfeld, Robert, Chm. Bd.--Ellwood City Forge, Ellwood City, PA, pg. 378
Barge, Alvin, Chm. Bd.--Barge-Wagener, Inc., Atlanta, GA, pg. 119
Barker, Paul, Chm. Bd.--McLaughlin Mfg. Company, Greenville, SC, pg. 731
Barkley, Rufus C., Jr., Chm. Bd.--Cameron & Barkley Company, Inc., Charleston Heights, SC, pg. 212
Barlow, Witt, Chm., Pres. & Chief Exec. Officer--Great Lakes Dredge & Dock, Oak Brook, IL, pg. 481
Barnes, Bradford, Chm. Bd. & Chief Exec. Officer--Crouch Supply Company, Inc., Fort Worth, TX, pg. 301
Barnett, Cecil C., Chm. Bd., Pres., Chief Exec. Officer & Treas.--Algood Food Company, Louisville, KY, pg. 34
Barnett, Charles E., Chm. Bd.--Barnett Millworks, Inc., Theodore, AL, pg. 120
Barnette, P. H., Chm. Bd.--Greenwood Packing Plant, Greenwood, SC, pg. 486
Barnhard, Sherwood A., Chm. Bd.--Lasky Company, Millburn, NJ, pg. 660
Barnhardt, J.H., Chm. Bd.--Carolina Absorbent Cotton Co., Charlotte, NC, pg. 120
Barnhardt, James H., Sr., Chm. Bd.--Barnhardt Manufacturing Co., Charlotte, NC, pg. 120
Barnhill, R.E., Chm. Bd.--Barnhill Contracting Company, Tarboro, NC, pg. 121
Barnum, William M., Chm. Bd. & Chief Exec. Officer--Educational Publishing Corporation, Oak Lawn, IL, pg. 369
Barouh, Victor, Chm. Bd.--Barouh Eaton Allen Corporation, Brooklyn, NY, pg. 121
Barr, Thomas A., Chm. Bd.--Barr & Barr, Inc., New York, NY, pg. 121
Barre, Stephen A., Chm. Bd., Pres., Chief Exec. Officer & Sec.--Servo Corporation of America, Hicksville, NY, pg. 993
Bartholow, Peter, Chm. Bd., Pres. & Chief Oper. Officer--MCorp, Dallas, TX, pg. 732
Bartlett, Paul D., Jr., Chm. Bd.--Bartlett and Company, Kansas City, MO, pg. 122
Bartolone, Joseph F., Sr., Chm. & Chief Exec. Officer--Pancom International Corp., Stamford, CT, pg. 845
Barton, A.P., Jr., Chm. Bd., Pres. & Chief Exec. Officer--Mutual Manufacturing & Supply Co., Cincinnati, OH, pg. 778
Barton, L.G., Chm. Bd.--Buzz Barton & Associates, Inc., Oak Brook, IL, pg. 123
Bartscht, Karl G., Chm. Bd. & Chief Exec. Officer--Chi Systems, Inc., Ann Arbor, MI, pg. 244
Basha, Edward N., Jr., Chm. Bd.--Bashas, Chandler, AZ, pg. 124
Baskin, Shale, Chm. Bd.--Mark Shale, Willowbrook, IL, pg. 994
Basler, William L., Chm. Bd., Chief Exec. Officer & Treas.--Basler Electric Company, Highland, IL, pg. 125
Bass, Sid R., Chm. Bd.--Bass Enterprises Production Company, Fort Worth, TX, pg. 125
Bassett, H.W., Chm. Bd.--The W.E. Bassett Company, Shelton, CT, pg. 125
Bassett, James E., III, Chm. Bd.--Keeneland Assoc., Inc., Lexington, KY, pg. 620
Bastian, Bruce W., Chm. Bd.--WordPerfect Corporation, Orem, UT, pg. 1202
Bata, T.G., Chm. Bd.--CHB Corp., Belcamp, MD, pg. 201
Bateman, Edward D., Chm. Bd.--Bateman Brothers Lumber Co., Inc., New Britain, PA, pg. 125
Bates, Harold, Chm. Bd.--Affiliated Foods Cooperative Inc., Norfolk, NE, pg. 23
Bates, Robert D., Chm. Bd., Pres. & Chief Exec. Officer--Guarantee Mutual Life Co., Omaha, NE, pg. 491
Bates, Warren H., Chm. Bd.--Bates Container, Inc., North Richland Hills, TX, pg. 125
Bates, Wesley, Chm. Bd. & Pres.--Stanley Steemer International, Inc., Dublin, OH, pg. 1038
Batteast, Robert V., Chm. Bd. & Pres.--Batteast Construction Company, Inc., South Bend, IN, pg. 126
Batten, Frank, Chm. Bd.--Landmark Communications, Inc., Norfolk, VA, pg. 654
Baucom, W.E., Chm.--E-B Advertising Display Inc., Massillon, OH, pg. 358
Bauer, Phil, Chm. Bd. & Creative Dir.--Smyth, Bauer & Lewis Advertising Inc., Richmond, VA, pg. 1014
Bauerle, Donald C., Sr., Chm. Bd.--Codisco Inc., Sanford, FL, pg. 258
Baugh, Robert H., Chm. Bd. & Pres.--Baugh Construction Company, Seattle, WA, pg. 127
Baugher, Claude O., Chm. Bd.--Baugher Chevrolet-Buick-Geo, Inc., Waynesboro, VA, pg. 127
Baughman, Walter P., Chm. Bd.--Plastomer Corp., Livonia, MI, pg. 876
Baum, W.A., Jr., Chm. Bd.--W. A. Baum Company, Inc., Copiague, NY, pg. 127
Bauman, Edward J., Chm. Bd.--Draper Corporation, Greensboro, NC, pg. 348
Baute, Joseph A., Chm. Bd. & Chief Exec. Officer--Markem Corporation, Keene, NH, pg. 708
Baxter, Alfred X., Chm. & Chief Exec. Officer--J.H. Baxter & Company, San Mateo, CA, pg. 127
Bayer, Gary R., Chm. & Chief Exec. Officer--Bayer Bess Vanderwarker Inc., Chicago, IL, pg. 128
Bayley, Robert E., Chm. Bd. & Chief Exec. Officer--Robert E. Bayley Construction, Seattle, WA, pg. 128
Beach, William H., Chm. Bd., Pres., Chief Exec. & Oper. Officer--Beach Mold & Tool Inc., New Albany, IN, pg. 128
Beadles, Wayne, Chm. Bd. & Pres.--Woodruff Electrical Co-Op, Forest City, AR, pg. 1200
Beall, E.R., Chm. Bd.--Beall's, Inc., Bradenton, FL, pg. 129
Bean, Vernon J., Chm. Bd.--D. D. Bean & Sons Co., Jaffrey, NH, pg. 129
Beard, A.D., Chm. Bd. & Pres.--Formation, Inc., Moorestown, NJ, pg. 424
Beardall, James C., Chm. Bd., Pres. & Chief Exec. Officer--Anderson Lumber Company, Ogden, UT, pg. 73
Beardsley, John R., Chm. Bd. & Chief Exec. Officer--Padilla Speer Beardsley Inc., Minneapolis, MN, pg. 842
Beaton, Alfred T., Chm. Bd.--New England Newspaper Supply Company, Inc., Millbury, MA, pg. 800
Beauchamp, Patrick L., Chm. Bd., Pres. & Treas.--Beauchamp Distributing Company, Compton, CA, pg. 130
Beber, Joyce, Chm. Bd.--Beber Silverstein & Partners, Inc., Miami, FL, pg. 130
Bechen, Peter F., Chm. Bd., Pres. & Chief Oper. Officer--M & T Incorporated, Portland, OR, pg. 690

Beck, Emily C., Chm. Bd.--Precisionaire, Inc., Saint Petersburg, FL, pg. 886
Beck, Henry C., Jr., Chm. Bd.--HCB Contractors, Dallas, TX, pg. 496
Beck, James H., Chm. Bd. & Chief Exec. Officer--Precision Twist Drill Co., Crystal Lake, IL, pg. 885
Beck, James H., Chm. Bd. & Chief Exec. Officer--Mohawk Tools, Crystal Lake, IL, pg. 885
Beck, Jerry, Chm. Bd., Pres. & Chief Exec. Officer--Mighty Distributing System, Norcross, GA, pg. 752
Beck, Scott, Chm. & Chief Exec. Officer--Boston Chicken, Inc., Naperville, IL, pg. 167
Becker, Jochen, Chm. Bd--American Barmag Co., Charlotte, NC, pg. 49
Beckley, John L., Chm. Bd.--The Economics Press, Inc., Fairfield, NJ, pg. 367
Beckman, Richard N., Chm.--Partners Meany, Inc., Albany, NY, pg. 850
Beckwith, F. W., Chm. Bd., Pres. & Chief Exec. Officer--Fareway Stores, Inc., Boone, IA, pg. 399
Beckwith, James S. III, Chm. Bd.--Beckwith Machinery Company, Murrysville, PA, pg. 131
Beddor, William N., Chm. Bd.--Japs-Olson Company, Minneapolis, MN, pg. 590
Beeler, Donald, Chm. Bd., Pres. & Chief Exec. Officer--Snyder's Drug Stores, Inc., Minnetonka, MN, pg. 1015
Beggs, Lyman M., Chm., Pres, & Chief Exec. Officer--Sealy, Inc., Cleveland, OH, pg. 985
Beggs, Lymann M., Chm., Pres. & Chief Exec. Officer--Sealy Corporation, Cleveland, OH, pg. 985
Behan, William L., Jr., Chm. Bd.--Hill-Behan Lumber Company, Saint Louis, MO, pg. 534
Behnke, John F., Chm. Bd.--Fisher Broadcasting, Inc., Seattle, WA, pg. 415
Behr, Philip H., Chm. Bd.--Forster Mfg. Co., Inc., Wilton, ME, pg. 21
Behrens, Peter, Vice Chm.--Great Salt Lake Minerals & Chemicals Corp., Ogden, UT, pg. 482
Belk, John M., Chm. Bd. & Chief Exec. Officer--Belk Stores Services Inc., Charlotte, NC, pg. 134
Bell, Calvin, Chm. Bd.--Twin County Grocers, Inc., Edison, NJ, pg. 1122
Bell, John, Jr., Chm. Bd. & Chief Exec. Officer--Bell Packaging Corporation, Marion, IN, pg. 135
Bell, Ray, Chm. Bd., Pres. & Chief Exec. Officer--Atex Oil Co. of Texas, Inc., Amarillo, TX, pg. 93
Bell, Richard H., Chm. Bd.--Highlights for Children, Inc., Columbus, OH, pg. 534
Bellacicco, Vincent, Chm. Bd.--Bellacicco & Sons, Queens Village, NY, pg. 136
Belz, Philip, Chm. Bd.--Belz Enterprises, Memphis, TN, pg. 138
Bender, Robert, Chm. Bd., Pres. & Chief Exec. Officer--Megas Beauty Aids, Inc., Cleveland, OH, pg. 737
Bender, Thomas B., Jr., Chm. Bd. & Pres.--Bender Shipbuilding & Repair Company, Mobile, AL, pg. 138
Bendheim, C.H., Chm. Bd.--Philipp Brothers Chemicals, Inc., Fort Lee, NJ, pg. 867
Bendheim, C.H., Chm. Bd.--Mathieu Corporation, Riverdale, NJ, pg. 720
Benjamin, Colin, Chm., Pres. & Chief Exec. Officer--Associated Metals & Minerals Corp., White Plains, NY, pg. 91
Benjamin, Morley, Chm. Bd.--Morley Group, Santa Monica, CA, pg. 770
Bennett, David, Chm. Bd.--Omega Performance Group, San Francisco, CA, pg. 826
Bennett, Dick, Chm. Bd. & Production Dir.--Bennett Kuhn Varner, Inc., Atlanta, GA, pg. 139
Bennett, Donald H., Chm. Bd.--Oakhurst Dairy, Portland, ME, pg. 819
Bennett, Paul F., Chm. Bd. & Chief Exec. Officer--Utility Trailer Manufacturing Co., City of Industry, CA, pg. 1141
Benson, Gerald, Chm. Bd., Pres. & Chief Exec. Officer--The Benatty Corporation, Cambridge, OH, pg. 138
Benson, H. E., Chm. Bd.--Benson's, Inc., Bogart, GA, pg. 140
Benson, Tom, Jr., Chm. Bd. & Pres.--Benson Management Company, San Antonio, TX, pg. 140
Bent, Gardner L., Chm. Bd. & Pres.--S. Bent & Brothers, Inc., Gardner, MA, pg. 140
Bently, Donald E., Chm. Bd. & Chief Exec. Officer--Bently Nevada Corporation, Minden, NV, pg. 140
Benton, Virgil K., Chm. Bd.--Keystone Automotive Industries, Inc., Pomona, CA, pg. 627
Benton, William B., Chm. Bd., Chief Exec. Officer & Chief Fin. Officer--Mid South Sales, Helena, AR, pg. 750
Berdass, Fred P., Chm. Bd.--Bermo, Inc., Circle Pines, MN, pg. 143
Beren, S.O., Chm. Bd., Pres. & Chief Exec. Officer--Misco Industries, Wichita, KS, pg. 759
Berenson, Paul S., Chm., Pres. & Dir.-Creative--Berenson, Isham & Partners, Inc., Boston, MA, pg. 141
Berenter, Bill, Chm. Bd. & Co-Creative Dir.--Berenter Greenhouse & Webster, Inc., New York, NY, pg. 141
Beres, Donald R., Chm. Bd.--Crafty Beaver Home Center, Skokie, IL, pg. 295
Berg, Jeff, Chm. Bd. & Chief Exec. Officer--International Creative Management, Inc., New York, NY, pg. 607
Berg, R.W., Chm. Bd.--ITA Group, West Des Moines, IA, pg. 560
Bergen, Lee D., Chm. Bd. & Sec.--Peter Lumber Company, Pleasantville, NJ, pg. 864
Berger, Robert S., Chm. Bd.--Rittenhouse Inc., Park Ridge, IL, pg. 936
Bergman, Stanley M., Chm. Bd., Pres. & Chief Exec. Officer--Henry Schein, Inc., Port Washington, NY, pg. 975
Bergquist, Harold, Chm. & Chief Exec. Officer--Northland Container Corp., Plymouth, MI, pg. 814
Bergt, Neil G., Chm. Bd. & Chief Exec. Officer--Markair, Inc., Anchorage, AK, pg. 708
Berkley, E. Bertram, Chm. Bd.--Tension Envelope Corp., Kansas City, MO, pg. 1088
Berkowitz, Robert H., Chm. Bd.--Central Paper Company, Newark, NJ, pg. 233
Berlin, David N., Chm. Bd. & Pres.--Metalloy Corporation, Hudson, MI, pg. 742
Berman, Barry H., Chm. Bd. & Pres.--CRN International, Inc., Hamden, CT, pg. 203
Berman, Barton M., Chm. Bd., Pres. & Chief Exec. Officer--Amurcon Corporation, Southfield, MI, pg. 70
Berman, Larry S., Chm. Bd.--MNP Corp., Utica, MI, pg. 693
Berman, Milton I., Chm. Bd., Pres. & Treas.--Avibank Mfg., Inc., Burbank, CA, pg. 102
Berman, Ronald, Chm. Bd.--DKM Building Enterprises, L.P., Lawrenceville, NJ, pg. 357
Bernard, Norman, Chm. Bd. & Chief Exec. Officer--Master Industries Corp., New York, NY, pg. 719
Berndsen, Alfred C., Chm. Bd.--Frank Messer & Sons Construction Co., Cincinnati, OH, pg. 741
Bernhardt, John C., Chm. Bd.--Bernhardt Furniture Co., Lenoir, NC, pg. 144
Bernstein, Dr. Joel, Chm. Bd. & Chief Exec. Officer--GenDerm Corporation, Lincolnshire, IL, pg. 448
Bernstein, Howard, Chm. Bd.--Atlas Lift Truck Rentals & Sales, Inc., Schiller Park, IL, pg. 96
Bernstein, Jay, Chm. Bd.--Northville Industries Corp., Melville, NY, pg. 814
Bernstein, Joel E., Chm. Bd.--GalenPharma, Inc., Lincolnshire, IL, pg. 448
Bernstein, Robert, Chm. Bd., Pres. & Chief Exec. Officer--Bernstein-Rein Advertising, Inc., Kansas City, MO, pg. 144
Bernstein, S.J., Chm. Bd. & Chief Exec. Officer--The Biltrite Corporation, Waltham, MA, pg. 151
Bernstein, Zalman C., Chm. & Chief Exec. Officer--Sanford C. Bernstein & Co., Inc., New York, NY, pg. 144
Bernuth, Peter K., Chm. Bd., Pres. & Treas.--The Bernuth Corporation, Miami, FL, pg. 144
Berry, Claude A., Jr., Chm. Bd. & Pres.--Wehr Constructors Inc., Louisville, KY, pg. 1172
Berry, James J., Chm. Bd.--Smith & Gillespie Engineers, Inc., Jacksonville, FL, pg. 1012
Berry, Robert E., Chm. Bd.--Berry-Brown Advertising, Inc., Dallas, TX, pg. 144
Bertelli, Jay, Chm. Bd., Pres. & Chief Exec. Officer--Mercury Computer Systems, Inc., Lowell, MA, pg. 740
Berthold, James K., Chm. Bd. & Pres.--Sunnen Products Company, Saint Louis, MO, pg. 1061
Bertrand, Frederic H., Chm. Bd. & Chief Exec. Officer--National Life Insurance Company, Montpelier, VT, pg. 791
Berwind, C. Graham, Chm. Bd.--Berwind Pharmaceuticals Services, Inc., King of Prussia, PA, pg. 145
Berwind, C. Graham, Jr., Chm. Bd., Pres., Chief Exec. & Chief Oper. Officer--Berwind Corporation, Philadelphia, PA, pg. 145
Beutler, Gary, Chm. Bd.--Beutler Heating & Air Conditioning Inc., Sacramento, CA, pg. 148
Bever, C.C., Jr., Chm. Bd., Pres. & Chief Oper. Officer--B & B Cash Grocery Store, Tampa, FL, pg. 105
Bevevino, Frank, Chm. & Chief Exec. Officer--Unifax, Inc., Wilkes-Barre, PA, pg. 1126
Beyer, Sonya Z., Chm., Pres. & Chief Exec. Officer--Midco International Inc., Chicago, IL, pg. 751
Beyster, J.R., Chm. Bd. & Chief Exec. Officer--Science Applications International Corporation, San Diego, CA, pg. 981
Bibb, Robert L., Jr., Chm. Bd.--Nashville Machine Co. Inc., Nashville, TN, pg. 784
Biblowitz, Louis, Chm. Bd.--Masters, Inc., Westbury, NY, pg. 720
Bickford, John H., Chm. Bd. & Treas.--Transistor Devices, Inc., Cedar Knolls, NJ, pg. 1107
Biddinger, John, Chm. Bd.--Diamond Electronics, Inc., Lancaster, OH, pg. 335
Biederman, Barry, Chm. Bd. & Creative Dir.--Biederman, Kelly & Shaffer, Inc., New York, NY, pg. 149
Bierer, William, Chm. Bd. & Chief Exec. Officer--Essex Grain Products, Inc., Frazer, PA, pg. 389
Bing, Dave, Chm. Bd.--Bing Steel Inc., Detroit, MI, pg. 151
Binswanger, Frank G., Jr., Chm. Bd.--The Binswanger Company, Philadelphia, PA, pg. 151
Biondi, Frank J., Pres. & Chief Exec. Officer--Viacom International Inc., New York, NY, pg. 785
Birdsall, Don R., Chm. & Chief Exec. Officer--Birdsall Voss & Kloppenburg, Inc., Mequon, WI, pg. 152
Birdsong, T.H., III, Chm. Bd.--Birdsong Corporation, Sulfolk, VA, pg. 153
Birge, Clifford A., Chm. Bd.--Seymour Manufacturing Company, Seymour, IN, pg. 994
Birkhauser, Robert R., Chm.--Auto Glass Specialists, Madison, WI, pg. 100
Birle, James, Chm. Bd.--Collins & Aikman Textile Group, Charlotte, NC, pg. 262
Birle, James R., Co-Chm. & Co-Chief Exec. Officer--Collins & Aikman Group Inc., Santa Monica, CA, pg. 262
Bishop, B.H., Chm. Bd. & Co-Chief Exec. Officer--Pendleton Woolen Mills, Inc., Portland, OR, pg. 857
Bishop, Benjamin M., Chm. & Chief Exec. Officer--The Western Group, Saint Louis, MO, pg. 1179
Bishop, Vernon, Chm. Bd., Pres. & Chief Exec. Officer--Lebanon Chemical Corp., Lebanon, PA, pg. 665
Bissell, John, Chm. Bd.--Camp International, Jackson, MI, pg. 153
Bitter, Edwin W., Chm. Bd.--Scalamandre, Inc., Long Island City, NY, pg. 974
Bixby, B.C., Chm. Bd.--Bixby International Corp., Newburyport, MA, pg. 153
Black, James, Chm. Bd. & Pres.--Johnson County Farm Bureau Co-op, Franklin, IN, pg. 598
Black, Stuart M., Chm. Bd.--Black & Co., Decatur, IL, pg. 154
Black, T.M., Sr., Chm. Bd. & Editor-in-Chief--Walter J. Black, Inc., Port Washington, NY, pg. 154
Black, William H., II, Chm. Bd.--Black Cadillac Olds, Inc., Greensboro, NC, pg. 153
Blacker, Stanley, Chm. Bd. & Pres.--Stanley Blacker, Inc., Philadelphia, PA, pg. 155
Blackwell, Charles E., Chm. Bd.--Piedmont Mechanical, Inc., Spartanburg, SC, pg. 870
Blackwood, Howard, Chm. Bd.--Juhl Marketing Communications, Mishawaka, IN, pg. 608
Blair, Richard W., Jr., Chm. Bd.--Jones Blair Company, Dallas, TX, pg. 602
Blair, Stuart, Chm. Bd.--United Artists Theatre Circuit, Inc., Englewood, CO, pg. 1130
Blanchard, Kenneth E., Chm. Bd., Pres. & Chief Oper. Officer--Phonetics, Inc., Aston, PA, pg. 869
Blanchard, Kirk F., Chm. Bd.--Wyatt Inc., Branford, CT, pg. 1205
Blanchard, Roger, Chm. Bd.--ACR Industries Inc., Mount Clemens, MI, pg. 2
Bland, William W., Chm. Bd. & Pres.--Bland Cadillac Company, Houston, TX, pg. 155
Blank, Benjamin, Chm. & Chief Exec. Officer--Savemart Inc., Bronx, NY, pg. 973
Blank, Richard, Chm. Bd. & Pres.--Direct Communications Corporation, Bronxville, NY, pg. 339
Blattner, Joseph R., Chm. & Chief Exec. Officer--Blattner/ Brunner Inc., Pittsburgh, PA, pg. 156
Blethen, Frank A., Chm., Chief Exec. Officer & Publr.--Seattle Times Company, Seattle, WA, pg. 986
Block, Annabelle, Chm. Bd.--Annabelle Candy Company, Hayward, CA, pg. 75
Block, Sam, Sr., Chm. Bd.--Ideal Chemical & Supply Company, Memphis, TN, pg. 562
Block, William, Chm. Bd.--Blade Communications, Inc., Toledo, OH, pg. 155
Block, William Sr., Chm. Bd.--Toledo Blade Co., Toledo, OH, pg. 155
Blodgett, Mark, Chm. Bd.--Stocker & Yale, Inc., Beverly, MA, pg. 1050
Blodgett, Mark W., Chm. Bd.--MFE Instruments, Beverly, MA, pg. 1050
Bloem, H. J., Chm.--Atlas Tag & Label Inc., Neenah, WI, pg. 153
Bloomfield, Coleman, Chm. Bd. & Chief Exec. Officer--The Minnesota Mutual Life Insurance Company, Saint Paul, MN, pg. 757
Bloomhorst, Kenneth F., Chm. Bd. & Art Dir.--Bloomhorst Story O'Hara Inc., Indianapolis, IN, pg. 158
Blount, S. Robert, Chm.--Meadowcraft, Inc., Birmingham, AL, pg. 733
Blum, Michael, Chm. Bd. & Pres.--Heller International, Chicago, IL, pg. 526
Blumenthal, Herman, Chm. & Chief Exec. Officer--Radiator Specialty Company, Charlotte, NC, pg. 909
Blumenthal, Thomas A., Chm. Bd, Pres. & Chief Exec. Officer--Norwalk Powdered Metals, Inc., Norwalk, CT, pg. 816
Bobinchuck, William, Chm. Bd.--Par Industries, inc., Medina, OH, pg. 847
Bobinchuck, William R., Chm. Bd.--Flexible Flyer Inc., West Point, MS, pg. 847
Bobit, Edward J., Chm. Bd. & Chief Exec. Officer--Bobit Publishing Company, Redondo Beach, CA, pg. 161
Boddie, Ben Mayo, Chm. Bd. & Chief Exec. Officer--Boddie-Noell Enterprises Inc., Rocky Mount, NC, pg. 161
Bodgren, Russell, Chm. Bd.--Northwestern Drug Company, Minneapolis, MN, pg. 343
Bodine, Edward F., Chm. Bd. & Treas.--The Bodine Corp., Bridgeport, CT, pg. 161
Bodine, Paul J., Chm. Bd.--Bodine Electric Company, Chicago, IL, pg. 162
Bogle, Robert, Chm. Bd.--The Hercules Tire & Rubber Company, Findlay, OH, pg. 531
Bogle, Robert, Chm. Bd.--Hercules Tire & Rubber Company, Findlay, OH, pg. 531
Boh, Robert H., Chm. Bd., Pres. & Chief Exec. Officer--Boh Corporation, New Orleans, LA, pg. 162
Bohn, Daniel J., Jr., Chm. Bd.--Giffels Associates, Inc., Southfield, MI, pg. 457
Bohn, Daniel J., Jr., Chm. Bd.--Giffels Hoyem Basso, Inc., Troy, MI, pg. 457
Boland, David, Chm. Bd., Pres. & Chief Exec. Officer--David Boland, Inc., Titusville, FL, pg. 162
Bolch, Carl, Jr., Chm. Bd. & Chief Exec. Officer--Racetrac Petroleum, Inc., Smyrna, GA, pg. 909
Bolin, M.R., Chm. Bd. & Chief Exec. Officer--M. R. Bolin Inc., Minneapolis, MN, pg. 162
Bolin, Scott, Chm. & Chief Creative Officer--M. R. Bolin Inc., Minneapolis, MN, pg. 162
Bollerer, Fred L., Chm. Bd. & Chief Exec. Officer--First American Bank of Virginia, McLean, VA, pg. 412
Bollerer, Fred L., Chm. Bd. & Chief Exec. Officer--First American Metro Corp., McLean, VA, pg. 412
Bolliger, Richard, Chm. Bd.--Bolliger, Inc., Stamford, CT, pg. 163
Bollinger, Don M., Chm. Bd. & Chief Exec. Officer--The John C. Groub Company Inc., Seymour, IN, pg. 489
Bollinger, Donald T., Chm. Bd., Chief Exec. Officer & Dir.-Fin.--Bollinger Machine Shop And Shipyard, Inc., Lockport, LA, pg. 163
Bollinger, Glenn D., Chm. Bd. & Pres.--Bollinger Industries Inc., Irving, TX, pg. 163
Bolton, Charles P., Chm. Bd.--Brittany Corporation, Cleveland, OH, pg. 177
Bomstein, Howard, Chm. Bd., Pres. & Chief Exec. Officer--The Bomstein Agency, Washington, DC, pg. 164
Bonham, Donald L., Chm. Bd. & Chief Exec. Officer--Fiesta Mart Inc., Houston, TX, pg. 409
Boniface, Ernest, Chm. Bd.--Bonland Industries, Inc., Wayne, NJ, pg. 164
Bonney, Weston, Chm. Bd.--American Management Group, Westbrook, ME, pg. 57
Bonsib, Richard E., Chm. Bd. & Pres.--Bonsib Inc., Fort Wayne, IN, pg. 164
Bontrager, Bertha, Chm. Bd.--Jayco Inc., Middlebury, IN, pg. 590

Booth, Charles H., Jr., Chm. Bd., Pres. & Chief Exec. Officer--Burrell Group, New Kensington, PA, pg. 195
Booth, John L., Sr., Chm. Bd. & Chief Exec. Officer--Booth American, Detroit, MI, pg. 165
Borck, Chester E., Chm. Bd.--Country Home Bakery, Inc., Bridgeport, CT, pg. 290
Borden, Lorraine, Chm. Bd., Chief Exec. Officer, Chief Fin. Officer, Pres.--Great Scott Advertising Co. Inc., New York, NY, pg. 482
Boren, L.E., Chm. Bd. & Chief Exec. Officer--Badger Construction Equipment Co., Insley Div., Winona, MN, pg. 113
Boren, Leland E., Chm. Bd., Pres. & Chief Exec. Officer--Avis Industrial Corporation, Upland, IN, pg. 102
Borg, Malcolm A., Chm. Bd. & Pres.--Macromedia Inc., Hackensack, NJ, pg. 698
Borgelt, Burton C., Chm. & Chief Exec. Officer--Dentsply International Inc., York, PA, pg. 329
Borges, Joseph, Chm. Bd.--Delta Sugar Corporation, Clarksburg, CA, pg. 327
Borgo, Enrique, Chm. Bd.--Taca International Airlines, S. A., New Orleans, LA, pg. 1076
Born, Fred, Chm. Bd.--American Crystal Sugar Company, Moorhead, MN, pg. 51
Borowsky, I.J., Chm. Bd.--North American Publishing Company, Philadelphia, PA, pg. 811
Boscov, Albert, Chm. Bd.--Boscov's Department Stores, Inc., Reading, PA, pg. 167
Bose, Amar G., Dr., Chm. Bd. & Chief Exec. Officer--Bose Corporation, Framingham, MA, pg. 167
Botifoll, Luis, Chm. Bd. & Chief Exec. Officer--Republic National Bank Of Miami, Miami, FL, pg. 928
Bottner, Irving J., Chm.--Roux Laboratories, Inc., Jacksonville, FL, pg. 696
Bottum, C.E., Chm. Bd.--Townsend & Bottum, Inc., Ann Arbor, MI, pg. 1104
Bouchard, John E., III, Chm. Bd. & Pres.--John Bouchard & Sons Company, Nashville, TN, pg. 168
Bouche, George, Chm. Bd.--HP Direct, Indianapolis, IN, pg. 497
Boucher, Allen C., Chm. Bd.--Caldwell Manufacturing Company, Rochester, NY, pg. 208
Bourns, Gordon L., Chm. Bd.--Bourns, Inc., Riverside, CA, pg. 168
Bourns, Gordon L., Chm. Bd.--Recon/Optical, Inc., Barrington, IL, pg. 917
Bowers, Frederick, Chm. Bd.--NMC of North America, Inc., Zebulon, NC, pg. 781
Bowers, Paul D., Jr., Chm. Bd.--The WBDC Group, Grand Rapids, MI, pg. 1155
Bowes, John G., Chm. Bd.--Kransco, San Francisco, CA, pg. 644
Bowles, Crandall, Chm. Bd.--S. E. Huffman Corp., Clover, SC, pg. 551
Bowman, Brian, Chm. Bd. & Chief Fin. Officer--Ryan Herco Products Corp., Burbank, CA, pg. 958
Boyan, William L., Chm.--John Hancock Property and Casualty Holding Co., Boston, MA, pg. 596
Boyce, Frank L., Chm. Bd.--Sioux Falls Construction Company, Sioux Falls, SD, pg. 1008
Boyd, J.A., Chm. Bd., Pres. & Chief Exec. Officer--Fish Engineering & Construction, Inc., Houston, TX, pg. 414
Boyd, Roy T., III, Chm. Bd. & Chief Exec. Officer--Mark III Industries, Ocala, FL, pg. 708
Boyd, Thomas J., Chm. Bd. & Pres.--Navajo Forest Products Industries, Navajo, NM, pg. 796
Boyd, William W., Chmn. Bd. & Pres.--Sterling Plumbing Group, Inc., Schaumburg, IL, pg. 640
Boyle, Les, Chm. Bd., Pres. & Chief Exec. Officer--CRE, Inc., Indianapolis, IN, pg. 203
Boyle, R.E., Chm. Bd. & Chief Exec. Officer--Ohio River Associates, Inc., Hannibal, OH, pg. 822
Boyle, R.E., Chm. Bd., Pres. & Chief Exec. Officer--Ormet Corporation, Hannibal, OH, pg. 822
Brabson, John, Chm. Bd., Pres. & Chief Exec. Officer--Peoples Gas System, Inc., Tampa, FL, pg. 689
Bracey, Morris W., Chm. Bd., Pres., Chief Exec. & Chief Oper. Officer--Dealers Electrical Supply Co., Waco, TX, pg. 322
Bracey, William, Chm. Bd.--Affiliated Food Distributors, Scranton, PA, pg. 23
Bradburd, Arnold W., Chm. Bd., Pres. & Chief Exec. Officer--Interstate Steel Supply Co., Philadelphia, PA, pg. 580
Bradbury, David, Chm. Bd. & Pres.--Bradbury Company, Inc., Moundridge, KS, pg. 169
Braddock, James L., Chm. Bd., Pres. & Treas.--Fastec Industrial, Elkhart, IN, pg. 403
Bradford, Judson T., Chm. Bd. & Pres.--Bradford Company, Holland, MI, pg. 170
Bradley, Rodney C., Chm. & Chief Exec. Officer--Bradley Communications, Inc., Anchorage, AK, pg. 170
Braitmayer, J.W., Chm. Bd. & Chief Exec. Officer--Mona Industries, Inc., Paterson, NJ, pg. 764
Braka, Ivor, Chm. Bd.--United States Realty & Investment Co., Newark, NJ, pg. 1137
Braman, Norman, Chm.-Exec. Committee--National Football League Properties, Inc., New York, NY, pg. 788
Bramble, David A., Chm. Bd. & Chief Exec. Officer--David A. Bramble, Inc., Chestertown, MD, pg. 171
Bramble, Reba H., Chm. Bd. & Chief Exec. Officer--Gulf States Asphalt Company, Inc., South Houston, TX, pg. 493
Bransom, Richard, Chm. Bd.--Affiliated Food Stores, Keller, TX, pg. 23
Brant, Murray, Chm. Bd.--Brant Allen Industries, Inc., Greenwich, CT, pg. 172
Bratt, John A., Chm. Bd.--Yorktown Tool & Die Corporation, Yorktown, IN, pg. 1208
Brauman, Murray, Chm. Bd. & Chief Exec. Officer--Moss and Company, Inc., New York, NY, pg. 772
Braun, Neil S., Sr. V.P. & Chm. & Chief Exec. Officer-Viacom Entertainment--Viacom Inc., New York, NY, pg. 785
Braun, Neil S., Chm. & Chief Exec. Officer--Viacom Entertainment, New York, NY, pg. 785
Braunlich, H.P., Jr., Chm. Bd., Pres. & Chief Exec. Officer--Brammer Manufacturing Company, Davenport, IA, pg. 171
Brayton, Roswell, Sr., Chm. Bd.--Woolrich, Inc., Woolrich, PA, pg. 1201
Brehm, William K., Chm. Bd.--Systems Research And Applications Corporation, Arlington, VA, pg. 1071
Breiner, James M., Chm. Bd. & Treas.--First Connecticut SBIC, Bridgeport, CT, pg. 412
Brembeck, Howard S., Chm. Bd. & Chief Exec. Officer--CTB Inc., Milford, IN, pg. 205
Bren, Donald, Chm. Bd.--Irvine Company, Newport Beach, CA, pg. 582
Brenia, Paul S., Chm., Pres. & Chief Exec. Officer--Ancra Corporation, Hawthorne, CA, pg. 72
Brennan, Bernard F., Chm. Bd. & Chief Exec. Officer--Montgomery Ward & Co., Inc., Chicago, IL, pg. 767
Brennan, David L., Chm. Bd. & Chief Exec. Officer--The Brenlin Group, Akron, OH, pg. 173
Brennan, Norm, Chm. Bd.--Dimco-Gray Company, Dayton, OH, pg. 338
Brennan, Richard, Chm. Bd.--Greenway Co-Op Service, Rochester, MN, pg. 485
Bresnahan, William W., Chm. Bd.--Hynes Industries Inc., Youngstown, OH, pg. 557
Breuer, Adam A., Chm. Bd.--Breuer Electric Mfg. Co., Chicago, IL, pg. 174
Brewer, Jeffrey C., Chm. Bd.--Grandville Printing Company, Grandville, MI, pg. 476
Brickel, Mary L., Chm. Bd.--BEC Inc., Richmond, MI, pg. 106
Bridell, Robert J., Chm. Bd. & Chief Exec. Officer--American Tara Corporation, Atlanta, GA, pg. 63
Brierley, Harold M., Chm. Bd. & Pres.--Brierley & Partners, Dallas, TX, pg. 175
Briggs, Karl L., Chm. Bd.--Quincy Mutual Fire Insurance Company, Quincy, MA, pg. 905
Brigham, James R., Sr., Chm. Bd.--Diagraph Corporation, Earth City, MO, pg. 335
Brinton, Garrison W., Chm. Bd.--Label-Aire Inc., Fullerton, CA, pg. 649
Briukerhoff, Peter, Chm. Bd., Pres. & Chief Exec. Officer--Aqua Fab Industries, Inc., East Greenwich, RI, pg. 79
Brix, Peter J., Chm. Bd. & Chief Exec. Officer--Brix Maritime Co., Portland, OR, pg. 177
Broad, John W., Chm. Bd., Pres. & Chief Exec. Officer--Broad Vogt & Conant Inc., River Rouge, MI, pg. 177
Broadhurst, James, Chm., Pres. & Chief Exec. Officer--Eat N Park Restaurants, Pittsburgh, PA, pg. 364
Brock, Richard T., Chm. Bd. & Chief Exec. Officer--Brock Control Systems, Inc., Atlanta, GA, pg. 178
Brokaw, Norman, Chm. Bd. & Chief Exec. Officer--William Morris Agency, Inc., Beverly Hills, CA, pg. 771
Broll, Arthur G., Jr., Chm. Bd., Chief Fin. Officer & Treas.--Geographic Marketing Group (GMG), Philadelphia, PA, pg. 452
Brooke, Peter A., Chm. Bd & Chief Exec. Officer--Advent International, Boston, MA, pg. 21
Brookfield, Donald W., Chm. Bd.--Brookfield Engineering Laboratories, Inc., Stoughton, MA, pg. 179
Brooks, Ed, Chm. Bd.--Wisconsin Dairies Cooperative, Baraboo, WI, pg. 1197
Brooks, James W., Chm. & Chief Exec. Officer--Brooks Beverage Management, Inc., Holland, MI, pg. 179
Brooks, John W., Chm. Bd.--John W. Brooks Inc., Nelsonville, OH, pg. 180
Brookshire, Bruce G., Chm. & Chief Exec. Officer--Brookshire Grocery, Tyler, TX, pg. 180
Brookshire, Eugene, Chm. Bd.--Brookshire Bros., Inc., Lufkin, TX, pg. 180
Bross, Thomas, III, Chm. Bd.--Round Hill Foods, Inc., New Oxford, PA, pg. 952
Brotman, Jeff, Chm. Bd.--Jeffrey Michael, Kirkland, WA, pg. 591
Brown, A. Worley, Chm. Bd.--Rock-Tenn Company, Norcross, GA, pg. 941
Brown, Alfred Keith, Chm. Bd.--WYO-Ben, Inc., Billings, MT, pg. 1157
Brown, Allan, Co-Chm. Bd.--Simon Marketing, Inc., Los Angeles, CA, pg. 1006
Brown, Andy F., Chm. Bd.--Calcor Space Facility, Inc., Whittier, CA, pg. 208
Brown, C. Terry, Chm. Bd., Pres., Chief Exec. Officer & Chief Oper. Officer--Atlas Hotels, Inc., San Diego, CA, pg. 96
Brown, Charles, Chm. Bd., Pres. & Chief Exec. Officer--Bayou State Oil Corporation, Shreveport, LA, pg. 128
Brown, Charles T., Chm. Bd.--Browns Lumber & Supply Company, Fairmont, WV, pg. 183
Brown, Dave M., Chm. Bd.--Homes By Dave Brown, Tempe, AZ, pg. 542
Brown, E.H., Jr., Chm. Bd., Chief Exec. Officer & Partner--E.H. Brown Advertising, Inc., Chicago, IL, pg. 181
Brown, Earle Palmer, Chm. Bd. & Founder--Earle Palmer Brown, Bethesda, MD, pg. 182
Brown, Jack E., Chm. & Chief Exec. Officer--The Bases Group, Covington, KY, pg. 124
Brown, Jeremy, Vice Chm.--McConnaughy Stein Schmidt Brown, Chicago, IL, pg. 727
Brown, John, Chm. Bd. & Creative Dir.--Brown & Hadley & Partners, Seattle, WA, pg. 182
Brown, Lawrence A., Chm. Bd.--Agsco, Inc., Grand Forks, ND, pg. 4
Brown, Louis M., Jr., Chm. Bd.--Planning Systems Inc., McLean, VA, pg. 874
Brown, Stephen L., Chm. Bd. & Chief Exec. Officer--John Hancock Mutual Life Insurance Company, Boston, MA, pg. 595
Brown, Stephen L., Chm. Bd. & Chief Exec. Officer--John Hancock HealthPlans, Inc., West Chester, PA, pg. 596
Brown, Sylvan L., Chm. Bd., Pres. & Chief Exec. Officer--Mediacomp, Inc., Houston, TX, pg. 735
Browne, Steven B., Chm. Bd., Pres. & Chief Exec. Officer--All American Bottling Corp., Oklahoma City, OK, pg. 35
Browning, Peter C., Chm. & Chief Exec. Officer--National Gypsum Company, Charlotte, NC, pg. 790
Brownstein, Howard N., Chm. Bd.--National Property Analysts, Inc., Philadelphia, PA, pg. 792
Brubaker, Galen B., Chm. Bd.--Southern States Cooperative, Inc., Richmond, VA, pg. 1022
Bruce, David F., Chm. Bd & Chief Exec. Officer--Bruce-Andersen Company, Inc., Belgrade, MT, pg. 183
Bruce, Frank B., Chm. Bd.--Bruce Industries, Inc., Dayton, NV, pg. 183
Bruder, Tom, Chm. Bd.--M.A.B. Paints, Terre Haute, IN, pg. 184
Bruenger, Leona, Chm. Bd.--M. Bruenger & Co., Inc., Wichita, KS, pg. 184
Bruggeman, W.L., Chm. & Chief Exec. Officer--Diversified Dynamics Inc., Minneapolis, MN, pg. 340
Bruggeman, W.L., Chm. Bd. & Chief Exec. Officer--Cat Pumps Corporation, Minneapolis, MN, pg. 340
Bruhn, Richard L., Chm. Bd.--Dick Bruhn Inc., Salinas, CA, pg. 184
Brush, Richard F., Chm. Bd.--Sentry Group, Rochester, NY, pg. 990
Brutger, Larry, Chm. Bd & Pres.--Brutger Equities, Inc., Saint Cloud, MN, pg. 185
Bryan, R.A., Jr., Chm. Bd & Chief Exec. Officer--T. A. Loving Company, Goldsboro, NC, pg. 685
Bryant, W. Dexter, Chm. Bd.--Bead Industries Inc., Bridgeport, CT, pg. 129
Buchanan, Robert, Chm. Bd.--Rising Paper Company, Housatonic, MA, pg. 428
Buchanan, Vern, Chm. Bd.--American Speedy Printing Centers, Inc., Bloomfield Hills, MI, pg. 61
Buchbiner, Henry M., Chm. Bd. & Treas.--Ardco, Inc., Alsip, IL, pg. 81
Buck, Charles T., Chm. Bd., Pres. & Chief Exec. Officer--Buck Knives, Inc., El Cajon, CA, pg. 185
Buckler, Leroy M., Chm. Bd.--Intech Advanced Analog, Santa Clara, CA, pg. 572
Buckman, M.W., Chm. Bd. & Pres.--Bulab Holdings, Inc., Memphis, TN, pg. 188
Buckman, R.H., Chm. Bd. & Chief Exec. Officer--Buckman Laboratories, Memphis, TN, pg. 185
Buckman, Robert H., Chm Bd. & Chief Exec. Officer--Buckman Laboratories, International, Memphis, TN, pg. 188
Buckman, Steven B., Chm. Bd.--Buckman Laboratories, Inc., Memphis, TN, pg. 188
Bucksbaum, Martin, Chm. Bd. & Chief Exec. & Info. Officer--General Growth Companies, Inc., Des Moines, IA, pg. 449
Buda, Stan D., Chm.--BSB/Canada Inc., Toronto,, Canada, pg. 109
Buennagel, David, Chm. Bd.--Rolock, Inc., Fairfield, CT, pg. 944
Buescher, C.A., Chm. Bd.--Long Island Water Corporation, Lynbrook, NY, pg. 682
Buettner, Milton B., Chm. Bd.--Western Reinsurance Brokers, Inc., Los Angeles, CA, pg. 1181
Buhl, Tim, Pres. & Chief Exec. Officer--Aerco International Inc., Northvale, NJ, pg. 21
Buhse, Howard, Chm. Bd.--American Funds Advisor Inc., Garden City, NJ, pg. 55
Bullard, Arthur, Chm. Bd.--Champaign Landmark, Urbana, OH, pg. 238
Bumby, John E., Chm. Bd.--Ripon Foods, Inc., Ripon, WI, pg. 935
Bungey, Michael, Chm. & Chief Exec. Officer--BSB Dorland Limited, London,, United Kingdom, pg. 109
Bunn, George R., Chm. Bd.--Bunn-O-Matic Corporation, Springfield, IL, pg. 188
Burdick, Richard L., Chm., Pres., Chief Exec. & Chief Oper. Officer--Thermon Manufacturing Company, San Marcos, TX, pg. 1091
Burger, Herbert F., Chm. Bd.--The St. George Group, Inc., Pittsburgh, PA, pg. 966
Burkart, Walter, Chm. Bd.--Kingsbury Corporation, Keene, NH, pg. 631
Burke, Pauline E., Chm. Bd.--Burke Engineering Company, South El Monte, CA, pg. 190
Burke, Robert L., Chm. Bd.--Burke Communication Industries, Inc., Chicago, IL, pg. 190
Burkle, Joseph, Chm. Bd.--Falley's Inc., Topeka, KS, pg. 1214
Burkle, Ronald, Chm. Bd & Partner--The Yucaipa Companies, Claremont, CA, pg. 1214
Burnham, Malin, Chm. Bd.--John Burnham & Co., San Diego, CA, pg. 194
Burns, Stephen F., Chm. Bd., Pres. & Chief Exec. Officer--Wheaton Van Lines, Inc., Indianapolis, IN, pg. 1184
Burrell, Thomas J., Chm.--Burrell Communications Group Inc., Chicago, IL, pg. 195
Burress, Mark, Chm. Bd. & Pres.--Affiliates Group Inc., Nashville, TN, pg. 24
Burris, A.A., III, Chm. Bd. & Pres.--Burris Chemical Inc., Charleston, SC, pg. 195
Burris, John E., Chm. Bd.--Burris Foods, Inc., Milford, DE, pg. 195
Burroughs, Henry F., Jr., Chm. Bd.--First Gray Line Corporation, Beverly Hills, CA, pg. 413
Burrows, R.W., Jr., Chm. Bd. & Pres.--Burrows Paper Corporation, Little Falls, NY, pg. 195
Burson, Harold, Founder & Chm.--Burson-Marsteller, New York, NY, pg. 1210
Burt, W. E., Chm. Bd., Pres., & Chief Exec. Officer--Dairy Fresh Corp., Greensboro, AL, pg. 310
Burton, Betsy, Chm. Bd. & Chief Exec. Officer--Pip Printing, Agoura Hills, CA, pg. 616
Burwell, Rodney P., Chm. Bd.--Xerxes Corporation, Minneapolis, MN, pg. 1206
Bush, Condon, Chm. & Chief Exec. Officer--Bush Brothers & Company, Dandridge, TN, pg. 196

Bush, Robert G., Chm. Bd.--Schreiber Foods, Inc., Green Bay, WI, pg. 978
Butcher, Charles, Chm. Bd.--The Butcher Co., Marlborough, MA, pg. 196
Butcher, Jonathan, Chm. Bd. & Pres.--Butcher & Co., Inc., Philadelphia, PA, pg. 196
Butcher, McBee, Chm.--The Philadelphia Bourse, Inc., Lanham, MD, pg. 866
Butcher, McBee, Chm. & Chief Exec. Officer--Butcher & Singer, Philadelphia, PA, pg. 1184
Butcko, Joseph A., Chm. Bd.--Crescive Die & Tool, Inc., Saline, MI, pg. 298
Butler, D.R., Chm.--Delaware Charter Guarantee & Trust Co., Wilmington, DE, pg. 890
Butler, Richard A., Jr., Chm. Bd. & Chief Exec. Officer--Butler Automatic, Inc., Canton, MA, pg. 197
Butler, Stephen T., Chm. Bd. & Chief Exec. Officer--W. C. Bradley Co., Columbus, GA, pg. 170
Butler, William, Chm. Bd., Pres., Chief Exec. Officer & Treas.--Corporex Companies, Inc., Covington, KY, pg. 287
Buxton, C.I., II, Chm. Bd. & Chief Exec. Officer--Federated Mutual Insurance Company, Owatonna, MN, pg. 405
Buyers, J.W.A., Chm. & Chief Exec. Officer--Mauna Loa Resources Inc., Honolulu, HI, pg. 174
Buyers, John W.A., Chm. Bd.--C. Brewer & Company, Limited, Honolulu, HI, pg. 174
Byer, Allan G., Chm. Bd., Pres. & Chief Exec. Officer--Byer California, San Francisco, CA, pg. 197
Byron, Robert W., Chm. Bd.--Security Mutual Life Insurance Co. of New York, Binghamton, NY, pg. 987
Cafaro, William M., Chm. Bd.--The Cafaro Co., Youngstown, OH, pg. 207
Calafati, Gabriel R., Chm. Bd., Pres. & Treas.--Frank Briscoe Co. Inc., Roseland, NJ, pg. 176
Calamari, Herman R., Chm. Bd.--El Dorado Tire Co., Troy, MI, pg. 372
Calicchio, John, Chm. Bd.--Argo International Corp., New York, NY, pg. 81
Call, O. Jay, Chm. Bd.--Flying J. Inc., Brigham City, UT, pg. 421
Call, William, Chm., Pres. & Chief Exec. Officer--Maverik Country Stores, Inc., Afton, WY, pg. 722
Callaghan, Peter, Chm. Bd.--Panarco, Inc., Summit, NJ, pg. 845
Callahan, Ralph W., Jr., Chm. Bd., Pres. & Chief Exec. Officer--Henderson Advertising, Inc., Greenville, SC, pg. 528
Callier, Jim, Chm. Bd.--Century Products Co., Macedonia, OH, pg. 235
Calligaris, A.E., Chm. Bd., Pres. & Chief Exec. Officer--Stebbins Engineering & Mfg. Co., Watertown, NY, pg. 1043
Calton, Van C., Chm. Bd.--North Carolina Equipment Co., Raleigh, NC, pg. 812
Calvert, Sam J. Jr., Chm. Bd.--Austin Co., Inc., Greeneville, TN, pg. 98
Calvillo, Ricardo C., Chm. Bd. & Chief Exec. Officer--Calet, Hirsch & Ferrell, Inc., New York, NY, pg. 949
Cameron, Gerald T., Sr., Chm. Bd. & Chief Exec. Officer--Amray, Inc., Bedford, MA, pg. 68
Camp, Ben H., Chm. Bd. & Chief Exec. Officer--Hub Inc., Tucker, GA, pg. 548
Campbell, Argyle, Chm. Bd. & Pres.--Cambro Manufacturing Company, Huntington Beach, CA, pg. 211
Campbell, Chester K., Chm. Bd.--Campbell Oil Co., Massillon, OH, pg. 213
Campbell, J.T., Chm. Bd.--Paramount Petroleum Corp., Paramount, CA, pg. 848
Campbell, John J., III, Chm. Bd. & Pres.--John J. Campbell Co., Inc., Memphis, TN, pg. 212
Campbell, Newton A., Chm. Bd. & Treas.--Burns & McDonnell Engineers-Architects-Consultants, Kansas City, MO, pg. 194
Campbell, Robert M., Chm. Bd & Pres.--The Campbell Group, Baltimore, MD, pg. 213
Campbell, W. Arthur, Chm. Bd.--Camalloy, Inc., Washington, PA, pg. 211
Campbell, William A., Chm. Bd.--Campbell Construction Co., Sacramento, CA, pg. 213
Camuto, Vincent, Co-Chm. Bd.--Nine West Group, Inc., Stamford, CT, pg. 807
Canavan, Daniel B., Chm. Bd.--Triple S Technologies, Inc., Vicksburg, MI, pg. 1114
Canavan, William, Chm. Bd.--Congoleum Corporation, Mercerville, NJ, pg. 274
Canfield, Arthur, Sr., Chm. Bd.--A. J. Canfield Co., Chicago, IL, pg. 214
Cannon, John D., Chm.--Cannon, Grand Island, NY, pg. 214
Capizzi, Anthony, Chm. Bd., Pres. & Chief Exec. Officer--Quality Food Oils, Inc., New Milford, CT, pg. 903
Caplan, James A., Chm. Bd., Pres., Treas., Prod. Mgr. & Chief Engr.--Capp, Inc., Philadelphia, PA, pg. 216
Capon, Dale E., Chm. Bd. & Pres.--Rieth-Riley Construction Co. Inc., Goshen, IN, pg. 934
Cappy, Michael, Chm. Bd. & Pres.--Norcross Industries, Inc., Louisville, KY, pg. 809
Cappy, Mike, Chm. Bd.--Servus Footwear Company, Rock Island, IL, pg. 993
Carabini, Louis E., Chm. Bd. & Pres.--Monex International, Ltd., Newport Beach, CA, pg. 765
Carbonell, Robert J., Dr., Chm. Bd.--Del Monte Foods, San Francisco, CA, pg. 325
Cardamone, Louis J., Chm.--Marc Advertising, Pittsburgh, PA, pg. 706
Cardenas, Francisco, Chm., Pres. & Mng. Dir.--Leo Burnett S.A. de C.V., Mexico,, Mexico, pg. 193
Cardin, Judge Meyer, Chm. Bd.--B. Green & Co., Baltimore, MD, pg. 484
Carell, Monroe, Jr., Chm. Bd. & Chief Exec. Officer--Central Parking Corp., Nashville, TN, pg. 234
Carey, William P., Chm. Bd. & Mng. Dir.--W. P. Carey & Co., Inc., New York, NY, pg. 218
Cargill, John S., Chm.--Cargill Detroit Corp., Clawson, MI, pg. 219
Cargill, Robert E., Chm.--Cole Henderson Drake, Inc., Atlanta, GA, pg. 260
Carickhoff, John E., Jr., Chm. Bd.--Penn Colour Graphics, Inc., Huntingdon Valley, PA, pg. 857
Carl, Fred, Jr., Chm. Bd., Pres. & Chief Exec. Officer--Viking Range Corp., Greenwood, MS, pg. 1151
Carlisle, Brian, Chm. Bd. & Chief Exec. Officer--Adept Technology, Inc., San Jose, CA, pg. 17
Carlisle, L. T. III, Chm., Pres. & Chief Exec. Officer--Carlisle Retailers, Inc., Ashtabula, OH, pg. 220
Carlos, Michael C., Chm. Bd. & Chief Exec. Officer--National Distributing Co., Inc., Atlanta, GA, pg. 787
Carlow, Michael, Chm. Bd.--Pittsburgh Brewing Company, Pittsburgh, PA, pg. 873
Carlsen, David R., Chm. Bd., Sec. & Legal Counsel--Upper Midwest Industries, Inc., Minneapolis, MN, pg. 1140
Carlson, Bruce I., Chm. & Chief Exec. Officer--Grant/Jacoby, Inc., Chicago, IL, pg. 477
Carlson, C.L., Chm.--Carlson Marketing Group, Inc., Minneapolis, MN, pg. 221
Carlson, Curtis L., Chm. Bd., Pres. & Chief Exec. Officer--Carlson Companies, Inc., Minneapolis, MN, pg. 220
Carlson, Curtis L., Chm. Bd.--Radisson Hotel Corporation, Minneapolis, MN, pg. 221
Carlson, Richard N., Chm. Bd.--Park Construction Company, Minneapolis, MN, pg. 848
Carlson, Robert A., Chm. Bd. & Pres.--North Atlantic Industries, Inc., Hauppauge, NY, pg. 812
Carlson, Robert F., Sr., Chm. Bd., Chief Exec. Officer & Treas.--Channel Technologies, Inc., Santa Barbara, CA, pg. 239
Carlson, Robert W., Jr., Chm. & Chief Exec. Officer--Quadion Corporation, Minneapolis, MN, pg. 902
Carlton, Doyle E., Chm. Bd.--Havatampa Incorporated, Tampa, FL, pg. 517
Carlton, Doyle E., Chm. Bd.--H.A.T. Holding Company, Tampa, FL, pg. 517
Carpenter, Archie H., Chm. Bd.--Semac Industries Inc., Millersburg, OH, pg. 989
Carpenter, Judith, Chm. Bd.--National Welders Supply Co. Inc., Charlotte, NC, pg. 794
Carr, Oliver, Chm. Bd.--The Oliver Carr Co., Washington, DC, pg. 225
Carrafiello, A. Louis, Pres., Treas. & Chief Exec. Officer--Carrafiello, Diehl & Associates, Inc., Irvington, NY, pg. 225
Carroll, Mark, Co-Chm.--Bandy Carroll Hellige Advertising, Louisville, KY, pg. 117
Carson, James B., Jr., Chm. & Chief Exec. Officer--Carter, Atlanta, GA, pg. 226
Carson, William C., Chm. Bd. & Chief Exec. Officer--Instrument Specialties Company, Delaware Water Gap, PA, pg. 572
Carstarphen, J.M., Chm. Bd., Pres. & Chief Exec. Officer--Stowe-Pharr Mills, Inc., McAdenville, NC, pg. 1052
Carsten, Donald, Chm. Bd.--Union Steel Products, Incorporated, Albion, MI, pg. 1129
Carstens, Donald D., Chm. Bd.--Pullman Industries, Inc., Madison Heights, MI, pg. 900
Carter, Arthur L., Chm. Bd.--The Unimax Corporation, New York, NY, pg. 1127
Carter, Jerry C., Chm. Bd., Pres. & Chief Exec. Officer--Jerry C. Carter, Inc., Gainesville, GA, pg. 226
Carter, John M., Chm. Bd., & Chief Exec. Officer--Carco Electronics, Menlo Park, CA, pg. 217
Carter, Margaret R., Chm. Bd.--Reitman Industries, West Caldwell, NJ, pg. 924
Carter, Tim, Chm. Bd. & Chief Exec. Officer--Bell-Carter Foods, Inc., Lafayette, CA, pg. 134
Carus, M. Blouke, Chm. Bd., Pres., Chief Exec. & Chief Oper. Officer--Carus Corporation, Peru, IL, pg. 227
Carus, M. Blouke, Chm. Bd. & Chief Exec. Officer--Open Court Publishing Company, Chicago, IL, pg. 227
Carus, M. Blouke, Chm. Bd. & Chief Exec. Officer--Open Court Publishing Co.-General Books, Peru, IL, pg. 227
Cascino, Alfred M., Chm. Bd. & Chief Exec. Officer--Cascino Purcell Freebairn, Atlanta, GA, pg. 227
Casey, John A., Chm. Bd.--WGM Safety Corporation, Reading, PA, pg. 1156
Casey, Thomas J., Chm. Bd.--Thomas Engineering Inc., Hoffman Estates, IL, pg. 1093
Casey, William R., Chm. Bd. & Chief Exec. Officer--The Myers Group (U.S) Inc., Rouses Point, NY, pg. 780
Cashman, Eugene C., Chm. Bd.--Merchant Capital Group Ltd, Chicago, IL, pg. 739
Cashman, Robert L., Chm. Bd., Pres. & Chief Exec. Officer--Pacific Envelope Company, Anaheim, CA, pg. 840
Casper, Jack H., Chm. Bd., Chief Exec. Officer--The Alden Group Ltd., New York, NY, pg. 32
Cassano, Victor J., Jr., Chm. Bd.--Cassano's Inc., Dayton, OH, pg. 228
Cassels, W. Tobin, Jr., Chm. Bd.--Southeastern Freight Lines, Inc., Columbia, SC, pg. 1019
Cassens, Albert, Chm. Bd.--Cassens Transport Company, Edwardsville, IL, pg. 228
Cassese, Patrick J., Chm. Bd., Pres. & Chief Exec. Officer--Antares Group Inc., Cleveland, OH, pg. 76
Casteborn, Lars, Chm. Bd.--Brougher Agency, Inc., Indianapolis, IN, pg. 1146
Casteborn, Lars, Chm. Bd.--VASA Brougher, Inc., Indianapolis, IN, pg. 1146
Casteborn, Lars, Chm. Bd.--VASA North Atlantic Insurance Company, Indianapolis, IN, pg. 1146
Casteborn, Lars, Chm. Bd.--VASA Life Insurance Co., Indianapolis, IN, pg. 1146
Castello, Robert, Chm.--Commons Bros., Inc., Elmsford, NY, pg. 269
Castello, Robert, Chm. Bd.--Commons Metro Inc., Brooklyn, NY, pg. 269
Castle, Jim, Chm. Bd. & Chief Exec. Officer--U.S. Computer Services, Rancho Cordova, CA, pg. 1135
Castle, John, Chm. Bd.--Castle-Harlan, Inc., New York, NY, pg. 229
Castle, John K., Chm. Bd.--Jerrico, Inc., Lexington, KY, pg. 229
Castleberry, Randy, Co-Chm. Bd.--Southern Pump & Tank Co. Inc., Charlotte, NC, pg. 1022
Castro, Dorothy L., Chm. Bd. & Chief Exec. Officer--Superior Fast Freight, Irwindale, CA, pg. 1063
Casty, David, Chm. Bd.--American Snacks, Inc., Chelsea, MA, pg. 61
Catrambone, Gregory, Chm. Bd.--AJ Industries, Inc., El Monte, CA, pg. 971
Cavanaugh, Jim, Chm. Bd.--Jani King of California, Inc., La Palma, CA, pg. 589
Caye, Charles G., Sr., Chm. Bd.--W.C. Caye & Company, Inc., Atlanta, GA, pg. 230
Celentano, Domenick, Chm. Bd. & Pres.--Celentano Brothers, Verona, NJ, pg. 231
Centeno, Victor Lopes, Chm. & Chief Exec. Officer--BSB Portugal, Lisbon,, Portugal, pg. 110
Cerri, S.G., Chm. Bd.--Alinabal, Inc., Milford, CT, pg. 34
Chadwick, Winslow J., Chm. Bd.--Distributors Oil Company, Inc., Baton Rouge, LA, pg. 340
Chaiken, Eugene B., Chm., Pres. & Chief Exec. Officer--Almo Corp., Philadelphia, PA, pg. 43
Chalmers, David B., Chm. Bd., Pres. & Chief Exec. Officer--Coral Petroleum Corporation, Houston, TX, pg. 285
Chamberlain, Milton, Chm. Bd.--Athens Paper Co. Inc., Nashville, TN, pg. 93
Chambers, Danny M., Chm. Bd.--Kettle Restaurants, Houston, TX, pg. 626
Chambers, Evelyn, Chm. Bd.--Clipper Exxpress Co., Lemont, IL, pg. 256
Chambers, Merle, Chm. of the Exec. Committee--Clipper Exxpress Co., Lemont, IL, pg. 256
Chambers, William R., Chm. Bd. & Chief Exec. Officer--C.B. Fleet Company, Incorporated, Lynchburg, VA, pg. 417
Chan, S.Y., Chm. Bd.--AdLand Advertising, Inc., San Francisco, CA, pg. 17
Chance, Emma, Chm. Bd.--Iowa Lottery, Des Moines, IA, pg. 582
Chant, Dixon S., Chm. Bd.--Versa Services Ltd., Etobicoke,, Canada, pg. 7
Chapman, D.B., Chm. Bd--Columbian Rope Company, Guntown, MS, pg. 266
Chapman, Donald, Chm. Bd. & Chief Exec. Officer--Optiworld, Atlanta, GA, pg. 828
Chapman, R.N., Chm. Bd., Pres. & Chief Exec. Officer--Pneumatic Scale Corporation, Quincy, MA, pg. 122
Chapman, Robert H., Chm. & Pres.--Barry-Wehmiller Company, Saint Louis, MO, pg. 122
Chapman, W. Marshall, Chm. Bd. & Chief Exec. Officer--Inman Mills, Inman, SC, pg. 570
Chapoton, David, Chm. Bd.--De Novo Corporation, Utica, MI, pg. 321
Chapoton, David, Chm. Bd.--Tastee Freez Intl. Inc., Utica, MI, pg. 321
Charbin, Paul G., Chm. Bd.--J.B. Martin Company, New York, NY, pg. 715
Charles, R., Chm. Bd. & Pres.--Hydro Group, Inc., Bridgewater, NJ, pg. 556
Charlestein, Morton, Chm. Bd.--Premier Dental Products Company, Norristown, PA, pg. 886
Charton, Steve, Chm. Bd., Pres & Chief Exec. Officer--Alex Foods, Inc., Anaheim, CA, pg. 33
Chase, Francis H. III, Chm. Bd., Pres., Chief Exec., Chief Fin. Officer & Treas.--F. H. Chase, Inc., Foxboro, MA, pg. 240
Chase, Malcolm G., III, Chm. Bd.--Mossberg Industries, Inc., Cumberland, RI, pg. 772
Chase, William K., Chm. of Bd.--Chase Chevrolet Co., Stockton, CA, pg. 240
Chatman, James I., Chm. Bd. & Pres.--Technology Applications, Inc., Alexandria, VA, pg. 1083
Chavkin, Wallace, Chm. Bd. & Chief Exec. Officer--Biddle Sawyer Corporation, New York, NY, pg. 148
Checchi, Alfred, Co-Chm. Bd.--NWA, Inc., Saint Paul, MN, pg. 782
Checchi, Alfred, Co-Chm. Bd.--Northwest Airlines, Inc., Saint Paul, MN, pg. 782
Cheek, Ben F., III, Chm. Bd. & Pres.--1st Franklin Corporation, Toccoa, GA, pg. 413
Cheek, Ben F., III, Chm. Bd.--First Franklin Financial Corp., Toccoa, GA, pg. 413
Cheek, Carl W., Chm. Bd.--Specialty Industries, Inc., Red Lion, PA, pg. 1027
Cheema, Jasse, Chm. Bd. & Pres.--Theodore Barry & Associates, Los Angeles, CA, pg. 122
Chehab, Farid, Chm. Bd.--Radius Leo Burnett U.A.E, Dubai,, United Arab Emirates, pg. 193
Cheifetz, David, Chm. Bd.--Full Circle Media Corp., Norwalk, CT, pg. 436
Chen, Jeffrey C., Chm. Bd., Pres. & Chief Exec. Officer--General Sciences Corp., Laurel, MD, pg. 981
Cheney, William A., Chm. Bd.--United Air Specialists, Inc., Cincinnati, OH, pg. 1130
Cheney, William J., Chm. Bd., Pres. & Chief Exec. Officer--Steadly Company, Carthage, MO, pg. 1043
Chernick, Aubrey G., Chm. Bd. & Chief Exec. Officer--Candle Corporation, Santa Monica, CA, pg. 214
Chernoff, Marvin, Chm.--Chernoff/Silver & Associates, Columbia, SC, pg. 243
Cherry, Peter W., Chm. Bd.--PTA Corporation, Oxford, CT, pg. 837
Chesebro, R.E., Chm. Bd.--Wigwam Mills, Inc., Sheboygan, WI, pg. 1189
Chiat, Jay, Chm. Bd., Chief Exec. Officer (Worldwide)--Chiat/Day/Mojo Inc. Advertising, Venice, CA, pg. 244
Child, William H., Chm. Bd. & Chief Exec. Officer--R.C. Willey Home Furnishings, Salt Lake City, UT, pg. 1190
Childers, Bruce S., Chm., Chief Exec. Officer--Meldrum & Fewsmith Yellow Pages Inc., Cleveland, OH, pg. 737
Childers, Bruce S., Chm., Chief Exec. Officer--Excel Media Services Inc., Cleveland, OH, pg. 737

Chm. Bd., Chief Exec. Officer--Seminole Manufacturing Company, Columbus, MS, pg. 989
Cho, Y.K., Chm. Bd.--Inkel Corp., La Mirada, CA, pg. 569
Cho, Y.K., Chm.--Sherwood Corporation, Fremont, CA, pg. 570
Chopra, Deepak, Chm. Bd., Pres. & Chief Exec. Officer--UDT Sensors, Inc., Hawthorne, CA, pg. 1122
Christenson, Eric Jr., Chm. Bd.--Christenson Electric, Inc., Portland, OR, pg. 248
Christian, Betty S., Chm. Bd., Pres. & Chief Exec. Officer--Central Coca-Cola Bottling Company, Inc., Richmond, VA, pg. 232
Christiansen, Ron, Chm.--Christiansen & Fritsch, Inc., Seattle, WA, pg. 249
Christianson, Warren G., Chm. Bd.--Despatch Industries, Minneapolis, MN, pg. 332
Christie, Tom E., Chm. & Chief Exec. Officer--Christie Electric Corporation, Gardena, CA, pg. 249
Christopher, R. Craig, Chm. Bd.--Taylor Medical Inc., Beaumont, TX, pg. 1081
Church, Roy B., Chm. Bd.--Church & Church Inc., Utica, MI, pg. 249
Chute, Robert A., Chm. Bd., & Chief Exec. Officer--The Gage Company, Pittsburgh, PA, pg. 441
Ciciola, Emilio J., Exec. V.P. & Sec.--Lanman & Kemp-Barclay Co. Inc., Westwood, NJ, pg. 657
Cinader, A., Chm. Bd.--Arcinco, Inc., Garfield, NJ, pg. 81
Cinader, Arthur, Chm. Bd.--J. Crew Group, Inc., New York, NY, pg. 584
Ciociola, Mel, Chm. & Exec. Creative Dir.--Ciociola & Company Advertising, Inc., New York, NY, pg. 250
Circo, Sebastian A., Chm. Bd.--Precision Industries, Omaha, NE, pg. 885
Cisneros, Ricardo, Chm. Bd.--Spalding & Evenflo Companies, Inc., Tampa, FL, pg. 1024
Clancy, Joseph E., Chm. Bd., Pres. & Chief Oper. Officer--Bridgeport Machines, Inc., Bridgeport, CT, pg. 175
Clapp, Jeffrey W., Jr., Chm. & New Bus. Contact--Stan Merritt Inc./Advertising, New York, NY, pg. 741
Clark, A. James, Chm. Bd., Pres. & Chief Exec. Officer--Clark Construction Group, Bethesda, MD, pg. 252
Clark, A. James, Chm., Pres. & Chief Exec. Officer--CEI Construction, Inc., Bethesda, MD, pg. 200
Clark, Al, Chm. Bd. & Pres.--Southeastern Investment Properties Inc., Orlando, FL, pg. 1019
Clark, Barbara, Chm. Bd.--D.C. Lottery & Charitable Games Control Board, Washington, DC, pg. 308
Clark, Cyrus Jr., Chm. Bd.--Cyrus Clark Co., Inc., New York, NY, pg. 253
Clark, Donald R., Chm. Bd.--Atlantic Builders Group Inc., Baltimore, MD, pg. 94
Clark, Edwin, Chm. & Chief Exec. Officer--Lewis, Clark & Graham, Atlanta, GA, pg. 673
Clark, George A., Chm. Bd., Pres. & Chief Exec. Officer--Snap-Tite, Incorporated, Erie, PA, pg. 1014
Clark, Herbert H., Chm.--Clark & Pope, Inc., New York, NY, pg. 253
Clark, Lester, Chm. Bd.--States, Inc., Breckenridge, TX, pg. 1041
Clark, Raymond S., Chm. Exec. Committee--W. P. Carey & Co., Inc., New York, NY, pg. 218
Clark, William J., Chm. Bd.--Massachusetts Mutual Life Insurance Co., Springfield, MA, pg. 718
Clark, William P., Chm. Bd.--Wall Colmonoy Corp., Madison Heights, MI, pg. 1160
Clarke, Terence M., Chm.--Clarke Goward Fitts Matteson, Inc., Boston, MA, pg. 253
Claverie, Roy E., Chm. Bd.--Tennessee Insurance Co., Nashville, TN, pg. 569
Claverie, Roye E., Chm. Bd.--Permanent General Companies, Nashville, TN, pg. 569
Clay, Robert Earl, Chm. Bd. & Chief Exec. Officer--Pridgeon & Clay, Inc., Grand Rapids, MI, pg. 889
Clay, William, Chm. Bd.--Lake County Press, Waukegan, IL, pg. 651
Claypool, William, III, Chm. Bd.--Cotter & Company, Chicago, IL, pg. 288
Clayton, E. Don, Chm. Bd.--Putt Putt Golf Courses of America, Inc., Fayetteville, NC, pg. 901
Clayton, E.M. III, Chm. Bd.--Fair Lanes Inc., Hunt Valley, MD, pg. 396
Claytor, W. Graham, Jr., Chm. Bd., Pres. & Chief Exec. Officer--Amtrak-National Railroad Passenger Corp., Washington, DC, pg. 69
Cleary, William T., Pres.--CKS Partners, San Francisco, CA, pg. 202
Clemence, Robert U., Chm. Bd.--Hyde Manufacturing Co., Southbridge, MA, pg. 556
Clemens, William E., Chm. Bd. & Chief Exec. Officer--Bankers Systems Inc., Saint Cloud, MN, pg. 117
Clement, Gale W., Chm. Bd. & Pres.--Idahoan Foods, Lewisville, ID, pg. 561
Clements, Richard H., Chm. Bd., Pres. , & Chief Fin. Officer--Clements Foods Co., Oklahoma City, OK, pg. 254
Clements, W.M., Chm. Bd., Pres. & Chief Exec. Officer--Golden Eagle Distributors, Inc., Tucson, AZ, pg. 466
Cleveland, Ken, Pres. & Chm. Bd.--Cardis Corporation, Cerritos, CA, pg. 224
Clifford, William M., Chm., Pres. & Chief Exec. Officer--St. Johnsbury Trucking Co., Inc., Holliston, MA, pg. 966
Cline, Morgan E., Chm. Bd. & Pres.--Cline, Davis & Mann, Inc., New York, NY, pg. 255
Clinton, Gary, Chm. Bd., Pres. & Chief Exec. Officer--United Design, Noble, OK, pg. 1131
Cloud, Forrest R., Chm. Bd.--IBT, Inc., Shawnee Mission, KS, pg. 558
Coady, Todd M., Chm. Bd., Pres. & Chief Exec. Officer--Hicks Oil-Hicks Gas, Inc., Roberts, IL, pg. 533
Coakley, Neil T., Chm. Bd., Sec. & Treas.--Coakley & Williams Inc., Greenbelt, MD, pg. 256
Cockayne, Ronald J., Chm. Bd.--Valley Innovative Management Service, Jackson, MS, pg. 1109
Cocke, Bartlett, Jr., Chm. Bd. & Chief Exec. Officer--Bartlett Cocke Jr. Construction Co., San Antonio, TX, pg. 258
Coe, R.E., Vice Chm.--Electric Furnace Co., Salem, OH, pg. 373
Coffey, Bruce, Chm. & Chief Exec. Officer--Presto Food Products, Inc., City of Industry, CA, pg. 888
Coffey, Charles, Chm.--The Weightman Group, Philadelphia, PA, pg. 1173
Coffey, David, Chm. Bd.--Tennelec/Nucleus, Inc., Oak Ridge, TN, pg. 1087
Coffman, Kenneth M., Chm. Bd.--K & G Of Wisconsin, Inc., Milwaukee, WI, pg. 610
Coffman, Kenneth M., Chm. Bd.--Downey, Inc., Milwaukee, WI, pg. 610
Cogan, Marshall S., Chm. Bd., Pres. & Chief Exec. Officer--21 International Holdings, Inc., New York, NY, pg. 1121
Cogan, Marshall S., Chm. Bd. & Chief Exec. Officer--Knoll International, Inc., New York, NY, pg. 1121
Coghlin, Fritzmaurice, Chm. Bd.--Dock Foundry Company, Three Rivers, MI, pg. 342
Cogswell, Arnold, Chm. Bd.--Pittsburgh Tube Co., Monaca, PA, pg. 873
Cohen, Abraham D., Chm. Bd.--Duane Reade, Long Island City, NY, pg. 350
Cohen, Boris, Chm. Bd.--All-Luminum Products, Inc., Philadelphia, PA, pg. 35
Cohen, Donald, Chm. Bd., Pres., Chief Exec. Officer & Chief Fin. Officer--Tool King, Denver, CO, pg. 1101
Cohen, Herbert, Chm. Bd.--Warren/Kremer/CMP/Advertising/Inc., New York, NY, pg. 1165
Cohen, Howard, Chm. Bd. & Exec. Creative Dir.--Cohen/Johnson, Inc., Los Angeles, CA, pg. 259
Cohen, Irving, Chm. Bd.--Host Apparel, Inc., New York, NY, pg. 545
Cohen, Joseph A., Chm. Bd. & Pres.--Sunweave Linen Corporation, New York, NY, pg. 1062
Cohen, Joseph M., Chm.--Cowen & Company, New York, NY, pg. 291
Cohen, Lawrence M., Chm. Bd.--Carlyle & Co. Jewelers, Greensboro, NC, pg. 222
Cohen, Robert H., Chm. Bd. & Pres.--Beauty Enterprises Inc., Hartford, CT, pg. 130
Cohen, Robert L., Chm. Bd.--Foster Medical Supply, Inc., Waltham, MA, pg. 426
Cohen, Steven A., Chm. Bd. & Pres.--Andy Frain Services, Inc., Chicago, IL, pg. 428
Cohn, Ronald I., Chm.--Weber Cohn & Riley, Inc., Chicago, IL, pg. 1171
Cohoon, J.L., Chm. Bd.--Environetics, Branford, CT, pg. 383
Coker, Kenneth, Pres. of Bd. Dir.--Plains Electric Generation Transmission Co-Op, Inc., Albuquerque, NM, pg. 873
Colbert, E.M., Chm. Bd.--Data Instruments, Inc., Acton, MA, pg. 316
Cole, Galen L., Chm. Bd.--Coles Express, Bangor, ME, pg. 261
Cole, Irwin H., Deputy Chm. Bd.--Cole Taylor Financial Group, Wheeling, IL, pg. 260
Cole, Irwin H., Deputy Chm. Bd.--Cole Taylor/Yorktown, Lombard, IL, pg. 260
Cole, Jeffrey A., Chm. Bd. & Chief Exec. Officer--Cole National Corporation, Cleveland, OH, pg. 260
Cole, Jeffrey A., Chm. Bd.--Cole Key Corporation, Cleveland, OH, pg. 260
Cole, Jeffrey A., Chm. Bd.--Cole Vision Corporation, Cleveland, OH, pg. 260
Cole, Jeffrey A., Chm. Bd.--Things Remembered, Cleveland, OH, pg. 260
Cole, Jeffrey N., Chm.--Ferrous Processing & Trading Co., Detroit, MI, pg. 407
Cole, Lee, Chm. Bd.--Calavo Growers of California, Tustin, CA, pg. 208
Coleman, Allan, Chm. Bd.--Coleman Cable Systems, Inc., North Chicago, IL, pg. 260
Coleman, Elizabeth J., Chm.--Maidenform, Inc., New York, NY, pg. 701
Coleman, Sheldon, Chm. Bd.--Crosman Corporation, East Bloomfield, NY, pg. 695
Coleman, Walter C., Jr., Chm. Bd.--Coleman Dairy Inc., Little Rock, AR, pg. 261
Coleman, William H., Jr., Chm. Bd.--Coleman Cadillac Inc., Bethesda, MD, pg. 261
Colgan, Paul, Chm. Bd. & Pres.--Waldo Bros. Company, Boston, MA, pg. 1159
Colin, George, Chm. Bd.--Colin Service Systems, Inc., White Plains, NY, pg. 261
Collette, W.R., Chm. Bd.--Oak Rubber Company, Ravenna, OH, pg. 819
Collins, David E., Chm. Bd.--Schering-Plough Healthcare Products Advertising Corp., Liberty Corner, NJ, pg. 976
Collins, W., III, Chm. Bd. & Pres.--Warren E. Collins, Inc., Braintree, MA, pg. 263
Collman, Nicholas, Chm., Pres. & Chief Exec. Officer--John D. Lucas Printing Company, Baltimore, MD, pg. 263
Collman, Nicholas J., Chm., Pres. & Chief Exec. Officer--Collman Graphics, Inc., Baltimore, MD, pg. 263
Colomb, Gilles, Chm.--Wunderman Cato Johnson France, Boulogne,, France, pg. 1212
Colonna, Leonard, Chm. Bd.--Colonna Bros., Inc., North Bergen, NJ, pg. 264
Colton, Sol, Chm. Bd.--Domestic Linen Supply & Laundry Co., Detroit, MI, pg. 343
Columbus, Shanna J., Chm. Bd., Pres. & New Bus. Contact--Price Weber Marketing Communications, Inc., Louisville, KY, pg. 889
Colwell, Thomas G., Chm. Bd., Pres. & Chief Exec. Officer--Colwell Industries, Inc., Minneapolis, MN, pg. 267
Colyer, John M., Chm. Bd. Emeritus--Smith & Gillespie Engineers, Inc., Jacksonville, FL, pg. 1012
Combe, Ivan D., Chm. Bd.--Combe Incorporated, White Plains, NY, pg. 267
Combs, Julius, Chm. Bd. & Chief Exec. Officer--United American Healthcare Corp., Detroit, MI, pg. 826
Combs, William H., Chm. Bd.--Tamaqua Cable Products Corporation, Schuylkill Haven, PA, pg. 1077
Comstock, Harwood B., Chm. Bd.--Pratt-Read Corporation, Bridgeport, CT, pg. 884
Conese, Eugene P., Sr., Chm. Bd.--Greenwich Air Services, Miami, FL, pg. 485
Conley, James, Chm. Bd.--New England Dairies, Inc., Hartford, CT, pg. 800
Conlon, Robert, Chm. & Co-Creative Dir.--Gearon Hoffman Conlon & Nye Advertising, Inc., Garden City, NY, pg. 447
Connelly, Joseph F., Chm. Bd.--Central Pharmaceuticals, Inc., Seymour, IN, pg. 234
Connelly, Thomas S., Chm. Bd., Pres., Chief Exec. & Chief Oper. Officer--Connelly Containers, Inc., Bala-Cynwyd, PA, pg. 275
Connor, George X., Chm. Bd.--Opus South Corporation, Tampa, FL, pg. 828
Connor, Matthew, Chm.-Exec. Committee--Tucker Wayne/Luckie & Company, Birmingham, AL, pg. 1118
Conrad, E. Henry, Chm. Bd.--A-B Emblem Div. of Conrad Industries, Inc., Weaverville, NC, pg. 2
Conrad, John R., Chm. & Chief Exec. Officer--S & C Electric Company, Chicago, IL, pg. 958
Constantin, Gus, Chm. Bd., Pres. & Chief Exec. Officer--Phoenix American Incorporated, San Rafael, CA, pg. 868
Contadino, Joseph, Chm. Bd., Pres. & Treas.--Del Webb's Coventry, Phoenix, AZ, pg. 1171
Cook, Carl, Chm. Bd. & Pres.--Overland Transportation System, Inc., Indianapolis, IN, pg. 832
Cook, J. Michael, Chm. Bd. & Chief Exec. Officer--Deloitte & Touche, Wilton, CT, pg. 326
Cook, Jack P., Chm. Bd. & Pres.--Bon Ton Foods, Inc., York, PA, pg. 164
Cook, James D., Chm. Bd. & Chief Exec. Officer--Concord Litho Co., Inc., Concord, NH, pg. 272
Cook, John J., Jr., Chm. Bd. & Chief Exec. Officer--First Boston Asset Management Corporation, New York, NY, pg. 204
Cook, John J., Jr., Chm.--CS First Boston Asset Management Limited, London, United Kingdom, pg. 204
Cook, John S., Chm. Bd.--The Chicago Faucet Co., Des Plaines, IL, pg. 245
Cook, Martin, Chm. Bd.--American Metal & Plastics, Grand Rapids, MI, pg. 58
Cook, Peter C., Chm. Bd.--Transnational Motors Inc., Grand Rapids, MI, pg. 1107
Cook, Samuel R., Chm. Bd. & Chief Exec. Officer--Broughton Foods Company, Marietta, OH, pg. 180
Coombe, V. Anderson, Chm. Bd., Chief Exec. Officer, & Treas.--The Wm. Powell Company, Cincinnati, OH, pg. 882
Coombe, V.A., Chm. Bd.--The Starflo Corporation, Orangeburg, SC, pg. 883
Cooney, David M., Chm. Bd.--Goodwill Industries of America, Inc., Bethesda, MD, pg. 471
Cooper, John A., Jr., Chm. Bd.--Cooper Communities, Inc., Bella Vista, AR, pg. 283
Cooper, Joseph V., Chm. Bd. & Pres.--C. Weaver Chevrolet, Inc., New York Mills, NY, pg. 1170
Cooper, Marshall Y., Jr., Pres., Chief Exec. Officer & Chm. Bd.--Harriet & Henderson Yarns, Inc., Henderson, NC, pg. 511
Cooper, William R., Chm. Bd. & Pres.--Paragon Group, Inc., Dallas, TX, pg. 847
Cooperman, Harold, Chm. Bd.--United A G Co-op, Inc., Omaha, NE, pg. 1130
Cop, E.J., Chm. Bd.--Evangeline Medical & X-Ray Distributors, Baton Rouge, LA, pg. 390
Copeland, Alvin C., Chm. Bd.--Church's Fried Chicken, Inc., Jefferson, LA, pg. 284
Copeland, William B., Chm. Bd.--Ploof Truck Lines, Inc., Jacksonville, FL, pg. 877
Copley, Helen K., Chm. Bd. & Chief Exec. Officer--The Copley Press, Inc., La Jolla, CA, pg. 284
Copps, Michael W., Chm. Bd. & Chief Exec. Officer--The Copps Corp., Stevens Point, WI, pg. 285
Corbin, James E., Jr., Chm. Bd.--Metal Trades, Inc., Hollywood, SC, pg. 741
Corcoran, Philip, Chm., Chief Exec. & Chief Oper. Officer--Comark, Bloomingdale, IL, pg. 267
Corcoran, Thomas, Chm. Bd.--Display Technologies, Inc., Elgin, IL, pg. 339
Cordier, William K., Chm. Bd.--Canton Drop Forge, Canton, OH, pg. 214
Cordover, Ronald, Chm. Bd.--Corber Corporation, Wayne, NJ, pg. 285
Cordover, Ronald H., Chm. Bd.--The Berkline Corporation, Morristown, TN, pg. 285
Corkin, Herbert I., Chm. Bd., Pres., Chief Exec. & Chief Oper. Officer--The Entwistle Company, Hudson, MA, pg. 383
Corley, Carl D., Vice Chm.--Carco International, Inc., Fort Smith, AR, pg. 217
Corley, Carl M., Chm. Bd.--Carco International, Inc., Fort Smith, AR, pg. 217
Cornell, Alverin M., Chm. Bd. & Chief Exec. Officer--Cornell Forge Company, Chicago, IL, pg. 286
Cornelsen, Paul F., Chm. Bd. & Chief Exec. Officer--Mitek, Inc., Chesterfield, MO, pg. 762
Cornish, David A., Chm. Bd.--Collegeville/Imagineering L.P., Collegeville, PA, pg. 262
Corogin, John S., Chm. Bd., Sec. & Treas.--Lake Erie Electric, Inc., Westlake, OH, pg. 651
Corrao, Michael J., Chm. Bd., Pres. & Chief Exec. Officer--Gingiss International, Chicago, IL, pg. 460
Cosgrave, Gary D., Chm. & Chief Exec. Officer--Pro Hardware, Inc., Englewood, CO, pg. 891
Cotler, Howard, Chm. Bd.--H. Cotler Company, New York, NY, pg. 288
Cottrell, Comer J., Chm. Bd. & Pres.--Pro-Line Corporation, Dallas, TX, pg. 892
Coulombe, Raymond R., Chm. & Chief Exec. Officer--White Rock Distilleries Inc., Lewiston, ME, pg. 1186

Coulter, Wallace, Chm. Bd. & Chief Exec. Officer--Coulter Corporation, Hialeah, FL, pg. 289
Counsell, Paul S., Chm. Bd. & Chief Exec. Officer--Cramer-Krasselt, Milwaukee, WI, pg. 296
Counsell, Paul S., Chm. Bd. & Chief Exec. Officer--Cramer-Krasselt, Milwaukee, WI, pg. 296
Countryman, G.L., Chm.--Liberty Mutual Fire Insurance Co., Boston, MA, pg. 674
Countryman, Gary L., Chm. & Chief Exec. Officer--Liberty Mutual Insurance Co., Boston, MA, pg. 674
Courbey, Patrice, Chm. Bd. & Pres.--Meridian Technology Leasing Services, Deerfield, IL, pg. 740
Couri, George G., Chm. Bd.--Couristan Inc., Fort Lee, NJ, pg. 290
Cousins, G.A., Chm.--George Patterson Pty. Limited, North Sydney,, Australia, pg. 112
Cousteau, Capt. J. Y., Chm. Bd.--U.S. Divers Co., Inc., Santa Ana, CA, pg. 1135
Coverdale, Glen E., Chm. Bd. & Chief Exec. Officer--Cross & Brown Company, New York, NY, pg. 744
Coverdale, Glen E., Chm.--Metmor Financial, Inc., Overland Park, KS, pg. 745
Cowan, James R., Chm. Bd. & Chief Exec. Officer--Stonecutter Mills Corp., Spindale, NC, pg. 1051
Cowen, Philip R., Chm. Bd. & Chief Exec. Officer--Alpha Electronic Signal Technologies, Inc., Elizabeth, NJ, pg. 43
Cowin, John J., Chm. Bd., Pres. & Treas.--Cowin & Company, Inc., Birmingham, AL, pg. 291
Cowley, George, Chm. Bd. & Chief Exec. Officer--Alpha One Exchange, New Providence, NJ, pg. 43
Cox, Archibald, Jr., Chm. Bd.--First Boston (Puerto Rico), Inc., Hato Rey, PR, pg. 204
Cox, Archibald, Jr., Chm Bd.--CS First Boston USA, Inc., New York, NY, pg. 204
Cox, Audrey C., Chm. Bd.--First State Federal Savings & Loan, Hutchinson, MN, pg. 413
Cox, Bill, Chm. Bd. & Chief Exec. Officer--Dal-Tile Corp., Dallas, TX, pg. 312
Cox, Michael, Chm. Bd. & Chief Exec. Officer--Cox Advertising, New York, NY, pg. 292
Cox, William B., Chm. Bd.--Cox Wood Preserving Co., Orangeburg, SC, pg. 295
Cox, Winston H. (Tony), Chm. & Chief Exec. Officer-Showtime Networks--Viacom Inc., New York, NY, pg. 785
Coyne, Nancy, Chm. Bd., Chief Exec. Officer & Dir.-Creative Services--Serino Coyne Inc., New York, NY, pg. 991
Craft, Stanley, Chm., Pres. & Chief Exec. Officer--Essex Group, Inc., Fort Wayne, IN, pg. 389
Crain, Gertrude, Chm. Bd.--Advertising Age, Chicago, IL, pg. 295
Crain, Gertrude R., Chm. Bd.--Crain Communications, Inc., Detroit, MI, pg. 295
Cramer, James D., Chm. Bd.--Science & Engineering Associates, Albuquerque, NM, pg. 982
Crandall, David E., Chm. Bd. & Chief Exec. Officer--PPA Industries, Inc., Dallas, TX, pg. 836
Crane, Dale E., Chm. Bd.--Uniphase Corporation, San Jose, CA, pg. 1129
Crane, Lansing, E., Chm. Bd.--Crane & Co., Inc., Dalton, MA, pg. 296
Crane, Robert S., Jr., Chm. Bd.--Crane Plastics Company, Columbus, OH, pg. 296
Crane, William C., Chm. Bd.--Decatur News Publishing Company, Inc., Decatur, GA, pg. 323
Cranford, Wayne, Chm. & Chief Exec. Officer--Cranford Johnson Robinson Woods, Little Rock, AR, pg. 296
Crawford, Bernard K., Chm. Bd.--Standard Tool & Manufacturing Company, Lyndhurst, NJ, pg. 1037
Crawford, Edward, Chm. Bd.--The Crawford Group, Cleveland, OH, pg. 297
Crawford, Jerry, Chm. Bd.--Rome Manufacturing Co., Rome, GA, pg. 945
Crawford, Mike, Chm. Bd. & Pres.--McCommunications Inc., Dallas, TX, pg. 727
Cressey, Bryan C., Chm. Bd.--Intercole, Inc., Washington, PA, pg. 574
Crider, Joe D., Chm. Bd. & Chief Exec. Officer--Metalcenter, Inc., Santa Fe Springs, CA, pg. 742
Crone, W.G., Chm. Bd. & Chief Exec. Officer--Conley Frog & Switch Company, Memphis, TN, pg. 274
Cronin, William J., Sr., Chm. Bd.--Cronin & Company, Inc., Glastonbury, CT, pg. 300
Crosby, George, Chm. Bd.--Quad Systems Corporation, Horsham, PA, pg. 902
Cross, Joe D., Sr., Chm.--Cross Motors Corp., Louisville, KY, pg. 300
Cross, Raymond, Sr., Chm. Bd.--Federal Chicago Corporation, North Chicago, IL, pg. 404
Crossingham, James H., Jr., Chm. Bd. & Pres.--Spencer's Inc., Mount Airy, NC, pg. 1030
Crotty, L. William, Chm., Pres. & Chief Exec. Officer--Van Dyne-Crotty, Inc., Dayton, OH, pg. 1144
Crow, Howard M., Jr., Chm. Bd.--Broadcast Electronics, Inc., Quincy, IL, pg. 177
Crow, Trammell, Chm. Bd.--Trammell Crow Company, Dallas, TX, pg. 1106
Crowell, Raymond E., Chm. Bd. & Pres.--Glines & Rhodes, Inc., Attleboro, MA, pg. 463
Crowley, Ralph D., Chm. Bd.--Polar Corporation, Worcester, MA, pg. 878
Crowley, Thomas B., Chm. Bd & Chief Exec. Officer--Crowley Maritime Corporation, Oakland, CA, pg. 301
Crown, Lester, Chm. Bd.--CC Industries, Inc., Chicago, IL, pg. 199
Cubberly, Walter A., Chm. Bd. & Treas.--Kalas Manufacturing, Inc., Denver, PA, pg. 615
Cudlip, Brittain B., Co-Chm. Bd.--Bardes Corp., Cincinnati, OH, pg. 119
Cullen, John B., Chm. Bd. & Chief Exec. Officer--King Kullen Grocery Co., Inc., Westbury, NY, pg. 630
Cummings, Jack, Jr., Chm. Bd.--Battey Machinery Company, Rome, GA, pg. 127
Cummings, Thomas L., Jr., Chm. Bd. & Chief Exec. Officer--Cummings Inc., Nashville, TN, pg. 304
Cunniffe, Maurice J., Chm. Bd. & Chief Exec. Officer--American Optical Corp., Greenwich, CT, pg. 59
Curless, Larry, Chm. Bd.--Countrymark Cooperative, Inc., Indianapolis, IN, pg. 290
Curran, James B., Chm. Bd. & Chief Exec. Officer--Henry Bacon Building Materials, Inc., Issaquah, WA, pg. 113
Curtis, Jay, Chm. Bd.--Curtis Lumber Company, Ballston Spa, NY, pg. 305
Curtis, Roger William, Chm. Bd., Chief Exec. Officer & Sec.--L.N. Curtis & Sons, Oakland, CA, pg. 306
Curtola, Terry A., Jr., Chm. Bd.--Marine World Africa USA, Vallejo, CA, pg. 707
Cutler, Burton, Chm. Bd.--Educational Insights, Inc., Dominguez Hills, CA, pg. 369
Cutler, Richard F., Co-Chm. Bd.--H.H. Cutler Company, Grand Rapids, MI, pg. 306
Cutler, William F., Co-Chm. Bd.--H.H. Cutler Company, Grand Rapids, MI, pg. 306
Cutter, W.R., Chm. Bd. & Pres.--Cutter Flying Service, Inc., Albuquerque, NM, pg. 307
D'Agostino, Nichold, Jr., Chm. Bd.--D'Agostino Supermarkets Inc., Larchmont, NY, pg. 310
D'Amour, Gerald E., Chm. Bd. & Pres.--Big Y Foods Inc., Springfield, MA, pg. 149
Dabah, Ezra, Chm. Bd. & Chief Exec. Officer--The Children's Place Retail Stores, Inc., Pine Brook, NJ, pg. 247
Dabah, Morris, Chm. Bd.--Gitano Group Inc., New York, NY, pg. 460
Dadourian, Alexander A., Chm. Bd.--Interroyal Corporation, Warren, PA, pg. 580
Dahlem, Bernard A., Chm. Bd.--Dahlem Company, Inc., Louisville, KY, pg. 310
Dake, Leland E., Chm. Bd.--Pro-Log Corporation, Monterey, CA, pg. 892
Daley, James E., Co-Chm.--Price Waterhouse - U.S., New York, NY, pg. 888
Dalquist, H. David, Sr., Chm. Bd. & Chief Exec. Officer--Northland Aluminum Products, Inc., Minneapolis, MN, pg. 814
Daltner, John, Chm.--Gilbert, Whitney & Johns, Inc., Whippany, NJ, pg. 458
Dalton, James G., Chm. Bd.--Caraustar Industries, Inc., Austell, GA, pg. 217
Daly, Leo A., Chm. Bd., Pres. & Treas.--Leo A. Daly Company, Omaha, NE, pg. 313
Dancker, Paul W., Chm. Bd.--Dancker, Sellew & Douglas, Inc., New York, NY, pg. 314
Danforth, Douglas, Chm. Bd.--Pittsburgh Pirates Professional Baseball Club, Pittsburgh, PA, pg. 873
Dang, Dennis K., Chm. Bd.--Corporate Health Strategies, Inc., Westport, CT, pg. 744
Daniels, William A., Chm. Bd. & Pres.--Daniels Manufacturing Corporation, Orlando, FL, pg. 314
Daniels, William D., Chm. Bd. & Chief Exec. Officer--Penn-Daniels, Inc., Quincy, IL, pg. 857
Danis, Richard R., Vice Chm.--Danis Industries Corporation, Dayton, OH, pg. 314
Danis, Thomas J., Chm. Bd.--Danis Industries Corporation, Dayton, OH, pg. 314
Danna, Leon J., Chm. Bd. & Chief Exec. Officer--Network Real Estate of California, Inc., Soquel, CA, pg. 798
Danna, Leon J., Chm. Bd. & Chief Exec. Officer--Network Real Estate, Inc., Soquel, CA, pg. 798
Danna, Leon J., Chm. Bd. & Chief Exec. Officer--Network Home Services, Inc., Soquel, CA, pg. 798
Danziger, Lawrence, Pres./ML Div.--Deare Marketing Inc./Matthew-Lawrence Advertising & Sales Promotion Inc., New York, NY, pg. 323
Darling, Albert, Chm. Bd.--Darling Envelope Corporation, Shawnee Mission, KS, pg. 315
Darling, Robert, Chm. Bd & Chief Exec. Officer--Zollner Corporation, Fort Wayne, IN, pg. 1221
Dart, William A., Chm.--Dart Container Corp., Mason, MI, pg. 316
Datchary, Michel, Chm.--Programmes Marketing Annuaires (PMA), Paris,, France, pg. 1074
Daunhauer, John R., Jr., Chm. Bd. & Pres.--Byerly Ford-Nissan Inc., Louisville, KY, pg. 198
Davenport, R.B., III, Chm.-Exec. Comm.--Krystal Company, Chattanooga, TN, pg. 645
Davidson, Donald, Co-Chm. Bd. & Chief Exec. Officer--D&L Venture Corp., New Britain, CT, pg. 307
Davidson, Ian B., Chm. Bd. & Chief Exec. Officer--D.A. Davidson & Co., Great Falls, MT, pg. 318
Davidson, Phillip T., Co-Chm. Bd.--D&L Venture Corp., New Britain, CT, pg. 307
Davidson, William, Chm., Pres., Chief Exec. & Chief Oper. Officer--Guardian Industries Corp., Northville, MI, pg. 491
Davies, George P., Chm. Bd. & Pres.--Trico Electric Co-Op, Tucson, AZ, pg. 1113
Davies, John, Chm. Bd.--Enerfab Inc., Cincinnati, OH, pg. 381
Davis, Charles E., Sr., Chm. Bd. & Pres.--Laboratory Supply Company, Inc., Louisville, KY, pg. 649
Davis, DeForest P., Chm.--Knight Wendling AG, Zurich,, Switzerland, pg. 637
Davis, DeForest P., Jr., Chm. Bd. & Chief Exec. Officer--Lester B. Knight & Associates, Inc., Chicago, IL, pg. 637
Davis, DeForest P., Jr., Chm.--Knight Management Consulting, Inc., Chicago, IL, pg. 637
Davis, Greg, Chm.--Ravenswood Aluminum Corp., Ravenswood, WV, pg. 914
Davis, Harold, Chm.--Electrical Wholesale Supply Company, Inc., Idaho Falls, ID, pg. 374
Davis, Jeffrey G., Chm., Pres. & Chief Exec. Officer--Aetna Plywood, Inc., Arlington Heights, IL, pg. 23
Davis, Michael K., Chm. Bd. & Chief Oper. Officer--Lee Davis Ayer, Hong Kong,, Hong Kong, pg. 104
Davis, Norwood, Chm. Bd. & Chief Exec. Officer--Blue Cross & Blue Shield of Virginia, Richmond, VA, pg. 160
Davis, Reese B., Chm. Bd.--Westgate Fabrics, Inc., Grand Prairie, TX, pg. 1182
Davis, Richard, Chm. Bd. & Pres.-Davis Industries--Davis Industries Inc., Detroit, MI, pg. 318
Davis, Robert M., Chm., Sec. & Treas.--Davis, Ball & Colombatto Advertising, Inc., Los Angeles, CA, pg. 318
Davis, Troy, Chm. Bd.--Best Western International, Inc., Phoenix, AZ, pg. 146
Davis, W. Jack, Chm. Bd.--Austin Powder Co., Cleveland, OH, pg. 99
Davis, W. Jack, Chm. Bd.--Rish Equipment Company, Bluefield, WV, pg. 935
Davis, William Jack, Chm. Bd. & Pres.--Davis Mining & Manufacturing, Colburn, VA, pg. 319
Davison, Joan, Chm. Bd.--Dacor Corporation, Northfield, IL, pg. 310
Daw, Ronald W., Chm. Bd. & Chief Exec. Officer--Daw Technologies, Inc., Salt Lake City, UT, pg. 319
Dawshare, Oscar D., Acting Chm. Bd.--Dawahares, Inc., Lexington, KY, pg. 319
Day, Gerald, Chm. Bd.--Associated Food Stores Inc., Salt Lake City, UT, pg. 89
Dayan, Ari, Chm. Bd.--Bon Jour International Ltd., New York, NY, pg. 164
Dayan, Ari, Chm.--Licensing Div., New York, NY, pg. 164
Daylor, David J., Chm. Bd.--Ashworth Bros., Inc., Fall River, MA, pg. 88
De Forrest, James R., Chm. Bd.--American Lock & Supply Inc., Anaheim, CA, pg. 57
De Pasquale, John A., Chm. Bd.--The Direct Marketing Group Inc., New York, NY, pg. 339
de Rothschild, David, Co-Chm.--Rothschild North America Inc., New York, NY, pg. 951
de Rothschild, Evelyn, Chm.-Exec. Committee--Rothschild North America Inc., New York, NY, pg. 951
Dean, Frederick B., Chm. Bd.--Coordinated Apparel, Inc., New York, NY, pg. 283
Dean, Lester M., Sr., Chm. Bd. & Chief Exec. Officer--Dean Operations Inc., Kansas City, MO, pg. 322
Deardorf, David, Chm. Bd.--Silicon Valley Development, Santa Clara, CA, pg. 1004
DeArment, George S., Co-Chm. Bd.--Channellock, Inc., Meadville, PA, pg. 239
DeArment, William A., Co-Chm. Bd.--Channellock, Inc., Meadville, PA, pg. 239
DeArmond, R.J., Chm. Bd.--Idaho Forest Industry, Inc., Coeur D'Alene, ID, pg. 561
Deason, Darwin, Chm. Bd. & Chief Exec. Officer--Affiliated Computer Services, Inc., Dallas, TX, pg. 23
Deaver, Mike, Chm. Bd.--W-B Supply Co., Pampa, TX, pg. 1155
DeBartolo, Edward J., Chm. Bd. & Chief Exec. Officer--The Edward J. DeBartolo Corporation, Youngstown, OH, pg. 323
DeBlasio, Carl, Exec. V.P.--Planes Moving And Storage, Inc., Cincinnati, OH, pg. 874
Deborde, Shelby J., Sr., Chm. Bd.--Bearing Distributors, Inc., Columbia, SC, pg. 130
DeBruce, Paul, Chm. Bd.--DeBruce Grain Inc., North Kansas City, MO, pg. 323
DeCesaris, Geaton A., Sr., Chm. Bd.--Washington Homes, Inc., Landover, MD, pg. 1166
Decker, Hans, Chm. Bd.--Academy Insurance Group, Inc., Atlanta, GA, pg. 11
Decker, James, Chm. & Dir. Creative Services--Decker Rickard, Glastonbury, CT, pg. 324
Dedman, Robert H., Sr., Chm. Bd. & Chief Exec. Officer--Club Corporation International, Dallas, TX, pg. 256
Dedman, Robert Jr., Chm. Bd.--Club Corporation Of America, Dallas, TX, pg. 256
Dee, Edward, Chm. Bd.--Ce De Candy, Inc., Union, NJ, pg. 230
DeFrancisci, Ignatius, Chm. Bd.--De Francisci Machine Corp.(Demaco), Ridgewood, NY, pg. 321
DeGeorge, L., Chm. Bd. & Chief Exec. Officer--Times Fiber Communications, Inc., Wallingford, CT, pg. 648
DeGeorge, Lawrence J., Chm. Bd., Pres. & Chief Exec. Officer--LPL Technologies, Inc., Wallingford, CT, pg. 648
Degner, Harry, Chm. Bd.--Topa Insurance Company, Los Angeles, CA, pg. 1101
Dehaan, Christal, Chm. Bd., Pres. & Chief Exec. Officer--Resort Condominiums International, Indianapolis, IN, pg. 929
Dehmlow, Louis H.T., Chm. Bd. & Chief Exec. Officer--Great Lakes Terminal & Transport Corp., Chicago, IL, pg. 482
Dehmlow, Louis H.T., Chm. Bd.--Alpha Resin Supply, Chicago, IL, pg. 482
DeJoris, John Paul, Chm. Bd. & Pres.--John Paul Mitchell Systems, Beverly Hills, CA, pg. 762
Dekker, Marcel, Chm. Bd. & Pres.--Marcel Dekker, Inc., New York, NY, pg. 325
Dekko, Chester E., Chm. Bd., Pres. & Chief Exec. Officer--Group Dekko International Inc., Kendallville, IN, pg. 489
DeKruif, Jack H., Chm. Bd. & Chief Exec. Officer--Wayne Corporation, Richmond, IN, pg. 1169
Delaney, Robert, Chm. Bd.--McMaster Carr Supply Co. Inc., Elmhurst, IL, pg. 731
Delany, Logan, Chm. Bd.--Eastern Air Devices, Inc., Dover, NH, pg. 363
Delany, Logan, Jr., Chm. Bd.--Howard Industries, Inc., Milford, IL, pg. 547
Delman, Jacob J., Chm. Bd. & Chief Oper. Officer--Splendor Form International Inc., Long Island City, NY, pg. 1031
DeLoache, Frances S., Chm. Bd.--Shealy Electrical Wholesalers, Greenville, SC, pg. 996
DeLuca, Robert, Chm. Bd., Pres. & Chief Exec. Officer--Aero Data Metal Crafters, Bohemia, NY, pg. 22
DeMaria, Joseph A., Sr., Chm. Bd. & Chief Exec. Officer--DeMaria Building Co. Inc., Novi, MI, pg. 327
DeMars, Richard B., Chm. Bd.--The DeMars Corp., Indianapolis, IN, pg. 327

Demere, Robert H., Chm. Bd. & Chief Exec. Officer--Colonial Oil Industries, Savannah, GA, pg. 263
DeMeuse, Donald H., Chm. Bd. & Chief Exec. Officer--Fort Howard Corporation, Green Bay, WI, pg. 425
Denise, Robert, Chm., Pres., Chief Exec. Officer & Chief Fin. Officer--Bucilla Corporation, Hazleton, PA, pg. 185
Denison, Glen H., Chm. Bd.--Axelson, Inc., Longview, TX, pg. 103
Dennis, Robert F., Chm. Bd.--United Parking, Inc., Atlanta, GA, pg. 1134
Dent, Frederick B., Chm. Bd.--Mayfair Mills, Inc., Arcadia, SC, pg. 724
Dent, James R., Chm. Bd & Pres.--Crosby & Overton, Inc., Long Beach, CA, pg. 300
Derrow, David D., Chm. Bd.--Ohio Transmission Corporation, Columbus, OH, pg. 822
Derst, Edward J., Jr., Chm. Bd.--Derst Baking Company, Inc., Savannah, GA, pg. 331
Derusha, Roger H., Chm. Bd.--Marinette Marine Corporation, Marinette, WI, pg. 707
Desaigoudar, Chan, Chm. Bd.--California Micro Devices, Tempe, AZ, pg. 210
Desloge, George B., Chm. Bd.--Watlow Electric Manufacturing Company, Saint Louis, MO, pg. 1167
Detmer, Josephine H., Chm. Bd.--Diversified Communications, Portland, ME, pg. 340
Deutsch, Alex, Chm. Bd. & Chief Exec. Officer--The Deutsch Company, Santa Monica, CA, pg. 333
Deutsch, David, Chm. Bd.--Deutsch/Dworin, Inc., New York, NY, pg. 333
Devers, William J., Jr., Chm. Bd.--Global Turnkey Systems Inc., Waldwick, NJ, pg. 463
Deverse, Frank T., Chm. Bd., Pres., Chief Exec. Officer & Treas.--International Microcircuits, Inc., Milpitas, CA, pg. 579
DeVoe, James K., Chm. Bd., Chief Exec. Officer--The Jayme Organization, Inc., Cleveland, OH, pg. 591
Dew, Donald F., Chm. Bd., Pres. & Chief Exec. Officer--Diemolding Corp., Canastota, NY, pg. 336
Dhanani, Noorally K. J., Chm. Bd.--The Double-Cola Company, Chattanooga, TN, pg. 347
Di Zazzo, James G., Chm. Bd. & Pres.--Oomphies, Inc., Lawrence, MA, pg. 827
Diamond, Isadore, Chm. Bd., Treas. & Chief Fin. & Chief Acctg. Officer--Magnetic Technologies Corporation, Rochester, NY, pg. 701
Diamond, Lawrence, Chm. Bd., Pres., Chief Exec. & Chief Oper. Officer & Dir.-Pur.--Triangle Marketing Corp., New York, NY, pg. 1112
Diamond, Robert, Chm.--CS First Boston Australia (Holdings) Limited, Melbourne,, Australia, pg. 204
Diamond, Robert E., Jr., Chm.--First Boston (Japan) Limited, Tokyo, Japan, pg. 204
Diamond, Robert E., Jr., Chm.--CS First Boston (Hong Kong) Limited, Hong Kong,, Hong Kong, pg. 204
Diamond, Robert E., Jr., Chm., Pres. & Chief Exec. Officer--CS First Boston Pacific, Inc., New York, NY, pg. 204
Dibben, David, Chm. Bd.--Carolina Builders Corporation, Raleigh, NC, pg. 223
Dick, Dorsey W., Chm. Bd.--Dick Corporation, Large, PA, pg. 335
Dick, Louise H., Chm. Bd.--Trumbull Corporation, West Mifflin, PA, pg. 1117
Dickens, Bryam E., Chm. Bd.--VJ Growers, Inc., Apopka, FL, pg. 1141
Dickens, Chris, Grp. Chm.-UK--Young & Rubicam Holdings Ltd., London, United Kingdom, pg. 1213
Dickenson, H. Boyd, Chm. & Chief Exec. Officer--Hayes, Seay, Mattern & Mattern, Inc., Roanoke, VA, pg. 519
Dickerson, N.K. III, Chm. Bd.--The Dickerson Group, Inc., Monroe, NC, pg. 335
Didde, Carl, Chm. Bd.--Didde Web Press, Emporia, KS, pg. 336
Didion, James J., Co-Chm. Bd.--CB Commercial Real Estate Group, Inc., Los Angeles, CA, pg. 222
Diedrick, G. Vern, Chm. Bd., Chief Exec. Officer, & Pres.--Maecorp Inc., Chicago, IL, pg. 699
Diehl, Neil N., Chm. Bd. Emeritus--Ingram Barge Company, Nashville, TN, pg. 569
Diehl, William A., Chm. Bd.--Diehl Specialties Intl., Defiance, OH, pg. 336
Diem, John J., Chm. Bd.--Southern Agricultural Insecticides, Palmetto, FL, pg. 1020
Dienert, Fred, Chm.--Walter Bennett Communications, Fort Washington, PA, pg. 139
Dietz, W.R., Chm. Bd., Pres. & Chief Exec. Officer--American Savings Bank, White Plains, NY, pg. 60
DiFillippo, Thomas A., Chm. Bd. & Pres.--DeVault Foods, Devault, PA, pg. 333
DiJulius, Paul, Chm. Bd.--Lavelle Aircraft Company, Philadelphia, PA, pg. 661
Dillon, Mike, Chm. Bd. & Pres.--Tom's Foods, Columbus, GA, pg. 1101
DiLorenzo, James E., Chm. Bd., Pres. & Chief Exec. Officer--Quality Pontiac, Inc., Albuquerque, NM, pg. 904
DiMatteo, Dominick, Chm. Bd.--Dominick's Finer Foods, Northlake, IL, pg. 343
Dimeo, Thomas P., Chm. Bd.--Dimeo Construction Company, Providence, RI, pg. 338
Dimmick, Henry M., Chm. Bd. & Chief Exec. Officer--AGR International, Inc., Butler, PA, pg. 4
Dinger, Frank S., Chm. Bd.--William H. Sadlier, Inc., New York, NY, pg. 966
Dingman, Michael D., Chm. Bd. & Chief Exec. Officer--The Henley Group, Inc., Hampton, NH, pg. 529
Dingman, Michael D., Chm., Chief Fin. Officer & Mng. Dir.--New Hampshire Oak, Hampton, NH, pg. 800
Dippold, George J., Chm. Bd. & Pres.--Whittaker, Clark & Daniels, Inc., South Plainfield, NJ, pg. 1187
Dircks, R.D., Chm. Bd. & Chief Exec. Officer--Berger Transfer & Storage, Inc., Saint Paul, MN, pg. 141
Dittmer, Thomas H., Chm. Bd.--Refco Group Ltd., Chicago, IL, pg. 921
Dixon, Joseph A., Dr., Chm. Bd.--American Chemical Society, Washington, DC, pg. 50
Dobles, Arthur J., Chm. Bd.--Dobles Chevrolet, Inc., Manchester, NH, pg. 342
Dobson, Grace, Chm. Bd.--Whataburger, Inc., Corpus Christi, TX, pg. 1184
Dodson, Cathleen, Chm. Bd. & Chief Exec. Officer--Dodson Group, Kansas City, MO, pg. 342
Dohmen, Erwin, Chm. Bd.--The F. Dohmen Company, Germantown, WI, pg. 343
Dokmo, Harold B., Jr., Chm. Bd., Pres., Treas. & Sec.--Norcraft Companies, Inc., Saint Paul, MN, pg. 809
Dolan, John F., Chm. Bd. & Pres.--Fairfax Lumber & Millwork Company Inc., Springfield, VA, pg. 397
Dolan, William A., II, Chm. Bd.--High Point Financial Corp., Branchville, NJ, pg. 533
Don, Robert E., Chm. Bd. & Chief Exec. Officer--Edward Don & Company of Illinois, North Riverside, IL, pg. 344
Donahoe, Edward J., Chm. Bd., Pres. & Acct. Supvr.--Donahoe & Purohit, Inc., Rosemont, IL, pg. 344
Donahue, John, Chm. Bd.--Pet Life Foods, Inc., Willowbrook, IL, pg. 863
Donaldson, Daniel R., Chm. Bd.--Smith Metal Arts Company, Inc., Buffalo, NY, pg. 1013
Donegan, L. Edwin, Chm. Bd.--Heico Inc., Lisle, IL, pg. 525
Doonan, Thomas, Chm. Bd.--O/E Automation, Inc., Troy, MI, pg. 819
Doornick, James, Chm. Bd.--Snokist Growers, Yakima, WA, pg. 1015
Dopkins, Leonard A., Chm. Bd., Treas. & Sec.--Standard Electronics, Inc., Amherst, NY, pg. 1036
Doppelt, Lawrence, Exec. V.P.--Goldberger Doll Mfg. Company, Inc., Brooklyn, NY, pg. 466
Dorn, Edward G., Chm. Bd. & Pres.--Edward G. Dorn & Associates, Inc., Rolling Meadows, IL, pg. 346
Dortch, David D., Sr., Chm. Bd.--Humboldt Express, Inc., Nashville, TN, pg. 552
Dott, A. Eric, Chm. Bd. & Chief Exec. Officer--Monarch Avalon, Inc., Baltimore, MD, pg. 765
Douce, Patrice, Chm. Bd.--Seiler Corporation, Waltham, MA, pg. 987
Douglas, Walter E., Chm. Bd. & Pres.--Avis Ford Inc., Southfield, MI, pg. 102
Douglass, A. Stone, Chm. Bd. & Owner--Piper Aircraft Corporation, Vero Beach, FL, pg. 872
Douglass, Don, Chm. Bd.--Alamo Group, Inc., Seguin, TX, pg. 29
Doulton, Charles, Chm. Bd.--Simonds Industries Inc., Fitchburg, MA, pg. 1006
Douma, David L., Chm. Bd. & Pres.--Theradyne Corporation, Lakeville, MN, pg. 1065
Dowling, James H., Chm. Bd.--Burson-Marsteller, New York, NY, pg. 1210
Downey, David G., Chm. Bd. & Chief Exec. Officer--Downey Designs International, Inc., Indianapolis, IN, pg. 348
Downey, John M., Chm. Bd.--Downey Printing, Waukee, IA, pg. 348
Downs, Richard, Chm. Bd. & Chief Exec. Officer--Tony Downs Foods Company, Saint James, MN, pg. 348
Downs, William F., Chm. Bd.--The Downs Group, Inc., Charlotte, NC, pg. 348
Dowsett, William J., Chm. Bd.--East Moline Metal Products Company, East Moline, IL, pg. 363
Doyle, M.C., Chm. Bd.--Econolite Control Products, Inc., Anaheim, CA, pg. 367
Draft, Howard, Chm. Bd. & Chief Exec. Officer--Kobs & Draft Advertising, Inc., Chicago, IL, pg. 109
Dragone, Allan R., Chm. Bd.--New York Racing Association, Jamaica, NY, pg. 803
Dragotta, Robert, Chm. Bd. & Pres.--National Out-of-Home Media/Metro 8, New York, NY, pg. 792
Dreisbach, Thomas S., Chm. Bd. & Chief Oper. Officer--Dreisbach & Sons Cadillac Company, Detroit, MI, pg. 348
Drell, Leonard, Chm. Bd.--Heet Automotive, Westchester, IL, pg. 328
Drell, Leonard B., Chm. Bd., Pres., Chief Exec. & Chief Oper. Officer--DeMert & Dougherty, Inc., Westchester, IL, pg. 328
Drendel, Lee S., Chm. Bd.--Capitol Group, Springfield, IL, pg. 215
Drettmann, Henry, Chm. Bd., Chief Exec. Officer & Treas.--Active Tool & Manufacturing Co., Inc., Roseville, MI, pg. 15
Dreyer, John W., Chm. Bd., Pres. & Chief Exec. Officer--Harold M. Pitman Co., Inc., Totowa, NJ, pg. 872
Drinkall, W.H., Chm. Bd. & Chief Exec. Officer--South Bend Plastics, Inc., Mishawaka, IN, pg. 1019
Driscoll, Edward C., Chm. Bd., Chief Exec. Officer & Treas.--L.F. Driscoll Co., Bala-Cynwyd, PA, pg. 349
Driscoll, Peter, Chm. Bd.--Plastic Suppliers, Inc., Columbus, OH, pg. 875
Driscoll, W.J., Chm. Bd.--Dietzgen Corporation, Des Plaines, IL, pg. 337
Driver, Robert F., Chm. Bd. Emeritus--Robert F. Driver Co., Inc., San Diego, CA, pg. 349
Drobis, David R., Chm. & Chief Exec. Officer--Ketchum Public Relations/Corporate, New York, NY, pg. 625
Drumheller, Dan P., Chm. Bd.--Lane Press, Inc., South Burlington, VT, pg. 654
Drummond, Garry N., Chief Exec. Officer--Drummond Company, Inc., Jasper, AL, pg. 349
Dubin, Ronald N., Chm. Bd.--Dubin-Clark & Company, Greenwich, CT, pg. 350
DuBose, E.R., Chm. Bd.--White Electrical Construction Co., Atlanta, GA, pg. 1185
Duchossois, C.J., Chm. Bd.--Thrall Car Mfg. Co., Chicago Heights, IL, pg. 350
Duchossois, Richard L., Chm. Bd. & Chief Exec. Officer--Duchossois Industries, Inc., Elmhurst, IL, pg. 350
Duda, Edward D., Chm. Bd.--A. Duda & Sons Inc., Oviedo, FL, pg. 351
Dudek Schneider, Thersea, Chm. Bd.--Dudek & Bock Spring Manufacturing Company, Chicago, IL, pg. 351
Dudley, Dean F., Co-Chm.--Jack Lawlor Advertising, Inc., Pasadena, CA, pg. 661
Dudreck, Albert W., Chm. Bd. & Chief Exec. Officer--DDF&M Inc. Dudreck DePaul Ficco & Morgan Inc., Pittsburgh, PA, pg. 308
Duff, Charles, Chm. Bd. & Chief Exec. Officer--Farnam Companies, Inc., Phoenix, AZ, pg. 403
Duffy, E.W., Chm. Bd.--Columbus McKinnon Corp., Amherst, NY, pg. 266
Dugan, Francis R., Chm. & Chief Exec. Officer--Dugan & Meyers Interests, Inc., Cincinnati, OH, pg. 351
Dugan, Peter, Chm.--Dugan, Valva Associates, Morristown, NJ, pg. 351
Duggan, J. Roy, Chm. Bd.--King & Prince Seafood Corporation, Brunswick, GA, pg. 631
Duker, Brack, Chm. Bd.--Columbia Falls Aluminum Company, Columbia Falls, MT, pg. 265
Dunavant, W.B., Jr., Chm. Bd.--Dunavant Enterprises, Inc., Memphis, TN, pg. 352
Duncan, Dan L., Chm. Bd. & Chief Exec. Officer--Enterprise Products Company, Houston, TX, pg. 382
Duncan, Richard J., Chm. Bd.--Jerome-Duncan Ford, Sterling Heights, MI, pg. 593
Dungan, Thomas N., Chm. Bd.--Sunkist Growers, Inc., Sherman Oaks, CA, pg. 1060
Dungey, D., Sr. V.P.--Bergquist Company, Inc., Minneapolis, MN, pg. 141
Dunham, James I., Chm. Bd. & Pres.--American Liberty Financial Corp., Baton Rouge, LA, pg. 57
Dunlap, Edward B., Chm Bd., Pres., & Chief Exec. Officer--Centimark Corporation, Bethel Park, PA, pg. 231
Dunlap, Roy R., Chm. Bd.--SOR Inc., Lenexa, KS, pg. 963
Dunn, William H., Chm. Bd.--Dunn Industries Inc., Kansas City, MO, pg. 354
Dunn, William H., Chm. Bd.--J.E. Dunn Construction Co., Kansas City, MO, pg. 354
Dunne, Thomas P., Chm. Bd. & Chief Exec. Officer--Fred Weber Inc., Maryland Heights, MO, pg. 1171
Dunville, Joseph R., Chm. Bd., Pres., & Chief Exec. Officer--Idea Engineering & Fabricating, Detroit, MI, pg. 562
Dunwody, Kenneth W., Jr., Chm. Bd.--Cherokee Brick & Tile Co., Macon, GA, pg. 243
Dupey, Michael, Chm. Bd. & Chief Exec. Officer--Dupey Management Corp., Irving, TX, pg. 354
Dupuis, Frank J., Chm. Bd. & Chief Fin. Officer--Your Man Tours, Inc., Inglewood, CA, pg. 1214
Duren, David, Chm. Bd.--Nebraska Public Power District, Columbus, NE, pg. 796
Durocher, Francis W., Chm. Bd., Pres. & Treas.--Gust K. Newberg Construction Co., Chicago, IL, pg. 803
Durrett, William E., Chm. Bd., Pres. & Chief Exec. Officer--American Fidelity Corp., Oklahoma City, OK, pg. 52
Durward, John C., Chm. Bd.--Duary/J.F. Duncan Industries, Inc., Downey, CA, pg. 350
Dustman, Lloyd, Chm. & Pres.--CAC Microcircuits, Inc., Mount Carmel, IL, pg. 198
Dutmers, James E., Jr., Chm. Bd.--Empire National Bank, Traverse City, MI, pg. 379
Dworman, Alvin, Chm. Bd. & Pres.--Lee National Corporation, New York, NY, pg. 666
Dwyer, James G., Chm. Bd.--Dwyer Instruments Inc., Michigan City, IN, pg. 356
Dyer, R. Richard, Chm. Bd.--Peirce-Phelps, Inc., Philadelphia, PA, pg. 855
Dyke, James T., Chm. Bd.--Dyke Industry, Inc., Little Rock, AR, pg. 356
Dykes, Archie R., Chm. Bd.--First Pyramid Life Insurance Company of America, Little Rock, AR, pg. 1150
Dyson, Robert R., Chm. Bd.--Kearney-National, Inc., White Plains, NY, pg. 357
Dyson, Robert R., Chm. Bd.--CCC Conveyors, Inc., Dallas, TX, pg. 357
Eacott, James H., Jr., Chm. Bd.--Bartlett Brainard & Eacott, Inc., Bloomfield, CT, pg. 122
Eagle, J.M., Chm. Bd. & Chief Exec. Officer--Pipe Fabricating & Supply Company, Santa Fe Springs, CA, pg. 872
Eagle, Robert M., Chm. Bd. & Chief Exec. Officer--Eagle Lincoln Mercury Inc., Dallas, TX, pg. 362
Eaken, R. William, Chm. Bd.--R.W. Eaken, Inc., Leesport, PA, pg. 362
Eanhard, Hal J., Jr., Chm. Bd.--Earnhardt's Auto Center, Tempe, AZ, pg. 362
Earwood, J. Calvin, Chm. Bd.--Oglethorpe Power Corp., Tucker, GA, pg. 822
Easley, Dick L., Chm. Bd. & Pres.--Health America/CapitalCare, Inc., Lincoln, NE, pg. 779
Easley, Ronald L., Chm. Bd., Pres. & Chief Exec. Officer--System Planning Corp., Arlington, VA, pg. 1070
Easterly, Clark, Chm. Bd.--Johnstown Knitting Mill Co., Johnstown, NY, pg. 602
Eaton, Henry F., Chm. & Chief Exec. Officer--Dix & Eaton Incorporated, Cleveland, OH, pg. 341
Eberle, Bruce, Chm. Bd. & Chief Exec. Officer--Eberle Direct Marketing Group, Inc., Vienna, VA, pg. 365
Eby, Martin K., Chm. Bd. & Pres.--Eby Corporation, Wichita, KS, pg. 365
Eby, Martin K., Jr., Chm. Bd. & Chief Exec. Officer--Martin K. Eby Construction Company, Inc., Wichita, KS, pg. 365
Ecke, Paul, Jr., Chm. Bd.--Paul Ecke Ranch, Inc., Encinitas, CA, pg. 366
Eckhoff, Anders, Chm. Bd.--BSB Bates-Gruppen A/S, Oslo,, Norway, pg. 109
Eddins, Roy A., Chm. Bd.--Friendly Chevrolet Co. Inc., Dallas, TX, pg. 433
Edelbrock, Victor, Chm. Bd., Pres. & Chief Exec. Officer--Edelbrock Corp., Torrance, CA, pg. 367
Edelman, Irving, Chm. Bd.--Greater New York Box Co., Clifton, NJ, pg. 483
Edelstein, David, Chm. Bd. & Pres.--Edelstein Associates Advertising Inc., Seattle, WA, pg. 368
Edelstein, Sidney M., Dr., Chm. Bd.--Dexter Chemical Corp., Bronx, NY, pg. 334

Corporate Responsibilities Index

Edmonson, Allen S., Dr., Chm. Bd.--State Volunteer Mutual Insurance Co. Inc., Brentwood, TN, pg. 1041
Edmund, Norman W., Chm. Bd.--Edmund Scientific Company, Barrington, NJ, pg. 369
Edwards, James O., Chm. Bd.--Banner Associates Inc., Laramie, WY, pg. 118
Edwards, Joel, Chm. Bd. & Chief Exec. Officer--Edwards Baking Co., Atlanta, GA, pg. 369
Edwards, Merle W., Sr., Chm. Bd.--Coastal Wholesale, Inc., Kinston, NC, pg. 257
Edwards, Oral W., Chm. Bd. & Pres.--GES Inc., Marianna, AR, pg. 439
Edwards, Thomas P., Chm. Bd.--Pilot Air Freight Corp., Lima, PA, pg. 870
Edwards, William C., Chm. Bd.--Acurex Environmental Corporation, Mountain View, CA, pg. 15
Edwards, William E., Jr., Chm. Bd. & Chief Exec. Officer--Cardinal Aluminum Co., Louisville, KY, pg. 217
Egan, Michael S., Chm. Bd. & Chief Exec. Officer--Alamo Rent-A-Car Inc., Fort Lauderdale, FL, pg. 30
Eggert, Charles, Chm. Bd.--Pacific Foods, Inc., Kent, WA, pg. 840
Ehler, John, Chm. Bd.--Farmers Marketing Association, Denver, CO, pg. 704
Ehlers, William A., Chm. Bd.--Capital Development Co., Lacey, WA, pg. 215
Eichman, Frank, Chm. Bd. & Pres.--Alcom Printing Group, Inc., Bethlehem, PA, pg. 32
Eihusen, Virgil, Chm. Bd. & Chief Exec. Officer--Chief Industries, Inc., Grand Island, NE, pg. 247
Eisaman, Joe R., Chm. Emeritus--Eisaman, Johns & Laws Advertising, Inc., Los Angeles, CA, pg. 372
Eisenberg, James, Chm. Bd. & Chief Exec. Officer--Vienna Sausage Mfg. Co., Chicago, IL, pg. 1151
Eisenbrey, John R., Chm. Bd., Pres. & Chief Exec. Officer--Artesian Resources Corporation, Newark, DE, pg. 86
Eisenbrey, John R., Chm. Bd., Pres. & Chief Exec. Officer--Artesian Water Company, Inc., Newark, DE, pg. 86
Eisenstadt, Benjamin, Chm. Bd.--Cumberland Packing Corp., Brooklyn, NY, pg. 304
Eisner, Elaine B., Chm. Bd.--William Eisner & Associates Inc., Milwaukee, WI, pg. 372
Eisner, Henry W., Chm. Emeritus--Eisner & Associates, Inc., Baltimore, MD, pg. 372
Eklund, Louis, E., Jr., Chm. & Treas.--Fleet Engineers, Inc., Muskegon, MI, pg. 417
Eldon Wheeler, M.L., Chm. Bd. & Chief Exec. Officer--Jernberg Industries, Inc., Chicago, IL, pg. 593
Elias, Fred, Chm. Bd.--Elias Brothers Restaurants, Inc., Warren, MI, pg. 376
Elkman, Stanley, Chm. Bd.--Elkman Advertising & Public Relations, Bala-Cynwyd, PA, pg. 377
Elkman, Stanley, Chm.--Elkman Advertising, Public Relations Div., Bala-Cynwyd, PA, pg. 378
Ellingson, Chester W., Jr., Chm. Bd., Pres. & Chief Exec. Officer--Reese Enterprises, Inc., Rosemount, MN, pg. 920
Elliott, Robert M., Chm. Bd. & Chief Exec. Officer--LFC Holding Corporation, Boca Raton, FL, pg. 647
Elliott, Robert M., Chm. Bd. & Chief Exec. Officer--Levitz Furniture Corporation, Boca Raton, FL, pg. 647
Ellis, Frank P., IV, Chm. Bd.--Associated Equipment Company, Inc., Mobile, AL, pg. 89
Ellis, Joseph N., Chm. Bd.--LaSalle-Deitch Co., Inc., Elkhart, IN, pg. 660
Ellis, William D., Chm. Bd. & Chief Exec. Officer--Southern Mills, Inc., Union City, GA, pg. 1021
Ellis, William H., Chm. Bd., Pres. & Chief Oper. Officer--Farley Candy Company, Chicago, IL, pg. 399
Ellison, Ed, Chm. Bd.--Harvest States Cooperatives, Saint Paul, MN, pg. 514
Ellison, Ray, Chm. Bd. & Pres.--Rayco, San Antonio, TX, pg. 914
Ellstrom, Elmer, Jr., Chm. Bd. & Chief Exec. Officer--Dearborn Gage Company, Garden City, MI, pg. 322
Elman, Robert H., Chm. Bd. & Chief Exec. Officer--Desa International, Inc., Bowling Green, KY, pg. 331
Elmore, David, Chm. Bd. & Pres.--Olson-Travelworld Ltd., Manhattan Beach, CA, pg. 824
Elmquist, Ronald E., Chm. Bd. & Chief Exec. Officer--W S Holding Company, Euless, TX, pg. 1156
Elmquist, Ronald E., Chm. & Chief Exec. Officer--White Swan, Inc., Euless, TX, pg. 1156
Elsberry, Howard W., Chm., Pres. & Chief Exec. Officer--Westlake Hardware, Inc., Shawnee Mission, KS, pg. 1183
Else, Charles W., Chm. Bd.--V.G.S. Corp. d/b/a Southland Oil Company, Jackson, MS, pg. 1141
Elsperman, Robert P., P.E., Chm. Bd. & Chief Exec. Officer--Tarlton Corporation, Saint Louis, MO, pg. 1079
Emmerling, John A., Chm. Bd., Pres. & Chief Exec. Officer--John Emmerling Inc., New York, NY, pg. 379
Engel, Clyde W., Chm. Bd. & Pres.--Libco Corporation, Chicago, IL, pg. 674
Engelsma, Lloyd, Chm. Bd. & Chief Exec. Officer--Kraus-Anderson, Inc., Minneapolis, MN, pg. 644
Engelsted, J.N., Chm. Bd.--O. S. Walker Co. Inc., Worcester, MA, pg. 1160
Engelsted, John N., Chm. Bd. & Chief Exec. Officer--Walker Magnetics Group, Inc., Worcester, MA, pg. 1160
England, Jonathan S., Chm. Bd.--Devlin Lumber & Supply Corp., Rockville, MD, pg. 334
Engle, Clyde W., Chm. Bd., Pres. & Treas.--GSC Enterprises, Inc., Chicago, IL, pg. 440
Engle, Cody, Chm. Bd.--Delta Queen Steamboat Company, New Orleans, LA, pg. 385
Englefield, F.W., III, Chm. Bd.--Englefield, Inc., Newark, OH, pg. 382
Engler, Paul F., Chm. Bd. & Pres.--Cactus Feeders, Inc., Amarillo, TX, pg. 207
Eppley, Mark, Chm. & Chief Exec. Officer--Traveling Software Inc., Bothell, WA, pg. 1108
Epstein, Perez, Chm. Bd.--Perry Group, Inc., Hainesport, NJ, pg. 863
Epstein, Richard, Chm. Bd., Pres. & Chief Exec. Officer--Vesco Oil Corp., Southfield, MI, pg. 1149
Epstein, Sidney, Chm. Bd.--A. Epstein and Sons, Intl., Inc., Chicago, IL, pg. 384
Erb, Fred A., Chm., Pres. & Chief Exec. Officer--Erb Lumber Company, Birmingham, MI, pg. 360
Erdman, Marshall, Chm. Bd.--Marshall Erdman and Associates, Inc., Madison, WI, pg. 385
Erenberg, Ethan M., Chm. Bd. & Chief Exec. Officer--W. Braun Company, Chicago, IL, pg. 172
Erickson, Richard P., Chm. Bd. & Chief Exec. Officer--Lifetouch, Inc., Bloomington, MN, pg. 675
Ernst, Lois Geraci, Chm. & Chief Exec. Officer--Advertising To Women, Inc., New York, NY, pg. 21
Ershig, A. Herbert, Chm. Bd.--Ershigs, Inc., Bellingham, WA, pg. 387
Erskine, John E., Sr., Chm. Bd.--Racine Federated, Inc., Racine, WI, pg. 909
Escobar, Frank, Chm. & Gen. Mgr.--Joffko Philippines, Inc., Rizal,, Philippines, pg. 595
Eskandarian, Ed, Chm. & Chief Exec. Officer--Arnold Fortuna Lawner & Cabot, Boston, MA, pg. 84
Essig, Armand J., Chm. Bd. & Chief Exec. Officer--Allied Sporting Goods Inc., Louisville, KY, pg. 40
Essig, Otto, Chm. Bd.--Berkshire Industries, Inc., Westfield, MA, pg. 142
Estenson, Noel K., Chm. Bd.--National Cooperative Refinery Association, McPherson, KS, pg. 787
Estes, Alexandra H., Chm. Bd. & Pres.--Haeger Industries, Inc., Dundee, IL, pg. 499
Estes, Robey W., Sr., Chm. Bd. & Chief Exec. Officer--Estes Express Lines, Inc., Richmond, VA, pg. 389
Estopinal, Fred N., Jr., Chm. Bd.--MCC Group, Inc., Metairie, LA, pg. 691
Estrada, Jairo A., Chm. Bd. & Chief Exec. Officer--Garden Way, Inc., Troy, NY, pg. 443
Etkin, Alex J., Chm. Bd.--Alex J. Etkin, Inc., Farmington Hills, MI, pg. 389
Ettleson, Richard, Chm. Bd. & Pres.--Electro Brand, Inc., Chicago, IL, pg. 374
Eugene, Christie, Chm. Bd.--Credit Union National Association, Madison, WI, pg. 298
Eulich, John F., Chm. Bd. & Chief Exec. Officer--Vantage Companies, Dallas, TX, pg. 1145
Evans, J.C., Chm. Bd.--Gold Medal Products Co., Cincinnati, OH, pg. 465
Evans, Robert B., Sr., Chm. Bd. & Chief Exec. Officer--Evans Industries, Inc., Detroit, MI, pg. 390
Evans, Stewart E., Chm. Bd.--Stu Evans Lincoln-Mercury Inc., Southgate, MI, pg. 390
Evers, C.K., Chm. Bd.--Quality Bakers of America Cooperative, Inc., Greenwich, CT, pg. 903
Ewing, Al, Pres.--Cajun Electric Power Co-op, Baton Rouge, LA, pg. 207
Ezell, F. Miles, Sr., Chm. Bd.--Purity Dairies Inc., Nashville, TN, pg. 901
Faber, Esther, Chm. Bd.--Faber Enterprises, Inc., Canoga Park, CA, pg. 395
Fabick, John, Chm. Bd.--John Fabick Tractor Company, Fenton, MO, pg. 396
Fagan, Robert, Chm. Bd. & Pres.--Audio Specialist, Inc., Newington, CT, pg. 98
Fahlbush, Helmut, Chm. Bd.--Gemtron Corporation, Sweetwater, TN, pg. 3
Fail, James M., Chm. Bd. & Chief Exec. Officer--The Chesapeake Life Insurance Co., Lincoln, NE, pg. 243
Fain, John H., Chm., Pres., Chief Exec. & Chief Oper. Officer--Metro Information Services, Virginia Beach, VA, pg. 743
Fain, Norman M, Chm. Bd.--Teknor Apex Company, Pawtucket, RI, pg. 1084
Fain, Richard, Chm. Bd. & Chief Exec. Officer--Royal Caribbean Cruises Ltd., Miami, FL, pg. 953
Fairchild, Marcia, Chm. Bd.--Handy Wacks Corporation, Sparta, MI, pg. 505
Faith, Marshall E., Chm. Bd. & Chief Exec. Officer--The Scoular Company, Omaha, NE, pg. 983
Faller, Robert O., Chm. Bd., Pres.--FKQ Advertising Inc., Clearwater, FL, pg. 394
Falls, Glenn, Chm. Bd.--Pay Less Super Markets, Inc., Anderson, IN, pg. 852
Farber, John J., Dr., Chm. Bd.--ICC Industries, Inc., New York, NY, pg. 558
Farkas, Andrew L., Chm. & Chief Exec. Officer--Insignia Financial Group, Inc., Greenville, SC, pg. 571
Farley, James B., Chm. Bd.--The Mutual Life Insurance Company of New York (MONY), New York, NY, pg. 778
Farley, James N., Chm. Bd.--SpeedFam Corporation, Des Plaines, IL, pg. 398
Farley, William, Chm. Bd. & Chief Exec. Officer--West Point-Pepperell, Inc., West Point, GA, pg. 400
Farley, William F., Chm. Bd. & Chief Exec. Officer--Farley Industries, Chicago, IL, pg. 399
Farnsworth, Ken, Chm. Bd. & Pres.--Rhodes International, Inc., Salt Lake City, UT, pg. 931
Farver, Herb, Chm. Bd. & Pres.--Blissfield Manufacturing Company, Blissfield, MI, pg. 157
Farver, Joan, Co.-Chm. Bd.--Pella Corporation, Pella, IA, pg. 856
Fattaleh, Daniel L., Chm. Bd., Pres., Chief Exec. Officer & Treas.--The Delphi Glass Corp. Delphi Stained Glass Centers, Lansing, MI, pg. 326
Fawcett, Dr. Sherwood, Chm. Bd.--Transmet Corporation, Columbus, OH, pg. 1107
Fayfield, Robert, Pres., Chief Exec. Officer & Chm. Bd.--Banner Engineering Corp., Minneapolis, MN, pg. 118
Feathers, Vaughn, Chm. Bd. & Chief Exec. Officer--Avadyne, Inc., Monterey, CA, pg. 101
Fehr, William H., Chm. Bd. & Chief Exec. Officer--Berks Products Corporation, Reading, PA, pg. 142
Fehsenfeld, Frank B., Chm. Bd.--Crystal Flash Petroleum Corp., Indianapolis, IN, pg. 303
Feinberg, H., Chm. Bd.--I. Appel Corporation, New York, NY, pg. 78
Feinberg, Harry, Chm. Bd.--Duron, Inc., Beltsville, MD, pg. 355
Felker, G. Stephen, Chm. Bd. & Chief Exec. Officer--Avondale Mills, Inc., Sylacauga, AL, pg. 103
Fellowes, John, Chm. & Chief Exec. Officer--Fellowes Manufacturing Co., Itasca, IL, pg. 405
Felts, Richard E., Chm. Bd.--Hamilton Mutual Insurance Company Of Cincinnati, Cincinnati, OH, pg. 503
Ferguson, Ronald T., Chm. Bd.--Hamlin, Inc., Lake Mills, WI, pg. 503
Ferman, James L., Sr., Chm. Bd.--Ferman Oldsmobile, Tampa, FL, pg. 406
Fermon, Joseph C., Chm. Bd. & Chief Exec. Officer--Continental Eagle Corporation, Prattville, AL, pg. 278
Fern, Saul Alden, Chm. Bd. & Chief Exec. Officer--Fitzgerald & Company, Inc., Cranston, RI, pg. 416
Fernandez, Carlos C., Chm., Pres. & Chief Exec. Officer--Purity, Inc., Miami, FL, pg. 901
Ferrell, James E., Chm. Bd., Pres. & Chief Exec. Officer--Ferrell Companies Inc./Ferrellgas, Liberty, MO, pg. 407
Ferry, Richard M., Chm. Bd., Pres. & Chief Exec. Officer--Korn/Ferry International, Los Angeles, CA, pg. 642
Fesler, John L., Chm. Bd.--Lampert Yards, Inc., Saint Paul, MN, pg. 653
Fetter, Jane T., Chm. Bd. & Sec.--Kettenburg Marine Corporation, San Diego, CA, pg. 626
Fetterman, Annabelle L., Chm. Bd. & Chief Exec. Officer--Lundy Packing Co. Inc., Clinton, NC, pg. 687
Fiedler, Louis P., Chm. Bd.--Admiral Maintenance Service L.P., Lincolnwood, IL, pg. 18
Fiedler, Paula P., Chm. Bd. & Sec.--Crown Fence Co., Pasadena, CA, pg. 302
Field, Eli, Chm. Bd.--Field Container Company, L.P., Elk Grove Village, IL, pg. 409
Field, Robert E., Chm. Bd.--Great Lakes Financial Resources, Inc., Homewood, IL, pg. 481
Field, Robert E., Chm. Bd.--First National Bank of Blue Island, Blue Island, IL, pg. 481
Field, Robert E., Chm. Bd.--Community Bank of Homewood-Flossmoor, Homewood, IL, pg. 481
Field, Robert E., Chm. Bd.--Bank of Homewood, Homewood, IL, pg. 481
Field, Thomas W., Chm. Bd.--Abco Markets, Inc., Phoenix, AZ, pg. 10
Fields, Debra, Chm. Bd., Pres. & Chief Exec. Officer--Mrs. Fields' Inc., Park City, UT, pg. 761
Fields, Randall, Chm. Bd.--La Petite Boulangerie, Inc., Park City, UT, pg. 761
Fife, Kay, Vice Chm.--Cogsdill Tool Products, Inc., Lugoff, SC, pg. 259
Fike, Lester L., Jr., Chm. Bd. & Chief Exec. Officer--Fike Corporation, Blue Springs, MO, pg. 409
Filler, Gary, Chm Bd. & Chief Exec. Officer--Burke Industries, Inc., San Jose, CA, pg. 191
Filler, Gary, Chm. Bd. & Chief Exec. Officer--Burke Industries Inc., San Jose, CA, pg. 190
Filter, Patrick S., Chm. Bd.--Harrington & King, Chicago, IL, pg. 511
Fimbel, Edward, Jr., Chm. Bd. & Pres.--Fimbel Door Corporation, Whitehouse, NJ, pg. 409
Findlay, Cary, Chm. Bd. & Pres.--Conso Products Company, Union, SC, pg. 276
Fine, Leo, Chm. Bd.--M. Fine & Sons Manufacturing Co., Inc., New York, NY, pg. 411
Fine, Ralph, Chm. Bd.--Triangle Maintenance Corporation, Valley Stream, NY, pg. 1112
Fink, H. Bernerd, Chm. Bd.--CGF Industries, Topeka, KS, pg. 201
Finkelstein, Harold R., Chm. Bd.--Hughes-Treitler Manufacturing Corporation, Garden City, NY, pg. 552
Finkl, Charles W., Chm. Bd.--A. Finkl & Sons Co., Chicago, IL, pg. 411
Finlayson, John, Chm. Bd.--Louis Dreyfus Corporation, Wilton, CT, pg. 348
Finlayson, John, Chm. Bd.--Louis Dreyfus Natural Gas, Oklahoma City, OK, pg. 349
Finn, David, Chm. Bd. & Chief Exec. Officer--Ruder, Finn, Inc., New York, NY, pg. 954
Finn, E.J., Chm. Bd.--Dorr-Oliver Incorporated, Milford, CT, pg. 346
Finn, Peter, Chief Fin. Officer & Chm. Exec. Committee--Ruder, Finn, Inc., New York, NY, pg. 954
Finnegan, Lawrence J., Chm., Pres., Chief Exec. & Chief Oper. Officer--Boston Mutual Life Insurance Co., Canton, MA, pg. 167
Fioroni, Daniel J., Chm. Bd.--Thermal Technology Industries, N. Kansas City, MO, pg. 1091
Fischer, George, Chm. Bd.--Goodheart-Willcox Co., Inc., South Holland, IL, pg. 470
Fischer, Harry A., Jr., Chm. Bd.--Daubert Industries, Inc., Westchester, IL, pg. 317
Fischer, James M., Jr., Chm. Bd.--Standard Candy Co., Inc., Nashville, TN, pg. 1035
Fisher, Alfred J., Jr., Chm. Bd.--General Safety Corporation, Saint Clair Shores, MI, pg. 450
Fisher, Jerome, Chm. Bd.--Nine West Group, Inc., Stamford, CT, pg. 807
Fisher, John E., Gen. Chm.--Employers Insurance of Wausau a Mutual Co., Wausau, WI, pg. 380
Fisher, John E., Gen. Chm. & Chief Exec. Officer--Nationwide Mutual Insurance Company, Columbus, OH, pg. 795
Fisher, John E., Gen. Chm.--Employers Insurance of Wausau a Mutual Co., Wausau, WI, pg. 795
Fisher, John E., Gen. Chm.--Nationwide Corporation, Columbus, OH, pg. 795
Fisher, Mike, Sr., Chm. Bd.--Fisher Graphic Industries, Modesto, CA, pg. 415
Fisher, Paul C., Chm. Bd.--Fisher Pen Company, Franklin Park, IL, pg. 415
Fisher, Steven A., Chm. Bd. & Chief Exec. Officer--Brown & Caldwell Consulting Engineers, Pleasant Hill, CA, pg. 181

Fisher, Thomas Scott, Chm. Bd. & Chief Exec. Officer--Samelson-Leon Company, Inc., Memphis, TN, pg. 968
Fishman, Alan H., Co-Chm.--Best Products Co., Inc., Richmond, VA, pg. 17
Fishman, Bernard, Chm.-Exec. Committee--Fishman & Tobin, Inc., Philadelphia, PA, pg. 415
Fitch, David H., Chm. Bd.--Rugg Manufacturing Company, Greenfield, MA, pg. 955
Fitzgibbons, James M., Chm. Bd.--Howes Leather Company, Inc., Quincy, MA, pg. 548
Fizdale, Richard B., Chm. & Chief Exec. & Creative Officer--Leo Burnett Company, Inc., Chicago, IL, pg. 191
Flaherty, Lee, Chm. & Chief Exec. Officer--Flair Communications Agency, Inc., New York, NY, pg. 416
Flaherty, Lee F., Chm Bd. & Chief Exec. Officer--Flair Communications Agency, Inc., Chicago, IL, pg. 416
Flaherty, William E., Chm. Bd. & Chief Exec. Officer--Horsehead Industries, Inc., New York, NY, pg. 545
Flaherty, William E., Chm. Bd.--Great Lakes Carbon Corp., Briarcliff Manor, NY, pg. 545
Flanders, Don H., Chm. Bd.--Flanders Industries, Inc., Fort Smith, AR, pg. 416
Fleischaker, Frank W., Chm. Bd.--Paramount Foods Inc., Louisville, KY, pg. 848
Fleischli, Gus, Chm. Bd.--Fleischli Oil Company, Inc., Cheyenne, WY, pg. 417
Fleming, Mark Jack, Chm. Bd., Pres. & Chief Exec. Officer--Merchants Publishing Co., Kalamazoo, MI, pg. 739
Fleming, Thomas, Chm. Bd.--National Truck Leasing System, Oakbrook Terrace, IL, pg. 794
Fletcher, Art, Chm. Bd.--Straw Hat Cooperative Corp., Dublin, CA, pg. 1053
Fletcher, Dugald, Chm. Bd.--Binning's Building Products, Inc., Lexington, NC, pg. 151
Fletcher, James H., Chm. & Chief Exec. Officer--J. H. Fletcher & Co., Huntington, WV, pg. 418
Fletcher, Susan, Chm. Bd. & Pres.--Suzannah Farms, Pennsauken, NJ, pg. 1065
Flint, Robert H., Chm. Bd. & Chief Exec. Officer--Flint Ink Corp., Detroit, MI, pg. 419
Floathe, Maury, Chm. Bd. & Pres.--Floathe Johnson Associates, Inc., Kirkland, WA, pg. 419
Flodstrom, Sven G., Chm. Bd.--Flodstrom Construction Co., Deerfield, IL, pg. 419
Flood, Earl F., Chm. Bd.--The Flood Company, Hudson, OH, pg. 419
Floren, David, Chm. & Chief Exec. Officer--Martin Williams Advertising Inc., Minneapolis, MN, pg. 1191
Flori, Robert D., Chm. Bd. & Treas.--Flori Corp., Phoenix, AZ, pg. 420
Flowers, D.F., Chm. Bd.--Difco, Inc., Findlay, OH, pg. 337
Flowers, J. Russell, Chm. Bd.--Central States Diversified, Inc., Saint Louis, MO, pg. 234
Flummerfelt, J. Kent, Pres., Chief Exec. Officer & Chm.--Lechmere, Inc., Woburn, MA, pg. 665
Flynn, Timothy P., Chm. Bd. & Chief Exec. Officer--WestAir Holding Inc., Fresno, CA, pg. 1178
Foil, Martin B., Jr., Chm. Bd. & Chief Exec. Officer--Tuscarora Yarns Inc., Mount Pleasant, NC, pg. 1120
Foley, Paul J., Chm. Bd.--Foley Holding Company, Inc., Wichita, KS, pg. 422
Foley, Thomas C., Chm. Bd.--T.B. Wood's Sons Company, Chambersburg, PA, pg. 1200
Foley, Thomas H., Chm. Bd.--The Bibb Company, Macon, GA, pg. 781
Foley, Vicky L., Chm. Bd. & Pres.--V.F. Energies, Inc., Madisonville, KY, pg. 1141
Folger, Lee M., Chm. Bd.--Folger Nolan Fleming Douglas, Washington, DC, pg. 422
Follett, Robert J., Chm. Bd.--Follett Corporation, Chicago, IL, pg. 422
Fontenot, M.L., Chm. Bd. & Pres.--Perfect Fit Industries, Inc., Monroe, NC, pg. 861
Footer, Harold, Chm. Bd. & Chief Exec. Officer--Easy Day Manufacturing Company, Inc., Holliston, MA, pg. 364
Ford, J. Frank, Chm. Bd.--Arrowhead Mills, Inc., Hereford, TX, pg. 86
Ford, James Curtis, Chm. Bd.--Ford Steel Co., Inc., Maryland Heights, MO, pg. 423
Ford, John L., Jr., Chm. Bd.--Ford Meter Box Company, Wabash, IN, pg. 423
Ford, Kenneth, Chm. Bd.--Roseburg Forest Products Co., Dillard, OR, pg. 948
Forgione, Anthony, Chm. Bd. & Pres.--Boyer Bros. Inc., Altoona, PA, pg. 169
Forman, Barry, Chm. Bd.--Forman Brothers, Inc., Washington, DC, pg. 424
Forsythe, Gerald, Chm. Bd., Pres. & Chief Exec. Officer--Indeck Power Equipment Company, Wheeling, IL, pg. 564
Fortgang, Charles, Co.-Chm. Bd.--M. Fabrikant & Sons, Inc., New York, NY, pg. 396
Foss, Joseph E., Chm. Bd. & Chief Exec Officer--First American Bank, N.A., Washington, D.C., Washington, DC, pg. 412
Fossel, Jon A., Chm. Bd. & Chief Exec. Officer--Oppenheimer Management Corp., New York, NY, pg. 719
Foster, E.L., Chm. Bd.--Foster-Miller, Inc., Waltham, MA, pg. 426
Foster, John H., Chm. Bd.--Malcolm Pirnie, Inc., White Plains, NY, pg. 872
Foster, L.B., Chm. Bd.--Summit Corporation of America, Thomaston, CT, pg. 1058
Foster, Thomas, Chm. Bd. & Chief Exec. Officer--Foster & Gallagher Inc., Peoria, IL, pg. 426
Foster, Wm. B., Jr., Chm. Bd.--Hardwick Clothes Inc., Cleveland, TN, pg. 508
Fotheringham, Robert S., Chm.--Fotheringham & Associates, Salt Lake City, UT, pg. 427
Fowler, Earl B., Vice Adm., Chm. Bd.--SPD Technologies, Philadelphia, PA, pg. 963
Fowler, Frederick V., Jr., Chm. Bd., Pres. & Chief Exec. Officer--Fred V. Fowler Company, Inc., Newton, MA, pg. 427
Fox, Herbert C., Chm. Bd., Pres., Chief Exec. Officer & Dir.-Pub. Rels.--Active Electrical Supply Company, Chicago, IL, pg. 15
Fox, J.L., Chm. Bd.--Republic Industries, Inc., Harwood Heights, IL, pg. 928
Fox, John E., Sr., Chm. Bd.--Arkansas Oak Flooring, Pine Bluff, AR, pg. 83
Fox, John, Jr., Chm.--Doran Textiles Inc., Shelby, NC, pg. 346
Fox, John, Jr., Chm. Bd.--Doran Mill Co., Shelby, NC, pg. 346
Fox, Martin, Chm. Bd.--Deerskin Trading Post, Inc., Carlstadt, NJ, pg. 324
Fox, Sam, Chm. Bd. & Chief Exec. Officer--Harbour Group Ltd., Clayton, MO, pg. 506
Fox, Wayne F., Chm. Bd. & Chief Exec. Officer--Triple F, Inc., Des Moines, IA, pg. 1114
Fraenkel, Albert, Chm. Bd.--Fraenkel Company, Baton Rouge, LA, pg. 428
Franco, Anthony M., Chm. & Chief Exec. Officer--Anthony M. Franco Inc., Detroit, MI, pg. 950
Frandsen, Dennis, Chm. Bd. & Owner--Plastech Corporation, Forest Lake, MN, pg. 874
Frank, Elaine S., Chm. Bd.--Frank Consolidated Enterprises Inc., Des Plaines, IL, pg. 428
Frank, Richard N., Chm. & Chief Exec. Officer--Lawry's Restaurants, Inc., Los Angeles, CA, pg. 663
Frank, Ronald R., Chm. Bd. & Chief Exec. Officer--Frank Industries, Inc., Brown City, MI, pg. 429
Frankel, Bernard, Chm. & Chief Exec. Officer--Frankel & Company, Chicago, IL, pg. 429
Frankfurt, Steve, Chm.--Frankfurt Gips Balkind, Advertising, New York, NY, pg. 429
Franklin, E. Thomas, Chm., Pres. & Treas.--Franklin Baking Co., Inc., Goldsboro, NC, pg. 429
Franklin, Irving H., Chm. Bd. & Treas.--Franklin Sports Industries, Stoughton, MA, pg. 429
Franzen, Gayle M., Chm. Bd.--Regional Transportation Authority (RTA), Chicago, IL, pg. 922
Frazer, Nimrod T., Chm. & Pres.--The Enstar Group, Inc., Montgomery, AL, pg. 382
Frazier, John L.D., Chm. Bd. & Chief Exec. Officer--Full Service Beverage Company, Wichita, KS, pg. 436
Frazier, Richard M., Acting Chm. Bd. & Pres.--Hickman Williams & Co. Inc., Cincinnati, OH, pg. 532
Freedman, Eugene M., Chm. Bd. & Chief Exec. Officer--Coopers & Lybrand, New York, NY, pg. 283
Freeman, Carl M., Chm. Bd. & Chief Exec. Officer--Carl M. Freeman Associates, Inc., Potomac, MD, pg. 431
Freeman, D.S., Jr., Chm. Bd. & Chief Exec. Officer--Freeman Decorating Co., Dallas, TX, pg. 431
Freidheim, Edgar, Chm. Bd.--Cougle Commission Company, Inc., Chicago, IL, pg. 289
Frem, George N., Chm. Bd. & Chief Exec. Office--Interstate Resources, Inc., Rosslyn, VA, pg. 580
French, Morton R., Chm. Bd., Pres., Chief Exec. & Chief Fin. Officer--Commercial Plastics & Supplies Corp., Richmond Hill, NY, pg. 268
Freston, Tom, Chm. & Chief Exec. Officer-MTV Networks--Viacom Inc., New York, NY, pg. 785
Freundlich, Richard L., Chm. & Chief Exec. Officer--Bridal Originals, Inc., Collinsville, IL, pg. 175
Frey, Dale F., Chm. Bd. & Pres.--General Electric Master Retirement Trust, Stamford, CT, pg. 449
Frey, Eugene U., Chm. Bd. & Chief Exec. Officer--Waldorf Corporation, Saint Paul, MN, pg. 1159
Frey, John S., Chm. Bd. & Pres.--John S. Frey Enterprises, Los Angeles, CA, pg. 433
Fribourg, Michel, Chm. Bd.--Continental Grain Company, New York, NY, pg. 279
Fricchione, Frank, Chm. Bd.--Simplex Industries, Inc., Scranton, PA, pg. 1006
Fried, Herbert D., Chm. of Exec. Committee--W.B. Doner & Company, Southfield, MI, pg. 344
Friedl, Donald G., Chm. Bd., Pres. & Chief Exec. Officer--All Seasons Services, Inc., Braintree, MA, pg. 35
Friedlander, Alfred L., Chm. Bd. & Chief Exec. Officer--Rice Food Markets Inc., Houston, TX, pg. 931
Friedman, Irwin, Chm. Bd.--Friedman, Eisenstein, Raemer & Schwartz, Chicago, IL, pg. 433
Friedman, Isidore, Chm. Bd.--S. Rothchild & Co., Inc., New York, NY, pg. 951
Friedman, Steven M., Chm. Bd. & Chief Exec. Officer--JPS Textile Group, Inc., Greenville, SC, pg. 586
Friedson, Belvin, Chm. Bd.--Freeson Advertising Agency, Miami Lakes, FL, pg. 431
Friel, Wm. J., Chm. Bd.--Southtec, Inc., Albany, NY, pg. 1019
Frietsch, Herman, Chm. Bd.--Savage Arms Inc., Westfield, MA, pg. 973
Fritz, Lynn C., Chm. Bd., Pres. & Chief Exec. Officer--Fritz Companies, Inc., San Francisco, CA, pg. 434
Frohlich, Marie Bommer, Chm. Bd.--Bommer Industries, Inc., Landrum, SC, pg. 164
Fruman, Albert, Chm. Bd.--Dale Industries Inc., Dearborn, MI, pg. 312
Fuchs, Bernard, Chm. Bd., Pres. & Chief Exec. Officer--Specialty Retailers, Inc., Houston, TX, pg. 1029
Fuerbach, W.F., Jr., Chm. Bd., Pres. & Treas.--S. M. Frank & Co., Inc., Peekskill, NY, pg. 429
Fugazy, William D., Chm. Bd.--Fugazy International Corporation, New York, NY, pg. 435
Fukunaga, George J., Chm. Bd. & Chief Exec. Officer--Servco Pacific Inc., Honolulu, HI, pg. 991
Fuldner, William Terry, Chm. Bd. & Chief Exec. Officer--Efco Corporation, Monett, MO, pg. 359
Fultz, William J., Chm.--Creswell, Munsell, Fultz & Zirbel, Cedar Rapids, IA, pg. 1211
Fumagali, Luigi, Chm. Bd.--The Dee Howard Company, San Antonio, TX, pg. 547
Funk, Robert, Chm. Bd. & Chief Exec. Officer--Johnstown Corporation, Johnstown, PA, pg. 601
Furman, John R., Chm. Bd.--Furman Lumber Company, Billerica, MA, pg. 436
Fusz, Louis, Chm. Bd.--Lou Fusz Automotive Network, Saint Louis, MO, pg. 437
Futterman, Jack, Chm. Bd., Pres. & Chief Exec. Officer--Supermarkets General Corporation, Woodbridge, NJ, pg. 1064
Futterman, Jack, Chm. Bd., Pres. & Chief Exec. Officer--Pathmark, Woodbridge, NJ, pg. 1064
Gabbert, James D., Chm. Bd., Pres. & Chief Exec. Officer--Gabbert's, Inc., Minneapolis, MN, pg. 441
Gable, Robert E., Chm. Bd.--Stearns Enterprises, Inc., Lexington, KY, pg. 1043
Gabriel, George S., Chm. Bd.--Bio Medic Corporation, Maywood, NJ, pg. 152
Gaby, Dan, Chm. & Chief Exec. Officer--Keyes Martin, Springfield, NJ, pg. 627
Gaeke, Harry F., Chm. Bd., Chief Exec. & Fin. Officer--Shook National Corporation, Dayton, OH, pg. 1000
Gaeke, Harry F., Chm. Bd. & Chief Fin. Officer--Shook, Inc., Dayton, OH, pg. 1000
Gaffney, Tom, Chm. Bd.--Component Technology Corp., Erie, PA, pg. 270
Gaffney, Tom, Chm. Bd.--R & R Plastics, Swanton, OH, pg. 270
Gage, Edwin C., Vice Chm.--Carlson Companies, Inc., Minneapolis, MN, pg. 220
Gage, Edwin C., Chm. & Chief Exec. Officer--Gage Marketing Group, Minneapolis, MN, pg. 441
Gai, Phillip, Chm. Bd.--Langendorf Baking Company Of Seattle, Inc., Seattle, WA, pg. 441
Gai, Phillip H., Chm. Bd.--Gai's Seattle French Baking Co., Inc., Seattle, WA, pg. 441
Gal, Kenneth, Chm., Chief Exec. Officer--Italia/Gal Advertising, Los Angeles, CA, pg. 582
Galanis, Terry S., Sr., Chm. Bd.--Sealing Devices Inc., Lancaster, NY, pg. 984
Galardi, John N., Chm. Bd.--Galardi Group, Inc., Newport Beach, CA, pg. 441
Galbraith, J.C., Jr., Chm. Bd.--Foxworth-Galbraith Lumber Co., Dallas, TX, pg. 428
Galesi, Francesco, Chm. Bd., Pres. & Chief Exec. Officer--Rotterdam Ventures Inc., Guilderland Center, NY, pg. 951
Gallagher, Charles P., Chm. Bd. & Chief Exec. Officer--Applied Industrial Materials Corporation, Deerfield, IL, pg. 79
Gallo, Ernest, Chm. Bd.--E & J Gallo Winery, Modesto, CA, pg. 441
Gallo, Ernest, Chm. Bd.--Bartles & Jaymes, Modesto, CA, pg. 442
Gallucci, John, Chm. Bd., Pres. & Treas.--Concrete Construction Company, Columbus, OH, pg. 273
Galuten, Jerry, Chm. Bd. & Pres.--SGD International Corp., New York, NY, pg. 962
Games, Donald W., Chm. Bd.--Production Machinery Corporation, Mentor, OH, pg. 893
Gans, Robert J., Chm. Bd. & Pres.--Gans Ink & Supply Company, Inc., Los Angeles, CA, pg. 442
Gant, Edmund R., Chm. Bd. & Sec.--Glen Raven Mills, Inc., Glen Raven, NC, pg. 461
Gant, Roger, Jr., Chm.-Exec. Committee--Glen Raven Mills, Inc., Glen Raven, NC, pg. 461
Garay, Charles J., Chm. Bd. & Pres.--Laminaire Corporation, Rahway, NJ, pg. 652
Garberg, Dennis, Chm. Bd. & Chief Exec. Officer--The Sunflower Group, Overland Park, KS, pg. 1060
Garcia-Serra, Al, Chm. & Chief Exec. Officer--GS&B-Lintas Advertising, Coral Gables, FL, pg. 440
Garcia, Antonio, Chm. Bd.--Chemoil, San Francisco, CA, pg. 242
Gardiner, Scott, Chm. Bd., Pres., Chief Exec. & Chief Oper. Officer--Gardiner Metal Company, Chicago, IL, pg. 443
Gardini, Fausto, Chm.--Ayer Milano, Milan,, Italy, pg. 104
Gardner, Bernell Dale, Chm. Bd.--Penninsular Meat Company, Inc., Tampa, FL, pg. 858
Gardner, Betty A., Co-Chm. Bd. & Sec.--Soft Sheen Products, Inc., Chicago, IL, pg. 1016
Gardner, Edward G., Chm. Bd. & Chief Exec. Officer--Soft Sheen Products, Inc., Chicago, IL, pg. 1016
Gardner, Richard W., Chm. Bd.--Calumet Construction Corporation, Hammond, IN, pg. 211
Garman, M.L., Chm. Bd.--ECP Incorporated, Westchester, IL, pg. 317
Garney, Charles A., Chm. Bd.--Garney Holding Company, Inc., Kansas City, MO, pg. 443
Garrison, Morrow, Vice Chm.--CRL, Inc., Des Plaines, IL, pg. 203
Garrison, Morrow, Vice Chm.--International Metals & Machines, Inc., Des Plaines, IL, pg. 203
Garrison, Richard C., Chm. & Chief Exec. Officer--Ingalls, Quinn & Johnson, Boston, MA, pg. 567
Garrison, T. Paul, Chm., Chief Exec. Officer--Garrison-Lontine Advertising, Denver, CO, pg. 443
Gartner, Gideon I., Chm. Bd.--Gartner Group, Inc., Stamford, CT, pg. 443
Garvey, James S., Chm. Bd.--Garvey Elevators Inc., Hutchinson, KS, pg. 443
Garvey, John, Chm. Bd. & Chief Exec. Officer--Petroleum Inc., Wichita, KS, pg. 865
Garvey, Willard W., Chm. Bd., Pres. & Chief Exec. Officer--Garvey Industries, Inc., Wichita, KS, pg. 443
Garvey, Willard W., Chm. Bd. & Chief Exec. Officer--Petroleum, Inc., Wichita, KS, pg. 444
Garvin, David, Chm. Bd.--Camping World Holdings, Inc., Bowling Green, KY, pg. 213
Gary, Samuel, Chm. Bd.--The Gary-Williams Company, Denver, CO, pg. 444
Gates, Charles C., Chm. Bd. & Chief Exec. Officer--The Gates Corporation, Denver, CO, pg. 445
Gates, Charles C., Chm. Bd. & Chief Exec. Officer--The Gates Rubber Company, Denver, CO, pg. 445

Gates, Milo S., Chm. Bd. & Chief Exec. Officer--Swinerton & Walberg Co., San Francisco, CA, pg. 1068
Gaugler, Richard L., Chm. Bd.--Macklanburg-Duncan Co., Oklahoma City, OK, pg. 697
Gaylord, Edward G., Chm. Bd.--Gaylord Entertainment Co., Nashville, TN, pg. 446
Gaylord, Edward L., Chm. Bd. & Chief Exec. Officer--Gaylord Broadcasting Co., Dallas, TX, pg. 446
Gaylord, Edward L., Chm. Bd.--Opryland USA, Inc., Nashville, TN, pg. 446
Gee, Norman D., Chm. Bd. & Chief Exec. Officer--Atlas Van Lines, Inc., Evansville, IN, pg. 96
Gee, Robert, Chm. Bd.--Cass-Clay Creamery, Fargo, ND, pg. 228
Geiger, Arthur R., Chm. Bd.--Haden, Inc., Madison Heights, MI, pg. 499
Geiger, Raymond A., Chm. Bd.--Geiger Brothers, Lewiston, ME, pg. 447
Geiger, Thomas B., Chm. Bd.--Capital Tire, Inc., Toledo, OH, pg. 215
Geller, Ehud, Dr., Chm. & Chief Exec. Officer--Mennen Medical Inc., Clarence, NY, pg. 739
Geller, Frank W., Chm. Bd. & Chief Exec. Officer--Integrated Resources, Inc., New York, NY, pg. 573
Geller, Sheldon, Chm. Bd.--Key Food Stores Co-operative, Inc., Brooklyn, NY, pg. 626
Geller, Stephen L., Chm. & Chief Exec. Officer--CSI International Corporation, New York, NY, pg. 205
Geller, Sue, Chm. Bd. & New Bus. Contact--Stephen L. Geller Inc., New York, NY, pg. 447
Gellerstedt, L.L., Jr., Chm. Bd.--Beers Construction Company, Atlanta, GA, pg. 132
Geneen, Harold, Chm. Bd.--Finlay Enterprises, Inc., New York, NY, pg. 411
Genova, Joseph, Chm. & Chief Exec. Officer--Genova Hartwick Juliano, Inc., Greenwich, CT, pg. 452
Genshaft, Neil, Chm. Bd. & Chief Exec. Officer--Fresh Mark, Inc., Massillon, OH, pg. 432
Gentine, Leonard A., Sr., Chm. Bd.--Sargento Incorporated, Plymouth, WI, pg. 971
Gentine, Leonard A., Sr., Chm. Bd.--Sargento Cheese Co., Plymouth, WI, pg. 971
Gentry, Jack T., Chm. Bd. & Pres.--Positronic Industries, Inc., Springfield, MO, pg. 881
Gentry, Marvin D., Chm. Bd. & Pres.--New Fortis Corp., King, NC, pg. 800
George, Boyd, Chm. & Chief Exec. Officer--Alex Lee, Inc., Hickory, NC, pg. 33
George, Boyd, Chm. Bd.--Lowe's Food Stores, Inc., Winston-Salem, NC, pg. 33
George, Daniel, Chm. Bd.--Georgie Boy Manufacturing, Inc., Edwardsburg, MI, pg. 453
George, Ernest, Chm. Bd.--Southern California Bancorp, Laguna Beach, CA, pg. 1020
George, Ernest, Chm.--First American Capital Bank, Laguna Beach, CA, pg. 1020
George, Sharkey T., Chm. Bd.--Melody Foods, Inc., Farmington Hills, MI, pg. 738
Georgine, Robert A., Chm., Pres. & Chief Exec. Officer--ULLICO Inc., Washington, DC, pg. 1124
Georgoulis, Strattcn, Chm. Bd., Pres. & Chief Exec. Officer--TIC United Corporation, Dallas, TX, pg. 1073
Gerchenson, Emile H., Chm. Bd. & Chief Exec. Officer--Alva/Amco Pharmacal Companies, Inc., Chicago, IL, pg. 46
Gerdy, Harvey, Chm. Bd., Pres. & Chief Exec. Officer--International Seaway Trading Corporation, Mayfield Village, OH, pg. 579
Gerken, Edward, Chm. Bd. & Pres.--Norwalk Furniture Corporation, Norwalk, OH, pg. 816
Gerlach, Lloyd A., Chm. Bd.--Stolper-Fabralloy Co., Waukesha, WI, pg. 1050
Gerrity, J. Frank, II, Chm. Bd. & Treas.--Gerrity Co., Inc., Newton, MA, pg. 454
Gerrity, Joe W. Jr., Chm. Bd.--Saratoga Harness Racing, Inc., Saratoga Springs, NY, pg. 970
Gerry, Alan, Chm. & Chief Exec. Officer--Cablevision Industries Corp., Liberty, NY, pg. 206
Gerry, Eugene, Chm. Bd. & Sec.--Precision Carbide Tool Company, Inc., Niles, IL, pg. 885
Gerson, Irwin C., Chm. & Chief Exec. Officer--William Douglas McAdams Inc., New York, NY, pg. 726
Gerson, Max, Chm. Bd.--Gerson & Gerson, Inc., New York, NY, pg. 454
Gerst, C. Gary, Co-Chm.--LaSalle Partners, Chicago, IL, pg. 660
Gerstein, Irving, Chm. Bd.--Bailey Banks & Biddle, Irving, TX, pg. 1215
Gerter, Irving, Chm. Bd.--All American Home Center, Downey, CA, pg. 35
Gessner, Tom R., Chm. Bd.--Al Johnson Construction Co., Minneapolis, MN, pg. 597
Getman, D.S., Chm. Bd. & Pres.--Getman Corporation, Bangor, MI, pg. 455
Gettlefinger, Andrew J., Chm. Bd., Pres. & Chief Exec. Officer--Pride Oil Co., Inc., Knoxville, TN, pg. 622
Gettleman, Maurice H., Chm. Bd. & Pres.--IBM Foods, Inglewood, CA, pg. 558
Getz, William A., Chm. Bd.--Williams, White & Company, Moline, IL, pg. 1191
Ghaznavi, John, Chm. Bd.--Glenshaw Glass Co. Inc., Glenshaw, PA, pg. 462
Giacolini, Earl, Chm.--Sun-land Products of California, Pleasanton, CA, pg. 1058
Gianettino, Ronald J., Chm. Bd. & Chief Exec. Officer--Gianettino & Meredith Advertising, Short Hills, NJ, pg. 455
Gibb, Robert Sr., Chm. Bd.--Robert Gibb & Sons, Inc., Fargo, ND, pg. 456
Gibbs, Charles F., Chm.--Gibbs Wire & Steel Company, Inc., Southington, CT, pg. 456
Gibson, David W., Chm. Bd.--Wolcott & Lincoln, Inc., Kansas City, MO, pg. 1198
Gibson, William B., Chm., Pres. & Chief Exec. Officer--Sudler & Hennessey, New York, NY, pg. 1211
Giesen, Richard A., Chm. Bd., Pres. & Chief Exec. Officer--American Appraisal Associates, Inc., Milwaukee, WI, pg. 48
Gignac, Kenneth, Chm. Bd. & Pres.--Elgin-Honey Hill Corporation, Chicago, IL, pg. 376
Gignac, Robert J., Chm. Bd.--Thunderline Corporation, Belleville, MI, pg. 1096
Gilbane, William J., Chm. Bd.--Gilbane Building Company, Providence, RI, pg. 457
Gilbert, E.A., Chm. Bd.--East Kentucky Power Co-op, Winchester, KY, pg. 362
Gilbert, G.S.B., Chm. Bd.--Aetna Bearing Company, Chicago, IL, pg. 23
Gilbert, Jan G., Chm. Bd.--N. G. Gilbert Corporation, Muncie, IN, pg. 458
Gilbert, Paul H., Chm. Bd.--Parsons Brinckerhoff Quade & Douglas, Inc., New York, NY, pg. 850
Gilbert, Walter, Chm. Bd.--Spaulding Company, Inc., Stoughton, MA, pg. 989
Gilbert, Walter F., Chm. Bd., Pres., Chief Exec. Officer & Treas.--Semco Industries, Stoughton, MA, pg. 989
Gill, George, Chm. Bd. & Chief Exec. Officer--Milk Specialties Company, Dundee, IL, pg. 753
Gill, Harry R., II, Chm. Bd.--The National Latex Products Co., Ashland, OH, pg. 791
Gill, Merwyn C., Chm. Bd.--M.C. Gill Corporation, El Monte, CA, pg. 458
Gilleland, Richard A., Chm. Bd., Pres. & Chief Exec. Officer--Kendall Healthcare Products Co., Mansfield, MA, pg. 622
Gillen, Dick, Chm. Bd., Pres. & Chief Exec. Officer--Harbor Financial Mortgage Corp., Houston, TX, pg. 506
Gillett, George N., Jr., Chm. Bd.--Gillett Holdings, Inc., Denver, CO, pg. 458
Gillett, George, Jr., Chm. Bd.--Vail Associates, Inc., Vail, CO, pg. 459
Gillis, Wayne H., Chm. Bd. & Pres.--Gillis Advertising & Public Relations, Birmingham, AL, pg. 459
Gilman, Howard, Chm. Bd. & Chief Exec. Officer--Gilman Paper Co., Saint Marys, GA, pg. 459
Gilman, Steven F., Chm. Bd., Pres. & Chief Exec. Officer--Style Auto, Van Nuys, CA, pg. 1055
Gilmore, Lloyd M., Chm. Bd.--Riverside Press, Inc., Dallas, TX, pg. 937
Gilvin, Leon P., Chm. Bd.--Gilvin-Terrill Inc., Amarillo, TX, pg. 460
Gimbel, William T., Chm. Bd. & Chief Exec. Officer--Reliance Steel & Aluminum Co., Los Angeles, CA, pg. 925
Gin, Sue Ling, Chm. Bd. & Sec.--Flying Food Fare, Inc., Chicago, IL, pg. 421
Ginsberg, Morton A., Chm. Bd.--Ginsberg's Institutional Foods, Inc., Hudson, NY, pg. 460
Ginzberg, Marc, Chm. Bd., Pres. & Chief Exec. Officer--Primary Industries Corporation, New York, NY, pg. 889
Giraudo, Louis, Chm. & Co-Chief Exec. Officer--San Francisco French Bread Company, Oakland, CA, pg. 969
Glaser, Herbert O., Chm. Bd. & Chief Oper. Officer--The Elder-Beerman Stores Corp., Dayton, OH, pg. 373
Glaser, Herbert O., Chm. Bd. & Chief Oper. Officer--Elder-Beerman Stores Div., Dayton, OH, pg. 373
Glaser, Herbert O., Chm. Bd.--The El-Bee Chargit Corp., Dayton, OH, pg. 373
Glass, Sherwin, Chm. Bd.--Warehouse Home Furnishings Distributor, Dublin, GA, pg. 1163
Glaubinger, Lawrence D., Chm. Bd.--Stern & Stern Industries Inc., New York, NY, pg. 1048
Glazer, Robert S., Chm. Bd., Pres. & Chief Exec. Officer--Glazers Wholesale Drug Co. Inc., Dallas, TX, pg. 461
Gleason, Sheldon, Chm. Bd., Pres., Chief Exec. & Chief Fin. Officer & Controller--Genie Manufacturing Corp., Rush, NY, pg. 452
Glenn, John J., Chm. Bd., Chief Exec. Officer--Dunn Reber Glenn Marz, Reno, NV, pg. 354
Glick, Alvin, Chm. Bd.--Alro Group, Jackson, MI, pg. 44
Glickman, Stanley, Chm. Bd. & Treas.--Red Calliope & Associates, Inc., Los Angeles, CA, pg. 918
Glickman, Stuart, Chm., Pres. Chief Exec. & Chief Fin. Officer--Security Alarms & Fire Engineering Inc., Davie, FL, pg. 987
Glidden, Robert, Chm. Bd.--Robert James Sales Inc., Buffalo, NY, pg. 589
Glikbarg, Thomas S., Chm., Pres. & Chief Exec. Officer--Lyon's Restaurants, Inc., Foster City, CA, pg. 690
Glover, Cliff C., Chm. Bd. & Chief Exec. Officer--Batson-Cook Company, West Point, GA, pg. 126
Glynn, William C., Pres.--IGI Resources, Inc., Boise, ID, pg. 575
Godchaux, Frank A., III, Chm. Bd.--Riviana Foods Inc., Houston, TX, pg. 937
Godden, Tim, Chm.-UK, Mng. Dir.-Europe--Wunderman Worldwide Limited, London, United Kingdom, pg. 1212
Godfrey, Richard H., Chm. Bd.--Felton Brush Inc., Manchester, NH, pg. 406
Godfrey, William G., Chm. Bd., Pres. & Chief Exec. Officer--Tekra Corporation, New Berlin, WI, pg. 1084
Godwin, George W., Jr., Chm. & Chief Exec. Officer--Godwin Advertising Agency, Inc., Jackson, MS, pg. 464
Goedert, Philip H., Pres. & Dir.--RNL Facilities Corporation, Denver, CO, pg. 907
Goergen, Robert, Chm. Bd.--Candle Corporation of America, Oshkosh, WI, pg. 214
Goff, Walter, Chm. Bd.--Grocers Baking Co., Grand Rapids, MI, pg. 488
Gold, Aaron A., Chm. Bd. & Chief Exec. Officer--Oxford First Corporation, Philadelphia, PA, pg. 834
Gold, Aaron A., Chm.--Computer Information Services, Inc., Philadelphia, PA, pg. 834
Gold, Aaron A., Chm.--Oxford Communities, Inc., Philadelphia, PA, pg. 834
Gold, Aaron A., Chm. Bd. & Chief Exec. Officer--Oxford Finance Companies, Inc., Philadelphia, PA, pg. 835
Gold, Jeffrey M., Chm. Bd. & Chief Exec. Officer--Goldmark Partners, New York, NY, pg. 469
Goldband, Shefford S., Chm. Bd.--Totsy Manufacturing Company, Inc., Holyoke, MA, pg. 1103
Goldbath, Raymond, Chm. Bd. & Chief Exec. Officer--Marathon Cheese Corp., Marathon, WI, pg. 705
Goldberg, Arthur, Chm. Bd., Pres. & Chief Exec. Officer--Di Giorgio Corporation, Somerset, NJ, pg. 334
Goldberg, Arthur M., Chm. Bd.--White Rose Food, Long Island City, NY, pg. 335
Goldberg, Gertrude, Chm. Bd.--Bestform Foundations, Inc., Long Island City, NY, pg. 147
Goldberg, Gertrude, Chm. Bd.--Lily of France, Inc., New York, NY, pg. 147
Goldberg, Gertrude, Chm. Bd.--Poirette Corsets, Inc., New York, NY, pg. 147
Goldberg, Norman, Chm.--Goldberg Marchesano Kohlman Inc., Washington, DC, pg. 465
Goldfarb, Gene, Chm. Bd.--House of Perfection, Inc., New York, NY, pg. 546
Goldfarb, Robert, Pres.--Goldfarb & Company Advertising, Southfield, MI, pg. 467
Goldfine, Erwin L., Chm. Bd.--Northern Drug Company, Duluth, MN, pg. 814
Goldman, Harold A., Chm. Bd.--Iowa Paint Mfg. Company, Inc., Des Moines, IA, pg. 582
Goldman, Marvin I., Chm. Bd.--Gulf Distribution Inc., Miami, FL, pg. 493
Goldman, Mort, Chm. Bd.--Elek-Tek, Inc., Skokie, IL, pg. 375
Goldress, Jerry E., Chm. & Chief Exec. Officer--First Land & Development, Inc., Richmond, VA, pg. 18
Goldress, Jerry E., Co-Chm.--Best Products Co., Inc., Richmond, VA, pg. 17
Goldschmidt, David, Chm. Bd.--Henrys, Inc., Wichita, KS, pg. 530
Goldsmith, Gary, Chm. Bd., Sec. & Creative Dir.--Goldsmith/Jeffrey, Inc., New York, NY, pg. 469
Goldsmith, John, Chm. & Chief Exec. Officer--John Hancock Freedom Securities Corporation, Boston, MA, pg. 596
Goldstein, Samuel R., Chm. Bd. & Treas.--Apex Oil Company, Inc., Saint Louis, MO, pg. 78
Goldwasser, Donald L., Chm. Bd.--Security Van Lines, Inc., Kenner, LA, pg. 987
Golemo, Stanley M., Jr., Chm. Bd. & Pres.--Hood & Company, Hamburg, PA, pg. 542
Gollmar, Robert L., Chm. Bd.--Elyria Foundry Company, Elyria, OH, pg. 378
Golodetz, Michele, Chm. Bd.--Golodetz Corporation, New York, NY, pg. 469
Golub, Lewis, Chm. Bd. & Chief Exec. Officer--Golub Corporation, Schenectady, NY, pg. 469
Golub, Lewis, Chm. Bd. & Chief Exec. Officer--Price Chopper, Schenectady, NY, pg. 469
Gomez, Oscar J., Jr., Chm. Bd.--Ezon Products, Inc., Germantown, TN, pg. 393
Good, Robert F., Chm. Bd.--White, Good & Co., Lebanon, PA, pg. 1185
Good, Sheldon F., Chm. & Chief Exec. Officer--Sheldon Good & Co., Inc., Chicago, IL, pg. 470
Goodall, Richard B., Chm. Bd. & Chief Exec. Officer--Dixon Valve & Coupling Company, Chestertown, MD, pg. 341
Goodall, Richard B., Chm. Bd.--Predco, Inc., Pennsauken, NJ, pg. 341
Goodchild, John, Chm.--Weightman Public Relations, Philadelphia, PA, pg. 1173
Gooden, C. Michael, Chm. Bd. & Pres.--Integrated Systems Analysts, Inc., Arlington, VA, pg. 573
Goodman, Ellis M., Chm. Bd.--Barton Brands, Ltd., Chicago, IL, pg. 123
Goodman, Ellis M., Chm. Bd.--Barton Beers, Ltd., Chicago, IL, pg. 123
Goodman, Lawrence B., Chm. Bd. & Treas.--The Ormond Shops, Inc., North Bergen, NJ, pg. 830
Goodpasture, Molly, Chm. Bd.--Goodpasture, Inc., Brownfield, TX, pg. 471
Goodrum, Harold, Chm. & Chief Exec. Officer--Goodrum Leonard & Associates, Inc., Nashville, TN, pg. 471
Goodwin, Bill, Chm. Bd.--AMF Bakery Systems, Richmond, VA, pg. 5
Goodwin, Daniel L., Chm. Bd. & Chief Exec. Officer--The Inland Group, Inc., Oak Brook, IL, pg. 570
Gorde, Jerry, Chm. Bd. & Chief Exec. Officer--VATEX America, Inc., Richmond, VA, pg. 1141
Gordon, Harry, Chm. Bd. & Controller--Saul Bros. & Company, Inc., Norcross, GA, pg. 972
Gordon, Paul B., Chm. Bd. & Chief Exec. Officer--Gordon Food Service Inc., Grand Rapids, MI, pg. 472
Gordon, Peter, Chm. Bd.--Crystal Geyser, Calistoga, CA, pg. 303
Gordon, Philip, Chm. Bd.--Gordon Brothers, Boston, MA, pg. 471
Gorman, Alvin L., Chm Bd.--Power Contracting & Engineering Corp., Rolling Meadows, IL, pg. 883
Gorman, Kenneth, Chm. Bd.--IDC Services, Inc., Chicago, IL, pg. 559
Gorra, George M., Chm. Bd.--Chemical Specialties Corp., Springfield, MA, pg. 1069
Goss, Howard S., Chm., Chief Exec. Officer & Treas.--Transco Inc., Chicago, IL, pg. 1106
Gossett, Edward M., Chm. Bd.--Ermco, Inc., Indianapolis, IN, pg. 387
Gottschalk, Eldon W., Co-Chm., Sec. & Treas.--Jack Lawlor Advertising, Inc., Pasadena, CA, pg. 661
Gouchenour, C. Lee, Chm. & Chief Exec. Officer--Gouchenour Adv., Inc., Orlando, FL, pg. 473
Gould, Charles L., Chm. & Chief Exec. Officer--Deutsch, Shea & Evans, Inc., South San Francisco, CA, pg. 333
Gould, James C., Chm. Bd.--Challenge Graphics Equipment Co., Grand Haven, MI, pg. 238
Gould, Kingdon, Jr., Chm. Bd.--Globe Industries, Inc., Chicago, IL, pg. 464

Gould, Margaret Z., Chm. Bd.--Magnetic Analysis Corp., Mount Vernon, NY, pg. 700
Gould, Morley, Chm. Bd.--Asher/Gould Advertising, Inc., Los Angeles, CA, pg. 88
Gozia, Richard M., Chm. & Chief Exec. Officer--Wyatt Cafeterias Inc., Dallas, TX, pg. 1205
Grace, J.P., Chm. Bd.--Restaurant Enterprises Group, Inc., Irvine, CA, pg. 929
Grace, Roy, Chm. Bd.--Grace & Rothschild, New York, NY, pg. 474
Grado, John, Chm. Bd. & Chief Exec. Officer--Technographics, Inc., Stratton, PA, pg. 1083
Graf, Jerry N., Chm. Bd.--LePage's, Inc., Pittsburgh, PA, pg. 287
Grafstrom, William E., Chm. Bd.--CenterMark Properties, Inc., Saint Louis, MO, pg. 231
Graham, Billy, Chm. Bd.--Christianity Today, Inc., Carol Stream, IL, pg. 249
Graham, Donald G., Jr., Chm. Bd. & Chief Exec. Officer--Fisher Companies, Inc., Seattle, WA, pg. 414
Graham, George, Chm. Bd.--John H. Graham & Co., Inc., Oradell, NJ, pg. 475
Graham, J.J., Chm.--Continental National American Real Estate Inc., San Jose, CA, pg. 280
Graham, Jack W., Chm. Bd., Sec. & Treas.--Petty Company, Inc., Effingham, IL, pg. 866
Graham, John, Chm. Bd.--MacMillan Oil Co., Inc., Des Moines, IA, pg. 475
Granger, Alton L., Chm. & Chief Exec. Officer--Granger Construction Co., Lansing, MI, pg. 476
Grant, Donald B., Chm. Bd.--Voyager Emblems, Inc., Sanborn, NY, pg. 1155
Grant, F., Chm. Bd.--Abbott Electronics, Inc., Los Angeles, CA, pg. 9
Grant, H.L., Chm. Bd.--Grant-Lydick Beverage Co., San Antonio, TX, pg. 477
Grant, Howard C., Chm. & Pres.--Grant Marketing Communications Inc., Lafayette Hill, PA, pg. 477
Grant, William A., Jr., Co-Chm.-Opers.--Ernst & Young, New York, NY, pg. 387
Granum, Robert M., Chm. Bd. & Chief Exec. Officer--Panel Processing, Inc., Alpena, MI, pg. 846
Grau, Juan, Chm. Bd., Pres. & Chief Exec. Officer--Bacardi Imports, Inc., Miami, FL, pg. 108
Graunke, Terence, Chm. Bd. & Pres.--U.S. Communications Corporation, Minneapolis, MN, pg. 1135
Graves, Earl G., Chm. Bd., Pres. & Chief Exec. Officer--Earl G. Graves, Ltd., New York, NY, pg. 478
Gray, John, S., Sr., Chm. Bd. & Pres.--Jack Gray Transport, Inc., Gary, IN, pg. 479
Gray, Lois Howard, Chm. Bd.--James N. Gray Construction Co., Inc., Lexington, KY, pg. 479
Gray, Melvin, Chm. & Chief Exec. Officer--Graycor, Inc., Homewood, IL, pg. 479
Gray, Melvin, Chm. Bd. & Chief Exec. Officer--The Edward Gray Corp., Homewood, IL, pg. 480
Gray, Melvin, Chm. Bd. & Chief Exec. Officer--Inland Construction Company, Homewood, IL, pg. 480
Gray, Thomas M., Chm. Bd.--Gray Printing Co., Fostoria, OH, pg. 479
Green, Donald, Chm. Bd. & Sr. V.P. & Gen. Mgr.--Menu Foods, Inc., Pennsauken, NJ, pg. 739
Green, Les, Chm. Bd.--Agripac Inc., Salem, OR, pg. 25
Green, Stephen J., Chm. Bd.--E-II Holdings, Inc., New York, NY, pg. 358
Greenberg, Marvin, Chm. Bd.--Baltic Linen Company, Inc., Valley Stream, NY, pg. 116
Greenblatt, Maurice, Chm. Bd.--Unigroup, Inc., Fenton, MO, pg. 1126
Greenblatt, Maurice, Chm. Bd.--United Van Lines, Inc., Fenton, MO, pg. 1126
Greene, Randy, Chm. Bd. & Pres.--Blevins Concession Supply Co., Tampa, FL, pg. 156
Greenfield, Harley J., Chm., Pres. & Chief Exec. Officer--Jennifer Convertibles Inc., Paramus, NJ, pg. 592
Greenfield, Harvey, Chm. Bd.--Commonwealth Toy & Novelty Company, New York, NY, pg. 269
Greenlee, James V., Chm. Bd.--Weinbrenner Shoe Company, Inc., Merrill, WI, pg. 1173
Greenstone, Ronald, Chm. & Chief Exec. Officer--Greenstone Roberts Advertising, Melville, NY, pg. 485
Greenwald, James L., Chm. Bd.--Katz Communications, Inc., New York, NY, pg. 618
Greer, J. Barton, Jr., Chm. Bd.--Autry Greer & Sons, Inc., Prichard, AL, pg. 486
Gregg, Charles R., Chm. Bd.--Gregg Industries, Inc., El Monte, CA, pg. 486
Gregg, F. Browne, Chm. Bd. & Chief Exec. Officer--Florida Crushed Stone Company, Leesburg, FL, pg. 420
Gregory, David M., Chm. Bd.--Golden Gate University, San Francisco, CA, pg. 466
Gregory, E. John, Sr., Chm. Bd. & Pres.--J.T. Slocomb Company, South Glastonbury, CT, pg. 1010
Gregory, William H., Chm. Bd. & Pres.--Gregory Affiliates, Inc., Beaverton, OR, pg. 486
Grell, Larry, Chm. Bd.--Rice Growers Association of California, West Sacramento, CA, pg. 931
Grieb, Warren, Chm. & Chief Exec. Officer--Advertising Checking Bureau Incorporated, New York, NY, pg. 21
Grieve, G.P., Chm. Bd.--The Grieve Corporation, Round Lake, IL, pg. 486
Griffin, George G., Chm. Bd., Pres. & Treas.--Davis Advertising Inc., Philadelphia, PA, pg. 318
Griffin, Jeff, Chm. Bd., Pres. & Chief Exec. Officer--Mountain Air Delivery, Sparks, NV, pg. 773
Griffin, John L., Sr., Chm. Bd.--Griffin Industries, Inc., Cold Spring, KY, pg. 487
Griffin, Mark E., Chm. Bd., Pres. & Chief Exec. Officer--Lewis Drug, Inc., Sioux Falls, SD, pg. 673
Griffin, Martha, Chm. Bd.--Griffin Manufacturing Co., Muskogee, OK, pg. 487
Griffin, Paul E., Chm. Bd.--Griffin Homes, Inc., Calabasas, CA, pg. 487
Griffin, Tom, Co-Chm. & Chief Exec. Officer--Griffin Bacal Inc., New York, NY, pg. 486
Griffith, Dean L., Chm. Bd.--Griffith Laboratories Worldwide, Inc., Alsip, IL, pg. 487
Griffith, Richard L., Chm.--Amfac/JMB Hawaii, Inc., Honolulu, HI, pg. 585
Grimaud, Joseph A., Jr., Pres. & Chief Exec. Officer--Precision Tune, Inc., Leesburg, VA, pg. 885
Grimmer, James B., Chm. Bd.--Grimmer Realty Co. Inc., Birmingham, AL, pg. 488
Grinberg, Gedalio, Chm. Bd. & Chief Exec. Officer--North American Watch Corporation, Lyndhurst, NJ, pg. 812
Grizzard, Claude H., Sr., Chm. Bd.--Grizzard Advertising, Inc., Atlanta, GA, pg. 488
Grizzard, Claude T., Jr., Vice Chm.--Grizzard Advertising, Inc., Atlanta, GA, pg. 488
Groendyke, John, Chm. Bd.--Groendyke Transports, Inc., Enid, OK, pg. 489
Groenevelt, Aat, Chm. Bd. & Pres.--Provimi Veal Corporation, Waukesha, WI, pg. 896
Groff, Jon, Chm. Bd. & Chief Exec. Officer--Systems Engineering Associates Co. (SEACOR), Mount Laurel, NJ, pg. 320
Grogan, David R., Chm., Pres. & Chief Exec. Officer--Toter Incorporated, Statesville, NC, pg. 1103
Grohn, Fred, Chm. Bd.--MFA Oil Company, Columbia, MO, pg. 692
Gropper, Edward, Chm. Bd. & Pres.--Faber, Coe & Gregg, Inc., Secaucus, NJ, pg. 395
Gross, Howard, Chm. Bd. & Chief Exec. Officer--Snyder Industries, Inc., Lincoln, NE, pg. 1015
Grossberg, Ewel, Chm. Bd.--George Rice & Sons, Los Angeles, CA, pg. 931
Grossman, Louis, Chm. Bd.--Southern Container Corporation, Hauppauge, NY, pg. 1020
Grossman, Neil J., Chm. Bd. & Pres.--Reed Exhibition Companies, Boston, MA, pg. 920
Grossman, Sidney, Chm. Bd.--Grossman Iron & Steel Company, St. Louis, MO, pg. 489
Grosvenor, Gilbert M., Chm. Bd. & Pres.--National Geographic Society, Washington, DC, pg. 789
Groussman, Dean, Chm., Pres. & Chief Exec. Officer--Zale Corporation, Irving, TX, pg. 1215
Groves, Franklin N., Chm. Bd. & Chief Exec. Officer--S. J. Groves & Sons Company, Minneapolis, MN, pg. 490
Groves, Ray J., Chm. Bd.--Ernst & Young, New York, NY, pg. 387
Grudberg, Ronald, Chm. Bd.--Finlay Fine Jewelry, New York, NY, pg. 411
Grundy, William J., Chm. Bd.--Jomac, Inc., Warrington, PA, pg. 602
Grunnah, Thomas, Chm. Bd.--Reliance Elevator Company, Chicago, IL, pg. 925
Grunow, John E.D., Jr., Chm. Bd. & Chief Exec. Officer--International Marine Holdings, Inc., Stamford, CT, pg. 579
Guccione, Bob, Chm. Bd., Chief Exec. Officer & Publr.--General Media Publishing Group, New York, NY, pg. 450
Guccione, Bob, Chm., Editor & Publisher--Omni Publications International Ltd., New York, NY, pg. 450
Guertler, Walter E., Jr., Chm. Bd., Pres., Chief Exec. Officer--Systems Engineering & Manufacturing Corp., Stoughton, MA, pg. 1071
Gullickson, W.D., Chm. Bd.--McLaughlin Gormley King Company, Minneapolis, MN, pg. 731
Gummere, John, Chm. Bd. & Chief Exec. Officer--Phoenix Home Life Mutual Insurance Company, Hartford, CT, pg. 868
Gunder, Stephen, Chm. Bd. & Pres.--Gunder & Associates, Inc., Dublin, OH, pg. 494
Gunn, Curtis C., Jr., Chm. Bd.--Curtis C. Gunn, Inc., San Antonio, TX, pg. 494
Gupta, Vinod, Chm., Pres., Chief Exec. Officer--American Business Information, Inc., Omaha, NE, pg. 50
Gurasich, Steve, Chm.--GSD&M, Austin, TX, pg. 441
Gurewitz, Richard, Chm. Bd. & Chief. Exec. Officer--Poly Pak America, Inc., Los Angeles, CA, pg. 880
Gurley, C.E., Chm. Bd.--Gurley Motor Company, Gallup, NM, pg. 494
Gurney, Robert J., Jr., Chm. Bd., Pres. & Chief Exec. Officer--Gurney Industries Inc., Gastonia, NC, pg. 495
Gut, Rainer E., Chm. Bd.--CS First Boston Group, Inc., New York, NY, pg. 203
Gutterman, Manny, Chm. Bd.--Jelmar Company, Lincolnwood, IL, pg. 592
Gwaltney, John R., Chm. Bd., Pres. & Chief Exec. Officer--Forestry Suppliers, Inc., Jackson, MS, pg. 424
Gwinn, John Curt, Chm. Bd.--Congaree Construction Co., Inc., Columbia, SC, pg. 274
Gwinn, Robert P., Chm. Bd. & Chief Exec. Officer--Encyclopaedia Britannica, Inc., Chicago, IL, pg. 381
Haas, Alvin N., Chm. Bd.--Bud Industries, Inc., Willoughby, OH, pg. 186
Haas, Robert D., Chm. Bd. & Chief Exec. Officer--Levi Strauss & Co., San Francisco, CA, pg. 670
Hackl, A.J., Chm. Bd. & Chief Exec. Officer--Herff Jones Inc., Indianapolis, IN, pg. 531
Hackman, Roger, Vice Chm.--Grizzard Advertising, Inc., Atlanta, GA, pg. 488
Hackney, James A., III, Chm. Bd.--Hackney & Sons, Inc., Washington, NC, pg. 498
Hackney, Thomas J., Jr., Chm. Bd.--Hackney Brothers, Inc., Wilson, NC, pg. 498
Haddon, Harvey, Chm. Bd.--HLB Communications, Inc., Chicago, IL, pg. 496
Hadfield, Neil, Chm. Bd., Chief Fin. Officer & Sec.--Western Pacific Data Systems, San Diego, CA, pg. 1180
Haerther, Daniel P., Chm. Bd.--Semblex Corporation, Elmhurst, IL, pg. 989
Hagan, Tom, Co-Chm. & Chief Exec. Officer--Karsh & Hagan, Inc., Englewood, CO, pg. 617
Hagen, Thomas B., Chm. Bd. & Chief Exec. Officer--Erie Family Life Insurance Company, Erie, PA, pg. 386
Hagen, Thomas B., Chm. Bd. & Chief Exec. Officer--Erie Insurance Group, Erie, PA, pg. 386
Hagen, Thomas B., Chm. Bd. & Chief Exec. Officer--Erie Indemnity Company, Erie, PA, pg. 386
Hagen, Thomas B., Chm. Bd. & Chief Exec. Officer--Erie Insurance Exchange, Erie, PA, pg. 386
Hagen, Thomas B., Chm. Bd. & Chief Exec. Officer--Flagship City Insurance Company, Erie, PA, pg. 386
Haggai, Thomas S., Chm. Bd. & Chief Exec. Officer--IGA, Inc. (Independent Grocers Alliance), Chicago, IL, pg. 560
Haggar, J.M., Jr., Chm. Bd.--Haggar Apparel Company, Dallas, TX, pg. 499
Haggen, Donald E., Chm. Bd. & Chief Exec. Officer--Haggen's, Inc., Bellingham, WA, pg. 499
Hagie, R.W., Chm. Bd.--Hagie Manufacturing Co., Clarion, IA, pg. 499
Hagiwara, Kokichi, Chm. Bd. & Chief Exec. Officer--National Steel Corporation, Mishawaka, IN, pg. 793
Hagler, Thomas W., Jr., Chm. & Chief Exec. Officer--Georgia Iron Works Co., Grovetown, GA, pg. 453
Hahn, Norman, Pres. & Chm. Bd.--Conestoga Wood Specialties, Inc., Earl, PA, pg. 273
Hahn, Philip J., Co.-Chm. Bd.--M. Fabrikant & Sons, Inc., New York, NY, pg. 396
Hahn, Warren E., Chm. Bd.--J.R. Hahn Co., Inc., Indianapolis, IN, pg. 500
Haidinger, Robert N., Chm. Bd., Pres. & Chief Exec. Officer--Jac Jacobsen Industries, Inc., Greenwich, CT, pg. 587
Haigh, Robert B., Chm., Chief Exec. Officer & Treas.--Chicago Tube & Iron Co., Chicago, IL, pg. 246
Haines, W.K., Sr., Chm. Bd.--Haines & Co., Inc., North Canton, OH, pg. 500
Hakes, Ellen H., Chm. Bd.--Construction Specialties, Inc., Cranford, NJ, pg. 277
Hale, Guy A., Chm. Bd., Pres. & Chief Exec. Officer--The Alamo Learning Systems, Inc., San Ramon, CA, pg. 29
Hale, John, Chm. Bd. & Pres.--Telex Communications, Inc., Minneapolis, MN, pg. 1085
Haley, Clifton, Chm. Bd., Pres. & Chief Exec. Officer--Beech Holdings Corp., Chicago, IL, pg. 131
Haley, Daniel J., Jr., Chm. Bd.--Finnaren & Haley, Inc., Conshohocken, PA, pg. 411
Haley, F.T., Chm. Bd. & Chief Exec. Officer--Brown & Haley, Tacoma, WA, pg. 182
Haley, Russell J., Chm. Bd. & Pres.--Midwest Tire & Muffler, Inc., Rapid City, SD, pg. 752
Hall, Adrienne, Vice Chm.--Eisaman, Johns & Laws Advertising, Inc., Los Angeles, CA, pg. 372
Hall, Charles, Exec. V.P.--Fort Pitt Acquisitions Company, Inc., Coraopolis, PA, pg. 425
Hall, Donald J., Chm. Bd.--Hallmark Cards, Inc., Kansas City, MO, pg. 501
Hall, Donald J., Chm. Bd.--Ambassador Cards, Kansas City, MO, pg. 502
Hall, Kenneth E., Chm. Bd.--Hall Contracting Corp., Louisville, KY, pg. 501
Hall, L.G., Jr., Chm. Bd.--The Stackpole Corporation, Boston, MA, pg. 1034
Hall, Richard E., Chm. Bd. & Chief Exec. Officer--Underground Construction Company, Inc., Benicia, CA, pg. 1125
Hall, Roger M., Chm. Bd.--Arvida, Boca Raton, FL, pg. 586
Hallaker, Rune, Chm. Bd.--VASA Insurance Group, Inc., Indianapolis, IN, pg. 1146
Hallam, Robert, Chm. Bd. & Chief Exec. Officer--Ben E. Keith Company, Fort Worth, TX, pg. 620
Halle, Bruce T., Chm. Bd. & Pres.--Reinalt-Thomas Corp., Ann Arbor, MI, pg. 923
Halpam, Fred, Chm. Bd.--Brookhurst, Inc., Compton, CA, pg. 179
Halperin, Thomas C., Chm Bd., Pres. & Chief Exec. Officer--Commercial Light Company, Hillside, IL, pg. 268
Halpern, Colin, Chm. Bd. & Pres.--NPS Corporation, Elmwood Park, NJ, pg. 781
Halton, Dale F., Chm. Bd., Pres. & Chief Exec. Officer--Pepsi-Cola Bottling Company of Charlotte Inc., Charlotte, NC, pg. 860
Hamblett, Stephen, Chm. Bd., Chief Exec. Officer & Publr.--Providence Journal Company, Providence, RI, pg. 895
Hamburger, Jack D., Chm. Bd.--Parliament Co., Bingham Farms, MI, pg. 850
Hamister, Mark E., Chm. Bd., Pres. & Chief Exec. Officer--National Health Care Affiliates, Inc., Buffalo, NY, pg. 791
Hammer, William C., Chm. Bd.--Messenger Corporation, Phoenix, AZ, pg. 741
Hampton, John C., Chm. Bd., Pres. & Chief Exec. Officer--Hampton Resources Inc., Portland, OR, pg. 504
Hancock, K. David, Chm. Bd.--Hancock Lumber, Inc., Casco, ME, pg. 504
Handler, Mark S., Co-Chm. & Co- Chief Exec. Officer--R. H. Macy & Co., Inc., New York, NY, pg. 698
Handler, Mark S., Co-Chm. Bd. & Co-Chief Exec. Officer--Bullock's, Los Angeles, CA, pg. 699
Hanel, L. Sterling, Pres.--Hanel Lumber Co., Inc., Hood River, OR, pg. 505
Hank, B.J., Jr., Chm. Bd. & Chief Exec. Officer--Montgomery Elevator Company, Moline, IL, pg. 767
Hanley, Robert, Chm. Bd.--Federal Data Corporation, Bethesda, MD, pg. 404
Hann, S.A., Chm. Bd. & Pres.--Health Care Lodges, Coffeyville, KS, pg. 520
Hannay, George A., Chm. Bd.--Clifford B. Hannay & Son Inc., Westerlo, NY, pg. 505
Hano, George, Chm. Bd.--Hano Business Forms, Inc., Springfield, MA, pg. 505
Hano, George, Chm. Bd.--Technicarbon Company, Inc., Springfield, MA, pg. 1083
Hansberger, R.V., Chm. Bd.--RAM Golf Corporation, Melrose Park, IL, pg. 910
Hansen, Donald E., Chm. Bd.--H & H Distributing Company, Inc., West Union, IA, pg. 495
Hansen, Donald W., Chm. Bd. & Pres.--Delta Resins & Refractories, Inc., Milwaukee, WI, pg. 327

Hansen, K.W., Chm. Bd.--Crystal Cream & Butter Company, Sacramento, CA, pg. 303
Hansen, Kai Soborg, Chm.--Cato Johnson Copenhagen, Copenhagen, Denmark, pg. 1211
Hansen, R.W., Chm. Bd., Pres. & Chief Exec. Officer--Furnas Electric Company, Batavia, IL, pg. 437
Hansen, W.E., Chm. Bd. & Pres.--Brandywine Sports, Inc., Wilmington, DE, pg. 172
Hanson, George V., Chm. Bd., Pres. & Chief Exec. Officer--Old Home Foods, Inc., Saint Paul, MN, pg. 823
Haradine, Ed, Chm. Bd.--Carlton Manufacturing, Inc., Elkhart, IN, pg. 222
Harary, Ralph, Chm. Bd.--Jacques Moret, Inc., New York, NY, pg. 588
Harbert, John Murdoch, III, Chm. Bd.--Harbert Corporation, Birmingham, AL, pg. 506
Harberts, Thomas W., Pres. & Chief Exec. Officer--Byerly's Inc., Edina, MN, pg. 198
Harbour, I.C., Chm. Bd.--Harbour Contractors, Inc., Naperville, IL, pg. 506
Hardaway, B.H. III, Chm. Bd.--The Hardaway Company, Columbus, GA, pg. 507
Hardaway, L. H., Jr., Chm. Bd.--Hardaway Construction Company, Inc., Nashville, TN, pg. 508
Harden, David E., Chm.--Harden Furniture Company, McConnellsville, NY, pg. 508
Harding, Craig K., Chm. Bd. & Pres.--Majestic Molded Products, Inc., Holbrook, NY, pg. 702
Harding, John H., Chm. & Chief Exec. Officer--Administrative Services, Inc., Montpelier, VT, pg. 791
Harding, L. Wayne, Chm. Bd.--Santa Monica Ford Company, Santa Monica, CA, pg. 970
Hardy, Joseph A. Sr., Chm., Pres. & Chief Exec. Officer--84 Lumber Co., Eighty Four, PA, pg. 371
Hardy, R.B., Chm. Bd.--Russell Harrington Cutlery Inc., Southbridge, MA, pg. 556
Hargrove, G. Thomas, Chm. Bd.--Keith Clark, Sidney, NY, pg. 304
Hargrove, Jack L., Chm. Bd.--Intercounty Title Co. of Illinois, Chicago, IL, pg. 574
Harkins, Thomas P., Chm. Bd. & Chief Exec. Officer--Harkins Builders, Inc., Silver Spring, MD, pg. 509
Harlan, John M., Chm. Bd. & Pres.--Harlan Electric Co., Southfield, MI, pg. 509
Harlan, Leonard, Chm. Bd.--Long John Silver's, Inc., Lexington, KY, pg. 229
Harling, C. Gene, Chm. Bd., Pres. & Chief Exec. Officer--FirstFed Michigan Corporation, Detroit, MI, pg. 414
Harling, C. Gene, Chm. Bd., Pres. & Chief Exec. Officer--First Federal of Michigan, Detroit, MI, pg. 414
Harmon, David E., Chm. Bd., Pres., Chief Exec. & Chief Oper. Officer--El Camino Resources, Ltd., Northridge, CA, pg. 372
Harmon, James D., Chm. Bd.--Twin City Die Castings Co., Minneapolis, MN, pg. 1121
Harmon, Lowell D., Chm. Bd. & Pres.--Progressive Driver Services, Inc., Jacksonville, FL, pg. 894
Harney, J. Philip, Chm. Bd.--Hall, Haerr, Peterson & Harney, Inc., Peoria, IL, pg. 501
Harp, Donald L., Chm. Bd. & Pres.--Harp's Food Stores, Inc., Springdale, AR, pg. 510
Harper, Daniel R., Chm. Bd. & Pres.--Harper Bros., Inc., Fort Myers, FL, pg. 510
Harrell, Samuel M., Chm. Bd., Pres. & Chief Exec. Officer--EDI International, Inc., Cincinnati, OH, pg. 359
Harrington, R.L., Chm. Bd.--Dumore Corporation, Mauston, WI, pg. 352
Harris, D. George, Chm. Bd.--North American Salt Company, Overland Park, KS, pg. 812
Harris, Earl F., Chm. Bd.--Rodney Hunt Company, Orange, MA, pg. 553
Harris, John C., Chm. Bd., Pres. & Chief Exec. Officer--Harris Farms, Inc., Coalinga, CA, pg. 511
Harris, Richard M., Jr., Chm. Bd.--Alling & Cory Company, Rochester, NY, pg. 40
Harris, Robert M., Chm. Bd. & Chief Exec. Officer--GFA Brands, Inc., Cresskill, NJ, pg. 440
Harrison, Donald, Chm. Bd. & Gen. Counsel--PVS Chemicals, Inc., Detroit, MI, pg. 837
Harrison, Stephen, Chm. & Chief Exec. Officer--Welsco Inc., North Little Rock, AR, pg. 1175
Harrison, William H., Jr., Chm. Bd. & Chief Exec. Officer--Taylor Drug Stores, Inc., Louisville, KY, pg. 1081
Hart, William L., Chm. Bd. & Chief Exec. Officer--Hart Graphics Inc., Austin, TX, pg. 513
Harte, Houston H., Chm. Bd.--Harte-Hanks Communications, Inc., San Antonio, TX, pg. 513
Harter, Evan C., Chm. Bd.--The Harter Group, Sturgis, MI, pg. 513
Hartwell, Samuel A., Co-Chm. Bd. & Chief Fin. Officer--G.S. Blodgett Corporation, Burlington, VT, pg. 157
Hartwick, Sharon, Co-Chm.--Genova Hartwick Juliano, Inc., Greenwich, CT, pg. 452
Hartzell, Robert C., Chm. Bd. & Pres.--Hartzell Corporation, Saint Paul, MN, pg. 514
Harvey, David E., Chm. & Chief Exec. Officer--Rome Cable Corporation, Rome, NY, pg. 945
Harvey, Joseph H., Jr., Chm. Bd. & Chief Exec. Officer--J.H. Harvey Company, Nashville, GA, pg. 515
Harvie, James, Chm. Bd., Pres. & Chief Exec. Officer--General Ship Corporation, Boston, MA, pg. 450
Haselton, Philip H., Chm. Bd.--Detex Corporation, New Braunfels, TX, pg. 333
Haseotes, Demetrios B., Chm. Bd.--Cumberland Farms, Inc., Canton, MA, pg. 304
Haserjian, Ted, Chm. Bd. & Sec.--Carpeteria, Inc., Valencia, CA, pg. 224
Hatcher, Jack, Co-Chm. Bd.--Southern Pump & Tank Co. Inc., Charlotte, NC, pg. 1022
Hatfield, Joe, Chm. Bd. & Chief Exec. Officer--Fieldale Corporation, Baldwin, GA, pg. 409
Hatt, Peter M., Chm. & Chief Exec. Officer--Borders, Perrin & Norrander, Inc., Portland, OR, pg. 165
Hatt, Peter M., Chm. & Chief Exec. Officer--Borders, Perrin & Norrander, Seattle, WA, pg. 165
Hauber, W.M., Chm. Bd., Pres. & Chief Exec. Officer--Matthews International Corp., Pittsburgh, PA, pg. 721
Hauck, John M., Chm. Bd.--Tubular Steel Inc., Saint Louis, MO, pg. 1118
Havener, Gary, Chm. Bd.--Antenna Products Corp., Mineral Wells, TX, pg. 76
Havens, Fred R., Chm. Bd.--Havens Steel Co., Kansas City, MO, pg. 517
Haversat, Robert A., Chm. Bd., Pres. & Chief Exec. Officer--Essex Industries, New Haven, CT, pg. 361
Haviland, M.M., Chm. Bd.--Haviland Enterprises, Grand Rapids, MI, pg. 517
Hawk, Richard C., Chm. Bd. & Chief Exec. Officer--Help Management Corporation, Overland Park, KS, pg. 527
Hawley, Jean Gannet, Chm. Bd. & Publr.--Guy Gannett Publishing Company, Portland, ME, pg. 442
Haworth, C. Dale, Chm.--Haworth Group Inc., Minnetonka, MN, pg. 518
Haworth, G.W., Chm. Bd.--Haworth, Inc., Holland, MI, pg. 518
Hawthorne, Timothy R., Chm. Bd. & Pres.--Hawthorne Communications, Inc., Fairfield, IA, pg. 518
Hayden, Bill, Chm. Bd.--Compuadd Corporation, Austin, TX, pg. 271
Hayes, Walter, Chm., Pres. & Chief Exec. Officer--Aston Martin LaGonda of North America, Inc., Stamford, CT, pg. 92
Haynam, Harvey H., Chm. & Chief Exec. Officer--Target Stamped Products Corp., Kinsman, OH, pg. 1079
Hays, George, Chm. Bd.--Nooter Corporation, Saint Louis, MO, pg. 808
Hays, Howard H., Jr., Chm. Bd.--Press Enterprise Company, Riverside, CA, pg. 887
Hays, Spencer, Chm. Bd.--Southwestern/Great American Inc., Nashville, TN, pg. 1023
Hays, Spencer, Chm. Bd.--Tom James Of Atlanta, Inc., Atlanta, GA, pg. 589
Haysbert, Raymond V., Sr., Chm. Bd., Pres. & Chief Exec. Officer--Parks Sausage Company, Baltimore, MD, pg. 850
Hazlehurst, Thomas E., Chm. Bd.--Potter Hazlehurst Incorporated, East Greenwich, RI, pg. 882
Heagerty, David A., Chm. Bd. & Chief Exec. Officer--The Coakley Heagerty Companies, Ltd., San Jose, CA, pg. 256
Healey, Robert T., Chm. Bd.--Viking Yacht Co., New Gretna, NJ, pg. 1151
Healy, Sondra A., Chm. Bd.--Turtle Wax, Inc., Chicago, IL, pg. 1120
Hearn, Richard E., Chm. Bd.--Capital City Press, Inc., Montpelier, VT, pg. 214
Hearst, Randolph A., Chm. Bd.--The Hearst Corporation, New York, NY, pg. 521
Hearst, Randolph A., Chm. Bd.--Colonial Homes, New York, NY, pg. 523
Heath, Milton W., Jr., Chm. Bd., Chief Exec. Officer & Treas.--Heath Consultants Incorporated, Stoughton, MA, pg. 524
Heath, Robert E., Chm. Bd.--Associated Grocers of New England, Inc., Manchester, NH, pg. 90
Hecht, Jack L., Chm. Bd.--Queens Group, Inc., Long Island City, NY, pg. 904
Hedger, Dick, Chm.--Ayer Ltd., London,, United Kingdom, pg. 104
Hedger, Richard, Chm. & Dir.-Europe--N W Ayer Incorporated, New York, NY, pg. 103
Hedinger, Howard, Chm. Bd. & Treas.--American Industries Inc., Portland, OR, pg. 55
Hedlund, J.C., Chm. Bd. & Pres.--California Offset Printers, Inc., Glendale, CA, pg. 210
Heeringa, Donald G., Chm. Bd. & Pres.--Trendway Corporation, Holland, MI, pg. 1109
Heffner, Ralph H., Chm. Bd.--Agway, Inc., De Witt, NY, pg. 25
Hegnar, Trygve, Chm. Bd. & Chief Exec. Officer--Norwegian Cruise Line, Coral Gables, FL, pg. 816
Heidrich, James K., Jr., Chm. Bd., Pres. & Chief Exec. Officer--The Miami Margarine Co., Cincinnati, OH, pg. 746
Heil, Joseph F., Jr., Chm. Bd. & Chief Exec. Officer--The Heil Co., Chattanooga, TN, pg. 525
Heiman, Paul, Chm. Bd. & Chief Exec. Officer--Standard Textile Co., Inc., Cincinnati, OH, pg. 1037
Heimberg, Eugene, Chm.--The Prudential Realty Group, Newark, NJ, pg. 897
Heinz, Edward, Chm. Bd.--Bell Flavors & Fragrances, Northbrook, IL, pg. 134
Heldberg, Quentin, Chm. Bd.--Central Livestock Association, Inc., South St. Paul, MN, pg. 233
Helgeson, Donald P., Chm. Bd.--JFC Inc., Saint Cloud, MN, pg. 584
Hellberg, Clifford, Chm. Bd., Pres., Chief Exec. Officer--Creative Productions, Pittsburgh, PA, pg. 297
Hellenbrand, V.J., Chm. Bd. & Pres.--Research Products Corporation, Madison, WI, pg. 928
Heller, C.M., Jr., Vice Chm. & Treas.--Marquette Coppersmithing Co., Inc., Philadelphia, PA, pg. 713
Heller, James, Chm. Bd.--Heller Bros. Packing Corp., Winter Garden, FL, pg. 526
Heller, John R., Chm. Bd. & Pres.--Heller Seasonings & Ingredients, Inc., Bedford Park, IL, pg. 526
Hellige, Tim, Chm.--Bandy Carroll Hellige Advertising, Louisville, KY, pg. 117
Helmer, Elmer J., Chm. Bd.--The Commercial Bank, Delphos, OH, pg. 268
Helmick, Louis G., Chm. Bd.--Helmick Corporation, Fairmont, WV, pg. 527
Helms, W. Edd, Jr., Chm.--Edd Helms Electrical Contracting, Miami, FL, pg. 527
Helmsley, Harry B., Chm. Bd., Pres. & Chief Exec. Officer--Helmsley Enterprises, Inc., New York, NY, pg. 527
Helpern, David, Chm. Bd.--Helpern Joan & David, Inc., Everett, MA, pg. 528
Helton, Michael R., Chm. Bd.--E.J. Bartells Co., Renton, WA, pg. 122
Helzberg, Barnett C., Jr., Chm. Bd. & Chief Exec. Officer--Helzberg's Diamond Shops, Inc., North Kansas City, MO, pg. 528
Hemmer, Paul W., Sr., Chm. Bd.--Paul Hemmer Construction Company, Fort Mitchell, KY, pg. 528
Hemphill, Robert B., Chm., Pres. & Chief Exec. & Chief Oper. Officer--Barclay White Incorporated, Berwyn, PA, pg. 119
Hempt, Max C., Chm. Bd.--Hempt Brothers, Inc., Camp Hill, PA, pg. 528
Henderson, C. Max, Chm. Bd. & Chief Exec. Officer--Laroche Holdings, Inc., Atlanta, GA, pg. 659
Henderson, Robert J., Sr., Chm. Bd., Pres. & Chief Exec. Officer--Ford Development Corporation, Cincinnati, OH, pg. 423
Henderson, Rodney J., Chm. Bd.--Henderson Electric Co., Inc., Louisville, KY, pg. 529
Hendricks, Kenneth A., Chm. Bd., Pres. & Chief Exec. Officer--ABC Supply Company, Inc., Beloit, WI, pg. 2
Hendrix, Tom E., Chm. Bd., Pres. & Chief Exec. Officer--Henco, Inc., Selmer, TN, pg. 528
Henkel, David R., Chm. Bd. & Pres.--Johnson & Quin, Inc., Niles, IL, pg. 599
Henkels, Paul M., Chm. Bd.--Henkels & McCoy, Inc., Blue Bell, PA, pg. 529
Henley, A.B., Jr., Chm. Bd.--Henley Paper Company, Greensboro, NC, pg. 529
Henley, Doy B., Chm. Bd.--Cox Hobbies, Inc., Corona, CA, pg. 294
Hennesberry, William H., Chm. Bd.--Communications Diversified, New York, NY, pg. 269
Hennessy, John M., Chm. Bd.--The First Boston Corporation, New York, NY, pg. 203
Hennesy, Dan, Chm. Bd.--Hirsh Company, Skokie, IL, pg. 258
Hennesy, Thomas J., Chm. Bd. & Chief Exec. Officer--TSC Industries, Inc., Nashville, TN, pg. 1075
Henningsen, Victor W., Jr., Chm.--Henningsen Foods, Inc., White Plains, NY, pg. 629
Henry, Harry, Chm. Bd.--The Asher Winer Company, Fitchburg, MA, pg. 88
Henry, R.E., Sr., Chm. Bd.--Fostoria Industries, Inc., Fostoria, OH, pg. 427
Hensler, William, Chm. Bd.--Wickes Lumber Co., Vernon Hills, IL, pg. 1188
Hensley, Chad, Chm. Bd.--Midwest Mutual Insurance Co., West Des Moines, IA, pg. 886
Henson, J. Peter, Chm. Bd. & Chief Exec. Officer--Flexible Products Company, Marietta, GA, pg. 418
Herb, Marvin J., Chm. Bd. & Chief Exec. Officer--Coca-Cola Bottling Co. of Chicago, Niles, IL, pg. 257
Herbster, Charles, Chm. Bd. & Pres.--Conklin Co. Inc., Shakopee, MN, pg. 274
Hergenrader, W.J., Chm. Bd.--Cummins Mid-South, Inc., Memphis, TN, pg. 305
Herley, John R., Chm. Bd.--Atlas Wire Corporation, Schiller Park, IL, pg. 97
Herlin, Robert M., Chm. Bd. & Chief Exec. Officer--Herlin Press, West Haven, CT, pg. 531
Herman, Loeb, Jr., Chm. Bd.--Piknik Products Company, Inc., Montgomery, AL, pg. 870
Hermann, Ronald B., Chm. & Pres.--General Automotive Specialty Co., Inc., North Brunswick, NJ, pg. 449
Hermanson, Merril, Chm. Bd. & Chief Exec. Officer--Mr. Christmas Inc., New York, NY, pg. 761
Hernandez, Noel, Chm. Bd., Pres. & Chief Fin. Officer--Graphic Productions Company, Miami, FL, pg. 478
Hershbeger, Terry, Chm. Bd.--Sargent & Greenleaf, Inc., Nicholasville, KY, pg. 971
Herst, Douglas J., Chm. Bd. & Pres.--Peerless Lighting Corp., Berkeley, CA, pg. 855
Hertel, Al, Chm. Bd.--Drug Guild Distributors, Inc., Secaucus, NJ, pg. 349
Hertrich, Adolf, Chm. Bd.--Vanport Manufacturing, Inc., Boring, OR, pg. 1145
Hertz, Arthur, Chm. Bd. & Chief Exec. Officer--Wometco Enterprises, Inc., Coral Gables, FL, pg. 1199
Hess, Emil C., Chm. Bd.--Parisian, Inc., Birmingham, AL, pg. 848
Hess, Johann T., Chm. Bd.--Hess Engineering Inc., Niles, MI, pg. 532
Hess, Marshall, Chm. Bd.--Fishers Big Wheel Inc., New Castle, PA, pg. 415
Hess, Robert, Chm. Bd. & Pres.--Lancaster Malleable Castings Company, Lancaster, PA, pg. 653
Hesser, E. Grant, Chm. Bd.--Maescher Industries, Inc., Cincinnati, OH, pg. 699
Heston, W. Craig, Chm. & Chief Exec. Officer--Utica Mutual Insurance Company, New Hartford, NY, pg. 1140
Hetherwick, Fred B., Chm. Bd., Pres. & Chief Exec. Officer--Plastigage Corporation, Jackson, MI, pg. 876
Heyman, Leonard J., Chm. Bd., Pres., Chief Exec. & Chief Oper. Officer--Heyman Corporation, Niles, IL, pg. 532
Heyman, Samuel J., Chm. Bd. & Chief Exec. Officer--GAF Corporation, Wayne, NJ, pg. 438
Heyman, Samuel J., Chm. Bd.--GAF Building Materials Corporation, Wayne, NJ, pg. 438
Heyman, Samuel J., Chm. Bd.--International Specialty Products, Inc., Wilmington, DE, pg. 438
Hickerson, Ken, Chm.--Hickerson Phelps Kirtley & Associates, Kansas City, MO, pg. 532
Hickman, S. Martin, Chm. Bd. & Chief Exec. Officer--Blue Cross & Blue Shield of Illinois, Chicago, IL, pg. 160
Hicks, Donald J., Chm. Bd., Pres. & Chief Exec. Officer--Hicks & Associates Inc., Coral Gables, FL, pg. 982
Hiemenz, John F., Chm. Bd.--Lobdell-Emery Manufacturing Company, Alma, MI, pg. 680
Higdon, Allan K., Chm.--Sullivan Higdon & Sink Incorporated, Wichita, KS, pg. 1056

Corporate Responsibilities Index

Higgins, Larry B., Chm. Bd., Pres. & Chief Exec. Officer--H & H Tube & Manufacturing Co., Vanderbilt, MI, pg. 495
Hildreth, Charles L., Jr., Chm. Bd.--Emery Waterhouse Company, Portland, ME, pg. 379
Hill, George J., III, Chm.--Hill, Holliday, Connors, Cosmopulos, Inc., Boston, MA, pg. 534
Hill, Stephen R., Chm. & Pres.--Tone Commander Systems, Redmond, WA, pg. 1101
Hill, William L., Chm. Bd. & Exec. Dir.-Creative--Levenson & Hill, Inc., Irving, TX, pg. 670
Hillman, Henry, Chm. Bd.--Hillman Company, Pittsburgh, PA, pg. 535
Hilt, John, Chm. Bd. & Chief Exec. Officer--Quality Stores Inc., North Muskegon, MI, pg. 904
Himeles, Martin S., Chm. Bd. & Chief Exec. Officer--Standard Medical Imaging, Inc., Columbia, MD, pg. 1037
Himes, Michael B., Chm. Bd., Pres. & Chief Exec. Officer--Petroleum Traders Corporation, Fort Wayne, IN, pg. 865
Hinckley, Gordon B., Chm. Bd.--Deseret Management Corporation, Salt Lake City, UT, pg. 332
Hinckley, Gordon B., Chm.--Bonneville International Corp., Salt Lake City, UT, pg. 332
Hindman, Don J., Chm. Bd. & Chief Exec. Officer--Clark Foodservice, Inc., Elk Grove Village, IL, pg. 252
Hindson, M. Tal, Chm. & Chief Exec. Officer--Tal Inc., Erie, PA, pg. 1077
Hines, Milton, Chm. & Pres.--Atchison County Co-op Association, Atchison, KS, pg. 93
Hinkle, Donald, Chm.-Exec. Committee--Dunes Hotels and Casinos Inc., Las Vegas, NV, pg. 352
Hinton, James, Chm. Bd.--R.L. Ziegler Co. Inc., Tuscaloosa, AL, pg. 1218
Hippeau, Eric, Chm. Bd.--Ziff-Davis Publishing Company, New York, NY, pg. 1219
Hirsch, Charles L., Chm. Bd.--Charles Leonard, Inc., Glendale, NY, pg. 668
Hirsch, Gary D., Chm., Pres., Dir., & Treas.--Grand Union Holdings Corporation, Riverside, CT, pg. 475
Hirsch, Gary D., Chm. Bd.--The Grand Union Company, Wayne, NJ, pg. 476
Hiruma, T., Chm. Bd.--Hamamatsu Corp., Bridgewater, NJ, pg. 502
Hishmeh, Basem L., Chm. Bd. & Treas.--Aerco International Inc., Northvale, NJ, pg. 21
Hitchcock, Donald S., Chm. & Chief Exec. Officer--Knight Architects Engineers Planners, Inc., Chicago, IL, pg. 637
Hitchcock, Gregory T., Chm. Bd.--Hitchcock Industries, Inc., Bloomington, MN, pg. 536
Hitchcock, Robert, Chm. Bd.--Affiliated of Florida Inc., Tampa, FL, pg. 23
Hladky, Joseph, Jr., Chm. Bd.--Gazette Company, Inc., Cedar Rapids, IA, pg. 447
Hoard, Ralph G., Exec. V.P.--Icicle Seafoods, Inc., Seattle, WA, pg. 561
Hobart, W.H., Chm. Bd., Pres., Chief Exec. & Chief Oper. Officer--Hobart Brothers Co., Troy, OH, pg. 536
Hochfelder, J. Gene, Chm. & Chief Exec. Officer--Beldoch Industries Corporation, West Hempstead, NY, pg. 133
Hodes, Alan, Chm. Bd. & Pres.--Pen-Tab Industries, Inc., Glendale, NY, pg. 856
Hodges, James, Chm. Bd.--Town Square Furniture, Inc., Hillsboro, TX, pg. 1104
Hodin, Joseph, Chm., Pres. & Chief Exec. Officer--Giant Markets Inc., Scranton, PA, pg. 456
Hoelzer, Dennis, Chm. Bd., Pres. & Chief Exec. Officer--Sentinel Computer Services Inc., Oak Brook, IL, pg. 990
Hoffman, Ebba C., Chm., Pres., Chief Exec. & Chief Fin. Officer--Smead Manufacturing Company, Hastings, MN, pg. 1011
Hoffman, Edmund, Chm. Bd.--Coca-Cola Bottling Co. of the Southwest, San Antonio, TX, pg. 257
Hoffman, Eric, Chm. Bd.--Hoffman Corporation, Portland, OR, pg. 537
Hofmeister, George S., Chm. Bd. & Pres.--EWI, Inc., Salem, OH, pg. 361
Hogg, Michael, Chm. Bd. (Zimbabwe)--Young & Rubicam (Zambia) Ltd., Lusaka,, Zambia, pg. 1214
Hogg, William T., Jr., Chm. Bd.--Trend Line Corporation, Jackson, MS, pg. 1109
Hohn, Harry, Chm. Bd.--New York Life Foundation, New York, NY, pg. 803
Hohn, Harry G., Chm. Bd. & Chief Exec. Officer--New York Life Insurance Company, New York, NY, pg. 802
Hoke, Joe, Chm., Pres. & Chief Exec. Officer--Mintz & Hoke Inc., Avon, CT, pg. 759
Hokin, Richard, Chm. Bd.--Intermountain Industries, Inc., Boise, ID, pg. 575
Hokin, Richard, Chm. Bd.--Intermountain Gas Co., Boise, ID, pg. 575
Hokin, Richard, Chm. Bd.--IGI Resources, Inc., Boise, ID, pg. 575
Holden, Richmond Y., Sr., Chm. Bd.--J. L. Hammett Company, Braintree, MA, pg. 504
Holder, George H., Sr., Chm. Bd.--Hershey Creamery Company, Harrisburg, PA, pg. 531
Holder, Robert M., Jr., Chm. Bd.--Holder Corporation, Atlanta, GA, pg. 538
Holdstein, Sophie, Chm. Bd.--General Sportcraft Company Ltd., Bergenfield, NJ, pg. 450
Holland, Clive, Chm.--Young & Rubicam Holdings Ltd., London, United Kingdom, pg. 1213
Holland, John B., Chm. Bd. & Chief Exec. Officer--Union Underwear Co., Inc., Bowling Green, KY, pg. 400
Holland, Ron, Chm. Bd.--Ron Holland Advertising Inc., New York, NY, pg. 539
Hollander, Jules A., Chm. Bd. & Treas.--Hartford Distributors Inc., Manchester, CT, pg. 514
Hollander, Per M., Chm. Bd.--A. J. Hollander Co., Inc., New York, NY, pg. 539
Holleman, Matt, Chm. Bd.--Capitol Street Corp., Jackson, MS, pg. 216
Hollern, Michael P., Chm. Bd. & Pres.--Brooks Resources Corporation, Bend, OR, pg. 180
Holley, Jack, Chm. Bd.--Gramex Corporation, Bridgeton, MO, pg. 475
Hollister, Dean, Chm Bd.--SB Entertainment Inc., New Providence, NJ, pg. 960
Holloway, Caswell F., Jr., Chm. Bd.--Josam Company, Michigan City, IN, pg. 607
Holman, Brian F., Chm.--Kartridg Pak Co., Davenport, IA, pg. 122
Holman, Joseph S., Chm. Bd.--Holman Enterprises, Pennsauken, NJ, pg. 540
Holman, W. H., Jr., Chm. Bd., Pres. & Chief Exec. & Oper. Officers--Jitney-Jungle Stores of America, Inc., Jackson, MS, pg. 594
Holmes, Adrian, Chm.--Lowe Howard-Spink Limited, London,, United Kingdom, pg. 685
Holmes, Harold, Co-Chm. Bd.--Taco John's International, Inc., Cheyenne, WY, pg. 1076
Holmes, Neal H., Chm. Bd.--Allied Security, Inc., Pittsburgh, PA, pg. 39
Holmes, Robert M., Chm. Bd. & Chief Exec. Officer--Oltmans Construction Company, Whittier, CA, pg. 824
Holmgren, Richard S., Jr., Chm. Bd.--James M. Montgomery Consulting Engineers, Pasadena, CA, pg. 767
Holsapple, E., Chm. Bd.--Welsh Farms, Inc., Long Valley, NJ, pg. 1175
Holt, Dennis F., Chm., Chief Exec. Officer--Western International Merchandising, Los Angeles, CA, pg. 1180
Holt, Dennis F., Chm., Chief Exec. Officer--Western International Premiums, Los Angeles, CA, pg. 1180
Holt, Ralph M., Jr., Chm. Bd.--Holt Hosiery Mills, Inc., Burlington, NC, pg. 541
Holtz, Abel, Chm. Bd. & Pres.--Capital Bancorp, Miami, FL, pg. 214
Holtz, Abel, Chm. Bd.--Capital Factors, Inc., Fort Lauderdale, FL, pg. 214
Holtz, Abel, Chm. Bd.--Capital Bank, N.A., Washington, DC, pg. 214
Holzer, Herbert, Exec. V.P.--Publix Group, New York, NY, pg. 898
Homes, W.G., Chm. Bd.--Homes & Son Contractors, Inc., Phoenix, AZ, pg. 542
Homrighaus, William E., Chm.--Daniel Green Co., Dolgeville, NY, pg. 484
Honek, Joseph A., Chm. Bd.--Connecticut Drive Shaft, Inc., Milford, CT, pg. 274
Hooker, Gary R., Chm. Bd.--Hooker Industries, Ontario, CA, pg. 543
Hooker, J. Clyde, Jr., Chm. Bd. & Chief Exec. Officer--Hooker Furniture Corporation, Martinsville, VA, pg. 543
Hopkins, Robert E., Chm. & Chief Exec. Officer--Schneller, Inc., Kent, OH, pg. 977
Hopper, Victor D., Chm. Bd., Pres. & Chief Exec. Officer--Hopper Inc., Bakersfield, CA, pg. 543
Hopson, Thomas R., Sr., Chm. Bd.--Thomas R. Hopson Broker, Inc., Marietta, GA, pg. 544
Horn, G. Arthur, Chm. Bd.--Horn Packaging Corporation, Ayer, MA, pg. 544
Horn, Russell E., Sr., Chm. Bd.--Pace Resources, Inc., York, PA, pg. 838
Horowitz, Edward D., Chm. & Chief Exec. Officer--Viacom Broadcasting Inc., New York, NY, pg. 785
Horrigan, D. Greg, Chm. Bd. & Chief Exec. Officer--Silgan Corporation, Stamford, CT, pg. 1004
Hort, Robert, Chm. Bd. & Sec.--Enterprise Press, Inc., New York, NY, pg. 382
Hosch, Robert F., Chm. Bd. & Pres.--Harris Mechanical Contracting Co., Saint Paul, MN, pg. 512
Hosie, William, Chm. Bd.--Sun Diamond Growers of California, Pleasanton, CA, pg. 1058
Hoskins, John T., Chm.--Curtis Screw Co., Inc., Buffalo, NY, pg. 306
Hospodor, Andrew T., Chm. Bd. & Chief Exec. Officer--Arinc Inc., Annapolis, MD, pg. 82
Hospodor, Andrew T., Chm. & Chief Exec. Officer--ARINC Research Corp., Annapolis, MD, pg. 82
Hostetter, Amos B., Jr., Chm. Bd. & Chief Exec. Officer--Continental Cablevision, Boston, MA, pg. 278
Hostetter, Richard, Chm. Bd.--Century Boats By General Marine Industries, Panama City, FL, pg. 450
Hotovy, Robert, Chm. Bd.--Creation Windows of Indiana, Inc., Elkhart, IN, pg. 297
Hougan, Tom M., Chm.--Gerber Advertising, Portland, OR, pg. 453
Hougen, Everett D., Chm. Bd.--Hougen Manufacturing Inc., Flint, MI, pg. 546
Hough, Richard T., Chm. Bd.--CHEMCENTRAL Corporation, Bedford Park, IL, pg. 241
Houghton, Tony, Chm., Chief Exec. Officer--Leo Burnett Company Ltd., Toronto,, Canada, pg. 192
Houlihan, Lawrence, Chm. Bd., Pres., Chief Exec. & Chief Fin. Officer, Treas. & Sec.--Frank B. Ross Co. Inc., Jersey City, NJ, pg. 949
Housen, Charles B., Chm. Bd., Pres. & Chief Exec. Officer--Erving Paper Mills, Erving, MA, pg. 388
Houston, Douglas, Chm. Bd. & Chief Exec. Officer--Houston Effler & Partners, Boston, MA, pg. 546
Houston, Ivan J., Chm. Bd.--Golden State Mutual Life Insurance Company, Los Angeles, CA, pg. 467
Houston, Robert A., Chm. Bd.--Office Electronics, Inc., Itasca, IL, pg. 821
Hovekamp, George D., Sr., Chm. Bd.--Kruse Hardware Company, Fairfield, OH, pg. 645
Hovespian, Suren, Chm. Bd. & Pres.--Lafayette Steel Co., Detroit, MI, pg. 650
Howard, J.T., Chm.-Emeritus--Howard, Merrell & Partners, Inc., Raleigh, NC, pg. 547
Howard, William G., Chm. Bd.--Mercer Transportation Co., Louisville, KY, pg. 739
Howe, Harold, Jr., Chm. Bd., Chief Exec. Officer & Treas.--Howe Furniture Corporation, Trumbull, CT, pg. 547
Howell, James, Chm. Bd. & Dir.--Aetna Health Plans, San Bruno, CA, pg. 23
Howell, John S., Chm. Bd., Pres. & Chief Exec. Officer--Howell Instruments Corp., Fort Worth, TX, pg. 547
Howenstein, William K., Chm. Bd. & Chief Exec. Officer--Copper & Brass Sales, Inc., East Detroit, MI, pg. 284
Howk, Richard H., Chm. Bd. & Pres.--Mathews & Boucher, Rochester, NY, pg. 720
Howson, Robert E., Chm. & Chief Exec. Officer--The Babcock & Wilcox Company, New Orleans, LA, pg. 107
Hoyt, Bruce K., Chm. Bd.--Vinyl Therm, Inc., Bloomington, MN, pg. 1152
Hoyt, Leon G., Chm. & Chief Exec. Officer--Knight/Emerson Consulting, Inc., Chicago, IL, pg. 637
Hradko, Joe, Chm. Bd. & Pres.--Cragar Industries, Compton, CA, pg. 761
Hsu, Ronald, Chm. Bd.--Ronald Hsu Construction, Capitol Heights, MD, pg. 548
Hua, Xiong Yao, Chm.--Dentsu, Young & Rubicam/Beijing, Beijing, People's Republic of China, pg. 330
Hubbard, Martin, Chm. Bd.--Harley Industries, Inc., Tulsa, OK, pg. 509
Hubbard, R.D., Chm. Bd., Pres. & Chief Exec. Officer--AFG Industries, Inc., Fort Worth, TX, pg. 3
Hubbard, Robert A., Chm. Bd. & Pres.--Wilbur Smith Associates, Columbia, SC, pg. 1011
Hubbard, Stanley S., Chm., Pres., & Chief Exec. Officer--Hubbard Broadcasting, Inc., Saint Paul, MN, pg. 548
Hubbard, Stanley S., Chm. Bd. & Chief Exec. Officer--KSTP-TV, Saint Paul, MN, pg. 549
Huber, E. W., Chm. Bd.--Topflight Corp., York, PA, pg. 1102
Huber, M.W., Chm. Bd.--J.M. Huber Corporation, Edison, NJ, pg. 550
Huber, Ron, Chm. Bd., Pres. & Chief Exec. Officer--Time Systems, Inc., Phoenix, AZ, pg. 1097
Huber, Ron, Chm. Bd., Pres. & Chief Exec. Officer--Time Index, Inc., Phoenix, AZ, pg. 1097
Hubert, Edward, Chm. Bd.--Hubert Company, Harrison, OH, pg. 550
Hubner, Cornelius A., Chm. Bd.--Central/Shippee, Inc., Bloomingdale, NJ, pg. 234
Hubner, Cornelius A., Chm. Bd.--Allied Felt Group, Bloomingdale, NJ, pg. 234
Hubner, W., Chm. Bd.--Paramount Fitness Equipment Corp., Los Angeles, CA, pg. 848
Hudetz, Frank C., Chm. Bd. & Chief Exec. Officer--Solar Press, Inc., Naperville, IL, pg. 1016
Hudson, Chris, Chm. Bd., Pres. & Chief Exec. Officer--Automation Intelligence, Inc., Maitland, FL, pg. 101
Hudson, Keith B., Chm. Bd.--Maui Divers Of Hawaii, Ltd., Honolulu, HI, pg. 721
Hudson, Lester, Chm. Bd.--Wunda Weve Carpet Co., Greenville, SC, pg. 1205
Hudson, M. R., Chm. Bd. & Pres.--Fisca Oil Co., Inc., Westwood, KS, pg. 414
Hughes, George E., Sr., Chm. Bd.--E.H. Hughes Company, Inc., Louisville, KY, pg. 552
Hughes, Jim, Chm., Pres. & Creative Dir.--TH&M Advertising, Inc., Irvine, CA, pg. 1073
Hughes, Roger K., Chm. Bd.--Hughes Markets Inc., Irwindale, CA, pg. 552
Huitt, E. Larry, Chm. Bd., Sec. & Treas.--Huitt-Zollars, Inc., Dallas, TX, pg. 552
Hull, Lewis, Chm. Bd.--Hull Corporation, Hatboro, PA, pg. 552
Huls, Harrison, Chm. Bd.--Hale-Halsell Company, Tulsa, OK, pg. 500
Hultquist, Keith, Chm. Bd.--Evergreen Mills Inc., Ada, OK, pg. 1145
Hume, William J., Chm. Bd.--Basic American Foods, San Francisco, CA, pg. 124
Humphrey, G. Watts, Jr., Chm. Bd. & Chief Exec. Officer--The Conair Group, Inc., Pittsburgh, PA, pg. 272
Humphrey, John W., Chm. Bd.--The Forum Corporation, Boston, MA, pg. 425
Hunsberger, Ruby Moore, Chm. Bd.--Crown International, Inc., Elkhart, IN, pg. 302
Hunt, E.C., Jr., Chm. Bd. & Chief Exec. Officer--Thermo Industries Inc., Charlotte, NC, pg. 1091
Hunt, Frank M., Chm. Bd. & Pres.--Citrus World Inc., Lake Wales, FL, pg. 251
Hunt, L., Chm.--The Campaign Palace, Melbourne,, Australia, pg. 111
Hunt, Ray L., Chm. Bd. & Chief Exec. Officer--Hunt Oil Company, Dallas, TX, pg. 553
Hunt, Robert C., Chm. Bd. & Chief Exec. Officer--The Hunt Corporation, Indianapolis, IN, pg. 553
Hunte, Henry F., Chm. Bd. & Chief Exec. Officer--H.G. Fenton Material Company, San Diego, CA, pg. 406
Hunter, B.D., Chm. Bd.--Huntco Inc., Chesterfield, MO, pg. 554
Huntington, Lawrence S., Chm. Bd.--Fiduciary Trust Co. International, New York, NY, pg. 408
Huntington, Lawrence S., Chm. Bd. & Chief Exec. Officer--Fiduciary Trust Company International, New York, NY, pg. 408
Huntsinger, Jerald E., Chm. & Founder--Huntsinger & Jeffer, Richmond, VA, pg. 555
Huntsman, Jon M., Chm. Bd. & Chief Exec. Officer--Huntsman Chemical Corporation, Salt Lake City, UT, pg. 555
Hurd, G. David, Chm. Bd., Pres. & Chief Exec. Officer--The Principal Financial Group, Des Moines, IA, pg. 890
Hurley, Dr. William D., Chm. Bd. & Chief Exec. Officer--Harvard Industries, Inc., Farmingdale, NJ, pg. 514
Hurley, William D., Chm. Bd.--Fel Corporation, Farmingdale, NJ, pg. 405
Hurley, William D., Chm. Bd.--FEL Corporation, Farmingdale, NJ, pg. 394
Hurvis, Tom, Chm. Bd.--Old World Industries, Inc., Northbrook, IL, pg. 823
Hussman, Walter E., Jr., Chm. Bd., Pres. & Publr.--Wehco Media, Inc., Little Rock, AR, pg. 1172
Huston, Preston D., Chm. Bd. & Chief Exec. Officer--Associated Advertising Agency, Inc., Wichita, KS, pg. 89
Hutchins, Burleigh M., Chm. Bd.--Zymark Corporation, Hopkinton, MA, pg. 1221

Hvide, Hans J., Chm. Bd.--Hvide Shipping, Inc., Fort Lauderdale, FL, pg. 556
Hyatt, Frederick, Chm. Bd.--Marshall & Williams Co., Greenville, SC, pg. 714
Iacovelli, Guido, Chm. Bd. & Pres.--Chef Italia, Inc., Vestal, NY, pg. 241
Iarossi, Frank J., Chm. Bd. & Pres.--American Bureau of Shipping, New York, NY, pg. 50
Iason, Girard, Chm.--N. Erlanger, Blumgart & Company, Inc., New York, NY, pg. 387
Ibos, Robert J., Chm. Bd., Pres. & Chief Exec. Officer--National Engineering & Contracting Co., Strongsville, OH, pg. 788
Ibsen, Dr. Robert, Chm. Bd., Pres., Chief Exec. Officer & Treas.--Den-Mat Corporation, Santa Maria, CA, pg. 328
Icahn, Carl C., Chm. Bd. & Chief Exec. Officer--Icahn & Co., Inc., Mount Kisco, NY, pg. 561
Icahn, Carl C., Chm. Bd. & Chief Exec. Officer--Trans World Airlines, Inc., Mount Kisco, NY, pg. 561
Icahn, Carl C., Chm. Bd.--ACF Industries, Inc., Earth City, MO, pg. 561
Idelman, Steven A., Chm. Bd.--ITI Marketing Services, Inc., Omaha, NE, pg. 561
Ilaria, Peter V., Chm. Bd. & Pres.--Tropar Mfg. Co., Inc., Florham Park, NJ, pg. 1115
Ilitch, Michael, Chm. Bd. & Pres.--Little Caesar Enterprises, Inc., Detroit, MI, pg. 678
Imboden, Stefan, Chm.--Zweiniederlassung Zurich, Zurich,, Switzerland, pg. 204
Imperatore, Arthur E., Chm. Bd.--A-P-A Transport Corp., North Bergen, NJ, pg. 5
Indursky, Harry, Chm. Bd. & Pres.--Cambridge Street Metal Co., Inc., Allston, MA, pg. 211
Infusino, Thomas P., Chm. Bd.--Wakefern Food Corporation, Elizabeth, NJ, pg. 1158
Ing, Sheridan C.F., Chm. Bd.--Aloha Airgroup, Inc., Honolulu, HI, pg. 43
Ing, Sheridan C.F., Chm. Bd. & Dir.--Aloha Airlines, Inc., Honolulu, HI, pg. 43
Ingalls, Daniel H.H., Sr., Chm. Bd.--Virginia Hot Springs, Inc., Hot Springs, VA, pg. 1152
Ingle, R.P., Chm. & Chief Exec. Officer--Ingles Markets, Inc., Asheville, NC, pg. 568
Ingram, E.W., Jr., Chm. Bd.--White Castle System, Inc., Columbus, OH, pg. 1185
Ingram, John C., Chm. Bd.--Ingram Paper Company, City of Industry, CA, pg. 569
Ingram, Richard E., Chm. Bd., Chief Exec. & Chief Fin. Officer--Builder Marts of America, Greenville, SC, pg. 187
Inman, Frank, Jr., Chm. Bd.--Inman Construction Corporation, Memphis, TN, pg. 570
Inman, Paul, Chm. Bd.--Paul Inman Associates Inc., Farmington Hills, MI, pg. 570
Ireton, John F., Chm. Bd.--American Foodservice Corp., King of Prussia, PA, pg. 54
Isaias, Roberto, Co-Chm.--Republic National Bank Of Miami, Miami, FL, pg. 928
Isen, Harold, Chm. Bd. & Chief Exec. Officer--Paramount Packaging Corp., Chalfont, PA, pg. 848
Isherwood, Robert, Chm. Bd. & Pres.--Ambac International Corp., Columbia, SC, pg. 47
Isola, Alfred, Chm. Bd. & Pres.--Silver State Disposal Service, Inc., Las Vegas, NV, pg. 1004
Isom, W. Howard, Chm. Bd.--Blue Diamond Growers, Sacramento, CA, pg. 160
Isseleib, Lutz, Chm., Pres. & Chief Oper. Officer--Falstaff Brewing Corporation, Vancouver, WA, pg. 959
Issleib, Lutz, Chm. Bd. & Pres.--S & P Company, Mill Valley, CA, pg. 959
Issleib, Lutz E., Chm. Bd. & Pres.--Pabst Brewing Co., San Antonio, TX, pg. 959
Iwakiri, Brooks, Chm. Bd.--Trend Offset Printing Services, Los Alamitos, CA, pg. 1109
Iwasaki, Minoru, Chm. Bd.--Pioneer/Eclipse Corp., Sparta, NC, pg. 871
Jaccoma, George E., Chm. Bd.--Marshall Jaccoma Mitchell Advertising, New York, NY, pg. 714
Jackman, Joseph R., Chm. Bd., Pres. & Chief Exec. Officer--Reactive Metals & Alloys Corporation (REMACOR), West Pittsburg, PA, pg. 916
Jackson, Mary Anne, Chm., Pres. & Chief Oper. Officer--My Own Meals, Inc., Deerfield, IL, pg. 779
Jackson, Philip C., Chm. Bd., Pres. & Chief Exec. Officer--Ateron Corp., Parsippany, NJ, pg. 93
Jackson, Ron, Chm. & Creative Dir.--Communico, Indianapolis, IN, pg. 270
Jackson, Seaborn W., Jr., Chm. Bd.--Weldon, Williams & Lick, Inc., Fort Smith, AR, pg. 1175
Jackson, William H., Chm. Bd.--Humphrey Products Company, Kalamazoo, MI, pg. 553
Jacob, Herbert H., Chm. Bd. & Chief Exec. Officer--Ajax Paving Industries Inc., Madison Heights, MI, pg. 28
Jacobs, Burleigh E., Chm. Bd.--Grede Foundries, Inc., Milwaukee, WI, pg. 483
Jacobs, Eli, Chm. Bd. & Chief Exec. Officer--Triangle Pacific Corporation, Dallas, TX, pg. 1112
Jacobs, Eli S., Chm. Bd.--Baltimore Orioles, Inc., Baltimore, MD, pg. 116
Jacobs, Eli S., Chm. Bd.--Industrial General Corporation, Elyria, OH, pg. 566
Jacobs, Howard S., Chm. Bd.--Industrial Ceramics, Inc., Derry, PA, pg. 566
Jacobs, I.L., Chm. Bd.--Genmar Industries, Inc., Minneapolis, MN, pg. 759
Jacobs, Irwin L., Chm. Bd. & Chief Exec. Officer--Minstar, Inc., Minneapolis, MN, pg. 758
Jacobs, Irwin L., Chm. Bd.--Watkins Incorporated, Winona, MN, pg. 1167
Jacobs, Jeremy M., Chm. & Chief Exec. Officer--Delaware North Companies, Inc., Buffalo, NY, pg. 326
Jacobs, K.J., Chm. Bd.--E.J. Brach Corporation, Oakbrook Terrace, IL, pg. 169
Jacobs, Richard E., Chm. Bd. & Chief Exec. Officer--The Richard & David Jacobs Group, Westlake, OH, pg. 932
Jacobs, Robert Lee, Chm. Bd.--Frog Switch & Manufacturing Company, Carlisle, PA, pg. 434
Jacobson, Sidney, Chm. Bd.--Sid Tool Co. Inc., Plainview, NY, pg. 1002
Jacobson, Sidney, Chm. Bd.--MSC Industrial Supply Co., Plainview, NY, pg. 693
Jacobson, Tryg, Chm. Bd.--Jacobson Rost, Inc., Sheboygan, WI, pg. 588
Jacoff, Richard, Chm. Bd.--Great Neck Saw Manufacturers, Inc., Mineola, NY, pg. 482
Jagoda, Leonard J., Chm., Pres. & Chief Exec. Officer--American SelfCare Corporation, Columbus, GA, pg. 60
Jamboretz, Glennon D., Chm. Bd., Pres. & Chief Exec. Officer--The Glennon Companies, Saint Louis, MO, pg. 462
James, G.W., Jr., Chm. Bd.--T.L. James & Company, Ruston, LA, pg. 588
James, Gene A., Chm. Bd.--CF Industries, Inc., Long Grove, IL, pg. 200
James, John H., Chm. Bd.--Texas Steel Co., Inc., Fort Worth, TX, pg. 1090
Jamison, John Vincent, III, Chm. Bd.--Jamison Door Company, Hagerstown, MD, pg. 589
Jamison, Thomas J., Chm. Bd. & Chief Exec. Officer--Southern Radio Corporation, pg. 1022
Jansen, Henry, Chm. Bd.--Lynden Incorporated, Seattle, WA, pg. 689
Janssen, Dan W., Chm. & Sr. V.P., Canada--Ziebart International Corporation, Troy, MI, pg. 1217
Janssen, Gail, Chm. Bd.--Badger Northland Inc., Kaukauna, WI, pg. 113
Jaworski, Walter J., Chm. Bd., Pres. Chief Exec. Officer & Chief Oper. Officer--Miken Companies, Inc., Cheektowaga, NY, pg. 752
Jay, Morton, Chm. Bd.--Campmor Inc., Paramus, NJ, pg. 213
Jaynes, Jerald K., Chm. Bd.--Meco Corporation, Greeneville, TN, pg. 734
Jayson, Joseph M., Chm. Bd. & Chief Exec. Officer--J. M. Jayson & Co., Inc., Getsville, NY, pg. 591
Jeanloz, Claude, Chm. Bd.--The Renovator's Supply, Inc., Millers Falls, MA, pg. 927
Jemison, Frank Z., Sr., Chm. Bd.--Jemison, Inc., Memphis, TN, pg. 592
Jenkins, Howard, Chm. Bd. & Chief Exec. Officer--Publix Supermarkets Inc., Lakeland, FL, pg. 898
Jenkins, Tiny, Chm. Bd. & Chief Exec. Officer--PSI Group of Companies, Memphis, TN, pg. 637
Jenks, Mrs. M. M., Chm. Bd. & Chief Exec. Officer--Mississippi Lime Co., Alton, IL, pg. 760
Jensen, Diane P., Chm. Bd.--Jensen Electric Company, Reno, NV, pg. 592
Jensen, Irving F., Jr., Chm., Treas. & Sec.--Irving F. Jensen Co., Inc., Sioux City, IA, pg. 593
Jerome, Wallace H., Chm. Bd.--Jerome Foods Inc., Barron, WI, pg. 593
Jessup, Stewart E., Chm. Bd.--Riceland Foods, Inc., Stuttgart, AR, pg. 931
Jewell, Everett G., Chm. Bd., Pres., Chief Exec. Officer & Treas.--Jewell Building Systems, Dallas, NC, pg. 594
Jewell, Robert B., Chm. Bd.--Mason Company, Lexington, KY, pg. 718
Jewell, Robert B., Chm. Bd.--Mason Hanger-Silas Mason Co., Lexington, KY, pg. 718
Joa, Curt G., Chm. Bd.--Curt G. Joa, Inc., Sheboygan Falls, WI, pg. 594
Jobs, Steven P., Chm. & Chief Exec. Officer--Next, Inc., Redwood City, CA, pg. 805
Joel, Larry, Chm. Bd.--Duling Optical Corporation, Louisville, KY, pg. 352
Joel, Larry, Chm. & Pres.--D & K Optical, Inc., Louisville, KY, pg. 307
Johanson, Edna L., Chm. Bd.--Johanson Manufacturing Corporation, Boonton, NJ, pg. 595
Johnannessen, Paul, Chm. Bd. & Pres.--Megapulse, Inc., Bedford, MA, pg. 737
Johnson, A. Stanley, Chm. Bd., Pres. & Chief Exec. Officer--Van Leunens Inc., Cincinnati, OH, pg. 1144
Johnson, Al, Chm. Bd.--Dobson & Johnson, Inc., Nashville, TN, pg. 342
Johnson, Albin S., Chm. & Chief Exec. Officer--Columbia Farms Inc., Leesville, SC, pg. 265
Johnson, Crawford, III, Chm. Bd.--Coca Cola Bottling Co. United, Inc., Birmingham, AL, pg. 257
Johnson, David O., Chm. & Chief Exec. Officer--Johnson Acoustical & Supply Co., Portland, OR, pg. 597
Johnson, Edward C., III, Chm. & Chief Exec. Officer--Fidelity Investments (FMR Corp.), Boston, MA, pg. 408
Johnson, Eric D., Chm. Bd., Chief Exec. Officer--Rick Johnson & Company, Inc., Albuquerque, NM, pg. 597
Johnson, Glendon E., Chm. Bd., Pres. & Chief Exec. Officer--John Alden Financial Corporation, Miami, FL, pg. 32
Johnson, J.D., Co-Chm. Bd., Pres. & Chief Exec. Officer--G.S. Blodgett Corporation, Burlington, VT, pg. 157
Johnson, John H., Chm. Bd. & Chief Exec. Officer--Johnson Publishing Company, Inc., Chicago, IL, pg. 598
Johnson, John H., Chm. Bd. & Chief Exec. Officer--Fashion Fair Cosmetics, Chicago, IL, pg. 599
Johnson, John L., Chm. Bd. & Pres.--Thoroughbred Software International, Inc., Somerset, NJ, pg. 1095
Johnson, LaRee K., Chm. Bd.--LeGrand Johnson Construction Co., Logan, UT, pg. 598
Johnson, Marlene A., Chm. Bd.--Sealaska Corporation, Juneau, AK, pg. 984
Johnson, Orville D., Chm. Bd. & Chief Exec. Officer--UFE Incorporated, Stillwater, MN, pg. 1123
Johnson, Ruth, Chm. Bd. & Chief Exec. Officer--I.C. System, Inc., Vadnais Heights, MN, pg. 558
Johnson, Samuel C., Chm. Bd.--S. C. Johnson & Son, Inc., Racine, WI, pg. 599
Johnson, W.B., Chm. Bd. & Chief Exec. Officer--Ritz-Carlton Hotel Company, Atlanta, GA, pg. 598
Johnson, W.E., Chm. Bd.--American Excelsior Company, Arlington, TX, pg. 51
Johnson, Wesley S., Chm. Bd. & Pres.--Blue Boar Cafeteria Co., Louisville, KY, pg. 158
Johnson, Weston L., Chm. Bd. & Pres.--Good Stuff Food Company, Inc., Los Angeles, CA, pg. 470
Johnson, William B., Chm. Bd. & Chief Exec. Officer--W.B. Johnson Property, Inc., Atlanta, GA, pg. 598
Johnston, David E., Chm.--Ministers Life Insurance Company, Minneapolis, MN, pg. 757
Johnston, Ernest S., Chm.--Ernest S. Johnston Advertising, Inc., Washington, DC, pg. 601
Johnston, Paul, Chm. Bd.--Cabot Creamery Co-Operative Inc., Cabot, VT, pg. 25
Jones, Barbara R., Chm. Bd.--Baltimore Stationery Co., Baltimore, MD, pg. 116
Jones, Glenn R., Chm. Bd., Pres., Chief Exec. Officer & Sole Stockholder--Jones International Ltd., Englewood, CO, pg. 603
Jones, J.C., III, Chm. Bd.--Fuel South, Inc., Hazlehurst, GA, pg. 435
Jones, James, Chm. Bd. & Chief Exec. Officer--The American Stock Exchange, New York, NY, pg. 62
Jones, James C., Jr., Chm. Bd. & Chief Exec. Officer--Jones Company, Inc., Waycross, GA, pg. 603
Jones, Joann K., Chm. Bd.--Capital Electric Group, Inc., Phoenix, AZ, pg. 215
Jones, John E., Chm. Bd.--Cummins-American Corp., Mount Prospect, IL, pg. 304
Jones, John E., Chm. Bd. & Chief Exec. Officer--Glenview State Bank, Glenview, IL, pg. 305
Jones, Lawrence M., Chm. & Chief Exec. Oficer--The Coleman Company, Inc., Wichita, KS, pg. 695
Jones, R.B., Chm. Bd. & Chief Exec. Officer--Jones Chemicals, Inc., Le Roy, NY, pg. 603
Jones, Vernon T., Chm. Bd. & Chief Exec. Officer--Apco Argentina Inc., Tulsa, OK, pg. 77
Jones, Warren F., Chm. Bd.--Hehr International Inc., Los Angeles, CA, pg. 525
Jones, William F., Chm. Bd.--Nelson A. Taylor Co., Inc., Gloversville, NY, pg. 1080
Jones, William M., Chm. Bd.--Cleveland Machine Controls, Cleveland, OH, pg. 255
Jordan, James, Chm. Bd.--Jordan, McGrath, Case & Taylor Inc., New York, NY, pg. 604
Jordan, John W. II, Chm. Bd. & Chief Exec. Officer--Jordan Industries, Inc., Deerfield, IL, pg. 604
Jordan, Joseph C., Chm. Bd. & Chief Exec. Officer--Jordan's Meats, Portland, ME, pg. 605
Jordan, Richard E., Chm. Bd. & Chief Exec. Officer--L. B. Smith, Inc., Camp Hill, PA, pg. 1013
Jordan, Warren K., Chm. Bd. & Chief Exec. Officer--Jordan Associates, Oklahoma City, OK, pg. 604
Jorgensen, Earle M., Chm. Bd.--Earle M. Jorgensen Company, Brea, CA, pg. 605
Josendale, James, Chm. Bd.--Leschen Wire Rope, Saint Joseph, MO, pg. 1197
Joseph, Edwin, Chm. Bd. & Pres.--The Great Atlantic Companies, Hampton, VA, pg. 480
Joseph, Jerome, Chm. Bd., Pres. & Treas.--Uppco, Inc., Chicago, IL, pg. 1139
Joseph, Thomas, Chm., Pres. & Chief Exec. Officer--Markdata Inc., Pittston, PA, pg. 708
Josephson, Marvin, Chm. Bd., Pres. & Chief Exec. Officer--Josephson International Inc., New York, NY, pg. 607
Joy, John W., Chm. Bd.--The Davey Tree Expert Company, Kent, OH, pg. 317
Juday, D.W., Chm. Bd.--Ideal Industries, Inc., Sycamore, IL, pg. 562
Juett, J. Lee, Chm. Bd., Pres. & Chief Exec. Officer--J. Lee Hackett Co., Farmington, MI, pg. 498
Julian, Michael, Chm. Bd., Pres. & Chief Exec. Officer--Farm Fresh, Inc., Norfolk, VA, pg. 401
Jumonville, Dan, Chm. Bd. & Pres.--Group Insurance Inc., Baton Rouge, LA, pg. 490
Justiss, James F., Jr., Chm. Bd., Pres. & Chief Exec. Officer--Justiss Oil Co., Inc., Jena, LA, pg. 610
Juszkiewicz, Henry E., Chm. Bd. & Chief Exec. Officer--Gibson Guitar Corporation, Inc., Nashville, TN, pg. 456
Kahler, Jeff, Chm. Bd.--Kahler Friendt & Partners, Inc., Omaha, NE, pg. 613
Kahlor, Robert A., Chm. Bd.--Journal Communications--Milwaukee Sentinel, Milwaukee, WI, pg. 607
Kahn, Alan, Chm. Bd.--M. B. Kahn Construction Co., Inc., Columbia, SC, pg. 614
Kahn, D. Dan, Chm. Bd. & Chief Exec. Officer--Production Tool Supply Co., Warren, MI, pg. 893
Kahn, Robert H., Jr., Chm. Bd.--The Lewis Bear Company, Pensacola, FL, pg. 129
Kaiser, Joseph P., Jr., Chm.--Gallagher-Kaiser Corp., Detroit, MI, pg. 441
Kaiser, Michael, Chm. & Chief Exec. Officer--Kaiser McEuen Inc., Los Angeles, CA, pg. 615
Kalainov, S.C., Chm. Bd. & Chief Exec. Officer--American Mutual Life Insurance Company, Des Moines, IA, pg. 58
Kalebic, Thomas, Exec. V.P. & Chief Oper. Officer--Lane Industries, Inc., Northbrook, IL, pg. 656
Kallen, Thomas E., Chm. Bd. & Treas.--Bake-Line Products, Inc., Des Plaines, IL, pg. 114
Kaltenbacher, Philip D., Chm. Bd. & Chief Exec. Officer--Seton Company, Norristown, PA, pg. 993
Kamberos, Chris, Chm. Bd., Pres. & Chief Oper. Officer--Treasure Island Foodmarts Inc., Chicago, IL, pg. 1109
Kamenstein, David R., Chm. Bd. & Chief Exec. Officer--M. Kamenstein, Inc., White Plains, NY, pg. 615
Kaminski, R.S., Chm. & Pres.--Continental/Midland, Inc., Park Forest, IL, pg. 279
Kaminsky, Howard, Chm. & Chief Exec. Officer--Hearst Book Group, New York, NY, pg. 522
Kaminstein, Merwin F., Chm. Bd., Pres. & Chief Exec. Officer--Brookstone Company, Inc., Peterborough, NH, pg. 180

Kamm, J.O., Chm. & Chief Exec. Officer--Wilkinson Company, Inc., Stow, OH, pg. 373
Kamm, J.O., Chm.--Canefco Limited, Scarborough,, Canada, pg. 373
Kamm, Jacob O., Chm. Bd., Pres. & Chief Exec. Officer--Electric Furnace Co., Salem, OH, pg. 373
Kampouris, Emmanuel A., Chm. Bd, Pres. & Chief Exec. Officer--American Standard Inc., New York, NY, pg. 61
Kamstra, K.M., Chm. & Chief Exec. Officer--Kamstra Communications, Inc., Saint Paul, MN, pg. 615
Kane, Gibby, Chm. Bd. & Pres.--Marden-Kane, Inc., Lake Success, NY, pg. 706
Kane, Raymond P., Chm. Bd.--Alford Industries, Inc., Ridgefield Park, NJ, pg. 33
Kane, Robert J., Chm. Bd.--Western Regional Off Track Betting, Batavia, NY, pg. 1181
Kane, Sam, Chm. Bd., Chief Exec. & Chief Fin. Officer--Sam Kane Beef Processors, Inc., Corpus Christi, TX, pg. 616
Kane, Stanley B., Chm. & Sec.--Kane-Miller Corp., Tarrytown, NY, pg. 616
Kaneshiro, Eijiro, Chm. Bd.--Pacific Hawaiian Ltd., Hilo, HI, pg. 840
Kanter, Burton W., Chm.--Chicago Holdings, Inc., Pittsburgh, PA, pg. 245
Kaplan, Leonard D., Chm. & Treas.--Prime Tanning Co., Inc., Berwick, ME, pg. 889
Kaplan, Philip, Chm. Bd.--Loehmann's, Inc., Bronx, NY, pg. 681
Kaplanek, Charles, Sr., Chm. Bd.--Floral Glass & Mirror, Inc., Hauppauge, NY, pg. 420
Kapp, Dennis, Chm.--Martin F. Weber Company, Philadelphia, PA, pg. 716
Kappel, Joseph, Chm. Bd.--Coast Manufacturing Company, Yonkers, NY, pg. 257
Kaprielian, Walter, Chm. & Creative Dir.--Kaprielian/O'Leary, New York, NY, pg. 616
Kapson, Jordan H., Chm. Bd.--Jordan Motors, Inc., Mishawaka, IN, pg. 605
Karabots, Nick G., Chm. Bd.--S L C Graphics, Inc., Pittston, PA, pg. 963
Karges, Edwin, Chm. Bd. & Pres.--Karges Furniture Company, Evansville, IN, pg. 616
Karmanos, Peter, Jr., Chm. Bd. & Chief Exec. Officer--Compuware Corporation, Farmington Hills, MI, pg. 271
Karsh, Phil, Co-Chm. & Chief Exec. Officer--Karsh & Hagan, Inc., Englewood, CO, pg. 617
Karsten, Harry, Jr., Chm. Bd. & Pres.--Golden West Homes, Santa Ana, CA, pg. 467
Kasen, Stewart M., Co-Chm., Pres. & Chief Exec. Officer--Best Products Co., Inc., Richmond, VA, pg. 17
Kasle, Leonard, Chm. Bd. & Chief Exec. Officer--Kasle Steel Corporation, Dearborn, MI, pg. 617
Kaspar, Don G., Chm. Bd. & Pres.--Kaspar Wire Works, Inc., Shiner, TX, pg. 617
Kassab, Gregory E., Chm. Bd. & Chief Exec. Officer--Stainless Incorporated, Deerfield Beach, FL, pg. 1035
Kassouf, Elias, Chm. Bd.--Metropolitan Properties Inc., Cleveland, OH, pg. 745
Kathwari, M. Farooq, Chm., Pres. & Chief Exec. Officer--Green Mountain Holding Corporation, Danbury, CT, pg. 485
Katt, Ray, Chm. Bd.--Benjamin Sheridan Co., Racine, WI, pg. 300
Katz, Earl L., Chm. Bd. & Chief Exec. Officer--Encore Shoe Corporation, Rochester, NH, pg. 380
Katz, Ronald C., Chm. Bd. & Chief Exec. Officer--Elkay Manufacturing Company, Oak Brook, IL, pg. 377
Katzenbach, Nicholas deB., Chm. Bd.--First American Bankshares, Inc., Washington, DC, pg. 412
Katzman, Julius, Chm. Bd.--Mastercraft Furniture Corp., Omaha, NE, pg. 720
Katzman, Lawrence, Chm. Bd. & Chief Exec. Officer--Kaz, Inc., New York, NY, pg. 619
Katzoff, Ron, Chm. Bd.--Remington Apparel, Inc., Wilmington, NC, pg. 926
Kautz, J.H., Chm. Bd. & Chief Exec. Officer--Grain Processing Corp., Muscatine, IA, pg. 1145
Kautz, R.C., Co-Chm. Bd.--Kent Feeds Inc., Muscatine, IA, pg. 1146
Kay, Allen, Chm. Bd. & Chief Creative Officer--Korey, Kay & Partners, New York, NY, pg. 642
Kazarian, Paul, Chm. & Mng. Dir.--Sunbeam-Oster Company, Inc., Providence, RI, pg. 1059
Kean, Stuart B., Chm. Bd.--KCS Energy Inc., Edison, NJ, pg. 612
Kearns, Walter J., Chm. Bd. & Pres.--Data Documents Holdings, Inc., Omaha, NE, pg. 316
Keating, Daniel J., Jr., Chm. Bd., Pres. & Chief Exec. Officer--Daniel J. Keating Co., Villanova, PA, pg. 619
Keating, P. Warren, Chm. Bd.--P.J. Keating Company, Lunenburg, MA, pg. 619
Keating, William J., Chm. Bd.--The Associated Press, New York, NY, pg. 91
Keeley, G.P., Chm. Bd.--PQ Corporation, Valley Forge, PA, pg. 836
Keenan, James F., Chm. Bd. & Chief Exec. Officer--Pace Industries, Inc., Fayetteville, AR, pg. 838
Keene, Robert A., Chm. Bd., Sec. & Treas.--John Roberts Company, Minneapolis, MN, pg. 938
Keeney, Lafayette, Chm. Bd., Pres. & Chief Exec. Officer--Sage-Allen & Co., Inc., Hartford, CT, pg. 966
Keery, Frank, Chm. Bd. & Chief Exec. Officer--The Swanson Company Manufacturers, Phoenix, AZ, pg. 1066
Kehne, Richard M., Chm. Bd. & Pres.--Kehne Electric Company, Inc., Saint Paul, MN, pg. 620
Kelb, Edwin D., Chm. Bd.--High Point Oil Co., Indianapolis, IN, pg. 534
Keller, John, Chm. & Treas.--Meadville Forging Co., Meadville, PA, pg. 733
Keller, John J., Chm. Bd.--J. J. Keller & Associates, Inc., Neenah, WI, pg. 620
Keller, William H., Chm. Bd.--The Keller Manufacturing Co., Inc., Corydon, IN, pg. 621
Kelley, Austin P., Chm. & Chief Exec. Officer--Austin Kelley Advertising, Inc., Atlanta, GA, pg. 99
Kelley, Gary L., Chm. Bd., Pres. & Chief Exec. Officer--Kelley Bean Co., Inc., Morrill, NE, pg. 621
Kelller, George, Chm. Bd.--SRI International, Menlo Park, CA, pg. 964
Kellman, Joseph, Chm., Pres. & Chief Exec. Officer--Globe Glass & Mirror Co., Chicago, IL, pg. 463
Kellman, Mildred, Chm. Bd. & Pres.--Globe-Amerada Glass Company, Elk Grove Village, IL, pg. 463
Kellner, Jack F., Chm. Bd.--Western Industries, Inc., Milwaukee, WI, pg. 1179
Kelly, Donald P., Chm. Bd., Pres. & Chief Exec. Officer--Envirodyne Industries, Inc., Oak Brook, IL, pg. 383
Kelly, Paul E., Sr., Chm. Bd.--Superior Tube Company, Collegeville, PA, pg. 1064
Kelly, Paul E., Sr., Chm. Bd., Chief Exec. & Fin. Officer--Cawsl Corporation, Wynnewood, PA, pg. 229
Kelly, Peter G., Chm. Bd.--Servistar Corporation, East Butler, PA, pg. 992
Kelly, Robert J., Co-Chm.-Opers.--Ernst & Young, New York, NY, pg. 387
Kelly, Stephen J., Chm. Bd., Pres. & Chief Exec. Officer--South Chester Tube Co., Concordville, PA, pg. 1019
Kelm, George, Chm. Bd.--Sahara Coal Co., Chicago, IL, pg. 966
Kelsey, Eugene W. III, Chm. Bd.--Kelsey Construction, Inc., Orlando, FL, pg. 621
Kendall, Donald S., III, Chm. Bd. & Pres.--Mack Molding Company, Arlington, VT, pg. 697
Kennedy, Andrew G., Chm. & Pres.--Kentile Floors Inc., South Plainfield, NJ, pg. 623
Kennedy, David F., Chm. Bd. & Creative Dir.--Wieden & Kennedy, Inc., Portland, OR, pg. 1188
Kennedy, James C., Chm. & Chief Exec. Officer--Cox Enterprises, Inc., Atlanta, GA, pg. 292
Kennedy, Karen S., Chm. Bd., Pres., Treas. & New Bus. Contact--KSK Communications, Ltd., Vienna, VA, pg. 613
Kennedy, Robert S., Chm. Bd.--T. H. Rogers Lumber Co. Inc., Oklahoma City, OK, pg. 943
Kennedy, T.C., Chm. Bd.--BE & K, Inc., Birmingham, AL, pg. 106
Kennedy, W.J. III, Chm. Bd.--North Carolina Mutual Life Insurance Co., Durham, NC, pg. 813
Kent, J.H., Co-Chm. Bd.--Kent Feeds Inc., Muscatine, IA, pg. 1146
Kent, Warren T., Chm. & Chief Exec. Officer--The Kent Manufacturing Co., Pickens, SC, pg. 623
Kern, Frank, Jr., Chm. Bd.--Maxitrol Co., Southfield, MI, pg. 723
Kern, Richard M., Chm. Bd.--Jewelers Mutual Insurance Company, Neenah, WI, pg. 593
Kernan, Richard M., Chm.--NYLIFE Inc., New York, NY, pg. 802
Kerr, Howard J., Chm. Bd., Pres. & Chief Exec. Officer--Consolidated Pipe & Supply Company, Birmingham, AL, pg. 277
Kertz, James R., Chm. Bd.--National Bulk Carriers, Inc., New York, NY, pg. 786
Kervick, Paul J., Chm. Bd.--Kervick Enterprises, Inc., Worcester, MA, pg. 624
Kessler, Frank, Chm. Bd.--Esther Williams Swimming Pool Co., Delair, NJ, pg. 389
Kessler, Paul, Chm. Bd.--Cora Texas Manufacturing Co., White Castle, LA, pg. 285
Kestenbaum, Louis, Chm.--Elkay Plastics Company, Inc., Los Angeles, CA, pg. 377
Kesterson, Tommy, Chm. Bd. & Pres.--Kesterson Food Company, Inc., Paris, TN, pg. 624
Keye, Paul, Chm. & Exec. Creative Dir.--Livingston + Keye, Venice, CA, pg. 679
Keysor, James B., Chm. Bd.--Keysor Century Corporation, Saugus, CA, pg. 627
Khim, Dr. Jay W., Chm. Bd., Pres. & Chief Exec. Officer--JWK International Corp., Annandale, VA, pg. 586
Khoury, Tawfig N., Chm. Bd. & Chief Exec. Officer--Pacific Scene Inc., San Diego, CA, pg. 841
Kiam, Victor, II, Chm. Bd., Pres., Chief Exec. & Chief Oper. Officer--Remington Products Inc., Bridgeport, CT, pg. 926
Kidd, Kenneth, Chm. Bd. & Pres.--Superior Label Systems, Inc., Cincinnati, OH, pg. 1063
Kiefer, William C., Chm. Bd. & Pres.--Bel-Ray Company, Inc., Farmingdale, NJ, pg. 133
Kiggen, James D., Chm. Bd., Pres. & Chief Exec. Officer--Xtek, Inc., Cincinnati, OH, pg. 1206
Kilguss, Howard K., Chm. Bd., Pres. & Treas.--Excell Manufacturing Company, Providence, RI, pg. 392
Killinger, Kerry K., Chm. Bd., Chief Exec. Officer & Pres.--Washington Mutual Savings Bank, Seattle, WA, pg. 1166
Kim, James J., Chm. & Chief Exec. Officer--Amkor Electronics, Inc., West Chester, PA, pg. 67
Kim, Kenneth H., Chm., Pres., Chief Exec. Officer, Corp. Sec. & Treas.--Medieval Dinner & Tournament, Inc., Buena Park, CA, pg. 735
Kimbell, David A., Chm. Bd. & Pres.--Burk Royalty Co., Wichita Falls, TX, pg. 190
Kimbrel, Charles, Chm. Bd.--American Savings of Florida, ESB, Miami, FL, pg. 382
Kimbrell, W. Duke, Chm. Bd. & Chief Exec. Officer--Parkdale Mills, Gastonia, NC, pg. 849
Kimmel, Sidney, Chm. Bd. & Chief Exec. Officer--Jones Apparel Group, Inc., Bristol, PA, pg. 602
Kinderman, Larry, Chm. Bd.--Stockham Valves & Fittings, Inc., Birmingham, AL, pg. 1050
King, Henry L., Chm. Bd.--Western Trailer Equipment & Manufacturing Co., Abilene, TX, pg. 1182
King, John, Chm. & Chief Exec. Officer--Sunox, Inc., Charlotte, NC, pg. 1062
King, Leroy A. Jr., Chm Bd. & Chief Exec. Officer--Tighe Industries, Inc., York, PA, pg. 1097
King, W.M., Chm. Bd.--Green Holdings, Inc., Denver, CO, pg. 484
Kinney, Douglas M., Chm. Bd.--Intermatic Inc., Spring Grove, IL, pg. 575
Kinning, Ronald L., Chm. Bd. & Chief Exec. Officer--RK Mechanical, Inc., Lakewood, CO, pg. 907
Kiplinger, Austin H., Chm. Bd.--The Kiplinger Washington Editors, Inc., Washington, DC, pg. 632
Kirby, G.E., Chm. & Pres.--Atlanta Wire Works, Inc., Jonesboro, GA, pg. 94
Kirby, William, Chm. Bd.--Auburn Faith Community Hospital, Auburn, CA, pg. 97
Kirgis, Robert, Chm. Bd. & Pres.--Farmway Co-Op Inc., Beloit, KS, pg. 402
Kirk, Chester H., Chm. Bd. & Chief Exec. Officer--Amtrol Inc., West Warwick, RI, pg. 70
Kirk, Jesse, Chm. Bd. & Pres.--Dallas Peterbilt, Inc., Irving, TX, pg. 312
Kirk, Thomas L., Chm. Bd. & Pres. & Chief Exec. Office--Kirk-Mayer, Inc., Los Angeles, CA, pg. 633
Kirkpatrick, Don O., Chm. Bd. & Pres.--Quality Foods Inc., Little Rock, AR, pg. 903
Kirkwood, J.H., Chm., Pres. & Chief Exec. Officer--Edgewater Corporation, Oakmont, PA, pg. 368
Kirschman, Victor F., Chm. Bd.--Morris Kirschman & Company, Inc., New Orleans, LA, pg. 633
Kirschner, David, Chm.--Hanna-Barbera Productions, Inc., Los Angeles, CA, pg. 53
Kiser, Walter T., Chm. Bd. & Chief Exec. Officer--Law Engineering, Inc., Atlanta, GA, pg. 661
Kislevitz, Harry, Chm. Bd.--Colorforms, Ramsey, NJ, pg. 265
Kitchell, Samuel F., Chm. Bd.--Kitchell Corporation, Phoenix, AZ, pg. 634
Klammer, Ronald J., Chm. Bd.--Belgrave Industries, Santa Ana, CA, pg. 133
Klas, Robert C., Chm. Bd.--Tapemark, West St. Paul, MN, pg. 1078
Klaus, L. George, Chm. Bd., Pres. & Chief Exec. Officer--Integral Systems, Walnut Creek, CA, pg. 572
Klaussner, Hans, Chm. Bd.--Klaussner Corporation, Asheboro, NC, pg. 634
Klaussner, Hans, Chm. Bd.--Klaussner Furniture Industry, Asheboro, NC, pg. 634
Klein, Bernard, Chm. Bd., Sec. & Treas.--Alaron Inc., Troy, MI, pg. 30
Klein, Donald M., Chm. Bd. & Creative Dir.--MacNamara, Klein & Solin Inc., New York, NY, pg. 698
Klein, Lawrence R., Dr., Chm. Economic Policy Committee--W. P. Carey & Co., Inc., New York, NY, pg. 218
Klein, Michael S., Chm. Bd. & Chief Exec. Officer--Klein Tools Inc., Skokie, IL, pg. 635
Kleinrock, Dr. Leonard, Chm. Bd. & Chief Exec. Officer--Technology Transfer Institute, Santa Monica, CA, pg. 1084
Klemer, Richard J., Chm. Bd.--Faribault Woolen Mill Co., Faribault, MN, pg. 399
Klevay, Walter S., Sr., Chm. & Chief Exec. Officer--Kleco Corp., Brecksville, OH, pg. 634
Kline, Arnold W., Chm. Bd., Pres. & Chief Oper. Officer--Boston Trading Ltd. Inc., Lynn, MA, pg. 168
Kline, Bernard H., Chm. Bd.--Kline Iron & Steel Co., Inc., Columbia, SC, pg. 635
Kling, John J., Chm. Bd.--Southern Ohio Fabricators, Inc., Cincinnati, OH, pg. 1022
Klinger, Georgette, Chm. Bd.--Georgette Klinger, Inc., New York, NY, pg. 635
Klink, Edwin H., Chm. Bd. & Pres.--E & A Industries, Inc., Indianapolis, IN, pg. 358
Klink, Edwin H., Chm. Bd.--Car Brite, Inc., Indianapolis, IN, pg. 358
Klipsch, Fred S., Chm. Bd. & Pres.--Klipsch & Associates Inc., Hope, AR, pg. 635
Klosterman, Kenneth, Chm. Bd.--Klosterman's Baking Company, Cincinnati, OH, pg. 636
Kluener, James A., Sr., Chm. Bd. & Pres.--Kluener Packing Company, Cincinnati, OH, pg. 636
Kluft, Earl, Chm. Bd.--The Spring Air Company, Des Plaines, IL, pg. 1032
Kluge, John W., Chm. & Pres.--Metromedia Company, East Rutherford, NJ, pg. 743
Kluge, John W., Chm. Bd.--Ponderosa, Inc., Vandalia, OH, pg. 743
Klugy, John, Chm. Bd.--Metromedia Steakhouses, Inc., Vandalia, OH, pg. 744
Knapp, Cleon T., Chm. Bd. & Pres.--Knapp Communications Corporation, Los Angeles, CA, pg. 636
Knapp, Cleon T., Chm. & Chief Exec. Officer--Architectural Digest, Los Angeles, CA, pg. 636
Knapp, Cleon T., Chm. & Chief Exec. Officer--Bon Appetit Magazine, Los Angeles, CA, pg. 636
Knapp, Jules F., Chm. Bd., Pres. & Chief Exec. Officer--United Coatings, Inc., Kankakee, IL, pg. 1131
Knauss, Donald T., Chm. Bd. & Chief Exec. Officer--E.W. Knauss & Son, Inc., Quakertown, PA, pg. 636
Knight, Charles, Jr., Chm.Bd.--Concrete Technology Corp., Tacoma, WA, pg. 273
Knight, Dick, Chm. Bd.--TBWA Holmes Knight Ritchie, London,, United Kingdom, pg. 1072
Knight, Theodore H., Chm. Bd. & Pres.--Misener Marine Construction, Tampa, FL, pg. 759
Knipfing, G.R., Chm., Pres. & Chief Exec. Officer--Scheduling Technology Corporation, Hopkinton, MA, pg. 975
Knobbe, Urban, Chm. Bd. & Pres.--Ag Processing Inc A Cooperative, Omaha, NE, pg. 24
Knox, Lance L., Chm. Bd.--PBS Building Systems of America, Anaheim, CA, pg. 835
Knox, Marion A., Sr., Vice Chm.--Terminix Service, Inc., Columbia, SC, pg. 1088
Knox, T.P, Jr., Chm. Bd.--Terminix Service, Inc., Columbia, SC, pg. 1088
Kobacker, Arthur J., Chm. Bd. & Chief Exec. Officer--The Kobacker Company & Affiliates, Columbus, OH, pg. 638

Koch, Anthony H., Chm. Bd. & Pres.--Alamo Industrial Group, San Antonio, TX, pg. 29
Koch, Anthony H., Chm. Bd. & Pres.--Alamo Iron Works, San Antonio, TX, pg. 29
Koch, Charles G., Chm. Bd. & Chief Exec. Officer--Koch Industries, Incorporated, Wichita, KS, pg. 639
Koch, Robert L., II, Chm. Bd. & Chief Exec. Officer--Gibbs Diecasting Aluminum Corp., Henderson, KY, pg. 639
Koehl, Hans H., Chm. Bd. & Chief Exec. Officer--Spirol International Corp., Danielson, CT, pg. 1031
Koehl, Hans H., Chm. Bd.--C.E.M. Div. Spirol Intl. Corp., Danielson, CT, pg. 1031
Koenitzer, J.C., Chm. Bd.--Helwig Carbon Products, Inc., Milwaukee, WI, pg. 528
Koetters, Ronald A., Chm. Bd. & Chief Exec. Officer--Monarch Construction Company, Cincinnati, OH, pg. 765
Koffman, Burton I., Chm. Bd. & Pres.--Great American Industries, Inc., Vestal, NY, pg. 480
Kohler, Herbert V., Jr., Chm. Bd., Pres., Chief Oper. & Chief Exec. Officer--Kohler Company, Kohler, WI, pg. 639
Kohler, Michael, Pres.--Facemate Corporation, Chicopee, MA, pg. 396
Kohm, William, Chm. Bd.--Kohm Associates, Inc., Oradell, NJ, pg. 640
Kolb, John W., Chm. Bd.--Automotive Rentals, Inc., Mount Laurel, NJ, pg. 101
Kolikof, Robert A., Pres., Chief Exec. Officer & Chief Oper. Officer--Prudential Metal Supply Corp., East Dedham, MA, pg. 898
Koll, Donald M., Chm. Bd. & Chief Exec. Officer--Koll Co., Newport Beach, CA, pg. 641
Koller, Alois J., Sr., Chm. Bd.--Koller Enterprises, Inc., Fenton, MO, pg. 641
Komen, Richard B., Chm. Bd.--Restaurants Unlimited, Seattle, WA, pg. 929
Komline, Elizabeth M., Vice Chm.--Komline-Sanderson Engineering Corp., Peapack, NJ, pg. 641
Koop, Donald J., Chm. Bd.--Spartan Stores Inc., Grand Rapids, MI, pg. 1026
Kopelman, David W., Chm. Bd.--The W.B. Wood Company, New Providence, NJ, pg. 1199
Kopko, Edward M., Chm. Bd., Pres., Chief Exec. & Chief Oper. Officer--Butler International, Montvale, NJ, pg. 197
Korbel, Boris, Chm. Bd.--The Upper Deck Company, Carlsbad, CA, pg. 1140
Kornhauser, Henry, Chm.--Partners & Shevack, Inc., New York, NY, pg. 850
Kosloff, Alan, Chm. Bd., Chief Exec. Officer & Pres.--American Marketing Industries, Inc., Kansas City, MO, pg. 58
Kosloff, Irving S., Chm. Bd.--Roosevelt Paper Co., Philadelphia, PA, pg. 946
Kosta, Nicholas, Chm. Bd.--Advance Business Graphics, Mira Loma, CA, pg. 18
Kotkins, Henry L., Chm. Bd.--Skyway Luggage Co., Seattle, WA, pg. 1009
Kovalefsky, Edward V., V.P. & Chm.--United Community Insurance Co., Albany, NY, pg. 662
Kozakis, Achilles, Chm. Bd. & Mng. Dir.--Joffko International, Houston, TX, pg. 595
Kraft, Donald B., Chm. & Dir.--EvansGroup, Salt Lake City, UT, pg. 390
Kraft, Donald B., Chm. Bd.--EvansGroup, Seattle, WA, pg. 391
Kragie, Jack, Chm. Bd.--Kragie/Newell, Des Moines, IA, pg. 643
Kraines, Maurice H., Chm. Bd.--Kraco Enterprises, Inc., Compton, CA, pg. 643
Krakowiak, E.T., Chm. Bd.--Illinois Range Company, Mount Prospect, IL, pg. 563
Kramer, Gordon M., Chm. Bd., Pres. & Chief Exec. Officer--Continental Plastic Card Co., Coral Springs, FL, pg. 280
Kramer, Martin B., Chm. Bd.--Trimfit, Inc., Philadelphia, PA, pg. 1113
Krauss, Carl W., Chm. Bd.--Lakewood Engineering & Manufacturing Co., Chicago, IL, pg. 652
Kreisman, Herbert, Chm. Bd. & Treas.--Advance Mechanical Systems, Inc., Elk Grove Village, IL, pg. 19
Kreiter, Harry, Chm. Bd. & Pres.--Castcraft Industries, Inc., Skokie, IL, pg. 228
Kreitzberg, James S., Chm. Bd.--Microflect Company, Inc., Salem, OR, pg. 749
Kress, George F., Chm. Bd.--Green Bay Packaging Inc., Green Bay, WI, pg. 483
Kresser, Bob, Chm. & Chief Exec. Officer--Kresser/Craig, Santa Monica, CA, pg. 644
Kretsch, Jerold, Chm. Bd.--Sanborn Manufacturing Company, Springfield, MN, pg. 969
Krier, B. Bruce, Chm. Bd. & Pres.--Krier Foods, Inc., Brown Deer, WI, pg. 645
Krippaehne, William, Jr., Chm. Bd.--Fisher Properties Inc., Seattle, WA, pg. 415
Kroch, Carl A., Chm. Bd.--Kroch's & Brentano's, Inc., Chicago, IL, pg. 645
Kroetch, Arthur, Chm. Bd., Pres. & Chief Exec. Officer--Scotchman Industries, Inc., Philip, SD, pg. 982
Kroll, Alex, Chm. & Chief Exec. Officer--Young & Rubicam Inc., New York, NY, pg. 1210
Kroot, A. Jerome, Chm. Bd.--Foland's Jewelry Brokers, Warren, MI, pg. 421
Kroot, Hyman, Chm. Bd.--Northeastern Graphic Supply, Inc., Portland, ME, pg. 814
Krucks, William, Chm. Bd. & Pres.--Rauland-Borg Corporation, Skokie, IL, pg. 914
Krugel, Marius, Chm.--Sigma, Zurich,, Switzerland, pg. 1212
Kruidenier, David, Chm. Bd.--Cowles Media Company, Minneapolis, MN, pg. 291
Krulik, Lawrence, Chm. Bd.--United States Luggage Company, Hauppauge, NY, pg. 1136
Krumwiede, Robert, Chm. Bd. & Pres.--C-Line Products, Inc., Des Plaines, IL, pg. 198
Krupsha, Andrew, Chm. Bd. & Pres.--Kleer Pak Corporation, Berwick, PA, pg. 635
Kruse, Daniel J., Chm. Bd.--Superior Auctioneers & Marketing, Inc., San Antonio, TX, pg. 1063
Kruse, Ed F., Chm. & Chief Exec. Officer--Blue Bell Creameries, Inc., Brenham, TX, pg. 158
Kuebler, Thomas E., Chm. Bd.--Uniflow Manufacturing Co., Erie, PA, pg. 1126
Kughn, Richard P., Chm. Bd. & Chief Exec. Officer--Lionel Trains, Inc., Chesterfield, MI, pg. 677
Kugle, J. Alan, Chm. Bd.--Wailuku Agribusiness Co., Inc., Wailuku, HI, pg. 175
Kugle, J. Alan, Chm. Bd.--Kilauea Agronomics, Inc., Kilauea, HI, pg. 174
Kugle, J. Alan, Chm. Bd.--Superior Coffee & Foods/Hawaii, Aiea, HI, pg. 174
Kuhlman, Harvey G., Chm. Bd.--Kuhlman, Inc., Menomonee Falls, WI, pg. 646
Kuhn, Richard S., Co-Chm. Bd.--Kuhn & Wittenborn, Inc., Kansas City, MO, pg. 646
Kuhns, John D., Chm. Bd.--Arcadian Power Corp., Pleasanton, CA, pg. 80
Kuhns, Robert W., Jr., Chm. Bd.--Northwest Pipe Fittings, Inc., Billings, MT, pg. 815
Kuiper, Peter, Co.-Chm Bd.--Pella Corporation, Pella, IA, pg. 856
Kukla, Stanley J., Chm. Bd. & Chief Exec. Officer--Kukla Press, Inc., Elk Grove Village, IL, pg. 646
Kulkarni, Deepak, Chm. Bd.--Wolverine Massachusetts Corporation, Merrimac, MA, pg. 1199
Kummer, Fred S., Chm., Pres., Chief Exec. Officer, Treas. & Founder--HBE Corporation, Saint Louis, MO, pg. 495
Kunzler, Christian C., Jr., Chm. Bd. & Pres.--Kunzler & Company, Inc., Lancaster, PA, pg. 646
Kupta, Satish, Co-Chm. Bd.--Shoreline Products, Inc., Arlington, TX, pg. 1000
Kurdziel, Joseph, Chm. Bd. & Pres.--Kurdziel Industries, Inc., Muskegon, MI, pg. 646
Kurland, Rayfield B., Chm. Bd.--Handy Manufacturing Co., Inc., Newark, NJ, pg. 505
Kurz, Mitchell, Pres./N. America--Wunderman Cato Johnson, New York, NY, pg. 1211
Kurzweg, Victor J., III, Chm. Bd. & Chief Exec. Officer--Consolidated Companies Inc. (CONCO), Metairie, LA, pg. 276
Kuwahara, Frank M., Chm. Bd.--Fairfield Maxwell Ltd., New York, NY, pg. 397
Kvasnicka, Allan J., Chm. Bd.--FM Industries, Inc., Fort Worth, TX, pg. 394
La Marre, James V., Chm. Bd.--White Pigeon Paper Company, White Pigeon, MI, pg. 87
La Rosa, Donald S., Chm. Bd.--La Rosa's, Inc., Cincinnati, OH, pg. 649
LaBarge, Pierre III, Chm. Bd. & Pres.--LaBarge Pipe & Steel Company, Saint Louis, MO, pg. 649
Labovitz, George H., Dr., Chm. Bd., Pres. & Chief Exec. Officer--ODI, Burlington, MA, pg. 818
Lackey, A. Wayne, Chm. Bd. & Pres.--Dentec Corporation, Boca Raton, FL, pg. 329
Lacourciere, William J., Chief Exec. Officer, Chm. Bd., Pres.--Novametrix Medical Systems Inc., Wallingford, CT, pg. 817
LaCrosse, Jim, Chm. Bd.--NWS, Inc., Chicago, IL, pg. 782
Lacy, Andre B., Chm., Pres. & Chief Exec. Officer--LDI, Ltd., Indianapolis, IN, pg. 647
Lacy, Roane, Chm. Bd.--Plantation Foods Inc., Waco, TX, pg. 874
Ladish, John H., Chm. Bd. & Chief Exec. Officer--Ladish Malting Co., Milwaukee, WI, pg. 219
Lafton, Donald, Co-Chm. Bd.--TCC, Miami, FL, pg. 1072
Lainson, Hal, Chm. Bd.--Dutton-Lainson Co., Hastings, NE, pg. 356
Lakin, James E., Chm. Bd.--Timpte Industries, Inc., Denver, CO, pg. 1098
LaMarca, James, Chm. Bd., Pres. & Chief Exec. Officer--LaMarca Group Inc., New York, NY, pg. 652
Lamb, Isabelle S., Chm. Bd., Pres. & Treas.--Enterprises International Inc., Hoquiam, WA, pg. 382
Lambert, Dave, Chm. Bd.--G & L Products, Inc., New Berlin, WI, pg. 438
Lamoreux, F. Holmes, Chm. Bd., Pres. & Chief Exec. Officer--Sabreliner Corp., Chesterfield, MO, pg. 965
Lampton, Leslie B., Sr., Chm. Bd. & Pres.--Ergon, Inc., Jackson, MS, pg. 386
Land, John, Chm. Bd.--M. M. Cohn Co., Inc., Little Rock, AR, pg. 353
Landau, Roy, Chm. Bd., Pres. & Chief Exec. & Chief Fin. Officer--Landau Building Co., Wexford, PA, pg. 654
Landegger, George, Chm. Bd.--Parsons & Whittemore Enterprises, Rye Brook, NY, pg. 850
Landey, Martin H., Chm. & Chief Exec. Officer--Cox Landey and Partners, Inc., New York, NY, pg. 294
Landsberger, Kurt, Chm. Bd.--Bel-Art Products, Pequannock, NJ, pg. 133
Landsberger, Kurt, Chm. Bd.--Maddak Inc., Pequannock, NJ, pg. 133
Lane, Edward B., Chm. & Chief Exec. Officer--E. B. Lane & Associates, Inc., Phoenix, AZ, pg. 656
Lane, Leonard C., Chm. Bd. & Chief Exec. Officer--ILC Industries, Inc., Bohemia, NY, pg. 560
Lane, Philip A., Chm. Bd.--Aratex Services, Lawrenceville, GA, pg. 6
Lane, William N., III, Chm. Bd., Pres. & Chief Exec. Officer--Lane Industries, Inc., Northbrook, IL, pg. 656
Lane, William N., III, Chm. Bd.--General Binding Corporation, Northbrook, IL, pg. 656
Lang, Henry S., Chm. Bd., Pres. & Chief Exec. Officer--Home Juice Company, Melrose Park, IL, pg. 541
Lang, Robert C., Chm. Bd.--Valentine-Radford, Inc., Kansas City, MO, pg. 1142
Lange, Stephens J., Chm. Bd.--Owatonna Canning Company, Owatonna, MN, pg. 833
Langlois, John, Chm.--CSFB Fund Management Limited, Guernsey,, Channel Islands, pg. 204
Langone, Kenneth G., Chm. Bd. & Chief Exec. Officer--Salem National Corporation, Winston-Salem, NC, pg. 967
Lanier, J.L., Jr., Chm. Bd. & Chief Exec. Officer--Dan River Inc., Danville, VA, pg. 313
Lapeyre, J. M., Jr., Chm. & Pres.--The Laitram Corporation, Harahan, LA, pg. 650
Lapeyre, J.M., Jr., Chm. & Pres.--Intralox, Inc., Harahan, LA, pg. 651
Lapides, Morton M., Chm. Bd., Pres. & Chief Exec. Officer--Alleco Inc., Cheverly, MD, pg. 35
Lapides, Robert E., Chm.--United Aluminum Corporation, North Haven, CT, pg. 1130
Lapin, Aaron S., Chm. Bd.--Clayton Corporation, Fenton, MO, pg. 253
LaPointe, Robert E., Chm. & Chief Exec. Officer--Tallant LaPointe & Partners, Inc., San Francisco, CA, pg. 1077
Lappin, Gerald D., Chm. Bd.--Lappin Electric Company, Milwaukee, WI, pg. 658
Larkin, Frank, Chm. Bd. & Investor Rels. Dir.--North Shore Movers, Northbrook, IL, pg. 813
Larned, Gardner, Chm. Bd., Pres., & Chief Exec. Officer--Berry Bearing Co., Lyons, IL, pg. 144
LaRosa, Joseph, Chm. & Co-Chief Exec. Officer--Waring & LaRosa, Inc., New York, NY, pg. 1163
Larsen, Jack Lenor, Chm. Bd.--Jack Lenor Larsen, Inc., New York, NY, pg. 659
Lash, James A., Chm. Bd.--Reading Tube Corp., Reading, PA, pg. 916
Laskowski, Richard E., Chm. Bd.--Ace Hardware Corporation, Oak Brook, IL, pg. 12
Late, Frank M., Chm. Bd. & Pres.--Republic Supply Company, Dallas, TX, pg. 928
Laubach, John L., Chm. Bd. & Sec.--Medrad, Inc., Pittsburgh, PA, pg. 736
Lauder, Estee, Chm. Bd.--Estee Lauder, Inc., New York, NY, pg. 389
Lauren, Ralph, Chm. Bd.--Polo/Ralph Lauren Corporation, New York, NY, pg. 879
Lawler, John P., Chm. Bd.--Lawler-Havens Inc., Cleveland, OH, pg. 661
Lawrence, Albert W., Chm.--Lawrence Group, Inc., Schenectady, NY, pg. 662
Lawrence, Albert W., Chm. Bd.--Lawrence Insurance Group, Inc., New York, NY, pg. 662
Lawrence, E.W. III, Chm. Bd. & Chief Exec. Officer--Orbitair International Ltd., New York, NY, pg. 828
Lawrence, Michael, Chm. Bd.--Tri-State Motor Transit Co., Joplin, MO, pg. 1111
Lawson, H. Richard, Chm. Bd.--Lawson Associates Inc., Minneapolis, MN, pg. 663
Lawson, Sam, Chm. Bd.--United Farm Tools, Kentucky Div., Glasgow, KY, pg. 1132
Lay, Joe L., Jr., Chm. Bd., Pres. & Chief Exec. Officer--Lay Packing Company Inc., Knoxville, TN, pg. 663
Layden, A.J., Chm. Bd. & Chief Exec. Officer--Allright Corporation, Houston, TX, pg. 41
Layman, Wm. D., Chm. Bd.--Layman Candy Company, Inc., Salem, VA, pg. 663
Lea, George A. Jr., Chm. Bd., Pres. & Chief Exec. Officer--The Mad Butcher, Inc., Pine Bluff, AR, pg. 699
Leach, Philip F., Chm. Bd.--Leach & Garner Company, North Attleboro, MA, pg. 663
Leaf, Robert S., Chm.-Intl./London--Burson-Marsteller, New York, NY, pg. 1210
Leavell, Charles H., Chm. Bd.--The Leavell Company, El Paso, TX, pg. 664
Leavitt, Julian, Chm. Bd., Pres., Chief Exec. Officer & Treas.--Sweetlife Foods, Inc., Suffield, CT, pg. 1067
Lebensfeld, Harry, Chm. Bd. & Chief Exec. Officer--UIS, Inc., New York, NY, pg. 1123
Lechler, Howard, Chm. Bd.--Cives Corp., Roswell, GA, pg. 251
LeClerc, H. George, Chm. Bd.--Cox & Company, Inc., New York, NY, pg. 292
Lee, Andrew, Chm. Bd., Pres. & Chief Oper. Officer--Daniel Caron Ltd., New York, NY, pg. 224
Lee, Frank, Chm. Bd.--Valley Pontiac Buick GMC, Inc., Auburn, WA, pg. 1143
Lee, George L., Jr., Chm. Bd.--Red Devil Inc., Union, NJ, pg. 918
Lee, Harry F., Chm. Bd.--C.R. Daniels, Inc., Ellicott City, MD, pg. 314
Lee, James C., Jr., Chm. Bd.--Buffalo Rock Company, Birmingham, AL, pg. 187
Lee, James D., Chm. Bd. & Pres.--Hamilton, Carver & Lee, Inc., Chicago, IL, pg. 503
Lee, Leighton, II, Chm. Bd.--Lee Company, Westbrook, CT, pg. 665
Lee, Patrick P., Chm. Bd. & Pres.--Enidine Incorporated, Orchard Park, NY, pg. 382
Lee, Preston R., Chm. Bd. & Pres.--Besteel Industries, Irvine, CA, pg. 147
Lee, Rhoady R., Jr., Chm. Bd. & Chief Exec. Officer--Lakeside Industries, Redmond, WA, pg. 651
Lee, Richard, Dr., Chm. Bd.--The Apparel Group, Ltd., New York, NY, pg. 78
Lee, S.C., Chm. Bd.--Markwood Inc., High Point, NC, pg. 710
Lee, Thomas H., Chm. Bd.--Chadwick-Miller Inc., Canton, MA, pg. 237
Lee, W.H., Chm. Bd. & Chief Exec. Officer--Zimdar Enterprises, Wyoming, MI, pg. 1220
Leebow, Steven, Chm. Bd., Pres. & Chief Exec. Officer--Pacesetter Steel Service, Inc., Marietta, GA, pg. 839
Leedom, John N., Sr., Chm. Bd.--Wholesale Electronic Supply, Dallas, TX, pg. 1188
Leeds, Gerard G., Co-Chm. Bd.--C M P Publications, Inc., Manhasset, NY, pg. 202
Leeds, Lilo J., Co-Chm. Bd.--C M P Publications, Inc., Manhasset, NY, pg. 202
Leeds, Robert K., Chm. Bd. & Pres.--Jewelmont Corporation, Minneapolis, MN, pg. 594

Leef, George L., Chm. Bd. & Chief Exec. Officer--Industrial Towel & Uniform, New Berlin, WI, pg. 567
Leff, Joseph, Chm. Bd.--National Spinning Co., Inc., New York, NY, pg. 793
Leffingwell, Dean, Chm. & Chief Exec. Officer--RELA, Inc., Boulder, CO, pg. 924
Leffingwell, Dean A., Chm. Bd. & Chief Exec. Officer--RELA Product Development Div. (PDD), Boulder, CO, pg. 924
LeFort, Leo J., Chm., Chief Exec. Officer--Arocom Direct, Inc., Cleveland, OH, pg. 737
LeFort, Leo J., Chm., Chief Exec. Officer--Arocom Marketing Group, Inc., Cleveland, OH, pg. 737
LeFrak, Samuel J., Chm. Bd.--Lefrak Organization Inc., Rego Park, NY, pg. 666
Legum, Leslie, Chm. Bd.--The Park Circle Motor Co., Baltimore, MD, pg. 848
Legus, James P., Chm. Bd. & Chief Exec. Officer--Magnetic Data, Inc., Eden Prairie, MN, pg. 700
Lehman, Jessie J., Chm. Bd. & Sec.--Georgian Press, Inc., New York, NY, pg. 453
Lehman, Ken, Co-Chm. Bd.--Fel-Pro Incorporated, Skokie, IL, pg. 405
Lehmann, John, Chm. Bd., Pres. & Chief Exec. Officer--Butterick Company, Inc., New York, NY, pg. 197
Lehr, Don, Chm. Bd. & Chief Exec. Officer--Cubix Corporation, Carson City, NV, pg. 303
Lehr, Gustav J., Chm. Bd. & Chief Exec. Officer--Shelter Mutual Insurance Company, Columbia, MO, pg. 997
Leibinger, Berthold, Chm. Bd.--Trumpf Inc., Farmington, CT, pg. 1118
Leicht, Richard F., Chm. Bd.--Eclipse Manufacturing Company, Sheboygan, WI, pg. 367
Leinniger, David L., Chm. Bd. & Chief Exec. Officer--Club Corp Realty, Dallas, TX, pg. 256
Leipsner, Stephen R., Chm., Pres. & Chief Exec. Officer--S & A Restaurant Corp., Dallas, TX, pg. 958
Leisure, Joe, Chm. & Pres.--Rush County Farm Bureau Co-op, Rushville, IN, pg. 956
Lemman, Robert L., Chm. Bd.--North Coast Electric Company, Bellevue, WA, pg. 813
Lemon, James H., Jr., Chm. Bd. & Chief Exec. Officer--Johnston, Lemon & Co. Inc., Washington, DC, pg. 601
Lenz, Randolph W., Chm. Bd.--FWD Corporation, Clintonville, WI, pg. 395
Leonard, Bruce N., Chm. & Chief Exec. Officer--Leonard Monahan Lubars & Kelly, Providence, RI, pg. 668
Leonard, Lois, Chm. Bd. & Pres.--Young & Roehr, Inc., Portland, OR, pg. 1210
Leone, Lucas J., Chm. Bd.--Eggland's Best, Inc., King of Prussia, PA, pg. 371
Lepape, H. E., Chm. Bd. & Chief Exec. Officer--Pacific Enterprises Oil Company (USA), Dallas, TX, pg. 840
Lervick, Arne T., Chm. Bd. & Chief Exec. Officer--Twin City Foods, Inc., Stanwood, WA, pg. 1122
LeSaffre, Peter, Chm. Bd. & Pres.--R.W. Electronics, Andover, MA, pg. 908
LeSage, William A., Chm. Bd & Chief Exec. Officer--General Homes Corporation, Houston, TX, pg. 449
Lesh, Charles P., Chm., Pres. & Treas.--Holcomb & Hoke Mfg. Company, Inc., Indianapolis, IN, pg. 538
Lesswing, Grant, Chm. Bd. & Chief Exec. Officer--Nuttall Equipment Co. Inc., Sherman, NY, pg. 818
Lester, Kenneth O., Chm. Bd.--Performance Food Group, Inc., Nashville, TN, pg. 861
Letven, Edward, Chm. & Chief Exec. Officer--Letven-Diccicco, Inc., Horsham, PA, pg. 669
Leventhal, Kenneth, Chm. Bd.--Kenneth Leventhal & Company, Los Angeles, CA, pg. 670
Levi, Malcolm, Sr., Chm. Bd.--Mayer Myers Paper Company, Memphis, TN, pg. 724
Levin, Ronald J., Chm.--Horlick Levin Advertising Inc., Los Angeles, CA, pg. 544
Levine, Sol, Chm.--Revlon Research Center, Inc., Edison, NJ, pg. 696
Levitt, Mortimer, Chm. Bd.--Custom Shop Shirtmakers Inc., New York, NY, pg. 306
Levonian, Elia Y., Chm. Bd.--Levonian Brothers Inc., Troy, NY, pg. 671
Levy, Barry W., Chm. Bd., Chief Exec. Officer & Communications Dir.--Levy Security Consultants, Limited, Chicago, IL, pg. 672
Levy, Daniel H., Vice Chm. & Chief Oper. Officer--Montgomery Ward & Co., Inc., Chicago, IL, pg. 767
Levy, Isaac A., Chm. Bd.--Level Export Sales Corp., New York, NY, pg. 670
Levy, Lawrence F., Chm. Bd.--The Levy Organization, Chicago, IL, pg. 672
Levy, Michael R., Chm. & Pres.--Mediatex Communications Corporation, Austin, TX, pg. 735
Levy, Saul, Chm. Bd.--Nationwise Automotive, Inc., Columbus, OH, pg. 795
Levy, T.R., Chm. Bd.--Sharon Tube Company, Sharon, PA, pg. 995
Lewis, Byron E., Chm. & Chief Exec. Officer--Uniworld Group, Inc., New York, NY, pg. 1139
Lewis, Clive, Chm. & Chief Exec. Officer--Lewis & Gace, Inc., Fort Lee, NJ, pg. 673
Lewis, Edward, Chm. Bd.--New York City Off Track Betting Corp., New York, NY, pg. 802
Lewis, Gene L., Chm.--Lewis Advertising, Inc., Rocky Mount, NC, pg. 673
Lewis, George T., Chm. Bd. & Chief Exec. Officer--Cogentrix Incorporated, Charlotte, NC, pg. 258
Lewis, Harriet G., Chm. Bd.--Gerber Plumbing Fixtures Corporation, Chicago, IL, pg. 454
Lewis, Harriet G., Chm. Bd.--Kokomo Sanitary Pottery Corp., Chicago, IL, pg. 640
Lewis, Jesse, Chm. Bd., Pres. & Chief Exec. Officer--Consumers Markets Inc., Springfield, MO, pg. 277
Lewis, Jewell M., Chm.--Media America Corp., Phoenix, AZ, pg. 734
Lewis, John, Chm. Bd. & Chief Exec. Officer--AmeriServ Food Company, Dallas, TX, pg. 66
Lewis, John H., Jr., Chm. Bd. & Pres.--Lewis Communications, Inc., Mobile, AL, pg. 673
Lewis, John P., Chm. Bd.--Sonneveldt Company, Grand Rapids, MI, pg. 1018
Lewis, Leslie B., Chm. & Pres.--Asahi/America, Inc., Malden, MA, pg. 87
Lewis, R. Jack, Sr., Chm. Bd.--Lewis Brothers Bakeries, Inc., Evansville, IN, pg. 673
Lewis, Ralph M., Chm. Bd.--Lewis Homes Management Corp., Upland, CA, pg. 673
Lewis, William, Chm. Bd., Pres. & Chief Exec. Officer--Career Blazers Inc., New York, NY, pg. 218
Liautaud, James P., Chm. Bd. & Chief Exec. Officer--Capsonic Group, Inc., Elgin, IL, pg. 216
Liban, G., Chm. Bd. & Chief Exec. Officer--Heresite Protective Coatings Inc., Manitowoc, WI, pg. 531
Libby, Darald R., Chm. Bd. & Chief Fin. Officer--David Clark Company, Inc., Worcester, MA, pg. 252
Libby, Henry G., Chm. Bd. & Pres.--The Disston Co., Greensboro, NC, pg. 339
Libera, John, Chm. Bd. & Chief Exec. Officer--Victor Corporation, West Warwick, RI, pg. 1149
Lieberman, David A., Chm. Bd.--Superior Linen & Drapery Company, Hackensack, NJ, pg. 1064
Liebman, Lawrence, Chm. Bd.--U.S. Reduction Company, Munster, IN, pg. 1137
Lieske, C.F., Chm. Bd.--Elkins Constructors, Inc., Jacksonville, FL, pg. 377
Lifton, Robert, Chm. Bd.--American Printers & Lithographers, Chicago, IL, pg. 59
Ligon, Ed D., Chm. Bd. & Pres.--Orbit Valve International, Inc., Little Rock, AR, pg. 828
Lilienthal, E.R., Chm. Bd.--Haas Brothers, San Francisco, CA, pg. 498
Lima, Raul Cruz, Chm.--Denison/BSB, Sao Paulo,, Brazil, pg. 111
Lima, William, Chm. Bd. & Pres.--Russell-Stanley Corporation, Red Bank, NJ, pg. 957
Limpe, Anthony T., Chm. Bd.--Petro Chem Development Company, New York, NY, pg. 865
Lin, Fred, Chm. Bd.--Payless Car Rental System, Inc., Saint Petersburg, FL, pg. 853
Linbeck, Leo E., Jr., Chm. Bd. & Chief Exec. Officer--Linbeck Corp., Houston, TX, pg. 675
Lindahl, John, Chm. Bd. & Chief Exec. Officer--State Industries Inc., Ashland City, TN, pg. 1041
Lindblad, Steve, Vice Chm.--The Stiffel Company, Chicago, IL, pg. 1049
Linder, Robert D., Sr., Chm. Bd.--United Dairy Farmers, Inc., Cincinnati, OH, pg. 1131
Lindheim, James B., Chm., Burson Marsteller/Europe (Paris)--Burson-Marsteller, New York, NY, pg. 1210
Lindner, Carl H., Chm. Bd. & Chief Exec. Officer--American Financial Corporation, Cincinnati, OH, pg. 52
Lindner, Carl H., Chm. Bd. & Chief Exec. Officer--Chiquita Brands International, Inc., Cincinnati, OH, pg. 53
Lindner, Carl H., Chm. & Chief Exec. Officer--Great American Communications Company, Cincinnati, OH, pg. 53
Lindner, Carl H., Chm. Bd. & Chief Exec. Officer--Spelling Entertainment Group, Inc., Cincinnati, OH, pg. 54
Lindner, Richard E., Sr., Chm. Bd.--Thriftway, Inc., Cincinnati, OH, pg. 1095
Lindsay, Winston S., III, Chm. Bd. & Chief Exec. Officer--Lindsay Manufacturing Inc., Ponca City, OK, pg. 676
Lindsey, W. Fred, Chm. Bd.--Dixie Oil Company, Tifton, GA, pg. 341
Liniger, Dave, Chm. Bd.--RE/MAX International, Inc., Englewood, CO, pg. 915
Link, Norman, Chm. Bd. & Chief Exec. Officer--O.P. Link Handle Company, Salem, IN, pg. 676
Linsmayer, Robert M., Chm. Bd.--Villaume Industries, Inc., Saint Paul, MN, pg. 1151
Lintz, Robert H., Chm. Bd.--Sterling Homes Corp., Sparks, NV, pg. 1046
Linvill, John G., Chm. Bd.--Telesensory, Mountain View, CA, pg. 1085
Lipman, Harry, Chm. Bd. & Chief Exec. Officer--Jameco Industries, Inc., Wyandanch, NY, pg. 588
Lipman, Ira A., Chm. & Pres.--Guardsmark, Inc., Memphis, TN, pg. 492
Lipsky, Jeff, Chm. Bd.--October Films, Inc., New York, NY, pg. 821
Lisherness, Harley, Chm. Bd. & Pres.--Roofing Wholesale Co., Inc., Phoenix, AZ, pg. 946
Liskys, Al, Chm. Bd.--Converse Professional Group, Inc., Pasadena, CA, pg. 281
Litow, Merrill, Chm. Bd.--Bentley, Barnes & Lynn, Inc., Chicago, IL, pg. 140
Littlejohn, B.R., Jr., Chm. Bd.--Community Cash Stores, Spartanburg, SC, pg. 270
Litvak, Leonard, Chm. Bd., Pres. & Chief Exec. Officer--Champion Boxed Beef, Denver, CO, pg. 238
Livingston, Robert, Chm., Pres. & Chief Exec. Officer--Grand Banks Yachts, Ltd., Greenwich, CT, pg. 475
Ljungberg, Robert, Chm. Bd., Pres., Chief Exec. & Chief Oper. Officer--Ultra Tool & Plastics, Inc., Amherst, NY, pg. 1125
Llewellyn, J. Bruce, Chm. Bd.--Philadelphia Coca-Cola Bottling Co., Philadelphia, PA, pg. 866
Lloyd, Harold E., Chm. Bd.--Lloyd Controls, Inc., Mountlake Terrace, WA, pg. 679
Lobel, Henry K., Chm. Bd. & Pres.--Smith-Edwards-Dunlap Company, Philadelphia, PA, pg. 1012
Lockard, Wendell, Chm. Bd.--Lockard Construction, Inc., Waterloo, IA, pg. 680
Lodge, William, Chm, Australia & Mng. Dir., Adelaide--Wunderman Cato Johnson, Dulwich,, Australia, pg. 1214
Loeb, Jef, Chm. Bd.--Katsin/Loeb Advertising, San Francisco, CA, pg. 618
Loeffler, William G., Chm. & Treas.--Loeffler Ketchum Mountjoy, Charlotte, NC, pg. 680
Loewenberg, William A., Chm. Bd.--Southern Leather Company, Memphis, TN, pg. 1021
Loft, John D., Chm. Bd. & Pres.--Loft's Seeds, Inc., Bound Brook, NJ, pg. 681
Logli, John, Chm.--Central Grocers Co-op, Franklin Park, IL, pg. 232
Lois, George, Chm. & Chief Exec. Officer--Lois/USA, New York, NY, pg. 681
Lombardi, Guido, Chm. Bd.--Ranchers Cotton Oil, Fresno, CA, pg. 911
Long, C.D., Chm. Bd. & Chief Exec. Officer--Krystal Company, Chattanooga, TN, pg. 645
Long, Charles A. Jr., Chm. Bd. & Pres.--Sullivan Long & Hagerty, Inc., Birmingham, AL, pg. 1057
Long, Donald J., Chm. Bd. & Chief Exec. Officer--Imperial, Inc., Green Bay, WI, pg. 564
Longsworth, Charles, Chm., Pres. & Chief Exec. Officer--Colonial Williamsburg Foundation, Williamsburg, VA, pg. 264
Loos, A.W., Chm. Bd.--Loos & Co., Inc., Pomfret, CT, pg. 683
Loos, Arthur E., Chm. Bd.--Evans Adhesive Corp., Columbus, OH, pg. 390
Lorch, Ernest H., Chm. Bd. & Chief Exec. Officer--The Dyson-Kissner-Moran Corporation, New York, NY, pg. 357
Lorch, Ernest H., Chm. & Chief Exec. Officer--DKM, Ltd., New York, NY, pg. 357
Lorenz, Horzt, Chm. Bd.--Kanex, Cleveland, OH, pg. 616
Lorsch, Robert H., Chm. Bd.--Lorsch Creative Network, Los Angeles, CA, pg. 684
Lorton, Robert, Chm.--World Publishing Company, Tulsa, OK, pg. 1203
Lotman, Herbert, Chm. Bd.--Keystone Foods Corporation, Bala-Cynwyd, PA, pg. 628
Lotter, John G.H., Chm. Bd. & Chief Exec. Officer--H. C. Miller Company, Milwaukee, WI, pg. 754
Love, Robert G., Chm. Bd.--Harris and Love, Inc., Salt Lake City, UT, pg. 512
Lowe, David M., Chm.--Arian, Lowe, Travis & Gusick, Inc., Chicago, IL, pg. 82
Lowe, Don F., Chm. Bd.--Comprehensive Business Services Inc., Carlsbad, CA, pg. 612
Lowe, Frank, Chm.--The Lowe Group, New York, NY, pg. 685
Lowe, Roger, Chm. Bd.--Affiliated Foods, Inc., Amarillo, TX, pg. 24
Lowenstein, Beth E., Chm. Bd.--Acme Mills Co. Inc., Detroit, MI, pg. 13
Lower, Martin, Chm. Bd.--Commercial Printers Of Connecticut, Norwich, CT, pg. 268
Lowman, George F., Chm. Bd.--Farrell Lines Incorporated, New York, NY, pg. 403
Lowrey, W.A., Chm. Bd., Pres. & Chief Exec. Officer--DDC PerTec, Tucson, AZ, pg. 308
Lowther, Mike, Chm. Bd. & Pres.--World Title Company, Burbank, CA, pg. 1203
Lowy, Rudolph, Chm. Bd., Pres. & Chief Exec. Officer--Pacific States Casualty Co., Los Angeles, CA, pg. 841
Luckie, Robert E., Jr., Chm. Bd.--Tucker Wayne/Luckie & Company, Birmingham, AL, pg. 1118
Ludington, Ivan, Jr., Chm Bd. & Chief Exec. Officer--Ludington News Co. Inc., Detroit, MI, pg. 686
Ludwig, Melvin, Chm. Bd. & Pres.--Eagle Electric Mfg. Co., Inc., Long Island City, NY, pg. 362
Lugbill, Charles, Chm. Bd. & Pres.--Lugbill Brothers, Inc., Archbold, OH, pg. 686
Luhrs, Warren R., Chm.--Hunter Marine Corporation, Alachua, FL, pg. 555
Lummis, Fred, Chm. Bd., Pres. & Chief Exec. Officer--AppleTree Markets, Houston, TX, pg. 79
Lummis, William R., Chm. Bd.--Summa Corporation, Las Vegas, NV, pg. 1057
Lumpkin, Richard A., Chm. Bd. & Chief Exec. Officer--Illinois Consolidated Telephone Co., Mattoon, IL, pg. 563
Lunt, Denham C., Jr., Chm. Bd.--Rogers, Lunt & Bowlen Co., Greenfield, MA, pg. 943
Luntz, John, Chm. Bd.--Luntz Corporation, Canton, OH, pg. 687
Lurie, Robert A., Chm. Bd.--San Francisco Giants Baseball Club, San Francisco, CA, pg. 969
Luscombe, Kevin, Chm. Bd. & Mng. Dir.--Luscombe and Partners Pty. Ltd., Port Melbourne,, Australia, pg. 344
Lusk, John D., Chm. Bd.--The Lusk Company, Irvine, CA, pg. 687
Luskey, Louis, Chm. Bd. & Pres.--Luskeys Western Stores, Inc., Fort Worth, TX, pg. 688
Lustbader, Edward E., Chm. Bd., Pres., Chief Exec. Officer & Treas.--The P.J. Carlin Construction Company, New Rochelle, NY, pg. 220
Lustine, Burton, Chm.--Lustine Oldsmobile & Buick, Inc., Hyattsville, MD, pg. 688
Luthringshausen, Wayne, Chm. Bd.--Options Clearing Corp., Chicago, IL, pg. 63
Lutz, Edgar, Chm. Bd.--Hoechst Ceramtec North America, Inc., Mansfield, MA, pg. 537
Lynch, Harry, Chm. Bd.--Texas Metal Works, Inc., Beaumont, TX, pg. 1089
Lynch, John, Chm. & Pres.--Towers, Perrin, Forster & Crosby, Inc., New York, NY, pg. 1103
Lynch, Leland T., Chm. & Chief Exec. Officer--Carmichael Lynch, Inc., Minneapolis, MN, pg. 222
Lynn, Jeffrey G., Chm. Bd., Pres. & Chief Exec. Officer--Dunham's Athleisure Corporation, Waterford, MI, pg. 353
Lyon, James E., Chm. Bd. & Chief Exec. Officer--Ruska Instrument Corporation, Houston, TX, pg. 956
Lyon, William, Chm. Bd.--William Lyon Company, Newport Beach, CA, pg. 690
Lyons, Michael J., Chm. & Chief Exec. & Creative Officer--Dorritie Lyons & Nickel, Inc., New York, NY, pg. 347
Lyons, William P., Chm. Bd.--Pennex Products Co., Inc., Verona, PA, pg. 858
Lytle, R.D., Chm. Bd., Pres. & Chief Exec. Officer--Star Bronze Company, Alliance, OH, pg. 1039
Maas, Curtis N., Chm. Bd. & Chief Exec. Officer--RDI, Inc., Itasca, IL, pg. 906

Mabee, John C., Chm. Bd.--Big Bear Supermarkets No. 3, San Diego, CA, pg. 149
MacArthur, John R., Chm. Bd.--Hammacher, Schlemmer & Co., Inc., Chicago, IL, pg. 503
MacCready, Paul, Dr., Chm. Bd. & Chief Exec. Officer--Aerovironment, Inc., Monrovia, CA, pg. 22
MacDonald, E.B., Chm. Bd.--Faribault Foods Inc., Minneapolis, MN, pg. 399
MacDonald, William F., Jr., Chm. Bd., Pres., Chief Exec. & Chief Oper. Officer--E. F. Houghton & Co., Valley Forge, PA, pg. 546
Macfarlane, Iain, Chm. & Chief Exec. Officer--Rockwood Gardens, Ltd., Rockwood,, Canada, pg. 638
MacFarlane, Iain, Chm. & Chief Exec. Officer--Michigan Bulb Company, Grand Rapids, MI, pg. 638
MacGregor, Ian, Sir., Chm. Bd.--Holmes Protection Group, Inc., New York, NY, pg. 540
Machamer, J.Q., Chm. Bd. & Chief Exec. Officer--Dyatron/Bondo Corporation, Atlanta, GA, pg. 356
Mack, Paul F., Chm. Bd.--Monroe Printing Company, East Stroudsburg, PA, pg. 697
MacKenzie, Howard J., Chm. Bd.--Standard Manifold Company, Inc., Chicago, IL, pg. 1037
Mackin, J. Leo, Co-Chm. Bd.--Interlock Industries, Inc., Louisville, KY, pg. 574
MacMillan, Whitney, Chm. Bd. & Chief Exec. Officer--Cargill Inc., Wayzata, MN, pg. 219
MacNeil, Norman E., Chm. Bd. & Treas.--Ark-Les Corporation, Watertown, MA, pg. 82
MacPherson, Robert W., Chm. Bd. & Chief Exec. Officer--General Latex & Chemical Corporation, Cambridge, MA, pg. 449
Maddock, Thomas S., Chm. Bd.--Boyle Engineering Corp., Newport Beach, CA, pg. 169
Madigan, Joseph D., Jr., Chm. Bd.--Madigan Brothers, Inc., River Forest, IL, pg. 699
Madison, Harold N., Chm. Bd.--Madison Graham Colorgraphics, Inc., Los Angeles, CA, pg. 699
Madonna, Jon C., Chm. & Chief Exec. Officer--KPMG Peat Marwick, New York, NY, pg. 613
Magdovitz, Joe, Chm. Bd., Sec. & Treas.--Imperial Manufacturing Company, Memphis, TN, pg. 564
Magee, John F., Chm. Bd.--Arthur D. Little, Inc., Cambridge, MA, pg. 678
Maghielse, Craig, Chm. Bd., Pres. & Chief Exec. Officer--Maghielse Tool Corporation, Grand Rapids, MI, pg. 700
Magliocco, John, Chm. Bd. & Chief Exec. Officer--Peerless Importers, Inc., Brooklyn, NY, pg. 855
Maguire, Bruce J., Chm. Bd.--Spartan Oil Corp., Lansing, MI, pg. 1026
Maguire, Cary M., Chm. Bd.--Components Corporation Of America, Dallas, TX, pg. 270
Mahler, Henrietta E., Chm. Bd. & Treas.--Henri's Food Products Co., Inc., Milwaukee, WI, pg. 530
Mahowald, James, Chm. Bd.--Our Own Hardware Company, Burnsville, MN, pg. 832
Mahr, Malcolm, Chm. Bd.--Maryland Paper Box Company, Baltimore, MD, pg. 717
Mai, Klaus, Chm. Bd.--Southwest Research Institute, San Antonio, TX, pg. 1023
Maibach, Ben C., Jr., Chm. Bd.--Cloverdale Equipment Co., Oak Park, MI, pg. 256
Maibach, Benjamin C., Jr., Chm. Bd.--Barton-Malow Enterprises, Inc., Southfield, MI, pg. 123
Maizlish, Irv, Chm. Bd.--Leo Eisenberg & Co., Inc., Kansas City, MO, pg. 372
Makhani, Madan P., Chm. Bd., Pres., Chief Oper. Officer & Chief Fin. Officer--American Foundry Group, Inc., Bixby, OK, pg. 54
Malek, Frederic, Co-Chm. Bd.--CB Commercial Real Estate Group, Inc., Los Angeles, CA, pg. 222
Maleson, Howard S., Chm. Bd.--Maleson Naylor, Owings Mills, MD, pg. 702
Malkin, Judd, Chm. Bd.--Amfac, Inc., Chicago, IL, pg. 585
Malmo, John, Chm. Bd.--Archer/Malmo Adv., Inc., Memphis, TN, pg. 80
Malody, Dennis, Commission Chm.--California State Lottery, Sacramento, CA, pg. 210
Maltzman, Donald, Chm. Bd.--Tomco Auto Products, Inc., Vernon, CA, pg. 1100
Malzahn, Edwin, Chm. Bd. & Pres.--Charles Machine Works, Inc., Perry, OK, pg. 240
Mandor, Leonard, Chm. Bd. & Chief Exec. Officer--Concord Assets Group, Inc., Boca Raton, FL, pg. 272
Manes, Nella C., Chm. Bd.--Abramson Ehrlich Manes, Inc., Washington, DC, pg. 10
Manigault, Peter, Chm. Bd.--Evening Post Publishing Co., Charleston, SC, pg. 391
Mann, Marvin L., Chm. & Chief Exec. Officer--Lexmark International, Inc., Greenwich, CT, pg. 673
Mansfield, John E., Sr., Chm. Bd.--Mansfield Oil Company, Gainesville, GA, pg. 704
Marcalus, Robert L., Sr., Chm. Bd. & Chief Exec. Officer--Marcal Paper Mills, Inc., Elmwood Park, NJ, pg. 706
March, Perrin G. III, Chm. Bd. & Chief Exec. Officer--Cincinnati Incorporated, Harrison, OH, pg. 250
Marchitto, Al, Chm. Bd. & Chief Exec. Officer--Simunico, Inc., Rutherford, NJ, pg. 1007
Marcus, Alex, Chm. Bd.--Halsey Drug Co., Inc., Brooklyn, NY, pg. 502
Marcus, Donald H., Chm. & Chief Exec. Officer--Marcus Advertising, Inc., Cleveland, OH, pg. 706
Marcus, Samuel, Chm. Bd.--Marcus Brothers Textiles, Inc., New York, NY, pg. 706
Mardell, Fred R., Vice Chm., Exec. V.P. & Sec.--Barton Brands, Ltd., Chicago, IL, pg. 123
Mardell, Fred R., Vice Chm., V.P. & Sec.--Barton Beers, Ltd., Chicago, IL, pg. 123
Margalith, Ethan Harold, Chm. Bd., Chief Exec. Officer & Treas.--Starving Students, Inc., Los Angeles, CA, pg. 1040
Margolis, Milton J., Vice Chm.--Host Apparel, Inc., New York, NY, pg. 545
Margolis, Robert, Chm. & Chief Exec. Officer--The Cherokee Group, Sunland, CA, pg. 243
Marini, Robert C., Chm. Bd. & Chief Exec. Officer--Camp Dresser & McKee Inc., Cambridge, MA, pg. 212
Marion, James P., Jr., Chm. Bd.--Bloomsburg Mills Inc., New York, NY, pg. 158
Maritz, William E., Chm. Bd. & Chief Exec. Officer--Maritz Inc., Fenton, MO, pg. 707
Mark, Jon J., Chm. Bd.--Marketing Magic Inc., Fort Lauderdale, FL, pg. 709
Markey, James, Chm. Bd. & Pres.--Action Manufacturing Co., Philadelphia, PA, pg. 15
Markin, William R., Chm. & Chief Exec. Officer--Lauerer Markin Gibbs, Inc., Maumee, OH, pg. 660
Marks, Philip, Chm. Bd.--Kettering Advertising Display Co., Englewood Cliffs, NJ, pg. 626
Marling, Mark E., Chm. Bd. & Pres.--Ed Marling Stores, Inc., Topeka, KS, pg. 710
Marotta, Thomas S., Chm. Bd. & Pres.--Marotta Scientific Controls, Inc., Montville, NJ, pg. 713
Marram, Edward P., Dr., Chm. Bd., Pres., Chief Exec. Officer & Treas.--Geo-Centers, Inc., Newton Center, MA, pg. 452
Mars, Forrest E., Jr., Chm. Bd. & Co-Pres.--Mars, Incorporated, McLean, VA, pg. 713
Marsh, George M., Chm. Bd.--Marsh Furniture Company, High Point, NC, pg. 714
Marsiglia, A.J., Chm. & Pres.--Responsive Marketing Communications, Inc., Schaumburg, IL, pg. 929
Marsilius, Philip R., Chm. Bd.--The Producto Machine Co., Bridgeport, CT, pg. 893
Martell, C. Ron, Chm. Bd. & Pres.--Microdynamics, Inc., Dallas, TX, pg. 749
Martin O'Neill, Chm. Bd.--Bata Shoe Co., Inc., Belcamp, MD, pg. 201
Martin, Bob, Chm. Bd.--Martin & Bayley Inc., Carmi, IL, pg. 714
Martin, David N., Chm.--Fahlgren Martin, Inc., Parkersburg, WV, pg. 396
Martin, David N., Chm. Bd. & Dir.-Creative Plans--Hawley Martin Partners, Inc., Richmond, VA, pg. 518
Martin, David O., Chm. Bd.--Martin Door Mfg., Inc., Salt Lake City, UT, pg. 714
Martin, Elliot, Chm. Bd., Pres. & Chief Exec. Officer--Windsor Publications, Inc., Chatsworth, CA, pg. 1196
Martin, Gordon, Chm. Bd., Pres. & Chief Exec. Officer--Martin Forest Industries, Healdsburg, CA, pg. 715
Martin, Henry G., Chm. Bd.--Refrigeration Supplies Distributors, Monterey Park, CA, pg. 921
Martin, J. Landis, Chm. Bd., Pres. & Chief Exec. Officer--Tremont Corporation, Denver, CO, pg. 1109
Martin, Jerry, Chm. & Chief Exec. Officer--Slater Hanft Martin, Inc., New York, NY, pg. 1010
Martin, Lee, Chm. Bd.--Nibco, Inc., Elkhart, IN, pg. 806
Martin, Leonard, Chm. Bd.--Mustang Tractor & Equip. Co., Houston, TX, pg. 777
Martin, Ret, Chm. Bd. & Chief Exec. Officer--The Dunlap Companies, Fort Worth, TX, pg. 353
Martindale, William A., Chm. Bd., Pres. & Chief Exec. Officer--Martrade Ltd., Santa Fe Springs, CA, pg. 716
Martiny, Kim R., Chm. Bd., Pres. & Chief Exec. Officer--Martiny & Company, Cincinnati, OH, pg. 716
Martire, Robert, Chm. Bd. & Pres.--Atlantic to Pacific Bedding Corp., Bronx, NY, pg. 95
Martz, Carrie, Chm. Bd. & Pres.--Martz & Wadas, Scottsdale, AZ, pg. 716
Marvin, William S., Chm. Bd.--Marvin Lumber & Cedar Company, Warroad, MN, pg. 716
Marzano, A.M., Chm. Bd. & Chief Exec. Officer--Mosler Inc., Hamilton, OH, pg. 772
Masek, Fred F., Chm. Bd.--Masek Distributing Inc., Gering, NE, pg. 717
Maslow, Lester, Chm. Bd. & Pres.--Best Manufacturing, Inc., New York, NY, pg. 146
Mason, Elvis L., Chm. & Chief Exec. Officer--Safeguard Business Systems, Inc., Fort Washington, PA, pg. 966
Massingil, Charles L., Chm. Bd.--Dot Printer, Inc., Irvine, CA, pg. 347
Masters, Philip S., Chm. Bd.--Arthur Murray Intl., Inc., Coral Gables, FL, pg. 776
Matarese, James M., Chm., Pres. & Chief Exec. Officer--Phoenix International, Inc., Beverly, NJ, pg. 868
Matarese, James M., Chm. Bd.--Precision Metal Prods., Inc., El Cajon, CA, pg. 869
Matellini, Dante, Chm. Bd. & Pres.--Aero Peru Corporation, Miami, FL, pg. 22
Mathias, John H., Chm. Bd. & Chief Exec. Officer--JPM Company, Lewisburg, PA, pg. 586
Mathieu, A.H. Pete, Chm. Bd. & Creative Dir.--Mathieu, Donovan & Associates, Inc., Montgomery, NY, pg. 721
Mathile, Clay, Chm. Bd. & Chief Exec. Officer--Iams Company, Dayton, OH, pg. 561
Mathis, Allen W., Jr., Chm. Bd.--Griffin Corporation, Valdosta, GA, pg. 487
Mathwich, Dale, Chm. Bd. & Chief Exec. Officer--American Standard Insurance Company of Wisconsin, Madison, WI, pg. 52
Mathwich, Dale F., Chm. Bd. & Chief Exec. Officer--American Family Mutual Insurance Co., Madison, WI, pg. 51
Mathwich, Dale F., Chm. Bd. & Chief Exec. Officer--American Family Financial Services, Inc., Madison, WI, pg. 52
Mathwich, Dale F., Chm. Bd. & Chief Exec Officer--American Family Mutual Insurance Co., Madison, WI, pg. 52
Mathwich, Dale F., Chm. Bd. & Chief Exec. Officer--AmFam, Inc., Madison, WI, pg. 52
Matt, F.X., II, Chm. Bd.--The F. X. Matt Brewing Co., Utica, NY, pg. 721
Matthaei, Charles W.H., Chm. Bd.--Roman Meal Company, Tacoma, WA, pg. 945
Matthews, James, Chm. Bd. & Chief Exec. Officer--Capener, Matthews & Walcher, San Diego, CA, pg. 214
Matthews, Joyce Carroll, Chm. Bd., Sec. & Treas.--Carroll's Foods, Inc., Warsaw, NC, pg. 225
Mattingly, David, Chm.--Mattingly & Partners/Melbourne, Richmond,, Australia, pg. 331
Mattingly, David, Grp. Chm.--Mattingly & Partners Group Pty Ltd., Richmond,, Australia, pg. 330
Mattingly, Mark S., Chm. Bd. & Chief Exec. Officer--Evansville Brewing Company, Evansville, IN, pg. 391
Mattingly, Thomas F., Chm. Bd. & Pres.--Metro Foods, Inc., Memphis, TN, pg. 743
Mattioli, Leonard S., Chm. Bd.--American TV & Appliance of Madison, Inc., Madison, WI, pg. 65
Matts, Joseph, Jr., Chm. Bd. & Pres.--HWH Architects Engineers Planners Inc., Cleveland, OH, pg. 498
Maude, Michael, Chm. Bd.--Clark Gum Company, Barrington, IL, pg. 252
Maughan, Rex, Chm. Bd., Pres. & Chief Exec. Officer--Forever Living Products, Tempe, AZ, pg. 424
Mauney, William K., Jr., Chm. Bd.--Mauney Hosiery Mills, Inc., Kings Mountain, NC, pg. 722
Mauren, P. Reed, Chm. Bd., Pres., & Gen. Mgr.--Galaxy Business Products, Honolulu, HI, pg. 742
Maurer, P. Reed, Chm. Bd., Chief Exec. Officer & Pres.--Metpac, Ltd., Honolulu, HI, pg. 742
Maurey, Joseph E., Chm. Bd. & Pres.--Maurey Manufacturing Corp., Chicago, IL, pg. 722
Mautner, Henry, Chm. Bd.--Midwesco Inc., Niles, IL, pg. 751
Maxey, Thomas F., Vice Chm. & Chief Oper. Officer--N W Ayer Incorporated, New York, NY, pg. 103
Maxon, Harry R., III, Chm. Bd.--Maxon Corporation, Muncie, IN, pg. 723
May, Ernest N., Jr., Chm. Bd.--Universal Dynamics Inc., Woodbridge, VA, pg. 1138
May, John, Chm. Bd.--The May Apparel Group, Inc., Mebane, NC, pg. 723
May, Stan, Chm. & Chief Creative Officer-Leo Burnett International--Leo Burnett Company, Inc., Chicago, IL, pg. 191
May, Stan, Chm. & Chief Creative Officer & Chief Exec. Officer--Leo Burnett Connaghan & May Pty. Ltd., North Sydney,, Australia, pg. 192
Mayer, Peter A., Chm.--Peter A. Mayer Advertising, Inc., New Orleans, LA, pg. 724
Mayfield, Cecil W., Chm. Bd.--MBS Holding, Inc., Arlington, TX, pg. 691
Mayfield, Cecil W., Chm. Bd.--Mayfield Building Supply Co., Arlington, TX, pg. 691
Mayhorne, Kenneth E., Chm.--Gray Kirk/VanSant Advertising, Inc., Baltimore, MD, pg. 479
Maynard, James H., Chm. Bd., Chief Exec. Officer & Treas.--Investor's Management Corp., Raleigh, NC, pg. 581
Maynard, James H., Chm. Bd.--Golden Corral Corporation, Raleigh, NC, pg. 466
Mayo, G.E., Chm. Bd.--Midland Mutual Life Insurance Co., Columbus, OH, pg. 751
Mazaika, Robert J., Chm. Bd., Pres. & Chief Exec. Officer--Uniroyal Chemical Company, Inc., Middlebury, CT, pg. 1129
McAboy, Jack, Chm. Bd.--California Electric Service, Oakland, CA, pg. 209
McAdams, Brian, Chm. Bd.--McAdams, Richman & Ong, Inc., Bala-Cynwyd, PA, pg. 725
McAdams, H. Hall, III, Chm. Bd.--The Union of Arkansas Corp., Little Rock, AR, pg. 1127
McAdams, Herbert H, II, Chm. Emeritus & Chief Exec. Officer--The Union of Arkansas Corp., Little Rock, AR, pg. 1127
McAdams, Rolla E., Vice Chm.--Reilly Industries, Inc., Indianapolis, IN, pg. 923
McAfee, Roy E., Chm. Bd.--McAfee Consolidated Inc., Mesa, AZ, pg. 726
McAllister, Donald, Jr., Chm. Bd.--Geyer-McAllister Publications, Inc., New York, NY, pg. 455
McAnally, N.A., Chm. Bd. & Chief Fin. Officer--McAnally Enterprises, Inc., Yucaipa, CA, pg. 726
McAuliffe, John, Chm. Bd. & Pres.--Compendium Systems, New York, NY, pg. 270
McBeth, Robert D., Chm. Bd., Pres. & Chief Exec. Officer--Associated Industrial Supply, Inc., Columbia, SC, pg. 90
McCaffray, S.J., Chm. Bd. & Pres.--National Frozen Foods Corp., Seattle, WA, pg. 789
McCain, William B., Chm. Bd.--McCain Manufacturing Corp., Chicago, IL, pg. 726
McCall, Donald, Chm. Bd.--Warner Press, Inc., Anderson, IN, pg. 1164
McCall, W. Calder, Chm. Bd.--McCall Oil & Chemical Corp., Portland, OR, pg. 726
McCall, W.C., Chm.--McCall Properties, Inc., Portland, OR, pg. 727
McCall, W.C., Chm.--GWC Properties, Inc., Portland, OR, pg. 727
McCall, W.C., Chm. Bd.--McCall Oil Real Estate Corporation, Portland, OR, pg. 727
McCallin, John L., Chm. Bd.--Steel, Inc., Commerce City, CO, pg. 1044
McCandless, Donald E., Vice Chm.--Dodson Group, Kansas City, MO, pg. 342
McCarthy, Michael M., Chm. Bd.--McCarthy Building Companies, Saint Louis, MO, pg. 727
McCarty, H.F., Jr., Chm. Bd.--McCarty Farms, Magee, MS, pg. 727
McClelland, Norman P., Chief Exec. Officer--Shamrock Foods Co., Phoenix, AZ, pg. 994
McClinton, Donald G., Co-Chm. Bd.--Interlock Industries, Inc., Louisville, KY, pg. 574
McCluskey, Edward H., Chm. Bd.--Standard Brands of America, Inc., Pompano Beach, FL, pg. 1035
McCollister, Paul, Chm. Bd., Pres. & Chief Exec. Officer--Jackson Hole Ski Resort, Teton Village, WY, pg. 587
McCollow, Thomas J., Chm. Bd., Pres. & Chief Exec. Officer--Journal Communications Inc., Milwaukee, WI, pg. 607

McCollow, Thomas J., Chm. Bd.--Journal Communications--The Milwaukee Journal, Milwaukee, WI, pg. 607
McCollum, James, Chm. Bd.--Tingley Rubber Corporation, South Plainfield, NJ, pg. 1098
McCollum, Robert, Chm. Bd. & Chief Exec. Officer--R. S. Hughes Co., Inc., Los Angeles, CA, pg. 551
McConnaughy, Tom, Chm. & Chief Exec. Officer--McConnaughy Stein Schmidt Brown, Chicago, IL, pg. 727
McConnell, William R., Chm. Bd. & Pres.--McConnell Cabinets, Inc., El Monte, CA, pg. 727
McCormack, John, Chm. Bd.--Visible Changes, Houston, TX, pg. 1153
McCormack, Mark H., Chm. Bd., Pres. & Chief Exec. Officer--International Management Group (IMG), Cleveland, OH, pg. 578
McCoy, Curtis G., Chm. Bd. & Pres.--Fantastic Sam's International, Inc., Memphis, TN, pg. 398
McCulloch, A. Donald, Jr., Chm. Bd. & Chief Exec. Officer--Nutri/System Inc., Blue Bell, PA, pg. 818
McCune, William, Chm. Bd.--Macco Constructors, Inc., Paramount, CA, pg. 696
McCurdy, Gilbert G., Chm. Bd.--McCurdy & Co., Inc., Rochester, NY, pg. 728
McDaniel, Gary P., Chm., Chief Exec. Officer & Sec.--ROC Properties Inc., Englewood, CO, pg. 908
McDermott, Gen. Robert, Chm. Bd. & Chief Exec. Officer--United Services Automobile Association (USAA), San Antonio, TX, pg. 1134
McDonald, Charles R., Chm., Pres. & Chief Exec. Officer--McDonald Equipment Co., Willoughby, OH, pg. 728
McDonald, J.M., III, Chm. Bd., Pres. & Chief Exec. Officer--A. Y. McDonald Industries, Inc., Dubuque, IA, pg. 728
McDonald, J.M., III, Chm. Bd., Pres., Treas. & Chief Exec. Officer--Brock-McVey Company, Lexington, KY, pg. 728
McDonald, R.D., Chm. Bd., Pres. & Chief Exec. Officer--A.Y.M. Inc., Albia, IA, pg. 728
McDonald, Thomas C., Chm. Bd.--Grindmaster Corporation, Louisville, KY, pg. 488
McDougal, Alfred L., Chief Exec. Officer--McDougal, Littell & Company, Evanston, IL, pg. 728
McDougall, Michael J., Chm. Bd.--McDougall Associates, Inc., Peabody, MA, pg. 728
McEachern, James, Chm. Bd. & Chief Exec. Officer--Tom James Company, Arlington, TX, pg. 589
McElroy, John L., Jr., Chm. Bd.--Wheat, First Securities Inc., Richmond, VA, pg. 1184
McElwee, Arthur, Chm. Bd. & Pres.--Goshen Rubber Co., Inc., Goshen, IN, pg. 472
McEniry, Robert Q., Chm. Bd.--Standard Welders Supply Co., Memphis, TN, pg. 1038
McEwen, Joseph, Chm. Bd. & Chief Exec. Officer--Modern Group Ltd., Bristol, PA, pg. 762
McFall, Thomas, Chm. & Chief Exec. Officer--Hamburger Hamlets Inc., Sherman Oaks, CA, pg. 1169
McFarland, William C., Chm. Bd. & Treas.--McFarland & Drier, Inc., Miami, FL, pg. 729
McFarling, James W., Chm. Bd.--McFarling Foods, Inc., Indianapolis, IN, pg. 729
McGarry, John, Vice Chm., Pres. & Chief Exec. Officer-No. America--Young & Rubicam Inc., New York, NY, pg. 1210
McGehee, Frank S., Co-Chm. Bd.--Mac Papers, Inc., Jacksonville, FL, pg. 694
McGehee, Thomas R., Co-Chm Bd. & Chief Exec. Officer--Mac Papers, Inc., Jacksonville, FL, pg. 694
McGinnis, Arthur J., Jr., Chm. Bd., Pres., Chief Oper. Officer--Simmons-Boardman Publishing Corp., New York, NY, pg. 1005
McGlothlen, James W., Chm. Bd.--Virginia Metal Industries, Inc., Orange, VA, pg. 1152
McGovern, Patrick J., Chm. Bd.--International Data Group, Boston, MA, pg. 576
McGrath, J. Brian, Chm. Bd.--Executive Enterprises, Inc., New York, NY, pg. 393
McGuinan, Mr., Chm.--Baker & McKenzie International, Chicago, IL, pg. 115
McKee, O. D., Chm. Bd.--McKee Baking Co., Inc., Collegedale, TN, pg. 730
McKee, O.D., Chm. Bd.--McKee Foods Corporation, Collegedale, TN, pg. 730
McKelvey, Andrew J., Chm. & Pres.--TMP Worldwide, Inc., New York, NY, pg. 1073
McKenna, Andrew J., Chm., Pres. & Chief Exec. Officer--Schwarz Paper Company, Morton Grove, IL, pg. 980
McKenna, P.W., Chm. Bd., Pres. & Chief Oper. Officer--Plasti-Kote Company Inc., Medina, OH, pg. 875
McKenzie, Joe, Chm. Bd. & Chief Exec. Officer--Rangaire & Company, Cleburne, TX, pg. 912
McKenzie, Kenneth, Chm. Bd.--GSC Enterprises, Inc., Sulphur Springs, TX, pg. 440
McKenzie, W. Guy, Sr., Chm. Bd.--McKenzie Tank Lines, Inc., Tallahassee, FL, pg. 730
McKnight, Andrew D., Chm. Bd. & Chief Exec. Officer--Tri-Chem, Inc., Harrison, NJ, pg. 1110
McLauchlan, Cal, Chm.-The McLauchlan Group--Deacon Day Advertising and The McLauchlan Group, Toronto,, Canada, pg. 685
McLaughlin, E.H., Jr., Chm. Bd.--McLaughlin Industrial Distributors, Inc., Pico Rivera, CA, pg. 731
McLean, William L., III, Chm. Bd. & Pres.--Independent Publications, Inc., Bryn Mawr, PA, pg. 565
McLendon, John A., Chm. Bd.--Nationwide Homes, Inc., Martinsville, VA, pg. 795
McLeod, John, Chm. Bd.--Lone Star Corrugated Container Corporation, Irving, TX, pg. 682
McMahon, Robert B., Chm. Bd.,Chief Exec. Officer, Treas., & Sec.--City Meats & Provisions Co., Tucsan, AZ, pg. 251
McManus, James R., Chm. Bd., Pres. & Chief Exec. Officer--Marketing Corp. of America, Westport, CT, pg. 709
McMullen, Walter P., Sr., Chm. Bd. & Chief Exec. Officer--Lithograph Printing Company, Inc., Memphis, TN, pg. 678
McNally, Alan G., Chm. Bd.--Mastercard International, Inc., New York, NY, pg. 720
McNally, Andrew, III, Chm. Bd.--Rand McNally & Company, Skokie, IL, pg. 911
McNamara, John F., Chm. Bd., Pres. & Chief Exec. Officer--Alco Health Services Corporation, Malvern, PA, pg. 31
McNeel, Van L., Chm. Bd. & Chief Exec. Officer--McNeel International Corp., Tampa, FL, pg. 732
McNeill, Bruce, Chm. Bd., Pres. & Chief Exec. Officer--Superior Federal Bank, Fort Smith, AR, pg. 1063
McNeilus, Garwin, Chm. Bd.--McNeilus Companies, Dodge Center, MN, pg. 732
McQueen, Angus, Chm. Bd. & Chief Exec. Officer--Ackerman McQueen, Inc., Oklahoma City, OK, pg. 12
McRae, Richard, Sr., Chm. Bd.--McRae's, Inc., Jackson, MS, pg. 733
McTague, Jerome J., Chm. Bd.--Fauber Construction Company, Inc., Lafayette, IN, pg. 403
McVaney, C. Edward, Chm. Bd., Pres. & Chief Exec. Officer--J.D. Edwards & Company, Denver, CO, pg. 370
McWane, James R., Chm. Bd.--McWane, Inc., Birmingham, AL, pg. 733
McWane, James R., Chm. Bd.--Clow Corporation, Birmingham, AL, pg. 733
McWillie, James, Chm.-Bd. Commissioners--Memphis Light, Gas & Water, Memphis, TN, pg. 738
Mead, Robert L., Chm. Bd.--Associated Grocers, Inc., Seattle, WA, pg. 90
Meads, Richard, Chm. & Chief Exec. Officer--Knoth & Meads Company, San Diego, CA, pg. 637
Meagher, M., Chm. Bd.--Financial World Partners, New York, NY, pg. 410
Mears, Paul S., Sr., Chm. Bd.--Mears Transportation Group, Orlando, FL, pg. 734
Medina, Robert S., Dr., Chm. Bd.--International Systems & Controls Corp., Houston, TX, pg. 579
Mee, George, Chm. & Pres.--Mallery Lumber Corp., Emporium, PA, pg. 702
Meehan, John E., Chm. Bd.--Redken Laboratories, Inc., Canoga Park, CA, pg. 919
Meehan, Paula Kent, Chief Exec. Officer--Redken Laboratories, Inc., Canoga Park, CA, pg. 919
Meer, Richard H., Chm. Bd. & Chief Exec. Officer--Meer Corporation, North Bergen, NJ, pg. 736
Mehlis, David L., Chm. Bd., Pres. & Chief Exec. Officer--David C. Cook Publishing Co., Elgin, IL, pg. 282
Meijer, Doug, Co-Chm.--Meijer, Inc., Grand Rapids, MI, pg. 737
Meijer, Hank, Co-Chm.--Meijer, Inc., Grand Rapids, MI, pg. 737
Mele, Edward V., Chm. Bd.--Mele Manufacturing Co., Inc., Utica, NY, pg. 737
Mellon, Timothy, Chm. Bd. & Chief Exec. Officer--Guilford Transportation Industries Inc., Merrimack, NH, pg. 493
Melnuk, Paul, Chm. Bd.--Clark Oil & Refining Corporation, Saint Louis, MO, pg. 252
Melo, James, Chm. Bd. & Treas.--Dynamic Metal Products Company, Manchester, CT, pg. 356
Meloon, Ralph C., Sr., Chm. Bd.--Correct Craft, Inc., Orlando, FL, pg. 287
Meltzer, Steven, Chm. Bd. & Pres.--MI Fund Incorporated, New York, NY, pg. 692
Melvyn, London, Chm. Bd.--London Litho Aluminum Co., Inc., Lincolnwood, IL, pg. 681
Mendelson, Murry, Chm. Bd.--Murry's, Inc., Forestville, MD, pg. 777
Mendelson, Murry, Chm. Bd.--Murry's, Inc., Forestville, MD, pg. 777
Mendenhall, William, Chm.--Mendenhall & Leistra, Grand Rapids, MI, pg. 739
Menon, V.B., Chm. Bd.--Capitol Industries-EMI Inc., Hollywood, CA, pg. 216
Meoni, Ronald J., Chm. Bd.--RLJC, Inc., Meriden, CT, pg. 783
Mercer, Bernard, Chm. Bd.--Preferred Risk Mutual Insurance, West Des Moines, IA, pg. 886
Mercer, Bernard, Chm. Bd.--Preferred Risk Life Insurance Co., West Des Moines, IA, pg. 886
Merlav, K.A., Chm. Bd., Pres. & Chief Exec. Officer--Ottenheimer & Company, Inc., Bannockburn, IL, pg. 831
Mermelstein, Joseph, Chm. Bd.--Elgin Watch International, Inc., Long Island City, NY, pg. 376
Merriman, Joe Jack, Chm. Bd.--Ann Raskas Gourmet Confectioners, Edwardsville, KS, pg. 913
Merritt, Robert E., Chm. Bd.--Renfro Corp., Mount Airy, NC, pg. 926
Merson, Albert, Chm. Bd.--MacNaughton Einson Graphics, Fair Lawn, NJ, pg. 698
Meyer Ekberg, Marietta, Chm. Bd.--Meyer Broadcasting Company, Bismarck, ND, pg. 746
Meyer, Frederick R., Chm. Bd. & Pres.--Aladdin Industries, Incorporated, Nashville, TN, pg. 29
Meyer, Stanley F., Chm. & Chief Exec. Officer--Wendt Advertising, Inc., Great Falls, MT, pg. 1176
Meyerson, Robert F., Chm. Bd.--Basic Computer, Akron, OH, pg. 124
Meza, Gonzalo, Chm. & Pres.--BSB/Meza, Ltda., Bogota,, Colombia, pg. 110
Michael, Joseph, Chm.--Professional Apartment Management, Inc., Lodi, CA, pg. 893
Michaels, J. David, Chm. Bd. & Pres.--Michaels Group Inc., Latham, NY, pg. 747
Michalek, Edward T., Chm. Bd. & Chief Exec. Officer--Norwesco, Inc., Minneapolis, MN, pg. 816
Michalek, Richard C., Chm. Bd. & Chief Exec. Officer--Quality Control Corporation, Harwood Heights, IL, pg. 903
Michel, Henry L., Chm. Bd.--Parsons Brinckerhoff Inc., New York, NY, pg. 850
Middleton, Charles S., Chm. Bd., Pres. & Chief Exec. Officer--Cal-Air Inc., Whittier, CA, pg. 208
Mikelsons, J. George, Chm. Bd., Pres. & Chief Exec. Officer--Amtran, Inc., Indianapolis, IN, pg. 69
Milenthal, David, Chm. Bd.--Hameroff/Milenthal/Spence, Inc., Columbus, OH, pg. 503
Miles, Gordon H., Chm. Bd.--Green Leaf Ventures, Inc., San Diego, CA, pg. 484
Milhous, Robert E., Chm. Bd.--Treasure Chest Advertising Co., Inc., Glendora, CA, pg. 1108
Milidrag, George, Chm. Bd.--Engineering Technology Ltd. (E.T.), Troy, MI, pg. 382
Mill, Victor J., Jr., Chm. Bd.--Lawrence Pumps, Inc., Lawrence, MA, pg. 662
Millard, Dan, Chm. Bd., Pres., Chief Exec. & Chief Oper. Officer--Central Illinois Steel Company, Carlinville, IL, pg. 232
Millard, Suzanne T., Chm. Bd & Pres.--Turtle & Hughes, Inc., Linden, NJ, pg. 1119
Miller, Augustus C., Chm. Bd., Pres., Chief Exec. Officer--Miller Oil Co., Inc., Norfolk, VA, pg. 754
Miller, Bernard J., Jr., Chm. Bd.--Columbian Advertising Inc., Chicago, IL, pg. 266
Miller, Carl, Jr., Chm. Bd.--Wayne Wire Cloth Products, Inc., Kalkaska, MI, pg. 1169
Miller, David P., Chm. Bd.--Atlas Lederer Co., Cleveland, OH, pg. 265
Miller, David P., Chm. Bd.--Grant Steel Corp., Pittsburgh, PA, pg. 265
Miller, Donald B., Chm. Bd.--Horizon Media, Inc., New York, NY, pg. 544
Miller, Edward, Chm. Bd.--Time Oil Company, Seattle, WA, pg. 1097
Miller, Henry E., Sr., Chm. Bd.--Miller Building Corp., Wilmington, NC, pg. 753
Miller, Herbert, Chm. Bd. & Chief Exec. Officer--Western Development Corporation, Washington, DC, pg. 1179
Miller, Hilary B., Chm. Bd.--American Paper Products Group, Ltd., Youngstown, OH, pg. 59
Miller, Howard, Chm. Bd.--Howard Miller Clock Company, Zeeland, MI, pg. 754
Miller, James B., Chm. Bd. & Chief Exec. Officer--Miller Business Systems, Inc., Arlington, TX, pg. 753
Miller, James F., Chm. Bd.--MTI Vacations, Inc., Oak Brook, IL, pg. 694
Miller, John F., III, Chm. Bd. & Chief Exec. Officer--Miller & Long Co. Inc., Bethesda, MD, pg. 754
Miller, Larry, Chm. Bd., Pres. & Chief Exec. Officer--Corinthian Media, Inc., New York, NY, pg. 286
Miller, Leonard J., Chm. Bd.--Miller Advertising Agency Inc., New York, NY, pg. 753
Miller, Lester, Chm. Bd.--Contico International, Inc., Saint Louis, MO, pg. 278
Miller, Malcolm, Chm. & Chief Exec. Officer--Prentiss Incorporated, Floral Park, NY, pg. 887
Miller, Max, Chm. Bd. & Treas.--McInerney-Miller Brothers Inc., Detroit, MI, pg. 729
Miller, Opha H., Chm. Bd.--Miller & Co., Selma, AL, pg. 753
Miller, Richard G., Jr., Chm. Bd.--Elgin National Industries, Inc., Chicago, IL, pg. 609
Miller, Robert S., Chm. Bd. & Chief Exec. Officer--Better Baked Foods, Inc., North East, PA, pg. 148
Miller, Robert V., Chm.--Miller Meester Advertising Inc., Minneapolis, MN, pg. 754
Miller, Steven, Chm. Bd., Pres. & Chief Exec. Officer--Miller Personnel, Inc., North Brunswick, NJ, pg. 755
Miller, T.D., Chm. Bd.--ZMP, Inc., Glendale, CA, pg. 237
Miller, Tod, Chm. Bd. & Chief Exec. Officer--Rosewood Property Company, Dallas, TX, pg. 949
Milliken, Roger, Chm. Bd. & Chief Exec. Officer--Milliken & Co., Inc., Spartanburg, SC, pg. 755
Mills, Howard, Jr., Chm. Bd. & Chief Exec. Officer--Maplehurst Farms, Inc., Indianapolis, IN, pg. 705
Mills, James S., Chm. Bd. & Chief Exec. Officer--Medline Industries, Inc., Mundelein, IL, pg. 736
Mills, John M., Chm. Bd.--Gravymaster Inc., Branford, CT, pg. 478
Mills, Olan, III, Chm. Bd. & Sec.--Olan Mills, Inc., Chattanooga, TN, pg. 756
Mills, Walter G., Chm. Bd., Chief Exec. Officer & Treas.--W.G. Mills, Inc., Sarasota, FL, pg. 756
Millstein, Jack H., Sr., Chm. Bd.--Millstein Industries, Jeannette, PA, pg. 756
Millstein, Jack H., Sr., Chm. Bd.--National Plastics Corporation, Jeannette, PA, pg. 756
Milstein, Howard, Chm. & Pres.--The Milford Agency, New York, NY, pg. 753
Minard, Duane, Chm. Bd.--ATI Industries, Escondido, CA, pg. 8
Minarik, William, Chm. Bd.--Minarik Electric Company, Glendale, CA, pg. 756
Miniat, Ronald, Chm., Pres. & Chief Exec. Officer--Ed Miniat, Inc., Chicago, IL, pg. 757
Minnick, Terry, Chm. Bd., Pres. & Chief Exec. Officer--The Pro Corporation, Florence, MA, pg. 891
Minor, Henry H., Jr., Chm. Bd.--P.W. Minor & Son, Inc., Batavia, NY, pg. 758
Minyard, Lisbeth, Co-Chm. Bd. & Treas.--Minyard Food Stores, Coppell, TX, pg. 759
Miska, Steven M., Chm. Bd. & Chief Exec. Officer--Generra Sportswear Company, Inc., Tukwila, WA, pg. 451
Mitchel, Thomas L., Chm. Bd. & Pres.--Mitchel & Scot Machine Co., Inc., Indianapolis, IN, pg. 761
Mitchell, Doug, Chm. Bd. & Pres.--Perryton Equity, Perryton, TX, pg. 863
Mitchell, Robert E., Chm. Bd.--Dunn-Edwards Corporation, Los Angeles, CA, pg. 353
Mitchell, Ronald B., Chm. Bd. & Pres.--Mitchell & Assoc., Inc., Bethesda, MD, pg. 761
Mitchell, William F., Chm. Bd., Pres. & Chief Exec. Officer--Mitchell Corporation of Owosso, Owosso, MI, pg. 761
Mize, John, Chm. Bd.--Distribution America, Des Plaines, IL, pg. 340
Mockley, B.A., Chm. Bd. & Pres.--Anchor Gasoline Corporation, Tulsa, OK, pg. 71
Moddrell, Joe, Jr., Chm. Bd.--Insurance Management Associates, Wichita, KS, pg. 572

Modell, William, Chm. Bd.--Henry Modell & Company, Inc., Long Island City, NY, pg. 762
Modrovich, Ivan, Chm. Bd.--Medical Analysis Systems Inc., Camarillo, CA, pg. 735
Moeckel, Alfred J., Sr. V.P.--Seminole Manufacturing Company, Columbus, MS, pg. 989
Moeller, Albert, Chm. Bd.--Concordia Publishing House, Saint Louis, MO, pg. 272
Mohrman, Roy, Chm. Bd., Pres. & Chief Exec. Officer--Handling Systems Engineering, Jacksonville, FL, pg. 505
Mojden, Wallace W., Chm. Bd.--Fleetwood Systems, Inc., Countryside, IL, pg. 417
Molesphini, Arthur J., Chm. & Media Dir.--Molesphini & Tobin, Inc., New York, NY, pg. 764
Molin, Carl E., Jr., Chm. Bd.--Molin Auto Parts Inc., Buffalo, NY, pg. 764
Molinaro, Albert P., Jr., Chm.-Emeritus--Klemtner Advertising Inc., New York, NY, pg. 635
Moll, Curtis E., Chm. Bd. & Chief Exec. Officer--MTD Products, Inc., Valley City, OH, pg. 694
Moloney, Earl, Chm. Bd. & Chief Exec. Officer--Molon Motor & Coil Corp., Rolling Meadows, IL, pg. 764
Molz, Otis, Chm. Bd.--Farmland Industries, Inc., Kansas City, MO, pg. 402
Monaghan, Thomas S., Chm. Bd., Pres. & Chief Exec. Officer--Domino's Pizza Inc., Ann Arbor, MI, pg. 344
Monette, Edward A., Chm., Pres., Chief Exec. & Oper. Officer--St. Croix Press, Inc., New Richmond, WI, pg. 966
Monk, William C., Chm. Bd., Chief Exec. Officer & Treas.--A.C. Monk Co., Inc., Farmville, NC, pg. 766
Monkiewicz, Frank V., Chm. Bd.--Kayem Foods, Inc., Chelsea, MA, pg. 619
Montague, B.L., III, Chm. Bd. & Chief Exec. Officer--B. L. Montague Co., Sumter, SC, pg. 766
Montgomery, Mead, Chm. Bd. & Chief Exec. Officer--Treaty Co., Greenville, OH, pg. 1109
Montgomery, Robert L., Chm. & Chief Exec. Officer--Montgomery, Zukerman, Davis, Inc., Indianapolis, IN, pg. 768
Montgomery, W. Barton, Chm. Bd.--Nationwide Corporation, Columbus, OH, pg. 795
Montgomery, Walter S., Sr., Chm. Bd.--Spartan Mills, Spartanburg, SC, pg. 1026
Montgomery, William, Chm. Bd., Pres., & Chief Exec. Officer--The SArgent-SOwell Company, Grand Prairie, TX, pg. 971
Montgomery, William J., Chm. Bd. & Chief Exec. Officer--American Finance Group, Boston, MA, pg. 52
Montna, Alfred, Chm. Bd.--Farmers Rice Cooperative, Sacramento, CA, pg. 401
Mooar, William, Chm. Bd.--Imprint Products, L.P., Rockville Centre, NY, pg. 564
Moomjy, Walter, Chm. Bd.--Einstein Moomjy Inc., Pine Brook, NJ, pg. 371
Mooney, Cathi, Chm. Bd., Creative Dir.--Mandelbaum Mooney Ashley, San Francisco, CA, pg. 703
Mooney, James P., Chm. Bd. & Chief Exec. Officer--Mooney Chemicals, Cleveland, OH, pg. 768
Moore, Alfred A., Chm. Bd.--Chelsea Moore Company, Cincinnati, OH, pg. 241
Moore, E. Joseph, Chm. Bd. Emeritus--Invetech Co., Detroit, MI, pg. 581
Moore, Harold, Chm. Bd.--Harold Moore & Associates, Inc., Fayetteville, TN, pg. 768
Moore, Hillar, Jr., Chm. Bd.--Shurfine-Central Corp., Northlake, IL, pg. 1001
Moore, J. Michael, Chm. Bd. & Chief Exec. Officer--Invetech Co., Detroit, MI, pg. 581
Moore, Jerry W., Chm. Bd., Chief Exec. Officer & New Bus. Contact--The J.W. Moore Group, Greensboro, NC, pg. 768
Moore, Lee P., Chm..--Sunniland Corporation, Sanford, FL, pg. 1061
Moore, Michael J., Chm. Bd. & Pres.--Southland Industries, Long Beach, CA, pg. 1023
Moore, Norman, Chm. Bd.--Bepco, Inc., Winston-Salem, NC, pg. 141
Moore, Rex, Chm. Bd.--Rex Moore Electrical Contractors & Engineers, West Sacramento, CA, pg. 768
Moore, Ronald D., Chm. Bd.--Chivas Products Ltd., Sterling Heights, MI, pg. 248
Moore, Thomas F., Chm. Bd.--Moore Company, Westerly, RI, pg. 768
Moore, Thomas H., Chm. Bd.--Contractors Supplies, Inc., Lufkin, TX, pg. 280
Moore, Wayne R., Chm. Bd., Pres. & Chief Exec. Officer--Moore Special Tool Co., Inc., Bridgeport, CT, pg. 768
Moore, William E., Chm. Bd.--Kelly-Moore Paint Company, Inc., San Carlos, CA, pg. 621
Moore, Woodrow J., Jr., Sr. V.P.--Stanley Consultants, Inc., Muscatine, IA, pg. 961
Moorhouse, Virginia F., Chm. Bd. & Publr.--The Bakersfield Californian, Bakersfield, CA, pg. 115
Moos, J. Clifford, Chm., Pres. & Chief Exec. Officer--Economy Folding Box Corp., Chicago, IL, pg. 367
Moran, Dennis, Chm. Bd. & Chief Exec. Officer--Moran Industries, Inc., Midlothian, IL, pg. 769
Moran, James M., Chm. Bd.--JM Family Enterprises Inc., Deerfield Beach, FL, pg. 584
Moran, Thomas E., Chm. Bd.--Moran Towing & Transporation Co. Inc, Greenwich, CT, pg. 769
Morelli, Joseph, Chm. Bd., Pres. & Chief Exec. Officer--M. H. Rhodes, Inc., Avon, CT, pg. 931
Morey, James N., Chm.--Hutchins/Young & Rubicam, Rochester, NY, pg. 1211
Morgan, John S., Chm., Pres. & Chief Exec. Officer--Morgan Foods, Inc., Austin, IN, pg. 770
Morgan, Paul S., Chm. Bd.--Morgan Construction Company, Worcester, MA, pg. 769
Morgan, Robert, Chm. Bd., Pres. & Chief Exec. Officer--Morgan Industries Inc., Bala-Cynwyd, PA, pg. 770
Morgan, Ronald, Chm. Bd.--RMI Marketing & Advertising, Emerson, NJ, pg. 907
Morison, John H., Chm. Bd.--Hitchiner Manufacturing Company, Inc., Milford, NH, pg. 536
Moroch, Thomas F., Chm. Bd.--Moroch & Assoc., Inc., Dallas, TX, pg. 770
Morris, Earl L., Chm. Bd. & Chief Exec. Officer--Acorn Engineering Company, City of Industry, CA, pg. 14
Morris, James R., Chm. Bd. & Chief Exec. Officer--MADD (Mothers Against Drunk Driving), Irving, TX, pg. 691
Morris, Lester A., Chm. Bd.--Mesirow Financial, Chicago, IL, pg. 741
Morris, T.N., Jr., Chm., Pres. & Chief Exec. Officer--Calcasieu Lumber Company, Austin, TX, pg. 208
Morris, Thad J., Chm. Bd.--T.J. Morris Company, Inc., Statesboro, GA, pg. 771
Morris, Thomas B., Jr., Chm. Policy Committee, Mng. Ptnr. & Chief Exec. Officer)--Dechert Price & Rhoads, Philadelphia, PA, pg. 323
Morris, W.S., III, Chm. Bd. & Chief Exec. Officer--Morris Corporation, Augusta, GA, pg. 999
Morris, William C., Chm. Bd. & Pres.--J. & W. Seligman & Company, New York, NY, pg. 584
Morrisett, Lloyd M., Chm. Bd.--RAND, Santa Monica, CA, pg. 911
Morrison, J.M., Chm. Bd. & Pres.--Morrison, Inc., Hammond, IN, pg. 771
Morrison, John C., Jr., Chm. & Chief Exec. Officer--MetLife Capital Corporation, Bellevue, WA, pg. 744
Morrison, John C., Jr., Chm. Bd.--MetLife Capital Credit Corp., Stamford, CT, pg. 744
Morrison, Robert K., Chm. Bd.--Harvey Industries, Inc., Waltham, MA, pg. 515
Morrow, David W., Chm. Bd., Pres., Chief Exec. Officer & Chief Oper. Officer--Pueblo International, Inc., Pompano Beach, FL, pg. 899
Morrow, Robert C., Chm. Bd.--Walman Optical Company, Minneapolis, MN, pg. 1161
Morse, Edward J., Sr., Chm. Bd. & Pres.--Morse Operations Inc., Ft. Lauderdale, FL, pg. 772
Mortenson, M.A., Jr., Chm. Bd., Chief Exec. Officer & Pres.--M. A. Mortenson Company, Minneapolis, MN, pg. 772
Morton, Jerry W., Chm. Bd.--United Engines, Inc., Oklahoma City, OK, pg. 1131
Moser, Robert P., Chm. Bd.--Pacific Coast Producers, Lodi, CA, pg. 839
Moss, Cruse W., Chm. Bd.--The Flexible Corp., Delaware, OH, pg. 421
Moss, Cruse W., Chm. Bd. & Chief Exec. Officer--General Automotive Corporation, Ann Arbor, MI, pg. 448
Motch, Arthur E., Jr., Chm. Bd.--R. A. Jones & Co. Inc., Covington, KY, pg. 604
Mougey, Charles L., Chm. Bd., Treas. & Mgr.-Sls.--Puget Sound Plywood, Inc., Tacoma, WA, pg. 899
Mourry, Dennis, Chm. Bd. & Chief Exec. Officer--Roytex, Inc., New York, NY, pg. 953
Mow, William, Chm. Bd.--Bugle Boy Industries, Inc., Simi Valley, CA, pg. 187
Mower, Eric, Chm. & Chief Exec. Officer--Eric Mower and Associates, Inc., Syracuse, NY, pg. 774
Mower, Eric, Chm. & Chief Exec. Officer--Eric Mower and Associates/Buffalo, Inc., Buffalo, NY, pg. 774
Moyer, William C., Dr., Chm. Bd., Pres. & Chief Exec. Officer--SFA, Inc., Landover, MD, pg. 961
Moynahan, John D., Chm.--MetLife HealthCare Management Corp., St. Louis, MO, pg. 745
Mrozinski, Walter F., Chm. Bd.--Facemate Corporation, Chicopee, MA, pg. 396
Mueller, J.D., Chm. Bd.--G & W Electric Co., Blue Island, IL, pg. 438
Mueller, John S., Chm. & Chief Exec. Officer--Laidlaw Corporation, Scottsdale, AZ, pg. 650
Mueller, Warren A., Chm. Bd. & Treas.--C & M Corporation, Wauregan, CT, pg. 198
Muhlhauser, Barbara, Chm. Bd. & Creative Dir.--Muhlhauser & Young, San Francisco, CA, pg. 774
Mulach, Joseph F., Jr., Chm. Bd.--Mulach Steel Corporation, Bridgeville, PA, pg. 775
Mulder, Lawrence, Chm. Bd.--ODL Incorporated, Zeeland, MI, pg. 819
Mulhern, James A., Chm. Bd.--Mulhern Belting, Inc., Oakland, NJ, pg. 775
Mull, Jackie, Chm. Bd.--Plains Cotton Co-op Association, Lubbock, TX, pg. 873
Mullally, Timothy J., Chm. Bd.--Ann Sacks Tile & Stone, Inc., Portland, OR, pg. 640
Mullan, Paul, Chm. Bd. & Chief Exec. Officer--Fleer Corporation, Mount Laurel, NJ, pg. 695
Mullaney, Brian, Chm Bd. & New Bus. Contact--Schell/Mullaney, New York, NY, pg. 975
Mullaney, Thomas, Chm. Bd.--The Levolor Corporation, Sunnyvale, CA, pg. 671
Muller, David M., Chm. Bd.--Federal Farm Credit Banks Funding Corporation, Jersey City, NJ, pg. 404
Mullet, Roy, Chm. Bd.--Excel Industries, Inc., Hesston, KS, pg. 392
Mullet, Willis, Chm. Bd. & Chief Exec. Officer--Wayne Dalton Corporation, Mount Hope, OH, pg. 312
Mullis, Wayne, Chm. Bd.--Bryant Universal Roofers Inc., Phoenix, AZ, pg. 185
Mungo, Michael J., Chm. Bd.--Michael J. Mungo Company, Inc., Columbia, SC, pg. 775
Munier, Emile H., Chm. Bd.--Wolff & Munier, Inc., Hawthorne, NY, pg. 1199
Munro, Donald, Chm. Bd., Chief Exec. Officer & Treas.--Munro & Company, Inc., Hot Springs, AR, pg. 775
Murchison, C.W., Chm. Bd.--United Exposition Service Company, Chicago, IL, pg. 1102
Murdock, David H., Chm. Bd. & Chief Exec. Officer--Dole Food Company, Inc., Westlake Village, CA, pg. 840
Muro, Roy A., Chm. & Chief Exec. Officer--Vitt Media International, Inc., New York, NY, pg. 1153
Murphy, Kenneth T., Chm. Bd., Pres. & Chief Exec. Officer--First Abilene Bankshares, Inc., Abilene, TX, pg. 411
Murphy, Kenneth T., Chm. Bd. & Chief Exec. Officer--First National Bank of Abilene, Abilene, TX, pg. 412
Murphy, Peter, Jr., Chm. Bd., Pres. & Chief Exec. Officer--Murphy Company, Eugene, OR, pg. 776
Murphy, Steve, Chm. Bd.--Producers Co-op Association, Inc., Girard, KS, pg. 892
Murphy, Thomas N., Chm. Bd.--National Car Rental System, Inc., Minneapolis, MN, pg. 786
Murphy, Thomas, Sr., Chm. Bd.--Spring Arbor Distributors, Belleville, MI, pg. 1033
Murray, Norman J., Chm. Bd.--The Airolite Company, Marietta, OH, pg. 28
Muse, J. Melvin, Chm.--Muse Cordero Chen, Inc., Los Angeles, CA, pg. 777
Muselman, Carl H., Chm. Bd.--E.P. Graphics, Inc., Berne, IN, pg. 360
Musgrove, H.B., Chm. Bd., Pres. & Chief Exec. Officer--Frantz Manufacturing Co., Sterling, IL, pg. 429
Muskat, Irwin, Chm. Bd., Pres. & Chief Exec. Officer--Granite State Packing Co., Manchester, NH, pg. 476
Must, Meyer, Chm. Bd.--Detroit City Dairy, Inc., Highland Park, MI, pg. 333
Muth, Peter G., Chm. Bd.--Orco Block Company, Stanton, CA, pg. 828
Muzzy, Richard W., Jr., Chm. Bd. & Chief Exec. Officer--Binkley Company, Warrenton, MO, pg. 151
Myers, Edward, Chm. Bd. & Pres.--Tillamook County Creamery Assn., Tillamook, OR, pg. 1097
Myers, H.E., Jr., Chm. Bd.--BCM Engineers Inc., Plymouth Meeting, PA, pg. 106
Myers, Joseph E., Chm. Bd. & Pres.--Collins Oldsmobile Inc., Indianapolis, IN, pg. 263
Myers, L. Richard, Chm. Bd.--Nielsen Construction Company, San Diego, CA, pg. 807
Myers, Paul, Chm.--Javelin/Young & Rubicam, Dublin, Ireland, pg. 1212
Myers, Robert, Chm. Bd.--Kocolene Oil Corp., Seymour, IN, pg. 639
Myerson, Robert, Chm. Bd.--Ben Myerson Candy Company, Inc., Los Angeles, CA, pg. 780
Myhre, Leonard A., Chm. Bd.--Hallidie Machinery Company, Inc., Seattle, WA, pg. 501
Nabholz, Robert D., Chm. Bd.--Nabholz Construction Corp., Conway, AR, pg. 782
Naccarato, Vincent A., Chm. Bd., Pres. & Chief Exec. Officer--Wilton Industries, Inc., Woodridge, IL, pg. 1194
Nadel, Jack, Chm. Bd. & Pres.--Measured Marketing Services, Los Angeles, CA, pg. 734
Naegele, Robert O., Jr., Chm. Bd.--Rollerblade, Inc., Minnetonka, MN, pg. 944
Nagler, Stewart G., Chm. Bd.--Metropolitan Property & Casualty Insurance Co.(Met P&C), Warwick, RI, pg. 744
Nagler, Stewart G., Chm. Bd.--Metropolitan Insurance & Annuity Co., New York, NY, pg. 744
Nagler, Stewart G., Chm. Bd.--Metropolitan Tower Life Insurance Co., New York, NY, pg. 744
Naify, Marshall, Chm. Bd.--The Todd-AO Corporation, San Francisco, CA, pg. 1099
Najjar, William K., Chm. Bd.--Ranir Corporation, Grand Rapids, MI, pg. 912
Nakae, Howard, Chm. Bd.--Blue Anchor, Inc., Sacramento, CA, pg. 158
Nancarrow, David, Chm. Bd.--Bruner Corporation, Milwaukee, WI, pg. 184
Narans, Stephen, Chm. Bd.--Hostmark Management Group, Rowing Meadows, IL, pg. 545
Naritoni, T.A., Chm. Bd.--Steelox Systems, Inc., Mason, OH, pg. 1044
Narlinger, Dennis, Chm., Pres. & Chief Exec. Officer--Shugart Corporation, Irvine, CA, pg. 1001
Nason, Charles T., Chm. Bd., Pres. & Chief Exec. Officer--The Acacia Group, Washington, DC, pg. 10
Nason, Walton H., Jr., Chm. Bd.--Nason and Cullen, Inc., Wayne, PA, pg. 784
Nassau, Robert, Chm. Bd.--Waterous Company, South Saint Paul, MN, pg. 50
Naumann, George F., Chm. Bd. & Chief Exec. Officer--Victaulic Company of America, Easton, PA, pg. 1149
Nave, Edward, Chm. Bd.--Mercury Distributing Co., Inc., Chatsworth, CA, pg. 740
Neal, Edmond A., Jr., Pres. & Gen. Mgr.--Russell Harrington Cutlery Inc., Southbridge, MA, pg. 556
Neal, John F., Chm. Bd. & Creative Dir.--Neal & Stephens Advertising, Inc., Kettering, OH, pg. 796
Neal, John R., Chm. Bd. & Pres.--JRN, Inc., Columbia, TN, pg. 586
Neale, Bill R., Chm.--Point Communications, Inc., Dallas, TX, pg. 878
Neally, Philip, Chm. Bd. & Chief Exec. Officer--Aldi Inc., Batavia, IL, pg. 33
Neary, Robert D., Co-Chm.-Professional Services--Ernst & Young, New York, NY, pg. 387
Needham, Tom, Chm., Pres. & Chief Exec. Officer--Allen & Hoshall, Inc., Memphis, TN, pg. 36
Needle, Gilbert, Chm. Bd.--Atlantic Plumbing Supply Company, Washington, DC, pg. 95
Neerhout, John, Jr., Chm. & Exec. Sponsor--Bechtel Great Britain Ltd., London, United Kingdom, pg. 131
Nelsen, Clifford D., Chm. Bd. & Pres.--Nelsen Steel & Wire Co., Franklin Park, IL, pg. 797
Nelson, Alix, Chm. & Chief Exec. Officer--Franklin Spier, Inc., New York, NY, pg. 1031
Nelson, Dan, Chm. & Chief Exec. Officer--Nelson & Schmidt, Inc., Milwaukee, WI, pg. 797
Nelson, Gary R., Chm. Bd. & Chief Exec. Officer--Nelson Photo Supplies, San Diego, CA, pg. 797
Nelson, Harold P., Chm. Bd.--Nelson & Small Inc., Portland, ME, pg. 798
Nelson, John F., Chm. Bd.--Golden Gem Growers Inc., Umatilla, FL, pg. 466
Nelson, Kent C., Chm. Bd. & Chief Exec. Officer--United Parcel Service of America, Inc., Atlanta, GA, pg. 1133
Nelson, Wayne K., Chm. & Chief Exec. Officer--Nelson Communications, Inc., New York, NY, pg. 797
Nemanick, Kathryn S., Chm. Bd.--The Lorvic Corp., St. Louis, MO, pg. 684

Nerad, John, Chm. Bd.--TimeMed Labeling Systems, Inc., Burr Ridge, IL, pg. 1098
Nerland, Rick, Chm. Bd., Pres. & New Bus. Contact--The Nerland Agency, Inc., Anchorage, AK, pg. 798
Nethercutt, J.B., Chm. Bd. & Chief Exec. Officer--Merle Norman Cosmetics, Inc., Los Angeles, CA, pg. 740
Netter, Edward, Chm. Bd. & Pres.--Geneve Corporation, Stamford, CT, pg. 451
Netter, Edward, Chm. Bd. & Chief Exec. Officer--Independence Holding Company, Stamford, CT, pg. 451
Netzsch, Thomas, Chm. Bd.--Netzsch, Inc., Exton, PA, pg. 798
Neubauer, Joseph, Chm. Bd., Pres. & Chief Exec. Officer--ARA Group, Philadelphia, PA, pg. 5
Neubauer, Joseph, Chm. Bd. & Pres.--ARA Services, Inc., Philadelphia, PA, pg. 5
Neuhoff, James H., Chm. Bd., Pres. & Chief Exec. Officer--Valleydale Packers Inc., Bristol, VA, pg. 1143
Neuwirth, Frank, Chm. Bd. & Pres.--Unex Conveying Systems, Inc., Jackson, NJ, pg. 1126
Neville, Robert J., Chm. Bd., Pres. & Chief Exec. Officer--The North American Manufacturing Co., Cleveland, OH, pg. 811
Nevin, Crocker, Chm. Bd.--CF&I Steel Corporation, Pueblo, CO, pg. 201
Newhouse, S.I., Jr., Chm. Bd.--The Conde Nast Publications Inc., New York, NY, pg. 19
Newhouse, Samuel I., Jr., Chm. Bd. & Chief Exec. Officer--Advance Publications Inc., Staten Island, NY, pg. 19
Newman, Larry, Chm. Bd. & Chief Exec. Officer--Prism Integrated Sanitation Management, Inc., Miami, FL, pg. 599
Newman, Richard A., Chm. Bd.--New Mech Companies, Inc., Saint Paul, MN, pg. 802
Newman, Van, Chm. Bd. & Treas.--Newman, Saylor & Gregory, Columbia, SC, pg. 804
Newton, John T., Chm. Bd.--Dundee Mills, Inc., Griffin, GA, pg. 352
Neyer, Donald L., Chm. Bd. & Pres.--Al Neyer, Inc., Cincinnati, OH, pg. 805
Neyer, Jerome C., Chm. & Chief Exec. Officer--NTH Consultants, Ltd., Farmington Hills, MI, pg. 781
Nicholas, Donna H., Chm. Bd.--The Orr Felt Company, Piqua, OH, pg. 830
Nichols, J.D., Chm. Bd. & Chief Exec. Officer--NTS Corporation, Louisville, KY, pg. 781
Nickels, William C., Chm. Bd.--Replogle Globes, Inc., Broadview, IL, pg. 927
Nickerson, Joshua A., Jr., Chm. Bd. & Pres.--Nickerson Lumber Company, Orleans, MA, pg. 806
Nickles, Ernest, Chm. & Chief Exec. Officer--Nickles Bakery Inc., Lima, Lima, OH, pg. 807
Nickles, Ernest A., Chm. & Chief Exec. Officer--Alfred Nickles Bakery, Inc., Navarre, OH, pg. 806
Nickles, Ernest A., Chm. & Chief Exec. Officer--Nickles Bakery, Inc., Martins Ferry, OH, pg. 807
Nidiffer, Raymond, Chm. Bd.--United Grocers Inc., Portland, OR, pg. 1132
Nie, Norman H., Chm. Bd.--SPSS Inc., Chicago, IL, pg. 964
Niebla, J. Fernando, Chm. Bd. & Chief Exec. Officer--Infotec Development, Inc., Santa Ana, CA, pg. 567
Nielsen, Eric C., Chm. Bd.--The Nielsen Company, Cincinnati, OH, pg. 807
Nielsen, Joseph, Chm. Bd.--Norbest, Inc., Midvale, UT, pg. 809
Nielsen, Stanley, Chm. Bd.--Universal Cooperatives, Inc., Minneapolis, MN, pg. 1138
Nielson, Don, Chm. Bd.--Norpac Foods, Inc. Cooperative, Stayton, OR, pg. 810
Nies, Thomas M., Chm. Bd., Pres. & Chief Exec. Officer--Cincom Systems, Inc., Cincinnati, OH, pg. 250
Nissen, William, Chm. Bd. & Pres.--Apache Hose & Belting Company, Cedar Rapids, IA, pg. 77
Nixon, Allen, Chm. Bd.--E.C. Barton & Co., Jonesboro, AR, pg. 123
Nixon, Kenneth, Chm. Bd.--Tennessee Farmers Co-op, La Vergne, TN, pg. 1087
Nixon, P. Andrews, Chm. Bd., Pres. & Chief Exec. Officer--Dead River Company, Portland, ME, pg. 321
Noble, Robert B., Chm. & Chief Exec. Officer--Noble & Associates, Springfield, MO, pg. 808
Nolan, Alan T., Chm. Bd.--Union City Body Company, Inc., Union City, IN, pg. 1128
Noland, L.U., Jr., Chm. Bd.--Basic Construction Company, Newport News, VA, pg. 124
Nonnelly, Mark, Chm. Bd.--EduServ, Saint Paul, MN, pg. 369
Norberg, Dennis, Chm.--Wild's Baking Company, Englewood, NJ, pg. 1189
Norm Haberman, Chm. Bd.--El Torito Restaurants, Inc., Irvine, CA, pg. 372
Norman, Jack, Sr., Chm. Bd.--Norman Brothers Nissan Inc., Orlando, FL, pg. 810
Norrie, K. Peter, Chm. Bd.--Specialty Paperboard Inc., Brattleboro, VT, pg. 1027
Norris, John W., Jr., Chm. Bd. & Chief Exec. Officer--Lennox International Inc., Richardson, TX, pg. 667
Norris, Stephen L., Chm. Bd.--Carlyle Holding Corporation, Washington, DC, pg. 222
Norton, J. Patrick, Chm. Bd., Pres. & Chief Exec. Officer--Fabreeka International, Inc., Stoughton, MA, pg. 396
Norton, John R., III, Chm. Bd. & Chief Exec. officer--J. R. Norton Company, Phoenix, AZ, pg. 816
Norton, Kenneth R., Chm. Bd. & Chief Exec. Officer--PST Vans, Inc., Salt Lake City, UT, pg. 837
Norton, Peter B., Chm. Bd. & Chief Exec. Officer--American Learning Corp., Chicago, IL, pg. 381
Nunley, Richard L., Chm. Bd., Pres. & Treas.--Better Living Inc., Charlottesville, VA, pg. 148
Nusim, Joseph, Chm., Pres. & Chief Exec. Officer--Channel Home Centers Inc., Whippany, NJ, pg. 238
O'Brien, Clarence J., II, Chm.--O'Brien Machinery Company, Downingtown, PA, pg. 820
O'Brien, F.L., III, Chm., Pres. & Chief Exec. Officer--O'Brien Energy Systems Inc., Philadelphia, PA, pg. 820
O'Brien, John F., Chm. Bd. & Pres.--The Hanover Insurance Company, Worcester, MA, pg. 34
O'Brien, Raymond V., Jr., Chm. Bd.--Emigrant Savings Bank, New York, NY, pg. 379
O'Callaghan, Mike, Chm. Bd.--Las Vegas Sun, Inc., Las Vegas, NV, pg. 659
O'Connell, L.E., Chm. Bd. & Chief Exec. Officer--Bunton Company, Louisville, KY, pg. 188
O'Connell, Robert, Chm. Bd. & Chief Exec. Officer--Hess's Department Stores, Inc., Allentown, PA, pg. 302
O'Connor, Laurence P., Chm. Bd. & Chief Exec. Officer--Unigard Security Insurance Co., Bellevue, WA, pg. 596
O'Connor, Laurence P., Chm. Bd. & Chief Exec. Officer--Unigard Indemnity Co., Raleigh, NC, pg. 596
O'Connor, Laurence P., Chm. Bd. & Chief Exec. Officer--Unigard Insurance Co., Seattle, WA, pg. 596
O'Connor, Laurence P., Chm. Bd. & Chief Exec. Officer--Unigard Service Corp., Seattle, WA, pg. 596
O'Connor, Thomas D., Chm., Pres. & Chief Exec. Officer--Mohawk Paper Mills, Inc., Cohoes, NY, pg. 763
O'Connor, Thomas P., Chm. Bd.--Greystone Realty Corporation, Greenwich, CT, pg. 802
O'Daly, Fergus F., Chm. & Chief Exec. Officer--Poppe Tyson, New York, NY, pg. 880
O'Donnell, James E., Chm. Bd., Pres. & Chief Exec. Officer--Wheatland Tube Company, Collingswood, NJ, pg. 1184
O'Hara, John M., Chm. Bd. & Chief Exec. Officer--R. L. Polk & Co., Detroit, MI, pg. 879
O'Keefe, William B., Chm. Bd.--Symmons Industries Inc., Braintree, MA, pg. 1069
O'Leary, Dennis P., Chm. Bd. & Pres.--The F. D. Lawrence Electric Co., Cincinnati, OH, pg. 661
O'Malia, George Joe, Chm. Bd.--O'Malia Food Markets Inc., Noblesville, IN, pg. 825
O'Malley, Shaun F., Co-Chm. & Sr. Partner--Price Waterhouse - U.S., New York, NY, pg. 888
O'Mara, A. James, Chm. Bd. & Chief Exec. Officer--Greenhorne & O'Mara, Inc., Greenbelt, MD, pg. 485
O'Neal, Emmet, Chm. Bd. & Chief Exec. Officer--O'Neal Steel Inc., Birmingham, AL, pg. 827
O'Neal, William J., Chm.--O'Neal & Prelle, Hartford, CT, pg. 827
O'Neill, Donald F., Pres. & Chief Exec. Officer--P M Company, Philadelphia, PA, pg. 835
O'Neill, W. McKerall, Jr., Chm. Bd.--Berwick Bay Oil Co. Inc., Morgan City, LA, pg. 144
O'Reilly, C.H., Chm. Bd.--O'Reilly Auto Inc., Springfield, MO, pg. 829
O'Rourke, Ruth E., Chm. & Treas.--A & A Manufacturing Co., New Berlin, WI, pg. 1
O'Shaughnessy, Patrick E., Chm. Bd. & Chief Exec. Officer--Lario Oil & Gas Company, Wichita, KS, pg. 658
Oates, James G., Chm. & Reg. Mng. Dir.-Leo Burnett USA--Leo Burnett Company, Inc., Chicago, IL, pg. 191
Oben, Walter J., Jr., Chm. Bd.--Southgate Ford Inc., Southgate, MI, pg. 1023
Oberg, Donald E. II., Chm. Bd.--Oberg Industries Co., Freeport, PA, pg. 819
Odegard, Robert J., Chm. Bd.--American Hardware Mutual Insurance Co., Minnetonka, MN, pg. 55
Odom, John P., Co-Chm. Bd. & Chief Exec. Officer--The Odom Corporation, Seattle, WA, pg. 821
Odom, William, Co-Chm. Bd.--The Odom Corporation, Seattle, WA, pg. 821
Oertli, Charles W., Chm. Bd.--Guarantee Electrical Company, Saint Louis, MO, pg. 490
Ogden, J.H., Jr., Chm. Bd. & Chief Exec. Officer--Conestoga Holdings, Inc., Stamford, CT, pg. 273
Ogden, Roger H., Chm. Bd.--The Maurin-Odgen Companies, New Orleans, LA, pg. 722
Ogle, D. Clark, Chm. Bd., Pres., Chief Exec. & Chief Oper. Officer--Peter J. Schmitt Holdings, West Seneca, NY, pg. 976
Ohm, Karl F., Chm.--The Brady Company, Menomonee Falls, WI, pg. 171
Ohmatsu, S., Chm. Bd.--Leader Instruments Corporation, Hauppauge, NY, pg. 664
Ohsawa, Takashi, Chm.--Chuo Senko Advertising Co., Ltd., Tokyo, Japan, pg. 103
Olin, Burton H., Chm. Bd. & Chief Exec. Officer--Humiston-Keeling, Inc., Chicago, IL, pg. 552
Olin, Thomas F., Chm. Bd.--Archway Cookies, Inc., Battle Creek, MI, pg. 81
Olmstead, R.N., Chm. Bd. & Pres.--Modern Equipment Co., Inc., Port Washington, WI, pg. 32
Olsen, David A., Chm., Pres., Chief Exec. & Chief Oper. Officer--Johnson & Higgins, New York, NY, pg. 598
Olsen, Fred, Chm. Bd.--Timex Corporation, Middlebury, CT, pg. 1098
Olson, Dean A., II, Chm. Bd.--Rockford Acromatic Product Co., Rockford, IL, pg. 941
Olson, Frank A., Chm. Bd. & Pres.--Park Ridge Corporation, Park Ridge, NJ, pg. 849
Olson, Frank A., Chm. Bd., Chief Exec. & Oper. Officer--The Hertz Corporation, Park Ridge, NJ, pg. 849
Olson, Ken, Chm. & Chief Exec. Officer--Proxima Corporation, San Diego, CA, pg. 896
Olson, Oscar L., Chm. Bd. & Chief Exec. Officer--Olsonite Corporation, Detroit, MI, pg. 824
Olson, Paul, Pres.--Intercole, Inc., Washington, PA, pg. 574
Oman, Jack A., Chm. Bd. & Pres.--Oman Construction Co. Inc., Nashville, TN, pg. 825
Omer, Don C., Chm. Bd., Pres., Chief Exec. & Fin. Officer--Inland Associates, Inc., Olathe, KS, pg. 570
Onstead, Robert R., Chm. Bd. & Chief Exec. Officer--Randall's Food Markets, Inc., Houston, TX, pg. 911
Opler, Edmond, Jr., Chm. Bd., Pres. & Chief Exec. Officer--World's Finest Chocolate, Inc., Chicago, IL, pg. 1203
Orczyk, Stanley R., Chm. & Chief Oper. Officer--Meenan Oil Co. Limited Partnership, Syosset, NY, pg. 736
Orden, Ted, Chm. Bd. & Pres.--Thrifty Oil Company, Downey, CA, pg. 1096
Orders, William H., Chm. Bd., Chief Exec. Officer & Treas--Orders Distributing Co., Greenville, SC, pg. 829
Ordway, Peter S., Chm., Pres. & Chief Exec. Officer--Union Pump Company, Battle Creek, MI, pg. 1128
Oreffice, Paul, Chm. Bd.--American Enterprise Institute for Public Policy Research, Washington, DC, pg. 51
Oren, John R., Chm. Bd. & Chief Exec. Officer--Eastway Delivery Service of Houston, Inc., Houston, TX, pg. 364
Oren, John R., Chm. Bd. & Chief Exec. Officer--Eastway Delivery Service of Austin, Inc., Austin, TX, pg. 364
Oren, John R., Chm. Bd. & Chief Exec. Officer--Eastway Delivery Service of Dallas, Inc., Grapevine, TX, pg. 364
Oren, John R., Chm. Bd. & Chief Exec. Officer--Eastway Air Cartage, Inc., Houston, TX, pg. 364
Oresman, Roger B., Chm. Bd.--Yazoo Investment Corporation, Jackson, MS, pg. 1207
Oresman, Roger B., Chm. Bd.--Mississippi Valley Gas Co., Jackson, MS, pg. 1208
Orfalea, Paul, Chm. Bd.--Kinko's Corporation, Ventura, CA, pg. 632
Orgill, Joseph, III, Chm. Bd.--West Union Corp., Memphis, TN, pg. 1177
Oringer, Howard, Chm. Bd. & Chief Exec. Officer--Telesciences Co. Systems Inc., Moorestown, NJ, pg. 1085
Ormsby, Ann, Chm. Bd.--Recreational Equipment, Inc., Kent, WA, pg. 917
Orral, John H., Chm. Bd.--Winthrop Printing Company, Inc., Boston, MA, pg. 1197
Ortolani, Timothy S., Chm. Bd., Pres. & Chief Exec. Officer--Carton-Craft Corporation, Buffalo, NY, pg. 226
Orton, J. Roy, Chm. Bd.--Welch's, Concord, MA, pg. 789
Orullian, B. La Rae, Chm. & Chief Exec. Officer--The Women's Bank, N.A., Denver, CO, pg. 385
Osawa, Kuniko, Chairwoman--Chuo Senko Advertising Co., Ltd., Tokyo, Japan, pg. 103
Osherow, Allen J., Chm. Bd. & Pres.--Windart Holding Inc., Pico Rivera, CA, pg. 1195
Osherow, Allen J., Chm. Bd. & Pres.--Windsor Art Products, Inc., Pico Rivera, CA, pg. 1195
Ostrover, Harvey, Chm. Bd. & Chief Exec. Officer--American Fabrics Company, New York, NY, pg. 51
Otakie, Daniel A., Chm., Pres., Chief Exec. Officer & Treas.--Futures Personnel Services, Baltimore, MD, pg. 438
Otero, Richard J., Chm., Pres. & Chief Exec. Officer--RJO Enterprises, Inc., Lanham, MD, pg. 907
Ott, James H., Chm.--Novar Electronics, Barberton, OH, pg. 817
Ott, Jerry E., Chm. Bd.--Ott Communications, Inc., Louisville, KY, pg. 831
Ott, Robert B., Chm. Bd.--The Hennegan Company, Cincinnati, OH, pg. 529
Otto, R.E., Chm. Bd.--Home-Owners Insurance Co., Lansing, MI, pg. 100
Otto, R.E., Chm. Bd.--Property-Owners Insurance Co., Marion, IN, pg. 100
Otto, Richard E., Chm. Bd. & Chief Exec. Officer--Auto-Owners Insurance, Lansing, MI, pg. 100
Oudt, John, Chm. Bd.--Barq's, Inc., New Orleans, LA, pg. 121
Oudt, John, Chm. Bd.--Delaware Punch Co., New Orleans, LA, pg. 121
Ouimet, Emil R., Chm. Bd. & Treas.--Ouimet Industries, West Wareham, MA, pg. 831
Ouimet, Emil R., Chm. Bd. & Treas.--Ouimet Corp., Nashville, TN, pg. 831
Ounjian, Marilyn J., Chm. Bd. & Chief Exec. Officer--Careers USA Inc., Philadelphia, PA, pg. 218
Overholt, Rod E., Chm. Bd.--Harrison Construction Corp., Miami, FL, pg. 512
Owen, Dian G., Chm. Bd.--Owen Health Care, Houston, TX, pg. 833
Owen, Dorothy G., Chm. Bd.--Owen Steel Co., Inc., Columbia, SC, pg. 834
Owen, Robert E., Chm. Bd. & Pres.--Owen Industries, Inc., Carter Lake, IA, pg. 834
Owens, Bill M., Chm. Bd. & Chief Exec. Officer--Owens Pollick & Associates, Phoenix, Inc., Phoenix, AZ, pg. 834
Paddock, S. R., Jr., Chm., Chief Exec. Officer & Publr.--Paddock Publications, Inc., Arlington Heights, IL, pg. 842
Page, F. Roger, Chm. Bd., Pres., Chief Exec. & Fin. Officer--Pace Oil Co., Inc., Winston-Salem, NC, pg. 838
Page, Jack L., Chm. Bd.--Kalamazoo Label Co., Kalamazoo, MI, pg. 615
Paige, Norma, Chm. Bd.--Astronautics Corp. of America, Milwaukee, WI, pg. 93
Paisner, Bruce L., Chm. & Chief Exec. Officer--Hearst Entertainment, New York, NY, pg. 523
Palasthira, Teddy Spha, Chm.--Dentsu, Young & Rubicam/Bangkok, Bangkok, Thailand, pg. 330
Paletz, Lenn, Chm., Pres., Chief Exec. & Chief Oper. Officer--The Sportsman's Guide, Inc., Eagan, MN, pg. 1032
Pallone, J.L., Chm. Bd.--Maccabees Mutual Life Insurance, Southfield, MI, pg. 696
Palmer, Charles L., Chm. Bd. & Chief Exec. Officer--North American Company, Fort Lauderdale, FL, pg. 811
Palmer, Richard F., Chm. Bd.--Palmer Moving & Storage Co., Livonia, MI, pg. 844
Palmer, Richard M., Jr., Chm. Bd. & Pres.--R.M. Palmer Company, West Reading, PA, pg. 843
Palmer, Stephen T., Jr., Chm. Bd. & Chief Exec. Officer--Palmer International, Inc., Worcester, PA, pg. 844
Palmon, Dan, Chm. Bd.--G.L. Advertising, Dumont, NJ, pg. 440
Pamplin, R.B., Sr., Chm. Bd.--Mount Vernon Mills, Inc., Greenville, SC, pg. 844
Pamplin, Robert B., Sr., Chm. Bd. & Chief Exec. Officer--R. B. Pamplin Corp., Portland, OR, pg. 844
Pansini, Andrew L., Chm. Bd.--Jandy Industries, Novato, CA, pg. 589
Papadinis, James, Chm. Bd.--Univex Corporation, Salem, NH, pg. 1139

Paparo, Irving, Chm. Bd. & Pres.--House of Ronnie, Inc., New York, NY, pg. 546
Pappas, Ted, Chm. Bd.--Keyes Company, Miami, FL, pg. 627
Park, J. Leonard, Chm. Bd., Pres., Chief Exec. Officer & Treas.--George W. Park Seed Co., Inc., Greenwood, SC, pg. 849
Park, James C., Chm. Bd. & Chief Exec. Officer--Besser Company, Alpena, MI, pg. 146
Parke, F.H., Jr., Chm.--Democrat Printing & Lithograph Company, Little Rock, AR, pg. 328
Parker, B.L., Chm. Bd.--MacKinnon-Parker, Inc., Toledo, OH, pg. 697
Parker, David H., Chm. Bd., Pres. & Chief Exec. Officer--Pelican Products, Torrance, CA, pg. 856
Parker, David J., Chm. Bd. & Chief Exec. Officer--Blount Lumber Company, Lacona, NY, pg. 158
Parker, Earle N., Chm. Bd.--Fort Worth Lumber Company, Fort Worth, TX, pg. 425
Parker, JoAnn, Chm. Bd. & Chief Exec. Officer--Omniflight, Inc., Dallas, TX, pg. 826
Parker, Ronald I., Chm. Bd., Pres. & Chief Exec. Officer--Indian Head Industries Inc., Southfield, MI, pg. 565
Parks, Edgar E., Chm. Bd. & Chief Exec. Officer--Albert Kahn Associates, Inc., Detroit, MI, pg. 613
Parrotto, Anthony J., Chm.--Kingswood Advertising, Inc., Ardmore, PA, pg. 632
Parry, Robert A., Chm. Bd., Pres. & Chief Exec. Officer--Monroc, Inc., Salt Lake City, UT, pg. 766
Partridge, George F., Chm. Bd.--Smith-Emery Company, Los Angeles, CA, pg. 1012
Partridge, James E., Pres.--Smith-Emery Company, Los Angeles, CA, pg. 1012
Pasquerilla, Frank J., Chm. Bd. & Chief Exec. Officer--Crown American Corporation, Johnstown, PA, pg. 301
Passaro, Lanny A., Chm. Bd.--MidWest Body Corporation, Paris, IL, pg. 752
Patch, Glenn E., Chm. Bd.--Patch Communications, Titusville, FL, pg. 851
Pate, Sebert L., Chm. Bd.--Texas Refinery Corp., Fort Worth, TX, pg. 1089
Patel, Charles Sr., Chm. Bd.--Magic Pan International Inc., Burlingame, CA, pg. 700
Patenge, Kenneth E., Chm., Pres. & Chief Exec. Officer--Wohlert Corp., Lansing, MI, pg. 1198
Patrick, Joseph A., Chm. Bd.--Baird, Patrick & Co., Inc., New York, NY, pg. 114
Patten, Charles R., Chm. Bd. & Pres.--Colfax Envelope Corporation, Buffalo Grove, IL, pg. 261
Patton, T.V., Chm. Bd.--Triton Inc., Doraville, GA, pg. 1114
Paty, John C., Jr., Chm. Bd.--The Paty Company, Piney Flats, TN, pg. 852
Pauley, Stanley F., Chm. Bd. & Chief Exec. Officer--E. R. Carpenter Co., Richmond, VA, pg. 224
Paulson, Allen E., Chm. Bd.--Gulfstream Holdings Corporation, Savannah, GA, pg. 494
Paulucci, Jeno F., Chm. Bd.--J.F.P. & Associates of Florida, Inc., Sanford, FL, pg. 584
Payton, Earl E., Chm. Bd., Chief Exec. Officer & Sec.--Cowden Metal Specialties, Inc., Chino, CA, pg. 291
Peabody, Lester C., Chm. Bd.--Peabody Office Furniture Corporation, Boston, MA, pg. 853
Peale, Ruth Stafford, Chm.--Guideposts Associates, Inc., Carmel, NY, pg. 493
Pearce, Louis M., Jr., Chm. Bd.--Pearce Industries Inc., Houston, TX, pg. 853
Pearson, Ronald, Chm. Bd., Pres. & Chief Exec. Officer--Hy-Vee Food Stores Incorporated, Chariton, IA, pg. 556
Pease, David H., Jr., Chm. Bd. & Chief Exec. Officer--Pease Industries, Inc., Fairfield, OH, pg. 854
Pease, Donald E., Chm. Bd.--Curtice-Burns Foods, Inc., Rochester, NY, pg. 25
Peck, John Weld, Chm. Bd.--Chicago West Pullman Corporation, Cincinnati, OH, pg. 246
Peckham, Janet G., Chm. Bd.--Peckham Industries, Inc., White Plains, NY, pg. 854
Peltz, Nelson, Chm. & Chief Exec. Officer--Trian Group, New York, NY, pg. 1111
Pemberton, Marlin H., Chm. Bd., Pres. & Chief Exec. Officer--Acorn Building Components Inc., Detroit, MI, pg. 13
Pemble, John C., Chm. Bd.--Itran Corporation, Manchester, NH, pg. 583
Penchina, Steve, Chm. & Exec. Creative Dir.--Ketchum Advertising/New York, New York, NY, pg. 625
Pendleton, Alexander, Chm. Bd. & Chief Exec. Officer--Warren Tool Group, Hiram, OH, pg. 1165
Penner, Pete J., Chm. Bd.--Sun-Maid Growers of California, Kingsburg, CA, pg. 1058
Penny, Robert L., Chm. Bd.--Penny/Ohlmann/Neiman, Inc., Dayton, OH, pg. 858
Penske, Richard H., Chm. Bd., Pres. & Treas.--Piercing Pagoda, Inc., Bethlehem, PA, pg. 870
Penske, Roger, Chm. Bd.--Penske Truck Leasing Corp., Reading, PA, pg. 859
Penske, Roger S., Chm. & Chief Exec. Officer--Detroit Diesel Corp., Detroit, MI, pg. 859
Pentecost, J. Miller, Chm. Bd.--Power & Telephone Supply Company, Memphis, TN, pg. 883
Pepper, Harry C., Jr., Chm. Bd.--Harry Pepper & Associates, Jacksonville, FL, pg. 859
Peppler, Dan, Chm., Natl. Creative Dir., Chief Exec. Officer--Doner Schur Peppler, Toronto,, Canada, pg. 344
Pepys, Shirley, Chm., Pres. & Chief Exec. Officer--Noel-Joanna, Inc., Rancho Santa Margarita, CA, pg. 808
Percival, Charles, Chm. Bd.--Cash Plus, Inc., Minneapolis, MN, pg. 228
Percival, Richard R., Chm. Bd.--Zieman Manufacturing Company, Inc., Whittier, CA, pg. 1218
Percy, Leroy, Chm. Bd.--Newsprint South, Inc., Yazoo City, MS, pg. 760
Perdue, James A., Chm. Bd.--Perdue Farms Inc., Salisbury, MD, pg. 860
Perelman, Raymond G., Chm. Bd. & Chief Exec. Officer--Belmont Industries, Inc., Philadelphia, PA, pg. 136
Perelman, Ronald, Chm. & Chief Exec. Officer--Revlon Group Inc., New York, NY, pg. 695
Perelman, Ronald O., Chm. Bd. & Chief Exec. Officer--MacAndrews & Forbes Holdings Inc., New York, NY, pg. 694
Perelman, Ronald O., Chm. Bd. & Chief Exec. Officer--Revlon, Inc., New York, NY, pg. 696
Perelman, Ronald O., Chm. Bd. & Chief Exec. Officer--Andrews Group, Incorporated, New York, NY, pg. 74
Perez, Lombardo, Chm. Bd., Pres. & Chief Oper. Officer--Metro Ford Inc., Miami, FL, pg. 743
Perkins, Lawrence, Chm. Bd., Pres. & Treas.--Connecticut Container Corporation, North Haven, CT, pg. 274
Perks, A. Campbell, Chm. Bd. & Chief Exec. Officer--Eclipse, Inc., Rockford, IL, pg. 366
Perlmuter, Ernest A., Chm. Bd.--Perlmuter Printing Company, Cleveland, OH, pg. 862
Perrino, S. Ronald, Chm. Bd., Pres. & Chief Exec. Officer--S.T. Research, Newington, VA, pg. 964
Perrish, Albert, Chm. Bd.--Ferro Union, Inc., Torrance, CA, pg. 407
Perrish, Albert, Chm. Bd.--Samsteel, Inc., Torrance, CA, pg. 407
Perrott, Patrick, Chm. Bd.--Chip Supply Inc., Orlando, FL, pg. 248
Perry, Anthony J., Chm. Bd.--M M I Companies, Inc., Deerfield, IL, pg. 692
Perry, Chris N., Chm. Bd. & Chief Exec. Officer--Meldrum & Fewsmith Communications Inc., Cleveland, OH, pg. 737
Perry, Dale, Co-Chm. Bd.--Perry's Ice Cream Co., Inc., Akron, NY, pg. 863
Perry, M. Dunman, Jr., Chm. Bd. & Chief Exec. Officer--Perry Equipment Corporation, Mineral Wells, TX, pg. 863
Perry, Thomas, Co-Chm. Bd.--Perry's Ice Cream Co., Inc., Akron, NY, pg. 863
Pesaro, Roberto, Chm. Bd.--Quaker Fabric Corporation, Fall River, MA, pg. 903
Pesch, Alan J., Chm. Bd., Pres. & Chief Exec. Officer--Ship Analytics, Inc., North Stonington, CT, pg. 999
Peslar, Frank P., Chm. Bd.--Automotive Moulding Company, Warren, MI, pg. 101
Peters, Robert L., Chm. Bd., Pres. & Chief Exec. Officer--Holmquist Grain & Lumber Co., Oakland, NE, pg. 540
Petersen, Allen D., Chm. Bd., Pres. & Chief Exec. Officer--American Tool Companies, Inc., Lincoln, NE, pg. 64
Petersen, Eric, Chm. Bd. & Treas.--Petersen Graphics Group, South Bend, IN, pg. 864
Petersen, L.C., Chm. Bd. & Chief Exec. Officer--Kirkpatrick Pettis, Omaha, NE, pg. 779
Petersen, R.E., Chm. Bd.--Petersen Publishing Company, Los Angeles, CA, pg. 864
Peterso, Carl, Chm.--Agri-Mark, Inc., Lawrence, MA, pg. 25
Peterson, Alfred H., III, Chm. Bd.--Peterson American Corp., Southfield, MI, pg. 864
Peterson, Glen, Chm. Bd.--PC Distributing Inc., Mount Prospect, IL, pg. 835
Peterson, L.N., Co.-Chm. Bd.--Regal Ware, Inc., Kewaskum, WI, pg. 921
Peterson, Lloyd E., Chm. Bd.--Peterson Industries Inc., Decatur, AR, pg. 864
Peterson, Milton V., Chm. Bd.--Guest Services, Inc., Fairfax, VA, pg. 493
Peterson, Philip L., Chm. Bd.--Morning Glory Farms Region, Shawano, WI, pg. 770
Petriat, Jean-Louis, Chm. Bd.--CSE Corporation, San Francisco, CA, pg. 204
Petsche, Thomas, Chm. Bd. & Pres.--Rocky Mountain Mechanical, Inc., Salt Lake City, UT, pg. 942
Pew, Robert C., Chm. Bd.--Steelcase Inc., Grand Rapids, MI, pg. 1044
Peyton, Herbert H., Chm. Bd. & Pres.--Gate Petroleum Company, Jacksonville, FL, pg. 445
Pfaelzer, Ellard, Jr., Chm. Bd.--Bruss Company, Chicago, IL, pg. 184
Pfaff, Edward, Chm. Bd.--Anchor Tool & Die Company, Cleveland, OH, pg. 71
Pfeiffer, Robert G., Chm. Bd. & Chief Exec. Officer--Neill-LaVielle Supply Co., Louisville, KY, pg. 797
Phares, Elwood W., Chm. Bd.--Petron Corporation, New Berlin, WI, pg. 1172
Phares, Elwood W., Chm. Bd.--West Pentone Inc., Ville d'Anjou,, Canada, pg. 1172
Phares, Elwood W. II, Chm. Bd.--Penetone Corp., Tenafly, NJ, pg. 1172
Phares, Elwood W., II, Chm. Bd. & Pres.--Wechco, Inc., Princeton, NJ, pg. 1172
Phelps, Barry, Chm. & Chief Exec. Officer--MICOM Communications Corp., Simi Valley, CA, pg. 748
Phelps, Terry M., Chm. Bd., Pres. & Chief Exec. Officer--Petroleum Marketers, Inc., Roanoke, VA, pg. 865
Phillips, Bradford E., Chm.--Totes Incorporated, Loveland, OH, pg. 1103
Phillips, Carol, Chm. Bd.--Clinique Laboratories, Inc., New York, NY, pg. 389
Phillips, Charlie, Chm. Bd.--Hardware Wholesalers, Inc., Fort Wayne, IN, pg. 508
Phillips, David, Chm. Bd. & Chief Exec. Officer--Credit Card Service Corporation, Springfield, VA, pg. 410
Phillips, Edward E., Chm. Bd.--The New England, Boston, MA, pg. 799
Phillips, John B., Jr., Chm. Bd.--Young-Phillips Sales Co., Winston-Salem, NC, pg. 1210
Phillips, Stanley F., Vice Chm.--Delaware North Companies, Inc., Buffalo, NY, pg. 326
Phillips, Thomas L., Chm. Bd., Pres. & Chief Exec. Officer--Phillips Publishing Inc., Potomac, MD, pg. 868
Piccinini, Robert M., Chm. Bd. & Chief Exec. Officer & Pres.--Save Mart Supermarkets, Modesto, CA, pg. 973
Picini, Dan E., Chm. Bd., Pres. & Chief Oper. Officer--Duro-Test Corporation, Fairfield, NJ, pg. 355
Picken, Robert F., Chm. Bd. & Pres.--Peerless Confection Company, Chicago, IL, pg. 855
Pickens, Gene, Chm. Bd.--Alabama Farmers Co-op, Decatur, AL, pg. 28
Picknelly, Peter L., Chm. Emeritus--Peter Pan Bus Lines, Inc., Springfield, MA, pg. 864
Picower, Jeffry, Chm. Bd. & Chief Exec. Officer--Monroe Systems For Business, Inc., Morris Plains, NJ, pg. 766
Pierce, Daniel, Chm. Bd.--Scudder, Stevens & Clark, Inc., New York, NY, pg. 983
Pierce, Frederick G., II, Chm. Bd., Pres. & Chief Exec. Officer--Niagara Envelope Company, Inc., Buffalo, NY, pg. 805
Pierce, Milton, Chm. Bd.--Guardian Alarm Co., Southfield, MI, pg. 491
Pierce, Willard G., Chm. Bd.--Flexfab, Inc., Hastings, MI, pg. 418
Pikovsky, Eugene, Chm. & Chief Exec. Officerr--Hyman Freightways Inc., Moundsview, MN, pg. 557
Pin, Loh Shiew, Chm. Bd.--Code-A-Phone Corp., Clackamas, OR, pg. 258
Pincus, David, Chm. Bd. & Chief Exec. Officer--Pincus Bros., Inc., Philadelphia, PA, pg. 870
Pines, Isidore, Chm. Bd. & Chief Exec. Officer--National Foods Inc., Bronx, NY, pg. 788
Pingel, Paul, Chm. Bd. & Pres.--New Cooperative Inc., Fort Dodge, IA, pg. 799
Pinne, Robert A., Chm. Bd. & Chief Exec. Officer--Pinne/Herbers Advertising Inc., San Francisco, CA, pg. 871
Piper, Paul J., Chm. Bd.--Business Information Technology, Wilmington, DE, pg. 196
Piper, Paul P., Jr., Chm. & Chief Exec. Officer--Piper Industries, Inc., Dallas, TX, pg. 872
Pirie, Robert S, Co-Chm. Bd.--Rothschild North America Inc., New York, NY, pg. 951
Pirie, Robert S Chm. Bd., Pres. & Chief Exec. Officer--Rothschild Inc., New York, NY, pg. 951
Pirie, Robert S Chm. Bd.--Rothchild Asset Management Inc., New York, NY, pg. 951
Pisa, Michael A., Sr., Chm. Bd. & Chief Exec. Officer--Continental Paper & Supply Co., Detroit, MI, pg. 280
Piser, Donald H., Chm. Bd. & Chief Exec. Officer--Morse Diesel International, New York, NY, pg. 771
Pistilli, Frederick M., Chm. & Chief Exec. Officer--General Time Corp., Norcross, GA, pg. 451
Pitterich, Michael P., Chm. Bd. & Pres.--Moltrup Steel Products Company, Beaver Falls, PA, pg. 764
Pittman, Gary, Chm. Bd., Pres., Chief Exec., Chief Oper. & Chief Fin. Officer--PCI, Austin, TX, pg. 836
Pivar, Stuart, Chm. Bd.--Chem-Tainer Corporation, Brooklyn, NY, pg. 241
Plangere, Jules L., Jr., Chm. Bd.--Asbury Park Press, Inc., Neptune, NJ, pg. 801
Plangere, Jules, Jr., Chm. Bd.--New Jersey Press, Inc., Neptune, NJ, pg. 801
Plapinger, Allan R., Chm. Bd.--S. P. Dunham & Co., Lawrenceville, NJ, pg. 353
Plotkin, Ron, Chm. Bd.--YPMS/TMP Worldwide, Inc., Mequon, WI, pg. 1074
Plummer, James W., Chm. Bd.--The Aerospace Corporation, El Segundo, CA, pg. 22
Plummer, Walter A., Chm. Bd.--The Zippertubing Co., Los Angeles, CA, pg. 1220
Pogue, A. Mack, Chm. Bd., Pres. & Chief Exec. Officer--Lincoln Property Company, Dallas, TX, pg. 676
Pogue, David, Chm. Bd. & Chief Exec. Officer--Stackig, Sanderson & White, Inc., McLean, VA, pg. 1034
Poirot, James W., Chm. Bd.--CH2M Hill Companies, Ltd., Englewood, CO, pg. 202
Poitevint, A.L., Chm. Bd. & Pres.--Flint River Mills, Bainbridge, GA, pg. 419
Pol, Warren I., Chm. Bd.--Airtrol, Inc., Baton Rouge, LA, pg. 28
Polack, Morris, Chm. Bd.--Acme Poultry Company, Inc., Seattle, WA, pg. 13
Polansky, Gerald A., Chm. Bd.--American Institute of C.P.A.'s Inc., New York, NY, pg. 56
Polera, Vito, Chm. Bd.--Polera Building Corp., Scarsdale, NY, pg. 878
Polizos, Arthur G., Chm.--The Polizos Agency, Norfolk, VA, pg. 879
Pollak, James S., Chm. & Chief Exec. Officer--Pollak Levitt Chaiet, Advertising, Atlanta, GA, pg. 879
Pollnow, Charles, Chm. Bd., Chief Exec. & Oper. Officer--The Brulin Corporation, Indianapolis, IN, pg. 184
Pollock, William K., Chm. Bd. & Chief Exec. Officer--Key Industries, Inc., Fort Scott, KS, pg. 627
Pomeranz, Harold, Chm. Bd., Treas. & Sec.--Stanley Roberts, Inc., Lodi, NJ, pg. 939
Pons, Francisco, Chm. Bd. & Pres.--Atlantic Sugar Association, Inc., Belle Glade, FL, pg. 95
Poortvliet, William G., Chm.--Metropolitan Life Holdings, Ltd., Ottawa,, Canada, pg. 745
Pope, William H., Chm. Bd.--Pacific Capital Bancorp, Salinas, CA, pg. 839
Popek, Gerald J., Chm. Bd.--Locus Computing Corp., Inglewood, CA, pg. 680
Popp, John F., Chm. Bd. & Pres.--Perfection Bakeries Inc., Fort Wayne, IN, pg. 861
Poppel, Seth, Chm. Bd. & Pres.--American Vision Centers, Inc., New York, NY, pg. 65
Poppert, Claris, Chm. Bd. & Chief Exec. Officer--Benson Industries, Inc., Portland, OR, pg. 139
Porcaro, Michael F., Chm. Bd. & New Bus. Contact--Porcaro Blankenship Advertising, Anchorage, AK, pg. 881
Porteous, L. Robert, Jr., Chm. Bd., Sec. & Treas.--Porteous, South Portland, ME, pg. 353
Porter, Charles, Chm. & Dir.-Creative--Crispin & Porter Advertising Inc., Miami, FL, pg. 299
Porter, Irwin, Chm. Bd.--Giant Eagle, Inc., Pittsburgh, PA, pg. 455
Portman, Robert, Ph.D., Chm.--M.E.D. Communications, Woodbridge, NJ, pg. 692
Portman, Robert, Ph.D., Chm.--CHC Advertising, Woodbridge, NJ, pg. 201

Posner, Sidney, Chm. Bd., Chief Exec. Officer, Treas.--Newmark, Posner & Mitchell, Inc., New York, NY, pg. 804
Posner, Victor, Chm. Bd. & Chief Exec. Officer--Graniteville Co., Graniteville, SC, pg. 476
Posner, Victor, Chm. Bd., Pres. & Chief Exec. Officer--Chesapeake Financial Corp., Miami Beach, FL, pg. 243
Posner, Victor, Chm. Bd. & Pres.--Royal Crown Cola Co., Miami Beach, FL, pg. 243
Postal, Robert, Chm. Bd.--Judy Bond, Inc., New York, NY, pg. 608
Potack, Bernard, Chm. Bd.--Coat, Apron & Linen Supply, Bronx, NY, pg. 257
Poupore, John, Chm. Bd., Co-Pres. & Chief Exec. Officer--Helm, Inc., Highland Park, MI, pg. 527
Povah, Eleanor H., Chm. Bd.--Hamilton Stores, Inc., West Yellowstone, MT, pg. 503
Powell, Don G., Chm. Bd. & Pres.--American Capital Management & Research, Inc., Houston, TX, pg. 50
Powell, Harold H., Chm. Bd.--Powell Electronics Inc., Philadelphia, PA, pg. 882
Powell, Lawrence M., Chm. Bd.--L. Powell Co., Inc., Culver City, CA, pg. 882
Powell, Watson, Jr., Chm. Bd.--American Republic Insurance Co., Des Moines, IA, pg. 60
Power, J.D., III, Chm. Bd.--R&D/J.D. Power, Tokyo,, Japan, pg. 883
Power, Philip H., Chm. Bd.--Suburban Communications Corp., Livonia, MI, pg. 1055
Powers, Frederic B., Jr., Chm. Bd. & Pres.--The Rawlplug Company, Inc., New Rochelle, NY, pg. 914
Powers, Richard J., Chm. Bd.--Lyon Conklin & Company, Baltimore, MD, pg. 690
Powers, W.O., Chm. Bd.--Powers Construction Co., Inc., Florence, SC, pg. 883
Powning, M.W., Chm. & Chief Exec. Officer--Koehler Manufacturing Company, Marlborough, MA, pg. 639
Pozzi, Arthur A., Chm. Bd.--Arthur A. Pozzi Co., Inc., Portland, OR, pg. 883
Prange, Henry C., Chm. Bd.--H. C. Prange Company, Green Bay, WI, pg. 884
Prasse, Henry R., Chm. Bd. & Pres.--Out of Home Media Services, Inc., New York, NY, pg. 832
Prechter, Heinz C., Chm. & Chief Exec. Officer--ASC Incorporated, Southgate, MI, pg. 7
Prendergast, M. Raymond, Chm. Bd. & Chief Exec. Officer--Boston Distributors, Inc., Maple Heights, OH, pg. 167
Pressman, Harold B., Chm. Bd.--Pearl-Pressman-Liberty Communications Group, Philadelphia, PA, pg. 853
Pressman, Lynn, Chm. Bd.--Pressman Toy Corp., New York, NY, pg. 887
Previti, James, Chm. Bd, Pres. & Chief Exec. Officer--Forecast Mortgage Corporation, Rancho Cucamonga, CA, pg. 423
Prewitt, Michael D., Chm.--Dana Communications, Inc., Hopewell, NJ, pg. 313
Price, Charles R., Jr., Chm.--Price/McNabb, Inc., Asheville, NC, pg. 888
Price, David S., Chm. Bd.--Deans Photo Service, Inc., San Diego, CA, pg. 322
Price, Gayle B., Jr., Chm. Bd. & Chief Exec. Officer--Price Brothers Co., Dayton, OH, pg. 888
Price, M.S., Chm. Bd. & Chief Exec. Officer--Humphreys Price/Cochran & Sanford Advertising, Memphis, TN, pg. 553
Price, William H., Chm. Bd.--National Posters, Inc., Chattanooga, TN, pg. 790
Pridmore, John E., Chm. Bd.--George Sollitt Construction, Wood Dale, IL, pg. 1017
Priester, Wolfgang, Chm. Bd.--Michael Business Machines Corporation, North Charleston, SC, pg. 747
Prince, Edgar, Chm. Bd.--Prince Corporation, Holland, MI, pg. 890
Prischak, Joseph J., Chm. Bd.--Plastek Group, Erie, PA, pg. 874
Pritkzer, Jay, Chm. Bd.--The Marmon Group, Inc., Chicago, IL, pg. 711
Pritz, Benjamin L., Chm. Bd., Pres. & Chief Exec. Officer--Grandpa Brands Company, Cincinnati, OH, pg. 476
Pritzker, Jay, Chm. Bd. & Chief Exec. Officer--H. Group Holding Inc., Chicago, IL, pg. 495
Pritzker, Jay A., Chm. Bd.--The Marmon Group, Inc., Chicago, IL, pg. 710
Pritzker, Jay A., Chm. Bd.--Marmon Industrial Corporation, Chicago, IL, pg. 712
Pritzker, Jay A., Chm. Bd.--Marmon Corporation, Chicago, IL, pg. 711
Pritzker, Jay A., Chm. Bd.--Hyatt Corporation, Chicago, IL, pg. 495
Proctor, Truby G., Jr., Chm. Bd. & Chief Exec. Officer--The Pantry, Inc., Sanford, NC, pg. 846
Proctor, Truby G., Jr., Chm. Bd.--Lee-Moore Oil Co., Inc., Sanford, NC, pg. 665
Pronko, David, Chm. Bd., Pres. & Chief Exec. Officer--PE Systems, Reston, VA, pg. 836
Protzman, Jim, Chm. Bd.--FGI, Chapel Hill, NC, pg. 394
Pruim, E.G., Chm. Bd., Pres. & Chief Exec. Officer--Wrought Washer Mfg., Inc., Milwaukee, WI, pg. 1205
Pruitt, J. Doug, Chm. & Chief Exec. Officer--Ninteman Construction Company, Inc., San Diego, CA, pg. 1060
Psomas, George, Chm. Bd.--Psomas & Associates, Santa Monica, CA, pg. 898
Pucheu, John, Jr., Chm. Bd.--Calcot, Ltd., Bakersfield, CA, pg. 208
Pulitzer, Sidney C., Chm. Bd. & Chief Oper. Officer--Wemco, Inc., New Orleans, LA, pg. 1176
Pulliam, Robert F., Chm. Bd.--Pulliam Motor Company, Columbia, SC, pg. 899
Pulver, David, Chm. Bd.--Morse Shoe, Inc., Canton, MA, pg. 772
Pumpelly, Robert J., Chm. Bd.--Pumpelly Oil, Inc., Westlake, LA, pg. 900
Purcell, John R., Chm. Bd.--Carol Wright Sales, Inc., Stamford, CT, pg. 1011
Purvis, G. Frank, Jr., Chm. Bd.--Pan-American Life Insurance Company, New Orleans, LA, pg. 845
Purvis, Kathryn M., Chm. Bd.--A.C. Legg Packing Company, Inc., Birmingham, AL, pg. 666
Puschel, Philip P., Chm. Bd. & Chief Exec. Officer--F. Schumacher & Co., New York, NY, pg. 979
Puttner, Dr. Gerhard, Chm. & Pres.--Dr. Puttner & BSB Worldwide Werbegesellschaft m.b.H., Vienna,, Austria, pg. 111
Pyle, Thomas F., Chm. Bd., Pres. & Chief Exec. Officer--RAYOVAC Corporation, Madison, WI, pg. 915
Quadracci, H.R., Chm. Bd.--Quad/Graphics, Inc., Pewaukee, WI, pg. 902
Quinif, Edward, Chm. Bd. & Pres.--Walled Lake Door Company, Phoenix, AZ, pg. 1161
Quinlan, Donald P., Chm. Bd., Pres., Chief Exec. & Chief Oper. Officer--Graphic Controls Corporation, Buffalo, NY, pg. 478
Quinland, Donald P., Chm. Bd., Pres. & Chief Exec. Officer--Graphic Controls, Corp., Buffalo, NY, pg. 478
Quinn, Thomas, Chm. Bd.--Archibald Candy Company, Chicago, IL, pg. 604
Quinn, Tom, Chm. Bd.--American Safety Razor Company, Verona, VA, pg. 604
Raab, Max L., Chm. Bd. & Chief Exec. Officer--J. G. Hook, Inc., Philadelphia, PA, pg. 543
Rabison, Bruce, Chm. Bd.--Hampton Print Works, Inc., Johnson City, TN, pg. 504
Rackoff, S.R., Chm. Bd.--Asko, Inc, Homestead, PA, pg. 88
Radek, Edward, Sr., Co-Chm. Bd. & Pres.--Ready Metal Manufacturing Company, Chicago, IL, pg. 916
Radek, John R., Sr., Co-Chm. Bd.--Ready Metal Manufacturing Company, Chicago, IL, pg. 916
Radler, Louis, Chm. Bd., Pres. & Chief Exec. Officer--Chessco Industries, Inc., Westport, CT, pg. 243
Radwill, Alvera, Chm. Bd., Chief Fin. Officer & Treas.--Master Appliance Corp., Racine, WI, pg. 719
Ragland, David, Chm. Bd.--Duncan Equipment Company, Duncan, OK, pg. 352
Raiche, Leo G., Chm. Bd.--Network Capital Group, Campbell, CA, pg. 798
Raines, J.R., Chm. Bd.--San Angelo Electric Service Company, San Angelo, TX, pg. 969
Rakolta, John, Sr., Chm. Bd. & Sec.--Walbridge Aldinger Company, Detroit, MI, pg. 1158
Ramey, William F., Chm. Bd.--Jasper County Farm Bureau Co-op Association, Inc., Rensselaer, IN, pg. 590
Ramsey, Forrest G., Jr., Chm. Bd.--American Systems Corporation, Chantilly, VA, pg. 63
Ramsey, J.S., Jr., Chm. Bd.--Diamond Hill Plywood Company, Darlington, SC, pg. 316
Ramsey, William, Chm. Bd.--Auto Crane Company, Tulsa, OK, pg. 100
Randall, Ronald F., Chm. Bd., Pres. & Chief Exec. Officer--Randall Stores, Inc., Mitchell, SD, pg. 911
Randolph, William, Chm. Bd. & Chief Exec. Officer--Post Buckley Schuh & Jernigan, Miami, FL, pg. 881
Rankin, Thompson L., Chm. Bd. & Chief Exec. Officer--Lykes Energy, Inc., Tampa, FL, pg. 689
Ransburg, David P., Chm. Bd.--L. R. Nelson Corporation, Peoria, IL, pg. 797
Ransome, Ernest L., III, Chm. Bd.--Giles & Ransome, Inc., Bensalem, PA, pg. 458
Rao, Duane, Chm. Bd. & Chief Exec. Officer--Rao Wholesale Tire Centers, Inc., Detroit, MI, pg. 912
Rapp, Horst, Chm. Bd. & Pres.--Alloway Manufacturing, Fargo, ND, pg. 41
Rappeport, Don, Chm. Bd. & Chief Exec. Officer--Donlen Corp., Deerfield, IL, pg. 345
Rapport, Norman, Chm. Bd.--American Frozen Foods, Inc., Stratford, CT, pg. 55
Rasmussen, Leo T., Chm.--Farmers National Company, Omaha, NE, pg. 744
Rath, F.E., Chm. Bd.--Today's Kids, Booneville, AR, pg. 1025
Rath, Frank E., Chm. Bd.--Spang & Company, Butler, PA, pg. 1025
Ratner, Charles, Chm. Bd.--Richter & Ratner Contracting Corporation, Maspeth, NY, pg. 933
Ratner, S., Chm. Bd. & Dir-Acct. Services--McCaffery & Ratner, Inc., New York, NY, pg. 726
Rattigan, Thomas J., Chm. Bd., Pres. & Chief Exec. Officer--G. Heileman Brewing Co., Inc., La Crosse, WI, pg. 526
Rau, Howard C., Chm. Bd.--Edwin B. Stimpson Company, Inc., Bayport, NY, pg. 1049
Rauch, Francis, Chm. Bd. & Pres.--M & C Specialties Company, Southampton, PA, pg. 690
Rauenhorst, Gerald, Chm. Bd. & Chief Exec. Officer--OPUS Corp., Minnetonka, MN, pg. 828
Rauh, Robert B., Chm. Bd., Pres., Chief Fin. Officer & New Bus. Contact--Rauh, Good, Darlo & Barnes Advertising Associates, Inc., Los Gatos, CA, pg. 914
Ravizza, Eugene A., Chm. Bd. & Pres.--Synergism, Inc., Sunnyvale, CA, pg. 1069
Raymonds, John M., Chm. Bd. & Chief Exec. Officer--Captive Plastics, Piscataway, NJ, pg. 216
Rea, Samuel A., Chm. Bd.--Emkay, Inc., Itasca, IL, pg. 379
Read, Howard, Chm.--Marketforce Australia, West Perth, Australia, pg. 112
Read, R.T., Chm. Bd., Pres. & Chief Exec. Officer--Harwick Chemical Corp., Akron, OH, pg. 515
Reagan, Jeanne L., Chm. Bd.--Reagan Equipment Company, Inc., Gretna, LA, pg. 917
Reardon, O. Ashby, Jr., Chm. Bd.--Mico, Inc., Springfield, VA, pg. 748
Reardon, Robert J., Chm. Bd.--Bremer Financial Corporation, Saint Paul, MN, pg. 173
Recht, Robert, Chm. Bd.--Admarketing, Inc., Los Angeles, CA, pg. 18
Reddy, Prasad, Chm. Bd., Pres. & Chief Exec. Officer--Freeman Shoes Company, Beloit, WI, pg. 431
Redies, Robert D., Chm. Bd.--R & B Machine Tool Co., Saline, MI, pg. 906
Redmon, Charles E., Chm. Bd.--Jeffersonville Distribution Center, Jeffersonville, IN, pg. 832
Redmon, William L., Chm. Bd.--W. C. Redmon Co., Peru, IN, pg. 919
Redmond, Thomas, Sr., Chm. Bd.--Redmond Products, Inc., Chanhassen, MN, pg. 920
Redstone, Sumner M., Chm. Bd.--National Amusements, Inc., Dedham, MA, pg. 784
Redstone, Sumner M., Chm. Bd.--Viacom Inc., New York, NY, pg. 785
Reed, Alan C., Chm. Bd. & Chief Exec. Officer--Radix Corporation, Salt Lake City, UT, pg. 909
Reed, Earl, Chm. Bd.--Reed Grain & Bean Company, Buhl, ID, pg. 920
Reed, Larry E., Chm. Bd. & Chief Exec. Officer--Horizon Bancorp, Michigan City, IN, pg. 544
Reed, Larry E., Chm. Bd. & Chief Exec. Officer--First Citizens Bank, N.A., Michigan City, IN, pg. 544
Reed, Richard C., Chm Bd. & Pres.--Kova Fertilizer Inc., Greensburg, IN, pg. 643
Reed, Robert E., Chm. Bd.--Utica Boilers Inc., Utica, NY, pg. 1140
Reed, William G., Jr., Chm. Bd.--Simpson Investment Co., Seattle, WA, pg. 1007
Reed, William G., Jr., Chm. Bd.-SICO--Simpson Timber Co., Shelton, WA, pg. 1007
Reese, Michael R., Chm Bd., Pres. & Chief Exec. Officer--Pierce Manufacturing, Inc., Appleton, WI, pg. 870
Reese, Terry, Chm. Bd.--Overly Manufacturing Co., Greensburg, PA, pg. 833
Reese, Thomas W., Chm. & Chief Exec. Officer--Hickory Printing Group, Inc., Hickory, NC, pg. 533
Reeve, Janice M., Chm. Bd.--Reeve Aleutian Airways, Inc., Anchorage, AK, pg. 921
Reeves, Francis S., Co-Chm.--Skinner Corp., Lanett, AL, pg. 1009
Reichenstein, Marvin, Chm. Bd. & Pres.--Reichenstein Advertising Agency, Mountainside, NJ, pg. 922
Reid, Bruce S., Chm. Bd. & Chief Exec. Officer--Reid & O'Donahue Advertising, Inc., Montgomery, AL, pg. 923
Reid, Russ, Chm. Bd. & Chief Exec. Officer--Russ Reid Company, Inc., Pasadena, CA, pg. 923
Reid, Wendy B., Chm. Bd.--Sacramento Municipal Utility District, Sacramento, CA, pg. 965
Reidel, Arthur A., Chm. Bd. & Chief Exec. Officer--Willamette-Western Corporation, Portland, OR, pg. 1190
Reidy, John, Chm. Bd.--Southern Case, Inc., Raleigh, NC, pg. 1020
Reidy, William J., Chm. & Chief Exec. Officer--Fine Organics Corp., Lodi, NJ, pg. 411
Reifschneider, Darrel, Chm. Bd. & Chief Exec. Officer--Manchester Tank & Equipment Company, Lynwood, CA, pg. 703
Reigle, James D., Co.-Chm. Bd.--Regal Ware, Inc., Kewaskum, WI, pg. 921
Reilly, F. Ward, Jr., Chm. Bd.--Sherman & Reilly, Inc., Chattanooga, TN, pg. 998
Reilly, Peter C., Chm. Exec. Committee--Reilly Industries, Inc., Indianapolis, IN, pg. 923
Reilly, Thomas E., Jr., Chm. Bd. & Chief Exec. Officer--Reilly Industries, Inc., Indianapolis, IN, pg. 923
Reilly, Wayne R., Chm. Bd. & Chief Exec. Officer--John W. Danforth Co., Buffalo, NY, pg. 314
Reilly, William F., Chm. Bd.--K-III Communications Corporation, New York, NY, pg. 610
Reilly, William F., Chm. Bd.--Daily Racing Form, Inc., Hightstown, NJ, pg. 611
Reilly, William F., Chm. Bd.--Soap Opera Digest, New York, NY, pg. 611
Reilly, William F., Chm.--Seventeen Magazine, New York, NY, pg. 611
Reily, Timothy, Chm. Bd., Pres. & Chief Exec. Officer--Reily Electric Supply, Inc., Metairie, LA, pg. 923
Reiman, Joey, Chm. Bd. & Chief Exec. Officer--The Joey Reiman Agency, Atlanta, GA, pg. 923
Reinig, L.P., Chm. Bd. & Pres.--Los Alamos Technical Associates, Inc., Los Alamos, NM, pg. 684
Reisman, Sam, Chm. Bd.--The Equion Corporation, New Haven, CT, pg. 385
Remos, Gary, Chm. Bd., Pres. & Chief Exec. Officer--Advanced Manufacturing & Development, Willits, CA, pg. 20
Rentenbach, T.J., Chm. Bd.--Rentenbach Engineering Company, Knoxville, TN, pg. 927
Reny, L. Guy, Chm. Bd. & Pres.--Standard Duplicating Machines Corp., Andover, MA, pg. 1036
Resnick, Lynda, Chm. Bd.--Teleflora, Los Angeles, CA, pg. 60
Resnick, Lynda R., Vice Chm.--The Franklin Mint, Franklin Center, PA, pg. 60
Resnick, Stewart, Chm. Bd.--American Protection Industries, Inc., Los Angeles, CA, pg. 60
Resnick, Stewart, Chm. Bd. & Chief Exec. Officer--The Franklin Mint, Franklin Center, PA, pg. 60
Reynolds, Donald W., Chm. Bd.--Donrey Media Group, Fort Smith, AR, pg. 345
Reynolds, James G., Chm. Bd. & Pres.--Portland Food Products Company, Portland, OR, pg. 881
Reynolds, Merrilyn, Co-Chm. Bd.--Bardes Corp., Cincinnati, OH, pg. 119
Ricardo, Jose, Chm. Bd. & Chief Exec. Officer--RII (Ricards International Inc.), Silver Spring, MD, pg. 907
Rice, Richard, Chm. Bd.--Rice/Spector Inc., Venice, CA, pg. 931
Rice, Ted, Chm. Bd. & Co-founder--T. J. Cinnamons Ltd., Kansas City, MO, pg. 1073
Rice, William B., Chm. Bd.--Blue Grass Foods, Inc., Crescent Springs, KY, pg. 160
Rich, Francis P., Jr., Chm. Bd. & Pres.--Action Equipment, Londonderry, NH, pg. 14
Rich, Robert E., Chm. Bd.--Rich Products Corp., Buffalo, NY, pg. 932
Richard, J.E., Chm. Bd. & Chief Oper. Officer--Tennessee Wholesale Drug Company, Nashville, TN, pg. 1088

Richards, H. Lee, Chm. Bd. & Chief Exec. Officer--Hygeia Dairy Co., Inc., Harlingen, TX, pg. 557
Richardson, David, Chm. Bd.--Richardson Brothers Co., Sheboygan Falls, WI, pg. 932
Richardson, Joan, Chm. Bd.--Power Conversion, Inc., Saddle Brook, NJ, pg. 883
Richardson, John, Chm. Bd.--Royal Oldsmobile Mazda, Inc., Metairie, LA, pg. 953
Richardson, Joseph, II, Chm. Bd.--Richardson Industries, Inc., Shaboygan Falls, WI, pg. 932
Richardson, Thomas, Chm. Bd., Pres. & Chief Exec. Officer--Delta Education, Inc., Hudson, NH, pg. 326
Richer, Alvin, Chm., Pres. & Chief Exec. Officer--Arnold Machinery Co., Salt Lake City, UT, pg. 84
Richter, Irvin E., Chm. Bd. & Chief Exec. Officer--Hill International Inc., Willingboro, NJ, pg. 534
Ricke, Donald W., Chm. Bd. & Chief Exec. Officer--Motek Engineering & Manufacturing Company, Cambridge, MN, pg. 773
Riddell, John, Chm.--Credit Suisse First Boston UK Limited, London, United Kingdom, pg. 204
Riddell, John, Chm.--CSFB (Gilts) Limited, London, United Kingdom, pg. 204
Rider, Chuck, Chm., Pres. & Chief Exec. Officer--Automotive Marketing Assoc., Nashville, TN, pg. 224
Rider, Robert F., Chm., Chief Exec. Officer & Treas.--O. A. Newton & Son Co., Bridgeville, DE, pg. 805
Riegel, William M., Chm. Bd.--Bryce Corporation, Memphis, TN, pg. 185
Riemer, David, Chm. Bd., Pres. & Chief Exec. Officer--Arley Merchandise Corporation, Taunton, MA, pg. 83
Riemer, David I., Chm. Bd., Pres. & Chief Exec. Officer--Rops Textiles Inc., Taunton, MA, pg. 83
Rifkin, Leonard, Chm. Bd. & Pres.--Omni Source Corporation, Fort Wayne, IN, pg. 826
Rigg, John G., Chm. Bd. & Chief Exec. Officer--Redco Foods, Inc., Windsor, CT, pg. 919
Riggio, Leonard, Chm. Bd., Pres. & Chief Exec. Officer--Barnes & Noble Bookstores, Inc., New York, NY, pg. 120
Riggs, John A., Chm. Bd.--J. A. Riggs Tractor Co., Little Rock, AR, pg. 934
Riggs, Sidney W., Chm. Bd.--Riggs Industries, Inc., Stoystown, PA, pg. 934
Rigoli, Tom, Chm.--Rigoli Communications, Mountain View, CA, pg. 934
Rigoni, Joseph J., Chm. Bd.--Bacco Construction Co., Iron Mountain, MI, pg. 108
Riker, Harland A. Jr., Chm.--Cambridge Consultants Limited, Cambridge,, United Kingdom, pg. 679
Riklis, Meshulam, Chm. Bd. & Pres.--Riklis Family Corporation, New York, NY, pg. 934
Riney, Hal P., Chm. & Chief Exec. Officer--Hal Riney & Partners, Inc., San Francisco, CA, pg. 935
Ringer, Walter M., Jr., Chm. Bd. & Chief Exec. Officer--Foley-Belsaw Company, Minneapolis, MN, pg. 422
Ringer, Walter M., Jr., Chm. Bd.--Foley-PLP Company, Rochester, NY, pg. 422
Ripley, F. Fuller, Chm. Bd.--Troy Mills, Inc., Troy, NH, pg. 1116
Rippey, Mike, Chm. Bd.--Institutional Financing Services, Benicia, CA, pg. 571
Risk, J. Fred, Chm. Bd.--Sovereign Group Inc., Indianapolis, IN, pg. 1024
Ritchie, Hale D., Jr., Chm. Bd. & Chief Exec. Officer--Ritchie Corporation, Wichita, KS, pg. 936
Rivett, Ron, Chm. Bd.--Super 8 Motels, Inc., Aberdeen, SD, pg. 1062
Rob, Joseph M., Chm. Bd., Pres. & Chief Exec. Officer--Equity Services, Inc., Montpelier, VT, pg. 791
Robbins, Bruce M., Jr., Chm. Bd.--Robbins Manufacturing Company, Tampa, FL, pg. 938
Robbins, Sidney, Chm. Bd.--Robbins Auto Parts, Inc., Dover, NH, pg. 938
Robert, Dean E., Sr., Chm. Bd. & Pres.--Roberts Foods, Inc., Springfield, IL, pg. 938
Roberts, Abbott S., Chm. Bd.--F. L. Roberts & Co. Inc., Springfield, MA, pg. 938
Roberts, Charles, Jr., Chm. Bd. & Pres.--Chas Roberts Air Conditioning, Inc., Phoenix, AZ, pg. 938
Roberts, Joseph, Chm. Bd. & Chief Exec. Officer--Advanced Circuit Technology, Nashua, NH, pg. 20
Roberts, Walter R., Chm. Bd.--Roberts Communications Inc., East Rochester, NY, pg. 938
Robertson, Michael B., Chm., Chief Exec. Officer & Chief Creative Dir.--McCaffrey and McCall, New York, NY, pg. 726
Robins, Charles, Chm. Bd.--Michigan Wheel Corporation, Grand Rapids, MI, pg. 747
Robins, Frank, III, Chm. Bd.--Conway Corporation, Conway, AR, pg. 281
Robins, Gerald, Chm. Bd.--Roland International Corporation, Coconut Grove, FL, pg. 944
Robinson, Harry T., Jr., Chm. Bd. & Sec.--Top Flight, Inc., Chattanooga, TN, pg. 1101
Robinson, James W., Chm. Bd.--Caldwell Tanks, Inc., Louisville, KY, pg. 209
Robinson, John E., Jr., Chm. Bd.--Robinson, Yesawich & Pepperdine, Orlando, FL, pg. 940
Robinson, Richard, Chm. Bd., Pres. & Chief Exec. Officer--SI Holdings Inc., New York, NY, pg. 962
Robinson, Ronald, Chm. Bd. & Chief Exec. Officer--Denver Equipment Company, Colorado Springs, CO, pg. 331
Robinson, Samuel G., Sr., Chm. Bd.--Robinson Lumber & Export Company, New Orleans, LA, pg. 940
Robinson, William A., Chm. Bd. & Chief Exec. Officer--Robinson & St. John Advertising & Public Relations, Inc., Jacksonville, FL, pg. 940
Robinson, William A., Chm. Bd. & Chief Exec. Officer--Robinson & St. John Advertising & Public Relations, Public Relations Div., Jacksonville, FL, pg. 940
Robson, Edward J., Chm. Bd.--Sun Lakes Marketing, Sun Lakes, AZ, pg. 1059
Roche, Jack F., Chm. Bd., Pres. & Chief Exec. Officer--PMC Industries Inc., Wickliffe, OH, pg. 836
Rockefeller, Frederic L., Chm. Bd.--Cranston Print Works Company, Cranston, RI, pg. 296
Rockett, Howard, Chm. & Chief Exec. Officer--Rockett, Burkhead, Lewis & Winslow, Raleigh, NC, pg. 941
Rodale, Ardath, Chm. Bd. & Chief Exec. Officer--Rodale Press, Inc., Emmaus, PA, pg. 942
Rodgers, B.D., Chm. Bd.--Rodgers Builders, Inc., Charlotte, NC, pg. 942
Rodgers, Dan, Chm. Bd. & Pres.--Thompson Medical Company, Inc., West Palm Beach, FL, pg. 1094
Rodgers, Joe M., Chm. & Acting Chief Exec. Officer--Berlitz International, Inc., Princeton, NJ, pg. 142
Roe, K. Keith, Chm. Bd., Pres., Chief Exec. & Chief Oper. Officer--Burns & Roe Enterprises, Inc., Oradell, NJ, pg. 194
Roessner, John K. III, Chm. Bd. & Pres.--E. J. Brooks Company, Newark, NJ, pg. 179
Rogers, G.W., Chm. Bd.--Consolidated Systems, Inc., Columbia, SC, pg. 277
Rogers, Joe, Sr., Chm. Bd.--Waffle House, Inc., Norcross, GA, pg. 1157
Rogers, M. Weldon, III, Chm. Bd., Pres. & Chief Exec. Officer--EAC Corporation, Saint Louis, MO, pg. 359
Rogers, Richard R., Chm. Bd., Pres. & Chief Exec. Officer--Mary Kay Corporation, Dallas, TX, pg. 716
Rogers, Richard R., Chm. & Chief Exec. Officer--Mary Kay Cosmetics Inc., Dallas, TX, pg. 716
Rogers, S.H., Jr., Chm. Bd.--Wilkins-Rogers Incorporated, Ellicott City, MD, pg. 1190
Rogerson, Michael, Chm. Bd., Pres. & Chief Exec. Officer--Rogerson Aircraft Corporation, Irvine, CA, pg. 943
Rokop, Joseph, Chm. Bd.--Rokop Corporation, Bridgeville, PA, pg. 944
Rolla, M.F., Chm. Bd.--Global Steel Products Corporation, Deer Park, NY, pg. 463
Rollins, Clark, Chm. Bd.--Nashville Wire Product Co., Nashville, TN, pg. 784
Roloff, Jeffrey J., Chm. Bd. & Chief Exec. Officer--Central Data Corporation, Champaign, IL, pg. 232
Roney, Patrick E., Chm. Bd., Pres. & Chief Exec. Officer--Electro Mechanical Design Services, Inc., Gaithersburg, MD, pg. 375
Roob, R., Chm. Bd.--Benjamin Moore & Co., Montvale, NJ, pg. 139
Rooney, Francis, Chm. Bd.--Bill's Dollar Stores, Inc., Jackson, MS, pg. 150
Rooney, Francis C., Jr., Chm. Bd. & Chief Exec. Officer--H.H. Brown Shoe Company, Inc., Greenwich, CT, pg. 182
Root, L.D., Jr., Chm. Bd.--Root Corporation, Mount Wolf, PA, pg. 946
Roper, Leroy B., Chm. Bd.--Roper Bros. Lumber Co., Inc., Petersburg, VA, pg. 947
Rosanio, Linda, Chm. Bd. & Chief Exec. Officer--Rosanio, Bailets & Talamo, Inc., Cherry Hill, NJ, pg. 947
Rosasco, Nat C., Chm. Bd.--Northwestern Golf Company, Chicago, IL, pg. 815
Rosasco, Nat C., Chm. Bd.--Pro-Select, Broadview, IL, pg. 815
Rose, Kelly L., Chm. Bd.--Starcraft Automotive Corp., Goshen, IN, pg. 1040
Rose, Marvin H., Chm. Bd.--Cleveland Wrecking Company, Los Angeles, CA, pg. 255
Rose, William R., Chm. Bd., Pres. & Chief Exec. Officer--Rose Packing Company, South Barrington, IL, pg. 947
Rosedale, Miles, Chm. Bd., Pres. & Chief Exec. Officer--Monrovia Nursery Co., Azusa, CA, pg. 766
Rosen, Edward H., Chm. & Chief Exec. Officer--Raymond Rosen Co., Conshohocken, PA, pg. 948
Rosen, Frederick D., Chm. Bd.--Ticketmaster Corporation, Los Angeles, CA, pg. 1096
Rosen, Jack, Chm., Pres., Chief Exec. & Chief Oper. Officer--Hazel Bishop Corporation, Englewood Cliffs, NJ, pg. 520
Rosen, Jerome, Chm. Bd.--Star Children's Dress Company, Inc., New York, NY, pg. 1039
Rosen, Ludwig M., Chm. Bd.--Rosens, Inc., Fairmont, MN, pg. 948
Rosen, Ludwig M., Chm. Bd.--Long Prairie Packing Co., Long Prairie, MN, pg. 948
Rosen, Sydney, Chm. Bd.--Rose Art Industries, Orange, NJ, pg. 947
Rosen, William M., Chm. Bd.--Alaskan Copper Companies, Seattle, WA, pg. 30
Rosenbaum, Edward W., Chm. Bd. & Chief Exec. Officer--David Michael & Co. Inc., Philadelphia, PA, pg. 747
Rosenbaum, Jerrold, Chm. Bd.--Vogue & Body Shops, Inc., Jacksonville, FL, pg. 1154
Rosenberg, Charlotte, Chm. Bd.--Rose Printing Company, Inc., Tallahassee, FL, pg. 948
Rosenberg, Gerald, Chm.--Cortec Group, New York, NY, pg. 287
Rosenberg, Harold, Chm. Bd.--Octagon Process Inc., Edgewater, NJ, pg. 821
Rosenberg, Kenneth M., Chm. & Chief Exec. Officer--Pharmavite Corp., Mission Hills, CA, pg. 866
Rosenberg, Kurt, Chm. Bd.--Hubbs Importing Corp., Emerson, NJ, pg. 550
Rosenberg, Marvin, Chm. Bd. & Sec.--Towne Properties, Cincinnati, OH, pg. 1104
Rosendin, Bertha C., Chm. Bd.--Rosendin Electric, Inc., San Jose, CA, pg. 948
Rosenfield, James, Chm. Bd.--John Blair Communications, Inc., New York, NY, pg. 155
Rosenfield, James H., Chm. Bd.--Blair Television, New York, NY, pg. 155
Rosenfield, James R., Chm.--Rosenfield/Dentino, Inc., Jersey City, NJ, pg. 948
Rosenthal, Alexander B., Chm. Bd.--Greater New York Mutual Insurance Company, New York, NY, pg. 483
Rosenthal, George I., Chm. Bd. & Pres.--Raleigh Enterprises, Inc., Los Angeles, CA, pg. 910
Rosenthal, Michael J., Chm. Bd.--Northwestern Steel & Wire Co., Sterling, IL, pg. 815
Rosenzwog, N. Stanley, Chm. Bd.--Monumental Millwork, Inc., Westminster, MD, pg. 768
Ross, Darryl A., Chm. Bd. & Pres.--Ross Advertising, Inc., Saint Louis, MO, pg. 949
Ross, Harold M., Chm. Bd.--Allied Old English, Inc., Port Reading, NJ, pg. 38
Ross, Jules, Chm. Bd.--Reliable Stores, Inc., Columbia, MD, pg. 925
Ross, Kenneth, Chm. & Chief Exec. Officer--J H Collectibles, Milwaukee, WI, pg. 584
Ross, Robert I., Chm. Bd.--Charles Curtain Company, Inc., Dallas, TX, pg. 239
Ross, Robert L., Chm. Bd.--Black Fin Yacht Corporation, Fort Lauderdale, FL, pg. 154
Rosser, Paul C., Chm. Bd.--Rosser Fabrap International, Atlanta, GA, pg. 950
Rossi, Carlos R., Chm. Bd. & Chief Exec. Officer--Conill Advertising, Inc., New York, NY, pg. 274
Rosson, W.M., Chm. Bd.--Conwood Company L.P., Memphis, TN, pg. 281
Rotando, Lynn Andrew, Chm., Pres. & Chief Exec. Officer--Rotando Lerch & Iafeliece Advertising, Stamford, CT, pg. 950
Roth, Nat, Chm. & Chief Fin. Officer--Furman, Roth Adv., New York, NY, pg. 437
Roth, Stanley, Chm. Bd. & Pres.--Panorama Press, Inc., Clifton, NJ, pg. 846
Rothberg, Joan O., Chm. Bd., Chief Exec. Officer & New Bus. Contact--Masterson Rothberg Advertising, New York, NY, pg. 720
Rothwell, Bernard J., III, Chm. Bd.--Bay State Milling Co., Quincy, MA, pg. 127
Rott, Herbert F., Sr., Chm. Bd. & Chief Exec. Officer--Rott-Keller Supply Co., Fargo, ND, pg. 951
Rotter, Steve H., Chm. Bd.--Towne, Silverstein, Rotter Inc., New York, NY, pg. 1104
Rotunno, J.R., Chm. Bd.--O'Neil Industries Inc., Chicago, IL, pg. 827
Roudebush, James R., Chm. Bd.--Caldwell VanRiper Inc., Indianapolis, IN, pg. 209
Roullet, Michel, Chm. Bd.--IA Construction Corp., Concordville, PA, pg. 558
Rouse, Anthony, Chm. Bd.--Associated Grocers, Inc., Baton Rouge, LA, pg. 89
Rouse, Mitchell, Chm. Bd. & Chief Exec. Officer--Supershuttle International, Los Angeles, CA, pg. 1064
Roush, David P., Chm. Bd., Pres. & Chief Exec. Officer--Rocor Transportation Companies Inc., Oklahoma City, OK, pg. 942
Roussel, Louis J., Jr., Chm. Bd., Pres. & Chief Exec. Officer--Victory Financial Group, Inc., Metairie, LA, pg. 1150
Rowe, Jim, Chm. Bd.--Scoville Press, Inc., Minneapolis, MN, pg. 983
Rowe, Richard R., Chm. Bd., Pres. & Chief Exec. Officer--The Faxon Company, Inc., Westwood, MA, pg. 404
Rowell, L.J. , Jr., Chm. Bd., Pres. & Chief Exec. Officer--Provident Mutual Life Insurance Co., Philadelphia, PA, pg. 896
Rowley, Claude, Chm. Bd.--Intermountain Farmers Association, Salt Lake City, UT, pg. 575
Rubart, Perry, Chm. Bd.--Sunflower Electric Power Corporation, Hays, KS, pg. 1060
Rubie, Kerry M., Chm.-Leo Burnett International--Leo Burnett Company, Inc., Chicago, IL, pg. 191
Rubin, Irving A., Chm. Bd., Pres. & Chief Exec. Officer--Container Products Inc., Southfield, MI, pg. 278
Rubin, Joel, Chm. Bd., Pres. & Chief Exec. Officer--Phototype Color Graphics, Inc., Pennsauken, NJ, pg. 869
Rubin, Mel, Chm.--Rubin Ehrenthal & Associates, New York, NY, pg. 953
Rubin, Richard, Chm., Pres., Chief Exec. & Chief Oper. Officer--Donnkenny, Inc., New York, NY, pg. 345
Rubin, William S., Chm. Bd. & Pres.--Rubin Response Services, Inc., Schaumburg, IL, pg. 954
Rudeen, William, Chm. Bd.--Southern Minnesota Beet Sugar Cooperative, Renville, MN, pg. 1022
Rudloff, Hans-Joerg, Chm. Bd., Pres. & Chief Exec. Officer--Financiere Credit Suisse-First Boston, Zug,, Switzerland, pg. 204
Rudloff, Hans-Jorg, Chm.--Credit Suisse First Boston Czechoslovakia a.s., Prague, Czechoslovakia, pg. 204
Rudy, Raymond B., Chm. Bd.--New Hampton, Inc., New York, NY, pg. 801
Ruen, Richard W., Sr., Chm. Bd.--Cleaners Hanger Co., Palm Harbor, FL, pg. 254
Ruhlin, John, Jr., Chm. Bd., Pres. & Chief Exec. Officer--The Ruhlin Company, Sharon Center, OH, pg. 955
Ruhr, Charles F., Chm. Bd. & Chief Exec. Officer--Chuck Ruhr Advertising, Minneapolis, MN, pg. 955
Ruibal, Charles A., Chm. Bd.--Applied Solar Energy Corporation, City of Industry, CA, pg. 79
Ruiz, Louis, Chm. Bd.--Ruiz Food Products, Inc., Dinuba, CA, pg. 955
Rumsfeld, Donald H., Chm. & Chief Exec. Officer--General Instrument Corporation, New York, NY, pg. 425
Runyan, E.E., Chm. Bd.--Energy Minerals Corporation, Denver, CO, pg. 381
Runyon, Marvin T., Chm. Bd.--Tennessee Valley Authority, Knoxville, TN, pg. 1088
Ruppman, Charles T., Chm. Bd. & Chief Exec. Officer--Ruppman National Yellow Pages Service (RNYPS), Peoria, IL, pg. 956
Rusk, Gerald W., Chm. Bd.--Freeman Manufacturing & Supply Company, Cleveland, OH, pg. 431
Russell, H. Jerome, Chm. Bd.--City Beverage Co., Atlanta, GA, pg. 251
Russell, Herman J., Chm. Bd. & Chief Exec. Officer--H. J. Russell Corp., Atlanta, GA, pg. 957
Russell, Leo P., Chm. Bd. & Chief Exec. Officer--Russell Industries, Inc., Carnegie, PA, pg. 957

Russell, William K., Chm. Bd.--Knight Equipment Corp., Costa Mesa, CA, pg. 636
Rust, Edward B., Jr., Chm. Bd., Pres. & Chief Exec. Officer--State Farm Mutual Automobile Insurance Company, Bloomington, IL, pg. 1041
Rutherford, Clyde E., Chm. Bd. & Pres.--Dairylea Cooperative Inc., East Syracuse, NY, pg. 311
Rutherford, Jack D., Chm. & Chief Exec. Officer--ICM Industries, Inc., Chicago, IL, pg. 559
Ruting, Wayne, Chm. Bd.--Columbine Systems Inc., Golden, CO, pg. 266
Rutland, Robert J., Chm. Bd. & Chief Exec. Officer--Allied Systems, Ltd., Decatur, GA, pg. 40
Ryan, Charles P., Jr., Chm. Bd., Pres.--Charan Industries, Inc., Garden City, NY, pg. 239
Ryder, William, Chm. & Chief Exec. Officer--Ryder & Schild, Inc., Miami, FL, pg. 958
Rye, Walter L., Chm. Bd.--Cincinnati Gear Company, Cincinnati, OH, pg. 250
Ryno, Ronald P., Chm. Bd. & Pres.--Cuplex, Inc., Garland, TX, pg. 305
Sabath, Robert, Chm.--Knight PMD, Inc., Barrington, IL, pg. 637
Sabatino, Gregory K., Chm. Bd.--Flynn/Sabatino, Miamisburg, OH, pg. 421
Sabbeth, Stephen J., Chm. Bd. & Pres.--Sabbeth Industries Ltd, Deer Park, NY, pg. 965
Sachs, Louis S., Chm. Bd. & Pres.--Sachs Holding Company, Chesterfield, MO, pg. 965
Sacks, Barry, Chm. Bd.--Jazz Holding Corporation, Vernon, CA, pg. 591
Sahm, Roland R., Chm. Bd. & Chief Exec. Officer--Elixir Industries, Gardena, CA, pg. 376
Sakosits, John J., Chm. Bd., Chief Exec. & Chief Oper. Officer--Hoboken Wood Flooring Corporation, Wayne, NJ, pg. 537
Saldanha, Stephen, Chm. Bd.--Hiross Inc., Niagara Falls, NY, pg. 536
Salerno, Ronald, Sr. V.P.--Western Development Corporation, Washington, DC, pg. 1179
Sall, Maurice, Chm. Bd.--Atlantic Metals Corporation, Philadelphia, PA, pg. 95
Sally, Paul J., Jr., Chm. Bd.--American Mathematical Society, Inc., Providence, RI, pg. 58
Salmon, John L., Chm. Bd., Sec. & Treas.--TVESCO, Inc., Memphis, TN, pg. 1075
Salter, Maxwell H., Chm. Bd.--Beno's, Los Angeles, CA, pg. 139
Samburg, A. Gene, Chm. Bd., Pres. & Chief Exec. Officer--Kastle Systems, Inc., Arlington, VA, pg. 618
Sammons, E.D., Chm. Bd.--Sammons Enterprises, Inc., Dallas, TX, pg. 968
Samson, Bernice, Chm. & Pres .--Sterling Supply Company, Inc., Lisle, IL, pg. 1047
Samuels, Robert P., Chm. Bd., Chief Exec. Officer--Milton Samuels Advertising Agency, Inc., New York, NY, pg. 968
Sanborn, Bruce, Chm. Bd., Pres. & Chief Exec. Officer--North Central Life Insurance Companies, Saint Paul, MN, pg. 813
Sanborn, Bruce C., Chm. Bd., Pres. & Chief Exec. Officer--Financial Life Companies, Inc., St. Paul, MN, pg. 813
Sanders, Harris, Jr., Chm. Bd.--Saunders Incorporated, Birmingham, AL, pg. 972
Sanders, Max D., Chm. Bd. & Pres.--Ohmite Manufacturing Company, Skokie, IL, pg. 823
Sanders, O'Neil, Chm. Bd., Pres., Chief Exec. & Chief Oper. Officer--Associated Petroleum Carriers, Spartanburg, SC, pg. 91
Sanders, Richard B., Chm. Bd.--Cortland Line Co., Inc., Cortland, NY, pg. 287
Sandhu, M.S., Chm. Bd., Pres. & Chief Exec. Officer--SRS Technologies, Newport Beach, CA, pg. 964
Sandifer, Norwood H., Chm. Bd.--Cain & Bultman, Inc., Jacksonville, FL, pg. 207
Sandler, Rose, Chm. Bd.--Interstate Drug Exchange, Inc., Amityville, NY, pg. 580
Sandner, Jack, Chm. Bd.--Chicago Mercantile Exchange, Chicago, IL, pg. 245
Sanel, Henry, Chm. Bd.--Automotive Supply Assoc., Inc., Concord, NH, pg. 101
Sankes, Gary, Chm. Bd. & Pres.--Scrufari Construction Co. Inc., Niagara Falls, NY, pg. 983
Sansom, William B., Chm. Bd. & Chief Exec. Officer--The H. T. Hackney Co., Knoxville, TN, pg. 498
Santarlasci, Joseph, Chm. Bd.--Swirl, Inc., New York, NY, pg. 1068
Santheimer, Stephen L., Chm. Bd.--Bultman Funeral Home, New Orleans, LA, pg. 832
Santry, Christopher B., Chm. & Chief Exec. Officer--Christopher Thomas Associates Inc., Garden City, NY, pg. 249
Saras, James, Chm. Bd. & Chief Exec. Officer--Tri Valley Growers Inc., San Francisco, CA, pg. 1111
Sarckowsky, Herman, Chm. Bd.--Pace International Corporation, Kirkland, WA, pg. 838
Sargent, Charles L., Chm. Bd. & Chief Exec. Officer--Thetford Corporation, Ann Arbor, MI, pg. 357
Sargent, Warren B., Chm. Bd.--Todd & Sargent, Inc., Ames, IA, pg. 1100
Sarkisian, Norman, Chm. Bd.--Cavalier Corporation, Chattanooga, TN, pg. 229
Sarmanian, Peter, Chm. Bd. & Chief Exec. Officer--Printed Circuit Corporation, Woburn, MA, pg. 891
Saubert, Walter E., Chm. Bd.--Red Ball Corporation, Seattle, WA, pg. 918
Sauder, Erie J., Chm. Bd.--Sauder Woodworking Co., Archbold, OH, pg. 972
Sauder, Maynard, Chm. Bd.--Sauder Manufacturing Corporation, Archbold, OH, pg. 972
Sauey, W.R., Chm. Bd., Pres. & Treas.--Nordic Group of Companies, Ltd., Baraboo, WI, pg. 809
Sauey, W.R., Chm. Bd.--Flambeau Corporation, Baraboo, WI, pg. 809
Saul, William J., Chm. Bd.--Remmele Engineering, Inc., Saint Paul, MN, pg. 926
Saunders, Bruce T., Chm. Bd.--Saunders Brothers, Westbrook, ME, pg. 972
Saunders, Gregory, Chm. Bd.--Chicago Convention & Tourism Bureau, Chicago, IL, pg. 245
Saunders, John H., Sr., Chm. Bd. & Chief Exec. Officer--Palmetto Wholesale Co., Inc., Columbia, SC, pg. 844
Saunders, Manuel, Chm. Bd.--Camellia Food Stores Co-op Inc., Norfolk, VA, pg. 211
Saunders, Manuel, Chm. Bd.--Be-Lo Markets Inc., Norfolk, VA, pg. 212
Saunders, R.F., Chm. Bd. & Chief Exec. Officer--Dakco Distributors, Inc., Minot, ND, pg. 311
Saunders, R.F., Chm. Bd.--Nodak Distributor, Minot, ND, pg. 311
Saunders, R.F., Chm. Bd.--Northland Sports Inc., Minot, ND, pg. 311
Saunders, William C., Chm. & Creative Dir.--Saunders, Lubinski & White, Inc., Dallas, TX, pg. 973
Sawyer, Gordon, Chm. Bd.--Sawyer Riley Compton Inc., Atlanta, GA, pg. 973
Saxonmeyer, W.J., Chm. Bd.--Whiting Corporation, Harvey, IL, pg. 1187
Sayers, Hanley, Chm. Bd.--Globe Business Furniture, Inc., Hendersonville, TN, pg. 463
Saylors, Eddie, Chm. Bd. & Chief Exec. Officer--First National Bank in Cleburne, Cleburne, TX, pg. 412
Sazenski, Chester R., Chm. Bd. & Chief Exec. Officer--Jesco, Inc., Minneapolis, MN, pg. 593
Scaff, Lester, Chm. Bd.--Certified Grocers of Florida, Inc., Ocala, FL, pg. 237
Scangas, Angelo N., Chm. Bd.--Scangas Brothers Holdings, Inc., Lynn, MA, pg. 974
Scarff, Edward, Chm. Bd.--Arcata Corporation, San Francisco, CA, pg. 80
Scelba, Andrew, Chm.--SSD&W Integrated Marketing Communications, Montville, NJ, pg. 964
Schaaf, Gunther, Chm. Bd.--Micro Component Technology Inc., Saint Paul, MN, pg. 748
Schackow, Gerald D., Chm. Bd.--Athletic Attic Properties Inc., Gainesville, FL, pg. 94
Schad, Theodore G., Jr., Chm. Bd., Pres. & Chief Exec. Officer--Schad Industries, Inc., Lafayette, LA, pg. 974
Schad, Theodore G., Jr., Chm. Bd., Pres. & Chief Exec. Officer--Lou Ana Foods, Inc., Opelousas, LA, pg. 974
Schaedler, Thomas J., Sr., Chm. Bd.--Schaedler Brothers, Inc., Harrisburg, PA, pg. 974
Schafer, Gordon, Chm. Bd.--United Hardware Distributing Co., Plymouth, MN, pg. 1132
Schaffler, R.S., Chm. Bd.--UC Industries, Inc., Parsippany, NJ, pg. 1122
Schaible, Paul G., Jr., Chm. Bd., Pres. & Chief Exec. Officer--Chelsea State Bank, Chelsea, MI, pg. 241
Schaller, Christopher L., Chm., Pres. & Chief Exec. Officer--Forstmann & Company, Inc., New York, NY, pg. 424
Schardt, Ronald, Chm. Bd., Chief Exec. Officer & Chief Oper. Officer--Reinke Manufacturing Co., Inc., Deshler, NE, pg. 924
Scharff, Werner G., Chm. Bd & Pres.--Lanz, Inc., Culver City, CA, pg. 658
Schawk, Clarence W., Chm. Bd & Chief Exec. Officer--Schawk, Inc., Des Plaines, IL, pg. 974
Schecter, Leroy, Chm. Bd. & Chief Exec. Officer--American Strip Steel Inc., Kearny, NJ, pg. 63
Schenk, Tony, Chm. Bd., Pres. & Chief Exec. Officer--Enabling Technologies Company, Stuart, FL, pg. 380
Schepps, Phil J., Chm. Bd.--The Julius Schepps Co., Dallas, TX, pg. 975
Scher, Gerald J., Chm. Bd., Treas. & Sec.--Westchester Lace, Inc., North Bergen, NJ, pg. 1178
Scherer, Robert P., Jr., Chm. Bd.--Scherer Scientific, Ltd., Atlanta, GA, pg. 976
Schick, Joseph C., Chm. Bd., Pres., Chief Exec. Officer & Chief Oper. Officer--Raub Supply Company, Lancaster, PA, pg. 913
Schiefler, Roger, Chm. & Chief Oper. Officer--Dieline Corporation, Kentwood, MI, pg. 336
Schieg, Henry F., Chm. Bd.--Aid Association For Lutherans, Appleton, WI, pg. 26
Schierholz, William F., Chm. Bd.--Chemtech Industries, Inc., Saint Louis, MO, pg. 242
Schifter, Yvonne, Chm. Bd. & Chief Exec. Officer--Squire-Cogswell Company, Northbrook, IL, pg. 1034
Schildge, Adam T., Chm. Bd.--Precision Roll Grinders, Inc., Allentown, PA, pg. 885
Schinman, H.L., Chm. Bd., Treas., Sec. & Gen. Counsel--Bogue Electric Manufacturing Co., Paterson, NJ, pg. 162
Schlanger, Joseph, Chm. Bd.--United Envelope Company, Inc., New York, NY, pg. 1131
Schlatter, H.H., Chm. Bd.--Art Iron, Inc., Toledo, OH, pg. 86
Schlecht, Karl, Chm. Bd.--Putzmeister, Inc., Gardena, CA, pg. 901
Schlem, Paul M., Chm. Bd.--Vintners International Company, Inc., Gonzales, CA, pg. 1152
Schlesinger, James R., Chm. Bd.--Mitre Corporation, Bedford, MA, pg. 762
Schlessman, Lee E., Chm. Bd. & Pres.--Greeley Gas Co., Denver, CO, pg. 483
Schloemer, Bertrand A., Chm. Bd.--Stockton West Burkhart Inc., Cincinnati, OH, pg. 1050
Schlosser, Phillip D., Chm. Bd.--Schlosser Forge Company, Rancho Cucamonga, CA, pg. 976
Schlueter, John J., Chm. Bd. & Chief Exec. Officer--Knapp Shoes Inc., Brockton, MA, pg. 636
Schmidt, Robert F., Chm. Bd. & Chief Exec. Officer--Cosco Industries, Spring Valley, NY, pg. 288
Schmidt, Rolf D., Chm. Bd.--Surgical Specialties, Reading, PA, pg. 1065
Schmidt, Ronald D., Chm. Bd., Pres. & Chief Exec. Officer--Zytec Corp., Eden Prairie, MN, pg. 1221
Schmidt, Steven K., Chm. Bd. & Treas.--Rogers & Associates Advertising, Inc., Santa Clara, CA, pg. 943
Schmidt, William B., Chm. Bd., Pres. & Treas.--Coca-Cola Bottling Company of Elizabethtown, Elizabethtown, KY, pg. 258
Schmitt, Bertel, Chm. Bd. & Creative Dir.--Graf Bertel, New York, NY, pg. 474
Schmitt, Peter C., Chm. Bd.--Color Custom, Inc., Warren, MI, pg. 264
Schmitt, Robert, Chm. Bd.--Paul A. Schmitt Music Company, Minneapolis, MN, pg. 976
Schnadig, L.K., Chm. Bd.--Schnadig Corporation, Chicago, IL, pg. 977
Schneider, Charles, Chm. Bd.--Future Foam, Inc., Council Bluffs, IA, pg. 437
Schneider, Ernst, Chm.--Credit Suisse Financial Products, London,, United Kingdom, pg. 204
Schneider, Hans, Chm. Bd.--Citizens National Bancshares Inc., Hammond, LA, pg. 250
Schneider, Marvin, Chm. & Chief Exec. Officer--Sherwood & Schneider Advertising, New York, NY, pg. 999
Schnitzer, Dr. Leonard, Chm. Bd. & Chief Exec. Officer--Schnitzer Steel Industries, Inc., Portland, OR, pg. 977
Schnuck, Craig, Chm. Bd. & Chief Exec. Officer--Schnuck Markets, Inc., Maryland Heights, MO, pg. 977
Schnuck, Scott, Pres. & Chief Oper. Officer--Schnuck Markets, Inc., Maryland Heights, MO, pg. 977
Scholtens, Michael, Chm., & Chief Exec. Officer--Nutech, Inc., San Jose, CA, pg. 817
Scholz, Jurgen, Chm.--Scholz & Friends GmbH, Hamburg, Germany, pg. 112
Schonberger, Phillip, Chm. Bd.--Landau & Heyman Inc., Chicago, IL, pg. 654
Schottenstein, Jay, Chm. Bd.--Schottenstein Stores Corporation, Columbus, OH, pg. 978
Schottenstein, Jay, Chm. Bd.--Retail Ventures, Inc., Warrendale, PA, pg. 929
Schottland, S.A., Chm. Bd.--American Packaging Corporation, Philadelphia, PA, pg. 59
Schrafl, Anton E., Chm. Bd.--Hanes Companies, Inc., Winston-Salem, NC, pg. 505
Schrager, Phillip G., Chm. Bd. & Chief Exec. Officer--Pacesetter Corporation, Omaha, NE, pg. 839
Schramm, Bernard C., Jr., Chm. Bd.--The William Cook Agency, Inc., Jacksonville, FL, pg. 282
Schramm, Howard M., Jr., Chm. Bd. & Pres.--Turner Supply Company, Mobile, AL, pg. 1119
Schroeder, William, Chm. Bd. & Chief Exec. Officer--Ireland Coffee Tea, Inc., Pleasantville, NJ, pg. 582
Schron, Jack H. Sr., Chm. Bd.--Jergens Inc., Cleveland, OH, pg. 593
Schrott, John D., Jr., Chm. Bd., Pres. & Chief Exec. Officer--Reel-O-Matic Systems, Inc., Oklahoma City, OK, pg. 920
Schuenke, Donald J., Chm. Bd. & Chief Exec. Officer--Northwestern Mutual Life Insurance Co., Milwaukee, WI, pg. 815
Schulte, C., Chm. Bd.--L. G. Everist Inc., Sioux Falls, SD, pg. 392
Schultz, George E., Chm. Bd.--Great Lakes Lithograph Co., Cleveland, OH, pg. 481
Schumacher, Donald, Chm. Bd. & Pres.--Schumacher Electric Corporation, Chicago, IL, pg. 979
Schumacher, Kenneth H., Chm. Bd. & Pres.--Paradata Computer Networks, Inc., Farmington Hills, MI, pg. 847
Schuman, S. W., Jr., Chm. Bd. & Pres.--West Coast Growers & Packers, Inc., Selma, CA, pg. 1177
Schuman, Seymour, Chm. Bd. & Sec.--Propper Manufacturing Co., Inc., Long Island City, NY, pg. 895
Schumb, Morris, Chm. Bd.--Pyttronic Industries, Inc., Montgomeryville, PA, pg. 901
Schwab, Richard D., Chm. Bd.--S. Schwab Company, Cumberland, MD, pg. 980
Schwan, Marvin M., Chm. Bd., Pres. & Chief Exec. Officer--Schwan's Sales Enterprises, Marshall, MN, pg. 980
Schwank, Bernd H., Chm. Bd.--Perfection-Schwank Inc., Waynesboro, GA, pg. 861
Schwartz, Barry, Chm.--CRK Advertising, New York, NY, pg. 203
Schwartz, Barry, Chm. Bd. & Chief Exec. Officer--Doe Spun, Inc., New York, NY, pg. 343
Schwartz, Barry, Chm. Bd. & Chief Exec. Officer--Bambinaggine, New York, NY, pg. 343
Schwartz, Barry, Chm. Bd. & Chief Exec. Officer--Mia Bambini, New York, NY, pg. 343
Schwartz, Barry K., Chm. Bd. & Chief Oper. Officer--Calvin Klein, Inc., New York, NY, pg. 635
Schwartz, Bernard, Chm. Bd.--Jack Schwartz Shoes, Inc., New York, NY, pg. 980
Schwartz, Bernard, Chm. Bd.--British Knights, New York, NY, pg. 980
Schwartz, M.J., Chm. Bd., Pres. & Chief Exec. Officer--Quaker City Motor Parts Company, Middletown, DE, pg. 903
Schwartz, Marvin, Chm. Bd. & Chief Exec. Officer--Gannett Transit, New York, NY, pg. 442
Schwartz, Mel, Chm. Bd.--Digital Pathways Inc., Mountain View, CA, pg. 337
Schwartz, N.R., Chm. Bd.--Swivelier Co., Inc., Nanuet, NY, pg. 1068
Schwartz, Norman S., Chm. Bd. & Chief Oper. Officer--Charron, Schwartz & Partners, Inc., New York, NY, pg. 240
Schwartz, Robert G., Chm. Bd., Pres. & Chief Exec. Officer--Metropolitan Life Insurance Co., New York, NY, pg. 744
Schwartzstein, Samuel, Chm. Bd.--Sebastian & Cooke, Parsippany, NJ, pg. 986
Schwedel, Nat N., Chm. Bd.--Amerbelle Corporation, Rockville, CT, pg. 47
Schweiner, Jerry, Chm. Bd., Pres. & Chief Exec. Officer--Benco Industries, Inc., Fort Deposit, AL, pg. 138
Schweizer, Melvin, Chm. Bd. & Pres.--Prairie Farms Dairy, Inc., Carlinville, IL, pg. 884
Scobie, William M., Chm. Bd., Chief Exec. & Legal Officer--Mason Shoe Mfg. Co., Chippewa Falls, WI, pg. 718

Scopetta, John N., Chm. Bd., Pres. & Chief Exec. Officer--Power Engineering Co. Inc., Coral Gables, FL, pg. 883
Scordato, Emil A., Chm. & Chief Exec. Officer--Medical Laboratory Automation, Inc., Pleasantville, NY, pg. 735
Scott, Edward, Chm. Bd.--United States Cold Storage, Inc., Cherry Hill, NJ, pg. 1135
Scott, James T., Chm. Bd., Chief Exec. Officer & Treas.--Norcostco, Inc., Minneapolis, MN, pg. 809
Scott, Ronald H., Chm. Bd. & Chief Exec. Officer--Interform Corporation, Bridgeville, PA, pg. 574
Scott, Stuart L., Co-Chm.--LaSalle Partners, Chicago, IL, pg. 660
Scott, Walter, Jr., Chm. Bd. & Pres.--Peter Kiewit Sons Inc., Omaha, NE, pg. 629
Scoville, John A., Chm. Bd.--Harza Engineering Co., Chicago, IL, pg. 516
Scudder, Charles D., Chm. Bd. & Chief Exec. Officer--Charing Cross Group, Louisville, KY, pg. 239
Scudder, Richard B., Chm. Bd.--MediaNews Group Inc., Houston, TX, pg. 735
Seabrook, James H., Sr., Chm. Bd.--Seabrook Wallcoverings, Inc., Memphis, TN, pg. 984
Seabrook, James M., Chm. Bd. & Chief Exec. Officer--Seabrook Brothers & Sons, Inc., Seabrook, NJ, pg. 984
Seaton, Kenneth M., Chm. Bd., Pres. & Chief Exec. Officer-Family Inns of America, Inc., Pigeon Forge, TN, pg. 398
Seaver, Richard C., Chm. Bd.--Hydril Company, Los Angeles, CA, pg. 556
Sebree, Gary, Chm. Bd.--Producers Rice Mill Inc., Stuttgart, AR, pg. 892
Sechler, Scott I., Chm. Bd. & Pres.--Farmer's Pride, Inc., Fredericksburg, PA, pg. 401
Secrist, Richard, Chm. Bd., Pres. & Chief Exec. Officer--Blue Tee Corporation, New York, NY, pg. 161
Secrist, Roger E., Chm. & Chief Exec. Officer--ANGUS Chemical Company, Buffalo Grove, IL, pg. 75
Seder, Jeffrey A., Chm. Bd.--Craftex Mills Inc. of Pennsylvania, Blue Bell, PA, pg. 295
Seeger, John, Chm. Bd.--Dayton Rogers Mfg. Co., Minneapolis, MN, pg. 321
Segal, Myron, Chm. Bd., Pres. & Chief Exec. Officer--Premier Mill Corp., New York, NY, pg. 887
Segal, Steven A., Chm. Bd.--North American Products Corp., Jasper, IN, pg. 811
Segall, Samson, Chm. Bd., Pres. & Treas.--Sharon-Jay Togs, Inc., New Bedford, MA, pg. 995
Seibel, Morris H., Chm. Bd.--Seibel & Stern Corp., New York, NY, pg. 987
Seidman, Theodore M., Chm. Bd. & Pres.--Air Conditioning Co., Inc., Glendale, CA, pg. 26
Seigle, Jack M., Chm. & Chief Exec. Officer--Starr Seigle McCombs, Inc., Honolulu, HI, pg. 1040
Seitz, Edgar C., Jr., Chm. Bd. & Exec. V.P.-Pur.--Service Supply Co. Inc. of Indiana, Indianapolis, IN, pg. 992
Seitz, Tadd C., Chm. Bd. & Chief Exec. Officer--The Scott Company, Marysville, OH, pg. 982
Seldin, S.G., Chm. Bd.--Miss Elaine Inc., Saint Louis, MO, pg. 760
Self, J.C., Jr., Chm. & Chief Exec. Officer--Greenwood Mills, Inc., Greenwood, SC, pg. 485
Seligman, Irving R., Chm. Bd. & Treas.--Seligman & Associates, Inc., Bloomfield Hills, MI, pg. 988
Seltzer, Edwin C., Chm. Bd. & Pres.--Roller Derby Skate Company, Litchfield, IL, pg. 944
Seltzer, Samuel M., Chm. Bd. & Pres.--Allison Corporation, Livingston, NJ, pg. 40
Semler, Jerry D., Chm. Bd., Pres. & Chief Exec. Officer--American United Life Insurance Company, Indianapolis, IN, pg. 65
Sempere, Pedro, Chm.--Young & Rubicam, S.A., Madrid,, Spain, pg. 1213
Sensing, Wilbur, Jr., Chm. Bd.--Enco Materials, Inc., Nashville, TN, pg. 380
Senty, James A., Chm. Bd. & Pres.--Consolidated Midwest, Inc., La Crosse, WI, pg. 277
Senty, James A., Chm. Bd. & Pres.--Midwest Bottle Gas Company, La Crosse, WI, pg. 277
Seppala, Martin, Chm. Bd.--Seppala & AHO Construction Company, New Ipswich, NH, pg. 990
Servaas, Beurt, Chm. Bd. & Pres.--Servaas, Inc., Indianapolis, IN, pg. 991
Servaas, Beurt R., Chm. Bd.--Servaas Investments, Inc., Indianapolis, IN, pg. 991
SerVaas, Cory, M.D., Chm. Bd., Pres. & Chief Exec. Officer-Benjamin Franklin Literary & Medical Society, Inc., Indianapolis, IN, pg. 139
Service, Richard L., Chm. Bd.--Hardwoods Of Michigan, Inc., Clinton, MI, pg. 509
Settle, Larry G., Chm. Bd.--Chartway Technologies, Rockville, MD, pg. 240
Seuss, C. David, Chm., Pres., Chief Exec. Officer & Treas.--Spinnaker Software Corporation, Cambridge, MA, pg. 1031
Sevier, Helen, Chm. Bd., Pres., Chief Exec. & Chief Oper. Officer--B.A.S.S., Inc., Montgomery, AL, pg. 105
Sewell, I.F., Chm. Bd.--Lithotype Company, Inc., South San Francisco, CA, pg. 678
Seymour Heatley, Nancy, Chm. Bd.--Seymour of Sycamore, Inc., Sycamore, IL, pg. 994
Shacklett, James H., Jr., Chm. Bd.--National Label Company, Lafayette Hill, PA, pg. 791
Shah, Harry, Pres.--National Food Stores, Inc. T/A Krauszer's, Edison, NJ, pg. 788
Shaheen, John, Chm. Bd.--World Carpets, Inc., Dalton, GA, pg. 1202
Shak, Denesh, Co-Chm. Bd.--Shoreline Products, Inc., Arlington, TX, pg. 1000
Shaker, Joseph R., Chm. Bd.--Shaker Advertising Agency, Oak Park, IL, pg. 994
Shames, Sidney J., Chm. Bd., Pres., CEO, COO, CFO & Treas.--Melard Manufacturing Corporation, Passaic, NJ, pg. 737
Shanes, Abraham, Chm. Bd. & Treas.--Talk-A-Phone Co., Chicago, IL, pg. 1077
Shapero, J., Chm. Bd., Pres. & Chief Exec. Officer--Quael Corp., Detroit, MI, pg. 902
Shapira, David, Chm. Bd.--Phar-Mor, Inc., Youngstown, OH, pg. 866
Shapiro, Bernard J., Chm. Bd.--Shapco, Inc., Van Nuys, CA, pg. 995
Shapiro, Marc J., Chm. Bd.--Texas Commerce Bancshares, Inc., Houston, TX, pg. 1089
Shapiro, Richard B., Chm. Bd., Pres. & Chief Exec. Officer--Charles River Data Systems, Inc., Framingham, MA, pg. 240
Shapiro, Ted, Chm. Bd.--The Patrician Group, New York, NY, pg. 851
Shaw, R.W., Chm. Bd.--American Inks & Coatings Corp., Valley Forge, PA, pg. 56
Shaw, Robert, Chm. Bd.--M.S. Walker, Inc./Seacoast, Somerville, MA, pg. 1160
Shaw, Robert A., Chm. Bd. & Pres.--Allied Plywood Corp., Alexandria, VA, pg. 38
Shaykin, Leonard P., Co-Chm.--Best Products Co., Inc., Richmond, VA, pg. 17
Shea, James F., Chm. Bd.--Fairmont Homes, Inc., Nappanee, IN, pg. 397
Shea, Terence J., Chm. Bd. & Chief Exec. Officer--Bradner Central Company, Chicago, IL, pg. 170
Sheehan, Dennis W., Chm. Bd., Pres. & Chief Exec. Officer-AXIA Incorporated, Oak Brook, IL, pg. 8
Sheehy, John P., Chm. Bd.--The Architects Collaborative, Inc. (TAC), Cambridge, MA, pg. 80
Sheehy, William J., Chm. Bd.--Sheehy, Knopf & Shaver, Inc., Louisville, KY, pg. 996
Sheerr, Richard C., Chm. Bd., Pres & Chief Exec. Officer--Crown Textile Company, Blue Bell, PA, pg. 302
Sheffield, John W., Chm. Bd.--Sheffield Hardware Company, Americus, GA, pg. 996
Sheinbaum, Uri, Chm. Bd. & Pres.--Calmark Investment Company, Los Angeles, CA, pg. 211
Sheldon, J.M., Chm. Bd., Pres. & Chief Exec. Officer--Sheldons' Inc., Antigo, WI, pg. 996
Shell, Earl L., Chm. Bd. & Chief Exec. Officer--Hardin Construction Group, Inc., Atlanta, GA, pg. 508
Shepard, D. C., Chm. Bd.--Menasha Corporation, Neenah, WI, pg. 738
Shepherd, Donald R., Chm. Bd. & Chief Exec. Officer--Loomis, Sayles & Co., Boston, MA, pg. 799
Sherman, Glenn, Dr., Chm. Bd. & Chief Exec. Officer--Laser Power Corporation, San Diego, CA, pg. 660
Shewmake, C. B., Chm. Bd. & Chief Exec. Officer--Algernon Blair International, Montgomery, AL, pg. 155
Shields, Gerald N., Chm. Bd., Pres. & Chief Exec. Officer--Graymills Corp., Chicago, IL, pg. 480
Shields, James W., Chm. Bd.--Judd's Incorporated, Washington, DC, pg. 608
Shields, John, Chm. Bd., Pres. & Chief Exec. Officer--Trader Joes Co., South Pasadena, CA, pg. 1076
Shillestad, John G., Chm. Bd., Pres. & Chief Exec. Officer--Columbian Mutual Life Insurance Co., Binghamton, NY, pg. 266
Shine, Jack, Chm. Bd.--First Financial Group, Inc., Encino, CA, pg. 413
Shipley, William S. II, Chm. Bd., Pres. & Chief Exec. Officer-Shipley Oil Company, York, PA, pg. 999
Shirk, Russell O., Chm. Bd.--Beer Nuts, Inc., Bloomington, IL, pg. 132
Shisler, Arden, Chm. Bd.--Employers Insurance of Wausau a Mutual Co., Wausau, WI, pg. 380
Shisler, Arden, Chm. Bd.--Employers Insurance of Wausau a Mutual Co., Wausau, WI, pg. 795
Shoen, E.J., Chm. Bd. & Pres.--Amerco, A Nevada Corporation, Reno, NV, pg. 47
Short, William W., Jr., Chm. Bd.--Southern Apparel Corporation, Largo, FL, pg. 1020
Shorter, Frank C., Chm.--Battery St. Enterprises, Running Gear Div., Boulder, CO, pg. 670
Shostack, G. Lynn, Chm. Bd. & Pres.--Joyce International, Inc., New York, NY, pg. 608
Shuford, Harley F., Sr., Chm. Bd.--Century Furniture Industries, Hickory, NC, pg. 235
Shultz, Gerald, Chm. Bd., Pres. & Chief Exec. Officer--Micro-Met L Corp., Indianapolis, IN, pg. 748
Shure, Myron B., Chm. Bd.--Strombecker Corporation, Chicago, IL, pg. 1054
Shure, S.N., Chm. Bd.--Shure Brothers Incorporated, Evanston, IL, pg. 1001
Siano, Jerry J., Chm. & Chief Exec. Officer--N W Ayer Inc., New York, NY, pg. 104
Sibley, Earl A., Chm. Bd. & Pres.--Shannon & Wilson, Inc., Seattle, WA, pg. 995
Sicola, Tom, Chm. Bd., Pres. & New Bus. Contact--Sicola Martin Koons Frank, Inc., Austin, TX, pg. 1001
Siddall, John N., Chm. Bd. & Chief Exec. Officer--Siddall, Matus & Coughter, Inc. Advertising & Public Relations, Richmond, VA, pg. 1002
Sieber, James, Chm. Bd.--Wm. S. Trimble Company, Inc., Knoxville, TN, pg. 1113
Sieg, Madison, Chm. Bd. & Chief Exec. Officer--Sieg Company, Davenport, IA, pg. 1002
Siegal, Sol, Chm. Bd.--Olympic Steel Inc., Bedford Heights, OH, pg. 825
Siegel, Alan, Chm. & Chief Exec. Officer--Siegel & Gale, New York, NY, pg. 1002
Siegel, Jerome, Chm. Bd.--Titan Industrial Corp., New York, NY, pg. 1099
Siegel, Mark S., Chm. Bd.--Sound Warehouse, Inc., Dallas, TX, pg. 1018
Siegel, Mo, Chm. Bd. & Chief Exec. Officer--Celestial Seasonings, Boulder, CO, pg. 231
Siegel, Owen R., Chm. Bd. & Chief Exec. Officer--R.S. Owens, Chicago, IL, pg. 834
Siemer, Arnold B., Chm. Bd. & Pres.--Desco Corporation, Columbus, OH, pg. 332
Siemr, A.B., Chm. Bd.--Digitec, Marion, OH, pg. 1069
Siener, P. Robert, Jr., Chm. Bd.--Cooley, Inc., Pawtucket, RI, pg. 282
Sigal, Gerald R., Chm. Bd.--Sigal Construction, Washington, DC, pg. 1003
Sigel, Arthur R., Chm. Bd., Pres. & Chief Exec. Officer--Velsicol Chemical Corporation, Rosemont, IL, pg. 1147
Sigler, Russell, Chm. Bd.--Sigler & Reeves, Phoenix, AZ, pg. 1003
Sigurgeston, Hordur, Chm. Bd.--IceLandAir, New York, NY, pg. 561
Sill, Michael R., Chm. Bd. & Chief Exec. Officer--Road Machinery & Supplies Co., Savage, MN, pg. 937
Silver, J. Leonard, Chm. Bd., Pres. & Personnel Training & Devel.--Hoffritz for Cutlery, New York, NY, pg. 538
Silverberg, Joe, Chm. Bd.--Bigsby & Kruthers, Inc., Chicago, IL, pg. 150
Silverman, A.A., Chm. Bd., Pres. & Chief Exec. Officer--Vilter Manufacturing Corporation, Milwaukee, WI, pg. 1152
Silverman, Barry S., Chm. Bd.--The Jaydor Corporation, Millburn, NJ, pg. 591
Silverthorne, John H., Chm. Bd.--Pillowtex Corporation, Dallas, TX, pg. 870
Simkins, L.J., Chm. Bd., Pres., Chief Exec. & Chief Oper. Officer--Simkins Industries, Inc., New Haven, CT, pg. 1005
Simmons, Edward M., Chm. Bd. & Pres.--B. F. Trappey's Sons, Inc., New Iberia, LA, pg. 729
Simmons, Hardwick, Pres. & Chief Exec. Officer-Prudential Securities--The Prudential Insurance Company of America, Newark, NJ, pg. 896
Simmons, Harold C., Chm. Bd., Pres. & Chief Exec. Officer-Contran Corporation, Dallas, TX, pg. 281
Simmons, Jerry D., Chm. Bd. & Chief Exec. Officer--Simmons Oil Corp., Phoenix, AZ, pg. 1005
Simmons, John M., Chm. Bd.--Elberta Crate & Box Company, Bainbridge, GA, pg. 372
Simon, Alan D., Chm. Bd. & Pres.--Omaha Steaks International, Omaha, NE, pg. 825
Simon, Arthur, Chm. Bd. & Treas.--Eagle Button Co., Inc., Carlstadt, NJ, pg. 362
Simon, D., Chm. Bd.--Keiper Recaro, Inc., Clawson, MI, pg. 620
Simon, Donald A., Chm. Bd.--Kangaroos, USA Inc., Chesterfield, MO, pg. 616
Simon, Donald A., Chm. Bd.--Trans World Shoe Import Co., Inc., Chesterfield, MO, pg. 616
Simon, Donald R., Chm. Bd., Pres. & Treas.--Contractors Steel Company, Livonia, MI, pg. 280
Simon, Donald, Sr., Chm. Bd.--Serta Mattress Company, Vacaville, CA, pg. 991
Simon, Ernest M., Chm. & Chief Exec. Officer--Arrow Group Industries, Inc., Wayne, NJ, pg. 357
Simon, Frederick J., Chm. Bd. & Pres.--Omaha Creative Group, Omaha, NE, pg. 825
Simone, Michael J., Chm. Bd.--Ideal Forging Corporation, Southington, CT, pg. 562
Simons, Carl, Pres.--Gateway Apparel, Inc., Saint Louis, MO, pg. 445
Simonson, Edward A., Chm. Bd.--Mid America Steel, Inc., Fargo, ND, pg. 750
Simonson, Edward R., Chm. Bd.--Anson Industries, Inc., Melrose Park, IL, pg. 76
Simonson, Edward R., Chm.--Anning-Johnson Company, Melrose Park, IL, pg. 76
Simplot, J.R., Chm. Bd.--J.R. Simplot Company, Boise, ID, pg. 1007
Simpson, Roy, Chm. Bd.--Calico Corners, Kennett Square, PA, pg. 209
Singer, Sidney, Chm. Bd. & Chief Exec. Officer--Singers Supermarkets, Inc., North Bergen, NJ, pg. 1008
Sirotek, Robert L., Chm. Bd.--Illinois Auto Electric Co., Elmhurst, IL, pg. 562
Sirowitz, Leonard, Co-Chm. Bd. & Creative Dir.--Rosenfeld, Sirowitz, Humphrey & Strauss, Inc., New York, NY, pg. 948
Sitt, Celia, Chm. Bd.--Baby Togs, Inc., New York, NY, pg. 107
Sjogren, Walter R., Sr., Chm. Bd.--Whibco, Inc., Leesburg, NJ, pg. 1185
Skaggs, James B., Chm. Bd., Pres. & Chief Exec. Officer--Tracor, Inc., Austin, TX, pg. 1104
Skinner, Jas C., Chm. Bd.--Thomas & Skinner, Inc., Indianapolis, IN, pg. 1093
Skinner, Odie G., Chm. Bd. & Chief Exec. Officer--Skinner Corp., Lanett, AL, pg. 1009
Sklar, Irwin B., Chm. Bd.--Robert F. Driver Co., Inc., San Diego, CA, pg. 349
Skutt, Thomas J., Chm. Bd. & Chief Exec. Officer--Mutual of Omaha Insurance Company, Omaha, NE, pg. 779
Skutt, Thomas J., Chm. Bd.--Mutual of Omaha Fund Management Co., Omaha, NE, pg. 779
Skutt, Thomas J., Chm. Bd.--United World Life Insurance Company, Omaha, NE, pg. 779
Slade, Jarvis J., Chm. Bd.--MCRB Service Bureau, Inc., North Hollywood, CA, pg. 691
Slater, Elaine, Chm. Bd.--Wechsler Coffee Corp., Moonachie, NJ, pg. 1172
Slater, Thomas F., Chm., Pres. & Chief Exec. Officer--Actron Manufacturing Company, Cleveland, OH, pg. 15
Sleepec, William, Jr., Chm. Bd.--Sleepeck Printing Company, Bellwood, IL, pg. 1010
Sloan, Morton, Chm. Bd.--Inner Secrets, Inc., Hoboken, NJ, pg. 570
Sloan, O. Temple, Jr., Chm. Bd.--General Parts, Inc., Raleigh, NC, pg. 224
Slotkin, Roger, Chm. Bd.--Tuffy Associates Corp., Toledo, OH, pg. 1119
Slovin, Bruce, Chm.-Exec. Committee--Revlon, Inc., New York, NY, pg. 696
Small, Peter M., Chm. Bd.--Spaulding & Slye Company, Burlington, MA, pg. 1026
Smead, H.J., Chm. Bd., Pres., Chief Exec. & Chief Fin. Officer & Sec.--Kaiser Aerospace & Electronics Corp., Foster City, CA, pg. 614

Smilow, Joel E., Chm. Bd. & Chief Exec. Officer--Playtex FP Group Incorporated, Stamford, CT, pg. 877
Smilow, Joel E., Chm. & Chief Exec. Officer--Playtex Beauty Care, Inc., Stamford, CT, pg. 877
Smilow, Joel E., Chm. & Chief Exec. Officer--Playtex Family Products Corp., Stamford, CT, pg. 877
Smilowitz, Herbert, Chm. Bd.--Allied Building Products Corporation, East Rutherford, NJ, pg. 37
Smita, O.R., Chm. Bd. & Chief Exec. Officer--Marine Tech, Lancaster, PA, pg. 759
Smith, Anthony D., Chm. Bd.--Smith Valve Corporation, Whitinsville, MA, pg. 1014
Smith, Archie W., III, Chm. Bd.--Universal Construction Company, Kansas City, KS, pg. 1138
Smith, Arnold A., Chm. Bd.--Smith Pipe & Steel Co., Phoenix, AZ, pg. 1014
Smith, B.R., Jr., Chm. Bd. & Chief Exec. Officer--Sverdrup Corporation, Maryland Heights, MO, pg. 1065
Smith, B.R., Jr., Chm. Bd.--Sverdrup Investments, Inc., Maryland Heights, MO, pg. 1066
Smith, Dale E., Chm. Bd. & Pres.--Farm Journal, Inc., Philadelphia, PA, pg. 401
Smith, Daryl D., Pres. & Chief Exec. Officer--Troy Corporation, East Hanover, NJ, pg. 1116
Smith, David L., Chm. Bd. & Owner--Homestead House Inc., Broomfield, CO, pg. 542
Smith, Delford M., Chm. Bd.--Evergreen International Aviation, Inc., McMinnville, OR, pg. 392
Smith, Derrick A.M., Chm. Bd.--Whitin Roberts Mfg. Div., Sanford, NC, pg. 1187
Smith, Donald, Chm. Bd.--Tennessee Restaurant Corp., Itasca, IL, pg. 1087
Smith, Donald C., Chm. Bd.--Fitzgerald Advertising Inc., New Orleans, LA, pg. 416
Smith, Donald N., Chm. & Chief Exec. Officer--Perkins Family Restaurants, Memphis, TN, pg. 1088
Smith, E. G., Chm. Bd.--Terre Hill Concrete Products, Inc., Terre Hill, PA, pg. 1089
Smith, Edward C., Chm. Bd. & Chief Exec. Officer--Ben Venue Laboratories, Inc., Bedford, OH, pg. 138
Smith, Everett G., Chm. Bd.--Albert Trostel Packings, Ltd., Lake Geneva, WI, pg. 1116
Smith, Everett G., Chm. Bd.--Sivyer Steel Corporation, Bettendorf, IA, pg. 1013
Smith, Everett G. Smith, Chm. Bd.--Albert Trostel Packings Ltd., Lake Geneva, WI, pg. 1116
Smith, Ferdinand J., III, Chm. Bd., Pres., Chief Exec. Officer, Creative Dir.--Jay Incorporated, Rochester, NY, pg. 590
Smith, Gary W., Chm. Bd., Pres. & Chief Exec. Officer--Proto Systems of Atlanta, Alpharetta, GA, pg. 895
Smith, Gerald R., Chm. Bd. & New Bus. Contact--J. Richard Smith, Ltd., Melville, NY, pg. 1013
Smith, Gordon V., Chm. Bd.--Miller & Smith, Inc., McLean, VA, pg. 755
Smith, Gregory H., Chm. Bd. & Pres.--Maine Potato Growers, Inc., Presque Isle, ME, pg. 702
Smith, Harry, Chm. Bd.--Dealers Transport Company, Inc., Memphis, TN, pg. 322
Smith, Henry Dale, Chm. Bd.--J. M. Smith Corp., Spartanburg, SC, pg. 1012
Smith, Howard W., Chm. Bd.--Pawling Corporation, Pawling, NY, pg. 852
Smith, J. Morse, Chm. Bd. & Pres.--H.J. Baker & Bro., Inc., New York, NY, pg. 114
Smith, J. Neil, Chm. Bd., Pres. & Chief Exec. Officer--American Technical Services Group, Inc., Norcross, GA, pg. 63
Smith, James A., Jr., Chm. Bd.--Smith & Sons Foods, Inc., Macon, GA, pg. 1014
Smith, Joshua I., Chm. Bd. & Chief Exec. Officer--The Maxima Corporation, Lanham, MD, pg. 723
Smith, LeRoy T., Chm. Bd., Pres. & Chief Exec. Officer--S-T Industries, Inc., Saint James, MN, pg. 964
Smith, Michael L., Chm. Bd. & Chief Exec. Officer--Mayflower Transit, Inc., Carmel, IN, pg. 724
Smith, Michael L., Chm., Pres. & Chief Exec. Officer--Mayflower Transit, Inc., Carmel, IN, pg. 724
Smith, R. Scott, Chm. & Chief Exec. Officer--Mannington Mills, Inc., Salem, NJ, pg. 704
Smith, Russell G., Chm. Bd. & Pres.--Collegiate Concepts Inc., Tucker, GA, pg. 262
Smith, Stephen E., Chm. Bd. & Pres.--LSJ Sportswear Inc., Deerfield, WI, pg. 739
Smith, Stockton N., Chm. Bd. & Chief Exec. Officer--Atlantic Aviation Corp., New Castle, DE, pg. 94
Smith, Terrence L., Chm. Bd., Pres. & Chief Exec. Officer--California Hardware Co., City of Industry, CA, pg. 209
Smith, Thomas J., Chm. Bd.--Ketchum Advertising (Japan) Ltd., Tokyo, Japan, pg. 626
Smith, W.P., Chm. Bd.--Gold Kist, Inc., Atlanta, GA, pg. 465
Smith, William J., Chm. Bd., Pres. & Chief Exec. Officer--U.S. Can Company, Oak Brook, IL, pg. 1134
Smiy, Paul R., Chm. Bd. & Chief Exec. Officer--Elliott Company, Jeannette, PA, pg. 378
Smoler, Jerome, Chm. Bd.--Wicker Park L.P., Chicago, IL, pg. 1188
Smulowitz, William, Chm., Pres. & Chief Exec. Officer--The Lion, Inc. (Gibbons-Stegmaier Brewery), Wilkes-Barre, PA, pg. 677
Smyth, John M., Chm. Bd.--John M. Smyth Co., Downers Grove, IL, pg. 1014
Smythe, Thomas M., Chm Bd. & Pres.--Keller Crescent Co., Evansville, IN, pg. 620
Snarr, L. Glen, Chm., Exec. Comm. & Dir.--EvansGroup, Salt Lake City, UT, pg. 390
Snavely, Christian M., Chm. Bd.--Snavely Forest Products, Inc., Pittsburgh, PA, pg. 1015
Snediker, R.R., Chm. Bd.--Chicago Show Printing Co., Morton Grove, IL, pg. 246
Snodgrass, Jim, Chm. Bd. & Pres.--The Stiffel Company, Chicago, IL, pg. 1049
Snowden, William F., Chm. Bd., Pres. & Chief Exec. Officer--Topline Imports, Inc., Bellevue, WA, pg. 1102
Snowdon, Clive, Chm. Bd.--Teca Corporation, Pleasantville, NY, pg. 1082
Snyder, G. Whitney, Chm. Bd.--Shenango Furnace Company, Princeton, NJ, pg. 997
Snyder, H. Hammond, Chm. Bd.--Robinson Export-Import Corporation, Springfield, VA, pg. 748
Snyder, Louis H., Chm. Bd. & Chief Exec. Officer--Snyder-Diamond, Santa Monica, CA, pg. 1015
Snyder, Richard W., Chm. Bd. & Chief Exec. Officer--SnyderGeneral Corporation, Dallas, TX, pg. 1015
Snyder, Shirley M., Chm. Bd.--Snyder Brothers, Inc., Minneapolis, MN, pg. 1015
Snyder, Steve, Chm.--DSIC/TMP Worldwide, Clawson, MI, pg. 1074
Sobel, Seymour, Chm. Bd.--Land N Sea, Inc., New York, NY, pg. 653
Soehnlen, Leo, Chm. Bd.--Superior Dairy, Inc., Canton, OH, pg. 1063
Soesanto, Hendra, Chm. & Fin. Dir.--Metro, Jakarta,, Indonesia, pg. 331
Sohl, John F., Chm. Bd.--Auto Driveaway Co., Chicago, IL, pg. 100
Solloway, Erwine, Chm. Bd. & Pres.--ACR Mechanical Corporation, Orange, CA, pg. 2
Solombrino, Scott, Chm. Bd., Pres. & Chief Exec. Officer--Dav-El Services, Inc., New York, NY, pg. 317
Solomon, Jerry L., Chm. Bd.--American Fluorescent Corporation, Waukegan, IL, pg. 54
Solomon, Robert, Chm. Bd., Pres. & Chief Exec. Officer--Dakin, Inc., Burlingame, CA, pg. 311
Solomon, Robert B., Chm. Bd. & Pres.--Robert Solomon & Associates Adv. Inc., Bloomfield Hills, MI, pg. 1017
Sommers, Joseph F., Chm. Bd.--Allied Printing Services, Inc., Manchester, CT, pg. 38
Sondhi, Vir K., Chm. Bd. & Pres.--National Solvent Corporation, Medina, OH, pg. 793
Sorenson, E.R., Exec. V.P.--H.D. Hudson Manufacturing Company, Chicago, IL, pg. 551
Sorrentino, Stanley L., Chm. Bd., Chief Exec. Officer & Treas.--Uncas Manufacturing Company, Providence, RI, pg. 1125
Soultanian, Sarkis, Chm. & Pres.--National Utility Service, Inc., Park Ridge, NJ, pg. 794
Spangler, F. Earl, Chm. Bd.--Spangler, Inc., Kansas City, KS, pg. 1025
Spanos, Alex G., Chm. Bd.--A. G. Spanos Development, Inc., Stockton, CA, pg. 1025
Spatz, William, Chm. Bd. & Chief Exec. Officer--Spatz & Co., Northbrook, IL, pg. 1026
Spear, Kenneth H., Chm. Bd., Pres. & Chief Exec. Officer--Del-Val Manufacturing Company, Warminster, PA, pg. 325
Spector, Michael J., Chm. Bd. & Pres., & Chief Exec. Officer--Margo Nursery Farms, Inc., Miami, FL, pg. 706
Speh, Albert J., Jr., Chm. Bd. & Pres.--May & Speh, Inc., Downers Grove, IL, pg. 724
Spelde, M.E., Chm. Bd., Pres. & Chief Exec. Officer--Empire Airlines, Hayden Lake, ID, pg. 379
Spelleri, Richard, Chm. Bd.--A.P.S., Inc., Houston, TX, pg. 5
Spence, Charles L., Chm. Bd.--Pacific Lumber & Shipping Co., Seattle, WA, pg. 840
Spence, Jeffrey E., Chm. Bd., Pres., Controller & Chief Exec. & Fin. Officer--Controlled Systems of Wisconsin, Inc., Nashotah, WI, pg. 281
Spencer, Guy J., Jr., Chm. Bd., Pres. & Chief Exec. Officer--Spencer Companies Inc., Huntsville, AL, pg. 1030
Sperber, Burton S., Chm. Bd., Pres. , & Chief Exec. Officer--Environmental Industries, Inc., Calabasas, CA, pg. 383
Sperber, Martin, Chm. Bd. & Pres.--Schein Pharmaceutical, Inc., Port Washington, NY, pg. 975
Sperger, Courtland, Chm. Bd.--Alto Dairy Cooperative, Waupun, WI, pg. 45
Sperry, Allen M., Chm. Bd.--The Turner & Seymour Mfg. Company, Torrington, CT, pg. 1119
Speyer, Lester D., Chm. Bd.--Tennsco Corporation, Dickson, TN, pg. 1088
Spielvogel, Carl, Chm. & Chief Exec. Officer--Backer Spielvogel Bates Worldwide, Inc., New York, NY, pg. 108
Spielvogel, Carl, Chm. & Chief Exec. Officer (BSB Worldwide Inc.)--BSB Japan Ltd., Tokyo, Japan, pg. 110
Spiewak, Gerald, Chm. Bd.--I. Spiewak & Sons, Inc., New York, NY, pg. 1031
Spiro, Walter A., Chm.--Earle Palmer Brown & Spiro, Philadelphia, PA, pg. 182
Sport, Michael C., Chm. Bd., Pres. & Chief Exec. Officer--Production Management Companies, Inc., Harvey, LA, pg. 893
Springborn, Robert C., Chm. Bd., Pres. Chief Exec. Officer--Springborn Laboratories, Inc., Enfield, CT, pg. 1033
Springer, George E., Chm. Bd.--Springer Schmid Group, Beachwood, OH, pg. 1033
Sprole, Robert R., II, Chm. Bd. & Pres.--Therm, Inc., Ithaca, NY, pg. 1090
Srere, Linda J., Chm.--Earle Palmer Brown/New York, New York, NY, pg. 182
St. Jacques, Robert, Chm. Bd.--Ocean Spray Cranberries, Inc., Lakeville, MA, pg. 820
Staab, Walter, Chm. & Pres.--SFM Media Corporation, New York, NY, pg. 962
Stabler, Donald B., Chm. Bd.--Stabler Companies, Inc., Harrisburg, PA, pg. 1034
Stabler, Donald B., Chm. Bd. & Pres.--Stabler Construction Company, Harrisburg, PA, pg. 1034
Stadelman, Russell C., Sr., Chm. Bd. & Treas.--Russell Stadèlman & Company, Germantown, TN, pg. 1034
Stading, Donald C., Chm. Bd.--The William Bayley Co., Springfield, OH, pg. 128
Staffa, Donald J., Chm.--Quality Medical Adjudication, Inc., Rancho Cordova, CA, pg. 521
Stafford, John, Chm. Bd.--Printco, Inc., Greenville, MI, pg. 891
Stager, Donald K., Chm. Bd., Pres. & Chief Exec. Officer--Dillingham Construction Corporation, Pleasanton, CA, pg. 337
Stahmann, William J., Chm. Bd.--Stahmann Farms, Inc., Las Cruces, NM, pg. 1034
Stamatakis, Alex, Chm. & Pres.--Construction Machinery Company, Waterloo, IA, pg. 277
Standen, Michael, Chm., Pres. & Chief Exec. Officer--Metallurg, Inc., New York, NY, pg. 742
Standish, Jay C., Chm. Bd.--Classic Markets Corp., Norcross, GA, pg. 253
Stangl, Peter E., Chm. & Chief Exec. Officer--Metropolitan Transportation Authority, New York, NY, pg. 745
Stanley, David, Chm. Bd. & Chief Exec. Officer--Payless Cashways, Inc., Kansas City, MO, pg. 853
Stanley, John W., Chm. Bd.--Blue Ridge Transfer Co., Roanoke, VA, pg. 161
Stanley, Olin B., Chm. Bd.--Stanley Stores Inc., Bay City, TX, pg. 1038
Stanley, Richard H., Chm. Bd.--Stanley Consultants, Inc., Muscatine, IA, pg. 961
Stansberry, Warren H., Jr., Chm. Bd.--Stanco Metal Products, Inc., Grand Haven, MI, pg. 1035
Stanton, Eric, Co-Chm. Bd.--Simon Marketing, Inc., Los Angeles, CA, pg. 1006
Stanton, Ronald, Chm. Bd. & Chief Exec. Officer--Transammonia Inc., New York, NY, pg. 1106
Stark, Bill, Chm. Bd. & Pres.--Semco, Inc., Houston, TX, pg. 989
Stark, Douglas A., Chm. Bd. & Chief Exec. Officer--Thrifty Drug Stores, Inc., Minneapolis, MN, pg. 1096
Stashower, David L., Chm. & Chief Exec. Officer--Liggett-Stashower, Inc., Cleveland, OH, pg. 675
Stasior, William F., Chm. Bd. & Chief Exec. Officer--Booz Allen & Hamilton Inc., New York, NY, pg. 165
Staudt, Eugene, Chm. Bd. & Chief Exec. Officer--Castro Convertible Corporation, New Hyde Park, NY, pg. 229
Stauffer, John H., Chm. Bd. & Pres.--Stauffer Communications, Inc., Topeka, KS, pg. 1042
Stayer, Ralph, Chm. Bd.--Perri Sausage, Inc., New Haven, CT, pg. 601
Stayer, Ralph F., Chm. Bd.--Johnsonville Foods, Inc., Kohler, WI, pg. 601
Steadman, Jack, Chm. Bd.--Kansas City Chiefs Football Club, Kansas City, MO, pg. 616
Steedman, Donald, Chm. Bd. & Pres.--Littleford Day, Taylor-Stiles Division, Florence, KY, pg. 679
Steele, Carolyn S., Co-Chm.--Skinner Corp., Lanett, AL, pg. 1009
Steele, Lewis M., Chm. Bd.--W. L. Hailey & Company, Inc., Nashville, TN, pg. 500
Steen, A.B., Chm Bd.--T.D. Williamson, Inc., Tulsa, OK, pg. 1192
Steigerwaldt, Donna Wolf, Chm. & Chief Exec. Officer--Jockey International, Inc., Kenosha, WI, pg. 595
Stein, Dr. Sidney J., Chm. Bd., Chief Exec. Officer--Electro-Science Laboratories, Inc., King of Prussia, PA, pg. 375
Stein, Isaac, Chm. Bd.--Esprit de Corp., San Francisco, CA, pg. 388
Stein, Joan W., Chm. Bd.--Regency Group Inc., Jacksonville, FL, pg. 922
Steinback, Kenneth, Chm. Bd. & Chief Exec. Officer--Computer Sales International Inc., Saint Louis, MO, pg. 271
Steinhart, Ronald G., Chm. Bd. & Chief Exec. Officer--Team Bancshares, Inc., Dallas, TX, pg. 1082
Steinhauer, Frederick C., Chm. Bd. & Pres.--Madison Dairy Produce Company, Madison, WI, pg. 699
Steinmetz, William A., Chm. Bd.--Tiernay Metals, Inc., Redondo Beach, CA, pg. 1096
Steiny, John O., Chm. Bd.--Steiny & Company, Inc., Los Angeles, CA, pg. 1049
Stempler, Gerald L., Chm. Bd.--Textilease Corporation, Beltsville, MD, pg. 1090
Stephens, Elton B., Chm. Bd.--Ebsco Industries, Inc., Birmingham, AL, pg. 365
Stephens, Jackson T., Chm. Bd.--Stephens, Inc., Little Rock, AR, pg. 1046
Stephens, Stephen W., Chm. Bd.--Vernay Laboratories, Inc., Yellow Springs, OH, pg. 1148
Stephenson, James M. Jr., Chm. Bd. & Pres.--Kinetic Systems Corporation, Lockport, IL, pg. 630
Stephenson, Paul W., Chm. Bd.--United Tectonic Industry, Harrisburg, PA, pg. 1137
Stern, H. Peter, Chm. Bd.--Star Expansion Company, Mountainville, NY, pg. 1039
Stern, Leonard, Chm. Bd.--Hartz Group, New York, NY, pg. 514
Stern, Leonard, Chm.--Hartz Mountain Group, Harrison, NJ, pg. 514
Stern, Leonard N., Chm. Bd. & Chief Exec. Officer--The Hartz Mountain Corp., Harrison, NJ, pg. 514
Stern, Leonard N., Chm. Bd.--VV Publishing Corp., New York, NY, pg. 1142
Stern, Nelson M., Chm.--Stern Advertising, Inc., Pepper Pike, OH, pg. 1047
Sternberg, Sheldon, Chm. Bd. & Pres.--Best Kosher Sausage Co., Chicago, IL, pg. 146
Steuart, Curtis, Chm. Bd.--Steuart Investment Co., Washington, DC, pg. 1048
Steuart, Leonard P., Chm. Bd.--Steuart Petroleum Company, Washington, DC, pg. 1048
Steurer, Joe, Chm. & Chief Exec. Officer--Jofco Inc., Jasper, IN, pg. 595
Stevens, Deane, Chm. Bd.--International Cold Storage Co., Inc., Andover, KS, pg. 576
Stevens, Frank P., Chm. Bd., Pres., Treas., Chief Exec. Officer & Chief Fin. Officer--Professional Travel, Inc., Dalton, GA, pg. 894
Stevens, J.B., Chm. Bd.--Davis Electrical Constructors, Inc., Greenville, SC, pg. 318
Stevenson, Charles E., Jr., Chm., Pres. & Chief Exec. Officer--CEBCOR (Consolidated Employment Benefits Corp.), Chicago, IL, pg. 230

Steves, Marshall T., Sr., Chm. Bd.--Steves & Sons, San Antonio, TX, pg. 1048
Stewart, Andrew K., Chm. Bd., Pres. & Chief Exec. Officer--Computer Methods Corporation, Livonia, MI, pg. 271
Stewart, James, Chm. Bd. & Pres.--Consolidated Co-op, Gowrie, IA, pg. 276
Stewart, John D., Chm. Bd.--The Bureau of National Affairs, Inc., Washington, DC, pg. 189
Stewart, Richard, Chm., Pres. & Chief Exec. Officer--Praxis International Inc., Cambridge, MA, pg. 884
Stewart, Robert L., Chm. Bd. & Pres.--Honorbuilt Industries, Inc., Minneapolis, KS, pg. 542
Stewart, Robert M., Sr., Chm. Bd. & Chief Exec. Officer--Remarks, Inc., Dublin, OH, pg. 925
Stewart, Thomas J., Chm. Bd.--Food Services of America, Seattle, WA, pg. 423
Stiefel, W.K., Chm. & Pres.--Stiefel Laboratories, Inc., Coral Gables, FL, pg. 1048
Stihl, Hans Peter, Chm. Bd.--Stihl Inc., Virginia Beach, VA, pg. 1049
Stillman, Walter R., Chm. Bd. & Pres.--Stillman & Hoag, Inc., Englewood, NJ, pg. 1049
Stitzlein, H.P., Chm.--Malone Advertising, Inc., Akron, OH, pg. 703
Stockel, Neil, Chm. Bd.--Carquest Corporation, Tarrytown, NY, pg. 224
Stocks, Thomas D., III, Chm. & Chief Exec. Officer--Rustco Products Company, Denver, CO, pg. 957
Stocks, Thomas D., III, Chm. Bd. & Chief Exec. Officer--Park Corporation, Barrington, IL, pg. 849
Stogel, Philip, Chm.--The Stogel Companies Inc., New York, NY, pg. 1050
Stoll, Howard E., Chm. Bd.--Plymouth Creameries, Inc., Plymouth, WI, pg. 877
Stommen, Clair E., Chm. Bd.--Lutheran Brotherhood, Minneapolis, MN, pg. 688
Stone, Andrew L., Chm. Bd., Pres. & Chief Exec. Officer--K-D Lamp Company, Cincinnati, OH, pg. 612
Stone, Charles G., Chm., Pres. & Chief Exec. Officer--Stone & Simons Advertising, Inc., Southfield, MI, pg. 1051
Stone, Eugene E., III, Chm. Bd.--Stone Manufacturing Company, Inc., Greenville, SC, pg. 1051
Stone, Harold, Chm. Bd.--West Coast National Video, Philadelphia, PA, pg. 1177
Stone, James W., Chm. Bd.--Stones, Inc., Bainbridge, GA, pg. 1051
Stone, John McWilliams, Jr., Chm. Bd. & Chief Exec. Officer--Dukane Corporation, Saint Charles, IL, pg. 351
Stone, Ronald I., Chm.--Stone, August, Baker Communications Companies, Troy, MI, pg. 1050
Stork, H. Donald, Chm. Bd.--Stonhard, Inc., Maple Shade, NJ, pg. 1051
Stover, W. Robert, Chm. Bd. & Chief Exec. Officer--Western Temporary Services, Inc., Walnut Creek, CA, pg. 1181
Strachen, John R., Chm. Bd.--Pepsi-Cola Albany Bottling Co., Inc., Latham, NY, pg. 860
Strahman, Herman, Jr., Chm. Bd. & Pres.--Strahman Valves, Inc., Florham Park, NJ, pg. 1052
Strand, Roger, Chm. Bd.--Tree Top, Inc., Selah, WA, pg. 1109
Stratton, James W., Chm. Bd., Pres. & Chief Exec. Officer--Stratton Management Company, Plymouth Meeting, PA, pg. 1053
Stratton, James W., Chm. Bd. & Chief Exec. Officer--Stratton Growth Fund, Inc., Plymouth Meeting, PA, pg. 1053
Stratton, James W., Chm. Bd. & Chief Exec. Officer--Stratton Monthly Dividend Shares, Inc., Plymouth Meeting, PA, pg. 1053
Straube, Win, Chm. Bd.--Pegasus International Corporation, Pennington, NJ, pg. 855
Strauce, David, Chm. Bd. & Pres.--Key Container Corporation, Pawtucket, RI, pg. 626
Straus, David J., Chm. Bd. & Chief Exec. Officer--STRAFCO, Inc., San Antonio, TX, pg. 1052
Straus, Joseph, Jr., Chm. Bd.--Strouse Greenberg & Co., Inc., Philadelphia, PA, pg. 1054
Strauss, Harold L., Co-Chm. Bd. & Opers.--Rosenfeld, Sirowitz, Humphrey & Strauss, Inc., New York, NY, pg. 948
Street, Gordon P., Jr., Chm. Bd., Pres. & Chief Exec. & Chief Oper. Officer--North American Royalties, Inc., Chattanooga, TN, pg. 811
Streety, Keith, Chm. Bd.--Plains Co-op Oil Mill, Lubbock, TX, pg. 873
Streur, Harold, Chm. Bd.--Castex Industries Inc., Holland, MI, pg. 228
Strickland, Vernon B., Chm. Bd.--Hawthorne Corp., Charleston, SC, pg. 518
Strickler, R.H., Chm. Bd.--Rocco Inc., Harrisonburg, VA, pg. 940
Strike, George L., Chm. Bd.--American Laundry Machinery Inc., Cincinnati, OH, pg. 57
Strike, George L., Chm. Bd.--One Hour Martinizing Dry Cleaning Franchise (System), Cincinnati, OH, pg. 826
Strite, Lewis E., Chm. Bd. & Chief Exec. Officer--Shenandoah Mfg. Co. Inc., Harrisonburg, VA, pg. 997
Strmotich, George M., Chm. Bd.--Up-Right, Inc., Selma, CA, pg. 1139
Stroh, Peter W., Chm. Bd. & Chief Exec. Officer--The Stroh Brewery Company, Detroit, MI, pg. 1053
Stroud, Bill, Chm. Bd. & Chief Exec. Officer--Strouds, City of Industry, CA, pg. 1054
Stuart, Thomas, Chm. Bd. & Chief Exec. Officer--Bureau of Engraving, Minneapolis, MN, pg. 189
Stumpf, Charles T., Chm. Bd., Pres., Chief Exec. Officer & Treas.--Financial Associates, Overland Park, KS, pg. 410
Sturm, Arthur C., Jr., Chm. Bd. & Pres.--The Sturm Communications Group, Inc., Chicago, IL, pg. 1055
Stusser, Herbert C., Chm. Bd.--Stusser Electric Company, Seattle, WA, pg. 1055
Styslinger, Lee J., Jr., Chm. Bd.--Altec Industries, Inc., Birmingham, AL, pg. 45
Suddath, Stephen M., Chm. Bd.--The Suddath Companies, Jacksonville, FL, pg. 1055
Sugarman, Joseph, Chm. Bd.--JS&A Group, Inc., Las Vegas, NV, pg. 586
Sugarman, Leonard, Chm. Bd., Pres. & Chief Exec. Officer--Statler Industries, Medford, MA, pg. 1041
Suissa, David, Chm.--Suissa/Miller, Santa Monica, CA, pg. 1056
Sukenik, John, Chm. Bd.--Pike & Fischer, Bethesda, MD, pg. 190
Sullivan, B.J., Chm. & Chief Exec. Officer--Byron Weston Paper Co., Dalton, MA, pg. 296
Sullivan, Charles, Chm. Bd.--Association of Credit Union League Executives, Madison, WI, pg. 298
Sullivan, James, Chm. Bd., Pres. & Chief Exec. Officer--Sullivan Holding Company, Brentwood, TN, pg. 1056
Sullivan, James, Chm. Bd.--Sullivan Graphics, Brentwood, TN, pg. 1057
Sullivan, James E., Chm. Bd.--Pacor, Inc., Philadelphia, PA, pg. 842
Sullivan, Richard S., Chm. Bd.--Sullivan Paper Company, West Springfield, MA, pg. 1057
Sullivan, Robert E., Chm. & Chief Exec. Officer--Lord, Sullivan & Yoder, Inc. Advertising, Columbus, OH, pg. 683
Sullivan, Robert J., Chm. Bd. & Chief Exec. Officer--G. R. Herberger's, Inc., Saint Cloud, MN, pg. 530
Sultivan, John, Chm. Bd.--Prince Manufacturing, Inc., Lawrenceville, NJ, pg. 890
Summerfield, Arthur E., Jr., Chm. Bd. & Pres.--Summerfield Truck Co. Inc., Portage, IN, pg. 1057
Summerford, Harold C., Chm. Bd.--United Piece Dye Works, LP, Princeton Junction, NJ, pg. 1134
Sunderland, Neil, Chm. Bd.--Bridgewater Resources Corporation, Beverly Hills, CA, pg. 175
Sunderland, Robert, Chm. Bd.--Ash Grove Cement Company, Overland Park, KS, pg. 87
Sundt, H. Wilson, Chm. Bd. & Chief Exec. Officer--Sundt Corp., Tucson, AZ, pg. 1060
Surdam, John L., Chm. Bd.--Osmose Wood Preserving Co., Buffalo, NY, pg. 830
Sussen, Joseph J., Chm. Bd.--Sussen, Inc., Cleveland, OH, pg. 225
Sutherland, Donald, Chm. Bd.--Career Club Shirt Co., New York, NY, pg. 898
Sutter, C. Fain, Sr., Chm. Bd.--Fisheries Supply Company, Seattle, WA, pg. 415
Sutter, Lynn R., Chm. Bd. & Pres.--Sutter/Martin, Inc., Buffalo Grove, IL, pg. 1065
Sutton, Thomas C., Chm. Bd. & Chief Exec. Officer--Pacific Mutual Life Insurance Company, Newport Beach, CA, pg. 841
Swain, D. Billings, Chm. Bd.--KCL Corporation, Shelbyville, IN, pg. 611
Swain, Robert D., Chm. Bd.--Chroma Corporation, McHenry, IL, pg. 249
Swallen, Donald, Chm. Bd., Pres.& Chief Exec. Officer--Swallen's, Inc., Cincinnati, OH, pg. 1066
Swalm, Dave C., Chm. Bd. & Chief Exec. Officer--Texas Olefins Co., Houston, TX, pg. 1089
Swank, Richard B., Chm. Bd. & Chief Exec. Officer--Advanstar Communications, Cleveland, OH, pg. 21
Swank, Richard B., Chm. Bd.--Beckley-Cardy, Inc., Duluth, MN, pg. 21
Swanson, W.M. "Gus", Chm.--Swanson Russell Associates, Lincoln, NE, pg. 1066
Swartz, Thomas B., Chm. Bd. & Chief Exec. Officer--The Sierra Capital Companies, San Francisco, CA, pg. 1002
Swayne, Amos, Chm. Bd.--Case-Swayne Co. Inc., Santa Ana, CA, pg. 228
Sween, Tom, Chm. Bd. & Chief Exec. Officer--E.A. Sween Company, Eden Prairie, MN, pg. 1066
Sweig, Morton A, Chm. Bd. & Chief Exec. Officer--National Cleaning Contractors, Inc., New York, NY, pg. 786
Swift, Charles O., Chm. Bd. & Pres.--Swift Dodge Rolls Royce Inc., Sacramento, CA, pg. 1067
Swift, George P., Jr., Chm. Bd. & Chief Exec. Officer--Columbus Mills, Inc., Columbus, GA, pg. 267
Swift, M. Allen, Chm. Bd., Pres. & Treas.--M. Swift & Sons Inc., Hartford, CT, pg. 1068
Swift, Vince, Chm.--Leo Burnett Ltd. Thailand, Bangkok, Thailand, pg. 193
Swigert, Henry T., Chm. Bd.--Esco Corporation, Portland, OR, pg. 388
Swinehart, Keith, Sr., Chm. Bd., Chief Exec. Officer & Chief Fin. Officer--Vanguard Plastics, Inc., McPherson, KS, pg. 1145
Swisher, Glenn, Chm. Bd. & Chief Exec. Officer--Syndicate Systems, Inc., Indianapolis, IN, pg. 1069
Swope, Samuel G., Chm. Bd.--Swope Automotive Group, Inc., Louisville, KY, pg. 1068
Syar, C.M., Chm. Bd.--Syar Industries, Inc., Napa, CA, pg. 1068
Sym-Smith, Ian, Chm. Bd.--Rural Metro Corporation, Scottsdale, AZ, pg. 956
Synott, Lee, Chm. Bd., Pres. & Chief Exec. Officer--Ingram Book Company, La Vergne, TN, pg. 569
Tabor, Jon K., Chm. Bd., Pres. & Chief Exec. Officer--Allied Mineral Products, Inc., Columbus, OH, pg. 38
Taddei, Armando, Chm. Bd., Pres. & Treas.--Hunter Contracting Company, Gilbert, AZ, pg. 554
Tahan, W.N., Chm. & Chief Exec. Officer--Bromar Inc., Newport Beach, CA, pg. 179
Tait, John E., Chm. Bd., Pres. & Chief Exec. Officer--The Penn Mutual Life Insurance Company, Philadelphia, PA, pg. 858
Takatta, James, Chm. Bd.--Takatta Inc., Olympia Fields, IL, pg. 1076
Tako, Anthony, Chm. Bd. & Pres.--Gerrard and Company, Des Plaines, IL, pg. 454
Talley, Willie, Chm. Bd., Pres. & Chief Exec. Officer--ColorTyme, Inc., Athens, TX, pg. 265
Tallichet, David C., Jr., Chm. Bd., Pres. & Chief Exec. Officer--Specialty Restaurants Corporation, Anaheim, CA, pg. 1027
Talmage, Frank B., Chm. Bd. & Chief Exec. Officer--Superior Reprographics, Seattle, WA, pg. 1064
Tananbaum, Stanley, Chm. Bd. & Chief Exec. Officer--Century Business Credit Corporation, New York, NY, pg. 235
Tang, Cyrus, Chm. Bd., Pres., & Chief Exec. Officer--Tang Industries Inc., Elk Grove Village, IL, pg. 1078
Tang, Oscar L., Chm. & Pres.--KOA Holdings, New York, NY, pg. 612
Taniguchi, Hidetoshi, Chm. Bd.--Puna Plantation Hawaii Ltd., Hilo, HI, pg. 900
Tanner, H. Max, Chm. Bd.--Owners Insurance Co., Lima, OH, pg. 100
Tanner, Simpson B., III, Chm. Bd.--Tanner Co. Inc., Rutherfordton, NC, pg. 1078
Tarantino, Dominic A., Co-Chm.--Price Waterhouse - U.S., New York, NY, pg. 888
Taratoot, Louis J., Chm., Pres. & Chief Exec. Officer--Taracorp, Inc., Atlanta, GA, pg. 1078
Tarlow, Arthur S., Sr., Chm. Bd.--Alden Shoe Co., Inc., Middleboro, MA, pg. 33
Tarrant, R. Lane, Chm. Bd., Pres. & Chief Exec. Officer--Tarrant Service Agency, Inc., Louisville, KY, pg. 1079
Tash, Ralph, Chm. Bd.--Tash, Inc., Des Plaines, IL, pg. 1080
Tattersall, Keith, Chm. Bd., Pres. & Chief Exec. Officer--Amperif Corporation, Chatsworth, CA, pg. 68
Tauber, Joel D., Chm. Bd.--Keywell Corporation, Detroit, MI, pg. 629
Tauber, Joel D., Chm. Bd.--Key Manufacturing Group, Inc., Royal Oak, MI, pg. 627
Tauscher, William Y., Chm. Bd.--Regency Lincoln Mercury, Dallas, TX, pg. 922
Taylor, Benton E., Chm. Bd.--Taylor-Morley, Inc., Saint Louis, MO, pg. 1081
Taylor, Cyril J.H., Chm. Bd.--American Institute For Foreign Study, Greenwich, CT, pg. 56
Taylor, Cyril J.H., Chm. & Chief Exec. Officer--American Institute for Foreign Study, London, United Kingdom, pg. 56
Taylor, Glen A., Chm. Bd. & Chief Exec. Officer--Taylor Corporation, Mankato, MN, pg. 1081
Taylor, Harry, Chm. Bd. & Pres.--Republic Telcom Systems Corporation, Boulder, CO, pg. 928
Taylor, Jack, Chm. Bd.--Alabama Electric Cooperative, Inc., Andalusia, AL, pg. 28
Taylor, Jack C., Chm. Bd.--Enterprise Rent-A-Car Company, Saint Louis, MO, pg. 382
Taylor, John A., Chm. Bd.--Taylor Oil Co. Inc., Winston-Salem, NC, pg. 1082
Taylor, Kenneth N., Chm. Bd.--Tyndale House Publishers, Inc., Carol Stream, IL, pg. 1122
Taylor, Larry, Chm. Bd.--Taylor-Smith Group, Houston, TX, pg. 1082
Taylor, Lucian W., Chm. Bd.--Velcon Filters, Inc., San Jose, CA, pg. 1146
Taylor, Sidney J., Chm. Bd. & Chief Exec. Officer--Cole Taylor Financial Group, Wheeling, IL, pg. 260
Taylor, Sidney J., Chm. Bd. & Chief Exec. Officer--Cole Taylor/Yorktown, Lombard, IL, pg. 260
Taylor, Stanley R., Chm. Bd.--U.S. Furniture Industries, Inc., High Point, NC, pg. 1136
Taylor, W.A., Jr., Chm. Bd.--Taylor Machine Works, Inc., Louisville, MS, pg. 1081
Taylor, William W., Chm. Bd.--Taylor Associates, Cedar Rapids, IA, pg. 751
Teater, David, Chm. & Chief Exec. Officer--Sefton Associates Inc., Grand Rapids, MI, pg. 987
Tecot, Stephen L., Chm. Bd.--Tecot Electric Supply Company, New Castle, DE, pg. 1084
Teel, Edwin A., Chm. Bd.--Vita-Milk Dairy, Inc., Seattle, WA, pg. 1153
Teel, James E., Co-Chm. Bd. & Chief Oper. Officer--Raley's, West Sacramento, CA, pg. 910
Teel, Joyce N., Co-Chm. Bd.--Raley's, West Sacramento, CA, pg. 910
Teiger, David, Chm. Bd.--Gemini Consulting, Morristown, NJ, pg. 448
Templeton, John, Chm. Bd.--Templeton, Kenly & Co., Inc., Broadview, IL, pg. 1086
Tendler, Stanley, Chm. Bd. & Chief Exec. Officer--Kennington Ltd., Inc., Los Angeles, CA, pg. 623
Tenenbaum, Joseph M., Chm. Bd.--A. Tenenbaum Co. Inc., North Little Rock, AR, pg. 1087
Terlip, Robert, Chm. Bd.--Strongheart Products, Inc., Kansas City, KS, pg. 1054
Terlizzi, Nick, Jr., Chm. Bd.--Ballet Makers, Inc., Totowa, NJ, pg. 116
Terpak, John B., Sr., Chm. Bd.--York Barbell Co., Inc., York, PA, pg. 1208
Teruya, Harold S., Chm. Bd.--Armstrong Produce Ltd., Honolulu, HI, pg. 84
Teruya, Raymond, Chm. Bd. & Chief Exec. Officer--Teruya Bros., Ltd., Honolulu, HI, pg. 1089
Terwillger, Dennis, Chm. Bd. & Pres.--Condere Corporation, Hamden, CT, pg. 273
Teti, Joseph A., Jr., Chm. Bd.--La France Corporation, Philadelphia, PA, pg. 649
Thacher, Carter P., Chm. Bd.--Wilbur-Ellis Company & Connell Brothers Company, San Francisco, CA, pg. 1189
Thalheimer, Louis B., Chief Exec. Officer & Chm. Bd.--American Trading and Production Corporation, Baltimore, MD, pg. 64
Thatcher, J.W., Chm. Bd.--SCT Yarns, Inc., Chattanooga, TN, pg. 961
Theis, Willis C., Chm. Bd.--Simonds-Shields-Theis Grain Co., Kansas City, MO, pg. 1006
Theofilos, Steve P., Chm. Bd., Pres. & Chief Exec. Officer--Theochem Labs., Inc., Tampa, FL, pg. 1090
Thiele, Paul F., Chm. Bd. & Chief Exec. Officer--Thiele Kaolin Co., Sandersville, GA, pg. 1092

Thoma, Carl, Chm. Bd.--DIMAC Corporation, Bridgeton, MO, pg. 338
Thomas, Bob, Chm.--Bob Thomas & Associates, Inc. Public Relations, Venice, CA, pg. 244
Thomas, Bryan, Chm. Bd., Pres. & New Bus. Contact--Thomas & Perkins, Denver, CO, pg. 1093
Thomas, Charles F., Chm. Bd.--Charlie Thomas Auto World, Houston, TX, pg. 1092
Thomas, G. N., Chm. Bd., Pres., Chief Exec. Officer, Chief Fin. Officer & Treas.--A. Levy & J. Zentner Co., Sacramento, CA, pg. 671
Thomas, John W., Jr., Chm. Bd. & Chief Exec. Officer--Thomas Built Buses, Inc., High Point, NC, pg. 1092
Thomas, Terence W., Chm. Bd. & Pres.--Arizona Wholesale Supply Company, Phoenix, AZ, pg. 82
Thomas, Terry, Chm. Bd.--National Brands, Inc., Phoenix, AZ, pg. 786
Thomopulos, Gregs G., Chm. Bd. & Pres.--Middle West Service Company, Muscatine, IA, pg. 961
Thompson, Bryan.E., Chm. Bd. & Pres.--Quintron Systems, Inc., Santa Maria, CA, pg. 905
Thompson, Clarence, Chm. Bd.--Colle & McVoy, Inc., Minneapolis, MN, pg. 261
Thompson, D.T., Chm. Bd.--Whisper Soft Mills Inc., New York, NY, pg. 1185
Thompson, Dennis O., Chm. Bd.--Thompson Enterprises Inc., Minnetonka, MN, pg. 1094
Thompson, F.L., Chm. Bd.--Xebec Corporation, Kansas City, MO, pg. 1206
Thompson, F.L., Chm. Bd.--DIT-MCO Intl., Kansas City, MO, pg. 1206
Thompson, J.F., Chm. Bd.--Burlington Basket Co., Burlington, IA, pg. 191
Thompson, Kenneth W., Chm. Bd. & Pres.--Thompson/Marince Advertising, San Antonio, TX, pg. 1094
Thompson, LeRoy, Jr., Chm. & Chief Exec. Officer--Steelite, Inc., Pittsburgh, PA, pg. 1044
Thompson, Lloyd, Chm. Bd.--Border States Paving, Inc., Fargo, ND, pg. 165
Thompson, Scott, Chm. Bd., Pres., Chief Exec. & Chief Oper. Officer--Advanced Technology, Inc., Reston, VA, pg. 20
Thornburg, H. Andrew, Chm. Bd.--Peerless Chain Co., Winona, MN, pg. 855
Thornton, Dewey, Chm. Bd.--Associated Grocers of Alabama, Inc., Birmingham, AL, pg. 90
Thornton, James H., Chm. Bd.--Thornton Oil Corp., Louisville, KY, pg. 1095
Thorson, Milton Z., Chm. Bd.--Red Spot Paint & Varnish Co., Evansville, IN, pg. 918
Thorstenson, Robert M., Chm. Bd.--Icicle Seafoods, Inc., Seattle, WA, pg. 561
Thrall, J. Jeffrey, Chm. Bd. & Chief Exec. Officer--Naz-Dar Company, Chicago, IL, pg. 1095
Thrall, Jerome A., Chm. Bd.--Thrall Enterprises, Inc., Chicago, IL, pg. 1095
Thumann, Jurgen, Chm. Bd. & Chief Exec. Officer--Thomas Steel Strip Corp., Warren, OH, pg. 1094
Thurston, Ray, Chm. Bd. & Chief Exec. Officer--Sonicair, Scottsdale, AZ, pg. 1018
Tibbetts, Linton N., Chm. Bd. & Chief Exec. Officer--Cox Lumber Co., Saint Petersburg, FL, pg. 294
Tibbitts, Samuel J., Chm. Bd.--PacifiCare Health Systems, Inc., Cypress, CA, pg. 1127
Ticknor, Arthur W., Chm. Bd.--Union Switch & Signal Inc., Pittsburgh, PA, pg. 1129
Tideman, Philip, Chm. Bd., Pres. & Chief Exec. Officer--United Power Association, Elk River, MN, pg. 1134
Tillery, Gary, Chm. Bd. & Sec.--The Townsend Agency, Ltd., Rosemont, IL, pg. 1104
Tillinghast, William, Chm. Bd.--SENCORP, Newport, KY, pg. 989
Timble, Frank, Chm. Bd.--Headco Industries, Inc., Broadview, IL, pg. 520
Timmins, P.A., Chm. Bd.--Epoxylite Corporation, Irvine, CA, pg. 384
Tindal, Charles H., Chm. Bd., Pres. & Chief Exec. Officer--Palmer Electric Co., Winter Park, FL, pg. 843
Ting, Kenneth, Chm. Bd.--Bachmann Industries, Inc., Philadelphia, PA, pg. 108
Tinsley, Sandra C., Chm. Bd.--Tinsley Advertising, Miami, FL, pg. 1099
Tippins, George W., Chm. Bd.--Tippins Incorporated, Pittsburgh, PA, pg. 1099
Tipton, Betty J., Chm. Bd.--Warrens Waller Press, South San Francisco, CA, pg. 1165
Tishman, John L., Chm.--Tishman Realty & Construction Co., New York, NY, pg. 1099
Tobias, Bob, Chm. Bd.--California Avocado Commission, Santa Ana, CA, pg. 209
Tobin, Sylvan M., Chm. Bd.--Fishman & Tobin, Inc., Philadelphia, PA, pg. 415
Todd, J. L., Chm. Bd. & Pres.--J. L. Todd Auction Co., Rome, GA, pg. 1099
Toland, C. E., Chm. Bd. & Chief Exec. Officer--Affiliated Foods Southwest, Little Rock, AR, pg. 24
Tollman, Stanley S., Chm. Bd.--Tollman/Hundley Hotels, Valhalla, NY, pg. 1100
Toma, Carl D., Chm. Bd.--Haddon Craftsmen, Inc., Scranton, PA, pg. 499
Tombras, Charles P., Jr., Chm. Bd. & Pres.--Charles Tombras Advertising, Inc., Knoxville, TN, pg. 1100
Tomei, Vincent H., Chm. Bd.--John R. Hollingsworth Co., Phoenixville, PA, pg. 539
Tomjack, Thomas J., Chm Bd. & Pres.--North Pacific Lumber Company, Portland, OR, pg. 813
Tomsich, Robert J., Chm.--NESCO, Inc., Mayfield Heights, OH, pg. 798
Tomsick, Frank, Chm. & Chief Exec. Officer--MBT Associates, Inc., San Francisco, CA, pg. 691
Torcivia, Benedict, Chm. Bd. & Chief Exec. Officer--Torcon, Inc., Westfield, NJ, pg. 1102
Torras, Joseph H., Chm. Bd. & Pres.--Eastern Fine Paper, Incorporated, Brewer, ME, pg. 363
Torstenson, Robert H., Chm. Bd. & Pres.--Duo-Fast Corporation, Franklin Park, IL, pg. 354
Tortorello, Nicholas, Chm. Bd.--Research & Forecasts, Inc., New York, NY, pg. 954
Tortoriello, Anthony M., Chm. Bd. & Pres.--Torco Oil, Chicago, IL, pg. 1102
Toth, Alex S., Chm. Bd., Pres. & Chief Exec. Officer--PBM Office Products, Cleveland, OH, pg. 835
Totten, Marvin, Chm. Bd.--Totten Tubes, Inc., Los Angeles, CA, pg. 1103
Toussaint, Wayne E., Chm. Bd.--Vance Industries, Inc., Chicago, IL, pg. 1144
Towery, Maurice J., Chm. Bd. & Chief Exec. Officer--Color Graphics, Inc., Atlanta, GA, pg. 264
Townsend, Kenneth W., Chm. Bd.--Blue Cross and Blue Shield of Oklahoma, Tulsa, OK, pg. 159
Townsend, Ramon, Chm. Bd.--Townsend & O'Leary, Inc., Laguna Hills, CA, pg. 1104
Townsend, Ray T., Chm. Bd.--Townsend Engineering Co., Des Moines, IA, pg. 1104
Traeger, John E., Chm. Bd.--Artistic Carton Company, Elgin, IL, pg. 87
Trame, Charles E., Vice Chm.--Everbrite, Inc., Greenfield, WI, pg. 391
Trauth, Louis J., Jr., Chm. Bd.--Trauth Dairy Inc., Newport, KY, pg. 1108
Traylor, W. Leroy, Sr., Chm. Bd.--Traylor Chemical & Supply Co., Orlando, FL, pg. 1108
Traylor, William F., Chm. Bd.--Traylor Brothers, Inc., Evansville, IN, pg. 1108
Treis, Edward F., Chm Bd. & Chief Exec. Officer--Arandell-Schmidt Corporation, Menomonee Falls, WI, pg. 79
Trerice, Byron W., Jr., Chm. Bd. & Chief Exec. Officer--Trerice Tosto International, Bingham Farms, MI, pg. 1110
Tribble, James L., Chm. Bd. & Chief Exec. Officer--Tribble & Stephens Co., Houston, TX, pg. 1112
Tribull, Christoph, Chm. Bd., Pres., Chief Exec. & Chief Oper. Officer--Sierracin Corporation, Sylmar, CA, pg. 1003
Trinchero, Louis, Chm. & Chief Exec. Officer--Sutter Home Winery, Inc., Saint Helena, CA, pg. 1065
Triplett, William W., Chm. Bd. & Chief Exec. Officer--HDS Services, Farmington Hills, MI, pg. 496
Troncalli, Samuel, Chm. Bd.--Troncalli Motors, Inc., Decatur, GA, pg. 1115
Trueb, Kurt O., Chm. Bd.--Spinnerin Yarn Co., Inc., South Hackensack, NJ, pg. 1031
Trueman, Barbara, Chm. Bd.--Red Roof Inns, Inc., Hilliard, OH, pg. 918
Trump, Donald J., Chm. Bd.--The USAir Shuttle, Jackson Heights, NY, pg. 1118
Trump, Julius, Chm. Bd. & Chief Exec. Officer--The Trump Group, New York, NY, pg. 1117
Trump, Julius, Chm.--Northern Pacific Corporation, New York, NY, pg. 1118
Trump, Julius, Chm. Bd.--Northern Automotive Corporation, Phoenix, AZ, pg. 1118
Trusheim, H. Edwin, Chm. Bd.--General American Life Insurance Co., St. Louis, MO, pg. 448
Trygg, Steve, Chm. Bd. & New Bus. Contact--Anderson & Lembke Inc., New York, NY, pg. 73
Tryon, William A., II, Chm. Bd.--Trayer Products, Inc., Elmira, NY, pg. 1108
Tscheulin, Frederick R., Chm. Bd., Pres. & Chief Exec. Officer--The Highland Group, Inc., Southport, CT, pg. 534
Tucker, Richard B.C., Chm. Bd. & Pres.--Wm. T. Burnett & Co., Inc., Baltimore, MD, pg. 191
Tulley, Vincent F., Chm. Bd.--Tulley Buick-Pontiac Company, Inc., Nashua, NH, pg. 1119
Tullman, Howard A., Chm. Bd.--CCC Information Services, Chicago, IL, pg. 410
Turben, John F., Chm. Bd.--Bristol Products, L.P., Bristol, IN, pg. 176
Turner, H. Lee, Chm. Bd.--The Fuller Brush Company, Great Bend, KS, pg. 436
Turner, William, Chm. Bd., Pres., Chief Exec. & Chief Oper. Officer--The Pullman Company, Livingston, NJ, pg. 899
Turner, William, Chm. Bd., Pres., Chief Exec. & Chief Oper. Officer--Lear Siegler Diversified Holdings Corp., Livingston, NJ, pg. 424
Turner, William J., Chm. Bd., Pres. & Chief Exec. Officer--Lear Siegler Diversified Holdings Corp., Livingston, NJ, pg. 664
Turner, William J., Chm. Bd., Pres. & Chief Exec. Officer--Lear Siegler Diversified Holdings Corp., Livingston, NJ, pg. 424
Turpin, Tom, Chm. Bd.--BJ Acquisition Corp., Charlotte, NC, pg. 107
Turriff, Thomas J., Chm. Bd., Pres. & Treas.--Tab Chemicals, Inc., Chicago, IL, pg. 1075
Tuthill, Victor P., Chm. Bd.--Oliver Products Company, Grand Rapids, MI, pg. 824
Tway, Robert C., Jr., Chm. Bd.--Kentucky Manufacturing Co., Louisville, KY, pg. 624
Tway, Robert C., Jr., Chm. Bd.--R.C. Tway Coal Company, Louisville, KY, pg. 1120
Tweddle, Michael E., Chm. Bd. & Pres.--Tweddle Litho Company, St. Clair Shores, MI, pg. 1120
Tweten, Leonard M., Chm. Bd.--Magnolia Hi-Fi, Inc., Seattle, WA, pg. 701
Twigg-Smith, Thurston, Chm., Pres. & Chief Exec. Officer--Persis Corporation, Honolulu, HI, pg. 863
Tyler, Robert L., Chm. Bd.--Lincoln Electric Systems, Lincoln, NE, pg. 675
Tyner, Neal E., Chm. & Chief Exec. Officer--Ameritas Life Insurance Corp., Lincoln, NE, pg. 66
Typermass, Arthur G., Chm.--MetLife Funding Co., Houston, TX, pg. 744
Tyson, Dr. Thomas J., Chm. Bd., Pres. & Chief Exec. Officer--Energy & Environmental Research Corp., Irvine, CA, pg. 381
Ueno, Shinzo (Tokyo), Chm.--Dentsu, Young & Rubicam Partnerships, New York, NY, pg. 330
Uhlmann, Paul, Jr., Chm. Bd.--The Uhlmann Co., Kansas City, MO, pg. 1125
Ulbrich, Frederick C., Jr., Chm. Bd., Pres. & Chief Exec. Officer--Ulbrich Stainless Steels & Special Metals, Inc., North Haven, CT, pg. 1125
Ullenberg, Thomas H., Chm. Bd.--Ullenberg Corp., Chattanooga, TN, pg. 1125
Ullman, Myron E., III, Co-Chm. & Co- Chief Exec. Officer--R. H. Macy & Co., Inc., New York, NY, pg. 698
Ullman, Myron E., III, Co-Chm. Bd. & Co.-Chief Exec. Officer--Bullock's, Los Angeles, CA, pg. 699
Umphenour, Russ, Chm., Pres. & Chief Exec. Officer--Mrs. Winner's Chicken & Biscuit Restaurants, Atlanta, GA, pg. 761
Umphenour, Russell V., Chm. Bd.--Tausche Martin Lonsdorf, Atlanta, GA, pg. 1080
Umphenour, Russell, Jr., Chm. Bd., Pres. & Chief Exec. Officer--R.T.M. Winners, Atlanta, GA, pg. 908
Undercofler, J. Clayton, III, Chm. Bd.--Southeastern Pennsylvania Transportation Authority, Philadelphia, PA, pg. 1020
Underwood, Rodney, Chm. & Creative Dir.--Geer, DuBois Inc., New York, NY, pg. 447
Underwood, Vernon, Jr., Chm. Bd.--Young's Market Company, Los Angeles, CA, pg. 1214
Unger, Paul A., Chm. Bd.--Unger Company, Cleveland, OH, pg. 1126
Unger, Phillip W., Chm. Bd. & Pres.--Alliance America, Norcross, GA, pg. 37
Urrutia, Mike, Chm. Bd. & Pres.--Producers Livestock, North Salt Lake, UT, pg. 892
Urschel, Joe R., Chm. Bd.--Urschel Labs Inc., Valparaiso, IN, pg. 1140
Usibelli, Joseph E., Chm. Bd. & Chief Fin. Officer--Usibelli Coal Mine, Inc., Healy, AK, pg. 1140
Usinger, Frederick D., Chm. Bd.--Fred Usinger, Inc., Milwaukee, WI, pg. 1140
Utley, Robert K., III, Chm. Bd.--First Worthing, Dallas, TX, pg. 414
Utley, Robert K, III, Chm. Exec. Committee & Co-Chief Exec. Officer)--First Southwest Company, Dallas, TX, pg. 413
Utsman, Robert E., Chm., Sec. & Mktg. Dir.--Gold Coast Advertising, Miami, FL, pg. 465
Uytengsu, Wilfred, Chm. & Chief Exec. Officer--Sunshine Biscuits, Inc., Woodbridge, NJ, pg. 439
Uytengsu, Wilfred, Chm. & Chief Exec. Officer--Sunshine/Salerno (IL), Niles, IL, pg. 439
Vakil, Usman U., Chm. Bd., Pres. & Treas.--Lights Of America, Inc., Walnut, CA, pg. 675
Valentine, Joseph C., Chm. Bd., Pres. & Chief Exec. Officer--Lubrication Engineers, Inc., Fort Worth, TX, pg. 686
Valk, Richard, Chm. Bd.--Valk Manufacturing Company, New Kingstown, PA, pg. 1143
Vallely, W.F., Jr., Chm. Bd.--A.T. Clayton & Company, Inc., New York, NY, pg. 253
Van Andel, Jay, Chm. Bd.--Amway Corporation, Ada, MI, pg. 70
Van Camp, Robert, Chm. Bd.--KNOX International Corp., Knoxville, TN, pg. 638
Van Den Blink, N. Mooers, Chm. Bd., Chief Exec. Officer, & Treas.--Hilliard Corporation, Elmira, NY, pg. 535
Van Denburgh, John P., Jr., Chm. Bd., Pres. & Chief Exec. Officer--American Fence Company, Phoenix, AZ, pg. 52
Van Dyke, Dick, Chm.--Nick at Nite--Nickelodeon/Nick At Nite, New York, NY, pg. 785
Van Elsander, Art, Chm. Bd.--Art Van Furniture Inc., Warren, MI, pg. 86
Van Horne, Ralph, Chm. Bd.--GranTree Corporation, Beaverton, OR, pg. 477
van Kesteren, S.J., Chm. Bd.--BIW Cable Systems, Inc., North Dighton, MA, pg. 106
van Marle, Johan T., Chm.--CSFB Finance B.V., Amsterdam,, Netherlands, pg. 204
Van Metre, Albert G., Sr., Chm. & Pres.--The Van Metre Companies, Burke, VA, pg. 1144
Van Mollenberg, H., Chm. Bd., Pres. & Chief Exec. Officer--Mollenberg-Betz Inc., Buffalo, NY, pg. 764
Van Pelt, David B., Sr., Chm. Bd. & Chief Exec. Officer--Van Pelt Corporation, Detroit, MI, pg. 1144
Van Pelt, Donald C., Chm. Bd., Pres. & Chief Exec. Officer--Plymouth Tube Company, Warrenville, IL, pg. 877
Van Vleet, Wayne, Chm. Bd.--Trinidad/Benham Corporation, Denver, CO, pg. 1113
Van Winkle, Fritz, Chm. Bd. & Pres.--Van Winkle & Associates, Inc., Atlanta, GA, pg. 1144
Vance, Robert M., Chm. Bd.--Clinton Mills Inc., Clinton, SC, pg. 202
Vance, William C., Chm. Bd. & Chief Exec. Officer--Vance Publishing Corporation, Lincolnshire, IL, pg. 1144
Vandail, Allan, Chm. Bd.--U.S. Graphite, Inc., Saginaw, MI, pg. 1136
Vanderbilt, H.B., Chm. Bd. & Chief Exec. Officer--R. T. Vanderbilt Company, Inc., Norwalk, CT, pg. 1144
Vanderminden, Henry J., Jr., Chm. Bd.--Mettowee Lumber & Plastic Co., Inc., Granville, NY, pg. 1085
Vanderminden, Henry J.W., Jr., Chm. Bd.--Telescope Casual Furniture, Inc., Granville, NY, pg. 1085
Vandermoer, Herbert H., Chm. Bd.--Sterling Lumber & Investment Co., Denver, CO, pg. 1047
VanDerven, Hans, Chm. Bd.--Hoogovens Aluminum Corp., Secaucus, NJ, pg. 543
VanDine, Alan, Chm.--VanDine, Humphrey, Herbert, Alber & Manges, Inc., Pittsburgh, PA, pg. 1145
Varblow, Carl R., Chm. Bd. & Chief Fin. Officer--Veda International, Inc., Alexandria, VA, pg. 1146
Varblow, Carl R., Chm. Bd. & Chief Fin. Officer--Veda Incorporated, Alexandria, VA, pg. 1146
Vazzana, John D., Chm. Bd., Pres. & Chief Exec. Officer--NRM-Steelastic, Akron, OH, pg. 781

Venable, Richard M., Jr., Co-Chm. & V.P.--Trojan Steel Co., Charleston, WV, pg. 1115
Venet, Zal, Chm. Bd., Pres. & Chief Exec. Officer--The Venet Companies, Inc., Union, NJ, pg. 1147
Venetis, Petros, Chm.--Leo Burnett S.A., Athens,, Greece, pg. 193
Vengroff, Harvey, Chm. Bd. & Chief Exec. Officer--Vengroff Williams & Associates, Inc., Centerpoint, NY, pg. 1147
Ventre, John, Jr., Chm. Bd. & Chief Exec. Officer--Ventre Packing Company, Inc., Syracuse, NY, pg. 1147
Vermeer, Robert, Chm. Bd. & Chief Exec. Officer--Vermeer Manufacturing Company, Pella, IA, pg. 1148
Verni, Robert F., Chm. Bd. & Chief Exec. Officer--State Street Research & Management Company, Boston, MA, pg. 744
Vernon, Christopher M., Chm. Bd.--Andrews/Mautner, Inc., Milwaukee, WI, pg. 74
Viggiano, Victor A., Chm. Bd.--The Okonite Company, Ramsey, NJ, pg. 823
Vile, Joel, D., Chm. Bd. & Pres.--Vile-Goller, Fine Art Printing & Lithography, Kansas City, KS, pg. 1151
Villaret, Jean-Pierre, Chm.-Paris--Young & Rubicam France S.A., Boulogne,, France, pg. 1212
Vincent, Burton J., Chm. Bd, Pres. & Chief Exec. Officer--Vincent Food Industries, Inc., Chicago, IL, pg. 1152
Viola, Ronald J., Chm. Bd. & Chief Exec. Officer--Rapid Power Technologies, Inc., Brookfield, CT, pg. 913
Vitale, A., Chm. Bd.--Crown Publishers, Inc., New York, NY, pg. 20
Vitner, James C., Chm. Bd.--C.J. Vitner & Co., Inc., Chicago, IL, pg. 1153
Vitt, Sam B., Chm. Emeritus--Vitt Media International, Inc., New York, NY, pg. 1153
Vittoria, Joseph V., Chm. Bd. & Chief Exec. Officer--Avis, Inc., Garden City, NY, pg. 102
Vittorini, Carlo, Chm., Publisher & Chief Exec. Officer--Parade Publications Inc., New York, NY, pg. 847
Vituli, Alan, Chm. Bd.--Carrols Corporation, Syracuse, NY, pg. 225
Vivian, H. Melvin, Jr., Chm. Bd.--Vivian Millworks, Forty Fort, PA, pg. 1154
Vogl, Alex J., Chm. Bd. & Pres.--Wilton Corporation, Palatine, IL, pg. 1194
Vohs, James, Chm. Bd.--Kaiser Foundation Health & Hospitals Group, Oakland, CA, pg. 614
Volk, Kenneth G., Jr., Chm. Bd.--Public Storage, Inc., Glendale, CA, pg. 898
von Matthiessen, Malte, Chm. Bd. & Chief Exec. Officer--YSI Incorporated, Yellow Springs, OH, pg. 1207
Wachner, Brian Gary, Chm. Bd. & Pres.--BGW Systems, Inc., Hawthorne, CA, pg. 106
Wacker, Fred G., Jr., Chm. Bd.--Liquid Controls Corporation, Lake Bluff, IL, pg. 677
Waddell, Robert F., Chm. Bd.--Standard Locknut & Lockwasher, Carmel, IN, pg. 1037
Wade, Tom W., Jr., Chm. Bd. & Chief Exec. Officer--Tom Wade Co., Kenton, TN, pg. 1157
Wadsworth, Maurice A., Chm. & Pres.--Gannett Fleming Affiliates, Inc., Harrisburg, PA, pg. 442
Wadsworth, Stanley, Chm. Bd., Pres. & Chief Exec. Officer--Golf Hosts, Inc., Palm Harbor, FL, pg. 469
Waggoner, Donald E., Chm. Bd.--Waggoner Corp., Troy, MI, pg. 1158
Wagman, Michael, Chm. Bd. & Creative Dir.--Campbell and Wagman, Los Angeles, CA, pg. 213
Wagner, H.J., Chm. & Chief Exec. Officer--Setco Sales Company, Cincinnati, OH, pg. 993
Wagner, Judith B., Chm.--Equitable Bankshares of Colorado, Inc., Denver, CO, pg. 385
Wahl, Eugene A., Chm. Bd.--Vibra Screw Inc., Totowa, NJ, pg. 1149
Wahl, Robert L., Chm. Bd.--Wahl Clipper Corp., Sterling, IL, pg. 1158
Waite, Harley Jr., Chm. Bd., Pres. & Chief Exec. Officer--Eastern Technologies Ltd, Amesbury, MA, pg. 364
Wakley, James T., Chm. Bd.--Marmac Corporation, Parkersburg, WV, pg. 710
Walcher, Jack, Chm., Pres. & Chief Exec. Officer--Eddins-Walcher Company, Midland, TX, pg. 367
Walden, Thomas, Chm. Bd. & Chief Fin. Officer--Ris Paper Company, Long Island City, NY, pg. 935
Waldner, Daniel, Chm. Bd.--D. Waldner Company, Inc., Farmingdale, NY, pg. 1159
Waldorf, Robert, Chm. Bd. & Pres.--Idea Man, Inc., Los Angeles, CA, pg. 562
Walker, A. Maceo, Sr., Chm. Bd. & Chief Exec. Officer--Universal Life Insurance Company, Memphis, TN, pg. 1138
Walker, B., Chm. Bd.--Colonial Pipeline Company, Atlanta, GA, pg. 264
Walker, Charles M., Chm. Bd.--Evana Automation, Evansville, IN, pg. 390
Walker, Claud B., Chm. Bd.--Fibrebond Corporation, Minden, LA, pg. 408
Walker, John T., Chm. Bd., Pres. & Chief Exec. Officer--St. Paul Metalcraft, Inc., Saint Paul, MN, pg. 967
Wall, John Lyndon, Chm. Bd. & Pres.--Bryant Electric Company, Inc., High Point, NC, pg. 185
Wallace, C.S., Sr., Chm. Bd.--Wallace Co. Inc., Houston, TX, pg. 1160
Wallace, Len, Chm. Bd.--Condor D.C. Power Supplies Inc., Oxnard, CA, pg. 273
Wallach, Ira D., Chm. Bd.--Central National-Gottesman Inc., Purchase, NY, pg. 233
Waller, Frank, Chm. Bd.--Woodward-Clyde Group, Inc., Denver, CO, pg. 1200
Wallin, Eric, Chm. Bd.--Dinner Bell Foods, Inc., Cincinnati, OH, pg. 53
Wallis, Bernard J., Chm. Bd.--Livernois Engineering Company, Dearborn, MI, pg. 679
Walpert, H.E., Chm. Bd., Pres. & Chief Exec. Officer--Ed Walpert & Associates, Rancho Mirage, CA, pg. 1161
Walser, Robert J., Chm. Bd.--Walser Automotive Corporation, Richfield, MN, pg. 1161
Walter, James W., Chm. Bd.--Walter Industries, Inc., Tampa, FL, pg. 1161
Walter, Paul F., Chm. Bd., Pres. & Chief Exec. Officer--Thermo Electric Co., Inc., Saddle Brook, NJ, pg. 1091
Walter, Richard A., Chm. Bd. & Chief Exec. Officer--Scicom Data Services, Ltd., Minnetonka, MN, pg. 981
Walters, Margaret J., Chm. Bd.--Cogsdill Tool Products, Inc., Lugoff, SC, pg. 259
Walters, Roger A., Chm. Bd. & Pres.--Harrison Paint Corporation, Canton, OH, pg. 512
Walters, W. Lindsey, Chm. Bd. & Pres.--Flexel, Inc., Atlanta, GA, pg. 418
Waltman, Howard L., Chm. Bd. & Chief Exec. Officer--Sanus Corp. Health Systems, Fort Lee, NJ, pg. 803
Walton, R.O., Chm. Bd.--Crested Butte Mountain Resort, Inc., Mount Crested Butte, CO, pg. 299
Wamser, Carl H., Chm. Bd.--Everbrite, Inc., Greenfield, WI, pg. 391
Wang, Herbert, Chm. Bd.--Tech Industries, Inc., Woonsocket, RI, pg. 1083
Ward, G. William, Chm. Bd.--Ward Trucking Corp., Altoona, PA, pg. 1163
Ward, John S., Chm. Bd.--American Kennel Club, Inc., New York, NY, pg. 57
Ward, Louis L., Chm. Bd., Pres. & Chief Oper. Officer--Russell Stover Candies, Inc., Kansas City, MO, pg. 957
Ward, Patrick J., Chm. Bd., Pres. & Chief Exec. Officer--Caltex Petroleum Corporation, Irving, TX, pg. 211
Ward, W.F., Jr., Chm. Bd.--The Ward Machinery Company, Cockeysville, MD, pg. 1162
Warehime, John, Chm. Bd.--Myers Foods Company, Plumsteadville, PA, pg. 506
Warehime, John A., Chm. Bd. & Chief Exec. Officer--Hanover Foods Corporation, Hanover, PA, pg. 506
Warm, Alexander D., Chm. Bd.--Warm Brothers Construction Company, Cincinnati, OH, pg. 1163
Warmington, Edward G., Chm. Bd.--Warmington Homes, Costa Mesa, CA, pg. 1164
Warner, Jack, Chm. Bd. & Chief Exec. Officer--Gulf States Paper Corporation, Tuscaloosa, AL, pg. 494
Warner, John E., Chm. Bd., Chief Exec. Officer & Creative Dir.--Warner, Bicking, Morris & Partners, Inc., New York, NY, pg. 1164
Warner, Robert C., Chm. Bd.--International Business Interiors Inc., Chicago, IL, pg. 575
Warp, Harold, Chm. Bd.--Flex-O-Glass, Inc., Chicago, IL, pg. 418
Warren, Fred, Chm. Bd.--Mobile Technology Inc., Los Angeles, CA, pg. 762
Warren, Paul B., Chm. Bd. & Pres.--UVP, Inc., San Gabriel, CA, pg. 1124
Warren, Richard, Chm. & Chief Exec. Officer--The Giardini/Russell Group, Watertown, MA, pg. 456
Warry, Lowrance, Chm. Bd. & Treas.--AEA, Inc., Charlotte, NC, pg. 3
Warwick, John P., Hon. Chm.--Warwick Baker & Fiore Inc., New York, NY, pg. 1165
Washington, R. Peter, Chm. Bd. & Chief Exec. Officer--Lyon Metal Products, Inc., Montgomery, IL, pg. 690
Wasserstein, Bruce, Co-Chm & Co-Chief Exec. Officer--Collins & Aikman Group Inc., Santa Monica, CA, pg. 262
Wassman, Ernest, Chm. Bd.--Tallgrass Technologies Corp., Overland Park, KS, pg. 1077
Watase, Frank W., Chm. Bd.--Yum Yum Donut Shop, Inc., City of Industry, CA, pg. 1214
Watkins, Dwain J., Chm. Bd.--Watkins System Inc., Concordville, PA, pg. 1167
Watkins, Edward G., Chm. Bd., Pres. & Chief Exec. Officer--Simplex Time Recorder Co., Gardner, MA, pg. 1006
Watkins, William D., Chm. Bd. & Chief Exec. Officer--The Alpha Corporation Of Tennessee, Collierville, TN, pg. 43
Watson, Houston B., Chm. Bd., Chief Exec. Officer, Chief Fin. Officer & Treas.--Watson Electric Supply Inc., Dallas, TX, pg. 1168
Watson, John, Chm. Bd.--VMC Fiberglass Products Inc., Daleville, AL, pg. 1142
Watson, Paul, Chm., Pres. & Chief Exec. Officer--Farmers Co-op Market Inc., Frisco City, AL, pg. 401
Watt, Raymond A., Chm. Bd.--Watt Industries, Santa Monica, CA, pg. 1168
Watt, Ronald W., Chm. & Chief Exec. Officer--Watt, Roop & Co., Cleveland, OH, pg. 1168
Waugh, John T., Chm. Bd. & Chief Exec. Officer--CJC Holdings, Inc., Austin, TX, pg. 202
Weaner, Frank A., Chm. Bd.--Paradise Fruit Company, Inc., Plant City, FL, pg. 847
Wear, Frank J., Chm. Bd.--Omaha Public Power District, Omaha, NE, pg. 825
Weaver, Michael, Chm. Bd.--W.H. Weaver Construction Co., Greensboro, NC, pg. 1170
Weaver, Welcome I., Chm. Bd.--Weaver Popcorn Company, Inc., Van Buren, IN, pg. 1170
Webb, Charles B., Jr., Chm. Bd. & Chief Exec. Officer--Alabama Metal Industries Corporation, Birmingham, AL, pg. 28
Webb, George H., Chm. Bd.--Jervis B. Webb Company, Farmington Hills, MI, pg. 1170
Webb, Harley D., Chm. Bd. & Pres.--WBH Industries, Inc., Arlington, TX, pg. 1155
Webb, Jervis C., Chm. Bd. Emeritus--Jervis B. Webb Company, Farmington Hills, MI, pg. 1170
Webb, Jervis H., Asst. Chm. Bd.--Jervis B. Webb Company, Farmington Hills, MI, pg. 1170
Webb, John R., Chm.--Crowley Webb & Associates, Buffalo, NY, pg. 301
Webb, O. Glenn, Chm. Bd. & Pres.--Growmark, Inc., Bloomington, IL, pg. 490
Webbe, Scotson, Chm. Bd.--Handgards Inc., Northbrook, IL, pg. 504
Weber, Franz Kent, Chm. Bd., Pres. & Chief Exec. Officer--Modulite Corporation, Compton, CA, pg. 763
Weber, Joseph A, Sr., Chm. Bd.--Weber Marking Systems, Inc., Arlington Heights, IL, pg. 1171
Weber, Robin, Chm. Bd. & Pres.--Elastomeric Technologies, Inc., Hatboro, PA, pg. 372
Weber, Roy E., Chm. Bd.--Great Lakes Bancorp, Ann Arbor, MI, pg. 480
Webster, Elroy, Chm. Bd.--CENEX (Farmers Union Central Exchange, Inc.), Inver Grove Heights, MN, pg. 231
Weeder, Charles E., Chm. Bd. & Chief Exec. Officer--Homes of Merit Inc., Bartow, FL, pg. 542
Weeks, Sinclair, Chm. Bd.--Reed & Barton Corporation, Taunton, MA, pg. 920
Wegner, Joan M., Chm. Bd.--The Jel Sert Co., West Chicago, IL, pg. 591
Wehrle, Henry B., Jr., Chm. Bd. & Chief Exec. Officer--McJunkin Corporation, Charleston, WV, pg. 730
Wehrmann, Nick, Chm. Bd.--Ithaca Industries Inc., Wilkesboro, NC, pg. 582
Wehrung, Woodrow, Chm. Bd.--Modern Concrete Septic Tank Company, Ottsville, PA, pg. 762
Weider, Joseph, Chm. Bd.--Weider Health & Fitness, Woodland Hills, CA, pg. 1173
Weigandt, Fritz, Chm. Bd.--Tri-State Armature Electric Works, Memphis, TN, pg. 1110
Weiler, A.R., Chm. Bd. & Chief Exec. Officer--Chittenden & Eastman Co., Burlington, IA, pg. 248
Weinbach, Lawrence A., Mng. Partner & Chief Exec. Officer--Arthur Andersen & Co., S.C., New York, NY, pg. 72
Weinberg, David, Co-Chm.--Fel-Pro Incorporated, Skokie, IL, pg. 405
Weinberg, John L., Sr. Chm.--Goldman, Sachs & Co., New York, NY, pg. 468
Weinberg, Marsha, Chm. Bd.--Coast Grain Company, Inc., Ontario, CA, pg. 256
Weinberger, Alan D., Chm., Pres. & Chief Exec. Officer--The ASCII Group, Inc., Bethesda, MD, pg. 8
Weinstein, Gerald, Chm. Bd.--General Tools Mfg., New York, NY, pg. 451
Weinstein, Howard J., Chm., Pres. & Chief Exec. Officer--Adams Wine Co., Atlanta, GA, pg. 17
Weinstein, Ira P., Chm. Bd.--Temkin & Temkin, Northbrook, IL, pg. 1086
Weinstein, Stephen J., Chm. Bd., Chief Exec. Officer & Creative Dir.--SJ Weinstein Associates Inc., New York, NY, pg. 1173
Weintraub, Lawrence, Chm.--Weintraub and Associates, Inc., Saint Louis, MO, pg. 1174
Weir, Don, Chm.--JMCT Publicidad, New York, NY, pg. 604
Weisbart, Graig, Chm. Bd.--Sigman Meat Co. Inc., Arvada, CO, pg. 1003
Weisberg, A.A., Chm. Bd. & Treas.--Technic Incorporated, Cranston, RI, pg. 1083
Weisberg, Arthur, Chm. Bd.--State Electric Supply Co., Huntington, WV, pg. 1040
Weisend, C. Frederick, Chm. Bd., Pres. & Chief Exec. Officer--Fritz Chemical Company, Mesquite, TX, pg. 434
Weiser, Michael, Chm. Bd.--Weiser Minkus Walek Communications, Inc., Chicago, IL, pg. 1174
Weiser, Sherwood M., Co-Chm. Bd. & Chief Exec. Officer--TCC, Miami, FL, pg. 1072
Weisiger, Ed, Chm. Bd.--Carolina Tractor & Equipment Co., Charlotte, NC, pg. 223
Weiss, Larry, Chm. Bd., Pres., Chief Exec. Officer & Sec.--Save More Food Mart, Inc., Hobart, IN, pg. 973
Weiss, Louis P., Chm. Bd. Emeritus--William Morris Agency, Inc., Beverly Hills, CA, pg. 771
Weiss, Selwyn M., Chm. Bd. & Treas.--Weiss Packing Co., Inc., Donora, PA, pg. 1174
Weitz, Fred, Chm. Bd. & Chief Exec. Officer--The Weitz-Cohen Construction Co., Des Moines, IA, pg. 1174
Welch, Joseph F., Chm., Pres. & Chief Exec. Officer--Bachman Company, Reading, PA, pg. 108
Welge, M.W., Chm. Bd.--Millers' Mutual Insurance Assn. Of Illinois, Alton, IL, pg. 755
Welles, D.K., Sr., Founder & Chm.--Therma-Tru Corp., Maumee, OH, pg. 1090
Wellman, Richard, Chm. Bd. & Chief Exec. Officer--International Airline Support Group, Inc., Miami, FL, pg. 575
Wellman, W. Arvid, Chm. Bd.--Andersen Windows Inc., Bayport, MN, pg. 72
Wells, Daniel C., Chm. & Chief Exec. Officer--Stiegler, Wells & Brunswick, Inc., Bethlehem, PA, pg. 1049
Wells, William M., Chm. Bd.--Dunkirk Ice Cream Co., Inc., Dunkirk, NY, pg. 353
Welsh, Robert H., Chm. Bd. & Chief Exec. Officer--Ludlow Textiles Co., Inc., Ludlow, MA, pg. 686
Wendell, Janice, Chm.--Ericson Marketing Communications, Nashville, TN, pg. 386
Wendler, Glenn, Chm. Bd. & Pres.--Amana Society, Amana, IA, pg. 46
Wendt, Edward G., Jr., Chm. Bd.--CoMed Management Inc., Dublin, OH, pg. 802
Wendt, Richard, Chm. Bd.--Jeld-Wen, Inc., Klamath Falls, OR, pg. 591
Wendt, Richard, Chm. Bd.--Frank Paxton Company, Kansas City, MO, pg. 592
Wenger, Jerry, Chm. Bd. & Pres.--Wenger Corporation, Owatonna, MN, pg. 1176
Wentz, Howard B., Chm. Bd.--ESSTAR Incorporated, New Haven, CT, pg. 361
Wenzinger, Carl J., Jr., Chm. Bd.--Doron Precision Systems, Inc., Binghamton, NY, pg. 346
Werra, Robert, Chm., Pres. & Chief Exec. Officer--Amrecorp Realty Inc., Dallas, TX, pg. 68
West, Charles B., Chm. Bd.--West Lumber Co., Atlanta, GA, pg. 1177
Westlie, Charles, Chm. Bd.--Westlie Motor Company, Minot, ND, pg. 1183
Westin, Richard S., Chm. Bd., Pres. & Chief Exec. Officer--Westin, Inc., Omaha, NE, pg. 1183
Westlake, Christina, Chm. Bd.--Nana Regional Corporation, Inc., Anchorage, AK, pg. 783
Weston, Roger L., Chm. Bd., Pres. & Chief Exec. Officer--GreatBanc, Inc., Aurora, IL, pg. 482

Westphal, Byron, Chm. Bd., Pres. & Chief Exec. Officer--Integrated Energy Controls Corp., Minneapolis, MN, pg. 573
Wexler, Jerrold, Chm. Bd.--The Jupiter Corporation, Chicago, IL, pg. 609
Weyforth, Frank G., Jr., Chm. Bd., Chief Exec. Officer & Pres.--Marketing Resources of America, Inc., Overland Park, KS, pg. 709
Wharton, Clifton R., Jr., Chm. Bd. & Chief Exec. Officer--Teachers Insurance and Annuity Association-College Retirement Equities Fund, New York, NY, pg. 1082
Wheatly, Richard, Chm.--Leo Burnett Limited, London,, United Kingdom, pg. 193
Wheaton, Robert E., Chm. Bd., Pres., Chief Exec. & Chief Fin. Officer--The Bekins Company, Glendale, CA, pg. 132
Wheeler, E.O., Chm. Bd.--Wheeler Brothers Grain Co., Watonga, OK, pg. 1184
Wheeler, Steven E., Chm. & Chief Exec. Officer--Hancock Realty Investors, Inc., Boston, MA, pg. 596
Whitaker, Gary, Chm., Pres. & Chief Exec. Officer--Curtis Mathes Corporation, Athens, TX, pg. 720
White, Arthur K., Chm. Bd.--Rite-Hite Corporation, Milwaukee, WI, pg. 936
White, Carter H., Chm. Bd.--The Record-Journal Publishing Company, Meriden, CT, pg. 917
White, Dorset, Chm. Bd.--Tork, Inc., Mount Vernon, NY, pg. 1102
White, E. James, Chm. Bd. & Pres.--E. James White Company, Herndon, VA, pg. 1185
White, Robert G., Chm. Bd., Pres. & Chief Exec. Officer--New England Frozen Foods, Southborough, MA, pg. 800
White, Robert R., Jr., Chm. Bd.--Delta Pride Catfish, Inc., Indianola, MS, pg. 327
White, William, Chm. Bd.--Whitestar Graphics, Inc., Spring Grove, IL, pg. 1186
White, William J., Chm. Bd., Pres. & Chief Exec. Officer--Bell & Howell Company, Skokie, IL, pg. 134
White, William S., Chm. Bd.--United States Sugar Corporation, Clewiston, FL, pg. 1137
White, Willis S., Jr., Chm. Bd.--Battelle Memorial Institute, Columbus, OH, pg. 126
Whitehead, Richard L., Chm. Bd. & Chief Admin. Officer--The Berkshire Life Insurance Company, Pittsfield, MA, pg. 142
Whiteman, Jack W., Chm. Bd. & Chief Exec. Officer--Empire Southwest Co., Mesa, AZ, pg. 379
Whitfield, L. B. III, Chm. Bd.--Whitfield Foods, Inc., Montgomery, AL, pg. 1187
Whitfield, Willaim, Chm. Bd. & Pres.--GMI, Inc.-Glasstream, Panama City, FL, pg. 450
Whiting, A. Milton, Chm. Bd. & Chief Exec. Officer--Kaibab Industries, Phoenix, AZ, pg. 614
Whitney, Dickson L., Sr., Chm. Bd.--McGean-Rohco, Inc., Cleveland, OH, pg. 729
Whitsell, Helen J., Chm. Bd., Chief Exec. Officer & Treas.--Copeland Lumber Yard, Inc., Portland, OR, pg. 284
Whittington, Aven, Chm. Bd.--Staple Cotton Cooperative Association, Greenwood, MS, pg. 1038
Whittle, John J., Chm. Bd., Pres. & Chief Exec. Officer--Farmers and Traders Life Insurance Co., Syracuse, NY, pg. 401
Whyte, George C., Jr., Chm. Bd., Pres. & Chief Exec. Officer--Dakotah, Inc., Webster, SD, pg. 312
Wick, John F., Chm. Bd. & Chief Exec. Officer--Wick Building Systems, Mazomanie, WI, pg. 1188
Wicken, Mike, Chm. Bd.--The Robert E. Morris Company, Farmington, CT, pg. 771
Wickens, Donald L., Chm. & Pres.--The Benham Group, Oklahoma City, OK, pg. 138
Wickland, J.A., Jr., Chm. Bd. & Chief Exec. Officer--Wickland Corporation, Sacramento, CA, pg. 1188
Widlund, W.B., Chm. Bd.--Noville Essential Oil Co., Inc., North Bergen, NJ, pg. 817
Widmann, Anthony, Chm. & Chief Exec. Officer--Taylor-Gordon/Widmann & Co., Inc., New York, NY, pg. 1081
Wiedenbeck, Roger D., Chm. Bd. & Pres.--The Johnson Corporation, Three Rivers, MI, pg. 597
Wiedenmayer, Christopher M., Chm. Bd. & Chief Exec. Officer--Faber/Castell Corporation, Parsippany, NJ, pg. 395
Wieland, John F., Chm. Bd., Pres. & Chief Exec. Officer--John Wieland Homes Inc., Atlanta, GA, pg. 1188
Wiesner, John J., Chm. Bd. & Chief Exec. Officer--C. R. Anthony Company, Oklahoma City, OK, pg. 77
Wiggin, Blanton C., Chm. Bd.--Advanced Instruments, Inc., Needham Heights, MA, pg. 20
Wiggins, Clarence R., Chm. Bd., Pres. & Chief Exec. Officer--Century Data Systems, Raleigh, NC, pg. 235
Wildauer, Werner K., Chm. Bd. & Pres.--Leupold & Stevens, Inc., Beaverton, OR, pg. 669
Wilder, Robert O., Chm. Bd., Pres. & Chief Exec. Officer--National Forge Company, Irvine, PA, pg. 788
Wiley, Louis, Chm. Bd.--Superba, Inc., Los Angeles, CA, pg. 1063
Wilkie, Michael L., Chm. Bd., Pres., Chief Exec. & Chief Oper. Officer--DoAll Company, Des Plaines, IL, pg. 341
Wilkie, Walter, Chm. Bd.--Vic Manufacturing, Minneapolis, MN, pg. 1149
Willert, August W., Jr., Chm. Bd.--Willert Home Products, Inc., Saint Louis, MO, pg. 1190
Williams, Byron, Chm. Bd. & Sec.--Clayton, Williams & Sherwood, Inc., Newport Beach, CA, pg. 254
Williams, C.E., Chm. Bd.--The Bates Mfg. Co., Hackettstown, NJ, pg. 125
Williams, D. Anderson, Chm. Bd.--Williams Whittle Associates, Inc., Alexandria, VA, pg. 1191
Williams, George, Chm. Bd.--Arkansas Electric Cooperatives Inc., Little Rock, AR, pg. 83
Williams, Robert M., Chm., Chief Exec. Officer & Treas.--Genova Products, Inc., Davison, MI, pg. 452
Williams, T. Bayard, Jr., Chm. Bd.--George Transfer, Inc., Parkton, MD, pg. 453
Williams, William J., Chm. Bd. & Chief Exec. Officer--Western & Southern Life Insurance Co., Cincinnati, OH, pg. 1181
Williamson, Gail P., Chm. Bd.--Williamson-Dickie Mfg. Co., Fort Worth, TX, pg. 1192
Williamson, Hugh H., III, Chm. Bd., Pres. & Chief Exec. Officer--Carolina Steel Corporation, Greensboro, NC, pg. 223
Williangham, James A., Chm. Bd. & Chief Exec. Officer--Harbor Bancorp, Long Beach, CA, pg. 506
Wills, J. Blacklock, Chm. Bd.--Wills Group, Inc., La Plata, MD, pg. 1193
Wilson, A.C., Chm. Bd. & Chief Exec. Officer--Ernest Paper Products, Inc., Los Angeles, CA, pg. 387
Wilson, Dean G., Chm. Bd., Pres. & Chief Exec. Officer--Blaw Knox Corp., Pittsburgh, PA, pg. 156
Wilson, Frank F., Chm. Bd.--Spencer Turbine Co., Windsor, CT, pg. 1030
Wilson, Frank S., Chm. Bd.--The J. M. Ney Company, Bloomfield, CT, pg. 805
Wilson, Gary, Co-Chm. Bd.--NWA, Inc., Saint Paul, MN, pg. 782
Wilson, Gary, Co-Chm. Bd.--Northwest Airlines, Inc., Saint Paul, MN, pg. 782
Wilson, Ian R., Chm. Bd., Pres., & Chief Exec. Officer--Windmill Holdings Corp., San Francisco, CA, pg. 1195
Wilson, Johnny, Chm. Bd.--SF Services, North Little Rock, AR, pg. 961
Wilson, Kemmons, Sr., Chm. Bd. & Owner--Kemmons Wilson Companies, Memphis, TN, pg. 1194
Wilson, Lynn R., Chm. Bd.--Wilson Products Co., Salt Lake City, UT, pg. 1194
Wilson, Ralph C., Jr., Chm. Bd. & Pres.--Ralph C. Wilson Enterprises, Detroit, MI, pg. 1194
Wilson, Ralph C., Jr., Chm. Bd. & Pres.--Highwood Service, Inc., Detroit, MI, pg. 1194
Wilson, Valarie M., Chm. & Chief Exec. Officer--Wilson Sculley Associates, Saint Louis, MO, pg. 1194
Wilson, Wallace S., Chm. Bd., Pres. & Chief Exec. Officer--Wilson Industries Inc., Houston, TX, pg. 1193
Wimberly, Joseph J., III, Chm. Bd. & Pres.--I. C. Thomasson Associates, Inc., Nashville, TN, pg. 1094
Winch, Harold, Chm. Bd. & Chief Exec. Officer--The Minster Machine Company, Minster, OH, pg. 759
Wing, John A., Chm. Bd. & Chief Exec. Officer--Chicorp, Inc., Chicago, IL, pg. 247
Wing, John A., Chm. Bd., Pres. & Chief Exec. Officer--Chicago Corp., Chicago, IL, pg. 247
Winkelmann, Joe, Chm. Bd., Pres. & Chief Exec. Officer--Greenstripe Media, Inc., Newport Beach, CA, pg. 485
Winkler, Marvin, Chm. Bd.--American Marketing Works & International Corporation, Gardena, CA, pg. 58
Winship, Patricia C., Chm. Bd.--Transus Inc., Atlanta, GA, pg. 1108
Winston, Sam, Chm. Bd. & Chief Exec. Officer--Winston Tire Company, Burbank, CA, pg. 1197
Winter, W.B., Chm. Bd. & Chief Exec. Officer--Bucyrus-Erie Company, South Milwaukee, WI, pg. 186
Winter, W.B., Chm. & Chief Exec. Officer--B-E Holdings Inc., South Milwaukee, WI, pg. 106
Winters, Robert C., Chm. Bd. & Chief Exec. Officer--The Prudential Insurance Company of America, Newark, NJ, pg. 896
Wisne, Anthony, Chm. Bd.--Progressive Tool & Industries Co., Southfield, MI, pg. 894
Wisner, J.D., Chm. & Chief Exec. Officer--The Gerstenslager Company, Wooster, OH, pg. 454
Wisotsky, Jerry, Chm. Bd., Sec. & Treas.--Imperial Litho/Graphics, Inc., Phoenix, AZ, pg. 564
Withall, William E., Chm. Bd. & Chief Exec. Officer--Miner Enterprises Inc., Geneva, IL, pg. 756
Wittenborn, Dale, Co-Chm. Bd.--Kuhn & Wittenborn, Inc., Kansas City, MO, pg. 646
Wolf, Bob, Chm. Bd., Chief Exec. Officer (North America)--Chiat/Day/Mojo Inc. Advertising, Venice, CA, pg. 244
Wolfe, John W., Chm. Bd.--The Dispatch Printing Company, Columbus, OH, pg. 339
Wolfington, Harry A., Chm. Bd.--Wolfington Body Company, Exton, PA, pg. 1199
Wood, Charles, Chm. Bd.--Recording & Statistical Corporation, Norwalk, CT, pg. 917
Wood, James, Chm. Bd.--American Bible Society, New York, NY, pg. 49
Wood, R. Ray, Chm., Pres., Chief Exec. & Chief Oper. Officer--Rockford Products Corp., Rockford, IL, pg. 941
Woodard, J.F., Chm. Bd.--Woodward Direct, Inc., Skokie, IL, pg. 1201
Woodbeck, Milford E., Chm. Bd.--Overhead Conveyor Co., Ferndale, MI, pg. 832
Woodhall, J.A., Jr., Chm. Bd., Pres. & Chief Exec. Officer--Central Allied Enterprises, Canton, OH, pg. 232
Woodruff, Paul H., Chm. Bd., Pres. & Chief Exec. Officer--The ERM Group, Exton, PA, pg. 360
Woodson, James, Co-Chm. Bd.--Taco John's International, Inc., Cheyenne, WY, pg. 1076
Woodward, Joe D., Chm. Bd.--American Fuel Cell & Coated Fabrics Co. (Amfuel), Magnolia, AR, pg. 55
Woolworth, Richard, Chm. Bd. & Pres.--Blue Cross & Blue Shield of Oregon, Portland, OR, pg. 160
Workman, C.E., Chm. Bd. & Chief Exec. Officer--Tru-Fit Products Corp., Medina, OH, pg. 1117
Wornick, Ronald C., Chm. Bd. & Pres.--The Wornick Company, Burlingame, CA, pg. 1203
Worsley, Walter C., Jr., Chm. Bd. & Pres.--Worsley Companies Inc., Wilmington, NC, pg. 1204
Wright, H.D., Chm. Bd. & Chief Exec. Officer--Schenectady Chemicals, Inc., Schenectady, NY, pg. 975
Wright, Merrill W., Jr., Chm. Bd. & Pres.--G.F. Wright Steel & Wire Company, Worcester, MA, pg. 1205
Wright, Warren E., Chm Bd.--Renosol Corp., Saline, MI, pg. 927
Wuertz, Greg, Chm. Bd.--Arizona Grains Inc., Casa Grande, AZ, pg. 82
Wunderman, Lester, Chm. Bd.--Wunderman Cato Johnson, New York, NY, pg. 1211
Wurzel, Tom, Chm. Bd., Pres. & Chief Exec. Officer--ACL Technologies, Santa Ana, CA, pg. 2
Wyatt, B., Chm. Bd.--United Health Plan, Inglewood, CA, pg. 1133
Wyatt, W. Whitlow, Chm. Bd.--Altama Delta Corp., Darien, GA, pg. 45
Wyckaerk, Luke, Chm. Bd., Pres. & Chief Exec. Officer--Intertrade Industries, Huntington Beach, CA, pg. 581
Wydman, Mary Will, Chm. Bd. & Chief Exec. Officer--Witt Company, Cincinnati, OH, pg. 1198
Wyman, Timothy E., Chm.--Brubaker Tool Corp., Millersburg, PA, pg. 183
Wynne, John O., Chm. Bd.--The Weather Channel, Atlanta, GA, pg. 654
Wyse, Marc A., Chm. & Chief Exec. Officer--Wyse Advertising, Inc., Cleveland, OH, pg. 1206
Yamakoshi, Noby, Chm. Bd. & Chief Exec. Officer--Nobart, Inc., Chicago, IL, pg. 808
Yarhi, Nassin, Chm. Bd.--Bufkor, Inc., Clearwater, FL, pg. 187
Yasumura, Muts, Chm. & Exec. Design Dir.--CYB Yasumura Design, New York, NY, pg. 1210
Yates, A. P., Chm.--Bechtel, Inc., Houston, TX, pg. 131
Yates, A. P., Chm. Bd.--Bechtel Civil, Inc., San Francisco, CA, pg. 131
Yates, A. P., Chm.--Bechtel Eastern Power Corporation, Gaithersburg, MD, pg. 131
Yates, A. P., Chm. Bd.--Bechtel National, Inc., San Francisco, CA, pg. 131
Yates, A. P., Chm.--Bechtel, Inc Mining & Metals Special Operation, San Francisco, CA, pg. 131
Yates, Jim, Chm. Bd.--E-Z Mart Stores, Inc., Texarkana, TX, pg. 361
Yelverton, William F., Chm. & Chief Exec. Officer-New York Worldwide Holding, Inc.--New York Life Insurance Company, New York, NY, pg. 802
Yelverton, William F., Chm. & Chief Exec. Officer--New York Life Worldwide Holding, Inc., New York, NY, pg. 803
Yenkin, Bernard, Chm. Bd.--Yenkin-Majestic Paint Corporation, Columbus, OH, pg. 1208
Yerant, Gene S., Chm. & Pres.--Transport Insurance Co., Dallas, TX, pg. 54
Yerger, John R., Chm. Bd. & Pres.--Yerger Bros., Inc., Lititz, PA, pg. 1208
Yeshoua, Marco, Chm. Bd.--Lucky Winner, Inc., New York, NY, pg. 686
Yoh, Harold L., Jr., Chm. Bd., Pres. & Chief Exec. Officer--Day & Zimmermann, Inc., Radnor, PA, pg. 320
Yohman, Edward J., Chm. Bd. & Chief Exec. Officer--Cyberex, Inc., Mentor, OH, pg. 307
Yost, Frank A., Chm. Bd.--Hopkinsville Milling Co., Hopkinsville, KY, pg. 543
Yost, Wallace H., Chm. Bd. & Chief Exec. Officer--D.S.U.-Peterbilt & GMC, Inc., Portland, OR, pg. 309
Young, David, Chm. Bd. & Pres.--Young & Laramore, Indianapolis, IN, pg. 1209
Young, David, Chm. Bd. & Chief Exec. Officer--Aminco, Inc., Savannah, GA, pg. 67
Young, Donald A., Chm. Bd. & Chief Exec. Officer--Carson Products Company, Savannah, GA, pg. 67
Young, Dr. C.B.F., Chm. Bd. & Pres.--Young Refining Corp., Douglasville, GA, pg. 1210
Young, Edward, Chm. Bd.--Munroe, Inc., Pittsburgh, PA, pg. 776
Young, Edward D., Hon. Chm.--The Jayme Organization, Inc., Cleveland, OH, pg. 591
Young, Edward S., Chm. Bd.--Ken-Mac Metal, Inc., Cleveland, OH, pg. 622
Young, Ira L., Chm. Bd.--Malibu Grand Prix Corporation, Canoga Park, CA, pg. 702
Young, J. Givens, Chm. Bd. & Pres.--Young Pecan Shelling Co., Inc., Florence, SC, pg. 1209
Young, Jane H., Chm. Bd.--General Wholesale Company, Inc., Atlanta, GA, pg. 451
Young, John A., Sr., Chm. Bd.--Burd & Fletcher Company, Kansas City, MO, pg. 189
Young, Richard F., Chm. Bd., Pres. & Chief Exec. Officer--Sues, Young & Brown Inc., Baldwin Park, CA, pg. 1056
Young, Thomas, Jr., Chm. Bd.--Young Electric Sign Company, Salt Lake City, UT, pg. 1209
Young, Warren V., Vice Chm.--Automobile Auction Division, Atlanta, GA, pg. 293
Young, William P., Chm. Bd.--Plastipak Packaging Inc., Plymouth, MI, pg. 876
Yount, G. Stuart, Chm. Bd., Chief Exec. & Chief Fin. Officer--Fortifiber Corporation, Los Angeles, CA, pg. 425
Ysasmandi, J. Joaquin Ysasi, Chm. Bd.--Domecq Importers Inc., Old Greenwich, CT, pg. 343
Ytterberg, Ralph, Chm. Bd. & Chief Exec. Officer--INDRESCO, Inc., Dallas, TX, pg. 565
Yuzon, Virgilio A., Chm.--Hemisphere-Leo Burnett, Inc., Metro Manila,, Philippines, pg. 192
Zachry, H.B., Jr., Chm. Bd. & Chief Exec. Officer--H.B. Zachry, San Antonio, TX, pg. 1215
Zack, Christine, Chm. Bd. & Pres.--Zack Company, Chicago, IL, pg. 1215
Zambito, Steven, Pres. & Chief Exec. Officer--Talon, Inc., Meadville, PA, pg. 1077
Zamoiski, C. J., Jr., Chm. Bd., Pres. & Chief Exec. Officer--The Zamoiski Co., Baltimore, MD, pg. 1216
Zaransky, David, Chm. Bd.--Ridgeview Motors, Inc., Schiller Park, IL, pg. 934
Zaransky, David, Chm. Bd.--Airways Rent A Car, Schiller Park, IL, pg. 934
Zell, Samuel, Chm. Bd. & Pres.--Equity Group Investments, Chicago, IL, pg. 385
Zeman, Carl, Chm. Bd.--Certified Grocers Midwest, Inc., Hodgkins, IL, pg. 236
Zenegy, Louis, Chm. Bd., Pres. & Chief Exec. Officer--Polymer Development Laboratories, Inc., Orange, CA, pg. 880

Zenner, Merrill, Chm. Bd.--The Reliable Corp., Chicago, IL, pg. 924
Ziegler, Allen S., Chm. Bd.--Westco Products, Inc., Pico Rivera, CA, pg. 1178
Zieve, Morton, Chm. Bd.--Simons Michelson Zieve, Inc., Troy, MI, pg. 1006
Ziff, William B., Jr., Chm. Bd.--Ziff Communications Company, New York, NY, pg. 1218
Zilber, Joseph J., Chm. Bd.--Zilber, Ltd., Milwaukee, WI, pg. 1219
Zilkha, Ezra, Chm. Bd.--Union Holdings, Inc., New York, NY, pg. 1128
Zilkha, Selim K., Chm. Bd. & Chief Exec. Officer--Zilkha Energy Company, Houston, TX, pg. 1219
Zimmer, Edward M., Jr., Chm. Bd. & Chief Exec. Officer--Berkeley Industries Inc., Laguna Beach, CA, pg. 141
Zimmerman, John, Chm. Bd.--Sunline Coach Co., Inc., Denver, PA, pg. 1061
Zimmerman, Raymond, Chm. Bd.--Standard Advertising Agency, Brentwood, TN, pg. 1035
Zimmermann, F.N., Chm. Bd. & Pres.--March Manufacturing Inc., Glenview, IL, pg. 706
Zinbarg, Steven, Chm. Bd. & Creative Dir.--Sisti, Zinbarg & Howard, Inc., Paramus, NJ, pg. 1009
Zirkle, Robert H., Chm. Bd.--Plan International U.S.A., Warwick, RI, pg. 874
Zoeller, Robert F., Chm. Bd. & Chief Exec. Officer--Zoeller Co., Louisville, KY, pg. 1220
Zoller, Gerhard H., Chm. Bd.--J.H. Findorff & Son, Inc., Madison, WI, pg. 411
Zook, Woodrow J., Chm. Bd.--The Wooster Brush Company, Wooster, OH, pg. 1202
Zuckerman, Mortimer, Chm. Bd.--The Atlantic Monthly Magazine, Boston, MA, pg. 95
Zuckerman, Mortimer B., Chm. Bd. & Editor-in-Chief--U.S. News & World Report, New York, NY, pg. 1136
Zuckerwar, Richard J., Chm. Bd. & Pres.--The Grandoe Corporation, Gloversville, NY, pg. 476
Zumbiel, Charles W., Chm. Bd.--C. W. Zumbiel Company, Cincinnati, OH, pg. 1221
Zylstra, O.W., Chm. Bd. & Chief Exec. Officer--Rena-Ware Distributors Inc., Redmond, WA, pg. 926
Zylstra, Stan, Chm. Bd.--Land O'Lakes, Inc., Arden Hills, MN, pg. 653

CHIEF EXECUTIVE OFFICER

Abbey, Nelson Dan, Jr., Chm. Bd. & Chief Exec. Officer--Abbey Etna Machine Company, Perrysburg, OH, pg. 9
Abbott, Garry, Mng. Dir. & Creative Dir.--Ketchum Advertising Singapore, Singapore, Singapore, pg. 625
Abdalla, Herbert A., Pres. & Chief Exec. Officer--Abdalla's Lafayette, Inc., Lafayette, LA, pg. 10
Abplanalp, Robert H., Chm. Bd., Pres. & Chief Exec. Officer--Precision Valve Corporation, Yonkers, NY, pg. 885
Abraham, G.M., Chief Exec. Officer & Gen. Mgr.--Screw Conveyor Corp., Hammond, IN, pg. 983
Abraham, Lee, Chm. Bd. & Chief Exec. Officer--Associated Merchandising Corp., New York, NY, pg. 91
Abramson, David B., Pres. & Chief Exec. Officer--Abramson Ehrlich Manes, Inc., Washington, DC, pg. 10
Ach, Roger W., II, Pres. & Chief Exec. Officer--Chicago West Pullman Corporation, Cincinnati, OH, pg. 246
Acker, Stanley, Chm., Pres. & Chief Exec. Officer--Pavion Ltd., Nyack on Hudson, NY, pg. 852
Ackerman, Roy A., Chm. Bd. & Chief Exec. Officer--Astre Corporate Group, Alexandria, VA, pg. 92
Acklen, Charles, Pres. & Chief Exec. Officer--Bill's Dollar Stores, Inc., Jackson, MS, pg. 150
Acomb, James C., Pres. & Chief Exec. Officer--Restaurant Company, Inc., Birmingham, AL, pg. 929
Adams, Charles, Chief Exec. Officer--Package Service Company, Inc., Kansas City, MO, pg. 842
Adams, Fred, Chief Exec. Officer--Cal-Maine Foods, Inc., Jackson, MS, pg. 208
Adams, H. Mat, Chm. & Chief Exec. Officer--Adams Colway & Associates, Rochester, NY, pg. 16
Adams, Harry, Pres., Chief Exec. Officer, & Chief Fin. Officer--Pyttronic Industries, Inc., Montgomeryville, PA, pg. 901
Adams, Kirby, Pres. & Chief Exec. Officer--Titanium Metals Corporation, Denver, CO, pg. 1109
Adams, Robert E., Pres. & Chief Exec. Officer--MidSouth Ice Co., Huntsville, AL, pg. 1030
Adams, Robert J., Pres. & Chief Exec. Officer--R. P. Adams Company, Inc., Tonawanda, NY, pg. 16
Addison, E. Christopher, Chm. Bd.--Addison Steel Inc., Orlando, FL, pg. 17
Adelman, Sheldon G., Chm. Bd. & Chief Exec. Officer--Blue Coral, Inc., Cleveland, OH, pg. 159
Adelman, Sheldon G., Chm. Bd. & Chief Exec. Officer--McKay Chemical Co., Los Angeles, CA, pg. 159
Adelman, Sheldon G., Chm. Bd. & Chief Exec. Officer--Simoniz Canada Ltd., Cleveland, OH, pg. 159
Adelman, Sheldon G., Chm. Bd. & Chief Exec. Officer--Nic Sand, Cleveland, OH, pg. 159
Adelman, Sheldon G., Chm. Bd. & Chief Exec. Officer--Chemifax, City of Commerce, CA, pg. 159
Ades, Alan, Chm., Pres. & Chief Exec. Officer--A & E Stores, Inc., Ridgefield, NJ, pg. 1
Adler, Larry M., Pres. & Chief Exec. Officer--Adler Boschetto Peebles & Partners, Inc., New York, NY, pg. 17
Adler, Myron, Chief Exec. Officer--Myron Manufacturing Corporation, Maywood, NJ, pg. 780
Adolfson, David G., Chm. Bd., Pres. & Chief Exec. Officer--Adolfson & Peterson, Inc., Minneapolis, MN, pg. 18
Agan, R.E., Pres. & Chief Exec. Officer--Hardinge Brothers, Inc., Elmira, NY, pg. 508
Aginian, Richard D., Pres. & Chief Exec. Officer--Suburban Communications Corp., Livonia, MI, pg. 1055
Ahrens, Jay, Chm. Bd., Pres. & Chief Exec. Officer--Holly's Inc., Grand Rapids, MI, pg. 540
Aiken, William, Chm. Bd. & Chief Exec. Officer--ACO Inc., Farmington Hills, MI, pg. 2
Akers, James F., Pres. & Chief Exec. Officer--The Crystal Tissue Co., Middletown, OH, pg. 303
Akins, Perry S., Pres. & Chief Exec. Officer--ELS Educational Services, Culver City, CA, pg. 56
Albers, John R., Chm. Bd., Pres. & Chief Exec. Officer--Dr Pepper/Seven-Up Companies, Inc., Dallas, TX, pg. 342
Albers, John R., Chm. & Chief Exec. Officer--Dr Pepper Company, Dallas, TX, pg. 342
Albert, Andrew B., Pres. & Co-Chief Exec. Officer--Rittenhouse Inc., Park Ridge, IL, pg. 936
Albrecht, Steven, Pres. & Chief Exec. Officer--The Fred W. Albrecht Grocery Co., Akron, OH, pg. 31
Alcorn, David C., Chm. Bd. & Chief Exec. Officer--Donlee Technologies Inc., York, PA, pg. 344
Aldridge, Edward C., Pres. & Chief Exec. Officer--The Aerospace Corporation, El Segundo, CA, pg. 22
Alexander, Patrick D., Pres. & Chief Exec. Officer--Cold Spring Granite Company, Minnetonka, MN, pg. 259
Aley, Paul N., Pres. & Chief Exec. Officer--National Machinery Company, Tiffin, OH, pg. 792
Alford, J. Keith, Pres. & Chief Exec. Officer--Adam Meldrum & Anderson Co., Inc., Buffalo, NY, pg. 16
Allard, Jean Marc, Chm. Bd., Pres. & Chief Exec. Officer--Hubbard Construction Co., Winter Park, FL, pg. 549
Allbritton, Joe L., Chm. Bd. & Chief Exec. Officer--Perpetual Corporation, Washington, DC, pg. 862
Allegretto, Paul V., Pres. & Chief Exec. Officer--Alpha Q, Inc., Colchester, CT, pg. 5
Allen, Charles S., Pres. & Chief Exec. Officer--Sloan Valve Company, Franklin Park, IL, pg. 1010
Allen, David, Chm., Pres. & Chief Exec. Officer--AMD Industries Inc., Cicero, IL, pg. 5
Allen, Roderick, Chm. Bd. & Chief Exec. Officer--Allen Canning Company, Siloam Springs, AR, pg. 35
Allison, Gerald L., Chief Exec. Officer--AJC International, Inc., Atlanta, GA, pg. 4
Allison, James R., Sr., Chm. Bd. & Chief Exec. Officer--Allison-Erwin Co. Inc., Charlotte, NC, pg. 40
Allison, Robert S., Chm. & Chief Exec. Officer--Doe-Anderson Advertising Agency, Inc., Louisville, KY, pg. 342
Alpert, Norman R., Chm. Bd., Pres. & Chief Exec. Officer--Bio-Tek Instruments, Inc., Winooski, VT, pg. 152
Alter, James M., Chm. Bd. & Chief Exec. Officer--The Harry Alter Company, Chicago, IL, pg. 45
Alvarez, Paul H., Chm. Bd., Pres. & Chief Exec. Officer--Ketchum Communications Inc., Pittsburgh, PA, pg. 625
Ament, Werner E., Chm. Bd., Pres., Chief Exec. Officer & Sec.--Milex of America, Inc., Chicago, IL, pg. 753
Ames, Richard S., Chm. & Chief Exec. Officer--Command Plastic Corporation, Akron, OH, pg. 268
Ameye, Victor, Chief Exec. Officer--After Six, Incorporated, Philadelphia, PA, pg. 24
Ammann, Fritz, Pres. & Chief Exec. Officer--Esprit de Corp., San Francisco, CA, pg. 388
Amore, Joe, Chm. Bd., Pres. & Chief Exec. Officer--BeefAmerica Operating Co., Inc., Omaha, NE, pg. 131
Amoss, W. James, Jr., Chm. Bd. & Chief Exec. Officer--Lykes Bros. Steamship Co., Inc., New Orleans, LA, pg. 688
Anasto, John, Pres., Chief Exec. & Chief Oper. Officer--Strongheart Products, Inc., Kansas City, KS, pg. 1054
Anderson, E. Dean, Chm. Bd. & Chief Exec. Officer--Leslie Advertising, Greenville, SC, pg. 668
Anderson, G. D., Jr., Pres. & Chief Exec. Officer--Sherley Grain Company, Bovina, TX, pg. 998
Anderson, James, Chm. Bd. & Chief Exec. Officer--Anderson Brothers Construction Brainerd, Brainerd, MN, pg. 72
Anderson, James D., Pres. & Chief Exec. Officer--Central DuPage Health System, Naperville, IL, pg. 232
Anderson, John, Pres., Chief Exec. & Oper. Officer--Alabama Farmers Co-op, Decatur, AL, pg. 28
Anderson, Lee R., Sr., Chm. Bd. & Chief Exec. Officer--API Group Inc., Saint Paul, MN, pg. 5
Anderson, Mark R., Pres. & Chief Exec. Officer--Mark Anderson Associates, Inc., Arlington Heights, IL, pg. 73
Anderson, Noble, Chief Exec. Officer & Gen. Mgr.--Associated Milk Producers, Inc., San Antonio, TX, pg. 91
Anderson, Norm, Pres., Chief Exec. Officer--Anderson, Rothstein & Fiqua, San Francisco, CA, pg. 73
Anderson, Ralph, Chm Bd., Pres., & Chief Exec. Officer--Belcan Corporation, Cincinnati, OH, pg. 133
Anderson, Richard C., Pres. & Chief Exec. Officer--Fairfield Industries, Inc., Houston, TX, pg. 397
Anderson, Richard P., Pres. & Chief Exec. Officer--The Andersons, Maumee, OH, pg. 73
Anderson, Ruel L., Jr., Pres. & Chief Exec. Officer--Anco Insulations, Inc., Baton Rouge, LA, pg. 72
Anderson, Thomas G., Chief Oper. Officer, Chief Fin. Officer & V.P.--Gordy's, Inc., Worthington, MN, pg. 472
Andretta, Vincent J., Pres., Chief Exec. Officer & Treas.--Colony Liquor Distributors, Inc., Kingston, NY, pg. 264
Anfield, Frank, Pres. & Chief Exec. Officer Y&R New York--Young & Rubicam Inc., New York, NY, pg. 1210
Anfield, Frank A., Pres. & Chief Exec. Officer-Y&R New York--Young & Rubicam New York, New York, NY, pg. 1211
Anschutz, Philip, Pres.--Anschutz Corporation, Denver, CO, pg. 75
Anshell, J.G., Chm. Bd. & Chief Exec. Officer--Moses Anshell, Inc., Phoenix, AZ, pg. 76
Anthony, Harry S., Chief Exec. Officer--J. E. Higgins Lumber Co., Concord, CA, pg. 533
Antink, Grant S., Pres. & Chief Exec. Officer--Drafting Graphics, Inc., Elk Grove Village, IL, pg. 348
Appalucci, Joseph L., Chm. & Chief Exec. Officer--Lieberman-Appalucci, Allentown, PA, pg. 675
Appelwick, Robert A., Chm. Bd. & Chief Exec. Officer--Apple Lines, Inc., Madison, SD, pg. 79
Applegate, Leslie T., Chm. Bd. & Chief Exec. Officer--Surgical Appliance Industries, Inc., Cincinnati, OH, pg. 1065
Applequist, Dale M., Pres., Chief Exec. Officer & New Bus. Contact--Cash Plus, Inc., Minneapolis, MN, pg. 228
Arch, D.C., Chm. Bd. & Chief Exec. Officer--Blistex, Inc., Oak Brook, IL, pg. 157
Archer, Ward, Jr., Pres. & Chief Exec. Officer--Archer/Malmo Adv., Inc., Memphis, TN, pg. 80
Arenberg, William D., Pres. & Chief Exec. Officer--Columbia Pipe & Supply Company, Chicago, IL, pg. 266
Arend, John R., Chm. Bd. & Chief Exec. Officer--International Chemical Company, Tulsa, OK, pg. 576
Arends, Donald L., Chief Exec. Officer--Donald L. Arends Inc., Oak Brook, IL, pg. 81
Arens, Richard P., Chm. Bd., Pres., Chief Exec. & Fin. Officer--Alacon, Sunnyvale, CA, pg. 29
Armbrecht, Edward C., Jr., Chm. Bd. & Co-Chief Exec. Officer--Stone & Thomas, Wheeling, WV, pg. 1051
Armbruster, Allan P., Chief Exec. Officer--Hoffritz for Cutlery, New York, NY, pg. 538
Armstrong, M.H., Pres. & Chief Exec. Officer--Armstrong International, Inc., Three Rivers, MI, pg. 83
Armstrong, Peter, Mng. Dir.--Young & Rubicam (Zambia) Ltd., Lusaka,, Zambia, pg. 1214
Arnold, David, Pres. & Chief Exec. Officer--Pacific Northern Oil Corp., Seattle, WA, pg. 841
Arnold, Howard M., Pres. & Chief Exec. Officer--Chartway Technologies, Rockville, MD, pg. 240
Arnold, Steve, Pres. & Chief Exec. Officer--One Stop Supply, Tyler, TX, pg. 827
Aronoff, Leona, Chief Exec. Officer--Gate City Beverage Distributors, San Bernardino, CA, pg. 444
Aronson, Arnold, Chm. Bd. & Chief Exec. Officer--Woodward & Lothrop/John Wanamaker, Washington, DC, pg. 1201
Aronson, Arnold, Chm. Bd. & Chief Exec. Officer--John Wanamaker, Philadelphia, Philadelphia, PA, pg. 1201
Arpin, Paul G., Chief Exec. Officer--Paul Arpin Vanlines, Inc., East Greenwich, RI, pg. 85
Arst, Rodger M., Chief Exec. Officer--Goldsmiths, Inc., Wichita, KS, pg. 469
Asch, Peter, Pres. & Chief Exec. Officer--Twincraft, Inc., Winooski, VT, pg. 1122
Aschinger, Carl J., Jr., Chm. Bd., Pres. & Chief Exec. Officer--Columbus Show Case Company, Columbus, OH, pg. 267
Ash, Carroll L., Co-Chm., Pres. & Chief Exec. Officer--Trojan Steel Co., Charleston, WV, pg. 1115
Ashkenazi, Ely, Chm. Bd. & Chief Exec. Officer--Soundesign Corporation, Jersey City, NJ, pg. 1018
Aspland, Brian, Chm. Bd., Pres. & Chief Exec. Officer--Integral Systems, Inc., Sunnyvale, CA, pg. 573
Atols, John M., Chm. Bd. & Chief Exec. Officer--Atols Tool and Mold Corp., Schiller Park, IL, pg. 97
Auch, Frederick J., Jr., Chm. Bd. & Chief Exec. Officer--George W. Auch Co., Pontiac, MI, pg. 97
Augustine, James N., Chm. Bd. & Chief Exec. Officer--Insurance Corp. of America, Houston, TX, pg. 572
Aurichio, Joseph L., Pres. & Chief Exec. Officer--Kearney-National, Inc., White Plains, NY, pg. 357
Austad, Dave, Pres. & Chief Exec. Officer--The Austad Company, Sioux Falls, SD, pg. 98
Autry, Gene, Chm. Bd., Pres. & Chief Exec. Officer--Golden West Broadcasters, Los Angeles, CA, pg. 467
Aveni, Joseph T., Chm. Bd. & Chief Exec. Officer--Realty One, Cleveland, OH, pg. 917
Aversano, John, Chief Exec. Officer--Air Conditioning Co., Inc., Glendale, CA, pg. 26
Avrett, John G., Chm. & Chief Exec. Officer--Avrett, Free & Ginsberg, Inc., New York, NY, pg. 103
Awad, Dennis J., Pres., Chief Exec. & Fin. Officer & Treas.--Tele-Com Products, Inc., Duarte, CA, pg. 1084
Axelrad, James A., Pres. & Chief Exec. Officer--Pakula & Company, Chicago, IL, pg. 843
Babich, N., Pres. & Chief Exec. Officer--Hitchiner Manufacturing Company, Inc., Milford, NH, pg. 536
Bachman, John C., Chm. Bd., Pres., Chief Exec. & Oper. Officer--Automated Marketing Systems, Inc., Chicago, IL, pg. 100
Bachmann, Thomas M., Chm. Bd., Pres. & Chief Exec. Officer--Calico Cat Press, Inc., New Providence, NJ, pg. 209
Bacigalupo, John W., Chief Exec. Officer--Kelly-Moore Paint Company, Inc., San Carlos, CA, pg. 621
Backman, William D., Jr., Pres. & Chief Exec. Officer--Aurora Casket Company, Aurora, IN, pg. 98
Backus, Roberta, Chm. Bd., Chief Exec. Officer & New Bus. Contact--Backus Turner & Partners, Inc., Miami, FL, pg. 112
Bader, Ronald L., Pres. & Chief Exec. Officer--Bader Rutter & Assoc., Inc., Brookfield, WI, pg. 113
Baer, Albert, Chm. Bd. & Chief Exec. Officer--Imperial Schrade Corp., New York, NY, pg. 564
Baggett, W. Les, Pres. & Chief Exec. Officer--LePage's, Inc., Pittsburgh, PA, pg. 287
Bailey, Charles, Pres. & Chief Exec. Officer--Signet Industries, Fraser, MI, pg. 1003
Bailey, J.H., Chm. Bd. & Chief Exec. Officer--The Cretex Companies, Elk River, MN, pg. 299
Bailey, John, Chm. Bd., Pres., Chief Exec. & Fin. Officer & Treas.--Cal/Emblem Labels, Inc., Fresno, CA, pg. 208
Bailey, John H., Chm. Bd., Pres., Chief Exec. & Chief Oper. Officer--The Climatic Corp., Columbia, SC, pg. 255
Bailey, Richard W., Chm. & Chief Exec. Officer--Bailey Lauerman & Associates, Inc., Lincoln, NE, pg. 114
Baines, Paul Edward Alex, Chief Exec. Officer--CS First Boston New Zealand Holdings Limited, Wellington,, New Zealand, pg. 204
Baird, J. Allen, Pres. & Chief Exec. Officer--Mrs. Baird's Bakeries, Inc., Fort Worth, TX, pg. 760
Baker, Charles W., Pres. & Chief Exec. Officer--Jackson Paper Company, Jackson, MS, pg. 587

Corporate Responsibilities Index

Baker, F.C. Buzz, Pres. & Chief Exec. Officer--Creswell, Munsell, Fultz & Zirbel, Cedar Rapids, IA, pg. 1211
Baker, H.R., Pres. & Chief Exec. Officer--Marathon Electric Manufacturing Corp., Wausau, WI, pg. 705
Baker, Ken, Chief Exec. Officer & Gen. Mgr.-Plastics Div.--Newage Industries Inc., Willow Grove, PA, pg. 803
Baker, Kenneth D., Chief Exec. Officer & Gen. Mgr.-Plastics Div.--Newage Industries Inc., Plastics Division, Willow Grove, PA, pg. 803
Baker, Maurice W., Pres. & Chief Exec. Officer--Madison Grocery Co., Inc., Richmond, KY, pg. 699
Baker, Robert, Chief Exec. Office:--Skyway Freight Systems, Inc., Watsonville, CA, pg. 1009
Baker, Ronald, Chm. Bd., Pres. & Chief Exec. Officer--Millmaster Onyx Group, Inc., Westport, CT, pg. 755
Baker, Terry, Chief Exec. Officer--Showell Farms, Inc., Showell, MD, pg. 1000
Baker, W.G., Jr., Chm. Bd. & Chief Exec. Officer--Pachmayr Gun Works Inc., Monrovia, CA, pg. 839
Baker, Wilder D., Chm. & Chief Exec. Officer--Warwick Baker & Fiore Inc., New York, NY, pg. 1165
Bakke, Richard, Pres. & Chief Exec. Officer--Portland Glass/American Management Group, Westbrook, ME, pg. 58
Bakke, Richard M., Pres. & Chief Exec. Officer--American Management Group, Westbrook, ME, pg. 57
Baldwin, Dan D., Pres. & Chief Exec. Officer--Nautilus, Independence, VA, pg. 796
Baldwin, Everett N., Pres. & Chief Exec. Officer--Welch's, Concord, MA, pg. 789
Balkind, Aubrey, Chief Exec. Officer--Frankfurt Gips Balkind, Advertising, New York, NY, pg. 429
Ball, Jess, Pres. & Chief Exec. Officer--Alford Industries, Inc., Ridgefield Park, NJ, pg. 33
Ball, John H., Chm. Bd. & Chief Exec. Officer--R. M. Shoemaker Co., West Conshohocken, PA, pg. 1000
Ball, Rex M., Chm. Bd. & Chief Exec. Officer--HTB, Inc., Oklahoma City, OK, pg. 497
Ballard, Larry C., Chm. Bd., Pres. & Chief Exec. Officer--Sentry Insurance, A Mutual Company, Stevens Point, WI, pg. 990
Ballhagen, Lloyd, Pres. & Chief Exec. Officer--Harris Enterprises Inc., Hutchinson, KS, pg. 511
Balsamo, Salvatore, Chm. Bd., Pres. & Chief Exec. Officer--Technical Aid Corporation, Newton Upper Falls, MA, pg. 1083
Banducci, Barry, Pres. & Chief Exec. Officer--The Equion Corporation, New Haven, CT, pg. 385
Bank, Morton B., Pres. & Chief Exec. Officer--Bank M F & Company, Inc., Minneapolis, MN, pg. 117
Bank, William J., Chief Exec. Officer--Jonbil Inc., Chase City, VA, pg. 602
Bankston, William S., Pres. & Chief Exec. Officer--AmTran Corporation, Conway, AR, pg. 69
Bankuty, Geza E., Chm. Bd., Pres. & Chief Exec. Officer--New England Machinery, Inc., Bradenton, FL, pg. 800
Baranski, Dennis A., Chm. Bd., Pres. & Chief Exec. Officer--Barancorp, Lecompton, KS, pg. 118
Barash, Ralph, Pres. & Chief Exec. Officer--Polarome Mfg. Co. Inc., Jersey City, NJ, pg. 878
Barbee, Robert P., Chm. Bd. & Chief Exec. Officer--Pneumafil Corp., Charlotte, NC, pg. 878
Barber, Miles H., Chm. Bd. & Chief Exec. Officer--Commercial & Industrial Administration Co. inc, Santa Clara, CA, pg. 268
Barden, Thomas, Exec. V.P. & Chief Exec. Officer--Barden & Robeson Corporation, Middleport, NY, pg. 119
Barensfeld, David E., Chief Exec. Officer--Ellwood City Forge, Ellwood City, PA, pg. 378
Barge, John M., Chief Exec. Officer--Barge-Wagener, Inc., Atlanta, GA, pg. 119
Barger, Michael E., Chief Exec. Officer--Barger Builder & Developers, Saint Petersburg, FL, pg. 119
Barlow, Richard A., Pres. & Chief Exec. Officer--Bentley-Harris Manufacturing Co., Lionville, PA, pg. 140
Barlow, Witt, Chm., Pres. & Chief Exec. Officer--Great Lakes Dredge & Dock, Oak Brook, IL, pg. 481
Barnes, Bradford, Chm. Bd. & Chief Exec. Officer--Crouch Supply Company, Inc., Fort Worth, TX, pg. 301
Barnes, Daniel F., Chief Exec. Officer--Republic Fastener Products Corp., Great Falls, SC, pg. 928
Barnes, John E., Chief Exec. Officer--Small Parts, Inc., Logansport, IN, pg. 1010
Barnes, Robert, Chief Exec. Officer--Belle Tire Distributor Inc., Allen Park, MI, pg. 136
Barnes, William, Pres. & Chief Exec. Officer--Spectrulite Consortium, Inc., Madison, IL, pg. 1029
Barnett, Cecil C., Chm. Bd., Pres., Chief Exec. Officer & Treas.--Algood Food Company, Louisville, KY, pg. 34
Barnett, Richard M., Pres. & Chief Exec. Officer--Reliable Stores, Inc., Columbia, MD, pg. 925
Barnhardt, T.M. III, Pres. & Chief Exec. Officer--Barnhardt Manufacturing Co., Charlotte, NC, pg. 120
Barnum, William M., Chm. Bd. & Chief Exec. Officer--Educational Publishing Corporation, Oak Lawn, IL, pg. 369
Barr, Stephen, Chief Exec. Officer--Osborn & Barr Communications, Clayton, MO, pg. 830
Barrans, Terry, Pres. & Chief Exec. Officer--Fisher Mills, Inc., Seattle, WA, pg. 415
Barre, Stephen A., Chm. Bd., Pres., Chief Exec. Officer & Sec.--Servo Corporation of America, Hicksville, NY, pg. 993
Barrera, Jess, Pres. & Chief Exec. Officer--Southern California Bancorp, Laguna Beach, CA, pg. 1020
Bartell, George, Jr., Chief Exec. Officer--The Bartell Drug Company, Seattle, WA, pg. 122
Bartholomew, Charles R., Chief Exec. Officer (Los Angeles) & Dir.--EvansGroup, Salt Lake City, UT, pg. 390
Bartholomew, Charles R., Chief Exec. Officer--EvansGroup, Los Angeles, CA, pg. 391
Bartholomew, Charles R., Chief Exec. Officer--EvansGroup, Denver, CO, pg. 391
Bartholow, Peter, Chm. Bd., Pres. & Chief Oper. Officer--MCorp, Dallas, TX, pg. 732
Bartolone, Joseph F., Sr., Chm. & Chief Exec. Officer--Pancom International Corp., Stamford, CT, pg. 845
Barton, A.P., Jr., Chm. Bd., Pres. & Chief Exec. Officer--Mutual Manufacturing & Supply Co., Cincinnati, OH, pg. 778
Barton, Max E., Pres. & Chief Exec. Officer--Groendyke Transports, Inc., Enid, OK, pg. 489
Bartscht, Karl G., Chm. Bd. & Chief Exec. Officer--Chi Systems, Inc., Ann Arbor, MI, pg. 244
Basinait, Martin C., Pres. & Chief Exec. Officer--Western Regional Off Track Betting, Batavia, NY, pg. 1181
Basler, William L., Chm. Bd., Chief Exec. Officer & Treas.--Basler Electric Company, Highland, IL, pg. 125
Bateman, M. Joel, Chief Exec. Officer--Cameron & Barkley Company, Inc., Charleston Heights, SC, pg. 212
Bates, Robert D., Chm. Bd., Pres. & Chief Exec. Officer--Guarantee Mutual Life Co., Omaha, NE, pg. 491
Batt, James M., Pres. & Chief Exec. Officer--Peck Spring Company, Plainville, CT, pg. 854
Bauer, John A., Jr., Chm. Bd.--Pennock, Philadelphia, PA, pg. 858
Baute, Joseph A., Chm. Bd. & Chief Exec. Officer--Markem Corporation, Keene, NH, pg. 708
Bawden, John D., Chief Exec. Officer--Bawden Printing, Inc., Eldridge, IA, pg. 127
Baxter, Alfred X., Chm. & Chief Exec. Officer--J.H. Baxter & Company, San Mateo, CA, pg. 127
Bayer, Gary R., Chm. & Chief Exec. Officer--Bayer Bess Vanderwarker Inc., Chicago, IL, pg. 128
Bayley, Robert E., Chm. Bd. & Chief Exec. Officer--Robert E. Bayley Construction, Seattle, WA, pg. 128
Bayly, George V., Pres. & Chief Exec. Officer--Ivex Packaging Corporation, Lincolnshire, IL, pg. 583
Bazant, Stanley K., Exec. V.P., Chief Exec. Officer & Gen. Mgr.--Plains Electric Generation Transmission Co-Op, Inc., Albuquerque, NM, pg. 873
Beach, William H., Chm. Bd., Pres., Chief Exec. & Oper. Officer--Beach Mold & Tool Inc., New Albany, IN, pg. 128
Bean, Delcie D., Pres., Treas. & Chief Exec. Officer--D. D. Bean & Sons Co., Jaffrey, NH, pg. 129
Beardall, James C., Chm. Bd., Pres. & Chief Exec. Officer--Anderson Lumber Company, Ogden, UT, pg. 73
Beardsley, John R., Chm. Bd. & Chief Exec. Officer--Padilla Speer Beardsley Inc., Minneapolis, MN, pg. 842
Beart, D.B., Pres. & Chief Exec. Officer--Standard Lafarge, Canfield, OH, pg. 1036
Beaton, Bradford, Pres. & Chief Exec. Officer--New England Newspaper Supply Company, Inc., Millbury, MA, pg. 800
Beaver, Donald C., Pres., Chief Exec. Officer & Treas.--Brian Center Management Corporation, Hickory, NC, pg. 175
Beck, James H., Chm. Bd. & Chief Exec. Officer--Precision Twist Drill Co., Crystal Lake, IL, pg. 885
Beck, Jerry, Chm. Bd., Pres. & Chief Exec. Officer--Mighty Distributing System, Norcross, GA, pg. 752
Beck, Paul D., Pres. & Chief Exec. Officer--Tecknit, Cranford, NJ, pg. 1084
Beck, Scott, Chm. & Chief Exec. Officer--Boston Chicken, Inc., Naperville, IL, pg. 167
Becker, B. Frederick, Pres. & Chief Exec. Officer--M M I Companies, Inc., Deerfield, IL, pg. 692
Beckwith, F. W., Chm. Bd., Pres. & Chief Exec. Officer--Fareway Stores, Inc., Boone, IA, pg. 399
Beckwith, G. Nicholas III, Pres. & Chief Exec. Officer--Beckwith Machinery Company, Murrysville, PA, pg. 131
Beech, Robert A., Pres. & Chief Exec. Officer--T O Plastics, Inc., Minneapolis, MN, pg. 1074
Beeler, Donald, Chm. Bd., Pres. & Chief Exec. Officer--Snyder's Drug Stores, Inc., Minnetonka, MN, pg. 1015
Beggington, Andrew, Chief Exec. Officer--NESLAB Instruments, Inc., Newington, NH, pg. 798
Beggs, John, Pres. & Chief Exec. Officer--Topco Associates, Inc., Skokie, IL, pg. 1101
Beggs, Lyman M., Chm., Pres. & Chief Exec. Officer--Sealy, Inc., Cleveland, OH, pg. 985
Beggs, Lyman M., Chief Exec. Officer--Sealy Canada, Ltd., Edmonton,, Canada, pg. 986
Beggs, Lymann M., Chm., Pres. & Chief Exec. Officer--Sealy Corporation, Cleveland, OH, pg. 985
Behnke, Bruce, Pres. & Chief Exec. Officer--Stanley Fastening Systems, Worcester, MA, pg. 1038
Behr, Richard, Pres. & Chief Exec. Officer--Joseph Behr & Sons Inc., Rockford, IL, pg. 132
Beidas, Burhan S., Chief Exec. Officer & Mng. Partner--BSB Madco, Dubai,, United Arab Emirates, pg. 110
Belden, John, Pres. & Chief Exec. Officer--OCTus, San Diego, CA, pg. 818
Belgrad, D.A., Pres. & Chief Exec. Officer--Schnadig Corporation, Chicago, IL, pg. 977
Belk, John M., Chm. Bd. & Chief Exec. Officer--Belk Stores Services Inc., Charlotte, NC, pg. 134
Bell, A. Quinn, Pres. & Chief Exec. Officer--The Suddath Companies, Jacksonville, FL, pg. 1055
Bell, Gene, Pres., Chief Exec. Officer--Union-Tribune Publishing Company, San Diego, CA, pg. 284
Bell, John, Pres. & Chief Exec. Officer--Dixico, Inc., Dallas, TX, pg. 135
Bell, John, Jr., Chm. Bd. & Chief Exec. Officer--Bell Packaging Corporation, Marion, IN, pg. 135
Bell, Ray, Chm. Bd., Pres. & Chief Exec. Officer--Atex Oil Co. of Texas, Inc., Amarillo, TX, pg. 93
Bell, Ray L., Pres. & Chief Exec. Officer--Bell Gas, Inc., Roswell, NM, pg. 134
Bell, Richard E., Pres. & Chief Exec. Officer--Riceland Foods, Inc., Stuttgart, AR, pg. 931
Belle, Thomas V., Pres. & Chief Exec. Officer--Carlson Learning Company, Minneapolis, MN, pg. 221
Beltz, William A., Pres., Chief Exec. Officer & Editor-in-Chief--The Bureau of National Affairs, Inc., Washington, DC, pg. 189
Belz, Jack A., Pres. & Chief Exec. Officer--Belz Enterprises, Memphis, TN, pg. 138
Bender, Robert, Chm. Bd., Pres. & Chief Exec. Officer--Megas Beauty Aids, Inc., Cleveland, OH, pg. 737
Benedict, Robert, Chief Exec. Officer, Chief Fin. Officer & V.P.--R.W. Electronics, Andover, MA, pg. 908
Benjamin, Colin, Chm., Pres. & Chief Exec. Officer--Associated Metals & Minerals Corp., White Plains, NY, pg. 91
Benjamin, Mark, Pres. & Chief Exec. Officer--Morley Group, Santa Monica, CA, pg. 770
Bennack, Frank A., Jr., Pres. & Chief Exec. Officer--The Hearst Corporation, New York, NY, pg. 521
Bennack, Frank A., Jr., Pres. & Chief Exec. Officer--Colonial Homes, New York, NY, pg. 523
Bennett, Jeffrey, Pres. & Chief Exec. Officer--Nature's Recipe Pet Foods, Corona, CA, pg. 796
Bennett, Paul F., Chm. Bd. & Chief Exec. Officer--Utility Trailer Manufacturing Co., City of Industry, CA, pg. 1141
Bensen, Kent, Chief Exec. Officer--Conklin Co. Inc., Shakopee, MN, pg. 274
Benson, Alan, Chief Exec. Officer & V.P.--Linzer Products Corp., Flushing, NY, pg. 677
Benson, Donald W., Pres. & Chief Exec. Officer--Associated Grocers, Inc., Seattle, WA, pg. 90
Benson, Gerald, Chm. Bd., Pres. & Chief Exec. Officer--The Benatty Corporation, Cambridge, OH, pg. 138
Bently, Donald E., Chm. Bd. & Chief Exec. Officer--Bently Nevada Corporation, Minden, NV, pg. 140
Benton, William B., Chm. Bd., Chief Exec. Officer & Chief Fin. Officer--Mid South Sales, Helena, AR, pg. 750
Beren, S.O., Chm. Bd., Pres. & Chief Exec. Officer--Misco Industries, Wichita, KS, pg. 759
Beres, Louis H., Pres. & Chief Exec. Officer--Lou Beres & Associates, Inc., Chicago, IL, pg. 141
Berg, Jeff, Chm. Bd. & Chief Exec. Officer--International Creative Management, Inc., New York, NY, pg. 607
Berghash, Robert, Chief Exec. Officer--Brimms Inc., Tonawanda, NY, pg. 176
Bergman, Stanley M., Chm. Bd., Pres. & Chief Exec. Officer--Henry Schein, Inc., Port Washington, NY, pg. 975
Bergquist, Harold, Chm. & Chief Exec. Officer--Northland Container Corp., Plymouth, MI, pg. 814
Bergt, Neil G., Chm. Bd. & Chief Exec. Officer--Markair, Inc., Anchorage, AK, pg. 708
Beriker, Kerman, Chief Exec. Officer & Gen. Mgr.--The Beverly Hills Hotel, Beverly Hills, CA, pg. 148
Berk, Fred, Pres., Chief Exec. & Chief Oper. Officer--Huffman Koos Co., River Edge, NJ, pg. 551
Berkley, William, Pres. & Chief Exec. Officer--Tension Envelope Corp., Kansas City, MO, pg. 1088
Berman, Barton M., Chm. Bd., Pres. & Chief Exec. Officer--Amurcon Corporation, Southfield, MI, pg. 70
Bernard, Norman, Chm. Bd. & Chief Exec. Officer--Master Industries Corp., New York, NY, pg. 719
Bernon, Peter M., Chm. Bd. & Chief Exec. Officer--Garelick Farms, Inc., Franklin, MA, pg. 443
Bernstein, Dr. Joel, Chm. Bd. & Chief Exec. Officer--GenDerm Corporation, Lincolnshire, IL, pg. 448
Bernstein, Robert, Chm. Bd., Pres. & Chief Exec. Officer--Bernstein-Rein Advertising, Inc., Kansas City, MO, pg. 144
Bernstein, Saul H., Pres., Chief Exec. Officer & Treas.--Savoy Construction Co. Inc., Kensington, MD, pg. 973
Bernstein, Zalman C., Chm. & Chief Exec. Officer--Sanford C. Bernstein & Co., Inc., New York, NY, pg. 144
Bertelli, Jay, Chm. Bd., Pres. & Chief Exec. Officer--Mercury Computer Systems, Inc., Lowell, MA, pg. 740
Bertrand, Frederic H., Chm. Bd. & Chief Exec. Officer--National Life Insurance Company, Montpelier, VT, pg. 791
Berwind, C. Graham, Jr., Chm. Bd., Pres., Chief Exec. & Chief Oper. Officer--Berwind Corporation, Philadelphia, PA, pg. 145
Besse, William C., Chief Exec. Officer--Sanborn Manufacturing Company, Springfield, MN, pg. 969
Best, Ron, Pres. & Chief Exec. Officer--Totes Incorporated, Loveland, OH, pg. 1103
Besthoff, Sydney J., III, Chief Exec. Officer--K & B, Inc., New Orleans, LA, pg. 611
Bethel, James E., Pres. & Chief Exec. Officer--Western Federal Savings & Loan Association, Marina Del Rey, CA, pg. 1179
Betz, Frederic J., Pres. & Chief Exec. Officer--Nationwide Homes, Inc., Martinsville, VA, pg. 795
Bevan, L. Darrell, Pres. & Chief Exec. Officer--Vidicom, L.D. Bevan Company, Inc., Thousand Oaks, CA, pg. 1151
Bevevino, Frank, Chm. & Chief Exec. Officer--Unifax, Inc., Wilkes-Barre, PA, pg. 1126
Beville, Gene, Chief Exec. Officer--Farmers Marketing Association, Denver, CO, pg. 704
Bevington, John F., Pres. & Chief Exec. Officer--The National Super Service Co., Toledo, OH, pg. 794
Bevis, J. Wayne, Pres. & Chief Exec. Officer--Pella Corporation, Pella, IA, pg. 856
Beyer, Sonya Z., Chm., Pres. & Chief Exec. Officer--Midco International Inc., Chicago, IL, pg. 751
Beyster, J.R., Chm. Bd. & Chief Exec. Officer--Science Applications International Corporation, San Diego, CA, pg. 981
Bhutani, Raj, Dr., Pres. & Chief Exec. Officer--Alra Laboratories, Inc., Gurnee, IL, pg. 44
Bialo, Walter, Chief Exec. Officer--Ventura Travelware, Inc., Long Island City, NY, pg. 1147
Biddinger, Clay M., Pres. & Chief Exec. Officer--Sun Financial Group, Inc., Tampa, FL, pg. 1058
Biddle, James, Sr, Pres. & Chief Exec. Officer--Mader Construction Group Inc., Elma, NY, pg. 699
Bieber, William F., Chief Exec. Officer--Acrometal Companies, Inc., Brainerd, MN, pg. 14
Bierer, William, Chm. Bd. & Chief Exec. Officer--Essex Grain Products, Inc., Frazer, PA, pg. 389

Binns, James, Pres. & Chief Exec. Officer--Timex Corporation, Middlebury, CT, pg. 1098
Biondi, Frank J., Pres. & Chief Exec. Officer--Viacom International Inc., New York, NY, pg. 785
Biondi, Frank J., Jr., Pres. & Chief Exec. Officer--Viacom Inc., New York, NY, pg. 785
Birdsall, Don R., Chm. & Chief Exec. Officer--Birdsall Voss & Kloppenburg, Inc., Mequon, WI, pg. 152
Bisang, Frank, Pres. & Chief Exec. Officer--Garnac Grain Co., Inc., Overland Park, KS, pg. 810
Bishop, B.H., Chm. Bd. & Co-Chief Exec. Officer--Pendleton Woolen Mills, Inc., Portland, OR, pg. 857
Bishop, Benjamin M., Chm. & Chief Exec. Officer--The Western Group, Saint Louis, MO, pg. 1179
Bishop, Vernon, Chm. Bd., Pres. & Chief Exec. Officer--Lebanon Chemical Corp., Lebanon, PA, pg. 665
Bishop, William W., Chief Exec. Officer--CHC Advertising, Woodbridge, NJ, pg. 201
Bizzaro, Richard, Pres. & Chief Exec. Officer-Food Division--Weider Health & Fitness, Woodland Hills, CA, pg. 1173
Black, W.J. II, Pres., Chief Exec. Officer & Treas.--Walter J. Black, Inc., Port Washington, NY, pg. 154
Blagge, Timothy J., Pres. & Chief Exec. Officer--Tim & Diane Blagge Inc., Rancho Cordova, CA, pg. 155
Blair, Michael D., Pres. & Chief Exec. Officer--Cyborg Systems, Inc., Chicago, IL, pg. 307
Blair, R. Cary, Pres. & Chief Exec. Officer--Westfield Companies, Westfield Center, OH, pg. 1182
Blank, Benjamin, Chm. & Chief Exec. Officer--Savemart Inc., Bronx, NY, pg. 973
Blatt, L. Douglas, Pres. & Chief Exec. Officer--The ISI Manufacturing, Inc., Fraser, MI, pg. 560
Blattner, Joseph R., Chm. & Chief Exec. Officer--Blattner/Brunner Inc., Pittsburgh, PA, pg. 156
Blattner, Simon J., Jr., Co-Chief Exec. Officer--Rittenhouse Inc., Park Ridge, IL, pg. 936
Blau, Robert F., Chief Oper. Officer--The W.B. Wood Company, New Providence, NJ, pg. 1199
Blethen, Frank A., Chm., Chief Exec. Officer & Publr.--Seattle Times Company, Seattle, WA, pg. 986
Bliss, James C., Pres. & Chief Exec. Officer--Telesensory, Mountain View, CA, pg. 1085
Bloch, Federico, Pres. & Chief Exec. Officer--Taca International Airlines, S. A., New Orleans, LA, pg. 1076
Block, Edward L., Pres. & Chief Exec. Officer--Block Distributing Company, San Antonio, TX, pg. 157
Bloomfield, Coleman, Chm. Bd. & Chief Exec. Officer--The Minnesota Mutual Life Insurance Company, Saint Paul, MN, pg. 757
Blume, Robert L., Pres. & Chief Exec. Officer--Capital Development Co., Lacey, WA, pg. 215
Blumenthal, Herman, Chm. & Chief Exec. Officer--Radiator Specialty Company, Charlotte, NC, pg. 909
Blumenthal, Robert, Pres. & Chief Exec. Officer--Penn Emblem Co., Philadelphia, PA, pg. 857
Boasberg, Howard, Chm. Bd. & Chief Exec. Officer--Boasberg Valentine-Radford, Inc., Kansas City, MO, pg. 1143
Bobit, Edward J., Chm. Bd. & Chief Exec. Officer--Bobit Publishing Company, Redondo Beach, CA, pg. 161
Boddie, Ben Mayo, Chm. Bd. & Chief Exec. Officer--Boddie-Noell Enterprises Inc., Rocky Mount, NC, pg. 161
Bodine, John R., Pres. & Chief Exec. Officer--Bodine Electric Company, Chicago, IL, pg. 162
Bodner, Herbert, Pres. & Chief Exec. Officer--Fru-Con Construction Corporation, Ballwin, MO, pg. 435
Boes, Francis X., Pres. & Chief Exec. Officer--Oriel Corporation, Stratford, CT, pg. 829
Bogan, Thomas F., Pres.--Avatar Corporation, Hopkinton, MA, pg. 101
Bogrand, Randall, Pres. & Chief Exec. Officer--Tollycraft Yachts Corp., Kelso, WA, pg. 1100
Boh, Robert H., Chm. Bd., Pres. & Chief Exec. Officer--Boh Corporation, New Orleans, LA, pg. 162
Bohbot, Allen J., Pres. & Chief Exec. Officer--Bohbot Communications, Inc., New York, NY, pg. 162
Bokser, Stephen R., Pres. & Chief Oper. Officer--White Rose Food, Long Island City, NY, pg. 335
Boland, David, Chm. Bd., Pres. & Chief Exec. Officer--David Boland, Inc., Titusville, FL, pg. 162
Bolch, Carl, Jr., Chm. Bd. & Chief Exec. Officer--Racetrac Petroleum, Inc., Smyrna, GA, pg. 909
Bolin, M.R., Chm. Bd. & Chief Exec. Officer--M. R. Bolin Inc., Minneapolis, MN, pg. 162
Bollerer, Fred L., Chm. Bd. & Chief Exec. Officer--First American Bank of Virginia, McLean, VA, pg. 412
Bollerer, Fred L., Chm. Bd. & Chief Exec. Officer--First American Metro Corp., McLean, VA, pg. 412
Bollinger, Bob, Chief Exec. Officer--Bollinger Industries Inc., Irving, TX, pg. 163
Bollinger, Don M., Chm. Bd. & Chief Exec. Officer--The John C. Groub Company Inc., Seymour, IN, pg. 489
Bollinger, Donald T., Chm. Bd., Chief Exec. Officer & Dir.-Fin.--Bollinger Machine Shop And Shipyard, Inc., Lockport, LA, pg. 163
Bomstein, Howard, Chm. Bd., Pres. & Chief Exec. Officer--The Bomstein Agency, Washington, DC, pg. 164
Bonadies, Lewis M., Pres. & Chief Exec. Officer--Willis Case Harwood, Inc., Dayton, OH, pg. 1192
Bonfante, Michael, Pres. & Chief Exec. Officer--Nob Hill General Store, Inc., Gilroy, CA, pg. 807
Bonham, Donald L., Chm. Bd. & Chief Exec. Officer--Fiesta Mart Inc., Houston, TX, pg. 409
Bonifazio, J., Chief Exec. Officer--Jamison Plastic Corporation, Allentown, PA, pg. 589
Boniols, Charles, Chief Exec. Officer--Model Glass, Inc., Anaheim, CA, pg. 762
Bonn, Neal F., Pres. & Chief Exec. Officer--F.H. Bonn Company, Arlington Heights, IL, pg. 164
Bonn, Neal F., Pres. & Chief Exec. Officer--International Steel Wool Corporation, Springfield, OH, pg. 164
Bookshester, Dennis, Pres. & Chief Exec. Officer--Bailey Banks & Biddle, Irving, TX, pg. 1215
Booth, Charles H., Jr., Chm. Bd., Pres. & Chief Exec. Officer--Burrell Group, New Kensington, PA, pg. 195
Booth, John L., Sr., Chm. Bd. & Chief Exec. Officer--Booth American, Detroit, MI, pg. 165
Borck, Judith L., Chief Exec. Officer--Country Home Bakery, Inc., Bridgeport, CT, pg. 290
Bordelais, Jacques, Chief Exec. Officer--Bordelais, Lemeunier & Leo Burnett, Clichy,, France, pg. 192
Borden, Lorraine, Chm. Bd., Chief Exec. Officer, Chief Fin. Officer, Pres.--Great Scott Advertising Co. Inc., New York, NY, pg. 482
Boren, L.E., Chm. Bd. & Chief Exec. Officer--Badger Construction Equipment Co., Insley Div., Winona, MN, pg. 113
Boren, Leland E., Chm. Bd., Pres. & Chief Exec. Officer--Avis Industrial Corporation, Upland, IN, pg. 102
Borgelt, Burton C., Chm. & Chief Exec. Officer--Dentsply International Inc., York, PA, pg. 329
Borshoff, Thomas N., Pres. & Chief Exec. Officer--First Federal Savings and Loan Assn. of Rochester, Rochester, NY, pg. 413
Bosboom, Tony J., Pres. & Chief Exec. Officer--Fabric Wholesalers, Inc., Portland, OR, pg. 396
Bose, Amar G., Dr., Chm. Bd. & Chief Exec. Officer--Bose Corporation, Framingham, MA, pg. 167
Boso, James, Pres. & Chief Exec. Officer--SPI Holdings, Richardson, TX, pg. 318
Boso, James, Chief Exec. Officer--Spectradyne Inc., Richardson, TX, pg. 318
Bottendorf, Larry, Pres. & Chief Exec. Officer--ECP Incorporated, Westchester, IL, pg. 317
Bovaird, W.J., Pres. & Chief Exec. Officer--Bovaird Supply Co., Tulsa, OK, pg. 168
Bowen, Steve, Pres., Chief Exec. Officer--Geer, DuBois Inc., New York, NY, pg. 447
Boyd, Dennis, Pres. & Chief Exec. Officer--Royal Waterbeds, Maryland Heights, MO, pg. 953
Boyd, Roy T., III, Chm. Bd. & Chief Exec. Officer--Mark III Industries, Ocala, FL, pg. 708
Boyer, Rahn, Pres. & Chief Exec. Officer--Gem-Dandy, Inc., Madison, NC, pg. 447
Boyle, Les, Chm. Bd., Pres. & Chief Exec. Officer--CRE, Inc., Indianapolis, IN, pg. 203
Boyle, R.E., Chm. Bd. & Chief Exec. Officer--Ohio River Associates, Inc., Hannibal, OH, pg. 822
Boyle, R.E., Chm. Bd., Pres. & Chief Exec. Officer--Ormet Corporation, Hannibal, OH, pg. 822
Brabson, John, Chm. Bd., Pres. & Chief Exec. Officer--Peoples Gas System, Inc., Tampa, FL, pg. 689
Braby, James R., Pres. & Chief Oper. Officer--Octagon Process Inc., Edgewater, NJ, pg. 821
Bracey, Morris W., Chm. Bd., Pres., Chief Exec. & Chief Oper. Officer--Dealers Electrical Supply Co., Waco, TX, pg. 322
Bradburd, Arnold W., Chm. Bd., Pres. & Chief Exec. Officer--Interstate Steel Supply Co., Philadelphia, PA, pg. 580
Bradley, Rodney C., Chm. & Chief Exec. Officer--Bradley Communications, Inc., Anchorage, AK, pg. 170
Brady, Barrett, Pres. & Chief Exec. Officer--Dunn Industries Inc., Kansas City, MO, pg. 354
Brady, Frank, Pres. & Chief Exec. Officer--The Brady Marketing Company, Pacheco, CA, pg. 171
Braitmayer, J.W., Chm. Bd. & Chief Exec. Officer--Mona Industries, Inc., Paterson, NJ, pg. 764
Bramble, David A., Chm. Bd. & Chief Exec. Officer--David A. Bramble, Inc., Chestertown, MD, pg. 171
Bramble, Reba H., Chm. Bd. & Chief Exec. Officer--Gulf States Asphalt Company, Inc., South Houston, TX, pg. 493
Branch, William J., Jr., Pres. & Chief Exec. Officer--Masland Industries, Carlisle, PA, pg. 717
Brandeis, E.P., Chief Exec. Officer--Integra Technologies Corp., Waltham, MA, pg. 572
Brantlinger, F. Herbert, Pres. & Chief Exec. Officer--Lawrence Insurance Group, Inc., New York, NY, pg. 662
Brantlinger, F. Herbert, Pres. & Chief Exec. Officer--United Community Insurance Co., Albany, NY, pg. 662
Braswell, Gary, Pres. & Chief Exec. Officer--MPD, Inc., Owensboro, KY, pg. 693
Brauman, Murray, Chm. Bd. & Chief Exec. Officer--Moss and Company, Inc., New York, NY, pg. 772
Braun, Ed, Pres. & Chief Exec. Officer--Sloan Technology, Santa Barbara, CA, pg. 1146
Braun, Neil S., Sr. V.P. & Chm. & Chief Exec. Officer-Viacom Entertainment--Viacom Inc., New York, NY, pg. 785
Braun, Neil S., Chm. & Chief Exec. Officer--Viacom Entertainment, New York, NY, pg. 785
Braunlich, H.P., Jr., Chm. Bd., Pres. & Chief Exec. Officer--Brammer Manufacturing Company, Davenport, IA, pg. 171
Brawer, Robert A., Pres. & Chief Exec. Officer--Maidenform, Inc., New York, NY, pg. 701
Brazier, John M., Pres. & Chief Exec. Officer--Brazier Forest Industries, Inc., Seattle, WA, pg. 172
Brembeck, Howard S., Chm. Bd. & Chief Exec. Officer--CTB Inc., Milford, IN, pg. 205
Brenia, Paul S., Chm., Pres. & Chief Exec. Officer--Ancra Corporation, Hawthorne, CA, pg. 72
Brennan, Bernard F., Chm. Bd. & Chief Exec. Officer--Montgomery Ward & Co., Inc., Chicago, IL, pg. 767
Brennan, David L., Chm. Bd. & Chief Exec. Officer--The Brenlin Group, Akron, OH, pg. 173
Brennan, N., Chief Exec. Officer--Dimco-Gray Company, Dayton, OH, pg. 338
Brenner, Ronald D., Pres. & Chief Exec. Officer--Technology for Energy Corporation, Knoxville, TN, pg. 1084
Brewster, E. Billings, Chief Exec. Officer--Labelon Corporation, Canandaigua, NY, pg. 649
Brice, Joni, Chief Exec. Officer--Heil-Brice Retail Advertising, San Clemente, CA, pg. 525
Brick, Frank E., Pres. & Chief Exec. Officer--Basic Computer, Akron, OH, pg. 124
Brickel, Jack W., Pres., Chief Exec. & Chief Oper. Officer & Dir.-Personnel--BEC Inc., Richmond, MI, pg. 106
Bridell, Robert J., Chm. Bd. & Chief Exec. Officer--American Tara Corporation, Atlanta, GA, pg. 63
Brien, Louis, Chief Exec. Officer--Just Pants, Chicago, IL, pg. 610
Briggs, R. Michael, Pres. & Chief Exec. Officer--Certified Holding Corp., Everett, WA, pg. 237
Brilliant, James, Chief Exec. Officer--Sporto Corp., Boston, MA, pg. 1032
Brindell, Charlie, Pres. & Chief Exec. Officer--Trammell Crow Company, Dallas, TX, pg. 1106
Brink, Jay, Chief Exec. Officer--Brink Electric Construction Company, Rapid City, SD, pg. 176
Brinkley, D.R., Pres. & Chief Exec. Officer--Colonial Pipeline Company, Atlanta, GA, pg. 264
Briscoe, John R., Pres. & Chief Exec. Officer--Bergelectric Corporation, Los Angeles, CA, pg. 141
Briukerhoff, Peter, Chm. Bd., Pres. & Chief Exec. Officer--Aqua Fab Industries, Inc., East Greenwich, RI, pg. 79
Brix, Peter J., Chm. Bd. & Chief Exec. Officer--Brix Maritime Co., Portland, OR, pg. 177
Broad, John W., Chm. Bd., Pres. & Chief Exec. Officer--Broad Vogt & Conant Inc., River Rouge, MI, pg. 177
Broadhurst, James, Chm., Pres. & Chief Exec. Officer--Eat N Park Restaurants, Pittsburgh, PA, pg. 364
Broadus, Robert F., Chief Exec. Officer--R.F. Broadus & Associates, Inc., Atlanta, GA, pg. 177
Brock, Joseph C., Chief Exec. Officer--J. C. Brock Corp., Buffalo, NY, pg. 178
Brock, Paul K., Pres. & Chief Exec. Officer--Brock Candy Company, Chattanooga, TN, pg. 177
Brock, Richard T., Chm. Bd. & Chief Exec. Officer--Brock Control Systems, Inc., Atlanta, GA, pg. 178
Brodbeck, William J., Pres. & Chief Exec. Officer--Brodbeck Enterprises, Inc., Flatteville, WI, pg. 178
Brode, Harold, Pres. & Chief Exec. Officer--Broder Bros. Co., Plymouth, MI, pg. 178
Brode, Harold, Pres. & Chief Exec. Officer--Broder Bros. Co. Of Florida, Inc., Orlando, FL, pg. 178
Brokaw, Norman, Chm. Bd. & Chief Exec. Officer--William Morris Agency, Inc., Beverly Hills, CA, pg. 771
Bronner, Michael, Chief Exec. Officer & New Bus. Contact--Bronner Slosberg Humphrey, Boston, MA, pg. 179
Bronstein, David G., Pres. & Chief Exec. Officer--Big V Supermarkets, Inc., Florida, NY, pg. 149
Brooke, Peter A., Chm. Bd & Chief Exec. Officer--Advent International, Boston, MA, pg. 21
Brooks, James W., Chm. & Chief Exec. Officer--Brooks Beverage Management, Inc., Holland, MI, pg. 179
Brooks, Peter E., Chief Exec. Officer--Langert Golf Co., Inc., Carlsbad, CA, pg. 890
Brooks, Roger K., Chief Exec. Officer--Central Life Assurance Co., Des Moines, IA, pg. 232
Brookshire, Bruce G., Chm. & Chief Exec. Officer--Brookshire Grocery, Tyler, TX, pg. 180
Brost, Jay, Pres. & Chief Exec. Officer--Miniature Precision Components, Walworth, WI, pg. 757
Brotman, Phyllis B., Pres., Chief Exec. Officer & New Bus. Contact--Image Dynamics, Incorporated, Baltimore, MD, pg. 563
Broudski, Norman, Pres. & Chief Exec. Officer--City Postal, Inc., New York, NY, pg. 251
Brouillette, Donald G., Pres. & Chief Exec. Officer--Demeter, Inc., Fowler, IN, pg. 328
Brown, Bruce W., Pres. & Chief Exec. Officer--The Hubinger Company, Keokuk, IA, pg. 550
Brown, C. Terry, Chm. Bd., Pres., Chief Exec. Officer & Chief Oper. Officer--Atlas Hotels, Inc., San Diego, CA, pg. 96
Brown, Carter, Pres. & Chief Exec. Officer--Omega Performance Group, San Francisco, CA, pg. 826
Brown, Charles, Chm. Bd., Pres. & Chief Exec. Officer--Bayou State Oil Corporation, Shreveport, LA, pg. 128
Brown, David C., Pres. & Chief Exec. Officer--Browns Lumber & Supply Company, Fairmont, WV, pg. 183
Brown, Dennis, Pres. & Chief Exec. Officer--Diet Center, Inc., Pittsburgh, PA, pg. 55
Brown, E.H., Jr., Chm. Bd., Chief Exec. Officer & Partner--E.H. Brown Advertising, Inc., Chicago, IL, pg. 181
Brown, Jack E., Chm. & Chief Exec. Officer--The Bases Group, Covington, KY, pg. 124
Brown, Jeremy E., Chief Exec. Officer--Earle Palmer Brown, Bethesda, MD, pg. 182
Brown, Millard, Pres. & Chief Exec. Officer--Powell Electronics Inc., Philadelphia, PA, pg. 882
Brown, Robert W., Jr., Exec. V.P., Gen. Mgr. & Sec.--Brown Motors, Toledo, OH, pg. 182
Brown, Ronald A., Pres. & Chief Exec. Officer--Calcor Space Facility, Inc., Whittier, CA, pg. 208
Brown, Stephen L., Chm. Bd. & Chief Exec. Officer--John Hancock Mutual Life Insurance Company, Boston, MA, pg. 595
Brown, Stephen L., Chm. Bd. & Chief Exec. Officer--John Hancock HealthPlans, Inc., West Chester, PA, pg. 596
Brown, Thomas V., Pres. & Chief Exec. Officer--Caraustar Industries, Inc., Austell, GA, pg. 217
Browne, Steven B., Chm. Bd., Pres. & Chief Exec. Officer--All American Bottling Corp., Oklahoma City, OK, pg. 35
Browning, Peter C., Chm. & Chief Exec. Officer--National Gypsum Company, Charlotte, NC, pg. 790
Bruce, David F., Chm. Bd. & Chief Exec. Officer--Bruce-Andersen Company, Inc., Belgrade, MT, pg. 183
Bruggeman, W.L., Chm. & Chief Exec. Officer--Diversified Dynamics Inc., Minneapolis, MN, pg. 340
Bruggeman, W.L., Chm. Bd. & Chief Exec. Officer--Cat Pumps Corporation, Minneapolis, MN, pg. 340
Bryan, A. Chris, II, Pres., Chief Exec. Officer, Sec. & Treas.--BA Advertising, Dallas, TX, pg. 105
Bryan, F. Sibley, Jr., Pres. & Chief Exec. Officer--Chipman-Union, Inc., Union Point, GA, pg. 248
Bryan, R.A., Jr., Chm. Bd. & Chief Exec. Officer--T. A. Loving Company, Goldsboro, NC, pg. 685

Corporate Responsibilities Index

Brynes, Edward G., Jr., Pres. & Chief Exec. Officer--Byrnes & Kiefer Company, Callery, PA, pg. 198
Brzustewicz, Robert, Chief Exec. Officer & Sec.--Northern Wire & Cable, Inc., Troy, MI, pg. 814
Bucci, Anthony L., Pres. & Chief Exec. Officer--Marc Advertising, Pittsburgh, PA, pg. 706
Buchanan, Robert C., Pres. & Chief Exec. Officer--Fox Valley Corporation, Appleton, WI, pg. 427
Buchanan, Robert C., Pres. & Chief Exec. Officer--Howard Paper Mills, Urbana, OH, pg. 428
Buck, Charles T., Chm. Bd., Pres. & Chief Exec. Officer--Buck Knives, Inc., El Cajon, CA, pg. 185
Buckley, Maurice, Pres. & Chief Exec. Officer--Panarco, Inc., Summit, NJ, pg. 845
Buckman, R.H., Chm. Bd. & Chief Exec. Officer--Buckman Laboratories, Memphis, TN, pg. 185
Buckman, Robert H., Chm Bd. & Chief Exec. Officer--Buckman Laboratories, International, Memphis, TN, pg. 188
Buckman, Steven B., Pres. & Chief Oper. Officer--Buckman Laboratories, International, Memphis, TN, pg. 188
Bucksbaum, Martin, Chm. Bd. & Chief Exec. & Info. Officer--General Growth Companies, Inc., Des Moines, IA, pg. 449
Buha, Stephen, V.P., Gen. Mgr. & Chief Exec. Officer--Summerfield Truck Co. Inc., Portage, IN, pg. 1057
Buhl, Tim, Pres. & Chief Exec. Officer--Aerco International Inc., Northvale, NJ, pg. 21
Bull, William H., Pres., Chief Exec. Officer & Treas.--McNaughton-McKay Electric Co., Madison Heights, MI, pg. 732
Bulloch, Juanita A., Pres., Chief Exec. Officer & Treas.--Southeastern Steel Company, Florence, SC, pg. 1020
Bunn, Arthur H., Pres. & Chief Exec. Officer--Bunn-O-Matic Corporation, Springfield, IL, pg. 188
Burandt, Gary (NY), Pres. & Chief Exec. Officer--Dentsu, Young & Rubicam Partnerships, New York, NY, pg. 330
Burdick, Richard L., Chm., Pres., Chief Exec. & Chief Oper. Officer--Thermon Manufacturing Company, San Marcos, TX, pg. 1091
Burke, Gary W., Pres. & Chief Exec. Officer--Burke Engineering Company, South El Monte, CA, pg. 190
Burke, John, Pres. & Chief Exec. Officer--Cato Johnson-New York, New York, NY, pg. 1210
Burke, Lawrence J., II, Pres. & Chief Exec. Officer--Burke Communication Industries, Inc., Chicago, IL, pg. 190
Burkhardt, Ron, Chief Exec. Officer & Exec. Creative Dir.--Burkhardt & Christy Advertising, Inc., New York, NY, pg. 191
Burkhardt, William C., Pres. & Chief Exec. Officer--Bahlsen Inc., Cary, NC, pg. 114
Burkle, Joseph, Chief Exec. Officer--Almac's Inc., East Providence, RI, pg. 1214
Burns, Emmett, Chief Exec. Officer--Western Data Systems, Calabasas, CA, pg. 1178
Burns, Stephen F., Chm. Bd., Pres. & Chief Exec. Officer--Wheaton Van Lines, Inc., Indianapolis, IN, pg. 1184
Burris, J. Mark, Pres. & Chief Exec. Officer--The Burris Agency, Inc., High Point, NC, pg. 195
Burrow, Grady, Pres. & Chief Exec. Officer--National Computer Print, Inc., Birmingham, AL, pg. 786
Burt, W. E., Chm. Bd., Pres., & Chief Exec. Officer--Dairy Fresh Corp., Greensboro, AL, pg. 310
Burtman, Charles, Pres. & Chief Exec. Officer--Burtman Iron Works, Inc., Boston, MA, pg. 195
Burton, Betsy, Chm. Bd. & Chief Exec. Officer--Pip Printing, Agoura Hills, CA, pg. 616
Busch, Sondra L., Chief Exec. Officer--Admark, Inc., Topeka, KS, pg. 18
Bush, Condon, Chm. & Chief Exec. Officer--Bush Brothers & Company, Dandridge, TN, pg. 196
Buskirk, Ernest, Pres. & Chief Exec. Officer--Rock Hill Materials Company, Catasauqua, PA, pg. 941
Butcher, Andrew D.W., Pres., Chief Exec. Officer--International Communications Group, Inc., Los Angeles, CA, pg. 576
Butcher, C. Preston, Pres. & Chief Exec. Officer--Lincoln Property Co., Northern California, Foster City, CA, pg. 676
Butcher, McBee, Chm. & Chief Exec. Officer--Butcher & Singer, Philadelphia, PA, pg. 1184
Butler, Edmund R., Pres. & Chief Exec. Officer--Mississippi Valley Gas Co., Jackson, MS, pg. 1208
Butler, Reginald H., Chief Exec. Officer--Mid-States Petroleum Inc., Troy, MI, pg. 750
Butler, Richard A., Jr., Chm. Bd. & Chief Exec. Officer--Butler Automatic, Inc., Canton, MA, pg. 197
Butler, Stephan T., Chm. Bd. & Chief Exec. Officer--W. C. Bradley Co., Columbus, GA, pg. 170
Butler, William, Chm. Bd., Pres., Chief Exec. Officer & Treas.--Corporex Companies, Inc., Covington, KY, pg. 287
Buttle, Eugene H., Pres. & Chief Exec. Officer--American Inks & Coatings Corp., Valley Forge, PA, pg. 56
Buxton, C.I., II, Chm. Bd. & Chief Exec. Officer--Federated Mutual Insurance Company, Owatonna, MN, pg. 405
Buyers, J.W.A., Chm. & Chief Exec. Officer--Mauna Loa Resources Inc., Honolulu, HI, pg. 174
Byer, Allan G., Chm. Bd., Pres. & Chief Exec. Officer--Byer California, San Francisco, CA, pg. 197
Byrd, H.P., Chief Exec. Officer--Flavor House Products, Inc., Dothan, AL, pg. 417
Byrd, Robert, Pres. & Chief Exec. Officer--The Keller Manufacturing Co., Inc., Corydon, IN, pg. 621
Cabral, Gilbert, Pres. & Chief Exec. Officer--MICOM Communications Corp., Simi Valley, CA, pg. 748
Cafaro, Anthony M., Pres. & Chief Exec. Officer--The Cafaro Co., Youngstown, OH, pg. 207
Cafferata, Patricia A., Pres. & Chief Exec. Officer--Young & Rubicam Chicago, Chicago, IL, pg. 1211
Caiazza, D., Pres. & Chief Exec. Officer--Copperweld Steel Company, Warren, OH, pg. 284
Cain, Herman, Pres. & Chief Exec. Officer--Godfather's Pizza, Inc., Omaha, NE, pg. 464
Calano, James C., Pres. & Chief Exec. Officer--CareerTrack Inc., Boulder, CO, pg. 218
Call, William, Chm., Pres. & Chief Exec. Officer--Maverik Country Stores, Inc., Afton, WY, pg. 722
Callaghan, Howard, Pres.--Plastic Suppliers, Inc., Columbus, OH, pg. 875
Callahan, Frank W., Pres. & Chief Exec. Officer--McKinney Inc. Advertising & Public Relations, Philadelphia, PA, pg. 730
Callahan, Ralph W., Jr., Chm. Bd., Pres. & Chief Exec. Officer--Henderson Advertising, Inc., Greenville, SC, pg. 528
Callaway, Howard Bo, Chief Exec. Officer--Crested Butte Mountain Resort, Inc., Mount Crested Butte, CO, pg. 299
Calligaris, A.E., Chm. Bd., Pres. & Chief Exec. Officer--Stebbins Engineering & Mfg. Co., Watertown, NY, pg. 1043
Calvillo, Ricardo C., Chm. Bd. & Chief Exec. Officer--Calet, Hirsch & Ferrell, Inc., New York, NY, pg. 949
Calvitti, Raymond, Pres. & Chief Exec. Officer--KDI Sylvan Pools, Inc., Doylestown, PA, pg. 612
Cameron, Gerald T., Sr., Chm. Bd. & Chief Exec. Officer--Amray, Inc., Bedford, MA, pg. 68
Camosy, Raymond J., Pres. & Chief Exec. Officer--Camosy, Inc., Russell, IL, pg. 212
Camp, Ben H., Chm. Bd. & Chief Exec. Officer--Hub Inc., Tucker, GA, pg. 548
Campbell, Dick, Pres. & Chief Exec. Officer--BJ Acquisition Corp., Charlotte, NC, pg. 107
Campbell, R.S., Pres. & Chief Exec. Officer--Commercial & Architectural Products Inc., Dover, OH, pg. 268
Campbell, Robert, Pres. & Chief Exec. Officer--Pfaudler-U.S., Inc., Rochester, NY, pg. 866
Capriotti, Laurence, Pres. & Chief Exec. Officer--Intercounty Title Co. of Illinois, Chicago, IL, pg. 574
Carcara, P.J., Pres. & Chief Exec. Officer--Baldt, Inc., Chester, PA, pg. 115
Carell, Monroe, Jr., Chm. Bd. & Chief Exec. Officer--Central Parking Corp., Nashville, TN, pg. 234
Cargen, David, Pres. & Chief Exec. Officer--Power King Products Co., Beaver Dam, WI, pg. 883
Cargill, Don A., Pres. & Chief Exec. Officer--Cargill Detroit Corp., Clawson, MI, pg. 219
Carlberg, W. Charles, Pres. & Chief Exec. Officer--Rives Carlberg, Houston, TX, pg. 937
Carley, S.E., Pres. & Chief Exec. Officer--Fair Lanes Inc., Hunt Valley, MD, pg. 396
Carlisle, Brian, Chm. Bd. & Chief Exec. Officer--Adept Technology, Inc., San Jose, CA, pg. 17
Carlisle, L. T. III, Chm., Pres. & Chief Exec. Officer--Carlisle Retailers, Inc., Ashtabula, OH, pg. 220
Carlos, Michael C., Chm. Bd. & Chief Exec. Officer--National Distributing Co., Inc., Atlanta, GA, pg. 787
Carlson, Bruce I., Chm. & Chief Exec. Officer--Grant/Jacoby, Inc., Chicago, IL, pg. 477
Carlson, Curtis L., Chm. Bd., Pres. & Chief Exec. Officer--Carlson Companies, Inc., Minneapolis, MN, pg. 220
Carlson, E. Jerome, Pres. & Chief Exec. Officer--The Instant Web Companies, Chanhassen, MN, pg. 571
Carlson, Robert F., Sr., Chm. Bd., Chief Exec. Officer & Treas.--Channel Technologies, Inc., Santa Barbara, CA, pg. 239
Carlson, Robert W., Jr., Chm. & Chief Exec. Officer--Quadion Corporation, Minneapolis, MN, pg. 902
Carlton, Edward, Jr., Pres. & Chief Exec. Officer--Corrugated Metals, Inc., Chicago, IL, pg. 287
Carota, Richard J., Chm., Pres. & Chief Exec. Officer--Finch, Pruyn & Co., Inc., Glens Falls, NY, pg. 410
Carpenter, Richard M., Pres. & Chief Exec. Officer--S. C. Johnson & Son, Inc., Racine, WI, pg. 599
Carr, John, III, Pres. & Chief Exec. Officer--Central Supply Co., Inc., Indianapolis, IN, pg. 234
Carr, Michael T., Pres. & Chief Exec. Officer-Publishing Division--Weider Health & Fitness, Woodland Hills, CA, pg. 1173
Carr, Pat, Pres. & Chief Exec. Officer--Mayflower Transit, Inc., Carmel, IN, pg. 724
Carrafiello, A. Louis, Pres., Treas. & Chief Exec. Officer--Carrafiello, Diehl & Associates, Inc., Irvington, NY, pg. 225
Carraher, Richard, Chief Exec. Officer--Fragrance Resources, Inc., Keyport, NJ, pg. 428
Carroll, Jane, Chief Exec. Officer-Forum Europe & Forum Asia--The Forum Corporation, Boston, MA, pg. 425
Carruthers, George, Pres., Chief Exec. & Chief Fin. Officer, Controller--Polycoat Systems, Inc., Hudson Falls, NY, pg. 880
Carson, James B., Jr., Chm. & Chief Exec. Officer--Carter, Atlanta, GA, pg. 226
Carson, William C., Chm. Bd. & Chief Exec. Officer--Instrument Specialties Company, Delaware Water Gap, PA, pg. 572
Carstarphen, J.M., Chm. Bd., Pres. & Chief Exec. Officer--Stowe-Pharr Mills, Inc., McAdenville, NC, pg. 1052
Carstens, Donald, Chief Exec. Officer--United Steel & Wire Co., Battle Creek, MI, pg. 1137
Carter, Donald J., Pres., Treas. & Chief Exec. Officer--Home Interiors & Gifts, Inc., Dallas, TX, pg. 541
Carter, Jerry C., Chm. Bd., Pres. & Chief Exec. Officer--Jerry C. Carter, Inc., Gainesville, GA, pg. 226
Carter, John M., Chm. Bd., & Chief Exec. Officer--Carco Electronics, Menlo Park, CA, pg. 217
Carter, Tim, Chm. Bd. & Chief Exec. Officer--Bell-Carter Foods, Inc., Lafayette, CA, pg. 134
Carus, M. Blouke, Chm. Bd., Pres., Chief Exec. & Chief Oper. Officer--Carus Corporation, Peru, IL, pg. 227
Carus, M. Blouke, Chm. Bd. & Chief Exec. Officer--Open Court Publishing Company, Chicago, IL, pg. 227
Carus, M. Blouke, Chm. Bd. & Chief Exec. Officer--Open Court Publishing Co.-General Books, Peru, IL, pg. 227
Carus, M. Blouke, Chief Exec. Officer--Carus Publishing Company, Peru, IL, pg. 227
Carvelli, A.J., Vice Chm. & Chief Exec. Officer--Pannier Corporation, Pittsburgh, PA, pg. 846
Cascino, Alfred M., Chm. Bd. & Chief Exec. Officer--Cascino Purcell Freebairn, Atlanta, GA, pg. 227
Casey, Martin M., Pres. & Chief Exec. Officer--El Torito Restaurants, Inc., Irvine, CA, pg. 372
Casey, William R., Chm. Bd. & Chief Exec. Officer--The Myers Group (U.S) Inc., Rouses Point, NY, pg. 780
Casgrain, Timothy, Pres. & Chief Exec. Officer--SBN System Inc., Fort Wayne, IN, pg. 960
Cashman, Robert L., Chm. Bd., Pres. & Chief Exec. Officer--Pacific Envelope Company, Anaheim, CA, pg. 840
Casper, Jack H., Chm. Bd., Chief Exec. Officer--The Alden Group Ltd., New York, NY, pg. 32
Cassese, Patrick J., Chm. Bd., Pres. & Chief Exec. Officer--Antares Group Inc., Cleveland, OH, pg. 76
Cassetty, Fred, Chm. Bd., Pres. & Chief Exec. Officer--Alley-Cassetty Coal Co., Nashville, TN, pg. 37
Cassidy, William L., Pres. & Chief Oper. Officer--Administrative Services, Inc., Montpelier, VT, pg. 791
Cassner, Alvin B., Pres. & Chief Exec. Officer--Rotary Forms Press, Inc., Hillsboro, OH, pg. 950
Castellano, Ugo, Pres. & Chief Exec. Officer--Young & Rubicam Italia, S.p.A., Milan,, Italy, pg. 1213
Castle, Frank E., Pres. & Chief Exec. Officer--Components Corporation Of America, Dallas, TX, pg. 270
Castle, Jim, Chm. Bd. & Chief Exec. Officer--U.S. Computer Services, Rancho Cordova, CA, pg. 1135
Castro, Adolfo, Chief Exec. Officer--Lowe MBAC, Barcelona,, Spain, pg. 685
Castro, Adolfo, Chief Exec. Officer--Lowe FMS, Madrid,, Spain, pg. 685
Castro, Dorothy L., Chm. Bd. & Chief Exec. Officer--Superior Fast Freight, Irwindale, CA, pg. 1063
Cataland, James R., Pres. & Chief Exec. Officer--Arthur Treacher's, Inc., Youngstown, OH, pg. 87
Cataldo, C.A., Pres. & Chief Exec. Officer--Hostmark Management Group, Rowing Meadows, IL, pg. 545
Cerana, Nicoletta, Chief Exec. Officer--R.P. Partners SRL, Milan,, Italy, pg. 626
Cervenka, Robert, Chief Exec. Officer--Phillips Plastics Corporation, Phillips, WI, pg. 867
Chadsey, Jack, Pres., Chief Exec. & Oper. Officer--Sunglass Hut Corporation, Miami, FL, pg. 1060
Chaiken, Eugene B., Chm., Pres. & Chief Exec. Officer--Almo Corp., Philadelphia, PA, pg. 43
Chalek, Morton, Chief Exec. Officer--Chalek & Chalek, Inc., New York, NY, pg. 238
Chalmers, David B., Chm. Bd., Pres. & Chief Exec. Officer--Coral Petroleum Corporation, Houston, TX, pg. 285
Chambers, Harry L., Pres. & Chief Exec. Officer--Kettle Restaurants, Houston, TX, pg. 626
Chambers, William R., Chm. Bd. & Chief Exec. Officer--C.B. Fleet Company, Incorporated, Lynchburg, VA, pg. 417
Chapman, Donald, Chm. Bd. & Chief Exec. Officer--Optiworld, Atlanta, GA, pg. 828
Chapman, Lawrence, Pres. & Chief Exec. Officer--Manna Pro Corporation, Saint Louis, MO, pg. 704
Chapman, R.N., Chm. Bd., Pres. & Chief Exec. Officer--Pneumatic Scale Corporation, Quincy, MA, pg. 122
Chapman, W. Marshall, Chm. Bd. & Chief Exec. Officer--Inman Mills, Inman, SC, pg. 570
Charlestein, Gary, Chief Exec. Officer & Treas.--Premier Dental Products Company, Norristown, PA, pg. 886
Charron, Theodore, J., Pres., Chief Exec. Officer & Creative Dir.--Charron, Schwartz & Partners, Inc., New York, NY, pg. 240
Charton, Steve, Chm. Bd., Pres & Chief Exec. Officer--Alex Foods, Inc., Anaheim, CA, pg. 33
Chase, Francis H. III, Chm. Bd., Pres., Chief Exec., Chief Fin. Officer & Treas.--F. H. Chase, Inc., Foxboro, MA, pg. 240
Chavkin, Wallace, Chm. Bd. & Chief Exec. Officer--Biddle Sawyer Corporation, New York, NY, pg. 148
Checchi, Alfred, Co-Chm. Bd.--NWA, Inc., Saint Paul, MN, pg. 782
Chen, Jeffrey C., Chm. Bd., Pres. & Chief Exec. Officer--General Sciences Corp., Laurel, MD, pg. 981
Cheney, William J., Chm. Bd., Pres. & Chief Exec. Officer--Steadly Company, Carthage, MO, pg. 1043
Chenok, Philip B., Pres. & Chief Exec. Officer--American Institute of C.P.A.'s Inc., New York, NY, pg. 56
Chernick, Aubrey G., Chm. Bd. & Chief Exec. Officer--Candle Corporation, Santa Monica, CA, pg. 214
Cherry, Kenneth, Chief Exec. Officer--American Frozen Foods, Inc., Stratford, CT, pg. 55
Chesterton, James D., Pres. & Chief Exec. Officer--A.W. Chesterton Company, Stoneham, MA, pg. 244
Chiat, Jay, Chm. Bd., Chief Exec. Officer (Worldwide)--Chiat/Day/Mojo Inc. Advertising, Venice, CA, pg. 244
Chichester, Richard H.L., Chief Exec. Officer & Gen. Mgr.--Select Sires, Inc., Plain City, OH, pg. 988
Child, William H., Chm. Bd. & Chief Exec. Officer--R.C. Willey Home Furnishings, Salt Lake City, UT, pg. 1190
Childers, Bruce S., Chm., Chief Exec. Officer--Meldrum & Fewsmith Yellow Pages Inc., Cleveland, OH, pg. 737
Childers, Bruce S., Chm., Chief Exec. Officer--Excel Media Services Inc., Cleveland, OH, pg. 737
Chimenti, Ronald C., Pres. & Chief Exec. Officer--DCI Marketing, Milwaukee, WI, pg. 308
Chitwood, Harold, Chief Exec. Officer--Gold Kist, Inc., Atlanta, GA, pg. 465
Chopra, Deepak, Chm. Bd., Pres. & Chief Exec. Officer--UDT Sensors, Inc., Hawthorne, CA, pg. 1122
Christensen, Mahlon, Pres. & Chief Exec. Officer--Muska Electric Company, Saint Paul, MN, pg. 777
Christian, Betty S., Chm. Bd., Pres. & Chief Exec. Officer--Central Coca-Cola Bottling Company, Inc., Richmond, VA, pg. 232
Christianson, Stanley D., Pres. & Chief Exec. Officer--Thrall Enterprises, Inc., Chicago, IL, pg. 1095
Christie, Tom E., Chm. & Chief Exec. Officer--Christie Electric Corporation, Gardena, CA, pg. 249
Christmas, James W., Pres. & Chief Exec. Officer--KCS Energy Inc., Edison, NJ, pg. 612

Chryst, Steven L., Pres. & Chief Exec. Officer--Anchor Financial Corporation, Myrtle Beach, SC, pg. 71
Church, William R., Pres. & Chief Exec. Officer--Church & Church Inc., Utica, MI, pg. 249
Chute, Robert A., Chm. Bd., & Chief Exec. Officer--The Gage Company, Pittsburgh, PA, pg. 441
Cicio, Joseph, Chm. Bd. & Chief Exec. Officer--I. Magnin & Co., San Francisco, CA, pg. 699
Cilurao, Joe, Pres. & Chief Exec. Officer--Mobile Technology Inc., Los Angeles, CA, pg. 762
Ciminelli, Frank L., Chief Exec. Officer--Ciminelli Development Company, Inc., Williamsville, NY, pg. 249
Circo, Dennis P., Pres. & Chief Exec. Officer--Precision Industries, Omaha, NE, pg. 885
Clain, G., Pres., Chief Exec. & Chief Oper. Officer--J. Gerber & Co. Inc., New York, NY, pg. 453
Clark, A. James, Chm. Bd., Pres. & Chief Exec. Officer--Clark Construction Group, Bethesda, MD, pg. 252
Clark, A. James, Chm., Pres. & Chief Exec. Officer--CEI Construction, Inc., Bethesda, MD, pg. 200
Clark, Clinton A., Pres. & Chief Exec. Officer--Long John Silver's, Inc., Lexington, KY, pg. 229
Clark, Don, Pres. & Chief Exec. Officer--Mid America Steel, Inc., Fargo, ND, pg. 750
Clark, Edwin, Chm. & Chief Exec. Officer--Lewis, Clark & Graham, Atlanta, GA, pg. 673
Clark, Edwin J., Pres. & Chief Exec. Officer--Dwyer Instruments Inc., Michigan City, IN, pg. 356
Clark, George A., Chm. Bd., Pres. & Chief Exec. Officer--Snap-Tite, Incorporated, Erie, PA, pg. 1014
Clark, H.S., Pres. & Chief Exec. Officer--Jackson Packing Co. Inc., Jackson, MS, pg. 587
Clark, John P., Pres. & Chief Exec. Officer--Industrial Coatings Group, Inc., Chicago, IL, pg. 566
Clay, Larry D., Pres. & Chief Exec. Officer--Pacific Coast Producers, Lodi, CA, pg. 839
Clay, Larry D., Pres. & Chief Exec. Officer--Hoover Group, Inc., Alpharetta, GA, pg. 543
Clay, Robert Earl, Chm. Bd. & Chief Exec. Officer--Pridgeon & Clay, Inc., Grand Rapids, MI, pg. 889
Claytor, W. Graham, Jr., Chm. Bd., Pres. & Chief Exec. Officer--Amtrak-National Railroad Passenger Corp., Washington, DC, pg. 69
Cleberg, Harry C., Pres. & Chief Exec. Officer--Farmland Industries, Inc., Kansas City, MO, pg. 402
Clemens, Clair W., Pres. & Chief Exec. Officer--Hatfield Quality Meats, Inc., Hatfield, PA, pg. 517
Clemens, Jay, Pres. & Chief Exec. Officer--Turtledove Clemens, Inc., Portland, OR, pg. 1120
Clemens, William E., Chm. Bd. & Chief Exec. Officer--Bankers Systems Inc., Saint Cloud, MN, pg. 117
Clement, Coy, Pres. & Chief Exec. Officer--Leichtung, Inc., Cleveland, OH, pg. 666
Clements, Edward B., V.P. & Chief Exec. Officer--Clements Foods Co., Oklahoma City, OK, pg. 254
Clements, W.M., Chm. Bd., Pres. & Chief Exec. Officer--Golden Eagle Distributors, Inc., Tucson, AZ, pg. 466
Click, James E., Treas., Chief Exec. Officer & Sec.--Maryland & Virginia Milk Producers Association, Reston, VA, pg. 717
Clifford, William M., Chm., Pres. & Chief Exec. Officer--St. Johnsbury Trucking Co., Inc., Holliston, MA, pg. 966
Clinton, Gary, Chm. Bd., Pres. & Chief Exec. Officer--United Design, Noble, OK, pg. 1131
Coady, Todd M., Chm. Bd., Pres. & Chief Exec. Officer--Hicks Oil-Hicks Gas, Inc., Roberts, IL, pg. 533
Coatney, Doyle, Pres. & Chief Exec. Officer--Acme Truck Line, Inc., Harvey, LA, pg. 13
Cochill, Thomas, Pres. & Chief Exec. Officer--Webcraft Technologies, Inc., North Brunswick, NJ, pg. 1171
Cochran, Keith, Chief Exec. & Chief Fin. Officer--Johnson County Farm Bureau Co-op, Franklin, IN, pg. 598
Cochran, R.W., Pres. & Chief Exec. Officer--817
Cocke, Bartlett, Jr., Chm. Bd. & Chief Exec. Officer--Bartlett Cocke Jr. Construction Co., San Antonio, TX, pg. 258
Coffey, Bruce, Chm. & Chief Exec. Officer--Presto Food Products, Inc., City of Industry, CA, pg. 888
Cogan, Marshall S., Chm. Bd., Pres. & Chief Exec. Officer--21 International Holdings, Inc., New York, NY, pg. 1121
Cogan, Marshall S., Chm. Bd. & Chief Exec. Officer--Knoll International, Inc., New York, NY, pg. 1121
Coggin, Luther, Pres. & Chief Exec. Officer--Coggin-O'Steen Investment Corp., Jacksonville, FL, pg. 259
Coggin, Luther, Pres. & Chief Exec. Officer--Coggin Pontiac-GMC Inc., Jacksonville, FL, pg. 259
Cohan, Norman H., Pres. & Chief Exec. Officer--Security Plastics, Inc., Miami Lakes, FL, pg. 987
Cohen, Donald, Chm. Bd., Pres., Chief Exec. Officer & Chief Fin. Officer--Tool King, Denver, CO, pg. 1101
Cohen, John K., Pres. & Chief Exec. Officer--Carlyle & Co. Jewelers, Greensboro, NC, pg. 222
Cohen, Leonard, Pres. & Chief Exec. Officer--Kelly, Scott And Madison, Inc., Chicago, IL, pg. 621
Cohen, Lewis M., Pres. & Chief Exec. Officer--Acme Canvas Co., Inc., Malden, MA, pg. 13
Cohen, Louis D., Pres. & Chief Exec. Officer--Sheplers, Inc., Wichita, KS, pg. 998
Cohen, Peter J., Pres. & Chief Exec. Officer--Periphonics Corp., Bohemia, NY, pg. 862
Cohen, Russell, Vice Chm. & Co-Chief Exec. Officer--Carlyle & Co. Jewelers, Greensboro, NC, pg. 222
Cohen, W.C., Jr., Chief Exec. Officer--Insurance Management Associates, Wichita, KS, pg. 572
Colangelo, Larry A., Pres. & Chief Exec. Officer--SPD Technologies, Philadelphia, PA, pg. 963
Cole, Jeffrey A., Chm. Bd. & Chief Exec. Officer--Cole National Corporation, Cleveland, OH, pg. 260
Coleman, Jim, Pres. & Chief Exec. Officer--Coleman Cable Systems, Inc., North Chicago, IL, pg. 260
Colin, Lawrence, Pres. & Chief Exec. Officer--Colin Service Systems, Inc., White Plains, NY, pg. 261
Collette, Murray P., Pres. & Chief Exec. Officer--Oak Rubber Company, Ravenna, OH, pg. 819
Collings, Charles L., Pres. & Chief Exec. Officer--Raley's, West Sacramento, CA, pg. 910
Collins, Bert, Pres. & Chief Exec. Officer--North Carolina Mutual Life Insurance Co., Durham, NC, pg. 813
Collins, Christopher C., Chm. Bd., Pres. & Chief Exec. Officer--Nuttall Gear Corporation, Niagara Falls, NY, pg. 818
Collins, Kevin, Chief Oper. Officer & V.P.--Bill Collins Ford Inc., Louisville, KY, pg. 263
Collins, Nicholas P., Pres. & Chief Exec. Officer--Esco Corporation, Portland, OR, pg. 388
Collman, Nicholas, Chm., Pres. & Chief Exec. Officer--John D. Lucas Printing Company, Baltimore, MD, pg. 263
Collman, Nicholas J., Chm., Pres. & Chief Exec. Officer--Collman Graphics, Inc., Baltimore, MD, pg. 263
Colman, James A., Pres. & Chief Exec. Officer--Acme Mills Co. Inc., Detroit, MI, pg. 13
Colman, John, Chief Exec. Officer--Mother Earth News, New York, NY, pg. 773
Colonna, Peter, Pres., Chief Exec. Officer & Mng. Dir.--Colonna Bros., Inc., North Bergen, NJ, pg. 264
Colsky, Richard A., Pres. & Chief Exec. Officer--Colsky Media, Inc., San Francisco, CA, pg. 265
Colwell, Thomas G., Chm. Bd., Pres. & Chief Exec. Officer--Colwell Industries, Inc., Minneapolis, MN, pg. 267
Combs, Julius, Chm. Bd. & Chief Exec. Officer--United American Healthcare Corp., Detroit, MI, pg. 826
Compton, William, Pres., Chief Exec. Officer & Chief Oper. Officer--Tropical Garment Manufacturing Company, Tampa, FL, pg. 1116
Comstock, Harwood B., Chm. Bd.--Pratt-Read Corporation, Bridgeport, CT, pg. 884
Conant, Victor, Pres. & Chief Exec. Officer--Nightingale-Conant Corp., Niles, IL, pg. 807
Concannon, Bill, Pres. & Chief Exec. Officer--Trammell Crow Company, Dallas, TX, pg. 1106
Conde, Mike, Pres. & Chief Exec. Officer--Everfresh Beverages Inc., Franklin Park, IL, pg. 391
Condie, Richard, Pres. & Chief Exec. Officer--E.J. Brach Corporation, Oakbrook Terrace, IL, pg. 169
Conese, Eugene P., Jr., Pres. & Chief Exec. Officer--Greenwich Air Services, Miami, FL, pg. 485
Confer, Richard P., Pres. & Chief Exec. Officer--Hubbard Milling Company, Mankato, MN, pg. 549
Conklin, Charles E., Pres. & Chief Exec. Officer--Conklin Instrument Corporation, Pleasant Valley, NY, pg. 274
Connell, William F., Chm. Bd. & Chief Exec. Officer--Connell Limited Partnership, Boston, MA, pg. 275
Connelly, Thomas S., Chm. Bd., Pres., Chief Exec. & Chief Oper. Officer--Connelly Containers, Inc., Bala-Cynwyd, PA, pg. 275
Connor, David J., Pres. & Chief Exec. Officer--Carrols Corporation, Syracuse, NY, pg. 225
Connors, Charles W., Chief Exec. Officer & Sec.--Magneco/Metrel, Inc., Addison, IL, pg. 700
Connors, John M., Jr., Pres. & Chief Exec. Officer--Hill, Holliday, Connors, Cosmopulos, Inc., Boston, MA, pg. 534
Conrad, Carlton J., Jr., Pres. & Chief Exec. Officer--E. H. Titchener & Company, Binghamton, NY, pg. 1099
Conrad, John R., Chm. & Chief Exec. Officer--S & C Electric Company, Chicago, IL, pg. 958
Constantin, Gus, Chm. Bd., Pres. & Chief Exec. Officer--Phoenix American Incorporated, San Rafael, CA, pg. 868
Cook, J. Michael, Chm. Bd. & Chief Exec. Officer--Deloitte & Touche, Wilton, CT, pg. 326
Cook, James D., Chm. Bd. & Chief Exec. Officer--Concord Litho Co., Inc., Concord, NH, pg. 272
Cook, John J., Jr., Chm. Bd. & Chief Exec. Officer--First Boston Asset Management Corporation, New York, NY, pg. 204
Cook, Nicholas H., Pres. & Chief Exec. Officer--Brauns Fashions, Inc., Minneapolis, MN, pg. 172
Cook, Samuel R., Chm. Bd. & Chief Exec. Officer--Broughton Foods Company, Marietta, OH, pg. 180
Coombe, V. Anderson, Chm. Bd., Chief Exec. Officer, & Treas.--The Wm. Powell Company, Cincinnati, OH, pg. 882
Cooper, Marshall Y., Jr., Pres., Chief Exec. Officer & Chm. Bd.--Harriet & Henderson Yarns, Inc., Henderson, NC, pg. 511
Cooper, Norton J., Pres. & Chief Exec. Officer--Charles Jacquin et Cie, Inc., Philadelphia, PA, pg. 588
Cope, Larry W., Pres. & Chief Exec. Officer--Clear Springs Foods, Inc., Buhl, ID, pg. 254
Copland, James R., III, Pres., Chief Exec. Officer & Treas.--Copland Fabrics, Inc., Burlington, NC, pg. 284
Copley, Helen K., Chm. Bd. & Chief Exec. Officer--The Copley Press, Inc., La Jolla, CA, pg. 284
Copps, Michael W., Chm. Bd. & Chief Exec. Officer--The Copps Corp., Stevens Point, WI, pg. 285
Corcoran, Philip, Chm., Chief Exec. & Chief Oper. Officer--Comark, Bloomingdale, IL, pg. 267
Cordes, William O., Pres. & Chief Exec. Officer--Draper Corporation, Greensboro, NC, pg. 348
Cordova, Stephen, Chief Exec. Officer--Cordova Laboratories, San Fernando, CA, pg. 286
Cordova, Steve, Chief Exec. Officer--Cordova Enterprise, Sylmar, CA, pg. 285
Corkin, Herbert I., Chm. Bd., Pres., Chief Exec. & Chief Oper. Officer--The Entwistle Company, Hudson, MA, pg. 383
Cornell, Alverin M., Chm. Bd. & Chief Exec. Officer--Cornell Forge Company, Chicago, IL, pg. 286
Cornelsen, Paul F., Chm. Bd. & Chief Exec. Officer--Mitek, Inc., Chesterfield, MO, pg. 762
Cornfield, Stanley M., Chief Exec. Officer--Sharon Concepts, Inc., Union, NJ, pg. 995
Cornstein, David, Pres. & Chief Exec. Officer--Finlay Enterprises, Inc., New York, NY, pg. 411
Cornwall, John R., Pres. & Chief Exec. Officer--MetLife Capital Credit Corp., Stamford, CT, pg. 744
Corrao, Michael J., Chm. Bd., Pres. & Chief Exec. Officer--Gingiss International, Chicago, IL, pg. 460
Cosentino, Francis J., Pres. & Chief Exec. Officer--ICE Communications, Inc., Rochester, NY, pg. 559
Cosgrave, Gary D., Chm. & Chief Exec. Officer--Pro Hardware, Inc., Englewood, CO, pg. 891
Costello, Samuel A., Chief Exec. Officer--Arthur Murray Intl., Inc., Coral Gables, FL, pg. 776
Cotter, Daniel A., Pres. & Chief Exec. Officer & Dir.--Cotter & Company, Chicago, IL, pg. 288
Coulombe, Raymond, Chief Exec. & Chief Oper. Officer--Fairview Wine Co., Lewiston, ME, pg. 1186
Coulombe, Raymond R., Chm. & Chief Exec. Officer--White Rock Distilleries Inc., Lewiston, ME, pg. 1186
Coulombe, Raymond R., Chief Exec. Office--Lawrence & Company, Lewiston, ME, pg. 1186
Coulombe, Raymond R., Chief Exec. Officer--Maine Bottlers, Lewiston, ME, pg. 1186
Coulson, Robert, Pres. & Chief Exec. Officer--American Arbitration Association, New York, NY, pg. 49
Coulter, Wallace, Chm. Bd. & Chief Exec. Officer--Coulter Corporation, Hialeah, FL, pg. 289
Counsell, Paul S., Chm. Bd. & Chief Exec. Officer--Cramer-Krasselt, Milwaukee, WI, pg. 296
Counsell, Paul S., Chm. Bd. & Chief Exec. Officer--Cramer-Krasselt, Milwaukee, WI, pg. 296
Countryman, Gary L., Chm. & Chief Exec. Officer--Liberty Mutual Insurance Co., Boston, MA, pg. 674
Cousins, G.A., Chm.--George Patterson Pty. Limited, North Sydney,, Australia, pg. 112
Coverdale, Glen E., Chm. Bd. & Chief Exec. Officer--Cross & Brown Company, New York, NY, pg. 744
Covitz, William, Chief Exec. Officer--Acme Continental Foods, Inc., Chicago, IL, pg. 13
Cowan, Andrew, Chief Oper. Officer--SAIC UK Limited, Cambridge, United Kingdom, pg. 982
Cowan, James R., Chm. Bd. & Chief Exec. Officer--Stonecutter Mills Corp., Spindale, NC, pg. 1051
Cowan, R. Douglas, Pres. & Chief Exec. Officer--The Davey Tree Expert Company, Kent, OH, pg. 317
Cowen, Philip R., Chm. Bd. & Chief Exec. Officer--Alpha Electronic Signal Technologies, Inc., Elizabeth, NJ, pg. 43
Cowles, Alfred, Jr., Pres. & Chief Exec. Officer--Bluff City Distributing Co., Inc., Memphis, TN, pg. 161
Cowley, George, Chm. Bd. & Chief Exec. Officer--Alpha One Exchange, New Providence, NJ, pg. 43
Cox, Bill, Chm. Bd. & Chief Exec. Officer--Dal-Tile Corp., Dallas, TX, pg. 312
Cox, David C., Pres. & Chief Exec. Officer--Cowles Media Company, Minneapolis, MN, pg. 291
Cox, Michael, Chm. Bd. & Chief Exec. Officer--Cox Advertising, New York, NY, pg. 292
Cox, Winston H. (Tony), Chm. & Chief Exec. Officer-Showtime Networks--Viacom Inc., New York, NY, pg. 785
Coy, Doug, Chief Exec. Officer--Bridgeman's Restaurants Inc., Minneapolis, MN, pg. 175
Coyne, Nancy, Chm. Bd., Chief Exec. Officer & Dir.-Creative Services--Serino Coyne Inc., New York, NY, pg. 991
Cracraft, Thomas M., Pres. & Chief Exec. Officer--Computerland, Arlington, TX, pg. 271
Craft, Stanley, Chm., Pres. & Chief Exec. Officer--Essex Group, Inc., Fort Wayne, IN, pg. 389
Craig, Jack, Chief Exec. Officer--PTS Electronics Corporation, Bloomington, IN, pg. 837
Crandall, David E., Chm. Bd. & Chief Exec. Officer--PPA Industries, Inc., Dallas, TX, pg. 836
Cranford, Wayne, Chm. & Chief Exec. Officer--Cranford Johnson Robinson Woods, Little Rock, AR, pg. 296
Crawford, William, Pres. & Chief Exec. Officer--Memphis Light, Gas & Water, Memphis, TN, pg. 738
Crider, Joe D., Chm. Bd. & Chief Exec. Officer--Metalcenter, Inc., Santa Fe Springs, CA, pg. 742
Crilly, John H., Pres. & Chief Exec. Officer--Sun Data Inc., Norcross, GA, pg. 1058
Crisp, Donald W., Pres. & Chief Exec. Officer--Caroline Hunt Trust Estate, Dallas, TX, pg. 553
Crisp, Donald W., Pres. & Chief Exec. Officer--Rosewood Corporation, Dallas, TX, pg. 553
Crispin, Andre A., Pres. & Chief Exec. Officer--The Crispin Company, Houston, TX, pg. 299
Cristiano, Joseph P., Pres. & Chief Exec. Officer--Kelly-Moore Paint Company, Inc., San Carlos, CA, pg. 621
Crockett, R.J., Pres. & Chief Exec. Officer--Dexter Company, Fairfield, IA, pg. 334
Crone, W.G., Chm. Bd. & Chief Exec. Officer--Conley Frog & Switch Company, Memphis, TN, pg. 274
Cronin, Eugene F., Jr., Pres. & Chief Exec. Officer--CSE Corporation, San Francisco, CA, pg. 204
Cronin, Tim, Pres. & Chief Exec. Officer--Rumrill-Hoyt, Inc., Rochester, NY, pg. 955
Crook, Steven E., Pres. & Chief Exec. Officer--Crooks Supermarket Inc., Nashville, TN, pg. 300
Crossett, Donald S., Pres. & Chief Exec. Officer--IDC Services, Inc., Chicago, IL, pg. 559
Crotty, L. William, Chm., Pres. & Chief Exec. Officer--Van Dyne-Crotty, Inc., Dayton, OH, pg. 1144
Crowder, Otis A., Pres. & Chief Exec. Officer--Crowder Construction Co., Charlotte, NC, pg. 301
Crowley, J.J., Jr., Pres. & Chief Exec. Officer--Fuller O'Brien Paints, South San Francisco, CA, pg. 820
Crowley, Thomas B., Chm. Bd. & Chief Exec. Officer--Crowley Maritime Corporation, Oakland, CA, pg. 301
Crowser, John C., Chief Exec. Officer--Hart Crowser, Inc., Seattle, WA, pg. 512
Crum, David H., Pres., Chief Exec. & Chief Fin. Officer--Crum Electric Supply Co., Inc., Casper, WY, pg. 303
Crum, John K., Dr., Chief Exec. Officer--American Chemical Society, Washington, DC, pg. 50
Cullen, John B., Chm. Bd. & Chief Exec. Officer--King Kullen Grocery Co., Inc., Westbury, NY, pg. 630
Cullers, Vincent T., Pres., Chief Exec. Officer & Treas.--Vince Cullers Advertising Inc., Chicago, IL, pg. 304
Cullum, Kenneth H., Pres. & Chief Exec. Officer--Bristol Steel & Iron Works, Inc., Bristol, VA, pg. 176

Cummings, Terry M., Pres. & Chief Exec. Officer--Bremer Financial Corporation, Saint Paul, MN, pg. 173
Cummings, Thomas L., Jr., Chm. Bd. & Chief Exec. Officer--Cummings Inc., Nashville, TN, pg. 304
Cummins, Bernard J., Pres. & Chief Exec. Officer (San Francisco) & Dir.--EvansGroup, Salt Lake City, UT, pg. 390
Cummins, Mick, Pres. & Chief Exec. Officer--EvansGroup, San Francisco, CA, pg. 391
Curran, James B., Chm. Bd. & Chief Exec. Officer--Henry Bacon Building Materials, Inc., Issaquah, WA, pg. 113
Curran, John H., Chief Exec. Officer--Curran Contracting Co., Crystal Lake, IL, pg. 305
Currey, Bradley, Jr., Pres. & Chief Exec. Officer--Rock-Tenn Company, Norcross, GA, pg. 941
Curtis, Charles, Pres. & Chief Exec. Officer--Cramer Inc., Kansas City, KS, pg. 296
Curtis, Charles L., Chief Exec. Officer--Rice & Rice Inc., Minneapolis, MN, pg. 1143
Curtis, Chuck, Chief Exec. Officer & Pres.--Valentine-Radford, Inc., Kansas City, MO, pg. 1142
Curtis, Roger William, Chm. Bd., Chief Exec. Officer & Sec.--L.N. Curtis & Sons, Oakland, CA, pg. 306
Cypher, Victor, Pres. & Chief Exec. Officer--Caldwell Manufacturing Company, Rochester, NY, pg. 208
D'Amour, Donald H., Sr. V.P. & Chief Exec. Officer--Big Y Foods Inc., Springfield, MA, pg. 149
Dabah, Ezra, Chm. Bd. & Chief Exec. Officer--The Children's Place Retail Stores, Inc., Pine Brook, NJ, pg. 247
Dabah, Haim, Pres. & Chief Exec. Officer--Gitano Group Inc., New York, NY, pg. 460
Dalinsky, Frank, Chief Exec. Officer & Exec. V.P.--Philadelphia Reserve Supply Company, Croydon, PA, pg. 867
Dally, Scott, Pres. & Chief Exec. Officer--Dally Advertising, Inc., Fort Worth, TX, pg. 312
Dalquist, H. David, Sr., Chm. Bd. & Chief Exec. Officer--Northland Aluminum Products, Inc., Minneapolis, MN, pg. 814
Dalton, James, Jr., Pres. & Chief Exec. Officer--Quorum Health Group, Inc., Brentwood, TN, pg. 905
Dambra, Barton, Pres. & Chief Exec. Officer--Markin Tubing, Inc., Wyoming, NY, pg. 709
Daniels, Terry, Chief Exec. Officer--Bruner Corporation, Milwaukee, WI, pg. 184
Daniels, William D., Chm. Bd. & Chief Exec. Officer--Penn-Daniels, Inc., Quincy, IL, pg. 857
Danna, Leon J., Chm. Bd. & Chief Exec. Officer--Network Real Estate of California, Inc., Soquel, CA, pg. 798
Danna, Leon J., Chm. Bd. & Chief Exec. Officer--Network Real Estate, Inc., Soquel, CA, pg. 798
Danna, Leon J., Chm. Bd. & Chief Exec. Officer--Network Home Services, Inc., Soquel, CA, pg. 798
Darazsdi, James J., Chief Exec. Officer & Sr. V.P.--Rocco Inc., Harrisonburg, VA, pg. 940
Dargatz, Kenneth C., Pres. & Chief Exec. Officer--Haden, Inc., Madison Heights, MI, pg. 499
Darian, Ralph, Pres., Chief Exec. & Chief Fin. Officer--Levonian Brothers Inc., Troy, NY, pg. 671
Darling, R.M., Chief Exec. Officer--Ampco Metal Incorporated, Milwaukee, WI, pg. 67
Darling, Robert, Chm. Bd & Chief Exec. Officer--Zollner Corporation, Fort Wayne, IN, pg. 1221
Dasburg, John, Pres. & Chief Exec. Officer--Northwest Airlines, Inc., Saint Paul, MN, pg. 782
Dasburg, John H., Pres. & Chief Exec. Officer--NWA, Inc., Saint Paul, MN, pg. 782
David, Paul, Pres. & Chief Exec. Officer--Camelot Music, Inc., North Canton, OH, pg. 212
Davidson, Donald, Co-Chm. Bd. & Chief Exec. Officer--D&L Venture Corp., New Britain, CT, pg. 307
Davidson, F. Lee, Pres. & Chief Exec. Officer--Parks Corporation, Somerset, MA, pg. 849
Davidson, Ian B., Chm. Bd. & Chief Exec. Officer--D.A. Davidson & Co., Great Falls, MT, pg. 318
Davidson, Martin, Pres. & Chief Exec. Officer--Southern Pipe & Supply Co., Inc., Meridian, MS, pg. 1022
Davidson, William, Chm., Pres., Chief Exec. & Chief Oper. Officer--Guardian Industries Corp., Northville, MI, pg. 491
Davis, DeForest P., Jr., Chm. Bd. & Chief Exec. Officer--Lester B. Knight & Associates, Inc., Chicago, IL, pg. 637
Davis, George L., Pres. & Chief Exec. Officer--First American Bankshares, Inc., Washington, DC, pg. 412
Davis, James L., Chm. Bd. & Chief Exec. Officer--Davis Paint Company, Kansas City, MO, pg. 319
Davis, Jeffrey G., Chm., Pres. & Chief Exec. Officer--Aetna Plywood, Inc., Arlington Heights, IL, pg. 23
Davis, Norwood, Chm. Bd. & Chief Exec. Officer--Blue Cross & Blue Shield of Virginia, Richmond, VA, pg. 160
Davis, W.F., Jr., Pres., Chief Exec. Officer & Treas.--Palmetto Spinning Corp., Laurens, SC, pg. 844
Davis, William, Pres. & Chief Exec. Officer--Cabot Creamery Co-Operative Inc., Cabot, VT, pg. 25
Daw, Ronald W., Chm. Bd. & Chief Exec. Officer--Daw Technologies, Inc., Salt Lake City, UT, pg. 319
Day, Joseph C., Chief Exec. Officer--Freudenberg-NOK (MI), Plymouth, MI, pg. 432
Day, Timothy T., Pres. & Chief Exec. Officer--Bar-S Foods Co., Phoenix, AZ, pg. 118
Dayan, Charles, Chief Exec. Officer--Bon Jour International Ltd., New York, NY, pg. 164
De Arment, W.S., Chief Exec. Officer--Hold-E-Zee, Ltd., Rochester, NY, pg. 239
De Crescenzo, Tony, Chief Oper. Officer & Exec. V.P.--Commercial & Architectural Products Inc., Dover, OH, pg. 268
Dean, Lester M., Sr., Chm. Bd. & Chief Exec. Officer--Dean Operations Inc., Kansas City, MO, pg. 322
Dearden, Douglas E., Chief Exec. Officer & Personnel Dir.--Dearden's, Inc., Los Angeles, CA, pg. 322
Deason, Darwin, Chm. Bd. & Chief Exec. Officer--Affiliated Computer Services, Inc., Dallas, TX, pg. 23
Deaver, Dan, Pres. & Chief Exec. Officer--Franks Supply Company, Inc., Albuquerque, NM, pg. 429
DeBartolo, Edward J., Chm. Bd. & Chief Exec. Officer--The Edward J. DeBartolo Corporation, Youngstown, OH, pg. 323
DeCamp, D.A., Pres. & Chief Exec. Officer--Flexfab, Inc., Hastings, MI, pg. 418
DeCarlo, Anthony J., Pres. & Chief Exec. Officer--Lumbermens Merchandising Corporation, Wayne, PA, pg. 687
DeCastro, Howard, Pres. & Chief Exec. Officer--Northwest Aerospace Training Corporation, Saint Paul, MN, pg. 782
DeCesaris, Geaton A., Jr., Pres. & Chief Exec. Officer--Washington Homes, Inc., Landover, MD, pg. 1166
Decker, Gilbert F., Pres. & Chief Exec. Officer--Acurex Environmental Corporation, Mountain View, CA, pg. 15
Decker, Jack E., Pres. & Chief Exec. Officer--Campbell Oil Co., Massillon, OH, pg. 213
Dedman, Robert H., Sr., Chm. Bd. & Chief Exec. Officer--Club Corporation International, Dallas, TX, pg. 256
DeFrancisci, Leonard, Pres. & Chief Exec. Officer--De Francisci Machine Corp.(Demaco), Ridgewood, NY, pg. 321
DeGeorge, L., Chm. Bd. & Chief Exec. Officer--Times Fiber Communications, Inc., Wallingford, CT, pg. 648
DeGeorge, Lawrence J., Chm. Bd., Pres. & Chief Exec. Officer--LPL Technologies, Inc., Wallingford, CT, pg. 648
Dehaan, Christal, Chm. Bd., Pres. & Chief Exec. Officer--Resort Condominiums International, Indianapolis, IN, pg. 929
Dehmlow, Louis H.T., Chm. Bd. & Chief Exec. Officer--Great Lakes Terminal & Transport Corp., Chicago, IL, pg. 482
Dekko, Chester E., Chm. Bd., Pres. & Chief Exec. Officer--Group Dekko International Inc., Kendallville, IN, pg. 489
DeKruif, Jack H., Chm. Bd. & Chief Exec. Officer--Wayne Corporation, Richmond, IN, pg. 1169
Del Monte, Raymond, Pres. & Chief Exec. Officer--Wolff Associates, Inc., Rochester, NY, pg. 1199
Delaney, John W., Pres. & Chief Exec. Officer--TransCoastal Mortgage Company, Bellevue, WA, pg. 1107
DelGaldo, Joseph A., Pres. & Chief Exec. Officer--Carlson, DelGaldo, Hoag, Matthei Advertising, Inc., Stamford, CT, pg. 222
Delich, John M., Chief Exec. Officer--Mutual of Omaha Fund Management Co., Omaha, NE, pg. 779
Dellamano, Patricia, Pres. & Chief Exec. & Chief Fin. Officer--Patson's Press, Sunnyvale, CA, pg. 851
Delonis, Robert J., Pres. & Chief Exec. Officer--Great Lakes Bancorp, Ann Arbor, MI, pg. 480
DeLuca, Robert, Chm. Bd., Pres. & Chief Exec. Officer--Aero Data Metal Crafters, Bohemia, NY, pg. 22
DeMaria, Joseph A., Sr., Chm. Bd. & Chief Exec. Officer--DeMaria Building Co. Inc., Novi, MI, pg. 327
Dembinski, Jan A., Pres., Chief Exec. Officer & Treas.--M.J. Daly & Sons, Inc., Waterbury, CT, pg. 313
Demere, Robert H., Chm. Bd. & Chief Exec. Officer--Colonial Oil Industries, Savannah, GA, pg. 263
DeMeuse, Donald H., Chm. Bd. & Chief Exec. Officer--Fort Howard Corporation, Green Bay, WI, pg. 425
Demmer, John E., Chief Exec. Officer--Jack Demmer Ford, Inc., Wayne, MI, pg. 328
DeMoulas, Telemachus A., Pres. & Chief Exec. Officer--Demoulas Super Markets, Tewksbury, MA, pg. 328
Denise, Robert, Chm., Pres., Chief Exec. Officer & Chief Fin. Officer--Bucilla Corporation, Hazleton, PA, pg. 185
Denrich, Stephen, Chief Exec. Officer--So-Lo-Food, Inc., Baltimore, MD, pg. 1016
Derrey, Robert F., Pres. & Chief Exec. Officer--Barr Brothers & Co., Inc., New York, NY, pg. 121
Derst, Edward J., III, Pres. & Chief Exec. Officer--Derst Baking Company, Inc., Savannah, GA, pg. 331
Desperak, Jack, Pres. & Chief Exec. Officer--Splendor Form International Inc., Long Island City, NY, pg. 1031
Dessy, William J., Vice Chm., Pres. & Chief Exec. Officer--T.L. James & Company, Ruston, LA, pg. 588
Detlef, Vernon A., Chief Exec. Officer & V.P.-Opers--Thomas & Skinner, Inc., Indianapolis, IN, pg. 1093
Deutsch, Alex, Chm. Bd. & Chief Exec. Officer--The Deutsch Company, Santa Monica, CA, pg. 333
Deverse, Frank T., Chm. Bd., Pres., Chief Exec. Officer & Treas.--International Microcircuits, Inc., Milpitas, CA, pg. 579
DeVoe, James K., Chm. Bd., Chief Exec. Officer--The Jayme Organization, Inc., Cleveland, OH, pg. 591
Dew, Donald F., Chm. Bd., Pres. & Chief Exec. Officer--Diemolding Corp., Canastota, NY, pg. 336
Deweese, Mary Ann, Chief Exec. Officer--DeWeese Inc., Los Angeles, CA, pg. 334
Di Sorbo, James, Pres. & Chief Exec. Officer--Hoechst Ceramtec North America, Inc., Mansfield, MA, pg. 537
Diamond, Lawrence, Chm. Bd., Pres., Chief Exec. & Chief Oper. Officer & Dir.-Pur.--Triangle Marketing Corp., New York, NY, pg. 1112
Diamond, Robert E., Jr., Chm., Pres. & Chief Exec. Officer--CS First Boston Pacific, Inc., New York, NY, pg. 204
DiBattista, Raymond, Pres. & Chief Exec. Officer--United Metal Fabricators, Inc., Johnstown, PA, pg. 1133
DiBui, William J., Pres., Chief Exec. & Chief Oper. Officer--Rumsey Electric Co., Philadelphia, PA, pg. 956
Dick, Louise H., Chm. Bd.--Trumbull Corporation, West Mifflin, PA, pg. 1117
Dickenson, H. Boyd, Chm. & Chief Exec. Officer--Hayes, Seay, Mattern & Mattern, Inc., Roanoke, VA, pg. 519
Dickerson, Arthur J., Chm. Bd., Pres. & Chief Exec. Officer--Southwestern Petroleum Corporation, Fort Worth, TX, pg. 1024
Dickerson, Michael A., Pres. & Chief Exec. Officer--High Point Financial Corp., Branchville, NJ, pg. 533
Dickerson, Michael A., Vice Chm., Pres. & Chief Exec. Officer--The Pocono Bank, Milford, PA, pg. 534
Dickson, John R., Pres. & Chief Exec. Officer--Roundy's, Inc., Pewaukee, WI, pg. 952
Diedrick, G. Vern, Chm. Bd., Chief Exec. Officer, & Pres.--Maecorp Inc., Chicago, IL, pg. 699
Dierberg, Robert J., Pres., Chief Exec. Officer & Treas.--Dierbergs Markets Inc., Chesterfield, MO, pg. 337
Dietrich, Thomas W., Pres. & Chief Exec. Officer--Dietrich's Milk Products, Inc., Reading, PA, pg. 337
Dietz, W.R., Chm. Bd., Pres. & Chief Exec. Officer--American Savings Bank, White Plains, NY, pg. 60
DiLorenzo, James E., Chm. Bd., Pres. & Chief Exec. Officer--Quality Pontiac, Inc., Albuquerque, NM, pg. 904
DiMatteo, James, Vice Chm. & Chief Exec. Officer--Dominick's Finer Foods, Northlake, IL, pg. 343
Dimmick, Henry M., Chm. Bd. & Chief Exec. Officer--AGR International, Inc., Butler, PA, pg. 4
Dineen, R.J., Pres. & Chief Exec. Officer--The Marley Company, Mission Woods, KS, pg. 710
Dingman, Michael D., Chm. Bd. & Chief Exec. Officer--The Henley Group, Inc., Hampton, NH, pg. 529
Dingwell, Everett W., Pres. & Chief Exec. Officer--Certified Grocers Of California, Los Angeles, CA, pg. 237
Dircks, R.D., Chm. Bd. & Chief Exec. Officer--Berger Transfer & Storage, Inc., Saint Paul, MN, pg. 141
Dirkes, James V., Pres., Chief Exec. Officer & Treas.--Rapid Engineering Inc., Comstock Park, MI, pg. 913
Dishon, James, Pres. & Chief Exec. Officer--Agripac Inc., Salem, OR, pg. 25
Dixon, Robert P., Pres. & Chief Exec. Officer--SF Services, North Little Rock, AR, pg. 961
Dockweiler, Thomas L., Chm.-Exec. Committee & Chief Exec. Officer--First National Bank of Blue Island, Blue Island, IL, pg. 481
Dodson, Cathleen, Chm. Bd. & Chief Exec. Officer--Dodson Group, Kansas City, MO, pg. 342
Doehrman, Dale F., Chm. Bd. & Chief Exec. Officer--The Medical Protective Company, Fort Wayne, IN, pg. 735
Doherty, Robert C., Pres. & Chief Exec. Officer--McKinney & Silver, Raleigh, NC, pg. 730
Dolson, Robert A., Pres. & Chief Exec. Officer--Continental Water Company, Saint Louis, MO, pg. 280
Domecq, Michael, Pres. & Chief Exec. Officer--Domecq Importers Inc., Old Greenwich, CT, pg. 343
Don, Robert E., Chm. Bd. & Chief Exec. Officer--Edward Don & Company of Illinois, North Riverside, IL, pg. 344
Donahue, James C., Pres. & Chief Exec. Officer--Donahue, Inc., Advertising, Hartford, CT, pg. 344
Donaldson, Darrell, Pres., Chief Exec. & Fin. Officer--Hot Shot Delivery Inc., Houston, TX, pg. 545
Donaldson, J. Bennett, Pres., Chief Exec. Officer & Sec.--Cunningham-Limp Development Co., Troy, MI, pg. 305
Donino, Frank, Pres. & Chief Exec. Officer--Donino & Partners, Inc., Atlanta, GA, pg. 344
Donnelly, Gerald K., Chief Exec. Officer--H. C. Prange Company, Green Bay, WI, pg. 884
Donnelly, James, Pres. & Chief Exec. Officer--Baxter Hodell Donnelly Preston Inc., Cincinnati, OH, pg. 127
Donofrio, Hal, Pres. & Chief Exec. Officer--Richardson, Myers & Donofrio, Inc., Baltimore, MD, pg. 933
Donovan, Richard P., Pres., Chief Exec. & Fin. Officer--World Jai-alai, Miami, FL, pg. 1202
Donsky, Ervin, Chief Exec. Officer--Sterling Jewelry & Distributing Co., Dallas, TX, pg. 1047
Dorris, Al, Pres. & Chief Exec. Officer--Xerxes Corporation, Minneapolis, MN, pg. 1206
Dott, A. Eric, Chm. Bd. & Chief Exec. Officer--Monarch Avalon, Inc., Baltimore, MD, pg. 765
Downey, David G., Chm. Bd. & Chief Exec. Officer--Downey Designs International, Inc., Indianapolis, IN, pg. 348
Downs, Beverly B., Vice Chm., Chief Exec. Officer & Treas.--The Downs Group, Inc., Charlotte, NC, pg. 348
Downs, Richard, Chm. Bd. & Chief Exec. Officer--Tony Downs Foods Company, Saint James, MN, pg. 348
Draeger, Ken, Pres. & Chief Exec. Officer--Decision Data Inc., Horsham, PA, pg. 323
Draft, Howard, Chm. Bd. & Chief Exec. Officer--Kobs & Draft Advertising, Inc., Chicago, IL, pg. 109
Drasner, Fred, Vice Chm. & Chief Exec. Officer--The Atlantic Monthly Magazine, Boston, MA, pg. 95
Drasner, Fred, Pres. & Chief Exec. Officer--U.S. News & World Report, New York, NY, pg. 1136
Drebes, Charles F., Pres. & Chief Exec. Officer--Gaylord Printing, Inc., Detroit, MI, pg. 446
Drell, Leonard B., Chm. Bd., Pres., Chief Exec. & Chief Oper. Officer--DeMert & Dougherty, Inc., Westchester, IL, pg. 328
Drettmann, Henry, Chm. Bd., Chief Exec. Officer & Treas.--Active Tool & Manufacturing Co., Inc., Roseville, MI, pg. 15
Dreusike, Don, Pres. & Chief Exec. Officer--Dinwiddie Construction Co., San Francisco, CA, pg. 338
Dreyer, John W., Chm. Bd., Pres. & Chief Exec. Officer--Harold M. Pitman Co., Inc., Totowa, NJ, pg. 872
Drinkall, W.H., Chm. Bd. & Chief Exec. Officer--South Bend Plastics, Inc., Mishawaka, IN, pg. 1019
Driscoll, Edward C., Chm. Bd., Chief Exec. Officer & Treas.--L.F. Driscoll Co., Bala-Cynwyd, PA, pg. 349
Drobis, David R., Chm. & Chief Exec. Officer--Ketchum Public Relations/Corporate, New York, NY, pg. 625
Drongowski, Steve, Sr. Exec. Partner--Fahlgren Martin, Inc., Parkersburg, WV, pg. 396
Drummond, Garry N., Chief Exec. Officer--Drummond Company, Inc., Jasper, AL, pg. 349
Drury, John R., Chief Exec. Officer--Harris Drury Cohen, Fort Lauderdale, FL, pg. 511
Drutt, William, Pres., Chief Exec. Officer & Sec.--Harris & Drutt Inc., Philadelphia, PA, pg. 511
Duchossois, Richard L., Chm. Bd. & Chief Exec. Officer--Duchossois Industries, Inc., Elmhurst, IL, pg. 350
Dudreck, Albert W., Chm. Bd. & Chief Exec. Officer--DDF&M Inc. Dudreck DePaul Ficco & Morgan Inc., Pittsburgh, PA, pg. 308
Dueser, Fred F., Chief Exec. Officer--States, Inc., Breckenridge, TX, pg. 1041
Dugan, Francis R., Chm. & Chief Exec. Officer--Dugan & Meyers Interests, Inc., Cincinnati, OH, pg. 351

Dugan, J. Patrick, Pres. & Chief Exec. Officer--Microband Companies, Inc., Fairfield, NJ, pg. 748
DuJardin, Neil A., Chief Oper. Officer--Dart Transit Company, Inc., Eagan, MN, pg. 316
Duncan, Dan L., Chm. Bd. & Chief Exec. Officer--Enterprise Products Company, Houston, TX, pg. 382
Dunlap, Edward B., Chm Bd., Pres., & Chief Exec. Officer--Centimark Corporation, Bethel Park, PA, pg. 231
Dunlap, William D., Worldwide Chief Exec. Officer--CME-KHBB Advertising, Minneapolis, MN, pg. 202
Dunn, Charles O., Vice Chm. & Chief Exec. Officer--Newsprint South, Inc., Yazoo City, MS, pg. 760
Dunne, Thomas P., Chm. Bd. & Chief Exec. Officer--Fred Weber Inc., Maryland Heights, MO, pg. 1171
Dunville, Joseph R., Chm. Bd., Pres., & Chief Exec. Officer--Idea Engineering & Fabricating, Detroit, MI, pg. 562
Dupey, Michael, Chm. Bd. & Chief Exec. Officer--Dupey Management Corp., Irving, TX, pg. 354
Durham, G.R., Pres. & Chief Exec. Officer--Walter Industries, Inc., Tampa, FL, pg. 1161
Durham, Timothy S., Pres. & Chief Exec. Officer--Carpenter Manufacturing, Inc., Mitchell, IN, pg. 991
Durrett, William E., Chm. Bd., Pres. & Chief Exec. Officer--American Fidelity Corp., Oklahoma City, OK, pg. 52
Dusenbery, John F., Chief Exec. Officer--John Dusenbery Co., Inc., Randolph, NJ, pg. 355
Duvall, Sharon B., Co-Chief Exec. Officer--San Francisco French Bread Company, Oakland, CA, pg. 969
Duvall, Sharon B., Pres. & Chief Exec. Officer--Andre-Boudin Bakeries, Inc., San Francisco, CA, pg. 969
Dym, Morrie, Pres. & Chief Exec. Officer--Five Dollar Clothing Stores, Los Angeles, CA, pg. 416
Eagle, J.M., Chm. Bd. & Chief Exec. Officer--Pipe Fabricating & Supply Company, Santa Fe Springs, CA, pg. 872
Eagle, Robert M., Chm. Bd. & Chief Exec. Officer--Eagle Lincoln Mercury Inc., Dallas, TX, pg. 362
Easley, Ronald L., Chm. Bd., Pres. & Chief Exec. Officer--System Planning Corp., Arlington, VA, pg. 1070
Eastland, Woods E., Pres. & Chief Exec. Officer--Staple Cotton Cooperative Association, Greenwood, MS, pg. 1038
Eaton, Henry F., Chm. & Chief Exec. Officer--Dix & Eaton Incorporated, Cleveland, OH, pg. 341
Eaves, Hayden, Pres. & Chief Exec. Officer--Trammell Crow Company, Dallas, TX, pg. 1106
Eberle, Bruce, Chm. Bd. & Chief Exec. Officer--Eberle Direct Marketing Group, Inc., Vienna, VA, pg. 365
Echevarria, Angel, Pres. & Chief Exec. Officer--Echevarria Angel Co., Inc., Los Angeles, CA, pg. 365
Echevarria, Michael, Chief Oper. Officer & Exec. V.P.--Echevarria Angel Co., Inc., Los Angeles, CA, pg. 365
Eckert, Michael J., Chief Exec. Officer--The Weather Channel, Atlanta, GA, pg. 654
Eckert, Wesley, Pres. & Chief Exec. Officer--Darigold, Inc., Seattle, WA, pg. 315
Eckhoff, Gilbert B., Pres. & Chief Exec. Officer--Henningsen Foods, Inc., White Plains, NY, pg. 629
Eddings, J. Carson, Pres. & Chief Exec. Officer--The William Cook Agency, Inc., Jacksonville, FL, pg. 282
Eddings, J. Carson, Pres., Chief Exec. Officer--William Cook Public Relations, Inc., Jacksonville, FL, pg. 282
Eddins, Mark A., Pres. & Chief Exec. Officer--Friendly Chevrolet Co. Inc., Dallas, TX, pg. 433
Edelson, Kenneth J., Pres. & Chief Exec. Officer--General Sportcraft Company Ltd., Bergenfield, NJ, pg. 450
Edinger, Daniel J., Pres. & Chief Oper. Officer--Telmark, Inc., Syracuse, NY, pg. 25
Edwards, Joel, Chm. Bd. & Chief Exec. Officer--Edwards Baking Co., Atlanta, GA, pg. 369
Edwards, T.L., Chief Exec. Officer--Coastal Wholesale, Inc., Kinston, NC, pg. 257
Edwards, Wesley, Pres. & Chief Exec. Officer--Spinnerin Yarn Co., Inc., South Hackensack, NJ, pg. 1031
Edwards, William E., Jr., Chm. Bd. & Chief Exec. Officer--Cardinal Aluminum Co., Louisville, KY, pg. 217
Egan, Gerald L., Pres. & Chief Exec. Officer--Egan Cos., Minneapolis, MN, pg. 371
Egan, Michael S., Chm. Bd. & Chief Exec. Officer--Alamo Rent-A-Car Inc., Fort Lauderdale, FL, pg. 30
Egan, Richard W., Pres. & Chief Exec. Officer--The Levolor Corporation, Sunnyvale, CA, pg. 671
Egbert, John C., Pres. & Chief Exec. Officer--McCourt Label Co., Lewis Run, PA, pg. 727
Egizii, Robert, Pres. & Chief Exec. Officerf--Egizii Electric, Inc., Springfield, IL, pg. 371
Eichler, Franklin R., Pres. & Chief Exec. Officer--The Sico Company, Mount Joy, PA, pg. 1001
Eihusen, Virgil, Chm. Bd. & Chief Exec. Officer--Chief Industries, Inc., Grand Island, NE, pg. 247
Eisele, Ed, Pres. & Chief Exec. Officer--Holsum Bakery, Inc., Phoenix, AZ, pg. 541
Eisenberg, James, Chm. Bd. & Chief Exec. Officer--Vienna Sausage Mfg. Co., Chicago, IL, pg. 1151
Eisenbrey, John R., Chm. Bd., Pres. & Chief Exec. Officer--Artesian Resources Corporation, Newark, DE, pg. 86
Eisenbrey, John R., Chm. Bd., Pres. & Chief Exec. Officer--Artesian Water Company, Inc., Newark, DE, pg. 86
Eisner, Bill, Pres., Chief Exec. Officer & Creative Dir.--William Eisner & Associates Inc., Milwaukee, WI, pg. 372
Eisner, Steven C., Pres. & Chief Exec. Officer--Eisner & Associates, Inc., Baltimore, MD, pg. 372
Eizenberg, Michael I., Pres.--American Council for International Studies, Boston, MA, pg. 56
Eldon Wheeler, M.L., Chm. Bd. & Chief Exec. Officer--Jernberg Industries, Inc., Chicago, IL, pg. 593
Ellingson, Chester W., Jr., Chm. Bd., Pres. & Chief Exec. Officer--Reese Enterprises, Inc., Rosemount, MN, pg. 920
Elliott, Charles A., Chm. Bd., Pres. & Chief Exec., Officer--Crenlo, Inc., Rochester, MN, pg. 298
Elliott, J.C., Chief Exec. Officer--Mrs. Alison's Cookie Company, Saint Louis, MO, pg. 760
Elliott, Robert M., Chm. Bd. & Chief Exec. Officer--LFC Holding Corporation, Boca Raton, FL, pg. 647
Elliott, Robert M., Chm. Bd. & Chief Exec. Officer--Levitz Furniture Corporation, Boca Raton, FL, pg. 647
Ellis, William D., Chm. Bd. & Chief Exec. Officer--Southern Mills, Inc., Union City, GA, pg. 1021
Ellstrom, Elmer, Jr., Chm. Bd. & Chief Exec. Officer--Dearborn Gage Company, Garden City, MI, pg. 322
Elman, Robert H., Chm. Bd. & Chief Exec. Officer--Desa International, Inc., Bowling Green, KY, pg. 331
Elmquist, Ronald E., Chm. Bd. & Chief Exec. Officer--W S Holding Company, Euless, TX, pg. 1156
Elsberry, Howard W., Chm., Pres. & Chief Exec. Officer--Westlake Hardware, Inc., Shawnee Mission, KS, pg. 1183
Elsener, Frank, Pres. & Chief Exec. Officer--Tree Top, Inc., Selah, WA, pg. 1109
Elsperman, Robert P., P.E., Chm. Bd. & Chief Exec. Officer--Tarlton Corporation, Saint Louis, MO, pg. 1079
Engel, Arthur, Pres. & Chief Exec. Officer--Southwest Marine, Inc., San Diego, CA, pg. 1023
Engelsma, Lloyd, Chm. Bd. & Chief Exec. Officer--Kraus-Anderson, Inc., Minneapolis, MN, pg. 644
Engelsted, John N., Chm. Bd. & Chief Exec. Officer--Walker Magnetics Group, Inc., Worcester, MA, pg. 1160
England-Markun, Mark W., Chief Exec. Officer & Mgr. Dir.--Cadence Capital Management, Boston, MA, pg. 841
England-Markun, Mark W., Chief Exec. Officer & Mng. Dir.--Parametric Portfolio Associates, Inc., Seattle, WA, pg. 841
Englefield, F.W., IV, Co-Pres., Chief Exec. & Chief Fin. Officer--Englefield, Inc., Newark, OH, pg. 382
Eppley, Mark, Chm. & Chief Exec. Officer--Traveling Software Inc., Bothell, WA, pg. 1108
Epstein, Martin, Pres., Chief Exec. & Chief Fin. Officer--Associated Machinecraft Corporation, Los Angeles, CA, pg. 90
Epstein, Richard, Chm. Bd., Pres. & Chief Exec. Officer--Vesco Oil Corp., Southfield, MI, pg. 1149
Erb, Fred A., Chm., Pres. & Chief Exec. Officer--Erb Lumber Company, Birmingham, MI, pg. 360
Erenberg, Ethan M., Chm. Bd. & Chief Exec. Officer--W. Braun Company, Chicago, IL, pg. 172
Erickson, Chuck, Pres. & Chief Exec. Officer--Digital Pathways Inc., Mountain View, CA, pg. 337
Erickson, Richard P., Chm. Bd. & Chief Exec. Officer--Lifetouch, Inc., Bloomington, MN, pg. 675
Ernst, Lois Geraci, Chm. & Chief Exec. Officer--Advertising To Women, Inc., New York, NY, pg. 21
Ernst, Paul W., Pres. & Chief Exec. Officer--Carter Day Industries, Inc., Minneapolis, MN, pg. 226
Erokan, Dennis, Pres. & Editor-in-Chief--Bam Publications, Inc., Pleasant Hill, CA, pg. 117
Ervin, William W., Pres. & Chief Exec. Officer--O'Neal & Prelle, Hartford, CT, pg. 827
Esak, J. Ronald, Pres. & Chief Exec. Officer--Nexus Plastics, Inc., Hawthorne, NJ, pg. 805
Esculier, Jacques, Chief Exec. Officer--Mooney Aircraft Corporation, Kerrville, TX, pg. 768
Eskandarian, Ed, Chm. & Chief Exec. Officer--Arnold Fortuna Lawner & Cabot, Boston, MA, pg. 84
Essig, Armand J., Chm. Bd. & Chief Exec. Officer--Allied Sporting Goods Inc., Louisville, KY, pg. 40
Estenson, Noel, Pres. & Chief Exec. Officer-Cenex Inc.--Cenex/Land O'Lakes, Inc., Saint Paul, MN, pg. 653
Estenson, Noel, Pres. & Chief Exec. Officer-Cenex Inc.--Cenex/Land O'Lakes, Inc., Saint Paul, MN, pg. 231
Estes, Robey W., Sr., Chm. Bd. & Chief Exec. Officer--Estes Express Lines, Inc., Richmond, VA, pg. 389
Estrada, Jairo A., Chm. Bd. & Chief Exec. Officer--Garden Way, Inc., Troy, NY, pg. 443
Eulich, John F., Chm. Bd. & Chief Exec. Officer--Vantage Companies, Dallas, TX, pg. 1145
Evans, Jim, Pres. & Chief Exec. Officer--Evans, Hardy & Young, Inc., Santa Barbara, CA, pg. 390
Evans, John E., Chm. Bd. & Chief Exec. Officer--Allied Mutual Insurance Company, Des Moines, IA, pg. 38
Evans, John R., Chief Exec. Officer--Evans Brothers Company, Inc., Waukesha, WI, pg. 390
Evans, Kenneth L., Pres. & Chief Exec. Officer--Oberdorfer Industries, Inc., Syracuse, NY, pg. 819
Evans, Robert B., Sr., Chm. Bd. & Chief Exec. Officer--Evans Industries, Inc., Detroit, MI, pg. 390
Evans, Ronald, Pres. & Chief Exec. Officer-Best Western Intl.--B-W Advertising Agency, Phoenix, AZ, pg. 107
Evans, Ronald A., Pres. & Chief Exec. Officer--Best Western International, Inc., Phoenix, AZ, pg. 146
Fabian, John M., Pres. & Chief Exec. Officer--Anser (Analytic Services Inc.), Arlington, VA, pg. 76
Fagan, A.L., Exec. V.P.--Charter House Group, New York, NY, pg. 240
Fagel, Harold, Pres. & Chief Exec. Officer--Aurora Packing Co., Inc., North Aurora, IL, pg. 98
Fahey, John R., Chief Exec. Officer--Balcrank Products, Weaverville, NC, pg. 801
Fahlgren, H. Smoot, Chief Exec. Officer--Fahlgren Martin, Inc., Parkersburg, WV, pg. 396
Fail, James M., Chm. Bd. & Chief Exec. Officer--The Chesapeake Life Insurance Co., Lincoln, NE, pg. 243
Fain, John H., Chm., Pres., Chief Exec. & Chief Oper. Officer--Metro Information Services, Virginia Beach, VA, pg. 743
Fain, Richard, Chm. Bd. & Chief Exec. Officer--Royal Caribbean Cruises Ltd., Miami, FL, pg. 953
Faith, Marshall E., Chm. Bd. & Chief Exec. Officer--The Scoular Company, Omaha, NE, pg. 983
Famalette, Joseph, Pres. & Chief Exec. Officer--American Crystal Sugar Company, Moorhead, MN, pg. 51
Farina, Robert E., Pres.& Chief Exec. Officer--Global Turnkey Systems Inc., Waldwick, NJ, pg. 463
Farkas, Andrew L., Chm. & Chief Exec. Officer--Insignia Financial Group, Inc., Greenville, SC, pg. 571
Farley, James N., Pres. & Chief Exec. Officer--FamTec International, Inc., Des Plaines, IL, pg. 398
Farley, T.M., Mng. Partner & Chief Exec. Officer--Brown Brothers, Harriman & Co., New York, NY, pg. 181
Farley, William, Chm. Bd. & Chief Exec. Officer--West Point-Pepperell, Inc., West Point, GA, pg. 400
Farley, William F., Chm. Bd. & Chief Exec. Officer--Farley Industries, Chicago, IL, pg. 399
Farnsworth, Jack, Pres. & Chief Exec. Officer--Daily Racing Form, Inc., Hightstown, NJ, pg. 611
Farrell, Hugh J., Chief Exec. Officer & Creative Dir.--Hammond Farrell Inc., New York, NY, pg. 504
Fawcett, John, Chief Exec. Officer--George Patterson Pty. Limited, North Sydney,, Australia, pg. 112
Fayfield, Robert, Pres., Chief Exec. Officer & Chm. Bd.--Banner Engineering Corp., Minneapolis, MN, pg. 118
Federico, Andrew, Pres. & Chief Exec. Officer--Novar Electronics, Barberton, OH, pg. 817
Fedrick, C. Richard, Chief Exec. Officer--C. R. Fedrick, Inc., Novato, CA, pg. 1060
Fehr, William H., Chm. Bd. & Chief Exec. Officer--Berks Products Corporation, Reading, PA, pg. 142
Feinberg, Hill, Vice Chm. & Co-Chief Exec. Officer--First Southwest Company, Dallas, TX, pg. 413
Feldman, Joel D., Exec. V.P. & Chief Oper. Officer--Byer California, San Francisco, CA, pg. 197
Feldman, Joseph, Pres. & Chief Exec. Officer--Isfel Company, Inc., Rahway, NJ, pg. 582
Felker, G. Stephen, Chm. Bd. & Chief Exec. Officer--Avondale Mills, Inc., Sylacauga, AL, pg. 103
Fellowes, John, Chm. & Chief Exec. Officer--Fellowes Manufacturing Co., Itasca, IL, pg. 405
Felts, Jeffrey E., Pres. & Chief Exec. Officer--Hamilton Mutual Insurance Company Of Cincinnati, Cincinnati, OH, pg. 503
Fenning, W.M., Pres.--Cleveland Wrecking Company, Los Angeles, CA, pg. 255
Ferguson, Robert L., Pres. & Chief Exec. Officer--CenterMark Properties, Inc., Saint Louis, MO, pg. 231
Ferguson, Sam, Pres., Chief Exec. & Chief Oper. Officer--Ferguson Industries, Dallas, TX, pg. 406
Fermon, Joseph C., Chm. Bd. & Chief Exec. Officer--Continental Eagle Corporation, Prattville, AL, pg. 278
Fern, Saul Alden, Chm. Bd. & Chief Exec. Officer--Fitzgerald & Company, Inc., Cranston, RI, pg. 416
Fernandez, Carlos C., Chm., Pres. & Chief Exec. Officer--Purity, Inc., Miami, FL, pg. 901
Fernandez, Castor A., Pres. & Chief Exec. Officer--Castor Advertising Corp., New York, NY, pg. 229
Fernandez, Manuel, Pres. & Chief Exec. Officer--Gartner Group, Inc., Stamford, CT, pg. 443
Fernandez, Nestor, Pres. & Chief Exec. Officer--Digitron Tool Co., Inc., Miamisburg, OH, pg. 337
Ferran, David J., Pres. & Chief Exec. Officer--Tylan General, Inc., San Diego, CA, pg. 1122
Ferrara, Arthur V., Pres. & Chief Exec. Officer--The Guardian Life Insurance Company of America, New York, NY, pg. 492
Ferrell, James E., Chm. Bd., Pres. & Chief Exec. Officer--Ferrell Companies Inc./Ferrellgas, Liberty, MO, pg. 407
Ferrera, Harold, Chief Exec. Officer--James Ferrera & Sons, Inc., Canton, MA, pg. 407
Ferry, Richard M., Chm. Bd., Pres. & Chief Exec. Officer--Korn/Ferry International, Los Angeles, CA, pg. 642
Fesenmyer, D. Kennedy, Pres. & Chief Exec. Officer--Lobdell-Emery Manufacturing Company, Alma, MI, pg. 680
Fetterman, Annabelle L., Chm. Bd. & Chief Exec. Officer--Lundy Packing Co. Inc., Clinton, NC, pg. 687
Feuer, Irwin, Pres. & Chief Exec. Officer--Feuer Leather Corporation, Hawthorne, NY, pg. 407
Feuerstein, Aaron, Pres. & Chief Exec. Officer--Malden Mills Industries, Inc., Lawrence, MA, pg. 702
Field, Kenneth W., Pres. & Chief Exec. Officer--Continental Web Press, Inc., Itasca, IL, pg. 280
Field, Lawrence, Pres. & Chief Exec. Officer--Field Container Company, L.P., Elk Grove Village, IL, pg. 409
Fields, Catherine M., Pres. & Chief Exec. Officer--P. S. International Inc., Indianapolis, IN, pg. 837
Fields, Debra, Chm. Bd., Pres. & Chief Exec. Officer--Mrs. Fields' Inc., Park City, UT, pg. 761
Fike, John T., Pres. & Chief Exec. Officer--Northwest Paper Converting Company, Vancouver, WA, pg. 814
Fike, Lester L., Jr., Chm. Bd. & Chief Exec. Officer--Fike Corporation, Blue Springs, MO, pg. 409
Filler, Gary, Chm. Bd. & Chief Exec. Officer--Burke Industries Inc., San Jose, CA, pg. 190
Finn, David, Chm. Bd. & Chief Exec. Officer--Ruder, Finn, Inc., New York, NY, pg. 954
Finnegan, Lawrence J., Chm., Pres., Chief Exec. & Chief Oper. Officer--Boston Mutual Life Insurance Co., Canton, MA, pg. 167
Firestone, Dan, Chief Exec. Officer--Century Computer Marketing, Marina Del Rey, CA, pg. 235
Firestone, Sue, Pres. & Chief Exec. Officer--Design 1 Interiors, Los Angeles, CA, pg. 332
Fisch, Michael J., Pres. & Cheif Exec. Officer--The Bakersfield Californian, Bakersfield, CA, pg. 115
Fischer, Charlotte G., Pres. & Chief Exec. Officer--Parklane Hosiery Co., Inc., Hasbrouck Heights, NJ, pg. 849
Fisher, David G., Pres. & Chief Exec. Officer--Pioneer Engineering & Manufacturing Co., Warren, MI, pg. 871
Fisher, David G., Chief Exec. Officer--Pioneer Industrial Engineering Div., Madison Heights, MI, pg. 871
Fisher, John E., Gen. Chm. & Chief Exec. Officer--Nationwide Mutual Insurance Company, Columbus, OH, pg. 795
Fisher, Mike, Jr., Pres. & Chief Exec. Officer--Fisher Graphic Industries, Modesto, CA, pg. 415
Fisher, Steven A., Chm. Bd. & Chief Exec. Officer--Brown & Caldwell Consulting Engineers, Pleasant Hill, CA, pg. 181
Fisher, Thomas Scott, Chm. Bd. & Chief Exec. Officer--Samelson-Leon Company, Inc., Memphis, TN, pg. 968
Fisk, Wallace K., Pres. & Chief Exec. Officer--AmClyde Engineered Products, Inc., Saint Paul, MN, pg. 47

Fitch, Robert, Chief Exec. Officer--Home Innovations, Inc., New York, NY, pg. 541
Fitzgerald, Duane D., Pres. & Chief Exec. Officer--Bath Iron Works, Bath, ME, pg. 126
Fizdale, Richard B., Chm. & Chief Exec. & Creative Officer--Leo Burnett Company, Inc., Chicago, IL, pg. 191
Flaherty, Lee, Chm. & Chief Exec. Officer--Flair Communications Agency, Inc., New York, NY, pg. 416
Flaherty, Lee F., Chm Bd. & Chief Exec. Officer--Flair Communications Agency, Inc., Chicago, IL, pg. 416
Flaherty, William E., Chm. Bd. & Chief Exec. Officer--Horsehead Industries, Inc., New York, NY, pg. 545
Flanders, Allen F., Pres. & Chief Exec. Officer--Hope Design Group, San Diego, CA, pg. 543
Fleischer, Morton H., Pres., Chief Exec. Officer & Treas.--Franchise Finance Corp. of America, Scottsdale, AZ, pg. 428
Fleischman, Marvin H., Pres., Chief Exec. & Chief Fin. Officer--Lakeside Refining Co. Inc., Southfield, MI, pg. 651
Fleming, Mark Jack, Chm. Bd., Pres. & Chief Exec. Officer--Merchants Publishing Co., Kalamazoo, MI, pg. 739
Fletcher, Andy, Pres. & Chief Exec. Officer--Fletcher Hunt Wirth Associates, Inc., Kansas City, MO, pg. 418
Fletcher, Donald J., Pres.--George S. May International Company, Park Ridge, IL, pg. 723
Fletcher, James H., Chm. & Chief Exec. Officer--J. H. Fletcher & Co., Huntington, WV, pg. 418
Flint, Robert H., Chm. Bd. & Chief Exec. Officer--Flint Ink Corp., Detroit, MI, pg. 419
Flood, Lawrence P., Pres. & Chief Exec. Officer--Owen Steel Co., Inc., Columbia, SC, pg. 834
Flood, Peter E., Pres. & Chief Exec. Officer--The Flood Company, Hudson, OH, pg. 419
Floren, David, Chm. & Chief Exec. Officer--Martin Williams Advertising Inc., Minneapolis, MN, pg. 1191
Flori, John R., Pres. & Chief. Exec. Officer--Flori Corp., Phoenix, AZ, pg. 420
Floum, Robert, Pres. & Chief Exec. Officer--Fishers Big Wheel Inc., New Castle, PA, pg. 415
Flummerfelt, J. Kent, Pres., Chief Exec. Officer & Chm.--Lechmere, Inc., Woburn, MA, pg. 665
Flynn, Timothy P., Chm. Bd. & Chief Exec. Officer--WestAir Holding Inc., Fresno, CA, pg. 1178
Fogg, A.S., Chief Exec. Officer--Farm Stores, Inc., Miami, FL, pg. 401
Fogg, F.W., Pres. & Chief Exec. Officer--Southeastern Medequip, Inc., Jacksonville Beach, FL, pg. 1019
Fohrman, Neal, Pres., Chief Exec. & Chief Fin. Officer & Controller--Red Calliope & Associates, Inc., Los Angeles, CA, pg. 918
Foil, Martin B., Jr., Chm. Bd. & Chief Exec. Officer--Tuscarora Yarns Inc., Mount Pleasant, NC, pg. 1120
Foley, Bill, Chief Exec. Officer--Greeff Fabrics, Port Chester, NY, pg. 262
Foley, John, Chief Exec. Officer, Dir.-Client Services & New Bus. Contact--Case Foley Sackett, Inc., Minneapolis, MN, pg. 227
Foley, Patrick, Chm., Pres. & Chief Exec. Officer--DHL Corporation, Redwood City, CA, pg. 309
Foley, Stephen X., Jr., Chief Oper. Officer--Steve Foley Cadillac, Northbrook, IL, pg. 422
Foley, Thomas C., Chm. Bd. & Chief Exec. Officer--NTC Group, Greenwich, CT, pg. 781
Folkert, Rod, Pres. & Chief Exec. Officer--Grocers Baking Co., Grand Rapids, MI, pg. 488
Folz, Theodore W., Pres. & Chief Exec. Officer--Consolidated Cigar Corporation, Fort Lauderdale, FL, pg. 276
Fontana, Jeanne, Chief Exec. Officer--Topline Advertising, Ronkonkoma, NY, pg. 1102
Footer, Harold, Chm. Bd. & Chief Exec. Officer--Easy Day Manufacturing Company, Inc., Holliston, MA, pg. 364
Forbes, Malcolm S., Jr., Pres., Chief Exec. & Editor-in-Chief--Forbes, Inc., New York, NY, pg. 423
Ford, Elinor R., Dr., Chief Exec. Officer--William H. Sadlier, Inc., New York, NY, pg. 966
Ford, Fred, Chief Exec. Officer--Tabs Associates, Abingdon, MD, pg. 1076
Forgione, Anthony, Chm. Bd. & Pres.--Boyer Bros. Inc., Altoona, PA, pg. 169
Forman, Willis M., Pres., Chief Exec. Officer & Treas.--Paper Calmenson & Co., Saint Paul, MN, pg. 847
Forsythe, Gerald, Chm. Bd., Pres. & Chief Exec. Officer--Indeck Power Equipment Company, Wheeling, IL, pg. 564
Fortinberry, Glen W., Chm. & Chief Exec. Officer--Ross Roy Group, Inc., Bloomfield Hills, MI, pg. 949
Fortinberry, Glen W., Chm. Bd., Pres. & Chief Exec. Officer--Ross Roy Inc., Bloomfield Hills, MI, pg. 950
Foss, Joseph E., Chm. Bd. & Chief Exec Officer--First American Bank, N.A., Washington, D.C., Washington, DC, pg. 412
Fossel, Jon A., Chm. Bd. & Chief Exec. Officer--Oppenheimer Management Corp., New York, NY, pg. 719
Foster, Boyd, Pres. & Chief Exec. Officer--Arrowhead Mills, Inc., Hereford, TX, pg. 86
Foster, John H., Chm. Bd.--Malcolm Pirnie, Inc., White Plains, NY, pg. 872
Foster, Neil, Pres. & Chief Exec. Officer--Star Sales Co., Inc., Knoxville, TN, pg. 1040
Foster, Thomas, Chm. Bd. & Chief Exec. Officer--Foster & Gallagher Inc., Peoria, IL, pg. 426
Foster, Willett S., IV, Pres. & Chief Exec. Officer--Edlund Company, Inc., Burlington, VT, pg. 368
Fowler, Frederick V., Jr., Chm. Bd., Pres. & Chief Exec. Officer--Fred V. Fowler Company, Inc., Newton, MA, pg. 427
Fowler, Theodore M., Jr., Pres. & Chief Exec. Officer--Golden Corral Corporation, Raleigh, NC, pg. 466
Fox, Herbert C., Chm. Bd., Pres., Chief Exec. Officer & Dir.-Pub. Rels.--Active Electrical Supply Company, Chicago, IL, pg. 15
Fox, Sam, Chm. Bd. & Chief Exec. Officer--Harbour Group Ltd., Clayton, MO, pg. 506
Fox, Wayne F., Chm. Bd. & Chief Exec. Officer--Triple F, Inc., Des Moines, IA, pg. 1114
Franco, Anthony M., Chm. & Chief Exec. Officer--Anthony M. Franco Inc., Detroit, MI, pg. 950
Franden, Robert A., Chief Exec. Officer--American Gilsonite Co., Salt Lake City, UT, pg. 55
Frank, H. Alan, Chief Exec. Officer--Admiral Packaging, Inc., Providence, RI, pg. 1128
Frank, Richard N., Chm. & Chief Exec. Officer--Lawry's Restaurants, Inc., Los Angeles, CA, pg. 663
Frank, Ronald R., Chm. Bd. & Chief Exec. Officer--Frank Industries, Inc., Brown City, MI, pg. 429
Frankel, Bernard, Chm. & Chief Exec. Officer--Frankel & Company, Chicago, IL, pg. 429
Frankel, Robert, Chief Exec. & Chief Fin. Officer--Construction Counsellors, Inc., Park Ridge, NJ, pg. 277
Franklin, Larry, Pres. & Chief Exec. Officer--Harte-Hanks Communications, Inc., San Antonio, TX, pg. 513
Frazier, John L.D., Chm. Bd & Chief Exec. Officer--Full Service Beverage Company, Wichita, KS, pg. 436
Frazier, Warner, Pres. & Chief Exec. Officer--Simplicity Manufacturing, Inc., Port Washington, WI, pg. 1006
Frechette, Peter L., Pres. & Chief Exec. Officer--Patterson Dental Company, Minneapolis, MN, pg. 851
Frederic, Rand, Pres. & Chief Exec. Officer--Frederic Printing Company, Aurora, CO, pg. 430
Freedman, Eugene M., Chm. Bd. & Chief Exec. Officer--Coopers & Lybrand, New York, NY, pg. 283
Freeman, A. James, Vice Chm. & Chief Exec. Officer--Lord Corporation, Erie, PA, pg. 683
Freeman, Carl M., Chm. Bd. & Chief Exec. Officer--Carl M. Freeman Associates, Inc., Potomac, MD, pg. 431
Freeman, D.S., Jr., Chm. Bd. & Chief Exec. Officer--Freeman Decorating Co., Dallas, TX, pg. 431
Freeman, David S., Chief Exec. Officer & Gen. Mgr.--Sacramento Municipal Utility District, Sacramento, CA, pg. 965
Freeman, Larry J., Pres. & Chief Exec. Officer--Freeman Cosmetic Corp., Los Angeles, CA, pg. 431
Frem, George N., Chm. Bd. & Chief Exec. Office--Interstate Resources, Inc., Rosslyn, VA, pg. 580
French, Morton R., Chm. Bd., Pres., Chief Exec. & Chief Fin. Officer--Commercial Plastics & Supplies Corp., Richmond Hill, NY, pg. 268
French, Philip, Pres. & Chief Exec. Officer--Countrymark Cooperative, Inc., Indianapolis, IN, pg. 290
Freston, Tom, Chm. & Chief Exec. Officer-MTV Networks--Viacom Inc., New York, NY, pg. 785
Freundlich, Richard L., Chm. & Chief Exec. Officer--Bridal Originals, Inc., Collinsville, IL, pg. 175
Frew, Bud L., Pres. & Chief Exec Officer--MFA Incorporated, Columbia, MO, pg. 692
Frey, Eugene U., Chm. Bd. & Chief Exec. Officer--Waldorf Corporation, Saint Paul, MN, pg. 1159
Frey, Thomas W., Pres. & Chief Exec. Officer--Amano Cincinnati, Inc., Cincinnati, OH, pg. 46
Friberg, John R., Pres., Chief Exec. Officer & Sec.--Eastern Smelting & Refining Corporation, Lynn, MA, pg. 363
Fricchione, Patrick, Sr., Chief Exec. Officer--Simplex Industries, Inc., Scranton, PA, pg. 1006
Frick, Frank J., Chief Oper. & Chief Exec. Officer & Sec.--Takatta Inc., Olympia Fields, IL, pg. 1076
Fried, Herbert D., Chm. of Exec. Committee--W.B. Doner & Company, Southfield, MI, pg. 344
Friederich, Jan, Chief Exec. Officer--Furr's Supermarkets, Albuquerque, NM, pg. 437
Friedheim, Louis, Pres. & Chief Exec. Officer--Cougle Commission Company, Inc., Chicago, IL, pg. 289
Friedl, Donald G., Chm. Bd., Pres. & Chief Exec. Officer--All Seasons Services, Inc., Braintree, MA, pg. 35
Friedland, Thomas S., Pres. & Chief Exec. Officer--Harper Industries, Inc., New York, NY, pg. 510
Friedland, Thomas S., Pres. & Chief Exec. Officer--Harper Shirt Company, New York, NY, pg. 510
Friedlander, Alfred L., Chm. Bd. & Chief Exec. Officer--Rice Food Markets Inc., Houston, TX, pg. 931
Friedlander, Sam, Pres. & Chief Exec. Officer--Production Machinery Corporation, Mentor, OH, pg. 893
Friedman, Reuben, Pres. & Chief Exec. Officer--Arrow Typographers, Inc., Newark, NJ, pg. 326
Friedman, Stephen Z., Chief Exec. Officer--Friedman Benjamin Inc. Adv., New York, NY, pg. 433
Friedman, Steven M., Chm. Bd. & Chief Exec. Officer--JPS Textile Group, Inc., Greenville, SC, pg. 586
Friedson, David, Pres. & Chief Exec. Officer--Freeson Advertising Agency, Miami Lakes, FL, pg. 431
Friendland, Thomas S., Pres. & Chief Exec. Officer--Midland Shirt Company, New York, NY, pg. 510
Friendt, Glenn, Pres. & Chief Exec. Officer--Kahler Friendt & Partners, Inc., Omaha, NE, pg. 613
Frieze, Michael, Chief Exec. Officer--Gordon Brothers, Boston, MA, pg. 471
Fritz, Lynn C., Chm. Bd., Pres. & Chief Exec. Officer--Fritz Companies, Inc., San Francisco, CA, pg. 434
Fryml, J.S., Pres. & Chief Exec. Officer--American Fast Print, Limited, Spartanburg, SC, pg. 52
Fuchs, Bernard, Chm. Bd., Pres. & Chief Exec. Officer--Specialty Retailers, Inc., Houston, TX, pg. 1029
Fuchs, Karl, Chief Exec. Officer--Liberty Tool Corporation, Rochester, NY, pg. 674
Fukunaga, George J., Chm. Bd. & Chief Exec. Officer--Servco Pacific Inc., Honolulu, HI, pg. 991
Fuldner, William Terry, Chm. Bd. & Chief Exec. Officer--Efco Corporation, Monett, MO, pg. 359
Fulwiler, Terrance, Chief Exec. Officer--Wisconsin Label Corporation, Algoma, WI, pg. 1198
Funk, Robert, Chm. Bd. & Chief Exec. Officer--Johnstown Corporation, Johnstown, PA, pg. 601
Futter, Bernard, Pres. & Chief Exec. Officer--Futter Lumber Corporation, Rockville Centre, NY, pg. 437
Futterman, Jack, Chm. Bd., Pres. & Chief Exec. Officer--Supermarkets General Corporation, Woodbridge, NJ, pg. 1064
Futterman, Jack, Chm. Bd., Pres. & Chief Exec. Officer--Pathmark, Woodbridge, NJ, pg. 1064
Gabbert, James D., Chm. Bd., Pres. & Chief Exec. Officer--Gabbert's, Inc., Minneapolis, MN, pg. 441
Gaby, Dan, Chm. & Chief Exec. Officer--Keyes Martin, Springfield, NJ, pg. 627
Gaeke, Harry F., Chm. Bd., Chief Exec. & Fin. Officer--Shook National Corporation, Dayton, OH, pg. 1000
Gaffin, Seth, Pres. & Chief Exec. Officer--Baris Shoe Company, Inc., New York, NY, pg. 119
Gage, Edwin C., Chm. & Chief Exec. Officer--Gage Marketing Group, Minneapolis, MN, pg. 441
Gagne, Lawrence, Sr., Chief Exec. Officer--Rex Lumber Company, Acton, MA, pg. 930
Gaillard, Roger R., Pres., Chief Oper. & Chief Exec. Officer--Williams & Company, Inc., Pittsburgh, PA, pg. 230
Gal, Kenneth, Chm., Chief Exec. Officer--Italia/Gal Advertising, Los Angeles, CA, pg. 582
Galesi, Francesco, Chm. Bd., Pres. & Chief Exec. Officer--Rotterdam Ventures Inc., Guilderland Center, NY, pg. 951
Galex, Martin, Pres. & Chief Exec. Officer--Therapedic Associates, Inc., Boca Raton, FL, pg. 1090
Gallagher, Charles P., Chm. Bd. & Chief Exec. Officer--Applied Industrial Materials Corporation, Deerfield, IL, pg. 79
Gambaccini, Louis J., Chief Exec. Officer & Gen. Mgr.--Southeastern Pennsylvania Transportation Authority, Philadelphia, PA, pg. 1020
Gambino, Joseph L., Pres. & Chief Exec. Officer--The Atlas Construction Co., Stamford, CT, pg. 96
Gandrud, Robert P., Pres. & Chief Exec. Officer--Lutheran Brotherhood, Minneapolis, MN, pg. 688
Gant, Edmund R., Chm. Bd. & Sec.--Glen Raven Mills, Inc., Glen Raven, NC, pg. 461
Garberg, Dennis, Chm. Bd. & Chief Exec. Officer--The Sunflower Group, Overland Park, KS, pg. 1060
Garcia-Serra, Al, Chm. & Chief Exec. Officer--GS&B-Lintas Advertising, Coral Gables, FL, pg. 440
Gardiner, Scott, Chm. Bd., Pres., Chief Exec. & Chief Oper. Officer--Gardiner Metal Company, Chicago, IL, pg. 443
Gardner, Edward G., Chm. Bd. & Chief Exec. Officer--Soft Sheen Products, Inc., Chicago, IL, pg. 1016
Gardner, Philip D., Pres. & Chief Exec. Officer--Findlay Industries, Inc., Findlay, OH, pg. 410
Garman, M. Lawrence, Pres. & Chief Exec. Officer--Daubert Industries, Inc., Westchester, IL, pg. 317
Garman, M. Lawrence, Pres. & Chief Exec. Officer--Daubert Coated Products, Inc., Westchester, IL, pg. 317
Garner, H. Richard, Chief Exec. Officer--Haviland Enterprises, Grand Rapids, MI, pg. 517
Garnett, Gerald, Exec. V.P. & Chief Exec. Officer--Southern Farm Bureau Casualty Insurance Company, Ridgeland, MS, pg. 1021
Garrison, Richard C., Chm. & Chief Exec. Officer--Ingalls, Quinn & Johnson, Boston, MA, pg. 567
Garrison, T. Paul, Chm., Chief Exec. Officer--Garrison-Lontine Advertising, Denver, CO, pg. 443
Garvey, John, Chm. Bd. & Chief Exec. Officer--Petroleum Inc., Wichita, KS, pg. 865
Garvey, Willard W., Chm. Bd., Pres. & Chief Exec. Officer--Garvey Industries, Inc., Wichita, KS, pg. 443
Garvey, Willard W., Chm. Bd. & Chief Exec. Officer--Petroleum, Inc., Wichita, KS, pg. 444
Gassman, John, Pres., Chief Exec. Officer & Chief Fin. Officer--Townsend & Bottum, Inc., Ann Arbor, MI, pg. 1104
Gates, Charles C., Chm. Bd. & Chief Exec. Officer--The Gates Corporation, Denver, CO, pg. 445
Gates, Charles C., Chm. Bd. & Chief Exec. Officer--The Gates Rubber Company, Denver, CO, pg. 445
Gates, Milo S., Chm. Bd. & Chief Exec. Officer--Swinerton & Walberg Co., San Francisco, CA, pg. 1068
Gaunt, John C., Pres. & Chief Exec. Officer--Ellerbe Becket, Inc., Minneapolis, MN, pg. 378
Gaylord, Edward L., Chm. Bd. & Chief Exec. Officer--Gaylord Broadcasting Co., Dallas, TX, pg. 446
Gearon, Dan, Vice Chm. & Chief Exec. Officer--Gearon Hoffman Conlon & Nye Advertising, Inc., Garden City, NY, pg. 447
Gebert, Kenton R., Pres., Chief Exec. & Chief Oper. Officer--The Dickerson Group, Inc., Monroe, NC, pg. 335
Gee, Norman D., Chm. Bd. & Chief Exec. Officer--Atlas Van Lines, Inc., Evansville, IN, pg. 96
Geer, Joseph R., Pres., Chief Exec. Officer--PMC Partnership, Ltd., Westport, CT, pg. 836
Gehring, Heinrich, Partner & Chief Exec. Officer--ATAG Allgemeine Treuhand AG, Zurich,, Switzerland, pg. 387
Geiger, Ron, Pres. & Chief Exec. Officer--Harker's Inc., Le Mars, IA, pg. 509
Geisler, Henry O., Chief Exec. Officer--Gem Top Mfg., Inc., Clackamas, OR, pg. 448
Geller, Anthony, Pres. & Chief Exec. Officer--Union Holdings, Inc., New York, NY, pg. 1128
Geller, Ehud, Dr., Chm. & Chief Exec. Officer--Mennen Medical Inc., Clarence, NY, pg. 739
Geller, Frank W., Chm. Bd. & Chief Exec. Officer--Integrated Resources, Inc., New York, NY, pg. 573
Geller, Larry, Pres. & Chief Exec. Officer--Rosauer's Supermarkets, Inc., Spokane, WA, pg. 947
Geller, Stephen L., Chm. & Chief Exec. Officer--CSI International Corporation, New York, NY, pg. 205
Gellerstedt, L.L., III, Pres. & Chief Exec. Officer--Beers Construction Company, Atlanta, GA, pg. 132
Gellert, Jay, Pres., Chief Exec. Officer & Dir.--Aetna Health Plans, San Bruno, CA, pg. 23
Genova, Joseph, Chm. & Chief Exec. Officer--Genova Hartwick Juliano, Inc., Greenwich, CT, pg. 452
Genshaft, Neil, Chm. Bd. & Chief Exec. Officer--Fresh Mark, Inc., Massillon, OH, pg. 432

Gentine, Louis P., Pres. & Chief Exec. Officer--Sargento Incorporated, Plymouth, WI, pg. 971
Genuardi, Charles A., Pres. & Chief Exec. Officer--Genuardi Super Markets Inc., Norristown, PA, pg. 452
George, Boyd, Chm. & Chief Exec. Officer--Alex Lee, Inc., Hickory, NC, pg. 33
George, Ken, Chief Exec. Officer--Epic Healthcare Group, Dallas, TX, pg. 384
Georgine, Robert A., Chm., Pres. & Chief Exec. Officer--ULLICO Inc., Washington, DC, pg. 1124
Georgoulis, Stratton, Chm. Bd., Pres. & Chief Exec. Officer--TIC United Corporation, Dallas, TX, pg. 1073
Gerard, Stephen, Pres., Chief Exec. Officer & Treas.--Bolliger, Inc., Stamford, CT, pg. 163
Gerbig, Robert L., Pres. & Chief Exec. Officer--Gerbig, Snell/Weisheimer & Assoc., Inc., Worthington, OH, pg. 454
Gerchenson, Emile H., Chm. Bd. & Chief Exec. Officer--Alva/Amco Pharmacal Companies, Inc., Chicago, IL, pg. 46
Gerdy, Harvey, Chm. Bd., Pres. & Chief Exec. Officer--International Seaway Trading Corporation, Mayfield Village, OH, pg. 579
Gero, Robert L., Chief Exec. Officer & Creative Dir.--Shapson Gero & Sommers, Inc., Philadelphia, PA, pg. 995
Gerrity, James F., III, Pres. & Chief Exec. Officer--Gerrity Co., Inc., Newton, MA, pg. 454
Gerry, Alan, Chm. & Chief Exec. Officer--Cablevision Industries Corp., Liberty, NY, pg. 206
Gerson, Irwin C., Chm. & Chief Exec. Officer--William Douglas McAdams Inc., New York, NY, pg. 726
Gerstein, David M., Chief Exec. Officer--K & R Delivery, Inc., Hinsdale, IL, pg. 610
Gettlefinger, Andrew J., Chm. Bd., Pres. & Chief Exec. Officer--Pride Oil Co., Inc., Knoxville, TN, pg. 622
Gherty, Jack, Pres. & Chief Exec. Officer--Land O'Lakes, Inc., Arden Hills, MN, pg. 653
Gherty, John, Pres. & Chief Exec. Officer-Land O'Lakes Inc.--Cenex/Land O'Lakes, Inc., Saint Paul, MN, pg. 653
Gherty, John, Pres. & Chief Exec. Officer-Land O'Lakes Inc.--Cenex/Land O'Lakes, Inc., Saint Paul, MN, pg. 231
Giacoio, Anthony, Chief Exec. Officer--Ballet Makers, Inc., Totowa, NJ, pg. 116
Gianettino, Ronald J., Chm. Bd. & Chief Exec. Officer--Gianettino & Meredith Advertising, Short Hills, NJ, pg. 455
Giaquinta, Jerry, Pres./Chief Exec. Officer--Bob Thomas & Associates, San Francisco, CA, pg. 244
Giaquinta, Jerry, Pres./Chief Exec Officer--Bob Thomas Associates, Toronto, Canada, pg. 244
Gibson, William B., Chm., Pres. & Chief Exec. Officer--Sudler & Hennessey, New York, NY, pg. 1211
Giesen, Richard A., Chm. Bd., Pres. & Chief Exec. Officer--American Appraisal Associates, Inc., Milwaukee, WI, pg. 48
Gilbert, Walter F., Chm. Bd., Pres., Chief Exec. Officer & Treas.--Semco Industries, Stoughton, MA, pg. 989
Gill, George, Chm. Bd. & Chief Exec. Officer--Milk Specialties Company, Dundee, IL, pg. 753
Gill, Stephen E., Pres. & Chief Exec. Officer--M.C. Gill Corporation, El Monte, CA, pg. 458
Gilleland, Richard A., Chm. Bd., Pres. & Chief Exec. Officer--Kendall Healthcare Products Co., Mansfield, MA, pg. 622
Gillen, Dick, Chm. Bd., Pres. & Chief Exec. Officer--Harbor Financial Mortgage Corp., Houston, TX, pg. 506
Gilman, Howard, Chm. Bd. & Chief Exec. Officer--Gilman Paper Co., Saint Marys, GA, pg. 459
Gilman, Steven F., Chm. Bd., Pres, & Chief Exec. Officer--Style Auto, Van Nuys, CA, pg. 1055
Gilmartin, Gene, Pres. & Chief Exec. Officer--Hoffman York & Compton, Milwaukee, WI, pg. 538
Gilmore, John F., Chief Exec. Office--Life Sciences International, Philadelphia, PA, pg. 320
Gimbel, William T., Chm. Bd. & Chief Exec. Officer--Reliance Steel & Aluminum Co., Los Angeles, CA, pg. 925
Gingg, Conrad, Pres. & Chief Exec. Officer--United Dairymen of Arizona, Tempe, AZ, pg. 1131
Ginsberg, Robert I., Pres. & Chief Exec. Officer--Carol Wright Sales, Inc., Stamford, CT, pg. 1011
Ginzberg, Marc, Chm. Bd., Pres. & Chief Exec. Officer--Primary Industries Corporation, New York, NY, pg. 889
Girard, Chris, Pres. & Chief Exec. Officer--Plaid Pantries, Inc., Beaverton, OR, pg. 873
Giraudo, Louis, Chm. & Co-Chief Exec. Officer--San Francisco French Bread Company, Oakland, CA, pg. 969
Givens, Susie, Pres. & Chief Exec. Officer--The Thompson Group Companies, Henderson, KY, pg. 1094
Glas, Don ald A., Pres. & Chief Exec. Officer--First State Federal Savings & Loan, Hutchinson, MN, pg. 413
Glaske, Paul E., Pres. & Chief Exec. Officer--Blue Bird Corporation, Fort Valley, GA, pg. 158
Glatz, Simon, Pres. & Chief Exec. Officer--Advanced Marine Enterprises, Inc., Arlington, VA, pg. 20
Glazer, Robert S., Chm. Bd., Pres. & Chief Exec. Officer--Glazers Wholesale Drug Co. Inc., Dallas, TX, pg. 461
Gleason, Sheldon, Chm. Bd., Pres., Chief Exec. & Chief Fin. Officer & Controller--Genie Manufacturing Corp., Rush, NY, pg. 452
Glenn, John J., Chm. Bd., Chief Exec. Officer--Dunn Reber Glenn Marz, Reno, NV, pg. 354
Glick, Robert, Pres. & Chief Exec. Officer--Martin Paint Stores, Jamaica, NY, pg. 715
Glickman, Marshall L., Pres. & Chief Exec. Officer--Ruslander & Sons, Inc., Buffalo, NY, pg. 956
Glickman, Marshall L., Pres. & Chief Exec. Officer--The Jewett Refrigerator Co., Inc., Buffalo, NY, pg. 957
Glickman, Stuart, Chm., Pres. Chief Exec. & Chief Fin. Officer--Security Alarms & Fire Engineering Inc., Davie, FL, pg. 987
Glikbarg, Thomas S., Chm., Pres. & Chief Exec. Officer--Lyon's Restaurants, Inc., Foster City, CA, pg. 690
Glover, Cliff C., Chm. Bd. & Chief Exec. Officer--Batson-Cook Company, West Point, GA, pg. 126
Glover, Keith, Pres. & Gen. Mgr.--Producers Rice Mill Inc., Stuttgart, AR, pg. 892
Godbersen, Byron, Chief Exec. Officer--Midwest Industries, Inc., Ida Grove, IA, pg. 752
Godfrey, William G., Chm. Bd., Pres. & Chief Exec. Officer--Tekra Corporation, New Berlin, WI, pg. 1084
Godwin, George W., Jr., Chm. & Chief Exec. Officer--Godwin Advertising Agency, Inc., Jackson, MS, pg. 464
Goeller, William A., Pres. & Chief Exec. Officer--Hatzel & Buehler, Inc., Wilmington, DE, pg. 277
Goetz, Lew, Pres. & Chief Exec. Officer--SOR Inc., Lenexa, KS, pg. 963
Gogol, Gary J., Pres. & Chief Exec. Officer--Annabelle Candy Company, Hayward, CA, pg. 75
Gold, Aaron A., Chm. Bd. & Chief Exec. Officer--Oxford First Corporation, Philadelphia, PA, pg. 834
Gold, Aaron A., Chm. Bd. & Chief Exec. Officer--Oxford Finance Companies, Inc., Philadelphia, PA, pg. 835
Gold, Jeffrey M., Chm. Bd. & Chief Exec. Officer--Goldmark Industries, Ltd., New York, NY, pg. 468
Gold, Jeffrey M., Chm. Bd. & Chief Exec. Officer--Goldmark Partners, New York, NY, pg. 469
Goldbath, Raymond, Chm. Bd. & Chief Exec. Officer--Marathon Cheese Corp., Marathon, WI, pg. 705
Goldberg, Arthur, Chm. Bd., Pres. & Chief Exec. Officer--Di Giorgio Corporation, Somerset, NJ, pg. 334
Goldberg, Fred., Pres. & Chief Exec. Officer--Goldberg Moser O'Neill, San Francisco, CA, pg. 465
Golden, Michael, Pres.--Stephen Gould Paper Co., Inc., Whippany, NJ, pg. 473
Goldfarb, Andrew, Pres. & Chief Exec. Officer--HCC Industries, Rosemead, CA, pg. 496
Goldman, Steve, Pres. & Chief Exec. Officer--Power-One, Inc., Camarillo, CA, pg. 883
Goldress, Jerry E., Chm. & Chief Exec. Officer--First Land & Development, Inc., Richmond, VA, pg. 18
Goldring, Norman M., Pres. & Chief Exec. Officer--CPM, Inc., Chicago, IL, pg. 203
Goldsmith, John, Chm. & Chief Exec. Officer--John Hancock Freedom Securities Corporation, Boston, MA, pg. 596
Goldwyn, Sandra, V.P. & Chief Exec. Officer--Culver Textile Corporation, West New York, NJ, pg. 304
Golenberg, Gary, Pres. & Chief Exec. Officer--The Gibson-Homans Company, Twinsburg, OH, pg. 457
Golias, Tipton L., Pres. & Chief Exec. Officer--Helena Laboratories Corporation, Beaumont, TX, pg. 526
Golub, Lewis, Chm. Bd. & Chief Exec. Officer--Golub Corporation, Schenectady, NY, pg. 469
Golub, Lewis, Chm. Bd. & Chief Exec. Officer--Price Chopper, Schenectady, NY, pg. 469
Gonnella, Robert, Chief Exec. Officer & Sec.--Gonnella Baking Co., Chicago, IL, pg. 469
Good, Sheldon F., Chm. & Chief Exec. Officer--Sheldon Good & Co., Inc., Chicago, IL, pg. 470
Goodall, Richard B., Chm. Bd. & Chief Exec. Officer--Dixon Valve & Coupling Company, Chestertown, MD, pg. 341
Goodart, Tyrone G., Pres. & Chief Exec. Officer--Carus Chemical Company, Chemical Div., Ottawa, IL, pg. 227
Goodchild, John, Pres. & Chief Exec. Officer--The Weightman Group, Philadelphia, PA, pg. 1173
Gooding, Terrance, Pres. & Chief Exec. Officer--Wavetek Corporation, San Diego, CA, pg. 1168
Goodman, Cary C., Chief Exec. Officer--Howard Needles Tammen & Bergendoff, Kansas City, MO, pg. 547
Goodman, Elis, Chief Exec. Officer--Monarch Import Co., Inc., New York, NY, pg. 765
Goodman, Gilbert, Chief Exec. Officer--J. Josephson, Inc., South Hackensack, NJ, pg. 607
Goodman, James F., Pres. & Chief Exec. Officer--Capitol Broadcasting Co., Inc., Raleigh, NC, pg. 215
Goodman, John M., Chief Exec. Officer--Lewis Homes Management Corp., Upland, CA, pg. 673
Goodnight, James H., Chief Exec. Officer--SAS Institute Inc., Cary, NC, pg. 959
Goodrum, Harold, Chm. & Chief Exec. Officer--Goodrum Leonard & Associates, Inc., Nashville, TN, pg. 471
Goolsby, John L., Pres. & Chief Exec. Officer--Summa Corporation, Las Vegas, NV, pg. 1057
Gorde, Jerry, Chm. Bd. & Chief Exec. Officer--VATEX America, Inc., Richmond, VA, pg. 1141
Gordon, Paul B., Chm. Bd. & Chief Exec. Officer--Gordon Food Service Inc., Grand Rapids, MI, pg. 472
Gore, Robert W., Pres. & Chief Exec. Officer--W. L. Gore & Associates, Inc., Newark, DE, pg. 472
Gorman, Patrick J., Co-Pres. & Chief Exec. Officer--Encore Marketing International, Lanham, MD, pg. 380
Gorra, William, Pres. & Chief Exec. & Chief Fin. Officer--Chemical Specialties Corp., Springfield, MA, pg. 1069
Gorsun, Barry R., Pres. & Chief Exec. Officer--Summa Four, Inc., Manchester, NH, pg. 1057
Gosnell, Robert A., Chief Exec. Officer--Gosnell Builders, Phoenix, AZ, pg. 472
Goss, Howard S., Chm., Chief Exec. Officer & Treas.--Transco Inc., Chicago, IL, pg. 1106
Gottschalk, Gary, Pres. & Chief Exec. Officer--The Harter Group, Sturgis, MI, pg. 513
Gouchenour, C. Lee, Chm. & Chief Exec. Officer--Gouchenour Adv., Inc., Orlando, FL, pg. 473
Gougion, Dennis H., Chief Exec. Officer--Budget Marketing, Inc., Des Moines, IA, pg. 186
Goulazian, Peter, Pres. & Chief Exec. Officer--Katz Communications, Inc., New York, NY, pg. 618
Gould, Charles L., Chm. & Chief Exec. Officer--Deutsch, Shea & Evans, Inc., South San Francisco, CA, pg. 333
Gould, James C., Chief Exec. Officer--Challenge Technologies, Grand Haven, MI, pg. 238
Gould, Peter J., Pres. & Chief Exec. Officer--Aldine Technologies, Carlstadt, NJ, pg. 33
Goulooze, Gene D., Vice Chm. & Chief Exec. Officer--Sonneveldt Company, Grand Rapids, MI, pg. 1018
Gozia, Richard M., Chm. & Chief Exec. Officer--Wyatt Cafeterias Inc., Dallas, TX, pg. 1205
Grace, John R., Chief Exec. Officer--Spring Engineers, Inc., Houston, TX, pg. 1033
Grado, John, Chm. Bd. & Chief Exec. Officer--Technographics, Inc., Stratton, PA, pg. 1083
Graf, Hubert, Chief Exec. Officer, Creative Dir. & New Bus. Contact--Graf Bertel, New York, NY, pg. 474
Graham, Donald G., Jr., Chm. Bd. & Chief Exec. Officer--Fisher Companies, Inc., Seattle, WA, pg. 414
Graham, James, Pres. & Chief Exec. Officer--Versa Services Ltd., Etobicoke,, Canada, pg. 7
Grandy, Jay F., Pres. & Chief Exec. Officer--Snokist Growers, Yakima, WA, pg. 1015
Granger, Alton L., Chm. & Chief Exec. Officer--Granger Construction Co., Lansing, MI, pg. 476
Granik, Russell, Deputy Commissioner & Chief Oper. Officer--National Basketball Association, New York, NY, pg. 786
Grant, Berl, Pres. & Chief Exec. Officer--Seymour Manufacturing Company, Seymour, IN, pg. 994
Grant, Walter L., Pres. & Chief Exec. Officer--Camellia Food Stores Co-op Inc., Norfolk, VA, pg. 211
Granum, Robert M., Chm. Bd. & Chief Exec. Officer--Panel Processing, Inc., Alpena, MI, pg. 846
Grau, Juan, Chm. Bd., Pres. & Chief Exec. Officer--Bacardi Imports, Inc., Miami, FL, pg. 108
Graves, Earl G., Chm. Bd., Pres. & Chief Exec. Officer--Earl G. Graves Ltd., New York, NY, pg. 478
Gray, James H., Pres. & Chief Exec. Officer--Harbor Bancorp, Long Beach, CA, pg. 506
Gray, John T., Pres. & Chief Exec. Officer--The Genie Company, Alliance, OH, pg. 452
Gray, Melvin, Chm. & Chief Exec. Officer--Graycor, Inc., Homewood, IL, pg. 479
Gray, Melvin, Chm. Bd. & Chief Exec. Officer--The Edward Gray Corp., Homewood, IL, pg. 480
Gray, Melvin, Chm. Bd. & Chief Exec. Officer--Inland Construction Company, Homewood, IL, pg. 480
Gray, Roger L., Pres. & Chief Exec. Officer--Gray Kirk/VanSant Advertising, Inc., Baltimore, MD, pg. 479
Greely, William C., Pres. & Chief Exec. Officer--Keeneland Assoc., Inc., Lexington, KY, pg. 620
Green, James M., Pres. & Chief Exec. Officer--FWD Corporation, Clintonville, WI, pg. 395
Green, John, Pres. & Chief Exec. Officer--Bauerlein Inc., New Orleans, LA, pg. 127
Green, Lester, Chief Exec. Officer--Capitol Chevrolet Cadillac GEO, Inc., Salem, OR, pg. 215
Green, Stanley, Pres., Chief Exec. & Chief Fin. Officer--DAQ Electronics Inc., Middlesex, NJ, pg. 308
Green, Stephen, Chief Exec. Officer--Lark Luggage Company, Inc., Denver, CO, pg. 359
Greenfield, Harley J., Chm., Pres. & Chief Exec. Officer--Jennifer Convertibles Inc., Paramus, NJ, pg. 592
Greenfield, Kenneth, Exec. V.P.--Federal Distributing Corporation, Maspeth, NY, pg. 404
Greenstone, Ronald, Chm. & Chief Exec. Officer--Greenstone Roberts Advertising, Melville, NY, pg. 485
Greenwald, James L., Chm. Bd.--Katz Communications, Inc., New York, NY, pg. 618
Grefenstette, Carl, Pres. & Chief Exec. Officer--Hillman Company, Pittsburgh, PA, pg. 535
Gregg, F. Browne, Chm. Bd. & Chief Exec. Officer--Florida Crushed Stone Company, Leesburg, FL, pg. 420
Gregory, Bruce, Pres. & Chief Exec. Officer--Ready Systems, Sunnyvale, CA, pg. 916
Grieb, Warren, Chm. & Chief Exec. Officer--Advertising Checking Bureau Incorporated, New York, NY, pg. 21
Griesdorn, Donald, Chief Exec. Officer--BKM Enterprises, Inc., East Hartford, CT, pg. 107
Griffen, Donald K., Pres. & Chief Exec. Officer--INTEGRATEC, Atlanta, GA, pg. 573
Griffin, Dennis B., Pres. & Chief Exec. Officer--Griffin Industries, Inc., Cold Spring, KY, pg. 487
Griffin, Jeff, Chm. Bd., Pres. & Chief Exec. Officer--Mountain Air Delivery, Sparks, NV, pg. 773
Griffin, Mark E., Chm. Bd., Pres. & Chief Exec. Officer--Lewis Drug, Inc., Sioux Falls, SD, pg. 673
Griffin, Rutledge A., Jr., Chief Exec. Officer--Griffin Corporation, Valdosta, GA, pg. 487
Griffin, Tom, Co-Chm. & Chief Exec. Officer--Griffin Bacal Inc., New York, NY, pg. 486
Griffis, W.I., Pres. & Chief Exec. Officer--T.J. Morris Company, Inc., Statesboro, GA, pg. 771
Griggs, David, Pres., Chief Exec. & Chief Fin. Officer & Treas.--Jack Griggs Inc., Exeter, CA, pg. 488
Grimaldi, Joseph M., Chief Oper. Officer--Mullen Advertising, Inc., Wenham, MA, pg. 775
Grimaud, Joseph A., Jr., Pres. & Chief Exec. Officer--Precision Tune, Inc., Leesburg, VA, pg. 885
Grinberg, Gedalio, Chm. Bd. & Chief Exec. Officer--North American Watch Corporation, Lyndhurst, NJ, pg. 812
Grinder, Dan, Pres. & Chief Exec. Officer--Hood Communications, Inc., Grand Terrace, CA, pg. 543
Grisanti, Michael J., Pres. & Chief Exec. Officer--Grisanti, Inc., Louisville, KY, pg. 488
Groendyke, Jay, Pres. & Chief Exec. Officer--Dieline Corporation, Kentwood, MI, pg. 336
Grogan, David R., Chm., Pres. & Chief Exec. Officer--Toter Incorporated, Statesville, NC, pg. 1103
Gromer, Richard H., Pres. & Chief Exec. Officer--Gromer Super Markets, Inc., Elgin, IL, pg. 489
Gross, Emerick, Pres. & Chief Exec. Officer--Dan's Supreme Super Markets Inc., Hempstead, NY, pg. 314
Gross, Howard, Chm. Bd. & Chief Exec. Officer--Snyder Industries, Inc., Lincoln, NE, pg. 1015
Groussman, Dean, Chm., Pres. & Chief Exec. Officer--Zale Corporation, Irving, TX, pg. 1215
Groves, Franklin N., Chm. Bd. & Chief Exec. Officer--S. J. Groves & Sons Company, Minneapolis, MN, pg. 490
Grua, Rudolph, Pres. & Chief Exec. Officer--General Binding Corporation, Northbrook, IL, pg. 656

Grua, Rudolph, Pres. & Chief Exec. Officer--VeloBind, Inc., Northbrook, IL, pg. 657
Grunow, John E.D., Jr., Chm. Bd. & Chief Exec. Officer--International Marine Holdings, Inc., Stamford, CT, pg. 579
Guccione, Bob, Chm. Bd., Chief Exec. Officer & Publr.--General Media Publishing Group, New York, NY, pg. 450
Guerrein, Richard, Co.-Chief Exec. Officer--Full Circle Media Corp., Norwalk, CT, pg. 436
Guertler, Walter E., Jr., Chm. Bd., Pres., Chief Exec. Officer--Systems Engineering & Manufacturing Corp., Stoughton, MA, pg. 1071
Guizzetti, Joseph, Chief Exec. Officer & Gen. Mgr.--Buffelen Woodworking Company, Tacoma, WA, pg. 187
Gulbas, Bruce, Pres. & Chief Exec. Officer--National Restaurant Supply Company, El Paso, TX, pg. 793
Gulley, Richard B., Chief Exec. Officer--Robert F. Driver Co., Inc., San Diego, CA, pg. 349
Gulling, Daniel L., Pres. & Chief Exec. Officer--Marinette Marine Corporation, Marinette, WI, pg. 707
Gummere, John, Chm. Bd. & Chief Exec. Officer--Phoenix Home Life Mutual Insurance Company, Hartford, CT, pg. 868
Gunderson, Richard L., Pres. & Chief Exec. Officer--Aid Association For Lutherans, Appleton, WI, pg. 26
Gupta, Vinod, Chm., Pres., Chief Exec. Officer--American Business Information, Inc., Omaha, NE, pg. 50
Gurewitz, Richard, Chm. Bd. & Chief. Exec. Officer--Poly Pak America, Inc., Los Angeles, CA, pg. 880
Gurney, Robert J., Jr., Chm. Bd., Pres. & Chief Exec. Officer--Gurney Industries Inc., Gastonia, NC, pg. 495
Gurnitz, Robert N., Pres. & Chief Exec. Officer--Northwestern Steel & Wire Co., Sterling, IL, pg. 815
Gustafson, Robert F., Chief Exec. Officer--Formac Corporation, Minneapolis, MN, pg. 424
Gustavsen, J., Chief Exec. Officer--Amspec Chemical Corporation, Gloucester City, NJ, pg. 5
Gutterman, Arthur, Pres., Chief Oper. & Chief Exec. Officer--Jelmar Company, Lincolnwood, IL, pg. 592
Gwaltney, John R., Chm. Bd., Pres. & Chief Exec. Officer--Forestry Suppliers, Inc., Jackson, MS, pg. 424
Gwinn, Robert P., Chm. Bd. & Chief Exec. Officer--Encyclopaedia Britannica, Inc., Chicago, IL, pg. 381
Haas, Robert D., Chm. Bd. & Chief Exec. Officer--Levi Strauss & Co., San Francisco, CA, pg. 670
Haass, Thomas, Chief Exec. Officer--American Legend Corporate, Seattle, WA, pg. 57
Habecker, Eugene B., Pres. & Chief Exec. Officer--American Bible Society, New York, NY, pg. 49
Habermann, N.N., Pres. & Chief Exec. Officer--Restaurant Enterprises Group, Inc., Irvine, CA, pg. 929
Hacker, Joshua, Chm. Bd., Pres., Chief Exec. & Chief Fin. Officer--Seaboard Electronics Co., Carlsbad, CA, pg. 983
Hackl, A.J., Chm. Bd. & Chief Exec. Officer--Herff Jones Inc., Indianapolis, IN, pg. 531
Hackney, Robert H., Pres. & Chief Exec. Officer--Hackney Brothers, Inc., Wilson, NC, pg. 498
Hadley, Jacquelyn, Chief Exec. Officer--Caswell/Massey Co. Ltd., Edison, NJ, pg. 229
Haeseker, Henry W., Pres. & Chief Exec. Officer--Boyle Engineering Corp., Newport Beach, CA, pg. 169
Hafner, Joseph A., Pres. & Chief Exec. Officer--Riviana Foods Inc., Houston, TX, pg. 937
Hagan, Tom, Co-Chm. & Chief Exec. Officer--Karsh & Hagan, Inc., Englewood, CO, pg. 617
Hagen, Thomas B., Chm. Bd. & Chief Exec. Officer--Erie Family Life Insurance Company, Erie, PA, pg. 386
Hagen, Thomas B., Chm. Bd. & Chief Exec. Officer--Erie Insurance Group, Erie, PA, pg. 386
Hagen, Thomas B., Chm. Bd. & Chief Exec. Officer--Erie Indemnity Company, Erie, PA, pg. 386
Hagen, Thomas B., Chm. Bd. & Chief Exec. Officer--Erie Insurance Exchange, Erie, PA, pg. 386
Hagen, Thomas B., Chm. Bd. & Chief Exec. Officer--Flagship City Insurance Company, Erie, PA, pg. 386
Haggai, Thomas S., Chm. Bd. & Chief Exec. Officer--IGA, Inc. (Independent Grocers Alliance), Chicago, IL, pg. 560
Haggar, Joe, III, Pres. & Chief Exec. Officer--Haggar Apparel Company, Dallas, TX, pg. 499
Haggen, Donald E., Chm. Bd. & Chief Exec. Officer--Haggen's Inc., Bellingham, WA, pg. 499
Hagiwara, Kokichi, Chm. Bd. & Chief Exec. Officer--National Steel Corporation, Mishawaka, IN, pg. 793
Hagler, Thomas W., Jr., Chm. & Chief Exec. Officer--Georgia Iron Works Co., Grovetown, GA, pg. 453
Hahn, Horst, Chief Exec. Officer & Gen. Mgr.--Multimatic Corporation, Northvale, NJ, pg. 775
Haigh, Robert B., Chm., Chief Exec. Officer & Treas.--Chicago Tube & Iron Co., Chicago, IL, pg. 246
Hale, Guy A., Chm. Bd., Pres. & Chief Exec. Officer--The Alamo Learning Systems, Inc., San Ramon, CA, pg. 29
Hale, Rodney L., Pres. & Chief Exec. Officer--Academy Insurance Group, Inc., Atlanta, GA, pg. 11
Haley, Clifton, Chm. Bd., Pres. & Chief Exec. Officer--Beech Holdings Corp., Chicago, IL, pg. 131
Haley, Clifton, Chm.Bd., Pres. & Chief Exec. Officer--Budget Rent A Car Corporation, Lisle, IL, pg. 131
Haley, F.T., Chm. Bd. & Chief Exec. Officer--Brown & Haley, Tacoma, WA, pg. 182
Hall, Alvin D., Pres. & Chief Exec. Officer--Miller & Smith, Inc., McLean, VA, pg. 755
Hall, Richard E., Chm. Bd. & Chief Exec. Officer--Underground Construction Company, Inc., Benicia, CA, pg. 1125
Hallam, Robert, Chm. Bd. & Chief Exec. Officer--Ben E. Keith Company, Fort Worth, TX, pg. 620
Halper, Steven, Chief Oper. Officer--Seaman Furniture Co., Inc., Woodbury, NY, pg. 986
Halperin, Thomas C., Chm Bd., Pres. & Chief Exec. Officer--Commercial Light Company, Hillside, IL, pg. 268
Halton, Dale F., Chm. Bd., Pres. & Chief Exec. Officer--Pepsi-Cola Bottling Company of Charlotte Inc., Charlotte, NC, pg. 860
Hamblett, Stephen, Chm. Bd., Chief Exec. Officer & Publr.--Providence Journal Company, Providence, RI, pg. 895
Hamilton, Jack H., Chief Exec. Officer--CGF Industries, Topeka, KS, pg. 201
Hamilton, Sherman, Pres. & Chief Exec. Officer--Hamilton Sweeney Advertising, Inc., Denver, CO, pg. 503
Hamister, Mark E., Chm. Bd., Pres. & Chief Exec. Officer--National Health Care Affiliates, Inc., Buffalo, NY, pg. 791
Hammond, Joseph M., Pres. & Chief Exec. Officer--Jervis B. Webb Company, Farmington Hills, MI, pg. 1170
Hampton, John C., Chm. Bd., Pres. & Chief Exec. Officer--Hampton Resources Inc., Portland, OR, pg. 504
Hand, Paul E., Chief Exec. Officer--Atlantic Dairy Cooperative, Southampton, PA, pg. 94
Handler, Mark S., Co-Chm. & Co- Chief Exec. Officer--R. H. Macy & Co., Inc., New York, NY, pg. 698
Handler, Mark S., Co-Chm. Bd. & Co-Chief Exec. Officer--Bullock's, Los Angeles, CA, pg. 699
Handler, Sheryl, Pres. & Chief Exec. Officer--Thinking Machines Corporation, Cambridge, MA, pg. 1092
Hank, B.J., Jr., Chm. Bd. & Chief Exec. Officer--Montgomery Elevator Company, Moline, IL, pg. 767
Hanlin, Russel L., Pres. & Chief Exec. Officer--Sunkist Growers, Processed Products, Ontario, CA, pg. 1061
Hanlin, Russell L., Pres., Chief Exec. & Chief Oper. Officer--Sunkist Growers, Inc., Sherman Oaks, CA, pg. 1060
Hanman, Gary, Chief Exec. Officer--Mid-America Dairymen, Inc., Springfield, MO, pg. 750
Hanna, Allan C., Pres. & Chief Exec. Officer--Zephyr Inc., North Muskegon, MI, pg. 1217
Hannah, Thomas E., Pres. & Chief Exec. Officer--Collins & Aikman Textile Group, Charlotte, NC, pg. 262
Hannay, Roger A., Pres. & Chief Exec. Officer--Clifford B. Hannay & Son Inc., Westerlo, NY, pg. 505
Hannebrink, Dave, Pres. & Chief Exec. Officer--Covalent Systems Corporation, Fremont, CA, pg. 290
Hano, Frank, Pres. & Chief Exec. Officer--Technicarbon Company, Inc., Springfield, MA, pg. 1083
Hano, Philip, Chief Exec. Officer--Hano Business Forms, Inc., Springfield, MA, pg. 505
Hansen, Charles M., Pres. & Chief Exec. Officer--Pillowtex Corporation, Dallas, TX, pg. 870
Hansen, R.W., Chm. Bd., Pres. & Chief Exec. Officer--Furnas Electric Company, Batavia, IL, pg. 437
Hanson, Allan D., Pres. & Chief Exec. Officer--Harvest States Cooperatives, Saint Paul, MN, pg. 514
Hanson, George V., Chm. Bd., Pres. & Chief Exec. Officer--Old Home Foods, Inc., Saint Paul, MN, pg. 823
Haraldson, Bill, Chief Oper. Officer & Exec. V.P.-Mktg.--Rosauer's Supermarkets, Inc., Spokane, WA, pg. 947
Harberts, Thomas W., Pres. & Chief Exec. Officer--Byerly's Inc., Edina, MN, pg. 198
Harden, Gregory, Chief Exec. Officer--Harden Furniture Company, McConnellsville, NY, pg. 508
Harder, Ronald R., Pres. & Chief Exec. Officer--Jewelers Mutual Insurance Company, Neenah, WI, pg. 593
Harding, John H., Chm. & Chief Exec. Officer--Administrative Services, Inc., Montpelier, VT, pg. 791
Hardy, Joseph A. Sr., Chm., Pres. & Chief Exec. Officer--84 Lumber Co., Eighty Four, PA, pg. 371
Hardy, Richard B., Pres., Chief Exec. & Chief Oper. Officer--Hyde Manufacturing Co., Southbridge, MA, pg. 556
Hare, Donald E., Pres. & Chief Exec. Officer--Coppus Engineering Corp., Millbury, MA, pg. 285
Harkins, Thomas P., Chm. Bd. & Chief Exec. Officer--Harkins Builders, Inc., Silver Spring, MD, pg. 509
Harling, C. Gene, Chm. Bd., Pres. & Chief Exec. Officer--FirstFed Michigan Corporation, Detroit, MI, pg. 414
Harling, C. Gene, Chm. Bd., Pres. & Chief Exec. Officer--First Federal of Michigan, Detroit, MI, pg. 414
Harmon, Austin, Pres. & Chief Exec. Officer--Harmon Smith Inc., Kansas City, MO, pg. 510
Harmon, David E., Chm. Bd., Pres., Chief Exec. & Chief Oper. Officer--El Camino Resources, Ltd., Northridge, CA, pg. 372
Harmon, Steven J., Pres. & Chief Exec. Officer--Twin City Die Castings Co., Minneapolis, MN, pg. 1121
Harrell, Samuel M., Chm. Bd., Pres. & Chief Exec. Officer--EDI International, Inc., Cincinnati, OH, pg. 359
Harris, Donald C., Chief Exec. Officer--Chip Supply Inc., Orlando, FL, pg. 248
Harris, Michael S., Pres. & Chief Exec. Officer--Deck House Inc., Acton, MA, pg. 324
Harris, Robert M., Chm. Bd. & Chief Exec. Officer--GFA Brands, Inc., Cresskill, NJ, pg. 440
Harrison, Stephen, Chm. & Chief Exec. Officer--Welsco Inc., North Little Rock, AR, pg. 1175
Harrison, William H., Jr., Chm. Bd. & Chief Exec. Officer--Taylor Drug Stores, Inc., Louisville, KY, pg. 1081
Hart, Alex W., Pres. & Chief Exec. Officer--Mastercard International, Inc., New York, NY, pg. 720
Hart, William L., Chm. Bd. & Chief Exec. Officer--Hart Graphics Inc., Austin, TX, pg. 513
Hartley, Milton E., Pres. & Chief Exec. Officer--The Elder-Beerman Stores Corp., Dayton, OH, pg. 373
Hartman, Carl C., Pres., Chief Oper. & Chief Exec. Officer--Trinidad/Benham Corporation, Denver, CO, pg. 1113
Hartshorn, Terry, Pres. & Chief Exec. Officer--PacifiCare Health Systems, Inc., Cypress, CA, pg. 1127
Harty, John B., Pres. & Chief Exec. Officer--PBS Building Systems of America, Anaheim, CA, pg. 835
Harvey, David E., Chm. & Chief Exec. Officer--Rome Cable Corporation, Rome, NY, pg. 945
Harvey, Joseph H., Jr., Chm. Bd. & Chief Exec. Officer--J.H. Harvey Company, Nashville, GA, pg. 515
Harvie, James, Chm. Bd., Pres. & Chief Exec. Officer--General Ship Corporation, Boston, MA, pg. 450
Harvieux, Ron, Pres. & Chief Exec. Officer--M&H Advertising, Minneapolis, MN, pg. 690
Hasler, Joseph W., Pres. & Chief Exec. Officer--Illinois Cereal Mills, Inc., Paris, IL, pg. 562
Hatfield, Joe, Chm. Bd. & Chief Exec. Officer--Fieldale Corporation, Baldwin, GA, pg. 409
Hatt, Peter M., Chm. & Chief Exec. Officer--Borders, Perrin & Norrander, Inc., Portland, OR, pg. 165
Hatt, Peter M., Chm. & Chief Exec. Officer--Borders, Perrin & Norrander, Seattle, WA, pg. 165
Hauber, W.M., Chm. Bd., Pres. & Chief Exec. Officer--Matthews International Corp., Pittsburgh, PA, pg. 721
Hauck, L. Christian, Pres. & Chief Exec. Officer--Sunflower Electric Power Corporation, Hays, KS, pg. 1060
Hauck, L. Christian, Pres. & Chief Exec. Officer--Holcomb Station, Holcomb, KS, pg. 1060
Haversat, Robert A., Pres. & Chief Exec. Officer--ESSTAR Incorporated, New Haven, CT, pg. 361
Haversat, Robert A., Chm. Bd., Pres. & Chief Exec. Officer--Essex Industries, New Haven, CT, pg. 361
Havlam, Douglas, Chief Exec. Officer--Menu Foods, Inc., Pennsauken, NJ, pg. 739
Hawk, Richard C., Chm. Bd. & Chief Exec. Officer--Help Management Corporation, Overland Park, KS, pg. 527
Hawk, Robert, Pres. & Chief Exec. Officer--Hale-Halsell Company, Tulsa, OK, pg. 500
Hawkins, Arthur M., Pres. & Chief Exec. Officer--Exide Corporation, Reading, PA, pg. 393
Hawley, Alan, Pres. & Chief Exec. Officer--The Griffith Laboratories Ltd., Scarborough,, Canada, pg. 488
Haworth, Richard G., Pres. & Chief Exec. Officer--Haworth, Inc., Holland, MI, pg. 518
Hayden, Donald C., Chief Exec. Officer--Transco Inc., Wayne, MI, pg. 1107
Hayes, Dennis C., Pres.--Hayes Microcomputer Products, Inc., Norcross, GA, pg. 519
Hayes, J. Michael, Pres. & Chief Exec. Officer--C. B. Ragland Company, Nashville, TN, pg. 909
Hayes, Matthew, Pres., Chief Exec. Officer & Treas.--Hayes/Harwood, Stowe, VT, pg. 519
Hayes, R. Dixon, Pres. & Chief Exec. Officer--Shenango Furnace Company, Princeton, NJ, pg. 997
Hayes, Walter, Chm., Pres. & Chief Exec. Officer--Aston Martin LaGonda of North America, Inc., Stamford, CT, pg. 92
Haynam, Harvey H., Chm. & Chief Exec. Officer--Target Stamped Products Corp., Kinsman, OH, pg. 1079
Haysbert, Raymond V., Sr., Chm. Bd., Pres. & Chief Exec. Officer--Parks Sausage Company, Baltimore, MD, pg. 850
Heagerty, David A., Chm. Bd. & Chief Exec. Officer--The Coakley Heagerty Companies, Ltd., San Jose, CA, pg. 256
Healey, William J., Pres. & Chief Exec. Officer--Viking Yacht Co., New Gretna, NJ, pg. 1151
Hearn, John, Pres. & Chief Exec. Officer--Tennelec/Nucleus, Inc., Oak Ridge, TN, pg. 1087
Heath, Milton W., Jr., Chm. Bd., Chief Exec. Officer & Treas.--Heath Consultants Incorporated, Stoughton, MA, pg. 524
Hecht, Robert, Chief Exec. Officer--Trumbull Corporation, West Mifflin, PA, pg. 1117
Heider, David, Pres. & Chief Exec. Officer--United Hardware Distributing Co., Plymouth, MN, pg. 1132
Heidrich, James K., Jr., Chm. Bd., Pres. & Chief Exec. Officer--The Miami Margarine Co., Cincinnati, OH, pg. 746
Heikens, Burdette N., Exec. V.P. & Chief Oper. Officer--American Republic Insurance Co., Des Moines, IA, pg. 60
Heil, Joseph F., Jr., Chm. Bd. & Chief Exec. Officer--The Heil Co., Chattanooga, TN, pg. 525
Heim, Greg, Exec. V.P. & Chief Exec. Officer--Modern Drop Forge Co., Blue Island, IL, pg. 762
Heiman, Paul, Chm. Bd. & Chief Exec. Officer--Standard Textile Co., Inc., Cincinnati, OH, pg. 1037
Heine, Spencer, Pres. & Chief Exec. Officer--The Signature Group, Schaumburg, IL, pg. 768
Heininger, Jeff, Chief Exec. Officer--Allsop, Inc., Bellingham, WA, pg. 43
Heins, Richard M., Pres. & Chief Exec. Officer--CUNA Mutual Insurance Society, Madison, WI, pg. 205
Heins, Richard M., Chief Exec. Officer--League Life Insurance Co., Southfield, MI, pg. 205
Heiser, Edward R., Pres. & Chief Exec. Officer--Wells Aluminum Corp., South Bend, IN, pg. 1175
Helgason, Sigurdur, Pres. & Chief Exec. Officer--IceLandAir, New York, NY, pg. 561
Hellberg, Clifford, Chm. Bd., Pres., Chief Exec. Officer--Creative Productions, Pittsburgh, PA, pg. 297
Heller, Chester M., Sr., Chm. Bd., Pres. & Chief Exec. Officer--Marquette Coppersmithing Co., Inc., Philadelphia, PA, pg. 713
Helliwell, John, Exec. Dir.-Mngmt. Information Systems--Ziff Communications Company, New York, NY, pg. 1218
Helm, Greg J., Chief Exec. Officer--Stein Robaire Helm, Inc., Los Angeles, CA, pg. 1045
Helmsley, Harry B., Chm. Bd., Pres. & Chief Exec. Officer--Helmsley Enterprises, Inc., New York, NY, pg. 527
Helzberg, Barnett C., Jr., Chm. Bd. & Chief Exec. Officer--Helzberg's Diamond Shops, Inc., North Kansas City, MO, pg. 528
Helzer, James A., Pres. & Chief Exec. Officer--Unicover Corporation, Cheyenne, WY, pg. 1126
Hemmer, Paul W., Jr., Pres. & Chief Exec. Officer--Paul Hemmer Construction Company, Fort Mitchell, KY, pg. 528
Hemphill, Robert B., Chm., Pres. & Chief Exec. & Chief Oper. Officer--Barclay White Incorporated, Berwyn, PA, pg. 119
Henderson, C. Max, Chm. Bd. & Chief Exec. Officer--Laroche Holdings, Inc., Atlanta, GA, pg. 659
Henderson, Don, Exec. V.P. & Chief Exec. Officer--United Farm Bureau Family Life Insurance Co., Indianapolis, IN, pg. 1131
Henderson, John N., III, Pres. & Chief Exec. Officer--Mid-West Paper Products Company, Warren, MI, pg. 750
Henderson, Richard, Chief Exec. Officer & Creative Dir.--Cole Henderson Drake, Inc., Atlanta, GA, pg. 260

Corporate Responsibilities Index

Henderson, Richard L., Pres.--Drug Emporium of Arizona, Inc., Scottsdale, AZ, pg. 349
Henderson, Robert J., Sr., Chm. Bd., Pres. & Chief Exec. Officer--Ford Development Corporation, Cincinnati, OH, pg. 423
Hendricks, Kenneth A., Chm. Bd., Pres. & Chief Exec. Officer--ABC Supply Company, Inc., Beloit, WI, pg. 2
Hendrix, Tom E., Chm. Bd., Pres. & Chief Exec. Officer--Henco, Inc., Selmer, TN, pg. 528
Hennessy, John M., Pres. & Chief Exec. Officer--CS First Boston Group, Inc., New York, NY, pg. 203
Hennesy, Thomas J., Chm. Bd. & Chief Exec. Officer--TSC Industries, Inc., Nashville, TN, pg. 1075
Henning, Peter H., Pres. & Chief Exec. Officer--Plano Molding Co., Plano, IL, pg. 874
Henry, James C., Jr., Pres. & Chief Exec. Officer--E.P. Henry Corporation, Woodbury, NJ, pg. 530
Hensley, Thomas L., Pres. & Chief Exec. Officer--Druther's International, Inc., Louisville, KY, pg. 350
Henson, J. Peter, Chm. Bd. & Chief Exec. Officer--Flexible Products Company, Marietta, GA, pg. 418
Herb, Marvin J., Chm. Bd. & Chief Exec. Officer--Coca-Cola Bottling Co. of Chicago, Niles, IL, pg. 257
Herbert, Richard, Pres., Chief Exec. & Fin. Officer--VanDine, Humphrey, Herbert, Alber & Manges, Inc., Pittsburgh, PA, pg. 1145
Herbison, J. Steve, Pres. & Chief Exec. Officer--U.R.M. Stores, Inc., Spokane, WA, pg. 1124
Herlin, Robert M., Chm. Bd. & Chief Exec. Officer--Herlin Press, West Haven, CT, pg. 531
Herman, Paula, Chief Exec. Officer--Herman Associates, Inc., New York, NY, pg. 531
Hermanson, Merril, Chm. Bd. & Chief Exec. Officer--Mr. Christmas Inc., New York, NY, pg. 761
Hermesdorf, J., Pres. & Chief Exec. Officer--Teepak, Inc., Westchester, IL, pg. 535
Herring, James, Pres. & Chief Exec. Officer--Friona Industries, L.P., Amarillo, TX, pg. 434
Herschend, Jack, Chm. Bd.--Silver Dollar City, Inc., Branson, MO, pg. 1004
Hertz, Arthur, Chm. Bd. & Chief Exec. Officer--Wometco Enterprises, Inc., Coral Gables, FL, pg. 1199
Hess, Donald E., Pres. & Chief Exec. Officer--Parisian, Inc., Birmingham, AL, pg. 848
Heston, W. Craig, Chm. & Chief Exec. Officer--Utica Mutual Insurance Company, New Hartford, NY, pg. 1140
Hetherwick, Fred B., Chm. Bd., Pres. & Chief Exec. Officer--Plastigage Corporation, Jackson, MI, pg. 876
Heyman, Leonard J., Chm. Bd., Pres., Chief Exec. & Chief Oper. Officer--Heyman Corporation, Niles, IL, pg. 532
Heyman, Samuel J., Chm. Bd. & Chief Exec. Officer--GAF Corporation, Wayne, NJ, pg. 438
Hickey, R. Michael, Pres. & Chief Exec. Officer--Bioproducts, Inc., Brecksville, OH, pg. 152
Hickey, William M., Pres. & Chief Exec. Officer--Lapham-Hickey Steel Corp., Chicago, IL, pg. 658
Hickman, S. Martin, Chm. Bd. & Chief Exec. Officer--Blue Cross & Blue Shield of Illinois, Chicago, IL, pg. 160
Hicks, Donald J., Chm. Bd., Pres. & Chief Exec. Officer--Hicks & Associates Inc., Coral Gables, FL, pg. 982
Hietala, Allan, Chief Exec. Officer--Colle & McVoy, Inc., Minneapolis, MN, pg. 261
Higginbotham, Alton, Chief Exec. Officer & Gen. Mgr.--First Electric Cooperative, Jacksonville, AR, pg. 412
Higginbotham, J.L., Pres. & Chief Exec. Officer--Higginbotham-Bartlett Co., Lubbock, TX, pg. 533
Higgins, Larry B., Chm. Bd., Pres. & Chief Exec. Officer--H & H Tube & Manufacturing Co., Vanderbilt, MI, pg. 495
Hilbert, William M., Sr., Chief Exec. Officer--PHB Parker Die Castings, Beaufort, SC, pg. 836
Hill, D.J., Pres. & Chief Exec. Officer--Micro Component Technology Inc., Saint Paul, MN, pg. 748
Hill, EdwardG., Jr., Pres. & Chief Exec. Officer--Abco Markets, Inc., Phoenix, AZ, pg. 10
Hillerich, John A., III, Pres. & Chief Exec. Officer--Hillerich & Bradsby Co., Inc., Louisville, KY, pg. 535
Hilt, John, Chm. Bd. & Chief Exec. Officer--Quality Stores Inc., North Muskegon, MI, pg. 904
Himeles, Martin S., Chm. Bd. & Chief Exec. Officer--Standard Medical Imaging, Inc., Columbia, MD, pg. 1037
Himes, Michael B., Chm. Bd., Pres. & Chief Exec. Officer--Petroleum Traders Corporation, Fort Wayne, IN, pg. 865
Hindman, Don J., Chm. Bd. & Chief Exec. Officer--Clark Foodservice, Inc., Elk Grove Village, IL, pg. 252
Hindson, M. Tal, Chm. & Chief Exec. Officer--Tal Inc., Erie, PA, pg. 1077
Hinman, Kirk, Pres., Chief Exec. Officer, Chief Fin. Officer & Treas.--Rome Strip Steel Co., Inc., Rome, NY, pg. 946
Hirsch, Gary D., Chm. Bd.--The Grand Union Company, Wayne, NJ, pg. 476
Hirschauer, Tom F., Pres. & Chief Exec. Officer--Bloomhorst Story O'Hara Inc., Indianapolis, IN, pg. 158
Hirschfeld, David L., Pres., Chief Exec. Officer & Treas.--Hirschfeld, Inc., San Angelo, TX, pg. 536
Hitchcock, Donald S., Chm. & Chief Exec. Officer--Knight Architects Engineers Planners, Inc., Chicago, IL, pg. 637
Hitchcock, Timothy R., Pres. & Chief Exec. Officer--Hitchcock Industries, Inc., Bloomington, MN, pg. 536
Hively, Charles, Pres., Chief Exec. Officer & Creative Dir.--The Hively Agency Inc., Houston, TX, pg. 536
Hobart, W.H., Chm. Bd., Pres., Chief Exec. & Chief Oper. Officer--Hobart Brothers Co., Troy, OH, pg. 536
Hochfelder, J. Gene, Chm. & Chief Exec. Officer--Beldoch Industries Corporation, West Hempstead, NY, pg. 133
Hockaday, Irvine O., Jr., Pres. & Chief Exec. Officer--Hallmark Cards, Inc., Kansas City, MO, pg. 501
Hodin, Joseph, Chm., Pres. & Chief Exec. Officer--Giant Markets Inc., Scranton, PA, pg. 456
Hoelzer, Dennis, Chm. Bd., Pres. & Chief Exec. Officer--Sentinel Computer Services Inc., Oak Brook, IL, pg. 990
Hoffer, Robert A., Sr., Pres. & Chief Exec. Officer--Hoffer Plastics Corporation, South Elgin, IL, pg. 537
Hoffman, Ebba C., Chm., Pres., Chief Exec. & Chief Fin. Officer--Smead Manufacturing Company, Hastings, MN, pg. 1011
Hoffman, Henry P., Chief Exec. Officer--Tri-State Motor Transit Co., Joplin, MO, pg. 1111
Hoffman, Ken, Pres. & Chief Exec. Officer--Coast to Coast, Denver, CO, pg. 993
Hoffman, Ken, Chief Exec. Officer--Coast To Coast Stores, Inc., Denver, CO, pg. 257
Hogan, Frank J., Pres. & Chief Exec. Officer--Overseas Service Corporation, West Palm Beach, FL, pg. 833
Hogarty, Daniel J. Jr., Pres. & Chief Exec. Officer--The Troy Savings Bank, Troy, NY, pg. 1116
Hogentogler, Don, Exec. V.P./Chief Exec. Officer--Gunnebo Fastening Corp., York, PA, pg. 494
Hogg, Robert H., III, Chief Exec. Officer & Pres.--Better Brands Of Atlanta, Inc., Atlanta, GA, pg. 148
Hohn, Harry G., Chm. Bd. & Chief Exec. Officer--New York Life Insurance Company, New York, NY, pg. 802
Hoke, Joe, Chm., Pres. & Chief Exec. Officer--Mintz & Hoke Inc., Avon, CT, pg. 759
Hokin, Myron, Pres. & Chief Exec. Officer--Century America Corporation, Chicago, IL, pg. 234
Holas, Frank W., Pres. & Chief Exec. Officer--Rich SeaPak Corp., Saint Simons Island, GA, pg. 932
Holding, R. E., Pres. & Chief Exec. Officer--Sinclair Oil Corp., Salt Lake City, UT, pg. 1008
Holding, R. Earl, Chief Exec. Officer--Little America Hotels, Salt Lake City, UT, pg. 1008
Holec, Kenneth, Pres. & Chief Exec. Officer--Lawson Associates Inc., Minneapolis, MN, pg. 663
Holford, Jay, Chief Exec. Officer--Seald-Sweet Growers, Inc., Vero Beach, FL, pg. 984
Holland, John, Chief Exec. Officer--Fruit of the Loom, Bowling Green, KY, pg. 400
Holland, John B., Chm. Bd. & Chief Exec. Officer--Union Underwear Co., Inc., Bowling Green, KY, pg. 400
Holland, Richard F., Pres. & Chief Exec. Officer--AEI Holding Co., Inc., Fullerton, CA, pg. 3
Holland, Richard F., Pres. & Chief Exec. Officer--American Electronics, Inc., Fullerton, CA, pg. 3
Hollister, Dean, Pres. & Chief.Exec. Officer--Hollister Advertising, New Providence, NJ, pg. 539
Holloway, M.E., Chief Exec. Officer--Cornnuts Inc., Alameda, CA, pg. 286
Holman, W. H., Jr., Chm. Bd., Pres. & Chief Exec. & Oper. Officers--Jitney-Jungle Stores of America, Inc., Jackson, MS, pg. 594
Holmes, George B., Pres., Chief Exec. & Chief Fin. Officer--Dombrowski & Holmes, Inc., Chicago, IL, pg. 343
Holmes, Robert M., Chm. Bd. & Chief Exec. Officer--Oltmans Construction Company, Whittier, CA, pg. 824
Holt, Dennis F., Pres. & Chief Exec. Officer--Western International Media Corporation, Los Angeles, CA, pg. 1179
Holt, Dennis F., Chief Exec. Officer--Western International Media Corporation, New York, NY, pg. 1180
Holt, Dennis F., Chm., Chief Exec. Officer--Western International Merchandising, Los Angeles, CA, pg. 1180
Holt, Dennis F., Chm., Chief Exec. Officer--Western International Premiums, Los Angeles, CA, pg. 1180
Honan, Terry, Pres. & Chief Exec. Officer--SAE-Pinkerton & Laws Inc., Atlanta, GA, pg. 966
Honroth, Dale K., Pres. & Chief Exec. Officer--Kendale Industries, Inc., Valley View, OH, pg. 622
Hood, Frank J., Pres. & Chief Exec. Officer--Welsh Farms, Inc., Long Valley, NJ, pg. 1175
Hooker, J. Clyde, Jr., Chm. Bd. & Chief Exec. Officer--Hooker Furniture Corporation, Martinsville, VA, pg. 543
Hoover, Herbert A., Pres. & Chief Exec. Officer--Acheson Industries, Inc., Port Huron, MI, pg. 12
Hopkins, Robert E., Chm. & Chief Exec. Officer--Schneller, Inc., Kent, OH, pg. 977
Hopper, Victor D., Chm. Bd., Pres. & Chief Exec. Officer--Hopper Inc., Bakersfield, CA, pg. 543
Hopson, Steve M., Pres. & Chief Exec. Officer--Thomas R. Hopson Broker, Inc., Marietta, GA, pg. 544
Hopton, David, Pres. & Chief Exec. Officer--U.S. Metalsource Corporation, Coraopolis, PA, pg. 1136
Hord, Fenton N., Pres. & Chief Exec. Officer--Carolina Builders Corporation, Raleigh, NC, pg. 223
Horn, Tom L., Jr., Pres. & Chief Exec. Officer--Kanawha Steel & Equipment Co., Charleston, WV, pg. 615
Horne, Timothy B., Chief Exec. Officer-Charbroil Div.--W. C. Bradley Co., Columbus, GA, pg. 170
Horowitz, Barry M., Dr., Pres. & Chief Exec. & Oper. Officer--Mitre Corporation, Bedford, MA, pg. 762
Horowitz, Edward D., Chm. & Chief Exec. Officer--Viacom Broadcasting Inc., New York, NY, pg. 785
Horrigan, D. Greg, Chm. Bd. & Chief Exec. Officer--Silgan Corporation, Stamford, CT, pg. 1004
Horton, D. Vernon, Chief Exec. Officer--Pacific Capital Bancorp, Salinas, CA, pg. 839
Horwitz, Susan, Pres. & Chief Exec. Officer--Aurora National Bank, Aurora, IL, pg. 483
Hosokawa, David, Chief Exec. Officer--TMP Worldwide, Inc., New York, NY, pg. 1073
Hospodor, Andrew T., Chm. Bd. & Chief Exec. Officer--Arinc Inc., Annapolis, MD, pg. 82
Hospodor, Andrew T., Chm. & Chief Exec. Officer--ARINC Research Corp., Annapolis, MD, pg. 82
Hospodor, Andrew T., Chm. Bd. & Chief Exec. Officer--Aeronautical Radio, Inc., Annapolis, MD, pg. 82
Hostetter, Amos B., Jr., Chm. Bd. & Chief Exec. Officer--Continental Cablevision, Boston, MA, pg. 278
Houck, Peter, Pres. & Chief Exec. Officer--Houck Industries, Inc., Tulare, CA, pg. 545
Hougen, Randall, Pres. & Chief Exec. Officer--Hougen Manufacturing Inc., Flint, MI, pg. 546
Houghton, Tony, Chm., Chief Exec. Officer--Leo Burnett Company Ltd., Toronto,, Canada, pg. 192
Houlihan, Lawrence, Chm. Bd., Pres., Chief Exec. & Chief Fin. Officer, Treas. & Sec.--Frank B. Ross Co. Inc., Jersey City, NJ, pg. 949
Housen, Charles B., Chm. Bd., Pres. & Chief Exec. Officer--Erving Paper Mills, Erving, MA, pg. 388
Houston, Douglas, Chm. Bd. & Chief Exec. Officer--Houston Effler & Partners, Boston, MA, pg. 546
Howalt, F. Harvey, Jr., Pres. & Chief Exec. Officer--Textile Rubber & Chemical Company, Dalton, GA, pg. 1090
Howard, Ron, Pres. & Chief Exec. Officer--Datability, Inc., Carlstadt, NJ, pg. 316
Howe, Michael V., Pres. & Chief Exec. Officer--Young & Rubicam Detroit, Detroit, MI, pg. 1211
Howell, Blair, Chief Exec. Officer--Compendium Systems, New York, NY, pg. 270
Howell, John S., Chm. Bd., Pres. & Chief Exec. Officer--Howell Instruments Corp., Fort Worth, TX, pg. 547
Howenstein, William K., Chm. Bd. & Chief Exec. Officer--Copper & Brass Sales, Inc., East Detroit, MI, pg. 284
Howson, Robert E., Chm. & Chief Exec. Officer--The Babcock & Wilcox Company, New Orleans, LA, pg. 107
Hoy, Thomas P., Pres. & Chief Exec. Officer--Geo. H. Lehleitner & Co., Inc., Harahan, LA, pg. 666
Hoyt, David P., Pres. & Chief Exec. Officer--Virginia Metal Industries, Inc., Orange, VA, pg. 1152
Hoyt, Leon G., Chm. & Chief Exec. Officer--Knight/Emerson Consulting, Inc., Chicago, IL, pg. 637
Hozik, John, Pres. & Chief Exec. Officer--The Philadelphia Bourse, Inc., Lanham, MD, pg. 866
Hozik, John, Chief Exec. Officer--E. C. Ernst, Capitol Heights, MD, pg. 866
Hroblak, Gerald, Chief Exec. Officer & Pres.--United Broadcasting Inc., Bethesda, MD, pg. 1131
Hubbard, Henry H., III, Pres. & Chief Exec. Officer--Madigan Brothers, Inc., River Forest, IL, pg. 699
Hubbard, R.D., Chm. Bd., Pres. & Chief Exec. Officer--AFG Industries, Inc., Fort Worth, TX, pg. 3
Hubbard, Samuel T., Pres. & Chief Exec. Officer--Alling & Cory Company, Rochester, NY, pg. 40
Hubbard, Stanley S., Chm., Pres., & Chief Exec. Officer--Hubbard Broadcasting, Inc., Saint Paul, MN, pg. 548
Huber, Ron, Chm. Bd., Pres. & Chief Exec. Officer--Time Systems, Inc., Phoenix, AZ, pg. 1097
Huber, Ron, Chm. Bd., Pres. & Chief Exec. Officer--Time Index, Inc., Phoenix, AZ, pg. 1097
Hudetz, Frank C., Chm. Bd. & Chief Exec. Officer--Solar Press, Inc., Naperville, IL, pg. 1016
Hudson, Chris, Chm. Bd., Pres. & Chief Exec. Officer--Automation Intelligence, Inc., Maitland, FL, pg. 101
Huey, Barry, Chm. Bd. & Chief Exec. Officer--Barry Huey, Bullock & Cook Advertising, Inc., Birmingham, AL, pg. 551
Huggins, David, Pres. & Chief Exec. Officer--RMS Techs, Inc., Marlton, NJ, pg. 907
Hughes, B. Wayne, Pres. & Chief Exec. Officer--Public Storage, Inc., Glendale, CA, pg. 898
Hughes, Richard, Pres. & Chief Exec. Officer--Hinderliter Industries, Inc., McKinney, TX, pg. 535
Hughes, Roger T., Pres. & Chief Exec. Officer--DonTech, Chicago, IL, pg. 345
Hughes, T.D., Chief Exec. & Chief Fin. Officer--La Rosa's, Inc., Cincinnati, OH, pg. 649
Hulseman, Robert L., Pres.--SCC Holding Co., Highland Park, IL, pg. 961
Hulsey, Neven, Pres. & Chief Exec. Officer--Earle M. Jorgensen Company, Brea, CA, pg. 605
Humphrey, G. Watts, Jr., Chm. Bd. & Chief Exec. Officer--The Conair Group, Inc., Pittsburgh, PA, pg. 272
Humphrey, John W., Chm. Bd.--The Forum Corporation, Boston, MA, pg. 425
Hunt, Bruce W., Pres. & Chief Exec. Officer--Petro-Hunt Corporation, Dallas, TX, pg. 865
Hunt, E.C., Jr., Chm. Bd. & Chief Exec. Officer--Thermo Industries Inc., Charlotte, NC, pg. 1091
Hunte, Henry F., Chm. Bd. & Chief Exec. Officer--H.G. Fenton Material Company, San Diego, CA, pg. 406
Huntington, Lawrence S., Chm. Bd. & Chief Exec. Officer--Fiduciary Trust Company International, New York, NY, pg. 408
Huntsman, Jon M., Chm. Bd. & Chief Exec. Officer--Huntsman Chemical Corporation, Salt Lake City, UT, pg. 555
Huntting, J.G., Jr., Chief Exec. & Chief Fin. Officer--Huntting Elevator Co., Austin, MN, pg. 555
Hurd, G. David, Chm. Bd., Pres. & Chief Exec. Officer--The Principal Financial Group, Des Moines, IA, pg. 890
Hurd, W. Russell, Pres. & Chief Exec. Officer--F.N. Burt Company, Inc., Buffalo, NY, pg. 195
Hurley, Dr. William D., Chm. Bd. & Chief Exec. Officer--Harvard Industries, Inc., Farmingdale, NJ, pg. 514
Huss, Jack, Pres. & Chief Exec. Officer--Briggs Industries, Inc., Tampa, FL, pg. 175
Hussar, Joseph, Chief Exec. Officer--Astro Wire & Cable Corporation, Worcester, MA, pg. 92
Hussey, Philip W., Jr., Pres. & Chief Exec. Officer--Hussey Corporation, North Berwick, ME, pg. 555
Huston, Preston D., Chm. Bd. & Chief Exec. Officer--Associated Advertising Agency, Inc., Wichita, KS, pg. 89
Ibos, Robert J., Chm. Bd., Pres. & Chief Exec. Officer--National Engineering & Contracting Co., Strongsville, OH, pg. 788
Ibsen, Dr. Robert, Chm. Bd., Pres., Chief Exec. Officer & Treas.--Den-Mat Corporation, Santa Maria, CA, pg. 328
Icahn, Carl C., Chm. Bd. & Chief Exec. Officer--Icahn & Co., Inc., Mount Kisco, NY, pg. 561
Icahn, Carl C., Chm. Bd. & Chief Exec. Officer--Trans World Airlines, Inc., Mount Kisco, NY, pg. 561
Ingersoll, Gary R., Pres. & Chief Exec. Officer--Bradley Printing Company, Des Plaines, IL, pg. 478
Ingle, R.P., Chm. & Chief Exec. Officer--Ingles Markets, Inc., Asheville, NC, pg. 568
Ingram, Donald C., Pres. & Chief Exec. Officer--Ingram Paper Company, City of Industry, CA, pg. 569
Ingram, E.W., III, Pres. & Chief Exec. Officer--White Castle System, Inc., Columbus, OH, pg. 1185

Ingram, Richard E., Chm. Bd., Chief Exec. & Chief Fin. Officer--Builder Marts of America, Greenville, SC, pg. 187
Inman, Gerald, Pres. & Chief Exec. Officer--Paul Inman Associates Inc., Farmington Hills, MI, pg. 570
Isemoto, Larry, Chief Exec. Officer--Isemoto Contracting Co. Ltd., Hilo, HI, pg. 582
Isen, Harold, Chm. Bd. & Chief Exec. Officer--Paramount Packaging Corp., Chalfont, PA, pg. 848
Iskra, Gary, Pres. & Chief Exec. Officer--Koolvent Aluminum Products, Inc., Pittsburgh, PA, pg. 841
Israel, Maureen, Chief Exec. Officer & Controller--Wright-Schuchart, Inc., Seattle, WA, pg. 1204
Israel, Steve, Chief Exec. Officer--B & B Motor & Control Corporation, Long Island City, NY, pg. 105
Issleib, Lutz, Chm. Bd., Pres., Chief Exec. & Chief Oper. Officer--General Brewing Company, Vancouver, WA, pg. 959
Jackman, Joseph R., Chm. Bd., Pres. & Chief Exec. Officer--Reactive Metals & Alloys Corporation (REMACOR), West Pittsburg, PA, pg. 916
Jackson, David J., Pres. & Chief Exec. Officer--Tupman Thurlow Co. Inc., New Rochelle, NY, pg. 1119
Jackson, Philip C., Chm. Bd., Pres. & Chief Exec. Officer--Ateron Corp., Parsippany, NJ, pg. 93
Jacob, Herbert H., Chm. Bd. & Chief Exec. Officer--Ajax Paving Industries Inc., Madison Heights, MI, pg. 28
Jacober, Jeffrey M., Pres. & Chief Exec. Officer--SGI Inc., Cranston, RI, pg. 962
Jacobs, Eli, Chm. Bd. & Chief Exec. Officer--Triangle Pacific Corporation, Dallas, TX, pg. 1112
Jacobs, Gilbert, Pres. & Chief Exec. Officer--Planning Systems Inc., McLean, VA, pg. 874
Jacobs, Irwin L., Chm. Bd. & Chief Exec. Officer--Minstar, Inc., Minneapolis, MN, pg. 758
Jacobs, Jeremy M., Chm. & Chief Exec. Officer--Delaware North Companies, Inc., Buffalo, NY, pg. 326
Jacobs, Richard E., Chm. Bd. & Chief Exec. Officer--The Richard & David Jacobs Group, Westlake, OH, pg. 932
Jacobson, Mitchell, Pres., Treas. & Chief Exec. Officer--Sid Tool Co. Inc., Plainview, NY, pg. 1002
Jacobson, Mitchell, Pres. & Chief Exec. Officer--MSC Industrial Supply Co., Plainview, NY, pg. 693
Jagoda, Leonard J., Chm., Pres. & Chief Exec. Officer--American SelfCare Corporation, Columbus, GA, pg. 60
Jamboretz, Glennon D., Chm. Bd., Pres. & Chief Exec. Officer--The Glennon Companies, Saint Louis, MO, pg. 462
James, Artis E., Jr., Pres. & Chief Exec. Officer--Purcell Co., Inc., Bay Saint Louis, MS, pg. 900
James, Gene A., Pres. & Chief Exec. Officer--Southern States Cooperative, Inc., Richmond, VA, pg. 1022
Jamison, Thomas J., Chm. Bd. & Chief Exec. Officer--Southern Radio Corporation, pg. 1022
Janik, Richard A., Pres. & Chief Exec. Officer--Janik & Associates, Inc., Los Angeles, CA, pg. 589
Jankowski, Richard, Chief Exec. Officer--Warrens Waller Press, South San Francisco, CA, pg. 1165
Jansen, James H., Pres., Chief Exec. & Oper. Officer--Lynden Incorporated, Seattle, WA, pg. 689
Janzem, Glen N., Pres. & Chief Exec. Officer--Ranchers Cotton Oil, Fresno, CA, pg. 911
Jaques, Chris, Chief Exec. Officer--BSB Hong Kong, Hong Kong, Hong Kong, pg. 110
Jasper, Paul T., Pres. & Chief Exec. Officer--Shurfine-Central Corp., Northlake, IL, pg. 1001
Jaworski, Walter J., Chm. Bd., Pres. Chief Exec. Officer & Chief Oper. Officer--Miken Companies, Inc., Cheektowaga, NY, pg. 752
Jay, Dan, Pres., Chief Exec. & Chief Fin. Officer--Campmor Inc., Paramus, NJ, pg. 213
Jayson, Joseph M., Chm. Bd. & Chief Exec. Officer--J. M. Jayson & Co., Inc., Getsville, NY, pg. 591
Jelenic, Robert M., Pres. & Chief Exec. Officer--Journal Register Company, Trenton, NJ, pg. 608
Jemison, Frank Z., Jr., Pres., Chief Exec. & Chief Oper. Officer--Jemison, Inc., Memphis, TN, pg. 592
Jenkins, Howard, Chm. Bd. & Chief Exec. Officer--Publix Supermarkets Inc., Lakeland, FL, pg. 898
Jenkins, Tiny, Chm. Bd. & Chief Exec. Officer--PSI Group of Companies, Memphis, TN, pg. 837
Jenks, Mrs. M. M., Chm. Bd. & Chief Exec. Officer--Mississippi Lime Co., Alton, IL, pg. 760
Jensen, Elizabeth D., V.P. & Chief Exec. Officer--Jensen Electric Company, Reno, NV, pg. 592
Jensen, Steven, Pres. & Chief Exec. Officer--Norbest, Inc., Midvale, UT, pg. 809
Jewell, Everett G., Chm. Bd., Pres., Chief Exec. Officer & Treas.--Jewell Building Systems, Dallas, NC, pg. 594
Jobs, Steven P., Chm. & Chief Exec. Officer--Next, Inc., Redwood City, CA, pg. 805
Johnson, A. Stanley, Chm. Bd., Pres. & Chief Exec. Officer--Van Leunens Inc., Cincinnati, OH, pg. 1144
Johnson, Albin S., Chm. & Chief Exec. Officer--Columbia Farms Inc., Leesville, SC, pg. 265
Johnson, Carl A., Pres., Chief Exec. & Chief Oper. Officer--Berlin Steel Construction Co., Berlin, CT, pg. 142
Johnson, David O., Chm. & Chief Exec. Officer--Johnson Acoustical & Supply Co., Portland, OR, pg. 597
Johnson, Edward C., III, Chm. & Chief Exec. Officer--Fidelity Investments (FMR Corp.), Boston, MA, pg. 408
Johnson, Eric D., Chm. Bd., Chief Exec. Officer--Rick Johnson & Company, Inc., Albuquerque, NM, pg. 597
Johnson, Gary S., Pres. & Chief Exec. Officer--Superior Oil Co. Inc., Indianapolis, IN, pg. 1064
Johnson, Glendon E., Chm. Bd., Pres. & Chief Exec. Officer--John Alden Financial Corporation, Miami, FL, pg. 32
Johnson, J.D., Co-Chm. Bd., Pres. & Chief Exec. Officer--G.S. Blodgett Corporation, Burlington, VT, pg. 157
Johnson, John C., Co-Chief Exec. Officer--Steuart Petroleum Company, Washington, DC, pg. 1048
Johnson, John H., Chm. Bd. & Chief Exec. Officer--Johnson Publishing Company, Inc., Chicago, IL, pg. 598
Johnson, John H., Chm. Bd. & Chief Exec. Officer--Fashion Fair Cosmetics, Chicago, IL, pg. 599
Johnson, Jon L., Pres., Chief Exec. Officer & Dir.--EvansGroup, Salt Lake City, UT, pg. 390
Johnson, Orville D., Chm. Bd. & Chief Exec. Officer--UFE Incorporated, Stillwater, MN, pg. 1123
Johnson, Richard W., Pres. & Chief Exec. Officer--Johnson Bros. Corp., Litchfield, MN, pg. 597
Johnson, Ruth, Chm. Bd. & Chief Exec. Officer--I.C. System, Inc., Vadnais Heights, MN, pg. 558
Johnson, Sam J., Chief Exec. Officer--Point Communications, Inc., Dallas, TX, pg. 878
Johnson, W.B., Chm. Bd. & Chief Exec. Officer--Ritz-Carlton Hotel Company, Atlanta, GA, pg. 598
Johnson, Warren, Pres. & Chief Exec. Officer--ATI Industries, Escondido, CA, pg. 8
Johnson, William B., Chm. Bd. & Chief Exec. Officer--W.B. Johnson Property, Inc., Atlanta, GA, pg. 598
Johnston, Fred B., II, Pres. & Chief Exec. Officer--Fred B. Johnston Company, Inc., Chapin, SC, pg. 601
Jolly, Roy H., Pres. & Chief Exec. Officer--E.C. Barton & Co., Jonesboro, AR, pg. 123
Jones, Alan C., Pres., Chief Exec. Officer & Sec.--United Grocers Inc., Portland, OR, pg. 1132
Jones, Chester, Pres. & Chief Exec. Officer--Hunter Corp., Portage, IN, pg. 554
Jones, Glenn R., Chm. Bd., Pres., Chief Exec. Officer & Sole Stockholder--Jones International Ltd., Englewood, CO, pg. 603
Jones, James, Chm. Bd. & Chief Exec. Officer--The American Stock Exchange, New York, NY, pg. 62
Jones, James C., Jr., Chm. Bd. & Chief Exec. Officer--Jones Company, Inc., Waycross, GA, pg. 603
Jones, Jerve M., Chief Exec. Officer--Peck Jones Construction, Los Angeles, CA, pg. 854
Jones, John, Chief Exec. Officer--Cummins-Allison Corp., Mount Prospect, IL, pg. 305
Jones, John E., Chm. Bd.--Cummins-American Corp., Mount Prospect, IL, pg. 304
Jones, John E., Chm. Bd. & Chief Exec. Officer--Glenview State Bank, Glenview, IL, pg. 305
Jones, Lawrence M., Chm. & Chief Exec. Oficer--The Coleman Company, Inc., Wichita, KS, pg. 695
Jones, R.B., Chm. Bd. & Chief Exec. Officer--Jones Chemicals, Inc., Le Roy, NY, pg. 603
Jones, Stanley, Pres., Chief Exec. Officer & Gen. Mgr.--Buhrman-Pharr Hardware Company, Texarkana, AR, pg. 187
Jones, Vernon T., Chm. Bd. & Chief Exec. Officer--Apco Argentina Inc., Tulsa, OK, pg. 77
Jones, Wilbur S., Jr., Pres. & Co-Chief Exec. Officer--Stone & Thomas, Wheeling, WV, pg. 1051
Jones, William W., Jr., Pres. & Chief Exec. Officer--Baltimore Stationery Co., Baltimore, MD, pg. 116
Jordan, John W. II, Chm. Bd. & Chief Exec. Officer--Jordan Industries, Inc., Deerfield, IL, pg. 604
Jordan, Joseph C., Chm. Bd. & Chief Exec. Officer--Jordan's Meats, Portland, ME, pg. 605
Jordan, Richard E., Chm. Bd. & Chief Exec. Officer--L. B. Smith, Inc., Camp Hill, PA, pg. 1013
Jordan, Warren K., Chm. Bd. & Chief Exec. Officer--Jordan Associates, Oklahoma City, OK, pg. 604
Joseph, Thomas, Chm., Pres. & Chief Exec. Officer--Markdata Inc., Pittston, PA, pg. 708
Josephson, Marvin, Chm. Bd., Pres. & Chief Exec. Officer--Josephson International Inc., New York, NY, pg. 607
Joshi, Krishan K., Pres. & Chief Exec. Officer--UES, Inc., Dayton, OH, pg. 1122
Juanarena, Douglas B., Pres. & Chief Exec. Officer--Pressure Systems, Hampton, VA, pg. 888
Judge, Jerry, Chief Exec. Officer--Young & Rubicam Holdings Ltd., London, United Kingdom, pg. 1213
Judy, S. Wade, Pres. & Chief Exec. Officer--Woolrich, Inc., Woolrich, PA, pg. 1201
Juett, J. Lee, Chm. Bd., Pres. & Chief Exec. Officer--J. Lee Hackett Co., Farmington, MI, pg. 498
Juilfs, George, Pres. & Chief Exec. Officer--SENCORP, Newport, KY, pg. 989
Julian, Michael, Chm. Bd., Pres. & Chief Exec. Officer--Farm Fresh, Inc., Norfolk, VA, pg. 401
Juodis, Walter, Pres. & Chief Exec. Officer--American Manufacturing Company, Inc. (LA), Lafayette, LA, pg. 58
Jura, James, Chief Exec. Officer--Associated Electric Co-op Inc., Springfield, MO, pg. 89
Jurgens, Thomas, Pres. & Chief Exec. Officer--ODL Incorporated, Zeeland, MI, pg. 819
Jurock, Oswald, Chm. Bd. & Chief Exec. Officer--Red Carpet Real Estate Services, Inc., San Diego, CA, pg. 918
Justiss, James F., Jr., Chm. Bd., Pres. & Chief Exec. Officer--Justiss Oil Co., Inc., Jena, LA, pg. 610
Juszkiewicz, Henry E., Chm. Bd. & Chief Exec. Officer--Gibson Guitar Corporation, Inc., Nashville, TN, pg. 456
Kahn, D. Dan, Chm. Bd. & Chief Exec. Officer--Production Tool Supply Co., Warren, MI, pg. 893
Kaiser, Marshall, Pres. & Chief Exec. Officer--Safe Harbor Water Power Corporation, Conestoga, PA, pg. 966
Kaiser, Michael, Chm. & Chief Exec. Officer--Kaiser McEuen Inc., Los Angeles, CA, pg. 615
Kalainov, S.C., Chm. Bd. & Chief Exec. Officer--American Mutual Life Insurance Company, Des Moines, IA, pg. 58
Kaltenbacher, Philip D., Chm. Bd. & Chief Exec. Officer--Seton Company, Norristown, PA, pg. 993
Kaltman, Eric, Chief Exec. Officer--Queens Group, Inc., Long Island City, NY, pg. 904
Kamberos, Chris, Chm. Bd., Pres. & Chief Oper. Officer--Treasure Island Foodmarts Inc., Chicago, IL, pg. 1109
Kamenstein, David R., Chm. Bd. & Chief Exec. Officer--M. Kamenstein, Inc., White Plains, NY, pg. 615
Kaminstein, Merwin F., Chm. Bd., Pres. & Chief Exec. Officer--Brookstone Company, Inc., Peterborough, NH, pg. 180
Kamm, Jacob O., Chm. Bd., Pres. & Chief Exec. Officer--Electric Furnace Co., Salem, OH, pg. 373
Kampouris, Emmanuel A., Chm. Bd, Pres. & Chief Exec. Officer--American Standard Inc., New York, NY, pg. 61
Kamstra, K.M., Chm. & Chief Exec. Officer--Kamstra Communications, Inc., Saint Paul, MN, pg. 615
Kane, Sam, Chm. Bd., Chief Exec. & Chief Fin. Officer--Sam Kane Beef Processors, Inc., Corpus Christi, TX, pg. 616
Kaplan, Samuel, Pres., Chief Exec. Officer, Sec. & Dir.-Sls. & Pur.--Admiration Hosiery Mills, Inc., Charlotte, NC, pg. 534
Kaplan, V. Jerome, Chief Exec. Officer--The Apparel Group, Ltd., New York, NY, pg. 78
Kapp, Dennis R., Chief Exec. Officer--Martin Universal Design, Inc., Westland, MI, pg. 715
Karmanos, Peter, Jr., Chm. Bd. & Chief Exec. Officer--Compuware Corporation, Farmington Hills, MI, pg. 271
Karol, Steven E., Pres. & Chief Exec. Officer--H M K Enterprises, Inc., Waltham, MA, pg. 497
Karp, Leonard, V.P., Chief Exec. Officer & Treas.--Best Provision Co., Inc., Newark, NJ, pg. 146
Karsh, Phil, Co-Chm. & Chief Exec. Officer--Karsh & Hagan, Inc., Englewood, CO, pg. 617
Karsten, Harry, Jr., Chm. Bd. & Pres.--Golden West Homes, Santa Ana, CA, pg. 467
Kasen, Stewart M., Co-Chm., Pres. & Chief Exec. Officer--Best Products Co., Inc., Richmond, VA, pg. 17
Kasle, Leonard, Chm. Bd. & Chief Exec. Officer--Kasle Steel Corporation, Dearborn, MI, pg. 617
Kassab, Gregory E., Chm. Bd. & Chief Exec. Officer--Stainless Incorporated, Deerfield Beach, FL, pg. 1035
Kassouf, James, Pres., Chief Exec. Officer & Treas.--Metropolitan Properties Inc., Cleveland, OH, pg. 745
Kathwari, M. Farooq, Chm., Pres. & Chief Exec. Officer--Green Mountain Holding Corporation, Danbury, CT, pg. 485
Kathwari, M. Farooq, Chm., Pres. & Chief Exec. Officer--Ethan Allen, Inc., Danbury, CT, pg. 485
Katsoulis, Tom, Chief Exec. Officer--GNWC Wire, Cable & Network Producers, Downers Grove, IL, pg. 440
Katz, Earl L., Chm. Bd. & Chief Exec. Officer--Encore Shoe Corporation, Rochester, NH, pg. 380
Katz, Lewis, Pres. & Chief Exec. Officer--Kinney System, Inc., New York, NY, pg. 632
Katz, Ronald C., Chm. Bd. & Chief Exec. Officer--Elkay Manufacturing Company, Oak Brook, IL, pg. 377
Katzen, Dr. Cyrus, Pres. & Chief Exec. Officer--Mozel Development Corp., Baileys Crossroads, VA, pg. 774
Katzman, Lawrence, Chm. Bd. & Chief Exec. Officer--Kaz, Inc., New York, NY, pg. 619
Kauffman, Richard N., Chm. Bd. & Chief Exec. Officer--H. S. Crocker Co., Inc., King of Prussia, PA, pg. 299
Kayne, Fred, Chief Exec. Officer--Fortune Fashion, Los Angeles, CA, pg. 425
Kearns, Joseph G., Chief Exec. Officer--Daniel F. Young, Inc., New York, NY, pg. 1209
Keating, Daniel J., Jr., Chm. Bd., Pres. & Chief Exec. Officer--Daniel J. Keating Co., Villanova, PA, pg. 619
Keats, Douglas E., Chief Exec. Officer--STS Holdings, Inc., Northbrook, IL, pg. 964
Keenan, James F., Chm. Bd. & Chief Exec. Officer--Pace Industries, Inc., Fayetteville, AR, pg. 838
Keener, J.W., Jr., Pres., Chief Exec. Officer & Treas.--The Chardon Rubber Co., Chardon, OH, pg. 239
Keener, Wayne, Chief Exec. Officer--Keeners, Inc., Seattle, WA, pg. 620
Keeney, Cecil M., Chief Exec. Officer--Walle Corporation, Jefferson, LA, pg. 1161
Keeney, Lafayette, Chm. Bd., Pres. & Chief Exec. Officer--Sage-Allen & Co., Inc., Hartford, CT, pg. 966
Keersmaeker, Charles A., Pres.--The John Johnson Co., Detroit, MI, pg. 597
Keery, Frank, Chm. Bd. & Chief Exec. Officer--The Swanson Company Manufacturers, Phoenix, AZ, pg. 1066
Kelley, Austin P., Chm. & Chief Exec. Officer--Austin Kelley Advertising, Inc., Atlanta, GA, pg. 99
Kelley, Gary L., Chm. Bd., Pres. & Chief Exec. Officer--Kelley Bean Co., Inc., Morrill, NE, pg. 621
Kellman, Joseph, Chm., Pres. & Chief Exec. Officer--Globe Glass & Mirror Co., Chicago, IL, pg. 463
Kellogg, Charles T., Pres., Chief Exec. Officer & Treas.--Hubbard Hall Inc., Waterbury, CT, pg. 549
Kelly, Austin, Mng. Dir.--Chiat/Day/Mojo Pty. Ltd., Kangaroo Point, Australia, pg. 245
Kelly, Donald P., Chm. Bd., Pres. & Chief Exec. Officer--Envirodyne Industries, Inc., Oak Brook, IL, pg. 383
Kelly, J. Fredrick, Jr., Pres. & Chief Exec. Officer--Aeroglide Corporation, Cary, NC, pg. 22
Kelly, J. Fredrick, Jr., Pres. & Chief Exec. Officer--Aeroglide Americas International, Inc., Raleigh, NC, pg. 22
Kelly, John D., Pres. & Chief Exec. Officer--Na-Churs Plant Food Company, Marion, OH, pg. 782
Kelly, Paul E., Sr., Chm. Bd., Chief Exec. & Fin. Officer--Cawsl Corporation, Wynnewood, PA, pg. 229
Kelly, Robert L., Pres. & Chief Exec. Officer--Kelly Michener Inc., Lancaster, PA, pg. 621
Kelly, Stephen J., Chm. Bd., Pres. & Chief Exec. Officer--South Chester Tube Co., Concordville, PA, pg. 1019
Kelso, R.W., Pres. & Chief Exec. Officer--PQ Corporation, Valley Forge, PA, pg. 836
Kendall, Stephen F., Pres. & Chief Exec. Officer--Aluminum Shapes, Inc., Delair, NJ, pg. 46
Kendall, Steve, Chief Exec. Officer--Electrical Insulation Suppliers, Hillside, IL, pg. 374
Kennedy, Bill, Chief Exec. Officer--Griffin Manufacturing Co., Muskogee, OK, pg. 487
Kennedy, James C., Chm. & Chief Exec. Officer--Cox Enterprises, Inc., Atlanta, GA, pg. 292
Kenney, G. Dickson, Pres. & Chief Exec. Officer--Kenney Manufacturing Company, Warwick, RI, pg. 623
Kenny, James C., Pres. & Chief Exec. Officer--Harbour Industries, Inc., Shelburne, VT, pg. 507
Kern, Martin H., Chief Exec. Officer--National Food Stores, Inc. T/A Krauszer's, Edison, NJ, pg. 788

Kerr, Howard J., Chm. Bd., Pres. & Chief Exec. Officer--Consolidated Pipe & Supply Company, Birmingham, AL, pg. 277
Kerr, Stephen R., Chief Exec. Officer--Holstein Association of America, Brattleboro, VT, pg. 541
Khoury, Tawfig N., Chm. Bd. & Chief Exec. Officer--Pacific Scene Inc., San Diego, CA, pg. 841
Kiam, Victor, II, Chm. Bd., Pres., Chief Exec. & Chief Oper. Officer--Remington Products Inc., Bridgeport, CT, pg. 926
Kies, A.M., Pres. & Chief Exec. Officer--Erico International, Cleveland, OH, pg. 386
Kiggen, James D., Chm. Bd., Pres. & Chief Exec. Officer--Xtek, Inc., Cincinnati, OH, pg. 1206
Killinger, Kerry K., Chm. Bd., Chief Exec. Officer & Pres.--Washington Mutual Savings Bank, Seattle, WA, pg. 1166
Kim, Edward, Pres., Chief Oper. & Chief Exec. Officer--Ronald Hsu Construction, Capitol Heights, MD, pg. 548
Kim, James J., Chm. & Chief Exec. Officer--Amkor Electronics, Inc., West Chester, PA, pg. 67
Kim, Kenneth H., Chm., Pres., Chief Exec. Officer, Corp. Sec. & Treas.--Medieval Dinner & Tournament, Inc., Buena Park, CA, pg. 735
Kimbrell, W. Duke, Chm. Bd. & Chief Exec. Officer--Parkdale Mills, Gastonia, NC, pg. 849
Kimmel, Sidney, Chm. Bd. & Chief Exec. Officer--Jones Apparel Group, Inc., Bristol, PA, pg. 602
King, Arthur, Chief Exec. Officer--Circle A.W. Products, Co., Portland, OR, pg. 250
King, John, Chm. & Chief Exec. Officer--Sunox, Inc., Charlotte, NC, pg. 1062
King, Leroy A. Jr., Chm Bd. & Chief Exec. Officer--Tighe Industries, Inc., York, PA, pg. 1097
King, Tommy, Pres. & Chief Exec. Officer--Western Trailer Equipment & Manufacturing Co., Abilene, TX, pg. 1182
Kinning, Ronald L., Chm. Bd. & Chief Exec. Officer--RK Mechanical, Inc., Lakewood, CO, pg. 907
Kipping, Arthur, Pres. & Chief Exec. Officer--Ray-Carroll County Grain Co-op, Richmond, MO, pg. 914
Kirk, Chester H., Chm. Bd. & Chief Exec. Officer--Amtrol Inc., West Warwick, RI, pg. 70
Kirk, Thomas L., Chm. Bd. & Pres. & Chief Exec. Office--Kirk-Mayer, Inc., Los Angeles, CA, pg. 633
Kirkwood, J.H., Chm., Pres. & Chief Exec. Officer--Edgewater Corporation, Oakmont, PA, pg. 368
Kiser, Walter T., Chm. Bd. & Chief Exec. Officer--Law Engineering, Inc., Atlanta, GA, pg. 661
Kittedge, Joseph B., Pres. & Exec. Oper. Officer--Tilcon, Inc., New Britain, CT, pg. 1097
Klaus, L. George, Chm. Bd., Pres. & Chief Exec. Officer--Integral Systems, Walnut Creek, CA, pg. 572
Klaus, Robert, Pres. & Chief Exec. Officer--Klaus Radio Inc., Peoria, IL, pg. 634
Klein, Calvin, Pres. & Chief Exec. Officer--Calvin Klein, Inc., New York, NY, pg. 635
Klein, Margaret, Chief Exec. Officer & Chief Fin. Officer--Wyatt Inc., Branford, CT, pg. 1205
Klein, Michael S., Chm. Bd. & Chief Exec. Officer--Klein Tools Inc., Skokie, IL, pg. 635
Kleinrock, Dr. Leonard, Chm. Bd. & Chief Exec. Officer--Technology Transfer Institute, Santa Monica, CA, pg. 1084
Klevay, Walter S., Sr., Chm. & Chief Exec. Officer--Kleco Corp., Brecksville, OH, pg. 634
Klibert, Jeffery M., Pres. & Chief Exec. Officer--Lift-All Co., Inc., Manheim, PA, pg. 675
Kling, Thomas R., Pres.--Philadelphia Gear Corp., King of Prussia, PA, pg. 866
Klink, Patricia W. DeBlank, Pres. & Chief Exec. Officer--Advisers Capital Management Inc., New York, NY, pg. 21
Klym, Richard W., Pres. & Chief Exec. Officer--Kirkwood Industries, Inc., Cleveland, OH, pg. 633
Knape, Anthony, Chief Exec. Officer--Knape & Knape, Dallas, TX, pg. 636
Knapp, Betsy Wood, Pres. & Chief Exec. Officer--Wood Knapp & Co., Inc., Los Angeles, CA, pg. 636
Knapp, Cleon T., Chm. & Chief Exec. Officer--Architectural Digest, Los Angeles, CA, pg. 636
Knapp, Cleon T., Chm. & Chief Exec. Officer--Bon Appetit Magazine, Los Angeles, CA, pg. 636
Knapp, Jules F., Chm. Bd., Pres. & Chief Exec. Officer--United Coatings, Inc., Kankakee, IL, pg. 1131
Knauss, Donald T., Chm. Bd. & Chief Exec. Officer--E.W. Knauss & Son, Inc., Quakertown, PA, pg. 636
Knauss, E. William, Pres., Chief Oper. Officer & Treas.--E.W. Knauss & Son, Inc., Quakertown, PA, pg. 636
Knight, J.A., Chief Exec. Officer--Heat Controller, Inc., Jackson, MI, pg. 524
Knight, Michael, Exec. V.P. & Chief Oper. Officer--SBN Systems Inc.-Corporate, Mississauga,, Canada, pg. 960
Knighton, Ernest S., Chief Exec. Officer--United Piece Dye Works, LP, Princeton Junction, NJ, pg. 1134
Knipfing, G.R., Chm., Pres. & Chief Exec. Officer--Scheduling Technology Corporation, Hopkinton, MA, pg. 975
Knoll, James B., Pres. & Chief Exec. Officer--Specialty Equipment Companies Inc., Belvidere, IL, pg. 1027
Knudson, Gerald, Pres. & Chief Exec. Officer--Resonex, Inc., Sunnyvale, CA, pg. 929
Kobacker, Arthur J., Chm. Bd. & Chief Exec. Officer--The Kobacker Company & Affiliates, Columbus, OH, pg. 638
Koch, Charles G., Chm. Bd. & Chief Exec. Officer--Koch Industries, Incorporated, Wichita, KS, pg. 639
Koch, Robert L. II, Pres. & Chief Exec. Officer--George Koch Sons, Inc., Evansville, IN, pg. 639
Koch, Robert L., II, Chm. Bd. & Chief Exec. Officer--Gibbs Diecasting Aluminum Corp., Henderson, KY, pg. 639
Koehl, Hans H., Chm. Bd. & Chief Exec. Officer--Spirol International Corp., Danielson, CT, pg. 1031
Koehlinger, A.W., Pres. & Chief Exec. Officer--R. A. Jones & Co. Inc., Covington, KY, pg. 604
Koenigsberg, William A., Pres. & Chief Exec. Officer--Horizon Media, Inc., New York, NY, pg. 544
Koenitzer, John E., Pres. & Chief Exec. Officer--Helwig Carbon Products, Inc., Milwaukee, WI, pg. 528
Koeppel, Martin, Chief Exec. Officer--Hughes-Treitler Manufacturing Corporation, Garden City, NY, pg. 552
Koetters, Ronald A., Chm. Bd. & Chief Exec. Officer--Monarch Construction Company, Cincinnati, OH, pg. 765
Koffman, Robert G., Pres. & Chief Exec. Officer--United Stores, Bay City, MI, pg. 1137
Kohler, Freya, Chief Exec. Officer--Komplettburo GmbH, Internationale Kommunikation, Munich, Germany, pg. 625
Kohler, Herbert V., Jr., Chm. Bd., Pres., Chief Oper. & Chief Exec. Officer--Kohler Company, Kohler, WI, pg. 639
Kohn, Eric F., Vice Chm. & Chief Exec. Officer--Holmes Protection Group, Inc., New York, NY, pg. 540
Kohtz, Alan, Chief Exec. Officer--Consolidated Co-op, Gowrie, IA, pg. 276
Kolikof, Robert A., Pres., Chief Exec. Officer & Chief Oper. Officer--Prudential Metal Supply Corp., East Dedham, MA, pg. 898
Koll, Donald M., Chm. Bd. & Chief Exec. Officer--Koll Co., Newport Beach, CA, pg. 641
Kolvenbach, Donald M., Pres., Chief Exec. Officer & Chief Oper. Officer--Affiliated of Florida Inc., Tampa, FL, pg. 23
Komar, Charles E., Pres. & Chief Exec. Officer--Charles Komar & Sons, Inc., New York, NY, pg. 641
Komar, David L., Exec. V.P.--Charles Komar & Sons, Inc., New York, NY, pg. 641
Konheim, B. Brad, Pres. & Chief Exec. Officer--Kobra International Ltd, New York, NY, pg. 638
Konig, Thomas, Pres. & Chief Exec. Officer--Meritcare, Inc., Pittsburgh, PA, pg. 740
Koontz, James L., Pres. & Chief Exec. Officer--Kingsbury Corporation, Keene, NH, pg. 631
Kopelman, David W., Chm. Bd.--The W.B. Wood Company, New Providence, NJ, pg. 1199
Kopko, Edward M., Chm. Bd., Pres., Chief Exec. & Chief Oper. Officer--Butler International, Montvale, NJ, pg. 197
Kopp, Charles G., Chief Exec. Officer--Wolf, Block, Schorr & Solis-Cohen, Philadelphia, PA, pg. 1199
Korn, Mel R., Pres. & Chief Exec. Officer--Geographic Marketing Group (GMG), Philadelphia, PA, pg. 452
Korsmeier, Gary, Chief Exec. Officer--California Milk Producers, Artesia, CA, pg. 210
Kosack, Eugene, Chief Exec. Officer--NBO Stores Inc., Fair Lawn, NJ, pg. 780
Kosel, Howard E., Chief Exec. Officer--Sathers Inc., Round Lake, MN, pg. 972
Koshizawa, Shoji, Pres., Chief Exec. Officer--Chuo Senko Advertising Co., Ltd., Tokyo, Japan, pg. 103
Kosloff, Alan, Chm. Bd., Chief Exec. Officer & Pres.--American Marketing Industries, Inc., Kansas City, MO, pg. 58
Kovac, F. Peter, Pres., Chief Exec. Officer--NKH&W, Inc., Kansas City, MO, pg. 781
Kramer, Arnold A., Pres. & Chief Exec. Officer--Trimfit, Inc., Philadelphia, PA, pg. 1113
Kramer, Dale, Pres. & Chief Exec. Officer--ShopKo Stores, Inc., Green Bay, WI, pg. 1000
Kramer, Gordon M., Chm. Bd., Pres. & Chief Exec. Officer--Continental Plastic Card Co., Coral Springs, FL, pg. 280
Krantz, John F., Chief Exec. Officer & Treas.--Adventure Lands of America, Inc., Des Moines, IA, pg. 21
Krasne, Charles A., Pres. & Chief Exec. Officer--Krasdale Foods Inc., Bronx, NY, pg. 644
Krebel, Albert D., Pres. & Chief Exec. Officer--Reed & Barton Corporation, Taunton, MA, pg. 920
Kreitzberg, Richard A., Pres. & Chief Exec. Officer--Microflect Company, Inc., Salem, OR, pg. 749
Kreitzer, Roderick G., Pres. & Chief Exec. Officer--Baker Knapp & Tubbs Inc., Grand Rapids, MI, pg. 640
Kress, James F., Pres. & Chief Exec. Officer--Green Bay Packaging Inc., Green Bay, WI, pg. 483
Kresser, Bob, Chm. & Chief Exec. Officer--Kresser/Craig, Santa Monica, CA, pg. 644
Kroetch, Arthur, Chm. Bd., Pres. & Chief Exec. Officer--Scotchman Industries, Inc., Philip, SD, pg. 982
Kroll, Alex, Chm. & Chief Exec. Officer--Young & Rubicam Inc., New York, NY, pg. 1210
Krommenhoek, William, Chief Exec. Officer--Krommenhoek McKeown Associates, San Diego, CA, pg. 645
Kronfeld, Fred N., Chief Exec. & Chief Fin. Officer & Treas.--Spirite Industries, Inc., Englewood, NJ, pg. 1031
Krueger, Robert A., Pres., Chief Exec. Officer & Treas.--Tri-Mark Metal Corp., Detroit, MI, pg. 1110
Krulik, Lawrence, Chm. Bd.--United States Luggage Company, Hauppauge, NY, pg. 1136
Krum, Frank, Pres. & Chief Exec. Officer--Golden Cat Corporation, South Bend, IN, pg. 637
Kruse, Ed F., Chm. & Chief Exec. Officer--Blue Bell Creameries, Inc., Brenham, TX, pg. 158
Kruse, Mitchell, Pres., Chief Exec. Officer & Auctioneer--Kruse International, Auburn, IN, pg. 645
Krusha, Kenneth J., Pres. & Chief Exec. Officer--J.H. Findorff & Son, Inc., Madison, WI, pg. 411
Kuban, William G., Pres., Chief Exec. Officer & Treas.--Kurt Manufacturing Co. Inc., Fridley, MN, pg. 646
Kubovic, John W., Pres. & Chief Exec. Officer--The Nash Engineering Company, Norwalk, CT, pg. 783
Kuehne, Carl, Chief Exec. Officer--American Foods Group, Green Bay, WI, pg. 54
Kuehne, Carl W., Pres. & Chief Exec. Officer--American Foods Group, Inc., Minneapolis, MN, pg. 54
Kughn, Richard P., Chm. Bd. & Chief Exec. Officer--Lionel Trains, Inc., Chesterfield, MI, pg. 677
Kujovich, L., Pres. & Chief Exec. Officer--Dietzgen Corporation, Des Plaines, IL, pg. 337
Kukla, Stanley J., Chm. Bd. & Chief Exec. Officer--Kukla Press, Inc., Elk Grove Village, IL, pg. 646
Kummer, Fred S., Chm., Pres., Chief Exec. Officer, Treas. & Founder--HBE Corporation, Saint Louis, MO, pg. 495
Kupperman, Melvin, Pres. & Chief Exec. Officer--A. Epstein and Sons, Intl., Inc., Chicago, IL, pg. 384
Kurz, Kelli McDonald, Pres. & Chief Oper. Officer (Denver) & Dir.--EvansGroup, Salt Lake City, UT, pg. 390
Kurz, Milton, Chief Exec. Officer--Apex Mills Corporation, Inwood, NY, pg. 78
Kurzweg, Victor J., III, Chm. Bd. & Chief Exec. Officer--Consolidated Companies Inc. (CONCO), Metairie, LA, pg. 276
Kwader, Alex, Pres., Chief Exec. Officer & Gen. Mgr.--Specialty Paperboard Inc., Brattleboro, VT, pg. 1027
LaBarba, Lucian M., Pres. & Chief Exec. Officer--American Produce & Vegetable Co., Dallas, TX, pg. 59
Labovitz, George H., Dr., Chm. Bd., Pres. & Chief Exec. Officer--ODI, Burlington, MA, pg. 818
Lacomis, Bernard J., Pres. & Chief Exec. Officer--Arthur D. Little Enterprises, Inc., Cambridge, MA, pg. 679
Lacourciere, William J., Chief Exec. Officer, Chm. Bd., Pres.--Novametrix Medical Systems Inc., Wallingford, CT, pg. 817
Lacy, Andre B., Chm., Pres. & Chief Exec. Officer--LDI, Ltd., Indianapolis, IN, pg. 647
Lacy, Roane, Jr., Chief Exec. Officer--Plantation Foods Inc., Waco, TX, pg. 874
Ladds, H.P., Jr., Pres. & Chief Exec. Officer--Columbus McKinnon Corp., Amherst, NY, pg. 266
Ladish, John H., Chm. Bd. & Chief Exec. Officer--Ladish Malting Co., Milwaukee, WI, pg. 219
Lafaye, Jean-Paul, Pres. & Chief Exec. Officer-Worldwide--Cato Johnson Worldwide, New York, NY, pg. 1210
Lafayette, Maurice, Jr., Pres. & Chief Exec. Officer--Lafayette Manufacturing, Inc., Hayward, CA, pg. 650
LaFlamme, Lon, Pres. & Chief Exec. Officer (Seattle) & Dir.--EvansGroup, Salt Lake City, UT, pg. 390
Lafleur, Georges, Pres. & Chief Exec. Officer--Lowe Troost S.A., Brussels,, Belgium, pg. 685
LaFond, Jerry, Chief Exec. Officer--The Asher Winer Company, Fitchburg, MA, pg. 88
Lahr, Angela, Treas, Controller, Chief Exec. & Fin. Officer--CAC Microcircuits, Inc., Mount Carmel, IL, pg. 198
LaMantia, Charles R., Pres. & Chief Exec. Officer--Arthur D. Little, Inc., Cambridge, MA, pg. 678
LaMarca, James, Chm. Bd., Pres. & Chief Exec. Officer--LaMarca Group Inc., New York, NY, pg. 652
Lamb, Joseph S., Pres. & Chief Exec. Officer--Bank Of North Dakota, Bismarck, ND, pg. 117
Lambesis, Nicholas, Pres. & Chief Exec. Officer--Lambesis Communications, San Diego, CA, pg. 652
Lammie, J.L., Pres. & Chief Exec. Officer--Parsons Brinckerhoff Inc., New York, NY, pg. 850
Lamoreux, F. Holmes, Chm. Bd., Pres. & Chief Exec. Officer--Sabreliner Corp., Chesterfield, MO, pg. 965
Landau, Roy, Chm. Bd., Pres. & Chief Exec. & Chief Fin. Officer--Landau Building Co., Wexford, PA, pg. 654
Landel, Michael, Pres. & Chief Exec. Officer--Seiler Corporation, Waltham, MA, pg. 987
Landey, Martin H., Chm. & Chief Exec. Officer--Cox Landey and Partners, Inc., New York, NY, pg. 294
Lane, Edward B., Chm. & Chief Exec. Officer--E. B. Lane & Associates, Inc., Phoenix, AZ, pg. 656
Lane, Leonard C., Chm. Bd. & Chief Exec. Officer--ILC Industries, Inc., Bohemia, NY, pg. 560
Lane, William N., III, Chm. Bd., Pres. & Chief Exec. Officer--Lane Industries, Inc., Northbrook, IL, pg. 656
Lang, Henry S., Chm. Bd., Pres. & Chief Exec. Officer--Home Juice Company, Melrose Park, IL, pg. 541
Lang, Robert H., Jr., Pres. & Chief Exec. Officer--Horn Packaging Corporation, Ayer, MA, pg. 544
Lange, Chadwick S., Pres.--Owatonna Canning Company, Owatonna, MN, pg. 833
Langer, David, Pres., Chief Exec. & Chief Oper. Officer & Treas.--David Langer & Co., Inc., Hollywood, CA, pg. 657
Langone, Kenneth G., Chm. Bd. & Chief Exec. Officer--Salem National Corporation, Winston-Salem, NC, pg. 967
Lanier, J.L., Jr., Chm. Bd. & Chief Exec. Officer--Dan River Inc., Danville, VA, pg. 313
Lapides, Morton M., Chm. Bd., Pres. & Chief Exec. Officer--Alleco Inc., Cheverly, MD, pg. 35
LaPointe, Robert E., Chm. & Chief Exec. Officer--Tallant LaPointe & Partners, Inc., San Francisco, CA, pg. 1077
Larned, Gardner, Chm. Bd., Pres., & Chief Exec. Officer--Berry Bearing Co., Lyons, IL, pg. 144
LaRosa, Joseph, Chm. & Co-Chief Exec. Officer--Waring & LaRosa, Inc., New York, NY, pg. 1163
Lash, James A., Chm. Bd.--Reading Tube Corp., Reading, PA, pg. 916
Lass, E. Donald, Pres., Editor & Chief Exec. Officer--New Jersey Press, Inc., Neptune, NJ, pg. 801
Lauder, Leonard, Pres. & Chief Exec. Officer--Estee Lauder, Inc., New York, NY, pg. 389
Lauren, Ralph, Chm. Bd.--Polo/Ralph Lauren Corporation, New York, NY, pg. 879
Laverdiere, Stephen, Pres. & Chief Exec. Officer--Laverdiere's Enterprises, Winslow, ME, pg. 661
Laviers, Harry, Jr., Pres. & Chief Exec. Officer--South East Coal Co., Irvine, KY, pg. 1019
Lavin, Ed., Jr., Chief Exec. Officer--Wiltel Communications Systems, Inc., The Woodlands, TX, pg. 1194
Lawernce, W. Larry Jr., Pres. & Chief Exec. Officer--Sunline Coach Co., Inc., Denver, PA, pg. 1061
Lawrence, David, Dr., Chief Exec. Officer--Kaiser Foundation Health & Hospitals Group, Oakland, CA, pg. 614
Lawrence, E.W. III, Chm. Bd. & Chief Exec. Officer--Orbitair International Ltd., New York, NY, pg. 828
Lay, Joe L., Jr., Chm. Bd., Pres. & Chief Exec. Officer--Lay Packing Company Inc., Knoxville, TN, pg. 663
Layden, A.J., Chm. Bd. & Chief Exec. Officer--Allright Corporation, Houston, TX, pg. 41
Lea, George A. Jr., Chm. Bd., Pres. & Chief Exec. Officer--The Mad Butcher, Inc., Pine Bluff, AR, pg. 699
Leary, William, Chief Exec. Officer & V.P.--Pen-Tab Industries, Inc., Glendale, NY, pg. 856
Leasure, George, Pres., Chief Exec. & Chief Fin. Officer & Treas.--Ghent Manufacturing, Inc., Lebanon, OH, pg. 455

Leavitt, Julian, Chm. Bd., Pres., Chief Exec. Officer & Treas.--Sweetlife Foods, Inc., Suffield, CT, pg. 1067
Lebel, Alfred J., Pres. & Chief Exec. Officer--Bates Fabrics, Inc., Lewiston, ME, pg. 125
Lebensfeld, Harry, Chm. Bd. & Chief Exec. Officer--UIS, Inc., New York, NY, pg. 1123
Lecamp, Yannick, Gen. Mgr.--Cargill Petroleum, Inc., Chelsea, MA, pg. 219
Lechmann, Ewald, Pres. & Chief Exec. Officer--Wollin Products, Inc., Stevensville, MI, pg. 1199
Leckinger, Robert, Chief Exec. Officer--DeWolfe & Fiske Inc., Canton, MA, pg. 237
Leckinger, Robert, Chief Exec. Officer--Lauriat Inc., Canton, MA, pg. 237
Lee, Andrew, Chief Exec. Officer--Lee Davis Ayer, Hong Kong,, Hong Kong, pg. 104
Lee, John E., Pres. & Chief Exec. Officer--Carver, Inc., Garden City, GA, pg. 227
Lee, John E., Pres. & Chief Exec. Officer--Murray-Carver, East Bridgewater, MA, pg. 776
Lee, Rhoady R., Jr., Chm. Bd. & Chief Exec. Officer--Lakeside Industries, Redmond, WA, pg. 651
Lee, W.H., Chm. Bd. & Chief Exec. Officer--Zimdar Enterprises, Wyoming, MI, pg. 1220
Lee, Weldon A., Pres., Chief Exec. Officer--Atlantic Builders Group Inc., Baltimore, MD, pg. 94
Leeds, Michael S., Pres. & Chief Exec. Officer--C M P Publications, Inc., Manhasset, NY, pg. 202
Leef, George L., Chm. Bd. & Chief Exec. Officer--Industrial Towel & Uniform, New Berlin, WI, pg. 567
Leffingwell, Dean, Chm. & Chief Exec. Officer--RELA, Inc., Boulder, CO, pg. 924
Lefkowitz, Abraham, Chief Exec. Officer--Crystal Clear Industries Company, Ridgefield Park, NJ, pg. 303
Lefler, R. Stephen, Pres. & Chief Exec. Officer--Williamson-Dickie Mfg. Co., Fort Worth, TX, pg. 1192
LeFort, Leo J., Chm., Chief Exec. Officer--Arocom Direct, Inc., Cleveland, OH, pg. 737
LeFort, Leo J., Chm., Chief Exec. Officer--Arocom Marketing Group, Inc., Cleveland, OH, pg. 737
Lefton, Al Paul Jr., Pres. & Chief Exec. Officer--Al Paul Lefton Co., Inc., Philadelphia, PA, pg. 666
Legus, James P., Chm. Bd. & Chief Exec. Officer--Magnetic Data, Inc., Eden Prairie, MN, pg. 700
Lehmann, John, Chm. Bd., Pres. & Chief Exec. Officer--Butterick Company, Inc., New York, NY, pg. 197
Lehmer, Thomas W., Chief Exec. Officer--Prepco, Los Angeles, CA, pg. 887
Lehr, Don, Chm. Bd. & Chief Exec. Officer--Cubix Corporation, Carson City, NV, pg. 303
Lehr, Gustav J., Chm. Bd. & Chief Exec. Officer--Shelter Mutual Insurance Company, Columbia, MO, pg. 997
Leinniger, David L., Chm. Bd. & Chief Exec. Officer--Club Corp Realty, Dallas, TX, pg. 256
Leinweber, John L., Pres. & Chief Exec. Officer--American Office Equipment, La Grange, IL, pg. 58
Leipsner, Stephen R., Chm., Pres. & Chief Exec. Officer--S & A Restaurant Corp., Dallas, TX, pg. 958
Lemon, James H., Jr., Chm. Bd. & Chief Exec. Officer--Johnston, Lemon & Co. Inc., Washington, DC, pg. 601
Leonard, Bruce N., Chm. & Chief Exec. Officer--Leonard Monahan Lubars & Kelly, Providence, RI, pg. 668
Leonsis, Ted, Chm. Bd., Chief Exec. Officer, Pres. & New Bus. Contact--Redgate Communications Corp., Vero Beach, FL, pg. 919
Lepape, H. E., Chm. Bd. & Chief Exec. Officer--Pacific Enterprises Oil Company (USA), Dallas, TX, pg. 840
Lepore, Alfred, Pres.--Ferrara Foods & Confections, Inc., New York, NY, pg. 407
Lervick, Arne T., Chm. Bd. & Chief Exec. Officer--Twin City Foods, Inc., Stanwood, WA, pg. 1122
LeSage, William A., Chm. Bd & Chief Exec. Officer--General Homes Corporation, Houston, TX, pg. 449
Lescroart, Emmett J., Chief Exec. Officer--Cooperheat, Inc., Piscataway, NJ, pg. 283
Lesswing, Grant, Chm. Bd. & Chief Exec. Officer--Nuttall Equipment Co. Inc., Sherman, NY, pg. 818
Letven, Edward, Chm. & Chief Exec. Officer--Letven-Diccicco, Inc., Horsham, PA, pg. 669
Levenson, Barbara L., Pres. & Chief Exec. Officer--Levenson & Hill, Inc., Irving, TX, pg. 670
Levenson, Stanley R., Chief Exec. Officer & Dir.-Pub. Rels.--Levenson & Hill, Inc., Irving, TX, pg. 670
Levin, Jerry W., Pres. & Chief Exec. Officer--Revlon, Inc., New York, NY, pg. 696
Levin, Michael S., Pres. & Chief Exec. Officer--Titan Industrial Corp., New York, NY, pg. 1099
Levine, Richard, Pres. & Chief Exec. Officer--Alleson of Rochester, Inc., Rochester, NY, pg. 37
Leviton, H., Pres.--Leviton Mfg. Co., Inc., Little Neck, NY, pg. 671
Levy, Barry W., Chm. Bd., Chief Exec. Officer & Communications Dir.--Levy Security Consultants, Limited, Chicago, IL, pg. 672
Levy, Frank L., Pres. & Chief Exec. Officer--L & L Oil Company, Inc., Metairie, LA, pg. 647
Levy, Nessim, Pres. & Chief Exec. Officer--Level Export Sales Corp., New York, NY, pg. 670
Levy, Sam, Chief Exec. Officer--Mactavish Machine Manufacturing Company, Richmond, VA, pg. 698
Lewis, Alan G., Chief Exec. Officer--Gerber Plumbing Fixtures Corporation, Chicago, IL, pg. 454
Lewis, Alan G., Chief Exec. Officer--Kokomo Sanitary Pottery Corp., Chicago, IL, pg. 640
Lewis, Byron E., Chm. & Chief Exec. Officer--Uniworld Group, Inc., New York, NY, pg. 1139
Lewis, Clive, Chm. & Chief Exec. Officer--Lewis & Gace, Inc., Fort Lee, NJ, pg. 673
Lewis, Donald D., Pres. & Chief Exec. Officer--Donald D. Lewis Advertising, Burbank, CA, pg. 672
Lewis, George T., Chm. Bd. & Chief Exec. Officer--Cogentrix Incorporated, Charlotte, NC, pg. 258
Lewis, Jesse, Chm. Bd., Pres. & Chief Exec. Officer--Consumers Markets Inc., Springfield, MO, pg. 277
Lewis, John, Chm. Bd. & Chief Exec. Officer- AmeriServ Food Company, Dallas, TX, pg. 66
Lewis, R. Jack, Jr., Pres. & Chief Exec. Officer--Lewis Brothers Bakeries, Inc., Evansville, IN, pg. 673
Lewis, William, Chm. Bd., Pres. & Chief Exec. Officer--Career Blazers Inc., New York, NY, pg. 218
Liautaud, James P., Chm. Bd. & Chief Exec. Officer--Capsonic Group, Inc., Elgin, IL, pg. 216
Liban, G., Chm. Bd. & Chief Exec. Officer--Heresite Protective Coatings Inc., Manitowoc, WI, pg. 531
Libera, John, Chm. Bd. & Chief Exec. Officer--Victor Corporation, West Warwick, RI, pg. 1149
Lichter, Robert, Pres. & Chief Exec. Officer--John Burnham & Co., San Diego, CA, pg. 194
Liddy, Richard A., Pres. & Chief Exec. Officer--General American Life Insurance Co., St. Louis, MO, pg. 448
Liebenow, Larry, Pres. & Chief Exec. Officer--Quaker Fabric Corporation, Fall River, MA, pg. 903
Lieberman, Stephen, Pres., Chief Exec. & Chief Oper. Officer--Carousel Snack Bars Of Minnesota, Minneapolis, MN, pg. 224
Liebermann, Thomas R., Chm Bd., Pres, & Chief Oper. Officer--Kaye Instruments, Inc., Bedford, MA, pg. 619
Lienau, Anthony, Chief Exec. Officer--Trend Offset Printing Services, Los Alamitos, CA, pg. 1109
Lieppe, Charles, Pres. & Chief Exec. Officer--Pen Holdings, Inc., Brentwood, TN, pg. 856
Lilly, Ed, Pres. & Chief Exec. Officer--Serta, Inc., Des Plaines, IL, pg. 991
Linbeck, Leo E., Jr., Chm. Bd. & Chief Exec. Officer--Linbeck Corp., Houston, TX, pg. 675
Lindahl, John, Chm. Bd. & Chief Exec. Officer--State Industries Inc., Ashland City, TN, pg. 1041
Lindemann, D.L., Pres. & Chief Exec. Officer--Citizens Gas & Coke Utility, Indianapolis, IN, pg. 250
Linder, S. Craig, Chief Exec. Officer-Spelling Entertainment Inc.--American Financial Corporation, Cincinnati, OH, pg. 52
Lindner, Carl H., Chm. Bd. & Chief Exec. Officer--American Financial Corporation, Cincinnati, OH, pg. 52
Lindner, Carl H., Chm. Bd. & Chief Exec. Officer--Chiquita Brands International, Inc., Cincinnati, OH, pg. 53
Lindner, Carl H., Chm. & Chief Exec. Officer--Great American Communications Company, Cincinnati, OH, pg. 53
Lindner, Carl H., Chm. Bd. & Chief Exec. Officer--Spelling Entertainment Group, Inc., Cincinnati, OH, pg. 54
Lindsay, James W., Chief Exec. Officer--Ag Processing Inc A Cooperative, Omaha, NE, pg. 24
Lindsay, Marsha, Pres. & Chief Exec. Officer--Lindsay, Stone & Briggs Advertising, Inc., Madison, WI, pg. 676
Lindsay, Winston S., III, Chm. Bd. & Chief Exec. Officer--Lindsay Manufacturing Inc., Ponca City, OK, pg. 676
Lindsey, Harold D., Chief Oper. Officer, Chief Fin. Officer, & V.P.--Bader & Co., Ipava, IL, pg. 113
Ling, John, Pres. & Chief Exec. Officer--Bettcher Manufacturing Corp., Cleveland, OH, pg. 148
Liniger, Gail, Chief Exec. Officer--RE/MAX International, Inc., Englewood, CO, pg. 915
Linsalata, Frank, Chief Exec. Officer--Somerset Technologies, Inc., Somerset, NJ, pg. 1017
Lipari, Francis J., Pres. & Chief Exec. Officer--Communication & Design Agency Inc., Latham, NY, pg. 269
Lipke, Brian J., Pres. & Chief Exec. Officer--Gibraltar Steel Corp., Buffalo, NY, pg. 456
Lipman, Harry, Chm. Bd. & Chief Exec. Officer--Jameco Industries, Inc., Wyandanch, NY, pg. 588
Lipner, William E., Pres. & Chief Exec. Officer--NFO Research, Inc., Greenwich, CT, pg. 780
Lippe, George, Pres. & Chief Exec. Officer--Trammell Crow Company, Dallas, TX, pg. 1106
Lipscomb, Michael S., Pres. & Chief Exec. Officer--Argo-Tech Corporation, Cleveland, OH, pg. 82
Lipsky, Jeff, Chm. Bd.--October Films, Inc., New York, NY, pg. 821
Lipton, Harry, Pres. & Chief Exec. Officer--American Aircraft Parts Manufacturing Co., Dearborn, MI, pg. 48
Lisker, Lawrence, Chief Exec. Officer & Treas.--Antwerp Diamond Distributors Inc., New York, NY, pg. 77
Litewka, Albert, Pres. & Chief Exec. Officer--Jacobs & Gerber, Inc., Los Angeles, CA, pg. 587
Littlejohn, B.R., III, Pres. & Chief Exec. Officer--Community Cash Stores, Spartanburg, SC, pg. 270
Litvak, Leonard, Chm. Bd., Pres. & Chief Exec. Officer--Champion Boxed Beef, Denver, CO, pg. 238
Litzsinger, Paul R., Pres. & Chief Exec. Officer--Follett Corporation, Chicago, IL, pg. 422
Liuzzi, R.C., Pres. & Chief Exec. Officer--CF Industries, Inc., Long Grove, IL, pg. 200
Livingston, Phil K., Pres. & Chief Exec. Officer--Citizens National Bancshares Inc., Hammond, LA, pg. 250
Livingston, Robert, Chm., Pres. & Chief Exec. Officer--Grand Banks Yachts, Ltd., Greenwich, CT, pg. 475
Livingston, Roger, Pres. & Chief Exec. Officer--Livingston & Company, Seattle, WA, pg. 679
Livingston, Roger, Pres. & Chief Exec. Officer--Livingston + Keye, Venice, CA, pg. 679
Ljungberg, Robert, Chm. Bd., Pres., Chief Exec. & Chief Oper. Officer--Ultra Tool & Plastics, Inc., Amherst, NY, pg. 1125
Llewellyn, John S., Jr., Pres. & Chief Exec. Officer--Ocean Spray Cranberries, Inc., Lakeville, MA, pg. 820
Lloyd, David R., Vice Chm. & Chief Exec. Officer--Putt Putt Golf Courses of America, Inc., Fayetteville, NC, pg. 901
Lloyd, David R., Vice Chm., Chief Exec. Officer & Commissioner--Professional Putters Association, Fayetteville, NC, pg. 901
Lockwood, Earl F., Pres. & Chief Exec. Officer--Betac International Corporation, Alexandria, VA, pg. 147
Lockwood, Robert, Pres.& Chief Exec. Officer--Our Sunday Visitor, Inc., Huntington, IN, pg. 832
Lohman, Gordon R., Pres. & Chief Exec. Officer--Amsted Industries Incorporated, Chicago, IL, pg. 68
Lois, George, Chm. & Chief Exec. Officer--Lois/USA, New York, NY, pg. 681
Long, C.D., Chm. Bd. & Chief Exec. Officer--Krystal Company, Chattanooga, TN, pg. 645
Long, David R., Pres. & Chief Exec. Officer--Rice Growers Association of California, West Sacramento, CA, pg. 931
Long, Donald J., Chm. Bd. & Chief Exec. Officer--Imperial, Inc., Green Bay, WI, pg. 564
Longacre, Kenneth A., Chief Exec. Officer--Farm & Home Oil Company, Telford, PA, pg. 401
Longsworth, Charles, Chm., Pres. & Chief Exec. Officer--Colonial Williamsburg Foundation, Williamsburg, VA, pg. 264
Lorch, Ernest H., Chm. Bd. & Chief Exec. Officer--The Dyson-Kissner-Moran Corporation, New York, NY, pg. 357
Lorch, Ernest H., Chm. & Chief Exec. Officer--DKM, Ltd., New York, NY, pg. 357
Lotter, John G.H., Chm. Bd. & Chief Exec. Officer--H. C. Miller Company, Milwaukee, WI, pg. 754
Loughlin, Richard J., Pres. & Chief Exec. Officer--Century 21 Real Estate Corp., Irvine, CA, pg. 744
Lowe, Thomas P., Pres.--Lyman Lumber Company, Excelsior, MN, pg. 689
Lowenstein, G.W., Chief Exec. Officer--Harlan Electric Co., Southfield, MI, pg. 509
Lowrey, W.A., Chm. Bd., Pres. & Chief Exec. Officer--DDC PerTec, Tucson, AZ, pg. 308
Lowy, Rudolph, Chm. Bd., Pres. & Chief Exec. Officer--Pacific States Casualty Co., Los Angeles, CA, pg. 841
Lozelle, James R., Pres. & Chief Exec. Officer--Edgewood Tool & Manufacturing Company, Romulus, MI, pg. 368
Lozier, Allan, Chief Exec. Officer--Lozier Corporation, Omaha, NE, pg. 686
Luddy, Robert, Pres. & Chief Exec. Officer--Captive-Aire Systems, Inc., Youngsville, NC, pg. 216
Ludington, Ivan, Jr., Chm Bd. & Chief Exec. Officer--Ludington News Co. Inc., Detroit, MI, pg. 686
Ludt, S.G., Pres., Chief Exec. Officer & Treas.--Columbian Rope Company, Guntown, MS, pg. 266
Luecke, David A., Pres. & Chief Exec. Officer--Riemeier Lumber Company, Inc., Cincinnati, OH, pg. 934
Lumpkin, Richard A., Chm. Bd. & Chief Exec. Officer--Illinois Consolidated Telephone Co., Mattoon, IL, pg. 563
Lundeen, Mark, Pres. & Chief Exec. Officer--Buzz Barton & Associates, Inc., Oak Brook, IL, pg. 123
Luntz, John, Chm. Bd.--Luntz Corporation, Canton, OH, pg. 687
Lustbader, Edward E., Chm. Bd., Pres., Chief Exec. Officer & Treas.--The P.J. Carlin Construction Company, New Rochelle, NY, pg. 220
Lyman, James M., Pres. & Chief Exec. Officer--Industrial General Corporation, Elyria, OH, pg. 566
Lynch, Joseph E., Exec. V.P., Chief Exec. & Fin. Officer--Boston Trading Ltd. Inc., Lynn, MA, pg. 168
Lynch, Leland T., Chm. & Chief Exec. Officer--Carmichael Lynch, Inc., Minneapolis, MN, pg. 222
Lynn, Jeffrey G., Chm. Bd., Pres. & Chief Exec. Officer--Dunham's Athleisure Corporation, Waterford, MI, pg. 353
Lyon, James E., Chm. Bd. & Chief Exec. Officer--Ruska Instrument Corporation, Houston, TX, pg. 956
Lyons, Michael J., Chm. & Chief Exec. & Creative Officer--Dorritie Lyons & Nickel, Inc., New York, NY, pg. 347
Lytle, L. Ben, Pres. & Chief Exec. Officer--The Associated Group, Indianapolis, IN, pg. 90
Lytle, R.D., Chm. Bd., Pres. & Chief Exec. Officer--Star Bronze Company, Alliance, OH, pg. 1039
Maas, Curtis N., Chm. Bd. & Chief Exec. Officer--RDI, Inc., Itasca, IL, pg. 906
Maca, Allen Leigh, Chief Exec. Officer--Sommer & Maca Industries, Inc., Chicago, IL, pg. 1017
MacCready, Paul, Dr., Chm. Bd. & Chief Exec. Officer--Aerovironment, Inc., Monrovia, CA, pg. 22
MacDaniels, John Scott, Chief Exec. Officer & Creative Dir.--MacDaniels, Henry & Sproul, Inc., San Francisco, CA, pg. 696
Macdonald, A. Ewan, Pres. & Chief Exec. Officer--Del Monte Foods, San Francisco, CA, pg. 325
MacDonald, Reid V., Pres. & Chief Exec. Officer--Faribault Foods Inc., Minneapolis, MN, pg. 399
MacDonald, William F., Jr., Chm. Bd., Pres., Chief Exec. & Chief Oper. Officer--E. F. Houghton & Co., Valley Forge, PA, pg. 546
Macfarlane, Iain, Pres. & Chief Exec. Officer--KNOX International Corp., Knoxville, TN, pg. 638
Macfarlane, Iain, Chm. & Chief Exec. Officer--Rockwood Gardens, Ltd., Rockwood,, Canada, pg. 638
MacFarlane, Iain, Chm. & Chief Exec. Officer--Michigan Bulb Company, Grand Rapids, MI, pg. 638
Machado, Gus, Pres. & Chief Exec. Officer--Gus Machado Enterprises, Hialeah, FL, pg. 696
Machamer, J.Q., Chm. Bd. & Chief Exec. Officer--Dyatron/Bondo Corporation, Atlanta, GA, pg. 356
Mackler, Paul, Co.-Chief Exec. Officer--Full Circle Media Corp., Norwalk, CT, pg. 436
MacLeod, Malcolm W., Pres. & Chief Exec. Officer--Moran Towing & Transporation Co. Inc, Greenwich, CT, pg. 769
MacMillan, Whitney, Chm. Bd. & Chief Exec. Officer--Cargill Inc., Wayzata, MN, pg. 219
MacPherson, Angus, Pres. & Chief Exec. Officer--Breton Construction, Inc., Irvine, CA, pg. 174
MacPherson, Donald R., Pres. & Chief Exec. Officer--Red Devil Inc., Union, NJ, pg. 918
MacPherson, Robert W., Chm. Bd. & Chief Exec. Officer--General Latex & Chemical Corporation, Cambridge, MA, pg. 449
MacVittie, Paula R., Pres. & Chief Exec. Officer--Caldwell VanRiper Inc., Indianapolis, IN, pg. 209
Madonna, Jon C., Chm. & Chief Exec. Officer--KPMG Peat Marwick, New York, NY, pg. 613
Madson, Paul C., Chief Exec. Officer--Border States Industries, Inc., Fargo, ND, pg. 165
Maghielse, Craig, Chm. Bd., Pres. & Chief Exec. Officer--Maghielse Tool Corporation, Grand Rapids, MI, pg. 700

Magliocco, John, Chm. Bd. & Chief Exec. Officer--Peerless Importers, Inc., Brooklyn, NY, pg. 855
Magnano, Louis A., Pres. & Chief Exec. Officer--Blue Bird Coach Lines Inc., Olean, NY, pg. 158
Maher, Jeffrey, Pres. & Chief Exec. Officer--MCC, Inc., Essex, CT, pg. 691
Mahoney, Stephen J., Pres. & Chief Exec. Officer--McInnes Steel Company, Corry, PA, pg. 729
Maley, John H.P., Pres. & Chief Exec. Officer--Chattanooga Group, Hixson, TN, pg. 241
Malin, Amir J., Co-Pres. & Chief Exec. Officer--October Films, Inc., New York, NY, pg. 821
Malinsky, Aaron, Pres. & Chief Exec. Officer--Victory Markets Inc., Norwich, NY, pg. 1150
Malkani, Roma, Pres. & Chief Exec. Officer--Information Systems & Network Corporation, Bethesda, MD, pg. 567
Mallott, Bryon I., Pres. & Chief Exec. Officer--Sealaska Corporation, Juneau, AK, pg. 984
Malmberg, John, Chief Oper. Officer & Exec. V.P.--Bank Of North Dakota, Bismarck, ND, pg. 117
Malone, B.L., Chief Exec. Officer--Malone Advertising, Inc., Akron, OH, pg. 703
Maloos, Vic, Pres. & Chief Exec. Officer--Bovay, Houston, TX, pg. 169
Manasco, David, Pres. & Chief Exec. Officer--Trina, Inc., Fall River, MA, pg. 1113
Mandelbaum, Ken, Chief Exec. Officer--Mandelbaum Mooney Ashley, San Francisco, CA, pg. 703
Mandell, Lester, Chief Exec. Officer--Greater Construction Corp., Altamonte Springs, FL, pg. 483
Mandor, Leonard, Chm. Bd. & Chief Exec. Officer--Concord Assets Group, Inc., Boca Raton, FL, pg. 272
Mango, Wilfred G., Jr., Pres. & Chief Exec. Officer--George A. Fuller Company, New York, NY, pg. 436
Mann, Marvin L., Chm. & Chief Exec. Officer--Lexmark International, Inc., Greenwich, CT, pg. 673
Manning, Thomas J., Sr., Chief Exec. Officer--Fabex Inc., Novi, MI, pg. 395
Mannlein, William J., Pres. & Chief Exec. Officer--Fleming Packaging Corp., Peoria, IL, pg. 417
Manzi, James, Pres. & Chief Exec. Officer--Lotus Publishing Corporation, Cambridge, MA, pg. 576
Marberg, Edwin, Pres., Chief Exec. Officer & Treas.--MCM Enterprises, Inc., Crawfordsville, IN, pg. 691
Marble, Stephen C., Pres. & Chief Exec. Officer--Nielsen Construction Company, San Diego, CA, pg. 807
Marcalus, Robert L., Sr., Chm. Bd. & Chief Exec. Officer--Marcal Paper Mills, Inc., Elmwood Park, NJ, pg. 706
March, Perrin G. III, Chm. Bd. & Chief Exec. Officer--Cincinnati Incorporated, Harrison, OH, pg. 250
Marchitto, Al, Chm. Bd. & Chief Exec. Officer--Simunico, Inc., Rutherford, NJ, pg. 1007
Marciano, George, Chief Exec. Officer--Guess ?, Inc., Los Angeles, CA, pg. 493
Marconi, Robert C., Chief Exec. Officer--RCM Industries, Franklin Park, IL, pg. 906
Marcus, Donald H., Chm. & Chief Exec. Officer--Marcus Advertising, Inc., Cleveland, OH, pg. 706
Margalith, Ethan Harold, Chm. Bd., Chief Exec. Officer & Treas.--Starving Students, Inc., Los Angeles, CA, pg. 1040
Margolin, Sam S., Pres. & Chief Exec. Officer--National Mortgage Company, Memphis, TN, pg. 792
Margolis, Robert, Chm. & Chief Exec. Officer--The Cherokee Group, Sunland, CA, pg. 243
Margus, Albert F., Chief Exec. Officer--Kitchens Of The Ocean, Inc., Deerfield Beach, FL, pg. 634
Marini, Robert C., Chm. Bd. & Chief Exec. Officer--Camp Dresser & McKee Inc., Cambridge, MA, pg. 212
Marion, James P., III, Pres. & Chief Exec. Officer--Bloomsburg Mills Inc., New York, NY, pg. 158
Markel, John D., Pres., Chief Exec. Officer & Treas.--Smartstar Corporation, Goleta, CA, pg. 1011
Markin, William R., Chm. & Chief Exec. Officer--Lauerer Markin Gibbs, Inc., Maumee, OH, pg. 660
Markos, Dennis, Chief Exec. Officer--Penda Corporation, Portage, WI, pg. 857
Marks, Marilyn, Pres. & Chief Exec. Officer--Dorsey Trailers, Inc., Atlanta, GA, pg. 347
Marram, Edward P., Dr., Chm. Bd., Pres., Chief Exec. Officer & Treas.--Geo-Centers, Inc., Newton Center, MA, pg. 452
Marriner, E. Randolph, Pres., Chief Exec. Officer--Marriner Marketing Communications, Inc., Columbia, MD, pg. 713
Mars, John F., Co-Pres. & Chief Exec. Officer--Mars, Incorporated, McLean, VA, pg. 713
Marsh, Water G., Chief Exec. Officer--Tapco Products Company, Plymouth, MI, pg. 1078
Marshall, Lowell R., Pres. & Chief Exec. Officer--Republic Storage Systems Company Inc., Canton, OH, pg. 928
Marshburn, Joseph D., Chief Exec. Officer--Citrus World Inc., Lake Wales, FL, pg. 251
Martin, David, Chief Exec. Officer--Martin, Cole, Dando & Robertson, Memphis, TN, pg. 714
Martin, Elliot, Chm. Bd., Pres. & Chief Exec. Officer--Windsor Publications, Inc., Chatsworth, CA, pg. 1196
Martin, Gordon, Chm. Bd., Pres. & Chief Exec. Officer--Martin Forest Industries, Healdsburg, CA, pg. 715
Martin, J. Landis, Chm. Bd., Pres. & Chief Exec. Officer--Tremont Corporation, Denver, CO, pg. 1109
Martin, Jerry, Chm. & Chief Exec. Officer--Slater Hanft Martin, Inc., New York, NY, pg. 1010
Martin, R.S., Jr., Chief Exec. Officer--Martin Gas Corporation, Kilgore, TX, pg. 715
Martin, Ret, Chm. Bd. & Chief Exec. Officer--The Dunlap Companies, Fort Worth, TX, pg. 353
Martin, Roy C., Sr., Chief Exec. Officer & Sec.--Triangle Electric Company, Madison Heights, MI, pg. 1112
Martin, Stephen H., Vice Chm. & Chief Exec. Officer--Hawley Martin Partners, Inc., Richmond, VA, pg. 518
Martin, Wayne, Pres. & Chief Exec. Officer--Plains Co-op Oil Mill, Lubbock, TX, pg. 873
Martindale, William A., Chm. Bd., Pres. & Chief Exec. Officer--Martrade Ltd., Santa Fe Springs, CA, pg. 716
Martiny, Kim R., Chm. Bd., Pres. & Chief Exec. Officer--Martiny & Company, Cincinnati, OH, pg. 716
Marx, Gilda, Co-Chief Exec. Officer--Gilda Marx Inc., Los Angeles, CA, pg. 716
Marx, Robert, Co-Chief Exec. Officer--Gilda Marx Inc., Los Angeles, CA, pg. 716
Marzano, A.M., Chm. Bd. & Chief Exec. Officer--Mosler Inc., Hamilton, OH, pg. 772
Mason, Albert D., Chief Exec. Officer & New Bus. Contact--Decker Rickard, Glastonbury, CT, pg. 324
Mason, David D. S., Pres., Chief Exec. Officer, Chief Fin. Officer & Treas.--Mason Oil Company, Ione, CA, pg. 718
Mason, Elvis L., Chm. & Chief Exec. Officer--Safeguard Business Systems, Inc., Fort Washington, PA, pg. 966
Mason, William T., Pres. & Chief Exec. Officer--Adra Systems, Inc., Lowell, MA, pg. 18
Matarese, James M., Chm., Pres. & Chief Exec. Officer--Phoenix International, Inc., Beverly, NJ, pg. 868
Mather, William J., Pres. & Chief Exec. Officer--Lawrence Agency Corporation, Schnectady, NY, pg. 662
Mathias, John H., Chm. Bd. & Chief Exec. Officer--JPM Company, Lewisburg, PA, pg. 586
Mathile, Clay, Chm. Bd. & Chief Exec. Officer--Iams Company, Dayton, OH, pg. 561
Mathot, Henk, Pres. & Chief Exec. Officer--Cargill Fertilizer, Inc., Riverview, FL, pg. 219
Mathwich, Dale, Chm. Bd. & Chief Exec. Officer--American Standard Insurance Company of Wisconsin, Madison, WI, pg. 52
Mathwich, Dale F., Chm. Bd. & Chief Exec. Officer--American Family Mutual Insurance Co., Madison, WI, pg. 51
Mathwich, Dale F., Chm. Bd. & Chief Exec. Officer--American Family Financial Services, Inc., Madison, WI, pg. 52
Mathwich, Dale F., Chm. Bd. & Chief Exec. Officer--American Family Mutual Insurance Co., Madison, WI, pg. 52
Mathwich, Dale F., Chm. Bd. & Chief Exec. Officer--AmFam, Inc., Madison, WI, pg. 52
Matteson, William C., Pres. & Chief Exec. Officer--Clarke Goward Fitts Matteson, Inc., Boston, MA, pg. 253
Matthaei, William L., Pres. & Chief Exec. Officer--Roman Meal Company, Tacoma, WA, pg. 945
Matthews, James, Chm. Bd. & Chief Exec. Officer--Capener, Matthews & Walcher, San Diego, CA, pg. 214
Matthewson, Edwin, Pres. & Chief Exec. Officer--Pullman Industries, Inc., Madison Heights, MI, pg. 900
Mattingly, Mark S., Chm. Bd. & Chief Exec. Officer--Evansville Brewing Company, Evansville, IN, pg. 391
Maughan, Rex, Chm. Bd., Pres. & Chief Exec. Officer--Forever Living Products, Tempe, AZ, pg. 424
Maurer, P. Reed, Chm. Bd., Chief Exec. Officer & Pres.--Metpac, Ltd., Honolulu, HI, pg. 742
Maxwell, R. L., Pres. & Chief Exec. Officer--The Lathrop Company, Toledo, OH, pg. 660
May, Stan, Chm. & Chief Creative Officer & Chief Exec. Officer--Leo Burnett Connaghan & May Pty. Ltd., North Sydney,, Australia, pg. 192
May, Van, Pres. & Chief Exec. Officer--Plains Cotton Co-op Association, Lubbock, TX, pg. 873
Mayer, William, Chief Exec. Officer--Jones & Lamson Waterbury Farrel Corp., Cheshire, CT, pg. 468
Mayfield, John D., III, Pres. & Chief Exec. Officer--Texas Life Insurance Company, Waco, TX, pg. 745
Maynard, James H., Chm. Bd., Chief Exec. Officer & Treas.--Investor's Management Corp., Raleigh, NC, pg. 581
Mazaika, Robert J., Chm. Bd., Pres. & Chief Exec. Officer--Uniroyal Chemical Company, Inc., Middlebury, CT, pg. 1129
Maziarka, Donald, Pres., Chief Exec. & Chief Oper. Officer--George Sollitt Construction, Wood Dale, IL, pg. 1017
McAdams, Herbert H, II, Chm. Emeritus & Chief Exec. Officer--The Union of Arkansas Corp., Little Rock, AR, pg. 1127
McAuliff, Timothy M., Pres. & Chief Exec. Officer--John Blair Communications, Inc., New York, NY, pg. 155
McAuliff, Timothy M., Pres. & Chief Exec. Officer--Blair Television, New York, NY, pg. 155
McAvoy, Jim, Pres. & Chief Exec. Officer-Chicago--Ruder, Finn, Inc., Chicago, IL, pg. 954
McBeth, Robert D., Chm. Bd., Pres. & Chief Exec. Officer--Associated Industrial Supply, Inc., Columbia, SC, pg. 90
McBride, John H., Pres. & Chief Exec. Officer--Porcelain Metals Corp., Louisville, KY, pg. 881
McBride, Robert D., Pres. & Chief Exec. Officer--McLouth Steel, Trenton, MI, pg. 731
McCaig, Joseph J., Pres. & Chief Exec. Officer--The Grand Union Company, Wayne, NJ, pg. 476
McCall, Robert H., Pres. & Chief Exec. Officer--McCall Oil & Chemical Corp., Portland, OR, pg. 726
McCall, Ronald L., Vice Chm., Chief Exec. Officer, Chief Fin. Officer & Treas.--M. B. Kahn Construction Co., Inc., Columbia, SC, pg. 614
McCallum, Elkin, Pres. & Chief Exec. Officer--Joan Fabrics Corp., Tyngsboro, MA, pg. 594
McCarter, William J., Pres. & Chief Exec. Officer--WTTW (Channel 11), Chicago, IL, pg. 1156
McCarty, H.F., Jr., Chm. Bd.--McCarty Farms, Magee, MS, pg. 727
McCarty, John R., Pres., Chief Exec. Officer & Chief Fin. Officer--McCarty Farms, Magee, MS, pg. 727
McCleary, James K., Chief Exec. Officer--AmeriData, Inc., Minneapolis, MN, pg. 66
McClelland, Mike, Pres. & Chief Exec. Officer--Hardware Wholesalers, Inc., Fort Wayne, IN, pg. 508
McClelland, Norman P., Chief Exec. Officer--Shamrock Foods Co., Phoenix, AZ, pg. 994
McClung, J. David, Pres. & Chief Exec. Officer--Green Holdings, Inc., Denver, CO, pg. 484
McClurg, Douglas G., Pres. & Chief Exec. Officer--Mossberg Industries, Inc., Cumberland, RI, pg. 772
McCollister, Paul, Chm. Bd., Pres. & Chief Exec. Officer--Jackson Hole Ski Resort, Teton Village, WY, pg. 587
McCollow, Thomas J., Chm. Bd., Pres. & Chief Exec. Officer--Journal Communications Inc., Milwaukee, WI, pg. 607
McConnaughy, Tom, Chm. & Chief Exec. Officer--McConnaughy Stein Schmidt Brown, Chicago, IL, pg. 727
McCormack, John J., III, Pres. & Chief Exec. Officer--Accurate Bushing Co., Inc., Garwood, NJ, pg. 11
McCormack, Mark H., Chm. Bd., Pres. & Chief Exec. Officer--International Management Group (IMG), Cleveland, OH, pg. 578
McCoy, Duncan, Pres. & Chief Exec. Officer--New Texas Tumbleweed, Houston, TX, pg. 802
McCracken, A. Keith, Pres. & Chief Exec. Officer--McCracken Brooks Communications, Inc., Minneapolis, MN, pg. 728
McCroskey, V.D., Pres. & Chief Exec. Officer--WGM Safety Corporation, Reading, PA, pg. 1156
McCulloch, A. Donald, Jr., Chm. Bd. & Chief Exec. Officer--Nutri/System Inc., Blue Bell, PA, pg. 818
McCune, Tom, Exec. V.P., Chief Exec. Officer-Building Div.--M. A. Mortenson Company, Minneapolis, MN, pg. 772
McCurdy, Ken, Pres. & Chief Exec. Officer--McCurdy & Co., Inc., Rochester, NY, pg. 728
McDaniel, Gary P., Chm., Chief Exec. Officer & Sec.--ROC Properties Inc., Englewood, CO, pg. 908
McDermitt, Edward A., Jr., Pres. & Chief Exec. Officer--National Bulk Carriers, Inc., New York, NY, pg. 786
McDermott, Gen. Robert, Chm. Bd. & Chief Exec. Officer--United Services Automobile Association (USAA), San Antonio, TX, pg. 1134
McDermott, Joseph, Jr., Pres. & Chief Exec. Officer--EBM Systems, Inc., Greenbelt, MD, pg. 359
McDivitt, Kris, Pres. & Chief Exec. Officer--Lost Arrow Corporation, Ventura, CA, pg. 684
McDonald, Charles R., Chm., Pres. & Chief Exec. Officer--McDonald Equipment Co., Willoughby, OH, pg. 728
McDonald, J.M., III, Chm. Bd., Pres. & Chief Exec. Officer--A. Y. McDonald Industries, Inc., Dubuque, IA, pg. 728
McDonald, J.M., III, Chm. Bd., Pres., Treas. & Chief Exec. Officer--Brock-McVey Company, Lexington, KY, pg. 728
McDonald, James H., Chief Exec. Officer--Paramount Petroleum Corp., Paramount, CA, pg. 848
McDonald, Lawrence, Pres. & Chief Exec. Officer--Gai's Seattle French Baking Co., Inc., Seattle, WA, pg. 441
McDonald, R.D., Chm. Bd., Pres. & Chief Exec. Officer--A.Y.M. Inc., Albia, IA, pg. 728
McDonald, Richard E., Pres. & Chief Exec. Officer--McDonald Davis & Associates, Inc., Milwaukee, WI, pg. 728
McDonald, Stuart R., Pres., Chief Exec. Officer & Treas.--Marshall & Williams Co., Greenville, SC, pg. 714
McDonnell, Dennis P., Pres. & Chief Exec. Officer--Trace Products, San Jose, CA, pg. 1104
McDonnell, Michael, Pres. & Chief Exec. Officer--West Union Corp., Memphis, TN, pg. 1177
McDougal, Alfred L., Chief Exec. Officer--McDougal, Littell & Company, Evanston, IL, pg. 728
McDowell, Frank, Pres. & Chief Exec. Officer--Cardinal Realty Services Inc., Reynoldsburg, OH, pg. 218
McDowell, James W., Exec. V.P. & Chief Exec. Officer--Dairymen, Inc., Louisville, KY, pg. 311
McEachern, James, Chm. Bd. & Chief Exec. Officer--Tom James Company, Arlington, TX, pg. 589
McEwen, Joseph, Chm. Bd. & Chief Exec. Officer--Modern Group Ltd., Bristol, PA, pg. 762
McFall, George E., Pres. & Chief Exec. Officer--Western Linen Corp., Phoenix, AZ, pg. 1180
McFall, Thomas, Chm. & Chief Exec. Officer--Hamburger Hamlets Inc., Sherman Oaks, CA, pg. 1169
McGarry, John P., Pres. & Chief Exec. Officer-Y&R North America--Young & Rubicam New York, New York, NY, pg. 1211
McGehee, Thomas R., Co-Chm Bd. & Chief Exec. Officer--Mac Papers, Inc., Jacksonville, FL, pg. 694
McGinnis, Arthur J., Sr., Chm.-Exec. Committee & Chief Exec. Officer--Simmons-Boardman Publishing Corp., New York, NY, pg. 1005
McGrath, Roger G., Pres. & Chief Exec. Officer--V.G.S. Corp. d/b/a Southland Oil Company, Jackson, MS, pg. 1141
McHugh, James P., Pres. & Chief Exec. Officer--James McHugh Construction Co., Chicago, IL, pg. 729
McIntyre, Douglas A., Pres. & Chief Exec. Officer--Financial World Partners, New York, NY, pg. 410
McIvor, Patrick J., Pres. & Chief Exec. Officer--Simms & McIvor Marketing Communications, Somerville, NJ, pg. 1005
McKay, Carl, Pres. & Chief Exec. Officer--Sioux Manufacturing Corp., Fort Totten, ND, pg. 1008
McKee, R. Ellsworth, Pres. & Chief Exec. Officer--McKee Baking Co., Inc., Collegedale, TN, pg. 730
McKeel, Sam S., Pres., Chief Exec. Officer & Publr.--Chicago Sun Times, Chicago, IL, pg. 18
McKellar, Christopher S., Chief Exec. Officer--McKellar Developers of La Jolla, San Diego, CA, pg. 730
McKenna, Andrew J., Chm., Pres. & Chief Exec. Officer--Schwarz Paper Company, Morton Grove, IL, pg. 980
McKenzie, Craig, Pres. & Chief Exec. Officer (Phoenix) & Dir.--EvansGroup, Salt Lake City, UT, pg. 390
McKenzie, Joe, Chm. Bd. & Chief Exec. Officer--Rangaire & Company, Cleburne, TX, pg. 912
McKnight, Andrew D., Chm. Bd. & Chief Exec. Officer--Tri-Chem, Inc., Harrison, NJ, pg. 1110
McLean, Victor H., Pres. & Chief Exec. Officer--Davis-Newman-Payne, Knoxville, TN, pg. 319
McMahon, John J. Jr., Pres. & Chief Exec. Officer--Clow Corporation, Birmingham, AL, pg. 733
McMahon, Robert B., Chm. Bd.,Chief Exec. Officer, Treas., & Sec.--City Meats & Provisions Co., Tucsan, AZ, pg. 251

McManus, James R., Chm. Bd., Pres. & Chief Exec. Officer--Marketing Corp. of America, Westport, CT, pg. 709
McMennamy, Roger N., Pres. & Chief Exec. Officer--Cooper Communities, Inc., Bella Vista, AR, pg. 283
McMillen, Robert B., Pres. & Chief Exec. Officer--Totem Resources Corporation, Seattle, WA, pg. 1103
McMorris, Jerry, Pres. & Chief Exec. Officer--N.W. Transport Service, Inc., Commerce City, CO, pg. 781
McMullen, Walter P., Sr., Chm. Bd. & Chief Exec. Officer--Lithograph Printing Company, Inc., Memphis, TN, pg. 678
McNally, Andrew, IV, Pres. & Chief Exec. Officer--Rand McNally & Company, Skokie, IL, pg. 911
McNamara, Austin, Pres. & Chief Exec. Officer--Dinner Bell Foods, Inc., Cincinnati, OH, pg. 53
McNamara, James, Pres. & Chief Exec. Officer--New World Entertainment, Inc., Los Angeles, CA, pg. 74
McNamara, John F., Chm. Bd., Pres. & Chief Exec. Officer--Alco Health Services Corporation, Malvern, PA, pg. 31
McNeel, Van L., Chm. Bd. & Chief Exec. Officer--McNeel International Corp., Tampa, FL, pg. 732
McNeil, Gordon H., Pres. & Chief Exec. Officer--Magnetic Technologies Corporation, Rochester, NY, pg. 701
McNeill, Bruce, Chm. Bd., Pres. & Chief Exec. Officer--Superior Federal Bank, Fort Smith, AR, pg. 1063
McPhail, Douglas J., Pres., Chief Exec. & Fin. Officer & Treas.--Indiana Records Managers, Indianapolis, IN, pg. 565
McQueen, Angus, Chm. Bd. & Chief Exec. Officer--Ackerman McQueen, Inc., Oklahoma City, OK, pg. 12
McQuillen, Harry A., Pres. & Chief Exec. Officer--K-III Magazines Corporation, New York, NY, pg. 611
McRae, Richard, Jr., Pres. & Chief Exec. Officer--McRae's, Inc., Jackson, MS, pg. 733
McRae, Richard, Sr., Chm. Bd.--McRae's, Inc., Jackson, MS, pg. 733
McSweene, Michael T., Pres. & Chief Exec. Officer--DIMAC Corporation, Bridgeton, MO, pg. 338
McSweeney, Michael T., Pres. & Chief Exec. Officer--DIMAC DIRECT, Bridgeton, MO, pg. 338
McSwiney, Ben L., Pres. & Chief Exec. Officer--Whitestar Graphics, Inc., Spring Grove, IL, pg. 1186
McTague, Michael, Pres. & Chief Exec. Officer--Fauber Construction Company, Inc., Lafayette, IN, pg. 403
McVaney, C. Edward, Chm. Bd., Pres. & Chief Exec. Officer--J.D. Edwards & Company, Denver, CO, pg. 370
Meads, Richard, Chm. & Chief Exec. Officer--Knoth & Meads Company, San Diego, CA, pg. 637
Meag, Jack, Pres. & Chief Exec. Officer--Schreiber Foods, Inc., Green Bay, WI, pg. 978
Meagher, Joseph B., Pres. & Chief Exec. Officer--Yankee Publishing Incorporated, Dublin, NH, pg. 1207
Meagher, Joseph B., Pres. & Chief Exec. Officer--Alaska Publishing Properties, Inc., Anchorage, AK, pg. 1207
Meany, Kevin C., Pres., Chief Exec. & New Bus. & Merger/Aquisition Contact--Partners Meany, Inc., Albany, NY, pg. 850
Medary, William, Pres. & Chief Exec. Officer--Bass Enterprises Production Company, Fort Worth, TX, pg. 125
Meehan, Paula Kent, Chief Exec. Officer--Redken Laboratories, Inc., Canoga Park, CA, pg. 919
Meer, Richard H., Chm. Bd. & Chief Exec. Officer--Meer Corporation, North Bergen, NJ, pg. 736
Mehlis, David L., Chm. Bd., Pres. & Chief Exec. Officer--David C. Cook Publishing Co., Elgin, IL, pg. 282
Mellon, Timothy, Chm. Bd. & Chief Exec. Officer--Guilford Transportation Industries Inc., Merrimack, NH, pg. 493
Mellott, Paul C., Chief Exec. Officer--H.B. Mellott Estate, Inc., McConnellsburg, PA, pg. 738
Meloon, Walter N., Pres. & Chief Exec. Officer--Correct Craft, Inc., Orlando, FL, pg. 287
Mendoza, R.V., Pres. & Chief Exec. Officer--Sterling Homes Corp., Sparks, NV, pg. 1046
Mendoza, V., Chief Fin. Officer & Chief Info. Officer & Treas. & Dir.-Data Pr--Gator Industries Inc., Hialeah, FL, pg. 446
Mentzer, Edward, Pres. & Chief Exec. Officer--Plastic Engineering Components Inc., New Berlin, WI, pg. 875
Menzer, G.W., Chief Exec. Officer--CAE Link Allen Division, Alexandria, VA, pg. 198
Meoni, Ronald J., Pres. & Chief Exec. Officer--The Napier Company, Meriden, CT, pg. 783
Mercandte, Frank, Pres. & Chief Exec. Officer--Franklin Federal Savings Association, Ottawa, KS, pg. 429
Meredith, Allen, Pres. & Chief Exec. Officer--Trammell Crow Company, Dallas, TX, pg. 1106
Merkel, Roberta A., Chief Exec. Officer--The Marketing Continuum, Inc., Dallas, TX, pg. 709
Merlav, K.A., Chm. Bd., Pres. & Chief Exec. Officer--Ottenheimer & Company, Inc., Bannockburn, IL, pg. 831
Mermelstein, Bernard, Pres. & Chief Exec. Officer--Elgin Watch International, Inc., Long Island City, NY, pg. 376
Merrell, John K., Pres., Chief Exec. Officer & Chief Oper. Officer--Industrial Dielectrics, Inc., Noblesville, IN, pg. 566
Merrick, P.R., Exec. V.P.--Charter House Group, New York, NY, pg. 240
Merrill, Thomas L., Pres. & Chief Exec. Officer--Altec Industries, Inc., Birmingham, AL, pg. 45
Merritt, Stanley S., Pres. & Chief Exec. Officer--Stan Merritt Inc./Advertising, New York, NY, pg. 741
Merson, Robert, Pres. & Chief Exec. Officer--Southern Electric Supply Co., Inc., Meridian, MS, pg. 1020
Meshberg, Emil, Chief Exec. Officer--Emson Research, Inc., Bridgeport, CT, pg. 380
Metropoulos, Evan D., Chief Exec. Officer--International Cheese Company Limited Partnership, Hinesburg, VT, pg. 575
Meyer, Robert D., Pres. & Chief Exec. Officer--Midwest Mutual Insurance Co., West Des Moines, IA, pg. 886
Meyer, Stanley F., Chm. & Chief Exec. Officer--Wendt Advertising, Inc., Great Falls, MT, pg. 1176
Meyocks, Richard, Pres. & Chief Exec. Officer--Meyocks Benkstein Associates, Des Moines, IA, pg. 746
Michalek, Edward, Pres. & Chief Exec. Officer--Advance Machine Company, Plymouth, MN, pg. 18
Michalek, Edward T., Chm. Bd. & Chief Exec. Officer--Norwesco, Inc., Minneapolis, MN, pg. 816
Michalek, Richard C., Chm. Bd. & Chief Exec. Officer--Quality Control Corporation, Harwood Heights, IL, pg. 903
Michel, George E., Pres. & Chief Exec. Officer--A & W Restaurants, Inc., Livonia, MI, pg. 1
Middleton, Charles S., Chm. Bd., Pres. & Chief Exec. Officer--Cal-Air Inc., Whittier, CA, pg. 208
Mikelsons, J. George, Chm. Bd., Pres. & Chief Exec. Officer--Amtran, Inc., Indianapolis, IN, pg. 69
Mikon, Arnold, Pres. & Chief Exec. Officer--The Smith Group, Inc., Detroit, MI, pg. 1012
Millard, Dan, Chm. Bd., Pres., Chief Exec. & Chief Oper. Officer--Central Illinois Steel Company, Carlinville, IL, pg. 232
Millenson, Elliott, Pres. & Chief Exec. Officer--Pollenex Corporation, Chicago, IL, pg. 879
Miller, Augustus C., Chm. Bd., Pres., Chief Exec. Officer--Miller Oil Co., Inc., Norfolk, VA, pg. 754
Miller, Bill, Pres., Chief Exec. & Chief Oper. Officer--Contico International, Inc., Saint Louis, MO, pg. 278
Miller, David, Pres. & Chief Exec. Officer--Columbia National Group, Inc., Cleveland, OH, pg. 265
Miller, Don, Pres. & Chief Exec. Officer--Ederer Inc., Seattle, WA, pg. 368
Miller, Duane L., Exec. V.P. & Chief Exec. Officer--Country Companies Insurance Group, Bloomington, IL, pg. 289
Miller, Duane L., Exec. V.P. & Chief Exec. Officer--Country Life Insurance Company, Bloomington, IL, pg. 289
Miller, Duane L., Exec. V.P. & Chief Exec. Officer--Country Mutual Insurance Company, Bloomington, IL, pg. 289
Miller, Duane L., Exec. V.P. & Chief Exec. Officer--CC Services, Bloomington, IL, pg. 289
Miller, Gary, Pres. & Chief Exec. Officer--Chadwick-Miller Inc., Canton, MA, pg. 237
Miller, Gary R., Chief Exec. Officer--Cannon, Grand Island, NY, pg. 214
Miller, George D., Pres. & Chief Exec. Officer--National Fire Protection Association, Quincy, MA, pg. 788
Miller, Herbert, Chm. Bd. & Chief Exec. Officer--Western Development Corporation, Washington, DC, pg. 1179
Miller, James B., Chm. Bd. & Chief Exec. Officer--Miller Business Systems, Inc., Arlington, TX, pg. 753
Miller, James H., Pres. & Chief Exec. Officer--Plastics Manufacturing Company, Dallas, TX, pg. 876
Miller, Jim, Pres. & Chief Exec. Officer--J P Foodservice, Inc., Hanover, MD, pg. 586
Miller, John F., III, Chm. Bd. & Chief Exec. Officer--Miller & Long Co. Inc., Bethesda, MD, pg. 754
Miller, John S., Pres. & Chief Exec. Officer--Tencarva Machinery Co., Inc., Greensboro, NC, pg. 1086
Miller, Larry, Chm. Bd., Pres. & Chief Exec. Officer--Corinthian Media, Inc., New York, NY, pg. 286
Miller, Leigh B., Pres. & Chief Exec. Officer--Freedman, Gibson & White Inc., Cincinnati, OH, pg. 430
Miller, Lewis, Pres. & Chief Exec. Officer--Industrial Ceramics, Inc., Derry, PA, pg. 566
Miller, Malcolm, Chm. & Chief Exec. Officer--Prentiss Incorporated, Floral Park, NY, pg. 887
Miller, Richard C., Pres. & Chief Exec. Officer--YPMS/TMP Worldwide, Inc., Mequon, WI, pg. 1074
Miller, Richard G., Jr., Chm. Bd.--Elgin National Industries, Inc., Chicago, IL, pg. 609
Miller, Robert S., Chm. Bd. & Chief Exec. Officer--Better Baked Foods, Inc., North East, PA, pg. 148
Miller, Steven, Chm. Bd., Pres. & Chief Exec. Officer--Miller Personnel, Inc., North Brunswick, NJ, pg. 755
Miller, Tod, Chm. Bd. & Chief Exec. Officer--Rosewood Property Company, Dallas, TX, pg. 949
Millgard, V. Dennis, Pres. & Chief Exec. Officer--The Millgard Corp., Livonia, MI, pg. 755
Milliken, Roger, Chm. Bd. & Chief Exec. Officer--Milliken & Co., Inc., Spartanburg, SC, pg. 755
Millner, Guy W., Chm. & Chief Exec. Officer--Norrell Corporation, Atlanta, GA, pg. 810
Mills, Howard, Jr., Chm. Bd. & Chief Exec. Officer--Maplehurst Farms, Inc., Indianapolis, IN, pg. 705
Mills, James S., Chm. Bd. & Chief Exec. Officer--Medline Industries, Inc., Mundelein, IL, pg. 736
Mills, Walter G., Chm. Bd., Chief Exec. Officer & Treas.--W.G. Mills, Inc., Sarasota, FL, pg. 756
Mims, T.J., Pres., Chief Exec. & Chief Oper. Officer--Canal Insurance Co., Greenville, SC, pg. 213
Miniat, Ronald, Chm., Pres. & Chief Exec. Officer--Ed Miniat, Inc., Chicago, IL, pg. 757
Minihan, John M., Pres. & Chief Exec. Officer--Louisville Bedding Company, Louisville, KY, pg. 684
Minnick, Terry, Chm. Bd., Pres. & Chief Exec. Officer--The Pro Corporation, Florence, MA, pg. 891
Miranda, Guillermo, Jr., Chm. Bd. & Chief Exec. Officer & Pres.--Gator Industries Inc., Hialeah, FL, pg. 446
Misch, Donald L., Chief Exec. Officer & Gen. Mgr.--Jasper County Farm Bureau Co-op Association, Inc., Rensselaer, IN, pg. 590
Miska, Steven M., Chm. Bd. & Chief Exec. Officer--Generra Sportswear Company, Inc., Tukwila, WA, pg. 451
Missett, Judi, Pres. & Chief Exec. Officer--Jazzercise, Inc., Carlsbad, CA, pg. 591
Mitchell, R.B., Pres., Chief Exec. Officer--Marshall Jaccoma Mitchell Advertising, New York, NY, pg. 714
Mitchell, William F., Chm. Bd., Pres. & Chief Exec. Officer--Mitchell Corporation of Owosso, Owosso, MI, pg. 761
Moe, Henrik, Pres., Chief Oper. & Exec. Officer--DEC International, Inc., Madison, WI, pg. 308
Mogas, V. Louis, Pres. & Chief Exec. Officer--Mogas Industries, Inc., Houston, TX, pg. 763
Mohre, David L., Chief Exec. Officer & Exec. V.P.--Cajun Electric Power Co-op, Baton Rouge, LA, pg. 207
Mohrman, Roy, Chm. Bd., Pres. & Chief Exec. Officer--Handling Systems Engineering, Jacksonville, FL, pg. 505
Moilanen, Thomas A., Pres. & Chief Exec. Officer--Cloverdale Equipment Co., Oak Park, MI, pg. 256
Moll, Curtis E., Chm. Bd. & Chief Exec. Officer--MTD Products, Inc., Valley City, OH, pg. 694
Moller, John J., Pres. & Chief Exec. Officer--USA Petroleum Corporation, Santa Monica, CA, pg. 1124
Moloney, Earl, Chm. Bd. & Chief Exec. Officer--Molon Motor & Coil Corp., Rolling Meadows, IL, pg. 764
Monaghan, Thomas S., Chm. Bd., Pres. & Chief Exec. Officer--Domino's Pizza Inc., Ann Arbor, MI, pg. 344
Monahan, William D., Pres. & Chief Exec. Officer--Edward V. Monahan Inc., Eastpointe, MI, pg. 765
Mondin, Galliano, Chief Exec. Officer--Diadora America, Inc., Kent, WA, pg. 335
Monette, Edward A., Chm., Pres., Chief Exec. & Oper. Officer--St. Croix Press, Inc., New Richmond, WI, pg. 966
Monks, Richard, Pres., Chief Exec. Officer & Chief Oper. Officer--ConTec International, Schenectady, NY, pg. 278
Montague, B.L., III, Chm. Bd. & Chief Exec. Officer--B. L. Montague Co., Sumter, SC, pg. 766
Montgomery, Mead, Chm. Bd. & Chief Exec. Officer--Treaty Co., Greenville, OH, pg. 1109
Montgomery, Robert L., Chm. & Chief Exec. Officer--Montgomery, Zukerman, Davis, Inc., Indianapolis, IN, pg. 768
Montgomery, Walter S., Jr., Pres., Treas., Chief Exec. & Chief Fin. Officer--Spartan Mills, Spartanburg, SC, pg. 1026
Montgomery, William, Chm. Bd., Pres., & Chief Exec. Officer--The SArgent-SOwell Company, Grand Prairie, TX, pg. 971
Montgomery, William J., Chm. Bd. & Chief Exec. Officer--American Finance Group, Boston, MA, pg. 52
Mooney, James P., Chm. Bd. & Chief Exec. Officer--Mooney Chemicals, Cleveland, OH, pg. 768
Moore, Edwin, Chief Exec. Officer--Crown International, Inc., Elkhart, IN, pg. 302
Moore, Hillar C., Jr., Pres. & Chief Exec. Officer--Associated Grocers, Inc., Baton Rouge, LA, pg. 89
Moore, J. Michael, Chm. Bd. & Chief Exec. Officer--Invetech Co., Detroit, MI, pg. 581
Moore, Jerry W., Chm. Bd., Chief Exec. Officer & New Bus. Contact--The J.W. Moore Group, Greensboro, NC, pg. 768
Moore, John O., Pres. & Chief Exec. Officer--Duncan Equipment Company, Duncan, OK, pg. 352
Moore, M.H., Pres. & Chief Exec. Officer--Longyear Company, Salt Lake City, UT, pg. 682
Moore, Richard, Pres. & Chief Exec. Officer--Kingswood Advertising, Inc., Ardmore, PA, pg. 632
Moore, Thomas R., Pres. & Chief Exec. Officer--Remmele Engineering, Inc., Saint Paul, MN, pg. 926
Moore, Wayne R., Chm. Bd., Pres. & Chief Exec. Officer--Moore Special Tool Co., Inc., Bridgeport, CT, pg. 768
Moorman, John R., Chief Exec. Officer--Mrs. Goochs Natural Food Markets, Sherman Oaks, CA, pg. 761
Moos, J. Clifford, Chm., Pres. & Chief Exec. Officer--Economy Folding Box Corp., Chicago, IL, pg. 367
Moram, Robert J., Pres. & Chief Exec. Officer--Ludlow Composites Corporation, Fremont, OH, pg. 686
Moran, Dennis, Chm. Bd. & Chief Exec. Officer--Moran Industries, Inc., Midlothian, IL, pg. 769
Moran, Dennis, Pres. & Chief Exec. Officer--U.S. Transparts, Midlothian, IL, pg. 769
Moran, Gordon W., Pres. & Chief Exec. Officer--Hollingsworth & Vose Co., East Walpole, MA, pg. 539
Moran, Patricia, Pres. & Chief Exec. Officer--JM Family Enterprises Inc., Deerfield Beach, FL, pg. 584
Morath, Paul, Chief Exec. Officer--Cold Heading Co., Detroit, MI, pg. 259
Morgan, John S., Chm., Pres. & Chief Exec. Officer--Morgan Foods, Inc., Austin, IN, pg. 770
Morgan, Phillip R., Pres. & Chief Exec. Officer--Morgan Construction Company, Worcester, MA, pg. 769
Morgan, Robert, Chm. Bd., Pres. & Chief Exec. Officer--Morgan Industries Inc., Bala-Cynwyd, PA, pg. 770
Moriarty, Kevin, Pres. & Chief Exec. Officer--Del Taco, Inc., Costa Mesa, CA, pg. 325
Morley, Harry T., Pres. & Chief Exec. Officer--Taylor-Morley, Inc., Saint Louis, MO, pg. 1081
Morris, Earl L., Chm. Bd. & Chief Exec. Officer--Acorn Engineering Company, City of Industry, CA, pg. 14
Morris, G. Ronald, Pres. & Chief Exec. Officer--Western Industries, Inc., Milwaukee, WI, pg. 1179
Morris, James R., Chm. Bd. & Chief Exec. Officer--MADD (Mothers Against Drunk Driving), Irving, TX, pg. 691
Morris, T.N., Jr., Chm., Pres. & Chief Exec. Officer--Calcasieu Lumber Company, Austin, TX, pg. 208
Morris, Thomas B., Jr., Chm. Policy Committee, Mng. Ptnr. & Chief Exec. Officer)--Dechert Price & Rhoads, Philadelphia, PA, pg. 323
Morris, W.S., III, Chm. Bd. & Chief Exec. Officer--Morris Corporation, Augusta, GA, pg. 999
Morrison, John C., Jr., Chm. & Chief Exec. Officer--MetLife Capital Corporation, Bellevue, WA, pg. 744
Morrison, Richard S., Pres. & Chief Exec. Officer--Molded Fiber Glass Companies, Ashtabula, OH, pg. 763
Morrow, David W., Chm. Bd., Pres., Chief Exec. Officer & Chief Oper. Officer--Pueblo International, Inc., Pompano Beach, FL, pg. 899
Mortenson, M.A., Jr., Chm. Bd., Chief Exec. Officer & Pres.--M. A. Mortenson Company, Minneapolis, MN, pg. 772
Morton, Jay W., Pres. & Chief Exec. Officer--United Engines, Inc., Oklahoma City, OK, pg. 1131
Mosley, Ralph, Vice Chm. & Chief Exec. Officer--Southwestern/Great American Inc., Nashville, TN, pg. 1023
Moss, Cruse W., Chm. Bd. & Chief Exec. Officer--General Automotive Corporation, Ann Arbor, MI, pg. 448

Mossberg, Alan I., Pres., Chief Exec. & Chief Oper. Officer & Treas.--O. F. Mossberg & Sons, Inc., North Haven, CT, pg. 773
Motta, Philip A., Chief Exec. Officer (Dallas) & Dir.--EvansGroup, Salt Lake City, UT, pg. 390
Motta, Philip A., Chief Exec. Officer--EvansGroup, Dallas, TX, pg. 391
Mourry, Dennis, Chm. Bd. & Chief Exec. Officer--Roytex, Inc., New York, NY, pg. 953
Mower, Eric, Chm. & Chief Exec. Officer--Eric Mower and Associates, Inc., Syracuse, NY, pg. 774
Mower, Eric, Chm. & Chief Exec. Officer--Eric Mower and Associates/Buffalo, Inc., Buffalo, NY, pg. 774
Moyer, William C., Dr., Chm. Bd., Pres. & Chief Exec. Officer--SFA, Inc., Landover, MD, pg. 961
Muck, Philip F., Pres., Chief Exec. Officer & Treas.--Munroe, Inc., Pittsburgh, PA, pg. 776
Mueller, John S., Chm. & Chief Exec. Officer--Laidlaw Corporation, Scottsdale, AZ, pg. 650
Muldrow, Ken, Pres. & Chief Exec. Officer--Goodpasture, Inc., Brownfield, TX, pg. 471
Mullan, Paul, Chm. Bd. & Chief Exec. Officer--Fleer Corporation, Mount Laurel, NJ, pg. 695
Mullane, Denis F., Pres. & Chief Exec. Officer--Connecticut Mutual Life Insurance Company, Hartford, CT, pg. 274
Mullen, James X., Pres. & Chief Exec. Officer--Mullen Advertising, Inc., Wenham, MA, pg. 775
Mullet, Willis, Chm. Bd. & Chief Exec. Officer--Wayne Dalton Corporation, Mount Hope, OH, pg. 312
Mullins, Roy L., Jr., Pres. & Chief Exec. Officer--Beacon Sales Corporation, Jacksonville, FL, pg. 129
Mundt, G. Henry, III, Pres. & Chief Exec. Officer--Cirrus System, Inc., Westchester, IL, pg. 720
Munro, Donald, Chm. Bd., Chief Exec. Officer & Treas.--Munro & Company, Inc., Hot Springs, AR, pg. 775
Murdock, David H., Pres. & Chief Exec. Officer--Pacific Holding Corporation, Los Angeles, CA, pg. 840
Murdock, David H., Chm. Bd. & Chief Exec. Officer--Dole Food Company, Inc., Westlake Village, CA, pg. 840
Muro, Roy A., Chm. & Chief Exec. Officer--Vitt Media International, Inc., New York, NY, pg. 1153
Murphy, Kenneth T., Chm. Bd., Pres. & Chief Exec. Officer--First Abilene Bankshares, Inc., Abilene, TX, pg. 411
Murphy, Peter, Jr., Chm. Bd., Pres. & Chief Exec. Officer--Murphy Company, Eugene, OR, pg. 776
Murray, Charles C., Pres., Chief Exec. Officer--Apparel America, Inc., New Haven, CT, pg. 78
Murray, N. Leight, Pres. & Chief Exec. Officer--The Airolite Company, Marietta, OH, pg. 28
Muse, Albert C., Pres. & Chief Exec. Officer--Crown Coal & Coke Co. Inc., Pittsburgh, PA, pg. 302
Musgrove, H.B., Chm. Bd., Pres. & Chief Exec. Officer--Frantz Manufacturing Co., Sterling, IL, pg. 429
Muskat, Irwin, Chm. Bd., Pres. & Chief Exec. Officer--Granite State Packing Co., Manchester, NH, pg. 476
Muzzy, Richard W., Jr., Chm. Bd. & Chief Exec. Officer--Binkley Company, Warrenton, MO, pg. 151
Myers, A. Maurice, Pres., Chief Exec. Officer & Dir.--Aloha Airgroup, Inc., Honolulu, HI, pg. 43
Myers, Garry C., Chief Exec. Officer--Highlights for Children, Inc., Columbus, OH, pg. 534
Myers, Howard B., Pres. & Chief Exec. Officer--Triumph*Lor, Inc., Houston, TX, pg. 1115
Myers, Jerry K., Pres. & Chief Exec. Officer--Steelcase Inc., Grand Rapids, MI, pg. 1044
Myers, L.G., Pres., Chief Exec. Officer & Admin. Dir.--LubeCon Systems, Inc., Fremont, MI, pg. 686
Myers, Norman S., Pres., Treas., Chief Exec. & Fin. Officers--IDM Controls, Houston, TX, pg. 560
Myra, Harold, Chief Exec. Officer--Christianity Today, Inc., Carol Stream, IL, pg. 249
Nabholz, Robert D., Jr., Chief Exec. Officer--Nabholz Construction Corp., Conway, AR, pg. 782
Naccarato, Vincent A., Chm. Bd., Pres. & Chief Exec. Officer--Wilton Industries, Inc., Woodridge, IL, pg. 1194
Nachman, David K., Pres. & Chief Exec. Officer--The Spohn Corporation, Cleveland, OH, pg. 1032
Nachman, David K., Pres. & Chief Exec. Officer--Emerald Corporation, Cleveland, OH, pg. 378
Nagy, Bob, Pres. & Chief Exec. Officer--Vernay Laboratories, Inc., Yellow Springs, OH, pg. 1148
Nahey, Brian L., Pres. & Chief Exec. Officer--Venturedyne, Ltd., Milwaukee, WI, pg. 1148
Nahser, F. Byron, Pres. & Chief Exec. Officer--Frank C. Nahser Inc., Chicago, IL, pg. 783
Nakahara, Asuka, Pres. & Chief Exec. Officer--Trammell Crow Company, Dallas, TX, pg. 1106
Nardizzi, Chuck, Chief Exec. Officer--Block & Nardizzi, Stamford, CT, pg. 157
Narlinger, Dennis, Chm., Pres. & Chief Exec. Officer--Shugart Corporation, Irvine, CA, pg. 1001
Nason, Charles T., Chm. Bd., Pres. & Chief Exec. Officer--The Acacia Group, Washington, DC, pg. 10
Nason, Robert E., Exec. Partner--Grant Thornton, Chicago, IL, pg. 477
Nattier, Robert, Chief Oper. Officer, Chief Fin. Officer & Gen. Mgr.--Mid-Kansas Co-op Association, Moundridge, KS, pg. 750
Naumann, George F., Chm. Bd. & Chief Exec. Officer--Victaulic Company of America, Easton, PA, pg. 1149
Neal, Gary M., Pres. & Chief Exec. Officer--Watlow Electric Manufacturing Company, Saint Louis, MO, pg. 1167
Neally, Philip, Chm. Bd. & Chief Exec. Officer--Aldi Inc., Batavia, IL, pg. 33
Needham, Tom, Chm., Pres. & Chief Exec. Officer--Allen & Hoshall, Inc., Memphis, TN, pg. 36
Neff, L., Chief Exec. Officer--American Foundry Group, Inc., Bixby, OK, pg. 54
Nei, Gary, Pres. & Chief Exec. Officer--Eon Labs, Inc., Lake Forest, IL, pg. 383
Neisel, Peter, Chief Exec. Officer--Schwab Corp., Lafayette, IN, pg. 980
Nelson, Alix, Chm. & Chief Exec. Officer--Franklin Spier, Inc., New York, NY, pg. 1031
Nelson, D., Chief Exec. Officer--Comlinear Corporation, Fort Collins, CO, pg. 268
Nelson, Dan, Chm. & Chief Exec. Officer--Nelson & Schmidt, Inc., Milwaukee, WI, pg. 797
Nelson, David, Chief Exec. Officer--Cellular Service, Inc., Glendale, CA, pg. 231
Nelson, Gary R., Chm. Bd. & Chief Exec. Officer--Nelson Photo Supplies, San Diego, CA, pg. 797
Nelson, Kent C., Chm. Bd. & Chief Exec. Officer--United Parcel Service of America, Inc., Atlanta, GA, pg. 1133
Nelson, Kirk N., Pres. & Chief Oper. Officer--Federated Mutual Insurance Company, Owatonna, MN, pg. 405
Nelson, Wayne K., Chm. & Chief Exec. Officer--Nelson Communications, Inc., New York, NY, pg. 797
Nemschoff, Mark, Pres., Chief Exec. Officer & Treas.--Nemschoff Chairs, Inc., Sheboygan, WI, pg. 798
Nethercutt, J.B., Chm. Bd. & Chief Exec. Officer--Merle Norman Cosmetics, Inc., Los Angeles, CA, pg. 740
Netter, Edward, Chm. Bd. & Chief Exec. Officer--Independence Holding Company, Stamford, CT, pg. 451
Neubauer, Joseph, Chm. Bd., Pres. & Chief Exec. Officer--ARA Group, Philadelphia, PA, pg. 5
Neuhoff, James H., Chm. Bd., Pres. & Chief Exec. Officer--Valleydale Packers Inc., Bristol, VA, pg. 1143
Neville, Robert J., Chm. Bd., Pres. & Chief Exec. Officer--The North American Manufacturing Co., Cleveland, OH, pg. 811
Nevin, John J., Pres. & Chief Exec. Officer--Broadcast Electronics, Inc., Quincy, IL, pg. 177
Newell, Ilse, Pres. & Chief Exec. Officer--Kragie/Newell, Des Moines, IA, pg. 643
Newgard, J. Richard, Pres. & Chief Exec. Officer--Henry Newgard & Company, Arlington Heights, IL, pg. 804
Newhouse, Samuel I., Jr., Chm. Bd. & Chief Exec. Officer--Advance Publications Inc., Staten Island, NY, pg. 19
Newman, Allen, Chief Exec. Officer--Key Food Stores Co-operative, Inc., Brooklyn, NY, pg. 626
Newman, Frank A., Pres. & Chief Exec. Officer--F & M Distributors Inc., Warren, MI, pg. 393
Newman, Larry, Chm. Bd. & Chief Exec. Officer--Prism Integrated Sanitation Management, Inc., Miami, FL, pg. 599
Newman, Michael, Pres. & Chief Exec. Officer--Polo/Ralph Lauren Corporation, New York, NY, pg. 879
Neyer, Jerome C., Chm. & Chief Exec. Officer--NTH Consultants, Ltd., Farmington Hills, MI, pg. 781
Nichols, J.D., Chm. Bd. & Chief Exec. Officer--NTS Corporation, Louisville, KY, pg. 781
Nichols, W.C., Pres. & Chief Exec. Officer--Renfro Corp., Mount Airy, NC, pg. 926
Nicholson, James B., Pres. & Chief Exec. Officer--PVS Chemicals, Inc., Detroit, MI, pg. 837
Nick, Dynn, Pres. & Chief Exec. Officer--Great Lakes Sportswear Manufacturing Industries, Detroit, MI, pg. 482
Nickel, Mark A., Chief Exec. Officer & Exec. Publr.--Sampler Publications Inc., Saint Charles, IL, pg. 968
Nickel, Mark A., Chief Exec. Officer--Country Sampler, Saint Charles, IL, pg. 968
Nickels, Robert T., Pres. & Chief Exec. Officer--Replogle Globes, Inc., Broadview, IL, pg. 927
Nickles, Ernest, Chm. & Chief Exec. Officer--Nickles Bakery Inc., Lima, Lima, OH, pg. 807
Nickles, Ernest A., Chm. & Chief Exec. Officer--Alfred Nickles Bakery, Inc., Navarre, OH, pg. 806
Nickles, Ernest A., Chm. & Chief Exec. Officer--Nickles Bakery, Inc., Martins Ferry, OH, pg. 807
Niebla, J. Fernando, Chm. Bd. & Chief Exec. Officer--Infotec Development, Inc., Santa Ana, CA, pg. 567
Nielsen, Claude B., Pres. & Chief Exec. Officer--Coca Cola Bottling Co. United, Inc., Birmingham, AL, pg. 257
Niemiec, Leo P., Pres. & Chief Exec. Officer--Lawnware Products, Inc., Morton Grove, IL, pg. 661
Nienstedt, William, Exec. V.P. & Chief Exec. Officer & Gen. Mgr.--Atchison County Co-op Association, Atchison, KS, pg. 93
Nierenberg, Bruce, Pres. & Chief Exec. Officer--Costa Cruise Lines, N.V., Miami, FL, pg. 288
Nies, Thomas M., Chm. Bd., Pres. & Chief Exec. Officer--Cincom Systems, Inc., Cincinnati, OH, pg. 250
Nixon, P. Andrews, Chm. Bd., Pres. & Chief Exec. Officer--Dead River Company, Portland, ME, pg. 321
Noble, Robert B., Chm. & Chief Exec. Officer--Noble & Associates, Springfield, MO, pg. 808
Noel, Marc, Pres. & Chief Exec. Officer--NMC of North America, Inc., Zebulon, NC, pg. 781
Noonan, Jack, Pres. & Chief Exec. Officer--SPSS Inc., Chicago, IL, pg. 964
Nordgren, Carl W., Chief Exec. Officer--FGI, Chapel Hill, NC, pg. 394
Nordquist, Ove, Pres. & Chief Exec. Officer--Commodore Cruise Line, Ltd., Coral Gables, FL, pg. 269
Nordquist, Ove, Pres. & Chief Exec. Officer--Crown Cruise Line, Coral Gables, FL, pg. 269
Norman, Reeve, Vice-Chm., Pres. & Chief Exec. Officer--Electrical Wholesale Supply Company, Inc., Idaho Falls, ID, pg. 374
Norris, John W., Jr., Chm. Bd. & Chief Exec. Officer--Lennox International Inc., Richardson, TX, pg. 667
Norton, J. Patrick, Chm. Bd., Pres. & Chief Exec. Officer--Fabreeka International, Inc., Stoughton, MA, pg. 396
Norton, John R., III, Chm. Bd. & Chief Exec. officer--J. R. Norton Company, Phoenix, AZ, pg. 816
Norton, Kenneth R., Chm. Bd. & Chief Exec. Officer--PST Vans, Inc., Salt Lake City, UT, pg. 837
Norton, Peter B., Chm. Bd. & Chief Exec. Officer--American Learning Corp., Chicago, IL, pg. 381
Novelly, Paul A., Pres. & Chief Exec. Officer--Apex Oil Company, Inc., Saint Louis, MO, pg. 78
Nucian, Lew, Chief Exec. Officer--Norman Levy Associates, Inc., Southfield, MI, pg. 672
Nulman, Louis, Pres. & Chief Exec. Officer--Alden Auto Parts Wholesale, Inc., Somerset, MA, pg. 32
Nusbaum, Irving, Pres. & Chief Exec. Officer--New York Carpet World Inc., Southfield, MI, pg. 802
Nusim, Joseph, Chm., Pres. & Chief Exec. Officer--Channel Home Centers Inc., Whippany, NJ, pg. 238
Nye, Mark, Chief Exec. Officer & V.P.--Niagara Therapy Mfg. Corp., Stanley, NC, pg. 806
O'Brien, F.L., III, Chm., Pres. & Chief Exec. Officer--O'Brien Energy Systems Inc., Philadelphia, PA, pg. 820
O'Brien, John F., Pres. & Chief Exec. Officer--All America Financial, Worcester, MA, pg. 34
O'Brien, John F., Pres. & Chief Exec. Officer--State Mutual Life Assurance Company of America, Worcester, MA, pg. 35
O'Brien, John F., Pres. & Chief Exec. Officer--All American Financial, Worcester, MA, pg. 34
O'Brien, Stephen J., Pres. & Chief Exec. Officer--Diversified Products Corporation, Opelika, AL, pg. 1193
O'Brien, Terry, Vice Chm. & Chief Exec. Officer--Ryan Herco Products Corp., Burbank, CA, pg. 958
O'Callaghan, R.A., Chief Exec. Officer--Universal Builders Supply, Inc., Mount Vernon, NY, pg. 1137
O'Connell, John, Pres. & Chief Exec. Officer--Garvin Fire Protection Systems, Orange, CA, pg. 444
O'Connell, L.E., Chm. Bd. & Chief Exec. Officer--Bunton Company, Louisville, KY, pg. 188
O'Connell, Robert, Chm. Bd. & Chief Exec. Officer--Hess's Department Stores, Inc., Allentown, PA, pg. 302
O'Connor, J.J., Chief Exec. Officer--Kores Nordic USA Corp., Summerville, SC, pg. 642
O'Connor, Laurence P., Chm. Bd. & Chief Exec. Officer--Unigard Security Insurance Co., Bellevue, WA, pg. 596
O'Connor, Laurence P., Chm. Bd. & Chief Exec. Officer--Unigard Indemnity Co., Raleigh, NC, pg. 596
O'Connor, Laurence P., Chm. Bd. & Chief Exec. Officer--Unigard Insurance Co., Seattle, WA, pg. 596
O'Connor, Laurence P., Chm. Bd. & Chief Exec. Officer--Unigard Service Corp., Seattle, WA, pg. 596
O'Connor, Thomas D., Chm., Pres. & Chief Exec. Officer--Mohawk Paper Mills, Inc., Cohoes, NY, pg. 763
O'Donnell, James E., Chm. Bd., Pres. & Chief Exec. Officer--Wheatland Tube Company, Collingswood, NJ, pg. 1184
O'Donnell, Owen, Pres. & Chief Exec. Officer--Management Dynamics, New Providence, NJ, pg. 703
O'Hara, John M., Chm. Bd. & Chief Exec. Officer--R. L. Polk & Co., Detroit, MI, pg. 879
O'Leary, Alice, Pres. & Chief Exec. Officer--Kaprielian/O'Leary, New York, NY, pg. 616
O'Malia, Daniel J., Pres. & Chief Exec. Officer--O'Malia Food Markets Inc., Noblesville, IN, pg. 825
O'Mara, A. James, Chm. Bd. & Chief Exec. Officer--Greenhorne & O'Mara, Inc., Greenbelt, MD, pg. 485
O'Neal, Emmet, Chm. Bd. & Chief Exec. Officer--O'Neal Steel Inc., Birmingham, AL, pg. 827
O'Neil, Gary M., Pres. & Chief Exec. Officer--O'Neil Griffin & Associates, Inc., Manchester, NH, pg. 827
O'Neill, Donald F., Pres. & Chief Exec. Officer--P M Company, Philadelphia, PA, pg. 835
O'Shaughnessy, Patrick E., Chm. Bd. & Chief Exec. Officer--Lario Oil & Gas Company, Wichita, KS, pg. 658
Oatway, Francis C., Pres. & Chief Exec. Officer--Hargro Enterprises, Inc., Stamford, CT, pg. 509
Ockels, Theodore S., Pres., Chief Exec. Officer, Chief Fin. Officer & Treas.--Up-Right Work Platforms Division, Selma, CA, pg. 1139
Oddy, Bill, Pres. & Chief Exec. Officer--California Electric Service, Oakland, CA, pg. 209
Oden, Clyde W., Dr., Pres. & Chief Exec. Officer--United Health Plan, Inglewood, CA, pg. 1133
Odom, John P., Co-Chm. Bd. & Chief Exec. Officer--The Odom Corporation, Seattle, WA, pg. 821
Ogden, J.H., Jr., Chm. Bd. & Chief Exec. Officer--Conestoga Holdings, Inc., Stamford, CT, pg. 273
Ogle, D. Clark, Chm. Bd., Pres., Chief Exec. & Chief Oper. Officer--Peter J. Schmitt Holdings, West Seneca, NY, pg. 976
Ohlmann, Walter, Pres. & Chief Exec. Officer--Penny/Ohlmann/Neiman, Inc., Dayton, OH, pg. 858
Okeleberry, Clair, Chief Exec. Officer, Treas. & Gen. Mgr.--Producers Livestock, North Salt Lake, UT, pg. 892
Okumura, Roy H., Chief Exec. Officer--Valley Isle Produce, Inc., Kahului, HI, pg. 1143
Olcott, Emery G., Pres. & Chief Exec. Officer--Canberra Industries, Inc., Meriden, CT, pg. 213
Oldenburg, Wayne C., Pres. & Chief Exec. Officer--The Oldenburg Group Companies, Milwaukee, WI, pg. 824
Oldenburg, Wayne C., Pres. & Chief Exec. Officer--Lake Shore, Inc., Kingsford, MI, pg. 824
Oldham, Noble, Pres. & Chief Exec. Officer--Artco-Bell Corporation, Temple, TX, pg. 86
Oleson, Dr. Douglas E., Pres. & Chief Exec. Officer--Battelle Memorial Institute, Columbus, OH, pg. 126
Olin, Burton H., Chm. Bd. & Chief Exec. Officer--Humiston-Keeling, Inc., Chicago, IL, pg. 552
Olsen, David A., Chm., Pres., Chief Exec. & Chief Oper. Officer--Johnson & Higgins, New York, NY, pg. 598
Olsen, George A., Pres. & Chief Exec. Officer--Kingsbury, Inc., Philadelphia, PA, pg. 632
Olsen, T. W., Pres. & Chief Exec. Officer--United A G Co-op, Inc., Omaha, NE, pg. 1130
Olson, Frank A., Chm. Bd., Chief Exec. & Oper. Officer--The Hertz Corporation, Park Ridge, NJ, pg. 849
Olson, Ken, Chm. & Chief Exec. Officer--Proxima Corporation, San Diego, CA, pg. 896
Olson, Kent F., Pres. & Chief Exec. Officer--Northwestern Drug Company, Minneapolis, MN, pg. 343
Olson, Oscar L., Chm. Bd. & Chief Exec. Officer--Olsonite Corporation, Detroit, MI, pg. 824
Omer, Don C., Chm. Bd., Pres., Chief Exec. & Fin. Officer--Inland Associates, Inc., Olathe, KS, pg. 570
Ommodt, Donald, Pres. & Chief Exec. Officer--Cass-Clay Creamery, Fargo, ND, pg. 228
Onderdonk, S.R., Pres. & Chief Exec. Officer--Econolite Control Products, Inc., Anaheim, CA, pg. 367
Onstead, Robert R., Chm. Bd. & Chief Exec. Officer--Randall's Food Markets, Inc., Houston, TX, pg. 911

Opler, Edmond, Jr., Chm. Bd., Pres. & Chief Exec. Officer--World's Finest Chocolate, Inc., Chicago, IL, pg. 1203
Opperman, Dwight D., Pres. & Chief Exec. Officer--West Publishing Co., Eagan, MN, pg. 1177
Ordway, Peter S., Chm., Pres. & Chief Exec. Officer--Union Pump Company, Battle Creek, MI, pg. 1128
Oren, John R., Chm. Bd. & Chief Exec. Officer--Eastway Delivery Service of Houston, Inc., Houston, TX, pg. 364
Oren, John R., Chm. Bd. & Chief Exec. Officer--Eastway Delivery Service of Austin, Inc., Austin, TX, pg. 364
Oren, John R., Chm. Bd. & Chief Exec. Officer--Eastway Delivery Service of Dallas, Inc., Grapevine, TX, pg. 364
Oren, John R., Chm. Bd. & Chief Exec. Officer--Eastway Air Cartage, Inc., Houston, TX, pg. 364
Orentzel, J., Chief Exec. Officer--American White Cross Laboratories, Inc., New Rochelle, NY, pg. 65
Oringer, Howard, Chm. Bd. & Chief Exec. Officer--Telesciences Co. Systems Inc., Moorestown, NJ, pg. 1085
Orlando, Maurice V., Chief Exec. Officer--Ortronics, Inc., Pawcatuck, CT, pg. 830
Ortolani, Timothy S., Chm. Bd., Pres. & Chief Exec. Officer--Carton-Craft Corporation, Buffalo, NY, pg. 226
Orullian, B. La Rae, Chm. & Chief Exec. Officer--The Women's Bank, N.A., Denver, CO, pg. 385
Osborne, Michael E., Pres. & Chief Exec. Officer--The Milnot Company, Saint Louis, MO, pg. 756
Ostendorf, Bob, Pres. & Chief Exec. Officer--VMC Fiberglass Products Inc., Daleville, AL, pg. 1142
Ostergard, Tonn, Pres. & Chief Exec. Officer--Crete Carrier Corp., Lincoln, NE, pg. 299
Ostrover, Harvey, Chm. Bd. & Chief Exec. Officer--American Fabrics Company, New York, NY, pg. 51
Otakie, Daniel A., Chm., Pres., Chief Exec. Officer & Treas.--Futures Personnel Services, Baltimore, MD, pg. 438
Otero, Richard J., Chm., Pres. & Chief Exec. Officer--RJO Enterprises, Inc., Lanham, MD, pg. 907
Otte, Stephen B., Pres. & Chief Exec. Officer--Florists' Mutual Insurance Co., Edwardsville, IL, pg. 421
Otto, Richard E., Chm. Bd. & Chief Exec. Officer--Auto-Owners Insurance, Lansing, MI, pg. 100
Ounjian, Marilyn J., Chm. Bd. & Chief Exec. Officer--Careers USA Inc., Philadelphia, PA, pg. 218
Overbeck, Joseph C., Chief Exec. Officer--Motor Wheel Corporation, Lansing, MI, pg. 773
Owens, Bill M., Chm. Bd. & Chief Exec. Officer--Owens Pollick & Associates, Phoenix, Inc., Phoenix, AZ, pg. 834
Owens, Phil, Pres. & Chief Oper. Officer--Top-Seal Corp., Phoenix, AZ, pg. 1083
Owens, Richard J., Pres. & Chief Exec. Officer--Manning & Lewis Engineering Co., Union, NJ, pg. 704
Packard Thomas M., Pres. & Chief Exec. Officer--Country Lake Foods, Inc., Saint Paul, MN, pg. 654
Paddock, S. R., Jr., Chm., Chief Exec. Officer & Publr.--Paddock Publications, Inc., Arlington Heights, IL, pg. 842
Padnos, Jeffrey S., Pres. & Chief Oper. Officer--Louis Padnos Iron & Metal Co., Holland, MI, pg. 842
Page, F. Roger, Chm. Bd., Pres., Chief Exec. & Fin. Officer--Pace Oil Co., Inc., Winston-Salem, NC, pg. 838
Pahl, Charles E., Pres. & Chief Exec. Officer--J.H. Larson Electrical Company, Golden Valley, MN, pg. 659
Paletz, Lenn, Chm., Pres., Chief Exec. & Chief Oper. Officer--The Sportsman's Guide, Inc., Eagan, MN, pg. 1032
Palmer, A. Robert, Pres. & Chief Exec. Officer--Eastern Color Printing Company, Avon, CT, pg. 363
Palmer, Charles L., Chm. Bd. & Chief Exec. Officer--North American Company, Fort Lauderdale, FL, pg. 811
Palmer, Eldon D., Pres. & Chief Exec. Officer--Kenworth of Indianapolis Inc., Indianapolis, IN, pg. 624
Palmer, Stephen T., Jr., Chm. Bd. & Chief Exec. Officer--Palmer International, Inc., Worcester, PA, pg. 844
Palmieri, Victor, Chief Exec. Officer--Mutual Benefit Life Insurance Company, Newark, NJ, pg. 778
Pamplin, Robert B., Sr., Chm. Bd. & Chief Exec. Officer--R. B. Pamplin Corp., Portland, OR, pg. 844
Pankow, Charles J., Jr., Pres. & Chief Exec. Officer--Charles Pankow Builders, Ltd., Altadena, CA, pg. 846
Pappenthenasi, Arthur J., Pres. & Chief Exec. Officer--Scangas Brothers Holdings, Inc., Lynn, MA, pg. 974
Parana, Gene T., Pres. & Chief Exec. Officer--Anderson Lithograph Company, Los Angeles, CA, pg. 73
Paridy, David R., Pres. & Chief Exec. Officer--Standard-Thomson Corporation, Waltham, MA, pg. 1037
Park, J. Leonard, Chm. Bd., Pres., Chief Exec. Officer & Treas.--George W. Park Seed Co., Inc., Greenwood, SC, pg. 849
Park, James C., Chm. Bd. & Chief Exec. Officer--Besser Company, Alpena, MI, pg. 146
Parker, David H., Chm. Bd., Pres. & Chief Exec. Officer--Pelican Products, Torrance, CA, pg. 856
Parker, David J., Chm. Bd. & Chief Exec. Officer--Blount Lumber Company, Lacona, NY, pg. 158
Parker, JoAnn, Chm. Bd. & Chief Exec. Officer--Omniflight, Inc., Dallas, TX, pg. 826
Parker, Larry L., Pres. & Chief Exec. Officer--Leach Corporation, Buena Park, CA, pg. 663
Parker, Ronald I., Chm. Bd., Pres. & Chief Exec. Officer--Indian Head Industries Inc., Southfield, MI, pg. 565
Parks, Edgar E., Chm. Bd. & Chief Exec. Officer--Albert Kahn Associates, Inc., Detroit, MI, pg. 613
Parrish, Paul G., Chief Exec. Officer & Exec. V.P.--Coble Dairy Products Co-op, Lexington, NC, pg. 257
Parry, Robert A., Chm. Bd., Pres. & Chief Exec. Officer--Monroc, Inc., Salt Lake City, UT, pg. 766
Parry, Tom C., Pres. & Chief Exec. Officer--Mississippi Chemical Corporation, Yazoo City, MS, pg. 760
Pasquarello, Theodore, Pres. & Chief Exec. Officer--Chiswick Trading Inc., Sudbury, MA, pg. 248
Pasquerilla, Frank J., Chm. Bd. & Chief Exec. Officer--Crown American Corporation, Johnstown, PA, pg. 301
Pastor, Irwin, Pres. & Chief Exec. Officer--W&F Manufacturing Corporation, Inc., Buffalo, NY, pg. 1155
Patch, Arthur, Pres. & Chief Exec. Officer--AppleTree Markets, Houston, TX, pg. 79
Patel, Charles, Jr., Vice Chm. & Chief Exec. Officer--Magic Pan International Inc., Burlingame, CA, pg. 700
Patenge, Kenneth E., Chm., Pres. & Chief Exec. Officer--Wohlert Corp., Lansing, MI, pg. 1198
Patrick, Stuart K., Pres. & Chief Exec. Officer--Baird, Patrick & Co., Inc., New York, NY, pg. 114
Patterson, Charles, Pres., Chief Exec. Officer & Chief Oper. Officer--Walman Optical Company, Minneapolis, MN, pg. 1161
Patterson, Ray, Chief Exec. Officer--Esskay Manufacturing Co., San Antonio, TX, pg. 389
Pauley, Stanley F., Chm. Bd. & Chief Exec. Officer--E. R. Carpenter Co., Richmond, VA, pg. 224
Payne, Ronald G., Pres. & Chief Exec. Officer--Warehouse Home Furnishings Distributor, Dublin, GA, pg. 1163
Payne, Walter F., Pres. & Chief Exec. Officer--Blue Diamond Growers, Sacramento, CA, pg. 160
Payton, Earl E., Chm. Bd., Chief Exec. Officer & Sec.--Cowden Metal Specialties, Inc., Chino, CA, pg. 291
Peardon, Thomas, Pres. & Chief Exec. Officer--Brunschwig & Fils, Inc., White Plains, NY, pg. 184
Pearson, Ronald, Chm. Bd., Pres. & Chief Exec. Officer--Hy-Vee Food Stores Incorporated, Chariton, IA, pg. 556
Pease, David H., Jr., Chm. Bd. & Chief Exec. Officer--Pease Industries, Inc., Fairfield, OH, pg. 854
Peavey, Hartley D., Chief Exec. Officer--Peavey Electronic Corp., Meridian, MS, pg. 854
Pedone, Michael F., Pres. & Chief Exec. Officer--Pedone & Partners Inc., New York, NY, pg. 854
Pellegrini, Donald P., Pres. & Chief Exec. Officer--The Spring Air Company, Des Plaines, IL, pg. 1032
Pellegrino, John B., Pres. & Chief Exec. Offcier--Ridg-U-Rak, Inc., North East, PA, pg. 933
Peltz, Nelson, Chm. & Chief Exec. Officer--Trian Group, New York, NY, pg. 1111
Pemberton, Marlin H., Chm. Bd., Pres. & Chief Exec. Officer--Acorn Building Components Inc., Detroit, MI, pg. 13
Pemble, John C., Pres. & Chief Exec. Officer--Itran Corporation, Manchester, NH, pg. 583
Pena, Luis X., Pres., Chief Exec. Officer & Chief Fin. Officer--Gulf States Asphalt Company, Inc., South Houston, TX, pg. 493
Pendleton, Alexander, Chm. Bd. & Chief Exec. Officer--Warren Tool Group, Hiram, OH, pg. 1165
Penny, Dick, Chm. & Chief Exec. Officer--Penny & Speier Inc., Houston, TX, pg. 858
Penske, Roger S., Chm. & Chief Exec. Officer--Detroit Diesel Corp., Detroit, MI, pg. 859
Pentz, Paul, Pres. & Chief Exec. Officer--Servistar Corporation, East Butler, PA, pg. 992
Pepper, Richard S., Chief Exec. Officer--The Pepper Companies, Inc., Chicago, IL, pg. 859
Peppers, Don, Pres. & Chief Exec. Officer--Perkins/Butler Direct Marketing, New York, NY, pg. 244
Peppler, Dan, Chm., Natl. Creative Dir., Chief Exec. Officer--Doner Schur Peppler, Toronto,, Canada, pg. 344
Pepys, Shirley, Chm., Pres. & Chief Exec. Officer--Noel-Joanna, Inc., Rancho Santa Margarita, CA, pg. 808
Perconti, Paul J., Pres. & Chief Exec. Officer--Thornton Oil Corp., Louisville, KY, pg. 1095
Perelman, Ronald, Chm. & Chief Exec. Officer--Revlon Group Inc., New York, NY, pg. 695
Perelman, Ronald O., Chm. Bd. & Chief Exec. Officer--MacAndrews & Forbes Holdings Inc., New York, NY, pg. 694
Perelman, Ronald O., Chm. Bd. & Chief Exec. Officer--Revlon, Inc., New York, NY, pg. 696
Perelman, Ronald O., Chm. Bd. & Chief Exec. Officer--Andrews Group, Incorporated, New York, NY, pg. 74
Perez, Jean-Yves, Pres. & Chief Exec. Officer--Woodward-Clyde Group, Inc., Denver, CO, pg. 1200
Perez, John, Pres. & Chief Exec. Officer--Perez Trading Co. Inc., Miami, FL, pg. 860
Peritz, Richard, Chief Exec. Officer--Archibald Candy Company, Chicago, IL, pg. 604
Perkins, C.M., Gen. Mgr.--Salt River Project Agricultural Improvement and Power District, Tempe, AZ, pg. 967
Perkins, Leigh H., Chief Exec. Officer--The Orvis Company, Inc., Manchester, VT, pg. 830
Perko, Paul E., Chief Exec. Officer--North Coast Electric Company, Bellevue, WA, pg. 813
Perks, A. Campbell, Chm. Bd. & Chief Exec. Officer--Eclipse, Inc., Rockford, IL, pg. 366
Perrino, S. Ronald, Chm. Bd., Pres. & Chief Exec. Officer--S.T. Research, Newington, VA, pg. 964
Perry, Chris N., Chm. Bd. & Chief Exec. Officer--Meldrum & Fewsmith Communications Inc., Cleveland, OH, pg. 737
Perry, Chris N., Chm., Chief Exec. Officer & Exec. Creative Dir.--Meldrum & Fewsmith Advertising Inc., Cleveland, OH, pg. 737
Perry, M. Dunman, Jr., Chm. Bd. & Chief Exec. Officer--Perry Equipment Corporation, Mineral Wells, TX, pg. 863
Perry, William H., Chief Exec. Officer--Detecto Scale Company, Webb City, MO, pg. 332
Pesch, Alan J., Chm. Bd., Pres. & Chief Exec. Officer--Ship Analytics, Inc., North Stonington, CT, pg. 999
Peters, A. Clark, Pres. & Chief Exec. Officer--LaSalle-Deitch Co., Inc., Elkhart, IN, pg. 660
Peters, Robert L., Chm. Bd., Pres. & Chief Exec. Officer--Holmquist Grain & Lumber Co., Oakland, NE, pg. 540
Peters, Roger, Pres. & Chief Exec. Officer--Kold Kist Brands, Inc., Los Angeles, CA, pg. 641
Petersen, Allen D., Chm. Bd., Pres. & Chief Exec. Officer--American Tool Companies, Inc., Lincoln, NE, pg. 64
Petersen, Fred M., Pres., Chief Exec. Officer & Chief Oper. Officer--Omaha Public Power District, Omaha, NE, pg. 825
Petersen, L.C., Chm. Bd. & Chief Exec. Officer--Kirkpatrick Pettis, Omaha, NE, pg. 779
Petersen, Maurice R., Chief Exec. Officer--Petersen Aluminum Corporation, Elk Grove Village, IL, pg. 864
Peterson, Donald V., Chief Exec. Officer--North Carolina Mutual Wholesale Drug Co., Durham, NC, pg. 813
Peterson, Jim L., Pres. & Chief Exec. Officer--Whataburger, Inc., Corpus Christi, TX, pg. 1184
Peterson, Ralph R., Pres. & Chief Exec. Officer--CH2M Hill Companies, Ltd., Englewood, CO, pg. 202
Peterson, Roger E., Pres. & Chief Exec. Officer--Ace Hardware Corporation, Oak Brook, IL, pg. 12
Petrocine, Thomas M., Pres. & Chief Oper. Officer--Christopher Thomas Associates Inc., Garden City, NY, pg. 249
Pfeiffer, Robert G., Chm. Bd. & Chief Exec. Officer--Neill-LaVielle Supply Co., Louisville, KY, pg. 797
Phares, Elwood W., II, Chm. Bd., Pres. & Chief Exec. Officer--West Chemical Products, Inc., Princeton, NJ, pg. 1172
Phelps, Barry, Chm. & Chief Exec. Officer--MICOM Communications Corp., Simi Valley, CA, pg. 748
Phelps, Jon, Pres. & Chief Exec. Officer--Hickerson Phelps Kirtley & Associates, Kansas City, MO, pg. 532
Phelps, Norman, Pres. & Chief Exec. Officer--National Liberty, Frazer, PA, pg. 791
Phelps, Terry M., Chm. Bd., Pres. & Chief Exec. Officer--Petroleum Marketers, Inc., Roanoke, VA, pg. 865
Phillips, David, Chm. Bd. & Chief Exec. Officer--Credit Card Service Corporation, Springfield, VA, pg. 410
Phillips, Thomas L., Chm. Bd., Pres. & Chief Exec. Officer--Phillips Publishing Inc., Potomac, MD, pg. 868
Piccinini, Robert M., Chm. Bd. & Chief Exec. Officer & Pres.--Save Mart Supermarkets, Modesto, CA, pg. 973
Picini, Dan E., Chm. Bd., Pres. & Chief Oper. Officer--Duro-Test Corporation, Fairfield, NJ, pg. 355
Pickering, Allen, Chief Exec. Officer, Treas. & Sec.--Pickering Industries Inc., Tacoma, WA, pg. 869
Picknelly, Peter A., Jr., Pres. & Chief Exec. Officer--Peter Pan Bus Lines, Inc., Springfield, MA, pg. 864
Picower, Jeffry, Chm. Bd. & Chief Exec. Officer--Monroe Systems For Business, Inc., Morris Plains, NJ, pg. 766
Pierce, Brian, Pres. & Chief Exec. Officer--Peirce-Phelps, Inc., Philadelphia, PA, pg. 855
Pierce, Douglas, V.P. & Chief Exec. Officer--Guardian Alarm Co., Southfield, MI, pg. 491
Pierce, Frederick G., II, Chm. Bd., Pres. & Chief Exec. Officer--Niagara Envelope Company, Inc., Buffalo, NY, pg. 805
Pifer, Kevin D., Exec. V.P. & Chief Exec. Officer--Nodak Mutual Insurance Company, Fargo, ND, pg. 808
Pike, Larry R., Chm. Bd., Pres. & Chief Exec. Officer--The Union Central Life Insurance Co., Cincinnati, OH, pg. 1127
Pikovsky, Eugene, Chm. & Chief Exec. Officerr--Hyman Freightways Inc., Moundsview, MN, pg. 557
Pincus, David, Chm. Bd. & Chief Exec. Officer--Pincus Bros., Inc., Philadelphia, PA, pg. 870
Pines, Isidore, Chm. Bd. & Chief Exec. Officer--National Foods Inc., Bronx, NY, pg. 788
Pinkerton, Fred H., Jr., Pres. & Chief Exec. Officer--Allied Foods, Inc., Atlanta, GA, pg. 38
Pinne, Robert A., Chm. Bd. & Chief Exec. Officer--Pinne/Herbers Advertising Inc., San Francisco, CA, pg. 871
Pinto, James J., Pres. & Chief Exec. Officer--Action Instruments, Inc., San Diego, CA, pg. 14
Piper, Paul P., Jr., Chm. & Chief Exec. Officer--Piper Industries, Inc., Dallas, TX, pg. 872
Pirie, Robert S, Chm. Bd., Pres. & Chief Exec. Officer--Rothschild Inc., New York, NY, pg. 951
Pirrong, J., Pres. & Chief Exec. Officer--BIW Cable Systems, Inc., North Dighton, MA, pg. 106
Pisa, Michael A., Sr., Chm. Bd. & Chief Exec. Officer--Continental Paper & Supply Co., Detroit, MI, pg. 280
Piser, Donald H., Chm. Bd. & Chief Exec. Officer--Morse Diesel International, New York, NY, pg. 771
Pistilli, Frederick M., Chm. & Chief Exec. Officer--General Time Corp., Norcross, GA, pg. 451
Pittman, Gary, Chm. Bd., Pres., Chief Exec., Chief Oper. & Chief Fin. Officer--PCI, Austin, TX, pg. 836
Platania, Philip, Pres., Chief Exec. & Chief Fin. Officer--Andmore Sportswear Corporation, Port Jervis, NY, pg. 74
Plunk, Robert, Pres. & Chief Exec. Officer--Preferred Risk Mutual Insurance, West Des Moines, IA, pg. 886
Podlich, William F., Chief Exec. Officer & Mng. Dir.--Pacific Investment Management Co., Newport Beach, CA, pg. 841
Poehlmann, Karl M., Pres. & Chief Exec. Officer--George Uhe Co., Inc., Paramus, NJ, pg. 1125
Pogue, A. Mack, Chm. Bd., Pres. & Chief Exec. Officer--Lincoln Property Company, Dallas, TX, pg. 676
Pogue, David, Chm. Bd. & Chief Exec. Officer--Stackig, Sanderson & White, Inc., McLean, VA, pg. 1034
Polera, Anthony, Chief Exec., Chief Oper. & Info. Officer--Polera Building Corp., Scarsdale, NY, pg. 878
Pollack, Glenn, Chief Exec. Officer--A & W Foods, Inc., Cleveland, OH, pg. 1
Pollak, James S., Chm. & Chief Exec. Officer--Pollak Levitt Chaiet, Advertising, Atlanta, GA, pg. 879
Pollnow, Charles, Chm. Bd., Chief Exec. & Oper. Officer--The Brulin Corporation, Indianapolis, IN, pg. 184
Pollock, William K., Chm. Bd. & Chief Exec. Officer--Key Industries, Inc., Fort Scott, KS, pg. 627
Poppert, Claris, Chm. Bd. & Chief Exec. Officer--Benson Industries, Inc., Portland, OR, pg. 139
Posey, Lee, Pres. & Chief Exec. Officer--Palm Harbor Homes, Inc., Dallas, TX, pg. 843
Posey, Sam, Chief Exec. Officer--B & B Cash Grocery Store, Tampa, FL, pg. 105
Posner, Sidney, Chm. Bd., Chief Exec. Officer, Treas.--Newmark, Posner & Mitchell, Inc., New York, NY, pg. 804
Posner, Victor, Chm. Bd. & Chief Exec. Officer--Graniteville Co., Graniteville, SC, pg. 476
Posner, Victor, Chm. Bd., Pres. & Chief Exec. Officer--Chesapeake Financial Corp., Miami Beach, FL, pg. 243

Post, James R., Pres., Chief Exec. Officer, Chief Fin. Officer--Ostarr Corporation, Chicago, IL, pg. 831
Potamkin, Victor, Pres. & Chief Exec. Officer--Potamkin Manhattan, New York, NY, pg. 882
Poupore, John, Chm. Bd., Co-Pres. & Chief Exec. Officer--Helm, Inc., Highland Park, MI, pg. 527
Powell, Richard M., Pres. & Chief Exec. Officer--L. Powell Co., Inc., Culver City, CA, pg. 882
Powell, Watson, III, Chief Exec. Officer--American Republic Insurance Co., Des Moines, IA, pg. 60
Powning, M.W., Chm. & Chief Exec. Officer--Koehler Manufacturing Company, Marlborough, MA, pg. 639
Prairie, Duane, Pres. & Chief Exec. Officer--Park Construction Company, Minneapolis, MN, pg. 848
Prechter, Heinz C., Chm. & Chief Exec. Officer--ASC Incorporated, Southgate, MI, pg. 7
Preece, Tony, Chief Exec. Officer--Batey/Poindexter, Los Angeles, CA, pg. 126
Prendergast, M. Raymond, Chm. Bd. & Chief Exec. Officer--Boston Distributors, Inc., Maple Heights, OH, pg. 167
Pressman, Gene, V.P. & Chief Exec. Officer--Barneys New York, New York, NY, pg. 120
Preston, Donald, Pres. & Chief Exec. Officer--Bijur Lubricating Corporation, Bennington, VT, pg. 150
Previdi, Melissa, Pres. & Chief Exec. Officer--Danbury Printing & Lithograph, Inc., Danbury, CT, pg. 313
Previti, James, Chm. Bd, Pres. & Chief Exec. Officer--Forecast Mortgage Corporation, Rancho Cucamonga, CA, pg. 423
Price, Gayle B., Jr., Chm. Bd. & Chief Exec. Officer--Price Brothers Co., Dayton, OH, pg. 888
Price, M.S., Chm. Bd. & Chief Exec. Officer--Humphreys Price/Cochran & Sanford Advertising, Memphis, TN, pg. 553
Price, Thomas P., Jr., Pres. & Chief Exec. Officer--Sabin Robbins Paper Co., Cincinnati, OH, pg. 965
Pritz, Benjamin L., Chm. Bd., Pres. & Chief Exec. Officer--Grandpa Brands Company, Cincinnati, OH, pg. 476
Pritzker, Jay, Chm. Bd. & Chief Exec. Officer--H. Group Holding Inc., Chicago, IL, pg. 495
Pritzker, Robert A., Pres. & Chief Exec. Officer--The Marmon Group, Inc., Chicago, IL, pg. 710
Proctor, Barbara G., Pres. & Chief Exec. Officer--Proctor & Gardner Advertising, Inc., Chicago, IL, pg. 892
Proctor, Truby G., Jr., Chm. Bd. & Chief Exec. Officer--The Pantry, Inc., Sanford, NC, pg. 846
Proiss, Mike, Chief Exec. Officer/Taren--Cole of California, Los Angeles, CA, pg. 1079
Pronko, David, Chm. Bd., Pres. & Chief Exec. Officer--PE Systems, Reston, VA, pg. 836
Prout, Stephen, Pres. & Chief Exec. Officer--AQHI, Inc., Colchester, CT, pg. 5
Puccini, Robert S., Pres. & Chief Exec. Officer--Head Sports, Inc., Boulder, CO, pg. 520
Purcell, Frank, Pres. & Chief Exec. Officer--Purcell International Group, Inc., Los Angeles, CA, pg. 900
Puris, Martin, Pres. & Chief Exec. Officer--Ammirati & Puris Inc., New York, NY, pg. 67
Puschel, Philip P., Chm. Bd. & Chief Exec. Officer--F. Schumacher & Co., New York, NY, pg. 979
Pyle, Thomas F., Chm. Bd., Pres. & Chief Exec. Officer--RAYOVAC Corporation, Madison, WI, pg. 915
Quadracci, H.V., Pres. & Chief Exec. Officer--Quad/Graphics, Inc., Pewaukee, WI, pg. 902
Quick, J. Douglas, Pres. & Chief Exec. Officer--Oceana Foods, Shelby, MI, pg. 651
Quinlan, Donald P., Chm. Bd., Pres., Chief Exec. & Chief Oper. Officer--Graphic Controls Corporation, Buffalo, NY, pg. 478
Quinland, Donald P., Chm. Bd., Pres. & Chief Exec. Officer--Graphic Controls, Corp., Buffalo, NY, pg. 478
Quinn, Patrick M., Pres., Chief Exec. Officer & Chief Oper. Officer--Spartan Stores Inc., Grand Rapids, MI, pg. 1026
Quinn, Terrence J., Pres. & Chief Exec. Officer--LINC Scientific Leasing Inc., Chicago, IL, pg. 648
Quirk, John E., Pres. & Chief Exec. Officer--Village Car Company, Bangor, ME, pg. 1151
Raab, Max L., Chm. Bd. & Chief Exec. Officer--J. G. Hook, Inc., Philadelphia, PA, pg. 543
Rabil, Richard J., Chief Exec. Officer & Exec. V.P.--The Van Metre Companies, Burke, VA, pg. 1144
Radler, Louis, Chm. Bd., Pres. & Chief Exec. Officer--Chessco Industries, Inc., Westport, CT, pg. 243
Radwill, Scott, Pres., Chief Exec. & Chief Oper. Officer--Export--Master Appliance Corp., Racine, WI, pg. 719
Ragel, Jack, Chm., Pres. & Chief Exec. Officer--Stephan & Brady, Incorporated, Madison, WI, pg. 1046
Raimo, Thomas M., Pres. & Chief Exec. Officer--Hudson & Affiliated Co., Shawnee Mission, KS, pg. 551
Raimondo, A.F., Pres. & Chief Exec. Officer--Behlen Mfg. Co., Columbus, NE, pg. 132
Rainville, Dewey, Chief Exec. Officer--Universal Dynamics Inc., Woodbridge, VA, pg. 1138
Rainville, Dewey, Chief Exec. Officer--Universal Dynamics Inc., North Plainfield, NJ, pg. 1138
Rainville, Dewey, Chief Exec. Officer--Universal Dynamics, Inc., Woodbridge, VA, pg. 1138
Raisbeck, Peter, Pres. & Chief Exec. Officer--Institutional Financing Services, Benicia, CA, pg. 571
Rakolta, John, Jr., Pres., Chief Exec. Officer & Treas.--Walbridge Aldinger Company, Detroit, MI, pg. 1158
Rakow, Thomas S., Pres., Chief Exec. Officer & Treas.--Illinois Hydraulic Construction Company, South Elgin, IL, pg. 563
Randall, Ronald F., Chm. Bd., Pres. & Chief Exec. Officer--Randall Stores, Inc., Mitchell, SD, pg. 911
Randazzo, Carmen T., Chief Oper. Officer--Thoroughbred Software International, Inc., Somerset, NJ, pg. 1095
Randolph, William, Chm. Bd. & Chief Exec. Officer--Post Buckley Schuh & Jernigan, Miami, FL, pg. 881
Rangen, Chirstopher, Chief Exec. Officer--Rangen, Inc., Buhl, ID, pg. 912
Rankin, Claiborne, Pres. & Chief Exec. Officer--Bruning Paint Company, Baltimore, MD, pg. 184
Rankin, Thompson L., Chm., Pres. & Chief Exec. Officer--Lykes Brothers Inc. of Florida, Tampa, FL, pg. 688
Rankin, Thompson L., Chm. Bd. & Chief Exec. Officer--Lykes Energy, Inc., Tampa, FL, pg. 689
Rao, Duane, Chm. Bd. & Chief Exec. Officer--Rao Wholesale Tire Centers, Inc., Detroit, MI, pg. 912
Rapelje, Ronald D., Pres. & Chief Exec. Officer--Ebeling & Reuss Company, Allentown, PA, pg. 365
Rappaport, Dr. Allan, Chm. Bd., Pres. & Chief Exec. Officer--National Emergency Services, Inc., Tiburon, CA, pg. 788
Rappeport, Don, Chm. Bd. & Chief Exec. Officer--Donlen Corp., Deerfield, IL, pg. 345
Rattigan, Thomas J., Chm. Bd., Pres. & Chief Exec. Officer--G. Heileman Brewing Co., Inc., La Crosse, WI, pg. 526
Rauch, C. Dixon, III, Pres. & Chief Exec. Officer--Rundel Products, Inc., Portland, OR, pg. 956
Rauenhorst, Gerald, Chm. Bd. & Chief Exec. Officer--OPUS Corp., Minnetonka, MN, pg. 828
Ray, Bill F., Pres., Chief Exec. Officer & Chief Oper. Officer--Binning's Building Products, Inc., Lexington, NC, pg. 151
Ray, Bingham, Co-Chief Exec. Officer--October Films, Inc., New York, NY, pg. 821
Raydon, Max E., Pres. & Chief Exec. Officer--Homeland Stores, Inc., Oklahoma City, OK, pg. 542
Raymonds, John M., Chm. Bd. & Chief Exec. Officer--Captive Plastics, Piscataway, NJ, pg. 216
Rayve, Robert G., Pres. & Chief Exec. Officer--The Spencer Turbine Co., Windsor, CT, pg. 1030
Rayve, Robert G., Pres. & Chief Exec. Officer--Spencer Turbine Co., Windsor, CT, pg. 1030
Read, R.T., Chm. Bd., Pres. & Chief Exec. Officer--Harwick Chemical Corp., Akron, OH, pg. 515
Rebuffat, Fausto, Chief Exec. Officer--Ayer Milano, Milan,, Italy, pg. 104
Reddy, Prasad, Chm. Bd., Pres. & Chief Exec. Officer--Freeman Shoes Company, Beloit, WI, pg. 431
Reed, Alan C., Chm. Bd. & Chief Exec. Officer--Radix Corporation, Salt Lake City, UT, pg. 909
Reed, Brad, Chief Oper. Officer, Sec. & Treas.--Kova Fertilizer Inc., Greensburg, IN, pg. 643
Reed, Joel L., Pres. & Chief Exec. Officer--Insilco Corporation, Midland, TX, pg. 571
Reed, Larry E., Chm. Bd. & Chief Exec. Officer--Horizon Bancorp, Michigan City, IN, pg. 544
Reed, Larry E., Chm. Bd. & Chief Exec. Officer--First Citizens Bank, N.A., Michigan City, IN, pg. 544
Reese, Michael R., Chm Bd., Pres. & Chief Exec. Officer--Pierce Manufacturing, Inc., Appleton, WI, pg. 870
Reese, Thomas W., Chm. & Chief Exec. Officer--Hickory Printing Group, Inc., Hickory, NC, pg. 533
Regan, John, Pres. & Chief Exec. Officer--Regan Holding Corporation, Petaluma, CA, pg. 921
Reich, Mort, Pres. & Chief Exec. Officer--The Reich Group, Inc., Philadelphia, PA, pg. 922
Reid, Bruce S., Chm. Bd. & Chief Exec. Officer--Reid & O'Donahue Advertising, Inc., Montgomery, AL, pg. 923
Reid, Daniel S., Pres., Chief Oper. Officer--McCaffrey and McCall, New York, NY, pg. 726
Reid, Russ, Chm. Bd. & Chief Exec. Officer--Russ Reid Company, Inc., Pasadena, CA, pg. 923
Reidel, Arthur A., Chm. Bd. & Chief Exec. Officer--Willamette-Western Corporation, Portland, OR, pg. 1190
Reidy, William J., Chm. & Chief Exec. Officer--Fine Organics Corp., Lodi, NJ, pg. 411
Reifschneider, Darrel, Chm. Bd. & Chief Exec. Officer--Manchester Tank & Equipment Company, Lynwood, CA, pg. 703
Reigle, Jeffrey A., Pres. & Chief Exec. Officer--Regal Ware, Inc., Kewaskum, WI, pg. 921
Reilly, Kevin, Jr., Pres. & Chief Exec. Officer--Lamar Corporation, Baton Rouge, LA, pg. 652
Reilly, Michael K., Pres. & Chief Exec. Officer--Ziegler Coal Holding Co., Fairview Heights, IL, pg. 1218
Reilly, Thomas E., Jr., Chm. Bd. & Chief Exec. Officer--Reilly Industries, Inc., Indianapolis, IN, pg. 923
Reilly, Wayne R., Chm. Bd. & Chief Exec. Officer--John W. Danforth Co., Buffalo, NY, pg. 314
Reily, Timothy, Chm. Bd., Pres. & Chief Exec. Officer--Reily Electric Supply, Inc., Metairie, LA, pg. 923
Reiman, Joey, Chm. Bd. & Chief Exec. Officer--The Joey Reiman Agency, Atlanta, GA, pg. 923
Reiman, Stephen W., Pres. & Chief Exec. Officer--W.A. Roosevelt Co., La Crosse, WI, pg. 946
Reimer, Kenneth F., Pres. & Chief Exec. Officer--Roma Holdings, Dallas, TX, pg. 945
Rein, Morrison, Pres. & Chief Exec. Officer--Standard Security Life Insurance Company of New York, New York, NY, pg. 452
Reister, Mark S., Chief Oper. Officer & Sec.--Wohlert Corp., Lansing, MI, pg. 1198
Remos, Gary, Chm. Bd., Pres. & Chief Exec. Officer--Advanced Manufacturing & Development, Willits, CA, pg. 20
Renfroe, Royce, Pres. & Chief Exec. Officer--Bentley Mills, Inc., City of Industry, CA, pg. 140
Renken, Carl E., Pres. & Chief Exec. Officer--Renken Boat Manufacturing Co., Charleston, SC, pg. 927
Rennert, Ira Leon, Pres. & Chief Exec. Officer--Renco Group, New York, NY, pg. 926
Rentenbach, T.M., Pres. & Chief Exec. Officer--Rentenbach Engineering Company, Knoxville, TN, pg. 927
Resnick, Stewart, Chm. Bd. & Chief Exec. Officer--The Franklin Mint, Franklin Center, PA, pg. 60
Reynolds, Byron, Jr., Chief Exec. Officer--Bandini Fertilizer Company, Los Angeles, CA, pg. 117
Rhoades, Ralph S., Pres. & Chief Exec. Officer--Blue Cross and Blue Shield of Oklahoma, Tulsa, OK, pg. 159
Rhodes, Brent, Pres. & Chief Exec. Officer--Carter Chambers Supply, Inc., Baton Rouge, LA, pg. 226
Rhodes, Hedric E., Pres. & Chief Exec. Officer--Griffith Laboratories Worldwide, Inc., Alsip, IL, pg. 487
Riberat, Jean-Charles, Chief Exec. Officer--IG Conseil S.A., Paris,, France, pg. 625
Ricardo, Jose, Chm. Bd. & Chief Exec. Officer--RII (Ricards International Inc.), Silver Spring, MD, pg. 907
Ricciardi, Ronald, V.P. & Gen. Mgr.--Acrison, Inc., Moonachie, NJ, pg. 14
Richards, H. Lee, Chm. Bd. & Chief Exec. Officer--Hygeia Dairy Co., Inc., Harlingen, TX, pg. 557
Richards, Robert J., Pres. & Chief Exec. Officer--SKR Resources, Inc., New York, NY, pg. 963
Richards, Roy, Chief Exec. Officer--Southwire Company, Inc., Carrollton, GA, pg. 1024
Richardson, Joe E., Chief Exec. Officer--Clayson Knitting Co. Inc., Star, NC, pg. 253
Richardson, John S., Pres., Chief Exec. & Chief Fin. Officer--Sugar Creek Packing Co., Mason, OH, pg. 1056
Richardson, Thomas, Chm. Bd., Pres. & Chief Exec. Officer--Delta Education, Inc., Hudson, NH, pg. 326
Richer, Alvin, Chm., Pres. & Chief Exec. Officer--Arnold Machinery Co., Salt Lake City, UT, pg. 84
Richey, Van L., Pres. & Chief Exec. Officer--American Cast Iron Pipe Co., Birmingham, AL, pg. 50
Richter, Irvin E., Chm. Bd. & Chief Exec. Officer--Hill International Inc., Willingboro, NJ, pg. 534
Ricke, Donald W., Chm. Bd. & Chief Exec. Officer--Motek Engineering & Manufacturing Company, Cambridge, MN, pg. 773
Riddleberger, Hensel D., Jr., Chief Exec. Officer--Riddleberger Brothers, Inc., Mount Crawford, VA, pg. 933
Rider, C.G., Pres. & Chief Exec. Officer--AEA, Inc., Charlotte, NC, pg. 3
Rider, Robert F., Chm., Chief Exec. Officer & Treas.--O. A. Newton & Son Co., Bridgeville, DE, pg. 805
Riedel, Dan, Chief Exec. Officer & Pres.-Benchmark Communities Inc.--Benchmark Homes, Inc., Brookville, OH, pg. 138
Riemer, David, Chm. Bd., Pres. & Chief Exec. Officer--Arley Merchandise Corporation, Taunton, MA, pg. 83
Riemer, David I., Chm. Bd., Pres. & Chief Exec. Officer--Rops Textiles Inc., Taunton, MA, pg. 83
Rigg, John G., Chm. Bd. & Chief Exec. Officer--Redco Foods, Inc., Windsor, CT, pg. 919
Riggio, Leonard, Chm. Bd., Pres. & Chief Exec. Officer--Barnes & Noble Bookstores, Inc., New York, NY, pg. 120
Riggs, Louis V., Pres. & Chief Exec. Officer--A. Teichert & Son, Inc., Sacramento, CA, pg. 1084
Riklis, Meshulam, Pres. & Chief Exec. Officer--McCrory Corporation, New York, NY, pg. 934
Riney, Hal P., Chm. & Chief Exec. Officer--Hal Riney & Partners, Inc., San Francisco, CA, pg. 935
Ringer, Walter M., Jr., Chm. Bd. & Chief Exec. Officer--Foley-Belsaw Company, Minneapolis, MN, pg. 422
Rink, Robert A., Pres. & Chief Exec. Officer--Prestige Stamping, Inc., Warren, MI, pg. 888
Riodan, Thomas W., Pres. & Chief Exec. Officer--Ferro Union, Inc., Torrance, CA, pg. 407
Ripich, Lawrence, Chief Exec. Officer--American Tank & Fabricating Co., Cleveland, OH, pg. 63
Ripley, Barrett F., Pres. & Chief Exec. Officer--Troy Mills, Inc., Troy, NH, pg. 1116
Riskind, Kenneth J., Pres. & Chief Exec. Officer--Fullerton Metals Co., Northbrook, IL, pg. 436
Rist, Robert G., Pres. & Chief Exec. Officer--Warner Press, Inc., Anderson, IN, pg. 1164
Ritchie, Hale D., Jr., Chm. Bd. & Chief Exec. Officer--Ritchie Corporation, Wichita, KS, pg. 936
Rob, Joseph M., Chm. Bd., Pres. & Chief Exec. Officer--Equity Services, Inc., Montpelier, VT, pg. 791
Robbins, L.C., Pres. & Chief Exec. Officer--Star Food Processing, Inc., San Antonio, TX, pg. 1039
Roberts, Dorothy H., Chief Exec. Officer--Echo Design Group, Inc., New York, NY, pg. 365
Roberts, Harry, Pres. & Chief Exec. Officer (Portland) & Dir.--EvansGroup, Salt Lake City, UT, pg. 390
Roberts, John H., Pres. & Chief Exec. Officer--J. H. Roberts Industries Inc., Des Plaines, IL, pg. 938
Roberts, John K., Jr., Pres. & Chief Exec. Officer--Pan-American Life Insurance Company, New Orleans, LA, pg. 845
Roberts, Joseph, Chm. Bd. & Chief Exec. Officer--Advanced Circuit Technology, Nashua, NH, pg. 20
Roberts, Stephen M., Pres., Chief Exec. Officer & Treas.--F. L. Roberts & Co. Inc., Springfield, MA, pg. 938
Robertson, G. Bruce, Pres. & Chief Exec. Officer--Robertson Marketing Inc., Charlotte, NC, pg. 939
Robertson, Michael B., Chm., Chief Exec. Officer & Chief Creative Dir.--McCaffrey and McCall, New York, NY, pg. 726
Robertson, Robert G., Pres. & Chief Exec. Officer--White Hen Pantry, Inc., Elmhurst, IL, pg. 1185
Robertson, Scott V., Pres. & Chief Exec. Officer--Robertson's Auto Salvage, Wareham, MA, pg. 939
Robinson, Bob, Pres. & Chief Exec. Officer--Doane Products Co., Branded Sales Div., Joplin, MO, pg. 342
Robinson, Claude D., Pres. & Chief Exec. Officer--Sivyer Steel Corporation, Bettendorf, IA, pg. 1013
Robinson, H. Ivens, Pres. & Chief Exec. Officer--Robinson Lumber & Export Company, New Orleans, LA, pg. 940
Robinson, Richard, Chm. Bd., Pres. & Chief Exec. Officer--SI Holdings Inc., New York, NY, pg. 962
Robinson, Ronald, Chm. Bd. & Chief Exec. Officer--Denver Equipment Company, Colorado Springs, CO, pg. 331
Robinson, William A., Chm. Bd. & Chief Exec. Officer--Robinson & St. John Advertising & Public Relations, Inc., Jacksonville, FL, pg. 940
Robinson, William A., Chm. Bd. & Chief Exec. Officer--Robinson & St. John Advertising & Public Relations, Public Relations Div., Jacksonville, FL, pg. 940
Roche, Jack F., Chm. Bd., Pres. & Chief Exec. Officer--PMC Industries Inc., Wickliffe, OH, pg. 836
Rochon, John, Chief Exec. Officer--Mary Kay Cosmetics Inc., Dallas, TX, pg. 716
Rockett, Howard, Chm. & Chief Exec. Officer--Rockett, Burkhead, Lewis & Winslow, Raleigh, NC, pg. 941

Rodale, Ardath, Chm. Bd. & Chief Exec. Officer--Rodale Press, Inc., Emmaus, PA, pg. 942
Rodell, Rick, Pres. & Chief Exec. Officer--Manufacturers Consolidation Service, Memphis, TN, pg. 705
Rodgers, Joe M., Chm. & Acting Chief Exec. Officer--Berlitz International, Inc., Princeton, NJ, pg. 142
Rodman, Stuart, Chief Exec. Officer--Alliance Automation Systems, Rochester, NY, pg. 37
Rodriguez, Ray, Pres. & Chief Exec. Officer--Univision Holdings, Inc., New York, NY, pg. 502
Roe, K. Keith, Chm. Bd., Pres., Chief Exec. & Chief Oper. Officer--Burns & Roe Enterprises, Inc., Oradell, NJ, pg. 194
Roelofs, Pieter, Pres. & Chief Exec. Officer--Taco John's International, Inc., Cheyenne, WY, pg. 1076
Roesler, Mark, Pres. & Chief Exec. Officer--Curtis Management Group, Indianapolis, IN, pg. 306
Rogan, Richard M., Pres. & Chief Exec. Officer--Burlington Motor Carriers Inc., Daleville, IN, pg. 191
Rogenski, Theodore J., Pres. & Chief Exec. Officer--John Hancock Leasing Corporation, Boston, MA, pg. 596
Rogers, Lloyd F., Pres. & Chief Exec. Officer--Wells Lamont, Niles, IL, pg. 712
Rogers, M. Weldon, III, Chm. Bd., Pres. & Chief Exec. Officer--EAC Corporation, Saint Louis, MO, pg. 359
Rogers, Richard R., Chm. Bd., Pres. & Chief Exec. Officer--Mary Kay Corporation, Dallas, TX, pg. 716
Rogers, Richard R., Chm. & Chief Exec. Officer--Mary Kay Cosmetics Inc., Dallas, TX, pg. 716
Rogerson, Michael, Chm. Bd., Pres. & Chief Exec. Officer--Rogerson Aircraft Corporation, Irvine, CA, pg. 943
Rogness, Kurt E., Chief Exec. Officer--Hammel, Green & Abrahamson, Inc., Minneapolis, MN, pg. 504
Roller, Thomas B., Pres. & Chief Exec. Officer--Plywood Panels, Inc., New Orleans, LA, pg. 878
Rollins, David, Pres. & Chief Exec. Officer--Nashville Wire Product Co., Nashville, TN, pg. 784
Roloff, Jeffrey J., Chm. Bd. & Chief Exec. Officer--Central Data Corporation, Champaign, IL, pg. 232
Romer, Klaus, Pres. & Chief Exec. Officer--McGean-Rohco, Inc., Cleveland, OH, pg. 729
Roney, Patrick E., Chm. Bd., Pres. & Chief Exec. Officer--Electro Mechanical Design Services, Inc., Gaithersburg, MD, pg. 375
Ronzoni, Robert, Chief Exec. Officer--Bellacicco & Sons, Queens Village, NY, pg. 136
Rooney, Francis C., Jr., Chm. Bd. & Chief Exec. Officer--H.H. Brown Shoe Company, Inc., Greenwich, CT, pg. 182
Roper, Gerald, Pres. & Chief Exec. Officer--Chicago Convention & Tourism Bureau, Chicago, IL, pg. 245
Roper, John L. III, Pres. & Chief Exec. Officer--Norfolk Shipbuilding & Drydock Corporation, Norfolk, VA, pg. 810
Rosanio, Linda, Chm. Bd. & Chief Exec. Officer--Rosanio, Bailets & Talamo, Inc., Cherry Hill, NJ, pg. 947
Rose, Kenneth L., Pres. & Chief Exec. Officer--Henkels & McCoy, Inc., Blue Bell, PA, pg. 529
Rose, Robert C., III, Pres. & Chief Exec. Officer--Altama Delta Corp., Darien, GA, pg. 45
Rose, William R., Chm. Bd., Pres. & Chief Exec. Officer--Rose Packing Company, South Barrington, IL, pg. 947
Rosen, David, Pres. & Chief Exec. Officer--CB North America, Inc., Glens Falls, NY, pg. 199
Rosen, Edward H., Chm. & Chief Exec. Officer--Raymond Rosen Co., Conshohocken, PA, pg. 948
Rosen, Jack, Chm., Pres., Chief Exec. & Chief Oper. Officer--Hazel Bishop Corporation, Englewood Cliffs, NJ, pg. 520
Rosenbaum, Edward W., Chm. Bd. & Chief Exec. Officer--David Michael & Co. Inc., Philadelphia, PA, pg. 747
Rosenberg, Alan, Pres. & Chief Exec. Officer--Seaman Furniture Co., Inc., Woodbury, NY, pg. 986
Rosenberg, Kenneth M., Chm. & Chief Exec. Officer--Pharmavite Corp., Mission Hills, CA, pg. 866
Ross, Fred C., Vice Chm., Pres. & Chief Exec. Officer--Allied Old English, Inc., Port Reading, NJ, pg. 38
Ross, Gerald, Pres., Chief Exec. & Chief Fin. Officer & Treas.--MGR Equipment Corp., Inwood, NY, pg. 692
Ross, Joseph, Pres. & Chief Exec. Officer--Entron Industries Limited Partnership, Glendale, NY, pg. 383
Ross, Kenneth, Chm. & Chief Exec. Officer--J H Collectibles, Milwaukee, WI, pg. 584
Ross, Marc S., Pres. & Chief Exec. Officer--Veda International, Inc., Alexandria, VA, pg. 1146
Ross, Marc S., Pres. & Chief Exec. Officer--Veda Incorporated, Alexandria, VA, pg. 1146
Ross, Marc S., Chief Exec. Officer--Veda Systems, Incorporated, California, MD, pg. 1146
Ross, Marc S., Chief Exec. Officer--Chameleon Technologies Incorporated, Alexandria, VA, pg. 1146
Ross, Robert, Chief Exec. Officer--Swiss-M-Tex, L.P., Travelers Rest, SC, pg. 1068
Rossi, Carlos R., Chm. Bd. & Chief Exec. Officer--Conill Advertising, Inc., New York, NY, pg. 274
Rossin, Jack, Chm. & Chief Exec. Officer--Rossin Greenberg Seronick, Boston, MA, pg. 950
Rossio, Robert D., Pres. & Chief Exec. Officer--Lindsay Olive Growers, Lindsay, CA, pg. 676
Rotando, Lynn Andrew, Chm., Pres. & Chief Exec. Officer--Rotando Lerch & Iafeliece Advertising, Stamford, CT, pg. 950
Roth, Ernie, Pres. & New Bus. Contact--Furman, Roth Adv., New York, NY, pg. 437
Roth, Jack, Pres. & Chief Exec. Officer--Admarketing, Inc., Los Angeles, CA, pg. 18
Roth, Michael I., Pres., Chief Oper. Officer & Chief Exec. Officer--The Mutual Life Insurance Company of New York (MONY), New York, NY, pg. 778
Rothbaum, Michael, Pres. & Chief Exec. Officer--The Harwood Companies, Inc., New York, NY, pg. 515
Rothberg, Joan O., Chm. Bd., Chief Exec. Officer & New Bus. Contact--Masterson Rothberg Advertising, New York, NY, pg. 720
Rothwell, Brian G., Pres. & Chief Exec. Officer--Bay State Milling Co., Quincy, MA, pg. 127
Rott, Herbert F., Sr., Chm. Bd. & Chief Exec. Officer--Rott-Keller Supply Co., Fargo, ND, pg. 951
Rouse, Mitchell, Chm. Bd. & Chief Exec. Officer--Supershuttle International, Los Angeles, CA, pg. 1064
Roush, David P., Chm. Bd., Pres. & Chief Exec. Officer--Rocor Transportation Companies Inc., Oklahoma City, OK, pg. 942
Roussel, Louis J., Jr., Chm. Bd., Pres. & Chief Exec. Officer--Victory Financial Group, Inc., Metairie, LA, pg. 1150
Rowan, Frederick J., Pres. & Chief Exec. Officer--The William Carter Company, New York, NY, pg. 226
Rowe, James W., Pres. & Chief Exec. Officer--Defense Credit Union Council, Washington, DC, pg. 298
Rowe, Richard R., Chm. Bd., Pres. & Chief Exec. Officer--The Faxon Company, Inc., Westwood, MA, pg. 404
Rowell, L.J., Jr., Chm. Bd., Pres. & Chief Exec. Officer--Provident Mutual Life Insurance Co., Philadelphia, PA, pg. 896
Rubin, Harold R., Pres. & Chief Exec. Officer--Stevens-Lee Company, Minneapolis, MN, pg. 1048
Rubin, Irving A., Chm. Bd., Pres. & Chief Exec. Officer--Container Products Inc., Southfield, MI, pg. 278
Rubin, Joel, Chm. Bd., Pres. & Chief Exec. Officer--Phototype Color Graphics, Inc., Pennsauken, NJ, pg. 869
Rubin, Richard, Chm., Pres., Chief Exec. & Chief Oper. Officer--Donnkenny, Inc., New York, NY, pg. 345
Rudloff, Hans-Joerg, Chm. Bd., Pres. & Chief Exec. Officer--Financiere Credit Suisse-First Boston, Zug,, Switzerland, pg. 204
Rueden, Jim Von, Chief Fin. Officer & Controller--Wausau Homes, Inc., Rothschild, WI, pg. 1168
Ruhl, Frank, Pres. & Chief Exec. Officer--Ruhl Companies, Inc., Valhalla, NY, pg. 955
Ruhlin, John, Jr., Chm. Bd., Pres. & Chief Exec. Officer--The Ruhlin Company, Sharon Center, OH, pg. 955
Ruhlman, Jon R., Pres. & Chief Exec. Officer--Preformed Line Products, Cleveland, OH, pg. 886
Ruiz, Fred, Pres. & Chief Exec. Officer--Ruiz Food Products, Inc., Dinuba, CA, pg. 955
Rumsfeld, Donald H., Chm. & Chief Exec. Officer--General Instrument Corporation, New York, NY, pg. 425
Rupp, Glenn, Pres. & Chief Exec. Officer--Simmons Upholstered Furniture, Inc., Saint Louis, MO, pg. 1005
Ruppman, Charles T., Chm. Bd. & Chief Exec. Officer--Ruppman National Yellow Pages Service (RNYPS), Peoria, IL, pg. 956
Russell, Dick, Pres. & Chief Exec. Officer--Guaranteed Products, Inc., City of Industry, CA, pg. 491
Russell, Herman J., Chm. Bd. & Chief Exec. Officer--H. J. Russell Corp., Atlanta, GA, pg. 957
Russell, Leo P., Chm. Bd. & Chief Exec. Officer--Russell Industries, Inc., Carnegie, PA, pg. 957
Russeth, Gerald, Pres. & Chief Exec. Officer--Coken Company, Inc., Providence, RI, pg. 259
Rust, Edward B., Jr., Chm. Bd., Pres. & Chief Exec. Officer--State Farm Mutual Automobile Insurance Company, Bloomington, IL, pg. 1041
Ruth, John, Chief Exec. Officer--Amana Society, Amana, IA, pg. 46
Rutherford, J. Larry, Pres. & Chief Exec. Officer--Atlantic Gulf Communities Corporation, Miami, FL, pg. 95
Rutherford, Jack D., Chm. & Chief Exec. Officer--ICM Industries, Inc., Chicago, IL, pg. 559
Ruting, Wayne, Pres. & Chief. Exec. Officer--Columbine Systems Inc., Golden, CO, pg. 266
Rutland, Robert J., Chm. Bd. & Chief Exec. Officer--Allied Systems, Ltd., Decatur, GA, pg. 40
Ryan, George T., Chief Exec. Officer--Thompson Steel Co., Inc., Canton, MA, pg. 1094
Ryan, John D., Pres. & Chief Exec. Officer--Worldvision Enterprises, New York, NY, pg. 54
Ryder, William, Chm. & Chief Exec. Officer--Ryder & Schild, Inc., Miami, FL, pg. 958
Rygh, Ole B., Pres. & Chief Exec. Officer--IDAB International Incorporated, Hampton, VA, pg. 559
Rynone, Thomas E., Chief Exec. Officer--Rynone Manufacturing Corporation, Sayre, PA, pg. 958
Ryser, Frank, Chm. Bd., Pres., Chief Exec. Officer & Treas.--Ryser Brothers Inc., Chicago, IL, pg. 958
Ryzman, Zvi, Pres.--Ardell International, Inc., City of Commerce, CA, pg. 81
Sabbatino, Anthony, Pres., Chief Oper. & Chief Exec. Officer--Bogue Electric Manufacturing Co., Paterson, NJ, pg. 162
Sack, Thomas F., Pres., Chief Exec. & Oper. Officer--Haddon Craftsmen, Inc., Scranton, PA, pg. 499
Safiol, George E., Pres. & Chief Exec. Officer--General Instrument Corporation, New York, NY, pg. 425
Sahm, Roland R., Chm. Bd. & Chief Exec. Officer--Elixir Industries, Gardena, CA, pg. 376
Sakosits, John J., Chm. Bd., Chief Exec. & Chief Oper. Officer--Hoboken Wood Flooring Corporation, Wayne, NJ, pg. 537
Salvati, Philip J., Pres. & Chief Exec. Officer--Salvati Montgomery Sakoda, Inc., Costa Mesa, CA, pg. 967
Samburg, A. Gene, Chm. Bd., Pres. & Chief Exec. Officer--Kastle Systems, Inc., Arlington, VA, pg. 618
Samis, Michael S., Pres. & Chief Exec. Officer--Macklanburg-Duncan Co., Oklahoma City, OK, pg. 697
Samsill, Mark, Pres. & Chief Exec. Officer--Samsill Corporation, Fort Worth, TX, pg. 968
Samuels, Robert P., Chm. Bd., Chief Exec. Officer--Milton Samuels Advertising Agency, Inc., New York, NY, pg. 968
Sanborn, Bruce, Chm. Bd., Pres. & Chief Exec. Officer--North Central Life Insurance Companies, Saint Paul, MN, pg. 813
Sanborn, Bruce C., Chm. Bd., Pres. & Chief Exec. Officer--Financial Life Companies, Inc., St. Paul, MN, pg. 813
Sandberg, A.L., Pres. & Chief Exec. Officer--Delta Sugar Corporation, Clarksburg, CA, pg. 327
Sanders, John, Pres. & Chief Exec. Officer WW (New York & Detroit)--Wunderman Cato Johnson, New York, NY, pg. 1211
Sanders, O'Neil, Chm. Bd., Pres., Chief Exec. & Chief Oper. Officer--Associated Petroleum Carriers, Spartanburg, SC, pg. 91
Sanderson, Sandra B., Pres. & Chief Exec. Officer--Sanderson Plumbing Products Inc., Columbus, MS, pg. 970
Sandhu, M.S., Chm. Bd., Pres. & Chief Exec. Officer--SRS Technologies, Newport Beach, CA, pg. 964
Sandifer, Thomas N., Pres. & Chief Exec. Officer--Cain & Bultman, Inc., Jacksonville, FL, pg. 207
Sandler, Ernest, Pres. & Chief Exec. Officer--Interstate Drug Exchange, Inc., Amityville, NY, pg. 580
Sanguinetti, Pat, Pres. & Chief Exec. Officer--Blue Anchor, Inc., Sacramento, CA, pg. 158
Sansom, William B., Chm. Bd. & Chief Exec. Officer--The H. T. Hackney Co., Knoxville, TN, pg. 498
Santry, Christopher B., Chm. & Chief Exec. Officer--Christopher Thomas Associates Inc., Garden City, NY, pg. 249
Sapos, Mary Ann, Pres. & Chief Exec. Officer--Hutchins/Young & Rubicam, Rochester, NY, pg. 1211
Saras, James, Chm. Bd. & Chief Exec. Officer--Tri Valley Growers Inc., San Francisco, CA, pg. 1111
Sargent, Charles L., Chm. Bd. & Chief Exec. Officer--Thetford Corporation, Ann Arbor, MI, pg. 357
Sargent, Lee M., Pres. & Chief Exec. Officer--Todd & Sargent, Inc., Ames, IA, pg. 1100
Sarkisian, Norman,, Owner, Pres. & Chief Exec. Officer--Beacon Group, Bloomfield, CT, pg. 128
Sarmanian, Peter, Chm. Bd. & Chief Exec. Officer--Printed Circuit Corporation, Woburn, MA, pg. 891
Sauder, Maynard, Pres. & Chief Exec. Officer--Sauder Woodworking Co., Archbold, OH, pg. 972
Sauer, Mark, Pres. & Chief Exec. Officer--Pittsburgh Pirates Professional Baseball Club, Pittsburgh, PA, pg. 873
Saul, Charles F., Pres. & Chief Exec. Officer--Agway, Inc., De Witt, NY, pg. 25
Saunders, John H., Sr., Chm. Bd & Chief Exec. Officer--Palmetto Wholesale Co., Inc., Columbia, SC, pg. 844
Saunders, R.F., Chm. Bd. & Chief Exec. Officer--Dakco Distributors, Inc., Minot, ND, pg. 311
Saunders, Richard F., Chief Exec. Officer--Dakota Drug, Inc., Minot, ND, pg. 311
Saunders, Robert H., Jr., Pres. & Chief Exec. Officer--The J. M. Ney Company, Bloomfield, CT, pg. 805
Savastomo, Ted, Chief Exec. Officer--Summit Environmental Group, Canton, OH, pg. 1058
Sazenski, Chester R., Chm. Bd. & Chief Exec. Officer--Jesco, Inc., Minneapolis, MN, pg. 593
Scanlan, Thomas M., Jr., Pres. & Chief Exec. Officer--The Ward Machinery Company, Cockeysville, MD, pg. 1162
Scelba, David F., Chief Exec. Officer--SSD&W Integrated Marketing Communications, Montville, NJ, pg. 964
Schad, Theodore G., Jr., Chm. Bd., Pres. & Chief Exec. Officer--Schad Industries, Inc., Lafayette, LA, pg. 974
Schad, Theodore G., Jr., Chm. Bd., Pres. & Chief Exec. Officer--Lou Ana Foods, Inc., Opelousas, LA, pg. 974
Schaible, Paul G., Jr., Chm. Bd., Pres. & Chief Exec. Officer--Chelsea State Bank, Chelsea, MI, pg. 241
Schaller, Christopher L., Chm., Pres. & Chief Exec. Officer--Forstmann & Company, Inc., New York, NY, pg. 424
Schardt, Ronald, Chm. Bd., Chief Exec. Officer & Chief Oper. Officer--Reinke Manufacturing Co., Inc., Deshler, NE, pg. 924
Scharer, Vivian, V.P, Chief Exec. Officer--Scharer Associates, Inc., Great Neck, NY, pg. 974
Scharfberg, Sheldon, Pres., Chief Exec. Officer, Treasurer & New Bus. Contact--Scharfberg & Associates, Ltd. Adv., Jenkintown, PA, pg. 974
Schatz, Douglas S., Pres. & Chief Exec. Officer--Advanced Energy Industry, Fort Collins, CO, pg. 20
Schawk, Clarence W., Chm. Bd. & Chief Exec. Officer--Schawk, Inc., Des Plaines, IL, pg. 974
Schecter, Leroy, Chm. Bd. & Chief Exec. Officer--American Strip Steel Inc., Kearny, NJ, pg. 63
Scheideler, Albert, Pres. & Chief Exec. Officer--McNally Industries, Inc., Grantsburg, WI, pg. 731
Scheinman, Tom, Pres. & Chief Exec. Officer--The Unimax Corporation, New York, NY, pg. 1127
Schenk, George, Pres. & Chief Exec. Officer--J.M. Huber Corporation, Edison, NJ, pg. 550
Schenk, Tony, Chm. Bd., Pres. & Chief Exec. Officer--Enabling Technologies Company, Stuart, FL, pg. 380
Scherbing, Gordon K., Pres. & Chief Exec. Officer--Farmers Union Marketing & Processing Association, Redwood Falls, MN, pg. 402
Schiavone, Phillip, Pres. & Chief Exec. Officer--E. W. Howell Company, Inc., Port Washington, NY, pg. 547
Schiavone, Ronald, Pres. & Chief Exec. Officer--Schiavone Construction Co., Secaucus, NJ, pg. 976
Schick, Joseph C., Chm. Bd., Pres., Chief Exec. Officer & Chief Oper. Officer--Raub Supply Company, Lancaster, PA, pg. 913
Schifter, Yvonne, Chm. Bd. & Chief Exec. Officer--Squire-Cogswell Company, Northbrook, IL, pg. 1034
Schimpf, Glenn P., Pres. & Chief Exec. Officer--Danis Industries Corporation, Dayton, OH, pg. 314
Schlatter, Donald A., Pres., Chief Exec. Officer & Gen. Counsel--Art Iron, Inc., Toledo, OH, pg. 86
Schlemmer, Robert E., Pres. & Chief Exec. Officer--United States Ceramic Tile Co., East Sparta, OH, pg. 1135
Schlottfeldt, Walter, Pres. & Chief Exec. Officer--Badger Air Brush Company, Franklin Park, IL, pg. 113
Schlueter, John J., Chm. Bd. & Chief Exec. Officer--Knapp Shoes Inc., Brockton, MA, pg. 636
Schmid, James A., Pres. & Chief Exec. Officer--Crescent Electric Supply Co., East Dubuque, IL, pg. 298
Schmidt, John, Co-Chief Exec. Officer--October Films, Inc., New York, NY, pg. 821

Corporate Responsibilities Index

Schmidt, Marcus, Pres. & Chief Exec. Officer--Atlas Tool Inc., Roseville, MI, pg. 96
Schmidt, P.G., Chief Exec. Officer--Marco Seattle, Inc., Seattle, WA, pg. 707
Schmidt, Peter G., Pres. & Chief Exec. Officer--Marine Construction & Design Co., Seattle, WA, pg. 707
Schmidt, Robert F., Chm. Bd. & Chief Exec. Officer--Cosco Industries, Spring Valley, NY, pg. 288
Schmidt, Ronald, Pres. & Chief Exec. Officer--I B Diffusion, LP, Chicago, IL, pg. 558
Schmidt, Ronald D., Chm. Bd., Pres. & Chief Exec. Officer--Zytec Corp., Eden Prairie, MN, pg. 1221
Schneider, Isidore, Pres. & Chief Exec. Officer--Schneider Mills, Inc., New York, NY, pg. 977
Schneider, Marvin, Chm. & Chief Exec. Officer--Sherwood & Schneider Advertising, New York, NY, pg. 999
Schnitzer, Dr. Leonard, Chm. Bd. & Chief Exec. Officer--Schnitzer Steel Industries, Inc., Portland, OR, pg. 977
Schoenecker, Guy, Pres. & Chief Exec. Officer--Guy Schoenecker, Inc., Minneapolis, MN, pg. 977
Schofield, Robert, Pres. & Chief Exec. Officer--Affiliated Food Distributors, Scranton, PA, pg. 23
Scholtens, Michael, Chm., & Chief Exec. Officer--Nutech, Inc., San Jose, CA, pg. 817
Schoonover, Steven L., Pres. & Chief Exec. Officer--Fibrebond Corporation, Minden, LA, pg. 408
Schorr, Roger J., Pres. & Chief Exec. Officer--The Crosset Company Inc., Cincinnati, OH, pg. 300
Schott, Owen W., Pres. & Chief Exec. Officer--Schott Corporation, Wayzata, MN, pg. 978
Schrager, Phillip G., Chm. Bd. & Chief Exec. Officer--Pacesetter Corporation, Omaha, NE, pg. 839
Schroeder, William, Chm. Bd. & Chief Exec. Officer--Ireland Coffee Tea, Inc., Pleasantville, NJ, pg. 582
Schroeder, William, Chief Exec. Officer--The Lenson Corporation, Pleasantville, NJ, pg. 582
Schrott, John D., Jr., Chm. Bd., Pres. & Chief Exec. Officer--Reel-O-Matic Systems, Inc., Oklahoma City, OK, pg. 920
Schrum, E.P., Pres., Chief Exec. Officer & Treas.--Carolina Mills, Inc., Maiden, NC, pg. 223
Schube, Frank W., Pres. & Chief Exec. Officer--Dualite Inc., Williamsburg, OH, pg. 350
Schubert, William C., Pres., Treas., & Chief Exec. Officer--Kitchell Corporation, Phoenix, AZ, pg. 634
Schuenke, Donald J., Chm. Bd. & Chief Exec. Officer--Northwestern Mutual Life Insurance Co., Milwaukee, WI, pg. 815
Schuette, Marvin, Pres. & Chief Exec. Officer--Wausau Homes, Inc., Rothschild, WI, pg. 1168
Schultz, James R., Pres. & Chief Exec. Officer--Great Lakes Lithograph Co., Cleveland, OH, pg. 481
Schultz, William, Pres. & Chief Exec. Officer--Fender Musical Instruments, Scottsdale, AZ, pg. 406
Schumacher, Donald, Pres. & Chief Exec. Officer--Spurgeon Mercantile Company, Chicago, IL, pg. 1034
Schutte, Alden F., Pres. & Chief Exec. Officer--Schutte & Company, Buffalo, NY, pg. 979
Schwab, Samuel C., Pres. & Chief Exec. Officer--S. Schwab Company, Cumberland, MD, pg. 980
Schwan, Marvin M., Chm. Bd., Pres. & Chief Exec. Officer--Schwan's Sales Enterprises, Marshall, MN, pg. 980
Schwartz, Barry, Chm. Bd. & Chief Exec. Officer--Doe Spun, Inc., New York, NY, pg. 343
Schwartz, Barry, Chm. Bd. & Chief Exec. Officer--Bambinaggine, New York, NY, pg. 343
Schwartz, Barry, Chm. Bd. & Chief Exec. Officer--Mia Bambini, New York, NY, pg. 343
Schwartz, M.J., Chm. Bd., Pres. & Chief Exec. Officer--Quaker City Motor Parts Company, Middletown, DE, pg. 903
Schwartz, Marvin, Chm. Bd. & Chief Exec. Officer--Gannett Transit, New York, NY, pg. 442
Schwartz, Robert G., Chm. Bd., Pres. & Chief Exec. Officer--Metropolitan Life Insurance Co., New York, NY, pg. 744
Schwarz, Carl, Exec. V.P. & Chief Exec. Officer--Kentile Floors Inc., South Plainfield, NJ, pg. 623
Schwedel, Alan R., Pres. & Chief Exec. Officer--Amerbelle Corporation, Rockville, CT, pg. 47
Schwegmann, John, Chief Exec. Officer & Chm.--Schwegmann Giant Super Markets, New Orleans, LA, pg. 980
Schweiner, Jerry, Chm. Bd., Pres. & Chief Exec. Officer--Benco Industries, Inc., Fort Deposit, AL, pg. 138
Sciame, Frank, Pres., Treas., Chief Exec. & Chief Fin. Officer--F.J. Sciame Construction, New York, NY, pg. 981
Scibelli, R.M., Pres. & Chief Exec. Officer--Yardney Technical Products, Inc., Pawcatuck, CT, pg. 1207
Scobie, William M., Chm. Bd., Chief Exec. & Legal Officer--Mason Shoe Mfg. Co., Chippewa Falls, WI, pg. 718
Scobie, William M., Chm. Bd., Chief Exec. & Legal Officer--Wissota Trader & B.A. Mason, Chippewa Falls, WI, pg. 718
Scopetta, John N., Chm. Bd., Pres. & Chief Exec. Officer--Power Engineering Co. Inc., Coral Gables, FL, pg. 883
Scordato, Emil A., Chm. & Chief Exec. Officer--Medical Laboratory Automation, Inc., Pleasantville, NY, pg. 735
Scott, Harry, Pres. & Chief Exec. Oper.--Corporate Travel Services, Oakland, CA, pg. 287
Scott, James T., Chm. Bd., Chief Exec. Officer & Treas.--Norcostco, Inc., Minneapolis, MN, pg. 809
Scott, Patrick, Pres. & Chief Exec. Officer--Fisher Broadcasting, Inc., Seattle, WA, pg. 415
Scott, Richard J., Chief Exec. Officer & Creative Dir.--Edelmann Scott, Inc., Richmond, VA, pg. 368
Scott, Ronald H., Chm. Bd. & Chief Exec. Officer--Interform Corporation, Bridgeville, PA, pg. 574
Scotti, Gavin A., Pres. & Chief Exec. Officer--Klemtner Advertising Inc., New York, NY, pg. 635
Scudder, Charles D., Chm. Bd. & Chief Exec. Officer--Charing Cross Group, Louisville, KY, pg. 239
Seabrook, James H., Jr., Pres. & Chief Exec. Officer--Seabrook Wallcoverings, Inc., Memphis, TN, pg. 984
Seabrook, James M., Chm. Bd. & Chief Exec. Officer--Seabrook Brothers & Sons, Inc., Seabrook, NJ, pg. 984
Searle, George, Pres. & Chief Exec. Officer--IA Construction Corp., Concordville, PA, pg. 558
Seaton, Kenneth M., Chm. Bd., Pres. & Chief Exec. Officer--Family Inns of America, Inc., Pigeon Forge, TN, pg. 398
Secrist, Richard, Chm. Bd., Pres. & Chief Exec. Officer--Blue Tee Corporation, New York, NY, pg. 161
Secrist, Roger E., Chm. & Chief Exec. Officer--ANGUS Chemical Company, Buffalo Grove, IL, pg. 75
Seelert, Robert, Pres. & Chief Exec. Officer--Kayser-Roth Hosiery, Inc., Greensboro, NC, pg. 262
Segal, Gordon I., Pres. & Chief Exec. Officer--Euromarket Designs, Inc., Northbrook, IL, pg. 390
Segal, Myron, Chm. Bd., Pres. & Chief Exec. Officer--Premier Mill Corp., New York, NY, pg. 887
Seigle, Jack M., Chm. & Chief Exec. Officer--Starr Seigle McCombs, Inc., Honolulu, HI, pg. 1040
Seitz, Tadd C., Chm. Bd. & Chief Exec. Officer--The Scott Company, Marysville, OH, pg. 982
Selders, Wim, H.J., Pres. & Chief Exec. Officer--Ortel Corporation, Alhambra, CA, pg. 830
Self, J.C., Jr., Chm. & Chief Exec. Officer--Greenwood Mills, Inc., Greenwood, SC, pg. 485
Selzer, William H., Pres. & Chief Exec. Officer--Cox Hobbies, Inc., Corona, CA, pg. 294
Semler, Jerry D., Chm. Bd., Pres. & Chief Exec. Officer--American United Life Insurance Company, Indianapolis, IN, pg. 65
Semrae Thomas, V.P.-Gen. Mgr. & Chief Exec. Officer--Rite-Hite Corporation (IA), Dubuque, IA, pg. 936
Serff, Paul, Chief Exec. Officer & Sr. V.P.-Human Resources--Tom's Foods, Columbus, GA, pg. 1101
Sertillange, Jean Marie, Chief Exec. Officer--Aero Peru Corporation, Miami, FL, pg. 22
SerVaas, Cory, M.D., Chm. Bd., Pres. & Chief Exec. Officer--Benjamin Franklin Literary & Medical Society, Inc., Indianapolis, IN, pg. 139
SerVaas, Cory, M.D., Pres. & Chief Exec. Officer--The Saturday Evening Post Society, Indianapolis, IN, pg. 139
Setzer, Leonard, Pres. & Chief Exec. Officer--National Merchandise Co., Inc., Jacksonville, FL, pg. 792
Seuss, C. David, Chm., Pres., Chief Exec. Officer & Treas.--Spinnaker Software Corporation, Cambridge, MA, pg. 1031
Sevier, Helen, Chm. Bd., Pres., Chief Exec. & Chief Oper. Officer--B.A.S.S., Inc., Montgomery, AL, pg. 105
Seward, John E., Jr., Pres. & Chief Exec. Officer--The Paty Company, Piney Flats, TN, pg. 852
Sewell, J. Carl, Jr., Chief Exec. Officer--Sewell Village Cadillac Co., Dallas, TX, pg. 993
Sexton, Edward W., Jr., Pres. & Chief Exec. Officer--Sexton Can Co., Inc., Cambridge, MA, pg. 993
Sexton, Thomas, Chief Exec. Officer--First Boston (Puerto Rico), Inc., Hato Rey, PR, pg. 204
Shacklett, James, III, Chief Exec. Officer--National Label Company, Lafayette Hill, PA, pg. 791
Shade, Tom, Pres. & Chief Exec. Officer--Moorman Mfg. Company, Quincy, IL, pg. 769
Shafer, Byron A., Pres. & Chief Exec. Officer--Shafer Commercial Seating Inc., Denver, CO, pg. 994
Shafer, Gary, Pres. & Chief Exec. Officer--Trammell Crow Company, Dallas, TX, pg. 1106
Shaffer, James B., Pres. & Chief Exec. Officer--Guy Gannett Publishing Company, Portland, ME, pg. 442
Shafto, Robert A., Pres. & Chief Exec. Officer--The New England, Boston, MA, pg. 799
Shah, Harry, Pres.--National Food Stores, Inc. T/A Krauszer's, Edison, NJ, pg. 788
Shah, Satish, Pres. & Chief Exec. Officer--Accra Pac Group, Elkhart, IN, pg. 11
Shaheen, David, Vice Chm. & Chief Exec. Officer--World Carpets, Inc., Dalton, GA, pg. 1202
Shames, Sidney J., Chm. Bd., Pres., CEO, COO, CFO & Treas.--Melard Manufacturing Corporation, Passaic, NJ, pg. 737
Shanahan, James P., Pres. & Chief Exec. Officer--Kranco, Inc., Houston, TX, pg. 643
Shanaman, Sam, Chief Exec. Officer--D. M. Management Company, Hingham, MA, pg. 309
Shank, Glen L., Pres., Chief Exec. & Oper. Officer--Duckwall-Alco Stores, Inc., Abilene, KS, pg. 351
Shanks, John, Chief Exec. Officer--Dobbs Brothers Management, Memphis, TN, pg. 342
Shapell, Nathan, Chm. Bd., Pres. & Chief Exec. Officer--Shapell Industries, Inc., Beverly Hills, CA, pg. 995
Shapero, J., Chm. Bd., Pres. & Chief Exec. Officer--Quael Corp., Detroit, MI, pg. 902
Shapira, David, Chief Exec. Officer--Giant Eagle, Inc., Pittsburgh, PA, pg. 455
Shapiro, Richard B., Chm. Bd., Pres. & Chief Exec. Officer--Charles River Data Systems, Inc., Framingham, MA, pg. 240
Sharbel, Patrick, Pres. & Chief Exec. Officer--Humboldt Express, Inc., Nashville, TN, pg. 552
Share, Harvey, Pres. & Chief Exec. Officer--Bobst Group Inc., Roseland, NJ, pg. 161
Sharp, Gene, Pres. & Chief Exec. Officer--Affiliated Food Stores, Keller, TX, pg. 23
Shaughnessy, William J., Pres. & Chief Exec. Officer--Wilbur Chocolate Co., Inc., Lititz, PA, pg. 219
Shaw, Ronald W., Pres. & Chief Exec. Officer--Cives Corp., Roswell, GA, pg. 251
Shea, Terence J., Chm. Bd. & Chief Exec. Officer--Bradner Central Company, Chicago, IL, pg. 170
Shearer, Martin P., Pres. & Chief Exec. Officer--Southern Belle Dairy Company, Inc., Somerset, KY, pg. 1020
Sheehan, David F., Mng. Partner & Chief Exec. Officer--Eire Partners, Inc., Chicago, IL, pg. 372
Sheehan, Dennis W., Chm. Bd., Pres. & Chief Exec. Officer--AXIA Incorporated, Oak Brook, IL, pg. 8
Sheerr, Richard C., Chm. Bd., Pres & Chief Exec. Officer--Crown Textile Company, Blue Bell, PA, pg. 302
Sheinbaum, Uri, Chm. Bd. & Pres.--Calmark Investment Company, Los Angeles, CA, pg. 211
Sheldon, J.M., Chm. Bd., Pres. & Chief Exec. Officer--Sheldons' Inc., Antigo, WI, pg. 996
Shell, Earl L., Chm. Bd. & Chief Exec. Officer--Hardin Construction Group, Inc., Atlanta, GA, pg. 508
Sheperd, Jeff, Pres. & Chief Exec. Officer--Pic'n Pay Stores, Inc., Charlotte, NC, pg. 201
Shepherd, J. Harold, Chief Exec. Officer--Shepherd Construction Co., Inc., Atlanta, GA, pg. 998
Sheridan, Edward J., Pres. & Chief Exec. Officer--Edwin B. Stimpson Company, Inc., Bayport, NY, pg. 1049
Sheridan, R. Champlin, Chm. Bd. & Chief Exec. Officer--The Sheridan Group, Hanover, PA, pg. 998
Sheridan, R. Champlin, Chief Exec. Officer--The Sheridan Press, Inc., Hanover, PA, pg. 998
Sherman, Glenn, Dr., Chm. Bd. & Chief Exec. Officer--Laser Power Corporation, San Diego, CA, pg. 660
Sherman, Malcolm, Pres. & Chief Exec. Officer--Morse Shoe, Inc., Canton, MA, pg. 772
Shevack, Brett, Pres. & Chief Exec. Officer--Partners & Shevack, Inc., New York, NY, pg. 850
Shewmake, C. B., Chm. Bd. & Chief Exec. Officer--Algernon Blair International, Montgomery, AL, pg. 155
Shields, Gerald N., Chm. Bd., Pres. & Chief Exec. Officer--Graymills Corp., Chicago, IL, pg. 480
Shields, John, Chm. Bd., Pres. & Chief Exec. Officer--Trader Joes Co., South Pasadena, CA, pg. 1076
Shiffman, Milton S., Pres. & Chief Exec. Officer--Shiffman/Fergusson/Stone Advertising Inc., Fort Lee, NJ, pg. 999
Shillestad, John G., Chm. Bd., Pres. & Chief Exec. Officer--Columbian Mutual Life Insurance Co., Binghamton, NY, pg. 266
Shipley, William S. II, Chm. Bd., Pres. & Chief Exec. Officer--Shipley Oil Company, York, PA, pg. 999
Shirazi, Mehdi, Pres. & Chief Exec. Officer--Sigman Meat Co. Inc., Arvada, CO, pg. 1003
Shlomm, Boris, Pres. & Chief Exec. Officer--Amicale Industries, Inc., New York, NY, pg. 66
Shlossman, Arthur, Pres. & Chief Exec. Officer--Jersey Printing Company, Inc., Bayonne, NJ, pg. 593
Sholtz, Gerald, Exec. V.P. & Chief Exec. Officer--H. Cotler Company, New York, NY, pg. 288
Shore, Lawrence A., Pres. & Chief Exec. Officer--United Republic Reinsurance Company, Houston, TX, pg. 662
Shuford, A. Pope, Pres. & Chief Exec. Officer--Shuford Mills, Inc., Hickory, NC, pg. 1001
Shultz, Gerald, Chm. Bd., Pres. & Chief Exec. Officer--Micro-Met L Corp., Indianapolis, IN, pg. 748
Siano, Jerry J., Chm. & Chief Exec. Officer--N W Ayer Incorporated, New York, NY, pg. 103
Siano, Jerry J., Chm. & Chief Exec. Officer--N W Ayer Inc., New York, NY, pg. 104
Siddall, John N., Chm. Bd. & Chief Exec. Officer--Siddall, Matus & Coughter, Inc. Advertising & Public Relations, Richmond, VA, pg. 1002
Sieb, Robert N., Exec. V.P. & Chief Oper. Officer--Henry Newgard & Company, Arlington Heights, IL, pg. 804
Sieg, Madison, Chm. Bd. & Chief Exec. Officer--Sieg Company, Davenport, IA, pg. 1002
Siegal, Michael D., Pres. & Chief Exec. & Chief Oper. Officer--Olympic Steel Inc., Bedford Heights, OH, pg. 825
Siegel, Alan, Chm. & Chief Exec. Officer--Siegel & Gale, New York, NY, pg. 1002
Siegel, Mo, Chm. Bd. & Chief Exec. Officer--Celestial Seasonings, Boulder, CO, pg. 231
Siegel, Owen R., Chm. Bd. & Chief Exec. Officer--R.S. Owens, Chicago, IL, pg. 834
Sigal, Ellen V., Chief Exec. Officer--Sigal/Zuckerman Co., Chevy Chase, MD, pg. 1003
Sigel, Arthur R., Chm. Bd., Pres. & Chief Exec. Officer--Velsicol Chemical Corporation, Rosemont, IL, pg. 1147
Silk, Steven, Chief Exec. Officer--The Estee Corporation, Parsippany, NJ, pg. 389
Sill, Michael R., Chm. Bd. & Chief Exec. Officer--Road Machinery & Supplies Co., Savage, MN, pg. 937
Silver, Ira, Chief Exec. Officer--Silver's Inc., Detroit, MI, pg. 1005
Silver, Phil, Chief Exec. Officer--Sweetheart Cup Co., Inc., Chicago, IL, pg. 1067
Silverman, A.A., Chm. Bd., Pres. & Chief Exec. Officer--Vilter Manufacturing Corporation, Milwaukee, WI, pg. 1152
Simkins, L.J., Chm. Bd., Pres., Chief Exec. & Chief Oper. Officer--Simkins Industries, Inc., New Haven, CT, pg. 1005
Simmons, Hardwick, Pres. & Chief Exec. Officer-Prudential Securities--The Prudential Insurance Company of America, Newark, NJ, pg. 896
Simmons, Hardwick, Pres. & Chief Exec. Officer--Prudential Securities Inc., New York, NY, pg. 897
Simmons, Harold C., Chm. Bd., Pres. & Chief Exec. Officer--Contran Corporation, Dallas, TX, pg. 281
Simmons, Jerry D., Chm. Bd. & Chief Exec. Officer--Simmons Oil Corp., Phoenix, AZ, pg. 1005
Simon, David A., Pres. & Chief Exec. Officer--Prime Hospitality Corp., Fairfield, NJ, pg. 889
Simon, Ernest M., Chm. & Chief Exec. Officer--Arrow Group Industries, Inc., Wayne, NJ, pg. 357
Simon, Melvin, Chief Exec. Officer--Melvin Simon & Associates, Indianapolis, IN, pg. 1006
Simpson, John, Pres. & Chief Exec. Officer--H. E. Sargent, Inc., Stillwater, ME, pg. 971
Sinclair, Stephen, Pres. & Chief Exec. Officer--Orix Real Estate Equities, Inc., Chicago, IL, pg. 829
Singer, Sidney, Chm. Bd. & Chief Exec. Officer--Singers Supermarkets, Inc., North Bergen, NJ, pg. 1008
Singleton, William Dean, Vice Chm. & Chief Exec. Officer--MediaNews Group Inc., Houston, TX, pg. 735
Sisti, Michael, Chief Exec. Officer--Sisti, Zinbarg & Howard, Inc., Paramus, NJ, pg. 1009
Skaggs, James B., Chm. Bd., Pres. & Chief Exec. Officer--Tracor, Inc., Austin, TX, pg. 1104

Skinner, Odie G., Chm. Bd. & Chief Exec. Officer--Skinner Corp., Lanett, AL, pg. 1009
Skutt, Thomas J., Chm. Bd. & Chief Exec. Officer--Mutual of Omaha Insurance Company, Omaha, NE, pg. 779
Slater, Thomas F., Chm., Pres. & Chief Exec. Officer--Actron Manufacturing Company, Cleveland, OH, pg. 15
Slifka, Alfred A., Pres. & Chief Exec. Officer--Global Petroleum Corp., Waltham, MA, pg. 463
Sloss, Lynes, Pres. & Chief Exec. Officer--Bellwether Technology Corporation, New Orleans, LA, pg. 136
Small, Robert, Pres. & Chief Exec. Officer--The Fairmont Hotels, San Francisco, CA, pg. 397
Smead, H.J., Chm. Bd., Pres., Chief Exec. & Chief Fin. Officer & Sec.--Kaiser Aerospace & Electronics Corp., Foster City, CA, pg. 614
Smilow, Joel E., Chm. Bd. & Chief Exec. Officer--Playtex FP Group Incorporated, Stamford, CT, pg. 877
Smilow, Joel E., Chm. & Chief Exec. Officer--Playtex Family Products Corp., Stamford, CT, pg. 877
Smit, James H., Pres. & Chief Exec. Officer--Spartan Oil Corp., Lansing, MI, pg. 1026
Smita, O.R., Chm. Bd. & Chief Exec. Officer--Marine Tech, Lancaster, PA, pg. 759
Smita, O.R., Chief Exec. Officer--Marine Tech, Lancaster, PA, pg. 758
Smith, B.R., Jr., Chm. Bd. & Chief Exec. Officer--Sverdrup Corporation, Maryland Heights, MO, pg. 1065
Smith, Corey, Chief Exec. Officer--Central Point Software, Inc., Beaverton, OR, pg. 234
Smith, Daryl D., Pres. & Chief Exec. Officer--Troy Corporation, East Hanover, NJ, pg. 1116
Smith, David, Chief Exec. Officer--Quad Systems Corporation, Horsham, PA, pg. 902
Smith, Donald N., Chm. & Chief Exec. Officer--Perkins Family Restaurants, Memphis, TN, pg. 1088
Smith, Edward C., Chm. Bd. & Chief Exec. Officer--Ben Venue Laboratories, Inc., Bedford, OH, pg. 138
Smith, Ferdinand J., III, Chm. Bd., Pres., Chief Exec. Officer, Creative Dir.--Jay Incorporated, Rochester, NY, pg. 590
Smith, Fred W., Pres. & Chief Exec. Officer--Donrey Media Group, Fort Smith, AR, pg. 345
Smith, Gary, Pres. & Chief Exec. Officer--Hercules Engines, Inc., Canton, OH, pg. 531
Smith, Gary W., Chm. Bd., Pres. & Chief Exec. Officer--Proto Systems of Atlanta, Alpharetta, GA, pg. 895
Smith, George E., Pres. & Chief Exec. Officer--Alco Industries, Inc., Valley Forge, PA, pg. 32
Smith, Gordon C., Pres., Chief Exec. & Chief Oper. Officer--J.R. Simplot Company, Boise, ID, pg. 1007
Smith, J. Neil, Chm. Bd., Pres. & Chief Exec. Officer--American Technical Services Group, Inc., Norcross, GA, pg. 63
Smith, Joshua I., Chm. Bd. & Chief Exec. Officer--The Maxima Corporation, Lanham, MD, pg. 723
Smith, Lee Allan, Pres. & Exec. Creative Dir.--Ackerman McQueen, Inc., Oklahoma City, OK, pg. 12
Smith, LeRoy T., Chm. Bd., Pres. & Chief Exec. Officer--S-T Industries, Inc., Saint James, MN, pg. 964
Smith, Lonnie L., Pres. & Chief Exec. Officer--Cumberland-Swan, Inc., Smyrna, TN, pg. 304
Smith, Michael, Pres., Chief Exec. Officer & Creative Dir.--J. Richard Smith, Ltd., Melville, NY, pg. 1013
Smith, Michael L., Chm. Bd. & Chief Exec. Officer--Mayflower Transit, Inc., Carmel, IN, pg. 724
Smith, Michael L., Chm., Pres. & Chief Exec. Officer--Mayflower Transit, Inc., Carmel, IN, pg. 724
Smith, R. Scott, Chm. & Chief Exec. Officer--Mannington Mills, Inc., Salem, NJ, pg. 704
Smith, Richard P., Exec. V.P. & Chief Exec. Officer--Dairylea Cooperative Inc., East Syracuse, NY, pg. 311
Smith, Robert E., Pres. & Chief Exec. Officer--Chicago West Pullman Transportation Corporation, Chicago, IL, pg. 246
Smith, Robin, Pres. & Chief Exec. Officer--Publishers Clearing House, Port Washington, NY, pg. 898
Smith, Roland, F., Pres. & Chief Exec. Officer--Jamison Door Company, Hagerstown, MD, pg. 589
Smith, Stockton N., Chm. Bd. & Chief Exec. Officer--Atlantic Aviation Corp., New Castle, DE, pg. 94
Smith, Terrence L., Chm. Bd., Pres. & Chief Exec. Officer--California Hardware Co., City of Industry, CA, pg. 209
Smith, Wally, Pres. & Chief Exec. Officer--Recreational Equipment, Inc., Kent, WA, pg. 917
Smith, William D., Pres. & Chief Exec. Officer--Brown & Bigelow, Inc., Saint Paul, MN, pg. 181
Smith, William J., Chm. Bd., Pres. & Chief Exec. Officer--U.S. Can Company, Oak Brook, IL, pg. 1134
Smitson, Robert M., Pres. & Chief Exec. Officer--Maxon Corporation, Muncie, IN, pg. 723
Smiy, Paul R., Chm. Bd. & Chief Exec. Officer--Elliott Company, Jeannette, PA, pg. 378
Smulowitz, William, Chm., Pres. & Chief Exec. Officer--The Lion, Inc. (Gibbons-Stegmaier Brewery), Wilkes-Barre, PA, pg. 677
Snoddon, Larry E., Pres. & Chief Exec. Officer--Burson-Marsteller, New York, NY, pg. 1210
Snowden, David, Pres. & Chief Exec. Officer--Tarco, North Little Rock, AR, pg. 1078
Snowden, William F., Chm. Bd., Pres. & Chief Exec. Officer--Topline Imports, Inc., Bellevue, WA, pg. 1102
Snyder, Eugene, Pres. & Chief Exec. Officer--Snyder Brothers, Inc., Minneapolis, MN, pg. 1015
Snyder, Fred J., Jr., Pres. & Chief Exec. Officer--Fiske Brothers Refining Company, Newark, NJ, pg. 415
Snyder, Louis H., Chm. Bd. & Chief Exec. Officer--Snyder-Diamond, Santa Monica, CA, pg. 1015
Snyder, Richard W., Chm. Bd. & Chief Exec. Officer--SnyderGeneral Corporation, Dallas, TX, pg. 1015
Softness, John, Chief Exec. Officer--The Siesel Company, New York, NY, pg. 1003
Soliman, Anwar, Pres. & Chief Exec. Officer--American Restaurant Group, Inc., Newport Beach, CA, pg. 60
Solin, Darrol B., Pres. & Chief Exec. Officer--MacNamara, Klein & Solin Inc., New York, NY, pg. 698
Soloff, Lawrence L., Pres. & Chief Exec. Officer--Century Seafood Inc., Philadelphia, PA, pg. 235
Solombrino, Scott, Chm. Bd., Pres. & Chief Exec. Officer--Dav-El Services, Inc., New York, NY, pg. 317
Solomon, Edward D., Chief Exec. Officer--Shoe-Town, Inc., Totowa, NJ, pg. 999
Solomon, Robert, Chm. Bd., Pres. & Chief Exec. Officer--Dakin, Inc., Burlingame, CA, pg. 311
Solomon, Russell S., Pres. & Chief Exec. Officer--MTS, Inc., West Sacramento, CA, pg. 694
Solomon, Russell S., Pres. & Chief Exec. Officer--Pulse Magazine, West Sacramento, CA, pg. 694
Solomon, William T., Chm. Bd., Pres. & Chief Exec. Officer--Austin Industries, Inc., Dallas, TX, pg. 99
Somerset, H.R., Pres. & Chief Exec. Officer--California & Hawaiian Sugar Company, Concord, CA, pg. 210
Somrock, J.D., Pres. & Chief Exec. Officer--E.F. Johnson Company, Eden Prarie, MN, pg. 598
Sorokwasz, Michael, Pres. & Chief Exec. Officer--TST/Impreso, Inc., Coppell, TX, pg. 1075
Sorrentino, Stanley L., Chm. Bd., Chief Exec. Officer & Treas.--Uncas Manufacturing Company, Providence, RI, pg. 1125
Southwell, Leonard, Chief Exec. Officer--Prairie Farms Dairy, Inc., Carlinville, IL, pg. 884
Spain, W.J., Jr., Pres. & Chief Exec. Officer--Birdsong Corporation, Suffolk, VA, pg. 153
Spear, Kenneth H., Chm. Bd., Pres. & Chief Exec. Officer--Del-Val Manufacturing Company, Warminster, PA, pg. 325
Spector, Michael J., Chm. Bd. & Pres., & Chief Exec. Officer--Margo Nursery Farms, Inc., Miami, FL, pg. 706
Spelde, M.E., Chm. Bd., Pres. & Chief Exec. Officer--Empire Airlines, Hayden Lake, ID, pg. 379
Spence, Robert L., Pres. & Chief Exec. Officer--Pacific Lumber & Shipping Co., Seattle, WA, pg. 840
Spencer, Guy J., Jr., Chm. Bd., Pres. & Chief Exec. Officer--Spencer Companies Inc., Huntsville, AL, pg. 1030
Sperber, Burton S., Chm. Bd., Pres. , & Chief Exec. Officer--Environmental Industries, Inc., Calabasas, CA, pg. 383
Spielvogel, Carl, Chm. & Chief Exec. Officer--Backer Spielvogel Bates Worldwide, Inc., New York, NY, pg. 108
Spielvogel, Carl, Chm. & Chief Exec. Officer (BSB Worldwide Inc.)--BSB Japan Ltd., Tokyo, Japan, pg. 110
Spiewak, Michael, Pres. & Chief Exec. Officer--I. Spiewak & Sons, Inc., New York, NY, pg. 1031
Spigai, Daniel J., Chief Exec. Officer--Howard Needles Tammen & Bergendoff, Kansas City, MO, pg. 547
Spires, Charles, Chief Exec. Officer--Hunter Marine Corporation, Alachua, FL, pg. 555
Spires, Keith, Pres. & Chief Exec. Officer--Osco Industries Inc., Portsmouth, OH, pg. 830
Sport, Michael C., Chm. Bd., Pres. & Chief Exec. Officer--Production Management Companies, Inc., Harvey, LA, pg. 893
Spradley, James W., Jr., Pres. & Chief Exec. Officer--Standard Candy Co., Inc., Nashville, TN, pg. 1035
Spradlin, Robert, Pres. & Chief Exec. Officer--Contract Interiors Inc., Southfield, MI, pg. 280
Spranger, Hanno W., Pres. & Chief Exec. Officer--Netzsch, Inc., Exton, PA, pg. 798
Springborn, Robert C., Chm. Bd., Pres. Chief Exec. Officer--Springborn Laboratories, Inc., Enfield, CT, pg. 1033
Sprott, H.B., Jr., Pres. & Chief Exec. Officer--Sprott Oil Co., Inc., Manning, SC, pg. 1034
Spurck, Fredric C., Pres. & Chief Exec. Officer--Webster Industries Inc., Tiffin, OH, pg. 1171
Stadelman, Pete, Pres., Chief Exec. & Fin. Officer--Stadelman Fruit Inc., Yakima, WA, pg. 1034
Stafford, Randy, Pres. & Chief Exec. Officer--The Court Company, Memphis, TN, pg. 290
Stager, Donald K., Chm. Bd., Pres. & Chief Exec. Officer--Dillingham Construction Corporation, Pleasanton, CA, pg. 337
Staheli, Donald L., Pres. & Chief Exec. Officer--Continental Grain Company, New York, NY, pg. 279
Stalcup, Winston, Chief Exec. Officer--RS Electronics, Livonia, MI, pg. 908
Standen, Michael, Chm., Pres. & Chief Exec. Officer--Metallurg, Inc., New York, NY, pg. 742
Stangl, Peter E., Chm. & Chief Exec. Officer--Metropolitan Transportation Authority, New York, NY, pg. 745
Stanko, Gary, Pres., Chief Exec. Officer--Marketing Alternatives, Inc., Arlington Heights, IL, pg. 709
Stanley, David, Chm. Bd. & Chief Exec. Officer--Payless Cashways, Inc., Kansas City, MO, pg. 853
Stanley, John W., Jr., Pres., Chief Exec. Officer & Sec.--Blue Ridge Transfer Co., Roanoke, VA, pg. 161
Stanton, Ronald, Chm. Bd. & Chief Exec. Officer--Transammonia Inc., New York, NY, pg. 1106
Starer, Robert L., Chief Exec. Officer--Computer Dynamics, Inc., Virginia Beach, VA, pg. 271
Starnes, Thomas, Chief Exec. Officer--The Auchter Company, Jacksonville, FL, pg. 98
Starvel, Frank A., Pres. & Chief Exec. Officer--New England Dairies, Inc., Hartford, CT, pg. 800
Stashower, David L., Chm. & Chief Exec. Officer--Liggett-Stashower, Inc., Cleveland, OH, pg. 675
Stasior, William F., Chm. Bd. & Chief Exec. Officer--Booz Allen & Hamilton Inc., New York, NY, pg. 165
Staudt, Eugene, Chm. Bd. & Chief Exec. Officer--Castro Convertible Corporation, New Hyde Park, NY, pg. 229
Stayer, Ralph C., Pres. & Chief Exec. Officer--Johnsonville Foods, Inc., Kohler, WI, pg. 601
Stearns, Neele E., Jr., Pres. & Chief Exec. Officer--CC Industries, Inc., Chicago, IL, pg. 199
Steele, Loren, Vice Chm., Chief Exec. Officer & Pres.--Super 8 Motels, Inc., Aberdeen, SD, pg. 1062
Steeley, Charles B., Pres. & Chief Exec. Officer--United Graphics, Inc., Seattle, WA, pg. 1132
Steigerwaldt, Donna Wolf, Chm. & Chief Exec. Officer--Jockey International, Inc., Kenosha, WI, pg. 595
Steil, Gordon E., Pres. & Chief Exec. Officer--Harrington & King, Chicago, IL, pg. 511
Stein, Dr. Sidney J., Chm. Bd., Chief Exec. Officer--Electro-Science Laboratories, Inc., King of Prussia, PA, pg. 375
Stein, Martin, Pres. & Chief Exec. Officer--Dawn Joy Fashions, Inc., New York, NY, pg. 319
Stein, Martin E., Jr., Pres. & Chief Exec. Officer--Regency Group Inc., Jacksonville, FL, pg. 922
Steinback, Kenneth, Chm. Bd. & Chief Exec. Officer--Computer Sales International Inc., Saint Louis, MO, pg. 271
Steinberg, Lawrence, Pres. & Chief Exec. Officer--Unisystems, Inc., New York, NY, pg. 1130
Steinberg, S. Ty, Pres. & Chief Exec. Officer--M. Buten & Sons Inc., Philadelphia, PA, pg. 196
Steiner, Lawrence G., Pres. & Chief Exec. Officer--American Linen Supply Company, Minneapolis, MN, pg. 57
Steiner, Richard R., Pres. & Chief Exec. Officer--Steiner Corporation, Salt Lake City, UT, pg. 1045
Steinhart, Ronald G., Chm. Bd. & Chief Exec. Officer--Team Bancshares, Inc., Dallas, TX, pg. 1082
Stempler, Charles J., Exec. V.P.--Charles Komar & Sons, Inc., New York, NY, pg. 641
Stephan, Walter, Pres. & Chief Exec. Officer--Uvex Safety, Inc., Smithfield, RI, pg. 1141
Stephens, J.M., Pres. & Chief Exec. Officer--Davis Electrical Constructors, Inc., Greenville, SC, pg. 318
Stephens, J.T., Pres., Chief Exec. Officer & Chief Oper. Officer--Ebsco Industries, Inc., Birmingham, AL, pg. 365
Stephens, Warren A., Pres. & Chief Exec. Officer--Stephens, Inc., Little Rock, AR, pg. 1046
Stephenson, Joseph E., Pres. & Chief Exec. Officer--Shenandoah Life Insurance Company, Roanoke, VA, pg. 997
Stern, Leonard N., Chm. Bd. & Chief Exec. Officer--The Hartz Mountain Corp., Harrison, NJ, pg. 514
Steuart, Leonard P., Chm. Bd.--Steuart Petroleum Company, Washington, DC, pg. 1048
Steurer, Joe, Chm. & Chief Exec. Officer--Jofco Inc., Jasper, IN, pg. 595
Stevens, Claude, Pres. & Chief Exec. Officer--Haworth Group Inc., Minnetonka, MN, pg. 518
Stevens, Frank P., Chm. Bd., Pres., Treas., Chief Exec. Officer & Chief Fin. Officer--Professional Travel, Inc., Dalton, GA, pg. 894
Stevens, Philip L., Pres. & Chief Exec. Officer--Gerber Advertising, Portland, OR, pg. 453
Stevenson, Charles E., Jr., Chm., Pres. & Chief Exec. Officer--CEBCOR (Consolidated Employment Benefits Corp.), Chicago, IL, pg. 230
Steves, Edward Galt, Vice Chm. & Chief Exec. Officer--Steves & Sons, San Antonio, TX, pg. 1048
Stewart, Andrew K., Chm. Bd., Pres. & Chief Exec. Officer--Computer Methods Corporation, Livonia, MI, pg. 271
Stewart, Richard, Chm., Pres. & Chief Exec. Officer--Praxis International Inc., Cambridge, MA, pg. 884
Stewart, Robert A., Owner & Chief Exec. Officer--Advance Steel Co., Detroit, MI, pg. 20
Stewart, Robert M., Sr., Chm. Bd. & Chief Exec. Officer--Remarks, Inc., Dublin, OH, pg. 925
Stiefel, W.K., Pres. & Chief Exec. Officer--Stiefel Laboratories, Inc., Oak Hill, Oak Hill, NY, pg. 1048
Stiff, P. Enoch, Pres. & Chief Exec. Officer--Trak International, Inc., Port Washington, WI, pg. 1106
Stiffler, Carolyn S., Pres. & Chief Exec. Officer--Classic Markets Corp., Norcross, GA, pg. 253
Stimpson, Fred T., Pres. & Chief Exec. Officer--Gulf Lumber Company, Inc., Mobile, AL, pg. 493
Stockham, Herbert, Pres. & Chief Exec. Officer--Stockham Valves & Fittings, Inc., Birmingham, AL, pg. 1050
Stocks, Thomas D., III, Chm. & Chief Exec. Officer--Rustco Products Company, Denver, CO, pg. 957
Stocks, Thomas D., III, Chm. Bd. & Chief Exec. Officer--Park Corporation, Barrington, IL, pg. 849
Stoehr, James H., Jr., Pres. & Chief Exec. Officer--Robbins, Inc., Cincinnati, OH, pg. 938
Stone, Albert, Pres. & Chief Exec. Officer--Sterlite Corporation, Townsend, MA, pg. 1047
Stone, Andrew L., Chm. Bd., Pres. & Chief Exec. Officer--K-D Lamp Company, Cincinnati, OH, pg. 612
Stone, Charles G., Chm., Pres. & Chief Exec. Officer--Stone & Simons Advertising, Inc., Southfield, MI, pg. 1051
Stone, Eugene E., IV, Chief Exec. Officer--Stone Manufacturing Company, Inc., Greenville, SC, pg. 1051
Stone, John McWilliams, Jr., Chm. Bd. & Chief Exec. Officer--Dukane Corporation, Saint Charles, IL, pg. 351
Stone, Robert, Exec. V.P.--Wasserstrom Company, Columbus, OH, pg. 1167
Storms, Charles D., Pres. & Chief Exec. Officer--Red Spot Paint & Varnish Co., Evansville, IN, pg. 918
Stout, Everett E., Pres., Chief Exec. Officer, Chief Fin. Officer & Controller--Metaltech, Inc., Kirkwood, MO, pg. 742
Stover, W. Robert, Chm. Bd. & Chief Exec. Officer--Western Temporary Services, Inc., Walnut Creek, CA, pg. 1181
Stratton, James W., Chm. Bd., Pres. & Chief Exec. Officer--Stratton Management Company, Plymouth Meeting, PA, pg. 1053
Stratton, James W., Chm. Bd. & Chief Exec. Officer--Stratton Growth Fund, Inc., Plymouth Meeting, PA, pg. 1053
Stratton, James W., Chm. Bd. & Chief Exec. Officer--Stratton Monthly Dividend Shares, Inc., Plymouth Meeting, PA, pg. 1053
Straus, David J., Chm. Bd. & Chief Exec. Officer--STRAFCO, Inc., San Antonio, TX, pg. 1052
Straus, Roger W., Jr., Pres. & Chief Exec. Officer--Farrar, Straus & Giroux, Inc., New York, NY, pg. 403
Strause, Richard, Chief Exec. Officer--Key Container Corporation, Pawtucket, RI, pg. 626

Street, Gordon P., Jr., Chm. Bd., Pres. & Chief Exec. & Chief Oper. Officer--North American Royalties, Inc., Chattanooga, TN, pg. 811

Strite, Lewis E., Chm. Bd. & Chief Exec. Officer--Shenandoah Mfg. Co. Inc., Harrisonburg, VA, pg. 997

Stroh, Peter W., Chm. Bd. & Chief Exec. Officer--The Stroh Brewery Company, Detroit, MI, pg. 1053

Strong, Warren R., Chief Exec. Officer, Chief Oper. Officer, & Pres.--Macco Constructors, Inc., Paramount, CA, pg. 696

Stroud, Bill, Chm. Bd. & Chief Exec. Officer--Strouds, City of Industry, CA, pg. 1054

Strubel, Richard P., Pres. & Chief Exec. Officer--MICRODOT, Inc., Chicago, IL, pg. 749

Strugatz, Peter, Chief Exec. Officer--Austin Sculpture, Holbrook, NY, pg. 99

Stuart, Thomas, Chm. Bd. & Chief Exec. Officer--Bureau of Engraving, Minneapolis, MN, pg. 189

Stumpf, Charles T., Chm. Bd., Pres., Chief Exec. Officer & Treas.--Financial Associates, Overland Park, KS, pg. 410

Suart, Dawn, Chief Exec. Officer--Olson-Travelworld Ltd., Manhattan Beach, CA, pg. 824

Sugarman, Joseph, Chm., Creative & Mktg. Dir.--JS&A Advertising, Las Vegas, NV, pg. 586

Sugarman, Leonard, Chm. Bd., Pres. & Chief Exec. Officer--Statler Industries, Medford, MA, pg. 1041

Suhowatsky, Stephen J., Pres. & Chief Exec. Officer--Syracuse Supply Company, Syracuse, NY, pg. 1070

Suitt, T. Howard, Pres. & Chief Exec. Officer--Suitt Construction Company, Inc., Greenville, SC, pg. 1056

Sullivan, B.J., Chm. & Chief Exec. Officer--Byron Weston Paper Co., Dalton, MA, pg. 296

Sullivan, James, Chm. Bd., Pres. & Chief Exec. Officer--Sullivan Holding Company, Brentwood, TN, pg. 1056

Sullivan, Kenneth R., Pres. & Chief Exec. Officer--Sullivan Oil Company, Baton Rouge, LA, pg. 1057

Sullivan, Robert E., Chm. & Chief Exec. Officer--Lord, Sullivan & Yoder, Inc. Advertising, Columbus, OH, pg. 683

Sullivan, Robert J., Chm. Bd. & Chief Exec. Officer--G. R. Herberger's, Inc., Saint Cloud, MN, pg. 530

Summers, Cary, Pres. & Chief Exec. Officer--Silver Dollar City, Inc., Branson, MO, pg. 1004

Sun, David, Pres. & Chief Exec. Officer--Sun Computers, Inc., Carson, CA, pg. 1058

Sundet, Johnson, Pres. & Chief Exec. Officer--Rollerblade, Inc., Minnetonka, MN, pg. 944

Sundt, H. Wilson, Chm. Bd. & Chief Exec. Officer--Sundt Corp., Tucson, AZ, pg. 1060

Sutton, Roy V., Pres. & Chief Exec. Officer--W. B. Goode Company, Inc., Richmond, VA, pg. 470

Sutton, Thomas C., Chm. Bd. & Chief Exec. Officer--Pacific Mutual Life Insurance Company, Newport Beach, CA, pg. 841

Suzio, Len, Pres. & Chief Exec. Officer--New England Corporation, Hamden, CT, pg. 800

Swalm, Dave C., Chm. Bd. & Chief Exec. Officer--Texas Olefins Co., Houston, TX, pg. 1089

Swaner, Keith, Chief Exec. Officer--Swaner Hardwood Company, Inc., Burbank, CA, pg. 1066

Swank, Richard B., Chm. Bd. & Chief Exec. Officer--Advanstar Communications, Cleveland, OH, pg. 21

Swanson, Jim, Chief Exec. Officer--Esco Elevators, Inc., Fort Worth, TX, pg. 388

Swartz, Thomas B., Chm. Bd. & Chief Exec. Officer--The Sierra Capital Companies, San Francisco, CA, pg. 1002

Sween, Tom, Chm. Bd. & Chief Exec. Officer--E.A. Sween Company, Eden Prairie, MN, pg. 1066

Sweig, Morton A, Chm. Bd. & Chief Exec. Officer--National Cleaning Contractors, Inc., New York, NY, pg. 786

Swift, George P., Jr., Chm. Bd. & Chief Exec. Officer--Columbus Mills, Inc., Columbus, GA, pg. 267

Swinehart, Keith, Sr., Chm. Bd., Chief Exec. Officer & Chief Fin. Officer--Vanguard Plastics, Inc., McPherson, KS, pg. 1145

Swisher, Glenn, Chm. Bd. & Chief Exec. Officer--Syndicate Systems, Inc., Indianapolis, IN, pg. 1069

Switzenbaum, Samuel, Pres. & Chief Exec. Officer--Strouse Greenberg & Co., Inc., Philadelphia, PA, pg. 1054

Synott, Lee, Chm. Bd., Pres. & Chief Exec. Officer--Ingram Book Company, La Vergne, TN, pg. 569

Sze, Andy, Pres. & Chief Exec. Officer--Clipper Exxpress Co., Lemont, IL, pg. 256

Szmulewitz, Armend, Chief Exec. Officer--Rexall Group, Fort Lauderdale, FL, pg. 1060

Szydlowski, T., Chief Exec. Officer--The ISI Manufacturing, Inc., Fraser, MI, pg. 560

Tabor, Jon K., Chm. Bd., Pres. & Chief Exec. Officer--Allied Mineral Products, Inc., Columbus, OH, pg. 38

Taddei, Armando, Chm. Bd., Pres. & Treas.--Hunter Contracting Company, Gilbert, AZ, pg. 554

Tait, John E., Chm. Bd., Pres. & Chief Exec. Officer--The Penn Mutual Life Insurance Company, Philadelphia, PA, pg. 858

Talley, Willie, Chm. Bd., Pres. & Chief Exec. Officer--ColorTyme, Inc., Athens, TX, pg. 265

Tallichet, David C., Jr., Chm. Bd., Pres. & Chief Exec. Officer--Specialty Restaurants Corporation, Anaheim, CA, pg. 1027

Tamski, Thomas J., Pres. & Chief Exec. Officer--Global Marketing Resources, New York, NY, pg. 463

Tananbaum, Stanley, Chm. Bd. & Chief Exec. Officer--Century Business Credit Corporation, New York, NY, pg. 235

Tang, Cyrus, Chm. Bd., Pres., & Chief Exec. Officer--Tang Industries Inc., Elk Grove Village, IL, pg. 1078

Tannenberg, Dieter E.A., Pres. & Chief Exec. Officer--Bell & Howell Document Management Products Company, Chicago, IL, pg. 135

Tanner, James T., Pres. & Chief Exec. Officer--Tanner Co. Inc., Rutherfordton, NC, pg. 1078

Taratoot, Louis J., Chm., Pres. & Chief Exec. Officer--Taracorp, Inc., Atlanta, GA, pg. 1078

Targett, William J., Pres. & Chief Exec. Officer--Meier Metal Service Centers, Inc., Hazel Park, MI, pg. 737

Tarrant, R. Lane, Chm. Bd., Pres. & Chief Exec. Officer--Tarrant Service Agency, Inc., Louisville, KY, pg. 1079

Tassani, Sally M., Pres. & Chief Exec. Officer--Tassani Communications, Chicago, IL, pg. 1080

Tatman, Richard M., Chm. Bd. & Pres.--Acme Foundry, Inc., Coffeyville, KS, pg. 13

Tattersall, Keith, Chm. Bd., Pres. & Chief Exec. Officer--Amperif Corporation, Chatsworth, CA, pg. 68

Tauber, Orner J., Jr., Pres. & Chief Exec. Officer--Tauber Oil Company, Houston, TX, pg. 1080

Tauscher, William Y., Pres. & Chief Exec. Officer--ComputerLand Corporation, Pleasanton, CA, pg. 271

Taylor, Cyril J.H., Chm. & Chief Exec. Officer--American Institute for Foreign Study, London, United Kingdom, pg. 56

Taylor, Dale, Pres. & Chief Exec. Officer--Abelson-Taylor, Inc., Chicago, IL, pg. 10

Taylor, Glen A., Chm. Bd. & Chief Exec. Officer--Taylor Corporation, Mankato, MN, pg. 1081

Taylor, James W., Pres. & Chief Exec. Officer--Nelson A. Taylor Co., Inc., Gloversville, NY, pg. 1080

Taylor, John, Pres. & Chief Exec. Officer--Ingram Entertainment Inc., La Vergne, TN, pg. 569

Taylor, John A., Chm. Bd.--Taylor Oil Co. Inc., Winston-Salem, NC, pg. 1082

Taylor, Sidney J., Chm. Bd. & Chief Exec. Officer--Cole Taylor Financial Group, Wheeling, IL, pg. 260

Taylor, Sidney J., Chm. Bd. & Chief Exec. Officer--Cole Taylor/Yorktown, Lombard, IL, pg. 260

Taylor, Stephen D., Pres. & Chief Exec. Officer--American Savings of Florida, ESB, Miami, FL, pg. 382

Taylor, Thomas H., Jr., Pres. & Chief Exec. Officer--Ohio Machinery Co., Cleveland, OH, pg. 822

Taylor, William, Pres. & Chief Exec. Officer--S. E. Huffman Corp., Clover, SC, pg. 551

Teague, Robert M., Pres. & Chief Exec. Officer--Thermo Industries Inc., Charlotte, NC, pg. 1091

Teasley, Larkin, Pres. & Chief Exec. Officer--Golden State Mutual Life Insurance Company, Los Angeles, CA, pg. 467

Teater, David, Chm. & Chief Exec. Officer--Sefton Associates Inc., Grand Rapids, MI, pg. 987

Teets, John B., Pres. & Chief Exec. Officer--Dunn-Edwards Corporation, Los Angeles, CA, pg. 353

Teller, Louis L., Vice Chm. & Chief Exec. Officer--Octagon Process Inc., Edgewater, NJ, pg. 821

Temple, John, Pres. & Chief Exec. Officer--Guideposts Associates, Inc., Carmel, NY, pg. 493

Tendler, Jonathan, Chief Exec. Officer--Commons Bros., Inc., Elmsford, NY, pg. 269

Tendler, Stanley, Chm. Bd. & Chief Exec. Officer--Kennington Ltd., Inc., Los Angeles, CA, pg. 623

Tepas, Gary L., Pres. & Chief Exec. Officer--Emkay, Inc., Itasca, IL, pg. 379

Terborgh, Eliot, Pres. & Chief Exec. Officer--Selectone Corporation, Hayward, CA, pg. 988

Terlato, Anthony, Pres. & Chief Exec. Officer--Paterno Imports Limited, Chicago, IL, pg. 851

Terral, Thomas F., Pres. & Chief Exec. Officer--Terral-Norris Seed Co., Inc., Lake Providence, LA, pg. 1088

Teruya, Raymond, Chm. Bd. & Chief Exec. Officer--Teruya Bros., Ltd., Honolulu, HI, pg. 1089

Teslow, Paul, Pres. & Chief Exec. Officer--UniHealth America, Burbank, CA, pg. 1126

Tessereau, Herbert L., Vice Chm. & Chief Exec. Officer--Doane Products Co., Joplin, MO, pg. 342

Testwuide, Thomas R., Pres. & Chief Exec. Officer--Schreier Malting Co., Sheboygan, WI, pg. 978

Thalheimer, Louis B., Chief Exec. Officer & Chm. Bd.--American Trading and Production Corporation, Baltimore, MD, pg. 64

Theisen, Claude I., Pres. & Chief Exec. Officer--T & S Brass & Bronze Works, Inc., Travelers Rest, SC, pg. 1074

Thenappan, Vis, Pres. & Chief Exec. Officer--San Angelo Electric Service Company, San Angelo, TX, pg. 969

Theofilos, Steve P., Chm. Bd., Pres. & Chief Exec. Officer--Theochem Labs., Inc., Tampa, FL, pg. 1090

Thiele, Paul F., Chm. Bd. & Chief Exec. Officer--Thiele Kaolin Co., Sandersville, GA, pg. 1092

Thielman, David, Chief Exec. Officer--E Z Loader Boat Trailers, Inc., Spokane, WA, pg. 361

Thomas, Carl M., Chief Exec. Officer--The Orr Felt Company, Piqua, OH, pg. 830

Thomas, David G., Chief Exec. Officer (Salt Lake City) & Dir.--EvansGroup, Salt Lake City, UT, pg. 390

Thomas, David G., Chief Exec. Officer--EvansGroup, Salt Lake City, UT, pg. 391

Thomas, G. N., Chm. Bd., Pres., Chief Exec. Officer, Chief Fin. Officer & Treas.--A. Levy & J. Zentner Co., Sacramento, CA, pg. 671

Thomas, Gary, Pres. & Chief Oper. Officer--RTMX-Uniflex Inc., Chapel Hill, NC, pg. 908

Thomas, Howard, Pres. & Chief Exec. Officer--Hubert Company, Harrison, OH, pg. 550

Thomas, John E., Pres. & Chief Exec. Officer--Tippins Incorporated, Pittsburgh, PA, pg. 1099

Thomas, Joseph H., Chief Exec. Officer--Allison Payment Systems Div., Indianapolis, IN, pg. 305

Thomas, Mark, Pres. & Chief Exec. Officer--Standard Communications Corporation, Carson, CA, pg. 1036

Thomas, Richard C., Chief Exec. Officer--Northeast Texas Farmers Co-Op, Sulphur Springs, TX, pg. 813

Thomas, S. Denis, Pres. & Chief Exec. Officer--Berol Corporation, Brentwood, TN, pg. 856

Thompson, Jack B., Chief Exec. Officer--Athletic Attic Properties Inc., Gainesville, FL, pg. 94

Thompson, John C., Chief Exec. Officer--The Hall China Company, East Liverpool, OH, pg. 501

Thompson, John Larkin, Chief Exec. Officer--Blue Cross and Blue Shield of Massachusetts, Boston, MA, pg. 159

Thompson, LeRoy, Jr., Chm. & Chief Exec. Officer--Steelite, Inc., Pittsburgh, PA, pg. 1044

Thompson, Michael D., Pres. & Chief Exec. Officer--Thompson Tractor Company, Birmingham, AL, pg. 1095

Thompson, Scott, Chm. Bd., Pres., Chief Exec. & Chief Oper. Officer--Advanced Technology, Inc., Reston, VA, pg. 20

Thomson, James A., Pres. & Chief Exec. Officer--RAND, Santa Monica, CA, pg. 911

Thomson, Robert G., Chief Exec. Officer--Furnival/State Machinery Co., Lancaster, PA, pg. 437

Thomson, Robert H., Pres. & Chief Exec. Officer--Construction Specialties, Inc., Cranford, NJ, pg. 277

Thorbeck, John, Chief Exec. Officer & Pres.--Geo. E. Keith Company, Bridgewater, MA, pg. 620

Thornburg, H.A., Chief Exec. Officer--Bridgewater Resources Corporation, Beverly Hills, CA, pg. 175

Thornton, Neil, Pres. & Chief Exec. Officer--American Industries Inc., Portland, OR, pg. 55

Thrall, J. Jeffrey, Chm. Bd. & Chief Exec. Officer--Naz-Dar Company, Chicago, IL, pg. 1095

Throgmartin, William G., Chief Exec. Officer--Gregg Appliances Inc., Indianapolis, IN, pg. 486

Thrush, Richard P., Chief Exec. Officer--Block Industries, Inc., Wilmington, NC, pg. 157

Thumann, Jurgen, Chm. Bd. & Chief Exec. Officer--Thomas Steel Strip Corp., Warren, OH, pg. 1094

Thurston, Amy, Chief Exec. Officer--Sonic Messenger Service, Phoenix, AZ, pg. 1018

Thurston, Ray, Chm. Bd. & Chief Exec. Officer--Sonicair, Scottsdale, AZ, pg. 1018

Tibbetts, Linton N., Chm. Bd. & Chief Exec. Officer--Cox Lumber Co., Saint Petersburg, FL, pg. 294

Tideman, Philip, Chm. Bd., Pres. & Chief Exec. Officer--United Power Association, Elk River, MN, pg. 1134

Tietjen, James J., Pres. & Chief Exec. Officer--SRI International, Menlo Park, CA, pg. 964

Timble, James N., Pres. & Chief Exec. Officer--Headco Industries, Inc., Broadview, IL, pg. 520

Timperman, Ernest J., Pres. & Chief Exec. Officer--Random Corporation, Cincinnati, OH, pg. 912

Tinberg, Richard W., Chief Exec. Officer--Hammacher, Schlemmer & Co., Inc., Chicago, IL, pg. 503

Tinberg, Richard W., Pres. & Chief Exec. Officer--Bradford Exchange Ltd., Niles, IL, pg. 170

Tindal, Charles H., Chm. Bd., Pres. & Chief Exec. Officer--Palmer Electric Co., Winter Park, FL, pg. 843

Tober, Lester V., Pres. & Chief Exec. Officer--Tober Industries, Inc., Saint Louis, MO, pg. 1099

Tobey, Joel N., Pres. & Chief Exec. Officer--Amica Mutual Insurance Co., Providence, RI, pg. 66

Toland, C. E., Chm. Bd. & Chief Exec. Officer--Affiliated Foods Southwest, Little Rock, AR, pg. 24

Tolaney, Murly, Pres. & Chief Exec. Officer--James M. Montgomery Consulting Engineers, Pasadena, CA, pg. 767

Tomasso, Angelo, Jr., Chief Exec. Officer--Tilcon, Inc., New Britain, CT, pg. 1097

Tomlin, Eugene B., Pres. & Chief Exec. Officer--I. H. French & Co. Inc., Champaign, IL, pg. 432

Tompkins, States D., Pres. & Chief Exec. Officer--Cresmer, Woodward, O'Mara & Ormsbee, New York, NY, pg. 298

Tomsick, Frank, Chm. & Chief Exec. Officer--MBT Associates, Inc., San Francisco, CA, pg. 691

Tongen, Richard W., Pres. & Chief Exec. Officer--American Hardware Mutual Insurance Co., Minnetonka, MN, pg. 55

Tongen, Richard W., Pres. & Chief Exec. Officer--American Merchants Life Insurance Co., Minnetonka, MN, pg. 55

Torcivia, Benedict, Chm. Bd. & Chief Exec. Officer--Torcon, Inc., Westfield, NJ, pg. 1102

Toth, Alex S., Chm. Bd., Pres. & Chief Exec. Officer--PBM Office Products, Cleveland, OH, pg. 835

Towery, Maurice J., Chm. Bd. & Chief Exec. Officer--Color Graphics, Inc., Atlanta, GA, pg. 264

Trabert, J.E., Chief Exec. Officer--ITA Group, West Des Moines, IA, pg. 560

Trad, Raja, Chief Exec. Officer--Radius Leo Burnett U.A.E, Dubai,, United Arab Emirates, pg. 193

Tragos, William G., Founder, Chm. & Chief Exec. Officer-WW--TBWA Advertising, Inc., New York, NY, pg. 1071

Trauscht, Donald C., Pres. & Chief Exec. Officer--Borg-Warner Corporation, Chicago, IL, pg. 165

Trauth, David E., Jr., Pres. & Chief Exec. Officer--Trauth Dairy Inc., Newport, KY, pg. 1108

Traylor, W. Leroy, Jr., Pres. & Chief Exec. Officer--Traylor Chemical & Supply Co., Orlando, FL, pg. 1108

Trees, Michael, Chief Exec. Officer--B&W Co-op, Inc., Breckenridge, MI, pg. 107

Treis, Edward F., Chm Bd. & Chief Exec. Officer--Arandell-Schmidt Corporation, Menomonee Falls, WI, pg. 79

Trenkamp, Robert, Pres. & Chief Exec. Officer--Varityper, Inc., East Hanover, NJ, pg. 1146

Trerice, Byron W., Jr., Chm. Bd. & Chief Exec. Officer--Trerice Tosto International, Bingham Farms, MI, pg. 1110

Tribble, James L., Chm. Bd. & Chief Exec. Officer--Tribble & Stephens Co., Houston, TX, pg. 1112

Tribull, Christoph, Chm. Bd., Pres., Chief Exec. & Chief Oper. Officer--Sierracin Corporation, Sylmar, CA, pg. 1003

Trinchero, Louis, Chm. & Chief Exec. Officer--Sutter Home Winery, Inc., Saint Helena, CA, pg. 1065

Triplett, William W., Chm. Bd. & Chief Exec. Officer--HDS Services, Farmington Hills, MI, pg. 496

Trofholz, LeRoy, Pres. & Chief Exec. Officer--Wagner Mills Inc., Schuyler, NE, pg. 1158

Troger, Jay R., Pres. & Chief Exec. Officer--Hackney & Sons, Inc., Washington, NC, pg. 498

Trotter, J. Don, Pres. & Chief Exec. Officer--SCT Yarns, Inc., Chattanooga, TN, pg. 961

Trotter, W.M., Pres. & Chief Exec. Officer--Consolidated Systems, Inc., Columbia, SC, pg. 277

Truchi, David, Pres. & Chief Exec. Officer--Trucchis Markets, Raynham, MA, pg. 1117

True, H.A., Jr., Pres. & Chief Exec. Officer--True Companies, Casper, WY, pg. 1117

Trump, Julius, Chm. Bd. & Chief Exec. Officer--The Trump Group, New York, NY, pg. 1117
Tscheulin, Frederick R., Chm. Bd., Pres. & Chief Exec. Officer--The Highland Group, Inc., Southport, CT, pg. 534
Tucker, Arlie, Chief Exec. Officer--Komatsu Dresser Company, Lincolnshire, IL, pg. 565
Tuckerman, Donald M., Pres. & Chief Exec. Officer--Elkman Advertising & Public Relations, Bala-Cynwyd, PA, pg. 377
Tuckerman, Donald M., Pres. & Chief Exec. Officer--Elkman Advertising, Public Relations Div., Bala-Cynwyd, PA, pg. 378
Tuozzolo, James A., Chief Exec. Officer--The Pyramid Companies, Syracuse, NY, pg. 901
Turcotte, Norman J., Pres. & Chief Exec. Officer--Associated Grocers of New England, Inc., Manchester, NH, pg. 90
Turley, Robert W., Pres. & Chief Exec. Officer--Intermountain Farmers Association, Salt Lake City, UT, pg. 575
Turley, Stewart, Chm. Bd., Pres. & Chief Exec. Officer--Jack Eckerd Corporation, Largo, FL, pg. 366
Turner, James A., Jr., Chief Exec. Officer--National Welders Supply Co. Inc., Charlotte, NC, pg. 794
Turner, Roger, Pres., Chief Exec. & Fin. Officer--Western Controls, North Salt Lake, UT, pg. 1178
Turner, Tom, Pres. & Chief Exec. Officer--Associated Druggists, Wichita, KS, pg. 304
Turner, William, Chm. Bd., Pres., Chief Exec. & Chief Oper. Officer--The Pullman Company, Livingston, NJ, pg. 899
Turner, William, Chm. Bd., Pres., Chief Exec. & Chief Oper. Officer--Lear Siegler Diversified Holdings Corp., Livingston, NJ, pg. 424
Turner, William, Chief Exec. Officer--Thomas & Betts Holdings, Inc., Memphis, TN, pg. 425
Turner, William J., Chm. Bd., Pres. & Chief Exec. Officer--Lear Siegler Diversified Holdings Corp., Livingston, NJ, pg. 664
Turner, William J., Chm. Bd., Pres. & Chief Exec. Officer--Lear Siegler Diversified Holdings Corp., Livingston, NJ, pg. 424
Turrell, Clifford, Pres., Chief Exec. Officer & Chief Fin. Officer--Cogifer Inc., Cincinnati, OH, pg. 259
Tushman, J. Lawrence, Chief Exec. Officer & Sec.--Orleans International, Inc., Bloomfield Hills, MI, pg. 829
Tuthill, James G., Jr., Pres. & Chief Exec. Officer--Tuthill Corporation, Hinsdale, IL, pg. 1120
Tutor, Ronald N., Pres. & Chief Exec. Officer--Tutor-Saliba Corporation, Sylmar, CA, pg. 1120
Tuttle, Robert H., Chief Exec. Officer--Holmes Tuttle Ford, Inc., Tucson, AZ, pg. 540
Tway, Robert C., III, Pres. & Chief Exec. Officer--Kentucky Manufacturing Co., Louisville, KY, pg. 624
Twigg-Smith, Thurston, Chm., Pres. & Chief Exec. Officer--Persis Corporation, Honolulu, HI, pg. 863
Tyner, Neal E., Chm. & Chief Exec. Officer--Ameritas Life Insurance Corp., Lincoln, NE, pg. 66
Tyree, James C., Chief Exec. Officer--Mesirow Financial, Chicago, IL, pg. 741
Tyrrell, Thomas, Pres. & Chief Exec. Officer--American Steel & Wire Corporation, Cuyahoga Heights, OH, pg. 246
Tyson, Dr. Thomas J., Chm. Bd., Pres. & Chief Exec. Officer--Energy & Environmental Research Corp., Irvine, CA, pg. 381
Uhl, Richard J., Pres. & Chief Exec. Officer--Chicago Holdings, Inc., Pittsburgh, PA, pg. 245
Ulbrich, Frederick C., Jr., Chm. Bd., Pres. & Chief Exec. Officer--Ulbrich Stainless Steels & Special Metals, Inc., North Haven, CT, pg. 1125
Ulery, Byron, Chief Exec. Officer & Gen. Mgr.--Farmway Co-Op Inc., Beloit, KS, pg. 402
Ullman, Myron E., III, Co-Chm. & Co- Chief Exec. Officer--R. H. Macy & Co., Inc., New York, NY, pg. 698
Ullman, Myron E., III, Co-Chm. Bd. & Co.-Chief Exec. Officer--Bullock's, Los Angeles, CA, pg. 699
Ulrich, Lloyd, Pres. & Chief Exec. Officer--Chicago Mechanical, Inc., Chicago, IL, pg. 245
Umans, A.R., Pres., Chief Exec. Officer & Treas.--RHC/Spacemaster Corporation, Melrose Park, IL, pg. 906
Umphenour, Russ, Chm., Pres. & Chief Exec. Officer--Mrs. Winner's Chicken & Biscuit Restaurants, Atlanta, GA, pg. 761
Umphenour, Russell, Jr., Chm. Bd., Pres. & Chief Exec. Officer--R.T.M. Winners, Atlanta, GA, pg. 908
Unger, Gerald F., Pres. & Chief Exec. Officer--Unger Company, Cleveland, OH, pg. 1126
Unger, Les, Pres. & Chief Exec. Officer--Bufkor, Inc., Clearwater, FL, pg. 187
Unroe, Brad, Pres. & Chief Exec. Officer--Communico, Indianapolis, IN, pg. 270
Utick, David, Pres. & Chief Exec.. Officer--Hehr International Inc., Los Angeles, CA, pg. 525
Utley, Robert K, III, Chm. Exec. Committee & Co-Chief Exec. Officer)--First Southwest Company, Dallas, TX, pg. 413
Uytengsu, Wilfred, Chm. & Chief Exec. Officer--Sunshine Biscuits, Inc., Woodbridge, NJ, pg. 439
Uytengsu, Wilfred, Chm. & Chief Exec. Officer--Sunshine/Salerno (IL), Niles, IL, pg. 439
Valade, Robert C., Pres. & Chief Exec. Officer--Carhartt, Inc., Dearborn, MI, pg. 220
Valentine, Joseph C., Chm. Bd., Pres. & Chief Exec. Officer--Lubrication Engineers, Inc., Fort Worth, TX, pg. 686
Van Buren, David, Pres. & Chief Exec. Officer--Applied Solar Energy Corporation, City of Industry, CA, pg. 79
Van Den Blink, N. Mooers, Chm. Bd., Chief Exec. Officer, & Treas.--Hilliard Corporation, Elmira, NY, pg. 535
Van Denburgh, John P., Jr., Chm. Bd., Pres. & Chief Exec. Officer--American Fence Company, Phoenix, AZ, pg. 52
Van Der Kamp, Jerry, Chief Exec. Officer & Exec. V.P.--American Grain & Related Industries, West Des Moines, IA, pg. 55
Van Fossen, Jack, Pres. & Chief Exec. Officer--Red Roof Inns, Inc., Hilliard, OH, pg. 918
Van Gorder, Terry, Pres. & Chief Exec. Officer--Knott's Berry Farm, Buena Park, CA, pg. 637
Van Houten, James F., Pres. & Chief Exec. Officer--MSI Insurance Companies, Arden Hills, MN, pg. 693
Van Hulst, Jack, Pres. & Chief Exec. Officer--Pennex Products Co., Inc., Verona, PA, pg. 858
Van Mollenberg, H., Chm. Bd., Pres. & Chief Exec. Officer--Mollenberg-Betz Inc., Buffalo, NY, pg. 764
Van Pelt, David B., Sr., Chm. Bd. & Chief Exec. Officer--Van Pelt Corporation, Detroit, MI, pg. 1144
Van Pelt, Donald C., Chm. Bd., Pres. & Chief Exec. Officer--Plymouth Tube Company, Warrenville, IL, pg. 877
Van Wyk, Brooke, Pres. & Chief Exec. Officer--Pace International Corporation, Kirkland, WA, pg. 838
Vance, William C., Chm. Bd. & Chief Exec. Officer--Vance Publishing Corporation, Lincolnshire, IL, pg. 1144
Vanderbilt, H.B., Chm. Bd. & Chief Exec. Officer--R. T. Vanderbilt Company, Inc., Norwalk, CT, pg. 1144
Vanderminden, Robert D., Sr., Chief Exec. Officer--Telescope Casual Furniture, Inc., Granville, NY, pg. 1085
Vangelos, Allen J., Pres. & Chief Exec. Officer--Calavo Growers of California, Tustin, CA, pg. 208
Varat, Joshua E., Pres. & Chief Exec. Officer--Varat Enterprises, Inc., Piedmont, SC, pg. 1145
Vaughn, A., Pres. & Chief Exec. Officer--Maryland & Virginia Milk Producers Association, Reston, VA, pg. 717
Vaughn, David L., Chief Exec. Officer--New York City Off Track Betting Corp., New York, NY, pg. 802
Veghte, Robert I., Pres. & Chief Exec. Officer--Wheaton Inc., Millville, NJ, pg. 1184
Velasquez, ArthurR., Pres. & Chief Exec. Officer--Azteca Foods, Incorporated, Chicago, IL, pg. 105
Venet, Zal, Chm. Bd., Pres. & Chief Exec. Officer--The Venet Companies, Inc., Union, NJ, pg. 1147
Vengroff, Harvey, Chm. Bd. & Chief Exec. Officer--Vengroff Williams & Associates, Inc., Centerpoint, NY, pg. 1147
Vensel, John, Chm. Bd., Pres. & Chief Exec. Officer--Crucible Materials Corp., Syracuse, NY, pg. 302
Vera, Alan D., Pres. & Chief Exec. Officer--The Quest Business Agency, Inc., Houston, TX, pg. 904
Verble, C. Michael, Pres. & Chief Exec. Officer--North American Roofing Company, Inc., Carmel, IN, pg. 811
Verdoorn, Sid, Pres., Chief Exec. & Chief Oper. Officer--C. H. Robinson Co. Inc., Eden Prairie, MN, pg. 939
Vereen, W.J., Pres., Treas., & Chief Exec. Officer--Riverside Manufacturing Co., Moultrie, GA, pg. 937
Vermeer, Robert, Chm. Bd. & Chief Exec. Officer--Vermeer Manufacturing Company, Pella, IA, pg. 1148
Verner, George C., Jr., Chief Exec. Officer--Acousti Engineering Co. of Florida, Orlando, FL, pg. 14
Verni, Ralph F., Pres. & Chief Exec. Officer, New England Investment Companies--The New England, Boston, MA, pg. 799
Verni, Robert F., Chm. Bd. & Chief Exec. Officer--State Street Research & Management Company, Boston, MA, pg. 744
Verrette, Louis C., Chm. Bd. & Chief Exec. Officer--Champion, Inc., Iron Mountain, MI, pg. 238
Vincent, Burton J., Chm. Bd. Pres. & Chief Exec. Officer--Vincent Food Industries, Inc., Chicago, IL, pg. 1152
Vinyard, Leon E., Pres. & Chief Exec. Officer--Intermatic Inc., Spring Grove, IL, pg. 575
Viola, Ronald J., Chm. Bd. & Chief Exec. Officer--Rapid Power Technologies, Inc., Brookfield, CT, pg. 913
Vitale, Alberto, Chm., Pres. & Chief Exec. Officer--Random House, Inc., New York, NY, pg. 19
Vittoria, Joseph V., Chm. Bd. & Chief Exec. Officer--Avis, Inc., Garden City, NY, pg. 102
Vittorini, Carlo, Chm., Publisher & Chief Exec. Officer--Parade Publications Inc., New York, NY, pg. 847
Vollrath, Walter III, Pres. & Chief Exec. Officer--Polar Ware Company, Sheboygan, WI, pg. 878
von Matthiessen, Malte, Chm. Bd. & Chief Exec. Officer--YSI Incorporated, Yellow Springs, OH, pg. 1207
von Riesen, Dietrich, Vice Chm. & Chief Exec. Officer--Pegasus International Corporation, Pennington, NJ, pg. 855
Vosburg, N.E., Pres. & Chief Exec. Officer--Pacific Hide & Fur Depot, Great Falls, MT, pg. 840
Wachstein, Barbara, Pres. & Chief Exec. Officer--Great Lakes Recreation Co., Livonia, MI, pg. 481
Wade, Tom W., Jr., Chm. Bd. & Chief Exec. Officer--Tom Wade Co., Kenton, TN, pg. 1157
Wadsworth, Stanley, Chm. Bd., Pres. & Chief Exec. Officer--Golf Hosts, Inc., Palm Harbor, FL, pg. 469
Waggoner, Donald E., Jr., Chief Exec. Officer--Waggoner Corp., Troy, MI, pg. 1158
Wagner, H.J., Chm. & Chief Exec. Officer--Setco Sales Company, Cincinnati, OH, pg. 993
Wagner, Jack, Pres. & Chief Exec. Officer--Hiross Inc., Niagara Falls, NY, pg. 536
Wahlert, Robert H., Chm. Bd., Pres. & Chief Exec. Officer--FDL Foods, Inc., Dubuque, IA, pg. 394
Waingrow, F.R., Pres.--Petersen Publishing Company, Los Angeles, CA, pg. 864
Waite, Harley Jr., Chm. Bd., Pres. & Chief Exec. Officer--Eastern Technologies Ltd, Amesbury, MA, pg. 364
Walcher, Jack, Chm., Pres. & Chief Exec. Officer--Eddins-Walcher Company, Midland, TX, pg. 367
Waldbillig, William J., Pres. & Chief Exec. Officer--Waldbillig & Besteman, Inc., Madison, WI, pg. 1159
Waldner, Stephen, Chief Exec. Officer--D. Waldner Company, Inc., Farmingdale, NY, pg. 1159
Walker, A. Maceo, Sr., Chm. Bd. & Chief Exec. Officer--Universal Life Insurance Company, Memphis, TN, pg. 1138
Walker, Philip R., Pres. & Chief Exec. Officer--Tennessee Farmers Co-op, La Vergne, TN, pg. 1087
Wall, John E., Chief Exec. Officer--Demco Inc., Madison, WI, pg. 328
Wallace, Dan, Chief Exec. Officer--Citation Companies, Inc., Birmingham, AL, pg. 250
Wallace, John W., Chief Exec. Officer--Wallace Co. Inc., Houston, TX, pg. 1160
Wallach, James G., Pres. & Chief Exec. Officer--Central National-Gottesman Inc., Purchase, NY, pg. 233
Wallentine, Robert, Chief Exec. Officer & Gen. Mgr.--New Cooperative Inc., Fort Dodge, IA, pg. 799
Waller, Jim, Chief Exec. Officer--Ithaca Industries Inc., Wilkesboro, NC, pg. 582
Walmsley, Jerry T., Chief Exec. Officer--Norweco, Inc., Spokane, WA, pg. 816
Walpert, H.E., Chm. Bd., Pres. & Chief Exec. Officer--Ed Walpert & Associates, Rancho Mirage, CA, pg. 1161
Walsworth, Don O., Pres. & Chief Exec. Officer--Walsworth Publishing Company, Inc., Marceline, MO, pg. 1161
Walter, Paul F., Chm. Bd., Pres. & Chief Exec. Officer--Thermo Electric Co., Inc., Saddle Brook, NJ, pg. 1091
Walter, Richard A., Chm. Bd. & Chief Exec. Officer--Scicom Data Services, Ltd., Minnetonka, MN, pg. 981
Waltman, Howard L., Chm. Bd. & Chief Exec. Officer--Sanus Corp. Health Systems, Fort Lee, NJ, pg. 803
Walton, Charles W., Pres. & Chief Exec. Officer--Dempster, Inc., Toccoa, GA, pg. 328
Walts, Harry P., Pres. & Chief Exec. Officer--Winston Steel Products Co., Detroit, MI, pg. 1197
Ward, Patrick J., Chm. Bd., Pres. & Chief Exec. Officer--Caltex Petroleum Corporation, Irving, TX, pg. 211
Warehime, John A., Chm. Bd. & Chief Exec. Officer--Hanover Foods Corporation, Hanover, PA, pg. 506
Waring, Saul, Vice Chm. & Co-Chief Exec. Officer--Waring & LaRosa, Inc., New York, NY, pg. 1163
Warkocki, Norbert M., Chief Exec. Officer--Griswold Industries, Inc., Costa Mesa, CA, pg. 488
Warn, Michael T., Pres. & Chief Exec. Officer--Warn Industries, Inc., Milwaukie, OR, pg. 1164
Warner, D. Gill, Pres., Chief Exec. Officer & Gen Mgr.--Associated Food Stores Inc., Salt Lake City, UT, pg. 89
Warner, Jack, Chm. Bd. & Chief Exec. Officer--Gulf States Paper Corporation, Tuscaloosa, AL, pg. 494
Warner, John E., Chm. Bd., Chief Exec. Officer & Creative Dir.--Warner, Bicking, Morris & Partners, Inc., New York, NY, pg. 1164
Warren, Gene A., Pres. & Chief Exec. Officer--Anson Industries, Inc., Melrose Park, IL, pg. 76
Warren, Richard, Chm. & Chief Exec. Officer--The Giardini/Russell Group, Watertown, MA, pg. 456
Warrenfeltz, Steven, Pres. & Chief Exec. Officer--Old World Industries, Inc., Northbrook, IL, pg. 823
Warrenfeltz, Steven, Chief Exec. Officer--Old World Automotive Products, Northbrook, IL, pg. 824
Washington, R. Peter, Chm. Bd. & Chief Exec. Officer--Lyon Metal Products, Inc., Montgomery, IL, pg. 690
Wasserman, Gerald, Pres. & Chief Exec. Officer--Weider Health & Fitness, Woodland Hills, CA, pg. 1173
Wasserstein, Bruce, Co-Chm & Co-Chief Exec. Officer--Collins & Aikman Group Inc., Santa Monica, CA, pg. 262
Wasserstrom, Rodney, Pres. & Chief Exec. Officer--Wasserstrom Company, Columbus, OH, pg. 1167
Watkins, Edward G., Chm. Bd., Pres. & Chief Exec. Officer--Simplex Time Recorder Co., Gardner, MA, pg. 1006
Watkins, James H., Chief Exec. & Oper. Officer--ATCOM, Inc., Research Triangle Park, NC, pg. 93
Watkins, Ronald W., Pres. & Chief Exec. Officer--Nebraska Public Power District, Columbus, NE, pg. 796
Watkins, William D., Chm. Bd. & Chief Exec. Officer--The Alpha Corporation Of Tennessee, Collierville, TN, pg. 43
Watson, Don, Pres./Chief Exec. Officer-New York--Chiat/Day/Mojo/New York, New York, NY, pg. 244
Watson, Houston B., Chm. Bd., Chief Exec. Officer, Chief Fin. Officer & Treas.--Watson Electric Supply Inc., Dallas, TX, pg. 1168
Watson, John D., Pres. & Chief Exec. Officer--Display Technologies, Inc., Elgin, IL, pg. 339
Watson, Paul, Chm., Pres. & Chief Exec. Officer--Farmers Co-op Market Inc., Frisco City, AL, pg. 401
Waugh, John T., Chm. Bd. & Chief Exec. Officer--CJC Holdings, Inc., Austin, TX, pg. 202
Weaver, Michael E., Pres., Chief Exec. Officer & Chief Oper. Officer--Weaver Popcorn Company, Inc., Van Buren, IN, pg. 1170
Weaver, Wayne, Pres. & Chief Exec. Officer--Nine West Group, Inc., Stamford, CT, pg. 807
Webb, Charles B., Jr., Chm. Bd. & Chief Exec. Officer--Alabama Metal Industries Corporation, Birmingham, AL, pg. 28
Webb, J. Fred, Pres. & Chief Exec. Officer--Fred Webb Inc., Greenville, NC, pg. 1170
Weber, Franz Kent, Chm. Bd., Pres. & Chief Exec. Officer--Modulite Corporation, Compton, CA, pg. 763
Weber, R.W., Chief Exec. Officer--Normark Corporation, Minneapolis, MN, pg. 810
Webster, Mark, Chief Exec. Officer, Chief Fin. Officer & Gen. Counsel--Rush County Farm Bureau Co-op, Rushville, IN, pg. 956
Weed, Mark A., Pres. & Chief Exec. Officer--Fisher Properties Inc., Seattle, WA, pg. 415
Weeder, Charles E., Chm. Bd. & Chief Exec. Officer--Homes of Merit Inc., Bartow, FL, pg. 542
Weeks, Ralph W., Pres. & Chief Exec. Officer--Quality Petroleum Corp., Lakeland, FL, pg. 903
Wehrle, Henry B., Jr., Chm. Bd. & Chief Exec. Officer--McJunkin Corporation, Charleston, WV, pg. 730
Weider, Eric, Pres. & Chief Exec. Officer-Equipment Division--Weider Health & Fitness, Woodland Hills, CA, pg. 1173
Weil, David S., Pres., Chief Exec. & Chief Oper. Officer--Ampacet Corporation, Tarrytown, NY, pg. 67
Weiler, A.R., Chm. Bd. & Chief Exec. Officer--Chittenden & Eastman Co., Burlington, IA, pg. 248
Weiler, Gerhard, Pres. & Chief Exec. Officer--Automatic Liquid Packaging, Inc., Woodstock, IL, pg. 100

Weinbach, Lawrence A., Mng. Partner & Chief Exec. Officer--Arthur Andersen & Co., S.C., New York, NY, pg. 72
Weinberger, Alan D., Chm., Pres. & Chief Exec. Officer--The ASCII Group, Inc., Bethesda, MD, pg. 8
Weinberger, Leon J., Pres. & Chief Exec. Officer--Employers Insurance of Wausau a Mutual Co., Wausau, WI, pg. 380
Weinberger, Leon J., Pres. & Chief Exec. Officer--Employers Insurance of Wausau a Mutual Co., Wausau, WI, pg. 795
Weinhart, Martin, Chm. Bd., Chief Exec. Officer & Treas.--Master Molded Products Corporation, Elgin, IL, pg. 720
Weinstein, Howard J., Chm., Pres. & Chief Exec. Officer--Adams Wine Co., Atlanta, GA, pg. 17
Weinstein, Stephen J., Chm. Bd., Chief Exec. Officer & Creative Dir.--SJ Weinstein Associates Inc., New York, NY, pg. 1173
Weis, Dick, Pres. & Chief Exec. Officer--Food Services of America, Seattle, WA, pg. 423
Weisend, C. Frederick, Chm. Bd., Pres. & Chief Exec. Officer--Fritz Chemical Company, Mesquite, TX, pg. 434
Weiser, Sherwood M., Co-Chm. Bd. & Chief Exec. Officer--TCC, Miami, FL, pg. 1072
Weiss, Larry, Chm. Bd., Pres., Chief Exec. Officer & Sec.--Save More Food Mart, Inc., Hobart, IN, pg. 973
Weiss, Stanley, Jr., Chief Exec. Officer & Treas.--Charles River Foods, Inc., Boston, MA, pg. 240
Weiss, W.D., Chief Exec. Officer--Medtech Laboratories, Inc., Jackson, WY, pg. 736
Weitz, Fred, Chm. Bd. & Chief Exec. Officer--The Weitz-Cohen Construction Co., Des Moines, IA, pg. 1174
Welch, David C., Chm.--CME-KHBB Advertising, Minneapolis, MN, pg. 202
Welch, Joseph F., Chm., Pres. & Chief Exec. Officer--Bachman Company, Reading, PA, pg. 108
Wellek, Richard L., Pres. & Chief Exec. Officer--Varlen Corp., Naperville, IL, pg. 358
Welles, D.K., Jr., Pres. & Chief Exec. Officer--Therma-Tru Corp., Maumee, OH, pg. 1090
Wellman, Richard, Chm. Bd. & Chief Exec. Officer--International Airline Support Group, Inc., Miami, FL, pg. 575
Wells, Daniel C., Chm. & Chief Exec. Officer--Stiegler, Wells & Brunswick, Inc., Bethlehem, PA, pg. 1049
Welsh, Robert H., Chm. Bd. & Chief Exec. Officer--Ludlow Textiles Co., Inc., Ludlow, MA, pg. 686
Wendell, Earl W., Pres. & Chief Exec. Officer--Gaylord Entertainment Co., Nashville, TN, pg. 446
Wendell, Janice, Chm.--Ericson Marketing Communications, Nashville, TN, pg. 386
Wendling, Erhard, Chief Exec. Officer--Knight Wendling AG, Zurich,, Switzerland, pg. 637
Wenstrup, H.D., Pres. & Chief Exec. Officer--CHEMCENTRAL Corporation, Bedford Park, IL, pg. 241
Werner, Marc, Pres. & Chief Exec. Officer--Amarlite Architectural Products, Atlanta, GA, pg. 47
Werra, Robert, Chm., Pres. & Chief Exec. Officer--Amrecorp Realty Inc., Dallas, TX, pg. 68
Westin, Richard S., Chm. Bd., Pres. & Chief Exec. Officer--Westin, Inc., Omaha, NE, pg. 1183
Weston, Roger L., Chm. Bd., Pres. & Chief Exec. Officer--GreatBanc, Inc., Aurora, IL, pg. 482
Westphal, Byron, Chm. Bd., Pres. & Chief Exec. Officer--Integrated Energy Controls Corp., Minneapolis, MN, pg. 573
Weyforth, Frank G., Jr., Chm. Bd., Chief Exec. Officer & Pres.--Marketing Resources of America, Inc., Overland Park, KS, pg. 709
Weyrens, J., Pres. & Chief Exec. Officer--Our Own Hardware Company, Burnsville, MN, pg. 832
Whalen, John D., Pres. & Chief Exec. Officer--Pennsylvania Crusher Corp., Broomall, PA, pg. 858
Whaling, George, Pres. & Chief Exec. Officer--Petty Company, Inc., Effingham, IL, pg. 866
Wharton, Clifton R., Jr., Chm. Bd. & Chief Exec. Officer--Teachers Insurance and Annuity Association-College Retirement Equities Fund, New York, NY, pg. 1082
Wheat, Allen, Chief Exec. Officer--Credit Suisse Financial Products, London,, United Kingdom, pg. 204
Wheatley, Charles N., Pres. & Chief Exec. Officer--Sahara Coal Co., Chicago, IL, pg. 966
Wheaton, Robert E., Chm. Bd., Pres., Chief Exec. & Chief Fin. Officer--The Bekins Company, Glendale, CA, pg. 132
Wheeler, Steven E., Chm. & Chief Exec. Officer--Hancock Realty Investors, Inc., Boston, MA, pg. 596
Wheeler, Thomas B., Pres. & Chief Exec. Officer--Massachusetts Mutual Life Insurance Co., Springfield, MA, pg. 718
Whelan, William A., Pres. & Chief Exec. Officer--Roseburg Forest Products Co., Dillard, OR, pg. 948
Whitaker, Gary, Chm., Pres. & Chief Exec. Officer--Curtis Mathes Corporation, Athens, TX, pg. 720
White, Charles R., Exec. V.P. & Chief Exec. Officer--Fastec Industrial, Elkhart, IN, pg. 403
White, Donald J., Pres. & Chief Oper. Officer--The Saugatuck Marketing Group, Westport, CT, pg. 972
White, Michael H., Pres. & Chief Exec. Officer--Rite-Hite Corporation, Milwaukee, WI, pg. 936
White, Robert C., Pres. & Chief Exec. Officer--Industrial Rubber Products Company, Charleston, WV, pg. 566
White, Robert G., Chm. Bd., Pres. & Chief Exec. Officer--New England Frozen Foods, Southborough, MA, pg. 800
White, Thomas A., Pres. & Chief Exec. Officer--Crane & Co., Inc., Dalton, MA, pg. 296
White, William J., Chm. Bd., Pres. & Chief Exec. Officer--Bell & Howell Company, Skokie, IL, pg. 134
Whiteford, Russell E., Pres. & Chief Exec. Officer--Buxton Company, Chicopee, MA, pg. 197
Whiteman, Jack W., Chm. Bd. & Chief Exec. Officer--Empire Southwest Co., Mesa, AZ, pg. 379
Whiting, A. Milton, Chm. Bd. & Chief Exec. Officer--Kaibab Industries, Phoenix, AZ, pg. 614
Whitsell, Helen J., Chm. Bd., Chief Exec. Officer & Treas.--Copeland Lumber Yard, Inc., Portland, OR, pg. 284
Whittenberg, Joseph, Pres. & Chief Exec. Officer--Kurfees Coatings, Inc., Louisville, KY, pg. 646
Whittenburg, Scott D., Pres. & Chief Exec. Officer--Graham Magnetics, Inc., Bedford, TX, pg. 475
Whittle, John J., Chm. Bd., Pres. & Chief Exec. Officer--Farmers and Traders Life Insurance Co., Syracuse, NY, pg. 401
Whyte, George C., Jr., Chm. Bd., Pres. & Chief Exec. Officer--Dakotah, Inc., Webster, SD, pg. 312
Wick, John F., Chm. Bd. & Chief Exec. Officer--Wick Building Systems, Mazomanie, WI, pg. 1188
Wickersham, John, Pres. & Chief Exec. Officer--Bill Communications, Inc., New York, NY, pg. 150
Wickland, J.A., Jr., Chm. Bd. & Chief Exec. Officer--Wickland Corporation, Sacramento, CA, pg. 1188
Widmann, Anthony, Chm. & Chief Exec. Officer--Taylor-Gordon/Widmann & Co., Inc., New York, NY, pg. 1081
Wiedenmayer, Christopher M., Chm. Bd. & Chief Exec. Officer--Faber/Castell Corporation, Parsippany, NJ, pg. 395
Wieland, John F., Chm. Bd., Pres. & Chief Exec. Officer--John Wieland Homes Inc., Atlanta, GA, pg. 1188
Wiesner, John J., Chm. Bd. & Chief Exec. Officer--C. R. Anthony Company, Oklahoma City, OK, pg. 77
Wiggins, Clarence R., Chm. Bd., Pres. & Chief Exec. Officer--Century Data Systems, Raleigh, NC, pg. 235
Wilbur, Brayton Jr., Pres. & Chief Exec. Officer--Wilbur-Ellis Company & Connell Brothers Company, San Francisco, CA, pg. 1189
Wilder, Robert O., Chm. Bd., Pres. & Chief Exec. Officer--National Forge Company, Irvine, PA, pg. 788
Wilkie, Michael L., Chm. Bd., Pres., Chief Exec. & Chief Oper. Officer--DoAll Company, Des Plaines, IL, pg. 341
Wilkinson, Howard W., V.P., Chief Exec. Officer, & Treas.--Fisher Broadcasting, Inc., Seattle, WA, pg. 415
Williams, Dan, Pres. & Chief Exec. Officer--DMI The Healthcare Agency, Chicago, IL, pg. 309
Williams, G.T., Chief Exec. Officer--CMI Industries, Inc., Columbia, SC, pg. 202
Williams, James E., Pres. & Chief Exec. Officer--Golden State Foods Corp., Pasadena, CA, pg. 466
Williams, Kathleen, Pres. & Chief Exec. Officer--Williams Television Time, Inc., Santa Monica, CA, pg. 1191
Williams, Larry E., Pres. & Chief Exec. Officer--National Cooperative Refinery Association, McPherson, KS, pg. 787
Williams, Robert M., Chm., Chief Exec. Officer & Treas.--Genova Products, Inc., Davison, MI, pg. 452
Williams, Ronald, Pres. & Chief Exec. Officer--The Gary-Williams Company, Denver, CO, pg. 444
Williams, Ronald, Pres. & Chief Exec. Officer--Gary-Williams Energy Corporation, Denver, CO, pg. 444
Williams, Steven C., Chief Exec. Officer--State Volunteer Mutual Insurance Co. Inc., Brentwood, TN, pg. 1041
Williams, William J., Chm. Bd. & Chief Exec. Officer--Western & Southern Life Insurance Co., Cincinnati, OH, pg. 1181
Williamson, Hugh H., III, Chm. Bd., Pres. & Chief Exec. Officer--Carolina Steel Corporation, Greensboro, NC, pg. 223
Williamson, Richard B., Pres. & Chief Exec. Officer--T.D. Williamson, Inc., Tulsa, OK, pg. 1192
Willingham, James A., Chm. Bd. & Chief Exec. Officer--Harbor Bancorp, Long Beach, CA, pg. 506
Willingham, Tom, Pres. & Chief Exec. Officer--Interstate Distributors Inc., Norcross, GA, pg. 580
Williome, Jack H., Chief Exec. Officer & V.P.--Rayco, San Antonio, TX, pg. 914
Willis, RobertF., Pres. & Chief Exec. Officer--Maine Printing & Business Forms Co., Portland, ME, pg. 702
Wills, Graeme, Chief Exec. Officer--Chiat/Day/Mojo, Auckland,, New Zealand, pg. 245
Wilson, A.C., Chm. Bd. & Chief Exec. Officer--Ernest Paper Products, Inc., Los Angeles, CA, pg. 387
Wilson, Dean G., Chm. Bd., Pres. & Chief Exec. Officer--Blaw Knox Corp., Pittsburgh, PA, pg. 156
Wilson, Ian R., Chm. Bd., Pres., & Chief Exec. Officer--Windmill Holdings Corp., San Francisco, CA, pg. 1195
Wilson, J. Steven, Chief Exec. Officer--Wickes Lumber Co., Vernon Hills, IL, pg. 1188
Wilson, J.S., Jr., Pres. & Chief Exec. Officer--Conwood Company L.P., Memphis, TN, pg. 281
Wilson, Lawrence A., Pres. & Chief Exec. Officer--HCB Contractors, Dallas, TX, pg. 496
Wilson, Valarie M., Chm. & Chief Exec. Officer--Wilson Sculley Associates, Saint Louis, MO, pg. 1194
Wilson, Wallace S., Chm. Bd., Pres. & Chief Exec. Officer--Wilson Industries Inc., Houston, TX, pg. 1193
Wilson, William, Pres. & Chief Exec. Officer--Pioneer/Eclipse Corp., Sparta, NC, pg. 871
Winch, Harold, Chm. Bd. & Chief Exec. Officer--The Minster Machine Company, Minster, OH, pg. 759
Wing, John A., Chm. Bd. & Chief Exec. Officer--Chicorp, Inc., Chicago, IL, pg. 247
Wing, John A., Chm. Bd., Pres. & Chief Exec. Officer--Chicago Corp., Chicago, IL, pg. 247
Winkelmann, Joe, Chm. Bd., Pres. & Chief Exec. Officer--Greenstripe Media, Inc., Newport Beach, CA, pg. 485
Winn, Elwood, Pres. & Chief Exec. Officer--Certified Grocers Midwest, Inc., Hodgkins, IL, pg. 236
Winship, Blanton C., Pres. & Chief Exec. Officer--Transus Inc., Atlanta, GA, pg. 1108
Winston, Sam, Chm. Bd. & Chief Exec. Officer--Winston Tire Company, Burbank, CA, pg. 1197
Winter, W.B., Chm. Bd. & Chief Exec. Officer--Bucyrus-Erie Company, South Milwaukee, WI, pg. 186
Winter, W.B., Chm. & Chief Exec. Officer--B-E Holdings Inc., South Milwaukee, WI, pg. 106
Winters, Robert C., Chm. Bd. & Chief Exec. Officer--The Prudential Insurance Company of America, Newark, NJ, pg. 896
Winters, Steve D., Pres. & Chief Exec. Officer--Bepco, Inc., Winston-Salem, NC, pg. 141
Wisne, Lawrence A., Pres. & Chief Exec. Officer--Progressive Tool & Industries Co., Southfield, MI, pg. 894
Wisner, J.D., Chm. & Chief Exec. Officer--The Gerstenslager Company, Wooster, OH, pg. 454
Withall, William E., Chm. Bd. & Chief Exec. Officer--Miner Enterprises Inc., Geneva, IL, pg. 756
Witmer, Thomas H., Pres. & Chief Exec. Officer--Medrad, Inc., Pittsburgh, PA, pg. 736
Witwer, Paul, Chief Exec. Officer--Kalas Manufacturing, Inc., Denver, PA, pg. 615
Wojnowich, Saul, Pres. & Chief Exec. Officer--Highland Mills Inc., Charlotte, NC, pg. 534
Wolf, Bob, Chm. Bd., Chief Exec. Officer (North America)--Chiat/Day/Mojo Inc. Advertising, Venice, CA, pg. 244
Wolfe, John F., Pres., Chief Exec. Officer & Publisher--The Dispatch Printing Company, Columbus, OH, pg. 339
Wolfe, Ronald J., Pres. & Chief Exec. Officer--Restaurant Developers Corp., Independence, OH, pg. 929
Wolken, Hal, Pres. & Chief Exec. Officer--A. W. Mendenhall Co., Inc., Elk Grove Village, IL, pg. 739
Wolstein, Bert L., Chief Exec. Officer--Developers Diversified, Moreland Hills, OH, pg. 333
Wood, Bruce, Pres. & Chief Exec. Officer--Lockwood Corporation, Gering, NE, pg. 680
Wood, R. Ray, Chm., Pres., Chief Exec. & Chief Oper. Officer--Rockford Products Corp., Rockford, IL, pg. 941
Woodhall, J.A., Jr., Chm. Bd., Pres. & Chief Exec. Officer--Central Allied Enterprises, Canton, OH, pg. 232
Woodrick, Bob, Chief Exec. Officer--D & W Food Centers, Inc., Grand Rapids, MI, pg. 308
Woodruff, Paul H., Chm. Bd., Pres. & Chief Exec. Officer--The ERM Group, Exton, PA, pg. 360
Woods, Gregory R., Pres. & Chief Exec. Officer--Science & Engineering Associates, Albuquerque, NM, pg. 982
Woodward, Stephen, Chief Exec. Officer--Ayer Ltd., London,, United Kingdom, pg. 104
Workman, C.E., Chm. Bd. & Chief Exec. Officer--Tru-Fit Products Corp., Medina, OH, pg. 1117
Worrell, Terry N., Pres. & Chief Exec. Officer--Sound Warehouse, Inc., Dallas, TX, pg. 1018
Wortman, J. John, Pres. & Chief Exec. Officer--Amerisure Companies, Detroit, MI, pg. 66
Wozniak, Edward F., Pres. & Chief Exec. Officer--Wozniak Industries, Inc., Oakbrook Terrace, IL, pg. 1204
Wratten, John, Pres. & Chief Exec. Officer--Seattle Lighting Fixture Co., Seattle, WA, pg. 986
Wright, H.D., Chm. Bd. & Chief Exec. Officer--Schenectady Chemicals, Inc., Schenectady, NY, pg. 975
Wright, Jerry, Pres. & Chief Exec. Officer--Placid Oil Company, Dallas, TX, pg. 873
Wright, William E., Chief Exec. Officer--H.O. Trerice Company, Oak Park, MI, pg. 1110
Wulf, Jerold W., Pres. & Chief Exec. Officer--Andersen Windows Inc., Bayport, MN, pg. 72
Wurm, Robert, Chm. Bd. & Chief Exec. Officer--La Belle Industries, Inc., Oconomowoc, WI, pg. 648
Wurzel, Tom, Chm. Bd., Pres. & Chief Exec. Officer--ACL Technologies, Santa Ana, CA, pg. 2
Wyckaert, Luke, Chm. Bd., Pres. & Chief Exec. Officer--Intertrade Industries, Huntington Beach, CA, pg. 581
Wydman, Mary Will, Chm. Bd. & Chief Exec. Officer--Witt Company, Cincinnati, OH, pg. 1198
Wyse, Marc A., Chm. & Chief Exec. Officer--Wyse Advertising, Inc., Cleveland, OH, pg. 1206
Yaffe, Fred, Chm. Bd. & Chief Exec. Officer--Yaffe & Co., Southfield, MI, pg. 1207
Yager, Vincent C., Pres. & Chief Exec. Officer--Great Lakes Financial Resources, Inc., Homewood, IL, pg. 481
Yaguda, Jerome D., Pres. & Chief Exec. Officer--Wakefern Food Corporation, Elizabeth, NJ, pg. 1158
Yaklich, Frank J., Jr., Pres. & Chief Exec. Officer--CF&I Steel Corporation, Pueblo, CO, pg. 201
Yamakoshi, Noby, Chm. Bd. & Chief Exec. Officer--Nobart, Inc., Chicago, IL, pg. 808
Yamaura, Shun, Pres. & Chief Exec. Officer--PhoneMate, Inc., Torrance, CA, pg. 869
Yelverton, William F., Chm. & Chief Exec. Officer-New York Worldwide Holding, Inc.--New York Life Insurance Company, New York, NY, pg. 802
Yelverton, William F., Chm. & Chief Exec. Officer--New York Life Worldwide Holding, Inc., New York, NY, pg. 803
Yesawich, Peter C., Ph.D., Pres. & Chief Exec. Officer--Robinson, Yesawich & Pepperdine, Orlando, FL, pg. 940
Yoh, Harold L., Jr., Chm. Bd., Pres. & Chief Exec. Officer--Day & Zimmermann, Inc., Radnor, PA, pg. 320
Yohman, Edward J., Chm. Bd. & Chief Exec. Officer--Cyberex, Inc., Mentor, OH, pg. 307
Yost, Wallace H., Chm. Bd. & Chief Exec. Officer--D.S.U.-Peterbilt & GMC, Inc., Portland, OR, pg. 309
Youmans, Peter, Owner & Chief Exec. Officer--Connecticut Spring & Stamping Corporation, Farmington, CT, pg. 275
Young, David, Chm. Bd. & Chief Exec. Officer--Aminco, Inc., Savannah, GA, pg. 67
Young, Donald A., Chm. Bd. & Chief Exec. Officer--Carson Products Company, Savannah, GA, pg. 67
Young, Jack, Chief Exec. Officer--Pocono Knits, Inc., Hazleton, PA, pg. 1209
Young, Richard D., Pres. & Chief Exec. Officer--Topa Thrift & Loan Association, Los Angeles, CA, pg. 1101
Young, Richard F., Chm. Bd., Pres. & Chief Exec. Officer--Sues, Young & Brown Inc., Baldwin Park, CA, pg. 1056
Young, William D., Sr., Pres. & Chief Exec. Officer--General Wholesale Company, Inc., Atlanta, GA, pg. 451
Yount, G. Stuart, Chm. Bd., Chief Exec. & Chief Fin. Officer--Fortifiber Corporation, Los Angeles, CA, pg. 425
Ytterberg, Ralph, Chm. Bd. & Chief Exec. Officer--INDRESCO, Inc., Dallas, TX, pg. 565
Yu, Eleanor N., Pres.--AdLand Advertising, Inc., San Francisco, CA, pg. 17

Zachry, H.B., Jr., Chm. Bd. & Chief Exec. Officer--H.B. Zachry, San Antonio, TX, pg. 1215
Zaks, Rodnay, Pres. & Chief Exec. Officer--Sybex Group, Alameda, CA, pg. 1069
Zamoiski, C. J., Jr., Chm. Bd., Pres. & Chief Exec. Officer--The Zamoiski Co., Baltimore, MD, pg. 1216
Zaricki, Tom, Pres. & Chief Exec. Officer--Arizona Supermarkets, Inc., Phoenix, AZ, pg. 82
Zarrow, Henry, Pres. & Chief Exec. Officer--Sooner Pipe & Supply Corp., Tulsa, OK, pg. 1018
Zattosky, S.M., Pres., Chief Exec. Officer & Treas.--Cortland Line Co., Inc., Cortland, NY, pg. 287
Zayed, Charles, Chief Exec. Officer--May & Speh, Inc., Downers Grove, IL, pg. 724
Zelazo, N.K., Chief Exec. Officer--Astronautics Corp. of America, Milwaukee, WI, pg. 93
Zemenick, Carl, Pres. & Chief Exec. & Chief Oper. Officer--GF Office Furniture Ltd., Gallatin, TN, pg. 439
Zenegy, Louis, Chm. Bd., Pres. & Chief Exec. Officer--Polymer Development Laboratories, Inc., Orange, CA, pg. 880
Zickler, Leo E., Pres. & Chief Exec. Officer--Oxford Realty Services Corp., Bethesda, MD, pg. 835
Zifferer, Morton F., Jr., Pres. & Chief Exec. Officer--New Standard Corporation, Mount Joy, PA, pg. 802
Zilkha, Selim K., Chm. Bd. & Chief Exec. Officer--Zilkha Energy Company, Houston, TX, pg. 1219
Zimmer, Edward M., Jr., Chm. Bd. & Chief Exec. Officer--Berkeley Industries Inc., Laguna Beach, CA, pg. 141
Zimmerli, Kurt, Chm. Bd., Pres., Chief Exec. Officer & Chief Oper. Officer--Zima Corp., Spartanburg, SC, pg. 1219
Zimmerman, Ann, Chief Exec. Officer--Fashion Shop of Kentucky Inc., Louisville, KY, pg. 403
Zimmerman, Martin E., Pres. & Chief Exec. Officer--The LINC Group, Inc., Chicago, IL, pg. 648
Zinbarg, Benson, Pres., Chief Exec. & Chief Fin. Officer & Treas.--Sun Hill Industries, Stamford, CT, pg. 1059
Zito, Paul M., Pres. & Chief Exec. Officer--Bacharach Inc., Pittsburgh, PA, pg. 108
Zitterkopf, Irvin L., Pres. & Chief Exec. Officer--Southern Minnesota Beet Sugar Cooperative, Renville, MN, pg. 1022
Zoeller, Robert F., Chm. Bd. & Chief Exec. Officer--Zoeller Co., Louisville, KY, pg. 1220
Zunenshine, David, Chief Exec. Officer--SLM, Inc., Gloversville, NY, pg. 963
Zurilla, Tom, Pres. & Chief Exec. Officer--G B Stores, Johnstown, PA, pg. 978
Zylstra, O.W., Chm. Bd. & Chief Exec. Officer--Rena-Ware Distributors Inc., Redmond, WA, pg. 926

CHIEF FINANCIAL OFFICER

Abbrederis, D.E., Sr. V.P. & Chief Fin. Officer--Unigard Security Insurance Co., Bellevue, WA, pg. 596
Abbrederis, D.E., Sr. V.P. & Chief Fin. Officer--Unigard Indemnity Co., Raleigh, NC, pg. 596
Abbrederis, D.E., Sr. V.P. & Chief Fin. Officer--Unigard Insurance Co., Seattle, WA, pg. 596
Abbrederis, D.E., Sr. V.P. & Chief Fin. Officer--Unigard Service Corp., Seattle, WA, pg. 596
Abrahamson, Mary Jo, Sr. V.P., Chief Fin. Officer & Treas.--Zapiecki & Partners Inc., Toledo, OH, pg. 1216
Abrams, Jerry, Treas. & Chief Fin. Officer--Hoogovens Aluminum Corp., Secaucus, NJ, pg. 543
Abroneaux, Jesse P., Chief Fin. Officer--Bultman Funeral Home, New Orleans, LA, pg. 832
Accardo, Jack P., V.P. & Chief Fin. Officer, Treas. & Sec.--Kasper Machine Company, Madison Heights, MI, pg. 618
Acker, H., Chief Fin. Officer--Gentex Optics, Inc., Simpson, PA, pg. 452
Ackerman, Sanford S., Sr. V.P. & Chief Fin. Officer--John Blair Communications, Inc., New York, NY, pg. 155
Acquinaldo, Wayne, Chief Fin. Officer--Gulf Exploration, Houston, TX, pg. 493
Adam, Dave, Chief Fin. Officer--GMI, Inc.-Glasstream, Panama City, FL, pg. 450
Adam, David P., Chief Fin. Officer--Century Boats By General Marine Industries, Panama City, FL, pg. 450
Adami, Gary, Exec. V.P., Chief Fin. Officer--Ruppman National Yellow Pages Service (RNYPS), Peoria, IL, pg. 956
Adams, Charles H., Sr. V.P. & Chief Fin. Officer--Omni Hotels, Hampton, NH, pg. 826
Adams, Donald L., V.P.-Fin. & Admin. & Chief Fin. Officer--American Institute of C.P.A.'s Inc., New York, NY, pg. 56
Adams, Harry, Pres., Chief Exec. Officer, & Chief Fin. Officer--Pyttronic Industries, Inc., Montgomeryville, PA, pg. 901
Adams, Richard B., Exec. V.P., Sec. & Treas.--R. P. Adams Company, Inc., Tonawanda, NY, pg. 16
Adante, David E., V.P., Chief Fin. Officer & Sec.--The Davey Tree Expert Company, Kent, OH, pg. 317
Adelstein, Stanford M., Chm. Bd. & Treas.--Hills Materials Co., Rapid City, SD, pg. 815
Adkins, Marshall, Sec. & Treas.--United Feeds, Inc., Sheridan, IN, pg. 1132
Adler, Jack, Sec. & Treas.--Bridal Originals, Inc., Collinsville, IL, pg. 175
Aebel, Charles, Chief Fin. Officer--Central States Diversified, Inc., Saint Louis, MO, pg. 234
Aelis, Gary, Sr. V.P. & Chief Fin. Officer--Consolidated Cigar Corporation, Fort Lauderdale, FL, pg. 276
Agler, Thomas S., V.P. & Chief Fin. Officer--Great Lakes Financial Resources, Inc., Homewood, IL, pg. 481
Agosinelli, Richard J., Sr. V.P. & Chief Fin. Officer--Continental Graphics Corporation, Los Angeles, CA, pg. 279
Agostinelli, Albert A., Chief Fin. Officer & Exec. V.P.--Fishers Big Wheel Inc., New Castle, PA, pg. 415
Ahrens, W.C. Jr., Treas.--HPM Corporation, Mount Gilead, OH, pg. 497
Aimone, Michael V., Chief Fin. Officer & V.P.--Mississippi Lime Co., Alton, IL, pg. 760
Ajami, Ana Marie, Chief Fin. Officer--New England Stone Industries, Inc., Esmond, RI, pg. 800
Albers, Mike, Chief Fin. Officer--SAIC Engineering, Inc., Lakeville, MA, pg. 982
Albracht, K.L., Chief Fin. Officer & V.P.--International Systems & Controls Corp., Houston, TX, pg. 579
Albright, James C., V.P. & Controller--Monier Roof Tile, Inc., Orange, CA, pg. 765
Alden, Richard, Chief Fin. Officer & Exec. V.P.--Joan Fabrics Corp., Tyngsboro, MA, pg. 594
Aldrich, Clif, Chief Fin. Officer--Richardson, Myers & Donofrio, Inc., Baltimore, MD, pg. 933
Alexander, Bill, V.P., Treas. & Chief Fin. Officer--Purcell Co., Inc., Bay Saint Louis, MS, pg. 900
Alexander, Ed, Chief Fin. Officer--Windmill Corp. d/b/a Martha White Foods, Inc., Brentwood, TN, pg. 1195
Alford, Jason, Treas. & Sec.--Rainbow Home Rentals, Canfield, OH, pg. 910
Allardyce, Fred A., V.P. & Chief Fin. Officer--American Standard Inc., New York, NY, pg. 61
Allen, Clinton, Sec. & Treas.--Bill Heard Leasing, Inc., Columbus, GA, pg. 521
Allen, W. Dean, Chief Fin. Officer & Treas.--Expo Industries, Inc., San Diego, CA, pg. 393
Alles, Charles, Treas.--Windemuller Electric Inc., Grandville, MI, pg. 1195
Allison, Theresa, Fin. V.P.--Hallmark Advertising, Inc., Pittsburgh, PA, pg. 501
Allmon, Diane, Controller--Gemtron Corporation, Sweetwater, TN, pg. 3
Allsup, Jay, Chief Fin. Officer--Fey Mfg. Co., Inc., Irwindale, CA, pg. 1038
Allsup, Jay M., Chief Fin. Officer & Treas.--Standun, Inc., Irwindale, CA, pg. 1038
Altherr, Jack R., Chief Fin. Officer, V.P. & Sec.--Avondale Mills, Inc., Sylacauga, AL, pg. 103
Altstadt, Manfred, Chief Fin. Officer & Sr. V.P.--Mutual of America, New York, NY, pg. 777
Amato, Larry, Chief Fin. Officer, Treas. & Sec.--Elkay Products, Inc., Shrewsbury, MA, pg. 377
Amstutz, Gary, Chief Fin. Officer--Energy and Technology Management Corporation, Germantown, MD, pg. 981
Andersen, Lynn, Treas.--Simmons Outdoor Corp., Miami, FL, pg. 1005
Andersen, Ross, V.P. & Chief Fin. Officer--Berry Bearing Co., Lyons, IL, pg. 144
Anderson, Bob, Sec. & Treas.--Telsco Industries, Garland, TX, pg. 1085
Anderson, Charlie, Chief Fin. Officer & Mng. Partner--Carmichael Lynch, Inc., Minneapolis, MN, pg. 222
Anderson, Donald, V.P.-Fin.--Simpson Electric Co., Elgin, IL, pg. 1007
Anderson, George, Chief Fin. Officer & V.P.--Juhl Marketing Communications, Mishawaka, IN, pg. 608
Anderson, George W. II, Chief Fin. Officer--Columbus Show Case Company, Columbus, OH, pg. 267
Anderson, James R., V.P.-Fin., Sec. & Treas.--The Austin Company, Cleveland, OH, pg. 790
Anderson, Keith, Chief Fin. Officer--Holmes Protection Group, Inc., New York, NY, pg. 540
Anderson, Ken, Chief Fin. Officer--Freudenberg-NOK (MI), Plymouth, MI, pg. 432
Anderson, Lloyd L., Chief Fin. Officer--Cole Papers Inc., Fargo, ND, pg. 260
Anderson, Lyn, Chief Fin. Officer--Tom's Foods, Columbus, GA, pg. 1101
Anderson, M. D., Chief Fin. Officer--Copeland Lumber Yard, Inc., Portland, OR, pg. 284
Anderson, Marge, Chief Fin. Officer & V.P.--The Aerospace Corporation, El Segundo, CA, pg. 22
Anderson, Mike, V.P. & Chief Fin. Officer--Anderson Wholesale Company, Muskogee, OK, pg. 73
Anderson, R.W., Chief Fin. Officer--Flying J. Inc., Brigham City, UT, pg. 421
Anderson, Richard, V.P. & Chief Fin. Officer--Instrument Specialties Company, Delaware Water Gap, PA, pg. 572
Anderson, Thomas G., Chief Oper. Officer, Chief Fin. Officer & V.P.--Gordy's, Inc., Worthington, MN, pg. 472
Andrews, David, Chief Fin. Officer--Prepco, Los Angeles, CA, pg. 887
Andrews, Michael, Chief Fin. Officer--Sunbeam Corporation (Canada) Limited, Toronto, Canada, pg. 1059
Andrews, Sue, V.P., Chief Fin. Officer--Evans, Hardy & Young, Inc., Santa Barbara, CA, pg. 390
Andrus, Frederick, Chief Fin. Officer--San Diego Zoo, San Diego, CA, pg. 969
Andrus, Frederick, Chief Fin. Officer--San Diego Wild Animal Park, Escondido, CA, pg. 969
Angart, Robert F., Chief Oper. Officer, Chief Fin. Officer, V.P.-Fin.--Perlmuter Printing Company, Cleveland, OH, pg. 862
Angelo, Thomas, Exec. V.P.-Fin.--Dribeck Importers, Inc., Greenwich, CT, pg. 349
Angelone, Fred, Chief Fin. Officer--U.S. Repeating Arms Company, New Haven, CT, pg. 1137
Anglin, Rick, Chief Fin. Officer--Mark Shale, Willowbrook, IL, pg. 994
Ansted, James P., Chief Fin. Officer, Treas., Sec.--Plastic Suppliers, Inc., Columbus, OH, pg. 875
Anstett, Joseph L., Chief Fin. Officer, Exec. V.P. & Sec.--Silver State Disposal Service, Inc., Las Vegas, NV, pg. 1004
Anzellotti, Diane, Chief Fin. Officer--Hitchcock Chair Company LTD, Riverton, CT, pg. 536
Aquilina, Robert, Sr. V.P. & Chief Fin. Officer--Estee Lauder, Inc., New York, NY, pg. 389
Arboneaux, Jesse P., V.P., Chief Fin. Officer, Treas. & Sec.--Ourso Investment Corporation, Donaldsonville, LA, pg. 832
Arboneaux, Jesse P., V.P., Treas. & Sec.--Security Industrial Insurance Co., Inc., Donaldsonville, LA, pg. 832
Archibald, Rae W., Chief Fin. Officer & V.P.--RAND, Santa Monica, CA, pg. 911
Arfmann, Bruce, Chief Fin. Officer & Treas.--RELA, Inc., Boulder, CO, pg. 924
Arfmann, Bruce L., Chief Fin. Officer--RELA Product Development Div. (PDD), Boulder, CO, pg. 924
Arlotta, Terry, Chief Fin. Officer--Peerless Importers, Inc., Brooklyn, NY, pg. 855
Armato, Michael, Chief Fin. Officer--Knutson Construction Co., Minneapolis, MN, pg. 638
Arnholt, John, Sr. V.P., Chief Fin. Officer--McFarland & Drier, Inc., Miami, FL, pg. 729
Arnold, Bill, V.P.-Fin.--Delta & Pine Land Company, Scott, MS, pg. 1024
Arnold, H.G., Chm. Bd. & Chief Fin. Officer--Venta Inc., Denver, CO, pg. 1147
Arnold, Mark S., V.P., Chief Fin. Officer & Controller--Sterling Plumbing Group, Inc., Schaumburg, IL, pg. 640
Aro, Jeanne, V.P.-Fin & Admin.--Mini Mart, Inc., Casper, WY, pg. 757
Aronaho, Kauko, Sr. V.P. & Chief Fin. Officer--ComputerLand Canada Ltd., Brampton,, Canada, pg. 271
Aronovitz, Alan, Sr. V.P. & Chief Fin. Officer--National Foods Inc., Bronx, NY, pg. 788
Arpe, James F., Chief Fin. Officer--Draper Corporation, Greensboro, NC, pg. 348
Arrigo, Joseph F., V.P., Treas. & Sec.--UIS, Inc., New York, NY, pg. 1123
Artz, F.J., Treas.--Today's Kids, Booneville, AR, pg. 1025
Ashley, Kenneth, Chief Fin. Officer, Sec. & Treas.--National R.V., Inc., Perris, CA, pg. 792
Ashman, Stephen, Exec. V.P. & Chief Fin. Officer--Capital Bank, Miami, FL, pg. 214
Ashton, Robert L., V.P., Chief Fin. Officer & Controller--All Seasons Services, Inc., Braintree, MA, pg. 35
Atkin, William W., Exec. V.P. & Chief Fin. Officer--Security Mutual Life Insurance Co. of New York, Binghamton, NY, pg. 987
Atko, Karen, Controller--Braun-Brumfield, Inc., Ann Arbor, MI, pg. 998
Attebury, Ronald L., Chief Fin. Officer & Treas.--Norbest, Inc., Midvale, UT, pg. 809
Au, Simon, Chief Fin. Officer--Lee Davis Ayer, Hong Kong,, Hong Kong, pg. 104
Aubuchon, David, Chief Fin. Officer--A. Pomerantz & Co., Philadelphia, PA, pg. 880
Augustine, Richard J., V.P.-Fin. & Chief Fin. Officer--Atwood Industries, Inc., Rockford, IL, pg. 97
Auriemma, Samuel, Chief Fin. Officer--Locus Computing Corp., Inglewood, CA, pg. 680
Ausing, Alan, Chief Fin. Officer--Farallon Computing, Inc., Emeryville, CA, pg. 399
Austin, William F., Pres., Sec. & Treas.--Starkey Laboratories, Inc., Eden Prairie, MN, pg. 1040
Autry, Jacqueline, Exec. V.P., Treas. & Chief Fin. Officer--Golden West Broadcasters, Los Angeles, CA, pg. 467
Auwaerter, John, Sr. V.P., Chief Fin. Officer--Asher/Gould Advertising, Inc., Los Angeles, CA, pg. 88
Averitt, Dewey, Chief Fin. Officer--Whitin Roberts Co., Sanford, NC, pg. 1187
Averitt, Dewey, Chief Fin. Officer--Whitin Roberts Mfg. Div., Sanford, NC, pg. 1187
Avery, Ken, Sr. V.P.-Finance--Yardney Technical Products, Inc., Pawcatuck, CT, pg. 1207
Awad, Dennis J., Pres., Chief Exec. & Fin. Officer & Treas.--Tele-Com Products, Inc., Duarte, CA, pg. 1084
Ayabe, Takato, Controller--Japan Travel Bureau International, Inc., New York, NY, pg. 590
Bachman, Lee W., V.P.-Fin. & Treas.--Bachman's, Inc., Minneapolis, MN, pg. 108
Bachmeier, Ronald M., V.P.-Fin., Chief Fin. Officer & Treas.--Xerxes Corporation, Minneapolis, MN, pg. 1206
Bailey, Bill, Chief Fin. Officer--Lykes Brothers Inc. of Florida, Tampa, FL, pg. 688
Bailey, D. Warren, Chief Fin. Officer & Sr. V.P.-Fin.--Parisian, Inc., Birmingham, AL, pg. 848
Bailey, Geraldine, Chief Fin. Officer--Charles Tombras Advertising, Inc., Knoxville, TN, pg. 1100
Bailey, Jack, V.P. & Treas.--Smith-Lee Co., Inc., Oneida, NY, pg. 1013
Bailey, John, Chm. Bd., Pres., Chief Exec. & Fin. Officer & Treas.--Cal/Emblem Labels, Inc., Fresno, CA, pg. 208
Bailey, Richard W., V.P.-Fin. & Chief Fin. Officer--Tree Top, Inc., Selah, WA, pg. 1109
Bailey, Tom, Chief Fin. Officer--Gordon Bailey & Associates, Inc., Stone Mountain, GA, pg. 114
Bair, Clinton, Sec. & Controller--Republic Die & Tool Company, Belleville, MI, pg. 928
Baird, Anna, Controller--Black Box Corporation, Lawrence, PA, pg. 748
Baird, Donn, Treas.--Kalsec, Inc., Kalamazoo, MI, pg. 615
Baird, M. Rex, Sr. V.P., Treas. & Chief Fin. Officer--Summa Corporation, Las Vegas, NV, pg. 1057
Baker, Alfred, V.P.-Fin.--Pro-Line Corporation, Dallas, TX, pg. 892
Baker, Bret, Chief Fin. Officer--Efco Corporation, Monett, MO, pg. 359
Baker, Diane P., Sr. V.P.-Fin. & Chief Fin. & Info. Officer--R. H. Macy & Co., Inc., New York, NY, pg. 698
Baker, John E., Chief Fin. Officer, Treas. & Controller--Steuart Investment Co., Washington, DC, pg. 1048
Baker, Peter G., Chief Exec. Officer--Seko-Air Freight, Elk Grove Village, IL, pg. 988
Baker, Robert M., Chief Fin. Officer & V.P.--Robinson & St. John Advertising & Public Relations, Inc., Jacksonville, FL, pg. 940
Baker, Russell, Controller--Chattanooga Choo-Choo Holiday Inn, Chattanooga, TN, pg. 241
Baker, Stan, Chief Fin. Officer--Colonial Homes, New York, NY, pg. 523
Baker, T.F., Sr. V.P.-Fin., Treas. & Chief Fin. Officer--Harvest States Cooperatives, Saint Paul, MN, pg. 514
Baker, W. Kendall, V.P., Treas., Chief Fin. & Acctg. Officer--Jim Walter Homes, Inc., Tampa, FL, pg. 1162
Ball, John, V.P. & Chief Fin. Officer--Golden Sun Feeds, Inc., Estherville, IA, pg. 467

Bamber, Anthony P., V.P. & Chief Fin. Officer--Decision Data Inc., Horsham, PA, pg. 323
Bamibery, John, Chief Fin. Officer--Engineering Technology Ltd. (E.T.), Troy, MI, pg. 382
Banks, Ken, V.P.-Fin., Sec. & Treas.--Grove Valve & Regulator Company, Oakland, CA, pg. 490
Barbeau, David, Chief Fin. Officer--A.P.S., Inc., Houston, TX, pg. 5
Barbour, Rodney, Chief Fin. Officer & Gen. Counsel--Lawson Mechanical Contractors, Sacramento, CA, pg. 663
Barclay, Fred, Chief Fin. Officer--The Spencer Turbine Co., Windsor, CT, pg. 1030
Barclay, Frederick B., Chief Fin. Officer & V.P.--Spencer Turbine Co., Windsor, CT, pg. 1030
Barda, Barbara, V.P.-Fin. & Admin.--Berkeley Industries Inc., Laguna Beach, CA, pg. 141
Bare, Richard, V.P.-Fin.--Walker Wire & Steel Company, Ferndale, MI, pg. 1160
Barfelt, Bruce, Chief Fin. Officer--Rainfair, Inc., Racine, WI, pg. 910
Bargull, Raymond C., Exec. V.P.-Real Estate Officer & Chief Fin. Officer--Sundt Corp., Tucson, AZ, pg. 1060
Barker, D.W., Treas. & Chief Fin. Officer--Maescher Industries, Inc., Cincinnati, OH, pg. 699
Barlow, Charles, Comptroller--Little America Refining, Salt Lake City, UT, pg. 1008
Barnes, James, V.P., Treas. & Chief Fin. Officer--Wohlert Corp., Lansing, MI, pg. 1198
Barnes, Swift C., Chief Fin. Officer--Harbert Corporation, Birmingham, AL, pg. 506
Barnet, John H., Chief Fin. Officer--Acurex Environmental Corporation, Mountain View, CA, pg. 15
Barnhill, Richard D., Chief Fin. Officer, Treas. & Sec.--Idea Engineering & Fabricating, Detroit, MI, pg. 562
Baroevich, Diane, Chief Fin. Officer--Summerfield Truck Co. Inc., Portage, IN, pg. 1057
Baron, Norbert, Chief Fin. Officer--American Barmag Co., Charlotte, NC, pg. 49
Barr, David, Chief Fin. Officer--PacifiCare of California, Cypress, CA, pg. 1127
Barraut, Guillaume, Chief Fin. Officer--Wunderman Cato Johnson France, Boulogne,, France, pg. 1212
Barrett, Dennis, Chief Fin. Officer--Minnesota Brewing Company, Saint Paul, MN, pg. 757
Barrett, Paul, Sr. V.P.-Fin., Treas., & Chief Fin. Officer--Bill's Dollar Stores, Inc., Jackson, MS, pg. 150
Barrick Paul W., Chief Fin. Officer--Hidden Valley Resort, Hidden Valley, PA, pg. 626
Barrick, Paul W., Chief Fin. Officer--Kettler Brothers, Inc., Montgomery Village, MD, pg. 626
Bartis, Brian, Controller--Wolverine Packing Co., Detroit, MI, pg. 1199
Barton, Faye, Chief Fin. Officer--Backus Turner & Partners, Inc., Miami, FL, pg. 112
Barton, Margaret, Chief Fin. Officer--Universal Steel Tube Co. Limited, Birmingham,, United Kingdom, pg. 878
Basar, John, Chief Fin. Officer & Controller--Red Carpet Real Estate Services, Inc., San Diego, CA, pg. 918
Basile, Frank, V.P.-Fin.--Rau Fasteners, Inc., Providence, RI, pg. 913
Bateman, Christopher H., V.P. & Sec.--HCC Industries, Rosemead, CA, pg. 496
Bates, D.W., V.P. & Treas.--J. H. France Refractories Co., Snow Shoe, PA, pg. 428
Bates, James C., V.P. & Chief Fin. Officer--ACF Industries, Inc., Earth City, MO, pg. 561
Baudais, Jean-Pierre, Chief Fin. Officer & Corp. Sec.--TBWA de Plas, Paris,, France, pg. 1072
Bauer, James P., V.P.-Fin. & Treas.--Small Parts, Inc., Logansport, IN, pg. 1010
Bauers, Barton, Jr., V.P.-Fin.--Standard-Knapp, Inc., Portland, CT, pg. 1036
Bauman, B. Kent, Pres. & Chief Fin. Officer--Condon Oil Company, Inc., Ripon, WI, pg. 273
Bauman, Mary Ellen, V.P.-Fin. & Chief Fin. Officer--Microband Companies, Inc., Fairfield, NJ, pg. 748
Baumann, Michael, Chief Fin. Officer--Ernst Home Center, Inc., Seattle, WA, pg. 387
Baumgardner, David, V.P.-Fin.--H.M. Smyth Co., Saint Paul, MN, pg. 1014
Baumhober, Roger, V.P. & Chief Fin. Officer--AmClyde Engineered Products, Inc., Saint Paul, MN, pg. 47
Bavely, Donald, Treas.--Rosenthal Chevrolet Co., Arlington, VA, pg. 949
Bax, Simon, Exec. V.P., Chief Fin. Officer-Worldwide--Chiat/Day/Mojo Inc. Advertising, Venice, CA, pg. 244
Bayley, Ronald E., Treas.--Programmed Maintenance Services, Inc., Kirkland, WA, pg. 128
Bean, Richard E., Chief Fin. Officer & Exec. V.P.-Fin.--Pearce Industries Inc., Houston, TX, pg. 853
Beard, Thomas, Sr. V.P., Chief Fin. Officer, Treas. & Controller--Petroleum Inc., Wichita, KS, pg. 865
Beattie, Ralph, Exec. V.P. & Chief Fin. Officer--Haggar Apparel Company, Dallas, TX, pg. 499
Beavais, Robert, Chief Fin. Officer--J. Austin Oil Co., Flint, MI, pg. 99
Bechtel, Jim, V.P. & Chief Fin. Officer--Hausted, Medina, OH, pg. 1008
Beck, Michael, Sr. V.P.-Fin.--Westat Inc., Rockville, MD, pg. 1178
Beck, Mike, Chief Fin. Officer--Bollinger Industries Inc., Irving, TX, pg. 163
Beck, Thomas E., V.P. & Treas.--Beck Manufacturing, Inc., Waynesboro, PA, pg. 153
Beck, William, V.P.-Fin. & Controller--Zena Jeans, New York, NY, pg. 1217
Becker, Carolyn, Chief Fin. Officer--L. L. Olds Seed Company, Madison, WI, pg. 824
Becker, Jerry, Controller--Hoof Products Company, Chicago, IL, pg. 543
Beckman, Dick, V.P.-Fin.--Yorktowne, Inc., Red Lion, PA, pg. 1208
Beckoff, Marc, Chief Fin. Officer--Leonard Wholesale, Inc., Elizabeth, NJ, pg. 668
Beckstead, Roger, V.P., Chief Fin. Officer--Fogarty & Klein/Winius Brandon, Houston, TX, pg. 421
Beckstead, Roger, Chief Fin. Officer--Fogarty & Klein Yellow Pages, Inc., Austin, TX, pg. 421
Beckstead, Roger, Chief Fin. Officer--Fogarty & Klein Public Relations, Houston, TX, pg. 421
Beda, Bruce A., V.P., Treas., Chief Fin. Officer & Sec.--Venturedyne, Ltd., Milwaukee, WI, pg. 1148
Beda, Bruce A., V.P. & Treas. & Chief Fin. Officer--Carnes Company, Inc., Milwaukee, WI, pg. 1148
Bedford, Bryan K., V.P. & Chief Fin. Officer--WestAir Holding Inc., Fresno, CA, pg. 1178
Bee, Dennis E., Treas.--United Refining Company, Warren, PA, pg. 1130
Beffa, T.G., V.P. & Chief Fin. Officer--DIMAC Corporation, Bridgeton, MO, pg. 338
Beffa, Timothy G., Sr. V.P., Fin., Chief Fin. Officer--DIMAC DIRECT, Bridgeton, MO, pg. 338
Behne, Don, V.P. & Treas.--National Savings Life Insurance Company, Murfreesboro, TN, pg. 1150
Behne, Donald L., Treas.--Kennesaw Life & Accident Insurance Company, Atlanta, GA, pg. 921
Behnen, Phillip, V.P., Chief Fin. Officer--The Puckett Group, Saint Louis, MO, pg. 899
Behner, Barbara, Chief Fin. Officer, Sec. & Treas.--Harmon Smith Inc., Kansas City, MO, pg. 510
Beihl, Bill, Sr. V.P., Chief Fin. Officer--Griffin Bacal Inc., New York, NY, pg. 486
Belew, W.B., Jr., Chief Fin. Officer--ITI Marketing Services, Inc., Omaha, NE, pg. 561
Bell, Howard, Controller-Florida Region--Specialty Restaurants Corporation, Anaheim, CA, pg. 1027
Bell, Patrick, Chief Fin. Officer--Weatherby, Inc., South Gate, CA, pg. 1169
Bell, Robert P., Exec. V.P., Sec. & Treas.--Harry H. Bell & Sons, Inc., Saint Petersburg, FL, pg. 134
Bell, Sam, Sr. V.P.-Fin. & Chief Fin. Officer--Newbridge Communications, New York, NY, pg. 611
Belsly, John C., Exec. V.P.-Fin. & Chief Fin. Officer--Graham Magnetics, Inc., Bedford, TX, pg. 475
Bembenista, Walter J., Sr. V.P. & Chief Fin. Officer--Goldmark Industries, Ltd., New York, NY, pg. 468
Benedict, Robert, Chief Exec. Officer, Chief Fin. Officer & V.P.--R.W. Electronics, Andover, MA, pg. 908
Benedict, Shirley, V.P.-Fin.--Winona Knits, Winona, MN, pg. 1196
Bennett, James D., Chief Fin. Officer & Treas.--V.G.S. Corp. d/b/a Southland Oil Company, Jackson, MS, pg. 1141
Bennett, Michael, Chief Fin. Officer & V.P.-Fin.--Midwesco Inc., Niles, IL, pg. 751
Bennett, Phillip R., Chief Fin. Officer--Refco Group Ltd., Chicago, IL, pg. 921
Bennett, Wycliff F., Chief Fin. Officer--Mormac Marine Transport, Inc., Stamford, CT, pg. 770
Bennion, Richard E., V.P.-Fin. & Chief Fin. Officer--Rowe Corp., Charlotte, NC, pg. 952
Benno, Eli, V.P., Treas. & Sec.--Trading Port, Inc., Albany, NY, pg. 1105
Bensimon, Rachel, Pres. & Chief Fin. Officer--Dearden's, Inc., Los Angeles, CA, pg. 322
Benson, Donald E., Exec. V.P. & Chief Fin. Officer--Globe Industries, Inc., Chicago, IL, pg. 464
Benton, William B., Chm. Bd., Chief Exec. Officer & Chief Fin. Officer--Mid South Sales, Helena, AR, pg. 750
Benveniste, Eric, Chief Fin. Officer--UniHealth America, Burbank, CA, pg. 1126
Benway, Joseph C., Exec. V.P., Chief Fin. Officer--Burson-Marsteller, New York, NY, pg. 1210
Berchem, Allen R., V.P.-Fin. & Pur.--Torke Coffee Company, Inc., Sheboygan, WI, pg. 1102
Berg, Adolph, Chief Fin. Officer--Alpha Shirt Co., Philadelphia, PA, pg. 44
Berger, Morris E., Chief Fin. Officer--Careers USA Inc., Philadelphia, PA, pg. 218
Bergsma, S., Chief Fin. Officer--BSB Amsterdam, Amsterdam,, Netherlands, pg. 109
Berlinger, Harvey, Controller--Remco Toys, New York, NY, pg. 926
Berman, Jay, Sr. V.P. & Chief Fin. Officer--The William Carter Company, New York, NY, pg. 226
Bernadet, Hubert, Chief Fin. Officer--Michael Conrad & Leo Burnett GmbH & Co. KG, Frankfurt/Main, Germany, pg. 192
Bernat, S.C., V.P.-Fin.--The Rotor Tool Company, Cleveland, OH, pg. 951
Berner, Wilber, Chief Fin. Officer--The Aarque Companies, Jamestown, NY, pg. 9
Bernhaut, Nancy, Exec. V.P. & Chief Fin. Officer--Zephyr Baskets & Balloons, New Providence, NJ, pg. 1217
Bernstein, Brian A., Chief Fin. Officer & Treas.--American Chemical Society, Washington, DC, pg. 50
Bernstein, Harvey, Chief Fin. Officer--Junior Gallery Ltd., New York, NY, pg. 609
Berry, Walter, Chief Fin. Officer--Algiers Iron Works & Dry Dock, Inc., New Orleans, LA, pg. 163
Bersch, Neil R., Sr. V.P. & Chief Fin. Officer--American Protection Industries, Inc., Los Angeles, CA, pg. 60
Berson, Selma, Sec. & Treas.--B & B Motor & Control Corporation, Long Island City, NY, pg. 105
Bertolini, Arthur G., Sr. V.P.-Fin. & Admin., Treas. & Sec.--Rocor Transportation Companies Inc., Oklahoma City, OK, pg. 942
Best, Jerry, Chief Fin. Officer--Louis London Advertising & Sales Promotion, Saint Louis, MO, pg. 684
Best, Michael, V.P. & Chief Fin. Officer--J H Collectibles, Milwaukee, WI, pg. 584
Best, Randy, Chief Fin. Officer--Allied Plywood Corp., Alexandria, VA, pg. 38
Bewley, Carl, Mgr.-Fiscal--Oregon State Lottery, Salem, OR, pg. 829
Beyer, Allan, V.P.-Fin. & Sec.--Basler Electric Company, Highland, IL, pg. 125
Beyer, William J., Sr. V.P. & Chief Fin. Officer--White Swan, Inc., Euless, TX, pg. 1156
Biacci, Tony, Chief Fin. Officer--Fabianac, Stropes & Armstrong, Inc., San Francisco, CA, pg. 395
Bickman, James, Pres. & Treas.--Stocker & Yale, Inc., Beverly, MA, pg. 1050
Bidelman, Jewell M., V.P.-Treas.--Northridge Industries, Inc., Las Vegas, NV, pg. 495
Biegel, Paul, Chief Fin. Officer--Ateron Corp., Parsippany, NJ, pg. 93
Biegler, Jack, Chief Fin. Officer & V.P.--Rayco, San Antonio, TX, pg. 914
Biemeck, Bruce J., V.P. & Chief Fin. Officer--Great Lakes Dredge & Dock, Oak Brook, IL, pg. 481
Bierer, Alice, Pres. & Chief Fin. Officer--Essex Grain Products, Inc., Frazer, PA, pg. 389
Biggs, John, Sr. V.P.-Fin. Admin.--Hyatt Hotels Corporation, Chicago, IL, pg. 495
Bigham, James J., Exec. V.P. & Chief Fin. Officer--Continental Grain Company, New York, NY, pg. 279
Billings, E.C., Chief Fin. Officer--Sequentia Inc., Strongsville, OH, pg. 990
Billings, Edwin, Sec. & Treas.--Sequentia Inc. Reinforced Plastics Div., Strongsville, OH, pg. 990
Billingsley, Ralph, V.P.-Fin.--Sanderson Plumbing Products Inc., Columbus, MS, pg. 970
Billison, Brad, Controller--Vic Manufacturing, Minneapolis, MN, pg. 1149
Bingenheimer, Charles G., Jr., V.P.-Fin.--Potrait Industries Corporation, Chesapeake, VA, pg. 675
Bischoff, Frederic J., Jr., V.P. & Chief Fin. Officer--SI Holdings Inc., New York, NY, pg. 962
Bischoff, Frederic J., Exec. V.P. & Chief Fin. Officer--Scholastic Inc., New York, NY, pg. 962
Bisson, Edwin, Chief Fin. Officer--Shape Inc., Biddeford, ME, pg. 995
Bizarro, Angelo D., Chief Fin. Officer--Caterair Holdings Corp., Potomac, MD, pg. 229
Bjarnson, Gary, V.P. & Chief Fin. Officer--Pollenex Corporation, Chicago, IL, pg. 879
Bjerg, Nils, Sec. & Chief Fin. Officer--Monrovia Nursery Co., Azusa, CA, pg. 766
Blackwell, Don W., Chief Fin. Officer, V.P. & Treas.--VASA Insurance Group, Inc., Indianapolis, IN, pg. 1146
Blair, Ian D., V.P. & Treas.--A.M. Todd Company, Kalamazoo, MI, pg. 1100
Blair, Kevan, Chief Fin. Officer--Daw Technologies, Inc., Salt Lake City, UT, pg. 319
Blaker, A. L., Sec., Treas. & Mktg. Dir.--King Bear Enterprises, Inc., North Merrick, NY, pg. 630
Blanchard, Craig A., Chief Fin. Officer, Treas. & Controller--Sheldons' Inc., Antigo, WI, pg. 996
Blank, George, Exec. V.P. & Chief Fin. Officer--Univision Holdings, Inc., New York, NY, pg. 502
Blattner, Simon J., III, Chief Fin. Officer--Rittenhouse Inc., Park Ridge, IL, pg. 936
Blattner, Stephen C., Sec., Treas. & Chief Fin. Officer--D.H. Blattner & Sons, Inc., Avon, MN, pg. 156
Blaxton, J. Cooper, Treas.--Lampert Yards, Inc., Saint Paul, MN, pg. 653
Blaydes, Tom H., V.P.-Admin.--W. B. Roddenbery Company, Inc., Cairo, GA, pg. 942
Bleck, Dale W., Controller-Denver--Western Dairymen Cooperative, Inc., Thornton, CO, pg. 1178
Bleiweis, Sol, V.P.-Fin.--Saxon Paint & Home Care Centers Inc., Chicago, IL, pg. 973
Blickens, Robert, V.P.-Fin., Treas. & Comptroller--Komline-Sanderson Engineering Corp., Peapack, NJ, pg. 641
Bliggi, Andy, Chief Fin. Officer--Cox Furniture, Maxton, NC, pg. 294
Bloom, David B., Chief Fin. Officer & Treas.--Bloom Electric Services, Inc., Oklahoma City, OK, pg. 157
Blount, Daniel J., Sr. V.P.-Fin.--Montgomery Elevator Company, Moline, IL, pg. 767
Blount, David, Chief Fin. Officer--The Forum Corporation, Boston, MA, pg. 425
Blum, Bernard, Chief Fin. Officer--Colin Service Systems, Inc., White Plains, NY, pg. 261
Blumenfrucht, J., V.P. & Chief Fin. Officer--Isfel Company, Inc., Rahway, NJ, pg. 582
Bo., Maria Ines, Chief Fin. Officer--Cicero/BSB Publicidad S.A., Buenos Aires,, Argentina, pg. 111
Boatwright, J.K, III, Treas.--Woodbury Business Forms, Inc., La Grange, GA, pg. 1200
Boeve, Roger L., Chief Fin. Officer & Exec. V.P.--Performance Food Group, Inc., Nashville, TN, pg. 861
Bogard, Richard, V.P.-Opers. & Fin.--Cherry Central Cooperative, Traverse City, MI, pg. 243
Boggess, Mark, Chief Fin. Officer--Hypro Corporation, New Brighton, MN, pg. 557
Bohman, Terrance, V.P.-Fin.--Universal Cooperatives, Inc., Minneapolis, MN, pg. 1138
Bonacci, Frank, Controller--Scott Lumber Company, Bridgeport, OH, pg. 983
Bonahoom, Roger, V.P. & Treas.--Wolverine Packing Co., Detroit, MI, pg. 1199
Bone, Steve, Chief Fin. Officer--Hurd Lock & Manufacturing Co., Greeneville, TN, pg. 102
Bonen, James J., Chief Fin. Officer--Sonicair, Scottsdale, AZ, pg. 1018
Boness, Jerry, Chief Fin. Officer--United States Bakery, Portland, OR, pg. 1134
Bonfini, Peter A., V.P. & Treas.--Stanley Steemer International, Inc., Dublin, OH, pg. 1038
Bonini, Victor, Chief Fin. Officer & V.P.-Fin.--Twin County Grocers, Inc., Edison, NJ, pg. 1122
Booth, John L., II, Pres. & Chief Fin. Officer--Booth American, Detroit, MI, pg. 165
Booth, Richard, Chief Fin. Officer & Exec. V.P.--McAdams, Richman & Ong, Inc., Bala-Cynwyd, PA, pg. 725
Booth, Thomas E., Sec. & Treas.--Woolverton Oldsmobile-G.M.C. Truck, Inc., Jacksonville, FL, pg. 1201
Boppe, Larry, Chief Fin. Officer & V.P.-Opers.--Toter Incorporated, Statesville, NC, pg. 1103

Borden, Lorraine, Chm. Bd., Chief Exec. Officer, Chief Fin. Officer, Pres.--Great Scott Advertising Co. Inc., New York, NY, pg. 482
Bordignon, Agostino, Chief Fin. Officer--Gariboldi Parisi Verga/Interad, Milan,, Italy, pg. 685
Boren, Robert P., Chief Fin. Officer--State Volunteer Mutual Insurance Co. Inc., Brentwood, TN, pg. 1041
Boresi, Janet, V.P. & Chief Fin. Officer--Amana Society, Amana, IA, pg. 46
Boroviak, Edwin, Chief Fin. Officer & Controller--Zyntec GmbH, Vienna,, Austria, pg. 1221
Borton, Ronald, Sec. & Treas.--Sauder Manufacturing Corporation, Archbold, OH, pg. 972
Bosfflub, Lance F., Chief Fin. Officer--T.L. James & Company, Ruston, LA, pg. 588
Bosley, Larry, V.P.-Admin. & Chief Fin. Officer--One Hour Martinizing Dry Cleaning Franchise (System), Cincinnati, OH, pg. 826
Bosnak, Gary D., Chief Fin. Officer--Tallgrass Technologies Corp., Overland Park, KS, pg. 1077
Bosshard, Otto, Sr. V.P. & Treas.--Westfield Companies, Westfield Center, OH, pg. 1182
Botte, Sam, Chief Fin. Officer, V.P.-Fin., Treas. & Controller--Raub Supply Company, Lancaster, PA, pg. 913
Boucher, Jonathan F., Chief Fin. Officer--Jordan Industries, Inc., Deerfield, IL, pg. 604
Bouchez, Jacques, V.P. & Chief Oper. Officer--The Crispin Company, Houston, TX, pg. 299
Bouillon, D.J., Treas. & Chief Fin. Officer--Fostoria Industries, Inc., Fostoria, OH, pg. 427
Bourne, Richard, Dir.-Fin. & Admin.--ASICS Tiger Corporation, Fountain Valley, CA, pg. 8
Bowab, Kenneth, Chief Fin. Officer--Computer Dynamics, Inc., Virginia Beach, VA, pg. 271
Bower, Robert R., Sr. V.P.--S.T. Research, Newington, VA, pg. 964
Bowers, Dave, Chief Fin. Officer--Crown International, Inc., Elkhart, IN, pg. 302
Bowker, Clayton K., V.P.-Fin.--Superior Industries of Nebraska, Inc., Omaha, NE, pg. 1063
Bowley, Donald W., Chief Fin. Officer--Manhattan Electric Cable Corporation, Rye, NY, pg. 370
Bowman, Brian, Chm. Bd. & Chief Fin. Officer--Ryan Herco Products Corp., Burbank, CA, pg. 958
Bowman, Fred, V.P. & Chief Fin. Officer--Seessel Holdings, Inc., Memphis, TN, pg. 987
Boxer, Shelley, Exec. V.P. & Chief Fin. Officer--Kinney System, Inc., New York, NY, pg. 632
Boyce, Charles, Sr. V.P. & Chief Fin. Officer--Capital Bank of California, Los Angeles, CA, pg. 214
Boyd, Luther I., V.P., Treas.--H. B. Zachry Company, San Antonio, TX, pg. 1215
Boyer, Norman L., Dir.-Fin. & Acct.--United McGill Corp., Groveport, OH, pg. 1133
Boyle, Brian, Chief Fin. Officer--SJ Weinstein Associates Inc., New York, NY, pg. 1173
Boyle, John W., Sr. V.P.-Fin. & Admin.--Jack Eckerd Corporation, Largo, FL, pg. 366
Brace, James, V.P.-Treasurer & CFO--Littelfuse, Inc., Des Plaines, IL, pg. 678
Bradley, Henry H., Chm., Treas. & Publisher--News-Press & Gazette Company, St. Joseph, MA, pg. 804
Bradway, Stewart, V.P.-Fin.--The W.B. Wood Company, New Providence, NJ, pg. 1199
Brady, Barrett, Exec. V.P.-Admin. & Treas.--J.E. Dunn Construction Co., Kansas City, MO, pg. 354
Brady, William, Treas.--Brady Enterprises, Inc., East Weymouth, MA, pg. 171
Brame, Grady K., Chief Fin. Officer--The Maurin-Odgen Companies, New Orleans, LA, pg. 722
Brandin, Seymour, Chief Fin. Officer & Treas.--Heyman Corporation, Niles, IL, pg. 532
Brands, James E., Exec. V.P., Sec. & Treas.--Scherer Scientific, Ltd., Atlanta, GA, pg. 976
Brandt, Thomas M., Jr., Chief Fin. Officer--U.S. Metalsource Corporation, Coraopolis, PA, pg. 1136
Brasher, Timonty, V.P. & Chief Fin. Officer--Hinderliter Industries, Inc., McKinney, TX, pg. 535
Braswell, Steven C., V.P.-Fin. & Chief Fin. Officer--Meadowcraft, Inc., Birmingham, AL, pg. 733
Braud, Peter, Chief Fin. Officer--Standard Advertising Agency, Brentwood, TN, pg. 1035
Braun, James, Sr. V.P. & Chief Fin. Officer--Safeguard Business Systems, Inc., Fort Washington, PA, pg. 966
Braun, Leonard, Treas.--CGS Industries, Inc., Long Island City, NY, pg. 201
Brazener, Ronald D., V.P. & Chief Fin. Officer--General American Door Company, Montgomery, IL, pg. 739
Brazinski, Al, Chief Fin. Officer--E. H. Titchener & Company, Binghamton, NY, pg. 1099
Breckenridge, James, Controller--Rodefeld Co., Inc., Richmond, IN, pg. 942
Bremer, Jim, V.P.-Credit--Starkey Laboratories, Inc., Eden Prairie, MN, pg. 1040
Brennan, Michael J., V.P. & Chief Fin. Officer--The Binswanger Company, Philadelphia, PA, pg. 151
Brenner, James F., V.P. & Chief Fin. Officer--Margo Nursery Farms, Inc., Miami, FL, pg. 706
Brenner, Ronald D., Pres. & Chief Exec. Officer--Technology for Energy Corporation, Knoxville, TN, pg. 1084
Brewer, Jackie W., V.P.-Fin. & Chief Fin. Officer--Affiliated Food Stores, Keller, TX, pg. 23
Brewster, James, V.P. & Chief Fin. Officer--New Hampton, Inc., New York, NY, pg. 801
Briggs, K. Douglas, V.P., Treas. & Sec.--Quincy Mutual Fire Insurance Company, Quincy, MA, pg. 905
Brinegar, Dee A., Chief Fin. Officer--Gay Johnson's Inc., Grand Junction, CO, pg. 446
Brininger, Thomas, Chief Fin. Officer--Lovejoy Inc., Downers Grove, IL, pg. 685
Brink, Duane, Chief Fin. Officer--Brink Electric Construction Company, Rapid City, SD, pg. 176
Brinkman, Anthony, Chief Fin. Officer--Accra Pac Group, Elkhart, IN, pg. 11
Brino, E., V.P.-Fin.--Cornell Dubilier Electronics, Wayne, NJ, pg. 616
Brittelli, Brenda S., Chief Fin. Officer, Sec.,Treas. & Controller--Adams Wine Co., Atlanta, GA, pg. 17
Brock, Frank E., Sec. & Treas.--Williamson-Dickie Mfg. Co., Fort Worth, TX, pg. 1192
Brocklehurst, David, Fin. Dir. & Sec.--Luscombe and Partners Pty. Ltd., Port Melbourne,, Australia, pg. 344
Brode, Edward, Chief Fin. Officer--Mastercard International, Inc., New York, NY, pg. 720
Broderick, William H. III, Principal-Syndicate Dept.--Edward D. Jones & Co., Maryland Heights, MO, pg. 603
Broll, Arthur G., Jr., Chm. Bd., Chief Fin. Officer & Treas.--Geographic Marketing Group (GMG), Philadelphia, PA, pg. 452
Brooks, H. Edward, Jr., Chief Fin. Officer & V.P.--Morris Newspaper Corporation, Savannah, GA, pg. 771
Brooks, Kenneth, V.P.-Fin.--Wells Mfg. Corp., Dond Du Lac, WI, pg. 1123
Brooksby, Brandt, Chief Fin. Officer--The Alamo Learning Systems, Inc., San Ramon, CA, pg. 29
Brostoff, George, Chm. Bd. & Treas.--Symplex Communications Corp., Ann Arbor, MI, pg. 1069
Brothers, Delores, Sec., Treas. & Chief Fin. Officer--Evana Automation, Evansville, IN, pg. 390
Brouilette, Alan, Chief Fin. Officer--Strombecker Corporation, Chicago, IL, pg. 1054
Brouillard, Jack, Chief Fin. Officer & Chief Admin. Officer--H. E. Butt Grocery Co., San Antonio, TX, pg. 197
Brown, Allen, Sec. & Treas.--Riverside Central Services, Inc., Natchez, MS, pg. 937
Brown, D.S., Chief Fin. Officer, V.P., Treas. & Gen. Counsel--United Laboratories, Inc., Itasca, IL, pg. 1133
Brown, Donald, Exec. V.P. & Treas.--Slant/Fin Corporation, Greenvale, NY, pg. 1010
Brown, Jerri, Chief Fin. Officer--Reference Software International, San Francisco, CA, pg. 921
Brown, Julius, Chief Fin. Officer--Queens Group, Inc., Long Island City, NY, pg. 904
Brown, Julius, Chief Fin. Officer--Queens Group Design, New York, NY, pg. 904
Brown, Keith C., Chief Fin. Officer--Lincoln Electric Systems, Lincoln, NE, pg. 675
Brown, Kirk D., Chief Fin. Officer & Exec. V.P.-Systems--EBM Systems, Inc., Greenbelt, MD, pg. 359
Brown, Lonnie, V.P.-Fin.--Sanborn Manufacturing Company, Springfield, MN, pg. 969
Brown, Patricia, Financial Dir.--Leo Burnett Co., Inc. Sucursal Argentina, Buenos Aires,, Argentina, pg. 192
Brown, Scott, Controller-Salt Lake City--Western Dairymen Cooperative, Inc., Thornton, CO, pg. 1178
Brown, Susan, Chief Fin. Officer & Treas.--American Tara Corporation, Atlanta, GA, pg. 63
Brue, Keith, Chief Fin. Officer & V.P.--Republic Telcom Systems Corporation, Boulder, CO, pg. 928
Brumleve, David, Chief Fin. Officer, Treas., & Sec.--Siemer Milling Company, Teutopolis, IL, pg. 1002
Brumm, Gregg, Chief Fin. Officer--Acme Mills Co. Inc., Detroit, MI, pg. 13
Brummond, Brad, Chief Fin. Officer & Treas.--Super 8 Motels, Inc., Aberdeen, SD, pg. 1062
Brunich, Theodre R., V.P. & Chief Fin. Officer--Hope Design Group, San Diego, CA, pg. 543
Brunner, James E., Dir.-Fin. Services & Investor Rels.--Wenger Corporation, Owatonna, MN, pg. 1176
Brunner, Paul, Chief Fin. Officer--United Dairy Farmers, Inc., Cincinnati, OH, pg. 1131
Brustein, Lawrence, Chief Fin. Officer, Sec. & Treas.--Henry Modell & Company, Inc., Long Island City, NY, pg. 762
Bryan, Larry J., Exec. V.P. & Chief Fin. Officer--Norrell Corporation, Atlanta, GA, pg. 810
Bucheister, James R., Chief Fin. Officer--Martin Forest Industries, Healdsburg, CA, pg. 715
Bucholz, Dave, Chief Fin. Officer--Ritchie Corporation, Wichita, KS, pg. 936
Buckingham, Douglas A., Treas. & Controller--WYO-Ben, Inc., Billings, MT, pg. 1157
Buckley, Alan, Chief Fin. Officer, Sec., Treas. & Legal Officer--Pease Industries, Inc., Fairfield, OH, pg. 854
Buckley, Mark R., Chief Fin. Officer--Leach & Garner Company, North Attleboro, MA, pg. 663
Buddhdev, Sharad N., Chief Fin. Officer & Asst. Sec.--Swallen's, Inc., Cincinnati, OH, pg. 1066
Buehrle, John G., V.P.-Fin. & Chief Fin. Officer--National Cooperative Refinery Association, McPherson, KS, pg. 787
Buffone, Luigi, Chief Fin. Officer--Sokol & Company, Countryside, IL, pg. 1016
Bukala, Robert J., Chief Fin. Officer--American Finance Group, Boston, MA, pg. 52
Bull, Jeremy, Chief Fin. Officer--Arrington-Hillgate International, London,, United Kingdom, pg. 85
Bulmer, Gary, Controller--Solon Manufacturing Company, Solon, ME, pg. 1017
Bunce, Leonard, Sr. V.P.-Fin. & Treas.--Schmidt Baking Co., Inc., Baltimore, MD, pg. 976
Buonfiglio, Nat, Treas.--Applied Graphics Technologies, Oceanside, NY, pg. 1136
Burden, Keith, Chief Fin. Officer--Dexter Shoe Company, Dexter, ME, pg. 334
Burgart, Richard H., Chief Fin. Officer--First State Federal Savings & Loan, Hutchinson, MN, pg. 413
Burk, Kenneth, Chief Fin. Officer & V.P.--Tutor-Saliba Corporation, Sylmar, CA, pg. 1120
Burke, Donald F., Chief Fin. Officer--Frank C. Nahser Inc., Chicago, IL, pg. 783
Burke, Jim, Chief Fin. Officer--H.D. Hudson Manufacturing Company, Chicago, IL, pg. 551
Burke, Ron, Chief Fin. Officer--Covalent Systems Corporation, Fremont, CA, pg. 290
Burke, William B., Treas. & Chief Fin. Officer--Wahl Clipper Corp., Sterling, IL, pg. 1158
Burkhart, Richard, Comptroller--Mid-Continent Screw Products Co., Lincolnwood, IL, pg. 750
Burman, Richard, V.P., Chief Fin. Officer--CRN International, Inc., Hamden, CT, pg. 203
Burmeister, James T., V.P. & Chief Fin. Officer--Tapemark, West St. Paul, MN, pg. 1078
Burne, Thomas, Chief Fin. Officer--Redco Foods, Inc., Windsor, CT, pg. 919
Burnett, Russ, V.P. & Chief Fin. Officer--Independent Insurance Agents of America, Alexandria, VA, pg. 565
Burns, R.J., V.P., Sec. & Chief Fin. Officer--Grede Foundries, Inc., Milwaukee, WI, pg. 483
Burnstad, Kent, Chief Fin. Officer--Burnstad Brothers, Inc., Tomah, WI, pg. 194
Burtch, W., V.P. & Controller--Jeffrey Division, Columbus, OH, pg. 565
Busboom, Larry D., Pres. & Chief Fin. Officer--Sun Diamond Growers of California, Pleasanton, CA, pg. 1058
Busby, Mike, Chief Fin. Officer, Treas. & Controller--Crested Butte Mountain Resort, Inc., Mount Crested Butte, CO, pg. 299
Bush, Raymond T., Sr. V.P. & Chief Fin. Officer--Maguire Group Inc., Foxboro, MA, pg. 701
Bussier, Bill, Chief Fin. Officer/Taren--Cole of California, Los Angeles, CA, pg. 1079
Bussiere, William, Chief Fin. Officer--Taren Holdings, Inc., Los Angeles, CA, pg. 1078
Buti, Bob, V.P.-Fin.--National Van Lines, Inc., Broadview, IL, pg. 794
Butler, William, Chief Fin. Officer--Giumarra Vineyards, Bakersfield, CA, pg. 460
Byerly, Stanley W., Chief Fin. Officer--New England Confectionery Co., Cambridge, MA, pg. 1123
Byers, Dennis W., Chief Fin. Officer, V.P.-Fin. & Treas.--Quality Stores Inc., North Muskegon, MI, pg. 904
Bylund, Daniel, Chief Fin. Officer--Green Leaf Ventures, Inc., San Diego, CA, pg. 484
Byrd, Tim, Chief Fin. Officer--Mary Kay Cosmetics Inc., Dallas, TX, pg. 716
Byrne, John D., V.P., Sec. & Treas.--Restaurants Unlimited, Seattle, WA, pg. 929
Cabrera, Louis, Sr. V.P.-Fin.--County Seat Stores, Inc., Dallas, TX, pg. 290
Cady, Ed, Sr. V.P.-Fin.--Unistrut Corporation, Ann Arbor, MI, pg. 1130
Cady, George, Chief Fin. Officer--Titan Industrial Corp., New York, NY, pg. 1099
Cafarchio, L., Sec. & Controller--Swivelier Co., Inc., Nanuet, NY, pg. 1068
Cafarella, Ronald F., Chief Fin. Officer--Joan & David, Inc., Everett, MA, pg. 528
Cagalj, Mike, Chief Fin. Officer, V.P. & Controller--Atlas Hotels, Inc., San Diego, CA, pg. 96
Cage, Gary W., Exec. V.P. & Chief Fin. Officer--Team Bancshares, Inc., Dallas, TX, pg. 1082
Cage, Gary W., Exec. V.P. & Chief Fin. Officer--Team Bank, Fort Worth, TX, pg. 1082
Cahill, Greg, Sr. V.P., Chief Fin. Officer--Fitzgerald & Co., Atlanta, GA, pg. 416
Cahoon, Arthur, Chief Fin. Officer--Cain & Bultman, Inc., Jacksonville, FL, pg. 207
Calderone, Thomas S., Treas.--Unifoil Corporation, Passaic, NJ, pg. 1126
Calhoun, Lynn, Chief Fin. Officer & Controller--Prime Technology, Inc., Grand Rapids, MI, pg. 889
Call, Lawrence M., V.P., Chief Fin. Officer--Amway Corporation, Ada, MI, pg. 70
Callahan, T. E., V.P.-Fin.--Welch's, Concord, MA, pg. 789
Callender, DeLisle, Sr. V.P., Chief Fin. Officer--The Mingo Group, Inc., New York, NY, pg. 757
Callentine, Ronald, Exec. V.P.--Guest Quarters Suite Hotels, Boston, MA, pg. 493
Calvin, Boyd, Chief Fin. Officer--Clayton Industries Co., El Monte, CA, pg. 253
camerota, Louis, Chief Fin. Officer--Arburg, Inc., Berlin, CT, pg. 79
Camp, William C., Treas. & Chief Fin. Officer--Science & Engineering Associates, Albuquerque, NM, pg. 982
Campbell, Andrew, Chief Fin. Officer, V.P., Treas. & Sec.--Simmons Upholstered Furniture, Inc., Saint Louis, MO, pg. 1005
Campbell, Bruce A., Chief Fin. Officer--Wilton Industries, Inc., Woodridge, IL, pg. 1194
Campbell, Gerald, Chief Fin. Officer--World Computer Corp., Auburn Hills, MI, pg. 1202
Campbell, J.H., Jr., Chief Fin. Officer, Treas. & Legal Counsel--Associated Grocers, Inc., Baton Rouge, LA, pg. 89
Campbell, Jack T., Treas., Asst. Sec. & Chief Fin. Officer--The Kent Manufacturing Co., Pickens, SC, pg. 623
Campbell, Joseph, V.P. & Treas.--Associated Wholesale Grocers, Inc., Kansas City, KS, pg. 92
Campbell, Mark, V.P. & Chief Fin. Officer--Farmstead Foods, Inc., Albert Lea, MN, pg. 402
Campbell, Robert W., Exec. V.P.-Fin. & Admin.--Wakefern Food Corporation, Elizabeth, NJ, pg. 1158
Campbell, Steven B., Pres. & Chief Fin. Officer--H. S. Crocker Co., Inc., King of Prussia, PA, pg. 299
Cantlin, John, V.P.-Fin.--Stockham Valves & Fittings, Inc., Birmingham, AL, pg. 1050
Cantrell, Ron, Chief Fin. Officer, Exec. V.P. & Controller--The Mad Butcher, Inc., Pine Bluff, AR, pg. 699
Capobianco, Ernie, V.P., Chief Fin. Officer--Valentine-Radford, Inc., Kansas City, MO, pg. 1142
Caponigro, Ralph A., Sr. V.P.-Fin. & Chief Fin. Officer--Compuware Corporation, Farmington Hills, MI, pg. 271
Cappon, Paul A., V.P. & Treas.--Camillus Cutlery Co., Camillus, NY, pg. 212
Capute, Joseph, Chief Fin. Officer--Service America Corporation, Stamford, CT, pg. 992
Caputo, Carmen M., Chief Fin. Officer, V.P.-Fin. & Treas.--Tork, Inc., Mount Vernon, NY, pg. 1102
Caralhido, Mike, Dir.-Finance--Daily Racing Form, Inc. (Midwest), Chicago, IL, pg. 611

Carbone, Gene, V.P.-Fin., Chief Fin. Officer & Sec.--Calavo Growers of California, Tustin, CA, pg. 208
Carbone, Michael F., V.P. & Chief Fin. Officer--Cardinal Realty Services Inc., Reynoldsburg, OH, pg. 218
Card, Wesley, Chief Fin. Officer--Jones Apparel Group, Inc., Bristol, PA, pg. 602
Carlsberg, Ralph, Chief Fin. Officer--E Z Loader Boat Trailers, Inc., Spokane, WA, pg. 361
Carlson, Gerald K., Pres., Treas. & Chief Fin. Officer--Bureau of Engraving, Minneapolis, MN, pg. 189
Carlson, H. Bill, Chief Fin. Officer--The Instant Web Companies, Chanhassen, MN, pg. 571
Carlson, J.C., V.P. & Chief Fin. Officer--Carlson Marketing Group Japan Co. Ltd., Tokyo, Japan, pg. 221
Carlson, Jane, Sec. & Treas.--Midcoast Industrial Services Corporation, Cedar Rapids, IA, pg. 751
Carlson, Jane, Treas.--Taylor Associates, Cedar Rapids, IA, pg. 751
Carlson, Jane R., Sec. & Treas.--D. C. Taylor Co., Cedar Rapids, IA, pg. 751
Carlson, Philip, Sr. V.P., Chief Fin. Officer--Biederman, Kelly & Shaffer, Inc., New York, NY, pg. 149
Carnahan, John M., Sec. & Treas.--Woodfin-Smith Pontiac, Inc., Baton Rouge, LA, pg. 1200
Carns, Charles E., Jr., V.P., Treas. & Chief Fin. Officer--Mears Transportation Group, Orlando, FL, pg. 734
Carpenter, Clay, V.P.-Fin. & Chief Fin. Officer--Best Western International, Inc., Phoenix, AZ, pg. 146
Carraziolo, Frank, Treas.--United Food Service Distributors, Inc., Albany, NY, pg. 1132
Carroll, Jim, Treas., Chief Fin. Officer & Sec.--The Chicago Faucet Co., Des Plaines, IL, pg. 245
CArroll, Michael, V.P.-Fin. & Chief Fin. Officer--The Millgard Corp., Livonia, MI, pg. 755
Carroll, Michael W., Grp. V.P. & Chief Fin. Officer--Walbridge Aldinger Company, Detroit, MI, pg. 1158
Carruthers, George, Pres., Chief Exec. & Chief Fin. Officer, Controller--Polycoat Systems, Inc., Hudson Falls, NY, pg. 880
Carter, Albert B., Sr. V.P. & Treas.--Farmers Mutual Hail Insurance Co., Des Moines, IA, pg. 401
Carter, Foster, Chief Fin. Officer--Joffko International, Houston, TX, pg. 595
Carter, Sam R., Chief Fin. Officer & Treas.--Farmers Co-op Market Inc., Frisco City, AL, pg. 401
Carteris, George, Chief Fin. Officer & V.P.--William Douglas McAdams Inc., New York, NY, pg. 726
Cartwright, William Y., Pres., Chief Exec., Chief Fin. Officer & Treas.--Cartwright Communications Co., Cincinnati, OH, pg. 227
Carvalhido, Michael, Dir.-Finance--Daily Racing Form, Inc. (Northwest), Seattle, WA, pg. 611
Carvalho, Dennis J., Exec. V.P. & Chief Fin. Officer--SGI Inc., Cranston, RI, pg. 962
Carvin, Connie, Chief Fin. Officer--Crest Cadillac Company, Nashville, TN, pg. 298
Casey, David, Chief Fin. Officer & Sr. V.P.--M.E.D. Communications, Woodbridge, NJ, pg. 692
Casey, James, Controller--H. B. Ives, Wallingford, CT, pg. 583
Casey, M.M., Exec. V.P. & Chief Fin. Officer--Restaurant Enterprises Group, Inc., Irvine, CA, pg. 929
Cassady, Michael, Dir., Fin.--Jessica Dee Communications Public Relations, New York, NY, pg. 244
Cassel, Bryan, Chief Fin. Officer--Farm & Home Oil Company, Telford, PA, pg. 401
Casselman, David, Controller--Westclox, Norcross, GA, pg. 451
Casselman, David A., V.P.-Fin., Controller, Sec. & Treas.--General Time Corp., Norcross, GA, pg. 451
Cassels, Leon H., Chief Fin. Officer & V.P.-Fin.--Printing House, Inc., Quincy, FL, pg. 891
Cassidy, Brian, Chief Fin. Officer--Krasdale Foods Inc., Bronx, NY, pg. 644
Cassner, Jon H., Sec. & Treas.--Rotary Forms Press, Inc., Hillsboro, OH, pg. 950
Castaldi, Alexander R., Sr. V.P.-Fin. & Chief Fin. Officer--Kendall Healthcare Products Co., Mansfield, MA, pg. 622
Castiglioni, Ezio, Chief Fin. Officer--BSB Italia, Milan,, Italy, pg. 110
Caston, George, Chief Fin. Officer--Camp International, Jackson, MI, pg. 153
Catenza, G.J., V.P. & Controller--Gulf Oil, Westborough, MA, pg. 304
Catsimatidis, John A., Pres. & Treas.--United Refining Inc., Warren, PA, pg. 1130
Caulkins, Susan, Controller--The Shane Group Inc., Hillsdale, MI, pg. 995
Cavalieri, Anthony, Chief Fin. Officer--Duro-Test Corporation, Fairfield, NJ, pg. 355
Ceithaml, Carl, Chief Fin. Officer--The Harter Group, Sturgis, MI, pg. 513
Cernahouz, Ralph, Chief Fin. Officer & Treas.--Schumacher Electric Corporation, Chicago, IL, pg. 979
Cerullo, John J., V.P.-IBM Mid-Range--Lawson Associates Inc., Minneapolis, MN, pg. 663
Chabot, Roland, Chief Fin. Officer--Stinson Seafood Company, Prospect Harbor, ME, pg. 1049
Chadwick, Winslow, Jr., Pres. & Chief Fin. Officer--Consolidated Companies Inc. (CONCO), Metairie, LA, pg. 276
Chalk, Bradford M., Chief Fin. Officer--Betac International Corporation, Alexandria, VA, pg. 147
Challenger, Walter W., V.P.-Fin. & Sec.--Princeville Corporation, Princeville, HI, pg. 890
Chamberlain, Thomas H., Chief Fin. Officer--Price Waterhouse - U.S., New York, NY, pg. 888
Chambers, Ed, Sr. V.P. & Chief Fin. Officer--Wawa, Inc., Wawa, PA, pg. 1169
Chambers, T. L., Sec. & Treas.--Rumsey Electric Co., Philadelphia, PA, pg. 956
Chamblin, Dale, Exec. V.P. & Sec.--California Electric Service, Oakland, CA, pg. 209
Chambliss, Richard, Chief Fin. Officer--Ancra Corporation, Hawthorne, CA, pg. 72
Chan, David M., V.P. & Chief Fin. Officer--Quik Wok Corporation, Dallas, TX, pg. 905
Chandler, Clark T., V.P. & Controller--American Tool Companies, Inc., Lincoln, NE, pg. 64
Chandler, Howard B., 1st. V.P. & Chief Fin. Officer--Universal Life Insurance Company, Memphis, TN, pg. 1138
Chappell, Robert E., Jr., Sr. Exec. V.P. & Chief Fin. Officer--Metropolitan Life Insurance Co., New York, NY, pg. 744
Charboneau, Darrell, Chief Fin. Officer--Faribault Foods Inc., Minneapolis, MN, pg. 399
Charkiewicz, Nancy, Chief Fin. Officer & Controller--Manufacturers Technologies, Inc., West Springfield, MA, pg. 705
Chawdowsky, Ronald, Chief Fin. Officer & V.P.-Fin.--Columbia National Group, Inc., Cleveland, OH, pg. 265
Chen, Dr. Lily C., Exec. V.P., Treas. & Chief Fin. Officer--General Sciences Corp., Laurel, MD, pg. 981
Chen, Terry, Chief Fin. Officer & Sr. V.P.--Allright Corporation, Houston, TX, pg. 41
Chenoweth, James, Chief Fin. Officer & V.P.-Fin.--Citizens Gas & Coke Utility, Indianapolis, IN, pg. 250
Chenoweth, JanR., Chief Fin. Officer--Young Automotive Group, Indianapolis, IN, pg. 1209
Cheong, T.C., Chief Fin. Officer--PMC, Inc., Sun Valley, CA, pg. 836
Chesterman, Paul, V.P., Chief Fin. Officer & Sec.--Trace Products, San Jose, CA, pg. 1104
Chick, Alice, V.P.-Fin. & Controller--Richard Young Office Products, Inc., Deerfield Beach, FL, pg. 535
Childers, Richard D., Chief Fin. Officer & V.P.--L & L Oil Company, Inc., Metairie, LA, pg. 647
Ching, Patrick D., Treas.--Servco Pacific Inc., Honolulu, HI, pg. 991
Chisum, David E., Chief Fin. Officer & Sec.--Piper Industries, Inc., Dallas, TX, pg. 872
Chitwood, T. Charles, Chief Fin. Officer--Dorsey Trailers, Inc., Atlanta, GA, pg. 347
Choksi, Paritosh K., Sr. V.P., Chief Fin. Officer & Treas.--Phoenix American Incorporated, San Rafael, CA, pg. 868
Chow, Shirley, V.P.-Fin. & Sec.--Bachmann Industries, Inc., Philadelphia, PA, pg. 108
Chraime, C., Sr. V.P. & Treas.--Soundesign Corporation, Jersey City, NJ, pg. 1018
Christensen, Kurt V., V.P. & Dir.-Fin. Services--Oxford Finance Companies, Inc., Philadelphia, PA, pg. 835
Christensen, Lee R., Chief Fin. Officer & V.P.--Moran Towing & Transporation Co. Inc, Greenwich, CT, pg. 769
Chua, Dennis, V.P.-Fin.--Newbridge Communications, New York, NY, pg. 611
Chung, Ray, Exec. V.P., Chief Fin. Officer & Treas.--Windmill Holdings Corp., San Francisco, CA, pg. 1195
Cialella, Toni, Chief Fin. Officer--Acess Energy Corporation, Dublin, OH, pg. 12
Ciepiel, Anthony, Exec. V.P., Chief Fin. Officer--Griswold, Inc., Cleveland, OH, pg. 950
Cioci, Jerry, Chief Fin. Officer & Corp. Sec.--Maecorp Inc., Chicago, IL, pg. 699
Ciofani, Peter, Chief Fin. Officer--Formu-3 International, Inc., Canton, OH, pg. 424
Ciotti, John, Exec. V.P., Chief Fin. Officer--Eisner & Associates, Inc., Baltimore, MD, pg. 372
Cipoletti, A.G., Chief Fin. Officer--Denver Equipment Company, Colorado Springs, CO, pg. 331
Clapp, Norman, Chief Fin. Officer--Conquest Carpet Mills, Dalton, GA, pg. 276
Clark, H.S., Pres. & Chief Exec. Officer--Jackson Packing Co. Inc., Jackson, MS, pg. 587
Clark, James A., Chief Fin. Officer & Treas.--Integral Systems, Walnut Creek, CA, pg. 572
Clark, Ralph, Controller--KBF Foods Division, Placentia, CA, pg. 637
Clark, Terry, Controller--Benjamin Franklin Literary & Medical Society, Inc., Indianapolis, IN, pg. 139
Clark, William, V.P.-Fin. & Treas.--Rex Lumber Company, Acton, MA, pg. 930
Clarke, Edwin R., Chief Fin. Officer, Treas. & Sec.--Letts Industries, Inc., Detroit, MI, pg. 668
Clarke, Michael J., Chief Fin. Officer, Exec. V.P.--Prime Hospitality Corp., Fairfield, NJ, pg. 889
Clauser, Fred, Pres.--Koh-I-Noor, Inc., Bloomsbury, NJ, pg. 639
Clay, Larry E., Exec. V.P. & Chief Fin. Officer--UES, Inc., Dayton, OH, pg. 1122
Clegg, Russ, Chief Fin. Officer--Food & Gas, Inc., Decatur, GA, pg. 423
Cleland, John, Treas.--Western Dairymen Cooperative, Inc., Thornton, CO, pg. 1178
Cleland, Mark, A., Chief Fin. Officer--Roney & Co., Detroit, MI, pg. 946
Clemens, Peter, V.P. & Chief Fin. Officer--T C Manufacturing Company, Inc., Evanston, IL, pg. 1072
Clement, Gloria, Chief Fin. Officer--Love Mortgage Company, St. Louis, MO, pg. 685
Clement, Robert, Chief Fin. Officer & Sec.--Excelsior Manufacturing & Supply Corp., Itasca, IL, pg. 392
Clements, Richard H., Chm. Bd., Pres. , & Chief Fin. Officer--Clements Foods Co., Oklahoma City, OK, pg. 254
Clifford, Linda J., Chief Fin. Officer, Treas. & Real Estate Dir.--C. C. Myers, Inc., Rancho Cordova, CA, pg. 780
Clifton, David, Treas. & Chief Fin. Officer--Young & Laramore, Indianapolis, IN, pg. 1209
Clifton, Jean B., Exec. V.P. & Chief Fin. Officer--Journal Register Company, Trenton, NJ, pg. 608
Cline, Lynn, Chief Fin. Officer--Rudolph Foods Company, Lima, OH, pg. 954
Cline, Philip E., Sr. V.P. & Chief Fin. Officer--J. H. Fletcher & Co., Huntington, WV, pg. 418
Clinton, Robert, V.P.-Fin.--United Design, Noble, OK, pg. 1131
Clock, Douglas G., Exec. V.P. & Chief Fin. Officer--Byerly's Inc., Edina, MN, pg. 198
Clonts, Richard, Chief Fin. Officer, V.P.-Fin. & Sec.--Sewell Village Cadillac Co., Dallas, TX, pg. 993
Clothier, G.S., Sr. V.P.-Fin.--The Phillies-A Limited Partnership, Philadelphia, PA, pg. 867
Cobb, Alton H., Jr., Chief Fin. Officer--Long MFG. NC, Inc., Tarboro, NC, pg. 682
Cobb, Alton H., Jr., Chief Fin. Officer--Long Equipment Co., Tarboro, NC, pg. 682
Cobb, Larry, V.P.-Fin., Treas. & Sec.--Ed Taylor Construction Co., Tucker, GA, pg. 1081
Cobb, William R., Mgr.-Bus.--Seattle Post-Intelligencer, Seattle, WA, pg. 524
Cochran, Barbara R., V.P. & Controller--Westfield Companies, Westfield Center, OH, pg. 1182
Cochran, Keith, Chief Exec. & Chief Fin. Officer--Johnson County Farm Bureau Co-op, Franklin, IN, pg. 598
Cocquyt, Ronald A., Sec. & Treas.--Wilmorite Inc., Rochester, NY, pg. 1193
Cogossi, Alfred, Chief Fin. Officer--Hameroff/Milenthal/Spence, Inc., Columbus, OH, pg. 503
Cohen, Alan H., Chief Fin. Officer & Treas.--George Uhe Co., Inc., Paramus, NJ, pg. 1125
Cohen, David, Treas.--Empire Diamond Corporation, New York, NY, pg. 379
Cohen, Donald, Chm. Bd., Pres., Chief Exec. Officer & Chief Fin. Officer--Tool King, Denver, CO, pg. 1101
Cohen, Harry, Chief Fin. Officer, Treas. & Sec.--Mozel Development Corp., Baileys Crossroads, VA, pg. 774
Cohen, Ira, Chief Fin. Officer & V.P.-Opers.--All-Luminum Products, Inc., Philadelphia, PA, pg. 35
Cohen, Matthew, Controller--Standard Brands of America, Inc., Pompano Beach, FL, pg. 1035
Colantoni, Alfred D., V.P. & Chief Fin. Officer--Press Broadcasting Co., Neptune, NJ, pg. 801
Cole, Stephen, V.P.-Fin.--S&D Coffee Inc., Concord, NC, pg. 959
Colgan, Frank, V.P.-Admin. & Chief Fin. Officer--Penn Emblem Co., Philadelphia, PA, pg. 857
Colligan, Jack J., Chief Fin. Officer & V.P.-Fin. & Admin.--Red Devil Inc., Union, NJ, pg. 918
Collings, Brian N., Chief Fin. Officer--Autoswage Products, Inc., Shelton, CT, pg. 101
Collins, Don, Controller--St. Louis Music, Inc., Saint Louis, MO, pg. 967
Collins, Douglas, Chief Fin. Officer--Days Inns of America, Inc., Atlanta, GA, pg. 1100
Collins, Robert E., V.P. & Chief Fin. Officer--Leach Corporation, Buena Park, CA, pg. 663
Collins, Tim, Chief Fin. Officer, Treas. & Controller--Capital Electric Group, Inc., Phoenix, AZ, pg. 215
Collison, Thomas G., Sr. V.P. & Chief Fin. Officer--TMP Worldwide, Inc., New York, NY, pg. 1073
Collova, J. James, Chief Fin. Officer & Sec.--Paper Calmenson & Co., Saint Paul, MN, pg. 847
Colway, David E., Pres. & Chief Fin. Officer--Adams Colway & Associates, Rochester, NY, pg. 16
Colwell, Jerry, Treas. & Chief Fin. Officer--Advanced Manufacturing & Development, Willits, CA, pg. 20
Combs, Kevin, Treas., Chief Fin. Officer & Sec.--Symons Corporation, Pasadena, CA, pg. 1069
Commisso, Rocco, Exec. V.P. & Chief Fin. Officer--Cablevision Industries Corp., Liberty, NY, pg. 206
Comollo, Thomas, V.P.-Fin.--Russell-Stanley Corporation, Red Bank, NJ, pg. 957
Conant, Mary, Chief Fin. Officer--Cass-Clay Creamery, Fargo, ND, pg. 228
Conaway, J. Michael, Chief Fin. Officer & V.P.--National Gypsum Company, Charlotte, NC, pg. 790
Concha, Alan, Chief Fin. Officer--Meehan Tooker, East Rutherford, NJ, pg. 736
Coneys, Robert, V.P.-Fin.--National Fire Protection Association, Quincy, MA, pg. 788
Confer, Ogden W., Sr. V.P., Sec. & Chief Fin. Officer--Hubbard Milling Company, Mankato, MN, pg. 549
Conlisk, K.M., Chief Fin. Officer--Alinabal, Inc., Milford, CT, pg. 34
Conner, George V., Jr., Treas.--Kyanite Mining Corporation, Dillwyn, VA, pg. 647
Conner, Wayne, Chief Fin. Officer--Elgin National Industries, Inc., Chicago, IL, pg. 609
Conway, J. W., Sec. & Treas.--Atlas Tag & Label Inc., Neenah, WI, pg. 153
Conway, Michael M., V.P.-Fin. & Chief Fin. Officer--Arrow Industries, Inc., Carrollton, TX, pg. 85
Conwell, Duane, Controller--Carstens Health Industries, Inc., Chicago, IL, pg. 225
Conzemius, Peter, V.P. & Chief Fin. Officer--M. A. Mortenson Company, Minneapolis, MN, pg. 772
Cook, Daniel L., V.P. & Chief Fin. Officer--Overland Transportation System, Inc., Indianapolis, IN, pg. 832
Cook, J.M., V.P., Chief Fin. Officer & Treas.--American Cast Iron Pipe Co., Birmingham, AL, pg. 50
Cook, R.H., Sr., Treas. & Sec.--B.C. Cook & Sons Enterprises, Inc., Haines City, FL, pg. 282
Cook, T., Chief Fin. Officer--Leo Burnett Company Ltd., Toronto,, Canada, pg. 192
Cooksey, David C., V.P., Chief Fin. Officer & Sec.--Contico International, Inc., Saint Louis, MO, pg. 278
Cookson, John S., V.P.-Fin., Treas., Chief Fin. Officer, Sec. & Dir.-Investor Rels.--Kingsbury Corporation, Keene, NH, pg. 631
Coomer, Ralph, Treas. & Sec.--Ziniz Inc., Louisville, KY, pg. 1220
Cooper, Antoinette, V.P. & Chief Fin. Officer--Cascino Purcell Freebairn, Atlanta, GA, pg. 227
Cooper, Cary D., Exec. V.P. & Chief Fin. Officer--The Cherokee Group, Sunland, CA, pg. 243
Cooper, J. Michael, Chief Fin. Officer--Noble & Associates, Springfield, MO, pg. 808
Cooperman, Michael, Chief Fin. Officer, V.P. & Treas.--Josephson International Inc., New York, NY, pg. 607

Coppersmith, Jack, Sr. V.P. & Chief Fin. Officer--Chesapeake Financial Corp., Miami Beach, FL, pg. 243
Corcoran, John S., Exec. V.P. & Chief Fin. Officer--Envirodyne Industries, Inc., Oak Brook, IL, pg. 383
Cordek, Lawrence D., Chief Fin. Officer & Corp. Sec.--G B Stores, Johnstown, PA, pg. 978
Corlett, Glenn E., Exec. V.P., Chief Fin. Officer--N W Ayer Incorporated, New York, NY, pg. 103
Corlett, Glenn E., Exec. V.P., Chief Fin. Officer--N W Ayer Inc., New York, NY, pg. 104
Cornutt, C.E., Exec. V.P. & Chief Fin. Officer--Hunt Oil Company, Dallas, TX, pg. 553
Cornwall, Lyle E., Exec. V.P. & Chief Fin. Officer--Management Dynamics, New Providence, NJ, pg. 703
Corredor, Martha, Chief Fin. Officer--Young & Rubicam, S.A. de C.V., Mexico,, Mexico, pg. 1213
Corrigan, Wilfred, Treas.--Silicon Power Cube Corporation, Long Beach, CA, pg. 1004
Corwin, Richard S., Chief Fin. Officer & Exec. V.P.--Adams Business Forms, Topeka, KS, pg. 16
Cosky, Stanley W., Controller--YSD Industries, Youngstown, OH, pg. 1207
Costa, Francisco, Chief Fin. Officer--Leo Burnett Publicidade, Ltda., Sao Paulo,, Brazil, pg. 193
Costa, Michael, Chief Fin. Officer--Arley Merchandise Corporation, Taunton, MA, pg. 83
Costantino, Basil, Chief Fin. Officer--F. Schumacher & Co., New York, NY, pg. 979
Costello, L.E., V.P.-Fin. & Chief Fin. Officer--J.R. Simplot Company, Boise, ID, pg. 1007
Coti, Anthony J., Exec. V.P. & Chief Fin. Officer--Pathmark, Woodbridge, NJ, pg. 1064
Cotton, Gary, Chief Fin. Officer--Sundown Vitamin Co., Inc., Fort Lauderdale, FL, pg. 1060
Cottrell, John, Chief Fin. Officer--Gene B. Glick Company, Inc., Indianapolis, IN, pg. 462
Countryman, Peter J., Chief Fin. Officer, Treas. & Controller--Sabin Robbins Paper Co., Cincinnati, OH, pg. 965
Cousins, George A., Treas.--HDS Services, Farmington Hills, MI, pg. 496
Coutts, Pamela, Deputy Dir.-Fin.--Maine State Lottery Commission, Augusta, ME, pg. 702
Couturier, Normand, V.P.-Fin.--U.S. Divers Co., Inc., Santa Ana, CA, pg. 1135
Cowan, Richard, Sec., Treas., Controller & Chief Fin. Officer--Wheeler Brothers Grain Co., Watonga, OK, pg. 1184
Cowles, H.B., Chief Fin. Officer, Treas. & Controller--Bluff City Distributing Co., Inc., Memphis, TN, pg. 161
Cox, Anne H., Mng. Partner & Chief Fin. Officer--Eire Partners, Inc., Chicago, IL, pg. 372
Cox, Charles D., III, V.P. & Chief Fin. Officer--Shenandoah Life Insurance Company, Roanoke, VA, pg. 997
Cox, Lawrence, Exec. V.P. & Chief Fin. Officer--Mary Kay Cosmetics Inc., Dallas, TX, pg. 716
Cox, Tom, Exec. V.P. & Chief Fin. Officer--Wing Industries, Inc., Dallas, TX, pg. 1196
Coyle, Kevin P., Treas.--Jones Spacelink, Ltd., Englewood, CO, pg. 603
Craft, Carl, V.P. & Chief Fin. Officer--Erb Lumber Company, Birmingham, MI, pg. 360
Crai, Richard, Chief Fin. Officer--A.T. Clayton & Company, Inc., New York, NY, pg. 253
Craigmile, Cynthia S., Chief Fin. Officer & V.P.--Downey Printing, Waukee, IA, pg. 348
Crane, Mary, V.P.-Fin. & Controller--ZBS Industries, Inc., Mayfield Village, OH, pg. 1215
Crane, Stephen, Treas. & Commissioner--New Jersey State Lottery, Trenton, NJ, pg. 801
Crane, Stephen D., V.P.--Stebbins Engineering & Mfg. Co., Watertown, NY, pg. 1043
Crass, Charles E., V.P.-Fin. & Chief Fin. Officer--Triumph*Lor, Inc., Houston, TX, pg. 1115
Creagh, Richard P., Controller, Treas. & Chief Fin. Officer--Hoffman Brothers Packing Co., Los Angeles, CA, pg. 537
Creevy, Edward, Chief Fin. Officer--Donnkenny, Inc., New York, NY, pg. 345
Crews, Hilliard, Chm. Bd., Pres., Chief Exec. Officer & Chief Fin. Officer--Shelby Group International, Inc., Memphis, TN, pg. 996
Cribbs, Francis J., Exec. V.P., Chief Fin. Officer & Treas.--Lloyd Properties, Los Angeles, CA, pg. 680
Cripe, Richard L., Treas. & Controller--Gohmann Asphalt & Construction of KY., Inc., Louisville, KY, pg. 465
Criqui, Robert, V.P.-Fin.--National Basketball Association, New York, NY, pg. 786
Crneckiy, Marty, Exec. V.P.-Fin.--The Vollrath Company Inc., Sheboygan, WI, pg. 1154
Crocker, Frederick G., Jr., V.P. & Chief Fin. Officer & Treas.--Springborn Laboratories, Inc., Enfield, CT, pg. 1033
Cromer, Vicki, Chief Fin. Officer--Bayou State Oil Corporation, Shreveport, LA, pg. 128
Cronan, James E., Sr. V.P. & Chief Fin. Officer--Harvey Industries, Inc., Waltham, MA, pg. 515
Cronin, John J., Jr., Controller--Vectura Group, Inc., Pittsburgh, PA, pg. 1146
Cross, John, Chief Fin. Officer & V.P.--Burris Foods, Inc., Milford, DE, pg. 195
Cross, William L., Chief Fin. Officer & Sr. V.P.--ULLICO Inc., Washington, DC, pg. 1124
Crothers, Regina, Controller--Puritan/Churchill Chemical Company, Atlanta, GA, pg. 900
Crotty, Thomas, Controller--Welsbach Electric Corp., Long Island City, NY, pg. 1175
Crowley, J.C., V.P.-Fin. & Chief Fin. Officer--Aladdin Industries, Incorporated, Nashville, TN, pg. 29
Cruickshank, D.J., V.P. & Chief Fin. Officer--Flexible Products Company, Marietta, GA, pg. 418
Crum, David H., Pres., Chief Exec. & Chief Fin. Officer--Crum Electric Supply Co., Inc., Casper, WY, pg. 303
Cruz, Lamberto, Sr. V.P., Chief Fin. Officer--Greenstone Roberts Advertising, Melville, NY, pg. 485
Crysdale, Jim, Chief Fin. Officer--ColorTyme, Inc., Athens, TX, pg. 265
Cudzewicz, Alexander, Dir.-Fin., Treas. & Chief Fin. Officer--Sargent & Lundy, Chicago, IL, pg. 971
Cullen, Richard, Chief Fin. Officer--Overseas Service Corporation, West Palm Beach, FL, pg. 833
Culp, David G., Controller--Knoll Intl., Inc., East Greenville, PA, pg. 1121
Cummings, Richard, Chief Fin. Officer--Southern California Bancorp, Laguna Beach, CA, pg. 1020
Cunningham, Patricia, V.P., Chief Fin. Officer , & Sec.--INPUT, Mountain View, CA, pg. 571
Cupp, Frank, Treas.--Smith Frozen Foods, Inc., Weston, OR, pg. 1012
Curci, Frank, Sr. V.P.-Fin.--Mayfair Super Markets, Inc., Elizabeth, NJ, pg. 724
Curci, Joseph E., Chief Fin. Officer--A. Finkl & Sons Co., Chicago, IL, pg. 411
Curci, Nicholas, Chief Fin. Officer--Full Circle Media Corp., Norwalk, CT, pg. 436
Curciarello, Gerry, Chief Fin. Officer--Landau & Heyman Inc., Chicago, IL, pg. 654
Current, Richard R., Chief Fin. Officer--The Shane Group Inc., Hillsdale, MI, pg. 995
Curry, Jeffrey, Chief Fin. Officer--Kenworth of Indianapolis Inc., Indianapolis, IN, pg. 624
Curtin, Thomas A., Exec. V.P. & Chief Fin. Officer--Simplex Time Recorder Co., Gardner, MA, pg. 1006
Cussigh, Richard, V.P. & Chief Fin. Officer--DonTech, Chicago, IL, pg. 345
Cuti, Anthony, Chief Fin. Officer--Supermarkets General Corporation, Woodbridge, NJ, pg. 1064
Cutler, George, Chief Fin. Officer & V.P.--Brown & Caldwell Consulting Engineers, Pleasant Hill, CA, pg. 181
Cutrali, A., V.P.-Fin.--PTC Aerospace, Inc., Litchfield, CT, pg. 837
Cyphers, Stanley P., Comptroller--The Uhlmann Co., Kansas City, MO, pg. 1125
D'Amato, Frederick, V.P.-Fin. & Admin.--Mayfair Industries, Inc., New York, NY, pg. 78
D'Haeze, T.M., V.P.-Fin. & Acctg., Treas. & Sec.--Dwyer Instruments Inc., Michigan City, IN, pg. 356
Dabbs, Karl, Chief Fin. Officer--Fishing Tackle Retailer, Montgomery, AL, pg. 105
Dabbs, Karl, Chief Fin. Officer--Southern Outdoors Magazine, Montgomery, AL, pg. 105
Dabbs, Karl, Chief Fin. Officer--Bassmaster Magazine, Montgomery, AL, pg. 105
Dabbs, Karl, Chief Fin. Officer--Southern Saltwater Magazine, Montgomery, AL, pg. 106
Daddario, Richard, Sr. V.P. & Chief Fin. Officer--The Mutual Life Insurance Company of New York (MONY), New York, NY, pg. 778
Dajani, A.T., Chief Fin. Officer--Burns & Roe Enterprises, Inc., Oradell, NJ, pg. 194
Dalluhn, Susan, Controller--Mallory, Inc., Carson City, NV, pg. 703
Damiano, Gary, Chief Fin. Officer & Controller--Triangle Marketing Corp., New York, NY, pg. 1112
Dammann, Jean Pierre, Chief Fin. Officer--Dubin-Clark & Company, Greenwich, CT, pg. 350
Daniel, Larry, Pres. & Chief Exec. & Chief Fin. Officer--The Daniel Co. of Springfield, Springfield, MO, pg. 314
Dannelly, Robert B., Sr., Chief Fin. Officer & V.P.-Fin.--Piedmont Mechanical, Inc., Spartanburg, SC, pg. 870
Darian, Ralph, Pres., Chief Exec. & Chief Fin. Officer--Levonian Brothers Inc., Troy, NY, pg. 671
Darnell, Nancy, Treas.--Health Care Distributors of Indiana, Inc., South Bend, IN, pg. 520
Darwin, Allen, V.P. & Treas.--Cardinal Inc., Port Reading, NJ, pg. 217
Daughtery, David B., Dir.-Intl. Fin.--A.M. Todd Company, Kalamazoo, MI, pg. 1100
David, George F., Chief Fin. Officer--Technic Incorporated, Cranston, RI, pg. 1083
Davies, Ernest, Chief Fin. Officer--Quadrangle Development Corporation, Washington, DC, pg. 902
Davies, Zachary M., Controller & Sec.--Tweddle Litho Company, St. Clair Shores, MI, pg. 1120
Davis, Bonnie, Sec. & Treas.--O.P. Link Handle Company, Salem, IN, pg. 676
Davis, Cheryl D., Chief Fin. Officer, V.P.-Taxes & Sec.--The Enstar Group, Inc., Montgomery, AL, pg. 382
Davis, Michael, Chief Fin. Officer--Crouch Supply Company, Inc., Fort Worth, TX, pg. 301
Davis, Michael C., Chief Fin. Officer--The Read Corporation, Middleboro, MA, pg. 916
Davis, Steve, Chief Fin. Officer--Midland Grocery, Westville, IN, pg. 952
Davis, Warren A., Exec. V.P. & Chief Fin. Officer--Gateway Apparel, Inc., Saint Louis, MO, pg. 445
Davis, William F., Chief Fin. Officer--Barnhill Contracting Company, Tarboro, NC, pg. 121
Davy, Nicholas, Chief Fin. Officer--Cooperheat, Inc., Piscataway, NJ, pg. 283
Day, Donald A., Sr. V.P.-Fin., Chief Fin. Officer & Sec.--St. Johnsbury Trucking Co., Inc., Holliston, MA, pg. 966
Day, James L., Chief Fin. Officer & Controller--The Miami Margarine Co., Cincinnati, OH, pg. 746
Day, Mark, Dir.-Fin.--Arkansas Industrial Development Commission, Little Rock, AR, pg. 83
Day, William H., Chief Fin. Officer--Joseph Behr & Sons Inc., Rockford, IL, pg. 132
de Bello, David, Chief Fin. Officer & Comptroller--Advertising To Women, Inc., New York, NY, pg. 21
de la Cruz, Isabel, Chief Fin. Officer--Aero Peru Corporation, Miami, FL, pg. 22
De Mento, Robert, Sec. & Treas.--Brooks Provisions Inc., Philadelphia, PA, pg. 180
De Rose, Louis, V.P. & Chief Fin. Officer--Schwarz Paper Company, Morton Grove, IL, pg. 980
Dean, Gary, Chief Fin. Officer--LePage's, Inc., Pittsburgh, PA, pg. 287
Dean, Jim, Chief Fin. Officer--Federal Data Corporation, Bethesda, MD, pg. 404
Dean, John, V.P. & Chief Fin. Officer--Solar Press, Inc., Naperville, IL, pg. 1016
DeAngelis, John, Sr. V.P., Chief Fin. Officer--Tarlow Advertising, New York, NY, pg. 1079
DeAngelis, Rudy, V.P.-Fin.--Timex Corporation, Middlebury, CT, pg. 1098
DeBerge, John, Chief Fin. Officer--Continental Web Press, Inc., Itasca, IL, pg. 280
DeCius, Dennis A., Chief Fin. Officer, Exec. V.P. & Asst. Sec.--Pacific Capital Bancorp, Salinas, CA, pg. 839
DeCius, Dennis A., Chief Fin. Officer & Sr. V.P.--First National Bank of Central California, Salinas, CA, pg. 839
Decker, Michael B., Chief Fin. Officer--Trammell Crow Company, Dallas, TX, pg. 1106
DeCordova, Bryan, V.P. & Chief Fin. Officer--Duckwall-Alco Stores, Inc., Abilene, KS, pg. 351
Deeb, Susan, Sec. & Treas.--Tamaroff Buick Inc., Southfield, MI, pg. 1077
Deeney, Gerald D., V.P., Chief Fin. Officer & Treas.--Hubbard Broadcasting, Inc., Saint Paul, MN, pg. 548
Deering, John R., Exec. V.P.-Fin., Chief Oper. Officer & Legal Officer--Production Machinery Corporation, Mentor, OH, pg. 893
DeGregory, Alfred D., V.P.-Fin., Treas. & Chief Fin. Officer--Blue Diamond Growers, Sacramento, CA, pg. 160
DeGroot, Don, Chief Fin. Officer & Sr. V.P.--Biggs Gilmore Communications, Kalamazoo, MI, pg. 149
Deitchle, Gerald W., Sr. V.P.-Fin. & Chief Fin. Officer--Jerrico, Inc., Lexington, KY, pg. 229
Deitchle, Gerald W., Exec. V.P.-Fin. & Chief Fin. Officer--Long John Silver's, Inc., Lexington, KY, pg. 229
Del Castillo, Henry Del, Chief Fin. Officer--Powerine Oil Company Holdings, Santa Fe Springs, CA, pg. 883
Del Rio, Gonzalo Martinez, Fin. Dir.--Lebrija Rubio Publicidad S.A., Mexico,, Mexico, pg. 104
Del Rio, Luz, Chief Fin. Officer & Asst. Sec.--Arthur Murray Intl., Inc., Coral Gables, FL, pg. 776
DelDuce, Gregory J., Treas.--Sealing Devices Inc., Lancaster, NY, pg. 984
Della Franco, Thomas, V.P.-Fin.--Zenith Products Corp., Aston, PA, pg. 1217
Dellamano, Patricia, Pres. & Chief Exec. & Chief Fin. Officer--Patson's Press, Sunnyvale, CA, pg. 851
Dellinger, J.B., III, V.P.-Fin.--Rodgers Builders, Inc., Charlotte, NC, pg. 942
Delman, Richard, Chief Fin. Officer, Treas., Sec. & Controller--Splendor Form International Inc., Long Island City, NY, pg. 1031
Demarest, John D., Chief Fin. Officer, V.P. & Treas.--Production Management Companies, Inc., Harvey, LA, pg. 893
Demartino, John A., V.P.-Data Processing & Fin.--Windsor Service, Inc., Reading, PA, pg. 1196
DeMasi, Dominick, V.P.-Fin. & Admin.--Malco Products, Inc., Barberton, OH, pg. 702
Demers, Norbert, V.P., Comptroller & Chief Fin. Officer--The Hilsinger Corp., Plainville, MA, pg. 535
Demetrakakis, D., Chief Fin. Officer--Geo-Young & Rubicam, Athens,, Greece, pg. 1212
Dempsey, Mike, Chief Fin. Officer--Club Resorts, Inc., Dallas, TX, pg. 256
Denaro, J., V.P., Chief Fin. Officer & Treas.--R. T. Vanderbilt Company, Inc., Norwalk, CT, pg. 1144
Denbo, Lawrence R., Chief Fin. Officer--Wabash Magnetics, Wabash, IN, pg. 357
Denise, Robert, Chm., Pres., Chief Exec. Officer & Chief Fin. Officer--Bucilla Corporation, Hazleton, PA, pg. 185
Dennis, David M., Sr. V.P., Chief Fin. Officer & Treas.--SBC Advertising, Columbus, OH, pg. 960
Denson, J., Controller--E-Z Serve Corp., Houston, TX, pg. 361
Deutcher, Klaus, Chief Fin. Officer & Controller--Bio-Tek Instruments, Inc., Winooski, VT, pg. 152
Deutsch, Louis G., Chief Fin. Officer & Human Resources--Jay Incorporated, Rochester, NY, pg. 590
Devareaux, Vance A., Exec. V.P., Sec., Treas. & Chief Fin. Officer--Arrowhead Mills, Inc., Hereford, TX, pg. 86
Dever, Doug, Controller--Brodhead-Garrett Co., Mansfield, OH, pg. 178
DeVille, Paul, V.P. & Chief Fin. Officer--Persis Corporation, Honolulu, HI, pg. 863
Devine, Donald, Chief Fin. Officer--Harris Farms, Inc., Coalinga, CA, pg. 511
Devona, Thomas C., Pres. & Treas.--Rite-Way, Inc., Saddle Brook, NJ, pg. 936
DeVourzi, Michael, Chief Fin. Officer--Budget Marketing, Inc., Des Moines, IA, pg. 186
Dhole, Gulab, Chief Fin. Officer & Controller--West Chemical Products, Inc., Princeton, NJ, pg. 1172
Diamond, Isadore, Chm. Bd., Treas. & Chief Fin. & Chief Acctg. Officer--Magnetic Technologies Corporation, Rochester, NY, pg. 701
Diamond, William, Chief Fin. Officer--Movado Watch Co., Lyndhurst, NJ, pg. 812
Diamond, William, Exec. V.P. & Chief Fin. Officer--North American Watch Corporation, Lyndhurst, NJ, pg. 812
Dicaro, Dan, Controller--CCC Information Services, Chicago, IL, pg. 410
Dicke, Larry, Chief Fin. Officer--E.J. Brach Corporation, Oakbrook Terrace, IL, pg. 169
Dickey, Sam, Sec. & Treas.--O'Neil Data Systems, Inc., Los Angeles, CA, pg. 827
Diedrich, John C., Chief Fin. Officer & Treas.--Cummins-American Corp., Mount Prospect, IL, pg. 304
Diesel, Wayne, Chief Fin. Officer--Lawrence Management Group, Inc., Albany, NY, pg. 662
Dietrich, Kerry, Chief Fin. Officer & Treas.--Dietrich's Milk Products, Inc., Reading, PA, pg. 337
Dietz, Henry, V.P., Chief Fin. Officer--Mills Hall Walborn & Associates, Mayfield Heights, OH, pg. 756

Dillon, John R., Chief Fin. Officer & Sr. V.P.--Cox Enterprises, Inc., Atlanta, GA, pg. 292
Dillon, Robert C., V.P. & Treas.--Zantop International Airlines, Inc., Ypsilanti, MI, pg. 1216
Dimond, Timothy P., Dir.-Fin. Reporting--The Marmon Group, Inc., Chicago, IL, pg. 710
Dinges, James A., V.P.-Fin.--Golden Cat Corporation, South Bend, IN, pg. 637
Dingman, Michael D., Chm., Chief Fin. Officer & Mng. Dir.--New Hampshire Oak, Hampton, NH, pg. 800
DioGuardi, Raymond T., V.P.-Fin. & Chief Fin. Officer--Nathan's Famous Inc., Westbury, NY, pg. 784
Dion, Ron, Chief Fin. Officer & Sec.--Kenco, Middlebury, IN, pg. 1025
Dion, Ronald, Sr. V.P.-Fin.--Sparkomatic Corporation, Milford, PA, pg. 1025
DiPietro, Al, Chief Fin. Officer & Sr. V.P.--LaMarca Group Inc., New York, NY, pg. 652
DiPietro, Al, Chief Fin. Officer--The Radio Group, New York, NY, pg. 652
DiPietro, Frank, Sr. V.P.-Fin. & Chief Fin. Officer--Sipex Corporation, Billerica, MA, pg. 1009
Diresta, Tony, Controller & Treas.--N. Erlanger, Blumgart & Company, Inc., New York, NY, pg. 387
Disler, D.S., Chief Fin. Officer--CAE Link Allen Division, Alexandria, VA, pg. 198
Divin, Charles, Controller--Walker-Pioneer Moss, New York, NY, pg. 1160
Dixon, J. E., V.P.-Fin.--Sturtevant Div., Boston, MA, pg. 547
Dobbs, Byron K., Chief Fin. Officer--Park Place Motorcars, Dallas, TX, pg. 849
Dobroff, Larry, Chief Fin. Officer--Austin Sculpture, Holbrook, NY, pg. 99
Dodds, William, Chief Fin. Officer & Sec.--Sunclipse, Inc., Montebello, CA, pg. 1059
Dodson, Larry S., Chief Fin. Officer & Sr. V.P.--Zimmerman Holdings, Inc., San Marino, CA, pg. 1220
Doerr, Jack A., Chief Fin. Officer, V.P. & Treas.--F.B. Wright Co., Dearborn, MI, pg. 1204
Doherty, John F., Pres. & Chief Exec. Officer--Sequentia Inc., Strongsville, OH, pg. 990
Doherty, John F., Pres. & Chief Exec. Officer--Sequentia Inc. Reinforced Plastics Div., Strongsville, OH, pg. 990
Dohler, D. Gary, Chief Fin. Officer--Atlantic Builders Group Inc., Baltimore, MD, pg. 94
Dolan, Maureen, Sec. & Treas.--Cargill Salt, Newark, CA, pg. 219
Dolan, Vincent T., Chief Fin. Officer--Superior Tube Company, Collegeville, PA, pg. 1064
Dominioni, Valerie, Sec. & Treas.--Bel Paese Sales Company, Inc., Lakewood, NJ, pg. 133
Donahoe, Michael P., V.P., Chief Fin. Officer & Treas.--Perkins Family Restaurants, Memphis, TN, pg. 1088
Donahue, Jack, Chief Fin. Officer--Paul Stuart, Inc., New York, NY, pg. 1054
Donald, John, Chief Fin. Officer & V.P.--Laverdiere's Enterprises, Winslow, ME, pg. 661
Donaldson, Darrell, Pres., Chief Exec. & Fin. Officer--Hot Shot Delivery Inc., Houston, TX, pg. 545
Donato, Joseph M., Chief Fin. Officer--Gilbane Building Company, Providence, RI, pg. 457
Donavan, Doug, Chief Fin. & Info. Officer, Treas., Controller & Sec.--Campbell Oil Co., Massillon, OH, pg. 213
Doner, Cliff, Chief Fin. Officer--American Gilsonite Co., Salt Lake City, UT, pg. 55
Donovan, Raymond J., V.P. & Chief Fin. Officer--Schiavone Construction Co., Secaucus, NJ, pg. 976
Dooling, Jack, Chief Fin. Officer--The Gradall Co., New Philadelphia, OH, pg. 559
Dorn, S.B., V.P. & Treas.--Zippo Manufacturing Company, Bradford, PA, pg. 1220
Dorsch, C.R., V.P.-Fin.--Today's Kids, Booneville, AR, pg. 1025
Dorsch, Charles R., V.P.-Fin. & Chief Fin. Officer--Spang & Company, Butler, PA, pg. 1025
Doss, Robert D., V.P.-Fin. & Chief Fin. Officer--Continental Eagle Corporation, Prattville, AL, pg. 278
Dossenbach, William R., V.P.-Fin. & Chief Fin. Officer--R. A. Jones & Co. Inc., Covington, KY, pg. 604
Dougherty, Thomas, Chief Fin. Officer & V.P.--Hoboken Wood Flooring Corporation, Wayne, NJ, pg. 537
Douglas, John, Chief Fin. Officer--Clemco Industries, Washington, MO, pg. 254
Douglas, Jon A., Pres. & Chief Exec. Officer--Jon Douglas Company, Beverly Hills, CA, pg. 347
Dow, Robert, Controller--Haviland/Wilbur-Ellis Agricultural, Sparta, MI, pg. 517
Dowell, James, Mgr.-Office--Heckethorn Mfg. Company, Dyersburg, TN, pg. 524
Downey, Chuck, Chief Fin. Officer--Warren Distribution, Inc., Omaha, NE, pg. 1164
Downey, James, Jr., Chief Fin. Officer--Dynamic Metal Products Company, Manchester, CT, pg. 356
Downey, Mortimer L. III, Exec. Dir. & Chief Fin. Officer--Metropolitan Transportation Authority, New York, NY, pg. 745
Downey, Tom, Treas.--The Maxima Corporation, Lanham, MD, pg. 723
Downie, Robert, V.P. & Chief Fin. Officer--James Austin Co., Mars, PA, pg. 99
Downs, Robert G., V.P.-Fin. & Admin.--Southern Frozen Foods, Montezuma, GA, pg. 26
Dowsett, Connie, Chief Fin. Officer & Treas.--East Moline Metal Products Company, East Moline, IL, pg. 363
Doyle, Patrick, Exec V.P. & Chief Fin. Officer--Commodore Cruise Line, Ltd., Coral Gables, FL, pg. 269
Doyle, Peter G., Chief Fin. Officer & Exec. V.P.--Linbeck Corp., Houston, TX, pg. 675
Doyle, Rick, Controller--Telescope Casual Furniture, Inc., Granville, NY, pg. 1085
Draghi, Ronald L., Chief Fin. Officer & V.P.-Fin. & MIS--Distribution America, Des Plaines, IL, pg. 340
Drago, Joseph, Chief Fin. Officer--The Dartnell Corporation, Chicago, IL, pg. 316
Drake, Don, Chief Fin. Officer--William O'Neil & Co., Inc., Los Angeles, CA, pg. 827
Drake, John, Chief Fin. Officer--North Central Life Insurance Companies Saint Paul, MN, pg. 813
Draper, Tim, Chief Fin. Officer--Radix Corporation, Salt Lake City, UT, pg. 909
Dressen, Scott, Chief Fin. Officer--Jewelmont Corporation, Minneapolis, MN, pg. 594
Drewry, George, Chief Fin. Officer--Karsten Manufacturing Corporation, Phoenix, AZ, pg. 617
Drewry, John T., V.P., Chief Oper. & Chief Fin. Officer & Treas.--Advanced Marine Enterprises, Inc., Arlington, VA, pg. 20
Dreyling, Robert, Controller--Spencer Industries, Inc., New Brunswick, NJ, pg. 1030
Dries, William J., Sr. V.P. & Chief Fin. Officer--Charter Oak Financial Corporation, Cincinnati, OH, pg. 491
Driver, Bob, Chief Fin. Officer--Sturgis Iron & Metal Company, Inc., Sturgis, MI, pg. 1055
Drucker, Herbert J., Chief Fin. Officer & V.P.--Harper Shirt Company, New York, NY, pg. 510
Drury, Anthony R., Chief Fin. Officer & V.P.--Quad Systems Corporation, Horsham, PA, pg. 902
Drury, David, Chief Fin. Officer & Exec. V.P.--The Oldenburg Group Companies, Milwaukee, WI, pg. 824
Dubrowski, Jerome, V.P., Treas. & Chief Fin. Officer--Louis Dreyfus Corporation, Wilton, CT, pg. 348
Ducich, Dan, V.P. & Chief Fin. Officer--Recreational Equipment, Inc., Kent, WA, pg. 917
Duffy, Robert E., V.P.-Fin., Sec. & Chief Fin. Officer--American Industries Inc., Portland, OR, pg. 55
Dugan, Darrell, Chief Fin. Officer & Chief Info. Officer--Conley Frog & Switch Company, Memphis, TN, pg. 274
Dukes, R.R., Chief Fin. Officer--O'Neil Industries Inc., Chicago, IL, pg. 827
Dumke, William E., V.P.-Fin. & Chief Fin. Officer--Henningsen Foods, Inc., White Plains, NY, pg. 629
Duncan, Nena, Controller--American Military Arms Corporation, Jacksonville, AR, pg. 58
Duncan, Pola, Chief Fin. Officer--Basso & Associates Inc. Adv. & Public Relations, Costa Mesa, CA, pg. 125
Dunleavy, Karen, Treas.--Georgetown Partners, Inc., Great Neck, NY, pg. 473
Dupuis, Frank J., Chm. Bd. & Chief Fin. Officer--Your Man Tours, Inc., Inglewood, CA, pg. 1214
Duran, Ramon, Controller--Wolfberg, Alvarez & Associates Inc., Miami, FL, pg. 1199
Durrett, Ken, Chief Fin. Officer--Coast To Coast Stores, Inc., Denver, CO, pg. 257
Dyer, J. Rodney, V.P.-Taxation--Jones Intercable, Inc., Englewood, CO, pg. 604
Dykema, Scot, Chief Fin. Officer--The Richards Group, Inc., Dallas, TX, pg. 932
Dymond, D.S., V.P. & Chief Fin. Officer--Mauna Loa Resources Inc., Honolulu, HI, pg. 174
Dziedzic, John, Treas.--Warren Equities Inc., New York, NY, pg. 1164
Dziedzic, John, Treas.--Warex Petroleum Corporation, Providence, RI, pg. 1165
Dziedzic, John T., Treas.--Mid-Valley Petroleum Corporation, Newburgh, NY, pg. 1165
Easley, Thomas L., Chief Fin. Officer & V.P.--The Granada Group, Houston, TX, pg. 475
East, F. Howard, Pres., Chief Oper. & Chief Fin. Officer--Bell Packaging Corporation, Marion, IN, pg. 135
Easterman, Dave, Chief Fin. Officer & Controller--B & B Cash Grocery Store, Tampa, FL, pg. 105
Eaton, Mark R., V.P.-Fin.--Children's World Learning Centers, Inc., Golden, CO, pg. 7
Ebel, George, Chief Fin. Officer--Moltrup Steel Products Company, Beaver Falls, PA, pg. 764
Eberle, Katherine M., Treas.--Bruce W. Eberle & Associates, Vienna, VA, pg. 365
Eble, Martin J., Chief Fin. Officer--Ashman Enterprises, Inc., Brecksville, OH, pg. 88
Eckstein, Darrell, Chief Fin. Officer--National Emergency Services, Inc., Tiburon, CA, pg. 788
Eckstein, Helene, Chief Fin. Officer, Treas., Sec. & Mktg. Coord.--Spectrum Color Center, Golden, CO, pg. 1029
Edwards, Joseph, Sr. V.P. & Chief Fin. Officer--Superior Federal Bank, Fort Smith, AR, pg. 1063
Egbert, Bradley, Chief Fin. Officer--Weaver Popcorn Company, Inc., Van Buren, IN, pg. 1170
Egertson, Darrell J., Chief Fin. Officer--Dart Transit Company, Inc., Eagan, MN, pg. 316
Eggebrecht, David L., Chief Fin. Officer & Treas.--Phillips Plastics Corporation, Phillips, WI, pg. 867
Egley, Thomas, Chief Fin. Officer--Southland Industries, Long Beach, CA, pg. 1023
Ehren, James B., Chief Fin. Officer & Sr. V.P.--Applied Industrial Materials Corporation, Deerfield, IL, pg. 79
Eich, Kenneth P, Chief Fin. Officer--Oppenheimer Management Corp., New York, NY, pg. 719
Eichler, Franklin R., Pres. & Chief Exec. Officer--The Sico Company, Mount Joy, PA, pg. 1001
Eilert, Norman E., Sr. V.P. & Chief Fin. Officer--A. Teichert & Son, Inc., Sacramento, CA, pg. 1084
Eitze, William O., V.P.-Fin., Chief Fin. Officer, Controller & Treas.--Carl M. Freeman Associates, Inc., Potomac, MD, pg. 431
Ekart, Conrad, Chief Fin. Officer--Charles Jacquin et Cie, Inc., Philadelphia, PA, pg. 588
Ekle, Tom, Chief Fin. Officer--AMI Industries, Inc., Colorado Springs, CO, pg. 5
Elder, Douglas P., Sr. V.P. & Chief Fin. Officer--Fellowes Manufacturing Co., Itasca, IL, pg. 405
Elgin, John E., Sr. V.P. & Chief Fin. Officer--Thrifty Oil Company, Downey, CA, pg. 1096
Ellenoff, Theodore, Treas. & Sec.--Voit Sports, Inc., Fairport, NY, pg. 1154
Ellenoff, Theodore, Sec. & Treas.--Voit Corp., Fairport, NY, pg. 1154
Ellingson, Sarah S., Chief Fin. Officer & Sec.--Reese Enterprises, Inc., Rosemount, MN, pg. 920
Ellison, Gary L., V.P.-Fin.--Emkay, Inc., Itasca, IL, pg. 379
Ellisor, David R., V.P.-Fin. & Admin.--Benson's, Inc., Bogart, GA, pg. 140
Ellwein, Leonard, Chief Fin. Officer & Controller--Randall Stores, Inc., Mitchell, SD, pg. 911
Elznic, Tom, Chief Fin. Officer & Controller--Majestic Molded Products, Inc., Holbrook, NY, pg. 702
Emde, Richard, V.P.-Fin.--Sun-Maid Growers of California, Kingsburg, CA, pg. 1058
Emma, Ronald F., V.P.-Fin.--Hill International Inc., Willingboro, NJ, pg. 534
Engel, Willard, Chief Fin. Officer--May & Speh, Inc., Downers Grove, IL, pg. 724
Engelman, Irwin, Exec. V.P. & Chief Fin. Officer--MacAndrews & Forbes Co., Camden, NJ, pg. 694
Engelsma, Bruce W., V.P. & Chief Fin. Officer--Kraus-Anderson, Inc., Minneapolis, MN, pg. 644
Engelson, David, Pres. & Chief Fin. Officer--First Connecticut SBIC, Bridgeport, CT, pg. 412
Englefield, F.W., IV, Co-Pres., Chief Exec. & Chief Fin. Officer--Englefield, Inc., Newark, OH, pg. 382
English, Chris, Chief Fin. Officer & Treas.--Webster Industries Inc., Tiffin, OH, pg. 1171
Ennis, E. L., Chief Fin. Officer, Treas. & Controller--Strachan Shipping Co., Garden City, GA, pg. 1052
Ensor, Phillip E., Exec. V.P.-Fin. & Admin.--Marine World Africa USA, Vallejo, CA, pg. 707
Epperlein, Richard, Treas. & Comptroller--A. Zeregas Sons, Inc., Fair Lawn, NJ, pg. 1217
Epstein, Corey, Sec./Treas.--Wallich Lumber Co., Detroit, MI, pg. 1161
Epstein, Martin, Pres., Chief Exec. & Chief Fin. Officer--Associated Machinecraft Corporation, Los Angeles, CA, pg. 90
Epstein, Mel, Exec. V.P., Chief Fin. Officer--Backer Spielvogel Bates, Inc., New York, NY, pg. 108
Erath, David, Chief Fin. Officer--Schwegmann Giant Super Markets, New Orleans, LA, pg. 980
Erb, Jeffrey L., Chief Fin. Officer--Owensboro Grain Co., Inc., Owensboro, KY, pg. 834
Erickson, Jerry L., Chief Fin. Officer--Padilla Speer Beardsley Inc., Minneapolis, MN, pg. 842
Erickson, Kenneth B., Sr. V.P. & Chief Fin. Officer--Treasure Chest Advertising Co., Inc., Glendora, CA, pg. 1108
Erickson, LeRoy L., Sec., Treas. & Chief Fin. Officer--D.C.I., Inc., Saint Cloud, MN, pg. 308
Erlick, Lance, Chief Fin. Officer & Controller--Component Technology Corp., Erie, PA, pg. 270
Erlick, Lance, Chief Fin. Officer & Controller--R & R Plastics, Swanton, OH, pg. 270
Estes, Larry, Chief Fin. Officer--Noel Canning Corporation, Yakima, WA, pg. 808
Ethridge, Joseph A., Sr. V.P.-Fin. & Chief Fin. Officer--Sammons Enterprises, Inc., Dallas, TX, pg. 968
Ettl, Al, Chief Fin. Officer & Controller--Putzmeister, Inc., Gardena, CA, pg. 901
Eubank, Don, Chief Fin. Officer--BA Advertising, Dallas, TX, pg. 105
Evans, Duane R., V.P.-Fin.--Watkins Incorporated, Winona, MN, pg. 1167
Evans, J.T., Treas.--Rubatex Corporation, Bedford, VA, pg. 480
Evans, Kenneth, Chief Fin. Officer--Just Born, Inc., Bethlehem, PA, pg. 610
Evans, Peter W., Vice Chm., Chief Fin. Officer--Ingalls, Quinn & Johnson, Boston, MA, pg. 567
Everett, Addison L., V.P. & Chief Fin. Officer--Syracuse Supply Company, Syracuse, NY, pg. 1070
Evons, Kenneth, Chief Fin. Officer--Just Born, Inc., Bethlehem, PA, pg. 610
Ewton, Floyd, Chief Fin. Officer--4Day Tire Stores, Irvine, CA, pg. 427
Eyster, Donald, Vice Chm. & Chief Fin. Officer--Donlee Technologies Inc., York, PA, pg. 344
Ezerski, Ronald E., Chief Fin. Officer--Direct Dental Supply Co., Sparks, NV, pg. 851
Fabianac, Donna, Chief Fin. Officer--Katsin/Loeb Advertising, San Francisco, CA, pg. 618
Fagot, William, Chief Fin. Officer--Weatherly Frozen Foods Group, Inc., St. Petersburg, FL, pg. 1169
Faircloth, Phillip, V.P. & Chief Fin. Officer--Warehouse Home Furnishings Distributor, Dublin, GA, pg. 1163
Falanga, Lou, V.P.-Fin.--The William Carter Company, New York, NY, pg. 226
Falcon, Eleanor, Chief Fin. Officer & V.P.-Fin.--Magic Pan International Inc., Burlingame, CA, pg. 700
Falconi, Robert, Chief Fin. Officer, Treas. & Sec.--Planning Systems Inc., McLean, VA, pg. 874
Farina, Andy, Chief Fin. Officer--WinCup, Phoenix, AZ, pg. 1195
Farley, Sheryl, Controller--United Laboratories, Inc., Itasca, IL, pg. 1133
Farmer, Richard, Exec. V.P. & Chief Fin. Officer--Garvin Fire Protection Systems, Orange, CA, pg. 444
Farrell, Neal F., Mng. Partner, V.P., Gen. Counsel & Chief Fin. Officer--Borg-Warner Corporation, Chicago, IL, pg. 165
Fasino, P., Chief Fin. Officer & Controller--Red L Foods, Pomfret Center, CT, pg. 1128
Feeney, James P., Chief Fin. Officer & V.P.--New England Coffee Company, Malden, MA, pg. 800
Fehsenfeld, Fred M., V.P. & Treas.--Crystal Flash Petroleum Corp., Indianapolis, IN, pg. 303
Feist, Howard N., V.P.-Fin.--Congoleum Corporation, Mercerville, NJ, pg. 274
Feldner, Ronald A., Chief Fin. Officer--Bill Heard Enterprises, Inc., Columbus, GA, pg. 521
Felt, Joel, Treas.--Southern Leather Company, Memphis, TN, pg. 1021
Fenu, Pietro, Chief Oper. Officer & Chief Fin. Officer--Andes Candies, Inc., Delavan, WI, pg. 169
Ferenzy, Lawrence, Exec. V.P. & Chief Fin. Officer--Avis, Inc., Garden City, NY, pg. 102

Corporate Responsibilities Index

Ferguson, Jack, V.P. & Chief Fin. Officer--Ingles Markets, Inc., Asheville, NC, pg. 568
Fermano,Joseph, Chief Fin. Officer--Blue Cross and Blue Shield of Massachusetts, Boston, MA, pg. 159
Fernandez, Claude, Chief Fin. Officer, V.P. & Mng. Dir.--W. P. Carey & Co., Inc., New York, NY, pg. 218
Fernandez, Frank L., Treas. & Sec.--Saratoga Harness Racing, Inc., Saratoga Springs, NY, pg. 970
Ferreira, Richard S., Exec. V.P. & Chief Fin. Officer--Golf Hosts, Inc., Palm Harbor, FL, pg. 469
Fertell, Paul A., Pres., Chief Oper. & Chief Fin. Officer--Seton Company, Norristown, PA, pg. 993
Fessler, Stan, Chief Fin. Officer--Goldsmith/Jeffrey, Inc., New York, NY, pg. 469
Feuz, Simon, Chief Fin. Officer--Electric Specialty & Supply Corp., Boston, MA, pg. 374
Feyen, Pat, Chief Fin. Officer--PacifiCare of Oregon, Inc., Lake Oswego, OR, pg. 1127
Fiacre, Albert E., Jr., Exec. V.P.-Treas & Chief Fin. Officer--Society for Savings Bancorp, Inc., Hartford, CT, pg. 1016
Fickenscher, Gerald H., V.P. & Chief Fin. Officer--Uniroyal Chemical Company, Inc., Middlebury, CT, pg. 1129
Ficks, Lee B., Pres., Chief Exec. Officer, & Treas.--Ficks Reed Company, Cincinnati, OH, pg. 408
Fields, C.S., Chief Fin. Officer--Ottenheimer & Company, Inc., Bannockburn, IL, pg. 831
Fiely, Charles, Controller--H. Koch & Sons, Anaheim, CA, pg. 262
Fierce, Robert, Chief Fin. Officer--G.C. Thorsen, Inc., Rockford, IL, pg. 609
Figge, Fred H., Jr., Exec. V.P. & Chief Fin. Officer--Encyclopaedia Britannica, Inc., Chicago, IL, pg. 381
Filanowski, Mark, Sr. V.P. & Chief Fin. Officer--Marine Transport Lines, Inc., Secaucus, NJ, pg. 707
Fineman, Evan L., Treas. & Chief Fin. Officer--Atlantic Dairy Cooperative, Southampton, PA, pg. 94
Fingel, James R., V.P. & Controller--Shamrock Broadcasting, Inc., Burbank, CA, pg. 994
Finn, Peter, Chief Fin. Officer & Chm. Exec. Committee--Ruder, Finn, Inc., New York, NY, pg. 954
Finnigan, Mike, Exec. V.P. & Chief Fin. Officer--Hollywood Park, Inc., Inglewood, CA, pg. 540
Fiorentini, Walter J., Sr. V.P., Chief Fin. Officer--Hoffman York & Compton, Milwaukee, WI, pg. 538
Firestone, Donald L., V.P. & Treas.--Tru-Weld Grating, Inc., Wexford, PA, pg. 1117
First, Harold, V.P. & Chief Fin. Officer--Trans World Airlines, Inc., Mount Kisco, NY, pg. 561
Fischer, Ken, Dir.-Fin.--Woodfin-Smith Pontiac, Inc., Baton Rouge, LA, pg. 1200
Fisher, G. David, Chief Fin. Officer, V.P. & Controller--SOR Inc., Lenexa, KS, pg. 963
Fisher, Joseph, Chief Fin. Officer & V.P.--Big Y Foods Inc., Springfield, MA, pg. 149
Fisher, McLane, Exec. V.P., Sec. & Chief Fin. Officer--CH2M Hill Companies, Ltd., Englewood, CO, pg. 202
Fitzgerald, Ken, Chief Fin. Officer & Sec.--R.L. Ziegler Co. Inc., Tuscaloosa, AL, pg. 1218
Fitzpatrick, Mike, Chief Fin. Officer & V.P.--TD Industries Inc., Dallas, TX, pg. 1072
Fiume, Orest J., V.P. & Fin. Administrator--The Wiremold Company, West Hartford, CT, pg. 1197
Flatley, William M., Sr. V.P. & Chief Fin. Officer--Horsehead Industries, Inc., New York, NY, pg. 545
Fleischman, Marvin H., Pres., Chief Exec. & Chief Fin. Officer--Lakeside Refining Co. Inc., Southfield, MI, pg. 651
Fleisher, David L., Sr. Exec. V.P. & Chief Fin. Officer--Maritz Inc., Fenton, MO, pg. 707
Fleming, William, Treas.--A.I. Root Company, Medina, OH, pg. 946
Flint, John E., V.P.-Acctg.--Gibraltar Steel Corp., Buffalo, NY, pg. 456
Flint, Mark, Sr. V.P. & Chief Fin. Officer--Peter J. Schmitt Holdings, West Seneca, NY, pg. 976
Flint, Mark A., Sr. V.P. & Chief Fin. Officer--Peter J. Schmitt Co., Inc., West Seneca, NY, pg. 977
Flintosh, Steve, Controller--Dorman-Roth Foods, Inc., Moonachie, NJ, pg. 346
Flippin, Mike, Chief Fin. Officer--PSI Group of Companies, Memphis, TN, pg. 837
Flood, Thomas, V.P.-Admin. & Fin. & Treas.--TSC Industries, Inc., Nashville, TN, pg. 1075
Floyd, Chuck, Chief Fin. Officer--Inland Associates, Olathe, KS, pg. 570
Floyd, Robert K., V.P.-Fin. & Chief Fin. Officer--Tracor, Inc., Austin, TX, pg. 1104
Fluegeman, Raymond W., Chief Fin. Officer, Treas., Controller & Dir.-Data Processing--Robbins, Inc., Cincinnati, OH, pg. 938
Fluker, E. Michael, Exec. V.P. & Chief Fin. Officer--MediaNews Group Inc., Houston, TX, pg. 735
Fobes, C., V.P.-Fin.--Air-O-Matic Power Steer Co., Marion, OH, pg. 1069
Fogg, William, III, Chief Fin. Officer & Treas.--Southeastern Medequip, Inc., Jacksonville Beach, FL, pg. 1019
Fohrman, Neal, Pres., Chief Exec. & Chief Fin. Officer & Controller--Red Calliope & Associates, Inc., Los Angeles, CA, pg. 918
Foley, Thomas, Chief Fin. Officer & V.P.--Print Northwest, Fife, WA, pg. 891
Folk, R. H., Exec. V.P.--L. B. Smith, Inc., Camp Hill, PA, pg. 1013
Folkerth, Bob, Chief Fin. Officer--Digitron Tool Co., Inc., Miamisburg, OH, pg. 337
Follman, John P., Chief Fin. Officer & Sr. V.P.-Fin.--Day & Zimmermann, Inc., Radnor, PA, pg. 320
Folwell, Jean, Chief Fin. Officer & Asst. Treas.--MADD (Mothers Against Drunk Driving), Irving, TX, pg. 691
Fong, Harry M., Treas.--Fugro-McClelland, Inc., Houston, TX, pg. 435
Fontenazza, Frank, Chief Fin. Officer & Controller--Monarch Avalon, Inc., Baltimore, MD, pg. 765
Forester, Scott, Chief Fin. Officer--Tiger Electronics, Inc., Vernon Hills, IL, pg. 1097
Fornella, Norman G., Sr. V.P. & Chief Fin. Officer--Morse Diesel International, New York, NY, pg. 771
Forster, Maria, Chief Fin. Officer & V.P.--Pro Hardware, Inc., Englewood, CO, pg. 891
Fortmuller, George A., Chief Fin. Officer, Treas. & Sec.--Edwin B. Stimpson Company, Inc., Bayport, NY, pg. 1049
Fossum, Jeffrey J., V.P. & Chief Fin. Officer--Effective Management Systems, Milwaukee, WI, pg. 370
Foster, Betty F., Treas.--The Long & Foster Real Estate, Inc., Fairfax, VA, pg. 682
Foster, David, Controller--Snyder Tank Corp., Buffalo, NY, pg. 1015
Fowler, William J., V.P.-Fin.--Melody Foods, Inc., Farmington Hills, MI, pg. 738
Fox, Harold, Exec. V.P. & Chief Fin. Officer--Del Taco, Inc., Costa Mesa, CA, pg. 325
Fox, Harold, Exec. V.P.-Fin. & Treas.--Del Taco/Naugles, Costa Mesa, CA, pg. 325
Fox, William J., Exec. V.P. & Chief Fin. Officer--Revlon, Inc., New York, NY, pg. 696
Frade, Madalena, Acctg. Asst.--BSB Portugal, Lisbon,, Portugal, pg. 110
Francis, Kent, Chief Fin. Officer & Treas.--O'Malia Food Markets Inc., Noblesville, IN, pg. 825
Francis, William, Treas., Controller & Chief Fin. Officer--Captive-Aire Systems, Inc., Youngsville, NC, pg. 216
Frank, Charles M., V.P.-Fin. & Chief Fin. Officer--Radionics, Inc., Salinas, CA, pg. 909
Frank, Douglas, Chief Fin. Officer--Dealers Manufacturing Company, Minneapolis, MN, pg. 322
Frank, H. Alan, Pres., Chief Fin. Officer & Treas.--Union Industries, Inc., Providence, RI, pg. 1128
Frank, Ken, Chief Fin. Officer--Mid-States Petroleum Inc., Troy, MI, pg. 750
Frank, L.C., V.P.-Fin. & Chief Fin. Officer--Duraco Products, Inc., Streamwood, IL, pg. 354
Frank, Sandy, Sr. V.P., Chief Fin. Officer--Berenter Greenhouse & Webster, Inc., New York, NY, pg. 141
Frank, William H., V.P. & Treas.--D.V.F. Inc., New York, NY, pg. 695
Frankel, Ernst D., Chief Fin. Officer, Treas., Controller & Sec.--Standard Textile Co., Inc., Cincinnati, OH, pg. 1037
Frankel, Robert, Chief Exec. & Chief Fin. Officer--Construction Counsellors, Inc., Park Ridge, NJ, pg. 277
Franklin, R.J., Pres. & Chief Fin. Officer--McMaster Carr Supply Co. Inc., Elmhurst, IL, pg. 731
Franklin, T.R., V.P.-Fin. & Treas.--Neenah Foundry Company, Neenah, WI, pg. 797
Fraser, Doug, Dir.-Fin.--Platt Saco Lowell Corporation, Greenville, SC, pg. 876
Frazier, William R., Chief Fin. Officer & V.P.-Fin.--FM Industries, Inc., Fort Worth, TX, pg. 394
Frederick, Edward F., Controller--Ruscon Corp., Charleston, SC, pg. 956
Frederick, Scott, Chief Fin. Officer & Treas.--American Appraisal Associates, Inc., Milwaukee, WI, pg. 48
Freedman, Leslie, Pres. & Chief Fin. Officer--FMS Management Systems, Inc., North Miami Beach, FL, pg. 394
Freeman, Dennis, Chief Fin. Officer--Imperial Die Casting, Easley, SC, pg. 906
Freeman, Jeff E., Sr. V.P.-Fin., Sec. & Treas.--H.A.T. Holding Company, Tampa, FL, pg. 517
Freeman, John, Chief Fin. Officer, V.P., Treas. & Sec.--Robert F. Driver Co., Inc., San Diego, CA, pg. 349
Freimark, Jeffrey P., Exec. V.P., Chief Fin. Officer & Gen. Counsel & Sec.--Pueblo International, Inc., Pompano Beach, FL, pg. 899
French, Morton R., Chm. Bd., Pres., Chief Exec. & Chief Fin. Officer--Commercial Plastics & Supplies Corp., Richmond Hill, NY, pg. 268
Freriks, Donald, V.P.-Fin.--O'Neal Steel Inc., Birmingham, AL, pg. 827
Frescoln, Leonard D., V.P.-Fin. & Admin.--Williams International, Walled Lake, MI, pg. 1191
Fried, R.I., Chief Fin. Officer--Stiefel Laboratories, Inc., Coral Gables, FL, pg. 1048
Friedl, Thomas, Controller--American Louver Co., Skokie, IL, pg. 57
Friedline, William, Controller--Riggs Industries, Inc., Stoystown, PA, pg. 934
Friedline, William, Controller--Somerset Welding & Steel, Inc., Somerset, PA, pg. 934
Friedman, Bruce, Chief Fin. Officer--Valcor Engineering Corp., Springfield, NJ, pg. 1142
Friedman, Lillian, Treas.--Vogue & Body Shops, Inc., Jacksonville, FL, pg. 1154
Friedman, Marty, Chief Fin. Officer, Treas, & Controller--Power Contracting & Engineering Corp., Rolling Meadows, IL, pg. 883
Friedrichsen, B.T., Sec. & Treas.--Wagner Mills Inc., Schuyler, NE, pg. 1158
Frigon, Henry F., Exec. V.P.-Devel./Strategy & Chief Fin. Officer--Hallmark Cards, Inc., Kansas City, MO, pg. 501
Friou, Roger P., Vice Chm. & Chief Fin. Officer--Jitney-Jungle Stores of America, Inc., Jackson, MS, pg. 594
Fritz, W.J., V.P.-Fin. & Treas.--Benjamin Moore & Co., Montvale, NJ, pg. 139
Froeliger, E.L., Sec., Treas. & Chief Fin. Officer--Frantz Manufacturing Co., Sterling, IL, pg. 429
Froemming, Herb, Sr. V.P. & Chief Fin. Officer--Brauns Fashions, Inc., Minneapolis, MN, pg. 172
Frojd, Tim, V.P., Chief Fin. Officer--Martin Williams Advertising Inc., Minneapolis, MN, pg. 1191
Frost, George, Chief Fin. Officer & Treas.--UFE Incorporated, Stillwater, MN, pg. 1123
Fuchs, Rita, Head Bookkeeper--Rosen Associates Management Corp., Jericho, NY, pg. 948
Fuentes, Juanita, Fin. Dir.--Leo Burnett Chile, Santiago,, Chile, pg. 192
Fuentes, Lutz, Controller--Young & Rubicam de Chile Ltda., Santiago,, Chile, pg. 1213
Fuette, Kenneth R., V.P. & Controller--Foam Product Corporation, Eddystone, PA, pg. 1121
Fugett, Hubert D., Chief Fin. Officer--Affiliated Foods Southwest, Little Rock, AR, pg. 24
Fuller, H. Thomas, Chief Fin. Officer & Sr. V.P.--Tucker Wayne/Luckie & Company, Birmingham, AL, pg. 1118
Fullerton, Germaine, Chief Fin. Officer & Controller--Schneider Commercial Real Estate, Orange, CA, pg. 977
Fullerton, Lola, Chief Fin. Officer--San Miguel (U.S.A.) Inc., San Mateo, CA, pg. 969
Furbush, Douglas, III, Chief Fin. Officer--Trans National Travel, Boston, MA, pg. 1106
Furlow, Mack, Sr. V.P. & Chief Fin. Officer--The Hunt Corporation, Indianapolis, IN, pg. 553
Furst, Rafael, Pres. & Treas.--The El-Bee Chargit Corp., Dayton, OH, pg. 373
Fusco, Joseph V., V.P. & Chief Fin. Officer--Monroe Systems For Business, Inc., Morris Plains, NJ, pg. 766
Fuss, Michael, Chief Fin. Officer--Boye Needle, Chicago, IL, pg. 1205
Fuss, Michael D., Chief Fin. Officer & V.P.--Wm. E. Wright Limited Partnership, West Warren, MA, pg. 1205
Gaebler, Walter, II, Chief Fin. Officer & Asst. Gen. Mgr.-Fin.--Sacramento Municipal Utility District, Sacramento, CA, pg. 965
Gaeke, Harry F., Chm. Bd., Chief Exec. & Fin. Officer--Shook National Corporation, Dayton, OH, pg. 1000
Gaeke, Harry F., Chm. Bd. & Chief Fin. Officer--Shook, Inc., Dayton, OH, pg. 1000
Gaffney, Edward J., Pres. & Treas.--Ortho-Kinetics, Inc., Waukesha, WI, pg. 830
Gagliardi, J.J., V.P.-Fin. & Chief Fin. Officer--Harvard Industries, Inc., Farmingdale, NJ, pg. 514
Gaidano, D.J., Chief Fin. Officer & Exec. V.P.--Bromar Inc., Newport Beach, CA, pg. 179
Gaines, Terry, V.P.-Fin.--W-B Supply Co., Pampa, TX, pg. 1155
Gaitzsch, Thomas, Chief Fin. Officer--Battelle-Institut E.V., Frankfurt/Main, Germany, pg. 126
Galbraith, John R., Sr. V.P. & Chief Fin. Officer--Liberty Northwest Insurance Corp., Portland, OR, pg. 674
Gallagher, Frank W., Chief Fin. Officer & Treas.--Paramount Packaging Corp., Chalfont, PA, pg. 848
Gallagher, John J., Controller--New Jersey State Lottery, Trenton, NJ, pg. 801
Gallucci, Joseph, Chief Fin. Officer & Sr. V.P.--John Wanamaker, Philadelphia, Philadelphia, PA, pg. 1201
Gallucci, Joseph F., Chief Fin. Officer--Woodward & Lothrop/John Wanamaker, Washington, DC, pg. 1201
Galvez, Matthew S., Chief Fin. Officer--Manufacturers Products Company, Warren, MI, pg. 705
Galvin, R. Terence, Sr. V.P. & Chief Fin. Officer--The Grand Union Company, Wayne, NJ, pg. 476
Gani, Marcel, Chief Fin. Officer--Next, Inc., Redwood City, CA, pg. 805
Gantt, G. Russell, V.P., Treas. & Asst. Sec.--Glen Raven Mills, Inc., Glen Raven, NC, pg. 461
Garceau, Albert A., V.P., Chief Fin. Officer & Treas.--Mr. Gasket Company, Cleveland, OH, pg. 761
Garcema, Albert, Chief Fin. Officer & Treas.--Cragar Industries, Compton, CA, pg. 761
Garcia, Carlos L., Dir.-Corp. Fin.--Playtex Family Products Corp., Stamford, CT, pg. 877
Garcia, Roberto M., Controller--Crisa Corporation, Plano, TX, pg. 299
Gardner, Hugh, Chief Fin. Officer--The Thompson Group Companies, Henderson, KY, pg. 1094
Gardner, John W., V.P. & Chief Fin. Officer--Fabwel Inc., Elkhart, IN, pg. 396
Gargaro, Timothy, Treas.--Ring Screw Works, Madison Heights, MI, pg. 935
Garibaldi, John L., Sr. V.P.-Fin., Chief Fin. Officer & Treas.--Aloha Airgroup, Inc., Honolulu, HI, pg. 43
Garibaldi, John L., Sr. V.P.-Fin., Chief Fin. Officer & Treas.--Aloha Airlines, Inc., Honolulu, HI, pg. 43
Garrett, C. L., Sr. V.P.-Fin. & Chief Fin. Officer--SENCORP, Newport, KY, pg. 989
Garrow, Ralph, V.P.-Fin.--The Selmer Co., Elkhart, IN, pg. 573
Gartin, Robert E., V.P. & Chief Fin. Officer--Automobile Auction Division, Atlanta, GA, pg. 293
Garvey, Robert A., Chief Fin. Officer--Ausherman Construction Company, Frederick, MD, pg. 98
Gasca, Peter, Treas.--Wards Cove Packing Company, Seattle, WA, pg. 1163
Gash, C. Ray, Chief Fin. Officer, Sr. V.P., Treas. & Sec.--Stephens, Inc., Little Rock, AR, pg. 1046
Gassman, John, Pres., Chief Exec. Officer & Chief Fin. Officer--Townsend & Bottum, Inc., Ann Arbor, MI, pg. 1104
Gaston, John, Sr. V.P.-Corp. Services & Chief Fin. Officer--SF Services, North Little Rock, AR, pg. 961
Gates, William C., Chief Fin. Officer, V.P. & Treas.--Graphic Controls, Corp., Buffalo, NY, pg. 478
Gates, William C., V.P., Treas. & Chief Fin. Officer--Graphic Controls Corporation, Buffalo, NY, pg. 478
Gates, William S., Treas. & Sec.--Preferred Risk Life Insurance Co., West Des Moines, IA, pg. 886
Gaudio, Anthony Del, Chief Fin. Officer--The Haband Co., Paterson, NJ, pg. 498
Gaudreau, Dan, Chief Fin. Officer, V.P.-Fin. & Dir.-Opers.--Ready Systems, Sunnyvale, CA, pg. 916
Gavin, Pat, V.P.-Fin. & Chief Fin. Officer--General Media Publishing Group, New York, NY, pg. 450
Gavinski, C. Martin, Chief Fin. Officer--Penda Corporation, Portage, WI, pg. 857
Gaw, Ed, Chief Fin. Officer, Treas. & Sec.--Griffin Corporation, Valdosta, GA, pg. 483
Gaylord, E.K. II, V.P. & Asst. Sec.--The Daily & Sunday Oklahoman, Oklahoma City, OK, pg. 446
Gazarek, Celeste, V.P.-Fin. & Treas.--National Frozen Foods Corp., Seattle, WA, pg. 789

Geiger, Denise, V.P., Chief Fin. Officer & Controller--The Atkins Agency, San Antonio, TX, pg. 94
Geiger, Jerry, Controller--West Coast Growers & Packers, Inc., Selma, CA, pg. 1177
Gejoff, Louis, Treas., Controller, Sec. & Chief Fin. Officer--Carver, Inc., Garden City, GA, pg. 227
Gejoff, Louis, Chief Fin. Officer, Treas., Controller & Sec.--Murray-Carver, East Bridgewater, MA, pg. 776
Geldmacher, Kenneth K., Treas. & Controller--Centrifugal & Mechanical Industries, Saint Louis, MO, pg. 609
Gelfeld, Mark, V.P. & Chief Fin. Officer--Century America Corporation, Chicago, IL, pg. 234
Gelman, Howard, Exec. V.P., Chief Fin. Officer--Adler Boschetto Peebles & Partners, Inc., New York, NY, pg. 17
Gemmo, Joseph, Chief Fin. Officer--General Aerospace Materials Corporation, Plainview, NY, pg. 448
Gencarelli, Angelo, Chief Fin. Officer & Sec.--Bess Eaton Donut Flour Co., Inc., Westerly, RI, pg. 146
Gendron, William, Asst. Controller--United Thermal Corporation, New York, NY, pg. 1137
Genesen, Louis, Chief Fin. Officer & V.P.--Humiston-Keeling, Inc., Chicago, IL, pg. 552
Gennrich, James N., V.P.-Fin.--Weasler Engineering Inc., West Bend, WI, pg. 1169
Genschaw, David A., Exec. V.P., Chief Fin. Officer--Waldbillig & Besteman, Inc., Madison, WI, pg. 1159
George, Michael, Controller--George E. Warren Corp., Vero Beach, FL, pg. 1164
Gerard, Joseph, Sr. V.P., Chief Fin. Officer--SFM Media Corporation, New York, NY, pg. 962
Gerdes, Michael, Exec. V.P. & Chief Fin. Officer--Vintners International Company, Inc., Gonzales, CA, pg. 1152
Gerrard, David, Chief Fin. Officer & Mktg. Dir.--National Truck Leasing System, Oakbrook Terrace, IL, pg. 794
Gerstein, Mel, Treas. & Dir.-Mktg., Adv. & Pub. Rels.--Thermwell Products Co., Inc., Paterson, NJ, pg. 1092
Gervasio, Thomas, Controller--Zemco Industries, Inc., Buffalo, NY, pg. 1217
Gesinski, Robert, V.P.-Fin. & Chief Fin. Officer--Andis Company, Racine, WI, pg. 74
Gettlefinger, Earl, Treas.--Superior Label Systems, Inc., Cincinnati, OH, pg. 1063
Gettlegfinger, Herman E., Chief Fin. Officer, Treas. & Sec.--Pride Oil Co., Inc., Knoxville, TN, pg. 622
Getz, Thomas, Treas.--Williams-White & Co., Moline, IL, pg. 1191
Ghazey, Ken, Exec. V.P. & Chief Fin. Officer--Darling-Delaware Co., Inc., Irving, TX, pg. 315
Gibbons, Peter, V.P. & Chief Fin. Officer--Gold Kist, Inc., Atlanta, GA, pg. 465
Gibney, Charles W., Sr. V.P. & Chief Fin. Officer--Macromedia Inc., Hackensack, NJ, pg. 698
Gibson, S.P., Chief Fin. Officer--Armstrong International, Inc., Three Rivers, MI, pg. 83
Gibson, T.J., Exec. V.P. & Chief Fin. Officer--The Gates Rubber Company, Denver, CO, pg. 445
Gibson, Thomas, Exec. V.P., Chief Fin. Officer, Sec. & Gen. Counsel--The Gates Rubber Company, Denver, CO, pg. 445
Giesler, James, Chief Oper. & Chief Fin. Officer--The Fuller Brush Company, Great Bend, KS, pg. 436
Gilbert, Gwen, Chief Fin. Officer--Briggs Weaver, Dallas, TX, pg. 968
Gilboy, Thomas V., Chief Fin. Officer & V.P.-Fin.--Troy Corporation, East Hanover, NJ, pg. 1116
Gilbride, Joseph, Exec. V.P., Chief Fin. Officer--The Lowe Group, New York, NY, pg. 685
Giles, James R., Chief Fin. Officer--Hickinbotham Bros., Ltd, Stockton, CA, pg. 532
Gill, Mark, Chief Fin. Officer--Krause's Sofa Factory, Inc., Brea, CA, pg. 644
Gilleland, Laura, Chief Fin. Officer & Controller--Gessner Industries, Concord, NC, pg. 455
Gillespie, Ray, Sec. & Treas.--Ford Meter Box Company, Wabash, IN, pg. 423
Gillon, William, Controller--Riverside Central Services, Inc., Natchez, MS, pg. 937
Gillula, E. William, Chief Fin. Officer & Sr. V.P.--Computer Sales International Inc., Saint Louis, MO, pg. 271
Gilmore, James R., V.P.-Fin.--Pawnee Extrusions, Grand Prairie, TX, pg. 852
Gilpin, John D., Sr. V.P.--Lyman Lumber Company, Excelsior, MN, pg. 689
Gingrich, Kenneth R., Jr., V.P. & Controller--Oxford Finance Companies, Inc., Philadelphia, PA, pg. 835
Ginnel, Casey, Chief Fin. Officer--JM Family Enterprises Inc., Deerfield Beach, FL, pg. 584
Gioiofo, George, Chief Fin. Officer--C-B Corporation, Charlotte, NC, pg. 198
Girata, Joseph, Chief Fin. Officer--Integral Systems, Inc., Sunnyvale, CA, pg. 573
Giroux, Beverly, V.P. & Chief Fin. Officer--Universal Dynamics Inc., Woodbridge, VA, pg. 1138
Giroux, Beverly, Chief Fin. Officer--Universal Dynamics Inc., North Plainfield, NJ, pg. 1138
Giroux, Beverly, V.P.-Fin.--Universal Dynamics, Inc., Woodbridge, VA, pg. 1138
Gissleman, Dave, Chief Fin. Officer & Controller--Weinbrenner Shoe Company, Inc., Merrill, WI, pg. 1173
Glasier, R., Chief Fin. Officer--Royal Caribbean Cruises Ltd., Miami, FL, pg. 953
Glass, William, Chief Fin. Officer--Advanced Controls, Inc., Irvine, CA, pg. 20
Glennie, Fred P., Sec. & Controller--Capital-Gazette Communications, Inc., Annapolis, MD, pg. 656
Glickman, Stuart, Chm., Pres. Chief Exec. & Chief Fin. Officer--Security Alarms & Fire Engineering Inc., Davie, FL, pg. 987
Glotzbecker, Paul G., Chief Fin. Officer--The Grandoe Corporation, Gloversville, NY, pg. 476
Gluth, Robert C., Chief Fin. Officer--The Marmon Group, Inc., Chicago, IL, pg. 710
Goddard, John W., Sr. V.P., Pres. & Chief Exec. Officer/Viacom Cable--Viacom Inc., New York, NY, pg. 785
Goedert, Philip H., Sec./Treas.--Design-Build West, Denver, CO, pg. 907
Goforth, James, Treas.--Renosol Corp., Saline, MI, pg. 927
Goforth, Mack, Chief Fin. Officer--MCorp, Dallas, TX, pg. 732
Goldberg, Arthur, Chief Fin. Officer, V.P.-Fin & Treas.--Forster Mfg. Co., Inc., Wilton, ME, pg. 21
Goldberg, Steven A., Chief Fin. Officer, V.P.-Fin. & Admin.--Prime Tanning Co., Inc., Berwick, ME, pg. 889
Goldberger, Seymour, Treas. & Adv. Dir.--Goldberger Doll Mfg. Company, Inc., Brooklyn, NY, pg. 466
Golden, David, Chief Fin. Officer, Treas. & Sec.--Stephen Gould Paper Co., Inc., Whippany, NJ, pg. 473
Golden, David M., V.P.-Fin & Admin., Chief Fin. Officer--Apparel America, Inc., New Haven, CT, pg. 78
Golden, J.M., V.P.-Fin.--Hub Inc., Tucker, GA, pg. 548
Golden, Jim, Chief Fin. Officer--Lillie Rubin Affiliates Inc., Miami, FL, pg. 954
Goldman, Zachary C., V.P., Chief Fin. Officer & Sec.--Londontown Corporation, Eldersburg, MD, pg. 682
Goldstein, Seija, Chief Fin. Officer--Communications International, New York, NY, pg. 269
Goldstein, Stanley, Chief Fin. Officer--Therapedic Associates, Inc., Boca Raton, FL, pg. 1090
Golinger, Robert, Chief Fin. Officer--Licensing Div., New York, NY, pg. 164
Gonnella, Ken, Chief Fin. Officer--Gonnella Frozen Products, Schaumburg, IL, pg. 470
Gonzalez, C., Sec., Treas. & Pur. Agent--Villazon Company Inc., Tampa, FL, pg. 1152
Gonzalez, Elias, Chief Fin. Officer--Transammonia Inc., New York, NY, pg. 1106
Good, Charles E., V.P.-Fin., Sec. & Treas.--Snyder's of Hanover, Inc., Hanover, PA, pg. 1015
Good, Fran, Chief Fin. Officer--MICOM Communications Corp., Simi Valley, CA, pg. 748
Good, Valeria, V.P.-Fin.--Whiting Manufacturing Co., Inc., Cincinnati, OH, pg. 1187
Goodman, Bernard, Chm. Bd. & Treas.--Sherwood Lumber Corporation, Islandia, NY, pg. 999
Goodman, Fredric, V.P.-Fin.--Welsbach Electric Corp., Long Island City, NY, pg. 1175
Goodman, Leonard, V.P.-Fin.--GAF Building Materials Corporation, Wayne, NJ, pg. 438
Goodman, Philip, Chief Fin. Officer--Dynabilt Products, Boston, MA, pg. 196
Goodwin, Janice, Chief Fin. Officer--Patten-Beers Constructors, Nashville, TN, pg. 132
Goolsbee, Arthur L., Chief Fin. Officer--Utility Trailer Manufacturing Co., City of Industry, CA, pg. 1141
Gordonson, Robert, Treas. & Chief Fin. Officer--Masters, Inc., Westbury, NY, pg. 720
Gorra, William, Pres. & Chief Exec. & Chief Fin. Officer--Chemical Specialties Corp., Springfield, MA, pg. 1069
Gottlieb, Lawrence, Exec. V.P.-Fin. & Admin.--Worldvision Enterprises, New York, NY, pg. 54
Gould, Maxine, Controller--Ventura Coastal Corporation, Ventura, CA, pg. 1147
Gould, Robin W., Chief Fin. Officer--E & J Gallo Winery, Modesto, CA, pg. 441
Grab, John M. Jr., Sr. V.P. & Chief Fin. Officer--Equity Services, Inc., Montpelier, VT, pg. 791
Grace, Don, V.P.-Fin.--Ventura Coastal Corporation, Ventura, CA, pg. 1147
Grady, Daniel A., Chief Fin. Officer--Bose Corporation, Framingham, MA, pg. 167
Graeff, Rodney J., V.P.-Fin. & Treas.--Walter H. Weaber Sons, Inc., Lebanon, PA, pg. 1169
Graf, Edward L., Vice Chm. & Chief Fin. Officer--Ketchum Communications Inc., Pittsburgh, PA, pg. 625
Graham, Glen, Treas. & Controller--Taco Inc., Cranston, RI, pg. 1076
Grant, Edward, Comptroller--Zoeller Co., Louisville, KY, pg. 1220
Grant, Michael, Sec. & Treas.--Grant-Lydick Beverage Co., San Antonio, TX, pg. 477
Grant, Paul, Chief Fin. Officer & Controller--Bergquist Company, Inc., Minneapolis, MN, pg. 141
Grathwohl, Joseph A., Treas.--Jake Sweeney Auto Leasing Inc., Cincinnati, OH, pg. 1066
Grathwohl, Joseph A., Treas.--Jake Sweeney Automotive Inc., Cincinnati, OH, pg. 1067
Gray, Brent J., Sr. V.P. & Chief Fin. Officer--Bremer Financial Services, Inc., St. Paul, MN, pg. 173
Gray, F. D., V.P.-Admin. & Controller--Home Fashions Div., New York, NY, pg. 400
Gray, Gardner, Jr., V.P. & Chief Fin. Officer--CSE Corporation, San Francisco, CA, pg. 204
Gray, Gardner, Jr., V.P. & Chief Fin. Officer--Civil Service Employees Insurance Co., San Francisco, CA, pg. 205
Gray, Gardner, Jr., V.P. & Chief Fin. Officer--Civil Service Employees Life Insurance Co., San Francisco, CA, pg. 205
Gray, George, Chief Fin. Officer--Furman Lumber Company, Billerica, MA, pg. 436
Gray, Gerald R., Chief Fin. Officer--Vinson Supply Co., Tulsa, OK, pg. 968
Gray, John, Comptroller & Asst. Sec.-Treas.--Sugar Cane Growers Cooperative of Florida, Belle Glade, FL, pg. 1056
Greathouse, Richard, Sr. V.P. & Treas.--Motorists Mutual Insurance Co., Columbus, OH, pg. 773
Greaves, J. Randal, Exec. V.P. & Chief Fin. Officer--Insilco Corporation, Midland, TX, pg. 571
Green, David, Chief Fin. Officer & Dir.-Investor Rels.--Coca-Cola Bottling Co. of the Southwest, San Antonio, TX, pg. 257
Green, Dick, Chief Fin. Officer--Purcell International Group, Inc., Los Angeles, CA, pg. 900
Green, James R., Chief Fin. Officer--Bearden Lumber Company, Inc., Bearden, AR, pg. 129
Green, Louis R., Chief Fin. Officer--Conestoga Wood Specialties, Inc., Earl, PA, pg. 273
Green, Stanley, Pres., Chief Exec. & Chief Fin. Officer--DAQ Electronics Inc., Middlesex, NJ, pg. 308
Greenburg, Arthur A., Sr. V.P & Chief Fin. Officer--Equity Group Investments, Chicago, IL, pg. 385
Greenburg, Mark D., V.P.-Fin. & Admin.--Robby Len Fashions, New York, NY, pg. 78
Greene, David, Exec. V.P., Chief Fin. Officer--Young & Rubicam Inc., New York, NY, pg. 1210
Greenler, Paul J., V.P.-Fin.--United Foam Plastics Corporation, Georgetown, MA, pg. 1132
Gregg, Dennis, Sr. V.P., Chief Fin. Officer--EvansGroup, Seattle, WA, pg. 391
Gregory, Carl, Chief Fin. Officer, V.P.-Fin. & Treas.--Preformed Line Products, Cleveland, OH, pg. 886
Gregory, Dennis, V.P.-Fin. & Chief Fin. Officer--Woodcraft Industries, Inc., Saint Cloud, MN, pg. 1200
Gregson, Alan, V.P.-Fin.--Levi Strauss & Co., San Francisco, CA, pg. 670
Grener, Darwin, Chief Fin. Officer--Brendamour's Sporting Goods Co., Cincinnati, OH, pg. 173
Grewe, Joseph, V.P.-Oper. & Chief Fin. Officer--Advance Machine Company, Plymouth, MN, pg. 18
Gricus, Michael J., Chief Fin. Officer & V.P.--Headco Industries, Inc., Broadview, IL, pg. 520
Griffin, Darrell, Chief Oper. Officer & Chief Fin. Officer--Williams Television Time, Inc., Santa Monica, CA, pg. 1191
Griffith, Dan L., Chief Fin. Officer & Exec. V.P.--Bridgeport Machines, Inc., Bridgeport, CT, pg. 175
Griffith, Jerry L., Sec. & Controller--J. A. Riggs Tractor Co., Little Rock, AR, pg. 934
Griffith, William C., V.P. & Chief Fin. Officer--Menasha Corporation, Neenah, WI, pg. 738
Griffith, William J., Chief Fin. Officer & Controller--Baldwin Construction, Inc., Fort Collins, CO, pg. 115
Griffiths, Barclay H., Chief Fin. Officer--White Rock Products Corp., White Stone, NY, pg. 1186
Grigg, Edward, Chief Fin. Officer--Acorn Building Components Inc., Detroit, MI, pg. 13
Griggs, David, Pres., Chief Exec. & Chief Fin. Officer & Treas.--Jack Griggs Inc., Exeter, CA, pg. 488
Grimm, Hans, Chief Fin. Officer--Lowe Luerzer GmbH, Frankfurt/Main, Germany, pg. 685
Grimm, Robert, Chief Fin. Officer--Dock Foundry Company, Three Rivers, MI, pg. 342
Grippo, John, Exec. V.P. & Chief Fin. Officer--Integrated Resources, Inc., New York, NY, pg. 573
Grismer, George, Chief Fin. Officer & Exec. V.P.--Winston Tire Company, Burbank, CA, pg. 1197
Griswold, Nannette, Chief Fin. Officer--Dakin, Inc., Burlingame, CA, pg. 311
Grob, Timothy J., V.P., Chief Fin. & Admin. Officer--Grant/Jacoby, Inc., Chicago, IL, pg. 477
Gronda, Richard, Pres.--Farrell Lines Incorporated, New York, NY, pg. 403
Grootveld, John, V.P.-Fin.--Laidlaw Corporation, Scottsdale, AZ, pg. 650
Gross, Jim, Sr. V.P. & Chief Fin. Officer--J. I. Kislak Inc., Miami Lakes, FL, pg. 633
Grossman, Bernard, V.P.-Sls., Mktg. & Fin.--M. Grossman Son, Inc., Passaic, NJ, pg. 489
Grossman, Morton, Chief Fin. Officer & Treas.--Waring & LaRosa, Inc., New York, NY, pg. 1163
Groves, D.D., V.P. & Chief Fin. Officer--SCT Yarns, Inc., Chattanooga, TN, pg. 961
Grubbe, Kenneth S., V.P.-Fin.--Ag Processing Inc A Cooperative, Omaha, NE, pg. 24
Grueter, Frank, Chief Fin. Officer & V.P.--George W. Prescott Publishing Co., Quincy, MA, pg. 887
Gruhl, Robert H., Chief Fin. Officer, Sr. V.P. & Treas.--Liberty Mutual Insurance Co., Boston, MA, pg. 674
Guarnieri, Don J., Exec. V.P., Chief Fin. Officer--Carrafiello, Diehl & Associates, Inc., Irvington, NY, pg. 225
Guccione, Anthony J., Sec. & Treas.--Omni Publications International Ltd., New York, NY, pg. 450
Guercio, Thomas R., V.P., Treas. & Chief Fin. Officer--Reliable Stores, Inc., Columbia, MD, pg. 925
Gugliotta, R., V.P.-Fin.--Uniflex, Inc., Hicksville, NY, pg. 1126
Guimond, A. Roger, Chief Fin. Officer--1st Franklin Corporation, Toccoa, GA, pg. 413
Guimond, A. Roger, Chief Fin. Officer--First Franklin Financial Corp., Toccoa, GA, pg. 413
Guimond, A. Roger, Chief Fin. Officer--Frandisco Life Insurance Co., Toccoa, GA, pg. 413
Guimond, A. Roger, Chief Fin. Officer--Franklin Securities, Inc., Toccoa, GA, pg. 413
Guimond, A. Roger, Chief Fin. Officer--Frandisco Property & Casualty Insurance, Toccoa, GA, pg. 413
Guinasso, Vic, Chief Oper. Officer--DHL Corporation, Redwood City, CA, pg. 309
Gustavson, Hakan, Treas--Young & Rubicam Sweden AB (Holding), Stockholm,, Sweden, pg. 1213
Guy, John F., V.P.-Fin. & Chief Fin. Officer--Altair Corporation, Lincolnshire, IL, pg. 45
Guzick, Louis M., Chief Fin. Officer & Sr. V.P.--Insurance Corp. of America, Houston, TX, pg. 572
Haack, Arthur L., V.P., Sec. & Chief Fin. Officer--Hickman Williams & Co. Inc., Cincinnati, OH, pg. 532
Haakenson, Paul, V.P. & Chief Fin. Officer--Freeman Shoes Company, Beloit, WI, pg. 431
Haberman, Alan L., Exec. V.P. & Chief Fin. Officer--Buxton Company, Chicopee, MA, pg. 197
Hacker, Joshua, Chm. Bd., Pres., Chief Exec. & Chief Fin. Officer--Seaboard Electronics Co., Carlsbad, CA, pg. 983
Hackerman, Willard, Pres. & Treas.--Whiting-Turner Contracting Co., Baltimore, MD, pg. 1187
Hadfield, Neil, Chm. Bd., Chief Fin. Officer & Sec.--Western Pacific Data Systems, San Diego, CA, pg. 1180
Hadley, Gary L., Treas. & Chief Exec. Officer--World Aerospace Corporation, Maple Grove, MN, pg. 1202
Haffner, Oscar H., Sr. V.P., Fin. & Chief Fin. Officer--Smith/Greenland, Incorporated, New York, NY, pg. 1012

Hafner, Tom, Chief Fin. Officer--Continental/Midland, Inc., Park Forest, IL, pg. 279
Hafstead, Christian C., Chief Fin. Officer--Bank M F & Company, Inc., Minneapolis, MN, pg. 117
Haga, Bruce, Chief Fin. Officer--Fargo Clinic Ltd., Fargo, ND, pg. 399
Hagan, James A., V.P. & Treas.--Roll Forming Corporation, Shelbyville, KY, pg. 944
Hagemann, Doug, Grp. Dir.-Fin.--FTD/Florists' Transworld Delivery Association, Southfield, MI, pg. 395
Hagen, Larry, Controller--Denver Wholesale Florists Company, Denver, CO, pg. 331
Hagopian, Comptroller--Western Reinsurance Brokers, Inc., Los Angeles, CA, pg. 1181
Hain, Bruce G., Chief Fin. Officer & V.P.--Geo-Centers, Inc., Newton Center, MA, pg. 452
Hake, J.J., Chief Fin. Officer--Duke Manufacturing Co., Inc., Saint Louis, MO, pg. 352
Hall, John L., V.P.-Fin., Treas. & Chief Fin. Officer--Schwab Corp., Lafayette, IN, pg. 980
Hall, Michael J., Sr. V.P., Treas., Chief Fin. & Admin. Officer--T.D. Williamson, Inc., Tulsa, OK, pg. 1192
Halleen, David, V.P.-Fin.--T.B. Wood's Sons Company, Chambersburg, PA, pg. 1200
Haller, W. E., V.P.-Fin., Chief Fin. Officer & Treas.--The Deutsch Company, Santa Monica, CA, pg. 333
Halpern, David, V.P., Chief Fin. Officer--Castor Advertising Corp., New York, NY, pg. 229
Halverstadt, Robert D., Treas.--ASM International, Materials Park, OH, pg. 8
Hamer, Rick, Sr. V.P.- Fin.--Penny/Ohlmann/Neiman, Inc., Dayton, OH, pg. 858
Hamilton James T., Sec. & Treas.--Independent Insurance Agents and Brokers of California, San Francisco, CA, pg. 565
Hamilton, Douglas, V.P.-Admin. & Chief Fin. Officer--USA Network, New York, NY, pg. 1124
Hamm, Lotuce L., Jr., Sr. V.P. & Treas.--Mutual Savings Life Insurance Company, Decatur, AL, pg. 1150
Hammel, Robert E., Chief Fin. Officer, Treas. & Sec.--Ohio Machinery Co., Cleveland, OH, pg. 822
Hammon, Dennis, V.P., Controller & Chief Fin. Officer--Young's Market Company, Los Angeles, CA, pg. 1214
Hammond, Jerry, V.P., Treas. & Sec.--Cargill Fertilizer, Inc., Riverview, FL, pg. 219
Hampel, Robert E., Sr. Exec. Chief Fin. Officer, Treas. & Sec.--Keller Crescent Co., Evansville, IN, pg. 626
Hanna, Allan C., Pres. & Chief Exec. Officer--Zephyr Inc., North Muskegon, MI, pg. 1217
Hannah, David, Chief Fin. Officer--Metalcenter, Inc., Santa Fe Springs, CA, pg. 742
Hannah, David H., Chief Fin. Officer & Exec. V.P.--Reliance Steel & Aluminum Co., Los Angeles, CA, pg. 925
Hansen, Jeffery, Chief Fin. Officer--Horizon Paper Co., Inc., New York, NY, pg. 544
Hanson, Dale S., Chief Fin. Officer, V.P.-Fin. & Treas.--C. H. Robinson Co. Inc., Eden Prairie, MN, pg. 939
Hantak, Susan, Exec. V.P. & Controller--Willert Home Products, Inc., Saint Louis, MO, pg. 1190
Harbottle, John, Controller--Wham-O Div. of Kransco, San Gabriel, CA, pg. 644
Harbottle, John, Chief Fin. Officer & V.P. Fin.--Institutional Financing Services, Benicia, CA, pg. 571
Hardaway, R.K., Chief Fin. Officer & Sr. V.P.--Ingram Micro Inc., Santa Ana, CA, pg. 569
Hardin, Donald M., V.P. & Chief Fin. Officer--CCI Corporation, Tulsa, OK, pg. 200
Harding, Marvin E., V.P., Chief Fin. Officer, Treas. & Sec.--Artesian Development Corporation, Newark, DE, pg. 86
Hardwick, Anthony, Controller--Collins & Aikman Textile Group, Charlotte, NC, pg. 262
Hardy, J.D., V.P.-Fin.--Farmhand, Inc., Excelsior, MN, pg. 402
Hardy, Richard T., Jr., V.P.-Mortgage Lending--First National Bank of Blue Island, Blue Island, IL, pg. 481
Harkleroad, Fred A., Treas., Controller & Chief Fin. Officer--Cleveland Group, Inc., Atlanta, GA, pg. 255
Harmon, Linda L., Chief Fin. Officer & Treas.--Progressive Driver Services, Inc., Jacksonville, FL, pg. 894
Harmon, Michael E., Chief Fin. Officer--The Western Group, Saint Louis, MO, pg. 1179
Harms, Daniel C., V.P.-Fin.--JII/Sales Promotion Associates, Inc., Coshocton, OH, pg. 604
Harnass, R. Ray, Partner & Chief Fin. Officer--J. C. Bradford & Co., Nashville, TN, pg. 170
Harney, Dwayne, Chief Fin. Officer--Allied Security, International, Spokane, WA, pg. 40
Harr, Richard, Sr. V.P.-Fin.--NRM-Steelastic, Akron, OH, pg. 781
Harr, Richard K., V.P.-Fin. & Treas.--NRM Corporation, Columbiana, OH, pg. 781
Harrah, Glen, Treas.--Goodkind & O'Dea, Inc., Rutherford, NJ, pg. 334
Harrah, Glen R., Chief Fin. Officer--Dewberry & Davis, Fairfax, VA, pg. 334
Harris, Anna M., Asst. Cashier--The National Bank of Sussex County, Branchville, NJ, pg. 534
Harris, Brian, Chief Fin. Officer-Worldwide--Cato Johnson Worldwide, New York, NY, pg. 1210
Harris, George, Pres. & Chief Fin. Officer--Harris, Baio & McCullough Inc., Philadelphia, PA, pg. 511
Harris, Jay, Chief Fin. Officer & Treas.--Aetna Health Plans, San Bruno, CA, pg. 23
Harrison, Carl W., Sec. & Treas.--Lincoln Steel, Lincoln, NE, pg. 834
Harrison, Douglas M., V.P.-Fin., Chief Fin. Officer & Treas.--Lyon Metal Products, Inc., Montgomery, IL, pg. 690
Harrison, Sandra, Sec. & Treas.--Bill Wink Chevrolet & GEO, Dearborn, MI, pg. 1196
Hart, Wayne, V.P., Chief Fin. Officer--Barkley & Evergreen Advertising, Inc., Shawnee Mission, KS, pg. 120
Hartig, Donald E., V.P. & Controller--Safelite Autoglass, Wichita, KS, pg. 664
Hartleb, E.G., Chief Fin. Officer & V.P.--The Georgia Marble Company, Kennesaw, GA, pg. 453
Hartley, George S., V.P. & Chief Fin. Officer--Romanoff International, Inc., Charlotte, NC, pg. 945
Hartman, Lawrence M., Chief Fin. Officer & Exec. V.P.--Velsicol Chemical Corporation, Rosemont, IL, pg. 1147
Hartman, Robert J., V.P. & Treas.--Central-United Life Insurance Co., Sioux City, IA, pg. 233
Hartman, William, Chief Fin. Officer--International Airline Support Group, Inc., Miami, FL, pg. 575
Hartung, Steven L., Chief Fin. Officer & V.P.--Markair, Inc., Anchorage, AK, pg. 708
Hartwell, Samuel A., Co-Chm. Bd. & Chief Fin. Officer--G.S. Blodgett Corporation, Burlington, VT, pg. 157
Harvey, Curtis R., Exec. V.P. & Chief Fin. Officer--First Abilene Bankshares, Inc., Abilene, TX, pg. 411
Haskins, Luther, V.P.-Fin.--Clear Shield National, Inc., Wheeling, IL, pg. 383
Hatcher, Stephen R., Sr. V.P.-Admin. & Chief Fin. Officer--The Union Central Life Insurance Co., Cincinnati, OH, pg. 1127
Hatcher, Steve, Chief Fin. Officer--Houck Industries, Inc., Tulare, CA, pg. 545
Hatt, Peter M., Chm. & Chief Exec. Officer--Borders, Perrin & Norrander, Inc., Portland, OR, pg. 165
Hattox, Brock A., Sr. V.P. & Chief Fin. Officer--The Babcock & Wilcox Company, New Orleans, LA, pg. 107
Haugen, Corky, Mgr.-Admin. & Fin.--North Dakota Mill & Elevator Association, Grand Forks, ND, pg. 813
Haupt, Roger A., Vice Chm. & Chief Fin. Officer--Leo Burnett Company, Inc., Chicago, IL, pg. 191
Hautamaki, Bob, Chief Fin. Officer--Martin Universal Design, Inc., Westland, MI, pg. 715
Hautamaki, Robert, Chief Fin. Officer--Martin F. Weber Company, Philadelphia, PA, pg. 716
Havner, Ronald, Chief Fin. Officer--Public Storage, Inc., Glendale, CA, pg. 898
Hawes, Don, V.P. & Chief Fin. Officer--Allfast Fastening Systems, Inc., City of Industry, CA, pg. 37
Hawkins, Arthur O., V.P., Chief Fin. Officer & Treas.--U.S. Computer Services, Rancho Cordova, CA, pg. 1135
Hawkins, Jonathan A., Sr. V.P. & Chief Fin. Officer--Southern States Cooperative, Inc., Richmond, VA, pg. 1022
Hawkins, Robert E., Chief Fin. Officer, Treas., Controller & Sec.--West Union Corp., Memphis, TN, pg. 1177
Hawkins, William F., Sr. V.P.-Fin. & Admin.--Mississippi Chemical Corporation, Yazoo City, MS, pg. 760
Hawley, Gary, V.P.-Fin. & Chief Fin. Officer--Snyder's Drug Stores, Inc., Minnetonka, MN, pg. 1015
Hay, James F., Chief Fin. Officer & V.P.--Valk Manufacturing Company, New Kingstown, PA, pg. 1143
Hay, Lewis, Chief Oper. & Chief Fin. Officer--J P Foodservice, Inc., Hanover, MD, pg. 586
Haydel, Agatha M., Treas.--Walk, Haydel & Associates, Inc., New Orleans, LA, pg. 1159
Hayes, Bill, V.P.-Fin.--Varel Manufacturing Co., Dallas, TX, pg. 1145
Hayes, Forrest, Chief Fin. Officer--Dempster, Inc., Toccoa, GA, pg. 328
Hayes, Kathleen A., Sec. & Treas.--Kennington Properties, Inc., Los Angeles, CA, pg. 623
Hays, Don L., Chief Fin. Officer & Treas.--Diemakers, Inc., Monroe City, MO, pg. 336
Hays, Gloria A., Treas.--Town & Country Ford Inc., Louisville, KY, pg. 1103
Hayward, Charles W., V.P.-Fin. & Admin. & Chief Fin. Officer--Amtrak-National Railroad Passenger Corp., Washington, DC, pg. 69
Hazan, Craig M., Chief Fin. Officer & Controller--The Jaydor Corporation, Millburn, NJ, pg. 591
Hazan, Mark, Controller--Trizec Properties, Inc., Encino, CA, pg. 1115
Heeke, Ron, Contr.--Supreme Feeders, Inc., Liberal, KS, pg. 1128
Heerey, Dan, Chief Fin. Officer--La Belle Industries, Inc., Oconomowoc, WI, pg. 648
Heery, Joseph, V.P. & Chief Fin. Officer--Cyborg Systems, Inc., Chicago, IL, pg. 307
Heinrichs, Chief Fin. Officer--Western Data Systems, Calabasas, CA, pg. 1178
Heiserman, Hewitt, V.P., Treas. & Sec.--Kingsbury, Inc., Philadelphia, PA, pg. 632
Heist, Gary A., Chief Fin. Officer & Treas.--Continental Machines, Inc., Savage, MN, pg. 279
Heistand, Mark A., Chief Fin. Officer--Union City Body Company, Inc., Union City, IN, pg. 1128
Heit, Stephen A., Chief Fin. Officer & Treas.--Pavion Ltd., Nyack on Hudson, NY, pg. 852
Helber, Larry C., Chief Fin. Officer--R. L. Polk & Co., Detroit, MI, pg. 879
Held, John R., Treas.--Princeville Corporation, Princeville, HI, pg. 890
Held, K. Lars, Treas. & Sec.--Overly Manufacturing Co., Greensburg, PA, pg. 833
Helen Nielsen, Chief Fin. Officer--Ed Walpert & Associates, Rancho Mirage, CA, pg. 1161
Hellreigel, Michael C., V.P., Controller & Asst. Sec.--Butler Service Group, Inc., Montvale, NJ, pg. 197
Helman, Herb, Treas.--Murry's, Inc., Forestville, MD, pg. 777
Helmbrecht, Glen V., Chief Fin. Officer & Sec.--Mayville Engineering Co., Inc., Mayville, WI, pg. 725
Hels, Michael, Chief Fin. Officer--Transilwrap Company, Inc., Chicago, IL, pg. 1107
Helt, John, Treas.--Wisconsin Dairies Cooperative, Baraboo, WI, pg. 1197
Hemminger, Kent, Dir.-Fin. Services--Eco Water Systems, Saint Paul, MN, pg. 367
Hempel, Kathleen J., Sr. Exec. V.P. & Chief Fin. Officer--Fort Howard Corporation, Green Bay, WI, pg. 425
Henderson, Jerome, Controller--Brooks Beverages Inc., Columbus, OH, pg. 179
Hendrix, William J., Chief Fin. Officer & V.P.-Fin.--Home Interiors & Gifts, Inc., Dallas, TX, pg. 541
Hengels, Charles F., Chief Fin. Officer--System Planning Corp., Arlington, VA, pg. 1070
Henley, Dale, Sr. V.P.-Fin. & Chief Fin. Officer--Haggen's, Inc., Bellingham, WA, pg. 499
Hennessey, Edward, Chief Fin. Officer--Littleton Coin Co., Inc., Littleton, NH, pg. 679
Hennessy, Dennis J., Chief Fin. Officer, Treas. & V.P.-Fin.--The Nash Engineering Company, Norwalk, CT, pg. 783
Hennigan, Gerald J., Chief Fin. Officer--Rotterdam Ventures Inc., Guilderland Center, NY, pg. 951
Henry, Joseph C., V.P., Treas. & Chief Fin. Officer--The Hanover Insurance Company, Worcester, MA, pg. 34
Henry, Joseph P., V.P.-Fin. & Admin.--Wheelock Inc., Long Branch, NJ, pg. 1185
Henry, Robert M., Vice Chm., Chief Fin. Officer--McCaffrey and McCall, New York, NY, pg. 726
Henry, Roy, Chief Acctg. Officer--Remington Products Inc., Bridgeport, CT, pg. 926
Henseler, Udo, Chief Fin. Officer--Coulter Corporation, Hialeah, FL, pg. 289
Hensley, Tom, V.P. & Chief Fin. Officer--Fieldale Corporation, Baldwin, GA, pg. 409
Herbert, Richard, Pres., Chief Exec. & Fin. Officer--VanDine, Humphrey, Herbert, Alber & Manges, Inc., Pittsburgh, PA, pg. 1145
Herbert, Steven, Chief Fin. Officer & V.P.--Riverside Millwork Company, Inc., Panacook, NH, pg. 937
Hermier, Patrick, Chief Fin. Officer--Spirit Cruises, Norfolk, VA, pg. 1031
Hernandez, Noel, Chm. Bd., Pres. & Chief Fin. Officer--Graphic Productions Company, Miami, FL, pg. 478
Herreid, Mark, V.P.-Fin.--Carlson Real Estate Company, Minneapolis, MN, pg. 221
Herrmann, Harold, Chief Fin. Officer & Controller--William B. Reily & Co., Inc., New Orleans, LA, pg. 923
Hertel, Janie, Controller--West Central Co-op, Ralston, IA, pg. 1176
Hess, Frank, Chief Fin. Officer--National Bulk Carriers, Inc., New York, NY, pg. 786
Hess, Gerald, Comptroller--Rutt Custom Cabinetry, Goodville, PA, pg. 957
Hess, R. Gene, V.P. & Controller--Doane Products Co., Joplin, MO, pg. 342
Hess, R. Gene, Chief Fin. Officer--Doane Products Co., Branded Sales Div., Joplin, MO, pg. 342
Hesselschwerdt, Paul, Chief Fin. Officer & V.P.--ODI, Burlington, MA, pg. 818
Hessler, David J., Sec. & Treas.--MTD Products Limited, Kitchener,, Canada, pg. 694
Hetzell, Jack H., II, V.P.-Fin.--Systech Computer Corporation, San Diego, CA, pg. 1071
Heuman, M., Sr. V.P. & Treas.--Uniflex, Inc., Hicksville, NY, pg. 1126
Hewett, Jack A., Sr. V.P.-Admin., Chief Fin. Officer & Treas.--VASA North Atlantic Insurance Company, Indianapolis, IN, pg. 1146
Hicks, Carroll C., Asst. Treas.--News-Press & Gazette Company, St. Joseph, MA, pg. 804
Hielke, William E., Controller, Admin. Sec. & Chief Fin. Officer--Bata Shoe Co., Inc., Belcamp, MD, pg. 201
Hieronymus, James, Chief Fin. Officer--Time Index, Inc., Phoenix, AZ, pg. 1097
Hieronymus, James A., Chief Fin. Officer--Time Systems, Inc., Phoenix, AZ, pg. 1097
High, Malcolm, Controller--TAD Technical Services Corp., Cambridge, MA, pg. 1071
Hightower, Linda, Controller--Dean Sellers Ford Inc., Troy, MI, pg. 988
Hilberg, Steve, Chief Fin. Officer--Orchard Supply Hardware, San Jose, CA, pg. 828
Hilbert, Steve, Controller--Berkeley Industries Inc., Laguna Beach, CA, pg. 141
Hildebrand, Sheryl, Chief Fin. Officer, Dir.-Human Resources & Employee Benefits--Pace International Corporation, Kirkland, WA, pg. 838
Hilger, Kenneth, Treas. & Chief Fin. Officer--Gardiner Metal Company, Chicago, IL, pg. 443
Hill, John P., Jr., Chief Fin. Officer--Heery International, Inc., Atlanta, GA, pg. 525
Hill, Justin, Jr., Sec. & Treas.--Lawrence Paper Company, Lawrence, KS, pg. 662
Hill, Max E., Chief Fin. Officer, V.P.-Fin. & Sec.--I.C. System, Inc., Vadnais Heights, MN, pg. 558
Hill, Michael O., Chief Fin. Officer--Andersen Consulting, Chicago, IL, pg. 72
Hillegeist, Willard, Chief Fin. Officer--SAIC Canada, Ottawa,, Canada, pg. 982
Hinderer, H. William III, Chief Fin. Officer & V.P.-Fin. & Admin.--Tacony Corporation, Fenton, MO, pg. 1076
Hindman, Robert A., Chief Fin. Officer--Brix Maritime Barging, Inc., Portland, OR, pg. 177
Hinds, Dan J., V.P. & Chief Fin. Officer--N. G. Gilbert Corporation, Muncie, IN, pg. 458
Hinds, Ron, V.P.-Credits & Collections--Texas Refinery Corp., Fort Worth, TX, pg. 1089
Hinkle, Max E., Chm. Bd., Pres., Chief Exec. Officer & Treas.--Rowtronics Company Inc., Indianapolis, IN, pg. 953
Hinman, Kirk, Pres., Chief Exec. Officer, Chief Fin. Officer & Treas.--Rome Strip Steel Co., Inc., Rome, NY, pg. 946
Hirman, Arland E., V.P., Sec. & Treas.--Advanstar Communications, Cleveland, OH, pg. 21
Hirsch, J.E., Exec. V.P. & Treas.--Mid-Continent Screw Products Co., Lincolnwood, IL, pg. 750
Hirsch, Leonard, V.P.-Fin. & Chief Fin. Officer--General Tools Mfg., New York, NY, pg. 451
Hixon, Maxine, V.P.-Fin.--Tri-State Wholesale Associated Grocers, El Paso, TX, pg. 1111
Hober, Calvin, Comptroller--Atlas Tag & Label Inc., Neenah, WI, pg. 153
Hoblett, Tom, Chief Fin. Officer--Bridgeman's Restaurants Inc., Minneapolis, MN, pg. 175

Hocking, Scott T., V.P. & Chief Fin. Officer--Insignia Financial Group, Inc., Greenville, SC, pg. 571
Hocum, Kevin, Chief Fin. Officer--The Electron Corp., Littleton, CO, pg. 375
Hocum, Kevin, Controller--RELA, Inc., Boulder, CO, pg. 924
Hodge, William W., V.P.-Fin. & Chief Fin. Officer--American Fast Print, Limited, Spartanburg, SC, pg. 52
Hodges, Steve, Sec. & Treas.--Varel Manufacturing Co., Dallas, TX, pg. 1145
Hoelterhoff, Ernest R., Treas. & Chief Fin. Officer--Harza Engineering Co., Chicago, IL, pg. 516
Hoff, George H., Exec. V.P. & Chief Fin. Officer--Sargento Incorporated, Plymouth, WI, pg. 971
Hoff, George H., Sec. & Treas.--Sargento Food Service Corp., Plymouth, WI, pg. 971
Hoff, George H., V.P.-Fin. & Admin.--Sargento Cheese Co., Plymouth, WI, pg. 971
Hoffman, Ebba C., Chm., Pres., Chief Exec. & Chief Fin. Officer--Smead Manufacturing Company, Hastings, MN, pg. 1011
Hoffman, Mark E., Chief Fin. Officer--Globe International Inc., Buffalo, NY, pg. 464
Hoffman, N., Fin. Admin.--Rainbow Apparel Distribution Center, Brooklyn, NY, pg. 910
Hoh, Shinsure, Chief Fin. Officer--Steelox Systems, Inc., Mason, OH, pg. 1044
Hojer, Susan, Chief Fin. Officer--Stocker & Yale, Inc., Beverly, MA, pg. 1050
Hojer, Susan, Chief Fin. Officer, Controller & Mgr.-Personnel--MFE Instruments, Beverly, MA, pg. 1050
Holbrook, Sandra, Chief Fin. Officer--Dalfort Corp., Dallas, TX, pg. 312
Holcomb, Fred A., Chief Fin. Officer--Beckwith Machinery Company, Murrysville, PA, pg. 131
Holden, Shirley, Treas., Sec. & Controller--Royal Oldsmobile Mazda, Inc., Metairie, LA, pg. 953
Holding, Carol, Treas.--Little America Refining, Salt Lake City, UT, pg. 1008
Hollingsworth, Linda, Sec. & Treas.--Sun Bulb Company, Inc., Arcadia, FL, pg. 1058
Hollis, Rob, Chief Fin. Officer & V.P.--Atlanta Market Center, Atlanta, GA, pg. 94
Hollowell, Mike, Chief Fin. Officer--Circle A.W. Products, Co., Portland, OR, pg. 250
Holman, Robert, V.P.-Fin.--Reinalt-Thomas Corp., Ann Arbor, MI, pg. 923
Holmes, George B., Pres., Chief Exec. & Chief Fin. Officer--Dombrowski & Holmes, Inc., Chicago, IL, pg. 343
Holson, Philip L., Sr. V.P. & Chief Fin. Officer--Associated Industrial Supply, Inc., Columbia, SC, pg. 90
Honeycutt, Mark, V.P.-Admin. & Chief Fin. Officer--PBM Office Products, Cleveland, OH, pg. 835
Hong, Hughie, Chief Fin. Officer--Teachers Management & Investment Corporation, Newport Beach, CA, pg. 1082
Honig, Burton A., Chief Fin. Officer--Freeson Advertising Agency, Miami Lakes, FL, pg. 431
Honzl, John J., V.P. & Chief Fin. Officer--Scicom Data Services, Ltd., Minnetonka, MN, pg. 981
Hood, Robert, Sr. V.P. & Chief Fin. Officer--Crowley Maritime Corporation, Oakland, CA, pg. 301
Hooker, Bruce, Sr. V.P. & Chief Fin. Officer--Amperif Corporation, Chatsworth, CA, pg. 68
Hope, David W., Chief Fin. Officer & V.P. Fin.--Red Ball Corporation, Seattle, WA, pg. 918
Horan, Dennis, Sec. & Treas.--U.R.M. Stores, Inc., Spokane, WA, pg. 1124
Horan, Don, Sr. V.P.-Fin., Chief Fin. Officer, Sec. & Treas.--Macklanburg-Duncan Co., Oklahoma City, OK, pg. 697
Horberg, Jane, Controller--Best Kosher Sausage Co., Chicago, IL, pg. 146
Horn, Richard, Pres. & Treas.--Mulberry Metal Products, Inc., Union, NJ, pg. 775
Horowitz, Kenneth J., V.P.-Fin.--Scott Printing Corporation, Jersey City, NJ, pg. 983
Horsley, Douglas M., Chief Fin. Officer--Altama Delta Corp., Darien, GA, pg. 45
Horsman, Raymond D., V.P. & Chief Fin. Officer--Mulach Steel Corporation, Bridgeville, PA, pg. 775
Horton, Ron, Controller--Rochester Gauges Inc. Of Texas, Dallas, TX, pg. 444
Hotchman, John, V.P.-Fin.--Central Point Software, Inc., Beaverton, OR, pg. 234
Hough, Tom, Chief Fin. Officer--Gregg Industries, Inc., El Monte, CA, pg. 486
Houlihan, Lawrence, Chm. Bd., Pres., Chief Exec. & Chief Fin. Officer, Treas. & Sec.--Frank B. Ross Co. Inc., Jersey City, NJ, pg. 949
Houseman, James E., Pres. & Treas.--Harrop Industries, Inc., Columbus, OH, pg. 512
Hov, Don, Chief Fin. Officer, Fin. & Admin.--Anderson & Lembke Inc., New York, NY, pg. 244
Howard, Gregory, V.P.-Opers.--Polaris Pool Systems, Inc., San Marcos, CA, pg. 878
Howard, James H., Chief Fin. Officer & Corp. Sec.--Stowe-Pharr Mills, Inc., McAdenville, NC, pg. 1052
Howe, Harold, Jr., Chm. Bd., Chief Exec. Officer & Treas.--Howe Furniture Corporation, Trumbull, CT, pg. 547
Howell, Danny, Loan Officer--Wieland Financial Services, Inc., Atlanta, GA, pg. 1188
Howell, Ken, Chief Fin. Officer--Clayton, Williams & Sherwood, Inc., Newport Beach, CA, pg. 254
Hoy, Patrick, Chief Fin. Officer & V.P.--Pacesetter Corporation, Omaha, NE, pg. 839
Hubbard, Allan B., Treas.--Technicare Cleaning Systems Inc., Indianapolis, IN, pg. 359
Hubbard, Jim, Chief Fin. Officer--Sun Lakes Marketing, Sun Lakes, AZ, pg. 1059
Hubbard, Sonja, Treas. & Sec.--Yates Enterprises Inc., Texarkana, TX, pg. 1207
Huber, Michael J., Chief Fin. Officer--The Bases Group, Covington, KY, pg. 124
Huddilston, Robert P., Chief Fin. Officer & Exec. V.P.--Meldrum & Fewsmith Communications Inc., Cleveland, OH, pg. 737
Hudson, John K., Chief Fin. Officer--Young Refining Corp., Douglasville, GA, pg. 1210
Huebner, Donald F., Chief Fin. Officer, Treas. & Controller--Active Electrical Supply Company, Chicago, IL, pg. 15
Huettl, Thomas R., Sr. V.P., Chief Oper. Officer, Treas. & Sec.--Steenberg Homes, Inc., Fond du Lac, WI, pg. 1045
Huey, Brenda, Exec. V.P., Chief Fin. Officer--Barry Huey, Bullock & Cook Advertising, Inc., Birmingham, AL, pg. 551
Huffman, Dale, Controller--Larkin, Inc., Atlanta, GA, pg. 667
Hughes, Nick, Chief Fin. Officer, Treas. & Controller--TV Host Inc., Harrisburg, PA, pg. 1075
Hughes, T.D., Chief Exec. & Chief Fin. Officer--La Rosa's, Inc., Cincinnati, OH, pg. 649
Huisman, Bruce, Acct. Mgr.--Preferred Risk Life Insurance Co., West Des Moines, IA, pg. 886
Hull, Kenneth J., Chief Fin. Officer--Follett Corporation, Chicago, IL, pg. 422
Humphrey, Gene, Chief Fin. Officer--Taylor Medical Inc., Beaumont, TX, pg. 1081
Hunceker, Jay, V.P.-Fin.--Cal/Emblem Labels, Inc., Fresno, CA, pg. 208
Hunger, John E., Chief Fin. Officer & Treas.--World Shipping, Inc., Lakewood, OH, pg. 1203
Hunger, John E., Chief Fin. Officer--Container Port Group, Cleveland, OH, pg. 1203
Hungler, Charles, Chief Fin. Officer--Granite State Packing Co., Manchester, NH, pg. 476
Hunt, William, Chief Fin. Officer--Spirol International Corp., Danielson, CT, pg. 1031
Huntoon, Christopher L., Chief Fin. Officer & Sr. V.P.-Fin.--Hollingsworth & Vose Co., East Walpole, MA, pg. 539
Huntting, J.G., Jr., Chief Exec. & Chief Fin. Officer--Huntting Elevator Co., Austin, MN, pg. 555
Hurst, Larry, Chief Fin. Officer--Messenger Corporation, Phoenix, AZ, pg. 741
Hutchings, Peter, Exec. V.P. & Chief Fin. Officer--The Guardian Life Insurance Company of America, New York, NY, pg. 492
Hyland, Robert J., Chief Fin. Officer & Treas.--Barclay White Incorporated, Berwyn, PA, pg. 119
Hymonitz, Mitchell, Chief Fin. Officer--American Passage Media Corporation, Seattle, WA, pg. 59
Ihle, Herbert, Sr. V.P.-Fin. & Controller--NWA, Inc., Saint Paul, MN, pg. 782
Imp, Raymond A., V.P.-Fin. & Chief Fin. Officer--ICM Industries, Inc., Chicago, IL, pg. 559
Infalvi, Daman, V.P.-Fin. & Chief Fin. Officer--Fibre Glass-Evercoat Company Inc., Cincinnati, OH, pg. 408
Ingram, James G., Chief Fin. Officer & V.P.--Ingram Paper Company, City of Industry, CA, pg. 569
Isaacs, Debbie, V.P.-Fin. & Controller--AmTran Corporation, Conway, AR, pg. 69
Isaacson, Steve, Chief Fin. Officer--Delta Queen Steamboat Company, New Orleans, LA, pg. 385
Jablonski, James J., Chief Fin. Officer & Sec.--BCM Engineers Inc., Plymouth Meeting, PA, pg. 106
Jackson, C.T., V.P. & Chief Fin. Officer--Maguire Oil Co., Dallas, TX, pg. 701
Jackson, Gilda, Dir.-Acctng.--Seattle Packaging Corporation, Seattle, WA, pg. 986
Jackson, Kathy, Chief Fin. Officer--Communico, Indianapolis, IN, pg. 270
Jackson, Robert R., Chief Fin. Officer--Zippo Manufacturing Company, Bradford, PA, pg. 1220
Jackson, Tom, Chief Fin. Officer & Controller--Blitz U.S.A., Inc., Miami, OK, pg. 157
Jacobs, David, Chief Fin. Officer--Rosewood Property Company, Dallas, TX, pg. 949
Jacobs, Frank D., V.P. & Chief Fin. Officer--Golden West Homes, Santa Ana, CA, pg. 467
Jacobson, Hugh N., Exec. V.P.-Treas.--Wexner & Jacobson, Inc., Memphis, TN, pg. 1183
Jacobson, Robert N., V.P.-Fin., Treas., Sec. & Chief Fin. Officer--The Atlas Construction Co., Stamford, CT, pg. 96
Jacobstein, David M., V.P.-Fin.--Wilmorite Inc., Rochester, NY, pg. 1193
Jacoby, Andrea, Chief Fin. Officer--MBT Associates, Inc., San Francisco, CA, pg. 691
Jadick, Anne, Chief Fin. Officer--Devon Direct Marketing & Advertising, Inc., Berwyn, PA, pg. 334
Jaeger, Stuart, Controller--Henry I. Siegel Company, Inc., New York, NY, pg. 1002
Jaeschke, Bob, Chief Fin. Officer--Arian, Lowe, Travis & Gusick, Inc., Chicago, IL, pg. 82
James, George, Sr. V.P. & Chief Fin. Officer--Levi Strauss & Co., San Francisco, CA, pg. 670
Janavey, Harry, V.P., Chief Fin. Officer--Geer, DuBois Inc., New York, NY, pg. 447
Janofsky, William, Controller--Van Son Holland Ink Corp. of America, Mineola, NY, pg. 1144
Janulis, John R., Chief Fin. Officer--Thomas & Betts Holdings, Inc., Memphis, TN, pg. 425
Jarvin, Frances M., Sec. & Treas.--Geo. F. Schuler, Inc., Stockton, CA, pg. 979
Jarzembinski, Peter P., V.P.-Fin. & Chief Fin. Officer--Journal Communications Inc., Milwaukee, WI, pg. 607
Jastrem, John F., Sr. V.P. & Chief Fin. Officer--Knapp Communications Corporation, Los Angeles, CA, pg. 636
Jastren, John, Chief Fin. Officer--Bon Appetit Magazine, Los Angeles, CA, pg. 636
Javage, Dan, V.P.-Fin.--MCRB Service Bureau, Inc., North Hollywood, CA, pg. 691
Jay, Dan, Pres., Chief Exec. & Chief Fin. Officer--Campmor Inc., Paramus, NJ, pg. 213
Jeffris, Ronald D., V.P. & Chief Fin. Officer--Apco Argentina Inc., Tulsa, OK, pg. 77
Jenkins, Gary E., Chief Fin. Officer & Treas.--Academy Insurance Group, Inc., Atlanta, GA, pg. 11
Jenkins, M., Treas.--Thruway Fasteners Inc., North Tonawanda, NY, pg. 1096
Jenning, William, V.P.-Fin.--Tanning Research Labs., Inc., Ormond Beach, FL, pg. 1078
Jensen, David H., V.P.-Fin., Opers. & Real Estate--Smith Frozen Foods, Inc., Weston, OR, pg. 1012
Jensen, Jon, Controller & Treas.--Philadelphia Gear Corp., King of Prussia, PA, pg. 866
Jepsen, Edward G., Exec. V.P., Chief Fin. Officer & Controller--LPL Technologies, Inc., Wallingford, CT, pg. 648
Jeske, Steve, Chief Fin. Officer--PetCare Plus, Inc., Addison, IL, pg. 863
Jett, Marvin, V.P. & Treas.--Dualite Inc., Williamsburg, OH, pg. 350
Jewell, Stanley R., Chief Fin. Officer & V.P.-Fin.--RHC/Spacemaster Corporation, Melrose Park, IL, pg. 906
Johansson, Nils A., Sr. V.P. & Chief Fin. Officer--Bell & Howell Company, Skokie, IL, pg. 134
John, David, Chief Fin. Officer--HP Direct, Indianapolis, IN, pg. 497
Johnsey, Walter, Exec. V.P.-Admin., Chief Fin. Officer & Treas.--Drummond Company, Inc., Jasper, AL, pg. 349
Johnson, Greg A., Treas. & Controller--F.H. Stoltze Land & Lumber Company, Stillwater, MN, pg. 1050
Johnson, James R., Chief Fin. Officer--Premier Industries, Inc., Tacoma, WA, pg. 887
Johnson, John C., Co-Chief Exec. Officer--Steuart Petroleum Company, Washington, DC, pg. 1048
Johnson, Joyce, Controller-West Region--Specialty Restaurants Corporation, Anaheim, CA, pg. 1027
Johnson, Lee R., Chief Fin. Officer--Gator Freightways, Inc., Wilmington, OH, pg. 446
Johnson, Michael, Chief Fin. Officer--Jemison, Inc., Memphis, TN, pg. 592
Johnson, Peter, Chief Fin. Officer--Deacon Day Advertising and The McLauchlan Group, Toronto,, Canada, pg. 685
Johnson, Robert A., Dir.-Fin.--Ridg-U-Rak, Inc., North East, PA, pg. 933
Johnson, Roger J., Sr. V.P.-Corp. Info. Services, Chief Fin. Officer & Treas.--Aid Association For Lutherans, Appleton, WI, pg. 26
Johnson, Victor, Chief Fin. Officer, V.P.-Fin. & Treas.--Reinke Manufacturing Co., Inc., Deshler, NE, pg. 924
Johnson, Walter D., Exec. V.P., Chief Fin. Officer & Sec.--Johnson Bros. Corp., Litchfield, MN, pg. 597
Johnson, William, Exec. V.P. & Chief Fin. Officer--Camping World Holdings, Inc., Bowling Green, KY, pg. 213
Jonas, John M., Chief Fin. Officer, V.P. & Sec.--Syar Industries, Inc., Napa, CA, pg. 1068
Jones, A. Ray, Controller--Custom Fabrics Div., West Point, GA, pg. 400
Jones, Andy, Chief Fin. Officer--Dupey Management Corp., Irving, TX, pg. 354
Jones, Don, Chief Fin. Officer--Gebo Distributing Co., Inc., Plainview, TX, pg. 447
Jones, Gordon, V.P. & Chief Fin. Officer--Arcade Inc., Chattanooga, TN, pg. 80
Jones, J. Gregory, Pres. & Chief Fin. Officer--Peck Jones Construction, Los Angeles, CA, pg. 854
Jones, James E., Chief Fin. Officer, Sec. & Treas.--Modern Welding Co., Inc., Owensboro, KY, pg. 763
Jones, Jean, Comptroller--Rome Manufacturing Co., Rome, GA, pg. 945
Jones, Jim, Chief Fin. Officer--The Reliable Corp., Chicago, IL, pg. 924
Jones, Kenneth, Exec. V.P., Chief Fin. Officer, Sec. & Treas.--Hatfield Quality Meats, Inc., Hatfield, PA, pg. 517
Jones, Lamar S., Sr. V.P., Chief Fin. Officer, Sec. & Dir.-Admin.--Kirkpatrick Pettis, Omaha, NE, pg. 779
Jones, Larry L., Treas. & Sec.--Rieth-Riley Construction Co. Inc., Goshen, IN, pg. 934
Jones, Margaret L., Controller--Grant-Lydick Beverage Co., San Antonio, TX, pg. 477
Jones, Richard F., V.P.-Fin. & Chief Fin. Officer--Arinc Inc., Annapolis, MD, pg. 82
Jones, Robert, Chief Fin. Officer--I Ski Ski Goggles, City of Commerce, CA, pg. 557
Jones, Russell B., Sr. V.P.-Fin., Treas., Chief Fin. Officer & Sec.--GranTree Corporation, Beaverton, OR, pg. 477
Jones, Sara, Controller & Chief Fin. Officer--The Criterion Group, Inc., Atlanta, GA, pg. 299
Jones, Thomas E., Jr., Chief Oper. & Chief Fin. Officer--Steadly Company, Carthage, MO, pg. 1043
Joyce, Michael D., Chief Fin. Officer--Echevarria Angel Co., Inc., Los Angeles, CA, pg. 365
Judson, Christopher M., Chief Fin. Officer--McKellar Developers of La Jolla, San Diego, CA, pg. 730
Jungwirth, Philip R., Chief Fin. Officer--Brown & Bigelow, Inc., Saint Paul, MN, pg. 181
Jurek, Steve, Chief Fin. Officer--Gold'n Plump, Inc., Saint Cloud, MN, pg. 584
Kabay, John K., Sr. V.P., Chief Fin. Officer & Treas.--Calvin Klein, Inc., New York, NY, pg. 635
Kaczor, Walt, Sr. V.P. & Chief Fin. Officer--Professional Healthcare Systems, Inc., Los Angeles, CA, pg. 894
Kadenbach, Axel, Chief Fin. Officer--Dr. Puttner & BSB Worldwide Werbegesellschaft m.b.H., Vienna, Austria, pg. 111
Kagan, Donald, Chief Fin. Officer--Jos. J. Pietrafesa Co., Inc., Liverpool, NY, pg. 870
Kahn, Jeffrey, Chief Fin. Officer--Malibu Grand Prix Corporation, Canoga Park, CA, pg. 702
Kahn, Jeffrey L., Exec. V.P. & Chief Fin. Officer--Whiting Corporation, Harvey, IL, pg. 1187
Kairys, A.M., Chief Fin. Officer--Industrial Ceramics, Inc., Derry, PA, pg. 566
Kaiser, Juerger, Exec. V.P. & Chief Fin. Officer--Fru-Con Construction Corporation, Ballwin, MO, pg. 435
Kakaty, Kenneth, Treas.--Rome Sentinel Co., Rome, NY, pg. 946
Kalanges, Nick, Chief Fin. Officer--Pacific Coast Building Products Inc., Sacramento, CA, pg. 839
Kalish, David, Chief Fin. Officer--Georgetown Partners, Inc., Great Neck, NY, pg. 473
Kalsoukis, Larry, V.P.-Fin.--Duff-Norton, Charlotte, NC, pg. 1032

Kamenick, Duaine, Chief Fin. Officer & V.P.-Fin.--Wisconsin Dairies Cooperative, Baraboo, WI, pg. 1197
Kamm, C.P., Mgr.-Pension Admin. & Risk Mngmt.--Electric Furnace Co., Salem, OH, pg. 373
Kamm, J.O., Chief Fin. Officer--Electric Furnace Co., Salem, OH, pg. 373
Kamm, J.O., Chief Fin. Officer--Industrial Products Division, Salem, OH, pg. 373
Kammer, Al, V.P.-Fin., Controller & Chief Fin. Officer--American Laundry Machinery Inc., Cincinnati, OH, pg. 57
Kandris, Michael D., Sr. V.P.-Fin. & Treas.--Burlington Motor Carriers Inc., Daleville, IN, pg. 191
Kane, Sam, Chm. Bd., Chief Exec. & Chief Fin. Officer--Sam Kane Beef Processors, Inc., Corpus Christi, TX, pg. 616
Kangas, Ron, Chief Fin. Officer--Setzer Forest Products, Sacramento, CA, pg. 993
Karl, Susan Gamson, V.P. & Chief Fin. Officer--Annabelle Candy Company, Hayward, CA, pg. 75
Karlovitz, Jim, Controller--McCain Citrus Inc., Chicago, IL, pg. 726
Karpuk, A., Treas.--New Haven Mfg. Corp., New Haven, CT, pg. 801
Kaseff, Fred, Sr. V.P., Chief Fin. Officer--Barry Blau & Partners, Inc., Fairfield, CT, pg. 156
Kassouf, James, Pres., Chief Exec. Officer & Treas.--Metropolitan Properties Inc., Cleveland, OH, pg. 745
Kasufkin, Gary, V.P.-Fin.--The Segerdahl Corp., Wheeling, IL, pg. 987
Katz, Leon, V.P.-Fin.--Weider Health & Fitness, Woodland Hills, CA, pg. 1173
Kaufman, Marvin, Chief Fin. Officer--Scharfberg & Associates, Ltd. Adv., Jenkintown, PA, pg. 974
Kaufmann, Joseph L., Chief Fin. Officer & Treas.--FWD Corporation, Clintonville, WI, pg. 395
Kaufmann, Joseph L., Treas. & Chief Fin. Officer--Seagrave Fire Apparatus, Inc., Clintonville, WI, pg. 395
Kautz, Walter J., Sec. & Treas.--Sugar Cane Growers Cooperative of Florida, Belle Glade, FL, pg. 1056
Kayser, John P., Chief Fin. Partner & Mgr.--William Blair & Company, Chicago, IL, pg. 155
Kec, Janet, Sec. & Treas.--Western States Petroleum Inc., Phoenix, AZ, pg. 1181
Kedrowski, Len W., Chief Fin. Officer, Treas. & Controller--Andersen Windows Inc., Bayport, MN, pg. 72
Keefe, Thomas G., Chief Fin. Officer--The Great Atlantic Companies, Hampton, VA, pg. 480
Kees, Ray, Chief Fin. Officer, Corp. Sec. & Tres.--Gem-Dandy, Inc., Madison, NC, pg. 447
Kees, Stan, Chief. Fin. Officer--West Point-Pepperell, Inc., West Point, GA, pg. 400
Kelley, Joseph G., Jr., Pres., Treas. & Chief Fin. Officer--Jordan's Meats, Portland, ME, pg. 605
Kellner, Douglas E., Chief Fin. Officer & Mng. Partner--Schutte & Company, Buffalo, NY, pg. 979
Kellner, Lawrence, Chief Fin. Officer--Koll Co., Newport Beach, CA, pg. 641
Kells, Peter C., Vice Chm., Chief Fin. & Chief Oper. Officer--Gitano Group Inc., New York, NY, pg. 460
Kelly, Carolyn, V.P. & Chief Fin. Officer--Seattle Times Company, Seattle, WA, pg. 986
Kelly, D.T., V.P.-Fin. & Admin.--Potters Industries, Inc., Parsippany, NJ, pg. 837
Kelly, Daniel F., Chief Fin. Officer--Gosnell Builders, Phoenix, AZ, pg. 472
Kelly, Dennis P., V.P. & Chief Fin. Officer--Titanium Metals Corporation, Denver, CO, pg. 1109
Kelly, Don, Chief Fin. Officer & Treas.--KSG Inc., Guntersville, AL, pg. 613
Kelly, Edward W., Jr., Exec. V.P. & Chief Fin. Officer--Cottman Transmission Systems, Inc., Fort Washington, PA, pg. 288
Kelly, Paul E., Sr., Chm. Bd., Chief Exec. & Fin. Officer--Cawsl Corporation, Wynnewood, PA, pg. 229
Kelsky, Richard B., V.P. & Gen. Counsel--Monroe Systems For Business, Inc., Morris Plains, NJ, pg. 766
Kemp, Mike, Chief Fin. Officer & Controller--Fantastic Sam's International, Inc., Memphis, TN, pg. 398
Kendall, Laura, Chief Fin. Officer--F & M Distributors Inc., Warren, MI, pg. 393
Kendall, Richard H., Pres. & Treas.--Indiana Financial Investors, Inc., Chicago, IL, pg. 674
Kendrick, Karen, V.P.-Fin.--Miller Business Systems, Inc., Arlington, TX, pg. 753
Kendrick, Mike, Controller--Kern's Bakeries, Incorporated, Knoxville, TN, pg. 624
Kenevan, Kenneth K., V.P., Chief Fin. Officer--Dunn Reber Glenn Marz, Reno, NV, pg. 354
Kenneally, Mary, Treas. & Sec.--Town Pump, Inc., Butte, MT, pg. 1104
Kennedy, C. Thomas, Chief Fin. Officer--A & W Foods, Inc., Cleveland, OH, pg. 1
Kennedy, J. Donald, Chief Fin. Officer, V.P.-Fin. & Admin.--King Kullen Grocery Co., Inc., Westbury, NY, pg. 630
Kennedy, John J. Jr., Exec. V.P., Chief Fin. Officer--Henderson Advertising, Inc., Greenville, SC, pg. 528
Kennedy, Mark, Sr. V.P. & Chief Fin. Officer--ShopKo Stores, Inc., Green Bay, WI, pg. 1000
Kennedy, Stephen, Chief Fin. Officer & V.P.--Glico Harmony Foods Corporation, Santa Cruz, CA, pg. 462
Kenny, Jack, Controller--Market Forge Company, Everett, MA, pg. 1027
Kenny, John T., Exec. V.P.-Fin. & Oper.--Specialty Restaurants Corporation, Anaheim, CA, pg. 1027
Kenton, James, Chief Fin. Officer--Eon Labs, Inc., Lake Forest, IL, pg. 383
Keolker, Ronald H., Chief Fin. Officer, V.P., Treas. & Controller--Twin City Foods, Inc., Stanwood, WA, pg. 1122
Kephart, R., V.P.-Treas. & Sec.--Slaughter Bros., Inc., Dallas, TX, pg. 436
Kepuraitis, Elizabeth, Chief Fin. Officer--Graphisphere Holding Company, Des Plaines, IL, pg. 478
Kepuraitis, Elizabeth, Chief Fin. Officer & V.P.--Bradley Printing Company, Des Plaines, IL, pg. 478
Kerr, Stephen R., V.P. & Chief Fin. Officer--All American Bottling Corp., Oklahoma City, OK, pg. 35
Kessler, Michael, Controller--K-D Lamp Company, Cincinnati, OH, pg. 612
Kessler, PhyllisK., Chief Fin. Officer--Kalin Enterprises, Inc., Sarasota, FL, pg. 615
Kessler, Steven, Chief Oper. & Chief Fin. Officer--Strouse Greenberg & Co., Inc., Philadelphia, PA, pg. 1054
Ketteler, Thomas R., V.P.-Fin.--Schottenstein Stores Corporation, Columbus, OH, pg. 978
Kevern, John, V.P.-Fin. & Chief Fin. Officer--General Alum & Chemical, Holland, OH, pg. 448
Keyser, Michael, On-Line Game Controller--Pennsylvania State Lottery, Middletown, PA, pg. 858
Keyser, S.A., Chief Fin. Officer--Burrows Paper Corporation, Little Falls, NY, pg. 195
Kibbon, Larry J., Treas. & Sec.--Walsh Construction Co. of Illinois, Chicago, IL, pg. 1161
Kiefer, Carl O., V.P.-Fin., Sec. & Treas.--Don E. Williams Co., Rock Island, IL, pg. 1190
Kiefer, Charles, Exec. V.P., Chief Fin. Officer--Arnold Fortuna Lawner & Cabot, Boston, MA, pg. 84
Kienzle, Gary M., Exec. V.P. & Chief Fin. Officer--WW Engineering & Science Inc., Grand Rapids, MI, pg. 1058
Kilby, Andrew, Chief Fin. Officer & V.P.--Renfro Corp., Mount Airy, NC, pg. 926
Kiley, Michael T., Chief Fin. Officer--Media That Works, Cincinnati, OH, pg. 735
Kilson, Greg, Chief Fin. Officer--Fleer Corporation, Mount Laurel, NJ, pg. 695
Kinerk, Toby, V.P.-Fin.--Zemco Industries, Inc., Buffalo, NY, pg. 1217
King, James A., Chief Fin. Officer & V.P.--Valley Asphalt Corporation, Cincinnati, OH, pg. 1143
King, Jim A., Chief Fin. Officer--Fred Webb Inc., Greenville, NC, pg. 1170
King, William, Treas.--Alimak Elevator Company, Bridgeport, CT, pg. 34
Kinn, Frank, V.P.-Fin. & Sec.--Roppe Corp., Fostoria, OH, pg. 947
Kinnebrew, Jim, Chief Fin. Officer--Rocky Mountain Bank Note Company, Lakewood, CO, pg. 942
Kinney, Thomas J., Controller--Mele Manufacturing Co., Inc., Utica, NY, pg. 737
Kinslow, Kevin C., Chief Fin. Officer--John Burnham & Co., San Diego, CA, pg. 194
Kinsvatter, Jim, Chief Fin. Officer--Cogifer Inc., Cincinnati, OH, pg. 259
Kipnis, Ira, Chief Fin. Officer--Mark Fabricks, Inc., Los Angeles, CA, pg. 708
Kirby, Kerry, V.P. & Chief Fin. Officer--Cotter & Company, Chicago, IL, pg. 288
Kirby, Shelby J., Chief Fin. Officer, Treas. & Controller--T.S. Ragsdale Company, Incorporated, Lake City, SC, pg. 910
Kirchoff, Phillip, Chief Fin. Officer & Controller--Farmway Co-Op Inc., Beloit, KS, pg. 402
Kistler, Patrick, Dir.-Fin. & Data Processing--U.S. Construction Co., Inc., Columbia, SC, pg. 1135
Kitchell, William, Chief Fin. Officer--The Zamoiski Co., Baltimore, MD, pg. 1216
Klaasen, John, Chief Fin. Officer, V.P.-Fin. & Treas.--DoAll Company, Des Plaines, IL, pg. 341
Klaasen, Keith, Controller--Koch Engineering Company, Inc., Akron, OH, pg. 638
Klatt, Gregg, Chief Fin. Officer--Midwest Coast Transport L.P., Sioux Falls, SD, pg. 752
Klein, Margaret, Chief Exec. Officer & Chief Fin. Officer--Wyatt Inc., Branford, CT, pg. 1205
Klein, Michael, Chief Fin. Officer--Murray's Discount Auto Stores, Taylor, MI, pg. 777
Kleinberg, Mindy, Chief Fin. Officer--United States Realty & Investment Co., Newark, NJ, pg. 1137
Klipper, Mitchell, Exec. V.P. & Chief Fin. Officer--B. Dalton Bookseller, Inc., New York, NY, pg. 120
Kluck, Patricia, Chief Fin. Officer--Classic Chevrolet, Waukegan, IL, pg. 674
Kluver, D., V.P. & Chief Fin. Officer--Magna-Pow'r Inc., Franklin Park, IL, pg. 559
Knapp, Greg, Dir.-Fin.--Upstate Milk Cooperatives Inc., Le Roy, NY, pg. 1140
Knatz, Michael, Chief Fin. Officer--Parklane Hosiery Co., Inc., Hasbrouck Heights, NJ, pg. 849
Knedlik, Ronald, Chief Fin. Officer, Treas. & Sec.--Alex Lee, Inc., Hickory, NC, pg. 33
Knoll, Patrick, V.P. & Chief Fin. Officer--Spectrulite Consortium, Inc., Madison, IL, pg. 1029
Knoth, Richard, Vice Chm. & Chief Fin. Officer--Knoth & Meads Company, San Diego, CA, pg. 637
Knox, Marion A., Jr., V.P., Treas. & Sec.--Terminix Service, Inc., Columbia, SC, pg. 1088
Knox, Rick, Treas. & Controller--Shelby Group International, Inc., Memphis, TN, pg. 996
Knueven, Gerald R., Chief Fin. Officer, Treas. & Controller--Harold M. Pitman Co., Inc., Totowa, NJ, pg. 872
Knust, Achim, V.P. & Chief Fin. Officer--Lexmark International, Inc., Greenwich, CT, pg. 673
Kobay, Seth, V.P.-Opers. & Controller--Georgetown Partners, Inc., Great Neck, NY, pg. 473
Koch, Timothy J., Chief Fin. Officer--Chernoff/Silver & Associates, Columbia, SC, pg. 243
Kocher, Herb, Mgr.-Credit--U.S. Reduction Company, Munster, IN, pg. 1137
Koedel, John G., Jr., V.P. & Chief Fin. Officer--National Forge Company, Irvine, PA, pg. 788
Koen, Phil, Chief Fin. Officer--The Levolor Corporation, Sunnyvale, CA, pg. 671
Koester, Ken, Controller--ALP/Freddy's, Rochester, NY, pg. 4
Koh, Kay Yew, Acting Pres. & Chief Fin. Officer--Shakey's Incorporated, South San Francisco, CA, pg. 994
Kolar, Susan, Sr. V.P. & Chief Fin. Officer--Viacom Entertainment, New York, NY, pg. 785
Koler, Gerald, Chief Fin. Officer--Hill-Behan Lumber Company, Saint Louis, MO, pg. 534
Kolesar, Barbara J., V.P.-Fin.--American Paper Products Group, Ltd., Youngstown, OH, pg. 59
Kolk, Fritz D., V.P.-Fin. & Chief Fin. Officer--Meijer, Inc., Grand Rapids, MI, pg. 737
Kolovson, Mark, V.P. & Treas.--Blue Bell/King Koil, Inc., Windsor, CT, pg. 158
Kolsted, Darrell, V.P.-Fin. & Oper.--Wick Building Systems, Mazomanie, WI, pg. 1188
Kontich, Michael J., Chief Fin. Officer & Treas.--Leupold & Stevens, Inc., Beaverton, OR, pg. 669
Koonce, Joel, V.P.-Fin. & Chief Fin. Officer--Cenex/Land O'Lakes, Inc., Saint Paul, MN, pg. 653
Koonce, Joel, Grp. V.P.-Fin. & Chief Fin. Officer--CENEX (Farmers Union Central Exchange, Inc.), Inver Grove Heights, MN, pg. 231
Koonce, Joel, V.P.-Fin. & Chief Fin. Officer--Cenex/Land O'Lakes, Inc., Saint Paul, MN, pg. 231
Kopatz, Margaret, Sr. Corp. Accountant--Valu Discount, Inc., Louisville, KY, pg. 1143
Kopchik, John, Exec. V.P. & Chief Fin. Officer--Viacom Cable, Pleasanton, CA, pg. 785
Kopfer, Frank J., V.P.-Fin. & Chief Fin. Officer--Gaymar Industries, Inc., Orchard Park, NY, pg. 447
Koputich, Richard M., Chief Fin. Officer--Plastic Engineering Components Inc., New Berlin, WI, pg. 875
Korphage, George J., V.P. & Chief Fin. Officer--The Bureau of National Affairs, Inc., Washington, DC, pg. 189
Koscielak, David, Chief Fin. Officer--Supershuttle International, Los Angeles, CA, pg. 1064
Kosloff, Theodore L., Pres. & Treas.--Roosevelt Paper Co., Philadelphia, PA, pg. 946
Koster, Michael, Treas.--Williams Distributing Company, Grand Rapids, MI, pg. 1190
Kotek, William, Chief Fin. Officer--Raffi & Swanson, Inc., Wilmington, MA, pg. 909
Koukias, Erene, Chief Fin. Officer--Muro Pharmaceutical, Inc., Tewksbury, MA, pg. 776
Kousantanou, John, Vice Chm. & Chief Fin. Officer--Kaprielian/O'Leary, New York, NY, pg. 616
Kovalchuk, Brian, V.P.-Fin.--Waldorf Corporation, Saint Paul, MN, pg. 1159
Koven, Michael A., Chief Fin. Officer--Purity, Inc., Miami, FL, pg. 901
Kowack, Jeffrey M., Sr. V.P. & Chief Fin. Officer--Sonneveldt Company, Grand Rapids, MI, pg. 1018
Kowal, W., Chief Fin. Officer--Flexonics Inc., Bartlett, IL, pg. 419
Kowalsky, William, V.P.-Fin. & Plng. & Chief Fin. Officer--Advertising Checking Bureau Incorporated, New York, NY, pg. 21
Kramer, Richard, Acting Chief Fin. Officer--Channel Home Centers Inc., Whippany, NJ, pg. 238
Kramer, Roger H., Chief Fin. Officer--Carroll's Foods, Inc., Warsaw, NC, pg. 225
Kraus, Larry, Sr. V.P. & Chief Fin. Officer--Nation's Business, Washington, DC, pg. 794
Krause, Larry, Chief Fin. Officer--Ithaca Industries Inc., Wilkesboro, NC, pg. 582
Kreiter, Fredric J., Chief Fin. Officer & Legal Counsel--Castcraft Industries, Inc., Skokie, IL, pg. 228
Kreter, Charles R., Chief Fin. Officer--Ellicott Machine Corp., Baltimore, MD, pg. 378
Kreusch, Paul P., Pres. & Chief Exec. Officer--Leonard Kreusch, Inc., Moonachie, NJ, pg. 645
Kroeger, Ron, V.P. & Treas.--Town & Country Food Markets, Inc., Wichita, KS, pg. 1103
Kromer, Alan C., Chief Fin. Officer & Controller--Takatta Inc., Olympia Fields, IL, pg. 1076
Kromer, Dennis R., Chief Fin. Officer, Treas. & Controller--Dunn-Edwards Corporation, Los Angeles, CA, pg. 353
Kronenberger, Robert, Chief Fin. Officer, Sr. V.P. & Treas.--Petty Company, Inc., Effingham, IL, pg. 866
Kronfeld, Fred N., Chief Exec. & Chief Fin. Officer & Treas.--Spirite Industries, Inc., Englewood, NJ, pg. 1031
Krueger, Robert E., V.P.-Fin. & Admin.--Shade Computer Forms Co., Green Bay, WI, pg. 994
Krugman, Mark, Chief Fin. Officer, V.P. & Treas.--Lee National Corporation, New York, NY, pg. 666
Kruml, Robert J., Chief Fin. Officer & Treas.--Health America/CapitalCare, Inc., Lincoln, NE, pg. 779
Krysevig, Walter, V.P. & Chief Fin. Officer--Sunglass Hut Corporation, Miami, FL, pg. 1060
Kryshak, Thomas E., Exec. V.P.-Fin.--Nationwide Corporation, Columbus, OH, pg. 795
Kryz, Duane, Chief Fin. Officer--National Engineering & Contracting Co., Strongsville, OH, pg. 788
Ksansnak, James, Exec. V.P.-Fin. & Chief Fin. Officer--ARA Services, Inc., Philadelphia, PA, pg. 5
Ku, Grace, Fin. Dir.--Leo Burnett Company, Ltd.-Taiwan Branch, Taipei., Taiwan, pg. 192
Kubiak, Robert, V.P.-Fin., Chief Fin. Officer & Sec.--Globe Glass & Mirror Co., Chicago, IL, pg. 463
Kubicek, R.T., Sr. V.P. & Chief Fin. Officer--AppleTree Markets, Houston, TX, pg. 79
Kucka, Barbara A., Chief Fin. Officer--Don Massey Cadillac Inc., Plymouth, MI, pg. 719
Kuhar, Martin J., V.P., Sec. & Treas.--Creation Windows of Indiana, Inc., Elkhart, IN, pg. 297
Kuhns, Glen, Controller--Esskay Manufacturing Co., San Antonio, TX, pg. 389
Kuieies, Robert, V.P.-Opers. & Treas.--Amstore Corporation, Muskegon, MI, pg. 69
Kullman, Timothy E., Chief Fin. Officer--Farm Fresh, Inc., Norfolk, VA, pg. 401
Kumf, Scott, Chief Fin. Officer--Polar Corporation, Worcester, MA, pg. 878
Kunkel, William, Sr. V.P. & Chief Fin. Officer--Weinstock's Flowers & Gifts, Atlanta, GA, pg. 638
Kunkel, William, Chief Fin. Officer--Rockwood Gardens, Ltd., Rockwood,, Canada, pg. 638

Kunkel, William, Sr. V.P. & Chief Fin. Officer--Michigan Bulb Company, Grand Rapids, MI, pg. 638
Kunkel, William M., Sr. V.P. & Chief Fin. Officer--KNOX International Corp., Knoxville, TN, pg. 638
Kuptsis, Steve, V.P.-Admin. & Chief Fin. Officer--Chadwick-Miller Inc., Canton, MA, pg. 237
Kuroda, Reiko, Chief Fin. Officer--Leader Instruments Corporation, Hauppauge, NY, pg. 664
Kurpis, L., Chief Fin. Officer--Eastern Technologies Ltd, Amesbury, MA, pg. 364
Kurtenbach, Don, Chief Fin. Officer--Michael R. Ellison Inc., Phoenix, AZ, pg. 378
Kurtz, Georgianna, Chief Fin. Officer & Bus. Mgr.--SJL of Kansas Corp., Wichita, KS, pg. 962
Kutner, Ben, Chief Fin. Officer, Treas. & Sec.--VATEX America, Inc., Richmond, VA, pg. 1141
Kuyers, David J., Exec. V.P.-Fin., Admin., Sec. & Treas.--American Seating Company, Grand Rapids, MI, pg. 60
Kuykendall, David, V.P. & Chief Fin. Officer--Freedom Newspapers Inc., Irvine, CA, pg. 431
Kwosniewski, Charlotte, Treas.--All Nation Insurance Co., Saint Paul, MN, pg. 35
LaBatte, Phillip W., Chief Fin. Officer--Mohawk Paper Mills, Inc., Cohoes, NY, pg. 763
Lacey, Daniel A., Chief Fin. Officer & Dir.-Admin.--The Bakersfield Californian, Bakersfield, CA, pg. 115
Lacroix, Raymond J., Sr. V.P.-Fin. & Chief Fin. Officer--Butler Service Group, Inc., Montvale, NJ, pg. 197
Ladecky, Robert, Chief Fin. Officer--Capsonic Group, Inc., Elgin, IL, pg. 216
LaDue, Jack W., Pres. & Treas.--Rochester Gauges Inc. Of Texas, Dallas, TX, pg. 444
Lagowski, Lawrence A., V.P. & Chief Fin. Officer--Indeck Power Equipment Company, Wheeling, IL, pg. 564
Lahr, William, Sr. V.P., Chief Fin. Officer--Avrett, Free & Ginsberg, Inc., New York, NY, pg. 103
Laiken, L., Controller--Rainbow Apparel Distribution Center, Brooklyn, NY, pg. 910
Laine, R., Pres., Chief Fin. Officer & Treas.--Telechron, Inc., Ashland, MA, pg. 1085
Lam, Steven, V.P.-Fin.--Star Video Entertainment, L.P., Jersey City, NJ, pg. 1040
LaMagna, Joseph, Exec. V.P. & Chief Fin. Officer--American Savings Bank, White Plains, NY, pg. 60
Lamb, Frank, Exec. V.P.-Fin.--J B Labs, Inc., Holland, MI, pg. 584
Lambert, Burton W., Chief Fin. Officer & V.P., Opers.--Creative Marketing Alliance Inc., Princeton Junction, NJ, pg. 297
Lambesis, Vicki, Chief Fin. Officer--Lambesis Communications, San Diego, CA, pg. 652
Lamdert, Greg, Sec. & Treas.--H.H. Cutler Company, Grand Rapids, MI, pg. 306
Lameka, Nolan L., V.P.-Fin.--WICO Corporation, Niles, IL, pg. 1156
Lampugnano, Phil, V.P.-Fin. & Chief Fin. Officer--American Office Equipment, La Grange, IL, pg. 58
Lamsey, D.L., V.P.-Fin.--American Manufacturing Co. (TN), Chattanooga, TN, pg. 58
Landau, Roy, Chm. Bd., Pres. & Chief Exec. & Chief Fin. Officer--Landau Building Co., Wexford, PA, pg. 654
Landry, James E., Chief Fin. Officer, Exec. V.P. & Sec.--United Piece Dye Works, LP, Princeton Junction, NJ, pg. 1134
Landry, Joe, Chief Fin. Officer--ITS: Intertrade Scientific, Inc., Vernon, CT, pg. 748
Lane, Daniel, V.P. & Chief Fin. Officer--Quality Food Oils, Inc., New Milford, CT, pg. 903
Lane, Leman G., Controller--Stanley Roberts, Inc., Lodi, NJ, pg. 939
Lane, Stan, Chief Fin. Officer--Floral Glass & Mirror, Inc., Hauppauge, NY, pg. 420
Lanfre, Melissa, V.P. & Chief Fin. Officer--Harbor Bancorp, Long Beach, CA, pg. 506
Lang, Sandra J., Chief Fin. Officer--Brutger Equities, Inc., Saint Cloud, MN, pg. 185
Langer, David, Pres., Chief Exec. & Chief Oper. Officer & Treas.--David Langer & Co., Inc., Hollywood, CA, pg. 657
Langos, R., Pres. & Treas.--Harco Technologies Corporation, Medina, OH, pg. 507
Lanier, Joseph V., Chief Fin. Officer & V.P.-Fin.--State Industries Inc., Ashland City, TN, pg. 1041
Lanka, Alan, Chief Fin. Officer--Resonex, Inc., Sunnyvale, CA, pg. 929
LaPaglia, Joseph T., V.P.-Fin. & Chief Fin. Officer--Faber/Castell Corporation, Parsippany, NJ, pg. 395
Lapina, John J., Chief Fin. Officer & V.P.-Fin.--Elliott Company, Jeannette, PA, pg. 378
Lapp, Saul, V.P.-Fin.--JCI Data Processing, Inc., Delran, NJ, pg. 584
Laret, Robert, Chief Fin. Officer--Lanz, Inc., Culver City, CA, pg. 658
Larsen, Jeffrey, Chief Fin. Officer--Faribault Woolen Mill Co., Faribault, MN, pg. 399
Larson, Jack, Chief Fin. Officer--Hirsh Company, Skokie, IL, pg. 258
Lasko, John C., Chm. Bd., Pres. & Treas.--Republic Die & Tool Company, Belleville, MI, pg. 928
Latman, Martin, Chief Fin. Officer--Caswell/Massey Co. Ltd., Edison, NJ, pg. 229
Latta, John M., Natl. Dir.-Tax Practice--Grant Thornton, Chicago, IL, pg. 477
Lavin, Nick, Chief Fin. Officer--Sithe Energies, U.S.A., Inc., San Diego, CA, pg. 1009
Law, Irving D., Jr., Chm. Bd. & Chief Fin. Officer--Broadcast Supply West, Tacoma, WA, pg. 177
Lawrence, Robert A., Treas.--Sullivan & Cozart Inc., Louisville, KY, pg. 1056
Lawson, Chris A., Exec. V.P., Chief Fin. Officer--Ross Roy Group, Inc., Bloomfield Hills, MI, pg. 949
Lawson, Chris A., Exec. V.P., Chief Fin. Officer--Ross Roy Inc., Bloomfield Hills, MI, pg. 950
Lay, F. Edwin, Jr., Chief Fin. Officer & Treas.--Lay Packing Company Inc., Knoxville, TN, pg. 663
Layfield, Brian, V.P. & Chief Fin. Officer--Carpeteria, Inc., Valencia, CA, pg. 224
Lazarc, John, Chief Fin. Officer & V.P.-Fin.--Leichtung, Inc., Cleveland, OH, pg. 666
Leach, J., Jr., V.P.-Fin.--William B. Reily & Co., Inc., New Orleans, LA, pg. 923
Lebens, Jeffrey K., V.P., Treas. & Chief Fin. Officer--Intermountain Industries, Inc., Boise, ID, pg. 575
Lebens, Jeffrey K., Sr. V.P.-Fin., Admin. & Treas.--Intermountain Gas Co., Boise, ID, pg. 575
Lebens, Jeffrey K., V.P., Treas. & Chief Fin. Officer--IGI Resources, Inc., Boise, ID, pg. 575
Lebovitz, Brad, Chief Oper. Officer & Chief Fin. Officer--Kanex, Cleveland, OH, pg. 616
Lee, Gary, V.P.-Fin.--Great Plains Manufacturing, Inc., Assaria, KS, pg. 482
Lee, James, Chief Fin. Officer--La Victoria Foods, Inc., City of Industry, CA, pg. 649
Lee, Mei, Treas., Controller & Chief Fin. Officer--Ronald Hsu Construction, Capitol Heights, MD, pg. 548
Lee, William H., Treas., Controller & Sec.--Zimdar Enterprises, Wyoming, MI, pg. 1220
Leef, Donald N., V.P., Chief Fin. Officer & Treas.--BIW Cable Systems, Inc., North Dighton, MA, pg. 106
Lefferts, E.A., Chief Fin. Officer--Golden Eagle Distributors, Inc., Tucson, AZ, pg. 466
Leffingwell, William, Chief Fin. Officer--Channellock, Inc., Meadville, PA, pg. 239
Legere, Ron, V.P.-Finance & Chief Fin. Officer--Hackney & Sons, Inc., Washington, NC, pg. 498
Lehde, Sue, Chief Fin. Officer--Economy Mechanical Industries, Inc., Wheeling, IL, pg. 609
Lehmann, James J., V.P.-Fin.--Haworth, Inc., Holland, MI, pg. 518
Leiferman, Ronald, Sr. V.P. & Chief Fin. Officer--Leo A. Daly Company, Omaha, NE, pg. 313
Leimkuhler, Lyle, V.P.-Fin. & Sec.--News-Press & Gazette Company, St. Joseph, MA, pg. 804
Lempert, Seymour, Comptroller--Service Web Offset Corporation, Chicago, IL, pg. 992
Lenhart, Mag. Peter, Fin. Dir.--Young & Rubicam Vienna Werbegesellschaft m.b.H., Vienna,, Austria, pg. 1213
Lenk, John C., Sec. & Treas.--Campbell Construction Co., Sacramento, CA, pg. 213
Lentin, Joseph, Jr., Chief Fin. Officer--Rau Fasteners, Inc., Providence, RI, pg. 913
Leo, James J., Corp. Controller--Wegmans Food Markets, Inc., Rochester, NY, pg. 1172
Leong, Margaret, V.P.-Fin. Services--Shapell Industries, Inc., Beverly Hills, CA, pg. 995
Lesh, Rodger L., Chief Fin. Officer, V.P. & Treas.--Lewis Brothers Bakeries, Inc., Evansville, IN, pg. 673
Lesser, Seymour H., Exec. V.P., Chief Fin. & Chief Admin. Officer--Arts & Entertainment Network, New York, NY, pg. 523
Letendre, Peter, Controller--Roma Holdings, Dallas, TX, pg. 945
Leung, Stephen, Chief Fin. Officer--Green Spot Packaging Inc., Claremont, CA, pg. 485
LeVasseur, Gerald, Chief Fin. Officer--Pratt-Read Corporation, Bridgeport, CT, pg. 884
Levin, Binnie J., Chief Fin. Officer & Sr. V.P.--Towne, Silverstein, Rotter Inc., New York, NY, pg. 1104
Levin, Bruce, Chief Fin. Officer & Controller--Adworks, Inc., Washington, DC, pg. 21
Levin, Henry, Legal Officer--Just Pants, Chicago, IL, pg. 610
Levine, H. Barry, Sr. V.P. & Chief Fin. Officer--W.B. Doner & Company, Southfield, MI, pg. 344
Levitt, Lawrence, Chief Fin. Officer--Odyssey Partners, New York, NY, pg. 821
Levy, Steven A., Exec. V.P. & Treas.--Titan Industrial Corp., New York, NY, pg. 1099
Lewis, Jim, V.P., Chief Fin. Officer, Sec. & Treas.--Hale-Halsell Company, Tulsa, OK, pg. 500
Lewis, John D., Mng. Partner & Chief Fin. Officer--Arthur Andersen & Co., S.C., New York, NY, pg. 72
Lewis, Robert, Chief Fin. Officer, V.P. & Sec.--Lockwood Corporation, Gering, NE, pg. 680
Lewy, Stephen H., Sr. V.P. & Treas.--Omni Hotels, Hampton, NH, pg. 826
Libby, Darald R., Chm. Bd. & Chief Fin. Officer--David Clark Company, Inc., Worcester, MA, pg. 252
Lick, David, Chief Fin. Officer & Sr. V.P.--Western Development Corporation, Washington, DC, pg. 1179
Lieberg, Eric N., Chief Fin. Officer & Exec. V.P.--Rundel Products, Inc., Portland, OR, pg. 956
Lieberman, David, Chief Fin. Officer--Falcon Safety Products Inc., Branchburg, NJ, pg. 398
Liebrer, Mark, Chief Fin. Officer & V.P.--Rural Metro Corporation, Scottsdale, AZ, pg. 956
Liem, James, V.P. & Chief Fin. Officer--Schuck & Sons Construction Co., Glendale, AZ, pg. 979
Lightstone, Stephen, Sr. V.P.-Fin. & Chief Fin. Officer--Payless Cashways, Inc., Kansas City, MO, pg. 853
Liken, Lloyd T., V.P.-Fin.--Midland National Life Insurance Co., Sioux Falls, SD, pg. 968
Limon, Patricia, Chief Fin. Officer--Freeman Cosmetic Corp., Los Angeles, CA, pg. 431
Lindner, Richard, Chief Fin. Officer--The Giardini/Russell Group, Watertown, MA, pg. 456
Lindsey, Harold D., Chief Oper. Officer, Chief Fin. Officer, & V.P.--Bader & Co., Ipava, IL, pg. 113
Linfante, Charles V., Chief Fin. Officer--Amalloy, Goshen, NY, pg. 46
Lingg, Joseph F., Chief Fin. Officer & Controller--Mosler Inc., Hamilton, OH, pg. 772
Lipoff, Steven, Pres., Treas. & Chief Fin. Officer--Butler Foods, Inc., Philadelphia, PA, pg. 197
Lis, Brad, Dir.-Investments--Carlson Real Estate Company, Minneapolis, MN, pg. 221
Lista, Leslie, Controller--Scholastic Inc., New York, NY, pg. 962
Littell, Ray, Chief Fin. Officer--Bauerlein Inc., New Orleans, LA, pg. 127
Little, William, V.P.-Treas. & Controller--Worzalla Publishing Co., Inc., Stevens Point, WI, pg. 1204
Littman, Jeffrey C., Chief Fin. Officer--Highwood Service, Inc., Detroit, MI, pg. 1194
Littmann, Jeffrey C., Chief Fin. Officer & V.P.--Ralph C. Wilson Enterprises, Detroit, MI, pg. 1194
Ljungberg, Robert, Chm. Bd., Pres., Chief Exec. & Chief Oper. Officer--Ultra Tool & Plastics, Inc., Amherst, NY, pg. 1125
Lockwood, Kent, Chief Fin. Officer & V.P.-Fin.--Producers Rice Mill Inc., Stuttgart, AR, pg. 892
Loer, James E., Jr., Treas.--Walpole Woodworkers, Inc., Walpole, MA, pg. 1161
Lofgren, Frederick, Chief Fin. Officer, Treas., Sec. & V.P.-Fin. & Admin.--Hitchiner Manufacturing Company, Inc., Milford, NH, pg. 536
Loftis, Harry E., V.P. & Chief Fin. Officer--Riceland Foods, Inc., Stuttgart, AR, pg. 931
Lofton, A.L., Jr., V.P. & Treas.--Utilities Construction Co., Inc. Of South Carolina, Charleston, SC, pg. 1141
Lohne, Peter, V.P.--Tilcon, Inc., New Britain, CT, pg. 1097
Lomen, A.J., V.P., Treas. & Chief Fin. Officer--Genmar Industries, Inc., Minneapolis, MN, pg. 759
Lomen, Arlyn J., V.P., Treas. & Chief Fin. Officer--Minstar, Inc., Minneapolis, MN, pg. 758
London, TerryE., V.P. & Chief Fin. Officer--Gaylord Entertainment Co., Nashville, TN, pg. 446
Long, Claranne R., Chief Fin. Officer--Synergism, Inc., Sunnyvale, CA, pg. 1069
Long, Jonathan R., Pres. & Chief Fin. Officer--J. E. Higgins Lumber Co., Concord, CA, pg. 533
Long, William, Jr., Comptroller--Robbins Manufacturing Company, Tampa, FL, pg. 938
Longbrake, William A., Sr. Exec. V.P. & Chief Fin. Officer--Washington Mutual Savings Bank, Seattle, WA, pg. 1166
Longstreet, Elizabeth, V.P., Chief Fin. Officer--Siddall, Matus & Coughter, Inc. Advertising & Public Relations, Richmond, VA, pg. 1002
Looper, Tommy E., Exec. V.P., Chief Fin. Officer & Sec.--Anchor Financial Corporation, Myrtle Beach, SC, pg. 71
Lorenz, Donald N., Chief Fin. Officer & V.P.-Fin.--Price Brothers Co., Dayton, OH, pg. 888
Lorenz, Richard B., Controller--U.S. Manufacturing Corp., Roseville, MI, pg. 1136
Loss, Stuart, Exec. V.P., Chief Fin. Officer--TBWA Advertising, Inc., New York, NY, pg. 1071
Loth, Jerry, Sec. & Treas.--Richardson Brothers Co., Sheboygan Falls, WI, pg. 932
Lotz, Jim, Chief Fin. Officer--Ortho-Kinetics, Inc., Waukesha, WI, pg. 830
Loux, Alvin H., V.P.-Fin.--Sigallo, Ltd., New York, NY, pg. 1003
Lovett, M.F., Chief Fin. Officer & V.P.--Ingram Distribution Group Inc., La Vergne, TN, pg. 569
Lovett, M.F., Chief Fin. Officer & Sr. V.P.--Ingram Book Company, La Vergne, TN, pg. 569
Lowe, Joan, Controller--Battery St. Enterprises, Running Gear Div., Boulder, CO, pg. 670
Lowell, Wayne, Sr. V.P., Chief Fin. Officer & Treas.--PacifiCare Health Systems, Inc., Cypress, CA, pg. 1127
Lowrey, John, Chief Fin. Officer--DDC PerTec, Tucson, AZ, pg. 308
Lowry, Bill, V.P.-Fin.--Servus Footwear Company, Rock Island, IL, pg. 993
Loyer, Dennis, V.P.-Fin.--Vernay Laboratories, Inc., Yellow Springs, OH, pg. 1148
Lozano, Joe J., Controller--H. B. Zachry Company, San Antonio, TX, pg. 1215
Lubliner, William, Treas.--Helmsley-Spear Inc., New York, NY, pg. 527
Lucien, Kent T., Exec. V.P., Chief Fin. Officer & Treas.--C. Brewer & Company, Limited, Honolulu, HI, pg. 174
Luckey, Dennis N., V.P. & Controller--Baker Commodities, Inc., Los Angeles, CA, pg. 115
Ludkiewicz, William, V.P., Chief Fin. Officer--Decker Rickard, Glastonbury, CT, pg. 324
Ludwig, Andreas, Exec. V.P. & Chief Fin. Officer--Zale Corporation, Irving, TX, pg. 1215
Lue, Connie, Controller--Pride Products, Inc., Elizabeth, NJ, pg. 889
Luebberman, Thomas M., V.P. & Treas.--Seppala & AHO Construction Company, New Ipswich, NH, pg. 990
Lueck, Allan, Chief Fin. Officer--Northwestern Drug Company, Minneapolis, MN, pg. 343
Lugar, Todd, Sec. & Treas.--Thomas L. Green & Co., Inc., Indianapolis, IN, pg. 484
Lugbill, Jerry, Treas. & Sec.--Lugbill Brothers, Inc., Archbold, OH, pg. 686
Luker, Robert C., V.P. & Chief Fin. Officer--Gerber Plumbing Fixtures Corporation, Chicago, IL, pg. 454
Luker, Robert C., Chief Fin. Officer & V.P.--Kokomo Sanitary Pottery Corp., Chicago, IL, pg. 640
Lumpkins, Robert L., V.P. & Chief Fin. Officer--Cargill Inc., Wayzata, MN, pg. 219
Lund, Brian, Controller--Wellens & Co., Inc., Minneapolis, MN, pg. 1175
Lund, Vic, V.P.-Fin. & Acctg.--Sioux Honey Association, Sioux City, IA, pg. 1008
Luntz, Gregory W., Chief Fin. Officer & Treas.--Luntz Corporation, Canton, OH, pg. 687
Lupino, Tony, Chief Fin. Officer--Pepsi-Cola Albany Bottling Co., Inc., Latham, NY, pg. 860
Lurie, Hil, Chief Fin. Officer--Struthers-Dunn Inc., Pitman, NJ, pg. 693
Lurus, Steven A., Chief Fin. Officer & Dir.-Fin., Treas.--Metro Information Services, Virginia Beach, VA, pg. 743
Luxenberg, Irwin, Controller--Jacques Moret, Inc., New York, NY, pg. 588
Luzum, James A., Chief Fin. Officer, Treas. & Controller--Villaume Industries, Inc., Saint Paul, MN, pg. 1151
Luzum, William J., V.P. & Treas.--Tyler Limited Partnership, Benson, MN, pg. 1122
Lyke, Audrey R., Chief Fin. Officer & Treas.--Lyke Corporation, Ripon, WI, pg. 688

Lynch, Brian A., Chief Fin. Officer--Rehrig Pacific Company, Los Angeles, CA, pg. 922
Lynch, Joe, V.P. & Chief Fin. Officer--Boston Traders Div., Lynn, MA, pg. 168
Lynch, Joseph E., Exec. V.P., Chief Exec. & Fin. Officer--Boston Trading Ltd. Inc., Lynn, MA, pg. 168
MacDonald, H., V.P. Fin. & Chief Fin. Officer--Versa Services Ltd., Etobicoke,, Canada, pg. 7
MacDonald, Thomas E., Chief Fin. Officer--Ernst W. Dorn Co., Inc., Gardena, CA, pg. 346
MacFadyen, Alex, V.P.-Fin.--National Football League Properties, Inc., New York, NY, pg. 788
MacInnes, Donald A., Chief Fin. Officer & V.P.--Morse Operations Inc., Ft. Lauderdale, FL, pg. 772
MacIntyre, Susan, Chief Fin. Officer--California Cedar Products, Inc., Stockton, CA, pg. 209
Mackay, Thomas C., Chief Fin. Officer--Nelson Communications, Inc., New York, NY, pg. 797
Macke, Bruce A., Chief Fin. Officer & Exec. V.P.--The Elder-Beerman Stores Corp., Dayton, OH, pg. 373
Macke, Bruce A., Exec. V.P. & Chief Fin. Officer--Elder-Beerman Stores Div., Dayton, OH, pg. 373
MacKee, Julie, Chief Fin. Officer--QLM Associates, Inc., Princeton, NJ, pg. 902
MacLeay, Thomas H., Sr. V.P. & Chief Fin. Officer--National Life Insurance Company, Montpelier, VT, pg. 791
Macleod, Robert W., Chief Fin. Officer--Foster Medical Supply, Inc., Waltham, MA, pg. 426
Madacsi, Pierre, V.P., Chief Fin. Officer--Steinert & Associates, Inc., New York, NY, pg. 1045
Madlinger, Steven R., V.P., Chief Fin. Officer & Treas.--GreatBanc, Inc., Aurora, IL, pg. 482
Maduza, Carolyn, Sr. V.P., Chief Fin. Officer--U.S. Communications Corporation, Minneapolis, MN, pg. 1135
Magaw, Roger W., Exec. V.P. & Treas.--Union Boiler Co., Nitro, WV, pg. 273
Magdol, Michael O., Vice Chm.-Chief Fin. Officer--Fiduciary Trust Co. International, New York, NY, pg. 408
Magdol, Michael O., Exec. V.P. & Chief Fin. Officer--Fiduciary Trust Company International, New York, NY, pg. 408
Maginn, James, Chief Fin. Officer & Sr. V.P.--Watt Industries, Santa Monica, CA, pg. 1168
Magnus, Art, Chief Fin. Officer--Bam Publications, Inc., Pleasant Hill, CA, pg. 117
Maguire, Frank, Comptroller--Rynone Manufacturing Corporation, Sayre, PA, pg. 958
Maharry, Anne, Pres. & Chief Fin. Officer--Bull, Inc., San Diego, CA, pg. 981
Mahood, Jeri, Acctg. Mgr.--Berkeley Industries Inc., Laguna Beach, CA, pg. 141
Mailler, W., Chief Fin. Officer & V.P.--Kentile Floors Inc., South Plainfield, NJ, pg. 623
Mains, Donald A., Pres. & Treas.--Tradehome Shoe Stores, Inc., Saint Paul, MN, pg. 1105
Makhani, Madan P., Chm. Bd., Pres., Chief Oper. Officer & Chief Fin. Officer--American Foundry Group, Inc., Bixby, OK, pg. 54
Maksel, E.A., V.P. & Controller--Wilbur Chocolate Co., Inc., Lititz, PA, pg. 219
Malcolm, Richard B., Chief Fin. Officer--Mathews & Boucher, Rochester, NY, pg. 720
Malec, William F., Sr. V.P. & Chief Fin. Officer--Tennessee Valley Authority, Knoxville, TN, pg. 1088
Malesevich, Michael, Chief Fin. Officer--Miller-St. Nazianz, Inc., Saint Nazianz, WI, pg. 755
Malkani, Roma, Pres. & Chief Exec. Officer--Information Systems & Network Corporation, Bethesda, MD, pg. 567
Mallen, David J., Chief Fin. Officer & Sr. V.P.-Employee Benefits--Wilder Management Associates, Waltham, MA, pg. 1189
Malliet, James, V.P.-Fin.--S. C. Johnson & Son, Limited, Brantford,, Canada, pg. 600
Mallon, Daniel J., Controller--Simplex Construction Co. Inc., Scranton, PA, pg. 1006
Maloney, Raymond, V.P.-Fin.--Intertec Publishing, Overland Park, KS, pg. 611
Mancuso, Richard, Sr. V.P. & Chief Fin. Officer--Associated Merchandising Corp., New York, NY, pg. 91
Mandeville, Robert, Chief Fin. Officer & Treas.--Cranston Print Works Company, Cranston, RI, pg. 296
Maness, George, Controller--Ritchie Corporation, Wichita, KS, pg. 936
Mangan, Chris, V.P. & Treas.--Orbitair International Ltd., New York, NY, pg. 828
Mangin, Joseph A., V.P., Chief Oper. & Chief Fin. Officer--Barr Brothers & Co., Inc., New York, NY, pg. 121
Mangum, Harleigh J., V.P.-Fin.--Standard Plywood, Inc., Clinton, SC, pg. 1037
Maniscalco, Diane, Chief Fin. Officer-Admin./Opers.-Sec. & Treas.--Colonna Bros., Inc., North Bergen, NJ, pg. 264
Manke, Victor, Controller--National Beef Packing Company, Liberal, KS, pg. 1128
Mann, Michael F., Exec. V.P. & Chief Fin. Officer--Florasynth Inc., New York, NY, pg. 420
Manukas, George, Sr. V.P. & Chief Fin. Officer--DKM Building Enterprises, L.P., Lawrenceville, NJ, pg. 357
Manzon, Peter E., V.P. & Chief Fin. Officer--Standard-Thomson Corporation, Waltham, MA, pg. 1037
Maples, Larry, V.P.-Fin. & Chief Fin. Officer--Peterson Builders, Inc., Sturgeon Bay, WI, pg. 864
Marach, Roger, Chief Fin. Officer & Treas.--FamTec International, Inc., Des Plaines, IL, pg. 398
Marchuk, Raymond, V.P.-Fin. Opers.--Scholastic Inc., New York, NY, pg. 962
Marcucci, Frank J., V.P.-Fin. & Admin.--Amkor Electronics, Inc., West Chester, PA, pg. 67
Marcucci, George, Chief Fin. Officer & Treas.--Gonnella Baking Co., Chicago, IL, pg. 469
Marek, Alan J., Treas. & Chief Fin. Officer--Vincent Food Industries, Inc., Chicago, IL, pg. 1152
Margolin, Norm, Chief Fin. Officer--Triumph Twist Drill Co., Crystal Lake, IL, pg. 885
Margolin, Norman, Chief Fin. Officer & Exec. V.P.-Fin.--Precision Twist Drill Co., Crystal Lake, IL, pg. 885
Margolin, Norman, Exec. V.P. & Chief Fin. Officer--Mohawk Tools, Crystal Lake, IL, pg. 885
Margolis, David, Chief Fin. Officer--Broder Bros. Co., Plymouth, MI, pg. 178
Marion, T.D., Treas.--TTX Co., Chicago, IL, pg. 1075
Maris, Edward G., Sr. V.P. & Chief Fin. Officer--Northwestern Steel & Wire Co., Sterling, IL, pg. 815
Markel, Lynn, Exec. V.P.-Fin. & Chief Fin. Officer--Koch Industries, Incorporated, Wichita, KS, pg. 639
Markham, Grigsby C., Chief Fin. Officer--Gartner Group, Inc., Stamford, CT, pg. 443
Markiewicz, Margaret V., Treas.--Van Son Holland Ink Corp. of America, Mineola, NY, pg. 1144
Markol, Larry, Comptroller & Sec.--J. H. France Refractories Co., Snow Shoe, PA, pg. 428
Marlow, James, Sr. V.P. & Chief Fin. Officer--Varityper, Inc., East Hanover, NJ, pg. 1146
Marohn, Edward, Chief Fin. Officer--I D E Associates, Billerica, MA, pg. 560
Marquardt, R.R., Chief Fin. Officer, Sec. & Treas.--Miller Electric Mfg. Co., Appleton, WI, pg. 754
Marscovetra, Bob, V.P., Dir. Finance--Chiat/Day/Mojo Inc. Advertising, San Francisco, CA, pg. 244
Marshall, David, Chief Oper. Officer & V.P.-Fin.--Bigsby & Kruthers, Inc., Chicago, IL, pg. 150
Marshall, Debbie, Controller--Richmond Technology Inc., Redlands, CA, pg. 933
Marshall, Jeff, Chief Fin. Officer--Maurin-Ogden Management Corporation, New Orleans, LA, pg. 722
Marshall, Robin L., Pres. & Chief Exec. Officer--Great Lakes Technologies Corp., Kalamazoo, MI, pg. 482
Martin, A.K., Mgr.-Credit--True Companies, Casper, WY, pg. 1117
Martin, Arthur L., Controller--Asbury Ferst, Inc., Atlanta, GA, pg. 87
Martin, Brian K., Treas.--Equity Services, Inc., Montpelier, VT, pg. 791
Martin, Charles A., Chief Fin. Officer--Bommer Industries, Inc., Landrum, SC, pg. 164
Martin, Gladys, Chief Fin. Officer, Treas., Sec. & Dir.-Personnel--Welsco Inc., North Little Rock, AR, pg. 1175
Martin, Gloria A., Sec. & Treas.--Williams International Industries, Inc., Richmond, VA, pg. 1191
Martin, Marvin, Chief Fin. Officer--Standard Shoe Company, Inglewood, CA, pg. 1037
Martin, Robert L., Sec. & Controller--Longyear Company, Salt Lake City, UT, pg. 682
Martin, Ronald, Sr. V.P. & Chief Fin. Officer--Mayflower Transit, Inc., Carmel, IN, pg. 724
Martin, Ronald W., Sr. V.P. & Chief Fin. Officer--Mayflower Transit, Inc., Carmel, IN, pg. 724
Martin, Ronald W., Chief Fin. Officer--Advantage Moving & Storage Co., Inc., Carmel, IN, pg. 724
Martin, Steve, Treas. & Sec.--Russell Chevrolet Company, Sherwood, AR, pg. 957
Martin, Timothy I., V.P. & Chief Fin. Officer--Country Lake Foods, Inc., Saint Paul, MN, pg. 654
Martin, Weldon, Treas.--E-Z Serve Corp., Houston, TX, pg. 361
Martone, Anthony J., V.P.-Fin. & Admin.--Metropolitan Sunday Newspapers, Inc., New York, NY, pg. 745
Martone, Anthony J., V.P.-Fin. & Admin.--Metro-Puck Comics Network, New York, NY, pg. 745
Martone, Anthony J., V.P.-Fin. & Admin.--Sunday Magazine Network, New York, NY, pg. 745
Marvelley, Brian, V.P.-Fin.--Battenfeld Gloucester Engineering Co. Inc., Gloucester, MA, pg. 126
Marvin, Jake, Chief Fin. Officer--Marvin Lumber & Cedar Company, Warroad, MN, pg. 716
Masinton, Richard, Sr. V.P.-Fin. & Chief Fin. Officer--Westlake Hardware, Inc., Shawnee Mission, KS, pg. 1183
Maslick, Joseph R., Sr. V.P., Chief Fin. Officer & Sec.--Griffith Laboratories Worldwide, Inc., Alsip, IL, pg. 487
Maslowski, Clem, Chief Fin. Officer--Rite-Hite Corporation, Milwaukee, WI, pg. 936
Mason, Chip, V.P.-Fin. & Chief Fin. Officer--Gulf States Toyota, Houston, TX, pg. 494
Mason, Fred, Treas., Sec. & Mgr.-Pur.--J.B. Rodgers Mechanical Contractors, Phoenix, AZ, pg. 943
Mason, Wallace, V.P., Sec. & Chief Fin. Officer--Temkin & Temkin, Northbrook, IL, pg. 1086
Masquelier, Jacques, Treas--BSB France, Puteaux, France, pg. 109
Massey, Les, Controller--Whitfield Foods, Inc., Montgomery, AL, pg. 1187
Matarese, James M., Chm., Pres. & Chief Exec. Officer--Phoenix International, Inc., Beverly, NJ, pg. 868
Matcuk, James R., V.P., Controller & Treas.--Cerro Copper Products Co., Sauget, IL, pg. 711
Mathews, H. Cannon, V.P.-Fin. & Chief Fin. Officer--Rogerson Aircraft Corporation, Irvine, CA, pg. 943
Mathieu, Barbara, V.P., Chief Fin. Officer--Mathieu, Donovan & Associates, Inc., Montgomery, NY, pg. 721
Mathieu, Raymond M., Chief Fin. Officer & Treas.--Narragansett Capital Inc., Providence, RI, pg. 783
Matlock, Kenneth J., Exec. V.P. & Chief Fin. Officer--Walter Industries, Inc., Tampa, FL, pg. 1161
Matre, Steven R., V.P.-Fin., Chief Fin. Officer & Sec.--Energy Minerals Corporation, Denver, CO, pg. 381
Matsumoto, Raymond, Chief Fin. Officer--Rice Growers Association of California, West Sacramento, CA, pg. 931
Matsushima, John, Chief Fin. Officer--Micro Component Technology Inc., Saint Paul, MN, pg. 748
Mattes, Ray, V.P.-Fin.--White Storage & Retrieval Systems, Inc., Kenilworth, NJ, pg. 1186
Matthes, Lesa, Controller--Champion Laboratories, Inc., Albion, IL, pg. 1123
Maurer, J., Sec. & Treas.--Rich Products Dayton, Dayton, OH, pg. 932
Maurer, Ken, V.P.-Admin. & Chief Fin. Officer--Hoffco, Inc., Richmond, IN, pg. 537
Maurer, Ken, V.P.-Acct. & Chief Fin. Officer--Comet Industries, Richmond, IN, pg. 537
Mavor, Thomas J., V.P.-Fin. & Chief Fin. Officer--McLouth Steel, Trenton, MI, pg. 731
May, Alison, Chief Fin. Officer--Lost Arrow Corporation, Ventura, CA, pg. 684
Mayberry, Ainslie, Chief Fin. Officer--Digital Pathways Inc., Mountain View, CA, pg. 337
Mayberry, Steve, Chief Fin. Officer--Pacific States Casualty Co., Los Angeles, CA, pg. 841
Mayland, Wes, Chief Fin. Officer--AmeriServ Food Company, Dallas, TX, pg. 66
Mayo, Jennifer, V.P. & Chief Fin. Officer--Swift Dodge Rolls Royce Inc., Sacramento, CA, pg. 1067
Mazza, Thomas J., Exec. V.P. & Chief Fin. Officer--Simunico, Inc., Rutherford, NJ, pg. 1007
McAlester, Pat, Sec. & Treas.--Texas Electric Cooperatives, Inc., Austin, TX, pg. 1089
McAllister, K. David, Chief Fin. Officer--Brim, Inc., Portland, OR, pg. 176
McAnally, David, Chief Fin. Officer--Unifax, Inc., Wilkes-Barre, PA, pg. 1126
McAuliffe, Joan, Chief Fin. Officer & Gen. Counsel--Compendium Systems, New York, NY, pg. 270
McAuliffe, Lawrence, Controller--Whitney Blake Company of Vermont, Inc., Bellows Falls, VT, pg. 155
McCabe, James B., Chief Fin. Officer & V.P.-Fin.--Chick-Fil-A, Inc., Atlanta, GA, pg. 247
McCaffrey, William, Chief Fin. Officer--American Restaurant Group, Inc., Newport Beach, CA, pg. 60
McCall, Ronald L., Vice Chm., Chief Exec. Officer, Chief Fin. Officer & Treas.--M. B. Kahn Construction Co., Inc., Columbia, SC, pg. 614
McCann, Jeff, Chief Fin. Officer--Nashville Wire Product Co., Nashville, TN, pg. 784
McCann, Vince, Chief Fin. Officer--Mother Earth News, New York, NY, pg. 773
McCarthy, Denis, Sr. V.P. & Chief Fin. Officer--Fidelity Investments (FMR Corp.), Boston, MA, pg. 408
McCarthy, Joe, Chief Fin. Officer--Case-Swayne Co. Inc., Santa Ana, CA, pg. 228
McCarthy, Michael W., Chief Exec. Officer & Treas.--Williams Steel & Hardware Company, Minneapolis, MN, pg. 1191
McCarty, John R., Pres., Chief Exec. Officer & Chief Fin. Officer--McCarty Farms, Magee, MS, pg. 727
McClelland, Frances H., Treas., Sec. & Chief Fin. Officer--Shamrock Foods Co., Phoenix, AZ, pg. 994
McClelland, John R., Exec. V.P. & Chief Fin. Officer--Provident Mutual Life Insurance Co., Philadelphia, PA, pg. 896
McCluskey, R.T., V.P. & Treas.--Lubriplate Div. of Fiske Bros. Refining Co., Newark, NJ, pg. 416
McCorkle, Martha A., Chief Fin. Officer & V.P.-Fin.--World Carpets, Inc., Dalton, GA, pg. 1202
McCormick, Scot M., Chief Fin. Officer--Whitestar Graphics, Inc., Spring Grove, IL, pg. 1186
McCormick, Susan Konn, Treas.--Scholastic Inc., New York, NY, pg. 962
McCoy, James P., Jr., Chief Fin. Officer--Club Corporation International, Dallas, TX, pg. 256
McCoy, John, Chief Fin. Officer--Muelhens, Inc., Orange, CT, pg. 774
McCoy, Michael J., Chief Fin. Officer & V.P.--The Flecto Co., Inc., Oakland, CA, pg. 417
McCrary, Dennie L., V.P.-Fin. & Sec.--Sea Island Company, Sea Island, GA, pg. 983
McCreery, Harry, V.P.-Fin.--Brown Disc Products Company, Colorado Springs, CO, pg. 451
McCreery, Mike, Exec. V.P. & Chief Fin. Officer--C. R. Anthony Company, Oklahoma City, OK, pg. 77
McCusker, Francis C., Chief Fin. Officer--Marmac Corporation, Parkersburg, WV, pg. 710
McDavid, Randall S., Asst. to Pres.-Fin. & Sec.--Union Boiler Co., Nitro, WV, pg. 273
McDermott, Robert J., V.P. & Chief Fin. Officer--Charan Industries, Inc., Garden City, NY, pg. 239
McDevitt, Larry, V.P. & Controller--Levitz Furniture Corporation, Boca Raton, FL, pg. 647
McDonald, Barbara, Chief Fin. Officer--Ford Development Corporation, Cincinnati, OH, pg. 423
McDonald, S. J., Controller & Systems Mgr.--Spectrum Color Center, Golden, CO, pg. 1029
McDonald, Thomas, Chief Fin. Officer & Treas.--Jernberg Industries, Inc., Chicago, IL, pg. 593
McDougal, Carmi, Mgr.-Office--Norbest, Inc., Midvale, UT, pg. 809
McDowell, Robbyn, Chief Fin. Officer--Earnhardt's Auto Center, Tempe, AZ, pg. 362
McElderry, C.J., Chief Fin. Officer & V.P.-Fin.--Rosauer's Supermarkets, Inc., Spokane, WA, pg. 947
McElligott, Frederick T., Treas.--Arthur D. Little of Canada Ltd., Toronto,, Canada, pg. 679
Mcelligott, Frederick T., Treas.--Arthur D. Little Far East, Inc., Singapore, Singapore, pg. 679
McFarland, Howard C., III, Chief Oper. Officer & Chief Fin. Officer--Mid-West Paper Products Company, Warren, MI, pg. 750
McGafferty, Patrick J., Sec., Treas. & Chief Fin. Officer--Grisanti, Inc., Louisville, KY, pg. 488
McGee, James E., Chief Fin. Officer, Treas. & Controller--Weil Brothers Cotton Inc., Montgomery, AL, pg. 1173
McGeough, Peter, Chief Fin. Officer--Seaman Furniture Co., Inc., Woodbury, NY, pg. 986
McGill, Edmund R., V.P. & Chief Fin. Officer--Marketing Corp. of America, Westport, CT, pg. 709
McGinnis, Lewis, Chief Fin. Officer--Die Cast Products, Inc., Gardena, CA, pg. 336
McGlone, James, V.P.-Acctg.--Vienna Sausage Mfg. Co., Chicago, IL, pg. 1151
McGlone, John F., V.P. & Chief Fin. Officer--Chicago Tube & Iron Co., Chicago, IL, pg. 246
McGraime, Douglas, V.P. & Controller--Combe Incorporated, White Plains, NY, pg. 267

McGrath, Brent P., Chief Fin. Officer, Treas. & Sec.--Mico Inc., North Mankato, MN, pg. 748
McGrath, George, V.P.-Fin.--Lane Limited, Tucker, GA, pg. 657
McGregor, Peter, Chief Fin. Officer--Affiliated of Florida Inc., Tampa, FL, pg. 23
McHugh, Michael P., V.P., Chief Fin. Officer--J. Crew Group, Inc., New York, NY, pg. 584
Mcisaac, Steve, Controller--Vesco Oil Corp., Southfield, MI, pg. 1149
McKaig, William D., Treas. & Sec.--Maaco Enterprises Inc., King of Prussia, PA, pg. 694
McKelvey, Patrick M., Treas.--RNL/Interplan, Los Angeles, CA, pg. 908
McKenna, Steve, Chief Fin. Officer/WW (New York)--Wunderman Cato Johnson, New York, NY, pg. 1211
McLamb, George T., Exec. V.P., Treas. & Chief Fin. Officer--Kingsdown, Inc., Mebane, NC, pg. 632
McLean, Bernard, Chief Fin. Officer--Bayer Bess Vanderwarker Inc., Chicago, IL, pg. 128
McLeish, Gordon, Comptroller--Semblex Corporation, Elmhurst, IL, pg. 989
McLeod, John, Jr., V.P. & Chief Fin. Officer--Lone Star Corrugated Container Corporation, Irving, TX, pg. 682
McMachon, William D., Treas. & Sec.--Walker Wire & Steel Company, Ferndale, MI, pg. 1160
McManimon, Bilol, Chief Fin. Officer/Comptroller--NJ Transit, Newark, NJ, pg. 801
McManus, Edward, Chief Fin. Officer--Diemolding Corp., Canastota, NY, pg. 336
McManus, T.K., Jr., V.P.-Fin.--Underground Construction Company, Inc., Benicia, CA, pg. 1125
McMillan, Bruce, Chief Fin. Officer--Cogentrix Incorporated, Charlotte, NC, pg. 258
McMillan, Peter, Chief Fin. Officer--CenterMark Properties, Inc., Saint Louis, MO, pg. 231
McNair, Joe, Exec. V.P.-Fin.--Whitfield Foods, Inc., Montgomery, AL, pg. 1187
McNamara, William B., Chief Fin. Officer, Treas. & Asst. Sec.--Air Conditioning Co., Inc., Glendale, CA, pg. 26
McNea, D., Chief Fin. Officer--Hiniker Company, Mankato, MN, pg. 535
McNeil, W.R., V.P., Treas. & Sec.--Carolina Mirror Company, North Wilkesboro, NC, pg. 223
McNulty, Edward J., V.P. & Chief Fin. Officer--General Binding Corporation, Northbrook, IL, pg. 656
McPhail, Douglas J., Pres., Chief Exec. & Fin. Officer & Treas.--Indiana Records Managers, Indianapolis, IN, pg. 565
McShea, Kevin, Exec. V.P. & Chief Fin. Officer--Budget Rent A Car Corporation, Lisle, IL, pg. 131
McVeigh, Robert A., Chief Fin. Officer & Sr. V.P.--Lockhart & Pettus, Inc., New York, NY, pg. 680
Meador, Charles Edwin, V.P.-Fin.--TST/Impreso, Inc., Coppell, TX, pg. 1075
Meagher, Ellen, Chief Fin. Officer & Treas.--Paisano Publications, Inc., Agoura, CA, pg. 843
Mears, William C., Chief Fin. Officer--Action Equipment, Londonderry, NH, pg. 14
Meckfessel, William R., Chief Fin. Officer--Carco Electronics, Menlo Park, CA, pg. 217
Meehan, Gregory W.A., V.P., Chief Fin. Officer & Treas.--High Point Financial Corp., Branchville, NJ, pg. 533
Meehan, Gregory, W.A., Exec. V.P. & Chief Fin. Officer--The National Bank of Sussex County, Branchville, NJ, pg. 534
Meglaughlin, William T., Jr., Sec. & Treas.--Asbury Graphite Mills, Inc., Asbury, NJ, pg. 87
Mehra, Ajay, Sec., Treas. & Controller--UDT Sensors, Inc., Hawthorne, CA, pg. 1122
Mehta, Shanti, Chief Fin. Officer--W. L. Gore & Associates, Inc., Newark, DE, pg. 472
Mei, Charlie, Fin. Dir.--Ayer Vazquez S.A. de Publicidad, Buenos Aires,, Argentina, pg. 104
Meiers, Charles W., Jr., Chief Fin. Officer & V.P.--Trinidad/Benham Corporation, Denver, CO, pg. 1113
Meilahn, J.E., Sr. V.P. & Chief Fin. Officer & Treas.--Federated Mutual Insurance Company, Owatonna, MN, pg. 405
Meinhardt, Ronald L., V.P. & Chief Fin. Officer--Penske Truck Leasing, Chesterfield, MO, pg. 859
Meister, Paul M., Mng. Dir. & Chief Fin. Officer--The Henley Group, Inc., Hampton, NH, pg. 529
Mellert, Donald, Chief Fin. Officer--Candle Corporation, Santa Monica, CA, pg. 214
Mellos, Steven P., Chief Fin. Officer, V.P. & Treas.--Invetech Co., Detroit, MI, pg. 581
Melton, Cindy, Chief Fin. Officer--DGWB, Inc., Irvine, CA, pg. 309
Melton, Gary, Chief Fin. Officer--Lake Region Manufacturing Company, Inc., Chaska, MN, pg. 651
Meltzner, Sidney, Chief Fin. Officer--Condor Pacific Industries, Inc., Canoga Park, CA, pg. 273
Mendela, Paul, Chief Fin. Officer & Corp. Sec.--Margeotes Fertitta & Weiss, Inc., New York, NY, pg. 706
Mendoza, V., Chief Fin. Officer & Chief Info. Officer & Treas. & Dir.-Data Pr--Gator Industries Inc., Hialeah, FL, pg. 446
Meng, J., Chief Fin. Officer--David Langer & Co., Inc., Hollywood, CA, pg. 657
Mennis, John F., Chief Fin. Officer--Mintz & Hoke Inc., Avon, CT, pg. 759
Menzie, David, Chief Fin. Officer & V.P.-Fin.--Essex Group, Inc., Fort Wayne, IN, pg. 389
Mereschuck, Jeffrey A., V.P. & Chief Fin. Officer--ESSTAR Incorporated, New Haven, CT, pg. 361
Mereschuk, Jeffrey A., V.P. & Chief Fin. Officer--Essex Industries, New Haven, CT, pg. 361
Mergy, Thomas J., Chief Fin. Officer--U.S. Turbine Corporation, Maineville, OH, pg. 1137
Merrillees, Bette, Controller--DeWeese Inc., Los Angeles, CA, pg. 334
Merriman, Michael, Chief Fin. Officer--Ann Raskas Gourmet Confectioners, Edwardsville, KS, pg. 913
Merriman, William, V.P., Fin. & Chief Fin. Officer--Donald D. Lewis Advertising, Burbank, CA, pg. 672
Merry, Bonnie, Treas.--Dormeyer Industries, Chicago, IL, pg. 346
Merz, John Frederick, Jr., Chm. Bd., Pres. & Treas.--Scott Specialty Gases, Inc., Plumsteadville, PA, pg. 983
Meserole, C.V., Exec. V.P. & Chief Fin. Officer--American Steel & Wire Corporation, Cuyahoga Heights, OH, pg. 246
Messmer, Steven E., Controller--Weston Paper & Manufacturing Co., Terre Haute, IN, pg. 1183
Meth, Joseph, Treas. & Chief Fin. Officer--F. Schumacher & Co., New York, NY, pg. 979
Metzinger, Leon, Chief Fin. Officer--Chance Operations, Inc., Wichita, KS, pg. 238
Metzinger, Leon, Chief Fin. Officer--Chance Rides, Inc., Wichita, KS, pg. 238
Meyer, Alan, V.P.-Fin.--Concordia Publishing House, Saint Louis, MO, pg. 272
Meyer, Carl, V.P.-Acctg.--Motorists Mutual Insurance Co., Columbus, OH, pg. 773
Meyer, Don, Controller--Lake to Lake Dairy, Kiel, WI, pg. 653
Meyer, Frederick G., Controller--Geneve Corporation, Stamford, CT, pg. 451
Meyer, Gary, Controller--Schnuck Markets, Inc., Maryland Heights, MO, pg. 977
Meyer, Gary, Sec. & Treas.--Sloans Supermarkets, Inc., New York, NY, pg. 1010
Meyer, James B., Chief Fin. Officer & Sr. V.P.--Spartan Stores Inc., Grand Rapids, MI, pg. 1026
Meyer, Robert, V.P.-Fin.--Iams Company, Dayton, OH, pg. 561
Meyer, Ron, Chief Fin. Officer--The John C. Groub Company Inc., Seymour, IN, pg. 489
Meyers, David L., Sr. V.P. & Chief Fin. Officer--Del Monte Foods, San Francisco, CA, pg. 325
Meza, Catalina, Chief Oper. Officer, Mng. Dir. & Chief Fin. Officer--BSB/Meza, Ltda., Bogota,, Colombia, pg. 110
Michalek, John S., V.P.-Fin. & Chief Fin. Officer--Plaid Enterprises Inc., Norcross, GA, pg. 357
Michelson, Maurice, Sr. V.P., Chief Fin. Officer, & Dir.-Admin. & Pur.--Burkhardt & Christy Advertising, Inc., New York, NY, pg. 191
Michie, Bob, Chief Fin. Officer, Treas. & Sec.--Archer/Malmo Adv., Inc., Memphis, TN, pg. 80
Mickelson, Arnold, V.P.-Fin. & Chief Fin. Officer--Holiday Companies, Minneapolis, MN, pg. 539
Mickey, Bob, Chief Fin. Officer--Old American Pottery Company, Howe, TX, pg. 823
Midkiff, Everett L., Chief Fin. Officer--American Marketing Industries, Inc., Kansas City, MO, pg. 58
Miehl, Peter, Chief Fin. Officer--Heet Automotive, Westchester, IL, pg. 328
Miehl, Peter C., V.P.-Fin. & Treas.--DeMert & Dougherty, Inc., Westchester, IL, pg. 328
Mielcuszny, Albert J., Chief Fin. Officer & Sr. V.P.--Servistar Corporation, East Butler, PA, pg. 992
Miido, Endel, V.P.-Fin. & Admin.--Seabrook Brothers & Sons, Inc., Seabrook, NJ, pg. 984
Mikelonis, Rudy, Controller--Zima Corp., Spartanburg, SC, pg. 1219
Mikolajczak, Robert, Chief Fin. Officer--Piper Aircraft Corporation, Vero Beach, FL, pg. 872
Milco, Ed, Chief Fin. Officer--Young & Rubicam (Zambia) Ltd., Lusaka,, Zambia, pg. 1214
Miles, John C., Controller & Asst. Treas.--Petroleum Inc., Wichita, KS, pg. 865
Miles, Rod, Chief Fin. Officer--Cappelli Miles Wiltz & Kelly, Portland, OR, pg. 216
Mileson, Glenna, V.P. & Chief Fin. Officer--Livingston & Company, Seattle, WA, pg. 679
Mileusnic, George, Sr. V.P. & Chief Fin. Officer--The Coleman Company, Inc., Wichita, KS, pg. 695
Mileusnie, George, Chief Fin. Officer--Coleman Outdoor Products, Wichita, KS, pg. 695
Milhizer, Robert, V.P., Chief Fin. Officer--Wardrop Murtaugh Temple, Chicago, IL, pg. 1163
Miller, Barry, Chief Fin. Officer--NBO Stores Inc., Fair Lawn, NJ, pg. 780
Miller, Bill, V.P. & Controller--Network Services Company of Chicago, Mount Prospect, IL, pg. 798
Miller, Clayton, Chief Fin. Officer--Washington Homes, Inc., Landover, MD, pg. 1166
Miller, Donald L., V.P.-Fin. & Treas.--Weston Paper & Manufacturing Co., Terre Haute, IN, pg. 1183
Miller, G.G., V.P.-Fin., Chief Fin. Officer & Treas.--AFG Industries, Inc., Fort Worth, TX, pg. 3
Miller, Gary L., Chief Fin. Officer--Enterprise Products Company, Houston, TX, pg. 382
Miller, Helen B., Treas. & Sec.--Washington Corporation, Missoula, MT, pg. 1165
Miller, John, V.P. & Controller--F. R. Manufacturing Corporation, Stockton, CA, pg. 395
Miller, John, V.P. & Chief Fin. Officer--Brim, Inc., Portland, OR, pg. 176
Miller, John, Chief Fin. Officer, Treas. & Controller--RJO Enterprises, Inc., Lanham, MD, pg. 907
Miller, Kenneth I., Chief Fin. Officer, Treas. & Sr. V.P.--Johnston, Lemon & Co. Inc., Washington, DC, pg. 601
Miller, Kirk, Treas.--Buff Whelan Chevrolet & GEO, Inc., Sterling Heights, MI, pg. 1185
Miller, Lester, Controller--Times Printing Company, Inc., Random Lake, WI, pg. 1098
Miller, Mike J., Chief Fin. Officer--Miller Oil Co., Inc., Norfolk, VA, pg. 754
Miller, Neil, Exec. V.P., Chief Fin. Officer--Partners & Shevack, Inc., New York, NY, pg. 850
Miller, Raymond J., Sr. V.P. Fin. & Chief Fin. Officer--Carlisle Retailers, Inc., Ashtabula, OH, pg. 220
Miller, Richard, V.P.-Fin. & Chief Fin. Officer--McInerney-Miller Brothers Inc., Detroit, MI, pg. 729
Miller, Steven, Chief Fin. Officer, Treas. & Controller--Resort Condominiums International, Indianapolis, IN, pg. 929
Miller, Wayne, Chief Fin. Officer--Career Club Shirt Co., New York, NY, pg. 898
Miller, Wayne E., Chief Fin. Officer--Publix Group, New York, NY, pg. 898
Miller,Chuck, Comptroller--Swift-Cor Tool Engineering, Gardena, CA, pg. 1067
Milliken, Minot, Chief Fin. Officer--Milliken & Co., Inc., Spartanburg, SC, pg. 755
Millikin, C.W., Chief Fin. Officer--Affiliated Foods, Inc., Amarillo, TX, pg. 24
Mills, Daniel J., Chief Fin. Officer & V.P.--Lebhar-Friedman, Inc., New York, NY, pg. 665
Mills, Dean, Chief Fin. Officer & Treas.--Brooks Products, Inc., El Monte, CA, pg. 180
Mills, Nancy M., Chief Fin. Officer & V.P.--Downey Designs International, Inc., Indianapolis, IN, pg. 348
Milota, Bernard F., High Sec. & Treas.--Catholic Order of Foresters, Naperville, IL, pg. 229
Minami, Wesley D., Sr. V.P. & Chief Fin. Officer--Oxford Realty Services Corp., Bethesda, MD, pg. 835
Minard, John D., V.P., Controller & Chief Fin. Officer--Manna Pro Corporation, Saint Louis, MO, pg. 704
Mineart, Carol J., Chief Fin. Officer & Treasurer--Avis Industrial Corporation, Upland, IN, pg. 102
Miniat, Edmund, Chief Fin. Officer & Treas.--Ed Miniat, Inc., Chicago, IL, pg. 757
Miniutti, Patrick, Chief Fin. Officer--Crown American Corporation, Johnstown, PA, pg. 301
Minkus, Leslie, V.P. & Chief Fin. Officer--Newly Weds Foods Inc., Chicago, IL, pg. 804
Minsky, Robert, V.P. & Chief Fin. Officer--Berlitz International, Inc., Princeton, NJ, pg. 142
Minsky, Robert, V.P. & Chief Fin. Officer--Berlitz Publishing Company Inc., New York, NY, pg. 142
Mintz, Murray, Chief Fin. Officer--Tropar Mfg. Co., Inc., Florham Park, NJ, pg. 1115
Mitchell, Alan, Sec. & Treas.--Service Web Offset Corporation, Chicago, IL, pg. 992
Mitchell, B.G., V.P. & Chief Fin. Officer--Adept Technology, Inc., San Jose, CA, pg. 17
Mitchell, Randy, Sec. & Treas.--The Hotsy Corporation, Englewood, CO, pg. 545
Mitlyng, Errol P., Sr. V.P.-Fin., Treas. & Chief Fin. Officer--The Marley Company, Mission Woods, KS, pg. 710
Mixtacki, Steven B., V.P. & Chief Fin. Officer--American TV & Appliance of Madison, Inc., Madison, WI, pg. 65
Mize, E.J., Jr., V.P.-Fin., Treas., Chief Fin. & Acctg. Officer--United States Pipe & Foundry Company, Birmingham, AL, pg. 1162
Mize, Mike, V.P.-Corp. Plng. & Devel., Chief Fin. Officer, Sec. & Treas.--GSC Enterprises, Inc., Sulphur Springs, TX, pg. 440
Mizenko, Michael, Chief Fin. Officer--After Six, Incorporated, Philadelphia, PA, pg. 24
Mizeur, David, Deputy Dir.-Audit & Fin.--Illinois State Lottery, Springfield, IL, pg. 563
Mock, C. A., V.P., Sec. & Chief Fin. Officer--Consolidated Pipe & Supply Company, Birmingham, AL, pg. 277
Mogas, V. Louis, Pres. & Chief Exec. Officer--Mogas Industries, Inc., Houston, TX, pg. 763
Mogul, Charles G., Chief Fin. Officer--Richter & Ratner Contracting Corporation, Maspeth, NY, pg. 933
Molden, Fred, Chief Fin. Officer--Pilot Air Freight Corp., Lima, PA, pg. 870
Moloney, Thomas E., Chief Fin. Officer--John Hancock Mutual Life Insurance Company, Boston, MA, pg. 595
Moloney, Thomas E., Chief Fin. Officer--John Hancock HealthPlans, Inc., West Chester, PA, pg. 596
Monaco, Dominick J., V.P.-Fin.--American Electronics, Inc., Fullerton, CA, pg. 3
Montgomery, R.L., Chief Fin. Officer, Exec. V.P. & Treas.--Columbus McKinnon Corp., Amherst, NY, pg. 266
Moodhe, Vernell E., Chief Fin. Officer--Johnson Acoustical & Supply Co., Portland, OR, pg. 597
Moore, Brant R., Chief Fin. Officer, Treas. & Sec.--I. H. French & Co. Inc., Champaign, IL, pg. 432
Moore, Bruce, Chief Fin. Officer & V.P.--Specialty Paperboard Inc., Brattleboro, VT, pg. 1027
Moore, Leonard D., Controller--Dean Operations Inc., Kansas City, MO, pg. 322
Moore, Leroy E., Sec. & Treas.--Thrifty Drug Stores, Inc., Minneapolis, MN, pg. 1096
Moore, P.J., Sr. V.P., Chief Oper. Officer, Chief Fin. Officer, Sec. & Treas.--Green Holdings, Inc., Denver, CO, pg. 484
Moore, P.J., Sr. V.P., Chief Fin. Officer, Sec. & Treas.--Green International, Inc., Denver, CO, pg. 484
Moore, Thomas, V.P. & Chief Fin. Officer--Wicker Park L.P., Chicago, IL, pg. 1188
Moran, David K., V.P., Chief Fin. Officer--Bradley Communications, Inc., Anchorage, AK, pg. 170
Moran, John, Controller--Rogers Markets Inc., Fort Wayne, IN, pg. 943
Moran, Kevin, Treas. & Sec.--TSI Industries, Inc., Landover, MD, pg. 1075
Moran, Thomas J., Chief Exec. Officer--Mutual of America, New York, NY, pg. 777
More, Dominick D., Chief Fin. Officer--Eastern Air Devices, Inc., Dover, NH, pg. 363
Morford, John A., V.P. & Chief Fin. Officer--V.T. Inc., Merriam, KS, pg. 1142
Morgan, Donna, Treas. & Sec.--Southgate Ford Inc., Southgate, MI, pg. 1023
Morgan, Nigel, Chief Fin. Officer--Ventura Associates, Inc., New York, NY, pg. 1147
Morgante, Paul, Exec. V.P. & Chief Fin. Officer--Dominick & Dominick, Incorporated, New York, NY, pg. 343
Morgrette, John, Sr. V.P. & Chief Fin. Officer--Wickes Lumber Co., Vernon Hills, IL, pg. 1188
Moroz, Kenneth, Controller--Harry H. Bell & Sons, Inc., Saint Petersburg, FL, pg. 134

Morrell, Jenny, V.P., Chief Fin. Officer--The Bomstein Agency, Washington, DC, pg. 164
Morris, Donna R., Dir.-Investor Rels., Asst. Sec. & Treas.--Walk, Haydel & Associates, Inc., New Orleans, LA, pg. 1159
Morris, Thomas F., Exec. V.P. & Chief Fin. Officer--World's Finest Chocolate, Inc., Chicago, IL, pg. 1203
Morrissey, John, Exec. V.P. & Chief Fin. Officer--Ferrous Processing & Trading Co., Detroit, MI, pg. 407
Morse, Robert, Controller--McDowell Mfg. Co., Du Bois, PA, pg. 32
Mortensen, Lee W., Chief Fin. Officer--Western Dairymen Cooperative, Inc., Thornton, CO, pg. 1178
Moser, Eugene R., Sec. & Treas.--Sioux Falls Construction Company, Sioux Falls, SD, pg. 1008
Moser, Martin, Chief Fin. Officer--Abramson Ehrlich Manes, Inc., Washington, DC, pg. 10
Moser, Ron, Chief Fin. Officer--Crane Construction Co., Northbrook, IL, pg. 296
Mosley, John, Chief Fin. Officer & Exec. V.P.--Sheplers, Inc., Wichita, KS, pg. 998
Mossberg, Alan I., Pres., Chief Exec. & Chief Oper. Officer & Treas.--O. F. Mossberg & Sons, Inc., North Haven, CT, pg. 773
Motola, Joseph C., Chief Fin. Officer, V.P.-Fin. & Sec.--Farnam Companies, Inc., Phoenix, AZ, pg. 403
Motzer, William R., V.P., Chief Fin. Officer & Sec.--Berwind Pharmaceuticals Services, Inc., King of Prussia, PA, pg. 145
Mucciolo, Michael R., Chief Fin. Officer & Sr. V.P.--Brooks Beverage Management, Inc., Holland, MI, pg. 179
Muegge, Lyn, Exec. V.P., Chief Fin. Officer--Hal Riney & Partners, Inc., San Francisco, CA, pg. 935
Mueller, James E., Sr. V.P. & Chief Fin. Officer--Dairymen, Inc., Louisville, KY, pg. 311
Mullen, David B., Chief Fin. Officer--CCC Information Services, Chicago, IL, pg. 410
Mullineaux, John, V.P.-Fin. & Gen. Mgr.--Fenner Manheim, Manheim, PA, pg. 406
Mullis, Elbert N., Jr., Exec. V.P. & Chief Admin. & Fin. Officer--Coca Cola Bottling Co. United, Inc., Birmingham, AL, pg. 257
Mumford, C.G., Exec. V.P., Treas. & Chief Fin. Officer--Arcata Corporation, San Francisco, CA, pg. 80
Mungcal, Edward, Controller--Wells Manufacturing Company, Verdi, NV, pg. 1027
Mungle, D., V.P.-Fin.--Layne & Bowler, Memphis, TN, pg. 710
Munier, Robert S.C., Exec. V.P. & Treas.--Wolff & Munier, Inc., Hawthorne, NY, pg. 1199
Murch, Karl, Chief Fin. Officer--Phoenix Steel, Inc., Eau Claire, WI, pg. 869
Murdock, Jack C., V.P.-Fin., Sec. & Treas.--Transus Inc., Atlanta, GA, pg. 1108
Murillo, Jeff, V.P., Treas., Controller & Chief Fin. Officer--MacMillan Oil Co., Inc., Des Moines, IA, pg. 475
Murphy, Dennis R., V.P.-Fin. & Chief Fin. Officer--Symmons Industries Inc., Braintree, MA, pg. 1069
Murphy, George E., Chief Fin. Officer & V.P.--Jupiter Industries, Inc., Chicago, IL, pg. 609
Murphy, Jeremiah T., V.P.-Fin.--A. G. Spanos Development, Inc., Stockton, CA, pg. 1025
Murphy, Karen, V.P., Sec. & Treas.--California Pacific Research, Inc., Reno, NV, pg. 210
Murphy, Kevin M., Chief Fin. Officer & Treas.--Rama Group of Companies, Cheektowaga, NY, pg. 910
Murphy, Kevin s., Sec. & Treas.--Michael Foods, Inc., Minneapolis, MN, pg. 747
Murphy, M., V.P. & Chief Fin. Officer--Franklin Steel Company, Franklin, PA, pg. 429
Murphy, Robert E., V.P. & Chief Fin. Officer--Creative Playthings Ltd., Framingham, MA, pg. 297
Murphy, Steve, V.P. & Chief Fin. Officer--A.B.P. Midwest, Inc., Madison, WI, pg. 2
Murphy, Tim, Chief Fin. Officer--Charles Pankow Builders, Ltd., Altadena, CA, pg. 846
Murray, John J., V.P.-Fin., Sec. & Treas.--Electro-Wire Products, Inc., Rochester Hills, MI, pg. 375
Murray, R.W., Chief Fin. Officer, Sr. V.P., Treas., Controller & Sec.--Webb, Murray & Associates, La Porte, TX, pg. 1170
Murrer, Thomas, Chief Fin. Officer--Sportsystems Corporation, Buffalo, NY, pg. 326
Muscarello, Diane, Sec. & Treas.--Westgate Inc., Port Allen, LA, pg. 1182
Muse, Charles H., Jr., Treas. & Chief Fin. Officer--Crown Coal & Coke Co. Inc., Pittsburgh, PA, pg. 302
Mutman, Danyal, V.P. & Chief Fin. Officer--Egizii Electric, Inc., Springfield, IL, pg. 371
Myers, H.J., Chief Fin. Officer--LubeCon Systems, Inc., Fremont, MI, pg. 686
Myers, Larry F., Sr. V.P., Chief Fin. Officer, Sec. & Treas.--Mitre Corporation, Bedford, MA, pg. 762
Myers, Leland, Controller--The Double-Cola Company, Chattanooga, TN, pg. 347
Myers, Norman S., Pres., Treas., Chief Exec. & Fin. Officers--IDM Controls, Houston, TX, pg. 560
Myers, Richard G., Exec. V.P. & Treas.--Seaboard Corporation, Newton, MA, pg. 984
Myers, Robert, Chief Fin. Officer--Capitol Chevrolet Cadillac GEO, Inc., Salem, OR, pg. 215
Myers, Ronald W., V.P.-Fin. & Admin. & Chief Fin. Officer--GF Office Furniture Ltd., Gallatin, TN, pg. 439
Myers, Vaughn, V.P.-Fin.--The Chas. H. Lilly Co., Portland, OR, pg. 675
Myhre, Paul, V.P. & Treas.--Wright-Schuchart, Inc., Seattle, WA, pg. 1204
Nadel, Kenneth, V.P.-Fin.--The Magee Carpet Company, Bloomsburg, PA, pg. 700
Nadorf, Ben J., Pres. & Treas.--Everlast Sports Manufacturing Corp., Bronx, NY, pg. 392
Nakamura, James, Chief Fin. Officer & Sr. V.P.--Southwest Marine, Inc., San Diego, CA, pg. 1023
Nannicelli, John J., Jr., Exec. V.P.-Fin. & Opers.--Lowell Shoe, Inc., Hudson, NH, pg. 772
Naporano, Joe, Chief. Fin. Officer--Wieden & Kennedy, Inc., Portland, OR, pg. 1188
Nash, James S., Treas., Chief Fin. Officer & Controller--E.P. Henry Corporation, Woodbury, NJ, pg. 530
Nassar, Kam, Exec. V.P.-Fin., Admin. & Chief Fin. Officer--Arby's, Inc., Miami Beach, FL, pg. 243
Nathan, Bala, Chief Fin. Officer--Wallace Co. Inc., Houston, TX, pg. 1160
Nattier, Robert, Chief Oper. Officer, Chief Fin. Officer & Gen. Mgr.--Mid-Kansas Co-op Association, Moundridge, KS, pg. 750
Needleman, Hyman, Chief Fin. Officer--Duane Reade, Long Island City, NY, pg. 350
Neff, Richard, Chief Fin. Officer--Di Giorgio Corporation, Somerset, NJ, pg. 334
Negomeir, George R., V.P.-Fin., Treas. & Sec.--Sigman Meat Co. Inc., Arvada, CO, pg. 1003
Neilsen, M., Chief Fin. Officer--AGEMA Infrared Systems, Inc., Secaucus, NJ, pg. 24
Neis, Arthur V., Treas.--The Weitz Corporation, Des Moines, IA, pg. 1174
Neis, Arthur V., Chief Fin. Officer & Treas.--Life Care Services Corporation, Des Moines, IA, pg. 1174
Nelson, Conrad, V.P.-Fin. & Chief Fin. Officer--Alloy Products Corporation, Waukesha, WI, pg. 41
Nelson, Grant E., Chief Fin. Officer--West Publishing Co., Eagan, MN, pg. 1177
Nelson, Jeff, V.P.-Fin.--Saladmaster, Arlington, TX, pg. 967
Nelson, Robert, Chief Fin. Officer--21 International Holdings, Inc., New York, NY, pg. 1121
Neskey, David A., Chief Fin. Officer & Sr. V.P.-Fin.--Spaulding & Slye Company, Burlington, MA, pg. 1026
Neto, Teresa, Acctg. Chief--BSB Portugal, Lisbon,, Portugal, pg. 110
Neu, Richard W., Exec. V.P. & Chief Fin. Officer--First Federal of Michigan, Detroit, MI, pg. 414
Neves, Faye, Chief Fin. Officer--Clayton-Davis & Associates, Incorporated, Saint Louis, MO, pg. 253
Nevins, Jay, V.P.-Fin.--Field Container Company, L.P., Elk Grove Village, IL, pg. 409
Newburger, John, Controller--American Marking Systems, Clifton, NJ, pg. 58
Newgard, James H., Sec. & Treas.--Henry Newgard & Company, Arlington Heights, IL, pg. 804
Newton, John W., Chief Fin. Officer--Morgan Construction Company, Worcester, MA, pg. 769
Nicholson, Bruce J., Chief Fin. Officer & Exec. V.P.--Lutheran Brotherhood, Minneapolis, MN, pg. 688
Nick, Richard, Chief Fin. Officer--North American Salt Company, Overland Park, KS, pg. 812
Nieboer, James, V.P.-Fin.--Liberty Tool Corporation, Rochester, NY, pg. 674
Niemiec, Thom, Treas. & Sec.--The Tech Group, Scottsdale, AZ, pg. 1082
Niewahner, Edward, Treas.--Van Leunens Inc., Cincinnati, OH, pg. 1144
Nikkel, Robert F., Pres. & Chief Fin. Officer--The Nikkel Corporation, Sacramento, CA, pg. 807
Nitsche, John, Chief Fin. Officer, V.P. & Treas.--United Hardware Distributing Co., Plymouth, MN, pg. 1132
Nobles, Herbert, Treas.--Upstate Milk Cooperatives Inc., Le Roy, NY, pg. 1140
Noell, Nick, Pres.-Intl. & Chief Fin. Officer--Samsonite Corporation, Denver, CO, pg. 358
Nofziger, Hope, Mgr.-Credit--Toledo Blade Co., Toledo, OH, pg. 155
Nolan, Patrick J., Sr. V.P., Chief Fin. Officer & Treas.--LFC Holding Corporation, Boca Raton, FL, pg. 647
Nolan, Patrick J., Sr. V.P. & Treas.--Levitz Furniture Corporation, Boca Raton, FL, pg. 647
Nolen, I.R., V.P.-Fin.--Sivalls, Inc., Odessa, TX, pg. 1009
Norberg, Joseph, Chief Fin. Officer & Treas.--Hill, Holliday, Connors, Cosmopulos, Inc., Boston, MA, pg. 534
Norberg, Paul A., Chief Fin. Officer & Exec. V.P.--Western Temporary Services, Inc., Walnut Creek, CA, pg. 1181
Nordgren, Bradley J., Sr. V.P. & Chief Fin. Officer--EvansGroup, Salt Lake City, UT, pg. 390
Nordstrom, William, Chief Fin. Officer & Sec.--Amana-Nordstrom Motel Co., Amana, IA, pg. 46
Norman, Dennis C., Sr. V.P. & Chief Fin. Officer--Mayflower Transit, Inc., Carmel, IN, pg. 724
Norton, Robert R., Jr., Exec. V.P., Chief Oper. & Fin. Officer--BeefAmerica Operating Co., Inc., Omaha, NE, pg. 131
Noselli, Charles, Chief Fin. Officer--Lensclean, Inc., Carlstadt, NJ, pg. 33
Nottleson, Neal R., V.P.-Fin.-U.S. Consumer Prods.--S. C. Johnson & Son, Inc., Racine, WI, pg. 599
Novak, Alex, Chief Fin. Officer--Remington Products Inc., Bridgeport, CT, pg. 926
Novak, Jeff, V.P., Chief Fin. Officer--Chuck Ruhr Advertising, Minneapolis, MN, pg. 955
Novak, Ronald, Chief Fin. Officer--Weider Health & Fitness, Woodland Hills, CA, pg. 1173
Novak, Rosina, Controller--Beck Manufacturing, Inc., Waynesboro, PA, pg. 153
Nowacki, Kajetan, Sec. & Treas.--Velcon Filters, Inc., San Jose, CA, pg. 1146
Noyce, Jeffrey P., Exec. V.P. & Chief Fin. Officer--Chicago West Pullman Corporation, Cincinnati, OH, pg. 246
Noyd, Mark R., Chief Fin. Officer--Brock Control Systems, Inc., Atlanta, GA, pg. 178
Nussbaum, Mark, Chief Fin. Officer--Western Federal Savings & Loan Association, Marina Del Rey, CA, pg. 1179
Nussdorf, Lawrence, Chief Fin. Officer & Treas.--CEI Construction, Inc., Bethesda, MD, pg. 200
O'Brien, Dennis, V.P. & Chief Fin. Officer--Tate Access Floors, Inc., Jessup, MD, pg. 1080
O'Brien, J.J., Sr. V.P. & Chief Fin. Officer--Gulf States Paper Corporation, Tuscaloosa, AL, pg. 494
O'Brien, John, Chief Fin. Officer& Dir.-F & I--Charles River Data Systems, Inc., Framingham, MA, pg. 240
O'Bryan, Thomas W., Sr. V.P. & Chief Fin. Officer--Taylor Drug Stores, Inc., Louisville, KY, pg. 1081
O'Callaghan, R.A., Chief Exec. Officer--Universal Builders Supply, Inc., Mount Vernon, NY, pg. 1137
O'Connell, Edward J., Chief Fin. Officer--GenDerm Corporation, Lincolnshire, IL, pg. 448
O'Connell, J., V.P.-Fin.--Spencer Industries, Inc., New Brunswick, NJ, pg. 1030
O'Connell, Joseph, V.P.-Fin.--Casual Sportswear Co., Inc., Dunmore, PA, pg. 1030
O'Connell, Mike, Chief Fin. Officer & Comptroller--Thomas & Skinner, Inc., Indianapolis, IN, pg. 1093
O'Connor, John, Chief Fin. Officer & Controller--Marketing Communications, Lenexa, KS, pg. 709
O'Connor, Patrick M., Chief Fin. Officer & V.P.--Maclean-Fogg Co., Mundelein, IL, pg. 697
O'Connor, Paul R., Sec., Treas. & Chief Fin. Officer--F.A. Wilhelm Construction Co., Inc., Indianapolis, IN, pg. 1189
O'Dell, Jane, Pres. & Treas.--Westfall GMC Truck Inc., North Kansas City, MO, pg. 1182
O'Hara, Eugene M., Sr. V.P., Comptroller & Chief Fin. Officer--The Prudential Insurance Company of America, Newark, NJ, pg. 896
O'Hara, Paul M., Exec. V.P. & Chief Fin. Officer--Farley Industries, Chicago, IL, pg. 399
O'Leary, Thomas M., Chief Fin. Officer & Gen Counsel--The Pepper Companies, Inc., Chicago, IL, pg. 859
O'Mally, John, V.P.-Fin.--Dayton Rogers Mfg. Co., Minneapolis, MN, pg. 321
O'Neal, Rex, Treas.--Spencer's Inc., Mount Airy, NC, pg. 1030
O'Neil, Joseph F., Chief Fin. Officer & Controller--The Harodite Finishing Company Inc., North Dighton, MA, pg. 510
O'Neil, William J., Chm. Bd., Pres. & Treas.--O'Neil Data Systems, Inc., Los Angeles, CA, pg. 827
O'Rourke, Dennis, Sr. V.P. & Chief Fin. Officer--Goldberg Moser O'Neill, San Francisco, CA, pg. 465
O'Shea, Martin, Sr. V.P.-Fin.--Tucson Realty & Trust Co., Tucson, AZ, pg. 1118
Oakford, S.I., V.P. & Chief Fin. Officer--Hesston, Norcross, GA, pg. 4
Oakson, John J., Chief Fin. Officer & V.P.--SRI International, Menlo Park, CA, pg. 964
Obst, J.C., Treas.--Schenectady Chemicals, Inc., Schenectady, NY, pg. 975
Ockels, Theodore S., Pres., Chief Exec. Officer, Chief Fin. Officer & Treas.--Up-Right Work Platforms Division, Selma, CA, pg. 1139
Odom, James M., V.P.-Fin. & Admin.--Superior Machine Company Of South Carolina, Inc., Florence, SC, pg. 1064
Oertling, Lawrence P., Chief Fin. Officer--The Laitram Corporation, Harahan, LA, pg. 650
Oertling, Lawrence P., Chief Fin. Officer--Intralox, Inc., Harahan, LA, pg. 651
Ogden, Jeff, V.P.-Admin. & Chief Fin. Officer--Despatch Industries, Minneapolis, MN, pg. 332
Ohl, Glen J., Treas. & Chief Fin. Officer--Great Lakes Bancorp, Ann Arbor, MI, pg. 480
Okin, Robert, Chief Fin. Officer--Webcraft Technologies, Inc., North Brunswick, NJ, pg. 1171
Okonow, Dale, Chief Fin. Officer & Sr. V.P.--H M K Enterprises, Inc., Waltham, MA, pg. 497
Oldfather, Grayson W., Exec. V.P.-Corp. Services & Chief Fin. Officer--Tristate Electrical Supply Co., Inc., Hagerstown, MD, pg. 1114
oliver, Paul, Chief Fin. Officer--Chicorp, Inc., Chicago, IL, pg. 247
Oliver, Robert, Chief Fin. Officer--Wilkins Outdoor Network, Inc., Atlanta, GA, pg. 1189
Olsen, Lawrence G., V.P., Treas. & Chief Fin. Officer--Golub Corporation, Schenectady, NY, pg. 469
Olsen, Lawrence G., V.P.-Fin., Treas. & Chief Fin. Officer--Price Chopper, Schenectady, NY, pg. 469
Olsen, Richard B., V.P.-Fin.--International Specialty Products, Inc., Wilmington, DE, pg. 438
Olsson, J. P., Sr. V.P.-Fin. & Chief Fin. Officer--Austin Industries, Inc., Dallas, TX, pg. 99
Omlor, Jack, Chief Fin. Officer & Treas.--P M Company, Philadelphia, PA, pg. 835
Opler, Edmond, Jr., Chm. Bd., Pres. & Chief Exec. Officer--World's Finest Chocolate, Inc., Chicago, IL, pg. 1203
Oppegaard, Larry B., Chief Fin. Officer & Exec. V.P.--Old Home Foods, Inc., Saint Paul, MN, pg. 823
Orbegzo, Luis, Chief Fin. Officer--Perdomo-Ted Bates/ Publicidad, Lima,, Peru, pg. 112
Oremland, Stanley, Chief Fin. Officer--Doe Spun, Inc., New York, NY, pg. 343
Orenstein, Steve, Chief Fin. Officer--Davis, Ball & Colombatto Advertising, Inc., Los Angeles, CA, pg. 318
Orlowski, Ronald J., Chief Fin. Officer & V.P.-Admin.--Osmose Wood Preserving Co., Buffalo, NY, pg. 830
Ormsby, Clarence, Sec. & Treas.--The Curtis Publishing Company, Indianapolis, IN, pg. 306
Ormsby, Clarence, Sec. & Treas.--Servaas Investments, Inc., Indianapolis, IN, pg. 991
Orr, Barbara, V.P. & Chief Fin. Officer--Jon Douglas Company, Beverly Hills, CA, pg. 347
Orr, Ed, V.P.-Fin.--Cramer Inc., Kansas City, KS, pg. 296
Osborne, Monica, V.P. & Chief Fin. Officer--Tollycraft Yachts Corp., Kelso, WA, pg. 1100
Oscherwitz, Jerry, V.P., Asst. Treas. & Sec.--Best Kosher Sausage Co., Chicago, IL, pg. 146
Ossmann, Robert E., Chief Fin. Officer, Treas. & Sec.--Heller Seasonings & Ingredients, Inc., Bedford Park, IL, pg. 526
Ostby, Ron, Grp. V.P. & Chief Fin. Officer--Land O'Lakes, Inc., Arden Hills, MN, pg. 653
Osusky, Frank, Chief Fin. Officer & V.P.-Fin.--Wechsler Coffee Corp., Moonachie, NJ, pg. 1172

Ott, Ellen, V.P., Chief Fin. Officer--Crowley Webb & Associates, Buffalo, NY, pg. 301
Ott, John, V.P. & Chief Fin. Officer--The Fairmont Hotels, San Francisco, CA, pg. 397
Otten, Leslie B., Pres. & Treas.--Sunday River Skiway Corporation, Bethel, ME, pg. 1059
Ottis, O.M., III, Chief Fin. Officer--Autry Greer & Sons, Inc., Prichard, AL, pg. 486
Otto, Henry James, Pres. & Chief Fin. Officer--Sid Harvey Inc., Valley Stream, NY, pg. 515
Ouimet, Emil R., Treas.--Ouimet Stay & Leather Co., Nashville, TN, pg. 831
Outlan, John H., Sec. & Treas.--Winter Park Leasing, Inc., Winter Park, FL, pg. 882
Ovenden, J.A., Chief Fin. Officer & Treas.--Clinton Mills Inc., Clinton, SC, pg. 202
Ovenden, James A., Chief Fin. Officer--CMI Industries, Inc., Columbia, SC, pg. 202
Overlock, Bill, Sr. V.P. & Chief Fin. Officer--Western International Media Corporation, Los Angeles, CA, pg. 1179
Owen, Gary, Chief Fin. Officer & Controller--Design 1 Interiors, Los Angeles, CA, pg. 332
Owen, Gary, Chief Fin. Officer--Century Computer Marketing, Marina Del Rey, CA, pg. 235
Owen, Sharyl, Sec., Treas. & Chief Fin. Officer--Power-One, Inc., Camarillo, CA, pg. 883
Owens, Brenda, Chief Fin. Officer--Ricart Ford Inc., Groveport, OH, pg. 931
Owens, C. Richard, Sr. V.P. & Chief Fin. Officer--The Dyson-Kissner-Moran Corporation, New York, NY, pg. 357
Owens, C. Richard, Sr. V.P. & Chief Fin. Officer--DKM, Ltd., New York, NY, pg. 357
Oyler, W. Kent, III, Treas.--Henry Vogt Machine Co., Louisville, KY, pg. 1154
Ozmun, Robert, Chief Fin. Officer & Controller--Grocers Supply Co. Inc., Houston, TX, pg. 488
Ozur, Ronald, Chief Fin. Officer--Gilda Marx Inc., Los Angeles, CA, pg. 716
Paffect, Chris, Chief Fin. Officer--Adelphia Lamp & Shade Inc., Philadelphia, PA, pg. 17
Page, F. Roger, Chm. Bd., Pres., Chief Exec. & Fin. Officer--Pace Oil Co., Inc., Winston-Salem, NC, pg. 838
Palazzo, Phil, Exec. V.P., Chief Fin. Officer--Ammirati & Puris Inc., New York, NY, pg. 67
Paletz, Lenn, Chm., Pres., Chief Exec. & Chief Oper. Officer--The Sportsman's Guide, Inc., Eagan, MN, pg. 1032
Pallat, Daniel J., Chief Fin. Officer, V.P., Treas. & Sec.--Home Juice Company, Melrose Park, IL, pg. 541
Palley, Thomas E., Chief Fin. Officer--Curtis Mathes Corporation, Athens, TX, pg. 720
Palmer, Douglas E., Pres. & Chief Fin. Officer--Terminal Grain Corp., Sioux City, IA, pg. 1088
Palmer, Edward, V.P. Opers.--Howden Sirocco inc., Hyde Park, MA, pg. 547
Paolin, Dolores, Chief Fin. Officer--Paolin & Sweeney, Cherry Hill, NJ, pg. 847
Papai, Jacki, Chief Fin. Officer, Sec. & Treas.--Ventre Packing Company, Inc., Syracuse, NY, pg. 1147
Pape, Eldon C., Chief Fin. Officer, Chief Plng. Officer & Exec. V.P.--Omaha Public Power District, Omaha, NE, pg. 825
Pardue, Coley, V.P.-Fin.--Tennelec/Nucleus, Inc., Oak Ridge, TN, pg. 1087
Parfit, Gavin J., Chief Fin. Officer--Primary Industries Corporation, New York, NY, pg. 889
Parfit, Gavin J., Chief Fin. Officer--Golodetz Corporation, New York, NY, pg. 469
Park, Charles, Chief Fin. Officer & V.P.-Fin.--Briggs Industries, Inc., Tampa, FL, pg. 175
Park, Sungho, Chief Fin. Officer--Westgate Fabrics, Inc., Grand Prairie, TX, pg. 1182
Parker, D.E., Chief Fin. Officer--The Black Clawson Co., New York, NY, pg. 154
Parker, Dave, Chief Fin. Officer--Molded Fiber Glass Co., Ashtabula, OH, pg. 764
Parker, Howard E., Sr. V.P.-Fin. & Admin. & Chief Fin. Officer--Atlas Van Lines, Inc., Evansville, IN, pg. 96
Parker, Stan, Chief Fin. Officer--Flambeau Products Corp., Middlefield, OH, pg. 809
Parkinson, Terry, Sec. & Treas.--Corn States Hybrid Service, Incorporated, Des Moines, IA, pg. 286
Parrish, Henry N., V.P. & Treas.--Chicago West Pullman Heavy Industries, Cincinnati, OH, pg. 246
Parrish, Neil, Treas. & Project Mgr.--Underground Construction Company, Inc., Benicia, CA, pg. 1125
Parsons, D., V.P.-Fin.--Curtis-Toledo, Inc., Saint Louis, MO, pg. 306
Parsons, Gregg, V.P.-Fin.--The Julius Schepps Co., Dallas, TX, pg. 975
Partridge, Fred, Exec. V.P. & Chief Fin. Officer--Smith-Emery Company, Los Angeles, CA, pg. 1012
Parzanese, Paul, Treas.--Keuffel & Esser, Rockaway, NJ, pg. 105
Pas, Greg, V.P., Chief Fin. Officer & Treas.--Squire-Cogswell Company, Northbrook, IL, pg. 1034
Pascuzzi, Bob, Chief Fin. Officer & Sec.--The Dorris Lumber & Moulding Co., Sacramento, CA, pg. 347
Pasquinelli, Arthur W., Chief Fin. Officer--Pro-Log Corporation, Monterey, CA, pg. 892
Pastor, Michael C., Chief Fin. Mgr.--Ebco Mfg. Company, Columbus, OH, pg. 365
Patnod, Lynda, Chief Fin. Officer--Ship Analytics, Inc., North Stonington, CT, pg. 999
Patterson, E.H., Exec. V.P. & Chief Fin. Officer--Donrey Media Group, Fort Smith, AR, pg. 345
Patterson, Gary, Controller--X-A Cabinet Corporation, La Mirada, CA, pg. 1206
Patterson, Raymond A., Chief Fin. Officer--Mac Papers, Inc., Jacksonville, FL, pg. 694
Pattinson, Michael, Chief Fin. Officer--Teca Corporation, Pleasantville, NY, pg. 1082
Paul, Tom, Controller--Sargento Cheese Co., Plymouth, WI, pg. 971
Paulson, Lawrence, Chief Fin. Officer--Valley Forest Resources Co., Marcell, MN, pg. 1152
Paxton, William, V.P. & Chief Fin. Officer--Advance Business Graphics, Mira Loma, CA, pg. 18
Payne, George N., Exec. V.P. & Chief Fin. Officer--Interstate Distributor Company, Tacoma, WA, pg. 580
Pearce, Dennis, V.P.-Fin.--Prism Integrated Sanitation Management, Inc., Miami, FL, pg. 599
Peary, Stephen K., Chief Fin. Officer--Dick Corporation, Large, PA, pg. 335
Pease, Steven, Chief Fin. Officer & Fin. Dir.--Ceras Johnson Ltda., Rio de Janeiro,, Brazil, pg. 599
Peck, John, V.P., Chief Fin. & Admin. Officer--Sahara Coal Co., Chicago, IL, pg. 966
Pedlar, Mindy, Chief Fin. Officer--Mrs. Goochs Natural Food Markets, Sherman Oaks, CA, pg. 761
Pedro, Joe, Chief Fin. Officer--Wayne Dalton Corporation, Mount Hope, OH, pg. 312
Peiken, Joseph, V.P. & Chief Fin. Officer--Mohawk Distilled Products, North Miami, FL, pg. 763
Pellisero, William C., V.P.-Fin. & Admin.--Signet Systems, Inc., Harrodsburg, KY, pg. 385
Pellizzon, Jerrold, Exec. V.P. & Chief Fin. Officer--Breton Construction, Inc., Irvine, CA, pg. 174
Peltier, Robert L., V.P.-Fin.--U.S. Manufacturing Corp., Roseville, MI, pg. 1136
Pemstein, Bernard L., Chief Fin. Officer--Astro Wire & Cable Corporation, Worcester, MA, pg. 92
Pena, Luis X., Pres., Chief Exec. Officer & Chief Fin. Officer--Gulf States Asphalt Company, Inc., South Houston, TX, pg. 493
Pender, David, V.P.-Fin.--Voit Sports, Inc., Fairport, NY, pg. 1154
Pender, David M., V.P.-Fin.--Voit Corp., Fairport, NY, pg. 1154
Pendrey, J.C., Jr., Sr. V.P., Chief Fin. Officer, Sec. & Treas.--Holder Corporation, Atlanta, GA, pg. 538
Pennington, Robert L., V.P. & Controller--Union Boiler Co., Nitro, WV, pg. 273
Penno, D. Bruce, Chief Fin. Officer & Treas.--Pridgeon & Clay, Inc., Grand Rapids, MI, pg. 889
Penny, Phil, V.P.-Fin.--Cowles Magazines, Inc., Harrisburg, PA, pg. 291
Penzes, Josefina, Sr. V.P., Chief Fin. Officer--Uniworld Group, Inc., New York, NY, pg. 1139
Peo, Richard, Chief Fin. Officer & Controller--Boyer Bros. Inc., Altoona, PA, pg. 169
Pepski, Kathleen P., Chief Fin. Officer & V.P.-Fin.--E.F. Johnson Company, Eden Prairie, MN, pg. 598
Perkins, Daniel, Chief Fin. Officer--Masland Industries, Carlisle, PA, pg. 717
Perkins, Mark, Chief Fin. Officer--Handgards Inc., Northbrook, IL, pg. 504
Perkins, Robert, V.P.-Fin. & Chief Fin. Officer--Super Club Music Corp., Marietta, GA, pg. 1062
Perkins, Thomas T., Sec. & Treas.--Thomas & Howard, Columbia, SC, pg. 1093
Perlman, Leonard, V.P., Chief Fin. Officer & Controller--W. Braun Company, Chicago, IL, pg. 172
Perocci, William, Chief Fin. Officer--Guest Quarters Suite Hotels, Boston, MA, pg. 493
Perry, Brian M., Chief Fin. Officer & Treas.--Interface Electronics Corporation, Hopkinton, MA, pg. 574
Pescosolido, Vin, V.P.-Fin.--J. A. Sexauer, Scarsdale, NY, pg. 357
Pesek, Tom, Chief Fin. Officer--Plastech Corporation, Forest Lake, MN, pg. 874
Peters, Gary, Controller--Tuckerman Optical Co., Columbus, OH, pg. 1118
Peters, Joe, Controller--Keiper Recaro, Inc., Clawson, MI, pg. 620
Peters, Laurie, Controller--R.J. Corr Naturals, Inc., Posen, IL, pg. 287
Petersen, Daniel L., Chief Fin. Officer & Corp. Sec.--J.H. Findorff & Son, Inc., Madison, WI, pg. 411
Petersen, John M., Pres., Chief Fin. Officer & Treas.--Erie Family Life Insurance Company, Erie, PA, pg. 386
Petersen, John M., Pres., Chief Fin. Officer & Treas.--Erie Insurance Group, Erie, PA, pg. 386
Petersen, John M., Pres., Chief Fin. Officer & Treas.--Erie Indemnity Company, Erie, PA, pg. 386
Petersen, John M., Pres., Chief Fin. Officer & Treas.--Erie Insurance Exchange, Erie, PA, pg. 386
Peterson, Charles, Chief Fin. Officer & Mng. Dir.--Cowen & Company, New York, NY, pg. 291
Peterson, Ed, Sr. V.P. & Chief Fin. Officer--Pacific Scene Inc., San Diego, CA, pg. 841
Peterson, Jeri, Controller--Western Metal Finishing Division, South Gate, CA, pg. 1073
Petit, Charles E., Exec. V.P., Chief Fin. Officer & Treas.--Fitzgerald & Company, Inc., Cranston, RI, pg. 416
Petrin, Robert M., Chief Fin. Officer--Weatherking Products, Inc., East Greenwich, RI, pg. 79
Petry, Paul E., Exec. V.P., Chief Fin. Officer & Treas.--Connecticut Mutual Life Insurance Company, Hartford, CT, pg. 274
Pettey, John, Treas. & Chief Fin. Officer--Kemmons Wilson Companies, Memphis, TN, pg. 1194
Pfeifer, Greg, Treas. & Chief Fin. Officer--Rochester-Midland ICL, Omaha, NE, pg. 941
Pfeil, Robert J., Sr. V.P., Chief Fin. Officer & Treas.--H. C. Prange Company, Green Bay, WI, pg. 884
Pfister, Terry W., V.P.-Fin., Chief Fin. Officer, Sec. & Treas.--Enerfab Inc., Cincinnati, OH, pg. 381
Phelps, Mike, Controller--J-Starr Industries, Inc., Fort Atkinson, WI, pg. 1040
Philby, Richard A., Chief Fin. Officer & V.P.-Fin.--Topline Imports, Inc., Bellevue, WA, pg. 1102
Philipp, Werner, V.P. & Chief Fin. Officer--Union Switch & Signal Inc., Pittsburgh, PA, pg. 1129
Phillips, Brad, Chief Fin. Officer--Uniflow Manufacturing Co., Erie, PA, pg. 1126
Phillips, Mary C., Sec. & Treas.--Young-Phillips Sales Co., Winston-Salem, NC, pg. 1210
Phillips, Ronald M., V.P.-Fin., Treas. & Sec.--J. J. Keller & Associates, Inc., Neenah, WI, pg. 620
Phillis, T.J., V.P. & Chief Fin. Officer--Omega Transworld, Inc, Utah, New Kensington, PA, pg. 195
Phipps, Howard R., V.P. & Chief Fin. Officer--Primacare Health Resources, Inc., Syracuse, NY, pg. 1070
Piani, Brian, V.P.-Fin. & Treas.--Yankee Publishing Incorporated, Dublin, NH, pg. 1207
Piani, Brian, Chief Fin. Officer--Alaska Publishing Properties, Inc., Anchorage, AK, pg. 1207
Pickral, Percy E., Controller--Hohner/HSS Inc., Ashland, VA, pg. 538
Picon, John, Chief Fin. Officer & Treas.--RE/MAX International, Inc., Englewood, CO, pg. 915
Pierce, A. Kenneth, Jr., V.P. & Chief Fin. Officer--The Dispatch Printing Company, Columbus, OH, pg. 339
Pierce, John, V.P. & Chief Fin. Officer--Beacon Mfg. Co., Swannanoa, NC, pg. 129
Pilarczyk, R.R., Pres., Chief Exec. Officer & Treas.--General Computer Corp. Inc., Twinsburg, OH, pg. 449
Pitney, William J., V.P. & Chief Fin. Officer--P/A Industries, Inc., Bloomfield, CT, pg. 835
Pittman, Gary, Chm. Bd., Pres., Chief Exec., Chief Oper. & Chief Fin. Officer--PCI, Austin, TX, pg. 836
Piva, Gary, V.P.-Fin.--Waremart Inc., Boise, ID, pg. 1163
Pivik, Robert W., Chief Fin. Officer--Deloitte & Touche, Wilton, CT, pg. 326
Pizel, Ken, Chief Fin. Officer & Treas.--Wenger Corporation, Owatonna, MN, pg. 1176
Place, Douglas N., V.P.-Fin. & Chief Fin. Officer--Asahi/America, Inc., Malden, MA, pg. 87
Plageman, Ronald, Exec. V.P., Chief Fin. Officer--Bailey Lauerman & Associates, Inc., Lincoln, NE, pg. 114
Plamann, Alfred, Sr. V.P.-Fin. & Chief Fin. Officer--Certified Grocers Of California, Los Angeles, CA, pg. 237
Platania, Philip, Pres., Chief Exec. & Chief Fin. Officer--Andmore Sportswear Corporation, Port Jervis, NY, pg. 74
Platt, Douglas G., Chief Fin. Officer--Kurdziel Industries, Inc., Muskegon, MI, pg. 646
Poe, David H., Chief Fin. Officer--Schein Pharmaceutical, Inc., Port Washington, NY, pg. 975
Polera, Catherine, Pres., Chief Fin. Officer, Sec. & Treas.--Polera Building Corp., Scarsdale, NY, pg. 878
Poli, Joseph B., V.P.-Fin.--I. Rokeach & Sons, Inc., Paramus, NJ, pg. 944
Pomares, Jim, Sec., Treas. & Personnel Mgr.--Von Housen Motors, Sacramento, CA, pg. 1155
Ponder, Daniel S., Sr. V.P., Chief Fin. Officer--Anthony M. Franco Inc., Detroit, MI, pg. 950
Pope, Frank M., Sr. V.P.-Fin.--Knoll International, Inc., New York, NY, pg. 1121
Pope, Fred, Chief Fin. Officer & Controller--Walker & Associates, Inc., Welcome, NC, pg. 1159
Porte, Charmaine, Chief Fin. Officer & Sec.--Advance Steel Co., Detroit, MI, pg. 20
Porter, Marc A., Chief Fin. Officer, V.P. & Treas.--The Law Company, Inc., Wichita, KS, pg. 661
Portman, Mark, Chief Fin. Officer--Dallas & Mavis Forwarding Co., Inc. (D & M), Kenosha, WI, pg. 609
Portman, Mark, Chief Fin. Officer--Jupiter Transportation Corp., Kenosha, WI, pg. 609
Portman, Mark, Chief Fin. Officer--Boat Transit, Inc., Costa Mesa, CA, pg. 609
Portman, Mark, Chief Fin. Officer--Jupiter Corp. Transportation System, Kenosha, WI, pg. 609
Porzio, Patrick F., V.P. & Chief Fin. Officer--H.J. Baker & Bro., Inc., New York, NY, pg. 114
Posey, Marianne, Chief Fin. Officer--Planes Moving And Storage, Inc., Cincinnati, OH, pg. 874
Postnicks, Andy, Chief Fin. Officer--Wellington Industries Inc., Paterson, NJ, pg. 1175
Postnicks, Andy, Chief Fin. Officer--Wellington Home Products, Paterson, NJ, pg. 1175
Potash, Paul D., V.P. & Controller--Spaulding & Slye Company, Burlington, MA, pg. 1026
Potter, Jim, Controller--Rice Food Markets Inc., Houston, TX, pg. 931
Potter, Joel, Brand Controller--Rado Watch Company, Inc., New York, NY, pg. 909
Potts, W. L., Jr., Chief Fin. Officer, Treas. & Controller--Nutech, Inc., San Jose, CA, pg. 817
Poulin, Tracey K., Chief Fin. Officer--Avatar Corporation, Hopkinton, MA, pg. 101
Powell, Daniel T., Chief Fin. Officer--F & B Manufacturing Co., Chicago, IL, pg. 393
Powell, Daniel T., Chief Fin. Officer--Filko/Cobra, Inc., Chicago, IL, pg. 393
Powell, Deborah D., Chief Fin. Officer & Sec.--Robert C. Powell Developments, Incorporated, Sacramento, CA, pg. 882
Powell, Roy, Chief. Fin. Officer--Standley Burridge Collings Ltd., London, United Kingdom, pg. 112
Powell, William, V.P.-Fin. & Chief Fin. Officer--Components Corporation Of America, Dallas, TX, pg. 270
Power, J., Chief Fin. Officer--Integra Technologies Corp., Waltham, MA, pg. 572
Powers, Michael, Chief Fin. Officer--Garden Way, Inc., Troy, NY, pg. 443
Powers, Patrick, Chief Fin. Officer--Donley's, Inc., Cleveland, OH, pg. 345
Poxom, James, V.P.-Pur.--Rapid Mounting & Finishing Co., Chicago, IL, pg. 913
Pozezinski, Ray, Dir.-Fin.--McKee Door, Inc., Aurora, IL, pg. 730
Pozzo, Jim Dal, Chief Fin. Officer--Jacmar Companies, Inc., Alhambra, CA, pg. 587
Prairie, Greg, V.P. & Chief Fin. Officer--Inland Printing Co., Inc., La Crosse, WI, pg. 570
Pratten, Robert, Chief Fin. Officer--Regency Associates Limited Partnership, Evansville, IN, pg. 922
Previti, F.J., Controller--TTX Co., Chicago, IL, pg. 1075

Price, John A., Chief Fin. Officer--Fuji TruColor Foto, San Diego, CA, pg. 322
Price, Robert J., V.P., Treas. & Pur. Mgr.--The Suddath Companies, Jacksonville, FL, pg. 1055
Pricola, Vito, Chief Fin. Officer--Jones Chemicals, Inc., Le Roy, NY, pg. 603
Prinzo, Felix J., Sr. V.P. & Chief Fin. Officer--Laroche Holdings, Inc., Atlanta, GA, pg. 659
Prinzo, Felix J., Sr. V.P. & Chief Fin. Officer--LaRoche Chemicals Inc., Baton Rouge, LA, pg. 659
Proat, L. Steven, Chief Fin. Officer--Alpha Q, Inc., Colchester, CT, pg. 5
Prockow, Eric, V.P. & Chief Fin. Officer--Sun Data Inc., Norcross, GA, pg. 1058
Profitt, Morris, Chief Fin. Officer & V.P.--Werthan Packaging, Inc., Nashville, TN, pg. 1176
Pronko, Elizabeth A., Chief Fin. Officer, V.P. & Controller--PE Systems, Reston, VA, pg. 836
Pruitt, Cheryl, Exec. V.P. & Treas.--Tremont Foods, Linthicum Heights, MD, pg. 1109
Psaropoulos, Alecos, Fin. Dir.--Leo Burnett S.A., Athens,, Greece, pg. 193
Purcell, Robert, Chief Oper. Officer & Chief Fin. Officer--ERA Real Estate, Overland Park, KS, pg. 360
Puricelli, Dick, Chief Fin. Officer--Scangas Brothers Holdings, Inc., Lynn, MA, pg. 974
Purpura, Salvatore, Chief Fin. Officer & Controller--Associated Metals & Minerals Corp., White Plains, NY, pg. 91
Pye, Ian, Chief Fin. Officer--Meridian Technology Leasing Services, Deerfield, IL, pg. 740
Qualmann, Gary, Chief Fin. Officer & Exec. V.P.--Red Roof Inns, Inc., Hilliard, OH, pg. 918
Quam, D.L., Controller--Venta Inc., Denver, CO, pg. 1147
Quarles, W. Greyson, Chief Fin. Officer & V.P.--SAS Institute Inc., Cary, NC, pg. 959
Quicksall, Doug, V.P., Chief Fin. Officer & Treas.--Central Freight Lines Inc., Waco, TX, pg. 232
Quigley, Joseph J., V.P.-Fin. & Chief Fin. Officer--Kitchell Corporation, Phoenix, AZ, pg. 634
Quigley, Keith, V.P. & Chief Fin. Officer--Clear Springs Foods, Inc., Buhl, ID, pg. 254
Quinn, David, V.P.-Fin.--Bruning Paint Company, Baltimore, MD, pg. 184
Quinn, James W., Chief Fin. Officer--Allen & Company Incorporated, New York, NY, pg. 35
Quinn, Roy, Pres. & Controller--Pompeian, Inc., Baltimore, MD, pg. 880
Rabinowitz, Sheldon B., Sr. V.P. & Chief Fin. Officer--Hanna-Barbera Productions, Inc., Los Angeles, CA, pg. 53
Raborg, Christopher H., Chief Fin. Officer--Ruiz Food Products, Inc., Dinuba, CA, pg. 955
Race, William S., Chief Fin. Officer--Cole Taylor Bank, Chicago, IL, pg. 260
Radler, Jeffrey, V.P.-Fin. & Chief Fin. Officer--Chessco Industries, Inc., Westport, CT, pg. 243
Radoff, Perry, Chief Fin. Officer--Joiner Rowland Serio Koeppel, Dallas, TX, pg. 602
Radus, Philip, Pres. & Treas.--Ribbon Narrow Fabric Company, Secaucus, NJ, pg. 931
Radwill, Alvera, Chm. Bd., Chief Fin. Officer & Treas.--Master Appliance Corp., Racine, WI, pg. 719
Radwin, Edward, Controller--Vacudyne Inc., Chicago Heights, IL, pg. 45
Rae, Rick, V.P.-Corp. Fin.--Nob Hill General Store, Inc., Gilroy, CA, pg. 807
Ragin, Luther M., Jr., Chief Fin. Officer--Earl G. Graves, Ltd., New York, NY, pg. 478
Rahausen, Susan B., V.P., Chief Fin. Officer--Gianettino & Meredith Advertising, Short Hills, NJ, pg. 455
Rains, Gladys, Chief Fin. Officer--Davis Paint Company, Kansas City, MO, pg. 319
Raker, James W., Sr. V.P. & Chief Fin. Officer--First Advantage Mortgage Corporation, Columbia, MD, pg. 412
Rakers, Harry B., V.P.-Fin.--M&W Gear Company, Gibson City, IL, pg. 690
Ramirez, Robert, Controller--Vita Food Products, Inc., Chicago, IL, pg. 1153
Rammohan, Seshan, Chief Fin. Officer--Dry Storage Corporation, Des Plaines, IL, pg. 350
Ramon, David, V.P. & Chief Fin. Officer--Gillett Holdings, Inc., Denver, CO, pg. 458
Ramsden, Geoffrey, Chief Fin. Officer--Ferrell Companies Inc./Ferrellgas, Liberty, MO, pg. 407
Randolph, E. Merle, Chief Fin. Officer--Syratech Corporation, East Boston, MA, pg. 1070
Randolph, E. Merle, V.P. & Chief Fin. Officer--Wallace International Silversmiths, Inc., East Boston, MA, pg. 1070
Rankin, Jr. Harley, Exec. V.P. & Chief Fin. Officer--Silgan Corporation, Stamford, CT, pg. 1004
Ranus, Robert D., V.P. & Chief Fin. Officer--Roundy's, Inc., Pewaukee, WI, pg. 952
Rapaport, Jonathan, Chief Fin. Officer, V.P. & Treas.--Pacesetter Steel Service, Inc., Marietta, GA, pg. 839
Raposa, Donald, Controller--Whaling Industries, Inc., Fall River, MA, pg. 1183
Rauh, Robert B., Chm. Bd., Pres., Chief Fin. Officer & New Bus. Contact--Rauh, Good, Darlo & Barnes Advertising Associates, Inc., Los Gatos, CA, pg. 914
Raval, Praful, Comptroller--Health Care Distributors of Indiana, Inc., South Bend, IN, pg. 520
Ravio, Richard, Chief Fin. Officer--Pac Paper, Inc., Vancouver, WA, pg. 815
Ray, E. Wayne, Jr., V.P.-Fin.--Riviana Foods Inc., Houston, TX, pg. 937
Ready, George W., Treas. & Sec.--Watkins Associated Industries Inc., Atlanta, GA, pg. 1167
Reagan, Larry, Treas.--Pascoe Building Systems, Inc., Columbus, GA, pg. 851
Reardon, Leonard, V.P.-Fin. & Treas., Chief Fin. Officer--Hobart Brothers Co., Troy, OH, pg. 536
Rector, Harry, V.P.-Fin.--Infotec Development, Inc., Santa Ana, CA, pg. 567
Rediehs, Richard L., Dir.-Fin.--Griffith Micro Science International Inc., Burr Ridge, IL, pg. 487
Reed, Don, Sr. Exec. V.P. & Chief Fin. Officer--The SArgent-SOwell Company, Grand Prairie, TX, pg. 971
Reed, Glenn, Chief Fin. Officer--800-Flowers, Westbury, NY, pg. 371
Reed, Jim, Chief Fin. Officer--Sommer Metalcraft Corporation, Crawfordsville, IN, pg. 1018
Reed, Ward, Chief Fin. Officer--Campus Point Realty Corporation, La Jolla, CA, pg. 981
Reed, William, V.P. & Chief Fin. Officer--Praxis International Inc., Cambridge, MA, pg. 884
Reedy, John D., Chief Fin. Officer--Michael Foods, Inc., Minneapolis, MN, pg. 747
Reego, William, Sr. V.P.-Fin. & Chief Fin. Officer--Topco Associates, Inc., Skokie, IL, pg. 1101
Reeher, Bill, Chief Fin. Officer--Muse Cordero Chen, Inc., Los Angeles, CA, pg. 777
Rees, Burton S., V.P. & Treas.--Salz Leathers, Inc., Santa Cruz, CA, pg. 968
Rees, John, Sec. & Treas.--Silver Springs Citrus Co-op, Ocoee, FL, pg. 1004
Reeves, Charles, Chief Fin. Officer & Treas.--Tennessee Farmers Co-op, La Vergne, TN, pg. 1087
Regala, John, Treas. & Chief Fin. Officer--Antares Group Inc., Cleveland, OH, pg. 76
Rege, Thomas J., Chief Fin. Officer, Sec., Treas. & Controller--Chartway Technologies, Rockville, MD, pg. 240
Register, John R., Sr. V.P., Chief Fin. Officer & Treas.--Technology Applications, Inc., Alexandria, VA, pg. 1083
Rehm, D. F., V.P.-Fin.--Wells Lamont, Niles, IL, pg. 712
Reichborn, P.K., Pres. & Treas.--Goodway Tool Corporation, Stamford, CT, pg. 471
Reichwein, John H., Chm. Bd. & Treas.--Revcor, Inc., Carpentersville, IL, pg. 930
Reid, Dal C., V.P. & Chief Fin. Officer--Friona Industries, L.P., Amarillo, TX, pg. 434
Reid, Mike, Controller--Eco Water Systems, Saint Paul, MN, pg. 367
Reidbord, Gilda P., Exec. V.P., Sec. & Treas.--Reidbord Bros., Inc., Pittsburgh, PA, pg. 923
Reif, David P., Chief Fin. Officer--Stonhard, Inc., Maple Shade, NJ, pg. 1051
Reiher, Nancy, Chief Fin. Officer, Controller--Newmark, Posner & Mitchell, Inc., New York, NY, pg. 804
Reilly, Robert J., Chief Fin. Officer--Parkway Fabricators, Inc., South Amboy, NJ, pg. 480
Reiss, Clifford E. II, Sec. & Asst. To Pres.--R.C.A. Rubber Company, Akron, OH, pg. 906
Reiswig, George C., V.P.-Fin. & Chief Fin. Officer--Perdue Farms Inc., Salisbury, MD, pg. 860
Remes, Audrey, Treas. & Chief Fin. Officer--Deerskin Trading Post, Inc., Carlstadt, NJ, pg. 324
Remley, Scott A., V.P. & Chief Fin. Officer--Health Management Systems, Inc., New York, NY, pg. 521
Resnick, Frank, Chief Fin. Officer--Medline Industries, Inc., Mundelein, IL, pg. 736
Retcher, M.F., Chief Fin. Officer & Treas.--Art Iron, Inc., Toledo, OH, pg. 86
Reymond, Kevin L., V.P. & Chief Fin. Officer--Viacom Broadcasting Inc., New York, NY, pg. 785
Reynen, John D., Treas. & Sec.--Reynen, Bardis & Winn, Sacramento, CA, pg. 930
Reynolds, James K., V.P.-Fin. & Chief Fin. Officer--Baker Commodities, Inc., Los Angeles, CA, pg. 115
Rhudy, Huey J., Treas. & Sec.--STRAFCO, Inc., San Antonio, TX, pg. 1052
Rice, Bobby, Chief Fin. Officer--Western Linen Corp., Phoenix, AZ, pg. 1180
Rice, Kenneth L., V.P. & Chief Fin. Officer--Zymark Corporation, Hopkinton, MA, pg. 1221
Rich, Jeff, Chief Fin. Officer & V.P.--Affiliated Computer Services, Inc., Dallas, TX, pg. 23
Richards, Daniel, Chief Fin. Officer--Ideal Chemical & Supply Company, Memphis, TN, pg. 562
Richards, Gerald, Treas.--United Power Association, Elk River, MN, pg. 1134
Richards, Harry, Controller--Wallace Leisure Products, Inc., Philadelphia, PA, pg. 1160
Richardson, Brian, V.P. & Chief Fin. Officer--Sullivan Holding Company, Brentwood, TN, pg. 1056
Richardson, Brian, Chief Fin. Officer--Sullivan Graphics, Brentwood, TN, pg. 1057
Richardson, Bryan D., Sr. V.P. & Chief Fin. Officer--Haddon Craftsmen, Inc., Scranton, PA, pg. 499
Richardson, Clayton H., Jr., Sec., Treas. & Gen. Mgr.--Gulf States Manufacturers, Inc., Starkville, MS, pg. 494
Richardson, John S., Pres., Chief Exec. & Chief Fin. Officer--Sugar Creek Packing Co., Mason, OH, pg. 1056
Rife, Teresa A., Chief Fin. Officer & Sr. V.P.--Roma Holdings, Dallas, TX, pg. 945
Rigaud, Didier, Chief Fin. Officer--Bordelais, Lemeunier & Leo Burnett, Clichy,, France, pg. 192
Riggs, Jere, Chief Fin. Officer--Syracuse China Corp., Syracuse, NY, pg. 1065
Riggs, Sidney W., Chm. Bd., Sec. & Treas.--Somerset Welding & Steel, Inc., Somerset, PA, pg. 934
Riley, James, V.P., Chief Fin. Officer & Treas.--Republic Engineered Steels, Inc., Massillon, OH, pg. 928
Riley, Jeremiah A., Exec. V.P. & Chief Fin. Officer--Horizon Media, Inc., New York, NY, pg. 544
Rilla, J.M., V.P.-Fin. & Admin.--Koehler Manufacturing Company, Marlborough, MA, pg. 639
Rinke, Roland, Pres., Treas. & Chief Exec. Officer--Rinke Pontiac-GMC Co., Warren, MI, pg. 935
Ripka, Sy, Pres., Chief Fin. Officer--The Alden Group Ltd., New York, NY, pg. 32
Ripp, Peter, Sr. V.P. & Chief Fin. Officer--Northville Industries Corp., Melville, NY, pg. 814
Ritchason, Marvin, Chief Oper. Officer & Gen. Mgr.--Ray-Carroll County Grain Co-op, Richmond, MO, pg. 914
Ritchie, Richard L., Sr. V.P. & Chief Fin. Officer--Harte-Hanks Communications, Inc., San Antonio, TX, pg. 513
Rittmann, Ron, V.P.-Fin. & Admin.--Somerset Technologies, Inc., Somerset, NJ, pg. 1017
Rizer, E. Lloyd, Sr. V.P.-Fin.--The Hotsy Corporation, Englewood, CO, pg. 545
Roach, J. Thurston, V.P. & Chief Fin. Officer--Simpson Investment Co., Seattle, WA, pg. 1007
Roach, J. Thurston, V.P., Sec. & Chief Fin. Officer-SICO--Simpson Timber Co., Shelton, WA, pg. 1007
Robb, Mary Susan, Corp. Sec. & Treas.--Blue Cross and Blue Shield of Oklahoma, Tulsa, OK, pg. 159
Robbins, Charlie, Treas.--Robbins Manufacturing Company, Tampa, FL, pg. 938
Robbins, Joseph H., Sr. V.P. & Treas.--Robbins Manufacturing Company, Tampa, FL, pg. 938
Roberts, Gary, Sr. V.P., Chief Fin. Officer, Admin. & Sec.--Sierracin Corporation, Sylmar, CA, pg. 1003
Roberts, Jim, Treas.--Transamerican Refining Corporation, Houston, TX, pg. 1106
Roberts, Michael V., V.P.-Fin, & Treas.--Soft Sheen Products, Inc., Chicago, IL, pg. 1016
Robertson, Philip S., Sr. V.P. & Treas.--Robertson Factories, Inc., Taunton, MA, pg. 939
Robertson, William A., V.P.-Opers. & Chief Fin. Officer--Smartstar Corporation, Goleta, CA, pg. 1011
Robinette, Gary, Chief Fin. Officer & V.P.--Carolina Builders Corporation, Raleigh, NC, pg. 223
Robinson, Barbara, Chief Fin. Officer & Treas.--Robinson Helicopter Company, Inc., Torrance, CA, pg. 940
Robinson, Charles K., Jr., Pres. & Treas.--Swayne Robinson & Company, Richmond, IN, pg. 939
Robinson, Clark, Pres. & Treas.--Streech Electric Company, Anaheim, CA, pg. 1053
Robinson, E. Montgomery, Pres. & Treas.--Top Flight, Inc., Chattanooga, TN, pg. 1101
Robinson, Fran, Chief Fin. Officer & Treas.--National Mortgage Company, Memphis, TN, pg. 792
Robinson, Jerry D., Chief Fin. Officer, V.P. & Treas.--SFA, Inc., Landover, MD, pg. 961
Robinson, W.S., Chief Fin. Officer & Treas.--The Lathrop Company, Toledo, OH, pg. 660
Robles, Ricardo, Chief Fin. Officer--La Reina, Inc., Los Angeles, CA, pg. 649
Robohm, Donald, V.P. & Chief Fin. Officer--Seaboard Corporation, Newton, MA, pg. 984
Roche, Michael, Chief Fin. Officer--GF Industries, Inc., Oakland, CA, pg. 439
Rochon, John P., Vice Chm. & Chief Fin. Officer--Mary Kay Corporation, Dallas, TX, pg. 716
Rodnar, M., Chief Fin. Officer--Blaw Knox - Duraloy Division, Scottdale, PA, pg. 156
Roedl, Suzanne, Chief Fin. Officer--Condor D.C. Power Supplies Inc., Oxnard, CA, pg. 273
Rogan, Patricia M., Chief Fin. Officer--Daxus Corporation, Pittsburgh, PA, pg. 319
Rogers, Darrell, Treas. & Sec.--Turner Dairies, Inc., Covington, TN, pg. 1119
Rogers, Dick, Chief Fin. Officer--SGD International Corp., New York, NY, pg. 962
Rogers, Jack, Chief Fin. Officer--Camelot Music, Inc., North Canton, OH, pg. 212
Rogers, Jo, Treas. & Sec.--Royal Jeep Eagle & Chrysler Plymouth, Casselberry, FL, pg. 953
Rogers, John, Chief Fin. Officer--I B Diffusion, LP, Chicago, IL, pg. 558
Rogers, John Baird, Chief Fin. Officer, V.P. & Treas.--Zytec Corp., Eden Prairie, MN, pg. 1221
Rogers, John C., Chief Fin. Officer--Continental National American Real Estate Inc., San Jose, CA, pg. 280
Rogers, John W., V.P., Treas. & Sec.--Rogers Markets Inc., Fort Wayne, IN, pg. 943
Rogoff, Alice, Sr. V.P.-Fin. & Chief Fin. Officer--U.S. News & World Report, New York, NY, pg. 1136
Rogoski, Patricia D., Sr. V.P., Treas. & Chief Fin. Officer--Guardsmark, Inc., Memphis, TN, pg. 492
Rohloff, William M., Chief Fin. Officer, Treas. & Sec.--Stebbins Engineering & Mfg. Co., Watertown, NY, pg. 1043
Rohr, Raymond C., Treas.--Russell Harrington Cutlery Inc., Southbridge, MA, pg. 556
Rohrer, Joanne M., Sec. & Treas.--Rohrer Corporation, Wadsworth, OH, pg. 944
Rollins, Royce L., Exec. V.P. & Chief Fin. Officer--Fleishman Hillard Inc., Saint Louis, MO, pg. 417
Romaniuk, Stefan, V.P.-Fin. & Sec.--VCA Teletronics Inc., Leonia, NJ, pg. 1141
Romano, Joseph J., V.P. & Chief Fin. Officer--Zilkha Energy Company, Houston, TX, pg. 1219
Romig, Michael V., V.P. & Chief Fin. Officer--Marine Construction & Design Co., Seattle, WA, pg. 707
Rones, Gail, Sec. & Treas.--Americo Manufacturing Co., Inc., Acworth, GA, pg. 66
Roof, Donald C., Chief Fin. Officer, Treas. & Comptroller--Spreckles Industries, Inc., Pleasanton, CA, pg. 1032
Rooney, George W., Jr., V.P.-Fin.--Ketchum, Inc., Pittsburgh, PA, pg. 626
Roos, John, Chief Fin. Officer--Duling Optical Corporation, Louisville, KY, pg. 352
Roos, Mark D., V.P., Treas. & Chief Fin. Officer--The Airolite Company, Marietta, OH, pg. 28
Roper, W.A., Jr., Chief Fin. Officer--Science Applications International Corporation, San Diego, CA, pg. 981
Rose, David, Exec. V.P. & Chief Fin. Officer--Environmental Industries, Inc., Calabasas, CA, pg. 383
Rose, Estelle, Chief Fin. Officer--Kobra International Ltd, New York, NY, pg. 638
Rose, Howard, V.P.-Fin.--Candle Corporation of America, Oshkosh, WI, pg. 214
Rose, Susan T., Treas.--Roman Electric Company, Inc., Milwaukee, WI, pg. 945
Rosen, Florence, Exec. V.P. & Controller--Rosen Associates Management Corp., Jericho, NY, pg. 948

Rosenberg, Donald M., Exec. V.P., Treas. & Chief Fin. Officer--Oxford First Corporation, Philadelphia, PA, pg. 834
Rosenberg, Donald M., Exec. V.P. & Chief Fin. Officer--Computer Information Services, Inc., Philadelphia, PA, pg. 834
Rosenberg, Donald M., Exec. V.P. & Chief Fin. Officer--Oxford Communities, Inc., Philadelphia, PA, pg. 834
Rosenberg, Donald M., Exec. V.P., Treas. & Chief Fin. Officer--Oxford Finance Companies, Inc., Philadelphia, PA, pg. 835
Rosenberger, Fred R., V.P.-Fin.--Hutchens Industries Inc., Springfield, MO, pg. 555
Rosenbloom, Sidney, V.P., Chief Fin. Officer & Treas.--McCurdy & Co., Inc., Rochester, NY, pg. 728
Rosenblum, Robert H., Chief Fin. Officer--Host Apparel, Inc., New York, NY, pg. 545
Rosendin, Raymond J., Pres. & Treas.--Rosendin Electric, Inc., San Jose, CA, pg. 948
Rosenstein, Ira M., Exec. V.P. & Chief Fin. Officer--Dr Pepper/Seven-Up Companies, Inc., Dallas, TX, pg. 342
Rosenthal, Irv, Chief Fin. Officer--Barneys New York, New York, NY, pg. 120
Ross, Gerald, Pres., Chief Exec. & Chief Fin. Officer & Treas.--MGR Equipment Corp., Inwood, NY, pg. 692
Ross, Janice, Treas.--T & R Electric Supply Company, Inc., Colman, SD, pg. 1071
Rossel, Cary, V.P., Chief Fin. Officer & Admin.--Glazers Wholesale Drug Co. Inc., Dallas, TX, pg. 461
Rossen, James R., V.P.-Fin. & Treas.--Union Pump Company, Battle Creek, MI, pg. 1128
Roth, Jeffrey R., Chief Fin. Officer--Frigid Food Products, Inc., Detroit, MI, pg. 433
Roth, Nat, Chm. & Chief Fin. Officer--Furman, Roth Adv., New York, NY, pg. 437
Rouner, Michael, Controller--GreatBanc, Inc., Aurora, IL, pg. 482
Rousset, Alain (Hong Kong), Sr. Exec. V.P., Chief Fin. Officer--Dentsu, Young & Rubicam Partnerships, New York, NY, pg. 330
Rowen, Barry, Chief Fin. Officer--Comlinear Corporation, Fort Collins, CO, pg. 268
Rowley, Donald W., Chief Fin. Officer--Seacoast Electric Company, Rye, NY, pg. 370
Roxe, Joseph D., Chief Fin. Officer--Johnson & Higgins, New York, NY, pg. 598
Royal, Stephen A., Chief Fin. Officer--Omega Performance Group, San Francisco, CA, pg. 826
Rozea, John M., Chief Fin. Officer--Falcon Associates, Ltd., McLean, VA, pg. 981
Ruark, Roger, Pres., Chief Fin. Officer--Garrison-Lontine Advertising, Denver, CO, pg. 443
Rubin, Georgette, Treas. & Sec.--Lillie Rubin Affiliates Inc., Miami, FL, pg. 954
Rubzin, Todd, Chief Fin. Officer--Power Plastics Inc., Paterson, NJ, pg. 1097
Rucker, Adin H., Jr., Pres. & Treas.--Stonecutter Mills Corp., Spindale, NC, pg. 1051
Rudzik, John A., Sr. V.P.-Fin., Chief Fin. Officer, & Treas.--Centimark Corporation, Bethel Park, PA, pg. 231
Rue, Richard, Sr. V.P. & Chief Fin. Officer--ITA Group, West Des Moines, IA, pg. 560
Ruffing, Paul J., Chief Fin. Officer & V.P.--The Cincinnati Cordage & Paper Company, Cincinnati, OH, pg. 249
Rufus, Greg, V.P.-Fin.--Kearney, Tucker, GA, pg. 357
Ruggerio, Tom, Chief Fin. Officer--The Estee Corporation, Parsippany, NJ, pg. 389
Ruiz, Rodolfo, V.P.-Fin. & Chief Fin. Officer--Bacardi Imports, Inc., Miami, FL, pg. 108
Rumble, Clayton T., V.P.-Fin. & Chief Fin. Officer--Sunox, Inc., Charlotte, NC, pg. 1062
Runk, Fred J., V.P. & Chief Fin. Officer--Chiquita Brands International, Inc., Cincinnati, OH, pg. 53
Runk, Fred J., V.P., Treas. & Chief Fin. Officer--Spelling Entertainment Group, Inc., Cincinnati, OH, pg. 54
Russell, Barron Jeff, Treas. & Sec.--Food & Gas, Inc., Decatur, GA, pg. 423
Russell, James F., V.P.-Fin., Chief Fin. Officer & Sec.--HCB Contractors, Dallas, TX, pg. 496
Russell, Jeanne Y., Sr. V.P.-Investment--Fiduciary Trust Co. International, New York, NY, pg. 408
Russell, Richard C., Sr. V.P., Chief Fin. Officer & Treas.--Danis Industries Corporation, Dayton, OH, pg. 314
Russell, Richard L., V.P. & Chief Fin. Officer--Lord Corporation, Erie, PA, pg. 683
Russell, T. Alan, Exec. V.P., Sec. & Treas.--Illinois Cereal Mills, Inc., Paris, IL, pg. 562
Russin, F., Controller--Selecto-Flash, Inc., West Orange, NJ, pg. 988
Rutherford, Donald E., V.P. & Controller--A.M. Todd Company, Kalamazoo, MI, pg. 1100
Rutherford, Greg, Controller--Washington Corporation, Missoula, MT, pg. 1165
Rutkay, Wayne, Chief Fin. Officer & Controller--Young Stuff Apparel Group, Inc., New York, NY, pg. 1214
Ryan, Mary L., Chief Fin. Officer & V.P.--Thompson Steel Co., Inc., Canton, MA, pg. 1094
Ryan, Michael A., Chief Fin. Officer & V.P.--Cleveland Brothers Equipment Co., Harrisburg, PA, pg. 255
Ryan, W.J., Sr. V.P. & Chief Fin. Officer--J.M. Huber Corporation, Edison, NJ, pg. 550
Ryder, Larry, Sr. V.P.-Fin. & Admin.--Hooker Furniture Corporation, Martinsville, VA, pg. 543
Rydin, Wes, V.P. & Chief Fin. Officer--Malden Mills Industries, Inc., Lawrence, MA, pg. 702
Rye, Alton, V.P., Treas. & Controller--Sammons Communications, Inc., Dallas, TX, pg. 968
Rynn, John A., V.P. & Treas.--Berol Corporation, Brentwood, TN, pg. 856
Rzicznek, Frank, V.P.-Fin. & Chief Fin. Officer--NESCO, Inc., Mayfield Heights, OH, pg. 798
Sabatini, Ralph, Chief Fin. Officer & V.P.--Publishers Clearing House, Port Washington, NY, pg. 898
Sabbag, Albert, Chief Fin. Officer--Gerrity Co., Inc., Newton, MA, pg. 454
Saggisi, Joe, Chief Fin. Officer--L.F. Driscoll Co., Bala-Cynwyd, PA, pg. 349
Saji, Mark, Chief Fin. Officer & V.P.--Linzer Products Corp., Flushing, NY, pg. 677
Saling, Robert, Controller--IBT, Inc., Shawnee Mission, KS, pg. 558
Salwasser, Dennis, V.P.-Fin. & Real Estate--Salwasser Manufacturing Company, Inc., Reedley, CA, pg. 968
Salwasser, Margaret, Sec. & Treas.--Salwasser Manufacturing Company, Inc., Reedley, CA, pg. 968
Salzano, James, Chief Fin. Officer, Sec. & Treas.--Altier & Sons Shoes Inc., Rochester, NY, pg. 45
Samayoa, John F., Exec. V.P.-Mktg. Mgr. & Treas.--Lanman & Kemp-Barclay Co. Inc., Westwood, NJ, pg. 657
Samonek, Kenneth, Chief Fin. Officer--The Producto Machine Co., Bridgeport, CT, pg. 893
Sampson, Jim, Treas.--Western Grain, Inc., Wichita, KS, pg. 1179
Samuelson, Marjorie, Partner & Chief Fin. Officer--J.D. Power and Associates, Agoura Hills, CA, pg. 883
Sanchez, Manuel, V.P. & Chief Fin. Officer--Capital Bank, N.A., Washington, DC, pg. 214
Sanchez, Raul de Jesus, Chief Fin. Officer--Laboratories Griffith de Mexico, S.A. de C.V., Monterrey,, Mexico, pg. 488
Sandberg, Dale H., V.P. & Chief Fin. Officer--Norwesco, Inc., Minneapolis, MN, pg. 816
Sander, William C., Exec. V.P., Sec. & Treas.--Hunt Building Corporation, El Paso, TX, pg. 553
Sanderman, Debbie, Comptroller--Pick's Cove Marina, Tacoma, WA, pg. 870
Sandin, Jose Luis, Fin. Mgr.--TAPSA Ayer, Madrid,, Spain, pg. 104
Sandlow, Richard, Chief Fin. Officer--Dudek & Bock Spring Manufacturing Company, Chicago, IL, pg. 351
Santina, John, Exec. V.P. & Chief Fin. Officer--Milton Industries, Inc., Chicago, IL, pg. 756
Sardone, Vince P., V.P.-Fin. & Chief Fin. Officer--Ervin Industries, Inc., Ann Arbor, MI, pg. 387
Sartori, Silvio, Treas.--Lee Myles Associates Corporation, Maywood, NJ, pg. 666
Sasjack, Charles, Jr., Chief Fin. Officer--General Sportcraft Company Ltd., Bergenfield, NJ, pg. 450
Saunders, James, Sr. V.P., Chief Fin. Officer--The Weightman Group, Philadelphia, PA, pg. 1173
Sawicki, Richard, Comptroller--Warren Equities Inc., New York, NY, pg. 1164
Sawicki, Richard J., Treas.--Drake Petroleum Company, Inc., Providence, RI, pg. 1165
Sawicki, Richard J., Treas.--Puritan Oil Company, Inc., Bellmawr, NJ, pg. 1165
Sawicki, Richard J., Treas.--Warren Oil Company, Providence, RI, pg. 1165
Saxton, R.D., Controller--The Union Fork & Hoe Co., Columbus, OH, pg. 1128
Scalfaro, Frank, Chief Fin. Officer--NavCom Defense Electronics, Inc., El Monte, CA, pg. 796
Scalia, Frank, Chief Fin. Officer--Coopers & Lybrand, New York, NY, pg. 283
Scangamor, Joe, Chief Fin. Officer--Media Buying Services Intl. Inc., New York, NY, pg. 734
Scanlan, Janette, Chief Fin. Officer & Dir.-Pur.--Fowler Tools of Canada, Kitchener,, Canada, pg. 427
Scanlon, Raymond, Chief Fin. Officer & V.P.--Al Paul Lefton Co., Inc., Philadelphia, PA, pg. 666
Scearce, C.B., Chief Fin. Officer, V.P., Sec. & Controller--Krystal Company, Chattanooga, TN, pg. 645
Schade, Edward P., V.P. & Chief Fin. Officer--Ethan Allen, Inc., Danbury, CT, pg. 485
Schaefer, John L., V.P.-Fin., Chief Fin. Officer & Sec.--The Wm. Powell Company, Cincinnati, OH, pg. 882
Schaejbe, Robert, Chief Fin. Officer--H. P. Hood Inc., Boston, MA, pg. 25
Schaer, Dennis, V.P.-Fin.--John S. Barnes Corp., Rockford, IL, pg. 120
Schafer, Glenn S., Exec. V.P. & Chief Fin. Officer--Pacific Mutual Life Insurance Company, Newport Beach, CA, pg. 841
Schafer, Robert W., V.P.-Admin. & Fin.--Haas Brothers, San Francisco, CA, pg. 498
Schanll, Carol, V.P. & Chief Fin. Officer--United States Luggage Company, Hauppauge, NY, pg. 1136
Schecter, Scott M., Sr. V.P., Chief Fin. Officer & Treas.--American Vision Centers, Inc., New York, NY, pg. 65
Schefelker, Wayne F., Sec. & Treas.--Fiberesin Industries Inc., Oconomowoc, WI, pg. 408
Scheller, Jim, V.P. & Gen. Mgr.--Roller Derby Skate Company, Litchfield, IL, pg. 944
Schellinger, Frank, Chief Fin. Officer--Kukla Press, Inc., Elk Grove Village, IL, pg. 646
Schenk, Leslie E., V.P. & Chief Fin. Officer--Ampex Corporation, Redwood City, CA, pg. 998
Scherer, Gary M., V.P.-Fin.--Scherer Bros. Lumber Company, Minneapolis, MN, pg. 976
Scherer, George, Chief Fin. Officer & Controller--McCarthy Building Companies, Saint Louis, MO, pg. 727
Scheuer, James, Sr. V.P. & Chief Fin. Officer--Hickory Farms, Inc., Maumee, OH, pg. 532
Schiavone, James, Chief Fin. Officer & Exec. V.P.--Financial World Partners, New York, NY, pg. 410
Schieber, Phil, Chief Fin. Officer--Berry-Brown Advertising, Inc., Dallas, TX, pg. 144
Schiess, John, V.P. & Chief Fin. Officer--Pabst Brewing Co., San Antonio, TX, pg. 959
Schimmoller, John, Sec. & Treas.--Renaissance Publishing Co., Inc., Auburn, IN, pg. 926
Schindler, E., V.P.-Fin.--Columbia Paint Co., Spokane, WA, pg. 265
Schirmang, William P., Pres., Treas. & Sls. Mgr.--Skokie Valley Beverage Co., Wheeling, IL, pg. 1009
Schloss, Marcel, V.P.-Fin.--Parade Publications Inc., New York, NY, pg. 847
Schlosser, P., Sec. & Treas.--Robins Engineers & Constructors, Inc., Englewood, CO, pg. 939
Schmalhoser, Bruno, Chief Fin. Officer--Farmer's Pride, Inc., Fredericksburg, PA, pg. 401
Schmidt, Donald O., Gen. Mgr., Treas. & Sec.--Walla Walla Grain Growers, Inc., Walla Walla, WA, pg. 1160
Schmidt, Leslie, Sec. & Treas.--Warrens Waller Press, South San Francisco, CA, pg. 1165
Schmidt, Robert, Sr. V.P. & Chief Fin. Officer--The Charles Levy Company, Chicago, IL, pg. 672
Schmidt, Robert J., Sr. V.P.-Fin. & Admin.--Wyandot Inc., Marion, OH, pg. 1205
Schneeberger, R. Louis, V.P. & Chief Fin. Officer--Olympic Steel Inc., Bedford Heights, OH, pg. 825
Schneider, Forrest M., Sr. V.P. & Chief Fin. Officer--Lane Industries, Inc., Northbrook, IL, pg. 656
Schneider, Paul L., Sr. V.P. & Chief Fin. Officer--The Acacia Group, Washington, DC, pg. 10
Schneider, Robert E., Exec. V.P. & Chief Fin. Officer--The New England, Boston, MA, pg. 799
Schneidewind, Bruce W., Chief Fin. Officer--Euromarket Designs, Inc., Northbrook, IL, pg. 390
Schnuck, Todd R., V.P. & Chief Fin. Officer--Schnuck Markets, Inc., Maryland Heights, MO, pg. 977
Schocke, Robert P., Chief Fin. Officer, Treas., Controller & Sec.--Greenhorne & O'Mara, Inc., Greenbelt, MD, pg. 485
Schoeck, Raymond, Chief Fin. Officer--DVC Industries, Bay Shore, NY, pg. 310
Schoepke, William F., V.P.-Production--Paddock Publications, Inc., Arlington Heights, IL, pg. 842
Schofield, Bob, Chief Fin. Officer--L'Ermitage Hotels, West Hollywood, CA, pg. 668
Scholler, Bernice, Sec. & Treas.--Times Printing Company, Inc., Random Lake, WI, pg. 1098
Schordock, R.A., Chief Fin. Officer, Treas. & Controller--Radix Wire Company, Cleveland, OH, pg. 909
Schott, Wendell, V.P. & Chief Fin. Officer--Schott Corporation, Wayzata, MN, pg. 978
Schram, C.R., V.P.-Fin.--RAM Golf Corporation, Melrose Park, IL, pg. 910
Schrank, Douglas R., Chief Fin. Officer & Sr. V.P.--Sealy Corporation, Cleveland, OH, pg. 985
Schrank, Douglas R., Sr. V.P. & Chief Fin. Officer--Sealy Mattress Company of Puerto Rico, Rio Piedras, PR, pg. 985
Schrank, Douglas R., Sr. V.P. & Chief Fin. Officer--The Stearns & Foster Upholstery Furniture Company, Cleveland, OH, pg. 985
Schrank, Douglas R., Chief Fin. Officer--Sealy Canada, Ltd., Edmonton,, Canada, pg. 986
Schrank, Douglas R., Sr. V.P. & Chief Fin. Officer--Stearns & Foster Upholstery Furniture Co., Columbiana, OH, pg. 985
Schrank, Douglas R., Sr. V.P. & Chief Fin. Officer--Stearns & Foster Upholstery Furniture Co., Pontotoc, MS, pg. 985
Schulak, Donald, Exec. V.P. & Chief Fin. Officer--Tri Valley Growers Inc., San Francisco, CA, pg. 1111
Schuller, James, V.P.-Fin.--Sathers Inc., Round Lake, MN, pg. 972
Schulte, Dennis, Chief Fin. Officer & V.P.-Fin.--United A G Co-op, Inc., Omaha, NE, pg. 1130
Schulte, J., Chief Fin. Officer & V.P.--Nelson A. Taylor Co., Inc., Gloversville, NY, pg. 1080
Schultz, Jay, Treas. & Sec.--ZBS Industries, Inc., Mayfield Village, OH, pg. 1215
Schultz, Robert J., Chief Fin. Officer, Treas. & Sec.--Great Lakes Lithograph Co., Cleveland, OH, pg. 481
Schulz, Lee A., Sec. & Treas.--Wine & Schulz Inc., Louisville, KY, pg. 1196
Schulz, Paul J., V.P.-Fin. & Controller--Wrought Washer Mfg., Inc., Milwaukee, WI, pg. 1205
Schulze, Max H., V.P., Sec., Treas. & Gen. Counsel--MCRB Service Bureau, Inc., North Hollywood, CA, pg. 691
Schumacher, Bill, Sr. V.P. & Chief Fin. Officer--Kemmerer Bottling Group Inc., Joliet, IL, pg. 622
Schumacher, D.A., Chief Fin. Officer & Treas.--The Cretex Companies, Elk River, MN, pg. 299
Schumacher, Norbert, Sr. V.P., Controller & Chief Fin. Officer--Marathon Cheese Corp., Marathon, WI, pg. 705
Schumacher, Roy J., Chief Fin. Officer, V.P.-Fin., Treas.--Fair Lanes Inc., Hunt Valley, MD, pg. 396
Schuster, Graig, Chief Fin. Officer--Weatherly Consumer Products, Inc., Lexington, KY, pg. 1169
Schwallie, Edward H., Sr. V.P. & Chief Fin. Officer--Booz Allen & Hamilton Inc., New York, NY, pg. 165
Schwartz, Curtis B., Exec. V.P.-Fin.--The Hartz Mountain Corp., Harrison, NJ, pg. 514
Schwartz, Earl, Treas.--Trans National Travel, Boston, MA, pg. 1106
Schwartz, Gary A., Chief Fin. Officer--Byer California, San Francisco, CA, pg. 197
Schwartz, Robert, Chief Fin. Officer & Controller--La Salle County Farm Supply, Ottawa, IL, pg. 649
Schwarz, Jeffrey D., V.P. & Chief Fin. Officer--Della Construction Co. Inc., Enfield, CT, pg. 326
Schwarz, William S., Exec. V.P. & Chief Fin. Officer--Telesensory, Mountain View, CA, pg. 1085
Sciame, Frank, Pres., Treas., Chief Exec. & Chief Fin. Officer--F.J. Sciame Construction, New York, NY, pg. 981
Scocchio, Jeffrey V., Chief Fin. Officer--Mathieu Corporation, Riverdale, NJ, pg. 720
Scott, Charles, Chief Fin. Officer & Controller--Mr. Christmas Inc., New York, NY, pg. 761
Scott, John L., Sr. V.P. & Chief Fin. Officer--Calmark Investment Company, Los Angeles, CA, pg. 211
Scribner, John, V.P. & Chief Fin. Officer--Paterno Imports Limited, Chicago, IL, pg. 851
Scribner, John, V.P. & Chief Fin. Officer--Pacific Wine Co., Chicago, IL, pg. 851
Scruggs, Walter L., Chief Fin. Officer--Electrocatalytic, Inc., Union, NJ, pg. 375

Scully, William T., Chief Fin. Officer--Partners Meany, Inc., Albany, NY, pg. 850
Searfoss, David W., Sr. V.P., Chief Fin. Officer & Treas.--Phoenix Home Life Mutual Insurance Company, Hartford, CT, pg. 868
Sears, L.D., Chief Fin. Officer & V.P.--Perfect Fit Industries, Inc., Monroe, NC, pg. 861
Sebastian, Paul E., Pres. & Chief Fin. Officer--Jockey International, Inc., Kenosha, WI, pg. 595
Seder, Steve D., V.P. & Chief Exec. Officer--Certified Grocers Midwest, Inc., Hodgkins, IL, pg. 236
Sedlack, Jeffery, Chief Fin. Officer--Colony Press Inc., Northbrook, IL, pg. 609
Seeley, Raynor M. Jr., V.P., Chief Fin. Officer & Sec.--PTA Corporation, Oxford, CT, pg. 837
Seem, David, Chief Fin. Officer--Alliance America, Norcross, GA, pg. 37
Seery, Patrick, Chief Fin. Officer, Treas. & Controller--James McHugh Construction Co., Chicago, IL, pg. 729
Seiffert, Robert, Sr. V.P. & Chief Fin. Officer--The Levy Organization, Chicago, IL, pg. 672
Seiser, Ronald, Chief Fin. Officer & Dir.-Opers.--Independent Metals, Germantown, WI, pg. 565
Seligman, Irving R., Treas.--Sterling Savings & Loan, Southfield, MI, pg. 988
Seligson, Stan, V.P., Chief Fin. Officer--Bernstein-Rein Advertising, Inc., Kansas City, MO, pg. 144
Sellberg, Steven, Chief Fin. Officer--Blue Bird Coach Lines Inc., Olean, NY, pg. 158
Sellers, Robert P., Sec. & Treas.--Dean Sellers Ford Inc., Troy, MI, pg. 988
Sellin, Douglas, Sr. V.P.-Opers. & Fin.--Seattle Pacific Industries, Inc., Seattle, WA, pg. 986
Senie, Kevin, Exec. V.P. & Chief Fin. Officer--Landmark Communications, Inc., Norfolk, VA, pg. 654
Seppala, Paul, Chief Fin. Officer--S. J. Groves & Sons Company, Minneapolis, MN, pg. 490
Serge, Anthony F., Chief Fin. Officer--HCC Industries, Rosemead, CA, pg. 496
Sergio, George, Exec. V.P. & Chief Fin. Officer--WWF Paper Corporation, Bala-Cynwyd, PA, pg. 1157
Severs, Gerard, Chief Fin. Officer--Lowe Troost S.A., Brussels,, Belgium, pg. 685
Severson, Sid, Chief Fin. Officer & Sr. V.P.--Sunflower Electric Power Corporation, Hays, KS, pg. 1060
Sevick, Daniel M., Chief Fin. Officer & Treas.--The ERM Group, Exton, PA, pg. 360
Sha, J., Sec. & Treas.--Fyrnetics, Inc., Roselle, IL, pg. 438
Shackford, Paul, V.P.-Fin. & Admin.--Equitable Bag Company, Long Island City, NY, pg. 385
Shae, Dennis, Chief Fin. Officer--Plymouth Lamston Stores, Corp., Saddle Brook, NJ, pg. 877
Shafer, Ernst S., Pres., Chief Exec., Chief Oper. & Chief Fin. Officer--Smith-Shafer Oil Co., Rockford, IL, pg. 1014
Shaffer, Jack M., Treas.--Just Born, Inc., Bethlehem, PA, pg. 610
Shaffer, John A., V.P. & Chief Fin. Officer--Finch, Pruyn & Co., Inc., Glens Falls, NY, pg. 410
Shah, Dipak, Sec. & Treas.--Village Ford Inc., Dearborn, MI, pg. 1151
Shah, Mayur, Treas.--H. Freeman & Son, Inc., Philadelphia, PA, pg. 431
Shaka, Douglas, Controller--Applied Graphics Technologies, Oceanside, NY, pg. 1136
Shames, Sidney J., Chm. Bd., Pres., CEO, COO, CFO & Treas.--Melard Manufacturing Corporation, Passaic, NJ, pg. 737
Shanahan, Martin, Exec. V.P., Chief Fin. Officer--Lewis & Gace, Inc., Fort Lee, NJ, pg. 673
Shao, Shiu, Chief Fin. Officer & Sr. V.P.--Oroamerica, Inc., Burbank, CA, pg. 830
Shapiro, David, Pres. & Treas.--Tamarkin Co., Inc., Pittsburgh, PA, pg. 456
Shapiro, Robert, Sec. & Controller--Weiners Enterprises, Inc., Houston, TX, pg. 1173
Shapiro, Ronald, Sr. V.P., Comptroller--Vitt Media International, Inc., New York, NY, pg. 1153
Shapria, David, Pres. & Treas.--Giant Eagle Market Co., Pittsburgh, PA, pg. 456
Sharkey, Kenneth C., V.P. & Treas.--Farmers and Traders Life Insurance Co., Syracuse, NY, pg. 401
Sharma, Anil, V.P. & Chief Fin. Officer--Raleigh Enterprises, Inc., Los Angeles, CA, pg. 910
Sharp, Robert R., V.P. & Chief Fin. Officer--Gusso Manufacturing, Inc., Brooklyn, NY, pg. 495
Shavelson, Kenneth, Chief Fin. Officer, Exec. V.P., Dir.-Intl. Fin. & Treas.--Weksler Instruments Corp., Freeport, NY, pg. 1174
Shaw, Ned W., V.P.-Fin., Treas. & Chief Fin. Officer--Bristol Steel & Iron Works, Inc., Bristol, VA, pg. 176
Shaykin, Robert H., Chief Fin. Officer--Adler & Shaykin, New York, NY, pg. 17
Shea, B.F., V.P.-Fin. & Chief Fin. Officer--Dan River Inc., Danville, VA, pg. 313
Shea, Kevin, Sr. V.P. & Chief Fin. Officer--Beech Holdings Corp., Chicago, IL, pg. 131
Shean, Steve, Chief Fin. Officer--United Health Plan, Inglewood, CA, pg. 1133
Shearer, William L., III, Chm. Bd. & Treas.--Paine Furniture Co., Norwood, MA, pg. 843
Sheffield, Tyler W., Chief Fin. Officer & Treas.--Burnham Broadcasting Company, Chicago, IL, pg. 193
Shepperd, Richard M., Chief Fin. Officer--Zenith Laboratories, Inc., Northvale, NJ, pg. 1217
Sheridan, Patrick M., Exec. V.P. & Chief Fin. Officer--The Associated Group, Indianapolis, IN, pg. 90
Sherman, Sheron, Controller--The Benson Music Group, Nashville, TN, pg. 140
Sherman, William H., V.P.-Fin. & Admin--The Royal China & Porcelain Companies Inc., Moorestown, NJ, pg. 953
Sherwood, R. C., Exec. V.P. & Chief Fin. Officer--L. B. Smith, Inc., Camp Hill, PA, pg. 1013
Shields, Wayne L., Chief Fin. Officer & Treas.--IBT, Inc., Shawnee Mission, KS, pg. 558
Shikles, Dale, Sr. V.P. & Controller--J.E. Dunn Construction Co., Kansas City, MO, pg. 354
Shimer, D.J., Exec. V.P. & Chief Fin. Officer--PQ Corporation, Valley Forge, PA, pg. 836
Shipengrover, Donald R., Treas. & Sec.--Watkins System Inc., Concordville, PA, pg. 1167
Shipp, B.B., Exec. V.P. & Chief Fin. Officer--Thermalloy, Inc., Farmers Branch, TX, pg. 1091
Shouldis, George, V.P.-Opers. & Fin.--Dri-Print Foils, Rahway, NJ, pg. 349
Shovlin, Gary, Sr. V.P. & Chief Fin. Officer--American Speedy Printing Centers, Inc., Bloomfield Hills, MI, pg. 61
Sichler, Joseph E., Chief Fin. Officer--C M P Publications, Inc., Manhasset, NY, pg. 202
Sider, William, Exec. V.P. & Chief Fin. Officer--The Hertz Corporation, Park Ridge, NJ, pg. 849
Sieben, Horst O., Chief Fin. Officer--Sterling, Inc., Milwaukee, WI, pg. 1047
Siegal, Bob, Controller--Universal Builders Supply, Inc., Mount Vernon, NY, pg. 1137
Siegel, Charles J., V.P. & Chief Fin. Officer--Topa Savings Bank, Los Angeles, CA, pg. 1101
Siegel, Charles J., Chief Fin. Officer & Treas.--Topa Thrift & Loan Association, Los Angeles, CA, pg. 1101
Siegel, Leonard, V.P. & Treas.--Anglo Fabrics Company, Inc., New York, NY, pg. 75
Siegel, Terry, Treas.--Siegel Corp., Fort Worth, TX, pg. 1002
Siegel, Terry, Treas.--Legis Corporation, Ft. Worth, TX, pg. 1002
Siegert, Marvin G., Sr. V.P. & Chief Fin. Officer--RAYOVAC Corporation, Madison, WI, pg. 915
Siekert, Harold R., V.P.-Fin.--Flambeau Corporation, Baraboo, WI, pg. 809
Sievert, Frederick, Sr. V.P. & Chief Fin. Officer--New York Life Insurance Company, New York, NY, pg. 802
Signori, J., Chief Fin. Officer & Treas.--Galaxy Business Products, Honolulu, HI, pg. 742
Signorini, J.E., Exec. V.P., Treas. & Chief Fin. Officer--The F.A. Bartlett Tree Expert Co., Stamford, CT, pg. 123
Silhacek, Bob, Chief Fin. Officer--Acrometal Companies, Inc., Brainerd, MN, pg. 14
Silles, Victor, Chief Fin. Officer & Treas.--Thetford Corporation, Ann Arbor, MI, pg. 357
Simkus, P.J., V.P.-Fin.--Flavor House Products, Inc., Dothan, AL, pg. 417
Simon, Charles E., Sr. V.P. & Chief Fin. Officer--Farm Family Mutual Insurance Co., Glenmont, NY, pg. 401
Simon, Laurence B., Treas.--Accelerated Claims Processing, Inc., New York, NY, pg. 521
Simon, Norman, V.P., Sec. & Treas.--Joseph Simon & Sons, Inc., Tacoma, WA, pg. 1006
Simon, Paul S., Pres. & Chief Fin. Officer--Morris Corporation, Augusta, GA, pg. 999
Simonsen, Eric A., V.P. & Chief Fin. Officer--State Mutual Life Assurance Company of America, Worcester, MA, pg. 35
Simpson, Frank, Chief Fin. Officer & Controller--Plywood Plastics Inc., Buffalo, NY, pg. 878
Simpson, Joe B., Jr., V.P.-Fin., Chief Fin. Officer & Treas.--The Alpha Corporation Of Tennessee, Collierville, TN, pg. 43
Simpson, Randy, Chief Fin. Officer & V.P.--Florida Crushed Stone Company, Leesburg, FL, pg. 420
Sims, Barry, V.P. & Chief Fin. Officer--Taco John's International, Inc., Cheyenne, WY, pg. 1076
Sims, Bernard J., V.P.-Fin.--Snokist Growers, Yakima, WA, pg. 1015
Sims, James M., V.P., Chief Fin. & Acctg. Officer--Jim Walter Resources, Inc., Brookwood, AL, pg. 1162
Sims, James M., V.P., Chief Fin. & Chief Acctg. Officer--Mining Div., Brookwood, AL, pg. 1162
Singer, Max E., Chief Fin. Officer, V.P. & Treas.--U.S. Engineering Company, Kansas City, MO, pg. 1135
Singer, Sharon, Chief Fin. Officer & V.P.--Singers Supermarkets, Inc., North Bergen, NJ, pg. 1008
Sisk, Raymond, Chief Fin. Officer--Blue Cross & Blue Shield of Virginia, Richmond, VA, pg. 160
Sislak, Elizabeth L., V.P., Chief Fin. Officer--Dix & Eaton Incorporated, Cleveland, OH, pg. 341
Skelton, Ronald E., Chief Fin. Officer & V.P.-Fin.--Zilber, Ltd., Milwaukee, WI, pg. 1219
Skubas, Charles E., Chief Fin. Officer & Sec.--Herlin Press, West Haven, CT, pg. 531
Slabas, Stanley F., V.P.-Fin.--S & C Electric Company, Chicago, IL, pg. 958
Slack, Paul, V.P & Controller--Mullen Advertising, Inc., Wenham, MA, pg. 775
Slezak, Dominic, Controller--Harford Systems, Inc., Aberdeen, MD, pg. 152
Sloan, Kerry, V.P.-Fin., Treas. & Chief Fin. Officer--Hardaway Construction Company, Inc., Nashville, TN, pg. 508
Slocum, Jack, Chief Fin. Officer--Molded Fiber Glass Co., Union City, PA, pg. 764
Slusarczyk, Eve, Chief Fin. Officer--Mesirow Financial, Chicago, IL, pg. 741
Smead, H.J., Chm. Bd., Pres., Chief Exec. & Chief Fin. Officer & Sec.--Kaiser Aerospace & Electronics Corp., Foster City, CA, pg. 614
Smelas, Robert, V.P.-Fin.--Flexel, Inc., Atlanta, GA, pg. 418
Smisor, Bradley, Sec. & Treas.--Builders Development Inc., Wichita, KS, pg. 444
Smith, Allen, Chief Fin. Officer, Treas. & Sec.--The Benham Group, Oklahoma City, OK, pg. 138
Smith, C.M., V.P. & Chief Fin. Officer--BE & K, Inc., Birmingham, AL, pg. 106
Smith, Edward C., Chief Fin. Officer & V.P.--Savoy Construction Co. Inc., Kensington, MD, pg. 973
Smith, Ellen M., Chief Fin. Officer & Comptroller--Transco Inc., Chicago, IL, pg. 1106
Smith, George S., Sr. V.P. & Chief Fin. Officer--Viacom International Inc., New York, NY, pg. 785
Smith, George S., Jr., Sr. V.P. & Chief Fin. Officer--National Amusements, Inc., Dedham, MA, pg. 784
Smith, George S., Jr., Sr. V.P. & Chief Fin. Officer--Viacom Inc., New York, NY, pg. 785
Smith, Glenn, Treasurer, Chief Fin. Officer--Haworth Group Inc., Minnetonka, MN, pg. 518
Smith, J. Michael, V.P. & Chief Fin. Officer--Horizon Bancorp, Michigan City, IN, pg. 544
Smith, James, Chief Fin. Officer--Wang's International, Inc., Memphis, TN, pg. 1162
Smith, Jerry, Chief Fin. Officer & Controller--Coble Dairy Products Co-op, Lexington, NC, pg. 257
Smith, Kelly E., Chief Fin. Officer--The Hoyt Group, Shawnee Mission, KS, pg. 548
Smith, Leon, Sr. V.P. & Chief Fin. Officer--American Hardware Mutual Insurance Co., Minnetonka, MN, pg. 55
Smith, Linda, Corp. Controller & Sec.--Standard Gravure Corp./Shea Communications, Atlanta, GA, pg. 1036
Smith, Matthew, Sr. V.P. & Chief Fin. Officer--CW Publishing, Inc., Framingham, MA, pg. 576
Smith, P. Jeremy, Jr., V.P.-Fin.--Gate Petroleum Company, Jacksonville, FL, pg. 445
Smith, Richard, Chief Fin. Officer--National Liberty, Frazer, PA, pg. 791
Smith, Thomas C., Exec. V.P.-Fin.--Jonbil Inc., Chase City, VA, pg. 602
Smith, William, Chief Fin. Officer, Treas. & Controller--Hoffritz for Cutlery, New York, NY, pg. 538
Smith, William, Chief Fin. Officer--Hoffritz International, New York, NY, pg. 538
Smyre, Dane, Sec. & Treas.--Diamond Hill Plywood Company, Darlington, SC, pg. 316
Smyth, Jeff A., V.P. & Chief Fin. Officer--Bovaird Supply Co., Tulsa, OK, pg. 168
Sneider, Chuck, Chief Fin. Officer--SAE Engineering, Inc., Santa Clara, CA, pg. 959
Snider, Terry L., V.P. & Comptroller--Atlas Foundry & Machine Co., Tacoma, WA, pg. 1073
Snover, Karl, Sr. V.P.-Fin.--West Coast Life Insurance Co., San Francisco, CA, pg. 795
Sny, Sharon, Chief Fin. Officer & Treas.--Duro-Last Roofing, Inc., Saginaw, MI, pg. 355
Snyder, Alex, Chief Fin. Officer--BSB Japan Ltd., Tokyo, Japan, pg. 110
Snyder, Ross B., Sr. V.P. & Chief Fin. Officer--Blue Cross & Blue Shield of Texas, Inc., Richardson, TX, pg. 160
Snyder, Tom, Chief Fin. Officer--The Hammerblow Corp., Wausau, WI, pg. 504
Sobczyk, John S., V.P.-Fin. & Chief Fin. Officer--Jervis B. Webb Company, Farmington Hills, MI, pg. 1170
Sobina, Donald E., V.P. & Controller--United Refining Company, Warren, PA, pg. 1130
Sobyak, Larry, V.P., Treas. & Personnel Mgr.--Demco Inc., Madison, WI, pg. 328
Soehnlen, Joseph, V.P.--Quality Chekd Dairy Products Association, Naperville, IL, pg. 903
Solheim, Bob, Grp. V.P.-Fin. & Admin.--Solvay Pharmaceuticals, Inc., Marietta, GA, pg. 1017
Solomon, Steven L., V.P. Fin., Chief Fin. Officer & Treas.--Elixir Industries, Gardena, CA, pg. 376
Solove, Sandra M., Chief Fin. Officer & Controller--Champion Boxed Beef, Denver, CO, pg. 238
Sommer, James, Pres., Chief Oper. & Fin. Officer & Treas.--Service Motor Company, Dale, WI, pg. 992
Sorensen, Nico Schou, Chief Fin. Officer--Young & Rubicam Copenhagen, Copenhagen, Denmark, pg. 1213
Sorrentino, Ralph, Exec. V.P., Chief Fin. & Admin. Officer--Bohbot Communications, Inc., New York, NY, pg. 162
Sortwell, Christopher, Sr. V.P. & Chief Fin. Officer--The Stroh Brewery Company, Detroit, MI, pg. 1053
Sosne, Marshall A., Chief Fin. Officer & V.P.--Dunham's Athleisure Corporation, Waterford, MI, pg. 353
Sosnoski, Donald S., Chief Fin. Officer, V.P. & Treas.--PVS Chemicals, Inc., Detroit, MI, pg. 837
Sotos, Hercules P., Vice Chm.--Playtex FP Group Incorporated, Stamford, CT, pg. 877
Soule, Charles, Chief Fin. Officer--Ullenberg Corp., Chattanooga, TN, pg. 1125
Soule, Edward, Principal & Chief Fin. Officer--Edward D. Jones & Co., Maryland Heights, MO, pg. 603
Sovich, Andrew, Treas.--Creative Productions, Pittsburgh, PA, pg. 297
Spacht, David B., Chief Fin. Officer & Asst. Treas.--Artesian Resources Corporation, Newark, DE, pg. 86
Spacht, David B., Chief Fin. Officer & Asst. Treas.--Artesian Water Company, Inc., Newark, DE, pg. 86
Spackler, J. Keith, Mgr.-Bus. Analysis--Ag Processing Inc A Cooperative, Omaha, NE, pg. 24
Spaman, Robert, Chief Fin. Officer & Treas.--Aves Advertising, Inc., Grand Rapids, MI, pg. 102
Spangler, John, Chief Fin. Officer--JPM Company, Lewisburg, PA, pg. 586
Spano, Michael, Chief Fin. Officer--Milton Samuels Advertising Agency, Inc., New York, NY, pg. 968
Sparler, D. John, Exec. V.P. & Treas.--Yorktowne Paper Mills, Inc., York, PA, pg. 1208
Spaulding, Richard, Exec. V.P. & Chief Fin. Officer--SI Holdings Inc., New York, NY, pg. 962
Specht, Dennis, Chief Fin. Officer--Food Services of America, Seattle, WA, pg. 423
Speer, R., Chief Fin. Officer--The Union Fork & Hoe Co., Columbus, OH, pg. 1128
Speicher, Mitch, Chief Fin. Officer--Vinyl Therm, Inc., Bloomington, MN, pg. 1152
Speicher, Mitch, Chief Fin. Officer--The Hoyt Company, Bloomington, MN, pg. 1152
Spence, Jeffrey E., Chm. Bd., Pres., Controller & Chief Exec. & Fin. Officer--Controlled Systems of Wisconsin, Inc., Nashotah, WI, pg. 281
Spencer, R.W., Chief Fin. Officer--W.A. Roosevelt Co., La Crosse, WI, pg. 946
Spendiff, James A., Chief Fin. Officer & V.P.--Freedom Forge Corporation, Burnham, PA, pg. 430

Spicer, Wm. V., Sr. Exec. V.P. & Chief Fin. Officer--Willamette-Western Corporation, Portland, OR, pg. 1190
Spiegel, John, Sec. & Treas.--Bucyrus Blades Inc., Bucyrus, OH, pg. 388
Spies, Robert J., Sr. V.P. & Chief Fin. Officer--Berol Corporation, Brentwood, TN, pg. 856
Spivak, Stuart, Chief Fin. Officer--Red Apple Companies, New York, NY, pg. 917
Spokane, Earl, Sr. V.P. & Chief Fin. Officer--Morse Shoe, Inc., Canton, MA, pg. 772
Spowart, Jay R., V.P.-Fin. & Corp. Sec.--PhoneMate, Inc., Torrance, CA, pg. 869
Spradling, William R., Exec. V.P. & Chief Fin. Officer--First American Bank of Georgia, N.A., Atlanta, GA, pg. 412
Springer, A., Controller--M. H. Rhodes, Inc., Avon, CT, pg. 931
Springer, Branch J., V.P., Chief Fin. Officer, Treas. & Sec.--Abbey Etna Machine Company, Perrysburg, OH, pg. 9
Sprow, Bob, Sec., Treas. & Controller--Ryan Herco Products Corp., Burbank, CA, pg. 958
Sprung, Joseph, Chief Fin. Officer--Muscum Boutique Intercontinental, Ltd., New York, NY, pg. 777
Squires, Robert, V.P.-Fin.--Scott Specialty Gases, Inc., Plumsteadville, PA, pg. 983
St. Hudson, Mark, Chief Fin. Officer--Swope Automotive Group, Inc., Louisville, KY, pg. 1068
St. Martin, Paul, Chief Oper. Officer & Chief Fin. Officer--The Allan R. Hackel Organization, Newton Center, MA, pg. 498
Stack, Alan, Chief Fin. Officer--Phototype Color Graphics, Inc., Pennsauken, NJ, pg. 869
Stadelman, Pete, Pres., Chief Exec. & Fin. Officer--Stadelman Fruit Inc., Yakima, WA, pg. 1034
Stafford, Lou, Internal Audit--Virginia State Lottery Department, Richmond, VA, pg. 1153
Stahlin, Kurt, Chief Fin. Officer--Knight Wendling AG, Zurich,, Switzerland, pg. 637
Stalder, Ruedi, Chief Fin. & Admin. Officer--CS First Boston Group, Inc., New York, NY, pg. 203
Stalzer, Robert J., Sr. V.P. Admin., Fin., Treas. & Asst. Sec.--Servo Corporation of America, Hicksville, NY, pg. 993
Stanek, John G., Sr. V.P. & Chief Fin. Officer--Burrell Communications Group Inc., Chicago, IL, pg. 195
Stanger, Yamna M., Chief Fin. Officer--McCormick Paint Works Company, Rockville, MD, pg. 727
Stangler, Kevin J., Sr. V.P., Chief Oper. & Fin. Officer & Treas.--Ministers Life Insurance Company, Minneapolis, MN, pg. 757
Stanislaw, Richard, Chief Fin. Officer--Collegeville Flag Mfg. Company, Collegeville, PA, pg. 261
Stanislaw, Richard, Chief Fin. Officer--Collegeville/Imagineering L.P., Collegeville, PA, pg. 262
Stark, Douglas A., Chm. Bd. & Chief Exec. Officer--Thrifty Drug Stores, Inc., Minneapolis, MN, pg. 1096
Statz, J.J., V.P. & Treas.--The Shaler Company, Waupun, WI, pg. 793
Stauff, Michael F., V.P.-Fin. & Chief Fin. Officer--International Marine Holdings, Inc., Stamford, CT, pg. 579
Stefano, Brian R., Chief Fin. Officer & Controller--Peter Pan Bus Lines, Inc., Springfield, MA, pg. 864
Steichem, Charles, V.P. & Chief Fin. Officer--Penhall International, Anaheim, CA, pg. 857
Steiger, Alan, Dir.-Fin.--A-Dec, Inc., Newberg, OR, pg. 1
Stein, David, V.P.-Fin., Chief Fin. Officer & Controller--T. J. Cinnamons Ltd., Kansas City, MO, pg. 1073
Stein, Jay, Chief Fin. Officer--Butterick Company, Inc., New York, NY, pg. 197
Steinberg, Mike, Chief Fin. Officer--Nelson Brothers Furniture Co., Chicago, IL, pg. 797
Steiner, Robert L., Treas.--Par Beverage Co., Cincinnati, OH, pg. 476
Steinhilber, Jeff R., Treas., Fin. Mgr. & Chief Fin. Officer--Austin Powder Co., Cleveland, OH, pg. 99
Stelling, James M., Exec. V.P., Treas. & Sec.--Ruscon Corp., Charleston, SC, pg. 956
Steltmann, Harry F., V.P., Chief Fin. Officer, Treas & Sec.--Eclipse, Inc., Rockford, IL, pg. 366
Stembridge, Alan B., V.P.-Admin. & Fin.--The P.J. Carlin Construction Company, New Rochelle, NY, pg. 220
Stepanek, Mark, Chief Fin. Officer--Moroch & Assoc., Inc., Dallas, TX, pg. 770
Sterbenz, Joanne, Chief Fin. Officer & Treas.--Olson-Travelworld Ltd., Manhattan Beach, CA, pg. 824
Stern, Jonathan H., V.P. & Treas.--GAF Export Corp., Wayne, NJ, pg. 438
Stern, Jonathan H., Treas.--GAF International Corp., Wayne, NJ, pg. 438
Sterrett, W.E., Exec. V.P. & Treas.--Wheaton Van Lines, Inc., Indianapolis, IN, pg. 1184
Stevens, Frank P., Chm. Bd., Pres., Treas., Chief Exec. Officer & Chief Fin. Officer--Professional Travel, Inc., Dalton, GA, pg. 894
Stevens, Richard, Chief Fin. Officer--Ritz-Carlton Hotel Company, Atlanta, GA, pg. 598
Stevenson, Allan J., Sr. V.P., Chief Fin. Officer & Controller--Parsons Brinckerhoff Inc., New York, NY, pg. 850
Stevenson, Dan, V.P.-Fin.--The Vernon Company, Newton, IA, pg. 1148
Stewart, Andrew, Sr. V.P., European Fin. Dir.--Ayer Europe, London,, United Kingdom, pg. 104
Stewart, Ronald G., Chief Fin. Officer--North Coast Electric Company, Bellevue, WA, pg. 813
Stiles, James E., V.P. & Chief Fin. Officer--Tom Thumb Food & Drugs, Inc., Dallas, TX, pg. 912
Stiles, Thomas E., Exec. V.P. & Chief Fin. Officer--The Penn Mutual Life Insurance Company, Philadelphia, PA, pg. 858
Stilper, Frank, Chief Fin. Officer & Treas.--Cummins Intermountain Diesel, Salt Lake City, UT, pg. 305
Stimpson, Ronald, Chief Fin. Officer & Exec. V.P.--Leader Federal Bank For Savings, Memphis, TN, pg. 663
Stimson, Charlie, Chief Fin. Officer--International Microcircuits, Inc., Milpitas, CA, pg. 579
Stinchcomb, G.M., V.P. & Treas.--The Daily & Sunday Oklahoman, Oklahoma City, OK, pg. 446
Stinson, Max L., Chief Fin. Officer--Reilly Industries, Inc., Indianapolis, IN, pg. 923
Stinson, Ruth Ann, Treas. & Dir.-Personnel--Young Supply Company, Detroit, MI, pg. 1214
Stitt, David R., Sr. V.P.-Fin. & Admin.--General Computer Corp. Inc., Twinsburg, OH, pg. 449
Stoefen, Gary E., Treas. & Investments Mgr.--Modern Woodmen of America, Rock Island, IL, pg. 763
Stoga, Len, V.P.-Fin.--Hyatt International Corporation, Chicago, IL, pg. 495
Stoloff, Robert, Sr. V.P., Chief Fin. Officer--Bronner Slosberg Humphrey, Boston, MA, pg. 179
Stone, Daniel T., V.P. & Treas.--STS Holdings, Inc., Northbrook, IL, pg. 964
Stone, David, Chief Fin. Officer & Treas.--Tylan General, Inc., San Diego, CA, pg. 1122
Stone, Robert M., Treas. & Chief Fin. Officer--Wil-Freds Construction, Inc., Aurora, IL, pg. 1189
Stonich, T.W., Sr. V.P.-Fin. & Chief Fin. Officer--U.S. Can Company, Oak Brook, IL, pg. 1134
Storm, June, V.P., Sec. & Treas.--Storm Products Company, Inc., Inglewood, CA, pg. 1052
Stout, Everett E., Pres., Chief Exec. Officer, Chief Fin. Officer & Controller--Metaltech, Inc., Kirkwood, MO, pg. 742
Stout, Paul D., Jr., V.P., Chief Fin. Officer & Treas.--McArdle Printing Co., Inc., Upper Marlboro, MD, pg. 189
Stover, D., Controller--ABB Environmental Systems, Knoxville, TN, pg. 2
Strachan, Randy, Chief Fin. Officer, V.P. & Controller--Ziebart Canada, Inc., Downsview,, Canada, pg. 1218
Straff, John J., Chief Fin. Officer--Steves & Sons, San Antonio, TX, pg. 1048
Strafford, William F., Sr. V.P.-Fin., Treas. & Chief Fin. Officer--Sealaska Corporation, Juneau, AK, pg. 984
Straka, Allen B., V.P., Chief Fin. Officer--The Jayme Organization, Inc., Cleveland, OH, pg. 591
Strande, Steve, Chief Fin. Officer--Miller Meester Advertising Inc., Minneapolis, MN, pg. 754
Strasma, Edward J., Exec. V.P., Chief Fin. Officer & Controller--Interstate Producers Livestock Association, Peoria, IL, pg. 580
Strauss, William D., Exec. V.P.-Admin. & Fin.--The American Stock Exchange, New York, NY, pg. 62
Streich, Gordon, Chief Fin. Officer--RK Mechanical, Inc., Lakewood, CO, pg. 907
Streich, Gordon, Chief Fin. Officer--Kinning & Reil of Wyoming, Lohewood, CO, pg. 907
Streich, William J., Treas. & Sec.--Resco Products, Inc., Conshohocken, PA, pg. 928
Strobel, Oren J., Pres. & Treas.--O. J. Strobel Oil & Tire Co., Inc., Summerville, SC, pg. 1053
Strole, Jon, Accountant--Tuffy Associates Corp., Toledo, OH, pg. 1119
Stromvall, Gil F., Chief Fin. Officer--Omega World Travel, Inc., Falls Church, VA, pg. 826
Stroud, Marie, Acctg. Mgr.--Alamo Group, Inc., La Grange, IL, pg. 29
Struzinski, Allan, Chief Fin. Officer--A. Pomerantz & Co., Philadelphia, PA, pg. 880
Stryker, James W., Chief Fin. Officer--El Torito Restaurants, Inc., Irvine, CA, pg. 372
Stuart, Ron, Comptroller--S. Schwab Company, Cumberland, MD, pg. 980
Stuhlmann, Eric, V.P. & Chief Fin. Officer--Shurfine-Central Corp., Northlake, IL, pg. 1001
Stull, Frank B., Chief Fin. Officer--Kayser-Roth Hosiery, Inc., Greensboro, NC, pg. 262
Sudhoff, Robert, Chief Fin. Officer & Sec.--The Minster Machine Company, Minster, OH, pg. 759
Suleman, Farid, Chief Fin. Officer & V.P.-Fin.--Infinity Broadcasting Corporation, New York, NY, pg. 567
Sullivan, A., Sr. V.P.-Fin.--I. Magnin & Co., San Francisco, CA, pg. 699
Sullivan, Charles J., V.P.-Fin.--Wehr Constructors Inc., Louisville, KY, pg. 1172
Sullivan, Eugene, Chief Fin. Officer--Spencer Press, Inc., Wells, ME, pg. 1030
Sullivan, Peter P., V.P.-Fin.--Brooks Beverages Inc., Columbus, OH, pg. 179
Sullivan, Sylvia, Chief Fin. Officer--McDonald Equipment Co., Willoughby, OH, pg. 728
Sullivan, Thomas C., Pres. & Chief Fin. Officer--Sullivan Paper Company, West Springfield, MA, pg. 1057
Sumrall, O. Malcolm, Chief Fin. Officer, Sec. & Treas.--Associated Equipment Company, Inc., Mobile, AL, pg. 89
Sundal, Rick, Chief Fin. Officer--Best Brands, St. Paul, MN, pg. 146
Suokko, Ronald, Chief Fin. Officer--SAIC Commercial Enterprises, Inc., San Diego, CA, pg. 982
Surma, Ronald F., Chief Fin. Officer & Controller--Processed Plastic Company, Montgomery, IL, pg. 892
Sutliff, Richard, Chief Fin. Officer--Dudnyk Advertising, Horsham, PA, pg. 351
Suzuki, Tak, Exec. V.P. & Chief Fin. Officer--PhoneMate, Inc., Torrance, CA, pg. 869
Svitek, John, Controller--Slant/Fin Corporation, Greenvale, NY, pg. 1010
Swallow, George, Controller--Luxor Corporation, Waukegan, IL, pg. 365
Swanson, Robert, V.P.-Fin., Sec., Treas. & Chief Fin. Officer--Danfoss Dukes Fluid Power Inc., Saint Charles, IL, pg. 314
Swartz, Jesse, Chief Fin. Officer--B. Green & Co., Baltimore, MD, pg. 484
Swinehart, Keith, Sr., Chm. Bd., Chief Exec. Officer & Chief Fin. Officer--Vanguard Plastics, Inc., McPherson, KS, pg. 1145
Swissa, David, Controller & Chief Fin. Officer--Dan's Supreme Super Markets Inc., Hempstead, NY, pg. 314
Switzer, Larry K., Sr. V.P. & Chief Fin. Officer--S. C. Johnson & Son, Inc., Racine, WI, pg. 599
Sykes, Darrell I., Sr. V.P. & Chief Fin. Officer--Ellerbe Becket, Inc., Minneapolis, MN, pg. 378
Sylvia, Joseph, Treas. & Dir.-Fin.--Simonds Industries Inc., Fitchburg, MA, pg. 1006
Symington, A.E., V.P.-Investments--Simpson Investment Co., Seattle, WA, pg. 1007
Szpotek, Gerald, Vice Chm.--ASC Incorporated, Southgate, MI, pg. 7
Taber, David, Chief Fin. Officer & V.P.-Fin.--National Health Care Affiliates, Inc., Buffalo, NY, pg. 791
Tadda, Thomas A., Chief Fin. Officer & V.P.-Fin.--Interform Corporation, Bridgeville, PA, pg. 574
Taff, Phillip W., Sr. V.P. & Chief Fin. Officer--American Trading and Production Corporation, Baltimore, MD, pg. 64
Taggart, Richard, V.P.-Fin. & Chief Fin. Officer--Brodbeck Enterprises, Inc., Platteville, WI, pg. 178
Taglianetti, Richard, Controller--Helmsley-Spear Inc., New York, NY, pg. 527
Tallent, Tom, V.P.-Fin.--Gemtron Corporation, Sweetwater, TN, pg. 3
Tamburro, Louis, V.P.-Fin. & Admin.--Patient Care, Inc., West Orange, NJ, pg. 851
Tananbaum, Andrew, Pres. & Chief Fin. Officer--Century Business Credit Corporation, New York, NY, pg. 235
Tannura, Frank V., Chief Fin. Officer--Ivex Packaging Corporation, Lincolnshire, IL, pg. 583
Tantalo, Daniel, Chief Fin. Officer--W&F Manufacturing Corporation, Inc., Buffalo, NY, pg. 1155
Tappan, James, Chief Fin. Officer & Treas.--United Dairymen of Arizona, Tempe, AZ, pg. 1131
Taradash, Elliott, V.P.-Production, Sec. & Treas.--M. Grossman Son, Inc., Passaic, NJ, pg. 489
Tarnay, Dennis, Chief Fin. Officer & Treas.--Lake Erie Electric, Inc., Westlake, OH, pg. 651
Tarren, Michael, V.P.-Fin.--Cole Business Furniture, York, PA, pg. 608
Tate, John B., V.P.-Fin.--CUNA Mutual Insurance Society, Madison, WI, pg. 205
Tate, Linda, Chief Fin. Officer--The Sunflower Group, Overland Park, KS, pg. 1060
Tate, R.L., Chm. Bd., Sec. & Treas.--Tate Access Floors, Inc., Jessup, MD, pg. 1080
Tate, Roy, Chief Fin. Officer--Ficks Reed Company, Cincinnati, OH, pg. 408
Tavel, Mark K., Pres. & Chief Investment Officer--Rothchild Asset Management Inc., New York, NY, pg. 951
Tawil, Theodore, Treas.--Tawil Associates Inc., Carteret, NJ, pg. 1080
Tayler, Phyllis, Chief Fin. Officer--Handel & Company, Inc., Pennsauken, NJ, pg. 504
Taylor, Chuck, Chief Fin. Officer & Controller--Maywood, Inc., Amarillo, TX, pg. 725
Taylor, Don R., Sr., Chief Fin. Officer, Treas. & Sec.--Homeland Stores, Inc., Oklahoma City, OK, pg. 542
Taylor, Ellen, Chief Fin. Officer--Charron, Schwartz & Partners, Inc., New York, NY, pg. 240
Taylor, Gerald R., Jr., Chief Fin. Officer & V.P.--Howe Furniture Corporation, Trumbull, CT, pg. 547
Taylor, James H., Jr., Partner, Chief Fin. Officer--Kupper Parker Communications Inc., Saint Louis, MO, pg. 646
Taylor, Meredith, V.P.-Fin. & Admin.--Stuart Anderson's Black Angus/Cattle Company Restaurants, Los Altos, CA, pg. 60
Taylor, Robert S., Chief Fin. Officer--Plywood Panels, Inc., New Orleans, LA, pg. 878
Teeple, William W., V.P., Chief Fin. Officer & Treas.--The Stackpole Corporation, Boston, MA, pg. 1034
Tell, Martin T., Chief Fin. Officer & Treas.--Jac Jacobsen Industries, Inc., Greenwich, CT, pg. 587
Temling, Peter, Chief Fin. Officer & Exec. V.P.-Fin.--TCC, Miami, FL, pg. 1072
Tepperman, Fred L., Exec. V.P. & Chief Fin. Officer--MacAndrews & Forbes Holdings Inc., New York, NY, pg. 694
Tepperman, Fred L., Sr. Exec. V.P. & Chief Fin. Officer--Andrews Group, Incorporated, New York, NY, pg. 74
Terrell, Charles, Pres., Treas. & Chief Exec. Officer--New Haven Savings Bank, New Haven, CT, pg. 801
Terrill, John R., V.P.-Credit & Internal Audit--Stone & Thomas, Wheeling, WV, pg. 1051
Terry, Thomas, Treas. & Sec.--Zimmer Paper Products Inc., Indianapolis, IN, pg. 1220
Teruya, Wayne, Exec. V.P.-Fin.--Times Super Market Ltd., Honolulu, HI, pg. 1089
Terwilliger, Mary, Dir.-Acctg. & Pur.--Spreckles Industries, Inc., Pleasanton, CA, pg. 1032
Tessmer, James, Chief Estimator--Walbridge Aldinger Company, Detroit, MI, pg. 1158
Thatcher, Gerald D., Sr. V.P., Chief Fin. Officer & Treas.--Central Mutual Insurance Co., Van Wert, OH, pg. 233
Thatcher, Gerald D., Sr. V.P. & Treas.--Cafco, Van Wert, OH, pg. 233
Theisen, Clifford R., V.P.-Fin. & Dir.-Data Processing--T & S Brass & Bronze Works, Inc., Travelers Rest, SC, pg. 1074
Theisen, Thomas G., V.P.-Fin. & Chief Fin. Officer--W. B. Goode Company, Inc., Richmond, VA, pg. 470
Thois, William, Chief Fin. Officer, Treas., Sec. & Dir.-Admin. & Opers.--Empire Airlines, Hayden Lake, ID, pg. 379
Thomas, G. N., Chm. Bd., Pres., Chief Exec. Officer, Chief Fin. Officer & Treas.--A. Levy & J. Zentner Co., Sacramento, CA, pg. 671
Thomas, Greg, Sr. V.P.-Fin. & Chief Fin. Officer--Great American Broadcasting Company, Cincinnati, OH, pg. 53
Thomas, Gregory, Exec. V.P. & Chief Fin. Officer--Great American Broadcasting Company, Cincinnati, OH, pg. 52
Thomas, Gregory C., Exec. V.P. & Chief Fin. Officer--Great American Communications Company, Cincinnati, OH, pg. 53

Thomas, Jesse G., Treas., Sec., Chief Fin. & Chief Information Officer--Allen & Hoshall, Inc., Memphis, TN, pg. 36
Thomas, Richard L., Treas. & Sec.--Mannington Ceramic Tile, Lexington, NC, pg. 704
Thomas, S.A., Asst. Sec. & Controller--York Wallcoverings Inc., York, PA, pg. 1208
Thompson, Gale, Chief Fin. Officer & Corp. Sec.--Thompson/Marince Advertising, San Antonio, TX, pg. 1094
Thompson, H.D., Chief Fin. Officer, V.P., Treas. & Sec.--Our Own Hardware Company, Burnsville, MN, pg. 832
Thompson, James G., Treas.--Hollytex, Saddle Brook, NJ, pg. 1121
Thompson, Patrick, V.P.-Fin. & Chief Fin. Officer--Modern Drop Forge Co., Blue Island, IL, pg. 762
Thompson, Richard, Treas.--Office Connection, Inc., Fort Lauderdale, FL, pg. 821
Thompson, Robert P., V.P.-Fin.--Cargocaire Engineering Corporation, Amesbury, MA, pg. 220
Thompson, Theodore J., Natl. Dir.-Fin. & Admin.--Grant Thornton, Chicago, IL, pg. 477
Thompson, Wayne, Pres. & Treas.--Tank Service, Inc., Knoxville, TN, pg. 526
Thomson, Mark, Chief Fin. Officer--Welsh Company, Saint Louis, MO, pg. 1175
Thomson, William H., V.P. & Trust Officer--First National Bank of Blue Island, Blue Island, IL, pg. 481
Thorne, Mark J., Chief Fin. Officer & V.P.-Fin.--TLC Beatrice International Holdings Inc., New York, NY, pg. 1073
Thrash, H. Lee, III., V.P.-Planning & Devel. & Chief Fin. Officer--Caraustar Industries, Inc., Austell, GA, pg. 217
Thurlow, Robin T., V.P., Chief Fin. Officer, Treas. & Sec.--Artesian Laboratories, Inc., Newark, DE, pg. 86
Tichenor, John A., Chief Fin. Officer, Treas. & Sec.--Allied Sporting Goods Inc., Louisville, KY, pg. 40
Tighe, Robert, Controller--Mustang Manufacturing Company, Inc., Owatonna, MN, pg. 777
Till, Alan, Sec. & Treas.--Carquest, Andalusia, AL, pg. 224
Timm, William C., Chief Fin. Officer & V.P.-Fin.--Contran Corporation, Dallas, TX, pg. 281
Tingle, Dan, Controller--Samtec Inc., New Albany, IN, pg. 968
Tipps, Gay, Treas. & Chief Fin. Officer--Wilson Pugh Inc., Portland, AR, pg. 1194
Tittle, David E., Chief Fin. Officer--Cosco Industries, Spring Valley, NY, pg. 288
Toberman, David, Treas. & Sec.--Toberman, Saint Louis, MO, pg. 1099
Todd, Curt, Chief Fin. Officer--Omaha Steaks International, Omaha, NE, pg. 825
Todd, Doris, Treas.--J. L. Todd Auction Co., Rome, GA, pg. 1099
Tolly, David H., V.P., Sec. & Gen. Counsel--Savage Arms Inc., Westfield, MA, pg. 973
Tolocka, Frank, Chief Fin. Officer--Datability, Inc., Carlstadt, NJ, pg. 316
Tomaszewski, Gerald E., V.P. & Chief Fin. Officer--A. Epstein and Sons, Intl., Inc., Chicago, IL, pg. 384
Tomchak, Leonard, Controller--Muskin Leisure Products, Inc., Wilkes-Barre, PA, pg. 777
Tomney, Douglas, V.P.-Fin.--National Oats Co., Cedar Rapids, IA, pg. 25
Torke, Marcella B., Sec. & Treas.--Torke Coffee Company, Inc., Sheboygan, WI, pg. 1102
Torres, Hiram, V.P. & Credit Mgr.--The Times-Picayune Publishing Corp., New Orleans, LA, pg. 1098
Toulmin, H.A., Jr., Pres. & Treas.--Central Pharmaceuticals, Inc., Seymour, IN, pg. 234
Touve, Richard L., Chief Fin. Officer--Exide Corporation, Reading, PA, pg. 393
Towne, William B., Exec. V.P. & Chief Fin. Officer--Forstmann & Company, Inc., New York, NY, pg. 424
Townsend, Arthur T., Chief Fin. Officer & Chief Oper. Officer--Lat Purser & Associate, Charlotte, NC, pg. 901
Townsend, Wayne, Chief Fin. Officer & Controller--Hygeia Dairy Co., Inc., Harlingen, TX, pg. 557
Trabold, John J., V.P.-Fin.--Superba, Inc., Los Angeles, CA, pg. 1063
Trabucco, Robert, Sr. V.P., Chief Fin. Officer, & Treas.--Lechmere, Inc., Woburn, MA, pg. 665
Traendly, Frank, Sr. V.P.-Fin.--Steinbach, White Plains, NY, pg. 1045
Traenkle, Jeffrey W., Chief Fin. Officer--Arthur D. Little, Inc., Cambridge, MA, pg. 678
Traversi, Philip, Mgr.-Acctg.--Strahman Valves, Inc., Florham Park, NJ, pg. 1052
Travis, Ronald O., V.P. & Chief Fin. Officer--McWane, Inc., Birmingham, AL, pg. 733
Treffiletti, Anthony J., Sec. & Treas.--J. Treffiletti & Sons, Inc., Albany, NY, pg. 1109
Trego, Charles, Jr., Sr. V.P. & Chief Fin. Officer--Rich Products Corp., Buffalo, NY, pg. 932
Trippel, Joe, V.P.-Fin.--Creation Windows of Indiana, Inc., Elkhart, IN, pg. 297
Truchi, James, Chief Fin. Officer, Treas. & Controller--Trucchis Markets, Raynham, MA, pg. 1117
Trumpore, Theresa, Treas.--Minor Rubber Co., Inc., Bloomfield, NJ, pg. 758
Tschoepe, Paul, V.P.-Fin.--Kaepa Inc., San Antonio, TX, pg. 613
Tuchalski, R.M., V.P., Chief Fin. Officer, Controller--YPMS/TMP Worldwide, Inc., Mequon, WI, pg. 1074
Tucker, Louhon, V.P.-Fin. & Chief Fin. Officer--Bekins Van Lines Co., Hillside, IL, pg. 133
Tuning, Joseph F., V.P.-Fin.--Virginia Hot Springs, Inc., Hot Springs, VA, pg. 1152
Tunmore, Edward E., Chm. Bd. & Treas.--Tunmore Oldsmobile Inc., Buffalo, NY, pg. 1119
Turfitt, Myron, Exec. V.P.-Fin.--United Refining Company, Warren, PA, pg. 1130
Turk, Michael G., Chief Fin. Officer--Simoniz Canada Ltd., Cleveland, OH, pg. 159
Turk, Michael G., Chief Fin. Officer--Nic Sand, Cleveland, OH, pg. 159
Turk, Michael G., Chief Fin. Officer--Chemifax, City of Commerce, CA, pg. 159
Turnbull, Alexander W., Sr. V.P. & Chief Fin. Officer--Ocean Spray Cranberries, Inc., Lakeville, MA, pg. 820
Turner, John L., Exec. V.P. & Gen. Mgr.--Allied Mineral Products, Inc., Columbus, OH, pg. 38
Turner, Lee, Exec. V.P. & Chief Fin. Officer--IVI Travel, Northbrook, IL, pg. 428
Turner, Roger, Pres., Chief Exec. & Fin. Officer--Western Controls, North Salt Lake, UT, pg. 1178
Turrell, Clifford, Pres., Chief Exec. Officer & Chief Fin. Officer--Cogifer Inc., Cincinnati, OH, pg. 259
Tyler, Judy, Instant Game Controller--Pennsylvania State Lottery, Middletown, PA, pg. 858
Tyson, Jane P., Sr. V.P., Chief Fin. Officer--O'Neil Griffin & Associates, Inc., Manchester, NH, pg. 827
Uddenberg, Eugenia M., Sec. & Treas.--Keith Uddenberg, Inc., Gig Harbor, WA, pg. 1125
Ulman, John, Controller--Fisher Broadcasting, Inc., Seattle, WA, pg. 415
Underhill, Stephen M., Chief Fin. Officer, Controller & Dir.-Personnel--Rowtronics Company Inc., Indianapolis, IN, pg. 953
Underwood, David, Chief Fin. Officer--AGI Inc., Melrose Park, IL, pg. 4
Underwood, Jerry, Comptroller--Frank Paxton Company, Kansas City, MO, pg. 592
Unterreiner, Ronald J., V.P.-Fin. & Chief Fin. Officer--HBE Corporation, Saint Louis, MO, pg. 495
Unverzagt, Phillip, Chief Fin. Officer & V.P.--Oregon Freeze Dry, Inc., Albany, OR, pg. 829
Updegraff, Judy, V.P. & Chief Fin. Officer--Madison Graham Colorgraphics, Inc., Los Angeles, CA, pg. 699
Urich, William, V.P.-Fin.--Dorman-Roth Foods, Inc., Moonachie, NJ, pg. 346
Ursini, Edilio, Exec. V.P.-Admin.--Savoy Construction Co. Inc., Kensington, MD, pg. 973
Usibelli, Joseph E., Chm. Bd. & Chief Fin. Officer--Usibelli Coal Mine, Inc., Healy, AK, pg. 1140
Uveges, George, Chief Fin. Officer--Industrial General Corporation, Elyria, OH, pg. 566
Uzolins, Uldis, Chief Fin. Officer & V.P.--Fred V. Fowler Company, Inc., Newton, MA, pg. 427
Vaccarella, J., V.P.-Chief Fin. Officer--Bead Industries Inc., Bridgeport, CT, pg. 129
Valdes, Alfredo, V.P.-Fin., Opers., Corp. Sec. & Treas.--Domecq Importers Inc., Old Greenwich, CT, pg. 343
Valdiva, Eunice, Exec. V.P.-Mktg. & Fin.--Clinique Laboratories, Inc., New York, NY, pg. 389
Van Caneghem, A., V.P.-Fin.--Rail Europe Inc., White Plains, NY, pg. 910
Van Luven, G.A., Vice Chm., Chief Fin. Officer, Treas. & Controller--The Gage Company, Pittsburgh, PA, pg. 441
Van Rijn, Bernard, Chief Fin. Officer, Treas. & Sec.--Kirk-Mayer, Inc., Los Angeles, CA, pg. 633
Vanaria, R. J., V.P.-Fin., Treas. & Sec.--Foamex L.P., East Providence, RI, pg. 1121
Vander Pol, Daryl L., V.P., Treas. & Sec.--Vita-Milk Dairy, Inc., Seattle, WA, pg. 1153
Vanderstelt, Mark J., Chief Fin. Officer & Treas.--Maxon Corporation, Muncie, IN, pg. 723
Vanderwal, Richard, Chief Fin. Officer & V.P.-Fin.--Gingiss International, Chicago, IL, pg. 460
Varblow, Carl R., Chm. Bd. & Chief Fin. Officer--Veda International, Inc., Alexandria, VA, pg. 1146
Varblow, Carl R., Chm. Bd. & Chief Fin. Officer--Veda Incorporated, Alexandria, VA, pg. 1146
Varblow, Carl R., Chief Fin. Officer--Veda Systems, Incorporated, California, MD, pg. 1146
Varblow, Carl R., Chief Fin. Officer--Chameleon Technologies Incorporated, Alexandria, VA, pg. 1146
Vargis, George, V.P.-Admin. & Chief Fin. Officer--Modulite Corporation, Compton, CA, pg. 763
Vastaris, Anthony, Chief Fin. Officer & V.P.--Wozniak Industries, Inc., Oakbrook Terrace, IL, pg. 1204
Vazquez, Jose Luis, Chief Fin. Officer--Arthur Andersen, Chicago, IL, pg. 72
Veale, Kenny, V.P., Mgr. Financial Services--Vitt Media International, Inc., New York, NY, pg. 1153
Vecchiolla, Joseph, Exec. V.P., Chief Fin. Officer & Sec.--Educational Publishing Corporation, Oak Lawn, IL, pg. 369
Verville, N.J., Chief Fin. Officer & Treas.--Bucyrus-Erie Company, South Milwaukee, WI, pg. 186
Vesci, Joseph V., Chief Fin. Officer--Interstate Steel Supply Co., Philadelphia, PA, pg. 580
Vicari, Yolande, V.P., Dir. Quality Control--Vitt Media International, Inc., New York, NY, pg. 1153
Vickers, John, V.P.-Fin.--Pharmavite Corp., Mission Hills, CA, pg. 866
Vieille, Bernard, Controller--Newage Industries Inc., Plastics Division, Willow Grove, PA, pg. 803
Viera, James J., V.P. & Chief Fin. Officer--Cowles Media Company, Minneapolis, MN, pg. 291
Viezens, Hans, Chief Fin. Officer--Fire Control Instruments, Inc., Newton, MA, pg. 411
Villamater, Henry, Chief Fin. Officer--Rocket Industries, Inc./Excel, The Excense Company, Pico Rivera, CA, pg. 941
Vitro, Thomas D., Dir.-Data Processing & Controller--Springborn Laboratories, Inc., Enfield, CT, pg. 1033
Vlahakis, Glenda, Sec. & Treas.--Trailer Wheel & Frame Company, Houston, TX, pg. 1105
Voge, Roger, V.P.-Fin--Star Lumber & Supply Company, Inc., Wichita, KS, pg. 1039
Vogel, Jack H., Chief Fin. Officer--Clay-Park Labs, Inc., Bronx, NY, pg. 253
Vogt, Richard, Dir.-Fin.--Cubix Corporation, Carson City, NV, pg. 303
Voigt, Richard, Controller--Wick Bldg. Systems Inc. Manufactured Homes Div., Marshfield, WI, pg. 1188
Volz, Larry H., Chief Fin. Officer--Carver Boat Corp., Pulaski, WI, pg. 758
von Luhrte, Richard L., Sec. & Treas.--RNL Technical Services, Denver, CO, pg. 908
von Luhrte, Richard L., Sec. & Treas.--Space Management Systems, Denver, CO, pg. 908
von Trapp, George, V.P. & Treas.--Trapp Family Lodge, Inc., Stowe, VT, pg. 1108
Vranek, William, Chief Fin. Officer--Coleman Cable Systems, Inc., North Chicago, IL, pg. 260
Vuckovich, Mitchell, Chief Fin. Officer--Friendly Chevrolet Co. Inc., Dallas, TX, pg. 433
Wabler, Bob, V.P. & Chief Fin. Officer--The Athlete's Foot Group, Inc., Kennesaw, GA, pg. 94
Waddell, Gregory A., Chief Fin. Officer & V.P. Fin.--Allied Paper Incorporated, Dayton, OH, pg. 38
Wade, Malcolm R., V.P.-Fin. & Chief Fin. Officer--Basic Construction Company, Newport News, VA, pg. 124
Wadsworth, Gary, V.P. & Chief Fin. Officer--Bernards Brothers, Inc., San Fernando, CA, pg. 143
Waetzman, Ron, Chief Fin. Officer--PacifiCare of Oklahoma Inc., Tulsa, OK, pg. 1127
Waggoner, Caroll, Treas.--Sunflower Electric Power Corporation, Hays, KS, pg. 1060
Waggoner, William, Pres. & Treas.--Waggoner Corp., Troy, MI, pg. 1158
Wagner, Christina B., V.P. & Chief Fin. Officer--K-III Magazines Corporation, New York, NY, pg. 611
Wagner, George W., Chief Fin. Officer & Comptroller--Western Regional Off Track Betting, Batavia, NY, pg. 1181
Wahlman, Mark M., V.P.-Fin.--Pacific Coast Producers, Lodi, CA, pg. 839
Waite, Karl A., V.P.-Fin.--Central Mutual Insurance Co., Van Wert, OH, pg. 233
Wakeland, Ralph, Exec. V.P.-Fin.--Fruit of the Loom, Bowling Green, KY, pg. 400
Wakeman, Fred J., Chief Fin. Officer--Green Bay Packaging Inc., Green Bay, WI, pg. 483
Waldbillig, Ron, Asst. V.P.-Mngmt. Information Systems--Hy-Vee Food Stores Incorporated, Chariton, IA, pg. 556
Walden, Thomas, Chm. Bd. & Chief Fin. Officer--Ris Paper Company, Long Island City, NY, pg. 935
Waldron, Mark, V.P. & Controller--Belvedere Company, Belvidere, IL, pg. 138
Waletzko, Don, Chief Fin. Officer--ACI Financial Corp., Minnetonka, MN, pg. 2
Waligurski, Raymond, Controller--Noma-International, Inc., Forest Park, IL, pg. 808
Walkenshaw, Philip S., Pres., Chief Exec. Officer & Treas.--The Townsend Agency, Ltd., Rosemont, IL, pg. 1104
Walker, Bob, Exec. V.P. & Chief Fin. Officer--Fiesta Mart Inc., Houston, TX, pg. 409
Walker, Chris, Treas.--Walker & Associates, Inc., Welcome, NC, pg. 1159
Walker, James P., Chief Fin. Officer--Codisco Inc., Sanford, FL, pg. 258
Wallace, Juanita, Pres., Chief Fin. Officer, Treas. & Sec.--Wallace & Wallace Fuel Oil, St. Albans, NY, pg. 1160
Wallace, Linda, Chief Fin. Officer & Treas.--Forecast Mortgage Corporation, Rancho Cucamonga, CA, pg. 423
Wallestad, Ruth, Asst. V.P. & Treas.--Zenith Laboratories, Inc., Northvale, NJ, pg. 1217
Wallis, W. Mark, Exec. V.P. & Chief Fin. Officer--Lincoln Property Company, Dallas, TX, pg. 676
Walsh, Chuck, Exec. V.P., Chief Fin. Officer--Earle Palmer Brown, Bethesda, MD, pg. 182
Walsh, Harry, Chief Fin. Officer--San Francisco French Bread Company, Oakland, CA, pg. 969
Walsh, Harry, Chief Fin. Officer--Calico Corners, Kennett Square, PA, pg. 209
Walsh, Thomas B., V.P. & Chief Fin. Officer--Turtle Wax, Inc., Chicago, IL, pg. 1120
Walsworth, James A., Chief Fin. Officer--Sloan Valve Company, Franklin Park, IL, pg. 1010
Walter, Gerald K., V.P. & Chief Fin. Officer--Amsted Industries Incorporated, Chicago, IL, pg. 68
Walter, Malcolm, Chief Fin. Officer--Ensoniq Corporation, Malvern, PA, pg. 382
Walters, Dave, Chief Fin. Officer--Abco Markets, Inc., Phoenix, AZ, pg. 10
Walters, Robert, Exec. V.P. & Chief Fin. Officer--Norwegian Cruise Line, Coral Gables, FL, pg. 816
Ward, Charles C., Jr., Treas.--Sunniland Corporation, Sanford, FL, pg. 1061
Wareham, L.J., V.P.-Fin.--The Elwell-Parker Electric Co., Cleveland, OH, pg. 378
Wark, Dale A., V.P.-Fin., Chief Fin. Officer, Treas. & Sec.--R. M. Shoemaker Co., West Conshohocken, PA, pg. 1000
Warner, Carol, Chief Fin. Officer--Johnstown Corporation, Johnstown, PA, pg. 601
Warner, Kathy, V.P.-Chief Fin. Officer--American SelfCare Corporation, Columbus, GA, pg. 60
Warner, Kathy, Chief Fin. Officer--American Health & Security Insurance Co., Inc., Columbus, GA, pg. 61
Warner, Lynne, Treas. & Sec.--Warner Vineyards, Paw Paw, MI, pg. 1164
Warniack, Tom, Sr. V.P. & Chief Fin. Officer--Contract Interiors Inc., Southfield, MI, pg. 280
Wascher, William J., Chief Fin. Officer--Seko-Air Freight, Elk Grove Village, IL, pg. 988
Wasinger, Charles, V.P.-Fin.--Revcor, Inc., Carpentersville, IL, pg. 930
Watkins, Paul E., Chief Fin. Officer--The LINC Group, Inc., Chicago, IL, pg. 648
Watson, Houston B., Chm. Bd., Chief Exec. Officer, Chief Fin. Officer & Treas.--Watson Electric Supply Inc., Dallas, TX, pg. 1168
Watson, John, V.P.-Fin.--Luzianne Blue Plate Foods, New Orleans, LA, pg. 923
Watson, John, Chm. Bd.--VMC Fiberglass Products Inc., Daleville, AL, pg. 1142

Watson, Laura, Chief Fin. Officer & Controller--Pachmayr Gun Works Inc., Monrovia, CA, pg. 839
Watson, Robbie, Controller--Binning's Building Products, Inc., Lexington, NC, pg. 151
Watson, T. Mitchell, Chief Fin. Officer & Treas.--B. L. Montague Co., Sumter, SC, pg. 766
Watts, Robert, Chief Fin. Officer--Electrical Insulation Suppliers, Hillside, IL, pg. 374
Way, T.L., V.P.-Fin.--Miller Chemical & Fertilizer Corp., Hanover, PA, pg. 32
Weaver, Michael, Comptroller--The Orange County Register, Santa Ana, CA, pg. 431
Weaver, Richard T., Treas., Sec. & Chief Fin. Officer--Hamburg Brothers Inc., Pittsburgh, PA, pg. 502
Weaver, Stephen D., Chief Fin. Officer & V.P. Fin.--The Carbide/Graphite Group, Inc., Pittsburgh, PA, pg. 217
Webb, Jerry, V.P.-Fin.--Tekra Corporation, New Berlin, WI, pg. 1084
Webb, Randy, Chief Fin. Officer--Griffin Manufacturing Co., Muskogee, OK, pg. 487
Webb, Richard, Chief Fin. Officer--Ambac International Corp., Columbia, SC, pg. 47
Webber, Jeff, V.P. & Chief Fin. Officer--Geo. E. Keith Company, Bridgewater, MA, pg. 620
Weber, Donald, Chief Fin. Officer--Rosco Manufacturing Co., Madison, SD, pg. 947
Weber, John R., V.P.-Fin. & Chief Fin. Officer--The Chardon Rubber Co., Chardon, OH, pg. 239
Weber, Rick, Sr. V.P. & Chief Fin. Officer--Dominick's Finer Foods, Northlake, IL, pg. 343
Webster, Mark, Chief Exec. Officer, Chief Fin. Officer & Gen. Counsel--Rush County Farm Bureau Co-op, Rushville, IN, pg. 956
Weeks, Shirley, Chief Fin. Officer & Dir.-Data Processing--Bill Woeste Dealer Group, Cincinnati, OH, pg. 1198
Wegman, Robert B., Chm. Bd., Chief Exec. Officer & Treas.--Wegmans Food Markets, Inc., Rochester, NY, pg. 1172
Wehrle, Michael H., Chief Fin. Officer & Treas.--McJunkin Corporation, Charleston, WV, pg. 730
Weibel, Fred E., Jr., Exec. V.P., Sec. & Treas.--Weibel Vineyards, Mission San Jose, CA, pg. 1173
Weidler, Allen, V.P.-Fin. & Sec.--Fred Usinger, Inc., Milwaukee, WI, pg. 1140
Weiner, Eugene L., Exec. V.P., Sec. & Treas.--Paradise Fruit Company, Inc., Plant City, FL, pg. 847
Weinstein, Abe, Chief Fin. Officer & V.P.--Hughes-Treitler Manufacturing Corporation, Garden City, NY, pg. 552
Weintraub, Irving J., Chief Fin. Officer & Sr. V.P.--William Morris Agency, Inc., Beverly Hills, CA, pg. 771
Weiss, David W., Treas.--Towers, Perrin, Forster & Crosby, Inc., New York, NY, pg. 1103
Weiss, Michael, V.P.-Fin. & Admin.--Federal Distributing Corporation, Maspeth, NY, pg. 404
Weldon, Robert W., V.P.-Fin. & Treas.--Country Life Insurance Company, Bloomington, IL, pg. 289
Weldon, W.N., V.P.-Chief Fin. officer--Mid-State Homes, Inc., Tampa, FL, pg. 1162
Wellborn, Susan E., V.P., Chief Fin. Officer, Controller, & Asst. Sec.--DKM Resources, Inc., Houston, TX, pg. 357
Wellens, Leroy, Chm. Bd., Pres., Chief Exec. & Chief Fin. Officer & Treas.--Wellens & Co., Inc., Minneapolis, MN, pg. 1175
Werner, David, V.P., Chief Fin. & Chief Information Officer--Microdot Aerospace Fastening Systems Group, Fullerton, CA, pg. 749
Werner, David A., Chief Fin. Officer & V.P.--MICRODOT, Inc., Chicago, IL, pg. 749
Werner, Ron, Mgr.-Fin. & Admin.--Alloway Manufacturing, Fargo, ND, pg. 41
Wessel, Paul C., V.P. & Chief Fin. Officer--Rodale Press, Inc., Emmaus, PA, pg. 942
West, Harry, Chief Fin. Officer & V.P.--Snap-Tite, Incorporated, Erie, PA, pg. 1014
Westmeyer, E.A., V.P.-Treas. & Sec.--Zeller Corp., Defiance, OH, pg. 1216
Whalen, Rita, Chief Fin. Officer--Beltone Electronics Corporation, Chicago, IL, pg. 137
Wheaton, Robert E., Chm. Bd., Pres., Chief Exec. & Chief Fin. Officer--The Bekins Company, Glendale, CA, pg. 132
Wheeler, C., Asst. Treas., Asst. Sec. & Controller--American Welding & Manufacturing Co., Warren, OH, pg. 431
Wheeler, Mike, Chief Fin. Officer, V.P. & Treas.--Hy-Vee Food Stores Incorporated, Chariton, IA, pg. 556
Whetson, Linda, Chief Fin. Officer & Controller--Life Line Nutritionals, Inc., Hayward, CA, pg. 675
Whipps, George, V.P. & Chief Fin. Officer--Whipps, Athol, MA, pg. 1185
White, H.G., V.P.-Fin.--Howell Instruments Corp., Fort Worth, TX, pg. 547
White, Jim, V.P., Treas. & Chief Fin. Officer--Tele-Trip Co., Omaha, NE, pg. 779
White, John W., Chief Fin. Officer & Asst. Treas.--United Grocers Inc., Portland, OR, pg. 1132
White, L.F., Chief Fin. Officer & V.P.--Sverdrup Corporation, Maryland Heights, MO, pg. 1065
White, Rock E., Chief Fin. Officer & Treas.--Rome Cable Corporation, Rome, NY, pg. 945
Whiteman, Jon, V.P. & Chief Fin. Officer--Morris Coupling Co., Erie, PA, pg. 771
Whiteside, Carol W., V.P., Sec. & Treas.--Rowe Corp., Charlotte, NC, pg. 952
Whiting, Paul L., Sr. V.P. & Chief Fin. Officer--Spalding & Evenflo Companies, Inc., Tampa, FL, pg. 1024
Whitley, Mark, Dir.-Fin.--Walker & Associates, Inc., Welcome, NC, pg. 1159
Whitten, Earl, Chief Fin. Officer, Treas. & Controller--Sherley Grain Company, Bovina, TX, pg. 998
Whyte, Len, Chief Fin. Officer--Columbia General Life Insurance Co., Laguna Hills, CA, pg. 1127
Wickhan, Robert, Treas. & Sec.--Wigwam Mills, Inc., Sheboygan, WI, pg. 1189
Wiesenthal, Richard S., Exec. V.P. & Chief Fin. Officer--The Unimax Corporation, New York, NY, pg. 1127
Wiesenthal, Richard S., Sr. V.P. & Chm.-Fin. Committee--Shepaug Corporation, New York, NY, pg. 997
Wiezel, Dave, Chief Fin. Officer--Gump's, Inc., San Francisco, CA, pg. 494
Wilcox, Jann Ozzello, V.P. & Chief Fin. Officer--Bank Shares, Inc., Minneapolis, MN, pg. 117
Wilcox, Jann Ozzello, Sr. V.P. & Chief Fin. Officer--Marquette Bank Minneapolis, National Association, Minneapolis, MN, pg. 117
Wilder, Duane, Chm. Bd., Pres. & Treas.--WDP, Inc., New York, NY, pg. 1156
Wilhelm, Robert, Deputy Dir.-Fin. & Admin.--West Virginia Lottery, Charleston, WV, pg. 1178
Wilhelmi, Dennis, Sr. V.P., Chief Fin. Officer--The Glennon Companies, Saint Louis, MO, pg. 462
Wilk, Ernest, Treas.--Kenyon Oil Company, Inc., North Grosvenordale, CT, pg. 1165
Wilk, Ernest J., Treas.--Mid-Valley Oil Company, Inc., New Windsor, NY, pg. 1165
Wilkins, Robin, Chief Fin. Officer--Jazzercise, Inc., Carlsbad, CA, pg. 591
Wilkinsom, James., Chief Fin. Officer & Gen. Counsel--Meritcare, Inc., Pittsburgh, PA, pg. 740
Wilkinson, GeorgeS., Chief Fin. Officer & Exec. V.P.--Modern Group Ltd., Bristol, PA, pg. 762
Wilkinson, Howard W., V.P., Chief Exec. Officer, & Treas.--Fisher Broadcasting, Inc., Seattle, WA, pg. 415
Willert, William D., Pres. & Treas.--Willert Home Products, Inc., Saint Louis, MO, pg. 1190
Williams, Belton R., Chief Fin. Officer, Treas. & Sec.--George W. Auch Co., Pontiac, MI, pg. 97
Williams, Belton R., Sec. & Treas.--GenCon Services, Inc., Pontiac, MI, pg. 98
Williams, Bruce E., Pres., Chief Exec. Officer & Treas.--Williams Company Of Orlando, Inc., Orlando, FL, pg. 1190
Williams, Chris, Chief Fin. Officer--Beers Construction Company, Atlanta, GA, pg. 132
Williams, David, Exec. V.P.--Hanna Car Wash International, Inc., Portland, OR, pg. 505
Williams, David, Chief Fin. Officer--National Academy Sciences USA, Washington, DC, pg. 784
Williams, David H., V.P.-Fin.--TVESCO, Inc., Memphis, TN, pg. 1075
Williams, Delon W., V.P., Controller, Chief Fin. Officer--Bonneville Communications, Salt Lake City, UT, pg. 164
Williams, Glen E., Jr., Exec. V.P. & Chief Fin. Officer--Dodson Group, Kansas City, MO, pg. 342
Williams, H. E., Controller--Levlad, Inc., Chatsworth, CA, pg. 671
Williams, J. Don, V.P.-Fin. & Admin.--Altec Industries, Inc., Birmingham, AL, pg. 45
Williams, Jay, Chief Fin. Officer & Treas.--Pacific Lumber & Shipping Co., Seattle, WA, pg. 840
Williams, Jimmie D., Exec. V.P., Chief Fin. Officer, Treas. & Sec.--Belz Enterprises, Memphis, TN, pg. 138
Williams, Joe V. III, Pres. & Treas.--Hardwick Clothes Inc., Cleveland, TN, pg. 508
Williams, John, Chief Fin. Officer--Rocco Inc., Harrisonburg, VA, pg. 940
Williams, Mary S., Comptroller--B.C. Cook & Sons Enterprises, Inc., Haines City, FL, pg. 282
Williams, Michael, Controller--Young Supply Company, Detroit, MI, pg. 1214
Williams, Mike, Chief Fin. Officer--Aeroglide Corporation, Cary, NC, pg. 22
Williams, Robert, Sr. V.P., Chief Fin. Officer--Keyes Martin, Springfield, NJ, pg. 627
Williams, Robert M., Pres. & Treas.--Williams Patent Crusher and Pulverizer Co., Saint Louis, MO, pg. 1191
Williams, Roger, Chief Fin. Officer--Little Lady Foods, Inc., Elk Grove Village, IL, pg. 679
Williams, Samuel M., V.P., Chief Fin. Officer--Sullivan Higdon & Sink Incorporated, Wichita, KS, pg. 1056
Williamson, Bob, Chief Fin. Officer--Wright Brand Foods, Inc., Vernon, TX, pg. 1204
Williamson, Scott, Chief Fin. Officer & Gen. Counsel--Plasti-Kote Company Inc., Medina, OH, pg. 875
Willims, Fred, V.P.-Fin.--Capitol Industries-EMI Inc., Hollywood, CA, pg. 216
Wilson, David E., V.P.-Opers. & Fin.--Shipley Oil Company, York, PA, pg. 999
Wilson, Jimmy, Chief Fin. Officer, Treas. & Controller--J. M. Smith Corp., Spartanburg, SC, pg. 1012
Wilson, John, V.P. & Chief Fin. Officer--Theodore Barry & Associates, Los Angeles, CA, pg. 122
Wilson, Kent, V.P.-Fin. & Chief Fin. Officer--Full Service Beverage Company, Wichita, KS, pg. 436
Wilson, Lawrence, Controller--Southern Container Corporation, Hauppauge, NY, pg. 1020
Wilson, R.K., Chief Fin. & Chief Admin. Officer--Woodward-Clyde Group, Inc., Denver, CO, pg. 1200
Wilson, Stephen R., Sr. V.P. & Chief Fin. Officer--CF Industries, Inc., Long Grove, IL, pg. 200
Wilson, Tony H., V.P.-Fin. & Sec.--PPA Industries, Inc., Dallas, TX, pg. 836
Wilton, Douglas H., Chief Fin. Officer--Unigroup, Inc., Fenton, MO, pg. 1126
Windell, Steve A., Mng. Partner & Chief Fin. Officer--R. W. Beck & Associates, Inc., Seattle, WA, pg. 131
Winkler, Gary M., V.P. & Chief Fin. Officer--Key Manufacturing Group, Inc., Royal Oak, MI, pg. 627
Winn, Elwood F., Sec., Treas. & Chief Fin. Officer--Certified Grocers Midwest, Inc., Hodgkins, IL, pg. 236
Winslow, Richard H., Chief Fin. Officer, V.P.-Fin., Controller & Treas.--Norfolk Shipbuilding & Drydock Corporation, Norfolk, VA, pg. 810
Wirtz, Norman, V.P.-Fin. & Chief Fin. Officer--TAD Technical Services Corp., Cambridge, MA, pg. 1071
Wisinski, Frank, Exec. V.P., Chief Fin. Officer--Campbell and Wagman, Los Angeles, CA, pg. 213
Wisner, Roland, Chief Fin. Officer--Omniflight, Inc., Dallas, TX, pg. 826
Wisser, William P., V.P.-Fin.--Narrow Fabric Industries, Inc., West Reading, PA, pg. 783
Witmer, James, Chief Fin. Officer--Avis Ford Inc., Southfield, MI, pg. 102
Wittstock, John, Chief Fin. Officer--American Printers & Lithographers, Chicago, IL, pg. 59
Wohleber, D., Exec. V.P.-Fin.--Eat N Park Restaurants, Pittsburgh, PA, pg. 364
Wolande, Charles, Pres. & Chief Fin. Officer--Comark, Bloomingdale, IL, pg. 267
Wolbers, Linda, Comptroller--Williams-White & Co., Moline, IL, pg. 1191
Wolf, Lawrence, Pres., Chief Exec. Officer, Sec. & Treas.--Leonard Wholesale, Inc., Elizabeth, NJ, pg. 668
Wolfe, T.E., Sr. V.P. & Treas.--Ziebart International Corporation, Troy, MI, pg. 1217
Wolff, Kenneth K., Exec. V.P. & Chief Fin. Officer--Amtran, Inc., Indianapolis, IN, pg. 69
Wolfgang, Donald R., Chief Fin. Officer & V.P.--Wells Aluminum Corp., South Bend, IN, pg. 1175
Wolford, B., Credit Mgr.--The Union Fork & Hoe Co., Columbus, OH, pg. 1128
Wolforth, Dennis L., Sr. V.P. & Chief Fin. Officer--The Bibb Company, Macon, GA, pg. 781
Wolfson, Alan, Chief Fin. Officer--Benderson Development Co., Inc., Buffalo, NY, pg. 138
Wolpert, Robert, Chief Fin. Officer--Lorsch Creative Network, Los Angeles, CA, pg. 684
Wolthausen, Reed, Sr. V.P. & Chief Fin. Officer--Burke Industries Inc., San Jose, CA, pg. 190
Wolthawen, Reed, Chief Fin. Officer--Burke Industries, Inc., San Jose, CA, pg. 191
Womack, Scott, V.P. & Chief Fin. Officer--Tanner Co. Inc., Rutherfordton, NC, pg. 1078
Wong, Alan, Chief Fin. Officer--Gordon Brothers Corporation, Boston, MA, pg. 471
Wong, Calvin, Chief Fin. Officer & V.P.--Pacific Steel Casting Co., Berkeley, CA, pg. 841
Wonowich, Simon, V.P. & Chief Fin. Officer--Admiration Hosiery Mills, Inc., Charlotte, NC, pg. 534
Wood, Bob, Chief Fin. Officer--Goodmans, Inc., Phoenix, AZ, pg. 471
Wood, Carol S., Treas., Sec., Controller & Chief Fin. Officer--Higginbotham-Bartlett Co., Lubbock, TX, pg. 533
Wood, R.B., Pres. & Treas.--Timec Company, Vallejo, CA, pg. 1097
Wood, Rene M., V.P.-Fin. & Sec.--McNeel International Corp., Tampa, FL, pg. 732
Wood, Robert C., Chief Fin. Officer, Treas. & Sec.--Xtek, Inc., Cincinnati, OH, pg. 1206
Woodard, Donald M., V.P.-Fin. Services--National Financial Insurance Company, Dallas, TX, pg. 788
Woodfill, John F., V.P.-Fin. & Chief Fin. Officer--Ash Grove Cement Company, Overland Park, KS, pg. 87
Woodhouse, Michael, Exec. V.P. & Chief Fin. Officer--Metromedia Steakhouses, Inc., Vandalia, OH, pg. 744
Woodhouse, Mike, Exec. V.P. & Chief Fin. Officer--Ponderosa, Inc., Vandalia, OH, pg. 743
Wooding, John, Mgr.-Credit--Howe Furniture Corporation, Trumbull, CT, pg. 547
Woodington, D., V.P.-Fin.--Cutler Manufacturing Corporation, Highland City, FL, pg. 307
Woods, Karen, Chief Fin. Officer, Dir.-MIS, & Mgr.-Opers.--Gordon & Smith, Inc., San Diego, CA, pg. 472
Woodward, Gary L., Chief Fin. Officer--Besteel Industries, Irvine, CA, pg. 147
Woodworth, Rodney, Chief Fin. Officer--Merchants Publishing Co., Kalamazoo, MI, pg. 739
Woolsey, James C., Exec. V.P. & Comptroller--Emigrant Savings Bank, New York, NY, pg. 379
Workman, Stephan, Chief Fin. Officer & V.P.-Fin.--Ortel Corporation, Alhambra, CA, pg. 830
Worley, Dana, Sr. V.P., Chief Fin. Officer--Black Gillock & Langberg, Houston, TX, pg. 154
Wornom, Samuel, V.P. & Chief Fin. Officer--Pace Resources, Inc., York, PA, pg. 838
Worthy, W. Craig, Chief Fin. Officer & Sr. V.P.--Boddie-Noell Enterprises Inc., Rocky Mount, NC, pg. 161
Wright, James, V.P.-Fin.--Hayden, Inc., Corona, CA, pg. 385
Wright, John, Chief Fin. Officer--Harbor Financial Mortgage Corp., Houston, TX, pg. 506
Wright, John R., Jr., Chief Fin. Officer--United Power Association, Elk River, MN, pg. 1134
Wright, Keith, Chief Fin. Officer--WEN Products, Inc., Chicago, IL, pg. 1156
Wright, Richard, Chief Fin. Officer & V.P.--Henkels & McCoy, Inc., Blue Bell, PA, pg. 529
Wulz, Jack, V.P.-Fin. & Admin.--Hollytex Carpet Mills, Inc., Ontario, CA, pg. 540
Wurtz, Ken, Chief Fin. Officer & Controller--Century Data Systems, Raleigh, NC, pg. 235
Wurtzler, Stephen, Chief Fin. Officer--Leschen Wire Rope, Saint Joseph, MO, pg. 1197
Wurtzler, Stephen D., Treas. & Chief Fin. Officer--Wire Rope Corp. of America, Inc., Saint Joseph, MO, pg. 1197
Wyckaerk, Veronica M., Chief Fin. Officer & Treas.--Intertrade Industries, Huntington Beach, CA, pg. 581
Wykes, Neil, Chief Fin. Officer--Convenient Food Mart, Inc., Schaumburg, IL, pg. 281
Wynne, Diana S., V.P.-Internal Audit--Ponderosa, Inc., Vandalia, OH, pg. 743
Yablon, Leonard H., Exec. V.P. & Chief Fin. Officer--Forbes, Inc., New York, NY, pg. 423
Yamamoto, Joyce, Supvr.-Acctng.--IBM Foods, Inglewood, CA, pg. 558
Yanotta, Patrick P., V.P.-Fin.--Conair Corporation, Stamford, CT, pg. 272
Yashida, Takao, V.P.-Fin. & Admin.--Seabrook Foods, Inc., Fresno, CA, pg. 984
Yates, Thos. H., Sec. & Treas.--Hopkinsville Milling Co., Hopkinsville, KY, pg. 543

Yeager, Leah B., Chief Fin. Officer, Treas. & Controller--Automation Intelligence, Inc., Maitland, FL, pg. 101
Yeager, Paul D., Chief Fin. Officer & Exec. V.P.--The Scott Company, Marysville, OH, pg. 982
Yeager, Robert A., Chief Fin. Officer--Quorum Health Group, Inc., Brentwood, TN, pg. 905
Yenish, James R., V.P.-Admin. & Treas.--Watkins Incorporated, Winona, MN, pg. 1167
Yeung, Donald, V.P. & Chief Fin. Officer--The Apparel Group, Ltd., New York, NY, pg. 78
Yilling, J. Louie, Chief Fin. Officer--Southern Case, Inc., Raleigh, NC, pg. 1020
Yoder, Kent, Pres., Chief Exec. Officer, Chief Fin. Officer & Treas.--Yoder Oil Company Inc., Elkhart, IN, pg. 1208
Yoder, Kent A., Chief Fin. Officer--Jayco Inc., Middlebury, IN, pg. 590
York, E. Malcolm, Chief Fin. Officer & Exec. V.P.--Paul Inman Associates Inc., Farmington Hills, MI, pg. 570
Young, Jack, Chm. Bd., Pres., Chief Exec. & Chief Fin. Officer--Jack Young Associates, Hazleton, PA, pg. 1209
Young, James G., Jr., Chief Fin. Officer & Treas.--Schurz Communications, Inc., South Bend, IN, pg. 979
Young, John E., V.P.-Fin. & Chief Fin. Officer--Alco Industries, Inc., Valley Forge, PA, pg. 32
Young, Mary G., Treas.--R.S. Young Excavating, Inc., Flint, MI, pg. 1209
Young, Patrick H., V.P.-Fin. & Admin.--League General Insurance Co., Detroit, MI, pg. 205
Yount, G. Stuart, Chm. Bd., Chief Exec. & Chief Fin. Officer--Fortifiber Corporation, Los Angeles, CA, pg. 425
Yu, Kenneth P., Exec. V.P., Treas. & Res. Dir.--AdLand Advertising, Inc., San Francisco, CA, pg. 17
Zaberer, Ronald, V.P.-Fin.--KDI Sylvan Pools, Inc., Doylestown, PA, pg. 612
Zabinski, A. F., Jr., Chief Fin. Officer, Treas. & Controller--George Sollitt Construction, Wood Dale, IL, pg. 1017
Zahn, Jack, Treas.--Uniseal, Inc., Evansville, IN, pg. 639
Zapisek, John R., Sr. V.P., Chief Fin. Officer & Treas.--Utica Mutual Insurance Company, New Hartford, NY, pg. 1140
Zary, Jerome E., V.P., Sec., Chief Fin. Officer & Treas.--Frog Switch & Manufacturing Company, Carlisle, PA, pg. 434
Zaske, Gene H., Chief Fin. Officer--CME-KHBB Advertising, Minneapolis, MN, pg. 202
Zaun, Darek, Chief Fin. Officer--Westlie Motor Company, Minot, ND, pg. 1183
Zieger, Claus D., Pres. & Treas.--Interbath, Inc., City of Industry, CA, pg. 574
Ziegler, Douglas, Sec. & Treas.--Westco Products, Inc., Pico Rivera, CA, pg. 1178
Zigray, Frank, Sec. & Treas.--The Fremont Co., Fremont, OH, pg. 432
Zimdar, William L., V.P. & Chief Fin. Officer--Zimdar Enterprises, Wyoming, MI, pg. 1220
Zimmer, Richard, Chief Fin. Officer & Dir.-Acctg.--Active Tool & Manufacturing Co., Inc., Roseville, MI, pg. 15
Zimmer, Robert J., V.P.-Fin. & Chief Fin. Officer & Sec.--Acheson Industries, Inc., Port Huron, MI, pg. 12
Zimmerman, Frank, Treas., Controller & Chief Fin. Officer--Hudson & Affiliated Co., Shawnee Mission, KS, pg. 551
Zimmerman, R.E., V.P. & Chief Fin. Officer--TTX Co., Chicago, IL, pg. 1075
Zimmerman, Ronald, Chief Fin. Officer--The Todd-AO Corporation, San Francisco, CA, pg. 1099
Zimmerman, Thomas, Chief Fin. Officer & V.P.--Unger Company, Cleveland, OH, pg. 1126
Zinbarg, Benson, Pres., Chief Exec. & Chief Fin. Officer & Treas.--Sun Hill Industries, Stamford, CT, pg. 1059
Zinbarg, Edward D., Exec. V.P.--The Prudential Insurance Company of America, Newark, NJ, pg. 896
Zinser, Kenneth R., Chief Fin. Officer--Bryant Universal Roofers Inc., Phoenix, AZ, pg. 185
Zirnkilton, Frank C., Jr., Chief Fin. Officer & Sr. V.P.--Atlantic Aviation Corp., New Castle, DE, pg. 94
Zlotnik, Judy, Chief Fin. Officer--Unsmoke International, Braddock, PA, pg. 1065
Zolot, Stuart M., Sr. V.P., Chief Fin. Officer--Marc Advertising, Pittsburgh, PA, pg. 706
Zook, Thomas W., V.P.-Admin, Asst. Treas. & Asst. Sec.--The Wooster Brush Company, Wooster, OH, pg. 1202
Zore, Edward J., Sr. V.P.-Chief Fin. Officer & Investments--Northwestern Mutual Life Insurance Co., Milwaukee, WI, pg. 815
Zucker, Arthur, Chief Fin. Officer--Superior Linen & Drapery Company, Hackensack, NJ, pg. 1064
Zucker, Murray J., V.P., Chief Fin. Officer & Treas.--The RAL Corporation, Fairfield, NJ, pg. 357
Zuckerman, Leon, Chm. Bd. & Treas.--Zuckerman-Honickman Inc., King of Prussia, PA, pg. 1221
Zurilla, Thomas, Treas. & Chief Fin. Officer--Glosser Brothers, Inc., Johnstown, PA, pg. 978
Zylstra, Ken, Chief Fin. Officer--Schuff Steel Co., Phoenix, AZ, pg. 979

CHIEF OPERATING OFFICER

Abbey, Nelson D., III, Pres. & Chief Oper. Officer--Abbey Etna Machine Company, Perrysburg, OH, pg. 9
Abroms, Harold L., Chief Oper. Officer, Exec. V.P., Treas. & Sec.--Parisian, Inc., Birmingham, AL, pg. 848
Acker, Stanley, Chm., Pres. & Chief Exec. Officer--Pavion Ltd., Nyack on Hudson, NY, pg. 852
Adams, J.D., V.P. & Chief Oper. Officer--Actron Manufacturing Company, Cleveland, OH, pg. 15
Adams, Paul G., III, Exec. V.P. & Chief Oper. Officer--First American Bankshares, Inc., Washington, DC, pg. 412
Adams, Robert E., Exec. V.P. & Chief Oper. Officer--Spencer Companies Inc., Huntsville, AL, pg. 1030
Alcorn, Charles S., Pres. & Chief Oper. Officer--Donlee Technologies Inc., York, PA, pg. 344
Alexander, Charles M., Exec. V.P. & Chief Oper. Officer--A. Teichert & Son, Inc., Sacramento, CA, pg. 1084
Allbritten, G.R., Chief Oper. Officer--Ferry-Morse Seed Company, Modesto, CA, pg. 407
Allen, Calhoun, Sr. V.P., Dir.-Mktg. Services/Opers.--The Atkins Agency, San Antonio, TX, pg. 94
Allen, R. Todd, Pres. & Chief Oper. Officer--The Harry Alter Company, Chicago, IL, pg. 45
Allen, Rick, V.P.- Fin., Admin. & Chief Fin. Officer--J.D. Edwards & Company, Denver, CO, pg. 370
Allred, Barry L., Pres., Chief Oper. Officer & Treas.--Elkins Constructors, Inc., Jacksonville, FL, pg. 377
Altholz, Thomas I., Pres. & Chief Oper. Officer--Inlander-Steindler Paper, Vernon Hills, IL, pg. 570
Altier, Richard J., Pres. & Chief Oper. Officer--Altier & Sons Shoes Inc., Rochester, NY, pg. 45
Alvarez, Antonio C., Pres. & Chief Oper. Officer--Phar-Mor, Inc., Youngstown, OH, pg. 866
Alyea, G. Mark, Pres. & Chief Oper. Officer--Alro Group, Jackson, MI, pg. 44
Anasto, John, Pres., Chief Exec. & Chief Oper. Officer--Strongheart Products, Inc., Kansas City, KS, pg. 1054
Anderson, Charles M., Pres. & Chief Oper. Officer--Stamler Corporation, Millersburg, KY, pg. 1035
Anderson, Conway M., Chief Oper. Officer--Young Automotive Group, Indianapolis, IN, pg. 1209
Anderson, John, Pres., Chief Exec. & Oper. Officer--Alabama Farmers Co-op, Decatur, AL, pg. 28
Anderson, Winston H., Chief Oper. Officer--Piedmont Mechanical, Inc., Spartanburg, SC, pg. 870
Andringa, Mary, Pres. & Chief Oper. Officer--Vermeer Manufacturing Company, Pella, IA, pg. 1148
Angelo, John, Exec. V.P.-Opers.--Angelo Brothers Co., Philadelphia, PA, pg. 74
Anhut, Francie, Pres. & Chief Oper. Officer--MarketPulse, Cambridge, MA, pg. 884
Anthony, Ronald T., Chief Oper. Officer & Exec. V.P.--Interform Corporation, Bridgeville, PA, pg. 574
Applebach, Chuck, Pres. & Chief Oper. Officer--The Polizos Agency, Norfolk, VA, pg. 879
Applegate, L. Thomas, Pres. & Chief Oper. Officer--Surgical Appliance Industries, Inc., Cincinnati, OH, pg. 1065
Arana, Alejandra, Chief Oper. Officer & Acct. Supvr.--Perdomo-Ted Bates/Publicidad, Lima,, Peru, pg. 112
Arbuckle, James E., Pres. & Chief Oper. Officer--Besser Company, Alpena, MI, pg. 146
Aretsky, Kenneth, Chm. & Chief Oper. Officer--The "21" Club, Inc., New York, NY, pg. 1121
Armstrong, T.K., Jr., Pres. & Chief Oper. Officer--Texas Steel Co., Inc., Fort Worth, TX, pg. 1090
Armstrong, Thomas R., Chief Oper. Officer, Exec. V.P.--Advent International, Boston, MA, pg. 21
Arndt, Walde, Chief Oper. Officer--Lawrence Pumps, Inc., Lawrence, MA, pg. 662
Arnold, George L., Pres. & Chief Oper. Officer (Dallas) & Dir.--EvansGroup, Salt Lake City, UT, pg. 390
Arnold, George L., Pres. & Chief Oper. Officer--EvansGroup, Dallas, TX, pg. 391
Arnold, Greg, Chief Oper. Officer & V.P.--Truman Arnold Companies, Texarkana, TX, pg. 84
Arras, Richard K., Pres. & Chief Oper. Officer--Perkins Family Restaurants, Memphis, TN, pg. 1088
Arth, Lawrence J., Pres. & Chief Oper. Officer--Ameritas Life Insurance Corp., Lincoln, NE, pg. 66
Auch, G. William, III, Chief Oper. Officer & V.P.--George W. Auch Co., Pontiac, MI, pg. 97
Bahler, Earl, Exec. V.P., Mng. Dir.--Communications Plus, Inc., New York, NY, pg. 269
Bailey, John H., Chm. Bd., Pres., Chief Exec. & Chief Oper. Officer--The Climatic Corp., Columbia, SC, pg. 255
Bailey, Ted, Chief Oper. Officer & V.P.--Heavy Machines, Inc., Memphis, TN, pg. 524
Bain, Mike, V.P.-Opers.--GSC Distributing Companies Division, Sulphur Springs, TX, pg. 440
Baird, William S., Pres. & Chief Oper. Officer--Alabama Metal Industries Corporation, Birmingham, AL, pg. 28
Baker, F., V.P.-Opers.--Perry Equipment Corporation, Mineral Wells, TX, pg. 863
Baker, Gene, Chief Oper. Officer--Excelsior Manufacturing & Supply Corp., Itasca, IL, pg. 392
Baker, Ken, Chief Oper. Officer--Newage Industries Inc., Testing Instruments Division, Willow Grove, PA, pg. 803
Baldwin, Mike, Chief Oper. Officer--H & H Distributing Company, Inc., West Union, IA, pg. 495
Ball, John K., Pres. & Chief Oper. Officer--R. M. Shoemaker Co., West Conshohocken, PA, pg. 1000
Barnes, C.W., III, Chief Oper. Officer--NKH&W, Inc., Kansas City, MO, pg. 781
Barnes, Richard A., Pres. & Chief Oper. Officer--Republic Fastener Products Corp., Great Falls, SC, pg. 928
Barnes, Robert L., Pres. & Chief Oper. Officer--Knight Architects Engineers Planners, Inc., Chicago, IL, pg. 637
Barnhardt, T.M., III, Pres. & Chief Oper. Officer--Carolina Absorbent Cotton Co., Charlotte, NC, pg. 120
Barnhart, Terry L., Pres. & Chief Oper. Officer--Barnhart Advertising, Marketing & Public Relations, Inc., Denver, CO, pg. 120
Barr, Allen, Chief Oper. Officer--Hippocrates Partners, San Francisco, CA, pg. 535
Barr, Greg, Exec. V.P. & Chief Oper. Officer--Nob Hill General Store, Inc., Gilroy, CA, pg. 807
Barr, Lynn E., V.P. & Chief Oper. Officer--Underground Construction Company, Inc., Benicia, CA, pg. 1125
Barrett, John F., Pres. & Chief Oper. Officer--Western & Southern Life Insurance Co., Cincinnati, OH, pg. 1181
Bartels, Juergen, Pres. & Chief Oper. Officer--Carlson Hospitality Group, Inc., Minneapolis, MN, pg. 221
Bartlett, Richard C., Pres. & Chief Oper. Officer--Mary Kay Cosmetics Inc., Dallas, TX, pg. 716
Battaglia, Michael S., Pres. & Chief Oper. Officer--Mosler Inc., Hamilton, OH, pg. 772
Bauknight, Harry L., Pres. & Chief Oper. Officer--Palmetto Wholesale Co., Inc., Columbia, SC, pg. 844
Baumann, Daniel E., Pres. & Chief Oper. Officer--Paddock Publications, Inc., Arlington Heights, IL, pg. 842
Beach, William H., Chm. Bd., Pres., Chief Exec. & Oper. Officer--Beach Mold & Tool Inc., New Albany, IN, pg. 128
Beall, Edward S., Pres. & Chief Oper. Officer--Brix Maritime Co., Portland, OR, pg. 177
Beattie, William, Chief Oper. Officer--Northwest Parking Services Inc., Seattle, WA, pg. 42
Bechen, Peter F., Chm. Bd., Pres. & Chief Oper. Officer--M & T Incorporated, Portland, OR, pg. 690
Beck, Art, Pres. & Chief Oper. Officer--Triumph Twist Drill Co., Crystal Lake, IL, pg. 885
Beck, Arthur R., Pres. & Chief Oper. Officer--Precision Twist Drill Co., Crystal Lake, IL, pg. 885
Beck, Henry C., III, Chief Oper. Officer--HCB Contractors, Dallas, TX, pg. 496
Beckner, Kerrie, Pres. & Chief Oper. Officer--Alpha One Exchange, New Providence, NJ, pg. 43
Beecham, R. Thomas, Pres. & Chief Oper. Officer--Jernberg Industries, Inc., Chicago, IL, pg. 593
Beldham, Paul, Chief Oper. Officer--Knight Equipment Corp., Costa Mesa, CA, pg. 636
Bell, Thomas D., Jr., Vice Chm. & Chief Operating Officer Worldwide (Washington)--Burson-Marsteller, New York, NY, pg. 1210
Bell, William, Chief Oper. Officer & V.P.--Randall Stores, Inc., Mitchell, SD, pg. 911
Belmondo, Craig, V.P. & Chief Oper. Officer-WestAir Commuter Airlines, Inc.--WestAir Holding Inc., Fresno, CA, pg. 1178
Belz, Martin S., Exec. V.P. & Chief Oper. Officer--Belz Enterprises, Memphis, TN, pg. 138
Bendzin, Leonard J., Exec. V.P. & Chief Oper. Officer--Globe Mortgage Company, Hackensack, NJ, pg. 464
Bennett, Craig, Chief Oper. Officer & V.P.-Sls. & Mktg.--Utility Trailer Manufacturing Co., City of Industry, CA, pg. 1141
Berendt, William E., Exec. V.P. & Chief Oper. Officer--Triple A Specialty Company, Bedford Park, IL, pg. 1114
Beresford, Jan, Chief Oper. Officer--Meritcare, Inc., Pittsburgh, PA, pg. 740
Bergt, Neil G., Chm. Bd. & Chief Exec. Officer--Markair, Inc., Anchorage, AK, pg. 708
Berk, Fred, Pres., Chief Exec. & Chief Oper. Officer--Huffman Koos Co., River Edge, NJ, pg. 551
Berwind, C. Graham, Jr., Chm. Bd., Pres., Chief Exec. & Chief Oper. Officer--Berwind Corporation, Philadelphia, PA, pg. 145
Bess, Ron, Pres. & Chief Oper. Officer--Bayer Bess Vanderwarker Inc., Chicago, IL, pg. 128
Bever, C.C., Jr., Chm. Bd., Pres. & Chief Oper. Officer--B & B Cash Grocery Store, Tampa, FL, pg. 105
Beyland, L.S., Pres. & Chief Oper. Officer--Rome Cable Corporation, Rome, NY, pg. 945
Bezousek, Richard, V.P.-Production & Chief Oper. Officer--Omaha Steaks International, Omaha, NE, pg. 825
Bianconi, Giorgio, Co-Chief Exec. Officer--Steuart Petroleum Company, Washington, DC, pg. 1048
Biblowitz, Joshua, Pres. & Chief Oper. Officer--Masters, Inc., Westbury, NY, pg. 720
Biggs, John H., Pres. & Chief Oper. Officer--Teachers Insurance and Annuity Association-College Retirement Equities Fund, New York, NY, pg. 1082
Billing, Mitchell G., Chief Oper. Officer--National Emergency Services, Inc., Tiburon, CA, pg. 788
Bishop, C.M., Jr., Pres. & Co-Chief Exec. Officer--Pendleton Woolen Mills, Inc., Portland, OR, pg. 857
Bishop, William L., Pres. & Chief Oper. Officer--The Western Group, Saint Louis, MO, pg. 1179
Bittinger, Randy, Chief Oper. Officer--McCourt Label Co., Lewis Run, PA, pg. 727
Bittner, Clarence J., Pres. & Chief Oper. Officer--Shook National Corporation, Dayton, OH, pg. 1000
Blake, Jerry A., Pres. & Chief Oper. Officer--Active Tool & Manufacturing Co., Inc., Roseville, MI, pg. 15
Blanchard, Kenneth E., Chm. Bd., Pres. & Chief Oper. Officer--Phonetics, Inc., Aston, PA, pg. 869
Blicher, Bert, Pres. & Chief Oper. Officer--Oxford First Corporation, Philadelphia, PA, pg. 834
Blount, Dan S., Pres. & Chief Oper. Officer--Montgomery Elevator Company, Moline, IL, pg. 767
Bobis, Arthur H., Pres.-Metal Div.--RHC/Spacemaster Corporation, Melrose Park, IL, pg. 906
Boccitto, Elio, Pres. & Chief Oper. Officer--Berlitz International, Inc., Princeton, NJ, pg. 142
Bocksch, David, Pres. & Chief Oper. Officer--Monroe Systems For Business, Inc., Morris Plains, NJ, pg. 766
Bodine, Jeffrey P., Chief Oper. Officer & Exec. V.P.--Bodine Electric Company, Chicago, IL, pg. 162
Bodman, James W., Pres. & Chief Oper. Officer--Vienna Sausage Mfg. Co., Chicago, IL, pg. 1151
Boehm, Josef F., Pres. & Chief Oper. Officer--Alaska Industrial Hardware Inc., Anchorage, AK, pg. 30
Boesenberg, Charles M., Pres. & Chief Oper. Officer--Central Point Software, Inc., Beaverton, OR, pg. 234
Bohan, Gloria, Pres. & Chief Oper. Officer--Omega World Travel, Inc., Falls Church, VA, pg. 826
Bolen, David E., Chief Oper. Officer--LeeWards Creative Crafts, Inc., Elgin, IL, pg. 666
Bolin, Todd, Pres. & Chief Oper. Officer--M. R. Bolin Inc., Minneapolis, MN, pg. 162
Bond, Geoff, Pres. & Chief Oper. Officer--Cooperheat, Inc., Piscataway, NJ, pg. 283
Bonk, James E., Exec. V.P. & Chief Oper. Officer--Camelot Music, Inc., North Canton, OH, pg. 212
Bores, Stephen J., Exec. V.P. & Chief Oper. Officer--Therma-Tru Corp., Maumee, OH, pg. 1090
Borges, John P., Chief Oper. Officer--Selectone Corporation, Hayward, CA, pg. 988
Borowsky, Ned S., Pres. & Chief Oper. Officer--North American Publishing Company, Philadelphia, PA, pg. 811
Botifoll, Luis, Chm. Bd. & Chief Exec. Officer--Republic National Bank Of Miami, Miami, FL, pg. 928
Bouchez, Jacques, V.P. & Chief Oper. Officer--The Crispin Company, Houston, TX, pg. 299
Boulton, Samuel R., Pres. & Chief Oper. Officer--Taylor Drug Stores, Inc., Louisville, KY, pg. 1081

Bovaird, W.J., Pres. & Chief Exec. Officer--Bovaird Supply Co., Tulsa, OK, pg. 168

Boyan, William L., Jr., Pres. & Chief Oper. Officer--John Hancock Mutual Life Insurance Company, Boston, MA, pg. 595

Boyce, Michael, Chief Oper. Officer--North American Salt Company, Overland Park, KS, pg. 812

Boyd, Robert A., Pres. & Chief Oper. Officer--J.H. Baxter & Company, San Mateo, CA, pg. 127

Boyden, James, Pres. & Chief Exec. Officer--Teachers Management & Investment Corporation, Newport Beach, CA, pg. 1082

Boykin, C.W. Jr., Chief Oper. Officer--National Financial Insurance Company, Dallas, TX, pg. 788

Bracey, Morris W., Chm. Bd., Pres., Chief Exec. & Chief Oper. Officer--Dealers Electrical Supply Co., Waco, TX, pg. 322

Bradfield, William, Pres. & Chief Oper. Officer--Sathers Inc., Round Lake, MN, pg. 972

Bradford, Claude, Chief Oper. Officer--Hopper Inc., Bakersfield, CA, pg. 543

Brady, John, Pres. & Chief Oper. Officer--Excelsior Manufacturing & Supply Corp., Itasca, IL, pg. 392

Bramble, David C., Pres. & Chief Oper. Officer--David A. Bramble, Inc., Chestertown, MD, pg. 171

Brennan, Robert J., Vice Chm. & Chief Oper. Officer--American Institute For Foreign Study, Greenwich, CT, pg. 56

Brennan, Robert J., Pres. & Chief Oper. Officer--American Institute for Foreign Study, London, United Kingdom, pg. 56

Brian, Richard, Chief Oper. Officer & V.P.-Residential Division--Robbins, Inc., Cincinnati, OH, pg. 938

Brickel, Jack W., Pres., Chief Exec. & Chief Oper. Officer & Dir.-Personnel--BEC Inc., Richmond, MI, pg. 106

Brindley, Thomas M., Chief Oper. Officer & Exec. V.P.--W.A. Roosevelt Co., La Crosse, WI, pg. 946

Brisk, David, Exec. V.P.-Opers.--The Western Group, Saint Louis, MO, pg. 1179

Brodbeck, Robert J., Sr. V.P. & Chief Oper. Officer--Brodbeck Enterprises, Inc., Platteville, WI, pg. 178

Broderick, Fred J., Pres. & Chief Oper. Officer--Haskel, Inc., Burbank, CA, pg. 516

Brody, June E., Vice Chm. & Chief Oper. Officer--CSI International Corporation, New York, NY, pg. 205

Brown, C. Terry, Chm. Bd., Pres., Chief Exec. Officer & Chief Oper. Officer--Atlas Hotels, Inc., San Diego, CA, pg. 96

Brown, Dave, Chief Oper. Officer--The William Carter Company, New York, NY, pg. 226

Brunner, Michael J., Pres. & Chief Oper. Officer--Blattner/Brunner Inc., Pittsburgh, PA, pg. 156

Brunswick, Paul E., Pres. & Chief Oper. Officer--Stiegler, Wells & Brunswick, Inc., Bethlehem, PA, pg. 1049

Bryden, Jeffrey H., Vice Chm. & Chief Oper. Officer--Meldrum & Fewsmith Communications Inc., Cleveland, OH, pg. 737

Bucksbaum, Matthew, Pres., Treas. & Sec.--General Growth Companies, Inc., Des Moines, IA, pg. 449

Buescher, James, Chief Oper. Officer--Idea Man, Inc., Los Angeles, CA, pg. 562

Burdette, Karen E., Exec. V.P. & Chief Oper. Officer--Robinson & St. John Advertising & Public Relations, Inc., Jacksonville, FL, pg. 940

Burdick, Richard L., Chm., Pres., Chief Exec. & Chief Oper. Officer--Thermon Manufacturing Company, San Marcos, TX, pg. 1091

Burgess, Bill, Pres. & Chief Oper. Officer--AmeriServ Food Company, Dallas, TX, pg. 66

Burris, J.D., Pres. & Chief Oper. Officer--The Alpha Corporation Of Tennessee, Collierville, TN, pg. 43

Burris, Robert D., Pres. & Chief Oper. Officer--Burris Foods, Inc., Milford, DE, pg. 195

Burroughs, James R., Pres. & Chief Oper. Officer--First Gray Line Corporation, Beverly Hills, CA, pg. 413

Burton, James, Pres. & Chief Oper. Officer--Reading Tube Corp., Reading, PA, pg. 916

Busca, G.P., Sr. V.P.-Sls. & Mktg. & Chief Oper. Officer--Energy Brokers Guild, Stevensville, MI, pg. 381

Busch, Dr. Paul L., Pres. & Chief Exec. Officer--Malcolm Pirnie, Inc., White Plains, NY, pg. 872

Bustillo, Oscar, Jr., Pres. & Chief Oper. Officer--Republic National Bank Of Miami, Miami, FL, pg. 928

Butler, Michael A., Chief Oper. Officer & Exec. V.P.--Kruse International, Auburn, IN, pg. 645

Byers, Stan J., Pres. & Chief Oper. Officer--Bunton Company, Louisville, KY, pg. 188

Byrnes, Donald J., Pres. & Chief Oper. Officer--Spalding & Evenflo Companies, Inc., Tampa, FL, pg. 1024

Cafiero, Eugene A., Chm. Bd., Pres., Chief Exec. & Oper. Officer--KDI Corporation, Cincinnati, OH, pg. 612

Calandruccio, Robert, Pres. & Chief Oper. Officer--Vitt Media International, Inc., New York, NY, pg. 1153

Cambridge, Edward F., Sr. V.P. & Chief Oper. Officer--Leo A. Daly Company, Omaha, NE, pg. 313

Campbell, John E., Chief Oper. Officer & Exec. V.P.--Red Roof Inns, Inc., Hilliard, OH, pg. 918

Campbell, John M., Chief Oper. Officer--E & A Industries, Inc., Indianapolis, IN, pg. 358

Capizzi, Frank, V.P. & Chief Oper. Officer--Quality Food Oils, Inc., New Milford, CT, pg. 903

Carlsen, Charles, Pres. & Chief Oper. Officer--Upper Midwest Industries, Inc., Minneapolis, MN, pg. 1140

Carney, Michael, V.P. & Chief Oper. Officer--Boury Incorporated, Wheeling, WV, pg. 168

Carr, Patrick F., Pres. & Chief Oper. Officer--Mayflower Transit, Inc., Carmel, IN, pg. 724

Carroll, James E., Exec. V.P. & Chief Oper. Officer--Bradley Corporation, Menomonee Falls, WI, pg. 170

Carroll, Robert J., Pres. & Chief Oper. Officer--National Cleaning Contractors, Inc., New York, NY, pg. 786

Carus, Andre W., Pres. & Chief Oper. Officer--Carus Publishing Company, Peru, IL, pg. 227

Carus, M. Blouke, Chm. Bd., Pres., Chief Exec. & Chief Oper. Officer--Carus Corporation, Peru, IL, pg. 227

Caruso, George C., Chief Oper. Officer--Alco Management, Inc., Memphis, TN, pg. 592

Caruso, Stephen M., Chief Oper. Officer--Citrus World Inc., Lake Wales, FL, pg. 251

Casper, Charles D., Pres. & Chief Oper. Officer--The Chesapeake Life Insurance Co., Lincoln, NE, pg. 243

Castro, Richard, Pres. & Chief Oper. Officer--Superior Fast Freight, Irwindale, CA, pg. 1063

Cavin, Terry, Sr. V.P., Chief Oper. Officer--Russ Reid Company, Inc., Pasadena, CA, pg. 923

Cei, Jay, Pres. & Chief Oper. Officer--Ulbrich Wire, Inc., North Haven, CT, pg. 1125

Cerreta, Ralph, Sr. V.P. & Chief Oper. Officer--The Atlas Construction Co., Stamford, CT, pg. 96

Chadsey, Jack, Pres., Chief Exec. & Oper. Officer--Sunglass Hut Corporation, Miami, FL, pg. 1060

Chambo, William, V.P.-Admin.--Gaylord Printing, Inc., Detroit, MI, pg. 446

Chapman, Michael M., Exec. V.P. & Co-Chief Oper. Officer--U.S. Divers Co., Inc., Santa Ana, CA, pg. 1135

Chazanoff, Jay D., Sr. Exec. V.P. & Chief Oper. Officer--Integrated Resources, Inc., New York, NY, pg. 573

Cheloha, Kenneth L., Chief Oper. Officer--American Tool Companies, Inc., Lincoln, NE, pg. 64

Chief Oper. Officer, Exec. V.P.--Morse Diesel International, New York, NY, pg. 771

Childs, Brian D., Pres. & Chief Oper. Officer--ComputerLand Canada Ltd., Brampton,, Canada, pg. 271

Christofferson, Tim, Chief Oper. Officer--Resonex, Inc., Sunnyvale, CA, pg. 929

Christy, Judy, Chief Oper. Officer & Mng. Dir.--Burkhardt & Christy Advertising, Inc., New York, NY, pg. 191

Clain, G., Pres., Chief Exec. & Chief Oper. Officer--J. Gerber & Co. Inc., New York, NY, pg. 453

Clancy, Joseph E., Chm. Bd., Pres. & Chief Oper. Officer--Bridgeport Machines, Inc., Bridgeport, CT, pg. 175

Clanton, Fred, V.P.-Opers.--Colfax Envelope Corporation, Buffalo Grove, IL, pg. 261

Clark, Charles, Pres. & Chief Oper. Officer--Dukane Corporation, Saint Charles, IL, pg. 351

Clark, Stephen S., Chief Oper. Officer & Exec. V.P.--Dwyer Instruments Inc., Michigan City, IN, pg. 356

Claudon, Ronald C., Sr., Pres. & Chief Oper. Officer--Valley Pontiac Buick GMC, Inc., Auburn, WA, pg. 1143

Clay, Robert Edwin, Pres. & Chief Oper. Officer--Pridgeon & Clay, Inc., Grand Rapids, MI, pg. 889

Clemente, Chuck, Chief Oper. Officer--Redgate Communications Corp., Vero Beach, FL, pg. 919

Clinton, Jean M., Chief Oper. Officer--United Design, Noble, OK, pg. 1131

Close, Graham, Chief Oper. Officer--Aladdin Industries Pty. Ltd., Westgate, Australia, pg. 29

Cloud, Bruce B., Pres. & Chief Oper. Officer--H.B. Zachry, San Antonio, TX, pg. 1215

Clymer, John A., Pres. & Chief Oper. Officer--The Minnesota Mutual Life Insurance Company, Saint Paul, MN, pg. 757

Coale, William, Chief Oper. Officer--Alcom Printing Group, Inc., Bethlehem, PA, pg. 32

Cochran, R.E., V.P. & Chief Oper. Officer--817

Coffey, Frank, Exec. V.P. & Chief Oper. Officer--Quality Bakers of America Cooperative, Inc., Greenwich, CT, pg. 903

Cohen, Eli D., Pres., Chief Oper. Officer & Treas.--Duane Reade, Long Island City, NY, pg. 350

Cohen, Philip E., Chief Oper. Officer & Dir.-Client Services--Harris Drury Cohen, Fort Lauderdale, FL, pg. 511

Cohen, Steve, Chief Oper. Officer--A. G. Spanos Development, Inc., Stockton, CA, pg. 1025

Cole, Catherine P., Chief Oper. Officer & Sec.--Columbine Systems Inc., Golden, CO, pg. 266

Coleman, Richard J., Exec. V.P.--Florasynth Inc., New York, NY, pg. 420

Colianni, Albert J., Jr., Exec. V.P. & Chief Oper. Officer--Marquette Bank Minneapolis, National Association, Minneapolis, MN, pg. 117

Collins, Marilyn, Pres. & Chief Exec. Officer--Valley Innovative Management Service, Jackson, MS, pg. 1109

Colman, Thomas E, Ph.D., Chief Oper. Officer & Exec. V.P.--Scott Specialty Gases, Inc., Plumsteadville, PA, pg. 983

Colonna, Mark, Exec. V.P., Chief Oper. Officer-Mktg, Dir.Sls. Promo & Mgr.-Adv.--Colonna Bros., Inc., North Bergen, NJ, pg. 264

Compton, William, Pres., Chief Exec. Officer & Chief Oper. Officer--Tropical Garment Manufacturing Company, Tampa, FL, pg. 1116

Condon, Leon J., Pres., Chief Oper. Officer & Treas.--Kennington Ltd., Inc., Los Angeles, CA, pg. 623

Connelly, Thomas S., Chm. Bd., Pres., Chief Exec. & Chief Oper. Officer--Connelly Containers, Inc., Bala-Cynwyd, PA, pg. 275

Constalbe, Philip, Chief Oper. Officer--Wolverine Massachusetts Corporation, Merrimac, MA, pg. 1199

Cook, Greg, Pres. & Chief Oper. Officer--Cook Manufacturing Corporation, Duncan, OK, pg. 282

Cook, Ken W., Pres. & Chief Oper. Officer--Barry Huey, Bullock & Cook Advertising, Inc., Birmingham, AL, pg. 551

Cook, Lyndol, Pres. & Chief Exec. Officer--Polaris Pool Systems, Inc., San Marcos, CA, pg. 878

Cook, Stephen A., V.P. & Chief Oper. Officer--Overland Transportation System, Inc., Indianapolis, IN, pg. 832

Coon, Miles A., Pres., Chief Oper. Officer & Treas.--Red Wing Products, Inc., Plainview, NY, pg. 919

Cooper, Terri, Vice Chm. & Chief Oper. Officer--Ardell International, Inc., City of Commerce, CA, pg. 81

Coppola, Alfred C., Pres. & Chief Oper. Officer--The Okonite Company, Ramsey, NJ, pg. 823

Corcoran, Philip, Chm., Chief Exec. & Chief Oper. Officer--Comark, Bloomingdale, IL, pg. 267

Corkin, Herbert I., Chm. Bd., Pres., Chief Exec. & Chief Oper. Officer--The Entwistle Company, Hudson, MA, pg. 383

Cornell, Linda, Sr. V.P., Chief Oper. Officer--Wolf Blumberg Krody Inc., Cincinnati, OH, pg. 1199

Cornwall, John R., Pres. & Chief Oper. Officer--MetLife Capital Corporation, Bellevue, WA, pg. 744

Corsini, John M., Pres. & Chief Oper. Officer--Uncas Manufacturing Company, Providence, RI, pg. 1125

Costello, Richard N., Pres. & Chief Oper. Officer--TBWA Advertising, Inc., New York, NY, pg. 1071

Coughlin, Richard, Chief Oper. Officer--Allright Springfield, Springfield, MA, pg. 42

Coulombe, Raymond, Chief Exec. & Chief Oper. Officer--Fairview Wine Co., Lewiston, ME, pg. 1186

Craigmile, David F., Pres.--Elkay Manufacturing Company, Oak Brook, IL, pg. 377

Crider, Joe D., Pres. & Chief Oper. Officer--Reliance Steel & Aluminum Co., Los Angeles, CA, pg. 925

Crimmins, Richard, Chief Oper. Officer--The Texwipe Co., Inc., Upper Saddle River, NJ, pg. 1090

Crosby, Samuel C., Chief Oper. Officer--Astre Corporate Group, Alexandria, VA, pg. 92

Crossley, Donald W., Chief Oper. Officer--Central Michigan Container Corporation, Jackson, MI, pg. 19

Cummings, Thomas L., III, Pres. & Chief Oper. Officer--Cummings Inc., Nashville, TN, pg. 304

Currey, R.J., Pres. & Chief Oper. Officer--Illinois Consolidated Telephone Co., Mattoon, IL, pg. 563

Curry, Charles H., Pres. & Chief Oper. Officer--Burrell Communications Group Inc., Chicago, IL, pg. 195

Curtis, Paul F., Pres., Chief Oper. Officer & Treas.--L.N. Curtis & Sons, Oakland, CA, pg. 306

Cwiok, Jerome J., Exec. V.P. & Chief Oper. Officer--Academy Insurance Group, Inc., Atlanta, GA, pg. 11

Dabagia, Robert C., Pres. & Chief Admin. Officer--Horizon Bancorp, Michigan City, IN, pg. 544

Dabagia, Robert C., Pres. & Chief Admin. Officer--First Citizens Bank, N.A., Michigan City, IN, pg. 544

Dadd, Ronald F., Chief Oper. Officer--Construction Specialties, Inc., Cranford, NJ, pg. 277

Dahl, H.D., Pres. & Chief Oper. Officer--Drummond Company, Inc., Jasper, AL, pg. 349

Dalton, Robert E., Exec. V.P. & Chief Oper Officer--Dunmore Corporation, Newtown, PA, pg. 353

Daniels, David P., Pres. & Chief Oper. Officer--Penn-Daniels, Inc., Quincy, IL, pg. 857

Darducci, Larry, Chief Oper. Officer--Molded Fiber Glass Co., Ashtabula, OH, pg. 764

Davenport, R.B., IV, Pres. & Chief Oper. Officer--Krystal Company, Chattanooga, TN, pg. 645

Davidson, William, Chm., Pres., Chief Exec. & Chief Oper. Officer--Guardian Industries Corp., Northville, MI, pg. 491

Davis, Alan V., Pres. & Chief Oper. Officer--The Bibb Company, Macon, GA, pg. 781

Davis, Edgar E., Pres. & Chief Oper. Officer--West Point-Pepperell, Inc., West Point, GA, pg. 400

Davis, Jay M., Pres. & Chief Oper. Officer--National Distributing Co., Inc., Atlanta, GA, pg. 787

Davis, Jerry, Pres. & Chief Oper. Officer--Affiliated Foods Southwest, Little Rock, AR, pg. 24

Davis, Mark D., Pres. (Even Days)--Davis, Ball & Colombatto Advertising, Inc., Los Angeles, CA, pg. 318

Davis, Michael K., Chm. Bd. & Chief Oper. Officer--Lee Davis Ayer, Hong Kong,, Hong Kong, pg. 104

Davis, Robert A., Chief Oper. Officer & Sec.--Swallen's, Inc., Cincinnati, OH, pg. 1066

Davis, Roger W., Pres.--Frank Paxton Company, Kansas City, MO, pg. 592

Davis, Tom I., III, Exec. V.P.--Brian Center Management Corporation, Hickory, NC, pg. 175

Davis, William H., Pres. & Chief Oper. Officer--Gilman Paper Co., Saint Marys, GA, pg. 459

De Stigter, Glenn H., Pres. & Chief Oper. Officer--The Weitz-Cohen Construction Co., Des Moines, IA, pg. 1174

Deandoff, Harold, Chief Operating Officer--Garvey Elevators Inc., Hutchinson, KS, pg. 443

DeBlase, Thomas E., Pres. & Chief Oper. Officer--Binkley Company, Warrenton, MO, pg. 151

DeCamp, Ronald L., Chief Oper. Officer--Plastic Engineering Components Inc., New Berlin, WI, pg. 875

Dedman, Robert H., Jr., Pres. & Chief Oper. Officer--Club Corporation International, Dallas, TX, pg. 256

Deering, John R., Exec. V.P.-Fin., Chief Oper. Officer & Legal Officer--Production Machinery Corporation, Mentor, OH, pg. 893

DeFabis, Mike, Exec. V.P. & Chief Oper. Officer--Associated Wholesale Grocers, Inc., Kansas City, KS, pg. 92

Degenhardt, Robert, Exec. V.P. & Chief Oper. Officer--Ellerbe Becket, Inc., Minneapolis, MN, pg. 378

DeGrazia, Nicholas J., Pres. & Chief Oper. Officer--Lionel Trains, Inc., Chesterfield, MI, pg. 677

Dehmlow, Steven L., Pres. & Chief Oper. Officer--Great Lakes Terminal & Transport Corp., Chicago, IL, pg. 482

Delman, Jacob J., Chm. Bd. & Chief Oper. Officer--Splendor Form International Inc., Long Island City, NY, pg. 1031

DeMarco, Albert J., Pres. & Chief Oper. Officer--Nutri/System Inc., Blue Bell, PA, pg. 818

Dembowczyk, Margaret P., Exec. V.P., Chief Oper. Officer--Geographic Marketing Group (GMG), Philadelphia, PA, pg. 452

Demere, Robert H., Jr., Pres. & Chief Oper. Officer--Colonial Oil Industries, Savannah, GA, pg. 263

Denenberg, Robert, Chief Oper. Officer & V.P.--Adelphia Lamp & Shade Inc., Philadelphia, PA, pg. 17

DePriest, Ted, Pres. & Chief Oper. Officer--Pacific Sound Resources, Seattle, WA, pg. 841

Desens, Joe, Chief Oper. Officer--Rocket Industries, Inc./Excel, The Exercise Company, Pico Rivera, CA, pg. 941

Desmond, Daniel J., Exec. V.P. & Chief Oper. Officer--Central Pharmaceuticals, Inc., Seymour, IN, pg. 234

DeTitta, Louis, Jr., Pres., Chief Oper. Officer--SSD&W Integrated Marketing Communications, Montville, NJ, pg. 964
Diamond, Lawrence, Chm. Bd., Pres., Chief Exec. & Chief Oper. Officer & Dir.-Pur.--Triangle Marketing Corp., New York, NY, pg. 1112
Dibb, John C., V.P.-Opers.--Blue Anchor, Inc., Sacramento, CA, pg. 158
DiBui, William J., Pres., Chief Exec. & Chief Oper. Officer--Rumsey Electric Co., Philadelphia, PA, pg. 956
Diehl, Michelle, Exec. V.P. & Chief Oper. Officer--Kragie/Newell, Des Moines, IA, pg. 643
Dille, Steven B., Pres. & Chief Oper. Officer--Scicom Data Services, Ltd., Minnetonka, MN, pg. 981
Dixon, John, Pres. & Chief Oper. Officer--Columbus Mills, Inc., Columbus, GA, pg. 267
Dmytryk, Ed, Chief Oper. Officer--Bollinger Industries Inc., Irving, TX, pg. 163
Doerr, Ronald H., Pres. & Chief Oper. Officer--National Steel Corporation, Mishawaka, IN, pg. 793
Dolan, Lawrence R., Exec. V.P. & Chief Oper. Officer--Commercial Light Company, Hillside, IL, pg. 268
Dolan, Vincent T., Chief Fin. Officer--Superior Tube Company, Collegeville, PA, pg. 1064
Doss, David, Chief Oper. Officer--Fairfax Lumber & Millwork Company Inc., Springfield, VA, pg. 397
Drake, Ann M., Chief Exec. Officer--Dry Storage Corporation, Des Plaines, IL, pg. 350
Dreisbach, Thomas S., Chm. Bd. & Chief Oper. Officer--Dreisbach & Sons Cadillac Company, Detroit, MI, pg. 348
Drell, Leonard B., Chm. Bd., Pres., Chief Exec. & Chief Oper. Officer--DeMert & Dougherty, Inc., Westchester, IL, pg. 328
Drell, Steven, Chief Oper. Officer--Heet Automotive, Westchester, IL, pg. 328
Drew, Walter H., Pres. & Chief Exec. Officer--Menasha Corporation, Neenah, WI, pg. 738
Drewry, John T., V.P., Chief Oper. & Chief Fin. Officer & Treas.--Advanced Marine Enterprises, Inc., Arlington, VA, pg. 20
Driver, George F., Pres. & Chief Oper. Officer--Robert F. Driver Co., Inc., San Diego, CA, pg. 349
Dudek, John, Chief Oper. Officer--Dudek & Bock Spring Manufacturing Company, Chicago, IL, pg. 351
Duecker, Kurt C., Exec. V.P. & Chief Opers. Officer--Schreier Malting Co., Sheboygan, WI, pg. 978
Duff, Charles, Chm. Bd. & Chief Exec. Officer--Farnam Companies, Inc., Phoenix, AZ, pg. 403
Duffy, Brian, Pres. & Chief Oper. Officer--C.B. Fleet Company, Incorporated, Lynchburg, VA, pg. 417
Dunn, Charles O., Exec. V.P. & Chief Oper. Officer--Mississippi Chemical Corporation, Yazoo City, MS, pg. 760
Dye, Michael H., Pres. & Chief Oper. Officer--Post Buckley Schuh & Jernigan, Miami, FL, pg. 881
Dyson, Robert R., Pres. & Chief Oper. Officer--The Dyson-Kissner-Moran Corporation, New York, NY, pg. 357
Eagle, John R., Pres. & Chief Oper. Officer--Eagle Lincoln Mercury Inc., Dallas, TX, pg. 362
East, F. Howard, Pres., Chief Oper. & Chief Fin. Officer--Bell Packaging Corporation, Marion, IN, pg. 135
Eastman, Dennis, Pres., Chief Oper. Officer--Barry Blau & Partners, Inc., Fairfield, CT, pg. 156
Ebihara, Yushi, Exec. V.P., Chief Oper. Officer--Kresser/Craig, Santa Monica, CA, pg. 644
Eckert, John P., Pres. & Chief Oper. Officer--The Babcock & Wilcox Company, New Orleans, LA, pg. 107
Edge, H. Arthur, Chief Oper. Officer--American Cast Iron Pipe Co., Birmingham, AL, pg. 50
Edmeades, Michael, Chief Oper. Officer--West & Company Marketing & Advertising, Tampa, FL, pg. 1177
Edwards, Steve, Chief Oper. Officer & V.P.--GES Inc., Marianna, AR, pg. 439
Edwards, William E., III, Pres. & Chief Oper. Officer--Cardinal Aluminum Co., Louisville, KY, pg. 217
Ehlke, J. David, Pres. & Chief Oper. Officer--Segue Partners, Cambridge, MA, pg. 885
Elhott, Edward W., Jr., Chief Oper. Officer--Ingrid-Sevko, Inc., Deerfield, IL, pg. 569
Elizalde, Hector F., Sr. Exec. V.P., Acct. Services & Chief Oper. Officer--Castor Advertising Corp., New York, NY, pg. 229
Ellis, William H., Chm. Bd., Pres. & Chief Oper. Officer--Farley Candy Company, Chicago, IL, pg. 399
Emerson, Richard B., Exec. V.P., Gen. Mgr. & Div. Oper.--Arnold Fortuna Lawner & Cabot, Boston, MA, pg. 84
Emmel, James, Chief Oper. Officer--Sentinel Computer Services Inc., Oak Brook, IL, pg. 990
Emmerling, John A., Chm. Bd., Pres. & Chief Exec. Officer--John Emmerling Inc., New York, NY, pg. 379
Engel, Herbert G., Exec. V.P. & Chief Oper.Officer--Southwest Marine, Inc., San Diego, CA, pg. 1023
Engelkes, Donald J., V.P. & Gen. Mgr.--Country Companies Insurance Group, Bloomington, IL, pg. 289
Ericson, James D., Pres. & Chief Oper. Officer--Northwestern Mutual Life Insurance Co., Milwaukee, WI, pg. 815
Esquibias, Gabriel, V.P. & Chief Oper. Officer--Raleigh Enterprises, Inc., Los Angeles, CA, pg. 910
Estey, John W., Pres. & Chief Oper. Officer--S & C Electric Company, Chicago, IL, pg. 958
Ethier, James B., Pres. & Chief Oper. Officer--Bush Brothers & Company, Dandridge, TN, pg. 196
Evans, Clarence, Chief Oper. Officer & Exec. V.P.-Personal Training & Devel.--The Mad Butcher, Inc., Pine Bluff, AR, pg. 699
Evans, Jack Jr., Pres. & Chief Oper. Officer--Tom Thumb Food & Drugs, Inc., Dallas, TX, pg. 912
Evans, Richard G., Jr., Exec. V.P.--The Cincinnati Cordage & Paper Company, Cincinnati, OH, pg. 249
Everett, Michael S., V.P. & Chief Oper. Officer--Wilkins-Rogers Incorporated, Ellicott City, MD, pg. 1190

Fabick, Harry, Pres. & Chief Oper. Officer--John Fabick Tractor Company, Fenton, MO, pg. 396
Fain, John H., Chm., Pres., Chief Exec. & Chief Oper. Officer--Metro Information Services, Virginia Beach, VA, pg. 743
Fairchild, Ronald, Chief Oper. Officer & Dir.-Grovery Distribution--Paul Inman Associates Inc., Farmington Hills, MI, pg. 570
Fancelli, Frank, Exec. V.P. & Chief Opers. Officer--Wasserstrom Company, Columbus, OH, pg. 1167
Farabi, Ralph, Co-Pres. & Chief Oper. Officer--Helm, Inc., Highland Park, MI, pg. 527
Farnsworth, Bruce W., Chief Oper. Officer--Cadet Manufacturing Company, Vancouver, WA, pg. 207
Farnsworth, Jack, Pres. & Chief Oper. Officer--Daily Racing Form, Inc. Pacific, Los Angeles, CA, pg. 611
Farnsworth, Jack, Pres. & Chief Oper. Officer--Daily Racing Form, Inc. (Midwest), Chicago, IL, pg. 611
Farnsworth, Jack, Pres. & Chief Oper. Officer--Daily Racing Form, Inc. (Northwest), Seattle, WA, pg. 611
Faron, M.J., Chief Oper. Officer--W. E. O'Neil Construction Company, Chicago, IL, pg. 827
Fassler, Leo, Chief Oper. Officer & Asst. Gen. Mgr.--Sacramento Municipal Utility District, Sacramento, CA, pg. 965
Felker, Steven, Chief Oper. Officer--Avondale, Monroe, GA, pg. 1162
Fellowes, James E., Pres. & Chief Oper. Officer--Fellowes Manufacturing Co., Itasca, IL, pg. 405
Ferguson, Sam, Pres., Chief Exec. & Chief Oper. Officer--Ferguson Industries, Dallas, TX, pg. 406
Fernstrom, H. Allen, Exec. V.P. & Chief Oper. Officer--Marine Construction & Design Co., Seattle, WA, pg. 707
Fernstrom, H. Allen, Exec. V.P. & Chief Oper. Officer--Marco Seattle, Inc., Seattle, WA, pg. 707
Fertell, Paul A., Pres., Chief Oper. & Chief Fin. Officer--Seton Company, Norristown, PA, pg. 993
Fertitta, George A., Pres. & Chief Oper. Officer--Margeotes Fertitta & Weiss, Inc., New York, NY, pg. 706
Fess, Margret, Exec. V.P., Chief Oper. Officer--Adams Colway & Associates, Rochester, NY, pg. 16
Ficco, James, Exec. V.P., Chief Oper. Officer--Ketchum Advertising/Pittsburgh, Pittsburgh, PA, pg. 625
Fiederlein, G.L., Pres. & Chief Oper. Officer--R. T. Vanderbilt Company, Inc., Norwalk, CT, pg. 1144
Fike, Robert M., Chief Oper. Officer--Pac Paper, Inc., Vancouver, WA, pg. 815
Filotto, Robert F., Chief Oper. Officer, V.P., & Controller--Kinetic Systems Corporation, Lockport, IL, pg. 630
Finkelstein, David, Exec. V.P.--Century Business Credit Corporation, New York, NY, pg. 235
Finnegan, Lawrence J., Chm., Pres., Chief Exec. & Chief Oper. Officer--Boston Mutual Life Insurance Co., Canton, MA, pg. 167
Finney, Donald, Chief Oper. Officer--Evergreen Healthcare Ltd., Carmel, IN, pg. 391
Fiore, Robert J., Pres., Chief Oper. Officer & Creative Dir.--Warwick Baker & Fiore Inc., New York, NY, pg. 1165
Fischer, Daniel J., Chief Oper. Officer--Manhattan Life Insurance Company, Cincinnati, OH, pg. 1128
Fish, James L., Chief Oper. Officer--Windsor Publications, Inc., Chatsworth, CA, pg. 1196
Fisk, Douglas R., Exec. V.P. & Chief Oper. Officer--Mustang Tractor & Equip. Co., Houston, TX, pg. 777
Fitzgerald, Robert, Chief Oper. Officer--Best Western Intl.--B-W Advertising Agency, Phoenix, AZ, pg. 107
Fitzgerald, Robert, Chief Oper. Officer--Best Western International, Inc., Phoenix, AZ, pg. 146
FitzGibbon, David A., V.P. & Chief Oper. Officer--Bardes Corp., Cincinnati, OH, pg. 119
FitzPatrick, Paul, Pres. & Chief Oper. Officer--The Weather Channel, Atlanta, GA, pg. 654
Fitzsimons, Michael J., Pres. & Chief Oper. Officer--Copper & Brass Sales, Inc., East Detroit, MI, pg. 284
Fleming, Donald R., Pres. & Chief Oper. Officer--Zoeller Co., Louisville, KY, pg. 1220
Fleming, Kenneth, Pres. & Chief Oper. Officer--World Publishing Company, Tulsa, OK, pg. 1203
Fletcher, Mike, Chief Oper. Officer--INTEGRATEC, Atlanta, GA, pg. 573
Flint, H. Howard, II, Pres. & Chief Oper. Officer--Flint Ink Corp., Detroit, MI, pg. 419
Fogg, A.S., Jr., Pres. & Chief Oper. Officer--Farm Stores, Inc., Miami, FL, pg. 401
Foltz, C. Henry, Pres. & Chief Oper. Officer--Liggett-Stashower, Inc., Cleveland, OH, pg. 675
Fontaine, R. Richard, Pres. & Chief Oper. Officer--B. Dalton Bookseller, Inc., New York, NY, pg. 120
Forde, John P., Pres. & Chief Oper. Officer--Times Fiber Communications, Inc., Wallingford, CT, pg. 648
Forgione, Anthony, Chm. Bd. & Pres.--Boyer Bros. Inc., Altoona, PA, pg. 169
Fox, Raymond A., V.P., Chief Oper. Officer & Sec.--Active Electrical Supply Company, Chicago, IL, pg. 15
Fraley, Marvin L., V.P. & Gen. Mgr.--Higginbotham-Bartlett Co., Lubbock, TX, pg. 533
France, B.E., Pres., Chief Oper. Officer & Treas.--The H. T. Hackney Co., Knoxville, TN, pg. 498
Frank, George, Exec. V.P., Chief Oper. Officer & Treas.--Sicola Martin Koons Frank, Inc., Austin, TX, pg. 1001
Frankel, Barry R., Pres., Chief Oper. Officer & New Bus. Contact--SJ Weinstein Associates Inc., New York, NY, pg. 1173
Fredericks, Wesley C., Jr., Pres. & Chief Oper. Officer--Manufacturers Products Company, Warren, MI, pg. 705
Freebairn, John C., Pres. & Chief Oper. Officer--Cascino Purcell Freebairn, Atlanta, GA, pg. 227
Freeman, Joshua M., Pres. & Chief Oper. Officer--Carl M. Freeman Associates, Inc., Potomac, MD, pg. 431
Freeman, Ray, Chief Oper. Officer--Remington Apparel, Inc., Wilmington, NC, pg. 926
Friant, Ray, Chief Oper. Officer--Mr. Gasket Company, Cleveland, OH, pg. 761

Fricchione, Patrick, Jr., Chief Oper. Officer--Simplex Construction Co. Inc., Scranton, PA, pg. 1006
Frick, Frank J., Chief Oper. & Chief Exec. Officer & Sec.--Takatta Inc., Olympia Fields, IL, pg. 1076
Friedman, Stephen, Co-Chm. & Sr. Partner--Goldman, Sachs & Co., New York, NY, pg. 468
Friend, Norma J., Exec. V.P., Chief Oper. Officer--Gianettino & Meredith Advertising, Short Hills, NJ, pg. 455
Fristedt, Hans, Pres. & Chief Oper. Officer--American Trading and Production Corporation, Baltimore, MD, pg. 64
Fritsch, Al, Chief Oper. Officer & V.P.--Flair Communications Agency, Inc., Chicago, IL, pg. 416
Fritz, Wayne, Chief Oper. Officer--Paxton Beautiful Woods, New Orleans, LA, pg. 592
Fry, Jim, Pres. & Chief Oper. Officer--Tuscarora Yarns Inc., Mount Pleasant, NC, pg. 1120
Fuerst, John, Chief Oper. Officer--Continental/Midland, Inc., Park Forest, IL, pg. 279
Fulton, Robert R., Exec. V.P. & Chief Oper. Officer--Doehler-Jarvis, Toledo, OH, pg. 559
Furman, Thomas D., Jr., Pres. & Chief Oper. Officer--Camp Dresser & McKee Inc., Cambridge, MA, pg. 212
Furst, Stephen J., Pres. & Chief Oper. Officer--Hess's Department Stores, Inc., Allentown, PA, pg. 302
Furzer, Simon, Mng. Dir.--Chiat/Day/Mojo Pty. Ltd., Nedlands,, Australia, pg. 245
Gaboury, D.R., Chief Oper. Officer--Woodward-Clyde Group, Inc., Denver, CO, pg. 1200
Gace, Francis, Pres. & Chief Oper. Officer--Lewis & Gace, Inc., Fort Lee, NJ, pg. 673
Gaffney, Michael, Chief Oper. Officer--Snyder Potato Chips, Berlin, PA, pg. 26
Gaffney, Michael, Pres. & Chief Oper. Officer--The Joey Reiman Agency, Atlanta, GA, pg. 923
Gaither, William H., Exec. V.P. & Chief Oper. Officer--J. H. Heafner Co. Inc., Lincolnton, NC, pg. 520
Galler, Anthony, Pres. & Chief Oper. Officer--Samelson-Leon Company, Inc., Memphis, TN, pg. 968
Gandhi, Bharat, Chief Oper. Officer--Pepper Construction Co., Chicago, IL, pg. 860
Gant, Allen E., Jr., Pres. & Asst. Treas.--Glen Raven Mills, Inc., Glen Raven, NC, pg. 461
Garahan, Peter L., V.P.--Chartway Technologies, Rockville, MD, pg. 240
Gardiner, Scott, Chm. Bd., Pres., Chief Exec. & Chief Oper. Officer--Gardiner Metal Company, Chicago, IL, pg. 443
Gardner, Gary E., Pres. & Chief Oper. Officer--Soft Sheen Products, Inc., Chicago, IL, pg. 1016
Garofano, Ken, V.P. & Chief Oper. Officer--Itran Corporation, Manchester, NH, pg. 583
Garratt, Reginald G., Pres. & Chief Oper. Officer--Knowles Electronics, Inc., Itasca, IL, pg. 637
Gartlan, Ronald B., Exec. V.P. & Chief Oper. Officer--Godfather's Pizza, Inc., Omaha, NE, pg. 464
Gebert, Kenton R., Pres., Chief Exec. & Chief Oper. Officer--The Dickerson Group, Inc., Monroe, NC, pg. 335
Gebhard, Mark S., Exec. V.P.-Chief Opers. Officer, Technology & Systems--ASC Incorporated, Southgate, MI, pg. 7
Gebhardt, Scott W., Chief Oper. Officer--Acess Energy Corporation, Dublin, OH, pg. 12
Genovese, Rocco C., Pres. & Chief Oper. Officer--Burke Industries Inc., San Jose, CA, pg. 190
Gerchenson, Jeffery H., Pres. & Chief Oper. Officer--Alva/Amco Pharmacal Companies, Inc., Chicago, IL, pg. 46
Gerling, Paul J., Pres. & Chief Oper. Officer--American Laundry Machinery Inc., Cincinnati, OH, pg. 57
Gerson, Sharon, Exec. V.P., Chief Oper. Officer--Global Marketing Resources, New York, NY, pg. 463
Gialanella, Philip T., Exec. V.P. & Chief Oper. Officer--Persis Corporation, Honolulu, HI, pg. 863
Gibson, Robert, Pres. & Chief Oper. Officer--The Medical Protective Company, Fort Wayne, IN, pg. 735
Giesler, James, Chief Oper. & Chief Fin. Officer--The Fuller Brush Company, Great Bend, KS, pg. 436
Gilman, Bill, Pres. & Chief Oper. Officer--McLaughlin Mfg. Company, Greenville, SC, pg. 731
Girvan, Garrett J., Exec. V.P. & Chief Oper Officer--Viacom Cable, Pleasanton, CA, pg. 785
Glaser, Herbert O., Chm. Bd. & Chief Oper. Officer--The Elder-Beerman Stores Corp., Dayton, OH, pg. 373
Glaser, Herbert O., Chm. Bd. & Chief Oper. Officer--Elder-Beerman Stores Div., Dayton, OH, pg. 373
Glasscock, Larry, Pres. & Chief Oper. Officer--First American Bank, N.A., Washington, D.C., Washington, DC, pg. 412
Glenn, Tyler E., Jr., Pres. & Chief Oper. Officer--The Downs Group, Inc., Charlotte, NC, pg. 348
Goldberg, Norman, Exec. V.P. & Chief Oper. Officer--Fortunoff, Westbury, NY, pg. 425
Goldsmith, Gerald, Pres. & Chief Oper. Officer--Rothschild North America Inc., New York, NY, pg. 951
Goldsmith, Gerald, Pres. & Chief Oper. Officer--Rothschild Inc., New York, NY, pg. 951
Golub, Neil M., Pres. & Chief Oper. Officer--Golub Corporation, Schenectady, NY, pg. 469
Gonnella, Louis, V.P. & Chief Oper. Officer--Torino Baking Co., Chicago, IL, pg. 470
Good, Richard L., Pres. & Chief Oper. Officer--NTS Corporation, Louisville, KY, pg. 781
Gorman, Martin D., Co-Pres. & Chief Oper. Officer--Encore Marketing International, Lanham, MD, pg. 380
Goss, John, Pres. & Chief Oper. Officer--Supershuttle International, Los Angeles, CA, pg. 1064
Goss, Robert M., Pres., Chief Oper. Officer--Transco Inc., Chicago, IL, pg. 1106
Gough, Thomas L., Pres. & Chief Oper. Officer--Integral Systems, Walnut Creek, CA, pg. 572
Goulston, Noel, Exec. V.P. & Chief Oper. Officer--Erb Lumber Company, Birmingham, MI, pg. 360
Grabbe, John, V.P.-Opers.--Producers Rice Mill Inc., Stuttgart, AR, pg. 892

Grace, Kevin, Pres. & Chief Oper. Officer--Spring Engineers, Inc., Houston, TX, pg. 1033
Graeber, George C., Chief Oper. Officer--Manhattan Electric Cable Corporation, Rye, NY, pg. 370
Graham, Stacey, Pres. & Chief Oper. Officer--Lewis, Clark & Graham, Atlanta, GA, pg. 673
Grams, Jerry, Pres. & Chief Oper. Officer--Freeway Corporation, Cleveland, OH, pg. 432
Granzon, Gary W., Pres. & Chief Oper. Officer--ANGUS Chemical Company, Buffalo Grove, IL, pg. 75
Gray, James P., II, Chief Oper. Officer--James N. Gray Construction Co., Inc., Lexington, KY, pg. 479
Gray, Lawrence F., Pres.--The Heil Co., Chattanooga, TN, pg. 525
Green, Richard K., Pres. & Chief Oper. Officer--Blistex, Inc., Oak Brook, IL, pg. 157
Green, Timothy T., Chief Oper. Officer--Clayton, Williams & Sherwood, Inc., Newport Beach, CA, pg. 254
Greenbaum, John, Pres. & Chief Oper. Officer--RELA, Inc., Boulder, CO, pg. 924
Greenbaum, John, Pres. & Chief Oper. Officer--RELA Product Development Div. (PDD), Boulder, CO, pg. 924
Greenblatt, Sherwin, Pres. & Chief Oper. Officer--Bose Corporation, Framingham, MA, pg. 167
Greenfield, Kenneth, Exec. V.P.--Federal Distributing Corporation, Maspeth, NY, pg. 404
Gresham, Edward R., Pres. & Chief Oper. Officer--Network Real Estate of California, Inc., Soquel, CA, pg. 798
Gresham, Edward R., Pres. & Chief Oper. Officer--Network Real Estate, Inc., Soquel, CA, pg. 798
Gresham, Edward R., Pres. & Chief Oper. Officer--Network Home Services, Inc., Soquel, CA, pg. 798
Griffin, Darrell, Chief Oper. Officer & Chief Fin. Officer--Williams Television Time, Inc., Santa Monica, CA, pg. 1191
Grinberg, Efraim, Pres. & Chief Oper. Officer--North American Watch Corporation, Lyndhurst, NJ, pg. 812
Grommes, John, V.P. & Chief Oper. Officer--Republic Die & Tool Company, Belleville, MI, pg. 928
Groszkruger, Fred, Chief Oper. Officer--San Francisco French Bread Company, Oakland, CA, pg. 969
Grubb, David H., Pres. & Chief Oper. Officer--Swinerton & Walberg Co., San Francisco, CA, pg. 1068
Gruenberg, Craig L., Exec. V.P., Chief Oper. Officer--William Eisner & Associates Inc., Milwaukee, WI, pg. 372
Guenther, John S., Sr. V.P.--Geo. J. Ball, Inc., West Chicago, IL, pg. 115
Guinasso, Vic A., Chief Oper. Officer--DHL Airways, Inc., Redwood City, CA, pg. 309
Gumkowski, Thomas J., Chief Oper. Officer--D. J. Mead-Hubbs & Howe, Buffalo, NY, pg. 1016
Gustafson, F. Edward, Exec. V.P. & Chief Oper. Officer--Envirodyne Industries, Inc., Oak Brook, IL, pg. 383
Gustafson, Ronald R., Chief Oper. Officer--Coast Packing Company, Vernon, CA, pg. 257
Gutterman, Arthur, Pres., Chief Oper. & Chief Exec. Officer--Jelmar Company, Lincolnwood, IL, pg. 592
Hackett, Lee P., V.P.-U.S. Opers.--American Appraisal Associates, Inc., Milwaukee, WI, pg. 48
Hagan, Bernard F., Chief Oper. Officer & Sr. V.P.--Henkels & McCoy, Inc., Blue Bell, PA, pg. 529
Haggen, Richard P., Pres. & Chief Oper. Officer--Haggen's, Inc., Bellingham, WA, pg. 499
Hall, Joe, V.P. & Chief Oper. Officer--Insta-Foam Products, Inc., Joliet, IL, pg. 419
Hall, Joe, Chief Oper. Officer & Sr. V.P.-Opers.--Central Freight Lines Inc., Waco, TX, pg. 232
Hall, Michael J., Sr. V.P., Treas., Chief Fin. & Admin. Officer--T.D. Williamson, Inc., Tulsa, OK, pg. 1192
Hallam, Howard, Pres. & Chief Oper. Officer--Ben E. Keith Company, Fort Worth, TX, pg. 620
Hallgren, Kenneth, Pres. & Chief Oper. Officer--Hurd Millwork Company, Inc., Medford, WI, pg. 1123
Halstead, William B., Chief Oper. Officer--Halstead Industries, Inc., Greensboro, NC, pg. 502
Halyburton, T., Chief Oper. Officer--American Fuel Cell & Coated Fabrics Co. (Amfuel), Magnolia, AR, pg. 55
Hamilton, Al, Chief Oper. Officer & Exec. V.P.--Southern Belle Dairy Company, Inc., Somerset, KY, pg. 1020
Hancock, Phil, Chief Oper. Officer--Molded Fiber Glass Co., Union City, PA, pg. 764
Handler, Mark S., Co-Chm. & Co- Chief Exec. Officer--R. H. Macy & Co., Inc., New York, NY, pg. 698
Hanft, Adam, Pres. & Chief Oper. Officer--Slater Hanft Martin, Inc., New York, NY, pg. 1010
Hanlon, Jack, Pres. & Chief Oper. Officer--Gerber Plumbing Fixtures Corporation, Chicago, IL, pg. 454
Hanlon, Jack, Pres. & Chief Oper. Officer--Kokomo Sanitary Pottery Corp., Chicago, IL, pg. 640
Hannay, Robert D., Exec. V.P. & Chief Oper. Officer--Clifford B. Hannay & Son Inc., Westerlo, NY, pg. 505
Hanson, Lee J., Chief Oper. Officer--Roman, Inc., Roselle, IL, pg. 945
Harding, Arthur J., Jr., Pres. & Chief Oper. Officer--PPA Industries, Inc., Dallas, TX, pg. 836
Harding, John H., Pres. & Chief Oper. Officer--National Life Insurance Company, Montpelier, VT, pg. 791
Hardy, Richard B., Pres., Chief Exec. & Chief Oper. Officer-Hyde Manufacturing Co., Southbridge, MA, pg. 556
Harker, Roger, Pres. & Chief Oper. Officer--Bently Nevada Corporation, Minden, NV, pg. 140
Harmon, David E., Chm. Bd., Pres., Chief Exec. & Chief Oper. Officer--El Camino Resources, Ltd., Northridge, CA, pg. 372
Harralson, James W., Exec. V.P. & Chief Oper. Officer--Chesapeake Financial Corp., Miami Beach, FL, pg. 243
Harris, James, Pres. & Chief Operating Officer--GFA Brands, Inc., Cresskill, NJ, pg. 440
Hart, Tim, Exec. V.P., Chief Oper. Officer--Ketchum Advertising/Los Angeles, Los Angeles, CA, pg. 625
Hartman, Carl C., Pres., Chief Oper. & Chief Exec. Officer--Trinidad/Benham Corporation, Denver, CO, pg. 1113
Hatt, Peter M., Chm. & Chief Exec. Officer--Borders, Perrin & Norrander, Inc., Portland, OR, pg. 165
Hatt, Peter M., Chm. & Chief Exec. Officer--Borders, Perrin & Norrander, Seattle, WA, pg. 165
Hatter, Kenneth, Chief Oper. Officer, Sr. V.P. & New Bus. Contact--Marriner Marketing Communications, Inc., Columbia, MD, pg. 713
Hawk, Robert, Pres. & Chief Exec. Officer--Hale-Halsell Company, Tulsa, OK, pg. 500
Hay, Lewis, Chief Oper. & Chief Fin. Officer--J P Foodservice, Inc., Hanover, MD, pg. 586
Haynes, Gary, Pres., Chief Exec. Officer--Ericson Marketing Communications, Nashville, TN, pg. 386
Haynes, Thomas J., Pres. & Chief Oper. Officer--HP Direct, Indianapolis, IN, pg. 497
Hays, Carl, Chief Oper. Officer--Al Copeland Enterprises, Inc., Jefferson, LA, pg. 283
Hays, Carl, Chief Oper. Officer--Church's Fried Chicken, Inc., Jefferson, LA, pg. 284
Hazard, Eric, Chief Oper. Officer--Campus Point Realty Corporation, La Jolla, CA, pg. 981
Heaney, Joe, Pres. & Chief Oper. Officer--Cornnuts Inc., Alameda, CA, pg. 286
Hebert, Lawrence I., Pres. & Chief Oper. Officer--Perpetual Corporation, Washington, DC, pg. 862
Hebert, Lawrence I., Pres. & Chief Oper. Officer--Allbritton Communications Company, Washington, DC, pg. 862
Heiman, Gary, Pres. & Chief Oper. Officer--Standard Textile Co., Inc., Cincinnati, OH, pg. 1037
Heisler, Emerson W., Pres. & Chief Oper. Officer--Price Brothers Co., Dayton, OH, pg. 888
Hellberg, C.E., Chief Oper. Officer--Creative Productions, Pittsburgh, PA, pg. 297
Helmig, Robert, V.P. & Chief Oper. Officer--United States Name Plate, Philadelphia, PA, pg. 649
Hemphill, Robert B., Chm., Pres. & Chief Exec. & Chief Oper. Officer--Barclay White Incorporated, Berwyn, PA, pg. 119
Hennessy, Michael W., Chief Oper. Officer--Fannie May Candy Shops, Inc., Chicago, IL, pg. 604
Henry, Thomas E., Chief Oper. Officer--MacDaniels, Henry & Sproul, Inc., San Francisco, CA, pg. 696
Henry, William L., Pres. & Chief Oper. Officer--The Stroh Brewery Company, Detroit, MI, pg. 1053
Hentges, Richard J., Pres. & Chief Oper. Officer--Foley-Belsaw Company, Minneapolis, MN, pg. 422
Herberg, Richard, Chief Oper. Officer & V.P.-Mktg.--Bachman's, Inc., Minneapolis, MN, pg. 108
Herbers, Donald, Pres. & Chief Oper. Officer--Pinne/Herbers Advertising Inc., San Francisco, CA, pg. 871
Herbst, Edward I., Chief Oper. Officer & Mng. Dir.--Cowen & Company, New York, NY, pg. 291
Herdemian, Gregory, Chief Oper. Officer--Empire Diamond Corporation, New York, NY, pg. 379
Herman, James A., Chief Oper. Officer, Chm. Exec. Comm., & Ptnr.--Woolpert Consultants, Dayton, OH, pg. 1201
Herres, Robert, Gen., Pres. & Chief Oper. Officer--United Services Automobile Association (USAA), San Antonio, TX, pg. 1134
Herring, Barry E., Pres. & Chief Oper. Officer--Spatz & Co., Northbrook, IL, pg. 1026
Herrman, Larry, Chief Oper. Officer--Integrated Systems Analysts, Inc., Arlington, VA, pg. 573
Heyman, Leonard J., Chm. Bd., Pres., Chief Exec. & Chief Oper. Officer--Heyman Corporation, Niles, IL, pg. 532
Hickson, Richard, Chief Oper. Officer, Sr. V.P. & Dir.--Holmes Protection Group, Inc., New York, NY, pg. 540
Higgins, Jonathan, Chief Opers. Officer--Bob Thomas & Associates, San Francisco, CA, pg. 244
Higgins, Jonathan, Chief Opers. Officer--Bob Thomas Associates, Toronto, Canada, pg. 244
Higgins, Jonathon, Chief Opers. Officer--Bob Thomas & Associates, Inc. Public Relations, Venice, CA, pg. 244
Hilbert, William M., Pres. & Chief Oper. Officer--PHB Parker Die Castings, Fairview, PA, pg. 836
Hilgendorf, Robert, V.P. & Chief Oper. Officer--The Johnson Industries Corp., Urbana, OH, pg. 598
Hirsch, Henry C. (Harry), Pres. & Chief Oper. Officer--Wiltel Communications Systems, Inc., The Woodlands, TX, pg. 1194
Hobart, W.H., Chm. Bd., Pres., Chief Exec. & Chief Oper. Officer--Hobart Brothers Co., Troy, OH, pg. 536
Hodin, Joseph, Chm., Pres. & Chief Exec. Officer--Giant Markets Inc., Scranton, PA, pg. 456
Hoffman, Roger P., Chief Oper. Officer--Green Bay Packaging Inc., Green Bay, WI, pg. 483
Hoffmaster, Jon, Exec. V.P. & Chief Oper. Officer--American Business Information, Inc., Omaha, NE, pg. 50
Holcombe, Hubert, Jr., Exec. V.P.-Sls. & Chief Oper. Officer--Arrowhead Mills, Inc., Hereford, TX, pg. 86
Holladay, J. Allen, Exec. V.P. & Chief Oper. Officer--American SelfCare Corporation, Columbus, GA, pg. 60
Hollis, Mark C., Pres. & Chief Oper. Officer--Publix Supermarkets Inc., Lakeland, FL, pg. 898
Holman, W. H., Jr., Chm. Bd., Pres. & Chief Exec. & Oper. Officers--Jitney-Jungle Stores of America, Inc., Jackson, MS, pg. 594
Holmes, John B., Jr., Pres. & Chief Oper. Officer--Zilkha Energy Company, Houston, TX, pg. 1219
Holter, Gary, Chief Oper. Officer & Exec. V.P.--Knapp Shoes Inc., Brockton, MA, pg. 636
Hoops, Alan, Exec. V.P., Chief Oper. Officer & Sec.--PacifiCare Health Systems, Inc., Cypress, CA, pg. 1127
Hopkins, Jerry W., Pres. & Chief Oper. Officer--Texas Refinery Corp., Fort Worth, TX, pg. 1089
Horne, Eugene B., Jr., Pres. & Chief Oper. Officer--The Pantry, Inc., Sanford, NC, pg. 846
Horowitz, Barry M., Dr., Pres. & Chief Exec. & Oper. Officer--Mitre Corporation, Bedford, MA, pg. 762
Horst, David L., Pres. & Chief Oper. Officer--The Sheridan Press, Inc., Hanover, PA, pg. 998
Horton, Adelaide, Sr. V.P., Chief Opers. Officer-Worldwide--Chiat/Day/Mojo/New York, New York, NY, pg. 244
Host, Theodore J., Pres. & Chief Oper. Officer--The Scott Company, Marysville, OH, pg. 982
Hoversen, Mike, V.P.-Fin. & Chief Oper. Officer--Bell-Carter Foods, Inc., Lafayette, CA, pg. 134
Howell, G.T., Pres. & Chief Oper. Officer--Universal Life Insurance Company, Memphis, TN, pg. 1138
Hoy. Daniel J., V.P. & Chief Oper. Officer--Summa Four, Inc., Manchester, NH, pg. 1057
Hudetz, Peter, Pres & Chief Oper. Officer--Solar Press, Inc., Naperville, IL, pg. 1016
Huettl, Thomas R., Sr. V.P., Chief Oper. Officer, Treas. & Sec.--Steenberg Homes, Inc., Fond du Lac, WI, pg. 1045
Hughes, Robert, Exec. V.P. & Chief Oper. Officer--California Offset Printers, Inc., Glendale, CA, pg. 210
Hunt, Robert C., Chm. Bd. & Chief Exec. Officer--The Hunt Corporation, Indianapolis, IN, pg. 553
Hunt, Ronald, V.P. & Chief Oper. Officer--Nationwide Health Care Corp., Columbus, OH, pg. 795
Hurd, James, Exec. V.P.--Lyman Lumber Company, Excelsior, MN, pg. 689
Hurt, Michael L., Pres. & Chief Oper. Officer--T.B. Wood's Sons Company, Chambersburg, PA, pg. 1200
Hutter, Heinz F., Pres. & Chief Oper. Officer--Cargill Inc., Wayzata, MN, pg. 219
Hyde, Kenneth R., Jr., Exec. V.P., Chief Opers. Officer & Treas.--Hackney Brothers, Inc., Wilson, NC, pg. 498
Idelman, Sheri, Chief Oper. Officer--ITI Marketing Services, Inc., Omaha, NE, pg. 561
Ingman, Tom, Pres. & Chief Oper. Officer--Condor D.C. Power Supplies Inc., Oxnard, CA, pg. 273
Ingram, Richard E., Chm. Bd., Chief Exec. & Chief Fin. Officer--Builder Marts of America, Greenville, SC, pg. 187
Isaac, Robert, Sr. V.P. & Chief Oper. Officer--Agripac Inc., Salem, OR, pg. 25
Isen, Irvin, Pres. & Chief Oper. Officer--Paramount Packaging Corp., Chalfont, PA, pg. 848
Isseleib, Lutz, Chm., Pres. & Chief Oper. Officer--Falstaff Brewing Corporation, Vancouver, WA, pg. 959
Issleib, Lutz, Chm. Bd., Pres., Chief Exec. & Chief Oper. Officer--General Brewing Company, Vancouver, WA, pg. 959
Issler, James E., Pres. & Chief Oper. Officer--H.H. Brown Shoe Company, Inc., Greenwich, CT, pg. 182
Ittner, George, Pres. & Chief Oper. Officer--New Hampton, Inc., New York, NY, pg. 801
Iversen, Leroy, Chief Oper. Officer--Yellowstone Transportation Service, Inc., Santa Fe Springs, CA, pg. 716
Jackson, Mary Anne, Chm., Pres. & Chief Oper. Officer--My Own Meals, Inc., Deerfield, IL, pg. 779
Jacobsen, Earl D., Pres. & Chief Oper. Officer--Central Data Corporation, Champaign, IL, pg. 232
Jalbert, Michael E., Exec. V.P.-Opers.--West Chemical Products, Inc., Princeton, NJ, pg. 1172
James, Evan R., Pres. & Chief Oper. Officer--Tal Inc., Erie, PA, pg. 1077
Jamison, R. Kenneth, Pres. & Chief Oper. Officer--Southern Radio Corporation, pg. 1022
Janning, James C., Pres. & Chief Oper. Officer--Harbour Group Ltd., Clayton, MO, pg. 506
Jaworski, Walter J., Chm. Bd., Pres. Chief Exec. Officer & Chief Oper. Officer--Miken Companies, Inc., Cheektowaga, NY, pg. 752
Jeansonne, R.L., Chief Oper. Officer--LaRoche Chemicals Inc., Baton Rouge, LA, pg. 659
Jemison, Frank Z., Jr., Pres., Chief Exec. & Chief Oper. Officer--Jemison, Inc., Memphis, TN, pg. 592
Jensen, Richard S., Exec. V.P., Chief Oper. Officer--Bader Rutter & Assoc., Inc., Brookfield, WI, pg. 113
Jewett, Harvey, Chief Oper. Officer--Super 8 Motels, Inc., Aberdeen, SD, pg. 1062
Jimenez, Carlos, Pres., Chief Oper. Officer & Dir.-Creative--Leslie Advertising, Greenville, SC, pg. 668
Johanneson, Gerald B., Chief Oper. Officer & Exec. V.P.--Haworth, Inc., Holland, MI, pg. 518
Johnson, Arthur E., Pres., Chief Oper. Officer & Gen. Mgr.--Basler Electric Company, Highland, IL, pg. 125
Johnson, Carl A., Pres., Chief Exec. & Chief Oper. Officer--Berlin Steel Construction Co., Berlin, CT, pg. 142
Johnson, Craig, Pres. & Chief Oper. Officer--Ris Paper Company, Long Island City, NY, pg. 935
Johnson, Dave, V.P. & Chief Oper. Officer--Cenex/Land O'Lakes, Inc., Saint Paul, MN, pg. 653
Johnson, Dave, V.P. & Chief Oper. Officer--Cenex/Land O'Lakes, Inc., Saint Paul, MN, pg. 231
Johnson, Donald M., V.P.-Opers. & Chief Oper. Officer--Energy Minerals Corporation, Denver, CO, pg. 381
Johnson, Karen, Chief Oper. Officer--Bull, Inc., San Diego, CA, pg. 981
Johnson, Luther, Sr. V.P. & Chief Oper. Officer--Millstone Coffee, Inc., Everett, WA, pg. 756
Johnson, Peter M., Chief Oper. Officer & V.P.--Johnson & Towers, Inc., Mount Laurel, NJ, pg. 601
Johnson, Peter N., Sr. V.P.-Chief Oper. Officer--Artesian Resources Corporation, Newark, DE, pg. 86
Johnson, Peter N., Sr. V.P.-Chief Oper. Officer--Artesian Water Company, Inc., Newark, DE, pg. 86
Johnson, Rodger L., Pres. & Chief Oper. Officer--Brock Control Systems, Inc., Atlanta, GA, pg. 178
Johnson, Ronald, Pres. & Chief Oper. Officer--Hoogovens Aluminum Corp., Secaucus, NJ, pg. 543
Johnson, Wesley, Jr., Chief Oper. Officer--Blue Boar Cafeteria Co., Louisville, KY, pg. 158
Johnston, Chap, Chief Oper. Officer--Tanner Co. Inc., Rutherfordton, NC, pg. 1078
Johnston, Doug, Chief Oper. Officer & Pres.--Ziebart Canada, Inc., Downsview, Canada, pg. 1218
Johnston, Sid D., Pres. & Chief Exec. Officer--Despatch Industries, Minneapolis, MN, pg. 332
Johnston, W. Douglas, Pres. & Chief Oper. Officer, Canada--Ziebart International Corporation, Troy, MI, pg. 1217
Jonas, Gary F., Pres. & Chief Oper. Officer--Earle Palmer Brown, Bethesda, MD, pg. 182
Jones, David, Pres. & Chief Oper. Officer--Gunnebo Fastening Corp., York, PA, pg. 494

Jones, Edward C., Exec. V.P. & Chief Oper. Officer--Jones Dairy Farm, Fort Atkinson, WI, pg. 603
Jones, J.C., III, Chm. Bd.--Fuel South, Inc., Hazlehurst, GA, pg. 435
Jones, James R., Pres. & Chief Oper. Officer--Dodson Group, Kansas City, MO, pg. 342
Jones, Larry, Chief Oper. Officer--Coleman Outdoor Products, Wichita, KS, pg. 695
Jones, Michael E., Pres. & Chief Oper. Officer--Capital Electric Group, Inc., Phoenix, AZ, pg. 215
Jones, Robert, Chief Fin. Officer--I Ski Ski Goggles, City of Commerce, CA, pg. 557
Jones, Thomas E., Jr., Chief Oper. & Chief Fin. Officer--Steadly Company, Carthage, MO, pg. 1043
Jorgensen, Erik, Pres. & Chief Oper. Officer--Faber/Castell Corporation, Parsippany, NJ, pg. 395
Jorgensen, Paul J., Chief Oper. Officer--SRI International, Menlo Park, CA, pg. 964
Josephs, Daniel, Pres. & Chief Oper. Officer--Dominick's Finer Foods, Northlake, IL, pg. 343
Judy, Aubrey E., Chief Oper. Officer--Farmers Telephone Co-Op, Kingstree, SC, pg. 402
Juelich, Richard J., Exec. V.P. & Chief Oper. Officer--AmClyde Engineered Products, Inc., Saint Paul, MN, pg. 47
Julius, George P., Jr., Pres. & Chief Oper. Officer--Brooks Beverage Management, Inc., Holland, MI, pg. 179
Junker, Paul J., Chief Oper. Officer--Food Services of America, Seattle, WA, pg. 423
Juris, Brett, Chief Oper. Officer--Magnasync Moviola Corporation, Hollywood, CA, pg. 586
Kaiser, Nicholas T., Pres. & Chief Oper. Officer--The Carbide/Graphite Group, Inc., Pittsburgh, PA, pg. 217
Kalebic, Thomas, Exec. V.P. & Chief Oper. Officer--Lane Industries, Inc., Northbrook, IL, pg. 656
Kalinowski, Sylvia J., Chief Oper. Officer & Controller--Tri-Mark Metal Corp., Detroit, MI, pg. 1110
Kalter, Alan, Pres. & Chief Oper. Officer--W.B. Doner & Company, Southfield, MI, pg. 344
Kamenstein, Peter D., Vice Chm., Pres. & Chief Oper. Officer--M. Kamenstein, Inc., White Plains, NY, pg. 615
Kanack, Ken, Chief Oper. Officer--Ortho-Kinetics, Inc., Waukesha, WI, pg. 830
Kane, Gary A., Pres. & Chief Oper. Officer--J. G. Hook, Inc., Philadelphia, PA, pg. 543
Karpik, Michael, Chief Oper. Officer-Mdse.--Bigsby & Kruthers, Inc., Chicago, IL, pg. 150
Kasen, Stewart M., Pres. & Chief Oper. Officer--First Land & Development, Inc., Richmond, VA, pg. 18
Kassab, Robert L., Vice Chm., Pres. & Chief Oper. Officer--Stainless Incorporated, Deerfield Beach, FL, pg. 1035
Katopodis, Louis, Pres. & Chief Oper. Officer--Fiesta Mart Inc., Houston, TX, pg. 409
Kaumeyer, Jeff, Pres. & Chief Oper. Officer--Hammond Farrell Inc., New York, NY, pg. 504
Kearney, E. James, Mng. Partner & Chief Oper. Officer--Eire Partners, Inc., Chicago, IL, pg. 372
Keating, Daniel J., III, Chief Oper. Officer--Daniel J. Keating Co., Villanova, PA, pg. 619
Keener, C. Robert, Exec. V.P. & Chief Oper. Officer--The Crystal Tissue Co., Middletown, OH, pg. 303
Keeney, Hilliard, Sr. V.P.-Opers.--Pella Corporation, Pella, IA, pg. 856
Keeton, Kathy, Pres. & Chief Oper. Officer--General Media Publishing Group, New York, NY, pg. 450
Keeton, Thomas, Chief Oper. Officer--Keller Construction Company Ltd., El Monte, CA, pg. 620
Keller, James J., Chief Oper. Officer & Exec. V.P.--J. J. Keller & Associates, Inc., Neenah, WI, pg. 620
Kelley, Terry, Pres. & Chief Oper. Officer--Team Bancshares, Inc., Dallas, TX, pg. 1082
Kellogg, Martin N., Pres., Chief Oper. Officer & Corp. Sec.--UFE Incorporated, Stillwater, MN, pg. 1123
Kells, Peter C., Vice Chm., Chief Fin. & Chief Oper. Officer--Gitano Group Inc., New York, NY, pg. 460
Kelly, Edmund F., Pres. & Chief Oper. Officer--Liberty Mutual Insurance Co., Boston, MA, pg. 674
Kelly, James P., St. V.P. & Chief Oper. Officer--United Parcel Service of America, Inc., Atlanta, GA, pg. 1133
Kelly, John, Pres. & Chief Oper. Officer--Biederman, Kelly & Shaffer, Inc., New York, NY, pg. 149
Kennedy, Bernard, Pres. & Chief Oper. Officer--King Kullen Grocery Co., Inc., Westbury, NY, pg. 630
Kenney, Joseph, Sec.--Provident Mutual Life Insurance Co., Philadelphia, PA, pg. 896
Kerr, Jill, Chief Oper. Officer & V.P.-Sls. & Mktg.--The ASCII Group, Inc., Bethesda, MD, pg. 8
Kessler, Steven, Chief Oper. & Chief Fin. Officer--Strouse Greenberg & Co., Inc., Philadelphia, PA, pg. 1054
Ketchman, Vic, Chief Oper. Officer--T-R Printing & Publishing, Irwin, PA, pg. 1113
Kiam, Victor, II, Chm. Bd., Pres., Chief Exec. & Chief Oper. Officer--Remington Products Inc., Bridgeport, CT, pg. 926
Kies, William S., Pres. & Chief Oper. Officer--IGA, Inc. (Independent Grocers Alliance), Chicago, IL, pg. 560
Kilb, Jerry L., Pres. & Chief Oper. Officer--GranTree Corporation, Beaverton, OR, pg. 477
Kilgore, Tom D., Pres. & Chief Exec. Officer--Oglethorpe Power Corp., Tucker, GA, pg. 822
Kim, Edward, Pres., Chief Oper. & Chief Exec. Officer--Ronald Hsu Construction, Capitol Heights, MD, pg. 548
King, Jim, Pres. & Chief Oper. Officer--Sunox, Inc., Charlotte, NC, pg. 1062
King, Robert J., Exec. Dir. & Chief Oper. Officer--MADD (Mothers Against Drunk Driving), Irving, TX, pg. 691
King, Stephen M., V.P. & Chief Oper. Officer--TGI Friday's, Inc., Addison, TX, pg. 221
Kingsmore, Harold D., Pres. & Chief Oper. Officer--Graniteville Co., Graniteville, SC, pg. 476
Kinning, Ronald L., Chief Oper. Officer--Kinning & Reil of Wyoming, Lohewood, CO, pg. 907
Kinser, Thomas, Exec. V.P. & Chief Oper. Officer--Blue Cross and Blue Shield Association, Chicago, IL, pg. 159
Kirk, Graham V., Sr. Exec. V.P., Chief Oper. Officer--Gray Kirk/VanSant Advertising, Inc., Baltimore, MD, pg. 479
Kirkland, D.L., Pres.-Glass Group & Chief Oper. Officer--AFG Industries, Inc., Fort Worth, TX, pg. 3
Klein, Richard T. Jr., Pres. & Chief Oper. Officer--Klein Tools Inc., Skokie, IL, pg. 635
Kline, Arnold W., Chm. Bd., Pres. & Chief Oper. Officer--Boston Trading Ltd. Inc., Lynn, MA, pg. 168
Knoth, Karl H., Pres. & Chief Oper. Officer, Mfg. & Assembly--ASC Incorporated, Southgate, MI, pg. 7
Knowles, True H., Chief Oper. Officer--Dr Pepper/Seven-Up Companies, Inc., Dallas, TX, pg. 342
Knowles, True H., Pres. & Chief Oper. Officer--Dr Pepper Company, Dallas, TX, pg. 342
Knudson, Knute S., Pres. & Chief Oper. Officer--Dixson, Inc., Grand Junction, CO, pg. 341
Koberg, Ronald L., V.P. & Chief Oper. Officer--Cox Hobbies, Inc., Corona, CA, pg. 294
Kobs, Duane, Chief Oper. Officer--La Belle Industries, Inc., Oconomowoc, WI, pg. 648
Koch, Craig R., Exec. V.P.--The Hertz Corporation, Park Ridge, NJ, pg. 849
Koci, Ludvik F., Pres. & Chief Oper. Officer--Detroit Diesel Corp., Detroit, MI, pg. 859
Koentopf, David D., Pres. & Chief Oper. Officer--Lifetouch, Inc., Bloomington, MN, pg. 675
Kohler, Herbert V., Jr., Chm. Bd., Pres., Chief Oper. & Chief Exec. Officer--Kohler Company, Kohler, WI, pg. 639
Kolikof, Robert A., Pres., Chief Exec. Officer & Chief Oper. Officer--Prudential Metal Supply Corp., East Dedham, MA, pg. 898
Kolvenbach, Donald M., Pres., Chief Exec. Officer & Chief Oper. Officer--Affiliated of Florida Inc., Tampa, FL, pg. 23
Koncelik, David G., Exec. V.P. & Chief Oper. Officer--California & Hawaiian Sugar Company, Concord, CA, pg. 210
Koon, Sandy, Asst. Sec.--The Florida Lottery, Tallahassee, FL, pg. 420
Kopko, Edward M., Chm. Bd., Pres., Chief Exec. & Chief Oper. Officer--Butler International, Montvale, NJ, pg. 197
Kouzuma, Makoto, V.P. & Chief Oper. Officer--FamTec International, Inc., Des Plaines, IL, pg. 398
Kraber, Dick, Chief Oper. Officer--Peerless Lighting Corp., Berkeley, CA, pg. 855
Kraft, Robert W., Exec. V.P., Chief Oper. Officer, POP Display & Mdsg. Systems Div.--DCI Marketing, Milwaukee, WI, pg. 308
Kravitz, Edward N., Pres. & Chief Oper. Officer--The Flexible Corp., Delaware, OH, pg. 421
Kreiter, Ned, Chief Oper. Officer, Treas. & Gen. Mgr.--Castcraft Industries, Inc., Skokie, IL, pg. 228
Kreitzer, Roderick G., Pres. & Chief Exec. Officer--Baker Knapp & Tubbs Inc., Grand Rapids, MI, pg. 640
Krida, Jeffrey, Exec. V.P. & Chief Oper. Officer--Delta Queen Steamboat Company, New Orleans, LA, pg. 385
Krissel, Robert A., Pres. & Chief Oper. Officer--Equitable Bag Company, Long Island City, NY, pg. 385
Krivkovich, Peter G., Pres. & Chief Oper. Officer--Cramer-Krasselt, Milwaukee, WI, pg. 296
Kuck, Duane, Chief Oper. Officer--Regal Marine Industries Inc., Orlando, FL, pg. 921
Kuhlman, David, Exec. V.P., Chief Oper. Officer & New Bus. Contact--The Hively Agency Inc., Houston, TX, pg. 536
Kukla, Robert J., Pres. & Chief Oper. Officer--Kukla Press, Inc., Elk Grove Village, IL, pg. 646
Kull, L.A., Pres. & Chief Oper. Officer--Science Applications International Corporation, San Diego, CA, pg. 981
Kullberg, Gary W., Pres. & Chief Oper. Officer--Pancom International Corp., Stamford, CT, pg. 845
Kullman, J.W., Exec. V.P. & Chief Oper. Officer--Orix Real Estate Equities, Inc., Chicago, IL, pg. 829
Kuntz, Dave, V.P. & Chief Oper. Officer--Interstate Distributors Inc., Norcross, GA, pg. 580
Kunz, Larry P., Pres. & Chief Oper. Officer--Payless Cashways, Inc., Kansas City, MO, pg. 853
Kutzmark, G.F., Exec. V.P. & Chief Oper. Officer--Edgewater Corporation, Oakmont, PA, pg. 368
Ladds, H.P., Jr., Pres. & Chief Exec. Officer--Columbus McKinnon Corp., Amherst, NY, pg. 266
Laesser, Jerry, V.P.-Mktg. & Franchise Devel. & Chief Oper. Officer--One Hour Martinizing Dry Cleaning Franchise (System), Cincinnati, OH, pg. 826
Landberg, George, Chief Oper. Officer--Valcor Engineering Corp., Springfield, NJ, pg. 1142
Lande, James, Pres. & Chief Oper. Officer--Quadion Corporation, Minneapolis, MN, pg. 902
Lander, Richard D., Exec. V.P. & Chief Oper. Officer--Marotta Scientific Controls, Inc., Montville, NJ, pg. 713
Laney, L.C., Pres. & Chief Oper. Officer--Ingles Markets, Inc., Asheville, NC, pg. 568
Langer, David, Pres., Chief Exec. & Chief Oper. Officer & Treas.--David Langer & Co., Inc., Hollywood, CA, pg. 657
Langhammer, Fred, Exec. V.P. & Chief Oper. Officer--Estee Lauder, Inc., New York, NY, pg. 389
Langmead, Jeffrey P., Sr. V.P. & Chief Oper. Officer--Blue Cross & Blue Shield of Texas, Inc., Richardson, TX, pg. 160
Lappin, Richard C., Pres. & Chief Oper. Officer--Farley Industries, Chicago, IL, pg. 399
Lauerer, Kenneth G., Pres. & Chief Oper. Officer--Lauerer Markin Gibbs, Inc., Maumee, OH, pg. 660
Lauerman, James M., Pres. & Chief Oper. Officer--Bailey Lauerman & Associates, Inc., Lincoln, NE, pg. 114
Lavelle, Thomas J., Exec. V.P. & Chief Oper. Officer--Industrial Coatings Group, Inc., Chicago, IL, pg. 566
Lavine, S.E., Pres. & Chief Oper. Officer--D&H Distributing Company, Harrisburg, PA, pg. 307
Lay, Ken, Chief Oper. Officer & Sec.--Lay Packing Company Inc., Knoxville, TN, pg. 663
Layton, Bill, Jr., Pres. & Chief Oper. Officer--Welsco Inc., North Little Rock, AR, pg. 1175
Leamer, Jim, Exec. V.P. & Chief Oper. Officer--McSwain Carpets Inc., Cincinnati, OH, pg. 733
Leary, Gary, Exec. V.P. & Chief Oper. Officer--UniHealth America, Burbank, CA, pg. 1126
LeBlanc, James J., Pres. & Chief Oper. Officer--K & B, Inc., New Orleans, LA, pg. 611
Lebovitz, Brad, Chief Oper. Officer & Chief Fin. Officer--Kanex, Cleveland, OH, pg. 616
Lee, Andrew, Chm. Bd., Pres. & Chief Oper. Officer--Daniel Caron Ltd., New York, NY, pg. 224
Lee, John W., Pres. & Chief Oper. Officer--Georgia Iron Works Co., Grovetown, GA, pg. 453
Lee, Weldon A., Pres., Chief Exec. Officer--Atlantic Builders Group Inc., Baltimore, MD, pg. 94
Leonard, Robert, Chief Oper. Officer--FMS Management Systems, Inc., North Miami Beach, FL, pg. 394
Leprevost, Rolf, Chief Oper. Officer--Medecine et Systemes Informatiques Intergres, Montpellier, France, pg. 982
Lerch, Allan, Chief Oper. Officer & V.P.--Porcelain Metals Corp., Louisville, KY, pg. 881
Levit, Max, V.P.--Grocers Supply Co. Inc., Houston, TX, pg. 488
Levy, Daniel H., Vice Chm. & Chief Oper. Officer--Montgomery Ward & Co., Inc., Chicago, IL, pg. 767
Levy, Robert, Pres. & Chief Oper. Officer--Norman Levy Associates, Inc., Southfield, MI, pg. 672
Licht, J.M., Pres. & Chief Exec. Officer--Duraco Products, Inc., Streamwood, IL, pg. 354
Lichtenstein, Howard, Pres. & Chief Oper. Officer--American Life Insurance Company of New York, New York, NY, pg. 778
Lieberman, Mark T., Pres. & Chief Oper. Officer--Lieberman-Appalucci, Allentown, PA, pg. 675
Lieberman, Stephen, Pres., Chief Exec. & Chief Oper. Officer--Carousel Snack Bars Of Minnesota, Minneapolis, MN, pg. 224
Liebermann, Thomas R., Chm Bd., Pres, & Chief Oper. Officer--Kaye Instruments, Inc., Bedford, MA, pg. 619
Light, L. L., Pres. & Chief Oper. Officer--L. B. Smith, Inc., Camp Hill, PA, pg. 1013
Lindahl, Herbert W., Pres. & Chief Oper. Officer--State Industries Inc., Ashland City, TN, pg. 1041
Lindberg, Dennis N., Exec. V.P. & Chief Oper. Officer--Chicago West Pullman Corporation, Cincinnati, OH, pg. 246
Linder, Keith E., Pres. & Chief Oper. Officer-Chiquita Brands Intl., Inc.--American Financial Corporation, Cincinnati, OH, pg. 52
Lindgren, James, Chief Oper. Officer & V.P.-Opers.--Micro-Met L Corp., Indianapolis, IN, pg. 748
Lindner, S. Craig, Pres. & Chief Oper. Officer--Spelling Entertainment Group, Inc., Cincinnati, OH, pg. 54
Lipsky, Len, Chief Opers. Officer--Kettering Advertising Display Co., Englewood Cliffs, NJ, pg. 626
Livermore, Curtis, Chief Opers. Officer--Laidlaw Corporation, Scottsdale, AZ, pg. 650
Livingston, Robert, Chief Oper. Officer--Allright Corporation, Wichita, KS, pg. 41
Ljungberg, Robert, Chm. Bd., Pres., Chief Exec. & Chief Oper. Officer--Ultra Tool & Plastics, Inc., Amherst, NY, pg. 1125
Logan, Oran, Pres. & Chief Oper. Officer--Alamo Group, Inc., Seguin, TX, pg. 29
Lolas, C. William, Chief Oper. Officer--Pony Sports & Leisure Inc., Warren, NJ, pg. 880
Long, James H., Exec. V.P. & Chief Oper. Officer--Long MFG. NC, Inc., Tarboro, NC, pg. 682
Looper, R.K., Pres. & Chief Oper. Officer--Cal-Maine Foods, Inc., Jackson, MS, pg. 208
Louttit, William A., Exec. V.P. & Chief Oper. Officer--The Grand Union Company, Wayne, NJ, pg. 476
Lovitz, David D., Pres. & Chief Oper. Officer--The Hartz Mountain Corp., Harrison, NJ, pg. 514
Lowe, William C., Pres., Chief Exec. & Chief Oper. Officer--Gulfstream Holdings Corporation, Savannah, GA, pg. 494
Lublin, Barry, Chief Oper. Officer--The Cherokee Group, Sunland, CA, pg. 243
Ludington, David, Pres. & Chief Oper. Officer--Ludington News Co. Inc., Detroit, MI, pg. 686
Ludlam, Roger J., Pres. & Chief Oper. Officer--S. J. Groves & Sons Company, Minneapolis, MN, pg. 490
Ludwick, John A., Chief Oper. Officer & Exec. V.P.--Realty One, Cleveland, OH, pg. 917
Ludwig, William, Chief Oper. Officer & V.P.--Rice Growers Association of California, West Sacramento, CA, pg. 931
Ludwig, William R., V.P.-Quality & Info. Systems--Lord Corporation, Erie, PA, pg. 683
Luedtke, Marc, Chief Oper. Officer--SJL of Kansas Corp., Wichita, KS, pg. 962
Lunder, Peter, Pres., Chief Oper. Officer & Sec.--Dexter Shoe Company, Dexter, ME, pg. 334
Lunderstadt, Carl, Pres. & Chief Oper. Officer--Florida Crushed Stone Company, Leesburg, FL, pg. 420
Lunoi, Ken, Chief Oper. Officer & Exec. V.P.--Delta Education, Inc., Hudson, NH, pg. 326
Luntz, Andrew M., Chief Oper. Officer--Luntz Corporation, Canton, OH, pg. 687
Lutz, Merritt, Pres. & Chief Oper. Officer--Candle Corporation, Santa Monica, CA, pg. 214
Lynch, Robert M., Exec. V.P., Chief Oper. Officer--Carrafiello, Diehl & Associates, Inc., Irvington, NY, pg. 225
Lynnes, R. Milton, Pres. & Chief Oper. Officer--Grant/Jacoby, Inc., Chicago, IL, pg. 477
Macaskill, Bridget, Pres. & Chief Oper. Officer--Oppenheimer Management Corp., New York, NY, pg. 719
MacDonald, William F., Jr., Chm. Bd., Pres., Chief Exec. & Chief Oper. Officer--E. F. Houghton & Co., Valley Forge, PA, pg. 546
MacKenzie, Brian S., Pres. & Chief Oper. Officer--Builder Marts of America, Greenville, SC, pg. 187
MacLeod, Daniel E., Chief Oper. Officer & Asst. Gen. Mgr.--Cajun Electric Power Co-op, Baton Rouge, LA, pg. 207

Madeod, Tom, Pres. & Chief Oper. Officer--Iams Company, Dayton, OH, pg. 561
Madsen, Dennis, Exec. V.P. & Chief Oper. Officer--Recreational Equipment, Inc., Kent, WA, pg. 917
Maged, Jack, Pres. & Chief Oper. Officer--Cox Advertising, New York, NY, pg. 292
Magill, Brad R., Exec. V.P. & Chief Oper. Officer--Direct Response Broadcasting Network, Inc., Philadelphia, PA, pg. 339
Makhani, Madan P., Chm. Bd., Pres., Chief Oper. Officer & Chief Fin. Officer--American Foundry Group, Inc., Bixby, OK, pg. 54
Malkani, Roma, Pres. & Chief Exec. Officer--Information Systems & Network Corporation, Bethesda, MD, pg. 567
Malone, Joe N., Sr. V.P. & Chief Oper. Officer--Sound Warehouse, Inc., Dallas, TX, pg. 1018
Mang, Robert B., Pres. & Chief Oper. Officer--Woodward & Lothrop/John Wanamaker, Washington, DC, pg. 1201
Mangin, Joseph A., V.P., Chief Oper. & Chief Fin. Officer--Barr Brothers & Co., Inc., New York, NY, pg. 121
Marano, William, Chief Oper. Officer--Creative Technical Services, Farmingdale, NY, pg. 339
Marcalus, Nicholas R., Pres. & Chief Oper. Officer--Marcal Paper Mills, Inc., Elmwood Park, NJ, pg. 706
March, Ronald E., Exec. V.P. & Chief Oper. Officer--Cliggot Publishing, Greenwich, CT, pg. 255
Markle, Lewis E., Pres. & Chief Oper. Officer--Cowper & Siegfried, Amherst, NY, pg. 291
Marlow, Alan, Pres. & Chief Oper. Officer--Harvey Industries, Inc., Waltham, MA, pg. 515
Marquis, Douglas P., Pres. & Chief Oper. Officer--Handgards Inc., Northbrook, IL, pg. 504
Marshall, David, Chief Oper. Officer & V.P.-Fin.--Bigsby & Kruthers, Inc., Chicago, IL, pg. 150
Marstiller, Phyllis C., Pres. & Chief Oper. Officer--Blue Cross & Blue Shield of Virginia, Richmond, VA, pg. 160
Martens, Willard, V.P.-Fin., Treas. & Chief Oper. Officer--TSR, Inc., Lake Geneva, WI, pg. 1075
Martin, Earl, V.P.--J. H. Heafner Co. Inc., Lincolnton, NC, pg. 520
Martin, Gerry L., Pres. & Chief Oper. Officer--Horizon Paper Co., Inc., New York, NY, pg. 544
Martin, Rex, Pres. & Chief Exec. Officer--Nibco, Inc., Elkhart, IN, pg. 806
Martosko, Don, Chief Oper. Officer--Plibrico Co., Chicago, IL, pg. 877
Masket, David C., Exec. V.P. & Chief Oper. Officer--Maidenform, Inc., New York, NY, pg. 701
Maslin, Harvey L., Pres. & Chief Oper. Officer--Western Temporary Services, Inc., Walnut Creek, CA, pg. 1181
Mason, Marc, Co-Pres. & Chief Oper. Officer-Production Sector--Flambeau Products Corp., Middlefield, OH, pg. 809
Massalone, Daniel, V.P.-Sls.--Eastway Delivery Service of Houston, Inc., Houston, TX, pg. 364
Massaro, Mike, Exec. V.P., Chief Oper. Officer--Goldberg Moser O'Neill, San Francisco, CA, pg. 465
Massicott, Andre J., Pres. & Chief Oper. Officer--Heath Consultants Incorporated, Stoughton, MA, pg. 524
Mauney, Charles F., Exec. V.P. & Chief Oper. Officer--Mauney Hosiery Mills, Inc., Kings Mountain, NC, pg. 722
Maupin, Robert W., Pres. & Chief Oper. Officer--Shelter Mutual Insurance Company, Columbia, MO, pg. 997
Maurer, Gilbert C., Chief Oper. Officer & Exec. V.P.--The Hearst Corporation, New York, NY, pg. 521
Maurer, Gilbert C., Chief Oper. Officer & Exec. V.P.--Colonial Homes, New York, NY, pg. 523
Maxey, Thomas F., Vice Chm. & Chief Oper. Officer--N W Ayer Incorporated, New York, NY, pg. 103
Maxey, Thomas F., Vice Chm. & Chief Oper. Officer--N W Ayer Inc., New York, NY, pg. 104
May, Edward, V.P.-Opers.--Esskay Manufacturing Co., San Antonio, TX, pg. 389
May, Peter W., Pres. & Chief Oper. Officer--Trian Group, New York, NY, pg. 1111
Maziarka, Donald, Pres., Chief Exec. & Chief Oper. Officer--George Sollitt Construction, Wood Dale, IL, pg. 1017
McAndrews, J.J., Pres. & Chief Oper. Officer--Mona Industries, Inc., Paterson, NJ, pg. 764
McCaskey, Raymond F., Pres. & Chief Oper. Officer--Blue Cross & Blue Shield of Illinois, Chicago, IL, pg. 160
McCleary, Paul F., Dr., Exec. Dir. & Chief Oper. Officer--Christian Children's Fund, Inc., Richmond, VA, pg. 248
McClung, J. David, Pres. & Chief Oper. Officer--Green International, Inc., Denver, CO, pg. 484
McCollum, James, Chief Oper. Officer--Warren E. Collins, Inc., Braintree, MA, pg. 263
McConnell, William, Chief Oper. Officer--Resort Condominiums International, Indianapolis, IN, pg. 929
McCormick, Rick, V.P. & Chief Oper. Officer--Eastway Transportation Services, Inc., Houston, TX, pg. 364
McCormick, Rick, Pres. & Chief Oper. Officer--Eastway Air Cartage, Inc., Houston, TX, pg. 364
McCready, James P., Pres. & Chief Oper. Officer--The Brenlin Group, Akron, OH, pg. 173
McCullough, R.L., Pres., Chief Oper. Officer & Partner--E.H. Brown Advertising, Inc., Chicago, IL, pg. 181
McDaniel, R. Leon, Pres. & Chief Oper. Officer--Pioneer Oil Company Inc., Fort Worth, TX, pg. 872
McDonald, Kelli, Pres., Chief Oper. Officer--EvansGroup, Denver, CO, pg. 391
McDonald, Scott, Chief Oper. Officer--McDonald Equipment Co., Willoughby, OH, pg. 728
McFarland, Howard C., III, Chief Oper. Officer & Chief Fin. Officer--Mid-West Paper Products Company, Warren, MI, pg. 750
McIntyre, William D., Chief Oper. Officer--American Speedy Printing Centers, Inc., Bloomfield Hills, MI, pg. 61
McKee, Jack C., Exec. V.P. & Chief Oper. Officer--McKee Baking Co., Inc., Collegedale, TN, pg. 730
McKenna, P.W., Chm. Bd., Pres. & Chief Oper. Officer--Plasti-Kote Company Inc., Medina, OH, pg. 875
McKenna, Robert J., Pres. & Chief Oper. Officer--National Car Rental System, Inc., Minneapolis, MN, pg. 786
McKenna, Tom, Chief Oper. Officer--Moorman Mfg. Company, Quincy, IL, pg. 769
McKeon, Joe, Chief Oper. Officer & Group Pres.--Ancra Corporation, Hawthorne, CA, pg. 72
McLean, Howard, V.P.-Opers.--FDL Foods, Inc., Dubuque, IA, pg. 394
McMillan, Douglas, Pres. & Chief Oper. Officer--Allison-Erwin Co. Inc., Charlotte, NC, pg. 40
McMullen, Thomas, Pres. & Chief Oper. Officer--Unifax, Inc., Wilkes-Barre, PA, pg. 1126
McNeeley, Donald R., Pres. & Chief Oper. Officer--Chicago Tube & Iron Co., Chicago, IL, pg. 246
McSally, Michael J., Sr. V.P. & Chief Oper. Officer--John Hancock Property and Casualty Holding Co., Boston, MA, pg. 596
Meer, E. Harvey, Pres., Chief Oper. Officer & Treas.--Meer Corporation, North Bergen, NJ, pg. 736
Meli, Stephen, Chief Oper. Officer--Muro Pharmaceutical, Inc., Tewksbury, MA, pg. 776
Melnuk, Paul D., Pres. & Chief Oper. Officer--Clark Oil & Refining Corporation, Saint Louis, MO, pg. 252
Mendelow, Clive G., Chief Oper. Officer--Binswanger Advisory Services, Philadelphia, PA, pg. 151
Mercurio, Frank, Chief Oper. Officer & Exec. V.P.--McAdams, Richman & Ong, Inc., Bala-Cynwyd, PA, pg. 725
Merrell, John K., Pres., Chief Exec. Officer & Chief Oper. Officer--Industrial Dielectrics, Inc., Noblesville, IN, pg. 566
Meyer, Bernard, Pres. & Chief Oper. Officer--Allright Corporation, Houston, TX, pg. 41
Mezo, Linda, Pres. & Chief Oper. Officer--Keyes Martin, Springfield, NJ, pg. 627
Micale, Vincent J., Sr. V.P. & Chief Oper. Officer--Gerrity Co., Inc., Newton, MA, pg. 454
Milbrandt, M. E., Chief Oper. Officer--Lawson Associates Inc., Minneapolis, MN, pg. 663
Miles, John C., Pres. & Chief Oper. Officer--Dentsply International Inc., York, PA, pg. 329
Millard, Dan, Chm. Bd., Pres., Chief Exec. & Chief Oper. Officer--Central Illinois Steel Company, Carlinville, IL, pg. 232
Miller, Amy, Chief Oper. Officer--GSC Enterprises, Inc., Chicago, IL, pg. 440
Miller, Bill, Pres., Chief Exec. & Chief Oper. Officer--Contico International, Inc., Saint Louis, MO, pg. 278
Miller, Donald E., Pres. & Chief Oper. Officer--The Gates Corporation, Denver, CO, pg. 445
Miller, Donald E., Pres. & Chief Oper. Officer--The Gates Rubber Company, Denver, CO, pg. 445
Miller, Jeffrey S., V.P.-Opers., Chief Oper. Officer--Prentiss Incorporated, Floral Park, NY, pg. 887
Mills, John, Pres. & Chief Oper. Officer--Medline Industries, Inc., Mundelein, IL, pg. 736
Mims, T.J., Pres., Chief Exec. & Chief Oper. Officer--Canal Insurance Co., Greenville, SC, pg. 213
Minson, Arthur T., Chief Oper. Officer & Gen. Mgr.--Georgette Klinger, Inc., New York, NY, pg. 635
Miranda, Jose J., Chief Oper. Officer & Exec. V.P.--Gator Industries Inc., Hialeah, FL, pg. 446
Mitchell, Danny, Pres. & Chief Oper. Officer--Godwin Advertising Agency, Inc., Jackson, MS, pg. 464
Mitchell, J., Exec. V.P. & Chief Oper. Officer--Versa Services Ltd., Etobicoke,, Canada, pg. 7
Mitchell, Stephen C., Pres. & Chief Oper. Officer--Lester B. Knight & Associates, Inc., Chicago, IL, pg. 637
Mockley, Michael E., Exec. V.P. & Chief Oper. Officer--Anchor Gasoline Corporation, Tulsa, OK, pg. 71
Modell, Mitchell B., Chief Oper. Officer--Henry Modell & Company, Inc., Long Island City, NY, pg. 762
Moe, Henrik, Pres., Chief Oper. & Exec. Officer--DEC International, Inc., Madison, WI, pg. 308
Moeller, Richard J., Pres.--Advanstar Communications, Cleveland, OH, pg. 21
Moffett, George, Chief Oper. Officer--Wolfer Printing Company, City of Commerce, CA, pg. 1199
Mollman, Robert E., Chief Oper. Officer--Molded Fiber Glass Companies, Ashtabula, OH, pg. 763
Monette, Edward A., Chm., Pres., Chief Exec. & Oper. Officer--St. Croix Press, Inc., New Richmond, WI, pg. 966
Monk, Albert C., III, Pres. & Chief Oper. Officer--A.C. Monk Co., Inc., Farmville, NC, pg. 766
Monk, Richard H., Jr., Pres. & Chief Oper. Officer--Avondale Mills, Inc., Sylacauga, AL, pg. 103
Monks, Richard, Pres., Chief Exec. Officer & Chief Oper. Officer--ConTec International, Schenectady, NY, pg. 278
Monnin, Michelle, Chief Oper. Officer--EMS-West, Irvine, CA, pg. 370
Moon, Wayne, Pres. & Chief Oper. Officer--Kaiser Foundation Health & Hospitals Group, Oakland, CA, pg. 614
Mooney, Edward P., V.P. & Chief Oper. Officer--Monsey Products Company, Kimberton, PA, pg. 766
Moore, Frank, Exec. V.P. & Chief Oper. Officer--McCall Oil & Chemical Corp., Portland, OR, pg. 726
Moore, George C., Chief Oper. Officer--Moore Company, Westerly, RI, pg. 768
Moore, James T., II, Pres. & Chief Oper. Officer--Invetech Co., Detroit, MI, pg. 581
Moore, Michael D., Exec. V.P. & Chief Oper. Officer--Capital Bank of California, Los Angeles, CA, pg. 214
Moore, P.J., Sr. V.P., Chief Oper. Officer, Chief Fin. Officer, Sec. & Treas.--Green Holdings, Inc., Denver, CO, pg. 484
Moorehead, George, V.P. & Chief Oper. Officer--Tollycraft Yachts Corp., Kelso, WA, pg. 1100
Mora, Dick, Chief Oper. Officer--Pharmavite Corp., Mission Hills, CA, pg. 866
Morchower, Donald L., Exec. V.P. & Chief Oper. Officer--Empire Blue Cross & Blue Shield, New York, NY, pg. 379
Morelli, Michael, Chief Oper. Officer--Littleton Coin Co., Inc., Littleton, NH, pg. 679
Morgan, Jerry, Pres. & Chief Oper. Officer--Sargent & Greenleaf, Inc., Nicholasville, KY, pg. 971
Morgan, Lloyd H., Pres. & Chief Oper. Officer--The Gage Company, Pittsburgh, PA, pg. 441
Morley, Francis W., Chief Oper. Officer--Midland Paper Co., Chicago, IL, pg. 751
Morris, Andrew, Pres. & Chief Oper. Officer--Warner, Bicking, Morris & Partners, Inc., New York, NY, pg. 1164
Morris, Glynn, Pres. & Chief Oper. Officer--Presto Food Products, Inc., City of Industry, CA, pg. 888
Morris, T.N., Jr., Chm., Pres. & Chief Exec. Officer--Calcasieu Lumber Company, Austin, TX, pg. 208
Morrow, David W., Chm. Bd., Pres., Chief Exec. Officer & Chief Oper. Officer--Pueblo International, Inc., Pompano Beach, FL, pg. 899
Morton, Sandi, V.P.-Opers.--Visible Changes, Houston, TX, pg. 1153
Mossberg, Alan I., Pres., Chief Exec. & Chief Oper. Officer & Treas.--O. F. Mossberg & Sons, Inc., North Haven, CT, pg. 773
Mosser, Thomas J., Vice Chm. & Chief Oper. Officer Worldwide (London)--Burson-Marsteller, New York, NY, pg. 1210
Muller, Frank, Exec. V.P. & Co-Chief Oper. Officer--U.S. Divers Co., Inc., Santa Ana, CA, pg. 1135
Mullin, Francis I., Pres. & Chief Oper. Officer--The Seven-Up Company, Dallas, TX, pg. 342
Mullinex, Travis, Pres. & Chief Oper. Officer--Tri Valley Growers Inc., San Francisco, CA, pg. 1111
Mullis, Elbert N., Jr., Exec. V.P. & Chief Admin. & Fin. Officer--Coca Cola Bottling Co. United, Inc., Birmingham, AL, pg. 257
Murphy, Cathy, Dir.-MIS--Octagon Process Inc., Edgewater, NJ, pg. 821
Murray, Ralph D., V.P.-Mktg. & Sls. & Chief Oper. Officer--Schwinn Bicycle Company, Chicago, IL, pg. 981
Murray, Vince, Pres. & Chief Oper. Officer--Fleer Corporation, Mount Laurel, NJ, pg. 695
Myhren, Trygve, Pres. & Chief Oper. Officer--Providence Journal Company, Providence, RI, pg. 895
Nally, Michael J., Exec. V.P. & Chief Oper. Officer--General Sportcraft Company Ltd., Bergenfield, NJ, pg. 450
Naszada, Hans, Chief Oper. Officer--Dr. Puttner & BSB Worldwide Werbegesellschaft m.b.H., Vienna,, Austria, pg. 111
Neely, Bill, Pres. & Chief Oper. Officer--M. B. Kahn Construction Co., Inc., Columbia, SC, pg. 614
Nelson, G. F., Pres.--Willamette-Western Corporation, Portland, OR, pg. 1190
Nelson, Jack, Pres. & Chief Oper. Officer--Allied Systems, Ltd., Decatur, GA, pg. 40
Nelson, Roscoe, Co-Chief Oper. Officer--Allright Carolina, Inc., Greensboro, NC, pg. 41
Nenno, David J., Exec. V.P. & Gen. Mgr.--Standard-Thomson Corporation, Waltham, MA, pg. 1037
Newberry, Richard A., Pres. & Chief Oper. Officer--Starcraft Automotive Corp., Goshen, IN, pg. 1040
Newell, Robert, Chief Oper. Officer--TV Host Inc., Harrisburg, PA, pg. 1075
Nickel, Albert G., Pres. & Chief Oper. Officer--Dorritie Lyons & Nickel, Inc., New York, NY, pg. 347
Niemiec, Edward W., Grp. V.P.-Opers. & Chief Oper. Officer--American Institute of C.P.A.'s Inc., New York, NY, pg. 56
Nienow, Lance, Chief Oper. Officer--Weinbrenner Shoe Company, Inc., Merrill, WI, pg. 1173
Nixon, James R., Exec. V.P. & Chief Oper. Officer--Shamrock Broadcasting, Inc., Burbank, CA, pg. 994
Norbitz, Wayne, Pres. & Chief Oper. Officer--Nathan's Famous Inc., Westbury, NY, pg. 784
Norris, T.H., V.P.-Opers.--Colonial Pipeline Company, Atlanta, GA, pg. 264
Norton, Robert R., Jr., Exec. V.P., Chief Oper. & Fin. Officer--BeefAmerica Operating Co., Inc., Omaha, NE, pg. 131
Noseworthy, Heber L., Pres. & Chief Oper. Officer--ACO Inc., Farmington Hills, MI, pg. 2
O'Donnell, Patrick J., Chief Oper. Officer, Treas. & Gen. Mgr.--National Grape Co-Op Association, Inc., Westfield, NY, pg. 789
O'Hagan, Mike, Exec. V.P. & Chief Oper. Officer--Combustion Power Company, Menlo Park, CA, pg. 267
O'Keefe, Tim, Chief Oper. Officer--Rangen Aquaculture Research, Buhl, ID, pg. 912
O'Neal, Emmet, III, Vice Chm. & Chief Oper. Officer--O'Neal Steel Inc., Birmingham, AL, pg. 827
O'Neill, Anthony, V.P. & Chief Oper. Officer--National Fire Protection Association, Quincy, MA, pg. 788
O'Reilly, Paul, Exec. V.P. & Chief Oper. Officer--Arley Merchandise Corporation, Taunton, MA, pg. 83
O'Shea, Daniel, Chief Oper. Officer--Bill Communications, Inc., New York, NY, pg. 150
Oberman, Larry, Exec. V.P. & Chief Oper. Officer--Aster Nut Products Inc., Newark, NJ, pg. 92
Oblom, Neil R., V.P.-Opers. & Chief Oper. Officer--Hold-E-Zee, Ltd., Rochester, NY, pg. 239
Ogilvie, Donald, Exec. V.P. & Chief Oper. Officer--The American Bankers Association, Washington, DC, pg. 49
Ogle, D. Clark, Chm. Bd., Pres., Chief Exec. & Chief Oper. Officer--Peter J. Schmitt Holdings, West Seneca, NY, pg. 976
Olin, Larry G., Pres., Chief Oper. Officer & Treas.--Humiston-Keeling, Inc., Chicago, IL, pg. 552
Olsen, David A., Chm., Pres., Chief Exec. & Chief Oper. Officer--Johnson & Higgins, New York, NY, pg. 598
Olsewski, Paul, V.P.-Opers. & Corp. Sec.--SB Entertainment Inc., New Providence, NJ, pg. 960
Olson, Frank A., Chm. Bd., Chief Exec. & Oper. Officer--The Hertz Corporation, Park Ridge, NJ, pg. 849
Orczyk, Stanley R., Chm. & Chief Oper. Officer--Meenan Oil Co. Limited Partnership, Syosset, NY, pg. 736
Orr, Donald, Exec. V.P., Chief Oper. Officer & Gen. Mgr.--Amperif Corporation, Chatsworth, CA, pg. 68

Ostendorf, Bob, Pres. & Chief Exec. Officer--VMC Fiberglass Products Inc., Daleville, AL, pg. 1142
Pachulski, Sheila, V.P.-Support Services--Prime Technology, Inc., Grand Rapids, MI, pg. 889
Paci, Gabriel, Chief Oper. Officer & V.P.--Raffi & Swanson, Inc., Wilmington, MA, pg. 909
Page, James, Co-Pres. & Chief Oper. Officer--Mission Industries, Santa Barbara, CA, pg. 760
Paglia, James A., Exec. V.P., Chief Oper. Officer--Tassani Communications, Chicago, IL, pg. 1080
Paige, Richard, Sr. V.P. & Chief Oper. Officer--Pro Hardware, Inc., Englewood, CO, pg. 891
Paletz, Lenn, Chm., Pres., Chief Exec. & Chief Oper. Officer--The Sportsman's Guide, Inc., Eagan, MN, pg. 1032
Palles, Allen P., Sr. V.P., Chief Oper. Officer & Gen. Counsel--The LINC Group, Inc., Chicago, IL, pg. 648
Pamplin, Dr. Robert B., Jr., Pres., Chief Oper. Officer & Sec.--R. B. Pamplin Corp., Portland, OR, pg. 844
Parks, Raymond F., Pres. & Chief Oper. Officer--J. H. Fletcher & Co., Huntington, WV, pg. 418
Parsons, Robert F., Pres. & Chief Oper. Officer--Hajoca Corp., Ardmore, PA, pg. 500
Parten, Steve, Pres. & Chief Oper. Officer--Bromar Inc., Newport Beach, CA, pg. 179
Patterson, Charles, Pres., Chief Exec. Officer & Chief Oper. Officer--Walman Optical Company, Minneapolis, MN, pg. 1161
Patterson, Kent E., Chief Oper. Officer--The ERM Group, Exton, PA, pg. 360
Patterson, William, Chief Oper. Officer & Sr. V.P.--Rundel Products, Inc., Portland, OR, pg. 956
Paul, Douglas, Pres. & Chief Oper. Officer--American Learning Corp., Chicago, IL, pg. 381
Payne, B.E., Exec. V.P. & Chief Oper. Officer--T. H. Rogers Lumber Co. Inc., Oklahoma City, OK, pg. 943
Pendergrast, Ross, Exec. V.P. & Chief Oper. Officer--Donrey Media Group, Fort Smith, AR, pg. 345
Perez, Jean-Yves, Pres. & Chief Exec. Officer--Woodward-Clyde International, Denver, CO, pg. 1201
Perez, Lombardo, Chm. Bd., Pres. & Chief Oper. Officer--Metro Ford Inc., Miami, FL, pg. 743
Perkins, C.M., Gen. Mgr.--Salt River Project Agricultural Improvement and Power District, Tempe, AZ, pg. 967
Perkins, Larry, Chief Oper. Officer--Redmond Products, Inc., Chanhassen, MN, pg. 920
Perks, Douglas,, Pres. & Chief Oper. Officer--Eclipse, Inc., Rockford, IL, pg. 366
Perlmuter, Richard M., Pres. & Chief Exec. Officer--Perlmuter Printing Company, Cleveland, OH, pg. 862
Perry, Dan, V.P. & Chief Oper. Officer--All American Bottling Corp., Oklahoma City, OK, pg. 35
Perry, Egbert L., Pres. & Chief Oper. Officer--H. J. Russell Corp., Atlanta, GA, pg. 957
Peters, Robert C., Pres. & Chief Oper. Officer--New World Entertainment, Inc., Los Angeles, CA, pg. 74
Petersen, Fred M., Pres., Chief Exec. Officer & Chief Oper. Officer--Omaha Public Power District, Omaha, NE, pg. 825
Petersen, K.C., Pres. & Chief Oper. Officer--Schenectady Chemicals, Inc., Schenectady, NY, pg. 975
Petrik, Alan W., Chief Oper. Officer--Archibald Candy Company, Chicago, IL, pg. 604
Petteway, Dave A., Chief Oper. Officer & Exec. V.P.--United Health Plan, Inglewood, CA, pg. 1133
Phillips, Delmar, V.P. & Chief Oper. Officer--Campbell Oil Co., Massillon, OH, pg. 213
Piatt, Lou, Exec. V.P. & Chief Oper. Officer--Jon Douglas Company, Beverly Hills, CA, pg. 347
Picini, Dan E., Chm. Bd., Pres. & Chief Oper. Officer--Duro-Test Corporation, Fairfield, NJ, pg. 355
Pierce, Harvey, Pres. & Chief Oper. Officer--American Family Mutual Insurance Co., Madison, WI, pg. 51
Pierce, James L., Chief Oper. Officer--ARINC Research Corp., Annapolis, MD, pg. 82
Pietila, Keith, Chief Oper. Officer--Acorn Building Components Inc., Detroit, MI, pg. 13
Pingree, Clyde, Chief Oper. Officer--Saunders Brothers, Westbrook, ME, pg. 972
Piper, Peter A., Pres. & Chief Oper. Officer--American Eagle Airlines, Chicago, IL, pg. 51
Pirrung, Mark, Chief Oper. Offcier--Atlanta Beverage Co., Atlanta, GA, pg. 94
Pittman, Gary, Chm. Bd., Pres., Chief Exec., Chief Oper. & Chief Fin. Officer--PCI, Austin, TX, pg. 836
Pittman, Gary, Chief Oper. Officer--Software Video Production, Austin, TX, pg. 836
Plamondon, William, Exec. V.P. & Chief Oper. Officer--Beech Holdings Corp., Chicago, IL, pg. 131
Platt, Charles, Pres. & Chief Oper. Officer--Alamo Rent-A-Car Inc., Fort Lauderdale, FL, pg. 30
Plodinec, Tim, Chief Oper. Officer--H. Salt Seafood Restaurants, Monterey Park, CA, pg. 967
Poehlmann, Karl M., Pres. & Chief Exec. Officer--George Uhe Co., Inc., Paramus, NJ, pg. 1125
Poignard, John M., V.P.-Opers. & Mfg. & Chief Oper. Officer--E.P. Henry Corporation, Woodbury, NJ, pg. 530
Pokarczyk, George, Pres. & Chief Oper. Officer--Duling Optical Corporation, Louisville, KY, pg. 352
Polera, Anthony, Chief Exec., Chief Oper. & Info. Officer--Polera Building Corp., Scarsdale, NY, pg. 878
Polk, Stephen R., Pres. & Chief Oper. Officer--R. L. Polk & Co., Detroit, MI, pg. 879
Pollaok, Robert, Chief Oper. Officer--Page Boy Company, Inc., Dallas, TX, pg. 843
Pollard, Frank, Pres. & Chief Oper. Officer--GenDerm Corporation, Lincolnshire, IL, pg. 448
Pollnow, Charles, Chm. Bd., Chief Exec. & Oper. Officer--The Brulin Corporation, Indianapolis, IN, pg. 184
Porress, Steve, Chief Oper. Officer & Mng. Dir.--Pacific States Casualty Co., Los Angeles, CA, pg. 841
Porter, Robert L., Pres. & Chief Oper. Officer--Oliver Products Company, Grand Rapids, MI, pg. 824
Portman, John C., Jr., Chief Oper. Officer--Atlanta Market Center, Atlanta, GA, pg. 94
Posinski, Frank J., Pres. & Chief Oper. Officer--Cincinnati Gear Company, Cincinnati, OH, pg. 250
Posner, Peter S., Pres., Chief Oper. Officer, New Bus. Contact--Newmark, Posner & Mitchell, Inc., New York, NY, pg. 804
Potkin, Harvey, Pres. & Chief Oper. Officer--National Foods Inc., Bronx, NY, pg. 788
Powell, John, Pres. & Chief Oper. Officer--P. Lawson Travel, Ltd., Islington,, Canada, pg. 221
Powers, James R., Chief Oper. Officer--CS First Boston Pacific, Inc., New York, NY, pg. 204
Prentice, Daniel F., Pres. & Chief Oper. Officer--Generra Sportswear Company, Inc., Tukwila, WA, pg. 451
Pressman, James R., Pres. & Chief Oper. Officer--Pressman Toy Corp., New York, NY, pg. 887
Pressman, Robert, V.P. & Chief Oper. Officer--Barneys New York, New York, NY, pg. 120
Prince, R.S., Pres. & Chief Oper. Officer--Central States Diversified, Inc., Saint Louis, MO, pg. 234
Pulitzer, Sidney C., Chm. Bd. & Chief Oper. Officer--Wemco, Inc., New Orleans, LA, pg. 1176
Pulk, Mike, Exec. V.P.--Winona Knits, Winona, MN, pg. 1196
Purcell, Robert, Chief Oper. Officer & Chief Fin. Officer--ERA Real Estate, Overland Park, KS, pg. 360
Purdon, Philip, Chief Oper. Officer--Bordelais, Lemeunier & Leo Burnett, Clichy,, France, pg. 192
Purpura, Vicment M., Pres. & Chief Oper. Officer--D.A. Davidson & Co., Great Falls, MT, pg. 318
Puschel, Gerald W., Pres. & Chief Oper. Officer--F. Schumacher & Co., New York, NY, pg. 979
Quinlan, Donald P., Chm. Bd., Pres., Chief Exec. & Chief Oper. Officer--Graphic Controls Corporation, Buffalo, NY, pg. 478
Quinn, Jay, Pres. & Chief Oper. Officer--Eric Mower and Associates, Inc., Syracuse, NY, pg. 774
Quinn, Patrick M., Pres., Chief Exec. Officer & Chief Oper. Officer--Spartan Stores Inc., Grand Rapids, MI, pg. 1026
Quinn, William, Pres. & Chief Oper. Officer--Dana Perfumes Corp., New York, NY, pg. 313
Radwill, Scott, Pres., Chief Exec. & Chief Oper. Officer-Export--Master Appliance Corp., Racine, WI, pg. 719
Ragains, Charles C., Exec. V.P. & Chief Oper. Officer--Anthony M. Franco Inc., Detroit, MI, pg. 950
Ragsdale, M. Terry, Exec. V.P. & Chief Oper. Officer--Southern States Cooperative, Inc., Richmond, VA, pg. 1022
Rainville, Donald, Pres. & Chief Oper. Officer--Universal Dynamics Inc., Woodbridge, VA, pg. 1138
Raisbeck, David W., Chief Oper. Officer--Cargill Financial Markets Div., Minneapolis, MN, pg. 219
Rankin, Jim, Chief Oper. Officer--Forecast Mortgage Corporation, Rancho Cucamonga, CA, pg. 423
Rasband, Ronald A., Pres. & Chief Oper. Officer--Huntsman Chemical Corporation, Salt Lake City, UT, pg. 555
Ratcliff, P.S., Sr. V.P.-Sls. & Opers.--Standard Lafarge, Canfield, OH, pg. 1036
Ratliff, Don, Pres. & Chief Oper. Officer--Gouchenour Adv., Inc., Orlando, FL, pg. 473
Ratliff, Robert J., Pres. & Chief Exec. Officer--Hesston, Norcross, GA, pg. 4
Rauenhorst, Mark, Pres. & Chief Oper. Officer--OPUS Corp., Minnetonka, MN, pg. 828
Rauenhorst, Neil, Pres.--Opus South Corporation, Tampa, FL, pg. 828
Ray, Bill F., Pres., Chief Exec. Officer & Chief Oper. Officer--Binning's Building Products, Inc., Lexington, NC, pg. 151
Rayner, Mitch A., V.P., Chief Oper. Officer & Sec.--Performance Contractors Inc., Baton Rouge, LA, pg. 861
Redies, R. Edward, Chief Oper. Officer--Saline Investment Co., Saline, MI, pg. 906
Reed, William D., Pres. & Chief Oper. Officer--Computer Corporation of America, Cambridge, MA, pg. 884
Reemer, Steven I., Pres. & Chief Oper. Officer--Radix Corporation, Salt Lake City, UT, pg. 909
Reeves, E.F., IV, Sr. V.P. & Gen. Mgr.--Pioneer/Eclipse Corp., Sparta, NC, pg. 871
Reid, Connie, Pres. & Chief Oper. Officer--Bradley Communications, Inc., Anchorage, AK, pg. 170
Reller, Charles E., Exec. V.P., Chief Oper. Officer--Hutchins/Young & Rubicam, Rochester, NY, pg. 1211
Remensperger, Thomas, Pres. & Chief Oper. Officer--Ninteman Construction Company, Inc., San Diego, CA, pg. 1060
Rhodes, Barry, Chief Oper. Officer--Turner Machine Company, Salem, OH, pg. 373
Rice, Linda Johnson, Pres. & Chief Oper. Officer--Johnson Publishing Company, Inc., Chicago, IL, pg. 598
Rice, Sam, Exec. V.P. & Chief Oper. Officer--T. J. Cinnamons Ltd., Kansas City, MO, pg. 1073
Richard, J.E., Chm. Bd. & Chief Oper. Officer--Tennessee Wholesale Drug Company, Nashville, TN, pg. 1088
Richard, Russell R., Pres. & Chief Oper. Officer--Pacific Scene Inc., San Diego, CA, pg. 841
Richards, Craig, Pres., Chief Oper. Officer & Treas.--Jeffrey Michael, Kirkland, WA, pg. 591
Richards, Penny, Chief Oper. Officer & Exec. V.P.--Joan Fabrics Corp., Tyngsboro, MA, pg. 594
Riegert, Theodore, V.P.-Opers.--Plastic Suppliers, Inc., Columbus, OH, pg. 875
Riggio, Stephen, Exec. V.P. & Chief Oper. Officer--B. Dalton Bookseller, Inc., New York, NY, pg. 120
Rinard, R. E., Pres. & Chief Oper. Officer--Pacific Enterprises Oil Company (USA), Dallas, TX, pg. 840
Rink, Robert J., Chief Oper. Officer--Prestige Stamping, Inc., Warren, MI, pg. 888
Riordan, Michael T., Pres. & Chief Oper. Officer--Fort Howard Corporation, Green Bay, WI, pg. 425
Ripley, Richard L., Pres. & Chief Oper. Officer--First American Bank of Virginia, McLean, VA, pg. 412
Ritchason, Marvin, Chief Oper. Officer & Gen. Mgr.--Ray-Carroll County Grain Co-op, Richmond, MO, pg. 914
Ritter, Michael J., Pres. & Chief Oper. Officer--Continental Cablevision, Boston, MA, pg. 278
Robb, D.H., Pres. & Chief Oper. Officer--Chittenden & Eastman Co., Burlington, IA, pg. 248
Robbins, Paul, Chief Oper. Officer--Christianity Today, Inc., Carol Stream, IL, pg. 249
Roberson, Gregg C., Sr. V.P. & Chief Oper. Officer--Drug Emporium of Arizona, Inc., Scottsdale, AZ, pg. 349
Roberts, C. J., Jr., Pres., Chief Oper. Officer & Treas.--The Leavell Company, El Paso, TX, pg. 664
Roberts, David, Pres. & Chief Oper. Officer--Doran Textiles Inc., Shelby, NC, pg. 346
Roberts, David, Pres. & Chief Oper. Officer--Doran Mill Co., Shelby, NC, pg. 346
Roberts, Gary, Pres., Chief Oper. Officer--Greenstone Roberts Advertising, Melville, NY, pg. 485
Roberts, James E., Exec. V.P. & Chief Oper. Officer--Avedis Zildjian Company, Norwell, MA, pg. 1219
Roberts, Paul J., Pres. & Chief Oper. Officer--Carco Electronics, Menlo Park, CA, pg. 217
Roberts, Tom, Chief Oper. Officer--Gator Freightways, Inc., Wilmington, OH, pg. 446
Robertson, Walter, Exec. V.P. & Chief Oper. Officer--American Steel & Wire Corporation, Cuyahoga Heights, OH, pg. 246
Robinson, Robert J., Exec. V.P. & Chief Oper. Officer--AXIA Incorporated, Oak Brook, IL, pg. 8
Robinson, Ron, Pres. & Chief Oper. Officer--Cranford Johnson Robinson Woods, Little Rock, AR, pg. 296
Roe, K. Keith, Chm. Bd., Pres., Chief Exec. & Chief Oper. Officer--Burns & Roe Enterprises, Inc., Oradell, NJ, pg. 194
Rogers, Kenneth R., Pres. & Chief Oper. Officer--Backer Spielvogel Bates, Inc., New York, NY, pg. 108
Rolla, M.F., Pres. & Chief Oper. Officer--Gem Industries Finance Corporation, Toccoa, GA, pg. 447
Rolla, M.F., Pres. & Chief Oper. Officer--Gem Industries, Inc., Gardner, MA, pg. 447
Ronco, Al, Chief Oper. Officer, Exec. V.P., & Sec.--Keystone Automotive Industries, Inc., Pomona, CA, pg. 627
Rork, Daniel R., V.P. & Chief Oper. Officer--Fabreeka International, Inc., Stoughton, MA, pg. 396
Rosen, Jack, Chm., Pres., Chief Exec. & Chief Oper. Officer--Hazel Bishop Corporation, Englewood Cliffs, NJ, pg. 520
Rosen, Theodore A., Pres. & Chief Oper. Officer--Raymond Rosen Co., Conshohocken, PA, pg. 948
Rosenbach, W.H., V.P.-Opers.--National Frozen Foods Corp., Seattle, WA, pg. 789
Rosskam, Skip, III, Pres. & Chief Oper. Officer--David Michael & Co. Inc., Philadelphia, PA, pg. 747
Roth, John, V.P.-Opers.--Action Instruments, Inc., San Diego, CA, pg. 14
Roth, Michael I., Pres., Chief Oper. Officer & Chief Exec. Officer--The Mutual Life Insurance Company of New York (MONY), New York, NY, pg. 778
Roy, Dennis, Chief Oper. Officer & Dir., Mktg. Services--BEC Advertising, Chicago, IL, pg. 106
Rubin, Richard, Chm., Pres., Chief Exec. & Chief Oper. Officer--Donnkenny, Inc., New York, NY, pg. 345
Rubin, Robert E., Co-Chm. & Sr. Partner--Goldman, Sachs & Co., New York, NY, pg. 468
Rucker, Adin H., Jr., Pres. & Treas.--Stonecutter Mills Corp., Spindale, NC, pg. 1051
Runk, Lee H., Pres. & Chief Oper. Officer--Harvard Industries, Inc., Farmingdale, NJ, pg. 514
Russick, John, V.P., Chief Oper. Officer--National Out-of-Home Media/Metro 8, New York, NY, pg. 792
Russillo, Thomas R., Pres. & Chief Oper. Officer--Ben Venue Laboratories, Inc., Bedford, OH, pg. 138
Ryals, Donald L., Pres. & Chief Oper. Officer--Network Capital Group, Campbell, CA, pg. 798
Ryan, John J., Pres. & Chief Oper. Officer--Charan Realty Group, Garden City, NY, pg. 239
Ryan, Kevin J., Pres. & Chief Oper. Officer--Bowling Corp. of America, Garden City, NY, pg. 239
Ryan, Tom, Exec. V.P.-Opers.--United Refrigerated Services, Atlanta, GA, pg. 1134
Sabath, Robert E., Pres. & Chief Oper. Officer--Knight/Emerson Consulting, Inc., Chicago, IL, pg. 637
Sabbatino, Anthony, Pres., Chief Oper. & Chief Exec. Officer--Bogue Electric Manufacturing Co., Paterson, NJ, pg. 162
Sachse, Richard, Chief Oper. Officer--Field Container Company, L.P., Elk Grove Village, IL, pg. 409
Sack, Thomas F., Pres., Chief Exec. & Oper. Officer--Haddon Craftsmen, Inc., Scranton, PA, pg. 499
Sadler, Ian, Chief Oper. Officer--Johnstown Corporation, Johnstown, PA, pg. 601
Saginaw, David, Pres. & Chief Oper. Officer--Roytex, Inc., New York, NY, pg. 953
Sakane, Masahiro, Pres. & Chief Oper. Officer--Komatsu Dresser Company, Lincolnshire, IL, pg. 565
Sakosits, John J., Chm. Bd., Chief Exec. & Chief Oper. Officer--Hoboken Wood Flooring Corporation, Wayne, NJ, pg. 537
Salanski, C.W., Chief Oper. Officer--Leschen Wire Rope, Saint Joseph, MO, pg. 1197
Salter, Michael, Pres. & Chief Oper. Officer--Beno's, Los Angeles, CA, pg. 139
Salway, Roger A., Chief Oper. Officer & Exec. V.P.--Paper Calmenson & Co., Saint Paul, MN, pg. 847
Sandalls, William T., Chief Oper. Officer--Mastercard International, Inc., New York, NY, pg. 720
Sander, Steven J., V.P.-Store Opers.--Dunham's Athleisure Corporation, Waterford, MI, pg. 353
Sanders, O'Neil, Chm. Bd., Pres., Chief Exec. & Chief Oper. Officer--Associated Petroleum Carriers, Spartanburg, SC, pg. 91
Sanderson, Sam, Chief Oper. Officer--Sanderson Plumbing Products Inc., Columbus, MS, pg. 970
Santelman, Roger D., Chief Oper. Officer--Hammel, Green & Abrahamson, Inc., Minneapolis, MN, pg. 504

Sardina, Eduardo M., Exec. V.P. & Chief Oper. Officer--Bacardi Imports, Inc., Miami, FL, pg. 108
Scarlett, Joseph, Pres. & Chief Oper. Officer--TSC Industries, Inc., Nashville, TN, pg. 1075
Schardt, Ronald, Chm. Bd., Chief Exec. Officer & Chief Oper. Officer--Reinke Manufacturing Co., Inc., Deshler, NE, pg. 924
Schenk, Tony, Chm. Bd., Pres. & Chief Exec. Officer--Enabling Technologies Company, Stuart, FL, pg. 380
Schichtel, Gerald F., Pres. & Chief Oper. Officer--Hilliard Corporation, Elmira, NY, pg. 535
Schick, Joseph C., Chm. Bd., Pres., Chief Exec. Officer & Chief Oper. Officer--Raub Supply Company, Lancaster, PA, pg. 913
Schiefler, Roger, Chm. & Chief Oper. Officer--Dieline Corporation, Kentwood, MI, pg. 336
Schimmenti, Michael R., Pres. & Chief Oper. Officer--Griffin Corporation, Valdosta, GA, pg. 487
Schindler, Mark, Chief Oper. Officer--Gem Southeast, Inc., Toccoa, GA, pg. 447
Schlotfeldt, Ken, V.P. & Chief Oper. Officer--Badger Air Brush Company, Franklin Park, IL, pg. 113
Schlueter, John J., Chm. Bd. & Chief Exec. Officer--Knapp Shoes Inc., Brockton, MA, pg. 636
Schmid, Charles W., Pres. & Chief Oper. Officer--Carlson Travel Group, Inc., Minneapolis, MN, pg. 221
Schneeberger, Donald G., Pres. & Chief Oper. Officer--H. C. Miller Company, Milwaukee, WI, pg. 754
Schnuck, Craig, Chm. Bd. & Chief Exec. Officer--Schnuck Markets, Inc., Maryland Heights, MO, pg. 977
Schnuck, Scott, Pres. & Chief Oper. Officer--Schnuck Markets, Inc., Maryland Heights, MO, pg. 977
Schofield, Dave, Sr. V.P.-Opers. & Chief Oper. Officer--Pip Printing, Agoura Hills, CA, pg. 616
Schrager, Harley, Pres. & Chief Oper. Officer--Pacesetter Corporation, Omaha, NE, pg. 839
Schreier, Bradley, Pres. & Chief Oper. Officer--Taylor Corporation, Mankato, MN, pg. 1081
Schriber, Maurice N., Chief Oper. Officer--System Planning Corp., Arlington, VA, pg. 1070
Schroeder, James, Exec. V.P. & Chief Oper. Officer--Sid Tool Co. Inc., Plainview, NY, pg. 1002
Schulte, Fred, Chief Oper. Officer--Cablevision Industries Corp., Liberty, NY, pg. 206
Schulte, Fred C., Pres. & Chief Exec. Officer--Elgin National Industries, Inc., Chicago, IL, pg. 609
Schultz, Randy, Exec. V.P. & Chief Oper. Officer--IGI Resources, Inc., Boise, ID, pg. 575
Schulze, Horst, Pres. & Chief Oper. Officer--W.B. Johnson Property, Inc., Atlanta, GA, pg. 598
Schwartz, Barry K., Chm. Bd. & Chief Oper. Officer--Calvin Klein, Inc., New York, NY, pg. 635
Schwartz, Norman S., Chm. Bd. & Chief Oper. Officer--Charron, Schwartz & Partners, Inc., New York, NY, pg. 240
Schwartz, Steven, Chief Oper. Officer--Doe Spun, Inc., New York, NY, pg. 343
Schwesig, N.L., Pres.--Maritz Inc., Fenton, MO, pg. 707
Scott, Billy D., Chief Oper. Officer--Allright Corporation of Delaware, Phoenix, AZ, pg. 41
Scott, John, Chief Oper. Officer--Allright Parking of Georgia, Inc., Savannah, GA, pg. 42
Scott, Michael D., Chief Oper. Officer & Creative Dir.--CoMed Communications Division, Philadelphia, PA, pg. 1092
Scroggin, Webster, Sr. V.P.-Opers.--Amperif Corporation, Chatsworth, CA, pg. 68
Seitz, Melvin C., Jr., Pres., Chief Exec. Officer, Chief Oper. Officer & Controller--Service Supply Co. Inc. of Indiana, Indianapolis, IN, pg. 992
Self, W.M., Pres. & Chief Oper. Officer--Greenwood Mills, Inc., Greenwood, SC, pg. 485
Serulneck, Lester, V.P.-Admin. & Sls.--Allmetal Screw Products Corp., Edgewood, NY, pg. 40
Sevier, Helen, Chm. Bd., Pres., Chief Exec. & Chief Oper. Officer--B.A.S.S., Inc., Montgomery, AL, pg. 105
Shacklett, Dean R., Chief Oper. Officer--National Label Company, Lafayette Hill, PA, pg. 791
Shames, Sidney J., Chm. Bd., Pres., CEO, COO, CFO & Treas.--Melard Manufacturing Corporation, Passaic, NJ, pg. 737
Shank, Glen L., Pres., Chief Exec. & Oper. Officer--Duckwall-Alco Stores, Inc., Abilene, KS, pg. 351
Shanks, Donald K., Pres. & Chief Oper. Officer--Unigard Security Insurance Co., Bellevue, WA, pg. 596
Shanks, Donald K., Pres. & Chief Oper. Officer--Unigard Indemnity Co., Raleigh, NC, pg. 596
Shanks, Donald K., Pres. & Chief Oper. Officer--Unigard Insurance Co., Seattle, WA, pg. 596
Shanks, Donald K., Pres. & Chief Oper. Officer--Unigard Service Corp., Seattle, WA, pg. 596
Sharff, John S., Exec. V.P. & Chief Oper. Officer--Baltimore Stationery Co., Baltimore, MD, pg. 116
Sharp, David L., Pres. & Chief Oper. Officer--Standun, Inc., Irwindale, CA, pg. 1038
Shea, Peter, Chief Oper. Officer-Meat Grp.--Chiquita Brands International, Inc., Cincinnati, OH, pg. 53
Shea, Peter, Chief Oper. Officer--John Morrell & Co., Cincinnati, OH, pg. 54
Shearer, Jeff, Pres. & Chief Oper. Officer--Boston Chicken, Inc., Naperville, IL, pg. 167
Sheiffer, Arnold, Sr. V.P. & Chief Oper. Officer--Katz Communications, Inc., New York, NY, pg. 618
Shepherd, Dan P., Chief Oper. Officer--Shepherd Construction Co., Inc., Atlanta, GA, pg. 998
Shepherd, Frank H., Exec. V.P. & Chief Oper. Officer--Stauffer Communications, Inc., Topeka, KS, pg. 1042
Sherman, Floyd, Pres. & Chief Oper. Officer--Triangle Pacific Corporation, Dallas, TX, pg. 1112
Shiu, Chester, Vice Chm.--A. Levy & J. Zentner Co., Sacramento, CA, pg. 671
Shnycer, William, Chief Oper. Officer & Exec. V.P.--Morgan Industries Inc., Bala-Cynwyd, PA, pg. 770
Sholakh, Marwan, V.P. & Chief Oper. Officer--Nexus Plastics, Inc., Hawthorne, NJ, pg. 805
Shuman, Willard E., Pres. & Chief Oper. Officer--Insurance Corp. of America, Houston, TX, pg. 572
Sibbel, Mick, Exec. V.P., Chief Oper. Officer--Swanson Russell Associates, Lincoln, NE, pg. 1066
Siebel, Gretchen, Pres., Chief Oper. Officer--Siebel/Mohr, Inc., New York, NY, pg. 1002
Siegal, Michael D., Pres. & Chief Exec. & Chief Oper. Officer--Olympic Steel Inc., Bedford Heights, OH, pg. 825
Siess, Robert D., P.E., Pres. & Chief Oper. Officer--Tarlton Corporation, Saint Louis, MO, pg. 1079
Silver, Mel, Pres. & Chief Oper. Officer--Knoll International, Inc., New York, NY, pg. 1121
Silver, Stan, Chief Oper. Officer & Exec. V.P.--The Children's Place Retail Stores, Inc., Pine Brook, NJ, pg. 247
Silverman, S.W., Exec. V.P. & Chief Oper. Officer--PQ Corporation, Valley Forge, PA, pg. 836
Simeus, Dumas M., Pres. & Chief Oper. Officer--TLC Beatrice International Holdings Inc., New York, NY, pg. 1073
Simkins, L.J., Chm. Bd., Pres., Chief Exec. & Chief Oper. Officer--Simkins Industries, Inc., New Haven, CT, pg. 1005
Slabe, James F., Pres. & Chief Oper. Officer--Executive Enterprises, Inc., New York, NY, pg. 393
Slaughter, Randy, V.P.-Franchise--Dr Pepper/Seven-Up Companies, Inc., Dallas, TX, pg. 342
Sloan, Robert B., Pres., Chief Oper. Officer & Treas.--Downey Designs International, Inc., Indianapolis, IN, pg. 348
Smith, Brian, Pres. & Chief Oper. Officer--Cole National Corporation, Cleveland, OH, pg. 260
Smith, C. Michael, Pres., Chief Oper. Officer & Sec.--Orders Distributing Co., Greenville, SC, pg. 829
Smith, Eric, Pres. & Chief Oper. Officer--Howe Furniture Corporation, Trumbull, CT, pg. 547
Smith, Gordon C., Pres., Chief Exec. & Chief Oper. Officer--J.R. Simplot Company, Boise, ID, pg. 1007
Smith, Gregory W., Exec. V.P., Chief Oper. Officer--Jay Incorporated, Rochester, NY, pg. 590
Smith, John, Pres.--Modern Group Ltd., Bristol, PA, pg. 762
Smith, Peter, Pres. & Chief Oper. Officer--W S Holding Company, Euless, TX, pg. 1156
Smith, Sandra, Chief Oper. Officer--J. Richard Smith, Ltd., Melville, NY, pg. 1013
Smith, Vince, Chief Oper. Officer--Allright Corporation, Omaha, NE, pg. 41
Smith, William E., Pres., Chief Oper. Officer & Sec.--Fitzgerald & Company, Inc., Cranston, RI, pg. 416
Solombrino, Scott, Chm. Bd., Pres. & Chief Exec. Officer--Dav-El Services, Inc., New York, NY, pg. 317
Solomon, Zachary, Pres. & Chief Oper. Officer--Associated Merchandising Corp., New York, NY, pg. 91
Sommer, James, Pres., Chief Oper. & Fin. Officer & Treas.--Service Motor Company, Dale, WI, pg. 992
Soper, Willard B., II, Chief Oper. Officer--J. I. Kislak Inc., Miami Lakes, FL, pg. 633
Soskin, David H., Pres. & Chief Oper. Officer--Communications Diversified, New York, NY, pg. 269
Southwell, Leonard, Chief Exec. Officer--Prairie Farms Dairy, Inc., Carlinville, IL, pg. 884
Speck, Robert, Chief Oper. Officer--Grandy's, Inc., Lewisville, TX, pg. 476
Speier, Stephen, Pres. & Chief Oper. Officer--Penny & Speier Inc., Houston, TX, pg. 858
Sponsler, James R., Pres. & Chief Oper. Officer--Rustco Products Company, Denver, CO, pg. 957
Spovale, Nancy L., Sr. V.P.-Opers.--Franklin Federal Savings Association, Ottawa, KS, pg. 429
Spring, H.L., Jr., V.P.-Opers.--Transus Inc., Atlanta, GA, pg. 1108
St. Martin, Paul, Chief Oper. Officer & Chief Fin. Officer--The Allan R. Hackel Organization, Newton Center, MA, pg. 498
Standlee, J. Mack, Chief Oper. Officer--American FoodService, Dallas, TX, pg. 60
Standlee, Mack, Chief Oper. Officer--American Produce & Vegetable Co., Dallas, TX, pg. 59
Stangler, Kevin J., Sr. V.P., Chief Oper. & Fin. Officer & Treas.--Ministers Life Insurance Company, Minneapolis, MN, pg. 757
Stanke, Mary, Pres. & Sec.--JS&A Advertising, Las Vegas, NV, pg. 586
Stanners, Bob, Chief Oper. Officer--A.I. Root Company, Medina, OH, pg. 946
Stansfield, Elaine, Pres. & Chief Oper. Officer--The Sunflower Group, Overland Park, KS, pg. 1060
Star, Howard D., Chief Oper. Officer--Engineering Service, Inc., Southfield, MI, pg. 382
Starr, John, Chief Oper. Officer--Koch Supplies Inc., Kansas City, MO, pg. 639
Stein, Michael Alan, Pres. & Chief Oper. Officer--Electro-Science Laboratories, Inc., King of Prussia, PA, pg. 375
Stein, Steven B., Pres. & Chief Oper. Officer--Allied Security, Inc., Pittsburgh, PA, pg. 39
Stein, William E., Pres. & Chief Oper. Officer--McConnaughy Stein Schmidt Brown, Chicago, IL, pg. 727
Stella, Walter M., Exec. V.P. & Chief Oper. Officer--New England Frozen Foods, Southborough, MA, pg. 800
Stemmier, Robert M., Exec. V.P. & Chief Oper. Officer--Sargent-Fletcher Co., El Monte, CA, pg. 970
Stepanian, Stephen, Pres. & Chief Oper. Officer--Printed Circuit Corporation, Woburn, MA, pg. 891
Stephen, Phillip L., Pres. & Chief Oper. Officer--Aid Auto Stores, Inc., Westbury, NY, pg. 26
Stephens, J.T., Pres., Chief Exec. Officer & Chief Oper. Officer--Ebsco Industries, Inc., Birmingham, AL, pg. 365
Stephens, Richard T., Pres. & Chief Oper. Officer--Delaware North Companies, Inc., Buffalo, NY, pg. 326
Stevens, Gus, Pres. & Chief Oper. Officer--Cyberex, Inc., Mentor, OH, pg. 307
Steves, Sam Bel, II, Pres. & Chief Oper. Officer--Steves & Sons, San Antonio, TX, pg. 1048
Stock, Brenda, Chief Oper. Officer--Southern Paving Co., Moab, UT, pg. 598
Stoddard, Nathaniel C., Pres. & Chief Oper. Officer--Garden Way, Inc., Troy, NY, pg. 443
Stone, Richard, Exec. V.P., Chief Oper. Officer--Lindsay, Stone & Briggs Advertising, Inc., Madison, WI, pg. 676
Stone, Richard B., Chief Oper. Officer--Capital Bank, N.A., Washington, DC, pg. 214
Strange, Don E., Pres. & Chief Oper. Officer--Schneller, Inc., Kent, OH, pg. 977
Straub, Gary F., Pres. & Chief Oper. Officer--Fine Organics Corp., Lodi, NJ, pg. 411
Street, Gordon P., Jr., Chm. Bd., Pres. & Chief Exec. & Chief Oper. Officer--North American Royalties, Inc., Chattanooga, TN, pg. 811
Strickler, Charles O., Pres.--Rocco Inc., Harrisonburg, VA, pg. 940
Strong, Warren R., Chief Exec. Officer, Chief Oper. Officer, & Pres.--Macco Constructors, Inc., Paramount, CA, pg. 696
Stryker, C. Samuel, Jr., Chief Oper. Officer, Exec. V.P., New Bus. Contact--PMC Partnership, Ltd., Westport, CT, pg. 836
Sullivan, Dennis F., Exec. V.P. & Chief Oper. Officer--Amtrak-National Railroad Passenger Corp., Washington, DC, pg. 69
Suma, Charles M., Pres. & Chief Oper. Officer--Piper Aircraft Corporation, Vero Beach, FL, pg. 872
Sundblad, Harry, Exec. V.P.--Action Instruments, Inc., San Diego, CA, pg. 14
Sussman, Alan, Chief Oper. Officer--H. Cotler Company, New York, NY, pg. 288
Sutter, Robert J., Pres.--Minstar, Inc., Minneapolis, MN, pg. 758
Sutter, Robert J., Pres. & Chief Oper. Officer--Genmar Industries, Inc., Minneapolis, MN, pg. 759
Sutton, D. R., Sec.--Tillamook County Creamery Assn., Tillamook, OR, pg. 1097
Swenson, Paul, Exec.V.P. & Chief Oper. Officer--Aetna Health Plans, San Bruno, CA, pg. 23
Swirsky, Morton, Chief Oper. Officer & Controller--Atlantic to Pacific Bedding Corp., Bronx, NY, pg. 95
Syar, James M., Pres. & Chief Oper. Officer--Syar Industries, Inc., Napa, CA, pg. 1068
Taddei, Armando, Chm. Bd., Pres. & Treas.--Hunter Contracting Company, Gilbert, AZ, pg. 554
Tahan, W.N., Chm. & Chief Exec. Officer--Bromar Inc., Newport Beach, CA, pg. 179
Tait, John E., Chm. Bd., Pres. & Chief Exec. Officer--The Penn Mutual Life Insurance Company, Philadelphia, PA, pg. 858
Talarico, Nancy, V.P., Chief Oper. Officer & Creative Dir.--Hank Forssberg, Inc., Hackensack, NJ, pg. 424
Tanimoto, Douglas, Dr., Pres. & Chief Oper. Officer--Laser Power Corporation, San Diego, CA, pg. 660
Tanis, Beth, Exec. V.P. & Chief Oper. Officer--Zephyr Baskets & Balloons, New Providence, NJ, pg. 1217
Tanner, James D., Chief Oper. Officer & Sr. V.P.--Warner Press, Inc., Anderson, IN, pg. 1164
Tassi, Michael J., Chief Fin. Officer & Treas.--Torco Oil, Chicago, IL, pg. 1102
Taylor, Bruce W., Pres. & Chief Oper. Officer--Cole Taylor Bank, Chicago, IL, pg. 260
Teague, Thomas L., Pres. & Chief Oper. Officer--Salem National Corporation, Winston-Salem, NC, pg. 967
Teel, James E., Co-Chm. Bd. & Chief Oper. Officer--Raley's, West Sacramento, CA, pg. 910
Tenhover, Robert, Chief Oper. Officer--Superior Label Systems, Inc., Cincinnati, OH, pg. 1063
Terlato, William A., V.P. & Chief Oper. Officer--Paterno Imports Limited, Chicago, IL, pg. 851
Terlato, William A., V.P. & Chief Oper. Officer--Pacific Wine Co., Chicago, IL, pg. 851
Terrell, James R., Pres. & Chief Oper. Officer-TV Stations--Gaylord Broadcasting Co., Dallas, TX, pg. 446
Terry, Lonnie R., Chief Oper. Officer & Exec. V.P.--Earle M. Jorgensen Company, Brea, CA, pg. 605
Teufel, Robert J., Pres. & Chief Oper. Officer--Rodale Press, Inc., Emmaus, PA, pg. 942
Theiss, George B., Pres. & Chief Operating Officer--Arthur Murray Intl., Inc., Coral Gables, FL, pg. 776
Tholey, James M., Chief Oper. Officer, Chief Fin. Officer, & Treas.--Peirce-Phelps, Inc., Philadelphia, PA, pg. 855
Thomas, John W., Jr., Chm. Bd. & Chief Exec. Officer--Thomas Built Buses, Inc., High Point, NC, pg. 1092
Thomas, Michael, V.P. & Chief Oper. Officer--Shape Inc., Biddeford, ME, pg. 995
Thompson, L. Dan, Chief Oper. Officer & Sr. V.P.--Schad Industries, Inc., Lafayette, LA, pg. 974
Thompson, L. Don, Chief Oper. Officer & Sr. V.P.--Lou Ana Foods, Inc., Opelousas, LA, pg. 974
Thompson, Ralph L., Pres. & Chief Oper. Officer--Fahlgren Martin, Inc., Parkersburg, WV, pg. 396
Thompson, Scott, Chm. Bd., Pres., Chief Exec. & Chief Oper. Officer--Advanced Technology, Inc., Reston, VA, pg. 20
Thompson, Wayne E., Chief Oper. Officer--Rish Equipment Company, Bluefield, WV, pg. 935
Thoms, Robert, Pres. & Chief Oper. Officer--Fortifiber Corporation, Los Angeles, CA, pg. 425
Thomson, Robert H., Pres. & Chief Exec. Officer--Construction Specialties, Inc., Cranford, NJ, pg. 277
Thornton, Dan, Chief Oper. Officer--Scoville Press, Inc., Minneapolis, MN, pg. 983
Thwing, K., V.P.-Chief Oper. Officer--Bead Industries Inc., Bridgeport, CT, pg. 129
Todilben, Carl, Chief Oper. Officer--Springfield Milling Corp., Springfield, MN, pg. 549
Tolone, Thomas A., Pres. & Chief Oper. Officer--Paoli, Inc., Paoli, IN, pg. 846

Tomlinson, Kendall, Sr. V.P. & Chief Oper. Officer--Lebanon Chemical Corp., Lebanon, PA, pg. 665
Townsend, Arthur T., Chief Fin. Officer & Chief Oper. Officer--Lat Purser & Associate, Charlotte, NC, pg. 901
Trachtenberg, Joseph M., Pres. & Chief Oper. Officer--Victaulic Company of America, Easton, PA, pg. 1149
Travis, James D., Pres. & Chief Oper. Officer--Hal Riney & Partners, Inc., San Francisco, CA, pg. 935
Treis, Donald J., Pres. & Chief Oper. Officer--Arandell-Schmidt Corporation, Menomonee Falls, WI, pg. 79
Tremblay, E., V.P. & Chief Oper. Officer--P/A Industries, Inc., Bloomfield, CT, pg. 835
Tribull, Christoph, Chm. Bd., Pres., Chief Exec. & Chief Oper. Officer--Sierracin Corporation, Sylmar, CA, pg. 1003
Trieschmann, Tim, Chief Oper. Officer--Amana-Nordstrom Motel Co., Amana, IA, pg. 46
Trosino, Vincent J., Chief Oper. Officer & Exec. V.P.--State Farm Mutual Automobile Insurance Company, Bloomington, IL, pg. 1041
Turk, Allen, Pres. & Chief Oper. Officer--S. E. Huffman Corp., Clover, SC, pg. 551
Turner, Ronald D.V., Pres. & Chief Oper. Officer--Elliott Company, Jeannette, PA, pg. 378
Turner, W.B., Jr., Pres. & Chief Oper. Officer--W. C. Bradley Co., Columbus, GA, pg. 170
Tusher, Thomas W., Pres. & Chief Oper. Officer--Levi Strauss & Co., San Francisco, CA, pg. 670
Ulewicz, Michael, Chief Oper. Officer--Kasle Steel Corporation, Dearborn, MI, pg. 617
Underhill, Robert L., Chief Oper. Officer & Sr. V.P.--Channing L. Bete Co., Inc., South Deerfield, MA, pg. 147
Unrine, Tom, Pres. & Chief Oper. Officer--Margo's La Mode, Inc., Dallas, TX, pg. 373
Upshaw, Lynn, Exec. V.P., Chief Oper. Officer--Ketchum Advertising/San Francisco, San Francisco, CA, pg. 625
Vacala, John, Chief Oper. Officer--Dann Dee Display Fixtures, Chicago, IL, pg. 314
Valentino, Harry, Pres. & Chief Oper. Officer--Fresh Mark, Inc., Massillon, OH, pg. 432
van Cuylenberg, Peter, Pres. & Chief Oper. Officer--Next, Inc., Redwood City, CA, pg. 805
Van Ort, Dale, Pres. & Chief Oper. Officer--Freeman Decorating Co., Dallas, TX, pg. 431
Vancelette, William D., Chief Oper. Officer & Exec. V.P.--Didde Web Press, Emporia, KS, pg. 336
Vann, James A., Jr., Pres. & Chief Oper. Officer--Alabama Electric Cooperative, Inc., Andalusia, AL, pg. 28
Vavasis, Andrew S., Exec. V.P. & Chief Oper. Officer--Vance Industries, Inc., Chicago, IL, pg. 1144
Ventre, John, Jr., Chm. Bd. & Chief Exec. Officer--Ventre Packing Company, Inc., Syracuse, NY, pg. 1147
Verdoorn, Sid, Pres., Chief Exec. & Chief Oper. Officer--C. H. Robinson Co. Inc., Eden Prairie, MN, pg. 939
Verner, James R., Pres. & Chief Oper. Officer--Acousti Engineering Co. of Florida, Orlando, FL, pg. 14
Veru, Theodore D., Co-Chm. & Chief Oper. Officer--Lois/USA, New York, NY, pg. 681
Vickers, David, Pres. & Chief Oper. Officer--H.G. Fenton Material Company, San Diego, CA, pg. 406
Vickers, David, Pres. & Chief Oper. Officer--Pre-Mix Concrete Co., San Diego, CA, pg. 406
Vincent, Philip S., Pres. & Chief Oper. Officer--Southern Mills, Inc., Union City, GA, pg. 1021
Vinson, Carol D., Pres. & Chief Oper. Officer--Insignia Financial Group, Inc., Greenville, SC, pg. 571
Vitale, Damon S., Pres. & Chief Oper. Officer--Desa International, Inc., Bowling Green, KY, pg. 331
Volland, Dan, Chief Oper. Officer--Mrs. Goochs Natural Food Markets, Sherman Oaks, CA, pg. 761
Volpara, Paolo, Chief Oper. Officer, Mng. Dir.--Markom/Leo Burnett A.S., Istanbul,, Turkey, pg. 193
Volpentesta, Frank, Chief Oper. Officer & Exec. V.P.--Headco Industries, Inc., Broadview, IL, pg. 520
Vornbrock, Robert, Chief Oper. Officer & Acct. Supvr.--Thompson & Company, Memphis, TN, pg. 1094
Wages, Terry W., Chief Oper. Officer--CGF Industries, Topeka, KS, pg. 201
Wagner, Lawrence M., Chief Oper. Officer & Exec. V.P.--Hillman Company, Pittsburgh, PA, pg. 535
Wahtola, Charles, Pres. & Chief Exec. Officer--Woodward-Clyde Consultants, Denver, CO, pg. 1201
Walker, Ronald F., Pres. & Chief Oper. Officer--American Financial Corporation, Cincinnati, OH, pg. 52
Wallace, William B., Vice Chm. & Chief Oper. Officer--Phoenix Home Life Mutual Insurance Company, Hartford, CT, pg. 868
Waller, Robert M., Chief Oper. Officer--Dry Storage Corporation, Des Plaines, IL, pg. 350
Waller, Stephen L., Sr. V.P.-Opers.--DHL Airways, Inc., Redwood City, CA, pg. 309
Walsh, W.J., Chief Oper. Officer--Channellock, Inc., Meadville, PA, pg. 239
Walstad, Dennis, Sr. V.P. & Chief Oper. Officer--Furnas Electric Company, Batavia, IL, pg. 437
Ward, Bill, Exec. V.P. & Gen. Mgr.--Golden West Broadcasters, Los Angeles, CA, pg. 467
Ward, Louis L., Chm. Bd., Pres. & Chief Oper. Officer--Russell Stover Candies, Inc., Kansas City, MO, pg. 957
Warmoth, Frank J., Pres. & Chief Oper. Officer--B. L. Montague Co., Sumter, SC, pg. 766
Warner, Jon, Pres. & Chief Oper. Officer--Gulf States Paper Corporation, Tuscaloosa, AL, pg. 494
Warrington, George, Chief Oper. Officer--NJ Transit, Newark, NJ, pg. 801
Watkins, James H., Chief Exec. & Oper. Officer--ATCOM, Inc., Research Triangle Park, NC, pg. 93
Weaver, Michael E., Pres., Chief Exec. Officer & Chief Oper. Officer--Weaver Popcorn Company, Inc., Van Buren, IN, pg. 1170
Weber, Philip P., Exec. V.P. & Chief Exec. Officer--Farm Family Mutual Insurance Co., Glenmont, NY, pg. 401
Webster, Mark, Chief Exec. Officer, Chief Fin. Officer & Gen. Counsel--Rush County Farm Bureau Co-op, Rushville, IN, pg. 956
Weekly, John W., Pres. & Chief Oper. Officer--Mutual of Omaha Insurance Company, Omaha, NE, pg. 779
Wehberg, Joyce, Chief Oper. Officer & Dir.-Pur.--Shillcraft, Inc., Baltimore, MD, pg. 999
Wehrle, Henry B. III, Pres. & Chief Oper. Officer--McJunkin Corporation, Charleston, WV, pg. 730
Weidaw, Robert F., Pres. & Chief Oper. Officer--Cogentrix Incorporated, Charlotte, NC, pg. 258
Weil, David S., Pres., Chief Exec. & Chief Oper. Officer--Ampacet Corporation, Tarrytown, NY, pg. 67
Weinbach, Lawrence A., Mng. Partner & Chief Exec. Officer--Arthur Andersen & Co., S.C., New York, NY, pg. 72
Weinberg, Martyn, Exec. V.P. & Chief Oper. Officer--Hanna-Barbera Productions, Inc., Los Angeles, CA, pg. 53
Weinberg, Thomas A., Pres. & Chief Oper. Officer (Los Angeles) & Dir.--EvansGroup, Salt Lake City, UT, pg. 390
Weinberg, Tom, Pres., Chief Oper. Officer--EvansGroup, Los Angeles, CA, pg. 391
Weiss, E., V.P. & Chief Oper. Officer--Beltone Electronics Corporation, Chicago, IL, pg. 137
Weiss, Lynn, Exec. V.P. & Chief Oper. Officer--Spinnaker Software Corporation, Cambridge, MA, pg. 1031
Weitzel, John P., Pres. & Chief Oper. Officer--Bankers Systems Inc., Saint Cloud, MN, pg. 117
Westerman, William, Pres. & Chief Oper. Officer--Cogsdill Tool Products, Inc., Lugoff, SC, pg. 259
Wevers, Pierre, Exec. V.P. & Chief Oper. Officer--Bigg's Hyper Shoppes, Inc., Milford, OH, pg. 150
White, Charles Y., Pres. & Chief Oper. Officer--Mississippi Lime Co., Alton, IL, pg. 760
White, Raymond W., Pres. & Chief Oper. Officer--Christie Electric Corporation, Gardena, CA, pg. 249
Whitehead, William J., Chief Exec. Officer--BSB/Canada Inc., Toronto,, Canada, pg. 109
Whitescarver, B., Exec. V.P. & Chief Oper. Officer--Dempster, Inc., Toccoa, GA, pg. 328
Whiting, R. Bruce, Pres. & Chief Oper. Officer--Kaibab Industries, Phoenix, AZ, pg. 614
Whitney, Nicholas, Exec. V.P. & Chief Oper. Officer--Management Dynamics, New Providence, NJ, pg. 703
Whitson, James N., Exec. V.P. & Chief Oper. Officer--Sammons Enterprises, Inc., Dallas, TX, pg. 968
Whitt, David, Pres. & Chief Oper. Officer--Elixir Industries, Gardena, CA, pg. 376
Wick, Jeff, Pres. & Chief Oper. Officer--Wick Building Systems, Mazomanie, WI, pg. 1188
Wieland, John, Chief Oper. Officer--Wieland Realty Associates, Inc., Atlanta, GA, pg. 1189
Wiggins, William H., Pres. & Chief Oper. Officer--Thiele Kaolin Co., Sandersville, GA, pg. 1092
Wilkie, Michael L., Chm. Bd., Pres., Chief Exec. & Chief Oper. Officer--DoAll Company, Des Plaines, IL, pg. 341
Wilkins, David G., Pres. & Chief Oper. Officer--Doe-Anderson Advertising Agency, Inc., Louisville, KY, pg. 342
Williams, George T., Pres. & Chief Exec. Officer--Clinton Mills Inc., Clinton, SC, pg. 202
Williams, James A., Pres. & Chief Oper. Officer--Petroleum Inc., Wichita, KS, pg. 865
Williams, Joanne King, Exec. V.P., Chief Oper. Officer--The Bomstein Agency, Washington, DC, pg. 164
Williams, R.L., Pres. & Chief Oper. Officer--Dan River Inc., Danville, VA, pg. 313
Williams, Steven C., Chief Oper. Officer--State Volunteer Mutual Insurance Co. Inc., Brentwood, TN, pg. 1041
Williamson, Philip, V.P.-Opers.--Williamson-Dickie Mfg. Co., Fort Worth, TX, pg. 1192
Willner, Michael, Exec. V.P. & Chief Oper. Officer--CPM, Inc., Chicago, IL, pg. 203
Wilson, Robin, Chief Oper. Officer--Trans World Airlines, Inc., Mount Kisco, NY, pg. 561
Wilson, Steven A., Pres. & Chief Oper. Officer--The Bases Group, Covington, KY, pg. 124
Winch, John J., Pres.--The Minster Machine Company, Minster, OH, pg. 759
Winkler, William F., Chief Oper. Officer, Sec. & Treas.--Ackerman McQueen, Inc., Oklahoma City, OK, pg. 12
Wirta, Ray, Pres. & Chief Oper. Officer--Koll Co., Newport Beach, CA, pg. 641
Wisdom, Daniel W., Exec. V.P. & Chief Oper. Officer--Leupold & Stevens, Inc., Beaverton, OR, pg. 669
Wissler, Robert C., Pres. & Chief Oper. Officer--Comprehensive Business Services Inc., Carlsbad, CA, pg. 612
Wolf, Michael A., Pres. & Chief Oper. Officer--Hobart Brothers Co., Troy, OH, pg. 536
Wolf, Sally, Chief Oper. Officer & V.P.--Leland A. Wolf & Associates, Foster City, CA, pg. 1199
Wolfson, B.J., Pres. & Chief Oper. Officer--Flexible Products Company, Marietta, GA, pg. 418
Wood, Brian, Chief Oper. Officer & V.P.--Paisano Publications, Inc., Agoura, CA, pg. 843
Wood, Jack T., Pres. & Chief Exec. Officer--Straw Hat Cooperative Corp., Dublin, CA, pg. 1053
Wood, R. Ray, Chm., Pres., Chief Exec. & Chief Oper. Officer--Rockford Products Corp., Rockford, IL, pg. 941
Woodson, Glen, II, Pres. & Chief Oper. Officer--Crouch Supply Company, Inc., Fort Worth, TX, pg. 301
Yahn, Clarence H., Pres. & Chief Oper. Officer--Blount Lumber Company, Lacona, NY, pg. 158
Yates, Jerry, Sr. V.P.-Opers.--Tropical Garment Manufacturing Company, Tampa, FL, pg. 1116
Yost, Jack, Dir.-Opers.--Moran Industries, Inc., Midlothian, IL, pg. 769
Young, Charles, Pres. & Chief Oper. Officer--Affiliated Computer Services, Inc., Dallas, TX, pg. 23
Young, James, Chief Oper. Officer--Reactive Metals & Alloys Corporation (REMACOR), West Pittsburg, PA, pg. 916
Zander, Glenn R., Chief Oper. Officer--Trans World Airlines, Inc., Mount Kisco, NY, pg. 561
Zemenick, Carl, Pres. & Chief Exec. & Chief Oper. Officer--GF Office Furniture Ltd., Gallatin, TN, pg. 439
Zenner, Ronald P., Exec. V.P. & Chief Oper. Officer--Wilton Industries, Inc., Woodridge, IL, pg. 1194
Zichlin, Sidney, Chief Oper. Officer & V.P.--Linzer Products Corp., Flushing, NY, pg. 677
Zifkin, Walter, Exec. V.P., Chief Oper. Officer & Sec.--William Morris Agency, Inc., Beverly Hills, CA, pg. 771
Zimm, John, Chief Oper. Officer--G B Stores, Johnstown, PA, pg. 978
Zimmerli, Kurt, Chm. Bd., Pres., Chief Exec. Officer & Chief Oper. Officer--Zima Corp., Spartanburg, SC, pg. 1219
Zollars, Robert L., Pres. & Chief Oper. Officer--Huitt-Zollars, Inc., Dallas, TX, pg. 552
Zukerman, Allan B., Pres. & Chief Oper. Officer--Montgomery, Zukerman, Davis, Inc., Indianapolis, IN, pg. 768
Zygulski, Robert, Pres. & Chief Opers. Officer--South Bend Plastics, Inc., Mishawaka, IN, pg. 1019

CONTROLLER

Abarquez, Jose, V.P., Controller--Rosenfeld, Sirowitz, Humphrey & Strauss, Inc., New York, NY, pg. 948
Abatino, Anthony, Controller--Polera Building Corp., Scarsdale, NY, pg. 878
Abbs, John, Controller--Clark Gum Company, Barrington, IL, pg. 252
Aberasturi, Paul, Controller & Mgr.-Traffic--Amicale Industries, Inc., New York, NY, pg. 66
Able, R. Bruce, V.P. & Controller--Whataburger, Inc., Corpus Christi, TX, pg. 1184
Abotomey, Darryl, V.P. & Controller--Sunclipse, Inc., Montebello, CA, pg. 1059
Abraham, John R., Controller--Stanchem Inc., East Berlin, CT, pg. 1035
Acocella, Susan, Controller--Vernon Sassos McGill, Inc., New York, NY, pg. 1148
Adams, Deborah, Controller--Amerco, A Nevada Corporation, Reno, NV, pg. 47
Adams, Doug, Controller--Paramount Foods Inc., Louisville, KY, pg. 848
Adams, Stephen, V.P.-Fin.--UniHealth America, Burbank, CA, pg. 1126
Adams, Todd, V.P. & Controller--Journal/Sentinel Inc., Milwaukee, WI, pg. 607
Adams, Todd, V.P. & Controller--Milwaukee Sentinel, Milwaukee, WI, pg. 607
Adams, Todd, V.P. & Controller--The Milwaukee Journal, Milwaukee, WI, pg. 607
Adams, W.C., Controller--Heller Bros. Packing Corp., Winter Garden, FL, pg. 526
Adelhardt, Joseph, V.P. & Controller--Pathmark, Woodbridge, NJ, pg. 1064
Adelhardt, Joseph W., V.P. & Controller--Supermarkets General Corporation, Woodbridge, NJ, pg. 1064
Adrian, Patricia M., Controller--Sivyer Steel Corporation, Bettendorf, IA, pg. 1013
Agnell, Bill, Controller--Reynen, Bardis & Winn, Sacramento, CA, pg. 930
Ahearn, M.J., Controller--C.R. Daniels, Inc., Ellicott City, MD, pg. 314
Aichele, William, Controller--Peabody Myers Corp., Streator, IL, pg. 900
Ainsworth, Richard, Controller--Mastercraft Corporation, Winnsboro, IA, pg. 759
Akers, Susan, Controller--Mr. Gasket Company, Cleveland, OH, pg. 761
Akers, Susan, Controller--Cragar Industries, Compton, CA, pg. 761
Alan, Arnold, Controller--Fisca Oil Co., Inc., Westwood, KS, pg. 414
Alberts, David E., Controller--G. E. Johnson Construction Co., Inc., Colorado Springs, CO, pg. 597
Alderman, Thomas E., Controller--Patterson Dental Company, Minneapolis, MN, pg. 851
Ales, S.J., Sec. & Controller--Brock-McVey Company, Lexington, KY, pg. 728
Alexander, Clayton, Controller--Alford Refrigerated Warehouse, Inc., Dallas, TX, pg. 34
Ali, Marge, Controller--Rubin Response Services, Inc., Schaumburg, IL, pg. 954
Allaby, Janet, Controller--Mayflower Transit, Inc., Carmel, IN, pg. 724
Allard, Maurice E., Treas. & Controller--Granite State Manufacturing Co., Manchester, NH, pg. 476
Allbers, Mark, V.P. & Controller--Old World Industries, Inc., Northbrook, IL, pg. 823
Alldian, David, V.P. & Controller--Blue Tee Corporation, New York, NY, pg. 161
Allen, Gordon, Treas. & Controller--Crown Fence Co., Pasadena, CA, pg. 302
Allen, John, Controller--Perry Equipment Corporation, Mineral Wells, TX, pg. 863
Allen, Joseph, Controller--Communications International, New York, NY, pg. 269
Allen, Lelan, Controller--Crosby & Overton, Inc., Long Beach, CA, pg. 300
Allen, Richard, Asst. V.P./Sr. Controller--Sentinel Consumer Products, Inc., Mentor, OH, pg. 990
Alley, Ramona C., Controller--Maine Potato Growers, Inc., Presque Isle, ME, pg. 702
Almanzo, Rita, Asst. Controller--J. Richard Smith, Ltd., Melville, NY, pg. 1013
Alp, Robert, Controller--Tribune Review Publishing Co., Greensburg, PA, pg. 1112
Alpers, Lynn, V.P. & Controller--Hamilton Stores, Inc., West Yellowstone, MT, pg. 503
Alseth, John, Controller--Anaheim Manufacturing Company, Anaheim, CA, pg. 71
Altman, Mery, Controller--Duane Reade, Long Island City, NY, pg. 350

Altscher, Stan, Controller--American Strip Steel Inc., Kearny, NJ, pg. 63
Amato, Ray, Controller--Mactavish Machine Manufacturing Company, Richmond, VA, pg. 698
Amborn, Kristine, V.P. & Controller--J H Collectibles, Milwaukee, WI, pg. 584
Ames, Frederick, V.P. & Controller--Artec Distributing, Inc., Shelburne, VT, pg. 86
Ametrano, Carmen S., Controller--Glenn O. Hawbaker, Inc., State College, PA, pg. 517
Amiri, Ray, Fin. Controller--NBS Limited-Card Systems Division, Surrey,, United Kingdom, pg. 960
Amundson, Gary, Controller--Bell Gardens Bicycle Club, Bell Gardens, CA, pg. 134
Andaya, Dante, Corp. Controller--Kelly-Moore Paint Company, Inc., San Carlos, CA, pg. 621
Andersen, Sandra L., Controller--Roffe, Inc., Seattle, WA, pg. 943
Anderson, Eric, Controller & Treas.--Spurgeon Mercantile Company, Chicago, IL, pg. 1034
Anderson, G.D., Controller--J.M. Huber, Calcium Carbonate Div., Quincy, IL, pg. 550
Anderson, Gunner, Controller & Asst. Sec.--Clements Foods Co., Oklahoma City, OK, pg. 254
Anderson, James, Controller--National Merchandise Co., Inc., Jacksonville, FL, pg. 792
Anderson, Joanne, Controller--Bell Flavors & Fragrances, Northbrook, IL, pg. 134
Anderson, Lynn, Controller--Allen Steel Co., Salt Lake City, UT, pg. 36
Anderson, Robert W., Sec., Treas. & Comptroller--Superior Oil Co. Inc., Indianapolis, IN, pg. 1064
Anderson, Ronald, Controller--Pyttronic Industries, Inc., Montgomeryville, PA, pg. 901
Andre, Diane, Comptroller--Bertrand Advertising Agency, Inc., Hollywood, CA, pg. 144
Andreacci, John, Controller--Duro-Test Corporation, Fairfield, NJ, pg. 355
Andreu, Cindy, Controller--The Weather Channel, Atlanta, GA, pg. 654
Andriz, Tom, Controller--Fort Pitt Acquisitions Company, Inc., Coraopolis, PA, pg. 425
Angart, Paul, Controller--Blue Coral, Inc., Cleveland, OH, pg. 159
Angelvich, David, Controller--John Williams & Associates, Ltd., Sausalito, CA, pg. 1190
Angulo, Rudy, Controller--World Jai-alai, Miami, FL, pg. 1202
Anstett, William J., Controller--Silver State Disposal Service, Inc., Las Vegas, NV, pg. 1004
Antes, Richard, Comptroller--Tetko, Inc., Briarcliff Manor, NY, pg. 1089
Anzuini, Renee, Controller--Genevar Enterprises, Colorado Springs, CO, pg. 451
Aoelizzi, Rob, Comptroller--Frank W. Winne & Son, Inc., Philadelphia, PA, pg. 1196
Aono, Sumi, Treas. & Sec.--Red Apple, Inc., Ontario, OR, pg. 918
Apesa, Mary, Controller--The Alden Group Ltd., New York, NY, pg. 32
Archard, Phillip, V.P. & Controller--Bridgeport Machines, Inc., Bridgeport, CT, pg. 175
Archer, John, V.P. & Controller--Stanley Knight Corporation, New Troy, MI, pg. 1038
Ariano, Martin G., Controller--Phelps Tointon Inc., Greeley, CO, pg. 866
Aris, Stanley, Controller--Amphenol Corporation, Wallingford, CT, pg. 648
Arlea, Mike, Controller & Mgr.-Personnel--Cardinal Inc., Port Reading, NJ, pg. 217
Arlen, Mary, Controller--Arlen Advertising, Los Angeles, CA, pg. 83
Arnesen, Jeff, Corp. Controller--Field Container Company, L.P., Elk Grove Village, IL, pg. 409
Arnett, Michael, V.P.-Fin.--Northern Wire & Cable, Inc., Troy, MI, pg. 814
Arnold, Mark S., V.P., Chief Fin. Officer & Controller--Sterling Plumbing Group, Inc., Schaumburg, IL, pg. 640
Arnott, Harold, Controller--Jensen Electric Company, Reno, NV, pg. 592
Arsenault, James, Treas. & Controller--The Asher Winer Company, Fitchburg, MA, pg. 88
Arterburn, Jim, V.P. & Controller--Sooner Pipe & Supply Corp., Tulsa, OK, pg. 1018
Aryan, Sako, Controller--Kold Kist Brands, Inc., Los Angeles, CA, pg. 641
Asbury, Allen, Controller--House of Raeford Farms, Inc., Raeford, NC, pg. 546
Asche, Ron D., Controller, Treas. & Div. Mgr.-Fin. & Acct.--Nebraska Public Power District, Columbus, NE, pg. 796
Ashburn, Edgar R., V.P. & Controller--Trans World Airlines, Inc., Mount Kisco, NY, pg. 561
Ashcraft, James, Comptroller--MD Pneumatics, Inc., Springfield, MO, pg. 1120
Ashton, Robert L., V.P., Chief Fin. Officer & Controller--All Seasons Services, Inc., Braintree, MA, pg. 35
Askins. Richard E., Controller--Franklin Baking Co., Inc., Goldsboro, NC, pg. 429
Atkinson, Gary, Controller--Sierracin Corporation, Sylmar, CA, pg. 1003
Atkinson, Gary, Controller--Harrison Div., Burbank, CA, pg. 1003
Atkinson, Ronald L., Controller--Tri-State Motor Transit Co., Joplin, MO, pg. 1111
Ausanka, John J., III, V.P. & Comptroller--The Record-Journal Publishing Company, Meriden, CT, pg. 917
Avery, Pat, Controller--Macklanburg-Duncan Co., Oklahoma City, OK, pg. 697
Awad, Dennis J., Pres., Chief Exec. & Fin. Officer & Treas.--Tele-Com Products, Inc., Duarte, CA, pg. 1084
Bachman, G.E., Controller--Diamond Chain Company, Indianapolis, IN, pg. 69
Bacic, Carol, Controller--The Unimax Corporation, New York, NY, pg. 1127
Back, Tom, Controller--H S Die & Engineering, Inc., Grand Rapids, MI, pg. 497
Baetens, Hedwig, Controller--Berlitz Schools of Languages B.V., Amsterdam,, Netherlands, pg. 143
Baetens, Hedwig, Controller--Berlitz Schools of Languages of Benelux S.A., Brussels,, Belgium, pg. 143
Bagnal, Jayne, Controller--Sprott Oil Co., Inc., Manning, SC, pg. 1034
Bailey, B.T., V.P. & Controller--Peoples Gas System, Inc., Tampa, FL, pg. 689
Bainbridge, Fran, Comptroller--Cox Landey and Partners, Inc., New York, NY, pg. 294
Baker, Avery D., V.P. & Comptroller--Pioneer Mutual Life Insurance Company, Fargo, ND, pg. 872
Baker, Donald W., Controller--Southwire Company, Inc., Carrollton, GA, pg. 1024
Baker, John E., Chief Fin. Officer, Treas. & Controller--Steuart Investment Co., Washington, DC, pg. 1048
Baker, Robert R., Controller--Faber/Castell Corporation, Parsippany, NJ, pg. 395
Baker, Russell, Controller--Chattanooga Choo-Choo Holiday Inn, Chattanooga, TN, pg. 241
Baker, Vicki, V.P., Controller--Borders, Perrin & Norrander, Inc., Portland, OR, pg. 165
Balaban, Eileen, Sr. V.P., Dir., Client Compensation--Young & Rubicam Inc., New York, NY, pg. 1210
Balasko, Jo-Ann, Controller--Marketing Support, Incorporated, Chicago, IL, pg. 709
Balcer, Brian, Controller--Lyman Lumber Company, Excelsior, MN, pg. 689
Balchunas, Donald F., V.P. & Controller--Arandell-Schmidt Corporation, Menomonee Falls, WI, pg. 79
Baldwin, H. Richard, V.P.-Admin. & Controller--Spartan Mills, Spartanburg, SC, pg. 1026
Baldwin, Larry, Controller--Lukenheimer Co.-Energo Valves, Cincinnati, OH, pg. 687
Baliga, Thomas, Controller--Chicago, Chicago, IL, pg. 656
Balk, Lavern, Controller--Don E. Williams Co., Rock Island, IL, pg. 1190
Balkit, Daniel, Controller--Amkor Electronics, Inc., West Chester, PA, pg. 67
Ball, Martha, Controller--Peck Sims Mueller, Inc., Honolulu, HI, pg. 854
Baloun, John, Controller--IGA, Inc. (Independent Grocers Alliance), Chicago, IL, pg. 560
Bamberger, David, Controller--Milton Shoe Manufacturing Company, Inc., Milton, PA, pg. 756
Bandel, Judy, Controller--Markair, Inc., Anchorage, AK, pg. 708
Bandusky, Drew M., Intl. Controller--Griffith Laboratories Worldwide, Inc., Alsip, IL, pg. 487
Bang, John, Controller--Computer Instruments Corporation, Westbury, NY, pg. 271
Bannell, Stephen G., Reg. Controller--Johnson's Wax (East Africa) Ltd., Nairobi,, Kenya, pg. 600
Banquer, C.S., Treas. & Controller--Acme Refrigeration Of Baton Rouge Inc., Baton Rouge, LA, pg. 13
Banse, Robert P., Chief Fin. Officer--Jim Lupient Enterprises, Golden Valley, MN, pg. 687
Barackman, Melody, Controller--Steuart Petroleum Company, Washington, DC, pg. 1048
Barber, John W., V.P. & Controller--General American Life Insurance Co., St. Louis, MO, pg. 448
Barcan, Ira, Treas.--The Cherenson Group, Livingston, NJ, pg. 243
Barefoot, James E., Chief Fin. Officer & Controller--Valleydale Packers Inc., Bristol, VA, pg. 1143
Barefoot, Wayne, Treas.--Victaulic Company of America, Easton, PA, pg. 1149
Barfuss, Sheldon K., Controller--Great Salt Lake Minerals & Chemicals Corp., Ogden, UT, pg. 482
Barger, Roger, Controller--Professional Apartment Management, Inc., Lodi, CA, pg. 893
Barker, Rhonda W., Controller--American Tara Corporation, Atlanta, GA, pg. 63
Barlow, Charles, Treas.--Sinclair Oil Corp., Salt Lake City, UT, pg. 1008
Barnard, Frank, Controller--Thunderline Corporation, Belleville, MI, pg. 1096
Barney, Chris, Controller--Schwinn Bicycle Company, Chicago, IL, pg. 981
Barney, D.D., Controller--Pennsylvania Petroleum Product Company, Southhampton, PA, pg. 858
Baron, Mark, Controller--Master Industries Corp., New York, NY, pg. 719
Baroni, Albert J., Controller--Malden Mills Industries, Inc., Lawrence, MA, pg. 702
Barr, Michael, Controller--Dietrich's Milk Products, Inc., Reading, PA, pg. 337
Barrientos, Emmanuel, Controller--John H. Graham & Co., Inc., Oradell, NJ, pg. 475
Barrier, Luther, Comptroller--S&D Coffee Inc., Concord, NC, pg. 959
Barry, Debby, Controller--Vance Industries, Inc., Chicago, IL, pg. 1144
Bartenstein, Jeff C., Sec., Treas. & Controller--Alaska Industrial Hardware Inc., Anchorage, AK, pg. 30
Barter, Art, Controller--Magnedyne Div., Carlsbad, CA, pg. 1003
Bartle, Richard, Controller--Economy Folding Box Corp., Chicago, IL, pg. 367
Bartley, Thomas, Controller--Modern Drop Forge Co., Blue Island, IL, pg. 762
Bartow, J.D., V.P. & Controller--Econocom-USA Inc., Memphis, TN, pg. 367
Baruch, Alex, Controller--Dairylea Cooperative Inc., East Syracuse, NY, pg. 311
Basar, John, Chief Fin. Officer & Controller--Red Carpet Real Estate Services, Inc., San Diego, CA, pg. 918
Bashir, Fraukh, Controller--Welsh Graphics, Pasadena, CA, pg. 1176
Basile, Vincent F., Controller--WWF Paper Corporation, Bala-Cynwyd, PA, pg. 1157
Batchelder, Herbert W., Controller--Bose Corporation, Framingham, MA, pg. 167
Bates, Susan, Controller, Chief Fin. Officer & Sec.--The Benatty Corporation, Cambridge, OH, pg. 138
Bath, David A., V.P. & Controller--Kleinschmidt Inc., Deerfield, IL, pg. 635
Batory, Lynn, Controller--Elgin National Industries, Inc., Chicago, IL, pg. 609
Batt, Bill, Controller--Kemmons Wilson Companies, Memphis, TN, pg. 1194
Batt, Jim, Controller--Sanborn Manufacturing Company, Springfield, MN, pg. 969
Battaglia, Gregg, Controller--Witt Company, Cincinnati, OH, pg. 1198
Battan, Thomas A., Treas. & Comptroller--W. L. Hailey & Company, Inc., Nashville, TN, pg. 500
Battles, Joe, Controller--Union Steel Products, Incorporated, Albion, MI, pg. 1129
Bauer, Joel, Controller--On-Cor Frozen Foods Inc., Chicago, IL, pg. 826
Baum, Kenneth, V.P. & Controller--The Grand Union Company, Wayne, NJ, pg. 476
Baum, Lynn, Controllor & Mgr.-Acct.--Idea Man, Inc., Los Angeles, CA, pg. 562
Baumkirchner, Raymond, Controller--The First Boston Corporation, New York, NY, pg. 203
Bauschka, Michael, V.P. & Controller--Montgomery Elevator Company, Moline, IL, pg. 767
Baydarian, Mark, Controller--Leviton Mfg. Co., Inc., Little Neck, NY, pg. 671
Baynee, April, Controller--Bruss Company, Chicago, IL, pg. 184
Beaman, Thomas E., Controller--Coastal Dairy Products, Inc., Wilson, NC, pg. 257
Beard, Thomas, Sr. V.P., Chief Fin. Officer, Treas. & Controller--Petroleum Inc., Wichita, KS, pg. 865
Beard, Thomas G., V.P.-Admin., Treas., Controller & Sec.--Palmer Electric Co., Winter Park, FL, pg. 843
Beasley, William, Controller--PTC Aerospace, Garden Grove, CA, pg. 837
Beauford, Richard, Controller--Coleman Dairy Inc., Little Rock, AR, pg. 261
Beauregard, Ron, Controller--Union Industries, Inc., Providence, RI, pg. 1128
Becker, Jerome, Controller--Masters, Inc., Westbury, NY, pg. 720
Becker, Mick, Controller--Interstate Distributors Inc., Norcross, GA, pg. 580
Beczkiewicz, Tom, Controller--Abbyland Foods, Inc., Abbotsford, WI, pg. 10
Beddingfield, Barbara, Controller--Hollingsworth & Vose Co., East Walpole, MA, pg. 539
Bedford, Brian C., Controller--Marketing Corp. of America, Westport, CT, pg. 709
Beeson, George, V.P. & Comptroller--Revere Electric Supply Co., Chicago, IL, pg. 930
Begue, J.S., Comptroller--Everlast Sports Manufacturing Corp., Bronx, NY, pg. 392
Behrendt, Don, Controller--A B C Appliance Inc., Pontiac, MI, pg. 2
Behrendt, Ken, Chief Fin. Officer, V.P.-Fin. & Controller--Lawson Associates Inc., Minneapolis, MN, pg. 663
Behymer, Jean M., Controller--Ghent Manufacturing, Inc., Lebanon, OH, pg. 455
Belardi, Donna, V.P., Controller--Letven-Diccicco, Inc., Horsham, PA, pg. 669
Beling, Gregory, Controller--Miner Enterprises Inc., Geneva, IL, pg. 756
Belitsky, Lee J., V.P., Treas. & Comptroller--Morse Shoe, Inc., Canton, MA, pg. 772
Bell, Bob, Asst. Treas. & Controller--Rose Packing Company, South Barrington, IL, pg. 947
Bell, Dennis, Controller & Treas.--Vernay Laboratories, Inc., Yellow Springs, OH, pg. 1148
Bell, Doug, Controller--Polaris Pool Systems, Inc., San Marcos, CA, pg. 878
Bell, Randy J., Sr. V.P. & Controller--Levy Security Consultants, Limited, Chicago, IL, pg. 672
Bell, Sharon H., Controller--RPR & Associates, Inc., Columbia, SC, pg. 908
Bellair, Robert, Controller--Harris-Kayot, Inc., Fort Wayne, IN, pg. 512
Bellis, W.J., Treas. & Controller--AGR International, Inc., Butler, PA, pg. 4
Belota, Al, Controller--MCKONE & CO., INC., Irving, TX, pg. 731
Belsky, Samuel, Dir.-Personnel & Controller--Spirite Industries, Inc., Englewood, NJ, pg. 1031
Belsly, J. Robert, Treas.--Nodak Mutual Insurance Co., Fargo, ND, pg. 808
Benapfl, William J., Controller--California Custom Foods, Lodi, CA, pg. 840
Bendelius, Ronald A., Sr. V.P. & Controller--Arnhold and S. Bleichroeder, Inc., New York, NY, pg. 84
Bender, Michael, Treas., Controller & Chief Accountant--Lewis Drug, Inc., Sioux Falls, SD, pg. 673
Bender, Ray A., Comptroller--Airguard Industries Inc., Louisville, KY, pg. 27
Benham, Barbara, Controller--Frederic Printing Company, Aurora, CO, pg. 430
Benka, Jim, Controller--Symons Corporation, Des Plaines, IL, pg. 1069
Benner, Kevin P., Controller, Sec. & Treas.--Jasper County Farm Bureau Co-op Association, Inc., Rensselaer, IN, pg. 590
Bennett, John, Comptroller--Quintron Systems, Inc., Santa Maria, CA, pg. 905
Bennett, Marvin, Controller--GF Industries, Inc., Oakland, CA, pg. 439
Bennett, Saul, Controller--Mark Fabricks, Inc., Los Angeles, CA, pg. 708
Benrus, Mark, Controller--The Jel Sert Co., West Chicago, IL, pg. 591

Benson, Bob, Controller (SEG)--Hallmark Cards, Inc., Kansas City, MO, pg. 501
Benson, Jan, Controller--Brown & Hadley & Partners, Seattle, WA, pg. 182
Benson, Robert, Controller--Komatsu Dresser Company, Lincolnshire, IL, pg. 565
Benson, Vera, Sec. & Controller--Ernst W. Dorn Co., Inc., Gardena, CA, pg. 346
Bentley, Al, Controller--Pearce Industries Inc., Houston, TX, pg. 853
Benz, Edward, Asst. Treas. & Controller--Wheaton Van Lines, Inc., Indianapolis, IN, pg. 1184
Berg, Jennifer, Controller--Al Neyer, Inc., Cincinnati, OH, pg. 805
Berger, Stan, Controller--Steinbach, White Plains, NY, pg. 1045
Bergman, Joseph, V.P. & Controller--Gould Paper Corporation, New York, NY, pg. 473
Bericopes, Tom, Controller--Amtran, Inc., Indianapolis, IN, pg. 69
Berkowski, Joe, Controller--Carhartt, Inc., Dearborn, MI, pg. 220
Berman, Alan R., V.P. & Controller--Bee-Gee Shoe Div., Dayton, OH, pg. 373
Berman, Lawrence, Controller--Transammonia Inc., New York, NY, pg. 1106
Berney, Linda, Controller--Chief Industries, Inc., Grand Island, NE, pg. 247
Bernstein, Minda, Controller--The Ad Team Of Florida Inc., North Miami, FL, pg. 16
Berry, Allen W., Controller--Wehco Media, Inc., Little Rock, AR, pg. 1172
Berry, Marci, Controller--Kroh Operating L.P., Overland Park, KS, pg. 645
Berry, Nancy, Controller--Jewell Instruments, Inc., Manchester, NH, pg. 594
Berton, Louis, Controller--Dena Corporation, Elk Grove Village, IL, pg. 329
Bertrand, Robert, V.P.-Fin.--Industrial Acoustics Company, Inc., Bronx, NY, pg. 565
Berube, Neal, Comptroller--Associated Food Stores Inc., Salt Lake City, UT, pg. 89
Betz, Michael, Controller--Allied Chucker & Engineering Company, Jackson, MI, pg. 37
Beutler, Tom, Sec., Treas. & Controller--Beutler Heating & Air Conditioning Inc., Sacramento, CA, pg. 148
Beverding, Steve, Controller--Oil & Gas Supply Company, Houston, TX, pg. 823
Beverly, Edith, Controller--Carter-Jones Lumber Company, Kent, OH, pg. 226
Bianchi, Robert, Controller--The Field Controls Company, Kinston, NC, pg. 525
Biegel, Russell Jr., Controller--William Morrow & Co., Inc., New York, NY, pg. 521
Biesmann, John, Controller--O'Brien Powder Products, Inc., Houston, TX, pg. 820
Biesmann, John, Controller--O'Brien Powder Products, Inc., Houston, TX, pg. 820
Bill Flatcher, Controller--Western Linen Corp., Phoenix, AZ, pg. 1180
Bindell, Jerry, Comptroller--Chester Gore Company Inc., New York, NY, pg. 472
Binkley, Ruth, Controller--Cummings Inc., Nashville, TN, pg. 304
Birdsall, Walt, V.P.-Fin. & Gen. Mgr.--Lafayette Manufacturing, Inc., Hayward, CA, pg. 650
Birdsong, Randall G., Controller--Spencer Companies Inc., Huntsville, AL, pg. 1030
Bishoff, John, Controller--Steiner Corporation, Salt Lake City, UT, pg. 1045
Bishop, Carl, Controller--Howell Laboratories, Inc., Bridgton, ME, pg. 548
Black, David R., Controller & Treas.--Jitney-Jungle Stores of America, Inc., Jackson, MS, pg. 594
Black, Douglas M., Controller--Bradley Printing Company, Des Plaines, IL, pg. 478
Blade, Kenneth L., Controller--Chicago Lock Company, Chicago, IL, pg. 245
Blaise, Gregor, Controller--Costa Cruise Lines, N.V., Miami, FL, pg. 288
Blake, Cynthia, Controller--Computer Methods Corporation, Livonia, MI, pg. 271
Blake, R.E., V.P. & Controller--Daubert Industries, Inc., Westchester, IL, pg. 317
Blake, Russell, F., Jr., Controller--Lee National Corporation, New York, NY, pg. 666
Blanchard, Craig A., Chief Fin. Officer, Treas. & Controller--Sheldons' Inc., Antigo, WI, pg. 996
Blanchette, Bob, Controller--American Mathematical Society, Inc., Providence, RI, pg. 58
Blanck, John P., Controller--Kuhn & Wittenborn, Inc., Kansas City, MO, pg. 646
Bleser, Howard, Controller--Wellcraft Marine, Sarasota, FL, pg. 759
Blickens, Robert, V.P.-Fin., Treas. & Comptroller--Komline-Sanderson Engineering Corp., Peapack, NJ, pg. 641
Blohm, Douglas L., Controller--Riceland Foods, Inc., Stuttgart, AR, pg. 931
Bloom, Ted, V.P. & Controller--International Data Group, Boston, MA, pg. 576
Blount, Aubrey, Controller--McKenzie Tank Lines, Inc., Tallahassee, FL, pg. 730
Blount, Jimmie, Sec., Treas. & Controller--Delta Pride Catfish, Inc., Indianola, MS, pg. 327
Blum, Michael, Controller--Utility Trailer Manufacturing Co., City of Industry, CA, pg. 1141
Blumberg, Richard, Controller--Titan Industrial Corp., New York, NY, pg. 1099
Blume, Jon, Controller--Bel-Art Products, Pequannock, NJ, pg. 133
Bobo, April, Sec. & Controller--Olen Corporation, Columbus, OH, pg. 641
Bobo, John D., Controller--Blissfield Manufacturing Company, Blissfield, MI, pg. 157
Bochniak, Ed, V.P. & Controller--Thybony Wall Coverings Co., Chicago, IL, pg. 1096
Bocklund, Scott R., Controller--E.F. Johnson Company, Eden Prarie, MN, pg. 598
Boe, Gerry, Controller--Enduro Industries, Inc., Addison, IL, pg. 939
Boedeker, Arnold, V.P. & Controller--Ludlow Composites Corporation, Fremont, OH, pg. 686
Boehmer, Doug, Controller--Associated Wholesale Grocers, Inc., Kansas City, KS, pg. 92
Boersma, Mark, Controller--Seton Company, Norristown, PA, pg. 993
Boeshart, Frank, V.P., Treas. & Controller--Terminal Grain Corp., Sioux City, IA, pg. 1088
Bogacki, Michael F., V.P. & Controller--Farley Industries, Chicago, IL, pg. 399
Bogart, Glenda, Controller--Kingsbridge Media & Marketing, Inc., Van Nuys, CA, pg. 631
Bohner, Dan A., Controller--Adventure Lands of America, Inc., Des Moines, IA, pg. 21
Boland, James, Dir.-Data Processing, Pension Admin., Controller & Sec.--Central Illinois Steel Company, Carlinville, IL, pg. 232
Bolce, Donn W., Controller--Hickman Williams & Co. Inc., Cincinnati, OH, pg. 532
Bonaivto, Paul, Controller--Perry Printing Corp., Waterloo, WI, pg. 607
Bonaker, Dave, Controller--Columbus Mills, Inc., Columbus, GA, pg. 267
Bondoc, Evelyn, Controller/Computer Operations--GWP, Inc., Los Angeles, CA, pg. 441
Bonelli, Ronald J., V.P. & Corp. Controller--Berol Corporation, Brentwood, TN, pg. 856
Bonelli, Steve, Controller--Ready Systems, Sunnyvale, CA, pg. 916
Bonifaci, John, Treas. & Controller--Old Home Foods, Inc., Saint Paul, MN, pg. 823
Bonk, Michael, V.P. & Controller--Bachman's, Inc., Minneapolis, MN, pg. 108
Bonkoski, Ken J., Controller--Menasha Corporation, Neenah, WI, pg. 738
Boone, Billy, Controller--Sunbeam Home Comfort, Shubuta, MS, pg. 1059
Boos, Robert V., Controller--American Institute of C.P.A.'s Inc., New York, NY, pg. 56
Boquist, John J., V.P. & Controller--MI-Jack Products, Inc., Hazel Crest, IL, pg. 746
Borgman, Jerry, Treas. & Controller--Lyon's Restaurants, Inc., Foster City, CA, pg. 690
Borlinghaus, Scott, Sec. & Controller--John Fabick Tractor Company, Fenton, MO, pg. 396
Born, Gary, Comptroller--National Live Stock & Meat Board, Chicago, IL, pg. 792
Boross, Steve, Comptroller--Pioneer Paper Corporation, Carlstadt, NJ, pg. 872
Borovíak, Edwin, Chief Fin. Officer & Controller--Zyntec GmbH, Vienna,, Austria, pg. 1221
Boschert, Judith T., Controller--Chelsea Moore Company, Cincinnati, OH, pg. 241
Botte, Sam, Chief Fin. Officer, V.P.-Fin., Treas. & Controller--Raub Supply Company, Lancaster, PA, pg. 913
Bottorff, Walter, Controller--Christianity Today, Inc., Carol Stream, IL, pg. 249
Boudreaux, Al, Comptroller--Sperling, New Orleans, LA, pg. 1030
Bouise, Crag, Treas. & Controller--Thermal Technology Industries, N. Kansas City, MO, pg. 1091
Boutros, Soad, Comptroller--Romann & Tannenholz Advertising, Inc., New York, NY, pg. 945
Bowen, Carl W., Controller--Ohio Machinery Co., Cleveland, OH, pg. 822
Bowen, James E., Sec. & Comptroller--Better Living Inc., Charlottesville, VA, pg. 148
Bowen, John, V.P.-Fin. & Controller--The Robert E. Morris Company, Farmington, CT, pg. 771
Bowers, Patrick, Controller--National Machinery Company, Tiffin, OH, pg. 792
Bowser, Dave, Controller-Seed--Land O'Lakes, Inc., Agricultural Services Div., Saint Paul, MN, pg. 653
Boyce, Craig D., Controller--Niagara Blower Company, Buffalo, NY, pg. 805
Boyd, Carolyn, Comptroller--Thompson & Company, Memphis, TN, pg. 1094
Boyd, Lester D., Controller & Mgr.-Office--Harrison Paint Corporation, Canton, OH, pg. 512
Boyd, Michael Delen, Controller--Avondale Mills, Inc., Sylacauga, AL, pg. 103
Boydston, Deanea, Controller--Marketing Resources of America, Inc., Overland Park, KS, pg. 709
Boyer, George W., Controller--Hamilton Equipment, Inc., Ephrata, PA, pg. 503
Boyer, Norman L., Dir.-Fin. & Acct.--United McGill Corp., Groveport, OH, pg. 1133
Boyer, Terry, Controller--Avibank Mfg., Inc., Burbank, CA, pg. 102
Boyet, Charles, Controller & Treas.--Sigmund Cohn Corp., Mount Vernon, NY, pg. 259
Boyette, John G., V.P. & Controller--Cox Enterprises, Inc., Atlanta, GA, pg. 292
Boyle, Steven L., Controller--Atwood Industries, Inc., Rockford, IL, pg. 97
Boza, Vivian, Controller--Athletic Attic Properties Inc., Gainesville, FL, pg. 94
Brace, John, Controller--Astre Corporate Group, Alexandria, VA, pg. 92
Bracken, Joseph, Controller--Precision Carbide Tool Company, Inc., Niles, IL, pg. 885
Brackman, Michael A., Controller--PMC Industries Inc., Wickliffe, OH, pg. 836
Bradly, Charles E., Treas. & Controller--Fabreeka International, Inc., Stoughton, MA, pg. 396
Bradshaw, Jim, Controller--Bruce Industries, Inc., Dayton, NV, pg. 183
Brady, Bill, Controller--Port of Houston Authority, Houston, TX, pg. 881
Brady, Robert T., Jr., Comptroller--Hopple Plastics, Inc., Florence, KY, pg. 544
Bram, Dana D., V.P.- Fin. & Controller--The American Companies, Inc., Topeka, KS, pg. 50
Branch, Kenneth A., Sec., Treas. & Controller--Randall's Food Markets, Inc., Houston, TX, pg. 911
Branch, Ruth, Controller--Darien & Kilburg, Inc., San Jose, CA, pg. 315
Brand, Ronald, Controller--Martin Exploration Management Company, Alsip, IL, pg. 715
Brassard, Mary, Corp. Sec. & Controller--F. H. Chase, Inc., Foxboro, MA, pg. 240
Braun, Margorie, Controller--Maryland Virginia Milk Producers Association, Inc., Reston, VA, pg. 717
Bray, David L., Controller--HPS, Inc., Indianapolis, IN, pg. 497
Bray, Stan, Controller--Bizzack Inc., Lexington, KY, pg. 153
Brayman, Mark, Controller--Electrical Insulation Suppliers, Hillside, IL, pg. 374
Brazeau, Richard, V.P. & Controller--Standard Manufacturing Company, Troy, NY, pg. 1037
Brennan, Arthur, Controller--Industrial Materials Technology, Andover, MA, pg. 789
Brennan, Arthur, Controller--National Forge Engineered Systems Div., Andover, MA, pg. 789
Brennan, Daniel V., Sec. & Controller--Frontier Lumber Company, Inc., Buffalo, NY, pg. 434
Brennan, Diane, Sec. & Controller--Thruway Fasteners Inc., North Tonawanda, NY, pg. 1096
Brennan, James, Comptroller--Christian Children's Fund, Inc., Richmond, VA, pg. 248
Brennan, John D., Controller--McAnally Enterprises, Inc., Yucaipa, CA, pg. 726
Brennan, Patrick, Controller--UFE Cal Tec Inc., Brea, CA, pg. 1123
Brenner, Jeff, Controller--Database America Companies, Montvale, NJ, pg. 316
Brenner, Michael D., Controller--Production Tool Supply Co., Warren, MI, pg. 893
Bridge, Paul W., Jr., Controller--Xtek, Inc., Cincinnati, OH, pg. 1206
Bridges, Maxine L., Sec., Treas. & Dir.-Personnel & Investor Rels.--Sterling Homes Corp., Sparks, NV, pg. 1046
Briggs, John, V.P., Sec. & Controller--Hy-Vee Food Stores Incorporated, Chariton, IA, pg. 556
Briggs, Steve, Controller--Star Lumber & Supply Company, Inc., Wichita, KS, pg. 1039
Bright, Cliff, Controller--Interform Corporation, Bridgeville, PA, pg. 574
Brinkman, Sue E., V.P. & Comptroller--Caddock Electronics, Inc., Riverside, CA, pg. 207
Brinson, Robert P., V.P. & Controller--Taylor-Morley, Inc., Saint Louis, MO, pg. 1081
Brisley, Peter, Controller--Klaussner Furniture Industry, Asheboro, NC, pg. 634
Brittelli, Brenda S., Chief Fin. Officer, Sec.,Treas. & Controller--Adams Wine Co., Atlanta, GA, pg. 17
Brockelmeyer, Donna, V.P. & Controller--David Boland, Inc., Titusville, FL, pg. 162
Brodzki, George, Exec. V.P., Chief Fin. Officer & Controller--Ryser Brothers Inc., Chicago, IL, pg. 958
Bromme, Mike, Comptroller--North Carolina Mutual Wholesale Drug Co., Durham, NC, pg. 813
Brown, Arnold, Controller--The Hively Agency Inc., Houston, TX, pg. 536
Brown, Charles, Controller--Engineered Polymers Corporation, Mora, MN, pg. 507
Brown, David, Controller-Canada--Ivex Packaging Corporation-Canadian Region, Toronto, Canada, pg. 583
Brown, Gayle, Controller--Crown Coat, Inc., Grand Rapids, MI, pg. 609
Brown, Gehr W., V.P.-Fin.--Mona Industries, Inc., Paterson, NJ, pg. 764
Brown, J. Gilbert, Controller--Stephen Gould Paper Co., Inc., Whippany, NJ, pg. 473
Brown, James E., Jr., V.P.-Finance--FMS Management Systems, Inc., North Miami Beach, FL, pg. 394
Brown, Leonard, Controller--The ERM Group, Exton, PA, pg. 360
Brown, Lyman R., Controller--United Grocers Inc., Portland, OR, pg. 1132
Brown, Mark, Controller--United Farm Tools, Inc., Glasgow, KY, pg. 1131
Brown, Mark, Controller--United Farm Tools, Kentucky Div., Glasgow, KY, pg. 1132
Brown, Paul,Jr., Controller--Willamette-Western Corporation, Portland, OR, pg. 1190
Brown, Raymond J., Asst. Controller--Gohmann Asphalt & Construction Inc., Clarksville, IN, pg. 465
Brown, Robert A., Controller--Air Conditioning Co., Inc., Glendale, CA, pg. 26
Brown, Ron, Controller--Pacific Forge, Inc., Fontana, CA, pg. 102
Brown, Saralyn, V.P. & Controller--Alex Foods, Inc., Anaheim, CA, pg. 33
Broz, James F., Controller & Asst. Treas.--Office Electronics, Inc., Itasca, IL, pg. 821
Bruce, Minette, Controller--Delta Queen Steamboat Company, New Orleans, LA, pg. 385
Bruce, Randy, Controller--Mar-Jac Inc., Gainesville, GA, pg. 705
Bruce, Sandra, Controller & Office Mgr.--Hall Contracting Corp., Louisville, KY, pg. 501
Brucker, David, Controller--Industrial Rubber Products Company, Charleston, WV, pg. 566
Brunton, David W., Controller--Phoenix American Incorporated, San Rafael, CA, pg. 868
Bruss, Nancy A., Controller--S.W. Jr. Enterprises, Inc., Santa Ana Heights, CA, pg. 965
Bryan, Robert, Controller--Osborn & Barr Communications, Clayton, MO, pg. 830

Bryant, David, Controller--Dealers Electrical Supply Co., Waco, TX, pg. 322
Bryen, G.E., V.P. & Controller--ASC Incorporated, Southgate, MI, pg. 7
Bubp, Greg, Controller--Eclipse, Inc., Rockford, IL, pg. 366
Bucci, Robert, Controller--Tupman Thurlow Co. Inc., New Rochelle, NY, pg. 1119
Buckingham, Douglas A., Treas. & Controller--WYO-Ben, Inc., Billings, MT, pg. 1157
Buczynski, Veronica, Controller--Gamma One, Inc., North Haven, CT, pg. 442
Budnick, David W., Controller--Hatfield Quality Meats, Inc., Hatfield, PA, pg. 517
Bukowski, Gary, V.P.-Fin., Controller & Sec.--Key Industries, Inc., Fort Scott, KS, pg. 627
Bullock, Judith A., Controller--Independent Metals, Germantown, WI, pg. 565
Buncher, S., Controller--Erico International, Cleveland, OH, pg. 386
Bunker, Theodore, Controller--Flint Manufacturing Co., Burton, MI, pg. 419
Bunn, Michael, Controller--Monroc, Inc., Salt Lake City, UT, pg. 766
Buonato, Richard T., V.P. & Controller--Icahn & Co., Inc., Mount Kisco, NY, pg. 561
Burch, J.E., V.P. & Controller--Guarantee Mutual Life Co., Omaha, NE, pg. 491
Burge, Michael D., Controller--Whiting Corporation, Harvey, IL, pg. 1187
BurKamper, Rick, Controller--Sieg Company, Davenport, IA, pg. 1002
Burke, Patrick, V.P., Controller & Treas.--Ziff Communications Company, New York, NY, pg. 1218
Burke, Steve, Controller--Butterick Company, Inc., New York, NY, pg. 197
Burkett, Thomas L., V.P. & Treas.--Golden Gem Growers Inc., Umatilla, FL, pg. 466
Burkey, Michelle, Controller & Treas.--Edgerton Forge, Inc., Edgerton, OH, pg. 102
Burley, Mark M., Controller--Joseph Simon & Sons, Inc., Tacoma, WA, pg. 1006
Burman, Donald P., Controller--Greeley Gas Co., Denver, CO, pg. 483
Burnett, Marti, Controller--Mid-America Dairymen, Inc., Springfield, MO, pg. 750
Burnham, B.E., Controller--J.M. Huber, Engineered Carbons Div., Borger, TX, pg. 550
Burns, John F., Controller & Principal Acctg. Officer--Arthur D. Little, Inc., Cambridge, MA, pg. 678
Burns, Michael, Controller--Davis Tool & Engineering Co., Detroit, MI, pg. 318
Burrell, Richard, Controller--Baroum Eaton Allen Corporation, Brooklyn, NY, pg. 121
Burton, Ann, Controller--The Monarch Company, Inc., Atlanta, GA, pg. 765
Burton, Ken, Comptroller--Anchor Continental Incorporated, Columbia, SC, pg. 71
Busam, Ray, Controller--L. R. Nelson Corporation, Peoria, IL, pg. 797
Busby, Mike, Chief Fin. Officer, Treas. & Controller--Crested Butte Mountain Resort, Inc., Mount Crested Butte, CO, pg. 299
Busch, Kevin E., Controller--Temp-Control Mechanical Corp., Portland, OR, pg. 1086
Bushweiler, Wayne, Controller--Morning Glory Farms Region, Shawano, WI, pg. 770
Busi, Maria-Luis, V.P. & Controller--Katz Communications, Inc., New York, NY, pg. 618
Buss, Scott, Controller--United Hardware Distributing Co., Plymouth, MN, pg. 1132
Bustros, Ryan, Chief Information Officer--Ferrara Foods & Confections, Inc., New York, NY, pg. 407
Butash, Carol, V.P., Comptroller--Mars Advertising Co., Southfield, MI, pg. 713
Butler, Alice, Controller--Byerly Ford-Nissan Inc., Louisville, KY, pg. 198
Butler, Frank J., Controller & Chief Info. Officer--Lyon Metal Products, Inc., Montgomery, IL, pg. 690
Butler, John, Controller--CC Services, Bloomington, IL, pg. 289
Butler, John, Controller--Producers Livestock, North Salt Lake, UT, pg. 892
Butler, Patricia, Controller--Willis Case Harwood, Inc., Dayton, OH, pg. 1192
Buttermelch, Bob, Controller--Florence Corporation, Huntington, NY, pg. 420
Bybee, O. Lynn, Treas. & Controller--Wick Building Systems, Mazomanie, WI, pg. 1188
Bye, Roger J., Controller--C B R Cement Corporation, San Mateo, CA, pg. 199
Byrd, Edward R., V.P. & Controller--Pacific Mutual Life Insurance Company, Newport Beach, CA, pg. 841
Byrnes, Gerald, Corp. Controller--DeBruce Grain Inc., North Kansas City, MO, pg. 323
Byruch, D.B., V.P. & Controller--J.E. Berkowitz, LP, Westville, NJ, pg. 142
Byrum, Lyndon, Controller--Alex Lee, Inc., Hickory, NC, pg. 33
Caboner, Gene, Division Controller--Ivex Packaging Corporation-Polymerization and Extrusion Division, Hazleton, PA, pg. 583
Cacchiotti, Don, Controller--Spelling Entertainment Group, Inc., Cincinnati, OH, pg. 54
Cagalj, Mike, Chief Fin. Officer, V.P. & Controller--Atlas Hotels, Inc., San Diego, CA, pg. 96
Cahill, Kirk, Controller--Chicago Extruded Metals Co., Cicero, IL, pg. 245
Cain, Robert, Controller--Cal/Emblem Labels, Inc., Fresno, CA, pg. 208
Cain, Robert O., Controller--Thompson-McCully Co., Belleville, MI, pg. 1094
Caiola, Vincent, Controller--The Lane Construction Corp., Meriden, CT, pg. 656
Caldwell, Jay, V.P.-Fin. & Admin.--Applied Microsystems Corporation, Redmond, WA, pg. 79
Calhoun, Lynn, Chief Fin. Officer & Controller--Prime Technology, Inc., Grand Rapids, MI, pg. 889
Call, Michael, Controller--Maverik Country Stores, Inc., Afton, WY, pg. 722
Camardo, Gina, Controller--Bradford Exchange Ltd., Niles, IL, pg. 170
Camarre, Jim, Controller & Dir.-Mngmt. Information Systems--Mollenberg-Betz Inc., Buffalo, NY, pg. 764
Campbell, Denise, Controller--Marontate & Co., Auburn Hills, MI, pg. 713
Campbell, Mike, Controller & Sec.--Fareway Stores, Inc., Boone, IA, pg. 399
Campbell, Scott, Controller--Lost Arrow Corporation, Ventura, CA, pg. 684
Campbell, Stephen, Mgr.-Financial Control--William Blair & Company, Chicago, IL, pg. 155
Canals, Gladys, Controller--American International Container, Inc., Miami, FL, pg. 56
Canfield, Darryl L., V.P. & Controller--Curtice-Burns Foods, Inc., Rochester, NY, pg. 25
Canipe, H.G., Jr., Controller--Rodgers Builders, Inc., Charlotte, NC, pg. 942
Cantrell, Ron, Chief Fin. Officer, Exec. V.P. & Controller--The Mad Butcher, Inc., Pine Bluff, AR, pg. 699
Capps, Joe, Comptroller--Ed Mullinax Ford, Inc., Amherst, OH, pg. 775
Carabetta, John, Comptroller & Dir.-Personnel & Investor Rels.--Beauty Enterprises Inc., Hartford, CT, pg. 130
Carey, Michael, Comptroller--Technology Applications, Inc., Alexandria, VA, pg. 1083
Carlovatto, Jeff, Treas. & Controller--QST Industries, Inc., Chicago, IL, pg. 902
Carlson, Bruce, Corp. Controller--Delaware North Companies, Inc., Buffalo, NY, pg. 326
Carlson, Carolyn, Controller--Micro-Aire Surgical Instruments, Inc., Valencia, CA, pg. 711
Carlson, Ronald, Controller--Wilson Machine Knife Co., Inc., Dayville, CT, pg. 556
Carlson, Ronald P., Controller--Hyde Manufacturing Co., Southbridge, MA, pg. 556
Carmany, Dave, V.P.-Fin., Treas. & Controller--Castleberry's Food Company, Augusta, GA, pg. 229
Carnes, Phyllis, Exec. V.P., Comptroller, Legal Officer & Dir.-Investor Rels.--Eagle Lincoln Mercury Inc., Dallas, TX, pg. 362
Carney, Kevin, Comptroller--The Carlyle Group, Washington, DC, pg. 222
Carroll, Chuck, Treas., Controller & Chief Fin. Officer--South East Coal Co., Irvine, KY, pg. 1019
Carpenter, Jan, Sr. V.P., Dir. Fin. & Admin.--Hal Riney & Partners, Inc., San Francisco, CA, pg. 935
Carpenter, Ransom A., Treas. & Controller--Mauney Hosiery Mills, Inc., Kings Mountain, NC, pg. 722
Carpenter, Scott J., Controller--Druther's International, Inc., Louisville, KY, pg. 350
Carpentier, Paul, Controller--Gordon Food Service Inc., Grand Rapids, MI, pg. 472
Carr, Katherine M., Controller--W.C. Caye & Company, Inc., Atlanta, GA, pg. 230
Carrico, F. Donald, Controller--Rapid Industries, Inc., Louisville, KY, pg. 913
Carrington, Norva, Sec. & Controller--Roland International Corporation, Coconut Grove, FL, pg. 944
Carro, Armando, Comptroller--Braum Ice Cream Stores Inc., Oklahoma City, OK, pg. 172
Carroll, Doug, Controller--Vernell's Candy Company, Bellevue, WA, pg. 1148
Carroll, Troy, Controller--Estes Industries, Inc., Penrose, CO, pg. 1011
Carruthers, George, Pres., Chief Exec. & Chief Fin. Officer, Controller--Polycoat Systems, Inc., Hudson Falls, NY, pg. 880
Carson, Bev, Controller--Iowa Assemblies, Inc., Osceola, IA, pg. 490
Carson, Donald, Controller--BGW Systems, Inc., Hawthorne, CA, pg. 106
Carson, William, Controller--South Chester Tube Co., Concordville, PA, pg. 1019
Cash, Lorene, Controller--Lone Star Corrugated Container Corporation, Irving, TX, pg. 682
Casper, Jack, Comptroller--Tecon Pacific, Sacramento, CA, pg. 1084
Cassella, Anthony, V.P.-Fin. & Controller--Croscill, Inc., New York, NY, pg. 300
Cassin, Gail, Controller--Cargocaire Engineering Corporation, Amesbury, MA, pg. 220
Castaldo, John, Controller--Music Sales Corporation, New York, NY, pg. 777
Caterbury, Larry, Comptroller--Algernon Blair International, Montgomery, AL, pg. 155
Catlett, Gary, Controller & V.P.--Winrock Enterprises, Inc., Little Rock, AR, pg. 1197
Cavellier, Thomas E., Controller--Gator Freightways, Inc., Wilmington, OH, pg. 446
Cebulski, James A., Asst. Controller--Applied Industrial Materials Corporation, Deerfield, IL, pg. 79
Celentano, Domenick A., Jr., V.P.-Mktg.--Celentano Brothers, Verona, NJ, pg. 231
Cella, Barbara T., Controller--Phonetics, Inc., Aston, PA, pg. 869
Centenail, Marie, Controller--Dad's Root Beer, Chicago, IL, pg. 765
Cetta, Anthony J., Mng. Dir. & Grp. Controller--CS First Boston Group, Inc., New York, NY, pg. 203
Chaddick, RoGene, Controller--Allsups Convenience Stores Inc., Clovis, NM, pg. 43
Chaiet, Howard, Controller--Fownes Brothers & Co., Inc., New York, NY, pg. 427
Chamberlin, Elizabeth, Controller--Sterling Paper Co., Philadelphia, PA, pg. 1047
Chan, Pam, Comptroller--Siebel/Mohr, Inc., New York, NY, pg. 1002
Chandler, Clark T., V.P. & Controller--American Tool Companies, Inc., Lincoln, NE, pg. 64
Chapell, Jeff, Controller--Prime Tanning Co., Inc., Berwick, ME, pg. 889
Chapin, John E., Controller--Kaiser Aerospace & Electronics Corp., Foster City, CA, pg. 614
Chapman, Julie, Controller--I Ski Ski Goggles, City of Commerce, CA, pg. 557
Charkiewicz, Nancy, Chief Fin. Officer & Controller--Manufacturers Technologies, Inc., West Springfield, MA, pg. 705
Chastain, Charity, V.P. & Controller--Gene Reed Chevrolet, Charleston Heights, SC, pg. 920
Chesen, Lisa, Controller--Pro Hardware, Inc., Englewood, CO, pg. 891
Chesmore, Mike, Controller--Tom Thumb Food & Drugs, Inc., Dallas, TX, pg. 912
Chiampa, Karen, Controller--Goldman Financial Group, Boston, MA, pg. 468
Chiesa, Nancy, Controller--Ziegler Chemical & Mineral Corp., Jericho, NY, pg. 1218
Childers, C. Scott, Controller--Ballenger Paving Company, Inc., Taylors, SC, pg. 116
Chin, Kenneth, V.P. & Controller--New Hermes Incorporated, Norwalk, CT, pg. 801
Chisnell, Lynn, Controller--Roni Hicks & Associates, Inc., San Diego, CA, pg. 533
Christiansen, Lawrence M., Controller--Concrete Technology Corp., Tacoma, WA, pg. 273
Christiansen, Timothy J., Controller--The Laitram Corporation, Harahan, LA, pg. 650
Christiansen, Timothy J., Controller--Intralox, Inc., Harahan, LA, pg. 651
Christianson, Dean, Controller--Owatonna Canning Company, Owatonna, MN, pg. 833
Christopher, Mark, Controller--Palmetto Wholesale Co., Inc., Columbia, SC, pg. 844
Chudnow, Randy, Controller--Jordache Enterprises, Inc., New York, NY, pg. 604
Cieply, Lucy, Controller & Sec.--Rama Group of Companies, Cheektowaga, NY, pg. 910
Cimini, Lee, Controller--Singers Supermarkets, Inc., North Bergen, NJ, pg. 1008
Cimo, David, Controller--Midwest Litho Arts, Des Plaines, IL, pg. 478
Cirillo, N.J., Asst. V.P. & Controller--The F.A. Bartlett Tree Expert Co., Stamford, CT, pg. 123
Clancy, Bob, Controller--Molon Motor & Coil Corp., Rolling Meadows, IL, pg. 764
Clancy, John P., Sr. V.P. & Controller--Douglas Elliman-Gibbons & Ives, Inc., New York, NY, pg. 347
Clarey, William, Controller--Flex-O-Glass, Inc., Chicago, IL, pg. 418
Clark, James A., Chief Fin. Officer & Treas.--Integral Systems, Walnut Creek, CA, pg. 572
Clark, John P., V.P. & Controller--Londontown Corporation, Eldersburg, MD, pg. 682
Clark, Robert, Controller--Maurice Electric Supply Company, Washington, DC, pg. 722
Clark, Steven, Exec. V.P.-Fin.--Trumbull Corporation, West Mifflin, PA, pg. 1117
Clark, Terry J., Controller--Maxon Corporation, Muncie, IN, pg. 723
Clarke, Ted, Chief Fin. Officer, Treas. & Controller--Hynes Industries Inc., Youngstown, OH, pg. 557
Clatzkin, Terry, Controller--Clark Construction Group, Bethesda, MD, pg. 252
Claverie, Roy E., Sr. V.P.--Ingram Industries Inc., Nashville, TN, pg. 568
Clay, Frank, Treas. & Controller--Pacific Hawaiian Ltd., Hilo, HI, pg. 840
Cleary, Paul, Controller--Butler Automatic, Inc., Canton, MA, pg. 197
Clegg, Ken, Controller--Anderson Advertising, Inc., San Antonio, TX, pg. 72
Clement, Erma, Sec. & Controller--Carden & Cherry, Inc., Nashville, TN, pg. 217
Clements, Marilyn, Controller--Freedman, Gibson & White Inc., Cincinnati, OH, pg. 430
Clifton, David, Treas. & Chief Fin. Officer--Young & Laramore, Indianapolis, IN, pg. 1209
Cling, Michael, Controller--Multi-Plex, Inc., Howe, IN, pg. 318
Closs, Willie, V.P. & Controller--North Carolina Mutual Life Insurance Co., Durham, NC, pg. 813
Clouser, Harry F., Comptroller--Ace Glass Incorporated, Vineland, NJ, pg. 11
Coanz, Howard, Controller--A. J. Hollander Co., Inc., New York, NY, pg. 539
Coats, W. John, V.P.-Fin.--Nutri/System Inc., Blue Bell, PA, pg. 818
Cobb, Tom, Controller--Buffelen Woodworking Company, Tacoma, WA, pg. 187
Cocheo, Paul, Controller--Simmons-Boardman Publishing Corp., New York, NY, pg. 1005
Cockrell, G.F., Controller--Black & Veatch, Kansas City, MO, pg. 154
Cockrell, Mel, Chief Fin. Officer, Treas., Controller & Sec.--Ben E. Keith Company, Fort Worth, TX, pg. 620
Cody, Mary, V.P., Controller--Alexander Marketing Services, Inc., Grand Rapids, MI, pg. 33
Coe, Roger, Controller--C. R. Anthony Company, Oklahoma City, OK, pg. 77
Coffey, Robert J., Controller--The Stackpole Corporation, Boston, MA, pg. 1034
Coffman, Michael W., Controller--Shenandoah Life Insurance Company, Roanoke, VA, pg. 997
Coffman, Michael W., Controller--Old Dominion Life Insurance Co., Roanoke, VA, pg. 997
Cofsky, Stewart, V.P. & Controller--Finora Company, Inc., New York, NY, pg. 810
Cohen, Herbert S., Controller--Arcata Graphics Company, Baltimore, MD, pg. 80

Cohen, Lewis, Treas. & Controller--Kastle Systems, Inc., Arlington, VA, pg. 618
Cohn, Steve, Controller--Jack Greenberg Inc., Philadelphia, PA, pg. 485
Coleman, Mike, Controller--The Coe Mfg. Co., Painesville, OH, pg. 258
Coleman, Richard D., V.P., Controller & Sec.--Kash N Karry Food Stores, Inc., Tampa, FL, pg. 617
Collett, Kenneth L., Controller--Keeney Manufacturing Co., Newington, CT, pg. 620
Collins, Charles, Controller--Cal-Maine Foods, Inc., Jackson, MS, pg. 208
Collins, G.M., Controller--J.M. Huber, Wood Products Div., Charlotte, NC, pg. 550
Collins, Grace, Asst. Controller--Bohbot Communications, Inc., New York, NY, pg. 162
Collins, James, Controller--American Rug Craftsmen Inc., Sugar Valley, GA, pg. 60
Collins, Jim, Controller--Whitin Roberts Co., Sanford, NC, pg. 1187
Collins, Sally, Controller--Land O'Lakes International Div., Minneapolis, MN, pg. 653
Collins, Sally, Controller--Ventures Group, Minneapolis, MN, pg. 654
Collins, Sheila, Controller--INPUT, Mountain View, CA, pg. 571
Collins, Stephen, Controller--California Artichoke & Vegetable Growers Corp., Castroville, CA, pg. 209
Collins, William, Controller--Ward Leonard Electric Company, Inc., Mount Vernon, NY, pg. 1127
Colucci, Catherine, V.P., Comptroller--Rotando Lerch & Iafeliece Advertising, Stamford, CT, pg. 950
Combs, Theodore, Controller--Spring Engineers, Inc., Houston, TX, pg. 1033
Comport, Bradley, Controller--The Davey Tree Expert Company, Kent, OH, pg. 317
Conard, Kim, Controller--B & G Wholesalers, Inc., Nashville, TN, pg. 106
Conley, Paul, Controller--Associated Machinecraft Corporation, Los Angeles, CA, pg. 90
Conley, Perry, Controller--Spartan Mills, Spartanburg, SC, pg. 1026
Conley, Suzanne, Controller--Starving Students, Inc., Los Angeles, CA, pg. 1040
Conlisk, Steve, Controller--Precision Echo, Inc., Santa Clara, CA, pg. 885
Conn, Richard, Controller--Ervin Industries, Inc., Ann Arbor, MI, pg. 387
Connell, Francis X., Controller--Finnaren & Haley, Inc., Conshohocken, PA, pg. 411
Connor, John M., Controller--Cives Corp., Roswell, GA, pg. 251
Conway, Gary, V.P. & Controller--First National Bank of Sweetwater, Sweetwater, TX, pg. 412
Conway, Jack, Sr. V.P. & Controller--Keystone Foods Corporation, Bala-Cynwyd, PA, pg. 628
Conyers, Brent, V.P. & Controller--Precision Metal Prods., Inc., El Cajon, CA, pg. 869
Cook, Tom, Controller--Marinette Marine Corporation, Marinette, WI, pg. 707
Cookson, Bernard, Controller--Mitre Corporation, Bedford, MA, pg. 762
Cooley, Robert, Comptroller--The F. X. Matt Brewing Co., Utica, NY, pg. 721
Coombs, Michael, Controller--Meer Corporation, North Bergen, NJ, pg. 736
Coomes, R.E., V.P. & Controller--Dorr-Oliver Incorporated, Milford, CT, pg. 346
Coon, Wm. Thomas, Controller--Esco Elevators, Inc., Fort Worth, TX, pg. 388
Cooper, Brian G., V.P.-Fin. & Controller--Cox Enterprises Newspaper Division, Atlanta, GA, pg. 292
Cooper, E.H., Controller--Colonial Pipeline Company, Atlanta, GA, pg. 264
Cooper, Laury L., Controller--Brix Maritime Co., Portland, OR, pg. 177
Copans, Philip, Natl. Controller--Coopers & Lybrand, New York, NY, pg. 283
Copass, Harvey, Controller--Franks Supply Company, Inc., Albuquerque, NM, pg. 429
Copp, Christine, Controller--Standard Shoe Company, Inglewood, CA, pg. 1037
Corcoran, Charles, Comptroller--Blue Bird Coach Lines Inc., Olean, NY, pg. 158
Corcoran, William B., Controller--Hapco/American Div., Abingdon, VA, pg. 357
Cordek, Lawrence D., Chief Fin. Officer & Corp. Sec.--G B Stores, Johnstown, PA, pg. 978
Cordes, William, Controller--Gaymar Industries, Inc., Orchard Park, NY, pg. 447
Cordle, Audra, Chief Fin. Officer, Treas. & Controller--Consolidated Co-op, Gowrie, IA, pg. 276
Corey, Wayne, V.P. & Controller--Pacesetter Corporation, Omaha, NE, pg. 839
Corley, Ken, Controller--Wilbur Smith Associates, Columbia, SC, pg. 1011
Corliss, Dennis, Controller--Encore Shoe Corporation, Rochester, NH, pg. 380
Corrigan, Denis, Controller--Pavion Ltd., Nyack on Hudson, NY, pg. 852
Corrigan, John, Asst. Controller--Ivex Packaging Corporation, Lincolnshire, IL, pg. 583
Corriveau, Robert, V.P. & Controller--Robertson Factories, Inc., Taunton, MA, pg. 939
Corso, Frank, Controller--Direct Response Broadcasting Network, Inc., Philadelphia, PA, pg. 339
Cote, Charles R., Controller--Carolina Biological Supply Co., Burlington, NC, pg. 222
Cothern, Carol, Controller--Precision Tune, Inc., Leesburg, VA, pg. 885
Cottrell, Paul, Jr., Controller--Pine State Tobacco & Candy Company, Augusta, ME, pg. 871
Coumbe, Frederick R., Controller--Denver Equipment Company, Colorado Springs, CO, pg. 331
Countryman, Peter J., Chief Fin. Officer, Treas. & Controller--Sabin Robbins Paper Co., Cincinnati, OH, pg. 965
Courtney, Doug, Controller--Ray-Carroll County Grain Co-op, Richmond, MO, pg. 914
Courtney, Thomas, Controller--Brennan College Service, Inc., Springfield, MA, pg. 422
Courtney, Wayne, Controller--Rangen, Inc., Buhl, ID, pg. 912
Covington, Michael A., Controller--Commtek Communications, Vienna, VA, pg. 269
Cowles, H.B., Chief Fin. Officer, Treas. & Controller--Bluff City Distributing Co., Inc., Memphis, TN, pg. 161
Cowles, Rick, Controller--Sullivan Paper Company, West Springfield, MA, pg. 1057
Cox, Ronald L., Controller--Chemtech Industries, Inc., Saint Louis, MO, pg. 242
Coyle, Leila, Controller--Paul A. De Jesse, Inc. Advertising, Freehold, NJ, pg. 321
Craft, Ronald K., V.P.-Fin., Treas. & Controller--CF&I Steel Corporation, Pueblo, CO, pg. 201
Cragen, John R., Controller--Schawk, Inc., Des Plaines, IL, pg. 974
Crane, Fred, Controller--Brooks Products, Inc., El Monte, CA, pg. 180
Crane, Jerry, V.P. & Controller--Harris Mechanical Contracting Co., Saint Paul, MN, pg. 512
Cravens, L.A., Controller--National Frozen Foods Corp., Seattle, WA, pg. 789
Crawford, Linda, Controller--Hickerson Phelps Kirtley & Associates, Kansas City, MO, pg. 532
Crawford, Norma, Controller--Michael Business Machines Corporation, North Charleston, SC, pg. 747
Creagh, Richard P., Controller, Treas. & Chief Fin. Officer--Hoffman Brothers Packing Co., Los Angeles, CA, pg. 537
Creviston, Cheryl, V.P., Controller--Admark, Inc., Topeka, KS, pg. 18
Cron, Norm, Controller--Dawahares, Inc., Lexington, KY, pg. 319
Crook, Orville, Controller--Farm Fresh, Inc., Norfolk, VA, pg. 401
Cross, Mary Lenore, V.P. & Controller--Federal Chicago Corporation, North Chicago, IL, pg. 404
Cross, Silas R., Controller--The Todd-AO Corporation, San Francisco, CA, pg. 1099
Croteau, Maurice, Controller--New England Newspaper Supply Company, Inc., Millbury, MA, pg. 800
Crotty, Mark W., Controller & Sec.--J. C. Brock Corp., Buffalo, NY, pg. 178
Crowell, M., Controller--Digitec, Marion, OH, pg. 1069
Crowell, Myron, Controller--Sycon Corporation, Marion, OH, pg. 1069
Crowley, Malvern D., V.P.-Fin. & Treas.--Drug Emporium of Arizona, Inc., Scottsdale, AZ, pg. 349
Crowley, Mark, Controller--American Speedy Printing Centers, Inc., Bloomfield Hills, MI, pg. 61
Crown, Jerome, Controller--Machado & Co. Inc., New York, NY, pg. 696
Cruger, Michael H., V.P.-Oper. & Controller--Henningsen Foods, Inc., White Plains, NY, pg. 629
Cruse, William, Controller--Wexner & Jacobson, Inc., Memphis, TN, pg. 1183
Cryer, Dave, Contorller--Yardney Technical Products, Inc., Pawcatuck, CT, pg. 1207
Cubberley, Robert, Controller--R. M. Shoemaker Co., West Conshohocken, PA, pg. 1000
Culbreth, Robert, Chief Fin. Officer, Treas. & Controller--Skinner Corp., Lanett, AL, pg. 1009
Cummings, Don, V.P. & Controller--Quality Bakers of America Cooperative, Inc., Greenwich, CT, pg. 903
Cummings, M. Laurie, Controller & Asst. Treas.--Windmill Holdings Corp., San Francisco, CA, pg. 1195
Cummins, Chris, Controller--Mayville Metal Products Division, Mayville, WI, pg. 275
Cummiskey, Thomas S., Controller--Twin County Grocers, Inc., Edison, NJ, pg. 1122
Cumptom, M.E., Controller--J.M. Huber, Clay Div., Macon, GA, pg. 550
Curly, Frank, Jr., Controller--Navajo Forest Products Industries, Navajo, NM, pg. 796
Currie, John L., Controller--G. Heileman Brewing Co., Inc., La Crosse, WI, pg. 526
Curry, James T., Controller--Miller Advertising Agency Inc., New York, NY, pg. 753
Curtis, John, Comptroller--Taylor Company, Rockton, IL, pg. 1027
Cutright, Brenda, V.P-Finance & Controller--Aloha Airgroup, Inc., Honolulu, HI, pg. 43
Czajka, Walter, Controller--Key Food Stores Co-operative, Inc., Brooklyn, NY, pg. 626
Czulno, John J., Comptroller--Naylor Pipe Company, Chicago, IL, pg. 796
D'Amico, John, V.P. & Controller--Wechsler Coffee Corp., Moonachie, NJ, pg. 1172
Dailey, Vincent M., Sr., Comptroller--Einstein Moomjy Inc., Pine Brook, NJ, pg. 371
Daily, John, Controller--Ultra Tool & Plastics, Inc., Amherst, NY, pg. 1125
Daitch, Herbert L., Controller--Idle Wild Management Corporation, Worcester, MA, pg. 1128
Dalal, Peter, Controller--General Welding Supply Corporation, Westbury, NY, pg. 451
Dalke, Gary, Controller--Phoenix Fuel Company, Inc., Phoenix, AZ, pg. 868
Dalmaso, Bruno, Controller & Leasing Dir.--Abbell Associates, Chicago, IL, pg. 9
Daly, Peter, Comptroller--Pedone & Partners Inc., New York, NY, pg. 854
Damiano, Gary, Chief Fin. Officer & Controller--Triangle Marketing Corp., New York, NY, pg. 1112
Dangelo, Jacqueline, Controller & Treas.--The Tobin Corporation, North Ridgeville, OH, pg. 102
Daniel, David B., Controller--Citizens National Bank, Hammond, LA, pg. 251
Daniel, Mark, Controller--Danly-Komatsu L.P., Cicero, IL, pg. 275
Daniel, Michael, Sec., Treas. & Controller--Field Packing Company, Owensboro, KY, pg. 409
Dankmyer, William, Controller--AFG Industries, Inc., Fort Worth, TX, pg. 3
Dannelly, Bruce, Controller--Piedmont Mechanical, Inc., Spartanburg, SC, pg. 870
Danner, Daniel G., Controller--Mid-West Paper Products Company, Warren, MI, pg. 750
Darden, Frankie F., Controller--Veda Incorporated, Alexandria, VA, pg. 1146
Darquea, Nelson, V.P. & Controller--Pacifica Services, Inc., Pasadena, CA, pg. 842
Darsow, David, Controller--Palm Beach Beauty Products Co., Minneapolis, MN, pg. 843
Darville, Christina, Asst. Controller--American Savings Bank, White Plains, NY, pg. 60
Dasaro, Steven, V.P.-Fin. & Admin.--Kaye Instruments, Inc., Bedford, MA, pg. 619
Datt, Gary, Controller--Pannier Corporation, Pittsburgh, PA, pg. 846
Daughtry, E.R., Controller--Perfection-Schwank Inc., Waynesboro, GA, pg. 861
Dauska, Walter J., Controller--Green Bay Packaging Inc., Green Bay, WI, pg. 483
Davenport, Eileen, Controller--Scicom Data Services, Ltd., Minnetonka, MN, pg. 981
David Culley, Controller--Dee Paper Company, Chester, PA, pg. 324
Davidson, James, Controller--Certified Grocers Of California, Los Angeles, CA, pg. 237
Davidson, William J., V.P., Sec. & Controller--Stevens Graphics, Inc., Atlanta, GA, pg. 136
Davis, Al, V.P. & Controller--Marley Pump Co., Mission, KS, pg. 710
Davis, Gary, Controller--Hunter Contracting Company, Gilbert, AZ, pg. 554
Davis, James N., Controller--Nibco, Inc., Elkhart, IN, pg. 806
Davis, Jo, Controller--Krause, Nadurek & Eickmeyer, Dallas, TX, pg. 644
Davis, Kenneth, Comptroller--The Osterneck Co. Inc., Lumberton, NC, pg. 831
Davis, Robert, Controller--Fairfield Maxwell Ltd., New York, NY, pg. 397
Davis, Stephen, Controller--Farnam Companies, Inc., Phoenix, AZ, pg. 403
Day, James L., Chief Fin. Officer & Controller--The Miami Margarine Co., Cincinnati, OH, pg. 746
Day, Mark, Controller--United Broadcasting Inc., Bethesda, MD, pg. 1131
Day, Tom, Controller--Columbia Sussex Corporation, Fort Mitchell, KY, pg. 266
de Bello, David, Chief Fin. Officer & Comptroller--Advertising To Women, Inc., New York, NY, pg. 21
De Luca, Jeff, V.P. & Controller--After Six, Incorporated, Philadelphia, PA, pg. 24
Dean, Dolores M., Controller--Ellwood City Forge, Ellwood City, PA, pg. 378
DeBoth, Dale, Controller--AmClyde Engineered Products, Inc., Saint Paul, MN, pg. 47
Debrecht, Donald R., Sr. V.P., Treas. & Controller--Hill-Behan Lumber Company, Saint Louis, MO, pg. 534
DeBruyn, Barbara, Controller--LSI Truck Products Corp.-Neway/Anchor Lock, Muskegon, MI, pg. 664
DeCecco, Richard, Controller--Pennex Products Co., Inc., Verona, PA, pg. 858
Deemer, Nancy, Controller--Spectradyne Inc., Richardson, TX, pg. 318
Deese, Donald W., Sec. & Controller--Jim Hudson, Pontiac, Oldsmobile GMC, Columbia, SC, pg. 551
Deffet, Suzanne Tabor, Controller--Allied Mineral Products, Inc., Columbus, OH, pg. 38
DeGady, Sonny, Controller--Trainer Wortham & Company Incorporated, New York, NY, pg. 1106
DeGain, Marcy A., Controller--Standard Electronics, Inc., Amherst, NY, pg. 1036
DeGuzman, Renato, Controller--United Health Plan, Inglewood, CA, pg. 1133
Deiser, James, Controller--Auburn Faith Community Hospital, Auburn, CA, pg. 97
Deiter, Jon, Controller--Gerber Plumbing Fixtures Corporation, Chicago, IL, pg. 454
Deiter, Jon, Controller--Kokomo Sanitary Pottery Corp., Chicago, IL, pg. 640
Del Calvo, Teresita, Controller & Dir.-Data Processing--E & G Foods, Miami, FL, pg. 358
Del Rio, Luz, Chief Fin. Officer & Asst. Sec.--Arthur Murray Intl., Inc., Coral Gables, FL, pg. 776
Delaney, Thomas, Controller--ConTec International, Schenectady, NY, pg. 278
DelGaiso, Dave, Controller--Soap Opera Digest, New York, NY, pg. 611
Delisi, Patrick, Controller--Junior Gallery Ltd., New York, NY, pg. 609
Delman, Richard, Chief Fin. Officer, Treas., Sec. & Controller--Splendor Form International Inc., Long Island City, NY, pg. 1031
Deloach, Scott, Controller--Post Buckley Schuh & Jernigan, Miami, FL, pg. 881
Delrossi, John A., Controller--P.J. Keating Company, Lunenburg, MA, pg. 619
DeLuca, Susan, Exec. V.P., Controller & Chief Fin. Officer--Aero Data Metal Crafters, Bohemia, NY, pg. 22
Delventhal, R.H., Controller--Benjamin Moore & Co., Montvale, NJ, pg. 139
DeMaria, Peter J., V.P. & Controller--The Hearst Corporation, New York, NY, pg. 521
DeMent, Cindy, Controller--Keller Crescent Co., Irving, TX, pg. 621

Demers, Norbert, V.P., Comptroller & Chief Fin. Officer--The Hilsinger Corp., Plainville, MA, pg. 535
Dempsey, David W., Controller--Gate City Beverage Distributors, San Bernardino, CA, pg. 444
Den Braker, James, Controller--Louis Padnos Iron & Metal Co., Holland, MI, pg. 842
Dennison, John, Controller--Gaylord Printing, Inc., Detroit, MI, pg. 446
Denton, David, Controller--Farmers Investment Company, Inc., Horse Cave, KY, pg. 115
DePrimo, Richard C., Controller--Alpha Associates, Inc., Woodbridge, NJ, pg. 43
DeRito, J.L., Controller--PQ Corporation, Valley Forge, PA, pg. 836
Dermott, Nancy, Controller--Ocean Spray Cranberries, Inc., Lakeville, MA, pg. 820
DeRose, Douglas, Controller--All World Travel Service, Inc., Dayton, OH, pg. 373
Derrick, Al, Exec. V.P., Chief Fin. Officer & Controller--Cain & Bultman, Inc., Jacksonville, FL, pg. 207
Descoteaux, Mary, V.P. & Controller--Sundt Corp., Tucson, AZ, pg. 1060
Desjarlais, Don, Comptroller--Alto Dairy Cooperative, Waupun, WI, pg. 45
Deter, Robert, Controller--Peerless Chain Co., Winona, MN, pg. 855
Deters, Jim, Controller--Grand Prairie Co-op, Inc., Tolono, IL, pg. 475
Deutcher, Klaus, Chief Fin. Officer & Controller--Bio-Tek Instruments, Inc., Winooski, VT, pg. 152
Dhole, Gulab, Chief Fin. Officer & Controller--West Chemical Products, Inc., Princeton, NJ, pg. 1172
Dhole, Gulab S., V.P.-Fin. & Admin.--Penetone Corp., Tenafly, NJ, pg. 1172
Dhole, Gulab S., V.P.-Fin. & Admin. & Controller--West Pentone Inc., Ville d'Anjou,, Canada, pg. 1172
Di Carlo, Robert, Controller--The Ormond Shops, Inc., North Bergen, NJ, pg. 830
DiChello, Joseph, Controller--New England Corporation, Hamden, CT, pg. 800
Dickerson, Al, Controller--Nautilus, Independence, VA, pg. 796
Dickert, Trudi, V.P., Controller--Smyth, Bauer & Lewis Advertising Inc., Richmond, VA, pg. 1014
Dickhaus, Steve, Controller--Hypro Corporation, New Brighton, MN, pg. 557
Dickinson, Joe, V.P. & Controller--AVW Audiovisual, Inc., Dallas, TX, pg. 431
Dickinson, Nanci, V.P., Controller--Gerber Advertising, Portland, OR, pg. 453
Dickinson, Royce, Sec., Treas. & Controller--Power Process Piping, Inc., Plymouth, MI, pg. 883
Dieckrager, Loren, V.P. & Controller--Inland Printing Co., Inc., La Crosse, WI, pg. 570
Diekemper, Joseph, Controller--M. Bruenger & Co., Inc., Wichita, KS, pg. 184
Dillon, Glennon M., Controller--Zilkha Energy Company, Houston, TX, pg. 1219
Dillon, James T., V.P.-Fin.--Up-Right, Inc., Selma, CA, pg. 1139
Dillon, Jeff, Controller--Country Life Insurance Company, Bloomington, IL, pg. 289
Dillon, Jeffrey, Controller--Country Companies Insurance Group, Bloomington, IL, pg. 289
Dills, E. Anthony, Controller--Beckwith Machinery Company, Murrysville, PA, pg. 131
Dimond, Sue, Controller--Jordan Associates, Oklahoma City, OK, pg. 604
Dircks, Roberta, V.P., Controller--Gage Marketing Group, Minneapolis, MN, pg. 441
Dischler, Richard, Controller--Magnus Metals, Fremont, NE, pg. 400
Dise, Paul R., Controller--Erving Paper Mills, Erving, MA, pg. 388
Dixon, Marcus, Treas.--Dentsply International Inc., York, PA, pg. 329
Dizon, Romy, Controller--Your Man Tours, Inc., Inglewood, CA, pg. 1214
Dlugatch, Debra, Controller--Marketing Alternatives, Inc., Arlington Heights, IL, pg. 709
Dlugolecki, Walt, Controller--National Foods Inc., Bronx, NY, pg. 788
Dodd, Lanny R., Controller--Northeast Texas Farmers Co-Op, Sulphur Springs, TX, pg. 813
Dohler, D. Gary, Chief Fin. Officer--Atlantic Builders Group Inc., Baltimore, MD, pg. 94
Doiron, David, Controller--Gordon Bailey & Associates, Inc., Stone Mountain, GA, pg. 114
Dolce, Susan, V.P. & Controller--Viacom Cable, Pleasanton, CA, pg. 785
Dominguez, Candace, Controller--Educational Insights, Inc., Dominguez Hills, CA, pg. 369
Domke, Kerry L., Controller--National Cooperative Refinery Association, McPherson, KS, pg. 787
Donaldson, Todd, Controller--The Daniel Co. of Springfield, Springfield, MO, pg. 314
Donavan, Doug, Chief Fin. & Info. Officer, Treas., Controller & Sec.--Campbell Oil Co., Massillon, OH, pg. 213
Donavan, Paul, Controller--Powers Pharmaceutical, Brockton, MA, pg. 236
Donnellan, John J., Sec. & Controller--National Utility Service, Inc., Park Ridge, NJ, pg. 794
Donnelly, Richard, Controller--George Kovacs Lighting, Inc., Glendale, NY, pg. 643
Donovan, James, Controller--Azon Corporation, Johnson City, NY, pg. 105
Donovan, James, V.P. & Controller--J.B. Martin Company, New York, NY, pg. 715
Donovan, Tom, Controller--CHC Advertising, Woodbridge, NJ, pg. 201
Dore, Jim, Controller--Gloria Jean's Coffee Bean Corp., Buffalo Grove, IL, pg. 464
Doris, Michael A., Controller--Equitable Bag Company, Long Island City, NY, pg. 385
Dorrell, Carroll, Controller--Greengage Associates, Inc., New York, NY, pg. 485
Dorsey, Dennis, Controller--Leather Center, Inc., Carrollton, TX, pg. 664
Dosch, Donald A., V.P. & Corp. Controller--Victory Markets Inc., Norwich, NY, pg. 1150
Dossenbach, William R., V.P.-Fin. & Chief Fin. Officer--R. A. Jones & Co. Inc., Covington, KY, pg. 604
Doubles, Michael J., Controller--Alex J. Etkin, Inc., Farmington Hills, MI, pg. 389
Dougherty, Joe, Controller--Prospect Foundry, Inc., Minneapolis, MN, pg. 895
Dowd, Richard, V.P.-Logistics & Control & Controller--SK Hand Tool Corp., Chicago, IL, pg. 963
Doyle, Doug, Controller--Vallerie's Transport Service, Inc., Norwalk, CT, pg. 1143
Draper, Michael E., Controller--Tennessee Valley Authority, Knoxville, TN, pg. 1088
Dreher, Carolyn A., V.P. & Controller--S & A Restaurant Corp., Dallas, TX, pg. 958
Dreyling, Robert, Controller--Casual Sportswear Co., Inc., Dunmore, PA, pg. 1030
Drobeck, Sharon M., Controller--Mary Kay Cosmetics Inc., Dallas, TX, pg. 716
Drogaris, Thomas, Controller--Wakefern Food Corporation, Elizabeth, NJ, pg. 1158
Drossman, Gary, Controller--American Specialties Inc., Yonkers, NY, pg. 61
Drotar, Paul P., V.P., Corp. Controller & Sec.--Carrols Corporation, Syracuse, NY, pg. 225
Drucker, Howard, Controller--Furniture Consultants, New York, NY, pg. 437
Drury, Daniel, Treas. & Controller--Liquid Controls Corporation, Lake Bluff, IL, pg. 677
Drury, L. Wayne, Controller--Perkins Family Restaurants, Memphis, TN, pg. 1088
Druseikis, Raymond, V.P. & Controller--Red Roof Inns, Inc., Hilliard, OH, pg. 918
Dryer, Stephen J., V.P. & Controller--Spalding & Evenflo Companies, Inc., Tampa, FL, pg. 1024
Du Bois, Amy, Dir.-Admin. & Opers. & Comptroller--Norman Brothers Nissan Inc., Orlando, FL, pg. 810
Duane, Dave, Controller--Heat Controller, Inc., Jackson, MI, pg. 524
Dubrow, F., Controller--J.M. Huber, Solem Div., Norcross, GA, pg. 550
Ducat, Dale, Controller--Branch Cheese Company, Inc., Branch, WI, pg. 576
Duda, Frederick, Controller--Delta Rubber Company, Danielson, CT, pg. 327
Duerre, Peter R., Controller & Personnel Dir.--Transistor Devices, Inc., Cedar Knolls, NJ, pg. 1107
Duff, L.C., Corp. Controller--Schenectady Chemicals, Inc., Schenectady, NY, pg. 975
Duffie, Bill, Controller--Goolsby Foods, Inc., Columbus, GA, pg. 471
Duffy, Kristi L., Controller--Gordon & Ferguson of Delaware, Inc., Plymouth, MN, pg. 471
Duffy, William, Controller--Deluxe Homes Of Pennsylvania, Inc., Berwick, PA, pg. 327
Duley, Roslyn, Controller--The Myers Group (U.S) Inc., Rouses Point, NY, pg. 780
Dull, M. Jo, Grp. Controller--Group Dekko International Inc., Kendallville, IN, pg. 489
Dunaway, Amy M., Treas. & Controller--The Enstar Group, Inc., Montgomery, AL, pg. 382
Dunaway, Daniel J., Controller--George S. May International Company, Park Ridge, IL, pg. 723
Duncalf, David, Controller & Mgr.-Data Processing--Hagie Manufacturing Co., Clarion, IA, pg. 499
Duncan, J., Controller--Copperweld Steel Company, Warren, OH, pg. 284
Duncan, James, Controller--Smith-Emery Company, Los Angeles, CA, pg. 1012
Duncan, Willis P., Jr., V.P.-Fin. & Treas.--Thomas Built Buses, Inc., High Point, NC, pg. 1092
Dunham, Dave, Controller--Gillett Holdings, Inc., Denver, CO, pg. 458
Dunleavy, James J., Controller--The Binswanger Company, Philadelphia, PA, pg. 151
Dunleavy, Tom, Controller--Kraus-Anderson, Inc., Minneapolis, MN, pg. 644
Dunn, James, Controller--Wheatland Tube Company, Collingswood, NJ, pg. 1184
Dunn, Paul, Controller--Shealy Electrical Wholesalers, Greenville, SC, pg. 996
Dunnirvine, R., Controller--Telechron, Inc., Ashland, MA, pg. 1085
Durben, Larry, Controller--Taracorp, Inc., Atlanta, GA, pg. 1078
Durkee, Ted, Controller--Johnson Bros. Corp., Litchfield, MN, pg. 597
Dussault, Dennis, Controller--Parks Corporation, Somerset, MA, pg. 849
Dutton, Larry, Controller--Buffalo Rock Company, Birmingham, AL, pg. 187
Dwyer, Shaun, Controller--PTA Corporation, Oxford, CT, pg. 837
Dwyer, Tim, Controller--Kangaroos, USA Inc., Chesterfield, MO, pg. 616
Dyck, Christopher W., Controller-Food Service & Vending Div.--AVA-Automatic Vendors of America, Atlanta, GA, pg. 8
Dyckes, John, Controller--Dunkirk Ice Cream Co., Inc., Dunkirk, NY, pg. 353
Dyckman, Judy, Controller--B. Green & Co., Baltimore, MD, pg. 484
Dymond, D.S., Controller--C. Brewer & Company, Limited, Honolulu, HI, pg. 174
Eads, Janet, Controller--re:Source Marketing, Columbus, OH, pg. 929
Eads, Jerry, Controller--Shafer Commercial Seating Inc., Denver, CO, pg. 994
Eaken, Barbara J., Sec., Treas. & Comptroller--R.W. Eaken, Inc., Leesport, PA, pg. 362
Easterman, Dave, Chief Fin. Officer & Controller--B & B Cash Grocery Store, Tampa, FL, pg. 105
Eastman, Linda, Controller & Office Mgr.--R.W. Electronics, Andover, MA, pg. 908
Easton, Ray, V.P., Controller--Granger Construction Co., Lansing, MI, pg. 476
Easton, Stewart, Controller--Pacific Coast Producers, Lodi, CA, pg. 839
Eck, Joseph, Treas. & Controller--King Kullen Grocery Co., Inc., Westbury, NY, pg. 630
Eckardt, Dennis J., Controller--Colorforms, Ramsey, NJ, pg. 265
Eckstein, Michael, Controller--Kulite Semiconductor Products, Inc., Leonia, NJ, pg. 646
Edelman, Allan, V.P. & Controller--Greater New York Box Co., Clifton, NJ, pg. 483
Edelman, Laurie, Controller--Pro Clinica Inc., New York, NY, pg. 891
Edwards, Bill, V.P.-Finance & Controller--Sunbeam Outdoor Products Co., Neosho, MO, pg. 1059
Edwards, Jeff, Comptroller--Beaver Street Fisheries, Inc., Jacksonville, FL, pg. 130
Edwards, Melvin L., Comptroller--Vess Beverages, Inc., Maryland Heights, MO, pg. 1149
Edwards, Rodney, Controller--McCarty Farms, Magee, MS, pg. 727
Eftax, William P., Controller--Fullerton Metals Co., Northbrook, IL, pg. 436
Egan, William, V.P. & Controller--The Hartz Mountain Corp., Harrison, NJ, pg. 514
Egner, Michael, Controller--Powerine Oil Company Holdings, Santa Fe Springs, CA, pg. 883
Ehmann, Thomas R., Controller--The LINC Group, Inc., Chicago, IL, pg. 648
Ehni, Edwin, Controller--Boury Incorporated, Wheeling, WV, pg. 168
Eich, Margaret E., Mgr.-Acctg.--Tassani Communications, Chicago, IL, pg. 1080
Eisel, Mike, Controller & Mgr.-Pur.--Little Lady Foods, Inc., Elk Grove Village, IL, pg. 679
Eitze, William O., V.P.-Fin., Chief Fin. Officer, Controller & Treas.--Carl M. Freeman Associates, Inc., Potomac, MD, pg. 431
Elings, Gary, Controller--Brim, Inc., Portland, OR, pg. 176
Elizes, Merlie, Comptroller--DeWitt Media, Inc., New York, NY, pg. 334
Ely, Burton, Asst. Controller--Delta Pride Catfish, Inc., Indianola, MS, pg. 327
Elznic, Tom, Chief Fin. Officer & Controller--Majestic Molded Products, Inc., Holbrook, NY, pg. 702
Emma, Salvatore, Jr., Controller--Kervick Enterprises, Inc., Worcester, MA, pg. 624
Endres, John, V.P. & Controller--Golub Corporation, Schenectady, NY, pg. 469
Engelsgaard, David, Controller--Interplastic Corp., Saint Paul, MN, pg. 579
English, Stuart, Controller--Wyatt Inc., Branford, CT, pg. 1205
Ennis, E. L., Chief Fin. Officer, Treas. & Controller--Strachan Shipping Co., Garden City, GA, pg. 1052
Epifano, Robert, Sec. & Asst. Treas.--Nuarc Company, Inc., Niles, IL, pg. 817
Epler, J.L., V.P. & Controller--Unigard Security Insurance Co., Bellevue, WA, pg. 596
Epler, J.L., V.P. & Controller--Unigard Indemnity Co., Raleigh, NC, pg. 596
Epler, J.L., V.P. & Controller--Unigard Insurance Co., Seattle, WA, pg. 596
Epler, J.L., V.P. & Controller--Unigard Service Corp., Seattle, WA, pg. 596
Erickson, Diane, Controller--JFC Inc., Saint Cloud, MN, pg. 584
Erickson, Joyce, Controller--Marine World Africa USA, Vallejo, CA, pg. 707
Erickson, Keith, Controller--American Industries Inc., Portland, OR, pg. 55
Erlenbach, Brad, Asst. Controller & Dir.-Acctg.--William Morrow & Co., Inc., New York, NY, pg. 521
Erlenbush, William, Controller--Growmark, Inc., Bloomington, IL, pg. 490
Erlick, Lance, Chief Fin. Officer & Controller--Component Technology Corp., Erie, PA, pg. 270
Erlick, Lance, Chief Fin. Officer & Controller--R & R Plastics, Swanton, OH, pg. 270
Erstice, Kevin, Controller--Colad Group Inc., Buffalo, NY, pg. 259
Ertel, G.E., Controller--Grede Foundries, Inc., Milwaukee, WI, pg. 483
Erwin, John D., Sec.--Tolleson Lumber Company, Inc., Perry, GA, pg. 1100
Erwin, Walter, V.P.-Fin. & Admin.--The Pro Corporation, Florence, MA, pg. 891
Esak, Mary Lynn, Controller--Nexus Plastics, Inc., Hawthorne, NJ, pg. 805
Essex, Robert, Controller--George W. Cochran Co., Inc., Washington, DC, pg. 258
Ettl, Al, Chief Fin. Officer & Controller--Putzmeister, Inc., Gardena, CA, pg. 901
Ettling, Elizabeth, Controller--GranTree Corporation, Beaverton, OR, pg. 477
Eubel, Nancy, Controllor--Institutional Financing Services, Benicia, CA, pg. 571
Eugenio, Chuck, Controller--Gans Ink & Supply Company, Inc., Los Angeles, CA, pg. 442
Evans, J., Controller--Groendyk Mfg. Co., Inc., Buchanan, VA, pg. 480
Evans, Sidney H., V.P. & Controller--General Homes Corporation, Houston, TX, pg. 449
Evavold, Douglas, Controller--J. Hellman Produce, Inc., Los Angeles, CA, pg. 527
Ewald, Barry, Controller--Surgical Specialties, Reading, PA, pg. 1065

Fabrizius, Arthur L., Controller--Harris Enterprises Inc., Hutchinson, KS, pg. 511
Fair, B.R., V.P. & Controller--Broad Vogt & Conant Inc., River Rouge, MI, pg. 177
Fairbanks, William, Controller--C. H. Robinson Co. Inc., Eden Prairie, MN, pg. 939
Falgout, Eldon, Controller--Production Management Companies, Inc., Harvey, LA, pg. 893
Fanning, Parker, Controller--The SArgent-SOwell Company, Grand Prairie, TX, pg. 971
Farmer, Cecil, Controller--Stratmar Systems, Inc., Port Chester, NY, pg. 1053
Farmer, Robert L., Controller--H.O. Trerice Company, Oak Park, MI, pg. 1110
Farrar, Ann, Controller--Empire Airlines, Hayden Lake, ID, pg. 379
Farrell, Dianne, Sec. & Controller--McNally Industries, Inc., Grantsburg, WI, pg. 731
Fasino, P., Chief Fin. Officer & Controller--Red L Foods, Pomfret Center, CT, pg. 1128
Fattaleh, Alice C., Controller--The Delphi Glass Corp. Delphi Stained Glass Centers, Lansing, MI, pg. 326
Favreau, Joanne, Controller--Jordan's Meats, Portland, ME, pg. 605
Fawkes, Mary, Controller--Spiegel Meats, Inc., Miami, FL, pg. 1030
Fawkes, Mary, Controllller--RealCold Storage, Miami, FL, pg. 1031
Federicci, Joseph, Controller--The Lion, Inc. (Gibbons-Stegmaier Brewery), Wilkes-Barre, PA, pg. 149
Fehr, Lawrence F., V.P., Controller & Sec.--Herff Jones Inc., Indianapolis, IN, pg. 531
Fehring, Ann, Controller--United Dairy Farmers, Inc., Cincinnati, OH, pg. 1131
Feldkemp, Lynn E., Controller--The Coleman Company, Inc., Wichita, KS, pg. 695
Fellenstein, Mike, Sec., Treas. & Comptroller--Biddulph Oldsmobile, Glendale, AZ, pg. 149
Femenia, Selma, Controller--Star Container, Inc., Phoenix, AZ, pg. 1082
Fenske, Richard, Controller & Office Mgr.--Stanco Metal Products, Inc., Grand Haven, MI, pg. 1035
Fensterstock, Larry, Controller--Joyce International, Inc., New York, NY, pg. 608
Fentross, Mark, Controller--Greensboro News & Record, Greensboro, NC, pg. 655
Fergurson, Ron, Controller--GSC Distributing Companies Division, Sulphur Springs, TX, pg. 440
Ferguson, Gary R., Controller--Mountain States Pipe & Supply Company, Colorado Springs, CO, pg. 773
Fernandez, Carol, Controller--R & S Strauss, Inc., South River, NJ, pg. 1053
Fernino, Roselaine, Controller--Mark Lighting Fixture Co., Inc., Moonachie, NJ, pg. 708
Ferrera, James J., Controller & Treas.--James Ferrera & Sons, Inc., Canton, MA, pg. 407
Festenstein, Gerald, Controller--Universal Overall Company, Chicago, IL, pg. 1139
Feusse, Tom, Controller--The Scott Company, Marysville, OH, pg. 982
Feye, Lyle, Controller & Asst. Treas.--AXIA Incorporated, Oak Brook, IL, pg. 8
Fidler, Lynn, V.P., Controller--Price/McNabb, Inc., Asheville, NC, pg. 888
Fields, John, Controller--Homemaker Shops, Inc., Southfield, MI, pg. 542
Fields, W.O., Controller--Buffalo Color Corporation, Parsippany, NJ, pg. 187
Fields, William, Treas. & Controller--Sherborne Group, Inc., New York, NY, pg. 998
Fierke, Bob, Controller--Cosco, Inc., Columbus, IN, pg. 287
Figley, Mark, Controller--North Atlantic Industries Systems Division, Columbia, MD, pg. 812
Figueras, Julie, Comptroller--Zubi Advertising Services, Inc., Miami, FL, pg. 1221
Filipski, Tom, Controller--Cotter & Company, Chicago, IL, pg. 288
Filosa, Rolf, Controller--Multiple Allied Services, Inc., Hayward, CA, pg. 775
Filotto, Robert F., Chief Oper. Officer, V.P., & Controller--Kinetic Systems Corporation, Lockport, IL, pg. 630
Finch, James, Controller--Warren Distributing Corp., Raleigh, NC, pg. 1164
Finelli, Mary Lynn, V.P & Controller--Provident Mutual Life Insurance Co., Philadelphia, PA, pg. 896
Fink, Brenda, Mgr.-Acct.--The Apparel Group, Ltd., New York, NY, pg. 78
Fink, Charles J., V.P. & Controller--Atlas/Soundolier, Fenton, MO, pg. 64
Finney, Mike, Controller--Baugh Construction Company, Seattle, WA, pg. 127
Fiolet, R.A.H., Controller--Lowe Kuiper & Schouten B.V., Amsterdam,, Netherlands, pg. 685
Fioravante, Raymond, Controller--Fawn Industries, Inc., Hunt Valley, MD, pg. 404
Fischer, Sharon, Fin. & Controller--Spring, O'Brien & Co. Inc., New York, NY, pg. 1033
Fiscus, Barbara, Controller--Tremont Foods, Linthicum Heights, MD, pg. 1109
Fisher, G. David, Chief Fin. Officer, V.P. & Controller--SOR Inc., Lenexa, KS, pg. 963
Fisher, John J., Controller & Asst. Sec.--Tarlton Corporation, Saint Louis, MO, pg. 1079
Fisher, L.J., Controller--J.M. Huber, Polymer Services Div., Orange, TX, pg. 550
Fisher, M.C., Controller--Carolina Tractor & Equipment Co., Charlotte, NC, pg. 223
Fisher, Martha, Controller & Asst. Treas.--Prudential Metal Supply Corp., East Dedham, MA, pg. 898
Fisher, Norma Joe, Treas., Controller & Chief Fin. Officer--Fisher Graphic Industries, Modesto, CA, pg. 415
Fisher, R.H., Controller--Standard Alloys & Manufacturing, Port Arthur, TX, pg. 161
Fisher, Rosemarie, Controller--Tingley Rubber Corporation, South Plainfield, NJ, pg. 1098
Fitzgerald, Ann, Controller--Stu Evans Lincoln-Mercury Inc., Southgate, MI, pg. 390
Fitzgerald, J., Controller--Teepak, Inc., Westchester, IL, pg. 535
Fitzgerald, John, Controller--Halstead Industries, Inc., Greensboro, NC, pg. 502
Fitzpatrick, Mike, Controller--Aircap Industries Corp., Verona, MS, pg. 694
Fivecoat, William G., Controller--Fairbanks Morse Pump Corporaton, Kansas City, KS, pg. 397
Flanigan, Michael, Treas. & Comptroller--Jones Blair Company, Dallas, TX, pg. 602
Fleck, Donald C., V.P. & Controller--The Hennegan Company, Cincinnati, OH, pg. 529
Fledderman, J.H., Controller--AVEX Electronics, Inc., Huntsville, AL, pg. 550
Flegger, Allen, Treas. & Controller--Southern Apparel Corporation, Largo, FL, pg. 1020
Fleishell, John R., Controller--McArdle Printing Co., Inc., Upper Marlboro, MD, pg. 189
Fleming, Thomas, Controller--McKay Chemical Co., Los Angeles, CA, pg. 159
Flener, Michael, Controller--J. E. Higgins Lumber Co., Concord, CA, pg. 533
Fleury, John, V.P. & Controller--SPD Technologies, Philadelphia, PA, pg. 963
Flick, Elaine, Controller--Ingram Materials Co., Nashville, TN, pg. 569
Florence, Gary, Controller--Jeld-Wen, Inc., Klamath Falls, OR, pg. 591
Florio, Charles J., V.P. & Controller--Jac Jacobsen Industries, Inc., Greenwich, CT, pg. 587
Floyd, Allen, Controller--MFA Incorporated, Columbia, MO, pg. 692
Floyd, Charles A., Controller--Inland Associates, Inc., Olathe, KS, pg. 570
Floyd, Stacy, Asst. Controller--E-Z Mart Stores, Inc., Texarkana, TX, pg. 361
Flucker, Robert, V.P. & Controller--Edward C. Levy Co., Inc., Detroit, MI, pg. 672
Fluegeman, Raymond W., Chief Fin. Officer, Treas., Controller & Dir.-Data Processing--Robbins, Inc., Cincinnati, OH, pg. 938
Flynn, Patrick, Controller--SFM Media Corporation, New York, NY, pg. 962
Foecking, Leland R., Treas., Controller & Sec.--Joseph Behr & Sons Inc., Rockford, IL, pg. 132
Fohrman, Neal, Pres., Chief Exec. & Chief Fin. Officer & Controller--Red Calliope & Associates, Inc., Los Angeles, CA, pg. 918
Foley, Gene, Controller--Dugan, Valva Associates, Morristown, NJ, pg. 351
Folson, Fred, Controller--Indian Head Industries Inc., Southfield, MI, pg. 565
Fonacier, Andrew Lee, Asst. Controller--Young Automotive Group, Indianapolis, IN, pg. 1209
Fontenazza, Frank, Chief Fin. Officer & Controller--Monarch Avalon, Inc., Baltimore, MD, pg. 765
Ford, Bruce L., Controller--Pepper-Lawson, Katy, TX, pg. 860
Ford, LaDonna, Controller--City Meats & Provisions Co., Tucsan, AZ, pg. 251
Forero, Luis, Controller--Instituto de Idiomas Colombia, S.A., Bogota,, Colombia, pg. 143
Forstneger, Frank J., Controller--Home Juice Company, Melrose Park, IL, pg. 541
Forsythe, Dick, Controller--Leyse, Kewaunee, WI, pg. 1155
Fortelka, Bruce, Controller--Rollex Corporation, Elk Grove Village, IL, pg. 944
Fortney, David, Controller--York Barbell Co., Inc., York, PA, pg. 1208
Foshie, Harold, Comptroller--Family Inns of America, Inc., Pigeon Forge, TN, pg. 398
Foster, Don, Controller--Tidelands Oil Production Co., Long Beach, CA, pg. 1096
Foster, R.A., Treas./Controller--United States Bronze Powders, Inc., Flemington, NJ, pg. 1134
Fournier, Mitch, Controller--Duro-Last Roofing, Inc., Saginaw, MI, pg. 355
Fournier, Paul, Controller--Ivex Packaging Corporation-Industrial Products Division, Newton, MA, pg. 583
Fout, Charles, V.P.- Fin. & Human Resources--Gouchenour Adv., Inc., Orlando, FL, pg. 473
Fowler, Jack, Comptroller--Dixie Dairy Company, Gary, IN, pg. 341
Fox, Edward D., Controller--Massachusetts Envelope Co., Somerville, MA, pg. 718
Fox, Peter, Controller--ACL Technologies, Santa Ana, CA, pg. 2
Fox, Robert, V.P. & Controller--Burlington Motor Carriers Inc., Daleville, IN, pg. 191
Francis, Donetta, V.P. & Controller--Robert F. Driver Co., Inc., San Diego, CA, pg. 349
Francis, Tom, Controller--Westlake Hardware, Inc., Shawnee Mission, KS, pg. 1183
Francis, Trudy, Asst. Controller--Intelligent Controls Inc., Lynnwood, WA, pg. 573
Francis, William, Treas., Controller & Chief Fin. Officer--Captive-Aire Systems, Inc., Youngsville, NC, pg. 216
Franco, R.A., Controller--Rieth-Riley Construction Co. Inc., Goshen, IN, pg. 934
Frank, Harold D., Controller--Research Products Corporation, Madison, WI, pg. 928
Frank, Peter S., V.P. & Controller--The Edward J. DeBartolo Corporation, Youngstown, OH, pg. 323
Frankel, Ernst D., Chief Fin. Officer, Treas., Controller & Sec.--Standard Textile Co., Inc., Cincinnati, OH, pg. 1037
Franklin, Robert, Controller--Northland Aluminum Products, Inc., Minneapolis, MN, pg. 814
Frantzen, Ella, Controller--Berlitz International Danmark A/S, Copenhagen,, Denmark, pg. 142
Frederick, Gary, Asst. Controller--Fibre Glass-Evercoat Company Inc., Cincinnati, OH, pg. 408
Frediani, Mario J., Comptroller--Reidbord Bros., Inc., Pittsburgh, PA, pg. 923
Freed, Steve, Controller--Statler Industries, Medford, MA, pg. 1041
Freedmon, Mike, Controller--Power Conversion, Inc., Saddle Brook, NJ, pg. 883
Freeman, Ray Anne, Controller--The Brady Marketing Company, Pacheco, CA, pg. 171
Freeman, Richard, Controller--Berlitz Schools of Languages Ltd., London, United Kingdom, pg. 143
Frelan, Gary, Controller--Lapham-Hickey Steel Corp., Chicago, IL, pg. 658
French, R.G., Treas. & Controller--Sunkist Growers, Inc., Sherman Oaks, CA, pg. 1060
Freyberger, Larry, Controller--Wharfside Restaurants, Inc., Jasper, IN, pg. 1184
Frick, Walter, Controller--Danafilms, Inc., Westborough, MA, pg. 313
Fricks, Roy, Controller--The Tog Shop, Americus, GA, pg. 1100
Friedland, Richard, V.P. & Controller--General Instrument Corporation, New York, NY, pg. 425
Friedman, Marty, Chief Fin. Officer, Treas, & Controller--Power Contracting & Engineering Corp., Rolling Meadows, IL, pg. 883
Friel, James, Comptroller--Ajax Paving Industries Inc., Madison Heights, MI, pg. 28
Fritzen, Doris A., Controller & Sec.--C.F. Haglin & Sons, Minneapolis, MN, pg. 499
Frost, Kurt, Controller--Magnolia Hi-Fi, Inc., Seattle, WA, pg. 701
Fry, Darrel K., Controller--Stauffer Communications, Inc., Topeka, KS, pg. 1042
Fuller, Genie, Controller--Haskel, Inc., Burbank, CA, pg. 516
Fuller, Randy, Controller--Wellborn - DE Corp., Albuquerque, NM, pg. 354
Fullerton, Germaine, Chief Fin. Officer & Controller--Schneider Commercial Real Estate, Orange, CA, pg. 977
Funk, H. Nicholas, Controller--Furnas Electric Company, Batavia, IL, pg. 437
Funk, Joseph, Controller--Davis Mining & Manufacturing, Colburn, VA, pg. 319
Furey, Joseph, Controller--Bill Communications, Inc., New York, NY, pg. 150
Furrer, Ron, Treas. & Controller--Darigold, Inc., Seattle, WA, pg. 315
Fuss, Tony, Controller--Triton Industries, Inc., Chicago, IL, pg. 1114
Gabinet, John J., Controller--Fair Lanes Inc., Hunt Valley, MD, pg. 396
Gabriel, Doug, V.P., Treas. & Controller--Apperson Business Forms, Inc., Los Angeles, CA, pg. 78
Gaddie, Troy, Controller--Chemical Exchange Industries, Houston, TX, pg. 242
Gaffney, James, Controller--Triton Inc., Doraville, GA, pg. 1114
Gafford, Wade, Comptroller--Shoe City Corporation, Montgomery, AL, pg. 382
Gafney, Nark, Controller--Huron Valley Steel Corp., Belleville, MI, pg. 555
Gage, George E., Mgr. & Controller--Brown Brothers, Harriman & Co., New York, NY, pg. 181
Gager, Susan, Controller--Lawrence Agency Corporation, Schnectady, NY, pg. 662
Gagliano, Nancy, Controller--Imprint Products, L.P., Rockville Centre, NY, pg. 564
Gainer, T. R., Controller--State Industries Inc., Ashland City, TN, pg. 1041
Galan, Val F., Controller--Atlantic Sugar Association, Inc., Belle Glade, FL, pg. 95
Gallant, Steve, Controller--Markem Corporation, Keene, NH, pg. 708
Galvin, James, Controller & Chief Acctg. Officer--Simkins Industries, Inc., New Haven, CT, pg. 1005
Ganahl, John, Controller--Ganahl Lumber Company, Anaheim, CA, pg. 442
Ganbert, D.R., V.P. & Controller--The Babcock & Wilcox Company, New Orleans, LA, pg. 107
Gannon, Thomas A., Treas. & Controller--Reading Eagle Company, Reading, PA, pg. 916
Gantz, Ann M., Controller--Gregory & Clyburne, Inc., Stamford, CT, pg. 486
Garcia, Armando, Controller--Escuelas de Idiomas Berlitz de Espana, S.A., Madrid,, Spain, pg. 143
Gardiner, Tom, Controller--Pioneer Supermarkets, Los Angeles, CA, pg. 872
Gardner, Robert G., Controller--Shenango Furnace Company, Princeton, NJ, pg. 997
Garey, Elizabeth, Division Controller--The Crosset Company Inc., Cincinnati, OH, pg. 300
Garofolo, Gary, Controller--Harkins Builders, Inc., Silver Spring, MD, pg. 509
Garsombke, James, V.P. & Controller--ADD, Inc., Waupaca, WI, pg. 607
Gartland, H., Controller--R. T. Vanderbilt Company, Inc., Norwalk, CT, pg. 1144
Garvin, Bruce M., V.P.-Fin. & Controller--Sterlite Corporation, Townsend, MA, pg. 1047
Gasper, David, V.P., Comptroller--Image Dynamics, Incorporated, Baltimore, MD, pg. 563
Gatchel, R., Controller--Vari Tronics Company, Inc., Duarte, CA, pg. 1145
Gaughier, Albert R., Controller & Treas.--Oliver Products Company, Grand Rapids, MI, pg. 824
Gault, Donna, Controller--Karges Furniture Company, Evansville, IN, pg. 616
Gauntt, Edward, Controller--Ardell Industries inc., Union, NJ, pg. 604
Gearns, Janet, Controller--Wavetek Communications Div., Indianapolis, IN, pg. 1168
Gee, Pearl, Controller--Anderson, Rothstein & Fiqua, San Francisco, CA, pg. 73

Geiger, Denise, V.P., Chief Fin. Officer & Controller--The Atkins Agency, San Antonio, TX, pg. 94
Geiser, James, Controller--Kokosing Construction Company, Inc., Fredericktown, OH, pg. 640
Geisler, Michael, Controller--Burns International Security Services, Inc., Parsippany, NJ, pg. 166
Gejoff, Louis, Treas., Controller, Sec. & Chief Fin. Officer--Carver, Inc., Garden City, GA, pg. 227
Gejoff, Louis, Chief Fin. Officer, Treas., Controller & Sec.--Murray-Carver, East Bridgewater, MA, pg. 776
Gelinas, Roger, Controller--White Rock Distilleries Inc., Lewiston, ME, pg. 1186
Gemeinhart, John, Controller--Hamburg Brothers Inc., Pittsburgh, PA, pg. 502
Genschaw, David A., Exec. V.P., Chief Fin. Officer--Waldbillig & Besteman, Inc., Madison, WI, pg. 1159
George, Richard, Controller--The Andersons, Maumee, OH, pg. 73
Gerard, Antonia, Exec. V.P., Chief Fin. & Oper. Officer, Sec. & Controller--Bolliger, Inc., Stamford, CT, pg. 163
Gerard, Marc, Controller--The Beverly Hills Hotel, Beverly Hills, CA, pg. 148
Gerboth, Robert, Controller--F. Schumacher & Co., New York, NY, pg. 979
Gerencer, Diane, Controller--Pent Assemblies, Inc., Kendallville, IN, pg. 490
Germano, Anthony P., Controller--Tilcon, Inc., New Britain, CT, pg. 1097
Gerstenhaber, Lee, Controller, Mgr.-Office & Oper., Telecommunications--Clayton-Davis & Associates, Incorporated, Saint Louis, MO, pg. 253
Gerstman, Henry, Sec., Treas. & Controller--Century Business Credit Corporation, New York, NY, pg. 235
Getsay, Mary Ellen, Controller--Barge-Wagener, Inc., Atlanta, GA, pg. 119
Getz, Thomas G., Treas.--Williams, White & Company, Moline, IL, pg. 1191
Gianakos, John N., V.P.-Opers. & Controller--Virginia Metal Industries, Inc., Orange, VA, pg. 1152
Giangreco, Richard, Exec. V.P., Controller--C.F. Thompson Group, Inc., Windsor, CT, pg. 1094
Gibbons, John V., III, Controller--Dimeo Construction Company, Providence, RI, pg. 338
Gibson, Jack, Controller--American Foundry Group, Inc., Bixby, OK, pg. 54
Gibson, Lucy, Controller--Goodrum Leonard & Associates, Inc., Nashville, TN, pg. 471
Giebel, Terry, Asst. Controller--Erickson Diversified Corp., Hudson, WI, pg. 386
Giese, Pam, Controller--Thomas Engineering Inc., Hoffman Estates, IL, pg. 1093
Giger, James, Controller--Central DuPage Health System, Naperville, IL, pg. 232
Gignac, Edward, Controller & Dir.-Data Processing--Elgin-Honey Hill Corporation, Chicago, IL, pg. 376
Gildea, Hugh, Controller--F & W Publications, Inc., Cincinnati, OH, pg. 394
Gilleland, Laura, Chief Fin. Officer & Controller--Gessner Industries, Concord, NC, pg. 455
Gillespie, Larry, Controller--Creative Marketing Resource, Inc., Chicago, IL, pg. 297
Gillespie, Larry, Controller & Treas.--HLB Communications, Inc., Chicago, IL, pg. 496
Gilmore, Russell, Treas. & Controller--Hamilton Sweeney Advertising, Inc., Denver, CO, pg. 503
Gingrich, Kenneth R., Jr., V.P. & Controller--Oxford First Corporation, Philadelphia, PA, pg. 834
Giraffa, Pete, Controller--Myers Foods Company, Plumsteadville, PA, pg. 506
Giraffa, Pietro, Comptroller--Hanover Foods Corporation, Hanover, PA, pg. 506
Gissleman, Dave, Chief Fin. Officer & Controller--Weinbrenner Shoe Company, Inc., Merrill, WI, pg. 1173
Gitin, Herbert, Comptroller--Eagle Button Co., Inc., Carlstadt, NJ, pg. 362
Giuler, Robert C., Controller--Ward Trucking Corp., Altoona, PA, pg. 1163
Givens, Hugh, Controller & Asst. Sec.--National Steel Corporation, Mishawaka, IN, pg. 793
Glascock, Janet L., Controller--George W. Auch Co., Pontiac, MI, pg. 97
Glass, Jon P., Controller--William Eisner & Associates Inc., Milwaukee, WI, pg. 372
Gleason, Sheldon, Chm. Bd., Pres., Chief Exec. & Chief Fin. Officer & Controller--Genie Manufacturing Corp., Rush, NY, pg. 452
Glover, Suz-Ann, Controller--Plains Cotton Co-op Association, Lubbock, TX, pg. 873
Godfrey, Robert, Sec. & Treas.--Central States Enterprises, Inc., Heathrow, FL, pg. 234
Godlove, John, Controller--Ivex Packaging Corporation-Grove City, Grove City, PA, pg. 583
Godshall, Judee, Controller--Surco Products, Inc., Braddock, PA, pg. 1065
Godshall, Judee, Controller--Odomaster Canada, Mississauga,, Canada, pg. 1065
Goeke, Gerard, V.P.-Information Services & Controller--The Donohoe Companies, Inc., Washington, DC, pg. 345
Goffman, Stephen V., Controller--United States Sugar Corporation, Clewiston, FL, pg. 1137
Goforth, Charles, Controller--Macklanburg-Duncan Co., Oklahoma City, OK, pg. 697
Goggin, Daniel B., V.P. & Controller--Boston Mutual Life Insurance Co., Canton, MA, pg. 167
Gold, Barry, Controller--Victoria Packing Corporation, Brooklyn, NY, pg. 1149
Golden, Stephen D., V.P., Controller--The William Cook Agency, Inc., Jacksonville, FL, pg. 282
Goldman, Richard, Sr. V.P., Controller--TBWA Advertising, Inc., New York, NY, pg. 1071
Goldstein, Fred, Controller--Bentex Kiddie Corporation, New York, NY, pg. 140
Goodwin, Jamie, Controller--Airways Rent A Car, Schiller Park, IL, pg. 934
Gorczycki, Jim, Controller & Human Resources Dir.--The Sportsman's Guide, Inc., Eagan, MN, pg. 1032
Gordon, Harry, Chm. Bd. & Controller--Saul Bros. & Company, Inc., Norcross, GA, pg. 972
Gordon, Juanita, Controller--William H. Goodwin Trust, Richmond, VA, pg. 471
Gordon, Walter, Controller--Mac Papers, Inc., Jacksonville, FL, pg. 694
Gordon, William, Controller--Parks Sausage Company, Baltimore, MD, pg. 850
Gore, Richard, V.P. & Controller--Quorum Health Group, Inc., Brentwood, TN, pg. 905
Gorgone, Christopher, Controller--Global Petroleum Corp., Waltham, MA, pg. 463
Gorman, David J., V.P. & Controller--NFO Research, Inc., Greenwich, CT, pg. 780
Gormley, Charles, Controller--Philadelphia Reserve Supply Company, Croydon, PA, pg. 867
Goziker, Dora, Controller--Robert Towers Advertising, Inc., New York, NY, pg. 1103
Grabowski, Jim, Assoc. Controller--Wolff Associates, Inc., Rochester, NY, pg. 1199
Grace, P.W., V.P. & Controller--MacAndrews & Forbes Co., Camden, NJ, pg. 694
Graham, Brian, Controller--Michael J. Mungo Company, Inc., Columbia, SC, pg. 775
Graham, Joe, Controller--Netzsch, Inc., Exton, PA, pg. 798
Grainger, Michael, V.P. & Controller--Ingram Industries Inc., Nashville, TN, pg. 568
Grammer, Rob, Controller--Lakin General Corporation, Chicago, IL, pg. 652
Granger, Robert, Controller--Pitco Frialator Inc., Concord, NH, pg. 157
Grant, Paul, Chief Fin. Officer & Controller--Bergquist Company, Inc., Minneapolis, MN, pg. 141
Grant, R.R., V.P. & Controller-STCO--Simpson Timber Co., Shelton, WA, pg. 1007
Gray, Donald M., V.P. & Controller--MSI Insurance Companies, Arden Hills, MN, pg. 693
Gray, Jay, Controller--CSE Corporation, San Francisco, CA, pg. 204
Gray, Loren, Controller--Jones Dairy Farm, Fort Atkinson, WI, pg. 603
Gray, Timothy M., Controller--Ryan Properties Inc., Minneapolis, MN, pg. 958
Gray, Timothy M., Comptroller--Ryan Construction Company Of Minnesota, Hibbing, MN, pg. 958
Greco, James, Controller--National Cleaning Contractors, Inc., New York, NY, pg. 786
Greeley, Jolene T., Controller--Keith Uddenberg, Inc., Gig Harbor, WA, pg. 1125
Green, Patricia, Controller--Marx/Knoll, Denight & Dodge, Inc., Portland, OR, pg. 716
Green, R., Controller--Melard Manufacturing Corporation, Passaic, NJ, pg. 737
Greene, Luke, Controller--West & Company Marketing & Advertising, Tampa, FL, pg. 1177
Gregerson, Richard E., V.P.-Fin.--The Equion Corporation, New Haven, CT, pg. 385
Gregory, John, Controller--Joshua Meier Corp., North Bergen, NJ, pg. 737
Grex, Debbie, Controller--American Antenna Corp, Elgin, IL, pg. 216
Grietzer, Roland, Controller & Treas.--Alcom Printing Group, Inc., Bethlehem, PA, pg. 32
Griffin, Peter, Controller--Louis Dreyfus Corporation, Wilton, CT, pg. 348
Griffin, Tracy, V.P., Controller--Saunders, Lubinski & White, Inc., Dallas, TX, pg. 973
Griffith, Fred, V.P. & Controller--Ceramic Cooling Tower Co., Ft. Worth, TX, pg. 69
Griffith, William J., Chief Fin. Officer & Controller--Baldwin Construction, Inc., Fort Collins, CO, pg. 115
Grimwood, Charlotte, Controller--Linn Products, Inc., Charlotte, MI, pg. 677
Grinstead, B.M., Asst. V.P. & Controller--The H. T. Hackney Co., Knoxville, TN, pg. 498
Grisetti, Michael, Controller--Nationwide Homes, Inc., Martinsville, VA, pg. 795
Groski, Donald, Asst. Controller--Kelly, Scott And Madison, Inc., Chicago, IL, pg. 621
Grossman, Paul, V.P.-Controller--Sierracin/Sylmar Corporation, Sylmar, CA, pg. 1003
Groszek, James D., Controller--Velsicol Chemical Corporation, Rosemont, IL, pg. 1147
Groveman, Howard, Natl. Dir.-Acct. & Audit--Grant Thornton, Chicago, IL, pg. 477
Grubich, Mike, Controller--M&W Gear Company, Gibson City, IL, pg. 690
Gruenwald, John J., Comptroller--UES, Inc., Dayton, OH, pg. 1122
Grygorcewicz, Chester, Sr. V.P. & Controller--Marcal Paper Mills, Inc., Elmwood Park, NJ, pg. 706
Guarino, David A., V.P.-Controller--TLC Beatrice International Holdings Inc., New York, NY, pg. 1073
Guarnaccio, Frank J., Controller--Daxus Corporation, Pittsburgh, PA, pg. 319
Guber, A.M., Controller--John Dusenbery Co., Inc., Randolph, NJ, pg. 355
Gudmundsen, Ralph W., Sr. V.P. & Controller--Giffels Associates, Inc., Southfield, MI, pg. 457
Guimond, A. Roger, Controller--First Franklin Financial Corp., Toccoa, GA, pg. 413
Gulick, Cynthia, Controller--B&W Co-op, Inc., Breckenridge, MI, pg. 107
Gumpert, Peter, Controller--Beauchamp Distributing Company, Compton, CA, pg. 130
Gumtow, Nancy, Controller--RS Electronics, Livonia, MI, pg. 908
Gunderson, Joanne, Controller--Bridgeman's Restaurants Inc., Minneapolis, MN, pg. 175
Gunther, Christian H., Comptroller--Banner Associates Inc., Laramie, WY, pg. 118
Gutman, Dave, V.P. & Controller--The Charles Levy Company, Chicago, IL, pg. 672
Haas, Barbara, Controller--Linett & Harrison, Millburn, NJ, pg. 676
Haas, Joseph S., Treas. & Controller--CRL, Inc., Des Plaines, IL, pg. 203
Haberle, Don, Controller--Century Seafood Inc., Philadelphia, PA, pg. 235
Hackimer, Ed, Comptroller--Lotas Minard Patton McIver, New York, NY, pg. 684
Hadahan, Susan E., Controller--Charles River Data Systems, Inc., Framingham, MA, pg. 240
Haddock, Marlene, Comptroller--Beacon Sales Corporation, Jacksonville, FL, pg. 129
Hadley, Jeff, Controller--Correct Craft, Inc., Orlando, FL, pg. 287
Haesse, Victor, Controller--Republic Supply Company, Dallas, TX, pg. 928
Haesser, Inge, Controller--Berlitz Schools of Languages GmbH, Frankfurt/Main, Germany, pg. 143
Haesser, Inge, Controller--Berlitz Sprachschulen GmbH, Vienna,, Austria, pg. 143
Hagar, Gary, Controller--Ivex Packaging Corporation-Visalia, Visalia, CA, pg. 583
Hagemann, Maryanne, Controller--Super 8 Motels, Inc., Aberdeen, SD, pg. 1062
Haggerty, Tom, Controller--Levonian Brothers Inc., Troy, NY, pg. 671
Hailemichael, Tesfaye, Controller--Artecon, Inc., Carlsbad, CA, pg. 809
Haines, A.L., V.P., Treas., Controller & Chief Fin. Officer--CHEMCENTRAL Corporation, Bedford Park, IL, pg. 241
Hainsworth, Douglas, Controller--Dukane Canada Ltd., Kitchener,, Canada, pg. 352
Hajospek, John, Controller--W.W. Wallwork, Inc., Fargo, ND, pg. 1161
Halben, Robert A., Controller & Sec.--Almac's Inc., East Providence, RI, pg. 1214
Halcomb, Ken, Controller--The Brulin Corporation, Indianapolis, IN, pg. 184
Hale, Gordon, Controller--Yankee Publishing Incorporated, Dublin, NH, pg. 1207
Haley, Judy, Controller--Mears Transportation Group, Orlando, FL, pg. 734
Hall, C.W., Controller--Taylor-Evans Seed Co., Tulia, TX, pg. 1081
Hall, Gary F., V.P. & Controller--Cajun Electric Power Co-op, Baton Rouge, LA, pg. 207
Hall, John T., Controller--Dixie Electric Cooperative, Union Springs, AL, pg. 341
Hall, Steven, Controller--Cecil Saydah Company, Los Angeles, CA, pg. 973
Hallagan, Don, Controller--Pollenex Corporation, Chicago, IL, pg. 821
Hallier, Robert, Controller--American Finance Group, Boston, MA, pg. 52
Halligan, Howard, Asst. Controller--Soap Opera Digest, New York, NY, pg. 611
Halling, Steve, Controller--Red Spot Paint & Varnish Co., Evansville, IN, pg. 918
Halm, Thomas L., V.P. & Controller--Brown Motors, Toledo, OH, pg. 182
Halsell, Tom, Controller--Yum Yum Donut Shop, Inc., City of Industry, CA, pg. 1214
Hamblen, Dan, Controller--The Gilman Company, Chattanooga, TN, pg. 603
Hamby, Jess, Controller--Murphy Company, Eugene, OR, pg. 776
Hamel, Walter, Comptroller--C-B Corporation, Charlotte, NC, pg. 198
Hamilton, Barbara, Controller--The Venet Companies, Inc., Union, NJ, pg. 1147
Hamilton, Doug, Controller & Treas.--Spinnerin Yarn Co., Inc., South Hackensack, NJ, pg. 1031
Hamilton, Kenneth, Controller--Illinois Cereal Mills, Inc., Paris, IL, pg. 562
Hammell, Eva, Controller--Rocky Mountain Mechanical, Inc., Salt Lake City, UT, pg. 942
Hampton, John W., Sr. V.P. & Controller--NTS Corporation, Louisville, KY, pg. 781
Hanas, Diana, Comptroller--Shiffman/Fergusson/Stone Advertising Inc., Fort Lee, NJ, pg. 999
Hanauer, Linda H., Asst. Treas.--The First Boston Corporation, New York, NY, pg. 203
Hancock, Joyce K., Sr. V.P. & Controller--First Federal of Michigan, Detroit, MI, pg. 414
Handler, Marlene, Controller--Larsen Colby Advertising, Los Angeles, CA, pg. 659
Hanes, Andrew G., Controller & Sec.--Superior Container, Inc., Warrensville, OH, pg. 1063
Hanlin, Thomas W., Controller--Lockhart Cadillac Inc., Indianapolis, IN, pg. 680
Hanlin, Thomas W., Controller--Saturn of Indianapolis, Indianapolis, IN, pg. 680
Hanlon, Michael, Controller--Duron, Inc., Beltsville, MD, pg. 355
Hanna, Gregory, Controller--Horizon Media, Inc., New York, NY, pg. 544
Hannah, Bob, Controller--UVP, Inc., San Gabriel, CA, pg. 1124
Hanover, Randi, Controller & Mgr.-Office--NTC Group, Greenwich, CT, pg. 781
Hanselman, Allan C., V.P. & Comptroller--North American Company, Fort Lauderdale, FL, pg. 811
Harab, Paul, Controller & Sec.--Duron, Inc., Beltsville, MD, pg. 355
Harding, Ruth, Controller--Accurate Threaded Fasteners, Inc., Lincolnwood, IL, pg. 11
Hardwe, Angie, Controller--Theochem Labs., Inc., Tampa, FL, pg. 1090
Hardwick, Robert, Sec., Controller & Treas.--Axelson, Inc., Longview, TX, pg. 103
Harkins, Barbara, Sr. V.P., Controller--Ingalls, Quinn & Johnson, Boston, MA, pg. 567

Harmon, Davis, Controller--Polar Corporation, Worcester, MA, pg. 878
Harmon, John, V.P., Controller--McCracken Brooks Communications, Inc., Minneapolis, MN, pg. 728
Harmon, Linda L., Chief Fin. Officer & Treas.--Progressive Driver Services, Inc., Jacksonville, FL, pg. 894
Harrington, J., Sec.--Maryland & Virginia Milk Producers Association, Reston, VA, pg. 717
Harris, Charlotte R., Controller--Massey Cadillac, Inc., Orlando, FL, pg. 719
Harris, Dennis, V.P. & Controller--Korn/Ferry International, Los Angeles, CA, pg. 642
Harris, H. David, Asst. Treas. & Controller--Transus Inc., Atlanta, GA, pg. 1108
Harris, James H., Controller--Penske Corporation, Detroit, MI, pg. 859
Harris, Rick L., Treas.& Controller--Bader & Co., Ipava, IL, pg. 113
Harris, W. Douglass, V.P. & Controller--Shapell Industries, Inc., Beverly Hills, CA, pg. 995
Harrison, Roland, Controller--Earle Industries, Inc., Earle, AR, pg. 362
Harstine, Jay A., Controller--L. J. Smith, Inc., Bowerston, OH, pg. 710
Hart, David W., Controller--Ginsberg's Institutional Foods, Inc., Hudson, NY, pg. 460
Hart, Ray, Controller--Kanawha Steel & Equipment Co., Charleston, WV, pg. 615
Hartis, Norman, Controller--Myrick Construction Inc., Biscoe, NC, pg. 780
Hartline, Lee, Treas. & Controller--Greer Steel Co., Dover, OH, pg. 486
Hasche, Bruce, Controller--Sencore, Inc., Sioux Falls, SD, pg. 989
Hash, Dave, Controller--Tri Valley Growers Inc., San Francisco, CA, pg. 1111
Haskell, Richard, Controller--Systems Engineering & Manufacturing Corp., Stoughton, MA, pg. 1071
Hastings, G. Melvin, Sr. V.P. & Controller--Capital Development Co., Lacey, WA, pg. 215
Hattori, Gerald Y., Controller--Sipex Corporation, Billerica, MA, pg. 1009
Haugan, Karla, Comptroller--Lawrence & Schiller, Inc., Sioux Falls, SD, pg. 663
Hauser, Fred P., Sr. V.P. & Controller--Metropolitan Life Insurance Co., New York, NY, pg. 744
Havenga, Hester, Fin. Controller--NBS Limited-Card Services Division, Surrey,, United Kingdom, pg. 960
Havlik, Gregory C., Controller--Wm. T. Burnett & Co., Inc., Baltimore, MD, pg. 191
Havner, Ron, V.P. & Controller--Public Storage, Inc., Glendale, CA, pg. 898
Hawkins, Elvest, Controller--Crown Prince, Inc. (CA), City of Industry, CA, pg. 302
Hawkins, P., Controller--The Gerstenslager Company, Wooster, OH, pg. 454
Hawkins, Robert E., Chief Fin. Officer, Treas., Controller & Sec.--West Union Corp., Memphis, TN, pg. 1177
Hawkins, William R., Controller--Coastal Wholesale, Inc., Kinston, NC, pg. 257
Hawley, Tom, Controller--Poly Pak America, Inc., Los Angeles, CA, pg. 880
Hayes, James, Controller--David Brett, Inc., Easton, MA, pg. 174
Hayes, Kathleen A., Controller--Kennington Ltd., Inc., Los Angeles, CA, pg. 623
Hayes, Matthew, Pres., Chief Exec. Officer & Treas.--Hayes/Harwood, Stowe, VT, pg. 519
Hayes, Mike, Controller & Dir.-Data Processing--M. B. Kahn Construction Co., Inc., Columbia, SC, pg. 614
Hayes, Ronney L., Controller--Ruffin Building Systems, Inc., Oak Grove, LA, pg. 955
Haynes, Anthony, V.P. & Controller--Flav-O-Rich, Inc., Louisville, KY, pg. 311
Hays, Randy K., Sec., Controller, & Treas.--Masek Distributing Inc., Gering, NE, pg. 717
Hazan, Craig M., Chief Fin. Officer & Controller--The Jaydor Corporation, Millburn, NJ, pg. 591
Heacock, Richard, V.P.-Fin., Treas., Sec. & Controller--Apache Hose & Belting Company, Cedar Rapids, IA, pg. 77
Hebert, Bruce, Corp. Controller--SnyderGeneral Corporation, Dallas, TX, pg. 1015
Heenan, Edward S., V.P. & Comptroller--Western & Southern Life Insurance Co., Cincinnati, OH, pg. 1181
Hefferman, William, Controller--General Binding Corporation, Northbrook, IL, pg. 656
Hegstrand, Rich, Controller--Magnetic Data, Inc., Eden Prairie, MN, pg. 700
Heidelberg, Jerry, Controller--Target Sportswear, Inc., New York, NY, pg. 1079
Heil, Chris, Controller--The Hammerblow Corp., Wausau, WI, pg. 504
Heist, David C., V.P., Grp. Controller--Ross Roy Inc., Bloomfield Hills, MI, pg. 950
Hejnar, Gerald J., Controller, Sec. & Dir.-Employee Benefits--Regency Lincoln Mercury, Dallas, TX, pg. 922
Helfer, David, Controller--VJ Growers, Inc., Apopka, FL, pg. 1141
Helie, Ray, Controller--C & M Corporation, Wauregan, CT, pg. 198
Heller, Keith, Controller--Hitchcock Chair Company LTD, Riverton, CT, pg. 536
Heller, Rodney D., Comptroller--Marquette Coppersmithing Co., Inc., Philadelphia, PA, pg. 713
Helmer, W., Treas. & Controller--Republic Industries, Inc., Harwood Heights, IL, pg. 928
Helmig, Robert, Controller--La France Corporation, Philadelphia, PA, pg. 649
Helms, Helen, Controller--Renken Boat Manufacturing Co., Charleston, SC, pg. 927
Heltemes, Linda, Controller--Bermo, Inc., Circle Pines, MN, pg. 143
Heltsley, Tom A., Controller--Carlyle & Co. Jewelers, Greensboro, NC, pg. 222
Hemmerflag, Charles, V.P. & Controller--Meijer, Inc., Grand Rapids, MI, pg. 737
Henderson, Billie, Controller--Rangaire & Company, Cleburne, TX, pg. 912
Henderson, Ken, Controller--Futter Lumber Corporation, Rockville Centre, NY, pg. 437
Henderson, Ronald, Controller & Chief Fin. Officer--Klaus Radio Inc., Peoria, IL, pg. 634
Hendrickson, Stanley, Controller--Leon Hendrickson, Winchester, IN, pg. 529
Hensley, Tom, V.P. & Chief Fin. Officer--Fieldale Corporation, Baldwin, GA, pg. 409
Henss, Laurence R., V.P., Treas. & Controller--Industrial Dielectrics, Inc., Noblesville, IN, pg. 566
Herchenroder, Jan A., Controller--Ris Paper Company, Long Island City, NY, pg. 935
Herlihy, Tom, Controller--Pepsi-Cola Albany Bottling Co., Inc., Latham, NY, pg. 860
Herman, Randy, V.P., Controller & Sec.--Carter Day Industries, Inc., Minneapolis, MN, pg. 226
Herr, Craig, Controller--The Sico Company, Mount Joy, PA, pg. 1001
Herrmann, Harold, Chief Fin. Officer & Controller--William B. Reily & Co., Inc., New Orleans, LA, pg. 923
Herschuk, Michael J., Controller--Cine Magnetics, Inc., Mamaroneck, NY, pg. 250
Hershiser, Dave, Controller--Omaha Steaks International, Omaha, NE, pg. 825
Herstine, David, Controller--Panorama Press, Inc., Clifton, NJ, pg. 846
Herwald, Kurt A., V.P.-Fin.--NTC Group, Greenwich, CT, pg. 781
Hess, R. Gene, V.P. & Controller--Doane Products Co., Joplin, MO, pg. 342
Heumann, Peter L., Controller--The Scotsman Group, Inc., Baltimore, MD, pg. 982
Heurung, Bob, Controller--Scherer Bros. Lumber Company, Minneapolis, MN, pg. 976
Hewell, Mike, Retail Controller--Thrifty Oil Company, Downey, CA, pg. 1096
Hibma, Sam, Controller--Patterson Frozen Foods, Inc., Patterson, CA, pg. 851
Hibo, Henry P., V.P. & Controller--Annin & Company, Roseland, NJ, pg. 75
Hickman, Rickey, Controller--T.L. James & Company, Ruston, LA, pg. 588
Hielke, William E., Controller, Admin. Sec. & Chief Fin. Officer--Bata Shoe Co., Inc., Belcamp, MD, pg. 201
Higgins, Howard N., Controller--Pace Industries, Inc., Fayetteville, AR, pg. 838
Hileman, Steve, Controller--Mrs. Baird's Bakeries, Inc., Fort Worth, TX, pg. 760
Hill, Alan, Controller--Superior Federal Bank, Fort Smith, AR, pg. 1063
Hill, Curtis V., V.P. & Controller--Vogue & Body Shops, Inc., Jacksonville, FL, pg. 1154
Hill, Rick, Controller--Falconer Glass Industries, Inc., Falconer, NY, pg. 492
Hilliard, Anthony A., Controller--American Fuel Cell & Coated Fabrics Co. (Amfuel), Magnolia, AR, pg. 55
Hines, Shelley G., Controller--Zytec Corp., Eden Prairie, MN, pg. 1221
Hines, Zoe, Sr. V.P. & Controller--Stephens, Inc., Little Rock, AR, pg. 1046
Hinrichs, Tom, Controller--Micropump Corporation, Vancouver, WA, pg. 749
Hinrichs, Tom, Controller--Micropump, Concord, CA, pg. 749
Hinson, Robert, Controller--Columbus Steel Drum Company, Blacklick, OH, pg. 267
Hintz, Walter R., V.P. & Controller--The Stroh Brewery Company, Detroit, MI, pg. 1053
Hinzman, H.W., Controller--Midwest Tire & Muffler, Inc., Rapid City, SD, pg. 752
Hirji, Farokh, Controller--West Mill Clothes, Inc., Woodside, NY, pg. 1177
Hislop, Thomas W., Controller--Subway Franchisee Advertising Fund Trust, Milford, CT, pg. 1055
Hlade, Robert, Controller--California Pacific Research, Inc., Reno, NV, pg. 210
Hlas, Al, Controller--Brown & Haley, Tacoma, WA, pg. 182
Hobizon, Pamela A., Controller--Schutte & Company, Buffalo, NY, pg. 979
Hochstedler, Kevin, Controller & Asst. Treas.--Bristol Products, L.P., Bristol, IN, pg. 176
Hocking, Scott T., V.P. & Chief Fin. Officer--Insignia Financial Group, Inc., Greenville, SC, pg. 571
Hocum, Kevin, Controller--RELA Product Development Div. (PDD), Boulder, CO, pg. 924
Hodges, Bruce, Controller--Hopper Inc., Bakersfield, CA, pg. 543
Hodges, Charles, Treas. & Controller--Colonial Oil Industries, Savannah, GA, pg. 263
Hodgson, Dave, Controller--Perry's Ice Cream Co., Inc., Akron, NY, pg. 863
Hoeller, Diane, Controller--Texas Steel Co., Inc., Fort Worth, TX, pg. 1090
Hoese, Stephen, Controller--E.A. Sween Company, Eden Prairie, MN, pg. 1066
Hoff, Carl D., Treas. & Controller--Rice Growers Association of California, West Sacramento, CA, pg. 931
Hoffman, Gail, V.P., Controller--Christopher Thomas Associates Inc., Garden City, NY, pg. 249
Hoffstein, Richard, Sr. V.P. & Controller--Continental Cablevision, Boston, MA, pg. 278
Hofman, Henry J., Controller & Sec.--Reliance Elevator Company, Chicago, IL, pg. 925
Hogen, R., Controller--Thordarson Meissner, Inc., Mount Carmel, IL, pg. 270
Hohlman, R.J., V.P. & Controller--Hesston, Norcross, GA, pg. 4
Hojer, Susan, Chief Fin. Officer, Controller & Mgr.-Personnel--MFE Instruments, Beverly, MA, pg. 1050
Holbrook, Edgar, Controller--Romac Industries, Inc., Hays Division, Dallas, NC, pg. 945
Holden, Daisy L., Controller--Sullivan Oil Company, Baton Rouge, LA, pg. 1057
Holden, Shirley, Treas., Sec. & Controller--Royal Oldsmobile Mazda, Inc., Metairie, LA, pg. 953
Holland, Chris, V.P. & Controller--LeeWards Creative Crafts, Inc., Elgin, IL, pg. 666
Hollandsworth, Ronald, Controller--Donnkenny, Inc., New York, NY, pg. 345
Holmes, N.E., V.P. & Controller--The Marley Company, Mission Woods, KS, pg. 710
Holst, Peter, Controller & Dir.-Data Processing--Theradyne Corporation, Lakeville, MN, pg. 1065
Holtzhauser, John, Controller--Mooney Chemicals, Cleveland, OH, pg. 768
Holtzman, Robert J., Controller--Millers' Mutual Insurance Assn. Of Illinois, Alton, IL, pg. 755
Honeycutt, Mark, V.P.-Admin. & Chief Fin. Officer--PBM Office Products, Cleveland, OH, pg. 835
Honton, Angelyn M., V.P., Controller--Trone Advertising, Inc., Greensboro, NC, pg. 1115
Hood, Cecil G., Sec. & Controller--Batson-Cook Company, West Point, GA, pg. 126
Hood, Faye, Controller--B.A.S.S., Inc., Montgomery, AL, pg. 105
Hood, Osbert M., V.P. & Controller--John Hancock Mutual Life Insurance Company, Boston, MA, pg. 595
Hood, Philip, Controller--Enco Materials, Inc., Nashville, TN, pg. 380
Hoole, James, Controller--Winthrop Printing Company, Inc., Boston, MA, pg. 1197
Hooper, Davis L., Comptroller--Electro Mechanical Design Services, Inc., Gaithersburg, MD, pg. 375
Hoover, George N., III, Controller--The Columbia Corporation, Chatham, NY, pg. 1209
Hoover, Ralph E., Comptroller--Pacific Steel Casting Co., Berkeley, CA, pg. 841
Hopp, William A., Controller--The Ward Machinery Company, Cockeysville, MD, pg. 1162
Hopper, John, Controller--Piper Aircraft Corporation, Vero Beach, FL, pg. 872
Horberg, Jane, Controller--Bessin Corporation, Chicago, IL, pg. 146
Hordericki, Richard, Controller--Hermes Automotive Manufacturing Corp., Detroit, MI, pg. 531
Horning, John, Controller--SafetyMaster Corporation, Billings, MT, pg. 1053
Horton, Betty, Controller--Pic'n Pay Stores, Inc., Charlotte, NC, pg. 201
Horton, Ron, Controller--Gas Equipment Company, Inc., Dallas, TX, pg. 444
Hosack, Joseph V., Controller--Premier Dental Products Company, Norristown, PA, pg. 886
Hosenitz, Luke, Controller--Arrow Group Industries, Inc., Wayne, NJ, pg. 357
Houts, Beverly, Controller--Elyria Foundry Company, Elyria, OH, pg. 378
Hove, J. Norman, V.P. & Controller--American Linen Supply Company, Minneapolis, MN, pg. 57
Howard, Connie, Controller--U.S. Metalsource Corporation, Coraopolis, PA, pg. 1136
Howard, Judy, Asst. Controller--Grizzard Advertising, Inc., Atlanta, GA, pg. 488
Howard, Martin, V.P. & Controller--Ergon, Inc., Jackson, MS, pg. 386
Howard, Mike, Controller--Mark Andy, Inc., Chesterfield, MO, pg. 708
Howell, Fred, V.P. & Controller--Maritz Communications Co., Fenton, MO, pg. 707
Howell, G.J., Controller--Sverdrup Corporation, Maryland Heights, MO, pg. 1065
Howell, Joyce, Controller--First Electric Cooperative, Jacksonville, AR, pg. 412
Hower, Matthew J., Controller--Burgess-Norton Mfg. Co., Geneva, IL, pg. 69
Hoyer, David, Controller--North Park Lincoln Mercury Inc., San Antonio, TX, pg. 813
Hoyt, Linda, Controller--Toledo Blade Co., Toledo, OH, pg. 155
Hubbard, Roger, Controller--J.L. Lester & Son, Inc., Rockmart, GA, pg. 668
Hubbard, Sonja, Controller, Treas & Sec.--E-Z Mart Stores, Inc., Texarkana, TX, pg. 361
Huber, Richard G., V.P. & Controller--Freeman Decorating Co., Dallas, TX, pg. 431
Huber, Thomas, Comptroller--Long Island Water Corporation, Lynbrook, NY, pg. 682
Hudgin, Patrick, Controller--C.J. Vitner & Co., Inc., Chicago, IL, pg. 1153
Hudson, James, Controller--Taylor Drug Stores, Inc., Louisville, KY, pg. 1081
Huebner, Donald F., Chief Fin. Officer, Treas. & Controller--Active Electrical Supply Company, Chicago, IL, pg. 15
Huey, Charles, Controller--S L C Graphics, Inc., Pittston, PA, pg. 963
Huffman, Dale, Controller--Heatcraft, Inc., Stone Mountain, GA, pg. 667
Hughes, David, Treas.--Central Supply Co., Inc., Indianapolis, IN, pg. 234
Hughes, Massie E., Controller--Acme Visible Records, Crozet, VA, pg. 13
Huitsing, John, Controller & Dir.-Fin.--Michigan Bulb Company, Grand Rapids, MI, pg. 638
Hulbert, Robert, Controller--Diehl Specialties Intl., Defiance, OH, pg. 336
Hull, Richard C., Controller--Norpac Foods, Inc. Cooperative, Stayton, OR, pg. 810
Hullibarger, Gail R., Mgr.-Acct. Dept. & Controller--Sacramento Municipal Utility District, Sacramento, CA, pg. 965

Corporate Responsibilities Index

Humphrey, Thomas, V.P.-Fin. & Controller--Savage Arms Inc., Westfield, MA, pg. 973
Hund, Martin H., Controller--Meco Corporation, Greeneville, TN, pg. 734
Hundley, Pam, Controller--The Disston Co., Greensboro, NC, pg. 339
Hunt, Robert, Controller--E & A Industries, Inc., Indianapolis, IN, pg. 358
Hunter, David, Controller--All-Luminum Products, Inc., Philadelphia, PA, pg. 35
Hurley, Charles T., Sr. V.P. & Controller--Meldrum & Fewsmith Communications Inc., Cleveland, OH, pg. 737
Hurley, Jeannie, Controller--San Francisco Giants Baseball Club, San Francisco, CA, pg. 969
Hurt, Matt, Controller--Universal Vise & Tool Co., Parma, MI, pg. 103
Huston, John, Controller--Autoroll Machine Corp., Middleton, MA, pg. 101
Hutchens, Sharon, Comptroller--Blue Boar Cafeteria Co., Louisville, KY, pg. 158
Hutcherson, Cecil, Controller--Mayfair Mills, Inc., Arcadia, SC, pg. 724
Huth, Nancy, Controller--Green Leaf Ventures, Inc., San Diego, CA, pg. 484
Hutton, Nancy, Sec., Treas. & Controller--Crustbuster, Inc., Dodge City, KS, pg. 303
Hynes, Jack, Controller--Sommer & Maca Industries, Inc., Chicago, IL, pg. 1017
Hynes, Martin, Controller--Spraying Systems Co., Wheaton, IL, pg. 1032
Iacobucci, Al, Controller--Astro Wire & Cable Corporation, Worcester, MA, pg. 92
Iacuone, Nick A. Jr., Controller--O. F. Mossberg & Sons, Inc., North Haven, CT, pg. 773
Iannuzzi, Vito, Controller--Imperia Bros., Inc., Pelham Manor, NY, pg. 563
Ihle, Herbert, Sr. V.P.-Fin. & Controller--NWA, Inc., Saint Paul, MN, pg. 782
Ihle, Herbert D., Sr. V.P.-Fin. & Controller--Northwest Airlines, Inc., Saint Paul, MN, pg. 782
Innes, Jim, Controller--Superior Dairy, Inc., Canton, OH, pg. 1063
Inzitari, Frank, Controller--Frank Ix & Sons, Inc., New York, NY, pg. 584
Irvine, Terri, Controller--Manufacturers Products Company, Warren, MI, pg. 705
Isaacs, Debbie, V.P.-Fin. & Controller--AmTran Corporation, Conway, AR, pg. 69
Israel, Maureen, Chief Exec. Officer & Controller--Wright-Schuchart, Inc., Seattle, WA, pg. 1204
Ivia, Jay, Controller--Three Beall Brothers 3, Inc., Jacksonville, TX, pg. 1029
Izydorek, Ronald, Controller--Synchro-Start Products, Inc., Niles, IL, pg. 638
Jablonsky, Allan J., Treas. & Controller--Trak International, Inc., Port Washington, WI, pg. 1106
Jackson, Barbara, Controller--RHC/Spacemaster Corporation, Melrose Park, IL, pg. 906
Jackson, Jesse, Treas. & Controller--Cumberland-Swan, Inc., Smyrna, TN, pg. 304
Jackson, Thomas, Controller--National Forge Company, Irvine, PA, pg. 788
Jackson, Tom, Controller--Blitz USA, Miami, OK, pg. 157
Jackson, Tom, Chief Fin. Officer & Controller--Blitz U.S.A., Inc., Miami, OK, pg. 157
Jacob, Bob, Controller--Ivex Packaging Corporation-Hillside, Hillside, IL, pg. 583
Jacobs, Jay, Controller--Sunox, Inc., Charlotte, NC, pg. 1062
Jacobsen, Torben, Controller--Wunderman Worldwide A/S, Copenhagen, Denmark, pg. 1212
Jacobson, Darlene, Mill Controller--Ivex Packaging Corporation-Chagrin Falls, Chagrin Falls, OH, pg. 583
Jain, Karan, Controller--Interbath, Inc., City of Industry, CA, pg. 574
James, Henry D., V.P. & Worldwide Controller--Berlitz International, Inc., Princeton, NJ, pg. 142
Janes, Robert, Controller--John D. Lucas Printing Company, Baltimore, MD, pg. 263
Janice, Jo, Controller--National Bulk Carriers, Inc., New York, NY, pg. 786
Janikies, Cynthia, Controller--Jan-Co., Inc., Cranston, RI, pg. 589
Janiszewski, Andrew, Controller--World's Finest Chocolate Australia Pty. Ltd., Stanmore,, Australia, pg. 1203
Jankowski, Gerald, Controller--Georgie Boy Manufacturing, Inc., Edwardsburg, MI, pg. 453
Janssen, Dan, Controller--Sathers Inc., Round Lake, MN, pg. 972
Jatzlau, D.P., Controller--J.M. Huber, Flow Control Div., Tomball, TX, pg. 550
Jennings, Barbara, Controller--Sterling Builders, Inc., Irvine, CA, pg. 1047
Jennings, Mark, Controller--Spartan Oil Corp., Lansing, MI, pg. 1026
Jennrich, William F., V.P. & Controller--Brown-Minneapolis Tank & Fabricating Co., Eagan, MN, pg. 182
Jensen, Gordon E., V.P.-Comptroller, Treas. & Asst. Sec.--Omaha Property & Casualty, Omaha, NE, pg. 779
Jensen, Gordon E., V.P., Treas., Comptroller & Asst. Sec.--Omaha Property & Casualty Co., Omaha, NE, pg. 779
Jensen, Janeen, Controller--Capener, Matthews & Walcher, San Diego, CA, pg. 214
Jensen, Jon, Controller & Treas.--Philadelphia Gear Corp., King of Prussia, PA, pg. 866
Jensen, Owen, Treas. & Controller--M. A. Mortenson Company, Minneapolis, MN, pg. 772
Jenssen, Paul H., Controller--The Associated Press, New York, NY, pg. 91
Jepsen, Edward G., Exec. V.P., Chief Fin. Officer & Controller--LPL Technologies, Inc., Wallingford, CT, pg. 648
Jeremiah, Anthony, Controller--Swede Sportswear Company, Inc., Los Angeles, CA, pg. 1066
Jermanus, Paul, Controller--Michigan Milk Producers Association, Novi, MI, pg. 747
Jevahirian, Mary J., Controller--Contract Interiors Inc., Southfield, MI, pg. 280
Jobe, Russell, Controller--Hale-Halsell Company, Tulsa, OK, pg. 500
Johns, F. Ray, Controller--Birdsong Corporation, Sulfolk, VA, pg. 153
Johns, L.M., Jr., Controller--National Fruit Product Company, Winchester, VA, pg. 789
Johnson, Allan E., V.P. & Controller--American Bureau of Shipping, New York, NY, pg. 50
Johnson, Bruce, Controller--Elan Foods, Buffalo, NY, pg. 372
Johnson, Charles, Controller--TimeMed Labeling Systems, Inc., Burr Ridge, IL, pg. 1098
Johnson, Dale M., Controller--Medtech Laboratories, Inc., Jackson, WY, pg. 736
Johnson, Dave, Controller--Metabo Corporation, West Chester, PA, pg. 741
Johnson, David, Controller--Smith & Sons Foods, Inc., Macon, GA, pg. 1014
Johnson, David, Controller--Johnson & Towers, Inc., Mount Laurel, NJ, pg. 601
Johnson, Debbie, Controller--Point Communications, Inc., Dallas, TX, pg. 878
Johnson, Dorothy, Controller--Hoogovens Aluminum Corp., Secaucus, NJ, pg. 543
Johnson, Greg A., Treas. & Controller--F.H. Stoltze Land & Lumber Company, Stillwater, MN, pg. 1050
Johnson, H.M., Controller--American Trading & Production Corporation, Oil & Gas Div., Houston, TX, pg. 64
Johnson, Henry, Controller--Connors Brunswick, Inc., South Portland, ME, pg. 275
Johnson, J. Brent, V.P. & Controller--American Family Mutual Insurance Co., Madison, WI, pg. 51
Johnson, Jill, Controller--Flanagan Brothers, Bear Creek, WI, pg. 416
Johnson, Margaret, Controller--H. C. Miller Company, Milwaukee, WI, pg. 754
Johnson, Merlyn, Controller--Christie Electric Corporation, Gardena, CA, pg. 249
Johnson, Randall, Controller--Encyclopaedia Britannica, Inc., Chicago, IL, pg. 381
Johnson, Rich, Controller--Tash, Inc., Des Plaines, IL, pg. 1080
Johnson, Richard, Controller--Petersen Publishing Company, Los Angeles, CA, pg. 864
Johnson, Robert, Controller & Dir.-Data Processing--Treasure Island Foodmarts Inc., Chicago, IL, pg. 1109
Johnson, Robert, Controller--Chance Industries, Inc., Wichita, KS, pg. 238
Johnson, Ron, Controller--Airmaster Fan Co., Michigan Center, MI, pg. 28
Johnson, Ron, Controller--Bates Container, Inc., North Richland Hills, TX, pg. 125
Johnson, Sharon M., Controller & Sec.--Sauer Industries, Inc., Pittsburgh, PA, pg. 972
Johnson, Terry, Controller--Mersman Furniture, Celina, OH, pg. 741
Johnson, William L., Jr., Comptroller--Hillerich & Bradsby Co., Inc., Louisville, KY, pg. 535
Johnston, Scott, Controller--W. B. Goode Company, Inc., Richmond, VA, pg. 470
Johnston, Terry, Controller & Treas.--Sioux Manufacturing Corp., Fort Totten, ND, pg. 1008
Jones, Dan, Controller--Wyatt Cafeterias Inc., Dallas, TX, pg. 1205
Jones, Donald, Controller--Fleet Engineers, Inc., Muskegon, MI, pg. 417
Jones, Jeff, Controller--Placid Oil Company, Dallas, TX, pg. 873
Jones, John, Controller--Kline Iron & Steel Co., Inc., Columbia, SC, pg. 635
Jones, LouAnn, Controller--Remarks, Inc., Dublin, OH, pg. 925
Jones, P.E., V.P. & Controller--Hunt Oil Company, Dallas, TX, pg. 553
Jones, Paul, Controller--Pace Oil Co., Inc., Winston-Salem, NC, pg. 838
Jones, Robert M., Controller--Cablevision Industries Corp., Liberty, NY, pg. 206
Jones, Sara, Controller & Chief Fin. Officer--The Criterion Group, Inc., Atlanta, GA, pg. 299
Jones, William, Controller--DDC PerTec, Tucson, AZ, pg. 308
Jordan, J. Randal, Controller--Manke Lumber Company, Inc., Tacoma, WA, pg. 704
Jordan, Jerry C., Controller-Store Opers.--Montgomery Ward & Co., Inc., Chicago, IL, pg. 767
Jordan, Leon, Treas. & Controller--Harbor Financial Mortgage Corp., Houston, TX, pg. 506
Jordan, Toni, Sr. V.P., Controller--McKinney & Silver, Raleigh, NC, pg. 730
Joseph, Marsha, Controller--Showell Farms, Inc., Showell, MD, pg. 1000
Joshipura, Sukumar, Controller--Freedland Industries Corporation, Dearborn, MI, pg. 430
Jossart, C.L., Sr. V.P. & Controller--Marquette Bank Rochester, Rochester, MN, pg. 117
Joyce, Joseph, Controller--Gerrity Co., Inc., Newton, MA, pg. 454
Joyce, Norm, Controller--Intermatic Inc., Spring Grove, IL, pg. 575
Judkins, J., Controller--Wisconsin Dairies Cooperative, Baraboo, WI, pg. 1197
Julian, Stephen C., Controller--Steves & Sons, San Antonio, TX, pg. 1048
Jullehe, Joanne, Controller--The WBDC Group, Grand Rapids, MI, pg. 1155
June, David M., Sr. V.P. & Controller--Omni Hotels, Hampton, NH, pg. 826
Jury, James, Controller--H & H Tube & Manufacturing Co., Vanderbilt, MI, pg. 495
Just, Pam B., V.P. & Controller--Coca-Cola Bottling Company of Elizabethtown, Elizabethtown, KY, pg. 258
Kaczmarski, Michael J., Sr. V.P., Controller--Ketchum Communications Inc., Pittsburgh, PA, pg. 625
Kadera, Richard F., Comptroller--CUNA Mutual Insurance Society, Madison, WI, pg. 205
Kadish, Mark, Controller--Telesciences Co. Systems Inc., Moorestown, NJ, pg. 1085
Kahle, Rita D., V.P. & Controller--Ace Hardware Corporation, Oak Brook, IL, pg. 12
Kaiser, Norman, Controller--Kaspar Wire Works, Inc., Shiner, TX, pg. 617
Kaldubowski, M.G., V.P. & Controller--Clearing International, Inc., Chicago, IL, pg. 254
Kalinowski, Sylvia J., Chief Oper. Officer & Controller--Tri-Mark Metal Corp., Detroit, MI, pg. 1110
Kallio, S., Controller--Crankshaft Machine Company, Jackson, MI, pg. 102
Kammer, Al, V.P.-Fin., Controller & Chief Fin. Officer--American Laundry Machinery Inc., Cincinnati, OH, pg. 57
Kanter, G., Controller--Thermal American Fused Quartz Co., Louisville, KY, pg. 1091
Kao, Areen, Controller--City Beverage Co., Atlanta, GA, pg. 251
Kapanek, Margaret, Controller--Buffalo Hospital Supply Co., Inc., Amherst, NY, pg. 187
Kaplan, William, Controller--Tekni-Plex, Inc., Brooklyn, NY, pg. 1084
Kapp, Richard, Controller--Domecq Importers Inc., Old Greenwich, CT, pg. 343
Karst, Terry, Controller--Standun, Inc., Irwindale, CA, pg. 1038
Kaseman, Fred, Controller--Englefield, Inc., Newark, OH, pg. 382
Kaskey, Dale, Controller--The Akro Corporation, Canton, OH, pg. 262
Kaskovich, Nickolas, Controller--Geo. J. Ball, Inc., West Chicago, IL, pg. 115
Kasnicki, Ted, Controller--Publishers Clearing House, Port Washington, NY, pg. 898
Kates, Frank, Controller--Columbus Show Case Company, Columbus, OH, pg. 267
Kau, Alfonso, Controller--Aero Peru Corporation, Miami, FL, pg. 22
Kavanaugh, Edward F., V.P., Treas., Controller & Mng. Dir.--New Hampshire Oak, Hampton, NH, pg. 800
Kayton, Roxanna, Controller--The Orvis Company, Inc., Manchester, VT, pg. 830
Kazmarex, R., Controller--Stillman Seal, Carlsbad, CA, pg. 1049
Kazmierczak, Kenneth J., Treas., Controller & Sec.--Schreier Malting Co., Sheboygan, WI, pg. 978
Kean, James, Comptroller & Treas.--Henderson Electric Co., Inc., Louisville, KY, pg. 529
Keane, W., Controller--GFA Brands, Inc., Cresskill, NJ, pg. 440
Keating, William M., Controller--Lane Industries, Inc., Northbrook, IL, pg. 656
Keck, Elizabeth K., Controller--Broadcast Electronics, Inc., Quincy, IL, pg. 177
Kedrowski, Len W., Chief Fin. Officer, Treas. & Controller--Andersen Windows Inc., Bayport, MN, pg. 72
Keenahan, Michael, Controller--Hutchins/Young & Rubicam, Rochester, NY, pg. 1211
Kees, Ray, Chief Fin. Officer, Corp. Sec. & Tres.--Gem-Dandy, Inc., Madison, NC, pg. 447
Kegley, Don, Chief Fin. Officer & Controller--Cunningham-Limp Development Co., Troy, MI, pg. 305
Keilman, David W., Treas. & Controller--Comark, Bloomingdale, IL, pg. 267
Keiser, Sarah L., Controller--Seligman & Associates, Inc., Bloomfield Hills, MI, pg. 988
Keisler, Carl, Controller--Dewberry & Davis, Fairfax, VA, pg. 334
Keitel, Tom, Controller--Garney Holding Company, Inc., Kansas City, MO, pg. 443
Keller, August, Controller--Cosmetique, Inc., Vernon Hills, IL, pg. 288
Keller, Chris, Controller & Treasurer--Darda Inc. (USA), Baltimore, MD, pg. 315
Keller, James E., Treas. & Controller--Rapid Mounting & Finishing Co., Chicago, IL, pg. 913
Kelley, Candy, Controller--D. J. Mead-Hubbs & Howe, Buffalo, NY, pg. 1016
Kelly, Ike, Controller--California-Gym Equipment Co., Los Angeles, CA, pg. 163
Kelly, James, V.P., Gen. Mgr. & Controller--Animal Fair, Edina, MN, pg. 978
Kelly, Jim, V.P. & Controller--Harris Farms, Inc., Coalinga, CA, pg. 511
Kelly, Maria G., Controller--Kelly Michener Inc., Lancaster, PA, pg. 621
Kemp, Alan, Controller--Airtex Products, Fairfield, IL, pg. 1123
Kemp, Mike, Chief Fin. Officer & Controller--Fantastic Sam's International, Inc., Memphis, TN, pg. 398
Kempa, Steve, V.P. & Controller--M.L. Stern & Company, Inc., Beverly Hills, CA, pg. 1047
Kempen, Bud, Controller--Pabst Brewing Co., San Antonio, TX, pg. 959
Kempf, LeRoy, Controller & Sec.--Condon Oil Company, Inc., Ripon, WI, pg. 273
Kenehan, MichaelJ., Controller--Haddon Craftsmen, Inc., Scranton, PA, pg. 499
Keolker, Ronald H., Chief Fin. Officer, V.P., Treas. & Controller--Twin City Foods, Inc., Stanwood, WA, pg. 1122
Kerfoot, William, 2nd V.P. & Controller--Wetsel-Oviatt Lumber Company, Folsom, CA, pg. 1183
Kermode, Richard, Exec. V.P.-Admin. & Treas.--Misener Marine Construction, Tampa, FL, pg. 759
Kerr, Rose, Asst. Controller--Washington Homes, Inc., Landover, MD, pg. 1166

Kessler, Gary, Controller--American Color, Phoenix, AZ, pg. 1056
Kessler, Lee, Sec. & Controller--Stern & Stern Industries Inc., New York, NY, pg. 1048
Ketsdever, Matthew, Controller--Bromar Inc., Newport Beach, CA, pg. 179
Keuper, Robert, Controller--South Bend Plastics, Inc., Mishawaka, IN, pg. 1019
Keyes, Susan, Controller--The Dartnell Corporation, Chicago, IL, pg. 316
Keysvik, Mike, Controller--Pancom International Corp., Stamford, CT, pg. 845
Kezer, John, Controller--CEI Construction, Inc., Bethesda, MD, pg. 200
Khadan, Kelvin, Controller--Allied Systems, Ltd., Decatur, GA, pg. 40
Khalil, Nick, Controller--Cold Spring Granite Company, Minnetonka, MN, pg. 259
Khire, N.R., Controller--Chaitra Leo Burnett Advertising Private Ltd., Bombay, India, pg. 192
Khoury, E.R., Treas. & Controller--Morrison Textile Machinery Co., Fort Lawn, SC, pg. 771
Kierzek, Marty, V.P., Controller--Grant/Jacoby, Inc., Chicago, IL, pg. 477
Kile, Melinda G., Controller--Tree Top, Inc., Selah, WA, pg. 1109
Killoran, Michael F., Controller--Paul Arpin Vanlines, Inc., East Greenwich, RI, pg. 85
Kilts, Albert, Internal Auditor--Lawrence Management Group, Inc., Albany, NY, pg. 662
Kim, H., Controller--Sherwood Corporation, Fremont, CA, pg. 570
Kimaid, Paul, Controller--Prince Manufacturing, Inc., Lawrenceville, NJ, pg. 890
Kincaid, Mike, Controller--TSC Industries, Inc., Nashville, TN, pg. 1075
King, Dave, Controller--Dann Dee Display Fixtures, Chicago, IL, pg. 314
King, Larry, Controller--VMC Fiberglass Products Inc., Daleville, AL, pg. 1142
King, Lawrence R., Controller--Marine Construction & Design Co., Seattle, WA, pg. 707
Kirby, Shelby J., Chief Fin. Officer, Treas. & Controller--T.S. Ragsdale Company, Incorporated, Lake City, SC, pg. 910
Kirchoff, Phillip, Chief Fin. Officer & Controller--Farmway Co-Op Inc., Beloit, KS, pg. 402
Kiser, Jimmy, V.P.-Fin.--Kesterson Food Company, Inc., Paris, TN, pg. 624
Kish, Tom, V.P. & Comptroller--Raynor Garage Door Company, Dixon, IL, pg. 915
Kitamura, Kazumi, Controller--The Berlitz Schools of Languages (Japan) Inc., Tokyo, Japan, pg. 143
Kitchens, Michael, Controller--Associated Process Controls, Pleasanton, CA, pg. 92
Kitchens, Orman L., Treas. & Controller--Capeletti Bros., Inc., Miami Lakes, FL, pg. 214
Kittle, John, Controller--Nylon Corporation Of America, Manchester, NH, pg. 818
Kitts, Diane L., V.P. & Controller--Jerome-Duncan Ford, Sterling Heights, MI, pg. 593
Kiuenta, Bill, Controller--Microwave Networks Incorporated, Houston, TX, pg. 749
Klatt, David, Controller--Nodak Mutual Insurance Company, Fargo, ND, pg. 808
Klaus-Owens, Laura, Controller--North Shore Movers, Northbrook, IL, pg. 813
Klemm, Edwin, Controller--Hano Business Forms, Inc., Springfield, MA, pg. 505
Klerk, Willima J., Controller--McNeel International Corp., Tampa, FL, pg. 732
Klocek, Gary, Controller--Jones Apparel Group, Inc., Bristol, PA, pg. 602
Klomes, Joseph, Controller--Azteca Foods, Incorporated, Chicago, IL, pg. 105
Kmoch, Robert, Controller--DEC/Bou-Matic, Madison, WI, pg. 309
Knepp, Lynn E., Controller--Gannett Fleming Affiliates, Inc., Harrisburg, PA, pg. 442
Knesek, Mike, Controller--Enterprise Products Company, Houston, TX, pg. 382
Knight, Bob, Chief Fin. Officer, Controller & Sec.--Stadelman Fruit Inc., Yakima, WA, pg. 1034
Knight, Jim, Controller--Mount Vernon Mills, Inc., Greenville, SC, pg. 844
Knueven, Gerald R., Chief Fin. Officer, Treas. & Controller--Harold M. Pitman Co., Inc., Totowa, NJ, pg. 872
Kobylarz, Michael, V.P. & Controller--The Texwipe Co., Inc., Upper Saddle River, NJ, pg. 1090
Koch, Pam, Controller--Lindsay, Stone & Briggs Advertising, Inc., Madison, WI, pg. 676
Kochman, Karl, Sr. V.P. & Controller--D&L Venture Corp., New Britain, CT, pg. 307
Kocur, Ted, Chief Fin. Officer--Eberle Direct Marketing Group, Inc., Vienna, VA, pg. 365
Kodosky, Thomas M., Controller--Elkay Manufacturing Company, Oak Brook, IL, pg. 377
Koechley, L. Thomas, Controller--Kirkwood Industries, Inc., Cleveland, OH, pg. 633
Koenig, Kenneth, Controller--Creation Windows of Indiana, Inc., Elkhart, IN, pg. 297
Koenig, Mark, Controller--Williams Steel & Hardware Company, Minneapolis, MN, pg. 1191
Koennecke, Susan, Comptroller--S. R. Leon Company, Inc., Oyster Bay, NY, pg. 667
Koenning, George, Controller--Gus Machado Enterprises, Hialeah, FL. pg. 696
Koeserich, Ron, Asst. V.P. & Controller--Maidenform, Inc., New York, NY, pg. 701
Koh, Linda, Controller--Jupiter Industries, Inc., Chicago, IL, pg. 609
Kohl, Don, Controller--Crown Foods Inc., Saint Louis, MO, pg. 302
Kohler, Cliff, Plant Controller--Ivex Packaging Corporation-Joliet, Joliet, IL, pg. 583
Kolesar, Mary Alice, V.P. & Controller--Fry/Hammond/Barr Incorporated, Orlando, FL, pg. 435
Kollias, Ernie, Controller--North American Publishing Company, Philadelphia, PA, pg. 811
Kolodziej, Raymond P., V.P.-Corp. Controller & Treas.--Turtle Wax, Inc., Chicago, IL, pg. 1120
Kolsin, Jeffrey, Controller--Paramount Fitness Equipment Corp., Los Angeles, CA, pg. 848
Kometer, Clyde W., Controller--Kohler Company, Kohler, WI, pg. 639
Konas, Theodore V., Controller & Asst. Treas.--Yerger Bros., Inc., Lititz, PA, pg. 1208
Konczal, Raymond E., V.P. & Controller--Doehler-Jarvis, Toledo, OH, pg. 559
Kondzjolka, Dan, Controller--Daktronics, Inc., Brookings, SD, pg. 312
Koons, Kevin, Comptroller--Allied Building Products Corporation, East Rutherford, NJ, pg. 37
Koontz, Alexander H., Controller--Koolvent Aluminum Products, Inc., Pittsburgh, PA, pg. 641
Kopff, Matthew, Controller--Country Mutual Insurance Company, Bloomington, IL, pg. 289
Korber, Libby, Controller, Treas. & Sec.--J. Korber & Company, Albuquerque, NM, pg. 641
Korot, Cliff, Controller--M. Rubin & Sons Inc., New York, NY, pg. 954
Kos, Donaid J., Controller--Tradehome Shoe Stores, Inc., Saint Paul, MN, pg. 1105
Kosik, John, Controller--Olson Rug Company, Chicago, IL, pg. 824
Koucouthakis, George, V.P., Controller--The Quest Business Agency, Inc., Houston, TX, pg. 904
Koury, Don, Controller--Green Spot Packaging Inc., Claremont, CA, pg. 485
Koval, Thomas J., Treas. & Controller--Radiator Specialty Company, Charlotte, NC, pg. 909
Kowal, Chris, Controller--YSI Incorporated, Yellow Springs, OH, pg. 1207
Kowalski, Mary A., Controller--Antares Group Inc., Cleveland, OH, pg. 76
Kozel, Theresa, Comptroller--Hottman Edwards, Baltimore, MD, pg. 545
Kozma, M.J., Treas. & Controller--Maxitrol Co., Southfield, MI, pg. 723
Kraft, Ken, Controller--The Herald, Monterey, CA, pg. 155
Kramer, Cynthia S., Comptroller & Treas.--Seabrook Brothers & Sons, Inc., Seabrook, NJ, pg. 984
Kramer, Richard, Controller--Omni Lens Corporation, Forty Fort, PA, pg. 826
Kramer, William, III, V.P. & Controller--Reuland Electric Company, City of Industry, CA, pg. 930
Krampf, Ira, V.P. & Controller--Apparel Industries, Inc., New York, NY, pg. 78
Krasinski, Joe, Controller--Tri-K Industries, Inc., Emerson, NJ, pg. 1110
Krasna, Estelle, Sr. V.P., Controller, Corp. Sec.--Furman, Roth Adv., New York, NY, pg. 437
Krautstrunk, Steve, Controller--Dial Tube Company, Bedford Park, IL, pg. 939
Kreger, Joseph, Asst. Treas.--Preformed Line Products, Cleveland, OH, pg. 886
Kreiniker, Thomas J., Sec. & Controller--Standard Manifold Company, Inc., Chicago, IL, pg. 1037
Kretovic, Michael, Controller--Alleson of Rochester, Inc., Rochester, NY, pg. 37
Kretzmann, Walt, Controller--Mid-West Company, Burr Ridge, IL, pg. 939
Krill, Steve, Controller--Southtec, Inc., Albany, NY, pg. 1019
Kristiansen, Michelle, Controller--Harris Ford, Inc., Lynnwood, WA, pg. 512
Kromer, Alan C., Chief Fin. Officer & Controller--Takatta Inc., Olympia Fields, IL, pg. 1076
Kromer, Dennis R., Chief Fin. Officer, Treas. & Controller--Dunn-Edwards Corporation, Los Angeles, CA, pg. 353
Krueger, Michael B., Controller & Asst. Sec.--IDC Services, Inc., Chicago, IL, pg. 559
Krueger, Terry, Chief Fin. Officer & Controller--Associated Milk Producers, Inc., San Antonio, TX, pg. 91
Kruger, Jeffrey, Controller--Scott Printing Corporation, Jersey City, NJ, pg. 983
Kruis, Robert, Controller--Findley Adhesives, Inc., Wauwatosa, WI, pg. 410
Krumrei, Steve, Controller--The Hiebing Group, Inc., Madison, WI, pg. 533
Kruse, Jeffrey R., Exec. V.P. & Controller--Intelligent Controls Inc., Lynnwood, WA, pg. 573
Krzyminski, Richard, Sr. V.P.-Admin. & Controller--Corporex Companies, Inc., Covington, KY, pg. 287
Kubit, Kenneth, V.P. & Controller--Great Lakes Recreation Co., Livonia, MI, pg. 481
Kuechler, Karl, Controller--Brimms Inc., Tonawanda, NY, pg. 176
Kuehn, T., Controller--Transco Inc., Wayne, MI, pg. 1107
Kuhn, Rick, Controller--Game Time, Inc., Fort Payne, AL, pg. 442
Kung, Elisa, Controller--International Microcircuits, Inc., Milpitas, CA, pg. 579
Kunko, Rick, Controller--Wayne Dalton Corporation, Mount Hope, OH, pg. 312
Kunz, Ray, Controller--Watlow Electric Manufacturing Company, Saint Louis, MO, pg. 1167
Kuptsis, Steve, V.P.-Admin. & Chief Fin. Officer--Chadwick-Miller Inc., Canton, MA, pg. 237
Kurcik, John A., Jr., V.P. & Controller--Alco Health Services Corporation, Malvern, PA, pg. 31
Kurtis, Ron, Controller--WTMJ, Inc., Milwaukee, WI, pg. 608
Kuruhara, Raymond S., V.P. & Controller--Mauna Kea Agribusiness Co., Inc., Papaikou, HI, pg. 174
Kusner, Mark, Controller--The Lathrop Company, Toledo, OH, pg. 660
Kutys, James, Sec., Treas. & Controller--IA Construction Corp., Concordville, PA, pg. 558
Kutz, Dale L., Sr. Assoc. Controller--John Hancock Mutual Life Insurance Company, Boston, MA, pg. 595
Kuykendall, James S., Controller--Bar-S Foods Co., Phoenix, AZ, pg. 118
Kuzemchak, Raymond F., Controller--L. Robert Kimball & Associates, Ebensburg, PA, pg. 629
Labak, Joseph, V.P. & Controller--Globe Industries, Inc., Chicago, IL, pg. 464
LaChance, Georgette, Controller--Austin Associates, Inc., San Jose, CA, pg. 98
Lachey, G., Controller & Asst. Treas.--Neenah Foundry Company, Neenah, WI, pg. 797
Lada, Dolores, Comptroller--Dennis Chemical Company, Inc., Saint Louis, MO, pg. 329
LaDouceur, James, Controller--James Steel & Tube Company, Madison Heights, MI, pg. 102
LaFauci, Peter, Controller--Roberts Communications Inc., East Rochester, NY, pg. 938
Lagard, W., Controller--Hewitt-Robins Corp., West Caldwell, NJ, pg. 532
Lagoni, Susan, Controller--Carlisle Retailers, Inc., Ashtabula, OH, pg. 220
Lahiff, William, V.P. & Controller--Things Remembered, Cleveland, OH, pg. 260
Lahner, Kenneth, Controller--West Dairies, Inc., Spring City, PA, pg. 1177
Lahr, Angela, Treas, Controller, Chief Exec. & Fin. Officer--CAC Microcircuits, Inc., Mount Carmel, IL, pg. 198
Laibson, Alan, Controller--McGuffey's Restaurants, Inc., Asheville, NC, pg. 729
Laine, Gary, Controller--Iroquois Die & Mfg. Co., Warren, MI, pg. 582
Lam, Ho Chang, Controller--Colsky Media, Inc., San Francisco, CA, pg. 265
LaMarche, Gary D., Treas. & Controller--Welco Lumber Company, Marysville, WA, pg. 1175
Lambe, William T., Controller--National Label Company, Lafayette Hill, PA, pg. 791
Lambert, Eddie, Controller--Hardaway Construction Company, Inc., Nashville, TN, pg. 508
Lamberti, Nicholas, Controller--J. Crew Group, Inc., New York, NY, pg. 584
Lambros, Joseph, Controller--United Dairymen of Arizona, Tempe, AZ, pg. 1131
Lamers, Tim, Controller--Fred Usinger, Inc., Milwaukee, WI, pg. 1140
Lance, Walter C., Sr. V.P., Controller & Asst. Sec.--N W Ayer Incorporated, New York, NY, pg. 103
Lance, Walter C., Sr. V.P., Controller & Asst. Sec.--N W Ayer Inc., New York, NY, pg. 104
Landeck, John, Controller--Gromer Super Markets, Inc., Elgin, IL, pg. 489
Lane, Bill, Controller--Marvin Engineering Company, Inc., Inglewood, CA, pg. 716
Lang, Leonard, Dir.-Personnel & Controller--Kaz, Inc., New York, NY, pg. 619
Langis, George, V.P. & Controller--Rogers Group Inc., Nashville, TN, pg. 943
Langley, H.F., Controller--Mississippi Valley Gas Co., Jackson, MS, pg. 1208
Lantzer, Dale, Comptroller--Wayne Wire Cloth Products, Inc., Kalkaska, MI, pg. 1169
Larrowe, Nikki, Corp. Accountant--Pioneer/Eclipse Corp., Sparta, NC, pg. 871
Larsen, Barbara, Controller--Rex Moore Electrical Contractors & Engineers, West Sacramento, CA, pg. 768
Larsen, Edwin, Comptroller--Megapulse, Inc., Bedford, MA, pg. 737
Larson, Elliot J., Controller--Marvin Lumber & Cedar Company, Warroad, MN, pg. 716
Larson, Larry, Chief Fin. Officer, Treas., Sec. & Controller--Holmquist Grain & Lumber Co., Oakland, NE, pg. 540
Lascoe, John, Controller--Russell Stover Candies, Inc., Kansas City, MO, pg. 957
Lashner, Penny, Controller--Burnham Broadcasting Company, Chicago, IL, pg. 193
Latchford, Christopher, Controller--George Lithograph, San Francisco, CA, pg. 452
Laten, Steve, Controller--Invetech Co., Detroit, MI, pg. 581
Lau, Francis, Mgr.-Quality Control--Brown & Haley, Tacoma, WA, pg. 182
Lau, Lawrence S., V.P. & Controller--Klear Knit Inc., Clover, SC, pg. 634
Lauder, R. William, Treas. & Controller--Concrete Construction Company, Columbus, OH, pg. 273
Lauf, John, Controller--Modern Group Ltd., Bristol, PA, pg. 762
Launder, William H., Comptroller--Cook Moving Systems, Inc., Buffalo, NY, pg. 282
Lavan, Kevin C., V.P.-Controller & Chief Acctg. Officer--National Amusements, Inc., Dedham, MA, pg. 784
Lavan, Kevin C., V.P., Controller & Chief Acctg. Officer--Viacom Inc., New York, NY, pg. 785
Lavery, Brian K., Controller--Geo-Centers, Inc., Newton Center, MA, pg. 452
Lavett, Molla, V.P., Controller--Stauch Vetromile & Mitchell Advertising, Inc., East Providence, RI, pg. 1042
Lavoie, George, Controller & Dir.-Mngmt. Information Systems--Advanced Circuit Technology, Nashua, NH, pg. 20
Lavoie, Norman W., V.P.-Fin. & Controller--H.H. Brown Shoe Company, Inc., Greenwich, CT, pg. 182
Law-Smith, David J., Comptroller--Caltex Petroleum Corporation, Irving, TX, pg. 211
Lawless, Floyd J., Controller--Gray Printing Co., Fostoria, OH, pg. 479
Lawrence, Fred, Controller--Curtis Mathes Corporation, Athens, TX, pg. 720
Laws, Anna, Sec. & Controller--Eisaman, Johns & Laws Advertising, Inc., Los Angeles, CA, pg. 372
Lawson, Bruce, Reg. Controller--Country Mutual Insurance Company, Bloomington, IL, pg. 289
Lawson, C. Eugene, Controller--Tennelec/Nucleus, Inc., Oak Ridge, TN, pg. 1087

Lawson, Jim, Controller--Pneumatic Scale Corporation, Quincy, MA, pg. 122
Lazar, Allen, Controller--Kreher Steel Company, Inc., Melrose Park, IL, pg. 644
Leach, Allen, Controller--W.H. Weaver Construction Co., Greensboro, NC, pg. 1170
LeBlanc, Roger D., Controller--Pollack Corporation, Scarborough, ME, pg. 879
LeBrasseur, Phillip J., Controller--Diamond Brands, Inc., Cloquet, MN, pg. 335
Leccesse, Ken, V.P. & Controller--CB North America, Inc., Glens Falls, NY, pg. 199
Leckband, Brian, Controller--Peco Inc., Portland, OR, pg. 854
Ledebuhr, P.G., Controller--Thrall Car Mfg. Co., Chicago Heights, IL, pg. 350
Lee, David, V.P., Treas., Sec. & Controller--Dinwiddie Construction Co., San Francisco, CA, pg. 338
Lee, James, Controller--Spotnails Inc., Rolling Meadows, IL, pg. 1032
Lee, Mei, Treas., Controller & Chief Fin. Officer--Ronald Hsu Construction, Capitol Heights, MD, pg. 548
Lehman, Branden, Controller--Piercing Pagoda, Inc., Bethlehem, PA, pg. 870
Lehmann, Ralph, Treas. & Controller--Barq's, Inc., New Orleans, LA, pg. 121
Lekan, J.M., Comptroller--Cleveland Machine Controls, Cleveland, OH, pg. 255
Lellio, Rachel, V.P., Controller--Media Store Inc., New York, NY, pg. 735
Lemler, Bradley, Controller--Starcraft Automotive Corp., Goshen, IN, pg. 1040
Lemmer, Carole, Controller & Dir.-Human Resources--Shurfine-Central Corp., Northlake, IL, pg. 1001
Lempicki, Chester P., Sec. & Comptroller--Ardco, Inc., Alsip, IL, pg. 81
Lennox, Jeffery, Controller--Niagara Envelope Company, Inc., Buffalo, NY, pg. 805
Lenzen, Heinz, Controller--System Planning Corp., Arlington, VA, pg. 1070
Leonard, Coral, Controller--Security Alarms & Fire Engineering Inc., Davie, FL, pg. 987
Lerman, Robert, Controller--Isfel Company, Inc., Rahway, NJ, pg. 582
Lerner, Harry J., V.P. & Controller--Information Builders, New York, NY, pg. 567
Lessman, Steve, Controller--Northville Industries Corp., Melville, NY, pg. 814
Lester, Wayne, V.P. & Corp. Controller--George W. Park Seed Co., Inc., Greenwood, SC, pg. 849
Letier, Scott, V.P. & Controller--AmeriServ Food Company, Dallas, TX, pg. 66
LeTourneau, Karen, Asst. Comptroller--The Reeves Agency, Inc., Baltimore, MD, pg. 921
Lev, Karyn, Controller--The Dearborn Group, Chicago, IL, pg. 322
Levin, Alan, Controller--VV Publishing Corp., New York, NY, pg. 1142
Levin, Ann, Controller--John Emmerling Inc., New York, NY, pg. 379
Levin, Bruce, Chief Fin. Officer & Controller--Adworks, Inc., Washington, DC, pg. 21
Levine, Neil, Controller--Wills and Evans, New York, NY, pg. 1193
Levine, Sondra, Controller--SJ Weinstein Associates Inc., New York, NY, pg. 1173
Levy, Allan, V.P., Controller, Sec. & Data Processing Dir.--Level Export Sales Corp., New York, NY, pg. 670
Lewanda, Douglas M., Controller--Bartlett Brainard & Eacott, Inc., Bloomfield, CT, pg. 122
Lewis, M.J., Controller--Kendall-Futuro Company, Newport, KY, pg. 622
Lewis, Rick, Controller--Maguire Oil Co., Dallas, TX, pg. 701
Lewis, Robert L., Controller--Chicago Union Station Company, Washington, DC, pg. 69
Lewis, Robert L., III, Controller--Amtrak-National Railroad Passenger Corp., Washington, DC, pg. 69
Lewis, T.A., V.P. & Controller--A.C. Monk Co., Inc., Farmville, NC, pg. 766
Lewis, Terry, Controller--The Ruhlin Company, Sharon Center, OH, pg. 955
Ley, Steven, V.P.-Fin.--Pfaudler-U.S., Inc., Rochester, NY, pg. 866
Liban, G., Chm. Bd. & Chief Exec. Officer--Heresite Protective Coatings Inc., Manitowoc, WI, pg. 531
Libbe, Allan J., Sec., Treas. & Controller--Rudolph/Libbe, Inc., Walbridge, OH, pg. 955
Lieb, Doug, Controller--Aster Nut Products Inc., Newark, NJ, pg. 92
Lieberman, Harold, V.P. & Controller--Carousel Snack Bars Of Minnesota, Minneapolis, MN, pg. 224
Lieberman, Stuart T., V.P., Controller & Chief Acctg. Officer--Bell & Howell Company, Skokie, IL, pg. 134
Liebowitz, Mark, Controller--The Campbell Group, Baltimore, MD, pg. 213
Likens, Gordon, Controller--Commercial & Industrial Administration Co. inc, Santa Clara, CA, pg. 268
Lind, Ralph, Corp. Sec. & Controller--St. Croix Press, Inc., New Richmond, WI, pg. 966
Lindahl, Dennis, Controller--Holiday Companies, Minneapolis, MN, pg. 539
Lindahl, Susan, Controller & Asst. Treas.--McDougal, Littell & Company, Evanston, IL, pg. 728
Lindblad, John, Controller--Clark Oil & Refining Corporation, Saint Louis, MO, pg. 252
Linderman, Jerry, Controller--Orleans International, Inc., Bloomfield Hills, MI, pg. 829
Linehan, Gerald F., Exec. V.P., Chief Fin. Officer--Pelican Products, Torrance, CA, pg. 856
Lingg, Joseph F., Chief Fin. Officer & Controller--Mosler Inc., Hamilton, OH, pg. 772
Linn, H.A., Controller--Swiss-M-Tex, L.P., Travelers Rest, SC, pg. 1068
Linn, Thomas, R., Controller--Nova Power, Inc., Santa Ana, CA, pg. 816
Linsalato, Michael, Controller--Mintz & Hoke Inc., Avon, CT, pg. 759
Linton, Richard A., Controller & Asst. Treas.--Consolidated Midwest, Inc., La Crosse, WI, pg. 277
Linton, Richard A., Controller & Dir.-Personnel & Data Processing--Midwest Bottle Gas Company, La Crosse, WI, pg. 277
Linville, Lewis, V.P., Controller & Asst. Treas.--Farmland Industries, Inc., Kansas City, MO, pg. 402
Lipshitz, Nathan, Controller--Schneider Mills, Inc., New York, NY, pg. 977
Litke, Edward, Controller--American Office Equipment, La Grange, IL, pg. 58
Livermore, Richard, Controller--Adra Systems, Inc., Lowell, MA, pg. 18
Livigni, Roy, Controller--Alterman Transport Lines, Inc., Opa Locka, FL, pg. 45
Livingstone, John, Controller--Mexican Industries in Michigan, Detroit, MI, pg. 745
Lloyd, A., Controller--Drumheller Bag & Supply, Valdosta, GA, pg. 810
Lock, Larry B., Controller & Sec.--Enterprises International Inc., Hoquiam, WA, pg. 382
Lockyear, Pam, Controller--Rundel Products, Inc., Portland, OR, pg. 956
Loew, James P., V.P.-Fin. & Controller & Treas.--Modern Concrete Septic Tank Company, Ottsville, PA, pg. 762
Loftin, Jerry, V.P.-Treas. & Controller--National Bedding & Furniture Industries, Memphis, TN, pg. 786
Lofton, Darrell W., V.P., Treas. & Controller--Donrey Media Group, Fort Smith, AR, pg. 345
Long, Gary E., V.P. & Controller--Northwestern Mutual Life Insurance Co., Milwaukee, WI, pg. 815
Long, Joan M., Controller--Dunham's Athleisure Corporation, Waterford, MI, pg. 353
Long, Larry, Comptroller--Machining Enterprises Inc., Warren, MI, pg. 696
Longythorne, H. David, V.P. & Asst. Controller--M.L. Stern & Company, Inc., Beverly Hills, CA, pg. 1047
Lopez, Laura M., Controller--The Atlas Construction Co., Stamford, CT, pg. 96
Lopez, Roberto, Controller--Sanchez & Levitan, Inc., Miami, FL, pg. 970
Lopez, Vicente, Controller--JMC Creatividad Orientada/Young & Rubicam, Caracas,, Venezuela, pg. 1213
Lorenz, Eric J., Controller--Plastic Engineering Components Inc., New Berlin, WI, pg. 875
Lorwy, Ray, Controller--Sierra Pacific Industries, Redding, CA, pg. 1003
Lotman, Alan, V.P. & Controller--W-B Supply Co., Pampa, TX, pg. 1155
Louie, Keith, Controller--Donaldson Group, San Francisco, CA, pg. 344
Lovejoy, David W., Sr. V.P. & Controller--The Elder-Beerman Stores Corp., Dayton, OH, pg. 373
Lovell, B.J., Comptroller--Bruce Foods Corp., Saint Martinville, LA, pg. 183
Lovell, Bill, Controller--Tyler Elevator Products, Inc., Valley View, OH, pg. 1122
Lovvorn, Joseph, Treas. & Controller--Alabama Farmers Co-op, Decatur, AL, pg. 28
Lowery, Everet, Controller--Conbraco Industries Inc., Matthews, NC, pg. 272
Lowry, Gary W., V.P. & Controller--Duckwall-Alco Stores, Inc., Abilene, KS, pg. 351
Lozano, Joe, V.P. & Controller--H.B. Zachry, San Antonio, TX, pg. 1215
Lozier, Jackie, Treas.--Washington Homes, Inc., Landover, MD, pg. 1166
Lubarsky, Paul, V.P., Controller--Deutsch/Dworin, Inc., New York, NY, pg. 333
Lubinski, Jim, Controller--Chernin's Shoes, Chicago, IL, pg. 243
Lucarelli, Brian M., Comptroller--Alaskan Copper Companies, Seattle, WA, pg. 30
Lucien, Kent T., Exec. V.P., Chief Fin. Officer & Treas.--C. Brewer & Company, Limited, Honolulu, HI, pg. 174
Lucien, Kent T., Sr. V.P. & Treas.--Ka'u Agribusiness Co., Inc., Pahala, HI, pg. 174
Ludington, Christopher, Controller--Trapp Family Lodge, Inc., Stowe, VT, pg. 1108
Luhrs, Robert, Controller--Leo A. Daly Company, Omaha, NE, pg. 313
Lundquist, Bruce, Controller--Tillamook County Creamery Assn., Tillamook, OR, pg. 1097
Luse, Dick, V.P. & Controller--Payless Cashways, Inc., Kansas City, MO, pg. 853
Lutzen, William, Controller--Journal Communications Inc., Milwaukee, WI, pg. 607
Luzum, James A., Chief Fin. Officer, Treas. & Controller--Villaume Industries, Inc., Saint Paul, MN, pg. 1151
Lydic, John R., Sr. V.P., Dir.-Fin. & Controller--Harley Ellington Pierce Yee Associates, Inc., Southfield, MI, pg. 509
Lyke, H. Andersen, Controller--Lyke Corporation, Ripon, WI, pg. 688
Lynch, Ken, Controller--Abbott Laboratories/Ashland, Ashland, OH, pg. 9
Lyon, Terry, Controller--Metro Information Services, Virginia Beach, VA, pg. 743
Lyons, Dan, Controller, Mgr.-Personnel--Moran Industries, Inc., Midlothian, IL, pg. 769
Lyons, Ed, Controller--Bohbot Communications, Inc., New York, NY, pg. 162
Lyster, Larry, Controller--Auto Crane Company, Tulsa, OK, pg. 100
MacArthur, Allan, Controller--Mazo Lerch Company, Inc., Alexandria, VA, pg. 725
MacDonald, Bruce S., Controller--Cabot Creamery Co-Operative Inc., Cabot, VT, pg. 25
Mack, John, Controller--Miken Companies, Inc., Cheektowaga, NY, pg. 752
Mackin, Vincent J., Asst. V.P.-Fin.--Burns & Roe Enterprises, Inc., Oradell, NJ, pg. 194
Mackus, C.R., Controller--Bucyrus-Erie Company, South Milwaukee, WI, pg. 186
Macre, R., Controller--Elastic Stop Nut, Union, NJ, pg. 514
Madden, Bill, Controller--Marshall Erdman and Associates, Inc., Madison, WI, pg. 385
Madden, Catherine A., Controller--Goodman Equipment Corp., Bedford Park, IL, pg. 470
Magasko, John C., Controller--Interstate Steel Supply Co., Philadelphia, PA, pg. 580
Magenheim, Michael J., Controller--McCrory Corporation, New York, NY, pg. 934
Maggi, Joseph, Controller & Chief Fin. Officer--F. L. Roberts & Co. Inc., Springfield, MA, pg. 938
Magna, Barbara, Comptroller--Buzz Barton & Associates, Inc., Oak Brook, IL, pg. 123
Magnani, Joseph, Controller--New York City Off Track Betting Corp., New York, NY, pg. 802
Magnemi, Joe, Controller--Cline, Davis & Mann, Inc., New York, NY, pg. 255
Magrisso, Julio, V.P.-Fin. & Controller--Injection Footwear Corp., Miami, FL, pg. 569
Maher, Harry, Controller--AmeriData, Inc., Minneapolis, MN, pg. 66
Mahoney, Kathleen, Controller--Bailey, Klepinger & Medrich, Inc., Ann Arbor, MI, pg. 114
Major, Tom, Controller--Bluewater Marine, Mora, MN, pg. 161
Maki, William, Controller--Avis Industrial Corporation, Upland, IN, pg. 102
Malburg, Karen, Controller--Oakland Tool & Manufacturing Company, Fraser, MI, pg. 819
Malijan, Rod, Controller--Complex Industry Corporation, New York, NY, pg. 270
Malkani, Roma, Pres. & Chief Exec. Officer--Information Systems & Network Corporation, Bethesda, MD, pg. 567
Mallon, Daniel J., Controller--Simplex Industries, Inc., Scranton, PA, pg. 1006
Mallon, Daniel J., Controller--Simplex Construction Co. Inc., Scranton, PA, pg. 1006
Malls, Stephen, Controller--Monumental Millwork, Inc., Westminster, MD, pg. 768
Maltz, Margaret A., Sec. & Controller--Nason and Cullen, Inc., Wayne, PA, pg. 784
Mamach, Chuck, Controller--Moritz Cadillac-Saab Inc., Arlington, TX, pg. 770
Manburg, Rick, Controller--Concord Litho Co., Inc., Concord, NH, pg. 272
Mandell, Alan, Controller--J. Gerber & Co. Inc., New York, NY, pg. 453
Mangan, Carmen, Controller--Frank B. Ross Co. Inc., Jersey City, NJ, pg. 949
Mangan, Peter F., Controller--Kingsbury Corporation, Keene, NH, pg. 631
Mangum, L.W., Controller--Holt Hosiery Mills, Inc., Burlington, NC, pg. 541
Mann, James L., V.P. & Controller--Baird & Warner Inc., Chicago, IL, pg. 114
Mannarion, Mario R., Controller--CAE Link Allen Division, Alexandria, VA, pg. 198
Manso, Esther, Comptroller, Sec. & Treas.--Metro Ford Inc., Miami, FL, pg. 743
Manter, Thomas, Controller--Associated Grocers of New England, Inc., Manchester, NH, pg. 90
Mantineo, Mary, Comptroller--Media Management Associates, Fort Lee, NJ, pg. 734
Mantione, Russell R., Controller--Paramount Packaging Corp., Chalfont, PA, pg. 848
Maples, Ronald, Controller--Bush Brothers & Company, Dandridge, TN, pg. 196
Maracino, Art, Exec. Vice Pres.--T. L. Smith Machine, Springville, NY, pg. 1013
Marburger, Cynthia, Controller--Ross Engineering Co., Inc., Leola, PA, pg. 949
Marcelo, Bert, Controller--R.S. Owens, Chicago, IL, pg. 834
Marco, Alfred D., Controller--Ventre Packing Company, Inc., Syracuse, NY, pg. 1147
Marcusson, Reese, V.P.-Controller--WTTW (Channel 11), Chicago, IL, pg. 1156
Mardirossian, Olga, Sr. V.P. & Controller--Western International Media Corporation, Los Angeles, CA, pg. 1179
Marek, Wayne, Controller--Technicarbon Company, Inc., Springfield, MA, pg. 1083
Margiotta, Ken, Controller--Financial World Partners, New York, NY, pg. 410
Marglous, Steve, Controller--Miss Elaine Inc., Saint Louis, MO, pg. 760
Margolies, Mike, Controller--Ocean Chevrolet, Inc., Toms River, NJ, pg. 820
Margolis, David, Controller--Broder Bros. Co. Of Florida, Inc., Orlando, FL, pg. 178
Margolis, Ron, Controller--Bugle Boy Industries, Inc., Simi Valley, CA, pg. 187
Mariani, Albert, Jr., Controller--Precision Valve Corporation, Yonkers, NY, pg. 885
Marin, Lori, Controller--Dominick's Finer Foods, Northlake, IL, pg. 343
Marino, Joseph, Controller--Winston Tire Company, Burbank, CA, pg. 1197
Mario, Richard, Controller--JPS Elastomerics Corp., Northampton, MA, pg. 586
Marjeoti, Mike, Controller--Fitchburg Coated Products Inc., Scranton, PA, pg. 1083
Marker, Ron, Controller--Emrick Chevrolet Sales Corporation, Richmond, VA, pg. 380
Markevich, Fenton, Controller--Pip Printing, Agoura Hills, CA, pg. 616
Marquardt, Charles B., Jr., V.P. & Controller--Pearlstine Distributors Inc., Charleston, SC, pg. 853
Marrapodi, L.J., Controller--J.M. Huber, Chemicals Division, Havre de Grace, MD, pg. 550

Marshall, David, Controller--Continental Paper & Supply Co., Detroit, MI, pg. 280
Marshall, Liz, Controller--Fiesta Mart Inc., Houston, TX, pg. 409
Marshall, Ron, V.P. & Controller--Barnes & Noble Bookstores, Inc., New York, NY, pg. 120
Martello, June, Controller--The Long & Foster Companies, Inc., Fairfax, VA, pg. 682
Martin, Charles A., Controller--Bank Shares, Inc., Minneapolis, MN, pg. 117
Martin, Herbert W., V.P. & Controller--Massman Construction Company, Kansas City, MO, pg. 719
Martin, James L., Jr., Controller--Brian Center Management Corporation, Hickory, NC, pg. 175
Martin, James W., Controller--Evening Post Publishing Co., Charleston, SC, pg. 391
Martin, JoAnn, V.P. & Comptroller--Ameritas Life Insurance Corp., Lincoln, NE, pg. 66
Martin, Karen, Controller--Thomson MacConnell Cadillac, Inc., Cincinnati, OH, pg. 1095
Martin, Robert L., Sec. & Controller--Longyear Company, Salt Lake City, UT, pg. 682
Martin, Thomas, Controller--Dempster, Inc., Toccoa, GA, pg. 328
Martin, Tony, Controller--National Welders Supply Co. Inc., Charlotte, NC, pg. 794
Martinelli, R.M., Treas. & Controller--MPO Videotronics, Inc., New York, NY, pg. 693
Martinez, Andres A., V.P. & Controller--Environmental Industries, Inc., Calabasas, CA, pg. 383
Martinez, Bob, Controller--Wilson, Horne, McClelland & Gray, Inc., Atlanta, GA, pg. 1193
Martinez, Marcelino, Controller--Berlitz de Mexico, S.A. de C.V., Mexico,, Mexico, pg. 142
Maschmann, Michael, Controller--ATAPCO Office Products Group, Saint Louis, MO, pg. 64
Mason, Bruce, Controller--I. C. Thomasson Associates, Inc., Nashville, TN, pg. 1094
Mason, Robert E., V.P. & Controller--Treasure Chest Advertising Co., Inc., Glendora, CA, pg. 1108
Massa, Becky, Controller--Communico, Indianapolis, IN, pg. 270
Massad, Leo A., Jr., Controller--The Hertz Corporation, Park Ridge, NJ, pg. 849
Massad, Leo, Jr., V.P. & Controller--Park Ridge Corporation, Park Ridge, NJ, pg. 849
Masseth, Leroy, Controller--Quebedeaux Pontiac, Inc., Tucson, AZ, pg. 904
Massy, Brenda, V.P., Controller--Warren/Kremer/CMP/Advertising/Inc., New York, NY, pg. 1165
Mataya, Toni, Controller--Acme Poultry Company, Inc., Seattle, WA, pg. 13
Mathias, J., Controller--Hofley Manufacturing Company, Warren, MI, pg. 538
Mathieu, Jan T., Controller--Elkay Products, Inc., Shrewsbury, MA, pg. 377
Mathis, Robert, Controller--Pendleton Woolen Mills, Inc., Portland, OR, pg. 857
Matino, Frank, Controller--Sharon Concepts, Inc., Union, NJ, pg. 995
Matta, Daniel, Comptroller--The Guttman Group, Belle Vernon, PA, pg. 495
Matthews, McKay, Controller--WordPerfect Corporation, Orem, UT, pg. 1202
Mattingly, Mike, Treas., Controller & Chief Fin. Officer--The Court Company, Memphis, TN, pg. 290
Mauldin, W. Crayton, Sr. V.P. & Controller--Leslie Advertising, Greenville, SC, pg. 668
Maury, Elizabeth, Controller--Communication Trends, Inc., Atlanta, GA, pg. 269
Maxson, Albert T., V.P.-Fin. & Controller--Harbour Industries, Inc., Shelburne, VT, pg. 507
Maxwell, William E., V.P. & Controller--Stone & Thomas, Wheeling, WV, pg. 1051
May, Ralph E.F., Controller--The Taney Corporation, Taneytown, MD, pg. 1077
Mazur, Diane, Controller--Injectron Corporation, Plainfield, NJ, pg. 569
McAdams, Robert, Controller--Bobit Publishing Company, Redondo Beach, CA, pg. 161
McAfee, Nancy G., V.P., Treas. & Controller--Thrall Enterprises, Inc., Chicago, IL, pg. 1095
McAllister, Scott A., V.P. & Controller--J. Gibson McIlvain Co., White Marsh, MD, pg. 729
McAlpine, Laurie, Comptroller--Lumber Systems, Inc., Vancouver, WA, pg. 687
McArrhey, Dennis P., Controller--Phillips Plastics Corporation, Phillips, WI, pg. 867
McArthur, Carol, Controller--Mogas Industries, Inc., Houston, TX, pg. 763
McAuliffe, Hawley H., Controller--Compendium Systems, New York, NY, pg. 270
McBride, Timothy F., III, Controller--McWilliams Forge Co., Rockaway, NJ, pg. 733
McBurney, Robert, V.P.-Admin. & Controller--S. E. Huffman Corp., Clover, SC, pg. 551
McCaffrey, Doug, Sr. V.P. & Controller--Altus Federal Savings Bank, Mobile, AL, pg. 46
McCall, W.A., Sec., Treas., Controller & Data Processing Mgr.--Dixie Oil Company, Tifton, GA, pg. 341
McCarter, Arthur B., Controller--Replacements, Ltd., Greensboro, NC, pg. 927
McCartney, Bob, Controller--Electronics Stamping Corp., Rancho Dominguez, CA, pg. 375
McCausland, George J., Treas. & Controller--Ash Grove Cement Company, Overland Park, KS, pg. 87
McClure, Jeff, Controller--Valentine-Radford, Inc., Kansas City, MO, pg. 1142
McConnell, Donald A., V.P., Treas. & Controller--RTKL Associates Inc., Baltimore, MD, pg. 908
McConnell, Roger, Controller--BeefAmerica Operating Co., Inc., Omaha, NE, pg. 131
McCool, Michael, Controller--Exide Corporation, Reading, PA, pg. 393
McCormack, John, Controller--Active Tool & Manufacturing Co., Inc., Roseville, MI, pg. 15
McCormick, Robert, V.P.-Opers. & Controller--Paco Rabanne Parfums, New York, NY, pg. 842
McCormick, Steven, Controller--J.H. McCormick, Inc., Burbank, CA, pg. 727
McCoy, Richard, Controller--Random Corporation, Cincinnati, OH, pg. 912
McCoy, Robert S., Controller--Calcor Space Facility, Inc., Whittier, CA, pg. 208
McCracken, Alan L., Comptroller & Treas.--Baltimore Stationery Co., Baltimore, MD, pg. 116
McCreadie, K.G., V.P. & Controller--Columbus McKinnon Corp., Amherst, NY, pg. 266
McCullars, Michael, Controller--Garcy Corporation, Piedmont, AL, pg. 907
McCullers, Randy, V.P. & Controller--Federal Savings Bank, Fort Smith, AR, pg. 1194
McDaniel, Wayne, Controller--Pulliam Motor Company, Columbia, SC, pg. 899
McDevitt, Lawrence R., V.P. & Controller--LFC Holding Corporation, Boca Raton, FL, pg. 647
McElroy, Suzanne, Controller--The Brownstein Group, Philadelphia, PA, pg. 183
McEvoy, Thomas P., Treas. & Controller--New Standard Corporation, Mount Joy, PA, pg. 802
McFarland, Julie, Controller--McNaughton & Gunn, Inc., Saline, MI, pg. 732
McGaffin, Mark, Controller--Tech Poulson, Inc., Scottsdale, AZ, pg. 1083
McGaffin, Mark, Controller--Tech Medical Inc., Tempe, AZ, pg. 1083
McGill, J., Controller--J. L. Hammett Company, Braintree, MA, pg. 504
McGinnis, Steve, Asst. Controller--Package Service Company, Inc., Kansas City, MO, pg. 842
McGlamery, Kathy, Controller--Sir Speedy, Inc., Laguna Hills, CA, pg. 613
McGough, John. P., V.P.-Taxes--R. L. Polk & Co., Detroit, MI, pg. 879
McGovern, Donna, Controller--Noel-Joanna, Inc., Rancho Santa Margarita, CA, pg. 808
McGowan, J.R., V.P. & Controller--U.S. Can Company, Oak Brook, IL, pg. 1134
McGraime, Douglas, V.P. & Controller--Combe Incorporated, White Plains, NY, pg. 267
McGregor, Deborah S., V.P., Controller--Mitchell & Assoc., Inc., Bethesda, MD, pg. 761
McGregor, Peter, Chief Fin. Officer--Affiliated of Florida Inc., Tampa, FL, pg. 23
McGroarty, Ed, Comptroller--American Foodservice Corp., King of Prussia, PA, pg. 54
McHugh, Mike, Controller--Alpha Distributors Ltd., Madison, WI, pg. 66
McInerney, Carol, Controller--Bradley Corporation, Menomonee Falls, WI, pg. 170
McIntosh, Sharon, Controller--RII (Ricards International Inc.), Silver Spring, MD, pg. 907
McKay, Patricia A., V.P. & Controller--Dole Food Company, Inc., Westlake Village, CA, pg. 840
McKenna, Don, Controller--Bandini Fertilizer Company, Los Angeles, CA, pg. 117
McKenna, John, Controller--Robert James Sales Inc., Buffalo, NY, pg. 589
McKenzie, Laurel, Controller--The Giardini/Russell Group, Watertown, MA, pg. 456
McKeon, Barry J., Sr. V.P. & Comptroller--Fiduciary Trust Company International, New York, NY, pg. 408
McKeon, Bary J., Sr. V.P. & Comptroller--Fiduciary Trust Co. International, New York, NY, pg. 408
McKinney, Hiram Y., Sr. V.P., Sec., Treas. & Controller--Sullivan Long & Hagerty, Inc., Birmingham, AL, pg. 1057
McKinnon, Michael, Controller--General Ship Corporation, Boston, MA, pg. 450
McKnight, John, Controller--Abdalla's Lafayette, Inc., Lafayette, LA, pg. 10
McLouth, Richard, Controller--Quality Stores Inc., North Muskegon, MI, pg. 904
McManimon, Bilol, Chief Fin. Officer/Comptroller--NJ Transit, Newark, NJ, pg. 801
McManus, Terry, Exec. Dir.-Acctg. & Controller--Advanced Technology, Inc., Reston, VA, pg. 20
McMillen, R.W. III, Controller--Welch's, Concord, MA, pg. 789
McMurry, B.J., Controller--Canal Insurance Co., Greenville, SC, pg. 213
McNamara, Cynthia, Controller--NBO Stores Inc., Fair Lawn, NJ, pg. 780
McNamara, Linda, Controller--Strouds, City of Industry, CA, pg. 1054
McNamee, Ken, Controller--Memphis Publishing Company, Memphis, TN, pg. 738
McNaughton, G.L., Controller--MTD Products Limited, Kitchener,, Canada, pg. 694
McNew, Russel E., Controller--Bovaird Supply Co., Tulsa, OK, pg. 168
McPherson, Michael J., Sec. & Controller--Steadly Company, Carthage, MO, pg. 1043
McSherry, Andre J., Controller--Adler & Shaykin, New York, NY, pg. 17
McSpadden, Ron, V.P. & Controller--Benco Industries, Inc., Fort Deposit, AL, pg. 138
McVay, Daniel J., Comptroller--Centimark Corporation, Bethel Park, PA, pg. 231
Mebus, Christopher, Controller--Arrow Metal Products Corporation, Detroit, MI, pg. 85
Mebus, Philip K., Jr., Pres. & Treas.--Arrow Metal Products Corporation, Detroit, MI, pg. 85
Meckfessel, William R., Chief Fin. Officer--Carco Electronics, Menlo Park, CA, pg. 217
Medel, Ariel, Controller--Berkliff Corporation, New York, NY, pg. 142
Medukas, Terry, Contr.--Arcata Graphics Kingsport, Kingsport, TN, pg. 80
Meeker, Thomas C., Controller--Health Care Lodges, Coffeyville, KS, pg. 520
Megas, George, Controller--J P Foodservice, Inc., Hanover, MD, pg. 586
Meglaughlin, William T., Jr., Controller--Asbury Carbons, Inc., Asbury, NJ, pg. 87
Meierhans, Gil, Controller--Key Handling Systems, Inc., Hackensack, NJ, pg. 627
Meinkoth, Richard K., Treas. & Controller--Contico International, Inc., Saint Louis, MO, pg. 278
Meizlik, Leon, Controller--The Food Group, New York, NY, pg. 423
Melendes, D., Controller--Abbott Electronics, Inc., Los Angeles, CA, pg. 9
Meller, Barbara, Controller--Sally Lou Fashions Corporation, New York, NY, pg. 967
Meltzer, Ronni, V.P. & Controller--Morse Diesel International, New York, NY, pg. 771
Mendez, Olga, Comptroller--R.J. Palmer, Inc., New York, NY, pg. 844
Mente, Rich, V.P.-Fin. & Controller--Empire Southwest Co., Mesa, AZ, pg. 379
Merola, Dana, Controller--Williams Television Time, Inc., Santa Monica, CA, pg. 1191
Mesado, Sylvia, Controller--Centro de Idiomas Berlitz de Venezuela, Caracas,, Venezuela, pg. 143
Messina, Paul, Controller--North American Watch Corporation, Lyndhurst, NJ, pg. 812
Messing, Paul, Controller--Movado Watch Co., Lyndhurst, NJ, pg. 812
Messman, Mary C., Controller--The Bases Group, Covington, KY, pg. 124
Meyer, Jack, Controller--Yuba Heat Transfer Division, Tulsa, OK, pg. 275
Meyer, Russell J., Controller--White Castle System, Inc., Columbus, OH, pg. 1185
Michael, Tom, Controller--National Carriers, Inc., Liberal, KS, pg. 1128
Michalski, Sandra, Controller--Acme Mills Co. Inc., Detroit, MI, pg. 13
Mickiewicz, Laurie, Controller--Guardian Alarm Co., Southfield, MI, pg. 491
Middleton, B.J., Controller--Cassano's Inc., Dayton, OH, pg. 228
Middleton, Janice, Controller--Maryland Paper Box Company, Baltimore, MD, pg. 717
Midgette, Stephen, Controller--Newage Industries Inc., Willow Grove, PA, pg. 803
Midgette, Steve, Controller--Newage Industries Inc., Testing Instruments Division, Willow Grove, PA, pg. 803
Mignanelli, Thomas, Controller--Corham, Inc., White Plains, NY, pg. 286
Miller, Andrea, Controller--Nana Regional Corporation, Inc., Anchorage, AK, pg. 783
Miller, Brian, Controller--Ivex Packaging Corporation-Madison, Madison, GA, pg. 583
Miller, C., Controller--Schwab Corp., Lafayette, IN, pg. 980
Miller, Dallas, Controller--Laubeck Corporation/Cross, Carbondale, PA, pg. 660
Miller, Dan, Sec. & Controller--Ritchie Industries, Inc., Conrad, IA, pg. 936
Miller, Donald, Controller & Sec.--Schwan's Sales Enterprises, Marshall, MN, pg. 980
Miller, Gary, Controller--Landmark Community Newspapers, Inc., Shelbyville, KY, pg. 655
Miller, Greg, Controller--Kentile Floors Inc., South Plainfield, NJ, pg. 623
Miller, John, Chief Fin. Officer, Treas. & Controller--RJO Enterprises, Inc., Lanham, MD, pg. 907
Miller, Kathleen A., Controller--The Commercial Bank, Delphos, OH, pg. 268
Miller, Kenneth, Controller--Doe Spun, Inc., New York, NY, pg. 343
Miller, Larry S., Comptroller--De Vons Jewelers, Sacramento, CA, pg. 321
Miller, Robert, Controller--Normark Corporation, Minneapolis, MN, pg. 810
Miller, Steven, Chief Fin. Officer, Treas. & Controller--Resort Condominiums International, Indianapolis, IN, pg. 929
Miller, William, Controller & Treas.--Merle Norman Cosmetics, Inc., Los Angeles, CA, pg. 740
Miller, Wilson C., Opers. Controller--Price Brothers Co., Dayton, OH, pg. 888
Milligan, Barbara, Controller--Jack Gray Transport, Inc., Gary, IN, pg. 479
Mills, Craig V., Controller & Dir.-Data Processing--Lamb Engineering & Construction Co., Salt Lake City, UT, pg. 652
Mills, John, Controller--Affiliated Foods Southwest, Little Rock, AR, pg. 24
Mills, Michael, V.P. & Controller--Overland Transportation System, Inc., Indianapolis, IN, pg. 832
Mills, Stephen, Controller--Ferrell Companies Inc./Ferrellgas, Liberty, MO, pg. 407
Millwater, Don, Controller--Decorative Fabrics - Mastercraft, Spindale, NC, pg. 262
Miluka, Ida, Controller--Conklin Instrument Corporation, Pleasant Valley, NY, pg. 274
Minard, John D., V.P., Controller & Chief Fin. Officer--Manna Pro Corporation, Saint Louis, MO, pg. 704
Minella, Roberto, Controller--Berlitz Language Centers, S.R.L., Rome,, Italy, pg. 142
Miressi, Joseph V., V.P. & Controller--The Rawlplug Company, Inc., New Rochelle, NY, pg. 914
Mirski, Dan, Division Controller--Ivex Packaging Corporation-Industrial Products Division, Newton, MA, pg. 583
Mischak, Bob, Jr., Controller--Atlas Citron Haligman & Bedecarre, San Francisco, CA, pg. 96
Mishalanie, Phillip G., Controller--Barber Dairies, Inc., Birmingham, AL, pg. 119
Mitch, Sue, Controller--Instrumentarium Imaging, Inc., Milwaukee, WI, pg. 572

Mitchell, Maryilyn R., Comptroller--The Union Central Life Insurance Co., Cincinnati, OH, pg. 1127
Mitolo, Joseph J., Comptroller--DiFeo Automotive Network, Jersey City, NJ, pg. 337
Mitschele, George, Controller--Krasdale Foods Inc., Bronx, NY, pg. 644
Mocoghi, George, Controller--Alra Laboratories, Inc., Gurnee, IL, pg. 44
Moeller, Delbert H., Controller--Burlington Basket Co., Burlington, IA, pg. 191
Moll, Otto E., Controller--A. Finkl & Sons Co., Chicago, IL, pg. 411
Molton, John, Controller--Ed Miniat, Inc., Chicago, IL, pg. 757
Monacelli, Kevin J., Controller--Alling & Cory Company, Rochester, NY, pg. 40
Monaco, C.E., Controller--Wingfoot Films Corporation, Carrollton, OH, pg. 555
Monaghan, Robert, Controller--Lat Purser & Associate, Charlotte, NC, pg. 901
Monahan, Michael P., Controller--Edward V. Monahan Inc., Eastpointe, MI, pg. 765
Monday, Elizabeth, Controller--Fred Webb Inc., Greenville, NC, pg. 1170
Montgomery, Dorothy, Comptroller--Group Two Advertising, Inc., Philadelphia, PA, pg. 490
Montgomery, Gary B., Controller--Amsted Industries Incorporated, Chicago, IL, pg. 68
Mooney, Alan W., Controller--S. I. Goldman Co., Longwood, FL, pg. 467
Moore, Gary, Controller-Feed--Land O'Lakes, Inc., Agricultural Services Div., Saint Paul, MN, pg. 653
Moore, Gary W., Controller--Inman Construction Corporation, Memphis, TN, pg. 570
Moore, Sam, Controller--Warehouse Home Furnishings Distributor, Dublin, GA, pg. 1163
Mootoo, Alexis, Controller--Savoy Construction Co. Inc., Kensington, MD, pg. 973
Morabito, Richard, V.P.-Controller--Dawn Joy Fashions, Inc., New York, NY, pg. 319
Mordarski, Werner, Controller--Cablewave Systems, Inc., North Haven, CT, pg. 206
Morehead, Russell R., Controller--Haeger Industries, Inc., Dundee, IL, pg. 499
Morello, Eduardo, Controller--Berlitz Escuelas de Idiomas Ltda., Santiago,, Chile, pg. 142
Morena, Richard, Controller--New Jersey Press, Inc., Neptune, NJ, pg. 801
Moreno, William F., Treas.--Machado & Co. Inc., New York, NY, pg. 696
Morgan, Brad, Controller--Greenfield Industries Inc., Evans, GA, pg. 507
Morgan, Catherine, Controller--Paine Furniture Co., Norwood, MA, pg. 843
Morgan, Gayle, Controller--O'Neal Steel Inc., Birmingham, AL, pg. 827
Morgan, John K., Controller--Williamson-Dickie Mfg. Co., Fort Worth, TX, pg. 1192
Morgan, Thomas, Controller--Basic Food International Inc., Fort Lauderdale, FL, pg. 124
Morgione, Vincent, Controller--The Cafaro Co., Youngstown, OH, pg. 207
Morin, M., V.P. & Controller--Knapp Shoes Inc., Brockton, MA, pg. 636
Morissette, Art, Controller--Duo-Fast Corporation, Franklin Park, IL, pg. 354
Morowitz, M., Controller--Martin Paint Stores, Jamaica, NY, pg. 715
Morris, Paul, V.P.-Human Resources & Controller--Arcola Wire Company, Branford, CT, pg. 81
Morris, Peter, Controller--Georgette Klinger, Inc., New York, NY, pg. 635
Morris, Stephen A., V.P. & Controller--American Trading and Production Corporation, Baltimore, MD, pg. 64
Morrison, Edd, V.P.-Controller--Pony Express Courier Corp., Charlotte, NC, pg. 166
Morse, Janet, Controller--R.F. Broadus & Associates, Inc., Atlanta, GA, pg. 177
Morse, Linda, Sr. V.P., Controller--Kahler Friendt & Partners, Inc., Omaha, NE, pg. 613
Morton, Victoria C., Controller--Hollymatic Corporation, Countryside, IL, pg. 539
Mossman, Mike, Controller--Rena-Ware Distributors Inc., Redmond, WA, pg. 926
Most, Jeff, Controller--Marcus Brothers Textiles, Inc., New York, NY, pg. 706
Motley, Jackie, Controller--U.S. Broach & Machine Company, Sumter, SC, pg. 102
Motsinger, Janice, Controller--Mother Earth News, New York, NY, pg. 773
Mott, Jean, Controller--Meade Group, Inc., Detroit, MI, pg. 733
Mounsey, Ed, Comptroller--Cowtown Boot Company, El Paso, TX, pg. 291
Movine, Robert, Controller--Merchants Rent A Car, Inc., Hooksett, NH, pg. 739
Moyers, Donald L., Treas., Sec. & Controller--Riddleberger Brothers, Inc., Mount Crawford, VA, pg. 933
Moza, Jerome, Controller--Coca-Cola Bottling Co. of Chicago, Niles, IL, pg. 257
Mozzillo, Nick, Controller--Norwalk Powdered Metals, Inc., Norwalk, CT, pg. 816
Mrnak, Gerald, V.P. & Controller--Foley-Belsaw Company, Minneapolis, MN, pg. 422
Mrnak, Gerald D., Controller--Foley-PLP Company, Rochester, NY, pg. 422
Mrowka, James A., Controller--Detroit City Dairy, Inc., Highland Park, MI, pg. 333
Muccino, Robert D., Controller & Sec.--Frank Briscoe Co. Inc., Roseland, NJ, pg. 176
Mudd, Tony, Controller--Allied Oil & Supply, Inc., Omaha, NE, pg. 38
Mudry, George, Controller--United Exposition Service Company, Chicago, IL, pg. 1102
Mueller, Helga, Controller & Personnel Mgr.--Hoechst Ceramtec North America, Inc., Mansfield, MA, pg. 537
Mueller, Mike, Controller--Cardinal Aluminum Co., Louisville, KY, pg. 217
Muldowney, Terry, Controller--Javelin Electronics, Torrance, CA, pg. 64
Mulig, Mario, V.P.-Acctg. & Controller--Production Machinery Corporation, Mentor, OH, pg. 893
Mulligan, Donald, V.P. & Controller--Demoulas Super Markets, Tewksbury, MA, pg. 328
Mulrooney, Robert, Controller--Danbury Printing & Lithograph, Inc., Danbury, CT, pg. 313
Mumma, Glenn, Controller--Manning & Lewis Engineering Co., Union, NJ, pg. 704
Muratori, Mark, Controller--L'Ermitage Hotels, West Hollywood, CA, pg. 668
Murillo, Jess, V.P., Treas., Controller & Chief Fin. Officer--Graham Group, Inc., Des Moines, IA, pg. 475
Murphy, Ann, Controller--Paradata Computer Networks, Inc., Farmington Hills, MI, pg. 847
Murphy, Arthur, Controller--Jamison Plastic Corporation, Allentown, PA, pg. 589
Murphy, Christine, Controller--Marisa Christina Inc., New York, NY, pg. 707
Murphy, Diane, Controller--Sharp Hartwig, Inc., Seattle, WA, pg. 995
Murphy, P. Cornell, Controller--Progress Printing Company, Lynchburg, VA, pg. 894
Murphy, Robert F., Controller--Butler International, Montvale, NJ, pg. 197
Murphy, Sharon, Controller--Lance Camper Manufacturing Corporation, Pacoima, CA, pg. 653
Murphy, Thomas G., Controller--American Kennel Club, Inc., New York, NY, pg. 57
Murray, Bruce, Controller--Peter J. Schmitt Co., Inc., West Seneca, NY, pg. 977
Murray, Bruce W., V.P. & Controller--Peter J. Schmitt Holdings, West Seneca, NY, pg. 976
Murray, Doug, Mill Controller--IPMC, Inc.-Detroit, Detroit, MI, pg. 583
Murray, Eric, Controller--National Steel & Shipbuilding Company, San Diego, CA, pg. 794
Musachia, Sandra L., Controller--Envirodyne Industries, Inc., Oak Brook, IL, pg. 383
Musial, Dennis, Controller--Murdock, Inc., Compton, CA, pg. 776
Musil, Daniel, Controller--Heinen's Inc., Warrensville Heights, OH, pg. 526
Myer, Arthur D., Controller--Western Extrusions, Carrollton, TX, pg. 1179
Myers, Alan, Controller--Kearney, Tucker, GA, pg. 357
Myers, Joe N., Treas. & Sec.--T. H. Rogers Lumber Co. Inc., Oklahoma City, OK, pg. 943
Myers, Kurt, Controller--Honorbuilt Industries, Inc., Minneapolis, KS, pg. 542
Myers, Lisa A., Controller--Muro Pharmaceutical, Inc., Tewksbury, MA, pg. 776
Myers, Ronald W., V.P.-Fin. & Admin. & Chief Fin. Officer--GF Office Furniture Ltd., Gallatin, TN, pg. 439
Myers, Russell R., Controller--Geneva Corporation, Greensboro, NC, pg. 451
Myers, Stephen R., Asst. Controller--Bell & Howell Company, Skokie, IL, pg. 134
Myrick, Sue, Controller--Aetna Health Plans, San Bruno, CA, pg. 23
Nagata, Gerald T., V.P. & Controller--Mauna Loa Macadamia Nut Corporation, Hilo, HI, pg. 174
Nagem, Alex, Controller--Ohio River Associates, Inc., Hannibal, OH, pg. 822
Nagengast, Barbara A., Controller--Atlas Refinery, Newark, NJ, pg. 96
Nakama, Paul Y., Controller--Dillingham Construction Corporation, Pleasanton, CA, pg. 337
Napolez, Mario, Controllor--Gator Industries Inc., Hialeah, FL, pg. 446
Napoli, Eleanor, Asst. Treas. & Controller--Carelli, Glynn & Ward, Butler, NJ, pg. 218
Narazaki, Keiji, Controller--Berlitz Escola de Idiomas Ltda., Sao Paulo,, Brazil, pg. 142
Nardland, Robert, Controller--Crystal Cabinet Works, Inc., Princeton, MN, pg. 303
Nash, James S., Treas., Chief Fin. Officer & Controller--E.P. Henry Corporation, Woodbury, NJ, pg. 530
Nash, Thomas J., V.P.-Admin. & Controller--Tagsons Papers, Inc., Albany, NY, pg. 1076
Nash, Walter Stephen, Controller--The Bartell Drug Company, Seattle, WA, pg. 122
Nason, Conrad, Controller--Bob Sellers Pontiac GMC Truck Inc., Farmington Hills, MI, pg. 988
Naylor, Michael, Controller--Estee Lauder, Inc., New York, NY, pg. 389
Neany, John, Controller--Hamilton, Carver & Lee, Inc., Chicago, IL, pg. 503
Nease, Scott, V.P.-Corp. Controller--Littelfuse, Inc., Des Plaines, IL, pg. 678
Necorvo, Richard, Controller--Aladdin Synergetics, Inc., Nashville, TN, pg. 29
Neese, Johnnie, Controller--Capital City Manufacturing Company, West Columbia, SC, pg. 546
Neff, Terry A., Controller--Kissimmee Toyota Inc., Kissimmee, FL, pg. 633
Neill, Michael, Controller--Pacific Optical Division, Torrance, CA, pg. 917
Nellis, Kirk, Controller, Treas. & Sec.--Harley Industries, Inc., Tulsa, OK, pg. 509
Nelson, D.A., Controller--RAIL Company, Towson, MD, pg. 906
Nelson, Gary, Controller--Wilson Industries Inc., Houston, TX, pg. 1193
Nelson, L.L., Controller--CH2M Hill Companies, Ltd., Englewood, CO, pg. 202
Nelson, Tom, V.P.-Fin.--Petro-Hunt Corporation, Dallas, TX, pg. 865
Nelson, William F., Controller--Bodine Electric Company, Chicago, IL, pg. 162
Nerone, Maureen, V.P., Controller & Chief Fin. Officer--Colony Liquor Distributors, Inc., Kingston, NY, pg. 264
Neuman, Ronald W., Treas. & Controller--Allen-Edmonds Shoe Corp., Port Washington, WI, pg. 36
Newberry, Tom, Controller--Hubbard Broadcasting, Inc., Saint Paul, MN, pg. 548
Newell, Matthew, V.P. & Controller--Allied Advertising Agency, Boston, MA, pg. 37
Newell, W.F., V.P. & Controller--AP Parts Manufacturing Company, Toledo, OH, pg. 240
Nguyen, Rosalie N.H., Controller--Pike & Fischer, Bethesda, MD, pg. 190
Nice, Robert, Controller--Rosenbergers Dairies, Inc., Hatfield, PA, pg. 948
Nicholson, Faithe, Chief Acctg. Officer--Levenson & Hill, Inc., Irving, TX, pg. 670
Nicholson, Peter, Controller--Asher/Gould Advertising, Inc., Los Angeles, CA, pg. 88
Nieds, Ward, Controller--F & B Manufacturing Co., Chicago, IL, pg. 393
Nimnicht, Ann, Controller, Treas. & Sec.--Nimnicht Chevrolet Company, Jacksonville, FL, pg. 807
Nistendirk, Jack W., Controller--J. H. Fletcher & Co., Huntington, WV, pg. 418
Nitzberg, Gerry, Controllor--Linzer Products Corp., Flushing, NY, pg. 677
Niwinski, Richard, Controller--E. F. Houghton & Co., Valley Forge, PA, pg. 546
Nobles, R.L., Controller & Dir.-Data Processing--Blevins Inc., Nashville, TN, pg. 156
Noel, Steve, Controller--Superior Auctioneers & Marketing, Inc., San Antonio, TX, pg. 1063
Noga, John, Controller--The Chardon Rubber Co., Chardon, OH, pg. 239
Nolan, Liam, Controller--Universal Dynamics Inc., Woodbridge, VA, pg. 1138
Noll, Chris A., Controller, Asst. Sec. & Asst. Treas.--Carus Corporation, Peru, IL, pg. 227
Noonan, Tom, Div. Controller--Ivex Packaging Corporation-Food Packaging Division, Lincolnshire, IL, pg. 583
Novak, John, Controller--Woodward & Lothrop/John Wanamaker, Washington, DC, pg. 1201
Nowlin, Charles, Controller--McWane, Inc., Birmingham, AL, pg. 733
Numme, Kaare, Treas. & Controller--American White Cross Laboratories, Inc., New Rochelle, NY, pg. 65
O'Berg, Page, Controller--Consolidated Beverages, Inc., Auburn, MA, pg. 276
O'Brien, Leo, Controller--Bay State Milling Co., Quincy, MA, pg. 127
O'Day, Art T., Controller--Aircraft Gear Corporation, Chicago, IL, pg. 27
O'Donnell, Joseph, Controller--Daniel Caron Ltd., New York, NY, pg. 224
O'Hara, Eugene M., Sr. V.P., Comptroller & Chief Fin. Officer--The Prudential Insurance Company of America, Newark, NJ, pg. 896
O'Hara, Harriet, Controller--Pease Industries, Inc., Fairfield, OH, pg. 854
O'Haren, D.M., Controller--Holder Corporation, Atlanta, GA, pg. 538
O'Hop, Rick, Controller--Panel Prints, Inc., Old Forge, PA, pg. 846
O'Keefe, Carol, Controller--Bonland Industries, Inc., Wayne, NJ, pg. 164
O'Leary, Patricia, Controller--Townsend & O'Leary, Inc., Laguna Hills, CA, pg. 1104
O'Neal, Michael R., Controller--Davis & Phillips, Inc., Norfolk, VA, pg. 319
O'Neil, Joseph F., Chief Fin. Officer & Controller--The Harodite Finishing Company Inc., North Dighton, MA, pg. 510
O'Niel, Amy, Controller--Rayco, San Antonio, TX, pg. 914
O'Reilly, William, Controller--Contract Furnishings & Systems, Ltd., New York, NY, pg. 280
O'Shea, James B., Controller--A.D. Clark, Inc., Los Angeles, CA, pg. 252
Oakley, Robert A., V.P. & Controller--Nationwide Mutual Insurance Company, Columbus, OH, pg. 795
Oberhelman, Steve, Controller--Swepco Tube Corporation, Clifton, NJ, pg. 1067
Occicone, Michael J., Controller--Associated Air Freight, Inc., New Hyde Park, NY, pg. 89
Ochoa, Greg, Controller--C. A. Muer Corp., Detroit, MI, pg. 774
Odmark, Edward, V.P. & Controller--Dry Storage Corporation, Des Plaines, IL, pg. 350
Odom, Don, Controller--Conwood Company L.P., Memphis, TN, pg. 281
Oelmont, Ray, Controller--Northern Michigan Veneers, Inc., Gladstone, MI, pg. 814
Ogilvy, David, Controller--Electric Specialty & Supply Corp., Boston, MA, pg. 374
Oilschlager, Bob, Controller--Andes Candies, Inc., Delavan, WI, pg. 169
Olander, Stephen, Controller--Dynamic Metal Products Company, Manchester, CT, pg. 356
Oldham, Allen, V.P. & Controller--Ingram Barge Company, Nashville, TN, pg. 569
Oldhan, Debbie, Controller--Quality Foods Inc., Little Rock, AR, pg. 903
Oliver, Jeffrey L., Controller--Alley-Cassetty Coal Co., Nashville, TN, pg. 37
Oliver, Ray, V.P.-Opers. & Pur. & Comptroller--Tatum Farms, Dawsonville, GA, pg. 1080
Olsen, Jorn, V.P. & Controller--Dutton-Lainson Co., Hastings, NE, pg. 356
Olsen, Robert, Controller--Trafalgar/Ghurka, Norwalk, CT, pg. 1105
Olson, Alfred C., Jr., Controller--GAI Consultants, Inc., Monroeville, PA, pg. 439

Olson, Dale, Controller--Smead Manufacturing Company, Hastings, MN, pg. 1011
Olson, David, V.P. & Controller--Ruiz Food Products, Inc., Dinuba, CA, pg. 955
Olson, Ronald, Comptroller--The Fusco Corporation, New Haven, CT, pg. 437
Oney, Cindy, Controller--Realty One, Cleveland, OH, pg. 917
Oranowitz, Jay, Controller--Weiss, Whitten, Carroll, Stagliano Inc., New York, NY, pg. 1174
Ordogne, Rene, Controller--Andersen Consulting, Chicago, IL, pg. 72
Ordonez, Ramon A., Controller--Hydro-Mill Co., Chatsworth, CA, pg. 557
Orgeron, Aubrey, Controller--Bollinger Machine Shop And Shipyard, Inc., Lockport, LA, pg. 163
Orloff, Dale O., Controller--First State Federal Savings & Loan, Hutchinson, MN, pg. 413
Orme, Steven R., Controller--PST Vans, Inc., Salt Lake City, UT, pg. 837
Orr, L. Homer, Comptroller & Personnel Dir.--S-G Metals Industries, Inc., Kansas City, KS, pg. 962
Orr, Vernon R., V.P., Sec. & Controller--J.D. Diffenbaugh, Inc., Riverside, CA, pg. 337
Orsi, Mara, Controller--Lortz Direct Marketing Inc., Omaha, NE, pg. 684
Orth, Leroy, Controller--Lario Oil & Gas Company, Wichita, KS, pg. 658
Osborn, Robert, Controller--Sigler & Reeves, Phoenix, AZ, pg. 1003
Osiecki, Robert C., Controller--American Snacks, Inc., Chelsea, MA, pg. 61
Oskins, James C., Controller--George Koch Sons, Inc., Evansville, IN, pg. 639
Osterbauer, Bill, Controller--Lindsay International, Lindsay, CA, pg. 676
Ostroff, Arthur J., Treas. & Controller--Standard Medical Imaging, Inc., Columbia, MD, pg. 1037
Ott, William, Controller--Pullman Industries, Inc., Madison Heights, MI, pg. 900
Otte, Alfred Ray, Sr. V.P & Controller--United Services Automobile Association (USAA), San Antonio, TX, pg. 1134
Ottensmeyer, Richard C., Controller--Journal Register Company, Trenton, NJ, pg. 608
Oversmith, Blake, Controller--Union-Tribune Publishing Company, San Diego, CA, pg. 284
Overton, Samuel, Controller--Mattison Machine Works, Rockford, IL, pg. 721
Owen, Gary, Chief Fin. Officer & Controller--Design 1 Interiors, Los Angeles, CA, pg. 332
Owen, James, Controller--Brookfield Engineering Laboratories, Inc., Stoughton, MA, pg. 179
Owens, D.J., Controller--The Pollock Corp., Pottstown, PA, pg. 879
Owens, Tom, Controller--P/A Industries, Inc., Bloomfield, CT, pg. 835
Ozmun, Robert, Chief Fin. Officer & Controller--Grocers Supply Co. Inc., Houston, TX, pg. 488
Pace, James C., Jr., Controller--Inman Mills, Inman, SC, pg. 570
Packard, Katherine, Comptroller--Scharer Associates, Inc., Great Neck, NY, pg. 974
Packer, Wayne, Controller--Keysor Century Corporation, Saugus, CA, pg. 627
Padilla, Lourdes, Controller--Commodore Cruise Line, Ltd., Coral Gables, FL, pg. 269
Pageau, Philip, V.P. & Controller--CPS Corporation, Franklin, TN, pg. 428
Pajnic, Bill, Controller--Fletcher Hunt Wirth Associates, Inc., Kansas City, MO, pg. 418
Palesota, Peter, Controller, Treas. & Sec.--Plantation Foods Inc., Waco, TX, pg. 874
Palilla, Salvatore, Controller--Out of Home Media Services, Inc., New York, NY, pg. 832
Pallen, Michael, Controller--Gilman Paper Co., Saint Marys, GA, pg. 459
Palmer, John, Controller--City Postal, Inc., New York, NY, pg. 251
Palmer, Mary, Dir.-Fin. & Controller--American Fluorescent Corporation, Waukegan, IL, pg. 54
Palmer, Pauline, Controller--Ft. Dearborn Lithograph Graphic Arts Division, Fort Worth, TX, pg. 425
Paluska, Stephen M., Controller--Dav-El Services, Inc., New York, NY, pg. 317
Pantaliano, Robert, V.P., Controller--Gilbert, Whitney & Johns, Inc., Whippany, NJ, pg. 458
Pantzer, Robert T., Controller--Wilbur-Ellis Company & Connell Brothers Company, San Francisco, CA, pg. 1189
Paolozzi, Anthony, V.P. & Controller--Utica Mutual Insurance Company, New Hartford, NY, pg. 1140
Papa, Bernard, Controller--Troy Corporation, East Hanover, NJ, pg. 1116
Papiernick, Donald, Treas. & Controller--The Harwood Companies, Inc., New York, NY, pg. 515
Pappas, Dana, Controller--Johnny Appleseed's, Inc., Beverly, MA, pg. 597
Pardi, Richard, Controller--Western Data Systems, Calabasas, CA, pg. 1178
Park, Dwain S., Controller--True Companies, Casper, WY, pg. 1117
Park, John, Controller--Aquidneck Data Company, Middletown, RI, pg. 320
Parker, C.W., Controller--StacoEnergy Products Co., Dayton, OH, pg. 270
Parker, E., Controller--Acme Canvas Co., Inc., Malden, MA, pg. 13
Parker, Sandra, Sr. V.P., Controller--Lewis Advertising, Inc., Rocky Mount, NC, pg. 673
Partington, John, Controller--AJC International, Inc., Atlanta, GA, pg. 4
Parton, Joe, Controller--M.J. Daly & Sons, Inc., Waterbury, CT, pg. 313
Patane, Anthony, Controller--Roytex, Inc., New York, NY, pg. 953
Patel, Anil, Controller--J.M.P. Bakery Co., Inc., Brooklyn, NY, pg. 586
Paterline, Vicky, Controller--The May Apparel Group, Inc., Mebane, NC, pg. 723
Patrick, J.L., V.P. & Controller--Illinois Consolidated Telephone Co., Mattoon, IL, pg. 563
Patterson, David, Controller--Bike Athletic Co., Knoxville, TN, pg. 150
Patterson, Jeffrey, Controller--Truck World Inc., Hubbard, OH, pg. 1117
Patterson, Patricia, Controller--Road Machinery Company, Phoenix, AZ, pg. 937
Pattison, Sarah, Controller--Summit Communications, Inc., Atlanta, GA, pg. 1057
Paulsen, Bruce, V.P. & Controller--Carlson Companies, Inc., Minneapolis, MN, pg. 220
Paulsen, Dave, Controller & Dir.-Fin. & Treasury--Columbine Systems Inc., Golden, CO, pg. 266
Pavelik, Richard, Controller--Landau Building Co., Wexford, PA, pg. 654
Pawer, Terri, Comptroller--Label Products & Design Division, Green Bay, WI, pg. 608
Pawley, Thomas, V.P. & Controller--McSwain Carpets Inc., Cincinnati, OH, pg. 733
Pawlowski, D.A., Controller--Macwhyte Co., Kenosha, WI, pg. 69
Pawlowski, Walter, Treas. & Controller--H. B. Smith Co., Inc., Westfield, MA, pg. 1013
Paxton, Gary W., Controller--Trojan Steel Co., Charleston, WV, pg. 1115
Pearl, Ronald, Controller--Morgan Realty Associates, Englishtown, NJ, pg. 770
Peck, Robbie, Controller--Marlow Industries, Dallas, TX, pg. 710
Pedersen, Niels, Comptroller--Harmon City, Inc., West Valley City, UT, pg. 510
Pedley, Robert, Controller--Harvey Construction Company, Inc., Bedford, NH, pg. 515
Pekar, James, V.P. & Controller--Color Arts, Inc., Racine, WI, pg. 264
Pelak, Jerry, Controller & Mgr.-Opers.--Instructional Fair, Inc., Grand Rapids, MI, pg. 369
Pelisson, Edward, Controllor--Marcel Dekker, Inc., New York, NY, pg. 325
Pender, Terry, Controller--Windsor Publications, Inc., Chatsworth, CA, pg. 1196
Penn, Dan, Controller--Peck Jones Construction, Los Angeles, CA, pg. 854
Pennell, Donald G., Controller--Lauerer Markin Gibbs, Inc., Maumee, OH, pg. 660
Penner, W. Robert, Sr. V.P., Chief Fin. Officer & Asst. Treas.--Century 21 Real Estate Corp., Irvine, CA, pg. 744
Penno, D. Bruce, Chief Fin. Officer & Treas.--Pridgeon & Clay, Inc., Grand Rapids, MI, pg. 889
Pennoyer, Cynthia, Asst. Controller--Stauch Vetromile & Mitchell Advertising, Inc., East Providence, RI, pg. 1042
Peo, Richard, Chief Fin. Officer & Controller--Boyer Bros. Inc., Altoona, PA, pg. 169
Perdue, Sharon, Controller--Tropical Garment Manufacturing Company, Tampa, FL, pg. 1116
Perez, Louis, Controller--The Phillies-A Limited Partnership, Philadelphia, PA, pg. 867
Perigo, Mary, Controller--MPD, Inc., Owensboro, KY, pg. 693
Perlman, Leonard, V.P., Chief Fin. Officer & Controller--W. Braun Company, Chicago, IL, pg. 172
Perotti, Joseph, Controller--Dacor Corporation, Northfield, IL, pg. 310
Perritano, Anthony, Controller--Epec, Inc., New Bedford, MA, pg. 384
Perry, Carmen, Sec., Treas. & Controller--Outdoor Venture Corp., Stearns, KY, pg. 832
Perry, Jay, Sec., Treas. & Controller--Steiny & Company, Inc., Los Angeles, CA, pg. 1049
Perry, Wallace, Controller--Cooper Instrument Corp., Middlefield, CT, pg. 283
Perzyna, Steve, Controller--Keller Construction Company Ltd., El Monte, CA, pg. 620
Peterka, John, Controller--Rittenhouse Inc., Park Ridge, IL, pg. 936
Peters, Barbara, Controller--Brower Company, Kent, WA, pg. 127
Peters, Phillip H., Treas. & Comptroller--Continental Water Company, Saint Louis, MO, pg. 280
Peters, William, Controller--Pierce Manufacturing, Inc., Appleton, WI, pg. 870
Peterson, Craig P., V.P. & Controller--The Dunlap Companies, Fort Worth, TX, pg. 353
Peterson, Janet, Controller--Vitatech International, Inc., Tustin, CA, pg. 1153
Peterson, Kurt, Controller--Cummins Southwest Inc., Phoenix, AZ, pg. 305
Peterson, Norman, V.P. & Comptroller--Jonathan Manufacturing Corp., Fullerton, CA, pg. 602
Petruschin, Renee, Comptroller--Pool Communications, Los Angeles, CA, pg. 880
Petz, Joe, Controller--Grayline Housewares, Elgin, IL, pg. 480
Pfeifer, Greg, Treas. & Chief Fin. Officer--Rochester-Midland ICL, Omaha, NE, pg. 941
Phagans, T. M., Sec. & Treas.--Addison Steel Inc., Orlando, FL, pg. 17
Phekkekara, Jack, Controller--Inner Secrets, Inc., Hoboken, NJ, pg. 570
Phelan, James, Controller--The H. W. Wilson Co., Bronx, NY, pg. 1193
Phillips, David, Controller--Publix Supermarkets Inc., Lakeland, FL, pg. 898
Phillips, M.A., Controller--E.H. Brown Advertising, Inc., Chicago, IL, pg. 181
Phillips, Ron, Comptroller--Georgia Duck & Cordage Mills, Scottdale, GA, pg. 453
Phillips, Susan, Mgr., Acctg. & Fin., Controller--Brand, Shick & Wesley, Cleveland, OH, pg. 172
Philpot, Michael, Controller--G.L. Ness Agency, Inc., Fargo, ND, pg. 798
Piaget, Adamir, V.P. & Controller--Fiduciary Trust (International) S.A., Geneva, Switzerland, pg. 409
Pianki, Ed, Controller--Bekins Van Lines Co., Hillside, IL, pg. 133
Pick, Philip, Controller--Arrow Pneumatics Co. Inc., Lake Zurich, IL, pg. 85
Pick, Philip, Controller--Arrow Fluid Power, Broadview, IL, pg. 85
Pickus, R., Controller--Airline Hydraulics Corporation, Bensalem, PA, pg. 27
Pickus, Russell, V.P. & Controller--General Refractories Co., U. S. Refractories Div., Pittsburgh, PA, pg. 136
Pierce, Mary, Controller--SBS Products, Inc., Saginaw, MI, pg. 323
Pillsbury, Donald, Controller--IFP Hydraulics Inc., Franklin Park, IL, pg. 559
Ping, Al, Controller--Muhlhauser & Young, San Francisco, CA, pg. 774
Pini, Ralph, V.P.-Fin.--Nautilus, Independence, VA, pg. 796
Piraneo, Carl, Controller--Guideposts Associates, Inc., Carmel, NY, pg. 493
Pitelka, David L., Sr. V.P. & Controller--First American Bankshares, Inc., Washington, DC, pg. 412
Pitesa, Jan, Controller--Peter A. Mayer Advertising, Inc., New Orleans, LA, pg. 724
Pittman, Colleen, Controller--Landmark Communications, Inc., Norfolk, VA, pg. 654
Plack, Jeff, Treas., Controller & Corp. Sec.--Orix Real Estate Equities, Inc., Chicago, IL, pg. 829
Plamer, D., Controller--Econolite Control Products, Inc., Anaheim, CA, pg. 367
Plautz, Bill, V.P.-Bus. Devel. & Controller--Restaurant Developers Corp., Independence, OH, pg. 929
Plebani, Gabe, Controller--Cleveland Brothers Equipment Co., Harrisburg, PA, pg. 255
Plizga, Wayne, Controller--Energy & Environmental Research Corp., Irvine, CA, pg. 381
Ploaskier, Harry, Controller--The Dyson-Kissner-Moran Corporation, New York, NY, pg. 357
Plott, Mary F., V.P.-Fin.--Associated Grocers of Alabama, Inc., Birmingham, AL, pg. 90
Plunkett, Mike, Controller--Hajoca Corp., Ardmore, PA, pg. 500
Podjasek, Michael, Controller--Globe Glass & Mirror Co., Chicago, IL, pg. 463
Pohl, Jim, Controller--Kropp Forge Co., Chicago, IL, pg. 1073
Pohl, Walter F., Jr., Controller--Gold Kist, Inc., Atlanta, GA, pg. 465
Polivka, Fred, V.P. & Controller--Specialty Restaurants Corporation, Anaheim, CA, pg. 1027
Pollack, Robert, Controller--Elixir Industries, Gardena, CA, pg. 376
Pollock, Maurice, V.P., Treas. & Controller--Collin Street Bakery, Corsicana, TX, pg. 262
Ponath, Angelia, Controller--Bollinger Health Care, Lubbock, TX, pg. 163
Poncin, Mark, Controller--Schlosser Forge Company, Rancho Cucamonga, CA, pg. 976
Pope, Fred, Chief Fin. Officer & Controller--Walker & Associates, Inc., Welcome, NC, pg. 1159
Pope, James, Controller--Crown Textile Company, Blue Bell, PA, pg. 302
Popma, Tom, Controller--Kenwal Products Corp., Detroit, MI, pg. 624
Popp, Betty, Sec. & Controller--Red Wing Products, Inc., Plainview, NY, pg. 919
Porcelli, James A., Controller--Conair Corporation, Stamford, CT, pg. 272
Porpora, Peter, V.P. & Controller--Briggs Industries, Inc., Tampa, FL, pg. 175
Porta, Clarence J., Jr., Dir.-Comptroller & Data Processing--Eatel Corporation, Gonzales, LA, pg. 364
Porter, Mary, Controller--Ivex Packaging Corporation-Grant Park, Grant Park, IL, pg. 583
Posey, Jerome L., Controller--Quadion Corporation, Minneapolis, MN, pg. 902
Post, Jill, Controller--Goldberg Fossa Seid Advertising, Inc., New York, NY, pg. 465
Potash, Paul D., V.P. & Controller--Spaulding & Slye Company, Burlington, MA, pg. 1026
Poteraj, Robert S., Controller--Boyle Engineering Corp., Newport Beach, CA, pg. 169
Potts, Carol R., Controller--The Guthrie Group, Portland, ME, pg. 495
Potts, W. L., Jr., Chief Fin. Officer, Treas. & Controller--Nutech, Inc., San Jose, CA, pg. 817
Poulatian, Alek, Controller--Carpeteria, Inc., Valencia, CA, pg. 224
Poulos, Lori J., V.P., Treas., Controller & Sec.--Bridgewater Resources Corporation, Beverly Hills, CA, pg. 175
Poupard, J.J., V.P. & Controller--Haulpak Division, Komatsu Dresser Company, Peoria, IL, pg. 565
Pouttu, E.E., Controller--Harwick Chemical Corp., Akron, OH, pg. 515
Powell, John, Controller--Talon, Inc., Meadville, PA, pg. 1077
Powell, Rhonda, Controller--NTH Consultants, Ltd., Farmington Hills, MI, pg. 781
Pratt, Joel M., Comptroller--C.B. Fox Company, New Orleans, LA, pg. 427
Prekop, Lon, Controller--Lake Shore, Inc., Kingsford, MI, pg. 824
Prescott, Steve, Controller--Idaho Supreme Company, Firth, ID, pg. 561
Pressman, Martin, Controller--Dektas & Eger, Inc., Cincinnati, OH, pg. 325
Prestosa, Patrick, Controller--Industrial Wire Products Corporation, Pomona, CA, pg. 567

Price, Anthony, V.P., Acct. Services & Controller--TJ Clark Advertising/PR, Hingham, MA, pg. 251
Price, Charles, Comptroller--Empire Brushes, Inc., Greenville, NC, pg. 379
Price, Gary L., Treas. & Comptroller--Ben Venue Laboratories, Inc., Bedford, OH, pg. 138
Price, Gordon, Controller, Treas. & Sec.--Coleman Cadillac Inc., Bethesda, MD, pg. 261
Price, Richard, Controller--Associated Grocers, Inc., Baton Rouge, LA, pg. 89
Pries, Sue, Controller--Guth Lighting Company, Saint Louis, MO, pg. 588
Prindle, Cheryl, Controller--Restonic Corporation, Chicago, IL, pg. 929
Pritchett, Stanford, Controller--Humboldt Express, Inc., Nashville, TN, pg. 552
Privette, Herbert, Controller--Lowe's Food Stores, Inc., Winston-Salem, NC, pg. 33
Procik, John, Controller--Sheffield Steel Corporation-Joliet, Joliet, IL, pg. 996
Pronko, Elizabeth A., Chief Fin. Officer, V.P. & Controller--PE Systems, Reston, VA, pg. 836
Provost, Bob, Controller--Guest Quarters Suite Hotels, Boston, MA, pg. 493
Prowse, Rich, Controller--Ayer Chicago, Chicago, IL, pg. 104
Pucky, Timothy, Controller--Luntz Corporation, Canton, OH, pg. 687
Pugiello, Peter, Controller--Blonder-Tongue Laboratories, Inc., Old Bridge, NJ, pg. 157
Pulfipher, Allen, Controller--Norbest, Inc., Midvale, UT, pg. 809
Pulskamp, Jack, Controller--Miami Systems Corporation, Cincinnati, OH, pg. 746
Purpura, Salvatore, Chief Fin. Officer & Controller--Associated Metals & Minerals Corp., White Plains, NY, pg. 91
Quattro, Susanne, Controller--Servistar Corporation, East Butler, PA, pg. 992
Quinby, Charles, Controller--Omni Source Corporation, Fort Wayne, IN, pg. 826
Quinn, J. Paul, Controller--Arizona Supermarkets, Inc., Phoenix, AZ, pg. 82
Quirk, William, V.P.-Fin. & Chief Fin. Officer--ATI Industries, Escondido, CA, pg. 8
Rabe, Debbie, Controller--Wasserstrom Company, Columbus, OH, pg. 1167
Racavich, Carl, Controller--California Panel & Veneer Company, Cerritos, CA, pg. 210
Rackley, James, Controller--Justrite Manufacturing Company, Des Plaines, IL, pg. 610
Rackowski, Thomas, V.P. & Controller--The IDI Group Companies, Arlington, VA, pg. 560
Radermacher, Frank, V.P. & Controller--Ministers Life Insurance Company, Minneapolis, MN, pg. 757
Radtke, Eldon, Comptroller--Maze Nails, Peru, IL, pg. 725
Raffia, M.J., V.P.-Fin.--Kane-Miller Corp., Tarrytown, NY, pg. 616
Rager, Dennis, Controller--Snyder's of Hanover, Inc., Hanover, PA, pg. 1015
Ragsdale, John, Controller--Century Products Co., Macedonia, OH, pg. 235
Rahbar, Sherry, V.P., Controller--Davis, Ball & Colombatto Advertising, Inc., Los Angeles, CA, pg. 318
Raible, William, V.P. & Controller--Bacharach Inc., Pittsburgh, PA, pg. 108
Raiche, John T., Sec. & Controller--Divane Bros. Electric Co., Franklin Park, IL, pg. 340
Raivio, Richard, Controller--Northwest Paper Converting Company, Vancouver, WA, pg. 814
Ralph, David, Controller--Thermon Manufacturing Company, San Marcos, TX, pg. 1091
Ramaglia, Peter A., Controller--Global Insurance Company, Houston, TX, pg. 662
Ramberg, David, Controller--Big Horn Co-Op Marketing Association, Greybull, WY, pg. 149
Ramey, Peter, Chief Fin. Officer--Lou Fusz Automotive Network, Saint Louis, MO, pg. 437
Ramsey, Craig R., Exec. V.P.--Frank Paxton Company, Kansas City, MO, pg. 592
Ramus, David W., V.P., Controller, Treas. & Chief Fin. Officer--M & T Incorporated, Portland, OR, pg. 690
Ranazzissi, Tony, V.P., Chief Info. Officer & Controller--Burkhardt & Christy Advertising, Inc., New York, NY, pg. 191
Rapaport, Jonathan, Chief Fin. Officer, V.P. & Treas.--Pacesetter Steel Service, Inc., Marietta, GA, pg. 839
Raper, Jeff, Controller--United States Ceramic Tile Co., East Sparta, OH, pg. 1135
Rasmussen, Casey, Controller--Belgrave Industries, Santa Ana, CA, pg. 133
Rather, Jerome, V.P.-Fin. & Controller--Credit Union National Association, Madison, WI, pg. 298
Rather, Jerome, V.P.-Fin. & Controller--CUNA Service Group, Inc., Madison, WI, pg. 298
Rauzi, Henry, Controller--Sunbeam-Oster Company, Inc., Providence, RI, pg. 1059
Ravasio, Doris, Controller--Gibbs Wire & Steel Company, Inc., Southington, CT, pg. 456
Ray, Arnold S., V.P. & Controller--Connell Limited Partnership, Boston, MA, pg. 275
Rayback, Carolyn, Controller--Pacific Foods, Inc., Kent, WA, pg. 840
Raye, Charmane, Controller--Hayes/Harwood, Stowe, VT, pg. 519
Re, Michael, Controller--Swinerton & Walberg Co., San Francisco, CA, pg. 1068
Reagan, Terry, Controller--Metal Seal & Products, Inc., Willoughby, OH, pg. 741
Reardon, Gene, Controller--Guy Gannett Publishing Company, Portland, ME, pg. 442
Reba, Jay, Controller--Drug Guild Distributors, Inc., Secaucus, NJ, pg. 349
Reber, L., Controller--Stamco Industries Inc., Euclid, OH, pg. 1035
Rector, Douglas, Controller--Pioneer Press Newspapers Inc., Wilmette, IL, pg. 18
Reed, Robert, Chief Accountant--Laird & Company, Scobeyville, NJ, pg. 650
Reed, Thomas E., Controller--Schultz Steel Company, South Gate, CA, pg. 979
Reeves, Stuart, Controller--Guaranteed Products, Inc., City of Industry, CA, pg. 491
Regan, John, Controller--The Van Metre Companies, Burke, VA, pg. 1144
Regan, Rick, Controller, & Dir.-Data Processing--American Produce & Vegetable Co., Dallas, TX, pg. 59
Regan, William, Controller--Vindicator Corporation, Austin, TX, pg. 1152
Rege, Thomas J., Chief Fin. Officer, Sec., Treas. & Controller--Chartway Technologies, Rockville, MD, pg. 240
Rehaste, Enn, Controller--Griswold Industries, Inc., Costa Mesa, CA, pg. 488
Rehl, William M., Controller--United Air Specialists, Inc., Cincinnati, OH, pg. 1130
Reid, William B., V.P. & Controller--Chemstone Corp., Strasburg, VA, pg. 242
Reiher, Nancy, Chief Fin. Officer, Controller--Newmark, Posner & Mitchell, Inc., New York, NY, pg. 804
Reilly, Gerald E., V.P. & Controller--Laminaire Corporation, Rahway, NJ, pg. 652
Reinhart, J.W., Controller & Asst. Treas.--Logan & Kanawha Coal Co., Cincinnati, OH, pg. 681
Reiter, Frank, Controller--Redmond Products, Inc., Chanhassen, MN, pg. 920
Reith, Steve, Comptroller--Hudepohl-Schoenling Brewing Company, Cincinnati, OH, pg. 550
Reker, David, Controller--Bedford Industries, Inc., Worthington, MN, pg. 131
Relis, Murray, Controller--Primary Industries Corporation, New York, NY, pg. 889
Renda, Ben A., V.P. & Controller--American Envelope Company, Chicago, IL, pg. 199
Reppert, Tracy, Controller--Nature's Recipe Pet Foods, Corona, CA, pg. 796
Reyes, Joseph, Controller--Harper Industries, Inc., New York, NY, pg. 510
Reyes, Luis, Controller--Coulter Corporation, Hialeah, FL, pg. 289
Reyes, Rod, Controller--IDM Controls, Houston, TX, pg. 560
Reznick, Gary, Controller--The Sturm Communications Group, Inc., Chicago, IL, pg. 1055
Rice, James, Controller--Essex Group, Inc., Fort Wayne, IN, pg. 389
Richards, Cathy, Controller--Tucker Wayne/Luckie & Company, Atlanta, GA, pg. 1118
Richards, Dave, Treas. & Controller--Pacific Hide & Fur Depot, Great Falls, MT, pg. 840
Richardson, Thomas, V.P., Sec., Treas. & Controller--Aladdin Petroleum Corporation, Wichita, KS, pg. 29
Richter, Paul, Controller--Weilwood Industries, Inc., New York, NY, pg. 970
Rieger, James J., V.P. & Controller--Ponderosa, Inc., Vandalia, OH, pg. 743
Riegert, George, Controller--Robbins, Inc., Cincinnati, OH, pg. 938
Riesenbeck, Ronald, Controller--Save Mart Supermarkets, Modesto, CA, pg. 973
Riffert, Dennis, Controller & Treas.--Citizens Realty & Insurance Inc., Evansville, IN, pg. 251
Rimarcik, Joseph C., Sr. V.P.-Accounting & Admin.--Paul Inman Associates Inc., Farmington Hills, MI, pg. 570
Ringdahl, Paul, Controller--Press Enterprise Company, Riverside, CA, pg. 887
Ringel, James, Controller--Serfilco, Ltd., Northbrook, IL, pg. 990
Riodan, Mary Beth, Controller--Cyborg Systems, Inc., Chicago, IL, pg. 307
Rissman, Dennis, Controller--Bresler's Industries, Inc., Des Plaines, IL, pg. 174
Ritter, Rick, V.P. & Controller--Handley & Miller, Inc., Indianapolis, IN, pg. 505
Ritzel, Joseph, V.P. & Controller--Day & Zimmermann, Inc., Radnor, PA, pg. 320
Rivard, Peter A., Comptroller--D. D. Bean & Sons Co., Jaffrey, NH, pg. 129
Rivera, Jose A., Comptroller--Puerto Rico Tourism Company, New York, NY, pg. 899
Rizzi, Kenneth A., Controller--The Turner & Seymour Mfg. Company, Torrington, CT, pg. 1119
Roach, David, Controller--Speedling Incorporated, Sun City, FL, pg. 1029
Roberts, Keith, V.P., Controller--Karsh & Hagan, Inc., Englewood, CO, pg. 617
Roberts, Michael D., 1st V.P., Controller & Asst. Treas.--W. P. Carey & Co., Inc., New York, NY, pg. 218
Robertson, Gordy, Controller--Malt-O-Meal Company, Minneapolis, MN, pg. 703
Robins, R. Steven, Sec., Treas., Controller & Cash Mgr.--Builder Marts of America, Greenville, SC, pg. 187
Robinson, Eli E., Controller--Contractors Steel Company, Livonia, MI, pg. 280
Robinson, Greg, Controller--Russell-Stanley Corporation, Red Bank, NJ, pg. 957
Robinson, Jerry D., Chief Fin. Officer, V.P. & Treas.--SFA, Inc., Landover, MD, pg. 961
Robinson, Marc, Controller--PVS Chemicals, Inc., Detroit, MI, pg. 837
Robinson, Phil, Controller--Libco Corporation, Chicago, IL, pg. 674
Robison, Hal, Controller--Taylor Machine Works, Inc., Louisville, MS, pg. 1081
Rocco, Joseph, Controller--Blount Lumber Company, Lacona, NY, pg. 158
Rockhill, Ervin, Controller--Warner Press, Inc., Anderson, IN, pg. 1164
Roden, Jim, Controller--Crum Electric Supply Co., Inc., Casper, WY, pg. 303
Rodriguez, Gaspar, Asst. Controller--Simunico, Inc., Rutherford, NJ, pg. 1007
Rodriguez, Maria A., Controller--Garber, Goodman Advertising, Inc., Miami, FL, pg. 443
Rodriguez, Ray, Treas.--Fiesta Mart Inc., Houston, TX, pg. 409
Roe-Wentworth, Marcia, Controller--Craddock Development Co., Inc., Colorado Springs, CO, pg. 295
Roedl, Suzanne, Chief Fin. Officer--Condor D.C. Power Supplies Inc., Oxnard, CA, pg. 273
Roesnheim, John, Controller--FWD Corporation, Clintonville, WI, pg. 395
Rogers, Irwin W., V.P., Controller & Sec.--North Pacific Lumber Company, Portland, OR, pg. 813
Rogers, John, Treas. & Controller--Mallery Lumber Corp., Emporium, PA, pg. 702
Roland, R. Wayne, Controller--Brookstone Company, Inc., Peterborough, NH, pg. 180
Rold, Stephen K., V.P., Treas., Sec. & Controller--Roofing Wholesale Co., Inc., Phoenix, AZ, pg. 946
Romanczuk, Wayne, Sec. & Controller--P M Company, Philadelphia, PA, pg. 835
Romano, Linda, Controller--Mark Chevrolet Inc., Wayne, MI, pg. 708
Romer, John, Comptroller--Guest Services, Inc., Fairfax, VA, pg. 493
Romick, Frederick W., Dir.-Fin. & Controller--International Seaway Trading Corporation, Mayfield Village, OH, pg. 579
Romig, Michael V., V.P. & Chief Fin. Officer--Marine Construction & Design Co., Seattle, WA, pg. 707
Romine, Cynthia, Controller--CPM, Inc., Chicago, IL, pg. 203
Romine, Debbie, Controller--BA Advertising, Dallas, TX, pg. 105
Ronga, Neil, Controller--Judy Bond, Inc., New York, NY, pg. 608
Roof, Donald C., Chief Fin. Officer, Treas. & Comptroller--Spreckles Industries, Inc., Pleasanton, CA, pg. 1032
Rose, Estelle, Chief Fin. Officer--Kobra International Ltd, New York, NY, pg. 638
Rose, Loren, Dir.-Data Processing & Controller--Pyramid Mountain Lumber, Seeley Lake, MT, pg. 901
Rose, Meredith, Controller--Bearing Service Company, Pittsburgh, PA, pg. 130
Rosell, Ibrahim, Asst. V.P. & Controller--Bacardi Imports, Inc., Miami, FL, pg. 108
Rosemin, Neville N., Controller--Industrial Acoustics Company, Inc., Bronx, NY, pg. 565
Rosen, Harold, Controller--Fel-Pro Incorporated, Skokie, IL, pg. 405
Rosen, Martin, Controller--BLH Electronics, Canton, MA, pg. 107
Rosenberg, Harvey, Controller--Coat, Apron & Linen Supply, Bronx, NY, pg. 257
Rosenfeld, Robert, Controller--Barton Press, Inc., West Orange, NJ, pg. 123
Rosenfield, J., V.P., Controller & Chief Fin. Officer--Sweetlife Foods, Inc., Suffield, CT, pg. 1067
Rosenhaft, Martin, V.P. & Controller--Murry's, Inc., Forestville, MD, pg. 777
Rosinski, Henry J., Controller--Flint Ink Corp., Detroit, MI, pg. 419
Rosinski, Martin J., Controller--Rand McNally & Company, Skokie, IL, pg. 911
Rosloff, Cary S., Controller--Fine Organics Corp., Lodi, NJ, pg. 411
Rosloniec, James, V.P.-Audit & Contol--Amway Corporation, Ada, MI, pg. 70
Ross, D.R., V.P. & Controller--Pyle Inc., Chicago, IL, pg. 648
Ross, Lyle, Controller--Lan-O-Sheen, Inc., Saint Paul, MN, pg. 653
Ross, R.L., Sec., Treas. & Controller--Edgewater Corporation, Oakmont, PA, pg. 368
Rossmeisl, Shirley I., Controller--Hazen Paper Company, Holyoke, MA, pg. 520
Roth, Barbara J., Controller--Nielsen Construction Company, San Diego, CA, pg. 807
Rothwell, Ronnie E., Controller--Arrow Industries, Inc., Carrollton, TX, pg. 85
Rotolo, Jan, Controller--Harris, Baio & McCullough Inc., Philadelphia, PA, pg. 511
Rouse, John J., Jr., V.P. & Controller--Broadcast Division, Atlanta, GA, pg. 292
Routledge, Monty, Controller--Interstate Payco Seed Company, West Fargo, ND, pg. 580
Rowan, Eamond, Controller--AMF Bakery Systems, Richmond, VA, pg. 5
Rowe, Charles, Controller--Plywood Panels, Inc., New Orleans, LA, pg. 878
Rowe, David, Controller--American Stabilis, Inc., Lewiston, ME, pg. 61
Rowe, Jean, Controller--Carlton Manufacturing, Inc., Elkhart, IN, pg. 222
Rowell, Colie, Controller--Central Coca-Cola Bottling Company, Inc., Richmond, VA, pg. 232
Roy, Kathy, Controller--Heck Enterprises, Inc., Baton Rouge, LA, pg. 524
Roznowski, Jack, V.P.-Fin. & Controller--Trerice Tosto International, Bingham Farms, MI, pg. 1110
Rubar, W.H., Asst. Controller--BE & K, Inc., Birmingham, AL, pg. 106
Rubino, Marcia, Controller--Eire Partners, Inc., Chicago, IL, pg. 372
Rudolph, Carl J., V.P. & Controller--Aid Association For Lutherans, Appleton, WI, pg. 26
Rue, Eugene D., Controller & Mgr.-Credit--R.C.A. Rubber Company, Akron, OH, pg. 906
Rueden, Jim Von, Chief Fin. Officer & Controller--Wausau Homes, Inc., Rothschild, WI, pg. 1168
Ruffing, Robert H., Controller--American Financial Corporation, Cincinnati, OH, pg. 52

Ruhl, Robert, Controller--Ruhl Companies, Inc., Valhalla, NY, pg. 955
Ruic, Jay, Controller--AMI Industries, Inc., Colorado Springs, CO, pg. 5
Rumpp, Carl W., Controller--Marine Transport Lines, Inc., Secaucus, NJ, pg. 707
Ruscher, Stephen, V.P., Treas. & Controller--Columbia National Group, Inc., Cleveland, OH, pg. 265
Rush, Dave, V.P.-Controller--BJ Acquisition Corp., Charlotte, NC, pg. 107
Russell, Ronald, Controller--GenDerm Corporation, Lincolnshire, IL, pg. 448
Russo, Elaine, Controller--The Protector Corporation, Addison, IL, pg. 895
Rutkay, Wayne, Chief Fin. Officer & Controller--Young Stuff Apparel Group, Inc., New York, NY, pg. 1214
Rutledge, Connie, V.P. & Corp. Controller--Lincoln Property Company, Dallas, TX, pg. 676
Rutman, Robert, V.P. & Controller--Adam Meldrum & Anderson Co., Inc., Buffalo, NY, pg. 16
Ryan, Dennis, Controller--Menu Foods, Inc., Pennsauken, NJ, pg. 739
Ryan, Ed, Controller--Magnetic Analysis Corp., Mount Vernon, NY, pg. 700
Ryan, John W., Controller--D.S.U.-Peterbilt & GMC, Inc., Portland, OR, pg. 309
Ryan, Philip, Pres.--Taylor Oil Co. Inc., Winston-Salem, NC, pg. 1082
Ryan, William T., Controller--VASA Insurance Group, Inc., Indianapolis, IN, pg. 1146
Ryder, Fred, V.P. & Controller--PacifiCare Health Systems, Inc., Cypress, CA, pg. 1127
Saap, Clayton H., Sec. & Controller--Wurzburg, Inc., Memphis, TN, pg. 1205
Sacks, Randy, Controller & Sec.--Morton Goldberg Associates, Inc., New York, NY, pg. 465
Sacripanti, P., Controller--Standard Lafarge, Canfield, OH, pg. 1036
Sadler, A. James, Controller--Arinc Inc., Annapolis, MD, pg. 82
Sadoski, Charles, Controller--Stevedoring Services Of America, Seattle, WA, pg. 1048
Safer, Joel, Controller--Lebhar-Friedman, Inc., New York, NY, pg. 665
Sager, P.A., Controller--Science Applications International Corporation, San Diego, CA, pg. 981
Sajeski, Edmund, Jr., Sec., Treas. & Controller--A. H. Hoffman, Inc., Landisville, PA, pg. 538
Salazar, Yolanda, Controller--Taylor-Gordon/Widmann & Co., Inc., New York, NY, pg. 1081
Salberg, Greg, Controller--Quality Pontiac, Inc., Albuquerque, NM, pg. 904
Salo, James R., Controller--Fremont Forest Products, Whittier, CA, pg. 432
Salsbury, D.L., Controller--Eriez Magnetics, Erie, PA, pg. 386
Salzano, James, Chief Fin. Officer, Sec. & Treas.--Altier & Sons Shoes Inc., Rochester, NY, pg. 45
Sample, Donald L., Controller & Sec.--Thompson Tractor Company, Birmingham, AL, pg. 1095
Samuel, R. K., Controller--Pacific Enterprises Oil Company (USA), Dallas, TX, pg. 840
San Antonio, Thomas, Controller--Charan Industries, Inc., Garden City, NY, pg. 239
San Meguel, George B., V.P. & Comptroller--Graphic Productions Company, Miami, FL, pg. 478
Sanchez, Raymond, Controller, Treas. & Asst. Sec.--Hunter Engineering Co., Inc., Riverside, CA, pg. 554
Sanders, Angela, Controller--Barnhart Advertising, Marketing & Public Relations, Inc., Denver, CO, pg. 120
Sanderson, Deborah, Controller--Pickering Industries Inc., Tacoma, WA, pg. 869
Sands, Peter, Controller--Star Children's Dress Company, Inc., New York, NY, pg. 1039
Sanford, Joan, Controller-Ross Roy, Inc.--Ross Roy Inc., Bloomfield Hills, MI, pg. 950
Santacroce, John, Controller--Argo International Corp., New York, NY, pg. 81
Santos, Oliver, Controller--Albert C. Martin & Associates, Los Angeles, CA, pg. 714
Saperstein, Robert, Controller--Cosco Industries, Spring Valley, NY, pg. 288
Sarette, William, Controller & Asst. Treas.--Central Livestock Association, Inc., South St. Paul, MN, pg. 233
Sarmiento, Alice, Controller--Admiral Maintenance Service L.P., Lincolnwood, IL, pg. 18
Sartori, Dominic, V.P., Controller & Sec.--Service America Corporation, Stamford, CT, pg. 992
Sassin, Joe, Controller--Tauber Oil Company, Houston, TX, pg. 1080
Sato, Brian, Controller--Topco Associates, Inc., Skokie, IL, pg. 1101
Sauerwein, Robert A., V.P. & Controller--The Okonite Company, Ramsey, NJ, pg. 823
Saunders, Gene, Controller--Thomas Built Buses, Inc., High Point, NC, pg. 1092
Savage, Robert, Controller--Pressure Systems, Hampton, VA, pg. 888
Saville, Ralph, Controller--The Hercules Tire & Rubber Company, Findlay, OH, pg. 531
Savinsky, Sandy, Controller--Den-Mat Corporation, Santa Maria, CA, pg. 328
Saylor, Richard, Controller--American Crystal Sugar Company, Moorhead, MN, pg. 51
Scalia, Rebeka J., V.P. & Controller--Connecticut Mutual Life Insurance Company, Hartford, CT, pg. 274
Scalzi, Barbara, Controller--Chiswick Trading Inc., Sudbury, MA, pg. 248
Scardaci, Leslie, Controller--AVA-Automatic Vendors of America, Atlanta, GA, pg. 8
Scearce, C.B., Chief Fin. Officer, V.P., Sec. & Controller--Krystal Company, Chattanooga, TN, pg. 645
Schaeffer, Charles, Controller--Agripac Inc., Salem, OR, pg. 25
Schambach, Stanley L., Controller--Hoffer Plastics Corporation, South Elgin, IL, pg. 537
Schanot, Steve, Controller--Concordia Publishing House, Saint Louis, MO, pg. 272
Schaper, Martin W., V.P. & Controller--Fru-Con Construction Corporation, Ballwin, MO, pg. 435
Schario, Paul V., Controller--Canton Drop Forge, Canton, OH, pg. 214
Scheffy, Hubert, Jr., V.P. & Controller--Lewis Homes Management Corp., Upland, CA, pg. 673
Schelhaas, Glenn, Controller--Manna Pro Partners, Denver, CO, pg. 704
Schenck, Tim, Controller--Ivex Packaging Corporation-Troy, Troy, OH, pg. 583
Schenker, Leon, Controller--State-Wide Capital Corp., Uniondale, NY, pg. 1041
Scherer, George, Chief Fin. Officer & Controller--McCarthy Building Companies, Saint Louis, MO, pg. 727
Schertz, David, Controller--Smith/Greenland, Incorporated, New York, NY, pg. 1012
Schiess, John M., Exec. V.P.-Fin. & Controller--General Brewing Company, Vancouver, WA, pg. 959
Schilling, Ken, Controller--Affiliated Food Stores, Keller, TX, pg. 23
Schillman, Frank, Controller--Sharon-Jay Togs, Inc., New Bedford, MA, pg. 995
Schimp, Dan, Controller--Mohawk Paper Mills, Inc., Cohoes, NY, pg. 763
Schimpf, Barbara, Controller & Human Resources--Scharfberg & Associates, Ltd. Adv., Jenkintown, PA, pg. 974
Schipper, M.R., Asst. Sec. & Controller--Green Holdings, Inc., Denver, CO, pg. 484
Schlegel, Trish, Controller--Stiles Corporation, Fort Lauderdale, FL, pg. 1049
Schleiffer, Steve, V.P. & Controller--Soundesign Corporation, Jersey City, NJ, pg. 1018
Schliess, John, Controller--S & P Company, Mill Valley, CA, pg. 959
Schliessmann, John, Controller--Just Pants, Chicago, IL, pg. 610
Schlosser, P., Sec. & Treas.--Robins Engineers & Constructors, Inc., Englewood, CO, pg. 939
Schmidt, Brian L., Controller--Wayne Steel, Inc., Wooster, OH, pg. 1169
Schmidt, Cheryl A., Controller--Fitzpatrick & Weller, Inc., Ellicottville, NY, pg. 416
Schmidt, Dennis, Controller--Milwaukee Electric Tool Corp., Brookfield, WI, pg. 361
Schmidt, Don, Controller--Hay & Forage Industries, Hesston, KS, pg. 4
Schnurr, Joseph, Controller--Time Systems, Inc., Phoenix, AZ, pg. 1097
Schocke, Robert P., Chief Fin. Officer, Treas., Controller & Sec.--Greenhorne & O'Mara, Inc., Greenbelt, MD, pg. 485
Schoonenberg, Donald S., Sec. & Controller--Simplicity Manufacturing, Inc., Port Washington, WI, pg. 1006
Schoonover, Rod, Controller--Hyplains Dressed Beef, Inc., Dodge City, KS, pg. 557
Schor, Irwin, Controller--Antwerp Diamond Distributors Inc., New York, NY, pg. 77
Schordock, R.A., Chief Fin. Officer, Treas. & Controller--Radix Wire Company, Cleveland, OH, pg. 909
Schourek, Joseph E., Controller--Maryland & Virginia Milk Producers Association, Reston, VA, pg. 717
Schranz, James, Controller--Austin Industries, Inc., Dallas, TX, pg. 99
Schrieklin, Richard, Controller--Executive Car Leasing Company, Los Angeles, CA, pg. 393
Schuering, James A., Controller--J. D. Streett & Co., Inc., Maryland Heights, MO, pg. 1053
Schuler, Roberta, Controller--Edd Helms Electrical Contracting, Miami, FL, pg. 527
Schultheis, Pat, V.P.-Controller--Forsythe Marcelli Johnson Advertising, Inc., Newport Beach, CA, pg. 425
Schultz, Dennis, Controller & Mgr.-Acctg.--Cranford Johnson Robinson Woods, Little Rock, AR, pg. 296
Schultz, Gary, Controller--Lund Boats, New York Mills, MN, pg. 759
Schultz, Harry, Controller--Trimfit, Inc., Philadelphia, PA, pg. 1113
Schultz, Ron, Controller--Jack Ross Motors Inc., Tempe, AZ, pg. 949
Schumacher, Norbert, Sr. V.P., Controller & Chief Fin. Officer--Marathon Cheese Corp., Marathon, WI, pg. 705
Schussel, Robert, Controller--National Distributing Co., Inc., Atlanta, GA, pg. 787
Schuster, Ronald, V.P. & Controller--The Hunt Corporation, Indianapolis, IN, pg. 553
Schwartz, Gary A., Chief Fin. Officer--Byer California, San Francisco, CA, pg. 197
Schwartz, Jeffrey, Controller--The P.J. Carlin Construction Company, New Rochelle, NY, pg. 220
Schwartz, Robert, Chief Fin. Officer & Controller--La Salle County Farm Supply, Ottawa, IL, pg. 649
Schwartzkoff, Mike, Comptroller--CHF Industries, Inc., New York, NY, pg. 200
Schwedler, Pat, V.P., Controller--Marshall Jaccoma Mitchell Advertising, New York, NY, pg. 714
Sciberras, M., Sec., Treas. & Comptroller--Dearborn Gage Company, Garden City, MI, pg. 322
Scier, Edward J., Treas. & Controller--Camalloy, Inc., Washington, PA, pg. 211
Scinto, Teresa, Comptroller--Anson-Stoner, Inc., Winter Park, FL, pg. 76
Sciole, Domenick R., Controller--Pennock, Philadelphia, PA, pg. 858
Scoggins, Rex R., Controller--C & K Markets, Inc., Brookings, OR, pg. 198
Scott, Charles, Chief Fin. Officer & Controller--Mr. Christmas Inc., New York, NY, pg. 761
Scott, Jody, Controller--Edelbrock Corp., Torrance, CA, pg. 367
Scott, William H., V.P., Sec. & Controller--The Leavell Company, El Paso, TX, pg. 664
Scrivner, Patricia, Controller--Judson-Atkinson Candies, Inc., San Antonio, TX, pg. 608
Seaman, Thomas, Controller & Dir.-Personnel--Blauer Manufacturing Co., Inc., Boston, MA, pg. 156
Sears, Robert R., Controller & Sec.--Clark Foodservice, Inc., Elk Grove Village, IL, pg. 252
Seaton, John R., V.P. & Comptroller--Graybar Electric Company, Inc., Clayton, MO, pg. 479
Seay, Ronald F., V.P. & Controller--Coastal Lumber Company, Weldon, NC, pg. 257
Sebastian, D.J., Controller--J.M. Huber, Oil & Gas Div., Houston, TX, pg. 550
Seccarelli, Joe, Controller--Barneys New York, New York, NY, pg. 120
Sedin, David, Controller--Video Products Distributors, Inc., Sacramento, CA, pg. 1150
Seekely, Martin, Controller--Boston Distributors, Inc., Maple Heights, OH, pg. 167
Seeley, Paul J., Treas., Sec. & Controller--Lindsay Manufacturing Inc., Ponca City, OK, pg. 676
Seery, Patrick, Chief Fin. Officer, Treas. & Controller--James McHugh Construction Co., Chicago, IL, pg. 729
Segerson, Roger L., Treas. & Controller--Sterling Lumber & Investment Co., Denver, CO, pg. 1047
Seitz, Melvin C., Jr., Pres., Chief Exec. Officer, Chief Oper. Officer & Controller--Service Supply Co. Inc. of Indiana, Indianapolis, IN, pg. 992
Selby, Jolene D., Controller--The Bakersfield Californian, Bakersfield, CA, pg. 115
Selle, William, Controller--The Fred W. Albrecht Grocery Co., Akron, OH, pg. 31
Semel, Semel I., Controller--Calvin Klein, Inc., New York, NY, pg. 635
Semrad, Myron, Controller--Dr Pepper/Seven-Up Companies, Inc., Dallas, TX, pg. 342
Semrau, Char, Asst. Controller--ICE Communications, Inc., Rochester, NY, pg. 559
Senst, Bruce A., Controller--Reese Enterprises, Inc., Rosemount, MN, pg. 920
Serman, L.D., Controller--Raymark Friction Company, Manheim, PA, pg. 914
Serowik, Leo P., V.P. & Controller--Great American Industries, Inc., Vestal, NY, pg. 480
Sessanta, Sal, Controller--Structural Foam Plastics, Inc., North Branch, NJ, pg. 1054
Sexton, Terry, Comptroller--Ace Doran Hauling & Rigging Company, Cincinnati, OH, pg. 346
Seyhun, Michael, Controller--The Cherokee Group, Sunland, CA, pg. 243
Sgroi, S.B., Controller--Elkins Constructors, Inc., Jacksonville, FL, pg. 377
Shaih, Dan, Controller--Southern Ohio Fabricators, Inc., Cincinnati, OH, pg. 1022
Shane, Kenneth A., Controller--White Pigeon Paper Company, White Pigeon, MI, pg. 87
Shapiro, Ronald, Sr. V.P., Comptroller--Vitt Media International, Inc., New York, NY, pg. 1153
Shaputis, Brian, Controller--Ektelon Corp., San Diego, CA, pg. 890
Shatz, Art, Treas.--Amicale Industries, Inc., New York, NY, pg. 66
Shaw, Dennis M., Controller--Petroleum Products Corp., Middletown, PA, pg. 865
Shay, S.F., Controller-Mfg.--Citizens Gas & Coke Utility, Indianapolis, IN, pg. 250
Sheehan, Thomas J., Corp. Controller--H. S. Crocker Co., Inc., King of Prussia, PA, pg. 299
Shein, Paul D., Controller--Parsons Brinckerhoff Quade & Douglas, Inc., New York, NY, pg. 850
Shelhause, Glen, Controller--Manna Pro Partner L.P. (Limited Partnership), Denver, CO, pg. 704
Shelley, D.O., Controller--Georgetown Industries, Inc., Charlotte, NC, pg. 453
Shenton, Gary, Controller--Smartstar Corporation, Goleta, CA, pg. 1011
Shepard, Morry, Controller--Reeve Aleutian Airways, Inc., Anchorage, AK, pg. 921
Shepherd, Mardy, Controller--Alliance America, Norcross, GA, pg. 37
Sheridian, James E., Controller--Paper Enterprises, Inc., Bronx, NY, pg. 847
Sherif, Jack, Controller--George Rice & Sons, Los Angeles, CA, pg. 931
Sherman, Robert, Cntroller--Black Fin Yacht Corporation, Fort Lauderdale, FL, pg. 154
Sherry, Kenneth C., Sec. & Controller--Valk Manufacturing Company, New Kingstown, PA, pg. 1143
Shide, Mark, Controller--Rihm Motor Company, Saint Paul, MN, pg. 934
Shields, Charles, Controller--WEN Products, Inc., Chicago, IL, pg. 1156
Shields, Mark, Controller & Dir.-Data Processing--Atchison County Co-op Association, Atchison, KS, pg. 93
Shilling, Ken, Controller--Zycon Corporation, Santa Clara, CA, pg. 1221
Shipper, Jonathan, Controller--Donlee Technologies Inc., York, PA, pg. 344
Shneider, Jerry, Treas. & Controller--Kelly, Scott And Madison, Inc., Chicago, IL, pg. 621
Shom, Christine, Controller--Merling, Marx & Seidman, Inc., New York, NY, pg. 741
Shoul, Wilma, Controller--Yorktown Tool & Die Corporation, Yorktown, IN, pg. 1208
Shuman, Charles, Controller--Condor Pacific Industries, Inc., Canoga Park, CA, pg. 273
Siano, Michael J., Controller--Stratton Management Company, Plymouth Meeting, PA, pg. 1053
Sieben, Horst O., V.P.-Fin. & Controller--Alford Industries, Inc., Ridgefield Park, NJ, pg. 33
Sieg, George, Controller--Meadville Forging Co., Meadville, PA, pg. 733

Sieome, Guy, Controller--Web Food Products Corp., Jamaica, NY, pg. 1170
Sierens, Dennis, Controller--The Harter Group, Sturgis, MI, pg. 513
Sills, H.D., Controller--Bell Packaging Corporation, Marion, IN, pg. 135
Silman, Jay, Controller--Winner Communications, Inc., New York, NY, pg. 1196
Silverman, Harry, Controller--Domino's Pizza Inc., Ann Arbor, MI, pg. 344
Silverman, Harvey, Sec., Treas., Controller & Dir.-Mngmt. Information Systems--MI Fund Incorporated, New York, NY, pg. 692
Silverstein, Arthur, Controller--Advance Publications Inc., Staten Island, NY, pg. 19
Silzer, Frank S., V.P. & Controller--MTI Vacations, Inc., Oak Brook, IL, pg. 694
Simmons, R., Controller--Hardinge Brothers, Inc., Elmira, NY, pg. 508
Simmons, Tom, Controller--Bongards Creameries Inc., Norwood, MN, pg. 164
Simms, Donald G., Controller--United Piece Dye Works, LP, Princeton Junction, NJ, pg. 1134
Simon, Alan D., Treas.--Omaha Creative Group, Omaha, NE, pg. 825
Simon, David, Controller--National Property Analysts, Inc., Philadelphia, PA, pg. 792
Simon, Guy, Controller--Berlitz France S.A., Paris,, France, pg. 143
Simon, Ronald, V.P.-Controller--The Trane Company, La Crosse, WI, pg. 62
Simone, Gray, Controller--Bookazine Company, Inc., Bayonne, NJ, pg. 164
Simoneaux, Will, Controller--Carter Chambers Supply, Inc., Baton Rouge, LA, pg. 226
Simons, James W., Pres.--Mersman Furniture, Celina, OH, pg. 741
Simpson, Frank, Chief Fin. Officer & Controller--Plywood Plastics Inc., Buffalo, NY, pg. 878
Simpson, Kevin, Controller--Friedman, Eisenstein, Raemer & Schwartz, Chicago, IL, pg. 433
Sims, Barry, V.P. & Chief Fin. Officer--Taco John's International, Inc., Cheyenne, WY, pg. 1076
Sinclair, Joy M., Controller--Sinclair Printing & Litho, Inc., Los Angeles, CA, pg. 1008
Singletary, Bill, Controller--Cole of California, Los Angeles, CA, pg. 1079
Sink, Joseph S., Jr., Controller--Cooperheat, Inc., Piscataway, NJ, pg. 283
Sircy, Robert, Controller--Southwestern/Great American Inc., Nashville, TN, pg. 1023
Sitter, James J., Sec. & Controller--Plastek Group, Erie, PA, pg. 874
Sizemore, Dennis, V.P. & Controller--Summa Corporation, Las Vegas, NV, pg. 1057
Skamoto, Lester, Controller--Isemoto Contracting Co. Ltd., Hilo, HI, pg. 582
Skeffington, Edward F., Jr., Sr. V.P. & Controller--Revlon, Inc., New York, NY, pg. 696
Skelton, Rick, Controller--T & S Brass & Bronze Works, Inc., Travelers Rest, SC, pg. 1074
Skinner, Mark, Controller--Macklanburg-Duncan Co., Oklahoma City, OK, pg. 697
Skinner, Marlise C., Controller--Eastway Delivery Service of Houston, Inc., Houston, TX, pg. 364
Sklenicka, George, Sr. V.P.-Admin. & Controller--Vienna Sausage Mfg. Co., Chicago, IL, pg. 1151
Slade, William, Controller--Melling Forging Company, Lansing, MI, pg. 102
Slagle, Kathryn, Controller--Aydlotte & Cartwright, Inc., Atlanta, GA, pg. 103
Slamp, Jim, Controller--Ivex Packaging Corporation, Lincolnshire, IL, pg. 583
Slattery, John, Controller--Diagraph Corporation, Earth City, MO, pg. 335
Sleath, Alan, Controller--Sun Hill Industries, Stamford, CT, pg. 1059
Sledge, Brian, Controller--Utilities Construction Co., Inc. Of South Carolina, Charleston, SC, pg. 1141
Sloan, Ben, Asst. V.P. & Controller, Atlas Van Lines--Atlas Van Lines, Inc., Evansville, IN, pg. 96
Sloan, John E., Controller--Detroit Coil Company, Ferndale, MI, pg. 333
Slyman, J.K., Controller--Kleer Pak Corporation, Berwick, PA, pg. 635
Smaldone, Dennis, Comptroller & Asst. Sec.--Loft's Seeds, Inc., Bound Brook, NJ, pg. 681
Small, George, V.P. & Controller--Franklin Sports Industries, Stoughton, MA, pg. 429
Small, Stanley R., V.P. & Controller--Manhattan Electric Cable Corporation, Rye, NY, pg. 370
Smarto, Michael G., Controller--Tippins Incorporated, Pittsburgh, PA, pg. 1099
Smeenge, James J., Sec., Treas. & Comptroller--Amick Construction Ltd., Orlando, FL, pg. 67
Smith, Andra, Controller--JM Family Enterprises Inc., Deerfield Beach, FL, pg. 584
Smith, Dan, Comptroller--Montgomery, Zukerman, Davis, Inc., Indianapolis, IN, pg. 768
Smith, Darrell, Controller--Small Tube Products Co., Inc., Altoona, PA, pg. 1010
Smith, David R., Controller--Jerrico, Inc., Lexington, KY, pg. 229
Smith, Ellen M., Chief Fin. Officer & Comptroller--Transco Inc., Chicago, IL, pg. 1106
Smith, Gary A., V.P.-Distr. & Controller--Parisian, Inc., Birmingham, AL, pg. 848
Smith, Jack, Controller--Schaedler Brothers, Inc., Harrisburg, PA, pg. 974
Smith, Janet, Controller--Capitol Group, Springfield, IL, pg. 215
Smith, Jerry, Chief Fin. Officer & Controller--Coble Dairy Products Co-op, Lexington, NC, pg. 257
Smith, Kathleen, Controller--Algood Food Company, Louisville, KY, pg. 34
Smith, Patrick F., V.P & Controller--John Hancock Variable Life Insurance Co., Boston, MA, pg. 596
Smith, Priscilla, Controller--Anthony Forest Products Co., Inc., El Dorado, AR, pg. 77
Smith, Robert Lewis, Treas., Sec. & Controller--Hankins Lumber Company, Inc., Grenada, MS, pg. 505
Smith, Sharon A., Controller--Golden State Mutual Life Insurance Company, Los Angeles, CA, pg. 467
Smith, Walter C., Controller--Carlson, DelGaldo, Hoag, Matthei Advertising, Inc., Stamford, CT, pg. 222
Smith, William, Chief Fin. Officer, Treas. & Controller--Hoffritz for Cutlery, New York, NY, pg. 538
Snelling, Randy, Controller--Locus Computing Corp., Inglewood, CA, pg. 680
Snider, John, V.P.-Fin.--Hardware Wholesalers, Inc., Fort Wayne, IN, pg. 508
Snow, Barbara, Controller--Rhodes, Inc., Atlanta, GA, pg. 931
Snowden, David, Jr., Controller--Tarco, North Little Rock, AR, pg. 1078
Snyder, James M., Controller--Syracuse Supply Company, Syracuse, NY, pg. 1070
Snyder, Lance, Controller--McLaughlin Mfg. Company, Greenville, SC, pg. 731
Sobota, John J., Controller--CC Industries, Inc., Chicago, IL, pg. 199
Sobotik, Mark, V.P. & Controller--Alamo Industrial Group, San Antonio, TX, pg. 29
Soccio, Matthew, Controller--Empire Kosher Poultry, Inc., Mifflintown, PA, pg. 379
Sodestrom, Dirk, Controller--Western Temporary Services, Inc., Walnut Creek, CA, pg. 1181
Sokolowski, Anthony M., Controller--Jordan Tamraz Caruso Advertising, Inc., Chicago, IL, pg. 605
Sokup, Larry, Controller--J.H. Larson Electrical Company, Golden Valley, MN, pg. 659
Solomon, Peter, Controller--Del Taco, Inc., Costa Mesa, CA, pg. 325
Solomon, Terry, Controller--Best Western International, Inc., Phoenix, AZ, pg. 146
Solove, Sandra M., Chief Fin. Officer & Controller--Champion Boxed Beef, Denver, CO, pg. 238
Sommers, Michael, Controller--Cosmos Communications, Inc., Long Island City, NY, pg. 288
Somodi, Thomas, Controller--Albert Trostel & Sons Co., West Allis, WI, pg. 1116
Sonricker, Thomas K., Controller--Ferguson Electric Construction Co., Inc., Buffalo, NY, pg. 406
Soro, Linda, V.P., Comptroller--Slater Hanft Martin, Inc., New York, NY, pg. 1010
Soto-Castroman, Bebe, Controller--Horlick Levin Advertising Inc., Los Angeles, CA, pg. 544
Sou, Betty, Controller--Oroamerica, Inc., Burbank, CA, pg. 830
Soukup, George, Controller--Frankel & Company, Chicago, IL, pg. 429
Sourdiff, Jerald, Sr. V.P. & Controller--Lutheran Brotherhood, Minneapolis, MN, pg. 688
Sousoures, Chris, V.P.-Fin. & Controller--Cox Hobbies, Inc., Corona, CA, pg. 294
Soust, Dianna, V.P. & Controller--GNWC Wire, Cable & Network Producers, Downers Grove, IL, pg. 440
Southard, J. James, V.P., Controller & Treas.--Hoover Group, Inc., Alpharetta, GA, pg. 543
Sovinsky, Steven G., Controller--DeMaria Building Co. Inc., Novi, MI, pg. 327
Sowerby, Richard, Controller--Elliott Company, Jeannette, PA, pg. 378
Spafford, David, Asst. Controller--Tom Thumb Food & Drugs, Inc., Dallas, TX, pg. 912
Sparduto, John, Controller--Warren Properties, Rancho Santa Fe, CA, pg. 1165
Sparks, Christopher, Controller--John Burnham & Co., San Diego, CA, pg. 194
Sparks, Gary, Controller--Trauth Dairy Inc., Newport, KY, pg. 1108
Speas, John, Corp. Controller--Globe Business Furniture, Inc., Hendersonville, TN, pg. 463
Spence, Jeffrey E., Chm. Bd., Pres., Controller & Chief Exec. & Fin. Officer--Controlled Systems of Wisconsin, Inc., Nashotah, WI, pg. 281
Spencer, Colleen M., Controller--Marketing Displays International, Inc., Farmington Hills, MI, pg. 709
Speridakos, John D., Controller--ESSTAR Incorporated, New Haven, CT, pg. 361
Speridakos, John D., Controller--Essex Industries, New Haven, CT, pg. 361
Spielberger, Thomas, Controller--Jordan Industries, Inc., Deerfield, IL, pg. 604
Spiewak, Roy, Controller & Import Mgr.--I. Spiewak & Sons, Inc., New York, NY, pg. 1031
Spirko, Ed, Controller--Stanbee Company, Inc., Carlstadt, NJ, pg. 1035
Spitz, Randy J., Treas., Sec. & Controller--Hicks Oil-Hicks Gas, Inc., Roberts, IL, pg. 533
Spivey, Katherine, Comptroller--Carse Oil Co. Inc., Orlando, FL, pg. 225
Spivey, Richard, Controller--Sunnyland Refining Co., Inc., Birmingham, AL, pg. 616
Sponseller, Bob, V.P. & Controller--Golden West Broadcasters, Los Angeles, CA, pg. 467
Spowart, Jay R., V.P.-Fin. & Corp. Sec.--PhoneMate, Inc., Torrance, CA, pg. 869
Spradlin, Steve, Controller--American Ball Manufacturing, Carrollton, TX, pg. 890
Spratt, Lee, Controller--Blue Diamond Growers, Sacramento, CA, pg. 160
Springer, Branch J., V.P., Chief Fin. Officer, Treas. & Sec.--Abbey Etna Machine Company, Perrysburg, OH, pg. 9
St. Martin, William C., Controller--Morgan Construction Company, Worcester, MA, pg. 769
Stablein, L.R., Controller--Quintana Petroleum Corp., Houston, TX, pg. 905
Stack, Mark C., Controller--A & S Tribal Industries, Poplar, MT, pg. 1
Stahl, Edwin E., Controller--Microflect Company, Inc., Salem, OR, pg. 749
Stalkfleet, Rick, V.P., Controller & Dir.-Engrg.--Rauland-Borg Corporation, Skokie, IL, pg. 914
Stamp, Robert L., V.P.-Fin., Treas. & Controller--The Gates Corporation, Denver, CO, pg. 445
Stanford, Bob, Controller--Howard Industries, Inc., Milford, IL, pg. 547
Stanger, Rodney, V.P., Controller & Chief Fin. Officer--Allmetal Screw Products Corp., Edgewood, NY, pg. 40
Staplemin, Tim, Controller--J.H. Findorff & Son, Inc., Madison, WI, pg. 411
Staples, William, V.P., Treas. & Controller--Rodney Hunt Company, Orange, MA, pg. 553
Starcevich, John, Controller--The Jupiter Corporation, Chicago, IL, pg. 609
Starley, Barbara, Controller & Dir.-Personnel--Martz & Wadas, Scottsdale, AZ, pg. 716
Stasiewicz, David, Controller--Convenient Food Mart, Inc., Schaumburg, IL, pg. 281
Staszak, Stan, Controller--Spatz & Co., Northbrook, IL, pg. 1026
Stearns, Whit, Controller--Schein Pharmaceutical, Inc., Port Washington, NY, pg. 975
Steck, Vicki, Controller--Townsend & Bottum, Inc., Ann Arbor, MI, pg. 1104
Steele, James E., Sr. V.P. & Controller--Landmark Hotel Corporation, Topeka, KS, pg. 656
Stefano, Brian R., Chief Fin. Officer & Controller--Peter Pan Bus Lines, Inc., Springfield, MA, pg. 864
Stegall, Charles N., Controller--Stowe-Pharr Mills, Inc., McAdenville, NC, pg. 1052
Stein, David, V.P.-Fin., Chief Fin. Officer & Controller--T. J. Cinnamons Ltd., Kansas City, MO, pg. 1073
Stein, Donald L., V.P. & Controller--Gulf States Paper Corporation, Tuscaloosa, AL, pg. 494
Steinberg, Jack, Controller--De Francisci Machine Corp.(Demaco), Ridgewood, NY, pg. 321
Steinberg, Jan, Controller--Palm Iron & Bridge Works, Inc., Sacramento, CA, pg. 843
Steiner, Donald, Controller--Yoder Oil Company Inc., Elkhart, IN, pg. 1208
Steinhardt, J., Comptroller--Monarch Luggage Co. Inc., Brooklyn, NY, pg. 765
Steinig, Stephen N., Sr. V.P. & Controller & Chief Actuary--New York Life Insurance Company, New York, NY, pg. 802
Steinrock, Timothy, Comptroller--Carlos R. Leffler Inc., Richland, PA, pg. 666
Stephens, J. Michael, Controller, Div. Dir.-Admin. Services & Personnel Dir.--Goodwill Industries of America, Inc., Bethesda, MD, pg. 471
Stephens, Kathy, V.P. & Controller--Tollman/Hundley Hotels, Valhalla, NY, pg. 1100
Stern, Jonathan H., V.P. & Controller--GAF Corporation, Wayne, NJ, pg. 438
Stern, Jonathan H., V.P. & Controller--GAF Broadcasting Co., Inc., New York, NY, pg. 438
Stevens, B. Glynn, Comptroller--The Auchter Company, Jacksonville, FL, pg. 98
Stevens, David, Comptroller--Scott U.S.A., Ketchum, ID, pg. 983
Stevens, Doris E., Controller--Trimtex Co. Inc., Williamsport, PA, pg. 1113
Stevens, Fran, Controller--Star Video Entertainment, L.P., Jersey City, NJ, pg. 1040
Stevenson, Allan J., Sr. V.P., Chief Fin. Officer & Controller--Parsons Brinckerhoff Inc., New York, NY, pg. 850
Stewart, Marcia, Controller--Walker & Associates, Inc., Memphis, TN, pg. 1159
Stewart, William T., Controller--Master Collectors Inc., Atlanta, GA, pg. 719
Stievater, James E., V.P. & Controller--Steelcase Inc., Grand Rapids, MI, pg. 1044
Stiles, John, V.P., Admin. & Controller--Willoughby's, New York, NY, pg. 1193
Stiles, Sandra E., V.P. & Controller--Random House, Inc., New York, NY, pg. 19
Stillwagon, Greg, Controller--Emson Research, Inc., Bridgeport, CT, pg. 380
Stimpson, James R., Treas., Controller & Sec.--Channellock, Inc., Meadville, PA, pg. 239
Stimson, D.W., Controller--Crystal Cream & Butter Company, Sacramento, CA, pg. 303
Stine, John, Controller--Darling-Delaware Co., Inc., Irving, TX, pg. 315
Stock, Joyce, Controller--Siemer Milling Company, Teutopolis, IL, pg. 1002
Stocker, Mary Todd, V.P.-Fin. & Controller--The Acacia Group, Washington, DC, pg. 10
Stoegbauer, William J., Treas.--Jewelers Mutual Insurance Company, Neenah, WI, pg. 593
Stofka, John, Controller--Crispin & Porter Advertising Inc., Miami, FL, pg. 299
Stohler, Roger, Controller--Hoboken Wood Flooring Corporation, Wayne, NJ, pg. 537
Stoker, Gary, Controller--Celestial Seasonings, Boulder, CO, pg. 231
Stokes, John E., Controller--Riviana Foods Inc., Houston, TX, pg. 937
Stoll, James E., Controller--Hillman Company, Pittsburgh, PA, pg. 535
Stoll, Joseph, Controller--Sid Harvey Inc., Valley Stream, NY, pg. 515
Stone, Larry, Controller--Gates Energy Products, Inc., Alachua, FL, pg. 445
Stone, Lynn, Controller--Celebrity Boats, Inc., Benton, IL, pg. 609
Stone, Sylvia, Controller--H.O. Penn Machinery Co. Inc., Armonk, NY, pg. 857

Stooksbury, Hugh T., Controller--Pride Oil Co., Inc., Knoxville, TN, pg. 622
Storck, Bill, Controller--Fike Corporation, Blue Springs, MO, pg. 409
Storms, Tom, Controller & Dir.-Taxation--Rodale Press, Inc., Emmaus, PA, pg. 942
Story, Dirk, Controller--American Machinery Corp., Orlando, FL, pg. 22
Story, Kendra A., Treas. & Controller--ABC Supply Company, Inc., Beloit, WI, pg. 2
Stout, Everett E., Pres., Chief Exec. Officer, Chief Fin. Officer & Controller--Metaltech, Inc., Kirkwood, MO, pg. 742
Stovall, James, Controller--SRS Technologies, Newport Beach, CA, pg. 964
Stowe, Wilford, Controller & Sec.--JPS Converter & Industrial Corp., Greenville, SC, pg. 586
Strachan, Randy, Chief Fin. Officer, V.P. & Controller--Ziebart Canada, Inc., Downsview,, Canada, pg. 1218
Strasma, Edward J., Exec. V.P., Chief Fin. Officer & Controller--Interstate Producers Livestock Association, Peoria, IL, pg. 580
Strathman, Paul, Controller--Spires Restaurants Inc., Orange, CA, pg. 1031
Strawn, Timothy, V.P. & Controller--Hatteras Yachts, High Point, NC, pg. 758
Strayer, Norman, Controller--JII/Sales Promotion Associates, Inc., Coshocton, OH, pg. 604
Streamer, David, Controller--W&F Manufacturing Corporation, Inc., Buffalo, NY, pg. 1155
Stricko, Nancy, V.P., Controller--Ammirati & Puris Inc., New York, NY, pg. 67
Stringer, Larry, Controller--Dal-Tile Corp., Dallas, TX, pg. 312
Strong, Curt, Controller--Zieman Manufacturing Company, Inc., Whittier, CA, pg. 1218
Strong, Gregory S., V.P.-Fin. Mngmt.--The Minnesota Mutual Life Insurance Company, Saint Paul, MN, pg. 757
Strotman, Jim, Controller--The Wm. Powell Company, Cincinnati, OH, pg. 882
Struglia, Michael M., Controller--Korman Co., Trevose, PA, pg. 642
Struzzi, Peter, V.P. & Controller--The Kobacker Company & Affiliates, Columbus, OH, pg. 638
Stuckey, Ray, Controller--Harp's Food Stores, Inc., Springdale, AR, pg. 510
Stump, Ken, Controller--Brooks Beverage Management, Inc., Holland, MI, pg. 179
Sturgeon, John A., Sr. Exec. V.P. & Gen. Comptroller--Mutual of Omaha Insurance Company, Omaha, NE, pg. 779
Sturgeon, John A., Sr. Exec. V.P. & Gen. Comptroller--Mutual of Omaha, Omaha, NE, pg. 779
Subranni, Robert, P., Controller--Peirce-Phelps, Inc., Philadelphia, PA, pg. 855
Suherman, Timotheus, Controller--BSB Indonesia, Jakarta,, Indonesia, pg. 110
Sula, James, Controller--International Jensen Inc., Lincolnshire, IL, pg. 578
Sulich, Fred J., Controller--White Hen Pantry, Inc., Elmhurst, IL, pg. 1185
Sullivan, Brian, Controller & Sec.--Applied Solar Energy Corporation, City of Industry, CA, pg. 79
Sullivan, Debra, Controller--Johnstown Knitting Mill Co., Johnstown, NY, pg. 602
Sullivan, Gerald, Controller--DeMert & Dougherty, Inc., Westchester, IL, pg. 328
Sullivan, John L., Treas., Sec. & Controller--Totsy Manufacturing Company, Inc., Holyoke, MA, pg. 1103
Sullivan, Terry, Controller--Golub & Co., Chicago, IL, pg. 469
Summerlin, W.C., Controller--Carolina Steel Corporation, Greensboro, NC, pg. 223
Summers, C.D., V.P. & Controller--Stuart-Ironsides, Inc., Willowbrook, IL, pg. 1054
Summers, Cheryl, Controller & Asst. Sec.--McCall Oil & Chemical Corp., Portland, OR, pg. 726
Surace, Lee, V.P. & Controller--L.L. Bean, Inc., Freeport, ME, pg. 648
Surma, Ronald F., Chief Fin. Officer & Controller--Processed Plastic Company, Montgomery, IL, pg. 892
Suville, Ralph, Controller--Hercules Tire & Rubber Company, Findlay, OH, pg. 531
Swanson, Richard, Controller--Metron Steel Corp., Chicago, IL, pg. 744
Swanson, Ron, Controller--Alkota Cleaning Systems, Inc., Alcester, SD, pg. 34
Sweany, Larry, Controller--American United Life Insurance Company, Indianapolis, IN, pg. 65
Sweeney, Gerald, Controller--AMD Industries Inc., Cicero, IL, pg. 5
Sweeney, Stephen J., Controller--Parsons & Whittemore Enterprises, Rye Brook, NY, pg. 850
Sweeney, Tom, Treas. & Controller--Aetna Industries, Inc., Center Line, MI, pg. 23
Swink, J.M., Controller--Inland Tool & Manufacturing, Inc., Detroit, MI, pg. 1194
Swirsky, Morton, Chief Oper. Officer & Controller--Atlantic to Pacific Bedding Corp., Bronx, NY, pg. 95
Swissa, David, Controller & Chief Fin. Officer--Dan's Supreme Super Markets Inc., Hempstead, NY, pg. 314
Symon, Robert J., V.P. & Controller--Triangle Pacific Corporation, Dallas, TX, pg. 1112
Szabo, Bill, Controller--Niagara Cutter, Inc., North Tonawanda, NY, pg. 805
Szabo, Frank C., V.P. & Controller--First Federal Savings and Loan Assn. of Rochester, Rochester, NY, pg. 413
Szeglin, Irene, Controller--Enterprise Press, Inc., New York, NY, pg. 382
Szews, Charles L., Controller--Fort Howard Corporation, Green Bay, WI, pg. 425
Szywala, Dennis, Controller--Graphic Controls, Corp., Buffalo, NY, pg. 478
Tabano, Louis, V.P.-Acctng.--Alva/Amco Pharmacal Companies, Inc., Chicago, IL, pg. 46
Taglianetti, Richard, Controller--Helmsley Enterprises, Inc., New York, NY, pg. 527
Takata, Ryoko, Controller--Watt Industries, Santa Monica, CA, pg. 1168
Talbott, Thomas V., V.P. & Controller--Tracor, Inc., Austin, TX, pg. 1104
Talbott, Thomas V., V.P.-Fin. & Grp. Controller--Tracor Applied Sciences Inc., Rockville, MD, pg. 1105
Tallerico, Sam, III, V.P. & Controller--Harris and Love, Inc., Salt Lake City, UT, pg. 512
Talmage, Joseph M., Controller--Sunshine Biscuits, Inc., Woodbridge, NJ, pg. 439
Tang, Sam, Controller--NDAP/TMP Worldwide, Toronto,, Canada, pg. 1074
Tansellie, James, Comptroller--Cross Motors Corp., Louisville, KY, pg. 300
Tansey, James, Comptroller--Jaydon Incorporated, Rock Island, IL, pg. 590
Tanzola, Anthony J., V.P., Controller & Admin. Officer--ARA Group, Philadelphia, PA, pg. 5
Taretto, Len, Controller--Medico Industries, Inc., Wilkes-Barre, PA, pg. 735
Tarreto, Len, Controller--Action Lift, Wilkes-Barre, PA, pg. 735
Tarzwell, Jeff, Controller--Sasco/Valley Electric, Mountain View, CA, pg. 972
Tate, Chris, Asst. Controller--Ingram Merchandising Service Inc., La Vergne, TN, pg. 569
Taub, Carl, Controller--Main Brothers Oil Company, Inc., Albany, NY, pg. 702
Taylor, C.J., V.P. & Controller--S. C. Johnson & Son, Inc., Racine, WI, pg. 599
Taylor, Chuck, Chief Fin. Officer & Controller--Maywood, Inc., Amarillo, TX, pg. 725
Taylor, Harold L., Controller--RNL Facilities Corporation, Denver, CO, pg. 907
Taylor, Robert W., V.P. & Controller--Southern States Cooperative, Inc., Richmond, VA, pg. 1022
Teague, Roger D., Sec. & Controller--Worsley Companies Inc., Wilmington, NC, pg. 1204
Teague, Wayne, Controller--Arcata Graphics Fairfield Inc., Fairfield, PA, pg. 80
Tedesco, Mark S., Asst. V.P. & Controller--National Health Care Affiliates, Inc., Buffalo, NY, pg. 791
Teicher, Lawrence, Controller--Monitor Aerospace Corporation, Amityville, NY, pg. 765
Ten, Lim Cheng, Controller--American Furniture Company, Albuquerque, NM, pg. 55
Tengelly, Owen, Treas. & Controller--Walled Lake Door Company, Phoenix, AZ, pg. 1161
Terborg, Glenn, Controller--Humphrey Products Company, Kalamazoo, MI, pg. 553
Terrell, Dan, Controller--Peebles, Inc., South Hill, VA, pg. 855
Terrell, John, Controller--Del American Properties, Inc., Maitland, FL, pg. 325
Terrill, Charles, Controller--Deitsch Plastics Company, West Haven, CT, pg. 325
Terzigne, Dale, Controller--Collman Graphics, Inc., Baltimore, MD, pg. 263
Tessman, Tom, Controllor--Penda Corporation, Portage, WI, pg. 857
Teter, Dennis, Controller--Mid-Kansas Co-op Association, Moundridge, KS, pg. 750
Tews, Michael V., V.P. & Controller--John Roberts Company, Minneapolis, MN, pg. 938
Thibault, Chuck, Controller--Lazy Days R V Center, Inc., Tampa, FL, pg. 663
Thomas-Montgomery, J., V.P. & Controller--Contran Corporation, Dallas, TX, pg. 281
Thomas, Elmer A., Comptroller--Affiliated Food Distributors, Scranton, PA, pg. 23
Thomas, Joe, Treas.--Paramount Foods Inc., Louisville, KY, pg. 848
Thomas, John, V.P. & Controller--Blue Cross and Blue Shield of Oklahoma, Tulsa, OK, pg. 159
Thomas, John R., Controller--Judd's Incorporated, Washington, DC, pg. 608
Thomas, Judy, Controller--Edmund Scientific Company, Barrington, NJ, pg. 369
Thomas, Kevin, Controller--Econocom-USA Inc., Memphis, TN, pg. 367
Thomason, Joel, Controller--The Pepper Companies, Inc., Chicago, IL, pg. 859
Thompson, Ann, Comptroller--American Fast Print, Limited, Spartanburg, SC, pg. 52
Thompson, Curtis A., V.P.-Operational Finance & Controller--K-III Communications Corporation, New York, NY, pg. 610
Thompson, D. Kathryn, Controller--Great Lakes Bancorp, Ann Arbor, MI, pg. 480
Thompson, G.E., Controller--Lester Coggins Trucking, Okahumpka, FL, pg. 259
Thompson, George, Controller--Performance Contractors Inc., Baton Rouge, LA, pg. 861
Thompson, Lonnie J., Controller--Howell Instruments Corp., Fort Worth, TX, pg. 547
Thompson, Michael G., Corp. Controller--RAYOVAC Corporation, Madison, WI, pg. 915
Thompson, P.C., Controller--S & C Electric Company, Chicago, IL, pg. 958
Thompson, R.T., Controller--MidWest Body Corporation, Paris, IL, pg. 752
Thompson, Robert L., Controller--McCourt Label Co., Lewis Run, PA, pg. 727
Thompson, Ronnie D., Controller--Bearden Lumber Company, Inc., Bearden, AR, pg. 129
Thompson, Tony, Controller--Fotheringham & Associates, Salt Lake City, UT, pg. 427
Thomson, Doug, Dir.-Fin. & Accounting--Skyway Freight Systems, Inc., Watsonville, CA, pg. 1009
Thomson, Robert, Controller--Continental Plastic Card Co., Coral Springs, FL, pg. 280
Thornton, Bruce, V.P. & Controller--Employers Insurance of Wausau a Mutual Co., Wausau, WI, pg. 380
Thornton, Bruce, V.P. & Controller--Employers Insurance of Wausau a Mutual Co., Wausau, WI, pg. 795
Throm, Thomas, Controller--Golden State Foods Corp., Pasadena, CA, pg. 466
Tierney, William E., Jr., Controller--Facemate Corporation, Chicopee, MA, pg. 396
Tilton, Janet M., Controller--Brittany Corporation, Cleveland, OH, pg. 177
Tilton, Kenneth L., Exec. V.P. & Controller--Texas Commerce Bancshares, Inc., Houston, TX, pg. 1089
Tinka, M.L., Controller--Treaty Co., Greenville, OH, pg. 1109
Tipkin, Hubert, Controller--Philadelphia Coca-Cola Bottling Co., Philadelphia, PA, pg. 866
Titlebaum, Kenneth H., Controller--Kendall Healthcare Products Co., Mansfield, MA, pg. 622
Tochterman, Florence, Controller--International Components Corporation, Melville, NY, pg. 576
Todd, Curtis, V.P., Controller--Omaha Creative Group, Omaha, NE, pg. 825
Todd, Nancy, Controller--Farago Advertising, New York, NY, pg. 399
Todres, Harry, Controller--Roselle Paper Co., Inc., Roselle, NJ, pg. 948
Tomas, Gary, Controller--Richmond Screw Anchor Company, Fort Worth, TX, pg. 933
Tomek, Allen G., V.P. & Controller--Lykes Bros. Steamship Co., Inc., New Orleans, LA, pg. 688
Tompkins, J.R., Controller--M. D. Moody & Sons Inc., Jacksonville, FL, pg. 768
Toovey, Doug, Controller--Wilsey Bennett Co., San Francisco, CA, pg. 1193
Topmiller, Tom, Controller--Vinylweld Division, Chicago, IL, pg. 857
Torpie, Steve, Exec. V.P. & Controller--Hollister Advertising, New Providence, NJ, pg. 539
Torres, Rafael, V.P., Controller, Asst. Treas. & Asst. Sec.--Pueblo International, Inc., Pompano Beach, FL, pg. 899
Tortora, Dennis J., Controller & Asst. Treas.--Steinway & Sons, Long Island City, NY, pg. 1046
Tortorello, Peter W., V.P. & Controller--J.M. Huber Corporation, Edison, NJ, pg. 550
Toten, Tom, Controller--K & R Delivery, Inc., Hinsdale, IL, pg. 610
Toto, Joseph P., Controller--Karnak Corporation, Clark, NJ, pg. 617
Tousignant, Normand, Exec. V.P. & Controller--Harris Drury Cohen, Fort Lauderdale, FL, pg. 511
Townsend, Joseph, Controller--Ranir Corporation, Grand Rapids, MI, pg. 912
Townsend, Wayne, Chief Fin. Officer & Controller--Hygeia Dairy Co., Inc., Harlingen, TX, pg. 557
Trabold, Marie, Comptroller--Shapson Gero & Sommers, Inc., Philadelphia, PA, pg. 995
Trabucco, Robert, Sr. V.P., Chief Fin. Officer, & Treas.--Lechmere, Inc., Woburn, MA, pg. 665
Tracey, Steve, Controller--Chesco Products, Inc., Beatrice, NE, pg. 64
Trapani, Nick, Controller--Compuware Corporation, Farmington Hills, MI, pg. 271
Trares, Kevin, Controller--Midway Products Corporation, Monroe, MI, pg. 751
Travis,Susan, Controller--C-Line Products, Inc., Des Plaines, IL, pg. 198
Treacy, Dave, Controller--The Medical Protective Company, Fort Wayne, IN, pg. 735
Trefelner, Shirley, Controller--Burrell Group, New Kensington, PA, pg. 195
Treinen, James M., Controller--Romac Industries, Inc., Seattle, WA, pg. 945
Tremelling, Terrance, Comptroller--Bel Air Markets, Sacramento, CA, pg. 133
Trent, Joe, Controller--Bob Montgomery Chevrolet/Honda, Louisville, KY, pg. 767
Treynor, Sam, Sec., Treas. & Controller--Peck Road Ford Truck Sales, Whittier, CA, pg. 854
Tribby, P. G., V.P. & Controller--Bradner Central Company, Chicago, IL, pg. 170
Trier, James, Controller--Paul Stuart, Inc., New York, NY, pg. 1054
Trimbath, Leroy, Controller--Dick Corporation, Large, PA, pg. 335
Triplett, Preston, V.P. & Controller--Brookshire Grocery, Tyler, TX, pg. 180
Tropsa, Jon E., Controller--Hargro Enterprises, Inc., Stamford, CT, pg. 509
Troutman, W. Wilson, Controller & Asst. Treas.--Industrial Coatings Group, Inc., Chicago, IL, pg. 566
Truchi, James, Chief Fin. Officer, Treas. & Controller--Trucchis Markets, Raynham, MA, pg. 1117
Truitt, Lynn T., V.P., Controller--Hall, Haerr, Peterson & Harney, Inc., Peoria, IL, pg. 501
Trupiano, James, Controller--Champion Aluminum Corporation, Syosset, NY, pg. 238
Tsacalis, William A., V.P. & Controller--Chiquita Brands International, Inc., Cincinnati, OH, pg. 53
Tschumper, D.F., Controller--Badger Construction Equipment Co., Insley Div., Winona, MN, pg. 113
Tsou, Charles, Controller--Nady Systems, Inc., Emeryville, CA, pg. 783
Tucker, Lee, Controller--Douglas Steel Fabricating Corporation, Lansing, MI, pg. 347
Tucker, Sharon, Controller--Medical Laboratory Automation, Inc., Pleasantville, NY, pg. 735
Tukiendorf, T., Comptroller--United Coatings, Inc., Kankakee, IL, pg. 1131
Tummers, Nick, Controller--Sun Diamond Growers of California, Pleasanton, CA, pg. 1058
Turpin, Jayne A., Controller--Inverness Corp., Fair Lawn, NJ, pg. 581

Turret, Bernard, Controller & Chief Fin. Officer--Polarome Mfg. Co. Inc., Jersey City, NJ, pg. 878
Tushar, C.P., Treas. & Controller--Oak Rubber Company, Ravenna, OH, pg. 819
Tuthill, Janet, Controller--Joiner Rowland Serio Koeppel, Dallas, TX, pg. 602
Twede, Floyd, Controller--Air Industries Corporation, Garden Grove, CA, pg. 27
Tyler, Terese, Asst. Controller--Rundel Products, Inc., Portland, OR, pg. 956
Udasin, Seth, Controller--The Children's Place Retail Stores, Inc., Pine Brook, NJ, pg. 247
Uemura, Ken, Treas.--Persis Corporation, Honolulu, HI, pg. 863
Underhill, James F., Controller--McJunkin Corporation, Charleston, WV, pg. 730
Underwood, Bob, Controller--Fred B. Johnston Company, Inc., Chapin, SC, pg. 601
Unruh, V. Paul, V.P. & Controller--Bechtel Group, Inc., San Francisco, CA, pg. 130
Urban, William, V.P. & Controller--Wells Fargo Alarm Services, King of Prussia, PA, pg. 166
Urgo, Chris, Controller--PetCare Plus, Inc., Addison, IL, pg. 863
Vail, Dennis, Comptroller--Kendale Industries, Inc., Valley View, OH, pg. 622
Valenti, Peter, Controller--SRI International, Menlo Park, CA, pg. 964
Vallis, Mary Anne, Controller--Seventeen Magazine, New York, NY, pg. 611
Van Bogart, T. J., Controller & Asst. Sec.--Nutech, Inc., San Jose, CA, pg. 817
Van de Visser, Larry W., Controller--Dan River Inc., Danville, VA, pg. 313
Van Hook, Donald W., Controller--Strahman Valves, Inc., Florham Park, NJ, pg. 1052
Van Luven, G.A., Vice Chm., Chief Fin. Officer, Treas. & Controller--The Gage Company, Pittsburgh, PA, pg. 441
Vance, Craig, V.P., Controller--Culver & Associates, Inc., Omaha, NE, pg. 304
Vander Wey, Rita A., Comptroller--The National Bank of Sussex County, Branchville, NJ, pg. 534
Vanderburg, Scott, Controller--Russell Stadelman & Company, Germantown, TN, pg. 1034
Vandermeer, Diane C., Controller--Eastman Machine Co., Buffalo, NY, pg. 364
Varcalli, Patricia, Controller--Evans Industries, Inc., Detroit, MI, pg. 390
Vasel, Gregory M., V.P. & Treas.--Schiavone Construction Co., Secaucus, NJ, pg. 976
Vater, Thomas A., Controller & Sec.--Thompson Medical Company, Inc., West Palm Beach, FL, pg. 1094
Vaughn, Victor, Controller--Ancra Corporation, Hawthorne, CA, pg. 72
Vavrek, Michael, Controller--Fairview Construction, Inc, Auburn Hills, MI, pg. 397
Vega, Fernando, Controller--RNF Media Corporation Inc., Beverly Hills, CA, pg. 907
Venditti, J.M., Controller--J.M. Huber, Printing Ink Div., Edison, NJ, pg. 550
Venneman, Nicholas, Comptroller--Aurora Packing Co., Inc., North Aurora, IL, pg. 98
Venuti, Kenneth, Controller--Farm Journal, Inc., Philadelphia, PA, pg. 401
Verbrugge, Paul, Controller--WW Engineering & Science Inc., Grand Rapids, MI, pg. 1058
Verdoorn, Thomas, V.P. & Controller--Land O'Lakes, Inc., Arden Hills, MN, pg. 653
Verhage, Ron, Controller--Lee Grocery Company, Everett, WA, pg. 665
Verville, N.J., V.P., Treas. & Controller--B-E Holdings Inc., South Milwaukee, WI, pg. 106
Vetali, Vicki M., Treas. & Controller--Excelsior Manufacturing & Supply Corp., Itasca, IL, pg. 392
Vetere, Nicholas, Controller--Fishman & Tobin, Inc., Philadelphia, PA, pg. 415
Vic, Tom, V.P.-Fin. & Controller--World Dryer Corp., Berkeley, IL, pg. 1027
Vidal, K.J., Controller--Cairns & Brother, Inc., Clifton, NJ, pg. 207
Vied, B. Joe, Resident Controller--San Antonio Light, San Antonio, TX, pg. 524
Vieira, Rod, Controller--Lindsay Olive Growers, Lindsay, CA, pg. 676
Vietneer, Judy, Controller--Structural Industries, Inc., Hicksville, NY, pg. 1054
Vilagi, John, Controller & Chief Fin. Officer--Pacific Envelope Company, Anaheim, CA, pg. 840
Vitale, Judi A., Controller--Brock Control Systems, Inc., Atlanta, GA, pg. 178
Vitro, Thomas D., Dir.-Data Processing & Controller--Springborn Laboratories, Inc., Enfield, CT, pg. 1033
Vodily, Merril, Controller--Rolled Steel Products Corporation, Los Angeles, CA, pg. 944
Voelkel, Harold G., Controller--V.G.S. Corp. d/b/a Southland Oil Company, Jackson, MS, pg. 1141
Vogtman, Theodore W., Controller--Thomas & Betts Holdings, Inc., Memphis, TN, pg. 425
Volinski, Jack, Controller--The J. M. Ney Company, Bloomfield, CT, pg. 805
Vollan, James R., Controller & Chief Admin. Officer--The Flood Company, Hudson, OH, pg. 419
Von Haden, Shelley, Controller--Stark Candy Company, Pewaukee, WI, pg. 1123
Von Vital, Len, Controller--Decision Data Inc., Horsham, PA, pg. 323
Vondriska, Donald, Treas. & Controller--Bioproducts, Inc., Brecksville, OH, pg. 152
Vorhees, Ken, Controller--E Z Loader Boat Trailers, Inc., Spokane, WA, pg. 361
Wacnik, David J., Controller--Edgewood Tool & Manufacturing Company, Romulus, MI, pg. 368
Wade, Donnie, Controller, Treas. & Sec.--Goodpasture, Inc., Brownfield, TX, pg. 471
Wade, Mike, Controller--Tech Mold, Inc., Tempe, AZ, pg. 1083
Waggoner, Henry R., Controller & Asst. Sec.--Lakeside Industries, Redmond, WA, pg. 651
Wagner, Douglas A., Controller--Dothan Underwear, New York, NY, pg. 545
Wagner, George W., Chief Fin. Officer & Comptroller--Western Regional Off Track Betting, Batavia, NY, pg. 1181
Wagner, Sidney, Controller--House of Ronnie, Inc., New York, NY, pg. 546
Wait, Tim, Controller--UDL Laboratories, Inc., Rockford, IL, pg. 1072
Wakner, Kathy C., Asst. V.P.-Controller--American SelfCare Corporation, Columbus, GA, pg. 60
Walchirk, Nina, Controller--OMNI Superstores, Northlake, IL, pg. 344
Walde, Dave, Controller--D. M. Management Company, Hingham, MA, pg. 309
Waldman, Morris, Controller--Windsor Art Products, Inc., Pico Rivera, CA, pg. 1195
Walker, Baker, Treas., Controller, Sec. & Chief Fin. Officer--C. B. Ragland Company, Nashville, TN, pg. 909
Walker, Gary, Comptroller--Crooks Supermarket Inc., Nashville, TN, pg. 300
Walker, Kathy, Controller--Dana Communications, Inc., Hopewell, NJ, pg. 313
Walker, Philip R., Pres. & Chief Exec. Officer--Tennessee Farmers Co-op, La Vergne, TN, pg. 1087
Walker, Steven, Controller--McKean Oldsmobile Company, Pittsburgh, PA, pg. 730
Walker, Vernon W., V.P. & Comptroller--Blue Cross & Blue Shield of Texas, Inc., Richardson, TX, pg. 160
Walker, Vicki, Controller--The Heil Co., Chattanooga, TN, pg. 525
Wallace, Albert, V.P. & Controller--Georgia Iron Works Co., Grovetown, GA, pg. 453
Wallace, Chris, Controller--Doran Textiles Inc., Shelby, NC, pg. 346
Wallace, Chris, Controller--Doran Mill Co., Shelby, NC, pg. 346
Walsh, Brendan, Treas. & Controller--Monsey Products Company, Kimberton, PA, pg. 766
Walsh, Gary, Controller--Clayton, Williams & Sherwood, Inc., Newport Beach, CA, pg. 254
Walsh, James W., Controller--JRN, Inc., Columbia, TN, pg. 586
Walters, Jan, Controller--Moses Anshell, Inc., Phoenix, AZ, pg. 76
Walters, Thomas M., V.P. & Controller--Drummond Company, Inc., Jasper, AL, pg. 349
Walton, Bill R., Controller--Belk Stores Services Inc., Charlotte, NC, pg. 134
Walts, Loren W., Comptroller--Johnson Newspaper Corporation, Watertown, NY, pg. 598
Wandre, Bruce, Treas. & Controller--Crown Iron Works Company, Roseville, MN, pg. 302
Wanjek, Carl, Controller--Giles & Ransome, Inc., Bensalem, PA, pg. 458
Warady, Timothy S., Controller--Dentsply International Inc., York, PA, pg. 329
Ward, Richard L., V.P. & Controller--F.N. Burt Company, Inc., Buffalo, NY, pg. 195
Warner, Bob, V.P. & Controller--Newbridge Communications, New York, NY, pg. 611
Warner, Dottie, Controller--Stockton West Burkhart Inc., Cincinnati, OH, pg. 1050
Warner, Jeffrey D., V.P. & Controller--International Business Interiors Inc., Chicago, IL, pg. 575
Warner, Kathy, V.P.-Chief Fin. Officer--American SelfCare Corporation, Columbus, GA, pg. 60
Warren, Jim, Controller--HOH Associates, Alexandria, VA, pg. 882
Washatka, Mary Lou, Controller--The Copley Press, Inc., La Jolla, CA, pg. 284
Washko, John A., V.P. & Controller--Crown American Corporation, Johnstown, PA, pg. 301
Wassner, Judah, Controller--Arnav Industries, Inc., New York, NY, pg. 84
Waters, John, Controller--Consolidated Metco, Inc., Portland, OR, pg. 277
Watkins, Joe, V.P. & Controller--McLean Enterprises, Inc., Springfield, MO, pg. 731
Watkins, Kim A., Controller--Ohio Gas Company, Bryan, OH, pg. 822
Watkins, Timothy C., V.P. & Controller--Gilmore Bros., Inc., Kalamazoo, MI, pg. 459
Watson, Don, Controller--Northern Automotive Corporation, Phoenix, AZ, pg. 1118
Watson, Laura, Chief Fin. Officer & Controller--Pachmayr Gun Works Inc., Monrovia, CA, pg. 839
Watson, Neil, Controller--Mike Daugherty's Hurling Chevrolet, Inc., Sacramento, CA, pg. 555
Watson, Robbie, Controller--Binning's Building Products, Inc., Lexington, NC, pg. 151
Watson, Robert, Controller--S.T. Research, Newington, VA, pg. 964
Watts, Brian, V.P. & Controller--Educational Publishing Corporation, Oak Lawn, IL, pg. 369
Waxler, David, Controller--West Coast National Video, Philadelphia, PA, pg. 1177
Wear, Ray, Comptroller--Peterson Industries Inc., Decatur, AR, pg. 864
Weaver, Debbie, Controller--Royal Paper Box of California, Montebello, CA, pg. 953
Weaver, Robert L., V.P. & Controller--Cameron & Barkley Company, Inc., Charleston Heights, SC, pg. 212
Webb, Jerry, V.P.-Fin.--Tekra Corporation, New Berlin, WI, pg. 1084
Webb, Michael W., V.P., Controller & Asst. Treas.--Margo's La Mode, Inc., Dallas, TX, pg. 373
Webb, Robert D., Controller & Asst. Sec.--Lester B. Knight & Associates, Inc., Chicago, IL, pg. 637
Weber, R., Controller--Hobart Brothers Co., Troy, OH, pg. 536
Webne, Barry, Controller--Bettcher Manufacturing Corp., Cleveland, OH, pg. 148
Weeberg, Lynn, Controller--American Wyott Corporation, Cheyenne, WY, pg. 65
Weglarz, John, Controller--Pakula & Company, Chicago, IL, pg. 843
Wegleitner, Marcia, Controller--Plastech Corporation, Forest Lake, MN, pg. 874
Weimer, Larry, Controller--Porcelain Metals Corp., Louisville, KY, pg. 881
Weimer, Robert C., V.P. & Controller--Union City Body Company, Inc., Union City, IN, pg. 1128
Weinstein, Jeri, Comptroller--Easy Day Manufacturing Company, Inc., Holliston, MA, pg. 364
Weiss, Jim, Controller--Minstar, Inc., Minneapolis, MN, pg. 758
Weiss, Margaret, Controller--Save More Food Mart, Inc., Hobart, IN, pg. 973
Weiss, Michael, V.P.-Fin. & Admin.--Federal Distributing Corporation, Maspeth, NY, pg. 404
Welge, Michael W., Exec. V.P., Sec., Treas. & Comptroller--Gilster Mary Lee Corp., Chester, IL, pg. 460
Wellborn, Susan E., V.P., Chief Fin. Officer, Controller, & Asst. Sec.--DKM Resources, Inc., Houston, TX, pg. 357
Wells, A. Keith, Chief Fin. Officer & Controller--M. Swift & Sons Inc., Hartford, CT, pg. 1068
Wells, Barbara, V.P., Controller--Gray Kirk/VanSant Advertising, Inc., Baltimore, MD, pg. 479
Wells, Clyde, Controller & Treas.--Vestal Manufacturing, Sweetwater, TN, pg. 1162
Wells, ClydeL., Controller & Treas.--Vestal Manufacturing, Sweetwater, TN, pg. 1162
Wells, Gregory A., Treas. & Controller--Executive Telecom Systems, Inc., Indianapolis, IN, pg. 189
Wells, J.D., Controller--Infotec Development, Inc., Santa Ana, CA, pg. 567
Wells, Tim, Comptroller--Cummins Cumberland Inc., Louisville, KY, pg. 305
Welsh, Dale, Controller--Hill & Griffith Company, Cincinnati, OH, pg. 534
Welsh, Richard W., Controller--Allied Security, Inc., Pittsburgh, PA, pg. 39
Wempe, Joe, Controller--Dazey Corporation, Industrial Airport, KS, pg. 321
Wendeln, Richard V., Controller--The Orr Felt Company, Piqua, OH, pg. 830
Wendt, W.D., Controller--Southside Ford Truck Sales Inc., Chicago, IL, pg. 1023
Wensel, Deborah, Controller--Great Lakes Dredge & Dock, Oak Brook, IL, pg. 481
Wentz, Katherine, V.P., Controller--Wray-Ward-Laseter Advertising, Charlotte, NC, pg. 1204
Werner, Rick, Controller--York Building Products Co., Inc., York, PA, pg. 1208
Werner, William, Comptroller--Apache Plastics, L.P., Stockton, CA, pg. 77
Wertheimer, Merrill J., Sr. V.P. & Controller--Zale Corporation, Irving, TX, pg. 1215
Wertz, Carl, Controller--Westco Products, Inc., Pico Rivera, CA, pg. 1178
Wesorick, L., Controller--Rapid Engineering Inc., Comstock Park, MI, pg. 913
West, Alice, Controller--Soft Sheen Products, Inc., Chicago, IL, pg. 1016
West, Gabrele, Controller--A. Levy & J. Zentner Co., Sacramento, CA, pg. 671
West, Karen E., V.P. & Controller--The Vanguard Group, Inc., Wayne, PA, pg. 1145
West, Wilmer A., V.P. & Controller--Mays Chemical Company, Indianapolis, IN, pg. 725
Westbrook, Lloyd T., Controller--Broughton Foods Company, Marietta, OH, pg. 180
Westhoff, Joseph A., Controller--Atlantic Concrete Products, Inc., Tullytown, PA, pg. 94
Wetzel, Edward M., Controller--Standard Locknut & Lockwasher, Carmel, IN, pg. 1037
Wey, Walter, Controller--Fortifiber Corporation, Los Angeles, CA, pg. 425
Wharton, Joanne, Controller--The American Bankers Association, Washington, DC, pg. 49
Wheeler, Arnold F., Controller--Bartlett and Company, Kansas City, MO, pg. 122
Wheeler, C., Controller--American Welding & Manufacturing Co., Warren, OH, pg. 65
Wheeler, Mike, Chief Fin. Officer, V.P. & Treas.--Hy-Vee Food Stores Incorporated, Chariton, IA, pg. 556
Whetson, Linda, Chief Fin. Officer & Controller--Life Line Nutritionals, Inc., Hayward, CA, pg. 675
White, Debbie, Controller--John Paul Mitchell Systems, Beverly Hills, CA, pg. 762
Whitelsey, Stuart, Controller--Acurex Environmental, Mountain View, CA, pg. 16
Whitmore, David, Gen. Counsel & Controller--E. James White Company, Herndon, VA, pg. 1185
Whitten, Earl, Chief Fin. Officer, Treas. & Controller--Sherley Grain Company, Bovina, TX, pg. 998
Wichtoski, Alan, Controller--A.B. Data, Ltd., Milwaukee, WI, pg. 1
Widener, Judy, Controller--Summerfield Truck Co. Inc., Portage, IN, pg. 1057
Wieckert, W.B., V.P. & Controller--Miller Electric Mfg. Co., Appleton, WI, pg. 754
Wiell, Tim, V.P., Treas. & Controller--American Bread Company - Sunbeam Bakery, Nashville, TN, pg. 49
Wiepz, Ron, Controller--Pabst Brewing Co./Tumwater, Tumwater, WA, pg. 959
Wiest, Dale, Controller--Terre Hill Concrete Products, Inc., Terre Hill, PA, pg. 1089
Wiggins, Charles, Controller--Alpha Electronic Signal Technologies, Inc., Elizabeth, NJ, pg. 43
Wilaby, Katie, Controller--Mico Inc., North Mankato, MN, pg. 748

Wilbanks, Laura, Controller--Ghafari Associates, Inc., Dearborn, MI, pg. 455
Wilber, Larry, Controller--Hydril Company, Los Angeles, CA, pg. 556
Wilcox, Albert, Asst. Comptroller, Office Mgr.--Towne, Silverstein, Rotter Inc., New York, NY, pg. 1104
Wilcox, Betty, Controller & Dir.-Mngmt. Information Systems--Andmore Sportswear Corporation, Port Jervis, NY, pg. 74
Wild, Paul, Controller--Roman Electric Company, Inc., Milwaukee, WI, pg. 945
Wiley, George, Controller--Saratoga Harness Racing, Inc., Saratoga Springs, NY, pg. 970
Wilhelmsen, Harold J., V.P. & Controller, Intl.--S. C. Johnson & Son, Inc., Racine, WI, pg. 599
Wilkens, Walter J., Controller--Tri-Chem, Inc., Harrison, NJ, pg. 1110
Wilkerson, Bill, Treas., Controller & Sec.--Greenwood Packing Plant, Greenwood, SC, pg. 486
Wilkes, Dwayne, Controller--Big V Supermarkets, Inc., Florida, NY, pg. 149
Wilkins, Lowell, Controller--Foulds Inc., Libertyville, IL, pg. 427
Will, Larry L., Controller--The Law Company, Inc., Wichita, KS, pg. 661
Willhite, Donald H., V.P. & Comptroller--Atlantic Aviation Corp., New Castle, DE, pg. 94
William, Dorothy, Asst. Controller--Alford Refrigerated Warehouse, Inc., Dallas, TX, pg. 34
Williams, A.R., V.P.-Controller--Bill's Dollar Stores, Inc., Jackson, MS, pg. 150
Williams, Cathy, Controller--Dri Mark Products, Inc., Port Washington, NY, pg. 349
Williams, Chalmers, Controller--Harte-Hanks Communications, Inc., San Antonio, TX, pg. 513
Williams, David R., Controller--North American Royalties, Inc., Chattanooga, TN, pg. 811
Williams, Delon W., V.P., Controller, Chief Fin. Officer--Bonneville Communications, Salt Lake City, UT, pg. 164
Williams, Don, Controller--West Lumber Co., Atlanta, GA, pg. 1177
Williams, Earl, Controller--Belz Enterprises, Memphis, TN, pg. 138
Williams, Gary, Controller--Mitchel & Scot Machine Co., Inc., Indianapolis, IN, pg. 761
Williams, Jean, Asst. Controller--Fitzgerald Advertising Inc., New Orleans, LA, pg. 416
Williams, John, Controller--Gunnebo Fastening Corp., York, PA, pg. 494
Williams, John, Controller--Iowa Industrial Hydraulics, Inc., Pocahontas, IA, pg. 559
Williams, John, Controller--Country Fresh, Inc., Grand Rapids, MI, pg. 289
Williams, Phil, Controller--Tom James Company, Arlington, TX, pg. 589
Williams, Rogers, V.P., Treas. & Controller--White Stag Manufacturing Company, Van Nuys, CA, pg. 1186
Williams, Shenee, Controller--Tom's Foods, Columbus, GA, pg. 1101
Williams, Steven D., Treas. & Controller--Coca Cola Bottling Co. United, Inc., Birmingham, AL, pg. 257
Williams, Wgonda, Treas. & Controller--Handling Systems Engineering, Jacksonville, FL, pg. 505
Williamson, Dick, V.P.-Fin. & Grp. Controller--Tracor Aerospace, Inc., Austin, TX, pg. 1105
Williamson, Ed, Controller--Consolidated Pipe & Supply Company, Birmingham, AL, pg. 277
Williamson, Thomas, V.P. & Controller--Erickson Diversified Corp., Hudson, WI, pg. 386
Willis, Charlotte Y., Controller--Harrison Construction Corp., Miami, FL, pg. 512
Willocks, Laurie, V.P., Controller & Gen. Mgr.--The Schmidt/Westerdahl Group Ltd., Portland, OR, pg. 976
Wilson, James C., Controller--Stamler Corporation, Millersburg, KY, pg. 1035
Wilson, Jimmy, Chief Fin. Officer, Treas. & Controller--J. M. Smith Corp., Spartanburg, SC, pg. 1012
Wilson, Riley, Pres., Treas., Sec. & Controller--Rapid Power Technologies, Inc., Brookfield, CT, pg. 913
Wilson, Robert G., Controller--Kitchen Kompact, Inc., Jeffersonville, IN, pg. 634
Wilson, Teresa, Controller--Sugar Creek Packing Co., Mason, OH, pg. 1056
Winchell, Chuck, Controller--Schuck & Sons Construction Co., Glendale, AZ, pg. 979
Winchester, Glenda, Controller--Marshall & Williams Co., Greenville, SC, pg. 714
Winer, Michael, V.P. & Controller--Global Turnkey Systems Inc., Waldwick, NJ, pg. 463
Winslow, Richard H., Chief Fin. Officer, V.P.-Fin., Controller & Treas.--Norfolk Shipbuilding & Drydock Corporation, Norfolk, VA, pg. 810
Winter, Mitchel, Controller--McDonald Davis & Associates, Inc., Milwaukee, WI, pg. 728
Winters, David R., V.P.-Fin. & Controller--M. A. Bruder & Sons, Inc., Broomall, PA, pg. 184
Winton, Randy, Corp. Controller--Central Parking Corp., Nashville, TN, pg. 234
Wisdorf, Douglas G., Sr. V.P. & Controller--Washington Mutual Savings Bank, Seattle, WA, pg. 1166
Wise, Keith, Sr. V.P. & Controller--Allright Corporation, Houston, TX, pg. 41
Wise, Spence, Controller--Milliken & Co., Inc., Spartanburg, SC, pg. 755
Wissink, Stephen, Controller--Effingham-Clay Service Co., Effingham, IL, pg. 371
Witt, Joseph, V.P. & Controller--Kettering Advertising Display Co., Englewood Cliffs, NJ, pg. 626
Wittenberg, Carl, Controller--Puget Sound Plywood, Inc., Tacoma, WA, pg. 899
Wittensoldner, L.D., Controller--Gougler Industries, Inc., Kent, OH, pg. 473
Witty, Tim, Controller--Ag Processing Inc A Cooperative, Omaha, NE, pg. 24
Woehlke, Bill, Asst. Treas. & Controller--Pioneer Engineering & Manufacturing Co., Warren, MI, pg. 871
Wolbers, Linda K., Controller--Williams, White & Company, Moline, IL, pg. 1191
Wold, Dennis, Controller--The Cretex Companies, Elk River, MN, pg. 299
Wolf, Ann, Controller--Micro-Met L Corp., Indianapolis, IN, pg. 748
Wolf, Rosemary C., Controller--Brauns Fashions, Inc., Minneapolis, MN, pg. 172
Wolfe, Don, V.P. & Controller--Softool Corporation, Goleta, CA, pg. 1016
Wolfe, Nelson, Controller--Beach Mold & Tool Inc., New Albany, IN, pg. 128
Wolfe, Shana K., Controller--Tristate Electrical Supply Co., Inc., Hagerstown, MD, pg. 1114
Wolfe, Victor, Controller--Lithographix, Inc., Los Angeles, CA, pg. 678
Wolff, Renana, Controller--Ambassador Steel Co., Detroit, MI, pg. 47
Wolff, Robert, V.P. & Comptroller--Federal Business Products, Inc., Clifton, NJ, pg. 404
Wolfrom, Ed, Controller--Burns & McDonnell Engineers-Architects-Consultants, Kansas City, MO, pg. 194
Womble, Edgar, Controller--Perryton Equity, Perryton, TX, pg. 863
Wong, Bill, Controller--Signet Industries, Fraser, MI, pg. 1003
Wong, Gene, Controller--Bel Air Markets, Sacramento, CA, pg. 133
Wong, Jennifer, Treas. & Controller--Peter Wong & Associates, Inc., Richmond, VA, pg. 1199
Wood, Carol S., Treas., Sec., Controller & Chief Fin. Officer--Higginbotham-Bartlett Co., Lubbock, TX, pg. 533
Wood, Timothy M., V.P. & Controller--Borg-Warner Corporation, Chicago, IL, pg. 165
Woodcock, Herman, Controller--J. S. Alberici Construction Co., Inc., Saint Louis, MO, pg. 31
Woodfield, Grant, Controller--Griffin Envelope, Inc., Seattle, WA, pg. 487
Woods, Carlette, V.P. & Controller--Kettle Restaurants, Houston, TX, pg. 626
Woods, Thomas, Controller--Tool & Engineering Co., Chicago, IL, pg. 400
Worth, Larry, Controller--Wright-Schuchart, Inc., Seattle, WA, pg. 1204
Wright, George, Controller--Transamerican Refining Corporation, Houston, TX, pg. 1106
Wright, Samuel G., V.P. & Controller--Jack Eckerd Corporation, Largo, FL, pg. 366
Wu, Esther, Chief Fin. Officer, Treas. & Controller--Visible Changes, Houston, TX, pg. 1153
Wuest, Mary L., Controller--Rome Cable Corporation, Rome, NY, pg. 945
Wurdemann, Moran, Controller--Schwartz & Benjamin, Inc., New York, NY, pg. 980
Wurtz, Ken, Chief Fin. Officer & Controller--Century Data Systems, Raleigh, NC, pg. 235
Wyatt, William J. Sr., V.P.-Fin. & Controller--Rea Magnet Wire Company, Inc., Fort Wayne, IN, pg. 915
Y'Barbo, James, Controller--AppleTree Markets, Houston, TX, pg. 79
Yancek, Harold, Controller--Multimatic Corporation, Northvale, NJ, pg. 775
Yax, Vincent, V.P., Controller & Treas.--Fairfield International Corporation, New York, NY, pg. 397
Yeager, Dave, Controller--Aunt Nellie's Farm Kitchens, Inc., Clyman, WI, pg. 98
Yeager, Leah B., Chief Fin. Officer, Treas. & Controller--Automation Intelligence, Inc., Maitland, FL, pg. 101
Yelenic, Joseph J., Controller-Spec & Voltec--Sauer Industries, Inc., Pittsburgh, PA, pg. 972
Yelick, Frank, V.P. & Controller--Peter Kiewit Sons Inc., Omaha, NE, pg. 629
Yelpo, Beverly, Controller--Victaulic Company of America, Easton, PA, pg. 1149
Yohalem, Alan, V.P. & Controller--The Economics Press, Inc., Fairfield, NJ, pg. 367
Yolcomico, Evelyn, Comptroller--Dick Bruhn Inc., Salinas, CA, pg. 184
Yong, Milton C., V.P.-Fin.--NWS, Inc., Chicago, IL, pg. 782
Yordy, William R., Controller & Treas.--Brian Unlimited Distribution Company, Inc., Detroit, MI, pg. 175
York, Frank, Controller--Southern Pipe & Supply Co., Inc., Meridian, MS, pg. 1022
York, W.R., Controller--Flexible Products Company, Marietta, GA, pg. 418
Yost, Dale, V.P. & Controller--Dairymen, Inc., Louisville, KY, pg. 311
Yost, William H., Treas. & Controller--Maguire Group Inc., Foxboro, MA, pg. 701
Young, Frank, Controller--American Chemical Society, Washington, DC, pg. 50
Young, Gene, Controller--Swirl, Inc., New York, NY, pg. 1068
Young, Karen, Controller--Logghe Stamping Company, Fraser, MI, pg. 681
Young, Richard, V.P. & Controller--Bill Heard Enterprises, Inc., Columbus, GA, pg. 521
Younggren, Terry, Controller--Pizza Haven Inc., Seattle, WA, pg. 873
Zabinski, A. F., Jr., Chief Fin. Officer, Treas. & Controller--George Sollitt Construction, Wood Dale, IL, pg. 1017
Zajac, Dan, Controller--Smith System Manufacturing Company, Shoreview, MN, pg. 1014
Zarrelli, Joseph, Gen. Mgr. & Controller--Staveley Sensors, Inc., East Hartford, CT, pg. 1043
Zator, Cathy, Controller--Maecorp Inc., Chicago, IL, pg. 699
Zaweski, Richard, Controller--Meenan Oil Co. Limited Partnership, Syosset, NY, pg. 736
Zdebski, Susan M., Controller--Chicago Convention & Tourism Bureau, Chicago, IL, pg. 245
Zdon, Joseph P., Jr., Sr. V.P. & Controller--Atlantic Gulf Communities Corporation, Miami, FL, pg. 95
Zeek, Walter F., Jr., Controller--Superior Label Systems, Inc., Cincinnati, OH, pg. 1063
Zellers, W.L., Controller-Gas Opers.--Citizens Gas & Coke Utility, Indianapolis, IN, pg. 250
Zelno, Michael, Controller--Dunmore Corporation, Newtown, PA, pg. 353
Zemba, S., Controller--Munroe, Inc., Pittsburgh, PA, pg. 776
Zenofsky, Allan, Controller--Victor Corporation, West Warwick, RI, pg. 1149
Zerah, Patricia A., Asst. Controller--Publishers Clearing House, Port Washington, NY, pg. 898
Zervoudis, Evangeline, V.P., Controller--Griswold, Inc., Cleveland, OH, pg. 950
Ziegler, Richard, Controller--Metal Cutting Tools Corp., Rockford, IL, pg. 507
Zielinski, Maria E., Controller--Federal Farm Credit Banks Funding Corporation, Jersey City, NJ, pg. 404
Zikakis, Damian, Controller--Silver's Inc., Detroit, MI, pg. 1005
Zilinskas, Matthew J., Controller--Kearney-National, Inc., White Plains, NY, pg. 357
Zimbalatti, Gary, Controller--American Savings Bank, White Plains, NY, pg. 60
Zimbo, Theodore, Controller--ACO Inc., Farmington Hills, MI, pg. 2
Zimmerman, Frank, Treas., Controller & Chief Fin. Officer--Hudson & Affiliated Co., Shawnee Mission, KS, pg. 551
Zins, James, Controller--Desco Corporation, Columbus, OH, pg. 332
Zinter, Gary, Controller--Food Ingredients, Minneapolis, MN, pg. 653
Zipf, Bruce, Controller--Coldwell Bankers/Schlott Realtors, Wayne, NJ, pg. 260
Zitnay, Bob, Controller--The William Carter Company, New York, NY, pg. 226
Zofkie, Mike, Controller--Hirsh Company, Skokie, IL, pg. 258
Zolper, C.E., Controller--Dukane Corporation, Saint Charles, IL, pg. 351
Zuar, Robert D., V.P. & Controller--The New England, Boston, MA, pg. 799
Zuckerman, Bernie, Controller--Abbott Glass Co., Inc., Maspeth, NY, pg. 9
Zupnik, Rachelle, Controller--Proctor & Gardner Advertising, Inc., Chicago, IL, pg. 892
Zura, W., Controller--Summit Corporation of America, Thomaston, CT, pg. 1058
Zwart, Norma, Controller--Carol Wright Sales, Inc., Stamford, CT, pg. 1011
Zwrek, Lawrence, Controller--Humiston-Keeling, Inc., Chicago, IL, pg. 552
22hry, George, Controller--Hearst Business Communications, Inc., Garden City, NY, pg. 522

CORPORATE SECRETARY

Aarvig, Thora A., Sec.--Equitable Bankshares of Colorado, Inc., Denver, CO, pg. 385
Abair,Daniel, Sec. & Treas.--Park Motor Sales Company, Detroit, MI, pg. 849
Abbey, Richard, Sec. & Treas.--Automotive Moulding Company, Warren, MI, pg. 101
Abbot, Patricia, Treas. & Sec.--Metro Label Corp., Garland, TX, pg. 743
Abbott, Henry J., Sec.--Central Parking Corp., Nashville, TN, pg. 234
Abbott, Henry J., Sec.--Central Parking Corp., Nashville, TN, pg. 234
Abbott, John S., Sec.--Gaylord Printing, Inc., Detroit, MI, pg. 446
Abdalla, Carolyn, Sec.--Abdalla's Lafayette, Inc., Lafayette, LA, pg. 10
Abdalla, Gerald M., Exec. V.P., Gen. Counsel & Sec.--Croft Metal Inc., McComb, MS, pg. 300
Abernethy, Robert C., Sec.--Carolina Glove Co., Newton, NC, pg. 223
Abney, Delbert, V.P. & Sec.--Sunniland Corporation, Sanford, FL, pg. 1061
Abrams, Patricia, Sec.--Abrams Publishing Inc., Waterbury, CT, pg. 10
Abroms, Harold L., Chief Oper. Officer, Exec. V.P., Treas. & Sec.--Parisian, Inc., Birmingham, AL, pg. 848
Accardo, Jack P., V.P. & Chief Fin. Officer, Treas. & Sec.--Kasper Machine Company, Madison Heights, MI, pg. 618
Acker, Howard F., Sec.--The F.A. Bartlett Tree Expert Co., Stamford, CT, pg. 123
Acker, Karen, V.P.-International & Sec.--Pavion Ltd., Nyack on Hudson, NY, pg. 852
Ackerman, Sanford S., Sr. V.P. & Chief Fin. Officer--John Blair Communications, Inc., New York, NY, pg. 155
Ackerman, Susan D., V.P. & Sec.--Phoenix American Incorporated, San Rafael, CA, pg. 868
Acklie, Phyllis A., V.P. & Sec.--Crete Carrier Corp., Lincoln, NE, pg. 299
Adams, Al, Corp. Sec. & V.P.-Adams Div.--M. B. Kahn Construction Co., Inc., Columbia, SC, pg. 614
Adams, Betty, Sec.--Delta Life Corporation, Memphis, TN, pg. 327
Adams, Gail A., V.P. & Sec.--United Refrigerated Services, Atlanta, GA, pg. 1134
Adams, Grace, Sec.--O. A. Newton & Son Co., Bridgeville, DE, pg. 805
Adams, Richard B., Exec. V.P., Sec. & Treas.--R. P. Adams Company, Inc., Tonawanda, NY, pg. 16
Adante, David E., V.P., Chief Fin. Officer & Sec.--The Davey Tree Expert Company, Kent, OH, pg. 317
Adduce, Vicci, Sec.--Royle Systems Group, Pompton Lakes, NJ, pg. 953
Adelstein, Bruce S., Exec. V.P. & Sec.--Olympic Steel Inc., Bedford Heights, OH, pg. 825
Adelstein, Robert M., Sec.--Northwestern Engineering Co., Rapid City, SD, pg. 815
Adessi, Alfred, Treas. & Sec.--Mossberg Industries, Inc., Cumberland, RI, pg. 772

Adikes, Robert K., V.P., Sec. & Gen. Counsel--Spalding & Evenflo Companies, Inc., Tampa, FL, pg. 1024
Adkins, Marshall, Sec. & Treas.--United Feeds, Inc., Sheridan, IN, pg. 1132
Adler, Elaine, Sec.--Myron Manufacturing Corporation, Maywood, NJ, pg. 780
Adler, Richard J., V.P.-Sls. & Sec.--Fort Dearborn Lithograph Company, Niles, IL, pg. 425
Agler, Nancy L., Corp. Sec.--Guy Gannett Publishing Company, Portland, ME, pg. 442
Agnew, Charles D., V.P.-Pur. & Sec.--National Savings Life Insurance Company, Murfreesboro, TN, pg. 1150
Agnew, Charles D., Sec.--Kennesaw Life & Accident Insurance Company, Atlanta, GA, pg. 921
Ahlin, Thomas, Sec. & Treas.--Fargo Clinic Ltd., Fargo, ND, pg. 399
Ahto, Charles A., Exec. V.P. & Sec.--MPO Videotronics, Inc., New York, NY, pg. 693
Akins, Edwin E., Treas., Sec. & Dir.-Personnel--T.J. Morris Company, Inc., Statesboro, GA, pg. 771
Al-Talib, Dr. Hisham, Sec.--Mar-Jac Processing, Inc., Gainesville, GA, pg. 705
Alber, Stephen A., Sec.--VanDine, Humphrey, Herbert, Alber & Manges, Inc., Pittsburgh, PA, pg. 1145
Alberici, John S., Chief Fin. Officer, Sr. V.P. & Sec.--J. S. Alberici Construction Co., Inc., Saint Louis, MO, pg. 31
Albert, Billie, Treas. & Sec.--Farmway Co-Op Inc., Beloit, KS, pg. 402
Albert, Insulinde, Treas. & Sec.--R.L. Albert & Son, Inc., Greenwich, CT, pg. 31
Albertelli, George J., Sr. V.P. & Sec.--The Stellar Group Inc., Jacksonville, FL, pg. 1046
Alberts, Harold, Sec.--Sam Kane Beef Processors, Inc., Corpus Christi, TX, pg. 616
Alberts, Robert J., Corp. Sec. & Treas.--Templeton, Kenly & Co., Inc., Broadview, IL, pg. 1086
Albertson, Jack, Sec.--Jonbil Inc., Chase City, VA, pg. 602
Albrecht, Marilyn, Sec.--Red Wing Publishing Company, Red Wing, MN, pg. 919
Alcott, Jeanne, Sec.--Traco Advertising, Inc., Tulsa, OK, pg. 1104
Ales, S.J., Sec. & Controller--Brock-McVey Company, Lexington, KY, pg. 728
Alesso, Dominick, Sec. & Gen. Counsel--A-P-A Transport Corp., North Bergen, NJ, pg. 5
Alexander, James C., V.P., Sec. & Treas.--General Homes Corporation, Houston, TX, pg. 449
Alexander, John R., Sec.--Hilliard Corporation, Elmira, NY, pg. 535
Alexander, Rosemary, Sec.--Cold Spring Granite Company, Minnetonka, MN, pg. 259
Alflen, J., Treas. & Sec.--Torrance Nissan, Inc., Torrance, CA, pg. 1102
Alford, Jason, Treas. & Sec.--Rainbow Home Rentals, Canfield, OH, pg. 910
Alge, Jack, Sec.--Affiliated of Florida Inc., Tampa, FL, pg. 23
Allen, Charlotte D., Sec.--Allen Canning Company, Siloam Springs, AR, pg. 35
Allen, Clinton, Sec. & Treas.--Bill Heard Leasing, Inc., Columbus, GA, pg. 521
Allen, Clinton G., Sec. & Treas.--Bill Heard Chevrolet Inc., Columbus, GA, pg. 521
Allen, Elizabeth, Sec.--Pemco Die Casting Corporation, Bridgman, MI, pg. 856
Allen, Florence E., Sec.--Clark Enterprises, Inc., Bethesda, MD, pg. 252
Allen, Frank C., V.P., Sec. & Gen. Counsel--The Babcock & Wilcox Company, New Orleans, LA, pg. 107
Allen, Joseph, Exec. V.P., Treas. & Sec.--Brant Allen Industries, Inc., Greenwich, CT, pg. 172
Allen, Judith H., Sec.--Yankee Publishing Incorporated, Dublin, NH, pg. 1207
Allen, Kathleen, Sec.--California Panel & Veneer Company, Cerritos, CA, pg. 210
Allen, Mark, Sec.--O'Brien Powder Products, Inc., Houston, TX, pg. 820
Allen, Mark R., Sec.--The O'Brien Corporation, South San Francisco, CA, pg. 820
Allen, Mark R., V.P. & Sec.--Fuller O'Brien Paints, South San Francisco, CA, pg. 820
Allen, Robert J., Treas. & Sec.--Mason Shoe Mfg. Co., Chippewa Falls, WI, pg. 718
Allen, Robert J., Sec. & Treas.--Wissota Trader & B.A. Mason, Chippewa Falls, WI, pg. 718
Allen, Roger, Jr., Exec. V.P. & Sec.--Gore Graphics, Inc., Los Angeles, CA, pg. 472
Allen, Ronald, V.P. & Sec.--American Foodservice Corp., King of Prussia, PA, pg. 54
Allen, Sharon, Sec.--Republic Alloys, Inc., Charlotte, NC, pg. 927
Allen, Wayne, V.P.-Sls. & Mktg. & Sec.--Idaho Supreme Company, Firth, ID, pg. 561
Allison, Charles, V.P., Sec. & Gen. Counsel--Gulf States Paper Corporation, Tuscaloosa, AL, pg. 494
Allison, Lynette E., V.P.-Gen. Counsel & Sec.--Scholastic Inc., New York, NY, pg. 962
Allsup, Barbara J., V.P., Sec. & Treas.--Allsups Convenience Stores Inc., Clovis, NM, pg. 43
Allums, Mary B., Sec.--Buffalo Rock Company, Birmingham, AL, pg. 187
Alongi, Linda, Sec. & Treas.--American Furniture Company, Albuquerque, NM, pg. 55
Alperson, Lorraine, Sec.--Rolled Steel Products Corporation, Los Angeles, CA, pg. 944
Alphson, Howard C., Sec. & Gen. Counsel--M.C. Gill Corporation, El Monte, CA, pg. 458
Alteri, Sharon, Sec.--Airguard Industries Inc., Louisville, KY, pg. 27
Altherr, Jack R., Chief Fin. Officer, V.P. & Sec.--Avondale Mills, Inc., Sylacauga, AL, pg. 103
Altman, Micky D., Sec.--Equity Fund Advisors Inc., Houston, TX, pg. 385
Altmann, Howard J., 2nd V.P. & Asst. Sec.--W. P. Carey & Co., Inc., New York, NY, pg. 218
Alvey, Steven, V.P.-Fin. & Opers.--Shugart Corporation, Irvine, CA, pg. 1001
Amato, Larry, Chief Fin. Officer, Treas. & Sec.--Elkay Products, Inc., Shrewsbury, MA, pg. 377
Ament, Werner E., Chm. Bd., Pres., Chief Exec. Officer & Sec.--Milex of America, Inc., Chicago, IL, pg. 753
Ames, J.W., V.P.-Fin., Treas. & Sec.--Milwaukee Electric Tool Corp., Brookfield, WI, pg. 361
Amhowitz, Harris J., Deputy Chm.--Coopers & Lybrand, New York, NY, pg. 283
Amster, Kirk, V.P., Treas. & Sec.--A S H, Inc., Phoenix, AZ, pg. 8
Amsterdam, M., Sec. & Treas.--General Metalcraft, Inc., Dover, DE, pg. 450
Anderko, Frank, V.P.-Mfg. & Sec.--Worzalla Publishing Co., Inc., Stevens Point, WI, pg. 1204
Anderson, Betty Jo, Sec.--Andys Rental Inc., La Mirada, CA, pg. 1206
Anderson, Bob, Sec. & Treas.--Telsco Industries, Garland, TX, pg. 1085
Anderson, Douglas E., Exec. V.P. & Sec.--Boddie-Noell Enterprises Inc., Rocky Mount, NC, pg. 161
Anderson, Gary, Treas. & Sec.--X-A Cabinet Corporation, La Mirada, CA, pg. 1206
Anderson, George E., V.P. & Sec.--Crown Holdings, Inc., Roseville, MN, pg. 302
Anderson, George E., V.P. & Sec.--Crown Iron Works Company, Roseville, MN, pg. 302
Anderson, Gunner, Controller & Asst. Sec.--Clements Foods Co., Oklahoma City, OK, pg. 254
Anderson, James, V.P. & Gen. Counsel--Ingram Industries Inc., Nashville, TN, pg. 568
Anderson, James R., V.P.-Fin., Sec. & Treas.--The Austin Company, Cleveland, OH, pg. 790
Anderson, Linnea, Sec.--Anderson Brothers Construction Brainerd, Brainerd, MN, pg. 72
Anderson, Lorraine, Sec.--Burnside Construction Co., Downers Grove, WI, pg. 194
Anderson, Robert G., V.P., Sec. & Gen. Counsel--Boston Scientific Corp., Watertown, MA, pg. 167
Anderson, Robert W., Sec., Treas. & Comptroller--Superior Oil Co. Inc., Indianapolis, IN, pg. 1064
Anderson, T.I., V.P. & Sec.--W.J. Dennis Co., Elgin, IL, pg. 329
Anderson, Theodore C., Asst. Sec.--Macco Constructors, Inc., Paramount, CA, pg. 696
Anderson, Vivian L., Sr. V.P. & Sec.--Franchise Finance Corp. of America, Scottsdale, AZ, pg. 428
Anderson, William E. II, Sr. V.P., Sec. & Gen. Counsel--Jerrico, Inc., Lexington, KY, pg. 229
Anderson, William E., II, Sr. V.P., Sec. & Gen. Counsel--Long John Silver's, Inc., Lexington, KY, pg. 229
Anderson, William J., Sec. & Treas.--Pella Corporation, Pella, IA, pg. 856
Anderson, Willis M., Gen. Counsel & Sec.--Shenandoah Life Insurance Company, Roanoke, VA, pg. 997
Anderson, Willis M., Gen. Counsel & Sec.--Old Dominion Life Insurance Co., Roanoke, VA, pg. 997
Andonian, Hratch K., Exec. V.P., Sec. & Treas.--A K H Company, Inc., Los Angeles, CA, pg. 4
Andre, Wayne, Treas. & Sec.--Roseville Chrysler Plymouth Inc., Roseville, MI, pg. 949
Andrejkovics, Bernard, V.P. & Sec.--Hughes-Treitler Manufacturing Corporation, Garden City, NY, pg. 552
Andreola, A.V., Sec.--Holman Enterprises, Pennsauken, NJ, pg. 540
Ansted, James P., Chief Fin. Officer, Treas., Sec.--Plastic Suppliers, Inc., Columbus, OH, pg. 875
Anstett, Joseph L., Chief Fin. Officer, Exec. V.P. & Sec.--Silver State Disposal Service, Inc., Las Vegas, NV, pg. 1004
Anthony, Aubra, Jr., Treas., Sec. & Counsel--Anthony Forest Products Co., Inc., El Dorado, AR, pg. 77
Anzaldo, Marianne W., Sec., Adv. & Chief Information Officer--E.P. Henry Corporation, Woodbury, NJ, pg. 530
Aono, Sumi, Treas. & Sec.--Red Apple, Inc., Ontario, OR, pg. 918
Appelwick, Karen K., Sec. & Treas.--Apple Lines, Inc., Madison, SD, pg. 79
Applebaum, Arnie, V.P. & Sec.--Jackson Mills, Inc., Wellford, SC, pg. 587
Aquilino, Vincent, Sec.--Graymills Corp., Chicago, IL, pg. 480
Arakelian, Dorothy J., Treas. & Sec.--Standard Manufacturing Company, Troy, NY, pg. 1037
Arana, Cherly, Treas. & Sec.--Chase Chevrolet Co., Stockton, CA, pg. 240
Arboneaux, Jesse P., V.P., Chief Fin. Officer, Treas. & Sec.--Ourso Investment Corporation, Donaldsonville, LA, pg. 832
Arboneaux, Jesse P., V.P., Treas. & Sec.--Security Industrial Insurance Co., Inc., Donaldsonville, LA, pg. 832
Arcadi, Vincent, Sec. & Treas.--Depew Development Inc., Lancaster, NY, pg. 331
Arcaro, Teri, Corp. Sec.--The Crawford Group, Cleveland, OH, pg. 297
Archer, Ophelia, Treas. & Sec.--Stahmann Farms, Inc., Las Cruces, NM, pg. 1034
Archibald, Kathy R., Sec. & Treas.--Printing House, Inc., Quincy, FL, pg. 891
Archuleta, Maria, Sec.--National Systems & Research Co., Colorado Springs, CO, pg. 794
Arend, Patricia, Sec.--International Chemical Company, Tulsa, OK, pg. 576
Arens, Joel, Exec. V.P., Treas. & Sec.--Alacon, Sunnyvale, CA, pg. 29
Armstrong, Arthur O., Admin. Officer & Sec.--Merle Norman Cosmetics, Inc., Los Angeles, CA, pg. 740
Arndt, Ardean, V.P. & Sec.--Lincoln Industries, Lincoln, NE, pg. 676
Arnold, Gilbert S., Sec.--Windsor Shade Tobacco Company, Inc., Hartford, CT, pg. 1196
Arnold, Patricia L., Sec.--Bacco Construction Co., Iron Mountain, MI, pg. 108
Arnopolin, Judith, Sec.--Century Publishing Company, Evanston, IL, pg. 235
Aronson, Alan, Legal Officer & Sec.--Carus Corporation, Peru, IL, pg. 227
Arrigo, Joseph F., V.P., Treas. & Sec.--UIS, Inc., New York, NY, pg. 1123
Arst, Patricia L., Sec.--Goldsmiths, Inc., Wichita, KS, pg. 469
Arterbery, Vivian J., Sec.--RAND, Santa Monica, CA, pg. 911
Arthur, Margaret, Sec.--National Life Insurance Company, Montpelier, VT, pg. 791
Asch, David, Exec. V.P.-Treas. & Sec.--Twincraft, Inc., Winooski, VT, pg. 1122
Aselage, Susan Seabury, V.P. & Sec.--Sabreliner Corp., Chesterfield, MO, pg. 965
Ash, Eugene, Asst. Sec. & Dir.-Indus. Rels.--Walton Monroe Mills, Inc., Monroe, GA, pg. 1162
Ashburn, Joanna, Admin. Asst.--Ellwood City Forge, Ellwood City, PA, pg. 378
Ashby, Ralph, Treas. & Sec.--United Producers & Consumers Co-Op, Phoenix, AZ, pg. 1134
Ashe, Diane, Sec.--Bruce Industries, Inc., Dayton, NV, pg. 183
Ashkin, Anna, Sec. & Treas.--Rugby-Darby Group Of Cos., Rockville Centre, NY, pg. 955
Ashley, James W., Sec.--Chicago Tube & Iron Co., Chicago, IL, pg. 246
Ashley, Kenneth, Chief Fin. Officer, Sec. & Treas.--National R.V., Inc., Perris, CA, pg. 792
Ashmore, R.C., V.P. & Asst. Sec.--Ballenger Paving Company, Inc., Taylors, SC, pg. 116
Ashmun, R.E., Sec.--National Frozen Foods Corp., Seattle, WA, pg. 789
Asmuth, A. William, Jr., Sec.--Dickten & Masch Manufacturing Co., Nashotah, WI, pg. 336
Asplan, Donald J., Sec.--Western States Machine Co., Hamilton, OH, pg. 1181
Asplund, Anne, Sec--Young & Rubicam Sweden AB (Holding), Stockholm,, Sweden, pg. 1213
Astor, Z.H., Sec.--Apperson Business Forms, Inc., Los Angeles, CA, pg. 78
Astrup, Corrine, Treas. & Sec.--Astrup Drugs, Inc., Austin, MN, pg. 93
Atkins, Pat, Corp. Sec., Treas.--The Atkins Agency, San Antonio, TX, pg. 94
Attardi, Charles, Jr., Sec. & Treas.--North Carolina Equipment Co., Raleigh, NC, pg. 812
Atwood, Fern, Asst. Sec. & Treas.--Atwood Distributing, Inc., Enid, OK, pg. 97
Atwood, Johnnie, Sec.--Atwood Distributing, Inc., Enid, OK, pg. 97
Aus, Janice A., Sec.--Bremer Financial Corporation, Saint Paul, MN, pg. 173
Austin, Cornelia, Sec.--Gurney Industries Inc., Gastonia, NC, pg. 495
Austin, G. Kenneth, III, Sec.--A-Dec, Inc., Newberg, OR, pg. 1
Austin, Geanne, V.P. & Sec.--Keller Motor Car Company, Inc., Latham, NY, pg. 621
Austin, Laurence, V.P.-Fin., Sec. & Treas.--Miniature Precision Components, Walworth, WI, pg. 757
Austin, Michael, Dir.-Corp. Communications & Asst. Sec.--Utica Mutual Insurance Company, New Hartford, NY, pg. 1140
Austin, William F., Pres., Sec. & Treas.--Starkey Laboratories, Inc., Eden Prairie, MN, pg. 1040
Auten, David C., Asst. Sec.--W. P. Carey & Co., Inc., New York, NY, pg. 218
Avallone, Pamela, Sec.--Alpha Associates, Inc., Woodbridge, NJ, pg. 43
Avery, James, Treas. & Sec.--Schumacher-Dugan Construction, West Chester, OH, pg. 979
Avery, John, V.P. & Sec.--Southwire Company, Inc., Carrollton, GA, pg. 1024
Avery, O. Keith, Sec. & Treas.--Presto Food Stores, Inc., Plant City, FL, pg. 888
Axelband, Leonard, Exec. V.P., Sec.--Axelband & Brown & Associates Inc., Cleveland, OH, pg. 103
Axelrad, Marilyn, Sec.--Pakula & Company, Chicago, IL, pg. 843
Azar, Cyrus, Sec.--Symplex Communications Corp., Ann Arbor, MI, pg. 1069
Babb, Terry L., Sec.--Hidden Valley Resort, Hidden Valley, PA, pg. 626
Bachler, Bud, V.P.-Mktg./Communications--Winona Knits, Winona, MN, pg. 1196
Bachman, Alan, V.P. & Sec.--Bachman's, Inc., Minneapolis, MN, pg. 108
Bacigalupo, John W., Chief Exec. Officer--Kelly-Moore Paint Company, Inc., San Carlos, CA, pg. 621
Backer, Richard I., Exec. V.P.-Devel. & Asst. Sec.--Carlyle & Co. Jewelers, Greensboro, NC, pg. 222
Badcock Bader, Evelyn, Asst. Sec.--W.S. Badcock Corporation, Mulberry, FL, pg. 113
Badcock Pou, Malda, Asst. Sec.--W.S. Badcock Corporation, Mulberry, FL, pg. 113
Badcock, Henry C., Exec. V.P.-Dealer Opers. & Sec.--W.S. Badcock Corporation, Mulberry, FL, pg. 113
Baden, Marvin, V.P.-Mktg. & Sls., Sec. & Treas.--Producers Rice Mill Inc., Stuttgart, AR, pg. 892
Badofsky, Jack, V.P., Creative Dir. & Sec.--Smith, Badofsky & Raffel, Inc. Advertising, Chicago, IL, pg. 1011
Bahr, Mark A., Exec. V.P. & Sec.--Barton-Malow Enterprises, Inc., Southfield, MI, pg. 123
Bailey, A.C., Sec.--The Stackpole Corporation, Boston, MA, pg. 1034
Bailey, Kelly, Sec.--Moritz Cadillac-Saab Inc., Arlington, TX, pg. 770
Bailey, Mark, V.P. Sec & Gen Counsel--SENCORP, Newport, KY, pg. 989

Bailey, Norma R., Asst. Sec.--Global Insurance Company, Houston, TX, pg. 662
Bailey, R. Annette, Bd. Sec.--Nebraska Public Power District, Columbus, NE, pg. 796
Baines, Edith M., Sec.--Stop Shop Save, Baltimore, MD, pg. 1052
Bair, Clinton, Sec. & Controller--Republic Die & Tool Company, Belleville, MI, pg. 928
Baker, Bridget, Sec.--Guard Publishing Company, Eugene, OR, pg. 491
Baker, David, Corp. Counsel & Asst. Sec.--CENEX (Farmers Union Central Exchange, Inc.), Inver Grove Heights, MN, pg. 231
Baker, Marty, Sec.--Madison Grocery Co., Inc., Richmond, KY, pg. 699
Baker, Newell A., Jr., Exec. V.P. & Corp. Sec.--J. D. Streett & Co., Inc., Maryland Heights, MO, pg. 1053
Baker, Steven E., Sec.--W.G. Mills, Inc., Sarasota, FL, pg. 756
Balaban, Jay, Treas. & Sec.--Chorus Line, Inc., Vernon, CA, pg. 591
Baldauf, David, V.P. & Sec.--Benderson Development Co., Inc., Buffalo, NY, pg. 138
Baldwin, Cherlynn S., Sec.--Baldwin Construction, Inc., Fort Collins, CO, pg. 115
Baldwin, Ellen R., Sec.--David A. Bramble, Inc., Chestertown, MD, pg. 171
Baldwin, Janet, Sec.--Guaranty Corporation, Baton Rouge, LA, pg. 491
Ball, Alice, Treas. & Sec.--Air Power, Inc., High Point, NC, pg. 27
Ball, Leonard F., Sr. V.P., Gen. Counsel & Asst. Sec.--HTB, Inc., Oklahoma City, OK, pg. 497
Ballantine, J. C., V.P., Sec. & Treas.--Miller Building Corp., Wilmington, NC, pg. 753
Ballard, Augustus S., Sec.--The Kent Manufacturing Co., Pickens, SC, pg. 623
Ballew, Glenn, V.P.-Underwriting & Sec.--Midwest Mutual Insurance Co., West Des Moines, IA, pg. 886
Ballweg, Rose, Sec.--Mueller Sports Medicine, Inc., Prairie du Sac, WI, pg. 774
Bangs, Nelson A., V.P., Gen Counsel & Sec.--Dr Pepper/Seven-Up Companies, Inc., Dallas, TX, pg. 342
Bank, Malvin, Sec.--Columbia National Group, Inc., Cleveland, OH, pg. 265
Banks, Ada L., Sec.--Ritchie Corporation, Wichita, KS, pg. 936
Banks, Ken, V.P.-Fin., Sec. & Treas.--Grove Valve & Regulator Company, Oakland, CA, pg. 490
Banquer, C.S., Treas. & Controller--Acme Refrigeration Of Baton Rouge Inc., Baton Rouge, LA, pg. 13
Banstetter, Robert J., V.P., Gen. Counsel & Sec.--General American Life Insurance Co., St. Louis, MO, pg. 448
Baracaia, Erma, Corp. Sec.--Giant Markets Inc., Scranton, PA, pg. 456
Baracos, Victor, Sec.--Weilwood Industries, Inc., New York, NY, pg. 970
Barber, Dan, Sec. & Treas.--Barnett Millworks, Inc., Theodore, AL, pg. 120
Barberia, Anthony, Exec. V.P. & Sec.--Amloid Corporation, Saddle Brook, NJ, pg. 67
Barbieri, Stephen R., Sec. & Legal Counsel--Sunshine Biscuits, Inc., Woodbridge, NJ, pg. 439
Barbour, W. Robert, Sec.--Northwest Pipe Fittings, Inc., Billings, MT, pg. 815
Barkan, Lee, Sr. V.P. Sec. & Gen. Counsel--American Vision Centers, Inc., New York, NY, pg. 65
Barker, Everette, Asst. Sec.--Bankhead Enterprises Inc., Atlanta, GA, pg. 117
Barker, Mary, Admin. Sec.--Mid-State Wire Company, Crawfordsville, IN, pg. 691
Barlow, Carol Ann, Sec. & Treas.--Macristy Industries, Inc., New Britain, CT, pg. 698
Barlow, Cynthia, Sr. V.P.-Underwriting & Sec.--Insurance Corp. of America, Houston, TX, pg. 572
Barnes, Elaine, Sec.--Perdue Farms Inc., Salisbury, MD, pg. 860
Barnes, Phillip, Corporate Sec.--Spectrulite Consortium, Inc., Madison, IL, pg. 1029
Barnes, R. B., Jr., Sec. & Treas.--Austin Co., Inc., Greeneville, TN, pg. 98
Barnett, Gillian H., V.P. & Sec.--Algood Food Company, Louisville, KY, pg. 34
Barnette, Lea, Sec.--Tasco, Miami, FL, pg. 1079
Barnhardt, Sadler H., Sec. & Treas.--Barnhardt Manufacturing Co., Charlotte, NC, pg. 120
Barnhardt, Sadler H., Sec.--Carolina Absorbent Cotton Co., Charlotte, NC, pg. 120
Barnhill, Richard D., Chief Fin. Officer, Treas. & Sec.--Idea Engineering & Fabricating, Detroit, MI, pg. 562
Barocas, Leon, V.P., Treas. & Sec.--Santee Print Works, Inc., New York, NY, pg. 970
Baron, C.B., Sec.--Nixdorff Krein Industries Inc., Saint Louis, MO, pg. 807
Barone, Elaine, V.P., Sec. & Treas.--Coken Company, Inc., Providence, RI, pg. 259
Barone, Patricia A., Asst. Sec.--Unigard Security Insurance Co., Bellevue, WA, pg. 596
Barr, Marie, Sec.--Barr Electric Corporation, Wheeling, IL, pg. 122
Barre, Stephen A., Chm. Bd., Pres., Chief Exec. Officer & Sec.--Servo Corporation of America, Hicksville, NY, pg. 993
Barrett, Fred C., Treas. & Sec.--Ryan Oldsmobile, Billings, MT, pg. 958
Barrett, Paul L., Gen. Counsel & Sec.--Redman Industries, Inc., Dallas, TX, pg. 919
Barrier, Rick, Sec.--The Nerland Agency, Inc., Anchorage, AK, pg. 798
Barro, Dan, V.P. & Corp. Sec.--Lamp Post Franchise Corporation, Tustin, CA, pg. 652
Barrott, John C., Sec. & Asst. Treas.--Aurora Casket Company, Aurora, IN, pg. 98
Barry, Elizabeth T., Sec.--Gazette Company, Inc., Cedar Rapids, IA, pg. 447
Bartenstein, Jeff C., Sec., Treas. & Controller--Alaska Industrial Hardware Inc., Anchorage, AK, pg. 30
Bartlett, John L., Corp. Sec. & Gen. Counsel--Arinc Inc., Annapolis, MD, pg. 82
Bartlett, John L., Sec. & Gen. Counsel--ARINC Research Corp., Annapolis, MD, pg. 82
Bartlett, John L., Sec. & Gen. Counsel--Aeronautical Radio, Inc., Annapolis, MD, pg. 82
Barton, Graham G., Sec.--Thunderline Corporation, Belleville, MI, pg. 1096
Barton, John S., Corp. Sec.--Thiele Kaolin Co., Sandersville, GA, pg. 1092
Bartram, John C., Sec.--Lord, Sullivan & Yoder, Inc. Advertising, Columbus, OH, pg. 683
Bartzen, Robert, Sec.--Lappin Electric Company, Milwaukee, WI, pg. 658
Baseman, Harris, Sec.--Statler Industries, Medford, MA, pg. 1041
Basham, B.H., V.P. & Sec.--Industrial Rubber Products Company, Charleston, WV, pg. 566
Basile, Peter A., Pres.--Peter A. Basile Sons Inc., Livonia, MI, pg. 124
Basquin, Peter, Chm. Bd., Sec. & Treas.--Harmeson Manufacturing Company, Inc., Frankfort, IN, pg. 510
Bass, Norma, Treas. & Sec.--The Parman Corporation, Nashville, TN, pg. 850
Bassett, David M., Sec. & Project Mgr.--The W.E. Bassett Company, Shelton, CT, pg. 125
Bast, Bonnie R., V.P. & Sec.--Bast Chevrolet Inc., Seaford, NY, pg. 125
Batarseh, Gabriel, Sec. & Treas.--Filco, Inc., Sacramento, CA, pg. 409
Bateman, Christopher H., V.P. & Sec.--HCC Industries, Rosemead, CA, pg. 496
Bateman, George W., Sec.--Bateman Brothers Lumber Co., Inc., New Britain, PA, pg. 125
Bates, Dorothy G., Sec. & Treas.--Ring Technologies, Inc., Warren, MI, pg. 935
Bates, Susan, Controller, Chief Fin. Officer & Sec.--The Benatty Corporation, Cambridge, OH, pg. 138
Baubonis, Patricia, Sec. & Mgr.-Legal Services--Graphic Controls, Corp., Buffalo, NY, pg. 478
Baubonis, Patricia, Sec.--Graphic Controls Corporation, Buffalo, NY, pg. 478
Baudais, Jean-Pierre, Chief Fin. Officer & Corp. Sec.--TBWA de Plas, Paris,, France, pg. 1072
Bauder, Dixie A., Sec.--Coca Cola Bottling Co. United, Inc., Birmingham, AL, pg. 257
Bauer, Mimi, Treas. & Sec.--Basic Food International Inc., Fort Lauderdale, FL, pg. 124
Baugh, Thomas E., Jr., Sec.--Sands Investments, Inc., Myrtle Beach, SC, pg. 970
Baugher, Susie E., Sec.--Baugher Chevrolet-Buick-Geo, Inc., Waynesboro, VA, pg. 127
Baum, W.A., Sec. & Treas.--W. A. Baum Company, Inc., Copiague, NY, pg. 127
Baumgarte, Virginia, Sec. & Treas.--E.M. Wiegmann & Company, Inc., Freeburg, IL, pg. 1188
Bavido, Joe, Sec.--Associated Milk Producers, Inc., San Antonio, TX, pg. 91
Baxter, Derek, Asst. Sec.--Holmatic, Inc., Norcross, GA, pg. 122
Bayles, Mary, Sec.--Royal Waterbeds, Maryland Heights, MO, pg. 953
Bayley, Joanne, Treas. & Sec.--Robert E. Bayley Construction, Seattle, WA, pg. 128
Beach, Juanita, Sec. & Treas.--Beach Mold & Tool Inc., New Albany, IN, pg. 128
Beadie, William M., Sec.--API Group Inc., Saint Paul, MN, pg. 5
Beale, Horace, V.P. & Sec.--Control Systems Inc., Saint Paul, MN, pg. 281
Beard, C.L., V.P. & Sec.--Annin & Company, Roseland, NJ, pg. 75
Beard, Karen E., Sec. & Treas.--N. G. Gilbert Corporation, Muncie, IN, pg. 458
Beard, Thomas G., V.P.-Admin., Treas., Controller & Sec.--Palmer Electric Co., Winter Park, FL, pg. 843
Bearmon, Lee, V.P., Sec. & Gen. Counsel--Carlson Companies, Inc., Minneapolis, MN, pg. 220
Beatty, Leslie F., Corp. Sec.--Fredrickson Motor Express Corp., Charlotte, NC, pg. 430
Beauch, Steve, Sec. & Treas.--Veda Design Group, Alexandria, VA, pg. 1146
Beaudoin, Marc, Sec. & Treas.--Hancock Lumber, Inc., Casco, ME, pg. 504
Beavers, Robert F., Sec.--Maxon Corporation, Muncie, IN, pg. 723
Bechor, Sasson, V.P.-Fin. & Sec.--Allied Foods, Inc., Atlanta, GA, pg. 38
Beck, J. Edward, Jr., Sec.--Beck Manufacturing, Inc., Waynesboro, PA, pg. 153
Beck, Stephen, V.P. & Sec.--Bitrek Corporation, Waynesboro, PA, pg. 153
Beck, William, Sec.--Arkansas Electric Cooperatives Inc., Little Rock, AR, pg. 83
Becker, Debra, Sec.--Sullivan & Brownell, Inc., Randolph, VT, pg. 1056
Becker, Paul, V.P., Sec., Treas. & Gen. Counsel--Cosco Industries, Spring Valley, NY, pg. 288
Becker, Robert, Sec. & Treas.--Ershigs, Inc., Bellingham, WA, pg. 387
Beda, Bruce A., V.P., Treas., Chief Fin. Officer & Sec.--Venturedyne, Ltd., Milwaukee, WI, pg. 1148
Bedford, Hilda L., Sec.--Beckwith Elevator Co., Boston, MA, pg. 131
Beeby, Kenneth J., V.P., Sec. & Gen. Counsel--Ocean Spray Cranberries, Inc., Lakeville, MA, pg. 820
Beegan, Geraldine, Sec.--Cla-Val Div., Newport Beach, CA, pg. 488
Beggs, Robert W., Sr. V.P. & Sec.--Society for Savings Bancorp, Inc., Hartford, CT, pg. 1016
Behan, William L., III, V.P. & Sec.--Hill-Behan Lumber Company, Saint Louis, MO, pg. 534
Behner, Barbara, Chief Fin. Officer, Sec. & Treas.--Harmon Smith Inc., Kansas City, MO, pg. 510
Belcher, B.M., Jr., V.P.-Planning & Sec.--Benjamin Moore & Co., Montvale, NJ, pg. 139
Belk, Lowell, V.P.-Admin. & Sec.--The Bibb Company, Macon, GA, pg. 781
Bell, Arthur, V.P. & Sec.--Madison Graham Colorgraphics, Inc., Los Angeles, CA, pg. 699
Bell, Carmela Leone, Gen. Counsel & Sec.--Reliable Stores, Inc., Columbia, MD, pg. 925
Bell, Gail L., Corp. Sec.--Peter W. Smith & Company, Inc., Chicago, IL, pg. 1011
Bell, George L., V.P. & Sec.--Star Food Products, Inc., Burlington, NC, pg. 1039
Bell, Kayden, V.P., Sec. & Treas.--Arnold Machinery Co., Salt Lake City, UT, pg. 84
Bell, Peter, Sec.--Chicago Reader, Inc., Chicago, IL, pg. 245
Bell, Robert P., Exec. V.P., Sec. & Treas.--Harry H. Bell & Sons, Inc., Saint Petersburg, FL, pg. 134
Bell, Wayne L., V.P. & Sec.--Virginia Metal Industries, Inc., Orange, VA, pg. 1152
Benedetto, Josephine, Sec.--Affiliated Food Stores, Keller, TX, pg. 23
Benner, Kevin P., Controller, Sec. & Treas.--Jasper County Farm Bureau Co-op Association, Inc., Rensselaer, IN, pg. 590
Bennett, Annese, Asst. Sec.--HTB, Inc., Oklahoma City, OK, pg. 497
Bennett, George O., V.P. & Sec.--Bennett Brothers, Inc., Chicago, IL, pg. 139
Bennett, Ruby T., Corp. Sec.--Jemison, Inc., Memphis, TN, pg. 592
Bennett, Shirley O., Asst. Sec.--Bennett Brothers, Inc., Chicago, IL, pg. 139
Benno, Eli, V.P., Treas. & Sec.--Trading Port, Inc., Albany, NY, pg. 1105
Benson, Betty, Treas. & Sec.--Delaware Electric Co-Op, Greenwood, DE, pg. 325
Benson, Vera, Sec. & Controller--Ernst W. Dorn Co., Inc., Gardena, CA, pg. 346
Bentley, Alan, Sec. & Treas.--National Merchandise Co., Inc., Jacksonville, FL, pg. 792
Benua, P.L., Exec. V.P. & Sec.--Ebco Mfg. Company, Columbus, OH, pg. 365
Benvenuti, Joan A., V.P.-Admin. & Sec.--Octagon Process Inc., Edgewater, NJ, pg. 821
Berg, Carole L., V.P. & Sec.--Serfilco, Ltd., Northbrook, IL, pg. 990
Berg, S., Sec.--L.H. Sowles Company, Inc., Minneapolis, MN, pg. 1024
Berg, Thomas C., V.P., Gen. Counsel & Sec.--Amsted Industries Incorporated, Chicago, IL, pg. 68
Berg, W. Robert, Vice Chm., Treas. & Sec.--Bartlett and Company, Kansas City, MO, pg. 122
Bergen, Lee D., Chm. Bd. & Sec.--Peter Lumber Company, Pleasantville, NJ, pg. 864
Berger, Bryan, Sec. & Treas.--Smith Farms, Inc., Flatonia, TX, pg. 1012
Bergman, David R., Exec. V.P. & Sec.--Processed Plastic Company, Montgomery, IL, pg. 892
Berkley, Herbert R., Sec. & Treas.--Berkliff Corporation, New York, NY, pg. 142
Berkley, Richard L., Sec. & Treas.--Tension Envelope Corp., Kansas City, MO, pg. 1088
Berkman, Jerome, Sec.--Medical Laboratory Automation, Inc., Pleasantville, NY, pg. 735
Berkson, Stanley, Sec. & Treas.--Stanbee Company, Inc., Carlstadt, NJ, pg. 1035
Berlin, Alan, Treas. & Sec.--Potato Sales Company, Inc., Los Angeles, CA, pg. 882
Berlin, Marvin, Sec. & Treas.--New York Carpet World Inc., Southfield, MI, pg. 802
Berliner, Robert, Corp. Sec.--Jupiter Industries, Inc., Chicago, IL, pg. 609
Berlinsky, Jay S., Sec.--Transco Inc., Chicago, IL, pg. 1106
Berman, Robert, Sec. & Treas.--Metpar Corporation, Westbury, NY, pg. 742
Berman, Russell S., Sec.--John Emmerling Inc., New York, NY, pg. 379
Bernards, Jeffrey, V.P. & Sec.--Bernards Brothers, Inc., San Fernando, CA, pg. 143
Bernstein, Harvey, Pres. & Sec.--Spirite Industries, Inc., Englewood, NJ, pg. 1031
Bernstein, Jonathan, V.P., Treas. & Sec.--National Foods Inc., Bronx, NY, pg. 788
Bernstein, Sheldon, Sec. & Treas.--Milady Brassiere & Corset Co., Inc., New York, NY, pg. 753
Berry, Richard C., Legal Counsel--Hobart Brothers Co., Troy, OH, pg. 536
Bersoff, Marilyn, Sec. & Treas.--BTG, Inc., Vienna, VA, pg. 107
Berson, Joel, Sec. & Gen. Counsel--Tork, Inc., Mount Vernon, NY, pg. 1102
Berson, Selma, Sec. & Treas.--B & B Motor & Control Corporation, Long Island City, NY, pg. 105
Bertelsen, Anita M., Sec.--Waldorf Corporation, Saint Paul, MN, pg. 1159
Bertolini, Arthur G., Sr. V.P.-Fin. & Admin., Treas. & Sec.--Rocor Transportation Companies Inc., Oklahoma City, OK, pg. 942
Besse, Grey, Sec.--Northern Michigan Veneers, Inc., Gladstone, MI, pg. 814
Best, Philip C., V.P. & Sec.--STS Holdings, Inc., Northbrook, IL, pg. 964
Beutler, Tom, Sec., Treas. & Controller--Beutler Heating & Air Conditioning Inc., Sacramento, CA, pg. 148
Bewley, Linda L., Asst. Sec.--Kartridg Pak Co., Davenport, IA, pg. 122
Beyer, Allan, V.P.-Fin. & Sec.--Basler Electric Company, Highland, IL, pg. 125
Bibler, Laurie, Treas. & Sec.--Bibler Brothers, Inc., Russellville, AR, pg. 148

Bienvenu, Wayne, Sec.--Turnbull Enterprises, Inc., Baltimore, MD, pg. 1119
Bigler, Debra E., V.P., Dir.-Mktg. & Asst. Sec.--W. P. Carey & Co., Inc., New York, NY, pg. 218
Bikales, Norman A., Sec. & Clerk--BIW Cable Systems, Inc., North Dighton, MA, pg. 106
Billings, Edwin, Sec. & Treas.--Sequentia Inc. Reinforced Plastics Div., Strongsville, OH, pg. 990
Billings, K.W., Sec. & Treas.--Ranchers Cotton Oil, Fresno, CA, pg. 911
Billups, S. Keith, Sec.--Publix Supermarkets Inc., Lakeland, FL, pg. 898
Binder, Joe, Sec.--Acme Truck Line, Inc., Harvey, LA, pg. 13
Binder, Joseph, Sec.--Key Food Stores Co-operative, Inc., Brooklyn, NY, pg. 626
Bingle, Donald J., V.P., Gen. Counsel & Clerk--Boston Chicken, Inc., Naperville, IL, pg. 167
Bird, Patricia, Sec.--Inman Mills, Inman, SC, pg. 570
Birkanshaw, Ralph, Sec.--New England Dairies, Inc., Hartford, CT, pg. 800
Bishop, J. Randall, Sec. & Treas.--Cameron & Barkley Company, Inc., Charleston Heights, SC, pg. 212
Bishop, P.S., Treas. & Sec.--Rissler & McMurry Company, Casper, WY, pg. 936
Bistiline, Margi, Sec.--Rogerson Hiller Corporation, Port Angeles, WA, pg. 944
Bistricer, Nathan, Sec.--Philipp Brothers Chemicals, Inc., Fort Lee, NJ, pg. 867
Bjerg, Nils, Sec. & Chief Fin. Officer--Monrovia Nursery Co., Azusa, CA, pg. 766
Black, T.M., Jr., Sec. & Dir.-Research--Walter J. Black, Inc., Port Washington, NY, pg. 154
Blackburn, Lisa, Exec. Sec.--Carroll's Foods, Inc., Warsaw, NC, pg. 225
Blackstone, Franklin, Jr., Gen. Counsel & Sec.--Bearing Service Company, Pittsburgh, PA, pg. 130
Blackwell, Daisy S., Sec.--V.G.S. Corp. d/b/a Southland Oil Company, Jackson, MS, pg. 1141
Blackwell, Daisy S., Treas. & Sec.--Yazoo Investment Corporation, Jackson, MS, pg. 1207
Blair, David, Sec.--Seabrook Foods, Inc., Fresno, CA, pg. 984
Blaker, A. L., Sec., Treas. & Mktg. Dir.--King Bear Enterprises, Inc., North Merrick, NY, pg. 630
Blanchard, William C., Sec. & Treas.--Wm. Blanchard Co., Springfield, NJ, pg. 155
Blank, Jeffrey, Sec. & Dir.-Mktg.--Elastic Materials, Inc., Smithville, OH, pg. 372
Blankenship, Paula, Sec.--Bush Brothers & Company, Dandridge, TN, pg. 196
Blankinship, Scott F., Exec. V.P. & Sec.--Petroleum Marketers, Inc., Roanoke, VA, pg. 865
Blatt, Selma K., Sec.--Columbus Steel Drum Company, Blacklick, OH, pg. 267
Blattner, Stephen C., Sec., Treas. & Chief Fin. Officer--D.H. Blattner & Sons, Inc., Avon, MN, pg. 156
Bliley, J. Earle, Sec.--McInnes Steel Company, Corry, PA, pg. 729
Blinder, Alice D., Sec.--Nelson Brothers Furniture Co., Chicago, IL, pg. 797
Block, Ira, V.P., Gen. Counsel & Sec.--Wechsler Coffee Corp., Moonachie, NJ, pg. 1172
Block, Jed A., Dir.-Communications & Sec.--Jewelers Mutual Insurance Company, Neenah, WI, pg. 593
Block, Stephen A., V.P. & Sec.--GAF Broadcasting Co., Inc., New York, NY, pg. 438
Block, Stephen A., Sec.--GAF Export Corp., Wayne, NJ, pg. 438
Block, Stephen A., Sec.--GAF International Corp., Wayne, NJ, pg. 438
Blonkenmeyer, Gerald G., Treas. & Sec.--Lasting Products, Inc., Dallas, TX, pg. 660
Bloom, David B., Chief Fin. Officer & Treas.--Bloom Electric Services, Inc., Oklahoma City, OK, pg. 157
Bloomberg, Stanley, Exec. V.P. & Sec.--Glen Oaks Industries, Inc., New York, NY, pg. 461
Blount, Jimmie, Sec., Treas. & Controller--Delta Pride Catfish, Inc., Indianola, MS, pg. 327
Blunier, Doris, Sec.--DMI, Inc., Goodfield, IL, pg. 309
Bluth, Lawrence, V.P.- Sec. & Gen. Counsel--Penske Corporation, Detroit, MI, pg. 859
Blutstein, Barbara, Sec.--Reliable Knitting Works, Milwaukee, WI, pg. 924
Boasberg, Jack, V.P., Sec.--Sperling, New Orleans, LA, pg. 1030
Bobo, April, Sec. & Controller--Olen Corporation, Columbus, OH, pg. 641
Boda, Tammy, Sec.--Crossman Corp., East Bloomfield, NY, pg. 300
Bodifor, Lowell, Sec. & Treas.--Fort Worth Lumber Company, Fort Worth, TX, pg. 425
Bodine, David, V.P.-Admin. & Sec.--The Bodine Corp., Bridgeport, CT, pg. 161
Boehm, Hannes G., Sec.--Chatsworth Data Corporation, Chatsworth, CA, pg. 241
Bogenholm, Ellis, Sec.--Flex-O-Glass, Inc., Chicago, IL, pg. 418
Boger, Debra, Sec.--Ohio River Associates, Inc., Hannibal, OH, pg. 822
Boger, Debra J., Sec.--Ormet Corporation, Hannibal, OH, pg. 822
Bohan, Daniel P., Exec. V.P., Treas. & Sec.--Omega World Travel, Inc., Falls Church, VA, pg. 826
Bohm, Gerald, V.P., Corp. Counsel & Sec.--Prime Hospitality Corp., Fairfield, NJ, pg. 889
Boland, James, Dir.-Data Processing, Pension Admin., Controller & Sec.--Central Illinois Steel Company, Carlinville, IL, pg. 232
Boland, Michael, Sec. & Treas.--David Boland, Inc., Titusville, FL, pg. 162
Bolton, William J., V.P.-Fin. & Sec.--Carolina Steel Corporation, Greensboro, NC, pg. 223
Bonahoom, A. James, Jr., Pres. & Sec.--Wolverine Packing Co., Detroit, MI, pg. 1199
Bond, Robert J., Jr., Sec.--Altair Corporation, Lincolnshire, IL, pg. 45
Boneberger, Greg, Gen. Counsel & Corp. Sec.--Wyatt Inc., Branford, CT, pg. 1205
Bonn, Allan, Treas. & Sec.--F.H. Bonn Company, Arlington Heights, IL, pg. 164
Bonn, Patricia, Mgr.-Admin. & Employee Rels.--Bobst Group Inc., Roseland, NJ, pg. 161
Bonsib, Gretchen A., Sr. V.P., Sec. & Treas.--Bonsib Inc., Fort Wayne, IN, pg. 164
Booth, Richard W., Exec. V.P. & Sec.--Lennox International Inc., Richardson, TX, pg. 667
Booth, Thomas E., Sec. & Treas.--Woolverton Oldsmobile-G.M.C. Truck, Inc., Jacksonville, FL, pg. 1201
Bootz, Howard W., Treas. & Corp. Sec.--Red Spot Paint & Varnish Co., Evansville, IN, pg. 918
Borawski, Bob, Sec.--Silicon Power Cube Corporation, Long Beach, CA, pg. 1004
Borg, Sandra A., Vice Chm. & Asst. Sec.--Macromedia Inc., Hackensack, NJ, pg. 698
Borkhoder, Lloyd, Sec. & Controller--Pete Fall Ford Inc., Elkhart, IN, pg. 398
Borlinghaus, Scott, Sec. & Controller--John Fabick Tractor Company, Fenton, MO, pg. 396
Born, J. Ivan, V.P., Sec. & Treas.--Beaudry Ford, Inc., Atlanta, GA, pg. 130
Borod, Marx J., Sec.--Ideal Chemical & Supply Company, Memphis, TN, pg. 562
Borton, Ronald, Sec. & Treas.--Sauder Manufacturing Corporation, Archbold, OH, pg. 972
Bosch, Joel, Treas. & Sec.--Minot Builders Supply Association, Minot, ND, pg. 758
Bossio, Salvatore, Corp. Sec.--Swinerton & Walberg Co., San Francisco, CA, pg. 1068
Bost, Robert G., Sec.--Petroleum Products Corp., Middletown, PA, pg. 865
Boucher, Joyce J., Sec.--Caldwell Manufacturing Company, Rochester, NY, pg. 208
Bouchillon, J. Dan, Sec.--Town & Country Ford Inc., Louisville, KY, pg. 1103
Boughton, Sid, Sec.--Jacobsen Manufacturing, Inc., Safety Harbor, FL, pg. 588
Boulware, C. Diane, Sec.--Sunnen Products Company, Saint Louis, MO, pg. 1061
Bouthot, Kerry, Sec.--Beacon Group, Bloomfield, CT, pg. 128
Boutonnet, Edward, Gen. Mgr. & Sec.--California Artichoke & Vegetable Growers Corp., Castroville, CA, pg. 209
Bowden, C.E., V.P.-Grain/Traffic, Sec., & Treas.--Fisher Mills, Inc., Seattle, WA, pg. 415
Bowden, Douglas, Exec. V.P. & Sec.--Sencore, Inc., Sioux Falls, SD, pg. 989
Bowe, William J., V.P., Sec. & Gen. Counsel--Encyclopaedia Britannica, Inc., Chicago, IL, pg. 381
Bowen, James E., Sec. & Comptroller--Better Living Inc., Charlottesville, VA, pg. 148
Bower, Robert R., Sr. V.P.--S.T. Research, Newington, VA, pg. 964
Bowers, Hershey, Jr., Sec.--Nibble with Gibble's, Inc., Chambersburg, PA, pg. 806
Bowie, M.S., Asst. Sec.--Miller Advertising Agency Inc., New York, NY, pg. 753
Bowman, Elizabeth, Sec.--Homan Lumber Mart, Inc., Elkhart, IN, pg. 541
Boyd, James, Sec.--Goodkind & O'Dea, Inc., Rutherford, NJ, pg. 334
Boyd, Julius, Sec. & Treas.--Fairway Ford, Inc., Greenville, SC, pg. 397
Boyd, Julius, Sec. & Treas.--Heritage Lincoln-Mercury, Greenville, SC, pg. 398
Boyd, Sally, Sec.--Mark III Industries, Ocala, FL, pg. 708
Boyer, Vicki, Sec.--Angelo Brothers Co., Philadelphia, PA, pg. 74
Boyers, Charles F., Sr. V.P., Admin. & Sec.--Wills Group, Inc., La Plata, MD, pg. 1193
Boyle, Robert K., Sec. & Treas.--The Lewis Bear Company, Pensacola, FL, pg. 129
Bozof, Steve, Sec.--Bozof Dinettes, Inc., Olive Branch, MS, pg. 169
Bradford, J.W., V.P., Gen. Counsel & Sec.--AFG Industries, Inc., Fort Worth, TX, pg. 3
Bradley, Scott, Sec.--Topcor Financial Corporation, Chicago, IL, pg. 1101
Bradstock, N.E., Exec. V.P.-Sec.--Harrop Industries, Inc., Columbus, OH, pg. 512
Braig, Thomas, Sec.--Superior Label Systems, Inc., Cincinnati, OH, pg. 1063
Branch, Brenda, Sec.--House of Raeford Farms, Inc., Raeford, NC, pg. 546
Branch, Kenneth A., Sec., Treas. & Controller--Randall's Food Markets, Inc., Houston, TX, pg. 911
Brand, Robert, Treas. & Sec.--Performance Contracting Group, Charlotte, NC, pg. 861
Brand, Robert, Treas. & Sec.--Performance Contracting, Inc., Charlotte, NC, pg. 861
Brandon, Lynda, Sec. & Treas.--John J. Campbell Co., Inc., Memphis, TN, pg. 212
Brands, James E., Exec. V.P., Sec. & Treas.--Scherer Scientific, Ltd., Atlanta, GA, pg. 976
Brandt, Charles L., Exec. V.P.-Admin. & Sec.--Lubrication Engineers, Inc., Fort Worth, TX, pg. 686
Brannen, John T., Treas. & Sec.--Mid America International Trucks, Inc., Memphis, TN, pg. 750
Brassard, Mary, Corp. Sec. & Controller--F. H. Chase, Inc., Foxboro, MA, pg. 240
Braswell, Diana Callan, Sec.--Central Freight Lines Inc., Waco, TX, pg. 232
Braswell, Linda, Asst. Sec.--MADD (Mothers Against Drunk Driving), Irving, TX, pg. 691
Bratten, Carolyn, Legal Sec.--Wawa, Inc., Wawa, PA, pg. 1169
Braum, Mary, Sec.--Braum Ice Cream Stores Inc., Oklahoma City, OK, pg. 172
Brecht, Warren F., V.P., Treas. & Sec.--Butler International, Montvale, NJ, pg. 197
Breland, Nancy L., Sec.--Linbeck Corp., Houston, TX, pg. 675
Bremer, Craig W., Sec.--Susquehanna Pfaltzgraff, York, PA, pg. 1065
Bremer, John M., V.P., Gen. Counsel & Sec.--Northwestern Mutual Life Insurance Co., Milwaukee, WI, pg. 815
Brennan, Daniel V., Sec. & Controller--Frontier Lumber Company, Inc., Buffalo, NY, pg. 434
Brennan, Diane, Sec. & Controller--Thruway Fasteners Inc., North Tonawanda, NY, pg. 1096
Brennan, Walter, Sec. & Treas.--American Fabrics Company, New York, NY, pg. 51
Brenner, David L., Sec.--Children's World Learning Centers, Inc., Golden, CO, pg. 7
Brenton, Evelyn, Sec.--Autoswage Products, Inc., Shelton, CT, pg. 101
Brewer, Stan, V.P.-Opers., Sec. & Treas.--Associated Food Stores Inc., Salt Lake City, UT, pg. 89
Brewton, R. Gerald, Sec. & Treas.--Jerry Hamm Chevrolet Inc., Jacksonville, FL, pg. 503
Brice, Joni, Chief Exec. Officer--Heil-Brice Retail Advertising, San Clemente, CA, pg. 525
Bridge, John B., V.P.-Real Estate, Sec. & Gen. Counsel--VASA Insurance Group, Inc., Indianapolis, IN, pg. 1146
Bridge, John B., V.P., Gen. Counsel & Sec.--Brougher Agency, Inc., Indianapolis, IN, pg. 1146
Bridge, John B., V.P. & Sec.--VASA Brougher, Inc., Indianapolis, IN, pg. 1146
Bridge, John B., V.P. & Sec.--VASA North Atlantic Insurance Company, Indianapolis, IN, pg. 1146
Bridgeman, Robert E., Asst. Sec.--The Bibb Company, Macon, GA, pg. 781
Bridges, Deanne, Sec.--The Dee Howard Company, San Antonio, TX, pg. 547
Bridges, Harold R., V.P. & Sec.--Smith & Gillespie Engineers, Inc., Jacksonville, FL, pg. 1012
Bridges, Maxine L., Sec., Treas. & Dir.-Personnel & Investor Rels.--Sterling Homes Corp., Sparks, NV, pg. 1046
Briggs, John, V.P., Sec. & Controller--Hy-Vee Food Stores Incorporated, Chariton, IA, pg. 556
Briggs, K. Douglas, V.P., Treas. & Sec.--Quincy Mutual Fire Insurance Company, Quincy, MA, pg. 905
Brigham, Barbie, Sec.--Diagraph Corporation, Earth City, MO, pg. 335
Brinberg, Simeon, Sr. V.P. & Sec.--Georgetown Partners, Inc., Great Neck, NY, pg. 473
Brindle, Harold A., V.P. & Sec.--Wards Cove Packing Company, Seattle, WA, pg. 1163
Brink, James, Sec.--Concord Litho Co., Inc., Concord, NH, pg. 272
Brinkler, Kenneth C., Sec.--Fairmont Homes, Inc., Nappanee, IN, pg. 397
Brittelli, Brenda S., Chief Fin. Officer, Sec.,Treas. & Controller--Adams Wine Co., Atlanta, GA, pg. 17
Brock, Carolyn, Sec.--J. L. Todd Auction Co., Rome, GA, pg. 1099
Brock, Frank E., Sec. & Treas.--Williamson-Dickie Mfg. Co., Fort Worth, TX, pg. 1192
Brocke, Eugene, Sec.--George F. Brocke & Sons, Inc., Kendrick, ID, pg. 178
Brocklehurst, David, Fin. Dir. & Sec.--Luscombe and Partners Pty. Ltd., Port Melbourne,, Australia, pg. 344
Brocksher, Jean, Sec. & Asst. Treas.--Allright Corporation, Houston, TX, pg. 41
Broderick, John J., V.P., Sec. & Treas.--Judd's Incorporated, Washington, DC, pg. 608
Brodt, John D., Treas. & Sec.--Ohio Valley Electric Corporation, Piketon, OH, pg. 822
Brommels, Alyce M., Corp. Sec.--Bay State Milling Co., Quincy, MA, pg. 127
Brooks, Delcy, Sec.--Slant/Fin Corporation, Greenvale, NY, pg. 1010
Brooks, J.B., Sec. & Treas.--Flexel, Inc., Atlanta, GA, pg. 418
Brothers, Delores, Sec., Treas. & Chief Fin. Officer--Evana Automation, Evansville, IN, pg. 390
Broughton, Barbara K., Sec.--Diemakers, Inc., Monroe City, MO, pg. 336
Brountas, Paul, Sec.--Thinking Machines Corporation, Cambridge, MA, pg. 1092
Brown, Allen, Sec. & Treas.--Riverside Central Services, Inc., Natchez, MS, pg. 937
Brown, Bill G., V.P.-Estimating & Sec.--G. E. Johnson Construction Co., Inc., Colorado Springs, CO, pg. 597
Brown, David H., Sec.--Wyandot Inc., Marion, OH, pg. 1205
Brown, Gail, Sec. & Treas.--Mayfield Building Supply Co., Arlington, TX, pg. 691
Brown, Gordon S., Sec. & Treas.--Bruce Foods Corp., Saint Martinville, LA, pg. 183
Brown, Harvey J., Sec.--F.M. Brown Sons, Inc., Sinking Spring, PA, pg. 183
Brown, James D., Exec. V.P. & Sec.--Pacor, Inc., Philadelphia, PA, pg. 842
Brown, Katherine, Treas. & Sec.--Troncalli Motors, Inc., Decatur, GA, pg. 1115
Brown, Kimberly, Sec.--Field Container Company, L.P., Elk Grove Village, IL, pg. 409
Brown, Lynnea, Exec. Asst.--Ace Office Products, Rolling Meadows, IL, pg. 12
Brown, Nancy, Treas. & Sec.--Heintzelman's Truck Center Inc., Orlando, FL, pg. 526
Brown, Robert W., Jr., Exec. V.P., Gen. Mgr. & Sec.--Brown Motors, Toledo, OH, pg. 182
Brown, Rockwood, Sr. V.P., Sec. & Gen. Counsel--WYO-Ben, Inc., Billings, MT, pg. 1157
Brown, Susan, Sec.--Rex Marine Center, Inc., Norwalk, CT, pg. 930
Brown, Thomas H., Jr., Sec.--Molin Auto Parts Inc., Buffalo, NY, pg. 764

Brown, Timothy N., Corp. Counsel & Sec.--J. E. Higgins Lumber Co., Concord, CA, pg. 533
Brown, William R., Gen. Counsel & Sec.--American United Life Insurance Company, Indianapolis, IN, pg. 65
Browning, Jean, Treas. & Sec.--Browning Chemical Corporation, White Plains, NY, pg. 183
Broyles, Thomas M., V.P.-Fin. & Corp. Sec.--Peerless Pottery, Inc., Rockport, IN, pg. 855
Brubaker, Jerry L., Sec. & Treas.--Schneller, Inc., Kent, OH, pg. 977
Bruce, Rick, Corp. Sec.--SRS Technologies, Newport Beach, CA, pg. 964
Bruens, John, Treas. & Sec.--WRM, Inc., Mabscott, WV, pg. 1156
Bruggeman, G.F., Asst. Sec.--Al Johnson Construction Co., Minneapolis, MN, pg. 597
Brumber, K. Richard, Sec.--Jones Chemicals, Inc., Le Roy, NY, pg. 603
Brumby, David, Sec.--Pumpelly Oil, Inc., Westlake, LA, pg. 900
Brumleue, David L., Treas. & Sec.--Hodgson Mill, Inc., Gainesville, MO, pg. 1002
Brumleve, David, Chief Fin. Officer, Treas., & Sec.--Siemer Milling Company, Teutopolis, IL, pg. 1002
Bruskrud, Randy, Sec.--Bemco Inc., Simi Valley, CA, pg. 138
Brustein, Lawrence, Chief Fin. Officer, Sec. & Treas.--Henry Modell & Company, Inc., Long Island City, NY, pg. 762
Bryan, A. Chris, II, Pres., Chief Exec. Officer, Sec. & Treas.--BA Advertising, Dallas, TX, pg. 105
Bryan, Charles R., Exec. V.P., Sec. & Treas.--AVA-Automatic Vendors of America, Atlanta, GA, pg. 8
Bryant, Geraldine D., Treas. & Sec.--Lowell Packing Company, Fitzgerald, GA, pg. 685
Bryant, Richard J., Sec. & Treas.--Bryant Supply Company, Inc., Gastonia, NC, pg. 185
Bryce, William H., III, V.P. & Sec.--Bryce Corporation, Memphis, TN, pg. 185
Bryte, Deccie, Sec.--Ireland Coffee Tea, Inc., Pleasantville, NJ, pg. 582
Brzustewicz, Robert, Chief Exec. Officer & Sec.--Northern Wire & Cable, Inc., Troy, MI, pg. 814
Buchanan, Mary Jane, Sec. & Treas.--Heights Heating & Cooling, Auburn Hills, MI, pg. 525
Bucholtz, Barbara K., Sec.--T.D. Williamson, Inc., Tulsa, OK, pg. 1192
Buckley, Alan, Chief Fin. Officer, Sec., Treas. & Legal Officer--Pease Industries, Inc., Fairfield, OH, pg. 854
Buckman, M.W., Treas. & Asst. Sec.--Bulab Holdings, Inc., Memphis, TN, pg. 188
Bucksbaum, Matthew, Pres., Treas. & Sec.--General Growth Companies, Inc., Des Moines, IA, pg. 449
Buda, T.J., Sr. V.P., Sec. & Gen. Counsel--Auto-Owners Insurance, Lansing, MI, pg. 100
Buddhdev, Sharad N., Chief Fin. Officer & Asst. Sec.--Swallen's, Inc., Cincinnati, OH, pg. 1066
Budig, George J., V.P., Sec. & Treas.--Budco Group Inc., Cincinnati, OH, pg. 186
Buehler, Judith Stetter, Sec.--Wharfside Restaurants, Inc., Jasper, IN, pg. 1184
Buerger, Marie, Sec.--Brian Unlimited Distribution Company, Inc., Detroit, MI, pg. 175
Bukowski, Gary, V.P.-Fin., Controller & Sec.--Key Industries, Inc., Fort Scott, KS, pg. 627
Bull, Donald A., Exec. V.P. & Sec.--Goodway Tool Corporation, Stamford, CT, pg. 471
Bulman, Neil, Jr., Sec. & Gen. Counsel--Schottenstein Stores Corporation, Columbus, OH, pg. 978
Bunnell, Roderick, Sr. V.P., Sec. & Gen. Counsel--Blue Cross & Blue Shield of Oregon, Portland, OR, pg. 160
Burgiss, Wes, Exec. V.P., Sec.--Creative Alliance, Inc., Louisville, KY, pg. 297
Burgon, Barre G., V.P., Sec. & Corp. Counsel--Flying J. Inc., Brigham City, UT, pg. 421
Burgoyne, Mary Louise, Sec. & Treas.--Burgoyne, Inc., Philadelphia, PA, pg. 190
Burke, J. Terence, Sec. & Gen. Counsel--Realty One, Cleveland, OH, pg. 917
Burke, Margaret, Sec.--Hulman & Company, Terre Haute, IN, pg. 552
Burleson, Barbara E., Sec.--Pepsi-Cola Bottling Company of Charlotte Inc., Charlotte, NC, pg. 860
Burmaster, M.R., V.P.-Sec. & Head Legal Dept.--Clark Oil & Refining Corporation, Saint Louis, MO, pg. 252
Burns, John F., Sec.--HLC Industries, Farmington Hills, MI, pg. 496
Burns, John W., Exec. V.P., Sec. & Treas.--Consolidated Industrial Corporation, Birmingham, MI, pg. 276
Burns, R.J., V.P., Sec. & Chief Fin. Officer--Grede Foundries, Inc., Milwaukee, WI, pg. 483
Burnstad, Rita, V.P. & Sec.--Burnstad Brothers, Inc., Tomah, WI, pg. 194
Burnstead, Joan, Sec. & Treas.--Burnstead Construction Company, Bellevue, WA, pg. 194
Burnstein, Sumner, Sec.--Maine Printing & Business Forms Co., Portland, ME, pg. 702
Burr, Edward B., Pres. & Chief Exec. Officer--United Planners' Group, Inc., Scottsdale, AZ, pg. 841
Burris, Howard W., V.P. & Asst. Sec.--Burris Foods, Inc., Milford, DE, pg. 195
Burris, Steven Y., Sec. & Treas.--Burris Chemical Inc., Charleston, SC, pg. 195
Burrow, Sharon, Sec.--National Computer Print, Inc., Birmingham, AL, pg. 786
Burrows, Dennis A., Sr. V.P. & Sec.--Roper Bros. Lumber Co., Inc., Petersburg, VA, pg. 947
Burt, Victoria L., Asst. Sec.--Lampert Yards, Inc., Saint Paul, MN, pg. 653
Busby, Valerie S., Sec.--Pawling Corporation, Pawling, NY, pg. 852
Busch, William R., Jr., Sec.--Cowles Media Company, Minneapolis, MN, pg. 291
Buskirk, Glen, Sec. & Treas.--Rock Hill Materials Company, Catasauqua, PA, pg. 941
Buss, Cal, V.P., Sec. & Treas.--Vallet Food Serv Inc., Dubuque, IA, pg. 1143
Butcko, Mae Alice, Sec. & Treas.--Crescive Die & Tool, Inc., Saline, MI, pg. 298
Butler, William J., Sec.--Uforma Shelby Business Forms, Shelby, OH, pg. 746
Butner, Beverly B., V.P.-Admin. & Sec.--Proto Systems of Atlanta, Alpharetta, GA, pg. 895
Butterfield, Mark, Sec. & Treas.--Ausherman Construction Company, Frederick, MD, pg. 98
Butts, Teresa, V.P. & Sec.--Nulaid Foods, Ripon, CA, pg. 817
Buzzard, Michael, Sec.--Effingham-Clay Service Co., Effingham, IL, pg. 371
Byer, Marian, Treas. & Sec.--Byer California, San Francisco, CA, pg. 197
Byler, John, Exec. V.P. & Sec.--Carlos R. Leffler Inc., Richland, PA, pg. 666
Byrd, Mary S., Sec.--Southern Beverage Packers, Inc., Augusta, GA, pg. 1020
Byrne, John D., V.P., Sec. & Treas.--Restaurants Unlimited, Seattle, WA, pg. 929
Byrnes, Thomas, V.P., Sec. & Pur. Agent--Byrnes & Kiefer Company, Callery, PA, pg. 198
Byron, Richard J., V.P., Assoc. Gen. Counsel & Sec.--Employers Insurance of Wausau a Mutual Co., Wausau, WI, pg. 380
Byron, Richard J., V.P., Assoc. Gen. Counsel & Sec.--Employers Insurance of Wausau a Mutual Co., Wausau, WI, pg. 795
Byrum, Barbara, Sr. V.P., Opers., Sec. & Treas.--Gunder & Associates, Inc., Dublin, OH, pg. 494
Cafarchio, L., Sec. & Controller--Swivelier Co., Inc., Nanuet, NY, pg. 1068
Cagenello, Donald L., Sec. & Treas.--Graphic Center, Inc., Bloomfield, CT, pg. 478
Cahill, Kenneth, V.P. & Sec.--Larken Inc., Cedar Rapids, IA, pg. 659
Caldwell, Allen, Exec. V.P., Sec. & Gen. Counsel--Koch Industries, Incorporated, Wichita, KS, pg. 639
Calkins, Charles C., V.P. & Sec.--The Calkins Manufacturing Company, Spokane, WA, pg. 210
Calkins, William D., Sec.--Rice & Rice Inc., Minneapolis, MN, pg. 1143
Call, Val, V.P., Sec. & Treas.--Maverik Country Stores, Inc., Afton, WY, pg. 722
Calvert, Shirley, Sec.--Anderson Industries, Inc., Dallas, TX, pg. 72
Camarena, Karen, Asst. Corp. Sec.--Murdock, Inc., Compton, CA, pg. 776
Cameron, E. Colby, Sec.--Kervick Enterprises, Inc., Worcester, MA, pg. 624
Campbell, Alex, Sec.--Thornton Oil Corp., Louisville, KY, pg. 1095
Campbell, Andrew, Chief Fin. Officer, V.P., Treas. & Sec.--Simmons Upholstered Furniture, Inc., Saint Louis, MO, pg. 1005
Campbell, Cynthia, V.P., Gen. Counsel & Sec.--Transport Insurance Co., Dallas, TX, pg. 54
Campbell, Gerald, Chief Fin. Officer--World Computer Corp., Auburn Hills, MI, pg. 1202
Campbell, Jack T., Treas., Asst. Sec. & Chief Fin. Officer--The Kent Manufacturing Co., Pickens, SC, pg. 623
Campbell, Kimberly, Sec.--World Aerospace Corporation, Maple Grove, MN, pg. 1202
Campbell, Larry, Exec. V.P., Sec. & Treas.--Farm Journal, Inc., Philadelphia, PA, pg. 401
Campbell, Lela, Treas. & Sec.--Choctaw Electric Co-Op, Hugo, OK, pg. 248
Campbell, Mike, Controller & Sec.--Fareway Stores, Inc., Boone, IA, pg. 399
Campbell, Ronald, Sec.--Enco Materials, Inc., Nashville, TN, pg. 380
Campbell, William T., Exec. V.P., Sec.--Barker Campbell & Farley, Virginia Beach, VA, pg. 120
Caolo, Michael B., Sec. & Legal Officer--SnyderGeneral Corporation, Dallas, TX, pg. 1015
Caraway, Robert, Sec.--Lexington Co-Op Oil Co., Lexington, NE, pg. 673
Carbone, Gene, V.P.-Fin., Chief Fin. Officer & Sec.--Calavo Growers of California, Tustin, CA, pg. 208
Carey-Ranes, Marianne, Asst. Sec.--Health Care Lodges, Coffeyville, KS, pg. 520
Carey, Ronald, Corp. Sec.--Gator Freightways, Inc., Wilmington, OH, pg. 446
Carlsen, David R., Chm. Bd., Sec. & Legal Counsel--Upper Midwest Industries, Inc., Minneapolis, MN, pg. 1140
Carlson, Bruce, Sec.--Park Construction Company, Minneapolis, MN, pg. 848
Carlson, Eleanor, Mgr.-Shareholder Rels. & Asst. Sec.--GAF Corporation, Wayne, NJ, pg. 438
Carlson, Jane R., Sec. & Treas.--D. C. Taylor Co., Cedar Rapids, IA, pg. 751
Carlson, Lawrence S., Sec. & Treas.--Fleetwood Systems, Inc., Countryside, IL, pg. 417
Carlson, Ronald A., Sec. & Treas.--Helwig Carbon Products, Inc., Milwaukee, WI, pg. 528
Carlton, Dorothy, Sec. & Treas.--Corrugated Metals, Inc., Chicago, IL, pg. 287
Carmack, John M., Sec.--Amelco Corporation, Gardena, CA, pg. 47
Carnahan, John M., Sec. & Treas.--Woodfin-Smith Pontiac, Inc., Baton Rouge, LA, pg. 1200
Carpenter, Karen L., Exec. V.P. & Sec.--Curtis-Toledo, Inc., Saint Louis, MO, pg. 306
Carr, Barbara, V.P. & Sec.--Tiernay Metals, Inc., Redondo Beach, CA, pg. 1096
Carr, Joseph C., Jr., Sec. & Gen. Counsel--Mitek, Inc., Chesterfield, MO, pg. 762
Carrel, Clarence, Sec.--Remarks, Inc., Dublin, OH, pg. 925
Carrier, Arthur, Sec. & Treas.--Associated Electric Co-op Inc., Springfield, MO, pg. 89
Carrington, Norva, Sec. & Controller--Roland International Corporation, Coconut Grove, FL, pg. 944
Carroll, Jim, Treas., Chief Fin. Officer & Sec.--The Chicago Faucet Co., Des Plaines, IL, pg. 245
Carroll, Larry R., Sec.--Thompson-McCully Co., Belleville, MI, pg. 1094
Carse, Jimmie L., Sec. & Treas.--Carse Oil Co. Inc., Orlando, FL, pg. 225
Carstensen, Richard, Sec.--Carstensen Freight Line, Inc., Clinton, IA, pg. 226
Carter, E. Leo, V.P. & Asst. Sec.--SCC Holding Co., Highland Park, IL, pg. 961
Carter, Edward P., Exec. V.P. & Sec.--Reimel Carter Advertising, Inc., Philadelphia, PA, pg. 923
Carter, Helen D., Sec.--Carco Electronics, Menlo Park, CA, pg. 217
Carter, Nelson, Treas. & Chief Fin. Officer--Jerry C. Carter, Inc., Gainesville, GA, pg. 226
Carthaus, Richard W., Sr. V.P. & Sec.--Western Petroleum Company, Eden Prairie, MN, pg. 1181
Caruso, Jo Ann, Sec. & Treas.--Regency Dodge Inc., Jacksonville, FL, pg. 922
Caruso, John G., Exec. V.P., Loan Admin. & Sec.--Globe Mortgage Company, Hackensack, NJ, pg. 464
Casanova, Paul L., Pres., Sec. & New Bus. Contact--Casanova Pendrill Publicidad Inc., Irvine, CA, pg. 227
Casey, Karen L., Sec. & Treas.--Libertyville Lincoln-Mercury Sales, Inc., Libertyville, IL, pg. 674
Cashwell, Henry V., Sec. & Treas.--Tencarva Machinery Co., Inc., Greensboro, NC, pg. 1086
Casselman, David A., V.P.-Fin., Controller, Sec. & Treas.--General Time Corp., Norcross, GA, pg. 451
Cassens, Kay, Sec. & Treas.--Cassens Transport Company, Edwardsville, IL, pg. 228
Cassner, Jon H., Sec. & Treas.--Rotary Forms Press, Inc., Hillsboro, OH, pg. 950
Castanes, John, Sec.--Squire-Cogswell Company, Northbrook, IL, pg. 1034
Castiglione, Philip, Sec. & Treas.--Ray Laethem Pontiac GMC Truck Co., Detroit, MI, pg. 650
Castro, Dorothy, Sr. V.P., Treas. & Sec.--Superior Fast Freight, Irwindale, CA, pg. 1063
Cathey, O.D., Sec. & Treas.--Bearden Lumber Company, Inc., Bearden, AR, pg. 129
Cavalli, Caroline, Pres. & Sec.--Orbitair International Ltd., New York, NY, pg. 828
Cavender, William, Treas. & Sec.--Hallidie Machinery Company, Inc., Seattle, WA, pg. 501
Cejka, F.V., Treas. & Sec.--Ward Products Corporation, New Brunswick, NJ, pg. 1163
Celentano, Doris, Sec.--Celentano Brothers, Verona, NJ, pg. 231
Ceruzzi, Louis, V.P. & Sec.--Massachusetts Container Corporation, Marlborough, MA, pg. 274
Challenger, Walter W., V.P.-Fin. & Sec.--Princeville Corporation, Princeville, HI, pg. 890
Chambers, Rufus A., Sec.--W.B. Johnson Property, Inc., Atlanta, GA, pg. 598
Chambers, T. L., Sec. & Treas.--Rumsey Electric Co., Philadelphia, PA, pg. 956
Chamblin, Dale, Exec. V.P. & Sec.--California Electric Service, Oakland, CA, pg. 209
Chan, Paul, Sec. & Treas.--Generra Sportswear Company, Inc., Tukwila, WA, pg. 451
Chandler, Marcus, Asst. Sec.--LDI, Ltd., Indianapolis, IN, pg. 647
Chapek, Jane A., V.P.-Fin. & Sec.--American Lock & Supply Inc., Anaheim, CA, pg. 57
Chapman, Conrad D., Sec.--Davis Industries Inc., Detroit, MI, pg. 318
Charapp, Michael, Sec.--Rosenthal Chevrolet Co., Arlington, VA, pg. 949
Charlson, C.R., V.P. & Sec.--State Farm Life Insurance Co., Bloomington, IL, pg. 1041
Charpentier, Al, V.P.--Ensoniq Corporation, Malvern, PA, pg. 382
Charron, Carol, Sec. & Treas.--Art Moran Pontiac-GMC Inc., Southfield, MI, pg. 769
Chauvin, Hamilton J., Exec. V.P.-Admin. & Sec.--Consolidated Companies Inc. (CONCO), Metairie, LA, pg. 276
Chauvin, Hamilton J., Sec.--Distributors Oil Company, Inc., Baton Rouge, LA, pg. 340
Chawla, Vera, Exec. V.P.--Information Systems & Network Corporation, Bethesda, MD, pg. 567
Cheloha, Kenneth L., Chief Oper. Officer--American Tool Companies, Inc., Lincoln, NE, pg. 64
Chenoweth, R.A., Sec. & Gen. Counsel--Harwick Chemical Corp., Akron, OH, pg. 515
Chernin, Herbert, Sec.--Carpro, Inc., Totowa, NJ, pg. 217
Chervinak, Diane, Sec.--Lynden Incorporated, Seattle, WA, pg. 689
Chesson, Dave, Exec. V.P.-Opers. & Sec.--Leslie Advertising, Greenville, SC, pg. 668
Chesterman, Paul, V.P., Chief Fin. Officer & Sec.--Trace Products, San Jose, CA, pg. 1104
Child, Patricia, Sec.--R.C. Willey Home Furnishings, Salt Lake City, UT, pg. 1190
Childs, Freida, Sec.--WordPerfect Corporation, Orem, UT, pg. 1202
Ching, Han H., Vice Chm. & Sec.--Aloha Airgroup, Inc., Honolulu, HI, pg. 43
Ching, Han H., Vice Chm., Corp. Sec. & Dir.--Aloha Airlines, Inc., Honolulu, HI, pg. 43
Chisum, David E., Chief Fin. Officer & Sec.--Piper Industries, Inc., Dallas, TX, pg. 872
Chitwood, Frank W., Sr. V.P., Asst. Sec. & Mng. Principal-HTB/Tulsa--HTB, Inc., Oklahoma City, OK, pg. 497
Choate, A.G., Sec. & Gen. Counsel--American Trading and Production Corporation, Baltimore, MD, pg. 64
Chow, Shirley, V.P.-Fin. & Sec.--Bachmann Industries, Inc., Philadelphia, PA, pg. 108
Christ, Chris T., Sec.--Archway Cookies, Inc., Battle Creek, MI, pg. 81
Christian, Mark A., Plan V.P. & Sec.--Central Coca-Cola Bottling Company, Inc., Richmond, VA, pg. 232

Chrzanowski, Rebecca, Sec. & Treas.--Aldi Inc., Batavia, IL, pg. 33
Chuba, P.A., Sec.--AGR International, Inc., Butler, PA, pg. 4
Church, R.D., Sec. & Treas.--Erico International, Cleveland, OH, pg. 386
Chynoweth, Robert, Treas. & Sec.--Wyoming Machine Company, Casper, WY, pg. 1206
Ciccotelli, Teresa T., V.P., Legal Counsel & Sec.--Alco Health Services Corporation, Malvern, PA, pg. 31
Ciciola, Emilio J., Exec. V.P. & Sec.--Lanman & Kemp-Barclay Co. Inc., Westwood, NJ, pg. 657
Cicotte, Thomas, Sec. & Treas.--Shmina Construction, Inc., Livonia, MI, pg. 124
Cieply, Lucy, Controller & Sec.--Rama Group of Companies, Cheektowaga, NY, pg. 910
Cioci, Jerry, Chief Fin. Officer & Corp. Sec.--Maecorp Inc., Chicago, IL, pg. 699
Ciola, Marsha, Sec.--National Health Products, Orlando, FL, pg. 791
Ciolek, Walter, Sec.--The Lion, Inc. (Gibbons-Stegmaier Brewery), Wilkes-Barre, PA, pg. 677
Ciottone, R.T., Sec.--Continental Water Company, Saint Louis, MO, pg. 280
Cistone, Daniel, V.P.-Fin. & Admin., Sec. & Dir.-Real Estate--M & C Specialties Company, Southampton, PA, pg. 690
Claiborne, Jess, Sec.--Affiliated Foods, Inc., Amarillo, TX, pg. 24
Clark, Margaret, Treas. & Sec.--Covington Foods, Inc., Covington, IN, pg. 290
Clark, Robert, Sec.--Eagle Button Co., Inc., Carlstadt, NJ, pg. 362
Clark, Scott W., Sec. & Treas.--Construction Management Service, Wilmington, DE, pg. 277
Clark, Susan, V.P., Treas. & Asst. Sec.--HTB, Inc., Oklahoma City, OK, pg. 497
Clarke, Edwin R., Chief Fin. Officer, Treas. & Sec.--Letts Industries, Inc., Detroit, MI, pg. 668
Clarke, Thomas W., V.P.-Fin. & Treas.--Flint Ink Corp., Detroit, MI, pg. 419
Clarkson, Charles, Sec.--TLC Beatrice International Holdings Inc., New York, NY, pg. 1073
Clarkson, Janice, Sec.--Clarkson Construction Companies, Kansas City, MO, pg. 253
Claunch, Joe Howard, Sec. & Treas.--Somerset Refinery Inc., Somerset, KY, pg. 1017
Cleckner, Richard W., Sec.--United Tectonic Industry, Harrisburg, PA, pg. 1137
Clegg, Christopher, Sec.--M & T Incorporated, Portland, OR, pg. 690
Clement, Erma, Sec. & Controller--Carden & Cherry, Inc., Nashville, TN, pg. 217
Clement, Robert, Chief Fin. Officer & Sec.--Excelsior Manufacturing & Supply Corp., Itasca, IL, pg. 392
Clements, Edward B., V.P. & Chief Exec. Officer--Clements Foods Co., Oklahoma City, OK, pg. 254
Clements, Norman F., V.P., Sec. & Treas.--EAC Corporation, Saint Louis, MO, pg. 359
Cleveland, Beth, Sec.--Castleberry's Food Company, Augusta, GA, pg. 229
Cleveland, Van, Sec.--Cleveland Group, Inc., Atlanta, GA, pg. 255
Clifton, Harold, Treas., Sec. & Chief Fin. Officer--Hopper Inc., Bakersfield, CA, pg. 543
Clifton, Harold S., Sec.--The Bakersfield Californian, Bakersfield, CA, pg. 115
Clonts, Richard, Chief Fin. Officer, V.P.-Fin. & Sec.--Sewell Village Cadillac Co., Dallas, TX, pg. 993
Clyburne, Evelyn, Sec. & Treas.--Gregory & Clyburne, Inc., Stamford, CT, pg. 486
Coakley, Neil T., Chm. Bd., Sec. & Treas.--Coakley & Williams Inc., Greenbelt, MD, pg. 256
Coates, Glenn, Sec.--Racine Federated, Inc., Racine, WI, pg. 909
Coates, Michael R., Exec. V.P., Sec. & Dir. Client Services--The Coates Agency, Portland, OR, pg. 257
Coben, Carl G., V.P., Sec. & Legal--Aratex Services, Lawrenceville, GA, pg. 6
Cochran, Deryl E., Sec. & Treas.--Plastics Manufacturing Company, Dallas, TX, pg. 876
Cochran, Elizabeth, Sec.--Walker Die Casting, Inc., Lewisburg, TN, pg. 1160
Cochrane, E.G., II, Sec. & Gen. Counsel--Mount Vernon Mills, Inc., Greenville, SC, pg. 844
Cockrell, Karen, Sec.--UniHealth America, Burbank, CA, pg. 1126
Cockrell, Mel, Chief Fin. Officer, Treas., Controller & Sec.--Ben E. Keith Company, Fort Worth, TX, pg. 620
Cocquyt, Ronald A., Sec. & Treas.--Wilmorite Inc., Rochester, NY, pg. 1193
Coffey, John T., Jr., Sec. & Gen. Counsel--Maguire Group Inc., Foxboro, MA, pg. 701
Cogan, Juan, V.P.-Warehouse & Asst. Sec.--Pueblo International, Inc.-P.R. Div., Carolina, PR, pg. 899
Coggeshall, Bruce, Sec.--Forster Mfg. Co., Inc., Wilton, ME, pg. 21
Coggins, Lester, Jr., Sec. & Treas.--Lester Coggins Trucking, Okahumpka, FL, pg. 259
Cohane, Timothy, Sec.--Times Fiber Communications, Inc., Wallingford, CT, pg. 648
Cohen, Ezra, V.P., Sec. & Treas.--Sunweave Linen Corporation, New York, NY, pg. 1062
Cohen, Harry, Chief Fin. Officer, Treas. & Sec.--Mozel Development Corp., Baileys Crossroads, VA, pg. 774
Cohen, Isaac, Treas. & Sec.--First Computer Corporation, Los Angeles, CA, pg. 412
Cohen, Jack, Sec.--Duane Reade, Long Island City, NY, pg. 350
Cohen, Louis I., Asst. Treas. & Sec.--First Connecticut SBIC, Bridgeport, CT, pg. 412
Cohen, Stephen A., V.P., Sec. & Gen. Counsel--Academy Insurance Group, Inc., Atlanta, GA, pg. 11
Cohen, Steven, Sec.--Robbins Auto Parts, Inc., Dover, NH, pg. 938
Cohen, Steven A., Chm. Bd. & Pres.--Andy Frain Services, Inc., Chicago, IL, pg. 428
Cohen, Victor, V.P. & Gen. Counsel--Polo/Ralph Lauren Corporation, New York, NY, pg. 879
Cohen, Warren, V.P., Sec. & Treas.--Unisystems, Inc., New York, NY, pg. 1130
Cohn, Carol, Treas. & Sec.--Decorative Crafts, Inc., Greenwich, CT, pg. 324
Colantino, M.B., Sec.--Darlene Jewelry Manufacturing Company, Pawtucket, RI, pg. 315
Colburn, Rebecca, Sec.--Dahlstrom Manufacturing Company, Inc., Jamestown, NY, pg. 310
Cole, Betty, Sec.--Valley Innovative Management Service, Jackson, MS, pg. 1109
Cole, Catherine P., Chief Oper. Officer & Sec.--Columbine Systems Inc., Golden, CO, pg. 266
Cole, Glenda, Corp. Sec.--Bankhead Enterprises Inc., Atlanta, GA, pg. 117
Cole, Nadene R., Sec.--Barclay White Incorporated, Berwyn, PA, pg. 119
Colebatch, Philip, Sec. & Treas.--CS First Boston Financiere, Inc., New York, NY, pg. 204
Coleman, Bob, Gen. Mgr.-Sls. & Sec.--Coleman Dairy Inc., Little Rock, AR, pg. 261
Coleman, Joel C., V.P., Gen. Counsel & Sec.--Playtex FP Group Incorporated, Stamford, CT, pg. 877
Coleman, Richard D., V.P., Controller & Sec.--Kash N Karry Food Stores, Inc., Tampa, FL, pg. 617
Collat, Justin W., Dr., Sec.--American Chemical Society, Washington, DC, pg. 50
Collier, Evelyn L., Exec. Sec.--The Elder-Beerman Stores Corp., Dayton, OH, pg. 373
Collins, Donald F., Treas. & Sec.--Collins Electric Company, Inc., Chicopee, MA, pg. 263
Collins, Fred, V.P. & Sec.--Flint River Mills, Bainbridge, GA, pg. 419
Collins, Lawrence A., Sec. & Treas.--J. H. Roberts Industries Inc., Des Plaines, IL, pg. 938
Collova, J. James, Chief Fin. Officer & Sec.--Paper Calmenson & Co., Saint Paul, MN, pg. 847
Colnes, Martin B., Sec. & Treas.--Engineered Products, Inc., Pittsburgh, PA, pg. 382
Combs, Kevin, Treas., Chief Fin. Officer & Sec.--Symons Corporation, Pasadena, CA, pg. 1069
Como, John, Jr., V.P., Sec. & Treas.--Amco Folding Cartons, Inc., Towaco, NJ, pg. 47
Conant, Philip D., V.P. & Sec.--Golden Gem Growers Inc., Umatilla, FL, pg. 466
Coneglio, Vincent L., V.P.-Admin & Sec.--Carlisle Retailers, Inc., Ashtabula, OH, pg. 220
Confer, Ogden W., Sr. V.P., Sec. & Chief Fin. Officer--Hubbard Milling Company, Mankato, MN, pg. 549
Conforti, Sam, Sec. & Treas.--Bentley, Barnes & Lynn, Inc., Chicago, IL, pg. 140
Conklin, M.E., Corp. Sec.--Conklin Instrument Corporation, Pleasant Valley, NY, pg. 274
Conklin, Thomas J., Sr. V.P. & Sec.--The Mutual Life Insurance Company of New York (MONY), New York, NY, pg. 778
Connelly, Elizabeth K., Sr. V.P., Corp. Sec., Human Resources & Office Mngmt.--Adler Boschetto Peebles & Partners, Inc., New York, NY, pg. 17
Connelly, Thomas, Sec.--Washington Homes, Inc., Landover, MD, pg. 1166
Connon, Dana, Grp. V.P.--Welsh Company, Saint Louis, MO, pg. 1175
Connors, Charles W., Chief Exec. Officer & Sec.--Magneco/Metrel, Inc., Addison, IL, pg. 700
Conradsen, Jane, Sec.--Agri-Mark, Inc., Lawrence, MA, pg. 25
Conroy, David J., Sec.--C.B. Fox Company, New Orleans, LA, pg. 427
Consolati, Jay, Sec.--H W Electronics, Inc., Van Nuys, CA, pg. 497
Consolini, Michael G., Exec. V.P.-Opers. & Sec.--The Napier Company, Meriden, CT, pg. 783
Conway, J. W., Sec. & Treas.--Atlas Tag & Label Inc., Neenah, WI, pg. 153
Conway, Robert D., Treas. & Sec.--Schneider National, Inc., Green Bay, WI, pg. 977
Cook, Charlotte, Sec.--Coble Dairy Products Co-op, Lexington, NC, pg. 257
Cook, Debbie, Sec. & Treas.--Cook Manufacturing Corporation, Duncan, OK, pg. 282
Cook, Marsha Weir, Treas. & Sec.--Mediatex Communications Corporation, Austin, TX, pg. 735
Cook, Mike, Sec. & Treas.--Collins Oldsmobile Inc., Indianapolis, IN, pg. 263
Cook, R.H., Sr., Treas. & Sec.--B.C. Cook & Sons Enterprises, Inc., Haines City, FL, pg. 282
Cooke, La Nell, Sec.--Texas Olefins Co., Houston, TX, pg. 1089
Cooksey, David C., V.P., Chief Fin. Officer & Sec.--Contico International, Inc., Saint Louis, MO, pg. 278
Cookson, John S., V.P.-Fin., Treas., Chief Fin. Officer, Sec. & Dir.-Investor Rels.--Kingsbury Corporation, Keene, NH, pg. 631
Coombs, Eugene C., Sec. & Gen. Counsel--Town & Country Food Markets, Inc., Wichita, KS, pg. 1103
Coomer, Ralph, Treas. & Sec.--Ziniz Inc., Louisville, KY, pg. 1220
Cooper, Cary D., Exec. V.P. & Chief Fin. Officer--The Cherokee Group, Sunland, CA, pg. 243
Cooper, Maxine, Sec. & Treas.--Maxine Of Hollywood, Inc., Los Angeles, CA, pg. 723
Cooper, R. John, Exec. V.P., Gen. Counsel & Sec.--Young & Rubicam Inc., New York, NY, pg. 1210
Cooper, Scott, Sec.--The Hiebing Group, Inc., Madison, WI, pg. 533
Coopr, Jerome, Sec.--Green Bus Lines, Inc., Jamaica, NY, pg. 483
Cope, Ruth, Sec. & Office Mgr.--John Copes Food Products, Inc., Rheems, PA, pg. 284
Copeland, L.R., Sec.--Simmons, Durham & Associates, Saint Louis, MO, pg. 1005
Copelin, Deborah, Sec.--Tyndale House Publishers, Inc., Carol Stream, IL, pg. 1122
Copland, Ronald G., V.P. & Sec.--Copland Fabrics, Inc., Burlington, NC, pg. 284
Coppersmith, W. Louis, Sec. & Gen. Counsel--Glosser Brothers, Inc., Johnstown, PA, pg. 978
Coppola, Carl, Pres. & Sec.--Mark Lighting Fixture Co., Inc., Moonachie, NJ, pg. 708
Corbett, Grafton J., III, Sec.--Textile Rubber & Chemical Company, Dalton, GA, pg. 1090
Corbin, Richard F., Sec. & Treas.--Metal Trades, Inc., Hollywood, SC, pg. 741
Corcoran, John V., Sec.--Daniel F. Young, Inc., New York, NY, pg. 1209
Cordek, Lawrence D., Chief Fin. Officer & Corp. Sec.--G B Stores, Johnstown, PA, pg. 978
Cordle, Audra, Chief Fin. Officer, Treas. & Controller--Consolidated Co-op, Gowrie, IA, pg. 276
Corelli, Christopher, Treas. & Sec.--Corham, Inc., White Plains, NY, pg. 286
Corey, William, Sec.--American Frozen Foods, Inc., Stratford, CT, pg. 55
Coriden, Michael W., Corp. Attorney & Sec.--CF&I Steel Corporation, Pueblo, CO, pg. 201
Cornewll, Ed, Treas. & Asst. Sec.--U.S. Furniture Industries, Inc., High Point, NC, pg. 1136
Cornfield, Jane, Sec.--Sharon Concepts, Inc., Union, NJ, pg. 995
Cornish, H.L., Jr., Sr. V.P., Treas. & Sec.--Carson Products Company, Savannah, GA, pg. 67
Corogin, John S., Chm. Bd., Sec. & Treas.--Lake Erie Electric, Inc., Westlake, OH, pg. 651
Cosbey, J.R., V.P., Sec. & Treas.--Daubert Industries, Inc., Westchester, IL, pg. 317
Cosgrove, Hazel, Vice Chm., Treas., & Corp. Sec.--Pro Hardware, Inc., Englewood, CO, pg. 891
Costanzo, Arthur, Sec.--United Metal Fabricators, Inc., Johnstown, PA, pg. 1133
Cote, Gilman, Sec. & Treas.--Connecticut Spring & Stamping Corporation, Farmington, CT, pg. 275
Coughlin, Joseph, V.P. & Sec.--F.X. Coughlin Co., Taylor, MI, pg. 289
Coulombe, Cecile J., Pres., Treas. & Sec.--White Rock Distilleries Inc., Lewiston, ME, pg. 1186
Couri, Steven G., Sec.--Couristan Inc., Fort Lee, NJ, pg. 290
Cowan, Richard, Sec., Treas., Controller & Chief Fin. Officer--Wheeler Brothers Grain Co., Watonga, OK, pg. 1184
Cox, Arthur, Sec. & Treas.--The Knapheide Mfg. Co., Quincy, IL, pg. 636
Cox, Edward M., Sec.--Williams Foods Inc., Lenexa, KS, pg. 1191
Cox, Lynn E., Sec.--1st Franklin Corporation, Toccoa, GA, pg. 413
Cox, Lynn E., Sec.--First Franklin Financial Corp., Toccoa, GA, pg. 413
Cox, Richard, V.P. & Sec.--Cox Furniture, Maxton, NC, pg. 294
Coxwell, Frances, Sec. & Treas.--J.B. Coxwell Contract, Inc., Jacksonville, FL, pg. 295
Crabtree, William B., Sec. & Treas.--SCR, Inc., Lake Oswego, OR, pg. 961
Crafton, Leon, III, Sec.--Conway Corporation, Conway, AR, pg. 281
Crain, Merrilee P., Sec.--Crain Communications, Inc., Detroit, MI, pg. 295
Crane, Mary Louise, Treas. & Sec.--Decatur News Publishing Company, Inc., Decatur, GA, pg. 323
Cravens, Mary Ann, V.P.-Admin. & Sec.--Star Lumber & Supply Company, Inc., Wichita, KS, pg. 1039
Crawford, Christine, Sec. & Legal Officer--Henkels & McCoy, Inc., Blue Bell, PA, pg. 529
Crawford, Donna M., Sec.--The American Companies, Inc., Topeka, KS, pg. 50
Crawford, Randy, V.P. & Sec.--Adair Feed & Grain Company, Adair, IA, pg. 16
Creel, W.E., Treas. & Sec.--Michigan Tractor And Machinery Co., Novi, MI, pg. 747
Cremins, William T., Exec. V.P., Gen. Counsel & Sec.--Naugatuck Glass Company, Naugatuck, CT, pg. 796
Crews, Donald R., Sr. V.P., Legal & Sec.--Harte-Hanks Communications, Inc., San Antonio, TX, pg. 513
Crifasi, James, Sec. & Treas.--Hi Nabor Supermarket Inc., Baton Rouge, LA, pg. 532
Crig, Sam, Sec.--Ullenberg Corp., Chattanooga, TN, pg. 1125
Criso, Anthony, V.P., Legal Counsel & Sec.--Essex Group, Inc., Fort Wayne, IN, pg. 389
Crisp, Marlene, Sec.--The SArgent-SOwell Company, Grand Prairie, TX, pg. 971
Croll, Samuel W. III, Pres.--Croll-Reynolds Company, Westfield, NJ, pg. 300
Cromer, C. Jackson, Sec. & Gen. Counsel--Van Leunens Inc., Cincinnati, OH, pg. 1144
Cronen, Vin, Sec. & Treas.--Whittaker, Clark & Daniels, Inc., South Plainfield, NJ, pg. 1187
Cronin, S., Sec.--Donino & Partners, Inc., Atlanta, GA, pg. 344
Croone, Judy, Sec.--Pawtucket Fasteners Inc., Pawtucket, RI, pg. 852
Cross, John R., V.P.-Sls. & Sec.--The Chardon Rubber Co., Chardon, OH, pg. 239
Cross, Raymond, V.P. & Sec.--Federal Chicago Corporation, North Chicago, IL, pg. 404
Crotty, Mark W., Controller & Sec.--J. C. Brock Corp., Buffalo, NY, pg. 178
Croushore, Bruce J., V.P., Sec. & Gen. Counsel--Bender Shipbuilding & Repair Company, Mobile, AL, pg. 138
Crowley, Francis L., Sec.--Ship Analytics, Inc., North Stonington, CT, pg. 999

Crowley, Thomas V., Dir.-Mktg. & Sec.--Cadet Manufacturing Company, Vancouver, WA, pg. 207
Crowley, Timothy R., Treas. & Sec.--Health Care Lodges, Coffeyville, KS, pg. 520
Cruickshank, D.J., V.P. & Chief Fin. Officer--Flexible Products Company, Marietta, GA, pg. 418
Crum, Mary M., Treas. & Sec.--Crum Electric Supply Co., Inc., Casper, WY, pg. 303
Cruncleton, Barbara A., Treas., Sec. & Dir.--John S. Frey Enterprises, Los Angeles, CA, pg. 433
Crutcher, Richard E., Treas. & Sec.--East Kentucky Power Co-op, Winchester, KY, pg. 362
Crutcher, Shirley, Treas. & Sec.--Fojtasek Companies, Inc., Irving, TX, pg. 421
Crvarich, Gene, V.P., Sec. & Treas.--Al Larson Boat Shop, Inc., Terminal Island, CA, pg. 659
Cuff, Jean, Asst. Sec.--Moran Towing & Transporation Co. Inc, Greenwich, CT, pg. 769
Culbertson, Arthur C., Sec. & Gen. Counsel--Construction Specialties, Inc., Cranford, NJ, pg. 277
Cullers, Marian B., Exec. V.P. & Sec.--Vince Cullers Advertising Inc., Chicago, IL, pg. 304
Culver, Margaret S., Sec.--Henry Vogt Machine Co., Louisville, KY, pg. 1154
Cummings, R. C., Sec. & Gen. Counsel--Smith-Lee Co., Inc., Oneida, NY, pg. 1013
Cummins, Kenneth C., V.P., Sec. & Gen. Counsel--Morse Shoe, Inc., Canton, MA, pg. 772
Cunningham, Bob, Gen. Counsel & Sec.--Tennessee Farmers Co-op, La Vergne, TN, pg. 1087
Cunningham, John, Press Sec.--Metropolitan Transportation Authority, New York, NY, pg. 745
Cunningham, Patricia, V.P., Chief Fin. Officer , & Sec.--INPUT, Mountain View, CA, pg. 571
Cunningham, Robert, V.P.-Sec.--Dennis Chemical Company, Inc., Saint Louis, MO, pg. 329
Curci, Joseph E., Chief Fin. Officer--A. Finkl & Sons Co., Chicago, IL, pg. 411
Curran, Catherine, Sec.--Curran Contracting Co., Crystal Lake, IL, pg. 305
Curran, Kevin J., Sec. & Gen. Counsel--Parsons Brinckerhoff Inc., New York, NY, pg. 850
Curran, Kevin J., Sec.--Parsons Brinckerhoff Quade & Douglas, Inc., New York, NY, pg. 850
Currier, Ronald, Sec. & Treas.--Gilpatrick Construction Company, Riverton, WY, pg. 460
Curtin, Richard, Corp. Sec. & Gen. Counsel--Berry Bearing Co., Lyons, IL, pg. 144
Curtis, Fred M., Exec. V.P. & Sec.--The Hilsinger Corp., Plainville, MA, pg. 535
Curtis, Joyce H., Sec.--Curtis Lumber Company, Ballston Spa, NY, pg. 305
Curtis, Roger William, Chm. Bd., Chief Exec. Officer & Sec.--L.N. Curtis & Sons, Oakland, CA, pg. 306
Curtis, Stan, Asst. Sec. & Treas.--Continental Forge Company, Compton, CA, pg. 279
Curtis, Therese D., Sec.--Topa Equities Ltd, Inc., Los Angeles, CA, pg. 1101
Curto, Anthony, Treas. & Sec.--LaMarca Group Inc., New York, NY, pg. 652
Curto, Anthony, Sec. & Treas.--LaMarca Direct Marketing, New York, NY, pg. 652
Cutler, Diana, V.P. & Sec.--Educational Insights, Inc., Dominguez Hills, CA, pg. 369
Czerwinski, Connie, V.P., Sec. & Treas.--Cerwin Vega, Inc., Simi Valley, CA, pg. 237
Czuba, Daniel, Sec.--Display Technologies, Inc., Elgin, IL, pg. 339
D'Anna, Anthony S., V.P. & Sec.--Mars Super Markets, Inc., Baltimore, MD, pg. 714
D'Haeze, T.M., V.P.-Fin. & Acctg., Treas. & Sec.--Dwyer Instruments Inc., Michigan City, IN, pg. 356
Dabbs, Karl, V.P.-Fin., Treas. & Sec.--B.A.S.S., Inc., Montgomery, AL, pg. 105
Dabney, D., Sec. & Treas.--Chevy Chase Cars & Geo, Bethesda, MD, pg. 244
Dadds, Sara A., Sec.--Erin Group Administrators, Inc., Lancaster, PA, pg. 387
Dagnello, Sharon, Sec.--All America Financial, Worcester, MA, pg. 34
Dahl, Donald A., Sr. V.P. & Sec.--International Business Interiors Inc., Chicago, IL, pg. 575
Dahl, Valerie J., V.P. & Asst. Sec.--Stearns Enterprises, Inc., Lexington, KY, pg. 1043
Dahlem, Karen, Sec.--Dahlem Company, Inc., Louisville, KY, pg. 310
Dajer, Antonio, V.P.-Human Resources & Asst. Sec.--Pueblo International, Inc.-P.R. Div., Carolina, PR, pg. 899
Daledda, Enrico, Sec.--Abbott Glass Co., Inc., Maspeth, NY, pg. 9
Dalick, Marilynn, Sec.--Carris Reels, Inc., Rutland, VT, pg. 225
Daly, J.G., Corp. Sec.--Leo A. Daly Company, Omaha, NE, pg. 313
Daly, Kathleen C., Treas. & Sec.--Frank Messer & Sons Construction Co., Cincinnati, OH, pg. 741
Daly, Michael J., III, Sec.--M.J. Daly & Sons, Inc., Waterbury, CT, pg. 313
Damian, Walter, Sec.--Keuffel & Esser, Rockaway, NJ, pg. 105
Danello, Timothy, V.P., Gen. Counsel & Asst. Sec.--Oxford Realty Services Corp., Bethesda, MD, pg. 835
Danenhauer, Edwin H., Sec.--New Hampshire Oak, Hampton, NH, pg. 800
Daneri, Roxanne, Sec. & Gen. Counsel--Swift Dodge Rolls Royce Inc., Sacramento, CA, pg. 1067
Daniel, Michael, Sec., Treas. & Controller--Field Packing Company, Owensboro, KY, pg. 409
Daniel, Ron, V.P., Dir.-Personnel & Sec.--The Daniel Co. of Springfield, Springfield, MO, pg. 314
Daniel, William, Sec. & Dir.-Art--Equinox Advertising, Inc., Chicago, IL, pg. 384
Daniels, Pamela, Sec. & Production Dir.--Direct Communications Corporation, Bronxville, NY, pg. 339
Danko, Douglas B., Sec.--Stabler Companies, Inc., Harrisburg, PA, pg. 1034
Darnell, W. Reid, Sec. & Treas.--Florida Crushed Stone Company, Leesburg, FL, pg. 420
Darwin, Natalie, Sec.--Cardinal Inc., Port Reading, NJ, pg. 217
Daubney, John E., Sec.--T O Plastics, Inc., Minneapolis, MN, pg. 1074
Daunhauer, John Paul, Sec.--Byerly Ford-Nissan Inc., Louisville, KY, pg. 198
Davidson, David A., Sr. V.P. & Sec.--Liberty Northwest Insurance Corp., Portland, OR, pg. 674
Davidson, James, Sec.--Dancker, Sellew & Douglas, Inc., New York, NY, pg. 314
Davidson, William J., V.P., Sec. & Controller--Stevens Graphics, Inc., Atlanta, GA, pg. 136
Davies, Zachary M., Controller & Sec.--Tweddle Litho Company, St. Clair Shores, MI, pg. 1120
Davis, Adrienne, Sec. & Treas.--Clayton-Davis & Associates, Incorporated, Saint Louis, MO, pg. 253
Davis, Bonnie, Gen. Counsel & Sec.--Finlay Enterprises, Inc., New York, NY, pg. 411
Davis, Charles E., Jr., Sec. & Treas.--Laboratory Supply Company, Inc., Louisville, KY, pg. 649
Davis, Cheryl D., Chief Fin. Officer, V.P.-Taxes & Sec.--The Enstar Group, Inc., Montgomery, AL, pg. 382
Davis, Deborah Karen, Sec.--Davis Mining & Manufacturing, Colburn, VA, pg. 319
Davis, Edna R., Sec. & Treas.--South States Inc., Shreveport, LA, pg. 340
Davis, Edward E., Sec.--Moore Company, Westerly, RI, pg. 768
Davis, Gary K., Treas. & Sec.--Bud Davis Cadillac, Inc., Memphis, TN, pg. 318
Davis, George L., Pres. & Chief Exec. Officer--First American Bankshares, Inc., Washington, DC, pg. 412
Davis, Jo, Corp. Sec.--Conso Products Company, Union, SC, pg. 276
Davis, Lewis, Sec.--Crystal Flash Petroleum Corp., Indianapolis, IN, pg. 303
Davis, Louise M., Sec.--Carlisle Equipment Company, Louisville, KY, pg. 220
Davis, Martha O., Sec. & Treas.--Jimmy Davis Enterprises, Inc., Madison, FL, pg. 318
Davis, Mary, V.P. & Corp. Sec.--Palmetto Spinning Corp., Laurens, SC, pg. 844
Davis, Richard, Sec.--Waldo Bros. Company, Boston, MA, pg. 1159
Davis, Robert A., Chief Oper. Officer & Sec.--Swallen's, Inc., Cincinnati, OH, pg. 1066
Davis, Robert M., Chm., Sec. & Treas.--Davis, Ball & Colombatto Advertising, Inc., Los Angeles, CA, pg. 318
Davis, S. Wiley, Sec.--Piasa Motor Fuels Inc., Hartford, IL, pg. 869
Davis, Timothy M., Gen. Counsel & Sec.--Haddon Craftsmen, Inc., Scranton, PA, pg. 499
Davisson, Richard F., Sec. & Gen. Counsel--Pay Less Super Markets, Inc., Anderson, IN, pg. 852
Dawahare, Martin, Sec. & Treas.--Dawahares, Inc., Lexington, KY, pg. 319
Dawkins, George, Treas. & Sec.--Austin Industries, Inc., Dallas, TX, pg. 99
Dawson, Susan, Sec. & Dir.-Admin.--Information Systems & Network Corporation, Bethesda, MD, pg. 567
Day, Donald A., Sr. V.P.-Fin., Chief Fin. Officer & Sec.--St. Johnsbury Trucking Co., Inc., Holliston, MA, pg. 966
Day, James H., Sec. & Dir.-Admin.--Truman Arnold Companies, Texarkana, TX, pg. 84
Day, Sharon, Treas. & Sec.--Catalina Yachts, Inc., Woodland Hills, CA, pg. 229
De Jongh, Alberto J., V.P. & Sec.--Newtron Group Inc., Baton Rouge, LA, pg. 805
de la Garza, Stella, Sec.--Thompson/Marince Advertising, San Antonio, TX, pg. 1094
De Majistre, Robert, V.P. & Sec.--Seton Company, Norristown, PA, pg. 993
De Mento, Robert, Sec. & Treas.--Brooks Provisions Inc., Philadelphia, PA, pg. 180
Dean, John S., Sec. & Treas.--Oglethorpe Power Corp., Tucker, GA, pg. 822
Deane, James R., Exec. V.P., Gen. Counsel & Sec.--Fiduciary Trust Co. International, New York, NY, pg. 408
Deane, James R., Exec. V.P., Sec. & Gen. Counsel--Fiduciary Trust Company International, New York, NY, pg. 408
Deardorff, W.W., Jr., Mgr.-Sls. & Sec.--Deardorff-Jackson Company, Oxnard, CA, pg. 323
Dearinger, James E., Sec.--American Kennel Club, Inc., New York, NY, pg. 57
Dearking, Dean, V.P.-Admin. & Corp. Sec.--Sieg Company, Davenport, IA, pg. 1002
DeBlasio, Linda, Sec.--Planes Moving And Storage, Inc., Cincinnati, OH, pg. 874
DeBona, Ronald V., Sec.--H & H Tube & Manufacturing Co., Vanderbilt, MI, pg. 495
Dechnik, James, V.P.-Fin. & Sec.--The Johnson Corporation, Three Rivers, MI, pg. 597
DeCius, Dennis A., Chief Fin. Officer, Exec. V.P. & Asst. Sec.--Pacific Capital Bancorp, Salinas, CA, pg. 839
Deckelman, Bill, Sec.--Affiliated Computer Services, Inc., Dallas, TX, pg. 23
Dee, Jay, Treas. & Sec.--Dee Paper Company, Chester, PA, pg. 324
Deeb, Susan, Sec. & Treas.--Tamaroff Buick Inc., Southfield, MI, pg. 1077
Deegan, Mary, Sec.--H.J. Baker & Bro., Inc., New York, NY, pg. 114
Deen, Nancy, Sec. & Treas.--Deen Wholesale Meat Company, Inc., Fort Worth, TX, pg. 324
Deese, Donald W., Sec. & Controller--Jim Hudson, Pontiac, Oldsmobile GMC, Columbia, SC, pg. 551
DeFrancisci, Joseph, Jr., Sec.--De Francisci Machine Corp.(Demaco), Ridgewood, NY, pg. 321
Deihl, Richard, V.P. & Sec.--The Lusk Company, Irvine, CA, pg. 687
Deitsch, Sara, Sec.--Deitsch Plastics Company, West Haven, CT, pg. 325
Delaloye, John F., V.P., Sec. & Treas.--Hickey-Mitchell Company, Saint Louis, MO, pg. 795
Delfini, Joseph, Sec. & Treas.--Colonial Beef Co., Philadelphia, PA, pg. 263
Delman, Richard, Chief Fin. Officer, Treas., Sec. & Controller--Splendor Form International Inc., Long Island City, NY, pg. 1031
Demler, Lois, Sec.--Columbus McKinnon Corp., Amherst, NY, pg. 266
Dempster, Amelia R., Sec.--WDP, Inc., New York, NY, pg. 1156
Denhof, Ronnell P., Sec.--Owen-Ames-Kimball Co., Grand Rapids, MI, pg. 833
Denker, Michael, Sec. & Treas.--Arcon Construction Co., Inc., Mora, MN, pg. 81
Denlinger, Vera M., Exec. Sec.--Denlinger, Inc., Paradise, PA, pg. 329
Denniston, John, Sec.--Bobit Publishing Company, Redondo Beach, CA, pg. 161
Denny, Douglas, Sec.--World Shipping, Inc., Lakewood, OH, pg. 1203
Densley, Julie, Mngmt. Sec.--American Gilsonite Co., Salt Lake City, UT, pg. 55
Dent, Paul R., Sec.--Crosby & Overton, Inc., Long Beach, CA, pg. 300
Denton, David, Treas. & Sec.--Bale Of Kentucky, Inc., Horse Cave, KY, pg. 115
Denton, Leatha, Asst. Sec.--Denton Enterprises Inc., Grosse Pointe, MI, pg. 329
DePew, Marian J., Asst. Sec.--GreatBanc, Inc., Aurora, IL, pg. 482
Depolo, Robert A., Mgr.-Personnel, Treas. & Sec.--Monterey Mechanical Company, Oakland, CA, pg. 767
Deptula, George S., Sec.--Syracuse Supply Company, Syracuse, NY, pg. 1070
Derrico, Martin, Sec.--King Prime, Inc., Morgantown, WV, pg. 631
DeSabatino, Fred, Treas. & Sec.--Capital Pants Co., Philadelphia, PA, pg. 215
Desalvo, Joseph M., V.P. & Asst. Sec.--Converse Professional Group, Inc., Pasadena, CA, pg. 281
Desteian, Lucy, Recording Sec.--Colle & McVoy, Inc., Minneapolis, MN, pg. 261
Deutchman, Howard, V.P., Sec. & Treas.--Mark Fabricks, Inc., Los Angeles, CA, pg. 708
Devanney, William J., V.P., Sec. & Treas.--Meier Metal Service Centers, Inc., Hazel Park, MI, pg. 737
Devareaux, Vance A., Exec. V.P., Sec., Treas. & Chief Fin. Officer--Arrowhead Mills, Inc., Hereford, TX, pg. 86
Devine, David F., V.P. & Sec.--Boston Mutual Life Insurance Co., Canton, MA, pg. 167
Devine, Jack M., Sec. & Treas.--Associated Diesel Service & Equipment Company, Wilmington, CA, pg. 89
Dew, Bruce J., Sec.--Diemolding Corp., Canastota, NY, pg. 336
Dewey, Ronald L., Dir.-Fin. & Sec.--Erdle Perforating Co., Rochester, NY, pg. 385
DeYager, Betty J., Sec.--Foreign Candy Co., Inc., Huff, IA, pg. 424
Diamond, Clare W., Sec. & Treas.--T.L. Diamond Company, New York, NY, pg. 335
Diamond, Frederic, Exec. V.P., Sec. & Treas.--Diamond Chemical Co., Inc., Lyndhurst, NJ, pg. 335
Diamond, Irwin, Exec. V.P. & Sec.--Hoffman Brothers Packing Co., Los Angeles, CA, pg. 537
Diamond, Walter S., Sec. & Treas.--Snyder-Diamond, Santa Monica, CA, pg. 1015
Diaz, Saul, V.P. & Sec.--Med-Lab Supply Company, Inc., Miami, FL, pg. 734
Dibble, L.E., Treas. & Asst. Sec.--Bulab Holdings, Inc., Memphis, TN, pg. 188
Dickerson, Virginia, Sec.--Nelson Photo Supplies, San Diego, CA, pg. 797
Dickes, Glenn P., V.P. & Asst. Sec.--Revlon, Inc., New York, NY, pg. 696
Dickey, Sam, Sec. & Treas.--O'Neil Data Systems, Inc., Los Angeles, CA, pg. 827
Dickinson, Royce, Sec., Treas. & Controller--Power Process Piping, Inc., Plymouth, MI, pg. 883
Dickler, Gerard, Sec.--Guideposts Associates, Inc., Carmel, NY, pg. 493
Dickler, Herbert, Treas. & Sec.--Bankcrafters, Inc., Philadelphia, PA, pg. 117
Diehl, Harrison, Jr., Treas.--The Sico Company, Mount Joy, PA, pg. 1001
Diehl, Mary I., Sec.--Johnstown Corporation, Johnstown, PA, pg. 601
Diehl, Peter, V.P. & Sec.--Diehl Specialties Intl., Defiance, OH, pg. 336
Diem, Linda L., Sec. & Treas.--Southern Agricultural Insecticides, Palmetto, FL, pg. 1020
Diemer, Irving, Jr., V.P. & Sec.--Metal Seal & Products, Inc., Willoughby, OH, pg. 741
Dierberg, F. Roger, V.P. & Sec.--Dierbergs Markets Inc., Chesterfield, MO, pg. 337
DiFeo, Joseph C., Sec.--DiFeo Automotive Network, Jersey City, NJ, pg. 337
Dilatush, R.E., Jr., V.P. & Sec.--Staple Cotton Cooperative Association, Greenwood, MS, pg. 1038
DiMatteo, Lynne, Sec.--Chattanooga Choo-Choo Holiday Inn, Chattanooga, TN, pg. 241
Dimmer, Barbara, Sec.--Valu Discount, Inc., Louisville, KY, pg. 1143
Dimmers, Alan, Sec.--The Shane Group Inc., Hillsdale, MI, pg. 995
DiNinzio, Joseph A., Asst. Sec.--Artesian Water Company, Inc., Newark, DE, pg. 86
Dion, Ron, Chief Fin. Officer & Sec.--Kenco, Middlebury, IN, pg. 1025

Dirkes, Joanne E., Sec.--Rapid Engineering Inc., Comstock Park, MI, pg. 913
Distelrath, Julie, Sec.--Gulf States Toyota, Houston, TX, pg. 494
DiSylvester, Peter, Sec.--Credit Union National Association, Madison, WI, pg. 298
Ditcher, John, V.P. & Sec.--Atlantic Concrete Products, Inc., Tullytown, PA, pg. 94
Dockter, Rebecca L., Treas. & Sec.--Professional Book Distributors, Inc., Alpharetta, GA, pg. 894
Dodds, William, Chief Fin. Officer & Sec.--Sunclipse, Inc., Montebello, CA, pg. 1059
Dodelin, F.J., Sec.--The Hardaway Company, Columbus, GA, pg. 507
Dohmen, Robert, Sec.--The F. Dohmen Company, Germantown, WI, pg. 343
Dokmo, Harold B., Jr., Chm. Bd., Pres., Treas. & Sec.--Norcraft Companies, Inc., Saint Paul, MN, pg. 809
Dolan, Maureen, Sec. & Treas.--Cargill Salt, Newark, CA, pg. 219
Doll, David J., Chief Fin. Officer & Sr. V.P.--Bodine Electric Company, Chicago, IL, pg. 162
Dominioni, Valerie, Sec. & Treas.--Bel Paese Sales Company, Inc., Lakewood, NJ, pg. 133
Doms, Mary Anne, V.P. & Sec.--First Gray Line Corporation, Beverly Hills, CA, pg. 413
Donahue, John D., Sec.--Washers, Inc., Livonia, MI, pg. 1165
Donahue, John D., Sec.--Alpha Bolt Company, Madison Heights, MI, pg. 1165
Donaldson, D.J., Sec.--Jones Dairy Farm, Fort Atkinson, WI, pg. 603
Donaldson, George, Sec. & Treas.--Henco, Inc., Selmer, TN, pg. 528
Donaldson, J. Bennett, Pres., Chief Exec. Officer & Sec.--Cunningham-Limp Development Co., Troy, MI, pg. 305
Donavan, Doug, Chief Fin. & Info. Officer, Treas., Controller & Sec.--Campbell Oil Co., Massillon, OH, pg. 213
Donelan, Francis P., V.P., Sec. & Gen. Counsel--George A. Fuller Company, New York, NY, pg. 436
Donnellan, John J., Sec. & Controller--National Utility Service, Inc., Park Ridge, NJ, pg. 794
Donohoo, Richard G., V.P. & Sec.--The Gibson Group Inc., Cincinnati, OH, pg. 456
Donohue, Leonard, Treas. & Sec.--Steiner & Company, Milford, DE, pg. 1045
Dooley, Jo Ann C., V.P., Sec. & Treas.--Gardner Publications, Inc., Cincinnati, OH, pg. 443
Dopkins, Leonard A., Chm. Bd., Treas. & Sec.--Standard Electronics, Inc., Amherst, NY, pg. 1036
Doran, Michael W., Treas. & Sec.--Midway Ford Truck Center Inc., Kansas City, MO, pg. 751
Doremus, Peter, Sec.--Edlund Company, Inc., Burlington, VT, pg. 368
Dorman, Barry, Vice Chm., Sr. V.P. & Sec.--Omni Source Corporation, Fort Wayne, IN, pg. 826
Dorn, Cecilia A., Sec. & Treas.--Edward G. Dorn & Associates, Inc., Rolling Meadows, IL, pg. 346
Dortch, Ruth W., Sec.--Humboldt Express, Inc., Nashville, TN, pg. 552
Doster, Robert E., Treas. & Sec.--Lift-All Co., Inc., Manheim, PA, pg. 675
Dougan, Pauline V., Sec.--The J. M. Ney Company, Bloomfield, CT, pg. 805
Douglas, Robert, V.P. & Sec.--Warner Candy Company, Inc., Chicago, IL, pg. 1164
Douthit, R. E., V.P., Sec. & Treas.--Smith & Sons Foods, Inc., Macon, GA, pg. 1014
Dowie, Sandra L., Sec.--Freeman Decorating Co., Dallas, TX, pg. 431
Downey, Paul, Pres., Treas. & Sec.--Advanced Circuit Technology, Nashua, NH, pg. 20
Downie, John F., Sr. V.P., Sec. & Gen. Counsel--Cole National Corporation, Cleveland, OH, pg. 260
Downie, John F., Sec. & Gen. Counsel--Cole Vision Corporation, Cleveland, OH, pg. 260
Doyle, C.A., V.P., Sec. & Gen. Counsel--Burns & Roe Enterprises, Inc., Oradell, NJ, pg. 194
Doyle, Cecil G., Exec. V.P. & Sec.--Hayes, Seay, Mattern & Mattern, Inc., Roanoke, VA, pg. 519
Doyle, Elizabeth A., V.P.-Admin. & Production & Corp. Sec.-My Own Meals, Inc., Deerfield, IL, pg. 779
Drell, Steven, Exec. V.P. & Sec.--DeMert & Dougherty, Inc., Westchester, IL, pg. 328
Drenning, John, Legal Officer & Sec.--Smith Metal Arts Company, Inc., Buffalo, NY, pg. 1013
Drescher, Donald, Sec. & Treas.--Dazey Corporation, Industrial Airport, KS, pg. 321
Dressler, Abbott, W., Exec. V.P. & Sec.--Colfax, Inc., Pawtucket, RI, pg. 261
Drettmann, Margarete, Sec.--Active Tool & Manufacturing Co., Inc., Roseville, MI, pg. 15
Drew, W.J., Sec.--Kohler Company, Kohler, WI, pg. 639
Drewry, John T., V.P., Chief Oper. & Chief Fin. Officer & Treas.--Advanced Marine Enterprises, Inc., Arlington, VA, pg. 20
Dreyer, Dennis J., Sec.--Perry & Derrick Co., Cincinnati, OH, pg. 863
Drinkward, Robert, Exec. V.P. & Sec.--Bergelectric Corporation, Los Angeles, CA, pg. 141
Dropkin, Philip, Sec. & Gen. Counsel--Cablevision Industries Corp., Liberty, NY, pg. 206
Drotar, Paul P., V.P., Corp. Controller & Sec.--Carrols Corporation, Syracuse, NY, pg. 225
Drucker, N., V.P.-Fin., Treas. & Sec.--Weber Marking Systems, Inc., Arlington Heights, IL, pg. 1171
Drushel, W.H., Jr., V.P. & Sec.--Quintana Petroleum Corp., Houston, TX, pg. 905
Drutt, William, Pres., Chief Exec. Officer & Sec.--Harris & Drutt Inc., Philadelphia, PA, pg. 511
Dryden Hall, J.M., Jr., Sec.--The Sheridan Group, Hanover, PA, pg. 998
Dryden, Kay, Sr. V.P., Sec. & Legal Counsel--Del Monte Foods, San Francisco, CA, pg. 325
Dryer, Ned, Sec.--Arizona Wholesale Supply Company, Phoenix, AZ, pg. 82
Dryer, Ned, Sec. & Treas.--National Brands, Inc., Phoenix, AZ, pg. 786
Dubner, Miriam, Sec. & Treas.--Gerson & Gerson, Inc., New York, NY, pg. 454
Duckworth, Gary E., Sec.--Frederick Trading Company, Frederick, MD, pg. 430
Duckworth, William D., V.P., Corp. Treas. & Asst. Sec.--Stauffer Communications, Inc., Topeka, KS, pg. 1042
Duda, Luther, V.P. & Sec.--A. Duda & Sons Inc., Oviedo, FL, pg. 351
Duff, George M., Jr., Sec.--Transistor Devices, Inc., Cedar Knolls, NJ, pg. 1107
Duffy, Robert E., V.P.-Fin., Sec. & Chief Fin. Officer--American Industries Inc., Portland, OR, pg. 55
DuGan, Gordon F., V.P. & Asst. Sec.--W. P. Carey & Co., Inc., New York, NY, pg. 218
Dugan, Joel H., Sr. V.P.-Fin. & Admin.; Sec. & Treas.--Rhodes, Inc., Atlanta, GA, pg. 931
Dugan, Ruth, Exec. Admin. Assis.--Carpeteria, Inc., Valencia, CA, pg. 224
Duggan, Ruby, V.P. & Sec.--Duggan Industries, Inc., Dallas, TX, pg. 351
Dugger, Glenn, V.P. & Sec.--Queen Oxygen Company, Columbus, OH, pg. 904
Dula, C. Stephen, Sec.-Treas. & Chief Fin. Officer--Salem National Corporation, Winston-Salem, NC, pg. 967
Dumas, Dale H., Sec.--Technology Applications, Inc., Alexandria, VA, pg. 1083
Dun, David, Sec. & Gen. Counsel--Sierra Pacific Industries, Redding, CA, pg. 1003
Duncan, Linda, Sec.--HTB, Inc., Oklahoma City, OK, pg. 497
Duncan, Susan, Sec.--Greeley Gas Co., Denver, CO, pg. 483
Duncan, T.E., Sec.--Woodbury Business Forms, Inc., La Grange, GA, pg. 1200
Duncan, Walter, V.P.-Legal & Sec.--Southern Farm Bureau Casualty Insurance Company, Ridgeland, MS, pg. 1021
Dunham, Cynthia Harris, Owner, Treas. & Sec.--K-J Distributors, Inc., Glendale, AZ, pg. 612
Dunham, W. Lee H., Corp. Sec.--Continental Cablevision, Boston, MA, pg. 278
Dunn, Peter L., V.P.-Admin., Gen. Counsel & Sec.--Korn/Ferry International, Los Angeles, CA, pg. 642
Dunnavant, T. H., Sec.--Kyanite Mining Corporation, Dillwyn, VA, pg. 647
Duplesis, W.P., Sec.--American Liberty Financial Corp., Baton Rouge, LA, pg. 57
Dupps, David M., Treas. & Sec.--Dupps Company, Germantown, OH, pg. 354
DuPree, Billy, Sr. V.P., Gen. Counsel & Sec.--American Health Companies, Inc., Pittsburgh, PA, pg. 55
Durall, Keith, Sec.--Didde Web Press, Emporia, KS, pg. 336
Duran-Stock, June C., Sec.--Pacific Capital Bancorp, Salinas, CA, pg. 839
Durand, Mary K., Sec.--American Republic Insurance Co., Des Moines, IA, pg. 60
Durante, Katherine, Asst. Sec.--MADD (Mothers Against Drunk Driving), Irving, TX, pg. 691
Durfee, Barbara, Treas. & Sec.--Bethel Mills, Inc., Bethel, VT, pg. 148
Durkin, Alice, Sec.--Universal Photonics, Inc., Hicksville, NY, pg. 1139
Durnin, Jerry L., Sec. & Treas.--A. K. Durnin Chrysler Plymouth, Inc., Baton Rouge, LA, pg. 355
Dutton, C.B., Sec.--Sarkes Tarzian, Incorporated, Bloomington, IN, pg. 1079
Duwe, John, Sec. & Treas.--United States Bakery, Portland, OR, pg. 1134
Dwyer, Robert, Sec.--New England Frozen Foods, Southborough, MA, pg. 800
Dyson, Harry, Treas. & Sec.--Providence Journal Company, Providence, RI, pg. 895
Dzurick, Robert D., Sec.--Lloyd Controls, Inc., Mountlake Terrace, WA, pg. 679
Eacott, Susan H., Sec.--Bartlett Brainard & Eacott, Inc., Bloomfield, CT, pg. 122
Eagel, M.J., Sec. & Treas.--Pipe Fabricating & Supply Company, Santa Fe Springs, CA, pg. 872
Eaken, Barbara J., Sec., Treas. & Comptroller--R.W. Eaken, Inc., Leesport, PA, pg. 362
Eaker, Rusty, Sec.--Coble Dairy Products Co-op, Lexington, NC, pg. 257
Earle, J.B., Sec.--Lindsay Olive Growers, Lindsay, CA, pg. 676
Earle, Jim, Sec. & Distr. Mgr.--Lindsay International, Lindsay, CA, pg. 676
Early, William B., V.P. & Asst. Sec.--Jeld-Wen, Inc., Klamath Falls, OR, pg. 591
Earnhardt, Jim Babe, Sec. & Treas.--Earnhardt's Auto Center, Tempe, AZ, pg. 362
Earp, Marie, Sec. & Treas.--Earp Meat Company, Kansas City, KS, pg. 362
Easter, Steven, V.P.-Govt. Member Rels. & Sec.--Blue Diamond Growers, Sacramento, CA, pg. 160
Eaton, Robert L., Sec. & Treas.--Invincible Metal Furniture Co., Manitowoc, WI, pg. 582
Eaton, Scott, Sec.--Sasco Group, Cerritos, CA, pg. 971
Eaton, Scott, Sec. & Treas.--Sasco/Valley Electric, Mountain View, CA, pg. 972
Ebisa, J.M., Asst. Sec.--Green International, Inc., Denver, CO, pg. 484
Ebright, M. A., Sec.--Baker Commodities, Inc., Los Angeles, CA, pg. 115
Eccles, Margot L., V.P. & Sec.--LDI, Ltd., Indianapolis, IN, pg. 647
Eckberg, David, Gen. Counsel & Sec.--Hart Crowser, Inc., Seattle, WA, pg. 512
Eckenrod, Jeannie, Treas. & Sec.--FKG Oil Company, Belleville, IL, pg. 773
Eckstein, Helene, Chief Fin. Officer, Treas., Sec. & Mktg. Coord.--Spectrum Color Center, Golden, CO, pg. 1029
Edelbrock, Nancy, Sec.--Edelbrock Corp., Torrance, CA, pg. 367
Edelson, Jill, Sec.--General Sportcraft Company Ltd., Bergenfield, NJ, pg. 450
Edelstein, Nancy, Sec.--Edelstein Associates Advertising Inc., Seattle, WA, pg. 368
Edelstein, Stanley, Sec.--Pacesetter Corporation, Omaha, NE, pg. 839
Edreich, Jack, Treas. & Sec.--Brittany Dyeing & Printing Corporation, New Bedford, MA, pg. 177
Edson, Norman, Sec.--Streech Electric Company, Anaheim, CA, pg. 1053
Edwards, Bernard, Deputy Sec. & Mktg.--The Florida Lottery, Tallahassee, FL, pg. 420
Edwards, Jerry, Sr. V.P., Sec. & Treas.--Berry Companies, Inc., Wichita, KS, pg. 144
Edwards, Kenneth N., Sec.--Dunn-Edwards Corporation, Los Angeles, CA, pg. 353
Edwards, William F., Sec. & Treas.--Pilot Air Freight Corp., Lima, PA, pg. 870
Effstrom, Carroll E., Sec. & Treas.--Farmers Marine Copper Works, Galveston, TX, pg. 401
Egan, Charles J., Jr., V.P., Gen. Counsel & Sec.--Hallmark Cards, Inc., Kansas City, MO, pg. 501
Eggebrecht, David L., Chief Fin. Officer & Treas.--Phillips Plastics Corporation, Phillips, WI, pg. 867
Ehret, A.D., V.P., Sec. & Treas.--Dexter Company, Fairfield, IA, pg. 334
Ehrhard, Jan, Sec.--Clow Corporation, Birmingham, AL, pg. 733
Ehrhardt, Jan, Sec.--McWane, Inc., Birmingham, AL, pg. 733
Ehrle, J.S., Gen. Counsel & Sec.--North American Refractories Company, Cleveland, OH, pg. 811
Ehrlich, Henry, Sec. & Treas.--Bregg Data Forms, Inc., Hauppauge, NY, pg. 173
Einstein, Ernst, Sec. & Treas.--Einstein Moomjy Inc., Pine Brook, NJ, pg. 371
Eisele, Thomas, Sec. & Legal Counsel--Nibco, Inc., Elkhart, IN, pg. 806
Eisenmayer, Mildred F., Sec. & Asst. Treas.--Cullman Ventures, Inc., New York, NY, pg. 304
Eitzinger, Gisela, Treas. & Sec.--Mid-West Automation Systems, Buffalo Grove, IL, pg. 750
Ekdahl, Jon N., Sec. & Gen. Counsel--Arthur Andersen & Co., S.C., New York, NY, pg. 72
Ekdahl, Jon N., Sec.--Andersen Consulting, Chicago, IL, pg. 72
Eklund, Ann, Sec.--Fleet Engineers, Inc., Muskegon, MI, pg. 417
Eldridge, James F., Exec. V.P.-Legal & Sec.--American Family Mutual Insurance Co., Madison, WI, pg. 51
Ellenoff, Theodore, Treas. & Sec.--Voit Sports, Inc., Fairport, NY, pg. 1154
Ellenoff, Theodore, Sec. & Treas.--Voit Corp., Fairport, NY, pg. 1154
Ellingson, Sarah S., Chief Fin. Officer & Sec.--Reese Enterprises, Inc., Rosemount, MN, pg. 920
Elliott, R., Sec.--Mid-Am Building Supply, Inc., Moberly, MO, pg. 749
Ellis, Carol Cormier, Sec. & Treas.--Cormier Rice Milling Company, Inc., De Witt, AR, pg. 286
Ellis, E. John, Sec.--Western States Envelope Co., Butler, WI, pg. 1181
Ellison, Susan, Sec. & Treas.--Michael R. Ellison Inc., Phoenix, AZ, pg. 378
Ells, Theodore, Corp. Sec.--Lee Myles Associates Corporation, Maywood, NJ, pg. 666
Elmburg, Linda T., Sec.--Blitz USA, Miami, OK, pg. 157
Elwer, Ronald R., Exec. V.P. & Sec.--The Commercial Bank, Delphos, OH, pg. 268
Emerick, C., Sec.--Munroe, Inc., Pittsburgh, PA, pg. 776
Emery, John C., Jr., Sec.--Cargill Detroit Corp., Clawson, MI, pg. 219
Emily, Mary, Sec.--The John C. Groub Company Inc., Seymour, IN, pg. 489
Emrick, Charles, V.P. & Sec.--Ken-Mac Metal, Inc., Cleveland, OH, pg. 622
Endo, Edith M., Sec.--Servco Pacific Inc., Honolulu, HI, pg. 991
Engelman, Wayne, Sr. V.P., Sec. & Treas.--Colle & McVoy, Inc., Minneapolis, MN, pg. 261
Englefield, F.W., IV, Co-Pres., Chief Exec. & Chief Fin. Officer--Englefield, Inc., Newark, OH, pg. 382
Ensign, Gregory M., V.P., Sec. & Gen. Counsel--Kirkwood Industries, Inc., Cleveland, OH, pg. 633
Ensinger, James, Treas. & Sec.--Rudel Machinery Company, Inc., Shelton, CT, pg. 954
Epifano, Robert, Sec. & Asst. Treas.--Nuarc Company, Inc., Niles, IL, pg. 817
Epprecht, John W., V.P., Sec. & Treas.--The Great Lakes Cheese Co., Newbury, OH, pg. 481
Epstein, Corey, Sec./Treas.--Wallich Lumber Co., Detroit, MI, pg. 1161
Epstein, J. Earl, Sec.--Pennsylvania Petroleum Product Company, Southhampton, PA, pg. 858
Epstein, Lawrence, Sec. & Treas.--A J M Packaging Corporation, Detroit, MI, pg. 4
Erani, Albert, Exec. V.P. & Sec.--A & E Stores, Inc., Ridgefield, NJ, pg. 1
Erb, George L., Treas. & Sec.--Erb Lumber Company, Birmingham, MI, pg. 360
Erera, Larence E., Sec. & Treas.--American Funds Advisor Inc., Garden City, NJ, pg. 55
Erickson, Grant D., Sec.--Nelson Westerberg, Inc., Elk Grove Village, IL, pg. 1178
Erickson, Greg, Sec. & Gen. Counsel--Erickson Diversified Corp., Hudson, WI, pg. 386
Erickson, Leif V., Treas. & Sec.--Erickson Transport Corporation, Springfield, MO, pg. 386
Erickson, LeRoy L., Sec., Treas. & Chief Fin. Officer--D.C.I., Inc., Saint Cloud, MN, pg. 308
Erickson, Mel, Sr., Pres., Sec. & Treas.--Central Feed Mills, Inc., Snohomish, WA, pg. 232

Erickson, Suzanne, Exec. Sec.--Guest Quarters Suite Hotels, Boston, MA, pg. 493
Erwin, John D., Sec.--Tolleson Lumber Company, Inc., Perry, GA, pg. 1100
Eschbach, Reinhard, Sec.--Iroquois Die & Mfg. Co., Warren, MI, pg. 582
Eskilson, Arnold J., Sec. & Treas.--Dixie Dairy Company, Gary, IN, pg. 341
Essenberg, Ruth, Sec.--Douglas Steel Fabricating Corporation, Lansing, MI, pg. 347
Etkin, Toby, Sec.--Alex J. Etkin, Inc., Farmington Hills, MI, pg. 389
Ettelson, Stephen, V.P. & Sec.--Electro Brand, Inc., Chicago, IL, pg. 374
Etteridge, Timothy, Sec. & Treas.--Temps & Company, Washington, DC, pg. 1086
Etterling, Robert, Treas. & Sec.--Simonds-Shields-Theis Grain Co., Kansas City, MO, pg. 1006
Eugene, Donald, Sr. V.P. & Sec.--R. H. Macy & Co., Inc., New York, NY, pg. 698
Evangelidis, Randy, Corp. Sec.--Merchant Capital Group Ltd, Chicago, IL, pg. 739
Evans, Andrew J., Treas. & Sec.--Harrison Paint Corporation, Canton, OH, pg. 512
Evans, Gregg, Treas. & Sec.--Shield Security, Inc., Los Angeles, CA, pg. 999
Evans, Jody, Sec. & Treas.--Bell Construction Co. Inc., Brentwood, TN, pg. 134
Evans, Ronald L., Sec.--Charles Town Races, Inc., Charles Town, WV, pg. 240
Evans, Sue, Sec.--Jergens Inc., Cleveland, OH, pg. 593
Evans, Wayne C., V.P. & Sec.--EvansGroup, Salt Lake City, UT, pg. 391
Evergettis, Barry P., Sec.--Underground Construction Company, Inc., Benicia, CA, pg. 1125
Evers, Bradley W., V.P., Sec. & Gen. Counsel--Price Brothers Co., Dayton, OH, pg. 888
Evers, Linda, Sec. & Asst. Treas.--American Bread Company - Sunbeam Bakery, Nashville, TN, pg. 49
Ewell, Shirlee, Sec.--Wavetek Communications Div., Indianapolis, IN, pg. 1168
Eyster, Franklin S., II, Sr. V.P., Sec. & Gen. Counsel--Atlantic Aviation Corp., New Castle, DE, pg. 94
Ezell, Stan, V.P. & Sec.--Purity Dairies Inc., Nashville, TN, pg. 901
Ezratty, Joseph, Treas.--The Benatty Corporation, Cambridge, OH, pg. 138
Fagan, Larry, Gen. Mgr., Corp. Sec. & Treas.--Associated Machinecraft Corporation, Los Angeles, CA, pg. 90
Fagel, Marvin, V.P.-Investor Rels. & Sec.--Aurora Packing Co., Inc., North Aurora, IL, pg. 98
Falconi, Robert, Chief Fin. Officer, Treas. & Sec.--Planning Systems Inc., McLean, VA, pg. 874
Faller, Lisa M., Exec. V.P., Sec. & Client Services--FKQ Advertising Inc., Clearwater, FL, pg. 394
Fallon, Ann, Sec.--Ripon Foods, Inc., Ripon, WI, pg. 935
Falvey, Jim, Sec.--Pennock, Philadelphia, PA, pg. 858
Fankhauser, James R., Sr. Fin. Partner, Sec. & Treas.--Fahlgren Martin, Inc., Parkersburg, WV, pg. 396
Fanning, Laurene, Exec. Sec.--Harmon Smith Inc., Kansas City, MO, pg. 510
Fantich, Lawrence, Treas. & Sec.--Tool King, Denver, CO, pg. 1101
Faris, Jean, Corp. Sec.--Tri Valley Growers Inc., San Francisco, CA, pg. 1111
Farlik, Terry, Sec. & Treas.--Seco Warwick Corporation, Meadville, PA, pg. 987
Farrah, Elizabeth J., Sec.--School Apparel, Inc., San Francisco, CA, pg. 978
Farrell, Dianne, Sec. & Controller--McNally Industries, Inc., Grantsburg, WI, pg. 731
Farrell, James B., V.P., Gen. Counsel & Sec.--Minstar, Inc., Minneapolis, MN, pg. 758
Farrell, James B., V.P., Gen. Counsel & Sec.--Genmar Industries, Inc., Minneapolis, MN, pg. 759
Farrell, Katherine M., Sec.--Pan American Trade Development Corp., New York, NY, pg. 845
Fato, Martha, Sec. & Treas.--Par Enterprises, Inc., Wheeling, WV, pg. 847
Faude, William D., Sr. V.P., Sec.--Cramer-Krasselt, Milwaukee, WI, pg. 296
Faulk, Barbara D., Asst. Sec.--Standard Welders Supply Co., Memphis, TN, pg. 1038
Faulkner, Harry F., III, V.P.-Admin. & Sec.--North American Royalties, Inc., Chattanooga, TN, pg. 811
Faull, Linda, Sec.--Country Companies Insurance Group, Bloomington, IL, pg. 289
Faull, Linda, Sec.--Country Mutual Insurance Company, Bloomington, IL, pg. 289
Faull, Linda, Sec.--CC Services, Bloomington, IL, pg. 289
Faw, Thomas M., Sec.--Spencer's Inc., Mount Airy, NC, pg. 1030
Fawcett, Dwight J., Sec.--White Pigeon Paper Company, White Pigeon, MI, pg. 87
Fay, Thomas F., Treas. & Sec.--Overhead Conveyor Co., Ferndale, MI, pg. 832
Fedalen, Richard J., Sec.--The Acacia Group, Washington, DC, pg. 10
Fehr, Lawrence F., V.P., Controller & Sec.--Herff Jones Inc., Indianapolis, IN, pg. 531
Feibel, James B., Sec. & Gen. Counsel--Electric Power Equipment Co., Columbus, OH, pg. 373
Fekete, Roger, V.P. & Sec.--Peck Spring Company, Plainville, CT, pg. 854
Feld, Katherine P., Sec.--Oppenheimer Management Corp., New York, NY, pg. 719
Feldkamp, Joseph, Sec.--Jake Sweeney Auto Leasing Inc., Cincinnati, OH, pg. 1066
Feldkamp, Joseph, Sec.--Jake Sweeney Auto Leasing, Inc., Cincinnati, OH, pg. 1067
Feldman, Eugene, Sec. & Legal Officer--Doe Spun, Inc., New York, NY, pg. 343
Feldman, Shirley, Sec. & Treas.--Isfel Company, Inc., Rahway, NJ, pg. 582
Feles, Gust, Exec. V.P. & Sec.--Carhartt, Inc., Dearborn, MI, pg. 220
Fell, Lawrence M., Sec. & Gen. Counsel--Industrial General Corporation, Elyria, OH, pg. 566
Fellenstein, Mike, Sec., Treas. & Comptroller--Biddulph Oldsmobile, Glendale, AZ, pg. 149
Fellowes, Peter, Exec. V.P. & Sec.--Fellowes Manufacturing Co., Itasca, IL, pg. 405
Felsecker, James, Asst. Sec.--Duron, Inc., Beltsville, MD, pg. 355
Feltes, John, Sec. & Treas.--Automatic Liquid Packaging, Inc., Woodstock, IL, pg. 100
Fennell, John, V.P., Sec. & Dir.-Mktg.--Badger Air Brush Company, Franklin Park, IL, pg. 113
Fenster, Fred A., Treas. & Sec.--Capucci Creations International, Inc., Beverly Hills, CA, pg. 216
Fenton, Robert S., Exec. V.P. & Sec.--Collins & Aikman Group Inc., Santa Monica, CA, pg. 262
Fentress, Kenneth P., Treas. & Sec.--L & R Communications, Limited, Sioux City, IA, pg. 647
Ferguson, Scott, V.P.-Mktg. & Sec.--Hamlin, Inc., Lake Mills, WI, pg. 503
Ferman, Martha S., Sec. & Treas.--Ferman Oldsmobile, Tampa, FL, pg. 406
Fernandez, Frank L., Treas. & Sec.--Saratoga Harness Racing, Inc., Saratoga Springs, NY, pg. 970
Ferton, Michel, Sec.--Bordelais, Lemeunier & Leo Burnett, Clichy,, France, pg. 192
Fesler, Daniel L., V.P. & Sec.--Lampert Yards, Inc., Saint Paul, MN, pg. 653
Fetridge, Bonni Jean, Sec.--The Dartnell Corporation, Chicago, IL, pg. 316
Fetter, Jane T., Chm. Bd. & Sec.--Kettenburg Marine Corporation, San Diego, CA, pg. 626
Feuer, Myron, Sec.--Feuer Leather Corporation, Hawthorne, NY, pg. 407
Fibbe, R.E., Sec. & Pur. Agent--The Kirk & Blum Mfg. Co., Cincinnati, OH, pg. 633
Ficarra, Debbie, Sec.--The John Johnson Co., Detroit, MI, pg. 597
Fick, Jerry, Sec.--Standard Textile Co., Inc., Cincinnati, OH, pg. 1037
Ficks, Joy S., Sec.--Ficks Reed Company, Cincinnati, OH, pg. 408
Fiedler, Paula P., Chm. Bd. & Sec.--Crown Fence Co., Pasadena, CA, pg. 302
Fierle, Debra R., Sec.--Cook Moving Systems, Inc., Buffalo, NY, pg. 282
Fierle, R., V.P., Treas. & Sec.--Quackenbush Co. Inc., Buffalo, NY, pg. 902
Fikejs, John W., Treas. & Sec.--Plymouth Tube Company, Warrenville, IL, pg. 877
Filla, Roger, Sec.--A-G Co-op Creamery, Arcadia, WI, pg. 4
Fille, Roger, Sec.--Arcadia Fryers, Arcadia, WI, pg. 80
Fimbel, Edward III, Sec.--Fimbel Door Corporation, Whitehouse, NJ, pg. 409
Finanger, Dave, Sec.--Weinbrenner Shoe Company, Inc., Merrill, WI, pg. 1173
Fincher, Larry, Exec. V.P., Sec. & Treas.--Truman Arnold Companies, Texarkana, TX, pg. 84
Finegood, Freddi Sue, Sec.--Good Companies, Carson, CA, pg. 470
Fineman, C.P., Sec.--Caldwell Tanks, Inc., Louisville, KY, pg. 209
Fingerle, Larry, Sec. & Treas.--Fingerle Lumber Co., Ann Arbor, MI, pg. 411
Finkbeiner, James V., Sec.--Lobdell-Emery Manufacturing Company, Alma, MI, pg. 680
Finkel, Nathan, V.P. & Sec.--FMS Management Systems, Inc., North Miami Beach, FL, pg. 394
Finkelstein, Charles D., Sec.--Faber, Coe & Gregg, Inc., Secaucus, NJ, pg. 395
Finkelstein, Ronald W., Sec. & Treas.--Multi Media Services Corp., Alexandria, VA, pg. 775
Finn, Michael A., Sec.--Metallurg, Inc., New York, NY, pg. 742
Finnegan, Thomas J., Jr., V.P. & Sec.--Massachusetts Mutual Life Insurance Co., Springfield, MA, pg. 718
Fischer, Jerome, Sec. & Treas.--Buerkle Buick-Honda Co., Saint Paul, MN, pg. 186
Fischer, Klaus P., V.P., Gen. Counsel & Sec.--Elliott Company, Jeannette, PA, pg. 378
Fischer, Philip, Treas. & Sec.--Torcon, Inc., Westfield, NJ, pg. 1102
Fischer, Risa, Asst. Corp. Admin.--Electrical Insulation Suppliers, Hillside, IL, pg. 374
Fischman, Bernard D., Sec.--Shepaug Corporation, New York, NY, pg. 997
Fischman, Steven, Sec.--Helpern Joan & David, Inc., Everett, MA, pg. 528
Fischman, Steven F., Sec.--Joan & David, Inc., Everett, MA, pg. 528
Fish, Milton, Jr., V.P. & Sec.--L. Fish Corporation, Chicago, IL, pg. 414
Fisher, Arlene Lane, Sec.--ILC Industries, Inc., Bohemia, NY, pg. 560
Fisher, Harold, Sec. & Treas.--Hillerich & Bradsby Co., Inc., Louisville, KY, pg. 535
Fisher, John J., Controller & Asst. Sec.--Tarlton Corporation, Saint Louis, MO, pg. 1079
Fisher, Lisa, Sec.--Gray Printing Co., Fostoria, OH, pg. 479
Fisher, McLane, Exec. V.P., Sec. & Chief Fin. Officer--CH2M Hill Companies, Ltd., Englewood, CO, pg. 202
Fisher, Patricia, Sec.--Victaulic Company of America, Easton, PA, pg. 1149
Fisher, William, V.P.-Admin.--Butterick Company, Inc., New York, NY, pg. 197
Fissasloo, Bill, Dir.-Pur., Sec. & Treas.--Gress Foods Inc., Gainesville, GA, pg. 486
Fitts, Bill, Sec.--Braid Electric Company, Nashville, TN, pg. 171
Fitzgerald, Hope, Sec. & Sls. Admin.--Son Chief Electrics, Inc., Winsted, CT, pg. 1018
Fitzgerald, Jean, Asst. Sec. & Loan Officer--Wieland Financial Services, Inc., Atlanta, GA, pg. 1188
Fitzgerald, Ken, Chief Fin. Officer & Sec.--R.L. Ziegler Co. Inc., Tuscaloosa, AL, pg. 1218
Fitzpatrick, Gilbert L., Exec. V.P. & Sec.--The Curry Corporation, Scarsdale, NY, pg. 305
Fitzpatrick, Michael, V.P. & Sec.--Fitzpatrick & Weller, Inc., Ellicottville, NY, pg. 416
Fitzsimons, John H., Sec. & Gen. Counsel--The Dyson-Kissner-Moran Corporation, New York, NY, pg. 357
FitzSimons, John H., Sec.--Consolidated Group, Inc., Charlotte, NC, pg. 357
FitzSimons, John H., Sec.--Consolidated Engravers-East, Inc., Charlotte, NC, pg. 357
FitzSimons, John H., Sec.--Centre Foundry & Machine Co., Wheeling, WV, pg. 357
FitzSimons, John H., V.P. & Sec.--CCC Conveyors, Inc., Dallas, TX, pg. 357
Flechner, Neil, V.P.-Fin. & Sec.--The Ormond Shops, Inc., North Bergen, NJ, pg. 830
Fleischmann, Hartly, Sec.--George Lithograph, San Francisco, CA, pg. 452
Fleming, Gordon, Sec. & Treas.--Brock Candy Company, Chattanooga, TN, pg. 177
Fletcher, Shirley, Asst. Sec.--Graves-Humphreys Company, Roanoke, VA, pg. 592
Flippin, James C., V.P. & Sec.--Reading Eagle Company, Reading, PA, pg. 916
Flodstrom, Majken, Sec. & Treas.--Flodstrom Construction Co., Deerfield, IL, pg. 419
Flom, Gerald T., Sec.--Smith System Manufacturing Company, Shoreview, MN, pg. 1014
Floor, Richard, Sec.--Muro Pharmaceutical, Inc., Tewksbury, MA, pg. 776
Flori, James D., V.P. & Sec.--Flori Corp., Phoenix, AZ, pg. 420
Foecking, Leland R., Treas., Controller & Sec.--Joseph Behr & Sons Inc., Rockford, IL, pg. 132
Fogelsong, Linda, Sec.--Avibank Mfg., Inc., Burbank, CA, pg. 102
Foley, Mercedes, Vice Chm. & Sec.--Steve Foley Cadillac, Northbrook, IL, pg. 422
Folts, John B., Exec. V.P., Sec. & Treas.--Hargro Enterprises, Inc., Stamford, CT, pg. 509
Fong, Dean, Sec. & Treas.--Lucky Fruit & Produce, Inc., Sacramento, CA, pg. 686
Fontaine, Thomas P., Sec.--O'Neal & Prelle, Hartford, CT, pg. 827
Fontenelle, Scuddy F., Jr., Sec.--MCC Group, Inc., Metairie, LA, pg. 691
Fontenot, Sundra, Sec.--Fugro-McClelland, Inc., Houston, TX, pg. 435
Fooch, Kelly, Sec.--Temperature Equipment Corporation, Melrose Park, IL, pg. 1086
Ford, Elsa, Corp. Sec.--John Burnham & Co., San Diego, CA, pg. 194
Ford, James, Sec.--Rome Manufacturing Co., Rome, GA, pg. 945
Ford, Susan E., Sec.--Knight Architects Engineers Planners, Inc., Chicago, IL, pg. 637
Forgione, Dennis, Corp. Sec.--Boyer Bros. Inc., Altoona, PA, pg. 169
Fortmuller, George A., Chief Fin. Officer, Treas. & Sec.--Edwin B. Stimpson Company, Inc., Bayport, NY, pg. 1049
Fortune, Patricia, Sec.--American Legend Corporate, Seattle, WA, pg. 57
Fortunoff, Helene, Sec. & Treas.--Fortunoff, Westbury, NY, pg. 425
Fossom, Robert, Sec.--American Mathematical Society, Inc., Providence, RI, pg. 58
Foster, Marvin L., Sr. V.P. & Sec.--Nationwide Homes, Inc., Martinsville, VA, pg. 795
Foster, Mayson H., Sec. & Treas.--Citizens National Bancshares Inc., Hammond, LA, pg. 250
Foster, Robert J., V.P.-Fin.--National Machinery Company, Tiffin, OH, pg. 792
Foti, Frances, Sec. & Dir.-Personnel--ICC Industries, Inc., New York, NY, pg. 558
Fowler, Charlotte, Sec.--Paramount Foods Inc., Louisville, KY, pg. 848
Fowler, Eileen H., Sec.--Sunkist Growers, Inc., Sherman Oaks, CA, pg. 1060
Fowler, James L., V.P. & Sec.--Multiple Allied Services, Inc., Hayward, CA, pg. 775
Fowler, P.D., Sec.--International Systems & Controls Corp., Houston, TX, pg. 579
Fox, John, Sec. & Treas.--Presto Lock, Inc., Garfield, NJ, pg. 888
Fox, Randolph, V.P.-Fin., Treas. & Sec.--Metal Masters Foodservice Equipment, Smyrna, DE, pg. 741
Fox, Raymond A., V.P., Chief Oper. Officer & Sec.--Active Electrical Supply Company, Chicago, IL, pg. 15
Fox, Richard, Sec.--Green Construction of Indiana, Inc., Oaktown, IN, pg. 484
Fox, Stephen, V.P., Gen. Counsel & Sec.--Amperif Corporation, Chatsworth, CA, pg. 68
Fraedrich, David S., V.P., Sec. & Treas.--John W. Brooks Inc., Nelsonville, OH, pg. 180
Fraenkel, Eleanor, Sec.--Fraenkel Company, Baton Rouge, LA, pg. 428
Fralick, Millie, Sec. & Asst. Treas.--Behr Stores Inc., Louisville, KY, pg. 132
Francione, John, V.P., Sec. & Treas.--Aetna Plywood, Inc., Arlington Heights, IL, pg. 23
Franco, Frank J., Treas. & Sec.--Peckham Industries, Inc., White Plains, NY, pg. 854
Frangos, John E., V.P.-Mfg. & Sec.--C.R. Daniels, Inc., Ellicott City, MD, pg. 314
Frank, George, Exec. V.P., Chief Oper. Officer & Treas.--Sicola Martin Koons Frank, Inc., Austin, TX, pg. 1001
Frank, Harley, V.P. & Sec.--Union Industries, Inc., Providence, RI, pg. 1128

Frank, Judy, Sec.--Corner Pockets of America, Billings, MT, pg. 286
Franke, Thomas, V.P. & Sec.--Riemeier Lumber Company, Inc., Cincinnati, OH, pg. 934
Frankel, Ernst D., Chief Fin. Officer, Treas., Controller & Sec.--Standard Textile Co., Inc., Cincinnati, OH, pg. 1037
Frankel, Richard, Sec.--William Lyon Company, Newport Beach, CA, pg. 690
Franklin, Alice, Treas. & Sec.--Hickory Construction Company, Hickory, NC, pg. 532
Franz, Victor, V.P. & Sec.--Fenton Press, Inc., Addison, IL, pg. 406
Fraser, Margaret A., Sec.--Lester B. Knight & Associates, Inc., Chicago, IL, pg. 637
Frazen, Mary A., Exec. V.P., Sec. & Treas.--Ed Marling Stores, Inc., Topeka, KS, pg. 710
Frederick, Robert, Sec.--Henry Bacon Building Materials, Inc., Issaquah, WA, pg. 113
Freedland, Michael, Treas. & Sec.--Ambassador Steel Co., Detroit, MI, pg. 47
Freedland, Phyllis, Sec.--Homemaker Shops, Inc., Southfield, MI, pg. 542
Freedman, Marc D., Sr. V.P., Gen. Counsel & Sec.--Butler Service Group, Inc., Montvale, NJ, pg. 197
Freehling, Les, Sec.--Oberg Industries Co., Freeport, PA, pg. 819
Freeman, Barbara, Sec.--Guest Services, Inc., Fairfax, VA, pg. 493
Freeman, Jeff E., Sr. V.P.-Fin., Sec. & Treas.--Havatampa Incorporated, Tampa, FL, pg. 517
Freeman, Jeff E., Sr. V.P.-Fin., Sec. & Treas.--H.A.T. Holding Company, Tampa, FL, pg. 517
Freeman, John, Chief Fin. Officer, V.P., Treas. & Sec.--Robert F. Driver Co., Inc., San Diego, CA, pg. 349
Freeman, Mark S., Sec. & Dir.-Intl. Sls. & Mktg.--Freeman Cosmetic Corp., Los Angeles, CA, pg. 431
Freidheim, John, V.P. & Sec.--Cougle Commission Company, Inc., Chicago, IL, pg. 289
Freilich, Joseph, Treas. & Sec.--Icahn & Co., Inc., Mount Kisco, NY, pg. 561
Freimark, Jeffrey P., Exec. V.P., Chief Fin. Officer & Gen. Counsel & Sec.--Pueblo International, Inc., Pompano Beach, FL, pg. 899
Freitas, Noreen, Exec. V.P.--Den-Mat Corporation, Santa Maria, CA, pg. 328
French, Linda, Sr. V.P., Gen. Counsel & Sec.--Payless Cashways, Inc., Kansas City, MO, pg. 853
Freticelli, Teresa, Corp. Sec.--C. Brewer & Company, Limited, Honolulu, HI, pg. 174
Frey, James E., Sec.--Homewood Corporation, Columbus, OH, pg. 542
Frey, Robert L., Sec.--The National Latex Products Co., Ashland, OH, pg. 791
Frezel, William J., Exec. V.P. & Sec.--Premier Dental Products Company, Norristown, PA, pg. 886
Friberg, John R., Pres., Chief Exec. Officer & Sec.--Eastern Smelting & Refining Corporation, Lynn, MA, pg. 363
Frick, Frank J., Chief Oper. & Chief Exec. Officer & Sec.--Takatta Inc., Olympia Fields, IL, pg. 1076
Fried, Peter A., Treas. & Sec.--Rothschild North America Inc., New York, NY, pg. 951
Fried, Tamara, Sec.--B.T.F. Corporation, East Rutherford, NJ, pg. 107
Friedland, Laura S., V.P. & Sec.--Harper Industries, Inc., New York, NY, pg. 510
Friedman, Eric D., V.P. & Sec.--The Grandoe Corporation, Gloversville, NY, pg. 476
Friedman, Irwin, Asst. Sec.--Banner Wholesale Grocers, Inc., Chicago, IL, pg. 118
Friedman, Jerry, Exec. V.P., Treas. & Sec.--Marvin Engineering Company, Inc., Inglewood, CA, pg. 716
Friedrichsen, B.T., Sec. & Treas.--Wagner Mills Inc., Schuyler, NE, pg. 1158
Friesen, David, Treas. & Asst. Sec.--Clemens Markets Inc., Lansdale, PA, pg. 254
Friou, Roger P., Vice Chm. & Chief Fin. Officer--Jitney-Jungle Stores of America, Inc., Jackson, MS, pg. 594
Frisch, Benjamin P., V.P., Sec. & Treas.--Beaver Street Fisheries, Inc., Jacksonville, FL, pg. 130
Fritze, Kenneth, V.P. & Sec.--Philip Fritze & Sons, Inc., Whippany, NJ, pg. 434
Fritzen, Doris A., Controller & Sec.--C.F. Haglin & Sons, Minneapolis, MN, pg. 499
Froeliger, E.L., Sec., Treas. & Chief Fin. Officer--Frantz Manufacturing Co., Sterling, IL, pg. 429
Fry, David S., V.P., Sec. & Gen. Counsel--Steelcase Inc., Grand Rapids, MI, pg. 1044
Frye, Darrell, V.P.-Fin. & Sec.--Harriss & Covington Hosiery Mills, High Point, NC, pg. 512
Fudge, Dorothy, Treas. & Sec.--Tom James Of Atlanta, Inc., Atlanta, GA, pg. 589
Fuefing, Klans, Sec. & Treas.--American Barmag Co., Charlotte, NC, pg. 49
Fuerbach, D.S., Sec.--S. M. Frank & Co., Inc., Peekskill, NY, pg. 429
Fuller, Glenn, V.P. & Sec.--McKee Foods Corporation, Collegedale, TN, pg. 730
Fuller, Glenn, V.P. & Sec.--McKee Baking Co., Inc., Collegedale, TN, pg. 730
Fuller, Patricia, Sec.--Southwestern Petroleum Corporation, Fort Worth, TX, pg. 1024
Fulton, Marcelene F., Sec.--American Tara Corporation, Atlanta, GA, pg. 63
Furman, Granklin G., Sec.--Furman Foods, Inc., Northumberland, PA, pg. 436
Fusaro, Angelo, V.P.-Corp. Affairs--The Apparel Group, Ltd., New York, NY, pg. 78
Fushimi, V., Sec.--Dimco-Gray Company, Dayton, OH, pg. 338
Futrell, Tony, Sec.--E.C. Barton & Co., Jonesboro, AR, pg. 123
Futter, Kenneth, Sec. & Treas.--Futter Lumber Corporation, Rockville Centre, NY, pg. 437
Gabriel, George S., Chm. Bd.--Bio Medic Corporation, Maywood, NJ, pg. 152
Gaddis, L.L., V.P. & Sec.--National Posters, Inc., Chattanooga, TN, pg. 790
Gadon, S.F., Sec.--Simkins Industries, Inc., New Haven, CT, pg. 1005
Gaffin, Helen, Sec.--Baris Shoe Company, Inc., New York, NY, pg. 119
Gai, Donald P., V.P. & Sec.--Gai's Seattle French Baking Co., Inc., Seattle, WA, pg. 441
Gaidano, Don J., Sec.--Service Assets Corp., Newport Beach, CA, pg. 179
Gaier, J. Richard, Sec.--The Orr Felt Company, Piqua, OH, pg. 830
Gainer, Arthur, Treas. & Sec.--Champaign Landmark, Urbana, OH, pg. 238
Gajewski, J.L., V.P. & Sec.--Elkins Constructors, Inc., Jacksonville, FL, pg. 377
Galanis, Marian M., Sec.--Sealing Devices Inc., Lancaster, NY, pg. 984
Galante, Joyce M., Sec. & Legal Counsel--Tagsons Papers, Inc., Albany, NY, pg. 1076
Galey, Thomas, Sec.--Chicago Holdings, Inc., Pittsburgh, PA, pg. 245
Galiardao, Guy, Sec.--The National Enquirer, Lantana, FL, pg. 788
Gallagher, Cindy, Sec. & Treas.--Jim Fresard Pontiac Buick, Inc., Royal Oak, MI, pg. 432
Gallaher, James A., V.P.-Pub. Affairs/Pub. Rels. & Sec.--The New England, Boston, MA, pg. 799
Gallo, Samuel J., Sr. V.P., Sec. & Gen. Counsel--Arthur D. Little, Inc., Cambridge, MA, pg. 678
Gallo, Samuel J., Sec.--Arthur D. Little of Canada Ltd., Toronto,, Canada, pg. 679
Gallo, Samuel J., Sec.--Arthur D. Little Far East, Inc., Singapore, Singapore, pg. 679
Gallucci, Alfred, Exec. V.P., Sec. & Personnel Dir.--Concrete Construction Company, Columbus, OH, pg. 273
Galvin, R. Terence, Sr. V.P. & Chief Fin. Officer--The Grand Union Company, Wayne, NJ, pg. 476
Gamba, Jeanette L., Pres. & Sec.--Jordan Associates, Oklahoma City, OK, pg. 604
Gangitano, Sara, Sec.--Whisper Soft Mills Inc., New York, NY, pg. 1185
Gann, Sam H., Sec., Treas. & Dir.-Opers.--Pioneer Oil Company Inc., Fort Worth, TX, pg. 872
Gannon, Christopher R., Gen. Counsel & Sec.--G.S. Blodgett Corporation, Burlington, VT, pg. 157
Gant, Edmund R., Chm. Bd. & Sec.--Glen Raven Mills, Inc., Glen Raven, NC, pg. 461
Gant, Harry, Chief Fin. Officer, Treas. & Sec.--Young Radiator Company, Racine, WI, pg. 1210
Ganzi, Victor F., V.P., Gen. Counsel & Sec.--The Hearst Corporation, New York, NY, pg. 521
Garay, Marie, Sec.--Laminaire Corporation, Rahway, NJ, pg. 652
Garbarini, Rose, Sec.--Los Angeles Smoking Curing Company, Los Angeles, CA, pg. 684
Gardner, Betty A., Co-Chm. Bd. & Sec.--Soft Sheen Products, Inc., Chicago, IL, pg. 1016
Gardner, David A., Pres. & Sec.--Nickles Bakery, Inc., Martins Ferry, OH, pg. 807
Gardner, David E., Pres. & Sec.--Alfred Nickles Bakery, Inc., Navarre, OH, pg. 806
Gardner, Howard, Sec.--Cragar Industries, Compton, CA, pg. 761
Gardner, Howard B., Sec.--Mr. Gasket Company, Cleveland, OH, pg. 761
Garfinkle, Mark A., V.P., Gen. Counsel & Sec.--Alleco Inc., Cheverly, MD, pg. 35
Garonzik, Arnon E., Gen. Counsel & Sec.--The ERM Group, Exton, PA, pg. 360
Garrett, Ann, Sec.--The Mad Butcher, Inc., Pine Bluff, AR, pg. 699
Garrett, Steven, Sec.--Cimarron American Fidelity, Cimarron, KS, pg. 52
Garvey, Jean K., V.P. & Sec.--Garvey Industries, Inc., Wichita, KS, pg. 443
Garvin, Gail, Sec.--Garvin Fire Protection Systems, Orange, CA, pg. 444
Gary, Dorothea, V.P.-Sec.--Universal Molding Company, Lynwood, CA, pg. 1139
Gary, Elsa H., Exec. V.P., Sec., Acct. Supvr. & Media Dir.--The Gary Group, Culver City, CA, pg. 444
Gash, C. Ray, Chief Fin. Officer, Sr. V.P., Treas. & Sec.--Stephens, Inc., Little Rock, AR, pg. 1046
Gasparelli, Adeline, Sec. & Treas.--Wyse Advertising, Inc., Cleveland, OH, pg. 1206
Gass, Lauren, Sec.--The H. T. Hackney Co., Knoxville, TN, pg. 498
Gates, Deanna M., Sec.--Standard Plywood, Inc., Clinton, SC, pg. 1037
Gates, William S., Treas. & Sec.--Preferred Risk Life Insurance Co., West Des Moines, IA, pg. 886
Gatewood, Robert, Sr. Exec. V.P.-Legal Affairs & Sec.--Druther's International, Inc., Louisville, KY, pg. 350
Gattas, Andrew D., Treas. & Sec.--Fred P. Gattas Company, Inc., Memphis, TN, pg. 446
Gau, Jack, Sec. & Treas.--G. R. Herberger's, Inc., Saint Cloud, MN, pg. 530
Gaumont, Claire, Admin. Asst.--Harvey Construction Company, Inc., Bedford, NH, pg. 515
Gautnier, Alan E., V.P.-Fin. & Asst. Sec.--Exide Corporation, Reading, PA, pg. 393
Gaw, Ed, Chief Fin. Officer, Treas. & Sec.--Griffin Corporation, Valdosta, GA, pg. 487
Gay, Mickela D., V.P.-Opers. & Sec.--Kastle Systems, Inc., Arlington, VA, pg. 618
Gaylord, E.K. II, V.P. & Asst. Sec.--The Daily & Sunday Oklahoman, Oklahoma City, OK, pg. 446
Gaylord, Thomas M., Sec. & Treas.--Mack Molding Company, Arlington, VT, pg. 697
Gebo, L. Evelyn, V.P., Sec. & Treas.--Gebo Distributing Co., Inc., Plainview, TX, pg. 447
Gee, Edward, Treas. & Sec.--Cloverhill Bakery, Chicago, IL, pg. 256
Geisselbrecht, Elvin, Treas. & Sec.--YRJ Corporation, Houston, TX, pg. 1206
Gejoff, Louis, Treas., Controller, Sec. & Chief Fin. Officer--Carver, Inc., Garden City, GA, pg. 227
Gelder, John W., Sec.--Harlan Electric Co., Southfield, MI, pg. 509
Geller, Judith, Treas. & Asst. Sec.--Union Holdings, Inc., New York, NY, pg. 1128
Gelpi, John J., III, Sec.--Industrial Metals Of The South, New Orleans, LA, pg. 566
Gencarelli, Angelo, Chief Fin. Officer & Sec.--Bess Eaton Donut Flour Co., Inc., Westerly, RI, pg. 146
Genschaw, David A., Exec. V.P., Chief Fin. Officer--Waldbillig & Besteman, Inc., Madison, WI, pg. 1159
Genuardi, Joseph, Jr., Sec.--Genuardi Super Markets Inc., Norristown, PA, pg. 452
George, Dennis A., Treas. & Sec.--Sharon Tube Company, Sharon, PA, pg. 995
George, Leslie, Jr., Treas. & Sec.--King Group, Inc., Fenton, MI, pg. 630
George, Thomas A., Sec. & Treas.--Melody Foods, Inc., Farmington Hills, MI, pg. 738
Gerard, Antonia, Exec. V.P., Chief Fin. & Oper. Officer, Sec. & Controller--Bolliger, Inc., Stamford, CT, pg. 163
Gerber, Daryl, Sec.--Gerber Plumbing Fixtures Corporation, Chicago, IL, pg. 454
Gerber, Daryl E., Sec.--Kokomo Sanitary Pottery Corp., Chicago, IL, pg. 640
Gerber, Steven M., Gen. Counsel & Sec.--Gitano Group Inc., New York, NY, pg. 460
Geren, Tracey, Treas. & Sec.--Weldon, Williams & Lick, Inc., Fort Smith, AR, pg. 1175
Gerhart, Betty J., Sec.--High Industries Inc., Lancaster, PA, pg. 533
Gerland, Joseph P., Exec. V.P. & Sec.--Gerland Corp., Houston, TX, pg. 454
Gerry, Eugene, Chm. Bd. & Sec.--Precision Carbide Tool Company, Inc., Niles, IL, pg. 885
Gerstman, Henry, Sec., Treas. & Controller--Century Business Credit Corporation, New York, NY, pg. 235
Gertier, Tamar, V.P. & Sec.--All American Home Center, Downey, CA, pg. 35
Gertmenian, Russell M., Sec.--Desco Corporation, Columbus, OH, pg. 332
Gettlegfinger, Herman E., Chief Fin. Officer, Treas. & Sec.--Pride Oil Co., Inc., Knoxville, TN, pg. 622
Geyelin, Anthony, V.P., Asst. Sec. & Deputy Gen. Counsel--Academy Insurance Group, Inc., Atlanta, GA, pg. 11
Ghilardi, Louis J., Asst. Sec.--Park Ridge Corporation, Park Ridge, NJ, pg. 849
Ghiz, Sally, Sec.--Paddock Pool Construction Co., Scottsdale, AZ, pg. 842
Giarrusso, Raymond J., Sec. & Treas.--GAI Consultants, Inc., Monroeville, PA, pg. 439
Gibb, Bradley, Sec. & Treas.--Robert Gibb & Sons, Inc., Fargo, ND, pg. 456
Gibson, Cynthia, Sec.--Wolcott & Lincoln, Inc., Kansas City, MO, pg. 1198
Gibson, Kim, Exec. Sec.--Servus Footwear Company, Rock Island, IL, pg. 993
Gibson, Lauris H., Sec.--Westgate Fabrics, Inc., Grand Prairie, TX, pg. 1182
Gibson, Thomas, Exec. V.P., Chief Fin. Officer, Sec. & Gen. Counsel--The Gates Corporation, Denver, CO, pg. 445
Giesa, Jay, Exec. V.P.-Admin. & Sec.--Fisher Broadcasting, Inc., Seattle, WA, pg. 415
Gilbane, Robert V., Sec.--Gilbane Building Company, Providence, RI, pg. 457
Gilbert, Gary M., Asst. Sec.--Tighe Industries, Inc., York, PA, pg. 1097
Gill, Danny, V.P. & Sec.--Norden Fruit Company, Inc., Los Angeles, CA, pg. 809
Gillespie, Ray, Sec. & Treas.--Ford Meter Box Company, Wabash, IN, pg. 423
Gillogly, Roseanne L., Sec.--Gillogly Chevrolet Inc., West Seneca, NY, pg. 459
Gilman, Neil, V.P. & Sec.--Marty Gilman, Inc., Gilman, CT, pg. 459
Gilmer, Jay, Gen. Counsel & Sec.--Diet Center, Inc., Pittsburgh, PA, pg. 55
Gilmore, Bruce W., V.P. & Sec.--Bank Shares, Inc., Minneapolis, MN, pg. 117
Gimbel, Sidney, Sec.--General Drug Co., Chicago, IL, pg. 449
Gin, Sue Ling, Chm. Bd. & Sec.--Flying Food Fare, Inc., Chicago, IL, pg. 421
Ginsberg, Ira M., V.P. & Sec.--Ginsberg's Institutional Foods, Inc., Hudson, NY, pg. 460
Ginsburg, George B., Sec. & Gen. Mgr.--Money Point Diamond Co., Chesapeake, VA, pg. 765
Giordullo, Tony, Sec. & Treas.--Frazier-Williams Chevrolet GEO, Milford, OH, pg. 430
Gittelman, Milton, V.P, Treas. & Sec.--Triumph Pet Industries, Inc., Hillburn, NY, pg. 1115
Giuliani, John, Treas. & Sec.--Lodal, Inc., Kingsford, MI, pg. 680
Givens, Hugh, Controller & Asst. Sec.--National Steel Corporation, Mishawaka, IN, pg. 793
Glantz, Miles M., Sec. & Corp. Counsel--Wechco, Inc., Princeton, NJ, pg. 1172
Glantz, Miles M., Gen. Counsel & Sec.--West Chemical Products, Inc., Princeton, NJ, pg. 1172
Glascoe, Rosalyn B., Sec.--Mississippi Chemical Corporation, Yazoo City, MS, pg. 760
Glascoe, Roslyn, Sec.--Newsprint South, Inc., Yazoo City, MS, pg. 760
Glendening, R. Bradley, Sr. V.P., Gen. Counsel & Sec.--Mary Kay Cosmetics Inc., Dallas, TX, pg. 716
Glennie, Fred P., Sec. & Controller--Capital-Gazette Communications, Inc., Annapolis, MD, pg. 656
Globerson, Peter, Sec.--Windsor Art Products, Inc., Pico Rivera, CA, pg. 1195

Glotzon, Martin, Treas. & Sec.--PC Distributing Inc., Mount Prospect, IL, pg. 835
Gluck, Michelle H., Sec.--First Land & Development, Inc., Richmond, VA, pg. 18
Gluck, Michelle H., Sec.--Best Products Co., Inc., Richmond, VA, pg. 17
Gluckman, Gladyee, Sec.--Fownes Brothers & Co., Inc., New York, NY, pg. 427
Glynn, John J., Sec. & Treas.--Baird, Patrick & Co., Inc., New York, NY, pg. 114
Glynn, Terry, Treas. & Sec.--A. J. Canfield Co., Chicago, IL, pg. 214
Godfrey, Robert, Sec. & Treas.--Central States Enterprises, Inc., Heathrow, FL, pg. 234
Goebel, Janice R., Sec.--Kraus-Anderson, Inc., Minneapolis, MN, pg. 644
Goebel, Margaret E., Sec.--Goebel Art, Inc., Coon Rapids, MN, pg. 464
Goedert, Philip H., Sec./Treas.--Design-Build West, Denver, CO, pg. 907
Goeller, Michael C., Sec. & Gen. Counsel--Hatzel & Buehler, Inc., Wilmington, DE, pg. 277
Goelzer, D.M., Sec. & Gen. Counsel--B-E Holdings Inc., South Milwaukee, WI, pg. 106
Goelzer, David M., Sec. & Gen. Counsel--Bucyrus-Erie Company, South Milwaukee, WI, pg. 186
Goergen, Ronald M., V.P-International, Sec.--American Appraisal Associates, Inc., Milwaukee, WI, pg. 48
Goetz, W. Nicholas, Asst. Sec.--The Acacia Group, Washington, DC, pg. 10
Goguen, Paul A., Exec. V.P., Sec. & Treas.--Sexton Can Co., Inc., Cambridge, MA, pg. 993
Gohmann, John R., V.P., Chief Oper. Officer, Sec. & Dir.-Pur.--Gohmann Asphalt & Construction Inc., Clarksville, IN, pg. 465
Goldberg, Eve E., 2nd V.P. & Asst. Sec.--W. P. Carey & Co., Inc., New York, NY, pg. 218
Goldberg, Howard D., Corp. Sec.--Artec Distributing, Inc., Shelburne, VT, pg. 86
Golden, David, Chief Fin. Officer, Treas. & Sec.--Stephen Gould Paper Co., Inc., Whippany, NJ, pg. 473
Golden, J.M., V.P.-Fin.--Hub Inc., Tucker, GA, pg. 548
Goldenberg, Victoria, Sec. & Treas.--Fashion Shop of Kentucky Inc., Louisville, KY, pg. 403
Goldfine, John J., Sec.--Northern Drug Company, Duluth, MN, pg. 814
Goldings, Morris, Sec. & Gen. Counsel--Jet Spray Corp., Norwood, MA, pg. 593
Goldman, C. David, Sec. & Clerk--George E. Warren Corp., Vero Beach, FL, pg. 1164
Goldman, Carol, Sec.--Gulf Distribution Inc., Miami, FL, pg. 493
Goldman, Charles, Sec.--Seaboard Flour Corporation, Newton, MA, pg. 984
Goldman, Charles M., Sec. & Gen. Counsel--Seaboard Corporation, Newton, MA, pg. 984
Goldman, David, Legal Officer & Sec.--Duro-Test Corporation, Fairfield, NJ, pg. 355
Goldman, Jerome, Sec.--First Connecticut SBIC, Bridgeport, CT, pg. 412
Goldman, Marilyn S., Exec. V.P., Sec. & Treas.--S. I. Goldman Co., Longwood, FL, pg. 467
Goldman, Zachary C., Exec. V.P., Treas. & Sec.--Londontown Holdings Corporation, Eldersburg, MD, pg. 681
Goldman, Zachary C., V.P., Chief Fin. Officer & Sec.--Londontown Corporation, Eldersburg, MD, pg. 682
Goldsmith, Gary, Chm. Bd., Sec. & Creative Dir.--Goldsmith/Jeffrey, Inc., New York, NY, pg. 469
Goldsmith, Peter, V.P.-Import & Sec.--John H. Graham & Co., Inc., Oradell, NJ, pg. 475
Goldstein, Alan B., Exec. V.P., Sec. & Gen. Counsel--American Savings of Florida, ESB, Miami, FL, pg. 382
Goldstein, Mark L., Treas. & Sec.--Dexter Chemical Corp., Bronx, NY, pg. 334
Goldstein, Mary Jane, Sec.--Hampton Print Works, Inc., Johnson City, TN, pg. 504
Goldstein, Norman R., V.P., Treas. & Asst. Sec.--Barton Brands, Ltd., Chicago, IL, pg. 123
Goldstein, Norman R., Asst. Sec. & Asst. Treas.--Barton Beers, Ltd., Chicago, IL, pg. 123
Golias, Ann, Sec.--Helena Laboratories Corporation, Beaumont, TX, pg. 526
Golomb, D.I., Exec. V.P. & Sec.--Everlast Sports Manufacturing Corp., Bronx, NY, pg. 392
Gonge, Scott, Sec.--Troy Corporation, East Hanover, NJ, pg. 1116
Gonnella, Robert, Chief Exec. Officer & Sec.--Gonnella Baking Co., Chicago, IL, pg. 469
Gonnerman, Mary F., Sec.--MFA Incorporated, Columbia, MO, pg. 692
Gonzalez-Blanco, Roberto, V.P. & Sec.--Republic National Bank Of Miami, Miami, FL, pg. 928
Gonzalez, C., Sec., Treas. & Pur. Agent--Villazon Company Inc., Tampa, FL, pg. 1152
Good, Charles E., V.P.-Fin., Sec. & Treas.--Snyder's of Hanover, Inc., Hanover, PA, pg. 1015
Goodell, Brenda, Sec.--Willard Grain & Feed, Inc., Celina, TX, pg. 1190
Goodloe, Mary R., Sec.--Bulab Holdings, Inc., Memphis, TN, pg. 188
Goodman, Dorothy, Sec.--Goodmans, Inc., Phoenix, AZ, pg. 471
Goodman, James A., Gen. Counsel & Sec.--Day & Zimmermann, Inc., Radnor, PA, pg. 320
Goodman, Mark, Sec.--Burtman Iron Works, Inc., Boston, MA, pg. 195
Goodman, Michael R., V.P.-Fin. & Sec.--City Machine Tool & Die Company, Muncie, IN, pg. 251
Goodman, Rhea, Sec. & Treas.--Bonhomme Shirtmakers, Ltd., New York, NY, pg. 164
Goodrich, H.L., Sec. & Gen. Counsel--Dan River Inc., Danville, VA, pg. 313
Goolsby, Sharon, Asst. Sec.--Goolsby Foods, Inc., Columbus, GA, pg. 471
Gordan, Cynthia, Legal Counsel--Quaker Fabric Corporation, Fall River, MA, pg. 903
Gordon, Ada L., Sec.--Penobscot Frozen Foods, Inc., Belfast, ME, pg. 858
Gordon, John, V.P., Gen. Counsel & Sec.--Red Roof Inns, Inc., Hilliard, OH, pg. 918
Gore, Dr. Genevieve W., Treas. & Sec.--W. L. Gore & Associates, Inc., Newark, DE, pg. 472
Gore, G. H., Sec. & Gen. Counsel--North American Company, Fort Lauderdale, FL, pg. 811
Gorecki, Joseph, Corp. Sec.--The William Bayley Co., Springfield, OH, pg. 128
Gossett, Darrell, Exec. V.P., Sec. & Treas.--Ermco, Inc., Indianapolis, IN, pg. 387
Gotkin, Michael S., Sr. V.P. & Gen. Counsel--Farley Candy Company, Chicago, IL, pg. 399
Gottschalk, Eldon W., Co-Chm., Sec. & Treas.--Jack Lawlor Advertising, Inc., Pasadena, CA, pg. 661
Gottschalk, Gary, Pres. & Chief Exec. Officer--The Harter Group, Sturgis, MI, pg. 513
Gourde, R., Gen. Mgr. & Sec.--W.W. Wallwork, Inc., Fargo, ND, pg. 1161
Gowan, Anne L., Sec.--Community Cash Stores, Spartanburg, SC, pg. 270
Gowell, Joan, Sec.--Quality Stores Inc., North Muskegon, MI, pg. 904
Gowey, E.A., Sec.--Fisher Companies, Inc., Seattle, WA, pg. 414
Grabow, Laura M., V.P. & Sec.--Oxford Realty Services Corp., Bethesda, MD, pg. 835
Grady, Kevin, Mgr.-Credit & Asst. Treas.--Trak International, Inc., Port Washington, WI, pg. 1106
Graff, M., Treas. & Sec.--Douglas Stephen Plastics, Inc., Paterson, NJ, pg. 347
Graham, Anita, Corp. Sec.--Henco, Inc., Selmer, TN, pg. 528
Graham, Jack W., Chm. Bd., Sec. & Treas.--Petty Company, Inc., Effingham, IL, pg. 866
Graham, Malcolm C., Sec.--General Parts, Inc., Raleigh, NC, pg. 224
Graham, Wallace A., Vice Chm. & Sec.--Schenectady Chemicals, Inc., Schenectady, NY, pg. 975
Grandle, Pat, Mgr.-Mktg. & Sec.--Tricon Industries, Inc., Downers Grove, IL, pg. 1113
Granicher, John W., Sr. V.P. & Sec. & Treas.--Keller & Gannon, San Francisco, CA, pg. 637
Gransec, David H., Sec.--Vitarine Pharmaceuticals, Inc., Springfield Gardens, NY, pg. 383
Grant, Michael, Sec. & Treas.--Grant-Lydick Beverage Co., San Antonio, TX, pg. 477
Grant, Ronald D., V.P.-Data Processing Services--American SelfCare Corporation, Columbus, GA, pg. 60
Grant, Shirley, Sec. & Treas.--Grant Marketing Communications Inc., Lafayette Hill, PA, pg. 477
Gravely, Charles A., Sec.--Sigal/Zuckerman Co., Chevy Chase, MD, pg. 1003
Graves, John E., Sec.--Elkay Manufacturing Company, Oak Brook, IL, pg. 377
Graves, Ronald N., V.P., Sec. & Gen. Counsel--J.R. Simplot Company, Boise, ID, pg. 1007
Gravolet, Benjamin S., V.P. & Sec.--Mutual Savings Life Insurance Company, Decatur, AL, pg. 1150
Gray, Bernard, Sr. V.P.-Devel. & Sec.--Summit Communications, Inc., Atlanta, GA, pg. 1057
Green, John R., Sec. & Treas.--John E. Green Co., Highland Park, MI, pg. 484
Green, William S., Sec.--Granite State Packing Co., Manchester, NH, pg. 476
Greenberg, Fred, Exec. V.P., Sec. & Sls. Mgr.--Jack Greenberg Inc., Philadelphia, PA, pg. 485
Greene, Jerry W., Sec. & Treas.--Hanes Companies, Inc., Winston-Salem, NC, pg. 505
Greenfield, Betty, V.P. & Sec.--Commonwealth Toy & Novelty Company, New York, NY, pg. 269
Greenfield, Kenneth, Exec. V.P.--Federal Distributing Corporation, Maspeth, NY, pg. 404
Greenfield, Wesley, Sec.--Alto Dairy Cooperative, Waupun, WI, pg. 45
Greengard, Michael, V.P., Sec. & Treas.--Thompson Enterprises Inc., Minnetonka, MN, pg. 1094
Greenhaw, Karen, Sec.--Alabama Farmers Co-op, Decatur, AL, pg. 28
Greenman, Ronald L., Sec.--Portland Food Products Company, Portland, OR, pg. 881
Greenspan, Joseph, Sec.--Masters, Inc., Westbury, NY, pg. 720
Greenwell, Walter R., Sec.--Capeletti Bros., Inc., Miami Lakes, FL, pg. 214
Greer, Robert A., V.P. & Sec.--Autry Greer & Sons, Inc., Prichard, AL, pg. 486
Greever, Peggy, Sec.--Chattanooga Group, Hixson, TN, pg. 241
Gregory, Dennis, V.P.-Fin. & Chief Fin. Officer--Woodcraft Industries, Inc., Saint Cloud, MN, pg. 1200
Gremier, Nadine, Corp. Lib. & Sec.--Tarlton Corporation, Saint Louis, MO, pg. 1079
Gresham, Thomas, Asst. Sec.--Bankhead Enterprises Inc., Atlanta, GA, pg. 117
Grieve, H.W., Sec.--The Grieve Corporation, Round Lake, IL, pg. 486
Griffin, Marna W., Sec.--Mountain Air Delivery, Sparks, NV, pg. 773
Griffin, William E., Sec.--Precision Valve Corporation, Yonkers, NY, pg. 885
Griffith, James A., Sec.--Arthur Murray Intl., Inc., Coral Gables, FL, pg. 776
Griffith, Jerry L., Sec. & Controller--J. A. Riggs Tractor Co., Little Rock, AR, pg. 934
Griffith, Mike, Treas. & Sec.--Southern Radio Corporation, pg. 1022
Griffith, Robert, V.P., Sec. & Treas.--The Chas. H. Lilly Co., Portland, OR, pg. 675
Griggs, Forest, Jr., Sec.--Jack Griggs Inc., Exeter, CA, pg. 488
Grimley, Robert, Sec. & Treas.--Duo-Fast Corporation, Franklin Park, IL, pg. 354
Grimmer, Rose J., Sec.--Grimmer Realty Co. Inc., Birmingham, AL, pg. 488
Groce, David, V.P., Sec. & Gen. Counsel--Precision Tune, Inc., Leesburg, VA, pg. 885
Grogg, Mary, Sec. & Treas.--Mike Savoie Chevrolet Inc., Troy, MI, pg. 973
Grolnick, Herbert N., Sec.--The Guardian Life Insurance Company of America, New York, NY, pg. 492
Gromer, Bernice E., V.P. & Sec.--Gromer Super Markets, Inc., Elgin, IL, pg. 489
Gross, Donald, V.P., Treas. & Sec.--Dan's Supreme Super Markets Inc., Hempstead, NY, pg. 314
Grossenburg, Blanche, Sec.--Grossenburg Implements, Incorporated, Winner, SD, pg. 489
Grossman, Melvin, V.P., Sec. & Treas.--Lithographix, Inc., Los Angeles, CA, pg. 678
Grossman, Richard, Sec.--Therm, Inc., Ithaca, NY, pg. 1090
Grove, Ray, Sec.--California Apricot Advisory Board, Walnut Creek, CA, pg. 209
Growcott, Carm, Sec.--Streamlight Inc., Norristown, PA, pg. 1053
Grundman, Terry, Sec.--MICRODOT, Inc., Chicago, IL, pg. 749
Grupka, Richard A., Sec. & Treas.--John W. Danforth Co., Buffalo, NY, pg. 314
Guccione, Anthony, Sec. & Treas.--General Media Publishing Group, New York, NY, pg. 450
Guccione, Anthony J., Sec. & Treas.--Omni Publications International Ltd., New York, NY, pg. 450
Guerra, Jorge, Sec.--Real Holding Management Corp., Miami, FL, pg. 917
Guilford, Margaret, Sec.--Kentucky Manufacturing Co., Louisville, KY, pg. 624
Gulbas, Jacqueline, Sec. & Treas.--National Restaurant Supply Company, El Paso, TX, pg. 793
Gurewitz, Lorrie, Sec. & Treas.--Poly Pak America, Inc., Los Angeles, CA, pg. 880
Guriel, Florian, Asst. Sec. & Treas.--Whiting Equipment Canada, Inc., Welland,, Canada, pg. 1187
Gurka, Jane, Mgr.-Personnel & Sec.--M. Swift & Sons Inc., Hartford, CT, pg. 1068
Gusick, Dennis, V.P.-Fin., Treas. & Sec.--Helm, Inc., Highland Park, MI, pg. 527
Gustafson, Adele R., Asst. Sec.--Coast Packing Company, Vernon, CA, pg. 257
Gutknecht, James, Sec.--Wheaton Inc., Millville, NJ, pg. 1184
Gutterson, Gerald, Chief Fin. Officer, Treas. & Sec.--Martin Paint Stores, Jamaica, NY, pg. 715
Haag, Arliss, Sec.--First State Federal Savings & Loan, Hutchinson, MN, pg. 413
Haas, Fred Jr., Sec. & Treas.--National Band & Tag Co., Newport, KY, pg. 786
Haas, Stan, Asst. Sec.-East Region--G. Heileman Brewing Co., Inc., La Crosse, WI, pg. 526
Haase, Barbara S., V.P.-Admin. Services & Sec.--General Alum & Chemical, Holland, OH, pg. 448
Habegger, James L., Sec.--The Habegger Corporation, Cincinnati, OH, pg. 498
Haber, Bill, Exec. V.P. & Sec.--QST Industries, Inc., Chicago, IL, pg. 902
Hacking, Earl, Sec.--M. A. Mortenson Company, Minneapolis, MN, pg. 772
Hackney, Eugene W., Sec.--North Carolina Mutual Wholesale Drug Co., Durham, NC, pg. 813
Hada, Mutsumi M., Sec.--West Coast Life Insurance Co., San Francisco, CA, pg. 795
Haddon, James, Gen. Counsel & Sec.--Creative Marketing Resource, Inc., Chicago, IL, pg. 297
Hadfield, Neil, Chm. Bd., Chief Fin. Officer & Sec.--Western Pacific Data Systems, San Diego, CA, pg. 1180
Haft, Julie, Sec. & Treas.--Haywin Textile Products, Inc., Brooklyn, NY, pg. 520
Hagadorn, Robert E., Exec. V.P., Treas. & Sec.--Hazen & Sawyer, New York, NY, pg. 520
Hagemier, Robert, Sec.--Syndicate Systems, Inc., Indianapolis, IN, pg. 1069
Hager, Jean, Sec. & Treas.--Air Industries Corporation, Garden Grove, CA, pg. 27
Hagood, Derrill M., Sec.--William M. Bird & Co., Inc., Charleston, SC, pg. 152
Hahn, Elizabeth, Sec.--Conestoga Wood Specialties, Inc., Earl, PA, pg. 273
Haimes, Burt, Gen. Counsel & Sec.--National Cleaning Contractors, Inc., New York, NY, pg. 786
Haist, Dennis P., V.P., Gen. Counsel & Sec.--Dillingham Construction Corporation, Pleasanton, CA, pg. 337
Halben, Robert A., Controller & Sec.--Almac's Inc., East Providence, RI, pg. 1214
Hale, Bettyann, Admin. Asst. to Pres.--Basic Computer, Akron, OH, pg. 124
Hale, John, Sec.--Tarlton Corporation, Saint Louis, MO, pg. 1079
Hale, Kent, V.P. & Sec.--Intercole, Inc., Washington, PA, pg. 574
Hall, Debbie, Sec.--Miller Bros. Industries, Inc., Richmond, VA, pg. 753
Hall, Delvis A., V.P., Treas., Sec. & Gen. Mgr.--Lone Star Cadillac Co., Dallas, TX, pg. 682
Hall, John, V.P. & Sec.--Hydril Company, Los Angeles, CA, pg. 556
Hall, John B., Sr. V.P. & Sec.--Norbest, Inc., Midvale, UT, pg. 809
Hall, Kaye, Sec.--Linder & Associates, Inc., Wichita, KS, pg. 676
Hall, Priscilla, Corp. Sec.--All Seasons Services, Inc., Braintree, MA, pg. 35
Hall, Rosemary, Asst. Sec.--HTB, Inc., Oklahoma City, OK, pg. 497

Hall, William A., Sec. & Treas.--Tennessee Dressed Beef Company, Nashville, TN, pg. 1087
Halper, Melvyn H., Sec.--Southwide, Inc., New York, NY, pg. 1024
Halterman, Darlene F., Asst. Treas. & Sec.--The Sico Company, Mount Joy, PA, pg. 1001
Halterman, Darlene F., Sec. & Asst. Treas.--First Mount Joy Corporation, Mount Joy, PA, pg. 413
Halvorson, Lorraine, Sec. & Treas.--Prospect Motors, Inc., Jackson, CA, pg. 895
Halvorson, Melissa, Jo, Sec.--The Instant Web Companies, Chanhassen, MN, pg. 571
Hamburger, Jane, Sr. V.P., Sec. & Dir.-Personnel--Federal Farm Credit Banks Funding Corporation, Jersey City, NJ, pg. 404
Hamilton James T., Sec. & Treas.--Independent Insurance Agents and Brokers of California, San Francisco, CA, pg. 565
Hamilton, J. Richard, Sec.--Preformed Line Products, Cleveland, OH, pg. 886
Hamilton, Stephen G., V.P. & Sec.--Computer Sales International Inc., Saint Louis, MO, pg. 271
Hamister, Oliver C., V.P.-Admin., Treas. & Sec.--National Health Care Affiliates, Inc., Buffalo, NY, pg. 791
Hammel, Cindy, Sec. & Travel Planner--Juhl Marketing Communications, Mishawaka, IN, pg. 608
Hammel, Robert E., Chief Fin. Officer, Treas. & Sec.--Ohio Machinery Co., Cleveland, OH, pg. 822
Hammel, Robin, V.P. & Asst. Sec.--The Shane Group Inc., Hillsdale, MI, pg. 995
Hammer, Susan, Sec.--Oliver Products Company, Grand Rapids, MI, pg. 824
Hammond, Jerry, V.P., Treas. & Sec.--Cargill Fertilizer, Inc., Riverview, FL, pg. 219
Hammond, Michael, V.P.,Treas., & Sec.--H & H Advertising, Fort Worth, TX, pg. 496
Hampel, Robert E., Sr. Exec. Chief Fin. Officer, Treas. & Sec.--Keller Crescent Co., Evansville, IN, pg. 620
Hampton, Verne C., II, Sec.--Ross Roy Inc., Bloomfield Hills, MI, pg. 950
Hamrick, H. R., Sec., Treas. & Data Processing Mgr.--Haines City Citrus Growers Association, Haines City, FL, pg. 500
Hancey, Don, Sec.--LeGrand Johnson Construction Co., Logan, UT, pg. 598
Hancock, Dale D., V.P. & Sec.--Cowboy Oil Company, Pocatello, ID, pg. 290
Hancock, John C., Treas. & Sec.--Stanley Stores Inc., Bay City, TX, pg. 1038
Hand, John C., Sr. V.P., Gen. Counsel & Corp. Sec.--United Farm Bureau Family Life Insurance Co., Indianapolis, IN, pg. 1131
Hand, Paul E., Chief Exec. Officer--Atlantic Dairy Cooperative, Southampton, PA, pg. 94
Handelsman, H., Sec.--Northridge Industries, Inc., Las Vegas, NV, pg. 495
Handelsman, Harold, Sr. V.P., Sec. & Gen. Counsel--Hyatt Corporation, Chicago, IL, pg. 495
Handelsman, Harold S., V.P., Sec. & Gen. Counsel--Dalfort Corp., Dallas, TX, pg. 312
Hanel, Robert, Sec.--Hanel Lumber Co., Inc., Hood River, OR, pg. 505
Hanes, Andrew G., Controller & Sec.--Superior Container, Inc., Warrensville, OH, pg. 1063
Hanin, Francine, Treas. & Sec.--Allied Tire Sales, Orlando, FL, pg. 40
Hankins, David, V.P.-Admin. & Sec.--J.R. Hahn Co., Inc., Indianapolis, IN, pg. 500
Hanks, W. David, Exec. V.P. & Asst. Sec.--Riviana Foods Inc., Houston, TX, pg. 937
Hannenberg, Ruth C., Sec. & Legal Officer--Mesirow Financial, Chicago, IL, pg. 741
Hano, Philip III, V.P. & Sec.--Hano Business Forms, Inc., Springfield, MA, pg. 505
Hano, Phillip, III, Sec.--Technicarbon Company, Inc., Springfield, MA, pg. 1083
Hansen, J.G., Sec.--Furnas Electric Company, Batavia, IL, pg. 437
Hansen, Nancy S., V.P.-Admin. & Sec.--Pennsylvania Crusher Corp., Broomall, PA, pg. 858
Hansen, Ruth, Exec. V.P. & Sec.--H & H Distributing Company, Inc., West Union, IA, pg. 495
Hanson, Denise, V.P.-Admin. & Sec.--Aetna Health Plans, San Bruno, CA, pg. 23
Harab, Paul, Controller & Sec.--Duron, Inc., Beltsville, MD, pg. 355
Harbison, J.G., V.P.-Admin. & Sec.--Carolina Mills, Inc., Maiden, NC, pg. 223
Harcharek, Janice, Dir.-Human Resources & Sec.--Universal Dynamics Inc., Woodbridge, VA, pg. 1138
Harcharek, Janice, Sec.--Universal Dynamics, Inc., Woodbridge, VA, pg. 1138
Harding, Marvin E., Sec. & Treas.--Artesian Resources Corporation, Newark, DE, pg. 86
Harding, Marvin E., Sec. & Treas.--Artesian Water Company, Inc., Newark, DE, pg. 86
Harding, Marvin E., V.P., Chief Fin. Officer, Treas. & Sec.--Artesian Development Corporation, Newark, DE, pg. 86
Harding, Marvin E., Asst. Sec. & Asst. Treas.--Artesian Laboratories, Inc., Newark, DE, pg. 86
Harding, Marvin E., Sec. & Treas.--Churchmans Road Associates, L.P., Newark, DE, pg. 87
Harding, Marvin E., Sec. & Treas.--The Southwood Company, Newark, DE, pg. 87
Hardinge, Thomas H., III, V.P.-Sls. & Mktg., Treas. & Sec.--Statton Furniture Manufacturing Company, Hagerstown, MD, pg. 1042
Hardwick, Robert, Sec., Controller & Treas.--Axelson, Inc., Longview, TX, pg. 103
Hardy, Sophia, Sec. & Treas.--Barnhill Contracting Company, Tarboro, NC, pg. 121
Harmon, Dan, V.P. & Sec.--Hoffman Corporation, Portland, OR, pg. 537
Harp, Gerald L., V.P.-Opers., Sec. & Treas.--Harp's Food Stores, Inc., Springdale, AR, pg. 510
Harper, Daniel S., Sec.--Harper Bros., Inc., Fort Myers, FL, pg. 510
Harper, Dolores A., Sec.--The Guttman Group, Belle Vernon, PA, pg. 495
Harper, Edith Gaylord, Sec.--Oklahoma Publishing Company, Oklahoma City, OK, pg. 446
Harper, Edith Gaylord, Sec.--The Daily & Sunday Oklahoman, Oklahoma City, OK, pg. 446
Harper, Edith Gaylord, Sec.--Gaylord Broadcasting Co., Dallas, TX, pg. 446
Harrell, Paul, Jr., Sec. & Treas.--Long MFG. NC, Inc., Tarboro, NC, pg. 682
Harrington, John A., Sec. & Asst. Treas.--Geo. J. Ball, Inc., West Chicago, IL, pg. 115
Harris, Ann, Sec.--Horner Rausch Company, Nashville, TN, pg. 544
Harris, Cecily, Sec. & Treas.--GFA Brands, Inc., Cresskill, NJ, pg. 440
Harris, John G., Treas. & Sec.--Harris Enterprises Inc., Hutchinson, KS, pg. 511
Harris, June C., V.P. & Sec.--Old Home Foods, Inc., Saint Paul, MN, pg. 823
Harris, Karen J., Corp. Sec.--The Flood Company, Hudson, OH, pg. 419
Harris, R. Macy, III, Sec.--Alling & Cory Company, Rochester, NY, pg. 40
Harrison, Carl W., Sec. & Treas.--Lincoln Steel, Lincoln, NE, pg. 834
Harrison, Mitchell, Sec.--MHB Inc., Williamsport, PA, pg. 692
Harrison, Peggie T., Treas. & Sec.--Harco Drug, Inc., Tuscaloosa, AL, pg. 507
Harrison, Robert, V.P. & Gen. Counsel--Dominick & Dominick, Incorporated, New York, NY, pg. 343
Harrison, Ruth, Sec.--Anchor Gasoline Corporation, Tulsa, OK, pg. 71
Harrison, Sandra, Sec. & Treas.--Bill Wink Chevrolet & GEO, Dearborn, MI, pg. 1196
Harshaw, N.M., V.P. Human Res. & Sec.--YSI Incorporated, Yellow Springs, OH, pg. 1207
Hart, Owen, Sec.--Kalas Manufacturing, Inc., Denver, PA, pg. 615
Hart, Robert C., Sr. V.P., Sec. & Gen. Counsel--S. C. Johnson & Son, Inc., Racine, WI, pg. 599
Hartman, Pete, Treas. & Sec.--Chemung Ford, Inc., Elmira, NY, pg. 242
Hartog, Larry, Sec. & Asst. Treas.--R.C. Tway Coal Company, Louisville, KY, pg. 1120
Harton, Cynthia A., Sec.--Hawthorne Corp., Charleston, SC, pg. 518
Hartunian, Frieda, Sec.--A B C Appliance Inc., Pontiac, MI, pg. 2
Harvey, Jean, Sec. & Treas.--Combs & Heathcott, Little Rock, AR, pg. 267
Harvey, Michael L., Sr. V.P.-Law, Gen. Counsel & Sec.--Atlas Van Lines, Inc., Evansville, IN, pg. 96
Harwood, Brian, Exec. V.P. & Sec.--Hayes/Harwood, Stowe, VT, pg. 519
Haserjian, Ted, Chm. Bd. & Sec.--Carpeteria, Inc., Valencia, CA, pg. 224
Haskins, Betty, Sec.--Arrow Tank & Engineering Co., Minneapolis, MN, pg. 85
Haslam, George, Treas. & Sec.--Caltrol, Inc., Glendora, CA, pg. 211
Haslem, Cynthia, Sec.--Livernois Engineering Company, Dearborn, MI, pg. 679
Hasling, Robert J., V.P., Gen. Counsel & Sec.--The Minnesota Mutual Life Insurance Company, Saint Paul, MN, pg. 757
Hassell, Frances M., Sr. V.P. & Sec.--Universal Life Insurance Company, Memphis, TN, pg. 1138
Hassinger, Douglas, Treas. & Sec.--Perkasie Industries Corporation, Perkasie, PA, pg. 862
Hatcher, James A., Sec. & Gen. Counsel--Cox Enterprises, Inc., Atlanta, GA, pg. 292
Hatcher, James A., Sec.--Automobile Auction Division, Atlanta, GA, pg. 293
Hatcher, James A., Sec.--Cox Enterprises Newspaper Division, Atlanta, GA, pg. 292
Hatcher, James A., Sec.--Broadcast Division, Atlanta, GA, pg. 292
Hatcher, James A., Sec.--Cable Division, Atlanta, GA, pg. 294
Hathaway, Raeburn B., Jr., Sr. V.P. & Sec.--John Hancock Mutual Life Insurance Company, Boston, MA, pg. 595
Hatt, Peter M., Chm. & Chief Exec. Officer--Borders, Perrin & Norrander, Inc., Portland, OR, pg. 165
Haughton, Douglas, Sec.--Cello Bag Company, Inc., Tukwila, WA, pg. 231
Haupt, J. P., Corp. Sec., Treas. & Chief Fin. & Exec. Officer--Juniata Office Supplies, Altoona, PA, pg. 608
Hauser, F.J., Sec. & Treas.--Conley Frog & Switch Company, Memphis, TN, pg. 274
Haveman, Kenneth, Sec. & Asst. Treas.--Binkley Company, Warrenton, MO, pg. 151
Hawbaker, Alan, Sec. & Treas.--Glenn O. Hawbaker, Inc., State College, PA, pg. 517
Hawk, Louise, Sec. & Treas.--Gertrude Hawk Chocolates, Inc., Troop, PA, pg. 517
Hawkins, Betty, V.P. & Sec.--Hawkins Markets, Inc., Wooster, OH, pg. 518
Hawkins, Robert E., Chief Fin. Officer, Treas., Controller & Sec.--West Union Corp., Memphis, TN, pg. 1177
Hayes, Alan, Sec.--Tuscarora Yarns Inc., Mount Pleasant, NC, pg. 1120
Hayes, D.M., Sr. V.P., Sec. & Gen. Counsel--Agway, Inc., De Witt, NY, pg. 25
Hayes, Jere, V.P., Gen. Counsel & Sec.--Pacific Enterprises Oil Company (USA), Dallas, TX, pg. 840
Hayes, Kathleen A., Sec. & Treas.--Kennington Properties, Inc., Los Angeles, CA, pg. 623
Hayes, Vayle, V.P. & Sec.--Dahlsten Truck Line, Inc., Clay Center, NE, pg. 310
Hays, Barbara Sue, Sec.--Allen & Ohara, Inc., Memphis, TN, pg. 36
Hays, Helen C., Treas. & Sec.--Press Enterprise Company, Riverside, CA, pg. 887
Hays, Randy K., Sec., Controller, & Treas.--Masek Distributing Inc., Gering, NE, pg. 717
Haythe, Thomas M., Sec. & Gen. Counsel--Novametrix Medical Systems Inc., Wallingford, CT, pg. 817
Heacock, Richard, V.P.-Fin., Treas., Sec. & Controller--Apache Hose & Belting Company, Cedar Rapids, IA, pg. 77
Head, Alva, Exec. Asst.--Delta Queen Steamboat Company, New Orleans, LA, pg. 385
Heagney,, Larry, Sec. & Treas.--Milliken & Co., Inc., Spartanburg, SC, pg. 755
Heath, Frederick G., V.P., Sec. & Treas.--Brown Wood Preserving Company, Louisville, KY, pg. 183
Heck, Shirley A., Sec.--Heck Enterprises, Inc., Baton Rouge, LA, pg. 524
Heerman, William R., Sr. V.P.-Law & Communications, Sec. & Gen. Counsel--Aid Association For Lutherans, Appleton, WI, pg. 26
Heil, M., Sec. & Treas.--American Excelsior Company, Arlington, TX, pg. 51
Heil, Nelson, Treas. & Sec.--Ray-Carroll County Grain Co-op, Richmond, MO, pg. 914
Heilman, Emerson H., V.P.-Admin. & Sec.--Mack Printing Company, Easton, PA, pg. 697
Heilman, Emerson H., V.P. & Sec.--Monroe Printing Company, East Stroudsburg, PA, pg. 697
Heineman, Brett D., Sec. & Mgr.-East Reg. Sls.--Conway Import Co. Inc., Elmsford, NY, pg. 281
Heinman, Gregg J., V.P.-Opers., Sec. & Treas.--Conway Import Co. Inc., Elmsford, NY, pg. 281
Heinson, Ann, Sec.--Allied Oil & Supply, Inc., Omaha, NE, pg. 38
Heipt, J.D., Sec.--Science Applications International Corporation, San Diego, CA, pg. 981
Heiseke, F.H., Sec.--Federated Mutual Insurance Company, Owatonna, MN, pg. 405
Heiserman, Hewitt, V.P., Treas. & Sec.--Kingsbury, Inc., Philadelphia, PA, pg. 632
Hejnar, Gerald J., Controller, Sec. & Dir.-Employee Benefits--Regency Lincoln Mercury, Dallas, TX, pg. 922
Held, K. Lars, Treas. & Sec.--Overly Manufacturing Co., Greensburg, PA, pg. 833
Heldman, Barbara, Sec., Treas.--Northlich Stolley LaWarre, Cincinnati, OH, pg. 814
Heller, Edward, Sec.--Blumenthal Print Works, Inc., New Orleans, LA, pg. 161
Hellman, Murray, V.P., Treas. & Sec.--Pressman Toy Corp., New York, NY, pg. 887
Hellman, Tracy, Sec. & Treas.--J. Hellman Produce, Inc., Los Angeles, CA, pg. 527
Hellreigel, Michael C., V.P., Controller & Asst. Sec.--Butler Service Group, Inc., Montvale, NJ, pg. 197
Helman, Irving, Sec.--Prudential Metal Supply Corp., East Dedham, MA, pg. 898
Helmbrecht, Glen V., Chief Fin. Officer & Sec.--Mayville Engineering Co., Inc., Mayville, WI, pg. 725
Helmick, Susan T., Sec.--Helmick Corporation, Fairmont, WV, pg. 527
Helzing, Carl, Sec. & Treas.--Premier Coatings, Inc., Elk Grove Village, IL, pg. 886
Hemmer, Donald M., Treas. & Sec.--Paul Hemmer Construction Company, Fort Mitchell, KY, pg. 528
Hemmings, Wm. M., V.P.-Sls. & Mktg. & Corp. Sec.--Enger-Kress Company, West Bend, WI, pg. 381
Hempt, Gerald L., Sec. & Treas.--Hempt Brothers, Inc., Camp Hill, PA, pg. 528
Hemsted, Stephen, Sec. & Dir.-Fin.--The National Magazine Company Ltd., London, United Kingdom, pg. 524
Hemthill, John, Sec.--E-Z Serve Corp., Houston, TX, pg. 361
Henderson, Barbara, V.P. & Sec.--Drug Emporium of Arizona, Inc., Scottsdale, AZ, pg. 349
Henderson, David B., Sec.--Prospect Foundry, Inc., Minneapolis, MN, pg. 895
Henderson, Eugene L., Sec.--Indiana Financial Investors, Inc., Chicago, IL, pg. 674
Henderson, Genevieve C., Asst. Sec.--Shenandoah Life Insurance Company, Roanoke, VA, pg. 997
Henderson, Jeffery, Sec. & Treas.--Henderson Auctioneers, Livingston, LA, pg. 528
Henderson, Kenneth W., V.P. & Sec.--Malcolm Pirnie, Inc., White Plains, NY, pg. 872
Henderson, Lisa, V.P. & Sec.--James Austin Co., Mars, PA, pg. 99
Henderson, Marilyn, Sec.--Joseph J. Henderson & Son, Inc., Gurnee, IL, pg. 529
Hendon, Robert C., Jr., Gen. Counsel & Sec.--Berlitz International, Inc., Princeton, NJ, pg. 142
Hendricks, Diane M., V.P. & Sec.--ABC Supply Company, Inc., Beloit, WI, pg. 2
Hendricks, Ruth Ann, Corp. Sec.--Rose Acre Farms, Seymour, IN, pg. 947
Hendrickson, Orvil J., V.P. & Sec.--Industrial Contractors, Inc., Idaho Falls, ID, pg. 566
Hendrix, Nancy, Mktg. Services Coord.--Gast Mfg. Corp., Benton Harbor, MI, pg. 444
Henning, Robert V., Jr., Sec.--Belmont Metals, Inc., Brooklyn, NY, pg. 137
Henquinet, Wayne K., Sec. & Treas.--New Mech Companies, Inc., Saint Paul, MN, pg. 802
Henry, John C., V.P.-Gen. Counsel & Sec.--First American Bankshares, Inc., Washington, DC, pg. 412
Henry, Joseph P., V.P.-Fin. & Admin.--Wheelock Inc., Long Branch, NJ, pg. 1185
Hensley, Pat, Sec.--Burk Royalty Co., Wichita Falls, TX, pg. 190
Hepworth, John C., Sec.--Clear Springs Foods, Inc., Buhl, ID, pg. 254

Herald, Gwen, Sec.--TSC Industries, Inc., Nashville, TN, pg. 1075
Herald, James, V.P.-Fin., Sec & Treas.--Morgan Foods, Inc., Austin, IN, pg. 770
Herbert, John, Gen. Counsel & Sec.--Ace Doran Hauling & Rigging Company, Cincinnati, OH, pg. 346
Herman, Randy, V.P., Controller & Sec.--Carter Day Industries, Inc., Minneapolis, MN, pg. 226
Herman, W.A., III, Treas. & Sec.--Shivers Trading & Operating Co., Augusta, GA, pg. 999
Hermanson, Lydia, Sec.--Mr. Christmas Inc., New York, NY, pg. 761
Hernandez, Louis R., V.P., Treas. & Asst. Sec.--W. P. Carey & Co., Inc., New York, NY, pg. 218
Herner, Donald A., Gen. Counsel & Sec.--Jac Jacobsen Industries, Inc., Greenwich, CT, pg. 587
Herr, Philip C., Sec.--J. Gibson McIlvain Co., White Marsh, MD, pg. 729
Herschend, Peter, Vice Chm. & Exec. V.P.--Silver Dollar City, Inc., Branson, MO, pg. 1004
Hess, Gregory, Legal Counsel & Sec.--Barr & Barr, Inc., New York, NY, pg. 121
Hessler, D., Sec. & Gen. Counsel--Electric Furnace Co., Salem, OH, pg. 373
Hessler, David J., Sec. & Treas.--MTD Products Limited, Kitchener,, Canada, pg. 694
Heuer, Duane, Sec. & Treas.--Bongards Creameries Inc., Norwood, MN, pg. 164
Hewett, Dexter B., Pres.--Sonicair, Scottsdale, AZ, pg. 1018
Hewitt, Marsha A., Sec. & Assoc. Gen. Counsel--Trans World Airlines, Inc., Mount Kisco, NY, pg. 561
Hiatt, David A., Sec. & Treas.--The National Super Service Co., Toledo, OH, pg. 794
Hicks, Linda G., Sec.--Gardiner Metal Company, Chicago, IL, pg. 443
Hicks, Maude H., Sec. & Treas.--Horton Homes, Inc., Eatonton, GA, pg. 545
Hielke, William E., Controller, Admin. Sec. & Chief Fin. Officer--Bata Shoe Co., Inc., Belcamp, MD, pg. 201
Higbee, David M., Sec.--Apco Argentina Inc., Tulsa, OK, pg. 77
Higdon, James R., Dir.-Opers. & Sec.--Fine Organics Corp., Lodi, NJ, pg. 411
Higdon, Lawrence, V.P & Sec.--Ira Higdon Grocery, Inc., Cairo, GA, pg. 533
Higginbotham, Dorothy, Sec.--Ozark Motor Lines, Memphis, TN, pg. 835
Higgins, William, Sec. & Gen. Mgr.--Holland Mark Martin, Burlington, MA, pg. 539
Highley, Edward, Sec.--Alamo Group, Inc., La Grange, IL, pg. 29
Hildreth, Horace A., Jr., Pres. & Sec.--Diversified Communications, Portland, ME, pg. 340
Hill, Dorsey, Treas. & Sec.--Tallapoosa River Electric Co-Op, South Lafayette, AL, pg. 1077
Hill, Justin, Jr., Sec. & Treas.--Lawrence Paper Company, Lawrence, KS, pg. 662
Hill, Kathleen M., Sec.--Donald L. Arends Inc., Oak Brook, IL, pg. 81
Hill, Lewis, III, Sec.--Golf Hosts, Inc., Palm Harbor, FL, pg. 469
Hill, Lewis, III, Sec.--Golf Host Resorts, Inc., Tarpon Springs, FL, pg. 469
Hill, Max E., Chief Fin. Officer, V.P.-Fin. & Sec.--I.C. System, Inc., Vadnais Heights, MN, pg. 558
Hill, R.E., Sec. & Treas.--Democrat Printing & Lithograph Company, Little Rock, AR, pg. 328
Hill, Robert M., Sec. & Treas.--First Electric Cooperative, Jacksonville, AR, pg. 412
Hill, STeven H., Sr. V.P., Sec. & Dir.-Fin.--Southern Container Corporation, Hauppauge, NY, pg. 1020
Hilton, Ronald G., Corp. Treas. & Sec.--Inlander-Steindler Paper, Vernon Hills, IL, pg. 570
Himes, Andrew G., V.P.-Admin. & Sec.--Talon, Inc., Meadville, PA, pg. 1077
Hindman, Robert A., Sr. V.P.-Fin., Treas. & Sec.--Brix Maritime Co., Portland, OR, pg. 177
Hines, Edward J., V.P., Treas. & Sec.--Wolverine Massachusetts Corporation, Merrimac, MA, pg. 1199
Hines, John M., Exec. V.P. & Sec.--A.C. Monk Co., Inc., Farmville, NC, pg. 766
Hinker, Paul, Sec.--Argosy Electronics, Inc., Eden Prairie, MN, pg. 82
Hinman, Mark, V.P., Sec. & Mgr.-Sls.--Rome Strip Steel Co., Inc., Rome, NY, pg. 946
Hinton, Betty, Sec. & Treas.--Blue Grass Chrysler-Plymouth, Lexington, KY, pg. 156
Hinton, Helen L., Sec.--Broughton Foods Company, Marietta, OH, pg. 180
Hirman, Arland E., V.P., Sec. & Treas.--Advanstar Communications, Cleveland, OH, pg. 21
Hirschfeld, Dennis C., Exec. V.P. & Sec.--Hirschfeld, Inc., San Angelo, TX, pg. 536
Hirschfeld, Michael, Gen. Counsel & Asst. Sec.--Ficks Reed Company, Cincinnati, OH, pg. 408
Hitchcock, Emogene, Sec.--Hitchcock Industries, Inc., Bloomington, MN, pg. 536
Hitzelberger, Paul, Exec. V.P.-Mktg. & Sec.--Del Taco, Inc., Costa Mesa, CA, pg. 325
Hitzelberger, Paul, Exec. V.P.-Mktg. & Sec.--Del Taco/ Naugles, Costa Mesa, CA, pg. 325
Hobbs, Leon M., Jr., Sr. V.P. & Sec.--Rosser Fabrap International, Atlanta, GA, pg. 950
Hochberg, S., Sec.--L. Karp & Sons, Inc., Elk Grove Village, IL, pg. 617
Hodge, S.K., Sec.--Sterling Lumber & Investment Co., Denver, CO, pg. 1047
Hodges, Steve, Sec. & Treas.--Varel Manufacturing Co., Dallas, TX, pg. 1145
Hodges, Teresa, Sec.--Town Square Furniture, Inc., Hillsboro, TX, pg. 1104
Hoehn, Richard N., Asst. Sec.--Kingsbury Corporation, Keene, NH, pg. 631
Hoff, George H., Exec. V.P. & Chief Fin. Officer--Sargento Incorporated, Plymouth, WI, pg. 971
Hoff, George H., Sec. & Treas.--Sargento Food Service Corp., Plymouth, WI, pg. 971
Hoffer, Helen, Sec.--Hoffer Plastics Corporation, South Elgin, IL, pg. 537
Hoffman, Joyce, Sec.--The Principal Financial Group, Des Moines, IA, pg. 890
Hoffman, Julia A., Sec.--Weston Paper & Manufacturing Co., Terre Haute, IN, pg. 1183
Hoffman, William H., Sec. & Treas.--Jeffrey Buick-Nissan Inc., Roseville, MI, pg. 591
Hofman, Henry J., Controller & Sec.--Reliance Elevator Company, Chicago, IL, pg. 925
Hogan, Vicky, Sec.--Quik Print Inc., Wichita, KS, pg. 905
Hogan, William T., Sec.--Chicago Convention & Tourism Bureau, Chicago, IL, pg. 245
Hogg, G. Scott, Sec. & Treas.--Better Brands Of Atlanta, Inc., Atlanta, GA, pg. 148
Hohmann, Joseph, V.P. & Asst. Gen. Counsel--The LINC Group, Inc., Chicago, IL, pg. 648
Holcomb, Robert J., Sec. & Treas.--V.T. Inc., Merriam, KS, pg. 1142
Holdeman, R. Steven, Sec.--Atwood Industries, Inc., Rockford, IL, pg. 97
Holden, Shirley, Treas., Sec. & Controller--Royal Oldsmobile Mazda, Inc., Metairie, LA, pg. 953
Holler, Judy, Sec.--Roger Holler Chevrolet Co., Winter Park, FL, pg. 539
Hollingsworth, Linda, Sec. & Treas.--Sun Bulb Company, Inc., Arcadia, FL, pg. 1058
Hollon, Lyn, Dir.-Admin. & Corp. Sec.--Windmill Holdings Corp., San Francisco, CA, pg. 1195
Holloway, J. David, Sec.--American Technical Publishers, Inc., Homewood, IL, pg. 63
Holloway, Ronald L., Sec.--States, Inc., Breckenridge, TX, pg. 1041
Holly, Shirley, Sec.--Margo's La Mode, Inc., Dallas, TX, pg. 373
Holm, Joyce, Sec.--Your Man Tours, Inc., Inglewood, CA, pg. 1214
Holmes, Houston E., Jr., V.P., Sec. & Legal Counsel--Tom Thumb Food & Drugs, Inc., Dallas, TX, pg. 912
Holmes, Virginia, Sec.--Century Boats By General Marine Industries, Panama City, FL, pg. 450
Holmquist, Paul R., Gen. Counsel & Sec.--American Hardware Mutual Insurance Co., Minnetonka, MN, pg. 55
Holtz, Fana, Sec.--Capital Bancorp, Miami, FL, pg. 214
Holtzman, Morton, V.P., Sec. & Treas.--Harve Benard Ltd. Manufacturing, Secaucus, NJ, pg. 514
Holzman, Donald J., Sec. & Gen. Counsel--Dinaire Corp., Buffalo, NY, pg. 338
Homes, Gerald, Sec. & Treas.--Big Bear Supermarkets No. 3, San Diego, CA, pg. 149
Homes, Pat, V.P., Treas. & Sec.--Homes & Son Contractors, Inc., Phoenix, AZ, pg. 542
Honbarrier, Louise B., Sec. & Treas.--Central Transport Inc., High Point, NC, pg. 234
Honek, Anna B., Sec.--Connecticut Drive Shaft, Inc., Milford, CT, pg. 274
Hood, Cecil G., Sec. & Controller--Batson-Cook Company, West Point, GA, pg. 126
Hoopman, L. Elizabeth, Sec.--Burris Foods, Inc., Milford, DE, pg. 195
Hoops, Alan, Exec. V.P., Chief Oper. Officer & Sec.--PacifiCare Health Systems, Inc., Cypress, CA, pg. 1127
Hoover, Arthur, Sec. & Prod. Mgr.--T. Bruce Sales, Inc., West Middlesex, PA, pg. 183
Hopkins, Pearl, Sec. & Treas.--A & S Tribal Industries, Poplar, MT, pg. 1
Hopper, Tom, Sec.--Hardwick Clothes Inc., Cleveland, TN, pg. 508
Horan, Dennis, Sec. & Treas.--U.R.M. Stores, Inc., Spokane, WA, pg. 1124
Horan, Don, Sr. V.P.-Fin., Chief Fin. Officer, Sec. & Treas.--Macklanburg-Duncan Co., Oklahoma City, OK, pg. 697
Horn, Ann B., Sec.--Kanawha Steel & Equipment Co., Charleston, WV, pg. 615
Horn, B.D., Sec.--Oman Construction Co. Inc., Nashville, TN, pg. 825
Horn, Violet F., Sec.--Horn Packaging Corporation, Ayer, MA, pg. 544
Horowitz, Roberto, Sec.--Real Estate Corp. of Florida, Kissimmee, FL, pg. 917
Horowitz, William R., Sr. V.P & Asst. Sec.--Amerbelle Corporation, Rockville, CT, pg. 47
Hort, Robert, Chm. Bd. & Sec.--Enterprise Press, Inc., New York, NY, pg. 382
Horton, Brenda, Sec.--S&D Coffee Inc., Concord, NC, pg. 959
Horvat, Peter D., V.P., Sec. & Treas.--Lenape Forge, Inc., West Chester, PA, pg. 667
Horvath, Joseph J., Sr. V.P., Gen. Counsel & Sec.--The Penn Mutual Life Insurance Company, Philadelphia, PA, pg. 858
Hosek, LaVerne, Gen. Counsel & Sec.--Follett Corporation, Chicago, IL, pg. 422
Hoshizaki, Kotaro, Treas. & Sec.--Mutual Trading Co., Inc., Los Angeles, CA, pg. 779
Hosler, Darrell M., Exec. V.P. & Sec.--Burns & McDonnell Engineers-Architects-Consultants, Kansas City, MO, pg. 194
Hougen, Therese, V.P. & Sec.--Hougen Manufacturing Inc., Flint, MI, pg. 546
Houle, Patricia, Sec.--United Food Service Distributors, Inc., Albany, NY, pg. 1132
House, Randall, Sec. & Treas.--U.S. Creative, Inc., Austin, TX, pg. 1135
Howard, Annie W., Sec. & Treas.--Mercer Transportation Co., Louisville, KY, pg. 739
Howard, James H., Chief Fin. Officer & Corp. Sec.--Stowe-Pharr Mills, Inc., McAdenville, NC, pg. 1052
Howard, Thomas, V.P. & Sec.--Carl Weissman & Sons, Inc., Great Falls, MT, pg. 1174
Howell, Dolores, Exec. V.P. & Sec.--Moyer Packing Company, Souderton, PA, pg. 774
Howser, Ken, V. P., Sec.--Stephen Associates, Inc., New York, NY, pg. 1046
Hoxie, Henry, Sec. & Dir.-Human Resources--Atlas Hotels, Inc., San Diego, CA, pg. 96
Hoye, W.O., Exec. V.P. & Sec.--Century Fence Company, Pewaukee, WI, pg. 235
Hsieh, Stuart, Sec.--Owen Pacific, Los Angeles, CA, pg. 834
Hubbard, Bruce A., Corp. Sec.--Great Lakes Bancorp, Ann Arbor, MI, pg. 480
Hubbard, Sonja, Treas. & Sec.--Yates Enterprises Inc., Texarkana, TX, pg. 1207
Hubbard, Sonja, Controller, Treas & Sec.--E-Z Mart Stores, Inc., Texarkana, TX, pg. 361
Huber, Judy, Exec. V.P., Treas. & Sec.--Time Systems, Inc., Phoenix, AZ, pg. 1097
Hubert, George J., Jr., V.P. & Sec.--Hubert Company, Harrison, OH, pg. 550
Hudak, Irene, Sec.--Health Care Distributors of Indiana, Inc., South Bend, IN, pg. 520
Huenneken, Donovan D., Sec.--Lusk Interiors, Inc., Irvine, CA, pg. 688
Huerter, M. Jane, Exec. V.P. & Corp. Sec.--Mutual of Omaha Insurance Company, Omaha, NE, pg. 779
Huerter, M. Jane, Exec. V.P. & Corp. Sec.--Mutual of Omaha, Omaha, NE, pg. 779
Huettl, Thomas R., Sr. V.P., Chief Oper. Officer, Treas. & Sec.--Steenberg Homes, Inc., Fond du Lac, WI, pg. 1045
Huff, Donald R., Sr. V.P.-Underwriting & Asst. Sec.--Federated Mutual Insurance Company, Owatonna, MN, pg. 405
Huffman, Kip, Sec. & Treas.--Neil Huffman Nissan Inc., Louisville, KY, pg. 551
Hughes, J. Lowell, V.P. & Sec.--Davis Electrical Constructors, Inc., Greenville, SC, pg. 318
Hughes, Kay F., Sec.--Universal Securities Corporation, Birmingham, AL, pg. 1139
Hughes, Mary L., Sec.--Medtech Laboratories, Inc., Jackson, WY, pg. 736
Hughes, Paul, Sec.--Hughes Markets Inc., Irwindale, CA, pg. 552
Hughes, W. Alan, Treas. & Sec.--Fleischli Oil Company, Inc., Cheyenne, WY, pg. 417
Hughes, William, Exec. V.P. & Sec.--BeefAmerica Operating Co., Inc., Omaha, NE, pg. 131
Huitt, E. Larry, Chm. Bd., Sec. & Treas.--Huitt-Zollars, Inc., Dallas, TX, pg. 552
Hulseman, John, Exec. V.P. & Sec.--Solo Cup Company, Highland Park, IL, pg. 961
Hulseman, Paul F., Exec. V.P. & Sec.--SCC Holding Co., Highland Park, IL, pg. 961
Hult, F.A., Controller--Walter Industries, Inc., Tampa, FL, pg. 1161
Humbert, Jose, Sec. & Treas.--Direct Press Modern Litho Corporation, Huntington Station, NY, pg. 339
Humphrey, Biddy, Corp. Sec.--ATI Industries, Escondido, CA, pg. 8
Humphreys, Robert K., Sec. & Treas.--Valley Detroit Diesel Allison, City of Industry, CA, pg. 1143
Humphreys, Sandy, Sec.--Minor Rubber Co., Inc., Bloomfield, NJ, pg. 758
Humphreys, Susan, Sec.--The Gilman Company, Chattanooga, TN, pg. 603
Hunt, Bill, Sec. & Treas.--Keith Smith Farms, Inc., Hot Springs, AR, pg. 1012
Hunt, Walter L., V.P.-Human Resources & Sec.--Dead River Company, Portland, ME, pg. 321
Hupp, John W., Sec.--Knowles Electronics, Inc., Itasca, IL, pg. 637
Hurley, John W., Exec. V.P. & Sec.--Westin, Inc., Omaha, NE, pg. 1183
Hursh, Alan, Treas. & Sec.--Acousti Engineering Co. of Florida, Orlando, FL, pg. 14
Hutton, Nancy, Sec., Treas. & Controller--Crustbuster, Inc., Dodge City, KS, pg. 303
Hyde, Douglas W., Sr. V.P., Asst. Sec. & Mng. Principal-HTB/WDC--HTB, Inc., Oklahoma City, OK, pg. 497
Hyman, Susan, Sec.--Smarty Pants N Tops Too, Inc., City of Industry, CA, pg. 1011
Hysler, Lorraine, Sec.--KOA Holdings, New York, NY, pg. 612
Iacovelli, David, Sec. & Treas.--Chef Italia, Inc., Vestal, NY, pg. 241
Ichikawa, Susan, Corp. Sec.--Peck Jones Construction, Los Angeles, CA, pg. 854
Ilitch, Marian, Sec. & Treas.--Little Caesar Enterprises, Inc., Detroit, MI, pg. 678
Imperia, Joseph, Sec. & Treas.--Imperia Bros., Inc., Pelham Manor, NY, pg. 563
Infantino, T.C., Exec. V.P.-Opers.--Combe Incorporated, White Plains, NY, pg. 267
Ingram, Betty, Sec. & Treas.--B & B Homes Corporation, Casper, WY, pg. 105
Ingram, R.C., V.P. & Sec.--Traylor Brothers, Inc., Evansville, IN, pg. 1108
Ingram, Richard, Treas. & Sec.--T. A. Loving Company, Goldsboro, NC, pg. 685
Inserra, Laurence, Sec.--Wakefern Food Corporation, Elizabeth, NJ, pg. 1158
Ioos, George E., Treas. & Sec.--Shipley Oil Company, York, PA, pg. 999
Iorio, Frank, V.P., Treas. & Sec.--Torino Fashions, Inc., New York, NY, pg. 1102
Irvin, Robert H., Sr. V.P. & Gen. Counsel--Mayflower Transit, Inc., Carmel, IN, pg. 724
Irwin, Arlene G., Exec. Sec.--GAI Consultants, Inc., Monroeville, PA, pg. 439
Irwin, Cynthia, Corp. Sec.--Pacific Coast Producers, Lodi, CA, pg. 839
Isaac, Robert, Sec. & Gen. Counsel--Penrod Drilling Corporation, Dallas, TX, pg. 859

Corporate Responsibilities Index

Isemoto, Leslie, Sec.--Isemoto Contracting Co. Ltd., Hilo, HI, pg. 582
Isen, Robert, V.P. & Sec.--Paramount Packaging Corp., Chalfont, PA, pg. 848
Isom, Donna, Treas. & Sec.--Quality Foods Inc., Little Rock, AR, pg. 903
Izbicki, Anthony J., V.P. & Sec.--Hood & Company, Hamburg, PA, pg. 542
Jablonski, James J., Chief Fin. Officer & Sec.--BCM Engineers Inc., Plymouth Meeting, PA, pg. 106
Jackson, Eileen, Exec. Sec.--Shiffman/Fergusson/Stone Advertising Inc., Fort Lee, NJ, pg. 999
Jackson, James, Sec.--McNaughton-McKay Electric Co., Madison Heights, MI, pg. 732
Jackson, Peter H., Sec. & Mgr.-Special Projects--Humphrey Products Company, Kalamazoo, MI, pg. 553
Jackson, Wayne, Treas. & Sec.--G.I. Joe's Inc., Wilsonville, OR, pg. 440
Jacob, Loraine, Sec.--Sakrete, Inc., Cincinnati, OH, pg. 967
Jacobs, Frank D., V.P. & Chief Fin. Officer--Golden West Homes, Santa Ana, CA, pg. 467
Jacobs, Herbert V., Asst. Sec.--Rothchild Asset Management Inc., New York, NY, pg. 951
Jacobs, Jerry, V.P.-Fin., Treas. & Sec.--Pioneer Aluminum, Inc., Los Angeles, CA, pg. 871
Jacobs, Leonard, V.P. & Sec.--Perry Group, Inc., Hainesport, NJ, pg. 863
Jacobson, Harvey, Sec. & Treas.--Glencraft Lingerie, Inc., New York, NY, pg. 462
Jacobson, Robert N., V.P.-Fin., Treas., Sec. & Chief Fin. Officer--The Atlas Construction Co., Stamford, CT, pg. 96
Jacoff, Salem, V.P. & Sec.--Great Neck Saw Manufacturers, Inc., Mineola, NY, pg. 482
Jaffee, Daniel, V.P. & Sec.--Apparel Industries, Inc., New York, NY, pg. 78
James, David, Sec. & Treas.--Price Woods, Inc., Mesa, AZ, pg. 1200
Janes, David, V.P. & Sec.--California Manufacturing Enterprises, City of Industry, CA, pg. 210
Janger, Jerome, Sec. & Legal--Kennington Ltd., Inc., Los Angeles, CA, pg. 623
Jaqua, Frederick W., V.P., Gen. Counsel & Sec.--American Standard Inc., New York, NY, pg. 61
Jarries, Deb, Sec.--Flanagan Bros. Trucking Co., Bear Creek, WI, pg. 416
Jarvin, Frances M., Sec. & Treas.--Geo. F. Schuler, Inc., Stockton, CA, pg. 979
Jason, Floyd, V.P. & Sec.--Best Provision Co., Inc., Newark, NJ, pg. 146
Jasuiklo, Marcia, Sec.--Cresmer, Woodward, O'Mara & Ormsbee, New York, NY, pg. 298
Jayne, Neila, Sec.--Trinkle Sales, Inc., Cherry Hill, NJ, pg. 1114
Jedlinski, Diane M., Sec.--Roman, Inc., Roselle, IL, pg. 945
Jeffcoat, Peggy B., Sec.--Fairfield Electric Co-op, Winnsboro, SC, pg. 397
Jeffrey, Thomas W., Sr. V.P., Gen. Counsel & Corp. Sec.--Atlantic Gulf Communities Corporation, Miami, FL, pg. 95
Jehlen, Mary E., Sec. & Treas.--Arkansas Oak Flooring, Pine Bluff, AR, pg. 83
Jenkins, Bertha, Sec.--Tobacco Supply, Springfield, TN, pg. 1099
Jenkins, Mary, Sec. & Treas.--Coral Petroleum Corporation, Houston, TX, pg. 285
Jenny, Dawn, Sec.--Standard Brands of America, Inc., Pompano Beach, FL, pg. 1035
Jensen, D.M., Sec. & Treas.--Jensen Electric Company, Reno, NV, pg. 592
Jensen, Gary A., Pres. & Sec.--Jensen Electric Company, Reno, NV, pg. 592
Jensen, Gordon E., V.P.-Comptroller, Treas. & Asst. Sec.--Omaha Property & Casualty, Omaha, NE, pg. 779
Jensen, Gordon E., V.P., Treas., Comptroller & Asst. Sec.--Omaha Property & Casualty Co., Omaha, NE, pg. 779
Jensen, Harry, Sec.--The Elder-Beerman Stores Corp., Dayton, OH, pg. 373
Jensen, Harry A., Sec.--The El-Bee Chargit Corp., Dayton, OH, pg. 373
Jensen, Harry A., Sec.--All World Travel Service, Inc., Dayton, OH, pg. 373
Jensen, Irving F., Jr., Chm., Treas. & Sec.--Irving F. Jensen Co., Inc., Sioux City, IA, pg. 593
Jerneycic, Frank, Sec. & Treas.--F & M Distributors Inc., Warren, MI, pg. 393
Jett, Donald E., Sec.--TST/Impreso, Inc., Coppell, TX, pg. 1075
Jewell, Doris, V.P.-Fin, Treas. & Sec.--Wholesale Electronic Supply, Dallas, TX, pg. 1188
Jodun, Doris, Sec.--Woolrich, Inc., Woolrich, PA, pg. 1201
Joffe, Carl H., Sec. & Gen. Counsel--Purcell Co., Inc., Bay Saint Louis, MS, pg. 900
Johnson, Catherine C., V.P. & Sec.--Johnson Newspaper Corporation, Watertown, NY, pg. 598
Johnson, Chris, Sec. & Treas.--Fritz Co. Inc., Newport, MN, pg. 434
Johnson, Deanne, Treas. & Sec.--Elk Supply Company, Clinton, OK, pg. 376
Johnson, Ernest, Sr. V.P. & Sec.--La Victoria Foods, Inc., City of Industry, CA, pg. 649
Johnson, Eunice W., Treas. & Sec.--Johnson Publishing Company, Inc., Chicago, IL, pg. 598
Johnson, George R., Asst. Sec. & Gen. Counsel--Twin City Die Castings Co., Minneapolis, MN, pg. 1121
Johnson, Kathleen K., Corp. Sec.--SC Companies, Inc., Muscatine, IA, pg. 960
Johnson, Kathleen K., Sec.--Stanley Consultants, Inc., Muscatine, IA, pg. 961
Johnson, Kathleen M., Corp. Sec.--Thoroughbred Software International, Inc., Somerset, NJ, pg. 1095
Johnson, Kathy, Corp. Sec.--Aston Martin LaGonda of North America, Inc., Stamford, CT, pg. 92
Johnson, Larry, Sec.--Southern Minnesota Beet Sugar Cooperative, Renville, MN, pg. 1022
Johnson, Murray, V.P., Gen. Counsel & Sec.--H.B. Zachry, San Antonio, TX, pg. 1215
Johnson, Patricia M., Dir.-Fin., Treas. & Sec.--Tony Downs Foods Company, Saint James, MN, pg. 348
Johnson, R.E., V.P. & Sec.--Baton Rouge Water Works Company, Baton Rouge, LA, pg. 126
Johnson, Robert A., V.P.-Sec. & Gen. Counsel--Bonneville International Corp., Salt Lake City, UT, pg. 332
Johnson, Ronald, Sec. & Gen. Counsel--Bankers Systems Inc., Saint Cloud, MN, pg. 117
Johnson, Sharon M., Controller & Sec.--Sauer Industries, Inc., Pittsburgh, PA, pg. 972
Johnson, Stella, Sec.--Good Stuff Food Company, Inc., Los Angeles, CA, pg. 470
Johnson, Stewart H., V.P. & Sec.--Ballenger Paving Company, Inc., Taylors, SC, pg. 116
Johnson, Walter D., Exec. V.P., Chief Fin. Officer & Sec.--Johnson Bros. Corp., Litchfield, MN, pg. 597
Johnston, Evelyn, Sec.--Fred B. Johnston Company, Inc., Chapin, SC, pg. 601
Johnston, Gene, Sec.--Cass-Clay Creamery, Fargo, ND, pg. 228
Johnston, Richard C., Sec. & Treas.--Haden, Inc., Madison Heights, MI, pg. 499
Johnston, Richard C., Sec. & Treas.--Haden Equity, Ltd., Madison Heights, MI, pg. 499
Johnston, Richard C., Sec. & Treas.--Haden Investment, Ltd., Madison Heights, MI, pg. 499
Jolly, Terrance K., Sec.--Digital Electronic Automation, Livonia, MI, pg. 337
Jonas, John M., Chief Fin. Officer, V.P. & Sec.--Syar Industries, Inc., Napa, CA, pg. 1068
Jones, Carol Ann, Sec. & Treas.--Dealers Electrical Supply Co., Waco, TX, pg. 322
Jones, Diane R., Sec. & Dir.-Admin. Services--Jack Gray Transport, Inc., Gary, IN, pg. 479
Jones, Dorothy, Sec.--Magic Valley Foods, Inc., Rupert, ID, pg. 700
Jones, Gary, Treas. & Sec.--Rural Electric Co-op, Lindsay, OK, pg. 956
Jones, James E., Chief Fin. Officer, Sec. & Treas.--Modern Welding Co., Inc., Owensboro, KY, pg. 763
Jones, K., Corp. Sec.--Colonial Pipeline Company, Atlanta, GA, pg. 264
Jones, Kenneth, Exec. V.P., Chief Fin. Officer, Sec. & Treas.--Hatfield Quality Meats, Inc., Hatfield, PA, pg. 517
Jones, Kenneth J., Sec.--ESSTAR Incorporated, New Haven, CT, pg. 361
Jones, Lamar S., Sr. V.P., Chief Fin. Officer, Sec. & Dir.-Admin.--Kirkpatrick Pettis, Omaha, NE, pg. 779
Jones, Larry L., Treas. & Sec.--Rieth-Riley Construction Co. Inc., Goshen, IN, pg. 934
Jones, Linda, Sec. & Sr. Buyer--Cumberland-Swan, Inc., Smyrna, TN, pg. 304
Jones, Marvel C., Sec.--Dawn Food Products, Inc., Jackson, MI, pg. 319
Jones, Raymond E., V.P.-Admin. & Sec.--Shelter Mutual Insurance Company, Columbia, MO, pg. 997
Jones, Russell B., Sr. V.P.-Fin., Treas., Chief Fin. Officer & Sec.--GranTree Corporation, Beaverton, OR, pg. 477
Joplin, Jean, Treas. & Sec.--Oil & Gas Supply Company, Houston, TX, pg. 823
Jordan, Charles A., V.P. & Sec.--Jordan Tamraz Caruso Advertising, Inc., Chicago, IL, pg. 605
Jordan, Debra E., Asst. to Chm. Bd. & Asst. Sec.--W. P. Carey & Co., Inc., New York, NY, pg. 218
Jorgensen, Cheryl, Sec.--Buffelen Woodworking Company, Tacoma, WA, pg. 187
Joseph, Mark, Mgr.-Engrng. & Sec.--Uppco, Inc., Chicago, IL, pg. 1139
Jubelirer, Natalie, Sec.--John Reyer Company, Sharon, PA, pg. 930
Juda, Dennis, Sec.--Excelsior Manufacturing & Supply Corp., Itasca, IL, pg. 392
Jumonville, Carla, Sec.--Group Insurance Inc., Baton Rouge, LA, pg. 490
Jumonville, Francis, Sec. & Treas.--Airtrol, Inc., Baton Rouge, LA, pg. 28
Jungman, Charles J., Sec.--Remmele Engineering, Inc., Saint Paul, MN, pg. 926
Jurand, Henry A., V.P.-Corp. Plng. & Devel. & Sec.--KCS Energy Inc., Edison, NJ, pg. 612
Just, Lawrence E., Asst. Sec. & Gen. Counsel--Bradley Printing Company, Des Plaines, IL, pg. 178
Justesen, Wayne, V.P., Sec. & Gen. Counsel--Greenwood Mills, Inc., Greenwood, SC, pg. 485
Kadish, David A., Sec. & Gen. Counsel--Integral Systems, Walnut Creek, CA, pg. 572
Kaeser, Clifford R., Sr. Exec. V.P.--Delaware North Companies, Inc., Buffalo, NY, pg. 326
Kahlig, Sandra, Treas. & Sec.--North Park Lincoln Mercury Inc., San Antonio, TX, pg. 813
Kahn, Nelly, Sec.--Monico Alloys, Inc., Los Angeles, CA, pg. 765
Kahn, Simon, Sec.--Empire Steel Trading Company, New York, NY, pg. 380
Kahn, Stanley, V.P., Sec. & Treas.--Croscill, Inc., New York, NY, pg. 300
Kaiser, George E., Sec.--Kaiser Tobacco Company, Inc., New Albany, IN, pg. 615
Kaitz, Miriam Collins, Sec. & Treas.--Palm Beach Beauty Products Co., Minneapolis, MN, pg. 843
Kaizer, Karen, Sec.--Ridg-U-Rak, Inc., North East, PA, pg. 933
Kalin, Alyce, Sec.--Kalin Enterprises, Inc., Sarasota, FL, pg. 615
Kaltman, Martin, Sec.--Queens Group, Inc., Long Island City, NY, pg. 904
Kamimura, S., Sec.--KYB Corporation of America, Lombard, IL, pg. 613
Kamitaki, Wayne, Sec.--Maui Varieties, Ltd., Honolulu, HI, pg. 721
Kanarek, Arnold W., Sr. V.P. & Sec.--Industrial Acoustics Company, Inc., Bronx, NY, pg. 565
Kane, Alice T., Exec. V.P., Gen. Counsel & Sec.--New York Life Insurance Company, New York, NY, pg. 802
Kane, Stanley B., Chm. & Sec.--Kane-Miller Corp., Tarrytown, NY, pg. 616
Kane, William, V.P., Sec., Treas. & Chief Fin. Officer--Molded Fiber Glass Companies, Ashtabula, OH, pg. 763
Kanim, Elvira, Sec. & Treas.--Miss Elliette, Inc., Los Angeles, CA, pg. 760
Kant, Gabriele, Sec.--Wilkens Ayer, Hamburg,, Germany, pg. 104
Kaplan, Jarril F., Corp. Sec.--Smith Pipe & Steel Co., Phoenix, AZ, pg. 1014
Kaplan, Ronald N., Sr. Exec. V.P., Sec.--Smith, Kaplan, Allen & Reynolds, Inc., Omaha, NE, pg. 1013
Kaplan, Samuel, Pres., Chief Exec. Officer, Sec. & Dir.-Sls. & Pur.--Admiration Hosiery Mills, Inc., Charlotte, NC, pg. 534
Kaplanek, Rosemary, Sec. & Treas.--Floral Glass & Mirror, Inc., Hauppauge, NY, pg. 420
Kapson, Betty, Sec. & Tres.--Jordan Motors, Inc., Mishawaka, IN, pg. 605
Karr, David M., Sec. & Treas.--Norpac Foods, Inc. Cooperative, Stayton, OR, pg. 810
Karsian, Andrea, Sec.--Ocean Chevrolet, Inc., Toms River, NJ, pg. 820
Karwacki, Thomas J., Sec. & Treas.--The Park Circle Motor Co., Baltimore, MD, pg. 848
Kasle, Stephen, Sec.--Kasle Steel Corporation, Dearborn, MI, pg. 617
Katsampes, Theodore P., Sr. V.P.-Plng. Div., Gen. Counsel & Sec.--First Federal Savings and Loan Assn. of Rochester, Rochester, NY, pg. 413
Katz, Harry, Exec. V.P.-Sls. & Sec.--Stock Yards Packing Co., Inc., Chicago, IL, pg. 1049
Katz, S., Sec. & Treas.--Manhattan Store Interiors, Inc., Brooklyn, NY, pg. 704
Katzman, Gerald, Sec.--Bristol Industries, Brea, CA, pg. 176
Kaufelt, Florence, Sec.--Mayfair Super Markets, Inc., Elizabeth, NJ, pg. 724
Kauffman, Jeffery R., Asst. Treas. & Asst. Sec.--Lift-All Co., Inc., Manheim, PA, pg. 675
Kauffman, Patty, Sec.--Webster Industries Inc., Tiffin, OH, pg. 1171
Kaufman, Ronald P., Exec. V.P., Sec.--Media Power, Inc., Charlotte, NC, pg. 734
Kautz, Walter J., Sec. & Treas.--Sugar Cane Growers Cooperative of Florida, Belle Glade, FL, pg. 1056
Kawaguchi, Gary, V.P.-Prod. & Sec.--Fishking Processors, Inc., Los Angeles, CA, pg. 415
Kay Mebus Clara, Sec.--Arrow Metal Products Corporation, Detroit, MI, pg. 85
Kaynard, Gerald, Sec. & Legal Counsel--American Development Corporation, North Charleston, SC, pg. 51
Kazmierczak, Kenneth J., Treas., Controller & Sec.--Schreier Malting Co., Sheboygan, WI, pg. 978
Kean, Lawrence M., Sec.--A & A Manufacturing Co., New Berlin, WI, pg. 1
Kec, Janet, Sec. & Treas.--Western States Petroleum Inc., Phoenix, AZ, pg. 1181
Keck, Robert, Corp. Sec.--Schwinn Bicycle Company, Chicago, IL, pg. 981
Keeffe, Elmer C., Sec.--J.H. Harvey Company, Nashville, GA, pg. 515
Keen, Paul R., Gen. Counsel & Sec.--Argo-Tech Corporation, Cleveland, OH, pg. 82
Keene, Robert A., Chm. Bd., Sec. & Treas.--John Roberts Company, Minneapolis, MN, pg. 938
Keene, Stephen W., Sec.--Liberty Mutual Insurance Co., Boston, MA, pg. 674
Kees, Ray, Chief Fin. Officer, Corp. Sec. & Tres.--Gem-Dandy, Inc., Madison, NC, pg. 447
Kehne, Roma V., Sec.--Kehne Electric Company, Inc., Saint Paul, MN, pg. 620
Kehoe, Robert C., 2nd V.P. & Asst. Sec.--W. P. Carey & Co., Inc., New York, NY, pg. 218
Kelleher, Harry B., Sec.--Reagan Equipment Company, Inc., Gretna, LA, pg. 917
Keller, Thomas C., Treas. & Sec.--Schad Industries, Inc., Lafayette, LA, pg. 974
Keller, Thomas C., Treas. & Sec.--Lou Ana Foods, Inc., Opelousas, LA, pg. 974
Kelley, Charles A., Sec.--FamTec International, Inc., Des Plaines, IL, pg. 398
Kelley, Robert L., Exec. V.P. & Sec.--Kelley Bean Co., Inc., Morrill, NE, pg. 621
Kellhofer, Don, Sec. & Treas.--Efco Corporation, Monett, MO, pg. 359
Kellogg, Martin N., Pres., Chief Oper. Officer & Corp. Sec.--UFE Incorporated, Stillwater, MN, pg. 1123
Kelly, John A., Jr., Sec.--Peerless Confection Company, Chicago, IL, pg. 855
Kelly, John, Jr., V.P. & Sec.--Vanguard Energy Corp., Houston, TX, pg. 1145
Kelly, Paul E., Jr., Sec.--Anchor Darling Industries Inc., Rosemont, PA, pg. 230
Kelson, Christine, Sec.--Lena Chow, Inc., Palo Alto, CA, pg. 248
Kempf, LeRoy, Controller & Sec.--Condon Oil Company, Inc., Ripon, WI, pg. 273
Kendrick, Vicki, Sec., V.P.--Fresh Mark, Inc., Massillon, OH, pg. 432
Kenneally, Mary, Treas. & Sec.--Town Pump, Inc., Butte, MT, pg. 1104
Kenneally, William, V.P., Sec. & Gen. Counsel--Golub Corporation, Schenectady, NY, pg. 469
Kennedy, James C., Sec. & Dep. General Counsel--American Financial Corporation, Cincinnati, OH, pg. 52
Kenney, Joseph, Sec.--Provident Mutual Life Insurance Co., Philadelphia, PA, pg. 896
Kenward, John W., Sec.--Rice Growers Association of California, West Sacramento, CA, pg. 931
Kephart, R., V.P.-Treas. & Sec.--Slaughter Bros., Inc., Dallas, TX, pg. 436

Kerley, Marsha L., Treas. & Asst. Sec.--Peterson Builders, Inc., Sturgeon Bay, WI, pg. 864
Kermode, Richard, Exec. V.P.-Admin. & Treas.--Misener Marine Construction, Tampa, FL, pg. 759
Kerns, Judy, Sec.--Riley Creek Lumber Company, Laclede, ID, pg. 935
Kerr, Virginia, Sec.--California Hardware Co., City of Industry, CA, pg. 209
Kerz, Paul J., Sec.--Accelerated Claims Processing, Inc., New York, NY, pg. 521
Kessler, B.I., Exec. V.P. & Sec.--Formation, Inc., Moorestown, NJ, pg. 424
Kessler, Lee, Sec. & Controller--Stern & Stern Industries Inc., New York, NY, pg. 1048
Kessler, Paul B., Sec.--Cora Texas Manufacturing Co., White Castle, LA, pg. 285
Ketter, D.L., Sec.--Shenango Furnace Company, Princeton, NJ, pg. 997
Keuler, Lloyd J., Treas. & Sec.--Turner Supply Company, Mobile, AL, pg. 1119
Khoury, Richel G., Vice Chm., Sec. & Treas.--Pacific Scene Inc., San Diego, CA, pg. 841
Kibbon, Larry J., Treas. & Sec.--Walsh Construction Co. of Illinois, Chicago, IL, pg. 1161
Kick, John V., Treas. & Sec.--Barr Brothers & Co., Inc., New York, NY, pg. 121
Kiefer, Carl O., V.P.-Fin., Sec. & Treas.--Don E. Williams Co., Rock Island, IL, pg. 1190
Kiefer, Evelyn, Sec.--Bel-Ray Company, Inc., Farmingdale, NJ, pg. 133
Kieffer, D.A., Sec./Treas.--GWC Properties, Inc., Portland, OR, pg. 727
Kieffer, D.A., V.P.-Fin., Sec. & Treas.--McCall Oil & Chemical Corp., Portland, OR, pg. 726
Kieffer, D.A., Sec./Treas.--McCall Properties, Inc., Portland, OR, pg. 727
Kieffer, D.A., Sec. & Treas.--McCall Oil Real Estate Corporation, Portland, OR, pg. 727
Kieseman, John, Asst. Sec. & Asst. Treas.--Allied Mercantile Company, Philadelphia, PA, pg. 38
Kilgannon, Memma S., Sec. & Treas.--Amkor Electronics, Inc., West Chester, PA, pg. 67
Kim, Kenneth H., Chm., Pres., Chief Exec. Officer, Corp. Sec. & Treas.--Medieval Dinner & Tournament, Inc., Buena Park, CA, pg. 735
Kimelman, Martin, V.P. & Sec.--Lee National Corporation, New York, NY, pg. 666
Kimura, Mary, Sec.--Gurley Motor Company, Gallup, NM, pg. 494
Kinard, M. Mike, Sec.--American Fuel Cell & Coated Fabrics Co. (Amfuel), Magnolia, AR, pg. 55
King, F., Sec. & Treas.--Baird Ray Nissan, Inc., Longwood, FL, pg. 114
King, Harvey, Vice Chm., Fin. & Sec.--Brookshire Grocery, Tyler, TX, pg. 180
King, John, Sec. & Treas.--Greenway Co-Op Service, Rochester, MN, pg. 485
King, Lavinia K., Sec.--King Industries, Inc., Norwalk, CT, pg. 630
King, Thomas R., Sec.--Scicom Data Services, Ltd., Minnetonka, MN, pg. 981
Kinkade, Wallace R., Sec. & Treas.--Nashville Machine Co. Inc., Nashville, TN, pg. 784
Kinn, Frank, V.P.-Fin. & Sec.--Roppe Corp., Fostoria, OH, pg. 947
Kinneson, Danny, Sec. & Treas.--DBM Hatch, Inc., El Monte, CA, pg. 308
Kinning, Georgia, Sec.--RK Mechanical, Inc., Lakewood, CO, pg. 907
Kipnis, Ira A., V.P. & Sec.--The Jupiter Corporation, Chicago, IL, pg. 609
Kirbo, Bruce W., Sec.--Stones, Inc., Bainbridge, GA, pg. 1051
Kirk, J., Sec. & Treas.--Exact Equipment Corporation, Langhorne, PA, pg. 392
Kirk, Milo, Sec.--Dallas Peterbilt, Inc., Irving, TX, pg. 312
Kirkpatrick, Douglas, Sec. & Gen. Counsel--Miken Companies, Inc., Cheektowaga, NY, pg. 752
Kiser, Muriel, Sec.--Rehrig Pacific Company, Los Angeles, CA, pg. 922
Kish, David, V.P.-Admin. & Gen. Counsel--Delta Queen Steamboat Company, New Orleans, LA, pg. 385
Kitchens, Lovett, Sec.--Cox Wood Preserving Co., Orangeburg, SC, pg. 295
Klaasen, A.J., Sec.--Continental Machines, Inc., Savage, MN, pg. 279
Klapinsky, Raymond J., Sr. V.P. & Sec.--The Vanguard Group, Inc., Wayne, PA, pg. 1145
Klas, William L., Sec. & Treas.--Tapemark, West St. Paul, MN, pg. 1078
Klaszky, Carl W., Sec. & Treas.--A.N. Deringer, Inc., Saint Albans, VT, pg. 331
Kleban, Albert J., Sec. & Gen. Counsel--Chessco Industries, Inc., Westport, CT, pg. 243
Kleffman, Carolee S., Sec.--Florists' Mutual Insurance Co., Edwardsville, IL, pg. 421
Klein, Bernard, Chm. Bd., Sec. & Treas.--Alaron Inc., Troy, MI, pg. 30
Klein, Martin, Sec. & Treas.--Plascal Corporation, Farmingdale, NY, pg. 874
Klein, Richard M., Sec.--Baltimore Stationery Co., Baltimore, MD, pg. 116
Klein, Richard T. Jr., Pres. & Chief Oper. Officer--Klein Tools Inc., Skokie, IL, pg. 635
Kleinmanns, Robert, V.P., Sec. & Treas.--The Economics Press, Inc., Fairfield, NJ, pg. 367
Klemme, Kenneth E., Sec.--Demeter, Inc., Fowler, IN, pg. 328
Klenke, Barbara, Corp. Sec.--The Spencer Turbine Co., Windsor, CT, pg. 1030
Klenke, Barbara C., Sec.--Spencer Turbine Co., Windsor, CT, pg. 1030
Kline, Ralph H., Corp. Sec.--Raub Supply Company, Lancaster, PA, pg. 913
Klinefelter, Gary V., Sec. & Gen. Counsel--Amerco, A Nevada Corporation, Reno, NV, pg. 47
Kloempken, John, Corp. Sec.--Office Electronics, Inc., Itasca, IL, pg. 821
Knapp, Elizabeth W., Sec.--Knapp Communications Corporation, Los Angeles, CA, pg. 636
Knaup, Warren, Sr. V.P. & Sec.--Enterprise Rent-A-Car Company, Saint Louis, MO, pg. 382
Knedlik, Ronald, Chief Fin. Officer, Treas. & Sec.--Alex Lee, Inc., Hickory, NC, pg. 33
Kneissl, William L., Sr. V.P., Sec. & Treas.--The Troy Savings Bank, Troy, NY, pg. 1116
Knickerbocker, E. S., Sec.--United Power Association, Elk River, MN, pg. 1134
Kniffen, Janet A., Asst. Sec.--ACF Industries, Inc., Earth City, MO, pg. 561
Knipe, Rosella T., Sec.--David Clark Company, Inc., Worcester, MA, pg. 252
Knisely, Gary T., V.P.-Admin., Sec. & Counsel--Hanover Foods Corporation, Hanover, PA, pg. 506
Knispel, Isabel, Treas. & Sec.--Arrow Fastener Co., Inc., Saddle Brook, NJ, pg. 85
Knopke, Don P., V.P. & Sec.--Contractors Supply Company, Inc., Kansas City, MO, pg. 281
Knopp, Betty, Exec. Sec.--Holsum Bakery, Inc., Phoenix, AZ, pg. 541
Knox, Marion A., Jr., V.P., Treas. & Sec.--Terminix Service, Inc., Columbia, SC, pg. 1088
Knox, Richard, Exec. V.P., Sec. & Treas.--Knox Oil of Texas Inc., Dallas, TX, pg. 638
Kobulsky, Doris, V.P., Opers. & Sec.--The Phillips Agency, Horsham, PA, pg. 867
Koch, Jerome, Treas. & Sec.--Miles Sand & Gravel Company, Auburn, WA, pg. 753
Koch, Kenneth, Sec.--Jennifer Convertibles Inc., Paramus, NJ, pg. 592
Koch, W.O., Sec.--The Millgard Corp., Livonia, MI, pg. 755
Kocourek, Edward J., V.P., Sec. & Treas.--Egan Cos., Minneapolis, MN, pg. 371
Koehn, Donald L., Exec. V.P., Treas. & Sec.--Bradbury Company, Inc., Moundridge, KS, pg. 169
Koenings, Richard, V.P. & Sec.--Nordic Group of Companies, Ltd., Baraboo, WI, pg. 809
Koester, Alexis, Sec.--Smith Brothers Farms, Inc., Kent, WA, pg. 1011
Koffman, David L., V.P. & Asst. Sec.--Apparel America, Inc., New Haven, CT, pg. 78
Koffman, Richard, Sec.--Ben Arnold Co., Inc., Binghamton, NY, pg. 84
Koffman, Richard E., Vice Chm., Exec. V.P. & Sec.--Apparel America, Inc., New Haven, CT, pg. 78
Koffman, Robert G., Pres. & Chief Exec. Officer--United Stores, Bay City, MI, pg. 1137
Kogod, Marvin, Treas. & Sec.--Maurice Electric Supply Company, Washington, DC, pg. 722
Kohler, Dorothy, Sec.--The Bernuth Corporation, Miami, FL, pg. 144
Kohlscheen, Russel, Sec. & Treas.--Allen Samuels Chevrolet GEO, Waco, TX, pg. 969
Kolbe, William F., Sec.--Color Arts, Inc., Racine, WI, pg. 264
Kolkhorst, Steven, V.P., Sec. & Treas.--Hussey Corporation, North Berwick, ME, pg. 555
Koller, Marie, Treas. & Sec.--Koller Enterprises, Inc., Fenton, MO, pg. 641
Konheim, Colleen, Sec.--Kobra International Ltd, New York, NY, pg. 638
Kopelman, David W., Chm. Bd.--The W.B. Wood Company, New Providence, NJ, pg. 1199
Kopp, Joseph T., Treas. & Sec.--Massman Construction Company, Kansas City, MO, pg. 719
Kopp, Stephanie J., Exec. V.P. & Sec.--Mutual of America, New York, NY, pg. 777
Korallus, Guenther, V.P. & Sec.--Volvo Sales & Service Center, Lile, IL, pg. 1155
Korba, Robert, Sec.--Adventure Tours USA, Inc., Dallas, TX, pg. 21
Korber, Libby, Controller, Treas. & Sec.--J. Korber & Company, Albuquerque, NM, pg. 641
Korljan, Joan, Sec.--Kitchell Corporation, Phoenix, AZ, pg. 634
Korpela, Richard A., Sr. V.P., Sec. & Treas.--Lynden Incorporated, Seattle, WA, pg. 689
Korstad, Robert, Sec.--United Hardware Distributing Co., Plymouth, MN, pg. 1132
Kosek, Dave, Treas. & Sec.--Asplundh Tree Expert Co., Willow Grove, PA, pg. 88
Koslan, Spencer L., Sec.--Star Expansion Company, Mountainville, NY, pg. 1039
Kosloff, Irving S., Chm. Bd.--Roosevelt Paper Co., Philadelphia, PA, pg. 946
Kostek, J.R., V.P., Sec. & Treas.--Kelso-Burnett Company, Rolling Meadows, IL, pg. 622
Kotown, Kathy, Sec.--Tishman Realty & Construction Co., New York, NY, pg. 1099
Kotz, Robert, Sec.--ACR Industries Inc., Mount Clemens, MI, pg. 2
Koukouma, Olga, Sec.--Leo Burnett S.A., Athens,, Greece, pg. 193
Kovsky, Charles, Gen. Counsel & Sec.--Computer Methods Corporation, Livonia, MI, pg. 271
Kowalski, Linda, Sec.--Kowalski Sausage Co., Inc., Hamtramck, MI, pg. 643
Kramer, Worth A., V.P., Treas. & Corp. Sec.--Watlow Electric Manufacturing Company, Saint Louis, MO, pg. 1167
Kramme, Gerald A., Sec.--Ace Glass Incorporated, Vineland, NJ, pg. 11
Krantz, Byron, Sec.--Freeman Manufacturing & Supply Company, Cleveland, OH, pg. 431
Krantz, Mary Jan, V.P. & Sec.--Adventure Lands of America, Inc., Des Moines, IA, pg. 21
Krasna, Estelle, Sr. V.P., Controller, Corp. Sec.--Furman, Roth Adv., New York, NY, pg. 437
Krause, David A., V.P. & Sec.--The Pocono Bank, Milford, PA, pg. 534
Krause, Stephen H., Sec.--D. D. Bean & Sons Co., Jaffrey, NH, pg. 129
Krauss, Christine L., Exec. V.P. & Sec.--Lakewood Engineering & Manufacturing Co., Chicago, IL, pg. 652
Krauss, Helen, Sec. & Treas.--Spartan International, Holt, MI, pg. 1026
Kreher, Janit, Sec.--Kreher Steel Company, Inc., Melrose Park, IL, pg. 644
Kreiniker, Thomas J., Sec. & Controller--Standard Manifold Company, Inc., Chicago, IL, pg. 1037
Kremsdorf, Arlene, Sec.--Gusso Manufacturing, Inc., Brooklyn, NY, pg. 495
Kretschman, S.R., Sec.--Bissell Inc., Grand Rapids, MI, pg. 153
Kreusch, Anita E., Sec.--Leonard Kreusch, Inc., Moonachie, NJ, pg. 645
Kreusser, Judi, Exec. V.P., Sec. & Dir.-Human Resources--Handley & Miller, Inc., Indianapolis, IN, pg. 505
Krieble, John, V.P.-Opers. & Sec.--Capital Controls Company Inc., Colmar, PA, pg. 215
Kringel, J.H., Sec.--Wrought Washer Mfg., Inc., Milwaukee, WI, pg. 1205
Kritzer, Paul, Legal Officer & Corp. Sec.--Journal Communications Inc., Milwaukee, WI, pg. 607
Krivoshia, E., Jr., V.P., Gen. Counsel & Sec.--National Steel Corporation, Mishawaka, IN, pg. 793
Krommenhoek, Donna, V.P. & Sec.--Krommenhoek McKeown Associates, San Diego, CA, pg. 645
Kroneberg, Ingrid, Sec.--Wilbur-Ellis Company & Connell Brothers Company, San Francisco, CA, pg. 1189
Krumwiede, Gerald, Sec.--C-Line Products, Inc., Des Plaines, IL, pg. 198
Kruse, Dorthy M., Sec.--Empire Electric Association, Cortez, CO, pg. 379
Kruth, Harold E., Sec. & Gen. Counsel--SRI International, Menlo Park, CA, pg. 964
Kubes, Kathy, Sec. to the Chm.--Waldorf Corporation, Saint Paul, MN, pg. 1159
Kubiak, Robert, V.P.-Fin., Chief Fin. Officer & Sec.--Globe Glass & Mirror Co., Chicago, IL, pg. 463
Kuckowski, Joseph, V.P.-Estimating & Sec.--Joseph Davis, Inc., Buffalo, NY, pg. 318
Kuechle, Michael, Sec.--Mid-America Dairymen, Inc., Springfield, MO, pg. 750
Kuelthau, Jeanne C., Corp. Sec.--Quad/Graphics, Inc., Pewaukee, WI, pg. 902
Kuenzel, Donald D., Asst. Treas. & Sec.--Union Pump Company, Battle Creek, MI, pg. 1128
Kugler, Anthony, Mgr.-Fin. & Corp. Sec.--Hudson Valley Paper Company, Albany, NY, pg. 551
Kuhar, Martin J., V.P., Sec. & Treas.--Creation Windows of Indiana, Inc., Elkhart, IN, pg. 297
Kuhlman, Lou B., Sec.--Argiland Company, Byron, MN, pg. 81
Kuhlman, Ryan, Sec.--Kuhlman, Inc., Menomonee Falls, WI, pg. 646
Kuhn, Humberto G., Sec. & Legal Counsel--Wilson Industries Inc., Houston, TX, pg. 1193
Kulla, Raymond J., V.P., Gen. Counsel & Sec.--AXIA Incorporated, Oak Brook, IL, pg. 8
Kurdziel, Constance, Sec.--Kurdziel Industries, Inc., Muskegon, MI, pg. 646
Kuriyama, Yuko, Corp. Sec--BSB Japan Ltd., Tokyo, Japan, pg. 110
Kurkowski, Phillip, Sec.--North Electric Supply, Inc., Auburn Hills, MI, pg. 813
Kurten, George W., Sec. & Dir.-Personnel--Walsworth Publishing Company, Inc., Marceline, MO, pg. 1161
Kurtz, Dean, Treas. & Sec.--Midwest Tire & Muffler, Inc., Rapid City, SD, pg. 752
Kurtz, Stephen, Sec. & Treas.--Kulite Semiconductor Products, Inc., Leonia, NJ, pg. 646
Kusak, Sheri, Sec.--Yoakum Packing Company, Yoakum, TX, pg. 1208
Kushel, Stephen J., Sec.--Cine Magnetics, Inc., Mamaroneck, NY, pg. 250
Kusiak, Phil, Treas. & Sec.--Marsh Furniture Company, High Point, NC, pg. 714
Kutner, Ben, Chief Fin. Officer, Treas. & Sec.--VATEX America, Inc., Richmond, VA, pg. 1141
Kutys, James, Sec., Treas. & Controller--IA Construction Corp., Concordville, PA, pg. 558
Kuyers, David J., Exec. V.P.-Fin., Admin., Sec. & Treas.--American Seating Company, Grand Rapids, MI, pg. 60
Kvetko, Gloria Jean, Owner--Gloria Jean's Coffee Bean Corp., Buffalo Grove, IL, pg. 464
La Forte, Brian, Sec.--Polar Corporation, Worcester, MA, pg. 878
La Rue, Mary, Sec.--Berwind Corporation, Philadelphia, PA, pg. 145
LaBarba, James F., Sec.--American Produce & Vegetable Co., Dallas, TX, pg. 59
Labowe, Ronald, Sec. & Treas.--Trend Offset Printing Services, Los Alamitos, CA, pg. 1109
Lachenmayer, Gregg, V.P. & Sec.--Collegeville/Imagineering L.P., Collegeville, PA, pg. 262
Lachman, Betty, V.P.-Office Admin. & Computer Opers.--Kenneth Gordon New Orleans, Ltd., New Orleans, LA, pg. 472
Lackman, James, Sr. V.P. & Sec.--James M. Montgomery Consulting Engineers, Pasadena, CA, pg. 767
LaCross, Lisa, Corp. Sec.--Sefton Associates Inc., Grand Rapids, MI, pg. 987
Laddin, Howard, Sec., Treas.--Laddin & Company, Inc., New York, NY, pg. 650
LaDue, Jack R., Sec.--Rochester Gauges Inc. Of Texas, Dallas, TX, pg. 444
LaDue, M.J., III, V.P. & Sec.--Gas Equipment Company, Inc., Dallas, TX, pg. 444
Lainson, J.J., Sec.--Dutton-Lainson Co., Hastings, NE, pg. 356

Laird, M.L., Sec.--Laird & Company, Scobeyville, NJ, pg. 650
Laird, Marg E., Sec. & Treas.--Blockhouse Co., Inc., Red Lion, PA, pg. 157
Lamar, Charles W., III, Sec.--Lamar Corporation, Baton Rouge, LA, pg. 652
Lamb, Janice B., Sec. & Treas.--Lamb Engineering & Construction Co., Salt Lake City, UT, pg. 652
Lamdert, Greg, Sec. & Treas.--H.H. Cutler Company, Grand Rapids, MI, pg. 306
Lancaster, Tom, Treas. & Sec.--Atex Oil Co. of Texas, Inc., Amarillo, TX, pg. 93
Lancaster, Tom, Treas. & Sec.--Bell Gas, Inc., Roswell, NM, pg. 134
Lancaster, Wallace, Sec. & Treas.--Crown Buick, Inc., Metairie, LA, pg. 302
Lance, Walter C., Sr. V.P., Controller & Asst. Sec.--N W Ayer Incorporated, New York, NY, pg. 103
Lance, Walter C., Sr. V.P., Controller & Asst. Sec.--N W Ayer Inc., New York, NY, pg. 104
Lanchner, Bertrand M., Sr. V.P., Legal & Sec.--N W Ayer Incorporated, New York, NY, pg. 103
Lanchner, Bertrand M., Sr. V.P., Legal & Corp. Sec.--N W Ayer Inc., New York, NY, pg. 104
Landau, Jeffrey C., Sec.--Landau Building Co., Wexford, PA, pg. 654
Landergan, Walter L., Jr., Sec. & Legal--Components Corporation Of America, Dallas, TX, pg. 270
Landeut, Eliane, Corp. Sec.--Lowe Troost S.A., Brussels,, Belgium, pg. 685
Landolt, Jean K., Asst. Sec.--National Life Insurance Company, Montpelier, VT, pg. 791
Landry, James E., Chief Fin. Officer, Exec. V.P. & Sec.--United Piece Dye Works, LP, Princeton Junction, NJ, pg. 1134
Landsberger, Anny, Sec.--Bel-Art Products, Pequannock, NJ, pg. 133
Lane, Warren C., Jr., Sec.--Walker Magnetics Group, Inc., Worcester, MA, pg. 1160
Lange, Karen E., Sec.--Owatonna Canning Company, Owatonna, MN, pg. 833
Langenfelder, Katherine, Sec.--Standard Medical Imaging, Inc., Columbia, MD, pg. 1037
Langerman, D.L., Asst. Sec.--Green International, Inc., Denver, CO, pg. 484
Langston, Dudley I., Dir.-Pur., Personnel, Fin. & Sec.--Langston Companies, Memphis, TN, pg. 657
Lanier, Gale, V.P.-Client Services & Sec.--Encore Marketing International, Lanham, MD, pg. 380
Lanterman, A., Kirk, Treas. & Sec.--Usibelli Coal Mine, Inc., Healy, AK, pg. 1140
Lapiere, R.F., Sec.--Air Gage Company, Livonia, MI, pg. 27
Lapin, Philip L., Asst. Sec. & Asst. Treas.--Barton Brands, Ltd., Chicago, IL, pg. 123
Lapin, Philip L., Asst. Sec. & Asst. Treas.--Barton Beers, Ltd., Chicago, IL, pg. 123
Laramore, Jeff, Exec. V.P., Sec.--Young & Laramore, Indianapolis, IN, pg. 1209
Large, Robert O., V.P.-Fin., Sec. & Treas.--International Cold Storage Co., Inc., Andover, KS, pg. 576
Largent, Jackie, Sec.--Tele-Com Products, Inc., Duarte, CA, pg. 1084
Larkin, Patricia, Sec.--Niagara Envelope Company, Inc., Buffalo, NY, pg. 805
LaRocca, John Steven, Treas. & Sec.--Roberts Foods, Inc., Springfield, IL, pg. 938
LaRocque, James, Gen. Counsel & Sec.--James McHugh Construction Co., Chicago, IL, pg. 729
Larsen, Mary, Sec.--Specialty Paperboard Inc., Brattleboro, VT, pg. 1027
Larsens, Otto, Sec.--Atlantic Sugar Association, Inc., Belle Glade, FL, pg. 95
Larson, David J., Sr. V.P., Sec. & Gen. Counsel--Lutheran Brotherhood, Minneapolis, MN, pg. 688
Larson, Janet, Treas. & Sec.--United A G Co-op, Inc., Omaha, NE, pg. 1130
Larson, Lesly V., Asst. Sec.--Minstar, Inc., Minneapolis, MN, pg. 758
Larson, Lesly V., Asst. Sec.--Genmar Industries, Inc., Minneapolis, MN, pg. 759
Latrenta, Nicholas D., V.P. & Sec.--Metropolitan Life Insurance Co., New York, NY, pg. 744
Laubach, John L., Chm. Bd. & Sec.--Medrad, Inc., Pittsburgh, PA, pg. 736
Laukhuff, R.E., Mgr.-Human Resources & Sec.--Raymark Friction Company, Manheim, PA, pg. 914
Laulhere, Larry, Sec. & Treas.--Hood Corporation, Whittier, CA, pg. 542
Laurent, Louise, Treas. & Sec.--Custom Pak, Inc., Clinton, IA, pg. 306
Law, Betty J., V.P.-Treas. & Sec.--Broadcast Supply West, Tacoma, WA, pg. 177
Lawing, Jack L., V.P.-Law & Sec.--Gold Kist, Inc., Atlanta, GA, pg. 465
Lawrence, Barbara C., Sec.--Lawrence Group, Inc., Schenectady, NY, pg. 662
Lawrence, Barbara C., Sec.--Lawrence Insurance Group, Inc., New York, NY, pg. 662
Lawrence, Barbara C., Sec.--United Community Insurance Co., Albany, NY, pg. 662
Lawrence, Craig, V.P., Sec. & Treas.--Lawrence & Schiller, Inc., Sioux Falls, SD, pg. 663
Laws, Anna, Sec. & Controller--Eisaman, Johns & Laws Advertising, Inc., Los Angeles, CA, pg. 372
Lawson, William R., V.P. & Asst. Sec.--HTB, Inc., Oklahoma City, OK, pg. 497
Laxton, Ralph, V.P. & Sec.--Dualite Inc., Williamsburg, OH, pg. 350
Lay, Betty, Sec. & Treas.--San Angelo Electric Service Company, San Angelo, TX, pg. 969
Lay, Ken, Chief Oper. Officer & Sec.--Lay Packing Company Inc., Knoxville, TN, pg. 663
League, David, V.P., Gen. Counsel & Sec.--Ace Hardware Corporation, Oak Brook, IL, pg. 12
Leary, Elizabeth, Sec.--The Motorlease Corp., Farmington, CT, pg. 773
Leasch, George, Sec.--Holy Cross Electric Association, Glenwood Springs, CO, pg. 541
Leasure, Susan, Sec. & Dir. Admin. Services--Associated Advertising Agency, Inc., Wichita, KS, pg. 89
LeBovidge, Richard, V.P.-Quality Control--Chadwick-Miller Inc., Canton, MA, pg. 237
Lederer, Jan, Corp. Sec.--Blue Anchor, Inc., Sacramento, CA, pg. 158
Lederman, Michael G., Gen. Counsel & Sec.--Sunbeam-Oster Company, Inc., Providence, RI, pg. 1059
Ledlow, Verna E., V.P. & Sec.--Altus Federal Savings Bank, Mobile, AL, pg. 46
Lee, Alice H., Sec.--Georgia Iron Works Co., Grovetown, GA, pg. 453
Lee, David, V.P., Treas., Sec. & Controller--Dinwiddie Construction Co., San Francisco, CA, pg. 338
Lee, Dianna, Exec. V.P. & Sec.--Daniel Caron Ltd., New York, NY, pg. 224
Lee, Floyd, Sec.--Ploof Truck Lines, Inc., Jacksonville, FL, pg. 877
Lee, Jane T., V.P. & Sec.--Red Devil Inc., Union, NJ, pg. 918
Lee, Jeanne Marie, Sec. & Treas.--Lakeside Industries, Redmond, WA, pg. 651
Lee, Jesse, Chief Fin. Officer--The IDI Group Companies, Arlington, VA, pg. 560
Lee, Lian Ai, Sec.--Leo Burnett Pte. Ltd., Singapore, Singapore, pg. 193
Lee, Robert H., Sec. & Treas.--Wagstaff Inc., Spokane, WA, pg. 1158
Lee, Thomas H., Sec.--Border States Paving, Inc., Fargo, ND, pg. 165
Lee, William H., Treas., Controller & Sec.--Zimdar Enterprises, Wyoming, MI, pg. 1220
Leeb, Peter, Exec. V.P. & Corp. Sec.--Coleman Cable Systems, Inc., North Chicago, IL, pg. 260
Leef, Ruth L., Treas. & Sec.--Industrial Towel & Uniform, New Berlin, WI, pg. 567
Leeper, Ronald, Sec.--R.M. Palmer Company, West Reading, PA, pg. 843
Leeson, Sandra J., Sec.--Millers' Mutual Insurance Assn. Of Illinois, Alton, IL, pg. 755
Leffler, Darryl, Treas. & Asst. Sec.--National Cooperative Refinery Association, McPherson, KS, pg. 787
Leffler, Donald, Treas. & Sec.--Redburn Tire Company, Phoenix, AZ, pg. 919
Legg, James S., Gen. Counsel & Asst. Sec.--Griffith Laboratories Worldwide, Inc., Alsip, IL, pg. 487
Lehman, Jessie J., Chm. Bd. & Sec.--Georgian Press, Inc., New York, NY, pg. 453
Leibman, Libby, Sec.--Omni Lens Corporation, Forty Fort, PA, pg. 826
Leimkuhler, Gerard J., Jr., Exec. V.P., Sec. & Chief Admin. Officer--Oxford First Corporation, Philadelphia, PA, pg. 834
Leimkuhler, Gerard J., Jr., Exec. V.P., Sec. & Chief Admin. Officer--Oxford Finance Companies, Inc., Philadelphia, PA, pg. 835
Leimkuhler, Lyle, V.P.-Fin. & Sec.--News-Press & Gazette Company, St. Joseph, MA, pg. 804
Leitner, Virlyn, Sec.--Atlas Wire Corporation, Schiller Park, IL, pg. 97
Lemoyne, Stewart, Sec. & Gen. Counsel--Management Dynamics, New Providence, NJ, pg. 703
Lempicki, Chester P., Sec. & Comptroller--Ardco, Inc., Alsip, IL, pg. 81
Lenderman, Gaynell, Sec.--Gay Johnson's Inc., Grand Junction, CO, pg. 446
Lenhart, Miles L., V.P.-Fin., Treas. & Sec.--Reeves Southeastern Corporation, Tampa, FL, pg. 921
Lenk, John C., Sec. & Treas.--Campbell Construction Co., Sacramento, CA, pg. 213
Lentino, Leslie, Exec. V.P. & Sec.--Paterno Imports Limited, Chicago, IL, pg. 851
Lentino, Leslie, Exec. V.P. & Sec.--Pacific Wine Co., Chicago, IL, pg. 851
Leonard, Craig, Treas. & Sec.--Associated Company, Inc., Wichita, KS, pg. 89
Leong, Edith, Treas. & Sec.--Mutual Distributors Ltd., Honolulu, HI, pg. 778
Lester, James L., III, Sec. & Gen. Mgr.--J.L. Lester & Son, Inc., Rockmart, GA, pg. 668
Lester, Sandy, Sec.-Treas.--First Abilene Bankshares, Inc., Abilene, TX, pg. 411
Letica, Gudrun, Sec. & Treas.--Letica Corporation, Rochester Hills, MI, pg. 668
Lett, Denny L., Sec.--The Chesapeake Life Insurance Co., Lincoln, NE, pg. 243
Levenson, Donald, Sec.--Durlacher & Co., Inc., Long Island City, NY, pg. 354
Levin, Anne, Sec.--Midwest Petroleum Co., Saint Louis, MO, pg. 752
Levin, Morris J., Gen. Counsel & Sec.--Schiavone Construction Co., Secaucus, NJ, pg. 976
Levinson, Lawrence M., Sec.--Prime Tanning Co., Inc., Berwick, ME, pg. 889
Levit, Gerald, Sec. & Treas.--Grocers Supply Co. Inc., Houston, TX, pg. 488
Levitt, Harvey, Sec.--Strouse Greenberg & Co., Inc., Philadelphia, PA, pg. 1054
Levy, Allan, V.P., Controller, Sec. & Data Processing Dir.--Level Export Sales Corp., New York, NY, pg. 670
Levy, Kevin, Asst. Sec.--Darling-Delaware Co., Inc., Irving, TX, pg. 315
Levy, Peter, V.P. & Sec.--Rockville Fabrics Corporation, New York, NY, pg. 942
Lewis, Delores, Sec.--C. C. Myers, Inc., Rancho Cordova, CA, pg. 780
Lewis, Harry E., V.P. & Sec.--First Gray Line Corporation, Beverly Hills, CA, pg. 413
Lewis, Jim, V.P., Chief Fin. Officer, Sec. & Treas.--Hale-Halsell Company, Tulsa, OK, pg. 500
Lewis, Robert, Chief Fin. Officer, V.P. & Sec.--Lockwood Corporation, Gering, NE, pg. 680
Lewis, Sally, Sec.--Garsite/TSR, Inc., Kansas City, KS, pg. 443
Ley, Robert J., Sec.--Apollo Colors, Inc., Northbrook, IL, pg. 78
Libbe, Allan J., Sec., Treas. & Controller--Rudolph/Libbe, Inc., Walbridge, OH, pg. 955
Lichter, Mark, V.P. & Sec.--Baltic Linen Company, Inc., Valley Stream, NY, pg. 116
Lickert, W.R., Treas. & Sec.--Mason Company, Lexington, KY, pg. 718
Lieberg, Eric N., Chief Fin. Officer & Exec. V.P.--Rundel Products, Inc., Portland, OR, pg. 956
Liekar, John P., Jr., Sr. V.P. & Sec.--Centimark Corporation, Bethel Park, PA, pg. 231
Liekar, John P., Jr., Gen. Counsel & Sec.--Centimark Corporation, Bethel Park, PA, pg. 231
Lifland, Bill, V.P.-Circulation & Data Processing--PCI, Austin, TX, pg. 836
Light, Daniel T., Sec. & Treas.--Belle Tire Distributor Inc., Allen Park, MI, pg. 136
Light, Dorothy K., V.P. & Sec.--The Prudential Insurance Company of America, Newark, NJ, pg. 896
Lind, Ralph, Corp. Sec. & Controller--St. Croix Press, Inc., New Richmond, WI, pg. 966
Lind, Sheila, Sec.--Peerless Chain Co., Winona, MN, pg. 855
Linda, Gerald, Sec., Dir. Client & Mktg. Services--Kurtzman/Slavin/Linda, Inc., Northfield, IL, pg. 646
Linder, H. Willard, Pres. & Sec.--Minnesota Electric Supply Company, Willmar, MN, pg. 757
Linder, Harvey R., V.P., Sec. & Gen. Counsel--Laroche Holdings, Inc., Atlanta, GA, pg. 659
Lindway, Bernard S., V.P.-Fin., Treas. & Sec.--Sussen, Inc., Cleveland, OH, pg. 225
Linkous, Clare, Treas. & Sec.--Linkous Construction Company, Inc., Memphis, TN, pg. 677
Linnen, Thomas E., V.P.-Fin., Treas. & Sec.--Continental Circuits Corp., Phoenix, AZ, pg. 278
Lisker, Meshulam, Sec. & Mktg. Dir.--Antwerp Diamond Distributors Inc., New York, NY, pg. 77
List, Ruth, Sec. & Treas.--Alatec Products, Inc., North Hollywood, CA, pg. 30
Lite, Grace, Sec.--Belmont Industries, Inc., Philadelphia, PA, pg. 136
Litoff, Carol, Treas. & Sec.--Ronald Litoff, Ltd., New York, NY, pg. 678
Littell, Bettie, Sec. & Treas.--Metalcenter, Inc., Santa Fe Springs, CA, pg. 742
Lloyd, Donna, Sec.--Putt Putt Golf Courses of America, Inc., Fayetteville, NC, pg. 901
Lloyd, Ruth, Sec.--Keen Compressed Gas Co., Inc., Wilmington, DE, pg. 619
Lobel, Leonard J., Exec. V.P., Sec. & Treas.--Almo Corp., Philadelphia, PA, pg. 43
Locher, M.A., Sec.--Hydro Group, Inc., Bridgewater, NJ, pg. 556
Lock, Larry B., Controller & Sec.--Enterprises International Inc., Hoquiam, WA, pg. 382
Locke, Robert, Sr. V.P.-Plng. & Devel. & Asst. Sec.--Pueblo International, Inc., Pompano Beach, FL, pg. 899
Lodge, Susan M., Sec.--Delaware Ribbon Manufacturers, Inc., Philadelphia, PA, pg. 326
Loeb, Carl, Treas. & Sec.--Piknik Products Company, Inc., Montgomery, AL, pg. 870
Loeber, Paul, Sec. & Treas.--Loeber Motors, Inc., Chicago, IL, pg. 680
Lofgren, Frederick, Chief Fin. Officer, Treas., Sec. & V.P.-Fin. & Admin.--Hitchiner Manufacturing Company, Inc., Milford, NH, pg. 536
Lofgren, Raye M., Corp. Sec.--McAnally Enterprises, Inc., Yucaipa, CA, pg. 726
Logan, Muriel, Asst. to Pres.--Overseas Military Sales Corporation, Woodbury, NY, pg. 833
Logghe, Ronald M., V.P. & Sec.--Logghe Stamping Company, Fraser, MI, pg. 681
Loher, Brian H., Treas., Sec. & Dir.-Investor Rels.--Hall Contracting Corp., Louisville, KY, pg. 501
Lohman, Paul J., Treas. & Asst. Sec.--Sands Investments, Inc., Myrtle Beach, SC, pg. 970
Lombard, John J., Jr., Sec.--Airline Hydraulics Corporation, Bensalem, PA, pg. 27
Lomeli, Ann F., Corp. Sec.--Connecticut Mutual Life Insurance Company, Hartford, CT, pg. 274
London, Edith, Sec.--London Litho Aluminum Co., Inc., Lincolnwood, IL, pg. 681
Long, Gary R., Sec.--Sands Motor Company, Inc., Glendale, AZ, pg. 970
Long, Shirley, Sec.--Parrish Tire Company, Inc., Winston-Salem, NC, pg. 850
Looby, Lawrence J., V.P. & Sec.--Chicago West Pullman Transportation Corporation, Chicago, IL, pg. 246
Loomis, James, Asst. Sec.--Loomis Brothers, Inc., Cedar Rapids, IA, pg. 683
Looper, Tommy E., Exec. V.P., Chief Fin. Officer & Sec.--Anchor Financial Corporation, Myrtle Beach, SC, pg. 71
Loree, James H., Sec. & Legal Counsel--Zantop International Airlines, Inc., Ypsilanti, MI, pg. 1216
Lorenz, Barb, Sec.--H & D Steel Service, Inc., North Royalton, OH, pg. 495
Lorenzen, Shelley A., V.P., Sec. & Gen. Counsel--Arcata Corporation, San Francisco, CA, pg. 80
Lorinc, John, V.P., Sec. & Treas.--Grossman Iron & Steel Company, St. Louis, MO, pg. 489
Lorne, W.J., Sec.--East Jordan Iron Works, East Jordan, MI, pg. 362
LoStocco, Ralph J., V.P.-Admin.--Bridgeport Machines, Inc., Bridgeport, CT, pg. 175
Losurdo, Mary, Sec.--Losurdo Foods, Inc., Hackensack, NJ, pg. 684
Loth, Gerald, Treas. & Sec.--Richardson Industries, Inc., Shaboygan Falls, WI, pg. 932

Loth, Jerry, Sec. & Treas.--Richardson Brothers Co., Sheboygan Falls, WI, pg. 932
Louery, James M., Treas. & Sec.--Moto, Inc., Belleville, IL, pg. 773
Love, Jimmy, Sr. V.P. & Sec.--T.L. James & Company, Ruston, LA, pg. 588
Lovelace, Belle, Treas. & Sec.--Mar-Mac Manufacturing Company, Inc., McBee, SC, pg. 705
Lowe, Clifford, Treas. & Sec.--Star Food Processing, Inc., San Antonio, TX, pg. 1039
Lowenstam, Susan G., V.P., Gen. Counsel & Sec.--The Aerospace Corporation, El Segundo, CA, pg. 22
Lowrie, James, Sec.--Alcom Printing Group, Inc., Bethlehem, PA, pg. 32
Lowy, E., Sec.--Pacific States Casualty Co., Los Angeles, CA, pg. 841
Luchsinger, John, Sec.--Farmers and Traders Life Insurance Co., Syracuse, NY, pg. 401
Ludlow, Patricia, Sec.--Bedford Industries, Inc., Worthington, MN, pg. 131
Ludlum, Melissa, Sec.--Macromedia Inc., Hackensack, NJ, pg. 698
Ludwig, Melissa, Sec.--Gouchenour Adv., Inc., Orlando, FL, pg. 473
Luedeking, Peter C., Sec.--Gust K. Newberg Construction Co., Chicago, IL, pg. 803
Lugar, Todd, Sec. & Treas.--Thomas L. Green & Co., Inc., Indianapolis, IN, pg. 484
Lugbill, Jerry, Treas. & Sec.--Lugbill Brothers, Inc., Archbold, OH, pg. 686
Lukacs, Bela B., Exec. V.P. & Sec.--National Tool & Manufacturing Company, Kenilworth, NJ, pg. 794
Lummus, Brad, Sec.--Mrs. Baird's Bakeries, Inc., Fort Worth, TX, pg. 760
Lundberg, Larry T., Gen. Mgr. & Sec.--Trout Inc., Chelan, WA, pg. 1116
Lunder, Peter, Pres., Chief Oper. Officer & Sec.--Dexter Shoe Company, Dexter, ME, pg. 334
Lundquist, Gene A., V.P. & Corp. Sec.--Calcot, Ltd., Bakersfield, CA, pg. 208
Luongo, Ann Marie, Exec. Asst. & Asst. Sec.--W. P. Carey & Co., Inc., New York, NY, pg. 218
Luptak, John J., V.P.-Mktg. & Sec.--Niagara Therapy Mfg. Corp., Stanley, NC, pg. 806
Luskey, Alvin Leon, Sec.--Luskeys Western Stores, Inc., Fort Worth, TX, pg. 688
Lustbader, Brian G., Exec. V.P., Gen. Counsel & Sec.--The P.J. Carlin Construction Company, New Rochelle, NY, pg. 220
Lynch, Hal, Sec.--Sunrise Nissan of Orange Park, Orange Park, FL, pg. 1062
Lynch, William L., V.P. & Sec.--Washington Mutual Savings Bank, Seattle, WA, pg. 1166
Lynnett, Kaneshiro, Sec.--Pacific Hawaiian Ltd., Hilo, HI, pg. 840
Lyons, Robert P., Sec.--Xebec Corporation, Kansas City, MO, pg. 1206
Lyons, Stephen M., III, Asst. Sec.--W. P. Carey & Co., Inc., New York, NY, pg. 218
Lyons, Theresa, Sec.--North Carolina Mutual Life Insurance Co., Durham, NC, pg. 813
Mabanta, William, Corp. Sec.--Aero Data Metal Crafters, Bohemia, NY, pg. 22
MacConnell, Cynthia S., Sec. & Treas.--Bill Woeste Dealer Group, Cincinnati, OH, pg. 1198
Mace, Mike E., V.P. & Asst. Sec.--Ballenger Paving Company, Inc., Taylors, SC, pg. 116
Machado, Henry R., Sec.--Hollywood Alloy Casting Company, Compton, CA, pg. 540
Machida, Lois, Sec.--Del Mar Avionics, Irvine, CA, pg. 325
Macioce, S.F., Asst. Sec.--Commercial Light Company, Hillside, IL, pg. 268
Mackie, D.B., Sr. V.P., Gen. Counsel & Sec.--Great Lakes Dredge & Dock, Oak Brook, IL, pg. 481
MacKnight, Paul D., Sec. & Asst. Treas.--The Record-Journal Publishing Company, Meriden, CT, pg. 917
MacPartland, D., Sec.--Hubbard Hall Inc., Waterbury, CT, pg. 549
Maddox, Barbara T., Sec.--Lee-Moore Oil Co., Inc., Sanford, NC, pg. 665
Madigan, Carol M., Sec.--Madigan Brothers, Inc., River Forest, IL, pg. 699
Madison, Carolyn B., Sec.--Pace Industries, Inc., Fayetteville, AR, pg. 838
Magdovitz, Joe, Chm. Bd., Sec. & Treas.--Imperial Manufacturing Company, Memphis, TN, pg. 564
Maggiore, Cheryl, Corp. Sec.--Charles Holston, Inc., Jennings, LA, pg. 541
Magill, Michael D., Sec.--MCorp, Dallas, TX, pg. 732
Maher, John, Sec.--Bill Collins Ford Inc., Louisville, KY, pg. 263
Maher, Ray, Exec. V.P., Creative Dir. & Sec.--MCC, Inc., Essex, CT, pg. 691
Mahler, Glenn, V.P., Sec. & Treas.--Blue Cross Laboratories, Saugus, CA, pg. 160
Mahon, Dave, Sec. & Treas.--Alro Group, Jackson, MI, pg. 44
Mahoney, Terry W., Sec.--Trak International, Inc., Port Washington, WI, pg. 1106
Maier, Alden M., V.P. & Sec.--Morris Newspaper Corporation, Savannah, GA, pg. 771
Malik, Helen, Sec. & Treas.--Mitchell Corporation of Owosso, Owosso, MI, pg. 761
Malin, Herbert, Exec. V.P. & Sec.--Teknor Apex Company, Pawtucket, RI, pg. 1084
Mallendick, Carol, V.P. & Sec.--Empire Petroleum, Inc., Toledo, OH, pg. 379
Mallory, Richard, Treas. & Sec.--C. Weaver Chevrolet, Inc., New York Mills, NY, pg. 1170
Mallory, W.B. III, Vice Chm., Sec. & Gen. Counsel--Guardsmark, Inc., Memphis, TN, pg. 492
Mallory, W.B., III, Sec.--Peoplemark, Inc., Memphis, TN, pg. 493
Malloy, Edwin, Jr., Sec.--Cheraw Yarn Mills, Inc., Cheraw, SC, pg. 242
Maloney, Joseph J., Treas. & Sec.--Daniel J. Keating Co., Villanova, PA, pg. 619
Malstrom, Dan, Sec.--The Todd-AO Corporation, San Francisco, CA, pg. 1099
Maltz, Margaret A., Sec. & Controller--Nason and Cullen, Inc., Wayne, PA, pg. 784
Manchester, Lorraine, Admin. Sec.--SGI Inc., Cranston, RI, pg. 962
Maney, Norma, Sec.--Country Life Insurance Company, Bloomington, IL, pg. 289
Manger, Sandra, Sec.--Hamilton Stores, Inc., West Yellowstone, MT, pg. 503
Maniscalco, Diane, Chief Fin. Officer-Admin./Opers.-Sec. & Treas.--Colonna Bros., Inc., North Bergen, NJ, pg. 264
Manke, Virgil, Sec.--Manke Lumber Company, Inc., Tacoma, WA, pg. 704
Mann, David S., Sec.--Proctor & Gardner Advertising, Inc., Chicago, IL, pg. 892
Mann, Edmund S., Treas. & Corp. Sec.--Thermo Industries Inc., Charlotte, NC, pg. 1091
Mann, Fredric I., Exec. V.P., Sec. & Creative Dir.--Cline, Davis & Mann, Inc., New York, NY, pg. 255
Mansfield, Fred W., Sec. & Treas.--Great Lakes Financial Resources, Inc., Homewood, IL, pg. 481
Manso, Esther, Comptroller, Sec. & Treas.--Metro Ford Inc., Miami, FL, pg. 743
Manson, James J., V.P. & Sec.--National Concrete Products Company, Plymouth, MI, pg. 787
Manukas, George, V.P., Treas. & Asst. Sec.--DKM Properties Corporation, Lawrenceville, NJ, pg. 357
Manz, Terry K., V.P., Sec. & Treas.--Cactus Feeders, Inc., Amarillo, TX, pg. 207
Marchand, Darryl T., V.P., Gen. Counsel & Sec.--Triangle Pacific Corporation, Dallas, TX, pg. 1112
Marchisotto, Alan L., Sec. & Gen. Counsel--Moran Towing & Transporation Co. Inc, Greenwich, CT, pg. 769
Marcus, Arthur, V.P. & Sec.--Marcus Brothers Textiles, Inc., New York, NY, pg. 706
Marcus, Harriet, Sec. & Treas.--Harold Leonard & Company, Inc., Union, NJ, pg. 667
Mardell, Fred R., Vice Chm., Exec. V.P. & Sec.--Barton Brands, Ltd., Chicago, IL, pg. 123
Mardell, Fred R., Vice Chm., V.P. & Sec.--Barton Beers, Ltd., Chicago, IL, pg. 123
Marden, Robert, Sec.--Laverdiere's Enterprises, Winslow, ME, pg. 661
Mares, Virginia, Sec.--CH2M Hill Companies, Ltd., Englewood, CO, pg. 202
Margan, William D., Sec.--John Bouchard & Sons Company, Nashville, TN, pg. 168
Margulies, Joan, Sec.--Leather Warehouse, Inc., East Rutherford, NJ, pg. 664
Margulis, Irwin, Exec. V.P. & Sec.--Zemco Industries, Inc., Buffalo, NY, pg. 1217
Marino, Joseph R., Gen. Counsel & Sec.--Reactive Metals & Alloys Corporation (REMACOR), West Pittsburg, PA, pg. 916
Marinucci, Lisa W., Sec.--Marquette Coppersmithing Co., Inc., Philadelphia, PA, pg. 713
Maris, Edward G., Sr. V.P. & Chief Fin. Officer--Northwestern Steel & Wire Co., Sterling, IL, pg. 815
Mark, Carol, Sec., Treas., Sr. Art Dir.--Marketing Magic Inc., Fort Lauderdale, FL, pg. 709
Markey, Robert G., Corp. Sec.--Blue Coral, Inc., Cleveland, OH, pg. 159
Markey, Thomas, V.P., Treas. & Sec.--National Spinning Co., Inc., New York, NY, pg. 793
Markluis, John, V.P. & Sec.--Puritan Bakery, Inc., Carson, CA, pg. 900
Markol, Larry, Comptroller & Sec.--J. H. France Refractories Co., Snow Shoe, PA, pg. 428
Markowitz, Edwin, Sec.--Monitor Aerospace Corporation, Amityville, NY, pg. 765
Marks, Jay G., Acct. Services Dir., Corp. Sec.--Broyles, Allebaugh & Davis, Inc., Englewood, CO, pg. 183
Marks, Lorraine K., Sec.--G.B. DuPont Co., Inc., Troy, MI, pg. 354
Marks, Sam, Exec. V.P., Corp. Sec. & Dir.-Pur.--Triangle Marketing Corp., New York, NY, pg. 1112
Marlowe, Margaret H., Sec.--National Fruit Product Company, Winchester, VA, pg. 789
Marman, Charles, Sec. & Treas.--F.T. Reynolds Company, Glendive, MT, pg. 930
Marnane, Dana, Sec.--Newport/Cape Dory Yachts, Inc., Manorville, NY, pg. 804
Marriner, Ray M., Exec. V.P., Sec. & New Bus. Contact--Marriner Marketing Communications, Inc., Columbia, MD, pg. 713
Marsh, W.T., Sec.--Today's Kids, Booneville, AR, pg. 1025
Marsh, William A., V.P., Sec. & Gen. Counsel--Spang & Company, Butler, PA, pg. 1025
Marshal, Douglas, Sec. & Gen. Counsel--Darigold, Inc., Seattle, WA, pg. 315
Marshall, Douglas, Corp. Counsel & Sec.--Dairygold Inc., Seattle, WA, pg. 311
Marshall, J., Sec.--New Haven Mfg. Corp., New Haven, CT, pg. 801
Marshall, Jim, Sec.--Primus Inc., Dayton, OH, pg. 890
Marshall, Joananne, V.P. & Sec.--Marshall Contractors Inc., Rumford, RI, pg. 714
Marshall, Larry, Sec. & Gen. Counsel--MFA Oil Company, Columbia, MO, pg. 692
Marsilius, Richard A., Exec. V.P. & Sec.--The Producto Machine Co., Bridgeport, CT, pg. 893
Martell, Sandra, Corp. Sec. & Gen. Counsel--S. J. Groves & Sons Company, Minneapolis, MN, pg. 490
Martife, Mary, Sec.--Atlantic to Pacific Bedding Corp., Bronx, NY, pg. 95
Martin, Bill, Treas. & Sec.--I. C. Thomasson Associates, Inc., Nashville, TN, pg. 1094
Martin, Clarence, Exec. V.P., Treas. & Sec.--State Electric Supply Co., Huntington, WV, pg. 1040
Martin, D., V.P., Sec. & Gen. Counsel--Motor Wheel Corporation, Lansing, MI, pg. 773
Martin, Everett A., Sec.--Mid America Steel, Inc., Fargo, ND, pg. 750
Martin, Gary C., V.P. & Sec.--Martin Sprocket & Gear, Inc., Arlington, TX, pg. 715
Martin, Gladys, Chief Fin. Officer, Treas., Sec. & Dir.-Personnel--Welsco Inc., North Little Rock, AR, pg. 1175
Martin, Gloria A., Sec. & Treas.--Williams International Industries, Inc., Richmond, VA, pg. 1191
Martin, Harry, Sec.--Snap-Tite, Incorporated, Erie, PA, pg. 1014
Martin, Louanne, Exec. Sec.--Delta Life Corporation, Memphis, TN, pg. 327
Martin, Lynell, Treas. & Sec.--Martins Abbatoir & Wholesale Meats Inc., Godwin, NC, pg. 716
Martin, Phillip, Sec.--Wenger Corporation, Owatonna, MN, pg. 1176
Martin, Robert L., Sec. & Controller--Longyear Company, Salt Lake City, UT, pg. 682
Martin, Roy C., Sr., Chief Exec. Officer & Sec.--Triangle Electric Company, Madison Heights, MI, pg. 1112
Martin, Steve, Treas. & Sec.--Russell Chevrolet Company, Sherwood, AR, pg. 957
Martin, Terri, Treas. & Sec.--Martin Forest Industries, Healdsburg, CA, pg. 715
Martin, Virginia H., Sec. & Treas.--Martin Door Mfg., Inc., Salt Lake City, UT, pg. 714
Martiny, Lynn, Sec. & Treas.--Martiny & Company, Cincinnati, OH, pg. 716
Marx, Leo A., Jr., Sec. & Gen. Counsel--R. L. Polk & Co., Detroit, MI, pg. 879
Masco, Matt S., Exec. V.P., Treas. & Sec.--Pacific Wood Treating Coporation, Ridgefield, WA, pg. 842
Mashburn, Troy, Jr., Sec. & Treas.--Choctaw, Inc., Memphis, TN, pg. 248
Maslick, Joseph R., Sr. V.P., Chief Fin. Officer & Sec.--Griffith Laboratories Worldwide, Inc., Alsip, IL, pg. 487
Maslow, LarryN., V.P. & Sec.--George Uhe Co., Inc., Paramus, NJ, pg. 1125
Mason, David R., Jr., V.P. & Sec.--Mason Oil Company, Ione, CA, pg. 718
Mason, Fred, Treas., Sec. & Mgr.-Pur.--J.B. Rodgers Mechanical Contractors, Phoenix, AZ, pg. 943
Mason, Wallace, V.P., Sec. & Chief Fin. Officer--Temkin & Temkin, Northbrook, IL, pg. 1086
Massa, John A., Asst. Sec.--G. Heileman Brewing Co., Inc., La Crosse, WI, pg. 526
Massengale, John, Sec.--Wellington Industries Inc., Paterson, NJ, pg. 1175
Massengale, John, Sec.--Wellington Home Products, Paterson, NJ, pg. 1175
Masters, Sharon, Asst. Sec.--Woolrich, Inc., Woolrich, PA, pg. 1201
Matarese, Betty H., Sr. V.P. & Sec.--Phoenix International, Inc., Beverly, NJ, pg. 868
Mathis, Jim, V.P.-Mktg., Sec. & Treas.--Precision Parts Corp., Morristown, TN, pg. 885
Matthews, Joyce Carroll, Chm. Bd., Sec. & Treas.--Carroll's Foods, Inc., Warsaw, NC, pg. 225
Matthews, Paul, V.P. & Asst. Sec.--Tyndale House Publishers, Inc., Carol Stream, IL, pg. 1122
Matthis, Doris L., Sec. & Treas.--Kentucky Indiana Lumber Co. Inc., Louisville, KY, pg. 623
Mattielli, Louis D., Sec.--Thomas & Betts Holdings, Inc., Memphis, TN, pg. 425
Mattingly, Barbara A., Treas. & Sec.--Metro Foods, Inc., Memphis, TN, pg. 743
Mattison, P.L., Jr., V.P. & Sec.--Mattison Machine Works, Rockford, IL, pg. 721
Mauger, Samuel, Sec.--Berks Products Corporation, Reading, PA, pg. 142
Mauk, Patricia, Treas. & Sec.--Dudek & Bock Spring Manufacturing Company, Chicago, IL, pg. 351
Maupin, John W., V.P.-Gen. Counsel & Sec.--Fred Weber Inc., Maryland Heights, MO, pg. 1171
Maurer, J., Sec. & Treas.--Rich Products Dayton, Dayton, OH, pg. 932
Maurin, Lois J., Sec.--American Fence Company, Phoenix, AZ, pg. 52
Mauro, Ralph, Corp. Sec.--Willamette-Western Corporation, Portland, OR, pg. 1190
Mautz, Louise U., Sec.--Mautz Paint Company, Madison, WI, pg. 722
May, Jane Ballenger, Sec. & Treas.--Y.C. Ballenger Electrical Contractors, Spartanburg, SC, pg. 116
May, R.H., Sec.--Ziebart International Corporation, Troy, MI, pg. 1217
Mayer, Steven, Sec.--Davis Advertising Inc., Philadelphia, PA, pg. 318
Mayer, Sylvia, Sec. & Treas.--Mayer Berkshire Corporation, Wayne, NJ, pg. 724
Mayers, J. Thomas, V.P. & Sec.--The Hall China Company, East Liverpool, OH, pg. 501
Mayers, Lois E., Sec. & Treas.--Ace Novelty Company, Inc., Bellevue, WA, pg. 12
Mayle, David R., V.P., Sec. & Gen. Counsel--TIC United Corporation, Dallas, TX, pg. 1073
Mayo, James O., Vice Chm. & Sec.--The Kiplinger Washington Editors, Inc., Washington, DC, pg. 632
Maze, George H., V.P. & Sec.--Maze Nails, Peru, IL, pg. 725
Mazzuca, Joseph, Sec.--Central Grocers Co-op, Franklin Park, IL, pg. 232
Mc Curthan, Gordon E., Exec. V.P., Gen. Counsel Sec.--Nationwide Corporation, Columbus, OH, pg. 795
McAlester, Pat, Sec. & Treas.--Texas Electric Cooperatives, Inc., Austin, TX, pg. 1089
McBride, Beverly, Gen. Counsel & Corp. Sec.--The Andersons, Maumee, OH, pg. 73
McCaigue, Dan, Chief Fin. Officer--Showell Farms, Inc., Showell, MD, pg. 1000
McCall, W.A., Sec., Treas., Controller & Data Processing Mgr.--Dixie Oil Company, Tifton, GA, pg. 341

McCalla, Leonard, Sec.--Malloy Lithographing Inc., Ann Arbor, MI, pg. 703
McCann, Gregory, Corp. Counsel & Asst. Sec.--Danis Industries Corporation, Dayton, OH, pg. 314
McCann, Peter, V.P. & Sec.--Interstate Drug Exchange, Inc., Amityville, NY, pg. 580
McCarthy, Carol, Sec.--Servistar Corporation, East Butler, PA, pg. 992
McCarthy, Timothy, Sec. & Gen. Counsel--Western Regional Off Track Betting, Batavia, NY, pg. 1181
McCaskill, Beverly H., Sr. V.P., Chief Admin. Officer & Sec.--Texas Commerce Bancshares, Inc., Houston, TX, pg. 1089
McClelland, Frances H., Treas., Sec. & Chief Fin. Officer--Shamrock Foods Co., Phoenix, AZ, pg. 994
McClelland, George R., Sec.--Independent Can Company, Belcamp, MD, pg. 564
McCollister, Michael, V.P.-Opers.--Jackson Hole Ski Resort, Teton Village, WY, pg. 587
McConkey, Duane L., V.P.-Admin. & Sec.--C. H. Robinson Co. Inc., Eden Prairie, MN, pg. 939
McCormick, John, Corp. Sec.--Investor's Management Corp., Raleigh, NC, pg. 581
McCormick, John, Sec.--Golden Corral Corporation, Raleigh, NC, pg. 466
McCormick, John M., Sec.--SS Restaurant Corporation, Raleigh, NC, pg. 466
McCormick, Thomas P., Exec. V.P. & Sec.--Horizon Bancorp, Michigan City, IN, pg. 544
McCormick, Thomas P., Exec. V.P. & Sec.--First Citizens Bank, N.A., Michigan City, IN, pg. 544
McCoy, Janice, Sec. & Treas.--Fleetwood Aluminum Products, Corona, CA, pg. 417
McCoy, Phyllis, Corp. Sec.--United Dairy Farmers, Inc., Cincinnati, OH, pg. 1131
McCraine, Alice B., Sec. & Treas.--Bernhard Mechanical Contractor, Inc., Baton Rouge, LA, pg. 143
McCraney, Karen, Sec.--CSI Advertising Inc., Atlanta, GA, pg. 205
McCrary, Dennie L., V.P.-Fin. & Sec.--Sea Island Company, Sea Island, GA, pg. 983
McCrory, Kelly L., Sec. & Treas.--Steakley Chevrolet Subaru Inc., Dallas, TX, pg. 1043
McCullough, Bob, Exec. V.P., Sec. & Treas.--Harris, Baio & McCullough Inc., Philadelphia, PA, pg. 511
McCurdy, Robert D., V.P. & Sec.--SJL of Kansas Corp., Wichita, KS, pg. 962
McCutchan, Gordon E., Exec. V.P., Gen. Counsel & Sec.--Nationwide Mutual Insurance Company, Columbus, OH, pg. 795
McDaniel, Charles G., Sec.--Unigroup, Inc., Fenton, MO, pg. 1126
McDaniel, Charles G., Sec.--United Van Lines, Inc., Fenton, MO, pg. 1126
McDaniel, Elmer G., Sec. & Treas.--Alabama Electric Cooperative, Inc., Andalusia, AL, pg. 28
McDaniel, Gary P., Chm., Chief Exec. Officer & Sec.--ROC Properties Inc., Englewood, CO, pg. 908
McDavid, Randall S., Asst. to Pres.-Fin. & Sec.--Union Boiler Co., Nitro, WV, pg. 273
McDonald, J.D., Jr., Sec.--PHB Parker Die Castings, Fairview, PA, pg. 836
McDonald, M.B., Sr. V.P. & Corp. Sec.--A. Y. McDonald Industries, Inc., Dubuque, IA, pg. 728
McDowell, George E., V.P., Sec. & Treas.--Clayton Corporation, Fenton, MO, pg. 253
McDowell, Gloria A., Dir.-Human Resources & Sec.--Golden State Mutual Life Insurance Company, Los Angeles, CA, pg. 467
McDowell, John, Sec.--Lewis Drug, Inc., Sioux Falls, SD, pg. 673
McEwen, Anne L., Sec.--Modern Group Ltd., Bristol, PA, pg. 762
McFadden, J. Michael, Sec. & Corp. Fin. Mgr.--Monsey Products Company, Kimberton, PA, pg. 766
McFeeley, Patrick, V.P. & Sec.--Florig Equipment Company, Inc., Conshohocken, PA, pg. 421
McGafferty, Patrick J., Sec., Treas. & Chief Fin. Officer--Grisanti, Inc., Louisville, KY, pg. 488
McGarvey, John, Sec.--MacMillan Oil Co., Inc., Des Moines, IA, pg. 475
McGee, Dennis, Sec.--Tupman Thurlow Co. Inc., New Rochelle, NY, pg. 1119
McGill, Jayne F., Sec.--United McGill Corp., Groveport, OH, pg. 1133
McGinnis, Arthur J., Jr., Chm. Bd., Pres., Chief Oper. Officer--Simmons-Boardman Publishing Corp., New York, NY, pg. 1005
McGough, H.R., Gen. Counsel & Sec.--Unigard Security Insurance Co., Bellevue, WA, pg. 596
McGough, H.R., Gen. Counsel & Sec.--Unigard Indemnity Co., Raleigh, NC, pg. 596
McGough, H.R., Gen. Counsel & Sec.--Unigard Insurance Co., Seattle, WA, pg. 596
McGough, H.R., Sec.--Unigard Service Corp., Seattle, WA, pg. 596
McGowan, Gail, Corp. Sec.--The American Bankers Association, Washington, DC, pg. 49
McGrath, Brent P., Chief Fin. Officer, Treas. & Sec.--Mico Inc., North Mankato, MN, pg. 748
McGraw, Willard G., Sec.--Glines & Rhodes, Inc., Attleboro, MA, pg. 463
McGuire, Agnes A., Sec.--Fabreeka International, Inc., Stoughton, MA, pg. 396
McGuire, Brian, V.P. & Chief Financial Officer--The "21" Club, Inc., New York, NY, pg. 1121
McIlhenny, Paul C.P., V.P. & Sec.--McIlhenny Company, Avery Island, LA, pg. 729
McInnis, Judy, Sec. & Treas.--Southern Electric Supply Co., Inc., Meridian, MS, pg. 1020
McIntyre, Richard A., V.P.-Fin., Treas. & Sec.--Blaw Knox Corp., Pittsburgh, PA, pg. 156
McInvale, Willie K., Jr., Sec. & Treas.--McNamara Pontiac Inc., Orlando, FL, pg. 732
McKaig, William D., Treas. & Sec.--Maaco Enterprises Inc., King of Prussia, PA, pg. 694
McKenna, Thomas, Sr. V.P. & Corp. Sec.--Westat Inc., Rockville, MD, pg. 1178
McKenney, M.P., Sec. & Treas.--The Figaro Company, Inc., Mesquite, TX, pg. 409
McKenny, Alice, Sec.--List Industries, Inc., Deerfield Beach, FL, pg. 677
McKensie, Linda, Sec.--UniHealth America, Burbank, CA, pg. 1126
McKenzie, James D., Pres.-Petroleum Coke Grp.--Great Lakes Carbon Corp., Briarcliff Manor, NY, pg. 545
McKew, Laurie, Sec.--Scheduling Technology Corporation, Hopkinton, MA, pg. 975
McKinney, Bert, Sec. & Treas.--Contractors Supplies, Inc., Lufkin, TX, pg. 280
McKinney, Hiram Y., Sr. V.P., Sec., Treas. & Controller--Sullivan Long & Hagerty, Inc., Birmingham, AL, pg. 1057
McKnight, H. James, V.P. & Sec.--Vectura Group, Inc., Pittsburgh, PA, pg. 1146
McLaughlin, E.H., III, Exec. V.P., Treas. & Asst. Sec.--McLaughlin Industrial Distributors, Inc., Pico Rivera, CA, pg. 731
McLaughlin, Michael W., V.P. & Sec.--SCS Engineers, Long Beach, CA, pg. 961
McLaughlin, Stephen, Sec. & Gen. Counsel--Martin Exploration Management Company, Alsip, IL, pg. 715
McLean, Rodney A., Sec.--Interstate Distributor Company, Tacoma, WA, pg. 580
McMachon, William D., Treas. & Sec.--Walker Wire & Steel Company, Ferndale, MI, pg. 1160
McMahon, Marshall I., Jr., Sec.--Northwestern Industrial Piping, Niles, IL, pg. 815
McMahon, Michael P., Sec.--Polymer Development Laboratories, Inc., Orange, CA, pg. 880
McMahon, Robert B., Chm. Bd.,Chief Exec. Officer, Treas., & Sec.--City Meats & Provisions Co., Tucsan, AZ, pg. 251
McManigal, Robert M., Sec. & Gen. Counsel--Adams Rite Manufacturing Co., City of Industry, CA, pg. 16
McNabb, Frederick W., Jr., V.P. & Asst. Sec.--Charles of the Ritz Group Ltd., New York, NY, pg. 695
McNamara, William B., Chief Fin. Officer, Treas. & Asst. Sec.--Air Conditioning Co., Inc., Glendale, CA, pg. 26
McNeil, Donna, Sec.--Line Equipment Sales Co., Inc., Charleston, SC, pg. 1141
McNeil, Joan, Sec.--Romac Industries, Inc., Seattle, WA, pg. 945
McNeil, John, Sec.--Pridgeon & Clay, Inc., Grand Rapids, MI, pg. 889
McNeil, W.R., V.P., Treas. & Sec.--Carolina Mirror Company, North Wilkesboro, NC, pg. 223
McPherson, Michael J., Sec. & Controller--Steadly Company, Carthage, MO, pg. 1043
McPherson, Sara, Corp. Sec.--G.L. Advertising, Dumont, NJ, pg. 440
McQueen, Kenneth J., V.P.-Admin. & Asst. Sec.--Ag Processing Inc A Cooperative, Omaha, NE, pg. 24
McSwiney, C. Ronald, Gen. Counsel & Sec.--Danis Industries Corporation, Dayton, OH, pg. 314
McVety, James R., Sec.--Primacare Health Resources, Inc., Syracuse, NY, pg. 1070
Meaney, George, V.P.-Fin. & Sec.--Prince Manufacturing, Inc., Lawrenceville, NJ, pg. 890
Medico, Cataldo, Sec.--Medico Industries, Inc., Wilkes-Barre, PA, pg. 735
Meglaughlin, William T., Jr., Sec. & Treas.--Asbury Graphite Mills, Inc., Asbury, NJ, pg. 87
Mehra, Ajay, Sec., Treas. & Controller--UDT Sensors, Inc., Hawthorne, CA, pg. 1122
Meier, Karen, Sec.--S.B. Foot Tanning Co., Red Wing, MN, pg. 919
Meinck, Milton M., V.P., Gen. Mgr. & Sec.--Cox & Company, Inc., New York, NY, pg. 292
Melia, Edward A., Sec.--A. Levy & J. Zentner Co., Sacramento, CA, pg. 671
Melloy, Patrick C., V.P., Sec. & Treas.--Melloy Bros. Enterprises, Albuquerque, NM, pg. 738
Melnick, Jack, Sec. & Treas.--Young Stuff Apparel Group, Inc., New York, NY, pg. 1214
Memmel, Jan, Sec.--Arandell-Schmidt Corporation, Menomonee Falls, WI, pg. 79
Mendela, Paul, Chief Fin. Officer & Corp. Sec.--Margeotes Fertitta & Weiss, Inc., New York, NY, pg. 706
Mendello, William L., Exec. V.P., Sec. & Treas.--Fender Musical Instruments, Scottsdale, AZ, pg. 406
Mendelson, Herbert, V.P. & Asst. Sec.--Georgetown Partners, Inc., Great Neck, NY, pg. 473
Mendelson, Ida, Sec.--Murry's, Inc., Forestville, MD, pg. 777
Menke, Gerald T., Treas. & Sec.--The F. D. Lawrence Electric Co., Cincinnati, OH, pg. 661
Mereschuk, Jeff, Sec.--Curries Company, Mason City, IA, pg. 361
Mereschuk, Jeffrey A., V.P. & Chief Fin. Officer--Essex Industries, New Haven, CT, pg. 361
Merkef, Donald O., V.P., Sec. & Dir.-Pur. & Data Processing--E.W. Knauss & Son, Inc., Quakertown, PA, pg. 636
Merksamer, Jon R., V.P. & Sec.--De Vons Jewelers, Sacramento, CA, pg. 321
Merksamer, Steven A., Asst. Sec.--De Vons Jewelers, Sacramento, CA, pg. 321
Merritt, Terry, Asst. Corp. Sec. & Pub. Rels. Coord.--Walbridge Aldinger Company, Detroit, MI, pg. 1158
Merse, Lawrence A., V.P.-Fin. & Sec.--Federal Business Products, Inc., Clifton, NJ, pg. 404
Mertz, J. Doug, II, V.P., Sec. & Media Dir.--Meyocks Benkstein Associates, Des Moines, IA, pg. 746
Merwin, B.M., Sec.--Eriez Magnetics, Erie, PA, pg. 386
Messick, Alan, Sec. & Treas.--Palm Iron & Bridge Works, Inc., Sacramento, CA, pg. 843
Messick, Rose, Corp. Sec. & Dir., Acctg. Services--Bernstein-Rein Advertising, Inc., Kansas City, MO, pg. 144
Messmore, Larry, Sec. & Treas.--Curt Bullock Builders, Inc., Danville, IL, pg. 188
Metcalf, Robert, Sec. & Treas.--Smyth, Bauer & Lewis Advertising Inc., Richmond, VA, pg. 1014
Metcalfe, Walter L., Jr., Sec.--Hughes Advertising Inc., Saint Louis, MO, pg. 551
Mevs, Tracy P., Treas. & Corp. Sec.--Zilkha Energy Company, Houston, TX, pg. 1219
Meyer, Gary, Sec. & Treas.--Sloans Supermarkets, Inc., New York, NY, pg. 1010
Meyer, Tim, Sec.--Winters Welding Works, Inc., Winters, TX, pg. 1197
Meyerding, Charles E., Sec.--Villaume Industries, Inc., Saint Paul, MN, pg. 1151
Meyler, Frank M., V.P., Sec. & Gen. Counsel--American Bureau of Shipping, New York, NY, pg. 50
Mezan, Richard, Sec.--Bestform Foundations, Inc., Long Island City, NY, pg. 147
Micallef, J.S., Sec.--Dietzgen Corporation, Des Plaines, IL, pg. 337
Michel, Gary, Treas. & Sec.--Todd Pipe & Supply Hawthorne, Hawthorne, CA, pg. 1100
Michener, Sally R., Sec. & Dir.-Personnel & Pub. Rels.--Scott Specialty Gases, Inc., Plumsteadville, PA, pg. 983
Michie, Bob, Chief Fin. Officer, Treas. & Sec.--Archer/Malmo Adv., Inc., Memphis, TN, pg. 80
Mikovich, Fran, Sec. & Treas.--Orleans Materials & Equipment Co., Inc., New Orleans, LA, pg. 829
Milano, Sandro, Sec. & Treas.--Butera Finer Foods Inc., Elgin, IL, pg. 196
Milfs, Audrey L., V.P. & Sec.--Pacific Mutual Life Insurance Company, Newport Beach, CA, pg. 841
Miller, Carmen Strite, Sec.--Shenandoah Mfg. Co. Inc., Harrisonburg, VA, pg. 997
Miller, Charles, Corp. Sec.--American Management Group, Westbrook, ME, pg. 57
Miller, Charles L., Sr. V.P., Sec., & Pres.-Publications Div.--Roberts Communications Inc., East Rochester, NY, pg. 938
Miller, Dan, Sec. & Controller--Ritchie Industries, Inc., Conrad, IA, pg. 936
Miller, Donald, Controller & Sec.--Schwan's Sales Enterprises, Marshall, MN, pg. 980
Miller, Donald, Treas. & Sec.--Lee Grocery Company, Everett, WA, pg. 665
Miller, Edward, Sec.--Fremont Forest Products, Whittier, CA, pg. 432
Miller, Edwin L., Sec.--Broadcast Electronics, Inc., Quincy, IL, pg. 177
Miller, Floyd H., Sec. & Treas.--Valley Pontiac Buick GMC, Inc., Auburn, WA, pg. 1143
Miller, Harbaugh, Sec.--Steelite, Inc., Pittsburgh, PA, pg. 1044
Miller, Harvey L., Sec.--Quill Corp., Lincolnshire, IL, pg. 905
Miller, Helen B., Treas. & Sec.--Washington Corporation, Missoula, MT, pg. 1165
Miller, Helen P., Sec.--Intermountain Farmers Association, Salt Lake City, UT, pg. 575
Miller, Howard, Vice Chm. & Sec.--Dynamic Metal Products Company, Manchester, CT, pg. 356
Miller, James, Sec.--Ludington News Co. Inc., Detroit, MI, pg. 686
Miller, Jay, V.P.-Fin., Treas. & Sec.--Perfection Bakeries Inc., Fort Wayne, IN, pg. 861
Miller, Jill, Sec.--Channel Home Centers Inc., Whippany, NJ, pg. 238
Miller, Katherine, Sec. & Treas.--Pyromet, Inc., Aston, PA, pg. 901
Miller, Lawrence, Sr. V.P., Deputy Gen. Counsel & Asst. Sec.--Young & Rubicam Inc., New York, NY, pg. 1210
Miller, Lloyd A., V.P., Treas. & Sec.--Midway Products Corporation, Monroe, MI, pg. 751
Miller, Lucia, Sec.--Garden Way, Inc., Troy, NY, pg. 443
Miller, Margaret, Sec.--Farrar, Straus & Giroux, Inc., New York, NY, pg. 403
Miller, Neal D., V.P., Treas. & Sec.--Hasslocher Enterprises, Inc., d/b/a Frontier Enterprises, San Antonio, TX, pg. 516
Miller, Nicole, Sec.--Miller Advertising Agency Inc., New York, NY, pg. 753
Miller, Nina J., Sec.--Prentiss Incorporated, Floral Park, NY, pg. 887
Miller, Paul, Sec.--Nacoma Consolidated, Inc., Nacogdoches, TX, pg. 782
Miller, Richard H., Sec.--Meridian Industries, Inc., Milwaukee, WI, pg. 740
Miller, Richard L., Exec. V.P., Treas. & Sec.--Miller Transporters, Inc., Jackson, MS, pg. 334
Miller, Ross, Treas. & Sec.--Harris Steel Co., Chicago, IL, pg. 512
Millimet, Joseph, Sec.--Harvey Construction Company, Inc., Bedford, NH, pg. 515
Mills, Olan, III, Chm. Bd. & Sec.--Olan Mills, Inc., Chattanooga, TN, pg. 756
Mills, Stanley R., V.P., Gen. Counsel & Sec.--Delaware North Companies, Inc., Buffalo, NY, pg. 326
Milota, Bernard F., High Sec. & Treas.--Catholic Order of Foresters, Naperville, IL, pg. 229
Miner, Martin P., Sec.--Coat, Apron & Linen Supply, Bronx, NY, pg. 257
Minnaugh, Mark, V.P.-Fin. & Accounting--Giant Eagle, Inc., Pittsburgh, PA, pg. 455
Minnick, Terry, Chm. Bd., Pres. & Chief Exec. Officer--The Pro Corporation, Florence, MA, pg. 891
Minor, Karen, Exec. Sec.--McNeil & NRM., Inc., Akron, OH, pg. 732
Minori, Thomas M., Asst. Sec.--Stabler Companies, Inc., Harrisburg, PA, pg. 1034
Miranda, Gerald, Dir. & Corp. Sec.--BSB Malaysia Sdn. Bhd., Kuala Lumpur,, Malaysia, pg. 110
Miranda, Jose J., Chief Oper. Officer & Exec. V.P.--Gator Industries Inc., Hialeah, FL, pg. 446
Mistick, D. Thomas, Sec.--Bridges & Company, Inc., Pittsburgh, PA, pg. 175

Mistretta, F. David, V.P., Gen. Counsel & Sec.--Security Mutual Life Insurance Co. of New York, Binghamton, NY, pg. 987
Mitchel, Michael M., V.P.--Economy Folding Box Corp., Chicago, IL, pg. 367
Mitchel, Stephen, V.P., Sec. & Treas.--Mitchel & Scot Machine Co., Inc., Indianapolis, IN, pg. 761
Mitchell, Alan, Sec. & Treas.--Service Web Offset Corporation, Chicago, IL, pg. 992
Mitchell, Randy, Sec. & Treas.--The Hotsy Corporation, Englewood, CO, pg. 545
Mitchell, Robert J., Treas. & Asst. Sec.--ACF Industries, Inc., Earth City, MO, pg. 561
Mitchell, Ted, Treas. & Sec.--Columbia Sussex Corporation, Fort Mitchell, KY, pg. 266
Mitchell, William E., Sec.--Binning's Building Products, Inc., Lexington, NC, pg. 151
Mitchum, Billy E., Sec. & Treas.--Defender Services, Inc., Columbia, SC, pg. 324
Mitteness, Elaine, Sec.--Tyler Limited Partnership, Benson, MN, pg. 1122
Mize, Mike, V.P.-Corp. Plng. & Devel., Chief Fin. Officer, Sec. & Treas.--GSC Enterprises, Inc., Sulphur Springs, TX, pg. 440
Mock, C. A., V.P., Sec. & Chief Fin. Officer--Consolidated Pipe & Supply Company, Birmingham, AL, pg. 277
Moderow, Joseph, Sr. V.P. & Sec., Legal & Public Affairs--United Parcel Service of America, Inc., Atlanta, GA, pg. 1133
Mohl, Anthony S., V.P. & Asst. Sec.--W. P. Carey & Co., Inc., New York, NY, pg. 218
Mohr, John R., Sr. V.P., Gen. Counsel & Sec.--Ponderosa, Inc., Vandalia, OH, pg. 743
Moix, Norbert, Sec. & Treas.--Nabholz Construction Corp., Conway, AR, pg. 782
Mollenberg, Trudy, Sec.--Adam Meldrum & Anderson Co., Inc., Buffalo, NY, pg. 16
Monson, John, Sec.--Colonial Supply Corporation, Manchester, NH, pg. 264
Montgomery, Scott, Exec. V.P., Sec. & Creative Dir.--Salvati Montgomery Sakoda, Inc., Costa Mesa, CA, pg. 967
Mood, Alfred, Treas. & Sec.--Pyramid Mountain Lumber, Seeley Lake, MT, pg. 901
Moody, Catherine, Sec.--The Tog Shop, Americus, GA, pg. 1100
Moody, Marilyn S., Sec.--Thermal Technology Industries, N. Kansas City, MO, pg. 1091
Moon, Floyd, Treas. & Asst. Sec.--Deseret Management Corporation, Salt Lake City, UT, pg. 332
Moore, Anne, Sec.--Orbit Valve International, Inc., Little Rock, AR, pg. 828
Moore, Brant R., Chief Fin. Officer, Treas. & Sec.--I. H. French & Co. Inc., Champaign, IL, pg. 432
Moore, Charles, Corp. Sec.--Affiliated Foods Southwest, Little Rock, AR, pg. 24
Moore, Dan, V.P., Sec. & Gen. Counsel--Curtis Mathes Corporation, Athens, TX, pg. 720
Moore, Elizabeth, Sec.--Harold Moore & Associates, Inc., Fayetteville, TN, pg. 768
Moore, James O., V.P.-Fin., Treas. & Asst. Sec.--Cullman Ventures, Inc., New York, NY, pg. 304
Moore, Kenneth G., V.P. & Sec.--Banner Associates Inc., Laramie, WY, pg. 118
Moore, Kevin, Sec. & Treas.--Allsop, Inc., Bellingham, WA, pg. 43
Moore, Leroy E., Sec. & Treas.--Thrifty Drug Stores, Inc., Minneapolis, MN, pg. 1096
Moore, Lester W.B., Sr. V.P., Sec. & Sls.-Fast Food Service--E.A. Sween Company, Eden Prairie, MN, pg. 1066
Moore, P.J., Sr. V.P., Chief Oper. Officer, Chief Fin. Officer, Sec. & Treas.--Green Holdings, Inc., Denver, CO, pg. 484
Moore, P.J., Sr. V.P., Chief Fin. Officer, Sec. & Treas.--Green International, Inc., Denver, CO, pg. 484
Moore, P.J., Sr. V.P., Sec. & Treas.--Green Mining, Inc., Denver, CO, pg. 484
Moore, P.J., Sr. V.P., Treas. & Sec.--C.C. Conley & Sons, Inc., Denver, CO, pg. 484
Moore, P.J., Sr. V.P., Sec. & Treas.--Green International-Guyana, Inc., Denver, CO, pg. 484
Moore, Peter F., Deputy Sec.--Moore Company, Westerly, RI, pg. 768
Moore, Robert, V.P.-Fin. & Sec.--Roubin & Janeiro, Inc., Fairfax, VA, pg. 952
Moore, Samuel N., Sec.--Fairfax Lumber & Millwork Company Inc., Springfield, VA, pg. 397
Moore, Tom, Sec.--Electro-Matic Products Inc., Farmington Hills, MI, pg. 374
Mora, R. N., Sec. & Gen. Counsel--The HOH Organizations, Chicago, IL, pg. 497
Moran, G., Sec.--The Campaign Palace, Melbourne,, Australia, pg. 111
Moran, Henry A., Jr., Sec.--Berkshire Industries, Inc., Westfield, MA, pg. 142
Moran, John D., Sec. & Gen. Counsel--Sealy Corporation, Cleveland, OH, pg. 985
Moran, Kevin, Treas. & Sec.--TSI Industries, Inc., Landover, MD, pg. 1075
Morgan, Donna, Treas. & Sec.--Southgate Ford Inc., Southgate, MI, pg. 1023
Morgan, James A., V.P.-Fin. & Sec.--Tubular Steel Inc., Saint Louis, MO, pg. 1118
Morgan, Paul, Treas. & Sec.--F.P.A., Inc., Irving, TX, pg. 394
Morgan, Suzanne, V.P. & Sec.--Morgan Industries Inc., Bala-Cynwyd, PA, pg. 770
Morgan, V. Harley, Exec. V.P. & Sec.--Northwest Paper Converting Company, Vancouver, WA, pg. 814
Morgan, Virginia, Asst. Sec.--Lario Enterprises, Inc., Wichita, KS, pg. 659
Morrin, Nancy, V.P. & Asst. Sec.--ELS Educational Services, Culver City, CA, pg. 56
Morris, Ann P., Sec.--Peirce-Phelps, Inc., Philadelphia, PA, pg. 855
Morris, Ben F., V.P.-Admin. & Sec.--The Osterneck Co. Inc., Lumberton, NC, pg. 831
Morris, Donna R., Dir.-Investor Rels., Asst. Sec. & Treas.--Walk, Haydel & Associates, Inc., New Orleans, LA, pg. 1159
Morris, Dorothy M., Sec.--The Robert E. Morris Company, Farmington, CT, pg. 771
Morris, J. Malcolm, V.P., Gen. Counsel & Sec.--Ziff Communications Company, New York, NY, pg. 1218
Morris, Kathryn L., Sec. & Treas.--Acorn Engineering Company, City of Industry, CA, pg. 14
Morris, Margaret M., Asst. Sec.--Transus Inc., Atlanta, GA, pg. 1108
Morris, Melvin, Treas. & Sec.--Mountain States Constructors, Inc., Albuquerque, NM, pg. 773
Morris, Thomas F., Exec. V.P. & Chief Fin. Officer--World's Finest Chocolate, Inc., Chicago, IL, pg. 1203
Morris, Walter K., Sr. V.P.-Water Resources & Asst. Sec.--Gannett Fleming Affiliates, Inc., Harrisburg, PA, pg. 442
Morrison, Corinne, Asst. Sec.--CSE Corporation, San Francisco, CA, pg. 204
Morrison, Kathryn D., V.P., Sec., Treas. & Pub. Rels. Dir.--The Morrison Agency, Atlanta, GA, pg. 771
Morrison, Robert, Sec.--The Hercules Tire & Rubber Company, Findlay, OH, pg. 531
Morrison, Wyatt F., Asst. Sec. & Dir.--Shipley Oil Company, York, PA, pg. 999
Morrissey, Eugene, Sec.--Dana Perfumes Corp., New York, NY, pg. 313
Morrisson, A.S., V.P., Sec. & Gen. Counsel--Sverdrup Corporation, Maryland Heights, MO, pg. 1065
Morse, John H., Sec.--National Forge Company, Irvine, PA, pg. 788
Mortensen, Morris D., Sec.--Puget Sound Plywood, Inc., Tacoma, WA, pg. 899
Morton, Grant, Sec. & Treas.--E.H. Hughes Company, Inc., Louisville, KY, pg. 552
Morton, John H., Sec.--International Shoe Machine Corp., Nashua, NH, pg. 579
Moseley, Thomas J., V.P.-Acctg. & Sec.--Loxcreen Company, West Columbia, SC, pg. 686
Moser, Eugene R., Sec. & Treas.--Sioux Falls Construction Company, Sioux Falls, SD, pg. 1008
Moskowitz, Robert, Sec.--Sound Warehouse, Inc., Dallas, TX, pg. 1018
Moss, Victor, Pres. & Sec.--Tomco Auto Products, Inc., Vernon, CA, pg. 1100
Motola, Joseph C., Chief Fin. Officer, V.P.-Fin. & Sec.--Farnam Companies, Inc., Phoenix, AZ, pg. 403
Motzer, William R., V.P., Chief Fin. Officer & Sec.--Berwind Pharmaceuticals Services, Inc., King of Prussia, PA, pg. 145
Mount, Brian D., Exec. V.P., Creative Dir., Sec. & Treas.--Young & Roehr, Inc., Portland, OR, pg. 1210
Mowinski, Josephine, Sec.--Fabex Inc., Novi, MI, pg. 395
Moyers, Donald L., Treas., Sec. & Controller--Riddleberger Brothers, Inc., Mount Crawford, VA, pg. 933
Muccino, Robert D., Controller & Sec.--Frank Briscoe Co. Inc., Roseland, NJ, pg. 176
Mudd, Thomas A., Sec. & Treas.--Doe-Anderson Advertising Agency, Inc., Louisville, KY, pg. 342
Muehlbauer, James H., Exec. V.P. & Sec.--George Koch Sons, Inc., Evansville, IN, pg. 639
Mueller, Dorothy, Sec. & Treas.--Lombard Lincoln-Mercury & Leasing, Inc., Lombard, IL, pg. 681
Mueller, Lony, Sec.--Mulberry Metal Products, Inc., Union, NJ, pg. 775
Mueller, Paula, Sec.--Dualite Sales & Service, Inc., Williamsburg, OH, pg. 350
Muff, Walter, Sec.--Norfoods, Inc., Overland Park, KS, pg. 810
Muff, Walter, Sec.--Garnac Grain Co., Inc., Overland Park, KS, pg. 810
Mullen, Charles, Sec.--Pacific Sound Resources, Seattle, WA, pg. 841
Mullen, Larry J., V.P.-Sls., Sec. & Treas.--Terral-Norris Seed Co., Inc., Lake Providence, LA, pg. 1088
Mulliken, W.D., V.P., Sec. & Gen. Counsel--CHEMCENTRAL Corporation, Bedford Park, IL, pg. 241
Mullinix, H.M., V.P.-Admin. & Sec.--Ziegler Inc., Minneapolis, MN, pg. 1218
Mullins, Kay J., Treas. & Sec.--Rockford Acromatic Product Co., Rockford, IL, pg. 941
Muncy, Darlene, V.P., Dir. Acctg., Sec. & Treas.--Caldwell VanRiper Inc., Indianapolis, IN, pg. 209
Mundy, Gardner M., Gen. Counsel & Sec.--Johnson & Higgins, New York, NY, pg. 598
Munigle, Jo Ann, Sec.--Munigle Corporation, West Hartford, CT, pg. 775
Munita, Albert R., Asst. Sec.--Duron, Inc., Beltsville, MD, pg. 355
Munro, M. Vance, Sec.--Heath Consultants Incorporated, Stoughton, MA, pg. 524
Muratori, Jack R., Exec. V.P. & Sec.--King Kullen Grocery Co., Inc., Westbury, NY, pg. 630
Murdock, Jack C., V.P.-Fin., Sec. & Treas.--Transus Inc., Atlanta, GA, pg. 1108
Murdock, Joanne E., Corp. Sec.--Murdock, Inc., Compton, CA, pg. 776
Murphy, J. Lee, Sec.--Windemuller Electric Inc., Grandville, MI, pg. 1195
Murphy, John, Sec.--Murphy Company, Eugene, OR, pg. 776
Murphy, Joseph P., Sec.--Southwest Floor Covering Inc., San Diego, CA, pg. 1023
Murphy, Karen, V.P., Sec. & Treas.--California Pacific Research, Inc., Reno, NV, pg. 210
Murphy, Kevin s., Sec. & Treas.--Michael Foods, Inc., Minneapolis, MN, pg. 747
Murphy, Sheila E., Asst. to Pres., Office Mgr. & Asst. Sec.--W. P. Carey & Co., Inc., New York, NY, pg. 218
Murphy, Wayne, Sec.--Norcostco, Inc., Minneapolis, MN, pg. 809
Murray, D.D., Treas. & Asst. Sec.--Green Holdings, Inc., Denver, CO, pg. 484
Murray, D.D., Asst. Sec.--Green International, Inc., Denver, CO, pg. 484
Murray, John J., V.P.-Fin., Sec. & Treas.--Electro-Wire Products, Inc., Rochester Hills, MI, pg. 375
Murray, John T., Treas. & Sec.--Tinius Olsen Testing Machine Co., Inc., Willow Grove, PA, pg. 1098
Murray, R.W., Chief Fin. Officer, Sr. V.P., Treas., Controller & Sec.--Webb, Murray & Associates, La Porte, TX, pg. 1170
Murray, Virginia, Sec.--Ashworth Bros., Inc., Fall River, MA, pg. 88
Murtaugh, J. R., V.P.-Fin., Sec. & Treas.--Anser (Analytic Services Inc.), Arlington, VA, pg. 76
Muscarello, Diane, Sec. & Treas.--Westgate Inc., Port Allen, LA, pg. 1182
Muse, Charles H., Jr., Treas. & Chief Fin. Officer--Crown Coal & Coke Co. Inc., Pittsburgh, PA, pg. 302
Musgrove, Judith, Exec. Sec.--Muro Pharmaceutical, Inc., Tewksbury, MA, pg. 776
Muskus, John F., Corp. Sec.--Marketing Corp. of America, Westport, CT, pg. 709
Muth, Mary M., Sec.--Orco Block Company, Stanton, CA, pg. 828
Myer, Karen, Corp. Sec.--Corporex Companies, Inc., Covington, KY, pg. 287
Myers, Everett, Sec.--Monte Vista Co-Op Association, Inc., Monte Vista, CO, pg. 766
Myers, Joe N., Treas. & Sec.--T. H. Rogers Lumber Co. Inc., Oklahoma City, OK, pg. 943
Myers, John E., Sec.--Dixon Valve & Coupling Company, Chestertown, MD, pg. 341
Myers, Larry F., Sr. V.P., Chief Fin. Officer, Sec. & Treas.--Mitre Corporation, Bedford, MA, pg. 762
Myerson, James, Treas. & Sec.--Ben Myerson Candy Company, Inc., Los Angeles, CA, pg. 780
Myrick, B. Harold, Jr., V.P. & Sec.--Myrick Construction Inc., Biscoe, NC, pg. 780
Nackenson, Leon, Sec.--Louis Dreyfus Corporation, Wilton, CT, pg. 348
Nadel, Martin, Sec.--Measured Marketing Services, Los Angeles, CA, pg. 734
Najdzin, Jean, Sec.--Scott Printing Corporation, Jersey City, NJ, pg. 983
Nakash, Ralph, Treas. & Sec.--Jordache Enterprises, Inc., New York, NY, pg. 604
Nappo, Margot, Asst. Sec.--F. Schumacher & Co., New York, NY, pg. 979
Naquin, Gasper K., Sec. & Treas.--Intrepid Enterprises, Inc., Harvey, LA, pg. 581
Nash, Bedky, Sec. of the Authority--Regional Transportation Authority (RTA), Chicago, IL, pg. 922
Nathan, Stuart C., V.P.--JMB Realty Corporation, Chicago, IL, pg. 584
Naylor, Chuck, V.P. & Gen. Counsel--FDL Foods, Inc., Dubuque, IA, pg. 394
Naylor, John, Sec.--Kendale Industries, Inc., Valley View, OH, pg. 622
Nazarian, Robert G., Corp. Sec.--Levonian Brothers Inc., Troy, NY, pg. 671
Neff, William, Sec.--New Standard Corporation, Mount Joy, PA, pg. 802
Negomeir, George R., V.P.-Fin., Treas. & Sec.--Sigman Meat Co. Inc., Arvada, CO, pg. 1003
Nehrkorn, William H., V.P., Sec. & Gen. Counsel--The Heil Co., Chattanooga, TN, pg. 525
Neilson, L., Sec. & Gen. Counsel--L. B. Smith, Inc., Camp Hill, PA, pg. 1013
Nellen, James W., II, V.P., Gen. Counsel & Sec.--Fort Howard Corporation, Green Bay, WI, pg. 425
Nellis, Kirk, Controller, Treas. & Sec.--Harley Industries, Inc., Tulsa, OK, pg. 509
Nelson, F.C., V.P. & Sec.--Hershey Creamery Company, Harrisburg, PA, pg. 531
Nelson, Kenneth A., V.P.-Electrical & Asst. Sec.--The Benham Group, Oklahoma City, OK, pg. 138
Nelson, Lloyd, Sr. V.P., Dir.-Admin. & Asst. Sec.--Federated Mutual Insurance Company, Owatonna, MN, pg. 405
Nelson, Owen, Gen. Counsel & Sec.--Bergquist Company, Inc., Minneapolis, MN, pg. 141
Nelson, Ralph S., Exec. V.P., Sec. & Gen. Counsel--Burlington Motor Carriers Inc., Daleville, IN, pg. 191
Nelson, Rosemary, Sr. V.P., Gen. Counsel & Asst. Sec.--Young & Rubicam Inc., New York, NY, pg. 1210
Nelson, Wesley, V.P. & Sec.--H. E. Butt Grocery Co., San Antonio, TX, pg. 197
Nemschoff, Leonard, Chm. Bd. & Sec.--Nemschoff Chairs, Inc., Sheboygan, WI, pg. 798
Nestor, John G., Sec.--Bristol Products, L.P., Bristol, IN, pg. 176
Netzsch, Wolfgang, Sec. & Treas.--Netzsch, Inc., Exton, PA, pg. 798
Neubert, Marie, Sec.--North American Enclosures, Inc., Central Islip, NY, pg. 811
Neville, James D., Exec. V.P., Chief Fin. Officer, Treas. & Sec.--The North American Manufacturing Co., Cleveland, OH, pg. 811
Newallis, Eleanor, Sec.--Roselle Paper Co., Inc., Roselle, NJ, pg. 948
Newgard, James H., Sec. & Treas.--Henry Newgard & Company, Arlington Heights, IL, pg. 804
Newman, Sanders D., Sr. V.P., Sec. & Gen. Counsel--O'Brien Energy Systems Inc., Philadelphia, PA, pg. 820
Newsom, Jan R., Sr. V.P., Gen. Counsel & Sec.--Blue Cross & Blue Shield of Texas, Inc., Richardson, TX, pg. 160
Newton, Millie, Sec.--Waremart Inc., Boise, ID, pg. 1163
Newton, Stanley B., V.P., Treas. & Sec.--Holmes Tuttle Ford, Inc., Tucson, AZ, pg. 540
Neyer, William, Sec.--Al Neyer, Inc., Cincinnati, OH, pg. 805

Niarchos, Michael C., Sr. V.P., Gen. Counsel & Sec.--Summa Corporation, Las Vegas, NV, pg. 1057
Nicholas, Francine, Assoc. Counsel--Peter J. Schmitt Holdings, West Seneca, NY, pg. 976
Nicholas, Francine, Gen. Counsel & Corp. Sec.--Peter J. Schmitt Co., Inc., West Seneca, NY, pg. 977
Nichols, Jacques B., Treas. & Sec.--Fabric Wholesalers, Inc., Portland, OR, pg. 396
Nichols, John R., Sec.--Bradford Company, Holland, MI, pg. 170
Nichols, Wade H. III, V.P. & Sec.--Charles of the Ritz Group Ltd., New York, NY, pg. 695
Nicholson, David, V.P. & Sec.--Rock-Tenn Company, Norcross, GA, pg. 941
Nickerson, Louise, Sec.--Nickerson Lumber Company, Orleans, MA, pg. 806
Nickles, R., Treas. & Sec.--The Dickerson Group, Inc., Monroe, NC, pg. 335
Nicola, Shirley, Sec., Treas. & Office Mgr.--Penny & Speier Inc., Houston, TX, pg. 858
Nicolai, Ray, Sec.--Dakota Electric Association, Farmington, MN, pg. 312
Nicolaus, Penny, Sec. & Treas.--Plymouth Creameries, Inc., Plymouth, WI, pg. 877
Nidiffer, M. June, Treas. & Sec.--C & K Markets, Inc., Brookings, OR, pg. 198
Niedens, Douglas, Sec. & Treas.--Universal Construction Company, Kansas City, KS, pg. 1138
Nielsen, Roberta D., Sec.--Martin K. Eby Construction Company, Inc., Wichita, KS, pg. 365
Niemeyer, Vernon, Sec.--New Cooperative Inc., Fort Dodge, IA, pg. 799
Niemiec, Thom, Treas. & Sec.--The Tech Group, Scottsdale, AZ, pg. 1082
Nikkel, Margarita, Sec. & Treas.--The Nikkel Corporation, Sacramento, CA, pg. 807
Nimnicht, Ann, Controller, Treas. & Sec.--Nimnicht Chevrolet Company, Jacksonville, FL, pg. 807
Nohejl, Robert, V.P.-Fin. & Sec.--Imperial Pearl Company, Inc., Providence, RI, pg. 564
Nolan, Steve, Sec.--Grey Eagle Distributors Inc., Maryland Heights, MO, pg. 486
Nominees, Crislaw, Corp. Sec.--Insight Communications Ltd., Lagos,, Nigeria, pg. 111
Nonn, James C., Sec. & Treas.--Pemko Manufacturing Company, Ventura, CA, pg. 856
Noonan, John F., Sec.--Dreisbach & Sons Cadillac Company, Detroit, MI, pg. 348
Nordhougen, C.A., Sec. & Gen. Counsel--American Crystal Sugar Company, Moorhead, MN, pg. 51
Nordstrom, William, Chief Fin. Officer & Sec.--Amana-Nordstrom Motel Co., Amana, IA, pg. 46
Noren, Florence, Sec.--Marcal Paper Mills, Inc., Elmwood Park, NJ, pg. 706
Norman, James G., Sec. & Treas.--Norman Brothers Nissan Inc., Orlando, FL, pg. 810
Norris, Francis J., Treas. & Sec.--Mannington Mills, Inc., Salem, NJ, pg. 704
Norris, Robert N., Sec.--Harvey Industries, Inc., Waltham, MA, pg. 515
North, Richard J., V.P., Sec. & Treas.--Miller & Smith, Inc., McLean, VA, pg. 755
Norwood, Kevin, Sec. & Gen. Counsel--KNOX International Corp., Knoxville, TN, pg. 638
Norwood, Kevin, Sec.--Weinstock's Flowers & Gifts, Atlanta, GA, pg. 638
Norwood, Kevin, Sec.--Michigan Bulb Company, Grand Rapids, MI, pg. 638
Nothnagel, E., Sec.--Weinberger Werbehaus Ges.m.b.H & Co. KG, Vienna,, Austria, pg. 105
Nougus-Sans, Marquerite, Corp. Sec., Asst. Gen. Counsel--North American Watch Corporation, Lyndhurst, NJ, pg. 812
Nowacki, Kajetan, Sec. & Treas.--Velcon Filters, Inc., San Jose, CA, pg. 1146
Nower, Jay, Sec.--Atchison County Co-op Association, Atchison, KS, pg. 93
Null, Lester H., Sr., Treas. & Sec.--ULLICO Inc., Washington, DC, pg. 1124
Nunez, Olga M., Sec.--Northwestern Meats Inc., Miami, FL, pg. 815
Nussbaum, Patricia, Sec.--Southern Foods, Inc., Greensboro, NC, pg. 1021
O'Brien, J. Michael, V.P.-Sls. & Sec.--American Cast Iron Pipe Co., Birmingham, AL, pg. 50
O'Brien, Richard M., Sec. & Treas.--Gibraltar Steel Corp., Buffalo, NY, pg. 456
O'Callaghan, R.A., Chief Exec. Officer--Universal Builders Supply, Inc., Mount Vernon, NY, pg. 1137
O'Conner, Susan S., V.P. & Sec.--Silver's Inc., Detroit, MI, pg. 1005
O'Connor, John K., Sec.--Vincent Food Industries, Inc., Chicago, IL, pg. 1152
O'Connor, Paul R., Sec., Treas. & Chief Fin. Officer--F.A. Wilhelm Construction Co., Inc., Indianapolis, IN, pg. 1189
O'Dell, M.P., Sec.--Denver Equipment Company, Colorado Springs, CO, pg. 331
O'Donahue, Claudia, Exec. V.P., Sec. & Treas.--Reid & O'Donahue Advertising, Inc., Montgomery, AL, pg. 923
O'Hara, Michael, Sec.--Omaha Public Power District, Omaha, NE, pg. 825
O'Leary, John, V.P.-Fin., Treas. & Sec.--Republic Storage Systems Company Inc., Canton, OH, pg. 928
O'Leary, Thomas M., Chief Fin. Officer & Gen Counsel--The Pepper Companies, Inc., Chicago, IL, pg. 859
O'Neil, P.A., Treas. & Sec.--O'Neil Industries Inc., Chicago, IL, pg. 827
O'Neill, Robert B., V.P., Gen. Counsel & Sec.--Capitol Industries-EMI Inc., Hollywood, CA, pg. 216
O'Shaughnessy, Gerald E., V.P. & Sec.--Lario Oil & Gas Company, Wichita, KS, pg. 658
O'Shaughnessy, P., V.P. & Sec.--Lario Enterprises, Inc., Wichita, KS, pg. 659
Oakes, Gary D., Corp. Sec.--Estes Express Lines, Inc., Richmond, VA, pg. 389
Oakley, Milton V., Vice Chm. & Sec.--Yorktowne Paper Mills, Inc., York, PA, pg. 1208
Oakley, Roy, Sec.--Cornucopia, Inc., Irvine, CA, pg. 287
Oberembet, Jerome J., Sec. & Treas.--Consolidated Lumber Co., Stillwater, MN, pg. 276
Oberhauser, Louis B., Corp. Sec.--AmeriData, Inc., Minneapolis, MN, pg. 66
Obert, Paul R., V.P., Gen. Counsel & Sec.--CF Industries, Inc., Long Grove, IL, pg. 200
Oberweis, Marie, Sec.--Oberweis Dairy, Inc., Aurora, IL, pg. 820
Offen, Chris, V.P.-Mktg.--Solvay Pharmaceuticals, Inc., Marietta, GA, pg. 1017
Okinow, Harold, Sec.--Carousel Snack Bars Of Minnesota, Minneapolis, MN, pg. 224
Oldfield, Russell M., V.P.-Legal & Corp. Sec.--Rogers Group Inc., Nashville, TN, pg. 943
Olen, Gary, Sec. & Exec. V.P.--The Sportsman's Guide, Inc., Eagan, MN, pg. 1032
Olinde, Humphrey T., Jr., Treas. & Sec.--B. Olinde & Sons Company, Inc., Baton Rouge, LA, pg. 824
Oliveri, Elena, V.P., Sec. & Treas.--Alleson of Rochester, Inc., Rochester, NY, pg. 37
Oliveri, Theodore A., Sec. & Treas.--Penn Colour Graphics, Inc., Huntingdon Valley, PA, pg. 857
Olsewski, Paul, V.P.-Opers. & Corp. Sec.--SB Entertainment Inc., New Providence, NJ, pg. 960
Olson, D. Joseph, V.P., Gen. Counsel & Sec.--Citizens Insurance Company of America, Howell, MI, pg. 35
Olson, David, V.P.-Treas., Sec. & Data Processing--Jesco, Inc., Minneapolis, MN, pg. 593
Olson, Elaine L., Clerk--Danafilms, Inc., Westborough, MA, pg. 313
Olson, Gene L., V.P.-Fin. & Sec.--Golden State Foods Corp., Pasadena, CA, pg. 466
Olson, Mary Jean, V.P. & Sec.--Pioneer Mutual Life Insurance Company, Fargo, ND, pg. 872
Olson, R.F., V.P., Treas. & Sec.--Treadwell Corporation, Thomaston, CT, pg. 1108
Olson, Richard F., Sec. & Treas.--Elometa Corporation, Moonachie, NJ, pg. 1108
Olsrud, Wanda J., Sec.--Sherms Thunderbird Market, Medford, OR, pg. 998
Onderdonk, Phil, Sec.--HP Direct, Indianapolis, IN, pg. 497
Oneto, Evelyn, Sec.--Hickinbotham Bros., Ltd, Stockton, CA, pg. 532
Onraet, Robert, Chief Fin. Officer--Telesciences Co. Systems Inc., Moorestown, NJ, pg. 1085
Opdike, William, Sec.--Dearden's, Inc., Los Angeles, CA, pg. 322
Opper, Lewis, Treas. & Sec.--Jacob Levy & Bros., Inc., Louisville, KY, pg. 672
Opperman, Chuck, Sec.--Expo Industries, Inc., San Diego, CA, pg. 393
Oren, Karen, Sec.--Eastway Delivery Service of Houston, Inc., Houston, TX, pg. 364
Orentzel, B., Sec.--American White Cross Laboratories, Inc., New Rochelle, NY, pg. 65
Orgill, Joseph, III, Chm. Bd. & Sec.--Orgill Brothers & Company, Inc., Memphis, TN, pg. 1178
Orlando, Ida L., Treas. & Sec.--Ortronics, Inc., Pawcatuck, CT, pg. 830
Orlin, Jay, Sec.--Joan Fabrics Corp., Tyngsboro, MA, pg. 594
Ormsby, Clarence, Sec. & Treas.--The Curtis Publishing Company, Indianapolis, IN, pg. 306
Ormsby, Clarence, V.P., Sec. & Treas.--Servaas, Inc., Indianapolis, IN, pg. 991
Ormsby, Clarence, Sec. & Treas.--Servaas Investments, Inc., Indianapolis, IN, pg. 991
Oropeza, Anne, V.P. & Sec.--Transpo Electronics, Inc., Orlando, FL, pg. 1108
Orr, S.W., Jr., Sec.--Marathon Electric Manufacturing Corp., Wausau, WI, pg. 705
Orr, Vernon R., V.P., Sec. & Controller--J.D. Diffenbaugh, Inc., Riverside, CA, pg. 337
Orsi, Bernard, Exec. V.P. & Sec.--S & P Company, Mill Valley, CA, pg. 959
Orsi, Bernard A., Sec.--General Brewing Company, Vancouver, WA, pg. 959
Ortman, Elizabeth J., Treas. & Sec.--Kokomo Grain Co., Inc., Kokomo, IN, pg. 640
Ortner, Robert C., V.P. & Sec.--Berwick Freight Car Co., Berwick, PA, pg. 246
Ortolani, Thecly L., Sec. & Treas.--Carton-Craft Corporation, Buffalo, NY, pg. 226
Osborne, Carolyn, Sec. & Dir.-Personnel--Plastigage Corporation, Jackson, MI, pg. 876
Osborne, James F., Sec.--Selectone Corporation, Hayward, CA, pg. 988
Oscherwitz, Jerry, V.P., Asst. Treas. & Sec.--Best Kosher Sausage Co., Chicago, IL, pg. 146
Oshinski, Jerry P., Exec. V.P., Treas. & Sec.--Hunter Corp., Portage, IN, pg. 554
Oshiro, Kathleen F., Sec.--Mauna Loa Macadamia Nut Corporation, Hilo, HI, pg. 174
Oshiro, Kathleen F., Sec.--Ka'u Agribusiness Co., Inc., Pahala, HI, pg. 174
Oshiro, Kathleen F., Sec.--Mauna Kea Agribusiness Co., Inc., Papaikou, HI, pg. 174
Oshiro, Kathleen F., Sec.--Olokele Sugar Co., Limited, Kaumakani, HI, pg. 174
Oshiro, Kathleen F., Sec.--Wailuku Agribusiness Co., Inc., Wailuku, HI, pg. 175
Oshiro, Kathleen F., Sec.--HT&T Company, Inc., Hilo, HI, pg. 174
Oshiro, Kathleen F., Sec.--Kilauea Agronomics, Inc., Kilauea, HI, pg. 174
Oshiro, Kathleen F., Sec.--Mauna Loa Resources Inc., Honolulu, HI, pg. 174
Oshita, Hosen, V.P., Sec. & Treas.--Newly Weds Foods Inc., Chicago, IL, pg. 804
Oshrin, Martin, Sec. & Treas.--Junior Gallery Ltd., New York, NY, pg. 609
Osland, Dean, V.P. & Sec.--Harris Mechanical Contracting Co., Saint Paul, MN, pg. 512
Ossmann, Robert E., Chief Fin. Officer, Treas. & Sec.--Heller Seasonings & Ingredients, Inc., Bedford Park, IL, pg. 526
Ostdiek, Glen R., Sec. & Treas.--Tuthill Corporation, Hinsdale, IL, pg. 1120
Oster, Stephen, Sec.--Gulf Coast Lead Company, Inc., Tampa, FL, pg. 493
Osterhouse, Donald, Sec. & Gen. Counsel--King Milling Company, Lowell, MI, pg. 631
Ott, Susan, Sec.--Ott Communications, Inc., Louisville, KY, pg. 831
Ouellette, Pierre, Sec. & Dir. Creative Services--Karakas, VanSickle Ouellette Advertising & Public Relations, Portland, OR, pg. 616
Outlan, John H., Sec. & Treas.--Winter Park Leasing, Inc., Winter Park, FL, pg. 882
Overstreet, Dorothy M., Sr. V.P. & Sec.--Overstreet Paving Company, Largo, FL, pg. 833
Ovrut, Barnett D., Assoc. Gen. Counsel & Sec.--The Hanover Insurance Company, Worcester, MA, pg. 34
Owen, Dolores, Sec. & Treas.--Owen Industries, Inc., Carter Lake, IA, pg. 834
Owen, Elizabeth G., Sec.--Owen Steel Co., Inc., Columbia, SC, pg. 834
Owen, Judith E., V.P. & Sec.--Avis Industrial Corporation, Upland, IN, pg. 102
Owen, Sharyl, Sec., Treas. & Chief Fin. Officer--Power-One, Inc., Camarillo, CA, pg. 883
Owen, Shirley J., Sec.--AJC International, Inc., Atlanta, GA, pg. 4
Owens, Gary, Sec.--Peerless Lighting Corp., Berkeley, CA, pg. 855
Owings, Frank, Jr., Exec. V.P., Mng. Dir., Sec. & Treas.--Service Supply Co. Inc. of Indiana, Indianapolis, IN, pg. 992
Oyola, Margie, Mgr.-Office--SLM, Inc., Gloversville, NY, pg. 963
Ozuna, Rosemary, Treas. & Sec.--New Bedford Panoramex Corporation, Upland, CA, pg. 799
Packard, Scott D., Sec. & Treas.--Cloverdale Equipment Co., Oak Park, MI, pg. 256
Padegs, Juris, Sec.--Scudder, Stevens & Clark, Inc., New York, NY, pg. 983
Padnos, Barbara, Sec.--Louis Padnos Iron & Metal Co., Holland, MI, pg. 842
Page, Doris B., Treas. & Sec.--Pace Oil Co., Inc., Winston-Salem, NC, pg. 838
Page, Tom, Sec.--RDI, Inc., Itasca, IL, pg. 906
Page, V.J., Sec. & Treas.--Kalamazoo Label Co., Kalamazoo, MI, pg. 615
Page, William N., Mng. Dir.-Admin. & Sec.--Insignia Financial Group, Inc., Greenville, SC, pg. 571
Pagel, Edward O., Sec.--Waterous Company, South Saint Paul, MN, pg. 50
Pahidis, Peter, Exec. V.P. & Sec.--Cedar Farms Company, Inc., Philadelphia, PA, pg. 230
Painter, Benjamin D., Sec. & Treas.--Borchers Bros., San Jose, CA, pg. 165
Painton, Russell E., V.P., Gen. Counsel & Sec.--Tracor, Inc., Austin, TX, pg. 1104
Palagonia, Frances, Sec.--J.M.P. Bakery Co., Inc., Brooklyn, NY, pg. 586
Palaska, Y., Sec.--Geo-Young & Rubicam, Athens,, Greece, pg. 1212
Pallat, Daniel J., Chief Fin. Officer, V.P., Treas. & Sec.--Home Juice Company, Melrose Park, IL, pg. 541
Palmer, David, Treas. & Sec.--Farnsworth Companies, Mesa, AZ, pg. 403
Palmer, Elaine, Sec.--Kenworth of Indianapolis Inc., Indianapolis, IN, pg. 624
Palmer, John, Sec. & Gen. Counsel--Dunham's Athleisure Corporation, Waterford, MI, pg. 353
Palmer, Roberta, Sec.--Palmer International, Inc., Worcester, PA, pg. 844
Palmieri, Harlene S., Asst. Sec.--Tagsons Papers, Inc., Albany, NY, pg. 1076
Pamplin, Dr. R.B., Jr., Pres. & Sec.--Ross Island Sand & Gravel Co., Inc., Portland, OR, pg. 845
Pamplin, Dr. R.B., Jr., Pres. & Sec.--K.F. Jacobson Co., Portland, OR, pg. 845
Pamplin, Dr. Robert B., Jr., Pres., Chief Oper. Officer & Sec.--R. B. Pamplin Corp., Portland, OR, pg. 844
Pampush, Robert, Treas. & Asst. Sec.--The Sanymetal Products Co., Inc., Vanceburg, KY, pg. 970
Pangan, Alex, Sec. & Treas.--Santa Monica Ford Company, Santa Monica, CA, pg. 970
Panjabi, Deepak, Sec.--Taj International Hotels, Washington, DC, pg. 1076
Pannell, B. Coleman, V.P.-Admin. & Sec.--Walton Monroe Mills, Inc., Monroe, GA, pg. 1162
Pansini, David, Treas. & Sec.--Jandy Industries, Novato, CA, pg. 589
Panzarino, Laura, Corp. Sec.--The Stogel Companies Inc., New York, NY, pg. 1050
Papai, Jacki, Chief Fin. Officer, Sec. & Treas.--Ventre Packing Company, Inc., Syracuse, NY, pg. 1147
Papandrianos, Vaso, Sec.--Joffko International, Houston, TX, pg. 595
Papera, Michael F., Sec.--Allstate Can Corporation, Clifton, NJ, pg. 43
Paras, Richard S., Asst. Sec.--Butler Service Group, Inc., Montvale, NJ, pg. 197
Parfet, Ray T., Jr., Sec. & Treas.--Gilmore Bros., Inc., Kalamazoo, MI, pg. 459
Parisi, Alice, Sec.--Parisi, Inc., Philadelphia, PA, pg. 848
Parker, Carter, Treas. & Sec.--Louisiana Utilities Supply Company, Baton Rouge, LA, pg. 684
Parker, James L., V.P., Gen. Counsel & Sec.--Matthews International Corp., Pittsburgh, PA, pg. 721

Parker, Ron C., Treas., Sec. & Chief Fin. Officer--Roseburg Forest Products Co., Dillard, OR, pg. 948
Parkinson, Terry, Sec. & Treas.--Corn States Hybrid Service, Incorporated, Des Moines, IA, pg. 286
Parks, A.L., Sec. & Treas.--Parks Products, Inc., Hollywood, CA, pg. 850
Parks, Margaret A., Sec.--Western & Southern Life Insurance Co., Cincinnati, OH, pg. 1181
Parr, Phillis, V.P. & Sec.--Budget Marketing, Inc., Des Moines, IA, pg. 186
Parrish, Carol, Sec.--Fisher Skylights, Inc., West Nyack, NY, pg. 415
Parrish, Danny B., V.P.-Fin., Asst. Sec. & Asst. Treas.--James N. Gray Construction Co., Inc., Lexington, KY, pg. 479
Parrott, Charles, Sec.--Fred V. Fowler Company, Inc., Newton, MA, pg. 427
Pascal, Edward, Managing Partner, V.P. & Corp. Sec.--Kombi, Ltd., Naugatuck, CT, pg. 641
Pascuzzi, Bob, Chief Fin. Officer & Sec.--The Dorris Lumber & Moulding Co., Sacramento, CA, pg. 347
Paskal, Betty, Sec.--J & R Film Company, Los Angeles, CA, pg. 586
Paterson, William, Sec.--Whiting Equipment Canada, Inc., Welland,, Canada, pg. 1187
Patrasso, Frances, Sec.--Master Molded Products Corporation, Elgin, IL, pg. 720
Patterson, John, Sec.--Crowe Rope Company, Warren, ME, pg. 301
Paturzo, Michael R., Treas. & Sec.--Henningsen Foods, Inc., White Plains, NY, pg. 629
Paul, John H.L., Sec.--Sterling Paper Co., Philadelphia, PA, pg. 1047
Paulin, Ira J., Sec.--Carder, Inc., Lamar, CO, pg. 217
Paulson, Donald, Sec.--Goldman Financial Group, Boston, MA, pg. 468
Pawelko, Ron, Sec.--Superior Graphite Company, Chicago, IL, pg. 1063
Payton, Earl E., Chm. Bd., Chief Exec. Officer & Sec.--Cowden Metal Specialties, Inc., Chino, CA, pg. 291
Pearce, Louis, III, V.P. & Sec.--Pearce Industries Inc., Houston, TX, pg. 853
Pearce, Richard W., Jr., Sr. V.P. & Sec.--Amica Mutual Insurance Co., Providence, RI, pg. 66
Pearl, Manny, Sec. & Treas.--Pearl-Pressman-Liberty Communications Group, Philadelphia, PA, pg. 853
Pearlman, Ted, V.P., Sec. & Treas.--Atlite Lighting Equip, Inc., Maspeth, NY, pg. 97
Pearson, Julie, Sec.--Jim Lupient Enterprises, Golden Valley, MN, pg. 687
Peck, Aaron M., Treas. & Sec.--Peck Iron & Metal Company, Inc., Portsmouth, VA, pg. 854
Peeler, Nancy Carole, Treas. & Sec.--Peelers Rug Company, Inc., Gaffney, SC, pg. 855
Pekin, D. James, V.P., Gen. Counsel & Sec.--Redken Laboratories, Inc., Canoga Park, CA, pg. 919
Pelly, Jerry D., V.P.-Sls. , Customer Service & Sec.--Forestry Suppliers, Inc., Jackson, MS, pg. 424
Pendrey, J.C., Jr., Sr. V.P., Chief Fin. Officer, Sec. & Treas.--Holder Corporation, Atlanta, GA, pg. 538
Penera, Bonnie, Exec. Sec.--Display Technologies, Inc., Elgin, IL, pg. 339
Penn, Barbara, Sec.--Cummins Mid-South, Inc., Memphis, TN, pg. 305
Pentaris, George, Dir.-Admin. Services & Asst. Sec.--Industrial Coatings Group, Inc., Chicago, IL, pg. 566
Pepelnjak, James F., Sec. & Dir.-Human Resources--Great Lakes Terminal & Transport Corp., Chicago, IL, pg. 482
Pepper, J. David, Sec.--The Pepper Companies, Inc., Chicago, IL, pg. 859
Pepper, Martha, Sec.--Harry Pepper & Associates, Jacksonville, FL, pg. 859
Pepys, Eric C., Sec. & Treas.--Dot Printer, Inc., Irvine, CA, pg. 347
Peraldo, Leo, V.P.-Fin., Treas. & Sec.--Klaussner Corporation, Asheboro, NC, pg. 634
Peraldo, Leo, V.P.-Fin., Treas. & Sec.--Klaussner Furniture Industry, Asheboro, NC, pg. 634
Perez, Carl A., V.P. & Sec. Of Bd.--Perez Trading Co. Inc., Miami, FL, pg. 860
Perfido, Ruth S., Asst. Sec.--W. P. Carey & Co., Inc., New York, NY, pg. 218
Perkins, Arthur, Sec.--Patsy's, Inc., Concord, NH, pg. 851
Perkins, Jean A., Sec.--Blue Cross & Blue Shield of Texas, Inc., Richardson, TX, pg. 160
Perkins, Sara S., Sr. Mktg. Asst. & Asst. Sec.--W. P. Carey & Co., Inc., New York, NY, pg. 218
Perkins, Thomas T., Sec. & Treas.--Thomas & Howard, Columbia, SC, pg. 1093
Perlman, Charles H., Sec.--GreatBanc, Inc., Aurora, IL, pg. 482
Perlmuter, Bruce, Sec., Treas. & V.P.-Opers.--Perlmuter Printing Company, Cleveland, OH, pg. 862
Perrier, Art, Exec. V.P., Treas. & Sec.--Maryland Paper Box Company, Baltimore, MD, pg. 717
Perry, Carmen, Sec., Treas. & Controller--Outdoor Venture Corp., Stearns, KY, pg. 832
Perry, D., Sec.--Perry Equipment Corporation, Mineral Wells, TX, pg. 863
Perry, Jay, Sec., Treas. & Controller--Steiny & Company, Inc., Los Angeles, CA, pg. 1049
Perry, Marion E., Sec. & Treas.--Detecto Scale Company, Webb City, MO, pg. 332
Peske, Milian, Treas. & Sec.--Metric & Multistandard Components, Hawthorne, NY, pg. 743
Petermeyer, Kay, Sec.--Power Contracting & Engineering Corp., Rolling Meadows, IL, pg. 883
Peters, Ronald, Sec.--Josephson International Inc., New York, NY, pg. 607
Petersen, Ann R., Sec.--Petersen Aluminum Corporation, Elk Grove Village, IL, pg. 864
Petersen, Daniel L., Chief Fin. Officer & Corp. Sec.--J.H. Findorff & Son, Inc., Madison, WI, pg. 411
Petersen, March, Pres. & Sec.--Petersen Graphics Group, South Bend, IN, pg. 864
Peterson, Craig D., Gen. Counsel & Sec.--Xerxes Corporation, Minneapolis, MN, pg. 1206
Peterson, David, Grp. V.P. & Sec.--Rockford Products Corp., Rockford, IL, pg. 941
Peterson, Fred J., II, Sec.--Peterson Builders, Inc., Sturgeon Bay, WI, pg. 864
Peterson, J.R., Sr. V.P. & Sec.--United Parcel Service of America, Inc., Atlanta, GA, pg. 1133
Peterson, James, Sec.--Commercial Printers Of Connecticut, Norwich, CT, pg. 268
Peterson, Jean, Treas. & Sec.--Peterson Motor Company, Boise, ID, pg. 865
Peterson, Lorrayne L., Sec.--Peterson Industries Inc., Decatur, AR, pg. 864
Pettit, Mark F., Sec--Cambridge Consultants Limited, Cambridge,, United Kingdom, pg. 679
Petty, George O., Sec.--Sun Diamond Growers of California, Pleasanton, CA, pg. 1058
Pew, Patricia, Sec.--Full Service Beverage Company, Wichita, KS, pg. 436
Pfaff, Amelia, Sec.--Anchor Tool & Die Company, Cleveland, OH, pg. 71
Pfeifer, Greg, Treas. & Chief Fin. Officer--Rochester-Midland ICL, Omaha, NE, pg. 941
Pfister, JoAnne, Dir., Personnel, Asst. Sec.--Henderson Advertising, Inc., Greenville, SC, pg. 528
Pfister, Terry W., V.P.-Fin., Chief Fin. Officer, Sec. & Treas.--Enerfab Inc., Cincinnati, OH, pg. 381
Pflaster, Tina, Sec.--Arnold Steel Company, Inc., Lakewood, NJ, pg. 85
Phagans, T. M., Sec. & Treas.--Addison Steel Inc., Orlando, FL, pg. 17
Phillips, Dayton, Sec. & Treas.--Fischer Lime & Cement Company, Memphis, TN, pg. 414
Phillips, James E., Corp. Sec.--EWI, Inc., Salem, OH, pg. 361
Phillips, Mary C., Sec. & Treas.--Young-Phillips Sales Co., Winston-Salem, NC, pg. 1210
Phillips, Ronald M., V.P.-Fin., Treas. & Sec.--J. J. Keller & Associates, Inc., Neenah, WI, pg. 620
Phillips, Toni, Sec.--Quoizel Inc., Hauppauge, NY, pg. 905
Piacenti, Carol A., Sec.--Knight/Emerson Consulting, Inc., Chicago, IL, pg. 637
Piccirillo, Rocco, V.P.-Opers. & Sec.--Beauty Enterprises Inc., Hartford, CT, pg. 130
Pickering, Allen, Chief Exec. Officer, Treas. & Sec.--Pickering Industries Inc., Tacoma, WA, pg. 869
Pickering, Judith, Sec. & Legal Counsel--Woodward & Lothrop/John Wanamaker, Washington, DC, pg. 1201
Pickering, T. H., Sr. V.P. & Sec.--Westfield Companies, Westfield Center, OH, pg. 1182
Pickett, William S., V.P.-Fin. & Sec.--K & G Of Wisconsin, Inc., Milwaukee, WI, pg. 610
Pickett, William S., V.P.-Fin. & Sec.--Downey, Inc., Milwaukee, WI, pg. 610
Picou, Richard, V.P., Sec. & Treas.--Picou Brothers Construction Company, Gonzales, LA, pg. 870
Picus, Herbert, Sec.--M. Buten & Sons Inc., Philadelphia, PA, pg. 196
Pierce, A. Kenneth, Jr., V.P. & Chief Fin. Officer--The Dispatch Printing Company, Columbus, OH, pg. 339
Pierce, James, Exec. V.P.--Cyborg Systems, Inc., Chicago, IL, pg. 307
Pierce, Linda, Sec.-Human Resources--The Edward J. DeBartolo Corporation, Youngstown, OH, pg. 323
Pierce, Richard, Sec.--Guardian Alarm Co., Southfield, MI, pg. 491
Piercy, William H., Sec. & Treas.--Dunmore Corporation, Newtown, PA, pg. 353
Pieri, Albert, V.P., Sec. & Treas.--Artichoke Industries, Inc., Castroville, CA, pg. 87
Pifer, Glenn A., Treas. & Sec.--Allied Security, Inc., Pittsburgh, PA, pg. 39
Pike, Mary Anne, Treas. & Sec.--Elite Lamp, Inc., West Memphis, AR, pg. 376
Pilkington, Angela, Office Admin.--Correct Craft, Inc., Orlando, FL, pg. 287
Pindyck, Mary E., V.P. & Asst. Sec.--Meridian Industries, Inc., Milwaukee, WI, pg. 740
Piper, Harold E., V.P. & Asst. Sec.--SS Restaurant Corporation, Raleigh, NC, pg. 466
Pirtle, Lee, V.P., Fin., Sec. & Treas.--Responsive Marketing Communications, Inc., Schaumburg, IL, pg. 929
Pisa, Veronica, Sec.--Continental Paper & Supply Co., Detroit, MI, pg. 280
Pisani, Patricia, Sec. & Treas.--APG Security, Inc., Denver, CO, pg. 5
Pitzer, R. Knox, V.P.-Admin. & Sec.--Thermon Manufacturing Company, San Marcos, TX, pg. 1091
Plack, Jeff, Treas., Controller & Corp. Sec.--Orix Real Estate Equities, Inc., Chicago, IL, pg. 829
Placke, Roger, V.P. & Sec.--Vess Beverages, Inc., Maryland Heights, MO, pg. 1149
Platania, John, Sec.--Andmore Sportswear Corporation, Port Jervis, NY, pg. 74
Platt, Mervyn J., Vice Chm. & Sec.--S. P. Dunham & Co., Lawrenceville, NJ, pg. 353
Pleau, Gene, Sec. & Treas.--Future Ford/Hugo Inc., Roseville, CA, pg. 437
Plimpton, Conrad A., Sec.--PBS Building Systems of America, Anaheim, CA, pg. 835
Plotkin, B. William, Pres. & Sec.--The Fairfield Lumber & Supply Company, Fairfield, CT, pg. 397
Plum, Rosemary, Corp. Sec.--Frank Paxton Company, Kansas City, MO, pg. 592
Plummer, Frank, V.P. & Sec.--Markem Corporation, Keene, NH, pg. 708
Plunkett, Rick, V.P., Sec. & Treas.--Ivan Allen Company, Inc., Atlanta, GA, pg. 36
Poeschl, Gaylord, V.P. & Sec.--Tank Service, Inc., Knoxville, TN, pg. 526
Polera, Catherine, Pres., Chief Fin. Officer, Sec. & Treas.--Polera Building Corp., Scarsdale, NY, pg. 878
Poling, Kathy, Sec.--Electro-Coatings, Inc., Emeryville, CA, pg. 374
Polizos, Catherine, Sec.--The Polizos Agency, Norfolk, VA, pg. 879
Pollack, Michael B., 1st V.P. & Sec.--W. P. Carey & Co., Inc., New York, NY, pg. 218
Pollard, Boyd A., Sec. & Treas.--Power & Telephone Supply Company, Memphis, TN, pg. 883
Pollock, B.R., Sec. & Treas.--Morris Coupling Co., Erie, PA, pg. 771
Pomares, Jim, Sec., Treas. & Personnel Mgr.--Von Housen Motors, Sacramento, CA, pg. 1155
Pomeranz, Harold, Chm. Bd., Treas. & Sec.--Stanley Roberts, Inc., Lodi, NJ, pg. 939
Ponce, James F., Div. Pres., Sec. & Gen. Mgr.--YPMS/TMP Worldwide, Inc., Mequon, WI, pg. 1074
Poole, John, Sec. & Treas.--Daycon Products Company, Inc., Capitol Heights, MD, pg. 321
Pope, William, Sec.--Toter Incorporated, Statesville, NC, pg. 1103
Popov, Peter N., V.P., Gen. Counsel & Sec.--Marine Transport Lines, Inc., Secaucus, NJ, pg. 707
Popp, Betty, Sec. & Controller--Red Wing Products, Inc., Plainview, NY, pg. 919
Porte, Charmaine, Chief Fin. Officer & Sec.--Advance Steel Co., Detroit, MI, pg. 20
Porteous, L. Robert, Jr., Chm. Bd., Sec. & Treas.--Porteous, South Portland, ME, pg. 353
Porter, Edward A., V.P.-Admin., Gen. Counsel & Corp. Sec.--National Gypsum Company, Charlotte, NC, pg. 790
Porter, Henry M., Sec. & Gen. Counsel--Scipar, Buffalo, NY, pg. 982
Posen, Fay, Sec.--Beltone Electronics Corporation, Chicago, IL, pg. 137
Posner, E.G., V.P., Sec. & Gen. Counsel--PQ Corporation, Valley Forge, PA, pg. 836
Posner, Miriam, Corp. Sec.--Newmark, Posner & Mitchell, Inc., New York, NY, pg. 804
Posnock, Michelle, Sls. Rep.--Shofar Kosher Foods, Inc., Newark, NJ, pg. 1000
Post, G. Roger, V.P., Sec. & Gen Counsel--White Castle System, Inc., Columbus, OH, pg. 1185
Potamkin, Robert, Sec.--Potamkin Manhattan, New York, NY, pg. 882
Poteshman, Armand, Asst. Sec.--Ultimo Ltd., Chicago, IL, pg. 1125
Potratz, Dean C., Exec. V.P., Sec. & Pub. Rels. Dir.--Sargent & Potratz, Inc., Brookfield, WI, pg. 971
Pou, Evelyn Susan, Asst. Sec.--W.S. Badcock Corporation, Mulberry, FL, pg. 113
Pou, William K., Sr., Exec. V.P. & Asst. Sec. & Treas.--W.S. Badcock Corporation, Mulberry, FL, pg. 113
Poulin, Tracey K., Chief Fin. Officer--Avatar Corporation, Hopkinton, MA, pg. 101
Poulos, Lori J., V.P., Treas., Controller & Sec.--Bridgewater Resources Corporation, Beverly Hills, CA, pg. 175
Powell, Caroline E., Sec.--Carolina Biological Supply Co., Burlington, NC, pg. 222
Powell, Deborah D., Chief Fin. Officer & Sec.--Robert C. Powell Developments, Incorporated, Sacramento, CA, pg. 882
Powell, Joyce, V.P. & Sec.--L. Powell Co., Inc., Culver City, CA, pg. 882
Powers, Ann, Sec.--Powers Construction Co., Inc., Florence, SC, pg. 883
Powers, I.W., Sec.--The Rawlplug Company, Inc., New Rochelle, NY, pg. 914
Powers, J. William, Corp. Sec. & Chief Admin. Officer--Harbert Corporation, Birmingham, AL, pg. 506
Prahl, Richard D., V.P.-Industrial & Asst. Sec.--The Benham Group, Oklahoma City, OK, pg. 138
Prainito, Francis, Corp. Sec.--Acme Mills Co. Inc., Detroit, MI, pg. 13
Prater, Ronald, Sec.--Owensboro Grain Co., Inc., Owensboro, KY, pg. 834
Prather, Robert L., Exec. V.P., Sec. & Treas.--Kocolene Oil Corp., Seymour, IN, pg. 639
Pratt, Hazel, Sec.--Bradford Oil Company, Inc., Bradford, VT, pg. 170
Pratt, Sharon, Sec. & Treas.--Lou LaRiche Chevrolet-Subaru Inc., Plymouth, MI, pg. 658
Press, Myrna, Sec.--Hypro Corporation, New Brighton, MN, pg. 557
Preston, Charles, V.P. & Sec.--Larwin Company, Encino, CA, pg. 659
Price, Gordon, Controller, Treas. & Sec.--Coleman Cadillac Inc., Bethesda, MD, pg. 261
Price, Joseph, V.P.-Mfg. & Sec.--Dettra Flag Company, Oaks, PA, pg. 333
Price, Pamela J., V.P. & Sec.--Tucson Realty & Trust Co., Tucson, AZ, pg. 1118
Priebe, Kathy, Corp. Sec.--Laidlaw Corporation, Scottsdale, AZ, pg. 650
Printz, Victoria, Sec. & Treas.--Somerset Pontiac GMC Inc., Troy, MI, pg. 1017
Proudfit, Debe, Sec. & Treas.--Vanport Manufacturing, Inc., Boring, OR, pg. 1145
Pruiett, Norma, Mgr.-Admin.--Morgan Manufacturing Company, Inc., Paris, IL, pg. 770
Prunier, Gerald, Sec.--Seppala & AHO Construction Company, New Ipswich, NH, pg. 990
Pukering, Allen, Sec.--Pickering Industries Inc., Tacoma, WA, pg. 869
Purcell, Richard F., Sr. V.P. & Sec.--Connell Rice & Sugar Co., Westfield, NJ, pg. 275
Purcell, Sheryl I., Sec.--Carol Wright Sales, Inc., Stamford, CT, pg. 1011
Purmort, F.W. III, Res. V.P. & Sec.--Central Regional Office, Van Wert, OH, pg. 233
Purmort, F.W., III, V.P. & Sec.--Central Mutual Insurance Co., Van Wert, OH, pg. 233

Purvis, Sandra K., Exec. V.P. & Sec.--A.C. Legg Packing Company, Inc., Birmingham, AL, pg. 666
Putterman, Florence G., Sec.--Milton Shoe Manufacturing Company, Inc., Milton, PA, pg. 756
Quebedeaux, Carol, V.P., Sec. & Treas.--Quebedeaux Pontiac, Inc., Tucson, AZ, pg. 904
Quinn, Joellyn, V.P.-Corp. Rels. & Asst. Sec.--Credit Union National Association, Madison, WI, pg. 298
Quist, Gordon, Sec.--Transnational Motors Inc., Grand Rapids, MI, pg. 1107
Raber, James A., Sec.--Star Bronze Company, Alliance, OH, pg. 1039
Rabin, Erwin, Sec. & Treas.--Nationwide Beef, Inc., Chicago, IL, pg. 795
Racine, Phyllis R., Sec.--Spirol International Corp., Danielson, CT, pg. 1031
Rader, Larry, Sec. & Gen. Counsel--Marine Travelift, Inc., Sturgeon Bay, WI, pg. 707
Rades, Randolph, V.P. & Sec.--Finora Company, Inc., New York, NY, pg. 810
Radford, Enoch, V.P. & Sec.--Plant Maintenance Service Corporation, Memphis, TN, pg. 874
Radwill, Linda, V.P., Mgr.-Mktg. & Sec.--Master Appliance Corp., Racine, WI, pg. 719
Rafanello, Richard A., Treas. & Sec.--E.C.D., Inc., Hillside, NJ, pg. 359
Ragland, Judy, V.P. & Sec.--Duncan Equipment Company, Duncan, OK, pg. 352
Raiche, John T., Sec. & Controller--Divane Bros. Electric Co., Franklin Park, IL, pg. 340
Raifman, Stuart, Asst. Sec.--Systems Engineering & Manufacturing Corp., Stoughton, MA, pg. 1071
Raines, Bobby J., V.P. & Treas.--Cal-Maine Foods, Inc., Jackson, MS, pg. 208
Rainwater, Jay Earl, Sec. & Legal Counsel--Wm. S. Trimble Company, Inc., Knoxville, TN, pg. 1113
Rakolta, John, Sr., Chm. Bd. & Sec.--Walbridge Aldinger Company, Detroit, MI, pg. 1158
Rakow, May T., Sr. V.P.-Personnel & Sec.--Illinois Hydraulic Construction Company, South Elgin, IL, pg. 563
Raley, Ruth, Sec. & Treas.--The Thompson Group Companies, Henderson, KY, pg. 1094
Ralph, Donald, Sec.--Producers Co-op Association, Inc., Girard, KS, pg. 892
Ralph, Marvin G., Sec. & Treas.--Lumco Industries, Inc., Philadelphia, PA, pg. 687
Ramey, Peter, Chief Fin. Officer--Lou Fusz Automotive Network, Saint Louis, MO, pg. 437
Ramsey, Stewart P., Treas. & Sec.--LSJ Sportswear Inc., Deerfield, WI, pg. 739
Rands, Mary, Sec. & Treas.--Brush Research Manufacturing Company, Los Angeles, CA, pg. 184
Rao, Elizabeth, Sec.--Rao Wholesale Tire Centers, Inc., Detroit, MI, pg. 912
Rapp, Christian F., V.P.-Fin. & Sec.--Louisville Bedding Company, Louisville, KY, pg. 684
Rathblott, Paul, V.P., Sec. & Gen Counsel--Baker Industries, Inc., Parsippany, NJ, pg. 166
Rauh, Darlene A., Sec.--Rauh, Good, Darlo & Barnes Advertising Associates, Inc., Los Gatos, CA, pg. 914
Rayner, Mitch A., V.P., Chief Oper. Officer & Sec.--Performance Contractors Inc., Baton Rouge, LA, pg. 861
Ready, George W., Treas. & Sec.--Watkins Associated Industries Inc., Atlanta, GA, pg. 1167
Reaugh, O.H., Sr. V.P. & Asst. Sec.--States, Inc., Breckenridge, TX, pg. 1041
Redlin, Gerald, Corp. Sec.--Harvest States Cooperatives, Saint Paul, MN, pg. 514
Redmer, L., Sec.--ASC Incorporated, Southgate, MI, pg. 7
Redmond, Ellen, Sec.--Redmond Products, Inc., Chanhassen, MN, pg. 920
Reed, Brad, Chief Oper. Officer, Sec. & Treas.--Kova Fertilizer Inc., Greensburg, IN, pg. 643
Reed, Carol O., Sec.--Reed Grain & Bean Company, Buhl, ID, pg. 920
Reed, E.C., Pres. & Sec.--Utica Boilers Inc., Utica, NY, pg. 1140
Reed, Fred, V.P.-Fin. & Sec.--Smith-Edwards-Dunlap Company, Philadelphia, PA, pg. 1012
Reed, John, V.P. & Sec.--Wahl Instruments, Culver City, CA, pg. 1158
Reed, John J., Jr., Sec. & Gen. Mgr.--Reed Motors, Inc., Orlando, FL, pg. 920
Reed, Stephen, Sec.--Green Spot Packaging Inc., Claremont, CA, pg. 485
Rees, John, Sec. & Treas.--Silver Springs Citrus Co-op, Ocoee, FL, pg. 1004
Reese, Marva N., Sec.--Bland Cadillac Company, Houston, TX, pg. 155
Reeves, Julia, Sec.--Bayou State Oil Corporation, Shreveport, LA, pg. 128
Regan, Michael J., V.P. & Sec.--Amtrol Inc., West Warwick, RI, pg. 70
Regan, Tim, Treas.--The Scoular Company, Omaha, NE, pg. 983
Rege, Thomas J., Chief Fin. Officer, Sec., Treas. & Controller--Chartway Technologies, Rockville, MD, pg. 240
Reichlin, Lawrence S., Sec.--Zuckerman-Honickman Inc., King of Prussia, PA, pg. 1221
Reichwein, Mary, Sec.--Revcor, Inc., Carpentersville, IL, pg. 930
Reicke, Agnes T., Sr. V.P. & Sec.--Financiere Credit Suisse-First Boston, Zug,, Switzerland, pg. 204
Reily, Patrick, Sec.--Reily Electric Supply, Inc., Metairie, LA, pg. 923
Reinhard, Christopher J., V.P. & Sec.--General Chemical Corporation, Parsippany, NJ, pg. 801
Reishi, Alan, Corp. Sec.--Felton Brush Inc., Manchester, NH, pg. 406
Reisman, Kenneth, V.P., Gen. Counsel & Sec.--Technical Aid Corporation, Newton Upper Falls, MA, pg. 1083
Reister, Mark S., Chief Oper. Officer & Sec.--Wohlert Corp., Lansing, MI, pg. 1198
Reitz, Carl F., Sec.--Panel Processing, Inc., Alpena, MI, pg. 846
Rekward, Mildred, Sec.--Lockard Construction, Inc., Waterloo, IA, pg. 680
Reno, Carol L., Sec.--Stainless Incorporated, Deerfield Beach, FL, pg. 1035
Ressler, I., V.P. & Sec.--Aluminum Shapes, Inc., Delair, NJ, pg. 46
Reuscher, William, Sec.--Keystone Carbon Company, Saint Marys, PA, pg. 628
Reyes, Nora, Sec./Treas.--Communications Plus, Inc., New York, NY, pg. 269
Reynen, John D., Treas. & Sec.--Reynen, Bardis & Winn, Sacramento, CA, pg. 930
Reynolds, Jonathan P., V.P., Gen. Counsel & Sec.--Cosco, Inc., Columbus, IN, pg. 287
Reynolds, Robert H., Sec.--LDI, Ltd., Indianapolis, IN, pg. 647
Rhudy, Huey J., Treas. & Sec.--STRAFCO, Inc., San Antonio, TX, pg. 1052
Rhyne, Neal H., V.P.-Fin., Sec. & Treas.--Cochrane Furniture Co., Inc., Lincolnton, NC, pg. 258
Rice, Bernard J., Jr., Sec. & Treas.--Blue Grass Foods, Inc., Crescent Springs, KY, pg. 160
Rice, David, V.P.-Mktg. & Corp. Sec.--New Haven Savings Bank, New Haven, CT, pg. 801
Rice, Donald L., V.P. & Sec.--Warm Brothers Construction Company, Cincinnati, OH, pg. 1163
Rice, Roberta, V.P., Treas. & Sec.--Western Linen Corp., Phoenix, AZ, pg. 1180
Rich, David R., Sec.--Rich Products Corp., Buffalo, NY, pg. 932
Rich, Jynne, Exec. Sec. & Librarian--Tatum Toomey & Whicker, High Point, NC, pg. 1080
Richards, Lynn S., Sec.--Little America Refining, Salt Lake City, UT, pg. 1008
Richards, Olive, V.P. & Sec.--Richards Brothers of Mountain Grove, Mountain Grove, MO, pg. 932
Richards, Roger, Sec.--Brance Krachy Company, Inc., Houston, TX, pg. 171
Richardson, Clayton H., Jr., Sec., Treas. & Gen. Mgr.--Gulf States Manufacturers, Inc., Starkville, MS, pg. 494
Richardson, Terry L., V.P.-Admin. & Sec.--Riceland Foods, Inc., Stuttgart, AR, pg. 931
Richardson, Thomas, V.P., Sec., Treas. & Controller--Aladdin Petroleum Corporation, Wichita, KS, pg. 29
Richenthal, Arthur, Gen. Counsel, Corp. Sec.--Carrafiello, Diehl & Associates, Inc., Irvington, NY, pg. 225
Richert, Maxine, Corp. Sec.--Sealaska Corporation, Juneau, AK, pg. 984
Richert, Maxine H., Sec.--Sealaska Corporation, Juneau, AK, pg. 984
Richter, Lyle H., V.P., Treas. & Sec.--Fox Valley Corporation, Appleton, WI, pg. 427
Ricke, Beatrice, Sec. & Treas.--Motek Engineering & Manufacturing Company, Cambridge, MN, pg. 773
Riecke, Robert, Treas. & Sec.--Walle Corporation, Jefferson, LA, pg. 1161
Riely, Sandra, Sec. & Treas.--Hood Communications, Inc., Grand Terrace, CA, pg. 543
Rieman, Stephen R., Sec. & Treas.--Bard Mfg. Co., Bryan, OH, pg. 119
Riemer, Wolfgang J., Asst. Sec.--Lawrence Group, Inc., Schenectady, NY, pg. 662
Rifkin, Bernard, Exec. V.P. & Sec.--Ticor Title Guarantee Co., New York, NY, pg. 1096
Riggins, Larry D., Sec.--CGF Industries, Topeka, KS, pg. 201
Riggs, C. Daniel, Sec.--Riggs Industries, Inc., Stoystown, PA, pg. 934
Riggs, Sidney W., Chm. Bd., Sec. & Treas.--Somerset Welding & Steel, Inc., Somerset, PA, pg. 934
Riha, Frances, Sec. & Treas.--Office Equipment Company Of Chicago, Chicago, IL, pg. 821
Riker, Glenn, Sr. V.P.-Human Resources & Sec.--Holmes Protection Group, Inc., New York, NY, pg. 540
Riley, Ed, V.P. & Asst. Sec.--HTB, Inc., Oklahoma City, OK, pg. 497
Riley, Kim, Exec. Sec.--Brooks Foods, Mt. Summit, IN, pg. 26
Ringer, Walter M., III, Sec.--Foley-PLP Company, Rochester, NY, pg. 422
Rinke, Kevin, V.P. & Sec.--Rinke Pontiac-GMC Co., Warren, MI, pg. 935
Rintamaki, John, V.P. & Sec.--Park Ridge Corporation, Park Ridge, NJ, pg. 849
Riordan, Robert W., Sec.--The Conair Group, Inc., Pittsburgh, PA, pg. 272
Ritscher, Charles W., V.P.-Mktg., Sls. & Sec.--New Jersey Press, Inc., Neptune, NJ, pg. 801
Ritscher, Charles W., Sec.--Press Broadcasting Co., Neptune, NJ, pg. 801
Rittner, George, Sec.--Menu Foods, Inc., Pennsauken, NJ, pg. 739
Rivers, Richard D., V.P., Gen. Counsel & Asst. Sec.--Berwind Corporation, Philadelphia, PA, pg. 145
Rizzitello, Jack, Co. Sec.--W.W. Norton & Company, Inc., New York, NY, pg. 815
Rizzolo, Sara Lee, Sec.--Challenge Technologies, Grand Haven, MI, pg. 238
Roach, J. Thurston, V.P., Sec. & Chief Fin. Officer-SICO--Simpson Timber Co., Shelton, WA, pg. 1007
Roades, Jean, Sec.--American Electronics, Inc., Fullerton, CA, pg. 3
Roades, Jean M., Corp. Sec.--AEI Holding Co., Inc., Fullerton, CA, pg. 3
Robbins, Keith D., Corp. Sec.--Phoenix Home Life Mutual Insurance Company, Hartford, CT, pg. 868
Robbinson, R. Courtney, Sec.--Robinson Lumber Company, New Orleans, LA, pg. 940
Roberts, Gary, Sr. V.P., Chief Fin. Officer, Admin. & Sec.--Sierracin Corporation, Sylmar, CA, pg. 1003
Roberts, Leland D., Sec. & Dir.-Pur.--Elgin-Honey Hill Corporation, Chicago, IL, pg. 376
Roberts, Stephen W., Sec.--Triple F, Inc., Des Moines, IA, pg. 1114
Roberts, Xenia, Sec. & Treas.--Chas Roberts Air Conditioning, Inc., Phoenix, AZ, pg. 938
Robertson, William A., V.P.-Opers. & Chief Fin. Officer--Smartstar Corporation, Goleta, CA, pg. 1011
Robins, Charles, Corp. Sec.--Automation Intelligence, Inc., Maitland, FL, pg. 101
Robins, R. Steven, Sec., Treas., Controller & Cash Mgr.--Builder Marts of America, Greenville, SC, pg. 187
Robinson, Harry T., Jr., Chm. Bd. & Sec.--Top Flight, Inc., Chattanooga, TN, pg. 1101
Robinson, Michael D., V.P. & Sec.--King Louie International, Inc., Grandview, MO, pg. 631
Robinson, R. Courtney, Sec.--Robinson Lumber & Export Company, New Orleans, LA, pg. 940
Robinson, Steven, Sec.--Lakeside Refining Co. Inc., Southfield, MI, pg. 651
Robinson, Thomas E., Sr. V.P. & Sec.--The Entwistle Company, Hudson, MA, pg. 383
Robles, Estela, Sec. & Treas.--La Reina, Inc., Los Angeles, CA, pg. 649
Rocco, Deborah, V.P. & Asst. Sec.--Capital Bancorp, Miami, FL, pg. 214
Rocush, Peter, Sec. & Treas.--Gerrard and Company, Des Plaines, IL, pg. 454
Rodbell, Sidney P., V.P. & Sec.--Apex Supply Co. Inc., Atlanta, GA, pg. 78
Rodd, Allan K., Treas. & Asst. Sec.--The Wooster Brush Company, Wooster, OH, pg. 1202
Rodefeld, Gary H., V.P. & Sec.--Rodefeld Co., Inc., Richmond, IN, pg. 942
Rodriguez, Thelma, Grp. V.P. & Sec.--Graphic Productions Company, Miami, FL, pg. 478
Rodriguez, Ulijes E., Treas. & Sec.--Power Engineering Co. Inc., Coral Gables, FL, pg. 883
Roedl, Suzanne, Chief Fin. Officer--Condor D.C. Power Supplies Inc., Oxnard, CA, pg. 273
Roehl, Katherine S., Sec.--Lake Region Manufacturing Company, Inc., Chaska, MN, pg. 651
Roelof, Jay T., V.P. & Sec.--CS First Boston Group, Inc., New York, NY, pg. 203
Rogers, Darrell, Treas. & Sec.--Turner Dairies, Inc., Covington, TN, pg. 1119
Rogers, Irwin W., V.P., Controller & Sec.--North Pacific Lumber Company, Portland, OR, pg. 813
Rogers, Jo, Treas. & Sec.--Royal Jeep Eagle & Chrysler Plymouth, Casselberry, FL, pg. 953
Rogers, Joann, Corp. Sec.--Royal Jeep Eagle Chrysler Plymouth, Inc., Casselberry, FL, pg. 953
Rogers, John W., V.P., Treas. & Sec.--Rogers Markets Inc., Fort Wayne, IN, pg. 943
Rogers, Patricia, Sec.--RMS Techs, Inc., Marlton, NJ, pg. 907
Rohanna, John, Sec. & Treas.--Lumbermens Merchandising Corporation, Wayne, PA, pg. 687
Rohloff, William M., Chief Fin. Officer, Treas. & Sec.--Stebbins Engineering & Mfg. Co., Watertown, NY, pg. 1043
Rohrbacker, Raymond B., V.P., Sec. & Treas.--Nooter Corporation, Saint Louis, MO, pg. 808
Rohrer, Joanne M., Sec. & Treas.--Rohrer Corporation, Wadsworth, OH, pg. 944
Rojek, David, Sec.--Advance Mechanical Systems, Inc., Elk Grove Village, IL, pg. 19
Rold, Stephen K., V.P., Treas., Sec. & Controller--Roofing Wholesale Co., Inc., Phoenix, AZ, pg. 946
Rolla, M.F., Pres. & Chief Oper. Officer--Gem Industries Finance Corporation, Toccoa, GA, pg. 447
Romanczuk, Wayne, Sec. & Controller--P M Company, Philadelphia, PA, pg. 835
Romaniuk, Stefan, V.P.-Fin. & Sec.--VCA Teletronics Inc., Leonia, NJ, pg. 1141
Romano, John, V.P., Sec. & Adv. Mgr.--Stephen L. Geller Inc., New York, NY, pg. 447
Romans, John C., Sr. V.P. & Sec.--H.D. Hudson Manufacturing Company, Chicago, IL, pg. 551
Romig, Michael V., V.P. & Chief Fin. Officer--Marine Construction & Design Co., Seattle, WA, pg. 707
Rominski, Kathryn Hubbard, Sec. & Dir.-Hubbard Foundation--Hubbard Broadcasting, Inc., Saint Paul, MN, pg. 548
Romney, Frank M., Asst. Sec. & Treas.--Associated Food Stores Inc., Salt Lake City, UT, pg. 89
Ronco, Al, Chief Oper. Officer, Exec. V.P., & Sec.--Keystone Automotive Industries, Inc., Pomona, CA, pg. 627
Rones, Gail, Sec. & Treas.--Americo Manufacturing Co., Inc., Acworth, GA, pg. 66
Root, Stuart W., Mgr.-Personnel & Sec.--A.I. Root Company, Medina, OH, pg. 946
Roper, John L., IV, Exec. V.P.-Opers. & Sec.--Norfolk Shipbuilding & Drydock Corporation, Norfolk, VA, pg. 810
Rosania, John, Treas. & Sec.--Structural Foam Plastics, Inc., North Branch, NJ, pg. 1054
Rose, Cathryne G., Sec.--Roman Electric Company, Inc., Milwaukee, WI, pg. 945
Rose, Pamela S., Asst. V.P. & Corp. Sec.--Ministers Life Insurance Company, Minneapolis, MN, pg. 757
Rosen, Douglas C., Sec.--Alaskan Copper Companies, Seattle, WA, pg. 30
Rosen, Hermine, Sec.--Star Children's Dress Company, Inc., New York, NY, pg. 1039
Rosen, Jerald I., Sec.--Freeson Advertising Agency, Miami Lakes, FL, pg. 431
Rosen, Thomas, Sec.--Long Prairie Packing Co., Long Prairie, MN, pg. 948
Rosenberg, Benjamin, Esq., Exec. V.P., Gen. Counsel & Asst. Sec.--United Community Insurance Co., Albany, NY, pg. 662
Rosenberg, Marvin, Chm. Bd. & Sec.--Towne Properties, Cincinnati, OH, pg. 1104

Rosenberger, Marcus L., Treas. & Sec.--Rosenbergers Dairies, Inc., Hatfield, PA, pg. 948
Rosenblum, Howard, Sec.--Spinnaker Software Corporation, Cambridge, MA, pg. 1031
Rosendin, Louis M., Exec. V.P. & Sec.--Rosendin Electric, Inc., San Jose, CA, pg. 948
Rosenfeld, Alan, V.P. & Sec.--DAQ Electronics Inc., Middlesex, NJ, pg. 308
Rosenmeier, W.C., Jr., Sec. & Treas.--Geo. H. Lehleitner & Co., Inc., Harahan, LA, pg. 666
Rosenthal, Benjamin, Sec. & Treas.--Madison Electric Co., Detroit, MI, pg. 699
Rosenzwog, Edith, Sec.--Monumental Millwork, Inc., Westminster, MD, pg. 768
Rosner, Erwin, Treas. & Sec.--Boscov's Department Stores, Inc., Reading, PA, pg. 167
Ross, Bradley, Sec.--Science & Engineering Associates, Albuquerque, NM, pg. 982
Ross, John E., Sec.--Spelling Entertainment Group, Inc., Cincinnati, OH, pg. 54
Ross, Judy, Sec. & Treas.--Layman Candy Company, Inc., Salem, VA, pg. 663
Ross, R.L., Sec., Treas. & Controller--Edgewater Corporation, Oakmont, PA, pg. 368
Rossini, Edwin R., V.P.-Deputy Gen. Counsel & Asst. Sec.--S. C. Johnson & Son, Inc., Racine, WI, pg. 599
Rossiter, P.L., Sec.--Illinois Consolidated Telephone Co., Mattoon, IL, pg. 563
Rossler, John, V.P.-Fin., Treas. & Asst. Sec.--Shonac Corporation, Columbus, OH, pg. 1000
Roth, Alan, Sec.--Panorama Press, Inc., Clifton, NJ, pg. 846
Roth, Robert J., V.P. & Sec.--Tru-Weld Grating, Inc., Wexford, PA, pg. 1117
Rothe, John E., V.P. & Sec.--Turtle & Hughes, Inc., Linden, NJ, pg. 1119
Rothenberger, Eva, Sec. & Treas.--Vari Tronics Company, Inc., Duarte, CA, pg. 1145
Rothman, Henry, Sec.--House of Ronnie, Inc., New York, NY, pg. 546
Rothstein, Stanley, V.P.-Fin., Treas. & Asst. Sec.--Bestform Foundations, Inc., Long Island City, NY, pg. 147
Rott, Herbert, Jr., V.P., Sec. & Treas.--Rott-Keller Supply Co., Fargo, ND, pg. 951
Roubin, Richard, V.P. & Sec.--Roubinco, Inc., Fairfax, VA, pg. 952
Rowe, John E., Treas. & Sec.--Oltmans Construction Company, Whittier, CA, pg. 824
Rowland, T.W., Sr. V.P., Sec. & Gen. Counsel--California & Hawaiian Sugar Company, Concord, CA, pg. 210
Rubin, Benjamin H., Sec. & Treas.--Stevens-Lee Company, Minneapolis, MN, pg. 1048
Rubin, David M., Sec. & Gen. Counsel--CC Industries, Inc., Chicago, IL, pg. 199
Rubin, David M., Gen. Counsel & Sec.--American Envelope Company, Chicago, IL, pg. 199
Rubin, Georgette, Treas. & Sec.--Lillie Rubin Affiliates Inc., Miami, FL, pg. 954
Rubin, Milton, Sec. & Gen. Counsel--Argo International Corp., New York, NY, pg. 81
Rubin, Milton, Sec.--Decal Enterprises, Inc., New York, NY, pg. 323
Rubin, Robert, Exec. V.P. & Sec.--M. Rubin & Sons Inc., New York, NY, pg. 954
Rubin, Steven, V.P., Sec. & Gen. Counsel--General Binding Corporation, Northbrook, IL, pg. 656
Ruddy, Joanna, Sec.--General Welding Supply Corporation, Westbury, NY, pg. 451
Rudolph, Jim, Sec.--Boston Trading Ltd. Inc., Lynn, MA, pg. 168
Ruehlmann, Eugene P., Sec.--Ashley F. Ward, Inc., Cincinnati, OH, pg. 1162
Ruen, Daniel P., Sec.--Cleaners Hanger Co., Palm Harbor, FL, pg. 254
Ruffin, Pat, V.P., Treas. & Sec.--Ruffin Building Systems, Inc., Oak Grove, LA, pg. 955
Rufo, Beth Ann, Sec. & Meetings Plng.--Post Buckley Schuh & Jernigan, Miami, FL, pg. 881
Rugg, Jonathan, Sec.--Rugg Manufacturing Company, Greenfield, MA, pg. 955
Ruland, James, Treas. & Sec.--H.G. Fenton Material Company, San Diego, CA, pg. 406
Runk, Judith, Sec.--Directory Distributing Associates, Inc., Saint Louis, MO, pg. 339
Rusica, Dorothy, Sec.--Cooper Instrument Corp., Middlefield, CT, pg. 283
Rusinak, Ronald, Corp. Sec. & Gen. Counsel--Crown American Corporation, Johnstown, PA, pg. 301
Russell, Barron Jeff, Treas. & Sec.--Food & Gas, Inc., Decatur, GA, pg. 423
Russell, Beverly L., Sec.--Knight Management Consulting, Inc., Chicago, IL, pg. 637
Russell, George Earl, Treas. & Sec.--Russell Petroleum Corporation, Montgomery, AL, pg. 957
Russell, James F., V.P.-Fin., Chief Fin. Officer & Sec.--HCB Contractors, Dallas, TX, pg. 496
Russell, T. Alan, Exec. V.P., Sec. & Treas.--Illinois Cereal Mills, Inc., Paris, IL, pg. 562
Russo, Lori M., Asst. Sec.--The First Boston Corporation, New York, NY, pg. 203
Rutledge, William A., Sr. V.P. & Sec.--Farmers Mutual Hail Insurance Co., Des Moines, IA, pg. 401
Ruzicka, Leonard R., Sr. V.P., Sec. & Gen. Counsel--Fru-Con Construction Corporation, Ballwin, MO, pg. 435
Ryan, John F., V.P. & Sec.--Fleming Packaging Corp., Peoria, IL, pg. 417
Ryan, Kevin T., V.P. & Sec.--Charan Industries, Inc., Garden City, NY, pg. 239
Ryan, Russell J., V.P.-Sec. & Treas.--Ryan Construction Company Of Minnesota, Hibbing, MN, pg. 958
Ryan, Russell R., V.P., Treas. & Sec.--Ryan Properties Inc., Minneapolis, MN, pg. 958
Rybnick, W., Sec.--J. Gerber & Co. Inc., New York, NY, pg. 453
Rynn, John A., V.P. & Treas.--Berol Corporation, Brentwood, TN, pg. 856
Ryno, J. Jeff, Exec. V.P. & Sec.--Cuplex, Inc., Garland, TX, pg. 305
Rynone, William J., Sec. & Treas.--Rynone Manufacturing Corporation, Sayre, PA, pg. 958
Saap, Clayton H., Sec. & Controller--Wurzburg, Inc., Memphis, TN, pg. 1205
Saari, Paul, Treas. & Asst. Sec.--Rock-Tenn Company, Norcross, GA, pg. 941
Sachs, Arthur S., Sec.--O. F. Mossberg & Sons, Inc., North Haven, CT, pg. 773
Sachs, Donald, Sec.--Systems Parking, Inc., Pasadena, CA, pg. 1071
Sacks, Louis, Treas. & Sec.--S. Freedman & Sons, Inc., Landover, MD, pg. 430
Sacks, Randy, Controller & Sec.--Morton Goldberg Associates, Inc., New York, NY, pg. 465
Saculla, William F., Sec.--Arthur Treacher's, Inc., Youngstown, OH, pg. 87
Sadlowski, Dennis A., V.P., Sec. & Gen. Counsel--Millmaster Onyx Group, Inc., Westport, CT, pg. 755
Safchick, Jeff, Sec.--McCrory Corporation, New York, NY, pg. 934
Sajeski, Edmund, Jr., Sec., Treas. & Controller--A. H. Hoffman, Inc., Landisville, PA, pg. 538
Sakosits, Mildred, Pres. & Sec.--Hoboken Wood Flooring Corporation, Wayne, NJ, pg. 537
Saladen, Barbara, Asst. Sec.--Chief Industries, Inc., Grand Island, NE, pg. 247
Salamon, Robert, V.P., Sec. & Treas.--Pic N'pay Supermarkets, Inc., Dania, FL, pg. 869
Saliba, Naseeb M., Exec. V.P. & Sec.--Tutor-Saliba Corporation, Sylmar, CA, pg. 1120
Salit, Gary S., Asst. Sec.--Bell & Howell Company, Skokie, IL, pg. 134
Salmon, John L., Chm. Bd., Sec. & Treas.--TVESCO, Inc., Memphis, TN, pg. 1075
Saltz, Theodore, Sec.--McDonald Equipment Co., Willoughby, OH, pg. 728
Saltzman, Shirley, Sec.--Banner Wholesale Grocers, Inc., Chicago, IL, pg. 118
Salwasser, Margaret, Sec. & Treas.--Salwasser Manufacturing Company, Inc., Reedley, CA, pg. 968
Salzano, James, Chief Fin. Officer, Sec. & Treas.--Altier & Sons Shoes Inc., Rochester, NY, pg. 45
Samayoa, John F., Exec. V.P.-Mktg. Mgr. & Treas.--Lanman & Kemp-Barclay Co. Inc., Westwood, NJ, pg. 657
Sample, Donald L., Controller & Sec.--Thompson Tractor Company, Birmingham, AL, pg. 1095
Samsill, Loretta, Exec. V.P., Sec. & Treas.--Samsill Corporation, Fort Worth, TX, pg. 968
Sanbloom, Robert, Sec.--White County Farm Bureau Co-Op Association, Monticello, IN, pg. 1185
Sanborn, Barry, Asst. Sec.--John Hancock Mutual Life Insurance Company, Boston, MA, pg. 595
Sanborn, David, Sec. & Treas.--Financial Life Companies, Inc., St. Paul, MN, pg. 813
Sanchez, Raymond, Controller, Treas. & Asst. Sec.--Hunter Engineering Co., Inc., Riverside, CA, pg. 554
Sandberg, Joel, V.P, Sec., Fin. & Personnel--Jameco Industries, Inc., Wyandanch, NY, pg. 588
Sandberg, Oscar A., Sec.--Lincoln Electric Systems, Lincoln, NE, pg. 675
Sander, Duane E., Dr., Sec.--Daktronics, Inc., Brookings, SD, pg. 312
Sander, William C., Exec. V.P., Sec. & Treas.--Hunt Building Corporation, El Paso, TX, pg. 553
Sanders, Bernard, V.P.-Plng.--Farmland Industries, Inc., Kansas City, MO, pg. 402
Sanders, Bernard C., Corp. Sec.--Union Equity, Enid, OK, pg. 402
Sanders, Jim, Treas. & Asst. Sec.--Hickman Williams & Co. Inc., Cincinnati, OH, pg. 532
Sanders, Judith A., Sec.--Wil-Freds Construction, Inc., Aurora, IL, pg. 1189
Sanderson, James E., V.P., Gen. Counsel & Sec.--Brooks Beverage Management, Inc., Holland, MI, pg. 179
Sanford, Clara E., Sec.--Sanford & Hawley, Inc., Unionville, CT, pg. 970
Sanford, Robert, Corp. Sec.--Interform Corporation, Bridgeville, PA, pg. 574
Sang, Bernard G., Sec. & Gen. Counsel--Humiston-Keeling, Inc., Chicago, IL, pg. 552
Sankovitch, Jeffery, Sec.--Lewis Brothers Bakeries, Inc., Evansville, IN, pg. 673
Santo, James M., V.P.-Legal Affairs & Sec.--Jack Eckerd Corporation, Largo, FL, pg. 366
Santos, Dianne, Corp. Sec.--The Noteworthy Company, Amsterdam, NY, pg. 816
Saperstein, Carol, Sec.--Kraft Hardware, Inc., New York, NY, pg. 643
Sarai, Andre, V.P., Treas. & Sec.--Weiss Sheet Metal Company, Gardena, CA, pg. 1174
Sargent, Jean, Sec.--Todd & Sargent, Inc., Ames, IA, pg. 1100
Sargisson, Dwayne T., Sec.--Coppus Engineering Corp., Millbury, MA, pg. 285
Sarkisian, A. Alex, Sec.--Schawk, Inc., Des Plaines, IL, pg. 974
Sarmiento, Antonio A., Chm. Bd., Pres. & Sec.--Lumas Realty, Inc., Miami, FL, pg. 687
Sarosiek, James J., V.P., Gen. Counsel & Sec.--Menasha Corporation, Neenah, WI, pg. 738
Sarrail, J.L., Sec. & Treas.--McConnell Cabinets, Inc., El Monte, CA, pg. 727
Sartori, Dominic, V.P., Controller & Sec.--Service America Corporation, Stamford, CT, pg. 992
Sasser, Chris, Sec.--Health Vitamin Company, Inc., Yonkers, NY, pg. 521
Sasso, Claire, V.P. & Sec.--The Jason Group, Inc., Short Hills, NJ, pg. 590
Saterbo, Edith, Sec.--Colorado Boxed Beef Co., Auburndale, FL, pg. 265
Sauer, George D., Sec.--The Airolite Company, Marietta, OH, pg. 28
Saul, Les, Treas. & Sec.--Beach City Chevrolet Co., Long Beach, CA, pg. 128
Saunders, William B., Sec.--Murphy Farms Inc., Rose Hill, NC, pg. 776
Sawyer, Joyce M., Sec.--Congaree Construction Co., Inc., Columbia, SC, pg. 274
Saydah, John, V.P. & Sec.--Cecil Saydah Company, Los Angeles, CA, pg. 973
Scales, Gene, Treas. & Sec.--Allied Plywood Corp., Alexandria, VA, pg. 38
Scangas, James N., Sec.--Scangas Brothers Holdings, Inc., Lynn, MA, pg. 974
Scanlan, Arthur G., III, V.P., Sec. & Treas.--Eatel Corporation, Gonzales, LA, pg. 364
Scariot, Terry G., Sr., V.P.-Fin. & Sec.--Desa International, Inc., Bowling Green, KY, pg. 331
Scearce, C.B., Chief Fin. Officer, V.P., Sec. & Controller--Krystal Company, Chattanooga, TN, pg. 645
Schaake, Paul E., Sec.--Schaake Packing Company, Inc., Ellensburg, WA, pg. 974
Schaedler, Thomas J., Jr., Sec.--Schaedler Brothers, Inc., Harrisburg, PA, pg. 974
Schaefer, John D., Sec.--Plastipak Packaging Inc., Plymouth, MI, pg. 876
Schaefer, John L., V.P.-Fin., Chief Fin. Officer & Sec.--The Wm. Powell Company, Cincinnati, OH, pg. 882
Schafer, Seymour, Sec.--Asko, Inc, Homestead, PA, pg. 88
Schaffer, Lisa, Sec.--Rivers Trainor Doyle & Walsh, Inc., Providence, RI, pg. 937
Schall, Fred, Sec. & Treas.--Delair Group, Inc., Delair, NJ, pg. 46
Scharden, Ruth Dale, Sec.--Farmers Investment Company, Inc., Horse Cave, KY, pg. 115
Scharfberg, Doug, Sr. V.P., Sec., Market Res., Telecommunications, Res. & Devel.--Scharfberg & Associates, Ltd. Adv., Jenkintown, PA, pg. 974
Schaum, J. Michael, V.P., Sec. & Treas.--Calumet Construction Corporation, Hammond, IN, pg. 211
Schebo, Cindy, Treas., Sec. & Dir.-Personnel--Ostarr Corporation, Chicago, IL, pg. 831
Scheer, Steven E., Sr. V.P., Sec. & Treas.--Scheer Advertising Agency, South Orange, NJ, pg. 975
Schefelker, Wayne F., Sec. & Treas.--Fiberesin Industries Inc., Oconomowoc, WI, pg. 408
Schein, Ester, Sec. & Treas.--Henry Schein, Inc., Port Washington, NY, pg. 975
Schein, M., Sec.--Baltimore Orioles, Inc., Baltimore, MD, pg. 116
Schelhas, Peter M., V.P.-Sls., Sec. & Treas.--Chicago White Metal Casting, Inc., Bensenville, IL, pg. 246
Schell, Ivan, Sec. & Gen. Counsel--Roll Forming Corporation, Shelbyville, KY, pg. 944
Scher, Gerald J., Chm. Bd., Treas. & Sec.--Westchester Lace, Inc., North Bergen, NJ, pg. 1178
Scherer, Pete, Sec.--Scherer Bros. Lumber Company, Minneapolis, MN, pg. 976
Scherle, Arthur J., Sec. & Treas.--The Lorvic Corp., St. Louis, MO, pg. 684
Scherr, Ted, Sec. & Treas.--Dakota Drug, Inc., Minot, ND, pg. 311
Scheuer, Thomas, Legal Counsel & Asst. Sec.--Louis Dreyfus Corporation, Wilton, CT, pg. 348
Schey, Walter, Sec.--Putzmeister, Inc., Gardena, CA, pg. 901
Schildge, Ronald, Sec.--Precision Roll Grinders, Inc., Allentown, PA, pg. 885
Schilling, Rod, V.P.-Fin. & Sec.--Continental Coin Corporation, Van Nuys, CA, pg. 278
Schimmoller, John, Sec. & Treas.--Renaissance Publishing Co., Inc., Auburn, IN, pg. 926
Schinman, H.L., Chm. Bd., Treas., Sec. & Gen. Counsel--Bogue Electric Manufacturing Co., Paterson, NJ, pg. 162
Schiotis, Yvette M., Sec.--Reliance Steel & Aluminum Co., Los Angeles, CA, pg. 925
Schipall, Duane, Sec. & Treas.--Bawden Corporation, Eldridge, IA, pg. 127
Schipper, M.R., Asst. Sec. & Controller--Green Holdings, Inc., Denver, CO, pg. 484
Schipper, M.R., Asst. Sec.--Green International, Inc., Denver, CO, pg. 484
Schipper, M.R., V.P. & Asst. Sec.--Green Mining, Inc., Denver, CO, pg. 484
Schirmang, William A., V.P.-Data Processing & Sec.--Skokie Valley Beverage Co., Wheeling, IL, pg. 1009
Schlagenhauf, June A., Sec.--Badger Truck Center, Inc., Milwaukee, WI, pg. 113
Schlang, Alan L., Sec.--Guardian Industries Corp., Northville, MI, pg. 491
Schlanger, Richard, Exec. V.P. & Sec.--United Envelope Company, Inc., New York, NY, pg. 1131
Schleif, Lyle, Sec. & Treas.--AEC, Anoka, MN, pg. 3
Schlipf, Catherine, Asst. Sec.--Laird & Company, Scobeyville, NJ, pg. 650
Schlobohm, Jon, Sec. & Treas.--National Corset Supply House, Los Angeles, CA, pg. 787
Schlosser, Elaine, M., Treas. & Sec.--Schlosser Forge Company, Rancho Cucamonga, CA, pg. 976
Schlosser, P., Sec. & Treas.--Robins Engineers & Constructors, Inc., Englewood, CO, pg. 939
Schlott, Thelma, Corp. Sec.--Warren Distribution, Inc., Omaha, NE, pg. 1164
Schmalz, Robert L., V.P., Sec. & Gen. Counsel--Spreckles Industries, Inc., Pleasanton, CA, pg. 1032
Schmeller, Tanya, Sec.--Columbian Mutual Life Insurance Co., Binghamton, NY, pg. 266
Schmid, Daniel J., Jr., Exec. V.P.-Fin., Treas. & Asst. Sec.--G. Heileman Brewing Co., Inc., La Crosse, WI, pg. 526
Schmidt, Clifford, Sec.--Perry Brothers, Inc., Lufkin, TX, pg. 862
Schmidt, Donald O., Gen. Mgr., Treas. & Sec.--Walla Walla Grain Growers, Inc., Walla Walla, WA, pg. 1160

Schmidt, H.J., Sec. & Treas.--L. G. Everist Inc., Sioux Falls, SD, pg. 392
Schmidt, Leslie, Sec. & Treas.--Warrens Waller Press, South San Francisco, CA, pg. 1165
Schmit, James, Sec.--Robert James Sales Inc., Buffalo, NY, pg. 589
Schmitt, Mary M., Sec.--Farm Family Mutual Insurance Co., Glenmont, NY, pg. 401
Schnadig, R., Sec.--Schnadig Corporation, Chicago, IL, pg. 977
Schneeman, Donald J., Gen. Counsel & Sec.--American Institute of C.P.A.'s Inc., New York, NY, pg. 56
Schneible, William F., Sec. & Treas.--Brooklyn Bottling Co., Milton, NY, pg. 179
Schneider, James M., Sec.--Northwestern Drug Company, Minneapolis, MN, pg. 343
Schneider, Richard A., V.P.-Fin., Sec. & Treas.--North Atlantic Industries, Inc., Hauppauge, NY, pg. 812
Schnieber, Dorothy E., Sec.--Schnieber Fine Foods, Inc., Lincoln, NE, pg. 977
Schnomeier, Theodore, V.P. & Asst. Sec.--Jeld-Wen, Inc., Klamath Falls, OR, pg. 591
Schnuck, Terry, Sec. & Gen. Counsel--Schnuck Markets, Inc., Maryland Heights, MO, pg. 977
Schocke, Robert P., Chief Fin. Officer, Treas., Controller & Sec.--Greenhorne & O'Mara, Inc., Greenbelt, MD, pg. 485
Schoeber, Eldon, V.P., Sec. & Treas.--Site Oil Co. of Missouri, Clayton, MO, pg. 1009
Schoeneman, Cecil, Treas. & Sec.--Schoeneman Brothers Company, Sioux Falls, SD, pg. 978
Scholler, Bernice, Sec. & Treas.--Times Printing Company, Inc., Random Lake, WI, pg. 1098
Scholten, Heidi, Corp. Sec.--Muelhens, Inc., Orange, CT, pg. 774
Scholz, Gelaine, Treas. & Sec.--Walser Automotive Corporation, Richfield, MN, pg. 1161
Schomer, Marian E., Sec.--Nova Power, Inc., Santa Ana, CA, pg. 816
Schonwald, Gary A., Sec. & Legal Officer--Hollytex, Saddle Brook, NJ, pg. 1121
Schoonenberg, Donald S., Sec. & Controller--Simplicity Manufacturing, Inc., Port Washington, WI, pg. 1006
Schori, Jan, Gen. Counsel & Corp. Sec.--Sacramento Municipal Utility District, Sacramento, CA, pg. 965
Schottenstein, Saul, Sec.--Kroehler Furniture Manufacturing Company, Inc., Conover, NC, pg. 645
Schrimpf, R. William, Asst. Sec.--Hartford-Wood River Terminal, Hartford, IL, pg. 869
Schroeder, Jacquelyn M., Exec. Sec.--Sunbeam Casual Furniture Co., Portland, TN, pg. 1059
Schroeder, Mary Lou, Asst. Sec. & Asst. Treas.--Modern Group Ltd., Bristol, PA, pg. 762
Schroeder, Vernon, Treas. & Sec.--Big Cheese Pizza Corporation, Wichita, KS, pg. 464
Schuler, Mark J., V.P.-Fin. & Sec.--American Systems Corporation, Chantilly, VA, pg. 63
Schull, Johanna, Sec. & Treas.--Building Products Inc., Watertown, SD, pg. 188
Schultz, Jay, Treas. & Sec.--ZBS Industries, Inc., Mayfield Village, OH, pg. 1215
Schultz, Robert J., Chief Fin. Officer, Treas. & Sec.--Great Lakes Lithograph Co., Cleveland, OH, pg. 481
Schulz, Lee A., Sec. & Treas.--Wine & Schulz Inc., Louisville, KY, pg. 1196
Schulze, Max H., V.P., Sec., Treas. & Gen. Counsel--MCRB Service Bureau, Inc., North Hollywood, CA, pg. 691
Schumacher, D.A., Chief Fin. Officer & Treas.--The Cretex Companies, Elk River, MN, pg. 299
Schuman, Seymour, Chm. Bd. & Sec.--Propper Manufacturing Co., Inc., Long Island City, NY, pg. 895
Schurz, Mary, V.P. & Sec.--Schurz Communications, Inc., South Bend, IN, pg. 979
Schuster, Stephen M., V.P., Sec. & Gen. Counsel--Envirodyne Industries, Inc., Oak Brook, IL, pg. 383
Schwab, Doug, Sec. & Dir.-Data Processing--S. Schwab Company, Cumberland, MD, pg. 980
Schwab, Jerry L., Sec.--Farmland Foods, Inc., Kansas City, MO, pg. 402
Schwab, Morris, Sec.--D&H Distributing Company, Harrisburg, PA, pg. 307
Schwartz, Daniel L., V.P., Sec. & Treas.--Schwartz & Benjamin, Inc., New York, NY, pg. 980
Schwartz, Louis J., Sec.--Baker Concrete Construction, Inc., Monroe, OH, pg. 115
Schwarz, James N., Sec. & Gen. Counsel--Steuart Petroleum Company, Washington, DC, pg. 1048
Sciberras, M., Sec., Treas. & Comptroller--Dearborn Gage Company, Garden City, MI, pg. 322
Scola, Andrea, V.P.-Admin. & Sec.--Chicago West Pullman Corporation, Cincinnati, OH, pg. 246
Scott, Gary L., V.P.-Natl. Sls. Mgr. & Corp. Sec.--Alkota Cleaning Systems, Inc., Alcester, SD, pg. 34
Scott, John R., V.P., Sec. & Gen. Counsel--Hunt Oil Company, Dallas, TX, pg. 553
Scott, Milton C., Sec., Treas. & Exec. Office Mgr.--Georgia Duck & Cordage Mills, Scottdale, GA, pg. 453
Scott, Sherry, Sec. & Treas.--Texas Metal Works, Inc., Beaumont, TX, pg. 1089
Scott, William H., V.P., Sec. & Controller--The Leavell Company, El Paso, TX, pg. 664
Seabrook, Evelyn T., Sec.--Seabrook Brothers & Sons, Inc., Seabrook, NJ, pg. 984
Sealy, Carol T., Sec. & Treas.--Lewis Communications, Inc., Mobile, AL, pg. 673
Seaman, Janet W., Sec. & Treas.--Seaman Timber Company, Inc., Montevallo, AL, pg. 986
Searcy, Dan, Sec.--Cowin & Company, Inc., Birmingham, AL, pg. 291
Sears, Robert R., Controller & Sec.--Clark Foodservice, Inc., Elk Grove Village, IL, pg. 252
Sebastian, Paul E., Sr. Exec. V.P.-Fin. & Sec.--Jockey International, Inc., Kenosha, WI, pg. 595
Seberry, Therese M., Corp. Sec.--Zephyr Inc., North Muskegon, MI, pg. 1217
Secker, Joseph, V.P.-Fin.--Jordan Industries, Inc., Deerfield, IL, pg. 604
Seeley, Gregory D., Sec.--Boston Distributors, Inc., Maple Heights, OH, pg. 167
Seeley, James B., Sec.--Bison Canning Co., Inc., Angola, NY, pg. 474
Seeley, Paul J., Treas., Sec. & Controller--Lindsay Manufacturing Inc., Ponca City, OK, pg. 676
Seeley, Raynor M. Jr., V.P., Chief Fin. Officer & Sec.--PTA Corporation, Oxford, CT, pg. 837
Seeligman, Richard, Sec.--M M I Companies, Inc., Deerfield, IL, pg. 692
Segale, David S., Sec. & Treas.--Rapton Honda-GMC, Sacramento, CA, pg. 913
Segall, Mary Ann, Corp. Sec.--Sharon-Jay Togs, Inc., New Bedford, MA, pg. 995
Seidel, Thomas A., Sec.--Growmark, Inc., Bloomington, IL, pg. 490
Seigfreid, Jim, Sec.--Kansas City Chiefs Football Club, Kansas City, MO, pg. 616
Sellers, Alan B., Exec. V.P.-Admin. & Legal, Corp. Sec.--Dole Food Company, Inc., Westlake Village, CA, pg. 840
Sellers, Robert P., Sec. & Treas.--Dean Sellers Ford Inc., Troy, MI, pg. 988
Selover, Patricia W., Sec. & Treas.--Selover Buick, Inc., Billings, MT, pg. 988
Seltzer, Agatha, Sec.--Roller Derby Skate Company, Litchfield, IL, pg. 944
Seltzer, Mike, V.P. & Sec.--Red Apple Companies, New York, NY, pg. 917
Senne, Sandra, Sec.--Wetsel-Oviatt Lumber Company, Folsom, CA, pg. 1183
Sensing, Janice, Sec. & Treas.--Phoenix Enterprises Inc., Nashville, TN, pg. 868
Senty, John L., V.P. & Sec.--Consolidated Midwest, Inc., La Crosse, WI, pg. 277
Senty, John L., V.P., Sec. & Treas.--Midwest Bottle Gas Company, La Crosse, WI, pg. 277
Serr, Erik, Sec. & Gen. Counsel--R & B Machine Tool Co., Saline, MI, pg. 906
Serrano, George, V.P. & Sec.--Canberra Industries, Inc., Meriden, CT, pg. 213
Severino, Beverly, Sec. & Treas.--Great Scott Advertising Co. Inc., New York, NY, pg. 482
Sexson, Ward E., V.P.-Fin. & Sec.--Holcomb & Hoke Mfg. Company, Inc., Indianapolis, IN, pg. 538
Seyle, Jeanann, Sec. & Treas.--Mike Daugherty's Hurling Chevrolet, Inc., Sacramento, CA, pg. 555
Sha, J., Sec. & Treas.--Fyrnetics, Inc., Roselle, IL, pg. 438
Shafer, Evelyn, Sec. & Treas.--Shafer Commercial Seating Inc., Denver, CO, pg. 994
Shafer, Linda N., Sec.--Smith-Shafer Oil Co., Rockford, IL, pg. 1014
Shaffer, Harry Gard, Jr., Exec. Sec.--The Florists Assn. of Greater Cleveland, Inc., Cleveland, OH, pg. 421
Shah, Dipak, Sec. & Treas.--Village Ford Inc., Dearborn, MI, pg. 1151
Shaker, Helen, Sec.--Shaker Advertising Agency, Oak Park, IL, pg. 994
Shames, Harold, Exec. V.P. & Sec.--Melard Manufacturing Corporation, Passaic, NJ, pg. 737
Shanes, Samuel, Exec. V.P. & Sec.--Talk-A-Phone Co., Chicago, IL, pg. 1077
Shank, Robert K., Sec. & Asst. Treas.--Sisco Company, Mount Joy, PA, pg. 413
Shannon, Elizabeth O'Neal, Sec.--O'Neal Steel Inc., Birmingham, AL, pg. 827
Shapiro, Robert, Sec. & Controller--Weiners Enterprises, Inc., Houston, TX, pg. 1173
Sharp, John M., Sec.--Electrical Wholesale Supply Company, Inc., Idaho Falls, ID, pg. 374
Sharp, Vivian A., Sec. & Treas.--Texas Refinery Corp., Fort Worth, TX, pg. 1089
Shaver, Kenneth, Asst. Sec.--MCorp, Dallas, TX, pg. 732
Shaw, William J., Co. Sec.--Bently Nevada Corporation, Minden, NV, pg. 140
Shea, Cathy D., Asst. Sec.--Butler International, Montvale, NJ, pg. 197
Shearer, Peter, Sec.--Philadelphia Reserve Supply Company, Croydon, PA, pg. 867
Sheets, Mary J., Sec. & Treas.--Rapid Industries, Inc., Louisville, KY, pg. 913
Sheldon, Leone, Sec.--Sheldons' Inc., Antigo, WI, pg. 996
Shelton, David R., Sec.--Treaty Co., Greenville, OH, pg. 1109
Shelton, James, Sec. & Treas.--Apex Corporation, Indianapolis, IN, pg. 78
Shelton, John, Gen. Mgr. & Sec.--Denver Wholesale Florists Company, Denver, CO, pg. 331
Shepard, Robert L., Chief Fin. Officer, Dir.-Mngmt. Info. Systems, Sec. & Treas.--Acme Foundry, Inc., Coffeyville, KS, pg. 13
Shepherd, William Clyde, Jr., Sec. & Treas.--Shepherd Construction Co., Inc., Atlanta, GA, pg. 998
Sher, Pete, Sec. & Gen. Counsel--San Francisco French Bread Company, Oakland, CA, pg. 969
Sherrill, John, Treas. & Sec.--Howards Appliances, Inc., San Gabriel, CA, pg. 547
Sherry, Kenneth C., Sec. & Controller--Valk Manufacturing Company, New Kingstown, PA, pg. 1143
Shimala, Joseph C., Sec.--Morrison, Inc., Hammond, IN, pg. 771
Shine, Loretta, Treas. & Sec.--First Financial Group, Inc., Encino, CA, pg. 413
Shine, Philip J., Sec.--Peter Pan Bus Lines, Inc., Springfield, MA, pg. 864
Shinn, William R., Treas. & Sec.--Chicago Lock Company, Chicago, IL, pg. 245
Shipengrover, Donald R., Treas. & Sec.--Watkins System Inc., Concordville, PA, pg. 1167
Shipman, Tana, Sec.--Crowley Maritime Corporation, Oakland, CA, pg. 301
Shirk, Betty J., Treas. & Sec.--Beer Nuts, Inc., Bloomington, IL, pg. 132
Shoemaker, Kevin, V.P.-Fin., Sec. & Treas.--Seneca Wire & Manufacturing Co., Fostoria, OH, pg. 989
Shoff, Norman E., Sec.--Columbia Pipe & Supply Company, Chicago, IL, pg. 266
Shorey, Ginger, Sec. & Treas.--Magnolia Hi-Fi, Inc., Seattle, WA, pg. 701
Short, Roland T., Exec. V.P. & Sec.--Alabama Metal Industries Corporation, Birmingham, AL, pg. 28
Shott, John S., V.P. & Sec.--National Engineering & Contracting Co., Strongsville, OH, pg. 788
Shoup, Don, Exec. V.P. & Sec.--Amana Society, Amana, IA, pg. 46
Shuford, Arlene, Sec. & Treas.--Bowen Brothers Fruit Co., Inc., Winter Haven, FL, pg. 169
Shuman, Larry E., V.P. & Sec.--Walter H. Weaber Sons, Inc., Lebanon, PA, pg. 1169
Sica, Salvatore M., Sec. & Gen. Counsel--Interroyal Corporation, Warren, PA, pg. 580
Sicks, J.N., Asst. Sec.--Berwind Corporation, Philadelphia, PA, pg. 145
Siebel, Richard, Sec.--Woodwork Corporation of America, Chicago, IL, pg. 1201
Siecgrist, Linda L., Sr. V.P., Sec. & Treas.--Landmark Hotel Corporation, Topeka, KS, pg. 656
Siegel, Evelyn, Sec.--Siegel Corp., Fort Worth, TX, pg. 1002
Siegel, Evelyn, Sec.--Legis Corporation, Ft. Worth, TX, pg. 1002
Siegel, S.L., Treas. & Sec.--R.S. Owens, Chicago, IL, pg. 834
Siegfried, Peter, V.P., Gen. Counsel & Sec.--Central National-Gottesman Inc., Purchase, NY, pg. 233
Siegmund, John, Sec.--Land O'Lakes, Inc., Arden Hills, MN, pg. 653
Sigman, Benjamin L., V.P. & Sec.--B. Green & Co., Baltimore, MD, pg. 484
Sikorovsky, Eugene F., Sr. V.P., Gen. Counsel & Sec.--Bell & Howell Company, Skokie, IL, pg. 134
Silberstein, Dr. Jack, Sec.--Columbus Pipe & Equipment Company, Columbus, OH, pg. 267
Silva, Ed, V.P.-Fin. & Treas.--Cincinnati Incorporated, Harrison, OH, pg. 250
Silvera, Mike, Gen. Counsel--Save Mart Supermarkets, Modesto, CA, pg. 973
Silverman, Alan, V.P. & Sec.--Silverman Products & Textiles, New York, NY, pg. 1004
Silverman, Harvey, Sec., Treas., Controller & Dir.-Mngmt. Information Systems--MI Fund Incorporated, New York, NY, pg. 692
Silverman, Richard H., Asst. Gen. Mgr. & Sec.--Salt River Project Agricultural Improvement and Power District, Tempe, AZ, pg. 967
Silverman, Selma, V.P. & Sec.--White Rose Food, Long Island City, NY, pg. 335
Silvers, Robert, Sr. V.P., Assoc. Publisher & Sec.--Benjamin Franklin Literary & Medical Society, Inc., Indianapolis, IN, pg. 139
Simmons, Brian, V.P. & Sec.--M. Kamenstein, Inc., White Plains, NY, pg. 615
Simmons, D. Ramsay, III, V.P., Sec. & Treas.--Elberta Crate & Box Company, Bainbridge, GA, pg. 372
Simmons, Harvey O., III, Gen. Counsel & Sec.--Crucible Materials Corp., Syracuse, NY, pg. 302
Simon, Dolph B.H., V.P., Gen. Counsel & Sec.--Zale Corporation, Irving, TX, pg. 1215
Simon, Esther, Sec.--Contractors Steel Company, Livonia, MI, pg. 280
Simon, Sam, Gen. Counsel & Sec.--Great American Broadcasting Company, Cincinnati, OH, pg. 52
Simon, Samuel J., Gen. Counsel & Sec.--Great American Communications Company, Cincinnati, OH, pg. 53
Simon, Stephen H., Sec.--Omaha Creative Group, Omaha, NE, pg. 825
Simon, Susan, Sec.--Riccobon & Company, Inc., Santa Fe Springs, CA, pg. 931
Simpson, D.L., III, Sec. & Gen. Counsel--Conwood Company L.P., Memphis, TN, pg. 281
Sink, Barbara J., V.P., Sec. & Dir.-Personnel--Traders Supermarkets, Inc., Berrien Springs, MI, pg. 1105
Sink, George, Asst. Sec.--Graves-Humphreys Company, Roanoke, VA, pg. 592
Siragusa, John R., Exec. V.P. & Sec.--Game Time, Inc., Fort Payne, AL, pg. 442
Sirkin, Samuel, Sec.--Clay-Park Labs, Inc., Bronx, NY, pg. 253
Sirotkin, Martin, Sec.--Rapid Industrial Plastics Company, Jersey City, NJ, pg. 913
Sisley, G. William, Sec.--Silgan Corporation, Stamford, CT, pg. 1004
Sitter, James J., Sec. & Controller--Plastek Group, Erie, PA, pg. 874
Siviglia, Peter, Sec.--Fairfield International Corporation, New York, NY, pg. 397
Sjogren, Loriann, V.P. & Sec.--Whibco, Inc., Leesburg, NJ, pg. 1185
Skaff, Ramez G., Sec. & Treas.--Interstate Resources, Inc., Rosslyn, VA, pg. 580
Skiera, Dorothy A., Corp. Sec.--S & C Electric Company, Chicago, IL, pg. 958
Skogquist, Kenneth, Asst. Sec.--United Power Association, Elk River, MN, pg. 1134
Skolyan, Mary Rose, Corp. Sec.--Knight Equipment Corp., Costa Mesa, CA, pg. 636
Skrobola, A.W., Sr. V.P.-Fin., Sec. & Treas.--Thomas Steel Strip Corp., Warren, OH, pg. 1094
Skubas, Charles E., Chief Fin. Officer & Sec.--Herlin Press, West Haven, CT, pg. 531
Sladen, J.B., Sec.--Buckman Laboratories, Memphis, TN, pg. 185
Slater, Craig, Sec.--Anschutz Corporation, Denver, CO, pg. 75
Slavin, Stephen M., Sec.--Hess Engineering Inc., Niles, MI, pg. 532

Sloan, Patricia L., Sec. & Treas.--Stratton Growth Fund, Inc., Plymouth Meeting, PA, pg. 1053
Sloan, Patricia L., Sec. & Treas.--Stratton Monthly Dividend Shares, Inc., Plymouth Meeting, PA, pg. 1053
Sloan, William E. II, Exec. V.P., Treas. & Sec.--Sloan Valve Company, Franklin Park, IL, pg. 1010
Slote, Richard B., Sec.--King Fuels Inc., Troy, NY, pg. 630
Smagley, Norman, Treas., Sec. & Risk Mngmt.--GenDerm Corporation, Lincolnshire, IL, pg. 448
Smaldone, Dennis, Comptroller & Asst. Sec.--Loft's Seeds, Inc., Bound Brook, NJ, pg. 681
Small, J.R., Sec. & Treas.--Atlas Supply Company, Atlanta, GA, pg. 96
Smallenberger, James Andrew, V.P., Gen. Counsel & Sec.--Central Life Assurance Co., Des Moines, IA, pg. 232
Smart, Averyl, Sec.--VV Publishing Corp., New York, NY, pg. 1142
Smead, H.J., Chm. Bd., Pres., Chief Exec. & Chief Fin. Officer & Sec.--Kaiser Aerospace & Electronics Corp., Foster City, CA, pg. 614
Smeenge, James J., Sec., Treas. & Comptroller--Amick Construction Ltd., Orlando, FL, pg. 67
Smilowitz, Bernard, Sec. & Treas.--Allied Building Products Corporation, East Rutherford, NJ, pg. 37
Smisor, Bradley, Sec. & Treas.--Builders Development Inc., Wichita, KS, pg. 444
Smisor, Bradley K., Sec.--Builders Inc., Wichita, KS, pg. 444
Smith, A. Ledyard, Sec.--Rex Lumber Company, Acton, MA, pg. 930
Smith, Allen, Sec.--Valleydale Packers Inc., Bristol, VA, pg. 1143
Smith, Allen, Chief Fin. Officer, Treas. & Sec.--The Benham Group, Oklahoma City, OK, pg. 138
Smith, C. Michael, Pres., Chief Oper. Officer & Sec.--Orders Distributing Co., Greenville, SC, pg. 829
Smith, Christine J., V.P. & Sec.--Berol Corporation, Brentwood, TN, pg. 856
Smith, Cynthia, Sec.--Theochem Labs., Inc., Tampa, FL, pg. 1090
Smith, Delta E., Sec.--Header Products Inc., Romulus, MI, pg. 520
Smith, Ed, Treas. & Sec.--Martin & Bayley Inc., Carmi, IL, pg. 714
Smith, Ellen W., Sec.--American Technical Services Group, Inc., Norcross, GA, pg. 63
Smith, Gary V., Sec. & Treas.--Herman Hughes & Sons, Inc., North Salt Lake, UT, pg. 552
Smith, Gordon L., Jr., V.P.-Plng.--North American Royalties, Inc., Chattanooga, TN, pg. 811
Smith, H.A., Sr. V.P. & Sec.--Allison-Erwin Co. Inc., Charlotte, NC, pg. 40
Smith, Harold J., V.P. & Sec.--Tradehome Shoe Stores, Inc., Saint Paul, MN, pg. 1105
Smith, Jack, Sec.--Benson Management Company, San Antonio, TX, pg. 140
Smith, John, Jr., Sec.--Southeastern Equipment Company, Inc., Augusta, GA, pg. 1019
Smith, Klara, Sec.--Terre Hill Concrete Products, Inc., Terre Hill, PA, pg. 1089
Smith, Larry, V.P. & Sec.--Five Dollar Clothing Stores, Los Angeles, CA, pg. 416
Smith, Les, Treas. & Sec.--Buhrman-Pharr Hardware Company, Texarkana, AR, pg. 187
Smith, Linda, Corp. Controller & Sec.--Standard Gravure Corp./Shea Communications, Atlanta, GA, pg. 1036
Smith, Lois M., Sec. & Treas.--Davis-Moore Oldsmobile, Inc., Wichita, KS, pg. 319
Smith, Margaret, Sec.--WBH Industries, Inc., Arlington, TX, pg. 1155
Smith, Marie, Corp. Sec., Office Mgr.--Jay Incorporated, Rochester, NY, pg. 590
Smith, Marie, Sec.--Kohm Associates, Inc., Oradell, NJ, pg. 640
Smith, Mary R., V.P. & Sec.--Ben Venue Laboratories, Inc., Bedford, OH, pg. 138
Smith, Maureen, V.P.-Human Rels.--Yardney Technical Products, Inc., Pawcatuck, CT, pg. 1207
Smith, Michael, Sec.--Purity, Inc., Miami, FL, pg. 901
Smith, Mike, Sec. & Treas.--Kelsey Construction, Inc., Orlando, FL, pg. 621
Smith, Randy J., V.P., Gen. Counsel & Sec.--G. Heileman Brewing Co., Inc., La Crosse, WI, pg. 526
Smith, Robert, Sec.--O/E Automation, Inc., Troy, MI, pg. 819
Smith, Robert C., Sr. V.P., Sec. & Gen. Counsel--White Hen Pantry, Inc., Elmhurst, IL, pg. 1185
Smith, Robert J., Sec.--Welsh Farms, Inc., Long Valley, NJ, pg. 1175
Smith, Robert Lewis, Treas., Sec. & Controller--Hankins Lumber Company, Inc., Grenada, MS, pg. 505
Smith, Susan, Sec.--Landmark Communications, Inc., Norfolk, VA, pg. 654
Smith, Theodore B. III, Sec.--John Hassall, Inc., Westbury, NY, pg. 516
Smith, William E., Pres., Chief Oper. Officer & Sec.--Fitzgerald & Company, Inc., Cranston, RI, pg. 416
Smith, William N., Treas. & Sec.--Tell City Chair Co., Tell City, IN, pg. 1085
Smith, William S., Sec. & Gen. Counsel--Tasa Corporation, Pittsburgh, PA, pg. 1079
Smoak, Robert R., V.P., Sec. & Treas.--Bernhardt Furniture Co., Lenoir, NC, pg. 144
Smoliar, Burton B., Asst. Sec.--Park Ridge Corporation, Park Ridge, NJ, pg. 849
Smyre, Dane, Sec. & Treas.--Diamond Hill Plywood Company, Darlington, SC, pg. 316
Smyth, Anthony, Sec.--John M. Smyth Co., Downers Grove, IL, pg. 1014
Snapp, Robert B., Jr., Asst. Sec. & Treas.--Clarkson Construction Companies, Kansas City, MO, pg. 253
Snavely, Theresa V., Sec.--Snavely Forest Products, Inc., Pittsburgh, PA, pg. 1015
Snead, Elizabeth P., Sec.--The Paty Company, Piney Flats, TN, pg. 852
Snelling, Andrew P., Treas. & Sec.--The Shelburne Corporation, Shelburne, VT, pg. 996
Snelling, Guy, Sec. & Treas.--Edmonson Wheat Growers, Inc., Edmonson, TX, pg. 369
Snow, Mary C., Asst. Sec.--Walter Industries, Inc., Tampa, FL, pg. 1161
Snow, Richard G., Jr., V.P.- Gen. Counsel & Sec.--J.D. Edwards & Company, Denver, CO, pg. 370
Snyder, Colby H., V.P.-Fin. & Sec.--Namico, Inc., Philadelphia, PA, pg. 783
Snyder, E.L., Treas. & Sec.--In-N-Out Burgers, Baldwin Park, CA, pg. 564
Snyder, Herman, Sec.--Gordon Brothers Corporation, Boston, MA, pg. 471
Snyder, Judith, Sec.--McLean-Thomas Inc., Buffalo, NY, pg. 731
Snyder, Richard, Exec. V.P. & Sec.--Gateway 2000, Sioux City, SD, pg. 446
Soehnlen, Joseph, V.P.--Quality Chekd Dairy Products Association, Naperville, IL, pg. 903
Solan, Bob, Sec.--S & S Graphics, Inc., Laurel, MD, pg. 959
Solimsky, James A., V.P.-Fin. & Sec.--Phillips Plastics Corporation, Phillips, WI, pg. 867
Solombrino, Scott, Chm. Bd., Pres. & Chief Exec. Officer--Dav-El Services, Inc., New York, NY, pg. 317
Sommer, Nila, Sec.--Service Motor Company, Dale, WI, pg. 992
Sorden, Michael R., Sec. & Treas.--Commercial Light Company, Hillside, IL, pg. 268
Sorheim, Dennis, Sec. & Treas.--Peoples Electric Company, Inc., Saint Paul, MN, pg. 859
Sornstein, Anne, V.P.-Admin. & Asst. Treas. & Sec.--Central Paper Company, Newark, NJ, pg. 233
Sottile, Frances M., Sec.--Barrett Haentjens & Company, Hazleton, PA, pg. 499
Spahn, David T., Treas. & Asst.Sec.--Emerald Corporation, Cleveland, OH, pg. 378
Spahn, Dennis A., Sec.--Emerald Corporation, Cleveland, OH, pg. 378
Spaniol, Joseph F., V.P.-Contracts & Corp. Sec.--RJO Enterprises, Inc., Lanham, MD, pg. 907
Sparks, William B., V.P., Sec. & Treas.--Macco Constructors, Inc., Paramount, CA, pg. 696
Spear, Carol, Sec.--Del-Val Manufacturing Company, Warminster, PA, pg. 325
Spears, Jimmy, Sec.--Darlington Veneer Company, Darlington, SC, pg. 315
Spector, Margaret D., Sec.--Margo Nursery Farms, Inc., Miami, FL, pg. 706
Spector, Martin W., Exec. V.P. & Gen. Counsel--ARA Group, Philadelphia, PA, pg. 5
Spector, Martin W., Sr. V.P., Gen. Counsel & Sec.--ARA Services, Inc., Philadelphia, PA, pg. 5
Speer, Carlton, V.P. & Sec.--Oliver Oil Company, Inc., Chambersburg, PA, pg. 824
Spellberg, Vic, Sec.--Office Connection, Inc., Fort Lauderdale, FL, pg. 821
Spellman, Richard A., Sr. V.P., Gen. Counsel & Sec.--Guarantee Mutual Life Co., Omaha, NE, pg. 491
Spence, Brad, Sec.--Wilson Products Co., Salt Lake City, UT, pg. 1194
Spencer, Marilyn, Sec. & Treas.--Faber Enterprises, Inc., Canoga Park, CA, pg. 395
Speranza, Paul S., Gen. Counsel & Sec.--Wegmans Food Markets, Inc., Rochester, NY, pg. 1172
Sperry, A. R., Sr. V.P. & Sec.--Royal Oak Enterprises, Inc., Atlanta, GA, pg. 953
Speyer, Guy, V.P., Sec.--Phillips, Miller, Speyer & Frost, Inc., Amityville, NY, pg. 867
Spiegel, Gary J., Sec.--Southwark Metal Manufacturing Company, Philadelphia, PA, pg. 1023
Spiegel, John, Sec. & Treas.--Bucyrus Blades Inc., Bucyrus, OH, pg. 388
Spille, Lisa, Sec.--Union City Body Company, Inc., Union City, IN, pg. 1128
Spitalnick, Andrea, Sec. & Treas.--Wellmade Industries, Inc., New York, NY, pg. 1175
Spitz, Arnold J., Exec. V.P., Sec. & Treas.--International Seaway Trading Corporation, Mayfield Village, OH, pg. 579
Spitz, Randy J., Treas., Sec. & Controller--Hicks Oil-Hicks Gas, Inc., Roberts, IL, pg. 533
Spohn, Dennis A., Sec.--The Spohn Corporation, Cleveland, OH, pg. 1032
Spowart, Jay R., V.P.-Fin. & Corp. Sec.--PhoneMate, Inc., Torrance, CA, pg. 869
Spradley, James W., Jr., Pres. & Chief Exec. Officer--Standard Candy Co., Inc., Nashville, TN, pg. 1035
Spratling, B.B., Jr., Sec. & Treas.--Dixie Electric Cooperative, Union Springs, AL, pg. 341
Sprik, Harlan, V.P.-Fin., Treas. & Sec.--Trendway Corporation, Holland, MI, pg. 1109
Springer, Branch J., V.P., Chief Fin. Officer, Treas. & Sec.--Abbey Etna Machine Company, Perrysburg, OH, pg. 9
Springer, June, Sec. & Treas.--Smith Motors, Inc., Hammond, IN, pg. 1014
Sprott, H.B. III, V.P. & Sec.--Sprott Oil Co., Inc., Manning, SC, pg. 1034
Sprouse, Patricia A., Gen. Counsel & Asst. Sec.--Sierracin Corporation, Sylmar, CA, pg. 1003
Sprow, Bob, Sec., Treas. & Controller--Ryan Herco Products Corp., Burbank, CA, pg. 958
St. Claire, Joy, Sec.--Senator Ford, Sacramento, CA, pg. 989
Stachura, Raymond, V.P.-Fin. & Sec.--Northland Container Corp., Plymouth, MI, pg. 814
Stada, Terry, V.P. & Sec.--Herbal Enterprises Inc., Manchester, CT, pg. 530
Stadelman, Shirley M., Sec.--Russell Stadelman & Company, Germantown, TN, pg. 1034
Staebell, Gerald, Sec.--Waterloo Service Company, Waterloo, IA, pg. 1167
Staelens, Peter, Treas. & Asst. Sec.--Dawn Food Products, Inc., Jackson, MI, pg. 319
Stafford, Rose Ann, Sec. & Treas.--Equity Supply Company, Kalispell, MT, pg. 385
Stafford, Theresa, Sec.--Dinner Bell Foods, Inc., Cincinnati, OH, pg. 53
Stalla, Gloria D., Sec.--Quael Corp., Detroit, MI, pg. 902
Stalzer, Robert J., Sr. V.P. Admin., Fin., Treas. & Asst. Sec.--Servo Corporation of America, Hicksville, NY, pg. 993
Standaert, James V., Natl. Sec.--Modern Woodmen of America, Rock Island, IL, pg. 763
Standridge, W.L., Chief Fin. Officer, Treas. & Sec.--Spencer Companies Inc., Huntsville, AL, pg. 1030
Stanke, Mary, Pres. & Sec.--JS&A Advertising, Las Vegas, NV, pg. 586
Stanley, John W., Jr., Pres., Chief Exec. Officer & Sec.--Blue Ridge Transfer Co., Roanoke, VA, pg. 161
Stanton-Riesgo, Margaret P., Exec. V.P. & Copr. Sec.--Jazzercise, Inc., Carlsbad, CA, pg. 591
Stanton, Laura, V.P., Sec. & Treas.--Dunlap & Co. Inc., Columbus, IN, pg. 353
Stapleton, R.D., Exec. V.P.-Fin. & Admin., Sec. & Gen. Counsel--The Lane Construction Corp., Meriden, CT, pg. 656
Staskiel, James, V.P., Legal Counsel & Sec.--McCarthy Building Companies, Saint Louis, MO, pg. 727
Statter, Noelle, Sec.--Gregory Affiliates, Inc., Beaverton, OR, pg. 486
Stauffer, Jerry, V.P., Gen. Counsel & Sec.--The Alpha Corporation Of Tennessee, Collierville, TN, pg. 43
Stauffer, John H., Jr., Gen. Counsel & Corp. Sec.--Stauffer Communications, Inc., Topeka, KS, pg. 1042
Stauffer, Kimberly, V.P. & Sec.--Boyle Engineering Corp., Newport Beach, CA, pg. 169
Stavely, Richard W., V.P., Sec. & Gen. Counsel--Misco Industries, Wichita, KS, pg. 759
Stayer, Alice, V.P., Sec. & Treas.--Johnsonville Foods, Inc., Kohler, WI, pg. 601
Steele, Donald K., V.P.-Sls. & Sec.--Industrial Dielectrics, Inc., Noblesville, IN, pg. 566
Steele, Elizabeth M., Corp. Sec.--Jones Spacelink, Ltd., Englewood, CO, pg. 603
Steele, Marcia, V.P. & Sec.--H S Die & Engineering, Inc., Grand Rapids, MI, pg. 497
Steele, Russell F., Asst. Sec.--Tasa Corporation, Pittsburgh, PA, pg. 1079
Steenland, Douglas, V.P., Deputy Gen. Counsel & Sec.--NWA, Inc., Saint Paul, MN, pg. 782
Steenland, Douglas M., V.P., Deputy Gen. Counsel & Sec.--Northwest Airlines, Inc., Saint Paul, MN, pg. 782
Steiner, Philip, Sec.--Par Beverage Co., Cincinnati, OH, pg. 476
Steiner, Phillip, Sec.--Grandpa Brands Company, Cincinnati, OH, pg. 476
Steiner, Phillip, Sec.--A. J. Lehman Co., Cincinnati, OH, pg. 476
Steinhart, Conrad, Treas. & Sec.--Happy Holiday Tree Farms, Sheridan, MI, pg. 506
Steinhauer, Gary, Sec. & Treas.--Madison Dairy Produce Company, Madison, WI, pg. 699
Steinhauer, John S., Sec.--The Brenlin Group, Akron, OH, pg. 173
Steinhauer, John S., Sec.--The Cedarwood Companies, Akron, OH, pg. 230
Stelling, James M., Exec. V.P., Treas. & Sec.--Ruscon Corp., Charleston, SC, pg. 956
Steltmann, Harry F., V.P., Chief Fin. Officer, Treas & Sec.--Eclipse, Inc., Rockford, IL, pg. 366
Stempler, Deana, Sec.--Textilease Corporation, Beltsville, MD, pg. 1090
Stephenson, Louise S., Sec.--Capitol Broadcasting Co., Inc., Raleigh, NC, pg. 215
Stern, Herbert L., Jr., Chm.-Exec. Committee & Sec.--T C Manufacturing Company, Inc., Evanston, IL, pg. 1072
Stern, Judith, Sec.--Pollenex Corporation, Chicago, IL, pg. 879
Stern, Marion, Sec.--Hygrade Metal Moulding Mfg. Corp., Farmingdale, NY, pg. 557
Stern, Maxine E., Sec.--M.L. Stern & Company, Inc., Beverly Hills, CA, pg. 1047
Sterner, Gene E., Sec. & Treas.--Jordon Commercial Refrigerator Co., Philadelphia, PA, pg. 605
Sternheimer, Ross, Treas. & Sec.--Sternheimer Brothers Inc., Sandston, VA, pg. 1048
Steubben, Dorothy, Corp. Sec.--North Shore Movers, Northbrook, IL, pg. 813
Steuer, James C., Exec. V.P., Dir.-Res., & Sec.--Mintz & Hoke Inc., Avon, CT, pg. 759
Stevens, Gayle, Sec.--Associated Industrial Supply, Inc., Columbia, SC, pg. 90
Stevens, Jim, J., Jr., Treas. & Sec.--Lincoln Provision Company, Inc., Chicago, IL, pg. 676
Stewart, Barbara E., Sec.--Seligman & Associates, Inc., Bloomfield Hills, MI, pg. 988
Stewart, Greg, Sec.--Honorbuilt Industries, Inc., Minneapolis, KS, pg. 542
Stewart, Lever, Gen. Counsel & Asst. Sec.--Rock-Tenn Company, Norcross, GA, pg. 941
Stichter, Richard D., Sec.--Capital Tire, Inc., Toledo, OH, pg. 215
Stiefel, C.W., Vice Chm., Exec. V.P., Gen. Counsel & Corp. Sec.--Stiefel Laboratories, Inc., Coral Gables, FL, pg. 1048
Stillings, Robert, V.P.-Opers., Sls., Mktg. & Personnel Dir.--Presto Food Stores, Inc., Plant City, FL, pg. 888
Stillman, John C., Exec. V.P. & Sec.--Stillman & Hoag, Inc., Englewood, NJ, pg. 1049
Stimpson, Gordon S., Treas. & Sec.--Gulf Lumber Company, Inc., Mobile, AL, pg. 493
Stimpson, James R., Treas., Controller & Sec.--Channellock, Inc., Meadville, PA, pg. 239
Stinchfield, John E., Sec. & Gen. Counsel--The Donohoe Companies, Inc., Washington, DC, pg. 345
Stitt, David R., Sr. V.P.-Fin. & Admin.--General Computer Corp. Inc., Twinsburg, OH, pg. 449

Stockwell, Barbara, Sec.--Trico Electric Co-Op, Tucson, AZ, pg. 1113
Stoeckle, Marilyn, V.P. & Sec.--Bardes Corp., Cincinnati, OH, pg. 119
Stolarz-Fantino, Dr. Stephanie, Exec. V.P., Sec.--Bertrand Advertising Agency, Inc., Hollywood, CA, pg. 144
Stoll, Alan M., Clerk--Fallon Community Health Plan, West Boylston, MA, pg. 398
Stone, Edward B., V.P. & Sec.--W. O. Bankston Enterprises Inc., Dallas, TX, pg. 118
Stone, Howard S., Pres. & Sec.--Bake-Line Products, Inc., Des Plaines, IL, pg. 114
Stone, Kathy, V.P., Treas. & Sec.--Ergon, Inc., Jackson, MS, pg. 386
Stone, Martin S., Treas. & Sec.--Helmsley Enterprises, Inc., New York, NY, pg. 527
Stone, Rose, V.P. & Sec.--R. S. Hughes Co., Inc., Los Angeles, CA, pg. 551
Storm, June, V.P., Sec. & Treas.--Storm Products Company, Inc., Inglewood, CA, pg. 1052
Stowe, Wilford, Controller & Sec.--JPS Converter & Industrial Corp., Greenville, SC, pg. 586
Strassberg, Roslyn, Sec.--Anglers Roslyn Group Ltd., Flushing, NY, pg. 75
Strassler, Marc, Sec. & Gen. Counsel--Supermarkets General Corporation, Woodbridge, NJ, pg. 1064
Strassler, Marc, Sec. & Gen. Counsel--Pathmark, Woodbridge, NJ, pg. 1064
Straub, Donald A., Sec. & Gen. Counsel--Republic Industries, Inc., Harwood Heights, IL, pg. 928
Strauss, Jonathon, Corp. Sec.--Century America Corporation, Chicago, IL, pg. 234
Streck, James J., Sr. V.P.-Ins. Opers. & Sec.--American Mutual Life Insurance Company, Des Moines, IA, pg. 58
Streich, William J., Treas. & Sec.--Resco Products, Inc., Conshohocken, PA, pg. 928
Strickstein, Irvin, V.P. & Sec.--National Lumber Co., Warren, MI, pg. 792
Strobel, Lula Z., Sec.--O. J. Strobel Oil & Tire Co., Inc., Summerville, SC, pg. 1053
Stropple, Peter W., V.P.-Fin. & Sec.--Ris Paper Company, Long Island City, NY, pg. 935
Struthers, Archibald G., V.P.-Credit & Asst. Sec.--Wheatland Tube Company, Collingswood, NJ, pg. 1184
Strutt, David, V.P. & Sec.--The Weitz Corporation, Des Moines, IA, pg. 1174
Strutt, David S., Sec.--The Weitz-Cohen Construction Co., Des Moines, IA, pg. 1174
Stryker, Elsebeth Sexton, Sr. V.P. & Sec.--PMC Partnership, Ltd., Westport, CT, pg. 836
Stubblefield, William, Sec.--Dunavant Enterprises, Inc., Memphis, TN, pg. 352
Stucker, Robert J., Sec.--Industrial Coatings Group, Inc., Chicago, IL, pg. 566
Stucker, Robert J., Corp. Sec.--Lane Industries, Inc., Northbrook, IL, pg. 656
Stultz, Gardner M., Sec.--Concorp, Inc., Nitro, WV, pg. 272
Suard, Andrea Bollinger, Sec.--Bollinger Machine Shop And Shipyard, Inc., Lockport, LA, pg. 163
Suchor, Leo, Sec. & Treas.--Larrys, Inc., Gillette, WY, pg. 659
Sudhoff, Robert, Chief Fin. Officer & Sec.--The Minster Machine Company, Minster, OH, pg. 759
Sugarman, Alicia, Sec.--Pachmayr Gun Works Inc., Monrovia, CA, pg. 839
Suitt, Hilda, Sec.--Suitt Construction Company, Inc., Greenville, SC, pg. 1056
Sullivan, Barbara, Sec. & Treas.--Hesco Parts Corporation, Louisville, KY, pg. 531
Sullivan, Brian, Controller & Sec.--Applied Solar Energy Corporation, City of Industry, CA, pg. 79
Sullivan, Glenda D., Sec.--Sullivan Oil Company, Baton Rouge, LA, pg. 1057
Sullivan, John L., Treas., Sec. & Controller--Totsy Manufacturing Company, Inc., Holyoke, MA, pg. 1103
Sullivan, Laura P., V.P. & Sec.--State Farm Mutual Automobile Insurance Company, Bloomington, IL, pg. 1041
Summers, Cheryl, Controller & Asst. Sec.--McCall Oil & Chemical Corp., Portland, OR, pg. 726
Sumrall, O. Malcolm, Chief Fin. Officer, Sec. & Treas.--Associated Equipment Company, Inc., Mobile, AL, pg. 89
Sunderland, Kent W., Sec.--Ash Grove Cement Company, Overland Park, KS, pg. 87
Supcoe, Donald, V.P.-Admin.--Eastern American Energy Corporation, Charleston, WV, pg. 363
Surhan, Pat, Sec.--National Welders Supply Co. Inc., Charlotte, NC, pg. 794
Susco, John A., Sec. & Treas.--Ideal Forging Corporation, Southington, CT, pg. 562
Sutherland, Jerry, Sr. V.P., Treas. & Sec.--Consumers Markets Inc., Springfield, MO, pg. 277
Sutton, D. R., Sec.--Tillamook County Creamery Assn., Tillamook, OR, pg. 1097
Swallen, Jay, Sec. & Treas.--Haines & Co., Inc., North Canton, OH, pg. 500
Swaner, Beverly, Sec.--Swaner Hardwood Company, Inc., Burbank, CA, pg. 1066
Swanson, Elizabeth, Sec.--Patient Care, Inc., West Orange, NJ, pg. 851
Swanson, Robert, V.P.-Fin., Sec., Treas. & Chief Fin. Officer--Danfoss Dukes Fluid Power Inc., Saint Charles, IL, pg. 314
Swanson, Stanley, Sec. & Treas.--Minuteman Press International, Farmingdale, NY, pg. 759
Swartz, Sadie, Sec.--David Brett, Inc., Easton, MA, pg. 174
Swaze, Steven, Sec.--W-B Supply Co., Pampa, TX, pg. 1155
Swenson, Gordon, V.P.-Fin., Treas. & Sec.--The Odom Corporation, Seattle, WA, pg. 821
Swink, James W., Exec. V.P. & Sec.--Young Pecan Shelling Co., Inc., Florence, SC, pg. 1209
Switzer, Richard J., Sec. & Treas.--Drive Train Industries, Denver, CO, pg. 349
Swords, L. Frank, V.P., Treas. & Sec.--National Safety Associates, Memphis, TN, pg. 793
Sykes, Barbara, Treas. & Sec.--Sebastian & Cooke, Parsippany, NJ, pg. 986
Szabo, Bridget, Sec.--Rosanio, Bailets & Talamo, Inc., Cherry Hill, NJ, pg. 947
Szekely, Steven, Sec. & Treas.--Monarch Avalon, Inc., Baltimore, MD, pg. 765
Szidon, Bonnie Bixler, Sec.--Ranch-Way, Inc., Fort Collins, CO, pg. 911
Szulman-Jones, Marilyn, Sec. & Treas.--Airco Mechanical Inc., Sacramento, CA, pg. 27
Tabor, Jessie, V.P.-Admin. & Sec.--Kettle Restaurants, Houston, TX, pg. 626
Tack, Kim P., Sec. & Treas.--Kartridg Pak Co., Davenport, IA, pg. 122
Taddei, Mirian H., Sec.--Hunter Contracting Company, Gilbert, AZ, pg. 554
Takano, Eiichi, V.P. & Sec.--Glico Harmony Foods Corporation, Santa Cruz, CA, pg. 462
Takashima, Kenji, V.P., Sec., & Treas.--Pentax Precision Instruments Corp., Orangeburg, NY, pg. 859
Talcott, Joel D., V.P., Sec. & Gen. Counsel--Ampex Corporation, Redwood City, CA, pg. 998
Tallackson, Jeffrey S., Exec. V.P., Sec. & Gen. Counsel--American Savings Bank, White Plains, NY, pg. 60
Tang, Jane Y., Treas. & Corp. Sec.--Tekni-Plex, Inc., Brooklyn, NY, pg. 1084
Taniguchi, Lon, V.P. & Sec.--Puna Plantation Hawaii Ltd., Hilo, HI, pg. 900
Tapscott, James T., Sec. & Treas.--Columbus Mills, Inc., Columbus, GA, pg. 267
Taradash, Elliott, V.P.-Production, Sec. & Treas.--M. Grossman Son, Inc., Passaic, NJ, pg. 489
Tarica, Laurence, Exec. V.P. & Sec.--Jimlar Corporation, Great Neck, NY, pg. 594
Tarr, Peter, Sec.--Gaggenau USA Corporation, Norwood, MA, pg. 441
Tate, R.L., Chm. Bd., Sec. & Treas.--Tate Access Floors, Inc., Jessup, MD, pg. 1080
Taub, Jon, Sec.--PVS Chemicals, Inc., Detroit, MI, pg. 837
Tawil, Fred, Sec.--Tawil Associates Inc., Carteret, NJ, pg. 1080
Taylor, Arnold, Treas. & Sec.--Heather Crolie, Inc., Rochester, NY, pg. 300
Taylor, Becky, Admin. Asst.--Murry's, Inc., Forestville, MD, pg. 777
Taylor, Charles, Sec.--Graham Group, Inc., Des Moines, IA, pg. 475
Taylor, David H., Exec. V.P.-Fin. & Sec.--JPS Textile Group, Inc., Greenville, SC, pg. 586
Taylor, Don R., Sr., Chief Fin. Officer, Treas. & Sec.--Homeland Stores, Inc., Oklahoma City, OK, pg. 542
Taylor, Dorothy, Sec.--MADD (Mothers Against Drunk Driving), Irving, TX, pg. 691
Taylor, Michael, Sec.--Thunderbird Steel Corporation, Albuquerque, NM, pg. 1096
Taylor, Mike, Sec. & Treas.--White Electrical Construction Co., Atlanta, GA, pg. 1185
Taylor, R.T., V.P., Sec. & Asst. Treas.--Al Johnson Construction Co., Minneapolis, MN, pg. 597
Taylor, Robert M., Exec. V.P. & Sec.--Maui Divers Of Hawaii, Ltd., Honolulu, HI, pg. 721
Taylor, Terry, Sr. V.P., Gen. Counsel & Sec.--Club Corporation International, Dallas, TX, pg. 256
Taylor, Terry, Gen. Counsel, Sec. & Dir.--Club Corporation Of America, Dallas, TX, pg. 256
Teague, Roger D., Sec. & Controller--Worsley Companies Inc., Wilmington, NC, pg. 1204
Teasdale, Thomas, Sec.--Eastern Color Printing Company, Avon, CT, pg. 363
Tedone, Constantino, Sec.--J.T. Slocomb Company, South Glastonbury, CT, pg. 1010
Tellier, James P., Sec. & Treas.--Jefferson Chevrolet Co., Detroit, MI, pg. 591
Tellock, Wanda, Sec.--FWD Corporation, Clintonville, WI, pg. 395
Tellock, Wanda D., Corp. Sec.--Seagrave Fire Apparatus, Inc., Clintonville, WI, pg. 395
Temel, Selim, Sec.--Microphase Corporation, Norwalk, CT, pg. 749
Templeton, Nancy, Corp. Sec.--Pace International Corporation, Kirkland, WA, pg. 838
Tepoorten, Harold V., Treas. & Sec.--Steel, Inc., Commerce City, CO, pg. 1044
Terrell, Eddie, Sec. & Treas.--B. F. Trappey's Sons, Inc., New Iberia, LA, pg. 729
Terry, Thomas, Treas. & Sec.--Zimmer Paper Products Inc., Indianapolis, IN, pg. 1220
Teruya, Ethel, Sec.--Armstrong Produce Ltd., Honolulu, HI, pg. 84
Thanepohn, D.A., Sec.--Lyon Metal Products, Inc., Montgomery, IL, pg. 690
Theisen, Joan L., Sec.--T & S Brass & Bronze Works, Inc., Travelers Rest, SC, pg. 1074
Theurer, Jeffrey L., Sec.--PST Vans, Inc., Salt Lake City, UT, pg. 837
Thois, William, Chief Fin. Officer, Treas., Sec. & Dir.-Admin. & Opers.--Empire Airlines, Hayden Lake, ID, pg. 379
Thomas, Addie Joe, Sec. & Treas.--V. B. Hook & Co., Inc., Columbia, SC, pg. 543
Thomas, Doris, J., Sec.--National Group, Inc., Chattanooga, TN, pg. 789
Thomas, Eugene C., Sec. & Gen. Counsel--Intermountain Industries, Inc., Boise, ID, pg. 575
Thomas, Helen, Treas. & Sec.--Camino Real Chevrolet, Monterey Park, CA, pg. 212
Thomas, James W., Sec. & Gen. Mgr.--Anderson Wholesale Company, Muskogee, OK, pg. 73
Thomas, Jesse G., Treas., Sec., Chief Fin. & Chief Information Officer--Allen & Hoshall, Inc., Memphis, TN, pg. 36
Thomas, Marian A., Sec.--Citizens Realty & Insurance Inc., Evansville, IN, pg. 251
Thomas, Richard L., Treas. & Sec.--Mannington Ceramic Tile, Lexington, NC, pg. 704
Thomas, S.A., Asst. Sec. & Controller--York Wallcoverings Inc., York, PA, pg. 1208
Thompson, Dave, V.P. & Sec.--Burlington Basket Co., Burlington, IA, pg. 191
Thompson, Donnie, Sec.--Arcade Inc., Chattanooga, TN, pg. 80
Thompson, Gale, Chief Fin. Officer & Corp. Sec.--Thompson/Marince Advertising, San Antonio, TX, pg. 1094
Thompson, H.D., Chief Fin. Officer, V.P., Treas. & Sec.--Our Own Hardware Company, Burnsville, MN, pg. 832
Thompson, James B., Sec.--Pacific Coast Building Products Inc., Sacramento, CA, pg. 839
Thompson, Pam, Treas. & Sec.--Key Cadillac, Inc., Edina, MN, pg. 626
Thomsen, Stan K., Sr. V.P.-Admin. & Sec.--Golden Sun Feeds, Inc., Estherville, IA, pg. 467
Thomsen, Walter L., Sec. & Treas.--Schaeps Ice Cream Company, Madison, WI, pg. 974
Thornton, A.J., Sec. & Treas.--Consolidated Publishing Company, Anniston, AL, pg. 277
Thornton, Keith, Sec. & Treas.--Farmington Hills Holding Company, Farmington, MI, pg. 402
Thorpe, Donna, Sec.--Black & Co., Decatur, IL, pg. 154
Thorrez, Morris C., Sec.--Allied Chucker & Engineering Company, Jackson, MI, pg. 37
Thrall, Jerome Jeffrey, Exec. V.P. & Sec.--Thrall Enterprises, Inc., Chicago, IL, pg. 1095
Thurlow, Robin T., V.P., Chief Fin. Officer, Treas. & Sec.--Artesian Laboratories, Inc., Newark, DE, pg. 86
Tibus, Karen, Sec.--Don Massey Cadillac Inc., Plymouth, MI, pg. 719
Tichenor, John A., Chief Fin. Officer, Treas. & Sec.--Allied Sporting Goods Inc., Louisville, KY, pg. 40
Tiffany, John M., Sec.--Central Livestock Association, Inc., South St. Paul, MN, pg. 233
Tiffany, R.M., V.P. & Sec.--Plunkett-Webster, Inc., New Rochelle, NY, pg. 877
Tiffin, R. Alex, Sr., Treas. & Sec.--Tiffin Motor Homes, Inc., Red Bay, AL, pg. 1097
Till, Alan, Sec. & Treas.--Carquest, Andalusia, AL, pg. 224
Tillander, Thomas, V.P. & Sec.--Koret Givenchy, New York, NY, pg. 642
Tillery, Gary, Chm. Bd. & Sec.--The Townsend Agency, Ltd., Rosemont, IL, pg. 1104
Timm, Theodore, Sec. & Gen. Counsel--DoAll Company, Des Plaines, IL, pg. 341
Timma, Michael C., V.P.-Fin., Sec. & Treas.--M M Systems Corporation, Tucker, GA, pg. 692
Timmons, Linda, Sec.--Bates Container, Inc., North Richland Hills, TX, pg. 125
Tingle, Douglas R., Sec.--Dundee Mills, Inc., Griffin, GA, pg. 352
Tinius, Barry, Treas. & Sec.--Love Box Company, Inc., Wichita, KS, pg. 685
Tinker, T.F., V.P.-Opers. & Corp. Sec.--Hackney Brothers, Inc., Wilson, NC, pg. 498
Titus, William, Sec. & Pur. Agent--Panel Prints, Inc., Old Forge, PA, pg. 846
Toberman, David, Treas. & Sec.--Toberman, Saint Louis, MO, pg. 1099
Tobin, Michael, V.P. & Sec.--SGI Inc., Cranston, RI, pg. 962
Toburen, J.R., V.P. & Sec.--Flexfab, Inc., Hastings, MI, pg. 418
Todd, Jim, V.P.-Mfg. & Sec.--Preservative Paint Company, Seattle, WA, pg. 887
Todd, W.F., Sec.--TTX Co., Chicago, IL, pg. 1075
Tolkan, Victor K., Sec. & Treas.--Door Store, Inc., Washington, DC, pg. 346
Tolly, David H., V.P., Sec. & Gen. Counsel--Savage Arms Inc., Westfield, MA, pg. 973
Tomlinson, James F., V.P., Sec. & Asst. to the Pres.--The Associated Press, New York, NY, pg. 91
Tompkins, Polly, Sec. & Treas.--Burgess Pigment Co., Sandersville, GA, pg. 190
Toms, C.R., Sec. & Personnel Dir.--Rubatex Corporation, Bedford, VA, pg. 480
Toner, Edward J., Sec. & Legal Officer--Faber/Castell Corporation, Parsippany, NJ, pg. 395
Tonkin, William H., Treas. & Sec.--Safe Harbor Water Power Corporation, Conestoga, PA, pg. 966
Toothman, Mary Jane, Sec.--Trojan Steel Co., Charleston, WV, pg. 1115
Torke, Marcella B., Sec. & Treas.--Torke Coffee Company, Inc., Sheboygan, WI, pg. 1102
Tornberg, Edward, Sec.--Cyberex, Inc., Mentor, OH, pg. 307
Tornetta, Paul, Sec.--Reading Anthracite Co., Pottsville, PA, pg. 916
Torres, Rafael, V.P., Controller, Asst. Treas. & Asst. Sec.--Pueblo International, Inc., Pompano Beach, FL, pg. 899
Torres, Vera Trinchero, Sec. & Treas.--Sutter Home Winery, Inc., Saint Helena, CA, pg. 1065
Torres, William J., V.P., Sec., Treas., Legal Officer & Telecommunications Dir.--Gibbs Wire & Steel Company, Inc., Southington, CT, pg. 456
Tosch, John, V.P. & Corp. Counsel--American Speedy Printing Centers, Inc., Bloomfield Hills, MI, pg. 61
Tottino, Les, Treas. & Asst. Sec.--California Artichoke & Vegetable Growers Corp., Castroville, CA, pg. 209
Touhey, Charles L., V.P. & Sec.--Orange Motor Company Inc., Albany, NY, pg. 828
Towey, Ed, Sec.--Hammel, Green & Abrahamson, Inc., Minneapolis, MN, pg. 504
Towles, H.D., Sec.--Mayfair Mills, Inc., Arcadia, SC, pg. 724
Trabbuco, John E., Sec. & Gen. Counsel--Beckwith Machinery Company, Murrysville, PA, pg. 131
Tracy, James D., Sec.--Roy O'Brien Inc., St. Clair Shores, MI, pg. 820
Trador, Jack L., V.P. & Asst. Sec.--White Castle System, Inc., Columbus, OH, pg. 1185
Traeger, Ferne, Asst. Sec.--Plastoid Corporation, Hamburg, NJ, pg. 876

Trauth, Steven A., V.P.-Prod. & Sec.--Trauth Dairy Inc., Newport, KY, pg. 1108
Treffiletti, Anthony J., Sec. & Treas.--J. Treffiletti & Sons, Inc., Albany, NY, pg. 1109
Trevino, Julio C., Sec.--Arthur D. Little Mexicana, S.A. de C.V., Mexico, Mexico, pg. 679
Treynor, Sam, Sec., Treas. & Controller--Peck Road Ford Truck Sales, Whittier, CA, pg. 854
Tribble, Jay, Corp. Sec.--Tribble & Stephens Co., Houston, TX, pg. 1112
Trigg, Donald C., Sr. V.P.-Sec. & Gen. Counsel--The Associated Group, Indianapolis, IN, pg. 90
Truesdell, J. E., Jr., Pres. & Sec.--J. Austin Oil Co., Flint, MI, pg. 99
Truitt, Jim, Treas. & Sec.--Martin Industries (AL), Florence, AL, pg. 715
Trump, Arthur, Sec. & Gen. Counsel--Atlantic Builders Group Inc., Baltimore, MD, pg. 94
Tschirhart, Paul M., Sr. V.P., Gen. Counsel & Sec.--The Hertz Corporation, Park Ridge, NJ, pg. 849
Tschirhart, Paul M., V.P. & Sec.--Hertz Equipment Rental Corp., Park Ridge, NJ, pg. 849
Tsuchida, Ben, V.P. & Sec.--Time Oil Co., Los Angeles, CA, pg. 1097
Tsudis, Carol Cochran, Corp. Sec. & Treas.--817
Tucker, James D., Sec./Treas.--Network Real Estate of California, Inc., Soquel, CA, pg. 798
Tucker, James D., Sec./Treas.--Network Real Estate, Inc., Soquel, CA, pg. 798
Tucker, James L., Sr. V.P., Sec. & Gen. Counsel--OPUS Corp., Minnetonka, MN, pg. 828
Tucker, Rebbeca C., Corp. Sec.--Bovaird Supply Co., Tulsa, OK, pg. 168
Tudor, Michael S., Sec. & Gen. Counsel--Tudor Inc., Alexandria, LA, pg. 1118
Tujo, Patricia L., Asst. Corp. Sec.--Vincent Food Industries, Inc., Chicago, IL, pg. 1152
Tulloch, G.S., V.P., Sec. & Gen. Counsel--Graybar Electric Company, Inc., Clayton, MO, pg. 479
Tullos, Doris V., Sec.--McCarty Farms, Magee, MS, pg. 727
Tumminello, Theodore, Sr. V.P., Gen. Counsel & Sec.--Pan-American Life Insurance Company, New Orleans, LA, pg. 845
Tunmore, E. Roger, Pres. & Sec.--Tunmore Oldsmobile Inc., Buffalo, NY, pg. 1119
Turbville, John F., V.P.-Legal & Sec.--Walter Industries, Inc., Tampa, FL, pg. 1161
Turcott, Robert G., V.P., Sec. & Gen. Counsel--Roundy's, Inc., Pewaukee, WI, pg. 952
Turem, Lois, Sec.--Gabbert's, Inc., Minneapolis, MN, pg. 441
Turgeon, Nancy, Sec.--Robertson's Auto Salvage, Wareham, MA, pg. 939
Turk, Mike, Sr. V.P. & Chief Fin. Officer--Blue Coral, Inc., Cleveland, OH, pg. 159
Turkin, Todd, V.P., Sec. & Dir.-Telecommunications--Broder Bros. Co., Plymouth, MI, pg. 178
Turner, C.O., III, Sec. & Treas.--Manufacturers Consolidation Service, Memphis, TN, pg. 705
Turner, John L., Exec. V.P. & Gen. Mgr.--Allied Mineral Products, Inc., Columbus, OH, pg. 38
Turner, Judy, Corp. Sec.--Bureau of Engraving, Minneapolis, MN, pg. 189
Turriff, Patricia, Sec.--Tab Chemicals, Inc., Chicago, IL, pg. 1075
Tushman, J. Lawrence, Chief Exec. Officer & Sec.--Orleans International, Inc., Bloomfield Hills, MI, pg. 829
Tuttle, Myrna L., Sec.--Ohio Gas Company, Bryan, OH, pg. 822
Twigg-Smith, David, Vice Chm. & Sec.--Persis Corporation, Honolulu, HI, pg. 863
Twitchell, E., Sec.--Barton-Malow Company, Detroit, MI, pg. 123
Twitchell, Orman G., Sec.--Ocean Properties, Ltd., Boynton Beach, FL, pg. 820
Tyll, Betty, Treas. & Sec.--Sterling Heights Dodge, Inc., Sterling Heights, MI, pg. 1046
Uchiyama, Don, Exec. V.P. & Sec.--Tulip Corporation, Los Angeles, CA, pg. 1119
Uddenberg, Eugenia M., Sec. & Treas.--Keith Uddenberg, Inc., Gig Harbor, WA, pg. 1125
Underberg, Mark A., Mng. Dir., Sec. & Gen. Counsel--The Henley Group, Inc., Hampton, NH, pg. 529
Underwood, William E., Jr., Sec. & Gen. Counsel--AEA, Inc., Charlotte, NC, pg. 3
Unger, Sonja F., Sec.--Unger Company, Cleveland, OH, pg. 1126
Urland, Alice I., Asst. Sec.--LifeSurance Corporation, Atlanta, GA, pg. 921
Urschel, Elena V., V.P. & Sec.--Urschel Labs Inc., Valparaiso, IN, pg. 1140
Utsman, Robert E., Chm., Sec. & Mktg. Dir.--Gold Coast Advertising, Miami, FL, pg. 465
Vaccaro, Thomas S., V.P.-Fin. & Sec.--The Orvis Company, Inc., Manchester, VT, pg. 830
Vagnini, K.L., V.P., Sec. & Treas.--The Gerstenslager Company, Wooster, OH, pg. 454
Vahlsing, Donald W., V.P. & Sec.--Effective Management Systems, Milwaukee, WI, pg. 370
Vakil, Farooq U., Exec. V.P. & Sec.--Lights Of America, Inc., Walnut, CA, pg. 675
Valdes, Alfredo, V.P.-Fin., Opers., Corp. Sec. & Treas.--Domecq Importers Inc., Old Greenwich, CT, pg. 343
Valier, Glenn L., Sec.--Nebraska-Iowa Supply Company, Blair, NE, pg. 796
Van Allsburg,Dale, Sec.--American Metal & Plastics, Grand Rapids, MI, pg. 58
Van Gorder, Jan R., Exec. V.P., Sec. & Gen. Counsel--Erie Family Life Insurance Company, Erie, PA, pg. 386
Van Gorder, Jan R., Exec. V.P., Sec. & Gen. Counsel--Erie Insurance Group, Erie, PA, pg. 386
Van Gorder, Jan R., Exec. V.P., Sec. & Gen. Counsel--Erie Indemnity Company, Erie, PA, pg. 386
Van Gorder, Jan R., Exec. V.P., Sec. & Gen. Counsel--Erie Insurance Exchange, Erie, PA, pg. 386
Van Kanegan, Roy W., Jr., Pres., Treas. & Sec.--Target Stamped Products Corp., Kinsman, OH, pg. 1079
Van Rijn, Bernard, Chief Fin. Officer, Treas. & Sec.--Kirk-Mayer, Inc., Los Angeles, CA, pg. 633
Van Treeck, Dorothy, Sec. & Dir.-Data Processing--Gray-Pro, Inc., Boulder, CO, pg. 479
Van Vlack, Dudley, V.P. & Sec.--Coordinated Apparel, Inc., New York, NY, pg. 283
Van Vlierbergen, Brian R., V.P., Gen. Counsel & Sec.--Blue Cross & Blue Shield of Illinois, Chicago, IL, pg. 160
Vanaria, R. J., V.P.-Fin., Treas. & Sec.--Foamex L.P., East Providence, RI, pg. 1121
Vandenbergh, Robert A., Sec.--High Point Financial Corp., Branchville, NJ, pg. 533
Vander Boon, John, Sec. & Treas.--Ada Beef, Inc., Ada, MI, pg. 16
Vander Pol, Daryl L., V.P., Treas. & Sec.--Vita-Milk Dairy, Inc., Seattle, WA, pg. 1153
Vanderbilt, P., V.P.-Environmental & Sec.--R. T. Vanderbilt Company, Inc., Norwalk, CT, pg. 1144
Vanderminden, Henry J.W. III, Exec. V.P. & Sec.--Mettowee Lumber & Plastic Co., Inc., Granville, NY, pg. 1085
Vargo, James D., Sec. & Treas.--Daniels Manufacturing Corporation, Orlando, FL, pg. 314
Varona, Daniel, Chief Admin. Officer, Sec. & Gen. Counsel--Companion Life Insurance Co., Rye, NY, pg. 779
Vater, Thomas A., Controller & Sec.--Thompson Medical Company, Inc., West Palm Beach, FL, pg. 1094
Vaughan, Gaye, Sec.--The Van Metre Companies, Burke, VA, pg. 1144
Vaughn, Robert E., Treas., Sec. & Gen. Mgr.--Maryland Virginia Milk Producers Association, Inc., Reston, VA, pg. 717
Vecchiolla, Joseph, Exec. V.P., Chief Fin. Officer & Sec.--Educational Publishing Corporation, Oak Lawn, IL, pg. 369
Veligan, Daniel, V.P.-Fin., Sec. & Treas.--The Johnson Industries Corp., Urbana, OH, pg. 598
Ventura, M., Asst. Sec.--Quality Bakers of America Cooperative, Inc., Greenwich, CT, pg. 903
Vermylen, Mark E., V.P. & Sec.--A. Zeregas Sons, Inc., Fair Lawn, NJ, pg. 1217
Vermylen, Paul A., Jr., Pres., Treas. & Sec.--Meenan Oil Co. Limited Partnership, Syosset, NY, pg. 736
Vernick, Ruth, V.P. & Sec.--Universal Folding Box Company, Inc., Hoboken, NJ, pg. 1138
Vernon, Shirley A., Sec. & Treas.--Gilvin-Terrill Inc., Amarillo, TX, pg. 460
Vestrand, Donald A., Sec. & Treas.--Holmatic, Inc., Norcross, GA, pg. 122
Vetter, Charles R., V.P.-Fin. & Sec.--Osco Industries Inc., Portsmouth, OH, pg. 830
Vetter, Erich, Sr. V.P. & Sec.--Uniflex, Inc., Hicksville, NY, pg. 1126
Vetter, Sandra, Sec. & Treas.--Better Baked Foods, Inc., North East, PA, pg. 148
Vezza, Carlo, V.P. & Sec.--Aluma Shield Industries, Inc., Daytona Beach, FL, pg. 46
Viani, James, Sec.--Schutte Lumber Company, Kansas City, MO, pg. 980
Viator, Daniel, Corp. Sec.--SF Services, North Little Rock, AR, pg. 961
Vicsek, Sue, Corp. Sec.--South Bend Plastics, Inc., Mishawaka, IN, pg. 1019
Vile, Bella, Sec.--Vile-Goller, Fine Art Printing & Lithography, Kansas City, KS, pg. 1151
Villabona, America, Sec.--BSB/Meza, Ltda., Bogota,, Colombia, pg. 110
Vincent, Susan, Sec.--Amerisure Companies, Detroit, MI, pg. 66
Vinje, Ronald, Treas. & Sec.--Psomas & Associates, Santa Monica, CA, pg. 898
Viola, Roger, Sec.--First Pyramid Life Insurance Company of America, Little Rock, AR, pg. 1150
Visosky, Leonard M., V.P. & Sec.--Tapco Products Company, Plymouth, MI, pg. 1078
Vitus, Felicia J., V.P., Sec. & Treas.--Vitus Electrical Supply Company, Eugene, OR, pg. 1154
Vlahakis, Glenda, Sec. & Treas.--Trailer Wheel & Frame Company, Houston, TX, pg. 1105
Vogeter, Allan, Sec.--Kruse Hardware Company, Fairfield, OH, pg. 645
Voght, Judy, V.P.-Personnel & Human Resources & Sec.--Tennelec/Nucleus, Inc., Oak Ridge, TN, pg. 1087
Vogt, Doreen, Sec. & Treas.--De Nooyer Chevrolet Inc., Albany, NY, pg. 329
Voll, Ruth F., Sec.--Price Weber Marketing Communications, Inc., Louisville, KY, pg. 889
von Luhrte, Richard L., Exec. V.P., Sec. & Dir.--RNL Facilities Corporation, Denver, CO, pg. 907
von Luhrte, Richard L., Sec.--Interplan, Denver, CO, pg. 907
von Luhrte, Richard L., Sec.--RNL Design, Denver, CO, pg. 907
von Luhrte, Richard L., Sec.--RNL/Interplan, Los Angeles, CA, pg. 908
Von Wadden, Dennis C., Sec.--Twentieth Century Investors, Inc., Kansas City, MO, pg. 1121
VonHandorf, Donna, Sec. to the Pres.--C.S. Dent & Co., Cincinnati, OH, pg. 476
Vora, S.B., Sec.--The Smith Group, Inc., Detroit, MI, pg. 1012
Voss, Marianne, Treas. & Sec.--Voss Industries, Inc., Cleveland, OH, pg. 1155
Vrooman, Edward A., Gen. Counsel & Sec.--Tri-State Motor Transit Co., Joplin, MO, pg. 1111
Vumbacco, Joseph, Gen. Counsel & Sec.--The Lathrop Company, Toledo, OH, pg. 660
Wachner, Barbara Jo, Exec. V.P.-Mktg., Personnel & Sec.--BGW Systems, Inc., Hawthorne, CA, pg. 106
Wadas, Alicia, Exec. V.P. & Sec.--Martz & Wadas, Scottsdale, AZ, pg. 716
Waddington, Harold T., Sr. V.P.-Valuation, Rates & Sec.--Gannett Fleming Affiliates, Inc., Harrisburg, PA, pg. 442
Wade, Donnie, Controller, Treas. & Sec.--Goodpasture, Inc., Brownfield, TX, pg. 471
Wadler, Arnold, Sr. V.P., Gen. Counsel & Sec.--Metromedia Company, East Rutherford, NJ, pg. 743
Waggoner, Henry R., Controller & Asst. Sec.--Lakeside Industries, Redmond, WA, pg. 651
Wagner, M.J., Sec. & Treas.--American Inks & Coatings Corp., Valley Forge, PA, pg. 56
Wahl, C. Richard, Sr. V.P., Treas. & Sec.--Wheatland Tube Company, Collingswood, NJ, pg. 1184
Waite, Pamella D., V.P. & Corp. Sec.--Commtek Communications, Vienna, VA, pg. 269
Walborn, Earl J., V.P. & Sec.--Windsor Service, Inc., Reading, PA, pg. 1196
Walden, Susan L., Asst. Sec. & Treas.--Miller Electric Company, Jacksonville, FL, pg. 754
Waldman, David S., Sec.--MONY Life Insurance Co. of America, Teaneck, NJ, pg. 778
Waldman, Gary, Sec.--Service Packing Company, Los Angeles, CA, pg. 992
Waldschmidt, David, Sec.--Pacific Northern Oil Corp., Seattle, WA, pg. 841
Walk, Consuelo F., Sec.--Walk, Haydel & Associates, Inc., New Orleans, LA, pg. 1159
Walker, Anita, Treas.& Sec.--Fritz Chemical Company, Mesquite, TX, pg. 434
Walker, Baker, Treas., Controller, Sec. & Chief Fin. Officer--C. B. Ragland Company, Nashville, TN, pg. 909
Walker, C. Denny, Sec. & Dir.-Personnel--Draper Corporation, Greensboro, NC, pg. 348
Walker, John D., Sec. & Treas.--Anco Insulations, Inc., Baton Rouge, LA, pg. 72
Walker, Kandee Jo, Sec. & Treas.--Eldorado Chemical Company, San Antonio, TX, pg. 373
Walker, Max N., Treas. & Sec.--Gaston County Dyeing Machine Co., Stanley, NC, pg. 444
Walker, Robert, Sec.--American Snacks, Inc., Chelsea, MA, pg. 61
Walker, Ronald E., Pres. & Sec.--Lyon Conklin & Company, Baltimore, MD, pg. 690
Walker, T.J., Gen. Mgr. & Sec.--Electrical Equipment Company, Raleigh, NC, pg. 374
Walker, T.P., Sr. V.P. & Sec.--Stonecutter Mills Corp., Spindale, NC, pg. 1051
Walker, Virginia M., Sec.--Walker & Associates, Inc., Welcome, NC, pg. 1159
Wall, Hugh E., Jr., Sec.--Shook National Corporation, Dayton, OH, pg. 1000
Wall, Kay D., Sec. & Treas.--Bryant Electric Company, Inc., High Point, NC, pg. 185
Wallace, Donald W., V.P. & Sec.--Lazy Days R V Center, Inc., Tampa, FL, pg. 663
Wallace, Harry, Sec.--Albert Trostel Packings, Ltd., Lake Geneva, WI, pg. 1116
Wallace, Harry, Sec.--Everett Smith Investment Co. of Delaware, Milwaukee, WI, pg. 1013
Wallace, Harry L., Sec.--Albert Trostel & Sons Company, Milwaukee, WI, pg. 1116
Wallace, Juanita, Pres., Chief Fin. Officer, Treas. & Sec.--Wallace & Wallace Fuel Oil, St. Albans, NY, pg. 1160
Wallace, Leo A., Sec.--Dairyland Power Cooperative, La Crosse, WI, pg. 311
Wallace, Patricia, Sec.--Cowper & Siegfried, Amherst, NY, pg. 291
Wallens, E., Sec.--John Gross & Co., Baltimore, MD, pg. 489
Waller, William A., Sr. V.P., Gen. Counsel & Sec.--Petty Company, Inc., Effingham, IL, pg. 866
Walter, Anna C., V.P. & Sec.--Thermo Electric Co., Inc., Saddle Brook, NJ, pg. 1091
Waltersdorf, Margaret S., Sec.--Tristate Electrical Supply Co., Inc., Hagerstown, MD, pg. 1114
Walton, John, Sec.--S L C Graphics, Inc., Pittston, PA, pg. 963
Wampler, J., Sec.--Woodruff Electrical Co-Op, Forest City, AR, pg. 1200
Wander, Elyse G., V.P.-Plng. & Devel. & Sec.--Amtrak-National Railroad Passenger Corp., Washington, DC, pg. 69
Wannamaker, William, Sec.--Hardware Wholesalers, Inc., Fort Wayne, IN, pg. 508
Ward, Bill, Sr. V.P., Sec. & Treas.--N.W. Transport Service, Inc., Commerce City, CO, pg. 781
Ward, J. Richard, Sec. & Treas.--Ward Trucking Corp., Altoona, PA, pg. 1163
Ward, John P., V.P.-Fin. & Sec.--American Uniform Co., Cleveland, TN, pg. 1045
Ward, Nancy, Sec.--Carelli, Glynn & Ward, Butler, NJ, pg. 218
Ward, Taylor, Sec.--JM Family Enterprises Inc., Deerfield Beach, FL, pg. 584
Wardley, George, Sec.--Utica Mutual Insurance Company, New Hartford, NY, pg. 1140
Warford, David, V.P., Sec. & Treas.--Lenac, Warford, Stone, Inc., Newport Beach, CA, pg. 667
Wark, Dale A., V.P.-Fin., Chief Fin. Officer, Treas. & Sec.--R. M. Shoemaker Co., West Conshohocken, PA, pg. 1000
Warmington, Carole, Sec. & Treas.--Complete Interiors Inc., Altamonte Springs, FL, pg. 270
Warner, L., Sec.--Laubeck Corporation/Cross, Carbondale, PA, pg. 660
Warnick, Kenneth L., V.P.-Admin., Sec. & Treas.--Great Salt Lake Minerals & Chemicals Corp., Ogden, UT, pg. 482
Warnock, Inez, Sec.--Smith Frozen Foods, Inc., Weston, OR, pg. 1012
Warren, John F.T., Sec.--Rockwood Gardens, Ltd., Rockwood,, Canada, pg. 638
Warren, Robert S. III, Sec. & Treas.--Warren Distributing Corp., Raleigh, NC, pg. 1164
Waters, Shirley B., V.P. & Sec.--Rome Sentinel Co., Rome, NY, pg. 946

Watkins, L. Earl, Jr., Gen. Counsel & Sec.--Sunflower Electric Power Corporation, Hays, KS, pg. 1060
Watson, Anthony, V.P. & Asst. Sec.--Watson Electric Supply Inc., Dallas, TX, pg. 1168
Watson, Steven L., V.P. & Sec.--Contran Corporation, Dallas, TX, pg. 281
Watson, Steven L., V.P. & Sec.--Tremont Corporation, Denver, CO, pg. 1109
Weary, Daniel P., Sec.--Fairbanks Morse Pump Corporaton, Kansas City, KS, pg. 397
Weaver, Anna, Sec.--Adelphia Lamp & Shade Inc., Philadelphia, PA, pg. 17
Weaver, Richard T., Treas., Sec. & Chief Fin. Officer--Hamburg Brothers Inc., Pittsburgh, PA, pg. 502
Weaver, W.N., Jr., Sec.--GSC Enterprises, Inc., Chicago, IL, pg. 440
Webb, R.W., Sec. & Gen. Counsel--Fenestra Corporation, Erie, PA, pg. 711
Webb, R.W., V.P. & Sec.--Marmon Corporation, Chicago, IL, pg. 711
Webb, Robert, Sec.--The Marmon Group, Inc., Chicago, IL, pg. 711
Webb, Robert D., Controller & Asst. Sec.--Lester B. Knight & Associates, Inc., Chicago, IL, pg. 637
Webb, Robert D., Sec.--Lester B. Knight Cast Metals, Inc., Chicago, IL, pg. 637
Webb, Robert D., Sec. & Treas.--Knight PMD, Inc., Barrington, IL, pg. 637
Webb, Sandra, Treas. & Sec.--Delagra Corporation, Bridgeville, DE, pg. 325
Weber, Lynn B., Sec.--Modulite Corporation, Compton, CA, pg. 763
Webster, Gordon J., Sec. & Treas.--Cleveland Wrecking Company, Los Angeles, CA, pg. 255
Weeks, William D., Sec.--Reed & Barton Corporation, Taunton, MA, pg. 920
Wefer, Donald P., Sr. V.P., Gen. Counsel & Sec.--Associated Metals & Minerals Corp., White Plains, NY, pg. 91
Wege, Debbie, Sec.--Flanagan Brothers, Bear Creek, WI, pg. 416
Wege, Peter M., V.P. & Sec.--Steelcase Inc., Grand Rapids, MI, pg. 1044
Wehrung, S. Blanche, Sec.--Modern Concrete Septic Tank Company, Ottsville, PA, pg. 762
Weibel, Fred E., Jr., Exec. V.P., Sec. & Treas.--Weibel Vineyards, Mission San Jose, CA, pg. 1173
Weicht, Richard A., V.P. & Sec.--Adolfson & Peterson, Inc., Minneapolis, MN, pg. 18
Weidler, Allen, V.P.-Fin. & Sec.--Fred Usinger, Inc., Milwaukee, WI, pg. 1140
Weidman, Charlotte, Sr. V.P. & Sec.--Petroleum Inc., Wichita, KS, pg. 865
Weiler, Timothy, Sec.--Steiner Corporation, Salt Lake City, UT, pg. 1045
Weinberger, Laura, Sec.--The ASCII Group, Inc., Bethesda, MD, pg. 8
Weiner, Eugene L., Exec. V.P., Sec. & Treas.--Paradise Fruit Company, Inc., Plant City, FL, pg. 847
Weiner, Ronald, Gen. Counsel & Corp. Sec.--Radiator Specialty Company, Charlotte, NC, pg. 909
Weingarten, Sidney, V.P. & Sec.--A. J. Hollander Co., Inc., New York, NY, pg. 539
Weinstein, G., V.P. & Sec.--The Biltrite Corporation, Waltham, MA, pg. 151
Weinstein, Mark M., Sr. V.P.-Gen. Counsel & Sec.--National Amusements, Inc., Dedham, MA, pg. 784
Weisberg, David D., V.P. & Sec.--Technic Incorporated, Cranston, RI, pg. 1083
Weisberg, Jerome, V.P. & Sec.--Jacob Stern & Sons, Inc., Santa Barbara, CA, pg. 1047
Weisner, Charles L., V.P.-Fin. & Sec.--Electronic Data Magnetics, Inc., High Point, NC, pg. 375
Weiss, James A., Sec. & Treas.--James Chevrolet Inc., Mount Clemens, MI, pg. 588
Weiss, Larry, Chm. Bd., Pres., Chief Exec. Officer & Sec.--Save More Food Mart, Inc., Hobart, IN, pg. 973
Weiss, R.W., Sec.--Idaho Forest Industry, Inc., Coeur D'Alene, ID, pg. 561
Weiss, Seymour, V.P. & Sec.--Weiss Packing Co., Inc., Donora, PA, pg. 1174
Weitzenfeld, Marvin, Sec.--Globe-Amerada Glass Company, Elk Grove Village, IL, pg. 463
Welch, Cathy, Sec.--Ben Schwartz Market, Inc., Peoria, IL, pg. 980
Welge, Michael W., Exec. V.P., Sec., Treas. & Comptroller--Gilster Mary Lee Corp., Chester, IL, pg. 460
Wellman, Lynda, Sec./Treas.--International Airline Support Group, Inc., Miami, FL, pg. 575
Wells, Carol G., Corp. Sec.--Roche Constructors, Inc., Greeley, CO, pg. 940
Welsh, Michael T., Sec.--FirstFed Michigan Corporation, Detroit, MI, pg. 414
Welsh, Michael T., Sr. V.P. & Sec.--First Federal of Michigan, Detroit, MI, pg. 414
Welte, Wendy, Sec.--Twentieth Century Companies, Kansas City, MO, pg. 1121
Wenczel, Arthur R., Sec.--Wenczel Tile Co., Trenton, NJ, pg. 1176
Wender, Stanley L., Sec.--National Mortgage Company, Memphis, TN, pg. 792
Wendte, Ardyth L., Sec.--Dunn Industries Inc., Kansas City, MO, pg. 354
Wendte, Ardyth L., Sr. V.P. & Sec.--J.E. Dunn Construction Co., Kansas City, MO, pg. 354
Wenger, Carmon R., Sec.--CTB Inc., Milford, IN, pg. 205
Wenstrand, Thomas W., Co-Pres. & Sec.--Hawkeye Steel Products, Inc., Houghton, IA, pg. 518
Wentworth, Francis M., Jr., Sec.--Gaylord Entertainment Co., Nashville, TN, pg. 446
Wentz, Jack L., Assoc. Gen. Counsel & Corp. Sec.--Borg-Warner Corporation, Chicago, IL, pg. 165
Wermerskirchen, James, Sec. & Treas.--Huntting Elevator Co., Austin, MN, pg. 555
Werschky, Don, V.P. & Sec.--Maxcor Manufacturing, Inc., Colorado Springs, CO, pg. 722
Wesemann, Jeannie, Sec.--Affiliated Foods Cooperative Inc., Norfolk, NE, pg. 23
West, Elsie M., Sec.--West Dairies, Inc., Spring City, PA, pg. 1177
West, G. W., Chief Fin. Officer, Corp. Sec. & Treas.--Alley-Cassetty Coal Co., Nashville, TN, pg. 37
West, V.G., Sec.--Bush Development Corp., Williamsburg, VA, pg. 196
Westbrock, Leon, Sec. & Treas.--Universal Cooperatives, Inc., Minneapolis, MN, pg. 1138
Westerbeck, David F., V.P., Sec. & Gen. Counsel--The Union Central Life Insurance Co., Cincinnati, OH, pg. 1127
Westerhoff, Paul W., Sec.--Standun, Inc., Irwindale, CA, pg. 1038
Westfall, William C., Sec.--Westfall GMC Truck Inc., North Kansas City, MO, pg. 1182
Westlie, James H., Treas. & Sec.--Westlie Motor Company, Minot, ND, pg. 1183
Westmeyer, E.A., V.P.-Treas. & Sec.--Zeller Corp., Defiance, OH, pg. 1216
Westreich, Murray, Exec. V.P., Sec. & Treas.--West Mill Clothes, Inc., Woodside, NY, pg. 1177
Wetmore, Edward C., Sec. & Gen. Counsel--LPL Technologies, Inc., Wallingford, CT, pg. 648
Wharton, Garry, Sr. V.P., Corp. Counsel & Sec.--Motorists Mutual Insurance Co., Columbus, OH, pg. 773
Wheeler, C., Asst. Treas., Asst. Sec. & Controller--American Welding & Manufacturing Co., Warren, OH, pg. 431
White, H.G., V.P.-Fin.--Howell Instruments Corp., Fort Worth, TX, pg. 547
White, Ray, Exec. V.P. & Sec.--John R. Hollingsworth Co., Phoenixville, PA, pg. 539
White, Turner, Treas. & Sec.--Positronic Industries, Inc., Springfield, MO, pg. 881
White, Virginia, V.P. & Asst. Sec.--Staple Cotton Cooperative Association, Greenwood, MS, pg. 1038
White, Virginia L., Treas. & Sec.--Perpetual Corporation, Washington, DC, pg. 862
White, Virginia L., Sec. & Treas.--Allbritton Communications Company, Washington, DC, pg. 862
White, Virginia L., Sec. & Treas.--WJLA-TV, Washington, DC, pg. 862
Whitehouse, David, Sr. V.P. & Sec.--Ellerbe Becket Construction Services, Minneapolis, MN, pg. 378
Whitehouse, James K., Sec.--Metalloy Corporation, Hudson, MI, pg. 742
Whiteside, Carol W., V.P., Sec. & Treas.--Rowe Corp., Charlotte, NC, pg. 952
Whitlock, Lyndon, Sec. & Gen. Counsel--Velsicol Chemical Corporation, Rosemont, IL, pg. 1147
Whitmore, Margie, Mgr., Corp. Sec.--Ericson Marketing Communications, Nashville, TN, pg. 386
Whitney, Robert C., Sec. & Treas.--Frehner Construction Company, Inc., North Las Vegas, NV, pg. 432
Whitney, Stephen Q., V.P. & Sec.--Albert Kahn Associates, Inc., Detroit, MI, pg. 613
Whitsell, Helen J., Chm. Bd., Chief Exec. Officer & Treas.--Copeland Lumber Yard, Inc., Portland, OR, pg. 284
Whitt, John R., V.P.-Sls. & Sec.--Sherman & Reilly, Inc., Chattanooga, TN, pg. 998
Whitters, James P., III, Sec.--Robertson Factories, Inc., Taunton, MA, pg. 939
Wick, Harriett B., V.P. & Sec.--Zippo Manufacturing Company, Bradford, PA, pg. 1220
Wickhan, Robert, Treas. & Sec.--Wigwam Mills, Inc., Sheboygan, WI, pg. 1189
Wiege, Lloyd, V.P., Sec. & Treas.--Baugh Construction Company, Seattle, WA, pg. 127
Wiener, M.A., Co.-Chm. Bd. & Sec.--Infinity Broadcasting Corporation, New York, NY, pg. 567
Wilcox, Arthur M., Sec.--Evening Post Publishing Co., Charleston, SC, pg. 391
Wilcox, Jane T., Treas. & Sec.--Mountain States Pipe & Supply Company, Colorado Springs, CO, pg. 773
Wilcox, Terry, Treas. & Sec.--Charles Machine Works, Inc., Perry, OK, pg. 240
Wiley, Edwin P., Sec.--The Shaler Company, Waupun, WI, pg. 793
Wilhoit, T.A., Sec.--Phoenix Fuel Company, Inc., Phoenix, AZ, pg. 868
Wilkerson, Bill, Treas., Controller & Sec.--Greenwood Packing Plant, Greenwood, SC, pg. 486
Wilkerson, Dean, Asst. Sec.--MADD (Mothers Against Drunk Driving), Irving, TX, pg. 691
Wilkerson, Wayne, Sec.--Brookshire Bros., Inc., Lufkin, TX, pg. 180
Wilkins, Shirley J., Sec.--Montgomery Elevator Company, Moline, IL, pg. 767
Willemson, Mary Ann, Sec.--Frank B. Ross Co. Inc., Jersey City, NJ, pg. 949
Willert, Willmae C., V.P. & Sec.--Willert Home Products, Inc., Saint Louis, MO, pg. 1190
Willging, Jerry, Sec. & Treas.--Baxter Hodell Donnelly Preston Inc., Cincinnati, OH, pg. 127
Williams, A. Melton, V.P. & Sec.--Emrick Chevrolet Sales Corporation, Richmond, VA, pg. 380
Williams, Alan R., V.P. & Sec.--Williams Company Of Orlando, Inc., Orlando, FL, pg. 1190
Williams, Angie C., V.P. & Sec.--Camillus Cutlery Co., Camillus, NY, pg. 212
Williams, Belton R., Chief Fin. Officer, Treas. & Sec.--George W. Auch Co., Pontiac, MI, pg. 97
Williams, Belton R., Sec. & Treas.--GenCon Services, Inc., Pontiac, MI, pg. 98
Williams, Byron, Chm. Bd. & Sec.--Clayton, Williams & Sherwood, Inc., Newport Beach, CA, pg. 254
Williams, Carolyn, Sec.--Memphis Group, Inc., Memphis, TN, pg. 738
Williams, Dawn M., Dir.-Admin. & Sec.--Erving Paper Mills, Erving, MA, pg. 388
Williams, Doug, Sec.--Chernoff/Silver & Associates, Columbia, SC, pg. 243
Williams, Faye M., Treas. & Sec.--Northwest Tobacco & Candy Co., Fayetteville, AR, pg. 815
Williams, Gregory O., Sr. V.P., Sec. & Treas.--Rothchild Asset Management Inc., New York, NY, pg. 951
Williams, Gretchen, Co-Chm. Bd. & Sec.--Minyard Food Stores, Coppell, TX, pg. 759
Williams, Jerry D., Treas. & Sec.--Cajun Electric Power Co-op, Baton Rouge, LA, pg. 207
Williams, Jill L., Sec.--Genova Products, Inc., Davison, MI, pg. 452
Williams, Jimmie D., Exec. V.P., Chief Fin. Officer, Treas. & Sec.--Belz Enterprises, Memphis, TN, pg. 138
Williams, Joe, Sec.--Whitin Roberts Co., Sanford, NC, pg. 1187
Williams, Kathleen Hopson, Sec.--Thomas R. Hopson Broker, Inc., Marietta, GA, pg. 544
Williams, Mary, Sr. V.P., Sec. & Corp. Librarian--CSE Corporation, San Francisco, CA, pg. 204
Williams, Melvin, Sec. & Treas.--Besche Oil Company, Inc., Waldorf, MD, pg. 145
Williams, Nancy, Exec. Sec.--Lindsay Olive Growers, Lindsay, CA, pg. 676
Williams, Timothy, V.P., Treas. & Sec.--Spring Arbor Distributors, Belleville, MI, pg. 1033
Williams, Victor J., Sec. & Treas.--Select Sires, Inc., Plain City, OH, pg. 988
Williamson, Daphne, Sec. & Treas.--Airline Manufacturing Company, Inc., Columbus, MS, pg. 27
Willis, J.C., Treas. & Sec.--Cormier Chevrolet Company, Inc., Long Beach, CA, pg. 286
Wills, R.J., Sec. & Treas.--A. Tenenbaum Co. Inc., North Little Rock, AR, pg. 1087
Wilner, L., Sec.--Lensclean, Inc., Carlstadt, NJ, pg. 33
Wilsey, Alfred S., Jr., Sec.--Wilsey Bennett Co., San Francisco, CA, pg. 1193
Wilson, Albert J., V.P., Sec. & Chief Counsel--Teachers Insurance and Annuity Association-College Retirement Equities Fund, New York, NY, pg. 1082
Wilson, Logan J., V.P.-Legal Affairs & Sec.--Fike Corporation, Blue Springs, MO, pg. 409
Wilson, Lowell, Treas. & Sec.--Ag Processing Inc A Cooperative, Omaha, NE, pg. 24
Wilson, Riley, Pres., Treas., Sec. & Controller--Rapid Power Technologies, Inc., Brookfield, CT, pg. 913
Wilson, Rob, Sec. & Treas.--Hubler Chevrolet Inc., Indianapolis, IN, pg. 550
Wilson, Stanton E., Sec.--Monroc, Inc., Salt Lake City, UT, pg. 766
Wilson, Tony H., V.P.-Fin. & Sec.--PPA Industries, Inc., Dallas, TX, pg. 836
Winiarski, Victor A., Treas. & Sec.--Progressive Tool & Industries Co., Southfield, MI, pg. 894
Winkelman, Earl, V.P., Gen. Counsel & Asst. Sec.--Jockey International, Inc., Kenosha, WI, pg. 595
Winkels, Thomas, Sec. & Treas.--McNeilus Companies, Dodge Center, MN, pg. 732
Winkler, William F., Chief Oper. Officer, Sec. & Treas.--Ackerman McQueen, Inc., Oklahoma City, OK, pg. 12
Winn, Elwood F., Sec., Treas. & Chief Fin. Officer--Certified Grocers Midwest, Inc., Hodgkins, IL, pg. 236
Winslow, Muriel A., Sec.--Air Conditioning Co., Inc., Glendale, CA, pg. 26
Winter, Robert, Sec. & Treas.--Hastings Co-Op Creamery Company, Hastings, MN, pg. 516
Winters, Yvonne, Sec.--Bepco, Inc., Winston-Salem, NC, pg. 141
Wise, Bruce S., Sec. & Treas.--Global Insurance Company, Houston, TX, pg. 662
Wise, Chris, Sec.--Grand Prairie Co-op, Inc., Tolono, IL, pg. 475
Wise, Christine, Corp. Sec.--Davis Paint Company, Kansas City, MO, pg. 319
Wise, John A., Jr., Sec.--Suburban Communications Corp., Livonia, MI, pg. 1055
Wise, Ronald L., Treas. & Sec.--E & A Industries, Inc., Indianapolis, IN, pg. 358
Wise, Ronald L., Sec. & Treas.--H & K Realty Co. Inc., Indianapolis, IN, pg. 358
Wise, Ronald L., Sec. & Treas.--Car Brite, Inc., Indianapolis, IN, pg. 358
Wise, Ronald L., Sec.--Technicare Cleaning Systems Inc., Indianapolis, IN, pg. 359
Wiseman, Donald F., V.P., Gen. Counsel & Sec.--Perkins Family Restaurants, Memphis, TN, pg. 1088
Wisotsky, Jerry, Chm. Bd., Sec. & Treas.--Imperial Litho/Graphics, Inc., Phoenix, AZ, pg. 564
Woeste, Cynthia, V.P. & Sec.--Bill Woeste Dealer Group, Cincinnati, OH, pg. 1198
Wojcik, Paul N., V.P., Gen. Counsel & Sec.--The Bureau of National Affairs, Inc., Washington, DC, pg. 189
Wojnowski, Leon A., Sec., Treas. & Chief Fin. Officer--Connelly Containers, Inc., Bala-Cynwyd, PA, pg. 275
Wolchansky, Louise G., Sec.--Security Van Lines, Inc., Kenner, LA, pg. 987
Wolf, Lawrence, Pres., Chief Exec. Officer, Sec. & Treas.--Leonard Wholesale, Inc., Elizabeth, NJ, pg. 668
Wolf, Norman, Sec. & Treas.--Carole Wren, Inc., New York, NY, pg. 1204
Wolf, R.B., Sec.--Brunner & Lay, Inc., Franklin Park, IL, pg. 184
Wolf, Timothy W., Sec., Treas.--Fessel, Siegfriedt & Moeller, Inc., Louisville, KY, pg. 407
Wolfcale, A. D., V.P., Deputy Gen. Counsel & Sec.--The Edward J. DeBartolo Corporation, Youngstown, OH, pg. 323
Wolfe, Lawrence A., Exec. V.P. & Sec.--Production Tool Supply Co., Warren, MI, pg. 893
Wolfington, James E., Exec. V.P. & Sec.--Wolfington Body Company, Exton, PA, pg. 1199
Wood, Betty T., Sec.--J. M. Smith Corp., Spartanburg, SC, pg. 1012

Wood, Carol S., Treas., Sec., Controller & Chief Fin. Officer--Higginbotham-Bartlett Co., Lubbock, TX, pg. 533
Wood, Nell, Sec.--Chuck Hutton Chevrolet Company, Memphis, TN, pg. 556
Wood, Rene M., V.P.-Fin. & Sec.--McNeel International Corp., Tampa, FL, pg. 732
Wood, Robert C., Chief Fin. Officer, Treas. & Sec.--Xtek, Inc., Cincinnati, OH, pg. 1206
Wood, Robert L., Treas., Sec. & Chief Fin. Officer--Justiss Oil Co., Inc., Jena, LA, pg. 610
Woodard, Elizabeth B., V.P., Gen. Counsel & Sec.--Riviana Foods Inc., Houston, TX, pg. 937
Woodham, P.S., V.P.-Admin.--American Buildings Co., Eufaula, AL, pg. 49
Woodhatch, Maynard, Sec. & Treas.--Shearman Corporation, Lake Charles, LA, pg. 996
Woodruff, Sharon H., Office Mgr., Asst. Sec. & Treas.--Dentec Corporation, Boca Raton, FL, pg. 329
Woods, Marilyn, Sec.--The ISI Manufacturing, Inc., Fraser, MI, pg. 560
Woods, Nina Jo, Sec.--Joe E. Woods, Inc., Mesa, AZ, pg. 1200
Woods, Rondall G., Sec.--W. L. Hailey & Company, Inc., Nashville, TN, pg. 500
Woodward, David A., Sec. & Treas.--Certified Grocers Of California, Los Angeles, CA, pg. 237
Woodward, Fielden, Sec.--Kitchen Kompact, Inc., Jeffersonville, IN, pg. 634
Woolsey, Jerry, Exec. V.P., Sec.--CRE, Inc., Indianapolis, IN, pg. 203
Woolsten Crost, Janet, Sec.--Schott Corporation, Wayzata, MN, pg. 978
Worner, Meredith, Sec.--Menard Electric Cooperative, Petersburg, IL, pg. 738
Wosje, Walt, Sec. & Gen. Mgr.--Michigan Milk Producers Association, Novi, MI, pg. 747
Wright, Clancy, Exec. V.P., Treas. & Sec.--Bawden Printing, Inc., Eldridge, IA, pg. 127
Wright, James W., V.P.-Legal Affairs & Sec.--Lord Corporation, Erie, PA, pg. 683
Wright, James W., V.P. & Sec.--Bankmanagers Corp., Milwaukee, WI, pg. 118
Wright, P Jane, Sec.--Highwood Service, Inc., Detroit, MI, pg. 1194
Wright, P. Jane, Sec.--Ralph C. Wilson Enterprises, Detroit, MI, pg. 1194
Wright, Robert, Sec. & Treas.--W. C. Bradley Co., Columbus, GA, pg. 170
Wright, Robert W., Sec.--Cloud Corporation, Des Plaines, IL, pg. 256
Wright, Terry, V.P., Sec. & Treas.--Fones & Mann Inc., New York, NY, pg. 422
Wright, W. Kevin, V.P.-Gen. Counsel & Asst. Sec.--TLC Beatrice International Holdings Inc., New York, NY, pg. 1073
Wright, Wayne C., Chief Fin. Officer, Treas. & Sec.--Copper & Brass Sales, Inc., East Detroit, MI, pg. 284
Wright, William E., Sec.--Wright Brand Foods, Inc., Vernon, TX, pg. 1204
Wrobel, Robert F., Sr. V.P., Gen. Counsel & Chief Admin. Officer--The Marley Company, Mission Woods, KS, pg. 710
Wurst, William, Sec. & Treas.--Tamaroff Leasing Co., Southfield, MI, pg. 1077
Wurz, Jane, Sec. & Treas.--Accu-Sort Systems, Inc., Telford, PA, pg. 11
Wynn, Jane M., Exec. V.P., Sec. & Treas.--Miller Electric Company, Jacksonville, FL, pg. 754
Wysong, Charles N., V.P. & Sec.--Holbrook Lumber Company, Albany, NY, pg. 538
Wysong, Phil, V.P. & Treas.--Fuel South, Inc., Hazlehurst, GA, pg. 435
Wysong, Phil, V.P.-Treas. & Sec.--Jones Company, Inc., Waycross, GA, pg. 603
Yada, David, V.P. & Sec.--TACT Holding, South Pasadena, CA, pg. 1076
Yagi, Clyde H., Dir.-Data Processing, Sec. & Treas.--Mutual Welding Co., Ltd, Honolulu, HI, pg. 779
Yates, Thos. H., Sec. & Treas.--Hopkinsville Milling Co., Hopkinsville, KY, pg. 543
Yeargan, Victor B., Jr., Sec. & Treas.--Battey Machinery Company, Rome, GA, pg. 127
Yeshoua, Valentine, V.P. & Sec.--Lucky Winner, Inc., New York, NY, pg. 686
Yeung, William, Sec. & Treas.--Kroch's & Brentano's, Inc., Chicago, IL, pg. 645
Yoda, David, Sec. & Treas.--Trader Joes Co., South Pasadena, CA, pg. 1076
Yoder, Elvin D., V.P.-Fin. & Admin & Corp. Sec.--Sauder Woodworking Co., Archbold, OH, pg. 972
Yoder, Galen, Sec.--Milk Marketing Inc., Strongsville, OH, pg. 753
York, Frank, Controller--Southern Pipe & Supply Co., Inc., Meridian, MS, pg. 1022
Yost, Jan, Treas. & Sec.--D.S.U.-Peterbilt & GMC, Inc., Portland, OR, pg. 309
Young, Anita J.T., V.P. & Treas.--Lutheran Brotherhood, Minneapolis, MN, pg. 688
Young, James B., V.P. & Sec.--Zilber, Ltd., Milwaukee, WI, pg. 1219
Young, Jeffrey S., Sec.--Young Electric Sign Company, Salt Lake City, UT, pg. 1209
Young, Peter A., Sec. & Treas.--Burd & Fletcher Company, Kansas City, MO, pg. 189
Young, Rachel O., Sec.--Standard Industries, Inc., Salt Lake City, UT, pg. 1036
Young, W.E., Sec. & Treas.--George W. Cochran Co., Inc., Washington, DC, pg. 258
Young, William D., Jr., V.P. & Sec.--General Wholesale Company, Inc., Atlanta, GA, pg. 451
Youngblood, John F., Sec.--Meade Group, Inc., Detroit, MI, pg. 733
Youngchild, Linda L., Corp. Sec. & Asst. Treas.--The Metal Ware Corp., Two Rivers, WI, pg. 741
Youngren, Judith, Sec.--All Nation Insurance Co., Saint Paul, MN, pg. 35
Yraceburu, Vatinia, Sec.--United Engine & Machine Company, Carson City, NV, pg. 1131
Yuen, Lawren, Fin. Dir. & Sec.--BSB Hong Kong, Hong Kong,, Hong Kong, pg. 110
Yuen, William, V.P.-Fin., Sec. & Treas.--J.H. Baxter & Company, San Mateo, CA, pg. 127
Yusko, Dave, Sec.--Potamkin Toyota, Inc., Miami, FL, pg. 882
Zachrich, C.S., Sec.--Haeger Industries, Inc., Dundee, IL, pg. 499
Zacky, Robert, Pres. & Sec.--Zacky Farms, Inc., South El Monte, CA, pg. 1215
Zahner, Josephine, Sec. & Treas.--Carey Machinery & Supply Company, Baltimore, MD, pg. 218
Zakutney, Ray, Treas. & Sec.--McConnell Automotive, Mobile, AL, pg. 727
Zall, Betty, Treas. & Sec.--Paris Presents, Gurnee, IL, pg. 848
Zanders, Lorette, Sec.--Boury Incorporated, Wheeling, WV, pg. 168
Zaransky, Michael, Pres. & Sec.--Ridgeview Motors, Inc., Schiller Park, IL, pg. 934
Zary, Jerome E., V.P., Sec., Chief Fin. Officer & Treas.--Frog Switch & Manufacturing Company, Carlisle, PA, pg. 434
Zaugg, Christine, Sec.--Taylor Associates, Cedar Rapids, IA, pg. 751
Zeinger, Henry, Treas. & Sec.--King Wire & Cable Corporation, Jamaica, NY, pg. 631
Zekaria, Alice, Sec. & Mgr.-Gen. Mdse.--Windsor Fashions, Los Angeles, CA, pg. 1195
Zemanek, Louis M., Sec. & Treas.--Gate Petroleum Company, Jacksonville, FL, pg. 445
Zennedjian, Violet, Sec. & Treas.--Adray Appliance & Photo Center, Inc., Dearborn, MI, pg. 18
Zieger, Juscy, V.P. & Sec.--Interbath, Inc., City of Industry, CA, pg. 574
Ziegler, Dennis, Asst. Sec.--RHC/Spacemaster Corporation, Melrose Park, IL, pg. 906
Ziegler, William C., Treas. & Sec.--Ziegler Tire & Supply Company, Inc., Canton, OH, pg. 1218
Zifkin, Walter, Exec. V.P., Chief Oper. Officer & Sec.--William Morris Agency, Inc., Beverly Hills, CA, pg. 771
Zigmundt, Robert V., Sec. & Treas.--Kunzler & Company, Inc., Lancaster, PA, pg. 646
Zigray, Frank, Sec. & Treas.--The Fremont Co., Fremont, OH, pg. 432
Zilkha, Cecile, Sec.--Union Holdings, Inc., New York, NY, pg. 1128
Zilkha, Donald, V.P. & Asst. Sec.--Union Holdings, Inc., New York, NY, pg. 1128
Zimmer, Edward, Sr. V.P., Sec. & Gen. Counsel--LFC Holding Corporation, Boca Raton, FL, pg. 647
Zimmer, Edward, Sr. V.P., Sec. & Gen. Counsel--Levitz Furniture Corporation, Boca Raton, FL, pg. 647
Zimmer, Robert J., V.P.-Fin. & Chief Fin. Officer & Sec.--Acheson Industries, Inc., Port Huron, MI, pg. 12
Zimmerman, Edward, Sec., Treas. & Personnel Mgr.--Dobles Chevrolet, Inc., Manchester, NH, pg. 342
Zimmerman, Joyce I., Sec. & Treas.--Marval Industries, Inc., Mamaroneck, NY, pg. 716
Zimmerman, Lester, Sec.--Greater Construction Corp., Altamonte Springs, FL, pg. 483
Zimmermann, W.K., Treas. & Sec.--March Manufacturing Inc., Glenview, IL, pg. 706
Zink, Robby, Sec.--Schmieding Enterprises Inc., Springdale, AR, pg. 976
Zinn, Chester A., Jr., V.P., Sec. & Gen. Counsel--MSI Insurance Companies, Arden Hills, MN, pg. 693
Zinn, Thomas R., Pres. & Sec.--Stearns Enterprises, Inc., Lexington, KY, pg. 1043
Zipprich, R.A., V.P.-Plng. & Information Services--Mississippi Lime Co., Alton, IL, pg. 760
Zogg, Chris J., Sec. & Gen. Counsel--Kent Feeds Inc., Muscatine, IA, pg. 1146
Zoll, Steven, Sec.--Kassel & Zoll Provisions, Inc., Chicago, IL, pg. 618
Zook, Thomas W., V.P.-Admin, Asst. Treas. & Asst. Sec.--The Wooster Brush Company, Wooster, OH, pg. 1202
Zumbiel, Thomas J., Exec. V.P. & Sec.--C. W. Zumbiel Company, Cincinnati, OH, pg. 1221
Zumpkehr, Charles E., Sec.--Donley's, Inc., Cleveland, OH, pg. 345

EXECUTIVE VICE PRESIDENT

Aaronson, Don, Exec. V.P.--Laddin & Company, Inc., New York, NY, pg. 650
Abbott, Weyne, Exec. V.P.--Multiple Allied Services, Inc., Hayward, CA, pg. 775
Abdalla, Edward IV, Exec. V.P.--Abdalla's Lafayette, Inc., Lafayette, LA, pg. 10
Abdalla, Harold C., Exec. V.P.--Abdalla's Lafayette, Inc., Lafayette, LA, pg. 10
Abdo, Stephen P., Exec. V.P.--ACL Technologies, Santa Ana, CA, pg. 2
Abt, Richard, Exec. V.P.--West Coast National Video, Philadelphia, PA, pg. 1177
Adams, J. Phillip, Pres.--Flying J. Inc., Brigham City, UT, pg. 421
Adams, J.D., V.P. & Chief Oper. Officer--Actron Manufacturing Company, Cleveland, OH, pg. 15
Adams, James, Exec. V.P.--Samsill Corporation, Fort Worth, TX, pg. 968
Adelstein, Bruce S., Exec. V.P. & Sec.--Olympic Steel Inc., Bedford Heights, OH, pg. 825
Adler, Robert, Exec. V.P., Fin. & Admin--Franklin Spier, Inc., New York, NY, pg. 1031
Adrien, Dan, Exec. V.P.--Burgess Pigment Co., Sandersville, GA, pg. 190
Agnello, John, Exec. V.P.--National Cleaning Contractors, Inc., New York, NY, pg. 786
Akerson, Alan W., Exec. V.P.--Fleishman Hillard Inc., Saint Louis, MO, pg. 417
Akimoto, Takayoshi, Exec. V.P.--Dentsu, Sudler & Hennessey, Tokyo, Japan, pg. 330
Alahouzos, John, Jr., Exec. V.P.--Market Development Group Inc., Washington, DC, pg. 709
Alarcon, Horacio, Exec. V.P.--Leo Burnett Chile, Santiago,, Chile, pg. 192
Alayeto, George I., Exec. V.P.--Connell Rice & Sugar Co., Westfield, NJ, pg. 275
Albarelli, Joseph, Exec. V.P. & Treas.--Amloid Corporation, Saddle Brook, NJ, pg. 67
Albers, Thomas, Exec. V.P.--Trek Bicycle Corporation, Waterloo, WI, pg. 581
Albertson, Phyllis, Exec. V.P.-Intl. Opers.--Associated Merchandising Corp., New York, NY, pg. 91
Albright, Warren E., Exec. V.P. Dir.--N W Ayer Incorporated, New York, NY, pg. 103
Albright, Warren E., Exec. V.P., Dir.--N W Ayer Inc., New York, NY, pg. 104
Alesi, Charles, Exec. V.P.--Walker Magnetics Group, Inc., Worcester, MA, pg. 1160
Alexander, Charles M., Exec. V.P. & Chief Oper. Officer--A. Teichert & Son, Inc., Sacramento, CA, pg. 1084
Allen, Kenneth C., Jr., Exec. V.P.--Perlmuter Printing Company, Cleveland, OH, pg. 862
Allen, Mark, Exec. V.P., Dir. Acct. Services--Trahan, Burden & Charles, Inc., Baltimore, MD, pg. 1105
Allison, G., Exec. V.P.--McCormick Paint Works Company, Rockville, MD, pg. 727
Alred, Ken, Exec. V.P.--Timpte, Inc., Council Bluffs, IA, pg. 1098
Altiere, Daniel J., Exec. V.P.--Blonder-Tongue Laboratories, Inc., Old Bridge, NJ, pg. 157
Altilia, T., Exec. V.P.--Leo Burnett Company Ltd., Toronto,, Canada, pg. 192
Altstadt, Manfred, Chief Fin. Officer & Sr. V.P.--Mutual of America, New York, NY, pg. 777
Ambrose, Steven F., Exec. V.P.--Country Home Bakery, Inc., Bridgeport, CT, pg. 290
Anderson, Bruce, Exec. V.P., Treas. & Dir.-Mfg. & Quality Control--Integrated Energy Controls Corp., Minneapolis, MN, pg. 573
Anderson, Dana K., Exec. V.P.--The Macerich Co., Santa Monica, CA, pg. 696
Anderson, Douglas E., Exec. V.P. & Sec.--Boddie-Noell Enterprises Inc., Rocky Mount, NC, pg. 161
Anderson, Eric, Exec. V.P. & Treas.--The Conde Nast Publications Inc., New York, NY, pg. 19
Anderson, James A., Sr. V.P.--Thermo Industries Inc., Charlotte, NC, pg. 1091
Anderson, Will, Exec. V.P.--Karakas, VanSickle Ouellette Advertising & Public Relations, Portland, OR, pg. 616
Andonian, John, Exec. V.P.--A K H Company, Inc., Los Angeles, CA, pg. 4
Andrasick, James S., Exec. V.P.--C. Brewer & Company, Limited, Honolulu, HI, pg. 174
Andreas, Ursula E., Exec. V.P.--Lantzsch-Andreas Enterprises, Inc., Vienna, VA, pg. 658
Angelich, Mark, Exec. V.P.--Amelco Corporation, Gardena, CA, pg. 47
Angelos, Peter, Exec. V.P., Creative Dir.--Young & Rubicam San Francisco, San Francisco, CA, pg. 1211
Anhut, Francie, Exec. V.P.--Praxis International Inc., Cambridge, MA, pg. 884
Anstett, Joseph L., Exec. V.P.--Disposal Urban Maintenance Procession Co., Inc., Las Vegas, NV, pg. 1004
Anthony, James Norman, Exec. V.P.--Bearden Lumber Company, Inc., Bearden, AR, pg. 129
Anthony, Susan, Exec. V.P., Pub. Rels.--Richardson, Myers & Donofrio, Inc., Baltimore, MD, pg. 933
Anton, Paul, Exec. V.P., Mngmt. Supvr.--Kresser/Craig, Santa Monica, CA, pg. 644
Appel, Arthur S., Exec. V.P.--Fire Control Instruments, Inc., Newton, MA, pg. 411
Aquilina, Robert J., Exec. V.P.--Estee Lauder, Intl., New York, NY, pg. 389
Arams, Frank, Exec. V.P.--LNR Communications, Hauppauge, NY, pg. 648
Arenberg, Daniel R., Exec. V.P.--Columbia Pipe & Supply Company, Chicago, IL, pg. 266
Arender, Frank N., Exec. V.P.--Godwin Advertising Agency, Inc., Jackson, MS, pg. 464
Argyelan, Michael, Exec. V.P.--Whittaker, Clark & Daniels, Inc., South Plainfield, NJ, pg. 1187
Arlow, Arnold, Exec. V.P., Co-Creative Dir.-U.S.--TBWA Advertising, Inc., New York, NY, pg. 1071
Armstrong, Thomas R., Chief Oper. Officer, Exec. V.P.--Advent International, Boston, MA, pg. 21
Aro, Thomas W., Exec. V.P.--Tollman/Hundley Hotels, Valhalla, NY, pg. 1100
Arrell, Ralph, Exec. V.P.--Eddins-Walcher Company, Midland, TX, pg. 367
Asche, Phil, Exec. V.P., Area Dir.-Australia & New Zealand--Young & Rubicam New York, New York, NY, pg. 1211
Ash, Norman, Exec. V.P.--Perfection Automotive Products Corporation, Livonia, MI, pg. 861
Ashman, Stephen, Exec. V.P. & Chief Fin. Officer--Capital Bank, Miami, FL, pg. 214
Ashworth, R.C., III, Exec. V.P.--Ashworth Bros., Inc., Fall River, MA, pg. 88
Atchison, Rick, Exec. V.P.--Dunn Reber Glenn Marz, Reno, NV, pg. 354
Athanassiades, Ted, Sr. Exec. V.P.-Pensions--Metropolitan Life Insurance Co., New York, NY, pg. 744
Atkins, Susanne, Exec. V.P.--General Media Services, Inc., Westport, CT, pg. 450
Atols, James L., Exec. V.P.--Atols Tool and Mold Corp., Schiller Park, IL, pg. 97
Atwell, Michael J., Exec. V.P., Creative Dir.--Arocom Marketing Group, Inc., Cleveland, OH, pg. 737

Auer, David L., Exec. V.P.--WYO-Ben, Inc., Billings, MT, pg. 1157
Auerbach, Zev, Exec. V.P., Creative--The Ad Team Of Florida Inc., North Miami, FL, pg. 16
Ault, William C., Exec. V.P.--Thompson/Marince Advertising, San Antonio, TX, pg. 1094
Auriemma, Louis, Exec. V.P.--Haddon Craftsmen, Inc., Scranton, PA, pg. 499
Austad, Randall, Exec. V.P.--The Austad Company, Sioux Falls, SD, pg. 98
Avent, Sharon, Exec. V.P.--Smead Manufacturing Company, Hastings, MN, pg. 1011
Averbach, Larry, Exec. V.P.--William Morris Agency, Inc., Beverly Hills, CA, pg. 771
Awad, John, Exec. Vice Pres. & Dir.-Opers.--Tele-Com Products, Inc., Duarte, CA, pg. 1084
Bachman, Ed, Exec. V.P.--Remco Toys, New York, NY, pg. 926
Bacon, Bert, Exec. V.P.--Herlin Press, West Haven, CT, pg. 531
Badcock, Henry C., Exec. V.P.-Dealer Opers. & Sec.--W.S. Badcock Corporation, Mulberry, FL, pg. 113
Badcock, Mary R., Exec. V.P.--W.S. Badcock Corporation, Mulberry, FL, pg. 113
Badcock, Wogan S., III, Exec. V.P.-Admin.--W.S. Badcock Corporation, Mulberry, FL, pg. 113
Badenhop, Stephen, Exec. V.P.-Acct. Services--Jordan, McGrath, Case & Taylor Inc., New York, NY, pg. 604
Bag, Richard, Exec. V.P. & Adv. Mgr.--Apparel Industries, Inc., New York, NY, pg. 78
Bahr, Mark, Exec. V.P.--Barton-Malow Company, Detroit, MI, pg. 123
Bailey, Kirk, Exec. V.P.--Leader Federal Bank For Savings, Memphis, TN, pg. 663
Bailly, Richard L., Exec. V.P.--United Foam Plastics Corporation, Georgetown, MA, pg. 1132
Baird, F. Carroll, Exec. V.P.--Mrs. Baird's Bakeries, Inc., Fort Worth, TX, pg. 760
Baker, Dan, Exec. V.P. & Dir.-Quality Control & Res. & Devel.--Pace International Corporation, Kirkland, WA, pg. 838
Baker, Richard J., Exec. V.P., Treas.--The Highland Group, Inc., Southport, CT, pg. 534
Balakrishnan, V., Exec. V.P.--Republic Container Corp., Jersey City, NJ, pg. 927
Balaster, Ammon N., Dr., Exec. V.P.--RELA Product Development Div. (PDD), Boulder, CO, pg. 924
Balaster, Ammon, Dr., Exec. V.P.--RELA, Inc., Boulder, CO, pg. 924
Baldi, Joseph, Jr., Exec. V.P.--Baldi, Bloom & Whelan Advertising, New York, NY, pg. 115
Bandman, Donald, Exec. V.P., Grp. Acct. Dir.--Avrett, Free & Ginsberg, Inc., New York, NY, pg. 103
Bank, David L., Exec. V.P.--Bank M F & Company, Inc., Minneapolis, MN, pg. 117
Bank, Eliot, Exec. V.P.--Columbus Steel Drum Company, Blacklick, OH, pg. 267
Barbar, Anthony K.G., Exec. V.P.--The Barbar Group, Inc., Boca Raton, FL, pg. 119
Barland, David D., Exec. V.P.--Freedom Forge Corporation, Burnham, PA, pg. 430
Barnes, James, Exec. V.P., Creative Dir.--Rauh, Good, Darlo & Barnes Advertising Associates, Inc., Los Gatos, CA, pg. 914
Barnes, John L., Jr., Exec. V.P.--Graniteville Co., Graniteville, SC, pg. 476
Baroni, Tom, Exec. V.P., Creative Services--Marketing Magic Inc., Fort Lauderdale, FL, pg. 709
Barr, Greg, Exec. V.P. & Chief Oper. Officer--Nob Hill General Store, Inc., Gilroy, CA, pg. 807
Barrocas, Charles, Exec. V.P.--Injection Footwear Corp., Miami, FL, pg. 569
Barron, Richard B., V.P.--Barton Beers, Ltd., Chicago, IL, pg. 123
Barsky, David L., Exec. V.P.--Prime Hospitality Corp., Fairfield, NJ, pg. 889
Bartels, Juergen, Exec. V.P.--Carlson Companies, Inc., Minneapolis, MN, pg. 220
Bartleson, Charles, Exec. V.P.--Speer, Young & Hollander, Inc., Los Angeles, CA, pg. 1030
Bartley, David E., Exec. V.P.--Bunton Company, Louisville, KY, pg. 188
Bartolone, Joseph F., Jr., Exec. V.P.--Pancom International Corp., Stamford, CT, pg. 845
Battista, Richard, Exec. V.P.--Letven-Diccicco, Inc., Horsham, PA, pg. 669
Bauer, Lawrence R., Exec. V.P.--Arburg, Inc., Berlin, CT, pg. 79
Bauer, Tom, Exec. V.P.-Comml. Div.--Bureau of Engraving, Minneapolis, MN, pg. 189
Baum, David, Exec. V.P.--Arcon Construction Co., Inc., Mora, MN, pg. 81
Baum, Robert H., Vice Chm. & Gen. Counsel--The Inland Group, Inc., Oak Brook, IL, pg. 570
Bauman, Bill, Exec. V.P.--Great American Broadcasting Company, Cincinnati, OH, pg. 52
Baumann, William T., Exec. V.P.--Great American Communications Company, Cincinnati, OH, pg. 53
Bauroth, John W., Exec. V.P.--Amfac/JMB Hawaii, Inc., Honolulu, HI, pg. 585
Bayer, Mark, Exec. V.P.--Doyle McKenna Bayer Brown, Reno, NV, pg. 348
Bazant, Stanley K., Exec. V.P., Chief Exec. Officer & Gen. Mgr.--Plains Electric Generation Transmission Co-Op, Inc., Albuquerque, NM, pg. 873
Bealle, James, Exec. V.P.--Carter, Atlanta, GA, pg. 226
Beam, Gerald B., Exec. V.P.-Corp.--Provident Mutual Life Insurance Co., Philadelphia, PA, pg. 896
Beatty, Ralph, Jr., Exec. V.P.--RPR & Associates, Inc., Columbia, SC, pg. 908
Beber, Jennifer, Exec. V.P.--Beber Silverstein & Partners, Inc., Miami, FL, pg. 130
Becka, Michael M., Exec. V.P. & Gen. Mgr.--International Shoe Machine Corp., Nashua, NH, pg. 579
Beckley, Ken, Exec. V.P.--Gregg Appliances Inc., Indianapolis, IN, pg. 486
Beegle, William, Exec. V.P.--Columbia Sussex Corporation, Fort Mitchell, KY, pg. 266
Behrens, H.R., Exec. V.P.--Plano Molding Co., Plano, IL, pg. 874
Bell, Joseph, Exec. V.P.--Curtis Media Group Inc., Raleigh, NC, pg. 305
Bell, Robert, Exec. V.P.--Marden-Kane, Inc., Lake Success, NY, pg. 706
Bellucci, Eunice, Exec. V.P.--Arts & Entertainment Div.--Great Scott Advertising Co. Inc., New York, NY, pg. 482
Belz, Martin S., Exec. V.P. & Chief Oper. Officer--Belz Enterprises, Memphis, TN, pg. 138
Belz, Ronald A., Exec. V.P.-Special Projects--Belz Enterprises, Memphis, TN, pg. 138
Bender, James T., Exec. V.P.--Ziebart Corp., Troy, MI, pg. 1217
Benjamin, Gary, Exec. V.P.--Jamison, Cawdrey, Benjamin, San Francisco, CA, pg. 589
Bennett, Robert, Exec. V.P.--D. D. Bean & Sons Co., Jaffrey, NH, pg. 129
Bennett, Robert L., Exec. V.P.-Construction--Ruscon Corp., Charleston, SC, pg. 956
Bennett, Ron, Exec. V.P.--Leo Eisenberg & Co., Inc., Kansas City, MO, pg. 372
Benoit, David C., Exec. V.P.--Key Plastics, Inc., Livonia, MI, pg. 627
Benson, Donald E., Exec. V.P. & Chief Fin. Officer--Globe Industries, Inc., Chicago, IL, pg. 464
Benson, Donald E., Exec. V.P.--Bank Shares, Inc., Minneapolis, MN, pg. 117
Bento, James, Exec. V.P.--Trumpf Inc., Farmington, CT, pg. 1118
Benvenuto, Robert, Exec. V.P.--Harry Winston, Inc., New York, NY, pg. 1197
Benway, Joseph C., Exec. V.P., Chief Fin. Officer--Burson-Marsteller, New York, NY, pg. 1210
Beradinelli, C., Exec. V.P.--Hypertronics Corporation, Hudson, MA, pg. 557
Beren, Peter, Exec. V.P.--Misco Industries, Wichita, KS, pg. 759
Berendt, William E., Exec. V.P. & Chief Oper. Officer--Triple A Specialty Company, Bedford Park, IL, pg. 1114
Bergfalk, Addison, Exec. V.P.--Shade Foods, Inc., Union City, CA, pg. 810
Berghash, Mark, Exec. V.P.--Brimms Inc., Tonawanda, NY, pg. 176
Berkowitz, Victor, Exec. V.P.--Sillcocks Plastics International, Inc., Berkeley Heights, NJ, pg. 1004
Berkowitz, Victor, Exec. V.P.--Daylux, Inc., Berkeley Heights, NJ, pg. 1004
Berman, Charles L., Exec. V.P.--Contract Furnishings & Systems, Ltd., New York, NY, pg. 280
Bernon, Peter M., Chm. Bd. & Chief Exec. Officer--Garelick Farms, Inc., Franklin, MA, pg. 443
Bernstein, Martin M., Exec. V.P.-Real Estate--Carlyle & Co. Jewelers, Greensboro, NC, pg. 222
Berriman, Edward E., Exec. V.P. & Gen. Supt.--Gem Industries Finance Corporation, Toccoa, GA, pg. 447
Berriman, Edward E., Exec. V.P. & Gen. Supt.--Gem Industries, Inc., Gardner, MA, pg. 447
Berry, Claude A., III, Exec. V.P.--Wehr Constructors Inc., Louisville, KY, pg. 1172
Berry, Ira R., Exec. V.P.--Pharmacaps Inc., Elizabeth, NJ, pg. 866
Betker, Mark, Exec. V.P.--Windsor Industries, Inc., Englewood, CO, pg. 1195
Beumer, R.E., Exec. V.P.--Sverdrup Corporation, Maryland Heights, MO, pg. 1065
Bevers, Jerry W., Exec. V.P.-Dir. of Retail Banking--Team Bancshares, Inc., Dallas, TX, pg. 1082
Bhutani, Neelam, Exec. V.P.--Alra Laboratories, Inc., Gurnee, IL, pg. 44
Bieber, Paul D., Exec. V.P.--Floral Glass & Mirror, Inc., Hauppauge, NY, pg. 420
Biederman, Wayne, Exec. V.P.--Northern Wire & Cable, Inc., Troy, MI, pg. 814
Bienenfeld, Julius, Exec. V.P.--Bestform Foundations, Inc., Long Island City, NY, pg. 147
Bierman, Norman, Exec. V.P., Acct. Mngmt.--Backer Spielvogel Bates, Inc., New York, NY, pg. 108
Biggs, Jeremy, Vice Chm.--Fiduciary Trust Company International, New York, NY, pg. 408
Binstock, William, Exec. V.P.--Hallmark Advertising, Inc., Pittsburgh, PA, pg. 501
Bishop, Thomas, Exec. V.P.--Alaron Inc., Troy, MI, pg. 30
Bitter, E. Ward, Exec. V.P.--Scalamandre, Inc., Long Island City, NY, pg. 974
Bitter, Mark J., Exec. V.P.--Scalamandre, Inc., Long Island City, NY, pg. 974
Bitter, Robert Franco, Exec. V.P.--Scalamandre, Inc., Long Island City, NY, pg. 974
Blackham, J. William, Exec. V.P.--Corporex Companies, Inc., Covington, KY, pg. 287
Blais, Robert M., Exec. V.P.--Algood Food Company, Louisville, KY, pg. 34
Blaisdell, Deborah, Exec. V.P.--The U.S. Baird Corporation, Stratford, CT, pg. 114
Blaisdell, Deborah A., Exec. V.P.--The A. H. Nilson Machine Co., Stratford, CT, pg. 114
Blanco, Dianne, Exec. V.P.--MICRODOT, Inc., Chicago, IL, pg. 749
Blankinship, Scott F., Exec. V.P. & Sec.--Petroleum Marketers, Inc., Roanoke, VA, pg. 865
Blasko, Robert L., Exec. V.P.--SBS Products, Inc., Saginaw, MI, pg. 323
Blattner, Christopher J., Exec. V.P.--D.H. Blattner & Sons, Inc., Avon, MN, pg. 156
Blecker, Robert, Exec. V.P.--Carlos R. Leffler Inc., Richland, PA, pg. 666
Block, John, Exec. V.P., Co-Publr. & Editor-in Chief--Blade Communications, Inc., Toledo, OH, pg. 155
Blome, Anthony E., Exec. V.P.--Hopple Plastics, Inc., Florence, KY, pg. 544
Bloom, Richard, Exec. V.P.--TST/Impreso, Inc., Coppell, TX, pg. 1075
Bluemke, David, Exec. V.P.--Cream Products Co., Inc., Westchester, IL, pg. 297
Blume, Gary A., Exec. V.P.--Capital Development Co., Lacey, WA, pg. 215
Blumenfeld, Phillip, Exec. V.P.--American Savings Bank, White Plains, NY, pg. 60
Boardman, Donald, Exec. V.P.--Oxford Realty Services Corp., Bethesda, MD, pg. 835
Bodine, Jeffrey P., Chief Oper. Officer & Exec. V.P.--Bodine Electric Company, Chicago, IL, pg. 162
Bodnar, Emery J., Exec. V.P.--Grant-Lydick Beverage Co., San Antonio, TX, pg. 477
Bohan, Daniel P., Exec. V.P., Treas. & Sec.--Omega World Travel, Inc., Falls Church, VA, pg. 826
Bohny, Gene, Exec. V.P.--Texas Olefins Co., Houston, TX, pg. 1089
Bohrer, Thomas C., Exec. V.P.-Chemicals--GAF Corporation, Wayne, NJ, pg. 438
Bollman, William G., Exec. V.P.--Ferro Union, Inc., Torrance, CA, pg. 407
Bolt, Edward V., Exec. V.P.--PHB Parker Die Castings, Fairview, PA, pg. 836
Bonczyk, Robert, Exec. V.P.--Container Products Inc., Southfield, MI, pg. 278
Bond, Alice, Exec. V.P.-Acct. Services--Jordan, McGrath, Case & Taylor Inc., New York, NY, pg. 604
Boniface, Andrew, Exec. V.P.--Bonland Industries, Inc., Wayne, NJ, pg. 164
Bonnette, Dennis, Exec. V.P. & Chief Oper. Officer--Advanced Circuit Technology, Nashua, NH, pg. 20
Bonsaing, Edward G., Exec. V.P., Dir. Local Brdcst. & Field Opers.--Backer Spielvogel Bates, Inc., New York, NY, pg. 108
Bonser, Sidney H., Exec. V.P.--Marmon Corporation, Chicago, IL, pg. 711
Bontrager, Wilbur, Exec. V.P.--Jayco Inc., Middlebury, IN, pg. 590
Boost, Martin G., Exec. V.P.--Pacific States Casualty Co., Los Angeles, CA, pg. 841
Booth, Richard, Chief Fin. Officer & Exec. V.P.--McAdams, Richman & Ong, Inc., Bala-Cynwyd, PA, pg. 725
Bork, Steven E., Exec. V.P.--Mark Anderson Associates, Inc., Arlington Heights, IL, pg. 73
Boschetto, Laurence J., Exec. V.P., Dir. Acct. Mngmt.--Adler Boschetto Peebles & Partners, Inc., New York, NY, pg. 17
Botts, Thomas M., Exec. V.P.--National Emergency Services, Inc., Tiburon, CA, pg. 788
Bouckaert, G.P., Exec. V.P.--Nooter Corporation, Saint Louis, MO, pg. 808
Boughfman, L.B., Exec. V.P.--Lehigh-Leopold, Burlington, IA, pg. 608
Bourgeois, Ronald, Exec. V.P.--Anco Insulations, Inc., Baton Rouge, LA, pg. 72
Bovaird, J.R., Exec. V.P.--Bovaird Supply Co., Tulsa, OK, pg. 168
Bowden, Douglas, Exec. V.P. & Sec.--Sencore, Inc., Sioux Falls, SD, pg. 989
Boyd, Tom, Exec. V.P.--Kearney, Tucker, GA, pg. 357
Boyle, Allen D., Exec. V.P.--Dumore Corporation, Mauston, WI, pg. 352
Bradberry, Robert W., Exec. V.P.--Continental Ozark, Inc., Fayetteville, AR, pg. 280
Braden, G.F., Sr. V.P.--Central Allied Enterprises, Canton, OH, pg. 232
Bradshaw, John P., Exec. V.P.--Hayes, Seay, Mattern & Mattern, Inc., Roanoke, VA, pg. 519
Brady, John T., Exec. V.P. & Treas.--Worldvision Enterprises, New York, NY, pg. 54
Brady, Patrick, Exec. V.P.--Aurora Casket Company, Aurora, IN, pg. 98
Brady, Thomas, Exec. V.P.--Kobs & Draft Advertising, Inc., Chicago, IL, pg. 109
Braine, John W., Exec. V.P.-Fin. & Admin.--Randolph Medical Inc., Livonia, MI, pg. 912
Brandt, Robert C., Exec. V.P.--Carrafiello, Diehl & Associates, Inc., Irvington, NY, pg. 225
Brehm, Robert T., Exec. V.P.--Chicago Corp., Chicago, IL, pg. 247
Brener, Joshua L., Exec. V.P.--Heery International, Inc., Atlanta, GA, pg. 525
Breslin, Michael, Exec. V.P. & Gen. Counsel--Leo Burnett Company, Inc., Chicago, IL, pg. 191
Bressler, Harry, Exec. V.P., Creative--Steiner/Bressler Advertising, Birmingham, AL, pg. 1045
Brewer, Michael, Exec. V.P.--Linkous Construction Company, Inc., Memphis, TN, pg. 677
Briggs, Richard, Exec. V.P.--National Out-of-Home Media/Metro 8, New York, NY, pg. 792
Bright, Rebecca, Exec. V.P.--Harris Ford, Inc., Lynnwood, WA, pg. 512
Brindley, Thomas M., Chief Oper. Officer & Exec. V.P.--W.A. Roosevelt Co., La Crosse, WI, pg. 946
Brink, K. Robert, Exec. V.P. & Grp. Publishing Dir.--Hearst Magazines Division, New York, NY, pg. 523
Brink, K. Robert, Exec. V.P.--Colonial Homes, New York, NY, pg. 523
Brinling, John J., Jr., Exec. V.P.--Erie Family Life Insurance Company, Erie, PA, pg. 386
Britson, Wesley G., Sr. V.P. & Mng. Principal-HTB/OKC--HTB, Inc., Oklahoma City, OK, pg. 497
Britt, Glenn A., Exec. V.P.--State Farm Life Insurance Co., Bloomington, IL, pg. 1041
Britton, Dennis A., Exec. V.P. & Editor--Chicago Sun Times, Chicago, IL, pg. 18
Britton, Richard L., Exec. V.P., Gen Mgr.--Arnold Fortuna Lawner & Cabot, Boston, MA, pg. 84
Broccoli, Henry, Exec. V.P.--Best Manufacturing, Inc., New York, NY, pg. 146

Brock, Kathleen K., Exec. V.P.--EvansGroup, Denver, CO, pg. 391
Bromlow, Terry, Exec. V.P.--Hereford State Bank, Hereford, TX, pg. 412
Broome, H. Cuy, Jr., Exec. V.P.--Harry Pepper & Associates, Jacksonville, FL, pg. 859
Brosnan, Daryl, Exec. V.P.--Bel-Ray Company, Inc., Farmingdale, NJ, pg. 133
Brouillette, Marilyn S., Exec. V.P.--Demeter, Inc., Fowler, IN, pg. 328
Brown, Douglas S., Exec. V.P.--Enterprise Rent-A-Car Company, Saint Louis, MO, pg. 382
Brown, Edwin C., Exec. V.P.--Feed Service Corp., Crete, NE, pg. 405
Brown, Hugh J., Exec. V.P.--Dix & Eaton Incorporated, Cleveland, OH, pg. 341
Brown, Kirk D., Chief Fin. Officer & Exec. V.P.-Systems--EBM Systems, Inc., Greenbelt, MD, pg. 359
Brown, Michael I., Exec. V.P.-Corporate Mngmt. Serv. Admin.--The New England, Boston, MA, pg. 799
Brown, Ray, Exec. V.P.--Doyle McKenna Bayer Brown, Reno, NV, pg. 348
Brownfeld, Fred, Exec. V.P.--Rosenfeld, Sirowitz, Humphrey & Strauss, Inc., New York, NY, pg. 948
Brucchieri, James, Exec. V.P.--Greeff Fabrics, Port Chester, NY, pg. 262
Brucchieri, William, Exec. V.P.--Decorative Fabrics - Mastercraft, Spindale, NC, pg. 262
Bruder, James J., Exec. V.P.--M. A. Bruder & Sons, Inc., Broomall, PA, pg. 184
Brunelle, John, Exec. V.P.--The Conde Nast Publications Inc., New York, NY, pg. 19
Bruno, Joseph, Exec. V.P.--Dixie Brewing Co., Inc., New Orleans, LA, pg. 341
Bruskrud, Barry, Exec. V.P.--Bemco Inc., Simi Valley, CA, pg. 138
Bryant, Bob, Exec. V.P.--Bradshaw Associates in Advertising, Inc., Springfield, MO, pg. 171
Bryant, Harry M., Jr., Exec. V.P.--Bryant Supply Company, Inc., Gastonia, NC, pg. 185
Buchan, John, Exec. V.P.--Cloverdale Equipment Co., Oak Park, MI, pg. 256
Buchta, C.J., Sr. Exec. V.P.--American Savings Bank, White Plains, NY, pg. 60
Buck, C.B., Exec. V.P.--Buck Knives, Inc., El Cajon, CA, pg. 185
Buck, Max, Exec. V.P.--Vitt Media International, Inc., New York, NY, pg. 1153
Buck, Max, Exec. V.P.--Vitt Media International, Inc., New York, NY, pg. 1153
Bucksbaum, John, Exec. V.P.--General Growth Companies, Inc., Des Moines, IA, pg. 449
Buda, Stanley, Exec. V.P.--Hitchcock-Fleming & Associates, Inc., Akron, OH, pg. 536
Buenger, C.G., Exec. V.P.--Modern Equipment Co., Inc., Port Washington, WI, pg. 32
Buescher, C.A., Exec. V.P.--Continental Water Company, Saint Louis, MO, pg. 280
Buff, George, III, Exec. V.P.--Penny Plate, Inc., Cherry Hill, NJ, pg. 858
Buicko, David M., Exec. V.P.--Rotterdam Ventures Inc., Guilderland Center, NY, pg. 951
Bull, Clint, Exec. V.P.--Fellowes Manufacturing Co., Itasca, IL, pg. 405
Buns, Kenneth W., Exec. V.P.--Dualite Inc., Williamsburg, OH, pg. 350
Burden, Thomas L., Exec. V.P. & Pres.-TBC Direct--Trahan, Burden & Charles, Inc., Baltimore, MD, pg. 1105
Burickson, Sue, Exec. V.P.--G.L. Advertising, Dumont, NJ, pg. 440
Burleson, Milt, Exec. V.P.--Monterey Mechanical Company, Oakland, CA, pg. 767
Burnett, Russ, V.P. & Chief Fin. Officer--Independent Insurance Agents of America, Alexandria, VA, pg. 565
Burrell, Chester E., Exec. V.P.--The Associated Group, Indianapolis, IN, pg. 90
Butcher, Dick, Exec. V.P.--Anchor Continental Incorporated, Columbia, SC, pg. 71
Butler, Bill, Exec. V.P.--Girgenti, Hughes, Butler & McDowell, New York, NY, pg. 460
Butler, Harry P., Exec. V.P.--Mid-States Petroleum Inc., Troy, MI, pg. 750
Butler, I.E., Exec. V.P.--Stephens, Inc., Little Rock, AR, pg. 1046
Butler, Michael A., Chief Oper. Officer & Exec. V.P.--Kruse International, Auburn, IN, pg. 645
Butner, Eleanor, Exec. V.P.--Lawrence Butner Advertising, Inc., New York, NY, pg. 197
Butter, Dave, Exec. V.P.-Europe--Wunderman Worldwide Limited, London, United Kingdom, pg. 1212
Byall, Louis, Exec. V.P.--Mayer Myers Paper Company, Memphis, TN, pg. 724
Byington, Walt, Exec. V.P.--Klipsch & Associates Inc., Hope, AR, pg. 635
Caffrone, Douglas P., Exec. V.P.--Geyer-McAllister Publications, Inc., New York, NY, pg. 455
Cagan, Martin, Exec. V.P.--Admarketing, Inc., Los Angeles, CA, pg. 18
Caine, William, T., Exec. V.P.--Metal Seal & Products, Inc., Willoughby, OH, pg. 741
Calamari, Joseph, Exec. V.P.--Marvel Entertainment Group, New York, NY, pg. 695
Calkins, Harlan D., Chm. Bd. & Pres.--Rochester Midland Corporation, Rochester, NY, pg. 940
Callahan, Tim J., Exec. V.P.--Gulf States Asphalt Company, Inc., South Houston, TX, pg. 493
Callan, Sherri, Exec. V.P., Dir.-West Coast Div.--Great Scott Advertising Co. Inc., New York, NY, pg. 482
Callentine, Ronald, Exec. V.P.--Guest Quarters Suite Hotels, Boston, MA, pg. 493
Cameron, Doug, Exec. V.P.--JMB Realty Corporation, Chicago, IL, pg. 584
Cameron, Duane H., Exec. V.P.--Systems Parking, Inc., Pasadena, CA, pg. 1071
Cameron, Patricia, Exec. V.P., Dir. Planning & Research--TBWA Advertising, Inc., New York, NY, pg. 1071
Campbell, Charles H., Exec. V.P.--Peter Kiewit Sons Inc., Omaha, NE, pg. 629
Campbell, Chuck, Exec. V.P.--Cosmetique, Inc., Vernon Hills, IL, pg. 288
Campbell, Donald A., Exec. V.P.--Marcus Advertising, Inc., Cleveland, OH, pg. 706
Campbell, John E., Chief Oper. Officer & Exec. V.P.--Red Roof Inns, Inc., Hilliard, OH, pg. 918
Campbell, Keith, Exec. V.P.--Mannington Resilient Floors, Salem, NJ, pg. 704
Campbell, Robert E., Exec. V.P.--T. Bruce Sales, Inc., West Middlesex, PA, pg. 183
Canno, Jonathon S., Exec. V.P.--Equitable Bag Company, Long Island City, NY, pg. 385
Cantrell, Ron, Chief Fin. Officer, Exec. V.P. & Controller--The Mad Butcher, Inc., Pine Bluff, AR, pg. 699
Capstaff, Diane M., Exec. V.P.-Corp. Sector--John Hancock Mutual Life Insurance Company, Boston, MA, pg. 595
Carlson, Jim, Exec. V.P.--Laubeck Corporation/Cross, Carbondale, PA, pg. 660
Carlson, Robert E., Exec. V.P.-Agencies & Mktg.--Northwestern Mutual Life Insurance Co., Milwaukee, WI, pg. 815
Caron, James A., Exec. V.P.--Beno's, Los Angeles, CA, pg. 139
Caropino, Stephen, Exec. V.P.--Pacifica Services, Inc., Pasadena, CA, pg. 842
Carpender, Gary, Exec. V.P.--American International Container, Inc., Miami, FL, pg. 56
Carroll, James E., Exec. V.P. & Chief Oper. Officer--Bradley Corporation, Menomonee Falls, WI, pg. 170
Carroll, Thomas S., Exec. V.P.--Viking Yacht Co., New Gretna, NJ, pg. 1151
Cartwright, Jeane H., Exec. V.P., New Bus. Contact--Aydlotte & Cartwright, Inc., Atlanta, GA, pg. 103
Caruso, Raymond S., Exec. V.P.--Lord, Sullivan & Yoder, Inc. Advertising, Columbus, OH, pg. 683
Carver, Laurie A., Exec. V.P., Creative Dir.--Hamilton, Carver & Lee, Inc., Chicago, IL, pg. 503
Casabona, Joseph E., Exec. V.P.--Eastern American Energy Corporation, Charleston, WV, pg. 363
Case, Harry L., Exec. V.P.--Chaffee Case & Partners, Providence, RI, pg. 237
Casey, Robert E. Jr., Exec. V.P.--Robinhood Homes, Inc., San Diego, CA, pg. 939
Casper, Jack M., Exec. V.P.--Mitek, Inc., Chesterfield, MO, pg. 762
Casson, Joan M., Exec. V.P. & Chief Investment Officer--Mutual of America, New York, NY, pg. 777
Castagna, Patrick, Exec. V.P.--Carlos R. Leffler Inc., Richland, PA, pg. 666
Castro, Jose Luis, Exec. V.P. & New Business Contact--GS&B-Lintas Advertising, Coral Gables, FL, pg. 440
Casty, L. Roger, Exec. V. P.--CPM, Inc., Chicago, IL, pg. 203
Cataldo, Robert J., Exec. V.P.-Opers.--Hostmark Management Group, Rowing Meadows, IL, pg. 545
Cavanagh, John, Exec. Dir.--Morse Diesel International, New York, NY, pg. 771
Cavitt, Glen, Exec. V.P.--Eddins-Walcher Company, Midland, TX, pg. 367
Cawdrey, Marc, Exec. V.P.--Jamison, Cawdrey, Benjamin, San Francisco, CA, pg. 589
Cerny, Rodney D., Exec. V.P. & Chief Investment Officer--Kirkpatrick Pettis, Omaha, NE, pg. 779
Chaiken, Roslyn, Exec. V.P.--Almo Corp., Philadelphia, PA, pg. 43
Chalmers, D., Exec. V.P.--Leo Burnett Company Ltd., Toronto,, Canada, pg. 192
Chamberlain, J.J., Exec. V.P.--Stowe-Pharr Mills, Inc., McAdenville, NC, pg. 1052
Chandler, Steven L., Sr. V.P.--L.N. Curtis & Sons, Oakland, CA, pg. 306
Chapman, Michael M., Exec. V.P. & Co-Chief Oper. Officer--U.S. Divers Co., Inc., Santa Ana, CA, pg. 1135
Chapman, Robert, Exec. V.P.--Amfac, Inc., Chicago, IL, pg. 585
Chappell, Robert E., Jr., Sr. Exec. V.P. & Chief Fin. Officer--Metropolitan Life Insurance Co., New York, NY, pg. 744
Charappe, Mike, Exec. V.P.--Rosenthal Automotive Organization, Arlington, VA, pg. 949
Charles, Allan, Exec. V.P., Creative Dir.--Trahan, Burden & Charles, Inc., Baltimore, MD, pg. 1105
Chastain, Roger W., Exec. V.P. & Pres.- Riegel Textile Div.--Mount Vernon Mills, Inc., Greenville, SC, pg. 844
Chawla, Vera, Exec. V.P.--Information Systems & Network Corporation, Bethesda, MD, pg. 567
Chen, Janice B., Exec. V.P.--Significs, Inc., Rochester, NY, pg. 1004
Cherry, John R., III, Exec. V.P.--Carden & Cherry, Inc., Nashville, TN, pg. 217
Chervokas, John, Exec. V.P., Chief Creative Officer--Sudler & Hennessey, New York, NY, pg. 1211
Child, Mark W., Exec. V.P.--Sterling Savings & Loan, Irvine, CA, pg. 1047
Childers, James H., Exec. V.P.--Garvey Industries, Inc., Wichita, KS, pg. 443
Chororos, William, Exec. V.P., Grp. Creative Dir.--Backer Spielvogel Bates, Inc., New York, NY, pg. 108
Christie, Doris, Exec. V.P.--J. I. Kislak Inc., Miami Lakes, FL, pg. 633
Christoff, Dave, Exec. V.P., Production Dir.--TBWA Kerlick Switzer, Saint Louis, MO, pg. 1071
Chun, Rupert K., Exec. V.P.--Mutual Welding Co., Ltd, Honolulu, HI, pg. 779
Ciccone-Scott, Cynthia, Exec. V.P., Mngmt. Supvr.--Trahan, Burden & Charles, Inc., Baltimore, MD, pg. 1105
Ciepiel, Anthony M., Exec. V.P., Chief Oper. Officer--Teledira National Yellow Pages Service, Cleveland, OH, pg. 950
Cims, Donald V., Exec. V.P.--Nuarc Company, Inc., Niles, IL, pg. 817
Claeys, Jerry, Exec. V.P.--JMB Realty Corporation, Chicago, IL, pg. 584
Clark, James N., Exec. V.P.--Western & Southern Life Insurance Co., Cincinnati, OH, pg. 1181
Clark, MacDonald, Exec. V.P.--Alamo Rent-A-Car Inc., Fort Lauderdale, FL, pg. 30
Clark, Thomas, Exec. V.P.--Cosmopulos Crowley Daly/CKG, Boston, MA, pg. 288
Clark, Thomas H., Exec. V.P.--Guaranty Corporation, Baton Rouge, LA, pg. 491
Clarke, G., Exec. V.P.--Coldwater Seafood Corporation, Rowayton, CT, pg. 260
Clarke, Michael J., Chief Fin. Officer, Exec. V.P.--Prime Hospitality Corp., Fairfield, NJ, pg. 889
Clarkson, Sandy, Exec. V.P.--The Bergman Group, New York, NY, pg. 949
Clay, Larry E., Exec. V.P. & Chief Fin. Officer--UES, Inc., Dayton, OH, pg. 1122
Clayton, David, Exec. V.P.--Andy Frain Services, Inc., Chicago, IL, pg. 428
Clayton, Ronald J., Exec. V.P.--Consolidated Industries, Inc., Cheshire, CT, pg. 276
Cleary, Robert T., Exec. V.P.--Kinetic Systems Corporation, Lockport, IL, pg. 630
Clemens, John P., Sr. Exec. V.P.--Bankers Systems Inc., Saint Cloud, MN, pg. 117
Clifford, Thomas, Exec. V.P.--Cresmer, Woodward, O'Mara & Ormsbee, New York, NY, pg. 298
Clifton, Jean B., Exec. V.P. & Chief Fin. Officer--Journal Register Company, Trenton, NJ, pg. 608
Cluer, Allen, Exec. V.P. & Gen. Mgr.--Clayton Industries Co., El Monte, CA, pg. 253
Coakley, Terrance, Exec. V.P.--Coakley & Williams Inc., Greenbelt, MD, pg. 256
Coates, John C., Exec. V.P.--J. E. Higgins Lumber Co., Concord, CA, pg. 533
Cobb, Wm. A., Exec. V.P.--Sullivan Long & Hagerty, Inc., Birmingham, AL, pg. 1057
Cocboth, J.D., Exec. V.P.--The Lathrop Company, Toledo, OH, pg. 660
Coe, David L., Exec. V.P.--Central States Diversified, Inc., Saint Louis, MO, pg. 234
Cogger, William G., Exec. V.P.--Moore Special Tool Co., Inc., Bridgeport, CT, pg. 768
Cohen, L. Robert, Exec. V.P.--Lever Mfg. Corp., Paterson, NJ, pg. 1092
Cohen, Leon E., Exec. Sr. V.P.--Duane Reade, Long Island City, NY, pg. 350
Cohen, Peter J., Exec. V.P.--Hollytex, Saddle Brook, NJ, pg. 1121
Cohen, Steven, Exec. V.P.--Host Apparel, Inc., New York, NY, pg. 545
Cohenca, Philip, Exec. V.P.--Jason Industrial, Inc., Fairfield, NJ, pg. 590
Cohn, James, Exec. V.P.--Sigmund Cohn Corp., Mount Vernon, NY, pg. 259
Cohune, Paul, Exec. V.P., New Bus. Contact--Darien & Kilburg, Inc., San Jose, CA, pg. 315
Colbert, Christopher M., Exec. V.P. & New Bus. Contact--Holland Mark Martin, Burlington, MA, pg. 539
Cole, James J., Jr., Exec. V.P.--Alex J. Etkin, Inc., Farmington Hills, MI, pg. 389
Cole, James P., Exec. V.P.--Cole Henderson Drake, Inc., Atlanta, GA, pg. 260
Coleman, Richard, Exec. V.P.--World Shipping, Inc., Lakewood, OH, pg. 1203
Coleman, Richard J., Exec. V.P.--Florasynth Inc., New York, NY, pg. 420
Collesberry, Thomas, Exec. V.P.--Ruiz Food Products, Inc., Dinuba, CA, pg. 955
Collier, Joseph W., Exec. V.P.--Allied Systems, Ltd., Decatur, GA, pg. 40
Collins, James E., Exec. V.P.--Avis, Inc., Garden City, NY, pg. 102
Collop, Mark, Exec. V.P.--Vantage Companies, Dallas, TX, pg. 1145
Colman, Thomas E, Ph.D., Chief Oper. Officer & Exec. V.P.--Scott Specialty Gases, Inc., Plumsteadville, PA, pg. 983
Combe, Roger G., Exec. V.P.--Robert F. Driver Co., Inc., San Diego, CA, pg. 349
Comeau, R.L., Exec. V.P.-Grp. Div.--Guarantee Mutual Life Co., Omaha, NE, pg. 491
Conant, Mark, Exec. V.P.--USA Petroleum Corporation, Santa Monica, CA, pg. 1124
Conger, S.H., Exec. V.P.--Coastal Lumber Company, Weldon, NC, pg. 257
Conklin, David J., Exec. V.P.--Conklin Instrument Corporation, Pleasant Valley, NY, pg. 274
Conlan, Gary, Exec. V.P.--Neer Manufacturing Company, Lexington, OH, pg. 797
Conley, Terrence, Sr. V.P.--Kraco Enterprises, Inc., Compton, CA, pg. 643
Connell, Ted, Exec. V.P.--Connell Rice & Sugar Co., Westfield, NJ, pg. 275
Connelly, T.T., Exec. V.P.--Hardinge Brothers, Inc., Elmira, NY, pg. 508
Conners, John B., Exec. V.P.--Liberty Mutual Insurance Co., Boston, MA, pg. 674
Conners, William, Exec. V.P.--Pearl-Pressman-Liberty Communications Group, Philadelphia, PA, pg. 853
Connolly, R.C., Exec. V.P.--Connell Rice & Sugar Co., Westfield, NJ, pg. 275
Connolly, Richard S., Exec. V.P.--Tippins Incorporated, Pittsburgh, PA, pg. 1099
Conrad, E.T., Exec. V.P.--SCS Engineers, Long Beach, CA, pg. 961
Constantinoff, George, Exec. V.P., Dir. Scientific & Medical Affairs--Klemtner Advertising Inc., New York, NY, pg. 635
Conte, Leo, Exec. V.P.--Montebello Brands Inc., Baltimore, MD, pg. 767
Cook, Therese Marie, Exec. V.P.-A.I.A.--Scalamandre, Inc., Long Island City, NY, pg. 974

Cool, David H., Exec. V.P.--S. C. Johnson & Son, Inc., Racine, WI, pg. 599
Coon, C. Ed, Exec. V.P.--Martin K. Eby Construction Company, Inc., Wichita, KS, pg. 365
Cooney, Diane, Exec. V.P., Dir. of Creative Services--Sudler & Hennessey, New York, NY, pg. 1211
Cooper, David, Exec. V.P.--C. Weaver Chevrolet, Inc., New York Mills, NY, pg. 1170
Cooper, Gary, Exec. V.P.--Century 21 Real Estate Corp., Irvine, CA, pg. 744
Cooper, Michael, Exec. V.P.--Best Manufacturing, Inc., New York, NY, pg. 146
Cooper, R. John, Exec. V.P., Gen. Counsel & Sec.--Young & Rubicam Inc., New York, NY, pg. 1210
Cooper, Rick, Exec. V.P.--The SArgent-SOwell Company, Grand Prairie, TX, pg. 971
Cooper, William L., Exec. V.P.--Barnhill Contracting Company, Tarboro, NC, pg. 121
Coopersmith, Harold, Exec. V.P.--Smith-Edwards-Dunlap Company, Philadelphia, PA, pg. 1012
Copenhaver, Ed, Exec. V.P.--Atlanta Motor Lines, Inc., Conley, GA, pg. 94
Coppola, Arthur, Exec. V.P.--The Macerich Co., Santa Monica, CA, pg. 696
Copps, Frederick C., Exec. V.P.-Wholesale--The Copps Corp., Stevens Point, WI, pg. 285
Corbett, Thomas W., Exec. V.P. & Dir.-Newport Beach Office--Robert F. Driver Co., Inc., San Diego, CA, pg. 349
Corcoran, Joe, Exec. V.P.--Computer Dynamics, Inc., Virginia Beach, VA, pg. 271
Corcoran, John E., Exec. V.P. & Gen. Mgr.--Marine World Africa USA, Vallejo, CA, pg. 707
Cordial, C. Alan, Exec. V.P.--Creative Productions, Pittsburgh, PA, pg. 297
Corelitz, Richard, Exec. V.P. & Mng. Dir.--Bayer Bess Vanderwarker Inc., Chicago, IL, pg. 128
Corkran, James, Exec. V.P.--Cottman Transmission Systems, Inc., Fort Washington, PA, pg. 288
Corlett, Glenn E., Exec. V.P., Chief Fin. Officer--N W Ayer Incorporated, New York, NY, pg. 103
Coti, Anthony J., Exec. V.P. & Chief Fin. Officer--Pathmark, Woodbridge, NJ, pg. 1064
Coughlin, E., Exec. V.P.--Lake Shore, Inc., Kingsford, MI, pg. 824
Covney, Arlene, Exec. V.P.--Career Blazers Inc., New York, NY, pg. 218
Cox, Lawrence G., Exec. V.P.--Mary Kay Corporation, Dallas, TX, pg. 716
Craft, Donald B., Exec. V.P.--Wyatt Inc., Branford, CT, pg. 1205
Cramer, Robert, Exec. V.P.--Fareway Stores, Inc., Boone, IA, pg. 399
Crawford, Dave, Exec. V.P.-Bldg. Grp.--Sundt Corp., Tucson, AZ, pg. 1060
Crimmins, Robert J., Exec. V.P.-Personal Insurance--Metropolitan Life Insurance Co., New York, NY, pg. 744
Crisafulli, Frank, Exec. V.P.--Columbian Mutual Life Insurance Co., Binghamton, NY, pg. 266
Crittenden, Jack, Exec. V.P.--Misener Marine Construction, Tampa, FL, pg. 759
Cron, Kenneth, Exec. V.P.--C M P Publications, Inc., Manhasset, NY, pg. 202
Cross, J.L., Exec. V.P.--CAE Link Allen Division, Alexandria, VA, pg. 198
Crotty, Thomas, Exec. V.P., Treas.--Sudler & Hennessey, New York, NY, pg. 1211
Crouch, Robert F., Sr. V.P.--The Copley Press, Inc., La Jolla, CA, pg. 284
Crow, Howard M., Exec. V.P.--Broadcast Electronics, Inc., Quincy, IL, pg. 177
Cullers, Marian B., Exec. V.P. & Sec.--Vince Cullers Advertising Inc., Chicago, IL, pg. 304
Culver, Mary N., Corp. V.P.--Culver & Associates, Inc., Omaha, NE, pg. 304
Cunningham, R.C., Exec. V.P.--AFG Industries, Inc., Fort Worth, TX, pg. 3
Curtis, F.M., Exec. V.P.--Eyecessories, Plainville, MA, pg. 535
Cuskley, Stephanie, Exec. V.P.--Integrated Resources, Inc., New York, NY, pg. 573
Cutler, Gerald, Exec. V.P., Dir.-Plng. & Opers.--Ketchum Advertising/New York, New York, NY, pg. 625
Cwiok, Jerome J., Exec. V.P. & Chief Oper. Officer--Academy Insurance Group, Inc., Atlanta, GA, pg. 11
D'Amato, Victor W., Exec. V.P.--Ideal Forging Corporation, Southington, CT, pg. 562
D'Anna, Carmen V., Exec. V.P.--Mars Super Markets, Inc., Baltimore, MD, pg. 714
D'Anna, Lynn, Exec. V.P.--Pancom International Corp., Stamford, CT, pg. 845
Dahlman, Charles R., Exec. V.P.--Homestead House Inc., Broomfield, CO, pg. 542
Dale, Richard, Exec. V.P. & Mng. Dir.--Wills and Evans, New York, NY, pg. 1193
Daley, Edward J., Exec. V.P.--The In-House Agency, Weehawken, NJ, pg. 564
Dalton, Robert E., Exec. V.P. & Chief Oper Officer--Dunmore Corporation, Newtown, PA, pg. 353
Danberg, Kenneth, Exec. V.P.-Sls.--Harper Industries, Inc., New York, NY, pg. 510
Dardas, Charles L., Exec. V.P.--Lobdell-Emery Manufacturing Company, Alma, MI, pg. 680
Dardine, Warren A., Exec. V.P.--Roberts & Raymond Assoc., Inc., Bala-Cynwyd, PA, pg. 939
Daunhauer, Gregory, Exec. V.P.--Byerly Ford-Nissan Inc., Louisville, KY, pg. 198
Davis, Harry L., Exec. V.P.--Montgomery, Zukerman, Davis, Inc., Indianapolis, IN, pg. 768
Davis, Jim, Exec. V.P.--Lowell Packing Company, Fitzgerald, GA, pg. 685
Davis, John W., Exec. V.P.-Non-Textile Opers.--Greenwood Mills, Inc., Greenwood, SC, pg. 485
Davis, John T., Exec. V.P.--First American Bankshares, Inc., Washington, DC, pg. 412
Davis, Lawrence, Exec. V.P.--Seibel & Stern Corp., New York, NY, pg. 987
Davis, Roger, Exec. V.P.--William Morris Agency, Inc., Beverly Hills, CA, pg. 771
Davis, Scott, Exec. V.P.-Network Opers.--Viacom Inc., New York, NY, pg. 785
Davis, Scott, Exec. V.P.-Network Opers. & Gen. Mgr.-Nickelodeon Studios--MTV Networks, New York, NY, pg. 785
Davis, Tom I., III, Exec. V.P.--Brian Center Management Corporation, Hickory, NC, pg. 175
Davis, Troy W., Chm. Bd.-Best Western Intl.--B-W Advertising Agency, Phoenix, AZ, pg. 107
Day, Garry L., Exec. V.P.--Flynn/Sabatino, Miamisburg, OH, pg. 421
Day, Richard P., Exec. V.P.-Business Devel.--Ameritas Life Insurance Corp., Lincoln, NE, pg. 66
Day, Roy, Exec. V.P.--Essex Grain Products, Inc., Frazer, PA, pg. 389
De Deo, Joseph E., Exec. V.P., Chief Creative Officer--Young & Rubicam Inc., New York, NY, pg. 1210
De Vita, Lou, Exec. V.P.--Oh Boy Corporation, San Fernando, CA, pg. 822
Deal, David, Sr. Exec. V.P.--Little Caesar Enterprises, Inc., Detroit, MI, pg. 678
Dean, Alexander L., Exec. V.P.--Builders Inc., Wichita, KS, pg. 444
Dean, Art, Exec. V.P. & G.M.--Evergreen Mills Inc., Ada, OK, pg. 1145
Deane, James R., Exec. V.P., Sec. & Gen. Counsel--Fiduciary Trust Company International, New York, NY, pg. 408
DeCardenas, Jennie, Exec. V.P.--Cacique Cheese Co., Inc., City of Industry, CA, pg. 206
DeCius, Dennis A., Chief Fin. Officer, Exec. V.P. & Asst. Sec.--Pacific Capital Bancorp, Salinas, CA, pg. 839
Deehring, Walter, Exec. V.P.--Foster & Gallagher Inc., Peoria, IL, pg. 426
Deering, J., Exec. V.P.--Mentor AGVS, Inc., Mentor, OH, pg. 893
DeGraeve, Donald L., Exec. V.P.-Mdsg.--The Elder-Beerman Stores Corp., Dayton, OH, pg. 373
DeGreave, Doanld L., Exec. V.P.-Mdsg.--Elder-Beerman Stores Div., Dayton, OH, pg. 373
del Rivero, Eduardo, Exec. V.P.-Acct. Services--GS&B-Lintas Advertising, Coral Gables, FL, pg. 440
Delaney, James, Sr V.P.--Johnson & Higgins, New York, NY, pg. 598
Delgado, Robert M., Exec. V.P.--Hensley & Co., Phoenix, AZ, pg. 530
DeLoache, Bill, Exec. V.P.--Shealy Electrical Wholesalers, Greenville, SC, pg. 996
DeLorenzo, David A., Pres., Dole Food Co. & Exec. V.P., Dole Food Co., Inc.--Dole Food Company, Inc., Westlake Village, CA, pg. 840
Delp, George W., Exec. V.P.-U.S. Consumer Prods.--S. C. Johnson & Son, Inc., Racine, WI, pg. 599
DeMagistris, Manny, Sr. Exec. V.P., Creative Dir. on Ralston Cereals--Avrett, Free & Ginsberg, Inc., New York, NY, pg. 103
DeMaria, Joseph A., Jr., Exec. V.P.--DeMaria Building Co. Inc., Novi, MI, pg. 327
Denk, Gregory P., Exec. V.P.--Kitchell Corporation, Phoenix, AZ, pg. 634
DeRossett, Tommy, Exec. V.P.--Associated Aircraft Supply Company, Dallas, TX, pg. 89
Derton, H.E., Exec. V.P.--Centrifugal & Mechanical Industries, Saint Louis, MO, pg. 609
DeSantis, Damon, Exec. V.P.--Sundown Vitamin Co., Inc., Fort Lauderdale, FL, pg. 1060
Desmond, Daniel J., Exec. V.P. & Chief Oper. Officer--Central Pharmaceuticals, Inc., Seymour, IN, pg. 234
Deutsch, Lester, Exec. V.P.--The Deutsch Company, Santa Monica, CA, pg. 333
deYong, James L., Exec. V.P.--DGWB, Inc., Irvine, CA, pg. 309
Dickson, Ron, Exec. V.P., Pres.-Direct Mktg.r--Barkley & Evergreen Advertising, Inc., Shawnee Mission, KS, pg. 120
Dieffenbach, N., Exec. V.P.--Hauck Mfg. Co., Cleona, PA, pg. 517
Dietrich, William V., Exec. V.P.--Kastle Systems, Inc., Arlington, VA, pg. 618
DiFillippo, Lucy R., Exec. V.P.--DeVault Foods, Devault, PA, pg. 333
Digges, J.J., Exec. V.P.--Bush Development Corp., Williamsburg, VA, pg. 196
Dillahey, Frank, Exec. V.P.--TV Host Inc., Harrisburg, PA, pg. 1075
Dillon, R.I., Exec. V.P. & Treas.--Standard Lafarge, Canfield, OH, pg. 1036
Dinkins, Thomas A., III, Exec. V.P.--John Fabick Tractor Company, Fenton, MO, pg. 396
Diranna, Dave, V.P.-Franchise Services--Precision Tune, Inc., Leesburg, VA, pg. 885
Dishman, Charles, Exec. V.P.--Gump's, Inc., San Francisco, CA, pg. 494
Divine, Harold S., Exec. V.P.--McCrory Corporation, New York, NY, pg. 934
Dixler, Joseph M., Exec. V.P.--Nuarc Company, Inc., Niles, IL, pg. 817
Dixon, James M., Exec. V.P.--Tri-Mark Metal Corp., Detroit, MI, pg. 1110
Doan, Bruce, Sr. V.P.--W. M. Barr & Co., Inc., Memphis, TN, pg. 121
Dobrick, Glenn, Exec. V.P.--Kentucky Manufacturing Co., Louisville, KY, pg. 624
Dobrick, Glenn, Exec. V.P.--R.C. Tway Coal Company, Louisville, KY, pg. 1120
Dodds, John M., Exec. V.P.--U-Haul International, Inc., Phoenix, AZ, pg. 48
Dodge, Mark, Exec. V.P. & Gen. Counsel--Western International Media Corporation, Los Angeles, CA, pg. 1179
Dohmen, John, Exec. V.P.--The F. Dohmen Company, Germantown, WI, pg. 343
Dolan, Lawrence R., Exec. V.P. & Chief Oper. Officer--Commercial Light Company, Hillside, IL, pg. 268
Domantay, N.V. (Lito), Exec. V.P., Consumer Products--Simon Marketing, Inc., Los Angeles, CA, pg. 1006
Donley, Mac, Exec. V.P.--Donley's, Inc., Cleveland, OH, pg. 345
Donnelly, Andrew W., Exec. V.P.--Fort Howard Corporation, Green Bay, WI, pg. 425
Donnelly, John J., Exec. V.P.-Construction--L.F. Driscoll Co., Bala-Cynwyd, PA, pg. 349
Donofrio, Chuck, Exec. V.P.--Richardson, Myers & Donofrio, Inc., Baltimore, MD, pg. 933
Doolin, Wallace, Exec. V.P.-Franchise & Corp. Devel.--TGI Friday's, Inc., Addison, TX, pg. 221
Doshan, Jeffrey R., Exec. V.P.--Things Remembered, Cleveland, OH, pg. 260
Dowden, Albert L., Exec. V.P.--Park Ridge Corporation, Park Ridge, NJ, pg. 849
Downie, John F., Sr. V.P.--Things Remembered, Cleveland, OH, pg. 260
Doyle, Peter G., Chief Fin. Officer & Exec. V.P.--Linbeck Corp., Houston, TX, pg. 675
Drabb, Michael J., Exec. V.P.-Investment Mngmt.--The Mutual Life Insurance Company of New York (MONY), New York, NY, pg. 778
Dragan, Simon, Exec. V.P.-Scotsman Building Div.--The Scotsman Group, Inc., Baltimore, MD, pg. 982
Drake, J.S., Exec. V.P.--Camelot Communications, Inc., Dallas, TX, pg. 212
Drawe, Stephen L., Exec. V.P.--Fru-Con Construction Corporation, Ballwin, MO, pg. 435
Dreeben, Alan, Exec. V.P.--Block Distributing Company, San Antonio, TX, pg. 157
Dreisbach, Albert, Exec. V.P.--E. J. Brooks Company, Newark, NJ, pg. 179
Dressler, Robert, Exec. V.P.--Merle Norman Cosmetics, Inc., Los Angeles, CA, pg. 740
Driggers, R.W., Exec. V.P.--M M Systems Corporation, Tucker, GA, pg. 692
Driscoll, Karen, Exec. V.P., Acct. Dir.--Arnold Fortuna Lawner & Cabot, Boston, MA, pg. 84
Drury, David, Chief Fin. Officer & Exec. V.P.--The Oldenburg Group Companies, Milwaukee, WI, pg. 824
Dubin, Thomas G., Exec. V.P.--Manufacturers' News, Inc., Evanston, IL, pg. 705
Duda, Andrew L., Exec. V.P.--A. Duda & Sons Inc., Oviedo, FL, pg. 351
Dudley, David, Exec. V.P.--S. Gumpert Co., Inc., Columbus, OH, pg. 932
Duffield, Gary, Exec. V.P. & Gen. Mgr.-Mailroom Div.--IDAB International Incorporated, Hampton, VA, pg. 559
Duffy, Michael W., Exec. V.P. & Gen. Mgr.--American Red Ball World Wide Movers, Indianapolis, IN, pg. 918
Duggan, Edwin L., Sr., Exec. V.P.--Duggan Industries, Inc., Dallas, TX, pg. 351
Duggan, Michael, Exec. V.P.-Sls.--Melard Manufacturing Corporation, Passaic, NJ, pg. 737
Dumun, George, Jr., Exec. V.P.--Geo. H. Lehleitner & Co., Inc., Harahan, LA, pg. 666
Duncan, Bruce W., Exec. V.P.--JMB Realty Corporation, Chicago, IL, pg. 584
Dunham, Donald D., Exec. V.P., Acct. Service--Gillis Advertising & Public Relations, Birmingham, AL, pg. 459
Dunn, Charles O., Exec. V.P. & Chief Oper. Officer--Mississippi Chemical Corporation, Yazoo City, MS, pg. 760
Dunn, Melvin B., Exec. V.P. & Chief Mktg. Officer--Security Mutual Life Insurance Co. of New York, Binghamton, NY, pg. 987
Dupps, Frank N., Exec. V.P.--Dupps Company, Germantown, OH, pg. 354
Duvall, Claude W., Exec. V.P.--Jitney-Jungle Stores of America, Inc., Jackson, MS, pg. 594
Dwyer, Arthur A., Exec. V.P.--Communication Trends, Inc., Atlanta, GA, pg. 269
Dyer, Lex, III, Exec. V.P.-Capital Mkts.--International Airline Support Group, Inc., Miami, FL, pg. 575
Dzvonik, Michael D., Exec. V.P.--Grizzard Advertising, Inc., Atlanta, GA, pg. 488
Eagle, Paul H., Exec. V.P.--Greer Steel Co., Dover, OH, pg. 486
Eaken, Roderick, Exec. V.P.--R.M. Palmer Company, West Reading, PA, pg. 843
Eastham, John, Exec. V.P. (Seattle) & Dir.--EvansGroup, Salt Lake City, UT, pg. 390
Eberhart, Dan, V.P.--The Tog Shop, Americus, GA, pg. 1100
Ebihara, Yushi, Exec. V.P., Chief Oper. Officer--Kresser/Craig, Santa Monica, CA, pg. 644
Eby, Carl J., Exec. V.P.--Capital Tire, Inc., Toledo, OH, pg. 215
Eby, Charles K., Exec. V.P.--Martin K. Eby Construction Company, Inc., Wichita, KS, pg. 365
Eck, Robert L., Exec. V.P.--Albert Kahn Associates, Inc., Detroit, MI, pg. 613
Edelman, Jules, Exec. V.P.--Greater New York Box Co., Clifton, NJ, pg. 483
Egan, Joseph, Exec. V.P.--Strouse Greenberg & Co., Inc., Philadelphia, PA, pg. 1054
Eger, Donald L., Jr., Exec. V. P.--Dektas & Eger, Inc., Cincinnati, OH, pg. 325
Eggleston, Thomas W., Exec. V.P. & Gen. Counsel--Amway Corporation, Ada, MI, pg. 70
Ehlke, David, Exec. V.P.--Praxis International Inc., Cambridge, MA, pg. 884
Ehrle, R.W., Exec. V.P.--The Principal Financial Group, Des Moines, IA, pg. 890
Eidel, Paula, Exec. V.P.--Tri-City Electrical Contractors Inc., Altamonte Springs, FL, pg. 1110

Ek, F. Donald, Exec. V.P.--Tenax Corporation, Danbury, CT, pg. 1086
Elkins, George, Exec. V.P.--General Aerospace Materials Corporation, Plainview, NY, pg. 448
Ellis, Edwin E., Exec. V.P.--Chicago West Pullman Transportation Corporation, Chicago, IL, pg. 246
Ellstrom, Olof W., Exec. V.P.--Dearborn Gage Company, Garden City, MI, pg. 322
Elstner, Judy, Exec. V.P.--J. Korber & Company, Albuquerque, NM, pg. 641
Elwer, Ronald R., Exec. V.P. & Sec.--The Commercial Bank, Delphos, OH, pg. 268
Emanuel, Herbert E., Exec. V.P. & Chief Admin. Officer--United Services Automobile Association (USAA), San Antonio, TX, pg. 1134
Emerson, Richard B., Exec. V.P., Gen. Mgr. & Div. Oper.--Arnold Fortuna Lawner & Cabot, Boston, MA, pg. 84
Ensign, M. Dale, Exec. V.P.--Little America Refining, Salt Lake City, UT, pg. 1008
Epstein, Kenneth R., Exec. V.P.-Stores--The Elder-Beerman Stores Corp., Dayton, OH, pg. 373
Erani, Albert, Exec. V.P. & Sec.--A & E Stores, Inc., Ridgefield, NJ, pg. 1
Erani, Dennis, Exec. V.P. & G.M.--A & E Stores, Inc., Ridgefield, NJ, pg. 1
Erickson, David B., Exec. V.P.--Erickson Oil Products, Inc., Hudson, WI, pg. 386
Erickson, Mel E., Jr., Exec. V.P. & Gen. Mgr.--Central Feed Mills, Inc., Snohomish, WA, pg. 232
Erickson, S.K., Exec. V.P. & Treas.--Ziegler Inc., Minneapolis, MN, pg. 1218
Erickson, W.E., Exec. V.P.--National Forge Company, Irvine, PA, pg. 788
Erickson, Walter W., Exec. V.P.--Carlson Marketing Group, Inc., Minneapolis, MN, pg. 221
Ernest, Hal, Exec. V.P.--Lavidge & Associates Inc., Knoxville, TN, pg. 661
Erwin, Larry E., Exec. V.P.--New England Newspaper Supply Company, Inc., Millbury, MA, pg. 800
Esposito, Joseph, Exec. V.P.--Four Seasons Solar Products Corp., Holbrook, NY, pg. 427
Essary, David K., Exec. V.P.--Jitney-Jungle Stores of America, Inc., Jackson, MS, pg. 594
Evans, Benjamin, Exec. V.P. & Creative Dir.--Wills and Evans, New York, NY, pg. 1193
Evans, Clarence, Chief Oper. Officer & Exec. V.P.-Personal Training & Devel.--The Mad Butcher, Inc., Pine Bluff, AR, pg. 699
Evans, Gary, Exec. V.P.--Farmland Industries, Inc., Kansas City, MO, pg. 402
Evans, Michael B., Exec. V.P. & Chief Admin. Officer--G. Heileman Brewing Co., Inc., La Crosse, WI, pg. 526
Evans, Richard G., Jr., Exec. V.P.--The Cincinnati Cordage & Paper Company, Cincinnati, OH, pg. 249
Facchini, Mario, Exec. V.P.--Dynamic Metal Products Company, Manchester, CT, pg. 356
Fadiga, Antonio, Gen. Mgr.--Young & Rubicam Brasil, Sao Paulo,, Brazil, pg. 1213
Faherty, Michael J., Exec. V.P.-Radio--Broadcast Division, Atlanta, GA, pg. 292
Fairbrother, Jim, Exec. V.P., Creative Dir.--Cox Advertising, New York, NY, pg. 292
Falciani, Robert A., Exec. V.P.--Keller & Gannon, San Francisco, CA, pg. 637
Fallat, Dale, Exec. V.P.-Govt. Affairs--The Andersons, Maumee, OH, pg. 73
Fallenstein, Albert, Exec. V.P.--Taylor Corporation, Mankato, MN, pg. 1081
Fancelli, Frank, Exec. V.P. & Chief Opers. Officer--Wasserstrom Company, Columbus, OH, pg. 1167
Fantozzi, Anthony, Exec. V.P.--William Morris Agency, Inc., Beverly Hills, CA, pg. 771
Farley, A. Palmer, Exec. V.P., Treas.--Barker Campbell & Farley, Virginia Beach, VA, pg. 120
Farmer, Richard, Exec. V.P. & Chief Fin. Officer--Garvin Fire Protection Systems, Orange, CA, pg. 444
Faulhaber, Alan M., Exec. V.P.--The F. D. Lawrence Electric Co., Cincinnati, OH, pg. 661
Fausel, Charles E., Exec. V.P.--Lester B. Knight & Associates, Inc., Chicago, IL, pg. 637
Fee, Kevin T., Exec. V.P.--Reliable Automatic Sprinkler Co., Inc., Mount Vernon, NY, pg. 924
Fee, Paul F., Exec. V.P.--Cotter & Company, Chicago, IL, pg. 288
Feigenbaum, Jacob I., Exec. V.P.--Apparel America, Inc., New Haven, CT, pg. 78
Feldman, Clark, Exec. V.P.--Vita Food Products, Inc., Chicago, IL, pg. 1153
Feldman, Joel D., Exec. V.P. & Chief Oper. Officer--Byer California, San Francisco, CA, pg. 197
Feldman, Robert C., Exec. V.P., Dir.--Ketchum Public Relations/New York, New York, NY, pg. 625
Feldman, Trudy, Exec. V.P.--Careers USA Inc., Philadelphia, PA, pg. 218
Fellowes, Peter, Exec. V.P. & Sec.--Fellowes Manufacturing Co., Itasca, IL, pg. 405
Fenton, Gordon, Exec. V.P., Intl. Creative Dir.--Backer Spielvogel Bates, Inc., New York, NY, pg. 108
Ferguson, Clint S., Exec. V.P.--Eastland National Bank, Eastland, TX, pg. 412
Ferguson, Dick, Exec. V.P.--Creative Marketing International Corp., West Chicago, IL, pg. 297
Ferguson, R.A., Exec. V.P.--Setco Sales Company, Cincinnati, OH, pg. 993
Fermon, Roger, Exec. V.P.--Continental Eagle Corporation, Prattville, AL, pg. 278
Fernandez, Manuel, Exec. V.P.--Berlitz International, Inc., Princeton, NJ, pg. 142
Fernstrom, H. Allen, Exec. V.P. & Chief Oper. Officer--Marine Construction & Design Co., Seattle, WA, pg. 707
Fernstrom, H. Allen, Exec. V.P. & Chief Oper. Officer--Marco Seattle, Inc., Seattle, WA, pg. 707
Feron, David S., Sr. V.P.--Ruhl Companies, Inc., Valhalla, NY, pg. 955
Ferreira, Richard S., Exec. V.P. & Chief Fin. Officer--Golf Hosts, Inc., Palm Harbor, FL, pg. 469
Fiddler, Robert, Exec. V.P.--Lanz, Inc., Culver City, CA, pg. 658
Field, David O., Exec. V.P.--Petty Company, Inc., Effingham, IL, pg. 866
Fimiano, Andrew, Exec. V.P.--Southland Industries, Long Beach, CA, pg. 1023
Finkelstein, David, Exec. V.P.--Century Business Credit Corporation, New York, NY, pg. 235
Finkelstein, Harvey, Exec. V.P.--S. Schaffer Grocery Corporation, New Rochelle, NY, pg. 974
Finkelstein, M.L., Exec. V.P.--Iceland Seafood Corporation, Camp Hill, PA, pg. 561
Finneran, Tom, Exec. V.P.-Fin. Services--Jordan, McGrath, Case & Taylor Inc., New York, NY, pg. 604
Finnigan, Joseph T., Exec. V.P.--Fleishman Hillard Inc., Saint Louis, MO, pg. 417
Fiorillo, Shirley, Exec. V.P.--Robert Solomon & Associates Adv. Inc., Bloomfield Hills, MI, pg. 1017
Fiqua, Jim, Exec. V.P.--Anderson, Rothstein & Fiqua, San Francisco, CA, pg. 73
Fishberg, Bruce, Exec. V.P.--Pincus Bros., Inc., Philadelphia, PA, pg. 870
Fisher, Andrew S., Exec. V.P.-Affiliates--Broadcast Division, Atlanta, GA, pg. 292
Fisher, Thomas J., Exec. V.P.--Fisher Skylights, Inc., West Nyack, NY, pg. 415
Fisk, Douglas R., Exec. V.P. & Chief Oper. Officer--Mustang Tractor & Equip. Co., Houston, TX, pg. 777
Fitzgerald, John, Exec. V.P.--J. Josephson, Inc., South Hackensack, NJ, pg. 607
Fitzgerald, John A., Exec. V.P.--C&A Wallcoverings, Cleveland, OH, pg. 262
Flaherty, Joseph V., Exec. V.P.--Central National-Gottesman Inc., Purchase, NY, pg. 233
Flanders, Dudley K., Pres. & Chief Exec. Officer--Flanders Industries, Inc., Fort Smith, AR, pg. 416
Fletcher, William C., Exec. V.P.--Independence Investment Associates, Inc., Boston, MA, pg. 596
Flint, Dennis F., Exec. V.P.--Georgetown Industries, Inc., Charlotte, NC, pg. 453
Florence, David, Exec. V.P., Dir.-European Oper.--Kobs & Draft Advertising, Inc., Chicago, IL, pg. 109
Flores, Pat, Exec. V.P. & Dir.-Mfg.--Macklanburg-Duncan Co., Oklahoma City, OK, pg. 697
Flounders, Burtis C., Exec. V.P., Mngmt. Supvr.--McCaffrey and McCall, New York, NY, pg. 726
Fogg, S.M., Exec. V.P.--Farm Stores, Inc., Miami, FL, pg. 401
Foley, Jim, Exec. V.P.--Dentsu, Young & Rubicam/Seoul, Seoul,, Korea, pg. 330
Fooks, V. Thomas, Exec. V.P.--RMS Techs, Inc., Marlton, NJ, pg. 907
Ford, Charles, Exec. V.P.--Kehne Electric Company, Inc., Saint Paul, MN, pg. 620
Fortinberry, Glen W., Chm. & Chief Exec. Officer--Ross Roy Group, Inc., Bloomfield Hills, MI, pg. 949
Fortuna, Michael B., Exec. V.P., Creative Dir.--Arnold Fortuna Lawner & Cabot, Boston, MA, pg. 84
Foust, Larry, Exec. V.P. & Gen. Mgr.-Consolidated Wholesale Lumber Co.--Calcasieu Lumber Company, Austin, TX, pg. 208
Fox, David, Exec. V.P.--Hamburger Hamlets Inc., Sherman Oaks, CA, pg. 1169
Frailey, Jerry, Exec. V.P.--Petty Company, Inc., Effingham, IL, pg. 866
Frakes, Jack, Exec. V.P., Exec. Creative Dir.--Ross Roy Inc., Bloomfield Hills, MI, pg. 950
Frank, Stanley D., Exec. V.P. & Pres.-Compton's Multimedia Publ. Grp.--Encyclopaedia Britannica, Inc., Chicago, IL, pg. 381
Franklin, E. Thomas, Jr., Exec. V.P.--Franklin Baking Co., Inc., Goldsboro, NC, pg. 429
Franklin, William P., Exec. V.P.-Bldg. Div.--T. A. Loving Company, Goldsboro, NC, pg. 685
Franks, Richard M., Exec. V.P. & Gen. Mgr.--The Dispatch Printing Company, Columbus, OH, pg. 339
Franks, Richard M., Exec. V.P. & Gen. Mgr.--The Dispatch Printing Company, Columbus, OH, pg. 339
Fraoli, John, Exec. V.P.--Earle Palmer Brown/New York, New York, NY, pg. 182
Frascione, G., Sr. V.P., Acct. Dir.--Leo Burnett Company Ltd., Toronto,, Canada, pg. 192
Fraser, Steven, Exec. V.P.-Housewares--Regal Ware, Inc., Kewaskum, WI, pg. 921
Frazier, Ben, Exec. V.P.--Klaussner Corporation, Asheboro, NC, pg. 634
Frazier, Ben, Exec. V.P.--Klaussner Furniture Industry, Asheboro, NC, pg. 634
Frederick, Glen, Exec. V.P.--Harvey Industries, Inc., Waltham, MA, pg. 515
Frederick, Hank, Exec. V.P.--Zacky Farms, Inc., South El Monte, CA, pg. 1215
Freitag, Harry, Exec. V.P.--Heller Bros. Packing Corp., Winter Garden, FL, pg. 526
Frelich, Bennett E., Exec. V.P.--Tober Industries, Inc., Saint Louis, MO, pg. 1099
Fribourg, Paul J., Exec. V.P. & Grp. Pres.-World Grain & Oilseeds--Continental Grain Company, New York, NY, pg. 279
Friday, Timothy J., Exec. V.P., Gen. Mgr.--TTA/Newport, Inc., Newport Beach, CA, pg. 1092
Friedman, Irwin, Exec. V.P.--International Components Corporation, Melville, NY, pg. 576
Friedman, Jane Becker, Exec. V.P.--Alfred A. Knopf, Inc., New York, NY, pg. 20
Friedson, Barbara, Exec. V.P.--Freeson Advertising Agency, Miami Lakes, FL, pg. 431
Friehe, Bob, Exec. V.P.--Reinke Manufacturing Co., Inc., Deshler, NE, pg. 924
Frisch, Hans, Exec. V.P.--Beaver Street Fisheries, Inc., Jacksonville, FL, pg. 130
Froelich, Robert L., Exec. V.P., Grp. Creative Dir.--Backer Spielvogel Bates, Inc., New York, NY, pg. 108
Fromm, Claude, Exec. V.P., Media Dir.--TBWA Advertising, Inc., New York, NY, pg. 1071
Frons, Brian, Exec. V.P.-New World Televison--New World Entertainment, Inc., Los Angeles, CA, pg. 74
Fuchs, Joseph L., Exec. V.P.--The Conde Nast Publications Inc., New York, NY, pg. 19
Fueger, Frank, Vice Chm. & Exec. V.P.--Stephan & Brady, Incorporated, Madison, WI, pg. 1046
Fuhrer, Mark, Exec. V.P.-Admin.--Premier Mill Corp., New York, NY, pg. 887
Fujita, Koji, Exec. V.P.--Dentsu Wunderman Direct Inc., Tokyo,, Japan, pg. 1213
Fulmer, Gary C., Exec. V.P.--Crane Plastics Company, Columbus, OH, pg. 296
Fulton, Robert R., Exec. V.P. & Chief Oper. Officer--Doehler-Jarvis, Toledo, OH, pg. 559
Furlong, Daniel R., Exec. V.P., Treas.--Paradigm Communications, Tampa, FL, pg. 847
Furlong, Jerry E., Exec. V.P. & Asst. to Chm.--Mutual of Omaha Insurance Company, Omaha, NE, pg. 779
Furlong, Jerry E., Exec. V.P. & Asst. to Chm.--Mutual of Omaha, Omaha, NE, pg. 779
Furth, Yvonne, Exec. V.P., Gen. Mgr.--Kobs & Draft Advertising, Inc., Chicago, IL, pg. 109
Gagan, Dick, Exec. V.P.--Amity Leather Products Company, West Bend, WI, pg. 67
Gaidano, D.J., Chief Fin. Officer & Exec. V.P.--Bromar Inc., Newport Beach, CA, pg. 179
Gaines, Weaver H., Jr., Exec. V.P. & Gen. Counsel--The Mutual Life Insurance Company of New York (MONY), New York, NY, pg. 778
Gaines, William R., Jr., Exec. V.P.--Fred Weber Inc., Maryland Heights, MO, pg. 1171
Gaither, William H., Exec. V.P. & Chief Oper. Officer--J. H. Heafner Co. Inc., Lincolnton, NC, pg. 520
Galanos, Nicholas, Exec. V.P.-Opers.--TGI Friday's, Inc., Addison, TX, pg. 221
Galante, Nicholas T., III, Exec. V.P.--Tagsons Papers, Inc., Albany, NY, pg. 1076
Galante, Thomas A., II, Exec. V.P.--Tagsons Papers, Inc., Albany, NY, pg. 1076
Gallian, Robert, Exec. V.P.--Pet Life Foods, Inc., Willowbrook, IL, pg. 863
Gallivan, Michael D., Exec. V.P.--Harris and Love, Inc., Salt Lake City, UT, pg. 512
Galuten, Keith, Exec. V.P.--SGD International Corp., New York, NY, pg. 962
Galvin, Frank J., Exec. V.P.--U.S. Can Company, Oak Brook, IL, pg. 1134
Galvin, T.K., Jr., Exec. V.P.--Ellicott Machine Corp., Baltimore, MD, pg. 378
Gambill, Thomas K., Exec. V.P.--Braid Electric Company, Nashville, TN, pg. 171
Gammill, Lee M., Jr., Exec. V.P.-Individual Opers.--New York Life Insurance Company, New York, NY, pg. 802
Gann, L. Keith, Exec. V.P. & Gen. Mgr.--SOR Inc., Lenexa, KS, pg. 963
Gantman, David, Exec. V.P., Dir.--N W Ayer Incorporated, New York, NY, pg. 103
Gardner, Edward F., Exec. V.P.--SSD&W Integrated Marketing Communications, Montville, NJ, pg. 964
Gardner, Philip J., Exec. V.P.--Findlay Industries, Inc., Findlay, OH, pg. 410
Gardner, Stephen, Exec. V.P.--Ammirati & Puris Inc., New York, NY, pg. 67
Garoutte, Bill, Exec. V.P., Gen. Mgr.--Earle Palmer Brown/Atlanta, Atlanta, GA, pg. 182
Garratt, Graham, Exec. V.P. & Publr.--Marcel Dekker, Inc., New York, NY, pg. 325
Gartlan, Ronald B., Exec. V.P. & Chief Oper. Officer--Godfather's Pizza, Inc., Omaha, NE, pg. 464
Gartner, Elliott M., Exec. V.P.--New England Investment Marketing, Inc., Boston, MA, pg. 799
Gaspar, Alfred, Exec. V.P.-Mktg.--McKay Chemical Co., Los Angeles, CA, pg. 159
Gastman, Rhonda, Exec. V.P., Media--J. Richard Smith, Ltd., Melville, NY, pg. 1013
Gattas, James Wood, Exec. V.P.--Fred P. Gattas Company, Inc., Memphis, TN, pg. 446
Gatto, Dominick J., Exec. V.P.--Knight Architects Engineers Planners, Inc., Chicago, IL, pg. 637
Gaynor, Joseph P., Exec. V.P.--Chicago Sun Times, Chicago, IL, pg. 18
Gebhard, Mark S., Exec. V.P.-Chief Opers. Officer, Technology & Systems--ASC Incorporated, Southgate, MI, pg. 7
Gecowets, Jerry, Exec. V.P.--Gosiger Inc., Dayton, OH, pg. 472
Geething, Rick C., Exec. V.P.--The National Latex Products Co., Ashland, OH, pg. 791
Geller, Jeffrey, Exec. V.P.--Idle Wild Foods, Worcester, MA, pg. 1128
Genschaw, David A., Exec. V.P., Chief Fin. Officer--Waldbillig & Besteman, Inc., Madison, WI, pg. 1159
George, William D., Jr., Exec. V.P. & Chief Oper. Officer-Worldwide Consumer Prods.--S. C. Johnson & Son, Inc., Racine, WI, pg. 599
Gerhardstein, E. Michael, Exec. V.P.--Gerrard and Company, Des Plaines, IL, pg. 454
Germano, Julius, Exec. V.P.--Anderson Advertising, Inc., San Antonio, TX, pg. 72
Gerson, David, Exec. V.P.--American Enterprise Institute for Public Policy Research, Washington, DC, pg. 51
Getzoff, Mel H., Exec. V.P., Mngmt. Supvr.--SJ Weinstein Associates Inc., New York, NY, pg. 1173
Ghazey, Ken, Exec. V.P. & Chief Fin. Officer--Darling-Delaware Co., Inc., Irving, TX, pg. 315
Giangreco, Richard, Exec. V.P., Controller--C.F. Thompson Group, Inc., Windsor, CT, pg. 1094
Gilbane, Thomas F., Jr., Exec. V.P.--Gilbane Building Company, Providence, RI, pg. 457

Gillette, Vance, Exec. V.P.--Jandy Industries, Novato, CA, pg. 589
Gilsdorf, Russell, Exec. V.P., Creative Dir. & Media Dir.--Tarlow Advertising, New York, NY, pg. 1079
Ginn, David R., Exec. V.P.--Thiele Kaolin Co., Sandersville, GA, pg. 1092
Gladstone, Christopher, Exec. V.P.--Quadrangle Development Corporation, Washington, DC, pg. 902
Glasnapp, J., Exec. V.P.--Kragie/Newell, Des Moines, IA, pg. 643
Glazov, Burton E., Exec. V.P.--JMB Realty Corporation, Chicago, IL, pg. 584
Glover, John, Exec. V.P.--Lester Coggins Trucking, Okahumpka, FL, pg. 259
Gluth, R.C., Exec. V.P.--Marmon Corporation, Chicago, IL, pg. 711
Gluth, Robert, Exec. V.P.--The Marmon Group, Inc., Chicago, IL, pg. 711
Gnesda, Thomas A., Exec. V.P.--American Machinery Corp., Orlando, FL, pg. 22
Goff, Robert E., Exec. V.P.--Coleman & Christison, Inc., Saint Paul, MN, pg. 261
Goins, Charlynn, Exec. V.P.--Integrated Resources International, Ltd., New York, NY, pg. 573
Goldberd, Richard, Exec. V.P.--Coast Manufacturing Company, Yonkers, NY, pg. 257
Goldberg, Gary I., Exec. V.P.--Jack Gray Transport, Inc., Gary, IN, pg. 479
Golden, Annette, Exec. V.P.--Revlon Group Inc., New York, NY, pg. 695
Golden, Dale, Exec. V.P.--Stephen Gould Paper Co., Inc., Whippany, NJ, pg. 473
Golden, John, Exec. V.P.--Stephen Gould Paper Co., Inc., Whippany, NJ, pg. 473
Goldstein, Randall M., Exec. V.P.--Cumberland-Swan, Inc., Smyrna, TN, pg. 304
Golnick, Marshall, Exec. V.P.--Leon Shaffer Golnick Advertising, Inc., Fort Lauderdale, FL, pg. 469
Goodall, Douglas K., Exec. V.P.--Dixon Valve & Coupling Company, Chestertown, MD, pg. 341
Goodall, G. Brian, Exec. V.P. & Mng. Dir.--Bayer Bess Vanderwarker Inc., Chicago, IL, pg. 128
Goodby, Donald R., Exec. V.P.--Amica Mutual Insurance Co., Providence, RI, pg. 66
Gooding, Richard, Exec. V.P.--Commercial Printers Of Connecticut, Norwich, CT, pg. 268
Gorton, Roy, Exec. V.P.--Mannington Ceramic Tile, Lexington, NC, pg. 704
Gottlieb, Jerry, Exec. V.P., Acct. Mngmt.--Backer Spielvogel Bates, Inc., New York, NY, pg. 108
Gottlieb, Lawrence, Exec. V.P.-Fin.--Worldvision Enterprises, New York, NY, pg. 54
Gould, Keith B., Exec. V.P., Dir. Creative Services-NY--N W Ayer Incorporated, New York, NY, pg. 103
Graber, Jon P., Exec. V.P.--Kindel Furniture Company, Grand Rapids, MI, pg. 630
Graf, Robert, Exec. V.P.--Pacific Coast Producers, Lodi, CA, pg. 839
Grall, W.R., Exec. V.P.--Serigraph, Inc., West Bend, WI, pg. 991
Gramer, Arthur, Exec. V.P., Dir. Acct. Services--TBWA Kerlick Switzer, Saint Louis, MO, pg. 1071
Grary, William C., Exec. V.P.--Atlantic Plumbing Supply Company, Washington, DC, pg. 95
Graves, B.J., Exec. V.P.--Jackson Paper Company, Jackson, MS, pg. 587
Gray, Dave, Exec. V.P.--Lyke Corporation, Ripon, WI, pg. 688
Gray, Elizabeth, Exec. V.P., Dir. Client Services, New Bus. Contact--Farago Advertising, New York, NY, pg. 399
Gray, Franklin N., Exec. V.P.--James N. Gray Construction Co., Inc., Lexington, KY, pg. 479
Gray, Jack, Exec. V.P.--WBH Industries, Inc., Arlington, TX, pg. 1155
Gray, John H., Exec. V.P. & Chief Admin. Officer--Club Corporation International, Dallas, TX, pg. 256
Grebler, M.J., Exec. V.P.--Tony Lambert Company, New York, NY, pg. 652
Green, Benjamin L., Exec. V.P.--B. Green & Co., Baltimore, MD, pg. 484
Green, Robert D., Pres. & Chief Exec. Officer--Green Construction of Indiana, Inc., Oaktown, IN, pg. 484
Green, William, Exec. V.P., Grp. Dir.--Young & Rubicam New York, New York, NY, pg. 1211
Greene, David, Exec. V.P., Chief Fin. Officer--Young & Rubicam Inc., New York, NY, pg. 1210
Greene, Judye, Exec. V.P., Mktg. Dir.--Adair Greene Advertising, Atlanta, GA, pg. 16
Greenhalgh, Thomas J., Exec. V.P.-Admin.--Auto Glass Specialists, Madison, WI, pg. 100
Greenland, Drew, Exec. V.P.--Smith/Greenland, Incorporated, New York, NY, pg. 1012
Greenstein, Stanley, Exec. V.P.--Gitano Group Inc., New York, NY, pg. 460
Greenwald, William, Exec. V.P.--Marcus Advertising, Inc., Cleveland, OH, pg. 706
Griffin, John M., Exec. V.P.--Griffin Industries, Inc., Cold Spring, KY, pg. 487
Griffin, Patrick W., Exec. V.P.--O'Neil Griffin & Associates, Inc., Manchester, NH, pg. 827
Griffith, Gerald P., Exec. V.P.--The Alpha Corporation Of Tennessee, Collierville, TN, pg. 43
Grimes, Jim, Exec. V.P.--Golden Eagle Distributors, Inc., Tucson, AZ, pg. 466
Grismer, George, Chief Fin. Officer & Exec. V.P.--Winston Tire Company, Burbank, CA, pg. 1197
Gross, Jesse, Exec. V.P.--Harold Leonard & Company, Inc., Union, NJ, pg. 667
Gross, Lewis, Exec. V.P.--Pioneer Paper Corporation, Carlstadt, NJ, pg. 872
Grossman, Robert, Exec. V.P.--The Patrician Group, New York, NY, pg. 851
Grote, Roger, Exec. V.P.--Kragie/Newell, Des Moines, IA, pg. 643
Gruenberg, Craig L., Exec. V.P., Chief Oper. Officer--William Eisner & Associates Inc., Milwaukee, WI, pg. 372
Gruenhut, E., Exec. V.P.--Zim-American Israeli Shipping Co., New York, NY, pg. 1219
Grypp, Lawrence L., Exec. V.P.--Massachusetts Mutual Life Insurance Co., Springfield, MA, pg. 718
Guidotti, Bruce, Exec. V.P.-Acct. Services--Jordan, McGrath, Case & Taylor Inc., New York, NY, pg. 604
Guimond, Clarence, Exec. V.P.-Internal Affairs--Brown & Haley, Tacoma, WA, pg. 182
Gunn, Richard W., Exec. V.P.--Ira Thomas Associates, Inc., Youngstown, OH, pg. 1092
Gustafson, F. Edward, Exec. V.P. & Chief Oper. Officer--Envirodyne Industries, Inc., Oak Brook, IL, pg. 383
Gustafson, Gary, Exec. V.P.--Pepper West, Inc., Irvine, CA, pg. 860
Gutmann, Jay D., Exec. V.P.--Bee-Gee Shoe Div., Dayton, OH, pg. 373
Gutterman, Steven, Exec. V.P.--Jelmar Company, Lincolnwood, IL, pg. 592
Guttman, Maury S., Exec. V.P.--The Guttman Group, Belle Vernon, PA, pg. 495
Haag, Ron, Jr., Exec. V.P.--B.C. Cook & Sons Enterprises, Inc., Haines City, FL, pg. 282
Hackett, Randall W., Exec. V.P., Acct. Mngmt.--Backer Spielvogel Bates, Inc., New York, NY, pg. 108
Hackett, William F., Exec. V.P.--Barton Brands, Ltd., Chicago, IL, pg. 123
Hafer, Henry M., Exec. V.P.--Faber, Coe & Gregg, Inc., Secaucus, NJ, pg. 395
Hagadorn, Robert E., Exec. V.P., Treas. & Sec.--Hazen & Sawyer, New York, NY, pg. 520
Hager, Hampton C., Exec. V.P.--Colonial Petroleum Co., Cliffside, NC, pg. 264
Haggar, Thomas, Exec. V.P.--Premarc Corporation, Durand, MI, pg. 886
Hahn, H.P., Exec. V.P.--Thrall Car Mfg. Co., Chicago Heights, IL, pg. 350
Hale, Judson D., Sr., Sr. V.P.--Yankee Publishing Incorporated, Dublin, NH, pg. 1207
Haley, Robert A., Jr., Exec. V.P.--Finnaren & Haley, Inc., Conshohocken, PA, pg. 411
Hall, Alfred J., Exec. V.P.--Mills Hall Walborn & Associates, Mayfield Heights, OH, pg. 756
Hall, Derek, Exec. V.P.--Dentsu, Young & Rubicam/Tokyo, Tokyo, Japan, pg. 330
Hall, R.J., Exec. V.P.--The Coon-De Visser Co., Royal Oak, MI, pg. 282
Hamacher, Samuel, Exec. V.P.--Harbour Group Ltd., Clayton, MO, pg. 506
Hamilton, Al, Chief Oper. Officer & Exec. V.P.--Southern Belle Dairy Company, Inc., Somerset, KY, pg. 1020
Hamlin, Robert C., Exec. V.P.--The In-House Agency, Weehawken, NJ, pg. 564
Hancock, Michael, Exec. V.P.-Restaurant Devel.--Boddie-Noell Enterprises Inc., Rocky Mount, NC, pg. 161
Handel, George, Exec. V.P.--Handel & Company, Inc., Pennsauken, NJ, pg. 504
Hanks, W. David, Exec. V.P. & Asst. Sec.--Riviana Foods Inc., Houston, TX, pg. 937
Hannay, Robert D., Exec. V.P. & Chief Oper. Officer--Clifford B. Hannay & Son Inc., Westerlo, NY, pg. 505
Happel, Charles, Exec. V.P.--WBH Industries, Inc., Arlington, TX, pg. 1155
Hardy, Charles, Exec. V.P.--Atlanta Beverage Co., Atlanta, GA, pg. 94
Hargrove, G. Thomas, Exec. V.P.--Cullman Ventures, Inc., New York, NY, pg. 304
Harker, Gary, Exec. V.P.-Sls.--California Panel & Veneer Company, Cerritos, CA, pg. 210
Harker, John H., Exec. V.P.--Eastern Fine Paper, Incorporated, Brewer, ME, pg. 363
Harney, Larry, Exec. V.P.--Dormeyer Industries, Chicago, IL, pg. 346
Harp, Sidney, II, Exec. V.P. & Agency Dir.--Security Industrial Insurance Co., Inc., Donaldsonville, LA, pg. 832
Harralson, James W., Exec. V.P. & Chief Oper. Officer--Chesapeake Financial Corp., Miami Beach, FL, pg. 243
Harril, Don W., Exec. V.P.--Teachers Insurance and Annuity Association-College Retirement Equities Fund, New York, NY, pg. 1082
Harrington, W.J., Exec. V.P.--Zack Company, Chicago, IL, pg. 1215
Harris, Geoffrey, Exec. V.P.--Silvestri Corp., Chicago, IL, pg. 1005
Harris, John C., Exec. V.P.--Chicago Corp., Chicago, IL, pg. 247
Harris, Joseph M., Exec. V.P.--Heery International, Inc., Atlanta, GA, pg. 525
Harrison, R.W., Exec. V.P.--Kwik-Kopy Corp., Cypress, TX, pg. 647
Hart, Norman, Exec. V.P.--Idahoan Foods, Lewisville, ID, pg. 561
Hart, Tim, Exec. V.P., Chief Oper. Officer--Ketchum Advertising/Los Angeles, Los Angeles, CA, pg. 625
Hartman, Chris, Exec. V.P., Gen. Mgr.-RMD Pub. Affairs--Richardson, Myers & Donofrio, Inc., Baltimore, MD, pg. 933
Hartman, Lawrence M., Chief Fin. Officer & Exec. V.P.--Velsicol Chemical Corporation, Rosemont, IL, pg. 1147
Hartoch, R., Exec. V.P.--J. Gerber & Co. Inc., New York, NY, pg. 453
Harwood, Brian, Exec. V.P. & Sec.--Hayes/Harwood, Stowe, VT, pg. 519
Harwood, Herbert A., Exec. V.P.--Detecto Scale Company, Webb City, MO, pg. 332
Hasson, Raymond I., Exec. V.P.--Alba Forwarding Co., Inc., Jersey City, NJ, pg. 30
Hasten, Michael A., Exec. V.P.--Downey Designs International, Inc., Indianapolis, IN, pg. 348
Havener, Marlin R., Exec. V.P.-Hotel Div.--Crown American Corporation, Johnstown, PA, pg. 301
Haviland, Michael JD, Exec V.P.--RMI Marketing & Advertising, Emerson, NJ, pg. 907
Hayes, Geoff, Exec. V.P., Exec. Art Dir.--TBWA Advertising, Inc., New York, NY, pg. 1071
Heaslip, John G., Exec. V.P.--Harbour Industries, Inc., Shelburne, VT, pg. 507
Heathcott, Gary, Exec. V.P.--Combs & Heathcott, Little Rock, AR, pg. 267
Heatwole, Milton W., Exec. V.P.--Shenandoah Mfg. Co. Inc., Harrisonburg, VA, pg. 997
Hedemark, N.C., Exec. V.P.--Intermountain Gas Co., Boise, ID, pg. 575
Heide, Robert, Exec. V.P.--Vitt Media Direct, New York, NY, pg. 1154
Heide, Robert., Exec. V.P.--Vitt Media International, Inc., New York, NY, pg. 1153
Heim, Greg, Exec. V.P. & Chief Exec. Officer--Modern Drop Forge Co., Blue Island, IL, pg. 762
Heim, Richard, Exec. V.P.--Modern Drop Forge Co., Blue Island, IL, pg. 762
Heiman, Mark, Exec. V.P.--Standard Textile Co., Inc., Cincinnati, OH, pg. 1037
Heinrich, H.E., Exec. V.P.--Apex Broach & Machine Co., Detroit, MI, pg. 77
Heiser, John E., Exec. V.P.--CUMIS Insurance Society, Inc., Madison, WI, pg. 205
Heller, Andrew T., Exec. V.P.--Marquette Coppersmithing Co., Inc., Philadelphia, PA, pg. 713
Heller, Art, Exec. V.P., Dir. Media Services--Griffin Bacal Inc., New York, NY, pg. 486
Hempel, Kathleen J., Sr. Exec. V.P. & Chief Fin. Officer--Fort Howard Corporation, Green Bay, WI, pg. 425
Hemrich, Kurt J., Exec V.P.-Opers. & Admin.--Fender Musical Instruments, Scottsdale, AZ, pg. 406
Henderson, Don, Exec. V.P. & Chief Exec. Officer--United Farm Bureau Family Life Insurance Co., Indianapolis, IN, pg. 1131
Hendrix, John A., Exec. V.P. & Gen. Mgr.--Carolina Tractor & Equipment Co., Charlotte, NC, pg. 223
Henry, J.C., II, Exec. V.P.--E.P. Henry Corporation, Woodbury, NJ, pg. 530
Henry, J.C., III, Exec. V.P.-Sls. & Mktg.--E.P. Henry Corporation, Woodbury, NJ, pg. 530
Henson, Byron K., Exec. V.P.--Excel Industries, Inc., Hesston, KS, pg. 392
Herbst, James, Exec. V.P.--Kendale Industries, Inc., Valley View, OH, pg. 622
Herbst, Thomas A., Exec. V.P.--Bank Shares, Inc., Minneapolis, MN, pg. 117
Herbst, Thomas A., Exec. V.P.--Marquette Bank Minneapolis, National Association, Minneapolis, MN, pg. 117
Herchede, Bill, Exec. V.P.--R.L. Ziegler Co. Inc., Tuscaloosa, AL, pg. 1218
Herrmann, Mary, Exec. V.P.--Ammirati & Puris Inc., New York, NY, pg. 67
Hertog, Roger, Exec. V.P.--Sanford C. Bernstein & Co., Inc., New York, NY, pg. 144
Herz, Larry, Exec. V.P.--I. Appel Corporation, New York, NY, pg. 78
Herzog, Alan C., Exec. V.P., Assoc. Creative Dir.--McCaffrey and McCall, New York, NY, pg. 726
Hessan, Diane, Exec. V.P.-Corp.--The Forum Corporation, Boston, MA, pg. 425
Hetrick, C.N., Exec. V.P.--Maxon Corporation, Muncie, IN, pg. 723
Heyer, Steve, Exec. V.P.--Young & Rubicam Inc., New York, NY, pg. 1210
Heyer, Steven, Exec. V.P.--Young & Rubicam Inc., New York, NY, pg. 1210
Hicks, Art, Exec. V.P.--Northern Automotive Corporation, Phoenix, AZ, pg. 1118
Hill, Richard H., Exec. V.P.--Alexander Marketing Services, Inc., Grand Rapids, MI, pg. 33
Hill, Robert P., Exec. V.P.-Individual Insurance--The Prudential Insurance Company of America, Newark, NJ, pg. 896
Hill, Robert R., Exec. V.P.--Jacmar Companies, Inc., Alhambra, CA, pg. 587
Hill, Thomas A., Exec. V.P.--Kimray, Inc., Oklahoma City, OK, pg. 629
Hill, William, Exec. V.P.--Bubble-Up, Chicago, IL, pg. 765
Hillman, Douglas C., Exec. V.P.--Londontown Holdings Corporation, Eldersburg, MD, pg. 681
Hillman, Sandra S., Exec. V.P., Pub. Rels. Dir.--Trahan, Burden & Charles, Inc., Baltimore, MD, pg. 1105
Hinshaw, Morris E., Exec. V.P.--First National Bank of Sweetwater, Sweetwater, TX, pg. 412
Hirsch, David J., Exec. V.P.--Charles Leonard, Inc., Glendale, NY, pg. 668
Hirsch, Donald S., V.P.--Barton Beers, Ltd., Chicago, IL, pg. 123
Hirschman, Ray, Exec. V.P., Exec. Creative Dir.--Gillespie Advertising, Inc., Princeton, NJ, pg. 458
Hirshan, Leonard, Exec. V.P.--William Morris Agency, Inc., Beverly Hills, CA, pg. 771
Hitchcock, Donald S., Exec. V.P.--Lester B. Knight & Associates, Inc., Chicago, IL, pg. 637
Hlavacek, James H., Exec. V.P.--Amtran, Inc., Indianapolis, IN, pg. 69
Hoar, J. William, Exec. V.P.--Trans World Airlines, Inc., Mount Kisco, NY, pg. 561
Hoard, Ralph G., Exec. V.P.--Icicle Seafoods, Inc., Seattle, WA, pg. 561
Hodnik, David F., Exec. V.P.--Ace Hardware Corporation, Oak Brook, IL, pg. 12
Hoffine, Bruce, Exec. V.P.--The Zippertubing Co., Los Angeles, CA, pg. 1220
Hofnagel, Fred, Exec. V.P.--Billcom Exposition & Conference, Washington, DC, pg. 150
Hogan, Michael, Exec. Grp. V.P.-Life & Health--General American Life Insurance Co., St. Louis, MO, pg. 448
Hogebol, Jan, Exec. V.P.--BSB Bates-Gruppen A/S, Oslo,, Norway, pg. 109

Hogentogler, Don, Exec. V.P./Chief Exec. Officer--Gunnebo Fastening Corp., York, PA, pg. 494
Holdeman, R. Steven, Exec. V.P.--Anderson Industries Inc., Rockford, IL, pg. 73
Holland, Darrell M., Exec. V.P.--Pepsi-Cola Bottling Company of Charlotte Inc., Charlotte, NC, pg. 860
Holleman, Matthew L., Exec. V.P & Treas.--Mississippi Valley Gas Co., Jackson, MS, pg. 1208
Holmes, Frank E., Exec. V.P. & Reg. Mgr.--EB (NA), Chicago, IL, pg. 381
Holmes, John, Exec. V.P., Mktg. Dir. & Sec.--Paradigm Communications, Tampa, FL, pg. 847
Holmes, Lucinda, Exec. V.P., Gen. Mgr.--The Lowe Group, New York, NY, pg. 685
Holoubek, Terri, Exec. V.P.--Holoubek Inc., Waukesha, WI, pg. 540
Holster, Robert M., Exec. V.P.--Health Management Systems, Inc., New York, NY, pg. 521
Holston, Charles, Exec. V.P.--Charles Holston, Inc., Jennings, LA, pg. 541
Holter, Gary, Chief Oper. Officer & Exec. V.P.--Knapp Shoes Inc., Brockton, MA, pg. 636
Honkamp, Paul F., Exec. V.P.--Hydrite Chemical Company, Brookfield, WI, pg. 556
Hood, James, Exec. V.P., Dir. Bus. Devel.--Young & Rubicam New York, New York, NY, pg. 1211
Hooker, Robert, Exec. V.P.-Sls.--Purity, Inc., Miami, FL, pg. 901
Hopper, Carl, Exec. V.P.--Optiworld, Atlanta, GA, pg. 828
Hopper, Duane B., Exec. V.P.--Graphic Controls, Corp., Buffalo, NY, pg. 478
Hopper, Frank III, Exec. V.P.--Hopper Inc., Bakersfield, CA, pg. 543
Horn, Dwaine R., Exec. V.P.& Dir.-Grp. Pensions--Mutual of Omaha, Omaha, NE, pg. 779
Horner, Matina S., Exec. V.P.--Teachers Insurance and Annuity Association-College Retirement Equities Fund, New York, NY, pg. 1082
Hornsby, D. Wayne, Exec. V.P.--Jim Walter Homes, Inc., Tampa, FL, pg. 1162
Horowitz, Irving, Vice Chm., Exec. V.P.-Opers. & Engrng.--Amerbelle Corporation, Rockville, CT, pg. 47
Hoskins, Tom, Exec. V.P.--The Dunlap Companies, Fort Worth, TX, pg. 353
Howard, Bruce, Exec. V.P.--Flint Manufacturing Co., Burton, MI, pg. 419
Hoyle, Richard, Exec. V.P.--A.W. Chesterton Company, Stoneham, MA, pg. 244
Hoyt, R.L., Exec. V.P., Partner & Acct. Services--Howard, Merrell & Partners, Inc., Raleigh, NC, pg. 547
Huber, Richard C., Jr., Exec. V.P.--The Associated Group, Indianapolis, IN, pg. 90
Hubner, C.E., Jr., Exec. V.P.--Central/Shippee, Inc., Bloomingdale, NJ, pg. 234
Huey, Brenda, Exec. V.P., Chief Fin. Officer--Barry Huey, Bullock & Cook Advertising, Inc., Birmingham, AL, pg. 551
Hull, Cordell W., Exec. V.P. & Dir.--Bechtel Group, Inc., San Francisco, CA, pg. 130
Hunstad, Robert E., Exec. V.P.--The Minnesota Mutual Life Insurance Company, Saint Paul, MN, pg. 757
Hunt, Bruce, Exec. V.P.--Goodrum Leonard & Associates, Inc., Nashville, TN, pg. 471
Hunt, David A., Exec. V.P.--Biggs Gilmore Communications, Kalamazoo, MI, pg. 149
Hunt, Raymond, Exec. V.P.--Connecticut Spring & Stamping Corporation, Farmington, CT, pg. 275
Hunt, Robin R., Exec. V.P.--Allied Security, International, Spokane, WA, pg. 40
Hunter, George J., Exec. V.P.--Bonanza Bus Lines, Inc., Providence, RI, pg. 164
Hurd, James, Exec. V.P.--Lyman Lumber Company, Excelsior, MN, pg. 689
Huskey, James, Exec. V.P.-Fin.--National Group, Inc., Chattanooga, TN, pg. 789
Hussey, P.A., Exec. V.P.--Hussey Seating Company, North Berwick, ME, pg. 555
Hussey, Peter A., Exec. V.P.--Hussey Corporation, North Berwick, ME, pg. 555
Hussey, Robert J., Exec. V.P.--Dunavant Enterprises, Inc., Memphis, TN, pg. 352
Hutchinson, Robert, Exec. V.P.--Century 21 Real Estate Corp., Irvine, CA, pg. 744
Hutchison, T.M., Exec. V.P.--The Principal Financial Group, Des Moines, IA, pg. 890
Hyde, Kenneth R., Jr., Exec. V.P., Chief Opers. Officer & Treas.--Hackney Brothers, Inc., Wilson, NC, pg. 498
Hydorn, Vernon H., Exec. V.P.--Barber Dairies, Inc., Birmingham, AL, pg. 119
Iandoli, Michael, Exec. V.P.--Technical Aid Corporation, Newton Upper Falls, MA, pg. 1083
Ielmini, Angelo, Exec. V.P.--Patterson Frozen Foods, Inc., Patterson, CA, pg. 851
Inglett, Terris H., Exec. V.P.--C. Brewer & Company, Limited, Honolulu, HI, pg. 174
Ingram, John M., Exec. V.P.--Ingram Paper Company, City of Industry, CA, pg. 569
Ingram, Robert, Exec. V.P.--Corinthian Media, Inc., New York, NY, pg. 286
Inqui, Dennis, Exec. V.P.--Sasson Jeans for Men, New York, NY, pg. 972
Irish, Charles A., Exec. V.P.--Whiting-Turner Contracting Co., Baltimore, MD, pg. 1187
Irvine, Robert, Exec. V.P. & Mng. Dir.--Bayer Bess Vanderwarker Inc., Chicago, IL, pg. 128
Isaacs, Herb, Exec. V.P.--Kelly, Scott And Madison, Inc., Chicago, IL, pg. 621
Isham, Carolynn C., Exec. V.P.--Berenson, Isham & Partners, Inc., Boston, MA, pg. 141
Israel, Robert E., Exec. V.P.--Truck World Inc., Hubbard, OH, pg. 1117
Itkowitz, Mark, Exec. V.P. & Dir.-Creative--Jordan, McGrath, Case & Taylor Inc., New York, NY, pg. 604

Jackson, Robert, Exec. V.P.--Struthers-Dunn Inc., Pitman, NJ, pg. 693
Jackson, W.L., Exec. V.P.--Weil-McLain, Michigan City, IN, pg. 710
Jacobs, L. Lloyd, Exec. V.P.--McKinney & Silver, Raleigh, NC, pg. 730
Jacobs, Lambert, Exec. V.P.--Security Plastics, Inc., Miami Lakes, FL, pg. 987
Jacoby, J.E.M., Exec. V.P.--Stephens, Inc., Little Rock, AR, pg. 1046
Jacquinot, Bernard, Exec. V.P.-Field Oper.--J.E. Dunn Construction Co., Kansas City, MO, pg. 354
Jaffe, Marc, Exec. V.P. & Editor-In-Chief-Vallard--Random House, Inc., New York, NY, pg. 19
Jaffee, Steven B., Exec. V.P.--Acess Energy Corporation, Dublin, OH, pg. 12
Jagoda, Syd, Exec. V.P.--Don Jagoda Associates, Inc., Melville, NY, pg. 588
James, Bruce, Exec. V.P.--Foss Manufacturing Company Incorporated, Hampton, NH, pg. 426
James, Kenneth T., Exec. V.P.--Rauland-Borg Corporation, Skokie, IL, pg. 914
James, Kenneth T., Exec. V.P.--Rauland-Borg (Canada) Inc., Mississauga,, Canada, pg. 914
James, Tom, Sr. Exec. V.P., Dir. Client Services--Avrett, Free & Ginsberg, Inc., New York, NY, pg. 103
Janco, Gary, Exec. V.P.--C. C. Myers, Inc., Rancho Cordova, CA, pg. 780
Jardine, Larry L., Exec. V.P.--LeGrand Johnson Construction Co., Logan, UT, pg. 598
Jareske, Michael J., Exec. V.P. & Dir.-Grp. Fin. Reporting & Admin. Services--Mutual of Omaha Insurance Company, Omaha, NE, pg. 779
Jarowey, Peter M., Chief Exec. Officer--Raffi & Swanson, Inc., Wilmington, MA, pg. 909
Jeffe, Doug, Exec. V.P.--Braun/Ketchum Public Relations, Los Angeles, CA, pg. 625
Jefferson, Antwine, III, Exec. V.P.--New England Investment Marketing, Inc., Boston, MA, pg. 799
Jenkins, Richard P., Sr., Exec. V.P. & Pres.-Hardee's Opers. Grp.--Boddie-Noell Enterprises Inc., Rocky Mount, NC, pg. 161
Jennings, James B., Exec. V.P.--Hunt Oil Company, Dallas, TX, pg. 553
Jensen, Erik M., Exec. V.P.--Irving F. Jensen Co., Inc., Sioux City, IA, pg. 593
Jensen, Richard S., Exec. V.P., Chief Oper. Officer--Bader Rutter & Assoc., Inc., Brookfield, WI, pg. 113
Jentoft, Arthur P., Exec. V.P.--Wasco Products, Inc., Sanford, ME, pg. 1165
John, James W., Exec. V.P.--Mastercard International, Inc., New York, NY, pg. 720
Johns, R. Powell, Exec. V.P.--Arian, Lowe, Travis & Gusick, Inc., Chicago, IL, pg. 82
Johnson, Bill, Exec. V.P.--Farnam Companies, Inc., Phoenix, AZ, pg. 403
Johnson, Carl I., Jr., Exec. V.P.--Johnson Supply & Equipment Corp., Houston, TX, pg. 601
Johnson, James, Exec. V.P.--Calmark Hospitality Systems, San Diego, CA, pg. 211
Johnson, James P., Exec. V.P.--Sommer & Maca Industries, Inc., Chicago, IL, pg. 1017
Johnson, Jim, Exec. V.P.--Johnson Storage & Moving Company, Denver, CO, pg. 600
Johnson, Keith, Mgr.-Employee Benefits--Contran Corporation, Dallas, TX, pg. 281
Johnson, Mark, Exec. V.P.--Johnson Storage & Moving Company, Denver, CO, pg. 600
Johnson, William, Exec. V.P. & Chief Fin. Officer--Camping World Holdings, Inc., Bowling Green, KY, pg. 213
Jones, Alfred W., III, Exec. V.P.--Sea Island Company, Sea Island, GA, pg. 983
Jones, Barclay G., III, Exec. V.P. & Mng. Dir.--W. P. Carey & Co., Inc., New York, NY, pg. 218
Jones, Dick, Exec. V.P. & Design Dir.--Dorland Sweeney Jones, Philadelphia, PA, pg. 346
Jones, Edward C., Exec. V.P. & Chief Oper. Officer--Jones Dairy Farm, Fort Atkinson, WI, pg. 603
Jones, Steven M., Exec. V.P.--Dawn Food Products, Inc., Jackson, MI, pg. 319
Jones, Tom, Exec. V.P.--Nautilus, Independence, VA, pg. 796
Jones, Wiley, Exec. V.P.--Green Spot Packaging Inc., Claremont, CA, pg. 485
Jones, William F., Exec V.P.--Coppus Engineering Corp., Millbury, MA, pg. 285
Jorden, Edwin W., Exec. V.P.--Barclay White Incorporated, Berwyn, PA, pg. 119
Joseph, James R., Exec. V.P.--The Great Atlantic Companies, Hampton, VA, pg. 480
Joslyn, David E., Exec. V.P.--Air Gage Company, Livonia, MI, pg. 27
Juelich, Richard J., Exec. V.P. & Chief Oper. Officer--AmClyde Engineered Products, Inc., Saint Paul, MN, pg. 47
Justiss, Harry A., Exec. V.P.--Riverside Press, Inc., Dallas, TX, pg. 937
Kabins, Larry, Grp. Exec. V.P.--Birdsall Voss & Kloppenburg, Inc., Mequon, WI, pg. 152
Kadish, Gerald M., Exec. V.P.--The Helmsley Palace Hotel, New York, NY, pg. 527
Kaeser, Clifford R., Sr. Exec. V.P.--Delaware North Companies, Inc., Buffalo, NY, pg. 326
Kafka, Donald L., Exec. V.P.--Del American Properties, Inc., Maitland, FL, pg. 325
Kagan, Michael, Exec. V.P. & Chief Fin. Officer--Tropical Garment Manufacturing Company, Tampa, FL, pg. 1116
Kahn, Charles, Exec. V.P.--Things Remembered, Cleveland, OH, pg. 260
Kaisand, Duane E., Exec. V.P.--Webcraft Technologies, Inc., North Brunswick, NJ, pg. 1171
Kaiser, Juerger, Exec. V.P. & Chief Fin. Officer--Fru-Con Construction Corporation, Ballwin, MO, pg. 435

Kaitz, Richard A., Exec. V.P.--Palm Beach Beauty Products Co., Minneapolis, MN, pg. 843
Kalscheur, Denis, Exec. V.P.--Admarketing, Inc., Los Angeles, CA, pg. 18
Kalt, S. Richard, Exec. V.P.--CRN International, Inc., Hamden, CT, pg. 203
Kamen, Harry P., Sr. Exec. V.P.-Professional Service Opers.--Metropolitan Life Insurance Co., New York, NY, pg. 744
Kane, Kelly, Exec. V.P.--Gray & Kilgore, Inc., Troy, MI, pg. 950
Kaneft, Linda P., Exec. V.P.--Palmetto Wholesale Co., Inc., Columbia, SC, pg. 844
Kaplan, Barry, Exec. V.P.--Marvel Entertainment Group, New York, NY, pg. 695
Kaplan, Daniel I., Exec. V.P.-HERC--The Hertz Corporation, Park Ridge, NJ, pg. 849
Karam, Alan, Exec. V.P.--American Laundry Machinery Inc., Cincinnati, OH, pg. 57
Karler, Henry, Exec. V.P.--Karler Packing Company, Inc., Albuquerque, NM, pg. 617
Karmadi, Paul W., Exec. V.P., Dir. Opers. & Mktg. Services--Matari Advertising, Jakarta,, Indonesia, pg. 104
Karp, Jeff, Exec. V.P.--Power Contracting & Engineering Corp., Rolling Meadows, IL, pg. 883
Karpas, Alan, Exec. V.P.--Sharon-Jay Togs, Inc., New Bedford, MA, pg. 995
Karsch, Stephen E., Sr. Exec. V.P.--Sloans Supermarkets, Inc., New York, NY, pg. 1010
Karszes, Arthur J., Exec. V.P. & Pres.-Applied Physical Sciences Div.--Springborn Laboratories, Inc., Enfield, CT, pg. 1033
Kasch, James A., Exec. V.P.--M.W. Kasch Company, Mequon, WI, pg. 617
Kathol, Robert F., Exec. V.P. & Dir.-Investment Banking--Kirkpatrick Pettis, Omaha, NE, pg. 779
Katz, James E., Exec. V.P.--Katz, Inc., Honesdale, PA, pg. 618
Katz, Joel, Exec. V.P.--Windsor Publications, Inc., Chatsworth, CA, pg. 1196
Katz, Ronald A., Exec. V.P.--Encore Shoe Corporation, Rochester, NH, pg. 380
Katz, Stanley M., Exec. V.P.--Minuteman Press International, Farmingdale, NY, pg. 759
Kavanaugh, Lawrence R., Exec. V.P., Gen. Mgr.-Jayme Advertising--The Jayme Organization, Inc., Cleveland, OH, pg. 591
Kawashima, Yoshi, Exec. V.P.--BSB Japan Ltd., Tokyo, Japan, pg. 110
Kaylor, Barbara Brotman, Exec. V.P., Adv.--Image Dynamics, Incorporated, Baltimore, MD, pg. 563
Keane, Paul, Exec. V.P. & Gen. Mgr.--The Bates Mfg. Co., Hackettstown, NJ, pg. 125
Kearns, Robert F., Exec. V.P.--B. H. Aircraft Co., Inc., Farmingdale, NY, pg. 106
Keaton, William C., Jr., Exec. V.P.--H.H. Brown Shoe Company, Inc., Greenwich, CT, pg. 182
Keefus, Gary L., Exec. V.P.--Global Insurance Company, Houston, TX, pg. 662
Keegan, Terrence, Exec. V.P.--Baxter Advertising, Inc., Minneapolis, MN, pg. 127
Keller, James J., Chief Oper. Officer & Exec. V.P.--J. J. Keller & Associates, Inc., Neenah, WI, pg. 620
Kelly, Albert J., Exec. V.P.--Hyatt Hotels Corporation, Chicago, IL, pg. 495
Kelly, Mark J., Exec. V.P.--Adams Rite Manufacturing Co., City of Industry, CA, pg. 16
Kelsey, Richard W., Exec. V.P.--Tinsley Advertising, Miami, FL, pg. 1099
Kemp, Melvin T., Chief Exec. Officer--B & K Steel & Supply, Inc., Ogden, UT, pg. 105
Kenin, David, Exec. V.P.-Programming--USA Network, New York, NY, pg. 1124
Kennedy, Ian, Exec. V.P., Dir.-Pacific Rim Region--Kobs & Draft Advertising, Inc., Chicago, IL, pg. 109
Kennedy, John J. Jr., Exec. V.P., Chief Fin. Officer--Henderson Advertising, Inc., Greenville, SC, pg. 528
Kennedy, Neil, Exec. V.P.-BSB Europe--BSB Dorland Limited, London,, United Kingdom, pg. 109
Kennedy, Paul L., Exec. V.P.--Dominick & Dominick, Incorporated, New York, NY, pg. 343
Kennedy, Robert B., Exec. V.P.--YPMS/TMP Worldwide, Inc., Mequon, WI, pg. 1074
Kenyon, Robert, Exec. V.P.--Sleepeck Printing Company, Bellwood, IL, pg. 1010
Kerin, Joe, Exec. V.P.--Retail Ventures, Inc., Warrendale, PA, pg. 929
Kern, Frank, III, Exec. V.P.--Maxitrol Co., Southfield, MI, pg. 723
Kerr, Stephen R., Exec. V.P.--Holstein-Friesian Services, Inc., Brattleboro, VT, pg. 541
Kervick, Kevin M., Exec. V.P.--Kervick Enterprises, Inc., Worcester, MA, pg. 624
Keslo, Michael, Exec. V.P.-Opers.--Viacom Entertainment, New York, NY, pg. 785
Kesselhaut, Arthur M., Exec. V.P.-Individual Insurance--Pacific Mutual Life Insurance Company, Newport Beach, CA, pg. 841
Kessler, B.I., Exec. V.P. & Sec.--Formation, Inc., Moorestown, NJ, pg. 424
Ketterman, Alda, Exec. V.P.--York Barbell Co., Inc., York, PA, pg. 1208
Kettler, James M., Exec. V.P. & Gen. Mgr.--Kettler Brothers, Inc., Montgomery Village, MD, pg. 626
Kiddoo, Robert, Exec. V.P.--Kirk-Mayer, Inc., Los Angeles, CA, pg. 633
Kiefer, Charles, Exec. V.P., Chief Fin. Officer--Arnold Fortuna Lawner & Cabot, Boston, MA, pg. 84
Kienzle, Gary M., Exec. V.P. & Chief Fin. Officer--WW Engineering & Science Inc., Grand Rapids, MI, pg. 1058
Killeen, Laura Lee, Exec. V.P., Copy Dir.--Fitzgerald Advertising Inc., New Orleans, LA, pg. 416
Kimball, R. Jeffrey, Exec. V.P.--L. Robert Kimball & Associates, Ebensburg, PA, pg. 629

Kimmins, John, Exec. V.P.--Arthur Murray Intl., Inc., Coral Gables, FL, pg. 776
Kindseth, Gary A., Exec. V.P.--Faribault Foods Inc., Minneapolis, MN, pg. 399
King, Kenneth A., Exec. V.P.--Louisville Bedding Company, Louisville, KY, pg. 684
King, Lynne, Exec. V.P.--Stan Merritt Inc./Advertising, New York, NY, pg. 741
King, Stephen, Exec. V.P., Creative Services--Lewis & Gace, Inc., Fort Lee, NJ, pg. 673
King, William, Exec. V.P.--Sunbeam Outdoor Products Co., Neosho, MO, pg. 1059
Kircher, Robert R., Exec. V.P.--William J. Kircher & Associates, Washington, DC, pg. 633
Kirchhoff, William T., Exec. V.P.--Cleveland Brothers Equipment Co., Harrisburg, PA, pg. 255
Kirtley, Jeff, Exec. V.P.--Hickerson Phelps Kirtley & Associates, Kansas City, MO, pg. 532
Kistinger, Robert F., Exec. V.P.--Chiquita Brands, Inc., Cincinnati, OH, pg. 53
Kitch, Fred, Exec. V.P.--Keller Crescent Co., Evansville, IN, pg. 620
Kitei, Michael, Exec. V.P., Creative Dir.--Sive/Young & Rubicam, Cincinnati, OH, pg. 1211
Klein, E. Manny, Exec. V.P., Media Services Dir.--Trahan, Burden & Charles, Inc., Baltimore, MD, pg. 1105
Klein, Mathias A., III, Exec. V.P.--Klein Tools Inc., Skokie, IL, pg. 635
Klingman, Walter, Exec. V.P.--Alexandra De Markoff, Ltd., New York, NY, pg. 695
Kloppenburg, Jerry, Grp. Exec. V.P.--Birdsall Voss & Kloppenburg, Inc., Mequon, WI, pg. 152
Kluener, Kenneth, Exec. V.P.--Kluener Foods Co., Cincinnati, OH, pg. 636
Kluger, Lynne, Exec. V.P., Brdcst. Production--Avrett, Free & Ginsberg, Inc., New York, NY, pg. 103
Kluger, N., Exec. V.P.--Eagle Electric Mfg. Co., Inc., Long Island City, NY, pg. 362
Klumpp, Donald K., Exec. V.P.--Aldan Rubber Co., Philadelphia, PA, pg. 32
Knaisch, Michael C., Exec. V.P., Dir. Client Services--Earle Palmer Brown/Norfolk, Norfolk, VA, pg. 182
Knight, Michael, Exec. V.P. & Chief Oper. Officer--SBN Systems Inc.-Corporate, Mississauga,, Canada, pg. 960
Knispel, Barry, Exec. V.P.--Arrow Fastener Co., Inc., Saddle Brook, NJ, pg. 85
Knobloch, Peter, Exec. V.P.--R.J. Palmer, Inc., New York, NY, pg. 844
Knoth, Bill, Exec. V.P.--Leo Eisenberg & Co., Inc., Kansas City, MO, pg. 372
Knowldon, Maury, Exec. V.P.--National Bedding & Furniture Industries, Memphis, TN, pg. 786
Knox, Lawner L., Exec. V.P.--Knox Oil of Texas Inc., Dallas, TX, pg. 638
Knox, Robert, Exec. V.P.--Knox Oil of Texas Inc., Dallas, TX, pg. 638
Knutson, G.H., Exec. V.P., Partner & Creative Dir.--Howard, Merrell & Partners, Inc., Raleigh, NC, pg. 547
Koch, Craig R., Exec. V.P.--The Hertz Corporation, Park Ridge, NJ, pg. 849
Koch, Peter, Exec. V.P.--Plywood Plastics Inc., Buffalo, NY, pg. 878
Koehler, Charles F., Exec. V.P.-Opers.--Capital Bank, N.A., Washington, DC, pg. 214
Koelb, Clayton T., Sr. Exec. V.P.--Amica Mutual Insurance Co., Providence, RI, pg. 66
Koffman, Richard E., Vice Chm., Exec. V.P. & Sec.--Apparel America, Inc., New Haven, CT, pg. 78
Kohl, James F., Exec. V.P.--Furman Foods, Inc., Northumberland, PA, pg. 436
Kohlman, Kris, Exec. V.P.--Goldberg Marchesano Kohlman Inc., Washington, DC, pg. 465
Kole, Bernard, Exec. V.P.--Generation Metals Corp., Hauppauge, NY, pg. 451
Kopp, Stephanie J., Exec. V.P. & Sec.--Mutual of America, New York, NY, pg. 777
Korde, Satish, Exec. V.P., Dir., Consumer Res.-WW--Young & Rubicam Inc., New York, NY, pg. 1210
Korologos, Mike, Exec. V.P., Dir. Pub. Rels.--EvansGroup, Salt Lake City, UT, pg. 391
Kost, Joe, Exec. V.P.--Finger Furniture Company, Inc., Houston, TX, pg. 411
Kotar, Barry A., Sr. V.P.-Quality, Human Resources & Info. Services--Northwest Airlines, Inc., Saint Paul, MN, pg. 782
Kraft, Ken, Exec. V.P.--La Belle Industries, Inc., Oconomowoc, WI, pg. 648
Krant, Dick, Exec. V.P.--Safelite Autoglass, Wichita, KS, pg. 664
Kreiter, Abe E., Exec. V.P.--Castcraft Industries, Inc., Skokie, IL, pg. 228
Kremer, Murray, Exec. V.P.--Cipriani Kremer Design, Boston, MA, pg. 84
Krentzel, Theodore, Exec. V.P.--Granite State Packing Co., Manchester, NH, pg. 476
Kreusser, Judi, Exec. V.P., Sec. & Dir.-Human Resources--Handley & Miller, Inc., Indianapolis, IN, pg. 505
Krida, Jeffrey, Exec. V.P. & Chief Oper. Officer--Delta Queen Steamboat Company, New Orleans, LA, pg. 385
Kruse, Jeffrey R., Exec. V.P. & Controller--Intelligent Controls Inc., Lynnwood, WA, pg. 573
Krysa, E.M., Exec. V.P.--Illinois Range Company, Mount Prospect, IL, pg. 563
Kryshak, Thomas E., Exec. V.P.-Fin.--Employers Insurance of Wausau a Mutual Co., Wausau, WI, pg. 380
Kryshak, Thomas E., Exec. V.P.-Fin.--Employers Insurance of Wausau a Mutual Co., Wausau, WI, pg. 795
Kullman, J.W., Exec. V.P. & Chief Oper. Officer--Orix Real Estate Equities, Inc., Chicago, IL, pg. 829
Kuperschmid, Peter, Exec. V.P.--Broadcast Time, Inc., Roslyn, NY, pg. 177
Kuraner, Irving, Exec. V.P.--Twentieth Century Investors, Inc., Kansas City, MO, pg. 1121
Lackey, Bill, Exec. V.P.--Retail Ventures, Inc., Warrendale, PA, pg. 929
Lacourse, Julian, Exec. V.P.--Demoulas Super Markets, Tewksbury, MA, pg. 328
LaFayette, David R., Exec. V.P. & Chief Agent-Canada--Mutual of Omaha Insurance Company, Omaha, NE, pg. 779
LaFayette, David R., Exec. V.P. & Chief Agent-Canada--Mutual of Omaha, Omaha, NE, pg. 779
Lafferty, Richard F., Exec. V.P.--Parkway Fabricators, Inc., South Amboy, NJ, pg. 480
LaFleur, Gerald W., Exec. V.P.--Dole Food Company, Inc., Westlake Village, CA, pg. 840
LaFond, Jerry, Chief Exec. Officer--The Asher Winer Company, Fitchburg, MA, pg. 88
LaFontaine, Robert, Exec. V.P.--Cresmer, Woodward, O'Mara & Ormsbee, New York, NY, pg. 298
Lahey, Gerald F., Exec. V.P.--Duchossois Industries, Inc., Elmhurst, IL, pg. 350
Lakin, Ken, Exec. V.P.--Lakin General Corporation, Chicago, IL, pg. 652
Lala, D.J., Exec. V.P.--Gould Paper Corporation, New York, NY, pg. 473
Lamb, Anthony, Exec. V.P.--Chem-Tainer Corporation, Brooklyn, NY, pg. 241
Lamb, James R., Exec. V.P.--Lamb Engineering & Construction Co., Salt Lake City, UT, pg. 652
Lambright, Bernard, Sr. V.P.--Jayco Inc., Middlebury, IN, pg. 590
Lammert, Walter, Exec. V.P.--Microwave Networks Incorporated, Houston, TX, pg. 749
Lancaster, William G., Exec. V.P.--Lantech Inc., Louisville, KY, pg. 658
Landau, Richard, Exec. V.P.--Hosiery Sls.--Union Underwear Co., Inc., Bowling Green, KY, pg. 400
Landau, Richard, Exec. V.P.--Camp Hosiery, New York, NY, pg. 400
Lander, Richard D., Exec. V.P. & Chief Oper. Officer--Marotta Scientific Controls, Inc., Montville, NJ, pg. 713
Landry, James E., Chief Fin. Officer, Exec. V.P. & Sec.--United Piece Dye Works, LP, Princeton Junction, NJ, pg. 1134
Lane, Keith, Exec. V.P., Creative Dir.--Arnold Fortuna Lawner & Cabot, Boston, MA, pg. 84
Lang, Richard A., Sr., Exec. V.P.--Dad's Products Co., Inc., Meadville, PA, pg. 310
Langer, Robert, Exec. V.P.--Van Son Holland Ink Corp. of America, Mineola, NY, pg. 1144
Langhammer, Fred, Exec. V.P. & Chief Oper. Officer--Estee Lauder, Inc., New York, NY, pg. 389
Lankford, George, Exec. V.P.--Affiliated Foods, Inc., Amarillo, TX, pg. 24
Lanktree, Charles T., Exec. V.P.--Eggland's Best, Inc., King of Prussia, PA, pg. 371
Lannoye, Lee D., Exec. V.P.--Washington Mutual Savings Bank, Seattle, WA, pg. 1166
Lansciardi, James, Exec. V.P.--Robert E. Bayley Construction, Seattle, WA, pg. 128
Lansciardi, James, Exec. V.P.--Programmed Maintenance Services, Inc., Kirkland, WA, pg. 128
Lantzsch, Margarete G., Exec. V.P.--Lantzsch-Andreas Enterprises, Inc., Vienna, VA, pg. 658
Lanzerath, Geunter, Exec. V.P.-Europe--Steiber Div. der Borg-Warner GmbH, Heidelberg,, Germany, pg. 166
Larkin, James K., Exec. V.P., Dir. U.S. Opers.--Ketchum Advertising/USA, New York, NY, pg. 625
Larsen, Richard, Exec. V.P.-External Affairs--Blue Cross & Blue Shield of Oregon, Portland, OR, pg. 160
Larson, Lowell, Exec. V.P.--Klapmeier Management Company, Mora, MN, pg. 634
Laseter, James F., III, Exec. V.P.--Wray-Ward-Laseter Advertising, Charlotte, NC, pg. 1204
Laskey, Susan, Exec. V.P.--Media Management Associates, Fort Lee, NJ, pg. 734
Lassoff, Donald, Exec. V.P.--Integrated Resources, Inc., New York, NY, pg. 573
Laster, Owen, Exec. V.P.--William Morris Agency, Inc., Beverly Hills, CA, pg. 771
Latone, Sal, Exec. V.P.--Magnetic Technologies Corporation, Rochester, NY, pg. 701
Lauder, Evelyn, Exec. V.P.--Estee Lauder, Inc., New York, NY, pg. 389
Lausin, Gerald M., Exec. V.P.--Prestige Fragrances, Ltd., New York, NY, pg. 696
Lauterbach, Marvin, Exec. V.P.--National Utility Service, Inc., Park Ridge, NJ, pg. 794
Lavelle, Thomas J., Exec. V.P. & Chief Oper. Officer--Industrial Coatings Group, Inc., Chicago, IL, pg. 566
Lawton, Bradley L., Exec. V.P.--Star Cutter Co., Farmington Hills, MI, pg. 1039
Lebau, Joseph P., Exec. V.P.--Ben Schwartz Market, Inc., Peoria, IL, pg. 980
LeBlanc, Edward, Exec. V.P.--Macklanburg-Duncan Co., Oklahoma City, OK, pg. 697
LeBrasseur, Richard, Exec. V.P.--Weekly Reader Corp., Middletown, CT, pg. 611
LeBreux, E. George, Exec. V.P.--Farley Candy Company, Chicago, IL, pg. 399
Lee, Charles P., Exec. V.P.--Muralo Co., Inc., Bayonne, NJ, pg. 776
Lee, J. Daniel, Jr., Exec. V.P.--Teachers Insurance and Annuity Association-College Retirement Equities Fund, New York, NY, pg. 1082
Lee, Robert R., Exec. V.P.--Progressive Driver Services, Inc., Jacksonville, FL, pg. 894
Leener, Jack J., Exec. V.P.--Eisaman, Johns & Laws Advertising, Inc., Los Angeles, CA, pg. 372
Lefever, Terry, Exec. V.P.-Welding Prods.--Hobart Brothers Co., Troy, OH, pg. 536
Lefkowitz, Ira, Exec. V.P.--Hoboken Wood Flooring Corporation, Wayne, NJ, pg. 537
Legasey, Edward, Exec. V.P.--Systems Research And Applications Corporation, Arlington, VA, pg. 1071
Lehman, Eric A., Exec. V.P.--Communications Concepts, Toledo, OH, pg. 269
Leicht, Steve, Exec. V.P.--Communications Diversified, New York, NY, pg. 269
Leimkuhler, Gerard J., Jr., Exec. V.P.--Computer Information Services, Inc., Philadelphia, PA, pg. 834
Leiner, Neil, Exec. V.P., Grp. Dir.--Sudler & Hennessey, New York, NY, pg. 1211
Leitner, Robert, Exec. V.P.--Accurate Bushing Co., Inc., Garwood, NJ, pg. 11
Leitten, David, Exec. V.P.--Progress Casting Group, Inc., Plymouth, MN, pg. 894
Lekowitz, Joel, Exec. V.P.--Hoboken Wood Flooring Corporation, Wayne, NJ, pg. 537
Lelchuk, Marshall, Exec. V.P.--Leathers Best, Melville, NY, pg. 664
Lemon, David W., Exec. V.P.--American Hardware Mutual Insurance Co., Minnetonka, MN, pg. 55
Lenox, John W., Vice Chm. & Exec. V.P.--Shelter Mutual Insurance Company, Columbia, MO, pg. 997
Lenz, Scott, Exec. V.P.--Gunder & Associates, Inc., Dublin, OH, pg. 494
Leokum, Lenny, Exec. V.P., Creative Dir.--Griffin Bacal Inc., New York, NY, pg. 486
Leonard, Robert, Chief Oper. Officer--FMS Management Systems, Inc., North Miami Beach, FL, pg. 394
Leong, Calvin, Exec. V.P.--Maness Industries, Inc., Long Beach, CA, pg. 703
Lepore, Thomas F., Exec. V.P.--Della Construction Co. Inc., Enfield, CT, pg. 326
Lester, Nelle, Exec. V.P.--J.L. Lester & Son, Inc., Rockmart, GA, pg. 668
Levine, Kenneth M., Exec. V.P. & Chief Investment Officer--The Mutual Life Insurance Company of New York (MONY), New York, NY, pg. 778
Levine, Morton, Exec. V.P.-Fin.--Glamorise Foundations, Inc., New York, NY, pg. 460
Levy, D.G., Exec. V.P.--Levy Security Consultants, Limited, Chicago, IL, pg. 672
Levy, Lew, Exec. V.P.--United States Luggage Company, Hauppauge, NY, pg. 1136
Levy, Martin, Exec. V.P.--Landau & Heyman Inc., Chicago, IL, pg. 654
Lewis, Carol D., Exec. V.P.--Squire-Cogswell Company, Northbrook, IL, pg. 1034
Lewis, Carol D., Exec. V.P.--Aeros Instruments, Inc., Northbrook, IL, pg. 1034
Lewis, Goldy S., Exec. V.P.--Lewis Homes Management Corp., Upland, CA, pg. 673
Lewis, Randal W., Exec. V.P.--Lewis Homes Management Corp., Upland, CA, pg. 673
Lewis, Robert E., Pres. NV Opers. & Exec. V.P.--Lewis Homes Management Corp., Upland, CA, pg. 673
Lewis, Roger G., Exec. V.P.--Lewis Homes Management Corp., Upland, CA, pg. 673
Leyman, Donald W., Exec. V.P.--Swinerton & Walberg Co., San Francisco, CA, pg. 1068
Lia, Gary, Exec. V.P.--Liberty Mutual Insurance Co., Boston, MA, pg. 674
Lichtendahl, Charles, Exec. V.P.--Hudepohl-Schoenling Brewing Company, Cincinnati, OH, pg. 550
Lieb, James, Sr. V.P.--The Trump Group, New York, NY, pg. 1117
Liebenson, Sid, Exec. V.P., Dir. Mktg.--Kobs & Draft Advertising, Inc., Chicago, IL, pg. 109
Lieberg, Eric N., Chief Fin. Officer & Exec. V.P.--Rundel Products, Inc., Portland, OR, pg. 956
Lien, Richard C., Exec. V.P.--Bank M F & Company, Inc., Minneapolis, MN, pg. 117
Liff, Lawrence, Exec. V.P.--Collegeville/Imagineering L.P., Collegeville, PA, pg. 262
Limpe, Emily T., Exec. V.P.--Petro Chem Development Company, New York, NY, pg. 865
Linder, Allan, Exec. V.P.--Linder & Associates, Inc., Wichita, KS, pg. 676
Linder, Steven W., Exec. V.P.--Minnesota Electric Supply Company, Willmar, MN, pg. 757
Lindner, Alan B., Exec. V.P.--United Dairy Farmers, Inc., Cincinnati, OH, pg. 1131
Lindsey, James S., Exec. V.P.--Doe-Anderson Advertising Agency, Inc., Louisville, KY, pg. 342
Link, William P., Exec. V.P.--The Prudential Insurance Company of America, Newark, NJ, pg. 896
Lipke, Neil E., Exec. V.P.--Gibraltar Steel Corp., Buffalo, NY, pg. 456
Lipman, David, Exec. V.P.--Lipman, Richmond, Greene, New York, NY, pg. 677
Lipman, Donna, Exec. V.P.--Lipman, Richmond, Greene, New York, NY, pg. 677
Lipman, Richard, Exec. V.P.--Lipman, Richmond, Greene, New York, NY, pg. 677
Lites, Denise Ilitch, Sr. Exec. V.P.--Little Caesar Enterprises, Inc., Detroit, MI, pg. 678
Ljungberg, Susan L., Exec. V.P. & Gen. Mgr.--Ultra Tool & Plastics, Inc., Amherst, NY, pg. 1125
Lloyd, Gary, Exec. V.P.--Plymouth Tube Company, Warrenville, IL, pg. 877
Lobsinger, Michael, Exec. V.P.-Corp. Plng.--Compuware Corporation, Farmington Hills, MI, pg. 271
Locatelli, James, Exec. V.P.--McDonald Davis & Associates, Inc., Milwaukee, WI, pg. 728
Lodge, H. Cabot, III, Exec. V.P. & Mng. Dir.--W. P. Carey & Co., Inc., New York, NY, pg. 218
Logan, Robert, Exec. V.P.--Plastics Manufacturing Company, Dallas, TX, pg. 876
Lohrs, Eugene, Exec. V.P.--Lee Company, Westbrook, CT, pg. 665
Loizou, George, Exec. V.P.--Becon Construction Company, Inc., Houston, TX, pg. 131
Londen, Lars E., Exec. V.P.--Central National-Gottesman Inc., Purchase, NY, pg. 233
Long, Bernard J., Exec. V.P., Mngmt. Supvr.--McCaffrey and McCall, New York, NY, pg. 726

Longbrake, William A., Sr. Exec. V.P. & Chief Fin. Officer--Washington Mutual Savings Bank, Seattle, WA, pg. 1166
Longley, Steve, Exec. V.P.--Leo Burnett Publicidade, Ltda., Sao Paulo,, Brazil, pg. 193
Lonson, Tom, Exec. V.P.--Capitol Group, Springfield, IL, pg. 215
Losurdo, Mark, Exec. V.P.--Losurdo Foods, Inc., Hackensack, NJ, pg. 684
Losurdo, Michael, Jr., Exec. V.P.--Losurdo Foods, Inc., Hackensack, NJ, pg. 684
Loudermilk, Tim A., Exec. V.P. & Reg. Mgr.-Real Estate Lending--Team Bancshares, Inc., Dallas, TX, pg. 1082
Lovaas, John, Exec. V.P. & Gen. Mgr.--Harrington & King, Chicago, IL, pg. 511
Lowell, David, Exec. V.P.-Opers.--Diversified Communications, Portland, ME, pg. 340
Lowenstein, David C., Exec. V.P.--Reitman Industries, West Caldwell, NJ, pg. 924
Lozier, Robert D., Exec. V.P.--Freeman Decorating Co., Dallas, TX, pg. 431
Lubalin, Peter, Exec. V.P., Co-Creative Dir.-U.S.--TBWA Advertising, Inc., New York, NY, pg. 1071
Lucas, Maurice, Exec. V.P.--Conair Corporation, Stamford, CT, pg. 272
Luce, James W., Exec. V.P.--ULLICO Inc., Washington, DC, pg. 1124
Lucien, Kent T., Exec. V.P., Chief Fin. Officer & Treas.--C. Brewer & Company, Limited, Honolulu, HI, pg. 174
Luckey, Gene, Exec. V.P.--S&D Coffee Inc., Concord, NC, pg. 959
Lukman, John C., Exec. V.P.--Stanchem Inc., East Berlin, CT, pg. 1035
Lunde, Hilmar, Exec. V.P.--BSB Bates-Gruppen A/S, Oslo,, Norway, pg. 109
Lundeen, Kenneth C., Exec. V.P.--C.J. Langenfelder & Son, Inc., Baltimore, MD, pg. 657
Lunoi, Ken, Chief Oper. Officer & Exec. V.P.--Delta Education, Inc., Hudson, NH, pg. 326
Luscinski, Steven, Exec. V.P. & Gen. Mgr.--Accu-Sort Systems, Inc., Telford, PA, pg. 11
Lustbader, Brian G., Exec. V.P., Gen. Counsel & Sec.--The P.J. Carlin Construction Company, New Rochelle, NY, pg. 220
Lynch, Kevin, Exec. V.P.--HLB Communications, Inc., Chicago, IL, pg. 496
Lynch, Roger, Exec. V.P.--Kimstock, Inc., Santa Ana, CA, pg. 630
Lynn, Michael F., Exec. V.P.--Carl M. Freeman Associates, Inc., Potomac, MD, pg. 431
Mace, Tom, Exec. V.P.--Forever Living Products, Tempe, AZ, pg. 424
MacGregor, Alexander, Exec. V.P.-Admin.--Random House, Inc., New York, NY, pg. 19
Macke, Bruce A., Chief Fin. Officer & Exec. V.P.--The Elder-Beerman Stores Corp., Dayton, OH, pg. 373
MacPhail, Andy, Exec. V.P.--Minnesota Twins Baseball Club, Minneapolis, MN, pg. 758
Macy, Bill C., Exec. V.P.--Lincoln Industries, Lincoln, NE, pg. 676
Madden, ThomasA., Exec. V.P.--Daniel F. Young, Inc., New York, NY, pg. 1209
Madsen, Dennis, Exec. V.P. & Chief Oper. Officer--Recreational Equipment, Inc., Kent, WA, pg. 917
Maehler, Roger A., Exec. V.P.--Heller Seasonings & Ingredients, Inc., Bedford Park, IL, pg. 526
Magalska, James M., Exec. V.P.--Wausau Life Insurance Company, Wausau, WI, pg. 380
Magill, Brad R., Exec. V.P. & Chief Oper. Officer--Direct Response Broadcasting Network, Inc., Philadelphia, PA, pg. 339
Magrann, Robert P., Exec. V.P.--E.J. Brach Corporation, Oakbrook Terrace, IL, pg. 169
Maher, Ray, Exec. V.P., Creative Dir. & Sec.--MCC, Inc., Essex, CT, pg. 691
Mahoney, Art, Exec. V.P.--Sandler Communications Inc., New York, NY, pg. 970
Mahoney, Barbara E., Exec. V.P.-Retail Banking--American Savings of Florida, ESB, Miami, FL, pg. 382
Majka, Ken, Exec. V.P., Creative Dir.--Richardson, Myers & Donofrio, Inc., Baltimore, MD, pg. 933
Maloney, Therese A., Exec. V.P.--Liberty Mutual Insurance Co., Boston, MA, pg. 674
Mandarano, C. Patrick, Exec. V.P.--Carrafiello, Diehl & Associates, Inc., Irvington, NY, pg. 225
Mandelbaum, Howard, Exec. V.P.--William Douglas McAdams Inc., New York, NY, pg. 726
Maniatty, George, Exec. V.P.--Precision Roll Grinders, Inc., Allentown, PA, pg. 885
Manitsas, Nikitas C., Exec. V.P.--Lantzsch-Andreas Enterprises, Inc., Vienna, VA, pg. 658
Mann, Johnny, Exec. V.P.--Associated Aircraft Supply Company, Dallas, TX, pg. 89
Marciano, Armond, Exec. V.P.--Guess ?, Inc., Los Angeles, CA, pg. 493
Marconi, Joseph, Exec. V.P.--Weber Cohn & Riley, Inc., Chicago, IL, pg. 1171
Marcus, Barbara, Exec. V.P.-Children's Book Pblg.--Scholastic Inc., New York, NY, pg. 962
Marcus, Fred, Exec. V.P.--21 International Holdings, Inc., New York, NY, pg. 1121
Mardell, Fred R., Vice Chm., Exec. V.P. & Sec.--Barton Brands, Ltd., Chicago, IL, pg. 123
Marfuggi, Eugene, Exec. V.P.-Natl. Sls., Mktg. & Adv.--Ferrara Foods & Confections, Inc., New York, NY, pg. 407
Margolis, A.E., Exec. V.P.--Mallet & Co., Carnegie, PA, pg. 703
Marino, Samuel F., Exec. V.P.--Green Spot Packaging Inc., Claremont, CA, pg. 485
Mark, Margaret, Exec. V.P., Dir., Res.--Young & Rubicam Inc., New York, NY, pg. 1210
Mark, Margaret, Exec. V.P., Dir. Brand Plng.--Young & Rubicam New York, New York, NY, pg. 1211
Marks, Greg, Exec. V.P.--Allied Sporting Goods Inc., Louisville, KY, pg. 40
Marks, Harry, Exec. V.P.--Allied Sporting Goods Inc., Louisville, KY, pg. 40
Marks, Michael, Exec. V.P.--Allied Sporting Goods Inc., Louisville, KY, pg. 40
Marks, Sam, Exec. V.P., Corp. Sec. & Dir.-Pur.--Triangle Marketing Corp., New York, NY, pg. 1112
Marquis, Peter, Exec. V.P.--Sofco-Mead, Inc., Scotia, NY, pg. 1016
Marshall, Andrew, Exec. V.P.--National-General Supply, Inc., Great Falls, MT, pg. 1174
Martin, Brian, Sr. V.P., Dir.-New Bus.--Deutsch/Dworin, Inc., New York, NY, pg. 333
Martin, Earl, V.P.--J. H. Heafner Co. Inc., Lincolnton, NC, pg. 520
Martin, Edward K., Exec. V.P.--Sutter/Martin, Inc., Buffalo Grove, IL, pg. 1065
Martin, James S., Exec. V.P.--Teachers Insurance and Annuity Association-College Retirement Equities Fund, New York, NY, pg. 1082
Martin, Louis, Exec. V.P.--Sunline Coach Co., Inc., Denver, PA, pg. 1061
Martin, Peter, Exec. V.P.--Hyman Freightways Inc., Moundsview, MN, pg. 557
Martin, Samuel A., Exec. V.P.--Binkley Company, Warrenton, MO, pg. 151
Martin, Steve, Exec. V.P., Creative Dir.--Sicola Martin Koons Frank, Inc., Austin, TX, pg. 1001
Martin, Walter, Exec. V.P.--Tower Records, West Sacramento, CA, pg. 694
Martino, Michael, Exec. V.P. & Chief Investment Officer--Back Bay Advisors, Inc., Boston, MA, pg. 799
Marx, Sheldon H., Exec. V.P.--Merling, Marx & Seidman, Inc., New York, NY, pg. 741
Mashaua, John, Exec. V.P.--ALP/Freddy's, Rochester, NY, pg. 4
Masket, David C., Exec. V.P. & Chief Oper. Officer--Maidenform, Inc., New York, NY, pg. 701
Mason, Ron, Exec. V.P.--Kentucky Indiana Lumber Co. Inc., Louisville, KY, pg. 623
Masterson, Donald, Exec. V.P., Grp. Dir.--Sudler & Hennessey, New York, NY, pg. 1211
Mattingly, Thomas M., Exec. V.P.--Metro Foods, Inc., Memphis, TN, pg. 743
Matza, Bonnie, Exec V.P.--Muhlhauser & Young, San Francisco, CA, pg. 774
Matzell, Charles, Exec. V.P., Assoc. Creative Dir.--Arnold Fortuna Lawner & Cabot, Boston, MA, pg. 84
Mauney, Charles F., Exec. V.P. & Chief Oper. Officer--Mauney Hosiery Mills, Inc., Kings Mountain, NC, pg. 722
Maurer, Gilbert C., Chief Oper. Officer & Exec. V.P.--The Hearst Corporation, New York, NY, pg. 521
Maxfield, Michael G., Exec. V.P.--Universal Companies, Inc., Grand Rapids, MI, pg. 1138
May, Will E., Exec. V.P.--Leader Federal Bank For Savings, Memphis, TN, pg. 663
Mayer, Chester, Exec. V.P.--Mayer Berkshire Corporation, Wayne, NJ, pg. 724
Mayer, Michael, Exec. V.P.--Mayer Berkshire Corporation, Wayne, NJ, pg. 724
Mayer, Robert G., Sr. Exec. V.P.--Rosenfeld, Sirowitz, Humphrey & Strauss, Inc., New York, NY, pg. 948
McAlister, Jim, Exec. V.P.--The Saugatuck Marketing Group, Westport, CT, pg. 972
McAssey, Edward, Exec. V.P.--Lasko Metal Products, Inc., West Chester, PA, pg. 660
McAuvic, Karen, Exec. V.P., Retail Div.--Gianettino & Meredith Advertising, Short Hills, NJ, pg. 455
McCabe, Kathy, Exec. V.P.--Chaffee Case & Partners, Providence, RI, pg. 237
McCabe, Thomas F., Exec. V.P.--Union Industries, Inc., Providence, RI, pg. 1128
McCain, Elaine, Exec. V.P.-Relocation Services--RE/MAX International, Inc., Englewood, CO, pg. 915
McCall, Donald M., Exec. V.P.--Standard Gravure Corp./Shea Communications, Atlanta, GA, pg. 1036
McCammack, Donald R., Exec. V.P.--First Gray Line Corporation, Beverly Hills, CA, pg. 413
McCammon, David, Exec. V.P.--Park Ridge Corporation, Park Ridge, NJ, pg. 849
McCartan, Mike, Exec. V.P., Gen. Mgr.--Gillespie Advertising, Inc., Princeton, NJ, pg. 458
McCarthy, Michael, Exec. V.P.--Waffle House, Inc., Norcross, GA, pg. 1157
McCarthy, Michael P., Exec. V.P.--Harrison Paint Corporation, Canton, OH, pg. 512
McCloskey, W.D., Exec. V.P.--Baltimore Aircoil Company, Jessup, MD, pg. 69
McClure, James S., Exec. V.P.-Portfolio--Oppenheimer Management Corp., New York, NY, pg. 719
McCormack, John J., Exec. V.P.--Teachers Insurance and Annuity Association-College Retirement Equities Fund, New York, NY, pg. 1082
McCormick, Brendan K., Exec. V.P.--Thompson Steel Co., Inc., Canton, MA, pg. 1094
McCormick, Gary, Exec. V.P.--J.H. McCormick, Inc., Burbank, CA, pg. 727
McCormick, Robert, Exec. V.P.--Abelson-Taylor, Inc., Chicago, IL, pg. 10
McCulloch, G.F., Exec. V.P.--Hauenstein & Burmeister, Inc., Minneapolis, MN, pg. 517
McCullough, Bob, Exec. V.P., Sec. & Treas.--Harris, Baio & McCullough Inc., Philadelphia, PA, pg. 511
McCune, Tom, Exec. V.P., Chief Exec. Officer-Building Div.--M. A. Mortenson Company, Minneapolis, MN, pg. 772
McCusker, Thomas J., Exec. V.P. & Counsel to Chm. & Pres.--Mutual of Omaha Insurance Company, Omaha, NE, pg. 779
McCusker, Thomas J., Exec. V.P. & Counsel to Chm. & Pres.--Mutual of Omaha, Omaha, NE, pg. 779
McDavid, Oney, Exec. V.P.-Equip.--Union Boiler Co., Nitro, WV, pg. 273
McDonald, Charles, Jr., Exec. V.P.--McDonald Equipment Co., Willoughby, OH, pg. 728
McDonald, William F., Exec. V.P.--Sunnyland Refining Co., Inc., Birmingham, AL, pg. 616
McDowell, James W., Exec. V.P. & Chief Exec. Officer--Dairymen, Inc., Louisville, KY, pg. 311
McEnany, Rob, Exec. V.P.--Levenson & Hill, Inc., Irving, TX, pg. 670
McEneely, Kevin, Exec. V.P.--Nightingale-Conant Corp., Niles, IL, pg. 807
McEvoy, Charles, Exec. V.P.--Western Extrusions, Carrollton, TX, pg. 1179
McGarry, John, Exec. V.P., Pres. & Chief Exec. Officer-No. America--Young & Rubicam Inc., New York, NY, pg. 1210
McGehee, David S., Exec. V.P.--Mac Papers, Inc., Jacksonville, FL, pg. 694
McGill, Joanne, Exec. V.P.--Vernon Sassos McGill, Inc., New York, NY, pg. 1148
McGrath, Judith, Exec. V.P. & Dir.-Creative--MTV: Music Television, New York, NY, pg. 785
McKean, Evelyn C., Exec. V.P.--Breckenridge Material Company, Saint Louis, MO, pg. 173
McLane, Larry R., Exec. V.P.--Hughes Advertising Inc., Saint Louis, MO, pg. 551
McLarin, Ed, Assoc. Exec. Dir.-Publishing--American Library Association, Chicago, IL, pg. 57
McLaughlin, E.H., III, Exec. V.P., Treas. & Asst. Sec.--McLaughlin Industrial Distributors, Inc., Pico Rivera, CA, pg. 731
McLean, Porter, Exec. V.P.--Accurate Threaded Fasteners, Inc., Lincolnwood, IL, pg. 11
McLeod, Rod, Exec. V.P.--Royal Caribbean Cruises Ltd., Miami, FL, pg. 953
McMahill, James, Exec. V.P.--ACI Financial Corp., Minnetonka, MN, pg. 2
McMasters, R.G., Exec. V.P.--AFG Industries, Inc., Fort Worth, TX, pg. 3
McMillan, Bayne, Exec. V.P.--Cummins Intermountain Diesel, Salt Lake City, UT, pg. 305
McNally, John, Exec. V.P.--JM Family Enterprises Inc., Deerfield Beach, FL, pg. 584
McNamara, Robert, Exec. V.P.--Marshall Contractors Inc., Rumford, RI, pg. 714
Meadows, LaDonna, Exec. V.P.--Kwik-Kopy Corp., Cypress, TX, pg. 647
Meeder, Bill, Exec. V.P.--Larkin Meeder & Schweidel, Dallas, TX, pg. 659
Melcott Jr., Paul C., Exec. V.P.--H.B. Mellott Estate, Inc., McConnellsburg, PA, pg. 738
Melek, Al, Exec. V.P.--McNeil & NRM., Inc., Akron, OH, pg. 732
Mellott, Robert H., Exec. V.P.--Knight Architects Engineers Planners, Inc., Chicago, IL, pg. 637
Melo, Rafael, Exec. V.P.--Crisa Corporation, Plano, TX, pg. 299
Meranus, Arthur B., Exec. V.P., Assoc. Dir., Creative Services--N W Ayer Inc., New York, NY, pg. 104
Meranus, Arthur W., Exec. V.P., Dir.--N W Ayer Incorporated, New York, NY, pg. 103
Mercurio, Frank, Chief Oper. Officer & Exec. V.P.--McAdams, Richman & Ong, Inc., Bala-Cynwyd, PA, pg. 725
Merideth, Eddie, V.P.--Barton Beers, Ltd., Chicago, IL, pg. 123
Merola, Ralph, Exec. V.P.--House of Ronnie, Inc., New York, NY, pg. 546
Merrill, Eleanor, Exec. V.P.--Capital-Gazette Communications, Inc., Annapolis, MD, pg. 656
Merz, Kenneth, Exec. V.P. & New Business Contact--Sefton Associates Inc., Grand Rapids, MI, pg. 987
Meschery, Ann, Exec. V.P., Grp. Media Dir.--Backer Spielvogel Bates, Inc., New York, NY, pg. 108
Messinger, Herbert J., Exec. V.P., Agency Opers.--Botto, Roessner, Horne & Messinger, Inc., New York, NY, pg. 625
Metzger, William A., Exec. V.P., Mngmt. Supvr.--McCaffrey and McCall, New York, NY, pg. 726
Meyer, Richard E., Exec. V.P.--Johnson & Higgins, New York, NY, pg. 598
Meyers, Richard, Exec. V.P., Dir. Fin. & Treas.--Kobs & Draft Advertising, Inc., Chicago, IL, pg. 109
Miamis, James D., Exec. V.P.--Demoulas Super Markets, Tewksbury, MA, pg. 328
Michalec, Alice, Exec. V.P., Gen. Mgr.--Rives Carlberg, Houston, TX, pg. 937
Middleton, Tom, Exec. V.P.--Goodpasture, Inc., Brownfield, TX, pg. 471
Mignano, Richard A., Exec. V.P.--Inlander-Steindler Paper, Vernon Hills, IL, pg. 570
Mike, Czerwinski, Exec. V.P.--Eatel Corporation, Gonzales, LA, pg. 364
Milazzo, E.J., Exec. V.P.--Ward Products Corporation, New Brunswick, NJ, pg. 1163
Milenthal, Richard K., Exec. V.P.--Hameroff/Milenthal/Spence, Inc., Columbus, OH, pg. 503
Mileski, Alan S., Exec. V.P.--Nelson Westerberg, Inc., Elk Grove Village, IL, pg. 1178
Millard, Frank W., Exec. V.P.--Turtle & Hughes, Inc., Linden, NJ, pg. 1119
Miller, Don, Exec. V.P.--United Stores, Bay City, MI, pg. 1137
Miller, Duane L., Exec. V.P. & Chief Exec. Officer--Country Companies Insurance Group, Bloomington, IL, pg. 289
Miller, Duane L., Exec. V.P. & Chief Exec. Officer--CC Services, Bloomington, IL, pg. 289
Miller, George, Exec. V.P. & Supvr.-Mngmt.--Proctor & Gardner Advertising, Inc., Chicago, IL, pg. 892
Miller, George F., Sr. Exec. V.P.-Business Insurance Sector--John Hancock Mutual Life Insurance Company, Boston, MA, pg. 595
Miller, James E., Exec. V.P.--Massachusetts Mutual Life Insurance Co., Springfield, MA, pg. 718

Corporate Responsibilities Index

Miller, John, Exec. V.P.--Young Stuff Apparel Group, Inc., New York, NY, pg. 1214
Miller, Linn R., Exec. V.P.--Lat Purser & Associate, Charlotte, NC, pg. 901
Miller, Lloyd, Exec. V.P.--American Laubscher Corp., Farmingdale, NY, pg. 57
Miller, Nicole, Exec. V.P.--Kobra International Ltd, New York, NY, pg. 638
Miller, Raymond, Exec. V.P.--National Seating Co., Vonore, TN, pg. 793
Miller, Rodger M., Exec. V.P.--Spelling Entertainment Group, Inc., Cincinnati, OH, pg. 54
Miller, Sydell, Exec. V.P.--Matrix Essentials, Inc., Solon, OH, pg. 721
Millgard, C. Richard, Exec. V.P.--The Millgard Corp., Livonia, MI, pg. 755
Mills, Linda S., Exec. V.P.--Fleishman Hillard Inc., Saint Louis, MO, pg. 417
Milner, Bruce D., Exec. V.P.--International Communications Group, Inc., Los Angeles, CA, pg. 576
Miniat, Edmund, Jr., Exec. V.P.--Ed Miniat, Inc., Chicago, IL, pg. 757
Minkoff, Bruce, Exec. V.P.--Fraenkel Company, Baton Rouge, LA, pg. 428
Mintz, Stephen A., Exec. V.P.--Integrated Resources, Inc., New York, NY, pg. 573
Mitchell, Don, Exec. V.P.--Cogsdill Tool Products, Inc., Lugoff, SC, pg. 259
Mitchell, J., Exec. V.P. & Chief Oper. Officer--Versa Services Ltd., Etobicoke,, Canada, pg. 7
Mitchell, Perry, Exec. V.P., Creative Dir.--Bennett Kuhn Varner, Inc., Atlanta, GA, pg. 139
Mockley, Michael E., Exec. V.P. & Chief Oper. Officer--Anchor Gasoline Corporation, Tulsa, OK, pg. 71
Mody, Jane, Exec. V.P.-Investments--Rosewood Property Company, Dallas, TX, pg. 949
Moeller, Rudy F., Jr., Exec. V.P.--Fessel, Siegfriedt & Moeller, Inc., Louisville, KY, pg. 407
Mohre, David L., Chief Exec. Officer & Exec. V.P.--Cajun Electric Power Co-op, Baton Rouge, LA, pg. 207
Molesworth, Richard C., Exec. V.P.--Frederick Trading Company, Frederick, MD, pg. 430
Moloney, Raymond D., Exec. V.P.--Wyandot Inc., Marion, OH, pg. 1205
Moltz, Sanford, Exec. V.P., Exec. Creative Dir.--Kobs & Draft Advertising, Inc., Chicago, IL, pg. 109
Monaghan, William, Exec. V.P., Dir., Creative Services--Arnold Fortuna Lawner & Cabot, Boston, MA, pg. 84
Monahan, Grace, Exec. V.P.--C M P Publications, Inc., Manhasset, NY, pg. 202
Monda, Keith, Exec. V.P.--J. Crew Group, Inc., New York, NY, pg. 584
Monitto, Douglas, Exec. V.P.--Monitor Aerospace Corporation, Amityville, NY, pg. 765
Montagnino, Frank, Exec. V.P.--Peter A. Mayer Advertising, Inc., New Orleans, LA, pg. 724
Montalvo, Paco, Exec. V.P.--Lowe MBAC, Barcelona,, Spain, pg. 685
Montero, Fernan, Exec. V.P., Area Dir.-Latin America--Young & Rubicam Inc., New York, NY, pg. 1210
Montero, Fernan, Exec. V.P., Area Dir.-Latin America--Young & Rubicam New York, New York, NY, pg. 1211
Montgomery, Christian, Exec. V.P.-Mktg.--Andy Frain Services, Inc., Chicago, IL, pg. 428
Montgomery, David, Exec. V.P.--The Phillies-A Limited Partnership, Philadelphia, PA, pg. 867
Montgomery, R.L., Chief Fin. Officer, Exec. V.P. & Treas.--Columbus McKinnon Corp., Amherst, NY, pg. 266
Moody, Dan T., Exec. V.P.--Eddins-Walcher Company, Midland, TX, pg. 367
Moody, Michael, Exec. V.P.--Creative Marketing International Corp., West Chicago, IL, pg. 297
Moody, Raymond L., Jr., Exec. V.P.--Batson-Cook Company, West Point, GA, pg. 126
Mooers, Robert, Exec. V.P.--Wilshire Newport Inc., Burbank, CA, pg. 1193
Mooney, David W., Exec. V.P.-Consumer Banking--Texas Commerce Bancshares, Inc., Houston, TX, pg. 1089
Moore, Frank, Exec. V.P. & Chief Oper. Officer--McCall Oil & Chemical Corp., Portland, OR, pg. 726
Moore, Marianne, Exec. V.P. & Media Dir.--Moore, Epstein, Moore, Tampa, FL, pg. 768
Moore, Michael, Exec. V.P., Acct. Services--Chapman Direct Advertising, New York, NY, pg. 1210
Moore, Michael D., Exec. V.P. & Chief Oper. Officer--Capital Bank of California, Los Angeles, CA, pg. 214
Moore, Michael F., Exec. V.P.--Potter Hazlehurst Incorporated, East Greenwich, RI, pg. 882
Moore, Robert, Exec. V.P.--Hawthorne Communications, Inc., Fairfield, IA, pg. 518
Moore, Ted, Exec. V.P. & New Bus. Contact--Moore, Epstein, Moore, Tampa, FL, pg. 768
Mooth, Thomas A., Exec. V.P.--Trone Advertising, Inc., Greensboro, NC, pg. 1115
Moran, Thomas J., Chief Exec. Officer--Mutual of America, New York, NY, pg. 777
Morchower, Donald L., Exec. V.P. & Chief Oper. Officer--Empire Blue Cross & Blue Shield, New York, NY, pg. 379
Morello, Marianna, Exec. V.P.--Stephen L. Geller Inc., New York, NY, pg. 447
Morgan, V. Harley, Exec. V.P. & Sec.--Northwest Paper Converting Company, Vancouver, WA, pg. 814
Morgenstern, Barbara, Exec. V.P.--Nuarc Company, Inc., Niles, IL, pg. 817
Morice, James L., Exec. V.P.--Fleishman Hillard Inc., Saint Louis, MO, pg. 417
Morrell, Richard, Exec. V.P.--E B 5 Corporation, Portland, OR, pg. 359
Morris, Anna K., Exec. V.P. & Chief Creative Officer--Burrell Communications Group Inc., Chicago, IL, pg. 195
Morris, Davis L., Exec. V.P., Gen. Mgr.--Ross Advertising, Inc., Saint Louis, MO, pg. 949
Morris, James A., Exec. V.P.--Texas Electric Cooperatives, Inc., Austin, TX, pg. 1089
Morris, Mark R., Exec. V.P., Acct. Mngmt.--Backer Spielvogel Bates, Inc., New York, NY, pg. 108
Morris, Thomas F., Exec. V.P. & Chief Fin. Officer--World's Finest Chocolate, Inc., Chicago, IL, pg. 1203
Morrison, Don, Exec. V.P.-Mdse.--Retail Ventures, Inc., Warrendale, PA, pg. 929
Morrison, Robert, Exec. V.P. & Creative Dir.--Dorland Sweeney Jones, Philadelphia, PA, pg. 346
Morrissette, Arthur, Jr., Exec. V.P.--Interstate Van Lines, Inc., Springfield, VA, pg. 581
Morrissey, Mike, Exec. V.P.--Siemer Milling Company, Teutopolis, IL, pg. 1002
Morrow, Jack, Exec. V.P.--Dakin, Inc., Burlingame, CA, pg. 311
Morton, Richard, Exec. V.P.--Moran Industries, Inc., Midlothian, IL, pg. 769
Motch, David W., Exec. V.P.--R. A. Jones & Co. Inc., Covington, KY, pg. 604
Mountjoy, James W., Exec. V.P., Creative Dir.--Loeffler Ketchum Mountjoy, Charlotte, NC, pg. 680
Moynahan, John D., Jr., Exec. V.P.-Group Insurance--Metropolitan Life Insurance Co., New York, NY, pg. 744
Mueller, Donald R., Exec. V.P.--Peck Sims Mueller, Inc., Honolulu, HI, pg. 854
Mulchrone, Fergal, Exec. V.P.--Mama Tish's Italian Specialties, Chicago, IL, pg. 703
Muller, Frank, Exec. V.P. & Co-Chief Oper. Officer--U.S. Divers Co., Inc., Santa Ana, CA, pg. 1135
Muller, Henry J., Exec. V.P.--North American Safety Program Administrators, Schenectady, NY, pg. 662
Mulligan, Michael, Exec. V.P.--Berlitz International, Inc., Princeton, NJ, pg. 142
Mullin, Edward, Exec. V.P.--Steelite, Inc., Pittsburgh, PA, pg. 1044
Mullin, Thomas J., Sr. Exec. V.P.--First Federal Savings and Loan Assn. of Rochester, Rochester, NY, pg. 413
Mullis, Elbert N., Jr., Exec. V.P. & Chief Admin. & Fin. Officer--Coca Cola Bottling Co. United, Inc., Birmingham, AL, pg. 257
Mungo, Billy, Exec. V.P.--Michael J. Mungo Company, Inc., Columbia, SC, pg. 775
Murgio, Peter J., Exec. V.P.--BKM Enterprises, Inc., East Hartford, CT, pg. 107
Murphy, Blaine G., Exec. V.P.--Donahue, Inc., Advertising, Hartford, CT, pg. 344
Murphy, Peter, Exec. V.P., Grp. Creative Dir.--Backer Spielvogel Bates, Inc., New York, NY, pg. 108
Muschweck, Stanley, Exec. V.P.--The St. George Group, Inc., Pittsburgh, PA, pg. 966
Musgrave, William, Exec. V.P.--Hendrick Management Corporation, Charlotte, NC, pg. 529
Musselman, John, Exec. V.P.--G. Leblanc Corporation, Kenosha, WI, pg. 665
Myers, Roy, Exec. V.P.--Curtice-Burns Foods, Inc., Rochester, NY, pg. 25
Mykytyn, Russ B., Exec. V.P.--Creative Marketing Alliance Inc., Princeton Junction, NJ, pg. 297
Naber, Drew, Exec. V.P.--Pony Express Courier Corp., Charlotte, NC, pg. 166
Naess, Jan-Erik, Exec. V.P.--BSB Bates-Gruppen A/S, Oslo,, Norway, pg. 109
Nagler, Stewart G., Sr. Exec. V.P.-Insurance Opers.--Metropolitan Life Insurance Co., New York, NY, pg. 744
Naismith, Linda, Exec. V.P.--American Passage Media Corporation, Seattle, WA, pg. 59
Nakash, Avi, Exec. V.P.--Jordache Enterprises, Inc., New York, NY, pg. 604
Nally, Michael J., Exec. V.P. & Chief Oper. Officer--General Sportcraft Company Ltd., Bergenfield, NJ, pg. 450
Narvaez, Carlos, Exec. V.P.--Young & Rubicam, S.A. de C.V., Mexico,, Mexico, pg. 1213
Nash, Amelia J., Exec. V.P.--Universal Securities Corporation, Birmingham, AL, pg. 1139
Naughton, John M., Exec. V.P.--Massachusetts Mutual Life Insurance Co., Springfield, MA, pg. 718
Nayes, Richard A., Exec. V.P.--Jones Blair Company, Dallas, TX, pg. 602
Neeb, Philip, Pres.--Neeb Corporation, Bad Axe, MI, pg. 797
Neerhout, John, Jr., Exec. V.P. & Dir.--Bechtel Group, Inc., San Francisco, CA, pg. 130
Nees, Bernard J., Exec. V.P.--Johnston, Lemon & Co. Inc., Washington, DC, pg. 601
Nelsen, C. Davis, II, Exec. V.P.--Nelsen Steel & Wire Co., Franklin Park, IL, pg. 797
Nelson, Carl E., Exec. V.P.--Recording & Statistical Corporation, Norwalk, CT, pg. 917
Nelson, Gary, Exec. V.P.--Systems Research And Applications Corporation, Arlington, VA, pg. 1071
Nelson, Ralph S., Exec. V.P., Sec. & Gen. Counsel--Burlington Motor Carriers Inc., Daleville, IN, pg. 191
Nelson, Robert G., Exec. V.P.--Walton Monroe Mills, Inc., Monroe, GA, pg. 1162
Nenno, David J., Exec. V.P. & Gen. Mgr.--Standard-Thomson Corporation, Waltham, MA, pg. 1037
Nerby, Dennis, Exec. V.P.--PSI Group of Companies, Memphis, TN, pg. 837
Nerhood, Philip T., Exec. V.P.--Hawthorne Machinery Company, San Diego, CA, pg. 519
Nerlich, B.W., Exec. V.P.--Franklin Steel Company, Franklin, PA, pg. 429
Neu, Richard W., Exec. V.P. & Chief Fin. Officer--First Federal of Michigan, Detroit, MI, pg. 414
Neubner, Klaus, Vice Chm. & Exec. V.P.--George W. Park Seed Co., Inc., Greenwood, SC, pg. 849
Newell, William C., Exec. V.P.--Cameron-Newell Advertising, Inc., Van Nuys, CA, pg. 212
Newkirk, Gerry, Exec. V.P.--TSC Industries, Inc., Nashville, TN, pg. 1075
Newman, Gary L., Exec. V.P.--Cooper Communities, Inc., Bella Vista, AR, pg. 283
Newman, Martin C., Exec. V.P.--King Wire & Cable Corporation, Jamaica, NY, pg. 631
Nick, Harry, Exec. V.P.--Western Development Corporation, Washington, DC, pg. 1179
Nicolato, Joseph L., Exec. V.P.--Park Ridge Corporation, Park Ridge, NJ, pg. 849
Nicolosi, John, Exec. V.P.-Construction--The Kaempfer Company, Investment Builders, Washington, DC, pg. 613
Niederquell, Michael O., Exec. V.P.--Anthony M. Franco Inc., Detroit, MI, pg. 950
Nielsen, Richard, Exec. V.P.--Johnson & Higgins, New York, NY, pg. 598
Nienstedt, William, Exec. V.P. & Chief Exec. Officer & Gen. Mgr.--Atchison County Co-op Association, Atchison, KS, pg. 93
Nightingale, Geoffrey, Exec. V.P., Pres.-Synergenics--Burson-Marsteller, New York, NY, pg. 1210
Nixon, James R., Exec. V.P. & Chief Oper. Officer--Shamrock Broadcasting, Inc., Burbank, CA, pg. 994
Noble, John, Exec. V.P., Creative Dir.--Backer Spielvogel Bates, Inc., New York, NY, pg. 108
Noble, John, Exec. V.P., Creative Dir.--Backer Spielvogel Bates, Inc., Irvine, CA, pg. 108
Nolan, Donald D., Jr., Exec. V.P.--Williams Crane & Rigging, Inc., Richmond, VA, pg. 1191
Nolind, Dick, Exec. V.P.--Merle Norman Cosmetics, Inc., Los Angeles, CA, pg. 740
Norman, Larry, Exec. V.P. & Creative Dir.--EvansGroup, Denver, CO, pg. 391
Norman, Lewis G., III, Exec. V.P.--Bernhardt Furniture Co., Lenoir, NC, pg. 144
Norman, William S., Exec. V.P.--Amtrak-National Railroad Passenger Corp., Washington, DC, pg. 69
Norris, Norman, Exec. V.P.--Besche Oil Company, Inc., Waldorf, MD, pg. 145
North, William A., Exec. V.P.--C. R. Anthony Company, Oklahoma City, OK, pg. 77
Norton, Robert R., Jr., Exec. V.P., Chief Oper. & Fin. Officer--BeefAmerica Operating Co., Inc., Omaha, NE, pg. 131
Noskin, Steven, Exec. V.P.--Polymer Plastics Corporation, Hauppauge, NY, pg. 880
Noto, Peter, Exec. V.P., Creative Services (DTC)--Lewis & Gace, Inc., Fort Lee, NJ, pg. 673
Nowicki, John, Exec. V.P.--Advance Mechanical Systems, Inc., Elk Grove Village, IL, pg. 19
Nussbaum, Joseph, Exec. V.P. & Pres.-Cabinet Div.--Triangle Pacific Corporation, Dallas, TX, pg. 1112
Nussdorf, Lawrence, Exec. V.P.--Clark Construction Group, Bethesda, MD, pg. 252
O'Brien, Kevin P., Exec. V.P.-Independents--Broadcast Division, Atlanta, GA, pg. 292
O'Bryan, Henry E., Exec. V.P.--Owensboro Grain Co., Inc., Owensboro, KY, pg. 834
O'Connell, John D., Exec. V.P.--Topcor Financial Corporation, Chicago, IL, pg. 1101
O'Connor, Thomas P., Exec. V.P.-Pensions, Mutual Funds, Partnership Investments--New York Life Insurance Company, New York, NY, pg. 802
O'Donahue, Claudia, Exec. V.P., Sec. & Treas.--Reid & O'Donahue Advertising, Inc., Montgomery, AL, pg. 923
O'Hara, John C., Exec. V.P., Creative Dir.--Bloomhorst Story O'Hara Inc., Indianapolis, IN, pg. 158
O'Neill, Joe, Exec. V.P., Gen. Mgr. & Chief Creative Officer--Hal Riney & Partners, Inc., New York, NY, pg. 935
O'Reilly, Paul, Exec. V.P. & Chief Oper. Officer--Arley Merchandise Corporation, Taunton, MA, pg. 83
O'Shaughnessy, Joseph A., Sr. Exec. V.P.--Friendly Ice Cream Corp., Wilbraham, MA, pg. 1087
Oberman, Larry, Exec. V.P. & Chief Oper. Officer--Aster Nut Products Inc., Newark, NJ, pg. 92
Obernier, Robert, Exec. V.P.--Horizon Paper Co., Inc., New York, NY, pg. 544
Oberting, Gary, Exec. V.P.--Interstate Commodities Inc., Troy, NY, pg. 580
Oberting, V.A., Jr., Pres.--Interstate Commodities Inc., Troy, NY, pg. 580
Oblak, Robert, Jr., Exec. V.P.--American Louver Co., Skokie, IL, pg. 57
Oertli, Roger S., Exec. V.P.-Construction Div.--Guarantee Electrical Company, Saint Louis, MO, pg. 490
Offutt, James A., Exec. V.P.--Shelter Mutual Insurance Company, Columbia, MO, pg. 997
Ogilvie, Donald, Exec. V.P. & Chief Oper. Officer--The American Bankers Association, Washington, DC, pg. 49
Olen, Gary, Sec. & Exec. V.P.--The Sportsman's Guide, Inc., Eagan, MN, pg. 1032
Olinger, Jack, Exec. V.P.--The Hammerblow Corp., Wausau, WI, pg. 504
Oliver, Paul W., Jr., Exec. V.P.--Chicago Corp., Chicago, IL, pg. 247
Oliveri, Joe, Exec. V.P.--Sisti, Zinbarg & Howard, Inc., Paramus, NJ, pg. 1009
Olsen, David N., Exec. V.P.--Ralph C. Wilson Enterprises, Detroit, MI, pg. 1194
Olsen, Ernest, Exec. V.P.--Arnold Steel Company, Inc., Lakewood, NJ, pg. 85
Olsne, David N., Exec. V.P.--Highwood Service, Inc., Detroit, MI, pg. 1194
Olson, Norman E., Exec. V.P., Dir., Media Services--Griswold, Inc., Cleveland, OH, pg. 950
Oran, Frederic M., Exec. V.P.--Industrial Acoustics Company, Inc., Bronx, NY, pg. 565
Orn, Gerald, Exec. V.P. & Treas.--Central Allied Enterprises, Canton, OH, pg. 232
Orsi, Bernard, Exec. V.P.--Pabst Brewing Co., San Antonio, TX, pg. 959
Osawa, Yutaka, Exec. Sr. V.P.--Chuo Senko Advertising Co., Ltd., Tokyo, Japan, pg. 103
Oscherwitz, J., Exec. V.P.--Sinai 48 Kosher Foods Corp., Chicago, IL, pg. 146
Osgood, Dennis, Exec. V.P.--Cole Vision Corporation, Cleveland, OH, pg. 260
Oteri, James, Sr. V.P.--Nob Hill General Store, Inc., Gilroy, CA, pg. 807

Ott, Christopher J., Exec. V.P.--Ott Communications, Inc., Louisville, KY, pg. 831
Ott, Kevin D., Exec. V.P.--The Hennegan Company, Cincinnati, OH, pg. 529
Owen, David, Exec. V.P.--Cactus Feeders, Inc., Amarillo, TX, pg. 207
Owens, John, Exec. V.P.--Charles River Data Systems, Inc., Framingham, MA, pg. 240
Owens, M., Exec. V.P.--United Health Plan, Inglewood, CA, pg. 1133
Owings, Frank, Jr., Exec. V.P., Mng. Dir., Sec. & Treas.--Service Supply Co. Inc. of Indiana, Indianapolis, IN, pg. 992
Owsley, R.M., Exec. V.P.--Owsley & Sons, Inc., Fort Mill, SC, pg. 834
Paben, John M., Exec. V.P. & Gen. Mgr.--Lozier Store Fixtures, Inc., Omaha, NE, pg. 686
Page, Robert W., Exec. V.P. & Grp. Exec.--The Babcock & Wilcox Company, New Orleans, LA, pg. 107
Page, William N., Mng. Dir.-Admin. & Sec.--Insignia Financial Group, Inc., Greenville, SC, pg. 571
Paino, Robert, Exec. V.P.--Warren/Kremer/CMP/Advertising/Inc., New York, NY, pg. 1165
Paisner, Bruce L., Exec. V.P.--King Features Syndicate Division, New York, NY, pg. 524
Pajak, John J., Exec. V.P.--Massachusetts Mutual Life Insurance Co., Springfield, MA, pg. 718
Palagonia, Chris, Exec. V.P.--J.M.P. Bakery Co., Inc., Brooklyn, NY, pg. 586
Palermo, Anthony J., Exec. V.P.-Services--Brock Control Systems, Inc., Atlanta, GA, pg. 178
Palle, Robert J., Jr., Exec. V.P.--Blonder-Tongue Laboratories, Inc., Old Bridge, NJ, pg. 157
Pantano, Bruce, Exec. V.P.--Publishers Clearing House, Port Washington, NY, pg. 898
Papas, Mirka Giacoletto, Exec. V.P.--R.P. Partners SRL, Milan,, Italy, pg. 626
Parkinson, Richard, Exec. V.P. & Asst. Gen Mgr.--Associated Food Stores Inc., Salt Lake City, UT, pg. 89
Parkinson, Roger P., Exec. V.P.--Cowles Media Company, Minneapolis, MN, pg. 291
Parrinello, John, Jr., Exec. V.P.--Frank Briscoe Co. Inc., Roseland, NJ, pg. 176
Parrish, James, Exec. V.P.--North Carolina Mutual Life Insurance Co., Durham, NC, pg. 813
Parrish, Paul G., Chief Exec. Officer & Exec. V.P.--Coble Dairy Products Co-op, Lexington, NC, pg. 257
Partridge, Fred, Exec. V.P. & Chief Fin. Officer--Smith-Emery Company, Los Angeles, CA, pg. 1012
Pastor, Sydney, Exec. V.P.--W&F Manufacturing Corporation, Inc., Buffalo, NY, pg. 1155
Pastore, Robert, Exec. V.P.--Cine Magnetics, Inc., Mamaroneck, NY, pg. 250
Pastula, Joanne, Exec. V.P.--John Burnham & Co., San Diego, CA, pg. 194
Paszamant, David, Vice Chm., Exec. V.P. & Dir.-Mktg.--Adams Wine Co., Atlanta, GA, pg. 17
Patterson, Donald H. Jr., Exec. V.P.--Landmark Communications, Inc., Norfolk, VA, pg. 654
Patterson, James E., Exec. V.P. & Gen. Mgr.--Fred B. Johnston Company, Inc., Chapin, SC, pg. 601
Patterson, William, Exec. V.P.--Malibu Grand Prix Corporation, Canoga Park, CA, pg. 702
Patton, Steve, Exec. V.P.--Juhl Marketing Communications, Mishawaka, IN, pg. 608
Pavik, Malvin, Exec. V.P.-East Territory--Montgomery Ward & Co., Inc., Chicago, IL, pg. 767
Paydos, Charles J., Exec. V.P.--Phoenix Home Life Mutual Insurance Company, Hartford, CT, pg. 868
Payne, Philip D., Exec. V.P.--Doe-Anderson Advertising Agency, Inc., Louisville, KY, pg. 342
Peal, Leonard B., Exec. V.P.-Cost & Leased Depts.--The Elder-Beerman Stores Corp., Dayton, OH, pg. 373
Pearson, Douglas N., Exec. V.P.--Exide Corporation, Reading, PA, pg. 393
Pearson, Ford G., Exec. V.P.--Frank Consolidated Enterprises Inc., Des Plaines, IL, pg. 428
Peck, Richard, Exec. V.P.--Ranir Corporation, Grand Rapids, MI, pg. 912
Peckham, John R., Exec. V.P.--Peckham Industries, Inc., White Plains, NY, pg. 854
Peetz, Jack, Exec. V.P.--Crete Carrier Corp., Lincoln, NE, pg. 299
Pegan, Robert, Exec. V.P.--Central States Enterprises, Inc., Heathrow, FL, pg. 234
Peiss, Karen G., Exec. V.P.--Gardiner Metal Company, Chicago, IL, pg. 443
Peister, Milton, Exec. V.P.--David L. Peister Co., Inc., New York, NY, pg. 856
Pelton, Richard, Exec. V.P.--O. F. Mossberg & Sons, Inc., North Haven, CT, pg. 773
Pendergrast, Ross, Exec. V.P. & Chief Oper. Officer--Donrey Media Group, Fort Smith, AR, pg. 345
Penn, John, Exec. V.P.--Western Development Corporation, Washington, DC, pg. 1179
Penny, Dick, Chm. & Chief Exec. Officer--Penny & Speier Inc., Houston, TX, pg. 858
Perlis, Barry, Exec. V.P.--S. Freedman & Sons, Inc., Landover, MD, pg. 430
Perlman, Alan, Exec. V.P.--E. W. Howell Company, Inc., Port Washington, NY, pg. 547
Perlow, Irwin, Exec. V.P.--Baar & Beards, New York, NY, pg. 107
Perry, Steve, Exec. V.P. & G.M.--The Sanymetal Products Co., Inc., Vanceburg, KY, pg. 970
Pestillo, Peter J., Exec. V.P.--Park Ridge Corporation, Park Ridge, NJ, pg. 849
Peter, Hugh M., Sr., Exec. V.P.--Peter Lumber Company, Pleasantville, NJ, pg. 864
Peters, David, Exec. V.P.--Lockard Construction, Inc., Waterloo, IA, pg. 680
Peters, David, Exec. V.P.--Sellstrom Manufacturing Co., Palatine, IL, pg. 988
Petit, Charles E., Exec. V.P., Chief Fin. Officer & Treas.--Fitzgerald & Company, Inc., Cranston, RI, pg. 416
Petricca, Perric C., Exec. V.P.--Petricca Industries, Inc., Pittsfield, MA, pg. 865
Pettus, Theodore, Exec. V.P., Creative Dir.--McCaffrey and McCall, New York, NY, pg. 726
Pettus, Theodore D., Exec. V.P.--Lockhart & Pettus, Inc., New York, NY, pg. 680
Petty, J. William, Exec. V.P.--Curtice-Burns Foods, Inc., Rochester, NY, pg. 25
Pew, Robert III, Exec. V.P.-S/C Opers.--Steelcase Inc., Grand Rapids, MI, pg. 1044
Pfeffer, Philip Maurice, Exec. V.P.--Ingram Industries Inc., Nashville, TN, pg. 568
Pfersich, Gordon J., Exec. V.P.--Atlantic Gulf Communities Corporation, Miami, FL, pg. 95
Phelon, Phillip, Exec. V.P.--Telex Communications, Inc., Minneapolis, MN, pg. 1085
Philips, Dorothy, Dr., Exec. V.P., Health Care Div.--Gianettino & Meredith Advertising, Short Hills, NJ, pg. 455
Pierce, James, Exec. V.P.--Cyborg Systems, Inc., Chicago, IL, pg. 307
Pierce, Roger L., Exec. V.P.--Visa U.S.A. Inc., San Mateo, CA, pg. 1153
Pierce, Thomas, Exec. V.P.--Vienna Sausage Mfg. Co., Chicago, IL, pg. 1151
Pierson, J. David, Exec. V.P.--Cole Vision Corporation, Cleveland, OH, pg. 260
Pifer, Kevin, Exec. V.P.--Nodak Mutual Insurance Co., Fargo, ND, pg. 808
Pifer, Kevin D., Exec. V.P. & Chief Exec. Officer--Nodak Mutual Insurance Company, Fargo, ND, pg. 808
Pines, Wayne, Exec. V.P., Dir. Medical Issues (Washington)--Burson-Marsteller, New York, NY, pg. 1210
Pinnick, Larry V., Exec. V.P.--Spangler, Inc., Kansas City, KS, pg. 1025
Pinsky, Jerry, Exec. V.P.--Bestform Foundations, Inc., Long Island City, NY, pg. 147
Pitts, Tim, Exec. V.P.--Oppenheimer Management Corp., New York, NY, pg. 719
Piza, Stanley J., Exec. V.P.--Alloy Products Corporation, Waukesha, WI, pg. 41
Plamondon, Mark, Exec. V.P.--The Weightman Group, Philadelphia, PA, pg. 1173
Plamondon, Mark, Exec. V.P.--Weightman Advertising, Inc., Philadelphia, PA, pg. 1173
Plamondon, William, Exec. V.P. & Chief Oper. Officer--Beech Holdings Corp., Chicago, IL, pg. 131
Plangere, Jules, III, Exec. V.P.--New Jersey Press, Inc., Neptune, NJ, pg. 801
Platt, Richard, Exec. V.P.-Mktg. Div.--First Federal of Michigan, Detroit, MI, pg. 414
Pleasant, Richard, Exec. V.P.--Industrial Electronic Engineers, Inc., Van Nuys, CA, pg. 566
Plozaj, Lee, Exec V.P.-Construction--Gosnell Builders, Phoenix, AZ, pg. 472
Poe, Cynthia, Exec. V.P.--Advertiming Inc., Arlington, MA, pg. 1154
Pohlmann, Edwin G, Exec. V.P.-Stores & Fin.--Montgomery Ward & Co., Inc., Chicago, IL, pg. 767
Poiter, Mary Sue, Exec. V.P.--Bankers Systems Inc., Saint Cloud, MN, pg. 117
Polack, James, Exec. V.P.--Acme Poultry Company, Inc., Seattle, WA, pg. 13
Pollak, Lewis B., Sr., Exec. V.P.--The Lewis Bear Company, Pensacola, FL, pg. 129
Pollio, Lynnda, Exec. V.P., Corp. Devel.--McCaffrey and McCall, New York, NY, pg. 726
Pollock, Duncan, Exec. V.P.--Ammirati & Puris Inc., New York, NY, pg. 67
Pollok, John H., Exec. V.P.--Warren/Kremer/CMP/Advertising/Inc., New York, NY, pg. 1165
Pond, Donald H., Exec. V.P.-Individual Insurance--Connecticut Mutual Life Insurance Company, Hartford, CT, pg. 274
Poortvliet, William G., Exec. V.P.-International Operations--Metropolitan Life Insurance Co., New York, NY, pg. 744
Porco, Frank, Exec. V.P.--Shoreline Products, Inc., Arlington, TX, pg. 1000
Portnoy, Simon, Exec. V.P.--Capital Bancorp, Miami, FL, pg. 214
Posner, Fred I., Exec. V.P., Research & Mktg. Dir.--N W Ayer Incorporated, New York, NY, pg. 103
Postal, Elaine, Exec. V.P.--Judy Bond, Inc., New York, NY, pg. 608
Poure, Timothy, Exec. V.P.--General Alum & Chemical, Holland, OH, pg. 448
Powell, Robert L., Exec. V.P.--Custom Control Sensors, Inc., Chatsworth, CA, pg. 306
Prewitt, Robert F., Exec. V.P.--Dana Communications, Inc., Hopewell, NJ, pg. 313
Price, Donald H., Exec. V.P.--Wawa, Inc., Wawa, PA, pg. 1169
Price, W. Ralph, Exec. V.P.--Doron Precision Systems, Inc., Binghamton, NY, pg. 346
Prokopis, E.C. Mick, Exec. V.P.--Ziff Communications Company, New York, NY, pg. 1218
Pulk, Mike, Exec. V.P.--Winona Knits, Winona, MN, pg. 1196
Puls, Charles H., Exec. V.P.--Zylke & Associates, Northbrook, IL, pg. 1221
Pundyk, Bernard, Exec. V.P.--Glamorise Foundations, Inc., New York, NY, pg. 460
Purcell, Robert, Chief Oper. Officer & Chief Fin. Officer--ERA Real Estate, Overland Park, KS, pg. 360
Purvis, Ed, Exec. V.P.--Benjamin Metals Company, Gardena, CA, pg. 139
Putterman, Lawrence, Exec. V.P.--Milton Shoe Manufacturing Company, Inc., Milton, PA, pg. 756
Pyatt, Donald, Exec. V.P.--Quadion Corporation, Minneapolis, MN, pg. 902
Quaid, M.C., Exec. V.P.--Benjamin Moore & Co., Montvale, NJ, pg. 139
Quinn, J.M., Exec. V.P.--Spencer Industries, Inc., New Brunswick, NJ, pg. 1030
Quinn, James, Exec. V.P.--Casual Sportswear Co., Inc., Dunmore, PA, pg. 1030
Rabil, Richard J., Chief Exec. Officer & Exec. V.P.--The Van Metre Companies, Burke, VA, pg. 1144
Rabin, Ed, Exec. V.P.--Hyatt Hotels Corporation, Chicago, IL, pg. 495
Radigan, Bob, Sr. Exec. V.P.--Plasti-Kote Company Inc., Medina, OH, pg. 875
Raffel, William D., Exec. V.P., Treas.--Smith, Badofsky & Raffel, Inc. Advertising, Chicago, IL, pg. 1011
Rahmann, John, Exec. V.P.--WTTW (Channel 11), Chicago, IL, pg. 1156
Ramseth, Paul R., Exec. V.P.-Member Services--Lutheran Brotherhood, Minneapolis, MN, pg. 688
Ramsey, Craig R., Exec. V.P.--Frank Paxton Company, Kansas City, MO, pg. 592
Ramsey, James H., Exec. V.P.--Diamond Hill Plywood Company, Darlington, SC, pg. 316
Ramseyer, Bryon J., Exec. V.P.--Gamma One, Inc., North Haven, CT, pg. 442
Randall, Roger D., Sr. V.P. & Publr.--Farm Journal, Inc., Philadelphia, PA, pg. 401
Raniszeski, Edward L., Exec. V.P.-Sls. & Mktg.--AmTran Corporation, Conway, AR, pg. 69
Rankin, Jr. Harley, Exec. V.P. & Chief Fin. Officer--Silgan Corporation, Stamford, CT, pg. 1004
Rappaport, Stanley, Exec. V.P.--House of Ronnie, Inc., New York, NY, pg. 546
Rappaport, Steven N., Exec. V.P.--Metallurg, Inc., New York, NY, pg. 742
Rau, R. E., Jr., Exec. V.P.--Edwin B. Stimpson Company, Inc., Bayport, NY, pg. 1049
Raubacher, Charles V., Exec. V.P.--Heery International, Inc., Atlanta, GA, pg. 525
Rauch, Donald, Exec. V.P.--M & C Specialties Company, Southampton, PA, pg. 690
Ray, William D., Jr., Exec. V.P.--Baird Ray Nissan, Inc., Longwood, FL, pg. 114
Ready, James, Exec. V.P.--Ready Systems, Sunnyvale, CA, pg. 916
Redmon, Samuel C., Exec. V.P.--W. C. Redmon Co., Peru, IN, pg. 919
Reichow, Jim, Exec. V.P.--J & R Film Company, Los Angeles, CA, pg. 586
Reid, Michael, Exec. V.P., Creative Services (DTC)--Lewis & Gace, Inc., Fort Lee, NJ, pg. 673
Reilly, Butch, Exec. V.P.--CB North America, Inc., Glens Falls, NY, pg. 199
Reilly, Sharon S., Exec. V.P.--F/S Reilly, Media +, San Francisco, CA, pg. 923
Reilly, Thomas, Exec. V.P.--Support Systems Associates, Inc., Hauppauge, NY, pg. 1064
Reimers, Larry, Exec. V.P.--The Segerdahl Corp., Wheeling, IL, pg. 987
Reimnitz, Jurgen, Exec. V.P.--Park Ridge Corporation, Park Ridge, NJ, pg. 849
Rein, Catherine A., Exec. V.P.-Corp. Services--Metropolitan Life Insurance Co., New York, NY, pg. 744
Rein, Irwin "Skip", Exec. V.P.--Bernstein-Rein Advertising, Inc., Kansas City, MO, pg. 144
Reinfrank, Rudy, Exec. V.P., Capital Resources Group--Shamrock Holdings, Inc., Burbank, CA, pg. 994
Reis, R.J., Exec. V.P.--Serigraph, Inc., West Bend, WI, pg. 991
Reitman, Jerry, Exec. V.P. & Dir.-Integrated Communications--Leo Burnett Company, Inc., Chicago, IL, pg. 191
Reller, Charles E., Exec. V.P., Chief Oper. Officer--Hutchins/Young & Rubicam, Rochester, NY, pg. 1211
Reny, Timothy G., Exec. V.P.--Standard Duplicating Machines Corp., Andover, MA, pg. 1036
Reynolds, Richard D., Exec. V.P.--G.B. DuPont Co., Inc., Troy, MI, pg. 354
Reynolds, Robert, Exec. V.P.--Newsprint South Sales Corp., Dallas, TX, pg. 760
Ricca, Gregory, Exec. V.P. & Gen. Counsel--MTV Networks, New York, NY, pg. 785
Ricca, Gregory J., Exec. V.P.-Bus. Affairs & Networks Grps.--Viacom Inc., New York, NY, pg. 785
Ricca, Gregory J., Exec. V.P.-Business Affairs--Viacom Networks Inc., New York, NY, pg. 785
Ricca, Gregory J., Exec. V.P.-Bus. Affairs--Viacom International Inc., New York, NY, pg. 785
Rice, Glen E., Exec. V.P.--Blue Grass Foods, Inc., Crescent Springs, KY, pg. 160
Rice, James R., Exec. V.P.--United Mailing, Inc., Chanhassen, MN, pg. 571
Rice, Jamie, Exec. V.P.--Richardson, Myers & Donofrio, Inc., Baltimore, MD, pg. 933
Rice, Sam, Exec. V.P. & Chief Oper. Officer--T. J. Cinnamons Ltd., Kansas City, MO, pg. 1073
Rich, Lawrence, Exec. V.P.--JM Family Enterprises Inc., Deerfield Beach, FL, pg. 584
Richard, Ralph S., Exec. V.P.--Johnston, Lemon & Co. Inc., Washington, DC, pg. 601
Richards, Clarence A., Exec. V.P.--McCrory Construction Co., Inc., Columbia, SC, pg. 728
Richards, G. Robert, Exec. V.P.-Fin. & Admin.--General Automotive Corporation, Ann Arbor, MI, pg. 448
Richards, Penny, Chief Oper. Officer & Exec. V.P.--Joan Fabrics Corp., Tyngsboro, MA, pg. 594
Richards, Stanley, Exec. V.P. & Gen. Counsel--General Growth Companies, Inc., Des Moines, IA, pg. 449
Richardson, Mark, Exec. V.P., Dir. of Client Services--Houston Effler & Partners, Boston, MA, pg. 546
Richman, Bruce, Exec. V.P.--S.D. Richman Sons, Inc., Philadelphia, PA, pg. 933
Richmond James A., Exec. V.P.--Mortgate Loans--Globe Mortgage Company, Hackensack, NJ, pg. 464
Richmond, Bruce, Exec. V.P., Grp. Dir.--Sudler & Hennessey, New York, NY, pg. 1211

Riddle, Stephen, Exec. V.P.--Asbury Carbons, Inc., Asbury, NJ, pg. 87
Riegel, Larry, Exec. V.P., Grp. Acct. Dir.--Avrett, Free & Ginsberg, Inc., New York, NY, pg. 103
Rifkin, Daniel M., Exec. V.P.--Omni Source Corporation, Fort Wayne, IN, pg. 826
Riggio, Stephen, Exec. V.P. & Chief Oper. Officer--B. Dalton Bookseller, Inc., New York, NY, pg. 120
Rigoni, Robert J., Exec. V.P.--Bacco Construction Co., Iron Mountain, MI, pg. 108
Riley, Jeremiah A., Exec. V.P. & Chief Fin. Officer--Horizon Media, Inc., New York, NY, pg. 544
Riley, Richard, Exec. V.P.--Sawyer Riley Compton Inc., Atlanta, GA, pg. 973
Riley, Robert E., Exec. V.P.-Prudential Investment Corp. & Chm.-Prud. Realty Grp.--The Prudential Insurance Company of America, Newark, NJ, pg. 896
Ripich, John R., Exec. V.P.--American Tank & Fabricating Co., Cleveland, OH, pg. 63
Risdall, William, Exec V.P.--Smith System Manufacturing Company, Shoreview, MN, pg. 1014
Rizner, Michael J., Exec. V.P.--Southeastern Equipment Company, Inc., Augusta, GA, pg. 1019
Roach, John B., Jr., Exec. V.P. & Metroplex Region Retail Mgr.--Team Bancshares, Inc., Dallas, TX, pg. 1082
Robbins, Gerald H., Exec. V.P.--Lappin Electric Company, Milwaukee, WI, pg. 658
Roberts, Gary, Pres., Chief Oper. Officer--Greenstone Roberts Advertising, Melville, NY, pg. 485
Roberts, James E., Exec. V.P. & Chief Oper. Officer--Avedis Zildjian Company, Norwell, MA, pg. 1219
Robinson, Carol, Exec. V.P.--Presto Food Stores, Inc., Plant City, FL, pg. 888
Robinson, Donald A., Exec. V.P.--Fairbanks Morse Pump Corporaton, Kansas City, KS, pg. 397
Robinson, Robert J., Exec. V.P. & Chief Oper. Officer--AXIA Incorporated, Oak Brook, IL, pg. 8
Robinson, Timothy R., Exec. V.P.--Asahi/America, Inc., Malden, MA, pg. 87
Rocheleau, Ron, Exec. V.P.--Helm, Inc., Highland Park, MI, pg. 527
Rodman, Dale, Exec. V.P.--Excel Corp., Wichita, KS, pg. 219
Rodriguez, Mike, Exec. V.P., Dir. Acct. Services--EvansGroup, Salt Lake City, UT, pg. 391
Rogers, John M., Exec. V.P.--Douglas Steel Fabricating Corporation, Lansing, MI, pg. 347
Rogers, Ronni, Exec. V.P.-Florida--Rogers & Associates Advertising, Inc., Santa Clara, CA, pg. 943
Rogers, Terry D., Exec. V.P.--Capital Electric Group, Inc., Phoenix, AZ, pg. 215
Roggeman, Daniel J., Exec. V.P.--American Finance Group, Boston, MA, pg. 52
Rogich, Ed, Exec. V.P.--R & R Advertising, Las Vegas, NV, pg. 906
Rokop, Judith, Exec. V.P.-Pur.--Rokop Corporation, Bridgeville, PA, pg. 944
Roland, Michael D., Exec. V.P.--Metal Trades, Inc., Hollywood, SC, pg. 741
Rolla, Peter M., Exec. V.P.--American Specialties Inc., Yonkers, NY, pg. 61
Romanok, David, Exec. V.P.--L&R Manufacturing Co., Kearny, NJ, pg. 647
Ronco, Al, Chief Oper. Officer, Exec. V.P., & Sec.--Keystone Automotive Industries, Inc., Pomona, CA, pg. 627
Rooney, Steve, Exec. V.P.--Hoyt Corporation, Westport, MA, pg. 548
Root, Brad I., Exec. V.P.--A.I. Root Company, Medina, OH, pg. 946
Roper, John L., IV, Exec. V.P.-Opers. & Sec.--Norfolk Shipbuilding & Drydock Corporation, Norfolk, VA, pg. 810
Roppel, Frank, Exec. V.P.--Alaska Pulp Corporation, Seattle, WA, pg. 30
Rose, Marshall, Exec. Officer--Gould Investors, L.P., Great Neck, NY, pg. 473
Rosen, Arthur, Exec. V.P.--Pace Collection, Inc., Long Island City, NY, pg. 838
Rosen, Arthur M., Exec. V.P., Dir.--Sudler & Hennessey Consumer Group, New York, NY, pg. 1211
Rosen, Marcella, Exec. V.P., Mng. Dir. Media Services--N W Ayer Incorporated, New York, NY, pg. 103
Rosenbaum, Robert, Exec. V.P.--Bruckner Machine & Tool Corp., Port Washington, NY, pg. 183
Rosenberg, Benjamin, Esq., Exec. V.P., Gen. Counsel & Asst. Sec.--United Community Insurance Co., Albany, NY, pg. 662
Rosenberg, Bert, Exec. V.P.--Smith/Greenland, Incorporated, New York, NY, pg. 1012
Rosenberg, James, Exec. V.P. & Dir.-Mktg.--Berenson, Isham & Partners, Inc., Boston, MA, pg. 141
Rosenberg, Ronald E., Exec. V.P.--The Associated Group, Indianapolis, IN, pg. 90
Rosenfield, Sheryl, Exec. V.P.--Tasco, Miami, FL, pg. 1079
Rosenthal, Bruce, Exec. V.P.--Freedland Industries Corporation, Dearborn, MI, pg. 430
Ross, Alex, Exec. V.P.-Creative Services--Jordan, McGrath, Case & Taylor Inc., New York, NY, pg. 604
Ross, Anthony J., Exec. V.P.--The Cafaro Co., Youngstown, OH, pg. 207
Ross, Barry, Exec. V.P.--G. R. Herberger's, Inc., Saint Cloud, MN, pg. 530
Ross, H.G., Exec. V.P.--Gas Equipment Company, Inc., Dallas, TX, pg. 444
Ross, H.G., Exec. V.P.--Rochester Gauges Inc. Of Texas, Dallas, TX, pg. 444
Roth, Richard, Exec. V.P.-Sls. & mktg.--Queens Group Indiana, Inc., Indianapolis, IN, pg. 904
Rowe, Clifford R., Exec. V.P.--Trumbull Corporation, West Mifflin, PA, pg. 1117
Rowley, John F., Exec. V.P.--Fort Howard Corporation, Green Bay, WI, pg. 425
Rubin, Howard, Exec. V.P.--Shogyo International Corporation, Great Neck, NY, pg. 1000
Rubin, Mark S., Exec. V.P.--State-Wide Capital Corp., Uniondale, NY, pg. 1041
Rubin, Samuel, Exec. V.P.--Prime Tanning Co., Inc., Berwick, ME, pg. 889
Rubman, Marvin, Exec. V.P. & Adv. Dir.--Generation Metals Corp., Hauppauge, NY, pg. 451
Rubow, Steven, Exec. V.P.--Topco Associates, Inc., Skokie, IL, pg. 1101
Rudolph, Fred, Exec. V.P. & Chief Fin. Officer--Gramex Corporation, Bridgeton, MO, pg. 475
Ruff, Gary F., Exec. V.P.--CMI International Inc., Southfield, MI, pg. 202
Ruhl, Barry L., Exec. V.P.--A. G. Spanos Development, Inc., Stockton, CA, pg. 1025
Ruhr, Charles F., Chm. Bd. & Chief Exec. Officer--Chuck Ruhr Advertising, Minneapolis, MN, pg. 955
Rupp, Richard, Exec. V.P.--Datability, Inc., Carlstadt, NJ, pg. 316
Rusgis, Warren J., Exec. V.P.--Lapham-Hickey Steel Corp., Chicago, IL, pg. 658
Russell, John B., Exec. V.P.--Kissimmee Toyota Inc., Kissimmee, FL, pg. 633
Rutman, Charles, Exec. V.P., Grp. Media Dir.--Backer Spielvogel Bates, Inc., New York, NY, pg. 108
Ryan, P.A., Jr., Exec. V.P.--The Selmer Co., Elkhart, IN, pg. 573
Ryan, Rex, Exec. V.P.--Burke Communication Industries, Inc., Chicago, IL, pg. 190
Ryan, Thomas J., Exec. V.P.--Big Cheese Pizza Corporation, Wichita, KS, pg. 464
Sachter, Alan Z., Exec. V.P.--Darling-Delaware Co., Inc., Irving, TX, pg. 315
Sacks, A. L., Exec. V.P.--Arvida, Boca Raton, FL, pg. 586
Sadler, Robert A., Exec. V.P.--Mack Printing Company, Easton, PA, pg. 697
Salt, G.A., Exec. V.P.--Haeger Potteries of Macomb, Inc., Macomb, IL, pg. 499
Salwasser, Leslie, Exec. V.P.--Salwasser Manufacturing Company, Inc., Reedley, CA, pg. 968
Salway, Roger A., Chief Oper. Officer & Exec. V.P.--Paper Calmenson & Co., Saint Paul, MN, pg. 847
Samelman, Irwin, Exec. V.P.-Mktg.--Jones Apparel Group, Inc., Bristol, PA, pg. 602
Sampson, Terry, Exec. V.P.--Dakotah, Inc., Webster, SD, pg. 312
Sanders, D., Exec. V.P.--Kangaroos, USA Inc., Chesterfield, MO, pg. 616
Sanders, John, Exec. V.P.--Young & Rubicam Inc., New York, NY, pg. 1210
Sanders, Robert, Exec. V.P.--Eastern Technologies Ltd, Amesbury, MA, pg. 364
Sanders, William J., Exec. V.P.--Trans World Shoe Import Co., Inc., Chesterfield, MO, pg. 616
Sandlin, Judith F., Exec. V.P.--Newspaper Advertising Specialists, Inc. (N.A.S.), Chicago, IL, pg. 805
Sands, Rod, Exec. V.P.--Pace Foods, Inc., San Antonio, TX, pg. 838
Sans, Jose, Exec. V.P.--Medieval Dinner & Tournament, Inc., Buena Park, CA, pg. 735
Sargent, Joseph D., Exec. V.P.-Life Insurance--The Guardian Life Insurance Company of America, New York, NY, pg. 492
Sarrasin, Robert N., Exec. V.P.--Brimms Inc., Tonawanda, NY, pg. 176
Sartini, Alex L., Exec. V.P.--American Tara Corporation, Atlanta, GA, pg. 63
Saterbo, Stephen, Sr. V.P.-Sls. & Mktg.--Colorado Boxed Beef Co., Auburndale, FL, pg. 265
Sauls, Ronald K., Exec. V.P.--Printing House, Inc., Quincy, FL, pg. 891
Savage, Mary, Exec. V.P.--Clearpoint Research Corporation, Hopkinton, MA, pg. 254
Sawicz, Thomas T., Sr. Exec. V.P. & Dir.-Supplemental Distr.--Mutual of Omaha Insurance Company, Omaha, NE, pg. 779
Sawicz, Thomas T., Sr. Exec. V.P. & Dir.-Supplemental Distr.--Mutual of Omaha, Omaha, NE, pg. 779
Sawyer, Andrew T. Jr., Exec. V.P.--Park Bank, Milwaukee, WI, pg. 118
Sawyer, Louis, Exec. V.P.--Sawyer Riley Compton Inc., Atlanta, GA, pg. 973
Sawyer, Richard, Exec. V.P.--Earle Palmer Brown/New York, New York, NY, pg. 182
Scheinman, Tom, Exec. V.P.--Shepaug Corporation, New York, NY, pg. 997
Schenker, Leo, Sr. Exec. V.P.--Central National-Gottesman Inc., Purchase, NY, pg. 233
Schmid, Charles W., Exec. V.P.--Carlson Companies, Inc., Minneapolis, MN, pg. 220
Schneider, Perry, Exec. V.P.--Noel-Joanna, Inc., Rancho Santa Margarita, CA, pg. 808
Schneider, Thomas J., Exec. V.P.--Goodman Equipment Corp., Bedford Park, IL, pg. 470
Schoenecker, Larry, Sr. V.P.--Guy Schoenecker, Inc., Minneapolis, MN, pg. 977
Schoenfeld, Jay B., Exec. V.P., Media Dir.--Backer Spielvogel Bates, Inc., New York, NY, pg. 108
Schomer, William P., Exec. V.P.--Allied Chucker & Engineering Company, Jackson, MI, pg. 37
Schorr, Phillip A., Exec. V.P.-Individual--General American Life Insurance Co., St. Louis, MO, pg. 448
Schott, Roz, Exec. V.P.--Schott Brothers, Inc., Perth Amboy, NJ, pg. 978
Schreiber, John G., Exec. V.P.--JMB Realty Corporation, Chicago, IL, pg. 584
Schroeder, David L., Exec. V.P.--Atlas Refinery, Newark, NJ, pg. 96
Schroeder, James, Exec. V.P.--MSC Industrial Supply Co., Plainview, NY, pg. 693
Schroeder, Robert, Exec. V.P.--Argo-Tech Corporation, Cleveland, OH, pg. 82
Schuette, Tim, Exec. V.P.--Invincible Metal Furniture Co., Manitowoc, WI, pg. 582
Schull, Lester, Exec. V.P.--Building Products Inc., Watertown, SD, pg. 188
Schultz, James, Exec. V.P.--The Trane Company, La Crosse, WI, pg. 62
Schultz, Randy, Exec. V.P. & Chief Oper. Officer--IGI Resources, Inc., Boise, ID, pg. 575
Schur, Jeff, Exec. V.P.--Earle Palmer Brown/Bethesda, Bethesda, MD, pg. 182
Schutz, John, Exec. V.P.--Strombecker Corporation, Chicago, IL, pg. 1054
Schwab, Leonard C., Exec. V.P.--S. Schwab Company, Cumberland, MD, pg. 980
Schwartz, Larry, Exec. V.P.--Jack Schwartz Shoes, Inc., New York, NY, pg. 980
Schwartz, Stanley, Exec. V.P.--Rosco Laboratories, Inc., Port Chester, NY, pg. 947
Schwartzbard, Marvin, Exec. V.P.--J. I. Kislak Inc., Miami Lakes, FL, pg. 633
Schwarz, Carl, Exec. V.P. & Chief Exec. Officer--Kentile Floors Inc., South Plainfield, NJ, pg. 623
Schwarz, Robert, Exec. V.P.--Peter Pan Bus Lines, Inc., Springfield, MA, pg. 864
Scott, Odell A., Exec. V.P.--The Marketing Continuum, Inc., Dallas, TX, pg. 709
Scott, Walter, Jr., Exec. V.P.--Scott Printing Corporation, Jersey City, NJ, pg. 983
Scrivani, Francine, Exec. V.P.--Futter Lumber Corporation, Rockville Centre, NY, pg. 437
Sear, Peter W., Exec. V.P.--First Federal Savings and Loan Assn. of Rochester, Rochester, NY, pg. 413
Searcy, Phillip, Sr. Exec. V.P.-Tech. & Engrng.--Post Buckley Schuh & Jernigan, Miami, FL, pg. 881
Sears, Donald K., Exec. V.P.-Opers. & Sls.--Mayflower Transit, Inc., Carmel, IN, pg. 724
Seawright, Charles, Exec. V.P.--Flexible Flyer Inc., West Point, MS, pg. 847
Sellers, Allen, Exec. V.P.--Pacific Holding Corporation, Los Angeles, CA, pg. 840
Semel, Robert K., Exec. V.P.--Uniflex, Inc., Hicksville, NY, pg. 1126
Senter, Alan Z., Exec. V.P.--International Specialty Products, Inc., Wilmington, DE, pg. 438
Sergey, John M., Exec. V.P.-Bldg. Matls.--GAF Corporation, Wayne, NJ, pg. 438
Serlick, Joseph, Exec. V.P.--Lillie Rubin Affiliates Inc., Miami, FL, pg. 954
Serls, Phillip, Exec. V.P.--Colonial Metals Co., Columbia, PA, pg. 263
Serrianne, Mark A., Exec. V.P.--Northlich Stolley LaWarre, Cincinnati, OH, pg. 814
Shackleford, Robert M., Exec. V.P.--Gulf Lumber Company, Inc., Mobile, AL, pg. 493
Shadek, Keith, Exec. V.P.--Lyon Metal Products, Inc., Montgomery, IL, pg. 690
Shames, Harold, Exec. V.P. & Sec.--Melard Manufacturing Corporation, Passaic, NJ, pg. 737
Shames, Harold, Exec. V.P.- Mktg. & Sls.--Melard Plastics Inc., Passaic, NJ, pg. 737
Shanahan, Martin, Exec. V.P., Chief Fin. Officer--Lewis & Gace, Inc., Fort Lee, NJ, pg. 673
Shannon, Patrick J., Exec. V.P.--Communications Diversified, New York, NY, pg. 269
Shapell, David, Exec. V.P.--Shapell Industries, Inc., Beverly Hills, CA, pg. 995
Shapiro, Harold D., Exec. V.P.--Commander Oil Corporation, Oyster Bay, NY, pg. 268
Shapiro, Joseph G., Exec. V.P.--Commander Oil Corporation, Oyster Bay, NY, pg. 268
Shapiro, Larry, Exec. V.P., Grp. Dir.--Young & Rubicam New York, New York, NY, pg. 1211
Sharff, John S., Exec. V.P. & Chief Oper. Officer--Baltimore Stationery Co., Baltimore, MD, pg. 116
Shavelson, Kenneth, Chief Fin. Officer, Exec. V.P., Dir.-Intl. Fin. & Treas.--Weksler Instruments Corp., Freeport, NY, pg. 1174
Shaver, Mary Louise, Grp. Exec. V.P.--Birdsall Voss & Kloppenburg, Inc., Mequon, WI, pg. 152
Shaw, James M., Exec. V.P.--MTV Networks, New York, NY, pg. 785
Shaw, Norman, Exec. V.P.--Collin Street Bakery, Corsicana, TX, pg. 262
Shaw, Thomas N., Exec. V.P. & Dir.-Adv. & Sls.--Monarch Avalon, Inc., Baltimore, MD, pg. 765
Shear, Larry, Exec. V.P.--M. R. Bolin Inc., Minneapolis, MN, pg. 162
Sheldon, Alan J., Exec. V.P., Gen. Mgr.--Young & Rubicam Inc., New York, NY, pg. 1210
Sher, Robert K., Exec. V.P.--Donnelley Marketing, Inc., Stamford, CT, pg. 1011
Sheridan, Patrick M., Exec. V.P. & Chief Fin. Officer--The Associated Group, Indianapolis, IN, pg. 90
Sherman, Ken, Exec. V.P.--Charles Leonard, Inc., Glendale, NY, pg. 668
Shields, Edward J., Exec. V.P.--Dudnyk Advertising, Horsham, PA, pg. 351
Shiffman, Roger, Exec. V.P.--Tiger Electronics, Inc., Vernon Hills, IL, pg. 1097
Shimko, Robert A., Exec. V.P.--Geiger Brothers, Lewiston, ME, pg. 447
Shipp, B.B., Exec. V.P. & Chief Fin. Officer--Thermalloy, Inc., Farmers Branch, TX, pg. 1091
Shirley, Marvin A., Exec. V.P.--Allbritton Communications Company, Washington, DC, pg. 862
Shoen, Harry, Exec. V.P.--Decorative Fabrics - Mastercraft, Spindale, NC, pg. 262
Sholtz, Gerald, Exec. V.P. & Chief Exec. Officer--H. Cotler Company, New York, NY, pg. 288
Shore, Harvey, Exec. V.P.--Concord Assets Group, Inc., Boca Raton, FL, pg. 272
Shoup, Don, Exec. V.P. & Sec.--Amana Society, Amana, IA, pg. 46

Shropshire, Ronald T., Exec. V.P. & Chief Credit Officer--Bank of Homewood, Homewood, IL, pg. 481
Shryock, Larry L., Exec. V.P.-Comml. Banking--Texas Commerce Bancshares, Inc., Houston, TX, pg. 1089
Shultz, Stephen, Exec. V.P.--Schultz Steel Company, South Gate, CA, pg. 979
Shur, Walter, Exec. V.P.--New York Life Insurance Company, New York, NY, pg. 802
Sia, David, Exec. V.P. & Reg. Dir.-South & East Asia--Dentsu, Young & Rubicam/Bangkok, Bangkok, Thailand, pg. 330
Sibbel, Mick, Exec. V.P., Chief Oper. Officer--Swanson Russell Associates, Lincoln, NE, pg. 1066
Sibley, Gerry, Exec. V.P.--Eclipse, Inc., Rockford, IL, pg. 366
Sibley, Harold O., Exec. V.P.--The WBDC Group, Grand Rapids, MI, pg. 1155
Siegal, Frederick R., Exec. V.P., Exec. Creative Dir.--Ketchum Advertising/Philadelphia, Philadelphia, PA, pg. 625
Siemer, Paul J., Exec. V.P.--Fleishman Hillard Inc., Saint Louis, MO, pg. 417
Sifton, Elizabeth, Exec. V.P.--Alfred A. Knopf, Inc., New York, NY, pg. 20
Silberberg, Robert, Exec. V.P., Dir. Natl. Brdcst. & Programming--Backer Spielvogel Bates, Inc., New York, NY, pg. 108
Silver, A. Richard, Exec. V.P.--Chernoff/Silver & Associates, Columbia, SC, pg. 243
Silver, Martin, Exec. V.P.--National Foods Inc., Bronx, NY, pg. 788
Silver, Stan, Chief Oper. Officer & Exec. V.P.--The Children's Place Retail Stores, Inc., Pine Brook, NJ, pg. 247
Silverman, Rick, Exec. Dir.--The Milford Agency, New York, NY, pg. 753
Silverman, S.W., Exec. V.P. & Chief Oper. Officer--PQ Corporation, Valley Forge, PA, pg. 836
Simmers, John, Exec. V.P.--Financial Network Investment, Torrance, CA, pg. 410
Simon, Alan, Exec. V.P.--Allied Sporting Goods Inc., Louisville, KY, pg. 40
Simon, George A., Exec. V.P.--U.S. Manufacturing Corp., Roseville, MI, pg. 1136
Simon, Laurence P., Sr. V.P.--Health Management Systems, Inc., New York, NY, pg. 521
Simon, Loretta L., Exec. V.P.--Nason and Cullen, Inc., Wayne, PA, pg. 784
Simon, Paul S., Exec. V.P.--Shivers Trading & Operating Co., Augusta, GA, pg. 999
Simonton, Greer, Exec. V.P.-Mktg.--Archer/Malmo Adv., Inc., Memphis, TN, pg. 80
Sine, Philip, Exec. V.P.--Ziff Communications Company, New York, NY, pg. 1218
Singer, Jane, Dir., Mktg. & Strategic Plng.--Calet, Hirsch & Ferrell, Inc., New York, NY, pg. 949
Singer, Stephen H., Exec. V.P.--Merchants Rent A Car, Inc., Hooksett, NH, pg. 739
Sitver, Leonard A., Exec. V.P.--Dexter Chemical Corp., Bronx, NY, pg. 334
Slay, Ken, Exec. V.P.--Georgia Crown Distributing, Columbus, GA, pg. 453
Sleeper, Gordon C. III, Exec. V.P.--Grace & Rothschild, New York, NY, pg. 474
Sloan, Adam, Exec. V.P.--Hult Fritz Matuszak & Associates, Inc., Peoria, IL, pg. 552
Sloan, C. Hamilton, Exec. V.P.--General Parts, Inc., Raleigh, NC, pg. 224
Slott, Michael P., Exec. V.P.--Columbian Advertising Inc., Chicago, IL, pg. 266
Slotten, Nancy, Exec. V.P. & Treas.--Border States Paving, Inc., Fargo, ND, pg. 165
Small-Weil, Susan, Exec. V.P., Chief Plng. Officer--Warwick Baker & Fiore Inc., New York, NY, pg. 1165
Smelas, William A., Exec. V.P.--Horsehead Resource Development Company, Inc., Palmerton, PA, pg. 545
Smiley, Larry, Exec. V.P.--Reliable Castings Corporation, Cincinnati, OH, pg. 924
Smith, Allen J., Exec. V.P.--Oriel Corporation, Stratford, CT, pg. 829
Smith, B.E., Exec. V.P.--Auto-Owners Insurance, Lansing, MI, pg. 100
Smith, Calvin C., Exec. V.P.--David A. Bramble, Inc., Chestertown, MD, pg. 171
Smith, Carolyn, Exec. V.P., Acct. Dir.--Arnold Fortuna Lawner & Cabot, Boston, MA, pg. 84
Smith, Christopher, Exec. V.P.--H.J. Baker & Bro., Inc., New York, NY, pg. 114
Smith, David, Exec. V.P.--H.J. Baker & Bro., Inc., New York, NY, pg. 114
Smith, Dick, Exec. V.P.--Taylor-Smith Group, Houston, TX, pg. 1082
Smith, Elliott L., Exec. V.P.--General Binding Corporation, Northbrook, IL, pg. 656
Smith, Frank K., Exec. V.P.--McInnes Steel Company, Corry, PA, pg. 729
Smith, Gregory W., Exec. V.P., Chief Oper. Officer--Jay Incorporated, Rochester, NY, pg. 590
Smith, Jerry, Exec. V.P.--84 Lumber Co., Eighty Four, PA, pg. 371
Smith, John O., Exec. V.P.-Debit Card Services--Mastercard International, Inc., New York, NY, pg. 720
Smith, Lawrence, Exec. V.P.-Opers.--The Enro Shirt Company, Inc., Louisville, KY, pg. 78
Smith, Leslie, Exec. V.P.--Ruthman Pump & Engineering Co., Cincinnati, OH, pg. 957
Smith, R.C., Exec. V.P.--The Rotor Tool Company, Cleveland, OH, pg. 951
Smith, Richard F., Exec. V.P.--The Climatic Corp., Columbia, SC, pg. 255
Smith, Robert A., Exec. V.P.--Smith & Sons Foods, Inc., Macon, GA, pg. 1014
Smith, Steven J., Exec. V.P.--Journal Communications Inc., Milwaukee, WI, pg. 607
Snell, Christopher J., Exec. V.P.--Gerbig, Snell/Weisheimer & Assoc., Inc., Worthington, OH, pg. 454
Snell, Mark A., Exec. V.P.--World Oil Company, South Gate, CA, pg. 1203
Snider, Ronald, Exec. V.P.--Slane Hosiery Mills, Inc., High Point, NC, pg. 1010
Snoddon, Larry, Exec. V.P., Pres. & Chief Exec. Officer-Burson Marsteller--Young & Rubicam Inc., New York, NY, pg. 1210
Snyder, Gerald C., Exec. V.P.--G. E. Johnson Construction Co., Inc., Colorado Springs, CO, pg. 597
Snyder, Richard, Exec. V.P. & Sec.--Gateway 2000, Sioux City, SD, pg. 446
Snyder, Steven R., Exec. V.P.--Donnelley Marketing, Inc., Stamford, CT, pg. 1011
Soichet, Francis, Exec. V.P.--Jacques Jugeat, Inc., New York, NY, pg. 608
Solheim, Louise, Exec. V.P.--Karsten Manufacturing Corporation, Phoenix, AZ, pg. 617
Sollers, Joseph S., Exec. V.P. & Pres. Unifoam Div.--Wm. T. Burnett & Co., Inc., Baltimore, MD, pg. 191
Sommers, Bettina, Exec. V.P.--Allied Printing Services, Inc., Manchester, CT, pg. 38
Sommers, Gerald, Exec. V.P.--Allied Printing Services, Inc., Manchester, CT, pg. 38
Son, Daniel P., Dir.--First Southwest Company, Dallas, TX, pg. 413
Songy, Gerald E., Exec. V.P.--The Maurin-Odgen Companies, New Orleans, LA, pg. 722
Sonnenberg, Ronnie, Exec. V.P.--Ziff-Davis Publishing Company, New York, NY, pg. 1219
Sossin, Syd, Exec. V.P.--Universal Molding Company, Lynwood, CA, pg. 1139
Soulia, Joseph, Pres.--Infotec Development, Inc., Santa Ana, CA, pg. 567
Southern, William S., Jr., Exec. V.P.--Krause Plow Corp., Hutchinson, KS, pg. 644
Southwell, Leonard, Chief Exec. Officer--Prairie Farms Dairy, Inc., Carlinville, IL, pg. 884
Sowa, Jeanne M., Exec. V.P.--Beef Industry Council, Chicago, IL, pg. 792
Spaner, Mark, Exec. V.P.--Whitemyer Advertising, Inc., Zoar, OH, pg. 1186
Spanos, Michael A., Exec. V.P.--A. G. Spanos Development, Inc., Stockton, CA, pg. 1025
Spaulding, Richard M., Exec. V.P.-Scholastic, Inc.--Scholastic Inc., New York, NY, pg. 962
Specht, Ilon, Exec. V.P. & Dir.-Creative--Jordan, McGrath, Case & Taylor Inc., New York, NY, pg. 604
Speelman, Irving, Exec. V.P.--Propper Manufacturing Co., Inc., Long Island City, NY, pg. 895
Spencer, Rodney, Exec. V.P.--Leonard & Harral Packing Co., San Antonio, TX, pg. 667
Stahl, Bob, Exec. V.P.--Dealers Electrical Supply Co., Waco, TX, pg. 322
Stai, Harlan C., Exec. V.P.--Owen Health Care, Houston, TX, pg. 833
Stallard, Larry, Exec. V.P.--Feed Service Corp., Crete, NE, pg. 405
Stambaugh, Joe, Exec. V.P.--Henry Russell Bruce, Inc., Cedar Rapids, IA, pg. 530
Stanford, Arlyn, Exec. V.P.--Anderson Lithograph Company, Los Angeles, CA, pg. 73
Stansoucy, R.J., Exec. V.P.--The Presmet Corp., Worcester, MA, pg. 887
Stark, Daniel J., Exec. V.P.--Kinney System, Inc., New York, NY, pg. 632
Stark, Robert L., Exec. V.P. & Pres.-Personnal Communications Grp.--Hallmark Cards, Inc., Kansas City, MO, pg. 501
Steele, Coleman, Exec. V.P., Media Dir.--TBWA Kerlick Switzer, Saint Louis, MO, pg. 1071
Steele, Jeffrey D., Exec. V.P.--Bucilla Corporation, Hazleton, PA, pg. 185
Stefan, William, Exec. V.P.--Key Handling Systems, Inc., Hackensack, NJ, pg. 627
Steffensen, Donald D., Exec. V.P.--The Lusk Company, Irvine, CA, pg. 687
Stein-Townsend, Karen, Sr. V.P.--Johnson & Higgins, New York, NY, pg. 598
Stein, Robert L., Exec. V.P.--Regency Group Inc., Jacksonville, FL, pg. 922
Steinhart, Donald L., Exec. V.P.--Snavely Forest Products, Inc., Pittsburgh, PA, pg. 1015
Steinhauer, Chuck, Exec. V.P.--Madison Dairy Produce Company, Madison, WI, pg. 699
Steinhoff, Christopher B., Exec. V.P.--Fairbanks Morse Pump Corporaton, Kansas City, KS, pg. 397
Steinwandel, Charles, Exec. V.P.--Ross Island Sand & Gravel Co., Inc., Portland, OR, pg. 845
Steinwandel, Charles, Exec. V.P.--K.F. Jacobson Co., Portland, OR, pg. 845
Stelling, James M., Exec. V.P., Treas. & Sec.--Ruscon Corp., Charleston, SC, pg. 956
Stemmier, Robert M., Exec. V.P. & Chief Oper. Officer--Sargent-Fletcher Co., El Monte, CA, pg. 970
Stern, Bruce M., Exec. V.P.--Stern Advertising, Inc., Pepper Pike, OH, pg. 1047
Stern, Harvey, Exec. V.P.--Cleveland Wrecking Company, Los Angeles, CA, pg. 255
Stevens, James W., Exec. V.P.--The Prudential Insurance Company of America, Newark, NJ, pg. 896
Stevens, Leroy, Exec. V.P.--Pacific Hide & Fur Depot, Great Falls, MT, pg. 840
Stewart, Joseph J., Exec. V.P. & Grp. Exec.--The Babcock & Wilcox Company, New Orleans, LA, pg. 107
Stiefel, C.W., Vice Chm., Exec. V.P., Gen. Counsel & Corp. Sec.--Stiefel Laboratories, Inc., Coral Gables, FL, pg. 1048
Stiefel, Charles W., Exec. V.P.--Stiefel Laboratories, Inc., Oak Hill, Oak Hill, NY, pg. 1048
Stimpson, Ronald, Chief Fin. Officer & Exec. V.P.--Leader Federal Bank For Savings, Memphis, TN, pg. 663
Stimpson, William Sandy, Exec. V.P.--Gulf Lumber Company, Inc., Mobile, AL, pg. 493
Stocker, James E., Exec. V.P.--Murphy Farms Inc., Rose Hill, NC, pg. 776
Stoll, Larry, Exec. V.P., Client Services--Lewis & Gace, Inc., Fort Lee, NJ, pg. 673
Stone, Alan, Exec. V.P.--Sisti, Zinbarg & Howard, Inc., Paramus, NJ, pg. 1009
Stone, Richard, Exec. V.P., Chief Oper. Officer--Lindsay, Stone & Briggs Advertising, Inc., Madison, WI, pg. 676
Stoner, Mike, Exec. V.P.--Anson-Stoner, Inc., Winter Park, FL, pg. 76
Storey, Jane, Exec. V.P.--Marketing Support, Incorporated, Chicago, IL, pg. 709
Strackbein, Ronald G., Exec. V.P.--Geneve Corporation, Stamford, CT, pg. 451
Strait, Rick E., Exec. V.P.--Netzsch, Inc., Exton, PA, pg. 798
Straub, Gerard, Exec. V.P.--Viking Yacht Co., New Gretna, NJ, pg. 1151
Straus, Peter, Exec. V.P.--Superba, Inc., Los Angeles, CA, pg. 1063
Straus, Roger W., III, Exec. V.P.--Farrar, Straus & Giroux, Inc., New York, NY, pg. 403
Strauss, Ron, Exec. V.P.--Gordon Bailey & Associates, Inc., Stone Mountain, GA, pg. 114
Strawn, James, Exec. V.P.--Summit Communications, Inc., Atlanta, GA, pg. 1057
Strom, Fred, Exec. V.P.--Empire Brushes, Inc., Greenville, NC, pg. 379
Stukane, Edward F., Exec. V.P.--Keyes Martin, Springfield, NJ, pg. 627
Stulc, Dennis, Exec. V.P.--Berkley, Inc., Spirit Lake, IA, pg. 141
Stutts, Terrell E., Exec. V.P.--Loxcreen Company, West Columbia, SC, pg. 686
Subotnick, Stuart, Exec. V.P.--Metromedia Company, East Rutherford, NJ, pg. 743
Subotnick, Stuart, Exec. V.P.--METPON, Secaucus, NJ, pg. 743
Sugrue, Charles J., Exec. V.P.--Divane Bros. Electric Co., Franklin Park, IL, pg. 340
Suhre, Richard, Exec. V.P.--Cassens Transport Company, Edwardsville, IL, pg. 228
Sullivan, Robert W., Exec. V.P.--Eastern Fine Paper, Incorporated, Brewer, ME, pg. 363
Sullivan, Thomas, Exec. V.P.--Princeton Partners, Inc., Princeton, NJ, pg. 890
Sullivan, Thomas, Exec. V.P.--Princeton Partners, Inc., Princeton, NJ, pg. 1177
Sun, Betty Lee, Exec. V.P.--Sun Computers, Inc., Carson, CA, pg. 1058
Sundblad, Harry, Exec. V.P.--Action Instruments, Inc., San Diego, CA, pg. 14
Sutter, Suzanne, Exec. V.P.--Things Remembered, Cleveland, OH, pg. 260
Swan, John, Exec. V.P., Grp. Dir.--Young & Rubicam New York, New York, NY, pg. 1211
Swanger, Ronald, Exec. V.P.--Empire Kosher Poultry, Inc., Mifflintown, PA, pg. 379
Swanzey, Robert, Exec. V.P.--Century Data Services, Inc., New York, NY, pg. 235
Swenson, Alan D., Exec. V.P.--Dart Transit Company, Inc., Eagan, MN, pg. 316
Swenson, Brent, Exec. V.P. & V.P. Sls.--Linzer Products Corp., Flushing, NY, pg. 677
Swerdloff,Peter, Exec. V.P., Adv. Dir.--Siegel & Gale, New York, NY, pg. 1002
Swinden, David, Exec. V.P.--Imperial Schrade Corp., New York, NY, pg. 564
Swinden, David A., Exec. Pres.--Imperial Schrade Corp., Ellenville, NY, pg. 564
Swink, James W., Exec. V.P. & Sec.--Young Pecan Shelling Co., Inc., Florence, SC, pg. 1209
Sylvester, Norman, Exec. V.P.--Block & Nardizzi, Stamford, CT, pg. 157
Symmons, Kevin V., Exec. V.P.--Symmons Industries Inc., Braintree, MA, pg. 1069
Symon, Jim, Exec. V.P., Assoc. Creative Dir.--Avrett, Free & Ginsberg, Inc., New York, NY, pg. 103
Tall, Craig E., Exec. V.P.--Washington Mutual Savings Bank, Seattle, WA, pg. 1166
Tallman, Wesley C., Exec. V.P.--Visa U.S.A. Inc., San Mateo, CA, pg. 1153
Tamney, Joseph P., Exec. V.P.--Boyd, Tamney & Cross Advertising/Marketing, Wayne, PA, pg. 169
Tang, Michael, Exec. V.P.--Tang Industries Inc., Elk Grove Village, IL, pg. 1078
Tankersley, Ronald S., Exec. V.P.--Carlsberg Financial Corp., Santa Monica, CA, pg. 220
Tanner, Michael S., Exec. V.P.--Tanner Co. Inc., Rutherfordton, NC, pg. 1078
Taratoot, R. Kim, Exec. V.P.--Taracorp, Inc., Atlanta, GA, pg. 1078
Tatlock, Anne M., Exec. V.P.--Fiduciary Trust Company International, New York, NY, pg. 408
Tatum, Rick, Exec. V.P.--Tatum Farms, Dawsonville, GA, pg. 1080
Tauber, David, Exec. V.P.--Tauber Oil Company, Houston, TX, pg. 1080
Tauber, Richard, Exec. V.P.--Tauber Oil Company, Houston, TX, pg. 1080
Tawil, Isaac, Exec. V.P.--Tawil Associates Inc., Carteret, NJ, pg. 1080
Taylor, Dian C., Exec. V.P.--Artesian Resources Corporation, Newark, DE, pg. 86
Taylor, Dian C., Exec. V.P.--Artesian Water Company, Inc., Newark, DE, pg. 86
Taylor, Guy D., Exec. V.P.--Southern Electric Supply Co., Inc., Meridian, MS, pg. 1020
Taylor, H. David, Exec. V.P. & Dir.-Processing Services--Team Bancshares, Inc., Dallas, TX, pg. 1082
Taylor, James, Exec. V.P.--Semblex Corporation, Elmhurst, IL, pg. 989

Temple, John M., Exec. V.P.--Memphis Group, Inc., Memphis, TN, pg. 738
Tepperman, Fred L., Sr. Exec. V.P. & Chief Fin. Officer--Andrews Group, Incorporated, New York, NY, pg. 74
Terlizzi, Donald, Exec. V.P.--Ballet Makers, Inc., Totowa, NJ, pg. 116
Terry, Lonnie R., Chief Oper. Officer & Exec. V.P.--Earle M. Jorgensen Company, Brea, CA, pg. 605
Texeira, Joseph, Exec. V.P., Chief Admin. Officer--Arnold Fortuna Lawner & Cabot, Boston, MA, pg. 84
Theofilos, John S., Exec. V.P.--Theochem Labs., Inc., Tampa, FL, pg. 1090
Thomas, Gregory, Exec. V.P. & Chief Fin. Officer--Great American Broadcasting Company, Cincinnati, OH, pg. 52
Thomopulos, Greg G., Exec. V.P.--SC Companies, Inc., Muscatine, IA, pg. 960
Thompson, Elizabeth, Exec. V.P.--The Thompson Group Companies, Henderson, KY, pg. 1094
Thompson, James, Exec. V.P.--Jackson Paper Company, Jackson, MS, pg. 587
Thompson, Jeffrey L., Exec. V.P.--Edelbrock Corp., Torrance, CA, pg. 367
Thoms, Carl, Exec. V.P.--Fortifiber Corporation, Los Angeles, CA, pg. 425
Thye, Keith H., Exec. V.P.--Associated Grocers of New England, Inc., Manchester, NH, pg. 90
Tinsley, Stephen, Exec. V.P.--CB Commercial Real Estate Group, Inc., Los Angeles, CA, pg. 222
Tischler, Florence, Exec. V.P.--Kaprielian/O'Leary, New York, NY, pg. 616
Tobin, Timothy P., Exec. V.P.--Fairfax Lumber & Millwork Company Inc., Springfield, VA, pg. 397
Todd, James S., Exec. V.P.--A.M. Todd Company, Kalamazoo, MI, pg. 1100
Toland, R.F., Exec. V.P.--Temperature Equipment Corporation, Melrose Park, IL, pg. 1086
Tollman, Brett G., Exec. V.P.--Tollman/Hundley Hotels, Valhalla, NY, pg. 1100
Toran, Daniel J., Exec. V.P.-Agency Opers. Admin.--The New England, Boston, MA, pg. 799
Torano, Raul, Exec. V.P.--Univision Holdings, Inc., New York, NY, pg. 502
Torcivia, Benedict, Jr., Exec. V.P.--Torcon, Inc., Westfield, NJ, pg. 1102
Torcivia, Joseph A., Exec. V.P.--Torcon, Inc., Westfield, NJ, pg. 1102
Torrey, Tom, Exec. V.P.--Bawden, Torrey & Associates, Davenport, IA, pg. 127
Towers, Michael D., Exec. V.P.--Washington Mutual Savings Bank, Seattle, WA, pg. 1166
Townsend, David D., Exec. V.P. & Pres. Fibers Div.--Wm. T. Burnett & Co., Inc., Baltimore, MD, pg. 191
Traynor, Michael H., Exec. V.P.--Haws Drinking Faucet Co., Berkeley, CA, pg. 518
Treharne, William H., Exec. V.P.--Broad Vogt & Conant Inc., River Rouge, MI, pg. 177
Trimble, Charles E., Exec. V.P.--Ketchum, Inc., Pittsburgh, PA, pg. 626
Tripp, Montie, Exec. V.P.--Garney Holding Company, Inc., Kansas City, MO, pg. 443
Trivento, John, Exec. V.P.--Affiliated of Florida Inc., Tampa, FL, pg. 23
Troll, Christian M., Exec. V.P.--W. Atlee Burpee Co., Warminster, PA, pg. 116
Trull, G., Exec. V.P.--Flexible Flyer Inc., West Point, MS, pg. 847
Tucci, James, Exec. V.P.--Associated Air Freight, Inc., New Hyde Park, NY, pg. 89
Tucker, Bill, Exec. V.P., Grp. Acct. Dir.--Avrett, Free & Ginsberg, Inc., New York, NY, pg. 103
Tudisco, Len, Exec. V.P.--Out of Home Media Services, Inc., New York, NY, pg. 832
Turcotte, Jeff, Exec. V.P.--Forsythe Marcelli Johnson Advertising, Inc., Newport Beach, CA, pg. 425
Turf, Barbara, Exec. V.P.--Euromarket Designs, Inc., Northbrook, IL, pg. 390
Turner, John L., Exec. V.P. & Gen. Mgr.--Allied Mineral Products, Inc., Columbus, OH, pg. 38
Turner, Ronald D.V., Pres. & Chief Oper. Officer--Elliott Company, Jeannette, PA, pg. 378
Twiddy, David, Exec. V.P.--Post Buckley Schuh & Jernigan, Miami, FL, pg. 881
Tyson, Ted H., Exec. V.P.--The Dickerson Group, Inc., Monroe, NC, pg. 335
Underwood, Thomas, Exec. V.P.--Shepard Niles, Inc., Montour Falls, NY, pg. 997
Unger, Robert I., Exec. V.P.--Portland Food Products Company, Portland, OR, pg. 881
Upshaw, Lynn, Exec. V.P., Chief Oper. Officer--Ketchum Advertising/San Francisco, San Francisco, CA, pg. 625
Upton, E. David, Exec. V.P.--Ruska Instrument Corporation, Houston, TX, pg. 956
Usandizaga, Carlos, Exec. V.P.--Grupo BSB SA, Madrid,, Spain, pg. 111
Uselton, J.C., Exec. V.P.--Sverdrup Corporation, Maryland Heights, MO, pg. 1065
Vainisi, Julie T., Exec. V.P.-Gas. Div.--Torco Oil, Chicago, IL, pg. 1102
Valentine, Mark, Exec. V.P.--Cole Vision Corporation, Cleveland, OH, pg. 260
Vallee, Louis-Eric, Exec. V.P. & Mng. Dir.--Young & Rubicam, Ltee., Montreal,, Canada, pg. 1213
Vallely, Scott, Exec. V.P.--A.T. Clayton & Company, Inc., New York, NY, pg. 253
Van Der Kamp, Jerry, Chief Exec. Officer & Exec. V.P.--American Grain & Related Industries, West Des Moines, IA, pg. 55
Van Pelt, Donald C., Jr., Exec. V.P.--Plymouth Tube Company, Warrenville, IL, pg. 877
Van Slyke, Peter, Exec. V.P.--Stephen Gould Paper Co., Inc., Whippany, NJ, pg. 473
van Zandt, Pamela, Exec. V.P.--The Conde Nast Publications Inc., New York, NY, pg. 19
Vancelette, William D., Chief Oper. Officer & Exec. V.P.--Didde Web Press, Emporia, KS, pg. 336
Vandegrift, Richard, Exec. V.P.--McCarthy Building Companies, Saint Louis, MO, pg. 727
Vander Bie, Tom, Exec. V.P.--Castex Industries Inc., Holland, MI, pg. 228
VanderKloot, Barbara, Exec. V.P.--Carstens Health Industries, Inc., Chicago, IL, pg. 225
Vansice, Fred H., Exec. V.P.--F & B Manufacturing Co., Chicago, IL, pg. 393
Varnadore, Lon, Exec. V.P.--Western Reinsurance Brokers, Inc., Los Angeles, CA, pg. 1181
Varner, Maribett, Exec. V.P., Client Services--Bennett Kuhn Varner, Inc., Atlanta, GA, pg. 139
Vasholz, Lothar A., Exec. V.P. & Corp. Mktg. Officer--The Union Central Life Insurance Co., Cincinnati, OH, pg. 1127
Vaughan, William, Jr., Exec. V.P.--Standard Welders Supply Co., Memphis, TN, pg. 1038
Vavasis, Andrew S., Exec. V.P. & Chief Oper. Officer--Vance Industries, Inc., Chicago, IL, pg. 1144
Vaz, Madeline, Exec. V.P., Dir. Acct. Mngmt.--Gigante Vaz & Partners Advertising, Inc., Parsippany, NJ, pg. 457
Veil, Lynne C., Exec. V.P.--Media That Works, Cincinnati, OH, pg. 735
Velardi, Thomas J., Exec. V.P., Assoc. Creative Dir.-Art--Dorritie Lyons & Nickel, Inc., New York, NY, pg. 347
Velazquez, Gil, Exec. V.P.--Lackman Food Service, Woodbury, NY, pg. 650
Vereen, H.B., Exec. V.P.--Riverside Manufacturing Co., Moultrie, GA, pg. 937
Verrette, Louis C., Chm. Bd. & Chief Exec. Officer--Champion, Inc., Iron Mountain, MI, pg. 238
Vetowich, Peter C., Exec. V.P., Dir. Retail Opers.--Ross Roy Inc., Bloomfield Hills, MI, pg. 950
Vignone, Ronald J., Exec. V.P.--William Douglas McAdams Inc., New York, NY, pg. 726
Villarreal, Carlos C., Sr., Exec. V.P.--Wilbur Smith Associates, Columbia, SC, pg. 1011
Virvo, Deirdre J.P., Exec. V.P.--ADV Marketing Group, Inc., Stamford, CT, pg. 2
Vlamis, Betty, Exec. V.P.--Continental American Corp. d/b/a Pioneer Balloon Company, Wichita, KS, pg. 278
Volpentesta, Frank, Chief Oper. Officer & Exec. V.P.--Headco Industries, Inc., Broadview, IL, pg. 520
von Luhrte, Richard L., Exec. V.P., Sec. & Dir.--RNL Facilities Corporation, Denver, CO, pg. 907
Von Voightlander, T.R., Exec. V.P.--Reinalt-Thomas Corp., Ann Arbor, MI, pg. 923
Vyas, C.B., Exec. V.P.--Ziegler Coal Holding Co., Fairview Heights, IL, pg. 1218
Wachsman, Steven, Exec. V.P.--Marcus Brothers Textiles, Inc., New York, NY, pg. 706
Wachtel, W.W., Exec. V.P.--Jonathan Manufacturing Corp., Fullerton, CA, pg. 602
Wadas, Alicia, Exec. V.P. & Sec.--Martz & Wadas, Scottsdale, AZ, pg. 716
Wade, Thomas, Exec. V.P.--Jamison Bedding, Inc., Franklin, TN, pg. 589
Wagner, Bruce S., Exec. V.P.--Ross Roy Group, Inc., Bloomfield Hills, MI, pg. 949
Wagner, Erick, Exec. V.P.--Progress West, Omaha, NE, pg. 894
Wagner, James Allen, Exec. V.P.--City Machine Tool & Die Company, Muncie, IN, pg. 251
Wagner, James E., Exec. V.P.--Sullivan Paper Company, West Springfield, MA, pg. 1057
Wainwright, Frank, Exec. V.P.--Block & Nardizzi, Stamford, CT, pg. 157
Walden, Ronald L., Exec. V.P.--Craddock Development Co., Inc., Colorado Springs, CO, pg. 295
Walker, Fergus J., Exec. V.P.--Redman Industries, Inc., Dallas, TX, pg. 919
Walker, James C., Exec. V.P.--Ernst W. Dorn Co., Inc., Gardena, CA, pg. 346
Wallace, Eve S., Exec. V.P.--Mitchell & Assoc., Inc., Bethesda, MD, pg. 761
Wallace, James, Exec. V.P.--Mayfield Building Supply Co., Arlington, TX, pg. 691
Wallace, Joe, Exec. V.P.--Citizens Realty & Insurance Inc., Evansville, IN, pg. 251
Waller, Stephen L., Sr. V.P.-Opers.--DHL Airways, Inc., Redwood City, CA, pg. 309
Wallman, Howard, Exec. V.P.--The Vogel Communications Group, Los Angeles, CA, pg. 1154
Walsh, James, Exec. V.P.--Naz-Dar Company, Chicago, IL, pg. 1095
Walsh, Thomas G., Exec. V.P.--Teachers Insurance and Annuity Association-College Retirement Equities Fund, New York, NY, pg. 1082
Walters, Jess M., Exec. V.P.--Hall Contracting Corp., Louisville, KY, pg. 501
Wander, Philip, Exec. V.P.--National Spinning Co., Inc., New York, NY, pg. 793
Wang, Susie, Exec. V.P.--Wang's International, Inc., Memphis, TN, pg. 1162
Ward, David, Exec. V.P.--Namico, Inc., Philadelphia, PA, pg. 783
Ward, Dick, Exec. V.P.--Ross Roy Inc., Bloomfield Hills, MI, pg. 950
Ward, Michael E., Exec. V.P.--Ward Trucking Corp., Altoona, PA, pg. 1163
Wardell, Jay, Exec. V.P.--Beef Industry Council, Chicago, IL, pg. 792
Wardell, Jay H., Exec. V.P.-Beef Industry Council--National Live Stock & Meat Board, Chicago, IL, pg. 792
Warden, Herbert W., Exec. V.P., Mngmt. Supvr.--McCaffrey and McCall, New York, NY, pg. 726
Warner, Jay, Exec. V.P.--Uniflex, Inc., Hicksville, NY, pg. 1126
Waskiewicz, David F., Pres.--Rodney Hunt Company, Orange, MA, pg. 553
Watson, Richard P., Exec. V.P. & Chief Oper. Officer--H & H Tube & Manufacturing Co., Vanderbilt, MI, pg. 495
Watson, Robert, Exec. V.P.--Feuer Leather Corporation, Hawthorne, NY, pg. 407
Watts, David L., Exec. V.P.--Treaty Co., Greenville, OH, pg. 1109
Webb, Robert M., Exec. V.P.--The In-House Agency, Weehawken, NJ, pg. 564
Weber, Owen, Exec. V.P.-Radio--Summit Communications, Inc., Atlanta, GA, pg. 1057
Weckworth, Rodney R., Exec. V.P.--Rex Moore Electrical Contractors & Engineers, West Sacramento, CA, pg. 768
Weddle, John, Exec. V.P.--Spencer's Inc., Mount Airy, NC, pg. 1030
Weidemann, Bill, Exec. V.P.--Model Glass, Inc., Anaheim, CA, pg. 762
Weil, Adolph, III, Exec. V.P.--Weil Brothers Cotton Inc., Montgomery, AL, pg. 1173
Weil, Richard, Exec. V.P. & Gen. Mgr.--Homemaker Shops, Inc., Southfield, MI, pg. 542
Weinberg, Martyn, Exec. V.P. & Chief Oper. Officer--Hanna-Barbera Productions, Inc., Los Angeles, CA, pg. 53
Weinberg, Samuel, Exec. V.P.--A. Pomerantz & Co., Philadelphia, PA, pg. 880
Weinberger, S., Exec. V.P.--Weinberger Werbehaus Ges.m.b.H & Co. KG, Vienna,, Austria, pg. 105
Weiner, Jim, Exec. V.P.--LeDonne, Wilner & Weiner, Inc., New York, NY, pg. 665
Weingardt, Ronald, Exec. V.P.--Sun Process Converting Company, Elk Grove Village, IL, pg. 1059
Weinhart, Martin, Chm. Bd., Chief Exec. Officer & Treas.--Master Molded Products Corporation, Elgin, IL, pg. 720
Weinstein, Marta, Exec. V.P.--Logistix, Fremont, CA, pg. 681
Weinstein, Walter, Exec. V.P.--Levlad, Inc., Chatsworth, CA, pg. 671
Weir, Donald, Exec. V.P.-Acct. Services--Jordan, McGrath, Case & Taylor Inc., New York, NY, pg. 604
Weisfeld, Marty, Exec. V.P.--Zena Jeans, New York, NY, pg. 1217
Weisheimer, Richard A., Exec. V.P.--Gerbig, Snell/Weisheimer & Assoc., Inc., Worthington, OH, pg. 454
Weisman, Ben, Exec. V.P.--Americo Manufacturing Co., Inc., Acworth, GA, pg. 66
Weisser, Sidney, Exec. V.P.--Cine Magnetics, Inc., Mamaroneck, NY, pg. 250
Welch, Norman H., Jr., Exec. V.P.-Audio Sls.--Eva-Tone Inc., Clearwater, FL, pg. 390
Wells, James R., Exec. V.P. & Gen. Mgr--John Wanamaker, Philadelphia, Philadelphia, PA, pg. 1201
Welsh, Jerad, Exec. V.P.--Collman Graphics, Inc., Baltimore, MD, pg. 263
Welsh, Jerad, Exec. V.P.--John D. Lucas Printing Company, Baltimore, MD, pg. 263
Wendlandt, Gary E., Exec. V.P.--Massachusetts Mutual Life Insurance Co., Springfield, MA, pg. 718
Wendling, Erhard, Exec. V.P.--Lester B. Knight & Associates, Inc., Chicago, IL, pg. 637
Wendt, John, Exec. V.P.--Rudel Machinery Company, Inc., Shelton, CT, pg. 954
Wernette, Beverly F., Exec. V.P.--Ted Thomas Associates Inc., Advertising, Philadelphia, PA, pg. 1092
Westerman, Frank G., Exec. V.P.--A. J. Canfield Co., Chicago, IL, pg. 214
Wetter, Larry, Exec. V.P.--Jeld-Wen, Inc., Klamath Falls, OR, pg. 591
Wevers, Pierre, Exec. V.P. & Chief Oper. Officer--Bigg's Hyper Shoppes, Inc., Milford, OH, pg. 150
Wheeler, G.B., Exec. V.P.--Lensclean, Inc., Carlstadt, NJ, pg. 33
Wheeler, G.B., III, Exec. V.P.--Aldine Technologies, Carlstadt, NJ, pg. 33
Whelan, Nancy, Exec. V.P.--Baldi, Bloom & Whelan Advertising, New York, NY, pg. 115
Whelpton, P., Exec. V.P.--Royal Caribbean Cruises Ltd., Miami, FL, pg. 953
Whipple, Richard, Exec. V.P.--Kingsbury Corporation, Keene, NH, pg. 631
White, Charles R., Exec. V.P. & Chief Exec. Officer--Fastec Industrial, Elkhart, IN, pg. 403
White, Donald, Exec. V.P.--Compel Marketing, Inc., Greensboro, NC, pg. 270
White, Edward F., Exec. V.P.--Rosser Fabrap International, Atlanta, GA, pg. 950
White, Jim, Exec. V.P., Creative Dir.--Backer Spielvogel Bates, Inc., New York, NY, pg. 108
White, Morgan P., Exec. V.P.--Rite-Hite Corporation, Milwaukee, WI, pg. 936
White, Paul, Exec. V.P.--Tabs Associates, Abingdon, MD, pg. 1076
White, Paul H., Exec. V.P.--M.L. Stern & Company, Inc., Beverly Hills, CA, pg. 1047
White, W. Donald, Exec. V.P.--Trone Advertising, Inc., Greensboro, NC, pg. 1115
Whiteman, Michael, Exec. V.P.--Sheldon Good & Co., Inc., Chicago, IL, pg. 470
Whitescarver, B., Exec. V.P. & Chief Oper. Officer--Dempster, Inc., Toccoa, GA, pg. 328
Whitney, John K., Jr., Exec. V.P.--Gaymar Industries, Inc., Orchard Park, NY, pg. 447
Whittaker, Paul, Exec. V.P.--Oberdorfer Industries, Inc., Syracuse, NY, pg. 819
Whitworth, Robert, Exec. V.P.--Encyclopaedia Britannica Educational Corporation, Chicago, IL, pg. 380
Widman, Dale, Exec. V.P.--Kerrison Dry Goods Company, Inc., Charleston, SC, pg. 624
Wiebe, Kathy, Exec. V.P.--Associated Advertising Agency, Inc., Wichita, KS, pg. 89
Wier, Patricia A., Exec. V.P. & Pres.-EBNA--Encyclopaedia Britannica, Inc., Chicago, IL, pg. 381
Wiesenthal, Richard S., Exec. V.P. & Chief Fin. Officer--The Unimax Corporation, New York, NY, pg. 1127
Wiest, Leo H., Exec. V.P.--Charter Oak Financial Corporation, Cincinnati, OH, pg. 491
Wigand, Emeric, Jr., Exec. V.P.--Wigand Corporation, Colorado Springs, CO, pg. 1189

Wilder, Alfred Lee, Exec. V.P.--Kastle Systems, Inc., Arlington, VA, pg. 618
Wilhoit, William H., Exec. V.P.--Skyway Luggage Co., Seattle, WA, pg. 1009
Wilkie, Leighton A., Exec. V.P.--Continental Machines, Inc., Savage, MN, pg. 279
Wilkolak, Thomas N., Exec. V.P.--Carlson Marketing Group, Inc., Minneapolis, MN, pg. 221
Williams, D. Wayne, Exec. V.P.--Century Data Systems, Raleigh, NC, pg. 235
Williams, David, Exec. V.P.--Hanna Car Wash International, Inc., Portland, OR, pg. 505
Williams, Donald D., Exec. V.P., Grp. Dir.--Young & Rubicam Detroit, Detroit, MI, pg. 1211
Williams, Gary, Exec. V.P.--Coakley & Williams Inc., Greenbelt, MD, pg. 256
Williams, Glen E., Jr., Exec. V.P. & Chief Fin. Officer--Dodson Group, Kansas City, MO, pg. 342
Williams, Jimmie D., Exec. V.P., Chief Fin. Officer, Treas. & Sec.--Belz Enterprises, Memphis, TN, pg. 138
Williams, John A., Exec. V.P.--Seattle Times Company, Seattle, WA, pg. 986
Williams, Miles A., Exec. V.P.--Anschutz Corporation, Denver, CO, pg. 75
Williamson, James C., Sr., Exec. V.P. & Treas.--Smith & Gillespie Engineers, Inc., Jacksonville, FL, pg. 1012
Willner, Michael, Exec. V.P. & Chief Oper. Officer--CPM, Inc., Chicago, IL, pg. 203
Willnis, James A., Exec. V.P.--Unicover Corporation, Cheyenne, WY, pg. 1126
Wilmoth, E.J., Exec. V.P.--Peterson Industries Inc., Decatur, AR, pg. 864
Wilmoth, Gene, Exec. V.P.--Peterson Industries Inc., Decatur, AR, pg. 864
Wilner, Jon, Exec. V.P.--LeDonne, Wilner & Weiner, Inc., New York, NY, pg. 665
Wilson, H. Thomas, Exec. V.P., Media Dir.--McCaffrey and McCall, New York, NY, pg. 726
Wilson, James L., Exec. V.P.--United Van Lines, Inc., Fenton, MO, pg. 1126
Wilson, Jim, III, Exec. V.P.--Jim Wilson & Associates, Montgomery, AL, pg. 1193
Wilson, Julie, Exec. V.P.--Regian Advertising & Public Relations, Fort Worth, TX, pg. 922
Wilson, Kemmons, Jr., Exec. V.P.--Kemmons Wilson Companies, Memphis, TN, pg. 1194
Wilson, Robert, Exec. V.P.--Kemmons Wilson Companies, Memphis, TN, pg. 1194
Wilson, Russell, Exec. V.P.--Artco-Bell Corporation, Temple, TX, pg. 86
Wilson, S. Liane, Exec. V.P.--Washington Mutual Savings Bank, Seattle, WA, pg. 1166
Winninghoff, Albert, Chm.--Noordervliet & Winninghoff/Leo Burnett B.V., Amsterdam,, Netherlands, pg. 193
Winslow, Dave, Exec. V.P., Dir. Acct. Services--EvansGroup, Dallas, TX, pg. 391
Winters, James L., Exec. V.P., Exec. Creative Dir. (Dallas) & Dir.--EvansGroup, Salt Lake City, UT, pg. 390
Winters, Jim, Exec. V.P., Exec. Creative Dir.--EvansGroup, Dallas, TX, pg. 391
Wise, Michelle R., Exec. V.P.--Kreps-Wise Associates, Saint Louis, MO, pg. 644
Wiseman, Ed, Exec. V.P.--E.C. Barton & Co., Jonesboro, AR, pg. 123
Withall, Gary A., Exec. V.P.--Miner Enterprises Inc., Geneva, IL, pg. 756
Wittman, Mark, Exec. V.P.--OMNI Flight Helicopters, Inc., Janesville, WI, pg. 826
Woglom, Dorothy, Exec. V.P., Acct. Principal--Duval & Partners, Boston, MA, pg. 356
Wolf, Kevin M., Exec. V.P.--Leonard Wholesale, Inc., Elizabeth, NJ, pg. 668
Wolfe, Lawrence A., Exec. V.P. & Sec.--Production Tool Supply Co., Warren, MI, pg. 893
Wolfe, Lloyd, Exec. V.P., Creative Dir.--TBWA Kerlick Switzer, Saint Louis, MO, pg. 1071
Wolfe, T.J., Exec. V.P.--Welch's, Concord, MA, pg. 789
Wombacher, Klaus, Exec. V.P.--Costa Cruise Lines, N.V., Miami, FL, pg. 288
Wong, Fred, Exec. V.P.--Ansco Photo-Optical Products Corp., Elk Grove Village, IL, pg. 76
Wood, Guy, Exec. V.P.--Gloria Jean's Coffee Bean Corp., Buffalo Grove, IL, pg. 464
Woodbeck, Thomas M., Exec. V.P.--Overhead Conveyor Co., Ferndale, MI, pg. 832
Woodhouse, Michael, Exec. V.P. & Chief Fin. Officer--Metromedia Steakhouses, Inc., Vandalia, OH, pg. 744
Woodrick, Rob, Exec. V.P.-Sls. & Mktg.--D & W Food Centers, Inc., Grand Rapids, MI, pg. 308
Woods, Kevin J., Exec. V.P.--Gust K. Newberg Construction Co., Chicago, IL, pg. 803
Woods, Shelby, Exec. V.P. & Chm.-Exec. Committee--Cranford Johnson Robinson Woods, Little Rock, AR, pg. 296
Woolsey, Jerry, Exec. V.P., Sec.--CRE, Inc., Indianapolis, IN, pg. 203
Wooten, Rosalie, Exec. V.P.--O'Reilly Auto Inc., Springfield, MO, pg. 829
Wright, Clancy, Exec. V.P.--Bawden Corporation, Eldridge, IA, pg. 127
Wright, Gary K., Exec. V.P.-Corp. Banking--Texas Commerce Bancshares, Inc., Houston, TX, pg. 1089
Wright, Steve, Exec. V.P.--Citation Companies, Inc., Birmingham, AL, pg. 250
Wuestefeld, Norman H., Exec. V.P.--Wilbur Smith Associates, Columbia, SC, pg. 1011
Wurst, B.J., Exec. V.P.--Camelot Communications, Inc., Dallas, TX, pg. 212
Wynkoop, Roger D., Exec. V.P.--ACF Industries, Inc., Earth City, MO, pg. 561
Wysocki, Rick, Exec. V.P., Dir. Creative Services--Backer Spielvogel Bates, Inc., New York, NY, pg. 108
Yarmark, Martin J., Exec. V.P.--Triboro Electric Corp., Warminster, PA, pg. 1112
Yates, Jeffery M., Exec. V.P. & Gen. Counsel--Independent Insurance Agents of America, Alexandria, VA, pg. 565
Yeager, Paul D., Chief Fin. Officer & Exec. V.P.--The Scott Company, Marysville, OH, pg. 982
Yedor, Cyril, Exec. V.P.--Executive Car Leasing Company, Los Angeles, CA, pg. 393
Yollich, Lester, Exec. V.P.--Production Tool Supply Co., Warren, MI, pg. 893
Yonadi, Albert J., Exec. V.P.--Lasky Company, Millburn, NJ, pg. 660
Young, Bill, Exec. V.P.--Stiles Corporation, Fort Lauderdale, FL, pg. 1049
Young, Bobby R., Exec. V.P.--Century Data Systems, Raleigh, NC, pg. 235
Young, Bonney, Exec. V.P.--Lewis Advertising Agency, Newark, NJ, pg. 672
Young, James T., Exec. V.P.--Young Refining Corp., Douglasville, GA, pg. 1210
Young, John A., III, Exec. V.P.--Burd & Fletcher Company, Kansas City, MO, pg. 189
Young, John L., Exec. V.P.--Abbey Etna Machine Company, Perrysburg, OH, pg. 9
Young, Matthew, Exec. V.P.--Murry's, Inc., Forestville, MD, pg. 777
Young, Matthew, Exec. V.P.--Murry's, Inc., Forestville, MD, pg. 777
Youree, Joe F., Exec. V.P.--Tennsco Corporation, Dickson, TN, pg. 1088
Yu, Kenneth P., Exec. V.P., Treas. & Res. Dir.--AdLand Advertising, Inc., San Francisco, CA, pg. 17
Yurish, John L., Exec. V.P.--National Car Rental System, Inc., Minneapolis, MN, pg. 786
Yuzawa, Mikio, Exec. V.P., Domestic--Chuo Senko Advertising Co., Ltd., Tokyo, Japan, pg. 103
Zabek, Basil, Exec. V.P.--YSI Incorporated, Yellow Springs, OH, pg. 1207
Zagerman, Barry, Exec. V.P.--Broder Bros. Co., Plymouth, MI, pg. 178
Zagerman, Barry, Exec. V.P.--Broder Bros. Co. Of Florida, Inc., Orlando, FL, pg. 178
Zanotti, John P., Exec. V.P.--Great American Communications Company, Cincinnati, OH, pg. 53
Zara, Tom, Exec. V.P.--Gregory & Clyburne, Inc., Stamford, CT, pg. 486
Zarembra, Michael, Exec. V.P.--GSP Marketing Services, Inc., Chicago, IL, pg. 441
Zarrow, Jack, Exec. V.P.--Sooner Pipe & Supply Corp., Tulsa, OK, pg. 1018
Zehender, Barbara, Exec. V.P., Grp. Dir.--Dorland Sweeney Jones, Philadelphia, PA, pg. 346
Zeldman, Irving, Sr. Exec. V.P.--TCC, Miami, FL, pg. 1072
Zelin, Jerome, Exec. V.P.--Masters, Inc., Westbury, NY, pg. 720
Zeller, K.W., Exec. V.P.--Zeller Corp., Defiance, OH, pg. 1216
Zilinski, James W., Exec. V.P. & Chief Mktg. Officer--The New England, Boston, MA, pg. 799
Zilkha, Michael E. S., Exec. V.P.--Zilkha Energy Company, Houston, TX, pg. 1219
Zilovic, Alexandra, Exec. V.P.--Language Institute for English (L.I.F.E.), Rutherford, NJ, pg. 142
Zimmer, Delaine, Exec. V.P. & Chief Oper. Officer--Tighe Industries, Inc., York, PA, pg. 1097
Zimmermann, Keith, Exec. V.P.--Whitney Blake Company of Vermont, Inc., Bellows Falls, VT, pg. 155
Zlotnik, Cliff, Exec. V.P.--Surco Products, Inc., Braddock, PA, pg. 1065
Zuckerman, Alan M., Exec. V.P.--Chi Systems, Inc., Ann Arbor, MI, pg. 244
Zuerker, Jack A., Exec. V.P.--Sivalls, Inc., Odessa, TX, pg. 1009
Zwilling, Paul R., Exec. V.P. & Chief Actuary--Mutual of America, New York, NY, pg. 777

GENERAL COUNSEL

Abdalla, Gerald M., Exec. V.P., Gen. Counsel & Sec.--Croft Metal Inc., McComb, MS, pg. 300
Abernathy, Durant, Sr. V.P. & Gen. Counsel--Credit Union National Association, Madison, WI, pg. 298
Abowitz, Milton D., Gen. Counsel--Interstate Steel Supply Co., Philadelphia, PA, pg. 580
Abraham, Gary J., V.P.-Fin. & Gen. Counsel--Gaylord Printing, Inc., Detroit, MI, pg. 446
Ackerman, Bernard, Gen. Counsel--Stan Merritt Inc./ Advertising, New York, NY, pg. 741
Adams, Larry L., V.P. & Gen. Counsel--Tanning Research Labs., Inc., Ormond Beach, FL, pg. 1078
Adams, Philip E., Corp. Counsel--Cajun Electric Power Co-op, Baton Rouge, LA, pg. 207
Adams, Tim, Gen. Counsel--The Bibb Company, Macon, GA, pg. 781
Adikes, Robert K., V.P., Sec. & Gen. Counsel--Spalding & Evenflo Companies, Inc., Tampa, FL, pg. 1024
Adler, Jack, Sec. & Treas.--Bridal Originals, Inc., Collinsville, IL, pg. 175
Aids, Leland, Gen. Counsel--DDC PerTec, Tucson, AZ, pg. 308
Alekel, Dennis A., Sr. V.P. & Gen. Counsel--Lewis Homes Management Corp., Upland, CA, pg. 673
Alesso, Dominick, Sec. & Gen. Counsel--A-P-A Transport Corp., North Bergen, NJ, pg. 5
Alfaro, Vince, V.P.-Legal--Kitchell Corporation, Phoenix, AZ, pg. 634
Allen, Frank C., V.P., Sec. & Gen. Counsel--The Babcock & Wilcox Company, New Orleans, LA, pg. 107
Allgood, Joan, Gen. Counsel--Developers Diversified, Moreland Hills, OH, pg. 333
Allison, Charles, V.P., Sec. & Gen. Counsel--Gulf States Paper Corporation, Tuscaloosa, AL, pg. 494
Allison, Lynette E., V.P.-Gen. Counsel & Sec.--Scholastic Inc., New York, NY, pg. 962
Alphson, Howard C., Sec. & Gen. Counsel--M.C. Gill Corporation, El Monte, CA, pg. 458
Alterbaum, James, Gen. Counsel--Masters, Inc., Westbury, NY, pg. 720
Ames, Richard S., Chm. & Chief Exec. Officer--Command Plastic Corporation, Akron, OH, pg. 268
Amhowitz, Harris J., Deputy Chm.--Coopers & Lybrand, New York, NY, pg. 283
Ancarrow, N. Hopper, V.P. & Gen. Counsel--Southern States Cooperative, Inc., Richmond, VA, pg. 1022
Andereck, Eugene, Gen. Counsel--Associated Electric Co-op Inc., Springfield, MO, pg. 89
Anderson, C. R., Gen. Counsel--States, Inc., Breckenridge, TX, pg. 1041
Anderson, James, Legal Officer--Prairie Farms Dairy, Inc., Carlinville, IL, pg. 884
Anderson, James, V.P. & Gen. Counsel--Ingram Industries Inc., Nashville, TN, pg. 568
Anderson, Richard, V.P.-Deputy Gen. Counsel--NWA, Inc., Saint Paul, MN, pg. 782
Anderson, Robert G., V.P., Sec. & Gen. Counsel--Boston Scientific Corp., Watertown, MA, pg. 167
Anderson, Vincent P., Sr. V.P. & Legal Officer--Wawa, Inc., Wawa, PA, pg. 1169
Anderson, William E. II, Sr. V.P., Sec. & Gen. Counsel--Jerrico, Inc., Lexington, KY, pg. 229
Anderson, William E., II, Sr. V.P., Sec. & Gen. Counsel--Long John Silver's, Inc., Lexington, KY, pg. 229
Anderson, Willis M., Gen. Counsel & Sec.--Shenandoah Life Insurance Company, Roanoke, VA, pg. 997
Anderson, Willis M., Gen. Counsel & Sec.--Old Dominion Life Insurance Co., Roanoke, VA, pg. 997
Anthony, Aubra, Jr., Treas., Sec. & Counsel--Anthony Forest Products Co., Inc., El Dorado, AR, pg. 77
Anthony, Steven M., Gen. Counsel--Bearden Lumber Company, Inc., Bearden, AR, pg. 129
Apperson, Lawson, Gen. Counsel--National Bedding & Furniture Industries, Memphis, TN, pg. 786
Aprati, Robert L., Sr. V.P. & Gen. Counsel--Beech Holdings Corp., Chicago, IL, pg. 131
Aprati, Robert L., Sr. V.P. & Gen. Counsel--Budget Rent A Car Corporation, Lisle, IL, pg. 131
Argilla, Luke, Corp. Counsel--Swinerton & Walberg Co., San Francisco, CA, pg. 1068
Ark, John, Gen. Counsel--Jay Incorporated, Rochester, NY, pg. 590
Armstrong, Paul L., V.P. & Gen. Counsel--Brown & Caldwell Consulting Engineers, Pleasant Hill, CA, pg. 181
Aronson, Alan, Legal Officer & Sec.--Carus Corporation, Peru, IL, pg. 227
Aronson, Alan A., Gen. Counsel--Open Court Publishing Company, Chicago, IL, pg. 227
Asher, Anthony, Gen. Counsel--Stainless Incorporated, Deerfield Beach, FL, pg. 1035
Auton, J. Paul, Mng. Dir.--Cambridge Consultants Limited, Cambridge,, United Kingdom, pg. 679
Autry, Charles T., Sr. V.P.-Governmental Affairs & Gen. Counsel--Oglethorpe Power Corp., Tucker, GA, pg. 822
Avram, G.A., Gen. Counsel--Pioneer/Eclipse Corp., Sparta, NC, pg. 871
Babbin, Fred, Gen. Counsel--Orleans International, Inc., Bloomfield Hills, MI, pg. 829
Bacigalupo, Richard J., Gen. Counsel--Regional Transportation Authority (RTA), Chicago, IL, pg. 922
Bacon, Richard A., Sr. V.P. & Gen. Counsel--John Wieland Homes Inc., Atlanta, GA, pg. 1188
Bailey, Mark, V.P. Sec & Gen Counsel--SENCORP, Newport, KY, pg. 989
Baker, David, Corp. Counsel & Asst. Sec.--CENEX (Farmers Union Central Exchange, Inc.), Inver Grove Heights, MN, pg. 231
Baker, Jamie, Gen. Counsel--Joffko International, Houston, TX, pg. 595
Baker, Rhodes, Sr. V.P. & Gen. Counsel--Team Bancshares, Inc., Dallas, TX, pg. 1082
Baldave, David, Gen. Counsel--Benderson Development Co., Inc., Buffalo, NY, pg. 138
Balka, Sigmound, Gen. Counsel--Krasdale Foods Inc., Bronx, NY, pg. 644
Ball, Leonard F., Sr. V.P., Gen. Counsel & Asst. Sec.--HTB, Inc., Oklahoma City, OK, pg. 497
Ballard, Eugene H., V.P. & Gen. Counsel--Simplex Time Recorder Co., Gardner, MA, pg. 1006
Ballard, Richard, Gen. Counsel--Taylor Machine Works, Inc., Louisville, MS, pg. 1081
Balzano, John, Gen. Counsel--C. Weaver Chevrolet, Inc., New York Mills, NY, pg. 1170
Bangs, Nelson A., V.P., Gen Counsel & Sec.--Dr Pepper/ Seven-Up Companies, Inc., Dallas, TX, pg. 342
Banstetter, Robert J., V.P., Gen. Counsel & Sec.--General American Life Insurance Co., St. Louis, MO, pg. 448
Baray, H., V.P. & Gen. Counsel--Restaurant Enterprises Group, Inc., Irvine, CA, pg. 929
Barbieri, Stephen R., Sec. & Legal Counsel--Sunshine Biscuits, Inc., Woodbridge, NJ, pg. 439
Barbour, Rodney, Chief Fin. Officer & Gen. Counsel--Lawson Mechanical Contractors, Sacramento, CA, pg. 663
Barefield, Bob, Gen. Counsel--Honorbuilt Industries, Inc., Minneapolis, KS, pg. 542
Barkan, Lee, Sr. V.P, Sec. & Gen. Counsel--American Vision Centers, Inc., New York, NY, pg. 65
Barlin, Wayne, Gen. Counsel--Coulter Corporation, Hialeah, FL, pg. 289
Barnett, David, Legal--Sharon-Jay Togs, Inc., New Bedford, MA, pg. 995
Barnett, Sherie, Legal Counsel--Iowa Lottery, Des Moines, IA, pg. 582
Barrett, Paul L., Gen. Counsel & Sec.--Redman Industries, Inc., Dallas, TX, pg. 919
Bartlett, John L., Corp. Sec. & Gen. Counsel--Arinc Inc., Annapolis, MD, pg. 82
Bartlett, John L., Sec. & Gen. Counsel--ARINC Research Corp., Annapolis, MD, pg. 82
Bartlett, John L., Sec. & Gen. Counsel--Aeronautical Radio, Inc., Annapolis, MD, pg. 82

Bartz, Michael, Sr. V.P. & Gen. Counsel--Empire West Companies, Inc., Tucson, AZ, pg. 380
Batenhorst, Gary, V.P. & Gen. Counsel--Godfather's Pizza, Inc., Omaha, NE, pg. 464
Battaglia, Tim, Sr. V.P. & Gen. Counsel--Acess Energy Corporation, Dublin, OH, pg. 12
Baty, Lee, Gen. Counsel--Wahl Clipper Corp., Sterling, IL, pg. 1158
Bauch, Thomas J., Sr. V.P. & Gen. Counsel--Levi Strauss & Co., San Francisco, CA, pg. 670
Baum, Robert H., Vice Chm. & Gen. Counsel--The Inland Group, Inc., Oak Brook, IL, pg. 570
Bean, Christopher V., Gen. Counsel--D. D. Bean & Sons Co., Jaffrey, NH, pg. 129
Beard, Pat, Gen. Counsel--Artco-Bell Corporation, Temple, TX, pg. 86
Bearmon, Lee, V.P., Sec. & Gen. Counsel--Carlson Companies, Inc., Minneapolis, MN, pg. 220
Becker, Mitchel, Sr. V.P. & Gen. Counsel--Morse Diesel International, New York, NY, pg. 771
Becker, Paul, V.P., Sec., Treas. & Gen. Counsel--Cosco Industries, Spring Valley, NY, pg. 288
Beeby, Kenneth J., V.P., Sec. & Gen. Counsel--Ocean Spray Cranberries, Inc., Lakeville, MA, pg. 820
Beeson, Donald L., Gen. Counsel--Peerless Lighting Corp., Berkeley, CA, pg. 855
Bell, Carmela Leone, Gen. Counsel & Sec.--Reliable Stores, Inc., Columbia, MD, pg. 925
Bennett, Peter, Gen. Counsel--W.S. Libbey Company, Great Falls, SC, pg. 674
Bennett, Thomas F., Legal Counsel--Veda Incorporated, Alexandria, VA, pg. 1146
Berens, Sheldon L., Sr. V.P. & Gen. Counsel--Continental Grain Company, New York, NY, pg. 279
Berg, Thomas C., V.P., Gen. Counsel & Sec.--Amsted Industries Incorporated, Chicago, IL, pg. 68
Bergen, Robert, Gen. Counsel--Metropolitan Transportation Authority, New York, NY, pg. 745
Bergreen, Bernard, Gen. Counsel--Gilman Paper Co., Saint Marys, GA, pg. 459
Berrsard, N. Ray, Gen. Counsel--Standard Alloys & Manufacturing, Port Arthur, TX, pg. 161
Berry, Richard C., Legal Counsel--Hobart Brothers Co., Troy, OH, pg. 536
Berson, Joel, Sec. & Gen. Counsel--Tork, Inc., Mount Vernon, NY, pg. 1102
Bertolini, Arthur G., Sr. V.P.-Fin. & Admin., Treas. & Sec.--Rocor Transportation Companies Inc., Oklahoma City, OK, pg. 942
Bessozzi, John F., Jr., Gen. Counsel--Summit Corporation of America, Thomaston, CT, pg. 1058
Bettman, Gary B., Sr. V.P. & Gen. Counsel--National Basketball Association, New York, NY, pg. 786
Bingle, Donald J., V.P., Gen. Counsel & Clerk--Boston Chicken, Inc., Naperville, IL, pg. 167
Birn, S.R., Sr. V.P. & Assoc. Gen. Counsel--Auto-Owners Insurance, Lansing, MI, pg. 100
Birndorf, B., Gen. Counsel--Donlen Corp., Deerfield, IL, pg. 345
Bishop, Eric, Gen. Counsel--E-Z Mart Stores, Inc., Texarkana, TX, pg. 361
Bissey, Brian P., Gen. Counsel--Victaulic Company of America, Easton, PA, pg. 1149
Bitting, William M., Gen. Counsel--General Brewing Company, Vancouver, WA, pg. 959
Black, Natalie A., V.P. & Gen. Counsel--Kohler Company, Kohler, WI, pg. 639
Blackstone, Franklin, Jr., Gen. Counsel & Sec.--Bearing Service Company, Pittsburgh, PA, pg. 130
Blackwell, Katrina, V.P. & Gen. Mgr.--Red Ball Forwarders, Inc., Indianapolis, IN, pg. 918
Blackwell, Richard M., Sr. V.P. & Gen. Counsel--Metropolitan Life Insurance Co., New York, NY, pg. 744
Blake, Mona, Gen. Counsel--D.C. Lottery & Charitable Games Control Board, Washington, DC, pg. 308
Blanton, Amelia, Gen. Counsel--Fantastic Sam's International, Inc., Memphis, TN, pg. 398
Blaxter, H. Vaughan, III, Gen. Counsel--Hillman Company, Pittsburgh, PA, pg. 535
Block, Ira, V.P., Gen. Counsel & Sec.--Wechsler Coffee Corp., Moonachie, NJ, pg. 1172
Block, S. Lester, Sr. V.P.-Govt. Rels. & Labor Counsel--R. H. Macy & Co., Inc., New York, NY, pg. 698
Block, Stephen A., Sr. V.P. & Gen. Counsel--GAF Corporation, Wayne, NJ, pg. 438
Blomrosen, J.R., Gen. Counsel--Plains Cotton Co-op Association, Lubbock, TX, pg. 873
Blonkoff, Sharon A., Corp. Counsel--Ethan Allen, Inc., Danbury, CT, pg. 485
Bloom, Donald, Pres. & Chief Exec. Officer--Bloom Electric Services, Inc., Oklahoma City, OK, pg. 157
Blumberg, B., Gen. Counsel--Lensclean, Inc., Carlstadt, NJ, pg. 33
Blumrosen, J.R., Gen. Counsel--Plains Co-op Oil Mill, Lubbock, TX, pg. 873
Bluth, Lawrence, V.P.- Sec. & Gen. Counsel--Penske Corporation, Detroit, MI, pg. 859
Bogan, Charles E., V.P. & Gen. Counsel--Duckwall-Alco Stores, Inc., Abilene, KS, pg. 351
Bohm, Gerald, V.P., Corp. Counsel & Sec.--Prime Hospitality Corp., Fairfield, NJ, pg. 889
Bolis, John M., Sr. V.P. & Gen. Counsel--Omni Hotels, Hampton, NH, pg. 826
Bomar, Horace, Legal Officer--Zima Corp., Spartanburg, SC, pg. 1219
Bonaros, Thomas P., V.P. & Gen. Counsel--Utica Mutual Insurance Company, New Hartford, NY, pg. 1140
Boneberger, Greg, Gen. Counsel & Corp. Sec.--Wyatt Inc., Branford, CT, pg. 1205
Booker, Lewis, Gen. Counsel--Christian Children's Fund, Inc., Richmond, VA, pg. 248
Boris, Howard, Gen. Counsel--Lefrak Organization Inc., Rego Park, NY, pg. 666
Bouey, Pam, Legal Counsel--Aetna Health Plans, San Bruno, CA, pg. 23
Bowe, William J., V.P., Sec. & Gen. Counsel--Encyclopaedia Britannica, Inc., Chicago, IL, pg. 381
Bowen, Bill, Gen. Counsel & V.P.--Super 8 Motels, Inc., Aberdeen, SD, pg. 1062
Bowman, D. Craig, V.P. & Assoc. Gen. Counsel--The Pullman Company, Livingston, NJ, pg. 899
Bowman, D. Craig, V.P. & Assoc. Gen. Counsel--Lear Siegler Diversified Holdings Corp., Livingston, NJ, pg. 424
Bowman, David, V.P. & Gen. Counsel--Coast To Coast Stores, Inc., Denver, CO, pg. 257
Bownas, Jim, V.P. & Gen. Counsel--Cardinal Realty Services Inc., Reynoldsburg, OH, pg. 218
Bowns, Roland, Gen. Counsel--California State Lottery, Sacramento, CA, pg. 210
Bradford, David, V.P.-Legal--Bradford Exchange Ltd., Niles, IL, pg. 170
Bradford, J.W., V.P., Gen. Counsel & Sec.--AFG Industries, Inc., Fort Worth, TX, pg. 3
Bradley, Edward, Gen. Counsel--Frank C. Nahser Inc., Chicago, IL, pg. 783
Bradshaw, John, Gen. Counsel--Industrial Wire Products Corporation, Pomona, CA, pg. 567
Brady, Pat, Gen. Counsel--Wausau Homes, Inc., Rothschild, WI, pg. 1168
Brafman, Howard, Gen. Counsel--J. I. Kislak Inc., Miami Lakes, FL, pg. 633
Braman, James, Legal Officer--Michaels Group Inc., Latham, NY, pg. 747
Breckenridge, John, Gen. Counsel--Manchester Tank & Equipment Company, Lynwood, CA, pg. 703
Brecker, Robert John, Esq., Corp. Counsel--J. G. Hook, Inc., Philadelphia, PA, pg. 543
Breed, J.R., V.P. & Gen. Counsel-SICO--Simpson Timber Co., Shelton, WA, pg. 1007
Breed, Joseph, V.P. & Gen. Counsel--Simpson Investment Co., Seattle, WA, pg. 1007
Bremer, John M., V.P., Gen. Counsel & Sec.--Northwestern Mutual Life Insurance Co., Milwaukee, WI, pg. 815
Brenner, Stephen, Sr. V.P.-Bus. Affairs & Opers.; Gen. Counsel--USA Network, New York, NY, pg. 1124
Breslin, Michael, Exec. V.P. & Gen. Counsel--Leo Burnett Company, Inc., Chicago, IL, pg. 191
Bridge, John B., V.P.-Real Estate, Sec. & Gen. Counsel--VASA Insurance Group, Inc., Indianapolis, IN, pg. 1146
Bridge, John B., V.P., Gen. Counsel & Sec.--Brougher Agency, Inc., Indianapolis, IN, pg. 1146
Brinberg, Simeon, Gen. Counsel--Gould Investors, L.P., Great Neck, NY, pg. 473
Brinkley, Linster E., Gen. Counsel--Payless Car Rental System, Inc., Saint Petersburg, FL, pg. 853
Broderick, James, V.P. & Gen. Counsel--RAYOVAC Corporation, Madison, WI, pg. 915
Brooks, Randy, Legal Dept. Admin.--Family Inns of America, Inc., Pigeon Forge, TN, pg. 398
Brooks, Ronald J., Gen. Counsel--John Blair Communications, Inc., New York, NY, pg. 155
Brooks, Ronald J., Gen. Counsel--Blair Television, New York, NY, pg. 155
Brown, D.S., Chief Fin. Officer, V.P., Treas. & Gen. Counsel--United Laboratories, Inc., Itasca, IL, pg. 1133
Brown, Frank, Gen. Counsel--Dallas Peterbilt, Inc., Irving, TX, pg. 312
Brown, J. Walter, Gen. Counsel--Riverside Central Services, Inc., Natchez, MS, pg. 937
Brown, Lawrence R., Jr., Sr. V.P. & Corp. Counsel--Provident Mutual Life Insurance Co., Philadelphia, PA, pg. 896
Brown, Richard M., Esq., Gen. Counsel--Golden West Broadcasters, Los Angeles, CA, pg. 467
Brown, Robert M., Gen. Counsel--Interform Corporation, Bridgeville, PA, pg. 574
Brown, Rockwood, Sr. V.P., Sec. & Gen. Counsel--WYO-Ben, Inc., Billings, MT, pg. 1157
Brown, Timothy N., Corp. Counsel & Sec.--J. E. Higgins Lumber Co., Concord, CA, pg. 533
Brown, William R., Gen. Counsel & Sec.--American United Life Insurance Company, Indianapolis, IN, pg. 65
Browne, Larry W., Sr. V.P., Corp. Fin. Officer, & Gen. Counsel--Friendly Ice Cream Corp., Wilbraham, MA, pg. 1087
Bryson, Chris, Gen. Counsel--Pacific States Casualty Co., Los Angeles, CA, pg. 841
Buckley, Alan, Chief Fin. Officer, Sec., Treas. & Legal Officer--Pease Industries, Inc., Fairfield, OH, pg. 854
Buckstein, Mark, Sr. V.P.-External Affairs & Gen. Counsel--Trans World Airlines, Inc., Mount Kisco, NY, pg. 561
Buda, T.J., Sr. V.P., Sec. & Gen. Counsel--Auto-Owners Insurance, Lansing, MI, pg. 100
Buker, Robert H., Jr., V.P.-Legal Affairs--United States Sugar Corporation, Clewiston, FL, pg. 1137
Bukowski, Gerry, Gen. Counsel--Burns & McDonnell Engineers-Architects-Consultants, Kansas City, MO, pg. 194
Bullwinkel, George, Gen. Counsel--World's Finest Chocolate, Inc., Chicago, IL, pg. 1203
Bulman, Neil, Jr., Sec. & Gen. Counsel--Schottenstein Stores Corporation, Columbus, OH, pg. 978
Bunnell, Roderick, Sr. V.P., Sec. & Gen. Counsel--Blue Cross & Blue Shield of Oregon, Portland, OR, pg. 160
Burgon, Barre G., V.P., Sec. & Corp. Counsel--Flying J. Inc., Brigham City, UT, pg. 421
Burke, Edward O., Gen. Counsel--Double AA Builders, Ltd., Phoenix, AZ, pg. 347
Burke, J. Terence, Sec. & Gen. Counsel--Realty One, Cleveland, OH, pg. 917
Burke, Robert, Gen. Counsel--Tang Industries Inc., Elk Grove Village, IL, pg. 1078
Burkett, Lawrence V., Jr., Sr. V.P. & Deputy Gen. Counsel--Massachusetts Mutual Life Insurance Co., Springfield, MA, pg. 718
Burns, Daniel, V.P. & Gen. Counsel--Cotter & Company, Chicago, IL, pg. 288
Burns, Stephen F., Chm. Bd., Pres. & Chief Exec. Officer--Wheaton Van Lines, Inc., Indianapolis, IN, pg. 1184
Burton, Steven, Gen. Counsel--Sithe Energies, U.S.A., Inc., San Diego, CA, pg. 1009
Byrd, Ford, Sr. V.P.-Real Estate & Legal Affairs--Advanced Technology, Inc., Reston, VA, pg. 20
Byron, Richard J., V.P., Assoc. Gen. Counsel & Sec.--Employers Insurance of Wausau a Mutual Co., Wausau, WI, pg. 380
Byron, Richard J., V.P., Assoc. Gen. Counsel & Sec.--Employers Insurance of Wausau a Mutual Co., Wausau, WI, pg. 795
Cahoon, James P., Gen. Counsel--Central Mutual Insurance Co., Van Wert, OH, pg. 233
Caldwell, Allen, Exec. V.P., Sec. & Gen. Counsel--Koch Industries, Incorporated, Wichita, KS, pg. 639
Cambridge, Robert M., Gen. Counsel--American Systems Corporation, Chantilly, VA, pg. 63
Campbell, Cynthia, V.P., Gen. Counsel & Sec.--Transport Insurance Co., Dallas, TX, pg. 54
Campbell, Henry M., Gen. Counsel--HDS Services, Farmington Hills, MI, pg. 496
Campbell, J.H., Jr., Chief Fin. Officer, Treas. & Legal Counsel--Associated Grocers, Inc., Baton Rouge, LA, pg. 89
Caolo, Michael B., Sec. & Legal Officer--SnyderGeneral Corporation, Dallas, TX, pg. 1015
Carabillo, Joseph, Chief Legal Officer & V.P.--ULLICO Inc., Washington, DC, pg. 1124
Carlsen, David R., Chm. Bd., Sec. & Legal Counsel--Upper Midwest Industries, Inc., Minneapolis, MN, pg. 1140
Carmichael, David R., Sr. V.P. & Gen. Counsel--Pacific Mutual Life Insurance Company, Newport Beach, CA, pg. 841
Carnes, Phyllis, Exec. V.P., Comptroller, Legal Officer & Dir.-Investor Rels.--Eagle Lincoln Mercury Inc., Dallas, TX, pg. 362
Carney, Valerie, Sr. V.P. & Gen. Counsel--Sarkes Tarzian, Incorporated, Bloomington, IN, pg. 1079
Carpenter, Ernest A., V.P.-Admin. & Gen. Counsel--Tippins Incorporated, Pittsburgh, PA, pg. 1099
Carpenter, James W., V.P. & Sr. Counsel--Western & Southern Life Insurance Co., Cincinnati, OH, pg. 1181
Carr, Joseph C., Jr., Sec. & Gen. Counsel--Mitek, Inc., Chesterfield, MO, pg. 762
Carr, Oscar C., III, Legal Officer--Samelson-Leon Company, Inc., Memphis, TN, pg. 968
Carr, Stephen R., V.P. & Corp. Counsel--Growmark, Inc., Bloomington, IL, pg. 490
Carraway, A., Gen. Counsel--Guest Services, Inc., Fairfax, VA, pg. 493
Carreco, Alan, V.P. & Legal Counsel--Specialty Restaurants Corporation, Anaheim, CA, pg. 1027
Carretta, Thomas, Gen. Counsel--Control Systems Inc., Saint Paul, MN, pg. 281
Carrier, Bruce, V.P. & Corp. Counsel--Laverdiere's Enterprises, Winslow, ME, pg. 661
Carter, Jerry C., Chm. Bd., Pres. & Chief Exec. Officer--Jerry C. Carter, Inc., Gainesville, GA, pg. 226
Carter, John, Sr. V.P., Bechtel Group, Inc.--Bechtel Group, Inc., San Francisco, CA, pg. 130
Cartoon, Bernard, Gen. Counsel--Weider Health & Fitness, Woodland Hills, CA, pg. 1173
Cassetty, Fred, Chm. Bd., Pres. & Chief Exec. Officer--Alley-Cassetty Coal Co., Nashville, TN, pg. 37
Castillo, Angel, Gen. Counsel--Sanchez & Levitan, Inc., Miami, FL, pg. 970
Cerutti, P.B., Legal Counsel--U.R.M. Stores, Inc., Spokane, WA, pg. 1124
Chalifoux, Charles, V.P.-Mfg.--Bradley Printing Company, Des Plaines, IL, pg. 478
Chato, Genevieve, Gen. Counsel--Navajo Forest Products Industries, Navajo, NM, pg. 796
Chenoweth, Nick, V.P. & Gen. Counsel--Empire Airlines, Hayden Lake, ID, pg. 379
Chenoweth, R.A., Sec. & Gen. Counsel--Harwick Chemical Corp., Akron, OH, pg. 515
Cherrick, Lorraine, V.P. & Assoc. Gen. Counsel--Computer Sales International Inc., Saint Louis, MO, pg. 271
Chesley, Roger D., V.P. & Gen. Counsel--ESSTAR Incorporated, New Haven, CT, pg. 361
Chesley, Roger D., V.P. & Gen. Counsel--Essex Industries, New Haven, CT, pg. 361
Chilton, Charles, Gen. Counsel--Colorado Boxed Beef Co., Auburndale, FL, pg. 265
Choate, A.G., Sec. & Gen. Counsel--American Trading and Production Corporation, Baltimore, MD, pg. 64
Chozen, Richard, Gen. Counsel--Pumpelly Oil, Inc., Westlake, LA, pg. 900
Christenbury, Edward S., V.P. & Gen. Counsel--Tennessee Valley Authority, Knoxville, TN, pg. 1088
Christenson, James M., Gen. Counsel--Ministers Life Insurance Company, Minneapolis, MN, pg. 757
Christian, Betty S., Chm. Bd., Pres. & Chief Exec. Officer--Central Coca-Cola Bottling Company, Inc., Richmond, VA, pg. 232
Churna, Vic, Gen. Counsel--Dombrowski & Holmes, Inc., Chicago, IL, pg. 343
Ciccotelli, Teresa T., V.P., Legal Counsel & Sec.--Alco Health Services Corporation, Malvern, PA, pg. 31
Claccum, Jo Ann, Gen. Counsel--Meehan Tooker, East Rutherford, NJ, pg. 736
Clapman, Peter C., Sr. V.P. & Chief Counsel-Investments--Teachers Insurance and Annuity Association-College Retirement Equities Fund, New York, NY, pg. 1082
Clark, J. Patrick, Gen. Counsel--Dentsply International Inc., York, PA, pg. 329
Clark, John R., Gen. Counsel--Steuart Investment Co., Washington, DC, pg. 1048
Clayman, Raymond, Gen. Counsel--The Elder-Beerman Stores Corp., Dayton, OH, pg. 373

Clayton, D. Michael, Gen. Counsel--Samsonite Corporation, Denver, CO, pg. 358
Cleary, Stephen, Corp. Counsel--Gloria Jean's Coffee Bean Corp., Buffalo Grove, IL, pg. 464
Cline, Geffrey, Legal Officer--Lost Arrow Corporation, Ventura, CA, pg. 684
Clinton, Robert, V.P.-Fin.--United Design, Noble, OK, pg. 1131
Coben, Carl G., V.P., Sec. & Legal--Aratex Services, Lawrenceville, GA, pg. 6
Cochrane, E.G., II, Sec. & Gen. Counsel--Mount Vernon Mills, Inc., Greenville, SC, pg. 844
Coffey, John T., Jr., Sec. & Gen. Counsel--Maguire Group Inc., Foxboro, MA, pg. 701
Cohen, Allan, LLD, Medical & Legal--Paul A. De Jesse, Inc. Advertising, Freehold, NJ, pg. 321
Cohen, Herbert, Gen. Counsel--The Allan R. Hackel Organization, Newton Center, MA, pg. 498
Cohen, Stephen A., V.P., Sec. & Gen. Counsel--Academy Insurance Group, Inc., Atlanta, GA, pg. 11
Cohen, Victor, V.P. & Gen. Counsel--Polo/Ralph Lauren Corporation, New York, NY, pg. 879
Cohen, William N., V.P., Gen. Counsel, & Sec.--Environmental Industries, Inc., Calabasas, CA, pg. 383
Coleman, Joel C., V.P., Gen. Counsel & Sec.--Playtex FP Group Incorporated, Stamford, CT, pg. 877
Coleman, Joel C., Gen. Counsel--Playtex Family Products Corp., Stamford, CT, pg. 877
Collis, Foster J., Gen. Counsel--East Kentucky Power Co-op, Winchester, KY, pg. 362
Collyer, Macon, V.P. & Gen. Counsel--Sun Data Inc., Norcross, GA, pg. 1058
Collyer, William, V.P. & Gen. Counsel--Sun Data Inc., Norcross, GA, pg. 1058
Compton, Gregory A., Gen. Counsel--NTS Corporation, Louisville, KY, pg. 781
Connely, Peter, Sr. V.P. & Gen. Counsel--Hyatt Hotels Corporation, Chicago, IL, pg. 495
Connors, James, Gen. Counsel--Universal Builders Supply, Inc., Mount Vernon, NY, pg. 1137
Cook, Jeanne, Gen. Counsel--Hill International Inc., Willingboro, NJ, pg. 534
Cookerly, Ernest S., Gen. Counsel--David A. Bramble, Inc., Chestertown, MD, pg. 171
Coombs, Eugene C., Sec. & Gen. Counsel--Town & Country Food Markets, Inc., Wichita, KS, pg. 1103
Cooper, Cary D., Exec. V.P. & Chief Fin. Officer--The Cherokee Group, Sunland, CA, pg. 243
Cooper, R. John, Exec. V.P., Gen. Counsel & Sec.--Young & Rubicam Inc., New York, NY, pg. 1210
Copeland, Donald F., Gen. Counsel--Atlantic Dairy Cooperative, Southampton, PA, pg. 94
Copeland, Donald F., Gen. Counsel--Resco Products, Inc., Conshohocken, PA, pg. 928
Coppersmith, W. Louis, Sec. & Gen. Counsel--Glosser Brothers, Inc., Johnstown, PA, pg. 978
Cordaro, Robert, Gen. Counsel--William Brojack Lumber Company, pg. 179
Coriden, Michael W., Corp. Attorney & Sec.--CF&I Steel Corporation, Pueblo, CO, pg. 201
Costello, Thomas, Gen. Counsel--Compuware Corporation, Farmington Hills, MI, pg. 271
Cotter, William, V.P. & Gen. Counsel--American Optical Corp., Greenwich, CT, pg. 59
Covington, Kennedy, Gen. Counsel--Sunox, Inc., Charlotte, NC, pg. 1062
Cowan, William, Gen. Counsel--Creation Windows of Indiana, Inc., Elkhart, IN, pg. 297
Cox, Bill, Corp. Counsel--Willamette-Western Corporation, Portland, OR, pg. 1190
Cox, Garen, Gen. Counsel--Health Care Lodges, Coffeyville, KS, pg. 520
Cox, Robert T., V.P. & Gen. Counsel--Shelter Mutual Insurance Company, Columbia, MO, pg. 997
Coxe, Tench, Legal Officer--Ed Taylor Construction Co., Tucker, GA, pg. 1081
Craine, Katherine G., V.P. & Gen. Counsel--Kettle Restaurants, Houston, TX, pg. 626
Crane, Don, Gen. Counsel--UniHealth America, Burbank, CA, pg. 1126
Crawford, Christine, Sec. & Legal Officer--Henkels & McCoy, Inc., Blue Bell, PA, pg. 529
Cremins, William T., Exec. V.P., Gen. Counsel & Sec.--Naugatuck Glass Company, Naugatuck, CT, pg. 796
Crews, Donald R., Sr. V.P., Legal & Sec.--Harte-Hanks Communications, Inc., San Antonio, TX, pg. 513
Criso, Anthony, V.P., Legal Counsel & Sec.--Essex Group, Inc., Fort Wayne, IN, pg. 389
Cromer, C. Jackson, Sec. & Gen. Counsel--Van Leunens Inc., Cincinnati, OH, pg. 1144
Crossan, Jane, Gen. Counsel--W&F Manufacturing Corporation, Inc., Buffalo, NY, pg. 1155
Croushore, Bruce J., V.P., Sec. & Gen. Counsel--Bender Shipbuilding & Repair Company, Mobile, AL, pg. 138
Crowe, H., Gen. Counsel--American Foundry Group, Inc., Bixby, OK, pg. 54
Cruikshank, Ronald, Sr. V.P., Gen. Counsel--Ketchum Communications Inc., Pittsburgh, PA, pg. 625
Culbertson, Arthur C., Sec. & Gen. Counsel--Construction Specialties, Inc., Cranford, NJ, pg. 277
Cummings, R. C., Sec. & Gen. Counsel--Smith-Lee Co., Inc., Oneida, NY, pg. 1013
Cummins, Kenneth C., V.P., Sec. & Gen. Counsel--Morse Shoe, Inc., Canton, MA, pg. 772
Cunningham, Bob, Gen. Counsel & Sec.--Tennessee Farmers Co-op, La Vergne, TN, pg. 1087
Cunningham, Dale, Sr. V.P. & Gen. Counsel--Sunkist Growers, Inc., Sherman Oaks, CA, pg. 1060
Curran, Kevin J., Sec. & Gen. Counsel--Parsons Brinckerhoff Inc., New York, NY, pg. 850
Curtin, Richard, Corp. Sec. & Gen. Counsel--Berry Bearing Co., Lyons, IL, pg. 144
Cutler, Jim, Dir.-Contracts--Western Data Systems, Calabasas, CA, pg. 1178
D'Amour, Charles L., Sr. V.P. & Gen. Counsel--Big Y Foods Inc., Springfield, MA, pg. 149
Dadamo, Vincent M., V.P. & Legal Counsel--Decision Data Inc., Horsham, PA, pg. 323
Danello, Timothy, V.P., Gen. Counsel & Asst. Sec.--Oxford Realty Services Corp., Bethesda, MD, pg. 835
Daneri, Roxanne, Sec. & Gen. Counsel--Swift Dodge Rolls Royce Inc., Sacramento, CA, pg. 1067
Davis, Bonnie, Gen. Counsel & Sec.--Finlay Enterprises, Inc., New York, NY, pg. 411
Davis, Mark F., Gen. Counsel--Dewberry & Davis, Fairfax, VA, pg. 334
Davis, Thomas, Exec. Dir. & Gen. Counsel--Advanced Technology, Inc., Reston, VA, pg. 20
Davis, Timothy M., Gen. Counsel & Sec.--Haddon Craftsmen, Inc., Scranton, PA, pg. 499
Davis, Walter S., Gen. Counsel--Grede Foundries, Inc., Milwaukee, WI, pg. 483
Davisson, Richard F., Sec. & Gen. Counsel--Pay Less Super Markets, Inc., Anderson, IN, pg. 852
Dawahare, Joe, Dir.-Govt. Affairs & Gen. Counsel--Dawahares, Inc., Lexington, KY, pg. 319
Dawson, William R., Gen. Counsel--Glico Harmony Foods Corporation, Santa Cruz, CA, pg. 462
De Majistre, Robert, V.P. & Sec.--Seton Company, Norristown, PA, pg. 993
Deane, James R., Exec. V.P., Gen. Counsel & Sec.--Fiduciary Trust Co. International, New York, NY, pg. 408
Deane, James R., Exec. V.P., Sec. & Gen. Counsel--Fiduciary Trust Company International, New York, NY, pg. 408
DeCaro, Phil, Gen. Counsel--Micro Component Technology Inc., Saint Paul, MN, pg. 748
Deering, John R., Exec. V.P.-Fin., Chief Oper. Officer & Legal Officer--Production Machinery Corporation, Mentor, OH, pg. 893
DeJohn, Stephen E., Legal Counsel--Ohio Lottery Commission, Cleveland, OH, pg. 822
Delambo, Robert, Gen. Counsel--Countrymark Cooperative, Inc., Indianapolis, IN, pg. 290
Delmenico, Ronald, Legal Officer--Soft Sheen Products, Inc., Chicago, IL, pg. 1016
Derounian, Paul, Gen. Counsel--Reliable Automatic Sprinkler Co., Inc., Mount Vernon, NY, pg. 924
Derzaw, Richard, Gen. Counsel--MI Fund Incorporated, New York, NY, pg. 692
Desch, Theodore E., Sr. V.P.-Law & Corp. Affairs--Blue Cross & Blue Shield of Illinois, Chicago, IL, pg. 160
Devor, R.C., Jr., Legal Officer--Nashville Wire Product Co., Nashville, TN, pg. 784
DeVore, Thomas, Legal Officer--Acme Foundry, Inc., Coffeyville, KS, pg. 13
Diarla, Pamela,, Gen. Counsel--Chicago Holdings, Inc., Pittsburgh, PA, pg. 245
DiBenedetto, Tony, V.P.-Legal Counsel--ERA Real Estate, Overland Park, KS, pg. 360
Dickerson, B.R., Gen. Counsel--The Crispin Company, Houston, TX, pg. 299
Dickerson, L.C., III, Gen. Counsel--Bollinger Machine Shop And Shipyard, Inc., Lockport, LA, pg. 163
DiNicola, John W., V.P. & Gen. Counsel--Gilbane Building Company, Providence, RI, pg. 457
DiPaola, Robert, Gen. Counsel--Calvin Klein, Inc., New York, NY, pg. 635
Dobran, James, Chief Litigation & Devel. Counsel--The Cafaro Co., Youngstown, OH, pg. 207
Dodge, Mark, Exec. V.P. & Gen. Counsel--Western International Media Corporation, Los Angeles, CA, pg. 1179
Doherty, Richard M., Gen. Counsel--Camp Dresser & McKee Inc., Cambridge, MA, pg. 212
Donelan, Francis P., V.P., Sec. & Gen. Counsel--George A. Fuller Company, New York, NY, pg. 436
Donovan, John S., Exec. V.P.-Fin., Admin. & Gen. Counsel--Cives Corp., Roswell, GA, pg. 251
Dorson, Patricia Freeman, V.P. & Gen. Counsel--VASA Brougher, Inc., Indianapolis, IN, pg. 1146
Douglas, Gene, V.P.-Legal & Admin.--Hvide Shipping, Inc., Fort Lauderdale, FL, pg. 556
Downie, John F., Sr. V.P., Sec. & Gen. Counsel--Cole National Corporation, Cleveland, OH, pg. 260
Downie, John F., Sec. & Gen. Counsel--Cole Key Corporation, Cleveland, OH, pg. 260
Downie, John F., Sec. & Gen. Counsel--Cole Vision Corporation, Cleveland, OH, pg. 260
Downing, Walt, Gen. Counsel--RK Mechanical, Inc., Lakewood, CO, pg. 907
Doyle, C.A., V.P., Sec. & Gen. Counsel--Burns & Roe Enterprises, Inc., Oradell, NJ, pg. 194
Drenning, John, Legal Officer & Sec.--Smith Metal Arts Company, Inc., Buffalo, NY, pg. 1013
Dropkin, Philip, Sec. & Gen. Counsel--Cablevision Industries Corp., Liberty, NY, pg. 206
Dryden, Kay, Sr. V.P., Sec. & Legal Counsel--Del Monte Foods, San Francisco, CA, pg. 325
Duberstein, Gary K., V.P. & Gen. Counsel--Icahn & Co., Inc., Mount Kisco, NY, pg. 561
Dubow, R., V.P. & Gen. Counsel--Quality Bakers of America Cooperative, Inc., Greenwich, CT, pg. 903
Dudas, J., Gen. Counsel--Rite-Way, Inc., Saddle Brook, NJ, pg. 936
Duerr, Steve, Gen. Counsel--Jackson Hole Ski Resort, Teton Village, WY, pg. 587
Duffey, Kenta, Gen. Counsel--Blue Anchor, Inc., Sacramento, CA, pg. 158
Duffy, James F., Sr. V.P. & Gen. Counsel--The American Stock Exchange, New York, NY, pg. 62
Dun, David, Sec. & Gen. Counsel--Sierra Pacific Industries, Redding, CA, pg. 1003
Duncan, Walter, V.P.-Legal & Sec.--Southern Farm Bureau Casualty Insurance Company, Ridgeland, MS, pg. 1021
Dunn, Peter L., V.P.-Admin., Gen. Counsel & Sec.--Korn/Ferry International, Los Angeles, CA, pg. 642
DuPree, Billy, Sr. V.P., Gen. Counsel & Sec.--American Health Companies, Inc., Pittsburgh, PA, pg. 55
Dusenbury, James H., Gen. Counsel--Anchor Financial Corporation, Myrtle Beach, SC, pg. 71
Dwyer, Carrie, Sr. V.P. & Gen. Counsel--The American Stock Exchange, New York, NY, pg. 62
Dyer, Patrick, V.P. & Gen. Counsel--The Vagabond Inns, San Diego, CA, pg. 1142
Easton, Reed W., Gen. Counsel--Mona Industries, Inc., Paterson, NJ, pg. 764
Eckberg, David, Gen. Counsel & Sec.--Hart Crowser, Inc., Seattle, WA, pg. 512
Eckman, Amy, V.P. & Gen. Counsel--Eckman Construction Company, Bedford, NH, pg. 366
Edelstein, Stuart, Gen. Counsel--Commercial Light Company, Hillside, IL, pg. 268
Edwards, Carl, Jr., V.P. & Gen. Counsel--Lennox International Inc., Richardson, TX, pg. 667
Egan, Charles J., Jr., V.P., Gen. Counsel & Sec.--Hallmark Cards, Inc., Kansas City, MO, pg. 501
Egan, Mary, Legal Admin.--Esco Corporation, Portland, OR, pg. 388
Eggleston, Thomas W., Exec. V.P. & Gen. Counsel--Amway Corporation, Ada, MI, pg. 70
Eisele, Thomas, Sec. & Legal Counsel--Nibco, Inc., Elkhart, IN, pg. 806
Eisenstein, Lois, Sr. V.P.-Business Affairs & Gen. Counsel--MTV Networks, New York, NY, pg. 785
Eisenstein, Lois Peel, Sr. V.P.-Bus. Affairs & Gen. Counsel-MTV Networks--Viacom Inc., New York, NY, pg. 785
Ekdahl, Jon N., Sec. & Gen. Counsel--Arthur Andersen & Co., S.C., New York, NY, pg. 72
Ekeler, Kathryn, Legal Counsel--ITI Marketing Services, Inc., Omaha, NE, pg. 561
Eklund, Robert, Gen. Counsel--Fleet Engineers, Inc., Muskegon, MI, pg. 417
Eldridge, James F., Exec. V.P.-Legal & Sec.--American Family Mutual Insurance Co., Madison, WI, pg. 51
Ells, Craig, Gen. Counsel--Lee Myles Associates Corporation, Maywood, NJ, pg. 666
Emanuel, David, Gen. Counsel--Lillie Rubin Affiliates Inc., Miami, FL, pg. 954
Emmons, Melvin, Gen. Counsel--Grocers Supply Co. Inc., Houston, TX, pg. 488
Ensign, Gregory M., V.P., Sec. & Gen. Counsel--Kirkwood Industries, Inc., Cleveland, OH, pg. 633
Epstein, Martin, Pres., Chief Exec. & Chief Fin. Officer--Associated Machinecraft Corporation, Los Angeles, CA, pg. 90
Erickson, Greg, Sec. & Gen. Counsel--Erickson Diversified Corp., Hudson, WI, pg. 386
Erwin, Robert P., Gen. Counsel--Bartlett and Company, Kansas City, MO, pg. 122
Evanoff, Michael, V.P.-Devel. & Gen. Counsel--Hyatt International Corporation, Chicago, IL, pg. 495
Evans, James E., V.P. & Gen. Counsel--American Financial Corporation, Cincinnati, OH, pg. 52
Evers, Bradley W., V.P., Sec. & Gen. Counsel--Price Brothers Co., Dayton, OH, pg. 888
Eyster, Franklin S., II, Sr. V.P., Sec. & Gen. Counsel--Atlantic Aviation Corp., New Castle, DE, pg. 94
Ezra, Robert, Gen. Counsel--Style Auto, Van Nuys, CA, pg. 1055
Falick, Paul, V.P. & Gen. Counsel--ICC Industries, Inc., New York, NY, pg. 558
Farr, Thomas, V.P.-Claims & Gen. Counsel--Preferred Risk Mutual Insurance, West Des Moines, IA, pg. 886
Farrell, James B., V.P., Gen. Counsel & Sec.--Minstar, Inc., Minneapolis, MN, pg. 758
Farrell, James B., V.P., Gen. Counsel & Sec.--Genmar Industries, Inc., Minneapolis, MN, pg. 759
Farrell, Neal F., Mng. Partner, V.P., Gen. Counsel & Chief Fin. Officer--Borg-Warner Corporation, Chicago, IL, pg. 165
Farris, John, Gen. Counsel--Conley Frog & Switch Company, Memphis, TN, pg. 274
Faulkner, Harry F., III, V.P.-Admin. & Sec.--North American Royalties, Inc., Chattanooga, TN, pg. 811
Feibel, James B., Sec. & Gen. Counsel--Electric Power Equipment Co., Columbus, OH, pg. 373
Feldman, Eugene, Sec. & Legal Officer--Doe Spun, Inc., New York, NY, pg. 343
Fell, Lawrence M., Sec. & Gen. Counsel--Industrial General Corporation, Elyria, OH, pg. 566
Fennell, Mauryne, Legal Officer--Thrifty Oil Company, Downey, CA, pg. 1096
Ferdinand, Mark, Gen. Counsel--Triton Industries, Inc., Chicago, IL, pg. 1114
Field, Robert, Gen. Counsel--Greenhorne & O'Mara, Inc., Greenbelt, MD, pg. 485
Fiffer, James D., Legal Officer--American Fluorescent Corporation, Waukegan, IL, pg. 54
Fischer, Klaus P., V.P., Gen. Counsel & Sec.--Elliott Company, Jeannette, PA, pg. 378
Fisher, Evans W., V.P. & Gen. Counsel--Brian Center Management Corporation, Hickory, NC, pg. 175
Fisher, G. Robert, Legal Counsel--Jordan Industries, Inc., Deerfield, IL, pg. 604
Fisher, Joe, Legal Officer--CCC Information Services, Chicago, IL, pg. 410
Fisher, Rebecca Hope, V.P. & Corp. Counsel--Capital Bancorp, Miami, FL, pg. 214
Fitzgerald, Robert M., Esq., Legal Officer--Son Chief Electrics, Inc., Winsted, CT, pg. 1018
Fitzsimons, John H., Sec. & Gen. Counsel--The Dyson-Kissner-Moran Corporation, New York, NY, pg. 357
Flaggman, Steve, Gen. Counsel--Seligman & Associates, Inc., Bloomfield Hills, MI, pg. 988
Fleishaker, Aaron, Gen. Counsel--Henry Modell & Company, Inc., Long Island City, NY, pg. 762
Fleming, Gordon, Sec. & Treas.--Brock Candy Company, Chattanooga, TN, pg. 177
Flick, Sol E., Gen. Counsel--North American Watch Corporation, Lyndhurst, NJ, pg. 812

Flood, John, Exec. V.P. & Legal Counsel--National Football League Properties, Inc., New York, NY, pg. 788
Florence, Faye A., Gen. Counsel--Syratech Corporation, East Boston, MA, pg. 1070
Flynn, Gary, Exec. V.P., Treas. & Sec.--Rotary Multiforms, Inc., Detroit, MI, pg. 951
Forneris, Jeanne, V.P. & Gen. Counsel--M. A. Mortenson Company, Minneapolis, MN, pg. 772
Fortenbaugh, Samuel B., III, Gen. Counsel--Goodman Equipment Corp., Bedford Park, IL, pg. 470
Fox, Stephen, V.P., Gen. Counsel & Sec.--Amperif Corporation, Chatsworth, CA, pg. 68
Francis, William, Treas., Controller & Chief Fin. Officer--Captive-Aire Systems, Inc., Youngsville, NC, pg. 216
Frankel, Edward M., V.P. & Gen. Counsel--Standard Textile Co., Inc., Cincinnati, OH, pg. 1037
Franklin, Gary R., Corp. Counsel--The Maxima Corporation, Lanham, MD, pg. 723
Fraser, Brian G., V.P.-Admin. & Gen. Counsel--Clark Foodservice, Inc., Elk Grove Village, IL, pg. 252
Freedman, Marc D., Sr. V.P., Gen. Counsel & Sec.--Butler Service Group, Inc., Montvale, NJ, pg. 197
Freedman, Sanford, Exec. V.P. & Gen. Counsel--Tollman/Hundley Hotels, Valhalla, NY, pg. 1100
Freimark, Jeffrey P., Exec. V.P., Chief Fin. Officer & Gen. Counsel & Sec.--Pueblo International, Inc., Pompano Beach, FL, pg. 899
Frelinghuysen, Peter, Legal Counsel--KOA Holdings, New York, NY, pg. 612
French, Linda, Sr. V.P., Gen. Counsel & Sec.--Payless Cashways, Inc., Kansas City, MO, pg. 853
Friedman, Kathryn, Gen. Counsel--Convenient Food Mart, Inc., Schaumburg, IL, pg. 281
Fritz, Jerald N., V.P. & Gen. Counsel--Allbritton Communications Company, Washington, DC, pg. 862
Froeliger, E.L., Sec., Treas. & Chief Fin. Officer--Frantz Manufacturing Co., Sterling, IL, pg. 429
Frost, Thomas E., V.P. & Gen. Counsel--CenterMark Properties, Inc., Saint Louis, MO, pg. 231
Fry, David S., V.P., Sec. & Gen. Counsel--Steelcase Inc., Grand Rapids, MI, pg. 1044
Fuson, Harold W., Jr., V.P.-Legal Affairs--The Copley Press, Inc., La Jolla, CA, pg. 284
Gaines, Weaver H., Jr., Exec. V.P. & Gen. Counsel--The Mutual Life Insurance Company of New York (MONY), New York, NY, pg. 778
Gaither, Michael, Gen. Counsel--J. H. Heafner Co. Inc., Lincolnton, NC, pg. 520
Galante, Joyce M., Sec. & Legal Counsel--Tagsons Papers, Inc., Albany, NY, pg. 1076
Galli, Robert G., Exec. V.P.-Legal--Oppenheimer Management Corp., New York, NY, pg. 719
Gallo, Samuel J., Sr. V.P., Sec. & Gen. Counsel--Arthur D. Little, Inc., Cambridge, MA, pg. 678
Gannett, Herbert M., Gen. Counsel--Red Devil Inc., Union, NJ, pg. 918
Gannon, Christopher R., Gen. Counsel & Sec.--G.S. Blodgett Corporation, Burlington, VT, pg. 157
Gantner, F.J., Gen. Counsel--Rieth-Riley Construction Co. Inc., Goshen, IN, pg. 934
Ganzi, Victor F., V.P., Gen. Counsel & Sec.--The Hearst Corporation, New York, NY, pg. 521
Garfinkle, Mark A., V.P., Gen. Counsel & Sec.--Alleco Inc., Cheverly, MD, pg. 35
Garonzik, Arnon E., Gen. Counsel & Sec.--The ERM Group, Exton, PA, pg. 360
Garramone, Daniel, V.P. & Gen. Counsel--Schwinn Bicycle Company, Chicago, IL, pg. 981
Garten, David B., V.P. & Gen. Counsel--Tremont Corporation, Denver, CO, pg. 1109
Gartenberg, Irving L., Gen. Counsel--Inner Secrets, Inc., Hoboken, NJ, pg. 570
Gary, Thomas, Gen. Counsel--The Bernuth Corporation, Miami, FL, pg. 144
Gatewood, Robert, Sr. Exec. V.P.-Legal Affairs & Sec.--Druther's International, Inc., Louisville, KY, pg. 350
George, Armen S., Legal Officer--Up-Right, Inc., Selma, CA, pg. 1139
Gerber, Jody, Gen. Counsel--SGD International Corp., New York, NY, pg. 962
Gerber, Morris, Gen. Counsel--Connelly Containers, Inc., Bala-Cynwyd, PA, pg. 275
Gerber, Steven M., Gen. Counsel & Sec.--Gitano Group Inc., New York, NY, pg. 460
Gerchenson, Jeffery H., Pres. & Chief Oper. Officer--Alva/Amco Pharmacal Companies, Inc., Chicago, IL, pg. 46
Germine, Thomas J., V.P. & Gen. Counsel--General Chemical Corporation, Parsippany, NJ, pg. 801
Gerstman, George, Legal Officer--JS&A Group, Inc., Las Vegas, NV, pg. 586
Geyelin, Anthony, V.P., Asst. Sec. & Deputy Gen. Counsel--Academy Insurance Group, Inc., Atlanta, GA, pg. 11
Giblin, Pat, Legal Officer--Kampgrounds of America, Inc., Billings, MT, pg. 613
Gibson, Thomas, Exec. V.P., Chief Fin. Officer, Sec. & Gen. Counsel--The Gates Corporation, Denver, CO, pg. 445
Gilbert, M. Glenn, Exec. V.P. & Gen. Counsel--Zimmerman Holdings, Inc., San Marino, CA, pg. 1220
Gill, John J., Gen. Counsel--The American Bankers Association, Washington, DC, pg. 49
Gillen, James R., Sr. V.P. & Gen. Counsel--The Prudential Insurance Company of America, Newark, NJ, pg. 896
Gilmer, Jay, Gen. Counsel & Sec.--Diet Center, Inc., Pittsburgh, PA, pg. 55
Gilmore, Robert G., V.P. & Chief Counsel-Corp. Fin.--Teachers Insurance and Annuity Association-College Retirement Equities Fund, New York, NY, pg. 1082
Givant, Stephen, Gen. Counsel--Kearfott Guidance & Navigation Corp., Wayne, NJ, pg. 93
Glantz, Miles M., Sec. & Corp. Counsel--Wechco, Inc., Princeton, NJ, pg. 1172
Glantz, Miles M., Gen. Counsel & Sec.--West Chemical Products, Inc., Princeton, NJ, pg. 1172
Gleason, Owen, Gen. Counsel--C. H. Robinson Co. Inc., Eden Prairie, MN, pg. 939
Glendening, R. Bradley, Sr. V.P., Gen. Counsel & Sec.--Mary Kay Cosmetics Inc., Dallas, TX, pg. 716
Glennon, William, Gen. Counsel--Borchers Bros., San Jose, CA, pg. 165
Glover, Keith, Pres. & Gen. Mgr.--Producers Rice Mill Inc., Stuttgart, AR, pg. 892
Godson, John, Gen. Counsel--Capital Electric Group, Inc., Phoenix, AZ, pg. 215
Goeller, Michael C., Sec. & Gen. Counsel--Hatzel & Buehler, Inc., Wilmington, DE, pg. 277
Goelzer, D.M., Sec. & Gen. Counsel--B-E Holdings Inc., South Milwaukee, WI, pg. 106
Goelzer, David M., Sec. & Gen. Counsel--Bucyrus-Erie Company, South Milwaukee, WI, pg. 186
Goldammer, Vance, Gen. Counsel--The Austad Company, Sioux Falls, SD, pg. 98
Goldblatt, Thomas, Gen. Counsel--Strombecker Corporation, Chicago, IL, pg. 1054
Golder, Morton I., Gen. Counsel--Unigroup, Inc., Fenton, MO, pg. 1126
Golder, Morton I., Gen. Counsel--United Van Lines, Inc., Fenton, MO, pg. 1126
Goldfeld, Seymour, Legal Officer--Splendor Form International Inc., Long Island City, NY, pg. 1031
Goldin, Edward S., Legal Officer--Union Industries, Inc., Providence, RI, pg. 1128
Goldings, Morris, Sec. & Gen. Counsel--Jet Spray Corp., Norwood, MA, pg. 593
Goldman, Charles M., Sec. & Gen. Counsel--Seaboard Corporation, Newton, MA, pg. 984
Goldman, David, Legal Officer & Sec.--Duro-Test Corporation, Fairfield, NJ, pg. 355
Goldstein, Alan B., Exec. V.P., Sec. & Gen. Counsel--American Savings of Florida, ESB, Miami, FL, pg. 382
Gonzales, Ignacio, Gen. Counsel & Dir.-Data Processing--Cash & Carry Grocer Inc., Chicago, IL, pg. 228
Goodman, James A., Gen. Counsel & Sec.--Day & Zimmermann, Inc., Radnor, PA, pg. 320
Goodrich, H.L., Sec. & Gen. Counsel--Dan River Inc., Danville, VA, pg. 313
Gordan, Cynthia, Legal Counsel--Quaker Fabric Corporation, Fall River, MA, pg. 903
Gordon, John, V.P., Gen. Counsel & Sec.--Red Roof Inns, Inc., Hilliard, OH, pg. 918
Gordon, Richard S., Legal Officer--Pressure Systems, Hampton, VA, pg. 888
Gore, G. H., Sec. & Gen. Counsel--North American Company, Fort Lauderdale, FL, pg. 811
Gorlin, Robert H., Gen. Counsel--Guardian Industries Corp., Northville, MI, pg. 491
Gorman, Jeff, V.P. & Gen. Counsel--Adventure Tours USA, Inc., Dallas, TX, pg. 21
Gorski, Walter, Sr. V.P. & Gen. Counsel--Connecticut Mutual Life Insurance Company, Hartford, CT, pg. 274
Gotkin, Michael S., Sr. V.P. & Gen. Counsel--Farley Candy Company, Chicago, IL, pg. 399
Gottesman, M., Legal Officer--Antwerp Diamond Distributors Inc., New York, NY, pg. 77
Graff, Terry D., Legal Officer--Mountain Air Delivery, Sparks, NV, pg. 773
Graham, Alma, Gen. Counsel--United Health Plan, Inglewood, CA, pg. 1133
Graves, Ronald N., V.P., Sec. & Gen. Counsel--J.R. Simplot Company, Boise, ID, pg. 1007
Greeley, Walter F., Gen. Counsel--Raffi & Swanson, Inc., Wilmington, MA, pg. 909
Green, Doug, Sr. V.P. & Gen. Counsel--Ellerbe Becket, Inc., Minneapolis, MN, pg. 378
Green, Tom, Gen. Counsel--Trammell Crow Company, Dallas, TX, pg. 1106
Greenbaum, Kenneth, V.P. & Gen. Counsel--Farley Industries, Chicago, IL, pg. 399
Greene, James, Gen. Counsel--The Gary-Williams Company, Denver, CO, pg. 444
Greene, James, Gen. Counsel--Gary-Williams Energy Corporation, Denver, CO, pg. 444
Greenman, Charles, Gen. Counsel--Corinthian Media, Inc., New York, NY, pg. 286
Greensfelder, Ed, Gen. Counsel--Welsh Company, Saint Louis, MO, pg. 1175
Greenwood, Ramon, Gen. Counsel--Cranford Johnson Robinson Woods, Little Rock, AR, pg. 296
Groce, David, V.P., Sec. & Gen. Counsel--Precision Tune, Inc., Leesburg, VA, pg. 885
Gudgel, Thomas H., Sr. V.P. & Gen. Counsel--Blue Cross and Blue Shield of Oklahoma, Tulsa, OK, pg. 159
Gurion, Henry B., V.P. & Corp. Counsel--MI-Jack Products, Inc., Hazel Crest, IL, pg. 746
Haber, Irving, V.P.-Legal--R. H. Macy & Co., Inc., New York, NY, pg. 698
Haber, Marvin, V.P. & Legal Counsel--Federal Data Corporation, Bethesda, MD, pg. 404
Haddon, James, Gen. Counsel & Sec.--Creative Marketing Resource, Inc., Chicago, IL, pg. 297
Haimes, Burt, Gen. Counsel & Sec.--National Cleaning Contractors, Inc., New York, NY, pg. 786
Hain, Mark, V.P. & Gen. Counsel--Norrell Corporation, Atlanta, GA, pg. 810
Haist, Dennis P., V.P., Gen. Counsel & Sec.--Dillingham Construction Corporation, Pleasanton, CA, pg. 337
Hale, Guy A., Chm. Bd., Pres. & Chief Exec. Officer--The Alamo Learning Systems, Inc., San Ramon, CA, pg. 29
Hall, Robert, Gen. Counsel--International Cold Storage Co., Inc., Andover, KS, pg. 576
Hall, Tom, Legal Officer--LaSalle-Deitch Co., Inc., Elkhart, IN, pg. 660
Hallmark, Robert J., Sr. V.P.-Claims & Gen. Counsel--Insurance Corp. of America, Houston, TX, pg. 572
Hamlyn, Richard, Legal Officer--Elias Brothers Restaurants, Inc., Warren, MI, pg. 376
Hand, John C., Sr. V.P., Gen. Counsel & Corp. Sec.--United Farm Bureau Family Life Insurance Co., Indianapolis, IN, pg. 1131
Handelsman, Harold, Sr. V.P., Sec. & Gen. Counsel--Hyatt Corporation Chicago, IL, pg. 495
Handelsman, Harold S., V.P., Sec. & Gen. Counsel--Dalfort Corp., Dallas, TX, pg. 312
Handle, Ken, Gen. Counsel--Halsey Drug Co., Inc., Brooklyn, NY, pg. 502
Hannenberg, Ruth C., Sec. & Legal Officer--Mesirow Financial, Chicago, IL, pg. 741
Hanson, Tom, Gen. Counsel--Sieg Company, Davenport, IA, pg. 1002
Harpold, Lew W., Gen. Counsel--Randall's Food Markets, Inc., Houston, TX, pg. 911
Harr, Lawrence F., Exec. V.P. & Chief Counsel--Mutual of Omaha Insurance Company, Omaha, NE, pg. 779
Harr, Lawrence F., Exec. V.P. & Chief Counsel--Mutual of Omaha, Omaha, NE, pg. 779
Harrison, Donald, Chm. Bd. & Gen. Counsel--PVS Chemicals, Inc., Detroit, MI, pg. 837
Harrison, Robert, V.P. & Gen. Counsel--Dominick & Dominick, Incorporated, New York, NY, pg. 343
Hart, George E., V.P. & Corp. Counsel--National Health Care Affiliates, Inc., Buffalo, NY, pg. 791
Hart, Kenneth, Gen. Counsel--The Florida Lottery, Tallahassee, FL, pg. 420
Hart, Robert C., Sr. V.P., Sec. & Gen. Counsel--S. C. Johnson & Son, Inc., Racine, WI, pg. 599
Hartman, James O., Gen. Couns., Sec.--Up-Right Work Platforms Division, Selma, CA, pg. 1139
Harvey, Michael L., Sr. V.P.-Law, Gen. Counsel & Sec.--Atlas Van Lines, Inc., Evansville, IN, pg. 96
Harwood, Dennis W., Legal Officer--Label-Aire Inc., Fullerton, CA, pg. 649
Haskell, Charles L., Exec. V.P.-Fin. & Legal--Lettuce Entertain You Enterprises, Inc., Chicago, IL, pg. 668
Hasling, Robert J., V.P., Gen. Counsel & Sec.--The Minnesota Mutual Life Insurance Company, Saint Paul, MN, pg. 757
Hatcher, James A., Sec. & Gen. Counsel--Cox Enterprises, Inc., Atlanta, GA, pg. 292
Hatfield, Gus, V.P.-Legal Affairs--Solvay Pharmaceuticals, Inc., Marietta, GA, pg. 1017
Hawkes, Thomas, Sr. V.P.-Gen. Counsel--Beech Holdings Corp., Chicago, IL, pg. 131
Hayase, Paul, Gen. Counsel--Bon Appetit Magazine, Los Angeles, CA, pg. 636
Hayase, Paul H., Sr. V.P. & Gen. Counsel--Knapp Communications Corporation, Los Angeles, CA, pg. 636
Hayes, D.M., Sr. V.P., Sec. & Gen. Counsel--Agway, Inc., De Witt, NY, pg. 25
Hayes, David W., V.P.-Personnel & Gen. Counsel--Seiler Corporation, Waltham, MA, pg. 987
Hayes, Jere, V.P., Gen. Counsel & Sec.--Pacific Enterprises Oil Company (USA), Dallas, TX, pg. 840
Haythe, Thomas M., Sec. & Gen. Counsel--Novametrix Medical Systems Inc., Wallingford, CT, pg. 817
Hearnburg, William, Gen. Counsel--Southwire Company, Inc., Carrollton, GA, pg. 1024
Heerman, William R., Sr. V.P.-Law & Communications, Sec. & Gen. Counsel--Aid Association For Lutherans, Appleton, WI, pg. 26
Heiden, George F., V.P. & Gen. Counsel--Peter Kiewit Sons Inc., Omaha, NE, pg. 629
Heine, Spencer H., Exec. V.P.-Legal & Fin. Services--Montgomery Ward & Co., Inc., Chicago, IL, pg. 767
Hellman, Herbert M., Sr. V.P. & Gen. Counsel--R. H. Macy & Co., Inc., New York, NY, pg. 698
Hendon, Rob, V.P.-Corp. Counsel--Berlitz International, Inc., Princeton, NJ, pg. 142
Hendon, Robert C., Jr., Gen. Counsel & Sec.--Berlitz International, Inc., Princeton, NJ, pg. 142
Hendrick, T. Paul, Legal Officer--Edgar B. Furniture Co., Clemmons, NC, pg. 368
Hendrickson, R., Gen. Counsel--Standard Lafarge, Canfield, OH, pg. 1036
Henry, John C., V.P.-Gen. Counsel & Sec.--First American Bankshares, Inc., Washington, DC, pg. 412
Herbert, John, Gen. Counsel & Sec.--Ace Doran Hauling & Rigging Company, Cincinnati, OH, pg. 346
Herman, Robin A., V.P. & Gen. Counsel--Western Temporary Services, Inc., Walnut Creek, CA, pg. 1181
Herner, Donald A., Gen. Counsel & Sec.--Jac Jacobsen Industries, Inc., Greenwich, CT, pg. 587
Hess, Gregory, Legal Counsel & Sec.--Barr & Barr, Inc., New York, NY, pg. 121
Hess, Jerry, V.P. & Legal Counsel--Pony Express Courier Corp., Charlotte, NC, pg. 166
Hessler, D., Sec. & Gen. Counsel--Electric Furnace Co., Salem, OH, pg. 373
Hewitt, Marsha A., Sec. & Assoc. Gen. Counsel--Trans World Airlines, Inc., Mount Kisco, NY, pg. 561
Heyman, Ralph, Gen. Counsel--The Sportsman's Guide, Inc., Eagan, MN, pg. 1032
Hickey, Thomas J., V.P. & Gen. Counsel--Malcolm Pirnie, Inc., White Plains, NY, pg. 872
Hiltgen, Bill, Gen. Mgr.--TIC Investment Corp., Dallas, TX, pg. 1073
Hilts, Johnathan, Legal Counsel--Fairview Construction, Inc, Auburn Hills, MI, pg. 397
Hindman, Don J., Chm. Bd. & Chief Exec. Officer--Clark Foodservice, Inc., Elk Grove Village, IL, pg. 252
Hinman, Michael, Gen. Counsel--Basin Electric Power Co-Op, Bismarck, ND, pg. 125
Hirschfeld, Michael, Gen. Counsel & Asst. Sec.--Ficks Reed Company, Cincinnati, OH, pg. 408
Hirst, Ben, Sr. V.P.-Gen. Counsel--NWA, Inc., Saint Paul, MN, pg. 782
Hirst, Richard B., Exec. V.P. & Gen. Counsel--NWA, Inc., Saint Paul, MN, pg. 782
Hirst, Richard B., Exec. V.P. & Gen. Counsel--Northwest Airlines, Inc., Saint Paul, MN, pg. 782

Hitchens, Glenn, Gen. Counsel--Metal Masters Foodservice Equipment, Smyrna, DE, pg. 741
Hobbs, Kenneth, Gen. Counsel--Bush Brothers & Company, Dandridge, TN, pg. 196
Hoecker, Wayne, Gen. Counsel--MFA Incorporated, Columbia, MO, pg. 692
Hoellering, Michael F., Gen. Counsel--American Arbitration Association, New York, NY, pg. 49
Hofman, William K., Sr. V.P. & Gen. Counsel--Microband Companies, Inc., Fairfield, NJ, pg. 748
Hogan, Katherine A., Sr. V.P., Gen. Counsel/Entertainment--Viacom Inc., New York, NY, pg. 785
Hogan, Katherine A., Sr. V.P. & Gen. Counsel--Viacom Entertainment, New York, NY, pg. 785
Hogan, Tom, Gen. Counsel--Ranir Corporation, Grand Rapids, MI, pg. 912
Hollingsworth, Mark, Gen. Counsel--Contran Corporation, Dallas, TX, pg. 281
Holmes, Houston E., Jr., V.P., Sec. & Legal Counsel--Tom Thumb Food & Drugs, Inc., Dallas, TX, pg. 912
Holmquist, Paul R., Gen. Counsel & Sec.--American Hardware Mutual Insurance Co., Minnetonka, MN, pg. 55
Holzman, Donald J., Sec. & Gen. Counsel--Dinaire Corp., Buffalo, NY, pg. 338
Hopkins, Jacques, Gen. Counsel--American Mathematical Society, Inc., Providence, RI, pg. 58
Horn, Everett B., Jr., V.P. & Gen. Counsel--Boston Mutual Life Insurance Co., Canton, MA, pg. 167
Horowitz, Ira, Gen. Counsel--Webcraft Technologies, Inc., North Brunswick, NJ, pg. 1171
Horton, T., Gen. Counsel--Dimco-Gray Company, Dayton, OH, pg. 338
Horvath, Joseph J., Sr. V.P., Gen. Counsel & Sec.--The Penn Mutual Life Insurance Company, Philadelphia, PA, pg. 858
Hosek, LaVerne, Gen. Counsel & Sec.--Follett Corporation, Chicago, IL, pg. 422
Howe, Chester M., Gen. Counsel--A.W. Chesterton Company, Stoneham, MA, pg. 244
Howe, Richard K., Gen. Counsel--John Hancock Freedom Securities Corporation, Boston, MA, pg. 596
Hrusoff, Ronald, Gen. Counsel--John Burnham & Co., San Diego, CA, pg. 194
Huff, Thomas, Gen. Counsel--Aiken Electric Cooperative Inc., Aiken, SC, pg. 26
Huffman, H.V., Assoc. Counsel--Citizens Gas & Coke Utility, Indianapolis, IN, pg. 250
Hughes, David R., Gen. Counsel--Black Box Corporation, Lawrence, PA, pg. 748
Hunt, Brian, Gen. Counsel & Sec.--Amtran, Inc., Indianapolis, IN, pg. 69
Hurley, Maureen O., V.P. & Gen. Counsel--Rich Products Corp., Buffalo, NY, pg. 932
Hursh, Alan, Treas. & Sec.--Acousti Engineering Co. of Florida, Orlando, FL, pg. 14
Hurwitz, Laurence, Gen. Counsel--Ambac International Corp., Columbia, SC, pg. 47
Hutchins, Robert, Gen. Counsel--Pickering Industries Inc., Tacoma, WA, pg. 869
Hyman, Frank, Gen. Counsel--Astre Corporate Group, Alexandria, VA, pg. 92
Idzik, Daniel R., Sr. V.P. & Gen. Counsel--Booz Allen & Hamilton Inc., New York, NY, pg. 165
Ingham, Cranford A., V.P. & Gen. Counsel--State Farm Mutual Automobile Insurance Company, Bloomington, IL, pg. 1041
Irvin, Robert H., Sr. V.P. & Gen. Counsel--Mayflower Transit, Inc., Carmel, IN, pg. 724
Irving, R.H., V.P. & Gen. Counsel--Duchossois Industries, Inc., Elmhurst, IL, pg. 350
Isaac, Robert, Sec. & Gen. Counsel--Penrod Drilling Corporation, Dallas, TX, pg. 859
Isen, Robert, V.P. & Sec.--Paramount Packaging Corp., Chalfont, PA, pg. 848
Ivey, Reef C., III, Gen. Counsel--Nutri/System Inc., Blue Bell, PA, pg. 818
Jackson, Duane B., Exec. V.P. & Sr. Legal Counsel--Ideal Pool Corp., Atlanta, GA, pg. 562
Jackson, Greg, Gen. Counsel--Taylor Corporation, Mankato, MN, pg. 1081
Jackson, Kenneth, Gen. Counsel--Recon/Optical, Inc., Barrington, IL, pg. 917
Jacober, Jeffrey M., Pres. & Chief Exec. Officer--SGI Inc., Cranston, RI, pg. 962
Janger, Jerome, Sec. & Legal--Kennington Ltd., Inc., Los Angeles, CA, pg. 623
Janzen, Peter S., Assoc. Counsel--Land O'Lakes, Inc., Agricultural Services Div., Saint Paul, MN, pg. 653
Jaqua, Frederick W., V.P., Gen. Counsel & Sec.--American Standard Inc., New York, NY, pg. 61
Jardine, Thomas V., V.P.-Legal & Treas.--Atlas Refinery, Newark, NJ, pg. 96
Jay, Dan, Pres., Chief Exec. & Chief Fin. Officer--Campmor Inc., Paramus, NJ, pg. 213
Jay, Morton, Chm. Bd.--Campmor Inc., Paramus, NJ, pg. 213
Jeffrey, Thomas W., Sr. V.P., Gen. Counsel & Corp. Sec.--Atlantic Gulf Communities Corporation, Miami, FL, pg. 95
Jeffries, Jack, Gen. Counsel--Chicago Convention & Tourism Bureau, Chicago, IL, pg. 245
Jekel, Louis G., Legal Officer--Rural Metro Corporation, Scottsdale, AZ, pg. 956
Joffe, Carl H., Sec. & Gen. Counsel--Purcell Co., Inc., Bay Saint Louis, MS, pg. 900
Johnson, E. Peter, Sr. V.P. & Gen. Counsel--Sundt Corp., Tucson, AZ, pg. 1060
Johnson, George R., Asst. Sec. & Gen. Counsel--Twin City Die Castings Co., Minneapolis, MN, pg. 1121
Johnson, Horace A., Gen. Counsel--Hempt Brothers, Inc., Camp Hill, PA, pg. 528
Johnson, Joya, Gen. Counsel--H. J. Russell Corp., Atlanta, GA, pg. 957
Johnson, Murray, V.P., Gen. Counsel & Sec.--H.B. Zachry, San Antonio, TX, pg. 1215
Johnson, Robert A., V.P.-Sec. & Gen. Counsel--Bonneville International Corp., Salt Lake City, UT, pg. 332
Johnson, Ronald, Sec. & Gen. Counsel--Bankers Systems Inc., Saint Cloud, MN, pg. 117
Johnson, Steven, Gen. Counsel & Dir.-Legal Services--Norbest, Inc., Midvale, UT, pg. 809
Jones, James E., Chief Fin. Officer, Sec. & Treas.--Modern Welding Co., Inc., Owensboro, KY, pg. 763
Jones, K., Corp. Sec.--Colonial Pipeline Company, Atlanta, GA, pg. 264
Jones, Ken, Gen. Counsel--Jandy Industries, Novato, CA, pg. 589
Jones, Richard, V.P. & Gen. Counsel--Anschutz Corporation, Denver, CO, pg. 75
Jones, Robert E., Gen. Counsel--Mississippi Chemical Corporation, Yazoo City, MS, pg. 760
Joy, Harry, Mgr.-Legal--Encyclopaedia Britannica Educational Corporation, Chicago, IL, pg. 380
Joyce, Edward J., V.P. & Gen. Counsel--Connell Limited Partnership, Boston, MA, pg. 275
Judd, Peter, Gen. Counsel--Superior Reprographics, Seattle, WA, pg. 1064
June, Roy, Gen. Counsel--Knight Equipment Corp., Costa Mesa, CA, pg. 636
Just, Lawrence E., Asst. Sec. & Gen. Counsel--Bradley Printing Company, Des Plaines, IL, pg. 478
Justesen, Wayne, V.P., Sec. & Gen. Counsel--Greenwood Mills, Inc., Greenwood, SC, pg. 485
Kabak, Wayne, Legal Officer--Josephson International Inc., New York, NY, pg. 607
Kadish, David A., Sec. & Gen. Counsel--Integral Systems, Walnut Creek, CA, pg. 572
Kalnes, David M., Legal Officer--Amrecorp Realty Inc., Dallas, TX, pg. 68
Kalnins-Ghafari, Mara, Gen. Counsel--Ghafari Associates, Inc., Dearborn, MI, pg. 455
Kane, Alice T., Exec. V.P., Gen. Counsel & Sec.--New York Life Insurance Company, New York, NY, pg. 802
Kane, Edward K., Sr. V.P. & Gen. Counsel--The Guardian Life Insurance Company of America, New York, NY, pg. 492
Kaner, Harvey, Sr. V.P. & Gen. Counsel--Harvest States Cooperatives, Saint Paul, MN, pg. 514
Karaba, Frank, Gen. Counsel--Fuller O'Brien Paints, South San Francisco, CA, pg. 820
Katsampes, Theodore P., Sr. V.P.-Plng. Div., Gen. Counsel & Sec.--First Federal Savings and Loan Assn. of Rochester, Rochester, NY, pg. 413
Katz, Sidney M., Sr. V.P. & Gen. Counsel--National Mortgage Company, Memphis, TN, pg. 792
Kaufmann, Roy, Gen. Counsel--George W. Cochran Co., Inc., Washington, DC, pg. 258
Kaynard, Gerald, Sec. & Legal Counsel--American Development Corporation, North Charleston, SC, pg. 51
Keen, Paul R., Gen. Counsel & Sec.--Argo-Tech Corporation, Cleveland, OH, pg. 82
Kelliher, Daniel J., Jr., Sr. V.P. & Assoc. Gen. Counsel-Investments--The New England, Boston, MA, pg. 799
Kellogg, Martin N., Pres., Chief Oper. Officer & Corp. Sec.--UFE Incorporated, Stillwater, MN, pg. 1123
Kelly, John F., Sr. V.P.-Gen. Counsel--All America Financial, Worcester, MA, pg. 34
Kelly, John F., Sr. V.P. & Gen. Counsel--State Mutual Life Assurance Company of America, Worcester, MA, pg. 35
Kenneally, William, V.P., Sec. & Gen. Counsel--Golub Corporation, Schenectady, NY, pg. 469
Kennedy, Bernard, Pres. & Chief Oper. Officer--King Kullen Grocery Co., Inc., Westbury, NY, pg. 630
Kennedy, Bernard P., Gen. Counsel--King Kullen Grocery Co., Inc., Westbury, NY, pg. 630
Kennedy, Donald D., Jr., Sr. V.P. & Legal Counsel--National Liberty, Frazer, PA, pg. 791
Kennedy, James C., Sec. & Dep. General Counsel--American Financial Corporation, Cincinnati, OH, pg. 52
Kennedy, James C., V.P. & Gen. Counsel--Spelling Entertainment Group, Inc., Cincinnati, OH, pg. 54
Kenney, Thomas J., Gen. Counsel--John McKenzie Packing Co., Inc., Burlington, VT, pg. 730
Kessner, Theodore L., Legal Officer--The Chesapeake Life Insurance Co., Lincoln, NE, pg. 243
Kevorkian, Corinne, Gen. Counsel--F. Schumacher & Co., New York, NY, pg. 979
Keys, Carol F., Gen. Counsel--First Florida Equities, Ltd., Miami, FL, pg. 413
Keysor, Gus, Gen. Counsel--Linotype-Hell Company, Hauppauge, NY, pg. 677
Kiefer, J.B., Gen. Counsel--Kenneth Gordon New Orleans, Ltd., New Orleans, LA, pg. 472
Kilcur, James S., Gen. Counsel--Southeastern Pennsylvania Transportation Authority, Philadelphia, PA, pg. 1020
Kimmins, John, Exec. V.P.--Arthur Murray Intl., Inc., Coral Gables, FL, pg. 776
King, John L., Legal Officer--F.B. Wright Co., Dearborn, MI, pg. 1204
King, Kernan F., Exec. V.P.-Admin. & Gen. Counsel--The New England, Boston, MA, pg. 799
King, Kernan F., Gen. Counsel--The New England, Boston, MA, pg. 799
Kinne, Morris, V.P. & Gen. Counsel--Bar-S Foods Co., Phoenix, AZ, pg. 118
Kinney, Patrick J., Gen. Counsel--All-Phase Electric Supply Co. Inc., Benton Harbor, MI, pg. 35
Kirkpatrick, Douglas, Sec. & Gen. Counsel--Miken Companies, Inc., Cheektowaga, NY, pg. 752
Kirschbaum, Gerald S., V.P. & Gen. Counsel--The Hartz Mountain Corp., Harrison, NJ, pg. 514
Kish, David, V.P.-Admin. & Gen. Counsel--Delta Queen Steamboat Company, New Orleans, LA, pg. 385
Kitay, Harvey, Gen. Counsel--Ruhl Companies, Inc., Valhalla, NY, pg. 955
Kittner, Marc R., Sr. V.P. & Corp. Counsel--Washington Mutual Savings Bank, Seattle, WA, pg. 1166
Klausner, Jack, Gen. Counsel--Hunter Contracting Company, Gilbert, AZ, pg. 554
Kleban, Albert J., Sec. & Gen. Counsel--Chessco Industries, Inc., Westport, CT, pg. 243
Kleczka, Mark D., Gen. Counsel--National Food Stores, Inc. T/A Krauszer's, Edison, NJ, pg. 788
Kleva, Gregory A., Jr., Sr. V.P. & Deputy Gen. Counsel--Mutual of America, New York, NY, pg. 777
Klinefelter, Gary V., Sec. & Gen. Counsel--Amerco, A Nevada Corporation, Reno, NV, pg. 47
Kluger, Allan, Gen. Counsel--The Lion, Inc. (Gibbons-Stegmaier Brewery), Wilkes-Barre, PA, pg. 677
Knight, David A., Sr. V.P. & Gen. Counsel--Stephens, Inc., Little Rock, AR, pg. 1046
Knisely, Gary T., V.P.-Admin., Sec. & Counsel--Hanover Foods Corporation, Hanover, PA, pg. 506
Knobbe, Urban, Chm. Bd. & Pres.--Ag Processing Inc A Cooperative, Omaha, NE, pg. 24
Koester, Robert, Gen. Counsel--HBE Corporation, Saint Louis, MO, pg. 495
Kohn, Herbert, Treas. & Gen. Counsel--Bernstein-Rein Advertising, Inc., Kansas City, MO, pg. 144
Kolodny, Richard S., V.P. & Gen. Counsel--American Protection Industries, Inc., Los Angeles, CA, pg. 60
Komensky, Alan M., Gen. Counsel--EB (NA), Chicago, IL, pg. 381
Konowiecki, Joseph S., Gen. Counsel & Asst. Sec.--PacifiCare Health Systems, Inc., Cypress, CA, pg. 1127
Kovsky, Charles, Gen. Counsel & Sec.--Computer Methods Corporation, Livonia, MI, pg. 271
Kraus, William J., Gen. Counsel--Restaurant Developers Corp., Independence, OH, pg. 929
Kreiter, Fredric J., Chief Fin. Officer & Legal Counsel--Castcraft Industries, Inc., Skokie, IL, pg. 228
Kritzer, Paul, Legal Officer & Corp. Sec.--Journal Communications Inc., Milwaukee, WI, pg. 607
Krivosha, Norman M., Judge, Exec. V.P.-Admin. & Gen. Counsel--Ameritas Life Insurance Corp., Lincoln, NE, pg. 66
Krivoshia, E., Jr., V.P., Gen. Counsel & Sec.--National Steel Corporation, Mishawaka, IN, pg. 793
Krominga, Lynn, V.P.-Law--Revlon, Inc., New York, NY, pg. 696
Krominga, Lynn, V.P.-Law--Charles of the Ritz Group Ltd., New York, NY, pg. 695
Krongard, Howard J., Gen. Counsel--Deloitte & Touche, Wilton, CT, pg. 326
Kruth, Harold E., Sec. & Gen. Counsel--SRI International, Menlo Park, CA, pg. 964
Kuehn, George E., Sr. V.P., Sec. & Gen. Counsel--The Stroh Brewery Company, Detroit, MI, pg. 1053
Kugle, J. Alan, Exec. V.P. & Gen. Counsel--C. Brewer & Company, Limited, Honolulu, HI, pg. 174
Kuhn, Humberto G., Sec. & Legal Counsel--Wilson Industries Inc., Houston, TX, pg. 1193
Kulla, Raymond J., V.P., Gen. Counsel & Sec.--AXIA Incorporated, Oak Brook, IL, pg. 8
LaBau, Dave, V.P.-Legal--Northern Automotive Corporation, Phoenix, AZ, pg. 1118
LaBerge, Ellen, Gen. Counsel--Dairylea Cooperative Inc., East Syracuse, NY, pg. 311
LaCour, Barry, Gen. Counsel--The Laitram Corporation, Harahan, LA, pg. 650
LaCour, Barry, Gen. Counsel--Intralox, Inc., Harahan, LA, pg. 651
Lafon, Rene Armando, Gen. Mgr.--Keystone Automotive Industries, Inc.-Tijuana, Tijuana,, Mexico, pg. 628
Lahr, Guy, Gen. Counsel--Illinois State Lottery, Springfield, IL, pg. 563
Lamade, Barbara S., Gen. Counsel--Advanced Marine Enterprises, Inc., Arlington, VA, pg. 20
Lambert, George, V.P. & Gen. Counsel--Provident Mutual Life Insurance Co., Philadelphia, PA, pg. 896
Lanchner, Bertrand M., Sr. V.P., Legal & Sec.--N W Ayer Incorporated, New York, NY, pg. 103
Lanchner, Bertrand M., Sr. V.P., Legal & Corp. Sec.--N W Ayer Inc., New York, NY, pg. 104
Landau, Harriet, Legal Officer--Racetrac Petroleum, Inc., Smyrna, GA, pg. 909
Landergan, Walter L., Jr., Sec. & Legal--Components Corporation Of America, Dallas, TX, pg. 270
Landis, Edwin, Esq., Gen. Counsel--Tekni-Plex, Inc., Brooklyn, NY, pg. 1084
Langner, Kevan K., Legal Officer--KDI Corporation, Cincinnati, OH, pg. 612
Lansing, Andrew, Gen. Counsel--The Levy Organization, Chicago, IL, pg. 672
Lansky, Mitchell, V.P. & Gen. Counsel--Econocom-USA Inc., Memphis, TN, pg. 367
Lapacek, J.V., Patent & Liability Counsel--S & C Electric Company, Chicago, IL, pg. 958
Lario, Frank M., Jr., Gen. Counsel--Philadelphia Sign Company, Palmyra, NJ, pg. 867
LaRocque, James, Gen. Counsel & Sec.--James McHugh Construction Co., Chicago, IL, pg. 729
Larson, David J., Sr. V.P., Sec. & Gen. Counsel--Lutheran Brotherhood, Minneapolis, MN, pg. 688
Larson, Michelle, Gen. Counsel--Trak International, Inc., Port Washington, WI, pg. 1106
Lassiter, John, V.P. & Gen. Counsel--Belk Stores Services Inc., Charlotte, NC, pg. 134
Latham, David C., Gen. Counsel--Citrus World Inc., Lake Wales, FL, pg. 251
Lauderdale, Katherine, V.P.-Gen. Counsel--WTTW (Channel 11), Chicago, IL, pg. 1156
Lavinthal, Frederick, Gen. Counsel--Bogue Electric Manufacturing Co., Paterson, NJ, pg. 162
Law, Russell, Gen. Counsel--Stanley Stores Inc., Bay City, TX, pg. 1038
Lawing, Jack L., V.P.-Law & Sec.--Gold Kist, Inc., Atlanta, GA, pg. 465
Lawler, Thomas J., V.P. & Gen. Counsel--Duro-Last Roofing, Inc., Saginaw, MI, pg. 355
Lawson, William H., Jr., Gen. Counsel--Jemison, Inc., Memphis, TN, pg. 592

League, David, V.P., Gen. Counsel & Sec.--Ace Hardware Corporation, Oak Brook, IL, pg. 12
Ledbetter, Bureon E., V.P. & Gen. Counsel--Chick-Fil-A, Inc., Atlanta, GA, pg. 247
Lederman, Michael G., Gen. Counsel & Sec.--Sunbeam-Oster Company, Inc., Providence, RI, pg. 1059
Lee, John L., Exec. V.P. & Gen. Counsel--American Finance Group, Boston, MA, pg. 52
Lee, William P., Chief of Staff--AdLand Advertising, Inc., San Francisco, CA, pg. 17
Leff, Todd, Gen. Counsel--Cottman Transmission Systems, Inc., Fort Washington, PA, pg. 288
Legg, James S., Gen. Counsel & Asst. Sec.--Griffith Laboratories Worldwide, Inc., Alsip, IL, pg. 487
Lemery, John, Gen. Counsel--CB North America, Inc., Glens Falls, NY, pg. 199
Lemoyne, Stewart, Sec. & Gen. Counsel--Management Dynamics, New Providence, NJ, pg. 703
Lerman, Cathy, Gen. Counsel--Post Buckley Schuh & Jernigan, Miami, FL, pg. 881
Lerner, Martin, Gen. Counsel--Universal Photonics, Inc., Hicksville, NY, pg. 1139
Letica, Mara, Gen. Counsel--Letica Corporation, Rochester Hills, MI, pg. 668
LeVander, Harold, Jr., Gen. Counsel--Dakota Electric Association, Farmington, MN, pg. 312
Levien, Joy, V.P.-Legal--R. H. Macy & Co., Inc., New York, NY, pg. 698
Levin, Morris J., Gen. Counsel & Sec.--Schiavone Construction Co., Secaucus, NJ, pg. 976
Levin, Steve, Sr. V.P. & Gen. Counsel--The Kaempfer Company, Investment Builders, Washington, DC, pg. 613
Levine, Jeffrey, Gen. Counsel--Merchants Rent A Car, Inc., Hooksett, NH, pg. 739
Levitt, Matthew, Gen. Counsel--Patterson Dental Company, Minneapolis, MN, pg. 851
Levy, Ivan, Gen. Counsel--Interplastic Corp., Saint Paul, MN, pg. 579
Levy, Melvin, Gen. Counsel--Weiss Packing Co., Inc., Donora, PA, pg. 1174
Lewis, Edwin, V.P.-Law--Burns International Security Services, Inc., Parsippany, NJ, pg. 166
Lewis, Myron S., Gen. Counsel--Altier & Sons Shoes Inc., Rochester, NY, pg. 45
Liekar, John P., Jr., Gen. Counsel & Sec.--Centimark Corporation, Bethel Park, PA, pg. 231
Lifflander, Matthew, Gen. Counsel--Queens Group, Inc., Long Island City, NY, pg. 904
Liggio, Carl D., Gen. Counsel--Ernst & Young, New York, NY, pg. 387
Liles, Curtis, Gen. Counsel--National Computer Print, Inc., Birmingham, AL, pg. 786
Linder, Harvey R., V.P., Sec. & Gen. Counsel--Laroche Holdings, Inc., Atlanta, GA, pg. 659
Linder, Harvey R., Gen. Counsel--LaRoche Chemicals Inc., Baton Rouge, LA, pg. 659
Lindsay, Ronald, Chief Counsel--Collins & Aikman Textile Group, Charlotte, NC, pg. 262
Linton, John, Gen. Counsel--RE/MAX International, Inc., Englewood, CO, pg. 915
Lipani, John F., V.P. & Gen. Counsel--Boh Corporation, New Orleans, LA, pg. 162
Lipani, John F., V.P. & Gen. Counsel--Boh Brothers Construction Company, Inc., New Orleans, LA, pg. 162
Lipson, Alan, V.P. & Gen. Counsel--Remington Products Inc., Bridgeport, CT, pg. 926
Livingston, Calvin J., Gen. Counsel--A. Duda & Sons Inc., Oviedo, FL, pg. 351
Lloyd, R. Jay, Legal Counsel--Forever Living Products, Tempe, AZ, pg. 424
Lockwood, Mike, Gen. Counsel--El Camino Resources, Ltd., Northridge, CA, pg. 372
Long, William B., V.P. & Gen. Counsel--Drummond Company, Inc., Jasper, AL, pg. 349
Loomis, John, Gen. Counsel--Salwasser Manufacturing Company, Inc., Reedley, CA, pg. 968
Loree, James H., Sec. & Legal Counsel--Zantop International Airlines, Inc., Ypsilanti, MI, pg. 1216
Lorentz, Jack A., Gen. Counsel--U-Haul International, Inc., Phoenix, AZ, pg. 48
Lorenzen, Shelley A., V.P., Sec. & Gen. Counsel--Arcata Corporation, San Francisco, CA, pg. 80
Loritz, Richard, Gen. Counsel--C.J. Vitner & Co., Inc., Chicago, IL, pg. 1153
Lorona, Mary Kay, Corp. Counsel--Empire Southwest Co., Mesa, AZ, pg. 379
Loveland, Peter G., Pres., Treas. & Gen. Counsel--Maze Nails, Peru, IL, pg. 725
Lowe, L. Stanley, Gen. Counsel--True Companies, Casper, WY, pg. 1117
Lowell, Mark, Gen. Counsel--Sanford & Hawley, Inc., Unionville, CT, pg. 970
Lowell, Ron, Gen. Counsel--Humboldt Express, Inc., Nashville, TN, pg. 552
Lowenfels, Fred, Sr. V.P. & Gen. Counsel--Transammonia Inc., New York, NY, pg. 1106
Lowenstam, Susan G., V.P., Gen. Counsel & Sec.--The Aerospace Corporation, El Segundo, CA, pg. 22
Lozier, Richard, Gen. Counsel--American Mutual Life Insurance Company, Des Moines, IA, pg. 58
Lucas, James A., V.P. & Gen. Counsel--McGean-Rohco, Inc., Cleveland, OH, pg. 729
Luks, Jerome M., V.P. & Gen. Counsel--National Foods Inc., Bronx, NY, pg. 788
Lund, Robert T., V.P. & Assoc. Counsel--Bank Shares, Inc., Minneapolis, MN, pg. 117
Lunney, Kathryn, Gen. Counsel--Shape Inc., Biddeford, ME, pg. 995
Lustbader, Brian G., Exec. V.P., Gen. Counsel & Sec.--The P.J. Carlin Construction Company, New Rochelle, NY, pg. 220
Lyford, Bob, Gen. Counsel--Arkansas Electric Cooperatives Inc., Little Rock, AR, pg. 83
Lykins, C.B., V.P.-Customer Service & Rates--Citizens Gas & Coke Utility, Indianapolis, IN, pg. 250
Lynch, John J., V.P. & Gen. Counsel--Avis, Inc., Garden City, NY, pg. 102
Lyon, Clarke, Gen. Counsel--Hazen Paper Company, Holyoke, MA, pg. 520
Lyons, Ray, Gen. Counsel--Tri-K Industries, Inc., Emerson, NJ, pg. 1110
Mackie, D.B., Sr. V.P., Gen. Counsel & Sec.--Great Lakes Dredge & Dock, Oak Brook, IL, pg. 481
Madera, Cornelius J.J., Jr., Sr. V.P., Gen. Counsel & Corp. Devel.--Big V Supermarkets, Inc., Florida, NY, pg. 149
Magill, K.B., Gen. Counsel--The Marley Company, Mission Woods, KS, pg. 710
Magram, Saul, Sr. V.P. & Gen. Counsel--Estee Lauder, Inc., New York, NY, pg. 389
Mahone, Wm., Gen. Counsel--Red L Foods, Pomfret Center, CT, pg. 1128
Maine, Cliff, Corp. Counsel--Prime Technology, Inc., Grand Rapids, MI, pg. 889
Mallory, W.B. III, Vice Chm., Sec. & Gen. Counsel--Guardsmark, Inc., Memphis, TN, pg. 492
Mancuso, Tommy, Gen. Counsel--Whitfield Foods, Inc., Montgomery, AL, pg. 1187
Mansfield, Christopher C., Sr. V.P. & Gen. Counsel--Liberty Mutual Insurance Co., Boston, MA, pg. 674
Mansky, Terry, Gen. Counsel--Carpeteria, Inc., Valencia, CA, pg. 224
Marafioti, Robert, Gen. Counsel--C M P Publications, Inc., Manhasset, NY, pg. 202
Marchand, Darryl T., V.P., Gen. Counsel & Sec.--Triangle Pacific Corporation, Dallas, TX, pg. 1112
Marchisotto, Alan L., Sec. & Gen. Counsel--Moran Towing & Transporation Co. Inc, Greenwich, CT, pg. 769
Marcus, H. Gwen, Sr. V.P. & Gen. Counsel-Showtime Networks--Viacom Inc., New York, NY, pg. 785
Marino, Joseph R., Gen. Counsel & Sec.--Reactive Metals & Alloys Corporation (REMACOR), West Pittsburg, PA, pg. 916
Marks, Louis, Gen. Counsel--Scharfberg & Associates, Ltd. Adv., Jenkintown, PA, pg. 974
Marsh, William A., V.P., Sec. & Gen. Counsel--Spang & Company, Butler, PA, pg. 1025
Marshal, Douglas, Sec. & Gen. Counsel--Darigold, Inc., Seattle, WA, pg. 315
Marshall, Douglas, Corp. Counsel & Sec.--Dairygold Inc., Seattle, WA, pg. 311
Marshall, Richard J., V.P.-Opers. & Legal Counsel--Maverik Country Stores, Inc., Afton, WY, pg. 722
Martell, Sandra, Corp. Sec. & Gen. Counsel--S. J. Groves & Sons Company, Minneapolis, MN, pg. 490
Martenstein, Thomas E., V.P.-Legal Affairs--Blue Cross & Blue Shield of Virginia, Richmond, VA, pg. 160
Martha, J. Paul, Exec. V.P. & Gen. Counsel-Civic Arena--The Edward J. DeBartolo Corporation, Youngstown, OH, pg. 323
Martin, D., V.P., Sec. & Gen. Counsel--Motor Wheel Corporation, Lansing, MI, pg. 773
Martin, D.R., Gen. Counsel--Green Holdings, Inc., Denver, CO, pg. 484
Martin, Janet, Gen. Counsel--Sir Speedy, Inc., Laguna Hills, CA, pg. 613
Martin, Loren D., Gen. Counsel--Martin Door Mfg., Inc., Salt Lake City, UT, pg. 714
Martin, Philip O., Chief Oper. Officer & Gen. Mgr.--United Power Association, Elk River, MN, pg. 1134
Marx, Leo A., Jr., Sec. & Gen. Counsel--R. L. Polk & Co., Detroit, MI, pg. 879
Masket, Steven N., Sr. V.P. & Gen. Counsel--Maidenform, Inc., New York, NY, pg. 701
Matchan, Brent, V.P. & Gen. Counsel--Ziegler Coal Holding Co., Fairview Heights, IL, pg. 1218
Matre, Steven R., V.P.-Fin., Chief Fin. Officer & Sec.--Energy Minerals Corporation, Denver, CO, pg. 381
Mattews, Jim, V.P. & Gen. Counsel--Lear Siegler Diversified Holdings Corp., Livingston, NJ, pg. 664
Mattews, Jim, V.P. & Gen. Counsel--Lear Siegler Diversified Holdings Corp., Livingston, NJ, pg. 424
Matthews, Mibs, Corp. Counsel--Forecast Mortgage Corporation, Rancho Cucamoñga, CA, pg. 423
Maupin, John W., V.P.-Gen. Counsel & Sec.--Fred Weber Inc., Maryland Heights, MO, pg. 1171
Mayle, David R., V.P., Sec. & Gen. Counsel--TIC United Corporation, Dallas, TX, pg. 1073
Mc Curthan, Gordon E., Exec. V.P., Gen. Counsel Sec.--Nationwide Mutual Insurance Co., Columbus, OH, pg. 795
McAuliffe, Joan, Sr. V.P. & Gen. Counsel--Beauty Handbook Corporation, Los Angeles, CA, pg. 130
McAuliffe, Joan, Chief Fin. Officer & Gen. Counsel--Compendium Systems, New York, NY, pg. 270
McBride, Beverly, Gen. Counsel & Corp. Sec.--The Andersons, Maumee, OH, pg. 73
McCallie, S. Wyatt, Gen. Counsel--CH2M Hill Companies, Ltd., Englewood, CO, pg. 202
McCann, Gregory, Corp. Counsel & Asst. Sec.--Danis Industries Corporation, Dayton, OH, pg. 314
McCarthy, Frank, Gen. Counsel--North Central Life Insurance Companies, Saint Paul, MN, pg. 813
McCarthy, Timothy, Sec. & Gen. Counsel--Western Regional Off Track Betting, Batavia, NY, pg. 1181
McCaw, Ken, Jr., V.P. & Gen. Counsel--Esco Corporation, Portland, OR, pg. 388
McClure, William, Gen. Counsel--Hamilton, Carver & Lee, Inc., Chicago, IL, pg. 503
McCormack, William, Gen. Counsel--Schwan's Sales Enterprises, Marshall, MN, pg. 980
McCrae, William, Sr. V.P. & Gen. Counsel--United Services Automobile Association (USAA), San Antonio, TX, pg. 1134
McCune, John J., Gen. Counsel--Hamilton Co., Inc., Reno, NV, pg. 503
McCutchan, Gordon E., Exec. V.P. & Gen. Counsel--Employers Insurance of Wausau a Mutual Co., Wausau, WI, pg. 380
McCutchan, Gordon E., Exec. V.P., Gen. Counsel & Sec.--Nationwide Mutual Insurance Company, Columbus, OH, pg. 795
McCutchan, Gordon E., Exec. V.P. & Gen. Counsel--Employers Insurance of Wausau a Mutual Co., Wausau, WI, pg. 795
McDonald, George, Gen. Counsel--York Barbell Co., Inc., York, PA, pg. 1208
McDonough, John, Gen. Counsel--Hubbard Broadcasting, Inc., Saint Paul, MN, pg. 548
McDonough, John, Legal Counsel--KSTP-TV, Saint Paul, MN, pg. 549
McElveen, John, Gen. Counsel--Colonial Oil Industries, Savannah, GA, pg. 263
McGough, H.R., Gen. Counsel & Sec.--Unigard Security Insurance Co., Bellevue, WA, pg. 596
McGough, H.R., Gen. Counsel & Sec.--Unigard Indemnity Co., Raleigh, NC, pg. 596
McGough, H.R., Gen. Counsel & Sec.--Unigard Insurance Co., Seattle, WA, pg. 596
McGregor, Peter, Chief Fin. Officer--Affiliated of Florida Inc., Tampa, FL, pg. 23
McIntosh, Steven I., Gen. Counsel--Celestial Seasonings, Boulder, CO, pg. 231
McKenzie, James D., Pres.-Petroleum Coke Grp.--Great Lakes Carbon Corp., Briarcliff Manor, NY, pg. 545
McKessy, Steven W., Deputy Chm.--Coopers & Lybrand, New York, NY, pg. 283
McLaughlin, Michael J., Sr. V.P. & Deputy Gen. Counsel--New York Life Insurance Company, New York, NY, pg. 802
McLaughlin, Stephen, Sec. & Gen. Counsel--Martin Exploration Management Company, Alsip, IL, pg. 715
McMackin, John, Gen. Counsel--Howell Instruments Corp., Fort Worth, TX, pg. 547
McManigal, Robert M., Sec. & Gen. Counsel--Adams Rite Manufacturing Co., City of Industry, CA, pg. 16
McNeil, Chris E., Jr., Exec. V.P. & Gen. Counsel--Sealaska Corporation, Juneau, AK, pg. 984
McSwiney, C. Ronald, Gen. Counsel & Sec.--Danis Industries Corporation, Dayton, OH, pg. 314
Mendelson, Morley, Gen. Counsel--National R.V., Inc., Perris, CA, pg. 792
Meyer, A. David, Gen. Counsel--Rowtronics Company Inc., Indianapolis, IN, pg. 953
Meyer, Albert J., Gen. Counsel--The Grand Union Company, Wayne, NJ, pg. 476
Meyer, James R., V.P. & Gen. Counsel--W.S. Badcock Corporation, Mulberry, FL, pg. 113
Meyler, Frank M., V.P., Sec. & Gen. Counsel--American Bureau of Shipping, New York, NY, pg. 50
Miller, David, Pres. & Chief Exec. Officer--Columbia National Group, Inc., Cleveland, OH, pg. 265
Miller, James, Gen. Counsel--Pacesetter Corporation, Omaha, NE, pg. 839
Miller, Lawrence, Sr. V.P., Deputy Gen. Counsel & Asst. Sec.--Young & Rubicam Inc., New York, NY, pg. 1210
Miller, Neil, Gen. Counsel--Apex Oil Company, Inc., Saint Louis, MO, pg. 78
Miller, Richard M., Gen. Counsel--Prince Manufacturing, Inc., Lawrenceville, NJ, pg. 890
Miller, S. Ira, Gen. Counsel--MI-Jack Products, Inc., Hazel Crest, IL, pg. 746
Miller, Steve, Gen. Counsel--P/A Industries, Inc., Bloomfield, CT, pg. 835
Mills, Stanley R., V.P., Gen. Counsel & Sec.--Delaware North Companies, Inc., Buffalo, NY, pg. 326
Mistretta, F. David, V.P., Gen. Counsel & Sec.--Security Mutual Life Insurance Co. of New York, Binghamton, NY, pg. 987
Mitchell, Thompson, Gen. Counsel--Tober Industries, Inc., Saint Louis, MO, pg. 1099
Moderow, Joseph, Sr. V.P. & Sec., Legal & Public Affairs--United Parcel Service of America, Inc., Atlanta, GA, pg. 1133
Mohr, John R., Sr. V.P., Gen. Counsel & Sec.--Ponderosa, Inc., Vandalia, OH, pg. 743
Molina, Joseph, Gen. Counsel--The IDI Group Companies, Arlington, VA, pg. 560
Molino, Virginia L., Gen. Counsel--McKinsey & Company, Inc., New York, NY, pg. 731
Mollerus, Michael J., Gen. Counsel--Redmond Products, Inc., Chanhassen, MN, pg. 920
Moore, Dan, V.P., Sec. & Gen. Counsel--Curtis Mathes Corporation, Athens, TX, pg. 720
Moore, Tom, General Counsel--Pic'n Pay Stores, Inc., Charlotte, NC, pg. 201
Mora, R. N., Sec. & Gen. Counsel--The HOH Organizations, Chicago, IL, pg. 497
Moran, John D., Sec. & Gen. Counsel--Sealy Corporation, Cleveland, OH, pg. 985
Moravek, John, Sr. V.P. & Gen. Counsel--Century 21 Real Estate Corp., Irvine, CA, pg. 744
Morello, Steve, Gen. Counsel--ASC Incorporated, Southgate, MI, pg. 7
Morgan, Charles R., V.P. & Gen. Counsel--Chiquita Brands, Inc., Cincinnati, OH, pg. 53
Morgan, D. Russell, Gen. Counsel--Equity Services, Inc., Montpelier, VT, pg. 791
Morledge, W. Frank, Gen. Counsel--GES Inc., Marianna, AR, pg. 439
Morreale, Justin P., Gen. Counsel--All Seasons Services, Inc., Braintree, MA, pg. 35
Morris, Herman, Gen. Counsel--Memphis Light, Gas & Water, Memphis, TN, pg. 738
Morris, J. Malcolm, V.P., Gen. Counsel & Sec.--Ziff Communications Company, New York, NY, pg. 1218
Morris, T., Gen. Counsel--Armstrong International, Inc., Three Rivers, MI, pg. 83
Morris, T.N., Jr., Chm., Pres. & Chief Exec. Officer--Calcasieu Lumber Company, Austin, TX, pg. 208
Morrison, P.A., Attorney--Colonial Pipeline Company, Atlanta, GA, pg. 264

Morrisson, A.S., V.P., Sec. & Gen. Counsel--Sverdrup Corporation, Maryland Heights, MO, pg. 1065
Morse, Richard A., Gen. Counsel--Granite State Packing Co., Manchester, NH, pg. 476
Moskowitz, Robert, Sr. V.P. & Gen. Counsel--Shamrock Holdings, Inc., Burbank, CA, pg. 994
Mouw, John, Gen. Counsel--Bacco Construction Co., Iron Mountain, MI, pg. 108
Muchin, A., Gen. Counsel--Heresite Protective Coatings Inc., Manitowoc, WI, pg. 531
Mullen, Mary A., V.P. & Asst. Counsel--Fiduciary Trust Company International, New York, NY, pg. 408
Mulliken, W.D., V.P., Sec. & Gen. Counsel--CHEMCENTRAL Corporation, Bedford Park, IL, pg. 241
Mullman, Mike, Gen. Counsel--Furniture Consultants, New York, NY, pg. 437
Mulroy, Richard E., Sr. V.P. & Gen. Counsel--The Mutual Life Insurance Company of New York (MONY), New York, NY, pg. 778
Mundy, Gardner M., Gen. Counsel & Sec.--Johnson & Higgins, New York, NY, pg. 598
Muraro, Bob, Gen. Counsel--United States Sugar Corporation, Clewiston, FL, pg. 1137
Murphy, Jesse, Gen. Counsel--Rayco, San Antonio, TX, pg. 914
Murphy, William, Gen. Counsel--Washington Corporation, Missoula, MT, pg. 1165
Murray, Mike, V.P. & Gen. Counsel--Gator Freightways, Inc., Wilmington, OH, pg. 446
Muse, Albert C., Pres. & Chief Exec. Officer--Crown Coal & Coke Co. Inc., Pittsburgh, PA, pg. 302
Musgraves, Robert E., V.P. & Gen. Counsel--Titanium Metals Corporation, Denver, CO, pg. 1109
Myers, G. William, Sr. V.P. & Legal Counsel--L. Robert Kimball & Associates, Ebensburg, PA, pg. 629
Myers, Jess, V.P. & Gen. Counsel--Martin K. Eby Construction Company, Inc., Wichita, KS, pg. 365
Myers, Ronald W., V.P.-Fin. & Admin. & Chief Fin. Officer--GF Office Furniture Ltd., Gallatin, TN, pg. 439
Naclerio, Steven, Sr. V.P. & Gen. Counsel--Bacardi Imports, Inc., Miami, FL, pg. 108
Napoleon, Roger F., Sr. V.P. & Assoc. Gen. Counsel--Mutual of America, New York, NY, pg. 777
Narber, Gregg, V.P. & Gen. Counsel--The Principal Financial Group, Des Moines, IA, pg. 890
Nash, Gordon L., Sr. Exec. V.P.-Legal & Regulatory Affairs--The American Stock Exchange, New York, NY, pg. 62
Naylor, Chuck, V.P. & Gen. Counsel--FDL Foods, Inc., Dubuque, IA, pg. 394
Negomeir, George R., V.P.-Fin., Treas. & Sec.--Sigman Meat Co. Inc., Arvada, CO, pg. 1003
Nehra, Gerald, V.P.-Legal--The Fuller Brush Company, Great Bend, KS, pg. 436
Nehrkorn, William H., V.P., Sec. & Gen. Counsel--The Heil Co., Chattanooga, TN, pg. 525
Neilson, L., Sec. & Gen. Counsel--L. B. Smith, Inc., Camp Hill, PA, pg. 1013
Nellen, James W., II, V.P., Gen. Counsel & Sec.--Fort Howard Corporation, Green Bay, WI, pg. 425
Nelson, Elaine, Gen. Counsel--Austin Industries, Inc., Dallas, TX, pg. 99
Nelson, Owen, Gen. Counsel & Sec.--Bergquist Company, Inc., Minneapolis, MN, pg. 141
Nelson, Ralph S., Exec. V.P., Sec. & Gen. Counsel--Burlington Motor Carriers Inc., Daleville, IN, pg. 191
Nelson, Rosemary, Sr. V.P., Gen. Counsel & Asst. Sec.--Young & Rubicam Inc., New York, NY, pg. 1210
Nelson, Stuart K., Sr. V.P. & Gen. Counsel--Sanford C. Bernstein & Co., Inc., New York, NY, pg. 144
Nelson, W. Mike, V.P.-Human Resources & Legal--Brooks Beverages Inc., Columbus, OH, pg. 179
Netchvolodoff, Alexander V., V.P.-Govt. Affairs--Cox Enterprises, Inc., Atlanta, GA, pg. 292
Nettleton, Robert C., Gen. Counsel--Haines City Citrus Growers Association, Haines City, FL, pg. 500
Newbold, Robert, Gen. Counsel--Formu-3 International, Inc., Canton, OH, pg. 424
Newman, Eric H., V.P. & Legal Counsel--BJ Acquisition Corp., Charlotte, NC, pg. 107
Newman, Sanders D., Sr. V.P., Sec. & Gen. Counsel--O'Brien Energy Systems Inc., Philadelphia, PA, pg. 820
Newsom, Jan R., Sr. V.P., Gen. Counsel & Sec.--Blue Cross & Blue Shield of Texas, Inc., Richardson, TX, pg. 160
Niarchos, Michael C., Sr. V.P., Gen. Counsel & Sec.--Summa Corporation, Las Vegas, NV, pg. 1057
Nicastro, Frank J., Sr. V.P. & Gen. Counsel--Oxford First Corporation, Philadelphia, PA, pg. 834
Nicholas, Francine, Gen. Counsel & Corp. Sec.--Peter J. Schmitt Co., Inc., West Seneca, NY, pg. 977
Nichols, Georgia, Legal Officer--O. F. Mossberg & Sons, Inc., North Haven, CT, pg. 773
Nichols, Wade H., III, Sr. V.P. & Gen. Counsel--Revlon, Inc., New York, NY, pg. 696
Nikonovich-Kahn, Richard, Legal Officer--Heery International, Inc., Atlanta, GA, pg. 525
Noble, Richard, Gen. Counsel--Delta Pride Catfish, Inc., Indianola, MS, pg. 327
Nolan, Michael, Gen. Counsel--John W. Brooks Inc., Nelsonville, OH, pg. 180
Nordhougen, C.A., Sec. & Gen. Counsel--American Crystal Sugar Company, Moorhead, MN, pg. 51
Norris, Jerry, Gen. Counsel--Leo A. Daly Company, Omaha, NE, pg. 313
Norton, J., Gen. Counsel--E.J. Brach Corporation, Oakbrook Terrace, IL, pg. 169
Norton, Robert, Sr. V.P. & Gen. Counsel--Mastercard International, Inc., New York, NY, pg. 720
Norwood, Kevin, Sec. & Gen. Counsel--KNOX International Corp., Knoxville, TN, pg. 638
Nougus-Sans, Marquerite, Corp. Sec., Asst. Gen. Counsel--North American Watch Corporation, Lyndhurst, NJ, pg. 812
Novick, B., Gen. Counsel--American White Cross Laboratories, Inc., New Rochelle, NY, pg. 65
Novick, Jeffery, Legal Officer--I. Spiewak & Sons, Inc., New York, NY, pg. 1031
O'Brien, Dan, Gen. Counsel--Villaume Industries, Inc., Saint Paul, MN, pg. 1151
O'Brien, William K., Deputy Chm.--Coopers & Lybrand, New York, NY, pg. 283
O'Leary, Thomas M., Chief Fin. Officer & Gen Counsel--The Pepper Companies, Inc., Chicago, IL, pg. 859
O'Malia, David T., Exec. V.P. & Gen. Counsel--O'Malia Food Markets Inc., Noblesville, IN, pg. 825
O'Neil, Mike, Gen. Counsel--Red Apple Companies, New York, NY, pg. 917
O'Neil, Patrick J., Gen. Counsel--Thoroughbred Software International, Inc., Somerset, NJ, pg. 1095
O'Neill, Robert B., V.P., Gen. Counsel & Sec.--Capitol Industries-EMI Inc., Hollywood, CA, pg. 216
O'Reilly, Vincent M., Deputy Chm.--Coopers & Lybrand, New York, NY, pg. 283
Obert, Paul R., V.P., Gen. Counsel & Sec.--CF Industries, Inc., Long Grove, IL, pg. 200
Olander, R.G., Vice Chm. & Legal Officer--Bucyrus-Erie Company, South Milwaukee, WI, pg. 186
Oldfield, Russell M., V.P.-Legal & Corp. Sec.--Rogers Group Inc., Nashville, TN, pg. 943
Oleson, George T., Legal Officer--Allied Mutual Insurance Company, Des Moines, IA, pg. 38
Olian, Jeffrey H., Gen. Counsel--LaSalle Partners, Chicago, IL, pg. 660
Olson, D. Joseph, V.P., Gen. Counsel & Sec.--Citizens Insurance Company of America, Howell, MI, pg. 35
Olson, David A., Sr. V.P. & Gen. Counsel--John Alden Financial Corporation, Miami, FL, pg. 32
Olson, Eldon, Gen. Counsel--Price Waterhouse - U.S., New York, NY, pg. 888
Orlin, Jay, Sec.--Joan Fabrics Corp., Tyngsboro, MA, pg. 594
Orme, Ted, Gen. Counsel--DHL Corporation, Redwood City, CA, pg. 309
Ortiz, Carlos, Gen. Counsel--Goya Foods, Inc., Secaucus, NJ, pg. 474
Osterhouse, Donald, Sec. & Gen. Counsel--King Milling Company, Lowell, MI, pg. 631
Ovrut, Barnett D., Assoc. Gen. Counsel & Sec.--The Hanover Insurance Company, Worcester, MA, pg. 34
Owens-Murrell, Stella, Gen. Counsel--Golden State Mutual Life Insurance Company, Los Angeles, CA, pg. 467
Painton, Russell E., V.P., Gen. Counsel & Sec.--Tracor, Inc., Austin, TX, pg. 1104
Palmer, John, Sec. & Gen. Counsel--Dunham's Athleisure Corporation, Waterford, MI, pg. 353
Parga, Luis, Gen. Counsel--CAE Link Allen Division, Alexandria, VA, pg. 198
Parker, James L., V.P., Gen. Counsel & Sec.--Matthews International Corp., Pittsburgh, PA, pg. 721
Parks, Cynthia E., V.P. & Gen. Counsel--Phoenix American Incorporated, San Rafael, CA, pg. 868
Parlmutter, J.A., V.P. & Gen. Counsel--Kayser-Roth Hosiery, Inc., Greensboro, NC, pg. 262
Parr, Glenn E., Gen. Counsel--Piper Aircraft Corporation, Vero Beach, FL, pg. 872
Pasquarello, Theodore, Pres. & Chief Exec. Officer--Chiswick Trading Inc., Sudbury, MA, pg. 248
Patten, C.J., V.P. & Gen. Counsel--Dorr-Oliver Incorporated, Milford, CT, pg. 346
Patterson, Douglas, V.P.-Legal--Ivex Packaging Corporation, Lincolnshire, IL, pg. 583
Patzman, David, Gen. Counsel--Harmon Smith Inc., Kansas City, MO, pg. 510
Peck, Steven, Gen. Counsel--Spatz & Co., Northbrook, IL, pg. 1026
Pekin, D. James, V.P., Gen. Counsel & Sec.--Redken Laboratories, Inc., Canoga Park, CA, pg. 919
Perlmuter, Michael, Sr. V.P. & Gen. Counsel--Perlmuter Printing Company, Cleveland, OH, pg. 862
Perlowitz, Marc, Legal Counsel--Barneys New York, New York, NY, pg. 120
Perrin, Gregory J., Gen. Counsel--Crystal Clear Industries Company, Ridgefield Park, NJ, pg. 303
Pessia, Michael, Gen. Counsel--James Ferrera & Sons, Inc., Canton, MA, pg. 407
Peters, Roger J., Gen. Counsel--Dick Corporation, Large, PA, pg. 335
Peterson, Craig D., Gen. Counsel & Sec.--Xerxes Corporation, Minneapolis, MN, pg. 1206
Petry, Bill, V.P. & Legal Counsel--Milliken & Co., Inc., Spartanburg, SC, pg. 755
Petty, George O., Sec.--Sun Diamond Growers of California, Pleasanton, CA, pg. 1058
Philipp, Elizabeth, V.P. & Gen. Counsel--Collins & Aikman Group Inc., Santa Monica, CA, pg. 262
Philips, Ian, Legal Officer--SGD International Corp., New York, NY, pg. 962
Pickering, Gordon G., Chm. Bd., Pres. & Gen. Counsel--Pickering Industries Inc., Tacoma, WA, pg. 869
Pickering, Judith, Sec. & Legal Counsel--Woodward & Lothrop/John Wanamaker, Washington, DC, pg. 1201
Pittenger, Bradford, Legal Officer--V.T. Inc., Merriam, KS, pg. 1142
Platten, Steven T., Gen. Counsel--Action Equipment, Londonderry, NH, pg. 14
Polack, Robert, Corp. Counsel & V.P.--Reilly Industries, Inc., Indianapolis, IN, pg. 923
Pomerantz, Sanford E., Legal Counsel--National Emergency Services, Inc., Tiburon, CA, pg. 788
Ponto, Steven, Corp. Counsel--Quad/Graphics, Inc., Pewaukee, WI, pg. 902
Pope, James Arthur, V.P. & Gen. Counsel--Variety Wholesalers, Inc., Raleigh, NC, pg. 1146
Popov, Peter N., V.P., Gen. Counsel & Sec.--Marine Transport Lines, Inc., Secaucus, NJ, pg. 707
Porter, Edward A., V.P.-Admin., Gen. Counsel & Corp. Sec.--National Gypsum Company, Charlotte, NC, pg. 790
Porter, Henry M., Sec. & Gen. Counsel--Scipar, Buffalo, NY, pg. 982
Posner, E.G., V.P., Sec. & Gen. Counsel--PQ Corporation, Valley Forge, PA, pg. 836
Post, G. Roger, V.P., Sec. & Gen Counsel--White Castle System, Inc., Columbus, OH, pg. 1185
Potter, Thomas A., Gen. Counsel--Titan Industrial Corp., New York, NY, pg. 1099
Powell, Ben, Gen. Counsel--Port of Galveston, Galveston, TX, pg. 881
Powhatan, Becky, V.P. & Corp. Counsel--Landmark Communications, Inc., Norfolk, VA, pg. 654
Pozen, Robert C., Sr. V.P. & Gen. Counsel--Fidelity Investments (FMR Corp.), Boston, MA, pg. 408
Pryor, Joe, Gen. Counsel & Tech. Affairs Dir.--Alamo Group, Inc., Seguin, TX, pg. 29
Puhl, Frances Pellegrino, Gen. Counsel--Associated Wholesale Grocers, Inc., Kansas City, KS, pg. 92
Pulliam, Virgil, V.P.-Legal Affairs--Mary Kay Cosmetics Inc., Dallas, TX, pg. 716
Rader, Larry, Sec. & Gen. Counsel--Marine Travelift, Inc., Sturgeon Bay, WI, pg. 707
Rainwater, Jay Earl, Sec. & Legal Counsel--Wm. S. Trimble Company, Inc., Knoxville, TN, pg. 1113
Randall, Richard D., V.P. & Gen. Counsel--Petroleum Inc., Wichita, KS, pg. 865
Rapuano, Robert A., V.P. & Corp. Counsel--Kinney System, Inc., New York, NY, pg. 632
Rason, Jerry, Gen. Counsel--North Shore Movers, Northbrook, IL, pg. 813
Rathblott, Paul, V.P., Sec. & Gen Counsel--Baker Industries, Inc., Parsippany, NJ, pg. 166
Ray, Jean Cullinan, V.P. & Chief Counsel-Insurance--Teachers Insurance and Annuity Association-College Retirement Equities Fund, New York, NY, pg. 1082
Rayburn, Clyde J., Gen. Counsel--Dodson Group, Kansas City, MO, pg. 342
Rebane, John, V.P. & Gen. Counsel--Land O'Lakes, Inc., Arden Hills, MN, pg. 653
Reed, Frederick M., Gen. Counsel--Pitco Frialator Inc., Concord, NH, pg. 157
Reed, Kenneth D., Gen. Counsel--Hammond Lead Products, Inc., Hammond, IN, pg. 504
Reisman, Kenneth, V.P., Gen. Counsel & Sec.--Technical Aid Corporation, Newton Upper Falls, MA, pg. 1083
ReMine, Debra B., Dir.-Legal Counsel--Federated Mutual Insurance Company, Owatonna, MN, pg. 405
Rentz, Richard D., V.P. & Gen. Counsel--Farm Stores, Inc., Miami, FL, pg. 401
Reynolds, Jonathan P., V.P., Gen. Counsel & Sec.--Cosco, Inc., Columbus, IN, pg. 287
Rhinehart, June A., V.P. & Gen. Counsel--Johnson Publishing Company, Inc., Chicago, IL, pg. 598
Riale, Patti L., Mgr.-Corp. Stock Registar--Artesian Resources Corporation, Newark, DE, pg. 86
Riale, Patti L., Corp. Stock Registar--Artesian Water Company, Inc., Newark, DE, pg. 86
Ricca, Gregory, Exec. V.P. & Gen. Counsel--MTV Networks, New York, NY, pg. 785
Rich, Herbert R., Gen. Counsel--Cumberland-Swan, Inc., Smyrna, TN, pg. 304
Richards, G. Robert, V.P. & Gen. Counsel--The Flexible Corp., Delaware, OH, pg. 421
Richards, Stanley, Exec. V.P. & Gen. Counsel--General Growth Companies, Inc., Des Moines, IA, pg. 449
Richenthal, Arthur, Gen. Counsel, Corp. Sec.--Carrafiello, Diehl & Associates, Inc., Irvington, NY, pg. 225
Richman, Arlene, Gen. Counsel--Landau & Heyman Inc., Chicago, IL, pg. 654
Rieck, Kim A., V.P. & Deputy Gen. Counsel--The Edward J. DeBartolo Corporation, Youngstown, OH, pg. 323
Riggins, Russell, Exec. V.P.-Fin. & Legal Counsel--Generra Sportswear Company, Inc., Tukwila, WA, pg. 451
Riley, Robert, V.P. & Gen. Counsel--Meijer, Inc., Grand Rapids, MI, pg. 737
Rivers, Richard D., V.P., Gen. Counsel & Asst. Sec.--Berwind Corporation, Philadelphia, PA, pg. 145
Roach, Walter, Gen. Counsel--Petro-Hunt Corporation, Dallas, TX, pg. 865
Roads, Marvin, Gen. Counsel--Norman Brothers Nissan Inc., Orlando, FL, pg. 810
Roalli, Constantine P., Gen. Counsel--Fairfield Maxwell Ltd., New York, NY, pg. 397
Roberson, James E., Sec. & Treas.--Merchants Truck Line, Inc., New Albany, MS, pg. 740
Roberts, John J., Deputy Chm.--Coopers & Lybrand, New York, NY, pg. 283
Robins, Martin, V.P. & Gen. Counsel--Meridian Technology Leasing Services, Deerfield, IL, pg. 740
Robinson, Jean, Gen. Counsel--Goodwill Industries of America, Inc., Bethesda, MD, pg. 471
Robinson, Leroy, Gen. Counsel & Consultant--Belk Stores Services Inc., Charlotte, NC, pg. 134
Rockefeller, Frederic L., Chm. Bd.--Cranston Print Works Company, Cranston, RI, pg. 296
Rogers, Lawrence A., V.P. & Gen. Counsel--American Capital Management & Research, Inc., Houston, TX, pg. 50
Rogers, Shelby R., Sr. V.P. & Gen. Counsel--Texas Commerce Bancshares, Inc., Houston, TX, pg. 1089
Rogers, Stephen C., Gen. Counsel--Amtrak-National Railroad Passenger Corp., Washington, DC, pg. 69
Rogers, Yandell, Jr., Pres. & Gen. Counsel--YRJ Corporation, Houston, TX, pg. 1206
Roloff, Jeffrey J., Chm. Bd. & Chief Exec. Officer--Central Data Corporation, Champaign, IL, pg. 232
Roseberry, Darwin N., Gen. Counsel--BCM Engineers Inc., Plymouth Meeting, PA, pg. 106
Rosenberg, Benjamin, V.P. & Gen. Counsel--Lawrence Insurance Group, Inc., New York, NY, pg. 662
Rosenberg, Benjamin, Esq., Exec. V.P., Gen. Counsel & Asst. Sec.--United Community Insurance Co., Albany, NY, pg. 662

Rosenberg, Benjamin, Esq., V.P. & Gen. Counsel--United Republic Reinsurance Company, Houston, TX, pg. 662
Rosenberg, Benjamin, Esq., V.P. & Gen. Counsel--Global Insurance Company, Houston, TX, pg. 662
Rosenfeld, Nancy, V.P., Deputy Gen. Counsel/Corporate--Viacom Inc., New York, NY, pg. 785
Rosenthal, Mark, V.P. & Gen. Counsel--Raleigh Enterprises, Inc., Los Angeles, CA, pg. 910
Ross, Ford G., Gen. Counsel--Hawkins Markets, Inc., Wooster, OH, pg. 518
Ross, John H. III, V.P. & Gen. Counsel--Ash Grove Cement Company, Overland Park, KS, pg. 87
Ross, Ronald J., Chief Real Estate Counsel--The Cafaro Co., Youngstown, OH, pg. 207
Rossini, Edwin R., V.P.-Deputy Gen. Counsel & Asst. Sec.--S. C. Johnson & Son, Inc., Racine, WI, pg. 599
Roth, Peter, Gen. Counsel--Lucky Winner, Inc., New York, NY, pg. 686
Rothenberg, Peter, V.P., Gen. Counsel--Chiat/Day/Mojo Inc. Advertising, Venice, CA, pg. 244
Rothenberg, Peter, V.P., Corp. Gen. Counsel--Chiat/Day/Mojo/New York, New York, NY, pg. 244
Roti, Thomas, V.P. & Gen. Counsel--Dominick's Finer Foods, Northlake, IL, pg. 343
Rowland, T.W., Sr. V.P., Sec. & Gen. Counsel--California & Hawaiian Sugar Company, Concord, CA, pg. 210
Rowsey, Paul, III, Pres. & Gen. Counsel--Rosewood Property Company, Dallas, TX, pg. 949
Rubin, Burton, Gen. Counsel--The Direct Marketing Group Inc., New York, NY, pg. 339
Rubin, David M., Sec. & Gen. Counsel--CC Industries, Inc., Chicago, IL, pg. 199
Rubin, L. Anthony, V.P. & Gen. Counsel--Pip Printing, Agoura Hills, CA, pg. 616
Rubin, Milton, Sec. & Gen. Counsel--Argo International Corp., New York, NY, pg. 81
Rubin, Steven, V.P., Sec. & Gen. Counsel--General Binding Corporation, Northbrook, IL, pg. 656
Rubino, Pauli, Gen. Counsel--DeVault Foods, Devault, PA, pg. 333
Rusinak, Ronald, Corp. Sec. & Gen. Counsel--Crown American Corporation, Johnstown, PA, pg. 301
Ruzicka, Leonard R., Sr. V.P., Sec. & Gen. Counsel--Fru-Con Construction Corporation, Ballwin, MO, pg. 435
Ryan, Jim, Gen. Counsel--Hale-Halsell Company, Tulsa, OK, pg. 500
Ryan, Louis F., Exec. V.P. & Gen. Counsel--Landmark Communications, Inc., Norfolk, VA, pg. 654
Ryan, Michael, Gen. Counsel--Netzsch, Inc., Exton, PA, pg. 798
Ryan, Peter, Gen. Counsel--Lodal, Inc., Kingsford, MI, pg. 680
Ryder, John, Gen. Counsel--Metro Foods, Inc., Memphis, TN, pg. 743
Ryser, Philip R., V.P. & Legal Counsel--Stanley Steemer International, Inc., Dublin, OH, pg. 1038
Sadlowski, Dennis A., V.P., Sec. & Gen. Counsel--Millmaster Onyx Group, Inc., Westport, CT, pg. 755
Saito, Russell, Gen. Counsel--Galaxy Business Products, Honolulu, HI, pg. 742
Salamon, Diane, Legal Counsel--Pic N'pay Supermarkets, Inc., Dania, FL, pg. 869
Sanderson, James E., V.P., Gen. Counsel & Sec.--Brooks Beverage Management, Inc., Holland, MI, pg. 179
Sanderson, Lisa, Corp. Counsel--Buck Knives, Inc., El Cajon, CA, pg. 185
Sandifer, Thomas N., Pres. & Chief Exec. Officer--Cain & Bultman, Inc., Jacksonville, FL, pg. 207
Sands, Robert-John H., V.P. & Gen. Counsel--The Acacia Group, Washington, DC, pg. 10
Sanford, Kenneth, V.P. & Gen. Counsel--The Rio Grande Industries Inc., Denver, CO, pg. 75
Sanford, Larry, Sr. V.P.-Legal--The Coleman Company, Inc., Wichita, KS, pg. 695
Sang, Bernard G., Sec. & Gen. Counsel--Humiston-Keeling, Inc., Chicago, IL, pg. 552
Sanner, Paul J., Sr. V.P. & Gen. Counsel--Woodward-Clyde Group, Inc., Denver, CO, pg. 1200
Santilli, Paul T., V.P. & Gen. Counsel--Battelle Memorial Institute, Columbus, OH, pg. 126
Santo, James M., V.P.-Legal Affairs & Sec.--Jack Eckerd Corporation, Largo, FL, pg. 366
Sarff, Jon, Gen. Counsel--Kraus-Anderson, Inc., Minneapolis, MN, pg. 644
Sarkisian, A. Alex, Sec.--Schawk, Inc., Des Plaines, IL, pg. 974
Sarosiek, James J., V.P., Gen. Counsel & Sec.--Menasha Corporation, Neenah, WI, pg. 738
Saunders, Beulah, Sec. & Treas.--Dakco Distributors, Inc., Minot, ND, pg. 311
Schechter, Loren, Exec. V.P. & Gen. Counsel--Prudential Securities Inc., New York, NY, pg. 897
Schell, Ivan, Sec. & Gen. Counsel--Roll Forming Corporation, Shelbyville, KY, pg. 944
Scher, Meyer, Gen. Counsel--Byer California, San Francisco, CA, pg. 197
Scheuer, Thomas, Legal Counsel & Asst. Sec.--Louis Dreyfus Corporation, Wilton, CT, pg. 348
Schinman, H.L., Chm. Bd., Treas., Sec. & Gen. Counsel--Bogue Electric Manufacturing Co., Paterson, NJ, pg. 162
Schlack, David A., Legal Officer--Levy Security Consultants, Limited, Chicago, IL, pg. 672
Schlatter, Donald A., Pres., Chief Exec. Officer & Gen. Counsel--Art Iron, Inc., Toledo, OH, pg. 86
Schlyer, Lyle, Gen. Counsel--USA Petroleum Corporation, Santa Monica, CA, pg. 1124
Schmalz, Robert L., V.P., Sec. & Gen. Counsel--Spreckles Industries, Inc., Pleasanton, CA, pg. 1032
Schmid, James A., Pres. & Chief Exec. Officer--Crescent Electric Supply Co., East Dubuque, IL, pg. 298
Schmidt, Karl A., Gen. Counsel--John S. Frey Enterprises, Los Angeles, CA, pg. 433
Schneeman, Donald J., Gen. Counsel & Sec.--American Institute of C.P.A.'s Inc., New York, NY, pg. 56
Schneider, Laz, Gen. Counsel--Edd Helms Electrical Contracting, Miami, FL, pg. 527
Schneider, Thomas A., Chief Legal Counsel--Safeguard Business Systems, Inc., Fort Washington, PA, pg. 966
Schnuck, Terry, Sec. & Gen. Counsel--Schnuck Markets, Inc., Maryland Heights, MO, pg. 977
Schoenlaub, F.E., Legal Officer--Black & Veatch, Kansas City, MO, pg. 154
Schonwald, Gary A., Sec. & Legal Officer--Hollytex, Saddle Brook, NJ, pg. 1121
Schor, Edward N., Sr. V.P.-Gen. Counsel/Communications--Viacom Inc., New York, NY, pg. 785
Schor, Edward N., Sr. V.P. & Gen. Counsel/Communications--Viacom Broadcasting Inc., New York, NY, pg. 785
Schor, Edward N., Sr. V.P., Gen. Counsel/Communications--Viacom Cable, Pleasanton, CA, pg. 785
Schori, Jan, Gen. Counsel & Corp. Sec.--Sacramento Municipal Utility District, Sacramento, CA, pg. 965
Schotz, Cole, Gen. Counsel--Sharon Concepts, Inc., Union, NJ, pg. 995
Schoyer, E., Gen. Counsel--Munroe, Inc., Pittsburgh, PA, pg. 776
Schrager, Marvin L., Gen. Counsel--Don E. Williams Co., Rock Island, IL, pg. 1190
Schulze, Max H., V.P., Sec., Treas. & Gen. Counsel--MCRB Service Bureau, Inc., North Hollywood, CA, pg. 691
Schuster, Karl, Gen. Counsel--Christian Memorial Cultural Center, Rochester Hills, MI, pg. 249
Schuster, Stephen M., V.P., Sec. & Gen. Counsel--Envirodyne Industries, Inc., Oak Brook, IL, pg. 383
Schwan, Mark, Corp. Counsel--Schwan's Sales Enterprises, Marshall, MN, pg. 980
Schwartz, Barry F., V.P. & Chief Counsel-Litigation--MacAndrews & Forbes Co., Camden, NJ, pg. 694
Schwartz, Bart, Legal Officer--Werthan Packaging, Inc., Nashville, TN, pg. 1176
Schwartz, Lloyd A., Sr. V.P. & Gen. Counsel--Southwest Marine, Inc., San Diego, CA, pg. 1023
Schwarz, James N., Sec. & Gen. Counsel--Steuart Petroleum Company, Washington, DC, pg. 1048
Schwarzstein, Richard, Gen. Counsel--American Lock & Supply Inc., Anaheim, CA, pg. 57
Scipione, Richard S., Gen. Counsel--John Hancock Mutual Life Insurance Company, Boston, MA, pg. 595
Scobie, William M., Chm. Bd., Chief Exec. & Legal Officer--Mason Shoe Mfg. Co., Chippewa Falls, WI, pg. 718
Scobie, William M., Chm. Bd., Chief Exec. & Legal Officer--Wissota Trader & B.A. Mason, Chippewa Falls, WI, pg. 718
Scott, Doug, Gen. Counsel--Science Applications International Corporation, San Diego, CA, pg. 981
Scott, Harry, Gen. Counsel--New York City Off Track Betting Corp., New York, NY, pg. 802
Scott, John R., V.P., Sec. & Gen. Counsel--Hunt Oil Company, Dallas, TX, pg. 553
Scott, Michael, Gen. Counsel--Mooney Chemicals, Cleveland, OH, pg. 768
Scotton, William P., Pres.--Custom Decor, Inc., Dover, DE, pg. 306
Scrivner, Doug G., Mng. Partner-Litigation--Andersen Consulting, Chicago, IL, pg. 72
Sedler, Jordan B., V.P., Sec. & Treas.--Paper Enterprises, Inc., Bronx, NY, pg. 847
Seely, John J., V.P. & Gen. Counsel--Newly Weds Foods Inc., Chicago, IL, pg. 804
Seghezzi, Alan R., V.P. & Gen. Counsel--John Hancock Leasing Corporation, Boston, MA, pg. 596
Seiler, Bill, Gen. Counsel--Vanguard Plastics, Inc., McPherson, KS, pg. 1145
Seller, Victor P., Gen. Counsel--Scoville Press, Inc., Minneapolis, MN, pg. 983
Semple, Paul, Legal Officer--Summa Four, Inc., Manchester, NH, pg. 1057
Serr, Erik, Sec. & Gen. Counsel--R & B Machine Tool Co., Saline, MI, pg. 906
Shadowitz, Beth I., Gen. Counsel--SKR Resources, Inc., New York, NY, pg. 963
Shannon, Patrick J., Gen. Counsel--Ed Miniat, Inc., Chicago, IL, pg. 757
Shapiro, Louis, Gen. Counsel--Triton Industries, Inc., Chicago, IL, pg. 1114
Shapiro, Michael, Staff Counsel--San Francisco Giants Baseball Club, San Francisco, CA, pg. 969
Sheffer, Sandra, Gen. Counsel--Mosler Inc., Hamilton, OH, pg. 772
Shepard, Paul, Gen. Counsel--Weatherby, Inc., South Gate, CA, pg. 1169
Sher, Pete, Sec. & Gen. Counsel--San Francisco French Bread Company, Oakland, CA, pg. 969
Sherer, F., V.P. & Gen. Counsel--Timex Corporation, Middlebury, CT, pg. 1098
Shields, Craig, Esq., Gen. Counsel--Triangle Marketing Corp., New York, NY, pg. 1112
Shiller, Arthur, Gen. Counsel--Lane Industries, Inc., Northbrook, IL, pg. 656
Shinofield, Dick, V.P.-Legal--Carlson Retail Marketing, Minneapolis, MN, pg. 221
Shipley, P.L., V.P. & Assoc. Gen. Counsel--Guarantee Mutual Life Co., Omaha, NE, pg. 491
Shrot, David, V.P.-Legal & Gen. Counsel--Roma Holdings, Dallas, TX, pg. 945
Sica, Salvatore M., Sec. & Gen. Counsel--Interroyal Corporation, Warren, PA, pg. 580
Sicher, John D., Jr., V.P. & Gen. Counsel--The Unimax Corporation, New York, NY, pg. 1127
Siegfried, Peter, V.P., Gen. Counsel & Sec.--Central National-Gottesman Inc., Purchase, NY, pg. 233
Sikorovsky, Eugene F., Sr. V.P., Gen. Counsel & Sec.--Bell & Howell Company, Skokie, IL, pg. 134
Silhasek, James, Gen. Counsel--Reinalt-Thomas Corp., Ann Arbor, MI, pg. 923
Sills, John D., V.P. & Gen. Counsel--Don Massey Cadillac Inc., Plymouth, MI, pg. 719
Silvera, Mike, Gen. Counsel--Save Mart Supermarkets, Modesto, CA, pg. 973
Simmons, Harvey O., III, Gen. Counsel & Sec.--Crucible Materials Corp., Syracuse, NY, pg. 302
Simon, Dolph B.H., V.P., Gen. Counsel & Sec.--Zale Corporation, Irving, TX, pg. 1215
Simon, Gary, V.P. & Gen. Counsel--Pony Sports & Leisure Inc., Warren, NJ, pg. 880
Simon, Sam, Gen. Counsel & Sec.--Great American Broadcasting Company, Cincinnati, OH, pg. 52
Simon, Samuel J., Gen. Counsel & Sec.--Great American Communications Company, Cincinnati, OH, pg. 53
Simpson, D.L., III, Sec. & Gen. Counsel--Conwood Company L.P., Memphis, TN, pg. 281
Singer, Robert W., Gen. Counsel--Headco Industries, Inc., Broadview, IL, pg. 520
Sklamberg, Marvin, Gen. Counsel--Duane Reade, Long Island City, NY, pg. 350
Slater, William A., V.P. & Gen. Counsel--Carol Wright Sales, Inc., Stamford, CT, pg. 1011
Smallenberger, James Andrew, V.P., Gen. Counsel & Sec.--Central Life Assurance Co., Des Moines, IA, pg. 232
Smith, Edward, Gen. Counsel--The ASCII Group, Inc., Bethesda, MD, pg. 8
Smith, Gary, Dir.-Legal Affairs--Alabama Electric Cooperative, Inc., Andalusia, AL, pg. 28
Smith, P.B., Gen. Counsel--Leach & Garner Company, North Attleboro, MA, pg. 663
Smith, Randy J., V.P., Gen. Counsel & Sec.--G. Heileman Brewing Co., Inc., La Crosse, WI, pg. 526
Smith, Richard H., Sr. V.P. & Gen. Counsel--Cooper Communities, Inc., Bella Vista, AR, pg. 283
Smith, Robert C., Sr. V.P., Sec. & Gen. Counsel--White Hen Pantry, Inc., Elmhurst, IL, pg. 1185
Smith, Robert W., V.P. & Gen. Counsel--DEC International, Inc., Madison, WI, pg. 308
Smith, Thomas, V.P., Treas. & Gen. Counsel--Dry Storage Corporation, Des Plaines, IL, pg. 350
Smith, William S., Sec. & Gen. Counsel--Tasa Corporation, Pittsburgh, PA, pg. 1079
Snow, Richard G., Jr., V.P.- Gen. Counsel & Sec.--J.D. Edwards & Company, Denver, CO, pg. 370
Soifer, Lawrence, V.P.-Legal--R. H. Macy & Co., Inc., New York, NY, pg. 698
Sokolov, Richard S., Sr. V.P.-Devel. & Gen. Counsel--The Edward J. DeBartolo Corporation, Youngstown, OH, pg. 323
Solie, Emory, Legal Officer--Walman Optical Company, Minneapolis, MN, pg. 1161
Solomon, Mike, Sr. V.P.-Legal--Tower Records, West Sacramento, CA, pg. 694
Sowalsky, Jerome, Sr. V.P.-Corporate Counsel--Ringling Bros., Barnum & Bailey Combined Shows, Inc., Vienna, VA, pg. 935
Spanos, George G., Legal Counsel--A. G. Spanos Development, Inc., Stockton, CA, pg. 1025
Spar, H., Gen. Counsel--Spirite Industries, Inc., Englewood, NJ, pg. 1031
Spector, Martin W., Exec. V.P. & Gen. Counsel--ARA Group, Philadelphia, PA, pg. 5
Spector, Martin W., Sr. V.P., Gen. Counsel & Sec.--ARA Services, Inc., Philadelphia, PA, pg. 5
Speelman, Joseph, Gen. Counsel--Transamerican Refining Corporation, Houston, TX, pg. 1106
Spellman, Richard A., Sr. V.P., Gen. Counsel & Sec.--Guarantee Mutual Life Co., Omaha, NE, pg. 491
Speranza, Paul S., Gen. Counsel & Sec.--Wegmans Food Markets, Inc., Rochester, NY, pg. 1172
Sprague, Donald, Legal Officer--Giles & Ransome, Inc., Bensalem, PA, pg. 458
Sprouse, Patricia A., Gen. Counsel & Asst. Sec.--Sierracin Corporation, Sylmar, CA, pg. 1003
Staff, Kenneth, Gen. Counsel--WWF Paper Corporation, Bala-Cynwyd, PA, pg. 1157
Stamm, Charles H., Exec. V.P. & Gen. Counsel--Teachers Insurance and Annuity Association-College Retirement Equities Fund, New York, NY, pg. 1082
Stanfor, Victoria, Gen. Counsel--Farm Family Mutual Insurance Co., Glenmont, NY, pg. 401
Stapleton, R.D., Exec. V.P.-Fin. & Admin., Sec. & Gen. Counsel--The Lane Construction Corp., Meriden, CT, pg. 656
Staskiel, James, V.P., Legal Counsel & Sec.--McCarthy Building Companies, Saint Louis, MO, pg. 727
Stasz, Peter J., Gen. Counsel--H. B. Smith Co., Inc., Westfield, MA, pg. 1013
Stauffer, Jerry, V.P., Gen. Counsel & Sec.--The Alpha Corporation Of Tennessee, Collierville, TN, pg. 43
Stauffer, John H., Jr., Gen. Counsel & Corp. Sec.--Stauffer Communications, Inc., Topeka, KS, pg. 1042
Stauton, Marshal, V.P. & Counsel--United Refining Company, Warren, PA, pg. 1130
Stavely, Richard W., V.P., Sec. & Gen. Counsel--Misco Industries, Wichita, KS, pg. 759
Stecher, Jamie, Gen. Counsel--Florasynth Inc., New York, NY, pg. 420
Steele, Elizabeth M., V.P. & Gen. Counsel--Jones International Ltd., Englewood, CO, pg. 603
Steinberg, Daryl, Corp. Counsel--Darling-Delaware Co., Inc., Irving, TX, pg. 315
Stele, Kurt, Gen. Counsel--Rand McNally & Company, Skokie, IL, pg. 911
Stern, Fred, Legal Officer--David Langer & Co., Inc., Hollywood, CA, pg. 657
Stewart, James, Chm. Bd. & Pres.--Consolidated Co-op, Gowrie, IA, pg. 276
Stewart, Lever, Gen. Counsel & Asst. Sec.--Rock-Tenn Company, Norcross, GA, pg. 941
Stewart, Mark, Legal Officer--Countrymark Co-Op Inc., Delaware, OH, pg. 290
Stiefel, C.W., Vice Chm., Exec. V.P., Gen. Counsel & Corp. Sec.--Stiefel Laboratories, Inc., Coral Gables, FL, pg. 1048

Stinchfield, John E., Sec. & Gen. Counsel--The Donohoe Companies, Inc., Washington, DC, pg. 345
Stith, Michael, Gen. Counsel--The Ruhlin Company, Sharon Center, OH, pg. 955
Stitt, David R., Sr. V.P.-Fin. & Admin.--General Computer Corp. Inc., Twinsburg, OH, pg. 449
Stolar, Henry, Sr. V.P. & Gen. Counsel--Maritz Inc., Fenton, MO, pg. 707
Stopsky, David C., V.P.-Legal--R. H. Macy & Co., Inc., New York, NY, pg. 698
Stotler, John L., Sr. V.P. & Gen. Counsel--National Life Insurance Company, Montpelier, VT, pg. 791
Stotler, John L., V.P. & Gen. Counsel--National Life Insurance Company, Montpelier, VT, pg. 791
Strassler, Marc, Sec. & Gen. Counsel--Supermarkets General Corporation, Woodbridge, NJ, pg. 1064
Strassler, Marc, Sec. & Gen. Counsel--Pathmark, Woodbridge, NJ, pg. 1064
Straub, Donald A., Sec. & Gen. Counsel--Republic Industries, Inc., Harwood Heights, IL, pg. 928
Street, Paul, Gen. Counsel--Specialty Paperboard Inc., Brattleboro, VT, pg. 1027
Strickland, Barbara S., Gen. Counsel--The Suddath Companies, Jacksonville, FL, pg. 1055
Strother, James, Legal Officer--Kenneth Leventhal & Company, Los Angeles, CA, pg. 670
Stubbs, Donald F., V.P. & Trust Counsel--Fiduciary Trust Co. International, New York, NY, pg. 408
Stuhlmann, Eric, V.P. & Chief Fin. Officer--Shurfine-Central Corp., Northlake, IL, pg. 1001
Stutes, Darrell, V.P. & Gen. Counsel--Al Copeland Enterprises, Inc., Jefferson, LA, pg. 283
Stutes, Darrell, V.P. & Gen. Counsel--Church's Fried Chicken, Inc., Jefferson, LA, pg. 284
Sullivan, Mark, Gen. Counsel--Bose Corporation, Framingham, MA, pg. 167
Sullivan, W. Michael, Gen. Counsel--Brooks Beverages Inc., Columbus, OH, pg. 179
Sutter, Larry, Legal Officer--General Media Publishing Group, New York, NY, pg. 450
Swick, Michael F., Gen. Counsel--Hesston, Norcross, GA, pg. 4
Symyk, Irene, V.P. & Counsel--Service America Corporation, Stamford, CT, pg. 992
Talcott, Joel D., V.P., Sec. & Gen. Counsel--Ampex Corporation, Redwood City, CA, pg. 998
Tallackson, Jeffrey S., Exec. V.P., Sec. & Gen. Counsel--American Savings Bank, White Plains, NY, pg. 60
Tansler, Hans, III, Gen. Counsel--Mark III Industries, Ocala, FL, pg. 708
Tarajano, Jose, Gen. Counsel & Mgr.-Personnel--Pala Group, Inc., Baton Rouge, LA, pg. 843
Taranto, Thomas, Gen. Counsel--The Long Island Rail Road Co., Jamaica, NY, pg. 745
Tario, James, Gen. Counsel--Rosendin Electric, Inc., San Jose, CA, pg. 948
Tate, Troy, Gen. Counsel--S.W. Jr. Enterprises, Inc., Santa Ana Heights, CA, pg. 965
Taub, Kathy, Gen. Counsel--Clark Construction Group, Bethesda, MD, pg. 252
Taub, Kathy, Gen. Counsel--CEI Construction, Inc., Bethesda, MD, pg. 200
Taub, Melvin S., Sr. Exec. V.P. & Gen. Counsel--Prime Hospitality Corp., Fairfield, NJ, pg. 889
Taylor, Perry, Sr. V.P. & Corp. Counsel--Chicago Corp., Chicago, IL, pg. 247
Taylor, Terry, Sr. V.P., Gen. Counsel & Sec.--Club Corporation International, Dallas, TX, pg. 256
Terlato, John, V.P. & Asst. Legal Counsel--Paterno Imports Limited, Chicago, IL, pg. 851
Terlato, John, V.P. & Asst. Legal Counsel--Pacific Wine Co., Chicago, IL, pg. 851
Tetsujiro, Nakamura, Gen. Counsel--Mutual Trading Co., Inc., Los Angeles, CA, pg. 779
Theobald, John O., Gen. Counsel--Gosnell Builders, Phoenix, AZ, pg. 472
Thomas, Curt, Gen. Counsel--Sunclipse, Inc., Montebello, CA, pg. 1059
Thomas, Eugene C., Sec. & Gen. Counsel--Intermountain Industries, Inc., Boise, ID, pg. 575
Thomas, W. Lee, Gen. Counsel--The Ward Machinery Company, Cockeysville, MD, pg. 1162
Thompson, Bruce, Gen. Counsel--Foote & Davies Inc., Atlanta, GA, pg. 423
Thompson, R. Duff, V.P. & Gen. Counsel--WordPerfect Corporation, Orem, UT, pg. 1202
Thurston, David E., V.P. & Gen. Counsel--The Binswanger Company, Philadelphia, PA, pg. 151
Timm, Theodore, Sec. & Gen. Counsel--DoAll Company, Des Plaines, IL, pg. 341
Timmons, S.D., V.P.-Bus. Affairs & Legal--National Steel & Shipbuilding Company, San Diego, CA, pg. 794
Tishler, Louis B., Gen. Counsel--Lou Beres & Associates, Inc., Chicago, IL, pg. 141
Toal, John H., Gen. Counsel--Phonetics, Inc., Aston, PA, pg. 869
Tobin, Dave, V.P. & Gen. Counsel--The William Carter Company, New York, NY, pg. 226
Toegemann, Alfred C., Sr. V.P.-Legal--Amica Mutual Insurance Co., Providence, RI, pg. 66
Toler, Gene, Gen. Counsel--Pabst Brewing Co., San Antonio, TX, pg. 959
Toler, Gene, Gen. Counsel--Pearl Brewing Company, San Antonio, TX, pg. 959
Tolly, David H., V.P., Sec. & Gen. Counsel--Savage Arms Inc., Westfield, MA, pg. 973
Toner, Edward J., Sec. & Legal Officer--Faber/Castell Corporation, Parsippany, NJ, pg. 395
Torgerson, Robert, Gen. Counsel--Jewelers Mutual Insurance Company, Neenah, WI, pg. 593
Torres, William J., V.P., Sec., Treas., Legal Officer & Telecommunications Dir.--Gibbs Wire & Steel Company, Inc., Southington, CT, pg. 456
Tosch, John, V.P. & Corp. Counsel--American Speedy Printing Centers, Inc., Bloomfield Hills, MI, pg. 61
Towers, Robers, V.P. & Gen. Counsel--The Stellar Group Inc., Jacksonville, FL, pg. 1046
Trabbuco, John E., Sec. & Gen. Counsel--Beckwith Machinery Company, Murrysville, PA, pg. 131
Travis, Andrew D., V.P. & Legal Counsel--Allright Corporation, Houston, TX, pg. 41
Trigg, Donald C., Sr. V.P.-Sec. & Gen. Counsel--The Associated Group, Indianapolis, IN, pg. 90
Tringale, Steven, V.P.-Pub. Affairs--Blue Cross and Blue Shield of Massachusetts, Boston, MA, pg. 159
Tripp, David, V.P. & Gen. Counsel--Spectradyne Inc., Richardson, TX, pg. 318
Truly, Ethel, Gen. Counsel--Newsprint South, Inc., Yazoo City, MS, pg. 760
Trump, Arthur, Sec. & Gen. Counsel--Atlantic Builders Group Inc., Baltimore, MD, pg. 94
Tschirhart, Paul M., Sr. V.P., Gen. Counsel & Sec.--The Hertz Corporation, Park Ridge, NJ, pg. 849
Tseng, V., Dir.-Legal--Welch's, Concord, MA, pg. 789
Tucker, Bradford, Exec. V.P. & Gen. Counsel--Mustang Tractor & Equip. Co., Houston, TX, pg. 777
Tucker, James L., Sr. V.P., Sec. & Gen. Counsel--OPUS Corp., Minnetonka, MN, pg. 828
Tudor, Michael S., Sec. & Gen. Counsel--Tudor Inc., Alexandria, LA, pg. 1118
Tulloch, G.S., V.P., Sec. & Gen. Counsel--Graybar Electric Company, Inc., Clayton, MO, pg. 479
Tumminello, Theodore, Sr. V.P., Gen. Counsel & Sec.--Pan-American Life Insurance Company, New Orleans, LA, pg. 845
Turbville, John F., V.P.-Legal & Sec.--Walter Industries, Inc., Tampa, FL, pg. 1161
Turcott, Robert G., V.P., Sec. & Gen. Counsel--Roundy's, Inc., Pewaukee, WI, pg. 952
Turgeon, Nancy, Sec.--Robertson's Auto Salvage, Wareham, MA, pg. 939
Underberg, Mark A., Mng. Dir., Sec. & Gen. Counsel--The Henley Group, Inc., Hampton, NH, pg. 529
Underwood, William E., Jr., Sec. & Gen. Counsel--AEA, Inc., Charlotte, NC, pg. 3
Valentine, Stephen K., Jr., Gen. Counsel--Paul Inman Associates Inc., Farmington Hills, MI, pg. 570
Van Allen, Moore, Gen. Counsel--Long MFG. NC, Inc., Tarboro, NC, pg. 682
Van Gorder, Jan R., Exec. V.P., Sec. & Gen. Counsel--Erie Family Life Insurance Company, Erie, PA, pg. 386
Van Gorder, Jan R., Exec. V.P., Sec. & Gen. Counsel--Erie Insurance Group, Erie, PA, pg. 386
Van Gorder, Jan R., Exec. V.P., Sec. & Gen. Counsel--Erie Indemnity Company, Erie, PA, pg. 386
Van Gorder, Jan R., Exec. V.P., Sec. & Gen. Counsel--Erie Insurance Exchange, Erie, PA, pg. 386
Van Steenberg, Gus N., V.P. & Legal Counsel--Southwest Research Institute, San Antonio, TX, pg. 1023
Van Vlierbergen, Brian R., V.P., Gen. Counsel & Sec.--Blue Cross & Blue Shield of Illinois, Chicago, IL, pg. 160
Varona, Daniel, Chief Admin. Officer, Sec. & Gen. Counsel--Companion Life Insurance Co., Rye, NY, pg. 779
Vaughn, Thomas D., V.P. & Gen. Counsel--Penske Truck Leasing, Chesterfield, MO, pg. 859
Ventre, Frank Jr., Gen. Counsel--Ventre Packing Company, Inc., Syracuse, NY, pg. 1147
Ventress, Michelle, Asst. Gen. Counsel--The LINC Group, Inc., Chicago, IL, pg. 648
Verdon, William, Sr. V.P. & Gen. Counsel--Crowley Maritime Corporation, Oakland, CA, pg. 301
Verhagen, Timothy J., V.P.-Human Resources & Assoc. Gen. Counsel--The Marley Company, Mission Woods, KS, pg. 710
Vinocur, Peter A., Legal Counsel--NESCO, Inc., Mayfield Heights, OH, pg. 798
Violet, Timothy, V.P.-Legal--Hubbard Milling Company, Mankato, MN, pg. 549
Vitkus, Richard F., Sr. V.P., Gen. Counsel & Dir.-Devel.--ComputerLand Corporation, Pleasanton, CA, pg. 271
Vrooman, Edward A., Gen. Counsel & Sec.--Tri-State Motor Transit Co., Joplin, MO, pg. 1111
Vumbacco, Joseph, Gen. Counsel & Sec.--The Lathrop Company, Toledo, OH, pg. 660
Waak, Richard, Gen. Counsel--National Safety Associates, Memphis, TN, pg. 793
Wadler, Arnold, Sr. V.P., Gen. Counsel & Sec.--Metromedia Company, East Rutherford, NJ, pg. 743
Wadsworth, Edward N., Sr. V.P. & Assoc. Gen. Counsel--The New England, Boston, MA, pg. 799
Waggoner, John, Sr. V.P. & Gen. Counsel--CUNA Mutual Insurance Society, Madison, WI, pg. 205
Wagner, Barbara, V.P.-Legal--Dinner Bell Foods, Inc., Cincinnati, OH, pg. 53
Wagner, Norman B., Gen. Counsel--Janlynn Corporation, Indian Orchard, MA, pg. 589
Walk, Frank H., Jr., Legal Officer--Walk, Haydel & Associates, Inc., New Orleans, LA, pg. 1159
Wall, Hugh, III, Gen. Counsel--Gosiger Inc., Dayton, OH, pg. 472
Waller, William A., Sr. V.P., Gen. Counsel & Sec.--Petty Company, Inc., Effingham, IL, pg. 866
Walley, Craig D., V.P. & Legal Counsel--The Scott Company, Marysville, OH, pg. 982
Wallin, R.E., Gen. Counsel--Kemmons Wilson Companies, Memphis, TN, pg. 1194
Walls, David, Gen. Counsel--Long MFG. NC, Inc., Tarboro, NC, pg. 682
Walters, Bette J., V.P. & Gen. Counsel--Alco Industries, Inc., Valley Forge, PA, pg. 32
Walters, Leigh, Gen. Counsel--Valcor Engineering Corp., Springfield, NJ, pg. 1142
Ward, Jeff, Gen. Counsel--Sugar Cane Growers Cooperative of Florida, Belle Glade, FL, pg. 1056
Ward, Patrick J., Chm. Bd., Pres. & Chief Exec. Officer--Caltex Petroleum Corporation, Irving, TX, pg. 211
Warren, E.T., Gen. Counsel--Molded Fiber Glass Companies, Ashtabula, OH, pg. 763
Warshawsky, Stanford S., Vice Chm. & Legal Officer--Arnhold and S. Bleichroeder, Inc., New York, NY, pg. 84
Washburn, John H., Sr. V.P.-Legal & Gen. Counsel--Sammons Enterprises, Inc., Dallas, TX, pg. 968
Wassong, Dwight, Gen Counsel & Dir. Taxes & Legal Services--Butterick Company, Inc., New York, NY, pg. 197
Watkins, L. Earl, Jr., Gen. Counsel & Sec.--Sunflower Electric Power Corporation, Hays, KS, pg. 1060
Watson, Gene D., Gen. Counsel--Nebraska Public Power District, Columbus, NE, pg. 796
Watson, James, Gen. Counsel--Wakefern Food Corporation, Elizabeth, NJ, pg. 1158
Weaver, Stephen, Gen. Counsel--L'Ermitage Hotels, West Hollywood, CA, pg. 668
Webb, Chris, V.P. & Gen. Counsel--Jervis B. Webb Company, Farmington Hills, MI, pg. 1170
Webb, J.G., V.P. & Gen. Counsel--J.M. Huber Corporation, Edison, NJ, pg. 550
Webb, R.W., Sec. & Gen. Counsel--Fenestra Corporation, Erie, PA, pg. 711
Webster, Mark, Chief Exec. Officer, Chief Fin. Officer & Gen. Counsel--Rush County Farm Bureau Co-op, Rushville, IN, pg. 956
Wefer, Donald P., Sr. V.P., Gen. Counsel & Sec.--Associated Metals & Minerals Corp., White Plains, NY, pg. 91
Weil, Gary, Sr. Corp. Counsel--RE/MAX International, Inc., Englewood, CO, pg. 915
Weiner, Ronald, Gen. Counsel & Corp. Sec.--Radiator Specialty Company, Charlotte, NC, pg. 909
Weinstein, Gerald H., Legal Officer--Alliance America, Norcross, GA, pg. 37
Weinstein, Mark M., Sr. V.P.-Gen. Counsel & Sec.--National Amusements, Inc., Dedham, MA, pg. 784
Weinstein, Mark M., Sr. V.P. & Gen. Counsel--Viacom Inc., New York, NY, pg. 785
Weinstein, Mark M., Sr. V.P. & Gen. Counsel--Viacom International Inc., New York, NY, pg. 785
Weiser, John W., Sr. V.P. & Gen. Counsel--Bechtel Group, Inc., San Francisco, CA, pg. 130
Weiss, Cathlean G., Chief Legal Counsel--Ohio Lottery Commission, Cleveland, OH, pg. 822
Weiss, Howard J., Gen. Counsel--Hudson Valley Tree, Inc., Newburgh, NY, pg. 551
Weiss, Jerome, Gen. Counsel--Country Companies Insurance Group, Bloomington, IL, pg. 289
Weiss, Jerome, Gen. Counsel--Country Life Insurance Company, Bloomington, IL, pg. 289
Weiss, Jerome, Gen. Counsel--Country Mutual Insurance Company, Bloomington, IL, pg. 289
Weiss, Jerome, Gen. Counsel--CC Services, Bloomington, IL, pg. 289
Welch, Jim, Gen. Counsel--Correct Craft, Inc., Orlando, FL, pg. 287
Weldin, John, Gen. Counsel--RJO Enterprises, Inc., Lanham, MD, pg. 907
Wentz, Jack L., Assoc. Gen. Counsel & Corp. Sec.--Borg-Warner Corporation, Chicago, IL, pg. 165
Westerbeck, David F., V.P., Sec. & Gen. Counsel--The Union Central Life Insurance Co., Cincinnati, OH, pg. 1127
Wetmore, Edward, Gen. Counsel--Times Fiber Communications, Inc., Wallingford, CT, pg. 648
Wetmore, Edward C., Sec. & Gen. Counsel--LPL Technologies, Inc., Wallingford, CT, pg. 648
Wharton, Garry, Sr. V.P., Corp. Counsel & Sec.--Motorists Mutual Insurance Co., Columbus, OH, pg. 773
Whitlock, Lyndon, Sec. & Gen. Counsel--Velsicol Chemical Corporation, Rosemont, IL, pg. 1147
Whitmore, David, Gen. Counsel & Controller--E. James White Company, Herndon, VA, pg. 1185
Wiese, James D., V.P.-Legal--R. H. Macy & Co., Inc., New York, NY, pg. 698
Wiggins, Clarence R., Chm. Bd., Pres. & Chief Exec. Officer--Century Data Systems, Raleigh, NC, pg. 235
Wilkes, Jack, Counsel--HP Direct, Indianapolis, IN, pg. 497
Wilkinsom, James., Chief Fin. Officer & Gen. Counsel--Meritcare, Inc., Pittsburgh, PA, pg. 740
Wilkinson, Mike, Gen. Counsel--Daw Technologies, Inc., Salt Lake City, UT, pg. 319
Williams, Dennis, Gen. Counsel--Allsop, Inc., Bellingham, WA, pg. 43
Williams, John, Gen. Counsel--Bennington Iron Works, Inc., Bennington, VT, pg. 139
Williams, John H., Gen. Counsel--Mack Molding Company, Arlington, VT, pg. 697
Williams, Richard John, Legal Officer--Handgards Inc., Northbrook, IL, pg. 504
Williams, Robert J., V.P. & Gen. Counsel--TTX Co., Chicago, IL, pg. 1075
Williams, Steve, Gen. Counsel--Markair, Inc., Anchorage, AK, pg. 708
Williamson, Scott, Chief Fin. Officer & Gen. Counsel--Plasti-Kote Company Inc., Medina, OH, pg. 875
Willis, Albert, Gen. Counsel--North Carolina Mutual Life Insurance Co., Durham, NC, pg. 813
Wilson, Albert J., V.P., Sec. & Chief Counsel--Teachers Insurance and Annuity Association-College Retirement Equities Fund, New York, NY, pg. 1082
Wilson, H. James, Sr. V.P. & Assoc. Gen. Counsel-Insurance--The New England, Boston, MA, pg. 799
Wilson, Logan J., V.P.-Legal Affairs & Sec.--Fike Corporation, Blue Springs, MO, pg. 409
Wilson, Lowell, Treas. & Sec.--Ag Processing Inc A Cooperative, Omaha, NE, pg. 24
Wilson, Roger, Gen. Counsel--Blue Cross and Blue Shield Association, Chicago, IL, pg. 159
Winebarger, Paige, V.P. & Counsel--Bank Shares, Inc., Minneapolis, MN, pg. 117

Winebarger, Paige, V.P. & Corp. Sec.--Marquette Bank Minneapolis, National Association, Minneapolis, MN, pg. 117
Winkelman, Earl, V.P., Gen. Counsel & Asst. Sec.--Jockey International, Inc., Kenosha, WI, pg. 595
Winkler, Ron, Legal Officer--Information Systems & Network Corporation, Bethesda, MD, pg. 567
Winters, Steve D., Pres. & Chief Exec. Officer--Bepco, Inc., Winston-Salem, NC, pg. 141
Wise, Richard W., Legal Officer--Mississippi Valley Gas Co., Jackson, MS, pg. 1208
Wise, Warren R., Exec. V.P. & Gen. Counsel--Massachusetts Mutual Life Insurance Co., Springfield, MA, pg. 718
Wiseman, Donald F., V.P., Gen. Counsel & Sec.--Perkins Family Restaurants, Memphis, TN, pg. 1088
Wojcik, Paul N., V.P., Gen. Counsel & Sec.--The Bureau of National Affairs, Inc., Washington, DC, pg. 189
Wolfcale, A. D., V.P., Deputy Gen. Counsel & Sec.--The Edward J. DeBartolo Corporation, Youngstown, OH, pg. 323
Wood, David, Gen. Counsel--Martin Universal Design, Inc., Westland, MI, pg. 715
Wood, Dennis, Sr. V.P., Gen. Counsel & Personnel--Atari Games Corporation, Milpitas, CA, pg. 93
Woodard, Elizabeth B., V.P., Gen. Counsel & Sec.--Riviana Foods Inc., Houston, TX, pg. 937
Wright, James W., V.P.-Legal Affairs & Sec.--Lord Corporation, Erie, PA, pg. 683
Wright, W. Kevin, V.P.-Gen. Counsel & Asst. Sec.--TLC Beatrice International Holdings Inc., New York, NY, pg. 1073
Wrobel, Robert F., Sr. V.P., Gen. Counsel & Chief Admin. Officer--The Marley Company, Mission Woods, KS, pg. 710
Wuebbling, Donald J., V.P. & Gen. Counsel--Western & Southern Life Insurance Co., Cincinnati, OH, pg. 1181
Yates, Jeffery M., Exec. V.P. & Gen. Counsel--Independent Insurance Agents of America, Alexandria, VA, pg. 565
Young, Dona D., Sr. V.P. & Gen. Counsel--Phoenix Home Life Mutual Insurance Company, Hartford, CT, pg. 868
Young, Gary S., Gen. Counsel--Metabo Corporation, West Chester, PA, pg. 741
Young, Peter J., Gen. Counsel--Gerrity Co., Inc., Newton, MA, pg. 454
Young, Stewart, V.P.-Legal Affairs--United Broadcasting Inc., Bethesda, MD, pg. 1131
Zacharczyk, Jill, V.P.-Contracts & Gen. Counsel--Calico Cat Press, Inc., New Providence, NJ, pg. 209
Zak, Leonard E., V.P. & Gen. Counsel--Harza Engineering Co., Chicago, IL, pg. 516
Zeiss, Michael G., Mng. Dir. & Gen. Counsel--CS First Boston Group, Inc., New York, NY, pg. 203
Zeiss, Michael G., Gen. Counsel--The First Boston Corporation, New York, NY, pg. 203
Zeller, Randi E., Assoc. Gen. Counsel--McKinsey & Company, Inc., New York, NY, pg. 731
Zenk, Saul, V.P. & Treas.--Monico Alloys, Inc., Los Angeles, CA, pg. 765
Zimmer, Edward, Sr. V.P., Sec. & Gen. Counsel--LFC Holding Corporation, Boca Raton, FL, pg. 647
Zimmer, Edward, Sr. V.P., Sec. & Gen. Counsel--Levitz Furniture Corporation, Boca Raton, FL, pg. 647
Zimmer, Emanuel, Gen. Counsel--Rosen Associates Management Corp., Jericho, NY, pg. 948
Zimmerman, Doug, Legal Officer--Best Western International, Inc., Phoenix, AZ, pg. 146
Zinn, Chester A., Jr., V.P., Sec. & Gen. Counsel--MSI Insurance Companies, Arden Hills, MN, pg. 693
Zogg, Chris J., Sec. & Gen. Counsel--Kent Feeds Inc., Muscatine, IA, pg. 1146
Zuk, Nicholas W., Legal Officer--White Castle System, Inc., Columbus, OH, pg. 1185

MANUFACTURING

Abernethy, Fred, V.P.-Mfg.--Carolina Glove Co., Newton, NC, pg. 223
Aceto, T.J., V.P.-Opers., Metal Products Div.--Wesbar Corporation, West Bend, WI, pg. 1176
Acton, Stephanie, Mgr.-Mfg.--RELA Manufacturing Division, Boulder, CO, pg. 924
Acuff, Bill, Dir.-Mfg.--Ohmite Manufacturing Company, Skokie, IL, pg. 823
Adams, Bob, V.P. & Dir.-Production--Automotive News, Detroit, MI, pg. 101
Adams, Robert C., V.P.-Production--Crain Communications, Inc., Detroit, MI, pg. 295
Agness, Terry, Exec. V.P.-Mfg.--Ford Meter Box Company, Wabash, IN, pg. 423
Alden, Tom, Mgr.-Oper. & Mfg.--Security Products Company of Delaware, Inc., Minneapolis, MN, pg. 1138
Alderink, Roger, V.P.-Engrng.--Alvey Inc., Saint Louis, MO, pg. 46
Allen, Dan, Dir.-Engrng.--AmTran Corporation, Conway, AR, pg. 69
Allyn, John, V.P.-Opers.--Despatch Industries, Minneapolis, MN, pg. 332
Alsip, Charles, V.P.-Engrng.--Tyler Limited Partnership, Benson, MN, pg. 1122
Alvey, Steven, V.P.-Fin. & Opers.--Shugart Corporation, Irvine, CA, pg. 1001
Alworth, R.L., V.P.-Mfg.--S & C Electric Company, Chicago, IL, pg. 958
Amend, H., V.P.-Mfg.--Shure Brothers Incorporated, Evanston, IL, pg. 1001
Amlie, James H., V.P.-Production--Honeymead Products Co., Mankato, MN, pg. 542
Anderko, Frank, V.P.-Mfg. & Sec.--Worzalla Publishing Co., Inc., Stevens Point, WI, pg. 1204
Anderson, Bruce, Exec. V.P., Treas. & Dir.-Mfg. & Quality Control--Integrated Energy Controls Corp., Minneapolis, MN, pg. 573
Anderson, Charles, Dir.-Mfg.--Eco Water Systems, Saint Paul, MN, pg. 367
Anderson, David, V.P.-Mfg.--I. Spiewak & Sons, Inc., New York, NY, pg. 1031
Anderson, Jon, V.P.-Mfg.--Printco, Inc., Greenville, MI, pg. 891
Anderson, Marc, Plant Mgr.--X-A Cabinet Corporation, La Mirada, CA, pg. 1206
Andreotti, Richard, V.P.-Mfg.--George Lithograph, San Francisco, CA, pg. 452
Andrews, Al, Pres.-Retail & Tanner Div.--Tanner Co. Inc., Rutherfordton, NC, pg. 1078
Andrews, Christopher, V.P.-Engrng.--Delta Rubber Company, Danielson, CT, pg. 327
Andrews, Stephen W., V.P.-Engrng.--Wheelock Inc., Long Branch, NJ, pg. 1185
Andruk, Wayne, Dir.-Engrng.--Power Conversion, Inc., Saddle Brook, NJ, pg. 883
Angel, Marvin, Dir.-Engrng.--Cowden Metal Specialties, Inc., Chino, CA, pg. 291
Annas, A. Wayne, V.P.-Mfg.--Hickory Hill Furniture Corporation, Valdese, NC, pg. 816
Anthony, Aubra, Sr., V.P.-Mfg.--Anthony Forest Products Co., Inc., El Dorado, AR, pg. 77
Anthony, Dale, V.P.-Mfg.--Pacesetter Corporation, Omaha, NE, pg. 839
Antos, John M., V.P.-Engrng.--Thetford Corporation, Ann Arbor, MI, pg. 357
Appel, Jack, V.P.-Engrng.--Efco Corporation, Monett, MO, pg. 359
Applebaum, David, V.P.-Mfg.--Triangle Marketing Corp., New York, NY, pg. 1112
Armiento, Mike, V.P.-Mfg.--S. Schwab Company, Cumberland, MD, pg. 980
Arndorfer, Frank M., V.P.-Finishing Opers.--Quad/Graphics, Inc., Pewaukee, WI, pg. 902
Arnold, David W., V.P.-Engrng.--Newsprint South, Inc., Yazoo City, MS, pg. 760
Arthur, R.B., Jr., Mgr.-Mfg.--North State Pyrophyllite, Greensboro, NC, pg. 928
Artwohl, Paul, V.P.-Engrng.--Ardco, Inc., Alsip, IL, pg. 81
Ash, W.T., V.P.-Opers.--Broadcast Electronics, Inc., Quincy, IL, pg. 177
Ashton, Craig, V.P.-Mfg.--T & S Brass & Bronze Works, Inc., Travelers Rest, SC, pg. 1074
Atalla, Anwar, V.P.-Engrng.--Revcor, Inc., Carpentersville, IL, pg. 930
Atkins, Roger, V.P.-Mfg.--Formex, Inc. - Permanent Steel Forms, Richmond, VA, pg. 470
Atwell, William, V.P.-Mfg.--Glines & Rhodes, Inc., Attleboro, MA, pg. 463
Atwood, Stephen C., Jr., Dir.-Production--The Wiremold Company, West Hartford, CT, pg. 1197
Austin, Jack, Gen. Mgr.--Surco Products, Inc., Braddock, PA, pg. 1065
Austin, Wade, Mgr.-Plant--Kroehler Furniture Manufacturing Company, Inc., Conover, NC, pg. 645
Autrey, Ronald, V.P.-Estimating & Engrng.--Miller Electric Company, Jacksonville, FL, pg. 754
Avery, Larry, V.P.-Engrng. & Opers.--Alabama Electric Cooperative, Inc., Andalusia, AL, pg. 28
Ayoub, Selim J., V.P.-Mfg.--Automation Intelligence, Inc., Maitland, FL, pg. 101
Azari, Ahmad, V.P.-Engrng.--Alford Refrigerated Warehouse, Inc., Dallas, TX, pg. 34
Backus, James, V.P.-Engrng. & Construction--Wilmorite Inc., Rochester, NY, pg. 1193
Bagwell, Charles F., V.P. & Dir.-Mfg. & Pur.--The Kent Manufacturing Co., Pickens, SC, pg. 623
Bailey, Neil, V.P.-Opers. & Engrng.--Holsum Bakery, Inc., Phoenix, AZ, pg. 541
Bailey, Robert J., Sr. V.P.-Quality Assurance & Admin.--The Hertz Corporation, Park Ridge, NJ, pg. 849
Baker, Ray, V.P.-Mfg.--Uvex Safety, Inc., Smithfield, RI, pg. 1141
Baker, Tom, Dir.-Mfg.--Difco, Inc., Findlay, OH, pg. 337
Baker, William, V.P.-Mfg.--Nylon Corporation Of America, Manchester, NH, pg. 818
Baldwin, Ardell, Dir.-Mfg.--Old Home Foods, Inc., Saint Paul, MN, pg. 823
Balish, Frank, V.P.-Mfg.--United Gilsonite Laboratories, Scranton, PA, pg. 1132
Ball, David, V.P.-Mfg.--Mason Shoe Mfg. Co., Chippewa Falls, WI, pg. 718
Ball, David, V.P.-Mfg.--Wissota Trader & B.A. Mason, Chippewa Falls, WI, pg. 718
Ball, Thomas E., Dir.-Mfg.--Bioproducts, Inc., Brecksville, OH, pg. 152
Baraglia, Bill, V.P.-Mfg.--Chicago White Metal Casting, Inc., Bensenville, IL, pg. 246
Barbeau, Jack, V.P.-Mfg.--Wells Mfg. Corp., Dond Du Lac, WI, pg. 1123
Barber, Joe, Mgr.-Mfg.--Airguard Industries Inc., Louisville, KY, pg. 27
Barnard, Dale, V.P.-Mfg.--Pneumatic Scale Corporation, Quincy, MA, pg. 122
Barnes, Robert, Supvr.-Mfg.--Southern Ohio Fabricators, Inc., Cincinnati, OH, pg. 1022
Barnhart, Ralph, V.P.-Engrng.--E. H. Titchener & Company, Binghamton, NY, pg. 1099
Barnhill, Al, Exec. V.P.-Mfg.--Blumenthal Print Works, Inc., New Orleans, LA, pg. 161
Barnhill, J., V.P.-Mfg.--Goshen Rubber Co., Inc., Goshen, IN, pg. 472
Barr, Harry S., V.P.-Prod. Devel.--Pneumafil Corp., Charlotte, NC, pg. 878
Barrett, John, Dir.-Maintenance--Fredrickson Motor Express Corp., Charlotte, NC, pg. 430
Barrett, Robert L., Prod. Engineer--Marquette Coppersmithing Co., Inc., Philadelphia, PA, pg. 713
Barrocas, Jacob, V.P.-Mfg.--Injection Footwear Corp., Miami, FL, pg. 569
Barteau, John F., Sr. V.P.-Devel. & Mfg.--Church's Fried Chicken, Inc., Jefferson, LA, pg. 284
Barthel, J., Mgr.-Tech.--Stuart-Ironsides, Inc., Willowbrook, IL, pg. 1054
Bartosh, Kenneth R., Mgr.-Mfg.--Hanover Foods Corporation, Hanover, PA, pg. 506
Bason, Jim, Production Mgr.--Snyder Potato Chips, Berlin, PA, pg. 26
Batliner, Doug, Dir.-Production & Pur.--Beach Mold & Tool Inc., New Albany, IN, pg. 128
Batt, David, Mgr.-Mfg.--Muro Pharmaceutical, Inc., Tewksbury, MA, pg. 776
Bauer, Ray, Chief Engr.--Kranco, Inc., Houston, TX, pg. 643
Baughan, Harry, V.P.-Mfg.--Poly-Seal Corporation, Baltimore, MD, pg. 880
Baughman, Walter P., III, V.P.-Mfg.--Plastomer Corp., Livonia, MI, pg. 876
Baumgartner, John, Chief Engineer--T. Bruce Sales, Inc., West Middlesex, PA, pg. 183
Baxevane, Nicholas, V.P.-Men's Mdsg.--Hess's Department Stores, Inc., Allentown, PA, pg. 302
Baxter, David, V.P.-Engrng.--Adept Technology, Inc., San Jose, CA, pg. 17
Bayer, Chris, Dir.-Mfg.--Precision Valve Corporation, Yonkers, NY, pg. 885
Bayne, Gerald, V.P.-Mfg.--Interform Corporation, Bridgeville, PA, pg. 574
Bayne, William, Jr., Dir.-Mfg.--Cablewave Systems, Inc., North Haven, CT, pg. 206
Bazzy, Dennis, V.P.-Engrng., Research & Devel.--T & S Brass & Bronze Works, Inc., Travelers Rest, SC, pg. 1074
Beach, Henry M., Exec. V.P.-Mfg.--O. F. Mossberg & Sons, Inc., North Haven, CT, pg. 773
Beal, Doris, V.P.-Mfg.--Entron Industries Limited Partnership, Glendale, NY, pg. 383
Beale, Nathan, V.P.-Mfg.--Lee Company, Westbrook, CT, pg. 665
Bean, William E., V.P.-Mfg.--D. D. Bean & Sons Co., Jaffrey, NH, pg. 129
Beattie, Robert, Production Mgr.--BNA International Inc., London,, United Kingdom, pg. 190
Beaty, Virgil, V.P.-Engrng.--Fairbanks Morse Pump Corporaton, Kansas City, KS, pg. 397
Becht, Rudolph, V.P.-Sls. & Mdsg.--King Kullen Grocery Co., Inc., Westbury, NY, pg. 630
Becker, A. Carl, V.P.-Pur. & Engrng.--Nuttall Gear Corporation, Niagara Falls, NY, pg. 818
Beckwith, Scott, V.P.-Mfg.--Efco Corporation, Monett, MO, pg. 359
Beeson, Thomas, V.P.-Mfg.--Bose Corporation, Framingham, MA, pg. 167
Belisle, William D., V.P.-Engrng.--Edgewood Tool & Manufacturing Company, Romulus, MI, pg. 368
Benavides, Patrick R., V.P.-Engrng.--Bonney Forge Corporation, Allentown, PA, pg. 164
Benda, Brian, Dir.-Mfg.--Control Systems Inc., Saint Paul, MN, pg. 281
Benham, Webster Lance, III, Sr. V.P.-Mechanical--The Benham Group, Oklahoma City, OK, pg. 138
Benhase, M., Mgr.-Mfg..--Red L Foods, Pomfret Center, CT, pg. 1128
Bennett, Lester, Mgr.-Production--The Paty Company, Piney Flats, TN, pg. 852
Bensberg, Thomas, Dir.-Mfg.--Weatherly Consumer Products, Inc., Lexington, KY, pg. 1169
Beregescazy, B., V.P.-Mfg.--Telechron, Inc., Ashland, MA, pg. 1085
Berg, W., Dir.-Tech.--Dahlstrom Manufacturing Company, Inc., Jamestown, NY, pg. 310
Bergami, S.S., V.P.-Mfg.--Alinabal, Inc., Milford, CT, pg. 34
Berger, George, V.P.-Mfg.--American Manufacturing Company, Inc. (LA), Lafayette, LA, pg. 58
Berkey, Richard, V.P.-Mfg.--Universal Folding Box Company, Inc., Hoboken, NJ, pg. 1138
Berkshire, M., Dir.-Quality Assurance & Technical Srvcs.--Brooks Foods, Mt. Summit, IN, pg. 26
Bernard, John, Dir.-Mfg.--O. S. Walker Co. Inc., Worcester, MA, pg. 1160
Bernie, Logan, V.P.-Mfg.--American Wyott Corporation, Cheyenne, WY, pg. 65
Bernstein, Eric, V.P.-Mfg.--Applied Graphics Technologies, Oceanside, NY, pg. 1136
Berrett, Richard A., V.P.-Mfg. & Freestanding Opers.--Haworth, Inc., Holland, MI, pg. 518
Best, Alex B., Sr. V.P.-Engrng.--Cable Division, Atlanta, GA, pg. 294
Bethel, Ron, Dir.-Mfg.--Hercules Engines, Inc., Canton, OH, pg. 531
Bethray, Adrian, V.P.-Indus. & Export Sls.--Reading Anthracite Coal Co., Pottsville, PA, pg. 916
Bezousek, Richard, V.P.-Production & Chief Oper. Officer--Omaha Steaks International, Omaha, NE, pg. 825
Bhandari, Harry, V.P.-Mfg.--Replogle Globes, Inc., Broadview, IL, pg. 927
Biggs, David H., V.P.-Mfg. & Prod. Devel.--Bently Nevada Corporation, Minden, NV, pg. 140
Biller, Kenneth V., V.P.-Mfg.--RAYOVAC Corporation, Madison, WI, pg. 915
Billie, L. Clark, V.P.-Engrng. & Opers. Control--Trans World Airlines, Inc., Mount Kisco, NY, pg. 561
Billing, D.M., V.P.-Prod. & Gen. Mgr.--Roydon Wear, Inc., McRae, GA, pg. 283
Bingham, Lanning, V.P.-Mfg.--Sentinel Consumer Products, Inc., Mentor, OH, pg. 990
Binkley, Ray, Dir.-Mfg.--Coble Dairy Products Co-op, Lexington, NC, pg. 257
Bird, Alan R., V.P.-Engrng.--Sunshine Biscuits, Inc., Woodbridge, NJ, pg. 439
Bittel, Mary Ellen, Dir.-Prod.--Lotus Publishing Corporation, Cambridge, MA, pg. 576
Black, Don, Chief Engr.--King & Prince Seafood Corporation, Brunswick, GA, pg. 631
Black, Herbert, Chief Engr.--Gertrude Hawk Chocolates, Inc., Troop, PA, pg. 517

Corporate Responsibilities Index

Black, Joe, Dir.-Mfg.--Bike Athletic Co., Knoxville, TN, pg. 150
Blakely, J.M., Mgr.-Scheduling, Shipper Rels.--Colonial Pipeline Company, Atlanta, GA, pg. 264
Blakeman, Bill, Dir.-Engrng.--Columbus Steel Drum Company, Blacklick, OH, pg. 267
Blank, Art, V.P.-Pur. & Mfg.--All-Luminum Products, Inc., Philadelphia, PA, pg. 35
Blank, L.W., V.P.-Engrng. & Res.--Miller Electric Mfg. Co., Appleton, WI, pg. 754
Blauer, Michael, V.P.-Engrng.--Blauer Manufacturing Co., Inc., Boston, MA, pg. 156
Bledsoe, L. L., V.P.-Towel Mfg.--Home Fashions Div., New York, NY, pg. 400
Blennis, Dennis R., Mgr.-Mfg.--Clifford B. Hannay & Son Inc., Westerlo, NY, pg. 505
Bliss, Robert E., V.P.-Chair Div.--Century Furniture Industries, Hickory, NC, pg. 235
Blum, David B., Dr., V.P.-Engrng.--Electrocatalytic, Inc., Union, NJ, pg. 375
Blum, L.J., V.P.-Production--The Kirk & Blum Mfg. Co., Cincinnati, OH, pg. 633
Blume, Bob, Mgr.-Mfg.--Noel-Joanna, Inc., Rancho Santa Margarita, CA, pg. 808
Blutstein, Morton, V.P.-Mfg.--Penthouse Knitting Mills, Milwaukee, WI, pg. 925
Bock, Frank, Dir.-Production & Engrng.--Cardinal Aluminum Co., Louisville, KY, pg. 217
Bode, Udo, Dir.-Engrng.--Cablewave Systems, Inc., North Haven, CT, pg. 206
Bodendorfer, Carl, Mfg. Mgr.--Erie Press Systems, Erie, PA, pg. 386
Boehler, Robert, V.P.-Mfg.--The Ingersoll Milling Machine Co., Rockford, IL, pg. 568
Boeve, Wayne, V.P.-Mfg.--Castex Industries Inc., Holland, MI, pg. 228
Boing, J.D., Sr. V.P.-Pur. & Production--Sporlan Valve Company, Saint Louis, MO, pg. 1032
Bolte, John, V.P.-Mfg.--National Machinery Company, Tiffin, OH, pg. 792
Bonczar, Lawrence J., V.P.-Engrng.--Casket Shells, Inc., Eynon, PA, pg. 228
Bonner, Marvin S., V.P.-Opers.--Walton Monroe Mills, Inc., Monroe, GA, pg. 1162
Bordelon, Noreen Hogg, Pres.--Trend Line Corporation, Jackson, MS, pg. 1109
Bordewyk, Wayne, V.P.-Opers.--Brink Electric Construction Company, Rapid City, SD, pg. 176
Boswell, Gene, V.P. & Plant Mgr.--Stuhr Enterprises Inc., Wilton, IA, pg. 1055
Botts, Kenneth C., Dir.-Mfg.--Stowe-Pharr Mills, Inc., McAdenville, NC, pg. 1052
Bowen, Leon O., Jr., V.P.-Engrng.--Rangaire & Company, Cleburne, TX, pg. 912
Bowman, Bruce, Sr. V.P.-Mfg.--Tom's Foods, Columbus, GA, pg. 1101
Box, George, Dir.-Engrng.--Capital Industries, Inc., Seattle, WA, pg. 215
Boyd, Dale, V.P.-Greige Mfg.--Greenwood Mills, Inc., Greenwood, SC, pg. 485
Boyd, Merle, V.P.-Mfg.--Bates Container, Inc., North Richland Hills, TX, pg. 125
Boyea, Gary J., V.P.-Mfg.--Tagsons Papers, Inc., Albany, NY, pg. 1076
Boyer, Dale, Plant Supt.--John Copes Food Products, Inc., Rheems, PA, pg. 284
Boyle, Mike, Dir.-Mfg.--M & C Specialties Company, Southampton, PA, pg. 690
Boyter, R. Steve, Sr. V.P.-Mfg.--The Bibb Company, Macon, GA, pg. 781
Brace, David E., V.P.-Opers.--Carol Wright Sales, Inc., Stamford, CT, pg. 1011
Bracken, J.F., V.P.-Engrng.--Simplicity Manufacturing, Inc., Port Washington, WI, pg. 1006
Bradley, Edward, V.P.-Opers.--Certified Grocers Midwest, Inc., Hodgkins, IL, pg. 236
Brady, Gerald, V.P.-Mfg. & Distr.--Evergreen Mills Inc., Ada, OK, pg. 1145
Bragdon, R.M., V.P.-Engrng.--American Cast Iron Pipe Co., Birmingham, AL, pg. 50
Brand, Larry, V.P.-Oper.--IBT, Inc., Shawnee Mission, KS, pg. 558
Bratsis, Gus, V.P.-Engrng.--Keymark Corporation, Fonda, NY, pg. 627
Brauks, Craig, Mgr.-Mfg.--Guth Lighting Company, Saint Louis, MO, pg. 588
Braund, Darwin G., Dir.-Res. & Applied Technology--Agway, Inc., De Witt, NY, pg. 25
Brazeal, Russ, V.P.-Engrng.--Hutchens Industries Inc., Springfield, MO, pg. 555
Brennan, E.J., V.P.-Engrng.--PTC Aerospace, Inc., Litchfield, CT, pg. 837
Brenton, T., V.P.-Mfg.--Layne & Bowler, Memphis, TN, pg. 710
Brewer, Kevin, Dir.-Engrng.--New Standard Corporation, Mount Joy, PA, pg. 802
Brezezinski, John, Prod. Mgr.-Dari-Kool--DEC/Bou-Matic, Madison, WI, pg. 309
Bridwell, Joe, V.P.-Opers.--NWS, Inc., Chicago, IL, pg. 782
Briick, Gerald, Dir.-Mfg. & Customer Services-Midwest--W. Braun Company, Chicago, IL, pg. 172
Brisson, Randy, Chief Engr.--Lodal, Inc., Kingsford, MI, pg. 680
Britt, Ron, Sr. V.P.-Mfg.--Belvedere Company, Belvidere, IL, pg. 138
Britten, Roy, V.P.-Mfg.--Sullivan Paper Company, West Springfield, MA, pg. 1057
Broadwell, John C., V.P.-Mfg.--Spencer Turbine Co., Windsor, CT, pg. 1030
Brock, Paul, Jr., V.P.-Mfg.--Brock Candy Company, Chattanooga, TN, pg. 177
Brodsky, J. Leon, V.P.-Engrng.--Plastoid Corporation, Hamburg, NJ, pg. 876
Brohas, Robert, V.P.-Engrng.--Plastic Moldings Corp., Cincinnati, OH, pg. 875
Brookfield, David A., V.P.-Engrng.--Brookfield Engineering Laboratories, Inc., Stoughton, MA, pg. 179
Brooks, Ed, Dir.-Mfg.--WICO Corporation, Niles, IL, pg. 1156
Brorup, Carl, Mgr.-Engrng.--Horton Homes, Inc., Eatonton, GA, pg. 545
Broslat, Bill, Mgr.-Pkgng. Devel.--Empire Berol U.S.A., Brentwood, TN, pg. 856
Broth, William, Dir.-Mfg.--Meer Corporation, North Bergen, NJ, pg. 736
Brown, Bobby, Mgr.-Mfg.--Whitin Roberts Co., Sanford, NC, pg. 1187
Brown, Charles C., Mgr.-Mfg.--J. H. Fletcher & Co., Huntington, WV, pg. 418
Brown, Gerald, Mgr.-Production--Smith Frozen Foods, Inc., Weston, OR, pg. 1012
Bruce R. Cochrane, Exec. V.P.-Mfg.--Cochrane Furniture Co., Inc., Lincolnton, NC, pg. 258
Brumfield, Donald L., V.P.-Pur. & Engrng.--Treasure Chest Advertising Co., Inc., Glendora, CA, pg. 1108
Brummitt, S.W., V.P.-Mfg.--Harriet & Henderson Yarns, Inc., Henderson, NC, pg. 511
Bruninga, Ken, Mgr.-Engrng.--L. R. Nelson Corporation, Peoria, IL, pg. 797
Brunini, Frank, V.P.-Mfg.--Warrens Waller Press, South San Francisco, CA, pg. 1165
Bryan, Gary G., V.P.-Mfg.--Chroma Corporation, McHenry, IL, pg. 249
Bryant, Richard, V.P.-Mfg.--Sullivan Paper Company, West Springfield, MA, pg. 1057
Bucaro, Benjamin, Mgr.-Prod.--Mark Lighting Fixture Co., Inc., Moonachie, NJ, pg. 708
Buchholz, Ron, V.P.-Mfg.--American Buildings Co., Eufaula, AL, pg. 49
Buck, Thomas A., V.P.-Mfg.--Titanium Metals Corporation, Denver, CO, pg. 1109
Budd, Richard L., Chief Engr.--Pittsburgh Tube Co., Monaca, PA, pg. 873
Bue, Richard, V.P.-Engrng.--SICO INC., Minneapolis, MN, pg. 1001
Bugby, David S., V.P.-Mfg.--Victaulic Company of America, Easton, PA, pg. 1149
Bulter, D. Fred, Chief Engineer--Seattle City Light, Seattle, WA, pg. 986
Bumpus, Bruce, Dir.-Mfg.--Zymark Corporation, Hopkinton, MA, pg. 1221
Bumsted, Tom, V.P.-Mfg.--Capsonic Group, Inc., Elgin, IL, pg. 216
Bundy, William H., V.P.-Mfg.--Foamex L.P., East Providence, RI, pg. 1121
Bungert, John, IV, V.P.-Mfg.--Captive Plastics, Piscataway, NJ, pg. 216
Bunke, Herbert, V.P.-Mfg.--The Metal Ware Corp., Two Rivers, WI, pg. 741
Burbidge, Fred, Production Mgr.--Alloway Manufacturing, Fargo, ND, pg. 41
Burget, Clark, V.P.-Mfg.--Koolvent Aluminum Products, Inc., Pittsburgh, PA, pg. 641
Burgett, William Barth, V.P.-Equipment--Kokosing Construction Company, Inc., Fredericktown, OH, pg. 640
Burggraaf, J.D., V.P.-Mfg.--Bissell Inc., Grand Rapids, MI, pg. 153
Burhans, Peter, Mgr.-Mfg.--Electro Methods Inc., South Windsor, CT, pg. 375
Burkhammer, Stephen, V.P.-Mfg.--Lake Shore, Inc., Kingsford, MI, pg. 824
Burrack, Bob, Mgr.-Plant--Turner Dairies, Inc., Covington, TN, pg. 1119
Burrow, Jim, V.P.-Mfg. & Opers.--ATAPCO Office Products Group, Saint Louis, MO, pg. 64
Busha, George, V.P.-Mfg.--National Oats Co., Cedar Rapids, IA, pg. 25
Butchart, James, V.P.-Mfg.--Bunton Company, Louisville, KY, pg. 188
Butkus, Joseph, Chief Engr.--The Fairfield Lumber & Supply Company, Fairfield, CT, pg. 397
Butler, N.L., V.P.-Mfg.--Chittenden & Eastman Co., Burlington, IA, pg. 248
Bybee, Jim L., V.P.-Engrng.--ACL Technologies, Santa Ana, CA, pg. 2
Bynum, Hal, V.P.-Mfg.--Williamson-Dickie Mfg. Co., Fort Worth, TX, pg. 1192
Byrne, John J., V.P.-Mfg.--Hollytex, Saddle Brook, NJ, pg. 1121
Byrum, Robert, V.P.-Intl. Supply & Distr.--Wickland Corporation, Sacramento, CA, pg. 1188
Cabak, R., Mgr.-Engr.--Illinois Range Company, Mount Prospect, IL, pg. 563
Cacciatore, Jerry, Production Mgr.--Viking Graphics, Chicago, IL, pg. 1151
Caddock, Richard E. Jr., V.P.-Engrng.--Caddock Electronics, Inc., Riverside, CA, pg. 207
Cagle, David, V.P.-Inventory & Distr.--Welsco Inc., North Little Rock, AR, pg. 1175
Caldwell, Greg, Facility Engrng. Dir.--Lowe's Food Stores, Inc., Winston-Salem, NC, pg. 33
Callaghan, Joseph, V.P.-Opers.--Certified Corp., Brockton, MA, pg. 236
Callaway, Robert R., Chief Engr.--Microflect Company, Inc., Salem, OR, pg. 749
Cameron, Gordon, V.P.-Mfg.--Ce De Candy, Inc., Union, NJ, pg. 230
Campbell, Jack, V.P.-Mfg.--Medical Laboratory Automation, Inc., Pleasantville, NY, pg. 735
Canady, W. Parker, V.P.-Pur. & Engrng.--Myrick Construction Inc., Biscoe, NC, pg. 780
Candalore, Gene, Exec. V.P.-Opers.--OCTus, San Diego, CA, pg. 818
Cannito, Peter A., V.P.-Engrng.--Amtrak-National Railroad Passenger Corp., Washington, DC, pg. 69
Cantwell, John, Dir.-Engrng.--The Pierce Co., Inc., Upland, IN, pg. 102
Caple, George, Production Mgr.--American Electronics, Inc., Fullerton, CA, pg. 3
Caponigro, Leonard, V.P.-Mfg. & Personnel & Dir.-Pur.--Tork, Inc., Mount Vernon, NY, pg. 1102
Cappadona, Tom, Mgr.-Mfg.--Kaz, Inc., New York, NY, pg. 619
Capps, Roger, V.P.-Production--Prairie Farms Dairy, Inc., Carlinville, IL, pg. 884
Carbone, Vincent M., V.P.-Mfg.--Rogers, Lunt & Bowlen Co., Greenfield, MA, pg. 943
Carder, Dane L., Sr., Dir.-Mfg.--YSD Industries, Youngstown, OH, pg. 1207
Carey, Scott, Mgr.-Mfg.--Howe Furniture Corporation, Trumbull, CT, pg. 547
Carlsen, Steve, V.P.-Mfg.--Kurt Manufacturing Co. Inc., Fridley, MN, pg. 646
Carlton, Glenn W., Sr. V.P.-Mfg.--Western States Envelope Co., Butler, WI, pg. 1181
Carney, Keith, V.P.-Engrng.--Welsbach Electric Corp., Long Island City, NY, pg. 1175
Carrieri, Warren, Dir.-Engrng.--Johnson & Towers, Inc., Mount Laurel, NJ, pg. 601
Carter, Hugh D., V.P.-Mfg.--Carco Electronics, Menlo Park, CA, pg. 217
Carter, Marty, Chief Engineer--Jonbil Inc., Chase City, VA, pg. 602
Castagna, John, V.P.-Engrng.--Sparkomatic Corporation, Milford, PA, pg. 1025
Castillano, Marya, Acting Dir.-Conservation & Solar--Seattle City Light, Seattle, WA, pg. 986
Cebulski, Joseph, Gen. Mgr.-Mfg.--Mitchell Corporation of Owosso, Owosso, MI, pg. 761
Cerchiaro, Tom, V.P.-Mfg.--Kentile Floors Inc., South Plainfield, NJ, pg. 623
Cerra, Joseph M., V.P.-Mfg.--Rich Products Corp., Buffalo, NY, pg. 932
Chamberlain, Garry G., V.P.-Mfg.--Merchandising Equipment Group, Arlington Heights, IL, pg. 739
Chambers, Glenn, Plant Mgr.--Truck Equipment Div., Tishomingo, MS, pg. 525
Chambers, W.S., V.P.-Engrng.--Kingsbury, Inc., Philadelphia, PA, pg. 632
Chamblee, Paul, V.P.-Mfg.--Diversified Products Corporation, Opelika, AL, pg. 1193
Chandler, Doug, Dir.-Mfg.--Thomas R. Hopson Broker, Inc., Marietta, GA, pg. 544
Channell, Bob, V.P.-Mfg.--Keymark Corporation, Fonda, NY, pg. 627
Charles, Mike, Dir.-Mfg.--Daktronics, Inc., Brookings, SD, pg. 312
Charlson, G., V.P.-Mfg.--Simmons Juvenile Products Co., Inc., New London, WI, pg. 1008
Cherenson, Edward, V.P.-Engrng.--King Industries, Inc., Norwalk, CT, pg. 630
Cherry, R., Sr. V.P.-Engrng.--Del Mar Avionics, Irvine, CA, pg. 325
Chivellit, Gary, Mgr.-Mfg.--Kokomo Spring Company, Inc., Kokomo, IN, pg. 640
Chleboun, Robert, Mgr.-Engrng.--General Automation, Inc., Skokie, IL, pg. 448
Chmielowiec, Ronald, Mgr.-Production--Hinkley Lighting Inc., Cleveland, OH, pg. 535
Chrismer, V.E., V.P.-Container Div.--Bell Packaging Corporation, Marion, IN, pg. 135
Christianson, Rod, Mgr.-Mfg.--Cargill Salt, Newark, CA, pg. 219
Christopherson, J.E., Factory-Service Mgr.--Badger Construction Equipment Co., Insley Div., Winona, MN, pg. 113
Chu, James, Mgr.-Mfg.--Tekni-Plex, Inc., Brooklyn, NY, pg. 1084
Church, Richard, V.P.-Opers.--Markem Corporation, Keene, NH, pg. 708
Ciaccia, Nicholas, Dir.-Mfg.--Rapid Power Technologies, Inc., Brookfield, CT, pg. 913
Cieplak, John, Mgr.-Mfg.--Tricon Electromechanical Div., Downers Grove, IL, pg. 1113
Cilentro, Alex, Mgr.-Mfg.--Tropar Mfg. Co., Inc., Florham Park, NJ, pg. 1115
Cimaroli, Richard, Mgr.-Engrng.--Vacudyne Inc., Chicago Heights, IL, pg. 45
Claasen, Sally, V.P.-Mfg.--T C Manufacturing Company, Inc., Evanston, IL, pg. 1072
Claibourn, Bill, Mfg. Mgr.--Davis Paint Company, Kansas City, MO, pg. 319
Clark, John, V.P.-Mfg.--Emson Research, Inc., Bridgeport, CT, pg. 380
Clemence, Richard R., Exec. V.P.-Mfg.--Hyde Manufacturing Co., Southbridge, MA, pg. 556
Clifford, Robert, Dir.-Mfg.--Recon/Optical, Inc., Barrington, IL, pg. 917
Coben, John, V.P.-Engrng.--Nashville Machine Co. Inc., Nashville, TN, pg. 784
Coco, David, Chief Engineer--National Fruit Product Company, Winchester, VA, pg. 789
Coda, Andrea, Mgr.-Production--Self, New York, NY, pg. 19
Cohen, Jonathon, Dir.-OEM & New Prod. Devel.--Nady Systems, Inc., Emeryville, CA, pg. 783
Cohen, Sanford, Sr. V.P.-Technology--Sipex Corporation, Billerica, MA, pg. 1009
Cohen, Steve, V.P.-Mfg.--Applied Solar Energy Corporation, City of Industry, CA, pg. 79
Cohen, T., V.P.-Mfg.--Global Steel Products Corporation, Deer Park, NY, pg. 463
Colado, Joe, Mgr.-Plant--Symons Corporation, Des Plaines, IL, pg. 1069
Colcolough, Ted, Exec. V.P.-Mfg.--Greenwood Mills, Inc., Greenwood, SC, pg. 485
Coleman, Billy R., V.P.-Production--Kyanite Mining Corporation, Dillwyn, VA, pg. 647
Coleman, Cherb, Mgr.-Traffic & Distr.--Coleman Dairy Inc., Little Rock, AR, pg. 261
Coleman, Dennis, V.P.-Engrng.--Dixson, Inc., Grand Junction, CO, pg. 341

Coleman, Dennis, Mgr.-Engnrg.--Electronic Instruments, Grand Junction, CO, pg. 341
Coleman, R.L., V.P.-Mfg.--American Packaging Corporation, Philadelphia, PA, pg. 59
Collins, H., V.P.-Mfg.--Haulpak Division, Komatsu Dresser Company, Peoria, IL, pg. 565
Collins, J., V.P.-Mfg.--Aluminum Shapes, Inc., Delair, NJ, pg. 46
Collins, Richard, V.P.-Engnrg.--Marotta Scientific Controls, Inc., Montville, NJ, pg. 713
Coltart, Mike, Sr. V.P.-Mfg.--E.J. Brach Corporation, Oakbrook Terrace, IL, pg. 169
Comeau, Mark, Dir.-Mfg.--The Asher Winer Company, Fitchburg, MA, pg. 88
Compston, Daniel J., V.P.-Hwy. & Heavy Construction--Kokosing Construction Company, Inc., Fredericktown, OH, pg. 640
Compton, David D., Dir.-Opers.--Central Coca-Cola Bottling Company, Inc., Richmond, VA, pg. 232
Condon, Edward F., Jr., V.P.-Engnrg.--Intermatic Inc., Spring Grove, IL, pg. 575
Cone, Stanley, V.P.-Mfg.--Stern & Stern Industries Inc., New York, NY, pg. 1048
Conigliaro, Margie, V.P.-Admin. & Production--Marisa Christina Inc., New York, NY, pg. 707
Conklin, John G., V.P.-Mfg.--Triangle Pacific Corporation, Dallas, TX, pg. 1112
Conley, Bruce, Dir.-Industrial Rels.--Sun-Maid Growers of California, Kingsburg, CA, pg. 1058
Conley, Eldon, Dir.-Production & Inventory Control--Precision Twist Drill Co., Crystal Lake, IL, pg. 885
Connelly, Rick, Chief Engineer--Heil Bulk Trailer Div., Athens, TN, pg. 525
Conway, Arch, Dir.-Mfg.--Advanced Controls, Inc., Irvine, CA, pg. 20
Cook, C., Pres.-Mfg. Div.--CJC Holdings, Inc., Austin, TX, pg. 202
Cook, Charles, Dir.-Mfg.--A-Dec, Inc., Newberg, OR, pg. 1
Cook, Jack, Sr. V.P.-Devel.--Al Copeland Enterprises, Inc., Jefferson, LA, pg. 283
Cooley, William H., V.P.-Mfg.--Mack Molding Company, Arlington, VT, pg. 697
Coombes, Richard, V.P.-Engrng. Services--Joan Fabrics Corp., Tyngsboro, MA, pg. 594
Cooper, James, V.P.-Mfg.--George Rice & Sons, Los Angeles, CA, pg. 931
Cooper, James A., V.P.-Opers.--Cox Enterprises Newspaper Division, Atlanta, GA, pg. 292
Corich, George, V.P.-Mfg.--Rapid Mounting & Finishing Co., Chicago, IL, pg. 913
Cosey, Dahl, V.P.-Mfg.--Kold Kist Brands, Inc., Los Angeles, CA, pg. 641
Costantino, Stephen, V.P.-Mfg.--United Metal Fabricators, Inc., Johnstown, PA, pg. 1133
Cotler, Maynard L., Mgr.-Mfg./Jamestown--The Producto Machine Co., Bridgeport, CT, pg. 893
Cotton, Steve, V.P.-Engrng.--Telesciences Co. Systems Inc., Moorestown, NJ, pg. 1085
Couch, R., V.P.-Engrng.-Mechanical Systems--Ashman Enterprises, Inc., Brecksville, OH, pg. 88
Cough, Clay, Dir.-Engrng.--American Metal & Plastics, Grand Rapids, MI, pg. 58
Coulter, Jack, Mgr.-Engrng.--Grove Valve & Regulator Company, Oakland, CA, pg. 490
Coupland, Gary, Dir.-Mfg.--American Welding & Manufacturing Co., Warren, OH, pg. 65
Coupland, Gary, Dir.-Engrng.--American Welding & Manufacturing Co., Warren, OH, pg. 431
Couris, Jim, V.P.-Mfg.--Clear Shield National, Inc., Wheeling, IL, pg. 383
Coutts, Robert, Mgr.-Mfg.--The Electron Corp., Littleton, CO, pg. 375
Covert, G. Chris, V.P.-Mfg.--Simplicity Manufacturing, Inc., Port Washington, WI, pg. 1006
Cowan, Robert, Mgr.-Production--Ortho-Kinetics, Inc., Waukesha, WI, pg. 830
Coward, Ira E., Chief Engineer--Graniteville Co., Graniteville, SC, pg. 476
Cowell, Gary, V.P.-Production--Broughton Foods Company, Marietta, OH, pg. 180
Cox, Donald, V.P.-Mfg.--Hayden, Inc., Corona, CA, pg. 385
Craig, Ron, Dir.-Engrng.--Capital City Press, Inc., Montpelier, VT, pg. 214
Craven, Clarence, Mgr.-Mfg.--Badger Equipment Company, Winona, MN, pg. 102
Cravey, Sally, Dir.-Mfg.--Funk & Wagnalls Corp., Mahwah, NJ, pg. 611
Crawford, Donald, V.P.-Private Labels--Tanner Co. Inc., Rutherfordton, NC, pg. 1078
Crosby, James, V.P.-Mfg.--Gurney Industries Inc., Gastonia, NC, pg. 495
Crouch, Bob, Mgr.-Mfg.--KCL Corporation, Shelbyville, IN, pg. 611
Crowder, W.T., Jr., V.P.-Equip. & Fixed Assets--Crowder Construction Co., Charlotte, NC, pg. 301
Crowell, Richard J., V.P.-Mfg.--The Wooster Brush Company, Wooster, OH, pg. 1202
Crownover, Daniel, Chief Engr.--Apache Plastics, L.P., Stockton, CA, pg. 77
Cuddy, James A., Dir.-Mfg.--Troy Mills, Inc., Troy, NH, pg. 1116
Cummings, Edward, V.P.-Mfg.--Duff-Norton, Charlotte, NC, pg. 1032
Cummings, Mark, V.P.-Mfg.--Cray Communications Inc., Annapolis Junction, MD, pg. 297
Cummings, Thomas J., V.P.-Opers. & Chief Engr.--The Noteworthy Company, Amsterdam, NY, pg. 816
Cummings, Timothy J., V.P.-Engrng.--Cummings Inc., Nashville, TN, pg. 304
Cunningham, James, V.P.-Mfg.--The Stiffel Company, Chicago, IL, pg. 1049
Curry, Tom, Plant Mgr.--Whitfield Foods, Inc., Montgomery, AL, pg. 1187
Cushman, Alex, V.P.-Mfg.--American Machine & Tool Company, Royersford, PA, pg. 57
Cushman, Floyd E., V.P.-Steel & Wire Processing--MNP Corp., Utica, MI, pg. 693
Cushman, Frank, V.P.-Opers.--Miller Fluid Power Corp., Bensenville, IL, pg. 754
Cuthbertson, Don, Dir.-Mfg.--Excel Industries, Inc., Hesston, KS, pg. 392
Daley, Philip, Chief Engr.--Custom Control Sensors, Inc., Chatsworth, CA, pg. 306
Dalton, Ron, Quality Control Mgr.--American Electronics, Inc., Fullerton, CA, pg. 3
Daly, Edward P., V.P.-Opers.--The O'Brien Corporation, South San Francisco, CA, pg. 820
Danheiser, Scott, Mgr.-Mfg. Service-Eastern Reg.--W. Braun Co., Lyndhurst, NJ, pg. 172
Daniels, Brian, Exec. V.P.-Mfg.--Stevens Carpet Div., New York, NY, pg. 400
Dattomo, Lou, V.P.-Mfg.--The Segerdahl Corp., Wheeling, IL, pg. 987
Davenport, Bob, Mgr.-Production--Welco Lumber Company, Marysville, WA, pg. 1175
Davey, John A., Mgr.-Mfg.--Aircraft Gear Corporation, Chicago, IL, pg. 27
Davis, Gene, Mgr.-Mfg.--The SArgent-SOwell Company, Grand Prairie, TX, pg. 971
Davis, John, V.P.-Mfg.--Sommer & Maca Industries, Inc., Chicago, IL, pg. 1017
Davis, Lynn, V.P.-Sls., Mktg., Pur. & Mfg.--Lithotype Company, Inc., South San Francisco, CA, pg. 678
Davis, Robert, V.P.-Mfg.--Kauffman Products, Inc., Carmel, IN, pg. 618
Davis, S., Dir.-Mfg.--EvsWater Industrial Systems, Middletown, OH, pg. 712
Davis, T. Russell, V.P.-Engrng. (Hayward)--The Paxall Group, Inc., Skokie, IL, pg. 852
Dawson, G., Dir.-Engrng.--Hypertronics Corporation, Hudson, MA, pg. 557
Day, Eric, V.P.-Opers.--Zieman Manufacturing Company, Inc., Whittier, CA, pg. 1218
Dean, Al, Prod. Mgr.-E.C.I. Controls & Instruments--U.S. Enertek, Inc., Farmington, NM, pg. 1135
Dean, Tim, Mgr.-Production--R.C.A. Rubber Company, Akron, OH, pg. 906
Deary, Donald R., V.P.-Mfg.--Nor-Cal Beverage Co., Inc., West Sacramento, CA, pg. 808
Deason, Bill, Chief Engineer--Cold Heading Co., Detroit, MI, pg. 259
Debnam, Warren, V.P.-Mfg.--Hanover Foods Corporation, Hanover, PA, pg. 506
Debnam, Warren, V.P.-Mfg.--Myers Foods Company, Plumsteadville, PA, pg. 506
DeBow, Thomas, Mgr.-Fabrication--Newage Industries Inc., Plastics Division, Willow Grove, PA, pg. 803
Decesare, Tony, V.P.-Opers.--Sparkomatic Corporation, Milford, PA, pg. 1025
DeGray, Frank, Mgr.-Pur.--Wm. E. Wright Limited Partnership, West Warren, MA, pg. 1205
DeGroff, Charles, Dir.-Mfg.--Hamilton Co., Inc., Reno, NV, pg. 503
Deisenroth, Dick, Engr.--Liberty Tool Corporation, Rochester, NY, pg. 674
Delisle, Vic, V.P.-Mfg.--Milwaukee Electric Tool Corp., Brookfield, WI, pg. 361
Dellamano, Joseph, Mgr.-Production--Patson's Press, Sunnyvale, CA, pg. 851
Delmastro, Fred, V.P.-Engrng.--Kranco, Inc., Houston, TX, pg. 643
Delzell, Gary, V.P.-Mfg.--Findley Adhesives, Inc., Wauwatosa, WI, pg. 410
Denham, W.A., V.P.-Mfg.--Speakman Company, Wilmington, DE, pg. 1027
DePalma, Joann, Prod.--Incentive, New York, NY, pg. 150
Deshaies, M.J., V.P.-Engrng.--Whitin Roberts Co., Sanford, NC, pg. 1187
Desiere, Phil, Dir.-Mfg.--Concord Litho Co., Inc., Concord, NH, pg. 272
Devino, Dave, V.P.-Mfg.--Fitchburg Coated Products Inc., Scranton, PA, pg. 1083
Dew, Maurice, V.P.-Mfg.--FM Industries, Inc., Fort Worth, TX, pg. 394
Dewitt, Donald E., Dir.-Engrng.--Dwyer Instruments Inc., Michigan City, IN, pg. 356
Dickey, Terry, V.P.-Mfg.--Norcraft Companies, Inc., Saint Paul, MN, pg. 809
Dickinson, Michael, V.P.-Engrng.--Liberty Tool Corporation, Rochester, NY, pg. 674
Dicola, Anthony, V.P.-Mfg.--Wrought Washer Mfg., Inc., Milwaukee, WI, pg. 1205
Dihigo, Mario, Mgr.-Mfg.--Platt Saco Lowell Corporation, Greenville, SC, pg. 876
DiMinno, Frank S., Jr., V.P.-Indus. Opers.--Edmund Scientific Company, Barrington, NJ, pg. 369
Dinsky, Seth, V.P.-Mfg.--Baroum Eaton Allen Corporation, Brooklyn, NY, pg. 121
Dinsky, Seth, V.P.-Mfg.--Ko-Rec-Type, Brooklyn, NY, pg. 121
DiPretro, John J., Gen. Mgr.-Mfg.--Steelox Systems, Inc., Mason, OH, pg. 1044
Disabato, Joseph, V.P.-Mfg.--Charles River Data Systems, Inc., Framingham, MA, pg. 240
Dismuke, Randy, V.P.-Opers.--Delta & Pine Land Company, Scott, MS, pg. 1024
Dittig, C.W., V.P.-Mfg.--Edwards Engineering Corporation, Pompton Plains, NJ, pg. 370
Dobbs, Mike, V.P.-Warehousing--Shoe City Corporation, Montgomery, AL, pg. 382
Dobrozsi, John, Sr. V.P.-Res. & Engrng.--Farley Candy Company, Chicago, IL, pg. 399
Dodd, Dennis, V.P.-Mfg.--Harbour Industries, Inc., Shelburne, VT, pg. 507
Dohse, Jerry, Dir.-Mfg.--AMD Industries Inc., Cicero, IL, pg. 5
Doninger, Joseph E., V.P.-Mfg.--Superior Graphite Company, Chicago, IL, pg. 1063
Donnellan, Kevin G., V.P.-Mfg. Opers.--Grant-Lydick Beverage Co., San Antonio, TX, pg. 477
Donnelly, Patrick, V.P.-Engrng.--Gosnell Builders, Phoenix, AZ, pg. 472
Doorley, Tom, Production Control Mgr.--Cres-Cor/Crown-X, Cleveland, OH, pg. 298
Dorece, Bill, V.P.-Mfg. Solution Div.--Cincom Systems, Inc., Cincinnati, OH, pg. 250
Dorsey, Ken, Mgr.-Prod.--David Michael & Co. Inc., Philadelphia, PA, pg. 747
Dougherty, E.L., Mfr. Mgr.--The William Bayley Co., Springfield, OH, pg. 128
Dove, John G., V.P.-Quality & Prod. Engrng.--Praxis International Inc., Cambridge, MA, pg. 884
Dowling, Mike, Dir.-Matls. Mngmt.--Avadyne, Inc., Monterey, CA, pg. 101
Downs, W.C., Mfg. Mgr.--Pittsburgh Tube Monaca Div., Monaca, PA, pg. 873
Doyle, Dennis, V.P.-Mfg.--Dieline Corporation, Kentwood, MI, pg. 336
Doyle, Edward, V.P.-Engnrg.--Conair Corporation, Stamford, CT, pg. 272
Doyle, Roland M., Sr. V.P.-Mfg.--King Milling Company, Lowell, MI, pg. 631
Drake, Tom, Plant Mgr.--Central Illinois Steel Company, Carlinville, IL, pg. 232
Drapekin, Jerome, V.P.-Mfg.--Pollenex Corporation, Chicago, IL, pg. 879
Dray, Peter, Mgr.-Mfg.--GFA Brands, Inc., Cresskill, NJ, pg. 440
Dulton, Richard, Dir.-Mfg.--Guideposts Associates, Inc., Carmel, NY, pg. 493
Duncan, G., V.P.-Engrng.--Econolite Control Products, Inc., Anaheim, CA, pg. 367
Duncan, Harold K., V.P.-Electrical Supplies--Braid Electric Company, Nashville, TN, pg. 171
Dunlap, Tom, OEM Mgr.--Warn Industries, Inc., Milwaukie, OR, pg. 1164
Durso, Joseph, V.P.-Mfg.--Slant/Fin Corporation, Greenvale, NY, pg. 1010
Dusel, Martin C., V.P.-Mfg.--Citizens Gas & Coke Utility, Indianapolis, IN, pg. 250
Dvoretsky, William, V.P.-Mfg.--Royle Systems Group, Pompton Lakes, NJ, pg. 953
Dyndiuk, Paul R., Mgr.-Mfg.--Specialty Manufacturing Company, St. Paul, MN, pg. 1027
Eary, Chuck, V.P.-Mfg.--Rollex Corporation, Elk Grove Village, IL, pg. 944
Easton, Marie, Mgr.-Mfg.--Power Conversion, Inc., Saddle Brook, NJ, pg. 883
Eber, Dave, V.P.-Engrng.--The Trane Company, La Crosse, WI, pg. 62
Eberts, Jack, Dir.-Production Opers.--MICOM Communications Corp., Simi Valley, CA, pg. 748
Eckel, Phil, V.P.-Production--FCN Advertising, Milwaukee, WI, pg. 394
Eckloff, Donald E., Plant Engineer--Pabst Brewing Co./ Tumwater, Tumwater, WA, pg. 959
Economos, James J., V.P.-Opers.--Imperial Schrade Corp., Ellenville, NY, pg. 564
Eddy, Carson, Dir.-Engrng.--Aetna Bearing Company, Chicago, IL, pg. 23
Edsall, Richard, V.P.-Production--Petoseed Co., Saticoy, CA, pg. 116
Edwards, D.S., V.P.-Prod. Engrng.--Edwards Engineering Corporation, Pompton Plains, NJ, pg. 370
Eggert, Mark, Mktg. & Opers. Mgr.--Morning Glory Farms Region, Shawano, WI, pg. 770
Egmont, Steven, Dir.-Engrng.--Connecticut Container Corporation, North Haven, CT, pg. 274
Eichelberber, Dale, Dir.-Mfg.--Rama Group of Companies, Cheektowaga, NY, pg. 910
Eitel, Robert C., V.P.-Oper.--The C. P. Hall Company, Chicago, IL, pg. 501
Elder, Philip, V.P.-Mfg.--Love Box Company, Inc., Wichita, KS, pg. 685
Eldredge, Chris, Mgr.-Prods.--Illinois Cereal Mills, Inc., Paris, IL, pg. 562
Elliott, Harold, Dir.-Mfg.--Howard Miller Clock Company, Zeeland, MI, pg. 754
Ellis, David, V.P.-Engrng.--Williams-White & Co., Moline, IL, pg. 1191
Ellis, David L., V.P.-Engrng.--Williams, White & Company, Moline, IL, pg. 1191
Ellis, Robert, V.P.-Mfg. & Distr.-Lawn, Farm & Garden Chemicals--Universal Cooperatives, Inc., Minneapolis, MN, pg. 1138
Ellis, Robert, V.P.-Mfg.--Security Products Company of Delaware, Inc., Minneapolis, MN, pg. 1138
Ellsworth, Tom, V.P.-Mfg. & Fin.--Ivex Packaging Corporation-Mill Division, Joliet, IL, pg. 583
Elrod, Mike, V.P.-Prod.--Correct Craft, Inc., Orlando, FL, pg. 287
Emerson, Lon, V.P.-Opers., Southern California--Calcot, Ltd., Bakersfield, CA, pg. 208
Emery, Ron, V.P.-Mfg.--Croscill, Inc., New York, NY, pg. 300
Emmel, Don, Plant Mgr.--McGaw, Inc., Irvine, CA, pg. 729
Emmitt, Bert, Production Mgr.--American Military Arms Corporation, Jacksonville, AR, pg. 58
Engle, Bob, V.P.-Mfg.--Burke Industries Inc., San Jose, CA, pg. 190
Engle, Robert, V.P.-Mfg.--Burke Industries, Inc., San Jose, CA, pg. 191
Engleby, Malcolm, V.P.-Mfg.--CMI International Inc., Southfield, MI, pg. 202
Ennis, Robert, Sr. V.P.-Mfg.--Havatampa Incorporated, Tampa, FL, pg. 517
Ennis, Robert, Sr. V.P.-Mfg.--H.A.T. Holding Company, Tampa, FL, pg. 517
Erdei, Martin, V.P.-Mfg.--The Jewett Refrigerator Co., Inc., Buffalo, NY, pg. 957

Erdman, Rick, Gen. Mgr.-Mfg.--Tylan General, Inc.-Flow Division, Torrance, CA, pg. 1122
Erickson, Bill, V.P.-Opers. & Production Mgr.--Demco Inc., Madison, WI, pg. 328
Ertel, Rick, V.P.-Mfg.--M&W Gear Company, Gibson City, IL, pg. 690
Ester, Kenneth R., V.P.-Mfg. & Engrng.--Wagner Spray Tech Corp., Minneapolis, MN, pg. 1158
Evans, Al, V.P.-Mfg.--Buck Knives, Inc., El Cajon, CA, pg. 185
Evans, John, Sr. V.P. & Production Dir.--Omni Publications International Ltd., New York, NY, pg. 450
Everson, Howard, Dir.-Warehousing--B. Green & Co., Baltimore, MD, pg. 484
Faivre, James, Mgr.-Mfg.--Ventre Packing Company, Inc., Syracuse, NY, pg. 1147
Farelli, George C., Chief Engineer--Ford Products Corporation, Valley Cottage, NY, pg. 423
Farley, L.O., V.P.-Mfg.--Macwhyte Co., Kenosha, WI, pg. 69
Farr, Michael, V.P.-Production--Bureau of Engraving, Minneapolis, MN, pg. 189
Fask, Richard, V.P.-Mfg.--Elkay Products, Inc., Shrewsbury, MA, pg. 377
Fearon, Terry, III, V.P.-Mfg. Opers.--Singh Industries, Cedar Knolls, NJ, pg. 1008
Feehly, Michael, Prod. Mgr.--Massachusetts Container Corporation, Marlborough, MA, pg. 274
Feeney, James E., Sr. V.P.-Mfg.--Wheatland Tube Company, Collingswood, NJ, pg. 1184
Fenton, D.R., Dir.-Engrng.--Dexter Company, Fairfield, IA, pg. 334
Ferreira, John, Plant Mgr.--Bridgeport Fittings, Inc., Stratford, CT, pg. 175
Ferreira, Wayne, V.P.-Mfg.--Deck House Inc., Acton, MA, pg. 324
Ferry, John, Dir.-Mfg.--Mid-West Company, Burr Ridge, IL, pg. 939
Fiedler, Martin, Chief Engr.--Arrow Pneumatics Co. Inc., Lake Zurich, IL, pg. 85
Fife, W., V.P.-Engrng.--Jeffrey Division, Columbus, OH, pg. 565
Fila, Edward C., Mgr.-Mfg.--H. B. Smith Co., Inc., Westfield, MA, pg. 1013
Fillmore, Robert, V.P.-Processing--Koch Supplies Inc., Kansas City, MO, pg. 639
Fischer, Robert, V.P. & Chief Engineer--American Plastic Toys Inc., Walled Lake, MI, pg. 59
Fisher, John, V.P.-Engrng.--Alamo Group, Inc., Seguin, TX, pg. 29
Fitten, Tim, Dir.-Mfg.--Redmond Products, Inc., Chanhassen, MN, pg. 920
Fitzgerald, Neil, V.P.-Mfg.--Ames Safety Envelope Company, Inc., Somerville, MA, pg. 66
Fitzgibbon, Pat, V.P.-Mfg.--Duo-Fast Corporation, Franklin Park, IL, pg. 354
Fitzgibbons, Jack, V.P.-Materials--C & M Corporation, Wauregan, CT, pg. 198
Flannery, Wesely, Production Mgr.--Western States Machine Co., Hamilton, OH, pg. 1181
Flax, Edward J., V.P.-Mfg. & Opers.--Martin F. Weber Company, Philadelphia, PA, pg. 716
Fleck, W.E., V.P.-Mfg.--Pipe Div., Birmingham, AL, pg. 1162
Fleck, William E., V.P.-Mfg.--United States Pipe & Foundry Company, Birmingham, AL, pg. 1162
Fleischer, Paul, V.P.-Mfg. & Engrng.--Mattison Machine Works, Rockford, IL, pg. 721
Fleischhacker, Mark, V.P.-Mfg.--Lake Region Manufacturing Company, Inc., Chaska, MN, pg. 651
Flickinger, W., V.P.-Mfg.--HPM Corporation, Mount Gilead, OH, pg. 497
Flood, Thomas, V.P.-Engrng.--Bennington Iron Works, Inc., Bennington, VT, pg. 139
Flores, Pat, Exec. V.P. & Dir.-Mfg.--Macklanburg-Duncan Co., Oklahoma City, OK, pg. 697
Flournoy, Kenoth H., Mgr.-Prod. Engrng.--Maguire Oil Co., Dallas, TX, pg. 701
Floyd, C., Dir.-Plastic Opers.--Abbott Laboratories/Ashland, Ashland, OH, pg. 9
Ford, R., Dir.-Engrng.--Sommer & Maca Industries, Inc., Chicago, IL, pg. 1017
Forgiano, Joseph P., V.P.-Mfg.--Keith Clark, Sidney, NY, pg. 304
Fornadel, J.F., Mgr.-Engrng.--Detex Corporation, New Braunfels, TX, pg. 333
Fornasiero, Gary R., Chief Engr.--WSF Industries, Inc., Tonawanda, NY, pg. 1156
Forseth, Robert, Dir.-Mfg.--Gem Top Mfg., Inc., Clackamas, OR, pg. 448
Fosmire, John, Exec. V.P.-Mfg.--Anderson Lithograph Company, Los Angeles, CA, pg. 73
Foster, Bob, Plant Mgr.--Heil Bulk Trailer Div., Athens, TN, pg. 525
Foster, George, V.P.-Mfg.--Blitz USA, Miami, OK, pg. 157
Foster, George, V.P.-Mfg.--Blitz U.S.A., Inc., Miami, OK, pg. 157
Fox, Duane, Sr. V.P.-Mfg.--Spangler Candy Company, Bryan, OH, pg. 1025
Fox, Michael R., Mgr.-Mfg. Services--American Envelope Company, Chicago, IL, pg. 199
Francisco, John, V.P.-Mfg.--Norwalk Furniture Corporation, Norwalk, OH, pg. 816
Frangos, John E., V.P.-Mfg. & Sec.--C.R. Daniels, Inc., Ellicott City, MD, pg. 314
Frank, Chuck, V.P.-Mfg.--Flambeau Corporation, Baraboo, WI, pg. 809
Frankel, Paul, Dir.-Mfg.--Imperial Manufacturing Company, Memphis, TN, pg. 564
Franklin, John, V.P.-Des. & Engrng.--Arrow Group Industries, Inc., Wayne, NJ, pg. 357
Frankum, Darwin, Dir.-Sls. & Mktg.--Macklanburg-Duncan Co., Oklahoma City, OK, pg. 697
Franzen, Dick, V.P.-Opers., Chicago--Pakula & Company, Chicago, IL, pg. 843
Frederick, Don, Mgr.-Mfg.--K-D Lamp Company, Cincinnati, OH, pg. 612
Frediani, Steve, V.P.-Mfg.--Davis Wire Corporation, Irwindale, CA, pg. 319
Freedy, Paul W., V.P.-Engrng.--Trak International, Inc., Port Washington, WI, pg. 1106
Freeman, G., Sr. V.P.-Mfg.--Haskel, Inc., Burbank, CA, pg. 516
Freeman, W. Tony, V.P.-Mfg. Knits & Specialties--Apparel Fabrics Div., New York, NY, pg. 400
Frey, W. Steve, V.P.-Mfg.--Luzianne Blue Plate Foods, New Orleans, LA, pg. 923
Friend, D., Chief Engr.--E. R. Carpenter Co., Richmond, VA, pg. 224
Friese, W.C., V.P.-Engrng.--RAIL Company, Towson, MD, pg. 906
Frigo, Jack, Plant Mgr.--Hirsh Company, Skokie, IL, pg. 258
Frink, Carol, Production Mgr.--Jakson-A CHF Company, New York, NY, pg. 200
Fritts, A.W., Dir.-Bus. Mfg.--Harwick Chemical Corp., Akron, OH, pg. 515
Froemming, H., V.P.-Mfg.--Republic Industries, Inc., Harwood Heights, IL, pg. 928
Fry, John, V.P.-Mfg. Opers.--Red Devil Inc., Union, NJ, pg. 918
Frye, Jeff, V.P.-Mfg.--Schneller, Inc., Kent, OH, pg. 977
Fryml, Martin, V.P.-Mfg.--American Fast Print, Limited, Spartanburg, SC, pg. 52
Fulp, William, V.P.-Mfg.--Kingsdown, Inc., Mebane, NC, pg. 632
Furman, Earl A., Mgr.-Mfg. & Quality Control--Yerger Bros., Inc., Lititz, PA, pg. 1208
Furman, Sam, V.P.-Mfg.--Mogas Industries, Inc., Houston, TX, pg. 763
Furr, William J., V.P.-YHOC Production--Hunt Oil International Production-Fountain Place, Dallas, TX, pg. 554
Gabbe, Fred, V.P.-Production--Mr. Christmas Inc., New York, NY, pg. 761
Gage, John, Mgr.-Engrng.--Allison Corporation, Livingston, NJ, pg. 40
Gaiteri, Frank T., V.P.-Engrng.--Root Corporation, Mount Wolf, PA, pg. 946
Gallagher, George, Technical Supvr.--American Envelope of Philadelphia, Philadelphia, PA, pg. 199
Gameson, Gary, V.P.-Mfg.--Thermalloy, Inc., Farmers Branch, TX, pg. 1091
Garabedian, Robert, V.P.-Engrng.--Printed Circuit Corporation, Woburn, MA, pg. 891
Gardner, Jim, Plant Mgr.--Radix Wire Company, Cleveland, OH, pg. 909
Garvey, John, V.P.-Mfg.--Parade Publications Inc., New York, NY, pg. 847
Gatti, Robert, V.P.-Mfg.--Globe Industries, Inc., Chicago, IL, pg. 464
Geary, Dene, V.P.-Mfg.--Advanced Input Devices, Inc., Coeur D'Alene, ID, pg. 20
Geisen, Dick, Mgr.-Mfg.--Heat Controller, Inc., Jackson, MI, pg. 524
Geiser, Hal, V.P.-Tech. Service--Republic Industries, Inc., Harwood Heights, IL, pg. 928
Geisler, Walter, V.P.-Engrng.--Screw Conveyor Corp., Hammond, IN, pg. 983
Gelderloos, Mark I., Sr. Dir.-Engrng. Construction--White Castle System, Inc., Columbus, OH, pg. 1185
Genday, Richard E., Sr. V.P.-Engrng. Grp.--L. Robert Kimball & Associates, Ebensburg, PA, pg. 629
Gendreau, Peter, Mgr.-Technical--Specialty Paperboard Inc., Brattleboro, VT, pg. 1027
Gentry, Jon, Dir.-Engrng.-Dry Mix Plant--Continental Mills, Inc., Tukwila, WA, pg. 279
Gentry, Richard S., Dir.-Mfg. & Pur.--CTB Inc., Milford, IN, pg. 205
George, Julius, Mgr.-Construction--Stone & Hoover Contracting, Inc., Lorton, VA, pg. 470
Gerbo, Mike, Dir.-Engrng.--Ritchie Industries, Inc., Conrad, IA, pg. 936
Gerding, Ronald, Chief Engineer--Truck Equipment Div., Tishomingo, MS, pg. 525
Gessford, Leo, Chief Engineer--Colonial Beef Co., Philadelphia, PA, pg. 263
Gessner, Russell, V.P.-Mfg.--Mayville Metal Products Division, Mayville, WI, pg. 275
Ghobrial, H., Mgr.-Production--Voyager Emblems, Inc., Sanborn, NY, pg. 1155
Giannuzzi, Louis, V.P.-Engrng.--The Rawlplug Company, Inc., New Rochelle, NY, pg. 914
Giard, Ronald G., V.P.-Mfg.--Geiger Brothers, Lewiston, ME, pg. 447
Giauque, Steve, Mgr.-Mfg.--The Gerstenslager Company, Wooster, OH, pg. 454
Gibbons, Bob, V.P.-Mfg.--North American Publishing Company, Philadelphia, PA, pg. 811
Gibbs, David E., Jr., Exec. V.P.-Fin.--Pannier Corporation, Pittsburgh, PA, pg. 846
Giddings, S.A., V.P.-Mfg.--Congoleum Corporation, Mercerville, NJ, pg. 274
Gihlstorf, John, Mgr.-Mfg.--Samuel Cabot, Inc., Newburyport, MA, pg. 206
Gilardi, Sam, Dir.-Opers.--Thriftway, Inc., Cincinnati, OH, pg. 1095
Gilbertson, James, Dir.-Mfg.--McNaughton & Gunn, Inc., Saline, MI, pg. 732
Gildenzopf, Dave, Dir.-Pressure Sensitive Markings & Training--The Vernon Company, Newton, IA, pg. 1148
Gillam, T. Scott Jr., V.P. & Mfg. Mgr.--Glen Raven Mills, Inc.-Filament Fabrics Div., Burnsville, NC, pg. 462
Gillespey, C. Wayne, Sr. V.P.-Mfg.--Burks Pumps, Inc., Piqua, OH, pg. 507
Gillespey, Wayne, V.P.-Mfg.--Prosser/Enpo Industries, Piqua, OH, pg. 507
Gillespey, Wayne, V.P.-Mfg.--Barnes Pumps, Inc., Mansfield, OH, pg. 507
Gillespey, Wayne, V.P.-Mfg.--AMW Industries Inc., Conway, AR, pg. 507
Giraudo, Steve, Exec. V.P.-Production--San Francisco French Bread Company, Oakland, CA, pg. 969
Glass, Ernest J., Jr., V.P.-Component & Custom Prods.--E.F. Johnson Company, Eden Prarie, MN, pg. 598
Gleason, Daniel J., V.P.-Mfg.--Finch, Pruyn & Co., Inc., Glens Falls, NY, pg. 410
Glennon, G., V.P.-Mfg.--Abbott Ball Company, West Hartford, CT, pg. 9
Gobin, Jim, Dir.-Mfg.--Intech Advanced Analog, Santa Clara, CA, pg. 572
Godfrey, William T., V.P.-Mfg. & Mktg.--Morris Coupling Co., Erie, PA, pg. 771
Goelz, Werner, V.P.-Facilities--Heller Seasonings & Ingredients, Inc., Bedford Park, IL, pg. 526
Goerner, Gary, V.P.-Prod.--Lifetouch, Inc., Bloomington, MN, pg. 675
Gold, Robert, V.P.-Engrng.--Dayton Rogers Mfg. Co., Minneapolis, MN, pg. 321
Goldman, D., V.P.-New Technology--Integra Technologies Corp., Waltham, MA, pg. 572
Goldsby, T.K., V.P.-Mfg.--Harwick Chemical Corp., Akron, OH, pg. 515
Goldsby, T.K., V.P.-Mfg.--Republic Chemical Company, Akron, OH, pg. 515
Goldschmidt, Dr. Robert E., V.P.-Engrng.--Kaye Instruments, Inc., Bedford, MA, pg. 619
Gomez, Enidio, V.P.-Mfg.--Security Plastics, Inc., Miami Lakes, FL, pg. 987
Good, Brian, Dir.-Mfg.--GF Office Furniture Ltd., Gallatin, TN, pg. 439
Goodall, Gordon, Dir.-Engng.--Smead Manufacturing Company, Hastings, MN, pg. 1011
Goodwin, J.D., V.P.-Mfg.--Hallmark Cards, Inc., Kansas City, MO, pg. 501
Gorbold, Jonathan, V.P.-Engrng. & Mktg.--ENI, Rochester, NY, pg. 360
Gorcyca, Ray, V.P.-Mfg.--Orbit Valve Co., Little Rock, AR, pg. 828
Gorsd, J., Chief Engr.--Isfel Company, Inc., Rahway, NJ, pg. 582
Goughneour, Richard, Mgr.-Mfg. Services--T & S Brass & Bronze Works, Inc., Travelers Rest, SC, pg. 1074
Gould, R., V.P.-Mfg.--Treadwell Corporation, Thomaston, CT, pg. 1108
Gould, Robert, Mgr.-Engrng.--Jandy Industries, Novato, CA, pg. 589
Graber, Dave, Mgr.-Production--Panel Prints, Inc., Old Forge, PA, pg. 846
Graff, Ray, Mgr.-Mfg.--Hanna Car Wash International, Inc., Portland, OR, pg. 505
Graham, Dellas, Exec. V.P.-Production & Opers. Services--Keller Crescent Co., Evansville, IN, pg. 620
Graham, E.W., V.P.-Mfg.--Medrad, Inc., Pittsburgh, PA, pg. 736
Grainger, W., V.P.-Mfg. & Engrng.--Potters Industries, Inc., Parsippany, NJ, pg. 837
Grant, J. L., V.P.-Sheet Mfg.--Home Fashions Div., New York, NY, pg. 400
Grant, M., V.P.-Mfg.--Gem, Incorporated, Byhalia, MS, pg. 447
Granthan, James, V.P.-Mfg.--Blue Bird Corporation, Fort Valley, GA, pg. 158
Graves, John, V.P.-Mfg.--TST/Impreso, Inc., Coppell, TX, pg. 1075
Gray, Michael, V.P.-Mfg. & Dir.-Columbus Opers.--Columbus Show Case Company, Columbus, OH, pg. 267
Greeley, Joseph B., Sr. V.P.-Opers.--Sanford C. Bernstein & Co., Inc., New York, NY, pg. 144
Green, Ken, Mgr.-Loose Leaf Bindery--H. C. Miller Company, Milwaukee, WI, pg. 754
Green, M., V.P.-Mfg.--Bergquist Company, Inc., Minneapolis, MN, pg. 141
Green, Thomas, Dir.-Opers.--AMI Industries, Inc., Colorado Springs, CO, pg. 5
Grider, Jack, Plant Mgr.--Interface Electronics Corporation, Hopkinton, MA, pg. 574
Grieve, D.V., V.P.-Engrng.--The Grieve Corporation, Round Lake, IL, pg. 486
Griffin, Jack, Mgr.-Mfg.--Adams Wine Co., Atlanta, GA, pg. 17
Grimes, Paul, V.P.-Mfg.--R. A. Jones & Co. Inc., Covington, KY, pg. 604
Grobowski, Frank, V.P.-Book Mfg.--Scholastic Inc., New York, NY, pg. 962
Grossinger, Robert, V.P.-Mfg.--Elgin Watch International, Inc., Long Island City, NY, pg. 376
Grove, Jeffrey, Mgr.-Mfg.--Specialty Industries, Inc., Red Lion, PA, pg. 1027
Grubbs, George, Chief Engineer--American Bread Company - Sunbeam Bakery, Nashville, TN, pg. 49
Gruenling, Edwin, V.P.-Mfg.--Harrison Paint Corporation, Canton, OH, pg. 512
Guerra, G.A., V.P.-Mfg. Tech.--S & C Electric Company, Chicago, IL, pg. 958
Guiles, R., V.P.-Mfg., Res. & Devel.--Columbia Paint Co., Spokane, WA, pg. 265
Gulbrandsen, Dick, V.P.-Engrng.--Precision Twist Drill Co., Crystal Lake, IL, pg. 885
Gulluscio, J., Mfg. Mgr.--Yardney Technical Products, Inc., Pawcatuck, CT, pg. 1207
Gutkneckt, John, V.P.-Mfg.--Rauland-Borg Corporation, Skokie, IL, pg. 914
Guyer, Steve, V.P.-Mfg.--Red Calliope & Associates, Inc., Los Angeles, CA, pg. 918
Guynes, Terry, Mgr.-Quality Control--U.S. Rubber Reclaiming, Inc., Vicksburg, MS, pg. 306
Haadsma, David, V.P.-Mfg.--American Metal & Plastics, Grand Rapids, MI, pg. 58
Hafner, Volker W., V.P.-Engrng.--Acorn Engineering Company, City of Industry, CA, pg. 14
Hagen, Ty, Chief Engr.--Brown-Minneapolis Tank & Fabricating Co., Eagan, MN, pg. 182

Haggard, Robert W., Dir.-Construction--Sound Warehouse, Inc., Dallas, TX, pg. 1018
Haggerty, James A., V.P.-Mfg.--Shade Computer Forms Co., Green Bay, WI, pg. 994
Hajec, Richard G., V.P.-Engrng.--Spencer Turbine Co., Windsor, CT, pg. 1030
Hale, David, V.P.-Mfg.--Republic Telcom Systems Corporation, Boulder, CO, pg. 928
Hale, Jim R., Dir.-Mfg.--Rostone Corporation, Lafayette, IN, pg. 950
Hall, Eric K., V.P.-Mfg.--Trimtex Co. Inc., Williamsport, PA, pg. 1113
Hall, J.R., Pres.-Mfg.--AP Parts Manufacturing Company, Toledo, OH, pg. 240
Hallene, A.M., Jr., Sr. V.P.-Mfg.--Montgomery Elevator Company, Moline, IL, pg. 767
Hanker, Ed, Jr., Dir.-Engrng.--Struthers-Dunn Inc., Pitman, NJ, pg. 693
Hanks, Bob D., V.P.-Engrng.--Sabreliner Corp., Chesterfield, MO, pg. 965
Hanner, Cliff, V.P.-Engrng.--Brubaker Tool Corp., Millersburg, PA, pg. 183
Hansberger, W.L., V.P.-Mfg.--RAM Golf Corporation, Melrose Park, IL, pg. 910
Hansen, Eric R., V.P.-Technical Dir.--Ash Grove Cement Company, Overland Park, KS, pg. 87
Hansen, Jim, Mgr.-Mfg.--Tricon Brazing Alloys & Chemical Products Div., Downers Grove, IL, pg. 1113
Hansen, Ralph, Chief Engineer--Red Devil Inc., Union, NJ, pg. 918
Hardison, Douglas, Dir.-Production--Hyspan Precision Products, Inc., Chula Vista, CA, pg. 557
Hardman, Douglas R., Chief Engr.--J. H. Fletcher & Co., Huntington, WV, pg. 418
Hargrove, George, V.P.-Mfg.--Barnhardt Manufacturing Co., Charlotte, NC, pg. 120
Harley, Jim, V.P.-Mfg.--Bentley Mills, Inc., City of Industry, CA, pg. 140
Harley, Larry, Exec. V.P.-Distr. Group--Mary Kay Cosmetics Inc., Dallas, TX, pg. 716
Harold, Derek, V.P.-Mill Service--Luria Bros. Division, Cleveland, OH, pg. 275
Harper, Charles, Dir.-Matl. Procurement--Duo-Fast Corporation, Franklin Park, IL, pg. 354
Harris, D., Mgr.-Mfg.--Abbott Electronics, Inc., Los Angeles, CA, pg. 9
Harris, Dave, V.P.-Engrng. & Tech. Services--Flambeau Corporation, Baraboo, WI, pg. 809
Harris, Tom, V.P.-Engrng.--Hillerich & Bradsby Co., Inc., Louisville, KY, pg. 535
Harrison, Brian, V.P.-Industrial Gases--Welsco Inc., North Little Rock, AR, pg. 1175
Harrison, Doug, V.P.-Mfg.--Thomas Built Buses, Inc., High Point, NC, pg. 1092
Harrod, Allen, V.P.-Mfg.--Printing House, Inc., Quincy, FL, pg. 891
Hartman, Donn A., V.P.-Engrng.--Cloud Corporation, Des Plaines, IL, pg. 256
Hartmann, Annette, V.P.-Mfg.--The Estee Corporation, Parsippany, NJ, pg. 389
Haslanger, Paul A., V.P.-Mfg.--Foam Product Corporation, Eddystone, PA, pg. 1121
Hasselbring, Don, Dir.-Admin.--Humphrey Products Company, Kalamazoo, MI, pg. 553
Hasting, John, V.P.-Mfg.--Binney & Smith Inc., Easton, PA, pg. 502
Hauck, W.J., V.P.-Mfg.--East Jordan Iron Works, East Jordan, MI, pg. 362
Haught, Mel, V.P.-Mfg.--Pella Corporation, Pella, IA, pg. 856
Hawk, David W., V.P.-Mfg.--Gertrude Hawk Chocolates, Inc., Troop, PA, pg. 517
Hawkins, John, Dir.-Opers.--Serono Baker Diagnostics, Allentown, PA, pg. 991
Hazlett, Don, V.P.-Mfg.--Zippo Manufacturing Company, Bradford, PA, pg. 1220
Heacock, Bob, V.P.-Mfg.--Hull Corporation, Hatboro, PA, pg. 552
Heerwagen, Louie, V.P.-Mfg.--The Selmer Co., Elkhart, IN, pg. 573
Heffernan, Roger L., V.P.-Mfg.--General Instrument Corporation, New York, NY, pg. 425
Hehlinger, Volker, Dir.-Mfg.--National Label Company, Lafayette Hill, PA, pg. 791
Heidorn, Ed, Mgr.-Mfg.--ATAPCO Globe-Weis/Kosciusko, Kosciusko, MS, pg. 64
Heimbach, Paul A., Sr. V.P.-Engrng./Network Opers. Ctr.--MTV Networks, New York, NY, pg. 785
Heinol, Dennis, Pres.-Display Mfg.--Burke Communication Industries, Inc., Chicago, IL, pg. 190
Heitmiller, C.E., Mgr.-Engrng.--Carrier Vibrating Equipment, Inc., Louisville, KY, pg. 225
Hekker, Gerard, V.P.-Mfg.--Steelcase Inc., Grand Rapids, MI, pg. 1044
Held, Joseph, V.P.-Mfg.--Presto Lock, Inc., Garfield, NJ, pg. 888
Helms, Roger, V.P.-Web Mfg.--The Hennegan Company, Cincinnati, OH, pg. 529
Hemby, J. Ray, V.P.-Mfg.--Mar-Mac Manufacturing Company, Inc., McBee, SC, pg. 705
Hendrickson, Robert M., V.P.-Mfg.--Potrait Industries Corporation, Chesapeake, VA, pg. 675
Henninger, Eldon, Mgr.-Mfg.--Kearney Div., Fayetteville, AR, pg. 357
Henrichs, B.W., Sr. V.P.-Engrng.--The Hartwell Corporation, Placentia, CA, pg. 514
Hensch, Timothy, Dir.-Mfg.--North Atlantic Industries, Inc., Hauppauge, NY, pg. 812
Hernke, Keith G., V.P.-Prod.--Quad/Graphics, Inc., Pewaukee, WI, pg. 902
Herrera, Frank, V.P. & Dir.-Distr.--Hearst Magazines Division, New York, NY, pg. 523
Herrington, Robert, V.P.-Mfg.--Farallon Computing, Inc., Emeryville, CA, pg. 399
Herschbein, Irving, V.P.-Mfg. & Distr.--The Conde Nast Publications Inc., New York, NY, pg. 19
Hersey, Lester, Mgr.-Mfg.--Maine Potato Growers, Inc., Presque Isle, ME, pg. 702
Hess, George W., V.P.-Opers.--Midway Products Corporation, Monroe, MI, pg. 751
Hettervik, Erwin, V.P.-Mfg. Opers.--KBF Foods Division, Placentia, CA, pg. 637
Hevert, C.H., V.P.-Opers. Mfg.--Kearfott Guidance & Navigation Corp., Wayne, NJ, pg. 93
Higdon, Robert, V.P. & Gen. Mgr.--Toledo Blade Co., Toledo, OH, pg. 155
Hilkhuysen, Hans, V.P.-Technical--Omniflight, Inc., Dallas, TX, pg. 826
Hill, Dick, V.P.-Mfg.--Perlmuter Printing Company, Cleveland, OH, pg. 862
Hill, John, Sr. V.P.-Mktg. & Mfg. Services--Beacon Mfg. Co., Swannanoa, NC, pg. 129
Hinderager, Larry, V.P.-Mining & Mfg.--J.R. Simplot Co., Minerals & Chemicals Group, Pocatello, ID, pg. 1007
Hinds, J.H., V.P.-Engrng.--Ruska Instrument Corporation, Houston, TX, pg. 956
Hinshaw, Howard, V.P.-Engrng.--Thermalloy, Inc., Farmers Branch, TX, pg. 1091
Hirsch, David, Exec. V.P.-Mfg.--J H Collectibles, Milwaukee, WI, pg. 584
Hirsch, Jamie, V.P.-Mfg. & Pur.--Structural Industries, Inc., Hicksville, NY, pg. 1054
Hirschfeld, Dennis C., V.P.-Engrng.--Hirschfeld Steel Company, Inc., San Angelo, TX, pg. 536
Hiskett, Harry, V.P.-Mfg.--Associated Company, Inc., Wichita, KS, pg. 89
Hlinsky, Emil, V.P.-Engrng.--Maclean-Fogg Co., Mundelein, IL, pg. 697
Hoback, John, V.P.-Mfg.--The Keller Manufacturing Co., Inc., Corydon, IN, pg. 621
Hobson, Carroll D., Sr. V.P.-Mfg. & Engrng.--Goshen Rubber Co., Inc., Goshen, IN, pg. 472
Hodapp, Norbert, V.P.-Mfg.--Action Technology Company, Rockaway, NJ, pg. 15
Hodge, Lowrance, Sr. V.P.-Mfg. Opers. & Engrng.--Mary Kay Cosmetics Inc., Dallas, TX, pg. 716
Hodges, Trey, V.P.-Mfg.--Custom Fabrics Div., West Point, GA, pg. 400
Hodgins, Keith, Brewing Mgr.--Pabst Brewing Co., San Antonio, TX, pg. 959
Hoffman, Robert, Dir.-mfg.--Interplastic Corp., Saint Paul, MN, pg. 579
Hofher, Lynn, Asst. Managing Editor--Self, New York, NY, pg. 19
Hogan, Michael J., V.P.-Mfg.--R & G Sloane Mfg. Co., Inc., Sun Valley, CA, pg. 1010
Hogan, Thad, V.P.-Intl. Mfg.--Mary Kay Cosmetics Inc., Dallas, TX, pg. 716
Hoganson, R.B., Dir.-Engrng.--Macwhyte Co., Kenosha, WI, pg. 69
Hohmeier, John C., Dir.-Mfg.--MTD Products Limited, Kitchener,, Canada, pg. 694
Holder, L., V.P.-Mfg.--Cutler Manufacturing Corporation, Highland City, FL, pg. 307
Hollabaugh, William, V.P.-Mfg.--Lobdell-Emery Manufacturing Company, Alma, MI, pg. 680
Holland, Clint, V.P.-Mfg.--Butler Automatic, Inc., Canton, MA, pg. 197
Hollenbach, H., V.P.-Mfg.--Murdock, Inc., Compton, CA, pg. 776
Hollering, Edward J., V.P.-Mfg.--Hazen Paper Company, Holyoke, MA, pg. 520
Holloran, Thomas, Dir.-Engrng.--Tyler Elevator Products, Inc., Valley View, OH, pg. 1122
Holmberg, Carl, Chief Engr.--Peerless Confection Company, Chicago, IL, pg. 855
Holmes, Arleen N., Supervisor-Production & Distribution--Pike & Fischer, Bethesda, MD, pg. 190
Holmes, Fred W., Sr. V.P.-Mfg.--Jockey International, Inc., Kenosha, WI, pg. 595
Holton, John, Mgr.-Mfg.--Wilson Products Co., Salt Lake City, UT, pg. 1194
Holzhauser, Ronald, V.P.-Engrng.--Thomas Built Buses, Inc., High Point, NC, pg. 1092
Homanick, George, V.P.-Mfg.--Cargill Detroit Corp., Clawson, MI, pg. 219
Home, Mike, V.P.-Mfg.--Tamaqua Cable Products Corporation, Schuylkill Haven, PA, pg. 1077
Hood, J.D., Dir.-Mfg.--Franklin Baking Co., Inc., Goldsboro, NC, pg. 429
Hood, Von, V.P.-Mfg.--Carbide International Inc., Chicago, IL, pg. 507
Hood, Von, V.P.-Carbide Production--Rogers Tool Works, Inc., Rogers, AR, pg. 507
Hookway, Warren, Exec. V.P.-Mfg.--Labelon Corporation, Canandaigua, NY, pg. 649
Hoover, Harold, V.P.-Mfg.--Acorn Engineering Company, City of Industry, CA, pg. 14
Hoover, Michael, Dir.-Mfg.--F & W Publications, Inc., Cincinnati, OH, pg. 394
Hophen, Vern, Chief Engr.--Lone Star Brewing, San Antonio, TX, pg. 526
Hopp, Robert, V.P.-Opers.--Na-Churs Plant Food Company, Marion, OH, pg. 782
Hopp, Tony, Plant Mgr.--Rodman Industries, Marinette, WI, pg. 408
Hoppe, Bill, V.P.-Mfg.--Preformed Line Products, Cleveland, OH, pg. 886
Hornaday, Chuck, Mgr.-Prod.--Symons Corporation, Des Plaines, IL, pg. 1069
Horne, Joel, V.P.-Mfg.--Allied Paper Incorporated, Dayton, OH, pg. 38
Horneck, Richard, V.P.-Mfg.--Sweetheart Cup Co., Inc., Chicago, IL, pg. 1067
Horowitz, Irving, Vice Chm., Exec. V.P.-Opers. & Engrng.--Amerbelle Corporation, Rockville, CT, pg. 47
Horton, John D., Mgr.-Tech. Services--Osmose Wood Preserving Co., Buffalo, NY, pg. 830
Houghton, Benjamin T., V.P.-Engrng.--Enidine Incorporated, Orchard Park, NY, pg. 382
Houston, D., V.P.-Engrng.--Perry Equipment Corporation, Mineral Wells, TX, pg. 863
Hoveland, H.E., V.P.-Mfg.--Research Products Corporation, Madison, WI, pg. 928
Howanitz, Joseph J., V.P. & Tech. Dir.--Fine Organics Corp., Lodi, NJ, pg. 411
Howard, Jay, V.P.-Mfg.--Dazey Corporation, Industrial Airport, KS, pg. 321
Howard, John, V.P.-Power Prod.--Alabama Electric Cooperative, Inc., Andalusia, AL, pg. 28
Howard, Patrick, Exec. V.P.-Mfg. Grp.--Mary Kay Cosmetics Inc., Dallas, TX, pg. 716
Howe, Winfield W., V.P.-Mfg.--Namico, Inc., Philadelphia, PA, pg. 783
Howes, Benjamin, V.P.-Mfg.--Robertson Factories, Inc., Taunton, MA, pg. 939
Howse, Geoff, Assoc. Dir.-Engrng.--Industrial Acoustics Company, Ltd., Staines,, United Kingdom, pg. 566
Hricz, George M., V.P.-Opers.--C.B. Fleet Company, Incorporated, Lynchburg, VA, pg. 417
Hrudka, Tom, V.P.-Opers.--Mr. Gasket Company, Cleveland, OH, pg. 761
Huetsch, Larry C., V.P.-Mfg.--Unison Industries, Jacksonville, FL, pg. 1130
Huetsch, Larry C., V.P.-Mfg.--Unison Industries, Jacksonville, FL, pg. 1130
Hughes, Ivan, Sr. V.P.-Mfg.--Duro Paper Bag Manufacturing Co., Ludlow, KY, pg. 355
Hughes, John, Mgr.-Mfg.--Merriam-Webster, Inc., Springfield, MA, pg. 381
Humason, Steve, V.P.-Engrng.--Airco Mechanical Inc., Sacramento, CA, pg. 27
Hunich, Kenneth, Dir.-Distr.--Seattle City Light, Seattle, WA, pg. 986
Hunt, Bob, Dir.-Mfg.--Genova Products, Inc., Davison, MI, pg. 452
Hunter, Pat, Dir.-Engrng.--McKee Door, Inc., Aurora, IL, pg. 730
Huntley, Max, V.P.-Mfg.--Parkdale Mills, Gastonia, NC, pg. 849
Hurd, Fred, Dir.-Mfg.--Plascal Corporation, Farmingdale, NY, pg. 874
Hurless, Tom, Chief Engineer--National Engineering & Contracting Co., Strongsville, OH, pg. 788
Hyatt, Marvin, V.P.-Mfg.--Ruska Instrument Corporation, Houston, TX, pg. 956
Ingebretsen, Bud, V.P.-Opers.--Patterson Frozen Foods, Inc., Patterson, CA, pg. 851
Itahara, Seiji, V.P.-Mfg.--RHC/Spacemaster Corporation, Melrose Park, IL, pg. 906
Iverson, Dennis, Mgr.-Prod.--Barrel O'Fun Snack Foods Co., Perham, MN, pg. 122
Iwanisziw, Nick, V.P.-Mfg.--Menu Foods, Inc., Pennsauken, NJ, pg. 739
Izzo, William, Dir.-Production--Equinox Advertising, Inc., Chicago, IL, pg. 384
Jackson, Phillip, V.P.-Opers.--Kroch's & Brentano's, Inc., Chicago, IL, pg. 645
Jacod, Edward, V.P.-Converting--Marcal Paper Mills, Inc., Elmwood Park, NJ, pg. 706
Jacot, William, V.P.-Mfg.--California Offset Printers, Inc., Glendale, CA, pg. 210
Jaffe, Al, Chief Engineer--Aster Nut Products Inc., Newark, NJ, pg. 92
Jakobs, B., V.P.-Engrng.--Shure Brothers Incorporated, Evanston, IL, pg. 1001
Jakosz, William, V.P.-Mfg.--Harrington & King, Chicago, IL, pg. 511
Jakubovic, Jim, V.P.-Mfg.--American Paper Products Group, Ltd., Youngstown, OH, pg. 59
Janover, Andrew, V.P.-Mfg. & Distr.--National Foods Inc., Bronx, NY, pg. 788
Janowitz, Dorris, V.P. & Production Mgr.--Farrar, Straus & Giroux, Inc., New York, NY, pg. 403
Jarvis, Chris, Mgr.-Engrng.--H. B. Smith Co., Inc., Westfield, MA, pg. 1013
Jayne, Ronald C., Dir.-Technical Services--The Edward J. DeBartolo Corporation, Youngstown, OH, pg. 323
Jeffery, T., V.P.-Mfg.--Tuthill Pump, Alsip, IL, pg. 1120
Jenkins, Jeffrey, V.P.-Mfg.--Georgia Iron Works Co., Grovetown, GA, pg. 453
Jenkins, Kenneth, V.P.-Mfg.--Applied Microsystems Corporation, Redmond, WA, pg. 79
Jennings, Thomas G., V.P.-Applied Technology--American Systems Corporation, Chantilly, VA, pg. 63
Jensen, Dennis P., Plant Mgr.--Holcomb & Hoke Mfg. Company, Inc., Indianapolis, IN, pg. 538
Jent, Ron, Mgr.-Mfg.--Wavetek Communications Div., Indianapolis, IN, pg. 1168
Jeschelnig, Richard J., V.P.-Sls. & Engrng.--PMC Industries Inc., Wickliffe, OH, pg. 836
Johann, E.W., V.P.-Mktg. & Engrng.--Weil-McLain, Michigan City, IN, pg. 710
Johnson, David, V.P.-Mfg.--Commercial & Architectural Products Inc., Dover, OH, pg. 268
Johnson, Eric, V.P.-Engrng.--Great Plains Manufacturing, Inc., Assaria, KS, pg. 482
Johnson, Frank, V.P.-Strategic Plng.--Caravan Products Company, Inc., Totowa, NJ, pg. 217
Johnson, J., Chief Prod. Engr.--Marmon-Herrington Company, Louisville, KY, pg. 711
Johnson, John, V.P.-Mfg.--Best Manufacturing, Inc., New York, NY, pg. 146
Johnson, Ken, Mgr.-Mfg.--Fiberesin Industries Inc., Oconomowoc, WI, pg. 408
Johnson, Skip, V.P.-Mfr.--Alex Foods, Inc., Anaheim, CA, pg. 33
Johnson, Tim, Mgr.-Mfg.--East Moline Metal Products Company, East Moline, IL, pg. 363
Jonas, Nelson J., Sr. V.P.-Construction Opers.--Bartlett Cocke Jr. Construction Co., San Antonio, TX, pg. 258

Jones, Charlie J., V.P.-Electrical Engrng.--Abbey Etna Machine Company, Perrysburg, OH, pg. 9
Jones, Garr M., Sr. V.P.-Engrng. Design--Brown & Caldwell Consulting Engineers, Pleasant Hill, CA, pg. 181
Jones, Harold, V.P.-Mfg.--Knowles Electronics, Inc., Itasca, IL, pg. 637
Jones, John J., Plant Supt.--Perry & Derrick Co., Cincinnati, OH, pg. 863
Jones, Rex, Pres.--Schilling Motors, Inc., Memphis, TN, pg. 322
Jones, T., V.P.-Tech./Customer Service--Telechron, Inc., Ashland, MA, pg. 1085
Jones, William H., Sr. V.P.-Mfg.--Electronic Data Magnetics, Inc., High Point, NC, pg. 375
Joseph, Ed, Prod. Mgr.-Sanitation--DEC/Bou-Matic, Madison, WI, pg. 309
Joseph, Mark, Mgr.-Engrng. & Sec.--Uppco, Inc., Chicago, IL, pg. 1139
Josephson, Herbert, V.P.-Adv. & Mfg.--McNally Industries, Inc., Grantsburg, WI, pg. 731
Joyner, Al, Pres.-Mfg.--Tanner Co. Inc., Rutherfordton, NC, pg. 1078
Juneau, J. Bradley, V.P.-Exploration--Zilkha Energy Company, Houston, TX, pg. 1219
Junkert, Ken, Consulting Engineer--Wahl Instruments, Culver City, CA, pg. 1158
Kahl, Norman, Dir.-Engrng.--Narrow Fabric Industries, Inc., West Reading, PA, pg. 783
Kale, George, Mgr. Mfg.--Estes Industries, Inc., Penrose, CO, pg. 1011
Kamp, Al S., V.P.-Mfg.--Zytec Corp., Eden Prairie, MN, pg. 1221
Kanady, Joseph, Jr., Sr. V.P.-Construction--Oman Construction Co. Inc., Nashville, TN, pg. 825
Karr, Bob, Mgr.-Mfg.--Netzsch, Inc., Exton, PA, pg. 798
Kastelberry, Julian, V.P.-Mfg.--Ring Screw Works, Madison Heights, MI, pg. 935
Katkaveck, Frank, Dir.-Mfg.--Abbott Laboratories/Ashland, Ashland, OH, pg. 9
Kaye, Gilbert D., V.P.-Mfg.--The Hartz Mountain Corp., Harrison, NJ, pg. 514
Kayne, Jack, V.P.-Engrng.--Slant/Fin Corporation, Greenvale, NY, pg. 1010
Keeling, William S., Sr. V.P.-Production--Gateway Press, Inc., Louisville, KY, pg. 446
Keeney, Hilliard, Sr. V.P.-Opers.--Pella Corporation, Pella, IA, pg. 856
Keller, Harold, Dir.-Engrng. Opers.--Mader Construction Group Inc., Elma, NY, pg. 699
Kelly, James J., V.P.-Mfg. & Research--M. A. Bruder & Sons, Inc., Broomall, PA, pg. 184
Kelly, Mike, V.P.-Mfg.--Besser Company, Alpena, MI, pg. 146
Kelly, William M., Exec. V.P.-Oper.--Blue Tee Corporation, New York, NY, pg. 161
Keltz, Martin J., V.P.-Scholastic Production--Scholastic Inc., New York, NY, pg. 962
Keng, William, V.P.-Technical--Puritan/Churchill Chemical Company, Atlanta, GA, pg. 900
Kennedy, Thomas, Dir.-Engrng.--Daxus Corporation, Pittsburgh, PA, pg. 319
Kenney, Robert, Dir.-Mfg.--Northwest Paper Converting Company, Vancouver, WA, pg. 814
Kessler, Richard, V.P.-Mfg.--Leschen Wire Rope, Saint Joseph, MO, pg. 1197
Kessler, Robert, Plant Mgr.--Grit Printing Co., Williamsport, PA, pg. 1043
Kestler, Paul, Opers. Mgr.--Sycon Corporation, Marion, OH, pg. 1069
Kiefert, D.E., V.P.-Mfg. Services--Bradley Corporation, Menomonee Falls, WI, pg. 170
Killin, K. D., V.P.-Engrng.--U.S. Reduction Company, Munster, IN, pg. 1137
King, Brian, Dir.-Mfg.--Yorktown Tool & Die Corporation, Yorktown, IN, pg. 1208
King, John H., V.P.-Engrng.--E. D. Bullard Company, Cynthiana, KY, pg. 188
King, Wayne, V.P.-Mfg.--The Apparel Group, Ltd., New York, NY, pg. 78
Kinghorn, D.T., Mgr.-Plant--Orbel Corporation, Phillipsburg, NJ, pg. 828
Kingsbury, Gale, Exec. V.P.-Opers.--Gem Top Mfg., Inc., Clackamas, OR, pg. 448
Kingsbury, Warren, Chief Engr.--Hempt Brothers, Inc., Camp Hill, PA, pg. 528
Kink, J.S., Mgr.-Mfg.--Thrall Car Mfg. Co., Chicago Heights, IL, pg. 350
Kinman, Luther, Dir.-Engrng.--Burtman Iron Works, Inc., Boston, MA, pg. 195
Kinstler, J.R., Exec. V.P.-Mfg.--Motor Wheel Corporation, Lansing, MI, pg. 773
Kirkpatrick, William, V.P.-Mfg.--Reliable Automatic Sprinkler Co., Inc., Mount Vernon, NY, pg. 924
Kisiazek, J., V.P.-Mfg.--Spotnails Inc., Rolling Meadows, IL, pg. 1032
Kittredge, John, V.P.-Mfg.--Crane & Co., Inc., Dalton, MA, pg. 296
Klein, Thomas R., V.P.-Matls. Mgmnt.--Klein Tools Inc., Skokie, IL, pg. 635
Klein, Tom, V.P.-Mfg.--MNP Corp., Utica, MI, pg. 693
Klempner, Bernie, Sr. V.P.-Engrng.--Seaboard Electronics Co., Carlsbad, CA, pg. 983
Kleven, Larry, V.P.-Mfg.--Oregon Freeze Dry, Inc., Albany, OR, pg. 829
Kline, Cullen, Mgr.-Materials--Tricon Brazing Alloys & Chemical Products Div., Downers Grove, IL, pg. 1113
Kling, Paul, Plant Engineer--Pabst Brewing Co., San Antonio, TX, pg. 959
Klocke, H. Gene, V.P.-Engrng.--Champion Pneumatic Machinery Co., Inc., Princeton, IL, pg. 238
Kluska, John, V.P.-Products & Services--Cyborg Systems, Inc., Chicago, IL, pg. 307
Knecht, R.L., V.P.-Refinery Opers.--California & Hawaiian Sugar Company, Concord, CA, pg. 210
Kniebel, Chuck, V.P.-Engrng.--Sanborn Manufacturing Company, Springfield, MN, pg. 969
Knight, Paul D., Brewing Mgr.--Pabst Brewing Co./Tumwater, Tumwater, WA, pg. 959
Knoth, Karl H., Pres. & Chief Oper. Officer, Mfg. & Assembly--ASC Incorporated, Southgate, MI, pg. 7
Knott, Tim, Mfg. Mgr.--Dakotah, Inc., Webster, SD, pg. 312
Knowles, Edward S., V.P.-Opers.--Lafayette Manufacturing, Inc., Hayward, CA, pg. 650
Knupp, Richard, V.P.-Mfg.--Cornell Iron Works, Inc., Mountaintop, PA, pg. 286
Knuth, Stephen B., V.P.-Opers. & Engrng.--PhoneMate, Inc., Torrance, CA, pg. 869
Kochis, Joe, Mgr.-Plant--Hanel Lumber Co., Inc., Hood River, OR, pg. 505
Koehlein, Gregg, Pres., Chief Exec. Officer, Plant & Mfg. Mgr.--Mallory, Inc., Carson City, NV, pg. 703
Koehling, B., Plant Mgr.--Dukane Corporation, Saint Charles, IL, pg. 351
Koenig, Daniel, V.P.-Mfg.--Steinway & Sons, Long Island City, NY, pg. 1046
Koenitzer, J.D., V.P.-Engrng.--Helwig Carbon Products, Inc., Milwaukee, WI, pg. 528
Kohner, Peter, V.P.-Mfg.--Industrial Acoustics Company, Inc., Bronx, NY, pg. 565
Kolk, Art, V.P.-Production--A. J. Canfield Co., Chicago, IL, pg. 214
Kopjo, Jerry, Engrng. Dir.--Brencal Contractors Inc., Detroit, MI, pg. 106
Korman, Richard, V.P.-Merchandising--J H Collectibles, Milwaukee, WI, pg. 584
Kozuck, Charles, Dir.-Mfg.--Elkay Products, Inc., Shrewsbury, MA, pg. 377
Kranz, Richard, V.P.-Production--Tension Envelope Corp., Kansas City, MO, pg. 1088
Krasko, R., Chief Engr.--Practical Automation, Inc., Shelton, CT, pg. 34
Krenek, James J., V.P.-Mfg.--Petersen Publishing Company, Los Angeles, CA, pg. 864
Kress, Glenn, Mgr.-Mfg. & Engrng.--Wells Manufacturing Company, Verdi, NV, pg. 1027
Krieble, John, V.P.-Opers. & Sec.--Capital Controls Company Inc., Colmar, PA, pg. 215
Krill, Jake, Dir.-Production--Optical Corp. of America, Louisville, KY, pg. 827
Ksiaek, Joe, V.P.-Mfg.--Ace Office Products, Rolling Meadows, IL, pg. 12
Kuck, Tim, V.P.-Mfg.--Regal Marine Industries Inc., Orlando, FL, pg. 921
Kuhl, John H., Sr. V.P.-Construction & Engrng.--Calmark Development Corp., Los Angeles, CA, pg. 211
Kuhr, Richard R., V.P.-Mfg.--Templeton, Kenly & Co., Inc., Broadview, IL, pg. 1086
Kunihiro, Jane K., Dir.-Mfg.--Elastomeric Technologies, Inc., Hatboro, PA, pg. 372
Kvasnicka, James, V.P.-Mfg.--The George E. Failing Company, Enid, OK, pg. 161
Kwiatkowski, Gery, Dir.-Mfr. Services--Hirsh Company, Skokie, IL, pg. 258
L'Eplattenier, J.J., V.P.-Mfg.--Bobst Group Inc., Roseland, NJ, pg. 161
Lafferty, James F., Sr. V.P.-Equipment--Henkels & McCoy, Inc., Blue Bell, PA, pg. 529
Lamb, Dwight, Jr., V.P., Treas. & Production Mgr.-Post--Benjamin Franklin Literary & Medical Society, Inc., Indianapolis, IN, pg. 139
Lambert, Neal, Sr. V.P.-Mfg., West Coast--Sipex Corporation, Billerica, MA, pg. 1009
Landi, John, V.P.-Mfg.--Smith-Edwards-Dunlap Company, Philadelphia, PA, pg. 1012
Lange, James, V.P.-Mfg.--Ocean Spray Cranberries, Inc., Lakeville, MA, pg. 820
Langille, Paul, V.P.-Mfg.--Schulze & Burch Biscuit Company, Chicago, IL, pg. 979
Langley, Travis L., V.P.-Mfg.--Proto Systems of Atlanta, Alpharetta, GA, pg. 895
Langteau, Joe, Sr. V.P.-Opers.--Arby's, Inc., Miami Beach, FL, pg. 243
Langton, Robert, Dir.-Quality Assurance--JPM Company, Lewisburg, PA, pg. 586
Lantz, Richard K., V.P.-Mfg. & Special Sls.--Shenandoah Mfg. Co. Inc., Harrisonburg, VA, pg. 997
LaPalme, Donald, V.P.-Mfg.--GAF Building Materials Corporation, Wayne, NJ, pg. 438
Larkin, Daniel, V.P.-Mfg.--Talon, Inc., Meadville, PA, pg. 1077
Larkin, John, V.P.-Mfg.--J H Collectibles, Milwaukee, WI, pg. 584
LaRosa, Thomas, Dir.-Mfg., Spice Opers.--M. Kamenstein, Inc., White Plains, NY, pg. 615
Larose, Dale, V.P.-Mfg.--Pioneer Plastics Corp., Auburn, ME, pg. 872
Larue, Quint, V.P.-Mfg.--H.M. Smyth Co., Saint Paul, MN, pg. 1014
Lasky, Jack S., V.P.-Research & Engrng.--The Okonite Company, Ramsey, NJ, pg. 823
Lauffer, Leonard, Dir.-Mfg.--Austin Sculpture, Holbrook, NY, pg. 99
Laviolette, Rene, Sr. V.P.-Product Devel.--Manufacturers Technologies, Inc., West Springfield, MA, pg. 705
Lawler, Gene, Dir.-Mfg.--Jandy Industries, Novato, CA, pg. 589
Lawrence, Bill, Dir.-Engrng.--Media America Corp., Phoenix, AZ, pg. 734
Lawrence, Samuel C., V.P.-Prod.--Nationwide Homes, Inc., Martinsville, VA, pg. 795
Lawson, Allan P., V.P.-Mfg.--Triple S Plastics, Inc., Vicksburg, MI, pg. 1114
Lawson, John, Mgr.-Plant; Paulk, GA--United Farm Tools, Kentucky Div., Glasgow, KY, pg. 1132
Lawson, W.L., Mgr.-Prod. Environmental--Lawson Associates Inc., Minneapolis, MN, pg. 663
Lazar, Jay, Mgr.-Mfg.--All-Luminum Products, Inc., Philadelphia, PA, pg. 35
Lease, Michael, V.P.-Research & Devel.--FoodCraft Equipment Co., Inc., Lancaster, PA, pg. 860
Leath, Charles, Dir.-Engrng.--U.S. Construction Co., Inc., Columbia, SC, pg. 1135
Leckie, John, V.P.-Prod. & Mfg.--William H. Sadlier, Inc., New York, NY, pg. 966
Lee, Paul, Chief Engineer--American Electronics, Inc., Fullerton, CA, pg. 3
Leibold, Rick, V.P.-Matls.--Wyandot Inc., Marion, OH, pg. 1205
Leicht, Jeffrey, V.P.-Mfg.--Eclipse Manufacturing Company, Sheboygan, WI, pg. 367
Leighley, K.C., Chief Engr.--Spectronics Corporation, Westbury, NY, pg. 1029
Leinhart, Phil, Brewmaster--The Lion, Inc. (Gibbons-Stegmaier Brewery), Wilkes-Barre, PA, pg. 677
Lemen, Richard, Mgr.-Materials--Harford Systems, Inc., Aberdeen, MD, pg. 152
Leoff, Rick, V.P.-Tour Opers.--Amtran, Inc., Indianapolis, IN, pg. 69
Leon, Juan, Exec. V.P.-Mfg.--Leather Center, Inc., Carrollton, TX, pg. 664
Leonard, Charles, V.P.-Opers.--Cutter Flying Service, Inc., Albuquerque, NM, pg. 307
Leonard, Paul, V.P.-Mfg.--Horn Packaging Corporation, Ayer, MA, pg. 544
Leone, Sam, Dir.-Mfg.--Hudson Valley Tree, Inc., Newburgh, NY, pg. 551
Leonhart, Charles, V.P.-Engrng.--Nuarc Company, Inc., Niles, IL, pg. 817
Lesneski, Bernard, V.P.-Engrng. & Mktg.--McNeil & NRM., Inc., Akron, OH, pg. 732
Lester, Donald R., Sr. V.P.-Panel Prods.--North Pacific Lumber Company, Portland, OR, pg. 813
Letendre, Norman, V.P.-Engrng.--Dynamic Metal Products Company, Manchester, CT, pg. 356
Levey, Harry, V.P.-Mfg.--SICO INC., Minneapolis, MN, pg. 1001
Levstek, Frank J., V.P.-Mfg.--The Sanymetal Products Co., Inc., Vanceburg, KY, pg. 970
Lewallen, William J., V.P.-Engrng.--Sivalls, Inc., Odessa, TX, pg. 1009
Lewandowski, J., Chief Engr.--Stamco Industries Inc., Euclid, OH, pg. 1035
Lewen, Ronald, Dir.-Engrng.--Trilan Systems Corporation, Saint Charles, IL, pg. 352
Lewis, Cecil H., Dir.-Engrng.--Midway Products Corporation, Monroe, MI, pg. 751
Light, William, V.P.-Opers.--Pavey Envelope & Tag Corp., Jersey City, NJ, pg. 852
Lillevold, G., V.P.-Engrng.--S-T Industries, Inc., Saint James, MN, pg. 964
Lindley, Joe, V.P.-Opers.--C & M Corporation, Wauregan, CT, pg. 198
Lindsay, David, V.P.-Mfg.--King Louie International, Inc., Grandview, MO, pg. 631
Lindsey, Darryl, V.P.-Opers.--Plains Cotton Co-op Association, Lubbock, TX, pg. 873
Linn, Bob, Mgr.-Mfg.--Mersman Furniture, Celina, OH, pg. 741
Litsermeier, Joseph, Chief Engnr.--The Columbia Corporation, Chatham, NY, pg. 1209
Liu, Donald, Sr. V.P.-Tech. Services--American Bureau of Shipping, New York, NY, pg. 50
Lloyd, Spence, V.P.-Opers.--Intermountain Farmers Association, Salt Lake City, UT, pg. 575
Loewen, Wally, Chief Engr.--Salwasser Manufacturing Company, Inc., Reedley, CA, pg. 968
Loftin, Wayne, Chief Engineer--Affiliated Foods Southwest, Little Rock, AR, pg. 24
Logan, John, V.P.-Mfg.--Melard Manufacturing Corporation, Passaic, NJ, pg. 737
Logan, Tom, V.P.-Opers.--Publishers Clearing House, Port Washington, NY, pg. 898
Lohr, Cliff, V.P.-Mfg.--Seco Warwick Corporation, Meadville, PA, pg. 987
Long, Philip A., V.P.-Mfg.--Metalloy Corporation, Hudson, MI, pg. 742
Longino, Betsy, Dir.-Tech.--Atlanta Market Center, Atlanta, GA, pg. 94
Lonnebotn, Trygve, Sr. V.P.-Opers. & Tech.--RAYOVAC Corporation, Madison, WI, pg. 915
Looney, Mark E., V.P. & Gen. Mgr.--Chemtech Industries, Inc., Saint Louis, MO, pg. 242
Lopez, Manny, Mgr.-Prod.--Symons Corporation, Des Plaines, IL, pg. 1069
Lopez, Ramon, V.P.-Technical Services--Gilbane Building Company, Providence, RI, pg. 457
Loprest, Jay, Asst. V.P.-Mfg. & Purchasing--Naz-Dar Company, Chicago, IL, pg. 1095
Loughran, James, Chief Engineer--Arrow Fluid Power, Broadview, IL, pg. 85
Lowry, Marvin, V.P.-Oper.--Blevins Concession Supply Co., Tampa, FL, pg. 156
Lowry, William D., Dir.-Production--Sampler Publications Inc., Saint Charles, IL, pg. 968
Lucas, Dan, Dir.-Mfg.--Bud Industries, Inc., Willoughby, OH, pg. 186
Luhm, Ralph, V.P.-Engrng.--Allfast Fastening Systems, Inc., City of Industry, CA, pg. 37
Lundsted, Stephen, V.P.-Mfg.--Simplex Time Recorder Co., Gardner, MA, pg. 1006
Lundy, Frank, II, V.P. & Chief Engr.--Lundy Construction Co., Inc., Williamsport, PA, pg. 687
Luthro, John O., V.P.-Mfg., Products--Rochester Midland Corporation, Rochester, NY, pg. 940
Lutton, J.E., Mgr.-Mfg.--Eriez Magnetics, Erie, PA, pg. 386
Lutz, L.H., V.P.-Engrng.--Bliss-Salem, Inc., Salem, OH, pg. 156
Lynch, Mark, V.P.-Mfg.--Avatar Corporation, Hopkinton, MA, pg. 101
Lynch, Roger, Exec. V.P.--Kimstock, Inc., Santa Ana, CA, pg. 630

MacDonald, Wallace, Dir.-Engrng.--Pneumatic Scale Corporation, Quincy, MA, pg. 122
Macholt, Fred, V.P.-Mfg.--Key Handling Systems, Inc., Hackensack, NJ, pg. 627
Mackey, Gary T., Sr. V.P.-Mfg.--American Ball Manufacturing, Carrollton, TX, pg. 890
Macklin, John, Plant Mgr.--Magnus Metals, Fremont, NE, pg. 400
Macy, Dick, Dir.-Mfg.--Ft. Dearborn Lithograph Graphic Arts Division, Fort Worth, TX, pg. 425
Magill, M.J., V.P.-Engrng.--Howden Sirocco inc., Hyde Park, MA, pg. 547
Majesty, Raymond, V.P.-Mfg.--Encyclopaedia Britannica, Inc., Chicago, IL, pg. 381
Malin, William, V.P.-Mfg.--Oriel Corporation, Stratford, CT, pg. 829
Mallery, John L., V.P. & Plant Mgr.--Mallery Lumber Corp., Emporium, PA, pg. 702
Malliris, Richard E., V.P.-Mfg.--KB Alloys, Inc., Sinking Spring, PA, pg. 507
Malvaso, Jim, V.P.-Mfg.--Pfaudler-U.S., Inc., Rochester, NY, pg. 866
Manoway, Dina, Mgr.-Mfg.--Victaulic Company of America, Easton, PA, pg. 1149
March, Owen, Dir.-Engrng. Services--Burgess & Niple, Limited, Columbus, OH, pg. 190
Marchant, Albert, Chief Engr.--Alimak Elevator Company, Bridgeport, CT, pg. 34
Marion, Robert, V.P.-Prod.--Weldon, Williams & Lick, Inc., Fort Smith, AR, pg. 1175
Marsh, Arthur H., Sr. V.P.-Tech.--Montgomery Elevator Company, Moline, IL, pg. 767
Marsh, Carl P., V.P.-Mfg. & Pur.--Maui Divers Of Hawaii, Ltd., Honolulu, HI, pg. 721
Marshall, Pat, Head Engr.--L&R Manufacturing Co., Kearny, NJ, pg. 647
Marsico, Joseph, V.P.-Mfg.--A.W. Chesterton Company, Stoneham, MA, pg. 244
Marta, Francis, V.P.-Engrng.--Circle A.W. Products, Co., Portland, OR, pg. 250
Martin, Darrell G., V.P.-Construction & Production--Johnson Acoustical & Supply Co., Portland, OR, pg. 597
Martin, Joe, Dir.-Engrng.--H. Koch & Sons, Anaheim, CA, pg. 262
Martin, John A., V.P.-Engrng.--Precision Echo, Inc., Santa Clara, CA, pg. 885
Martin, Louis, V.P.-Engrng.--Martin Industries (AL), Florence, AL, pg. 715
Martin, Reg, V.P.-Mfg.--Bufkor, Inc., Clearwater, FL, pg. 187
Martin, Richard, V.P.-Construction--H. E. Sargent, Inc., Stillwater, ME, pg. 971
Martin, Wilmer C., V.P.-Prod. & Opers. & Real Estate Officer--Kinetic Systems Corporation, Lockport, IL, pg. 630
Marttila, Raymond, V.P.-Engrng.--CTB Inc., Milford, IN, pg. 205
Marturano, Gus, V.P.-Mfg.--Duralam, Inc., Appleton, WI, pg. 971
Massaro, Karl, V.P.-Engrng.--Ajax Manufacturing Company, Inc., Hillsborough, NJ, pg. 28
Massingill, Glynn, V.P.-PAC Mfg. & Distr.--Precision Tune, Inc., Leesburg, VA, pg. 885
Mast, Randall, V.P.-Production--Landmark Community Newspapers, Inc., Shelbyville, KY, pg. 655
Mastalski, Leo, V.P.-Mfg.--Freeway Corporation, Cleveland, OH, pg. 432
Masters, Geoff, Mgr.-Mfg. & Engrng.--International Gear Corporation, Cleveland, OH, pg. 578
Masters, William, Dir.-Engrng.--Homes of Merit Inc., Bartow, FL, pg. 542
Matheson, Fred D., Exec. V.P.-Mfg.--Forstmann & Company, Inc., New York, NY, pg. 424
Mathews, Claude L., V.P.-Mfg.--Ortel Corporation, Alhambra, CA, pg. 830
Mathiesen, John P., V.P.-Quality Control & Mfg.--Dealers Manufacturing Company, Minneapolis, MN, pg. 322
Matiasek, R., V.P.-Mfg.--Dynamic Controls Corp., South Windsor, CT, pg. 356
Mattia, Arthur, V.P.-Engrng.--Action Manufacturing Co., Philadelphia, PA, pg. 15
Matusin, Gary, Mgr.-Engrng.--Bruner Corporation, Milwaukee, WI, pg. 184
Mauger, David W., V.P.-Mfg. & Engrng.--Bradford Company, Holland, MI, pg. 170
Maunus, David, V.P.-Mfg.--Meadowcraft, Inc., Birmingham, AL, pg. 733
Mayer, Dave, V.P.-Mfg.--Advanstar Communications, Cleveland, OH, pg. 21
Mayer, Vince, Dir.-Mfg.--General Safety Corporation, Saint Clair Shores, MI, pg. 450
Maynard, Tom, V.P.-Production--Maywood, Inc., Amarillo, TX, pg. 725
McCarty, Dennis, Mgr.-Mfg.--D.C.I., Inc., Saint Cloud, MN, pg. 308
McClean, Jim, Mgr.-Engrng.--Gallagher-Kaiser Corp., Detroit, MI, pg. 441
McClelland, O., Mgr.-Mfg.-Clean Room--Laminaire Corporation, Rahway, NJ, pg. 652
McClimen, Tom, V.P.-Mfg.--Flexel, Inc., Atlanta, GA, pg. 418
McClure, E. Ray, Dir.-Technical--Moore Special Tool Co., Inc., Bridgeport, CT, pg. 768
McClure, George, Sr. V.P.-Engrng.--Bel-Art Products, Pequannock, NJ, pg. 133
McClure, Jim, V.P.-Sls. & Mfg.--International Cold Storage Co., Inc., Andover, KS, pg. 576
McCord, Ed, V.P. Engrng. & Mfg.--Komatsu Dresser Company, Lincolnshire, IL, pg. 565
McCormick, G., V.P.-Engrng.--Elastic Stop Nut, Union, NJ, pg. 514
McCullough, Kevin, V.P.-Mfg.--Dennis Chemical Company, Inc., Saint Louis, MO, pg. 329
McDonald, Timothy R., Dir.-Technology--Hazen Paper Company, Holyoke, MA, pg. 520
McDonnell, Kevin J., V.P.-Engrng.--Trace Products, San Jose, CA, pg. 1104
McFeely, John A., Jr., V.P.-Engrng. & Estimating--Triangle Electric Company, Madison Heights, MI, pg. 1112
McGaha, Ray, V.P.-Sls. & Engrng.--Continental Conveyor & Equipment Company, Winfield, AL, pg. 798
McGary, F.H., V.P.-Mfg.--Star Bronze Company, Alliance, OH, pg. 1039
McGauran, Richard, Exec. V.P.-Opers.--Pascoe Building Systems, Inc., Columbus, GA, pg. 851
McGehee, Bill, Mgr.-Mfg.--FWD Corporation, Clintonville, WI, pg. 395
McGehee, William, Mgr.-Mfg.--Seagrave Fire Apparatus, Inc., Clintonville, WI, pg. 395
McGhee, Charles, V.P. & Dir.-Mfg.--Croft Metal Inc., McComb, MS, pg. 300
McGill, A., Mgr.-Mfg.--Perry Products Corp., Hainesport, NJ, pg. 863
McGinley, Dan, V.P.-Opers.--Freeman Shoes Company, Beloit, WI, pg. 431
McGinnis, William W., Exec. V.P.-Opers.--Jewelers Mutual Insurance Company, Neenah, WI, pg. 593
McGlothlin, James E., V.P.-Opers.--Quintron Systems, Inc., Santa Maria, CA, pg. 905
McGovern, Joseph P., Chief Tech. Advisor--White Rock Distilleries Inc., Lewiston, ME, pg. 1186
McGuigen, William P., V.P.-Prod. Plng. & Mfg.--Lotus Carpet Division, Columbus, GA, pg. 267
McIntyre, William S., Chief Design Engr.--J. H. Fletcher & Co., Huntington, WV, pg. 418
McKeller, Charles, V.P.-Mfg. Services--Glen Raven Mills, Inc., Glen Raven, NC, pg. 461
McKenzie, John, Sr. V.P. & Chief Engr.--Key Handling Systems, Inc., Hackensack, NJ, pg. 627
McKew, Howard, V.P.-Engrng.--Balco, Inc. (MA), Boston, MA, pg. 115
McKimey, Allen, Dir.-Mfg. Services--Holt Hosiery Mills, Inc., Burlington, NC, pg. 541
McKinnon, Henry, Mgr.-Opers.--B & G Wholesalers, Inc., Nashville, TN, pg. 106
McKnatt, Gene, Supvr.-Telecommunications Engrng.--Memphis Light, Gas & Water, Memphis, TN, pg. 738
McLean, Tom, V.P.-System Software Div.--Cincom Systems, Inc., Cincinnati, OH, pg. 250
McMahon, George, Dir.-Engrng.--Pitco Frialator Inc., Concord, NH, pg. 157
McManus, H.S., V.P.-Mfg.--Morrison Textile Machinery Co., Fort Lawn, SC, pg. 771
McManus, R.T., V.P.-Distr. & Warehousing, Gen. Mgr. & Dir.-Personnel--Walter J. Black, Inc., Port Washington, NY, pg. 154
McNeilly, Ellen, V.P.-Production--Alfred A. Knopf, Inc., New York, NY, pg. 20
McPhedrain, Larry L., V.P.-Opers.--Mary Maxim, Inc., Port Huron, MI, pg. 722
McQuillen, Denis, Sr. V.P. Mfg.--Consolidated Cigar Corporation, Fort Lauderdale, FL, pg. 276
Meehan, David, V.P.-Sound Selector--Ensoniq Corporation, Malvern, PA, pg. 382
Meiland, Nico J., V.P.-Mfg., U.S.--S. C. Johnson & Son, Inc., Racine, WI, pg. 599
Meinert, Gregory, Mgr.-Production/Facilities--Pennex Products Co., Inc., Verona, PA, pg. 858
Melin, Robert D., V.P.-Mfg.--Trak International, Inc., Port Washington, WI, pg. 1106
Melton, James P., V.P.-Press Opers.--Quad/Graphics, Inc., Pewaukee, WI, pg. 902
Mench, John, V.P.-Constr. Engrng.--Big V Supermarkets, Inc., Florida, NY, pg. 149
Menke, Andrew G., V.P.-Mfg.--Ardco, Inc., Alsip, IL, pg. 81
Mentzer, Lawrence, V.P.-Engrng.--Signet Systems, Inc., Harrodsburg, KY, pg. 385
Merck, Fred, Dir.-Engrng.--Yorktowne Paper Mills, Inc., York, PA, pg. 1208
Mericle, Steve, Mgr.-Mfg.--Hagie Manufacturing Co., Clarion, IA, pg. 499
Merl, Murray, V.P.-Mfg.--Robby Len Fashions, New York, NY, pg. 78
Merrell, R., V.P.-Mfg.--MidWest Body Corporation, Paris, IL, pg. 752
Merrill, Douglas W., V.P.-Mfg. Opers.--Kelly-Moore Paint Company, Inc., San Carlos, CA, pg. 621
Merrill, Hardy, V.P.-Mfg.--U.S. Repeating Arms Company, New Haven, CT, pg. 1137
Mertens, Heinz, Plant Mgr.--Warrens Waller Press, South San Francisco, CA, pg. 1165
Meyer, Richard, Chief Engineer--Pawling Corporation, Pawling, NY, pg. 852
Meyer, Richard S., V.P.-Technical Services--Nalleys Fine Foods, Tacoma, WA, pg. 25
Meyer, Robert, V.P.-Sheetfed Mfg.--The Hennegan Company, Cincinnati, OH, pg. 529
Meyers, David R., V.P.-Opers.--Industrial Coatings Group, Inc., Chicago, IL, pg. 566
Michaels, Don, V.P.-Mfg.--T.B. Wood's Sons Company, Chambersburg, PA, pg. 1200
Michaels, Frank, Mgr.-Plant Engrng.--Sunnen Products Company, Saint Louis, MO, pg. 1061
Miller, Ben, V.P.-Engrng.--Remcor Products Co., Glendale Heights, IL, pg. 926
Miller, Charles, V.P.-Mfg.--Narrow Fabric Industries, Inc., West Reading, PA, pg. 783
Miller, David, V.P.-Mfg.--Roppe Corp., Fostoria, OH, pg. 947
Miller, Don, Pres. & Chief Exec. Officer--Ederer Inc., Seattle, WA, pg. 368
Miller, Don, V.P.-Opers.--Reliance Elevator Company, Chicago, IL, pg. 925
Miller, Doug, V.P.-Mfg.--Blissfield Manufacturing Company, Blissfield, MI, pg. 157
Miller, Fred D., V.P.-Mfg.--The Ward Machinery Company, Cockeysville, MD, pg. 1162
Miller, Mark, V.P.-Opers.--Pressure Systems, Hampton, VA, pg. 888
Miller, Marvin, V.P.-Engrng. & Sec.--The Keller Manufacturing Co., Inc., Corydon, IN, pg. 621
Miller, Michael G., Dir.-Engrng.--Duff-Norton, Charlotte, NC, pg. 1032
Miller, R., V.P.-Engrng.--Harbour Industries, Inc., Shelburne, VT, pg. 507
Miller, R.A., V.P.-Engrng.--United States Sugar Corporation, Clewiston, FL, pg. 1137
Miller, V.M., V.P.-Mfg.--National Fruit Product Company, Winchester, VA, pg. 789
Miller, William, Dir.-Opers.--Better Baked Foods, Inc., North East, PA, pg. 148
Minchello, Edward, V.P.- Mfg.--Statler Industries, Medford, MA, pg. 1041
Minor, Travis, V.P.-Mfg.--P.W. Minor & Son, Inc., Batavia, NY, pg. 758
Miskew, John, Asst. V.P.-Field Engrng.--Monroe Systems For Business, Inc., Morris Plains, NJ, pg. 766
Miskewitch, Michael, V.P.-Mfg.--Premier Coatings, Inc., Elk Grove Village, IL, pg. 886
Mitchel, David, V.P.-Mfg.--Mitchel & Scot Machine Co., Inc., Indianapolis, IN, pg. 761
Mitchell, Brent, V.P.-Mfg.--Amano Cincinnati, Inc., Cincinnati, OH, pg. 46
Mitchell, Charles, V.P.-Mfg.--World Carpets, Inc., Dalton, GA, pg. 1202
Mitchell, John B., V.P.-Engrng.--T.B. Wood's Sons Company, Chambersburg, PA, pg. 1200
Mitchell, Steve, V.P.-Mfg.--Southern Mills, Inc., Union City, GA, pg. 1021
Mitchell, Wayne, V.P.-Mfg.--United Graphics, Inc., Seattle, WA, pg. 1132
Mitter, Lawrence, V.P.-Engrng.--Young & Franklin, Inc., Liverpool, NY, pg. 1209
Mizer, Mike, V.P.-Engrng.--Carver, Inc., Garden City, GA, pg. 227
Moberly, Mike, Mgr.-Production--Handy Wacks Corporation, Sparta, MI, pg. 505
Moestue, Anders, V.P.-Mfg.--Winthrop Printing Company, Inc., Boston, MA, pg. 1197
Mohler, Douglas, V.P.-Tech. Services--Topco Associates, Inc., Skokie, IL, pg. 1101
Mohney, Steven, Mgr.-Mfg. Engrng.--Humphrey Products Company, Kalamazoo, MI, pg. 553
Moll, Dr. Sheldon H., Sr. V.P.-Tech.--Amray, Inc., Bedford, MA, pg. 68
Monks, William, V.P.-Mfg.--Mohawk Paper Mills, Inc., Cohoes, NY, pg. 763
Moody, L.J., Mgr.-Mfg.--Koehler Manufacturing Company, Marlborough, MA, pg. 639
Mooney, Joseph M., Sr. V.P.-Opers.--EAC Corporation, Saint Louis, MO, pg. 359
Moore, Bill, Prod. Mgr.--C.G. Sargents Sons, Cary, NC, pg. 22
Moore, Richard, V.P.-Engrng.--Atari Games Corporation, Milpitas, CA, pg. 93
Moore, Robert T., V.P.-Engrng.--Hydraulics International, Inc., Chatsworth, CA, pg. 556
Morgan, Dave, Mgr.-Production--Larson Manufacturing Company, Brookings, SD, pg. 659
Morgan, George B., III, V.P.-Prod. Engrng.--Texas Metal Works, Inc., Beaumont, TX, pg. 1089
Morgan, Russ, Mgr.-Mfr.--Dearborn Gage Company, Garden City, MI, pg. 322
Moriarty, Joseph, Dir.-Mfg.--Weksler Instruments Corp., Freeport, NY, pg. 1174
Morrill, Bob, V.P.-Oper.--Emery Waterhouse Company, Portland, ME, pg. 379
Morris, Mark, Dir.-Mfg.--Tone Commander Systems, Redmond, WA, pg. 1101
Morris, Mike, V.P.-Mfg.--Rangaire & Company, Cleburne, TX, pg. 912
Moulton, Chet, Plant Mgr.--Capital City Press, Inc., Montpelier, VT, pg. 214
Mozade, Stanley, Dir.-Engrng.--Tekni-Plex, Inc., Brooklyn, NY, pg. 1084
Mueller, Peter, Exec. V.P.-Mfg.--Stihl Inc., Virginia Beach, VA, pg. 1049
Mueller, Richard, V.P.-Engrng.--Vienna Sausage Mfg. Co., Chicago, IL, pg. 1151
Mueller, Richard A., V.P.-Engrng.--Cable Division, Atlanta, GA, pg. 294
Muir, S.L., V.P.-Mfg.--Formation, Inc., Moorestown, NJ, pg. 424
Mulcahy, M., Mgr.-Engrng.--Tuthill Pump, Alsip, IL, pg. 1120
Mulhall, R., Indus. Mgr.-Conductive Prods.--Potters Industries, Inc., Parsippany, NJ, pg. 837
Mullen, John, Dir.-Quality & Engrng.--The Genie Company, Alliance, OH, pg. 452
Murphree, Jerry, V.P.-Opers.--The Vagabond Inns, San Diego, CA, pg. 1142
Murphy, Thomas, V.P.-Mfg.--Root Corporation, Mount Wolf, PA, pg. 946
Murray, John, V.P.-Engrng.--Difco, Inc., Findlay, OH, pg. 337
Murray, Wayne, V.P.-Mfg.--Edelbrock Corp., Torrance, CA, pg. 367
Muselman, Thomas, V.P.-Mfg.--E.P. Graphics, Inc., Berne, IN, pg. 360
Musselman, Stan, Dir.-Engrng.--Yorktown Tool & Die Corporation, Yorktown, IN, pg. 1208
Myers, Douglas R., Chief Engineer--Kasper Machine Company, Madison Heights, MI, pg. 618
Myers, Larry L., V.P.--Preston Energy Inc., Kingwood, WV, pg. 888
Nagel, Kenneth, Dir.-Engrng.--E.M. Wiegmann & Company, Inc., Freeburg, IL, pg. 1188
Nangia, Charles, V.P.-Engrng. Services--Pascoe Building Systems, Inc., Columbus, GA, pg. 851
Narducci, Lawrence, Mgr.-Mfg.--Molded Fiber Glass Companies, Ashtabula, OH, pg. 763
Neal, Carlos, Mgr.-Prod.--MD Pneumatics, Inc., Springfield, MO, pg. 1120
Nechay, J., V.P.-Mfg.--Dukane Corporation, Saint Charles, IL, pg. 351

Nehrt, J., Chief Engineer--Willert Home Products, Inc., Saint Louis, MO, pg. 1190
Nelson, Carl S., Jr., V.P.-Engrng.--Magnasync Moviola Corporation, Hollywood, CA, pg. 586
Nelson, Donald, V.P.-Mfg.--The Okonite Company, Ramsey, NJ, pg. 823
Nelson, Keith, Mgr.-Products--Pentax Precision Instruments Corp., Orangeburg, NY, pg. 859
Nesheim, Robert, Sr. V.P.-Science & Technology--Avadyne, Inc., Monterey, CA, pg. 101
Neul, M.C., V.P.-Engrng.--Haulpak Division, Komatsu Dresser Company, Peoria, IL, pg. 565
Nevers, Leon, V.P.-Mfg.--Roll Forming Corporation, Shelbyville, KY, pg. 944
Newton, David L., Mgr.-Engrng.--Kingsbury Assembly Machine Div., Keene, NH, pg. 632
Newton, William, V.P.-Mfg.--R.M. Palmer Company, West Reading, PA, pg. 843
Nichols, John, V.P.-Mfg.--Therm, Inc., Ithaca, NY, pg. 1090
Nickerson, J.T., V.P.-Mfg.--Southern Ohio Fabricators, Inc., Cincinnati, OH, pg. 1022
Niebler, Carol, V.P.-Mfg.--Curtis Instruments, Inc., Mount Kisco, NY, pg. 305
Nielsen, Tim R., V.P.-Opers. & Engrng.--Farnsworth Construction, Mesa, AZ, pg. 403
Noel, Jim, Dir.-Process Instrumentation--Associated Process Controls, Pleasanton, CA, pg. 92
Nolden, K., Mgr.-Mfg.--Champion Pneumatic Machinery Co., Inc., Princeton, IL, pg. 238
Noll, John L., V.P.-Opers.--A. H. Hoffman, Inc., Landisville, PA, pg. 538
Norton, Douglas, V.P.-Distribution & Mfg.--American Management Group, Westbrook, ME, pg. 57
Norton, Douglas, V.P.-Mfg. & Distr.--Portland Glass/American Management Group, Westbrook, ME, pg. 58
Norton, John Phelps, V.P.-Prod.--J. R. Norton Company, Phoenix, AZ, pg. 816
Novak, Edward K., V.P.-Mfg.--PMC Industries Inc., Wickliffe, OH, pg. 836
Novak, John S., II, V.P.-Mfg.--Sokol & Company, Countryside, IL, pg. 1016
Novitsky, D., Dir.-Engrng.--Laubeck Corporation/Cross, Carbondale, PA, pg. 660
O'Brien, James, V.P.-Mfg.--Nalleys Fine Foods, Tacoma, WA, pg. 25
O'Connell, Bradley D., Dir.-Mfg.--Crenlo, Inc., Rochester, MN, pg. 298
O'Connell, Tim, Mgr.-Engrng.--Superior Linkage Division, New Haven, IN, pg. 1120
O'Connor, Thomas, Dir.-Warehouse & Distr.--Publix Super Markets, Inc., Miami, FL, pg. 899
O'Doherty, Roy, V.P.-Mfg.--Delta Resins & Refractories, Inc., Milwaukee, WI, pg. 327
O'Kane, Robert E., V.P.-Mfg.--R. P. Adams Company, Inc., Tonawanda, NY, pg. 16
O'Leary, James, V.P.-Mfg.--Breuer Electric Mfg. Co., Chicago, IL, pg. 174
O'Neil, James E., Jr., V.P.-Mfg.--Kingsbury Corporation, Keene, NH, pg. 631
O'Sullivan, Peter F., V.P.-Pur. & Production Coordination--G. Heileman Brewing Co., Inc., La Crosse, WI, pg. 526
Ohman, John F., V.P.-Vessel Engrng., Maint. & Repair--Lykes Bros. Steamship Co., Inc., New Orleans, LA, pg. 688
Olinger, Jerry, Mgr.-Mfg.--Jofco Inc., Jasper, IN, pg. 595
Oliveria, Milton, V.P.-Opers.--Delta Rubber Company, Danielson, CT, pg. 327
Olore, Paul, Mgr.-Mfg.--Cooper Instrument Corp., Middlefield, CT, pg. 283
Olsby, Richard W., Dir.-Manufacturing--John Roberts Company, Minneapolis, MN, pg. 938
Oney, Howard D., V.P.-Mfg.--Magnetic Data, Inc., Eden Prairie, MN, pg. 700
Opatik, Frank, V.P. & Dir.-Engrng.--Wausau Homes, Inc., Rothschild, WI, pg. 1168
Oppeneer, Steve, V.P.-Mfg.--Nemschoff Chairs, Inc., Sheboygan, WI, pg. 798
Orgeron, Clarence, Dir.-Mfg.--Bollinger Machine Shop And Shipyard, Inc., Lockport, LA, pg. 163
Osam, Duane, V.P.-Production--Coleman Dairy Inc., Little Rock, AR, pg. 261
Osborne, Edward, V.P. & Dir.-Engrng.--AMI Industries, Inc., Colorado Springs, CO, pg. 5
Overstreet, Jackson, V.P.-Mfg.--Rubatex Corporation, Bedford, VA, pg. 480
Owen, William T., V.P.-Mfg.--Leupold & Stevens, Inc., Beaverton, OR, pg. 669
Padilla, Ben, Chief Engr.--Berlin Steel Construction Co., Berlin, CT, pg. 142
Paffrath, E.G., V.P.-Opers., Electrical Products Div.--Wesbar Corporation, West Bend, WI, pg. 1176
Page, Fred, Dir.-Engrng.--Burke Industries, Inc., San Jose, CA, pg. 191
Paladino, Hugh, V.P.-Mfg.--King & Prince Seafood Corporation, Brunswick, GA, pg. 631
Paluch, Mark, Dir.-Opers.--RDI, Inc., Itasca, IL, pg. 906
Papera, Joseph F., V.P.-Mfg.--Allstate Can Corporation, Clifton, NJ, pg. 43
Paraboschi, Joseph, V.P.-Mfg.--Ark-Les Corporation, Watertown, MA, pg. 82
Parham, W. Howard, Exec. V.P.-Pur. & Mfg.--Columbus Mills, Inc., Columbus, GA, pg. 267
Paris, Robert, V.P.-Opers.--J. Crew Group, Inc., New York, NY, pg. 584
Parker, Denny S., Sr. V.P.-Process Engrng.--Brown & Caldwell Consulting Engineers, Pleasant Hill, CA, pg. 181
Parkin, James W., Sr. V.P.-Mfg.--Continental Machines, Inc., Savage, MN, pg. 279
Parks, Charles C., V.P.-Mfg.--Safelite Autoglass, Wichita, KS, pg. 664
Parris, Hugh G., V.P.-Production--Nebraska Public Power District, Columbus, NE, pg. 796
Parrott, John W., V.P.-Opers.--Parisian, Inc., Birmingham, AL, pg. 848
Paskal, Randy, V.P.-Mfg.--Magnasync Moviola Corporation, Hollywood, CA, pg. 586
Pasowicz, Paul, Plant Mgr.--Label Products & Design Division, Green Bay, WI, pg. 608
Passmore, R. S., Dir.-Engrng.--Davis Electrical Constructors, Inc., Greenville, SC, pg. 318
Pateet, George, V.P.-Mfg.--National Safety Associates, Memphis, TN, pg. 793
Patel, Arvind A., V.P.-Mfg.--Intermatic Inc., Spring Grove, IL, pg. 575
Patterson, Frank, V.P.-Mfg.--Globe Business Furniture, Inc., Hendersonville, TN, pg. 463
Patterson, Hugh, V.P.-Production--Esskay Manufacturing Co., San Antonio, TX, pg. 389
Paules, Mark R., V.P.-Fin. & Mfg.--C P Converters, Inc., York, PA, pg. 203
Pauls, Charles W., Chief Mech. Engr.--National Cooperative Refinery Association, McPherson, KS, pg. 787
Pavao, Manuel, Engr.--Whaling Industries, Inc., Fall River, MA, pg. 1183
Pavlak, Francis C., V.P.-Production--Walter J. Black, Inc., Port Washington, NY, pg. 154
Pawelski, Mark, Gen. Mgr.-Mfg.--Daubert Chemical Company, Inc., Chicago, IL, pg. 317
Pawlowsky, Hal, Mgr.-Engrng.--Fill-Rite Division, Fort Wayne, IN, pg. 1120
Payne, Eugene D., V.P.-Mfg.--U.S. Rubber Reclaiming, Inc., Vicksburg, MS, pg. 306
Peaden, Spurgeon, V.P.-Mfg.--Wing Industries, Inc., Dallas, TX, pg. 1196
Pearse, J., Grp. V.P.-Engrng.--Leviton Mfg. Co., Inc., Little Neck, NY, pg. 671
Pearson, R., V.P.-Mfg.--The Levolor Corporation, Sunnyvale, CA, pg. 671
Pearson, W.C., V.P.-Mfg.--Allied Foods, Inc., Atlanta, GA, pg. 38
Pease, David H., III, V.P.-Engrng. & Mfg.--Pease Industries, Inc., Fairfield, OH, pg. 854
Pedersen, Vern, Master Service Technician--Dacor Corporation, Northfield, IL, pg. 310
Pereira, Richard, V.P.-Mfg.--Univex Corporation, Salem, NH, pg. 1139
Peroni, Peter, V.P.-Engrng.--La France Corporation, Philadelphia, PA, pg. 649
Pervier, Michael C., Plant Supt.--Anderson Products, Worcester, MA, pg. 1194
Peterko, Joseph, Dir.-Mfg.--Star-Parts Inc., Hazleton, PA, pg. 1039
Peterman, John J., V.P.-Construction--Robert E. Lamb, Inc., Valley Forge, PA, pg. 652
Petersen, Gary L., V.P.-Mfg.--Powerine Oil Company, Santa Fe Springs, CA, pg. 883
Peterson, Dennis, Mgr.-Mfg.--EWI, Inc., Salem, OH, pg. 361
Peterson, Ernest L., V.P.-Opers.--Twin City Die Castings Co., Minneapolis, MN, pg. 1121
Petrei, Massino, Chief Engr.--Dunmore Corporation, Newtown, PA, pg. 353
Petrie, Dale, Engrng. Dir. & Prod. Mgr.--Sommer Metalcraft Corporation, Crawfordsville, IN, pg. 1018
Petschke, R.L., V.P.-Mfg.--Brown & Bigelow, Inc., Saint Paul, MN, pg. 181
Phelan, G., V.P.-Mfg.--Swivelier Co., Inc., Nanuet, NY, pg. 1068
Phillip, Jim, V.P.-Mfg. & Opers.--Desa International, Inc., Bowling Green, KY, pg. 331
Phillipi, J., V.P.-Mfg.--R.A. Industries, Inc., Lansdale, PA, pg. 906
Phillips, T. A., V.P.-Engrng.--Dynamic Controls Corp., South Windsor, CT, pg. 356
Piazza, Frank J., V.P.-Mfg.--Octagon Process Inc., Edgewater, NJ, pg. 821
Picata, Charles, Mgr.-Production--Pace Press, Inc., New York, NY, pg. 838
Piec, C.J., V.P.-Mfg.--Duraco Products, Inc., Streamwood, IL, pg. 354
Piecuch, Andrew J., Mgr.-Prod.--Hazen Paper Company, Holyoke, MA, pg. 520
Pierce, Fred J., V.P.-Refining--National Cooperative Refinery Association, McPherson, KS, pg. 787
Pierce, Kenny J., Sr. V.P.-Mfg.--Seminole Manufacturing Company, Columbus, MS, pg. 989
Pietrafesa, Joseph J., II, Dir.-Mfg.--Jos. J. Pietrafesa Co., Inc., Liverpool, NY, pg. 870
Pilcher, J., V.P.-Mfg.--Mosler Inc., Hamilton, OH, pg. 772
Pilot, Grover, V.P.-Engrng.--Anchor Continental Incorporated, Columbia, SC, pg. 71
Pipkin, Luther N., Jr., V.P.-Appliance & Electronics--W.S. Badcock Corporation, Mulberry, FL, pg. 113
Pipkin, Wayne M., Mgr.-Matls.--Superior Machine Company Of South Carolina, Inc., Florence, SC, pg. 1064
Plagens, Sig G., Brewmaster & Plant Mgr.--Minnesota Brewing Company, Saint Paul, MN, pg. 757
Pletcher, Timothy, V.P.-Mfg.--Greenfield Industries Inc., Evans, GA, pg. 507
Plunkett, C. L., Dir.-Engrng. Opers.--CAE Link Allen Division, Alexandria, VA, pg. 198
Podgurski, Chuck, Mgr.-Prod.--Symons Corporation, Des Plaines, IL, pg. 1069
Polhmann, Edgar, Mfg. Dir.--Ceras Johnson Ltda., Rio de Janeiro,, Brazil, pg. 599
Policky, Leslie, Dir.-Production Control--Foote & Davies Inc., Atlanta, GA, pg. 423
Pollansky, Emil, Dir.-Mfg. & Engrng.--Cortland Line Co., Inc., Cortland, NY, pg. 287
Polliam, Tony, V.P.-Engrng.--Cissell Manufacturing Company, Louisville, KY, pg. 357
Pollono, John, Chief Engr.--Nylon Corporation Of America, Manchester, NH, pg. 818
Polzin, James J., V.P.-Mfg.--Monarch Ware, Inc., Algoma, WI, pg. 742
Pombo, Eliseo, V.P.-Mfg.--Prime Tanning Co., Inc., Berwick, ME, pg. 889
Poradek, Frank, Mgr.-Mfg. & Plant Mgr.--R.S. Owens, Chicago, IL, pg. 834
Poremba, Charles A., V.P.-Mfg.--American Tool Companies, Inc., Lincoln, NE, pg. 64
Poskie, James, V.P.-Mfg.--Badger Northland Inc., Kaukauna, WI, pg. 113
Post, Terry, Mgr.-Mfg.--Hubbard Hall Inc., Waterbury, CT, pg. 549
Potts, John, Mfg. Mgr. & Pur. Dir.--World Dryer Corp., Berkeley, IL, pg. 1027
Powell, Andrew J., Sr. V.P.-Mfg. & Mfg. Services--The Berkline Corporation, Morristown, TN, pg. 285
Powell, David, Grp. V.P.-Mfg.--Solvay Pharmaceuticals, Inc., Marietta, GA, pg. 1017
Powell, Joe J., Jr., V.P.-Tech. Services--Mississippi Valley Gas Co., Jackson, MS, pg. 1208
Powell, Larry, V.P.-Mfg.--Candle Corporation of America, Oshkosh, WI, pg. 214
Power, Henry, Mgr.-Mfg.--C. W. Zumbiel Company, Cincinnati, OH, pg. 1221
Powers, John, Mgr.-Mfg.--MFE Instruments, Beverly, MA, pg. 1050
Powers, Steven, V.P.-Engrng.--O. S. Walker Co. Inc., Worcester, MA, pg. 1160
Powers, Tom, V.P.-Fleet--United States Bakery, Portland, OR, pg. 1134
Prehn, Hans, V.P.-Mfg.--Fred Usinger, Inc., Milwaukee, WI, pg. 1140
Prellwitz, Lee A., Dir.-Mfg.--Ripon Foods, Inc., Ripon, WI, pg. 935
Prewitt, Verlon, V.P.-Mfg.--Carhartt, Inc., Dearborn, MI, pg. 220
Price, Joseph, V.P.-Mfg. & Sec.--Dettra Flag Company, Oaks, PA, pg. 333
Price, R., V.P.-Rubber Chemicals & Mineral Grp.--R. T. Vanderbilt Company, Inc., Norwalk, CT, pg. 1144
Price, Stephen, V.P.-Engrng.--Hayden, Inc., Corona, CA, pg. 385
Prince, Thomas F., V.P.-Engrng.--Ark-Les Corporation, Watertown, MA, pg. 82
Prior, Kenneth, V.P.-Mfg.--Ervin Industries, Inc., Ann Arbor, MI, pg. 387
Prischak, Dennis J., V.P.-Engrng.--Plastek Group, Erie, PA, pg. 874
Protheroe, Alwyn, Chief Engineer--Cowin & Company, Inc., Birmingham, AL, pg. 291
Pruitt, Fred, V.P.-Mfg.--Advance Business Graphics, Mira Loma, CA, pg. 18
Pugel, Joe, V.P.-Mfg.--The Vernon Company, Newton, IA, pg. 1148
Pugh, Chris, V.P.-Mfg.--Spangler, Inc., Kansas City, KS, pg. 1025
Quadracci, Thomas A., V.P.-Mfg.--Quad/Graphics, Inc., Pewaukee, WI, pg. 902
Qualigari, Fred, Mgr.-Production--Nexus Plastics, Inc., Hawthorne, NJ, pg. 805
Quigley, Richard M., V.P.-Mfg.--Cogsdill Tool Products, Inc., Lugoff, SC, pg. 259
Rackard, T., Dir.-Prod. Planning & Devel.--Binning's Building Products, Inc., Lexington, NC, pg. 151
Rackow, Martin, Maintenance Engr.--Andes Candies, Inc., Delavan, WI, pg. 169
Radcliffe, Kenneth, V.P.-Aerosol Mfg.--Precision Valve Corporation, Yonkers, NY, pg. 885
Radivaj, Kostika, V.P.-Mfg.--Great Lakes Lithograph Co., Cleveland, OH, pg. 481
Raezler, Don, V.P.-Opers.--McCain Citrus Inc., Chicago, IL, pg. 726
Ragland, Bob, V.P.-Mfg.--Zoeller Co., Louisville, KY, pg. 1220
Ragogna, Don, V.P.-Mfg.--General Time Corp., Norcross, GA, pg. 451
Rahn, Bill, V.P.-Engrng.--Reading Body Works, Inc., Reading, PA, pg. 916
Ramsey, P., V.P.-Engrng.--Royle Systems Group, Pompton Lakes, NJ, pg. 953
Randall, Richard C., V.P.-Engrng. Services--Saunders Brothers, Westbrook, ME, pg. 972
Ranson, Dan L., V.P.-Mfg.--Clayton Corporation, Fenton, MO, pg. 253
Rasmussen, N.W., V.P.-Mfg.--Farm Stores, Inc., Miami, FL, pg. 401
Ream, Michael D., V.P.-Engrng.--Up-Right, Inc., Selma, CA, pg. 1139
Reardon, Hugh, V.P.-Quality Assurance--Marathon Electric Manufacturing Corp., Wausau, WI, pg. 705
Recker, Clair, V.P.-Mfg.--Renaissance Publishing Co., Inc., Auburn, IN, pg. 926
Redding, R.C., V.P.-Design--York Wallcoverings Inc., York, PA, pg. 1208
Reddy, Govi C., Sr. V.P. & Pres.-Film Prod. Div.--Lane Film Products Division, Addison, IL, pg. 657
Reenan, Thomas, Mgr.-Mfg.--Ficks Reed Company, Cincinnati, OH, pg. 408
Reese, Donald E., Sr. V.P.-Mfg.--ACF Industries, Inc., Earth City, MO, pg. 561
Reid, John C., Mgr.-Tech. Services--Cashco, Inc., Ellsworth, KS, pg. 228
Reilly, P., V.P.-Mfg.--Conley Frog & Switch Company, Memphis, TN, pg. 274
Reister, Mike, V.P.-Mfg.--Alloy Products Corporation, Waukesha, WI, pg. 41
Reitler, Russell W., Mgr.-Mfg.--Lancaster Malleable Castings Company, Lancaster, PA, pg. 653
Remec, Andrej A.B., Mgr.-Opers.--Vance Industries, Inc., Chicago, IL, pg. 1144
Remington, H.J., Sr. V.P.-Mfg.--Comstock Michigan Fruit, Rochester, NY, pg. 25
Remus, Ken, Mgr.-Prod.--Symons Corporation, Des Plaines, IL, pg. 1069
Rendleman, R. Terrence, V.P.-Tech. Opers.--NWA, Inc., Saint Paul, MN, pg. 782
Rendleman, Terrence, Sr. V.P.-Technical Opers.--Northwest Airlines, Inc., Saint Paul, MN, pg. 782

Corporate Responsibilities Index

Renken, Fred, Plant Mgr.--Renken Boat Manufacturing Co., Charleston, SC, pg. 927
Revell, Ronald F., Dir.-Mdsg.--White Hen Pantry, Inc., Elmhurst, IL, pg. 1185
Reynolds, Owen P., Dir.-Engrng.--H.O. Trerice Company, Oak Park, MI, pg. 1110
Reynolds, R. Vincent, Dir.-Prod.--Times-World Corporation, Roanoke, VA, pg. 656
Reynolds, Robert L., V.P.-Mfg.--Standard-Knapp, Inc., Portland, CT, pg. 1036
Rice, Les, Mgr.-Production--Hamilton Co., Inc., Reno, NV, pg. 503
Richardson, Al, Dir.-Mfg.--Dwyer Instruments Inc., Michigan City, IN, pg. 356
Riddett, Kevin E., V.P.-Mfg.--Union Switch & Signal Inc., Pittsburgh, PA, pg. 1129
Riegsecker, Richard, V.P.-Mfg.--Sauder Woodworking Co., Archbold, OH, pg. 972
Riemer, W. John, Sr. V.P.-Engrng.--Replogle Globes, Inc., Broadview, IL, pg. 927
Rigas, Augustas C., V.P.-Construction--The Cafaro Co., Youngstown, OH, pg. 207
Riley, H.P., Exec. V.P.-Production Opers.--Quintana Petroleum Corp., Houston, TX, pg. 905
Rinehart, William, V.P.-Mfg.--Data Documents, Inc., Omaha, NE, pg. 316
Rink, James A., V.P.-Sls. & Engrng.--Prestige Stamping, Inc., Warren, MI, pg. 888
Riordan, Tom, V.P.-Mfg.--Ivex Packaging Corporation, Lincolnshire, IL, pg. 583
Risimini, Ralph, V.P.-Mfg.--United Farm Tools, Inc., Glasgow, KY, pg. 1131
Roane, Kenneth I., V.P.-Supply & Transportation--National Cooperative Refinery Association, McPherson, KS, pg. 787
Roark, Dennis, Exec. V.P.-Engrng.--Power-One, Inc., Camarillo, CA, pg. 883
Robason, Jim, V.P.-Production--Allen Canning Company, Siloam Springs, AR, pg. 35
Roberts, Edmund, V.P.-Mfg.--Faber/Castell Corporation, Parsippany, NJ, pg. 395
Roberts, Johnny, Dir.-Engrng.--Esco Elevators, Inc., Fort Worth, TX, pg. 388
Roberts, Lesa, Production Coord.--WordPerfect Corporation, Orem, UT, pg. 1202
Roberts, P., V.P.-Mfg.--Gemtron Corporation, Sweetwater, TN, pg. 3
Robertson, Frank, V.P.-Engrng.--Greenwood Mills, Inc., Greenwood, SC, pg. 485
Robertson, James, V.P.-Mfg. & Dir.-Personnel--Bregg Data Forms, Inc., Hauppauge, NY, pg. 173
Robinson, Andy, V.P.-Mfg.--Tom's Snax Co., Columbus, GA, pg. 1101
Robinson, J., Mgr.-Mfg.--Quality Bakers of America Cooperative, Inc., Greenwich, CT, pg. 903
Robinson, Terry, V.P.-Engrng.--Production Machinery Corporation, Mentor, OH, pg. 893
Rodgers, Joyn, Mgr.-Engrng.--Nodak Electric Co-op, Grand Forks, ND, pg. 808
Rodich, Michael E., V.P.-Mfg.--Stevens-Lee Company, Minneapolis, MN, pg. 1048
Rodman, Jerry, Sr. V.P.-Mfg.--Maidenform, Inc., New York, NY, pg. 701
Rokop, Nik, V.P.-Engrng.--Rokop Corporation, Bridgeville, PA, pg. 944
Rokowski, Al, Chief Engr.--Eagle Button Co., Inc., Carlstadt, NJ, pg. 362
Roland, Roni, Mgr.-Production--Bregg Data Forms, Inc., Hauppauge, NY, pg. 173
Romero, Alvaro, V.P.-Mfg.--Conway Import Co. Inc., Franklin Park, IL, pg. 281
Rosa, Bruno, V.P.-Engrng. & Pur.--AP Parts Manufacturing Company, Toledo, OH, pg. 240
Rosales, Nancy, V.P.-Mfg.--Bollinger Health Care, Lubbock, TX, pg. 163
Rosenblatt, Saul, V.P.-Engrng.--Weksler Instruments Corp., Freeport, NY, pg. 1174
Roser, Russ, V.P.-Mfg.--Reading Body Works, Inc., Reading, PA, pg. 916
Rotando, Lou, Mfg. Mgr.--Market Forge Company, Everett, MA, pg. 1027
Rottenberg, J., V.P.-Mfg.--Isfel Company, Inc., Rahway, NJ, pg. 582
Rubin, Eric, V.P.-Mfg.--M. Rubin & Sons Inc., New York, NY, pg. 954
Ruff, Jim, Dir.-Engrng.--Radix Corporation, Salt Lake City, UT, pg. 909
Rugg, Dave, V.P.-Opers.--Blue Bird Coach Lines Inc., Olean, NY, pg. 158
Rugotzke, Tom, Sr. V.P. & Dir.-Mfg.--Bush Brothers & Company, Dandridge, TN, pg. 196
Ruiz, G., Dir. Mfr.--Gator Industries Inc., Hialeah, FL, pg. 446
Rushinsky, Michael J., V.P.-Mfg.--Small Parts, Inc., Logansport, IN, pg. 1010
Russell, Dick, V.P.-Mfg.--Peterson Builders, Inc., Sturgeon Bay, WI, pg. 864
Russell, Michael, Dir.-Mfg.--Henri's Food Products Co., Inc., Milwaukee, WI, pg. 530
Russey, Keith, Dir.-Mfg.--Mooney Aircraft Corporation, Kerrville, TX, pg. 768
Russo, Domenic, V.P.-Opers.--F. H. Chase, Inc., Foxboro, MA, pg. 240
Rust, Don, Mgr.-Mfg.--Broadcast Electronics, Inc., Quincy, IL, pg. 177
Ruth, Gary R., Dir.-Prod.--American Bible Society, New York, NY, pg. 49
Ruthenburg, Peter, V.P.-Opers.--Red Spot Paint & Varnish Co., Evansville, IN, pg. 918
Ruzicka, Jerry, V.P.-Mfg.--Starkey Laboratories, Inc., Eden Prairie, MN, pg. 1040
Ryan, Brigid, Mgr.-Mfg. & Pur.--American Technical Publishers, Inc., Homewood, IL, pg. 63
Rychlinski, Victor Z., Dir.-Engrng.--Brad Foote Gear Works, Inc., Cicero, IL, pg. 169
Saad, Natan, V.P.-Mfg.--Telesensory, Mountain View, CA, pg. 1085
Sabatini, Joseph, Dir.-Mfg. Services--Crown Textile Company, Blue Bell, PA, pg. 302
Sack, Marcus, Chief Engineer--Burgess Pigment Co., Sandersville, GA, pg. 190
Safran, F.S., V.P.-Engrg.--The Rotor Tool Company, Cleveland, OH, pg. 951
Salcedo, Ubaldo, V.P.-Mfg.--Krause's Sofa Factory, Inc., Brea, CA, pg. 644
Salucci, Anthony, V.P.-Mfg.--Hughes-Treitler Manufacturing Corporation, Garden City, NY, pg. 552
Salum, Joe, Dir.-Opers.--Clifford Metal, Providence, RI, pg. 658
Samant, Suresh, V.P.-Mfg.--American Saw & Manufacturing Co., East Longmeadow, MA, pg. 60
Sampson, Charles E., V.P.-Technical Services--American Systems Corporation, Chantilly, VA, pg. 63
Samuels, Howard, V.P.-Production--Uniflex, Inc., Hicksville, NY, pg. 1126
Sandoval, Sandy, V.P.-Mining & Processing--J.R. Simplot Co., Minerals & Chemicals Group, Pocatello, ID, pg. 1007
Santos, Kenneth, Exec. V.P.-Mfg.--Arley Merchandise Corporation, Taunton, MA, pg. 83
Sanz, Robert, V.P.-Supply & Distr.--Wickland Corporation, Sacramento, CA, pg. 1188
Sarrail, H.B., V.P.-Production--McConnell Cabinets, Inc., El Monte, CA, pg. 727
Sarubbi, Tony, V.P.-Mfg.--Panorama Press, Inc., Clifton, NJ, pg. 846
Sarver, Dick, Mgr.-Mfg.--T. L. Smith Machine, Springville, NY, pg. 1013
Sarver, Terry, V.P.-Mfg.--Bawden Printing, Inc., Eldridge, IA, pg. 127
Satienza, Anthony, V.P.-Opers.--Greeco Brothers, Inc., Lawrence, MA, pg. 483
Saucier, David, V.P.-Engrng.--D.C.I., Inc., Saint Cloud, MN, pg. 308
Saul, Robin, V.P. & Prod. Dir.--The Virginian-Pilot and The Ledger Star, Norfolk, VA, pg. 656
Saving, Frank, Chief Engineer--Airguard Industries Inc., Louisville, KY, pg. 27
Savoie, R., V.P.-Engrng.--Telesensory, Mountain View, CA, pg. 1085
Saxton, Edward B., V.P.-Mfg.--Industrial Acoustics Company S.C. Inc., Moncks Corner, SC, pg. 566
Sayers, T., V.P.-Mfg. Opers.--PTC Aerospace, Inc., Litchfield, CT, pg. 837
Scatoloni, Mark, Mgr.-Engrng.--Faber Enterprises, Inc., Canoga Park, CA, pg. 395
Schaefer, John, V.P.-Mfg.--Heller Seasonings & Ingredients, Inc., Bedford Park, IL, pg. 526
Schafer, Alan, V.P.-Mfg. & Distr.--Financial World Partners, New York, NY, pg. 410
Schafer, Alan, Mgr.-Mfg.--Financial World Partners, New York, NY, pg. 410
Schalk, Steve, V.P.-Engrng.--Miniature Precision Components, Walworth, WI, pg. 757
Schaller, Gus, Chief Engr.--Presto Lock, Inc., Garfield, NJ, pg. 888
Schelich, A.J., V.P.-Mfg.--Sporlan Valve Company, Saint Louis, MO, pg. 1032
Schenk, Eric S., V.P.-Upholstery Opers.--Century Furniture Industries, Hickory, NC, pg. 235
Schiewe, Dr. Arthur J., Grp. V.P.-Engrng. & Tech.--The Aerospace Corporation, El Segundo, CA, pg. 22
Schilling, Glen, Dir.-Mfg.--Wausau Homes, Inc., Rothschild, WI, pg. 1168
Schilling, William, V.P.-Mfg.--Rea Magnet Wire Company, Inc., Fort Wayne, IN, pg. 915
Schippert, Manfred A., Sr. V.P.-Engrng.--Amray, Inc., Bedford, MA, pg. 68
Schlaegel, Dan, Dir.-Engrng.--Steel, Inc., Commerce City, CO, pg. 1044
Schmehl, Rodney P., Mgr.-Plant--Parisi, Inc., Philadelphia, PA, pg. 848
Schmelzer, Jim, V.P.-Materials & Specialty Products--Globe Glass & Mirror Co., Chicago, IL, pg. 463
Schmertzler, Rick, Mgr.-Mfg.--The Gilman Company, Chattanooga, TN, pg. 603
Schmidt, Harvey W., V.P.-Mfg.--MI-Jack Products, Inc., Hazel Crest, IL, pg. 746
Schmidt, Robert, V.P.-Engrng.--Rogers Group Inc., Nashville, TN, pg. 943
Schmitt, Jack, Chief Engineer--C. W. Zumbiel Company, Cincinnati, OH, pg. 1221
Schmitt, Jerry, Mgr.-Mfg. & Quality Assurance--Newage Industries Inc., Plastics Division, Willow Grove, PA, pg. 803
Schneider, Barry, V.P.-Mfg.--Pressman Toy Corp., New York, NY, pg. 887
Schonbach, Bernard H., V.P.-Engrng.--Pennsylvania Crusher Corp., Broomall, PA, pg. 858
Schoonderwoerd, Jake, V.P.-Mfg.--Plastic Packaging, Inc., Hickory, NC, pg. 875
Schott, Greg, Mgr.-Production--Perry & Derrick Co., Cincinnati, OH, pg. 863
Schott, Michael, V.P.-Production--Schott Brothers, Inc., Perth Amboy, NJ, pg. 978
Schottelkotte, W.F., V.P.-Engrng.--Dupps Company, Germantown, OH, pg. 354
Schrad, Dale, V.P.-Mfg.--Brammer Manufacturing Company, Davenport, IA, pg. 171
Schramm, Jerry, V.P.-Stores--Brauns Fashions, Inc., Minneapolis, MN, pg. 172
Schramm, John, Chief Engr.--Gerrard and Company, Des Plaines, IL, pg. 454
Schreiber, Gallo, Dir.-Mfg.--Poly Pak America, Inc., Los Angeles, CA, pg. 880
Schreiner, Klaus, V.P.-Mfg.--Milton Shoe Manufacturing Company, Inc., Milton, PA, pg. 756
Schrock, David, Plant Engineer--Sauder Manufacturing Corporation, Archbold, OH, pg. 972
Schroeder, Robert, V.P.-Production--Cincinnati Sub-Zero Products, Inc., Cincinnati, OH, pg. 250
Schurter, Gary, V.P.-Engrng.--Marathon Electric Manufacturing Corp., Wausau, WI, pg. 705
Schwartzkopf, Roy, V.P.-Mfg.--Cosco, Inc., Columbus, IN, pg. 287
Schwarz, Steven, V.P.-Mfg. & New Products--Alleson of Rochester, Inc., Rochester, NY, pg. 37
Schweibinz, Joanne, Mgr.-Mfg.--Peerless Lighting Corp., Berkeley, CA, pg. 855
Schweitzer, E.F., V.P.-Engrng.--Bucyrus-Erie Company, South Milwaukee, WI, pg. 186
Schweizer, Leslie, V.P.-Engrng.--Schweizer Aircraft Corporation, Elmira, NY, pg. 981
Schwelm, Frederick, V.P.-Mfg.--BIW Cable Systems, Inc., North Dighton, MA, pg. 106
Schwer, Walter, Dir.-Engrng.--Ortronics, Inc., Pawcatuck, CT, pg. 830
Schwonke, Paul A., V.P. & Gen. Mgr.--Burrows Paper Corporation, Little Falls, NY, pg. 195
Scopes, Timothy, V.P.-Mfg.--Salz Leathers, Inc., Santa Cruz, CA, pg. 968
Scott, Gary L., Mgr.-Prod. Scheduling--Rundel Products, Inc., Portland, OR, pg. 956
Sculati, Mary, V.P.-Mfg.--Servus Footwear Company, Rock Island, IL, pg. 993
Seabeck, Scott, Production Mgr.--Ken-Mac Metal, Inc., Cleveland, OH, pg. 622
Seabrook, William E., V.P.-Engrng.--Seabrook Brothers & Sons, Inc., Seabrook, NJ, pg. 984
Seaman, Mike, Mgr.-Plant--Modern Concrete Septic Tank Company, Ottsville, PA, pg. 762
Searles, David, Dir.-Mfg.--Pace International Corporation, Kirkland, WA, pg. 838
Sears, Donald K., Exec. V.P.-Opers. & Sls.--Mayflower Transit, Inc., Carmel, IN, pg. 724
Sears, Kay, Chief Engineer--Entron Industries Limited Partnership, Glendale, NY, pg. 383
Sedlacek, James E., V.P.-Mfg.--Lozier Corporation, Omaha, NE, pg. 686
Seery, Christina, Dir.-Mfg. & Pur.--Imprint Products, L.P., Rockville Centre, NY, pg. 564
Sellers, Danny C., V.P.-Mfg. Support--Bender Shipbuilding & Repair Company, Mobile, AL, pg. 138
Semke, Richard T., Plant Supvr.--Microflect Company, Inc., Salem, OR, pg. 749
Semon, William, V.P.-Mfg.--Casket Shells, Inc., Eynon, PA, pg. 228
Sentivany, David, Mgr.-Engrng.--ATAPCO Office Products Group, Saint Louis, MO, pg. 64
Sernay, John C., V.P.-Engrng.--Swift-Cor Tool Engineering, Gardena, CA, pg. 1067
Shabla, George, Mfg. Supt.--Morris Coupling Co., Erie, PA, pg. 771
Shaffer, Dale, V.P.-Mfg.--Harmeson Manufacturing Company, Inc., Frankfort, IN, pg. 510
Shaffer, M. Todd, Dir.-Pur. & Mfg. Services--Tru-Weld Grating, Inc., Wexford, PA, pg. 1117
Shane, Ken, Dir.-Opers.--Brutger Equities, Inc., Saint Cloud, MN, pg. 185
Sharp, Bob, V.P.-Textiles--The Coleman Company, Inc., Wichita, KS, pg. 695
Shauf, Jack E., V.P.-Mfg.--The Rotor Tool Company, Cleveland, OH, pg. 951
Shaw, James W., Dir.-Corp. Mfg.--Country Home Bakery, Inc., Bridgeport, CT, pg. 290
Shaw, Kenneth C., V.P.-Engrng.--Black Box Corporation, Lawrence, PA, pg. 748
Shearer, Gerald, V.P.-Engrng.--The Fusco Corporation, New Haven, CT, pg. 437
Sheldon, John, Corp. Mfg.--Len Ron Mfg. Co. Inc., Melville, NY, pg. 389
Shepherd, Steve C., Dir-Mfg.--Aetna Bearing Company, Chicago, IL, pg. 23
Sheppard, Charles R., V.P.-Mfg.--North American Salt Company, Overland Park, KS, pg. 812
Sherman, John, Mgr.-Mfg.--Jones Dairy Farm, Fort Atkinson, WI, pg. 603
Shiels, Walter, V.P.-Mfg.--Arkay Packaging Corporation, Hauppauge, NY, pg. 83
Shiffer, Bruce, Mgr.-Prod.--Cashco, Inc., Ellsworth, KS, pg. 228
Shocker, Richard, V.P.-Mfg.--SpeedFam Corporation, Des Plaines, IL, pg. 398
Shook, Michael D., Sr. V.P.-Mfg. & Engrng.--Riceland Foods, Inc., Stuttgart, AR, pg. 931
Shuld, Cliff, V.P.-Mfg.--Miniature Precision Components, Walworth, WI, pg. 757
Shulick, Robert, V.P.-Opers.--Arrow Pneumatics Co. Inc., Lake Zurich, IL, pg. 85
Sickman, Jack D., V.P.-Mfg.--Swayne Robinson & Company, Richmond, IN, pg. 939
Sidell, Hans G., V.P.-Mfg.--Davis Walker Corp., Irwindale, CA, pg. 525
Siegel, Alvan, Sr. V.P.-Production--Murry's, Inc., Forestville, MD, pg. 777
Sielzkowski, Bruce, V.P.-Opers.--CasChem Inc., Bayonne, NJ, pg. 227
Sikes, William, V.P.-Production--Baker Commodities, Inc., Los Angeles, CA, pg. 115
Silver, Allan, V.P.-Mfg.--Triangle Pacific Corporation, Dallas, TX, pg. 1112
Simitoski, Paul, Mfg. Dir.--Barcolene Penn Champ, East Butler, PA, pg. 153
Simmons, Ron, V.P.-Mfg.--DVC Industries, Bay Shore, NY, pg. 310
Simon, LeRoy, V.P.-Mfg.--The Spring Air Company, Des Plaines, IL, pg. 1032
Simpson, Lee, V.P.- Mfg. & Opers.--Capitol Industries-EMI Inc., Hollywood, CA, pg. 216
Sims, Oney, V.P.-Mfg.--I. Rokeach & Sons, Inc., Paramus, NJ, pg. 944

Singh, Paramjit, V.P.-Engrng.--Dixon Valve & Coupling Company, Chestertown, MD, pg. 341
Sinka, George, V.P.-Mfg.--Sleepeck Printing Company, Bellwood, IL, pg. 1010
Skryness, Jack, Dir.-Contract Admin.--Advanced Circuit Technology, Nashua, NH, pg. 20
Slade, Tom, V.P.-Mfg.--Larkin, Inc., Atlanta, GA, pg. 667
Slade, Tom, V.P.-Mfg.--Heatcraft, Inc., Stone Mountain, GA, pg. 667
Slagel, Gerald L., V.P.-Engrng.--Stanco Metal Products, Inc., Grand Haven, MI, pg. 1035
Slagel, Steve, V.P.-Engrng.--Carpenter Manufacturing, Inc., Mitchell, IN, pg. 991
Slat, William, V.P.-Opers. & Mfg. Dir.--Plastipak Packaging Inc., Plymouth, MI, pg. 876
Slate, Burton, V.P.-Mfg.--Spencer's Inc., Mount Airy, NC, pg. 1030
Slater, Jerry, V.P.-Mfg.--Carter Day Industries, Inc., Minneapolis, MN, pg. 226
Slaybaugh, L., V.P.-Engrng.--Republic Industries, Inc., Harwood Heights, IL, pg. 928
Sloan, Dave, Dir.-Engrng.-Frozen Mix Plants--Continental Mills, Inc., Tukwila, WA, pg. 279
Sloane, George, Dir.-Tech.--Halsey Drug Co., Inc., Brooklyn, NY, pg. 502
Slocum, John D., Exec. V.P.-Admin. & Mfg.--Beverage Canners International Corp., Miami, FL, pg. 148
Slusher, Ronald J., Dir.-Facilities--Advanced Technology, Inc., Reston, VA, pg. 20
Smeader, William, Mgr.-Mfg.--Metrologic Instruments, Inc., Blackwood, NJ, pg. 743
Smith, A.R., V.P.-Mfg.--The Canadian Coleman Co., Ltd., Toronto,, Canada, pg. 695
Smith, Cindell, Dir.-Mfg.--Standard Gravure d/b/a Oklahoma Graphics, Oklahoma City, OK, pg. 1036
Smith, Dwight, V.P.-Matls. Mngmt.--Schnadig Corporation, Chicago, IL, pg. 977
Smith, John, V.P.-Mfg. Devel.--Fellowes Manufacturing Co., Itasca, IL, pg. 405
Smith, Ken J., Dir.-Engrng.--Metalloy Corporation, Hudson, MI, pg. 742
Smith, R.A., V.P.-Mfg.--Raynor Garage Door Company, Dixon, IL, pg. 915
Smith, Richard, V.P.-Engrng.--Litecontrol Corporation, Hanson, MA, pg. 677
Smith, Ruble, Dir.-Engrng.--Lay Packing Company Inc., Knoxville, TN, pg. 663
Smith, Russ, V.P.-Mfg.--Micro Component Technology Inc., Saint Paul, MN, pg. 748
Smith, Stan, V.P.-Mfg.--Mustang Manufacturing Company, Inc., Owatonna, MN, pg. 777
Smith, Steve, Dir.-Engrng.--Modern Wood Products, Inc., Chino, CA, pg. 291
Smith, Susan, V.P.-Mfg.--Solar Press, Inc., Naperville, IL, pg. 1016
Smith, Thomas M., V.P.-Valve Mfg.--Nibco, Inc., Elkhart, IN, pg. 806
Smith, Tom, Chief Engineer--Franklin Baking Co., Inc., Goldsboro, NC, pg. 429
Smolen, S. Robert, V.P.-Mfg.--Marotta Scientific Controls, Inc., Montville, NJ, pg. 713
Smythe, Phil, V.P.-Mfg.--Lithograph Printing Company, Inc., Memphis, TN, pg. 678
Snow, George K., Jr., V.P.-Case-Good Opers.--Century Furniture Industries, Hickory, NC, pg. 235
Snow, R., V.P.-Mfg.--Ideal Industries, Inc., Sycamore, IL, pg. 562
Snyder, Robert, V.P.-Mfg. & Engrng.--American Manufacturing Co. (TN), Chattanooga, TN, pg. 58
Soddors, Mark, Mgr.-Mfg.. Sls.--Cheney Company, New Berlin, WI, pg. 242
Somers, Gary, V.P.-Mfg.--Howell Laboratories, Inc., Bridgton, ME, pg. 548
Sommers, William, Dir.-Technical Services--Just Born, Inc., Bethlehem, PA, pg. 610
Sordo, Art, V.P.-Mfg.--Mitek, Inc., Chesterfield, MO, pg. 762
Sorenson, Mary, Mgr.- Production--Master Appliance Corp., Racine, WI, pg. 719
Sotok, Fred, V.P.-Mfg.--Prince Corporation, Holland, MI, pg. 890
Sowers, Kent, Mgr.-Production--Time Systems, Inc., Phoenix, AZ, pg. 1097
Spadafora, Loretta, Dir.-Mfg.--Electro-Science Laboratories, Inc., King of Prussia, PA, pg. 375
Spears, Ronald, V.P.-Mfg.--C-Line Products, Inc., Des Plaines, IL, pg. 198
Speice, B.D., V.P.-Opers.--Baltimore Aircoil Company, Jessup, MD, pg. 69
Spencer, Jack, Gen. Mgr.-Mfg.--Bliss-Salem, Inc., Salem, OH, pg. 156
Spencer, Pete, Dir.-Mfg.--Ranging, East Bloomfield, NY, pg. 300
Spinoso, Jose, Mgr.-Prod.--Cora Texas Manufacturing Co., White Castle, LA, pg. 285
Spitz, Joseph, Dir.-Engrng. & Mfg.--Lavelle Aircraft Company, Philadelphia, PA, pg. 661
Spotts, Jack, Mgr.-Production--Sauder Manufacturing Corporation, Archbold, OH, pg. 972
Spraggins, T. Wayne, V.P.-Mfg. Services--Avondale Mills, Inc., Sylacauga, AL, pg. 103
Stadtmiller, Martin B., V.P.-Mfg.--Edwards Brothers, Inc., Ann Arbor, MI, pg. 369
Stahl, Chester W., V.P.-Tech.--Yenkin-Majestic Paint Corporation, Columbus, OH, pg. 1208
Stalnaker, Larry, V.P.-Mfg. & Engrng.--Canton Drop Forge, Canton, OH, pg. 214
Stanford, Bruce, Chief Engr.--M.C. Gill Corporation, El Monte, CA, pg. 458
Staniec, Ted, V.P.-Mfg.--Synchro-Start Products, Inc., Niles, IL, pg. 638
Stansfield, Robert, Mgr.-Materials--Penobscot Frozen Foods, Inc., Belfast, ME, pg. 858
Stark, Gary, V.P.-Prod. Support--Hawthorne Lift Systems, Escondido, CA, pg. 519
Steinmann, Russ, V.P.-Mfg.--Minor Rubber Co., Inc., Bloomfield, NJ, pg. 758
Stephen, James, V.P.-Mfg.--Weber-Stephen Products, Palatine, IL, pg. 1171
Steven, J., V.P.-Engrng.--Recon/Optical, Inc., Barrington, IL, pg. 917
Stewart, Bill, V.P.-Mfg.--Triple S Technologies, Inc., Vicksburg, MI, pg. 1114
Stewart, Dennis, Chief Engr.--Phototype Color Graphics, Inc., Pennsauken, NJ, pg. 869
Stewart, K.R., Plant Mgr.--Amspec Chemical Corporation, Gloucester City, NJ, pg. 5
Stewart, William, V.P.-Mfg.--Conso Products Company, Union, SC, pg. 276
Stickels, Charles, V.P.-Mfg.--Print-O-Tape, Mundelein, IL, pg. 891
Stillabower, Merrill, Mgr.-Mfg.--KCL Corporation, Shelbyville, IN, pg. 611
Stockham, George, Dir.-Mfg. & Quality Control--Macklanburg-Duncan Co., Oklahoma City, OK, pg. 697
Stocks, J.M., V.P.-Mfg.--Peco Inc., Portland, OR, pg. 854
Stolzer, E., V.P.-Mfg.--Quality Bakers of America Cooperative, Inc., Greenwich, CT, pg. 903
Stone, Michael, Mgr.-Engrng.--MD Pneumatics, Inc., Springfield, MO, pg. 1120
Story, Robert W., Sr. V.P.-Field Operations--CUNA Mutual Insurance Society, Madison, WI, pg. 205
Stote, Fred, Mgr.-Mfg.--Thermo Electric Co., Inc., Saddle Brook, NJ, pg. 1091
Stoutenberg, Bob, V.P.-Mfg.--Progressive Tool & Industries Co., Southfield, MI, pg. 894
Strain, Lee, V.P.-Mfg.--Culligan International Company, Northbrook, IL, pg. 358
Street, Joe, Mgr.-Mfg.--The Vernon Company, Newton, IA, pg. 1148
Strode, Jim, V.P.-Mfg.--Scotsman Group, Inc., Long Beach, CA, pg. 982
Stroebel, Richard H., V.P.-Mfg.--U.S. Graphite, Inc., Saginaw, MI, pg. 1136
Struffer, Wally, V.P.-Produce--Shurfine-Central Corp., Northlake, IL, pg. 1001
Strutner, Raymond J., V.P.-Mfg.--Crane Plastics Company, Columbus, OH, pg. 296
Stuckert, J., V.P.-Mfg.--Republic Industries, Inc., Harwood Heights, IL, pg. 928
Studer, Doug, Mgr.-Business Prods.-Seat--National Seating Co., Vonore, TN, pg. 793
Stull, John, V.P.-Mfg.--Malt-O-Meal Company, Minneapolis, MN, pg. 703
Stump, Jeffery J., V.P.-Mfg.--Cowden Metal Specialties, Inc., Chino, CA, pg. 291
Stump, Jennine, Dir.-Mfg.--Electro Dynamics Crystal Corporation, Overland Park, KS, pg. 374
Sturart, Roger, Chief Engr.--Cogifer Inc., Cincinnati, OH, pg. 259
Sty, David, Mgr.-Mfg.--Azteca Foods, Incorporated, Chicago, IL, pg. 105
Suart, Dawn, Chief Exec. Officer--Olson-Travelworld Ltd., Manhattan Beach, CA, pg. 824
Sullivan, Michael T., V.P.-Mfg.--Dunmore Corporation, Newtown, PA, pg. 353
Sutliff, David R., V.P.-Engrng.--ACF Industries, Inc., Earth City, MO, pg. 561
Sutliff, John, Mgr.-Mfg.--Connecticut Container Corporation, North Haven, CT, pg. 274
Sutter, Ronald, Mgr.-Prod.--National R.V., Inc., Perris, CA, pg. 792
Sutton, Michael E., V.P.-Mfg.--North American Products Corp., Jasper, IN, pg. 811
Sutton, Rod, V.P.-Mfg.--Scoville Press, Inc., Minneapolis, MN, pg. 983
Swank, Gary, Sr. V.P.-Opers.--Haggar Apparel Company, Dallas, TX, pg. 499
Swanson, John F., V.P.-Engrng.--Broadcast Division, Atlanta, GA, pg. 292
Sydlowski, F., V.P.-Mfg.--UC Industries, Inc., Parsippany, NJ, pg. 1122
Sydorenko, Paul, Plant Mgr.--Blue Coral, Inc., Cleveland, OH, pg. 159
Sylvester, John E., Sr. V.P.-Opers.--Nutri/System Inc., Blue Bell, PA, pg. 818
Szymaszek, P.G., Exec. V.P.-Engrng.--Vilter Manufacturing Corporation, Milwaukee, WI, pg. 1152
Tait, C. Robert, Jr., V.P.-Mfg.--Tinius Olsen Testing Machine Co., Inc., Willow Grove, PA, pg. 1098
Talbert, J.E., V.P.-Engrng.--Morrison Textile Machinery Co., Fort Lawn, SC, pg. 771
Tandler, Paul, V.P.-Mfg.--Cerro Copper Products Co., Sauget, IL, pg. 711
Tassin, Edward, V.P.-Mfg.--Kores Nordic USA Corp., Summerville, SC, pg. 642
Taub, S.J., Sr. V.P.-Mfg.--MacAndrews & Forbes Co., Camden, NJ, pg. 694
Taylor, D.R., V.P.-Production--Texas Refinery Corp., Fort Worth, TX, pg. 1089
Taylor, Hal, Mgr.-Prod.--Universal Dynamics Inc., Woodbridge, VA, pg. 1138
Taylor, J.L., V.P.-Mfg.--Daubert Coated Products, Inc., Westchester, IL, pg. 317
Taylor, Kathleen, Gen. Mgr.-MtC Remco Tape Products--M & C Specialties Company, Southampton, PA, pg. 690
Taylor, Larry, V.P.-Engrng.--Taylor Corporation, Mankato, MN, pg. 1081
Taylor, Walt, V.P.-Mfg.--Western Extrusions, Carrollton, TX, pg. 1179
Taylor, William W., Chm. Bd., Chief Exec. Officer & Technical Dir.--D. C. Taylor Co., Cedar Rapids, IA, pg. 751
Tegeler, Vernon, V.P.-Prod.--Siemer Milling Company, Teutopolis, IL, pg. 1002
Tekker, Peter, V.P.-Mfg.--Gates Canada Inc., Brantford,, Canada, pg. 445
Temple, T.G., V.P.-Aluminum Opers.--Ormet Corporation, Hannibal, OH, pg. 822
Tenke, Joseph, V.P.-Construction--Century Fence Company, Pewaukee, WI, pg. 235
Ternus, John, V.P.-Mfg.--Industrial Wire Products Corporation, Pomona, CA, pg. 567
Terwilliger, Larry, V.P.-Mfg.--Sintel, Inc., Spring Lake, MI, pg. 1008
Thacker, Bob, V.P.-Engrng.--Flexible Flyer Inc., West Point, MS, pg. 847
Tharaldson, Jim, Chief Engineer--United Farm Tools, Inc., Glasgow, KY, pg. 1131
Tharaldson, Jim, Chief Engineer & IA Plant Mgr.--United Farm Tools, Kentucky Div., Glasgow, KY, pg. 1132
Tharpe, Larry, Mgr.-Special Projects--Heckethorn Mfg. Company, Dyersburg, TN, pg. 524
Theroux, Rob, V.P.-Mfg.--Accra Pac Group, Elkhart, IN, pg. 11
Thomas, David, V.P.-Mfg.--Williams, White & Company, Moline, IL, pg. 1191
Thomas, Michael, Dir.-Production--American Aircraft Parts Manufacturing Co., Dearborn, MI, pg. 48
Thomas, Roger, V.P.-Mfg.--Empire Berol U.S.A., Brentwood, TN, pg. 856
Thompson, Jimmy, V.P.-Greige Mfg.--Greenwood Mills, Inc., Greenwood, SC, pg. 485
Thorn, Ken, Mgr.-Consumer Products Mfg.--MTD Products Limited, Kitchener,, Canada, pg. 694
Thornton, Michael A., V.P.-Prod.--Progress Printing Company, Lynchburg, VA, pg. 894
Threadgill, Ron, V.P.-Mfg.--Hollytex Carpet Mills, Inc., Ontario, CA, pg. 540
Tidwell, Richard, Asst. Exec. Dir.-Opers.--Metra, Commuter Rail Service Board, Chicago, IL, pg. 922
Tilley, Julius, V.P.-Mfg.--Metal Masters Foodservice Equipment, Smyrna, DE, pg. 741
Tinkel, Gary, V.P.-Mfg.--Spangler Candy Company, Bryan, OH, pg. 1025
Todd, George, V.P.-Mfg.--Kalamazoo Holdings, Inc., Kalamazoo, MI, pg. 615
Todd, Jim, V.P.-Mfg. & Sec.--Preservative Paint Company, Seattle, WA, pg. 887
Todd, John, V.P.-Mfg.--Frank Ix & Sons, Inc., New York, NY, pg. 584
Todd, Russell, V.P.-Mfg.--Martin Industries (AL), Florence, AL, pg. 715
Tolsch, Robert, Dir.-Mfg.--Periphonics Corp., Bohemia, NY, pg. 862
Tombasco, Gary, Mgr.-Computer Services--Cornell Iron Works, Inc., Mountaintop, PA, pg. 286
Tomesko, Charles, Plant Mgr.--Stanbee Company, Inc., Carlstadt, NJ, pg. 1035
Tozun, Orhan, V.P.-Mktg., Sls. & Engrng.--International Microcircuits, Inc., Milpitas, CA, pg. 579
Trauth, Andrew, V.P.-Engrng.--Trauth Dairy Inc., Newport, KY, pg. 1108
Trauth, Steven A., V.P.-Prod. & Sec.--Trauth Dairy Inc., Newport, KY, pg. 1108
Troth, William L., V.P.-Mfg.--Office Electronics, Inc., Itasca, IL, pg. 821
Trumpy, R.C., V.P.-Mfg.--Furnas Electric Company, Batavia, IL, pg. 437
Trzecki, R., Mgr.-Production Control--Blaw Knox Food & Chemical Equipment Company, Buffalo, NY, pg. 156
Trzop, James M., V.P.-Mfg.--JII/Sales Promotion Associates, Inc., Coshocton, OH, pg. 604
Tsakiridis, Christos, V.P.-Mfg.--Sellstrom Manufacturing Co., Palatine, IL, pg. 988
Tschan, E.W., V.P.-Mfg.--Gold Medal Products Co., Cincinnati, OH, pg. 465
Tuason, Oscar A., Mgr.-Mfg.--Myers Foods Company, Plumsteadville, PA, pg. 506
Tuchman, Walter, Sr. V.P.-Engrng.--Amperif Corporation, Chatsworth, CA, pg. 68
Tucker, Robert L., Dir.-Production--The Dispatch Printing Company, Columbus, OH, pg. 339
Turner, Bert, V.P.-Mfg.--Morgan Foods, Inc., Austin, IN, pg. 770
Turner, Gene, V.P.-Mfg.--Diagraph Corporation, Earth City, MO, pg. 335
Turner, Joseph, V.P.-Mfg.--Pullman Industries, Inc., Madison Heights, MI, pg. 900
Tzoucalis, Thomas, Dir.-Mfg.--Bill Communications, Inc., New York, NY, pg. 150
Tzoucalis, Thomas, V.P. & Dir.-Mfg.--Institutional Distribution, New York, NY, pg. 150
Ungar, Emanuel, Exec. V.P.-Mfg.--Queens Group Indiana, Inc., Indianapolis, IN, pg. 904
Ungar, Manny, Exec. V.P.-Mfg.--Queens Group, Inc., Long Island City, NY, pg. 904
Unis, Jim, Dir.-Engrng.--Active Tool & Manufacturing Co., Inc., Roseville, MI, pg. 15
Urban, Michael, V.P.-Field Service & Mfg.--Global Turnkey Systems Inc., Waldwick, NJ, pg. 463
Urell, Bob, V.P.-Engrng.--FDL Foods, Inc., Dubuque, IA, pg. 394
Uritz, Carmen, Electrical Engr.--Medico Industries, Inc., Wilkes-Barre, PA, pg. 735
Urquhart, Clive, Assoc. Dir.-Mfg.--Industrial Acoustics Company, Ltd., Staines,, United Kingdom, pg. 566
Usherwood, John, Mgr.-Production--Dairygold Inc., Seattle, WA, pg. 311
Vale, Robert S., Mgr.-Mfg.--The Elwell-Parker Electric Co., Cleveland, OH, pg. 378
Van Andel, Dave, Dir.-Mfg. Opers.--Amway Corporation, Ada, MI, pg. 70
Van Dyke, Garritt, Mgr.-Engrng.--Bridgeport Fittings, Inc., Stratford, CT, pg. 175
Van Tatenhove, Craig, Dir.-Mfg.--Myron Manufacturing Corporation, Maywood, NJ, pg. 780
Van Vieet, Lyle, V.P.-Mfg.--Vile-Goller, Fine Art Printing & Lithography, Kansas City, KS, pg. 1151
Vancalbergh, Chris, Dir.-Production & Mfg.--Open Court Publishing Co.-General Books, Peru, IL, pg. 227
Vanderminden, R., Jr., V.P. & Mgr.-Plant--Telescope Casual Furniture, Inc., Granville, NY, pg. 1085

Vandy, K., Mgr.-Production--The Lorvic Corp., St. Louis, MO, pg. 684
Varella, Steve, Dir.-Mfg.--Life Line Nutritionals, Inc., Hayward, CA, pg. 675
Varga, John, Plant Mgr.--The A. H. Nilson Machine Co., Stratford, CT, pg. 114
Varty, E.L., Mgr.-Prod.--American Trading & Production Corp., Canadian Oil & Gas Operations, Calgary,, Canada, pg. 65
Vaughan, Gerald A., Sr. V.P.-Mfg. & Tech.--U.S. Can Company, Oak Brook, IL, pg. 1134
Vaughan, Tom, Chief Engineer--Baker Commodities, Inc., Los Angeles, CA, pg. 115
Veum, Doug, Sr. V.P.-Mfg.--Duron, Inc., Beltsville, MD, pg. 355
Vevanth, Joseph, V.P.-Engrng.--Bose Corporation, Framingham, MA, pg. 167
Vidyarthi, A.D., V.P.-Mfg.--Miller Chemical & Fertilizer Corp., Hanover, PA, pg. 32
Vincent, Richard F., V.P.-Mfg.--Riviana Foods Inc., Houston, TX, pg. 937
Vinson, Stan, Exec. V.P.-Mfg.--Union Underwear Co., Inc., Bowling Green, KY, pg. 400
Viola, Tony, Dir.-Mfg.--Quaker Industries Limited, Antioch, IL, pg. 903
Visconti, John E., Exec. V.P.-Mfg.--Pannier Corporation, Pittsburgh, PA, pg. 846
Vispi, Donald R., V.P.-Mfg. & Distr.--Haddon Craftsmen, Inc., Scranton, PA, pg. 499
Visser, Al, Mgr.-Mfg.--Ritchie Industries, Inc., Conrad, IA, pg. 936
Vitale, R.D., V.P.-Mfg.--Bucyrus-Erie Company, South Milwaukee, WI, pg. 186
Vittek, Louis, V.P.-Mfg.--Artco-Bell Corporation, Temple, TX, pg. 86
Volchoff, Boris, V.P.-Engrng.--Vulcan Iron Works, Inc., Detroit, MI, pg. 1155
Vollmer, Carl, Chief Engineer--Hopple Plastics, Inc., Florence, KY, pg. 544
Von Deylen, Larry, Mgr.-Mfg.--Oregon Freeze Dry, Inc., Albany, OR, pg. 829
Vruggink, Jay, Mgr.-Production--Trendway Corporation, Holland, MI, pg. 1109
Wacaser, James R., Mgr.-Mfg.--Hollymatic Corporation, Countryside, IL, pg. 539
Wade, Tom, V.P.-Mfg.--Harris-Kayot, Inc., Fort Wayne, IN, pg. 512
Wagner, Richard C., V.P.-Engrng. & Res. & Devel.--Hollymatic Corporation, Countryside, IL, pg. 539
Wagner, T.W., V.P.-Mfg.--Kingsbury, Inc., Philadelphia, PA, pg. 632
Wagner, Thomas, Sr. V.P.-Mfg.--Ocean Spray Cranberries, Inc., Lakeville, MA, pg. 820
Wahlgren, George, Chief Engr. & Factory Mgr.--National Tool & Manufacturing Company, Kenilworth, NJ, pg. 794
Wakeling, James T., Sr. V.P.-Opers.--Knoll International, Inc., New York, NY, pg. 1121
Walden, P. Wayne, V.P.-Mfg.--Robinson Helicopter Company, Inc., Torrance, CA, pg. 940
Walker, Gary T., V.P.-Engrng.--St. Paul Metalcraft, Inc., Saint Paul, MN, pg. 967
Walker, James E., V.P.-Opers.--Cassens Transport Company, Edwardsville, IL, pg. 228
Walker, James F., V.P.-Mfg.--Getman Corporation, Bangor, MI, pg. 455
Walker, Terry, Dir.-Mfg.--Sloan Technology, Santa Barbara, CA, pg. 1146
Wallitsch, Frank, V.P.-Mfg.--Pennsylvania Crusher Corp., Broomall, PA, pg. 858
Walsh, J., V.P.-Engrng.--Cornell Iron Works, Inc., Mountaintop, PA, pg. 286
Walstad, Dennis, Sr. V.P. & Chief Oper. Officer--Furnas Electric Company, Batavia, IL, pg. 437
Walters, Keith, V.P.-Mfg.--Atlas/Soundolier, Fenton, MO, pg. 64
Walton, Bruce, Mgr.-Mfg.--Ready Systems, Sunnyvale, CA, pg. 916
Walton, Lori, Mgr.-Mdsg.--Narrow Fabric Industries, Inc., West Reading, PA, pg. 783
Walton, T. Campbell, V.P.-Mfg.--Marathon Electric Manufacturing Corp., Wausau, WI, pg. 705
Wargo, Chris A., V.P.-Engrng.--Aeronautical Radio, Inc., Annapolis, MD, pg. 82
Warner, Joseph M., V.P.-Opers.--Romac Industries, Inc., Seattle, WA, pg. 945
Wasserman, Seymour, V.P.-Engrng. Services--Industrial Acoustics Company, Inc., Bronx, NY, pg. 565
Wasylko, Steve, V.P.-Mfg.--Par Industries, Inc., Medina, OH, pg. 847
Watkins, Tommy R., Sr. V.P.-Mfg.--Alliance America, Norcross, GA, pg. 37
Watkins, Wendell, V.P.-Mfg.--The Harwood Companies, Inc., New York, NY, pg. 515
Watson, George, Mgr.-Mfg.--Piper Aircraft Corporation, Vero Beach, FL, pg. 872
Watts, R.D., V.P.-Industrial & Commodity--Riviana Foods Inc., Houston, TX, pg. 937
Wawrzyniak, Steve, V.P.-Tech. Services--Doane Products Co., Joplin, MO, pg. 342
Webb, Maurice J., V.P.-Special Projects--Victaulic Company of America, Easton, PA, pg. 1149
Weber, Brad, V.P.-Mfg.--Weber Marking Systems, Inc., Arlington Heights, IL, pg. 1171
Weber, D., Chief Engnr.--American Crane & Equipment Corp., Douglassville, PA, pg. 51
Weber, Paul, Mgr.-Mfg.--Simpson Electric Co., Elgin, IL, pg. 1007
Webster, J.C., V.P. & Chief Engineer--Ohio Gas Company, Bryan, OH, pg. 822
Wehner, R., V.P.-Engrng.--Cramer Inc., Kansas City, KS, pg. 296
Weigard, Dennis, Mgr.-Mfg.--Miller-St. Nazianz, Inc., Saint Nazianz, WI, pg. 755
Weisser, Al, V.P.-Mfg. & Supvr.-Plant--Stanley Knight Corporation, New Troy, MI, pg. 1038
Welch, William E., V.P.-Mfg.--Lane Limited, Tucker, GA, pg. 657
Weller, Ronald, V.P.-Engrng.--McCain Manufacturing Corp., Chicago, IL, pg. 726
Wells, James, V.P.-Chemical Mfg.--Radiator Specialty Company, Charlotte, NC, pg. 909
Wempe, Roman, V.P.-Industrial Mfg.--Gates Canada Inc., Brantford,, Canada, pg. 445
Wenger, Ron, V.P.-Mfg.--Bard Mfg. Co., Bryan, OH, pg. 119
Wenner, Hal, Mgr.-Mfg.--Sunroc Corporation, Media, PA, pg. 1062
Weston, Roger L., Chm. Bd., Pres. & Chief Exec. Officer--GreatBanc, Inc., Aurora, IL, pg. 482
Wetterschneider, Stuart R., V.P.-Design & Engrng.--The Austin Company, Cleveland, OH, pg. 790
Whelan, George, Dir.-Maintenance--B. Green & Co., Baltimore, MD, pg. 484
Whetzel, Charlie, Exec. V.P.-Mfg. & Opers.--The William Carter Company, New York, NY, pg. 226
White, Tim, Mgr.-Mfg.--South Bend Plastics, Inc., Mishawaka, IN, pg. 1019
Whitlock, T.L., Plant Mgr.--Mount Vernon Mills, Inc., Riegel Consumer Products Div., Johnston, SC, pg. 844
Whittle, Danny J., V.P.-Mfg., Quality Assurance & Asst. Gen. Mgr.--Heckethorn Mfg. Company, Dyersburg, TN, pg. 524
Wichmann, William J., V.P.-Opers.--Noville Essential Oil Co., Inc., North Bergen, NJ, pg. 817
Widdows, R.L., Mgr.-Control Valve Production--Cashco, Inc., Ellsworth, KS, pg. 228
Wiedlin, Paul E., V.P.-Mfg.--General Binding Corporation, Northbrook, IL, pg. 656
Wiencek, Donald, Dir.-Mfg. & Pur.--Continental Web Press, Inc., Itasca, IL, pg. 280
Wiertsema, Gerry, Dir.-Engrng.--Midwest Industries, Inc., Ida Grove, IA, pg. 752
Wiesley, Bruce, V.P.-Mfg.--Revcor, Inc., Carpentersville, IL, pg. 930
Wiles, Jack, V.P.-Tech Services--Arby's, Inc., Miami Beach, FL, pg. 243
Wilkinson, Edgar, V.P.-Labels Production--Wurzburg, Inc., Memphis, TN, pg. 1205
Williams, Doug, Sr. V.P.-Mfg.--Hooker Furniture Corporation, Martinsville, VA, pg. 543
Williams, Michael P., II, Chief Tech. Officer--Cadillac Products, Inc., Troy, MI, pg. 207
Williams, Nancy, V.P.-Mfg. & Matls.--Magnetic Technologies Corporation, Rochester, NY, pg. 701
Williams, Roger, V.P.-Mfg.--Hercules Engines, Inc., Canton, OH, pg. 531
Williamson, George, V.P.-Engrng.--American Laundry Machinery Inc., Cincinnati, OH, pg. 57
Wills, Dan, Dir.-Engrng.--Gem Top Mfg., Inc., Clackamas, OR, pg. 448
Wilson, Don, V.P.-Mfg. Mgr.--Gem-Dandy, Inc., Madison, NC, pg. 447
Wilson, J., V.P.-Mfg.--New Balance Athletic Shoe, Inc., Boston, MA, pg. 798
Wilson, Stanley A., Exec. V.P.-Fin. & Mfg.--Park Corporation, Barrington, IL, pg. 849
Wilson, Steve, V.P.-Engrng.--Duo-Fast Corporation, Franklin Park, IL, pg. 354
Wilson, W., V.P.-Mfg.--Neenah Foundry Company, Neenah, WI, pg. 797
Wine, Raymond L., V.P.-Mfg.--Acheson Industries, Inc., Port Huron, MI, pg. 12
Winn, Terry, V.P.-Opers.--Radionics, Inc., Salinas, CA, pg. 909
Wireman, Jerry, Mgr.-Mfg.--Thetford Corporation, Ann Arbor, MI, pg. 357
Wodack, Howard, Sr. V.P.-Opers.--Automotive Rentals, Inc., Mount Laurel, NJ, pg. 101
Wolf, J., V.P.-Engrng.--Bacharach Inc., Pittsburgh, PA, pg. 108
Wolf, Lee, V.P.-Mfg.--Polar Ware Company, Sheboygan, WI, pg. 878
Wolfe, Don, V.P.-Mfg.--Wingfoot Films Corporation, Carrollton, OH, pg. 555
Wolfe, T. Robert, V.P.-Production--Alfred Nickles Bakery, Inc., Navarre, OH, pg. 806
Wolfe, T.R., V.P.-Production--Nickles Bakery, Inc., Martins Ferry, OH, pg. 807
Wolfers, Alan M., V.P. & Engrng. Dir.--Accurate Bushing Co., Inc., Garwood, NJ, pg. 11
Wolski, Frank, Matls. Mgr.--Ektelon Corp., San Diego, CA, pg. 890
Wood, C.S., V.P.-Mfg.--Suburban Communications Corp., Livonia, MI, pg. 1055
Wood, H. E., V.P. & Gen. Mgr.--Boyer Bros. Inc., Altoona, PA, pg. 169
Woodrow, David M., V.P.-Opers.--Cable Division, Atlanta, GA, pg. 294
Wratney, Donald, Chief Engr.--Cornell Forge Company, Chicago, IL, pg. 286
Wright, Michael, Mgr.-Engrng.--Wallace Leisure Products, Inc., Philadelphia, PA, pg. 1160
Wright, William, Mgr.-Prod.--Ultra Tool & Plastics, Inc., Amherst, NY, pg. 1125
Wroblewski, Joseph, Mgr.-Mfg.--WSF Industries, Inc., Tonawanda, NY, pg. 1156
Yarborough, V.A., Dir.-Engrng.--Colonial Pipeline Company, Atlanta, GA, pg. 264
Yeomans, Mike, Mgr.-Construction & Engrng.--Benderson Development Co., Inc., Buffalo, NY, pg. 138
Yoas, Russell E., Mgr.-Pur. & Production--Yorktowne Paper Mills, Inc., York, PA, pg. 1208
Young, Donald R., V.P.-Production--Ash Grove Cement Company, Overland Park, KS, pg. 87
Young, Henry, Construction Mgr.--W. B. Goode Company, Inc., Richmond, VA, pg. 470
Youtt, Stanley, V.P.-Mfg.--American Tank & Fabricating Co., Cleveland, OH, pg. 63
Zabron, F.S., V.P.-Engrng.--Globe International Inc., Buffalo, NY, pg. 464
Zane, Vince, V.P.-Mfg.--Air Gage Company, Livonia, MI, pg. 27
Zanzig, Jerald, Chief Engr.--Heil Solid Waste Div., Chattanooga, TN, pg. 525
Zarlenga, Louis A., V.P.-Engrng.--The Edward J. DeBartolo Corporation, Youngstown, OH, pg. 323
Zdrojkowski, Floyd J., V.P.-Constuction & Engrng. Pur. Divs.--The Edward J. DeBartolo Corporation, Youngstown, OH, pg. 323
Zecca, John J., V.P.-Mfg.--Triboro Electric Corp., Warminster, PA, pg. 1112
Zemar, John, V.P.-Mfg.--Del Mar Avionics, Irvine, CA, pg. 325
Ziegler, Larry, V.P.-Mfg. & Sls.--Multi-Ad Services, Inc., Peoria, IL, pg. 775
Ziemelis, Herbert, V.P.-Mfg.--The Napier Company, Meriden, CT, pg. 783
Zinno, W.C., V.P.-Mfg.--Miller Electric Mfg. Co., Appleton, WI, pg. 754
Zipparro, Vincent J., V.P. & Chief Engineer--Harza Engineering Co., Chicago, IL, pg. 516
Zoeller, Kenneth, V.P.-Engrng.--Zoeller Co., Louisville, KY, pg. 1220
Zoga, Chris, Exec. V.P.-Mfg.--Premier Mill Corp., New York, NY, pg. 887
Zonsius, David, Dir.-Mfg.--ACR Industries Inc., Mount Clemens, MI, pg. 2
Zurawski, Daryl T., V.P.-Buflovak Sls. & Engrng.--Blaw Knox Food & Chemical Equipment Company, Buffalo, NY, pg. 156
Zwick, R., V.P.-Mfg.--Jeffrey Division, Columbus, OH, pg. 565

MARKETING

Abbott, William J., Assoc. Publr.-Mktg.--Glamour, New York, NY, pg. 19
Abend, David, Mgr.-Mktg. Services--Leach Corporation, Buena Park, CA, pg. 663
Abruzzo, Joseph, Sr. V.P., Dir. Mktg. Plng.--N W Ayer Inc., New York, NY, pg. 104
Abusamra, Mark, Mktg. Dir.--American Water Works Association, Denver, CO, pg. 65
Accetta, Christine, Dir.-Corp. Mktg.--Broad Vogt & Conant Inc., River Rouge, MI, pg. 177
Accola, Richard M., V.P.-Sls. & Mktg.--Gravymaster Inc., Branford, CT, pg. 478
Accola, Richard M., V.P.-Sls. & Mktg.--Dryden & Palmer Company, Branford, CT, pg. 479
Ackles, Paul, V.P.-Mktg.--Cuisinarts Inc., Stamford, CT, pg. 272
Adams, Ernest R., Dir.-Sls. & Mktg.--Evening Post Publishing Co., Charleston, SC, pg. 391
Adams, Henry, V.P.-Sls., Mktg., Adv. & Tech. Services--Norwalk Powdered Metals, Inc., Norwalk, CT, pg. 816
Adams, Nate, V.P.-Mktg.--Christianity Today, Inc., Carol Stream, IL, pg. 249
Adams, Richard, Mgr.-Mktg. & Pub. Rels.--Great Lakes Dredge & Dock, Oak Brook, IL, pg. 481
Adams, Steve, Mktg. Mgr.--Madison, Inc., Tulsa, OK, pg. 433
Addison, B.R., V.P.-Consumer Prods.--The Georgia Marble Company, Kennesaw, GA, pg. 453
Adelman, Ann Pollock, V.P.-Mktg. Services--Ziff-Davis Publishing Company, New York, NY, pg. 1219
Adelman, Bennett, Exec. V.P.-Mktg.--David Brett, Inc., Easton, MA, pg. 174
Adkins, Gary, Mgr.-Mktg.--Civil Service Employees Life Insurance Co., San Francisco, CA, pg. 205
Adler, Howard, Sr. V.P.-Sls. Promo. & Mktg.--R. H. Macy & Co., Inc., New York, NY, pg. 698
Adler, Katherine, V.P.-Mktg.--Echo Design Group, Inc., New York, NY, pg. 365
Adler, Robert A., Dir.-Mktg.--Dixico, Inc., Dallas, TX, pg. 135
Adner, Ben, Prod. Mgr.--Autoroll Machine Corp., Middleton, MA, pg. 101
Agnew, James W., V.P.-Mktg.--American Mutual Life Insurance Company, Des Moines, IA, pg. 58
Agnew, John, Mktg. Services Coord.--Muse Cordero Chen, Inc., Los Angeles, CA, pg. 777
Ahlstrom, Craig, Mktg. Dir.--Farnsworth Construction, Mesa, AZ, pg. 403
Ahlstrom, Craig, Dir.-Adv., Mktg., Opers. & Sls.--Farnsworth Development Co., Mesa, AZ, pg. 403
Ahlstrom, Mike, Dir.-Mktg.--Vernell's Candy Company, Bellevue, WA, pg. 1148
Akerson, Dean W., V.P.-Mktg.--Diemakers, Inc., Monroe City, MO, pg. 336
Akerson, Steve, Sr. V.P., Mktg. Research Dir.--Colle & McVoy, Inc., Minneapolis, MN, pg. 261
Albinger, Kelly, Mgr.-Mktg. Services--Vidicom, L.D. Bevan Company, Inc., Thousand Oaks, CA, pg. 1151
Albonetti, Joseph G., Sr. V.P. & Dir.-Hispanic & Intl. Mktg.--Tinsley Advertising, Miami, FL, pg. 1099
Aldred, Derrick, Sr. V.P.-Standard Prods. Devel.--Haskel, Inc., Burbank, CA, pg. 516
Alexander, George, V.P.-Sls. & Mktg.--Thermon Manufacturing Company, San Marcos, TX, pg. 1091
Alexander, Lynn E., V.P.-Mktg. & Sales--Thoroughbred Software International, Inc., Somerset, NJ, pg. 1095
Alexander, R.E., Mgr.-Mktg. Services--Lord Corporation, Erie, PA, pg. 683
Alexy, R. James, Sr. V.P.-Mktg./Sls.--Sealy Mattress Company of Puerto Rico, Rio Piedras, PR, pg. 985
Alexy, R. James, Sr. V.P.-Mktg./Sls.--Ohio-Sealy Mattress Mfg. Co., Inc., Randolph, MA, pg. 985
Alexy, R. James, Sr. V.P.-Mktg./Sls.--Ohio-Sealy Mattress Manufacturing Co.-Fort Worth, Richland Hills, TX, pg. 985
Alexy, R. James, Sr. V.P.-Mktg./Sls.--Ohio-Sealy Mattress Manufacturing Co.-Houston, Brenham, TX, pg. 985

Alexy, R. James, Sr. V.P.-Mktg./Sls.--The Stearns & Foster Bedding Company, Cleveland, OH, pg. 985
Alexy, R. James, Sr. V.P.-Mktg. & Sls.--Sealy, Inc., Cleveland, OH, pg. 985
Alexy, R. James, Sr. V.P.-Mktg./Sls.--The Stearns & Foster Upholstery Furniture Company, Cleveland, OH, pg. 985
Alexy, R. James, Sr. V.P.-Mktg./Sls.--Sealy Mattress Company of Albany, Inc., Albany, NY, pg. 985
Alexy, R. James, Sr. V.P.-Mktg./Sls.--Sealy of Minnesota, Inc., Saint Paul, MN, pg. 985
Alexy, R. James, Sr. V.P.-Mktg./Sls.--Sealy Connecticut, Inc., Oakville, CT, pg. 985
Alexy, R. James, Sr. V.P.-Mktg./Sls.--Sealy of Maryland & Virginia, Inc., Williamsport, MD, pg. 985
Alexy, R. James, Sr. V.P.-Mktg./Sls.--Sealy Mattress Company of Illinois, Batavia, IL, pg. 985
Alexy, R. James, Sr. V.P.-Mktg./Sls.--Sealy Mattress Company of Kansas City, Inc., Kansas City, KS, pg. 985
Alexy, R. James, Sr. V.P.-Mktg./Sls.--Sealy Mattress Company of Memphis, Memphis, TN, pg. 985
Alexy, R. James, Sr. V.P.-Mktg./Sls.--The Ohio Mattress Company Licensing And Components Group, Cleveland, OH, pg. 985
Alexy, R. James, Sr. V.P.-Mktg./Sls.--Sealy Mattress Company of Michigan, Inc., Taylor, MI, pg. 985
Alexy, R. James, Sr. V.P.-Mktg./Sls.--Stearns & Foster Upholstery Furniture Co., Columbiana, OH, pg. 985
Alexy, R. James, Sr. V.P.-Mktg./Sls.--Stearns & Foster Upholstery Furniture Co., Pontotoc, MS, pg. 985
Alioto, Mario, Dir.-Mktg.--San Francisco Giants Baseball Club, San Francisco, CA, pg. 969
Allen, Beverly, Mktg. Dir.--New York Magazine Company, New York, NY, pg. 611
Allen, Brad, Mgr.-Mktg.--Keiper Recaro, Inc., Clawson, MI, pg. 620
Allen, Carolanne, Direct Mail Supvr.--Public Media Center, San Francisco, CA, pg. 898
Allen, Clark R., V.P. & Grp. Mktg. Dir.--Combe Incorporated, White Plains, NY, pg. 267
Allen, Darlene, Dir.-Health Care Mktg.--The Estee Corporation, Parsippany, NJ, pg. 389
Allen, Joel, V.P.-Sls., Mktg. & Adv.--Allen Foods, Inc., Saint Louis, MO, pg. 36
Allen, John C., V.P.-Sls. & Mktg.--Wrought Washer Mfg., Inc., Milwaukee, WI, pg. 1205
Allen, Meredith, V.P.-Mktg.--Staple Cotton Cooperative Association, Greenwood, MS, pg. 1038
Allen, Mike, Dir.-Sls. & Mktg.-C Stores, Airlines & New Business--Aladdin Synergetics, Inc., Nashville, TN, pg. 29
Allen, Scott, Mktg. Dir.--M.S. Walker, Inc./Seacoast, Somerville, MA, pg. 1160
Allen, Thomas G., V.P.-Sls. & Mktg.--Effective Management Systems, Milwaukee, WI, pg. 370
Allen, Wayne, V.P.-Sls. & Mktg. & Sec.--Idaho Supreme Company, Firth, ID, pg. 561
Allman, James, Mgr.-Sls. & Mktg.--The Computer Patch of Joplin, Joplin, MO, pg. 1043
Almond, Jeff, Dir.-Adv. & Mktg.--Larkin, Inc., Atlanta, GA, pg. 667
Almond, Jeff, Dir.-Adv. & Mktg.--Heatcraft, Inc., Stone Mountain, GA, pg. 667
Alt, Jeffrey C., Mgr.-Mktg.--Mustang Tractor & Equip. Co., Houston, TX, pg. 777
Altberg, Marla, V.P., Sls. & Mktg.--Ventura Associates, Inc., New York, NY, pg. 1147
Amatangelo, Paul C., V.P.-Mktg.--Kendall-Futuro Company, Newport, KY, pg. 622
Amberger, Tom, Dir.-Mktg.--Galardi Group, Inc., Newport Beach, CA, pg. 441
Ames, G. Ronald, Sr. Exec. V.P. & Dir.-Mktg. Opers.--Mutual of Omaha Insurance Company, Omaha, NE, pg. 779
Ames, G. Ronald, Sr. Exec. V.P. & Dir.-Mktg. Opers.--Mutual of Omaha, Omaha, NE, pg. 779
Amick, Richard C., V.P.-Mktg.--Curries Company, Mason City, IA, pg. 361
Amiss, Brooke, Dir.-Mktg.--Victaulic International, Easton, PA, pg. 1149
Amos, Steve, V.P.-Sls. & Mktg.--The Blodgett Oven Co., Inc., Burlington, VT, pg. 157
Anacone, Robert B., V.P.-Mktg. & Sls.--Serono Baker Diagnostics, Allentown, PA, pg. 991
Andersen, Douglas, V.P.-Adv., Pub. Rels. & Mktg.--Allied Mutual Insurance Company, Des Moines, IA, pg. 38
Anderson, Bill, Mgr.-Sls. & Mktg.--Snyder Industries, Inc., Lincoln, NE, pg. 1015
Anderson, David, Sr. V.P., Mktg. Services--Newman, Saylor & Gregory, Columbia, SC, pg. 804
Anderson, Donald C., Mgr.-Mktg. Opers. & Engrng.--Anderson Brothers Construction Brainerd, Brainerd, MN, pg. 72
Anderson, Gene R., Grp. V.P.-Sls. & Mktg.--Southern States Cooperative, Inc., Richmond, VA, pg. 1022
Anderson, Lynn, Mktg. Mgr.--Alloway Manufacturing, Fargo, ND, pg. 41
Anderson, M., V.P.-Mktg.--Frantz Manufacturing Co., Sterling, IL, pg. 429
Anderson, Mike, V.P.-Sls. & Mktg.--H.P.H. Industries Ltd., Lake Forest, IL, pg. 497
Anderson, Richard, Exec. V.P.-Retail Brands--Comstock Michigan Fruit, Rochester, NY, pg. 25
Anderson, Robin, V.P.-Sls. & Mktg.--The Metal Ware Corp., Two Rivers, WI, pg. 741
Anderson, William P., Asst. V.P.-Corp. Plng./MIS--Bacardi Imports, Inc., Miami, FL, pg. 108
Andre, Stan, Sr. V.P.-Mktg.--Nulaid Foods, Ripon, CA, pg. 817
Andrepont, James A., V.P.-Mktg.--The Acacia Group, Washington, DC, pg. 10
Andrews, Gordon, Dir.-Mktg.--Southern Saltwater Magazine, Montgomery, AL, pg. 106
Andrus, Nicholas, V.P.-Mktg.--McCain Citrus Inc., Chicago, IL, pg. 726
Anello, Patrick, Dir.-Mktg.--Wahl Clipper Corp., Sterling, IL, pg. 1158
Angell, Nicholas J., Dir.-Mktg.--Stratmar Systems, Inc., Port Chester, NY, pg. 1053
Angell, Nicholas J., Dir.-Mktg. & Adv.--Stratmar Fulfillment Corp., Stratford, CT, pg. 1053
Anthony, Laura, Dir.-Mktg.--Castex Industries Inc., Holland, MI, pg. 228
Anton, Bill, V.P.-Mktg.--WEN Products, Inc., Chicago, IL, pg. 1156
Antonelli, Maria, Mktg. Coord.--Rosanio, Bailets & Talamo, Inc., Cherry Hill, NJ, pg. 947
Apostole, Phyllis, Mgr.-Mktg.--Georgette Klinger, Inc., New York, NY, pg. 635
Appel, Kenneth, Dir.-Mktg.--Kaye Instruments, Inc., Bedford, MA, pg. 619
Appledy, Victor, Exec. V.P.-Sls. & Mktg.--Tollman/Hundley Hotels, Valhalla, NY, pg. 1100
Aravosis, George, Sr. V.P.-Mktg. & Engrng.--Magna-Pow'r Inc., Franklin Park, IL, pg. 559
Archer, David, V.P.-Bus. Devel.-Viacom World Wide--Viacom Enterprises, New York, NY, pg. 785
Arends, L., Mgr.-Mktg. Services--G & W Electric Co., Blue Island, IL, pg. 438
Arenstein, Ed, Non-Ferrous Mktg.--Sturgis Iron & Metal Company, Inc., Sturgis, MI, pg. 1055
Aretakis, A.M., Mgr.-Mktg. & Sls.--Yardney Technical Products, Inc., Pawcatuck, CT, pg. 1207
Argeroudis, Nick, V.P.-Sls. & Mktg., Distr.--Tekra Corporation, New Berlin, WI, pg. 1084
Arliskis, Carole, Dir.-Mktg. & Gen. Mgr.--Oberweis Dairy, Inc., Aurora, IL, pg. 820
Armstrong, Darryl, Dir.-Sls.& Mktg.--Granite State Packing Co., Manchester, NH, pg. 476
Armstrong, Federick, V.P.-Sls. & Mktg.--Pannier Corporation, Pittsburgh, PA, pg. 846
Armstrong, Gary E., Sr. V.P. & Dir.-Mktg.--Lord, Sullivan & Yoder, Inc. Advertising, Columbus, OH, pg. 683
Armstrong, Karine, V.P.-Mktg.--Royal Caribbean Cruises Ltd., Miami, FL, pg. 953
Armstrong, Karine, V.P.-Mktg., Resorts--Hyatt Hotels Corporation, Chicago, IL, pg. 495
Arndt, Joseph E., Mgr.-Mktg. Communications--Andersen Windows Inc., Bayport, MN, pg. 72
Arnold, Alicia, Dir.-Mktg. Services--Sealy Corporation, Cleveland, OH, pg. 985
Arnold, Alicia, Dir.-Mktg. Services--Sealy, Inc., Cleveland, OH, pg. 985
Arnold, Ben, V.P.-Sls. & Mktg.--Chance Rides, Inc., Wichita, KS, pg. 238
Arnold, Bill, V.P., Sls. & Intl. Mktg.--Garvey International, Inc., St. Charles, IL, pg. 444
Arnold, Blayne, Mktg. Mgr.--California Micro Devices, Tempe, AZ, pg. 210
Arnold, Rachelle, Dir.-Mktg.--Blue Coral, Inc., Cleveland, OH, pg. 159
Arnold, Rachelle, Dir.-Mktg.--Simoniz Canada Ltd., Cleveland, OH, pg. 159
Arnold, Victoria J., Mgr.-Corp. Mktg.--Arthur D. Little, Inc., Cambridge, MA, pg. 678
Arosteguy, David J., Exec. V.P.-Mktg. Admin.--Champion Laboratories, Inc., Albion, IL, pg. 1123
Arrington, Edward, V.P.-Mktg.--General Business Services, Inc., Columbia, MD, pg. 449
Arthur, Ralph W., Sr. V.P.-Mktg. & Sls.--Burlington Motor Carriers Inc., Daleville, IN, pg. 191
Arwady, Joseph, Dir.-Sls. & Mktg.--Burns International Security Services, Inc., Parsippany, NJ, pg. 166
Ash, Kenneth, Mgr.-Mktg.--ETL Testing Laboratories, Inc, Cortland, NY, pg. 361
Ashburn, Warren W., Sr. V.P. & Dir.-Mktg.--Kelly Michener Inc., Lancaster, PA, pg. 621
Aslip, Dan, Mgr.-Mktg.--Basic Computer, Akron, OH, pg. 124
Astorino, Michael, V.P.-Mktg. & Sls.--Kex Products, Inc., La Vergne, TN, pg. 145
Atchley, Ted M., V.P.-Mktg.--Wotco Inc., Mills, WY, pg. 1204
Atherton, Rick, Dir.-Mktg.--Breton Construction, Inc., Irvine, CA, pg. 174
Atkinson, David, V.P.-Mktg.--Petoseed Co., Saticoy, CA, pg. 116
Aubuchon, William E., III, Mgr.-Mktg.--W.E. Aubuchon Co., Inc., Westminster, MA, pg. 97
Augello, Mike, V.P.-Mktg. & Adv.--Reeves Southeastern Corporation, Tampa, FL, pg. 921
Augurt, Thomas A., V.P.-Product Plng.--Propper Manufacturing Co., Inc., Long Island City, NY, pg. 895
Augustine, Patrick, Mgr.-Natl. Mktg.--Eva-Tone Inc., Clearwater, FL, pg. 390
Augustyn, Richard, V.P.-Mktg. & Sls.--King Group, Inc., Fenton, MI, pg. 630
Auslander, D.L., V.P.-Sls. & Mktg.--Medtech Laboratories, Inc., Jackson, WY, pg. 736
Austin, John T., Jr., V.P.-Mktg.--James Austin Co., Mars, PA, pg. 99
Austin, Peter, Mgr.-Sls. & Mktg.--Kingsbury Assembly Machine Div., Keene, NH, pg. 632
Austin, Stewart, Mgr.-Mktg.--Action Instruments, Inc., San Diego, CA, pg. 14
Aylward, A., V.P.-Sls. & Mktg.--Neenah Foundry Company, Neenah, WI, pg. 797
Baach, Michael, V.P.-Mktg.--Harco Technologies Corporation, Medina, OH, pg. 507
Baasch, Don, V.P.-Mktg.--American Vision Centers, Inc., New York, NY, pg. 65
Babicz, Gregory, Supvr.-Mktg. Communications--Union Switch & Signal Inc., Pittsburgh, PA, pg. 1129
Babinski, John, V.P.-Mktg.--Belle Tire Distributor Inc., Allen Park, MI, pg. 136
Babrowski, Mike, Dir.-Mktg. & Sls.--Zoeller Co., Louisville, KY, pg. 1220
Bach, Douglas, V.P.-Mktg.--O'Brien Powder Products, Inc., Houston, TX, pg. 820
Bach, Richard, Dir.-Mktg. Services--Zechman & Associates Adv. Inc., Chicago, IL, pg. 1216
Bach, W. Douglas, V.P.-Mktg. & Bus. Devel.--O'Brien Powder Products, Inc., Houston, TX, pg. 820
Bachler, Bud, V.P.-Mktg./Communications--Winona Knits, Winona, MN, pg. 1196
Backman, William D., III, V.P.-Special Mkts.--Aurora Casket Company, Aurora, IN, pg. 98
Badcock, Ben M., V.P.-Dir.-Mktg. & Mdsg.--W.S. Badcock Corporation, Mulberry, FL, pg. 113
Baddorf, M., Dir.-Mktg.--Hercules Tire & Rubber Company, Findlay, OH, pg. 531
Baddorf, Mel, Dir.-Mktg.--The Hercules Tire & Rubber Company, Findlay, OH, pg. 531
Baden, Marvin, V.P.-Mktg. & Sls., Sec. & Treas.--Producers Rice Mill Inc., Stuttgart, AR, pg. 892
Badrick, John, Pres.--Glenayre Turnkey Technologies, Inc., Springfield, NJ, pg. 462
Baen, Peter, Dir.-Mktg. & Corp. Video Systems--Thermon Manufacturing Company, San Marcos, TX, pg. 1091
Bagger, Guy, Mgr.-Mktg.--Raynor Garage Door Company, Dixon, IL, pg. 915
Baglien, James, Mgr.-Mkt. Devel.--Oregon Freeze Dry, Inc., Albany, OR, pg. 829
Bagot, William A., V.P.-Mktg.--Superior Graphite Company, Chicago, IL, pg. 1063
Bahdaw, Carol, Dir.-Mktg. & Pub. Rels.--Van Cleef & Arpels, Inc., New York, NY, pg. 1144
Baiden, Tim, V.P.-Mktg. & Sls.--Polar Ware Company, Sheboygan, WI, pg. 878
Bailey, Barbara, Mgr.-Mktg./Communications--Robert E. Lamb, Inc., Valley Forge, PA, pg. 652
Bailey, Robert E., Exec. V.P.-Adv. & Mktg.--Thriftway, Inc., Cincinnati, OH, pg. 1095
Bailey, Ronald G., Dir.-Mktg.--Smith Wholesale Drug Div., Spartanburg, SC, pg. 1012
Bailey, Sarah, Mktg. Mgr.-Popeyes--Popeye's Famous Fried Chicken, Rosemont, IL, pg. 284
Bailey, Tim, Mgr.-Mkt. Devel.--Na-Churs Plant Food Company, Marion, OH, pg. 782
Bailly, Jim, Dir.-Mktg.-Consumer Prods. Div.--Rich SeaPak Corp., Saint Simons Island, GA, pg. 932
Baimel, Steven, V.P.-Mktg.-Gen. Trade--Siftco Canada, Inc., Mississauga, Canada, pg. 812
Bair, Daran, Dir.-Sls. & Mktg.--Martin Universal Design, Inc., Westland, MI, pg. 715
Baird, D. Glenn, Mktg. Officer--Texas Commerce Bancshares, Inc., Houston, TX, pg. 1089
Baisley, Bill, V.P.-Mktg.--Peterson Industries Inc., Decatur, AR, pg. 864
Baittinger, Kenneth, Sr. V.P.-Sls. & Mktg.--Automotive Rentals, Inc., Mount Laurel, NJ, pg. 101
Bajko, Robert P., V.P.-Sls. & Mktg.--Cleveland Machine Controls, Cleveland, OH, pg. 255
Baker, Linda, Dir.-Mktg. & Mdsg.--County Seat Stores, Inc., Dallas, TX, pg. 290
Baker, Martha, Dir.-Mktg. & Sls.--San Diego Zoo, San Diego, CA, pg. 969
Baker, Martha, Dir.-Sls. & Mktg.--San Diego Wild Animal Park, Escondido, CA, pg. 969
Baker, William, V.P. & Gen. Mgr.--Hearst Business Communications, Inc., Garden City, NY, pg. 522
Baldassare, J.E., Mgr.-Export Mktg.--American Gilsonite Co., Salt Lake City, UT, pg. 55
Baldo, Jim, V.P.-Sls. & Mktg.--Zippo Manufacturing Company, Bradford, PA, pg. 1220
Ball, Michael, Dir.-Mktg.--NBBJ, Columbus, OH, pg. 780
Ballard, Jerry, V.P.-Sls. & Mktg.--Sunox, Inc., Charlotte, NC, pg. 1062
Balodimas, Steve, V.P.-Mktg.--CSE Corporation, San Francisco, CA, pg. 204
Balodimas, Steven, V.P.-Mktg.--Civil Service Employees Insurance Co., San Francisco, CA, pg. 205
Balogh, Edward A., Mgr.-Mktg. & Sls.--Pyro Chem, Inc., Boonton, NJ, pg. 166
Balsdon, Robert, V.P.-Sls. & Mktg.--Pioneer/Eclipse Corp., Sparta, NC, pg. 871
Balthazor, Robert, V.P.-Mktg.--Quality Medical Adjudication, Inc., Rancho Cordova, CA, pg. 521
Bambrick, James E., Exec. V.P.--Farrell Lines Incorporated, New York, NY, pg. 403
Bandkau, Theresa, Mgr.-Mktg.--Genova Products, Inc., Davison, MI, pg. 452
Bankes, James, V.P.-Sls. & Mktg.--Samsill Corporation, Fort Worth, TX, pg. 968
Bankos, Ronald, Dir.-Sls.--Universal Dynamics Inc., Woodbridge, VA, pg. 1138
Banks, Daryl, Dir.-Mktg.--North Carolina Mutual Life Insurance Co., Durham, NC, pg. 813
Banks, Wendy, V.P.-Mktg.--Alexandra De Markoff, Ltd., New York, NY, pg. 695
Bannon, Theresa, Dir.-Mktg. & Adv.--Spirit Cruises, Norfolk, VA, pg. 1031
Banyas, Charles G., V.P.-Mktg.--Robertson Factories, Inc., Taunton, MA, pg. 939
Barbar, Philip G., V.P.-Mktg.--The Barbar Group, Inc., Boca Raton, FL, pg. 119
Barber, G. Lewis, Mgr.-Mktg.--National Welders Supply Co. Inc., Charlotte, NC, pg. 794
Barclay, Gerry, Mgr.-Mktg. Srvcs.--Crown International, Inc., Elkhart, IN, pg. 302
Bardele, Neal, V.P.- Dir. Acct. & Mktg. Services--Meyer & Wallis, Inc., Milwaukee, WI, pg. 746
Barden, Mark, V.P.-Mktg.--Barden & Robeson Corporation, Middleport, NY, pg. 119
Bardill, David, Mgr.-Mktg. & Adv.--Cincinnati Gear Company, Cincinnati, OH, pg. 250
Barhite, James T., V.P.-Sls. & Mktg.--Interface Electronics Corporation, Hopkinton, MA, pg. 574
Barnes, Martin, Dir.-Major Projects--Ellicott Machine Corp., Baltimore, MD, pg. 378
Barnett, David, V.P.-Mktg.--Farley Candy Company, Chicago, IL, pg. 399

Barnett, Philip, Exec. V.P.-Mtkg.--Hirsh Company, Skokie, IL, pg. 258
Barnthoose, Donald, Mgr.-Mktg.--Plymouth Locomotive International, Inc., Plymouth, OH, pg. 877
Barone, Moshe, V.P.-Sls. & Mktg.--Mennen Medical Inc., Clarence, NY, pg. 739
Barone, Richard, V.P.-Mktg. & Pub. Rels.--New York Racing Association, Jamaica, NY, pg. 803
Barr, Constance, Asst. V.P.-Sls. & Mktg.--Siemer Milling Company, Teutopolis, IL, pg. 1002
Barr, George M., V.P.-Mktg.--Houston Fearless 76 Inc., Compton, CA, pg. 546
Barr, Richard, V.P.-Mktg.--Danly Die Set Division, Cicero, IL, pg. 275
Barrch, Bob, Dir.-Mktg.--Bruce Hardwood Floors, Dallas, TX, pg. 1112
Barrell, Dave, Mgr.-Sls. & Mktg.--Glasteel Industrial Laminates, Duarte, CA, pg. 461
Barrise, Mary Anne, Mgr.-Mktg. & Communications--Veeco Instrumentations, Inc., Plainview, NY, pg. 1146
Barrocas, Jose E., V.P.-Mktg.--Injection Footwear Corp., Miami, FL, pg. 569
Barron, William, V.P.-Sls. & Mktg.--Littelfuse, Inc., Des Plaines, IL, pg. 678
Barrott, William E., III, V.P.-Mktg.--Aurora Casket Company, Aurora, IN, pg. 98
Barrows, James, Dir.-Mktg.--GF Office Furniture Ltd., Gallatin, TN, pg. 439
Barry, Frank, V.P.-Sls. & Mktg.--Inland Printing Co., Inc., La Crosse, WI, pg. 570
Barry, James P., V.P.-Sls. & Mktg.--Remcor Products Co., Glendale Heights, IL, pg. 926
Barsky, Richard, Dir.-Mktg. & Adv.--Field Packing Company, Owensboro, KY, pg. 409
Bartlett, Brad, Dir.-Mktg. & Adv.--Coleman Outdoor Products, Wichita, KS, pg. 695
Bartlett, Michael, Dir.-Mktg.--Acoustic Research, Canton, MA, pg. 578
Bartley, Kim K., Dir.-Mktg.--White Castle System, Inc., Columbus, OH, pg. 1185
Barton, J. Michael, V.P.-Mktg.--Ardco, Inc., Alsip, IL, pg. 81
Basche, Tony, Sr. V.P., Mktg. & Acct. Services--Taylor Advertising, Inc., Tucson, AZ, pg. 1080
Basil, F., Dir.-Mktg.--Exact Equipment Corporation, Langhorne, PA, pg. 392
Basilick, Linda F., Sr. V.P.-Mktg.--J. I. Kislak Inc., Miami Lakes, FL, pg. 633
Bass, George, V.P.-Cloth Prod.--Amicale Industries, Inc., New York, NY, pg. 66
Bassi, Brad, V.P.-Mktg.--Struthers-Dunn Inc., Pitman, NJ, pg. 693
Bastian, Robert R., Dir.-Mktg.--Powell Electronics Inc., Philadelphia, PA, pg. 882
Bate, Michael, Mng. Dir.--Totes U.K. Limited, Billericay, United Kingdom, pg. 1103
Bates, Bob, Mgr.-Mfg.--Diebel Manufacturing Co., Morton Grove, IL, pg. 336
Bates, Charles, V.P.-Sls. & Mktg.--Quality Technologies Corporation, Sunnyvale, CA, pg. 904
Bator, Joseph D., Sr. V.P., Bus. Devel. & Mktg.--ASC Incorporated, Southgate, MI, pg. 7
Batsilas, Mgr.-Pub. Rels. & Mktg.--Austin Sculpture, Holbrook, NY, pg. 99
Battaglia, Anthony, Grp. Exec. V.P.-Mktg.-Chiquita Brands, Inc.--Chiquita Brands International, Inc., Cincinnati, OH, pg. 53
Battaglia, Mark, V.P.-Mktg.--SPSS Inc., Chicago, IL, pg. 964
Battin, James D., Exec. V.P.-Adv. & Mktg.--EB (NA), Chicago, IL, pg. 381
Battle, A. George, Mng. Partner-Mktg. Devel.--Andersen Consulting, Chicago, IL, pg. 72
Baty, Curtis, Dir.-Mktg.--Affiliated Foods, Inc., Amarillo, TX, pg. 24
Bauer, Thaddeus, Dir.-Sls. & Mktg.--The Presmet Corp., Worcester, MA, pg. 887
Baughman, David O., V.P.-Mktg.--Plastomer Corp., Livonia, MI, pg. 876
Bauhofer, Robert J., V.P., Mktg. Res.--Elser & Aucone, Inc., New York, NY, pg. 378
Bauman, Richard F., V.P.-Mktg. & Sls. Acetylenes--International Specialty Products, Inc., Wilmington, DE, pg. 438
Baumann, John, V.P.-Mktg.--The Swiss Colony, Monroe, WI, pg. 1068
Baumer, Stacy, V.P.-Mktg.--Commonwealth Toy & Novelty Company, New York, NY, pg. 269
Baxter, John T., V.P.-Sls. & Mktg.--Alpha Associates, Inc., Woodbridge, NJ, pg. 43
Beaber, Bryan, V.P.-Mktg.--Carter Companies, Kansas City, MO, pg. 226
Beach, Katherine, Mgr.-Mktg.--Deck House Inc., Acton, MA, pg. 324
Beach, Rosemary, Mktg. Mgr.--NDAP/TMP Worldwide, Toronto,, Canada, pg. 1074
Beall, Terry D., Exec. V.P.-Mktg.--Academy Insurance Group, Inc., Atlanta, GA, pg. 11
Bealor, Tim A., Dir.-Mktg.--Broadcast Electronics, Inc., Quincy, IL, pg. 177
Bean, Mark C., V.P.-Sls.--D. D. Bean & Sons Co., Jaffrey, NH, pg. 129
Bear, Craig, Mgr.-Mktg. & Sls.--Alloy Products Corporation, Waukesha, WI, pg. 41
Beason, John, V.P.-Mktg.-Contract--Decorative Fabrics - Mastercraft, Spindale, NC, pg. 262
Beatrice, Joseph G., Exec. V.P., Mktg. Dir.--Grybauskas & Partners, New York, NY, pg. 490
Beattie, David, V.P.-Sls. & Mktg.--McNaughton-McKay Electric Co., Madison Heights, MI, pg. 732
Beattie, Douglas, V.P.-Mktg.--Liquid Controls Corporation, Lake Bluff, IL, pg. 677
Beatty, Robert L., V.P., Dir. Special Markets--Ross Roy Inc., Bloomfield Hills, MI, pg. 950
Beaver, William E., V.P.-Mktg.--Ziebart International Corporation, Troy, MI, pg. 1217
Bechert, Ellen, Dir.-Corp. Devel.--Freeman Decorating Co., Dallas, TX, pg. 431
Becht, Edward F., V.P.-Mktg.--Schultz Steel Company, South Gate, CA, pg. 979
Beck, Bob, Dir.-Mdsg. & Mktg.--Farm Fresh, Inc., Norfolk, VA, pg. 401
Beck, Dan, Grp. V.P.-Franchise Services--Sir Speedy, Inc., Laguna Hills, CA, pg. 613
Beck, Robert V., V.P.-Sls. & Mktg.--Precisionaire, Inc., Saint Petersburg, FL, pg. 886
Becker, Russ, Dir.-Sls. & Mktg.--Hobart Brothers Co., Troy, OH, pg. 536
Becker, Wendy E., Dir.-Mktg.--A & W Restaurants, Inc., Livonia, MI, pg. 1
Beckerman, Robert, V.P.-Mktg.--Country Home Bakery, Inc., Bridgeport, CT, pg. 290
Bedrosian, Peter, V.P.-Mktg.--National Utility Service, Inc., Park Ridge, NJ, pg. 794
Beers, Robert, V.P.-Sls. & Mktg.--Microdot Aerospace Fastening Systems Group, Fullerton, CA, pg. 749
Beeson, Laurie, V.P.-Mktg.--Hallmark Cards, Inc., Kansas City, MO, pg. 501
Begley, Amy, Mktg. Coodinator--Acurex Environmental Corporation, Mountain View, CA, pg. 15
Begley, Amy, Mktg. Communications Coord.--Acurex Environmental, Mountain View, CA, pg. 16
Behle, Ted, Sls. Mgr.-Lawn Chief & Snow Chief--General Power Equipment Co., Harvard, IL, pg. 288
Behle, Theodore R., V.P.-Mktg.--Atlas Power Equipment Company, Harvard, IL, pg. 96
Behling, Richard, V.P.-Mktg.--TSR, Inc., Lake Geneva, WI, pg. 1075
Behling, Roy, V.P.-Sls. & Mktg.--McNally Wellman Company, Pittsburgh, PA, pg. 732
Beier, Peter, V.P.-Mktg. & Sls.--Cole Business Furniture, York, PA, pg. 608
Beisswanger, David, Dir.-Mktg.--Alpha Electronic Signal Technologies, Inc., Elizabeth, NJ, pg. 43
Bell, Edward, Mktg. Dir.--Pennsylvania State Lottery, Middletown, PA, pg. 858
Bell, Richard, V.P.-Sls. & Mktg.--Cornnuts Inc., Alameda, CA, pg. 286
Bell, Robert, Mgr.-Mktg.--Lyon Metal Products, Inc., Montgomery, IL, pg. 690
Bell, Robert, V.P.-Mktg.--Flav-O-Rich, Inc., Louisville, KY, pg. 311
Bell, Tim, Mktg. Dir., New Bus. Contact--re:Source Marketing, Columbus, OH, pg. 929
Bellnap, J.K., V.P.-Mktg.--J.M. Huber, Clay Div., Macon, GA, pg. 550
Bellows, Charles C., Sr. V.P.-Mktg. & Sls.--Medieval Dinner & Tournament, Inc., Buena Park, CA, pg. 735
Belt, Don, Sr. V.P.-Mktg.--Servistar Corporation, East Butler, PA, pg. 992
Benedict, Monica L., Dir.-Sls. & Mktg.--Booth Newspapers, Inc., Grand Rapids, MI, pg. 165
Benison, John E., Exec. V.P.-Sls. Mktg. & Prod. Devel.--The Napier Company, Meriden, CT, pg. 783
Benjamin, Martin, V.P.-Sls. & Mktg.--Pueblo International, Inc.-P.R. Div., Carolina, PR, pg. 899
Bennett, Craig, Chief Oper. Officer & V.P.-Sls. & Mktg.--Utility Trailer Manufacturing Co., City of Industry, CA, pg. 1141
Bennett, Daniel, Dir.-Mktg. & Adv.--Kentucky Department of Travel Development, Frankfort, KY, pg. 623
Bennett, John C., V.P.-Plng., Mktg. & Mngmt. System--The Long Island Rail Road Co., Jamaica, NY, pg. 745
Bennett, John H., Sr. V.P.-Mktg.--Visa U.S.A. Inc., San Mateo. CA, pg. 1153
Bennett, Judith A., V.P.-Mktg. & Pub. Rels.--Fabric Wholesalers, Inc., Portland, OR, pg. 396
Bennett, R. M., V.P.-Sls. & Mktg.--Smith & Sons Foods, Inc., Macon, GA, pg. 1014
Bennett, Tom, Dir.-Mktg. Devel.--Goldfarb & Company Advertising, Southfield, MI, pg. 467
Benson, Ronald A., V.P.-Mktg.--Louisville Bedding Company, Louisville, KY, pg. 684
Benson, Scott, Mktg. Mgr.--Staveley Sensors, Inc., East Hartford, CT, pg. 1043
Benson, Steven, V.P.-Sls. & Mktg.--The Prudential Asset Management Co., Inc., Florham Park, NJ, pg. 897
Benstein, Robert, V.P.-Sls. & Mktg.--SCC Holding Co., Highland Park, IL, pg. 961
Bentson, Gordy, Asst. Mgr.-Mktg.--Thrifty Drug Stores, Inc., Minneapolis, MN, pg. 1096
Benyo, Joseph, V.P.-Sls.--John Dusenbery Co., Inc., Randolph, NJ, pg. 355
Beran, Don, V.P.-Sls. & Mktg.--Honorbuilt Industries, Inc., Minneapolis, KS, pg. 542
Berdine, Jamie, Mktg. Coord.--Steelite, Inc., Pittsburgh, PA, pg. 1044
Berenston, Lynne, Dir.-Mktg.--Seventeen Magazine, New York, NY, pg. 611
Berentson, Lynne G., Mktg. Dir.--Bon Appetit Magazine, Los Angeles, CA, pg. 636
Bergen, Peter, Sr. V.P.-Mktg.--Newbridge Communications, New York, NY, pg. 611
Bergman, David C., V.P.-Prod. Devel.--Processed Plastic Company, Montgomery, IL, pg. 892
Bergstein, Andrew, Dir.-Mktg.--Sparkomatic Corporation, Milford, PA, pg. 1025
Bergstein, Andrew, Dir.-Mktg.--Kenco, Middlebury, IN, pg. 1025
Bergstein, Andrew, Dir.-Mktg.--Altec Lansing Consumer Products, Milford, PA, pg. 1025
Berkey, Donald L., Mgr.-Mktg.--Hollymatic Corporation, Countryside, IL, pg. 539
Berkowitz, Donald A., Exec. V.P.-Sls. & Mktg.--Central Paper Company, Newark, NJ, pg. 233
Berkowitz, Nancy D., V.P. & Dir.-Mktg.--Mohawk Distilled Products, North Miami, FL, pg. 763
Berman, Dan, Dir.-Sls. & Mktg.--TST/Impreso, Inc., Coppell, TX, pg. 1075
Bernard, Stephen, Div. V.P.-Circulation & Mktg., Magazine Grp.--Scholastic Inc., New York, NY, pg. 962
Bernstein, David P., V.P.-Fresh Fruit Mktg.--Sunkist Growers, Inc., Sherman Oaks, CA, pg. 1060
Berrett, John C., V.P.-Mktg.--Haworth, Inc., Holland, MI, pg. 518
Berris, Brian, Partner & Mktg. Dir.--Brown Brothers, Harriman & Co., New York, NY, pg. 181
Berry, Michael J., Mktg. Mgr.--Transilwrap Company, Inc., Chicago, IL, pg. 1107
Berry, Todd, Dir.-Mktg.--Jones Dairy Farm, Fort Atkinson, WI, pg. 603
Bertges, Deborah, Mgr.-Mktg. Services--Samuel Cabot, Inc., Newburyport, MA, pg. 206
Bertuch, Michael, V.P.-Mktg.--DVC Industries, Bay Shore, NY, pg. 310
Besch, Andrew, Sr. V.P.-Mktg.--USA Network, New York, NY, pg. 1124
Bethel, Richard N., V.P.-Mktg. & Adv.--Voit Sports, Inc., Fairport, NY, pg. 1154
Betush, E.T., Jr., V.P.-Sls. & Mktg.--Pennex Products Co., Inc., Verona, PA, pg. 858
Beutel, Nina, Dir.-Mktg.--Gump's, Inc., San Francisco, CA, pg. 494
Bevilaqua, Vic, V.P.-Mktg.--National Foods Inc., Bronx, NY, pg. 788
Bevington, Mark, V.P.-Sls. & Mktg.--The National Super Service Co., Toledo, OH, pg. 794
Beyer, John H., V.P.-Mktg.--John R. Hollingsworth Co., Phoenixville, PA, pg. 539
Beyman, Michelle, V.P., Dir. Mktg.--Barry Blau & Partners, Inc., Fairfield, CT, pg. 156
Bhide, A., Mktg. Mgr.-Wintriss Products--Data Instruments, Inc., Acton, MA, pg. 316
Bial, Scott, V.P.-Sls. & Mktg.--Wallace International Silversmiths, Inc., East Boston, MA, pg. 1070
Bicknell, Katie, V.P., Dir. Mktg. Services--Blattner/Brunner Inc., Pittsburgh, PA, pg. 156
Biddison, Peggy, V.P.-Mktg.--Western Data Systems, Calabasas, CA, pg. 1178
Biddle, Sharon, V.P.-Mktg.--Jazzercise, Inc., Carlsbad, CA, pg. 591
Biderman, George, V.P.-Mktg.--Tarlton Corporation, Saint Louis, MO, pg. 1079
Bieber, David F., Sr. V.P.-Natl. Client Service & Mktg. Mgr.--The Bases Group, Covington, KY, pg. 124
Bienenfeld, Carol, Sls. & Mktg. Admin.--Admiral Packaging, Inc., Providence, RI, pg. 1128
Biggs, David H., V.P.-Mfg. & Prod. Devel.--Bently Nevada Corporation, Minden, NV, pg. 140
Biggs, Gary, Exec. V.P.-Mktg.--Cragar Industries, Compton, CA, pg. 761
Biggs, Seanapri, Asst.-Mktg.--Heil-Brice Retail Advertising, San Clemente, CA, pg. 525
Bigler, Debra E., V.P., Dir.-Mktg. & Asst. Sec.--W. P. Carey & Co., Inc., New York, NY, pg. 218
Billings, Brian, Sr. V.P.-Mktg. & Plng.--DHL Airways, Inc., Redwood City, CA, pg. 309
Billmon, Paula, Mgr.-Mktg. & Sls. Support--Liberty Tool Corporation, Rochester, NY, pg. 674
Bingle, Fred, V.P., Dir. Mktg. Research--Montgomery, Zukerman, Davis, Inc., Indianapolis, IN, pg. 768
Binzer, Howard, Mgr.-Mktg.--Burks Pumps, Inc., Piqua, OH, pg. 507
Binzer, Howard, Mktg. Mgr.--Prosser/Enpo Industries, Piqua, OH, pg. 507
Binzer, Howard, Mktg. Mgr.--Barnes Pumps, Inc., Mansfield, OH, pg. 507
Binzer, Howard, Mktg, Mgr.--AMW Industries Inc., Conway, AR, pg. 507
Birch, Larry, V.P.-Residential Mktg.--Nibco, Inc., Elkhart, IN, pg. 806
Birnbaum, Marc, Exec. V.P.-Sls. & Mktg.--Hazel Bishop Corporation, Englewood Cliffs, NJ, pg. 520
Bischoff, E.A., Export Mgr.--United States Machinery, Painesville, OH, pg. 258
Bishop, Bethany, Mgr.-Mktg.--Vermont Lottery Commission, Barre, VT, pg. 1148
Bishop, Don, Grp. V.P.-Sls. & Mktg.--Gulf States Toyota, Houston, TX, pg. 494
Bishop, John J., V.P.-Mktg.--Motorists Mutual Insurance Co., Columbus, OH, pg. 773
Bishop, Raymond, V.P.-Mktg.--Stevens-Lee Company, Minneapolis, MN, pg. 1048
Bixby, B.C., Chm. Bd.--Bixby International Corp., Newburyport, MA, pg. 153
Bixby, W.W., Jr., Sr. V.P.-Mktg.--Haskel, Inc., Burbank, CA, pg. 516
Black, Dawn A., Mgr.-Mktg. Services--Harley Ellington Pierce Yee Associates, Inc., Southfield, MI, pg. 509
Black, Dennis, V.P.-Mktg.--Weinbrenner Shoe Company, Inc., Merrill, WI, pg. 1173
Black, Randy, V.P.-Sls. & Mktg.--Bike Athletic Co., Knoxville, TN, pg. 150
Blackburn, R.D., V.P.-Mktg.--Integra Technologies Corp., Waltham, MA, pg. 572
Blackstock, Connie, Mktg. Mgr.--Cobra Tool, Inc., De Witt, NE, pg. 64
Blackstock, Hoyt, Dir.-Mktg.--J.R. Simplot Company, Boise, ID, pg. 1007
Blackstone, M.J., Dir.-Mktg.--Ebco Mfg. Company, Columbus, OH, pg. 365
Blackstone, Shelly, Mktg. Mgr.--Peter Wong & Associates, Inc., Richmond, VA, pg. 1199
Blackwell, Katrina, V.P.-Sls. & Mktg.--American Red Ball World Wide Movers, Indianapolis, IN, pg. 918
Blagaich, Alvin, V.P.-Sls. & Mktg.--Fenton Press, Inc., Addison, IL, pg. 406
Blais, Russell A., V.P.-Mktg. & Sls.--Naylor Pipe Company, Chicago, IL, pg. 796
Blake, Charles, Gen. Mgr.-Mktg.--Rea Magnet Wire Company, Inc., Fort Wayne, IN, pg. 915
Blaker, A. L., Sec., Treas. & Mktg. Dir.--King Bear Enterprises, Inc., North Merrick, NY, pg. 630

Blakeslee, Bill, Corp. V.P.- Mktg. & Plng.--Mid-America Dairymen, Inc., Springfield, MO, pg. 750
Blanck, Robert M., V.P.-Mktg.--Standard Duplicating Machines Corp., Andover, MA, pg. 1036
Blank, Jeffrey, Sec. & Dir.-Mktg.--Elastic Materials, Inc., Smithville, OH, pg. 372
Blaschke, James C., V.P.-Mktg.--Adra Systems, Inc., Lowell, MA, pg. 18
Blauer, Stephen, V.P.-Mktg.--Blauer Manufacturing Co., Inc., Boston, MA, pg. 156
Blazer, B.D., V.P.-Mktg. Services--Miller Electric Mfg. Co., Appleton, WI, pg. 754
Bleil, James V., V.P.-Mktg.--Michael's Development Company, Marlton, NJ, pg. 747
Blevins, G. Drew, V.P.-Adv. & Mktg.--GranTree Corporation, Beaverton, OR, pg. 477
Blevins, Jim, Mgr.-Product--Kern's Bakeries, Incorporated, Knoxville, TN, pg. 624
Blise, John, V.P.-Product Mngmt.--Warner Press, Inc., Anderson, IN, pg. 1164
Block, Gerold, Mgr.-Mktg.--Bruner Corporation, Milwaukee, WI, pg. 184
Bloom, Allen J., Exec. V.P.-Mktg & Sls.--Ringling Bros., Barnum & Bailey Combined Shows, Inc., Vienna, VA, pg. 935
Bloom, Allen J., Sr. V.P.-Mktg. & Sls.--Ice Follies & Holiday on Ice, Vienna, VA, pg. 935
Bloom, Richard A., Gen. Mgr.-Sls. & Mktg.--Bloom Electric Services, Inc., Oklahoma City, OK, pg. 157
Bloom, T., V.P.-Mktg. & Sls.--Elastic Stop Nut, Union, NJ, pg. 514
Blumberg, Leo, V.P., Mktg. Services--Anderson, Dusenbury & Alban, Atlanta, GA, pg. 72
Blumberg, Thomas A., Grp. V.P.-Mktg. & Sls.--Leviton Mfg. Co., Inc., Little Neck, NY, pg. 671
Blyth, Peter, Exec. V.P.-Devel.--Radisson Hotel Corporation, Minneapolis, MN, pg. 221
Bobinchuck, Mark, V.P.-Mktg.--Par Industries, inc., Medina, OH, pg. 847
Bobowski, Steve, V.P.-Mktg.--Iams Company, Dayton, OH, pg. 561
Bodmer, Bill, Sr. V.P.-Adv. & Sls.--Pathmark, Woodbridge, NJ, pg. 1064
Bodow, Don, V.P.-Mktg.--The Upper Deck Company, Carlsbad, CA, pg. 1140
Boehm, George R., V.P., Dir. Media & Mkt. Research--YPMS/TMP Worldwide, Inc., Mequon, WI, pg. 1074
Boehmler, Sarah P., Exec. V.P.-Market Devel.--The American Stock Exchange, New York, NY, pg. 62
Boehs, Kenneth R., V.P.-Mktg.--American Systems Corporation, Chantilly, VA, pg. 63
Bogart, Tom, Dir.-Intl. Mktg.--Best Western International, Inc., Phoenix, AZ, pg. 146
Bogut, L., Mgr.-Mktg.--Vari Tronics Company, Inc., Duarte, CA, pg. 1145
Bohling, Lavon O., V.P.-Mktg.--Reinke Manufacturing Co., Inc., Deshler, NE, pg. 924
Bohlman, Victor, Dir.-Mktg.--RHC/Spacemaster Corporation, Melrose Park, IL, pg. 906
Bohn, J., Mktg. Dir.--Tracor ELSIN, Sunnyvale, CA, pg. 1105
Bohrk, Betty, Intl. Mktg. Mgr.--California Avocado Commission, Santa Ana, CA, pg. 209
Boland, Kate, Mgr.-Mktg.--Hausted, Medina, OH, pg. 1008
Bolanowski, Stephen A., Jr., V.P. & Mktg. Dir.--Hammond Lead Products, Inc., Hammond, IN, pg. 504
Bolger, Tom, Principal/Mktg. Services--Michael, Bolger, Reinschmiedt, King (MBRK), Dallas, TX, pg. 746
Bollmann, Julie K., Mktg. Services Coord.--Servus Footwear Company, Rock Island, IL, pg. 993
Bonistalli, James, Dir.-Mktg.--Metra, Commuter Rail Service Board, Chicago, IL, pg. 922
Bonono, Mary, Dir.-Mktg. & Adv.--Gilbert/Robinson, Inc., Kansas City, MO, pg. 458
Boodjeh, David, V.P.-Mktg.--Discount Drug Mart Inc., Medina, OH, pg. 339
Boot, John, Mktg. Communications Mgr.--Attwood Corporation, Lowell, MI, pg. 1044
Booth, Neil, V.P.-Sls. & Mktg.--Brown & Haley, Tacoma, WA, pg. 182
Boozer, Larry, Mgr.-Mktg. & Sls.--Lancaster Malleable Castings Company, Lancaster, PA, pg. 653
Borak, Beverly, Mgr.-Institutional Mktg.--ASM International, Materials Park, OH, pg. 8
Borck, George, Exec. V.P.-Mktg.--Leather Center, Inc., Carrollton, TX, pg. 664
Bordeaux, Phillip, V.P.-Mktg.--Intermountain Gas Co., Boise, ID, pg. 575
Borden, Robert C., Jr., V.P.-Mktg.--Shipley Oil Company, York, PA, pg. 999
Borges, Bill, V.P.-Sls. & Mktg.--Ventura Coastal Corporation, Ventura, CA, pg. 1147
Born, Lewis F., V.P.-Reinsurance Mktg.--American United Life Insurance Company, Indianapolis, IN, pg. 65
Bose, Henry, Natl. Dir.-Adv. & Mktg. Programs--The Fairmont Hotels, San Francisco, CA, pg. 397
Boshkoff, Katherine, Dir.-Mktg.--Integral Systems, Walnut Creek, CA, pg. 572
Botelho, Tom, V.P., Acct. Services & Mktg. Dir.--Thomas & Perkins, Denver, CO, pg. 1093
Bottaro, Ron, Mgr.-Major Accts.--Hanna Car Wash International, Inc., Portland, OR, pg. 505
Bottega, Debra, Mktg. Coord.--Flexel, Inc., Atlanta, GA, pg. 418
Bottin, William, Mgr.-Direct Mktg.--Murdock, Inc., Compton, CA, pg. 776
Boughton, Deb, Mgr.-Mktg.--Labelon Corporation, Canandaigua, NY, pg. 649
Boulay, David, Dir.-Mktg.-Fats & Oils--Holsum Foods, Waukesha, WI, pg. 515
Bove, James V., Jr., Mktg. Mgr.-Consumer Prods.--Everpure Inc., Westmont, IL, pg. 358
Bovis, George S., Sr. V.P.-Mktg. Devel. & Growth Plng.--White Hen Pantry, Inc., Elmhurst, IL, pg. 1185
Bowden, Peter, Dir.-Mktg. & Adv. Mgr.--American SelfCare Corporation, Columbus, GA, pg. 60
Bowen, Mary, Dir.-Mktg. & Intl. Sls.--Power & Telephone Supply Company, Memphis, TN, pg. 883
Bowers, Kip, Mgr.-Prod. Devel.--Benjamin Ansehl Company, Saint Louis, MO, pg. 76
Bowie, Kathy, Mktg. Asst.--Howden Sirocco inc., Hyde Park, MA, pg. 547
Bowling, Gene H., V.P.-Mktg. & Sls.--Alkota Cleaning Systems, Inc., Alcester, SD, pg. 34
Bowman, Gary D., Mkt. Plng. Mgr.-Regulators--Grove Valve & Regulator Company, Oakland, CA, pg. 490
Boyce, Hugh, Dir.-Sls. & Mktg.--Flexfab, Inc., Hastings, MI, pg. 418
Boyd, Andrew E., V.P.-Mktg.--The Hilsinger Corp., Plainville, MA, pg. 535
Boyd, Bruce, Adv. & Mktg. Mgr.--AEC, Inc., Wood Dale, IL, pg. 1047
Boyd, D.E., V.P.-Mktg. & Sls., Pre-contract--ABB Environmental Systems, Knoxville, TN, pg. 2
Boyd, E., V.P.-Mktg.--Eyecessories, Plainville, MA, pg. 535
Boyd, Stan, V.P.-Sls. & Mktg.--The Fairmont Hotels, San Francisco, CA, pg. 397
Boyer, Robert A., V.P.-Sls. & Mktg.--Amarlite Architectural Products, Atlanta, GA, pg. 47
Boykin, George, Dir.-Mktg.--Vince Cullers Advertising Inc., Chicago, IL, pg. 304
Boyle, Bill, V.P.-Mktg.--Artec Distributing, Inc., Shelburne, VT, pg. 86
Boyle, Eric M., Sr. V.P.-Intl. Sls. & Mktg.--Lindsay Olive Growers, Lindsay, CA, pg. 676
Boyle, Neil, Dir.-Mktg.--Marboro Books Inc., New York, NY, pg. 120
Boyter, J. Earle, V.P.-Mktg. & Sls.--Piper Aircraft Corporation, Vero Beach, FL, pg. 872
Bracher, James, Dir.-Mktg.--Surgical Specialties, Reading, PA, pg. 1065
Bracken, Frank, Exec. V.P.-Mktg.--Haggar Apparel Company, Dallas, TX, pg. 499
Bradley, Guy F. II, V.P.-Mktg.--Patterson Dental Company, Minneapolis, MN, pg. 851
Bradley, Jean E., Mgr.-Mktg. Communications--Holland Mark Martin, Burlington, MA, pg. 539
Brady, James, Dir.-Mktg.--The Allan R. Hackel Organization, Newton Center, MA, pg. 498
Brady, Michael, V.P.-Sls. & Mktg.--M.S. Walker, Inc./ Seacoast, Somerville, MA, pg. 1160
Brady, Richard, V.P.-Mktg.--Suburban Communications Corp., Livonia, MI, pg. 1055
Brady, Robert E., Exec. V.P. & Dir.-Sls. & Mktg.--Kirkpatrick Pettis, Omaha, NE, pg. 779
Brady, Robert W., Exec. V.P.-Sls. & Mktg.--American Tool Companies, Inc., Lincoln, NE, pg. 64
Bramen, Bruce, Mktg. Dir.--William B. Reily & Co., Inc., New Orleans, LA, pg. 923
Bramen, Bruce B., V.P.-Mktg.--Luzianne Blue Plate Foods, New Orleans, LA, pg. 923
Brandenburg, Carol, Mktg. Mgr.--American Louver Co., Skokie, IL, pg. 57
Brander, Frank, Dir.-Business Mktg.--Trans World Airlines, Inc., Mount Kisco, NY, pg. 561
Branen, Rebecca, V.P.-Mktg.--Brian Center Management Corporation, Hickory, NC, pg. 175
Branton, Robert, V.P.-Sls. & Mktg.--United Hardware Distributing Co., Plymouth, MN, pg. 1132
Braswell, Karen, Mktg. Mgr.--BJ Acquisition Corp., Charlotte, NC, pg. 107
Braun, Grant H., Sr. V.P.-Mktg.--Great Salt Lake Minerals & Chemicals Corp., Ogden, UT, pg. 482
Breard, Jack H., Dir.-Mktg.--Ebsco Industries, Inc., Birmingham, AL, pg. 365
Breen, Don, V.P.-Sls. & Mktg.--John Morrell & Co., Cincinnati, OH, pg. 54
Brehm, Jack J., Sr. V.P.-Mktg.--Levitz Furniture Corporation, Boca Raton, FL, pg. 647
Breit, Toby L., V.P., Dir. Mktg. Services--Silverstone, Adkins & Breit, Inc., Stratford, CT, pg. 1005
Brennan, Andrew J., V.P.-Sls. & Mktg.--Everfresh Beverages Inc., Franklin Park, IL, pg. 391
Brennan, Beverly, Dir.-Adv. & Mktg.--Olson Rug Company, Chicago, IL, pg. 824
Brennan, Edward, V.P.-Mktg.--American Legend Corporate, Seattle, WA, pg. 57
Brenner, David H., Sr. V.P.-Mktg.--Amway Corporation, Ada, MI, pg. 70
Bressi, Joseph R., Sr. V.P.-Pur. & Mktg.--Camelot Music, Inc., North Canton, OH, pg. 212
Bressler, Marc, V.P., Dir., Mktg. Services--Siebel/Mohr, Inc., New York, NY, pg. 1002
Brew, Jon, Dir.-Mktg.--Andes Candies, Inc., Delavan, WI, pg. 169
Brewster, Graham, Sr. V.P.-Sls. & Mktg.--The Napier Company, Meriden, CT, pg. 783
Brewster, John, Mgr.-Mktg.--Henri's Food Products Co., Inc., Milwaukee, WI, pg. 530
Bridgforth, Stewart, V.P.-Mktg.--McCarty Farms, Magee, MS, pg. 727
Briggs, Mike, V.P.-Mktg. & Human Resources--Anchor Continental Incorporated, Columbia, SC, pg. 71
Bring, Gordon, V.P., Mktg. Dir. & New Bus. Contact--Out of Home Media Services, Inc., New York, NY, pg. 832
Brink, Lyle, V.P.-Mktg.--Brink Electric Construction Company, Rapid City, SD, pg. 176
Brior, Bill, Dir.-Mktg.--Star-Parts Inc., Hazleton, PA, pg. 1039
Brisbon, Eric, V.P.-Mktg.--Ambac International Corp., Columbia, SC, pg. 47
Briskie, George, V.P.-Mktg.--NWS, Inc., Chicago, IL, pg. 782
Britain, David, V.P. & Dir.-Plng.--Brock Candy Company, Chattanooga, TN, pg. 177
Britenbach, Bill, V.P.-Sls. & Mktg.--Tom's Foods, Columbus, GA, pg. 1101
Britt, Arie C., V.P.-Gas Mktg.--Hunt Oil Company, Dallas, TX, pg. 553
Brochu, Patrick, V.P.-Intl. Mktg.--Adra Systems, Inc., Lowell, MA, pg. 18
Brock, David, V.P.-Mktg.--Brock Candy Company, Chattanooga, TN, pg. 177
Brock, Kerri, Dir.-Channel Mktg.--WordPerfect Corporation, Orem, UT, pg. 1202
Brockman, Sue, Dir.-Mktg.--Recreational Equipment, Inc., Kent, WA, pg. 917
Brockmeyer, Don, V.P.-Mktg. & Engrng.--Hydreco, Augusta, GA, pg. 559
Broderick, Matthew, V.P.-Mktg.--Turtle Wax, Inc., Chicago, IL, pg. 1120
Brodt, Donald B., Mgr.-Materials--Aircraft Gear Corporation, Chicago, IL, pg. 27
Brokaw, A. Allen, V.P.-Mktg. & Sls.--The Airolite Company, Marietta, OH, pg. 28
Bromwell, Steven, V.P.-Sls.--Bay State Milling Co., Quincy, MA, pg. 127
Brondi, Dennis, Dir.-Mktg.--Power-One, Inc., Camarillo, CA, pg. 883
Brook, John T., Mgr.-Sls. & Mktg.--Overly Manufacturing Co., Greensburg, PA, pg. 833
Brooke, Ralston L., Sr. V.P.-Mktg. & Adv.--Wheat, First Securities Inc., Richmond, VA, pg. 1184
Brookhart, Michael, Dir.-Mktg.-Frozen Foods--Hanover Foods Corporation, Hanover, PA, pg. 506
Brooks, Bob, V.P.-Sls. & Mktg.--The Bureau of National Affairs, Inc., Washington, DC, pg. 189
Brooks, David A., V.P.-Sls. & Mktg.--General Chemical Corporation, Parsippany, NJ, pg. 801
Brooks, Lauren, Sr. Mgr.-Apparel Sls. & Mktg.--ASICS Tiger Corporation, Fountain Valley, CA, pg. 8
Brooks, Terry, V.P.-Distr.--Wells Lamont, Niles, IL, pg. 712
Brooks, W., Dir.-Mktg.--Miller Electric Mfg. Co., Appleton, WI, pg. 754
Brookshier, Larry, V.P.-Mktg.--Rubatex Corporation, Bedford, VA, pg. 480
Bross, Mike, Mgr.-Prod.--E. D. Bullard Company, Cynthiana, KY, pg. 188
Brothers, Carl W., Sr. V.P.-Mktg.--Riceland Foods, Inc., Stuttgart, AR, pg. 931
Broughton, George W., Exec. V.P. & Dir.-Mktg.--Broughton Foods Company, Marietta, OH, pg. 180
Brous, David, Dir.-Mktg.--Joshua Meier Corp., North Bergen, NJ, pg. 737
Brown, Doug, Pres., Dir.-Intl. Mktg.--The Atkins Agency, San Antonio, TX, pg. 94
Brown, E. Ken, Dir.-Mktg.--Parks Sausage Company, Baltimore, MD, pg. 850
Brown, Jeffrey, Dir.-Sls. & Mktg.--P M Company, Philadelphia, PA, pg. 835
Brown, Joseph D., Ph.D., Mktg. Research Dir.--Bonsib Inc., Fort Wayne, IN, pg. 164
Brown, Karen, Dir.-Mktg.--Vortec Corporation, Cincinnati, OH, pg. 246
Brown, Kelly, V.P.-Mktg.--Smith Frozen Foods, Inc., Weston, OR, pg. 1012
Brown, Larry L., Jr., Dir.-Mktg. & Adv.--Riverside Central Services, Inc., Natchez, MS, pg. 937
Brown, Loretta, Sls. & Mktg.--Boyer Bros. Inc., Altoona, PA, pg. 169
Brown, Malcolm P., Sr. V.P.-Mktg. & Communications--The Binswanger Company, Philadelphia, PA, pg. 151
Brown, Mary, Assoc. Dir.-Mktg.--Colorado Lottery, Denver, CO, pg. 265
Brown, Randy, V.P.-Sls. & Mktg.--Agsco, Inc., Grand Forks, ND, pg. 4
Brown, Renee C., V.P.-Mktg. & Sls.--Pro-Line Corporation, Dallas, TX, pg. 892
Brown, Richard A., V.P.-Mktg.--DMI, Inc., Goodfield, IL, pg. 309
Brown, Susan, Mktg. Coord.--Peter Pan Bus Lines, Inc., Springfield, MA, pg. 864
Brown, William J., V.P., Dir. Mktg.--Meldrum & Fewsmith Advertising Inc., Cleveland, OH, pg. 737
Browne, William T., Jr., Sr. V.P.-Mktg. & Sls.--Marotta Scientific Controls, Inc., Montville, NJ, pg. 713
Brownstein, Hy, Dir.-Mktg.--Uniflex, Inc., Hicksville, NY, pg. 1126
Bruckheim, Stan, Media Mktg. Mgr.--Russ Reid Company, Inc., Pasadena, CA, pg. 923
Bruder, Thomas A., III, Mgr.-Mktg.--M. A. Bruder & Sons, Inc., Broomall, PA, pg. 184
Brueske, Glenn D., V.P.-Mktg.--Crown Holdings, Inc., Roseville, MN, pg. 302
Bruno, Richard, Corp. V.P., Mktg.--Freeson Advertising Agency, Miami Lakes, FL, pg. 431
Brunton, Dale, Prod. Mgr.-Poultry--AJC International, Inc., Atlanta, GA, pg. 4
Brush, James, Exec. V.P.-Sls. & Mktg.--Sentry Group, Rochester, NY, pg. 990
Bruskotter, Thomas, V.P.-Supply, Distribution & Mktg.--Gary-Williams Energy Corporation, Denver, CO, pg. 444
Bryan, Michael B., V.P.-Sls. & Mktg.--Graham Magnetics, Inc., Bedford, TX, pg. 475
Bryan, Steve, V.P.-Mktg.--T. A. Loving Company, Goldsboro, NC, pg. 685
Bryant, Bill, V.P.-Mktg.-Atlanta Apparel Ctr.--Atlanta Market Center, Atlanta, GA, pg. 94
Bryant, Carlton, V.P.-Mktg.--American Passage Media Corporation, Seattle, WA, pg. 59
Bryant, Marsha, Mktg. Services Coord.--Flambeau Products Corp., Middlefield, OH, pg. 809
Brydger, Allen, Dir., Media & Mktg. Services--Sanchez & Levitan, Inc., Miami, FL, pg. 970
Brye, Cara, V.P.-Mktg.--Remco Enterprises, Inc., Houston, TX, pg. 926
Buccola, Tony, V.P.-Sls. & Mktg.--Cumberland Packing Corp., Brooklyn, NY, pg. 304
Buchler, Christina, V.P.-Mktg. & Human Resources--Citizens National Bank, Hammond, LA, pg. 251
Buck, Dave, Mktg. Rep.--The Phillies-A Limited Partnership, Philadelphia, PA, pg. 867

Corporate Responsibilities Index

Buckley, J.G., V.P.-Wholesale Mktg.--Gulf Oil, Westborough, MA, pg. 304
Buckner, Cole J., V.P.-Mktg.--George E. Warren Corp., Vero Beach, FL, pg. 1164
Buddig, Thomas R., V.P.-Sls. & Mktg.--Carl Buddig & Company, Homewood, IL, pg. 186
Budgen, Donald, V.P.-Mktg.--Magnetic Analysis Corp., Mount Vernon, NY, pg. 700
Budzak, Annette, Mktg. & New Bus. Dir.--Chernoff/Silver & Associates, Columbia, SC, pg. 243
Buhl, Edward R., V.P.-Mktg.--Central Mutual Insurance Co., Van Wert, OH, pg. 233
Buhl, Edward R., V.P.-Mktg.--All America Insurance Company, Van Wert, OH, pg. 233
Bullard, Steve, V.P.-Retail Mktg.--Dorman-Roth Foods, Inc., Moonachie, NJ, pg. 346
Bullock, Jack, V.P.-Mktg. & Sls.--Powers Pharmaceutical, Brockton, MA, pg. 236
Bullock, Ron, V.P.-Mktg.--Fill-Rite Division, Fort Wayne, IN, pg. 1120
Bumpus, Richard, V.P.-Mktg. & Training--North Coast Electric Company, Bellevue, WA, pg. 813
Bunker, Debbie, Buyer--Sensor Developments Inc., Orion, MI, pg. 990
Burbick, Ron L., V.P.-Mktg. & Sls.--Schneller, Inc., Kent, OH, pg. 977
Burd, Carolyn, Mktg. Mgr.--Experience in Software, Inc., Berkeley, CA, pg. 393
Burget, Bill, Mgr.-Mktg.--York Wallcoverings Inc., York, PA, pg. 1208
Burghard, Kay, Dir.-Mktg.--Dedert Corporation, Olympia Fields, IL, pg. 324
Burgher, Rex, V.P.-Mktg.--Benderson Development Co., Inc., Buffalo, NY, pg. 138
Burgman, William, V.P.-Mktg.--Standard Manifold Company, Inc., Chicago, IL, pg. 1037
Burgoyne, Paul F., V.P.-Mktg.--Edward Don & Company of Illinois, North Riverside, IL, pg. 344
Burkam, Jack, Dir.-Mktg.--Sonoma Mission Inn & Spa, Sonoma, CA, pg. 1018
Burke, H. Worth, Exec. V.P.-Capital Markets--Texas Commerce Bancshares, Inc., Houston, TX, pg. 1089
Burke, John, V.P.-Sls. & Mktg.--Trek Bicycle Corporation, Waterloo, WI, pg. 581
Burke, Terry, V.P., Mktg. Services--Shelby & Shane Marketing Communications, Cincinnati, OH, pg. 996
Burke, W.J., V.P.-Mktg.--Alvey Inc., Saint Louis, MO, pg. 46
Burkett, Walter, V.P.-Mktg.--Post Buckley Schuh & Jernigan, Miami, FL, pg. 881
Burkoff, Jim, V.P.-Mktg.--Lady Marlene Sales Corp., New York, NY, pg. 650
Burks, T., V.P.-Intl. Mktg. & Sls.--Shure Brothers Incorporated, Evanston, IL, pg. 1001
Burnhart, George, Mgr.-Natl. Mktg.--Longyear Company, Salt Lake City, UT, pg. 682
Burns, Bruce C., V.P.-Mktg. Support--Blue Cross and Blue Shield of Oklahoma, Tulsa, OK, pg. 159
Burns, Creg, V.P.-Grocery Mktg. Opers.--Homeland Stores, Inc., Oklahoma City, OK, pg. 542
Burns, Jack, Mgr.-Mktg. Plans--ASC Incorporated, Southgate, MI, pg. 7
Burns, Leslie A., Mgr.-Mktg.--Executive Telecom Systems, Inc., Indianapolis, IN, pg. 189
Burns, R. Allen, Mgr.-Mktg.--Itran Corporation, Manchester, NH, pg. 583
Burns, Robert, Mgr.-Sls. Promotion & Food Service Mktg.--Tri Valley Growers Inc., San Francisco, CA, pg. 1111
Burns, Robert D., V.P.-Sls. & Mktg.--Conway Import Co. Inc., Franklin Park, IL, pg. 281
Burrill, Ken, V.P.-Mktg.--H. E. Sargent, Inc., Stillwater, ME, pg. 971
Burson, Lourdes Martinez, Supvr.-Mktg.--Windsor Fashions, Los Angeles, CA, pg. 1195
Burton, Doug, Sr. V.P.-Mktg.--Westlake Hardware, Inc., Shawnee Mission, KS, pg. 1183
Burton, Richard I., Dir.-Sls. & Mktg.--Twin City Die Castings Co., Minneapolis, MN, pg. 1121
Burton, Robert, Sls. & Mktg. Dir.--Sterling Homes Corp., Sparks, NV, pg. 1046
Burton, Robert, Dir.-Sls. & Mktg.--Sterling Builders, Inc., Irvine, CA, pg. 1047
Burton, Tessa, V.P.-Viewer Mktg.--WTTW (Channel 11), Chicago, IL, pg. 1156
Busam, Jenny, Dir., Sports Mktg. & Promo.--Shelby & Shane Marketing Communications, Cincinnati, OH, pg. 996
Busca, G.P., Sr. V.P.-Sls. & Mktg. & Chief Oper. Officer--Energy Brokers Guild, Stevensville, MI, pg. 381
Busse, Bruce, Dir.-Mktg.--Enduro Industries, Inc., Addison, IL, pg. 939
Butler, Cindy, Mktg. Coord.--California Strawberry Advisory Board, Watsonville, CA, pg. 210
Butler, Dick, V.P.-Mktg.--El Torito Restaurants, Inc., Irvine, CA, pg. 929
Butler, Norman D., V.P.-Sls. & Mktg., Service Parts Div.--Foley-PLP Company, Rochester, NY, pg. 422
Butler, Richard, Exec. V.P.-Mktg.--El Torito Restaurants, Inc., Irvine, CA, pg. 372
Buxbaum, E., V.P.-Sls. & Mktg.--The Akro Corporation, Canton, OH, pg. 262
Buzanowski, Joe, Dir.-Mktg.--Continental Coin Corporation, Van Nuys, CA, pg. 278
Bybee, Steve, Dir.-Sls. & Mktg.--The Knapheide Mfg. Co., Quincy, IL, pg. 636
Bykerk, Larry, V.P.-Sls.--Apollo Colors, Inc., Northbrook, IL, pg. 78
Byrd, Russ, Mgr.-Mktg.--Wavetek Communications Div., Indianapolis, IN, pg. 1168
Byrnes, TerrenceJ., Dir.-Mktg.--Enerfab Inc., Cincinnati, OH, pg. 381
Byrnes, Thomas, V.P.-Mktg.--Decorative Fabrics - Mastercraft, Spindale, NC, pg. 262
Cagan Dennis, V.P.-Mktg. & Strategic Plng.--Century Computer Marketing, Marina Del Rey, CA, pg. 235
Cahill, Tony, V.P.-Indus. Prods.--National Oats Co., Cedar Rapids, IA, pg. 25
Caldwell, Bruce L., Exec. V.P.-Bus. Devel.--John Alden Financial Corporation, Miami, FL, pg. 32
Caldwell, Dale, V.P.-Mktg.--Edwards Baking Co., Atlanta, GA, pg. 369
Calengor, Jerry, Dir.-Mktg.--Normark Corporation, Minneapolis, MN, pg. 810
Calhoun, James D., Exec. Dir.-Mktg.--Citizens Gas & Coke Utility, Indianapolis, IN, pg. 250
Calio, Joseph, V.P.-Sls. & Mktg.--Exide Corporation, Reading, PA, pg. 393
Calkins, Suzanne B., V.P.-Mktg.--The William Carter Company, New York, NY, pg. 226
Callas, Chris, Chief Oper. Officer & Dir.-Sls. & Mktg.--Time Products, Inc., Atlanta, GA, pg. 1090
Calton, John, Mgr.-Mktg. Services--UC Industries, Inc., Parsippany, NJ, pg. 1122
Camarda, Bernard, V.P.-Sls. & Mktg.--Merchandising Equipment Group, Arlington Heights, IL, pg. 739
Camas, Walter, V.P.-Mktg.--Precision Valve Corporation, Yonkers, NY, pg. 885
Camens, Bernard, Sr. V.P.-Sls- Lighting Div.--Crystal Clear Industries Company, Ridgefield Park, NJ, pg. 303
Campbell, Alex, Dir.-Mktg.--Noma-International, Inc., Forest Park, IL, pg. 808
Campbell, Don, V.P. & Controller--Western Diesel Services Inc., Saint Louis, MO, pg. 1179
Campbell, Frank R., V.P.-Prod.--McAnally Enterprises, Inc., Yucaipa, CA, pg. 726
Campbell, Reg, Dir.-Mktg.--Kasle Steel Corporation, Dearborn, MI, pg. 617
Campbell, Thomas, V.P.-Mktg. & Sls.--KNOX International Corp., Knoxville, TN, pg. 638
Campbell, Thomas, V.P.-Sls. & Mktg.--Ranging, East Bloomfield, NY, pg. 300
Campbell, Thomas E., V.P.-Mktg. Mgr.--Weinstock's Flowers & Gifts, Atlanta, GA, pg. 638
Campbell, Tom, Prod. Mgr.--Crosman Corporation, East Bloomfield, NY, pg. 695
Canady, Ray, V.P.-Mktg.--Silver Dollar City, Inc., Branson, MO, pg. 1004
Canale, Cecil, V.P.-Mktg.-Fragrances--Revlon, Inc., New York, NY, pg. 696
Canaley, Virginia Brandreth, Mgr.-Mktg. Communications & Dir.-Coop Adv.--Sentry Group, Rochester, NY, pg. 990
Cange, Lorraine, Mktg. Asst.--Cerro Copper Products Co., Sauget, IL, pg. 711
Canning, John N., V.P.-Sls. & Mktg.--Pine State Tobacco & Candy Company, Augusta, ME, pg. 871
Cannon, Robert E., V.P.-Sls. & Mktg.--Channellock, Inc., Meadville, PA, pg. 239
Capauno, Anita, Dir.-Circulation & Mktg.--B.A.S.S., Inc., Montgomery, AL, pg. 105
Capitano, Joe, Dir.-Solar Cell Mktg.--Applied Solar Energy Corporation, City of Industry, CA, pg. 79
Capo, Barbara, Mgr.-Natl. Accts. & Foreign Sls.--Arrow Group Industries, Inc., Wayne, NJ, pg. 357
Caponi, Colleen, Mgr.-Adv. & Mktg.--Apple Vacations West Inc., Elk Grove Village, IL, pg. 79
Cappadocia, Ronald, Sr. V.P.-Mktg. & Sls.--Farley Candy Company, Chicago, IL, pg. 399
Caramela, Laurence M., Dir.-Sls. & Mktg., Bottle/Can--Central Coca-Cola Bottling Company, Inc., Richmond, VA, pg. 232
Carbone, Lou, V.P., Mktg. & Strategic Plng.--FKQ Advertising Inc., Clearwater, FL, pg. 394
Cardillo, Robert, V.P.-Sls. & Mktg.--Avis, Inc., Garden City, NY, pg. 102
Carey, Dallas, Mgr.-Adv. & Mktg.--Stratton Corp., South Londonderry, VT, pg. 1053
Carey, David, Dir.-Mktg. Services--Cosmopolitan, New York, NY, pg. 523
Carey, H. Augustus, 1st V.P. & Natl. Mktg. Coordinator--W. P. Carey & Co., Inc., New York, NY, pg. 218
Carey, Rita Ann, Mgr.-Mktg.--Rustco Products Company, Denver, CO, pg. 957
Carey, Verian, V.P.-Sls.--Kelly-Moore Paint Company, Inc., San Carlos, CA, pg. 621
Cariola, John, Dir.-Mktg.--Oto-Sonic, Inc., Chicago, IL, pg. 138
Cariolo, Cosimo, Dir.-Sls. & Mktg.--Warren E. Collins, Inc., Braintree, MA, pg. 263
Cark, Veda, V.P.-Mktg. & Sls.--Litecontrol Corporation, Hanson, MA, pg. 677
Carle, Ed, Prod. Mgr.-Consumer Products--Riceland Foods, Inc., Stuttgart, AR, pg. 931
Carlson, Robert E., Exec. V.P.-Agencies & Mktg.--Northwestern Mutual Life Insurance Co., Milwaukee, WI, pg. 815
Carlson, Rodney K., Dir.-Mktg.--Milk Marketing Inc., Strongsville, OH, pg. 753
Carlson, Rollie, V.P.-Mktg.--Coast To Coast Stores, Inc., Denver, CO, pg. 257
Carlton, Thomas J., V.P.-Sls. & Mktg.--Corrugated Metals, Inc., Chicago, IL, pg. 287
Carluccio, C., Div. Mgr.--Snow-Nabstedt Power Transmissions, Manchester, NH, pg. 476
Carney, Larry, V.P.-Sls. & Mktg.-Royalle Div.--Prince Gardner Incorporated, Saint Louis, MO, pg. 890
Carnival, John, V.P. & Dir.-Sls., Mktg., Direct Mktg., Adv. & Media--Weksler Instruments Corp., Freeport, NY, pg. 1174
Carolan, Douglas, Exec. V.P.-Mdsg. & Mktg.--Associated Wholesale Grocers, Inc., Kansas City, KS, pg. 92
Caron, Thomas, Dir.-Mktg.--Schwan's Sales Enterprises, Marshall, MN, pg. 980
Carpenter, Mike, V.P.-Sls. & Mktg.--The Vollrath Company Inc., Sheboygan, WI, pg. 1154
Carpenter, William R., Mktg. Mgr.--Erie Press Systems, Erie, PA, pg. 386
Carr, Chuck, Dir.-Mktg.--Pip Printing, Agoura Hills, CA, pg. 616
Carr, Gail A., Coord.-Mktg. Service--Microdot Aerospace Fastening Systems Group, Fullerton, CA, pg. 749
Carroll, Crawford, V.P. & Mktg. Services Dir.--The Times-Picayune Publishing Corp., New Orleans, LA, pg. 1098
Carroll, J.F., V.P.-Mktg.--Baltimore Aircoil Company, Jessup, MD, pg. 69
Carter, John, V.P.-Mktg.--Henschel Corp., Newburyport, MA, pg. 964
Carter, John M., Chm. Bd., & Chief Exec. Officer--Carco Electronics, Menlo Park, CA, pg. 217
Carter, Reid P., V.P., Mktg. & Research Dir.--Siddall, Matus & Coughter, Inc. Advertising & Public Relations, Richmond, VA, pg. 1002
Carter, W. D., VP-Mktg--Marion Power Shovel Division, Marion, OH, pg. 565
Cartier, Chuck, Dir.-Sls. & Mktg.--The Beverly Hills Hotel, Beverly Hills, CA, pg. 148
Cartwright, George R., Mgr.-Mktg.--The Columbia Corporation, Chatham, NY, pg. 1209
Cartwright, Marie Izzo, Asst. V.P.-Corp. Mktg. & Communications--The Edward J. DeBartolo Corporation, Youngstown, OH, pg. 323
Caruso, Vicky Kenyon, Dir.-Mktg. Services--Days Inns of America, Inc., Parsippany, NJ, pg. 1100
Casale, Ralph, Exec. V.P. & Chief Mktg. Officer--New York Life Worldwide Holding, Inc., New York, NY, pg. 803
Case, Dave, Div. V.P.-Mktg. Res.--Hallmark Cards, Inc., Kansas City, MO, pg. 501
Casey, J. Phillip, V.P.-Mktg. & Sls.--JII/Sales Promotion Associates, Inc., Coshocton, OH, pg. 604
Cash, Elaine, Mktg. Services Coord.--Burlington Motor Carriers Inc., Daleville, IN, pg. 191
Casper, Bert, V.P.-Mktg.--Remmele Engineering, Inc., Saint Paul, MN, pg. 926
Casper, Wayne, Mgr.-New Prod. Devel.--Sargento Cheese Co., Plymouth, WI, pg. 971
Cassano, William, V.P.-Mktg. & Sls.--Whaling Industries, Inc., Fall River, MA, pg. 1183
Cassidy, Joseph, V.P.-Mktg.--The Orvis Company, Inc., Manchester, VT, pg. 830
Cassin, Thomas C., V.P.-Mktg.--Pitco Frialator Inc., Concord, NH, pg. 157
Castaldo, Nicholas A., Sr. V.P.-Mktg.--S & A Restaurant Corp., Dallas, TX, pg. 958
Castle, Grant, Exec. V.P., Dir. Mktg. Services--TBWA Advertising, Inc., New York, NY, pg. 1071
Castner, C. Lloyd, Mgr.-Mktg.--Nebraska Public Power District, Columbus, NE, pg. 796
Castro, Mikki, Dir.-Mktg. & Mgr.-Adv.--Hoffritz for Cutlery, New York, NY, pg. 538
Castro, Mikki, Dir.-Mktg. & Mgr.-Adv.--Hoffritz International, New York, NY, pg. 538
Catalano, J.A., Mktg. Mgr.-Percussion--The Selmer Co., Elkhart, IN, pg. 573
Cates, Max, Dir.-Mtkg. Communications--Associated Electric Co-op Inc., Springfield, MO, pg. 89
Caulkins, William, Dir.-Mktg.--Sherman & Reilly, Inc., Chattanooga, TN, pg. 998
Cavallo, Doreen, Mgr., Mktg. Services--Arcinco, Inc., Garfield, NJ, pg. 81
Cavanagh, John, Mgr.-Mktg. Masking Prods.--Ivex Packaging Corporation-Industrial Products Division, Newton, MA, pg. 583
Cavanaugh, Martha, Mgr.-Mktg. Services--Yankee Publishing Incorporated, Dublin, NH, pg. 1207
Cavendish, James B., 2nd V.P.-Group Mktg.--Shenandoah Life Insurance Company, Roanoke, VA, pg. 997
Cayne, J.C., Mgr.-Mktg. Services--The Spencer Turbine Co., Windsor, CT, pg. 1030
Cecere, Thomas W., 2nd V.P.-Corp. Services--Shenandoah Life Insurance Company, Roanoke, VA, pg. 997
Celentano, Domenick A., Jr., V.P.-Mktg.--Celentano Brothers, Verona, NJ, pg. 231
Cerf, G., V.P.-Mktg.--Jack Lenor Larsen, Inc., New York, NY, pg. 659
Cerny, Richard H., Dir.-Reg. Mktg.--Master Collectors Inc., Atlanta, GA, pg. 719
Chalifour, Marcel O., V.P.-Sls. & Mktg.--Associated Grocers of New England, Inc., Manchester, NH, pg. 90
Chalmers, Deborah, Mgr.-Mktg. Communications--Ready Systems, Sunnyvale, CA, pg. 916
Chamberlain, Sargeant V., Dir.-Pur.--The Scott Company, Marysville, OH, pg. 982
Chambers, J.W., Sr. V.P.-Sls. & Mktg.--The Hartwell Corporation, Placentia, CA, pg. 514
Champion, Charles F., Sr. V.P.-Adv. Sls. & Mktg.--Chicago Sun Times, Chicago, IL, pg. 18
Champion, Greg, Dir.-Mktg.--Mattison Machine Works, Rockford, IL, pg. 721
Champion, Jeff, Product Mgr.--G.C. Thorsen, Inc., Rockford, IL, pg. 609
Champlin, Charles, Sr. V.P.-Special Mkts.--Faribault Woolen Mill Co., Faribault, MN, pg. 399
Chandis, Harry T., Sr. V.P.-Mktg.--Trans World Airlines, Inc., Mount Kisco, NY, pg. 561
Channell, Ken, V.P.-Mktg.--ERA Real Estate, Overland Park, KS, pg. 360
Chapman, Janice, Sls. Coord.--Kesterson Food Company, Inc., Paris, TN, pg. 624
Chapman, S.N., Mgr.-Sls. & Mktg.--Hall Sign, Inc., Bloomington, IN, pg. 501
Chappelear, W.T., Jr., V.P.-Mktg.--Flavor House Products, Inc., Dothan, AL, pg. 417
Chappell, H., Mgr.-Mfr.--Abbey Etna Machine Company, Perrysburg, OH, pg. 9
Chappell, John, V.P.-Mktg.--Levi Strauss & Co. (Canada), Inc., Markham,, Canada, pg. 670
Charaf, W., Dir.-Intl. Accounts--Komatsu Dresser Company, Lincolnshire, IL, pg. 565
Charbonneau, Elizabeth, Dir.-Retail Mktg. & Sls. Promotion--Congoleum Corporation, Mercerville, NJ, pg. 274
Charles, G.R., Dir.-Mktg.--National Forge Company, Irvine, PA, pg. 788

Charlton, Paul, Dir.-Mktg.--Littleton Coin Co., Inc., Littleton, NH, pg. 679
Charms, Iris, Dir.-Product Pricing & Supply--Octagon Process Inc., Edgewater, NJ, pg. 821
Charoen-Rajapark, Daranee, Mktg. Services Dir.--Leo Burnett Ltd. Thailand, Bangkok, Thailand, pg. 193
Chenoweth, David A., V.P.-Sls. & Mktg.--The Paxall Group, Inc., Skokie, IL, pg. 852
Chesler, R.K., Mgr.-Mktg. Communications--Wells Lamont, Niles, IL, pg. 712
Chess, Paul, Mgr.-Mktg. Communications--Schwinn Bicycle Company, Chicago, IL, pg. 981
Chevallier, Raymond, V.P.-Mktg.--F. Schumacher & Co., New York, NY, pg. 979
Chiesso, Salvador, V.P.-Mktg.--Creative Salon Furniture Inc., Brooklyn, NY, pg. 297
Childers, Bruce C., Exec. V.P., Mktg. Services--Meldrum & Fewsmith Advertising Inc., Cleveland, OH, pg. 737
Childs, Karl R., V.P.-Mktg.--Sabreliner Corp., Chesterfield, MO, pg. 965
Chin, Eddy, Dir.-Mktg.--Dentsu, Young & Rubicam/Kuala Lumpur, Kuala Lumpur,, Malaysia, pg. 330
Chinnici, J.A., Jr., V.P.-Sls.--Great Lakes Lithograph Co., Cleveland, OH, pg. 481
Chiostergi, Bob, V.P.-Mktg. & Sls.--Southern Mills, Inc., Union City, GA, pg. 1021
Chittick, S. Woodworth, V.P.-Plng. & Bus. Devel.--Ocean Spray Cranberries, Inc., Lakeville, MA, pg. 820
Chomakos, James, Sr. V.P. & Mgr.-Mktg. Admin.--First Federal of Michigan, Detroit, MI, pg. 414
Chopp, Jack L., V.P.-Mktg.--American Family Mutual Insurance Co., Madison, WI, pg. 51
Chouhy-Oria, Santiago, Dir.-Mktg.--S. C. Johnson & Son de Argentina S.A.I.C., Buenos Aires,, Argentina, pg. 599
Chriss, Jim, V.P.-Mktg.-Women's Wear--Levi Strauss & Co., San Francisco, CA, pg. 670
Christensen, Gary, Sr. V.P.-Mktg. & Sls.--Pella Corporation, Pella, IA, pg. 856
Christensen, Hal, Mktg. & Client Services Dir.--Fotheringham & Associates, Salt Lake City, UT, pg. 427
Christensen, Hal, Dir.-Mktg.--Idahoan Foods, Lewisville, ID, pg. 561
Christenson, Rich, V.P.-Mktg.--Winona Knitting Mills, Inc., Winona, MN, pg. 1196
Christoff, Greg, Dir.-Mktg.--Paterno Imports Limited, Chicago, IL, pg. 851
Christoff, Greg, Dir.-Mktg.--Pacific Wine Co., Chicago, IL, pg. 851
Christon, Dean, Mgr.-Mktg. Communications--DHL Airways, Inc., Redwood City, CA, pg. 309
Christopher, David, Sr. V.P.-Mktg. & Sls.--Commodore Cruise Line, Ltd., Coral Gables, FL, pg. 269
Christopherson, Terry, Grp. Mktg. Mgr.--G. Heileman Brewing Co., Inc., La Crosse, WI, pg. 526
Chun, Tai Vee, V.P.-Prod.--Mutual Welding Co., Ltd, Honolulu, HI, pg. 779
Chustak, T., Mgr.-Prod.--Mid-Continent Screw Products Co., Lincolnwood, IL, pg. 750
Ciabattoni, Christine B., Mktg. Services Supvr.--Willson Safety Products, Reading, PA, pg. 1193
Cianciaruso, C.J., Sr. V.P.-Mktg.-Special Projects--J.E. Dunn Construction Co., Kansas City, MO, pg. 354
Cimbolo, Salvatore, V.P.-Sls. & Mktg.--Monroe Systems For Business, Inc., Morris Plains, NJ, pg. 766
Citrin, Michael, Mktg., Res. & Devel. Dir.--Partners Meany, Inc., Albany, NY, pg. 850
Claassen, James G., Sr. V.P.-Mktg. & Sls.--Montgomery Elevator Company, Moline, IL, pg. 767
Clady, Barbara A., V.P. & Mgr.-Mktg.--Robert F. Driver Co., Inc., San Diego, CA, pg. 349
Clancy, Kevin, V.P.-Sls. & Mktg.--Homes of Merit Inc., Bartow, FL, pg. 542
Clark, Bernie, V.P.-Mktg.--Miller Fluid Power Corp., Bensenville, IL, pg. 754
Clark, David, V.P.-Mktg.--Empire Berol U.S.A., Brentwood, TN, pg. 856
Clark, John, Dir.-Mktg.--Bearden Lumber Company, Inc., Bearden, AR, pg. 129
Clark, Lance, V.P.-Mktg.--K & B, Inc., New Orleans, LA, pg. 611
Clark, Sarah F., Assoc. Mktg. Dir.--Yale University Press, New Haven, CT, pg. 1207
Clark, Terry, Dir.-Mktg.--Bearden Lumber Company, Inc., Bearden, AR, pg. 129
Clark, W.P., Jr., V.P.-Sls. & Mktg.--Wall Colmonoy Corp., Madison Heights, MI, pg. 1160
Clarke, John, Sr. V.P.-Mktg.--Dr Pepper Company, Dallas, TX, pg. 342
Claspell, Greg, Dir.-Mktg.--Evana Automation, Evansville, IN, pg. 390
Clausen, B.R., V.P.-Corp. Plng. & Mktg.--Alabama Electric Cooperative, Inc., Andalusia, AL, pg. 28
Clausing, Gordon, V.P.-Mktg. & Sls.--Times Printing Company, Inc., Random Lake, WI, pg. 1098
Clawson, James, V.P.-Legal--Sentry Insurance, A Mutual Company, Stevens Point, WI, pg. 990
Clegg, Tom, V.P.-Mktg.--Sargento Incorporated, Plymouth, WI, pg. 971
Cleveland, Colleen, V.P.-Mktg.--Prepco, Los Angeles, CA, pg. 887
Cline, J.W., V.P.-Indus. Prods.--The Georgia Marble Company, Kennesaw, GA, pg. 453
Clinton, Stephen P., V.P.-Business Devel.--Hayes, Seay, Mattern & Mattern, Inc., Roanoke, VA, pg. 519
Cloran, J.H., Mgr.-Bus. Devel.--The Kirk & Blum Mfg. Co., Cincinnati, OH, pg. 633
Coakley, James F., V.P., Bus. Devel.--Pedone & Partners Inc., New York, NY, pg. 854
Coalter, Rick, Dir.-Mktg. Communications--J. A. Sexauer, Scarsdale, NY, pg. 357
Coan, M.J., Dir.-Bus. Devel.--Elkins Constructors, Inc., Jacksonville, FL, pg. 377
Cobb, Bruce, V.P.-Mktg.--Powell Electronics Inc., Philadelphia, PA, pg. 882
Cobb, Earl, V.P. & Bus. Mgr.--The Times-Picayune Publishing Corp., New Orleans, LA, pg. 1098
Cobb, Gary, V.P.-Mktg.--Plains Co-op Oil Mill, Lubbock, TX, pg. 873
Cobian, Francis J., Production Dir.--Lake to Lake Dairy, Kiel, WI, pg. 653
Cochran, Ron, Dir.-Mktg.--Kokosing Construction Company, Inc., Fredericktown, OH, pg. 640
Coe, John, V.P., Gen. Mgr. & Direct Mktg.--Marcus Advertising, Inc., Cleveland, OH, pg. 706
Coenson, Barbara, Mktg. Coord.--American Automobile Association, National Travel Department, Heathrow, FL, pg. 49
Coffey, Patrick, V.P.-Mktg.--Citizens Insurance Company of America, Howell, MI, pg. 35
Coffman, Charles T., V.P.-Mktg.-Popeyes--Al Copeland Enterprises, Inc., Jefferson, LA, pg. 283
Coffman, Charles T., V.P.-Mktg.--Church's Fried Chicken, Inc., Jefferson, LA, pg. 284
Cogswell, Bob, V.P.-Mdsg. & Mktg.--White Swan, Inc., Euless, TX, pg. 1156
Cohen, Alan D., Sr. V.P., Mktg. Services & Devel.--The Reeves Agency, Inc., Baltimore, MD, pg. 921
Cohen, Elissa, Mktg. Dir. & Acct. Supvr.--Sperling, New Orleans, LA, pg. 1030
Cohen, Elizabeth, Dir.-Mktg.--Dana Perfumes Corp., New York, NY, pg. 313
Cohen, Jonathon, Dir.-OEM & New Prod. Devel.--Nady Systems, Inc., Emeryville, CA, pg. 783
Cohen, Louis D., V.P.-Mktg.--Allen Foods, Inc., Saint Louis, MO, pg. 36
Cohen, Mark J., V.P.-Sls. & Mktg.--All-Luminum Products, Inc., Philadelphia, PA, pg. 35
Cohen, Martin A., Dir.-Mktg.--Kaz, Inc., New York, NY, pg. 619
Cohen, Maurice, Dir.-Mktg.--Penetone Corp., Tenafly, NJ, pg. 1172
Cohen, Nina, V.P.-Mktg. Services--Costa Cruise Lines, N.V., Miami, FL, pg. 288
Cohen, Warren, V.P.-Sls. & Mktg.--Eagle Electric Mfg. Co., Inc., Long Island City, NY, pg. 362
Colburn, Lenita, Mktg. Services Dir.--Ektelon Corp., San Diego, CA, pg. 890
Cole, Adriene, Sr. Dir.-Mktg.--Freeman Cosmetic Corp., Los Angeles, CA, pg. 431
Cole, C. David, V.P.-Mktg.--RainSoft Water Conditioning Co., Elk Grove Village, IL, pg. 910
Cole, George, V.P.-Mktg.--Periphonics Corp., Bohemia, NY, pg. 862
Cole, Janet, Mgr.-Mktg.--Coles Express, Bangor, ME, pg. 261
Coleman, Bob, Gen. Mgr.-Sls. & Sec.--Coleman Dairy Inc., Little Rock, AR, pg. 261
Colen, Mary Leach, Sr. V.P.-Mktg.--L.F. Driscoll Co., Bala-Cynwyd, PA, pg. 349
Coles, Carl R., Mgr.-Mktg.--MD Pneumatics, Inc., Springfield, MO, pg. 1120
Colker, Jeff, Dir.-Sls. & Mktg.--Apollo Industries, Smyrna, GA, pg. 1090
Collier, D. Jack, Dir.-Port Devel.--Port of Galveston, Galveston, TX, pg. 881
Colman, Charles Lewis, Dir.-Mktg.--Ceras Johnson Ltda., Rio de Janeiro,, Brazil, pg. 599
Colon, Conrad O., V.P.-Mktg.--Goya Foods, Inc., Secaucus, NJ, pg. 474
Colonna, Mark, Exec. V.P., Chief Oper. Officer-Mktg, Dir.Sls. Promo & Mgr.-Adv.--Colonna Bros., Inc., North Bergen, NJ, pg. 264
Colucci, James, Sr. V.P. Sls. & Mktg.--Consolidated Cigar Corporation, Fort Lauderdale, FL, pg. 276
Colucci, James, Sr. V.P.-Sls. & Mktg.--Allied Products, Fort Lauderdale, FL, pg. 276
Coluccio, Shelly, Dir.-Mktg.--Tanning Research Labs., Inc., Ormond Beach, FL, pg. 1078
Colwell, Barbara, V.P.-Business Mktg.--Trans World Airlines, Inc., Mount Kisco, NY, pg. 561
Combe, Christopher B., V.P.-Mktg.--Combe Incorporated, White Plains, NY, pg. 267
Combs, Cindy Cameron, Dir.-Mktg.--Iowa Lottery, Des Moines, IA, pg. 582
Combs, George, V.P.-Mktg.--Tamaqua Cable Products Corporation, Schuylkill Haven, PA, pg. 1077
Combs, T.H., Prod. Mgr.-Tobacco Prods.--Conwood Company L.P., Memphis, TN, pg. 281
Compton, Sherre, Supvr.-Mktg.--Wells Manufacturing Company, Verdi, NV, pg. 1027
Comstock, Stacey, Dir.-Mktg.--Jacmar Companies, Inc., Alhambra, CA, pg. 587
Comyns, Bob, Mktg. Services Mgr.--Standard Duplicating Machines Corp., Andover, MA, pg. 1036
Conarroe, Richard, Mgr.-Sls. & Mktg. Devel.--Coleman International Operation, Wichita, KS, pg. 695
Condom, Mark, V.P.-Publications/Mktg.--CUNA Service Group, Inc., Madison, WI, pg. 298
Congleton, George L., V.P.-Mktg.--Baker Commodities, Inc., Los Angeles, CA, pg. 115
Conn, William, MRI Mktg. Mgr.--Instrumentarium Imaging, Inc., Milwaukee, WI, pg. 572
Connelly, Brian, V.P.-Sls. & Mktg.--Emson Research, Inc., Bridgeport, CT, pg. 380
Connelly, Michael, Gen. Mgr.-Sls. & Mktg.--Rea Magnet Wire Company, Inc., Fort Wayne, IN, pg. 915
Connon, Dana, Grp. V.P.--Welsh Company, Saint Louis, MO, pg. 1175
Connor, Richard J., V.P.-Mktg.--Macwhyte Co., Kenosha, WI, pg. 69
Conrad, James, V.P.-Mktg.--Industrial Ceramics, Inc., Derry, PA, pg. 566
Conroy, Michael W., Dir.-Mktg.--The J. M. Ney Company, Bloomfield, CT, pg. 805
Considine, Paul, V.P.-Sls. & Mktg.--American Fuel Cell & Coated Fabrics Co. (Amfuel), Magnolia, AR, pg. 55
Conte, James, V.P.-Intl. Mktg.--Northwest Airlines, Inc., Saint Paul, MN, pg. 782
Contino, H. Ray, Prod. Mgr.-Frozen Foods--AJC International, Inc., Atlanta, GA, pg. 4
Contreras, Tony, V.P.-Mktg.--Sugar Cane Growers Cooperative of Florida, Belle Glade, FL, pg. 1056
Converse, Stephen, Dir.-Mktg.--Keller Construction Company Ltd., El Monte, CA, pg. 620
Conway, Barry, Exec. V.P.-Sls. & Mktg.--Adams Business Forms, Topeka, KS, pg. 16
Conway, Martin B., V.P.-Mktg.--Baltimore Orioles, Inc., Baltimore, MD, pg. 116
Cook, Carey J., Mgr.-Engrng. Mktg.--S & C Electric Company, Chicago, IL, pg. 958
Cook, Don, V.P.-Mktg.--McGaw, Inc., Irvine, CA, pg. 729
Cook, Jack H., V.P.-Devel.--Children's World Learning Centers, Inc., Golden, CO, pg. 7
Cook, James F., Dir.-Mktg.--Eagle Electric Mfg. Co., Inc., Long Island City, NY, pg. 362
Cook, T.R., Mgr.-Mktg.--J.M. Huber, Solem Div., Norcross, GA, pg. 550
Cook, William G., V.P.-Mktg.--Faber/Castell Corporation, Parsippany, NJ, pg. 395
Cooke, William, V.P.-Strategic Plng. & Mktg.--DonTech, Chicago, IL, pg. 345
Cooksey, Thomas M., V.P.-Mktg. & Sls.--Bruner Corporation, Milwaukee, WI, pg. 184
Cooksey, William K., V.P.-Sls. & Mktg.--U.S. Manufacturing Corp., Roseville, MI, pg. 1136
Coombs, Whitney, V.P.-Mktg.--Hanover Foods Corporation, Hanover, PA, pg. 506
Coombs, Whitney, Dir.-Mktg.--Myers Foods Company, Plumsteadville, PA, pg. 506
Cooper, Bill, Dir.-Mktg. Programs--Atlas Van Lines, Inc., Evansville, IN, pg. 96
Cooper, Bob, Deputy Dir.-Mktg. & Information--Idaho Lottery, Boise, ID, pg. 561
Cooper, Carl, V.P.-Mktg.--Wagner Spray Tech Corp., Minneapolis, MN, pg. 1158
Cooper, Daryle, V.P.-Mktg. & Sls.--Eastern Air Devices, Inc., Dover, NH, pg. 363
Cooper, Jay, Dir.-Mktg.--Robbins, Inc., Cincinnati, OH, pg. 938
Cooper, Jonathan, V.P.-Sls. & Mktg.--Spectronics Corporation, Westbury, NY, pg. 1029
Cooper, William, Dir.-Sls. & Mktg.--Atlas Van Lines, Inc., Evansville, IN, pg. 96
Cope, David, Dir.-Adv. & Mktg.--Baltimore Orioles, Inc., Baltimore, MD, pg. 116
Copeland, William, Sr. Exec. V.P.-Franchising--Al Copeland Enterprises, Inc., Jefferson, LA, pg. 283
Corbett, James, Dir.-Sls. & Mktg.--Crown Prince, Inc. (CA), City of Industry, CA, pg. 302
Corden, Paul, Dir.-Mktg.--Beverage-Air Co., Spartanburg, SC, pg. 1027
Coriston, James M., Natl. Vice Chm.-Mktg.--Price Waterhouse - U.S., New York, NY, pg. 888
Corlett, Sandy, V.P.-Mktg.--Lexmark Canada Inc., North York,, Canada, pg. 674
Cornelison, Dave, Mgr.-Mktg. & Natl. Sls.--M & C Specialties Company, Southampton, PA, pg. 690
Cornwall, Dave, Dir.-Adv.--Press Enterprise Company, Riverside, CA, pg. 887
Coronado, Alex, Dir.-New Prod. Devel. & Natl. Sls. Mgr.--R.J. Corr Naturals, Inc., Posen, IL, pg. 287
Corrigan, Rob, V.P.-Mktg.--Ampex Corporation, Redwood City, CA, pg. 998
Costa, Roseann, Sls. & Mktg. Admin.--Toy Biz, Inc., New York, NY, pg. 1104
Costa, Steve, V.P.-Mktg.-Cosmetics & Treatment--Revlon, Inc., New York, NY, pg. 696
Costanzo, Donald J., Dir.-Mktg.--The Vernon Company, Newton, IA, pg. 1148
Costas, Peter, Dir.-Prod. Devel. & Mktg.--Elkay Products, Inc., Shrewsbury, MA, pg. 377
Costello, Steve, Mgr.-Mktg.--Celestial Seasonings, Boulder, CO, pg. 231
Cothren, J.W., V.P.-Mktg.--Conwood Company L.P., Memphis, TN, pg. 281
Cotten, Ray, V.P.-Mktg.--Microdynamics, Inc., Dallas, TX, pg. 749
Cotton, Judy, V.P.-Sls. & Mktg.--The Charles Levy Company, Chicago, IL, pg. 672
Coughlin, Neil P., V.P.-Sls. & Mktg.--Kingsbury Corporation, Keene, NH, pg. 631
Coulombe, Paul, V.P.-Mktg.--Lawrence & Company, Lewiston, ME, pg. 1186
Coulombe, Paul, V.P.-Mktg.--Maine Bottlers, Lewiston, ME, pg. 1186
Coulombe, Paul G., V.P.-Mktg.--White Rock Distilleries Inc., Lewiston, ME, pg. 1186
Coulton, Sally B., Mgr.-Sls. & Mktg.--BNA PLUS, Washington, DC, pg. 189
Courteau, Kevin, V.P.-Mktg.--National Oats Co., Cedar Rapids, IA, pg. 25
Courtney, D.W., V.P. & Dir.-Mktg.--CHEMCENTRAL Corporation, Bedford Park, IL, pg. 241
Coutu, John, V.P. & Resident Mgr.--Rising Paper Company, Housatonic, MA, pg. 428
Coville, James K., V.P.-Field Opers.--Citizens Insurance Company of America, Howell, MI, pg. 35
Cowan, Richard, V.P.-Mktg.--Little America Refining, Salt Lake City, UT, pg. 1008
Cowden, Jarrett, V.P.-Mktg.--Vermeer Manufacturing Company, Pella, IA, pg. 1148
Cowell, Carin, Coord.-Communications--IDAB International Incorporated, Hampton, VA, pg. 559
Cowell, John F., Mng. Dir. & Dir.-Mktg.--The First Boston Corporation, New York, NY, pg. 203
Cowell, John F., III, Mng. Dir. & Grp. Comm. Officer--CS First Boston Group, Inc., New York, NY, pg. 203
Cox, Basil, Exec. V.P.-Mktg.--Eat N Park Restaurants, Pittsburgh, PA, pg. 364
Cox, D.C., Mgr.-Mktg.--J.M. Huber, Polymer Services Div., Orange, TX, pg. 550

Cox, Gary L., Mgr.-Mktg. & Sls.--Mitchel & Scot Machine Co., Inc., Indianapolis, IN, pg. 761
Coyle, Bob, Principal & Mktg. Dir.--Sullivan Haas Coyle, Atlanta, GA, pg. 1056
Coyner, Russ, V.P.-Mktg.--Steelcase Inc., Grand Rapids, MI, pg. 1044
Crain, Bob, Dir.-Mktg. & Sls.--Steelcase Wood Div., Kentwood, MI, pg. 1044
Cramer, Conrad C., V.P.-Sls. & Mktg.--Pressed Steel Tank Co., Inc., West Allis, WI, pg. 887
Cramer, Richard, V.P.-Mktg. & Sls.--The Milnot Company, Saint Louis, MO, pg. 756
Crandell, Robert, V.P.-Sls. & Mktg.--Baker Material Handling Corp., Summerville, SC, pg. 115
Crane, Robert C., Mktg. Admin.--Williams-White & Co., Moline, IL, pg. 1191
Crane, Robert C., Mgr.-Mktg.--Williams, White & Company, Moline, IL, pg. 1191
Cranny, Mike, V.P.-Mktg.--Harker's Inc., Le Mars, IA, pg. 509
Creary, Brian, Reg. Mktg. Mgr.--The Jolt Company, Rochester, NY, pg. 602
Cress, Bill, Operating V.P., Adv. & Mktg.--Standard Advertising Agency, Brentwood, TN, pg. 1035
Crick, Robert, Mktg. Mgr.--Benmar, Santa Ana, CA, pg. 133
Criner, Douglas E., V.P.-Mktg.--Burns & McDonnell Engineers-Architects-Consultants, Kansas City, MO, pg. 194
Crockard, Craig S., V.P.-Plng. & Devel.--Avondale Mills, Inc., Sylacauga, AL, pg. 103
Cronin, Richard, Sr. V.P.-Mktg.--Nickelodeon/Nick At Nite, New York, NY, pg. 785
Crook, David, Mgr.-Mktg.--Aetna Bearing Company, Chicago, IL, pg. 23
Crorey, David, Exec. V.P.-Sls. & Mktg.--The ISI Manufacturing, Inc., Fraser, MI, pg. 560
Crosby, Jerry, V.P.-Intl. Licensing--Taren Holdings, Inc., Los Angeles, CA, pg. 1078
Crosby, Peter G., Sr. V.P.-Mktg. & Sls.--Belvedere Company, Belvidere, IL, pg. 138
Crotty, Robert S., V.P. & Dir.-Mktg.--Van Dyne-Crotty, Inc., Dayton, OH, pg. 1144
Crowell, Gaylan A., Dir.-Mktg.--Omniflight, Inc., Dallas, TX, pg. 826
Crowley, Bruce, V.P.-Mktg.--KDI Corporation, Cincinnati, OH, pg. 612
Crowley, Leo N., Exec. V.P.-Plng. & Admin.--Green Bay Packaging Inc., Green Bay, WI, pg. 483
Crowley, Patrick, Sr. V.P., Strategic Mktg., Media Grp. & New Bus. Contact--Lewis & Gace, Inc., Fort Lee, NJ, pg. 673
Crowley, Stephen, V.P.-Mktg. & Sls.--Rome Cable Corporation, Rome, NY, pg. 945
Crowley, Thomas V., Dir.-Mktg. & Sec.--Cadet Manufacturing Company, Vancouver, WA, pg. 207
Crump, Bob, Mktg. Dir.--Carlson Retail Marketing, Minneapolis, MN, pg. 221
Crump, Terry, V.P.-Mktg.--Conquest Carpet Mills, Dalton, GA, pg. 276
Crumpacker, Jim, Dir.-Mktg. & Adv.--Wharfside Restaurants, Inc., Jasper, IN, pg. 1184
Csehill, John, Mktg. Dir.--Admiral Maintenance Service L.P., Lincolnwood, IL, pg. 18
Csepregi, Roger, Mgr.-Mktg. Services--Gast Mfg. Corp., Benton Harbor, MI, pg. 444
Cubbage, William, V.P.-Animal Health & Nutrition--Universal Cooperatives, Inc., Minneapolis, MN, pg. 1138
Cugley, Derwyn, V.P.-Mktg.--VSI Fasteners, Inc., Stanton, CA, pg. 1142
Culbertson, Peter D., Sr. V.P.-Mktg. & Mdsg.--Woolrich, Inc., Woolrich, PA, pg. 1201
Culver, John A., Dir.-Sls. & Mktg. & Adv. Mgr.--Giumarra Vineyards, Bakersfield, CA, pg. 460
Culver, Karen, Mktg. Coord.--Moses Anshell, Inc., Phoenix, AZ, pg. 76
Cumbers, Blake, V.P. & Dir.-Mktg.--Hollywood Park, Inc., Inglewood, CA, pg. 540
Cummings, Andrea M., Dir., Mktg. Services--Fessel, Siegfriedt & Moeller, Inc., Louisville, KY, pg. 407
Cummings, Donald P., Dir.-Mktg.--Hyde Manufacturing Co., Southbridge, MA, pg. 556
Cummings, Robert, Dir.-Sls. & Mktg.--Wisconsin Label Corporation, Algoma, WI, pg. 1198
Cummins, Harold, Mgr.-Prod.--Rite-Way, Inc., Saddle Brook, NJ, pg. 936
Cummins, Marilyn, Dir. Mktg. Services, New Bus. Contact--Dudnyk Advertising, Horsham, PA, pg. 351
Cunningham, Tom, Sr. V.P.-Sls. & Mktg.--The Berkline Corporation, Morristown, TN, pg. 285
Curcio, Alida, V.P.-Mktg.-Toiletries--Revlon, Inc., New York, NY, pg. 696
Cureton, Renee, Mktg. Mgr.-Popeyes Fried Chicken--Al Copeland Enterprises, Inc., Atlanta, GA, pg. 283
Curtis, Alvin L., V.P.-Mktg.--Serigraph, Inc., West Bend, WI, pg. 991
Curtis, H.L., V.P.-Mktg.--J.M. Huber, Oil & Gas Div., Houston, TX, pg. 550
Curtis, James J., V.P.-Sls. & Mktg.--United Graphics, Inc., Seattle, WA, pg. 1132
Curtis, Joe, V.P.-Sls. & Mktg.--United Farm Tools, Inc., Glasgow, KY, pg. 1131
Curtis, Joe, V.P.-Sls. & Mktg.--United Farm Tools, Kentucky Div., Glasgow, KY, pg. 1132
Curtis, Kevin L., V.P.-Sls. & Mktg.--Besser Company, Alpena, MI, pg. 146
Curtis, Scott H., Product Application Mgr.--Anderson Products, Worcester, MA, pg. 1194
Curtis, William M., Dir.-Mktg.--L.N. Curtis & Sons, Oakland, CA, pg. 306
Cushna, Ralph A., Dir.-Sales & Mktg.--Burgess-Norton Mfg. Co., Geneva, IL, pg. 69
Cuttino, Phil, Exec. V.P., Creative Dir., Bus. Devel.--Pollak Levitt Chaiet, Advertising, Atlanta, GA, pg. 879
Cwikla, Mary, Mktg. Services Mgr.--Freeson Advertising Agency, Miami Lakes, FL, pg. 431
Czarnecki, Steve, Mgr., Intl. Mktg.--The Brady Company, Menomonee Falls, WI, pg. 171
Czirjak, Lianue, Dir.-Mktg.--Tiger Electronics, Inc., Vernon Hills, IL, pg. 1097
D'Agostino, Louis, Mgr.-Mktg.--Capital Controls Company Inc., Colmar, PA, pg. 215
D'Amour, Claire M., V.P.-Corp. Affairs--Big Y Foods Inc., Springfield, MA, pg. 149
D'Angelo, John, Dir.-Sls., Mktg., Purch.--Pyttronic Industries, Inc., Montgomeryville, PA, pg. 901
D'Ornellas, Robert W., Sr. V.P.-Mktg.--Del Monte Foods, San Francisco, CA, pg. 325
D'Ornellas, Robert W., Exec. V.P.-Mktg.--G. Heileman Brewing Co., Inc., La Crosse, WI, pg. 526
Daab, Joan, Mktg. Coord.--Jackes-Evans Mfg. Co., Saint Louis, MO, pg. 587
Dadiego, Sharon, Mktg. Admin.--Connors Brunswick, Inc., South Portland, ME, pg. 275
Dahl, Dennis, V.P.-Mktg.--Windmill Corp. d/b/a Martha White Foods, Inc., Brentwood, TN, pg. 1195
Dahlager, Ken, V.P.-Sls. & Mkgt.--Smith System Manufacturing Company, Shoreview, MN, pg. 1014
Daiger, Skip, Dir.-Adv. & Mktg.--FoodCraft Equipment Co., Inc., Lancaster, PA, pg. 860
Dalton, Dennis, V.P.-Intl. Mktg.--Buckman Laboratories, Memphis, TN, pg. 185
Dalvi, Ajit M., Sr. V.P.-Mktg.--Cable Division, Atlanta, GA, pg. 294
Dammeier, Kurt B., V.P.-Sls. & Mktg.--Print Northwest, Fife, WA, pg. 891
Damveld, Gary, Dir.-Mktg.--General Brewing Company, Vancouver, WA, pg. 959
Damveld, Gary, Dir.-Mktg.--Falstaff Brewing Corporation, Vancouver, WA, pg. 959
Danberg, Kenneth, Exec. V.P.-Sls.--Harper Industries, Inc., New York, NY, pg. 510
Dandurand, Curran, Sr. V.P.-Mktg.--Mary Kay Cosmetics Inc., Dallas, TX, pg. 716
Daniel, Michael, Mktg. Mgr.--Advance Seed Co., Fulton, KY, pg. 407
Daniels, William F., V.P.-Corp. Mktg.--U.S. Engineering Company, Kansas City, MO, pg. 1135
Dann-Gobin, Elene, Dir.-Mktg.--Dann Dee Display Fixtures, Chicago, IL, pg. 314
Danser, James, V.P.-Sls. & Mktg.--Topflight Corp., York, PA, pg. 1102
Darby, Mary Ann, Dir.-Mktg.--Warehouse Home Furnishings Distributor, Dublin, GA, pg. 1163
Darian, Ralph, Pres., Chief Exec. & Chief Fin. Officer--Levonian Brothers Inc., Troy, NY, pg. 671
Darveaux, Terry A., V.P.-Mktg. Services--First Federal Savings and Loan Assn. of Rochester, Rochester, NY, pg. 413
Daste, Cary, V.P.-Mktg.--Weibel Vineyards, Mission San Jose, CA, pg. 1173
Datlund, V.P.-Mktg--Sealy Corporation, Cleveland, OH, pg. 985
Daun, Dan, Dir.-Mktg.--Noma-International, Inc., Forest Park, IL, pg. 808
Dausey, W., V.P.-Sls. & Mktg.--PTC Aerospace, Inc., Litchfield, CT, pg. 837
Davidoff, Jennifer, Dir.-Mktg.--Weber-Stephen Products, Palatine, IL, pg. 1171
Davids, Michael, Natl. Sls. & Mktg. Mgr.--Koch Engineering Company, Inc., Akron, OH, pg. 638
Davidson, Irwin, V.P.-Mktg.--Ventura Travelware, Inc., Long Island City, NY, pg. 1147
Davidson, Scot, Aftermarket Mgr.--Warn Industries, Inc., Milwaukie, OR, pg. 1164
Davidson, Steven, Dir.-Products & Services--Carpeteria, Inc., Valencia, CA, pg. 224
Davies, Raymond A., V.P.-Sls. & MKtg.--Duff-Norton, Charlotte, NC, pg. 1032
Davis, David, V.P.-Mktg. & Transportation--Duro Paper Bag Manufacturing Co., Ludlow, KY, pg. 355
Davis, Doug, Asst. Chief Exec. Officer & Dir.-Mktg.--B & B Cash Grocery Store, Tampa, FL, pg. 105
Davis, Gordon O., Mgr.-Mktg.--Polar Corporation, Worcester, MA, pg. 878
Davis, Grady, V.P.-Sls. & Mktg.--Tolleson Lumber Company, Inc., Perry, GA, pg. 1100
Davis, Jim, Sr. V.P.-Mktg.--Quality Stores Inc., North Muskegon, MI, pg. 904
Davis, John, Dir.-Sls. & Mktg.--Simpson Dura-Vent Co., Inc., Vacaville, CA, pg. 1007
Davis, Lawrence C., Sr. V.P.-Mktg.--Greater New York Mutual Insurance Company, New York, NY, pg. 483
Davis, Lynn, V.P.-Sls., Mktg., Pur. & Mfg.--Lithotype Company, Inc., South San Francisco, CA, pg. 678
Davis, Park, Pres.-College Div.--CJC Holdings, Inc., Austin, TX, pg. 202
Davis, Philip, V.P.-Sls. & Mktg.--Stusser Electric Company, Seattle, WA, pg. 1055
Davis, Robert, Mgr.-Mktg. Communications--Sunnen Products Company, Saint Louis, MO, pg. 1061
Davis, Shelby, Mktg. Services Coord.--Leupold & Stevens, Inc., Beaverton, OR, pg. 669
Davis, Steve, V.P.-Sls. & Mktg.--Calavo Growers of California, Tustin, CA, pg. 208
Davis, Thomas C., V.P.-Sls. & Mktg.--The Ward Machinery Company, Cockeysville, MD, pg. 1162
Davis, William D., Sr. V.P.-Mktg.--Merchandising Equipment Group, National Marketing, Arlington Heights, IL, pg. 739
Davison, Lynn C., V.P.-Mktg. Resources--First Federal Savings and Loan Assn. of Rochester, Rochester, NY, pg. 413
Dawahare, A.F., Pres. & Dir.-Sls. & Mktg.--Dawahares, Inc., Lexington, KY, pg. 319
Day, Pat, V.P.-Mktg.--Hickory Construction Company, Hickory, NC, pg. 532
Dayton, William, Sr. V.P.-Mktg.--Trump's Castle Casino Resort, Atlantic City, NJ, pg. 1118
de Grasse, Cindy, Mktg. Dir.--D. M. Management Company, Hingham, MA, pg. 309
De Paszthory, Bob, Dir.-Export & Mktg. Plng.--Certified Grocers Of California, Los Angeles, CA, pg. 237
De Prima, Robert A., Reg. Mgr.-Intl.--The C. P. Hall Company, Chicago, IL, pg. 501
Dean, J. David, Sr. V.P.-Mktg.--Woodward-Clyde Group, Inc., Denver, CO, pg. 1200
Dean, Thomas H., Sr. V.P.-Corp. Devel.--Continental Grain Company, New York, NY, pg. 279
DeAngulo, Alan, Mgr.-Mktg.--Allied Paper Incorporated, Dayton, OH, pg. 38
Deaver, William, Dir.-Adv. & Promo.--United States Savings Bonds Division, Treasury Department, Washington, DC, pg. 1137
deBergeois, P., Dir.-Mktg.--Detex Corporation, New Braunfels, TX, pg. 333
DeBroux, Jim, V.P.-Mktg.-Vans--Anderson Trucking Service Inc., Saint Cloud, MN, pg. 73
Debruler, Jeanne, Mktg. Mgr.-Churches--Popeye's Famous Fried Chicken, Rosemont, IL, pg. 284
DeCesaro, Arthur F., Jr., Exec. V.P.-Mktg.& Nat'l. Sls.--Jockey International, Inc., Kenosha, WI, pg. 595
Decker Ward, James, Exec. V.P.-Mktg.--Encyclopaedia Britannica Educational Corporation, Chicago, IL, pg. 381
Decker-Ward, Jim, Exec. V.P.-Mktg.--Encyclopaedia Britannica Educational Corporation, Chicago, IL, pg. 380
Decker, Dave, Mktg. Coord.--Dwyer Instruments Inc., Michigan City, IN, pg. 356
Deer, Andy, Dir.-Mktg.--Farnam Companies, Inc., Phoenix, AZ, pg. 403
DeFrancisci, Joseph, Dir.-Mktg.--De Francisci Machine Corp.(Demaco), Ridgewood, NY, pg. 321
DeGood, Paul W., Mgr.-Mktg. Services--M.C. Gill Corporation, El Monte, CA, pg. 458
DeHoff, Jefferson L., Dir.-Mktg.--Dewberry & Davis, Fairfax, VA, pg. 334
Deichl, John, V.P.-Mktg. & Sls.--Simpson Electric Co., Elgin, IL, pg. 1007
Del Sesto, Richard, V.P.-Sls. & Mktg.--Red Devil Inc., Union, NJ, pg. 918
Delacroix, Chuck, V.P.-Mktg.--Gulf States Toyota, Houston, TX, pg. 494
DeLang, J.R., Dir.-Sls. & Mktg.--The Todd-AO Corporation, San Francisco, CA, pg. 1099
DeLash, James, Dir.-Direct Mktg.--W. Atlee Burpee Co., Warminster, PA, pg. 116
Deleenheer, Ronald V., V.P.-Mktg.--Ash Grove Cement Company, Overland Park, KS, pg. 87
Deliberato, Carmine J., Dir.-Mktg. & Sls.--Lavelle Aircraft Company, Philadelphia, PA, pg. 661
DeLime, Bridie, Dir.-Mktg.--Maddak Inc., Pequannock, NJ, pg. 133
Delman, Susan, Dir.-Mktg.--Ziff-Davis Publishing Company, New York, NY, pg. 1219
DeLora, Charles A., Sr. V.P.-Sls., Mktg., Adv. & Pub. Rels.--Service Supply Co. Inc. of Indiana, Indianapolis, IN, pg. 992
Delp, Mark, V.P.-Mktg. & Sls.--Gemtron Corporation, Sweetwater, TN, pg. 3
Delzio, Gerry, V.P.-Sls. & Mktg.--Bolliger, Inc., Stamford, CT, pg. 163
DeMain, Dominic P., V.P. & Grp. Mktg. Dir.--Combe Incorporated, White Plains, NY, pg. 267
DeMarino, Louis T., Sr. V.P.-Sls. & Mktg.--The Jaydor Corporation, Millburn, NJ, pg. 591
DeMell, Robert A., Natl. Mktg. Mgr.--McGean-Rohco, Inc., Cleveland, OH, pg. 729
Deming, Derrell, Dir.-Sls. & Mktg.--Thom Thumb Food Market Inc., Hastings, MN, pg. 879
Demond, John, V.P.-Sls. & Mktg.--TSC Carbide Co., Crystal Lake, IL, pg. 885
DeMond, John E., V.P.-Mktg. & Sls.--Precision Twist Drill Co., Crystal Lake, IL, pg. 885
Demond, John E., V.P.-Mktg. & Sls.--Mohawk Tools, Crystal Lake, IL, pg. 885
Dempsey, David, Dir.-Sales & Mktg.--Union Pump Company, Battle Creek, MI, pg. 1128
Denges, James, V.P.-Mktg. & Pur.--Central Grocers Co-op, Franklin Park, IL, pg. 232
Denison, William, V.P.-Sls. & Mktg.--Milk Specialties Company, Dundee, IL, pg. 753
Denny, Robert L., Dir.-Agency Sls., Devel. & Promo. Services--State Farm Mutual Automobile Insurance Company, Bloomington, IL, pg. 1041
Dent, Harold D., V.P.-Mktg.--Hesston, Norcross, GA, pg. 4
DePaolis, Dan, Natl. Sls. Mgr.--WEN Products, Inc., Chicago, IL, pg. 1156
Derasmo, Jack, V.P. Mktg. & Sls. Mgr.--Glen Raven Mills Marketing Corp., Pearl River, NY, pg. 461
Derasmo, Jack, V.P.-Mktg. & Sls. Mgr.--Glen Raven Marketing Corporation, Pearl River, NY, pg. 461
Derr, Tom, Dir.-Mktg.--Megas Beauty Aids, Inc., Cleveland, OH, pg. 737
Des Enfants, Laura, Mgr.-Mktg.--Mohawk Paper Mills, Inc., Cohoes, NY, pg. 763
Dethlefsen, Walt, Acting Pres. & V.P.-Adv. & Mktg.--Network Services Company of Chicago, Mount Prospect, IL, pg. 798
DeTour, Walter, V.P.-Mktg.--Universal Photonics, Inc., Hicksville, NY, pg. 1139
Dettmann, Robert J., V.P.-Sls. & Mktg.--Action Technology Company, Rockaway, NJ, pg. 15
Deuchars, Colin M., V.P.--Holmes Protection Group, Inc., New York, NY, pg. 540
Devilline, F.D., V.P.-Sls. & Mktg.--Columbus McKinnon Corp., Amherst, NY, pg. 266
Devine, Steve, Dir.-Mktg.--Whitmire Distribution, Folsom, CA, pg. 1187
Dewey, Brian G., Dir.-Mktg.--Lane Limited, Tucker, GA, pg. 657
Dewhirst, R.T., V.P.-Mktg.--Armstrong International, Inc., Three Rivers, MI, pg. 83

Dezek, R.J., Dir.-Sls. & Mktg.--Young Radiator Company, Racine, WI, pg. 1210
Di Pietro, Joan, V.P.-Mktg.--Norwegian Cruise Line, Coral Gables, FL, pg. 816
Diack, Lee, Dir.-Mktg.--Fownes Brothers & Co., Inc., New York, NY, pg. 427
Diamant, John R., Mgr.-Intl. Division--Victaulic Company of America, Easton, PA, pg. 1149
Diamantis, Diane G., Dir.-Mktg. Communications--Stiles Corporation, Fort Lauderdale, FL, pg. 1049
Diamond, Harold, Dir.-Mktg.--Diamond Chemical Co., Inc., Lyndhurst, NJ, pg. 335
Diamond, Harry, Dir.-Mktg.--Giffels Hoyem Basso, Inc., Troy, MI, pg. 457
Diamond, Heidi, V.P.-Mktg.--Nickelodeon/Nick At Nite, New York, NY, pg. 785
Dianich, Bev, Mgr.-Sls. & Mktg.--Pacific Wood Treating Coporation, Ridgefield, WA, pg. 842
Dick, Douglas P., Sr. V.P.-Sls. & Mktg.--Dick Corporation, Large, PA, pg. 335
Dick, Stephen, Exec. V.P., Mktg. Services--SSD&W Integrated Marketing Communications, Montville, NJ, pg. 964
Dickey, Jane, Dir.-Mktg.--Abbell Associates, Chicago, IL, pg. 9
Dickhoff, Bill, Dir.-Sls., Mktg. & Adv.--Roofing Wholesale Co., Inc., Phoenix, AZ, pg. 946
Dickleman, Tom, Mktg. Admin.--A. L. Hansen Mfg. Co., Waukegan, IL, pg. 506
Dickman, Marshall S., Dir., Mktg. & Acct. Mngmt.--Communication & Design Agency Inc., Latham, NY, pg. 269
Dicks, Tom, Dir.-Mktg. & Sls. Promo--American Fluorescent Corporation, Waukegan, IL, pg. 54
Dickson, Allan S., V.P.-Mktg.--Amphenol Corporation, Wallingford, CT, pg. 648
Dickson, Ron, Exec. V.P., Pres.-Direct Mktg.r--Barkley & Evergreen Advertising, Inc., Shawnee Mission, KS, pg. 120
Diedrich, Richard, Mgr.-Mktg. Services--Rite-Hite Corporation, Milwaukee, WI, pg. 936
Dietz, Dave, V.P.-Sls. & Mktg.--Hardware Wholesalers, Inc., Fort Wayne, IN, pg. 508
Dietz, Diane, Mgr.-Mkgt.--Malt-O-Meal Company, Minneapolis, MN, pg. 703
Difino, R.G., V.P.-Mktg. Services--United Laboratories, Inc., Itasca, IL, pg. 1133
DiGani, Jerry, Mktg. Res. Dir.--Shaker Advertising Agency, Oak Park, IL, pg. 994
Dilfer, Bill, Dir.-Mktg.--MICOM Communications Corp., Simi Valley, CA, pg. 748
Dillard, Steve, Exec. Dir.-Mdsg. & Mktg., Kansas City Div.--Associated Wholesale Grocers, Inc., Kansas City, KS, pg. 92
Dillihunt, Curtis L., V.P.-Customer Service & Mktg.--Memphis Light, Gas & Water, Memphis, TN, pg. 738
Dillingham, John, Sr. V.P.-Sls. & Mktg.--Garney Holding Company, Inc., Kansas City, MO, pg. 443
Dillon, Dan, Sr. V.P.-Mktg.--Replogle Globes, Inc., Broadview, IL, pg. 927
Dillon, E.V., V.P.-Mktg.--Thomas Publishing Co., New York, NY, pg. 1093
Dillon, Jim, V.P.-Sls. & Mktg.--Foster Refrigerator Corporation, Hudson, NY, pg. 426
Dilullo, Richard, Dir.-Mktg.--Southeastern Pennsylvania Transportation Authority, Philadelphia, PA, pg. 1020
DiMarco, Donna, Dir.-Mktg.--Carol Wright Sales, Inc., Stamford, CT, pg. 1011
DiMarco, James F., Sr. V.P.-Worldwide Consumer Prods., Res.--S. C. Johnson & Son, Inc., Racine, WI, pg. 599
Dimartini, F.M., V.P.-Prod. Devel, Raw Matls. & Pur.--Frank Ix & Sons, Inc., New York, NY, pg. 584
Dimon, Wanda, Mgr.-Adv., Mktg. Promo. & Pub. Rels.--Crested Butte Mountain Resort, Inc., Mount Crested Butte, CO, pg. 299
Dimond, Michael, V.P.-Mktg.--Gaylord Entertainment Co., Nashville, TN, pg. 446
Ding, Ian, Mgr.-Intl. Mktg.--Master Foods, Kings Lynn,, United Kingdom, pg. 713
Dinsmore, Stephen, Dir.-Mktg. Services--Ocean Spray Cranberries, Inc., Lakeville, MA, pg. 820
Dippel, John, Mgr.-Mktg.-Household Prods.--Turtle Wax, Inc., Chicago, IL, pg. 1120
Dircks, R.J., Exec. V.P.-Mktg., Sls. & Adv.--Berger Transfer & Storage, Inc., Saint Paul, MN, pg. 141
Dishman, Scott, Dir.-Mktg. & Adv.--I. Spiewak & Sons, Inc., New York, NY, pg. 1031
DiSipe, John, Exec. Dir.-Mktg.--William H. Sadlier, Inc., New York, NY, pg. 966
Dissinger, Scott, Mgr.-Mktg.--Remarks Co., Indianapolis, IN, pg. 926
DiStefano, Alan, Dir.-Mktg.--Hamilton Co., Inc., Reno, NV, pg. 503
Ditka, Ashton L., V.P.-Mktg. & Sls.--United Refining Company, Warren, PA, pg. 1130
Dittman, William, Dir.-Sls. & Mktg.--A. H. Hoffman, Inc., Landisville, PA, pg. 538
Dittoe, Richard, V.P.-Mktg.--Tyler Refrigeration Corp., Niles, MI, pg. 62
Diveley, L.R., V.P., Acct. Services & Mktg. Dir.--Simmons, Durham & Associates, Saint Louis, MO, pg. 1005
Dix, Ron, Sr. V.P.-Mktg. & Sls.--Bush Brothers & Company, Dandridge, TN, pg. 196
Dixon, Brian, V.P.-Mktg. Services--Long John Silver's, Inc., Lexington, KY, pg. 229
Dixon, Brian C., V.P.-Mktg. Services--Jerrico, Inc., Lexington, KY, pg. 229
Dixon, Jerry, V.P.-Sls. & Mktg.--Alma Industries, High Point, NC, pg. 43
Dixon, W.R., Deputy Dir.-Devel.--Christian Children's Fund, Inc., Richmond, VA, pg. 248
Dodge, Michael, V.P.-Mktg. & Sls.--Alleson of Rochester, Inc., Rochester, NY, pg. 37
Dodge, Robert, V.P.- Mktg.--The Renovator's-Fessel, Inc., Millers Falls, MA, pg. 927
Doehrer, Pat, Dir.-Mktg.--Star Lumber & Supply Company, Inc., Wichita, KS, pg. 1039
Doering, Roy, V.P.-Sls. & Mktg.--Hurd Millwork Company, Inc., Medford, WI, pg. 1123
Dolinar, Paul F., V.P.-Mktg.--Synchro-Start Products, Inc., Niles, IL, pg. 638
Dompke, Gerard, Mgr.-Mktg., Printing Paper--Cole Papers Inc., Fargo, ND, pg. 260
Donahue, J.T., V.P.-Mktg.--Pipe Div., Birmingham, AL, pg. 1162
Donahue, Joeseph T., V.P.-Mktg.--United States Pipe & Foundry Company, Birmingham, AL, pg. 1162
Donaldson, P. Kit, Dir.-Mktg.--Man-Gill Chemical Company, Cleveland, OH, pg. 703
Done, Brent, V.P.-Sls.--WordPerfect Corporation, Orem, UT, pg. 1202
Doninger, Donald R., Sr. Mktg. Consultant--Fessel, Siegfriedt & Moeller, Inc., Louisville, KY, pg. 407
Donnantuono, Michael, Dir.-Mktg.--Blistex, Inc., Oak Brook, IL, pg. 157
Dono, Joseph T., Sr. V.P.-Mktg. & Adv.--Nutri/System Inc., Blue Bell, PA, pg. 818
Donohue-Rolfe, Fay, Sr. V.P.-Mktg.--Blue Cross and Blue Shield of Massachusetts, Boston, MA, pg. 159
Donovan, Mary Ann, V.P.-Mktg.--M&M/Mars, Hackettstown, NJ, pg. 713
Doodson, K., Mgr.-Sls. & Mktg.--Metro Foods, Inc., Memphis, TN, pg. 743
Dorf, Noel, V.P.-Sls & Mktg.--The Harwood Companies, Inc., New York, NY, pg. 515
Dorhmann, William, V.P.-Mktg.--Tiger Electronics, Inc., Vernon Hills, IL, pg. 1097
Dorman, Ned, V.P.-Food Service-Mktg. & Sls.--Dorman-Roth Foods, Inc., Moonachie, NJ, pg. 346
Dorow, Duane, Dir.-Mktg. & Adv.--Barrel O'Fun Snack Foods Co., Perham, MN, pg. 122
DosSantos, Anthony, V.P.-Sls. & Mktg.--Pacific Optical Division, Torrance, CA, pg. 917
Dostal, Robert, Sr. V.P.-Mktg. & Adv.--Peter Pan Bus Lines, Inc., Springfield, MA, pg. 864
Doten, Bill, V.P.-Mktg.--Cablevision Industries Corp., Liberty, NY, pg. 206
Dougherty, Mike, Dir.-Mktg.--Minnesota Brewing Company, Saint Paul, MN, pg. 757
Dowdle, Liz, V.P.-Mktg., Mdsg. & Adv.--Spencer Industries, Inc., New Brunswick, NJ, pg. 1030
Dowdle, Liz, V.P.-Mktg., Mdsg. & Adv.--Casual Sportswear Co., Inc., Dunmore, PA, pg. 1030
Dowdy, Nancy S., Sr. V.P.-Adv. & Mktg.--Century Furniture Industries, Hickory, NC, pg. 235
Dowlen, Glenn, Dir.-Mktg.--Southern Frozen Foods, Montezuma, GA, pg. 26
Downing, John, Dir.-Mktg.--Guideposts Associates, Inc., Carmel, NY, pg. 493
Downs, Ryan A., V.P.-Sls. & Mktg.--Flanagan Brothers, Bear Creek, WI, pg. 416
Downs, Tom, V.P.-Corp. Plng. & Human Resources--Tanner Co. Inc., Rutherfordton, NC, pg. 1078
Downum, Bob, V.P.-Mktg. & Adv.--Harp's Food Stores, Inc., Springdale, AR, pg. 510
Doyer, Lee F., V.P.-Mktg.--Pennsylvania Crusher Corp., Broomall, PA, pg. 858
Doyle, Elizabeth A., V.P.-Admin. & Production & Corp. Sec.--My Own Meals, Inc., Deerfield, IL, pg. 779
Doyle, Timothy, Dir.-Mktg. Services--Family Pharmacy General Office, Columbus, OH, pg. 32
Dragoumis, Jim, Exec. V.P./Dir. Mktg. Services--Waring & LaRosa, Inc., New York, NY, pg. 1163
Drake, Dave, Mgr.-Mktg.--East Kentucky Power Co-op, Winchester, KY, pg. 362
Drennan, George V., V.P.-Sls. & Mktg.--Hiross Inc., Niagara Falls, NY, pg. 536
Drescher, David, Exec. V.P.-Mktg.--Fruit of the Loom, Bowling Green, KY, pg. 400
Drescher, David R., Exec. V.P.-Mktg.--Union Underwear Co., Inc., Bowling Green, KY, pg. 400
Dress, Stan, V.P.-Sls. & Mktg.--Rex Lumber Company, Acton, MA, pg. 930
Drexel-Bone, Janet, Dir.-Mktg.--Montana Lottery, Helena, MT, pg. 766
Drexler, Terri, Mgr.-Mktg. & Events--Datability, Inc., Carlstadt, NJ, pg. 316
Driscoll, Tom, Mgr.-Mktg.--Gerrard and Company, Des Plaines, IL, pg. 454
Drobny, Nancy, Mktg. Assoc.--Pioneer Engineering & Manufacturing Co., Warren, MI, pg. 871
Drozdow, Steve, V.P.-Sls. & Mktg.--Ohaus Corporation, Florham Park, NJ, pg. 822
Drum, S., V.P.-Mktg.--Cole Vision Corporation, Cleveland, OH, pg. 260
Dubas, Leonard, V.P.-Mktg.--Angelo Brothers Co., Philadelphia, PA, pg. 74
Dubreuil, Marc, Dir.-Mktg.--PTA Corporation, Oxford, CT, pg. 837
Duchaine, Terry A., Mktg. Communications Specialist--Ideal Industries, Inc., Sycamore, IL, pg. 562
Duffy, Patrick, Mktg. Mgr.--Auto Crane Company, Tulsa, OK, pg. 100
Dugan, Dick, Dir.-Mktg. Services--Oklahoma Publishing Company, Oklahoma City, OK, pg. 446
Duggan, Guy, Mgr.-Mktg.--Adams Extract Co., Inc., Austin, TX, pg. 16
Duistermars, Eric, Mgr.-Mktg. Communications--Candle Corporation, Santa Monica, CA, pg. 214
Duncan, James, Acting V.P.-Mktg.--Camp International, Jackson, MI, pg. 153
Duncan, Robert A., V.P.-Mktg.--Kearney, Tucker, GA, pg. 357
Duncan, Steve, V.P.-Sls. & Mktg.--Cold Spring Granite Company, Minnetonka, MN, pg. 259
Duncan, Terence, Sr. V.P.-Mktg.--Management Dynamics, New Providence, NJ, pg. 703
Duncheon, Charles S., V.P.-Mktg. & Sls.--Adept Technology, Inc., San Jose, CA, pg. 17
Dunlop, Tim, Mgr.-Mktg.--Utility Trailer Manufacturing Co., City of Industry, CA, pg. 1141
Dunn, George, V.P.-Mktg.--Tropitone Furniture Co. Inc., Sarasota, FL, pg. 1116
Dunn, Melvin B., Exec. V.P. & Chief Mktg. Officer--Security Mutual Life Insurance Co. of New York, Binghamton, NY, pg. 987
Dunn, Richard G., V.P.-Sls. & Mktg.--McIlhenny Company, Avery Island, LA, pg. 729
Dunn, Rick, Dir.-Adv. & Mktg.--B. F. Trappey's Sons, Inc., New Iberia, LA, pg. 729
Dunn, Robert, Dir.-Mktg.--J.H. Findorff & Son, Inc., Madison, WI, pg. 411
Dupuis, Alan, V.P.-Sls. & Mktg.--Quaker Industries Limited, Antioch, IL, pg. 903
Dupuy, Y., V.P.-Mktg.--Benjamin Moore & Co., Montvale, NJ, pg. 139
Duray, Gerald W., Dir.-Sls. & Mktg.--Power Contracting & Engineering Corp., Rolling Meadows, IL, pg. 883
Durden, Jeff, Dir.-Mktg. & Sls.--Dairymen, Inc., Louisville, KY, pg. 311
Durden, Jeff, Dir.-Mktg. Services--Flav-O-Rich, Inc., Louisville, KY, pg. 311
Durden, Listor, V.P.-Mktg. & Sls.--Viking Range Corp., Greenwood, MS, pg. 1151
Durell, David A., Mktg. Dir.--The Union Fork & Hoe Co., Columbus, OH, pg. 1128
Durlach, Chris L., V.P.-Mktg. & Intl. Div.--Ulbrich Stainless Steels & Special Metals, Inc., North Haven, CT, pg. 1125
Durocher, William G., V.P.-Sls. & Dir.-Mktg. & Intl. Sls.--Briggs Industries, Inc., Tampa, FL, pg. 175
Durrett, D.M., V.P.-Mktg.--Harriet & Henderson Yarns, Inc., Henderson, NC, pg. 511
Dusek, Glen, Dir.-Mktg. & Adv.--Contractors Steel Company, Livonia, MI, pg. 280
Dwight, Chris, Asst. Mgr.-Mktg. Services--Muse Cordero Chen, Inc., Los Angeles, CA, pg. 777
Dyer, Lowell, V.P.-Mktg.--Ripon Foods, Inc., Ripon, WI, pg. 935
Dyke, Kim, Mgr.-Mktg. Services--Anaheim Manufacturing Company, Anaheim, CA, pg. 71
Dykhouse, David, V.P.-Mktg. Devel.--Spring Arbor Distributors, Belleville, MI, pg. 1033
Eagles, Marion Edward, V.P.-Mktg.--The Babcock & Wilcox Company, New Orleans, LA, pg. 107
Eastin, Kim, Dir.-Mktg.--Lamp Post Franchise Corporation, Tustin, CA, pg. 652
Easton, Howard, Asst. Gen. Mgr.-Mktg. & Member Services--Basin Electric Power Co-Op, Bismarck, ND, pg. 125
Eaton, Mark, Mgr.-Natl. Sls. & Mktg.--Consolidated Metco, Inc., Portland, OR, pg. 277
Ebeck, Bill, Mgr.-Reg. Sls. & Mktg.--Ivex Packaging Corporation-Grove City, Grove City, PA, pg. 583
Eberline, Kathy, Gen. Mgr.-Mktg.--The Hubinger Company, Keokuk, IA, pg. 550
Ebert, Carol J., Dir.-Mktg. Communications & Pub. Rels.--Gates Energy Products, Inc., Alachua, FL, pg. 445
Eckert, Cece J., Mgr.-Mktg. & Food Standards--Lawry's Restaurants, Inc., Los Angeles, CA, pg. 663
Eckstein, Helene, Chief Fin. Officer, Treas., Sec. & Mktg. Coord.--Spectrum Color Center, Golden, CO, pg. 1029
Economos, George, Sr. V.P. & Dir.-Mktg.--The Dartnell Corporation, Chicago, IL, pg. 316
Edelmann, Edgar S., Pres. & Mktg. Dir.--Edelmann Scott, Inc., Richmond, VA, pg. 368
Edlund, John, Dir.-Mktg.--Molin Auto Parts Inc., Buffalo, NY, pg. 764
Edmund, Gwynne, V.P.-Mktg.--Edmund Scientific Company, Barrington, NJ, pg. 369
Edwards, A.L., Dir.-Mktg. & Sls.--Borg-Warner Automotive, Inc., Control Systems, Sterling Heights, MI, pg. 166
Edwards, Bernard, Deputy Sec. & Mktg.--The Florida Lottery, Tallahassee, FL, pg. 420
Edwards, Jim, Mgr.-Mktg. Services--Atlas/Soundolier, Fenton, MO, pg. 64
Edwards, Karen K., Dir.-Mktg, Sls. Promo., Mdse. & Communications--Applied Microsystems Corporation, Redmond, WA, pg. 79
Egan, James J., III, Assoc. Dir.-Mktg.--Fallon Community Health Plan, West Boylston, MA, pg. 398
Egan, Thomas, Deputy Commissioner-Mktg.--Michigan State Lottery Bureau, Lansing, MI, pg. 747
Egar, Jack, V.P.-Mktg.--Craftex Mills Inc. of Pennsylvania, Blue Bell, PA, pg. 295
Eggebrecht, Jim, Reg. Mktg. Mgr.--The Jolt Company, Rochester, NY, pg. 602
Eggert, Mark, Mktg. & Opers. Mgr.--Morning Glory Farms Region, Shawano, WI, pg. 770
Eglinton, Dave, Mgr.-Sls. & Mktg.--L. R. Nelson Corporation, Peoria, IL, pg. 797
Ego, Charles, Mgr.-Mktg.--Western States Envelope Co., Butler, WI, pg. 1181
Eichler, Larry, V.P.-Sls. & Mktg.--Prentiss Incorporated, Floral Park, NY, pg. 887
Eiriksson, Petur, Sr. V.P.-Mktg.--IceLandAir, New York, NY, pg. 561
Eisenbach, Arthur, Exec. V.P., Dir. Mktg./Media Services--Hill, Holliday, Connors, Cosmopulos, Inc., Boston, MA, pg. 534
Eisenhauer, Pat, V.P.-Sales & Mktg.--Crum Electric Supply Co., Inc., Casper, WY, pg. 303
Ekedahl, V. L., Exec. V.P.-Mktg.--Royal Oak Enterprises, Inc., Atlanta, GA, pg. 953
Elberg, Dale, Sr. V.P.-Sls. & Mktg.--Royal Oak Enterprises, Inc., Atlanta, GA, pg. 953
Eller, S. Heidi, Dir.-Mktg.--The Great Lakes Cheese Co., Newbury, OH, pg. 481
Elliott, Tom, Sr. V.P.-Sls. & Mktg.--Wiltel Communications Systems, Inc., The Woodlands, TX, pg. 1194

Ellis, Gary P., V.P.-Sls. & Mktg.--Crenlo, Inc., Rochester, MN, pg. 298
Ellis, Kendall, Adv. Mgr.--Stonhard, Inc., Maple Shade, NJ, pg. 1051
Ellish, F. Warren, V.P.-Mktg.--Boston Chicken, Inc., Naperville, IL, pg. 167
Elmaleh, Joseph, V.P.-Intl. Mktg. & Sls.--Eagle Electric Mfg. Co., Inc., Long Island City, NY, pg. 362
Elser, Stephen A., Sr. V.P., Mktg. & Bus. Devel.--Elser & Aucone, Inc., New York, NY, pg. 378
Elsey, John, Sr. V.P.-Mktg.--Sentry Insurance, A Mutual Company, Stevens Point, WI, pg. 990
Emanuel, William R., Jr., Dir.-Oper.--E. D. Bullard Company, Cynthiana, KY, pg. 188
Emerson, John, Dir.-Trade Mktg.--Ocean Spray Cranberries, Inc., Lakeville, MA, pg. 820
Emmerling, Paul E., V.P.-Sls. & Mktg.--American Welding & Manufacturing Co., Warren, OH, pg. 65
Emmerling, Paul E., V.P.-Sls. & Mktg.--American Welding & Manufacturing Co., Warren, OH, pg. 431
Emmert, Fred, V.P.-Sls. & Mktg.--Georgie Boy Manufacturing, Inc., Edwardsburg, MI, pg. 453
Engebretson, Duane, V.P.-Mktg.--Pioneer Mutual Life Insurance Company, Fargo, ND, pg. 872
Engels, Frank, Sr. V.P.-Mktg.--Crown Textile Company, Blue Bell, PA, pg. 302
England, Jim, Dir.-Mktg. & Sls.--Diversified Products Corporation, Opelika, AL, pg. 1193
Englander, K.H., V.P.-Mktg.--Central Paper Company, Newark, NJ, pg. 233
Engle, E.E., Dir.-Mktg.--Thrall Car Mfg. Co., Chicago Heights, IL, pg. 350
Engle, R.A., Dir.-Mktg., Comml. Hwy. & Military Prods.--Motor Wheel Corporation, Lansing, MI, pg. 773
Englert, Stan, Dir.-Mktg. & Sls.--Jofco Inc., Jasper, IN, pg. 595
English, Joel, Dir., Mktg. Services--McDonald Davis & Associates, Inc., Milwaukee, WI, pg. 728
English, Marc, V.P.-Mktg.--CPS Corporation, Franklin, TN, pg. 428
Engstrom, Rolf, Sr. V.P.-Mktg. & Admin.--E.A. Sween Company, Eden Prairie, MN, pg. 1066
Ennamorato, Robert J., Mktg. Mgr.--The Fibre-Metal Products Company, Concordville, PA, pg. 408
Epp, William H., Mgr.-Mktg. & Sls.--Penco Products, Oaks, PA, pg. 857
Epporly, Gary, Pres.-Highschool Div.--CJC Holdings, Inc., Austin, TX, pg. 202
Epstein, Elliot R., Exec. V.P.-Adv., Mktg. & Mdsg.--Marisa Christina Inc., New York, NY, pg. 707
Eqquiqfm, Hersey, Dir.-Mktg.--Domecq Importers Inc., Old Greenwich, CT, pg. 343
Erbland, R.M., Exec. V.P.-Mktg.--Miller Electric Mfg. Co., Appleton, WI, pg. 754
Erickson, Bert, Mgr.-Mktg. Communications--E.F. Johnson Company, Eden Prarie, MN, pg. 598
Erickson, Bill, Sr. V.P.-Sls. & Mktg.--Wellcraft Marine, Sarasota, FL, pg. 759
Erickson, Deanna, Dir.-Mktg.--De Novo Corporation, Utica, MI, pg. 321
Erickson, Deanna, Dir.-Mktg.--Tastee Freez Intl. Inc., Utica, MI, pg. 321
Erickson, Don, V.P.-Mktg.--McNally Industries, Inc., Grantsburg, WI, pg. 731
Erickson, Nancy, Asst. Mgr.-Mktg.--Schulze & Burch Biscuit Company, Chicago, IL, pg. 979
Erickson, Norm, Supvr.-Mktg. Services--Cargill Inc., Wayzata, MN, pg. 219
Erickson, Norm, Supvr.-Mktg. Services--Cargill Nutrena Feed, Minneapolis, MN, pg. 219
Erol, Robert R., V.P.-Sls. & Mktg.--Reading Tube Corp., Reading, PA, pg. 916
Erridge, Ian, V.P.-Sls. & Mktg.--Blue Diamond Growers, Sacramento, CA, pg. 160
Ervin, Mike, Dir.-Mktg. & Sls.--Hercules Engines, Inc., Canton, OH, pg. 531
Esberg, Guy, V.P.-Mktg.--Peerless Lighting Corp., Berkeley, CA, pg. 855
Esses, Michael, V.P.-Sls. & Mktg.--Pioneer Press Newspapers Inc., Wilmette, IL, pg. 18
Estep, Paul, Dir.-Mktg.--Beckley-Cardy, Inc., Duluth, MN, pg. 21
Esterling, Gary L., V.P.-Mktg.--Bodine Electric Company, Chicago, IL, pg. 162
Estreicher, Saul, Mgr.-Mktg. Support & Admin.--Bridgeport Machines, Inc., Bridgeport, CT, pg. 175
Etka, Jack L., V.P.-Prod. Service--Ardco, Inc., Alsip, IL, pg. 81
Euson, Greg, V.P.-Mktg.--Random House, Inc., New York, NY, pg. 19
Evangelatos, Themmi, Dir.-Mktg.--Muro Pharmaceutical, Inc., Tewksbury, MA, pg. 776
Evans, G., V.P.-Sls. & Mktg.--Waukesha Foundry Inc., Waukesha, WI, pg. 1168
Evans, Hank, V.P.-Mktg.--Pioneer Communications of America, Upper Saddle River, NJ, pg. 871
Evans, Steve, Dir.-Mktg.--Perdue Farms Inc., Salisbury, MD, pg. 860
Evans, Thomas, Mgr.-Sls. & Mktg.-Indus. Div.--Dumore Corporation, Mauston, WI, pg. 352
Evans, Tracy, Mgr.-Mktg. Services--Diagraph Corporation, Earth City, MO, pg. 335
Evans, William M., V.P.-Sls., Adv. & Mktg.--Evans Brothers Company, Inc., Waukesha, WI, pg. 390
Everette, Tony, V.P.-Mktg.--Sanborn Manufacturing Company, Springfield, MN, pg. 969
Ewoldt, Dean, Matl. Mgr.--Iowa Industrial Hydraulics, Inc., Pocahontas, IA, pg. 559
Fabiano, Francis, X., Mgr.-Intl. Mktg.--Star Expansion Company, Mountainville, NY, pg. 1039
Fabricius, Allen F., V.P.-Mktg.--Nodak Mutual Insurance Company, Fargo, ND, pg. 808
Fabricuis, Allen, V.P.-Mktg.--Nodak Mutual Insurance Co., Fargo, ND, pg. 808
Fajen, Steve, Exec. V.P., Dir. Media & Mktg. Services--Korey, Kay & Partners, New York, NY, pg. 642
Fajfar, V.P.-Mktg.--Popeye's Famous Fried Chicken, Alexandria, VA, pg. 283
Falk, Doug, Exec. V.P.-Sls. & Mktg.--Norwegian Cruise Line, Coral Gables, FL, pg. 816
Farace, Vince, Dir.-Sls. & Mktg.--B. Green & Co., Baltimore, MD, pg. 484
Farber, Bernard, Sr. V.P.-Mktg. & Sls.--West Mill Clothes, Inc., Woodside, NY, pg. 1177
Faria, Anthony J., V.P.-Mktg. & Sls.--Samuel Cabot, Inc., Newburyport, MA, pg. 206
Farland, Jim, V.P.-Sls. & Mktg.--The Union Fork & Hoe Co., Columbus, OH, pg. 1128
Farmer, Kevin, V.P., Sales & Mktg.--Adams Colway & Associates, Rochester, NY, pg. 16
Farmer, Mike, Mgr.-Contract Sls.--The Paty Company, Piney Flats, TN, pg. 852
Farrell, Michelle, Mktg. Coord.--Quality Bakers of America Cooperative, Inc., Greenwich, CT, pg. 903
Farrington, Dennis, Sr. V.P., Dir. Reg. Mktg.--Hill, Holliday/Los Angeles, Marina Del Rey, CA, pg. 534
Farrington, Renee, Dir., Mktg. Services--Carney/Mohlin & Company, Lynnfield, MA, pg. 222
Farris, Mark, V.P.-Mktg. & Sls.--E F Industries, Carson, CA, pg. 359
Fasano, Lorraine, Dir.-Mktg.--The National Bank of Sussex County, Branchville, NJ, pg. 534
Fasano, Tony, V.P.-Mktg. & Sls.--Neer Manufacturing Company, Lexington, OH, pg. 797
Feagans, Elizabeth W., V.P.-Mktg. & Communications--The Royal China & Porcelain Companies Inc., Moorestown, NJ, pg. 953
Federico, Nicholas, Sr., Sr. V.P.-Mktg.--Blue Coral, Inc., Cleveland, OH, pg. 159
Feeney, John R., Mgr.-Proprietary Prod.--Equity Services, Inc., Montpelier, VT, pg. 791
Feerer, Homer L., V.P.-Sls. & Mktg.--Finch, Pruyn & Co., Inc., Glens Falls, NY, pg. 410
Feierstein, Larry, V.P.-Mktg.--Nathan's Famous Inc., Westbury, NY, pg. 784
Felchner, Edward L., V.P. & Dir.-Prdouct Devel., Mktg. & Underwriting--Omaha Property & Casualty, Omaha, NE, pg. 779
Felchner, Edward L., V.P. & Dir.-Product Devel., Mktg. & Underwriting Opers.--Omaha Property & Casualty Co., Omaha, NE, pg. 779
Feldman, Nora, Dir.-Mktg.--I D E Associates, Billerica, MA, pg. 560
Feldmann, Thomas, Mgr.-Mktg.--West Central Co-op, Ralston, IA, pg. 1176
Fellbaum, Todd G., Dir.-Mktg.--Label Products & Design Division, Green Bay, WI, pg. 608
Fellman, Nelson, Pres., Sls. Promo.--Rosanio, Bailets & Talamo, Inc., Cherry Hill, NJ, pg. 947
Fellner, Peter, Mgr. Sls. & Mktg.--Zyntec GmbH, Vienna,, Austria, pg. 1221
Fenderson, A. P., Exec. V.P.-Mktg.--E & J Gallo Winery, Modesto, CA, pg. 441
Fenderson, A.P., Exec. V.P.-Mktg.--Carlo Rossi Vineyards, Modesto, CA, pg. 442
Fennell, John, V.P., Sec. & Dir.-Mktg.--Badger Air Brush Company, Franklin Park, IL, pg. 113
Fenniman, William W., Sr. V.P. & Chief Mktg. Officer--National Life Insurance Company, Montpelier, VT, pg. 791
Ferentinos, Terry, Products Line Mgr.--Repco Incorporated, Orlando, FL, pg. 927
Ferguson, Carolyn, Mgr.-Natl. Mktg.--Columbus Show Case Company, Columbus, OH, pg. 267
Ferguson, Donald J., V.P.-Mktg.--Intermatic Inc., Spring Grove, IL, pg. 575
Ferguson, Gerry H., V.P.-Mktg. & Sls.--Binning's Building Products, Inc., Lexington, NC, pg. 151
Ferguson, Mike, Exec. V.P.-Sls. & Mktg.--Colad Group Inc., Buffalo, NY, pg. 259
Ferguson, Sam Jr., Exec. V.P. & Dir.-Sls. & Mktg.--Ferguson Industries, Dallas, TX, pg. 406
Ferguson, Scott, V.P.-Mktg. & Sec.--Hamlin, Inc., Lake Mills, WI, pg. 503
Ferman, Don, V.P.-Mktg.--Maritz Communications Co., Fenton, MO, pg. 707
Fernandez, Juan, Dir.-Mktg. Analysis--Mission Industries, Santa Barbara, CA, pg. 760
Fernandi, Martin J., V.P.-Mktg.--Ampacet Corporation, Tarrytown, NY, pg. 67
Ferraris, Frank, V.P.-Mktg.--Sun-Maid Growers of California, Kingsburg, CA, pg. 1058
Ferraro, Karen L., Mgr.-Mktg.--Periphonics Corp., Bohemia, NY, pg. 862
Ferrie, Steve, Mktg. Dir.--Tecknit, Cranford, NJ, pg. 1084
Ferrucci, Anne, Asst. V.P.-Mktg.--The F.A. Bartlett Tree Expert Co., Stamford, CT, pg. 123
Fick, William J., Creative Dir.--Lyon Metal Products, Inc., Montgomery, IL, pg. 690
Fidler, Karen, Dir.-Mktg.--Bachman Company, Reading, PA, pg. 108
Fiegel, Kirby, V.P.-Equip. Mktg.--Phoenix American Incorporated, San Rafael, CA, pg. 868
Field, David, V.P.-Sls. & Mktg.--Trendway Corporation, Holland, MI, pg. 1109
Fielder, James, V.P.-Opers. & Mktg.--Robert B. Aikens & Associates Inc., Troy, MI, pg. 26
Fighter, Robert D., V.P.-Sls. & Mktg.--The Crocker-Fels Company, Cincinnati, OH, pg. 299
Fike, Robert M., Dir.-Mktg.--Northwest Paper Converting Company, Vancouver, WA, pg. 814
Filipelli, Tony, Sr. V.P., Mktg. Services--Rhea & Kaiser Advertising, Inc., Naperville, IL, pg. 930
Filippelli, Peter, V.P.-Mktg. & Sls.--Eli's Chicago's Finest, Inc., Chicago, IL, pg. 376
Fine, William, Pres.-Home Furnishings Mktg.--Dan River Inc.-Home Furnishings & Related Prods., Div. I, Danville, VA, pg. 313
Finigan, Nancy, Dir.-Mktg.--TimeMed Labeling Systems, Inc., Burr Ridge, IL, pg. 1098
Fink, Dick, V.P.-Mktg.--S & W Fine Foods, Inc., San Ramon, CA, pg. 1111
Finkbiener, Julia, Dir.-Telemarketing--Paradigm Communications, Tampa, FL, pg. 847
Finke, Daniel E., Group V.P.-Coding & Mktg. Systems--Diagraph Corporation, Earth City, MO, pg. 335
Finlay, Judith A., Mgr.-Adv. & Mktg.--Lindenmeyr Munroe, Peabody, MA, pg. 233
Finlayson, Bruce A., V.P.-Mktg.--Hawthorne Adv., Inc., Philadelphia, PA, pg. 518
Finley, Jon, Mgr.-Mktg. Support--Rundel Products, Inc., Portland, OR, pg. 956
Finley, Russell G., Sr. V.P., Mktg./Media--John Emmerling Inc., New York, NY, pg. 379
Finnegan, Bob, V.P.-Bus. Devel.--Handley & Miller, Inc., Indianapolis, IN, pg. 505
Finneran, Tom, Sr. V.P.-Mktg.--Quaker Fabric Corporation, Fall River, MA, pg. 903
Firesheets, William T., II, V.P.-Mktg.--Buquet & Le Blanc Inc., Baton Rouge, LA, pg. 189
Fischer, Dale, Dir.-Intl. Sls. & Mktg.--Metrologic Instruments, Inc., Blackwood, NJ, pg. 743
Fischioni, Phillip, Exec. V.P. & Corp. Dir.-Mktg.--Paul Inman Associates Inc., Farmington Hills, MI, pg. 570
Fisher, Bill, Dir.-Mktg.--Adventure Lands of America, Inc., Des Moines, IA, pg. 21
Fisher, James D., V.P.-Mktg.--Shakey's Incorporated, South San Francisco, CA, pg. 994
Fisher, Jim, V.P.-Mktg.--Monarch Foods, Inc., Tukwila, WA, pg. 994
Fisher, Kurt, V.P.-Mktg.--Transport Insurance Co., Dallas, TX, pg. 54
Fisher, Linda, Sr. Mgr.-Channel Mktg.--Spinnaker Software Corporation, Cambridge, MA, pg. 1031
Fisher, Marshall, Dir.-Mktg.--Carolina Glove Co., Newton, NC, pg. 223
Fisher, Millicent A., Mktg. Coord.--Unistrut Corporation, Ann Arbor, MI, pg. 1130
Fisher, Phelps K., V.P.-Mktg.--Fisher Broadcasting, Inc., Seattle, WA, pg. 415
Fitzgerald, Deborah, Mktg. & Sls. Specialist--Cooper Instrument Corp., Middlefield, CT, pg. 283
Fitzgerald, E.J., V.P.-Mktg.--Gold Bond Building Products, Charlotte, NC, pg. 790
Fitzgerald, Thomas, V.P.-Mktg.--ARA Services, Inc., Philadelphia, PA, pg. 5
Fitzpatrick, Donna, V.P., Mktg. Dir.--Borders, Perrin & Norrander, Inc., Portland, OR, pg. 165
Fitzsimmons, John, Dir.-Mktg.--DIT-MCO Intl., Kansas City, MO, pg. 1206
Flanagan, Kathleen, V.P.-Sls. & Mktg.--American Management Group, Westbrook, ME, pg. 57
Flathau, Robert, Dir.-New Prod. Devel.--Symons Corporation, Des Plaines, IL, pg. 1069
Flaugher, Teresa A., Mgr.-Mktg. Services--Weaver Popcorn Company, Inc., Van Buren, IN, pg. 1170
Fleischer, Barry, V.P.-Sls. & Mktg.--Aldan Rubber Co., Philadelphia, PA, pg. 32
Fleming, Paul, Sr. V.P., Mktg. Services--Duffy & Shanley, Inc., Providence, RI, pg. 351
Fleming, R.G., V.P.-Sls. & Mktg.--Sturtevant Div., Boston, MA, pg. 547
Fleming, Robin G., V.P.-Sls. & Mktg.--Howden Sirocco inc., Hyde Park, MA, pg. 547
Fletcher, Wendy, V.P., Mktg. Services--Fletcher Hunt Wirth Associates, Inc., Kansas City, MO, pg. 418
Fletcher, William, Dir.-Mktg.--California Custom Foods, Lodi, CA, pg. 840
Flick, Rocky, V.P.-Sls. & Mktg.--Blitz USA, Miami, OK, pg. 157
Flick, Rocky, V.P.-Mktg., Sls., Adv. & Export--Blitz U.S.A., Inc., Miami, OK, pg. 157
Flint, Bill, Jr., V.P.-Mktg.--Flambeau Corporation, Baraboo, WI, pg. 809
Florence, Terry L., Mgr.-Product--Triplett Electrical Instrument Corporation, Bluffton, OH, pg. 1114
Florey, Debi, V.P., Mktg., Adv. & New Bus. Contact--Bradley Communications, Inc., Anchorage, AK, pg. 170
Flory, Don, Mgr.-Mktg. Services--R. A. Jones & Co. Inc., Covington, KY, pg. 604
Flowers, Carol, Adv. & Mktg. Mgr.--Eager Beaver, Lake Wales, FL, pg. 362
Flynn, Dan, Prod. & Catalog Mgr.--Triple A Specialty Company, Bedford Park, IL, pg. 1114
Foerster, Stephen A., V.P.-Corp. Plng.--Tempel Steel Company, Skokie, IL, pg. 1086
Fogelson, Joel, V.P.-Mktg.--Rogerson Aircraft Corporation, Irvine, CA, pg. 943
Foley, Daniel P., Dir.-Mktg. Svcs.--Security Mutual Life Insurance Co. of New York, Binghamton, NY, pg. 987
Foley, Eugene T., Dir.-Mktg.--Pic'n Pay Stores, Inc., Charlotte, NC, pg. 201
Folk, James C., V.P.-Mktg. & Sls.--Jewell Instruments, Inc., Manchester, NH, pg. 594
Foote, Nathan, V.P.-Sls. & Mktg.--Blount Lumber Company, Lacona, NY, pg. 158
Footer, Eli, V.P.-Sls. & Mktg.--Schwartz & Benjamin, Inc., New York, NY, pg. 980
Ford, David, V.P.-Mktg.--Comlinear Corporation, Fort Collins, CO, pg. 268
Ford, John, V.P.-Mktg. & Sls.--UDL Laboratories, Inc., Rockford, IL, pg. 1072
Ford, Michael, Dir.-Mktg.--Swinerton & Walberg Co., San Francisco, CA, pg. 1068
Fording, William G., V.P.-Mktg.--Sussen, Inc., Cleveland, OH, pg. 225
Forgione, Anthony, Chm. Bd. & Pres.--Boyer Bros. Inc., Altoona, PA, pg. 169
Forgione, Deborah, Dir.-Mktg.--Boyer Bros. Inc., Altoona, PA, pg. 169
Forhan, Phillip, Dir.-Sls.--Active Tool & Manufacturing Co., Inc., Roseville, MI, pg. 15

Forlenza, William, Sr. V.P., Bus. Devel.--The Direct Marketing Group Inc., New York, NY, pg. 339
Formosa, Peter, V.P.-Mktg.--Frank Ix & Sons, Inc., New York, NY, pg. 584
Fornaro, Robert L., Sr. V.P.-Mkt. Plng.--Northwest Airlines, Inc., Saint Paul, MN, pg. 782
Foskey, Randall J., Dir.-Mktg.--Colonial Williamsburg Foundation, Williamsburg, VA, pg. 264
Fost, Dennis L., V.P.-Mktg. & Comml. Devel.--Mona Industries, Inc., Paterson, NJ, pg. 764
Foster, Donald, V.P.-Mktg.--The Garber Company, Ashland, OH, pg. 442
Foster, Jim, V.P.-Sls. & Mktg.--Tweddle Litho Company, St. Clair Shores, MI, pg. 1120
Foster, Torrey, Dir.-Mktg.--Carl Buddig & Company, Homewood, IL, pg. 186
Fosters, Jim V., V.P.-Mktg.--Florists' Mutual Insurance Co., Edwardsville, IL, pg. 421
Foti, Samuel J., Exec. V.P.-Insurance Opers.--The Mutual Life Insurance Company of New York (MONY), New York, NY, pg. 778
Fournier, Don B., Dir.-Mktg.--Cable Electric Products, Inc., Providence, RI, pg. 671
Fowler, Alan L., V.P.-Mktg.--James N. Gray Construction Co., Inc., Lexington, KY, pg. 479
Fowler, Phil, V.P.-Sls. & Mktg.--Hatteras Yachts, High Point, NC, pg. 758
Fox-Morris, Stephanie, Dir.-Mktg.--Thomas Publishing Co., New York, NY, pg. 1093
Fox, J.A., V.P.-Mktg.--Quintana Petroleum Services, Houston, TX, pg. 905
Fox, Laura, Dir.-Pub. Rels. & Mktg.--Williams Television Time, Inc., Santa Monica, CA, pg. 1191
Foy, Dwight D., V.P.-Mktg. & Transportation--North Pacific Lumber Company, Portland, OR, pg. 813
Fragman, Bonnie, Mktg. Coord.--Globus-Gateway/Cosmos Tourama, Rego Park, NY, pg. 464
Franceschino, Carmen, Mktg. Dir.--Roska Direct Marketing, Inc., North Wales, PA, pg. 949
Frangos, Cathy, Adv., Traffic & Media Planner--My Own Meals, Inc., Deerfield, IL, pg. 779
Frank, Tricia, V.P.-Sls. & Mktg.--American Eagle Airlines, Chicago, IL, pg. 51
Frankel, Norman, V.P.-Sls. & Mktg.--Standard Textile Co., Inc., Cincinnati, OH, pg. 1037
Franklin, John R., Mgr.-Mktg. & Adv.--Baltimore Stationery Co., Baltimore, MD, pg. 116
Franklin, Steve, V.P.-Mktg.--Humboldt Express, Inc., Nashville, TN, pg. 552
Franklin, Wayne, Dir.-Mktg.--The Parman Corporation, Nashville, TN, pg. 850
Frantz, David E., Dir.-Mktg. & Pub. Rels.--Developers Diversified, Moreland Hills, OH, pg. 333
Frash, Bill, V.P., Bus. Devel.--International Communications Group, Inc., Los Angeles, CA, pg. 576
Frasier, John, Dir.-Mktg.--Vanguard Plastics, Inc., McPherson, KS, pg. 1145
Frazier, Fritz, Dir.-Mktg.--RAM Golf Corporation, Melrose Park, IL, pg. 910
Frazier, Walter, V.P.-Sls. & Mktg.--Roller Derby Skate Company, Litchfield, IL, pg. 944
Frederickson, Joseph, Dir.-Mktg.--Toledo Blade Co., Toledo, OH, pg. 155
Fredrecks, Sally J., Mktg. Communications Specialist--Amano Cincinnati, Inc., Cincinnati, OH, pg. 46
Fredricksen, Heidi, Mgr.-Mktg.--Luxor Corporation, Waukegan, IL, pg. 365
Fredrickson, Joe, Dir.-Mktg.--Blade Communications, Inc., Toledo, OH, pg. 155
Freedman, Jennifer, Dir.-Mktg. Communications--Teca Corporation, Pleasantville, NY, pg. 1082
Freeman, Donald W., Sr. V.P.-Bus. Devel.--Rentenbach Engineering Company, Knoxville, TN, pg. 927
Freeman, Jill, Dir.-Mktg.--Freeman Cosmetic Corp., Los Angeles, CA, pg. 431
Freeman, Mark S., Sec. & Dir.-Intl. Sls. & Mktg.--Freeman Cosmetic Corp., Los Angeles, CA, pg. 431
Freiling, Walt, Dir.-Sls. & Mktg.--Jordon Commercial Refrigerator Co., Philadelphia, PA, pg. 605
French, Carolyn, Dir.-Mktg.--Dahlstrom Manufacturing Company, Inc., Jamestown, NY, pg. 310
French, Eddie, Natl. Sls. & Mktg. Mgr.--American Ball Manufacturing, Carrollton, TX, pg. 890
French, James, V.P.-Mktg.--Airguard Industries Inc., Louisville, KY, pg. 27
Frey, Marlene O., V.P.-Mktg.--Artesian Laboratories, Inc., Newark, DE, pg. 86
Friday, Sally, Dir.-Mktg.--Amurcon Corporation, Southfield, MI, pg. 70
Friebe, Joe, Dir.-Mktg.--The Sportsman's Guide, Inc., Eagan, MN, pg. 1032
Friedman, Mara, V.P., Dir. Research & Planning--Cohen/Johnson, Inc., Los Angeles, CA, pg. 259
Friedman, Reuben, Pres. & Chief Exec. Officer--Arrow Typographers, Inc., Newark, NJ, pg. 326
Friel, John P., V.P.-Sls. & Mktg.--Medrad, Inc., Pittsburgh, PA, pg. 736
Friend, Howard, Exec. V.P.-Sls. & Mktg.--On-Cor Frozen Foods Inc., Chicago, IL, pg. 826
Friend, Kent, Sr. V.P.-Sls. & Mktg.--Kraco Enterprises, Inc., Compton, CA, pg. 643
Friesen, Robert, Mgr.-Mktg. & Sls.--S-T Industries, Inc., Saint James, MN, pg. 964
Frisby, Owen, V.P.-Mktg.--Capital Bank, N.A., Washington, DC, pg. 214
Fritsch, Al, Dir.-Mktg.--Flair Communications Agency, Inc., Chicago, IL, pg. 416
Fritz, Bill, V.P.-Sls. & Mktg.--Illinois Auto Electric Co., Elmhurst, IL, pg. 562
Fritz, Gary, V.P.-Mktg.--Brodbeck Enterprises, Inc., Platteville, WI, pg. 178
Frohock, Christina M., Dir.-Mktg. & Communications--Advertising Age, Chicago, IL, pg. 295
Fross, Vern, Sr. V.P.-Sls. & Mktg.--Ingram Entertainment Inc., La Vergne, TN, pg. 569
Frost, Jerrold A., Staff V.P.-Mktg. Services--Michigan Tractor And Machinery Co., Novi, MI, pg. 747
Frost, Kai, Sr. V.P.-Mktg.--Woodward & Lothrop/John Wanamaker, Washington, DC, pg. 1201
Frost, Thomas C., V.P.-Mktg.--Frost Company, Andover, MA, pg. 435
Fruth, Steve, Dir.-Mktg.--Fostoria Industries, Inc., Fostoria, OH, pg. 427
Fuerstenberg, Gary, V.P.-Mktg.--Progress Casting Group, Inc., Plymouth, MN, pg. 894
Fujimoto, Dale, V.P.-Sls. & Mktg.--KNOX International Corp., Knoxville, TN, pg. 638
Fujimoto, Dale, V.P.-Mktg.--Michigan Bulb Company, Grand Rapids, MI, pg. 638
Fuldner, John E., Mgr.-Mktg. & Adv.--Efco Corporation, Monett, MO, pg. 359
Fulkerson, Gerald A., V.P.-Mktg.--The Buschman Co., Cincinnati, OH, pg. 196
Fullington, William, Dir.-Mktg. Services--The Richard & David Jacobs Group, Westlake, OH, pg. 932
Furlong, Mark, Mgr.-Mktg.--American Machine & Tool Company, Royersford, PA, pg. 57
Furman, Joel R., V.P.-Sls. & Mktg.--Furman Foods, Inc., Northumberland, PA, pg. 436
Furtsh, Kenneth W., Dir.-Mktg.--Justrite Manufacturing Company, Des Plaines, IL, pg. 610
Fusco, Lynn R., V.P.-Mktg.--The Fusco Corporation, New Haven, CT, pg. 437
Fynan, Peggy, V.P.-Mktg.--Stonhard, Inc., Maple Shade, NJ, pg. 1051
Gabe, Jon, V.P.-Sls. & Mktg.--Fred Usinger, Inc., Milwaukee, WI, pg. 1140
Gaffield, Christopher, V.P. & Dir.-Mktg.--Stone & Simons Advertising, Inc., Southfield, MI, pg. 1051
Gaffney, Orville E., V.P.-Mkt. Expansion--Na-Churs Plant Food Company, Marion, OH, pg. 782
Gagnassola, J.L., V.P.--Hydro Group, Inc., Bridgewater, NJ, pg. 556
Gagnon, Nicole, Mktg. Services Coord.--UC Industries, Inc., Parsippany, NJ, pg. 1122
Gainey, Harry, Dir.-Mktg. Communications--Draper Corporation, Greensboro, NC, pg. 348
Gaiss, Ralph, V.P.-Stores & Representative--Agway Petroleum Corp., De Witt, NY, pg. 25
Galadding, R. Daniel, V.P.-Mktg., Technical & Sourcing--Amalloy, Goshen, NY, pg. 46
Galante, Nancy, Dir. Mktg. & Media--Responsive Marketing Communications, Inc., Schaumburg, IL, pg. 929
Gale, Nelson, V.P.-Mktg. & Sls.--Interstate Distributors Inc., Norcross, GA, pg. 580
Galex, Martin, Pres. & Chief Exec. Officer--Therapedic Associates, Inc., Boca Raton, FL, pg. 1090
Gall, Robert E., V.P.-Sls. & Mktg.--Amtrak-National Railroad Passenger Corp., Washington, DC, pg. 69
Gallagher, Michael B., Exec. V.P.-Mktg.--Marine World Africa USA, Vallejo, CA, pg. 707
Gallagher, Shay, V.P.-Mktg.--Bradford Exchange Ltd., Niles, IL, pg. 170
Galler, Michelle I., V.P., Mktg.--Abramson Ehrlich Manes, Inc., Washington, DC, pg. 10
Galvin, James, Dir.-Adv. & Mktg. & Mgr.-Sls.--Media America Corp., Phoenix, AZ, pg. 734
Galvin, James J., Dir.-Mktg.--Symmons Industries Inc., Braintree, MA, pg. 1069
Gamache, Brian, Dir.-Resort Div. Sls. & Mktg.--Hyatt Hotels Corporation, Chicago, IL, pg. 495
Gambrell, James B., V.P.-Mktg. & Bus. Devel.--RPR & Associates, Inc., Columbia, SC, pg. 908
Ganey, Michael, V.P.-Mktg.--Bahlsen Inc., Cary, NC, pg. 114
Ganskopp, C. Robert, V.P.-Sls. & Mktg.--South Chester Tube Co., Concordville, PA, pg. 1019
Ganter, F.A., V.P.-Mktg.--Norfolk Shipbuilding & Drydock Corporation, Norfolk, VA, pg. 810
Gantt, Phillip L., Dir.-Sls. & Mktg.--Vidicom, L.D. Bevan Company, Inc., Thousand Oaks, CA, pg. 1151
GaNun, Joseph, V.P.-Sls. (Folding Carton Div.)--F.N. Burt Company, Inc., Buffalo, NY, pg. 195
Garber, Stan, Mktg. Mgr.-Brass & Woodwinds--The Selmer Co., Elkhart, IN, pg. 573
Garber, Van L., Dir.-Mktg. Services--Norandex Inc., Macedonia, OH, pg. 809
Garcia, Frank, V.P.-Mktg.--Good Companies, Carson, CA, pg. 470
Garder, Betsy, Mgr.-Mktg. Services--Forstmann & Company, Inc., New York, NY, pg. 424
Gardiner, Mark, Dir.-Sls. & Mktg.--Hinkley Lighting Inc., Cleveland, OH, pg. 535
Gardner, Denise, V.P.-Mktg.--Soft Sheen Products, Inc., Chicago, IL, pg. 1016
Garfield, Craig, Sls. & Mktg. Mgr.--Brodhead-Garrett Co., Mansfield, OH, pg. 178
Garfield, David G., Sr. V.P., Dir. Res. & Strategic Planning--Ross Roy Inc., Bloomfield Hills, MI, pg. 950
Garfinkel, Larry, V.P.-Devel.--The Fairmont Hotels, San Francisco, CA, pg. 397
Garms, Susan W., Mgr.-Mktg.--BNA Books Div., Washington, DC, pg. 189
Gaspar, Alfred, Exec. V.P.-Mktg.--McKay Chemical Co., Los Angeles, CA, pg. 159
Gast, K.C., Mgr.-Mktg. Devel.--Gast Mfg. Corp., Benton Harbor, MI, pg. 444
Gaston, P.A., Mktg. Service Rep.--Lord Corporation, Erie, PA, pg. 683
Gats, Robert J., V.P.-Mktg.--Park Corporation, Barrington, IL, pg. 849
Gattney, Tina, Mgr.-Mktg. Services--Thomas Publishing Co., New York, NY, pg. 1093
Gaube, Jerry, Dir.-Mktg.--Keuffel & Esser, Rockaway, NJ, pg. 105
Gaudio, Jeff, V.P.-Mktg. Opers.--Union Switch & Signal Inc., Pittsburgh, PA, pg. 1129
Gavallis, Leonora, Dir.-Mktg.--Zenith Laboratories, Inc., Northvale, NJ, pg. 1217
Gay, Glen, V.P.-Sls., Mktg. & Export--Pace International Corporation, Kirkland, WA, pg. 838
Gazaler, Ramsey, Dir.-Reseller Opers.--The ASCII Group, Inc., Bethesda, MD, pg. 8
Gazlay, Lawrence J., Dir.-Mktg.--General Sportcraft Company Ltd., Bergenfield, NJ, pg. 450
Geary, Gayle S., V.P., Dir. Mktg. Services--Gardner Communications, Inc., San Francisco, CA, pg. 443
Geers, Lisa, Dir. Media & Mktg.--Whitemyer Advertising, Inc., Zoar, OH, pg. 1186
Gefteas, Bill, Mgr.-Reg. Mkts.--Sentry Group, Rochester, NY, pg. 990
Geiger, Peter E., V.P.-Mktg. & Sls.--Geiger Brothers, Lewiston, ME, pg. 447
Geis, Carol, V.P.-Mktg.--The Levy Organization, Chicago, IL, pg. 672
Geiselman, R.D., Mgr.-Mktg. Services, Communications & Adv.--E.F. Houghton & Co., Valley Forge, PA, pg. 546
Geiserman, Otto, Dir.-Mktg. & Mgr.-Reg. Sls.--Digital Electronic Automation, Livonia, MI, pg. 337
Gemmel, Kari, Mktg. & Intl. Sls. Dir.--Jackson Hole Ski Resort, Teton Village, WY, pg. 587
Gentine, Lee M., Exec. V.P.-Mktg.--Sargento Cheese Co., Plymouth, WI, pg. 971
Genuser, Steve, V.P.-Mktg. & Sls.--Shugart Corporation, Irvine, CA, pg. 1001
Genuser, Steve, V.P.-Mktg. & Sls.--Kennedy Company, Irwindale, CA, pg. 1001
Geocaris, Dan, V.P.-Custom Products--Little Lady Foods, Inc., Elk Grove Village, IL, pg. 679
George, Paige, Mktg. Specialist--United Air Specialists, Inc., Cincinnati, OH, pg. 1130
George, Rodney M., V.P.-Mktg.--Melody Foods, Inc., Farmington Hills, MI, pg. 738
George, Stephen M., V.P.-Mktg.-Ice Cream Div.--Melody Foods, Inc., Farmington Hills, MI, pg. 738
Gerber, James L., Sr. V.P.-Mktg.--Alfred Nickles Bakery, Inc., Navarre, OH, pg. 806
Gerber, James L., V.P.-Mktg. & Distr.--Nickles Bakery, Inc., Martins Ferry, OH, pg. 807
Gerfen, Henry, Exec. V.P.-Mktg.--G. Heileman Brewing Co., Inc., La Crosse, WI, pg. 526
Germain, Bob, V.P.-Mktg.--Sloan Technology, Santa Barbara, CA, pg. 1146
German, James, V.P.-Mktg.--Delta Queen Steamboat Company, New Orleans, LA, pg. 385
Gerrard, David, Chief Fin. Officer & Mktg. Dir.--National Truck Leasing System, Oakbrook Terrace, IL, pg. 794
Gersch, Wayne, Dir.-Mktg.--UC Industries, Inc., Parsippany, NJ, pg. 1122
Gershaw, Gerald, Pres.-Intl. Div.--Therapedic Associates, Inc., Boca Raton, FL, pg. 1090
Gerstein, Mel, Treas. & Dir.-Mktg., Adv. & Pub. Rels.--Thermwell Products Co., Inc., Paterson, NJ, pg. 1092
Gerstein, Mel, V.P.-Mktg. & Adv.--Lever Mfg. Corp., Paterson, NJ, pg. 1092
Gerstl, Tibor, V.P.-Mktg. Communications--Leviton Mfg. Co., Inc., Little Neck, NY, pg. 671
Gertz, William, Sr. V.P.-Mktg.--American Institute For Foreign Study, Greenwich, CT, pg. 56
Getner, Bill, Mgr.-Mktg.--Kokomo Spring Company, Inc., Kokomo, IN, pg. 640
Gevorkian, Cindy, Mgr.-Mktg.--KBF Foods Division, Placentia, CA, pg. 637
Gezon, Bruce, V.P.-Mktg.--Helmick Corporation, Fairmont, WV, pg. 527
Giageos, Don, Mgr.-Human Resources--Simplicity Manufacturing, Inc., Port Washington, WI, pg. 1006
Giammarco, Ralph, Dir.-Mktg.--Tekra Corporation, New Berlin, WI, pg. 1084
Giamo, Kathy, Dir.-Sls. & Mktg.--Reckson Associates, Melville, NY, pg. 917
Gianfalla, Joe, Mktg. Mgr.--Intralox A/S, Hjorring,, Denmark, pg. 651
Giangiulio, MaryEllen, Mktg. Services Coord. & Corp. Travel Planner--Streamlight Inc., Norristown, PA, pg. 1053
Giannestras, James, V.P.-Mktg. & Sls.--Cherry Central Cooperative, Traverse City, MI, pg. 243
Gibbons, E.A., V.P.-Mktg. & Food Service Sls.--Presto Food Products, Inc., City of Industry, CA, pg. 888
Gibbs, Donald, V.P.-Sls. & Mktg.--Lawson Mechanical Contractors, Sacramento, CA, pg. 663
Giboney, Richard W., V.P.-Mktg.--Restaurants Unlimited, Seattle, WA, pg. 929
Giglis, Phil, V.P.-Mktg.--Apache Hose & Belting Company, Cedar Rapids, IA, pg. 77
Gilbert, George, Dir.-Mktg. Res. & Acct. Services--The Stogel Companies Inc., New York, NY, pg. 1050
Gilbert, John M., Sr. V.P.-Mktg.--State Volunteer Mutual Insurance Co. Inc., Brentwood, TN, pg. 1041
Gilbertson, O.B., V.P.-Mktg.--Wells Lamont, Niles, IL, pg. 712
Gilewicz, P. J., Mktg Service Mgr--Marion Power Shovel Division, Marion, OH, pg. 565
Gill, John E., V.P.-Sls. & Mktg.--American Paper Products Group, Ltd., Youngstown, OH, pg. 59
Gill, Phillip C., V.P.-Mktg.--M.C. Gill Corporation, El Monte, CA, pg. 458
Gillespie, Cary, Mktg. Mgr.--Colson Caster Corporation, Jonesboro, AR, pg. 711
Gillespie, Dennis G., Pres.-Worldwide Mktg. & Domestic Sls.--Viacom Enterprises, New York, NY, pg. 785
Gillespie, John C., Mktg. Dir.--Willson Safety Products, Reading, PA, pg. 1193
Gillespie, William G., Mgr.-Mktg.--J. L. Hammett Company, Braintree, MA, pg. 504
Gillett, Anthony F., V.P.-Mktg.--Monier Roof Tile, Inc., Orange, CA, pg. 765
Gilliam, Doyle, V.P.-Sls. & Mktg.--E.C. Barton & Co., Jonesboro, AR, pg. 123
Gilmore, Kathleen, Dir.-Mktg.--Gilmore Envelope Corp., Los Angeles, CA, pg. 460

Gilmore, Tim, Mgr.-Mktg. & Mdse.--Wunda Weve Carpet Co., Greenville, SC, pg. 1205
Gilsdorf, Paul E., V.P.-Sls. & Mktg.--A-B Emblem Div. of Conrad Industries, Inc., Weaverville, NC, pg. 2
Ginsberg, Kaye Wisecup, Dir.-Mktg.--Conde Nast Traveler, New York, NY, pg. 19
Gipson, Beverly, Mktg. Sls. Mgr.--American Water Works Association, Denver, CO, pg. 65
Gittens, Gregg, V.P.-Sls. & Mktg.--Labelon Corporation, Canandaigua, NY, pg. 649
Givens, Donald, V.P.-Mktg. & Sls.--Standco Industries, Inc., Houston, TX, pg. 1038
Glazer, Mark, V.P.-Sls. & Mktg.--Crisa Corporation, Plano, TX, pg. 299
Gleason, Joseph, V.P.-Mktg.--Academy Insurance Group, Inc., Atlanta, GA, pg. 11
Gleave, Pete, Mgr.-Mktg.--Solo Cup Company, Highland Park, IL, pg. 961
Gleaves, Leon R., V.P.-Mktg. & Sls.--Wilkins-Rogers Incorporated, Ellicott City, MD, pg. 1190
Glenn, Doug, Mktg. Services Coord.--Seco Warwick Corporation, Meadville, PA, pg. 987
Glisan, G.B., V.P.-Mktg. & Plng.--Illinois Consolidated Telephone Co., Mattoon, IL, pg. 563
Gloss, Gayl, Mgr.-Mktg.--Royal Oak Enterprises, Inc., Atlanta, GA, pg. 953
Glover, E. Alexander, Sr. V.P.-Mktg., Res. & Devel.--Kransco, San Francisco, CA, pg. 644
Glover, Jack, Dir.-Mktg.--Lester Coggins Trucking, Okahumpka, FL, pg. 259
Glover, P., V.P.-Mktg.--Versa Services Ltd., Etobicoke,, Canada, pg. 7
Glover, Tina, Dir.-Mktg.--The Levolor Corporation, Sunnyvale, CA, pg. 671
Glucksman,Roberta, V.P.-Mktg. Services--Myron Manufacturing Corporation, Maywood, NJ, pg. 780
Gmiter, Patrick J., V.P.-Mktg.--Broadcast Division, Atlanta, GA, pg. 292
Goble, Wayne, Dir.-Res. & Devel., Mkt. Res. & Librarian--B.A.S.S., Inc., Montgomery, AL, pg. 105
Goddard, Melanie L., Coord.-Mktg.--Koehler Manufacturing Company, Marlborough, MA, pg. 639
Godfrey, Mark, Dir.-Mktg.--Micro Component Technology Inc., Saint Paul, MN, pg. 748
Godfrey, William T., V.P.-Mfg. & Mktg.--Morris Coupling Co., Erie, PA, pg. 771
Goeb, Carl, Mgr.-Mktg. Services--LSI Truck Products Corp.-Neway/Anchor Lock, Muskegon, MI, pg. 664
Goedde, William R., V.P.-Mktg.--Hamilton Mutual Insurance Company Of Cincinnati, Cincinnati, OH, pg. 503
Goehring, Pamela, Dir.-Mktg. Services--Apparel Fabrics Div., New York, NY, pg. 400
Goeler, Tim, V.P.-Mktg.--Scripto-Tokai, Inc., Fontana, CA, pg. 983
Goerich, W. K., Dir.-Mktg.--Viskase Corporation, Bedford Park, IL, pg. 383
Goetsch, Tim, V.P.-Wholesale Opers.--Affiliated Foods Cooperative Inc., Norfolk, NE, pg. 23
Goetz, Tim, Dir.-Mktg.--Robinson Helicopter Company, Inc., Torrance, CA, pg. 940
Goff, Larry, Mgr.-Mktg.--Transnational Motors Inc., Grand Rapids, MI, pg. 1107
Goit, Whitney, II, Exec. V.P.-Sls. & Mktg.--Arts & Entertainment Network, New York, NY, pg. 523
Gold, Keith R., V.P.-Mktg.--Medical Analysis Systems Inc., Camarillo, CA, pg. 735
Goldfarb, David, Dir.-Mktg.--Consolidated Cigar Corporation, Fort Lauderdale, FL, pg. 276
Goldman, Lynne, Mktg. Coord.--The Levy Organization, Chicago, IL, pg. 672
Goldman, Martin R., Deputy Dir.-Mktg.--Maryland State Lottery, Baltimore, MD, pg. 717
Goldman, Richard B., V.P., Media & Mktg. Services--Ryder & Schild, Inc., Miami, FL, pg. 958
Goldsmith, Michelle, Dir.-Mktg. Services--Members Only By Europe Craft, New York, NY, pg. 738
Goldstein, Ephraim, Sr. V.P., Asst. Dir. Mktg. Plng.--N W Ayer Inc., New York, NY, pg. 104
Goldstein, John, Dir.-Mktg.--Jandy Industries, Novato, CA, pg. 589
Goldstein, Marcy, Dir.-Mktg.--American Speedy Printing Centers, Inc., Bloomfield Hills, MI, pg. 61
Goldstein, William L., V.P.-Mktg. & Sls.--Wheelock Inc., Long Branch, NJ, pg. 1185
Goltz, Colleen, Coord.-Mktg.--Demco Inc., Madison, WI, pg. 328
Gomeau, Mary Ellen, V.P.-Sls. & Mktg.--Phonetics, Inc., Aston, PA, pg. 869
Gonia, W.J., V.P.-Sls. & Mktg.--Flexonics Inc., Bartlett, IL, pg. 419
Gonzalez, Muriel, Sr. V.P.-Mktg.--Estee Lauder, Inc., New York, NY, pg. 389
Gooch, Sandra, Dir.-Mktg. & Admin.--Mrs. Goochs Natural Food Markets, Sherman Oaks, CA, pg. 761
Goodman, J.D., V.P.-Mktg.--E.F. Johnson Company, Eden Prarie, MN, pg. 598
Goodman, John, V.P.-Mktg.--Helzberg's Diamond Shops, Inc., North Kansas City, MO, pg. 528
Goodman, Marvin, V.P.-Sls. & Mktg.--Plastic Suppliers, Inc., Columbus, OH, pg. 875
Goodson, Buddy, Dir.-Mktg.--Pepper-Lawson, Katy, TX, pg. 860
Goodwin, James M., V.P.-Grp. Mktg., East--Blue Cross and Blue Shield of Oklahoma, Tulsa, OK, pg. 159
Goold, Peter, Dir.-Mktg. & Sls.--Just Born, Inc., Bethlehem, PA, pg. 610
Gorbett, Richard, V.P.-Mktg., Special Tran. Grp.--Atlas Specialized Transportation, Evansville, IN, pg. 97
Gorbold, Jonathan, V.P.-Engrng. & Mktg.--ENI, Rochester, NY, pg. 360
Gordon, Joanne, V.P., Dir. Mktg./Res.--Hill, Holliday/Los Angeles, Marina Del Rey, CA, pg. 534
Gordon, Lynn, Exec.-Mktg.--Reading Body Works, Inc., Reading, PA, pg. 916
Gordon, Mark, V.P.-Mktg. & Sls.--Lionel Trains, Inc., Chesterfield, MI, pg. 677
Goshien, Gerald, V.P.-Meat Mktg.--The Mad Butcher, Inc., Pine Bluff, AR, pg. 699
Gosnell, Ray, V.P. & Mktg. Mgr.--National Savings Life Insurance Company, Murfreesboro, TN, pg. 1150
Gould, Doyle, V.P.-Mktg.--Perry Equipment Corporation, Mineral Wells, TX, pg. 863
Gould, Jay, V.P., Bus. Devel. & Media--Kolesar & Hartwell Inc., Minneapolis, MN, pg. 641
Gould, Peter, Dir.-Mktg. & Sls.--Just Born, Inc., Bethlehem, PA, pg. 610
Gouwens, Bob, V.P.-Sls.--La Preferida, Inc., Chicago, IL, pg. 649
Grace, John, V.P.-Chicago Program Mktg.--WTTW (Channel 11), Chicago, IL, pg. 1156
Graessle, W., V.P.-Mktg.--Jeffrey Division, Columbus, OH, pg. 565
Graham, Michael, Sr. V.P.-Sls. & Mktg.--Pittsburgh Brewing Company, Pittsburgh, PA, pg. 873
Graham, Randall, Coord.-Mktg. Publicity--Mary Kay Cosmetics Inc., Dallas, TX, pg. 716
Graham, Robert E., Dir.-Mktg.--Tree Top, Inc., Selah, WA, pg. 1109
Grandinetti, Michael A., V.P.-Sls. & Mktg.--Tylan General, Inc., San Diego, CA, pg. 1122
Grandle, Pat, Mgr.-Mktg. & Sec.--Tricon Industries, Inc., Downers Grove, IL, pg. 1113
Granville, Paul, Sr. V.P.-Mkt. Plng. & Admin.--Newbridge Communications, New York, NY, pg. 611
Grass, Harry, Dir.-Sls. & Mktg.--Gordon Sign Company, Denver, CO, pg. 472
Graves, Earl G., Jr., Sr. V.P.-Sls. & Mktg.--Earl G. Graves, Ltd., New York, NY, pg. 478
Graves, Richard, V.P.-Mktg.-Aerospace & Comml. Fueling--J. C. Carter Company, Inc., Costa Mesa, CA, pg. 226
Gray, Allen, Mktg. Dir.--Fiesta Mart Inc., Houston, TX, pg. 409
Gray, Jeff, Dir.-Mktg. & Sls.--W. B. Roddenbery Company, Inc., Cairo, GA, pg. 942
Gray, Richard, V.P.-Sls. & Mktg.--Rochester-Midland ICL, Omaha, NE, pg. 941
Gray, Scott A., V.P.-Sls. & Mktg.--Gray Printing Co., Fostoria, OH, pg. 479
Gray, Steve, V.P., Dir. Mktg. Services--DRK Inc., Boston, MA, pg. 309
Greashaber, A., Mgr.-Adv. & Mktg.--Digitec, Marion, OH, pg. 1069
Greashaber, Anna, Mgr.-Mktg.--Desco Corporation, Columbus, OH, pg. 332
Greashaber, Anna, Mgr.-Mktg.--Desco Advertising & Marketing, Marion, OH, pg. 332
Greashaber, Anna, Mgr.-Adv. & Mktg.--Air-O-Matic Power Steer Co., Marion, OH, pg. 1069
Green, Lanny R., Sr. V.P.-Mktg.--VASA Brougher, Inc., Indianapolis, IN, pg. 1146
Green, Russ, V.P., Bus. Devel.--Godfrey Advertising, Lancaster, PA, pg. 464
Greenawalt, Jon, V.P.-Sls. & Mktg.--Lyon's Restaurants, Inc., Foster City, CA, pg. 690
Greenberg, E., Exec. V.P.-Sls. & Mktg.--Randolph Medical Inc., Livonia, MI, pg. 912
Greenberg, Joe, V.P., Media/Mktg.--Robert Elen & Associates, Los Angeles, CA, pg. 376
Greenberg, Steve, V.P.-Mktg.--Pittsburgh Pirates Professional Baseball Club, Pittsburgh, PA, pg. 873
Greene, Gilbert K., Mgr.-Mktg. Services--Victaulic Company of America, Easton, PA, pg. 1149
Greene, Judye, Exec. V.P., Mktg. Dir.--Adair Greene Advertising, Atlanta, GA, pg. 16
Greenhill, Anne, Mktg. Asst.--Ivex Packaging Corporation, Lincolnshire, IL, pg. 583
Greenisen, G., Dir.-Mktg.--Wilkinson Company, Inc., Stow, OH, pg. 373
Greenisen, Phil, Mktg.--Turner Machine Company, Salem, OH, pg. 373
Greenuk, John, Mgr.-Mktg.--Grisanti, Inc., Louisville, KY, pg. 488
Greenwood, Dan, Exec. V.P., Sports Mktg.--Simon Marketing, Inc., Los Angeles, CA, pg. 1006
Greer, David, Dir.-Universe Sls. & Mktg.--Charles River Data Systems, Inc., Framingham, MA, pg. 240
Greer, J. Kirkland, III, Sr. V.P.-Retail & Whls. Mktg.--Illinois Limited Partnership, Alsip, IL, pg. 715
Greer, Rita, V.P.-Design--Halper Bros., Milwaukee, WI, pg. 925
Greer, Rita, V.P.-Design--Penthouse Knitting Mills, Milwaukee, WI, pg. 925
Gregg, Karen, Mgr.-Sls. & Mktg. Services--Shade Computer Forms Co., Green Bay, WI, pg. 994
Gregory, Charlie, V.P.-Mktg. & Sls.--Buck Knives, Inc., El Cajon, CA, pg. 185
Grepp, D.W., Dir.-Mktg.--The Chardon Rubber Co., Chardon, OH, pg. 239
Grezelak, Dave, V.P.-Mktg.--Komatsu Dresser Company, Lincolnshire, IL, pg. 565
Grieco, John L., Dir.-Mktg.--Stratton Growth Fund, Inc., Plymouth Meeting, PA, pg. 1053
Grieco, John L., Dir.-Mktg.--Stratton Monthly Dividend Shares, Inc., Plymouth Meeting, PA, pg. 1053
Griesenauer, Quentin, Mgr.-Mktg. Communications--Diagraph Corporation, Earth City, MO, pg. 335
Grieshammer, Pat, V.P.-Mktg.--The Gibson-Homans Company, Twinsburg, OH, pg. 457
Griessel, Richard, V.P.-Mktg. & Sls.--National Fire Protection Association, Quincy, MA, pg. 788
Griffin, Clay, Mgr.-Sls. & Mktg.--Rustco Products Company, Denver, CO, pg. 957
Griffin, Simon, Dir.-Mktg., Instruments--Teca Corporation, Pleasantville, NY, pg. 1082
Griffith, Walt, V.P.-Mktg.--The Chas. H. Lilly Co., Portland, OR, pg. 675
Griggs, Louise, Mktg. Coord.--Mannington Mills, Inc., Salem, NJ, pg. 704
Griggs, Louise, Mktg. Coord.--Mannington Resilient Floors, Salem, NJ, pg. 704
Grindley, Mitchell P., V.P.-Mktg.--Plaskolite Inc., Columbus, OH, pg. 874
Grinley, Steven, Dir.-Direct Mktg.--Elkay Products, Inc., Shrewsbury, MA, pg. 377
Griswold, Richard B., Sr. V.P.-Plng. & Information Research--Utica Mutual Insurance Company, New Hartford, NY, pg. 1140
Grobstein, Michael, Vice Chm.-Plng., Mktg. & Industry Services--Ernst & Young, New York, NY, pg. 387
Grodd, K.E., V.P.-Mktg.--J.M. Huber, Engineered Carbons Div., Borger, TX, pg. 550
Groner, Norman, Mgr.-Prod.--Wayne Wire Cloth Products, Inc., Kalkaska, MI, pg. 1169
Grossman, Bernard, V.P.-Sls., Mktg. & Fin.--M. Grossman Son, Inc., Passaic, NJ, pg. 489
Grost, Michael, V.P.-Mktg.--The Shelburne Corporation, Shelburne, VT, pg. 996
Grot, Cindy, Coord.-Mktg.--Pascoe Building Systems, Inc., Columbus, GA, pg. 851
Grover, Richard L., V.P.-Mktg.--Diamond Electronics, Inc., Lancaster, OH, pg. 335
Gruen, Marsha, V.P.-Trade Relation--Stratmar Systems, Inc., Port Chester, NY, pg. 1053
Grupp, Lori, V.P.-Mktg.--Tiger Electronics, Inc., Vernon Hills, IL, pg. 1097
Gual, John, Dir.-Mktg.--Springborn Laboratories-Testing & QA Division, Enfield, CT, pg. 1033
Guaneri, Michael A., Dir.-Adv.--Aid Auto Stores, Inc., Westbury, NY, pg. 26
Guariniello, Art, Mgr.-Domestic Mktg.--Hanna Car Wash International, Inc., Portland, OR, pg. 505
Gudger, Charles, V.P.-Sls. & Mktg.--Universal Match Corp., Kenner, LA, pg. 335
Guerra, Peter M., Grp. V.P.--W&F Manufacturing Corporation, Inc., Buffalo, NY, pg. 1155
Guerrieri, Michael, V.P.-Sls. & Mktg.--Showell Farms, Inc., Showell, MD, pg. 1000
Guiney, Linda, Mktg. Mgr.--Crown Prince, Inc. (CA), City of Industry, CA, pg. 302
Gullickson, Roger, Grp. Dir.-Mktg.--FTD/Florists' Transworld Delivery Association, Southfield, MI, pg. 395
Gulliksen, J.E., V.P.-Mktg.--Koehler Manufacturing Company, Marlborough, MA, pg. 639
Gundacker, Janice, Mgr.-Mktg.--Press Broadcasting Co., Neptune, NJ, pg. 801
Gunn, Doug, Mgr.-Prod. Mktg.-Excavators--Komatsu Dresser Company, Lincolnshire, IL, pg. 565
Gunnoe, Tamara L., Deputy Dir.-Mktg.--West Virginia Lottery, Charleston, WV, pg. 1176
Gunther, Suzanne, Dir., New Bus. Devel.--Media Logic, Inc., Albany, NY, pg. 734
Gura, M., V.P., Dir., Special Mktg.--Weinstein Otterman & Associates, New York, NY, pg. 1173
Gushwa, Charles, V.P.-Mktg. & Sls.--Atlas/Soundolier, Fenton, MO, pg. 64
Guthrie, Jack H., Mgr.-Mktg. Services--Stihl Inc., Virginia Beach, VA, pg. 1049
Gyde, Richard J., Exec. V.P.-Mktg.--Nutri/System Inc., Blue Bell, PA, pg. 818
Gyenes, Ed, V.P.-Sls. & Mktg.--Beckley-Cardy, Inc., Duluth, MN, pg. 21
Gyori, Phil, Mgr.-Mktg.--Pollenex Corporation, Chicago, IL, pg. 821
Haas, B.K., Pres.--Bud Industries, Inc., Willoughby, OH, pg. 186
Haas, Jean, Dir.-Mktg.--MSC Industrial Supply Co., Plainview, NY, pg. 693
Haas, Stacy, Mgr.-Mktg. Services--Carden & Cherry, Inc., Nashville, TN, pg. 217
Haass, Jean, Dir.-Mktg.--Sid Tool Co. Inc., Plainview, NY, pg. 1002
Habernickel, Dana, Dir.-Mktg.--The Haband Co., Paterson, NJ, pg. 498
Hackett, Joseph, V.P.-Mktg. & Sls.--American Safety Razor Company, Verona, VA, pg. 604
Hackman, Roger D., V.P.-Mktg. & Sls.--Seymour Manufacturing Company, Seymour, IN, pg. 994
Hackney, R. Hodges, Exec. V.P.--Hackney & Sons, Inc., Washington, NC, pg. 498
Hadley, Jacquelyn, Chief Exec. Officer--Caswell/Massey Co. Ltd., Edison, NJ, pg. 229
Haerle, Karen, Mgr.-Sls. & Mktg.--Rose Printing Company, Inc., Tallahassee, FL, pg. 948
Hagan, James J., Dir.-Mktg.--Harza Environmental Services, Inc., Chicago, IL, pg. 516
Hagen, R., Mgr.-Intl. mktg.--Recon/Optical, Inc., Barrington, IL, pg. 917
Haggerty, David A., V.P.-Mktg.--Prince Manufacturing, Inc., Lawrenceville, NJ, pg. 890
Hahn, Douglas E., V.P.-Mktg., Pur. & Adv.--J.R. Hahn Co., Inc., Indianapolis, IN, pg. 500
Haight, Jerry L., V.P.-Mktg.--Thrifty Oil Company, Downey, CA, pg. 1096
Haines, C.L., V.P.-Mktg.--Riviana Foods Inc., Houston, TX, pg. 937
Hairston, Jim, Dir.-Sls. & Mktg.--Hooker Industries, Ontario, CA, pg. 543
Haley, Brian, Dir.-Mktg.--Johnny Appleseed's, Inc., Beverly, MA, pg. 597
Halford, Vicki, Mktg. Admin.--NavCom Defense Electronics, Inc., El Monte, CA, pg. 796
Hall, Anthony, V.P.-Mktg. & Sls.--Crown Textile Company, Blue Bell, PA, pg. 302
Hall, David, Sr. V.P.-Sls. & Mktg.--Time Systems, Inc., Phoenix, AZ, pg. 1097
Hall, David L., Mktg. Mgr.--Faraday, Inc., Tecumseh, MI, pg. 399
Hall, G.A. Corky, Exec. V.P., Mktg. Communications--Gage Marketing Group, Minneapolis, MN, pg. 441
Hall, George R., V.P.-Mktg.--Monex International, Ltd., Newport Beach, CA, pg. 765

Hall, James C., Sr. V.P.-Mktg.--Electronic Data Magnetics, Inc., High Point, NC, pg. 375
Hall, Marshall, Mgr.-Prod.--Vari Tronics Company, Inc., Duarte, CA, pg. 1145
Hall, Stephanie L., Dir.-Mktg.--Landau & Heyman Inc., Chicago, IL, pg. 654
Hall, Troy, Mgr.-Mktg.--Superior Machine Systems, Cincinnati, OH, pg. 1064
Hallstedt, Fred, Pres. & V.P.-Sls. & Mktg.--Sonneveldt Company, Grand Rapids, MI, pg. 1018
Hamann, Lori, Mktg. Services Coord.--J.R. Simplot Co., Minerals & Chemicals Group, Pocatello, ID, pg. 1007
Hamilton, Jerry, Sr. V.P., Dir., Mktg. Services--Ketchum Advertising/San Francisco, San Francisco, CA, pg. 625
Hamm, John, Dir.-Sls. & Mktg.--Codisco Inc., Sanford, FL, pg. 258
Hammer, Cheryl, Dir.-Mktg.--Dac Easy, Inc., Dallas, TX, pg. 571
Hammon, Bill, V.P.-Mktg.--Croscill, Inc., New York, NY, pg. 300
Hammond, Jeremy, V.P.-Mktg.--Capitol Records, Inc., Hollywood, CA, pg. 216
Hancock, James, V.P.-Mktg.--Knott's Berry Farm, Buena Park, CA, pg. 637
Handler, Howard, Sr. V.P.-Mktg. & Promotions--MTV: Music Television, New York, NY, pg. 785
Handley, John M., Sr. V.P.-Mkt. Devel.--Industrial Acoustics Company, Inc., Bronx, NY, pg. 565
Hange, Robert, V.P.-Sls. & Mktg.--Signet Systems, Inc., Harrodsburg, KY, pg. 385
Hanisko, Dean, Dir.-Mktg.--PREPLINK, Westlake, OH, pg. 481
Hanley, Paul, Sr. V.P.-Rooms Mngmt. & Mktg.--Omni Hotels, Hampton, NH, pg. 826
Hann, David, V.P.-Mktg. & Sls.--Micron Separations, Inc., Westborough, MA, pg. 749
Hanna, David E., Mgr.-Sls. & Mktg.--Owatonna Canning Company, Owatonna, MN, pg. 833
Hanna, Joe, Sr. V.P.-Mktg.--United Farm Bureau Family Life Insurance Co., Indianapolis, IN, pg. 1131
Hannah, Steve, V.P.-Mktg.--Peebles, Inc., South Hill, VA, pg. 855
Hannawacker, Joseph A., Dir.-Mktg.--Wenczel Tile Co., Trenton, NJ, pg. 1176
Hannes, Peter J., V.P.-Special Mkts.--Jockey International, Inc., Kenosha, WI, pg. 595
Hannigan, M.C., Dir.-Corp. Mktg.--Sverdrup Corporation, Maryland Heights, MO, pg. 1065
Hannikainen, Anna, Mktg. Mgr.--Masterfoods Oy, Helsinki,, Finland, pg. 714
Hanrahan, Michael, Mgr.-Mktg.--SJL of Kansas Corp., Wichita, KS, pg. 962
Hansberger, Allan, V.P.-Mktg.--RAM Golf Corporation, Melrose Park, IL, pg. 910
Hansbury, Ben, Dir.-Sls. & Mktg.--The Read Corporation, Middleboro, MA, pg. 916
Hansen, Dianne, Mktg. Mgr.--Levi Strauss (New Zealand) Ltd., Auckland, New Zealand, pg. 671
Hansen, John R., Mgr.-Mktg.-Social Stationery--Crane & Co., Inc., Dalton, MA, pg. 296
Hansen, R.M., V.P.-Mktg. & Sls.--Pyle Inc., Chicago, IL, pg. 648
Hansen, Ray N., V.P.-Mktg.--Forestry Suppliers, Inc., Jackson, MS, pg. 424
Hansill, Karen, V.P.-Sls.-Eastern Div.--Open Court Publishing Company, Chicago, IL, pg. 227
Hanson, Barbara, Dir.-Mktg.--Thomas Publishing Co., New York, NY, pg. 1093
Hanson, Gregory, V.P.-Mktg.--Cole Papers Inc., Fargo, ND, pg. 260
Hanson, Larry, Exec. V.P.-Mktg.--Minco Products, Inc., Minneapolis, MN, pg. 756
Hanzlovic, Jack, V.P.-Mktg.-West Region--G. Heileman Brewing Co., Inc., La Crosse, WI, pg. 526
Hanzlovic, Jack, V.P.-Mktg.--Rainier Brewing Co., Seattle, WA, pg. 526
Haraldson, Bill, Chief Oper. Officer & Exec. V.P.-Mktg.--Rosauer's Supermarkets, Inc., Spokane, WA, pg. 947
Harbaugh, W.L., V.P.-Mktg.--Omega Transworld Ltd., New Kensington, PA, pg. 195
Harbaugh, W.L., V.P.-Mktg.--Omega Transworld Inc., Utah, New Kensington, PA, pg. 195
Harbaugh, William L., V.P.-Mktg. & Sls.--Burrell Group, New Kensington, PA, pg. 195
Harbuck, John G., V.P., Sls. & Mktg.--Citation Companies, Inc., Birmingham, AL, pg. 250
Harding, Nancy Jenks, Mktg. Dir.--Mademoiselle, New York, NY, pg. 19
Hardinge, Thomas H., III, V.P.-Sls. & Mktg., Treas. & Sec.--Statton Furniture Manufacturing Company, Hagerstown, MD, pg. 1042
Hardy, Charles, Dir.-Mktg. & Sls.--Bollinger Machine Shop And Shipyard, Inc., Lockport, LA, pg. 163
Hare, Lori, V.P.-Sls. & Mktg.--Streamlight Inc., Norristown, PA, pg. 1053
Hare, Susan, Dir.-Mktg.--Warner Press, Inc., Anderson, IN, pg. 1164
Harl, James L., Sls. & Mktg. Mgr.--Dimco-Gray Company, Dayton, OH, pg. 338
Harlan, David M., V.P.-Natl. Sls. & Mktg.--United States Cold Storage, Inc., Cherry Hill, NJ, pg. 1135
Harman, Michael J., Exec. V.P.-Sls. & Mktg.--Consolidated Metco, Inc., Portland, OR, pg. 277
Harms, Jed, V.P.-Mktg. & Sls.--Triple F, Inc., Des Moines, IA, pg. 1114
Harp, Sidney, II, Exec. V.P. & Agency Dir.--Security Industrial Insurance Co., Inc., Donaldsonville, LA, pg. 832
Harper, Jeffrey, Mgr.-Mktg.--Countrymark Cooperative, Inc., Indianapolis, IN, pg. 290
Harper, Sharon, Mgr.-Mktg. Communications--ASM International, Materials Park, OH, pg. 8
Harple, Bob, Dir.-Mktg.--RE/MAX International, Inc., Englewood, CO, pg. 915
Harrell, Pamela A., Dir.-Mktg.--Seaboard Electronics Co., Carlsbad, CA, pg. 983
Harrell, Samuel D., Dir.-Mktg.--E & D Grain Marketing Co, Cincinnati, OH, pg. 359
Harridine, David, Mgr.-Mktg.--Metalcenter, Inc., Santa Fe Springs, CA, pg. 742
Harris, Albert, V.P.-Mktg. & Sls.--Johnson & Towers, Inc., Mount Laurel, NJ, pg. 601
Harris, Barry P., V.P.-Dir.-Mktg.--Corporate New Prods. & Tech.--S. C. Johnson & Son, Inc., Racine, WI, pg. 599
Harris, Don, Dir.-Mktg., Latin America--WordPerfect Corporation, Orem, UT, pg. 1202
Harris, Laurie L., V.P.-Mktg.--NFO Research, Inc., Greenwich, CT, pg. 780
Harris, Robert L., Mktg. Dir.--Creative Marketing International Corp., West Chicago, IL, pg. 297
Harris, Tim, Exec. V.P.-Products--Witt Company, Cincinnati, OH, pg. 1198
Harrison, Charles, Mgr.-Prod.--Telesensory, Mountain View, CA, pg. 1085
Hart, Chris, V.P.-Mktg.--Hart Graphics Inc., Austin, TX, pg. 513
Hart, Jim, Dir.-Mktg.--Chadwick-Helmuth Company, Inc., El Monte, CA, pg. 237
Hart, Peter, V.P.-Mktg.--New England Log Homes, Inc., Hamden, CT, pg. 800
Hart, S.S., V.P.-Mktg.--Welch's, Concord, MA, pg. 789
Hartan, Richard K., Mgr.-Sls., Mktg. & Adv.--E.W. Knauss & Son, Inc., Quakertown, PA, pg. 636
Hartge, Paul E., V.P.-Sls. & Mktg.--Wayne Corporation, Richmond, IN, pg. 1169
Hartman, Brooke, Dir. Mktg.--Abbott Electronics, Inc., Los Angeles, CA, pg. 9
Hartman, Martin, V.P.-Mktg.--United Health Plan, Inglewood, CA, pg. 1133
Hartman, Mary, Dir.-Mktg.--Drafting Graphics, Inc., Elk Grove Village, IL, pg. 348
Hartman, Mary E., Mgr.-Mktg. Devel.--Tassani Communications, Chicago, IL, pg. 1080
Hartman, Tracy L., Coord.-Mktg. & Adv.--Shape Inc., Biddeford, ME, pg. 995
Hartnett, Edward F., V.P., Mktg.--Horizon Media Inc., Germantown, TN, pg. 544
Hartranft, Debbie, Mktg. Mgr.--Reading Body Works, Inc., Reading, PA, pg. 916
Harvey, Larry Z., V.P.-Sls. & Mktg.--The Electron Corp., Littleton, CO, pg. 375
Harvey, Larry Z., V.P.-Sls. & Mktg.--Electron Corp., Blackwell, OK, pg. 375
Hassey, John, V.P.-Mktg.--Stanley Steemer International, Inc., Dublin, OH, pg. 1038
Hatch, Greg, Dir. Mktg.-Trade Sls.--Fuller O'Brien Paints, South San Francisco, CA, pg. 820
Hatch, Mark, V.P.-Mktg.--Data Instruments, Inc., Acton, MA, pg. 316
Hauser, Lawrence P., V.P.-Sls. & Mktg.--Cavalier Corporation, Chattanooga, TN, pg. 229
Hausler, Robert J., V.P.-Sls. & Mktg.--Mark Lighting Fixture Co., Inc., Moonachie, NJ, pg. 708
Haver, Dale, V.P.-Sls. & Mktg.--Ajax Paving Industries Inc., Madison Heights, MI, pg. 28
Haviland, D.E., Dir.-Mktg., Automotive Prods. Div.--Motor Wheel Corporation, Lansing, MI, pg. 773
Hawk, Hugh, Mgr.-New Business Devel.--Plymouth Tube Company, Warrenville, IL, pg. 877
Hawk, J.T., Dir.-Mktg.--J.M. Huber, Calcium Carbonate Div., Quincy, IL, pg. 550
Hawkins, Jayne G., Dir.-Mktg. & Export--Gulf States Asphalt Company, Inc., South Houston, TX, pg. 493
Hawkins, William J., V.P.-Mktg.--Republic Telcom Systems Corporation, Boulder, CO, pg. 928
Hawthorne, Josephine, Dir.-Mktg.--The Estee Corporation, Parsippany, NJ, pg. 389
Hay, John, Mgr.-Footwear Mktg.--ASICS Tiger Corporation, Fountain Valley, CA, pg. 8
Hayden, Julian G., Jr., V.P.-Mktg.--Owensboro Grain Co., Inc., Owensboro, KY, pg. 834
Hayes, Alexandria, V.P.-Mktg.--Delta Education, Inc., Hudson, NH, pg. 326
Hayes, C.A., Dir.-Pur., Adv. & Mktg.--Blevins Inc., Nashville, TN, pg. 156
Hayes, Karen, Mktg. Coord.--Chicago, Chicago, IL, pg. 656
Hayes, Kendall P., Mgr.-Adv. & Mktg. Consultant--Arrow Pneumatics Co. Inc., Lake Zurich, IL, pg. 85
Hays, Jennifer K., Mktg. Coord.--The Weitz-Cohen Construction Co., Des Moines, IA, pg. 1174
Haysey, M.R., Sr. V.P. & Mktg. Dir.--Aston Martin LaGonda of North America, Inc., Stamford, CT, pg. 92
Heald, Glenn, Dir.-Mktg.--Starving Students, Inc., Los Angeles, CA, pg. 1040
Heaney, Joe, Pres. & Chief Oper. Officer--Cornnuts Inc., Alameda, CA, pg. 286
Heaton, Nigel, V.P.-Circulation & Mktg. Devel.--Petersen Publishing Company, Los Angeles, CA, pg. 864
Heaton, Robert C., Mgr.-Mktg.--Petroleum, Inc., Wichita, KS, pg. 444
Heazlitt, Michael, V.P.-Sls. & Mktg.--Paoli, Inc., Paoli, IN, pg. 846
Heberle, Shelley, Mgr.-Mktg.--Video Products Distributors, Inc., Sacramento, CA, pg. 1150
Hebert, Judith, Mgr.-Mktg. Services--National Life Insurance Company, Montpelier, VT, pg. 791
Hecht, Alan, Dir.-Mktg.--NBO Stores Inc., Fair Lawn, NJ, pg. 780
Hecht, Len, V.P.-Mktg.--Queens Group, Inc., Long Island City, NY, pg. 904
Hecht, Stephen, Dir.-Sls.--Centimark Corporation, Bethel Park, PA, pg. 231
Hedge, Gary, Dir.-Mktg.--Taylor Medical Inc., Beaumont, TX, pg. 1081
Hedges, Helen, Dir.-Mktg.--Jack Schwartz Shoes, Inc., New York, NY, pg. 980
Hee, Richard K.C., V.P.-Mktg. & Services--Aloha IslandAir, Honolulu, HI, pg. 43
Heffernan, Paul, V.P.-Mktg.--New Balance Athletic Shoe, Inc., Boston, MA, pg. 798
Hegarty, Gerald, Mgr.-Mktg.--Fabreeka International, Inc., Stoughton, MA, pg. 396
Heifner, Thomas E., V.P.-Devel.--K & B, Inc., New Orleans, LA, pg. 611
Heilig, Michael, Dir.-Sls. & Mktg.--Flakt Inc., Bahnson Div., Winston-Salem, NC, pg. 416
Heilman, R., V.P.-Mktg.--Woodwork Corporation of America, Chicago, IL, pg. 1201
Heimlich, Amy, Mktg. Asst.--Continental Plastic Card Co., Coral Springs, FL, pg. 280
Heinemann, Kirsten, Dir.-Corp. Plng.--Schumacher & Forelle, Inc., Great Neck, NY, pg. 979
Held, Anita, Mgr.-Mktg.--Ingrid-Sevko, Inc., Deerfield, IL, pg. 569
Heldfond, Robert D., V.P.-Mktg.--E B 5 Corporation, Portland, OR, pg. 359
Helland, Bruce, Mgr.-Mktg. & Sls., Garden Div.--Specialty Manufacturing Company, St. Paul, MN, pg. 1027
Hellender, Mark, V.P.-Sls. & Mktg.--Kaiser Foundation Health & Hospitals Group, Oakland, CA, pg. 614
Helmer, Scott, Dir.-Mktg.-Sports Optics--Tasco, Miami, FL, pg. 1079
Helms, John R., Jr., Dir.-Mktg.--Viking Range Corp., Greenwood, MS, pg. 1151
Helsey, Brad, Dir.-Mktg. & Adv.--J.L. Lester & Son, Inc., Rockmart, GA, pg. 668
Hemmings, Wm. M., V.P.-Sls. & Mktg. & Corp. Sec.--Enger-Kress Company, West Bend, WI, pg. 381
Hemphill, Holly A., Dir.-Mktg.--Service America Corporation, Stamford, CT, pg. 992
Hench, Ellen, Mgr.-Mktg. Support--Tax Management, Inc., Washington, DC, pg. 190
Henderson-Hernandez, Susan E., V.P.-Mktg.--Perkins Family Restaurants, Memphis, TN, pg. 1088
Henderson, Amy, Mktg. Coord.--Magline, Inc., Pinconning, MI, pg. 700
Henderson, James, Dir.-Sls. & Mktg.--Fasfax Corporation, Nashua, NH, pg. 579
Henderson, Robert W., V.P.-Mktg.--Rodney Hunt Company, Orange, MA, pg. 553
Hendricks, John, V.P.-Rendering--Moyer Packing Company, Souderton, PA, pg. 774
Hendrix, Nancy, Mktg. Services Coord.--Gast Mfg. Corp., Benton Harbor, MI, pg. 444
Heneghan, Frank M., V.P.-Sls. & Mktg.--McArdle Printing Co., Inc., Upper Marlboro, MD, pg. 189
Henkel, Arnold D., Sr. V.P. & Chief Mktg. Officer--Ministers Life Insurance Company, Minneapolis, MN, pg. 757
Henken, Doug, Mgr.-Mktg.--Keith Uddenberg, Inc., Gig Harbor, WA, pg. 1125
Hennessey, R.J., V.P.-Sls. & Mktg.--Kentile Floors Inc., South Plainfield, NJ, pg. 623
Henning, Thomas G., V.P.-Retail Mktg.--Clark Oil & Refining Corporation, Saint Louis, MO, pg. 252
Hennington, Rolf, V.P.-Sls. & Mktg.--Industrial Coatings Group, Inc., Chicago, IL, pg. 566
Henry, Charles L., Jr., First V.P.-Mktg.--Great Lakes Bancorp, Ann Arbor, MI, pg. 480
Henry, J.C., III, Exec. V.P.-Sls. & Mktg.--E.P. Henry Corporation, Woodbury, NJ, pg. 530
Henry, R.D., Mgr.-Prod. Control--Hilliard Corporation, Elmira, NY, pg. 535
Hensel, Nancy, V.P.-Mktg. & Mdsg.--The Popcorn Factory, Lake Forest, IL, pg. 426
Herberg, Richard, Chief Oper. Officer & V.P.-Mktg.--Bachman's, Inc., Minneapolis, MN, pg. 108
Herker, Larry, V.P.& Mktg.--General American Door Company, Montgomery, IL, pg. 739
Herlihy, R., Dir.-Mktg.--Telechron, Inc., Ashland, MA, pg. 1085
Herman, William C., V.P.-Mktg.--Kransco, San Francisco, CA, pg. 644
Hermann, Bob, V.P., Mktg.--Martiny & Company, Cincinnati, OH, pg. 716
Hermann, D.T., Mgr.-Mktg.--Industrial Chemicals Div., Valley Forge, PA, pg. 837
Hermann, Jesse, V.P.-Sls. & Mktg.--General Automotive Specialty Co., Inc., North Brunswick, NJ, pg. 449
Hermann, William, Mktg. Dir.--John Zink Co., Tulsa, OK, pg. 639
Herrick, William, Dir.-Mktg. Svcs.--Michigan Wheel Corporation, Grand Rapids, MI, pg. 747
Herrmann, John, V.P.-Sls. & Mktg.--O. A. Newton & Son Co., Bridgeville, DE, pg. 805
Hertert, Dean, V.P.-Mktg.--Capital Controls Company Inc., Colmar, PA, pg. 215
Hertzeberg, Ed, V.P.-Mktg.--Rose Art Industries, Orange, NJ, pg. 947
Hervey, Frank Jr., Mgr.-Mktg.--Hyspan Precision Products, Inc., Chula Vista, CA, pg. 557
Hess, Williamrald A., Sr. V.P.-Mktg. & Sls.--Farmers and Traders Life Insurance Co., Syracuse, NY, pg. 401
Heuberger, Roger, V.P.-Mktg.--International Jensen Inc., Lincolnshire, IL, pg. 578
Hevn, Darrell, V.P.-Mktg. & Store Plng.--Builders Emporium, Irvine, CA, pg. 262
Hewgley, William M., Jr., V.P.-Sls. & Mktg.--American Manufacturing Co. (TN), Chattanooga, TN, pg. 58
Hickey, William III, V.P.-Mktg. & Sls.--H.M. Smyth Co., Saint Paul, MN, pg. 1014
Hickman, Dave, Dir.-Mktg.--IXL Furniture, Dallas, TX, pg. 1112
Hicks, Daniel C., Mgr.-Market Devel.--Heath Consultants Incorporated, Stoughton, MA, pg. 524
Hicks, Ken, Dir.-Mktg.--Argo-Tech Corporation, Cleveland, OH, pg. 82
Higgins, Becky, Dir.-Mktg.--Gordon Jewelry Corporation, Irving, TX, pg. 1215
Higgins, Hary, Mgr.-Prod. Devel.--Wigwam Mills, Inc., Sheboygan, WI, pg. 1189
Higgins, Walter R., V.P.-Mktg. & Sls.--Delta Sugar Corporation, Clarksburg, CA, pg. 327

Highberg, Peter, V.P.-Sls. & Mktg.--Black Box Corporation, Lawrence, PA, pg. 748
Hildebrand, James, V.P.-Sls. & Mktg.--GF Office Furniture Ltd., Gallatin, TN, pg. 439
Hildebrand, James, V.P.-Sls. & Mktg.--GF Office Furniture, Youngstown, OH, pg. 439
Hill, Andrew C., Mktg. Dir.--Sunbeam Casual Furniture Co., Portland, TN, pg. 1059
Hill, Andy, Dir.-Mktg.--Sunbeam Outdoor Products Co., Neosho, MO, pg. 1059
Hill, Douglas E., Principal-Mktg.--Edward D. Jones & Co., Maryland Heights, MO, pg. 603
Hill, Edward D., Partner & Dir.-Sls. & Mktg.--J. C. Bradford & Co., Nashville, TN, pg. 170
Hill, G. Stanley, Sr. V.P.-Mktg. & Customer Service--Oglethorpe Power Corp., Tucker, GA, pg. 822
Hill, George, Dir.-Mktg.--United Piece Dye Works, LP, Princeton Junction, NJ, pg. 1134
Hill, John, Sr. V.P.-Mktg. & Mfg. Services--Beacon Mfg. Co., Swannanoa, NC, pg. 129
Hill, Lee W., Mktg. Dir.--Clark & Pope, Inc., New York, NY, pg. 253
Hill, Louis, Dir.-Mktg.--PSB Co., Columbus, OH, pg. 1185
Hill, Lynda, Promo. & Mktg. Mgr.--Rowman & Littlefield Publishers, Inc., Lanham, MD, pg. 952
Hill, Mike, Exec. V.P., Mktg.--Dorland Sweeney Jones, Philadelphia, PA, pg. 346
Hill, Richard, V.P.-Natl. Mktg.--Barq's, Inc., New Orleans, LA, pg. 121
Hill, Richard, V.P.-Mktg.--Delaware Punch Co., New Orleans, LA, pg. 121
Hill, Timothy L., Dir.-Consumer Mktg. & Sls.--Gates Energy Products, Inc., Alachua, FL, pg. 445
Hill, Tom, Mgr. Mktg.-Feeds--Alabama Farmers Co-op, Decatur, AL, pg. 28
Hill, William C., V.P.-Mktg.--Dad's Root Beer, Chicago, IL, pg. 765
Hilliard-Jones, Amy, Sr. V.P. & Dir. Integrated Mktg. Services--Burrell Communications Group Inc., Chicago, IL, pg. 195
Hillman, Douglas C., Exec. V.P.-Mktg. & Sls.--Londontown Corporation, Eldersburg, MD, pg. 682
Hillman, Dwayne, Dir.-Mktg.--Stocker & Yale, Inc., Beverly, MA, pg. 1050
Hillman, Dwayne, Dir.-Mktg.--MFE Instruments, Beverly, MA, pg. 1050
Hills, C.R., V.P.-Mktg.--Crystal Cream & Butter Company, Sacramento, CA, pg. 303
Hills, Victoria, Mktg. Services Dir.--Devon Direct Marketing & Advertising, Inc., Berwyn, PA, pg. 334
Hilmoe, Karen, V.P.-Intl. Sls. & Mktg.--Code-A-Phone Corp., Clackamas, OR, pg. 258
Hilton, D. Andy, Sr. V.P.-Sls. & Mktg.--Tropical Garment Manufacturing Company, Tampa, FL, pg. 1116
Hindo, Kal R., Sr. V.P.-Corp. Devel.--NTH Consultants, Ltd., Farmington Hills, MI, pg. 781
Hinkle, Jane K., V.P.-Sls. & Mktg.--Octagon Process Inc., Edgewater, NJ, pg. 821
Hinner, John, Dir.-Sls. & Mktg.--Master Molded Products Corporation, Elgin, IL, pg. 720
Hinshaw, Dan, V.P.-Mktg. & Sls.--The Levolor Corporation, Sunnyvale, CA, pg. 671
Hipwell, Roger, Sr. V.P.-Sls. & Mktg.--Bay State Milling Co., Quincy, MA, pg. 127
Hirai, Kazuo, Mgr.-Mktg. & Plng.--Japan Travel Bureau International, Inc., New York, NY, pg. 590
Hird, Charles E., V.P.-Sls. & Mktg.--Bostrom Seating, Inc., Piedmont, AL, pg. 168
Hirou, Ann, Dir., Mktg.--Lambesis Communications, San Diego, CA, pg. 652
Hislop, W. Ross, V.P.-Mktg. Programs--Avis, Inc., Garden City, NY, pg. 102
Hite, Aubrey, Mgr.-Mktg.--Frederick Trading Company, Frederick, MD, pg. 430
Hitzelberger, Paul, Exec. V.P.-Mktg. & Sec.--Del Taco, Inc., Costa Mesa, CA, pg. 325
Hitzelberger, Paul, Exec. V.P.-Mktg. & Sec.--Del Taco/ Naugles, Costa Mesa, CA, pg. 325
Hoag, William K., Exec. V.P. & Dir. Media & Mktg. Services--Carlson, DelGaldo, Hoag, Matthei Advertising, Inc., Stamford, CT, pg. 222
Hodges, B., Mktg. Mgr.-Transducer Products--Data Instruments, Inc., Acton, MA, pg. 316
Hodgson, Ralph M., Dir.-Mktg.--Lotus Publishing Corporation, Cambridge, MA, pg. 576
Hoeferlia, Michelle, Dir.-Mktg.--Molded Fiber Glass Co., Ashtabula, OH, pg. 764
Hoey, John, Sr. V.P.-Mktg. & Adv.--National Liberty, Frazer, PA, pg. 791
Hoffelt, Greg, V.P.-Mktg.--Border States Industries, Inc., Fargo, ND, pg. 165
Hoffman, Alan, Mgr.-Mktg. & Promo.--Colorado Lottery, Denver, CO, pg. 265
Hoffman, Bob, Mgr.-Mktg.--New Jersey Press, Inc., Neptune, NJ, pg. 801
Hoffman, Joseph A., Mgr.-Mktg. & Prod. Devel.--Copperweld Steel Company, Warren, OH, pg. 284
Hoffman, Phyllis, V.P.-Sls. & Mktg.--Summa Four, Inc., Manchester, NH, pg. 1057
Hoffner, Heidi, Dir.-Mktg.--I Ski Ski Goggles, City of Commerce, CA, pg. 557
Hoffner, Katie, Dir.-Mktg. & Intl. Opers.--Kaepa Inc., San Antonio, TX, pg. 613
Hofmann, John, V.P.-Sls. & Mktg.--Pride Products, Inc., Elizabeth, NJ, pg. 889
Hogan, Francis P., V.P.-Mktg.--Unigard Indemnity Co., Raleigh, NC, pg. 596
Hogan, Francis P., V.P.-Mktg.--Unigard Insurance Co., Seattle, WA, pg. 596
Hogg, Wilgus Wade, Dir.-Mktg.--Fantastic Sam's International, Inc., Memphis, TN, pg. 398
Hogue, Charles, Mgr.-Mktg.--The O'Brien Corporation, South San Francisco, CA, pg. 820
Holcombe, Richard J., V.P.-Mktg.--Woolrich, Inc., Woolrich, PA, pg. 1201
Holder, Juanita, V.P.-Mktg.--Beauty Handbook Corporation, Los Angeles, CA, pg. 130
Holdmeyer, Kurt, Prod. Mgr.-Pork--AJC International, Inc., Atlanta, GA, pg. 4
Hollister, G.D., V.P.-Mktg.--Ideal Industries, Inc., Sycamore, IL, pg. 562
Hollister, Howard, V.P.-Food Services Sls. & Mktg.--Awrey Bakeries, Inc., Livonia, MI, pg. 103
Holloway, Altom, V.P.-Real Estate & Devel.--J.H. Harvey Company, Nashville, GA, pg. 515
Holloway, David, V.P.-Mktg.--American Technical Publishers, Inc., Homewood, IL, pg. 63
Hollowell, David, Dir.-Mktg.--Beacon Mfg. Co., Swannanoa, NC, pg. 129
Holm, Reagan, Dir.-Sls. & Mktg.--ATAPCO Office Products Group, Saint Louis, MO, pg. 64
Holmes, Diana, Dir.-Mktg.--GMI, Inc.-Glasstream, Panama City, FL, pg. 450
Holmes, Forest, Mgr.-Mktg. & Sls., Valves Div.--Specialty Manufacturing Company, St. Paul, MN, pg. 1027
Holmes, Irvin R., Jr., V.P.-Mktg., Fruits--Del Monte Foods, San Francisco, CA, pg. 325
Holmes, John, Exec. V.P., Mktg. Dir. & Sec.--Paradigm Communications, Tampa, FL, pg. 847
Holsinger, J.F., V.P.-Sls. & Mktg.--The Hubinger Company, Keokuk, IA, pg. 550
Holt, Ralph M., III, V.P.-Mktg.--Holt Hosiery Mills, Inc., Burlington, NC, pg. 541
Holt, Richard, Exec. V.P. & Gen. Mgr.-Decorative Prods.--Carolina Mirror Company, North Wilkesboro, NC, pg. 223
Holzberg, Joel M., V.P.-Mktg. & Sls.--Unifoil Corporation, Passaic, NJ, pg. 1126
Holzman, Larry, Adv. & Mktg. Dir.--Culligan International Company, Northbrook, IL, pg. 358
Hommel, Kady, Mgr.-Mktg.--Burns & McDonnell Engineers-Architects-Consultants, Kansas City, MO, pg. 194
Honan, Eleanor, Mktg. Admin.--Carl Buddig & Company, Homewood, IL, pg. 186
Honholt, Douglas, Exec. V.P.-Mktg.--Universal Companies, Inc., Grand Rapids, MI, pg. 1138
Hooper, D., Exec. V.P. & Dir.-Mktg.--McCaffery & Ratner, Inc., New York, NY, pg. 726
Hoover, Arthur, Sec. & Prod. Mgr.--T. Bruce Sales, Inc., West Middlesex, PA, pg. 183
Hoover, Robert, V.P.-Mktg. & Sls.--Iowa Industrial Hydraulics, Inc., Pocahontas, IA, pg. 559
Hope, F. Leeland, Dir.-Mktg.--Hope Design Group, San Diego, CA, pg. 543
Hopersberger, Paul, Mgr.-Mktg.--Jervis B. Webb Company, Farmington Hills, MI, pg. 1170
Hopkins, Allan, Dir.-Mktg.--Sunnen Products Company, Saint Louis, MO, pg. 1061
Hopkins, Charles, Dir.-Mktg.--Stratton Management Company, Plymouth Meeting, PA, pg. 1053
Hopkins, Lance, V.P., Mktg.--Godwin Advertising Agency, Inc., Jackson, MS, pg. 464
Hopkins, Wendy A., Mgr.-Communications--The Rawlplug Company, Inc., New Rochelle, NY, pg. 914
Hopper, Pat, Dir.-Mktg.--California Artichoke & Vegetable Growers Corp., Castroville, CA, pg. 209
Horrocks, Ted, Mktg. Mgr.--Ranging, East Bloomfield, NY, pg. 300
Horst, Lawrie O., V.P.-Mktg.--John Wieland Homes Inc., Atlanta, GA, pg. 1188
Horton, Ronald C., V.P.-Mktg.--John Hancock Variable Life Insurance Co., Boston, MA, pg. 596
Horwath, Mary, V.P.-Mktg. Services & Intl. Mktg.--Rollerblade, Inc., Minnetonka, MN, pg. 944
Hoshino, Karl, V.P.-Prod. Mktg.--Komatsu Dresser Company, Lincolnshire, IL, pg. 565
Hoskins, Rick, V.P.-Mktg.--Burke Industries, Inc., San Jose, CA, pg. 191
Hotchkin, W.F., Dir.-Mktg. & Sls.--Stamco Industries Inc., Euclid, OH, pg. 1035
Hough, Daniel, V.P.-Mktg. & Adv.--Best Products Co., Inc., Richmond, VA, pg. 17
House, Mary Helen, Dir.-Mktg., Adv., Art, Audio/Visual & Communication Services--Gold Medal Products Co., Cincinnati, OH, pg. 465
House, Randall F., V.P.-Mktg.--Poly-Seal Corporation, Baltimore, MD, pg. 880
House, Randall F., V.P.-Mktg.--Moldcraft Plastics Inc., Baltimore, MD, pg. 880
Houston, Kay H., V.P.-Mktg. Services--Insurance Corp. of America, Houston, TX, pg. 572
Howard, Chris, Dir.-Mktg.--Clear Springs Foods, Inc., Buhl, ID, pg. 254
Howard, Lee, V.P.-Mktg.--National Distributing Co., Inc., Atlanta, GA, pg. 787
Howard, Richard M., Dir.-Mktg.--Shafer Commercial Seating Inc., Denver, CO, pg. 994
Howard, Sharon H., Mgr.-Mktg. Services--Kirby Building Systems, Inc., Nashville, TN, pg. 632
Howard, Stephen, Dir.-Mktg. Services--Columbus Mills, Inc., Columbus, GA, pg. 267
Howard, Steve, Exec. V.P., Mktg.--Williams Television Time, Inc., Santa Monica, CA, pg. 1191
Howell, Edward, V.P.-Prod. Devel.--L.L. Bean, Inc., Freeport, ME, pg. 648
Howell, Robert, V.P.-Sls. & Mktg.--Wollin Products, Inc., Stevensville, MI, pg. 1199
Howell, William, V.P.-Mktg.--Howell Instruments Corp., Fort Worth, TX, pg. 547
Hrabina, Michael, V.P.-Sls. & Mktg.--Accu-Sort Systems, Inc., Telford, PA, pg. 11
Hredzak, John A., Mgr.-Mktg. Services--Stephens-Adamson, Pittsburgh, PA, pg. 732
Hubbard, Gary, V.P.-Sls. & Mktg.--PacifiCare of Oregon, Inc., Lake Oswego, OR, pg. 1127
Hudec, Michele, Mgr.-Mktg.--The Chicago Faucet Co., Des Plaines, IL, pg. 245
Hudson, Jerry, Mgr.-Mktg.--Seabrook Wallcoverings, Inc., Memphis, TN, pg. 984
Hudson, Randy J., V.P.-Sls. & Mktg.--Transus Inc., Atlanta, GA, pg. 1108
Huffines, Lawrence, V.P.-Mktg. & Sls.--Pickering Industries Inc., Tacoma, WA, pg. 869
Hughes, Bill, Sls. & Mktg. Mgr.--La Belle Industries, Inc., Oconomowoc, WI, pg. 648
Hughes, James J., V.P.-Sls. & Mktg.--Morse Shoe Leased Div., Canton, MA, pg. 772
Hughes, Jim, V.P.-Sls. & Mktg.--Star Container, Inc., Phoenix, AZ, pg. 1082
Hull, Randy L., V.P.-Sls. & Mktg. Admin.--G. Heileman Brewing Co., Inc., La Crosse, WI, pg. 526
Hulse, Doug, Dir.-Intl. Mktg.--Taylor Machine Works, Inc., Louisville, MS, pg. 1081
Hult, Kathy, Mgr.-Mktg. Plng.--Hypro Corporation, New Brighton, MN, pg. 557
Hult, Ron, Mgr.-Mktg.--John Fabick Tractor Company, Fenton, MO, pg. 396
Hultman, Jon E., Sr. V.P.-Mktg.--Replogle Globes, Inc., Broadview, IL, pg. 927
Hummel, William, V.P.-Mktg.--Highlights for Children, Inc., Columbus, OH, pg. 534
Humphrey, Lorraine, V.P.-Sls. & Mktg.--Hollytex Carpet Mills, Inc., Ontario, CA, pg. 540
Humphrey, Robert P., V.P.-Mktg. & Sls.--Humphrey Products Company, Kalamazoo, MI, pg. 553
Hundsdorfer, Rainer, V.P.-Mktg. & Sls.--Trumpf Inc., Farmington, CT, pg. 1118
Hundt, Paul, Mgr.-Sls.-Refrigeration & Mktg. Coord.--W.A. Roosevelt Co., La Crosse, WI, pg. 946
Huneke, Howard H., Acct. Exec.--American Selfcare Corporation, Glen Ellyn, IL, pg. 61
Huneycutt, Al, Dir.-Mktg.--Halsey Taylor, Oak Brook, IL, pg. 377
Hunsberger, Ronald, Dir.-Mktg.--Clemens Markets Inc., Lansdale, PA, pg. 254
Hunt, Valerie, Dir.-Mktg.--Lyon's Restaurants, Inc., Foster City, CA, pg. 690
Hunter, Stanley, V.P.-Mktg.--Hansen Coupling Division, Cleveland, OH, pg. 1120
Hunters, Cathleen, Coord.-Sls. & Mktg.--The Vagabond Inns, San Diego, CA, pg. 1142
Hupp, Michael G., V.P.-Mktg. & Sls.--Warner Press, Inc., Anderson, IN, pg. 1164
Hurley, Kenneth B., V.P.-Mktg. & Sls.--Kaye Instruments, Inc., Bedford, MA, pg. 619
Hurst, Charles W., V.P.-Sls. & Mktg.--Lay Packing Company Inc., Knoxville, TN, pg. 663
Husby, R.E., V.P.-Mktg.--Duraco Products, Inc., Streamwood, IL, pg. 354
Huser, Larry, V.P.-Sls. & Mktg.--Mayville Metal Products Division, Mayville, WI, pg. 275
Husko, Charles E., Mgr.-Indus. Div.--Bel-Ray Company, Inc., Farmingdale, NJ, pg. 133
Huston, C., V.P.-Mktg. & Sls.--Dixson, Inc., Grand Junction, CO, pg. 341
Huston, Harland W., Chm. & Pres.--Fiberesin Industries Inc., Oconomowoc, WI, pg. 408
Huston, Richard, Exec. V.P.-Mktg.--Monterey's Tex Mex Cafe, Irving, TX, pg. 767
Hutchinson, Alex, V.P.-Mktg.--Corporate Health Strategies, Inc., Westport, CT, pg. 744
Huttner, Gail, Dir.-Mktg. Services--The Alden Group Ltd., New York, NY, pg. 32
Hvide, Anders, V.P.-Mktg.--Hvide Shipping, Inc., Fort Lauderdale, FL, pg. 556
Iacchia, Flora, Dir.-Mktg. Communications--Softool Corporation, Goleta, CA, pg. 1016
Ibbott, David, V.P.-Mktg.-Highway & Chemical--Siftco Canada, Inc., Mississauga,, Canada, pg. 812
Iezzi, Bob, V.P.-Mktg.--Thornton Oil Corp., Louisville, KY, pg. 1095
Ignatovich, Dorrie, Mktg. Coord.--The Pro Corporation, Florence, MA, pg. 891
Iiams, Mike, V.P.-Mktg.--J.D. Edwards & Company, Denver, CO, pg. 370
Ilaria, Peter E., Dir.-Mktg. & Sls.--Tropar Mfg. Co., Inc., Florham Park, NJ, pg. 1115
Iles, Randy, V.P.-Mktg.--Pella Corporation, Pella, IA, pg. 856
Imler, Dan, Mgr.-Mtg. Communications--Tension Envelope Corp., Kansas City, MO, pg. 1088
Impey, William, V.P.-Mktg. & Prod. Devel.--Oregon Freeze Dry, Inc., Albany, OR, pg. 829
Ingmanson, Lance, Dir.-Sls. & Mktg.--Malibu Grand Prix Corporation, Canoga Park, CA, pg. 702
Ingram, Harry V. III, Dir.-Mktg.--I.B.C. Root Beer Company, Dallas, TX, pg. 342
Ingram, Robert F., V.P.-Sls. & Mktg.--Game Winner, Inc., Atlanta, GA, pg. 290
Irby, Mark, V.P.-Mktg. & Adv.--Publix Supermarkets Inc., Lakeland, FL, pg. 898
Irwin, Marie, Dir.-Mktg.--Carrols Corporation, Syracuse, NY, pg. 225
Isaacson, Scott, Sr. V.P.-Mktg.--Employers Insurance of Wausau a Mutual Co., Wausau, WI, pg. 380
Isaacson, Scott, Sr. V.P.-Mktg.--Employers Insurance of Wausau a Mutual Co., Wausau, WI, pg. 795
Isdell-Carpenter, Peter, European Mktg. Dir.--Young & Rubicam International European Hdqrs., London, United Kingdom, pg. 1213
Island, Joanne C., Mgr.-Mktg.--Howe Furniture Corporation, Trumbull, CT, pg. 547
Isola, Thomas, V.P.-Mktg. & Pub. Rels.--Silver State Disposal Service, Inc., Las Vegas, NV, pg. 1004
Israel, John, V.P.-Mktg. & Sls. Support--Safeguard Business Systems, Inc., Fort Washington, PA, pg. 966
Israel, Rich, Dir.-Mktg.--San Diego Chargers, San Diego, CA, pg. 969
Itkin, David, V.P.-Mktg.--Furniture Consultants, New York, NY, pg. 437
Iversen, Mary Ann, Dir.-Mktg. & Adv.--King Koil Licensing Company Inc., Saint Paul, MN, pg. 630

Corporate Responsibilities Index

Izzi, Suzanne, Mktg. Asst., Media Contact--Muhlhauser & Young, San Francisco, CA, pg. 774
Jaben, Ed, Sr. V.P.-Mktg. & Mdsg.--Bailey Banks & Biddle, Irving, TX, pg. 1215
Jablonski, Richard, Dir.-Mktg.--Ghafari Associates, Inc., Dearborn, MI, pg. 455
Jacino, John, 1st V.P.-Sls. & Mktg.--Wetsel-Oviatt Lumber Company, Folsom, CA, pg. 1183
Jack, Barbara, Sr. V.P., Bus. Devel.--Wunderman Cato Johnson, New York, NY, pg. 1211
Jackson, Cynthia A., Mktg. Coordinator--Baxter Hodell Donnelly Preston Inc., Cincinnati, OH, pg. 127
Jackson, Joe, Mktg. Dir.--Pallas Advertising, Inc., San Francisco, CA, pg. 843
Jackson, Karen, V.P.-Mktg. & Adv.--T. J. Cinnamons Ltd., Kansas City, MO, pg. 1073
Jackson, Peggy Fuller, Mgr.-Mktg. Services--Hardin Construction Group, Inc., Atlanta, GA, pg. 508
Jackson, Riley, V.P.-Mktg., Pur. & Adv.--Federal Savings Bank, Fort Smith, AR, pg. 1194
Jackson, Sharon P., Mgr.-Mktg. Services--Superior Tube Company, Collegeville, PA, pg. 1064
Jackson, Stevens P., Sr. V.P.-Direct Mktg.--LaMarca Direct Marketing, New York, NY, pg. 652
Jackson, William, V.P.-Prod. Opers.--Hardaway Concrete Co., Inc., Columbia, SC, pg. 507
Jacobi, C.M., V.P.-Sls. & Mktg.-World Wide--Timex Corporation, Middlebury, CT, pg. 1098
Jacobs, April, V.P.-Sls. & Mktg.--Mueller Sports Medicine, Inc., Prairie du Sac, WI, pg. 774
Jacobs, Daniel F., Dir.-Sls. & Mktg.--Albert C. Martin & Associates, Los Angeles, CA, pg. 714
Jacobsen, Dean, V.P.-Mktg.--Sweetheart Cup Co., Inc., Chicago, IL, pg. 1067
Jacobsen, Robert, Gen. Mgr.-Mktg.--U.S. Can Company, Oak Brook, IL, pg. 1134
Jacobson, Blaine, Dir.-Mktg.--J.R. Simplot Company, Boise, ID, pg. 1007
Jacobson, Jeanne, Mgr.-Mktg. Services--Harter Systems Div., Middlebury, IN, pg. 514
Jacoby, Roberto, Mktg. Dir.--Young & Rubicam Argentina, Buenos Aires,, Argentina, pg. 1213
Jacoby, Stephen M., Dir.-Mktg.--Vanity Fair, New York, NY, pg. 19
Jacoby, Ted, Dir.-Mktg.--Bongards Creameries Inc., Norwood, MN, pg. 164
Jaeb, Christopher, Dir.-Communications--Affiliated Computer Services, Inc., Dallas, TX, pg. 23
Jaffee, Theresa, Dir.-Mktg.--Arthur Andersen & Co., S.C., New York, NY, pg. 72
Jago, Rick, Mktg. Dir.--Old World Automotive Products, Northbrook, IL, pg. 824
Jago, Rick, Mktg. Dir.--Splitfire, Inc., Northbrook, IL, pg. 824
James, Howard, V.P.-Mktg.--Berol Corporation, Brentwood, TN, pg. 856
James, John E., V.P.-Mktg. & Sls.--Doehler-Jarvis, Toledo, OH, pg. 559
James, Michele, Mktg. Coord.--Snyder Potato Chips, Berlin, PA, pg. 26
Jameson, Jon, V.P.-Mktg. & Adv.--Big Boy Restaurant System, Washington, DC, pg. 376
Jamison, Lelan M., V.P.-Mktg.--UFE Incorporated, Stillwater, MN, pg. 1123
Janis, Roy M., Dir.-Business Plng.--Simplex Time Recorder Co., Gardner, MA, pg. 1006
Janner, Bill, Mktg. Mgr.--Benco Industries, Inc., Fort Deposit, AL, pg. 138
Jansen, Richard, V.P.-Mktg.--DVC Industries, Bay Shore, NY, pg. 310
Jantzi, Gerald P., V.P.-Mktg.--Sunshine Biscuits, Inc., Woodbridge, NJ, pg. 439
Jarvis, Kathy, Mktg. Analyst--Ivex Packaging Corporation, Lincolnshire, IL, pg. 583
Jaye, Edward, V.P.-Mktg. & Sls.--Elkay Products, Inc., Shrewsbury, MA, pg. 377
Jayson, Judith P., Dir.-Mktg.--J. M. Jayson & Co., Inc., Getsville, NY, pg. 591
Jefferson, Thomas DeQuincy, Dir.-Mktg.--Datability, Inc., Carlstadt, NJ, pg. 316
Jeffonsor, Robert F., V.P.-Mktg.--ARINC Research Corp., Annapolis, MD, pg. 82
Jeffrey, Jeanette P., Prod. Mgr.--Canned Foods--AJC International, Inc., Atlanta, GA, pg. 4
Jeffries, Lori L., Sls. Mgr.--Thordarson Meissner, Inc., Mount Carmel, IL, pg. 270
Jelinski, T.L., V.P.-Mktg.--Amspec Chemical Corporation, Gloucester City, NJ, pg. 5
Jenkins, James L., Exec. V.P.-Retail Sls. & Mktg.--Curtis Mathes Corporation, Athens, TX, pg. 720
Jennings, Karen P., Sr. V.P.-Mktg.--George W. Park Seed Co., Inc., Greenwood, SC, pg. 849
Jennings, Madeline, Dir.-Mktg.& Communications--Sellstrom Manufacturing Co., Palatine, IL, pg. 988
Jensen, Chris, Mgr.-Sls. & Mktg.--Jensen Electric Company, Reno, NV, pg. 592
Jensen, Richard, V.P.-New Bus. Dev.--Applied Microsystems Corporation, Redmond, WA, pg. 79
Jensen, Steve, Asst. V.P.-Mktg.--Pacesetter Corporation, Omaha, NE, pg. 839
Jensen, Terry, Mgr.-Mktg. Services--Xerxes Corporation, Minneapolis, MN, pg. 1206
Jeter, Kevin, Exec. V.P.-Sls. & Mktg.--Days Inns of America, Inc., Atlanta, GA, pg. 1100
Jewell, Douglas F., V.P.-Scholastic Mktg.--Herff Jones Inc., Indianapolis, IN, pg. 531
Jimencz, Clarisa, Dir.-Mktg.--Puerto Rico Tourism Company, New York, NY, pg. 899
Jindra, Martin, Dir.-Mktg.--Squire-Cogswell Company, Northbrook, IL, pg. 1034
Jindra, Martin, Dir.-Mktg.--Aeros Instruments, Inc., Northbrook, IL, pg. 1034
Jipp, Leona M., Mktg. Coordinator--Smith & Gillespie Engineers, Inc., Jacksonville, FL, pg. 1012
Joannou, Cindy, Shipping Mgr.--G. Joannou Cycle Co. Inc., Northvale, NJ, pg. 595
Jodzio, Greg, Mgr.-Mktg. Communications--Advance Machine Company, Plymouth, MN, pg. 18
Joesten, Nan, Dir.-Mktg.--Teleflora, Los Angeles, CA, pg. 60
Joffe, Philip L., Mktg. Mgr.--Radiator Specialty Company, Charlotte, NC, pg. 909
Johann, E.W., V.P.-Mktg. & Engrng.--Weil-McLain, Michigan City, IN, pg. 710
John D. Hedges, Dir.-Mktg. & Sls.--Hoffco, Inc., Richmond, IN, pg. 537
John, Caroline C., V.P.-New Ventures--Cox Enterprises Newspaper Division, Atlanta, GA, pg. 292
Johns, Michael, V.P.-Mktg.--Ward Trucking Corp., Altoona, PA, pg. 1163
Johnson, Bobbie, Corp. Librarian & Dir.-Mktg. Res.--Candle Corporation, Santa Monica, CA, pg. 214
Johnson, D., Mgr.-Mktg.--Felton Brush Inc., Manchester, NH, pg. 406
Johnson, Dave, V.P.-Sls. & Mktg.--Del Mar Avionics, Irvine, CA, pg. 325
Johnson, Don, Mgr.-Sls. & Mktg.--Juno Tool & Plastic Corporation, Minnetonka, MN, pg. 299
Johnson, Donald E., Dir.-Mktg.--Radix Corporation, Salt Lake City, UT, pg. 909
Johnson, Eileen, Mgr.-Mktg. Services--Walnut Grove-Nutrena Feed Div., Cargill, Inc., Atlantic, IA, pg. 219
Johnson, Frank, V.P.-Strategic Plng.--Caravan Products Company, Inc., Totowa, NJ, pg. 217
Johnson, Frank M., Sr. V.P.-Retail Mktg.--Associated Grocers, Inc., Seattle, WA, pg. 90
Johnson, Jerry, Mgr.-Mktg. Services--Eco Water Systems, Saint Paul, MN, pg. 367
Johnson, Jim, V.P.-Sls. & Mktg.--Midwest Mutual Insurance Co., West Des Moines, IA, pg. 886
Johnson, Lee K., Sr. V.P.-Engrng., Mktg. & Sls.--Thrall Car Mfg. Co., Chicago Heights, IL, pg. 350
Johnson, Mark E., V.P.-Mktg.--The Hartz Mountain Corp., Harrison, NJ, pg. 514
Johnson, N.R., V.P.-Mktg. & Sls.--Kettering Advertising Display Co., Englewood Cliffs, NJ, pg. 626
Johnson, Paul, Mgr.-Mktg.--Duo-Fast Corporation, Franklin Park, IL, pg. 354
Johnson, R. Mac, V.P.-Mktg.--Tom's Foods, Columbus, GA, pg. 1101
Johnson, R.E., V.P.-Reg. Baltimore--Tristate Electrical Supply Co., Inc., Hagerstown, MD, pg. 1114
Johnson, R.S., Mktg. Mgr.-Strings--The Selmer Co., Elkhart, IN, pg. 573
Johnson, Rob, V.P.-Sls. & Mktg.--Sunbeam Outdoor Products Co., Neosho, MO, pg. 1059
Johnson, Robert, Dor.-Mktg.--Production Tool Supply Co., Warren, MI, pg. 893
Johnson, Sherry, V.P.-Mktg.--The SArgent-SOwell Company, Grand Prairie, TX, pg. 971
Johnson, Stan, Dir.-Mktg. Devel.--Growmark, Inc., Bloomington, IL, pg. 490
Johnson, Timothy L., V.P. & Mktg. Dir.--MetLife Capital Corporation, Bellevue, WA, pg. 744
Johnston, S., V.P.-Mktg.--Wesbar Corporation, West Bend, WI, pg. 1176
Joles, Everett, V.P.-Sls. & Mktg.--Perry & Derrick Co., Cincinnati, OH, pg. 863
Jonap, Scott T., V.P.-Sls. & Mktg., Consumer Prods. Div.--Foley-PLP Company, Rochester, NY, pg. 422
Jones, Donald R., Mktg.--Victaulic Company of Canada Limited, Rexdale,, Canada, pg. 1149
Jones, Ian, Dir.-Mktg.--Gunnebo Fastening Corp., York, PA, pg. 494
Jones, J. Kevin, Exec. V.P.-Mktg.--Peck Jones Construction, Los Angeles, CA, pg. 854
Jones, J.B., V.P.-Sls. & Mktg.--Coldwater Seafood Corporation, Rowayton, CT, pg. 260
Jones, James, Sr. V.P.-Sls. & Mktg.--Mersman Furniture, Celina, OH, pg. 741
Jones, L.P., Dir.-Intl. Mktg.--Ideal Industries, Inc., Sycamore, IL, pg. 562
Jones, Maura, Mgr.-Mktg. Communications--Spinnaker Software Corporation, Cambridge, MA, pg. 1031
Jones, Pam, Mgr.-Mktg. Systems--I.B.C. Root Beer Company, Dallas, TX, pg. 342
Jones, Patrick, V.P.-Mktg.--Jones Company, Inc., Waycross, GA, pg. 603
Jones, Steve, Mgr.-Mktg.--Grey Eagle Distributors Inc., Maryland Heights, MO, pg. 486
Jones, Wini, Dir.-New Prod. Devel.--Roffe, Inc., Seattle, WA, pg. 943
Jordan, James, Dir.-Mktg. & Adv.--Multiple Allied Services, Inc., Hayward, CA, pg. 775
Jordan, James P., V.P.-Mktg.--Jewelers Mutual Insurance Company, Neenah, WI, pg. 593
Jordan, Lisa, Mgr.-Bus. Devel.--Ghafari Associates, Inc., Dearborn, MI, pg. 455
Jorgensen, Marty, V.P.-Mktg.--Ingram Entertainment Inc., La Vergne, TN, pg. 569
Jovanovski, Jovan, Dir.-Sls. & Intl. Mktg.--The Stroh Brewery Company, Detroit, MI, pg. 1053
Joyner, Barrett, Dir.-U.S. Mktg. & Sls.--SAS Institute Inc., Cary, NC, pg. 959
Juchem, Robert, V.P.-Sls. & Mktg.--Pyttronic Industries, Inc., Montgomeryville, PA, pg. 901
Juenger, Steven, Dir.-Mktg.--Reliance Medical Products, Inc., Mason, OH, pg. 925
Juhnke, Bruce, Dir.-Intl. Mktg. & Sls.--Behlen Mfg. Co., Columbus, NE, pg. 132
Jungquist, Jon A., V.P. & G.M.--Stiefel Laboratories, Inc., Coral Gables, FL, pg. 1048
Just, Cindy, Dir.-Mktg.--Great Lakes Lithograph Co., Cleveland, OH, pg. 481
Justice, Hal, Exec. V.P.-Mktg.--United Refrigerated Services, Atlanta, GA, pg. 1134
Kacvinsky, Ray C., V.P.-Mktg. & Sls.--Marathon Electric Manufacturing Corp., Wausau, WI, pg. 705
Kaffer, William J., V.P.-Mktg.--Theodore Barry & Associates, Los Angeles, CA, pg. 122
Kafka, Rick, Pres. & Dir.-Mktg.--Gosnell Builders, Phoenix, AZ, pg. 472
Kahle, Roger D., V.P.-Mktg.--Shenandoah Life Insurance Company, Roanoke, VA, pg. 997
Kahn, Randa, V.P.-Mktg.--Sportsystems Corporation, Buffalo, NY, pg. 326
Kahn, Ronald, V.P.-Mktg.--The National Latex Products Co., Ashland, OH, pg. 791
Kaidan, Daniel P., V.P.-Mktg.--Metropolitan Life Insurance Co., New York, NY, pg. 744
Kaiser, John K., Dir.-Mktg.--Strouse Greenberg & Co., Inc., Philadelphia, PA, pg. 1054
Kaiser, Karen E., Mgr.-Mktg. Research.--Clarity Coverdale Rueff Advertising, Minneapolis, MN, pg. 251
Kaiser, Mark, V.P.-Sls. & Mktg. Services--J P Foodservice, Inc., Hanover, MD, pg. 586
Kaiser, Steven, V.P.-Mktg.--David G. Steven, Inc., New York, NY, pg. 1048
Kalenbergm John C., Exec. V.P., Mktg. Services--Gage Marketing Group, Minneapolis, MN, pg. 441
Kalil, A.J., V.P.-Sls. & Mktg.--PHB Parker Die Castings, Fairview, PA, pg. 836
Kall, Terry J., V.P.-Sls. & Mktg.--Hollytex, Saddle Brook, NJ, pg. 1121
Kallenbach, Mary, Mktg. Mgr.--Marketing Services Unltd., Waukesha, WI, pg. 709
Kallenbach, Mary, Mgr.-Mktg.--Ortho-Kinetics, Inc., Waukesha, WI, pg. 830
Kalmuck, John, V.P.-Sls. & Mktg.--La Marche Mfg. Co., Des Plaines, IL, pg. 649
Kalous, Dave, V.P.-Mktg.--Duo-Fast Corporation, Franklin Park, IL, pg. 354
Kaloyanides, Jim, Dir.-Mktg.--New England Coffee Company, Malden, MA, pg. 800
Kalt, Robert, V.P.-Mktg.--H.B. Zachry, San Antonio, TX, pg. 1215
Kammersgard, Dana W., V.P.-Sls. & Mktg.--Artecon, Inc., Carlsbad, CA, pg. 809
Kamnikar, Michael A., V.P.-Mktg.--Ellwood City Forge, Ellwood City, PA, pg. 378
Kanas, Tom, V.P.-Sls. & Mktg.--Alto Shaam Inc., Menomonee Falls, WI, pg. 46
Kane, Jack, V.P.-Mktg.--The Wooster Brush Company, Wooster, OH, pg. 1202
Kannapell, Susan, V.P., Mktg.--Creative Alliance, Inc., Louisville, KY, pg. 297
Kaplan, Debbie, Dir.-Mktg.--Financial World Partners, New York, NY, pg. 410
Kaplan, Howard, Dir.-Mktg. & Asst. Publisher--The Goldhirsh Group Inc., Boston, MA, pg. 467
Kaplan, Michael M., V.P.-Sls. & Mktg.--Life Sciences International, Philadelphia, PA, pg. 320
Kaplan, Robert E., V.P.-Opers. & Mktg. Services--Greenwood Mills, Inc., New York, NY, pg. 486
Kaplowitz, Fred, Mgr.-Mktg.--Charan Industries, Inc., Garden City, NY, pg. 239
Kapp, James, Mktg. Communications Specialist--Countrymark Cooperative, Inc., Indianapolis, IN, pg. 290
Karasch, David, Dir.-Mktg., Tomatoes--Del Monte Foods, San Francisco, CA, pg. 325
Karleski, Thomas, Dir.-Sls. & Mktg.--Catholic Order of Foresters, Naperville, IL, pg. 229
Karmadi, Paul W., Exec. V.P., Dir. Opers. & Mktg. Services--Matari Advertising, Jakarta,, Indonesia, pg. 104
Karn, Harold G., Jr., V.P.-Mktg.--Toter Incorporated, Statesville, NC, pg. 1103
Karper, Donald J., V.P.-Sls. & Mktg.--Alva/Amco Pharmacal Companies, Inc., Chicago, IL, pg. 46
Karpinski, William, Business Mgr.--Aircraft Gear Corporation-Arizona Division, Chandler, AZ, pg. 27
Karrasch, Steven, Mgr.-Mktg. Services--The Vollrath Company Inc., Sheboygan, WI, pg. 1154
Karve, M.D., V.P.-Japan & Korean Mktg.--Buckman Laboratories, Memphis, TN, pg. 185
Kaspar, Dan A., Prod. Mgr.--Kaspar Wire Works, Inc., Shiner, TX, pg. 617
Kasperski, Ken, Dir.-Intl. Sls.--Spraying Systems Co., Wheaton, IL, pg. 1032
Kass, Ronald, Sr. V.P.-Mktg.--Knoll International, Inc., New York, NY, pg. 1121
Kassab, Thomas, Exec. V.P.-Mktg.--Stainless Incorporated, Deerfield Beach, FL, pg. 1035
Kaszubowski, E., Dir.-Intl. Mktg.--Recon/Optical, Inc., Barrington, IL, pg. 917
Katz, Alan, V.P.-Mktg. & Sls.--Empire Kosher Poultry, Inc., Mifflintown, PA, pg. 379
Katz, Gerald, Mgr.-Mktg.--Coventry Hotels Association, Saddle Brook, NJ, pg. 290
Katzman, Michael, V.P.-Mktg. & Sls.--Mastercraft Furniture Corp., Omaha, NE, pg. 720
Kauffman, T.G., V.P.-Mktg.--E. F. Houghton & Co., Valley Forge, PA, pg. 546
Kaufman, Bob, V.P.-Sls. & Mktg.--Mogas Industries, Inc., Houston, TX, pg. 763
Kaufman, Donald L., Pres. & Dir.-Sls. & Mktg., Alside Div.--Associated Materials Inc., Dallas, TX, pg. 91
Kaufman, Marion, Dir.-Mktg.--Greeff Fabrics, Port Chester, NY, pg. 262
Kaufmann, Michael, Dir.-Sls. & Mktg.--Ford Products Corporation, Valley Cottage, NY, pg. 423
Kavanagh, Jack, Dir.-Adv. & Mktg. Mgr.--Barton Brands, Ltd., Chicago, IL, pg. 123
Kavoukian, Jack C., Dir.-Mktg. Communications & Adv.--Hohner/HSS Inc., Ashland, VA, pg. 538
Kawaguchi, Kenneth K., V.P.-Mktg.--Fishking Processors, Inc., Los Angeles, CA, pg. 415
Kayser, John, Mktg. Promo. Mgr.--American Water Works Association, Denver, CO, pg. 65
Keane-Gillette, Denise, V.P.-Mktg.--Hammacher, Schlemmer & Co., Inc., Chicago, IL, pg. 503
Keane, Cary, V.P.-Mktg.--Royal Crown Cola Co., Miami Beach, FL, pg. 243

Corporate Responsibilities Index

Keane, Pat, Sr. Dir.-Mktg.--Redbook, New York, NY, pg. 523
Keating, John J., V.P.-Sls., Mktg. & Fin.--P.J. Keating Company, Lunenburg, MA, pg. 619
Keating, Paul J., II, Dir.-Sls. & Mktg. & Treas.--P.J. Keating Company, Lunenburg, MA, pg. 619
Keaveney, Vincent J., Mktg. Mgr.--Commercial Travelers Mutual Insurance Company, Utica, NY, pg. 269
Keefe, Steve, Mgr.-Natl. Sls.--Flambeau Products-Columbus, Columbus, IN, pg. 810
Keegan, Hugh, Dir.-Mktg.--Ventre Packing Company, Inc., Syracuse, NY, pg. 1147
Keehn, Andy, Sr. V.P., Dir. Planning--EvansGroup, Seattle, WA, pg. 391
Keeler, Robert, V.P.-Mktg.--WWF Paper Corporation, Bala-Cynwyd, PA, pg. 1157
Keenahan, Terry, Mgr.-Mktg.--Microdot Inserts, Placentia, CA, pg. 749
Kees, Thomas, Sr. V.P.-Mktg.--AppleTree Markets, Houston, TX, pg. 79
Kelberman, Murray, V.P.-Mktg.--Carnival Creations, New York, NY, pg. 222
Keller, Jacqueline, Sr. V.P.-Mktg. & Communications--Mayfair Super Markets, Inc., Elizabeth, NJ, pg. 724
Kelley, Jeanette, V.P., Mktg. Medical Grp.--Merling, Marx & Seidman, Inc., New York, NY, pg. 741
Kelley, Jim, Dir., Mktg. Hospitality/Travel & Leisure--Muhlhauser & Young, San Francisco, CA, pg. 774
Kellman, Jack, Exec. V.P.-Mktg. & Sls.--Globe Glass & Mirror Co., Chicago, IL, pg. 463
Kellogg, Jeanette, Dir.-Sls. & Mktg.--Genova Products, Inc., Davison, MI, pg. 452
Kelly, Gerard P., Sr. V.P.-Mktg.--John Hancock Leasing Corporation, Boston, MA, pg. 596
Kelly, J., Sr. V.P.-Special Prods. Devel.--Haskel, Inc., Burbank, CA, pg. 516
Kelly, Jack, Sr. V.P.-Comml. Mktg.--Preferred Risk Mutual Insurance, West Des Moines, IA, pg. 886
Kelly, John M., V.P.-Mktg. & Sls.--Desa International, Inc., Bowling Green, KY, pg. 331
Kelly, Karen, Mktg.--Alex J. Etkin, Inc., Farmington Hills, MI, pg. 389
Kelly, Michael D., V.P.-Mktg.--Friendly Ice Cream Corp., Wilbraham, MA, pg. 1087
Kelly, Mike, Dir.-Mktg. & Tech. Resources--The Alpha Corporation Of Tennessee, Collierville, TN, pg. 43
Kelly, Patrick T., V.P.-Sls. & Mktg.--Haws Drinking Faucet Co., Berkeley, CA, pg. 518
Kelly, S.W., Dir.-Sls. & Mktg.--The Crystal Tissue Co., Middletown, OH, pg. 303
Kemery, Frank, Dir.-Mktg.--Pace International Corporation, Kirkland, WA, pg. 838
Kemler, David, V.P.-Sls. & Mktg.--Information Builders, New York, NY, pg. 567
Kemph, Chris, V.P.-Mktg.--Site Oil Co. of Missouri, Clayton, MO, pg. 1009
Kempster, Michael, Sr. V.P.-Sls. & Mktg.--Weber-Stephen Products, Palatine, IL, pg. 1171
Kendall, Charles E., Exec. V.P.-Mktg. & Admin.--The DeMars Corp., Indianapolis, IN, pg. 327
Kennedy, Brian J., Exec. V.P.-Sls. & Mktg.--The Hertz Corporation, Park Ridge, NJ, pg. 849
Kennedy, Duane, Dir.-Consumer Sls.--Parker Fertilizer Co., Inc., Sylacauga, AL, pg. 849
Kennedy, Jon, V.P.-Mktg. & Adv.--Super 8 Motels, Inc., Aberdeen, SD, pg. 1062
Kennedy, Maureen, Mktg. Dir.--The Bornstein Agency, Washington, DC, pg. 164
Kennedy, Russell E., V.P.-Sls. & Mktg.--GAF Building Materials Corporation, Wayne, NJ, pg. 438
Kenney, Bob, Mgr.-Mktg.--Panduit Company, Tinley Park, IL, pg. 845
Kenney, Michael P., Sr. Supvr.-Mktg. Communications--J. J. Keller & Associates, Inc., Neenah, WI, pg. 620
Kenney, William D., V.P.-Mktg.--Kenney Manufacturing Company, Warwick, RI, pg. 623
Kent, David, Mgr.-Mktg. Support Services--Medrad, Inc., Pittsburgh, PA, pg. 736
Keon, Thomas, Dir.-Mktg.--Concession Air Corporation, Buffalo, NY, pg. 326
Keon, Thomas, Dir.-Mktg.--Sportservice Corporation, Buffalo, NY, pg. 326
Kerkhoff, Daniel W., V.P.-Mktg. & Sls.--The Pro Corporation, Florence, MA, pg. 891
Kerman, Richard, Dir.-Mktg.--Steiner Electric Co., Elk Grove Village, IL, pg. 1045
Kerr, Jill, Chief Oper. Officer & V.P.-Sls. & Mktg.--The ASCII Group, Inc., Bethesda, MD, pg. 8
Kerr, Norman, V.P., Dir. Mktg.--Hal Riney & Partners, Inc., Chicago, IL, pg. 935
Kesterson, Danny, Exec. V.P.-Sls. & Mktg.--Kesterson Food Company, Inc., Paris, TN, pg. 624
Ketter, Phillip, Dir.-Mktg. Services--Regal Ware, Inc., Kewaskum, WI, pg. 921
Kick, Alan, V.P.-Sls. & Mktg.--Dynamic Metal Products Company, Manchester, CT, pg. 356
Kidd, Wyndham, Sr. V.P.-Mktg.--Blue Cross & Blue Shield of Virginia, Richmond, VA, pg. 160
Kiely, E.J., II, V.P.-Mktg.--Montgomery Elevator Company, Moline, IL, pg. 767
Kilcollins, Raymond, Mgr.-Mktg.--Maine Potato Growers, Inc., Presque Isle, ME, pg. 702
Kilgore, Joe, Mgr.-Mktg. & Pub. Rels.--Chattanooga Choo-Choo Holiday Inn, Chattanooga, TN, pg. 241
Kilian, Emma, Mktg.--Brokay Products, Inc., Philadelphia, PA, pg. 217
Killian, James, Dir.-Mktg.--S L C Graphics, Inc., Pittston, PA, pg. 963
Killips, Ian, V.P., Chief Mktg. Officer--REMark Advertising, Honolulu, HI, pg. 999
Kimball, Don, V.P.-Sls. & Mktg.--Alex Foods, Inc., Anaheim, CA, pg. 33
Kimball, Jim, Mgr.-Mktg.--Huntsman Chemical Corporation, Salt Lake City, UT, pg. 555
Kimball, John R., Sr. V.P.-Mktg.--L. Robert Kimball & Associates, Ebensburg, PA, pg. 629
Kimberlin, Michele, Mktg. Services Mgr.--Sir Speedy, Inc., Laguna Hills, CA, pg. 613
Kimicata, Art, V.P.-Sls. & Mktg.--Sun Data Inc., Norcross, GA, pg. 1058
Kimmel, Donald L., V.P.-Mktg.--Delta & Pine Land Company, Scott, MS, pg. 1024
King, Alan, V.P.-Sls. & Mktg.--Carbide International Inc., Chicago, IL, pg. 507
King, Alan, V.P.-Sls. & Mktg.--Rogers Tool Works, Inc., Rogers, AR, pg. 507
King, Ann, Dir.-Mktg.--Weichert Realty, Inc., Alexandria, VA, pg. 1173
King, Darryl, Pres.--A. Grace Development, Houston, TX, pg. 474
King, Don, Dir.-Mktg.--PVS Chemicals, Inc., Detroit, MI, pg. 837
King, H. Alan, V.P.-Sls. & Mktg.--RTW, Rogers Tool Works, Inc., Rogers, AR, pg. 908
King, Jeffrey, Mgr.-Mktg.--The Milnot Company, Saint Louis, MO, pg. 756
King, Joe, V.P.-Mktg.--PTS Electronics Corporation, Bloomington, IN, pg. 837
King, John, Dir.-Mktg.--Perkins Family Restaurants, Memphis, TN, pg. 1088
King, Larry, Dir.-Sls. & Mktg.--Ryan Herco Products Corp., Burbank, CA, pg. 958
King, Robert C., Jr., V.P., Gen. Mgr., & Mgr.-Adv. & Mktg.--Richmond Motor Company, Richmond, VA, pg. 933
Kingham, E.E., Dir.-Mktg.--Venta Inc., Denver, CO, pg. 1147
Kinimonth, Barbara, V.P.-Mktg.--Hoffman Homes, Inc., Itasca, IL, pg. 516
Kinney, Edward, V.P.-Mktg.--Klaussner Furniture Industry, Asheboro, NC, pg. 634
Kinsley, Rick, V.P.-Sls. & Mktg.--Pfaudler-U.S., Inc., Rochester, NY, pg. 866
Kintz, Claudine, Mktg.--Mars Confectionery, Haguenau,, France, pg. 714
Kirby, Mike, V.P.-Mktg.--Magline, Inc., Pinconning, MI, pg. 700
Kirchner, W.L., Dir.-Mktg.--Nooter Corporation, Saint Louis, MO, pg. 808
Kirkland, Thurman, V.P.-Sls. & Mktg.--Long MFG. NC, Inc., Tarboro, NC, pg. 682
Kirkland, Thurman, V.P.-Sls. & Mktg.--Long Equipment Co., Tarboro, NC, pg. 682
Kirkman, Paul, Exec. V.P.-Mktg. & Sls.--Beverage Canners International Corp., Miami, FL, pg. 148
Kirsch, Gary, Dir.-Mktg.--Hydril Company, Houston, TX, pg. 556
Kiss, John, V.P.-Mktg.--The Paty Company, Piney Flats, TN, pg. 852
Kitchen, Douglas O., Partner & Dir.-Futures--J. C. Bradford & Co., Nashville, TN, pg. 170
Kitchen, W.T., Gen Sls. Mgr.--Carlisle Equipment Company, Louisville, KY, pg. 220
Kittel, John, V.P.-Mktg.--The Hanover Insurance Company, Worcester, MA, pg. 34
Kittelson, Edward, Mgr.-Mktg.--Harmony Engineering Corporation, Minneapolis, MN, pg. 510
Kittredge, George, V.P.-Mktg.--Rochester Midland Corporation, Rochester, NY, pg. 940
Kizer, C., Product Mgr.--Gemtron Corporation, Sweetwater, TN, pg. 3
Klaus, Mike, Dir.-Direct Mktg.--North Shore Movers, Northbrook, IL, pg. 813
Kleiman, Bruce, V.P.-Mdsg. & Mktg.--A & E Stores, Inc., Ridgefield, NJ, pg. 1
Klein, Bernard, Mgr.-Mktg. Devel.--Tension Envelope Corp., Kansas City, MO, pg. 1088
Klein, Beverly, Sr. V.P.-Mktg.--Journal/Sentinel Inc., Milwaukee, WI, pg. 607
Klein, Beverly, Sr. V.P.-Mktg.--Milwaukee Sentinel, Milwaukee, WI, pg. 607
Klein, Beverly A., Sr. V.P.-Mktg.--The Milwaukee Journal, Milwaukee, WI, pg. 607
Klein, Patty, V.P.-Mktg.--F & M Distributors Inc., Warren, MI, pg. 393
Klein, Russell, Sr. V.P.-Mktg.--The Seven-Up Company, Dallas, TX, pg. 342
Klien, Connie, Mgr.-Mktg. Services--Brown & Haley, Tacoma, WA, pg. 182
Kline, Jack, V.P.-Mktg.--Christie Electric Corporation, Gardena, CA, pg. 249
Klock, Dick, Mgr.-Mktg.--Sioux Steel Company, Sioux Falls, SD, pg. 1008
Kloman, Larry, V.P.-Mktg. & Sls.--PhoneMate, Inc., Torrance, CA, pg. 869
Klong, Lawrence A., Pres.--K & R Delivery, Inc., Hinsdale, IL, pg. 610
Klonne, Michael, V.P.-Mktg. & Sls.--Findley Adhesives, Inc., Wauwatosa, WI, pg. 410
Kloos, Roger, Dir.-Sls. & Mktg.--Conestoga Wood Specialties, Inc., Earl, PA, pg. 273
Kmon, Robert V., V.P.-Special Prods.--Spencer Turbine Co., Windsor, CT, pg. 1030
Knapp, Joy, V.P.-Mktg.--United Coatings, Inc., Kankakee, IL, pg. 1131
Knapp, S.R., V.P.-Sls. & Mktg.--R. A. Jones & Co. Inc., Covington, KY, pg. 604
Kneffel, Michael, V.P. & Assoc Dir.-Mktg.--W.B. Doner & Company, Southfield, MI, pg. 344
Knepple, George, Dir.-Mktg., Metal Prods.--Simonds Industries Inc., Fitchburg, MA, pg. 1006
Knerr, Chris, V.P.-Mktg.--Freeman Cosmetic Corp., Los Angeles, CA, pg. 431
Kniess, Thomas M., Mktg. Specialist--The Hammerblow Corp., Wausau, WI, pg. 504
Knipp, Don, Mgr.-Mktg.--Bandini Fertilizer Company, Los Angeles, CA, pg. 117
Knox, Doug, V.P.-Mktg. & Assoc. Publisher--Tyndale House Publishers, Inc., Carol Stream, IL, pg. 1122
Knox, Leslie H., Sr. V.P.-Sls. & Mktg.--Abco Markets, Inc., Phoenix, AZ, pg. 10
Knudsen, Dan, V.P.-Mktg.--National Car Rental System, Inc., Minneapolis, MN, pg. 786
Knudsen, K., V.P.-Mktg.--Bruning Paint Company, Baltimore, MD, pg. 184
Knudtson, Charles L., Sr. V.P.-Mktg., New Bus. Devel.--DCI Marketing, Milwaukee, WI, pg. 308
Kobel, Andrei, Dir.-Mktg.--Nihon Ready Systems, Tokyo,, Japan, pg. 916
Kobuse, Naoki (Tokyo), Sr. Exec. V.P., Dir. WW Mktg.--Dentsu, Young & Rubicam Partnerships, New York, NY, pg. 330
Koeller, Fred, V.P.-Mktg.--Andis Company, Racine, WI, pg. 74
Koenig, Carol, Mktg. Mgr.-Healthcare--Aladdin Synergetics, Inc., Nashville, TN, pg. 29
Koeniger, James K., V.P.-Sls. & Mktg.--Atlas Refinery, Newark, NJ, pg. 96
Koeppel, Peter S., Exec. V.P., Mktg. Dir.--Joiner Rowland Serio Koeppel, Dallas, TX, pg. 602
Kohen, Kenneth C., Sr. V.P. & Mktg. Dir.--Ticor Title Guarantee Co., New York, NY, pg. 1096
Kohls, Ellen P., Mgr.-Mktg.--Effective Management Systems, Milwaukee, WI, pg. 370
Kohoskie, Stephen E., Exec. V.P. & Dir.-Grp. Mktg.--Mutual of Omaha Insurance Company, Omaha, NE, pg. 779
Kohoskie, Stephen E., Exec. V.P. & Dir.-Grp. Mktg.--Mutual of Omaha, Omaha, NE, pg. 779
Kokias, Chris, V.P.-Mktg.--Phoenix Data Incorporated, Phoenix, AZ, pg. 630
Kolandjian, Vreij, V.P.-Mktg.--Kal Kan Foods, Inc., Vernon, CA, pg. 713
Kolkebeck, W. Charles, V.P.-Mktg. & Sls.--Nuttall Gear Corporation, Niagara Falls, NY, pg. 818
Kolkmeyer, R.A., Mgr.-Mktg.--The Miami Margarine Co., Cincinnati, OH, pg. 746
Koller, Barbara, Mktg. Dir.--CHF Industries, Inc., New York, NY, pg. 200
Kondos, J., Mgr.-Mktg.--Specialty Paperboard Inc., Brattleboro, VT, pg. 1027
Koontz, Mike, Dir.-Mktg. & Adv.--Tuffy Associates Corp., Toledo, OH, pg. 1119
Kopacz, Mike, Mgr.-Intl. Mktg.--Eco Water Systems, Saint Paul, MN, pg. 367
Koppe, Wayne, Mgr.-Prod.--Reliable Automatic Sprinkler Co., Inc., Mount Vernon, NY, pg. 924
Korthals, Doug, Mgr.-Natl. Sls. & Service--Bunton Company, Louisville, KY, pg. 188
Kortschak, Sepp A., V.P.-Quality Assurance & Regulatory Affairs--Mary Kay Cosmetics Inc., Dallas, TX, pg. 716
Kosar, Doug, Dir.-Mktg.--Cargocaire Engineering Corporation, Amesbury, MA, pg. 220
Kosier, Truman, Mgr.-Sls. & Mktg.--Schweizer Aircraft Corporation, Elmira, NY, pg. 981
Koski, Robert, V.P.-Mktg.--Central Data Corporation, Champaign, IL, pg. 232
Kossack, Susan, Dir.-Mktg.--California State Lottery, Sacramento, CA, pg. 210
Koster, Eugene S., Sr. V.P.-Mktg.--The Acacia Group, Washington, DC, pg. 10
Kotowski, Jack, Dir.-Mktg.--Mission Industries, Santa Barbara, CA, pg. 760
Kotz, Robert A., V.P.-Franchise Services--Comprehensive Business Services Inc., Carlsbad, CA, pg. 612
Kowalski, R. J., Mgr.-Mktg.--Dynamic Controls Corp., South Windsor, CT, pg. 356
Kowalsky, William, V.P.-Fin. & Plng. & Chief Fin. Officer--Advertising Checking Bureau Incorporated, New York, NY, pg. 21
Kozel, Edward, Mgr.-Mktg.--Medical Laboratory Automation, Inc., Pleasantville, NY, pg. 735
Kozel, Suzanne, Dir.-Mktg.--Ginsberg's Institutional Foods, Inc., Hudson, NY, pg. 460
Kozimor, George, Mgr.-Mktg.--E. J. Brooks Company, Newark, NJ, pg. 179
Kraft, Lee Jr., Mgr.-Quality Control--Jofco Inc., Jasper, IN, pg. 595
Kraft, Neil, Dir.-Image--Esprit de Corp., San Francisco, CA, pg. 388
Kraisinger, Gary, V.P.-RichMix Products--Ritchie Corporation, Wichita, KS, pg. 936
Kramer, Jay, V.P.-Mktg. Services--Darda Inc. (USA), Baltimore, MD, pg. 315
Kran, T., Mktg. Dir.--Levi Strauss France, S.A., Les Ulis,, France, pg. 671
Kranitz, John J., Mgr.-Mktg.--Microflect Company, Inc., Salem, OR, pg. 749
Kranz, Lisa, V.P.-Mktg.--Giant Eagle, Inc., Pittsburgh, PA, pg. 455
Krasin, Craig, V.P., Mktg.--Arcinco, Inc., Garfield, NJ, pg. 81
Kratz, Jack, Dir.-Grp. Exec. Mktg.--Pabst Brewing Co., San Antonio, TX, pg. 959
Kraus, John R., Dir.-Mktg.--Wilmorite Inc., Rochester, NY, pg. 1193
Krauss, Marvin, Dir.-Mktg.--Gourmet, New York, NY, pg. 19
Kravecas, M. Adler, V.P.-Mktg.--Myron Manufacturing Corporation, Maywood, NJ, pg. 780
Kravitz, Sheldon J., V.P.-Adv. & Consumer Mktg.--Trans World Airlines, Inc., Mount Kisco, NY, pg. 561
Krebs, Karen, Mktg. Coord.--American FoodService, Dallas, TX, pg. 60
Krecl, Bob L., V.P.-Mktg. & Sls.--General Time Corp., Norcross, GA, pg. 451
Krecl, Robert, Dir.-Mktg.--Westclox, Norcross, GA, pg. 451
Kremer, Harold, V.P.-Special Projects--Siemer Milling Company, Teutopolis, IL, pg. 1002
Kretzinger, D. Keith, Dir.-Mktg.--The Van Metre Companies, Burke, VA, pg. 1144
Krieg, Norm, Mktg. Dir.--Rogers & Associates Advertising, Inc., Santa Clara, CA, pg. 943
Kriskey, Nancy, Mktg. Asst.--The Goldhirsh Group Inc., Boston, MA, pg. 467

Kristie, Joe, V.P.-Corporate Mktg.--Cole Taylor Financial Group, Wheeling, IL, pg. 260
Kroetch, Jerry, V.P.-Sls. & Mktg.--Scotchman Industries, Inc., Philip, SD, pg. 982
Kroft, Gina, Mgr.-Pub. Rels. & Special Events--Crested Butte Mountain Resort, Inc., Mount Crested Butte, CO, pg. 299
Krone, Richard, V.P., Direct Mktg.--Letven-Diccicco, Inc., Horsham, PA, pg. 669
Kroshinsky, Frances, Mgr.-Mktg., Export Div.--Leviton Mfg. Co., Inc., Little Neck, NY, pg. 671
Krueger, Larry, Exec. V.P.-Mktg.--Arby's, Inc., Miami Beach, FL, pg. 243
Kruger, Holly, Dir.-Mktg.--Del Taco, Inc., Costa Mesa, CA, pg. 325
Krugler, Philip, Mgr.-Mktg. Services--Penco Products, Oaks, PA, pg. 857
Krump-Moss, Nan, Dir.-Mkt. Devel.--Hyatt Hotels Corporation, Chicago, IL, pg. 495
Krumwiede, James, V.P.-Sls. & Mktg.--C-Line Products, Inc., Des Plaines, IL, pg. 198
Krusiewicz, Betty, V.P.-Mktg.--Sun Computers, Inc., Carson, CA, pg. 1058
Kubiak, Rick, Mgr.-Mktg. & Communications--Carver Boat Corp., Pulaski, WI, pg. 758
Kuhn, Tom, V.P.-Mktg., Sheer Hosiery--Kayser-Roth Hosiery, Inc., Greensboro, NC, pg. 262
Kuhn, Tom, V.P.-Mktg.--Sheer Hosiery Div., Greensboro, NC, pg. 263
Kuhn, Wendy, Mktg. Services Mgr.--Barkley & Evergreen Advertising, Inc., Shawnee Mission, KS, pg. 120
Kujawa, Thomas R., Mktg. Services Mgr.--The Marlin Company, Springfield, MO, pg. 710
Kulbeda, James, Dir.-Mktg.-Indus. Prods. Group--Wilton Corporation, Palatine, IL, pg. 1194
Kulick, Tom, Mgr.-Sls.--Goebel Art, Inc., Coon Rapids, MN, pg. 464
Kulik, Paul, Dir.-Sls., Mktg. & Adv.--Hennells, Inc., Ferndale, MI, pg. 530
Kull, Michael J., Sr. Exec. V.P.-Mktg.--Druther's International, Inc., Louisville, KY, pg. 350
Kullmann, Don, V.P.-Mktg.--Prairie Farms Dairy, Inc., Carlinville, IL, pg. 884
Kulwicki, Chris, V.P.-Mktg.--The Keller Manufacturing Co., Inc., Corydon, IN, pg. 621
Kuncilo, Robert, Mgr.-Mktg./Communications--OCTus, San Diego, CA, pg. 818
Kupstas, Michael J., V.P.-Field Mktg. & Promo.--Jerrico, Inc., Lexington, KY, pg. 229
Kurdziel, Theodore, V.P.-Prod. & Treas.--Kurdziel Industries, Inc., Muskegon, MI, pg. 646
Kurie, E. J., V.P.-Ross Air Systems--Somerset Technologies, Inc., Somerset, NJ, pg. 1017
Kurinsky, Roger, V.P.-Mktg.--Ivex Packaging Corporation, Lincolnshire, IL, pg. 583
Kurkjy, Neil, Dir.-Sls. & Mktg.--Rapid Power Technologies, Inc., Brookfield, CT, pg. 913
Kurland, Richard M., V.P.-Mktg.--Handy Manufacturing Co., Inc., Newark, NJ, pg. 505
Kurtz, Jackie, V.P.-Mktg. & Admin.--Pioneer Engineering & Manufacturing Co., Warren, MI, pg. 871
Kurzman, Alan M., V.P.-Mktg.--Triangle Pacific Corporation, Dallas, TX, pg. 1112
Kurzman, Allen J., V.P.-Mktg. Services--Avis, Inc., Garden City, NY, pg. 102
Kusek, Ed, Dir.-Mktg.--Turtle Wax, Inc., Chicago, IL, pg. 1120
Kuszmaul, Marcia, Dir.-Mktg. Communications & Graphics--American Library Association, Chicago, IL, pg. 57
Kyle, Kurt, Sls. & Mktg. Coord.--McNeil & NRM, Inc., Akron, OH, pg. 732
LaBadie, Jim, Dir.-Sls. & Mktg.--Lancaster Host Resort, Lancaster, PA, pg. 653
LaBarre, M.Y., Grp. Mktg. Mgr.--Diamond Crystal Specialty Foods, Inc., Wilmington, MA, pg. 335
LaCalamita, Tony, Mgr.-Regional Sls. & Mktg.--Wayne Corporation, Richmond, IN, pg. 1169
Lachapelle, A. D., V.P.-Mktg.--Reed & Barton Corporation, Taunton, MA, pg. 920
Lackman, Jack G., V.P.-Mktg.--American Crystal Sugar Company, Moorhead, MN, pg. 51
Laesser, Jerry, V.P.-Mktg. & Franchise Devel. & Chief Oper. Officer--One Hour Martinizing Dry Cleaning Franchise (System), Cincinnati, OH, pg. 826
Laetz, Curtis J., V.P.-Mktg.--Trak International, Inc., Port Washington, WI, pg. 1106
LaForce, Barbara, Mktg. Coord.--Pawling Corporation, Pawling, NY, pg. 852
LaFrankie, J.L., V.P.-Mktg.--Farm Stores, Inc., Miami, FL, pg. 401
Lagano, Paul G. Lagano, V.P.-Sls. & Mktg.--Global Turnkey Systems Inc., Waldwick, NJ, pg. 463
Lagios, Arthur, V.P.- Mktg.--Harvey Construction Company, Inc., Bedford, NH, pg. 515
LaGrega, Andrew T., Sr. V.P.-Sls., Mktg., Adv. & Human Resources--Wilder Management Associates, Waltham, MA, pg. 1189
Laity, Daniel M., Mgr.-Mktg. Services--Ludlow Composites Corporation, Fremont, OH, pg. 686
Lakes, Carrie, Dir.-Mktg.--Jeff Wyler Dealer Group, Inc., Cincinnati, OH, pg. 1206
LaLiberty, Dennis, V.P.-Mktg.--Frank Consolidated Enterprises Inc., Des Plaines, IL, pg. 428
Laloggia, Mary, Mktg. Admin. Asst.--Green Leaf Ventures, Inc., San Diego, CA, pg. 484
Lamb, Robert, V.P.- Mktg./Strategic Plng.--TMP Worldwide, Inc., New York, NY, pg. 1073
Lamb, Vickie, Mgr.-Product--Sunshine/Salerno, Inc. (NJ), Sayreville, NJ, pg. 439
Lambert, John, Natl. Media Dir.--Leo Burnett Connaghan & May Pty. Ltd., North Sydney,, Australia, pg. 192
Lambert, Kurt, Dir.-Mktg.-Textured Yarns--Milliken & Co., Inc., Spartanburg, SC, pg. 755
Lamer, Allan, V.P.-Mktg. & Adv. Mgr.--Kewaunee Engineering Corp., Kewaunee, WI, pg. 707
Lamer, Allan, V.P.-Mktg.--MTI Leasing, Ltd., Sturgeon Bay, WI, pg. 707
Lamer, Allan, V.P.-Mktg. & Adv. Mgr.--Shuttlelift, Inc., Sturgeon Bay, WI, pg. 707
LaMonica, Michael, V.P.-Sls. & Mktg.--Bridgeport Machines, Inc., Bridgeport, CT, pg. 175
Lamson, Kerry P., Dir.-Mktg.--Daxus Corporation, Pittsburgh, PA, pg. 319
Lanahan, Christopher, V.P.-Sls. & Mktg., MRO--Carey Machinery & Supply Company, Baltimore, MD, pg. 218
Lancaster, Lisa, Mgr.-Mktg.--Grindmaster Corporation, Louisville, KY, pg. 488
Lancer, Mickey E., Mgr.-Customer & Mktg. Services--Oregon Freeze Dry, Inc., Albany, OR, pg. 829
Lanctot, Edmund W., Jr., V.P.-Sls. & Mktg.--J.W. Window Components, Inc., Tampa, FL, pg. 1162
Landisi, Ronald J., V.P.-Elect. Distr. & Dir.-Mktg.--Leviton Mfg. Co., Inc., Little Neck, NY, pg. 671
Landolfi, Tony, Dir.-Mktg. & Mgr.-Natl. Sls.--4C Foods Corporation, Brooklyn, NY, pg. 427
Landry, Bob, V.P.-Sls. & Marketing--Pioneer Aluminum, Inc., Los Angeles, CA, pg. 871
Landry, Marlon, V.P.-Mktg. & Estimating--Intrepid Enterprises, Inc., Harvey, LA, pg. 581
Landy, Thomas, V.P.-Sls. & Mktg.--World Dryer Corp., Berkeley, IL, pg. 1027
Lang, Karena, Mgr.-Mktg.--Besteel Industries, Irvine, CA, pg. 147
Lang, Richard A., Jr., V.P.-Adv., Sls. & Mktg.--Dad's Products Co., Inc., Meadville, PA, pg. 310
Lange, Eric, Dir.-Mktg.--Cincom Systems, Inc., Cincinnati, OH, pg. 250
Langenberger, Conrad, V.P.-N. American Sls. & Mktg.--Simplicity Manufacturing, Inc., Port Washington, WI, pg. 1006
Langla, Leslye, Dir.-Sls. & Mktg.--Markair, Inc., Anchorage, AK, pg. 708
Langston, Michael D., Sr. V.P.-Opers. & Mktg.--Atlantic Aviation Corp., New Castle, DE, pg. 94
Lankford, Mickey, V.P.-Mktg.--Walton Monroe Mills, Inc., Monroe, GA, pg. 1162
Lanman, Don, V.P., Dir. Database Mktg.--John Williams & Associates, Ltd., Sausalito, CA, pg. 1190
Lanz, Dennis D., V.P.-Mktg.--Hammel, Green & Abrahamson, Inc., Minneapolis, MN, pg. 504
Laos, A.G., Dir.-Mktg. & Sls.--Carter Day Co., Minneapolis, MN, pg. 226
Laos, A.G., Dir.-Sls. & Mktg.--Carter Day International, Inc., Minneapolis, MN, pg. 226
Lapides, James A., V.P.-Mktg. & Opers--United Aluminum Corporation, North Haven, CT, pg. 1130
LaPorta, Carol, Sr. V.P.-Mktg.--Pip Printing, Agoura Hills, CA, pg. 616
LaQuintano, T., V.P.-Sls. & Mktg.--Dietzgen Corporation, Des Plaines, IL, pg. 337
Larime, Michael W., V.P.-Sls. & Mktg.--Thetford Corporation, Ann Arbor, MI, pg. 357
Larison, Pamela, Mgr.-Mktg. & Personnel Devel.--Columbia Paint Co., Spokane, WA, pg. 265
Larkin, Steve, V.P.-Mktg. & Sls. Mgr.--Kluener Foods Co., Cincinnati, OH, pg. 636
Larsen, Johannes, Dir.-Mktg.--West Chemical Products, Inc., Princeton, NJ, pg. 1172
Larsen, Johannes, V.P.-Mktg.--Penetone Corp., Tenafly, NJ, pg. 1172
Larsen, Johannes, V.P.-Mktg.--West Pentone Inc., Ville d'Anjou,, Canada, pg. 1172
Larson, David, V.P.-Sls. & Mktg.--Wells Aluminum Corp., South Bend, IN, pg. 1175
Larson, Debra, V.P.-Mktg. & Training--Time Systems, Inc., Phoenix, AZ, pg. 1097
Lasse, Tom, Dir.-Plng.--ABC Supply Company, Inc., Beloit, WI, pg. 2
Lassers, Pam, V.P.-Adv. & Public Rels.--Marilyn Miglin, Inc., Chicago, IL, pg. 752
Latham, Cindy, Dir.-Mktg.--The Fuller Brush Company, Great Bend, KS, pg. 436
Latta, Stephen C., Sr. V.P.-Mktg.--Bioproducts, Inc., Brecksville, OH, pg. 152
Laufer, Dorris, V.P.-Mktg.--Kroch's & Brentano's, Inc., Chicago, IL, pg. 645
Laughter, Barbara, Dir.-Mktg.--Everbrite, Inc., Greenfield, WI, pg. 391
Lauter, Nancy A., Sr. V.P.-Mkt. Devel. & Intl. Sls.--McDougal, Littell & Company, Evanston, IL, pg. 728
Lavely, Anthony M., Exec. V.P.-Mktg.--Jerrico, Inc., Lexington, KY, pg. 229
Lavely, Anthony M., Exec. V.P.-Adv. & Mktg.--Long John Silver's, Inc., Lexington, KY, pg. 229
Lavin, Steven, V.P.-Mktg.--Kenneth Gordon New Orleans, Ltd., New Orleans, LA, pg. 472
Lawrence, Jim, V.P.-Corp. Communications--Earle M. Jorgensen Company, Brea, CA, pg. 605
Lawrence, Ralph G., Sr. V.P.-Sls. & Mktg.--Hyde Manufacturing Co., Southbridge, MA, pg. 556
Lawrence, Tom, Sr. V.P.-Sls. & Mktg.--Taco Inc., Cranston, RI, pg. 1076
Layne, James, Telemetry Products Mgr.--Repco Incorporated, Orlando, FL, pg. 927
Lazare, Peter, Dir.-Mktg.--Gurney Industries Inc., Gastonia, NC, pg. 495
Le Van, Sharon, Sr. V.P.-Mktg. & Creative Services--Aramis, Inc., New York, NY, pg. 389
Leach, Mike, Dir.-Mktg.--Carquest Corporation, Tarrytown, NY, pg. 224
Leach, Peter, Mgr.-Sls.--D. D. Bean & Sons Co., Jaffrey, NH, pg. 129
Leach, Thomas , Dir.-Sls. & Mktg.--Horton Homes, Inc., Eatonton, GA, pg. 545
Leadbetter, Pamela J., V.P.-Mktg.--Potrait Industries Corporation, Chesapeake, VA, pg. 675
Leaman, Donald H., Jr., Dir.-Mktg.--Rystan Company, Inc., Little Falls, NJ, pg. 222
Leaman, June, Sr. V.P.-Creative Mktg.--Estee Lauder, Inc., New York, NY, pg. 389
Leavitt, R. Alison, Mktg.-Communications--Medical Laboratory Automation, Inc., Pleasantville, NY, pg. 735
Leavsley, Ron, Dir., Mktg. & Strategic Plng.--Paul A. De Jesse, Inc. Advertising, Freehold, NJ, pg. 321
Leback, Elissa, Sr. V.P.-Mktg. Strategy--Viacom Enterprises, New York, NY, pg. 785
Lee, Richard, Dir.-Mktg.--Tone Commander Systems, Redmond, WA, pg. 1101
Lee, Richard E., Dir.-Mktg.--The Lathrop Company, Toledo, OH, pg. 660
Leeser, M.B., Sr. V.P.-Sls. & Mktg.--Thrall Car Mfg. Co., Chicago Heights, IL, pg. 350
LeFebvre, Timothy, V.P.-Domestic Sls. & Mktg.--NESLAB Instruments, Inc., Newington, NH, pg. 798
LeFevre, Robert M., Sr. V.P.-Mktg. & Sls.--The United States Playing Card Company, Cincinnati, OH, pg. 1136
Lehman, Mike, Dir.-Mktg.--Bard Mfg. Co., Bryan, OH, pg. 119
Lehmann, G.J., Mgr.-Sls. & Mktg.--Electronic Measurements, Inc., Neptune, NJ, pg. 145
Lehrer, Mames, Mgr.-Mktg.--Jeffersonville Distribution Center, Jeffersonville, IN, pg. 832
Leitgen, Loyal, Dir.-Intl. Mktg.--Universal Cooperatives, Inc., Minneapolis, MN, pg. 1138
Leitman, Jack, Dir.-Mktg.--W. Braun Distribution Center, Summit, IL, pg. 172
Leman, Jim, Dir.-Sls. & Mktg.--Meridian Technology Leasing Services, Deerfield, IL, pg. 740
LeMaster, Curt, V.P.-Mdsg.--Henry Bacon Building Materials, Inc., Issaquah, WA, pg. 113
Lembree, John A., V.P.-Mktg.--Foamex L.P., East Providence, RI, pg. 1121
Lemin, J., V.P.-Cameron Machine--Somerset Technologies, Inc., Somerset, NJ, pg. 1017
Lemm, Dick, Dir.-Mktg. & Adv.--Mini Mart, Inc., Casper, WY, pg. 757
Lemoyne, Herb, V.P.-Sls. & Mktg.--H.H. Brown Shoe Company, Inc., Greenwich, CT, pg. 182
Lenarth, Rick, V.P.-Sls.--Polymer Development Laboratories, Inc., Orange, CA, pg. 880
Lennertz, Carl, Dir.-Mktg.--Alfred A. Knopf, Inc., New York, NY, pg. 20
Lennon, John J., V.P.-Mktg.--Wisdom Imports Sales Co. Inc., Irvine, CA, pg. 1198
Leny, Sally, V.P.-Mktg.--Container Products Inc., Southfield, MI, pg. 278
Leon, Frank, Dir.-Mktg.--AMI Industries, Inc., Colorado Springs, CO, pg. 5
Leona, Ronald, V.P.-Mktg.--Pressman Toy Corp., New York, NY, pg. 887
Leonard, Jack, Mgr.-Mktg.--Quad Systems Corporation, Horsham, PA, pg. 902
Leonard, Michael, V.P., Mktg. Services--Larkin Meeder & Schweidel, Dallas, TX, pg. 659
Leong, James, V.P.-Sls., Mktg. & Adv.--Mutual Distributors Ltd., Honolulu, HI, pg. 778
Lepore, John, Mktg., Sls. & Adv. Mgr.--MFE Instruments, Beverly, MA, pg. 1050
Lescoe, Daniel, V.P.-Sls. & Mktg.--Big Y Foods Inc., Springfield, MA, pg. 149
Leshiniski, Bruce A., V.P.-Sls. & Mktg.--Newly Weds Foods Inc., Chicago, IL, pg. 804
Lesinki, Tom, V.P.-Mktg./Taren--Cole of California, Los Angeles, CA, pg. 1079
Lesinski, Tom, V.P.-Mktg.--Taren Holdings, Inc., Los Angeles, CA, pg. 1078
Leslie, James L., V.P.-Grp. Reinsurance Mktg. Services--American United Life Insurance Company, Indianapolis, IN, pg. 65
Leslie, Susan, Dir.-Mktg.--Merriam-Webster, Inc., Springfield, MA, pg. 381
Lesneski, Bernard, V.P.-Engrng. & Mktg.--McNeil & NRM., Inc., Akron, OH, pg. 732
Letten, Brian, Grp. V.P.-Mktg. & Sls.--Bata Shoe Co., Inc., Belcamp, MD, pg. 201
Leu, Dennis, V.P.-Mktg. & Sls.--Velsicol Chemical Corporation, Rosemont, IL, pg. 1147
LeVan, Sharon, Sr. V.P.-Creative Mktg. Devel.--Estee Lauder, Inc., New York, NY, pg. 389
Levenick, Tom, Dir.-Mktg. & Sls.--Brooks Beverages Inc., Columbus, OH, pg. 179
Levine, Daniel, Dir., Bus. Devel.--Romann & Tannenholz Advertising, Inc., New York, NY, pg. 945
Levine, Michael E., Exec. V.P.-Mktg.--Northwest Airlines, Inc., Saint Paul, MN, pg. 782
Levine, Steve, V.P.-Mktg.--Bel-Art Products, Pequannock, NJ, pg. 133
Levinson, Cara, Mgr.-Mktg. Services--LevLane Advertising, Inc., Bala-Cynwyd, PA, pg. 671
Levinson, Sara, Exec. V.P.-New Bus. Devel.--MTV Networks, New York, NY, pg. 785
Levis, Marcia, V.P.-Mktg./Sls.--Muelhens, Inc., Orange, CT, pg. 774
Levitt, Wayne M., V.P.-Mktg.--Gate Petroleum Company, Jacksonville, FL, pg. 445
Levy, Bruce, V.P.-Mktg.--O'Brien Energy Systems Inc., Philadelphia, PA, pg. 820
Levy, Harold L., Sr. V.P.-Sls. & Mktg. & New Bus. Contact--TMP Worldwide, Inc., New York, NY, pg. 1073
Lewin, G., Sr. V.P.-Mktg.--Jameco Industries, Inc., Wyandanch, NY, pg. 588
Lewis, Brad, V.P.-Sls. & Mktg.--Crystal Cabinet Works, Inc., Princeton, MN, pg. 303
Lewis, Harry D., V.P.-Mktg.--American Gilsonite Co., Salt Lake City, UT, pg. 55
Lewis, Lisa, Dir.-Sls, Mktg. & Adv.--Music Sales Corporation, New York, NY, pg. 777
Lewis, Mary, Mgr.-Mktg. Communications--Ingersoll International Inc., Rockford, IL, pg. 568

Corporate Responsibilities Index

Lewis, Mary, Mgr.-Mktg. Communications--The Ingersoll Milling Machine Co., Rockford, IL, pg. 568
Lewis, Michael E., Mgr.-Sls. & Mktg.--Ekstrom Industries, Inc., Farmington Hills, MI, pg. 180
Lewis, Paul J., V.P.-Sls. & Mktg.--Telesensory, Mountain View, CA, pg. 1085
Lewis, Randy, Dir.-Mktg. & Sls.--RTMX-Uniflex Inc., Chapel Hill, NC, pg. 908
Lewitzke, Ruth, Mgr.-Mktg. Services--Pabst Brewing Co., San Antonio, TX, pg. 959
Libby, Jackson A., Exec. V.P.-Mktg.--Eastern Fine Paper, Incorporated, Brewer, ME, pg. 363
Liberatore, R., V.P.-Corp. Sls. & Mktg.--Formation, Inc., Moorestown, NJ, pg. 424
Lichtenberg, Ronna G., Sr. V.P. & Dir.-Mktg.--Prudential Securities Inc., New York, NY, pg. 897
Liebenson, Sid, Exec. V.P., Dir. Mktg.--Kobs & Draft Advertising, Inc., Chicago, IL, pg. 109
Lieberman, Michael J., Exec. V.P., Bus. Devel.--Lieberman-Appalucci, Allentown, PA, pg. 675
Lieberman, Milton, Sr. V.P.-Mktg.--Parade Publications Inc., New York, NY, pg. 847
Liebman, Gary, V.P.-Mktg.--Carpeteria, Inc., Valencia, CA, pg. 224
Liebman, Paul, Mgr.-Mktg.--Coilcraft, Inc., Cary, IL, pg. 259
Lifson, Al, V.P.-Sls. & Mktg.--Standard Chlorine Chemical Company, Kearny, NJ, pg. 1035
Lightner, Roy, V.P. & Dir.-Mktg. Services--Carden & Cherry, Inc., Nashville, TN, pg. 217
Lincer, Walt, V.P.-Sls. & Mktg.--Citrus World Inc., Lake Wales, FL, pg. 251
Lind, Ted. C., V.P.-Sls. & Mktg.--Hull Corporation, Hatboro, PA, pg. 552
Linda, Gerald, Sec., Dir. Client & Mktg. Services--Kurtzman/Slavin/Linda, Inc., Northfield, IL, pg. 646
Linde, Keith, V.P.-Mktg. Services--Days Inns of America, Inc., Parsippany, NJ, pg. 1100
Lindeman, Gary, Dir.-Mktg. & Sls.--Microband Companies, Inc., Fairfield, NJ, pg. 748
Lindemulder, David, V.P.-Mktg.--MBT Associates, Inc., San Francisco, CA, pg. 691
Lindley, Peter, V.P.-Sls. & Mktg.--Sunroc Corporation, Media, PA, pg. 1062
Lindley, Peter M., V.P.-Sls. & Mktg.--Telkee Inc., Media, PA, pg. 1062
Lindsay, Mark, V.P.-Sls. & Mktg.--George Lithograph, San Francisco, CA, pg. 452
Lindsey, David, Mgr.-Mktg.--Doron Precision Systems, Inc., Binghamton, NY, pg. 346
Lindsey, Francis, V.P.-Consumer Appliance Mktg.--Conair Corporation, Stamford, CT, pg. 272
Lindsey, Ralph, V.P.-Mktg.--Barber Dairies, Inc., Birmingham, AL, pg. 119
Lindsey, Ralph, Mktg. Dir.--Barber Ice Cream Company, Birmingham, AL, pg. 119
Lindsey, Sam, Mgr.-Mktg.--J.L. Lester & Son, Inc., Rockmart, GA, pg. 668
Lindstrom, Riitta-Leena, Mktg Dir--Masterfoods Oy, Helsinki, , Finland, pg. 714
Linduska, Paul S., Mgr.-Sls. & Mktg.--Andersen Windows Inc., Bayport, MN, pg. 72
Linham, Linda Moore, V.P.-Mktg.--Renaissance Publishing Co., Inc., Auburn, IN, pg. 926
Linhart, Janette, Mgr.-Mktg.--CHEMCENTRAL Corporation, Bedford Park, IL, pg. 241
Link, Gary F., Dir.-Mktg. Services--Howard Needles Tammen & Bergendoff, Kansas City, MO, pg. 547
Linskey, Patrick M., Exec. V.P. & Dir.-Mktg.--The National Enquirer, Lantana, FL, pg. 788
Lipka, Carole, Dir.-Mktg.--Keeney Manufacturing Co., Newington, CT, pg. 620
Lipscomb, William, V.P.-Sls. & Mktg.--Plastic Packaging, Inc., Hickory, NC, pg. 875
Liscik, Raymond, V.P.-Adv., Mktg., Sls. & Pub. Rels.--JCI Data Processing, Inc., Delran, NJ, pg. 584
Lisker, Meshulam, Sec. & Mktg. Dir.--Antwerp Diamond Distributors Inc., New York, NY, pg. 77
Literski, Sally, Mgr.-Mktg.--Malt-O-Meal Company, Minneapolis, MN, pg. 703
Littfin, Jack, Mgr.-Mktg. & Pur.--Littfin Lumber Company, Winsted, MN, pg. 678
Little, John, Dir.-Mktg.--Rexall Group, Fort Lauderdale, FL, pg. 1060
Littleton, Connie, Dir.-Mktg. Services--Perdue Farms Inc., Salisbury, MD, pg. 860
Litwin, Frank J., Sr. V.P.-Mktg.--Society for Savings Bancorp, Inc., Hartford, CT, pg. 1016
Livecchi, Jim, Dir.-Bus. Devel.--Hameroff/Milenthal/Spence, Inc., Columbus, OH, pg. 503
Lively, Larry G., V.P.-Mktg.--Federal Compress & Warehouse Company, Inc., Memphis, TN, pg. 404
Livingston, Frederick C., Sr. V.P.-Mktg.--Continental Cablevision, Boston, MA, pg. 278
Livorsi, Joe, Sr. V.P.-Mktg.--Randall's Food Markets, Inc., Houston, TX, pg. 911
LLona, Tom, Mgr.-Intl. Sls. & Mktg.--Code-A-Phone Corp., Clackamas, OR, pg. 258
Locke, Ralph, V.P.-Mktg.--Syar Industries, Inc., Napa, CA, pg. 1068
Locke, Robert, Sr. V.P.-Plng. & Devel. & Asst. Sec.--Pueblo International, Inc., Pompano Beach, FL, pg. 899
Lockner, Jack, Sr. V.P.-Sls. & Mktg.--Bankers Systems Inc., Saint Cloud, MN, pg. 117
Loftis, Mike, Dir.-Mktg.--Lincoln Property Company, Dallas, TX, pg. 676
Loftus, Michael J., V.P.-Mktg.--Klein Tools Inc., Skokie, IL, pg. 635
Logie, James A., V.P.-Mktg.--J. L. Hammett Company, Braintree, MA, pg. 504
Lohmeyer, Donna, V.P., Mktg. Services--Lohmeyer Simpson Communications, Inc., Morristown, NJ, pg. 681
Lohr, D.G., V.P. & Dir.-Mktg. & Sls.-Paints--California Products Corp., Cambridge, MA, pg. 210
Lombardi, Michael, V.P.-Mktg.--PacifiCare of California, Cypress, CA, pg. 1127
Long, Nancy, V.P., Mktg. & Res. Dir.--Thomas & Perkins, Denver, CO, pg. 1093
Longino, Susie, V.P.-Mktg.-Atlanta Mdsg. & Gift Mkt.--Atlanta Market Center, Atlanta, GA, pg. 94
Longley, Russell, Dir.-Mktg.--SOR Inc., Lenexa, KS, pg. 963
Looyenga, R.L., Sr. V.P.-Mktg.--Auto-Owners Insurance, Lansing, MI, pg. 100
Lopez, Carlos, Dir.-Mktg.--Aero Peru Corporation, Miami, FL, pg. 22
Lorass, Dan, Dir.-Mktg.--Cold Spring Granite Company, Minnetonka, MN, pg. 259
Lorenz, Gerald, Dir.-Sales & Mktg.--Electro-Science Laboratories, Inc., King of Prussia, PA, pg. 375
Lorenz, Larry, V.P.-Mktg.--Cummins-Allison Corp., Mount Prospect, IL, pg. 305
Lorenze, A. John, V.P.-Mktg.--Standard-Knapp, Inc., Portland, CT, pg. 1036
Lotz, G.W., Dir.-Bus. Devel.--Dick Corporation, Large, PA, pg. 335
Loudon, Michael H., Dir.-Mktg.--Sunkist Growers, Processed Products, Ontario, CA, pg. 1061
Loughrey, Phil, V.P.-Mktg.--State Industries Inc., Ashland City, TN, pg. 1041
Loughridge, John, Mgr.-Mktg. & Intl. Mngmnt. Information Systems--Pacific Foods, Inc., Kent, WA, pg. 840
Louis, Francois, Dir.-Mktg.--National Banner Company, Dallas, TX, pg. 786
Love, Kelly, V.P.-Mktg.--Ohio Machinery Co., Cleveland, OH, pg. 822
Lovelace, H. E., V.P.-Mktg.--Ed Taylor Construction Co., Tucker, GA, pg. 1081
Lovell, Robert B., V.P.-Mktg. & Adv.--Coca Cola Bottling Co. United, Inc., Birmingham, AL, pg. 257
Lovoy, Cynthia, Publicity Mgr.--American Cast Iron Pipe Co., Birmingham, AL, pg. 50
Lowery, Roger L., V.P.-Mktg.--Alabama Metal Industries Corporation, Birmingham, AL, pg. 28
Loyd, Bill, V.P.-Sls. & Mktg.--Burks Prosser/Enpo Industries, Inc., Decatur, IL, pg. 507
Loyd, Bill, V.P.-Mktg. & Sls.--Burks Pumps, Inc., Piqua, OH, pg. 507
Loyd, Bill, V.P.-Sls. & Mktg.--Prosser/Enpo Industries, Piqua, OH, pg. 507
Loyd, Bill, V.P.-Sales & Mktg.--Barnes Pumps, Inc., Mansfield, OH, pg. 507
Loyd, Bill, V.P.-Sales & Mktg.--AMW Industries Inc., Conway, AR, pg. 507
Lucas, Karen, Mktg. Coord.--Whiting-Turner Contracting Co., Baltimore, MD, pg. 1187
Luchs, Kenneth, V.P.-Mktg., Sls. & Adv.--Reliable Stores, Inc., Columbia, MD, pg. 925
Ludlow, Ted, V.P.-Sls. & Mktg.--Bedford Industries, Inc., Worthington, MN, pg. 131
Ludwig, Bill, Dir.-Sls. & Mktg.--Polka Dot Dairy, Hastings, MN, pg. 879
Lueken, Tom, Mgr.-Sls. & Mktg., Retail Div.--R.S. Owens, Chicago, IL, pg. 834
Luis, Jose, Dir.-Human Resources & Mktg.--La Reina, Inc., Los Angeles, CA, pg. 649
Luiso, Sal, Dir.-Natl. Mktg.--Coopers & Lybrand, New York, NY, pg. 283
Lukas, Jerome J., V.P.-Mktg.--Harvard Industries, Inc., Farmingdale, NJ, pg. 514
Lund, Eric, V.P.-Mktg.--Great Plains Manufacturing, Inc., Assaria, KS, pg. 482
Lund, J., Mgr.-Sls. & Mktg.--Simmons Juvenile Products Co., Inc., New London, WI, pg. 1008
Lund, Jeffrey, V.P.-Process & Food Sls.--Lakeside Foods, Inc., Manitowoc, WI, pg. 651
Lund, Robert, Mgr.-Intl. Sls. & Mktg.--Hamilton Co., Inc., Reno, NV, pg. 503
Lundy, Dee, Dir.-Sls. & Mktg.--Family Inns of America, Inc., Pigeon Forge, TN, pg. 398
Lunt, Colby, V.P.-Mktg.--Rogers, Lunt & Bowlen Co., Greenfield, MA, pg. 943
Lunz, William, Dir.-Adv. & Mktg.--Plantation Foods Inc., Waco, TX, pg. 874
Luptak, John J., V.P.-Mktg. & Sec.--Niagara Therapy Mfg. Corp., Stanley, NC, pg. 806
Lurio, David, V.P.-Mktg.--Elbeco Incorporated, Reading, PA, pg. 372
Lushin, David, Gen. Mgr.-Mktg. Services--C&A Wallcoverings, Cleveland, OH, pg. 262
Lutter, A.W. Jr., Sr. V.P.-Mktg. & Bus. Affairs--National Steel & Shipbuilding Company, San Diego, CA, pg. 794
Lutz, Charles, Sr. V.P., Chief Mktg. Officer--Penny & Speier Inc., Houston, TX, pg. 858
Luxion, Clifford A., Mgr.-Business Devel.--Wil-Freds Construction, Inc., Aurora, IL, pg. 1189
Luzi, Armin L., Mgr.-Mktg.--Thetford Corporation, Ann Arbor, MI, pg. 357
Lynch, Bill, V.P.-Sls. & Mktg.--Dukane Ultrasonics Div., Saint Charles, IL, pg. 352
Lynch, Dan, V.P.-Mktg.--The Benson Music Group, Nashville, TN, pg. 140
Lynch, Edward, V.P.-Sls. & Intl. Mktg.--Ames Safety Envelope Company, Inc., Somerville, MA, pg. 66
Lynch, Pat, V.P.-Sls. & Mktg.--IDAB International Incorporated, Hampton, VA, pg. 559
Lynch, Scott, Mktg. Mgr.--Jomac, Inc., Warrington, PA, pg. 602
Lynch, Thomas, Mgr.-Mktg. Plng.--Flair Communications Agency, Inc., Chicago, IL, pg. 416
Lyon, David, Dir.-Mktg.--Macklanburg-Duncan Co., Oklahoma City, OK, pg. 697
Lyons, Eugene, Dir.-Mktg.--D.C. Lottery & Charitable Games Control Board, Washington, DC, pg. 308
Lytle, Francin M., V.P. & Dir., Mktg--Gianettino & Meredith Advertising, Short Hills, NJ, pg. 455
Lytle, Robert, V.P.-Sls. & Mktg.--Allied Paper Incorporated, Dayton, OH, pg. 38
Maas, Robert A., V.P.-Sls. & Mktg.--Kalmbach Publishing Co., Milwaukee, WI, pg. 615
MacCausland, Kathy, Adv. Mgr.--Viking Yacht Co., New Gretna, NJ, pg. 1151
MacConnell, Gregory L., V.P.-Mktg. & Plng.--The Myers Group (U.S) Inc., Rouses Point, NY, pg. 780
MacDonald, Roberta P., V.P.-Mktg.--Cabot Creamery Co-Operative Inc., Cabot, VT, pg. 25
Macerias, Leonardo, Dir.-Mktg.--Business Mens Insurance Corporation, Miami, FL, pg. 196
Macfarlane, Bud, V.P.-Sls. & Mktg.--Innovative Plastics Corporation, Orangeburg, NY, pg. 570
MacGregor, John A., Jr., V.P.-Sls. & Mktg.--The Kent Manufacturing Co., Pickens, SC, pg. 623
MacGuidwin, M. Reid, V.P.-Mktg.--Automotive News, Detroit, MI, pg. 101
Machamer, Lamont, V.P.-Sls. & Mktg.--Dyatron/Bondo Corporation, Atlanta, GA, pg. 356
MacKenzie, Warren, V.P.-Sls. & Mktg.--Pittsburgh Tube Co., Monaca, PA, pg. 873
Mackey, Bruce W., Sr. V.P., Dir. Plng. & Mktg. Services--Northlich Stolley LaWarre, Cincinnati, OH, pg. 814
Maddox, J.A., V.P.-Mktg. & Sls.--Wilbur Chocolate Co., Inc., Lititz, PA, pg. 219
Maddox, Richard, V.P.-Sls. & Mktg.--Bachmann Industries, Inc., Philadelphia, PA, pg. 108
Mader, John T., Dir.-Mktg.--Monsey Products Company, Kimberton, PA, pg. 766
Madigan, Lisa, Mktg. Asst.--American Mathematical Society, Inc., Providence, RI, pg. 58
Mager, Drew, Dir.-Mktg.--Molded Fiber Glass Co., Union City, PA, pg. 764
Magnacca, Scott, Mgr.-Sls./Mktg.--SBN Systems Inc.-Canadian Operations, Mississauga,, Canada, pg. 960
Magnarella, L.R., V.P.-Contracts & Mktg.--Yardney Technical Products, Inc., Pawcatuck, CT, pg. 1207
Maher, Larry, Mgr.-Sls. & Mkg.--Zappa Plastics, Phillipsburg, NJ, pg. 1216
Mahon, Dale, Dir.-Mktg. (Coated Prods.)--Ivex Packaging Corporation-Troy, Troy, OH, pg. 583
Mahoney, Tom, V.P.-Mktg.--ITA Group, West Des Moines, IA, pg. 560
Maibach, George, V.P.-Sls.--Bentley Mills, Inc., City of Industry, CA, pg. 140
Mailow, Anders E., V.P.-New Devel.--Graphic Controls Corporation, Buffalo, NY, pg. 478
Maiuccoro, Gary, Dir.-Sls. & Mktg.--Imperial Pools, Inc., Latham, NY, pg. 564
Makris, Joann, Sr. V.P.-Mktg.--Capital Bancorp, Miami, FL, pg. 214
Makris, Joann, Sr. V.P.-Mktg.--Capital Bank, Miami, FL, pg. 214
Malcolm, Peter, V.P.-Sls.--The Harter Group, Sturgis, MI, pg. 513
Malcolm, Richard G., V.P.-Direct Mkts. Div.--Blue Cross & Blue Shield of Illinois, Chicago, IL, pg. 160
Malehorn, Jack, Dir.-Mktg. & Consumer Res.--Country Companies Insurance Group, Bloomington, IL, pg. 289
Malehorn, Jack, Dir.-Mktg. & Consumer Res.--Country Mutual Insurance Company, Bloomington, IL, pg. 289
Mallett, Jeff, V.P.-Sls. & Mktg.--Reference Software International, San Francisco, CA, pg. 921
Malloy, Jim, Dir.-Mktg. & Sls.--Advanced Controls, Inc., Irvine, CA, pg. 20
Malone, Francis J., Sr. V.P.-Mktg. Services--The New England, Boston, MA, pg. 799
Malone, LaMar D., V.P.-Product Devel.--Goshen Rubber Co., Inc., Goshen, IN, pg. 472
Maloney, Donal P., V.P.-ESS Sls. & Mktg.--Elliott Company, Jeannette, PA, pg. 378
Maloney, Mark A., V.P.-Mktg.--ULLICO Inc., Washington, DC, pg. 1124
Maloney, Michael M., V.P.-Sls. & Mktg.--American Envelope Company, Chicago, IL, pg. 199
Maloney, William, Sr. V.P.-Mktg., College--Barnes & Noble Bookstores, Inc., New York, NY, pg. 120
Manby, Joel, Sr. V.P.-Mktg. & Sls.--Spring Arbor Distributors, Belleville, MI, pg. 1033
Manchem, Craig, Exec. V.P.-Sls. & Mktg.--Hurst Performances, Inc., Cleveland, OH, pg. 761
Mandel, Mark D., V.P.-Mktg.--Health Management Systems, Inc., New York, NY, pg. 521
Mandell, Alan, V.P.-Sls. & Mktg.--S. E. Huffman Corp., Clover, SC, pg. 551
Manganaro, Leslie, Asst. Dir.-Mktg.--Merriam-Webster, Inc., Springfield, MA, pg. 381
Mankamyer, Dick, Mktg. & Sls.--The Springwall Mattress Co., Akron, OH, pg. 1033
Mann, Barry, Dir.-Sls. & Mktg.--Enidine Incorporated, Orchard Park, NY, pg. 382
Mann, Christopher, V.P.-Sls. & Mktg.--CVC Products, Inc., Rochester, NY, pg. 206
Mann, Janet E., V.P.-Mktg.--ANGUS Chemical Company, Buffalo Grove, IL, pg. 75
Mannara, Joseph R., Dir.-Mktg. Communication--Pfaudler-U.S., Inc., Rochester, NY, pg. 866
Mannion, Dennis, Dir.-Mktg.--The Phillies-A Limited Partnership, Philadelphia, PA, pg. 867
Manno, Ted, Sls. & Mktg. Admin.--Delaware Lottery, Dover, DE, pg. 326
Manocchia, Robert A., V.P. & Reg. Bus. Devel. Mgr.-New England--Gilbane Building Company, Providence, RI, pg. 457
Manwaring, Brian, Mgr.-Mktg.--Marketing Displays International, Inc., Farmington Hills, MI, pg. 709
Manwarring, Mary, V.P.-Design Mktg.--Jerell, Inc., Dallas, TX, pg. 593
Marcantonio, Robert, V.P.-Mktg.--American Office Equipment, La Grange, IL, pg. 58
Marchak, John P., Dir.-Mktg. Admin.--Highlights for Children, Inc., Columbus, OH, pg. 534
Marchi, Graziano, Mgr.-Mktg.--Harold Leonard & Company, Inc., Union, NJ, pg. 667

Marco-Koehler, Antionette, Administrator-Sls. & Mktg.--Octagon Process Inc., Edgewater, NJ, pg. 821
Marconi, Allan P., Dir.-Mktg.--Manhattan Electric Cable Corporation, Rye, NY, pg. 370
Marcus, Bruce T., Sr. V.P.-Corp. Mktg. & Communications--WTTW (Channel 11), Chicago, IL, pg. 1156
Marcus, Paul, Exec. V.P., Entertainment Mktg.--Simon Marketing, Inc., Los Angeles, CA, pg. 1006
Marfuggi, Eugene, Exec. V.P.-Natl. Sls., Mktg. & Adv.--Ferrara Foods & Confections, Inc., New York, NY, pg. 407
Marinello, David, V.P.-Sls. & Mktg.-Branded Prods.--International Jensen Inc., Lincolnshire, IL, pg. 578
Maripa, M., Acct. Planner--J. N. Leoussis Advertising & Marketing S.A., Athens,, Greece, pg. 1072
Markey, Paul, Dir.-Mktg.--American Hardware Mutual Insurance Co., Minnetonka, MN, pg. 55
Marks, Art, V.P.-Mktg.--Resonex, Inc., Sunnyvale, CA, pg. 929
Marks, George V.; Sr. V.P.-Mktg.--Huitt-Zollars, Inc., Dallas, TX, pg. 552
Marks, Sam, Mktg. Consultant--Continental Plastic Card Co., Coral Springs, FL, pg. 280
Markus, Brian, Mgr.-Mktg.--Edelmann Div. of Stant, Inc., Deerfield, IL, pg. 368
Markwart, Robert, Dir.-Mktg.--The Chamberlain Group, Inc., Elmhurst, IL, pg. 350
Markwiese, Bob, Mgr.-Packaging--Pabst Brewing Co., San Antonio, TX, pg. 959
Marlieb, William, Pres.-Mktg. Div.--General Media Publishing Group, New York, NY, pg. 450
Marmion, Bridget, V.P. & Dir.-Mktg. & Sls.--Farrar, Straus & Giroux, Inc., New York, NY, pg. 403
Maroney, Debra, Mktg. Matls. Mgr.--Sentry Group, Rochester, NY, pg. 990
Marr, Clifford T., V.P.-Mktg. & Sls.--Pioneer Plastics Corp., Auburn, ME, pg. 872
Marra, Robert A., Sr. V.P.-Retail Mktg. & Prod. Devel.--John Hancock Mutual Life Insurance Company, Boston, MA, pg. 595
Marriott, Nina, Dir.-Mktg.--Blue Coral International, Newport, Saffron Walden, United Kingdom, pg. 159
Mars, Ann, Mgr.-Sls. & Mktg.--The Flood Company, Hudson, OH, pg. 419
Marsalla, Joe, V.P.-Mktg.--Sacramento Kings, Sacramento, CA, pg. 965
Marsh, D.P., Sr. V.P.-Life Mktg.--Auto-Owners Insurance, Lansing, MI, pg. 100
Marshall, Duff, Mgr.-Sls., Mktg. & Adv.--Marvin Lumber & Cedar Company, Warroad, MN, pg. 716
Marshall, Howard A., Sr. V.P.-Mktg.--Altec Industries, Inc., Birmingham, AL, pg. 45
Marshall, Michael J., V.P.-Sls.--Zymark Corporation, Hopkinton, MA, pg. 1221
Marshall, Walter, Mktg. Mgr.--New England Confectionery Co., Cambridge, MA, pg. 1123
Marshall, Wendy, Mktg. Admin.--Sudbury Consumer Products Company, Phoenix, AZ, pg. 403
Marshik, R.J., Mgr.-Mktg.--The Elwell-Parker Electric Co., Cleveland, OH, pg. 378
Martens, D. A., V.P.-Sls. & Mktg.--West Coast Growers & Packers, Inc., Selma, CA, pg. 1177
Martin, Bruce, V.P.-Pur. & Prods.--Ingram Micro Inc., Santa Ana, CA, pg. 569
Martin, Joel, Dir.-Mktg.--Mannington Wood Floors, High Point, NC, pg. 704
Martin, Kevin, Dir.-Mktg.--Walbridge Aldinger Company, Detroit, MI, pg. 1158
Martin, Kevin L., Dir.-Mktg.--NTH Consultants, Ltd., Farmington Hills, MI, pg. 781
Martin, Lawrence M., V.P.-Mktg. & Sls.--Hitchcock Industries, Inc., Bloomington, MN, pg. 536
Martin, Michael, V.P.-New Prod. Devel.--TSR, Inc., Lake Geneva, WI, pg. 1075
Martin, Michael, Dir.-Sls.--Dacor Corporation, Northfield, IL, pg. 310
Martin, Paul, Mgr.-Mktg.--B & B Motor & Control Corporation, Long Island City, NY, pg. 105
Martin, Phoebe, V.P.-Mktg.--1st Franklin Corporation, Toccoa, GA, pg. 413
Martin, Richard, V.P.-Sls. & Mktg., C&L--Tekra Corporation, New Berlin, WI, pg. 1084
Martinello, Tony, Dir.-Mktg.--Grayline Housewares, Elgin, IL, pg. 480
Martinez, Alicia, Dir.-Mktg. & Corp. Communications--Metropolitan Transportation Authority, New York, NY, pg. 745
Martinez, Paul, V.P.-Sls. & Mktg.--Label-Aire Inc., Fullerton, CA, pg. 649
Martino, Silvio M., Mgr.-Production--Goodman Equipment Corp., Bedford Park, IL, pg. 470
Martinolich, Michael, Mgr.-Medical Adv. & Promotion--Stiefel Laboratories, Inc., Oak Hill, Oak Hill, NY, pg. 1048
Martinsen, Mike, Dir.-Intl. Mktg.--Schwinn Bicycle Company, Chicago, IL, pg. 981
Martz, Robert L., V.P.-Mktg.--Consolidated Metal Products, Inc., Cincinnati, OH, pg. 276
Maskery, Tom, Dir.-Mktg.--Optyl Eyewear Fashion International Corp., Norwood, NJ, pg. 828
Mason, Richard R., Dir.-Mktg.--Prism Integrated Sanitation Management, Inc., Miami, FL, pg. 599
Mason, Sally, Dir.-Mktg.--W. Braun Company, Chicago, IL, pg. 172
Mason, Tom, Dir.-Sls. & Mktg.--Wausau Homes, Inc., Rothschild, WI, pg. 1168
Massey, Lee, Dir.-Mktg.--American Econo-Therm, Tulsa, OK, pg. 865
Massin, Jeff, V.P.-Mktg.--Fleer Corporation, Mount Laurel, NJ, pg. 695
Massini, David P., V.P.-Mktg.--The Universal Steel Co., Cleveland, OH, pg. 265
Masterson, J. E., Dir.-Mktg.--H. Koch & Sons, Anaheim, CA, pg. 262
Mastroianni, David, Dir.-Mktg.--Schiff Products, Inc., Salt Lake City, UT, pg. 1173
Mathews, Dana, Dir.-Mktg.--Interface Electronics Corporation, Hopkinton, MA, pg. 574
Mathews, Mike, Mktg. Mgr.--DIT-MCO Intl., Kansas City, MO, pg. 1206
Mathews, Richard, Mgr.-Mktg. & Sls.--Vacudyne Inc., Chicago Heights, IL, pg. 45
Mathis, Jim, V.P.-Mktg., Sec. & Treas.--Precision Parts Corp., Morristown, TN, pg. 885
Matt, Alfred D., Mgr.-Mktg.--The F. X. Matt Brewing Co., Utica, NY, pg. 721
Matter, Jean-Anne, Sr. V.P., Dir. Mktg. & Res.--Ketchum Advertising/Pittsburgh, Pittsburgh, PA, pg. 625
Mattes, Richard L., V.P.-Mktg.--Koh-I-Noor, Inc., Bloomsbury, NJ, pg. 639
Matteson, Raymond W., V.P.-New Bus. Devel. & Mktg.--U.S. Computer Services, Rancho Cordova, CA, pg. 1135
Matthews, Ken, Mgr.-Mktg.--S. I. Goldman Co., Longwood, FL, pg. 467
Matthews, Michael, Dir.-Mktg.--Sunbeam-Oster Household Products, Schaumburg, IL, pg. 1059
Matthews, Minda, Dir.-Mktg.--American Sign & Marketing Services, Inc., Florence, KY, pg. 61
Matthews, Paula, V.P., Food Mktg.--Ott Communications, Inc., Louisville, KY, pg. 831
Matthews, Trish, Dir.-Mktg.--Optiworld, Atlanta, GA, pg. 828
Mattingly, Joseph, Brand Mgr.--Luzianne Blue Plate Foods, New Orleans, LA, pg. 923
Matus, Michael, Mgr.-Mktg.--Rockford Products Corp., Rockford, IL, pg. 941
Mauro, Rich, V.P.-Mktg.-Inforum--Atlanta Market Center, Atlanta, GA, pg. 94
Maurstad, A.S., V.P.-Mktg.--Dalfort Corp., Dallas, TX, pg. 312
Maxey, Susan, Corp. Dir.-Mktg. Services--Mohawk Tools, Crystal Lake, IL, pg. 885
Maxey, Susan, Corp. Dir.-Mktg. Services--TSC Carbide Co., Crystal Lake, IL, pg. 885
Maxey, Susan, Corp. Dir., Mktg. Services--Triumph Twist Drill Co., Crystal Lake, IL, pg. 885
Maxey, Susan M., Dir.-Mktg. Services--Precision Twist Drill Co., Crystal Lake, IL, pg. 885
Maxon, J., Dir.-Mktg.--Technic Incorporated, Cranston, RI, pg. 1083
Maxwell, Charles, Dir.-Mktg.--Globus-Gateway/Cosmos Tourama, Rego Park, NY, pg. 464
Maxwell, John, V.P.-Sls. & Mktg.--Ivex Packaging Corporation-Polymerization and Extrusion Division, Hazleton, PA, pg. 583
Maxwell, Joseph D., V.P.-Mktg.--TSC Industries, Inc., Nashville, TN, pg. 1075
Maxwell, Susan K., Dir.-Mktg.--Pentax Precision Instruments Corp., Orangeburg, NY, pg. 859
Maxwell, William, Dir.-Mktg.--Boury Incorporated, Wheeling, WV, pg. 168
May, Andrew J., Dir.-Mktg--New England Machinery, Inc., Bradenton, FL, pg. 800
Mayer, Ridgeley, Dir.-Mktg.--Young Stuff Apparel Group, Inc., New York, NY, pg. 1214
Mayhall, Ruth, Dir.-Mktg.--C. A. Muer Corp., Detroit, MI, pg. 774
Maynard, T., Mgr.-Mktg.--Eagle Electric Mfg. Co., Inc., Long Island City, NY, pg. 362
Mayo, Susan T., V.P.-Pub. Rels. & Consumer Affairs--Farm Fresh, Inc., Norfolk, VA, pg. 401
Mazurco, Frank, V.P.-Sls. & Mktg.--Steinway & Sons, Long Island City, NY, pg. 1046
Mazzola, Ronald A., Exec. Dir.-Mktg. & Sls.--McNaughton & Gunn, Inc., Saline, MI, pg. 732
McAdam, Robert C., Sr. V.P.-Mktg. & Sls.--Facemate Corporation, Chicopee, MA, pg. 396
McAllister, Arnold B., Dir.-Mktg.--Monroe Systems For Business, Inc., Morris Plains, NJ, pg. 766
McBain, W.P., V.P.-Sls. & Mktg.--Daubert Coated Products, Inc., Westchester, IL, pg. 317
McCabe, Jerry, Dir.-Mktg. Services--Thompson Advertising Productions, Inc., Farmington Hills, MI, pg. 1094
McCabe, R.T., Dir.-Mktg.--Interplastic Corp., Saint Paul, MN, pg. 579
McCabe, Skip, Mgr.-Adv. & Mktg.--Nature's Recipe Pet Foods, Corona, CA, pg. 796
McCaffrey, Gene, Exec. V.P.-Mktg.--Montgomery Ward & Co., Inc., Chicago, IL, pg. 767
McCain, Laurel, Mktg. Coordinator--McCain Manufacturing Corp., Chicago, IL, pg. 726
McCamish, Bernie, V.P.-Sls. & Mktg.--Ward Leonard Electric Company, Inc., Mount Vernon, NY, pg. 1127
McCann, J.B., Natl. Mktg. Dir.--Atlanta Wire Works, Inc., Jonesboro, GA, pg. 94
McCarley, Bob, Mgr.-Mktg.--Electrical Insulation Suppliers, Hillside, IL, pg. 374
McCarthy, Charles, V.P.-Sls. & Mktg.--Syroco Inc., Baldwinsville, NY, pg. 1070
McCarthy, Francis J., V.P.-Mktg. & Sls.--A. Duda & Sons Inc., Oviedo, FL, pg. 351
McCarthy, Joyce L., Mgr.-Mktg. Services--Uvex Safety, Inc., Smithfield, RI, pg. 1141
McCarthy, Loretta, Sr. V.P.-Mktg. & Communications--Oppenheimer Management Corp., New York, NY, pg. 719
McCarthy, Patrick M., Grp. V.P.-Sls. & Mktg.--Ocean Spray Cranberries, Inc., Lakeville, MA, pg. 820
McCarthy, William J., Pres.-Stores & Mktg.--Montgomery Ward & Co., Inc., Chicago, IL, pg. 767
McCarty, Mike, Dir.-Mktg.--O.P. Link Handle Company, Salem, IN, pg. 676
McClain, Kenneth, Exec. V.P.-Mktg.--General Computer Corp. Inc., Twinsburg, OH, pg. 449
McClanahan, Kevin, V.P.-Mktg.--Crystal Geyser, Calistoga, CA, pg. 303
McClelland, Sue, V.P.-Media--E & J Gallo Winery, Modesto, CA, pg. 441
McClone, J.P., Dir.-Mktg.--Sterling Plumbing Group, Inc., Schaumburg, IL, pg. 640
McCloskey, Bill, Mgr.-New Bus. Devel.--Instrument Specialties Company, Delaware Water Gap, PA, pg. 572
McClure, Jim, V.P.-Sls. & Mfg.--International Cold Storage Co., Inc., Andover, KS, pg. 576
McClure, R.C., Mgr.-Sls. & Mktg., Hwy. Prods.--Potters Industries, Inc., Parsippany, NJ, pg. 837
McCollum, Bruce, Exec. V.P.--Tingley Rubber Corporation, South Plainfield, NJ, pg. 1098
McCoole, Robert, Dir.-Mktg. & Adv.--J. S. Alberici Construction Co., Inc., Saint Louis, MO, pg. 31
McCormack, Jack, V.P.-Sls. & Mktg.--Mission Industries, Santa Barbara, CA, pg. 760
McCormick, Christopher, V.P.-Adv. & Direct Mktg.--L.L. Bean, Inc., Freeport, ME, pg. 648
McCormick, Mariann, Dir., Mktg. & Market Res.--Jay Incorporated, Rochester, NY, pg. 590
McCormick, Tom, Mgr.-Mktg.--Kimray, Inc., Oklahoma City, OK, pg. 629
McCoun, Les, Dir.-Adv. & Mktg.--Wells Fargo Alarm Services, King of Prussia, PA, pg. 166
McCown, Fred E., V.P.-Sls. & Mktg.--ATAPCO Office Products Group, Saint Louis, MO, pg. 64
McCrackin, Mark, Dir., Mktg.--C.F. Thompson Group, Inc., Windsor, CT, pg. 1094
McCranie, James B., Exec. V.P.-Mktg.--Seald-Sweet Growers, Inc., Vero Beach, FL, pg. 984
McCreight, Allen, Dir.-Mktg.--Kraco Enterprises, Inc., Compton, CA, pg. 643
McCrocklin, Greg, V.P.-Mktg.--Manhattan Building Companies, Tulsa, OK, pg. 703
McCullan, Judy, Mgr.-Mktg.--American Buildings Co., Eufaula, AL, pg. 49
McCutchen, Richard D., Sr. V.P.-Mktg.--Blue Cross and Blue Shield of Oklahoma, Tulsa, OK, pg. 159
McDaniel, John L., V.P.-Sls. & Mktg.--Sunbeam Casual Furniture Co., Portland, TN, pg. 1059
McDonald, Eric, Dir., Alternative Mktg. Communications--McDonald Davis & Associates, Inc., Milwaukee, WI, pg. 728
McDonald, Jack, Dir.-Mktg.--The Thompson Group Companies, Henderson, KY, pg. 1094
McDonald, John F., V.P.-Mktg.--Plaid Enterprises Inc., Norcross, GA, pg. 357
McDow, Glenda, Mktg. Coord.--Game Time, Inc., Fort Payne, AL, pg. 442
McDowell, D.E., V.P.-Prod. Devel.--Bissell Inc., Grand Rapids, MI, pg. 153
McDowell, Scott A., V.P.-Reg. York, PA--Tristate Electrical Supply Co., Inc., Hagerstown, MD, pg. 1114
McEvoy, Annette M., Sr. V.P.-Mktg.--Revlon International Corporation, New York, NY, pg. 696
McGannon, Tom, V.P.-Mktg.--General Tools Mfg., New York, NY, pg. 451
McGavin, T.J., Exec. V.P., Mktg. & Sls.--Furnas Electric Company, Batavia, IL, pg. 437
McGee, John, Mgr.-Sls.--Ultra Tool & Plastics, Inc., Amherst, NY, pg. 1125
McGinley, John E., V.P.-Mktg.--Propper Manufacturing Co., Inc., Long Island City, NY, pg. 895
McGinnis, Joseph, Dir.-Mktg.--World's Finest Chocolate, Inc., Chicago, IL, pg. 1203
McGivern, Daniel M., Dir.-Mktg.--DoAll Company, Des Plaines, IL, pg. 341
McGlasson, Christine L., Dir.-Mktg.--Blue Diamond Growers, Sacramento, CA, pg. 160
McGlynn, Bill, Mktg. Mgr.--Information Systems, Montvale, NJ, pg. 316
McGonigle, Tom, Dir.-Mktg. Services--Komatsu Dresser Company, Lincolnshire, IL, pg. 565
McGorrin, Michael, V.P.-Mktg.--Children's World Learning Centers, Inc., Golden, CO, pg. 7
McGouldrick, J., Dir.-Mktg.--American Foundry Group, Inc., Bixby, OK, pg. 54
McGrail, Frank, Mgr.-Mktg. & Quality Control--Tab Chemicals, Inc., Chicago, IL, pg. 1075
McGrail, Robert, Sr. V.P.-Mktg.--Days Inns of America, Inc., Parsippany, NJ, pg. 1100
McGrath, Barry, Mgr.-Mktg.--The Garber Company, Ashland, OH, pg. 442
McGrath, D.P., V.P.-Mktg.--Weber Marking Systems, Inc., Arlington Heights, IL, pg. 1171
McGrath, John M., Sr. V.P.-Mktg. & Sls.--F.G. Montabert, Midland Park, NJ, pg. 766
McGrath, Michael, V.P.-Intl. Mktg.--Hillerich & Bradsby Co., Inc., Louisville, KY, pg. 535
McGrath, W.E., Sr. V.P.-Mktg.--American Mutual Life Insurance Company, Des Moines, IA, pg. 58
McGregor, Rod, Mgr.-Mktg.--Malco Products, Inc., Barberton, OH, pg. 702
McGushin, Terry, V.P.-Mktg.--Rite-Hite Corporation, Milwaukee, WI, pg. 936
McHenry, Brian, V.P.-Sls. & Mktg.--La France Corporation, Philadelphia, PA, pg. 649
McHugh, Patricia, Dir.-Mktg.--James McHugh Construction Co., Chicago, IL, pg. 729
McInerney, J. Barrett, V.P.-Mktg. & Sls.--Crane & Co., Inc., Dalton, MA, pg. 296
McInerney, John J., V.P.-Sls. & Mktg.--McInerney Inc., Oak Park, MI, pg. 729
McIntosh, Ardy, V.P.-Mktg.--Henco, Inc., Selmer, TN, pg. 528
McIntosh, Brice, Sr. V.P., Dir. Mktg. Services--The William Cook Agency, Inc., Jacksonville, FL, pg. 282
McKay, Alvin, Dir.-Mktg.--Cumberland Farms, Inc., Canton, MA, pg. 304
McKay, Donald, Dir.-Sls. & Mktg.--Colonial Beef Co., Philadelphia, PA, pg. 263
McKay, Gene, Dir., Automotive Mktg. Grp.--Steiner/Bressler Advertising, Birmingham, AL, pg. 1045
McKeithen, L.B., V.P.-Mktg. Services--Fruit of the Loom, Bowling Green, KY, pg. 400

Corporate Responsibilities Index

McKenna, Christine, Exec. V.P.-Mktg.--Plasti-Kote Company Inc., Medina, OH, pg. 875
McKeon, Patrick E., Exec. V.P.-Sls. & Mktg.--Spectrum Industries, Inc., Chippewa Falls, WI, pg. 1029
McKiever, Kevin T., V.P.-Mktg.--Cooper Communities, Inc., Bella Vista, AR, pg. 283
McKimmey, Chuck, V.P.-Sls. & Mktg.--Jayco Inc., Middlebury, IN, pg. 590
McKinley, Dave, Mgr.-Mktg.--Carver, Inc., Garden City, GA, pg. 227
McKnight, Jeffrey L., V.P.-Mktg. & Strategic Plng.--Aeronautical Radio, Inc., Annapolis, MD, pg. 82
McLain, Kristy, Mktg. Coord.--Root Corporation, Mount Wolf, PA, pg. 946
McLain, Scott A., V.P.-Natl. Sls. & Mktg.--Superior Industries of Nebraska, Inc., Omaha, NE, pg. 1063
McLaughlin, Dave, Forecasting Mgr.--Crown International, Inc., Elkhart, IN, pg. 302
McLean, Thomas I., V.P.-Mktg. & Research--Kingsdown, Inc., Mebane, NC, pg. 632
McLeod, John, V.P.-Mktg.--J.R. Simplot Co., Minerals & Chemicals Group, Pocatello, ID, pg. 1007
McLeod, John S., Jr., V.P.-Mktg.--Mar-Mac Manufacturing Company, Inc., McBee, SC, pg. 705
McLeod, Julie, Dir.-Mktg.--Marilyn Miglin, Inc., Chicago, IL, pg. 752
McMackin, Carl, V.P.-Mktg. Res.--M.E.D. Communications, Woodbridge, NJ, pg. 692
McMaken, Barbara, Mgr., Bus. Devel.--Pollak Levitt Chaiet, Advertising, Atlanta, GA, pg. 879
McManaman, Robert, V.P.-Mktg. & Mdsg.--Mary Maxim, Inc., Port Huron, MI, pg. 722
McMerty, Clarence J., Exec. V.P.-Mktg.-Baby Prods.--Dundee Mills, Inc., Griffin, GA, pg. 352
McMillan, Francis W., II, V.P.-Mktg.--Amerisure Companies, Detroit, MI, pg. 66
McMillan, Gloria, V.P.-Sls. & Mktg.--Kimstock, Inc., Santa Ana, CA, pg. 630
McMullen, Mark, Exec. V.P.-Mktg. Services--Walker & Associates, Inc., Memphis, TN, pg. 1159
McNabb, James, Dir.-Sls. & Mktg.--Associated Electric Co-op Inc., Springfield, MO, pg. 89
McNamara, Austin, V.P.-John Morrell Mktg.--John Morrell & Co., Cincinnati, OH, pg. 54
McNamara, J., Mgr.-Mktg.--Gentex Optics, Inc., Simpson, PA, pg. 452
McNamara, Karen, Mgr.-Bus. Devel.--Ghafari Associates, Inc., Dearborn, MI, pg. 455
McNicholas, David P., Exec. V.P.-Systems Mktg.--Avis, Inc., Garden City, NY, pg. 102
McNichols, Thomas A., Sr. V.P.-Mktg.--Barton Beers, Ltd., Chicago, IL, pg. 123
McQueen, Jeff, Mgr.-Mktg.--Schwab Corp., Lafayette, IN, pg. 980
McRoberts, Harold, Mgr.-Product--Franklin Baking Co., Inc., Goldsboro, NC, pg. 429
McRonald, Carol, V.P.-Mktg. & Creative Dir.--Royal Cruise Line Inc., San Francisco, CA, pg. 953
McShane, Brian, Exec. V.P. & Dir.-Mktg.--Advertising Checking Bureau Incorporated, New York, NY, pg. 21
McSpadden, Dan, Mgr.-Mktg.--Citrus World Inc., Lake Wales, FL, pg. 251
McSweeney, Pamela, Dir.-Mktg.-Executive Center, Woodland Hills, CA--Dakin, Inc., Burlingame, CA, pg. 311
McWilliams, Scott G., V.P.-Mktg.--McWilliams Forge Co., Rockaway, NJ, pg. 733
Meacham, Ronald G., V.P.-Sls. & Mktg.--Bachman Company, Reading, PA, pg. 108
Mead, R.J., Dir.-Export Mktg. Services--Sunkist Growers, Inc., Sherman Oaks, CA, pg. 1060
Meador, William A., V.P.-Mktg.--Lane Press, Inc., South Burlington, VT, pg. 654
Mechler, Brian, Mgr.-Mktg. Services--Hubbard Milling Company, Mankato, MN, pg. 549
Meddock, Larry, V.P.-Mktg.--Cocrest Craft, Inc., Orlando, FL, pg. 287
Meersschaert, Pieter, Dir.-Mktg. Services--Herman Associates, Inc., New York, NY, pg. 531
Mehtlan, David L., V.P.-Sls. & Mktg.--American Stone-Mix, Inc., Towson, MD, pg. 63
Mekus, Thomas, Dir.-Sls. & Mktg.--Diehl Specialties Intl., Defiance, OH, pg. 336
Mekus, Thomas A., Mgr.-Sls. & Mktg.--Diehl, Inc., Defiance, OH, pg. 336
Melko, Sophie, Dir.-Mktg.--The Stiffel Company, Chicago, IL, pg. 1049
Melko, Sophie A., Mgr.-Mktg. Services--Vance Industries, Inc., Chicago, IL, pg. 1144
Melody, Jay, V.P.-Mktg. & Adv.--Perfection Automotive Products Corporation, Livonia, MI, pg. 861
Melton, Lorraine D., V.P.-Mktg. & Special Events--New York City Off Track Betting Corp., New York, NY, pg. 802
Melum, R.S., Gen. Mgr.-Mktg.--Atlantic Steel Company, Atlanta, GA, pg. 95
Melvin, Robert, Dir.-Mktg.--Allen-Edmonds Shoe Corp., Port Washington, WI, pg. 36
Menard, Raymond, Dir.-Mktg. & Prod.--Vic Manufacturing, Minneapolis, MN, pg. 1149
Menard, Raymond, Dir.-Mktg.--Imparts, Minneapolis, MN, pg. 1149
Mendoza, Ray, V.P.-Natl. Accounts--Key Handling Systems, Inc., Hackensack, NJ, pg. 627
Mennen, Barnett, M.D., Sr. V.P., Medical & Mktg. Dir.--William Douglas McAdams Inc., New York, NY, pg. 726
Mente, Glen A., Sr. V.P.-Nutrition--Kent Feeds Inc., Muscatine, IA, pg. 1146
Merante, Joseph, Sr. V.P.-Mktg. & Sls.-No. America--Zim-American Israeli Shipping Co., New York, NY, pg. 1219
Merrick, George A., Exec. V.P.-Mktg., Sls. & Service--Ampex Corporation, Redwood City, CA, pg. 998
Meskell, Kevin, V.P. & Mktg. Agent--Quincy Mutual Fire Insurance Company, Quincy, MA, pg. 905
Metcalf, Virgil L., V.P.-Sls. & Mktg.--Waldes Truarc, Inc., Somerset, NJ, pg. 1159
Metcalfe, David D., V.P.-Mktg.--Guarantee Electrical Company, Saint Louis, MO, pg. 490
Methfessel, Louis D., Dir.-Mktg.--Boyd, Tamney & Cross Advertising/Marketing, Wayne, PA, pg. 169
Metts, William, Dir.-Mktg.--Taylor Machine Works, Inc., Louisville, MS, pg. 1081
Metz, Gene, V.P.-Sls. & Mktg.--Sauder Woodworking Co., Archbold, OH, pg. 972
Metzbower, Mike, V.P.-Mktg.--Tremont Foods, Linthicum Heights, MD, pg. 1109
Metzger, Daniel, V.P.-Mktg.--Lawson Associates Inc., Minneapolis, MN, pg. 663
Metzger, Donna, Dir.-Mktg.--Contract Interiors Inc., Southfield, MI, pg. 280
Meyer, Gerald L., V.P.-Mktg. & Exec. Devel.--D.A. Davidson & Co., Great Falls, MT, pg. 318
Meyer, Mark L., Dir.-Mktg.--Ward Manufacturing, Inc., Blassburg, PA, pg. 1163
Meyers, Jerome E. Jr., V.P.-Mktg. & Bus. Devel.--Dugan & Meyers Interests, Inc., Cincinnati, OH, pg. 351
Meyers, Lowell, Dir.-Mktg. & Adv.--Quill Corp., Lincolnshire, IL, pg. 905
Meyerson, Gerald, Prod. Dir.--American Journal Of Nursing Company, New York, NY, pg. 57
Miceli, Tom, V.P.-Mktg.--B & B Motor & Control Corporation, Long Island City, NY, pg. 105
Michaels, R. Alin, V.P., Mktg.--Buzz Barton & Associates, Inc., Oak Brook, IL, pg. 123
Michaels, Tony, Dir.-Mktg.--Elias Brothers Restaurants, Inc., Warren, MI, pg. 376
Michalak, John, Sr. V.P.-Mktg. & New Bus. Devel.--Food Services of America, Seattle, WA, pg. 423
Michalowski, Paul, Dir.-Mdse. & Mktg.--Distribution America, Des Plaines, IL, pg. 340
Michard, Laura, Dir.-Sls. & Mktg.--Beltone Electronics Corporation, Chicago, IL, pg. 137
Mickle, Robert, V.P.-Sls. & Mktg.--Wing Industries, Inc., Dallas, TX, pg. 1196
Middleton, Renee, Mgr.-Mktg. & Production--Taco John's International, Inc., Cheyenne, WY, pg. 1076
Middleton, Rob, Dir.-Community Devel.--Arkansas Industrial Development Commission, Little Rock, AR, pg. 83
Midlo, Maury, V.P.-Adv.--K & B, Inc., New Orleans, LA, pg. 611
Mikkelsen, Alice, Dir.-Mktg. Services--My Own Meals, Inc., Deerfield, IL, pg. 779
Mikulina, Tom, V.P.-Mktg. & Sls.--The Trane Company, La Crosse, WI, pg. 62
Milbauer, Kathy, Reg. Mgr.--Sonicair, Scottsdale, AZ, pg. 1018
Mild, E.E., Dir. Mktg. Devel.--Titanium Metals Corporation, Denver, CO, pg. 1109
Mildner, Curtis, V.P.-Mktg.--Hussey Seating Company, North Berwick, ME, pg. 555
Miller, Alton Wayne, Dir.-Sls. & Mktg.--Affiliated Foods Southwest, Little Rock, AR, pg. 24
Miller, Bob, Dir.-Mktg. & Communications Div.--East Kentucky Power Co-op, Winchester, KY, pg. 362
Miller, Bruce A., V.P.-Grp. Mktg.--American United Life Insurance Company, Indianapolis, IN, pg. 65
Miller, Carl E., V.P.-Sls. & Mktg.--Butler Automatic, Inc., Canton, MA, pg. 197
Miller, Daniel, Pres.-Mktg.--Dexter Shoe Company, Dexter, ME, pg. 334
Miller, David, Div. Mgr.-Sls.--Arizona Supermarkets, Inc., Phoenix, AZ, pg. 82
Miller, Dean A., V.P.-Industrial Rels.--BeefAmerica Operating Co., Inc., Omaha, NE, pg. 131
Miller, Dirk D., V.P.-Mfg. Services--Desa International, Inc., Bowling Green, KY, pg. 331
Miller, Edward H., V.P.-Bus. Devel.--Frank Messer & Sons Construction Co., Cincinnati, OH, pg. 741
Miller, Frank W., V.P.-Mktg. & Sls.--The H. W. Wilson Co., Bronx, NY, pg. 1193
Miller, Fred, Sr. V.P.-Mktg.--Kent Feeds Inc., Muscatine, IA, pg. 1146
Miller, Glenna A., Dir.-Mktg. & Sls.--Thermal American Fused Quartz Co., Louisville, KY, pg. 1091
Miller, J.J., Sr. V.P. & Chief Mktg. Officer--Western & Southern Life Insurance Co., Cincinnati, OH, pg. 1181
Miller, Janice, Communications Coord.--Triple F, Inc., Des Moines, IA, pg. 1114
Miller, Jerry, Mgr.-Mktg.--Fleet Engineers, Inc., Muskegon, MI, pg. 417
Miller, Jill, Mgr.-Mktg. & Promo.--Norwegian Cruise Line, Coral Gables, FL, pg. 816
Miller, Jim, Exec. V.P.-Sls. & Mktg.--Sutter Home Winery, Inc., Saint Helena, CA, pg. 1065
Miller, John, V.P.-Mktg.--Sealy Mattress Company, Memphis, TN, pg. 986
Miller, Joy, Dir.-Retail Devel.--Crown American Real Estate Division, Johnstown, PA, pg. 302
Miller, June, Mgr.-Mktg.--Red Spot Paint & Varnish Co., Evansville, IN, pg. 918
Miller, Maurice, V.P.-Mktg. Communications--CENEX (Farmers Union Central Exchange, Inc.), Inver Grove Heights, MN, pg. 231
Miller, Michael D., V.P.-Mktg.--SK Hand Tool Corp., Chicago, IL, pg. 963
Miller, Mike, Dir.-Mktg.--Griffin Manufacturing Co., Muskogee, OK, pg. 487
Miller, Nick, V.P.-Mktg. Radio Grp.--Great American Broadcasting Company, Cincinnati, OH, pg. 52
Miller, Paige, Dir.-Mktg. Services--Samsonite Corporation, Denver, CO, pg. 358
Miller, Richard B., Mktg. Services Mgr.--YPMS/TMP Worldwide, Inc., Mequon, WI, pg. 1074
Miller, Rick, V.P.-Mktg.--E. D. Bullard Company, Cynthiana, KY, pg. 188
Miller, Roger, Mgr.-Mktg.--The Bureau of National Affairs, Inc., Washington, DC, pg. 189
Mills, Jerry, Dir.-Mktg.--Karnak Corporation, Clark, NJ, pg. 617
Mills, Lea Ann, Dir.-Sls. & Mktg.--Replacements, Ltd., Greensboro, NC, pg. 927
Milner, Victor, Jr., V.P.-Mktg.--Rogerson Hiller Corporation, Port Angeles, WA, pg. 944
Mink, Gerald, V.P.-Mktg.--Columbia Iron & Metal Co., Cleveland, OH, pg. 265
Minkin, Mark, Sr. V.P., New Bus.--Hill, Holliday, Connors, Cosmopulos, Inc., Boston, MA, pg. 534
Minnihan, Richard L., Dir.-Mktg.--Medical Laboratory Automation, Inc., Pleasantville, NY, pg. 735
Mintzer, Elliot, Mgr.-Mktg. Services, Corp. Video Systems & Telecommunications--Tork, Inc., Mount Vernon, NY, pg. 1102
Misevicius, Milda, Exec. V.P., Dir. New Bus. Devel.--Korey, Kay & Partners, New York, NY, pg. 642
Missry, Herbert, V.P.-Mktg.--Baby Togs, Inc., New York, NY, pg. 107
Mitchell, Peter, V.P.-Mktg. Communications--Haggar Apparel Company, Dallas, TX, pg. 499
Mitchell, Vincent, Exec. V.P.-Sls. & Mktg.--Falcon Candy Company, Philadelphia, PA, pg. 398
Moeller, Wayne, V.P.-Sls. & Mktg.--Lozier Corporation, Omaha, NE, pg. 686
Moeller, Wayne A., V.P.-Sls. & Mktg.--Lozier Store Fixtures, Inc., Omaha, NE, pg. 686
Moerck, Rudi, Dr., V.P.-Mktg. & Sls.--Troy Corporation, East Hanover, NJ, pg. 1116
Moffatt, David L., Membership Devel. & Mktg.--ASM International, Materials Park, OH, pg. 8
Molendorp, Dayton H., V.P.-Individual Mktg.--American United Life Insurance Company, Indianapolis, IN, pg. 65
Mollet, Tom, Dir.-Mktg.--Game Time, Inc., Fort Payne, AL, pg. 442
Molnar, Thomas, V.P.-Mktg.--Gibbs Wire & Steel Company, Inc., Southington, CT, pg. 456
Mondello, Mike, V.P.-Mktg.--Celestial Seasonings, Boulder, CO, pg. 231
Monette, Robert W., Dir.-Mktg.--Operations Management International, Inc., Kingwood, TX, pg. 202
Monroe, Bruce B., Vice Chm. & V.P.-Mktg.--The Johnson Corporation, Three Rivers, MI, pg. 597
Monstvilas, Ruth, Dir.-Pkgng. Devel.--Dana Perfumes Corp., New York, NY, pg. 313
Montesano, Nick, V.P.-Sls., Mktg. & Mdse.--Quill Corp., Lincolnshire, IL, pg. 905
Montgomery, Christian, Exec. V.P.-Mktg.--Andy Frain Services, Inc., Chicago, IL, pg. 428
Montgomery, Dan, Dir.-Mktg. & Adv.--Van Dyne-Crotty, Inc., Dayton, OH, pg. 1144
Montgomery, Glenn, Natl. Sls. Mgr.--Flexible Flyer Inc., West Point, MS, pg. 847
Montgomery, Lloyd L., V.P.-Mktg.--The White Lily Foods Co., Knoxville, TN, pg. 1186
Monzyk, Debbie, Mgr.-Mktg. Opers.--ATAPCO Office Products Group, Saint Louis, MO, pg. 64
Moonjian, Donald, V.P.-Mktg.--Alamo Rent-A-Car Inc., Fort Lauderdale, FL, pg. 30
Moore, Arnold, Mgr.-Sls. & Mktg.--State Electric Supply Co., Huntington, WV, pg. 1040
Moore, Lindsay, Dir.-Mktg. Services--Celestial Seasonings, Boulder, CO, pg. 231
Moore, Ron, Mgr.-Mktg.--Thomas Built Buses, Inc., High Point, NC, pg. 1092
Moore, Theodore K., V.P.-Sls. & Mktg.--The Chicago Faucet Co., Des Plaines, IL, pg. 245
Moore, Thomas A., Exec. V.P., Dir. Mktg. Services--Liggett-Stashower, Inc., Cleveland, OH, pg. 675
Moore, Walter E., V.P. & Dir.-Sls.--Collegiate Concepts Inc., Tucker, GA, pg. 262
Moran, James M., Jr., Exec. V.P.-Mktg.--JM Family Enterprises Inc., Deerfield Beach, FL, pg. 584
Moran, John J., V.P. & Asst. Controller--Anchor Financial Corporation, Myrtle Beach, SC, pg. 71
Morano, Jerry, V.P.-Mktg. & Sls.--Quality Bakers of America Cooperative, Inc., Greenwich, CT, pg. 903
Morata, Eugene, V.P.-Professional Div. Mktg.--Conair Corporation, Stamford, CT, pg. 272
Moreley, Thomas S., V.P.-Sls. & Mktg.--Harrington & King, Chicago, IL, pg. 511
Morenberg, Edward, Sr. V.P.-Store Plng., Constr. & Admin.--R. H. Macy & Co., Inc., New York, NY, pg. 698
Morgan, Chas, V.P.-Mktg.--Sierracin/Sylmar Corporation, Sylmar, CA, pg. 1003
Morgan, Alex, V.P.-Mktg.--Sutter Home Winery, Inc., Saint Helena, CA, pg. 1065
Morgan, Brad, Exec. V.P.-Mktg.--Visa U.S.A. Inc., San Mateo, CA, pg. 1153
Morgan, H., Dir.-Teleconferencing Mktg. & Sls.--Shure Brothers Incorporated, Evanston, IL, pg. 1001
Morgan, Ken, Dir., Mktg. & Research--Tucker Wayne/Luckie & Company, Birmingham, AL, pg. 1118
Morgan, Mary, Dir.-Mktg.--Pollenex Corporation, Chicago, IL, pg. 821
Morgan, Philip, Dir.-Mktg.--Unifax, Inc., Wilkes-Barre, PA, pg. 1126
Morgan, W. Tommy III, Exec. V.P.-Adv., Mktg. & Sls.--H.A.T. Holding Company, Tampa, FL, pg. 517
Morgan, W. Tommy, III, Exec. V.P.-Adv., Mktg. & Sls.--Havatampa Incorporated, Tampa, FL, pg. 517
Morison, John, III, V.P.-Mktg. & Sls.--Hitchiner Manufacturing Company, Inc., Milford, NH, pg. 536
Morrell, E. Jean, Mgr.-Mktg. Services--Trak International, Inc., Port Washington, WI, pg. 1106
Morrill, Thomas, Dir.-Sls. & Mktg.--Atchison County Co-op Association, Atchison, KS, pg. 93
Morris, Ally, Dir.-Mktg.--Heil-Brice Retail Advertising, San Clemente, CA, pg. 525
Morris, Marvin, V.P.-Mktg.--Alamo Group, Inc., Seguin, TX, pg. 29
Morris, Marvin, V.P.-Mktg.--Alamo Group, Inc., La Grange, IL, pg. 29
Morris, Patrick, Sr. V.P.-Mktg. & Concept Strategic Plng.--Roma Holdings, Dallas, TX, pg. 945

Morris, Richard, V.P.-Mktg.--Pilot Air Freight Corp., Lima, PA, pg. 870
Morrison, Jerry E., Sr. Exec. V.P.-Mktg.--Cummings Inc., Nashville, TN, pg. 304
Morrison, John, Chief Mktg. Officer--Noble & Associates, Springfield, MO, pg. 808
Morrison, Sylvia, V.P., Direct Response Mktg. Gen. Mgr.--Liggett-Stashower, Inc., Cleveland, OH, pg. 675
Morrow, James, V.P.-Mktg.--W. C. Bradley Co., Columbus, GA, pg. 170
Morthanos, John, Dir.-Mktg.--TV Host Inc., Harrisburg, PA, pg. 1075
Morton, Craig, Dir.-Mktg. & Adv.--Paco Rabanne Parfums, New York, NY, pg. 842
Morton, Larry, Natl. Sls. & Mktg. Mgr.--Scott U.S.A., Ketchum, ID, pg. 983
Mosey, Mary K., Mgr.-Bus. Devel.--Ghafari Associates, Inc., Dearborn, MI, pg. 455
Mosier, George O., V.P.-Sls. & Mktg., Intl. Div.--Foley-PLP Company, Rochester, NY, pg. 422
Moss, Earl, Prod. Mgr.-Cameras--Ansco Photo-Optical Products Corp., Elk Grove Village, IL, pg. 76
Mosthof, Albert, Dir.-Mktg.--Ed Miniat, Inc., Chicago, IL, pg. 757
Motsay, John M., V.P.-Sls. & Mktg.--Canton Drop Forge, Canton, OH, pg. 214
Motsinger, Bill, Dir.-Mktg.--Montgomery Ward & Co., Inc., Chicago, IL, pg. 767
Mottley, M.L., V.P.-Sls. & Mktg., Compressors--Carey Machinery & Supply Company, Baltimore, MD, pg. 218
Moumousis, Michael F., V.P.-Mktg.--Automobile Auction Division, Atlanta, GA, pg. 293
Mowbray, Michael, Mktg. Dir.--Waldbillig & Besteman, Inc., Madison, WI, pg. 1159
Muckerman, John, Dir.-Mktg. & Adv.--Dierbergs Markets Inc., Chesterfield, MO, pg. 337
Mudd, Charles W., V.P.-Sls. & Mktg.--Dorsey Trailers, Inc., Atlanta, GA, pg. 347
Mudge, Rick, V.P.-Mktg. & Sls.--Cramer Inc., Kansas City, KS, pg. 296
Mueller, Brett, V.P.-Sls. & Mktg.--Mueller Sports Medicine, Inc., Prairie du Sac, WI, pg. 774
Mueller, Gerald C., Dir.-Sls. & Mktg.--Wenczel Tile Co., Trenton, NJ, pg. 1176
Mueller, Lawrence A., Exec. V.P.-Worldwide Sls. & Mktg.--J.D. Edwards & Company, Denver, CO, pg. 370
Mulcahy, Robert, Dir.-Mktg.--Clearpoint Research Corporation, Hopkinton, MA, pg. 254
Mulheirn, Judy, Mgr.-Creative Services--Fritz Chemical Company, Mesquite, TX, pg. 434
Mullen, George J., Sr. V.P.-Mktg.--Fiduciary Trust Co. International, New York, NY, pg. 408
Mullen, Terry, Dir.-Engrng. & Mktg.--DEC/Bou-Matic, Madison, WI, pg. 309
Mumma, J.S., Sr.-V.P.-Mktg. & Pub. Rels.--Atlas Van Lines, Inc., Evansville, IN, pg. 96
Mumper, Melanie, Mgr.-Mktg. Services--NFO Research, Inc., Greenwich, CT, pg. 780
Mundt, Bud, V.P.-Sls. & Mktg.--Miller Business Systems, Inc., Arlington, TX, pg. 753
Munhall, Charles R., Jr., Exec. V.P., Mktg. & Client Services--CSI Advertising Inc., Atlanta, GA, pg. 205
Munnis, Joseph W., V.P.-Sls. & Mktg.--Henkels & McCoy, Inc., Blue Bell, PA, pg. 529
Munro, Laura, Dir.-Mktg., Beverages--Del Monte Foods, San Francisco, CA, pg. 325
Murnin, Michael, V.P.-Sls. & Mktg.--Up-Right, Inc., Selma, CA, pg. 1139
Murphy, Ann, Div. Mgr.-Mktg.--Pace, Arlington Heights, IL, pg. 922
Murphy, Ann M., Div. Mgr.-Mktg.--Pace, Arlington Heights, IL, pg. 922
Murphy, Cleo, Sr. V.P.-Mktg.--First Pyramid Life Insurance Company of America, Little Rock, AR, pg. 1150
Murphy, Dan, V.P.-Mktg. & Prod. Devel.--Totes Incorporated, Loveland, OH, pg. 1103
Murphy, Frank, V.P.-Sls. & Mktg.--Cerro Copper Products Co., Sauget, IL, pg. 711
Murphy, Frank, Intl. Mktg. Mgr.--Micro-Aire Surgical Instruments, Inc., Valencia, CA, pg. 711
Murphy, J.J., U.S. Mktg. Mgr.--Dorr-Oliver Incorporated, Milford, CT, pg. 346
Murphy, L.D., V.P.-Mktg.--Commercial & Architectural Products Inc., Dover, OH, pg. 268
Murphy, Larry M., V.P.-Sls. & Mktg.--R & G Sloane Mfg. Co., Inc., Sun Valley, CA, pg. 1010
Murphy, Marian, Sr. V.P.-Mktg.--ComputerLand Corporation, Pleasanton, CA, pg. 271
Murphy, Michael J., V.P.-Mktg. & Sls.--Danly-Komatsu L.P., Cicero, IL, pg. 275
Murphy, Tom, Exec. V.P.-Sls. & Mktg.--Meehan Tooker, East Rutherford, NJ, pg. 736
Murray, Asa G., V.P.-Sls. & Mktg.--Philadelphia Coca-Cola Bottling Co., Philadelphia, PA, pg. 866
Murray, Bernadette, Mgr.-Sls. Devel.--Conde Nast Traveler, New York, NY, pg. 19
Murray, Edward A., V.P.-Sls. & Mktg.--Koh-I-Noor, Inc., Bloomsbury, NJ, pg. 639
Murray, George H., Sr. V.P.-Mktg. & Personnel Devel.--First Federal Savings and Loan Assn. of Rochester, Rochester, NY, pg. 413
Murray, Margaret, Dir.-Adv. & Pub. Rels.--Crosman Corporation, East Bloomfield, NY, pg. 695
Murray, Pamela, Mktg. & Adv. Mgr.--Alimak Elevator Company, Bridgeport, CT, pg. 34
Murzinski, Edward, V.P.-Mktg. & Sls.--Revcor, Inc., Carpentersville, IL, pg. 930
Mussbaun, Bob, V.P.-Sls. & Mktg.--Ireland Coffee Tea, Inc., Pleasantville, NJ, pg. 582
Muzyczko, T., Exec. V.P.--Bingham, Mt. Prospect, IL, pg. 151
Myer, Dave, Dir., Mktg. Services--TMP Worldwide, Inc., Miami, FL, pg. 1074
Myers, Chris, Dir.-Mktg.--American Enterprise Institute for Public Policy Research, Washington, DC, pg. 51
Myers, D., V.P.-Mktg.--Kleinschmidt Inc., Deerfield, IL, pg. 635
Myers, Daria, V.P.-Mktg.--Estee Lauder, Inc., New York, NY, pg. 389
Myers, Dyann, Mktg.-Coord.--OPUS Corp., Minnetonka, MN, pg. 828
Myers, James H., V.P.-Intl. Sls. & Product Mngmt.--Simplicity Manufacturing, Inc., Port Washington, WI, pg. 1006
Myers, Robert W., Mgr.-Sls. & Mktg.--Morris Coupling Co., Erie, PA, pg. 771
Myers, William K., Sr. V.P., Mktg.--DIMAC DIRECT, Bridgeton, MO, pg. 338
Myers, Wm. K., V.P.-Mktg.--DIMAC Corporation, Bridgeton, MO, pg. 338
Mylenki, Paula, Supvr.-Mktg. Communications--Ohaus Corporation, Florham Park, NJ, pg. 822
Myrick, Tom, Mgr.-Mktg.--Scherer Bros. Lumber Company, Minneapolis, MN, pg. 976
Nagy, Jack, Dir.-Mktg.--United Foam Plastics Corporation, Georgetown, MA, pg. 1132
Nairm, Brian, V.P.-Mktg.--Advanstar Communications, Cleveland, OH, pg. 21
Nakamura, Ken, V.P.-Mktg. Admin.--Komatsu Dresser Company, Lincolnshire, IL, pg. 565
Nall, Tom, V.P.-Sls. & Mktg.--Caliente Chili, Inc., Austin, TX, pg. 923
Nanfeldt, Suzan, V.P.-Mktg.--U.S. News & World Report, New York, NY, pg. 1136
Narayanan, P.G., V.P.-Engrng. & Mktg.--Cray Communications Inc., Annapolis Junction, MD, pg. 297
Nardella, A.N., Sr. V.P.-Distribution--Hubbard Hall Inc., Waterbury, CT, pg. 549
Nardelli, Rudy, Exec. V.P., Dir. Mktg. Services--Shiffman/Fergusson/Stone Advertising Inc., Fort Lee, NJ, pg. 999
Nash, Charlotte, Mgr.-Trade Shows & Mktg. Communications-OEM--Leviton Mfg. Co., Inc., Little Neck, NY, pg. 671
Natta, NAncy Van, Dir.-Mktg.--Computer Library, New York, NY, pg. 1219
Navota, Jim, Dir.-Mktg.--Sycamore Systems, Inc., Sycamore, IL, pg. 690
Nayak, P.R., Sr. V.P. & Dir.-Mktg.--Arthur D. Little, Inc., Cambridge, MA, pg. 678
Neal, Berni, Mgr.-Mktg. Services--Muse Cordero Chen, Inc., Los Angeles, CA, pg. 777
Neal, Normand, Exec. V.P.-Sls. & Mktg.--J H Collectibles, Milwaukee, WI, pg. 584
Nealis, Perry, Mgr.-Natl. Mktg.--Auto Glass Specialists, Madison, WI, pg. 100
Neff, Harry, V.P.-Sls. & Mktg.--Uvex Safety, Inc., Smithfield, RI, pg. 1141
Negreu, Dick, V.P.-Mktg.--Hehr International Inc., Los Angeles, CA, pg. 525
Neher, Ken, V.P.-Mktg.--Northwest Airlines, Inc., Saint Paul, MN, pg. 782
Nelson, Clayton M., Exec. V.P.-Bus. Opers.--American Family Mutual Insurance Co., Madison, WI, pg. 51
Nelson, G.L., V.P.-Sls. & Mktg.--Ampco Metal Incorporated, Milwaukee, WI, pg. 67
Nelson, Glen, V.P.-Sls. & Mktg.--Roll Forming Corporation, Shelbyville, KY, pg. 944
Nelson, James A., V.P.-Distribution--Dunham's Athleisure Corporation, Waterford, MI, pg. 353
Nelson, Jim, Dir.-Sls. & Mktg.--Ederer Inc., Seattle, WA, pg. 368
Nelson, Jim, Dir.-Sls. & Mktg.--Ederer Cranes, Seattle, WA, pg. 368
Nelson, Jim, Dir.-Sls. & Mktg.--Washington Cranes, Seattle, WA, pg. 368
Nelson, Jim, Dir.-Sls. & Mktg.--Star Cranes, Seattle, WA, pg. 368
Nelson, John L., V.P.-Sls. & Mktg.--Marlow Industries, Dallas, TX, pg. 710
Nelson, Randy, Mgr.-Intl. Mktg.--The Genie Company, Akron, OH, pg. 452
Nelson, Rodney E., V.P.-Mktg. & Sls.--Magnetic Data, Inc., Eden Prairie, MN, pg. 700
Nelson, Theodore, V.P.-Mktg. Devel.--Harkins Builders, Inc., Silver Spring, MD, pg. 509
Nenert, Ed, Mgr.-Mktg.--Artec Distributing, Inc., Shelburne, VT, pg. 86
Nessi, Toni, V.P.-Mktg.--Epstein Process Engineering, Inc., Chicago, IL, pg. 384
Neubauer, Allyn, Dir.-Mktg. & Adv.--Amana Society, Amana, IA, pg. 46
Neuschel, Robert F., Staff V.P.-Direct Mktg.--General Binding Corporation, Northbrook, IL, pg. 656
Neverman, Ken, Mgr.-Regional Sls. & Mktg.--Wayne Corporation, Richmond, IN, pg. 1169
Neville, Richard S., V.P.-Mktg.--Western Petroleum Company, Eden Prairie, MN, pg. 1181
Nevison, G., Sr. V.P.-Mktg. & Sls.--Eastern Technologies Ltd, Amesbury, MA, pg. 364
Newberg, Anthony, V.P.-Mktg. & Data Processing--Dealers Electrical Supply Co., Waco, TX, pg. 322
Newcombe, Arthur R., V.P.-Sls. & Mktg.--Parkdale Mills, Gastonia, NC, pg. 849
Newell, Jack, Dir.-Mktg., Communications & Adv.--The ERM Group, Exton, PA, pg. 360
Newhard, Susan, Mgr.-Corp. Mktg.--The Forum Corporation, Boston, MA, pg. 425
Newman, Douglas G., Asst. V.P.-Equity Mktg.--Equity Services, Inc., Montpelier, VT, pg. 791
Neyer, Thomas L., Jr., V.P.-Mktg.--Al Neyer, Inc., Cincinnati, OH, pg. 805
Nibbe, Warner, Dir.-Sls. & Mktg.--Paper Calmenson & Co., Saint Paul, MN, pg. 847
Nicas, Anthony, V.P.-Sls. & Mktg.--Security Products Company of Delaware, Inc., Minneapolis, MN, pg. 1138
Nicas, Pete, V.P.-Mktg. & Sls.-Security Prods.--Universal Cooperatives, Inc., Minneapolis, MN, pg. 1138
Nicas, Pete, V.P.-Sls. & Mktg.--Security Products Company, Minneapolis, MN, pg. 1138
Nicholishen, Dave, Mgr.-Sls. & Mktg.--Ivex Packaging Corporation-Canadian Region, Toronto, Canada, pg. 583
Nichols, Alexander, Dir.-Adv. & Mktg. Services--Sunshine Biscuits, Inc., Woodbridge, NJ, pg. 439
Nichols, Samuel J., Mktg. Dir.--Quality Chekd Dairy Products Association, Naperville, IL, pg. 903
Nicholson, David L., Dir.-Mktg.--Allen & Hoshall, Inc., Memphis, TN, pg. 36
Nicholson, Mary, Indus. Mktg. Specialist--Mallet & Co., Carnegie, PA, pg. 703
Nickel, D.A., Mgr.-Mktg. & Sls.--The Rotor Tool Company, Cleveland, OH, pg. 951
Nicolas, Francois, V.P.-Mktg.--Advance Seed Co., Fulton, KY, pg. 407
Nicoll, Rob, Dir.-Mktg. Communications--JPS Elastomerics Corp., Northampton, MA, pg. 586
Niebauer, Ron, Dir.-Mktg. & Direct Mktg.--SafetyMaster Corporation, Billings, MT, pg. 1053
Niemi, Frank, Dir.-Mktg.--Abbott Laboratories/Ashland, Ashland, OH, pg. 9
Nieves, John, Sr. V.P.-Mktg. & Sls.--New England Machinery, Inc., Bradenton, FL, pg. 800
Nightingale, Kathy, Dir.-Mammography Mktg.--Instrumentarium Imaging, Inc., Milwaukee, WI, pg. 572
Nikola, Richard J., Dir.-Sls.--Dietrich's Milk Products, Inc., Reading, PA, pg. 337
Nilson, John, Mgr.-Mktg.--Penrod Drilling Corporation, Dallas, TX, pg. 859
Niman, Mary, Dir.-Mktg.--Brock Control Systems, Inc., Atlanta, GA, pg. 178
Nishikawa, Morio, Mktg. Mgr.-Consumer Prods.--Johnson Company, Ltd., Yokohama, Japan, pg. 599
Nitz, Bruce E., V.P.-Sls. & Mktg.--Stanley Knight Corporation, New Troy, MI, pg. 1038
Nix, Gerald, Mgr.-Mktg. Services--Diversified Products Corporation, Opelika, AL, pg. 1193
Nizzere, Paul D., V.P.-Sls. & Mktg.--Pelouze Scale Co., Evanston, IL, pg. 856
Nocitra, Susan, Dir.-Mktg.--Fair Lanes Inc., Hunt Valley, MD, pg. 396
Nodelman, Edward, Asst. Mgr.-Mktg.--Falcon Safety Products Inc., Branchburg, NJ, pg. 398
Nontani, Anthony A., V.P.-Sls. & Mktg.--McInnes Steel Company, Corry, PA, pg. 729
Noone, John, Dir.-Agency Mktg.--Middlesex/Patriot General Insurance Companies, Concord, MA, pg. 751
Nordell, Peter, Dir.-Mktg. & Sls.--Edlund Company, Inc., Burlington, VT, pg. 368
Nordlander, Connie, Dir.-Mktg.--Bluewater Marine, Mora, MN, pg. 161
Noreen, Dan, Dir.-Mktg. & Sls.--Colorado Lottery, Denver, CO, pg. 265
North, Bob, Exec. Mktg. Dir.--Cargill Salt, Newark, CA, pg. 219
North, Bob, Dir.-Mktg.--Cargill Salt Division, Minneapolis, MN, pg. 219
North, Diane, Sr. V.P.-Direct Mktg.--Miller Meester Advertising Inc., Minneapolis, MN, pg. 754
Northup, Christopher, Dir.-Mktg.--Keystone Automotive Industries, Inc., Pomona, CA, pg. 627
Norton, Larry P., Dir.-Mktg.--Concrete Technology Corp., Tacoma, WA, pg. 273
Norton, Mary, V.P.-Mktg.--Thybony Wall Coverings Co., Chicago, IL, pg. 1096
Norton, Tim, Exec. V.P.-Sls. & Mktg.--AMD Industries Inc., Cicero, IL, pg. 5
Nova, Ben, Asst. Dir.-Mktg.--Arizona Lottery, Phoenix, AZ, pg. 82
Novacek, Art, Mgr.-Opers. & Mktg.--The Harry Alter Company, Chicago, IL, pg. 1086
Nover, Fred S., V.P.-Sls., Mktg. & Distr.--Empire Brushes, Inc., Greenville, NC, pg. 379
Novoselac, John, Mgr.-Mktg. & Sls.--Denver Equipment Company, Colorado Springs, CO, pg. 331
Nowak, Lynn, Mktg. Mgr.-Foodservice--Anderson Advertising, Inc., San Antonio, TX, pg. 72
Noyes, Gail, Div. V.P.-Mktg.--OMNI Industry, Denver, CO, pg. 463
Nubel, Edward, Dir.-Mktg.--Norrell Corporation, Atlanta, GA, pg. 810
Nulph, James L., Dir.-Mktg.--Virginia State Lottery Department, Richmond, VA, pg. 1153
Nunn, Dale E., V.P.-Corp. Mktg.--Golden Eagle Distributors, Inc., Tucson, AZ, pg. 466
Nusbaum, Dave, V.P.-Adv. & Pub. Rels. & Dir.-Mktg.--Kampgrounds of America, Inc., Billings, MT, pg. 613
Nussbaum, Robert, V.P.-Sls. & Mktg.--The Lenson Corporation, Pleasantville, NJ, pg. 582
O'Brian, Kevin, V.P.-Mktg.--Charles Jacquin et Cie, Inc., Philadelphia, PA, pg. 588
O'Brien, Donald, V.P.-Mktg.--Brookstone Company, Inc., Peterborough, NH, pg. 180
O'Brien, James, V.P.-Sls. & Mktg.--P M Company, Philadelphia, PA, pg. 835
O'Brien, Jim, V.P.-Sls. & Mktg.--P.M. Health Care Div., Philadelphia, PA, pg. 835
O'Brien, John, V.P.-Mktg.--Hickey-Mitchell Company, Saint Louis, MO, pg. 795
O'Brien, Michael, V.P.-Mktg.--Chiquita Brands, Inc., Cincinnati, OH, pg. 53
O'Connell, Edward, Mgr.-Mktg.--Pioneer Industrial Products Co., Willard, OH, pg. 871
O'Connor, Mary Lynn, Adv. & Mktg.--Xebec Corporation, Kansas City, MO, pg. 1206
O'Connor, Mike, Dir.-Direct Mktg.--LaMaster Farmer, Et Al, Minneapolis, MN, pg. 652
O'Connor, Patience, Sr. V.P.-Mktg.--Western Development Corporation, Washington, DC, pg. 1179
O'Connor, Ted, Mgr.-Sls.--Mohawk Paper Mills, Inc., Cohoes, NY, pg. 763
O'Day, Mark, Dir.-Mktg. Communications--Veryfine Products, Inc., Westford, MA, pg. 1148

O'Neil, P.A., Dir.-Mktg.--W. E. O'Neil Construction Company, Chicago, IL, pg. 827
O'Neill, Francis, Sr. V.P.-Sls. & Mktg.--Congoleum Corporation, Mercerville, NJ, pg. 274
O'Neill, Glenda W., Dir.-Mktg.--Diagraph Corporation, Earth City, MO, pg. 335
O'Neill, Stephen, Sr. V.P.-Mktg.--Alvey Inc., Saint Louis, MO, pg. 46
O'Shields, Betsy, Mgr.-Mktg.--Conso Products Company, Union, SC, pg. 276
Oakes, Marvin G., V.P.-Mktg.--Wilton Industries, Inc., Woodridge, IL, pg. 1194
Oates, Lynn, V.P.-Mktg.--Taylor Drug Stores, Inc., Louisville, KY, pg. 1081
Obey, Chris, Dir.-Mtkg.--MTD Products, Inc., Valley City, OH, pg. 694
Obey, Chris, Dir.-Mktg.--Aircap Industries Corp., Verona, MS, pg. 694
Oblak, Jim, Dir.-Mktg.--PhoneMate, Inc., Torrance, CA, pg. 869
Obrzut, Don, V.P.-Mktg.--National Food Stores, Inc. T/A Krauszer's, Edison, NJ, pg. 788
Oddo, Jim, V.P.-Mktg.--Atlas Hotels, Inc., San Diego, CA, pg. 96
Oeltjen, Ray, V.P.-Mktg.--Leupold & Stevens, Inc., Beaverton, OR, pg. 669
Oeschger, Gene, Sr. V.P.-Sls. & Mktg.--Wigwam Mills, Inc., Sheboygan, WI, pg. 1189
Okamoto, Takayuki, Dir.-Mktg. Services & Gen. Affairs--Leo Burnett-Kyodo Co. Ltd., Tokyo, Japan, pg. 192
Oldham, Darrell, Mgr.-Adv. & Mktg.--Seattle Times Company, Seattle, WA, pg. 986
Olerich, Richard B., Sr. V.P.-Sls. & Mktg.--Treasure Chest Advertising Co., Inc., Glendora, CA, pg. 1108
Olewnik, Richard L., V.P.-Mktg. Services--The Berkshire Life Insurance Company, Pittsfield, MA, pg. 142
Oligny, Vance, Dir.-Mktg.--Caddock Electronics, Inc., Riverside, CA, pg. 207
Olin, Thomas F. Jr., V.P.-Sls.--Archway Cookies, Inc., Battle Creek, MI, pg. 81
Olinger, Jerry, V.P.-Mktg.--Jofco Inc., Jasper, IN, pg. 595
Olinger, Michael L., V.P.-Intl. Mktg.--Telex Communications, Inc., Minneapolis, MN, pg. 1085
Oliver, Gregory, Sr. V.P.-Mktg.--Western Federal Savings & Loan Association, Marina Del Rey, CA, pg. 1179
Olmstead, David, V.P.-Sls. & Mktg.--Advance Machine Company, Plymouth, MN, pg. 18
Olsen, Donald, Exec. V.P.-Sls. & Mktg.--United States Ceramic Tile Co., East Sparta, OH, pg. 1135
Olson, E. Whitney, V.P.-Mktg.--Brix Maritime Co., Portland, OR, pg. 177
Olson, Gene, Sls. & Mktg. Mgr.--Dealers Manufacturing Company, Minneapolis, MN, pg. 322
Olson, Nobel D., V.P.-Mktg.--Rockford Acromatic Product Co., Rockford, IL, pg. 941
Olson, Thomas O., V.P.-Corp. Devel.--CUNA Mutual Insurance Society, Madison, WI, pg. 205
Ondras, Joseph G., Mktg. Dir.--Barge-Wagener, Inc., Atlanta, GA, pg. 119
Onigman, Sharon, Dir.-Mktg.--Advanced Instruments, Inc., Needham Heights, MA, pg. 20
Opheim, J.M., Mgr.-Sls. & Mktg.--Zephyr Baskets & Balloons, New Providence, NJ, pg. 1217
Opolko, Phyllis, Dir.-Mktg. & Pub. Rels.--Monarch Avalon, Inc., Baltimore, MD, pg. 765
Orall, John F., V.P.-Mktg.--Winthrop Printing Company, Inc., Boston, MA, pg. 1197
Orban, Rus, V.P.-Mktg.--Rutt Custom Cabinetry, Goodville, PA, pg. 957
Oringer, Hal, V.P.-Circulation & Mktg.--Cowles Magazines, Inc., Harrisburg, PA, pg. 291
Oris, D.C., Sr. V.P.-Mktg. & Sls.--Southern Pacific Lines, San Francisco, CA, pg. 1022
Orloff, Richard, Dir.-Mktg.--New Jersey Press, Inc., Neptune, NJ, pg. 801
Orlow, John, V.P.-Mktg.--Locks Advertising Agency, East Northport, NY, pg. 680
Orr, Doug, Dir.-Mktg. & Sls.--Iowa Lottery, Des Moines, IA, pg. 582
Ortonic, Frank, V.P.-Mktg.--Information Systems & Network Corporation, Bethesda, MD, pg. 567
Orvala, Lanny, Dir.-Mktg.--Lund Boats, New York Mills, MN, pg. 759
Osborn, Lee, Mgr.-Mktg.--Thrifty Drug Stores, Inc., Minneapolis, MN, pg. 1096
Osborn, Mike, V.P.-Mktg.--Sun Lakes Marketing, Sun Lakes, AZ, pg. 1059
Osborne, Brian, V.P.-Mktg.--Sentinel Computer Services Inc., Oak Brook, IL, pg. 990
Osborne, David, V.P.-Sls. & Mktg.--Uniphase Corporation, San Jose, CA, pg. 1129
Osborne, Robert C., V.P.-Health & Mkt. Devel.--Trans World Airlines, Inc., Mount Kisco, NY, pg. 561
Oseland, Bruce J., Sr. V.P.-Mktg.--Century 21 Real Estate Corp., Irvine, CA, pg. 744
Osowski, Kenneth, Dir.-Systems Mktg.--Charles River Data Systems, Inc., Framingham, MA, pg. 240
Ossip, Ronald, Dir.-Mktg.--Domecq Importers Inc., Old Greenwich, CT, pg. 343
Ostapowicz, Phil, V.P.-Mktg. & Sls.--Barry-Wehmiller Company, Saint Louis, MO, pg. 122
Osten, Gail, V.P.-Adv. & Mktg. Services--Chicago Mercantile Exchange, Chicago, IL, pg. 245
Oswall, Don, Mgr.-Mktg.--Tekni-Plex, Inc., Brooklyn, NY, pg. 1084
Ott, William F., Jr., Dir.-Mktg.--Watlow Electric Manufacturing Company, Saint Louis, MO, pg. 1167
Otti, John, V.P.-Mktg.--Smartstar Corporation, Goleta, CA, pg. 1011
Ouellette, Robert, Sr. V.P.-Mktg.--BCM Engineers Inc., Plymouth Meeting, PA, pg. 106
Owen, Michael, Dir.-Mktg.-Grocery Prods.--Uncle Ben's, Inc., Houston, TX, pg. 713
Owens, Howard, Mgr.-Prod.--Press Enterprise Company, Riverside, CA, pg. 887
Owens, Mary, Mktg. Coord.--A & W Restaurants, Inc., Livonia, MI, pg. 1
Owens, Park, Dir.-Mktg.--Fellowes Manufacturing Co., Itasca, IL, pg. 405
Ozimek, Sharon, Mgr.-Mktg. Services--Richco Plastics Company, Chicago, IL, pg. 933
Pacelli, Bob, Dir.-Mktg.--Dunn-Edwards Corporation, Los Angeles, CA, pg. 353
Pacifico, Joe, Exec. V.P.-Mktg.--The William Carter Company, New York, NY, pg. 226
Padnos, Mitchell W., V.P.-Sls. & Mktg.--Louis Padnos Iron & Metal Co., Holland, MI, pg. 842
Page, Janis, Dir.-Creative Service--Sampler Publications Inc., Saint Charles, IL, pg. 968
Paille', Ken, Mgr.-Mktg. Res.--L.L. Bean, Inc., Freeport, ME, pg. 648
Palante, Luke, V.P.-Sls. & Mktg.--Essex Grain Products, Inc., Frazer, PA, pg. 389
Palasciano, John, V.P.-Sls. & Mktg.--Harbour Industries, Inc., Shelburne, VT, pg. 507
Paley, William, Exec. V.P.-Mktg.--The Texwipe Co., Inc., Upper Saddle River, NJ, pg. 1090
Palisin, Edward F., V.P.-Mktg.--Venchurs Packaging, Inc., Adrian, MI, pg. 1147
Palmer, David, Sr. V.P.-Mktg. & Sls.--National Foods Inc., Bronx, NY, pg. 788
Palmer, David, V.P.-Sls.--Whitin Roberts Co., Sanford, NC, pg. 1187
Palmer, Stephanie, Mgr.-Mktg. Communications--Covalent Systems Corporation, Fremont, CA, pg. 290
Palmer, Steve, V.P.-Mktg.--Intermountain Farmers Association, Salt Lake City, UT, pg. 575
Palmer, Susan, Dir., List Mngmt.--Rubin Response Services, Inc., Schaumburg, IL, pg. 954
Palumbo, Mary, V.P.-Mktg.--Grandy's, Inc., Lewisville, TX, pg. 476
Pancoast, Robert, V.P.-Mktg.--MTI Vacations, Inc., Oak Brook, IL, pg. 694
Pape, Janet, Mktg. Analyst--Schwab Corp., Lafayette, IN, pg. 980
Papera, Richard D., V.P.-Sls. & Mktg.--Allstate Can Corporation, Clifton, NJ, pg. 43
Papi, Vincent J., V.P.-Mktg.--Allied Security, Inc., Pittsburgh, PA, pg. 39
Pardee, Richard L., Dir.-Mktg.--Preformed Line Products, Cleveland, OH, pg. 886
Pardue, Murray, V.P.-Mktg.--Post Buckley Schuh & Jernigan, Miami, FL, pg. 881
Parin, Floyd, V.P.-Mktg.--Microphase Corporation, Norwalk, CT, pg. 749
Pariza, George, V.P.-Plng. & Prod. Devel.--International Jensen Inc., Lincolnshire, IL, pg. 578
Park, Daryl Anne, Sr. V.P.-Mktg. & Sls.--Globe Business Furniture, Inc., Hendersonville, TN, pg. 463
Parke, Bob, V.P.-Mktg.--Ensoniq Corporation, Malvern, PA, pg. 382
Parker, Graham, Mgr.-Mktg.--J.T. Davenport & Sons, Inc., Sanford, NC, pg. 317
Parker, John, V.P.-Sls. & Mktg.--Aladdin Industries, Incorporated, Nashville, TN, pg. 29
Parker, W. Cary, V.P.-Food Mktg.--Riceland Foods, Inc., Stuttgart, AR, pg. 931
Parks, Michael, Mgr.-Mktg.--Security Products Company, Minneapolis, MN, pg. 1138
Parks, Michael, Mgr.-Mktg.--Security Products Company of Delaware, Inc., Minneapolis, MN, pg. 1138
Paro, John J., V.P.-Sls. & Mktg.--The C. P. Hall Company, Chicago, IL, pg. 501
Parrish, Stephen Bennett, V.P.-Mktg. Services--Central Life Assurance Co., Des Moines, IA, pg. 232
Partyka, Ed, Mgr.-Mktg.--Electrical Insulation Suppliers, Hillside, IL, pg. 374
Pasbach, L. R., V.P.-Mktg.--Lindenmeyr Munroe, Rutherford, NJ, pg. 233
Pash, J., V.P.-Kathabar Systems--Somerset Technologies, Inc., Somerset, NJ, pg. 1017
Pastor, Scott, Vice Chm.--W&F Manufacturing Corporation, Inc., Buffalo, NY, pg. 1155
Pastor, Todd, Pres.--W&F Manufacturing Corporation, Inc., Buffalo, NY, pg. 1155
Pasucci, Bob, V.P.-Sls. & Mktg.--Stegner Food Products Co., Cincinnati, OH, pg. 1045
Paszamant, David, Vice Chm., Exec. V.P. & Dir.-Mktg.--Adams Wine Co., Atlanta, GA, pg. 17
Pate, John G., V.P.-Prod. Devel.--Radionics, Inc., Salinas, CA, pg. 909
Paternack, Irene, Dir.-Mktg. Communications--Applied Microsystems Corporation, Redmond, WA, pg. 79
Patla, Mel, V.P.-Mktg. & Sls.--Chicago Convention & Tourism Bureau, Chicago, IL, pg. 245
Paton, Michael, Dir.-Mktg.--Peter Pan Bus Lines, Inc., Springfield, MA, pg. 864
Patterson, John, V.P.-Sls. & Mktg.--Mannington Wood Floors, High Point, NC, pg. 704
Patterson, Mel, Dir.-Mktg.--Moran Industries, Inc., Midlothian, IL, pg. 769
Patterson, Tom, Mgr.-Mktg.--Pip Printing, Agoura Hills, CA, pg. 616
Patton, Deborah, Dir.-Mktg.--Town & Country, New York, NY, pg. 523
Paul, Vincent, V.P.-Mktg.--Joanna, Charlotte, NC, pg. 200
Paulsen, Robert A., Mgr.-Mktg.--Albert Kahn Associates, Inc., Detroit, MI, pg. 613
Paulson, Christine, Promotion Coord.--Country Sampler, Saint Charles, IL, pg. 968
Pavelka, Ron, Dir.-Mktg.--Dacor Corporation, Northfield, IL, pg. 310
Pawlick, Thomas, Dir.-Mktg. Communications--Medline Industries, Inc., Mundelein, IL, pg. 736
Peabody, Charles, V.P.-Mktg.--Howell Laboratories, Inc., Bridgton, ME, pg. 548
Pearcy, D., V.P.-Sls. & Mktg.--Carpenter Manufacturing, Inc., Mitchell, IN, pg. 991
Pearsall, James R., V.P.-Mktg. & Sls.--Davis Walker Corp., Irwindale, CA, pg. 525
Pearsall, Roger, V.P.-Mktg.--National Safety Associates, Memphis, TN, pg. 793
Pearson, David, Dir.-Intl. PC Product Mktg.--WordPerfect Corporation, Orem, UT, pg. 1202
Pease, A.C., V.P.-Mktg.--National Welders Supply Co. Inc., Charlotte, NC, pg. 794
Peavey, Melia, Pres.--Peavey Electronic Corp., Meridian, MS, pg. 854
Pecha, Robert O., V.P.-Sls. & Mktg.--Chemstone Corp., Strasburg, VA, pg. 242
Peck, Richard, V.P.-Sls. & Mktg.--Levlad, Inc., Chatsworth, CA, pg. 671
Peck, Steven, Dir.-Mktg.--Bachman Company, Reading, PA, pg. 108
Pectros, M.J., V.P.-Mktg.--Academy Entertainment Inc., Beverly Hills, CA, pg. 86
Pede, Jacquie, Sr. Mkt. Analyst--J.R. Simplot Co., Minerals & Chemicals Group, Pocatello, ID, pg. 1007
Peill, Jerry C., Mgr.-Mktg.--American Felt & Filter, Newburgh, NY, pg. 52
Pelofsky, Mark, V.P., Internal Mktg. Mgr.--Barkley & Evergreen Advertising, Inc., Shawnee Mission, KS, pg. 120
Peloza, Susan, Dir.-Mktg.--Intercounty Title Co. of Illinois, Chicago, IL, pg. 574
Pelphrey, Gary, Dir.-Mktg.--Gourmet Foods Div., Omaha, NE, pg. 825
Pelton, Scott, V.P.-Mktg.--Metal Masters Foodservice Equipment, Smyrna, DE, pg. 741
Pendleton, Charles A., V.P.-Mktg.--Southeastern Freight Lines, Inc., Columbia, SC, pg. 1019
Pennavaria, Russell, Dir.-Mktg., Medical Div.--Cincinnati Sub-Zero Products, Inc., Cincinnati, OH, pg. 250
Pennell, Gary B., V.P.-Mktg.--Diamond Chain Company, Indianapolis, IN, pg. 69
Pennell, S.N., Dir.-Sls. & Mktg.--Romac Industries, Inc., Hays Division, Dallas, NC, pg. 945
Pennell, S.N., Dir.-Sls. & Mktg.--Hays Flood Controls, Dallas, NC, pg. 945
Pennick, Arthur, Dir.-Mktg.--Fox-Knapp Inc., New York, NY, pg. 427
Pensinger, Larry, Dir.-Mktg.--Hardware Wholesalers, Inc., Fort Wayne, IN, pg. 508
Peoples, Larry, Sr. V.P.-Mktg.--Riverside Manufacturing Co., Moultrie, GA, pg. 937
Peppler, Alice, Dir.-Mktg. Services--Augsburg Fortress, Publishers, Minneapolis, MN, pg. 98
Pepys, Renee, Dir.-Sls. & Mktg.--Noel-Joanna, Inc., Rancho Santa Margarita, CA, pg. 808
Perabo, James L., V.P., Dir.-Mktg. & New Bus. Contact--Kreps-Wise Associates, Saint Louis, MO, pg. 644
Perkins, Philip D., V.P.-Mktg.--Snyder's Drug Stores, Inc., Minnetonka, MN, pg. 1015
Perkins, Sara S., Sr. Mktg. Asst. & Asst. Sec.--W. P. Carey & Co., Inc., New York, NY, pg. 218
Perkins, Sherry, Dir.-Mktg.--J. E. Higgins Lumber Co., Concord, CA, pg. 533
Perkov, Adrian, Dir.-New Mkt. Devel.--J. Crew Group, Inc., New York, NY, pg. 584
Perks, Lachlen, V.P.-Mktg.--Eclipse, Inc., Rockford, IL, pg. 366
Perl, Allen S., V.P.--T.L. Diamond Company, New York, NY, pg. 335
Perlman, Milton, V.P.-Mktg. & Sls.--Schott Brothers, Inc., Perth Amboy, NJ, pg. 978
Peroutka, Michael S., V.P.-Sls. & Mktg.--Faribault Foods Inc., Minneapolis, MN, pg. 399
Perrella, Michael L., Dir.-Mktg.--Motor Boating & Sailing, New York, NY, pg. 523
Perrier, Gerald, V.P.-Mktg.--Welsco Inc., North Little Rock, AR, pg. 1175
Perry, Alfred J., V.P.-Sls. & Mktg.--Interstate Resources, Inc., Rosslyn, VA, pg. 580
Perry, R.D., V.P.-Mktg.--Millers' Mutual Insurance Assn. Of Illinois, Alton, IL, pg. 755
Perry, Robert J., V.P.-Mktg.--Heath Consultants Incorporated, Stoughton, MA, pg. 524
Pesavento, Gilbert, V.P.-Sls. & Mktg.--American Specialties Inc., Yonkers, NY, pg. 61
Pesch, Robert C., V.P.-Opers. & Prod. Devel.--Houston Foods Company, Chicago, IL, pg. 547
Pestovic, Edward J., Adv. Dir.--Steinbach, White Plains, NY, pg. 1045
Peters, Henry, V.P.-Mktg.--Miami Systems Corporation, Cincinnati, OH, pg. 746
Peters, Joseph M., V.P. & Dir.-Mktg.--Chamberlain Health & Beauty Aids Company, Des Moines, IA, pg. 238
Peters, Rich, 2nd V.P.-Mktg. Services & Pub. Rels.--Woodmen Accident & Life Co., Lincoln, NE, pg. 1200
Peters, Ron, V.P.-Mktg.--Hyman Freightways Inc., Moundsview, MN, pg. 557
Peterson, Kim T., V.P.-Mktg.--Regal Ware, Inc., Kewaskum, WI, pg. 921
Peterson, Ronald, Sr. V.P.-Mktg.--Jack Eckerd Corporation, Largo, FL, pg. 366
Peterson, Troy, Dir., Mktg. Services--Hoffman York & Compton, Milwaukee, WI, pg. 538
Petite, Joe, V.P.-Consumer Mktg.--The Scott Company, Marysville, OH, pg. 982
Petraitis, Paul, V.P.-Sls. & Mktg.--Premier Coatings, Inc., Elk Grove Village, IL, pg. 886
Pettersen, M., Dir.-Mixer Prods.--Shure Brothers Incorporated, Evanston, IL, pg. 1001
Pettis, Charles R., III, Sr. V.P. Mktg. & Business Development--Floathe Johnson Associates, Inc., Kirkland, WA, pg. 419
Petus, Charles, Mktg. Mgr.--Dukane Microrobotics Division, Saint Charles, IL, pg. 352
Peyer, Hans, Dir.-Mktg.-Greige Fine Goods--Milliken & Co., Inc., Spartanburg, SC, pg. 755

Pezold, Steve, Coord.-Direct Mail--Clayton-Davis & Associates, Incorporated, Saint Louis, MO, pg. 253
Pfeil, W., V.P.-Mktg.--Kenney Manufacturing Company, Warwick, RI, pg. 623
Phelan, J., Dir.-Intl. Mktg. & Sls.--Shure Brothers Incorporated, Evanston, IL, pg. 1001
Philbin, J. W., Dir.-Mktg. & Sls.--Altair Corporation, Lincolnshire, IL, pg. 45
Phillip, Wyatt, V.P.-Mktg.--QuikTrip Corporation, Tulsa, OK, pg. 905
Phillips, Bryant, Dir.-Mktg.--Hatteras Yachts, High Point, NC, pg. 758
Phillips, Dennis, V.P.-Mktg.--Cox & Company, Inc., New York, NY, pg. 292
Phillips, Donald P., Sr. V.P.-Sls. & Mktg.--Klein Tools Inc., Skokie, IL, pg. 635
Phillips, Neil, Mgr.-Retail--Be-Lo Markets Inc., Norfolk, VA, pg. 212
Phillips, Robert L., Mktg. Mgr.-West Coast--Grand Banks Yachts, Ltd., Greenwich, CT, pg. 475
Phillips, Scott, V.P.-Mktg.--W. Atlee Burpee Co., Warminster, PA, pg. 116
Phillips, Wayne, V.P.-Sls. & Mktg.--Pharmacaps Inc., Elizabeth, NJ, pg. 866
Piccola, Jay, V.P.-Sls. & Mktg.--Diadora America, Inc., Kent, WA, pg. 335
Pickett, Jerry, Sr. V.P.-Plng., Pur. & Distr.--Tropical Garment Manufacturing Company, Tampa, FL, pg. 1116
Piedra, Alfredo, Asst. V.P.-Mktg.--Bacardi Imports, Inc., Miami, FL, pg. 108
Pierce, Marc, V.P.-Sls. & Mktg.--Pentax Precision Instruments Corp., Orangeburg, NY, pg. 859
Pierce, Randy, Mgr.-Mktg. & Member Services--Cajun Electric Power Co-op, Baton Rouge, LA, pg. 207
Pierce, Walter, V.P.-Mktg.--Rau Fasteners, Inc., Providence, RI, pg. 913
Pierringer, Dean E., V.P.-Sls. & Mktg.--Research Products Corporation, Madison, WI, pg. 928
Pierson, Cathy, Mgr.-Mktg.--Didde Web Press, Emporia, KS, pg. 336
Pierson, Robert, V.P.-Sls. & Mktg.--Jervis B. Webb Company, Farmington Hills, MI, pg. 1170
Pierson, T.J., Dir.-Mktg.--Edwards Engineering Corporation, Pompton Plains, NJ, pg. 370
Pignone, Peter, V.P.-Tech. Service--Ark-Les Corporation, Watertown, MA, pg. 82
Pilchen, Bernie, Natl. Dir.-Mktg.--The Spring Air Company, Des Plaines, IL, pg. 1032
Pilchen, Dick, V.P.-Mktg.--Franchise World Headquarters, Milford, CT, pg. 1055
Pilz, Clayton, Mgr.-Sls. & Mktg.--Savage Arms Inc., Westfield, MA, pg. 973
Pimental, Frank, Exec. V.P.-Sls. & Mktg.--Weatherking Products, Inc., East Greenwich, RI, pg. 79
Pingue, Joe, Sr. V.P.-Mktg.--Phar-Mor, Inc., Youngstown, OH, pg. 866
Pinto, Stephen F., Mktg. Services Mgr.--Southwestern Industries, Inc., Rancho Dominguez, CA, pg. 1023
Pioch, Albert A., Mgr.-Sls. & Mktg.--WEN Products, Inc., Chicago, IL, pg. 1156
Pioppi, N. William, V.P.--Russell Harrington Cutlery Inc., Southbridge, MA, pg. 556
Pippin, Terry, Dir.-Mktg. & Pur.--Maverik Country Stores, Inc., Afton, WY, pg. 722
Pirnat, Alan, Mgr.-Sls.--Metal Seal & Products, Inc., Willoughby, OH, pg. 741
Pitman Schmidt, Robert, Dir.-Mktg.--Harold M. Pitman Co., Inc., Totowa, NJ, pg. 872
Pitney, Jim, Mgr.-Turbine Mktg.--Coppus Engineering Corp., Millbury, MA, pg. 285
Pittman, David, Sr. Mktg. Assoc.--SPSS Inc., Chicago, IL, pg. 964
Pitts, Denise A., Coordinator of Mktg.--Speakman Company, Wilmington, DE, pg. 1027
Pitzer, Randy, Mgr.-Mktg. Communications--SPSS Inc., Chicago, IL, pg. 964
Plaisier, Hank, V.P.-Sls. & Mktg.--Rauland-Borg Corporation, Skokie, IL, pg. 914
Plank, S. Craig, Mktg.--Sawyer Riley Compton Inc., Atlanta, GA, pg. 973
Plas, Raymond C., Exec. V.P.-Mktg. & Mdsg.--Gateway Apparel, Inc., Saint Louis, MO, pg. 445
Plath, R., V.P.-Mktg.--Selecto-Flash, Inc., West Orange, NJ, pg. 988
Platt, Richard, Exec. V.P.-Mktg. Div.--First Federal of Michigan, Detroit, MI, pg. 414
Plavocos, Alex, Dir.-Mktg.--Information Builders, New York, NY, pg. 567
Pless, Judy, V.P.-Bus. Devel.-Viacom World Wide--Viacom Enterprises, New York, NY, pg. 785
Plesser, Tully, Sr. V.P., Mkt. Plng. & Res.--Hal Riney & Partners, Inc., New York, NY, pg. 935
Pleszko, E.J., V.P.-Mktg.--Preformed Line Products, Cleveland, OH, pg. 886
Plews, Joe, Dir.-Intl. Mktg.--A-Dec, Inc., Newberg, OR, pg. 1
Plotkin, Loren, Dir.-Res. & Devel., Mktg. & Art--Macklanburg-Duncan Co., Oklahoma City, OK, pg. 697
Plowden, Amy L., Dir.-Mktg.--Arthur Treacher's, Inc., Youngstown, OH, pg. 87
Plympton, M., Mgr.-Mktg.--J.M. Huber, Flow Control Div., Tomball, TX, pg. 550
Podolski, Richard F., V.P.-Sls. & Mktg.--Serfilco, Ltd., Northbrook, IL, pg. 990
Poehling, Jim, V.P.-Sls. & Mktg.--Greenfield Industries Inc., Evans, GA, pg. 507
Poertner, Hank, Dir.-Mktg.--A-Dec, Inc., Newberg, OR, pg. 1
Poggenpohl, Teresa, Dir.-Mkt. Res.--Andersen Consulting, Chicago, IL, pg. 72
Pogorzelski, Dana, Dir.-Mktg.--The Bases Group, Covington, KY, pg. 124
Pohly, Diana, V.P., Bus. Devel.--Duval & Partners, Boston, MA, pg. 356
Poindexter, Randy, V.P.-Mktg.--BJ Acquisition Corp., Charlotte, NC, pg. 107
Polk, Harland L., V.P.-Sls.--Hughes Markets Inc., Irwindale, CA, pg. 552
Polston, Peter, V.P.-Sls. & Mktg.--Cowden Metal Specialties, Inc., Chino, CA, pg. 291
Pomianoski, Mike, V.P.-Mktg.--Congoleum Corporation, Mercerville, NJ, pg. 274
Pomplun, James, V.P.-Sls. & Mktg.--Cadet Manufacturing Company, Vancouver, WA, pg. 207
Pond, Nannette, Mgr.-Automotive Prods.--Dixson, Inc., Grand Junction, CO, pg. 341
Ponder, Linda, Project Coord.-Mktg.--Mrs. Fields' Inc., Park City, UT, pg. 761
Ponder, Linda, Project Coord.-Mktg.--Mrs. Fields Cookies Inc., Park City, UT, pg. 761
Ponte, James V., Dir.-Mktg. & Adv.--Cyrus Clark Co., Inc., New York, NY, pg. 253
Popp, Bohn, Dir.-Mktg.--Perfection Bakeries Inc., Fort Wayne, IN, pg. 861
Porter, Charles A., V.P.-Sls. & Mktg.--Peerless Pottery, Inc., Rockport, IN, pg. 855
Porter, Doug, V.P.-Mktg.--Spirit Cruises, Norfolk, VA, pg. 1031
Porter, Mark A., V.P.-Mktg.-Bedding--Sunbeam-Oster Household Products, Schaumburg, IL, pg. 1059
Porter, Michael C., V.P.-Mktg.--The Stroh Brewery Company, Detroit, MI, pg. 1053
Porterfield, Francis S., V.P.-Mktg.--Metropolitan Property & Casualty Insurance Co.(Met P&C), Warwick, RI, pg. 744
Porto, Barbara, Mktg. Coord.--Connecticut State Lottery, Newington, CT, pg. 275
Porto, John, V.P.-Sls. & Mktg.--Dri-Print Foils, Rahway, NJ, pg. 349
Posner, Fred I., Exec. V.P., Research & Mktg. Dir.--N W Ayer Incorporated, New York, NY, pg. 103
Posner, Fred I., Jr., Exec. V.P., Mng. Dir., Mktg. Plng. & Res.--N W Ayer Inc., New York, NY, pg. 104
Post, Charles, Dir.-Circulation--Kalmbach Publishing Co., Milwaukee, WI, pg. 615
Postma, Frank R., V.P.-Mktg.--The Okonite Company, Ramsey, NJ, pg. 823
Potter, Alfred K. II, V.P.-Mktg.--Gilbane Building Company, Providence, RI, pg. 457
Poulsen, Lance, V.P.-Sls. & Mktg.--Axelson, Inc., Longview, TX, pg. 103
Pountney, Dan, V.P.-Mktg.--Peoples Gas System, Inc., Tampa, FL, pg. 689
Powell, Jim, V.P.-Mktg. & Sls.--Sioux Honey Association, Sioux City, IA, pg. 1008
Powell, Ron, V.P.-Sls. & Mktg.--J & R Film Company, Los Angeles, CA, pg. 586
Powers, Dale, V.P.-Mktg. & Sls.--Deans Photo Service, Inc., San Diego, CA, pg. 322
Powers, J. Randal, V.P.-Mktg. & Agency Sls.--MSI Insurance Companies, Arden Hills, MN, pg. 693
Powers, J.E., V.P.-Mktg. & Sls.--Witt Company, Cincinnati, OH, pg. 1198
Powers, Jeffrey R., V.P.-Mktg.--The Rawlplug Company, Inc., New Rochelle, NY, pg. 914
Powers, Lynne, Sls. & Mktg. Coord.--Noel-Joanna, Inc., Rancho Santa Margarita, CA, pg. 808
Pozar, F., V.P.-Waldron Converting Machinery--Somerset Technologies, Inc., Somerset, NJ, pg. 1017
Pradetto, Richard V., Sr. V.P.-Mktg.--Cincinnati Incorporated, Harrison, OH, pg. 250
Pranses, Terrence J., V.P., Dir. Mktg. Devel.--Gilbert, Whitney & Johns, Inc., Whippany, NJ, pg. 458
Pratt, Roger P., V.P.-Mktg. & Sls.--Root Corporation, Mount Wolf, PA, pg. 946
Prazak, Joe, Mgr.-Farm-Lines Mktg.--DEC/Bou-Matic, Madison, WI, pg. 309
Presley, Rick, V.P.-Sls.--Cook Manufacturing Corporation, Duncan, OK, pg. 282
Pressler, Scott, Reg. Mktg. Mgr.--The Jolt Company, Rochester, NY, pg. 602
Pressman, Carol, Exec. V.P.-Sls. & Mktg.--Allied Old English, Inc., Port Reading, NJ, pg. 38
Prest, George, Mgr.-Mktg.--Prest Rack Inc., Warrenton, MO, pg. 151
Prettyman, Glenn C., V.P. Adv.--American Business Information, Inc., Omaha, NE, pg. 50
Prevatt, John W., V.P.-Sls. & Mktg.--Golden Gem Growers Inc., Umatilla, FL, pg. 466
Price, B., Dir.-New Products--Energy Brokers Guild, Stevensville, MI, pg. 381
Price, Bill, Mktg. Dir.--Your Man Tours, Inc., Inglewood, CA, pg. 1214
Price, Keith A., V.P.-Mktg.--The Hotsy Corporation, Englewood, CO, pg. 545
Price, Richard W., Mktg. Mgr.--Perfection Hy-Test Company, Florence, SC, pg. 711
Proto, Anthony, V.P.-Mktg. & Sls.--CEBCOR (Consolidated Employment Benefits Corp.), Chicago, IL, pg. 230
Proud, James D., Sr. V.P.-Sls. & Mktg.--The Hartz Mountain Corp., Harrison, NJ, pg. 514
Provencher, T.J., V.P.-Intl. Mktg.--Bodine Electric Company, Chicago, IL, pg. 162
Prues, John, Dir.-Mktg.--Dexol Industries, Inc., Torrance, CA, pg. 334
Pruzan, Ira, V.P.-Mktg.--Pollenex Corporation, Chicago, IL, pg. 879
Psaris, Georgette, V.P.-Mktg.--Trace Products, San Jose, CA, pg. 1104
Puglisi, Gerry, Dir.-Mktg. Services--Concordia Publishing House, Saint Louis, MO, pg. 272
Pugsley, John W., V.P.-Mktg. & Sls.--Edwards Brothers, Inc., Ann Arbor, MI, pg. 369
Pukering, Gordon, Dir.-Mktg.--Pickering Industries Inc., Tacoma, WA, pg. 869
Pulte, Earl F, Jr., Dir.-Sls. & Mktg.--Chicago Tube & Iron Co., Chicago, IL, pg. 246
Pundyk, Jon R., Dir.-Mktg.--Glamorise Foundations, Inc., New York, NY, pg. 460
Punton, Mike, Dir.-Mktg. & Adv.--Old Home Foods, Inc., Saint Paul, MN, pg. 823
Purser, Lat W., III, Pres. & Head of Devel.--Lat Purser & Associate, Charlotte, NC, pg. 901
Purvin, Thomas C., Mgr.-Mktg.--Aircraft Gear Corporation, Chicago, IL, pg. 27
Quesada, Juan, Exec. V.P.-Sls., Mktg. & Adv.--Cox Lumber Co., Saint Petersburg, FL, pg. 294
Quest, James H., Exec. V.P., Dir. Grp. Devel.--TBWA Advertising, Inc., New York, NY, pg. 1071
Quigley, William, V.P.-Mktg.--Fair Lanes Inc., Hunt Valley, MD, pg. 396
Quinlan, Robert M., V.P.-Mktg.--Gulf Oil, Westborough, MA, pg. 304
Quinlivan, William R., Mktg. Partner--Ad-Tech Communications, Miami Lakes, FL, pg. 16
Quitsch, Ciela, Group V.P., Adv./Mktg.--Esrock Advertising, Orland Park, IL, pg. 388
Rabadan, William, V.P.-Mktg.--Spinnerin Yarn Co., Inc., South Hackensack, NJ, pg. 1031
Rabeno, Lou, Mgr.-Mktg.--Lawrence Metal Products, Inc., Bay Shore, NY, pg. 662
Rader, James A., V.P.-Mktg.--The Pantry, Inc., Sanford, NC, pg. 846
Radler, Robert, Sr. V.P.-Mktg.--American Savings of Florida, ESB, Miami, FL, pg. 382
Radlicz, Dorothy, Mktg. Dir.-Estee--The Estee Corporation, Parsippany, NJ, pg. 389
Radomski, John, Gen. Mgr. & Mgr. Sls.--Sabbeth Industries Ltd, Deer Park, NY, pg. 965
Raebel, Richard, V.P.-Sls. & Mktg.--Republic Storage Systems Company Inc., Canton, OH, pg. 928
Raffaelli, Richard, V.P.-Sls. & Mktg.--Muskin Leisure Products, Inc., Wilkes-Barre, PA, pg. 777
Rager, Greg, V.P.-Sls. & Mktg.--Sporto Corp., Boston, MA, pg. 1032
Rahilly, D., Dir.-Mktg. & Sls.-U.S.A.--Timex Corporation, Middlebury, CT, pg. 1098
Raiskin, James, V.P.-Mktg. & Sls.--Winston Steel Products Co., Detroit, MI, pg. 1197
Raizman, Dir.-Mktg., Intl. Bus.--RELA, Inc., Boulder, CO, pg. 924
Raizman, Marc, Dir.-Mktg.--RELA Product Development Div. (PDD), Boulder, CO, pg. 924
Ramey, Tom, V.P.-Mktg.--Golden Cat Corporation, South Bend, IN, pg. 637
Ramey, William M., Sr. V.P.-Mktg.--Citizens Gas & Coke Utility, Indianapolis, IN, pg. 250
Ramsay, Bob, Prod. Mgr.--Crosman Corporation, East Bloomfield, NY, pg. 695
Ramsdell, Robert, V.P.-Mktg. & Sls.-Lawn, Farm & Garden--Universal Cooperatives, Inc., Minneapolis, MN, pg. 1138
Randolph, Ron, Dir.-Mktg.--American Laundry Machinery Inc., Cincinnati, OH, pg. 57
Raniszeski, Edward L., Exec. V.P.-Sls. & Mktg.--AmTran Corporation, Conway, AR, pg. 69
Rapaport, Michael, Dir.-Mktg.--Bresler's Industries, Inc., Des Plaines, IL, pg. 174
Rapaport, Michael, Dir.-Mktg.--Larry's Industries, Inc., Des Plaines, IL, pg. 174
Rapaport, Michael E., Dir.-Mktg.--Pro*Portion Industries, Inc., Des Plaines, IL, pg. 174
Rash, Douglas R., V.P.-Mktg.--Gaymar Industries, Inc., Orchard Park, NY, pg. 447
Rash, Edward, Dir.-Mktg. Communications--Clifford B. Hannay & Son Inc., Westerlo, NY, pg. 505
Rasmussen, J.A., V.P. & Dir.-Mktg.--The Uhlmann Co., Kansas City, MO, pg. 1125
Rather, Daniel B., Vice Chm. & Sr. Mktg. Dir.--Carter, Atlanta, GA, pg. 226
Rauss, William G., Dir.-Sls. & Mktg.--Edwin B. Stimpson Company, Inc., Bayport, NY, pg. 1049
Rawers, Mindy, Mktg. Mgr.--Union-Tribune Publishing Company, San Diego, CA, pg. 284
Rawlings, Robert L., V.P.-Sls. & Mktg.--John Zink Co., Tulsa, OK, pg. 639
Ray, David, V.P.-Mktg. & Pur.--Baird Ray Nissan, Inc., Longwood, FL, pg. 114
Ray, Lisa D., Sls. Coord., Public Rels. & Mktg.--Ray Communications, Inc., Elizabeth City, NC, pg. 914
Raymond, Eileen, Matl. Control Supvr.--IFP Hydraulics Inc., Franklin Park, IL, pg. 559
Raymond, Randy, V.P.-Mktg.--Cambridge Street Metal Co., Inc., Allston, MA, pg. 211
Razzetti, Gustavo, Mktg. Svcs. Dir.--Ayer Vazquez S.A. de Publicidad, Buenos Aires,, Argentina, pg. 104
Read, Robert O., Mgr.-Plng. & Human Resources--Matthews International Corp., Pittsburgh, PA, pg. 721
Readdy, William G., Dir.-Mktg.--Newly Weds Foods Inc., Chicago, IL, pg. 804
Reak, Ben, Sr. V.P.-Corp. Devel.--Weasler Engineering Inc., West Bend, WI, pg. 1169
Recca, Janet, Dir.-Mktg.--NJ Transit, Newark, NJ, pg. 801
Redensek, Ed, Asst. V.P.-Adv.--Decor Corporation, Columbus, OH, pg. 324
Redington, Brian, V.P.-Mktg.--Graycor, Inc., Homewood, IL, pg. 479
Reed, Russ, Dir.-Sls. & Mktg.--Aeroglide Corporation, Cary, NC, pg. 22
Rees, Michael, V.P.-Mktg.--The Sico Company, Mount Joy, PA, pg. 1001
Reese, Michael T., V.P.-Mktg.--Sisco Company, Mount Joy, PA, pg. 413
Reese, Monty, Sr. V.P.-Mktg.--Ernst Home Center, Inc., Seattle, WA, pg. 387
Rehling, Louise, Sr. V.P.-Devel.--SPSS Inc., Chicago, IL, pg. 964
Rehmert, Rory, V.P.-Mktg.--Meadowcraft, Inc., Birmingham, AL, pg. 733
Reichert, R.J., Mgr.-Mktg. Services--DEC/Bou-Matic, Madison, WI, pg. 309
Reicherter, Derek, V.P.-Mktg. Plng.--Newbridge Communications, New York, NY, pg. 611
Reichwald, William H., Exec. V.P.-Mktg.--Lutheran Brotherhood, Minneapolis, MN, pg. 688

Corporate Responsibilities Index

Reid, Garrett, Mktg. Dir.--Brodhead-Garrett Co., Mansfield, OH, pg. 178
Reider, Thomas D., V.P.-Sls. & Mktg.--The Jewett Refrigerator Co., Inc., Buffalo, NY, pg. 957
Reifeiss, Gary, V.P.-Mktg. & Consumer Prods.--Producers Rice Mill Inc., Stuttgart, AR, pg. 892
Reilly Dave, V.P.-Sls. & Mktg.--O'Brien Machinery Company, Downingtown, PA, pg. 820
Reinhardt, Dan, Strategic Mktg. Assoc.--Lewis & Gace, Inc., Fort Lee, NJ, pg. 673
Reis, R.J., Exec. V.P.--Serigraph, Inc., West Bend, WI, pg. 991
Reitzner, James A., V.P.-Mktg.--Steenberg Homes, Inc., Fond du Lac, WI, pg. 1045
Remstad, Michael, Mgr.-Mktg.--Tuff-Kote Dinol, Inc., Troy, MI, pg. 1217
Remstad, Michael, Mgr.-Mktg.--Tidy Car International, Inc., Troy, MI, pg. 1217
Renken, Ed, Dir.-Mktg.--Renken Boat Manufacturing Co., Charleston, SC, pg. 927
Renne, Randall, Dir.-Sls. & Mktg.--Raynor Garage Door Company, Dixon, IL, pg. 915
Renne, Virgil L., V.P.-Employer Prod. Mktg.--Northwestern Mutual Life Insurance Co., Milwaukee, WI, pg. 815
Reno, David, Mgr.-Mktg.--Kern's Bakeries, Incorporated, Knoxville, TN, pg. 624
Rensberger, Michael J., V.P.-Mktg. Support--The Acacia Group, Washington, DC, pg. 10
Resch, Ron, Mgr.-Opers.--Cartwright Communications Co., Cincinnati, OH, pg. 227
Resh, Edward, Dir.-Mktg.--Lone Star Corrugated Container Corporation, Irving, TX, pg. 682
Resnick, Dennis A., V.P.-Sls. & Mktg.--Reitman Industries, West Caldwell, NJ, pg. 924
Resnik, Robert, Dir.-Mktg.--L. Powell Co., Inc., Culver City, CA, pg. 882
Reszko, J., Dir.-Mktg.--Walter J. Black, Inc., Port Washington, NY, pg. 154
Rettke, Ralph P., V.P.-New Prod. Devel.--W. Braun Company, Chicago, IL, pg. 172
Retz, John R., V.P.-Mkt. Devel.--VASA Brougher, Inc., Indianapolis, IN, pg. 1146
Retzler, Kurt E., V.P.-Acquisitions Devel.--Carlson Companies, Inc., Minneapolis, MN, pg. 220
Reynolds, Barbara, V.P.-Mktg.--Realty One, Cleveland, OH, pg. 917
Reynolds, Laurence E., V.P., Mktg.--R.J. Palmer, Inc., New York, NY, pg. 844
Rhees, H., V.P.-Mktg.--Champion Pneumatic Machinery Co., Inc., Princeton, IL, pg. 238
Rhiver, Marc, V.P.-Sls. & Mktg.--Red Spot Paint & Varnish Co., Evansville, IN, pg. 918
Rhodenbaugh, Jeff P., Dir.-Mktg.--Specialty Equipment Companies Inc., Belvidere, IL, pg. 1027
Rhodes, Pam, Dir.-Mktg.--DHL Airways, Inc., Redwood City, CA, pg. 309
Rhodes, Paul, V.P.-Mktg.--Industrial Dielectrics, Inc., Noblesville, IN, pg. 566
Rhodes, Steve, V.P.-Mktg. & Sls.--Paramount Fitness Equipment Corp., Los Angeles, CA, pg. 848
Ricci, Victor, V.P.-Mdsg. & Mktg.--Camp Hosiery, New York, NY, pg. 400
Ricciarelli, Paul, Dir.-Mktg.--Empire Brushes, Inc., Greenville, NC, pg. 379
Rice, David, V.P.-Mktg. & Corp. Sec.--New Haven Savings Bank, New Haven, CT, pg. 801
Rice, Pat, V.P.-Corporate Devel.--The LINC Group, Inc., Chicago, IL, pg. 648
Rice, Steven, Dir.-Sls.--North Atlantic Industries Systems Division, Columbia, MD, pg. 812
Richards, Barbara, Sr. V.P.-Mktg.--Chicago Mercantile Exchange, Chicago, IL, pg. 245
Richards, John, Sr. V.P.--National Machinery Company, Tiffin, OH, pg. 792
Richardson, Jeff, Dir.-Mktg.--Children's Better Health Institute, Indianapolis, IN, pg. 139
Richelson, Joanne, Mktg. Dept.--Thompson Medical Company, Inc., West Palm Beach, FL, pg. 1094
Richert, G., V.P.-Sls. & Mktg.--Layne & Bowler, Memphis, TN, pg. 710
Richey, Alvan E. Jr., V.P.-Mktg.--American Buildings Co., Eufaula, AL, pg. 49
Richfield, Mark, Asst. Dir.-Mktg.--Vilter Manufacturing Corporation, Milwaukee, WI, pg. 1152
Richman, Steve, Dir.-Mktg.--Union Pen Company, Greenwich, CT, pg. 1128
Richman, Susan, Supvr., Direct Mktg.--Marquardt & Roche Inc., Stamford, CT, pg. 713
Richmond, Holly, V.P. & Dir.-Mktg.--Tele-Trip Co., Omaha, NE, pg. 779
Riedel, James F., V.P.-Mktg. & Adv.--Webster Industries Inc., Tiffin, OH, pg. 1171
Riesenberg, Ed, Mgr.-Prod.--Fishman & Tobin, Inc., Philadelphia, PA, pg. 415
Riggon, Mike, Exec. V.P.-Mktg. & Mdse.--PetCare Plus, Inc., Addison, IL, pg. 863
Riggs, Dennis, Mgr.-Mktg.--Cox Hobbies, Inc., Corona, CA, pg. 294
Riggs, Larry, Sr. V.P.-Sls. & Mktg.--Warmington Homes, Costa Mesa, CA, pg. 1164
Riley, Charles R., V.P.-Sls. & Mktg.--Meade Group, Inc., Detroit, MI, pg. 733
Riley, Daniel J., Sr. V.P.-Sls., Mktg. & Devel.--St. Johnsbury Trucking Co., Inc., Holliston, MA, pg. 966
Riley, William, Mgr.-Materials--Label-Aire Inc., Fullerton, CA, pg. 649
Rinehart, Rick, V.P.-Grp. Mktg. Sls., West--Blue Cross and Blue Shield of Oklahoma, Tulsa, OK, pg. 159
Ringland, Dennis, Dir.-Sls. & Mktg.--Granite State Manufacturing Co., Manchester, NH, pg. 476
Rissmeyer, Henry, Chief-Mktg. & Adv. Services--Metropolitan Transportation Authority, New York, NY, pg. 745
Ristaino, Bob, V.P.-Sls., Mktg. & Service--New England Coffee Company, Malden, MA, pg. 800
Ritscher, Charles W., V.P.-Mktg., Sls. & Sec.--New Jersey Press, Inc., Neptune, NJ, pg. 801
Rittenhouse, G.H., V.P.-Grp. Mktg.--Guarantee Mutual Life Co., Omaha, NE, pg. 491
Riviere, Donald, V.P.-Mktg. & Plng.--Menasha Corporation, Neenah, WI, pg. 738
Rizk, Amin, Mgr.-Mktg.--Muelhens, Inc., Orange, CT, pg. 774
Rizzuto, Ed, V.P.-Mktg., Acoustic Div.--Fender Musical Instruments, Scottsdale, AZ, pg. 406
Roache, Ned, Sr. V.P.-Sls. & Mktg.--Agripac Inc., Salem, OR, pg. 25
Roaman, Peter M., Exec. V.P.-Mktg.--Forstmann & Company, Inc., New York, NY, pg. 424
Robb, Chuck, Reg. Mktg. Mgr.--The Jolt Company, Rochester, NY, pg. 602
Robbs, Sherm, Mgr.-Mktg.--Farmland Foods, Inc., Kansas City, MO, pg. 402
Roberson, Donald, Dir.-Mktg. & Sls.--Theradyne Corporation, Lakeville, MN, pg. 1065
Roberts, Bill, V.P.-Mktg. & Sls.--J.R. Simplot Co. Food Group, Boise, ID, pg. 1007
Roberts, C.F., Dir.-Mktg. Services--Armstrong International, Inc., Three Rivers, MI, pg. 83
Roberts, Dale, V.P., Mktg.--Veda Design Group, Alexandria, VA, pg. 1146
Roberts, Dale R., Mktg. Dir.--Veda Incorporated, Alexandria, VA, pg. 1146
Roberts, Daniel, V.P.-Mktg. & Sls.--Crosman Corporation, East Bloomfield, NY, pg. 695
Roberts, Daniel, V.P.-Mktg.--Flexible Flyer Inc., West Point, MS, pg. 847
Roberts, David L., Dir.-Mktg. Admin.--Visa U.S.A. Inc., San Mateo, CA, pg. 1153
Roberts, Donald V., Dir.-Mktg.--CH2M Hill Companies, Ltd., Englewood, CO, pg. 202
Roberts, Harold, Sr. V.P.-Mktg.--OmniCare Health Plan, Detroit, MI, pg. 826
Roberts, Harold, Sr. V.P.-Mktg. & Sls.--United American Healthcare Corp., Detroit, MI, pg. 826
Roberts, J.W., Sr. V.P.-Mktg.--Hooker Furniture Corporation, Martinsville, VA, pg. 543
Roberts, Mary, Mgr.-Mktg.--Estes Industries, Inc., Penrose, CO, pg. 1011
Roberts, Ted, V.P.-Sls.--Dean Operations Inc., Kansas City, MO, pg. 322
Roberts, Tom, V.P.-Mktg.--C.F. Haglin & Sons, Minneapolis, MN, pg. 499
Roberts, W.I., V.P.-Mktg.--J.M. Huber, Printing Ink Div., Edison, NJ, pg. 550
Roberts, William J., V.P.-Mktg.--Houston Engineers, Houston, TX, pg. 1194
Robertson, C. Frank, Mgr.-Natl. Mktg.--Osmose Wood Preserving Co., Buffalo, NY, pg. 830
Robertson, Steve, V.P.-Mktg.--The Keller Manufacturing Co., Inc., Corydon, IN, pg. 621
Robertson, Vic, V.P.-Sls. & Mktg.--TimeMed Labeling Systems, Inc., Burr Ridge, IL, pg. 1098
Robichaux, David A., V.P.-Mktg. & Plng.--The Austin Company, Cleveland, OH, pg. 790
Robins, Bernard, Sr. V.P.-Mktg.--West Coast Life Insurance Co., San Francisco, CA, pg. 775
Robinson, Dan, Dir.-Mktg.--Top Flight, Inc., Chattanooga, TN, pg. 1101
Robinson, Dinah, V.P., Dir. Mktg. Services--Caroline Jones Advertising, Inc., New York, NY, pg. 603
Robinson, Donna Whalen, Dir.-Mktg.--BNA Electronic Media Div., Washington, DC, pg. 189
Robinson, George L., V.P.-Adv. & Mktg.--Spartan International, Holt, MI, pg. 1026
Robinson, J. Douglas, Sr. V.P.-Mktg.--Utica Mutual Insurance Company, New Hartford, NY, pg. 1140
Robinson, Larry M., V.P.-Life Mktg.--Nationwide Life Insurance Co., Columbus, OH, pg. 795
Robinson, Larry M., V.P.-Mktg.--Nationwide Health Care Corp., Columbus, OH, pg. 795
Robinson, Mike, V.P.-Sls. & Mktg.--General Marine Industries, Inc., Panama City, FL, pg. 449
Robinson, Steven A., V.P.-Mktg.--Chick-Fil-A, Inc., Atlanta, GA, pg. 247
Robnett, Phil, V.P.-Mktg. & Prod. Devel.--Ferry-Morse Seed Company, Modesto, CA, pg. 407
Robson, James, Gen. Mgr.-Sls. & Mktg.--Darigold, Inc., Seattle, WA, pg. 315
Robson, James, Gen. Mgr.-Sls. & Mktg.--Dairygold Inc., Seattle, WA, pg. 311
Rocca, F.H., V.P.-Mktg. & Sls.--Neapco, Inc., Pottstown, PA, pg. 1123
Rochester, Geof, V.P.-Mktg.--Radisson Hotel Corporation, Minneapolis, MN, pg. 221
Rockafellow, Al, V.P.-Mktg.--Aluma Shield Industries, Inc., Daytona Beach, FL, pg. 46
Rockwell, V.P.-Mktg.--U.S. Repeating Arms Company, New Haven, CT, pg. 1137
Roddenbery, Ralph J., Exec. V.P.-Sls. & Mktg.--W. B. Roddenbery Company, Inc., Cairo, GA, pg. 942
Rodgensack, Bartley E., V.P.-Mktg.--International Permalite, Inc., Ontario, CA, pg. 579
Rodgers, David, Mgr.-Mktg.--Digital Pathways Inc., Mountain View, CA, pg. 337
Rodgers, Dennis L., Dir.-Mktg.--RHS, Santa Fe Springs, CA, pg. 907
Rogal, Steve, Dir.-Mktg.--Attwood Corporation, Lowell, MI, pg. 1044
Rogalski, J.A., Mgr.-Mktg.--J.M. Huber, Wood Products Div., Charlotte, NC, pg. 550
Rogers, Bruce H., Dir.-Mkt. Devel.--Forbes, Inc., New York, NY, pg. 423
Rogers, Marshall, Sr. V.P., Dir. Mktg. Res. & Plng.--Hill, Holliday/Los Angeles, Marina Del Rey, CA, pg. 534
Rogers, Steve, Dir.-Mktg.--OCTus, San Diego, CA, pg. 818
Rogers, W.K., V.P.-Rates & Industrial Mktg.--Mississippi Valley Gas Co., Jackson, MS, pg. 1208
Rokos, Michelle, Coord.-Mktg.--Fair Lanes Inc., Hunt Valley, MD, pg. 396
Roland, Christopher, Exec. V.P.-Mktg.--Darling-Delaware Co., Inc., Irving, TX, pg. 315
Roll, Rick, Exec. V.P.-Sls. & Mktg.--Hackney & Sons, Inc., Washington, NC, pg. 498
Rolle, Ken, V.P.-Mktg.--Radionics, Inc., Salinas, CA, pg. 909
Rolls, D., V.P.-Mktg.--The Chamberlain Group, Inc., Elmhurst, IL, pg. 350
Roloff, Marvin, V.P.-Mktg.--Augsburg Fortress, Publishers, Minneapolis, MN, pg. 98
Roman, Patti, V.P.-Mktg.--Clemco Industries Corp., Washington, MO, pg. 254
Romanek, Joanne, Mktg. Services Mgr.--Intertec Publishing Corp., Edgemont, PA, pg. 611
Romeis, Chris, V.P.-Big A Program--A.P.S., Inc., Houston, TX, pg. 5
Romine, Russel, Mgr.-Mktg.--Mountain Air Delivery, Sparks, NV, pg. 773
Ronchetto, Dave, V.P.-Sls. & Adv.--Shoreline Products, Inc., Arlington, TX, pg. 1000
Ronidez, G.A., V.P.-Mktg.--Buckman Laboratories, Memphis, TN, pg. 185
Ronis, Marty, V.P.-Mktg.--Michigan Wheel Corporation, Grand Rapids, MI, pg. 747
Rooke, Donald B., Exec. V.P.-Mktg. & Sls.--American Saw & Manufacturing Co., East Longmeadow, MA, pg. 60
Rootberg, Philip, V.P.-Corp. Devel.--The Jupiter Corporation, Chicago, IL, pg. 609
Roppolo, Louis, V.P.-Mktg.--Roux Laboratories, Inc., Jacksonville, FL, pg. 696
Roppolo, Louis J., Sr. V.P.-Mktg.--Revlon-Realistic Professional Products, Inc., New York, NY, pg. 696
Rose, John, Dir.-Bus. Devel.--Accu-Sort Systems, Inc., Telford, PA, pg. 1[illegible]
Rosen, David, V.P.-Leasing, Mktg. & Adv.--Rosen Associates Management Corp., Jericho, NY, pg. 948
Rosen, Ralph J., V.P.-Sls. & Mktg.--Yerger Bros., Inc., Lititz, PA, pg. 1208
Rosenberg, James, Exec. V.P. & Dir.-Mktg.--Berenson, Isham & Partners, Inc., Boston, MA, pg. 141
Rosenberg, Michael, Dir.-Mktg.--Vienna Biscuit Co., Emerson, NJ, pg. 550
Rosenberger, Roger L., Sr. V.P.-Telemarketing--John Alden Financial Corporation, Miami, FL, pg. 32
Rosenblum, Mel, Mktg. Dir.--Goldberger Doll Mfg. Company, Inc., Brooklyn, NY, pg. 466
Rosendorf, Carl, Exec. V.P.-Mdse. & Mktg., College--Barnes & Noble Bookstores, Inc., New York, NY, pg. 120
Rosenthal, Mark, Exec. V.P.-Affil. Sls. & Mktg.--MTV Networks, New York, NY, pg. 785
Rosenthal, Steve, V.P.-Mktg.--Remco Toys, New York, NY, pg. 926
Rosenwald, James B., V.P.-OEM Mktg. & Dir.-Sls.--Leviton Mfg. Co., Inc., Little Neck, NY, pg. 671
Rosenzwog, Harvey, Exec. V.P.-Mktg.--Monumental Millwork, Inc., Westminster, MD, pg. 768
Roslow, Peter, V.P.-Sls. & Mktg.--Univision Holdings, Inc., New York, NY, pg. 502
Ross, Alan, V.P.-New Business Devel.--Cyborg Systems, Inc., Chicago, IL, pg. 307
Ross, Franklin, V.P.-Mktg.--Bollinger Industries Inc., Irving, TX, pg. 163
Ross, Mary, V.P., Direct Mktg. Dir.--Colle & McVoy, Inc., Minneapolis, MN, pg. 261
Ross, Michael, Dir.-Mktg.--D & W Food Centers, Inc., Grand Rapids, MI, pg. 308
Rossen, Elliot P., V.P.-Mktg.--Strombecker Corporation, Chicago, IL, pg. 1054
Rossi, Dave, V.P.-Mktg.--SGI Inc., Cranston, RI, pg. 962
Rossi, John, V.P.-Adv. & Mktg.--Seminole Manufacturing Company, Columbus, MS, pg. 989
Rosskam, Steve, Exec. V.P.-Sls. & Mktg.--David Michael & Co. Inc., Philadelphia, PA, pg. 747
Rossow, Robert W., V.P.-Sls. & Mktg.--Manufacturers Technologies, Inc., West Springfield, MA, pg. 705
Rost, Dan, Mgr.-Mktg.--Stock Yards Packing Co., Inc., Chicago, IL, pg. 1049
Rotatori, Enzo F., V.P.-Mktg.--Christy's Markets, Inc., Brockton, MA, pg. 249
Rotert, Kent, Mgr.-Mktg. Communications--Vermeer Manufacturing Company, Pella, IA, pg. 1148
Roth, Andrew, Dir.-Mktg.--ATAPCO Office Products Group, Saint Louis, MO, pg. 64
Roth, J.J., V.P.-Food & Bev. Mkt.--Sverdrup Corporation, Maryland Heights, MO, pg. 1065
Roth, Martin A., V.P.-Opers. Plng. & Research--U.S. Can Company, Oak Brook, IL, pg. 1134
Roth, Richard, Exec. V.P.-Sls. & Mktg.--Queens Group, Inc., Long Island City, NY, pg. 904
Roth, Richard, Exec. V.P.-Sls. & mktg.--Queens Group Indiana, Inc., Indianapolis, IN, pg. 904
Roth, Richard, Exec. V.P.-Sls. & Mktg.--Queens Group Design, New York, NY, pg. 904
Roth, Thomas, V.P., Mktg.--Stiegler, Wells & Brunswick, Inc., Bethlehem, PA, pg. 1049
Roths, Jim, Mktg. Mgr.--Telex Hy-gain Div., Lincoln, NE, pg. 1085
Rothschild, Martin, V.P.-Mktg.-Healthcare--Aladdin Synergetics, Inc., Nashville, TN, pg. 29
Rounce, J.R., V.P.-Mktg.--Biddle Instruments, Blue Bell, PA, pg. 148
Rouse, John, V.P.-Worldwide Sls. & Mktg.--MICOM Communications Corp., Simi Valley, CA, pg. 748
Roux, David J., Sr. V.P.-Mktg.--Central Point Software, Inc., Beaverton, OR, pg. 234
Rowan, Tom W., Jr., V.P.-Sls. & Mktg.--Johanson Manufacturing Corporation, Boonton, NJ, pg. 595
Rowekamp, David A., Sr. V.P.-Sls. & Mktg.--The Wooster Brush Company, Wooster, OH, pg. 1202
Rowley, J.M., V.P.-Contracts & Mktg.--Penrod Drilling Corporation, Dallas, TX, pg. 859

Rowse, Steven, V.P.-Mktg.--Veryfine Products, Inc., Westford, MA, pg. 1148
Roy, Dennis, Chief Oper. Officer & Dir., Mktg. Services--BEC Advertising, Chicago, IL, pg. 106
Roy, Dennis S., Dir.-Mktg. Services--Beltone Electronics Corporation, Chicago, IL, pg. 137
Roy, Mike, Dir.-Sls. & Mktg.--Kohler Ltd., Etobicoke,, Canada, pg. 640
Rozzi, S.J., Mgr.-Corp. Mktg.--Benjamin Moore & Co., Montvale, NJ, pg. 139
Ruback, Nancy, Mktg. & Sls. Coord.--Seymour of Sycamore, Inc., Sycamore, IL, pg. 994
Rubin, Bennett, V. P.-Mktg. & Sls.--The Genie Company, Alliance, OH, pg. 452
Rubin, Bennett, V.P.-Mktg. & Sls.--The Genie Company, Akron, OH, pg. 452
Rubin, Richard, V.P.-Mktg.--Dexter Shoe Company, Dexter, ME, pg. 334
Rubini, Roberto, V.P.-Mktg.--Cissell Manufacturing Company, Louisville, KY, pg. 357
Rubzin, Todd, Dir.-Mktg.--Tiffany Extruders, Inc., Paterson, NJ, pg. 1096
Rucker, Donna, Mktg. Dir.--BA Advertising, Dallas, TX, pg. 105
Ruddell, Brad, Dir.-Mktg.--Weatherby, Inc., South Gate, CA, pg. 1169
Rudolph, Richard M., V.P.-Mktg.--Rudolph Foods Company, Lima, OH, pg. 954
Ruediger, Brent E., V.P.-Mktg.--Troy Mills, Inc., Troy, NH, pg. 1116
Rueff, Bob, Chief Exec. Officer & Mktg. Dir.--Clarity Coverdale Rueff Advertising, Minneapolis, MN, pg. 251
Ruehlmann, Jim, V.P.-Brand Mktg.--John Morrell & Co., Cincinnati, OH, pg. 54
Ruga, Pat, V.P.-Mktg.--Acorn Engineering Company, City of Industry, CA, pg. 14
Ruggles, Patrick, V.P.-Mktg.--Sentinel Consumer Products, Inc., Mentor, OH, pg. 990
Ruhlman, Robert G., V.P.-Corp. Plng.--Preformed Line Products, Cleveland, OH, pg. 886
Rumsfield, Jean, Dir.-Mktg.--GenDerm Corporation, Lincolnshire, IL, pg. 448
Rupkey, Julie, Sls./Mktg. Analyst--Andes Candies, Inc., Delavan, WI, pg. 169
Rupp, Robert, Dir.-Mktg.--Shade Computer Forms Co., Green Bay, WI, pg. 994
Rusch, Don, Mgr.-Mktg.--Midwest Industries, Inc., Ida Grove, IA, pg. 752
Russ, Edmond V., Dir.-Mktg.--American Appraisal Associates, Inc., Milwaukee, WI, pg. 48
Russell, Cecil, Dir.-Mktg.--Save Mart Supermarkets, Modesto, CA, pg. 973
Russell, Ed, V.P.-Mktg.--Tree Top, Inc., Selah, WA, pg. 1109
Russell, Jeff, V.P.-Mktg. & Sls.--Xerxes Corporation, Minneapolis, MN, pg. 1206
Russell, R.W., V.P.-Mktg.--Mannington Resilient Floors, Salem, NJ, pg. 704
Russell, W., V.P.-Mktg.--Econolite Control Products, Inc., Anaheim, CA, pg. 367
Russo, Barry, Sr. V.P.-Mktg.--Arby's, Inc., Miami Beach, FL, pg. 243
Russo, Frank, V.P.-Mktg.--Acrison, Inc., Moonachie, NJ, pg. 14
Rutan, R.M., V.P.-Sls. & Mktg.--Teepak, Inc., Westchester, IL, pg. 535
Rutherford, Nathan R., V.P.-Mktg.--The Coe Mfg. Co., Painesville, OH, pg. 258
Rutkoski, Mary, Dir.-Shopping Center Mktg.--The Edward J. DeBartolo Corporation, Youngstown, OH, pg. 323
Rutledge, Scott, Mgr.-Mktg.--The Wooster Brush Company, Wooster, OH, pg. 1202
Ruvo/Everk, Linda, Mgr.-Channel Mktg.--Datability, Inc., Carlstadt, NJ, pg. 316
Ryan, Dan, V.P.-Mktg.--Unison Industries, Jacksonville, FL, pg. 1130
Ryan, Dan, V.P.-Mktg.--Unison Industries, Jacksonville, FL, pg. 1130
Ryan, Larry, V.P., Mktg. & Media--Esrock Advertising, Orland Park, IL, pg. 388
Ryan, Robert, V.P.-Mktg.--Ziff-Davis Press, Emeryville, CA, pg. 1219
Ryan, Robert E., Jr., V.P.-Mktg.--Mike Albert Leasing, Inc., Cincinnati, OH, pg. 31
Ryder, Charles, Dir.-Mktg. Services--Best Western International, Inc., Phoenix, AZ, pg. 146
Ryman, R.L., Sr. V.P.-Sls. & Mktg.--Prince Gardner Incorporated, Saint Louis, MO, pg. 890
Rynberg, Thomas, Mgr.-Mktg.--La-Co Industries, Inc., Chicago, IL, pg. 648
Ryon, Judy, Dir.-Sls. & Mktg.--C.B. Fleet Company, Incorporated, Lynchburg, VA, pg. 417
Rzemien, T., Dir.-Mktg. Services--Eyecessories, Plainville, MA, pg. 535
Sabo, Bill, V.P.-Mktg.--Advanced Technology, Inc., Reston, VA, pg. 20
Sacco, Jodi, Dir.-Mktg. Communications--Western Data Systems, Calabasas, CA, pg. 1178
Sacco, Paul, Sr. V.P.-Hotel Sls. & Mktg.--Omni Hotels, Hampton, NH, pg. 826
Sadler, Alan, V.P.-Sls. & Mktg., Europe--The Butcher Co., Marlborough, MA, pg. 196
Saffer, Don, V.P.-Mktg.--Colonial Metals Co., Columbia, PA, pg. 263
Sagaz, Gabriel, V.P.-Mktg. & Natl. Accts.--Domecq Importers Inc., Old Greenwich, CT, pg. 343
Sager, Dan, Dir., Mktg.--Patriot Direct Dial Systems, Los Angeles, CA, pg. 1180
Sair, Ralph A., Ph.D., Sr. V.P.-Worldwide Technical & Mktg.--Griffith Laboratories Worldwide, Inc., Alsip, IL, pg. 487
Sajovic, Frank, Dir.-Mktg.--Pharmavite Corp., Mission Hills, CA, pg. 866
Sakaduski, Nancy, Dir.-Healthcare Mktg.--Boyd, Tamney & Cross Advertising/Marketing, Wayne, PA, pg. 169
Sakharoff, Albert, V.P.-Sls. & Mktg.--Weiss Sheet Metal Company, Gardena, CA, pg. 1174
Sala, Jim, Dir.-Reg. Mktg.--Kresser/Craig, Santa Monica, CA, pg. 644
Salinas, Sergio, Dir.-Adv. & Mktg.--San Antonio Light, San Antonio, TX, pg. 524
Sallot, John, V.P.-Mktg. & Sls.--Mercer Transportation Co., Louisville, KY, pg. 739
Salois, Paul A., V.P.-Mktg.--Polar Corporation, Worcester, MA, pg. 878
Salsgiver, Paul, Exec. V.P.-Support & Dir.-Devel.--Integral Systems, Inc., Sunnyvale, CA, pg. 573
Salver, Henry A., V.P.-Corp. Devel.--GAI Consultants, Inc., Monroeville, PA, pg. 439
Salyers, David, Dir.-Store Mktg.--Chick-Fil-A, Inc., Atlanta, GA, pg. 247
Samayoa, John F., Exec. V.P.-Mktg. Mgr. & Treas.--Lanman & Kemp-Barclay Co. Inc., Westwood, NJ, pg. 657
Samelman, Irwin, Exec. V.P.-Mktg.--Jones Apparel Group, Inc., Bristol, PA, pg. 602
Sammis, F.M., Dir.-Mktg.--California & Hawaiian Sugar Company, Concord, CA, pg. 210
Samra, Ellen, V.P.-Sls. & Mktg.--Dri Mark Products, Inc., Port Washington, NY, pg. 349
San Martin, Richard, Dir.-Sls. & Mktg.--Meer Corporation, North Bergen, NJ, pg. 736
Sanford, Frank W., V.P.-Pur. & Mktg.--Sanford & Hawley, Inc., Unionville, CT, pg. 970
Sansolo, Jack, Dr., Vice Chm. & Mktg./Corp. Devel.--Hill, Holliday, Connors, Cosmopulos, Inc., Boston, MA, pg. 534
Santee, Richard, Dir.-Mktg.--A-P-A Transport Corp., North Bergen, NJ, pg. 5
Santercola, Rich, Dir.-Adv. & Mktg.--WICO Corporation, Niles, IL, pg. 1156
Santo, Frank, Pres.-Mktg.--Helm, Inc., Highland Park, MI, pg. 527
Santori, M., Mgr.-Mktg.--Tuthill Pump, Alsip, IL, pg. 1120
Saona, Raul, Mgr.-Intl. Sls. & Mktg.--Graphic Controls, Corp., Buffalo, NY, pg. 478
Saona, Raul, Mgr.-Intl. Sls. & Mktg.--Graphic Controls Corporation, Buffalo, NY, pg. 478
Sapin, Joy, Dir.-Mktg.--Rado Watch Company, Inc., New York, NY, pg. 909
Sarafian, Nancy, Mgr.-Sls. & Mktg.--Delta Surprenant Wire & Cable, Inc., Clinton, MA, pg. 327
Sargent, Bruce, V.P.-Sls. & Mktg.--Glastron Boats, Little Falls, MN, pg. 759
Sarlo, R.A., V.P.-Retail Stores--Chittenden & Eastman Co., Burlington, IA, pg. 248
Sarnei, Jean-Claude, V.P.-Mktg.--Ready Systems, Sunnyvale, CA, pg. 916
Sass, Gene J., Dir.-Mktg. & Intl. Mktg. Services--Sunkist Growers, Inc., Sherman Oaks, CA, pg. 1060
Saterbo, Stephen, Sr. V.P.-Sls. & Mktg.--Colorado Boxed Beef Co., Auburndale, FL, pg. 265
Sauder, Kevin, V.P.-Sls. & Mktg.--Sauder Woodworking Co., Archbold, OH, pg. 972
Sauers, R.S., Sr. V.P.-Mktg. & Sls.--Decatur News Publishing Company, Inc., Decatur, GA, pg. 323
Sauriol, Gary, Mgr.-Sls. & Mktg.--Tillamook County Creamery Assn., Tillamook, OR, pg. 1097
Savage, R., Sr. V.P.-Sls. & Mktg.--Bergquist Company, Inc., Minneapolis, MN, pg. 141
Sawch, Deborah, Sr. V.P., Bus. Devel.--Rotando Lerch & Iafeliece Advertising, Stamford, CT, pg. 950
Saxman, Scott, Mktg. Mgr.--Flexible Flyer Inc., West Point, MS, pg. 847
Saxon, Robert, Dir.-Mktg.--Energy Brokers Guild, Stevensville, MI, pg. 381
Saxton, Frank, V.P.-Mktg. Devel.--Puritan/Churchill Chemical Company, Atlanta, GA, pg. 900
Saylor, Don E., V.P.-Franchise Devel. & Real Estate--Druther's International, Inc., Louisville, KY, pg. 350
Sbezzi, Carmen, V.P.-Sls. & Mktg.--J. A. Sexauer, Scarsdale, NY, pg. 357
Scaglione, Jules, Mgr.-Mktg.--Arrow Pneumatics Co. Inc., Lake Zurich, IL, pg. 85
Scangas, Nicholas A., Exec. V.P.-Mktg. & Sls.--Scangas Brothers Holdings, Inc., Lynn, MA, pg. 974
Schaefer, Alan, Dir.-Mktg., Accessories--Teca Corporation, Pleasantville, NY, pg. 1082
Schaefer, John, Sls. & Mktg. Dir.--Acurex Environmental, Mountain View, CA, pg. 16
Schaefer, Lesly, Sr. V.P.-Mktg. & Promotions--VH-1/Video Hits One, New York, NY, pg. 785
Schaefer, Tom, V.P.-Mktg.--Farmhand, Inc., Excelsior, MN, pg. 402
Schafer, Gary, Mgr.-Sls.--Sunline Coach Co., Inc., Denver, PA, pg. 1061
Schaffer, Tony, V.P.-Mktg.--Starving Students, Inc., Los Angeles, CA, pg. 1040
Schaffner, Roger A., V.P., Mktg.--International Communications Group, Inc., Los Angeles, CA, pg. 576
Schalk, Don, Dir.-Mktg. & Sls.--Agway Petroleum Corp., De Witt, NY, pg. 25
Schaper, Mary Beth, V.P., Bus. Devel.--Gerbig, Snell/Weisheimer & Assoc., Inc., Worthington, OH, pg. 454
Scharf, Edward W., Dir.-Mktg., Adv. & Private Dealer Services--Southern States Cooperative, Inc., Richmond, VA, pg. 1022
Scharfberg, Doug, Sr. V.P., Sec., Market Res., Telecommunications, Res. & Devel.--Scharfberg & Associates, Ltd. Adv., Jenkintown, PA, pg. 974
Scharff, Christopher, V.P. & Dir.-Mktg.--Lanz, Inc., Culver City, CA, pg. 658
Schefter, Robert J., V.P.-Mktg.--Will & Baumer Incorporated, Liverpool, NY, pg. 1190
Scheib, Rody, Dir.-Mktg.-Churches--Al Copeland Enterprises, Inc., Jefferson, LA, pg. 283
Scheib, Rody, V.P.-Mktg.--Church's Fried Chicken, Inc., Jefferson, LA, pg. 284
Scheidemantel, Carrie, Dir.-Mktg.--Schawk, Inc., Des Plaines, IL, pg. 974
Scheidemantel, Carrie, Dir.-Mktg.--Schawkgraphics, Des Plaines, IL, pg. 975
Scheidt, Kay, Dir., Brand Mktg.--Mars Advertising Co., Southfield, MI, pg. 713
Schenk, Martin, V.P.-Sls. & Mktg.--Jackson Products Corp., Lexington, TN, pg. 587
Scherer, Gregory, V.P.-Personnel & Mktg.--Scherer Bros. Lumber Company, Minneapolis, MN, pg. 976
Schiller, John, V.P.-Mktg.--Concordia Publishing House, Saint Louis, MO, pg. 272
Schilling, Allan, Exec. V.P.-Sls. & Mktg.--Pannier Corporation, Pittsburgh, PA, pg. 846
Schimmel, Michael, Dir.-Mktg., Consumer Prods. Div.--Aladdin Industries, Incorporated, Nashville, TN, pg. 29
Schinsing, Terri, Mktg. Coord.--Ranging, East Bloomfield, NY, pg. 300
Schleier, Richard L., V.P.-Group Mkts. Specialty Prods.--Blue Cross & Blue Shield of Illinois, Chicago, IL, pg. 160
Schlesinger, Eric S., Chief Mktg. Officer--Empire Blue Cross & Blue Shield, New York, NY, pg. 379
Schlesinger, Mitchell, Sr. V.P.-Mktg.--Costa Cruise Lines, N.V., Miami, FL, pg. 288
Schlossberg, Alan, V.P., Media Devel.--Kelly, Scott And Madison, Inc., Chicago, IL, pg. 621
Schmid, Mike, Dir.-Sls. & Mktg.--John Copes Food Products, Inc., Rheems, PA, pg. 284
Schmidt, Al, V.P.-Mktg. & Sls.--Tulip Corporation, Los Angeles, CA, pg. 1119
Schmidt, Caryl, Mgr.-Mktg.--Mid Res Service Div., Niles, IL, pg. 751
Schmidt, Charles, V.P.-Feed--Land O'Lakes, Inc., Agricultural Services Div., Saint Paul, MN, pg. 653
Schmidt, H., Mgr.-Direct Mktg.--World's Finest Chocolate, Inc., Chicago, IL, pg. 1203
Schmidt, Jacob, V.P.-Mktg.--TST/Impreso, Inc., Coppell, TX, pg. 1075
Schmidt, Mike, V.P.-Mktg.--Milwaukee Electric Tool Corp., Brookfield, WI, pg. 361
Schmieder, Joseph, V.P.-Sls. & Mktg.--Oliver Products Company, Grand Rapids, MI, pg. 824
Schmiesing, Lane, Sr. V.P.-Mktg.--Bonanza Restaurants, Dallas, TX, pg. 744
Schmitt, Laurie A., V.P.-Consumer Mktg.--Candle Corporation of America, Oshkosh, WI, pg. 214
Schmitz, Robert, Mktg. Communications--DIT-MCO Intl., Kansas City, MO, pg. 1206
Schneebeli, Richard, Deputy Exec. Dir.-Sls. & Mktg.--United States Savings Bonds Division, Treasury Department, Washington, DC, pg. 1137
Schneider, Gretel M., Dir.-Mktg.--Self, New York, NY, pg. 19
Schneider, Hans, Mgr.-North America & Mgr.-Mktg.--Austrian Airlines, White Stone, NY, pg. 100
Schneider, John E., V.P.-Sls. & Mktg.--Dudek & Bock Spring Manufacturing Company, Chicago, IL, pg. 351
Schneider, L., Dir.-Mktg.--Delta Foremost Chemical Corp., Memphis, TN, pg. 327
Schneider, Michael J., V.P.-Bus. Devel.--Baker Concrete Construction, Inc., Monroe, OH, pg. 115
Schneider, Robert R., V.P.-Sls. & Mktg.--White Mop Wringer Company, Tampa, FL, pg. 1186
Schneider, Wayne, Dir.-Mktg.--Quintana Petroleum Corp., Houston, TX, pg. 905
Schneiderjohn, Diane, V.P.-Mktg.--Viacom Cable, Pleasanton, CA, pg. 785
Schnepper, Howard, Sls. & Mktg. Mgr.--Chipico Pickles, Chicago, IL, pg. 1151
Schnese, Kent A., V.P.-Sls. & Mktg.--Naz-Dar Company, Chicago, IL, pg. 1095
Schnitzer, George H., V.P.-Mktg.--Burns & Roe Enterprises, Inc., Oradell, NJ, pg. 194
Schnurr, Rodney, Dir.-Sls. & Mktg.--Snyder's of Hanover, Inc., Hanover, PA, pg. 1015
Schoenbacher, Robert N., V.P.-Sls. & Mktg.--Newhouse Newspapers Metro-Suburbia, Inc., New York, NY, pg. 19
Schoenberger, Jim, Sr. V.P.-Mktg.--Nationwise Automotive, Inc., Columbus, OH, pg. 795
Schoener, H., V.P.--Detecto Scale Company, Webb City, MO, pg. 332
Schoeninger, John W. Jr., Sr. V.P.-Individual Mktg.--Phoenix Home Life Mutual Insurance Company, Hartford, CT, pg. 868
Schoepke, William F., V.P.-Production--Paddock Publications, Inc., Arlington Heights, IL, pg. 842
Schofield, Colin, Dir.-Mktg.--Avedis Zildjian Company, Norwell, MA, pg. 1219
School, Robert, Mgr.-Mktg.--Badger Northland Inc., Kaukauna, WI, pg. 113
Schoun, Andy, Sr. V.P.-Music Programming & Promotions--MTV: Music Television, New York, NY, pg. 785
Schrader, Glen, Dir.-Sls. & Mktg.--Dukane Audio Visual Div., Saint Charles, IL, pg. 352
Schreiner, David, V.P.-Sls., Adv. & Mktg.--Del Webb's Coventry, Phoenix, AZ, pg. 1171
Schroeder, S., Dir.-Microphone Prods.--Shure Brothers Incorporated, Evanston, IL, pg. 1001
Schueler, V.C., Mgr.-Mktg. Services--Badger Construction Equipment Co., Insley Div., Winona, MN, pg. 113
Schuh, D.F., Mktg. Specialist--Neenah Foundry Company, Neenah, WI, pg. 797
Schulman, Sandra, Dir.-Mktg.--Weider Health & Fitness, Woodland Hills, CA, pg. 1173
Schultz, Art, Sr. V.P.-Sls. & Mktg.--Republic Telcom Systems Corporation, Boulder, CO, pg. 928
Schultz, Gary J., Dir.-Mktg.--LSI Truck Products Corp.-Neway/Anchor Lock, Muskegon, MI, pg. 664
Schultz, Judith, Exec. V.P.-Mktg.--Team Bank, Fort Worth, TX, pg. 1082
Schultz, K.R., Prod. Mgr.-Tobacco Prods.--Conwood Company L.P., Memphis, TN, pg. 281
Schultz, Robert G., V.P.-Mktg.--Plibrico Co., Chicago, IL, pg. 877
Schultz, Thomas A., V.P.-Mktg.--Great Lakes Lithograph Co., Cleveland, OH, pg. 481

Schuman, Nancy, V.P.-Mktg. & Opers.--Career Blazers Inc., New York, NY, pg. 218
Schumann, Willaim R., Jr., V.P.-Sls. & Mktg.--JM Clipper Corporation d/b/a Acadia, Roanoke, VA, pg. 507
Schuster, Dan, Dir.-Mktg.--SPD Technologies, Philadelphia, PA, pg. 963
Schuster, Elizabeth, Dir. Sls. & Mktg.--Berlitz Schools of Languages AG, Geneva,, Switzerland, pg. 143
Schwab, Lyn, Dir.-Mktg.--S. Schwab Company, Cumberland, MD, pg. 980
Schwain, David G., V.P.-Mktg.--Country Lake Foods, Inc., Saint Paul, MN, pg. 654
Schwalm, Thomas H., Exec. V.P.-Sls. & Mktg.--Dribeck Importers, Inc., Greenwich, CT, pg. 349
Schwartz, Irving, Sec. & Treas.-Intl. Opers.--S. Schaffer Grocery Corporation, New Rochelle, NY, pg. 974
Schwartz, Melissa, Dir.-Mktg.--Crystal Clear Industries Company, Ridgefield Park, NJ, pg. 303
Schwartz, R., Dir.-Mktg.--Monarch Luggage Co. Inc., Brooklyn, NY, pg. 765
Schwartz, William, Dir.-Mktg.--Bridges & Company, Inc., Pittsburgh, PA, pg. 175
Schwartzbeck, Tom, V.P.-Sls. & Mktg.--Duron, Inc., Beltsville, MD, pg. 355
Schwebel, Jim, V.P.-Mktg.--National Football League Properties, Inc., New York, NY, pg. 788
Schwieger, Tim, V.P.-Mktg.--Broadcast Supply West, Tacoma, WA, pg. 177
Scolaro, Michelle, Dir.-Sls. & Mktg.--California-Gym Equipment Co., Los Angeles, CA, pg. 163
Scoppechio, Debbie, Pres., New Bus. Contact & Mktg. Dir.--Creative Alliance, Inc., Louisville, KY, pg. 297
Scott, Bill, V.P.-Mktg.--Kemmerer Bottling Group Inc., Joliet, IL, pg. 622
Scott, Edward, V.P.-Sls. & Mktg.--Serta, Inc., Des Plaines, IL, pg. 991
Scott, J. Barrett, Mgr.-Mktg.--Bates Container, Inc., North Richland Hills, TX, pg. 125
Scott, Jack, V.P.-Retail--Camellia Food Stores Co-op Inc., Norfolk, VA, pg. 211
Scott, John M., Dir.-Mktg.--Eco Water Systems, Saint Paul, MN, pg. 367
Scott, Lesa, V.P.-Mktg.--McDougal, Littell & Company, Evanston, IL, pg. 728
Scott, Patricia H., Mgr.-Mktg.--Hackney Brothers, Inc., Wilson, NC, pg. 498
Scott, Robert, V.P.-Mktg.--Fort Pitt Acquisitions Company, Inc., Coraopolis, PA, pg. 425
Seaglione, Jules, Mgr.-Mktg.--Arrow Fluid Power, Broadview, IL, pg. 85
Sears, Ed, Mgr.-Mktg.--The Long & Foster Companies, Inc., Fairfax, VA, pg. 682
Sebastianelli, David, Mgr.-Natl. Sls.--Cooper Instrument Corp., Middlefield, CT, pg. 283
Sebastiao, A. Buddy, Mgr.-Mktg. & Intl. Sls.--Centrifugal & Mechanical Industries, Saint Louis, MO, pg. 609
Seehusen, Dave, V.P.-Seed--Land O'Lakes, Inc., Agricultural Services Div., Saint Paul, MN, pg. 653
Seelbach, William H., Dir.-Mktg.--Cardinal Aluminum Co., Louisville, KY, pg. 217
Segal, Amy, Coord.-Sls. & Mktg.--Premier Mill Corp., New York, NY, pg. 887
Seger, Charles F., III, V.P.-Sls. & Mktg.--Dennis Chemical Company, Inc., Saint Louis, MO, pg. 329
Seibold, Michael F., Sr. V.P.-Mktg.--Blue Cross & Blue Shield of Illinois, Chicago, IL, pg. 160
Seid, Lynne, Exec. V.P., Dir. Mktg. Services--Partners & Shevack, Inc., New York, NY, pg. 850
Seiglie, Carlos C., Strategic Mktg. Analyst--San Jose & Associates, Chicago, IL, pg. 969
Seiler, Carla, Mktg. Coord.--Dunkirk Ice Cream Co., Inc., Dunkirk, NY, pg. 353
Seinfeld, R.D., V.P.-Mktg.--Astronautics Corp. of America, Milwaukee, WI, pg. 93
Seipel, Paul E., V.P.-Sls. & Mktg.--Brad Foote Gear Works, Inc., Cicero, IL, pg. 169
Seiter, Karl, Dir.-Natl. Mktg. Communications--The O'Brien Corporation, South San Francisco, CA, pg. 820
Selina, Dave, Sr. V.P.-Mktg. & Sls.--World Computer Corp., Auburn Hills, MI, pg. 1202
Sellers, E. Gerald, V.P.-Mktg.--Shapell Industries, Inc., Beverly Hills, CA, pg. 995
Selzler, James, Mgr.-Sls. & Mktg.--McAnally Enterprises, Inc., Yucaipa, CA, pg. 726
Senkbeil, Robert C., V.P.-Mktg.--Eclipse Manufacturing Company, Sheboygan, WI, pg. 367
Sentell, Tom, Mktg. Mgr.--Madison Industries, Los Angeles, CA, pg. 433
Serenyi, Andrew, Mgr.-Mktg.--Laminaire Corporation, Rahway, NJ, pg. 652
Seurence, Mark, Dir.-Mktg. & Mkt. Res.--Horner Rausch Company, Nashville, TN, pg. 544
Seymour, Allen, V.P.-Sls. & Mktg.--Evenflo Juvenile Furniture Co., Piqua, OH, pg. 1024
Seymour, Michael, Dir.-Mktg.--Production Management Companies, Inc., Harvey, LA, pg. 893
Shadko, Noel S., V.P.-Mktg. & Strategic Plng.--Rollerblade, Inc., Minnetonka, MN, pg. 944
Shaevel, Evelyn, Dir.-Mktg.--American Library Association, Chicago, IL, pg. 57
Shafer, Alice, V.P.-Sls. & Mktg.--Alimed, Inc., Dedham, MA, pg. 34
Shaffer, Clyde H., Sr. V.P.-Sls. & Mktg.--Baltimore Stationery Co., Baltimore, MD, pg. 116
Shaffer, Donald P., V.P. Intl. Sls. & Mktg.--International Div., New York, NY, pg. 400
Shames, Harold, Exec. V.P.- Mktg. & Sls.--Melard Plastics Inc., Passaic, NJ, pg. 737
Shank, Gordon, V.P.-Mktg.--Levi Strauss & Co. (Canada), Inc., Rexdale,, Canada, pg. 670
Shannon, Kay, Dir.-Mktg.--Milliken & Co., Inc., Spartanburg, SC, pg. 755
Shapiro, Alan, V.P.-Adv. & Mktg.--Jacques Moret, Inc., New York, NY, pg. 588
Sharak, Robert L., Dir.-Mktg.--The USAir Shuttle, Jackson Heights, NY, pg. 1118
Sharp, Bette, Dir.-Mktg. Services--Royal Caribbean Cruises Ltd., Miami, FL, pg. 953
Sharpe, Ann, Mgr.-Mktg. Services--Veryfine Products, Inc., Westford, MA, pg. 1148
Sharpe, Rick, Dir.-Consumer Mktg.--FTD/Florists' Transworld Delivery Association, Southfield, MI, pg. 395
Shaw, C.E., Mgr.-Educational Services Mktg.--S & C Electric Company, Chicago, IL, pg. 958
Shaw, Ed, Dir.-Mktg.--Condor Pacific Industries, Inc., Canoga Park, CA, pg. 273
Shaw, John, Dir.-Mktg.--Summa Four, Inc., Manchester, NH, pg. 1057
Shaw, Tony, V.P.-Mktg.--Technology Transfer Institute, Santa Monica, CA, pg. 1084
Shea, Everett D., Jr., V.P.-Mktg. & Sls.--Keystone Carbon Company, Saint Marys, PA, pg. 628
Shea, Fred, Dir.-Midwest Div. Sls. & Mktg.--Hyatt Hotels Corporation, Chicago, IL, pg. 495
Shealy, Bruce, Exec. V.P.-Sls. & Mktg.--Allied Foods, Inc., Atlanta, GA, pg. 38
Shealy, Dennis G., V.P.-Bus. Devel.--McCrory Construction Co., Inc., Columbia, SC, pg. 728
Sheehy, JoAnn, Dir.-Mktg., Tomatoes & Vegetables--Del Monte Foods, San Francisco, CA, pg. 325
Sheehy, JoAnn, Dir.-Mktg., Vegetables--Del Monte Foods, San Francisco, CA, pg. 325
Sheep, Lloyd, V.P., Mktg.--U.S. Creative, Inc., Austin, TX, pg. 1135
Sheets, Ken, V.P.-Sls. & Mktg.--Rapid Industries, Inc., Louisville, KY, pg. 913
Shefa, Lori, Dir.-Adv. & Promotion--KSTP-TV, Saint Paul, MN, pg. 549
Sheidemantel, Carrie, Dir.-Mktg.--Process Color Plate, Chicago, IL, pg. 975
Sheidemantel, Carrie, Dir.-Mktg.--Color Data East, Armonk, NY, pg. 975
Sheidemantel, Carrie, Dir.-Mktg.--Robinson Industries, Huntley, IL, pg. 975
Sheilds, David, Dir.-Grp. Mktg.--The National Magazine Company Ltd., London, United Kingdom, pg. 524
Sheller, Keith A., V.P.-Sls. & Mktg.--Rustco Products Company, Denver, CO, pg. 957
Shelton, Lois, Deputy Dir. Mktg. & Sls.--Illinois State Lottery, Springfield, IL, pg. 563
Shemilt, Brian, Dir.-Mktg. & Engrng.--Decision Data Inc., Horsham, PA, pg. 323
Sherer, Betsy, Dir.-Mktg.--Funk & Wagnalls Corp., Mahwah, NJ, pg. 611
Sherlock, Michael, V.P.-Mktg.-Underwear & Hosiery--Fruit of the Loom, Bowling Green, KY, pg. 400
Sherman, Bill, V.P.-Sls. & Mktg.--Danbury Printing & Lithograph, Inc., Danbury, CT, pg. 313
Sherman, Don, Exec. V.P.-Mktg. Res.--Walker & Associates, Inc., Memphis, TN, pg. 1159
Sherman, James, Mgr.-Mktg. Communications, Electrical Distr.--Leviton Mfg. Co., Inc., Little Neck, NY, pg. 671
Sherrill, Thomas B., V.P.-Mktg.--The Dispatch Printing Company, Columbus, OH, pg. 339
Sherry, Shelly, Exec. V.P.-Sls. & Mktg.--Capital Pants Co., Philadelphia, PA, pg. 215
Sherwood, Patrick, Sr. V.P., Dir. Bus. Devel.--Goldberg Moser O'Neill, San Francisco, CA, pg. 465
Sheya, James P., V.P.-Mktg. & Sls.--Masland Industries, Carlisle, PA, pg. 717
Shields, H. Jay, Sr. V.P., Bus. Devel.--Austin Kelley Advertising, Inc., Atlanta, GA, pg. 99
Shields, Hank, Dir.-Buying/Mktg.--Associated Grocers of Alabama, Inc., Birmingham, AL, pg. 90
Shields, Pam, Mgr.-Mktg.--World's Finest Chocolate, Inc., Chicago, IL, pg. 1203
Shiff, Robert H., Mgr.-Mktg.--L&R Manufacturing Co., Kearny, NJ, pg. 647
Shiley, Kevin, Dir.-Mktg.--Roman Meal Company, Tacoma, WA, pg. 945
Shillman, Ronald, Mgr.-Mktg.--Shillcraft, Inc., Baltimore, MD, pg. 999
Shima, John F., Sr. V.P., Mktg. & Media--Taylor-Gordon/Widmann & Co., Inc., New York, NY, pg. 1081
Shind, Steve, V.P.-Sls. & Mktg.--Bon Ton Foods, Inc., York, PA, pg. 164
Shiner, Donald, V.P.--Deluxe Homes Of Pennsylvania, Inc., Berwick, PA, pg. 327
Shipley, L.C., V.P.-Mktg.--Coastal Lumber Company, Weldon, NC, pg. 257
Shirley, A., Dir.-Technical Mkts.--Shure Brothers Incorporated, Evanston, IL, pg. 1001
Shoaff, Victor, Dir.-Sls. & Mktg.--Magnetrol International, Downers Grove, IL, pg. 701
Shoemacher, J.C., Dir.-Mktg.--EvsWater Industrial Systems, Middletown, OH, pg. 712
Shoemaker, Robert, V.P.-Sls. & Mktg.--Yorktowne, Inc., Red Lion, PA, pg. 1208
Shoen, Mark, Mktg. Dir.--U-Haul International, Inc., Phoenix, AZ, pg. 48
Shoenhair, Dan, Dir.-Mktg.--Karsten Manufacturing Corporation, Phoenix, AZ, pg. 617
Shoffner, Harry, Dir.-Mktg. & Pub. Rels.--Carolina Biological Supply Co., Burlington, NC, pg. 222
Shortal, T. Michael, V.P.-Mktg.--Kastle Systems, Inc., Arlington, VA, pg. 618
Showich, Nick, Dir.-Mktg.--Seton Company, Norristown, PA, pg. 993
Shubat, Tom, Mgr.-Mktg.--Superior Linkage Division, New Haven, IN, pg. 1120
Shumite, Richard, Mgr.-Mktg.--Cutler Manufacturing Corporation, Highland City, FL, pg. 307
Shumway, Howard E., Mgr.-Mktg. Services--Shepard Niles, Inc., Montour Falls, NY, pg. 997
Shutty, Karen, Mgr.-Mktg.--The Popcorn Factory, Lake Forest, IL, pg. 426
Siagle, P.M., Mktg. Mgr.--Alloy Technology International Inc., West Nyack, NY, pg. 41
Sicheri, William, Prod. Mgr.--Melard Manufacturing Corporation, Passaic, NJ, pg. 737
Siciarz, Mary Ann, Dir.-Mktg.--Brown Derby, Inc., Cleveland, OH, pg. 181
Sido, John, Mgr.-Prod. Mktg.-Crawlers, Loaders & Trucks--Komatsu Dresser Company, Lincolnshire, IL, pg. 565
Siebrecht, Frank, V.P., Client Mktg. Plng.--Bader Rutter & Assoc., Inc., Brookfield, WI, pg. 113
Siembab, Kevin J., Mgr.-Sls. & Mktg.--Mele Manufacturing Co., Inc., Utica, NY, pg. 737
Siemer, Barbara J., Intl. Mktg. Coord.--Desco Corporation, Columbus, OH, pg. 332
Silmser, Anita, Mktg. Analyst--Time Systems, Inc., Phoenix, AZ, pg. 1097
Silver, Harold J., V.P.-Third Party Mktg.--EB (NA), Chicago, IL, pg. 381
Silverberg, Michael, V.P.-Beef--Moyer Packing Company, Souderton, PA, pg. 774
Silverman, Gene, V.P., Mktg.--Hawthorne Communications, Inc., Fairfield, IA, pg. 518
Silvertooth, Jerry, Dir.-Sls. & Mktg.--Hausted, Medina, OH, pg. 1008
Simmon, Jimmy, Dir.-Store Devel.--Affiliated Foods Southwest, Little Rock, AR, pg. 24
Simon, Frederick J., Exec. V.P.--Omaha Steaks International, Omaha, NE, pg. 825
Simon, Marc, Dir.-Mktg.--Bessin Corporation, Chicago, IL, pg. 146
Simonetto, Joseph A., V.P.-Mktg.--Calumet Construction Corporation, Hammond, IN, pg. 211
Simonich, Dennis, V.P.-Mktg.-Western Region--U.S. Engineering Company, Kansas City, MO, pg. 1135
Simonton, Greer, Exec. V.P.-Mktg.--Archer/Malmo Adv., Inc., Memphis, TN, pg. 80
Simpson, R., V.P.-Mktg.--StacoEnergy Products Co., Dayton, OH, pg. 270
Sims, Jay, Sls. Mgr. & Prod. Engr.--Standard Alloys & Manufacturing, Port Arthur, TX, pg. 161
Sims, Rich, Dir.-Mktg.--Life Line Nutritionals, Inc., Hayward, CA, pg. 675
Sinclair, H.M., Dir.-Pub. Rels.--Allright Corporation, Houston, TX, pg. 41
Sinclair, Sandy, Dir.-Mktg.--Ghafari Associates, Inc., Dearborn, MI, pg. 455
Singer, Jane, Dir., Mktg. & Strategic Plng.--Calet, Hirsch & Ferrell, Inc., New York, NY, pg. 949
Sirak, Rick, V.P.-Mktg.--MCRB Service Bureau, Inc., North Hollywood, CA, pg. 691
Sirridge, John, V.P.-Sls. & Mktg.--Bar-S Foods Co., Phoenix, AZ, pg. 118
Siskind, Allan, Dir.-Mktg.--Greater Orlando Auto Auction, Orlando, FL, pg. 483
Skapof, Jerome, V.P.-Mktg.--Cosmos Communications, Inc., Long Island City, NY, pg. 288
Skibo, Andrew D., Exec. V.P.-Sls. & Mktg.--Life Sciences International, Philadelphia, PA, pg. 320
Skiff, Lynda P., Mktg. Analyst--Larkin, Inc., Atlanta, GA, pg. 667
Skiff, Lynda P., Mktg. Analyst--Heatcraft, Inc., Stone Mountain, GA, pg. 667
Skorpinski, Casey J., V.P.-Customer Service, Sls. & Mktg.--Whiting Corporation, Harvey, IL, pg. 1187
Skunda, Robert T., Mng. Principal-Mktg.--Dewberry & Davis, Fairfax, VA, pg. 334
Slade, Mike, V.P.-Mktg.--Next, Inc., Redwood City, CA, pg. 805
Slade, Steve, V.P.-Mktg. Opers.--Homeland Stores, Inc., Oklahoma City, OK, pg. 542
Slater, Roger, Mgr.-Mktg. Services--Young Radiator Company, Racine, WI, pg. 1210
Slattery, J.J., Jr., Dir.-Sls. & Mktg.--Holder Corporation, Atlanta, GA, pg. 538
Slavick, David, V.P., Dir. Mktg. & Media Planning--Liggett-Stashower, Inc., Cleveland, OH, pg. 675
Slawson, Tom, V.P.-Mktg.--C.J. Vitner & Co., Inc., Chicago, IL, pg. 1153
Slifer, Anne M., Dir.-Personnel & Mktg.--Modern Concrete Septic Tank Company, Ottsville, PA, pg. 762
Sloan, Charles, Dir.-Mktg.--Arkansas Industrial Development Commission, Little Rock, AR, pg. 83
Slusarick, John, Dir.-Mktg.--Kendale Industries, Inc., Valley View, OH, pg. 622
Small, Lee, V.P.-Mktg.--Continental Circuits Corp., Phoenix, AZ, pg. 278
Smalley, Gary, Sr. V.P.-Sls. & Mktg.--Seattle Pacific Industries, Inc., Seattle, WA, pg. 986
Smart, Lee, Dir.-Adv., Pub. Rels. & Mktg. Services--Martin Industries (AL), Florence, AL, pg. 715
Smeall, Janice, Mgr.-Mktg.--Electro Dynamics Crystal Corporation, Overland Park, KS, pg. 374
Smetts, Stewart, Dir.-Mktg.--La Rosa's, Inc., Cincinnati, OH, pg. 649
Smith, Ann, Dir.-Mktg.--Professional Travel, Inc., Dalton, GA, pg. 894
Smith, Art, V.P.-Mktg.--John S. Barnes Corp., Rockford, IL, pg. 120
Smith, Brian M., Managing Dir.-Mktg. & Communications--Ferrell Companies Inc./Ferrellgas, Liberty, MO, pg. 407
Smith, Bruce J., V.P.-Mktg.--Proto Systems of Atlanta, Alpharetta, GA, pg. 895
Smith, Bruce W., V.P.-Mktg.--Smith Industries, Inc., Montgomery, AL, pg. 1013
Smith, Christopher, V.P.-Sls. & Mktg.--INPUT, Mountain View, CA, pg. 571
Smith, Dan, V.P.-Mktg., Electric Guitars--Fender Musical Instruments, Scottsdale, AZ, pg. 406
Smith, David, V.P.-Sls. & Mktg.--Metabo Corporation, West Chester, PA, pg. 741
Smith, Don, V.P.-Mktg.--Affiliated Food Stores, Keller, TX, pg. 23
Smith, Douglas, V.P.-Sls. & Mktg.--CAI, Barrington, IL, pg. 917
Smith, Glenn, sr. V.P.-Mktg.--C. R. Anthony Company, Oklahoma City, OK, pg. 77

Smith, Gordon G., Sr. V.P.-Mktg. & Sls.--The Heil Co., Chattanooga, TN, pg. 525
Smith, H.L., Rep.-Mktg. Services--Port of Galveston, Galveston, TX, pg. 881
Smith, Harold, Dir.-Sls. & Mktg.--MTD Products Limited, Kitchener,, Canada, pg. 694
Smith, J.E., V.P.-Mktg. & Sls.--Perfection-Schwank Inc., Waynesboro, GA, pg. 861
Smith, Jack, V.P.-Corp. Accts.--OPT Industries, Inc., Phillipsburg, NJ, pg. 819
Smith, Jake, V.P.-Sls. & Mktg.--Smith Enterprises, Rock Hill SC, pg. 1012
Smith, Jan, Dir.-Mktg.--Code-A-Phone Corp., Clackamas, OR, pg. 258
Smith, Jim, V.P.-Mktg.--YSI Incorporated, Yellow Springs, OH, pg. 1207
Smith, John, V.P.-Sls. & Mktg.--M&W Gear Company, Gibson City, IL, pg. 690
Smith, John, Dir.-Mktg.--Zephyr Baskets & Balloons, New Providence, NJ, pg. 1217
Smith, K.C., Asst. V.P.-Mktg.--Bacardi Imports, Inc., Miami, FL, pg. 108
Smith, Krysten, Dir.-Sls. & Mktg.--Acme Visible Records, Crozet, VA, pg. 13
Smith, Lynn, V.P.-Communication & Adv.--Mayflower Transit, Inc., Carmel, IN, pg. 724
Smith, M. Wayne, Exec. V.P.-Sls. & Mktg.--Ivan Allen Company, Inc., Atlanta, GA, pg. 36
Smith, Mary Beth, Asst. Mgr.-Mktg. Communications--Duo-Fast Corporation, Franklin Park, IL, pg. 354
Smith, Mary F., Dir. Mktg./Communications--Deloitte & Touche, Wilton, CT, pg. 326
Smith, Matthew, Dir.-Mktg.--Globe Industries, Inc., Chicago, IL, pg. 464
Smith, Matthew C., Mgr.- Mktg.--United States Ceramic Tile Co., East Sparta, OH, pg. 1135
Smith, Nancy, Dir.-Mktg. Services--O'Neal & Prelle, Hartford, CT, pg. 827
Smith, Rebecca J., V.P.-Mktg.--The Disston Co., Greensboro, NC, pg. 339
Smith, Richard, V.P.-Mktg. & Sales--S & C Electric Canada Ltd., Toronto,, Canada, pg. 959
Smith, Roger, V.P.-Distr.--C-B Corporation, Charlotte, NC, pg. 198
Smith, Steve, Adv. & Mktg. Dir.--Enterprise Rent-A-Car Company, Saint Louis, MO, pg. 382
Smith, Steve J., V.P.-Mktg.--Pawling Corporation, Pawling, NY, pg. 852
Smith, Tom, V.P.-Mktg.--U.S. Turbine Corporation, Maineville, OH, pg. 1137
Smith, Wanda Kenton, Dir.-Mktg.--Regal Marine Industries Inc., Orlando, FL, pg. 921
Smith, William, V.P.-Reg. Salisbury--Tristate Electrical Supply Co., Inc., Hagerstown, MD, pg. 1114
Smythe, Jerry, Dir., Sales & Mktg.--TMP/Telephone Marketing Programs, Ltd., Ilford,, United Kingdom, pg. 1074
Snediker, James M., Pres.--Chicago Show Printing Co., Morton Grove, IL, pg. 246
Snelgrove, Linda, Mktg. Coord.--Cirrus System, Inc., Westchester, IL, pg. 720
Snell, Robert E., Dir.-Mktg. Services--ATAPCO Office Products Group, Saint Louis, MO, pg. 64
Snider, Alan, V.P.-Sls. & Mktg.--Gusso Manufacturing, Inc., Brooklyn, NY, pg. 495
Snider, Richard, V.P.-Corp. Affairs--Thornton Oil Corp., Louisville, KY, pg. 1095
Snow, David, Dir.-Mktg.--Delta Queen Steamboat Company, New Orleans, LA, pg. 385
Snow, Dwight L., V.P.-Sls. & Mktg.--Screw Conveyor Corp., Hammond, IN, pg. 983
Snyder, C. C., V.P.-Mktg., Sls. & Adv.--California Hardware Co., City of Industry, CA, pg. 209
Snyder, Jean, Mgr., Direct Response & Media--BEC Advertising, Chicago, IL, pg. 106
Snyder, Merrill, Dir. Mktg. Resources--Calet, Hirsch & Ferrell, Inc., New York, NY, pg. 949
Snyder, Roger, Dir.-Mktg.--Adams Rite Products Inc., Glendale, CA, pg. 237
Soares, Joy, Mgr.-Mktg.--Ruiz Food Products, Inc., Dinuba, CA, pg. 955
Sobky, Assad, V.P.-Intl. Opers.--Marley Pump Co., Mission, KS, pg. 710
Sobozak, Michael T., V.P.-Mktg.--Malcolm Pirnie, Inc., White Plains, NY, pg. 872
Socozzo, Robert, Dir.-Mktg.--Standard Tag Mfg. Co., Jersey City, NJ, pg. 852
Sokolov, Richard S., Sr. V.P.-Devel. & Gen. Counsel--The Edward J. DeBartolo Corporation, Youngstown, OH, pg. 323
Sol, Mauricio, Dir.-Mktg. & Sls.--Taca International Airlines, S. A., New Orleans, LA, pg. 1076
Soldevilla, Jeremy, Dir.-Mktg.--American Mathematical Society, Inc., Providence, RI, pg. 58
Soles, Melanie, Dir.-Mktg.--Lat Purser & Associate, Charlotte, NC, pg. 901
Solis, Debra-Lynne, V.P. & Mktg. Dir.--Capital Bank of California, Los Angeles, CA, pg. 214
Sommer, Timothy P., Mgr.-Mktg.--Trayer Products, Inc., Elmira, NY, pg. 1108
Sooder, Karl, V.P.-Mktg.--The Double-Cola Company, Chattanooga, TN, pg. 347
Sorensen, Barbara, Dir.-Materials--Telesensory, Mountain View, CA, pg. 1085
Sorensen, Gordon, Direct Mktg.--Karakas, VanSickle Ouellette Advertising & Public Relations, Portland, OR, pg. 616
Sorenson, Kit, Dir.-Corp. Services--Neenah Foundry Company, Neenah, WI, pg. 797
Southerland, Terry, Dir.-Mktg.--Evansville Brewing Company, Evansville, IN, pg. 391
Southerland, Thomas, Mgr.-Mktg.--Gulf States Manufacturers, Inc., Starkville, MS, pg. 494
Sowa, Jeanne M., Exec. V.P.-Mktg.--National Live Stock & Meat Board, Chicago, IL, pg. 792
Spaeth, Sandra L., Assoc. Publisher & Dir.-Mktg.--Good Housekeeping, New York, NY, pg. 523
Spalding, Tom, V.P.-Sls. & Mktg.--Hospital Building & Equipment Co., Saint Louis, MO, pg. 496
Sparks, David, Sr. V.P.-Mrktg & Sls.--Beech Holdings Corp., Chicago, IL, pg. 131
Sparks, David J., Sr. V.P.-Sls. & Mktg.--Budget Rent A Car Corporation, Lisle, IL, pg. 131
Spath, Robert, Pres.--Templeton, Kenly & Co., Inc., Broadview, IL, pg. 1086
Spaulding, Susan, V.P., Direct Mktg. Dir.--Valentine-Radford, Inc., Kansas City, MO, pg. 1142
Spear, Bill, Dir.-Sls. & Mktg.--Arizona Supermarkets, Inc., Phoenix, AZ, pg. 82
Spear, Mike, V.P.-Mktg. & Sls.--Mustang Manufacturing Company, Inc., Owatonna, MN, pg. 777
Speck, Craig, V.P.-Prod. Mktg. & Systems Opers.--Haworth, Inc., Holland, MI, pg. 518
Spector, Barry, Exec. V.P., Mktg.--Maleson Naylor, Owings Mills, MD, pg. 702
Spence, G. C., Dir.-Mktg.--Pacific Enterprises Oil Company (USA), Dallas, TX, pg. 840
Spencer, Alan H., Sr. V.P.-Mktg.--Midland National Life Insurance Co., Sioux Falls, SD, pg. 968
Spencer, Craig, Mgr.-Mktg.--Triumph*Lor, Inc., Houston, TX, pg. 1115
Spenlinhauer, Stephen, V.P.-Mktg.--Spencer Press, Inc., Wells, ME, pg. 1030
Sperring, Don, European Mktg. Dir.--Young & Rubicam International European Hdqrs., London, United Kingdom, pg. 1213
Spiegelman, Edmond, Pres. & Dir.-Mktg.--General Metalcraft, Inc., Dover, DE, pg. 450
Spike, Lisa, Supvr.-Mktg.--Sun Process Converting Company, Elk Grove Village, IL, pg. 1059
Spinazzi, J., V.P.-Mktg.--Econolite Control Products, Inc., Anaheim, CA, pg. 367
Spino, Louis, V.P.-Mktg.--Metropolitan Sunday Newspapers, Inc., New York, NY, pg. 745
Spino, Louis, V.P. & Mktg. Dir.--Metro-Puck Comics Network, New York, NY, pg. 745
Spino, Louis, V.P. & Mktg. Dir.--Sunday Magazine Network, New York, NY, pg. 745
Spinola, Anthony, V.P.-Sls. & Mktg.--Sharon Concepts, Inc., Union, NJ, pg. 995
Spires, Rose, Mktg. Coord.--Timex Corporation, Middlebury, CT, pg. 1098
Spratford, Mitch, V.P.-Mktg.--Plano Molding Co., Plano, IL, pg. 874
Springstun, Carol, Dir.-Mktg.--Colonial Homes, New York, NY, pg. 523
Spurgeon, Lonni, V.P.-Refrigerated Dairy Prods.--Mid-America Dairymen, Inc., Springfield, MO, pg. 750
Squasoni, Harry, Exec. V.P., Mktg.--Block & Nardizzi, Stamford, CT, pg. 157
Squires, Genevieve, Dir.-Adv. & Mktg.--Bugle Boy Industries, Inc., Simi Valley, CA, pg. 187
Squires, W.K., V.P.-Mktg.--Edgewater Corporation, Oakmont, PA, pg. 368
Sramek, Robert, V.P.-Sls.--Dearborn Gage Company, Garden City, MI, pg. 322
St. Claire, Maggie, Dir.-Mktg. & Community Affairs--KSL Radio, Salt Lake City, UT, pg. 332
St. Onge, Claudette, Exec. V.P.-Sls. & Mktg.--Pharmavite Corp., Mission Hills, CA, pg. 866
Stacy, Bill, V.P.-Mktg.--Ambassador Cards, Kansas City, MO, pg. 502
Stadlen, Diane E., Sr. V.P., Dir. Mktg. Analysis & Media Services--Creswell, Munsell, Fultz & Zirbel, Cedar Rapids, IA, pg. 1211
Staff, R.H., Dir.-Mktg.--Hewitt-Robins Corp., West Caldwell, NJ, pg. 532
Stagliano, Adam, Dir., Acct. Plng.--Weiss, Whitten, Carroll, Stagliano Inc., New York, NY, pg. 1174
Stake, R.J., Mgr.-Mktg. Communications--Weber Marking Systems, Inc., Arlington Heights, IL, pg. 1171
Stamey, Roy, V.P.-Mktg.--S&D Coffee Inc., Concord, NC, pg. 959
Stang, Gary, V.P.-Sls. & Mktg.--Scoville Press, Inc., Minneapolis, MN, pg. 983
Stark, Dave, Sr. Mgr.-Mktg.--The Hotsy Corporation, Englewood, CO, pg. 545
Stark, Joel, V.P.-Mktg. & Sls.--Providence Journal Company, Providence, RI, pg. 895
Starling, Kenny, Dir.-Mktg.--House of Raeford Farms, Inc., Raeford, NC, pg. 546
Starnes, Jim, V.P.-Sls. & Mktg.--Miller Bros. Industries, Inc., Richmond, VA, pg. 753
Starrett, Frederick D., III, Pres., Treas., Sls. & Mktg.--Penobscot Frozen Foods, Inc., Belfast, ME, pg. 858
Starrett, K.E., V.P.-Mktg.--American Excelsior Company, Arlington, TX, pg. 51
Stasko, Mike, Mgr.-Mktg.--Mr. Gasket Company, Cleveland, OH, pg. 761
Stasko, Mike, Mgr.-Mktg.--Hurst Performances, Inc., Cleveland, OH, pg. 761
Statham, Peter B., V.P.-Mktg.--The Flood Company, Hudson, OH, pg. 419
Stearns, David, Sr. V.P.-Mktg.--The Coleman Company, Inc., Wichita, KS, pg. 695
Stearns, Doug, Dir.-Sls. & Mktg.--Seneca Wire & Manufacturing Co., Fostoria, OH, pg. 989
Stecklein, Leonard F., V.P.-Individual Prod. Mktg.--Northwestern Mutual Life Insurance Co., Milwaukee, WI, pg. 815
Steed, Frank, V.P.-Sls. & Mktg.--Samsonite Corporation, Denver, CO, pg. 358
Steel, John M., V.P.-Mktg. & Sls.--Zytec Corp., Eden Prairie, MN, pg. 1221
Steele, Cling, V.P.-Mktg.--Todd & Sargent, Inc., Ames, IA, pg. 1100
Steele, Jack F., V.P.-Sls. & Mktg.--Grede Foundries, Inc., Milwaukee, WI, pg. 483
Steele, Patricia A., Mktg. Communications--Team Bancshares, Inc., Dallas, TX, pg. 1082
Steele, Roger K., Dir.-Mtkg.--Laboratory Supply Company, Inc., Louisville, KY, pg. 649
Stein, Marshall, V.P.-Mktg.--Powerine Oil Company, Santa Fe Springs, CA, pg. 883
Steinbarth, David, V.P.-Adv. & Mktg.--La Preferida, Inc., Chicago, IL, pg. 649
Steinberg, Gary, V.P.-Mktg.--M. Buten & Sons Inc., Philadelphia, PA, pg. 196
Steinberg, Selwyn, Sr. V.P.-Mktg. Services--Slant/Fin Corporation, Greenvale, NY, pg. 1010
Steinbert, Garry, Dir.-Mktg.--American International Container, Inc., Miami, FL, pg. 56
Steinfield, Carl F., V.P.-Mktg.--Claremont Flock Corporation, Claremont, NH, pg. 251
Steinhauer, Wayne, V.P.-Mktg. Devel.--The Austad Company, Sioux Falls, SD, pg. 98
Steinman, Andrew, Dir.-Mktg. & Sls.--Falcon Safety Products Inc., Branchburg, NJ, pg. 398
Steinmiller, John, V.P.-Bus. Opers. & Mktg.--Milwaukee Bucks, Inc., Milwaukee, WI, pg. 756
Stejskal, William R., Sr. V.P. & Dir.-Mktg.--Buntin Advertising, Inc., Nashville, TN, pg. 188
Stemper, Robert, Dir.-Mktg.--American Savings Bank, White Plains, NY, pg. 60
Stensrud, Arlen, V.P.-Mktg.--Servus Footwear Company, Rock Island, IL, pg. 993
Stenstrom, E.E., Dir.-Mktg. Communications--Gold Bond Building Products, Charlotte, NC, pg. 790
Stephens, Buddy, Dir.-Mktg.--Hale-Halsell Company, Tulsa, OK, pg. 500
Stephens, Pam, Mktg. Coord.--Dixson, Inc., Grand Junction, CO, pg. 341
Stephens, Stella, Dir.-Adv. & Mktg.--Anchor Industries Inc., Evansville, IN, pg. 71
Stephenson, Jenny, Dir.-Mktg.--Huntsman Chemical Corporation, Salt Lake City, UT, pg. 555
Stephenson, John, V.P.-Mktg.--Yorktowne, Inc., Red Lion, PA, pg. 1208
Stern, Christoper, Dir.-Mktg.--Bloomfield Industries, Chicago, IL, pg. 1027
Sterry, Richard, V.P.-Mktg.--Avatar Corporation, Hopkinton, MA, pg. 101
Stertzer, D., V.P.-Distr.--Scholastic Inc., New York, NY, pg. 962
Steve Weiner, V.P.-Mktg.--IVI Travel, Northbrook, IL, pg. 428
Stevens, Andrew E., Chm. Bd., Pres., Mktg. & Pub. Rel. Dir.--GWP, Inc., Los Angeles, CA, pg. 441
Stevens, David, Prod. Mgr.--Setzer Forest Products, Sacramento, CA, pg. 993
Stevenson, Jeffrey, Mktg. & Adv. Mgr.--Talon, Inc., Meadville, PA, pg. 1077
Stevenson, Lloyd, V.P.-Mktg. & Sls.--Abbott Ball Company, West Hartford, CT, pg. 9
Steward, Toby, V.P.-Sls. & Mktg.--AMF Bakery Systems, Richmond, VA, pg. 5
Stewart, Cindy, Mktg. & Adv. Admin.--Tylan General, Inc., San Diego, CA, pg. 1122
Stewart, Glen, V.P.-Mktg.--Fayva, Canton, MA, pg. 772
Stewart, Jerry, V.P.-Mktg. & Poultry Grp.--Gold Kist, Inc., Atlanta, GA, pg. 465
Stewart, Joe, Dir.-Mktg.--Bar-S Foods Co., Phoenix, AZ, pg. 118
Stewart, Julia, V.P.-Mktg.--Stuart Anderson's Black Angus/ Cattle Company Restaurants, Los Altos, CA, pg. 60
Stibich, Ron, Sr. V.P.-Mktg. & Sls.--Fibre Glass-Evercoat Company Inc., Cincinnati, OH, pg. 408
Stickelmater, H. Charles, V.P.-Mktg.--Northwestern Golf Company, Chicago, IL, pg. 815
Stillings, Robert, V.P.-Opers., Sls., Mktg. & Personnel Dir.--Presto Food Stores, Inc., Plant City, FL, pg. 888
Stines, Scott, V.P., Data Base Mktg.--Kragie/Newell, Des Moines, IA, pg. 643
Stoddard, James, Dir.-Mktg.--Duro-Test Corporation, Fairfield, NJ, pg. 355
Stoddard, Jim, Mktg. Dir.--Duro Lite Lamps, Inc., Fairfield, NJ, pg. 355
Stoeckel, Howard, V.P.-Mktg.--Wawa, Inc., Wawa, PA, pg. 1169
Stokes, E. Donald, Sr. V.P., Dir. Mktg. Plng.--Ross Roy Inc., Bloomfield Hills, MI, pg. 950
Stokes, Jackie, Mgr.-Sls.--Dean Operations Inc., Kansas City, MO, pg. 322
Stone, David M., V.P.-Mktg.--Sterlite Corporation, Townsend, MA, pg. 1047
Stone, Donald, Mktg. Mgr.--Keith Clark, Sidney, NY, pg. 304
Stone, Harold, Jr., V.P.-Sls. & Mktg.--Renfro Corp., Mount Airy, NC, pg. 926
Stone, James E., V.P.-Mktg.--National Reproductions Corporation, Madison Heights, MI, pg. 793
Stoner, Parker, V.P., Media & Mktg. Devel.--Swanson Russell Associates, Lincoln, NE, pg. 1066
Stor, Richard, Dir.-Mktg., Sls. & Adv.--Atlantic Builders Group Inc., Baltimore, MD, pg. 94
Storseth, Jerry R., Chief Oper. Officer & Mktg. Dir.--Mediacomp, Inc., Houston, TX, pg. 735
Storseth, Jerry R., Dir.-Mktg.--Mediacomp Media Management Services, Houston, TX, pg. 735
Stotler, Roy G., V.P.-Reg. Hagerstown--Tristate Electrical Supply Co., Inc., Hagerstown, MD, pg. 1114
Stover, Kim R., Mgr.-Mktg.--T.D. Williamson, Inc., Tulsa, OK, pg. 1192
Strahan, Vicki, Mgr.-Mktg. Services--OPUS Corp., Minnetonka, MN, pg. 828
Strait, Rick E., Exec. V.P.--Netzsch, Inc., Exton, PA, pg. 798
Stranathan, Lee, V.P.-Mktg.--Igloo Corporation, Houston, TX, pg. 562
Strangis, Frank, V.P.-Mktg.--American Health Companies, Inc., Pittsburgh, PA, pg. 55

Strangis, Frank, V.P.-Mktg.--Diet Center, Inc., Pittsburgh, PA, pg. 55
Strangos, George, Dir., Remarketing Services--SKR Resources, Inc., New York, NY, pg. 963
Straton, Robert, Sr. V.P., Mktg.--Walter Bennett Communications, Fort Washington, PA, pg. 139
Strawbridge, K.W., Mgr.-Mkt. Research--Thrall Car Mfg. Co., Chicago Heights, IL, pg. 350
Stremba, Cynthia, V.P.-Mktg.--Almay, Inc., New York, NY, pg. 695
Striegel, Dave, Dir.-Mktg. Services--Growmark, Inc., Bloomington, IL, pg. 490
Stroh, Charles, Mgr.-Prod.--Toledo Blade Co., Toledo, OH, pg. 155
Strong, Dave, Dir.-Sls. & Mktg.--Integrated Energy Controls Corp., Minneapolis, MN, pg. 573
Strouber, Murray, V.P.-Consumer Mktg. & Dir.-Sls.--Leviton Mfg. Co., Inc., Little Neck, NY, pg. 671
Struve, Dee, Mgr.-Mktg. Services--National Oats Co., Cedar Rapids, IA, pg. 25
Stuart, John, Mgr.-Mktg.--Argo International Corp., New York, NY, pg. 81
Stuart, William, V.P.-Mktg. & Sls.--Schulze & Burch Biscuit Company, Chicago, IL, pg. 979
Stubbe, Allen, Mgr.-Sls. & Mktg.--E.R. Wagner Mfg. Co. Wagner Prods. Div., Hustisford, WI, pg. 1158
Stubbs, John M., V.P.-Mktg.--Dodson Group, Kansas City, MO, pg. 342
Stucky, Lynell, Mktg. Dir.--Sullivan Higdon & Sink Incorporated, Wichita, KS, pg. 1056
Stumpf, Robert, Mktg. Mgr.--Camillus Cutlery Co., Camillus, NY, pg. 212
Sturm, H., V.P.-Mktg. Services--Midwesco Filter Resources, Winchester, VA, pg. 751
Stutin, Jeff, Dir.-Mktg. Services--Norwegian Cruise Line, Coral Gables, FL, pg. 816
Suarez, Ken, Sr. Dir.-New Bus. Devel. & Program Mngmt.--Dalfort Corp., Dallas, TX, pg. 312
Sugarman, Joseph, Chm., Creative & Mktg. Dir.--JS&A Advertising, Las Vegas, NV, pg. 586
Sullivan, Barbara, Dir. Mktg. Services--Arvida, Boca Raton, FL, pg. 586
Sullivan, Barry, Pres.-Bridal Div.--CJC Holdings, Inc., Austin, TX, pg. 202
Sullivan, Beth, V.P., Mktg. Res. & Plng. Dir.--Hill, Holliday, Connors, Cosmopulos, Inc., Boston, MA, pg. 534
Sullivan, Brian J., Dir.-Mktg. & Adv.--F.A. Wilhelm Construction Co., Inc., Indianapolis, IN, pg. 1189
Sullivan, E. R., V.P.-Mktg.--Dean Operations Inc., Kansas City, MO, pg. 322
Sullivan, James, V.P.-Mktg.--Power Conversion, Inc., Saddle Brook, NJ, pg. 883
Sullivan, Jean, V.P.-Mktg.--Restaurant Developers Corp., Independence, OH, pg. 929
Sullivan, Marion, V.P.-Mktg.--Roundy's, Inc., Pewaukee, WI, pg. 952
Sullivan, Mary Pat, Dir.-Mktg.--Lettuce Entertain You Enterprises, Inc., Chicago, IL, pg. 668
Sullivan, Pat, V.P.-Specialty Prods.--William M. Bird & Co., Inc., Charleston, SC, pg. 152
Sullivan, Paul J., V.P.-Sls. & Mktg.--Lavelle Industries Inc., Burlington, WI, pg. 661
Sullivan, Timothy J., V.P.-Sls. & Mktg.--North American Salt Company, Overland Park, KS, pg. 812
Sultenfuss, John H., V.P.-Mktg.--CF Industries, Inc., Long Grove, IL, pg. 200
Summers, Doug, Mgr.-Mktg.--Carolina Tractor & Equipment Co., Charlotte, NC, pg. 223
Summers, Mike, V.P.-Mktg.--Bernea Food Service, Inc., Otsego, MI, pg. 143
Sunelay, Elizabeth, V.P.-Mktg.--The Forum Corporation, Boston, MA, pg. 425
Suntap, Belinda, Asst. Mgr.-Mtkg.--Samuel Cabot, Inc., Newburyport, MA, pg. 206
Supina, Susan, Mgr.-Mktg.--Kurt Manufacturing Co. Inc., Fridley, MN, pg. 646
Surgner, William H., V.P.-Mktg.--Barclay White Incorporated, Berwyn, PA, pg. 119
Surrette, Jack, V.P.-Mktg. & Product Devel.--Tanning Research Labs., Inc., Ormond Beach, FL, pg. 1078
Sutton, Donald R., Dir.-Mktg.--Benjamin Franklin Literary & Medical Society, Inc., Indianapolis, IN, pg. 139
Sutton, Donald R., Dir.-Mktg.--The Saturday Evening Post Society, Indianapolis, IN, pg. 139
Swain, Wink, Mgr.-Mktg. Communications--SAS Institute Inc., Cary, NC, pg. 959
Swearingen, David, Dir.-Mktg.--Memphis Publishing Company, Memphis, TN, pg. 738
Sweeney, Mark, V.P.-Sls., Mktg. & Pub. Rels.--Black Fin Yacht Corporation, Fort Lauderdale, FL, pg. 154
Sweetser, Cindy, V.P.-Mktg.-PSF Div.--Spinnaker Software Corporation, Cambridge, MA, pg. 1031
Sweger, Debra E., Dir.-Mktg.--Taylor Company, Rockton, IL, pg. 1027
Swegle, Tom, Dir.-Mktg.--Ritchie Industries, Inc., Conrad, IA, pg. 936
Syberg, Kenneth E., V.P.-Mktg.--Dualite Inc., Williamsburg, OH, pg. 350
Syberg, Kenneth E., V.P.-Mktg.--Dualite Sales & Service, Inc., Williamsburg, OH, pg. 350
Sylvia, Heidi P., Mgr.-Mktg. Communications--Avatar Corporation, Hopkinton, MA, pg. 101
Symon, Jeff, V.P.-Mktg.--ITI Marketing Services, Inc., Omaha, NE, pg. 561
Szabo, Dominique, V.P.-Makeup Mktg.--Estee Lauder, Inc., New York, NY, pg. 389
Szalkowski, Peter, Dir.-Mktg.--DonTech, Chicago, IL, pg. 345
Sze, Patricia M., Dir.-Mktg.--Berlitz International, Inc., Princeton, NJ, pg. 142
Sze, Patricia M., Dir.-Mktg.--Berlitz Publishing Company Inc., New York, NY, pg. 142
Szostak, Michael J., Dir.-Mktg. & Sls.--Douglas Steel Fabricating Corporation, Lansing, MI, pg. 347
Szostek, J., V.P.-Mktg.--BLH Electronics, Canton, MA, pg. 107
Tague, John, Sr. V.P.-Mktg. & Sls.--Amtran, Inc., Indianapolis, IN, pg. 69
Tague, John, Chief Mktg. Officer--American Trans Air, Inc., Indianapolis, IN, pg. 70
Taitz, Elbert, Dir.-Mktg.--Buyer Advertising, Inc., Newton, MA, pg. 197
Takekawa, Neil, V.P.-Customer Service--Aloha Airlines, Inc., Honolulu, HI, pg. 43
Talbott, Brian, Dir.-Prods.--Merle Norman Cosmetics, Inc., Los Angeles, CA, pg. 740
Talley, Betty P., Mgr.-Mktg. Services--American Tool Companies, Inc., Lincoln, NE, pg. 64
Tannebaum, Edward J., V.P.-Mktg.--Nason and Cullen, Inc., Wayne, PA, pg. 784
Tarkington, Stewart, V.P.-Mktg.--New Hampton, Inc., New York, NY, pg. 801
Tarlow, Leah, Mgr.-Mktg.--Cooperheat, Inc., Piscataway, NJ, pg. 283
Tashjian, Ed, V.P.-Mktg.--Institutional Distribution, New York, NY, pg. 150
Tashjy, Ken, Mgr.-Mktg.--Nexus Plastics, Inc., Hawthorne, NJ, pg. 805
Tasker, John, V.P.-Mktg. & Sls.--Frog Switch & Manufacturing Company, Carlisle, PA, pg. 434
Tassone, Tad, Mgr.-Mktg.--Aerolyte Systems, Washington, MO, pg. 254
Tassone, Tad, Mktg. Mgr.--Aerolyte Systems, Burlingame, CA, pg. 254
Tatum, Roger, Partner--Tatum Toomey & Whicker, High Point, NC, pg. 1080
Taweel, Ramsey, Dir.-Mktg.--Textilease Corporation, Beltsville, MD, pg. 1090
Taylor, Bill, V.P.-Mktg.--The Butcher Co., Marlborough, MA, pg. 196
Taylor, David J., Exec. V.P.-Mktg.--Dundee Mills, Inc., Griffin, GA, pg. 352
Taylor, David P. Jr., V.P.-Mktg.--Capital Industries, Inc., Seattle, WA, pg. 215
Taylor, Douglas, Sr. V.P.-Sls. & Mktg.--Spangler Candy Company, Bryan, OH, pg. 1025
Taylor, Jerry, V.P. & Dir.-Adv. & Mktg.--Jordache Advertising, New York, NY, pg. 604
Taylor, Karla, V.P.-Mktg. & Adv.--Pearlstine Distributors Inc., Charleston, SC, pg. 853
Taylor, Kathy, Dir.-Mktg. Services--Candle Corporation, Santa Monica, CA, pg. 214
Taylor, N.G., Sr. V.P.-Industrial Sls. & Mktg.--North American Refractories Company, Cleveland, OH, pg. 811
Taylor, R.B., V.P.-Sls. & Mktg.--Velcon Filters, Inc., San Jose, CA, pg. 1146
Taylor, Ronald B., Mgr.-Adv. & Mktg.--Telex Communications, Inc., Minneapolis, MN, pg. 1085
Taylor, Ted, Dir.-Mktg.--Swepco Tube Corporation, Clifton, NJ, pg. 1067
Teat, James, Mgr.-Mktg.--Alamo Industrial Group, San Antonio, TX, pg. 29
Teat, James, Mgr.-Mktg.--Alamo Iron Works, San Antonio, TX, pg. 29
Tebillcack, Jim, V.P.-Mktg.--Premier Beverages, Dallas, TX, pg. 342
Tedesco, Anthony, V.P.-Mktg. & Fantagraph Div.--Standard Textile Co., Inc., Cincinnati, OH, pg. 1037
Teeple, Andrew R., V.P.-Sls. & Mktg.--Haddon Craftsmen, Inc., Scranton, PA, pg. 499
Teeters, Clem, Mgr.-Consumer Products--Cargill Salt, Newark, CA, pg. 219
Teider, Tom, Mgr.-Engrng.--Marine Travelift, Inc., Sturgeon Bay, WI, pg. 707
Teller, Jeff, V.P.-Mktg.--Crystal Clear Industries Company, Ridgefield Park, NJ, pg. 303
Telsey, Mel, Dir.-Sls. & Mktg.--Peerless Importers, Inc., Brooklyn, NY, pg. 855
Temple, S.T., Corp. Communications Mgr.--The Black Clawson Co., New York, NY, pg. 154
Tenenbaum, Jay, Dir.-Mktg.--Rhodes, Inc., Atlanta, GA, pg. 931
Tennenhouse, Donald, V.P., Mktg. & Bus. Devel.--Adplan Associates, Evansville, IN, pg. 18
Tenura, David, Dir.-Sls. & Mktg.--Echevarria Angel Co., Inc., Los Angeles, CA, pg. 365
Terek, Lenore E., Mgr.-Mktg. Svcs.--Servaas Laboratories Inc., Indianapolis, IN, pg. 991
Terhune, Carolyn, Dir.-Mktg.--The Topeka Capital-Journal, Topeka, KS, pg. 1042
Terry, Alfred S., Sr. V.P.-Mktg.--Rapid Engineering Inc., Comstock Park, MI, pg. 913
Terry, Howard, Dir.-Mktg.--Metromedia Steakhouses, Inc., Vandalia, OH, pg. 744
Tesh, Theresa, Asst. Dir.-Sales & Mktg.--SAS Institute Inc., Cary, NC, pg. 959
Thaler, Bruce, V.P., Direct Mktg. Services--Moss and Company, Inc., New York, NY, pg. 772
Thalmann, Craig, V.P.-Mktg. & Sls.--National Utility Service, Inc., Park Ridge, NJ, pg. 794
Theesfeld, Donald A., Exec. V.P.-Sls. & Mktg.--Kettle Restaurants, Houston, TX, pg. 626
Theokas, Greg, Mktg. Mgr.--Stocker & Yale, Inc., Beverly, MA, pg. 1050
Theriot, Scott, Dir.-Sls. & Mktg.--Algiers Iron Works & Dry Dock, Inc., New Orleans, LA, pg. 163
Thielen, Lenore J., Mgr.-Mktg. & Pub. Rels.--Dillingham Construction Corporation, Pleasanton, CA, pg. 337
Thigpen, Martha S., Mgr.-Mktg.--Westgate Inc., Port Allen, LA, pg. 1182
Thomas, D.T., V.P.-Sls. & Mktg.--Ball Seed Co., West Chicago, IL, pg. 116
Thomas, Gary W., Dir.-Mktg. & Community Rels.--Fallon Community Health Plan, West Boylston, MA, pg. 398
Thomas, Greg, Mktg. Services Mgr.--Adplan Associates, Evansville, IN, pg. 18
Thomas, Greg, Dir.-Mktg.--Distribution America, Des Plaines, IL, pg. 340
Thomas, Greg, V.P.-Mktg.--Taco John's International, Inc., Cheyenne, WY, pg. 1076
Thomas, John E., V.P.-Mktg.--United World Life Insurance Company, Omaha, NE, pg. 779
Thomas, Tedd, V.P.-Mktg.--Charles of the Ritz Group Ltd., New York, NY, pg. 695
Thompsen, Terri, V.P.-Mktg.--Cable Division, Atlanta, GA, pg. 294
Thompson, Amy, Mktg. Services--Bonanza Restaurants, Dallas, TX, pg. 744
Thompson, Aubrey A., V.P.-Mktg. & Sls.--Graybar Electric Company, Inc., Clayton, MO, pg. 479
Thompson, Bert, Dir.-Sls. & Mktg.--Genmar Industries, Inc., Minneapolis, MN, pg. 759
Thompson, Bruce, Dir.-Mktg.--Binney & Smith Inc., Easton, PA, pg. 502
Thompson, Carla, Mgr.-Mktg. Services--Hart Crowser, Inc., Seattle, WA, pg. 512
Thompson, D.J., Mgr.-Mktg. Services--Cat Pumps Corporation, Minneapolis, MN, pg. 340
Thompson, Don, Dir.-Mktg. & Sls.--Telsco Industries, Garland, TX, pg. 1085
Thompson, George, Dir.-Mktg.--Hardaway Construction Company, Inc., Nashville, TN, pg. 508
Thompson, Gerry, V.P.-Mktg.--Blue Cross & Blue Shield of Oregon, Portland, OR, pg. 160
Thompson, James, V.P.-Mktg.--North Star Steel Co., Minneapolis, MN, pg. 219
Thompson, John, V.P.-Sls. & Mktg.--Mays Chemical Company, Indianapolis, IN, pg. 725
Thompson, Paulm, V.P.-Sls.--Duro Dyne Corporation, Farmingdale, NY, pg. 355
Thompson, Rick, V.P.-Mktg.--Burlington Basket Co., Burlington, IA, pg. 191
Thompson, William, V.P.-Mktg. & Devel.--Select Sires, Inc., Plain City, OH, pg. 988
Thor, Peter, Exec. V.P.-Mktg.--Tri Valley Growers Inc., San Francisco, CA, pg. 1111
Thornley, James, V.P.-Mktg. & Sls.--Talon, Inc., Meadville, PA, pg. 1077
Thornton, Dan, Mgr.-Mktg. Services--Tri Valley Growers Inc., San Francisco, CA, pg. 1111
Thornton, Daniel P., Sr. V.P.-Sls. & Mktg.--Progress Printing Company, Lynchburg, VA, pg. 894
Thornton, John M., V.P.-Consumer Mktg.--Forbes, Inc., New York, NY, pg. 423
Thurman, Mark, Dir.-Mktg.--Pepper West, Inc., Irvine, CA, pg. 860
Thurstone, Peter, Sls. Mgr.--Radix Wire Company, Cleveland, OH, pg. 909
Thybony, James D., Pres.--Thybony Wall Coverings Co., Chicago, IL, pg. 1096
Ticknor, William, Dir.-Franchise Devel. & Mktg.--Spring-Green Lawn Care Corporation, Plainfield, IL, pg. 1033
Tienanelli, Patrick, V.P.-Mktg.--Domestic Linen Supply & Laundry Co., Detroit, MI, pg. 343
Tiffany, A. L., V.P.-Sls. & Mktg.--KYB Corporation of America, Lombard, IL, pg. 613
Tilghman, Richard H., Sr V.P.-Mktg.--Pepper Construction Co., Chicago, IL, pg. 860
Tilles, Lois, Mktg. Dir.--Reference Software International, San Francisco, CA, pg. 921
Tillis, Arlen, V.P.-Sls. & Mktg.--Cox Lumber Co., Saint Petersburg, FL, pg. 294
Tillotson, Sandy, V.P.-Mktg.--Nu Skin International, Provo, UT, pg. 817
Timko, Joseph R., V.P.-Mktg. & Circulation--Yankee Publishing Incorporated, Dublin, NH, pg. 1207
Tinsky, James, Dir.-Mktg. & Sls. Promo.--Kettenburg Marine Corporation, San Diego, CA, pg. 626
Tippett, Debra L., Sr. V.P.-Mktg.--Wyatt Cafeterias Inc., Dallas, TX, pg. 1205
Tirey, Vernon J., V.P.-Database Mktg.--Holland Mark Martin, Burlington, MA, pg. 539
Tirone, George, V.P.-Mktg.--Fel Corporation, Farmingdale, NJ, pg. 405
Tison, Jackie, Dir., Mktg. Services--Williams Whittle Associates, Inc., Alexandria, VA, pg. 1191
Tobin, James, Sr. V.P.-Sls. & Mktg.--The Spring Air Company, Des Plaines, IL, pg. 1032
Toettcher, Fred, Sr. V.P. & Dir.-Mktg.--W.B. Doner & Company, Southfield, MI, pg. 344
Togher, Renee, Mgr.-Mktg.--Azteca Foods, Incorporated, Chicago, IL, pg. 105
Tolany, Bill, V.P.-Mktg. Services--Dr Pepper Company, Dallas, TX, pg. 342
Toma, Bernard, Dir.-Mktg.--Action Lift, Wilkes-Barre, PA, pg. 735
Tomczyk, Frederick A., Mgr.-Mktg. Services--Thetford Corporation, Ann Arbor, MI, pg. 357
Tomek, Warren, V.P.-Mktg. & Law Enforcement Sls.--O. F. Mossberg & Sons, Inc., North Haven, CT, pg. 773
Tomko, Donald R., Mgr.-Mktg.--Cleveland Machine Controls, Cleveland, OH, pg. 255
Tomlonovic, V., Dir.-Mktg.--Hiniker Company, Mankato, MN, pg. 535
Toms, J.L., V.P.-Admin. & Mktg.--Everlast Sports Manufacturing Corp., Bronx, NY, pg. 392
Toms, Michael, Catering Sls. & Dir.-Mktg.--Master Foods, Kings Lynn,, United Kingdom, pg. 713
Tomshay, Jeanen, V.P.-Mktg.--84 Lumber Co., Eighty Four, PA, pg. 371
Took, Jack L., 2nd V.P.-Grp. Sls. & Mktg.--Ameritas Life Insurance Corp., Lincoln, NE, pg. 66
Tooker, DAve, Exec. V.P.-Sls. & Mktg.--Golden Cat Corporation, South Bend, IN, pg. 637
Torke, Ward J., V.P.-Sls., Mktg. & Personnel Dir.--Torke Coffee Company, Inc., Sheboygan, WI, pg. 1102
Tortorelli, Frank, V.P.-Mktg., Military Prods.--North Atlantic Industries, Inc., Hauppauge, NY, pg. 812
Totino, Louis, Dir.-Mktg.--Massachusetts State Lottery, Braintree, MA, pg. 719
Totten, Tracy, V.P.-Sls. & Mktg.--Totten Tubes, Inc., Los Angeles, CA, pg. 1103

Toundas, Judith A., Sr. V.P., Gen. Mgr., Mktg. Support Services--Ross Roy Inc., Bloomfield Hills, MI, pg. 950
Tourtellott, Thomas E., Sr. V.P.-Mktg. & Admin.--Nielsen Construction Company, San Diego, CA, pg. 807
Tovell, W.W., V.P.-Mktg.--Bacardi Imports, Inc., Miami, FL, pg. 108
Townsend, Jack, V.P.-Sls. & Mktg.--Martin Industries (AL), Florence, AL, pg. 715
Townsend, Todd, Mktg. Service Mgr.--Rockford International Group, Rockford, IL, pg. 942
Tozun, Orhan, V.P.-Mktg., Sls. & Engrng.--International Microcircuits, Inc., Milpitas, CA, pg. 579
Tracy, Steve, Assoc. V.P.-Mktg. & Sls. Promo.--Post Buckley Schuh & Jernigan, Miami, FL, pg. 881
Traidman, Michael, V.P.-Sls. & Mktg.--Printco, Inc., Greenville, MI, pg. 891
Trapina, Joe, Mktg. Dir.--Glen Oaks Industries, Inc., New York, NY, pg. 461
Trauner, Stephen, Dir.-Mktg.--Colsky Media, Inc., San Francisco, CA, pg. 265
Trawinski, Eileen, V.P.-Mktg.--Emigrant Savings Bank, New York, NY, pg. 379
Tredi, Steve, Dir.-Mktg.--California Strawberry Advisory Board, Watsonville, CA, pg. 210
Trent, Jim, V.P.-Mktg.-Performance Grp.--Cragar Industries, Compton, CA, pg. 761
Trice, Albert M., V.P.-Mktg.--H. S. Crocker Co., Inc., King of Prussia, PA, pg. 299
Triggs, Jim, Dir.-Mktg. & Mdse.--Control Systems Inc., Saint Paul, MN, pg. 281
Triplett, Bobby, Mgr.-Mktg. Services--Taylor Machine Works, Inc., Louisville, MS, pg. 1081
Tromba, Ray, Dir.-Pub. Rels. & Mktg.--Louisiana Downs, Bossier City, LA, pg. 323
Trottman, Lanny, V.P.-Sls. & Mktg.--Desoto Hardwood Flooring Company, Memphis, TN, pg. 786
Troup, Daniel, V.P.-Mktg. & Sls.--National Fruit Product Company, Winchester, VA, pg. 789
Trumbore, John, Sr. V.P., Mktg. Research--Harris, Baio & McCullough Inc., Philadelphia, PA, pg. 511
Tschantz, Dale, Dir.-Mktg.--Harco Technologies Corporation, Medina, OH, pg. 507
Tsigrikes, Paul, Dir.-Mktg.--House Beautiful, New York, NY, pg. 523
Tubley, G.F., Dir.-Mktg. Opers. & Programs--Servo Corporation of America, Hicksville, NY, pg. 993
Tucker, A.F., V.P. & Dir.-Mktg. & Sls.-Sports Surfaces--California Products Corp., Cambridge, MA, pg. 210
Tucker, James E., V.P.-Sls. & Mktg.--R.M. Palmer Company, West Reading, PA, pg. 843
Tucker, L.W., V.P.-Sls. & Mktg.--Thermalloy, Inc., Farmers Branch, TX, pg. 1091
Tuerff, John, Dir.-Mktg.--Holsum Foods, Waukesha, WI, pg. 515
Tufts, Carl R., Mgr.-Sls. & Mktg.--Thomas & Skinner, Inc., Indianapolis, IN, pg. 1093
Tully, Paul R., V.P., New Bus. Devel.--Deutsch, Shea & Evans, Inc., South San Francisco, CA, pg. 333
Tults, Juri, V.P., New Bus. Contact & Devel.--CRE, Inc., Indianapolis, IN, pg. 203
Turner, David, Dir.-Sls. & Mktg.--Dobles Chevrolet, Inc., Manchester, NH, pg. 342
Turner, Jackie, Dir.-Mktg.--Thomas R. Hopson Broker, Inc., Marietta, GA, pg. 544
Turner, Ron L., V.P.-Mktg.--Kurtz Bros., Inc., Clearfield, PA, pg. 646
Turner, Stan, Dir.-Mktg. & Adv.--Davis Electrical Constructors, Inc., Greenville, SC, pg. 318
Turner, Steve, V.P.-Sls. & Mktg.--Micro Component Technology Inc., Saint Paul, MN, pg. 748
Turner, Steve, V.P.-Mktg. & Adv.--Turner Dairies, Inc., Covington, TN, pg. 1119
Tursi, Luke, Dir.-Mktg.--William H. Sadlier, Inc., New York, NY, pg. 966
Tutle, Danny, Dir.-Mktg.--Wyatt Cafeterias Inc., Dallas, TX, pg. 1205
Twombly, Paul, Dir.-Mktg.--L&J Technologies, Morton Grove, IL, pg. 647
Tyletki, Glenn, V.P.-Mktg.--United A G Co-op, Inc., Omaha, NE, pg. 1130
Tyndall, Marshall C., Exec. V.P.-Mktg.--Texas Commerce Bancshares, Inc., Houston, TX, pg. 1089
Tyszkiewizz, Joseph, Sr. V.P.-Mktg.--Blue Shield of California, San Francisco, CA, pg. 161
Uhler, Robert B., Dir.-Mktg.--James M. Montgomery Consulting Engineers, Pasadena, CA, pg. 767
Ulrich, Frank, V.P.-Sls.--Sauder Manufacturing Corporation, Archbold, OH, pg. 972
Underweiner, H., V.P.-Mktg. & Sls.--Farrell Lines Incorporated, New York, NY, pg. 403
Underwood, Ray, Dir.-Mktg. & Production--Walnut Grove-Nutrena Feed Div., Cargill, Inc., Atlantic, IA, pg. 219
Ungar, Andrew T., V.P.-Mktg.--Great Lakes Construction Co., Cleveland, OH, pg. 481
Unger, Richard, V.P.-Mktg. & Sls.--H. C. Prange Company, Green Bay, WI, pg. 884
Unsworth, Lisa, Sr. V.P., Mktg. Services Dir.--Houston Effler & Partners, Boston, MA, pg. 546
Upshaw, Kim, Dir.-Mktg., Sls., Adv. & Pub. Rels.--Empire Airlines, Hayden Lake, ID, pg. 379
Upton-Rowley, Brian, Asst. V.P.-Mktg. & Prod. Devel.--Unigard Security Insurance Co., Bellevue, WA, pg. 596
Upton, John, V.P., Nissan Reg. Mktg. Acct. Dir.--Chiat/Day/Mojo/San Francisco, San Francisco, CA, pg. 245
Ur, Joseph, Dir.-Sls. & Mktg.--Bison Foods Company, Buffalo, NY, pg. 1140
Urbani, Alexander M., V.P.-Sls. & Mktg.--Penske Truck Leasing, Chesterfield, MO, pg. 859
Urizzo, John, Mgr.-Product--Plascal Corporation, Farmingdale, NY, pg. 874
Urlwin, Robert, Mgr.-Mktg.--Telescope Casual Furniture, Inc., Granville, NY, pg. 1085
Urquhart, G.I., V.P.-Mktg. & Sls.--Bolton-Emerson, Inc., Lawrence, MA, pg. 163
Urquhart, Glenn I., V.P.-Mktg. & Sls.--Converting Machinery Div., Lawrence, MA, pg. 163
Usher, Steve, Dir.-Mktg.--Wagstaff Inc., Spokane, WA, pg. 1158
Utsman, Robert E., Chm., Sec. & Mktg. Dir.--Gold Coast Advertising, Miami, FL, pg. 465
Uttermohlen, Dee, Mktg. Service Coord.--Yorktowne, Inc., Red Lion, PA, pg. 1208
Uzpurvis, Horst, V.P.-Mktg.--Georgia Iron Works Co., Grovetown, GA, pg. 453
Vaagen, Dennis E., Mgr.-Sls. & Mktg.--Vaagen Brothers Lumber, Inc., Colville, WA, pg. 1142
Vabder Heiden, Jim, Dir.-Sls. & Mktg.--Sanitas Healthcare Div., Hastings, NE, pg. 356
Vaccaro, Sal Jr., V.P.-Mktg.--Sunbeam Outdoor Products Co., Neosho, MO, pg. 1059
Vail, Pat, Mgr.-Mktg.--Falcon Safety Products Inc., Branchburg, NJ, pg. 398
Vain, Rick, Dir.-Mktg.--Duron, Inc., Beltsville, MD, pg. 355
Valby, Mary Jane, Dir.-Sls. & Mktg.--Lucca Packing Div., Nalley's Fine Foods, South San Francisco, CA, pg. 25
Valdiva, Eunice, Exec. V.P.-Mktg. & Fin.--Clinique Laboratories, Inc., New York, NY, pg. 389
Valeiras, Luis, V.P.-Sls. , Mktg. & Adv., Dir.- Corp.Travel--Gator Industries Inc., Hialeah, FL, pg. 446
Valle, R., V.P.-Mktg.--Norandex Inc., Macedonia, OH, pg. 809
van Cauter, S., Dir.-Mktg.--Packard Instrument Co., Inc., Meriden, CT, pg. 213
Van Dover, Joe, Mktg. Mgr.--Madison Industries Inc. of Georgia, Conyers, GA, pg. 433
Van Erden, Don, Sr. V.P., Mktg.--Meridian Communications, Lexington, KY, pg. 740
van Hartesvelt, Mark, Sr. V.P.-Sls. & Mktg.--Guest Quarters Suite Hotels, Boston, MA, pg. 493
Van Tosh, David, Exec. V.P.-North American Adv. & Mktg.--Encyclopaedia Britannica, Inc., Chicago, IL, pg. 381
Van, Bob, V.P.-Mktg.--Carver Boat Corp., Pulaski, WI, pg. 758
Vance, David, Dir.-Corp. Mktg. & Communications--Austin Industries, Inc., Dallas, TX, pg. 99
Vance, Richard G., V.P.-Sls. & Mktg.--Bon Ton Foods, Inc., York, PA, pg. 164
VanderWeele, Julie, Sr. V.P.-Mktg.--Mesirow Financial, Chicago, IL, pg. 741
Vangilder, Linda, Mktg. & Admin. Asst.--Fitzgerald Advertising Inc., New Orleans, LA, pg. 416
Vann, Gary, V.P.-Sls. & Mktg.--Mighty Distributing System, Norcross, GA, pg. 752
Vara, Whittington P., Dir.-Mktg.--Graham Magnetics, Inc., Bedford, TX, pg. 475
Varakian, Robert, Sr. V.P.-Sls. & Mktg.--M. Kamenstein, Inc., White Plains, NY, pg. 615
Varian, Thomas J., V.P.-Mktg. Communications--ODI, Burlington, MA, pg. 818
Vasholz, Lothar A., Exec. V.P. & Corp. Mktg. Officer--The Union Central Life Insurance Co., Cincinnati, OH, pg. 1127
Vaughn, Chris, Mgr.-Portable Ventilator Mktg.--Coppus Engineering Corp., Millbury, MA, pg. 285
Vazzano, Andrew A., AIA Sr. V.P. & Dir.-Mktg.--Smith Hinchman Grylls Associates, Inc., Detroit, MI, pg. 1013
Veale, Ernest, V.P.-Sls., Mktg., Mdse. & Adv.--The Stellar Group Inc., Jacksonville, FL, pg. 1046
Veirs, William, V.P.-Sls. & Mktg.--Sonneveldt Company, Grand Rapids, MI, pg. 1018
Veit, Charles, V.P.-Mktg.--Office Electronics, Inc., Itasca, IL, pg. 821
Venturini, Martin, Sr. V.P.-Mktg.--Convenient Food Mart, Inc., Schaumburg, IL, pg. 281
Vermylen, Robert A., V.P.-Sls.--A. Zeregas Sons, Inc., Fair Lawn, NJ, pg. 1217
Vernon, Chris, Dir.-Product Lines--The Vernon Company, Newton, IA, pg. 1148
Verson, Richard N., Mgr.-Mktg. Communications--Everpure Inc., Westmont, IL, pg. 358
Vetterli, Michael O., V.P.-Mktg.--The Flecto Co., Inc., Oakland, CA, pg. 417
Vick, Terry, V.P.-Mktg.--Amarlite Architectural Products, Atlanta, GA, pg. 47
Vickers, William, V.P.-Mktg.--Overseas Service Corporation, West Palm Beach, FL, pg. 833
Vidmar, William J., V.P.-Wholesale Opers.--Snyder's Drug Stores, Inc., Minnetonka, MN, pg. 1015
Vient, John, Jr. Art Dir.--Hill, Holliday, Connors, Cosmopulos, Inc., Boston, MA, pg. 534
Vincent, Michael C., V.P.-Sls. & Mktg.--Interstate Electric Supply Company, Inc., Chantilly, VA, pg. 580
Vincent, Scott, Dir.-Mktg. & Adv.--Flying J. Inc., Brigham City, UT, pg. 421
Viola, Richard, Dir.-Mktg.--Furman Lumber Company, Billerica, MA, pg. 436
Virgo, Paul, Dir.-Mktg. & Adv.--Pro-Log Corporation, Monterey, CA, pg. 892
Visser, Sandra, Corp. Mktg. Mgr.--The Cafaro Co., Youngstown, OH, pg. 207
Vizzina, Tom, Dir.-Sls. & Mktg., Mgr.-Natl. Sls.--Theochem Labs., Inc., Tampa, FL, pg. 1090
Vocker, Robert, Dir.-Mktg.--Alra Laboratories, Inc., Gurnee, IL, pg. 44
Vogel, Robert, V.P.-Mktg.--Hardwoods Of Michigan, Inc., Clinton, MI, pg. 509
Voigt, John, V.P.-Mktg.--Forsythe Marcelli Johnson Advertising, Inc., Newport Beach, CA, pg. 425
Voisin, Bret, Dir.-Sls. & Mktg.--Mears Transportation Group, Orlando, FL, pg. 734
Volk, Stephen, V.P.-Mktg.--The Acacia Group, Washington, DC, pg. 10
Volk, Tim, Sr. V.P. & Dir.-Mktg. Services--Kelliher/Samets Marketing Communications, Burlington, VT, pg. 621
Volpe, Loretta, Exec. V.P., Dir. Media/Mktg. Services--Griffin Bacal Inc., New York, NY, pg. 486
von Juergenson, Janine, V.P.-Mktg., College--Barnes & Noble Bookstores, Inc., New York, NY, pg. 120
Voors, Jerry, Mgr.-Sls. & Mktg.--Cheney Company, New Berlin, WI, pg. 242
Voth, Herman, Dir.-Natl. Accts.--Komatsu Dresser Company, Lincolnshire, IL, pg. 565
Vr, Joe, Dir.-Sls. & Mktg.--Upstate Milk Cooperatives Inc., Le Roy, NY, pg. 1140
Vrabel, John, Dir.-Mktg.--Snyder's of Hanover, Inc., Hanover, PA, pg. 1015
Vroon, H., Dir.-Mktg.--Kores Nordic USA Corp., Summerville, SC, pg. 642
Vucovich, Doug, Mgr.-Gen. Mktg. & Sls.--Wingfoot Films Corporation, Carrollton, OH, pg. 555
Vukmanic, Frank, Sr. V.P.-Sls. & Mktg.--Amperif Corporation, Chatsworth, CA, pg. 68
Wade, James, Mgr.-Export & Intl. Mktg.--Battenfeld Gloucester Engineering Co. Inc., Gloucester, MA, pg. 126
Wade, Jim, V.P.-Sls. & Mktg.--Crane Carrier Company, Tulsa, OK, pg. 296
Wagar, Kenneth W., V.P.-Mktg.--Spartan Stores Inc., Grand Rapids, MI, pg. 1026
Wagner, Kim, Mgr.-Mktg.--Pevely Dairy Company, Saint Louis, MO, pg. 884
Wagner, Terry, V.P.-Mktg.--H.H. Cutler Company, Grand Rapids, MI, pg. 306
Wagnor, Ben, Mgr.-Mktg. & Admin. Opers.--Radix Corporation, Salt Lake City, UT, pg. 909
Wainwright, Julie, V.P.-Intl. Sls. & Mktg.--Spinnaker Software Corporation, Cambridge, MA, pg. 1031
Wait, Bud, Dir.-Sls.--Bibler Brothers, Inc., Russellville, AR, pg. 148
Waldron, Dan, v.P.-Sls. & Mktg.--Rangaire & Company, Cleburne, TX, pg. 912
Walker, Lisa, Mktg. Serv. Coord.--Vance Industries, Inc., Chicago, IL, pg. 1144
Walker, Norman, V.P.-Mktg.--Optical Corp. of America, Louisville, KY, pg. 827
Walker, Rebecca, Dir.-Promo. & Mktg.--Louisiana Downs, Bossier City, LA, pg. 323
Walker, Scott, Dir.-Western Div. Sls. & Mktg.--Hyatt Hotels Corporation, Chicago, IL, pg. 495
Wall, Patrick, V.P.-Mktg.--Demco Inc., Madison, WI, pg. 328
Wall, Richard M., Exec. V.P.-Mktg.--Chemical Exchange Industries, Houston, TX, pg. 242
Wallace, Cartina, V.P., Dir. Acct. Planning--Chiat/Day/Mojo Inc. Advertising, San Francisco, CA, pg. 244
Wallace, Thomas J., Dir.-Mktg.--Sunniland Corporation, Sanford, FL, pg. 1061
Wallace, Tim, Dir.-Mktg.--Glen Ellen Winery, Glen Ellen, CA, pg. 461
Wallich, Robin, V.P.-Mktg.--Locus Computing Corp., Inglewood, CA, pg. 680
Wallis, John, V.P.-Sls. & Mktg.--Hyatt International Corporation, Chicago, IL, pg. 495
Walsh, Betsy A., Mgr.-Mktg. Support--Packard Instrument Co., Inc., Meriden, CT, pg. 213
Walsh, James F., Sr. V.P.-Direct Mkts. Div. & Corp. Opers. Services--Blue Cross & Blue Shield of Illinois, Chicago, IL, pg. 160
Walsh, Mary, V.P.-Mktg.--Alban Tractor Co. Inc., Baltimore, MD, pg. 30
Walsh, Michael A., V.P.-Mktg.--Plan International U.S.A., Warwick, RI, pg. 874
Walsh, Robert, V.P.-Mktg. & Sls.--Rocco Inc., Harrisonburg, VA, pg. 940
Walsh, Robert, Dir.-Mktg. & Sls.--Rocco Further Processing, Timberville, VA, pg. 940
Walsworth, Gerald, V.P.-Mktg.--National Travelers Life Co., Des Moines, IA, pg. 794
Walter, Alan, V.P.-Mktg.--G.C. Thorsen, Inc., Rockford, IL, pg. 609
Walter, Bruce C., Chm. Bd., Pres. & Mktg. Dir.--Multi-Media Marketing Communications, Inc. (M.M.M.C., Inc.), Seal Beach, CA, pg. 775
Walters, Fred C., Dir.-Mktg.--Barq's, Inc., New Orleans, LA, pg. 121
Walters, Fred C., Dir.-Mktg.--Delaware Punch Co., New Orleans, LA, pg. 121
Walther, Lee, Dir.-Mktg. & Sls.--Piper Aircraft Corporation, Vero Beach, FL, pg. 872
Walton, Mark, Dir.-Mktg. & Sls.--Arrington Travel Center Inc., Chicago, IL, pg. 85
Wanke, Robert, V.P.-Mktg.--SLM, Inc., Gloversville, NY, pg. 963
Wankmiller, Albert, V.P.-Sls. & Mktg.--Print-O-Stat, Inc., York, PA, pg. 839
Ward, Brian P., V.P.-Sls. & Mktg.--Cortland Line Co., Inc., Cortland, NY, pg. 287
Ward, George, V.P.-Mktg.--Norwalk Co., Inc., South Norwalk, CT, pg. 816
Ward, Gregory, V.P.-Sls. & Mktg.--ACL Technologies, Santa Ana, CA, pg. 2
Wardford, Jeff, Dir.-Mktg.--Ludington News Co. Inc., Detroit, MI, pg. 686
Warner, Donald G., Mgr.-Mktg.--Newage Industries Inc., Willow Grove, PA, pg. 803
Warner, Donald G., Mgr.-Mktg.--Newage Industries Inc., Plastics Division, Willow Grove, PA, pg. 803
Warren, Walter, Mgr.-Sls. & Mktg.--Salwasser Manufacturing Company, Inc., Reedley, CA, pg. 968
Washington, Jeffrey M., Sr. V.P.-Mktg.--Team Bancshares, Inc., Dallas, TX, pg. 1082
Waterhouse, Jan, Dir.-Mktg.--Periphonics Voice Processing Systems Ltd., Camberley, United Kingdom, pg. 862
Waters, Bill, V.P.-Mktg.--World Carpets, Inc., Dalton, GA, pg. 1202
Watkins, Jim, V.P.-Mktg. Services--The Seven-Up Company, Dallas, TX, pg. 342
Watson, Bill, Dir.-Mktg.--Bennigan's, Dallas, TX, pg. 958
Watson, Jack, V.P.-Mktg.--Socks Division, Greensboro, NC, pg. 263
Watson, William, Sr. V.P.-Mktg., Best Western Intl.--B-W Advertising Agency, Phoenix, AZ, pg. 107

Watson, William S., Sr. V.P.-Worldwide Mktg.--Best Western International, Inc., Phoenix, AZ, pg. 146
Watts, James, Sr. V.P. & Dir.-Mktg.--Atlantic Gulf Communities Corporation, Miami, FL, pg. 95
Waugh, John, Dir.-Sls. & Mktg.--Porcelain Metals Corp., Louisville, KY, pg. 881
Weary, Sally, Dir.-Plng. & Mktg. Res.--Kelliher/Samets Marketing Communications, Burlington, VT, pg. 621
Weathers, Bruce, Investment Limited Partner & Mktg. Dir.--J. C. Bradford & Co., Nashville, TN, pg. 170
Weaver, Jeff, Dir.-Mktg.--ELE International, Inc., Lake Bluff, IL, pg. 359
Webb, Don, V.P.-Sls. & Mktg.--Central Transport Inc., High Point, NC, pg. 234
Webb, Eric, Mgr.-Mktg. Services--RainSoft Water Conditioning Co., Elk Grove Village, IL, pg. 910
Webb, Jack, Mgr.-Mktg.--Wavetek Communications Div., Indianapolis, IN, pg. 1168
Webb, James B., V.P.-Mktg.--Jetstream Systems, Hayward, CA, pg. 122
Webb, Mary Sue, Mgr. Mktg. Services--Evenflo Juvenile Furniture Co., Piqua, OH, pg. 1024
Webb, Robert, V.P.-Sls. & Mktg.--Saunders Brothers, Westbrook, ME, pg. 972
Webb, Susan, Dir.-Sls. Support & Mktg.--Varityper, Inc., East Hanover, NJ, pg. 1146
Webb, Thom E., V.P.-Adv. & Mktg.--ColorTyme, Inc., Athens, TX, pg. 265
Weber, Carol, Dir.-Sls. & Mktg.--Crown Textile Company, Blue Bell, PA, pg. 302
Weber, Dick H., V.P.-Mktg.--Doane Products Co., Joplin, MO, pg. 342
Weber, Dick H., V.P.-Sls. & Mktg.--Doane Products Co., Branded Sales Div., Joplin, MO, pg. 342
Weber, Thomas J., Exec. V.P.-Sls. & Mktg.--Automation Intelligence, Inc., Maitland, FL, pg. 101
Wecker, Richard A., Sr. V.P.-Mktg.--New York Life Insurance Company, New York, NY, pg. 802
Wedeward, Jeff, V.P., Indus. Grp.-Bader Rutter & Assoc., Inc., Brookfield, WI, pg. 113
Weeder, Mark, V.P.-Prod. Mktg.--Homes of Merit Inc., Bartow, FL, pg. 542
Weege, C.M., Dir.-Mktg.--Sloan Valve Company, Franklin Park, IL, pg. 1010
Weeks, Robert, V.P.-Sls. & Mktg.--Battenfeld Gloucester Engineering Co. Inc., Gloucester, MA, pg. 126
Wegelius, Curt, V.P.-Sls. & Mktg.--Roosevelt Paper Co., Philadelphia, PA, pg. 946
Weggeland, Bob, Dir.-Direct Mktg. Div.--Petersen Publishing Company, Los Angeles, CA, pg. 864
Weiler, Robert, Sr. V.P.-Mktg. & Sls.--Lotus Publishing Corporation, Cambridge, MA, pg. 576
Weill, Sheldon, V.P.-Mktg. & Sls.--Universal Folding Box Company, Inc., Hoboken, NJ, pg. 1138
Weinacht, Sue, Mktg. Coordinator--Lawson Associates Inc., Minneapolis, MN, pg. 663
Weiner, Tina C., Assoc. Dir. & Mktg. Mgr.--Yale University Press, New Haven, CT, pg. 1207
Weinstein, Paul, V.P.-Mktg. & Plng.--Countrymark Cooperative, Inc., Indianapolis, IN, pg. 290
Weirback, Terry, Mgr.-Sls. & Mktg.--Perkasie Industries Corporation, Perkasie, PA, pg. 862
Weiss, Andrew J., V.P.-Sls. & Mktg.--Stebbins Engineering & Mfg. Co., Watertown, NY, pg. 1043
Weiss, Ed, V.P.-Mktg.--Darda Inc. (USA), Baltimore, MD, pg. 315
Weiss, Henry, V.P.-Mktg.--Wheatland Tube Company, Collingswood, NJ, pg. 1184
Weiss, John W., V.P.-Mktg. & Adv.--The WBDC Group, Grand Rapids, MI, pg. 1155
Weist, Dan, Dir.-Mktg.--UDL Laboratories, Inc., Rockford, IL, pg. 1072
Weitz, C., V.P.-Mktg.-Intl. Tables--Schnadig Corporation, Chicago, IL, pg. 977
Weitz, Eric I., V.P.-Mktg. & Sls.--Robby Len Fashions, New York, NY, pg. 78
Weitzer, Andrew, Dir.-Mktg.--Gannett Transit, New York, NY, pg. 442
Weitzman, Sherrie, Dir.-Mktg. Services--Lionel Trains, Inc., Chesterfield, MI, pg. 677
Welch, Meredith, Dir.-Mktg.--The Atlantic Monthly Magazine, Boston, MA, pg. 95
Welch, Meredith, Dir.-Mktg.--The Atlantic Advertising Sales, New York, NY, pg. 95
Welfelt, Dave, Dir.-Sls. & Mktg.--Excel Industries, Inc., Hesston, KS, pg. 392
Welk, Tom, Dir.-Sls. & Mktg.--Lyke Corporation, Ripon, WI, pg. 688
Wellman, Mike, V.P.-Sls. & Mktg.--Wolfer Printing Company, City of Commerce, CA, pg. 1199
Wells, G.L., Dir.-Sls. & Mktg.--Claud S. Gordon Company, Richmond, IL, pg. 1167
Wells, John, Dir.-Sls. & Mktg.--The Bakersfield Californian, Bakersfield, CA, pg. 115
Welsh, John W., V.P.-Mktg.--Yorktowne Paper Mills, Inc., York, PA, pg. 1208
Wens, Richard, Mgr.-Mktg. Service--Red Devil Inc., Union, NJ, pg. 918
Wesley, Charles, V.P.-Sls. & Mktg.--Hyer Industries Inc./ Thayer Scale, Pembroke, MA, pg. 557
Wesling, Mark, V.P., Dir. Mktg. Services--Sive/Young & Rubicam, Cincinnati, OH, pg. 1211
West, W. Casey, V.P.-Sls. & Mktg.--Stanchem Inc., East Berlin, CT, pg. 1035
Westerhoff, Ralph, Sr. V.P., Direct Mktg.--Farago Advertising, New York, NY, pg. 399
Westerman, J.H., V.P.-Mktg.--Bucyrus-Erie Company, South Milwaukee, WI, pg. 186
Westerman, J.H., V.P.-Mktg.--B-E Holdings Inc., South Milwaukee, WI, pg. 106
Westhoff, Stacey, Dir.-Mktg. & Adv.--O'Keeffe's, Inc., San Francisco, CA, pg. 823
Wetterauer, Michael, Sr. V.P.-Sls. & Mktg.--Case-Swayne Co. Inc., Santa Ana, CA, pg. 228
Whaly, Billy, Dir.-Mktg.--Greenwood Mills, Inc., Greenwood, SC, pg. 485
Wheat, Zachary, Mktg. Mgr.--Pike & Fischer, Bethesda, MD, pg. 190
Wheeler, David, Sr. V.P.-Mktg.--LaMarca Direct Marketing, New York, NY, pg. 652
Whipple, Thomas A., Exec. V.P.-Mktg.--Kash N Karry Food Stores, Inc., Tampa, FL, pg. 617
White, Chuck, V.P.-Mktg.--Comprehensive Business Services Inc., Carlsbad, CA, pg. 612
White, Lawrence D., Exec. V.P.-Mktg.--NFO Research, Inc., Greenwich, CT, pg. 780
White, Mike, V.P.-Sls. & Mktg.--Hutchens Industries Inc., Springfield, MO, pg. 555
White, Robert C., Dir.-Mktg.--Superior Label Systems, Inc., Cincinnati, OH, pg. 1063
White, Simon, Dir.-Mktg.--Industrial Acoustics Company, Ltd., Staines,, United Kingdom, pg. 566
Whitelock, Ron, Mgr.-Mktg.--Boston Insulated Wire & Cable Co. Ltd., Burlington, Canada, pg. 107
Whitesell, Terry, V.P.-Mktg. & Corp. Devel.--Carpenter Manufacturing, Inc., Mitchell, IN, pg. 991
Whiteside, Robert E., Sr. V.P.-Mktg.--Wilbur Smith Associates, Columbia, SC, pg. 1011
Whiting, Lloyd, Mktg. Mgr.--Cargill Nutrena Feed, Minneapolis, MN, pg. 219
Whitley, Thomas, V.P.-Mktg.--Krystal Company, Chattanooga, TN, pg. 645
Whitney, Jim, V.P.-Sls. & Mktg.--Educational Insights, Inc., Dominguez Hills, CA, pg. 369
Wholihan, Steve E., V.P.-Sls. & Mktg.--Jones Dairy Farm, Fort Atkinson, WI, pg. 603
Wible, David, V.P.-Mktg. & Pub. Rels.--Red Roof Inns, Inc., Hilliard, OH, pg. 918
Wick, Alan, V.P.-Mktg.--Buffalo Hospital Supply Co., Inc., Amherst, NY, pg. 187
Wicker, David, V.P.-Mktg.--Things Remembered, Cleveland, OH, pg. 260
Widgodsky, John, V.P.-Mktg.-Activewear--Fruit of the Loom, Bowling Green, KY, pg. 400
Widlund, E., V.P.-Mktg.--Noville Essential Oil Co., Inc., North Bergen, NJ, pg. 817
Wienholz, Ken, V.P.-Sls & Mktg.--Bell-Carter Foods, Inc., Lafayette, CA, pg. 134
Wiesemes, Kurt, V.P.-Mktg. & Sls.--Quality Packaging Products, Inc., Benton Harbor, MI, pg. 903
Wiggin, N.C., Mgr.-Mktg. Services--J. H. France Refractories Co., Snow Shoe, PA, pg. 428
Wightman, Randel L., V.P.-Mktg.--Radix Corporation, Salt Lake City, UT, pg. 909
Wignall, David A., V.P., Database Mktg. Grp. Dir.--Creswell, Munsell, Fultz & Zirbel, Cedar Rapids, IA, pg. 1211
Wilberding, Frank D., Sr. V.P., Dir. Mktg. Services--Ross Roy Inc., Bloomfield Hills, MI, pg. 950
Wild, Robert, V.P.-Mktg.--Mayville Engineering Co., Inc., Mayville, WI, pg. 725
Wilde, Peter, Dir.-Mktg.--Gerrity Co., Inc., Newton, MA, pg. 454
Wiles, Ron, V.P.-Sls. & Mktg.--Therma-Tru Corp., Maumee, OH, pg. 1090
Wilkins, Gary, V.P.-Mktg.--Brandt, Inc., Bensalem, PA, pg. 1111
Wilkins, Katherine, Mktg. Mgr.--Daily Racing Form, Inc., Hightstown, NJ, pg. 611
Wilkins, Katherine, Mktg. Mgr.--Daily Racing Form, Inc. Pacific, Los Angeles, CA, pg. 611
Wilkins, Katherine, Mgr.-Mktg.--Daily Racing Form, Inc. (Midwest), Chicago, IL, pg. 611
Wilkins, Katherine, Mktg. Mgr.--Daily Racing Form, Inc. (Northwest), Seattle, WA, pg. 611
Willey, Glenn, V.P.-Mktg.--Allfast Fastening Systems, Inc., City of Industry, CA, pg. 37
Williams, Cliff, V.P.-Mktg. & Sls.--DAQ Electronics Inc., Middlesex, NJ, pg. 308
Williams, D.J., Jr., V.P.-Mktg. & Sls.--The Producto Machine Co., Bridgeport, CT, pg. 893
Williams, D.J., Jr., V.P.-Mktg.--Producto Machine Co. Ring Division, Jamestown, NY, pg. 893
Williams, Dale, Sr. V.P.-Mktg.--Pillowtex Corporation, Dallas, TX, pg. 870
Williams, David, Mktg.--Image Dynamics, Incorporated, Baltimore, MD, pg. 563
Williams, Donald K., V.P. & Dir.-Mktg.--Blair Television, New York, NY, pg. 155
Williams, Joe, Dir.-Sls. & Mktg.--The Uhlmann Co., Kansas City, MO, pg. 1125
Williams, John, V.P.-Mktg.--King & Prince Seafood Corporation, Brunswick, GA, pg. 631
Williams, Kathleen, Mktg. Dir.--Edward G. Dorn & Associates, Inc., Rolling Meadows, IL, pg. 346
Williams, Lyle, V.P.-Mktg.--Western Extrusions, Carrollton, TX, pg. 1179
Williams, Mark D., Dir.-Plng & Mktg. Devel.--The Equion Corporation, New Haven, CT, pg. 385
Williams, Phillip C., Dir.-Regional Sls. & Mktg.--Wayne Corporation, Richmond, IN, pg. 1169
Williams, R., V.P.-Intl. Mktg.--Lear Siegler Seating Corp., Southfield, MI, pg. 664
Williams, Steve, Mgr.-Mktg. & Adv.--Alvey Inc., Saint Louis, MO, pg. 46
Williams, Virginia M., Mgr.-Mktg. Services--Skyway Freight Systems, Inc., Watsonville, CA, pg. 1009
Williamson, David, V.P.-Mktg. & Sls.-Office Prods. Div.--Keith Clark, Sidney, NY, pg. 304
Willing, Judy, Mgr.-Mktg. Services--Snyder's of Hanover, Inc., Hanover, PA, pg. 1015
Willmann, Michael, Exec. V.P., Pub. Rels., Mktg. & Res. Dir., New Bus. Contact--Rosanio, Bailets & Talamo, Inc., Cherry Hill, NJ, pg. 947
Wilson, Anthony, V.P.-Sls. & Mktg.--Tippins Incorporated, Pittsburgh, PA, pg. 1099
Wilson, Bryan, Mgr.-Hospitality Sls. & Canada Sls.--Howe Furniture Corporation, Trumbull, CT, pg. 547
Wilson, C. Dewayne, V.P.-Grp. Pension Mktg.--American United Life Insurance Company, Indianapolis, IN, pg. 65
Wilson, Curt, Dir.-Mktg.--Folmar & Associates, Mobile, AL, pg. 422
Wilson, Don, Mng. Dir.--Totes Canada Ltd., Etobicoke,, Canada, pg. 1103
Wilson, James L., Dir.-Mktg. & Sales--First DataBank, San Bruno, CA, pg. 522
Wilson, John Seddon, III, Sr. V.P.-Mktg. & Media Plng.--Grant Marketing Communications Inc., Lafayette Hill, PA, pg. 477
Wilson, Sherry, V.P.-Mktg.--Sammons Communications, Inc., Dallas, TX, pg. 968
Windham, M.W., V.P.-Mktg.--MSD, Inc., Darlington, SC, pg. 693
Windsor, R. Dennis, Supvr.-Mktg. Services--BLH Electronics, Canton, MA, pg. 107
Winking, Kim, Mktg. Svc. Admin.--Broadcast Electronics, Inc., Quincy, IL, pg. 177
Winkler, Patricia, Mgr.-Mktg. Communications--The Fairmont Hotels, San Francisco, CA, pg. 397
Winn, Clive, V.P.-Mktg.--WordPerfect Corporation, Orem, UT, pg. 1202
Winston, Victoria, Dir.-Mktg. Communications--Praxis International Inc., Cambridge, MA, pg. 884
Winter, Richard, V.P.-Technical Mktg.--Praxis International Inc., Cambridge, MA, pg. 884
Wischermann, Roderick H., V.P.-Mktg. & Intl.--Kinetic Systems Corporation, Lockport, IL, pg. 630
Wise, Lynn, V.P.-Sls.--Admiral Packaging, Inc., Providence, RI, pg. 1128
Wise, Ronald, Exec. V.P.-Sls. & Mktg.--Continental Mills, Inc., Tukwila, WA, pg. 279
Wisner, James, V.P.-Mktg.--Topco Associates, Inc., Skokie, IL, pg. 1101
Wisniewski, Michael, Dir.-Mktg.--AJC International, Inc., Atlanta, GA, pg. 4
Witek, Steve A., V.P.-Mktg.--A. Finkl & Sons Co., Chicago, IL, pg. 411
Witte, S., Mgr.-Mktg.--J.M. Huber, Flow Control Div., Tomball, TX, pg. 550
Wittenberg, Robert, Sr. V.P.-Sls., Mktg. & Pur.--Video Products Distributors, Inc., Sacramento, CA, pg. 1150
Witwer, Walt, Mktg. Mgr.--Evenflo Juvenile Furniture Co., Piqua, OH, pg. 1024
Woessner, Tom, V.P.-Mktg. & sls.--Excelsior Manufacturing & Supply Corp., Itasca, IL, pg. 392
Wojtowicv, Ralph, Dir.-Mktg.--Holly's Inc., Grand Rapids, MI, pg. 540
Wolf, Fred, Mgr.-Mktg.--IDAB International Incorporated, Hampton, VA, pg. 559
Wolfe, Ray, Mgr.-Mktg.--Digitron Tool Co., Inc., Miamisburg, OH, pg. 337
Wolfe, Russ, V.P.-Meat Opers.--Topco Associates, Inc., Skokie, IL, pg. 1101
Wolfer, Carolyn, Coord.-Mktg.--Accu-Sort Systems, Inc., Telford, PA, pg. 11
Wolff, John, V.P.-Sls. & Mktg.--Crane Plastics Company, Columbus, OH, pg. 296
Wolfs, David, V.P.-Mktg.--El Camino Resources, Ltd., Northridge, CA, pg. 372
Wolgemuth, Lonny L., Mktg. Mgr.--Clinicare Systems, Inc., Orchard Park, NY, pg. 447
Wolters, William, Mgr.-Mktg. Opers.--Moorman Mfg. Company, Quincy, IL, pg. 769
Womack, Clydette, Mktg. Mgr.--The Daily & Sunday Oklahoman, Oklahoma City, OK, pg. 446
Wong, Bill, Dir.-Mktg.--Globe Business Furniture, Inc., Hendersonville, TN, pg. 463
Wood, Bill, Mgr.-Mktg.--Sensor Developments Inc., Orion, MI, pg. 990
Wood, Keith, Dir.-Mktg.--North Atlantic Industries Systems Division, Columbia, MD, pg. 812
Wood, Leonard E., Sr. V.P.-Mktg.--Blue Cross and Blue Shield Association, Chicago, IL, pg. 159
Wood, William, V.P.-Mktg.--Rogerson Kratos, Pasadena, CA, pg. 944
Woodbury, Dan, Sr. V.P., Dir. Mktg. Services--Martin Williams Advertising Inc., Minneapolis, MN, pg. 1191
Woodman, John, V.P.-Mktg. & Sls.--Florig Equipment Company, Inc., Conshohocken, PA, pg. 421
Woodrick, Rob, Exec. V.P.-Sls. & Mktg.--D & W Food Centers, Inc., Grand Rapids, MI, pg. 308
Woodrow, Gary, Dir.-Mktg.--Wiltel Communications Systems, Inc., The Woodlands, TX, pg. 1194
Woodruff, Laurie, V.P.-Devel. & Mktg.--The Vagabond Inns, San Diego, CA, pg. 1142
Woodruff, Laurie, V.P.-Mktg.--The Vagabond Inns, San Diego, CA, pg. 1142
Woodworth, N.B., V.P.-Mktg., Lightweight Fabrics--Dan River Apparel Fabrics Marketing Div., New York, NY, pg. 313
Woollacott, Robert, V.P.-Mktg.--Niagara Envelope Company, Inc., Buffalo, NY, pg. 805
Wooten, Sidney C., Jr., V.P.-Mktg. & Sls.--Lane Limited, Tucker, GA, pg. 657
Workman, Ron, Mgr.-Mktg. Communications--Ready Systems, Sunnyvale, CA, pg. 916
Wormley, Margaret, Dir.-Mktg.--Industrial Equipment News, New York, NY, pg. 1093
Worny, G.A., V.P.-Mktg.--AP Parts Manufacturing Company, Toledo, OH, pg. 240
Wrabel, George, V.P.-Sls. & Mktg.--N.B. Jackets Division, Marietta, GA, pg. 135
Wright, Carol F., Mgr.-Mktg. Services--Jetstream Systems, Hayward, CA, pg. 122
Wright, John, Mgr.-Mktg.--Rotary Forms Press, Inc., Hillsboro, OH, pg. 950
Wright, John E., Corp. Mktg. Mgr.--Rotary Forms Press, Inc., Hillsboro, OH, pg. 950
Wright, John W., Grp. V.P.-Employee Benefits Sls. & Mktg.--The New England, Boston, MA, pg. 799
Wright, L. C., V.P.-Sls. & Mktg.--Union City Body Company, Inc., Union City, IN, pg. 1128

Wright, Mark, Sr. V.P., Mktg. Services--Ericson Marketing Communications, Nashville, TN, pg. 386
Wright, Yates, V.P.-Sls. & Mktg.--Kirby Building Systems, Inc., Nashville, TN, pg. 632
Wurster, Hans C., Exec. V.P.-Mktg. & Sls.--Kaukauna Cheese, Little Chute, WI, pg. 619
Wyckoff, Paul, Exec. V.P.-Sls. & Mktg.--Maharam Fabric Corporation, Hauppauge, NY, pg. 701
Wygant, Pat, Mktg. Administrator & Corp. Travel Planner--Trendway Corporation, Holland, MI, pg. 1109
Wyman, Dell, Sr. V.P.-Mktg.--Farm Family Mutual Insurance Co., Glenmont, NY, pg. 401
Wyman, Robert, Jr., Mgr.-Adv., Mktg., Sls. & Sls. Promo.--Mallory, Inc., Carson City, NV, pg. 703
Yager, Mike, Dir.-Mktg.--Duling Optical Corporation, Louisville, KY, pg. 352
Yamakoshi, Warren, Pres.--Nobart, Inc., Chicago, IL, pg. 808
Yanda, David, V.P.-Frozen Food Sls.--Lakeside Foods, Inc., Manitowoc, WI, pg. 651
Yando, Gregory G., V.P.-Mktg.--Western Dairymen Cooperative, Inc., Thornton, CO, pg. 1178
Yanofsky, Marc, Sr. V.P.-Mktg.--Hyatt Hotels Corporation, Chicago, IL, pg. 495
Yarrington, James, Mgr.-Mktg.--JII/Sales Promotion Associates, Inc., Coshocton, OH, pg. 604
Yates, Michael, Mgr.-Mktg.--Young & Franklin, Inc., Liverpool, NY, pg. 1209
Yellig, C.B., V.P.-Mktg. & Sls.--Reliable Castings Corporation, Cincinnati, OH, pg. 924
Yelton, Lynn M., V.P.-Mktg.--Fox River Paper Company, Appleton, WI, pg. 428
Yingling, Sally, V.P.-Opers. & Mktg.--Patient Care, Inc., West Orange, NJ, pg. 851
Yoder, John, Dir.-Mktg. & European Sls.--Sauder Woodworking Co., Archbold, OH, pg. 972
Yorio, Frank, Sr. V.P.-Mktg. & Sls.--La Victoria Foods, Inc., City of Industry, CA, pg. 649
York, Marie Denise DeBartolo, Exec. V.P.-Corp. Mktg. & Communications--The Edward J. DeBartolo Corporation, Youngstown, OH, pg. 323
York, P.B., V.P.-Mktg.--Bradley Corporation, Menomonee Falls, WI, pg. 170
Yoshimoto, Henry, Mgr.-Mktg.--ACL Technologies, Santa Ana, CA, pg. 2
Young-sun, Kim, Mktg. Dir.--Diamond Ad Ltd., Seoul,, Korea, pg. 111
Young, Donald E., V.P.-Mktg. & Sls.--E. H. Titchener & Company, Binghamton, NY, pg. 1099
Young, Ellen, Mktg. Mgr.--Arrco Playing Card Co., Cincinnati, OH, pg. 1136
Young, Ellen S., Mgr.-Mktg.--The United States Playing Card Company, Cincinnati, OH, pg. 1136
Young, Gary T., V.P. & Dir.-Mktg.--Superior Auctioneers & Marketing, Inc., San Antonio, TX, pg. 1063
Young, Herb, Sr. V.P.-Mktg.--Dominick's Finer Foods, Northlake, IL, pg. 343
Young, John, V.P.-Sls. & Mktg.--Diamond Brands, Inc., Cloquet, MN, pg. 335
Young, William, V.P.-Retail Programs--Associated Grocers, Inc., Seattle, WA, pg. 90
Yow, Larry, V.P.-Mktg.-Glenspun Div.--Glen Raven Marketing Corp., New York, NY, pg. 461
Yow, Larry, V.P.-Mktg.-Glenspun Div.--Glen Raven Marketing Corporation, New York, NY, pg. 461
Yrigoyan, Daniel, Sr. V.P.-Sls. & Mktg.--Delta Resins & Refractories, Inc., Milwaukee, WI, pg. 327
Yudis, Charles S., Exec. V.P.-Sls. & Mktg.--Capp, Inc., Philadelphia, PA, pg. 216
Yurjevich, Glen S., V.P.-Sls. & Mktg.--Shade Computer Forms Co., Green Bay, WI, pg. 994
Zador, William, V.P.-Sls. & Mktg.--Sunbeam Home Comfort, Shubuta, MS, pg. 1059
Zager, Tom V., Mgr.-Sls. & Mktg.--Metron Steel Corp., Chicago, IL, pg. 744
Zakzeski, Jim, Dir.-Mktg.--Cubix Corporation, Carson City, NV, pg. 303
Zalarick, John, Mgr.-Mktg.--Panorama Press, Inc., Clifton, NJ, pg. 846
Zall, Raymond F., V.P.-Mktg.--HDS Services, Farmington Hills, MI, pg. 496
Zalla, Mary E., Mktg. Services Mgr.--Kendall-Futuro Company, Newport, KY, pg. 622
Zander, Tim, Coord.-Adv. & Mktg.--Zander's Creamery Inc., Cross Plains, WI, pg. 1216
Zangardi, J. Michael, Dir.-Sls. & Mktg.--Simplex Industries, Inc., Scranton, PA, pg. 1006
Zanitsch, Jerry, V.P.-Mktg.--New World Entertainment, Inc., Los Angeles, CA, pg. 74
Zarembo, Mark, V.P.-Intl. Sls. & Mktg.--NESLAB Instruments, Inc., Newington, NH, pg. 798
Zehr, Randy, Mgr.-Mktg. & Communications--TimeMed Labeling Systems, Inc., Burr Ridge, IL, pg. 1098
Zellmer, Gary, V.P.-Mktg.--Taylor Corporation, Mankato, MN, pg. 1081
Zemick, M., Exec. V.P.-Sls. & Mktg.--Industrial Steel & Wire Company, Chicago, IL, pg. 567
Zeno, Paul L., Sr. V.P., Mktg. & Sls.--Global Marketing Resources, New York, NY, pg. 463
Zeratsky, J. Bur, Mktg. Mgr.--The Shaler Company, Waupun, WI, pg. 793
Zickert, Steve, V.P.-Mktg.--Aunt Nellie's Farm Kitchens, Inc., Clyman, WI, pg. 98
Zielinski, Bella P., Dir.-Mktg. Communications--The Inland Group, Inc., Oak Brook, IL, pg. 570
Zielinski, Gary J., V.P.-Sls. & Mktg.--Heller Seasonings & Ingredients, Inc., Bedford Park, IL, pg. 526
Ziels, Larry, Sr. V.P.-Mktg.--Haggen's, Inc., Bellingham, WA, pg. 499
Zierke, David L., Mgr.-Mktg. & Sls.--Cotta Transmission Company, Rockford, IL, pg. 1062
Zierton, Lee, Mgr.-Sls. & Mktg.--Imperial Litho/Graphics, Inc., Phoenix, AZ, pg. 564
Zilinski, James W., Exec. V.P. & Chief Mktg. Officer--The New England, Boston, MA, pg. 799
Zilligen, Bill, Mgr.-Mktg.--A. J. Canfield Co., Chicago, IL, pg. 214
Zimmer, Lisa, Mgr.-Mktg.--Hyatt International Corporation, Chicago, IL, pg. 495
Zimmer, Mark E., V.P.-Mktg.--Shelter Mutual Insurance Company, Columbia, MO, pg. 997
Zimmerman, Curt, V.P.-Mktg.--Central Livestock Association, Inc., South St. Paul, MN, pg. 233
Zimmerman, Faye, Coord.-Sls. & Mktg.--Ferguson Manufacturing & Equipment Company, Dallas, TX, pg. 406
Zimmerman, Kent, V.P.-Mktg.--Kampgrounds of America, Inc., Billings, MT, pg. 613
Zimmerman, Robert W., V.P.-Mktg.--RAYOVAC Corporation, Madison, WI, pg. 915
Zimmerman, Ron, V.P.-Sls. & Mktg.--Leach Corporation, Buena Park, CA, pg. 663
Zimmet, Jane, Dir.-Mktg.--Colfax Envelope Corporation, Buffalo Grove, IL, pg. 261
Zingen, Patricia, Mktg. Coord.--Astronautics Corp. of America, Milwaukee, WI, pg. 93
Zizkuhr, Clyde, V.P.-Sls. & Mktg.--The Crocker-Fels Company, Cincinnati, OH, pg. 299
Zlotnik, A., Pres.--Odomaster Canada, Mississauga,, Canada, pg. 1065
Zlotnik, Arnold, Pres.--Surco Products, Inc., Braddock, PA, pg. 1065
Zona, Toni, Mktg. Asst.--Camillus Cutlery Co., Camillus, NY, pg. 212
Zschunke, Robert, V.P., Media & Mktg. Dir.--The Hively Agency Inc., Houston, TX, pg. 536
Zucchi, Daniel E., Sr. V.P. & Dir.-Consumer Mktg.--Hearst Magazines Division, New York, NY, pg. 523
Zuckerman, Ira, Dir., Bus. Devel.--Donaldson Group, San Francisco, CA, pg. 344

PERSONNEL

Abbott, Tom, Dir.-Human Resources--Zollner Corporation, Fort Wayne, IN, pg. 1221
Abramson, Betty, Dir.-Personnel & Acctg.--Starcrest Products of California, Perris, CA, pg. 1040
Abramson, Betty, Dir.-Personnel & Acctg.--Signatures, Perris, CA, pg. 1040
Abramson, Betty, Dir.-Personnel & Acctg.--Starcrest of California, Perris, CA, pg. 1040
Abramson, Betty, Dir.-Personnel & Acctg.--Handsome Rewards, Perris, CA, pg. 1040
Abramson, Fara, Personnel Mgr.--CHF Industries, Inc., New York, NY, pg. 200
Abreu, Robert, Dir.-Human Resources--Triangle Maintenance Corporation, Valley Stream, NY, pg. 1112
Adams, Anita, Dir.-Human Resources--Digitron Tool Co., Inc., Miamisburg, OH, pg. 337
Adams, Beth, V.P. & Mgr.-Personnel--The Times-Picayune Publishing Corp., New Orleans, LA, pg. 1098
Adams, Connie, Mgr.-Human Resources--Taylor Drug Stores, Inc., Louisville, KY, pg. 1081
Adams, Jo K., Dir.-Human Resources--Toledo Blade Co., Toledo, OH, pg. 155
Adams, Robert, Dir.-Personnel--MTD Products Limited, Kitchener,, Canada, pg. 694
Adkins, Bon, Mgr.-Employee Rels.--Placid Oil Company, Dallas, TX, pg. 873
Adler, James A., V.P.-Human Resources--Advanstar Communications, Cleveland, OH, pg. 21
Agor, Paula, Personnel Mgr.--Eastern Milk Producers Cooperative Assn., Inc., Syracuse, NY, pg. 363
Ahlfinger, R.E., Dir.-Human Resources--Colonial Pipeline Company, Atlanta, GA, pg. 264
Aiken, Barry H., Dir.-Human Res. & Public Affairs--Johnson Wax Limited, Camberley,, United Kingdom, pg. 600
Akins, Edwin E., Treas., Sec. & Dir.-Personnel--T.J. Morris Company, Inc., Statesboro, GA, pg. 771
Akright, Celeste, Mgr.-Personnel--G. Leblanc Corporation, Kenosha, WI, pg. 665
Alberts, Robert J., Corp. Sec. & Treas.--Templeton, Kenly & Co., Inc., Broadview, IL, pg. 1086
Albregts, Robert, V.P.-Human Resources--Pay Less Super Markets, Inc., Anderson, IN, pg. 852
Albright, Mary Ann, Dir.-Personnel--Connelly Containers, Inc., Bala-Cynwyd, PA, pg. 275
Aldworth, Patrick J., Mgr.-Human Resources--Humphrey Products Company, Kalamazoo, MI, pg. 553
Alesio, Dennis, V.P.-Personnel--Duckwall-Alco Stores, Inc., Abilene, KS, pg. 351
Alfano, Susan B., V.P.-Human Resources--Massachusetts Mutual Life Insurance Co., Springfield, MA, pg. 718
Allen, David, Dir.-Human Resources, Employee Benefits & Govt. Affairs--Specialty Paperboard Inc., Brattleboro, VT, pg. 1027
Allen, Larry L., V.P.-Human Resources--Soft Sheen Products, Inc., Chicago, IL, pg. 1016
Allen, Michael, V.P.-Human Resources--The Kobacker Company & Affiliates, Columbus, OH, pg. 638
Allen, Sally, V.P.-Admin. & Governmental Affairs--The Gary-Williams Company, Denver, CO, pg. 444
Allers, Patricia A., Mgr.-Personnel--Tarlton Corporation, Saint Louis, MO, pg. 1079
Alletag, Prentess, V.P.-Human Resources--Homeland Stores, Inc., Oklahoma City, OK, pg. 542
Allgood, Monty, V.P.-Indus. Rels.--Lozier Corporation, Omaha, NE, pg. 686
Almeida, E.M., III, Dir.-Personnel--Colonial Oil Industries, Savannah, GA, pg. 263
Alstad, Mille, Mgr., Personnel Dept.--BSB Bates-Gruppen A/S, Oslo,, Norway, pg. 109
Alverson, Carol, Dir.-Human Resources Mngmt.--Best Western International, Inc., Phoenix, AZ, pg. 146
Amann, D.C., V.P.-Human Resources--R. A. Jones & Co. Inc., Covington, KY, pg. 604
Amerman, Tom R., Sr. V.P.-Personnel & Loss Prevention--Parisian, Inc., Birmingham, AL, pg. 848
Ammons, Robert C., Exec. V.P. & Dir.-Human Resources--Team Bancshares, Inc., Dallas, TX, pg. 1082
Anderson, Barbara, Mgr.-Personnel--Stark Candy Company, Pewaukee, WI, pg. 1123
Anderson, Bradley, Personnel Dir.--Hamlin, Inc., Lake Mills, WI, pg. 503
Anderson, Bruce C., V.P.-Human Resources--State Mutual Life Assurance Company of America, Worcester, MA, pg. 35
Anderson, Donald E., V.P.-Human Resources--Lyon Metal Products, Inc., Montgomery, IL, pg. 690
Anderson, Georgene, V.P.-Personnel--Airco Mechanical Inc., Sacramento, CA, pg. 27
Anderson, Janet, Dir.-Employee Rels.--Periphonics Corp., Bohemia, NY, pg. 862
Anderson, Judy, Asst. Controller & Dir.-Personnel--Vogue & Body Shops, Inc., Jacksonville, FL, pg. 1154
Anderson, Lynn, V.P.-Admin/Human Resources--Candle Corporation, Santa Monica, CA, pg. 214
Anderson, Steve, Dir.-Personnel--Adventure Lands of America, Inc., Des Moines, IA, pg. 21
Anderson, Terry, Mgr.-Personnel--Andersen Windows Inc., Bayport, MN, pg. 72
Anderson, Vickie, Dir.-Human Resources--Computer Dynamics, Inc., Virginia Beach, VA, pg. 271
Andres, Richard, Mgr.-Personnel--Badger Northland Inc., Kaukauna, WI, pg. 113
Andriese, Ted, Mgr.-Pub. Rels.--Transnational Motors Inc., Grand Rapids, MI, pg. 1107
Ansted, James P., Chief Fin. Officer, Treas., Sec.--Plastic Suppliers, Inc., Columbus, OH, pg. 875
Anthony, Lynda, Mgr.-Human Resources--Anthony Forest Products Co., Inc., El Dorado, AR, pg. 77
Anthony, Sandy, Dir.-Corp. Communications--Quorum Health Group, Inc., Brentwood, TN, pg. 905
Apple, Larry G., Dir.-Personnel--Paoli, Inc., Paoli, IN, pg. 846
Aquilina, Gerald, V.P.-Personnel--Victoria Packing Corporation, Brooklyn, NY, pg. 1149
Aragon, Jose, V.P.-Human Resources--Bacardi Imports, Inc., Miami, FL, pg. 108
Arb, R.H., Dir.-Personnel--Nooter Corporation, Saint Louis, MO, pg. 808
Arendt, William, V.P.-Human Resources--Scoville Press, Inc., Minneapolis, MN, pg. 983
Arlea, Mike, Controller & Mgr.-Personnel--Cardinal Inc., Port Reading, NJ, pg. 217
Armitage, Rob, V.P.-Human Resources--Penn-Daniels, Inc., Quincy, IL, pg. 857
Armstrong, Connie, Dir.-Personnel--SJL of Kansas Corp., Wichita, KS, pg. 962
Armstrong, Sylvia, Dir.-Human Resources--Heavy Machines, Inc., Memphis, TN, pg. 524
Arnold, Linda, V.P.-Human Resources--Norrell Corporation, Atlanta, GA, pg. 810
Aruffo, Carol, Personnel Dir.--Zenith Products Corp., Aston, PA, pg. 1217
Asaro, Janice, Dir.-Personnel--Innovative Plastics Corporation, Orangeburg, NY, pg. 570
Ash, Barbara, Mgr.-Human Resources--O'Malia Food Markets Inc., Noblesville, IN, pg. 825
Asplund, Jennifer, Dir.-Personnel--Formac Corporation, Minneapolis, MN, pg. 424
Assante, Carole, V.P.-Human Resources--ULLICO Inc., Washington, DC, pg. 1124
Assis, Jane, Personnel Dir.--Ceras Johnson Ltda., Rio de Janeiro,, Brazil, pg. 599
Atwell, Sue, Dir.-Human Resources--Replacements, Ltd., Greensboro, NC, pg. 927
Atzert, Jill L., Admin.--Phoenix International, Inc., Beverly, NJ, pg. 868
Aubrey, Gary, V.P.-Human Resources--Komatsu Dresser Company, Lincolnshire, IL, pg. 565
Austin, Diane, Dir.-Personnel--Gress Foods Inc., Gainesville, GA, pg. 486
Avant, Roy, Dir.-Personnel--Burgess Pigment Co., Sandersville, GA, pg. 190
Averett, Claire, Dir.-Personnel--WordPerfect Corporation, Orem, UT, pg. 1202
Awad, Carmen, Dir.-Personnel--Tele-Com Products, Inc., Duarte, CA, pg. 1084
Axelrode, Julia, V.P.-Human Resources--Management Dynamics, New Providence, NJ, pg. 703
Axson, Pearl, Personnel Dir.--W.W. Norton & Company, Inc., New York, NY, pg. 815
Axtman, Judy, Office Mgr.--The Alamo Learning Systems, Inc., San Ramon, CA, pg. 29
Aydelotte, Julie, Mgr.-Human Resources--Icicle Seafoods, Inc., Seattle, WA, pg. 561
Ayles, Bill, Personnel Dir.--Alimak Elevator Company, Bridgeport, CT, pg. 34
Aylward, Patricia M., Dir.-Personnel--William Blair & Company, Chicago, IL, pg. 155
Baar, John, Dir.-Human Resources--Michigan Wheel Corporation, Grand Rapids, MI, pg. 747
Babb, Fred, V.P.-Admin. & Personnel--Redman Industries, Inc., Dallas, TX, pg. 919
Bachmann, Christine, Co-Dir.-Human Resources--Herff Jones Inc., Indianapolis, IN, pg. 531
Bacon, John, V.P.-Human Resources--Save Mart Supermarkets, Modesto, CA, pg. 973
Bacon, Kathy, Dir.-Personnel--The Austad Company, Sioux Falls, SD, pg. 98
Badke, John, Dir.-Logistics--La Preferida, Inc., Chicago, IL, pg. 649
Bagdonas, Ralph, Dir.-Human Resources--San Francisco French Bread Company, Oakland, CA, pg. 969
Baia, Pamela, Mgr.-Human Resources--D. J. Mead-Hubbs & Howe, Buffalo, NY, pg. 1016

Bailey, Bart, V.P.-Admin.--SnyderGeneral Corporation, Dallas, TX, pg. 1015
Bailey, Cindee, V.P.-Human Resources--The Climatic Corp., Columbia, SC, pg. 255
Bailey, Leon, V.P.-Opers.--American Vision Centers, Inc., New York, NY, pg. 65
Bailey, Lydia J., Mgr.-Personnel--Erving Paper Mills, Erving, MA, pg. 388
Baird, Thomas, Dir.-Employee Benefits--TIC United Corporation, Dallas, TX, pg. 1073
Baker, David, Mgr.-Personnel--Labelon Corporation, Canandaigua, NY, pg. 649
Baker, Dee Dee, Dir.-Human Resources--EWI, Inc., Salem, OH, pg. 361
Baker, Diane, Mgr.-Human Resources--J.W. Allen & Company, Wheeling, IL, pg. 36
Baker, Nancy, Dir., Human Resources--Asher/Gould Advertising, Inc., Los Angeles, CA, pg. 88
Baker, Pat, Asst. V.P.-Human Resources--Lackman Food Service, Woodbury, NY, pg. 650
Baker, William D., Dir.-Human Resources--E Z Loader Boat Trailers, Inc., Spokane, WA, pg. 361
Baldwin, Richard, Dir.-Human Resources--CENEX (Farmers Union Central Exchange, Inc.), Inver Grove Heights, MN, pg. 231
Ball, Pat, Mgr.-Personnel--Hanel Lumber Co., Inc., Hood River, OR, pg. 505
Ballagh, Dick, Mgr.-Human Resources--MICOM Communications Corp., Simi Valley, CA, pg. 748
Ballew, Dale, Dir.-Personnel--Koch Industries, Incorporated, Wichita, KS, pg. 639
Bane, Nancy, Dir.-Personnel & Bus. Mgr.--Nimnicht Chevrolet Company, Jacksonville, FL, pg. 807
Bank, Carl, Mgr.-Personnel--Rauland-Borg Corporation, Skokie, IL, pg. 914
Bannon, Marilyn, Mgr.-Human Resourses--ASC Incorporated, Southgate, MI, pg. 7
Baragona, Freddie J., Jr., Mgr.-Payroll & Employee Benefits--T.L. James & Company, Ruston, LA, pg. 588
Baravik, Andrew W., V.P.-Human Resources & Mngmt. Info. Systems--Quality Stores Inc., North Muskegon, MI, pg. 904
Barber, Joyce, Mgr.-Personnel--Millmaster Onyx Group, Inc., Westport, CT, pg. 755
Barclay, Don, Dir.-Human Resources--Affiliated Foods, Inc., Amarillo, TX, pg. 24
Bardgett, Ed, Dir.-Human Resources--H.B. Zachry, San Antonio, TX, pg. 1215
Barker, James, Mgr.-Human Resources--Specialty Paperboard Inc., Brattleboro, VT, pg. 1027
Barker, Ray, Dir.-Personnel--The Georgia Marble Company, Kennesaw, GA, pg. 453
Barna, Mike, Mgr.-Personnel--Powers Pharmaceutical, Brockton, MA, pg. 236
Barnes, Charles, Dir.-Labor Rels.--Illinois Cereal Mills, Inc., Paris, IL, pg. 562
Barnhardt, T.L., V.P.-Human Resources--Barnhardt Manufacturing Co., Charlotte, NC, pg. 120
Baron, Donald, Exec. V.P.-Personnel--Baron-Abramson, Inc., Medford, MA, pg. 121
Barr, L., Dir.-Personnel--American Cast Iron Pipe Co., Birmingham, AL, pg. 50
Barrett, Charles J., Sr. V.P.-Personnel--The Grand Union Company, Wayne, NJ, pg. 476
Barrett, Vicki, Dir.-Personnel & Benefits--Roni Hicks & Associates, Inc., San Diego, CA, pg. 533
Barrie, George R., Personnel Dir.--Lear Siegler Plastics Corp., Mendon, MI, pg. 664
Bartley, Joyce, Mgr.-Human Resources--South Bend Plastics, Inc., Mishawaka, IN, pg. 1019
Bartnett, John C., V.P.-Human Resources--J. S. Alberici Construction Co., Inc., Saint Louis, MO, pg. 31
Baschke, William, Dir.-Human Resources--Poly-Seal Corporation, Baltimore, MD, pg. 880
Baseman, Gerald, Dir.-Personnel--Auburn Faith Community Hospital, Auburn, CA, pg. 97
Baskerville, Lark, V.P., Dir. Human Resources--Rubin Postaer & Associates, Santa Monica, CA, pg. 954
Basore, Jay Neff, Jr., Sr. V.P.-Human Resources--Cooper Communities, Inc., Bella Vista, AR, pg. 283
Basso, Louis, Personnel Mgr.--Out of Home Media Services, Inc., New York, NY, pg. 832
Batchelor, Jeanne, Benefits Admin.--Effective Management Systems, Milwaukee, WI, pg. 370
Bates, Bonnie, Mgr.-Human Resources--Columbus Show Case Company, Columbus, OH, pg. 267
Bates, Mike, Dir.-Personnel--Remmele Engineering, Inc., Saint Paul, MN, pg. 926
Bates, Thomas, V.P.-Human Resources--Amperif Corporation, Chatsworth, CA, pg. 68
Battista, R., V.P.-Personnel--Stebbins Engineering & Mfg. Co., Watertown, NY, pg. 1043
Battjes, Kenneth, Dir.-Personnel--Guardian Industries Corp., Northville, MI, pg. 491
Bauer, Beth, Mgr.-Personnel--Dann Dee Display Fixtures, Chicago, IL, pg. 314
Baumgarten, Rodger W., Dir.-Personnel--K & B, Inc., New Orleans, LA, pg. 611
Beach, Jerry, Dir.-Human Resources--Oak Rubber Company, Ravenna, OH, pg. 819
Beach, Nancy, V.P.-Human Resources--Bel Air Markets, Sacramento, CA, pg. 133
Beagle, Fred, Dir.-Personnel--Progressive Tool & Industries Co., Southfield, MI, pg. 894
Beal, David, V.P.-Human Resources--Renfro Corp., Mount Airy, NC, pg. 926
Beal, Ruth, Dir.-Personnel--J. H. Heafner Co. Inc., Lincolnton, NC, pg. 520
Beale, Jane, Sr. V.P., Dir. Admin. & Human Resources--Wunderman Cato Johnson, New York, NY, pg. 1211
Beasley, John H., V.P.-Personnel--The Pepper Companies, Inc., Chicago, IL, pg. 859
Beasley, John H., Sr. V.P.-Personnel--Pepper Construction Co., Chicago, IL, pg. 860
Beauchman, Patrick, Mgr.-Personnel--A & S Tribal Industries, Poplar, MT, pg. 1
Beaudoin, Ken, Dir.-Personnel--World Carpets, Inc., Dalton, GA, pg. 1202
Beaulieu, John, Sr. V.P.-Human Resources--Beech Holdings Corp., Chicago, IL, pg. 131
Beavais, Robert, Chief Fin. Officer--J. Austin Oil Co., Flint, MI, pg. 99
Becella, Joyce, Mgr.-Human Resources--Pollenex Corporation, Chicago, IL, pg. 879
Becella, Joyce, Mgr.-Human Resources--Pollenex Corporation, Chicago, IL, pg. 821
Becka, Maria, Dir.-Personnel--Business Mens Insurance Corporation, Miami, FL, pg. 196
Becker, Hugo, V.P.-Personnel--Union Underwear Co., Inc., Bowling Green, KY, pg. 400
Beckman-Donley, Jill, Dir.-Human Resources--OCTus, San Diego, CA, pg. 818
Beckwith, Margaret, Dir.-Personnel--J. L. Hammett Company, Braintree, MA, pg. 504
Beckwith, Sandra J., Mgr.-Human Resources--Independent Metals, Germantown, WI, pg. 565
Beecher, R., Dir.-Personnel--L. B. Smith, Inc., Camp Hill, PA, pg. 1013
Begert, Jane, V.P.-Human Rels.--Guy Gannett Publishing Company, Portland, ME, pg. 442
Behrendt, Nancy L., Mgr.-Personnel--American Learning Corp., Chicago, IL, pg. 381
Beilfuss, Bob, V.P.-Human Resources & Admin.--Transilwrap Company, Inc., Chicago, IL, pg. 1107
Belasky, Michael, Exec. V.P.-Fin. & Personnel--Maharam Fabric Corporation, Hauppauge, NY, pg. 701
Bell, Brian, V.P.-Human Resources--National Utility Service, Inc., Park Ridge, NJ, pg. 794
Bell, Vilma M., V.P.-Employee Rels.--S & C Electric Company, Chicago, IL, pg. 958
Belsky, Samuel, Dir.-Personnel & Controller--Spirite Industries, Inc., Englewood, NJ, pg. 1031
Belton, Nancy, Dir.-Human Resources--Radionics, Inc., Salinas, CA, pg. 909
Benedict, Vincent P.A., Dir.-Human Resources--Henkels & McCoy, Inc., Blue Bell, PA, pg. 529
Benisek, J.P., V.P.-Human Resources--Ideal Industries, Inc., Sycamore, IL, pg. 562
Benjamin, F.L., V.P.-Pur., Opers., Personnel & Data Processing--Morris Kirschman & Company, Inc., New Orleans, LA, pg. 633
Bennett, Bruce, V.P.-Personnel--Esskay Manufacturing Co., San Antonio, TX, pg. 389
Bennett, Carl L., V.P.-Admin.--Quad/Graphics, Inc., Pewaukee, WI, pg. 902
Bennett, Duane, Dir.-Personnel--Alliance America, Norcross, GA, pg. 37
Benson, Earl, Dir.-Personnel--Building Products Inc., Watertown, SD, pg. 188
Benson, Gary, Mgr.-Personnel--Pendleton Woolen Mills, Inc., Portland, OR, pg. 857
Benson, Shirley, Personnel Mgr.--Duro-Test Corporation, Fairfield, NJ, pg. 355
Bentley, Larry, V.P.-Human Resources--International Jensen Inc., Lincolnshire, IL, pg. 578
Benton, Marty, V.P.-Human Resources--Flexel, Inc., Atlanta, GA, pg. 418
Benton, Murray, Dir.-Personnel & Treas.--Mid South Sales, Helena, AR, pg. 750
Benton, Robert R., V.P.-Human Resources--Connecticut Mutual Life Insurance Company, Hartford, CT, pg. 274
Berend, B.M., Dir.-Personnel--Science Applications International Corporation, San Diego, CA, pg. 981
Berg, Robert M., Dir.-Human Resources--Howard Needles Tammen & Bergendoff, Kansas City, MO, pg. 547
Berglund, Sharon, Mgr.-Personnel--AmeriData, Inc., Minneapolis, MN, pg. 66
Bergman, Walter, Personnel Dir--Zim-American Israeli Shipping Co., New York, NY, pg. 1219
Berkowitz, Mary Jane, Mgr.-Human Resources--Blair Television, New York, NY, pg. 155
Bernard, R.A., Dir.-Indus. Rels.--American Steel Foundries, Chicago, IL, pg. 69
Bernhard, Kathy, Dir.-Human Resources--C M P Publications, Inc., Manhasset, NY, pg. 202
Berry, F.K., Mgr.-Human Resources--CH2M Hill Companies, Ltd., Englewood, CO, pg. 202
Berry, Maxine, Human Resources Generalist--Regional Transportation Authority (RTA), Chicago, IL, pg. 922
Berry, Shirley, Dir.-Human Resources--Electronics Stamping Corp., Rancho Dominguez, CA, pg. 375
Bertelli, David, V.P.-Human Resources--Mercury Computer Systems, Inc., Lowell, MA, pg. 740
Bertsch, D.E., Dir.-Personnel--Ludlow Composites Corporation, Fremont, OH, pg. 686
Berwald, Joanne, Mgr.-Personnel--Buxton Company, Chicopee, MA, pg. 197
Beschorner, Roberta, Mgr.-Human Resources--Walnut Grove-Nutrena Feed Div., Cargill, Inc., Atlantic, IA, pg. 219
Bethel, William, Mgr.-Personnel--Hano Business Forms, Inc., Springfield, MA, pg. 505
Betts, Murray, Jr., Dir.-Personnel--STRAFCO, Inc., San Antonio, TX, pg. 1052
Bevilagua, D., Mgr.-Human Resources--American Welding & Manufacturing Co., Warren, OH, pg. 431
Bezdicek, Frank, Mgr.-Adv.--CENEX (Farmers Union Central Exchange, Inc.), Inver Grove Heights, MN, pg. 231
Bickley, B.M., Dir.-Human & Matl. Resources--Alinabal, Inc., Milford, CT, pg. 34
Bidese, John, Dir.-Human Resources--Globe Industries, Inc., Chicago, IL, pg. 464
Bielfeldt, Don, Mgr.-Personnel--M&W Gear Company, Gibson City, IL, pg. 690
Biery, Mike, Dir.-Human Resources--Celestial Seasonings, Boulder, CO, pg. 231
Bigler, Patsy, Personnel Admin.--Tighe Industries, Inc., York, PA, pg. 1097
Bilich, Joseph T., V.P.-Human Resources--Drummond Company, Inc., Jasper, AL, pg. 349
Billings, Gene P., Dir.-Personnel--Ash Grove Cement Company, Overland Park, KS, pg. 87
Birney, Donald M., V.P.-Personnel--American Bureau of Shipping, New York, NY, pg. 50
Bishop, Janet M., V.P.-Human Resources--White Rock Distilleries Inc., Lewiston, ME, pg. 1186
Bishop, Margaret, Dir.-Personnel--Hitchcock Chair Company LTD, Riverton, CT, pg. 536
Black, Jim, Mgr.-Personnel--Ross Engineering Co., Inc., Leola, PA, pg. 949
Blackwelder, Dedra, Dir.-Data Processing--Post Buckley Schuh & Jernigan, Miami, FL, pg. 881
Blackwell, Berman, Mgr.-Personnel--Norfoods, Inc., Overland Park, KS, pg. 810
Blankenship, Ernie, Dir.-Personnel--Rotary Forms Press, Inc., Hillsboro, OH, pg. 950
Blaschke, David C., Dir.-Personnel--Bernard Johnson Incorporated, Houston, TX, pg. 598
Blaugrund, Tracy, Dir.-Personnel--American Furniture Company, Albuquerque, NM, pg. 55
Blazer, Elizabeth, V.P., Human Resources--The Gillespie Organization, Inc., Princeton, NJ, pg. 458
Blickens, George, Dir.-Personnel--Haddon Craftsmen, Inc., Scranton, PA, pg. 499
Block, Jed A., Dir.-Communications & Sec.--Jewelers Mutual Insurance Company, Neenah, WI, pg. 593
Blois, Donald, Dir.-Personnel--Wilbur-Ellis Company & Connell Brothers Company, San Francisco, CA, pg. 1189
Blomberg, Joe, V.P.-Personnel--Microdot Aerospace Fastening Systems Group, Fullerton, CA, pg. 749
Blombers, Joseph, Dir.-Human Resources--MICRODOT, Inc., Chicago, IL, pg. 749
Blush, Ray, V.P.-Human Resources--Gaymar Industries, Inc., Orchard Park, NY, pg. 447
Board, William E., Dir.-Personnel--McJunkin Corporation, Charleston, WV, pg. 730
Boatright, Linda, Mgr.-Personnel--IDAB International Incorporated, Hampton, VA, pg. 559
Bobinet, Louis G., V.P. & Personnel Mgr.--Farmers Mutual Hail Insurance Co., Des Moines, IA, pg. 401
Bock, E., V.P.-Human Resources--Decision Data Inc., Horsham, PA, pg. 323
Boehm, H. Robert, V.P.-Human Resources--RJO Enterprises, Inc., Lanham, MD, pg. 907
Bogden, Patrice M., V.P.-Human Resources--Lionel Trains, Inc., Chesterfield, MI, pg. 677
Bohne, Chris, Dir.-Personnel--Sentinel Computer Services Inc., Oak Brook, IL, pg. 990
Bolivar, Mary, Dir.-Personnel--Injectron Corporation, Plainfield, NJ, pg. 569
Bonclarek, Lynda, Mgr.-Personnel--American Mathematical Society, Inc., Providence, RI, pg. 58
Bonfigio, Adriane, Mgr.-Personnel--Ain Plastics, Inc., Mount Vernon, NY, pg. 26
Bonheim, Frank W., V.P.-Personnel--Levitz Furniture Corporation, Boca Raton, FL, pg. 647
Bonhoff, Ali, Mgr.-Personnel--Mike Daugherty's Hurling Chevrolet, Inc., Sacramento, CA, pg. 555
Bonn, Patricia, Mgr.-Admin. & Employee Rels.--Bobst Group Inc., Roseland, NJ, pg. 161
Boone, Richard, Human Resources Dir.--Rutt Custom Cabinetry, Goodville, PA, pg. 957
Bordelon, Clarence J., V.P.-Sls. & Admin.--Tyler Elevator Products, Inc., Valley View, OH, pg. 1122
Boswell, S.M., Dir.-Employee Rels.--United States Pipe & Foundry Company, Birmingham, AL, pg. 1162
Bouchard, Clifford, Dir.-Personnel--Mohawk Paper Mills, Inc., Cohoes, NY, pg. 763
Boucher, Sandra, Dir.-Personnel--Felton Brush Inc., Manchester, NH, pg. 406
Bourgon, George M., Jr., Sr. V.P. & Dir.-Personnel--First Federal of Michigan, Detroit, MI, pg. 414
Bowen, Thomas H., Jr., V.P.-Admin. Services--Mississippi Valley Gas Co., Jackson, MS, pg. 1208
Bowers, John A., V.P.-Human Resources--Providence Journal Company, Providence, RI, pg. 895
Bowland, Wanda L., Mgr.-Human Resources--Cyber Systems, Inc., Anaheim, CA, pg. 307
Bowling, Virginia, Mgr.-Personnel--Educational Insights, Inc., Dominguez Hills, CA, pg. 369
Boykin, C.L., Personnel Mgr.--Coastal Dairy Products, Inc., Wilson, NC, pg. 257
Bradley, Charles F., Mgr.-Personnel--Summit Corporation of America, Thomaston, CT, pg. 1058
Bradley, Paul, Dir.-Human Resources--Hale-Halsell Company, Tulsa, OK, pg. 500
Bradner, Darlene A., V.P.-Human Resources--The Weitz Corporation, Des Moines, IA, pg. 1174
Bradshaw, Sandy, Dir.-Human Resources--CAE Link Allen Division, Alexandria, VA, pg. 198
Bragenberg, Albert, V.P.-Human Resources--Tyler Refrigeration Corp., Niles, MI, pg. 62
Bragg, Steve, V.P.-Human Resources--Pella Corporation, Pella, IA, pg. 856
Brandley, Norman, V.P.-Human Resources--Countrymark Cooperative, Inc., Indianapolis, IN, pg. 290
Brandson, Michael, V.P.-Human Resources--McGuffey's Restaurants, Inc., Asheville, NC, pg. 729
Brang, Barry, Mgr.-Personnel--Genova Products, Inc., Davison, MI, pg. 452
Brannon, Judy, V.P.-Personal Lines--Preferred Risk Mutual Insurance, West Des Moines, IA, pg. 886
Branz, Adell, Dir.-Personnel--Miss Elaine Inc., Saint Louis, MO, pg. 760
Bratz, Milton, Dir.-Personnel--Littleton Coin Co., Inc., Littleton, NH, pg. 679
Braun, Gene, Mgr.-Personnel--The Metal Ware Corp., Two Rivers, WI, pg. 741
Bray, Ann Marie, Dir.-Personnel--Kenco, Middlebury, IN, pg. 1025
Bray, Annemarie, Dir.-Personnel--Sparkomatic Corporation, Milford, PA, pg. 1025

Bray, Annemarie, Dir.-Human Resources--Altec Lansing Consumer Products, Milford, PA, pg. 1025
Brazik, Charles, Sr. V.P.-Human Resources--Dominick's Finer Foods, Northlake, IL, pg. 343
Breeze, Kathy, Dir.-Human Resources--Reliable Castings Corporation, Cincinnati, OH, pg. 924
Brennan, John, Dir.-Personnel--Quaker Fabric Corporation, Fall River, MA, pg. 903
Brenneman, Larry D., V.P.-Human Resources--Yorktowne Paper Mills, Inc., York, PA, pg. 1208
Brewer, Rob, Mgr.-Human Resources--Austin Industries, Inc., Dallas, TX, pg. 99
Brewer, Tina, Mgr.-Personnel--Allied Foods, Inc., Atlanta, GA, pg. 38
Brickel, Jack W., Pres., Chief Exec. & Chief Oper. Officer & Dir.-Personnel--BEC Inc., Richmond, MI, pg. 106
Brickman, Wayne, V.P.-Procurement & Human Resources--D.C.I., Inc., Saint Cloud, MN, pg. 308
Bridges, Maxine L., Sec., Treas. & Dir.-Personnel & Investor Rels.--Sterling Homes Corp., Sparks, NV, pg. 1046
Briggs, Mike, V.P.-Mktg. & Human Resources--Anchor Continental Incorporated, Columbia, SC, pg. 71
Brigham, Sarah, V.P.-Human Resources & Intl.--Diagraph Corporation, Earth City, MO, pg. 335
Brill, Roberta, Dir.-Personnel--Manostat Corporation, New York, NY, pg. 704
Brindley, Thomas M., Chief Oper. Officer & Exec. V.P.--W.A. Roosevelt Co., La Crosse, WI, pg. 946
Brinkerhoff, James W., Dir.-Human Resources--Potters Industries, Inc., Parsippany, NJ, pg. 837
Britt, Faye, Mgr.-Personnel--Long MFG. NC, Inc., Tarboro, NC, pg. 682
Britton, Harry, Dir.-Personnel--Affiliated of Florida Inc., Tampa, FL, pg. 23
Broadhead, D., Mgr.-Personnel--Astronautics Corp. of America, Milwaukee, WI, pg. 93
Brock, B.C., V.P.-Human Resources--U.S. Can Company, Oak Brook, IL, pg. 1134
Brockman, Lucy, Mgr.-Personnel--Apparel Ventures, Inc., Gardena, CA, pg. 78
Brodbeck, Barry, V.P.-Human Resources--Brodbeck Enterprises, Inc., Platteville, WI, pg. 178
Broderick, Mike, Dir.-Personnel--Ed Miniat, Inc., Chicago, IL, pg. 757
Brogan, Richard, V.P.-Human Resources--Kearney, Tucker, GA, pg. 357
Brogan, Steve, Mgr.-Personnel--Warner Press, Inc., Anderson, IN, pg. 1164
Bronsdard, George, Dir.-Human Resources--Bollinger Machine Shop And Shipyard, Inc., Lockport, LA, pg. 163
Brooks, Gail, Dir.-Employee Rels.--Maccabees Mutual Life Insurance, Southfield, MI, pg. 696
Brooks, Richard, Dir.-Human Resources--Ocean Spray Cranberries, Inc., Lakeville, MA, pg. 820
Brookshire, Tim, Exec. V.P.-Human Resources--Brookshire Grocery, Tyler, TX, pg. 180
Broome, Monnie, V.P.-Human Resources--JPS Textile Group, Inc., Greenville, SC, pg. 586
Brose, Brian, Mgr.-Personnel--Federated Mutual Insurance Company, Owatonna, MN, pg. 405
Brossart, Sue, Dir.-Pub. Rels.--Rural Metro Corporation, Scottsdale, AZ, pg. 956
Brown, A. David, Sr. V.P.-Human Resources--R. H. Macy & Co., Inc., New York, NY, pg. 698
Brown, Anthony, Dir.-Human Res.--Rocky Mountain Bank Note Company, Lakewood, CO, pg. 942
Brown, Bob, V.P.-Human Resources & Admin.--Capitol Industries-EMI Inc., Hollywood, CA, pg. 216
Brown, Cindy, Payroll Admin.--Dot Printer, Inc., Irvine, CA, pg. 347
Brown, Donna, Dir.-Personnel--Eastway Delivery Service of Houston, Inc., Houston, TX, pg. 364
Brown, Herb, Mgr.-Personnel--Efficient Engineering Co., Troy, MI, pg. 371
Brown, Joan, Dir.-Human Resources & Employee Benefits--Control Systems Inc., Saint Paul, MN, pg. 281
Brown, John, Mgr.-Personnel--Globe International Inc., Buffalo, NY, pg. 464
Brown, Larry, Personnel Dir.--Clow Corporation, Birmingham, AL, pg. 733
Brown, Larry L., Jr., Dir.-Mktg. & Adv.--Riverside Central Services, Inc., Natchez, MS, pg. 937
Brown, Rayna, V.P.-Human Resources--Capitol Records, Inc., Hollywood, CA, pg. 216
Brown, Robert K., Dir.-Human Resources--Spang & Company, Butler, PA, pg. 1025
Brown, Wayne H., Dir.-Personnel--Dundee Mills, Inc., Griffin, GA, pg. 352
Brownlie, Diane, Human Resources Rep.--Sipex Corporation, Billerica, MA, pg. 1009
Bruce, Doug, Dir.-Personnel Programs--Red Roof Inns, Inc., Hilliard, OH, pg. 918
Bruff, J.M., Personnel Mgr.--Toledo Commutator Co., Owosso, MI, pg. 633
Bruin, Linnea T., Dir.-Employee Rels.--Intermatic Inc., Spring Grove, IL, pg. 575
Bruscas, Angelo, V.P.-Human Resources--Associated Grocers, Inc., Seattle, WA, pg. 90
Brusher, Paul, V.P.-Human Resources--Pneumafil Corp., Charlotte, NC, pg. 878
Bryant, Tom, Dir.-Human Resources--Aladdin Industries, Incorporated, Nashville, TN, pg. 29
Buchler, Christina, V.P.-Mktg. & Human Resources--Citizens National Bank, Hammond, LA, pg. 251
Budai, Gabriella, Mgr.-Human Resources--Fishers Big Wheel Inc., New Castle, PA, pg. 415
Buehler, Walter P., Dir.-Personnel--Gannett Fleming Affiliates, Inc., Harrisburg, PA, pg. 442
Buhrow, Kim, Mgr.-Personnel--Olympic Steel Inc., Bedford Heights, OH, pg. 825
Bullard, Richard, Dir.-Personnel--Martins Abbatoir & Wholesale Meats Inc., Godwin, NC, pg. 716
Bulson, Nancy, Dir.-Human Resources--Castex Industries Inc., Holland, MI, pg. 228
Bundy, Phillip, V.P.-Personnel & Labor Rels.--Morgan Foods, Inc., Austin, IN, pg. 770
Bunn, Jack, Mgr.-Personnel--Doonan & Sons, Inc., Great Bend, KS, pg. 346
Burch, Candace S., V.P.-Human Resources--NFO Research, Inc., Greenwich, CT, pg. 780
Burch, Lisa, Mgr.-Personnel--Romac Industries, Inc., Hays Division, Dallas, NC, pg. 945
Burdette, Courtney B., Sr. V.P.-Cooperative Rels.--Agway, Inc., De Witt, NY, pg. 25
Burford, Kevin B., Dir.-Personnel--James N. Gray Construction Co., Inc., Lexington, KY, pg. 479
Burgess, Richard J., Dir.-Indus. Rels.--A. Finkl & Sons Co., Chicago, IL, pg. 411
Burkard, Walter, Dir.-Personnel--W&F Manufacturing Corporation, Inc., Buffalo, NY, pg. 1155
Burke, Tim, Dir.-Human Resources--Syratech Corporation, East Boston, MA, pg. 1070
Burlingame, Barry, Dir.-Human Resources--Kaiser Aerospace & Electronics Corp., Foster City, CA, pg. 614
Burnett, Kathy, Mgr.-Personnel--Insurance Management Associates, Wichita, KS, pg. 572
Burney, David, Personnel Mgr.--E. B. Kingman Company, Leominster, MA, pg. 631
Burns, Jon M., V.P.-Human Resources--Applied Industrial Materials Corporation, Deerfield, IL, pg. 79
Busch, David C., V.P.-Human Resources--Roundy's, Inc., Pewaukee, WI, pg. 952
Busch, Robert C., V.P.-Human Resources--Lord Corporation, Erie, PA, pg. 683
Bushore, John, Dir.-Human Resources--Lockwood Corporation, Gering, NE, pg. 680
Buss, William, Dir.-Human Resources--Victaulic Company of America, Easton, PA, pg. 1149
Butler, Clinton, Dir.-Personnel & Recruitment--Continental Conveyor & Equipment Company, Winfield, AL, pg. 798
Butler, Jeff, V.P.-Human Resources--Boston Chicken, Inc., Naperville, IL, pg. 167
Butner, Beverly B., V.P.-Admin. & Sec.--Proto Systems of Atlanta, Alpharetta, GA, pg. 895
Butorac, Terry, V.P.-Human Resources--Carlson Companies, Inc., Minneapolis, MN, pg. 220
Buxton, Mark, Dir.-Personnel--Del Monte Foods, San Francisco, CA, pg. 325
Byers, D.R., Mgr.-Personnel--AGR International, Inc., Butler, PA, pg. 4
Bylsma, Gary, Mgr.-Personnel--Bissell Inc., Grand Rapids, MI, pg. 153
Byrd, Doyle, Sr. V.P.-Human Resources & Devel.--Central Freight Lines Inc., Waco, TX, pg. 232
Byrd, Ronald D., Mgr.-Personnel--Hackney Brothers, Inc., Wilson, NC, pg. 498
Byrne, Cheryl, Dir.-Personnel--Niagara Envelope Company, Inc., Buffalo, NY, pg. 805
Byrnes, Gail, Dir.-Human Resources--Great Lakes Financial Resources, Inc., Homewood, IL, pg. 481
Caci, Mary, Dir.-Pur. & Personnel--Erin Group Administrators, Inc., Lancaster, PA, pg. 387
Cahill, Robert, Dir.-Human Resources--Mark III Industries, Ocala, FL, pg. 708
Cain, Mark, Mgr.-Personnel--Henry Vogt Machine Co., Louisville, KY, pg. 1154
Cain, Martin, V.P.-Human Resources--American Fuel Cell & Coated Fabrics Co. (Amfuel), Magnolia, AR, pg. 55
Callahan, Ed, Sr. V.P.-Human Resources-Worldwide--Estee Lauder, Inc., New York, NY, pg. 389
Calvert, Marilyn, Mgr.-Personnel--SENCORP, Newport, KY, pg. 989
Calzaretta, Carol, V.P.-Human Resources--DonTech, Chicago, IL, pg. 345
Camp, Richard O., Dir.-Human Resources--Freeman Decorating Co., Dallas, TX, pg. 431
Campanile, Connie, Dir.-Personnel--SRS Technologies, Newport Beach, CA, pg. 964
Campbell, Jeanneen, Mgr.-Personnel--Misco Industries, Wichita, KS, pg. 759
Campbell, Keith M., V.P.-Human Resources & Mngmt. Svcs.--The Minnesota Mutual Life Insurance Company, Saint Paul, MN, pg. 757
Campbell, Raymond, Dir.-Personnel--Sugar Cane Growers Cooperative of Florida, Belle Glade, FL, pg. 1056
Campbell, Tim, Dir.-Personnel--Tom's Foods, Columbus, GA, pg. 1101
Canada, John, Dir.-Human Resources--Gemtron Corporation, Sweetwater, TN, pg. 3
Canning, Arthur, Dir.-Personnel--Tempel Steel Company, Skokie, IL, pg. 1086
Cantreau, Eugene, Dir.-Personnel--Sierracin Corporation, Sylmar, CA, pg. 1003
Capdeville, Ralph, Dir.-Personnel--Production Management Companies, Inc., Harvey, LA, pg. 893
Caponigro, Leonard, V.P.-Mfg. & Personnel & Dir.-Pur.--Tork, Inc., Mount Vernon, NY, pg. 1102
Carabetta, John, Comptroller & Dir.-Personnel & Investor Rels.--Beauty Enterprises Inc., Hartford, CT, pg. 130
Carhart, Loretta, Dir.-Human Resources--Imprint Products, L.P., Rockville Centre, NY, pg. 564
Carioscia, Raymond, Personnel Dir.--J. A. Sexauer, Scarsdale, NY, pg. 357
Carlson, Linda, Dir.-Personnel--Swinerton & Walberg Co., San Francisco, CA, pg. 1068
Carlson, Suzanne, Mgr.-Employee Benefits--St. Johnsbury Trucking Co., Inc., Holliston, MA, pg. 966
Carnahan, M.L., V.P.-Human Resources--California & Hawaiian Sugar Company, Concord, CA, pg. 210
Carneal, Mark, V.P.-Human Resources--El Torito Restaurants, Inc., Irvine, CA, pg. 372
Caron, Richard, V.P.-Human Resources--Round Hill Foods, Inc., New Oxford, PA, pg. 952
Carozza, Regis, V.P.-Human Resources--Fishers Big Wheel Inc., New Castle, PA, pg. 415
Carpenter, Ernest A., V.P.-Admin. & Gen. Counsel--Tippins Incorporated, Pittsburgh, PA, pg. 1099
Carpenter, Joan, Personnel Dir.--Tenax Corporation, Danbury, CT, pg. 1086
Carr, R., Dir.-Personnel--Hercules Tire & Rubber Company, Findlay, OH, pg. 531
Carroccio, Joanne F., Mgr.-Personnel--Thermo Electric Co., Inc., Saddle Brook, NJ, pg. 1091
Cartagine, Sal, Human Resources Exec. Dir.--New York Racing Association, Jamaica, NY, pg. 803
Carter, Jack, Personnel Dir.--John Zink Co., Tulsa, OK, pg. 639
Carter, Nancy, Mgr.-Personnel--Five Dollar Clothing Stores, Los Angeles, CA, pg. 416
Carter, Robert, V.P.-Personnel--Penske Corporation, Detroit, MI, pg. 859
Casamento, Joseph, V.P.-Human Resources--Twin County Grocers, Inc., Edison, NJ, pg. 1122
Case, Raymond J., V.P.-Fin. & Human Resources--Bently Nevada Corporation, Minden, NV, pg. 140
Casey, John H., V.P.-Human Resources--Jockey International, Inc., Kenosha, WI, pg. 595
Casey, T.R., V.P.-Human Resources & Employee Benefits--Flexible Products Company, Marietta, GA, pg. 418
Cash, Glenn, Dir.-Personnel--American Fast Print, Limited, Spartanburg, SC, pg. 52
Caskey, Carol, Dir.-Employee Rels.--Long John Silver's, Inc., Lexington, KY, pg. 229
Casper, Daniel, Dir.-Personnel--Hiross Inc., Niagara Falls, NY, pg. 536
Cassidy, John J., Mgr.-Personnel--Franklin Sports Industries, Stoughton, MA, pg. 429
Casson, Helen, Dir.-Personnel--Saratoga Harness Racing, Inc., Saratoga Springs, NY, pg. 970
Caswell, Pat, Mgr.-Personnel--Cablewave Systems, Inc., North Haven, CT, pg. 206
Caughlin, T.F., V.P.-Industrial Rels.--Furnas Electric Company, Batavia, IL, pg. 437
Cauley, Kathleen P., Dir.-Personnel--United McGill Corp., Groveport, OH, pg. 1133
Cavellier, Thomas E., Controller--Gator Freightways, Inc., Wilmington, OH, pg. 446
Cawthon, Alex, Dir.-Human Resources--Thiele Kaolin Co., Sandersville, GA, pg. 1092
Celentano, Domenick A., Jr., V.P.-Mktg.--Celentano Brothers, Verona, NJ, pg. 231
Celli, Debbi, Supvr.-Employee Benefits--Pioneer Engineering & Manufacturing Co., Warren, MI, pg. 871
Chacana, Kathryn, Dir.-Human Resources--Hearst Business Communications, Inc., Garden City, NY, pg. 522
Chadburn, Carl T., V.P.-Human Resources--Phoenix Home Life Mutual Insurance Company, Hartford, CT, pg. 868
Chaddock, Paul H., Sr. V.P.-Human Resources--Lechmere, Inc., Woburn, MA, pg. 665
Chaffin, W.T., V.P.-Human Resources--Clinton Mills Inc., Clinton, SC, pg. 202
Chalfin, William D., V.P.-Human Resources--Wabash Alloys Division, Wabash, IN, pg. 275
Chamberlain, Paul, V.P.-Personnel--Porteous, South Portland, ME, pg. 353
Chandler, Joe, Dir.-Human Resources--Beacon Mfg. Co., Swannanoa, NC, pg. 129
Chandler, John, Dir.-Personnel--Venchurs Packaging, Inc., Adrian, MI, pg. 1147
Chandler, Russell, Dir.-Personnel--Camellia Food Stores Co-op Inc., Norfolk, VA, pg. 211
Chandler, W.S., Jr., V.P.-Devel.--Glen Raven Mills, Inc., Glen Raven, NC, pg. 461
Chapin, Ann, Mgr.-Human Resources--Unigard Security Insurance Co., Bellevue, WA, pg. 596
Chappell, Sarah S., Sr. V.P.-Personnel--Spencer Companies Inc., Huntsville, AL, pg. 1030
Chappell, Sheila, Mgr.-Personnel--A. L. Hansen Mfg. Co., Waukegan, IL, pg. 506
Chase, Tom, Mgr.-Personnel--Simpson Electric Co., Elgin, IL, pg. 1007
Chastain, Donna, Dir.-Personnel--Seabrook Wallcoverings, Inc., Memphis, TN, pg. 984
Chavance, Roberta, V.P.-Personnel--Strouds, City of Industry, CA, pg. 1054
Checchia, John, V.P., Treas., & Mgr.-Personnel & Data Processing--Media Printing Corporation, Miami, FL, pg. 734
Chenoweth, Joe, Mgr.-Personnel--Flambeau Plastics Co., Baraboo, WI, pg. 809
Cheppo, Nancy, Dir.-Human Resources--TMP Worldwide, Inc., New York, NY, pg. 1073
Chew, Albert, Sr. V.P.-Human Resources--Club Corporation International, Dallas, TX, pg. 256
Chiao, Elaine, Mgr.-Personnel--California State Lottery, Sacramento, CA, pg. 210
Chiappetta, Susan, 2nd V.P.-Human Resources--National Life Insurance Company, Montpelier, VT, pg. 791
Chick, Michal, Dir.-Human Resources--Tylan General, Inc., San Diego, CA, pg. 1122
Childers, Ron, Mgr.-Personnel--Golden State Foods Corp., Pasadena, CA, pg. 466
Chrismon, Eddie, Dir.-Human Resources--Carolina Biological Supply Co., Burlington, NC, pg. 222
Chrispen, Harry, Dir.-Human Resources--National Cleaning Contractors, Inc., New York, NY, pg. 786
Christensen, Pat, Mgr.-Human Resources--Accurate Threaded Fasteners, Inc., Lincolnwood, IL, pg. 11
Christian, Chip, V.P.-Human Res.--Rocco Inc., Harrisonburg, VA, pg. 940
Christian, Robert C., V.P.-Human Resources--Forstmann & Company, Inc., New York, NY, pg. 424
Christianson, David E., Dir.-Human Resources--Burns & McDonnell Engineers-Architects-Consultants, Kansas City, MO, pg. 194
Christie, Camille D., Mgr.-Acquisitions, Labor Rels. & Arbitration--BNA Books Div., Washington, DC, pg. 189
Christopher, Jeri, V.P.- Human Resources--Gordon Bailey & Associates, Inc., Stone Mountain, GA, pg. 114
Chukerman, H., V.P.-Human Resources--Schwarz Paper Company, Morton Grove, IL, pg. 980

Chun, JoAnne, Dir.-Personnel--The Shidler Group, San Francisco, CA, pg. 999
Chvala, Vicki, V.P.-Human Resources--American Family Mutual Insurance Co., Madison, WI, pg. 51
Cieslak, Daniel, Mng. Dir-Human Resources--Dunham's Athleisure Corporation, Waterford, MI, pg. 353
Clark, Major L., II, V.P.-Human Resources & Admin.--Maintain, Baltimore, MD, pg. 723
Clark, Major L., III, V.P.-Human Resources & Admin.--The Maxima Corporation, Lanham, MD, pg. 723
Clark, Major L., III, V.P.-Human Resources & Admin.--Maxima Business Systems, Rockville, MD, pg. 723
Clark, Major L., III, V.P.-Human Resources & Admin.--Maxima Computer Systems Corp., Upper Marlboro, MD, pg. 723
Clark, Major L., III, V.P.-Human Res. & Admin.--Maxima Data Systems, Rockville, MD, pg. 723
Clark, William, Mgr.-Personnel--Spangler Candy Company, Bryan, OH, pg. 1025
Claus, Bill, Dir.-Oper. & Training--Tuffy Associates Corp., Toledo, OH, pg. 1119
Claxton, Rick, Dir.-Human Resources--American Color, Phoenix, AZ, pg. 1056
Clay, William, V.P.-Personnel--SENCORP, Newport, KY, pg. 989
Claycomb, Deloris, Mgr.-Human Resources--Candle Corporation of America, Oshkosh, WI, pg. 214
Claypool, Jeffrey C., V.P.-Human Resources--Sealy Corporation, Cleveland, OH, pg. 985
Clegg, Jeanne, Personnel Mgr.--Ebco Mfg. Company, Columbus, OH, pg. 365
Clemens, Philip A., V.P.-Human Resources--Hatfield Quality Meats, Inc., Hatfield, PA, pg. 517
Clements, Larry, Dir.-Human Resources--Orr Safety Equipment Company, Louisville, KY, pg. 830
Cline, Cathy, Dir.-Human Resources--Aerovironment, Inc., Monrovia, CA, pg. 22
Cline, Ted J., Dir.-Human Resources--WW Engineering & Science Inc., Grand Rapids, MI, pg. 1058
Clinnin, Ted, V.P.-Human Resources--Certified Grocers Midwest, Inc., Hodgkins, IL, pg. 236
Clinton, Mark, Dir.-Personnel--Gemtron Corporation, Sweetwater, TN, pg. 3
Cloud, Corene, Dir.-Personnel--Howell Instruments Corp., Fort Worth, TX, pg. 547
Coatney, Betty, Dir.-Personnel--International Chemical Company, Tulsa, OK, pg. 576
Cobern, Jim, Dir.-Human Resources--Marcal Paper Mills, Inc., Elmwood Park, NJ, pg. 706
Cochran, Sherry, Gen. Mgr.--Professional Travel, Inc., Dalton, GA, pg. 894
Coe, James H., Dir.-Human Resources--Calvin Klein, Inc., New York, NY, pg. 635
Coffee, Richard P., V.P.-Human Resources--National Steel Corporation, Mishawaka, IN, pg. 793
Coffin, Dwight, V.P.-Human Resources--Continental Grain Company, New York, NY, pg. 279
Coffman, Jim, Dir.-Grp. Services--Redken Laboratories, Inc., Canoga Park, CA, pg. 919
Cohn, Thomas, V.P. & Dir.-Personnel & Communications--Sigmund Cohn Corp., Mount Vernon, NY, pg. 259
Coiter, Nancy, Dir.-Personnel--Academy Insurance Group, Inc., Atlanta, GA, pg. 11
Coleman, James, Jr., V.P.-Human Resources--Fru-Con Construction Corporation, Ballwin, MO, pg. 435
Coleman, M., V.P.-Personnel--Kal Kan Foods, Inc., Vernon, CA, pg. 713
Collen, Robert P., V.P.-Personnel--Rodney Hunt Company, Orange, MA, pg. 553
Collier, George, V.P.-Fin. & Personnel Mgr.--Streamlight Inc., Norristown, PA, pg. 1053
Collings, Kenneth, Dir.-Personnel--Raley's, West Sacramento, CA, pg. 910
Collins, Barry W., Mgr.-Personnel & Adv.--Peabody Myers Corp., Streator, IL, pg. 900
Collins, G. W., Dir.-Personnel--Buffalo Color Corporation, Parsippany, NJ, pg. 187
Collins, J., Dir.-Human Resources--Giffels Associates, Inc., Southfield, MI, pg. 457
Collins, Jim, Dir.-Personnel--Game Time, Inc., Fort Payne, AL, pg. 442
Collins, Karen, Mgr.-Personnel--James Austin Co., Mars, PA, pg. 99
Collins, Lonnie E., V.P.-Personnel--M. Bruenger & Co., Inc., Wichita, KS, pg. 184
Collins, Margaret, Dir.-Human Rels.--Hubbard Construction Co., Winter Park, FL, pg. 549
Collins, Theresa, Mgr.-Personnel--Grocery Supply Company Division, Sulphur Springs, TX, pg. 440
Collum, Roy, Dir. Personnel--W. M. Grace Development, Phoenix, AZ, pg. 474
Colo, Ann, Personnel Dir.--Brencal Contractors Inc., Detroit, MI, pg. 106
Combs, Conrey, Dir.-Human Resources--Preferred Risk Mutual Insurance, West Des Moines, IA, pg. 886
Commens, Diane, Mgr.-Human Resources--Diagraph Corporation, Earth City, MO, pg. 335
Commins, Julie, Mgr.-Personnel--J. E. Higgins Lumber Co., Concord, CA, pg. 533
Compton, David D., Dir.-Opers.--Central Coca-Cola Bottling Company, Inc., Richmond, VA, pg. 232
Compton, J.W., V.P.-Human Resources--Krystal Company, Chattanooga, TN, pg. 645
Conant, June, Dir.-Personnel--Delta Education, Inc., Hudson, NH, pg. 326
Conesa, Nidiam, Personnel Supvr.--Security Plastics, Inc., Miami Lakes, FL, pg. 987
Congdon, Kimberly, Dir.-Human Resources--Ortel Corporation, Alhambra, CA, pg. 830
Conger, K.W., V.P.-Human Resources--Kohler Company, Kohler, WI, pg. 639
Connelly, Elizabeth K., Sr. V.P., Corp. Sec., Human Resources & Office Mngmt.--Adler Boschetto Peebles & Partners, Inc., New York, NY, pg. 17
Connely, Bob, Mgr.-Personnel--Safeguard Business Systems, Inc., Fort Washington, PA, pg. 966
Connor, Winston H., V.P.-Human Resources--Huntsman Chemical Corporation, Salt Lake City, UT, pg. 555
Conrad, Roger C., Dir.-Personnel--Construction Specialties, Inc., Cranford, NJ, pg. 277
Conti, Anthony J., Vice Chm.-Human Resources--Coopers & Lybrand, New York, NY, pg. 283
Cook, Jim, Sr. V.P.-Opers. & Human Resources--Playtex Beauty Care, Inc., Stamford, CT, pg. 877
Cook, R.A., Mgr.-Personnel--Eriez Magnetics, Erie, PA, pg. 386
Cook, Suzanne J., Dir.-Human Resources--Ris Paper Company, Long Island City, NY, pg. 935
Cook, Tom, Dir.-Personnel--Carlisle Equipment Company, Louisville, KY, pg. 220
Cooke, Ralph M., Dir.-Human Resources--Pioneer/Eclipse Corp., Sparta, NC, pg. 871
Cooley, Harold E., V.P.--G B Stores, Johnstown, PA, pg. 978
Cooper, David, Dir.-Personnel--J. H. Fletcher & Co., Huntington, WV, pg. 418
Cooper, Jerry D., V.P.-Human Resources--HCB Contractors, Dallas, TX, pg. 496
Cooper, W., Dir.-Personnel--Quality Bakers of America Cooperative, Inc., Greenwich, CT, pg. 903
Coraci-McCann, Catherine, V.P., Human Resources Dir.--Young & Rubicam Detroit, Detroit, MI, pg. 1211
Corbett, Jay, Dir.-Human Resources--Pneumatic Scale Corporation, Quincy, MA, pg. 122
Corbin, Robert, Dir.-Human Resources--Charles River Data Systems, Inc., Framingham, MA, pg. 240
Corman, Joan, Dir.-Human Resources--W. Braun Company, Chicago, IL, pg. 172
Corman, Joan, Mgr.-Personnel--W. Braun Distribution Center, Summit, IL, pg. 172
Corr, Van, Mgr.-Personnel--Midwest Industries, Inc., Ida Grove, IA, pg. 752
Corrigan, Lee Ann, Dir.-Human Resources--Altus Federal Savings Bank, Mobile, AL, pg. 46
Cortez, Vicki, Dir.-Human Resources--Tropical Garment Manufacturing Company, Tampa, FL, pg. 1116
Cortise, Vicky L., V.P.-Personnel & Risk Mngmt.--Federal Compress & Warehouse Company, Inc., Memphis, TN, pg. 404
Cotter, Tim, Dir.-Human Resources--The Coleman Company, Inc., Wichita, KS, pg. 695
Cotterill, Fran, Human Resources--Hutchins/Young & Rubicam, Rochester, NY, pg. 1211
Cotton, Richard, Personnel Dir.--Broadmoor Hotel, Inc., Colorado Springs, CO, pg. 177
Cottrell, Lynn, V.P.-Admin. & Dir.-Personnel--Western Dairymen Cooperative, Inc., Thornton, CO, pg. 1178
Coughlin, Peg, Dir.-Human Resources--Sipex Corporation, Billerica, MA, pg. 1009
Coupey, P., V.P.-Human Resources--Versa Services Ltd., Etobicoke,, Canada, pg. 7
Courtney, Robert L., V.P.-Indus. Rels.--Safelite Autoglass, Wichita, KS, pg. 664
Couture, Robert, Dir.-Personnel--Tapemark, West St. Paul, MN, pg. 1078
Cowen, Ann, 2nd V.P.-Human Resources--Phoenix Home Life Mutual Insurance Company, Hartford, CT, pg. 868
Cowles, Leonard, Dir.-Indus. Rels.--Anchorlok Corp., Compton, CA, pg. 664
Cox, Sadie, Mgr.-Personnel--Carolina Steel Corporation, Greensboro, NC, pg. 223
Craft, Fred, Jr., Mgr.-Human Resources--Cheraw Yarn Mills, Inc., Cheraw, SC, pg. 242
Craft, Karen, Dir.-Human Resources--Proto Systems of Atlanta, Alpharetta, GA, pg. 895
Craig, Floyd, V.P.-Human Resources--SCT Yarns, Inc., Chattanooga, TN, pg. 961
Craig, Linda, Dir.-Personnel--Laboratory Supply Company, Inc., Louisville, KY, pg. 649
Craig, Robin, Human Resources Admin.--Pioneer Engineering & Manufacturing Co., Warren, MI, pg. 871
Cramer, Dale E., Dir.-Personnel--Howard Miller Clock Company, Zeeland, MI, pg. 754
Crandall, Dennis J., Dir.-Human Resources--Falconer Glass Industries, Inc., Falconer, NY, pg. 492
Crawford, Ellen, Office Mgr.--Cottman Transmission Systems, Inc., Fort Washington, PA, pg. 288
Crey, Russell, Dir.-Personnel--Smith Frozen Foods, Inc., Weston, OR, pg. 1012
Croonquist, Stan, V.P.-Human Resources--UniHealth America, Burbank, CA, pg. 1126
Cross, Jimmy L., V.P.-Customer Plng.--Tennessee Valley Authority, Knoxville, TN, pg. 1088
Cross, Karen, V.P.-Human Resources--Harmony House Records & Tapes, Troy, MI, pg. 510
Crowell, Barbara, Dir.-Personnel--Raffi & Swanson, Inc., Wilmington, MA, pg. 909
Crumlett, Bill, Dir.-Personnel--Southwest Research Institute, San Antonio, TX, pg. 1023
Crumley, Bob, Sr. V.P.-Personnel--Boddie-Noell Enterprises Inc., Rocky Mount, NC, pg. 161
Cubb, Vivian, Dir.-Human Resources--Chattanooga Choo-Choo Holiday Inn, Chattanooga, TN, pg. 241
Culver, Joe, Sr. V.P.-Personnel--Woodward & Lothrop/John Wanamaker, Washington, DC, pg. 1201
Culver, Joseph, Sr. V.P.-Human Resources--John Wanamaker, Philadelphia, Philadelphia, PA, pg. 1201
Cummings, Linda, V.P.-Human Resources--Super 8 Motels, Inc., Aberdeen, SD, pg. 1062
Cummings, Ruth J., Dir.-Human Resources--Code-A-Phone Corp., Clackamas, OR, pg. 258
Cunnigham, James M., V.P.-Human Resources--Argo-Tech Corporation, Cleveland, OH, pg. 82
Cunningham, Herbert E., V.P.-Human Resources--Nationwide Mutual Insurance Company, Columbus, OH, pg. 795
Cunningham, Maureen, V.P., Human Resources--Earle Palmer Brown, Bethesda, MD, pg. 182
Cuppett, Dona, Mgr.-Human Resources--Accu-Sort Systems, Inc., Telford, PA, pg. 11
Curran, Kathy, Dir.-Human Resources--Telex Communications, Inc., Minneapolis, MN, pg. 1085
Curry, James, Dir.-Personnel--Underground Construction Company, Inc., Benicia, CA, pg. 1125
Curtis, Michael, Personnel Mgr.--FoodCraft Equipment Co., Inc., Lancaster, PA, pg. 860
D'Agosta, Connye, V.P.-Employee Benefits & Personnel Admin.--Calvin Klein Sport, New York, NY, pg. 635
D'Aversa, Angela, Dir.-Human Resources & Office Admin.--Borg-Warner Corporation, Chicago, IL, pg. 165
Daily, James, Dir.-Human Resources--Cajun Electric Power Co-op, Baton Rouge, LA, pg. 207
Dajer, Antonio, V.P.-Human Resources & Asst. Sec.--Pueblo International, Inc.-P.R. Div., Carolina, PR, pg. 899
Dallal, Fortunate, V.P.-Personnel & Treas.--Windsor Fashions, Los Angeles, CA, pg. 1195
Damewood, Tom, V.P.-Human Resources--Tollman/Hundley Hotels, Valhalla, NY, pg. 1100
Danheiser, Marguerite, Dir.-Human Resources--Transammonia Inc., New York, NY, pg. 1106
Daniel, David A., Asst. to Exec. Dir.--American Chemical Society, Washington, DC, pg. 50
Daniel, Ron, V.P., Dir.-Personnel & Sec.--The Daniel Co. of Springfield, Springfield, MO, pg. 314
Danko-Koenig, Andrea, Dir.-Compensation & Benefits--Clark Construction Group, Bethesda, MD, pg. 252
Danley, Peggy L., Dir.-Personnel--Clark Oil & Refining Corporation, Saint Louis, MO, pg. 252
Darby, Patricia T., Dir.-Human Resources--Landmark Community Newspapers, Inc., Shelbyville, KY, pg. 655
Darian, Ralph, Pres., Chief Exec. & Chief Fin. Officer--Levonian Brothers Inc., Troy, NY, pg. 671
Dauk, R.A., V.P.-Human Resources--American Steel & Wire Corporation, Cuyahoga Heights, OH, pg. 246
Dauska, John B., Dir.-Personnel--Green Bay Packaging Inc., Green Bay, WI, pg. 483
Davidson, Steven A., V.P.-Personnel & Organization--General Instrument Corporation, New York, NY, pg. 425
Davis, Dan, Mgr.-Personnel--Conbraco Industries Inc., Matthews, NC, pg. 272
Davis, Donald R., V.P.-Corp. Rels.--Gate Petroleum Company, Jacksonville, FL, pg. 445
Davis, Gerry, Personnel Mgr.--The Gilman Company, Chattanooga, TN, pg. 603
Davis, Harold, Dir.-Personnel--Parkdale Mills, Gastonia, NC, pg. 849
Davis, Katherine, Dir.-Human Resources--American Management Group, Westbrook, ME, pg. 57
Davis, Rebecca M., Mgr.-Personnel--Mar-Mac Manufacturing Company, Inc., McBee, SC, pg. 705
Davis, Roberta, Dir.-Personnel--Rogers Markets Inc., Fort Wayne, IN, pg. 943
Davis, W. Stewart Jr., V.P.-Human Resources--Grede Foundries, Inc., Milwaukee, WI, pg. 483
Davis, William, Dir.-Personnel, Human Resources & Employee Benefits--Tennessee Farmers Co-op, La Vergne, TN, pg. 1087
Davitt, Charles, Dir.-Personnel--Gibraltar Steel Corp., Buffalo, NY, pg. 456
Dawdy, Sam, Dir.-Personnel--Dazey Corporation, Industrial Airport, KS, pg. 321
Dawson, Cindy, V.P.-Professional Rels.--Starkey Laboratories, Inc., Eden Prairie, MN, pg. 1040
Day, Wendy, V.P., Personnel Mgr.--Ammirati & Puris Inc., New York, NY, pg. 67
De Bruin, Wayne, Dir.-Indus. Rels.--Crenlo, Inc., Rochester, MN, pg. 298
De Chantal, RoJean, V.P.-Human Resources--The Fairmont Hotels, San Francisco, CA, pg. 397
De Marco, Patricia, Dir.-Personnel--Bradley Printing Company, Des Plaines, IL, pg. 478
De Segurintz, Gail, Dir.-Personnel--PE Systems, Reston, VA, pg. 836
Dean, Debby R., Dir.-Human Resources--Serono Baker Diagnostics, Allentown, PA, pg. 991
DeAndrea, C. A., Mgr.-Personnel--Dynamic Controls Corp., South Windsor, CT, pg. 356
DeAngelo, Joseph A., Treas.--Moran Towing & Transporation Co. Inc, Greenwich, CT, pg. 769
Dearden, Douglas E., Chief Exec. Officer & Personnel Dir.--Dearden's, Inc., Los Angeles, CA, pg. 322
Debiasi, Glenn, V.P.-Human Resources--Alex Lee, Inc., Hickory, NC, pg. 33
DeBruhl, Mike, Exec. Dir.-Employment--Advanced Technology, Inc., Reston, VA, pg. 20
DeFrancesco, Sal, Dir.-Personnel--Simkins Industries, Inc., New Haven, CT, pg. 1005
Delaney, Bob, Personnel Admin.--Foster Refrigerator Corporation, Hudson, NY, pg. 426
Delk, Melissa, Human Resources Asst.--Grizzard Advertising, Inc., Atlanta, GA, pg. 488
Dellinger, Kathy, Dir.-Human Resources--Williams Television Time, Inc., Santa Monica, CA, pg. 1191
DelNegro, Anthony T., V.P.-Human Resources--Berol Corporation, Brentwood, TN, pg. 856
Demeri, Ann, V.P., Personnel--Warwick Baker & Fiore Inc., New York, NY, pg. 1165
Demers, Eileen, Mgr.-Human Resources--Adra Systems, Inc., Lowell, MA, pg. 18
Demeter, Lynn, V.P.-Personnel--Sussen, Inc., Cleveland, OH, pg. 225
Denino, Daniel A., V.P.-Admin.--Camelot Music, Inc., North Canton, OH, pg. 212
Denny, Jim, V.P.-Human Resources--QuikTrip Corporation, Tulsa, OK, pg. 905
Depolo, Robert A., Mgr.-Personnel, Treas. & Sec.--Monterey Mechanical Company, Oakland, CA, pg. 767
DePuydt, Daniel G., V.P.-Human Resources--Titanium Metals Corporation, Denver, CO, pg. 1109
DeRose, Gabrielle, Dir.-Corp. Communications & Pub. Rels.--Rich Products Corp., Buffalo, NY, pg. 932

DeSantis, Joseph F., V.P.-Personnel--Ziebart International Corporation, Troy, MI, pg. 1217
Deutsch, Louis G., Chief Fin. Officer & Human Resources--Jay Incorporated, Rochester, NY, pg. 590
Devaney, Bill, Dir.-Player Personnel--San Diego Chargers, San Diego, CA, pg. 969
Devery, Gretchen, Coord.-Personnel--Systems Engineering & Manufacturing Corp., Stoughton, MA, pg. 1071
Dew, C. Eugene, Mgr.-Human Resources--Allied Mineral Products, Inc., Columbus, OH, pg. 38
DeWeerd, Norman, V.P.-Personnel & Opers.--Dickinson Press, Inc., Grand Rapids, MI, pg. 336
Dewitt, M., Dir.-Personnel--Fleet Engineers, Inc., Muskegon, MI, pg. 417
Dewosky, Suzanne, Mgr.-Human Resources--Tassani Communications, Chicago, IL, pg. 1080
Diacont, Steven, Dir.-Personnel--The Magee Carpet Company, Bloomsburg, PA, pg. 700
Diaz, Naomi, Mgr.-Personnel--UMI Data Courier, Louisville, KY, pg. 135
Dickenson, Susan, Mgr.-Human Resources--Allsop, Inc., Bellingham, WA, pg. 43
Dickson, K., Dir.- Human Resources--GS&B-Lintas Advertising, Coral Gables, FL, pg. 440
DiCrescenzo, N.A., Corp. Dir.-Human Resources--Laroche Holdings, Inc., Atlanta, GA, pg. 659
Didier, Howard C., V.P.-Personnel--Star Cutter Co., Farmington Hills, MI, pg. 1039
Diehl, V.S., Mgr.-Personnel--United States Bronze Powders, Inc., Flemington, NJ, pg. 1134
Diehm, Paul R., Dir.-Human Resources--Yerger Bros., Inc., Lititz, PA, pg. 1208
DiGeso, Amy, V.P.-Human Resources--Mary Kay Cosmetics Inc., Dallas, TX, pg. 716
Dilatush, R.E., Jr., V.P. & Sec.--Staple Cotton Cooperative Association, Greenwood, MS, pg. 1038
DiMiglio, Lucile, Dir.-Personnel & Pur.--Norwalk Powdered Metals, Inc., Norwalk, CT, pg. 816
Dimon, Gerry, V.P.-Corp. Resources--Ameritas Life Insurance Corp., Lincoln, NE, pg. 66
Dinkins, R. S., V.P.-Human Resources--Pacific Enterprises Oil Company (USA), Dallas, TX, pg. 840
Disbrow, Nancy M., Personnel Admin.--Liggett-Stashower, Inc., Cleveland, OH, pg. 675
Dixon, Andrew, Sr. V.P. -Human Resources--Continental Cablevision, Boston, MA, pg. 278
Dixon, Don, Personnel Dir.--Lehigh-Leopold, Burlington, IA, pg. 608
Dixon, Greg, Mgr.-Human Resources--J.D. Edwards & Company, Denver, CO, pg. 370
Dodd, Alan L., Dir.-Human Resources--Dewberry & Davis, Fairfax, VA, pg. 334
Dodson, Carol, Personnel Admin.--Production Machinery Corporation, Mentor, OH, pg. 893
Dodson, Jo Ann, Dir.-Personnel--Belgrave Industries, Santa Ana, CA, pg. 133
Doherty, Bruce, Dir.-Human Resources & Employee Benefits--Seton Company, Norristown, PA, pg. 993
Dombrowski, Regina C., V.P.-Personnel & Admin.--Bolton-Emerson, Inc., Lawrence, MA, pg. 163
Donahue, Kelly, Mgr.-Corp. Rels.--Redken Laboratories, Inc., Canoga Park, CA, pg. 919
Donavan, Doug, Chief Fin. & Info. Officer, Treas., Controller & Sec.--Campbell Oil Co., Massillon, OH, pg. 213
Donsbach, Don, Mgr.-Employment & Placement--Growmark, Inc., Bloomington, IL, pg. 490
Dorff, Gordon, V.P.-Human Resources--Ag Processing Inc A Cooperative, Omaha, NE, pg. 24
Dorman, Paul, Dir.-Personnel--Mayfair Mills, Inc., Arcadia, SC, pg. 724
Dornan, Sheila, V.P.-Human Resources--Spring Arbor Distributors, Belleville, MI, pg. 1033
Doudna, Greg, V.P.-Customer Support--Covalent Systems Corporation, Fremont, CA, pg. 290
Dougherty, Dan, Dir.-Personnel--Black Box Corporation, Lawrence, PA, pg. 748
Dougherty, Thomas, Dir.-Personnel--Smith-Edwards-Dunlap Company, Philadelphia, PA, pg. 1012
Dowd, Lois C., V.P.-Human Resources--The J. M. Ney Company, Bloomfield, CT, pg. 805
Dowden, C.P., Mgr.-Personnel--Thrall Car Mfg. Co., Chicago Heights, IL, pg. 350
Dowdy, Marianne, Mgr.-Personnel--The Vagabond Inns, San Diego, CA, pg. 1142
Downing, Brian, Mgr.-Personnel--The Chicago Faucet Co., Des Plaines, IL, pg. 245
Downs, Jane, Dir.-Human Resouces--Arcata Graphics Company, Baltimore, MD, pg. 80
Downs, Jane M., Dir.-Human Resources--Arcata Corporation, San Francisco, CA, pg. 80
Downs, Tom, V.P.-Corp. Plng. & Human Resources--Tanner Co. Inc., Rutherfordton, NC, pg. 1078
Doyle, Jere M., Dir.-Human Resources--Besser Company, Alpena, MI, pg. 146
Doyle, Jim, Dir.-Personnel--Chapman Printing Company, Huntington, WV, pg. 239
Drake, Larry R., V.P.-Human Resources & Information Services--Graphic Controls, Corp., Buffalo, NY, pg. 478
Drake, Larry R., V.P.-Human Resources & Information Services--Graphic Controls Corporation, Buffalo, NY, pg. 478
Drass, Juanita, Mgr.-Human Resources--Atlantic Builders Group Inc., Baltimore, MD, pg. 94
Drew, Robert E., Dir.-Personnel--Schawk, Inc., Des Plaines, IL, pg. 974
Drewicz, Mark, Mgr.-Personnel--Bentley-Harris Manufacturing Co., Lionville, PA, pg. 140
Dreyer, Jack, V.P.-Human Resources--Wakefern Food Corporation, Elizabeth, NJ, pg. 1158
Droege, John D. L., V.P.-Indus. Rels.--Green Bay Packaging Inc., Green Bay, WI, pg. 483
Drudy, Carole, Mgr.-Personnel--Haviland Enterprises, Grand Rapids, MI, pg. 517
Drury, Tom, Dir.-Human Resources--Penda Corporation, Portage, WI, pg. 857
Drydyk, Joe, Dir.-Personnel--DEC/Bou-Matic, Madison, WI, pg. 309
Drydyk, John, Mgr.-Personnel--DEC International, Inc., Madison, WI, pg. 308
Du Quette, Ernest A., V.P.-Human Res. & Admin.--American Optical Corp., Greenwich, CT, pg. 59
Dubish, Richard, V.P.-Personnel--Queens Group Indiana, Inc., Indianapolis, IN, pg. 904
Duca, Genevieve, Dir.-Personnel--Cortland Line Co., Inc., Cortland, NY, pg. 287
Duda, Andy, Dir.-Personnel--Kraus-Anderson, Inc., Minneapolis, MN, pg. 644
Duda, Michael J., V.P.-Personnel--Remington Products Inc., Bridgeport, CT, pg. 926
Duerre, Peter R., Controller & Personnel Dir.--Transistor Devices, Inc., Cedar Knolls, NJ, pg. 1107
Duey, Barb, Dir.-Personnel--Basic Computer, Akron, OH, pg. 124
Dugan, Regina, Mgr.-Personnel--Della Construction Co. Inc., Enfield, CT, pg. 326
Duggan, Pamela J., Dir.-Human Resources--Zymark Corporation, Hopkinton, MA, pg. 1221
Duke, Lonnie, Dir.-Human Resources--Wing Industries, Inc., Dallas, TX, pg. 1196
Duloc, Andrea, Dir.-Human Resources--S L C Graphics, Inc., Pittston, PA, pg. 963
Dumpert, Edwina, Mgr.-Personnel--The Pierce Co., Inc., Upland, IN, pg. 102
Dunbar, J.H., V.P., Dir. Human Resources--Sperling, New Orleans, LA, pg. 1030
Dunbar, Ronald H., Sr. V.P.-Human Resources--Revlon, Inc., New York, NY, pg. 696
Duncombe, Patricia, Dir.-Personnel--Replogle Globes, Inc., Broadview, IL, pg. 927
Dunlap, Bonnie, Dir.-Human Resources--Anchor Tool & Die Company, Cleveland, OH, pg. 71
Dunn, Betty, Mgr.-Personnel--Jones Blair Company, Dallas, TX, pg. 602
DuPlessis, Carol, Mgr.-Personnel--Cooper Instrument Corp., Middlefield, CT, pg. 283
Durant, Mary, Controller--LaMarca Group Inc., New York, NY, pg. 652
Dwerle, Leah, Mgr.-Personnel--A & E Stores, Inc., Ridgefield, NJ, pg. 1
Dyar, Bill, Dir.-Personnel--Davis Electrical Constructors, Inc., Greenville, SC, pg. 318
Dyjak, Carol A., Mgr.-Bus. Admin. & Human Resources--Springborn Laboratories, Inc., Enfield, CT, pg. 1033
Eade, Dennis H., V.P.-Human Resources--Beverage Management, Inc., Holland, MI, pg. 179
Eades, Paul, Dir.-Human Resources--Maritz Communications Co., Fenton, MO, pg. 707
Earp, Harlon, V.P.-Human Resources--Harp's Food Stores, Inc., Springdale, AR, pg. 510
Eastman, J.M., V.P.-Human Resources--E.F. Johnson Company, Eden Prarie, MN, pg. 598
Easton, Howard, Dir.-Personnel--Penco Products, Oaks, PA, pg. 857
Eatmon, Robert, Dir.-Personnel--Roppe Corp., Fostoria, OH, pg. 947
Ebertowski, Jo, Mgr.-Human Resources--Micro Component Technology Inc., Saint Paul, MN, pg. 748
Eck, Helen, Dir.-Personnel--Trimtex Co. Inc., Williamsport, PA, pg. 1113
Eckhardt, Gary, V.P.-Human Resources--American Tool Companies, Inc., Lincoln, NE, pg. 64
Ecklund, Andy, Mgr.-Human Resources--Sioux Manufacturing Corp., Fort Totten, ND, pg. 1008
Eder, Tom, Dir.-Personnel--A-Dec, Inc., Newberg, OR, pg. 1
Edgar, Tom, V.P.-Human Resources--Advanced Technology, Inc., Reston, VA, pg. 20
Edwards, Debbie, Dir.-Personnel & Corp. Video Systems--GES Inc., Marianna, AR, pg. 439
Eggemann, Marcella J., V.P.-Human & Admin. Resources--Millers' Mutual Insurance Assn. Of Illinois, Alton, IL, pg. 755
Ehrenstrom, James W., Sr. V.P.-Human Resources & Admin.--Northwestern Mutual Life Insurance Co., Milwaukee, WI, pg. 815
Eible, Kate, Mgr.-Sls. Admin. & Personnel--Furniture Consultants, New York, NY, pg. 437
Eichhold, Louis B., V.P.-Human Resources & Indus.--The United States Playing Card Company, Cincinnati, OH, pg. 1136
Eisenberg, Jamie, V.P.-Human Resources--Vienna Sausage Mfg. Co., Chicago, IL, pg. 1151
Eisle, Marilyn, Personnel Mgr.--Schneller, Inc., Kent, OH, pg. 977
Eisman, Bernard, Mgr.-Personnel--Lasko Metal Products, Inc., West Chester, PA, pg. 660
Elizondo, Juanita, Human Resources Dir.--Fiesta Mart Inc., Houston, TX, pg. 409
Elliott, G.A., Dir.-Employee Rels.--Danly-Komatsu L.P., Cicero, IL, pg. 275
Ellis, Donna, Dir.-Personnel--Teca Corporation, Pleasantville, NY, pg. 1082
Ellis, Jeff, V.P.-Personal Lines--VASA North Atlantic Insurance Company, Indianapolis, IN, pg. 1146
Ellis, Kay, Dir.-Human Resources--Kitchell Corporation, Phoenix, AZ, pg. 634
Ellis, O. L., Mgr.-Personnel--Wire Rope Corp. of America, Inc., Saint Joseph, MO, pg. 1197
Ellis, O.L., Mgr.-Personnel--Leschen Wire Rope, Saint Joseph, MO, pg. 1197
Elrod, Gene, Dir.-Personnel--Lewis Drug, Inc., Sioux Falls, SD, pg. 673
Emmett, Denis L., Treasurer--Erving Paper Mills, Erving, MA, pg. 388
Endter, Charlotte R., Mgr.-Admin. Services--BNA PLUS, Washington, DC, pg. 189
Enger, James F., Dir.-Personnel--Norpac Foods, Inc. Cooperative, Stayton, OR, pg. 810
Engfer, Robert T., V.P.-Human Resources--Agway, Inc., De Witt, NY, pg. 25
Englander, Joseph, V.P.-Personnel & Pur.--Central Paper Company, Newark, NJ, pg. 233
Engle, Susan, Sr. V.P., Corp. Human Resources/Facilities--Ketchum Communications Inc., Pittsburgh, PA, pg. 625
English, Greg, Dir.-Human Res.--Alamo Industrial Group, San Antonio, TX, pg. 29
Entrekin, Patricia M., Mgr.-Personnel--Converse Professional Group, Inc., Pasadena, CA, pg. 281
Epperson, Charles, V.P.-Human Resources--West Union Corp., Memphis, TN, pg. 1177
Epperson, William A., V.P.-Human Resources--Gold Kist, Inc., Atlanta, GA, pg. 465
Erb, D., Mgr.-Human Resources--Conley Frog & Switch Company, Memphis, TN, pg. 274
Erdei, Martin, V.P.-Human Resources--Ruslander & Sons, Inc., Buffalo, NY, pg. 956
Erdmann, Richard, Sr. V.P.-Human Resources--Serigraph, Inc., West Bend, WI, pg. 991
Ermeti, Frank, Dir.-Human Resources--Starcraft Automotive Corp., Goshen, IN, pg. 1040
Ernst, Paul, Mgr.-Personnel--Goodman Equipment Corp., Bedford Park, IL, pg. 470
Ertz, Caroline, Mgr.-Human Resources--Amana Society, Amana, IA, pg. 46
Erwin, Walter, V.P.-Fin. & Admin.--The Pro Corporation, Florence, MA, pg. 891
Ery, Jessica, Dir.-Personnel--Complete Interiors Inc., Altamonte Springs, FL, pg. 270
Eshleman, Bob, Personnel Dir.--Reading Body Works, Inc., Reading, PA, pg. 916
Estes, Sylvia D., Dir., Human Resources--Grizzard Advertising, Inc., Atlanta, GA, pg. 488
Euler, Rich, Dir.-Human Resources--Prime Tanning Co., Inc., Berwick, ME, pg. 889
Evans, Albert, Dir.-Personnel--Coulter Corporation, Hialeah, FL, pg. 289
Evans, Ellen, Mgr.-Personnel & Admin.--Carco Electronics, Menlo Park, CA, pg. 217
Evans, Jim, Mgr.-Human Resources--The Laitram Corporation, Harahan, LA, pg. 650
Evans, Jo, Dir.-Personnel--Varat Enterprises, Inc., Piedmont, SC, pg. 1145
Evans, Mark, Dir.-Human Resources--Eva-Tone Inc., Clearwater, FL, pg. 390
Evans, Randall, V.P.-Human Resources--Haworth, Inc., Holland, MI, pg. 518
Ewell, Barbara, Mgr.-Human Resources--Delta Queen Steamboat Company, New Orleans, LA, pg. 385
Ewing, C.W., Dir.-Personnel--T.B. Wood's Sons Company, Chambersburg, PA, pg. 1200
Ewing, Craig, Mgr.-Human Resources--Triangle Distributing Company, Santa Fe Springs, CA, pg. 1111
Ewing, Joe, Dir.-Personnel & Services--Mississippi Chemical Corporation, Yazoo City, MS, pg. 760
Fabel, Warren L., V.P.-Personnel--Employers Insurance of Wausau a Mutual Co., Wausau, WI, pg. 380
Fabel, Warren L., V.P.-Personnel--Employers Insurance of Wausau a Mutual Co., Wausau, WI, pg. 795
Fagin, Sherry, Dir.-Human Resources--Unigroup, Inc., Fenton, MO, pg. 1126
Fahey, Michael, V.P.-Labor Rels.--Northwest Airlines, Inc., Saint Paul, MN, pg. 782
Fairchild, F. Peter, V.P.-Human Resources--Camp Dresser & McKee Inc., Cambridge, MA, pg. 212
Fallon, Barbara, Dir.-Personnel & Investor Rels.--Chiswick Trading Inc., Sudbury, MA, pg. 248
Farfaglia, Charles, Dir.-Personnel--Ethan Allen, Inc., Danbury, CT, pg. 485
Farinacci, P. I., Personnel Dir.--Tri-State Motor Transit Co., Joplin, MO, pg. 1111
Farrar, Austin, V.P.-Human Resources--L.L. Bean, Inc., Freeport, ME, pg. 648
Farrell, John, Mgr.-Personnel--Emson Research, Inc., Bridgeport, CT, pg. 380
Fausher, Duane, Dir.-Personnel--Marvin Lumber & Cedar Company, Warroad, MN, pg. 716
Fautaz, Rudy, Dir.-Human Resources--Pillowtex Corporation, Dallas, TX, pg. 870
Fay, Peter P., V.P.-Human Resources--Chiquita Brands International, Inc., Cincinnati, OH, pg. 53
Federspiel, Dan, Mgr.-Personnel--Hardware Wholesalers, Inc., Fort Wayne, IN, pg. 508
Fee, Candida M., V.P.-Indus. Rels.--Reliable Automatic Sprinkler Co., Inc., Mount Vernon, NY, pg. 924
Fegelein, Brenda, Mgr.-Human Resources--The Texwipe Co., Inc., Upper Saddle River, NJ, pg. 1090
Feicke, Dennis, Dir.-Human Resources--Country Companies Insurance Group, Bloomington, IL, pg. 289
Feicke, Dennis, Dir.-Human Resources--Country Life Insurance Company, Bloomington, IL, pg. 289
Feicke, Dennis, Dir.-Human Resources--Country Mutual Insurance Company, Bloomington, IL, pg. 289
Feicke, Dennis, Dir.-Corp. Human Resources--CC Services, Bloomington, IL, pg. 289
Fein, Paul, Dir.-Human Resources--Ohaus Corporation, Florham Park, NJ, pg. 822
Feinman, Linda, Mgr.-Personnel--Jordache Enterprises, Inc., New York, NY, pg. 604
Feldman, Rudy, Dir.-Pro Personnel--San Diego Chargers, San Diego, CA, pg. 969
Fenn, Robert, Dir.-Personnel--Pedus Services, Inc., Los Angeles, CA, pg. 854
Ferber, James D., Dir.-Human Resources--Sunshine Biscuits, Inc., Woodbridge, NJ, pg. 439
Fergus, James V., Dir.-Personnel--Superior Tube Company, Collegeville, PA, pg. 1064
Ferla, Robert P., V.P.-Exec. Devel. & Training--The Grand Union Company, Wayne, NJ, pg. 476
Ferree, Larry, Dir.-Personnel--United Design, Noble, OK, pg. 1131
Ferrera, Diane, Dir.-Personnel--James Ferrera & Sons, Inc., Canton, MA, pg. 407

Ferretti, Gina, Dir.-Human Resources--Plastipak Packaging Inc., Plymouth, MI, pg. 876
Ferris, Donna, Dir.-Human Resources--Glico Harmony Foods Corporation, Santa Cruz, CA, pg. 462
Fiala, Brian, V.P.-Human Resources & MIS--Schwinn Bicycle Company, Chicago, IL, pg. 981
Ficks, Ronald, V.P.-Personnel & Admin. Services--Topco Associates, Inc., Skokie, IL, pg. 1101
Fiddler, John, Dir.-Personnel--Continental Eagle Corporation, Prattville, AL, pg. 278
Fikes, Howard, Dir.-Personnel--Orbit Valve Co., Little Rock, AR, pg. 828
Fineman, Evan L., Treas. & Chief Fin. Officer--Atlantic Dairy Cooperative, Southampton, PA, pg. 94
Fink, K.W., V.P.-Human Resources--The Hubinger Company, Keokuk, IA, pg. 550
Finkelstein, Al, Mgr.-Human Resources--Cerro Copper Products Co., Sauget, IL, pg. 711
Finn, Heidi, Mgr.-Personnel--American Passage Media Corporation, Seattle, WA, pg. 59
Fiore, Donald A., Treas. & Mgr.-Personnel--Palmer Manufacturing Company, Malden, MA, pg. 844
Fiscus, Laura, Mgr.-Human Relations--Dunmore Corporation, Newtown, PA, pg. 353
Fisher, John, Dir.-Personnel--Milk Marketing Inc., Strongsville, OH, pg. 753
Fisher, Nancy, Dir.-Personnel--The Kiplinger Washington Editors, Inc., Washington, DC, pg. 632
Fitzgerald, Patricia, Dir.-Personnel--Golden Gate University, San Francisco, CA, pg. 466
Fitzgerald, Regina, V.P.-Human Resources--Taco John's International, Inc., Cheyenne, WY, pg. 1076
Flachsmann, Joanne, Mgr.-Human Resources--Sonicair, Scottsdale, AZ, pg. 1018
Flagg, Ron, V.P.-Human Resources--Tree Top, Inc., Selah, WA, pg. 1109
Flanary, Bill, V.P.-Personnel--Tuscarora Yarns Inc., Mount Pleasant, NC, pg. 1120
Flaningham, E.G., Personnel Dir.--Diamond Chain Company, Indianapolis, IN, pg. 69
Fleck, V.B., V.P.-Human Resources--The F.A. Bartlett Tree Expert Co., Stamford, CT, pg. 123
Fleming, Ann, Mgr.-Personnel--Synchro-Start Products, Inc., Niles, IL, pg. 638
Flock, R. William, Sr. V.P.-Human Resources--Jerrico, Inc., Lexington, KY, pg. 229
Flock, William, Sr. V.P.-Human Resources--Long John Silver's, Inc., Lexington, KY, pg. 229
Flood, Edward, V.P.-Customer Rels.--Simmons Upholstered Furniture, Inc., Saint Louis, MO, pg. 1005
Flower, Beverlie, Dir.-Personnel--The National Magazine Company Ltd., London, United Kingdom, pg. 524
Floyd, Charles A., Controller--Inland Associates, Inc., Olathe, KS, pg. 570
Floyd, James S., Dir.-Human Resources--Cavalier Corporation, Chattanooga, TN, pg. 229
Flynn, James, V.P.-Personnel--Condere Corporation, Hamden, CT, pg. 273
Flynn, Jeff, V.P.-Human Resources--Service America Corporation, Stamford, CT, pg. 992
Flynn, Kim, Dir.-Personnel--Life Line Nutritionals, Inc., Hayward, CA, pg. 675
Flynn, Steve, Mgr.-Personnel--Pace Industries, Inc., Fayetteville, AR, pg. 838
Fodor, M., Mgr.-Human Resources--Rieth-Riley Construction Co. Inc., Goshen, IN, pg. 934
Fogelman, R., Dir.-Personnel--WGM Safety Corporation, Reading, PA, pg. 1156
Fogelman, Rodney, Dir.-Human Resources--WGM Safety Corporation, Reading, PA, pg. 1156
Fogelman, Rodney M., Personnel Dir.--Willson Safety Products, Reading, PA, pg. 1193
Fogerty, A.J., Sr. V.P.--Agway, Inc., De Witt, NY, pg. 25
Fogerty, Daniel, Dir.-Personnel & Employee Benefits--Peirce-Phelps, Inc., Philadelphia, PA, pg. 855
Fogerty, Thomas G., Personnel Dir.--South Chester Tube Co., Concordville, PA, pg. 1019
Follstad, Steve, Mgr.-Human Resources--Trak International, Inc., Port Washington, WI, pg. 1106
Fontana, Ovidio, Dir.-Personnel--Interplast Universal Industries, Inc., Lodi, NJ, pg. 579
Ford, Cooper, Dir.-Personnel--Fish Engineering & Construction, Inc., Houston, TX, pg. 414
Foreman, Gisela, Dir.-Human Resources--Guardian Alarm Co., Southfield, MI, pg. 491
Forristall, L.L., Dir.-Personnel--Frantz Manufacturing Co., Sterling, IL, pg. 429
Forsman, Terry, Dir.-Personnel--Carousel Snack Bars Of Minnesota, Minneapolis, MN, pg. 224
Forsythe, Suzanne, V.P.-Human Resources--Things Remembered, Cleveland, OH, pg. 260
Fortunato, Cheryl, Dir.-Human Resources & Office Admin.--The Binswanger Company, Philadelphia, PA, pg. 151
Foster, Cecilia, Sr. V.P., Human Resources--Uniworld Group, Inc., New York, NY, pg. 1139
Foti, Frances, Sec. & Dir.-Personnel--ICC Industries, Inc., New York, NY, pg. 558
Fout, Charles, V.P.- Fin. & Human Resources--Gouchenour Adv., Inc., Orlando, FL, pg. 473
Fouts, James, Dir.-Human Resources--Transnational Motors Inc., Grand Rapids, MI, pg. 1107
Fowler, S. Craig, Mgr.-Human Resources--Xtek, Inc., Cincinnati, OH, pg. 1206
Fox, Erwin J., V.P.-Indus. Rels.--Big V Supermarkets, Inc., Florida, NY, pg. 149
France, Richard E., V.P.-Human Resources--Caraustar Industries, Inc., Austell, GA, pg. 217
Franco, Georgette, Dir.-Human Resources--Graphic Productions Company, Miami, FL, pg. 478
Frank, D.K., Dir.-Personnel--Idaho Forest Industry, Inc., Coeur D'Alene, ID, pg. 561
Franke, J.C., V.P. & Dir.-Human Resources--Sverdrup Corporation, Maryland Heights, MO, pg. 1065
Frankovitz, Miriam, Dir.-Personnel--Zimmer Paper Products Inc., Indianapolis, IN, pg. 1220
Fraser, Brian G., V.P.-Admin. & Gen. Counsel--Clark Foodservice, Inc., Elk Grove Village, IL, pg. 252
Frauenhoffer, Gail, V.P.-Human Resources--LeeWards Creative Crafts, Inc., Elgin, IL, pg. 666
Frautschi, Deanna L., V.P.-Communications & Human Resources--Country Companies Insurance Group, Bloomington, IL, pg. 289
Frautschi, Deanna L., V.P.-Communications & Human Resources--Country Life Insurance Company, Bloomington, IL, pg. 289
Frautschi, Deanna L., V.P.-Communications & Human Resources--Country Mutual Insurance Company, Bloomington, IL, pg. 289
Freeman, Joan, Mgr.-Personnel--Republic Storage Systems Company Inc., Canton, OH, pg. 928
Freitag, Edwin W., V.P.-Personnel--Zantop International Airlines, Inc., Ypsilanti, MI, pg. 1216
Freudenthaler, Kris, Dir.-Personnel--Rain Bird Sprinkler Mfg. Corp., Glendora, CA, pg. 910
Frey, Marilyn, Dir.-Personnel--Basler Electric Company, Highland, IL, pg. 125
Frideres, Ken, Dir.-Personnel--Advance Machine Company, Plymouth, MN, pg. 18
Fritton, Paul F., Dir.-Personnel--Cannon, Grand Island, NY, pg. 214
Fritz, Anne C., Dir.-Human Resources--Thoroughbred Software International, Inc., Somerset, NJ, pg. 1095
Fromberg, Dixie, V.P. & Personnel Dir.--Calcasieu Lumber Company, Austin, TX, pg. 208
Frymoyer, William, Dir.-Personnel--Nibco, Inc., Elkhart, IN, pg. 806
Fuller, Rodney, Dir.-Human Resources--Columbus Mills, Inc., Columbus, GA, pg. 267
Funk, Roger, Dr., V.P.-Human & Technical Resources--The Davey Tree Expert Company, Kent, OH, pg. 317
Funk, Warren, Dir.-Personnel--Memphis Publishing Company, Memphis, TN, pg. 738
Fursman, David, Dir.-Indus. Rels.--Elastic Stop Nut, Union, NJ, pg. 514
Gaber, R., Dir.-Personnel--Isfel Company, Inc., Rahway, NJ, pg. 582
Gabriel, Jack, Dir.-Employee Rels.--Hallmark Cards, Inc., Kansas City, MO, pg. 501
Gabriel, S.G., Dir.-Personnel--Stonecutter Mills Corp., Spindale, NC, pg. 1051
Gaeth, W.A., V.P.-Human Resources--Daubert Industries, Inc., Westchester, IL, pg. 317
Gailey, Kim, Dir.-Personnel--Crested Butte Mountain Resort, Inc., Mount Crested Butte, CO, pg. 299
Gaines, Bob, Dir.-Personnel--Steinbach, White Plains, NY, pg. 1045
Galla, Marlene J., V.P.-Human Resources--Delaware North Companies, Inc., Buffalo, NY, pg. 326
Galla, Patrick, V.P.-Human Resources--Crown American Corporation, Johnstown, PA, pg. 301
Gallagher, A., V.P.-Human Resources--Pennex Products Co., Inc., Verona, PA, pg. 858
Gallagher, Chuck, Dir.-Personnel--The Andersons, Maumee, OH, pg. 73
Gallagher, Marilyn, V.P.-Human Resources--Pepsi-Cola Bottling Company of Charlotte Inc., Charlotte, NC, pg. 860
Gallaspy, Rhonda, V.P.-Human Resources--JM Family Enterprises Inc., Deerfield Beach, FL, pg. 584
Gallo, Maria, Dir.-Personnel--Injection Footwear Corp., Miami, FL, pg. 569
Gallucci, Alfred, Exec. V.P., Sec. & Personnel Dir.--Concrete Construction Company, Columbus, OH, pg. 273
Gappa, Mark, V.P.-Human Resources--Recreational Equipment, Inc., Kent, WA, pg. 917
Garb, Connie, Dir.-Human Rels.--The Cherenson Group, Livingston, NJ, pg. 243
Garcia, David, Dir.-Personnel--Paul Ecke Ranch, Inc., Encinitas, CA, pg. 366
Gardiner, Paulette, Dir.-Personnel--KCL Corporation, Shelbyville, IN, pg. 611
Gardner, Karen, Dir.-Human Resources--Louis Padnos Iron & Metal Co., Holland, MI, pg. 842
Garlock, Janice O., V.P.-Human Resources--Elliott Company, Jeannette, PA, pg. 378
Garner, Fran, Dir.-Human Resources--Pavion Ltd., Nyack on Hudson, NY, pg. 852
Garner, Richard, Sr. V.P.-Human Resources--Pic'n Pay Stores, Inc., Charlotte, NC, pg. 201
Garrett, Beth, Mgr.-Personnel--American Trading & Production Corporation, Oil & Gas Div., Houston, TX, pg. 64
Garrett, Debbie, Dir.-Human Resources--Microdynamics, Inc., Dallas, TX, pg. 749
Garrett, Nancy, Personnel Admin.--Thordarson Meissner, Inc., Mount Carmel, IL, pg. 270
Garrett, Tammy, Dir.-Personnel--Jake Sweeney Auto Leasing Inc., Cincinnati, OH, pg. 1066
Garrett, Tammy, Dir.-Personnel--Jake Sweeney Auto Leasing, Inc., Cincinnati, OH, pg. 1067
Garrison, Peggy, Dir.-Admin. Services--Burgess & Niple, Limited, Columbus, OH, pg. 190
Garsey, Connie, Human Resources & Office Mgr.--Shapson Gero & Sommers, Inc., Philadelphia, PA, pg. 995
Garver, Dean, Dir.-Human Resources--Doran Textiles Inc., Shelby, NC, pg. 346
Garver, Dean, Dir.-Human Resources--Doran Mill Co., Shelby, NC, pg. 346
Gaspar, David, Dir.-Human Resources--Auto Glass Specialists, Madison, WI, pg. 100
Gass, Jim, Personnel Mgr.--Sunkist Growers, Processed Products, Ontario, CA, pg. 1061
Gatewood, Char, Dir.-Personnel--Crystal Cabinet Works, Inc., Princeton, MN, pg. 303
Gatzke, Carla, Dir.-Human Resources--Daktronics, Inc., Brookings, SD, pg. 312
Gebhard, Bob, V.P.-Player Personnel--Minnesota Twins Baseball Club, Minneapolis, MN, pg. 758
Geczy, Paul C., V.P.-Human Resources--Jayco Inc., Middlebury, IN, pg. 590
Geiger, Denise, V.P., Chief Fin. Officer & Controller--The Atkins Agency, San Antonio, TX, pg. 94
Geis, Walter, V.P.-Human Devel. & Personnel Services--The Copps Corp., Stevens Point, WI, pg. 285
George, John, V.P.-Personnel--Bachman Company, Reading, PA, pg. 108
George, Patricia A., V.P.-Human Resources--U.S. Computer Services, Rancho Cordova, CA, pg. 1135
Geran, D.B., Mgr.-Personnel--Los Alamos Technical Associates, Inc., Los Alamos, NM, pg. 684
Gerard, Antonia, Exec. V.P., Chief Fin. & Oper. Officer, Sec. & Controller--Bolliger, Inc., Stamford, CT, pg. 163
Gerard, Ivan, V.P.-Human Resources--Pacesetter Corporation, Omaha, NE, pg. 839
Gerardo, Al M., Dir.-Personnel--Troy Corporation, East Hanover, NJ, pg. 1116
Gerner, David W., Dir.-Personnel--Ripon Foods, Inc., Ripon, WI, pg. 935
Gettig, T.E., V.P.-Human Resources--Welch's, Concord, MA, pg. 789
Giacini, Vivian P., Sr. V.P.-Human Resources--Mutual of America, New York, NY, pg. 777
Giageos, Don, Mgr.-Human Resources--Simplicity Manufacturing, Inc., Port Washington, WI, pg. 1006
Gibbs, Larry, Dir.-Personnel--Schwan's Sales Enterprises, Marshall, MN, pg. 980
Gibson, B.R., Dir.-Human Resources & Insurance--Sea Island Company, Sea Island, GA, pg. 983
Gibson, Charles, Jr., Mgr.-Admin. Services--Bovaird Supply Co., Tulsa, OK, pg. 168
Gibson, Toni, Dir.-Human Resources--Hirsh Company, Skokie, IL, pg. 258
Gifford, Patricia L., Sr. V.P.-Human Resources--The Elder-Beerman Stores Corp., Dayton, OH, pg. 373
Gifford, Patricia L., V.P. & Dir.-Human Resources--Elder-Beerman Stores Div., Dayton, OH, pg. 373
Gilbert, Rebecca, V.P. & Personnel Dir.--Sage-Allen & Co., Inc., Hartford, CT, pg. 966
Gilbertson, Dan, V.P.-Human Resources--Skyway Freight Systems, Inc., Watsonville, CA, pg. 1009
Gill, Barbara S., Mgr.-Human Resources--Westgate Inc., Port Allen, LA, pg. 1182
Gillen, Bunny, Mgr.-Personnel--Harbor Financial Mortgage Corp., Houston, TX, pg. 506
Gilles, James W., Mgr.-Human Resources--Leupold & Stevens, Inc., Beaverton, OR, pg. 669
Gillespie, Ed, V.P., Dir.-Human Resources--Lewis & Gace, Inc., Fort Lee, NJ, pg. 673
Gillespie, Jan, Dir.-Human Resources--Randall's Food Markets, Inc., Houston, TX, pg. 911
Gilligan, Janice, Dir.-Personnel--H.O. Penn Machinery Co. Inc., Armonk, NY, pg. 857
Gillman, Bruce, V.P.-Human Resources--Viacom Cable, Pleasanton, CA, pg. 785
Gillman, James N., V.P.-Federal Employee Program--Blue Cross and Blue Shield Association, Chicago, IL, pg. 159
Gilpin, Kathleen, Dir.-Personnel & Mngmt. Information Systems--Bio-Tek Instruments, Inc., Winooski, VT, pg. 152
Ginn, Kaye, V.P.-Personnel--Carson Products Company, Savannah, GA, pg. 67
Girata, Joseph, Chief Fin. Officer--Integral Systems, Inc., Sunnyvale, CA, pg. 573
Gittleson, Gail, V.P.-Human Resources--Barnes & Noble Bookstores, Inc., New York, NY, pg. 120
Gladstone, Myles, Dir.-Personnel--Miller & Long Co. Inc., Bethesda, MD, pg. 754
Glagola, Steve, V.P.-Personnel--Ellicott Machine Corp., Baltimore, MD, pg. 378
Glass, Gerbert, Mgr.-Human Resources--National Fruit Product Company, Winchester, VA, pg. 789
Gleckler, J. D., V.P.-Human Resources--SRI International, Menlo Park, CA, pg. 964
Gleed, Kenneth F., V.P.-Admin.--Burke Engineering Company, South El Monte, CA, pg. 190
Glickman, M.P., Treas.--Strombecker Corporation, Chicago, IL, pg. 1054
Glosser, Tom L., Dir.-Personnel--Gee Bee Department Stores, Johnstown, PA, pg. 978
Glover, Judy, Dir.-Personnel--Pine State Creamery Co., Raleigh, NC, pg. 871
Godwin, Diane, Mgr.-Personnel--Forms & Supply, Inc., Charlotte, NC, pg. 424
Gold, Lenore, Dir.-Personnel--Goldmark Industries, Ltd., New York, NY, pg. 468
Goldberg, Bella, Mgr.-Human Resources--Windsor Publications, Inc., Chatsworth, CA, pg. 1196
Goldberg, Lila, Mgr.-Human Resources--Information Builders, New York, NY, pg. 567
Goldberg, Lloyd, Exec. V.P.-Opers. & Personnel--Jersey Printing Company, Inc., Bayonne, NJ, pg. 593
Golodetz, Vicki, Dir.-Personnel--Primary Industries Corporation, New York, NY, pg. 889
Golomski, Russell, Dir.-Human Resources--Western States Envelope Co., Butler, WI, pg. 1181
Gonzalez, Irene, Mgr.-Human Resources--Up-Right, Inc., Selma, CA, pg. 1139
Goodman, Clifford, Dir.-Personnel--West Mill Clothes, Inc., Woodside, NY, pg. 1177
Goodman, Steve, Dir.-Personnel--Save Mart Supermarkets, Modesto, CA, pg. 973
Gorczycki, Jim, Controller & Human Resources Dir.--The Sportsman's Guide, Inc., Eagan, MN, pg. 1032
Gordon, H. Gray, V.P.-Personnel--Cargill Fertilizer, Inc., Riverview, FL, pg. 219
Gordon, Richard, Mgr.-Human Resources--J.T. Slocomb Company, South Glastonbury, CT, pg. 1010
Gordon, Sue, V.P.-Personnel--Radisson Hotel Corporation, Minneapolis, MN, pg. 221

Gordon, Sylvia, Dir.-Personnel--J.T. Davenport & Sons, Inc., Sanford, NC, pg. 317
Goring, Terry, V.P.-Personnel--Maritz Inc., Fenton, MO, pg. 707
Gossard, Thomas A., Mgr.-Human Resources--Union Pump Company, Battle Creek, MI, pg. 1128
Goya, Donna, Sr. V.P.-Human Resources--Levi Strauss & Co., San Francisco, CA, pg. 670
Grabler, Toni J., Dir.-Personnel--Brim, Inc., Portland, OR, pg. 176
Grady, Frank, Dir.-Personnel--Samsill Corporation, Fort Worth, TX, pg. 968
Graeber, Henry, Mgr.-Personnel--Sweeney & Company Division, San Antonio, TX, pg. 440
Grams, Jennifer, Mgr.-Personnel--Adams Rite Manufacturing Co., City of Industry, CA, pg. 16
Grand, Pam, Admin.--Ugly Duckling Rent-A-Car, Phoenix, AZ, pg. 1125
Grandle, Susan, Mgr.-Human Resources & Treas.--Tricon Industries, Inc., Downers Grove, IL, pg. 1113
Grandstaff, Ray, Personnel Mgr.--Reliance Medical Products, Inc., Mason, OH, pg. 925
Grant, P.A., V.P.-Human Resources--Columbus McKinnon Corp., Amherst, NY, pg. 266
Grant, Thomas E., V.P.-Human Resources--Geneva Corporation, Greensboro, NC, pg. 451
Gray, Elizabeth Ann, Dir.-Personnel--Wilson Industries Inc., Houston, TX, pg. 1193
Gray, Ellen M., Sr. V.P.-Admin. Services & Dir.-Human Resources--Stephens, Inc., Little Rock, AR, pg. 1046
Gray, Herbert, Dir.-Human Resources--Cranston Print Works Company, Cranston, RI, pg. 296
Green, Charles, V.P.-Data Processing--Coast To Coast Stores, Inc., Denver, CO, pg. 257
Green, Debbie, Office Mgr.--Top Billing Inc., Nashville, TN, pg. 1101
Greenbert, Jack M., V.P.-Personnel--Charles Curtain Company, Inc., Dallas, TX, pg. 239
Greene, H., Mgr.-Personnel--Armstrong International, Inc., Three Rivers, MI, pg. 83
Greene, Jeffrey R., Dir.-Human Resources--Equitable Bag Company, Long Island City, NY, pg. 385
Greenfield, Ann, V.P.-Human Resources--Lewis Brothers Bakeries, Inc., Evansville, IN, pg. 673
Greer, George, V.P.-Human Resources--Haggar Apparel Company, Dallas, TX, pg. 499
Gregory, Robert D., V.P.-Human Resources--Alco Health Services Corporation, Malvern, PA, pg. 31
Gregory, Roger, Mgr.-Personnel--North Carolina Mutual Life Insurance Co., Durham, NC, pg. 813
Greis, Ray, V.P.-Human Resources--Amano Cincinnati, Inc., Cincinnati, OH, pg. 46
Grenda, Kay, Dir.-Personnel--Energy & Environmental Research Corp., Irvine, CA, pg. 381
Griffey, J.I., Dir.-Personnel--HPM Corporation, Mount Gilead, OH, pg. 497
Griffin, Mike, Dir.-Matls. & Human Resources--GF Office Furniture Ltd., Gallatin, TN, pg. 439
Griffin, Mike, Dir.-Matls. & Human Resources--GF Office Furniture, Youngstown, OH, pg. 439
Griffith, James W., V.P.-Human Resources--Redken Laboratories, Inc., Canoga Park, CA, pg. 919
Griffith, Joseph H., V.P.-Human Resources & Corp. Services--Simplex Time Recorder Co., Gardner, MA, pg. 1006
Griggs, Al, Dir.-Human Resources--American Water Works Association, Denver, CO, pg. 65
Grimaldi, D.G., Dir.-Human Resources--Duraco Products, Inc., Streamwood, IL, pg. 354
Grimes, Thomas J., V.P.--The Hanover Insurance Company, Worcester, MA, pg. 34
Grimes, Tommy P., Mgr.-Admin.--Triumph*Lor, Inc., Houston, TX, pg. 1115
Grissom, Tom, Dir.-Personnel--County Seat Stores, Inc., Dallas, TX, pg. 290
Grose, Donald, Sr. V.P.-Human Resources--Certified Grocers Of California, Los Angeles, CA, pg. 237
Grothe, Dale, Dir.-Human Resources--Tony Downs Foods Company, Saint James, MN, pg. 348
Grove, G.E., V.P.-Fin. & Controller--Bud Industries, Inc., Willoughby, OH, pg. 186
Gruber, J.N., V.P.-Human Resources--Fair Lanes Inc., Hunt Valley, MD, pg. 396
Guercio, Thomas R., V.P., Treas. & Chief Fin. Officer--Reliable Stores, Inc., Columbia, MD, pg. 925
Guerrero, Claudia, Mgr.-Personnel--Costa Cruise Lines, N.V., Miami, FL, pg. 288
Guerrero, Dan, Mgr.-Human Resources--M.C. Gill Corporation, El Monte, CA, pg. 458
Guibert, Yolanda, V.P.-Human Resources--Case-Swayne Co. Inc., Santa Ana, CA, pg. 228
Gunderson, F.G., Dir.-Personnel--PSB Co., Columbus, OH, pg. 1185
Gunderson, Fred G., Dir.-Human Resources--White Castle System, Inc., Columbus, OH, pg. 1185
Gunderson, Kathy, Mgr.-Human Resources--Alra Laboratories, Inc., Gurnee, IL, pg. 44
Gunning, Barbara, Mgr.-Human Resources--Solar Press, Inc., Naperville, IL, pg. 1016
Gurka, Jane, Mgr.-Personnel & Sec.--M. Swift & Sons Inc., Hartford, CT, pg. 1068
Gusha, James, Mgr.-Personnel--The Presmet Corp., Worcester, MA, pg. 887
Guthrey, Nancy, Dir.-Personnel--Hyplains Dressed Beef, Inc., Dodge City, KS, pg. 557
Guthrie, Terry, Mgr.-Indus. Rels.--Century Furniture Industries, Hickory, NC, pg. 235
Guy, Monica, Mgr.-Human Resources--Case-Swayne Co. Inc., Santa Ana, CA, pg. 228
Haas, Barbara L., Personnel Admin.--Fine Organics Corp., Lodi, NJ, pg. 411
Haas, Randall J., V.P.-Human Resources & Admin.--Earle M. Jorgensen Company, Brea, CA, pg. 605
Haas, S.H., V.P.-Personnel--Bud Industries, Inc., Willoughby, OH, pg. 186
Habbart, Deborah J., Corp. Asst.--Stephen Gould Paper Co., Inc., Whippany, NJ, pg. 473
Hacker, David, V.P. & Dir.-Human Resources--Erickson Diversified Corp., Hudson, WI, pg. 386
Hackett, Harvey, Dir.-Personnel--Virginia Hot Springs, Inc., Hot Springs, VA, pg. 1152
Hackfeld, Sally, Mgr.-Personnel--Bates Container, Inc., North Richland Hills, TX, pg. 125
Hagen, Sharon, Mgr.-Personnel--Carpeteria, Inc., Valencia, CA, pg. 224
Hahn, Marilyn, Mgr.-Personnel--Andes Candies, Inc., Delavan, WI, pg. 169
Haines, Judith, Sr. V.P.-Human Resources--Spatz & Co., Northbrook, IL, pg. 1026
Hales, Patricia, Dir.-Personnel--Selectone Corporation, Hayward, CA, pg. 988
Hall, Frank, Dir.-Personnel--Raynor Garage Door Company, Dixon, IL, pg. 915
Hall, Gary, V.P.-Human Resources--Empire Berol U.S.A., Brentwood, TN, pg. 856
Hall, Sandra, Personnel Asst.--Warner Press, Inc., Anderson, IN, pg. 1164
Hallin, Liz, V.P.-Human Resources--Koll Co., Newport Beach, CA, pg. 641
Hallmark, Chris, Dir.-Personnel & Plant Mgr.--Thermalloy, Inc., Farmers Branch, TX, pg. 1091
Halloran, Jim, Dir.-Personnel--K & R Rentals, Inc., Hinsdale, IL, pg. 610
Halton, Bob, Dir.-Personnel & Safety--Crowder Construction Co., Charlotte, NC, pg. 301
Halverson, Elvin, Mgr.-Human Resources--Owatonna Canning Company, Owatonna, MN, pg. 833
Hamburger, Jane, Sr. V.P., Sec. & Dir.-Personnel--Federal Farm Credit Banks Funding Corporation, Jersey City, NJ, pg. 404
Hamilton, Bruce, Dir.-Human Resources--Philadelphia Gear Corp., King of Prussia, PA, pg. 866
Hamm, Jerald, V.P. & Dir.-Human Resources & Safety--Heckethorn Mfg. Company, Dyersburg, TN, pg. 524
Hammond, Gilbert P., Jr., V.P.-Human Resources--The DeMars Corp., Indianapolis, IN, pg. 327
Hammond, Renee, Mgr.-Human Resources--Velsicol Chemical Corporation, Rosemont, IL, pg. 1147
Hanks, Jim, V.P.-Employee Benefits & Human Resources--Sunflower Electric Power Corporation, Hays, KS, pg. 1060
Hanlon, T., Mgr.-Personnel--Swivelier Co., Inc., Nanuet, NY, pg. 1068
Hannon, Byron, V.P.-Human Resources--Crown Textile Company, Blue Bell, PA, pg. 302
Hanscom, Cathy, Dir.-Personnel--Nelson & Small Inc., Portland, ME, pg. 798
Hansen, Julien R., V.P.-Human Resources--Dillingham Construction Corporation, Pleasanton, CA, pg. 337
Hansen, Nancy S., V.P.-Admin. & Sec.--Pennsylvania Crusher Corp., Broomall, PA, pg. 858
Hanson, Gail, Mgr.-Personnel--Despatch Industries, Minneapolis, MN, pg. 332
Haraway, Terry, Dir.-Human Resources--The Disston Co., Greensboro, NC, pg. 339
Harcharek, Janice, Dir.-Human Resources & Sec.--Universal Dynamics Inc., Woodbridge, VA, pg. 1138
Harcourt, D., V.P.-Human Resources--Perry Equipment Corporation, Mineral Wells, TX, pg. 863
Harding, James C., V.P.-Human Resources--Uncle Ben's, Inc., Houston, TX, pg. 713
Hardwick, Ron, Dir.-Pub. Rels. & Personnel--Miniature Precision Components, Walworth, WI, pg. 757
Hardy, Kevin, Mgr.-Personnel--Idaho Supreme Company, Firth, ID, pg. 561
Harezga, Nancy M., Mgr.-Payroll--National Health Care Affiliates, Inc., Buffalo, NY, pg. 791
Harig, Robert J., Sr. V.P.-Human Resources--Ponderosa, Inc., Vandalia, OH, pg. 743
Harling, Frank, Personnel Dir.--Graniteville Co., Graniteville, SC, pg. 476
Harmon, Casandra, Dir.-Personnel--Communications International, Norcross, GA, pg. 269
Harmon, Mark A., Mgr.-Human Resources--Twin City Die Castings Co., Minneapolis, MN, pg. 1121
Harn, Pat, Dir.-Personnel--Sargent-Fletcher Co., El Monte, CA, pg. 970
Harned, Dave, Dir.-Personnel--E. R. Carpenter Co., Richmond, VA, pg. 224
Harper, Helen B., V.P., Human Resources--YPMS/TMP Worldwide, Inc., Mequon, WI, pg. 1074
Harrington, John, Dir.-Personnel--Oklahoma Publishing Company, Oklahoma City, OK, pg. 446
Harris, E.V., Dir.-Human Resources--AFG Industries, Inc., Fort Worth, TX, pg. 3
Harshaw, N.M., V.P. Human Res. & Sec.--YSI Incorporated, Yellow Springs, OH, pg. 1207
Harstad, Carmen, Dir.-Personnel--Freeman Shoes Company, Beloit, WI, pg. 431
Hart, Billie, Admin.-Personnel--OMCO Mould, Inc., Winchester, IN, pg. 819
Harte, Joseph M., Sr. V.P., Dir. Human Resources--N W Ayer Incorporated, New York, NY, pg. 103
Harte, Joseph M., Sr. V.P., Dir. Human Resources & Devel.-WW--N W Ayer Inc., New York, NY, pg. 104
Hartill, Jim, Dir.-Personnel--Gilmore Bros., Inc., Kalamazoo, MI, pg. 459
Hartley, Cynthia, V.P.-Human Resources--National Gypsum Company, Charlotte, NC, pg. 790
Hartmann, Barry, V.P.-Human Resources--Industrial Ceramics, Inc., Derry, PA, pg. 566
Hartwig, Jeanne, Dir.-Employee Benefits & Human Resources--Acme Foundry, Inc., Coffeyville, KS, pg. 13
Harvey, Edie, Mgr.-Personnel--Hamilton Co., Inc., Reno, NV, pg. 503
Haskell, Pat, Dir.-Personnel & Benefits--Witt Company, Cincinnati, OH, pg. 1198
Hasty, Jane, Dir.-Personnel--Americo Manufacturing Co., Inc., Acworth, GA, pg. 66
Hatlen, Erich, Dir.-Human Resources--MNP Corp., Utica, MI, pg. 693
Haukos, Carol, Dir.-Mktg. & Human Resources--First State Federal Savings & Loan, Hutchinson, MN, pg. 413
Hawkins, F. Ray, Dir.-Human Resources--Daw Technologies, Inc., Salt Lake City, UT, pg. 319
Hayden, Anne E., V.P.-Human Resources--Metropolitan Life Insurance Co., New York, NY, pg. 744
Hayes, David W., V.P.-Personnel & Gen. Counsel--Seiler Corporation, Waltham, MA, pg. 987
Hayes, Kris, Dir.-Human Resources--Kettenburg Marine Corporation, San Diego, CA, pg. 626
Hayes, Noreen J., V.P.-Human Resources--Western & Southern Life Insurance Co., Cincinnati, OH, pg. 1181
Hays, Randy K., Sec., Controller, & Treas.--Masek Distributing Inc., Gering, NE, pg. 717
Hayward, Troy E., V.P.-Human Resources--Bee-Gee Shoe Div., Dayton, OH, pg. 373
Hazekemp, Patricia, Dir.-Human Resources--Ranir Corporation, Grand Rapids, MI, pg. 912
Head, Michael, V.P.-Human Resources--Ingram Industries Inc., Nashville, TN, pg. 568
Heath, Charles, Mgr.-Personnel--Par Industries, inc., Medina, OH, pg. 847
Hebert, Patricia, Dir.-Human Resources--Michigan Milk Producers Association, Novi, MI, pg. 747
Heidelberg, Bill, Dir.-Personnel & Employee Benefits--Petro-Hunt Corporation, Dallas, TX, pg. 865
Heidrich, Robert, Dir.-Personnel--Broder Bros. Co., Plymouth, MI, pg. 178
Heimerdinger, William A., Sr. V.P.-Opers. & Human Resources--Playtex FP Group Incorporated, Stamford, CT, pg. 877
Heimerdinger, William A., V.P.-Opers. & Human Resources--Playtex Family Products Corp., Stamford, CT, pg. 877
Helberg, Penny, V.P.-Human Resources--Paper Calmenson & Co., Saint Paul, MN, pg. 847
Helderman, Carolyn, Dir.-Personnel--T & S Brass & Bronze Works, Inc., Travelers Rest, SC, pg. 1074
Helkey, Gail, Mgr.-Personnel--The Knapheide Mfg. Co., Quincy, IL, pg. 636
Heller, Maurice R., V.P.-Industrial Rels.--Connell Limited Partnership, Boston, MA, pg. 275
Helm, Donald F., V.P.-Personnel & Indus. Rels.--Rand McNally & Company, Skokie, IL, pg. 911
Hembrick, Dena, Mgr.-Human Resources--AMF Bakery Systems, Richmond, VA, pg. 5
Hempel, Stewart, Dir.-Personnel--Upstate Milk Cooperatives Inc., Le Roy, NY, pg. 1140
Henderson, Dorinda, Dir.-Personnel Svcs.--Sacramento Municipal Utility District, Sacramento, CA, pg. 965
Hendricks, Diane M., V.P. & Sec.--ABC Supply Company, Inc., Beloit, WI, pg. 2
Hendrix, R.L., Indus. Rels. Dir.--Griffin Pipe Products Co., Downers Grove, IL, pg. 69
Hendry, Lisa, Dir.-Personnel--Northern Wire & Cable, Inc., Troy, MI, pg. 814
Henke, Judy S., V.P.-Human Resources--Cable Division, Atlanta, GA, pg. 294
Hennen, Anne Y., Mgr.-Human Resoucres--The Cincinnati Cordage & Paper Company, Cincinnati, OH, pg. 249
Hennessey, Jack, V.P.-Human Resources--Modern Drop Forge Co., Blue Island, IL, pg. 762
Henning, David A., V.P.-Personnel--R. P. Adams Company, Inc., Tonawanda, NY, pg. 16
Hermann, Gerald W., V.P.-Employee Rels.--Walter Industries, Inc., Tampa, FL, pg. 1161
Hermes, Mike, Dir.-Personnel--Intercounty Title Co. of Illinois, Chicago, IL, pg. 574
Herr, John, Mgr.-Human Resources--Dove International, Inc., Burr Ridge, IL, pg. 713
Hershman, Mark E., V.P.-Corp. Communications & Admin. Services--VASA Insurance Group, Inc., Indianapolis, IN, pg. 1146
Hertz, Rodney, V.P.-Human Resources--The Acacia Group, Washington, DC, pg. 10
Heslin, Barbara, Dir.-Personnel--Spectronics Corporation, Westbury, NY, pg. 1029
Hess, Hans-Juergen, Personnel Dir.--Berlitz Sprachschulen GmbH, Vienna,, Austria, pg. 143
Hess, Hans-Jurgen, Personnel Dir.--Berlitz Schools of Languages GmbH, Frankfurt/Main, Germany, pg. 143
Hesser, H.G., V.P.-Personnel--American Fuel Cell & Coated Fabrics Co. (Amfuel), Magnolia, AR, pg. 55
Hetrick, Victor, Mgr.-Personnel--New Standard Corporation, Mount Joy, PA, pg. 802
Hettinger, Marc, V.P.-Human Resources--Channel Home Centers Inc., Whippany, NJ, pg. 238
Hettinger, Michelle, Mgr.-Personnel--Narrow Fabric Industries, Inc., West Reading, PA, pg. 783
Hettlinger, Bob, V.P., Human Resources--Colle & McVoy, Inc., Minneapolis, MN, pg. 261
Heying, Cathy, Mgr.-Human Resources--Fred Usinger, Inc., Milwaukee, WI, pg. 1140
Heyman, Jerry, V.P.-Human Resources--Colorado Boxed Beef Co., Auburndale, FL, pg. 265
Hickam, Clara, Mgr.-Personnel--Wilson Products Co., Salt Lake City, UT, pg. 1194
Hicks, R.W., Mgr.-Personnel--Horton Homes, Inc., Eatonton, GA, pg. 545
Hietikko, Donna, Mgr.-Personnel--Mary Maxim, Inc., Port Huron, MI, pg. 722
Higashi, Wallace S., Sr. V.P.-Staff Mngmt.--Servco Pacific Inc., Honolulu, HI, pg. 991
Higdon, Doug, V.P.-Personnel--Jerrico, Inc., Lexington, KY, pg. 229
Hildebrand, Sheryl, Chief Fin. Officer, Dir.-Human Resources & Employee Benefits--Pace International Corporation, Kirkland, WA, pg. 838
Hilgeneck, Joanne, Sr. V.P.-Human Resources--Great Lakes Bancorp, Ann Arbor, MI, pg. 480

Hill, Angie, Dir.-Human Resources--Century Boats By General Marine Industries, Panama City, FL, pg. 450
Hill, Angie, Dir.-Personnel--GMI, Inc.-Glasstream, Panama City, FL, pg. 450
Hill, Charlie, Mgr.-Employment & Benefits Admin.--Landmark Communications, Inc., Norfolk, VA, pg. 654
Hill, Dave, Mgr.-Personnel--Markem Corporation, Keene, NH, pg. 708
Hill, Monica L., Dir.-Human Resources--Pepper, Hamilton & Scheetz, Philadelphia, PA, pg. 860
Hill, Norman J., V.P.-Human Resources--Perkins Family Restaurants, Memphis, TN, pg. 1088
Himel, Steve, Human Resources Dir.--William B. Reily & Co., Inc., New Orleans, LA, pg. 923
Himel, Steve, Personnel Mgr.--Luzianne Blue Plate Foods, New Orleans, LA, pg. 923
Hinds, Phil H., Dir.-Personnel--Gateway Press, Inc., Louisville, KY, pg. 446
Hines, Chris, Dir.-Personnel--Elias Brothers Restaurants, Inc., Warren, MI, pg. 376
Hinthorn, Jim, Dir.-Human Resources--F. Schumacher & Co., New York, NY, pg. 979
Hite, Brenda, Personnel Mgr.--Virginia Hot Springs, Inc., Hot Springs, VA, pg. 1152
Hix, Kim, Payroll/Accounts Payable Coord.--Ivex Packaging Corporation, Lincolnshire, IL, pg. 583
Hodge, Carmi, V.P.-Human Resources--The Copley Press, Inc., La Jolla, CA, pg. 284
Hodge, Tommy, Dir.-Personnel--Milliken & Co., Inc., Spartanburg, SC, pg. 755
Hodgson, Robert, V.P.-Human Resources--GAF Building Materials Corporation, Wayne, NJ, pg. 438
Hofer, Rita, Mgr.-Personnel--L&J Technologies, Morton Grove, IL, pg. 647
Hoffman, Garth, V.P.-Human Resources--Yorktowne, Inc., Red Lion, PA, pg. 1208
Hoffman, P., Personnel Mgr.--Cable Electric Products, Inc., Providence, RI, pg. 671
Hoffman, Steven, V.P.--Sharon-Jay Togs, Inc., New Bedford, MA, pg. 995
Hogsven, Harlan J., Sr. V.P.-Human Resources--Lutheran Brotherhood, Minneapolis, MN, pg. 688
Hojer, Susan, Chief Fin. Officer, Controller & Mgr.-Personnel--MFE Instruments, Beverly, MA, pg. 1050
Holbert, Rick, Dir.-Human Res.--Thomas Built Buses, Inc., High Point, NC, pg. 1092
Holcomb, Marilyn, Dir.-Human Resources--Planning Systems Inc., McLean, VA, pg. 874
Holden, Rebecca, Dir.-Personnel--Sooner Pipe & Supply Corp., Tulsa, OK, pg. 1018
Holland, Donna M., Mgr.-Personnel--Eastern Fine Paper, Incorporated, Brewer, ME, pg. 363
Holloway, Cecelia, V.P.-Human Resources & Admin.--Viacom Entertainment, New York, NY, pg. 785
Holm, Rick, V.P.-Human Resources--Atwood Industries, Inc., Rockford, IL, pg. 97
Holmes, Bob, Dir.-Human Resources--Sun Computers, Inc., Carson, CA, pg. 1058
Holoboski, Ray, Dir.-Indus. Rels.--Tagsons Papers, Inc., Albany, NY, pg. 1076
Holt, Butch, Dir.-Personnel--Darda Inc. (USA), Baltimore, MD, pg. 315
Holzman, Ronald R., V.P.-Human Resources--Rudolph/Libbe, Inc., Walbridge, OH, pg. 955
Hooper, Fran, Chief-Admin. Staff--NJ Transit, Newark, NJ, pg. 801
Hoops, Barry, Dir.-Personnel--Jones Dairy Farm, Fort Atkinson, WI, pg. 603
Hopkins, Curt, Dir.-Personnel--Golub Corporation, Schenectady, NY, pg. 469
Hoplamazian, Marie, Admin. Dir.--Dechert Price & Rhoads, Philadelphia, PA, pg. 323
Hopper, Henrietta, Dir.-Human Resources--San Antonio Light, San Antonio, TX, pg. 524
Horne, George R., V.P.-Human Resources--Dole Food Company, Inc., Westlake Village, CA, pg. 840
Hornstein, Donald A., V.P.-Human Resources--Channellock, Inc., Meadville, PA, pg. 239
Horslev, Dave, Dir.-Human Resources--Culligan International Company, Northbrook, IL, pg. 358
Houghland, Fred, Dir.-Personnel--Dunes Hotels and Casinos Inc., Las Vegas, NV, pg. 352
Houston, Paula, Mgr.-Human Resources--Hart Crowser, Inc., Seattle, WA, pg. 512
Howard, Brian P., V.P.-Human Resources--The Ingersoll Milling Machine Co., Rockford, IL, pg. 568
Howard, James B., V.P.-Human Resources--First Federal Savings and Loan Assn. of Rochester, Rochester, NY, pg. 413
Howe, Anne, Dir.-Human Resources--Burke Industries, Inc., San Jose, CA, pg. 191
Howe, Anne, Dir.-Human Resources--Burke Industries Inc., San Jose, CA, pg. 190
Howell, Arden, V.P.-Human Resources--Lyon's Restaurants, Inc., Foster City, CA, pg. 690
Howes, Wayne, Personnel Dir.--National Oats Co., Cedar Rapids, IA, pg. 25
Hoxie, Henry, Sec. & Dir.-Human Resources--Atlas Hotels, Inc., San Diego, CA, pg. 96
Hoy, Debbra, Dir.-Human Resources--Lincoln Electric Systems, Lincoln, NE, pg. 675
Hoye, Janice, Mgr.-Human Resources--Diebel Manufacturing Co., Morton Grove, IL, pg. 336
Hoyt, Carol A., V.P.-Human Resources--Advance Packaging Corporation, Grand Rapids, MI, pg. 19
Hoyt, L.R., V.P.-Human Resources--Motor Wheel Corporation, Lansing, MI, pg. 773
Hubbard, Donald, Dir.-Indus. Rels.--Schmidt Baking Co., Inc., Baltimore, MD, pg. 976
Hubbard, Julie, Personnel Mgr.--DonTech, Chicago, IL, pg. 345
Hubbard, Roger, Controller--J.L. Lester & Son, Inc., Rockmart, GA, pg. 668
Huber, Ray, V.P.-Personnel & Labor Rels.--Giant Eagle, Inc., Pittsburgh, PA, pg. 455
Hughes, Carl M., Dir.-Personnel/Construction--Westgate Inc., Port Allen, LA, pg. 1182
Hughes, James, Dir.-Personnel--Barnhill Contracting Company, Tarboro, NC, pg. 121
Hughes, Timothy W., V.P.-Human Resources--Cox Enterprises, Inc., Atlanta, GA, pg. 292
Hughey, Nancy, Dir.-Human Resources--Applied Solar Energy Corporation, City of Industry, CA, pg. 79
Humphreys D., Dir.-Human Resources--Stamco Industries Inc., Euclid, OH, pg. 1035
Hunt, M.L., Pres. & Chief Exec. Officer--Hunt Building Corporation, El Paso, TX, pg. 553
Hunt, Sara, Dir.-Personnel--Dixson, Inc., Grand Junction, CO, pg. 341
Hunt, Walter L., V.P.-Human Resources & Sec.--Dead River Company, Portland, ME, pg. 321
Huntington, James F., V.P.-Admin.--JII/Sales Promotion Associates, Inc., Coshocton, OH, pg. 604
Hurley, John W., Exec. V.P. & Sec.--Westin, Inc., Omaha, NE, pg. 1183
Hurley, Sandra, V.P.-Indus. Rels.--Fel Corporation, Farmingdale, NJ, pg. 405
Hurst, Cynthia J., Dir.-Human Resources--H & H Tube & Manufacturing Co., Vanderbilt, MI, pg. 495
Hurst, Jack A., Sr. V.P.-Training & Human Resources--Rhodes, Inc., Atlanta, GA, pg. 931
Hurwitz, Betsy, Mgr.-Human Resources--S. Schwab Company, Cumberland, MD, pg. 980
Husmann, E., Dir.-Personnel--Vilter Manufacturing Corporation, Milwaukee, WI, pg. 1152
Hussko, Karen, Dir.-Personnel--Rex Moore Electrical Contractors & Engineers, West Sacramento, CA, pg. 768
Hyde, Don, Dir.-Opers. & Personnel--Battey Machinery Company, Rome, GA, pg. 127
Hyde, Joanne, Dir.-Human Resources--Summa Four, Inc., Manchester, NH, pg. 1057
Hyle, Ted, Jr., V.P.-Human Resources--American Laundry Machinery Inc., Cincinnati, OH, pg. 57
Ilardo, Marcia A., V.P.-Fin. & Dir.-Human Resources--ICE Communications, Inc., Rochester, NY, pg. 559
Imyak, Sandy, Dir.-Personnel--Bessin Corporation, Chicago, IL, pg. 146
Ingram, Kathy, Dir.-Personnel--Cain & Bultman, Inc., Jacksonville, FL, pg. 207
Iriart, Ken, V.P.-Personnel--In-N-Out Burgers, Baldwin Park, CA, pg. 564
Isbell, Phyllis, Dir.-Personnel--Westgate Fabrics, Inc., Grand Prairie, TX, pg. 1182
Isola, Thomas, V.P.-Mktg. & Pub. Rels.--Silver State Disposal Service, Inc., Las Vegas, NV, pg. 1004
Iverson, Patricia, V.P.-Human Resources--American Hardware Mutual Insurance Co., Minnetonka, MN, pg. 55
Jackman, Neil W., V.P.-Sls. & Human Resources--Pease Industries, Inc., Fairfield, OH, pg. 854
Jackson, Cecil, Dir.-Personnel--Bike Athletic Co., Knoxville, TN, pg. 150
Jackson, Dominick, Mgr.-Personnel--Meco Corporation, Greeneville, TN, pg. 734
Jackson, Steven P., V.P.--Johnson Bros. Corp., Litchfield, MN, pg. 597
Jackson, Sue, Dir.-Personnel--Racetrac Petroleum, Inc., Smyrna, GA, pg. 909
Jacobs, Carl, Dir.-Personnel--The American Bankers Association, Washington, DC, pg. 49
Jacobs, Les, Dir.-Human Resources--Insilco Corporation, Midland, TX, pg. 571
Jacobs, Nancy, Mgr.-Admin. Services--The Hennegan Company, Cincinnati, OH, pg. 529
Jacobs, Robert L., V.P.-Human Resources--Wells Mfg. Corp., Dond Du Lac, WI, pg. 1123
Jacobs, Verna, Personnel Dir.--UDT Sensors, Inc., Hawthorne, CA, pg. 1122
Jacobsen, Eric, V.P.-Admin.--Certified Grocers of Florida, Inc., Ocala, FL, pg. 237
Jacquet, Richard J., V.P.-Human Resources--Ampex Corporation, Redwood City, CA, pg. 998
Jaeger, Connie A., Asst. V.P. & Human Resources Dir.--The National Bank of Sussex County, Branchville, NJ, pg. 534
Jaenel, Sharon, Dir.-Human Resources--Barton Brands, Ltd., Chicago, IL, pg. 123
James, Ronald, Dir.-Human Resources--Heller Seasonings & Ingredients, Inc., Bedford Park, IL, pg. 526
Janies, Lee, Dir.-Personnel--Schwegmann Giant Super Markets, New Orleans, LA, pg. 980
Jaramillo, Alan M., V.P.-Human Resources--Woodward-Clyde Group, Inc., Denver, CO, pg. 1200
Jaramillo, Carol, Dir.-Personnel--PhoneMate, Inc., Torrance, CA, pg. 869
Jaros, Norman W., Dir.-Personnel--Transus Inc., Atlanta, GA, pg. 1108
Jaworski, Pauline, V.P.-Personnel--Miken Companies, Inc., Cheektowaga, NY, pg. 752
Jedinak, Audrey G., Dir.-Personnel--The Swanson Company Manufacturers, Phoenix, AZ, pg. 1066
Jenkins, Ezra, Mgr.-Employee Rels.--C.B. Fleet Company, Incorporated, Lynchburg, VA, pg. 417
Jenkins, Tiny, Chm. Bd. & Chief Exec. Officer--PSI Group of Companies, Memphis, TN, pg. 837
Jennerjahn, Rita Jo, Asst V.P.-Human Resources--CSE Corporation, San Francisco, CA, pg. 204
Jensen, Robert, V.P.-Human Resources & Pur.--Shape Inc., Biddeford, ME, pg. 995
Jensenius, Robert, Mgr.-Human Resources--Shipley Oil Company, York, PA, pg. 999
Jerue, Cherie, Mgr.-Personnel--Paul Inman Associates Inc., Farmington Hills, MI, pg. 570
Johnsen, Lenore, Dir.-Personnel--William Morrow & Co., Inc., New York, NY, pg. 521
Johnson, C., Dir.-Human Resources--Formation, Inc., Moorestown, NJ, pg. 424
Johnson, Duane, Sr. V.P.-Personnel--Bullock's, Los Angeles, CA, pg. 699
Johnson, Duane E., Dir.-Labor Rels.--Seattle Times Company, Seattle, WA, pg. 986
Johnson, Keith, Dir.-Human Resources--Denver Equipment Company, Colorado Springs, CO, pg. 331
Johnson, Michael, V.P.-Human Resources--Recon/Optical, Inc., Barrington, IL, pg. 917
Johnson, Nancy, Mgr., Human Resources--Silverstone, Adkins & Breit, Inc., Stratford, CT, pg. 1005
Johnson, Richard, Dir.-Human Resources--Mason Shoe Mfg. Co., Chippewa Falls, WI, pg. 718
Johnson, Richard, Dir.-Human Resources--Wissota Trader & B.A. Mason, Chippewa Falls, WI, pg. 718
Johnson, Richard, Dir.-Admin.--E.A. Sween Company, Eden Prairie, MN, pg. 1066
Johnson, Wayne C., Dir.-Personnel--C.B. Fleet Company, Incorporated, Lynchburg, VA, pg. 417
Johnson, Wiley, V.P.-Personnel--Orders Distributing Co., Greenville, SC, pg. 829
Johnston, B.M., V.P.-Human Resources--Dukane Corporation, Saint Charles, IL, pg. 351
Johnston, Debbie, Mgr.-Human Resources--Correct Craft, Inc., Orlando, FL, pg. 287
Johnston, Lee, V.P.-Human Resources--Holder Corporation, Atlanta, GA, pg. 538
Johnston, Robert, Personnel Dir--Atlanta Wire Works, Inc., Jonesboro, GA, pg. 94
Johnston, Vern, Dir.-Personnel--Allsups Convenience Stores Inc., Clovis, NM, pg. 43
Jones, Eric, Mgr.-Personnel--Vernay Laboratories, Inc., Yellow Springs, OH, pg. 1148
Jones, Gary, Dir.-Human Resources--Dunn-Edwards Corporation, Los Angeles, CA, pg. 353
Jones, J.A., Jr., Mgr.-Personnel--S & C Electric Company, Chicago, IL, pg. 958
Jones, Jerry L., Sr. V.P.-Human Res.--Jitney-Jungle Stores of America, Inc., Jackson, MS, pg. 594
Jones, Lisa, Mgr.-Personnel--Standard Communications Corporation, Carson, CA, pg. 1036
Jones, Sharon, Dir.-Personnel--Standard Candy Co., Inc., Nashville, TN, pg. 1035
Jones, William, V.P.-Human Resources--Schnuck Markets, Inc., Maryland Heights, MO, pg. 977
Joos, Lynn A., Personnel Mgr.--Artesian Resources Corporation, Newark, DE, pg. 86
Joos, Lynn A., Personnel Mgr.--Artesian Water Company, Inc., Newark, DE, pg. 86
Jordan, Betty, Dir.-Personnel--Better Brands Of Atlanta, Inc., Atlanta, GA, pg. 148
Joseph, John, Mgr.-Admin.--George W. Cochran Co., Inc., Washington, DC, pg. 258
Jouza, Rick, Dir.-Personnel & Pur. Agent--Just Pants, Chicago, IL, pg. 610
Joyce, Gerard J., Dir.-Human Resources--Kirkwood Industries, Inc., Cleveland, OH, pg. 633
Joyce, Robert, Sr. V.P.-Human Resources--Supermarkets General Corporation, Woodbridge, NJ, pg. 1064
Juhola, Andy, Dir.-Personnel--Molded Fiber Glass Companies, Ashtabula, OH, pg. 763
Julian, Rick, Mgr.-Human Resources--Sheffield Steel Corporation-Joliet, Joliet, IL, pg. 996
Junso, Gary, V.P.-Human Resources--John Morrell & Co., Cincinnati, OH, pg. 54
Kaczmarek, Bob, Dir.-Human Resources--Zippo Manufacturing Company, Bradford, PA, pg. 1220
Kafafian, Lori, V.P., Dir.-Human Resources--Dentsu, Young & Rubicam Partnerships, New York, NY, pg. 330
Kamer, Conard, Dir.-Human Resources--The Dartnell Corporation, Chicago, IL, pg. 316
Kana, Kiane, Dir.-Human Resources--Desco Corporation, Columbus, OH, pg. 332
Karalus, Jo-Ann B., V.P.-Human Resources--Brookstone Company, Inc., Peterborough, NH, pg. 180
Karapetian, David, V.P.-Human Resources--Suburban Communications Corp., Livonia, MI, pg. 1055
Karley, Sherry, Dir.-Employee Benefits--Costa Cruise Lines, N.V., Miami, FL, pg. 288
Karpinski, John, Mgr.-Indus. Rels.--MacAndrews & Forbes Co., Camden, NJ, pg. 694
Karriker, Richard G., V.P.-Human Resources--Rowe Corp., Charlotte, NC, pg. 952
Kasenter, Robert A., Exec. V.P.-Human Resources--Montgomery Ward & Co., Inc., Chicago, IL, pg. 767
Kates, Phillip, Dir.-Human Resources--Yuba Heat Transfer Division, Tulsa, OK, pg. 275
Katner, Terri, Dir.-Personnel--Graymills Corp., Chicago, IL, pg. 480
Kaufman, Seymour, Dir.-Personnel & Data Processing--I. Spiewak & Sons, Inc., New York, NY, pg. 1031
Kautz, E.T., Mgr.-Employee Rels.--PQ Corporation, Valley Forge, PA, pg. 836
Kay, Dwight, Dir.-Admin. Services--Cassens Transport Company, Edwardsville, IL, pg. 228
Kayse, Peggy, Dir.-Personnel--South East Coal Co., Irvine, KY, pg. 1019
Kearns, James E., Dir.-Personnel--Hynes Industries Inc., Youngstown, OH, pg. 557
Kearns, Richard P., Natl. Dir.-Human Resources--Price Waterhouse - U.S., New York, NY, pg. 888
Keating, Donna, Dir.-Personnel--Wheaton Van Lines, Inc., Indianapolis, IN, pg. 1184
Keating, John, Mgr.-Personnel Training & Devel.--Cray Communications Inc., Annapolis Junction, MD, pg. 297
Keehn, Roger, V.P.-Human Resources--Samsonite Corporation, Denver, CO, pg. 358
Keel, Jolene, Dir.-Personnel--Love Mortgage Company, St. Louis, MO, pg. 685
Keenan, Harry J., V.P.-Human Resources--Jac Jacobsen Industries, Inc., Greenwich, CT, pg. 587
Kehan, Kathleen, Mgr.-Human Resources--Dettra Flag Company, Oaks, PA, pg. 333
Kell, David, Mgr.-Personnel--Eco Water Systems, Saint Paul, MN, pg. 367

Keller, Mary Jo, Dir.-Personnel--Ingrid-Sevko, Inc., Deerfield, IL, pg. 569
Kelly, Dan M., V.P.-Human Resources--Gilbane Building Company, Providence, RI, pg. 457
Kelly, Helen, Dir.-Personnel--Sunniland Corporation, Sanford, FL, pg. 1061
Kelly, Joe, Dir.-Human Resources--Guideposts Associates, Inc., Carmel, NY, pg. 493
Kelly, John J., Sr. V.P.-Human Resources--United Parcel Service of America, Inc., Atlanta, GA, pg. 1133
Kelly, Kathleen, Personnel & Office Mgr.--Franklin Spier, Inc., New York, NY, pg. 1031
Kelly, M. Lyn, Mgr.-Personnel--La Victoria Foods, Inc., City of Industry, CA, pg. 649
Kelly, Ruthanne, Sr. V.P.-Human Resources--Unistrut Corporation, Ann Arbor, MI, pg. 1130
Kelm, S.E., Dir.-Indus. Rels.--Burgess-Norton Mfg. Co., Geneva, IL, pg. 69
Kenan, H.D., V.P.-Human Resources--Kayser-Roth Hosiery, Inc., Greensboro, NC, pg. 262
Kennedy, Bill, Mgr.-Personnel--Perkasie Industries Corporation, Perkasie, PA, pg. 862
Kennedy, Helen T., V.P.-Personnel--Torco Oil, Chicago, IL, pg. 1102
Kennedy, Jim, Dir.-Personnel--Kennedy Manufacturing Company, Van Wert, OH, pg. 623
Kennedy, Lois, Mgr.-Personnel--Muelhens, Inc., Orange, CT, pg. 774
Kennedy, Matthew, Dir.-Personnel--The Associated Group, Indianapolis, IN, pg. 90
Kennedy, Pam, Dir.-Personnel--Kern's Bakeries, Incorporated, Knoxville, TN, pg. 624
Kent, Van, V.P.-Human Resources--Thomas & Betts Holdings, Inc., Memphis, TN, pg. 425
Keown, Don G., V.P.-Human Resources--The Principal Financial Group, Des Moines, IA, pg. 890
Kern, Jane, Mgr.-Personnel--Reading Tube Corp., Reading, PA, pg. 916
Kerns, Jo, Dir.-Human Resources--Blade Communications, Inc., Toledo, OH, pg. 155
Kerr, D. Bruce, Mgr.-Personnel--Star Expansion Company, Mountainville, NY, pg. 1039
Kessler, Roberta R., Dir.-Human Resources--Air Conditioning Co., Inc., Glendale, CA, pg. 26
Khadivar, Michael R., Mgr.-Human Resources--CORS, Itasca, IL, pg. 203
Kiefer, Gerald J., V.P.-Human Resources & Safety--Rogers Group Inc., Nashville, TN, pg. 943
Kilbrydg, Linda, Personnel Mgr.--World Dryer Corp., Berkeley, IL, pg. 1027
Kilburn, Candace, Dir.-Human Rels.--Buck Knives, Inc., El Cajon, CA, pg. 185
Kilgore, Ginger, Dir.-Personnel--Jordan's Meats, Portland, ME, pg. 605
Kill, Stephen, V.P.-Human Resources--The Minster Machine Company, Minster, OH, pg. 759
Killian, Ray A., Sr., Exec. V.P.-Human Resources & Pub. Rels.--Belk Stores Services Inc., Charlotte, NC, pg. 134
Kilton, Wayne N., V.P.-Personnel--Central Mutual Insurance Co., Van Wert, OH, pg. 233
Kimball, James, Dir.-Human Resources--Geo-Centers, Inc., Newton Center, MA, pg. 452
Kimball, Richard T., Dir.-Personnel--Exide Corporation, Reading, PA, pg. 393
Kincaid, Bob, Mgr.-Personnel--Delta Industries, East Granby, CT, pg. 327
King, D., Personnel Dir.--The Canadian Coleman Co., Ltd., Toronto,, Canada, pg. 695
King, D.A., Dir.-Personnel--Wilbur Smith Associates, Columbia, SC, pg. 1011
King, Don, Dir.-Human Resources--Producers Rice Mill Inc., Stuttgart, AR, pg. 892
King, Richard, Dir.-Human Resources--Concord Litho Co., Inc., Concord, NH, pg. 272
Kinsey, Susan, V.P.-Human Resources--Atlantic Gulf Communities Corporation, Miami, FL, pg. 95
Kirker, Maureen, V.P.-Human Resources--Greenhorne & O'Mara, Inc., Greenbelt, MD, pg. 485
Kives, Sharon, Mgr.-Human Resources--Leichtung, Inc., Cleveland, OH, pg. 666
Klaiber, Dan, Dir.-Personnel--Freudenberg-NOK (MI), Plymouth, MI, pg. 432
Klain, Lisa Wolf, Dir.-Personnel--Leland A. Wolf & Associates, Foster City, CA, pg. 1199
Klammert, Mike, Dir.-Personnel--Maynard Steel Casting Company, Milwaukee, WI, pg. 725
Klein, James E., Sr. V.P.-Human Resources--Fiduciary Trust Co. International, New York, NY, pg. 408
Klein, James E., Sr. V.P.-Human Resources--Fiduciary Trust Company International, New York, NY, pg. 408
Kleman, Oscar D., Jr., V.P.-Human Resources--Anderson Trucking Service Inc., Saint Cloud, MN, pg. 73
Klingensmith, Les, Dir.-Personnel--Information Systems & Network Corporation, Bethesda, MD, pg. 567
Klosak, Robert J., V.P.-Data Processing & Personnel--L. Fish Corporation, Chicago, IL, pg. 414
Kluener, James A., Jr., Human Resources Dir.--Kluener Packing Company, Cincinnati, OH, pg. 636
Knez, Ronald, Corp. V.P.--National Car Rental System, Inc., Minneapolis, MN, pg. 786
Knighton, Linda, Dir.-Personnel--Insurance Corp. of America, Houston, TX, pg. 572
Knoernschild, Connie, Human Resources--S.T. Research, Newington, VA, pg. 964
Knors, Joe, Mgr.-Personnel, Office & Credit--Master Appliance Corp., Racine, WI, pg. 719
Knox, Terri, Dir.-Personnel--VMC Fiberglass Products Inc., Daleville, AL, pg. 1142
Knutson, David T., Dir.-Personnel--Hubbard Milling Company, Mankato, MN, pg. 549
Knutson, Deborah, Asst. V.P. & Dir-Human Resources--Robert F. Driver Co., Inc., San Diego, CA, pg. 349
Knutson, Steve, Mgr.-Human Resources--Grove Valve & Regulator Company, Oakland, CA, pg. 490
Koep, Donna, Dir.-Human Resources--Power-One, Inc., Camarillo, CA, pg. 883
Koesser, Susan, Mgr.-Human Resources--Liquid Controls Corporation, Lake Bluff, IL, pg. 677
Kogan, Barbara, Dir.-Human Resources--Tasco, Miami, FL, pg. 1079
Kohl, Edwin J., Dir.-Fin.--Electro-Science Laboratories, Inc., King of Prussia, PA, pg. 375
Kohl, Kermit K., Dir.-Personnel--Furman Foods, Inc., Northumberland, PA, pg. 436
Kohls, Ellen P., Mgr.-Mktg.--Effective Management Systems, Milwaukee, WI, pg. 370
Kolb, John P., V.P.-Human Resources--Philadelphia Coca-Cola Bottling Co., Philadelphia, PA, pg. 866
Kolk, Betsy, Dir.-Admin./Oper.--Pyttronic Industries, Inc., Montgomeryville, PA, pg. 901
Kolko, Ira, Personnel Mgr.--Gitano Group Inc., New York, NY, pg. 460
Komulainen, Marilyn, Dir.-Personnel--Muro Pharmaceutical, Inc., Tewksbury, MA, pg. 776
Konerman, John, Dir.-Personnel--Swallen's, Inc., Cincinnati, OH, pg. 1066
Konkel, Diane, Mgr.-Indus. Rels.--Waukesha Foundry Inc., Waukesha, WI, pg. 1168
Koons, Pat, Dir.-Personnel--American Fluorescent Corporation, Waukegan, IL, pg. 54
Koons, William, Dir.-Indus. Rels.--Standard Tool & Manufacturing Company, Lyndhurst, NJ, pg. 1037
Kopsa, Louis D., V.P.-Human Resources--Union Switch & Signal Inc., Pittsburgh, PA, pg. 1129
Korn, Donald L., Sr. V.P.-Human Resources--Avis, Inc., Garden City, NY, pg. 102
Kortes, Jeff, Dir.-Human Resources--Wigwam Mills, Inc., Sheboygan, WI, pg. 1189
Kosterman, Gayle P., V.P.-Human Resources-U.S. Consumer Prods.--S. C. Johnson & Son, Inc., Racine, WI, pg. 599
Kotar, Barry A., Sr. V.P.-Quality, Human Resources & Info. Services--Northwest Airlines, Inc., Saint Paul, MN, pg. 782
Kottkamp, Patti, Dir.-Human Resources--E & A Industries, Inc., Indianapolis, IN, pg. 358
Kotz, Lenard, Dir.-Personnel--Arinc Inc., Annapolis, MD, pg. 82
Kovaleski, John, Dir.-Personnel--Mayfair Super Markets, Inc., Elizabeth, NJ, pg. 724
Kovar, Nancy, Personnel Dir.--Associated Metals & Minerals Corp., White Plains, NY, pg. 91
Kozeny, JoAnn, V.P.-Human Resources--Omaha Steaks International, Omaha, NE, pg. 825
Kozuba, Karen, Mgr.-Corp. Personnel--Wing Industries, Inc., Dallas, TX, pg. 1196
Krafft, Ann, Dir.-Human Resource--Nashville Wire Product Co., Nashville, TN, pg. 784
Krahn, Kenneth L., V.P.-Indus. Rels.--Curries Company, Mason City, IA, pg. 361
Kramer, Richard A., V.P.-Personnel--Erb Lumber Company, Birmingham, MI, pg. 360
Kramer, Scott P., V.P.-Worldwide Human Resources Support--S. C. Johnson & Son, Inc., Racine, WI, pg. 599
Krammer, Kenneth, V.P.-Personnel--Nickerson Lumber Company, Orleans, MA, pg. 806
Kranford, Aileen, Mgr.-Personnel--Surgical Specialties, Reading, PA, pg. 1065
Kratz, Bruce, V.P.-Personnel--Hess's Department Stores, Inc., Allentown, PA, pg. 302
Kraun, Michael, Dir.-Human Resources--Continental Web Press, Inc., Itasca, IL, pg. 280
Kraunellis, Al, Dir.-Personnel--Malden Mills Industries, Inc., Lawrence, MA, pg. 702
Kraus, Howard, Dir.-Personnel--Saxon Paint & Home Care Centers Inc., Chicago, IL, pg. 973
Krause, M.E., Mgr.-Personnel--S & C Electric Company, Chicago, IL, pg. 958
Kravitz, Irving, Asst. V.P.-Human Resources--The Edward J. DeBartolo Corporation, Youngstown, OH, pg. 323
Krbec, James, V.P.-Human Resources--Big V Supermarkets, Inc., Florida, NY, pg. 149
Kreusser, Judi, Exec. V.P., Sec. & Dir.-Human Resources--Handley & Miller, Inc., Indianapolis, IN, pg. 505
Krische, Marilyn, Mgr.-Human Resources--Hollymatic Corporation, Countryside, IL, pg. 539
Krogmer, Sheila, Mgr.-Human Resources--Woodcraft Industries, Inc., Saint Cloud, MN, pg. 1200
Kroll, Jeannette, Dir.-Personnel--The Hammerblow Corp., Wausau, WI, pg. 504
Krout, Alfred L., V.P.-Human Resources--Clemens Markets Inc., Lansdale, PA, pg. 254
Krupka, Barbara, Dir.-Personnel--Petricca Industries, Inc., Pittsfield, MA, pg. 865
Ksansnak, James, Exec. V.P.-Fin. & Personnel--ARA Group, Philadelphia, PA, pg. 5
Kubina, N., Dir.-Human Resources--DeMert & Dougherty, Inc., Westchester, IL, pg. 328
Kuebler, Mary Ann, Mgr.-Human Resources--Whiting Corporation, Harvey, IL, pg. 1187
Kugler, William O., V.P.-Personnel & Wholesale Programs--Pro Hardware, Inc., Englewood, CO, pg. 891
Kuh, William, V.P.-Employee Rels. & Devel.--Tennessee Valley Authority, Knoxville, TN, pg. 1088
Kunkle, Tom, Mgr.-Indus. Rels.--Dexter Company, Fairfield, IA, pg. 334
Kurten, George W., Sec. & Dir.-Personnel--Walsworth Publishing Company, Inc., Marceline, MO, pg. 1161
Kurtzhals, William, V.P.-Personnel--Power Process Piping, Inc., Plymouth, MI, pg. 883
Kuzma, William, V.P.-Human Resources--Ziegler Coal Holding Co., Fairview Heights, IL, pg. 1218
Kyle, Trish, Dir.-Human Resources--Eric Mower and Associates, Inc., Syracuse, NY, pg. 774
LaCour, Jim, Dir.-Human Resources--Seattle City Light, Seattle, WA, pg. 986
Ladzinski, Greg, Dir.-Personnel & Indus. Rels.--Macwhyte Co., Kenosha, WI, pg. 69
Laehr, Mark, V.P.-Corp. Resources--Hydrite Chemical Company, Brookfield, WI, pg. 556
LaFontaine, Louis J., Sr. V.P.-Corp. Affairs--The Mutual Life Insurance Company of New York (MONY), New York, NY, pg. 778
Lager, Henry S., V.P.-Human Resources--Lear Siegler Diversified Holdings Corp., Livingston, NJ, pg. 664
Lager, Henry S., Sr. V.P.-Human Resources--The Pullman Company, Livingston, NJ, pg. 899
Lager, Henry S., V.P.-Human Resources--Lear Siegler Diversified Holdings Corp., Livingston, NJ, pg. 424
Lager, Henry S., Sr. V.P.-Human Resources--Lear Siegler Diversified Holdings Corp., Livingston, NJ, pg. 424
Laginess, Edward, V.P.-Employee Rels.--Genmar Industries, Inc., Minneapolis, MN, pg. 759
LaGrega, Andrew T., Sr. V.P.-Sls., Mktg., Adv. & Human Resources--Wilder Management Associates, Waltham, MA, pg. 1189
Lahman, A. Wayne, Indus. Rels. Mgr.--Union City Body Company, Inc., Union City, IN, pg. 1128
Laidlaw, Richard, Dir.-Human Resources--Active Tool & Manufacturing Co., Inc., Roseville, MI, pg. 15
Lalas, Janet, Personnel Admin.--Rapid Mounting & Finishing Co., Chicago, IL, pg. 913
Lamb, Russell W., Mgr.-Human Resources--Utilities Construction Co., Inc. Of South Carolina, Charleston, SC, pg. 1141
Lambert, John, Mgr.-Human Resources--Faber/Castell Corporation, Parsippany, NJ, pg. 395
Lambert, Lou Ann, Dir.-Human Resources--The Flood Company, Hudson, OH, pg. 419
Lamelas, Virginia, Mgr.-Personnel--Edmund Scientific Company, Barrington, NJ, pg. 369
Lamie, Theresa, Dir.-Personnel--Griffin Corporation, Valdosta, GA, pg. 487
LaMotte, Louise, Mgr.-Human Resources--RE/MAX International, Inc., Englewood, CO, pg. 915
Landes, Karen, Dir.-Personnel--Acme Visible Records, Crozet, VA, pg. 13
Landis, Drew W., V.P.-Human Resources--Binney & Smith Inc., Easton, PA, pg. 502
Landon, Marvin, V.P.-Personnel--Merle Norman Cosmetics, Inc., Los Angeles, CA, pg. 740
Landon, William, Dir.-Personnel--Pridgeon & Clay, Inc., Grand Rapids, MI, pg. 889
Landskron, Jerry, Sr. V.P.-Admin.--Pioneer Communications of America, Upper Saddle River, NJ, pg. 871
Lane, Kathy, V.P.-Personnel--Angelo Brothers Co., Philadelphia, PA, pg. 74
Lane, Lynda, Sr. V.P.-Admin. Corp. Communications--Koll Co., Newport Beach, CA, pg. 641
Lane, Richard W., V.P.-Indus. Rels.--Knowles Electronics, Inc., Itasca, IL, pg. 637
Lang, Leonard, Dir.-Personnel & Controller--Kaz, Inc., New York, NY, pg. 619
Lange, John P., Asst. V.P.-Labor Rels.--Amtrak-National Railroad Passenger Corp., Washington, DC, pg. 69
Langford, Robert, Personnel Dir.--Flying J. Inc., Brigham City, UT, pg. 421
Langlais, Jackie, Dir.-Personnel--Edelbrock Corp., Torrance, CA, pg. 367
Langston, Dudley I., Dir.-Pur., Personnel, Fin. & Sec.--Langston Companies, Memphis, TN, pg. 657
Lanigir, Joanne, Dir.-Personnel--Cubix Corporation, Carson City, NV, pg. 303
Larance, Larry, V.P.-Pub. Rels. & Human Resources--General American Life Insurance Co., St. Louis, MO, pg. 448
LaRew, Leo D., Dir.-Human Resources--Petersen Publishing Company, Los Angeles, CA, pg. 864
Large, James L., Dir.-Personnel--Van Leunens Inc., Cincinnati, OH, pg. 1144
Largent, Joy, Dir.-Human Resources--Strouse Greenberg & Co., Inc., Philadelphia, PA, pg. 1054
Larocca, Jay, Mgr.-Personnel--Interform Corporation, Bridgeville, PA, pg. 574
Larsen, Jack, Exec. Dir.-Human Res. & Organization--The Long Island Rail Road Co., Jamaica, NY, pg. 745
Larsen, Lawrence J., V.P.-Personnel--Waldorf Corporation, Saint Paul, MN, pg. 1159
Larson, Fred, Dir.-Personnel--Acorn Engineering Company, City of Industry, CA, pg. 14
Larson, Wayne, V.P.-Human Resources--Binkley Company, Warrenton, MO, pg. 151
Last, D., Dir.-Personnel--Illinois Range Company, Mount Prospect, IL, pg. 563
Lathrop, Shirley, Mgr.-Personnel--Quantic Industries, Inc., San Carlos, CA, pg. 904
Latimer, Matt, Mgr.-Human Resources--Jofco Inc., Jasper, IN, pg. 595
Laughlin, Shari, Mgr.-Human Resources--John Burnham & Co., San Diego, CA, pg. 194
Laukhuff, R.E., Mgr.-Human Resources & Sec.--Raymark Friction Company, Manheim, PA, pg. 914
Lavery, Jane, Mgr.-Personnel--Buck & Pulleyn, Inc., Rochester, NY, pg. 185
Lawrence, Jerry, V.P.-Human Resources--Ivex Packaging Corporation, Lincolnshire, IL, pg. 583
Lazar, Dan, Mgr.-Human Resources--Be-Lo Markets Inc., Norfolk, VA, pg. 212
Lazzaro, Linda, Dir.-Personnel--RHC/Spacemaster Corporation, Melrose Park, IL, pg. 906
Leach, Linda, Mgr.-Personnel--Capsonic Group, Inc., Elgin, IL, pg. 216
Lebel, Ernie, V.P.-Human Resources--Emery Waterhouse Company, Portland, ME, pg. 379
Leberfinger, John, V.P.-Human Resources--Parklane Hosiery Co., Inc., Hasbrouck Heights, NJ, pg. 849
Leblanc, Roger, Mgr.-Personnel--S. Bent & Brothers, Inc., Gardner, MA, pg. 140
Lebo, Mike, Dir.-Human Resources--Lowe's Food Stores, Inc., Winston-Salem, NC, pg. 33
Lebra, Nicholas L., Jr., V.P. & Dir.-Human Resources--MediaNews Group Inc., Houston, TX, pg. 735

Lee, Barbara, V.P.-Human Resources--INTEGRATEC, Atlanta, GA, pg. 573
Lee, James B., Mgr.-Human Resources--Alabama Electric Cooperative, Inc., Andalusia, AL, pg. 28
Lee, Jesse, Chief Fin. Officer--The IDI Group Companies, Arlington, VA, pg. 560
Lee, R.C., V.P.-Personnel & Community Affairs--United States Sugar Corporation, Clewiston, FL, pg. 1137
Lee, Susan, Mgr.-Human Resources--The ERM Group, Exton, PA, pg. 360
Leef, Ann, Dir.-Personnel--Industrial Towel & Uniform, New Berlin, WI, pg. 567
Lefevre, Russ, V.P.-Employee Rels.--RAYOVAC Corporation, Madison, WI, pg. 915
Leffler, Dennis, Mgr.-Personnel--The Keller Manufacturing Co., Inc., Corydon, IN, pg. 621
Lefkow, Frances, V.P.-Human Resources--The Charles Levy Company, Chicago, IL, pg. 672
Lehman, Edgar R., V.P.-Human Resources--Pacific Mutual Life Insurance Company, Newport Beach, CA, pg. 841
Lemeiux, Nancy, Mgr.-Personnel--Mulberry Metal Products, Inc., Union, NJ, pg. 775
Lemieux, Paul, Dir.-Personnel--Peter Pan Bus Lines, Inc., Springfield, MA, pg. 864
Lemmenes, Larry, Mgr.-Field Service--Alto Dairy Cooperative, Waupun, WI, pg. 45
Lemmer, Carole, Controller & Dir.-Human Resources--Shurfine-Central Corp., Northlake, IL, pg. 1001
Lenio, Bruce, V.P.-Human Resources--The Trane Company, La Crosse, WI, pg. 62
Lennon, Frank, Sr. V.P.-Admin.--Golub Corporation, Schenectady, NY, pg. 469
Leoncavallo, Phyllis A., Mgr.-Personnel--Lithograph Printing Company, Inc., Memphis, TN, pg. 678
Lerner, Bennett, V.P.-Personnel--Gateway Apparel, Inc., Saint Louis, MO, pg. 445
Leslie, Mary, Personnel Mgr.--Admiration Hosiery Mills, Inc., Charlotte, NC, pg. 534
Leurch, Frank, Mgr.-Personnel--K-D Lamp Company, Cincinnati, OH, pg. 612
Levenson, Mark, V.P.-Admin., Personnel & Adv.--CBM Industries, Inc., Minneapolis, MN, pg. 199
Levetown, Lewis D., V.P.-Human Resources--Health Management Systems, Inc., New York, NY, pg. 521
Levitt, V., Personnel Admin.--American Envelope of Philadelphia, Philadelphia, PA, pg. 199
Levy, Mara, Opers./Human Resources Dir.--Duval & Partners, Boston, MA, pg. 356
Lewin, R., Mgr.-Personnel--Edwards Engineering Corporation, Pompton Plains, NJ, pg. 370
Lewis, John, Dir.-Personnel--Wurzburg, Inc., Memphis, TN, pg. 1205
Lewison, John, Dir.-Human Resources--American Institute of C.P.A.'s Inc., New York, NY, pg. 56
Lewitzke, Gary, Asst. Corp. Dir.-Indus. Rels.--Pabst Brewing Co., San Antonio, TX, pg. 959
Liacopoulos, Kris, Mgr.-Human Resources--Radix Corporation, Salt Lake City, UT, pg. 909
Lickteig, Anita, Dir.-Personnel--Inland Associates, Olathe, KS, pg. 570
Licon, George, Dir.-Personnel--Clayton Industries Co., El Monte, CA, pg. 253
Lillard, D.H., Dir.-Personnel--Black & Veatch, Kansas City, MO, pg. 154
Lindberg, Charles, Dir.-Personnel--The Direct Marketing Group Inc., New York, NY, pg. 339
Lindgren, L.C., V.P.-Employee Rels.--Miller Electric Mfg. Co., Appleton, WI, pg. 754
Lindsey, Patricia, Dir.-Personnel--American Office Equipment, La Grange, IL, pg. 58
Lingenfelter, Norma J., Supvr.-Personnel--George Transfer, Inc., Parkton, MD, pg. 453
Linn, Don, Mgr.-Human Resources--Scherer Bros. Lumber Company, Minneapolis, MN, pg. 976
Linton, Patricia, Personnel Mgr.--Pioneer Communications of America, Upper Saddle River, NJ, pg. 871
Linton, Richard A., Controller & Dir.-Personnel & Data Processing--Midwest Bottle Gas Company, La Crosse, WI, pg. 277
Linville, Richard, V.P.-Personnel--Harriet & Henderson Yarns, Inc., Henderson, NC, pg. 511
Little, Thomas, Dir.-Human Resources--Sunnyland Foods, Inc., Thomasville, GA, pg. 1061
Lloyd, Spence, V.P.-Opers.--Intermountain Farmers Association, Salt Lake City, UT, pg. 575
Lobo, Fred, Dir.-Human Resources--Cotter & Company, Chicago, IL, pg. 288
Loesch, R.E., V.P.-Human Resources--Standard Lafarge, Canfield, OH, pg. 1036
Lofgren, Candace, Dir.-Personnel--Reed & Barton Corporation, Taunton, MA, pg. 920
Logan, Bonnie, V.P., Dir. Human Resources--Davis, Ball & Colombatto Advertising, Inc., Los Angeles, CA, pg. 318
Long, Ronald, Dir.-Personnel--4C Foods Corporation, Brooklyn, NY, pg. 427
Lopez, Eduardo, Dir.-Personnel--Perez Trading Co. Inc., Miami, FL, pg. 860
Lordon, Joseph, V.P.-Human Resources--Hamburger Hamlets Inc., Sherman Oaks, CA, pg. 1169
Loughlin, L., Sr. V.P.-Personnel--United Refining Company, Warren, PA, pg. 1130
Loughran, Roger, V.P.-Personnel--Amerisure Companies, Detroit, MI, pg. 66
Love, John, Dir.-Personnel--Gilman Paper Co., Saint Marys, GA, pg. 459
Lowe, Walter A., V.P. & Treas.--JRN, Inc., Columbia, TN, pg. 586
Loy, H. Steven, V.P.-Human Resources--Motorists Mutual Insurance Co., Columbus, OH, pg. 773
Lubeach, Norm, Mgr.-Personnel--P/A Industries, Inc., Bloomfield, CT, pg. 835
Lucas, Bill L., Sr. V.P.-Human Resources--Associated Merchandising Corp., New York, NY, pg. 91
Lucas, John, Dir.-Human Resources--Snyder's of Hanover, Inc., Hanover, PA, pg. 1015
Lucenta, Dominic, Dir.-Human Resources--Essex Group, Inc., Fort Wayne, IN, pg. 389
Ludeman, Cynthia, Dir.-Personnel--Nasco, Fort Atkinson, WI, pg. 452
Luis, Jose, Dir.-Human Resources & Mktg.--La Reina, Inc., Los Angeles, CA, pg. 649
Lunn, W., Dir.-Human Resources--Quintana Petroleum Corp., Houston, TX, pg. 905
Lunt, Terry, Dir.-Human Resources--Moorman Mfg. Company, Quincy, IL, pg. 769
Luppert, Eve, V.P., Personnel Dir.--Chiat/Day/Mojo/New York, New York, NY, pg. 244
Luppert, Eve, V.P., Personnel Mgr.--Perkins/Butler Direct Marketing, New York, NY, pg. 244
Lupu, Damon, V.P.-Human Resources--North American Watch Corporation, Lyndhurst, NJ, pg. 812
Luxon, Pam, Mgr.-Personnel--Smith Enterprises, Rock Hill, SC, pg. 1012
Luzzi, Jane, Mgr.-Personnel--McCourt Label Co., Lewis Run, PA, pg. 727
Lyford, Paul, V.P.-Human Resources--Roma Holdings, Dallas, TX, pg. 945
Lyles, Bonnie, V.P.-Admin. & Mngmt. Information Services--Bergquist Company, Inc., Minneapolis, MN, pg. 141
Lynch, Joseph E., Exec. V.P., Chief Exec. & Fin. Officer--Boston Trading Ltd. Inc., Lynn, MA, pg. 168
Lynch, K., Mgr.-Personnel--Oberdorfer Industries, Inc., Syracuse, NY, pg. 819
Lynch, Nancy, Dir.-Human Resources--Perry's Ice Cream Co., Inc., Akron, NY, pg. 863
Lynn, C.E., V.P.-Human Resources--CF Industries, Inc., Long Grove, IL, pg. 200
Lynn, Patrick J., Dir.-Human Resources--Bioproducts, Inc., Brecksville, OH, pg. 152
Lyons, Dan, Controller, Mgr.-Personnel--Moran Industries, Inc., Midlothian, IL, pg. 769
Lyons, Kimberly, Mgr.-Human Resources--Penetone Corp., Tenafly, NJ, pg. 1172
Lyons, Kimberly A., Dir.-Human Resources--West Chemical Products, Inc., Princeton, NJ, pg. 1172
Lyphout, Dan, Quality Process Mgr.--Don E. Williams Co., Rock Island, IL, pg. 1190
Mabile, Sidney, Dir.-Personnel/Maintenance--Westgate Inc., Port Allen, LA, pg. 1182
Mabry, Carlis, Dir.-Personnel--Spencer's Inc., Mount Airy, NC, pg. 1030
MacDonald, Luann, Mgr.-Human Resources--Levi Strauss & Co. (Canada), Inc., Markham,, Canada, pg. 670
Maciejewski, Elizabeth, Dir.-Personnel--Ohmite Manufacturing Company, Skokie, IL, pg. 823
MacKenzie, Vernon, Sr. V.P.-Admin. & Dir.-Human Resources, Personnel Training--Macklanburg-Duncan Co., Oklahoma City, OK, pg. 697
MacNeil, Bonnie, Dir.-Corp. H.R.--Candle Corporation, Santa Monica, CA, pg. 214
MacNichol, Malcolm, Dir.-Personnel--Betac International Corporation, Alexandria, VA, pg. 147
Maddock, Robert, Mgr.-Human Resources--Aquidneck Data Company, Middletown, RI, pg. 320
Madsen, Carolyn K., Mgr.-Human Resources--Kaye Instruments, Inc., Bedford, MA, pg. 619
Magness, Michael L., Mgr.-Personnel--Memphis Light, Gas & Water, Memphis, TN, pg. 738
Malano, Bernard J., Partner & Dir.-Human Resources--KPMG Peat Marwick, New York, NY, pg. 613
Malin, Dan, V.P.-Human Resources--Dalfort Corp., Dallas, TX, pg. 312
Maloy, Pat, Dir.-Personnel--Plasti-Kote Company Inc., Medina, OH, pg. 875
Malthie, Tina, Exec. Dir.-Human Resources & Admin.--Atlanta Market Center, Atlanta, GA, pg. 94
Manak, Donna M., Mgr.-Human Resources--Maecorp Inc., Chicago, IL, pg. 699
Manchester, Lorraine, Admin. Sec.--SGI Inc., Cranston, RI, pg. 962
Manes, Eunice C., V.P.-Human Resources--Blue Cross & Blue Shield of Texas, Inc., Richardson, TX, pg. 160
Manly, Marylyn, Mgr.-Personnel--Harmony Engineering Corporation, Minneapolis, MN, pg. 510
Mann, Donald C., Sr. V.P.-Human Resources--The Prudential Insurance Company of America, Newark, NJ, pg. 896
Mann, Neil David, Asst. V.P.-Personnel--Amtrak-National Railroad Passenger Corp., Washington, DC, pg. 69
Manning, J.D., Dir.-Personnel--Crane & Co., Inc., Dalton, MA, pg. 296
Marcello, Christine, Mgr.-Human Resources--Tropar Mfg. Co., Inc., Florham Park, NJ, pg. 1115
Marchio, Catherine, Mgr., Human Resources--Chuck Ruhr Advertising, Minneapolis, MN, pg. 955
Marcus, Jill, Mgr.-Personnel--Karnak Corporation, Clark, NJ, pg. 617
Marin, Kat, Dir.-Personnel--Sloan Technology, Santa Barbara, CA, pg. 1146
Markey, Arthur, Dir.-Human Resources--Azon Corporation, Johnson City, NY, pg. 105
Markham, Grigsby C., Chief Fin. Officer--Gartner Group, Inc., Stamford, CT, pg. 443
Marshall, Madria, Dir.-Personnel--United Health Plan, Inglewood, CA, pg. 1133
Marsilio, Dale, Dir.-Personnel--Great Scott Advertising Co. Inc., New York, NY, pg. 482
Martel, Lenice, Human Resources Admin.--Anderson Products, Worcester, MA, pg. 1194
Martels, Fred, Dir.-Personnel--Dierbergs Markets Inc., Chesterfield, MO, pg. 337
Martin, Betty, Dir.-Human Resources--Duff-Norton, Charlotte, NC, pg. 1032
Martin, Brent, Dir.-Human Resources--PST Vans, Inc., Salt Lake City, UT, pg. 837
Martin, Bruce, Mgr.-Personnel--G.C. Thorsen, Inc., Rockford, IL, pg. 609
Martin, Dixie, Mgr.-Personnel--Gem-Dandy, Inc., Madison, NC, pg. 447
Martin, George, Dir.-Personnel--Samelson-Leon Company, Inc., Memphis, TN, pg. 968
Martin, Gladys, Chief Fin. Officer, Treas., Sec. & Dir.-Personnel--Welsco Inc., North Little Rock, AR, pg. 1175
Martin, Jack, V.P.-Human Resources--Land O'Lakes, Inc., Arden Hills, MN, pg. 653
Martin, Roger L., V.P.-Human Resources & Community Rels.--Steelcase Inc., Grand Rapids, MI, pg. 1044
Martin, Steve, Dir.-Personnel--Red Spot Paint & Varnish Co., Evansville, IN, pg. 918
Martinelli, R.M., Treas. & Controller--MPO Videotronics, Inc., New York, NY, pg. 693
Martinez, Pat, Dir.-Personnel--Salz Leathers, Inc., Santa Cruz, CA, pg. 968
Mascia, Frank, Mgr.-Human Resources--United Aluminum Corporation, North Haven, CT, pg. 1130
Mason, Charles, V.P.-Human Resources--Sunclipse, Inc., Montebello, CA, pg. 1059
Mason, Dan, V.P.-Opers. & Dir.-Personnel--Capitol Group, Springfield, IL, pg. 215
Masoud, Keith, Dir.-Personnel--Beach Mold & Tool Inc., New Albany, IN, pg. 128
Massucco, R., Personnel Mgr.--Bryant Grinder Corp., Springfield, VT, pg. 468
Masulli, Denise, Coord.-Personnel--Bridgeport Machines, Inc., Bridgeport, CT, pg. 175
Mata, Rhonda, Personnel Admin.--California Hardware Co., City of Industry, CA, pg. 209
Matejka, Glen, Mgr.-Human Resources--Actron Manufacturing Company, Cleveland, OH, pg. 15
Mathias, Larry L., V.P.-Human Resources & Pub. Rels.--American Crystal Sugar Company, Moorhead, MN, pg. 51
Mathias, Susan K., Dir.-Human Resources--JPM Company, Lewisburg, PA, pg. 586
Mathis, Marnie, Dir.-Human Resources--Careers USA Inc., Philadelphia, PA, pg. 218
Matthews, Cyndy, Mgr.-Human Resources--Holt Hosiery Mills, Inc., Burlington, NC, pg. 541
Mattox, John, Dir.-Human Resources--AmTran Corporation, Conway, AR, pg. 69
Mattox, Kathleen, Dir.-Personnel--McDougal, Littell & Company, Evanston, IL, pg. 728
Matzko, Michael N., Dir.-Human Resources--Danis Industries Corporation, Dayton, OH, pg. 314
Maul, K., Dir.-Personnel--L. Robert Kimball & Associates, Ebensburg, PA, pg. 629
Mavro, Angela, V.P.-Human Resources--Rural Metro Corporation, Scottsdale, AZ, pg. 956
Maxey, Paula, Mgr.-Personnel--North American Products Corp., Jasper, IN, pg. 811
Maxwell, Will, Dir.-Personnel--Pawnee Industries, Inc., Wichita, KS, pg. 852
May, Janet, Dir.-Personnel--Texas Refinery Corp., Fort Worth, TX, pg. 1089
Mayer, Clark, Dir.-Human Resources--Speedling Incorporated, Sun City, FL, pg. 1029
Mayer, Steve, Mgr.-Human Resources--United States Bakery, Portland, OR, pg. 1134
Mayone, Lowell, V.P.-Personnel & Services--Hallmark Cards, Inc., Kansas City, MO, pg. 501
Mays, Ted, V.P.-Personnel--Mays Chemical Company, Indianapolis, IN, pg. 725
Mazza, Maxine, Dir.-Human Resources--Gray Printing Co., Fostoria, OH, pg. 479
McAfee, Don, Personnel Dir.--The George E. Failing Company, Enid, OK, pg. 161
McBride, Beverly, Coord.-Human Resources--Sooner Pipe & Supply Corp., Tulsa, OK, pg. 1018
McCaffray, C.M., Mgr.-Human Resources--National Frozen Foods Corp., Seattle, WA, pg. 789
McCarthy, Jean, Office Mgr.--Queen Oxygen Company, Columbus, OH, pg. 904
McCarthy, Michael, Mgr.-Personnel Services--East Kentucky Power Co-op, Winchester, KY, pg. 362
McCartney, W. Earl, V.P. & Treasurer--Peter J. Schmitt Holdings, West Seneca, NY, pg. 976
McCarty, Shirley, Gen. Mgr.-Human Resources Div.--The Aerospace Corporation, El Segundo, CA, pg. 22
McClain, James H., V.P.-Human Resources--Griffith Laboratories Worldwide, Inc., Alsip, IL, pg. 487
McClenahan, D.C., Dir.-Human Resources--Bodine Electric Company, Chicago, IL, pg. 162
McCluskey, M., Mgr.-Personnel--Monarch Luggage Co. Inc., Brooklyn, NY, pg. 765
McCormick, James H., Dir.-Personnel--Wenger Corporation, Owatonna, MN, pg. 1176
McCracken, Thomas F., V.P.-Human Resources--Cogentrix Incorporated, Charlotte, NC, pg. 258
McDade, William, V.P.-Human Resources--Sealy of Minnesota, Inc., Saint Paul, MN, pg. 985
McDade, William, V.P.-Human Resources--Sealy Connecticut, Inc., Oakville, CT, pg. 985
McDade, William J., V.P.-Human Resources--Sealy Mattress Company of Puerto Rico, Rio Piedras, PR, pg. 985
McDade, William J., V.P.-Human Resources--Ohio-Sealy Mattress Mfg. Co., Inc., Randolph, MA, pg. 985
McDade, William J., V.P.-Human Resources--Ohio-Sealy Mattress Manufacturing Co.-Fort Worth, Richland Hills, TX, pg. 985
McDade, William J., V.P.-Human Resources--Ohio-Sealy Mattress Manufacturing Co.-Houston, Brenham, TX, pg. 985
McDade, William J., V.P.-Human resources--The Stearns & Foster Bedding Company, Cleveland, OH, pg. 985
McDade, William J., V.P.-Human Resources--Sealy, Inc., Cleveland, OH, pg. 985
McDade, William J., V.P.-Human Resources--The Stearns & Foster Upholstery Furniture Company, Cleveland, OH, pg. 985
McDade, William J., V.P.-Human Resources--Sealy Mattress Company of Albany, Inc., Albany, NY, pg. 985

McDade, William J., V.P.-Human Resources--Sealy of Maryland & Virginia, Inc., Williamsport, MD, pg. 985
McDade, William J., V.P.-Human Resources--Sealy Mattress Company of Illinois, Batavia, IL, pg. 985
McDade, William J., V.P.-Human Resources--Sealy Mattress Company of Kansas City, Inc., Kansas City, KS, pg. 985
McDade, William J., V.P.-Human Resources--Sealy Mattress Company of Memphis, Memphis, TN, pg. 985
McDade, William J., V.P.-Human Resources--The Ohio Mattress Company Licensing And Components Group, Cleveland, OH, pg. 985
McDade, William J., V.P.-Huamn Resources--Sealy Mattress Company of Michigan, Inc., Taylor, MI, pg. 985
McDade, William J., V.P.-Human Resources--Stearns & Foster Upholstery Furniture Co., Columbiana, OH, pg. 985
McDade, William J., V.P.-Huaman Resources--Stearns & Foster Upholstery Furniture Co., Pontotoc, MS, pg. 985
McDermott, Ruth N., Mgr.-Personnel & Communications--Distribution America, Des Plaines, IL, pg. 340
McDonald, Charles H., V.P.-Human Resources--Allied Mutual Insurance Company, Des Moines, IA, pg. 38
McDonald, Joe, Mgr.-Personnel--Hoffco, Inc., Richmond, IN, pg. 537
McDonald, Joe, Mgr.-Personnel--Comet Industries, Richmond, IN, pg. 537
McDonald, Lynn, Mgr.-Personnel--Gertrude Hawk Chocolates, Inc., Troop, PA, pg. 517
McDowell, Gloria A., Dir.-Human Resources & Sec.--Golden State Mutual Life Insurance Company, Los Angeles, CA, pg. 467
McElfresh, Jim, Mgr.-Personnel--Behlen Mfg. Co., Columbus, NE, pg. 132
McEwen, Ellie, Mgr.-Human Resources--Forms Corporation Of America, Spring Grove, IL, pg. 1187
Mcfall, Carlyn, Dir.-Personnel--Barber Dairies, Inc., Birmingham, AL, pg. 119
McFall, Carlyn, Personnel Dir.--Barber Ice Cream Company, Birmingham, AL, pg. 119
McGee, Dennis, Sec.--Tupman Thurlow Co. Inc., New Rochelle, NY, pg. 1119
McGee, Gary C., Dir.-Personnel--North American Royalties, Inc., Chattanooga, TN, pg. 811
McGee, Gary C., Dir.-Personnel--The Wheland Foundry Div., Chattanooga, TN, pg. 812
McGovern, John R., Mgr.-Employee Benefits & Human Resources--Sunkist Growers, Inc., Sherman Oaks, CA, pg. 1060
McGraw, Kay, Dir.-Human Resources--The Virginian-Pilot and The Ledger Star, Norfolk, VA, pg. 656
McGregor, Bob, Dir.-Human Resources--Grandy's, Inc., Lewisville, TX, pg. 476
McGuin, Dennis, Dir.-Personnel--AGI Inc., Melrose Park, IL, pg. 4
McGuire, Bud, Mgr.-Human Resources--Comlinear Corporation, Fort Collins, CO, pg. 268
McGuirl, Joy A., Dir.-Personnel--George S. May International Company, Park Ridge, IL, pg. 723
McGurl, Maureen, V.P.-Human Resources--Pathmark, Woodbridge, NJ, pg. 1064
McHenry, Edith, V.P.-Admin. Services--Sealaska Corporation, Juneau, AK, pg. 984
McKain, Frank L., Mgr.-Human Resources--Steelox Systems, Inc., Mason, OH, pg. 1044
McKelvey, John, Dir.-Human Resources--WinCup, Phoenix, AZ, pg. 1195
McKenna, Joe, Dir.-Personnel--Medical Laboratory Automation, Inc., Pleasantville, NY, pg. 735
McKiernan, Robert E., V.P.-Human Resources--The American Stock Exchange, New York, NY, pg. 62
McKnight, William, V.P.-Human Resources--Bank Shares, Inc., Minneapolis, MN, pg. 117
McKowen, Elizabeth J., V.P.-Human Resources--The Commercial Bank, Delphos, OH, pg. 268
McLaughlin, Mike, Dir.-Adv. & Pub. Rels.--North Central Life Insurance Companies, Saint Paul, MN, pg. 813
McLean, Arlis A., V.P.-Human Resources--Fellowes Manufacturing Co., Itasca, IL, pg. 405
McLeod, Howard, V.P.-Human Resources--J.H. Harvey Company, Nashville, GA, pg. 515
McMahon, Jody, Dir.-Personnel--Apex Oil Company, Inc., Saint Louis, MO, pg. 78
McMahon, Margaret, Dir.-Pub. Rels. & Personnel--Shonac Corporation, Columbus, OH, pg. 1000
McManus, R.T., V.P.-Distr. & Warehousing, Gen. Mgr. & Dir.-Personnel--Walter J. Black, Inc., Port Washington, NY, pg. 154
McMorine, Wendy M., Mgr.-Human Resources--Brix Maritime Co., Portland, OR, pg. 177
McMullen, Dan, Dir.-Human Resources--Precision Twist Drill Co., Crystal Lake, IL, pg. 885
McMullen, R.W., V.P.-Human Resources--Bell Packaging Corporation, Marion, IN, pg. 135
McMurray, Dennis, Mgr.-Employee Relations--National Cooperative Refinery Association, McPherson, KS, pg. 787
McNally, Michael, V.P.-Human Resources--The Stiffel Company, Chicago, IL, pg. 1049
McNamara, Terri, Mgr.-Personnel--American TV & Appliance of Madison, Inc., Madison, WI, pg. 65
McNicholl, Anne, Dir.-Admin. Services--Friedman, Eisenstein, Raemer & Schwartz, Chicago, IL, pg. 433
McNish, Russ, Personnel Mgr.--First American Metro Corp., McLean, VA, pg. 412
McPhail, John R., Div. Mgr.-Human Resources--Nebraska Public Power District, Columbus, NE, pg. 796
McPherson, Sam, V.P.-Human Resources--Raley's, West Sacramento, CA, pg. 910
McWilliams, Marion J., Dir.-Human Resources--McWilliams Forge Co., Rockaway, NJ, pg. 733
Meador, Janice, V.P.-Corp. Services & Personnel Dir.--Kwik-Kopy Corp., Cypress, TX, pg. 647
Mechler, Ralph E., Dir.-Human Resources--Compuware Corporation, Farmington Hills, MI, pg. 271
Meehan, Carol, Dir., Human Resources--Sefton Associates Inc., Grand Rapids, MI, pg. 987
Mehler, Mark, Dir.-Personnel--Webcraft Technologies, Inc., North Brunswick, NJ, pg. 1171
Mehrhoff, Malinda, Dir.-Human Resources--Dakota Electric Association, Farmington, MN, pg. 312
Meier, Patty, Dir.-Personnel--Kingsley Machine Co., Hollywood, CA, pg. 632
Meinzer, Anita, Mgr.-Human Resources--Lavelle Aircraft Company, Philadelphia, PA, pg. 661
Melanson, Anne M., Exec. V.P., Dir. Human Resources--Backer Spielvogel Bates Worldwide, Inc., New York, NY, pg. 108
Melchi, Anne, Dir.-Personnel--The Harter Group, Sturgis, MI, pg. 513
Meliker, Gary, V.P.-Human Resources--Textilease Corporation, Beltsville, MD, pg. 1090
Melnick, Dean, Dir.-Personnel--Ingram Paper Company, City of Industry, CA, pg. 569
Melore, Neil A., V.P.-Human Resources--Uniroyal Chemical Company, Inc., Middlebury, CT, pg. 1129
Melton, Lou Ann, Mgr.-Payroll & Benefits--Electrical Insulation Suppliers, Hillside, IL, pg. 374
Mendoza, Ed, Supvr.-Payroll--Door Store, Inc., Washington, DC, pg. 346
Meng, J., Chief Fin. Officer--David Langer & Co., Inc., Hollywood, CA, pg. 657
Mercer, Danny, Dir.-Personnel & Safety--McCrory Construction Co., Inc., Columbia, SC, pg. 728
Merek, Steve, V.P.-Human Resources--Brian Center Management Corporation, Hickory, NC, pg. 175
Merrick, Frank, V.P.-Human Resources--Dry Storage Corporation, Des Plaines, IL, pg. 350
Merriweather, Donna, Dir.-Human Resources--Mountain Valley Spring Company, Hot Springs, AR, pg. 968
Meserve, Richard, Mgr.-Human Resources--Humiston-Keeling, Inc., Chicago, IL, pg. 552
Meske, Arthur M., Dir.-Personnel--Amsted Industries Incorporated, Chicago, IL, pg. 68
Messana, Stephen, Sr. V.P., Dir. Human Resources-WW--Young & Rubicam Inc., New York, NY, pg. 1210
Messner, Ronald E., V.P.-Human Resources--Luria Bros. Division, Cleveland, OH, pg. 275
Metcalf, Frank, Dir.-Employee Benefits--Monroc, Inc., Salt Lake City, UT, pg. 766
Metz, J.G., Dir.-Personnel--Conwood Company L.P., Memphis, TN, pg. 281
Metzler, David, V.P.-Human Resources--Bahlsen Inc., Cary, NC, pg. 114
Mewer, Wes, Dir.-Personnel--ACO Inc., Farmington Hills, MI, pg. 2
Meyer, John C., V.P.-Human Resources--Northwestern Steel & Wire Co., Sterling, IL, pg. 815
Meyer, Richard, V.P.-Human Resources--Amtran, Inc., Indianapolis, IN, pg. 69
Meyers, Charles A., V.P.-Human Resources--Blue Cross & Blue Shield of Illinois, Chicago, IL, pg. 160
Meyers, Jan, Mgr.-Personnel--UDL Laboratories, Inc., Rockford, IL, pg. 1072
Micelotti, Sandra, Dir.-Personnel--Jet Spray Corp., Norwood, MA, pg. 593
Michael, G. Clark, Dir.-Industrial Rels.--Collins & Aikman Textile Group, Charlotte, NC, pg. 262
Michaels, Thomas, Corp. Services Mngmt.--Judd's Incorporated, Washington, DC, pg. 608
Michalak, Norbert, V.P. & Dir.-Human Resources--Baird & Warner Inc., Chicago, IL, pg. 114
Michalcewicz, Joseph H., V.P.-Human Resources--Duchossois Industries, Inc., Elmhurst, IL, pg. 350
Michel, Charles, Dir.-Human Resources--Southern Ohio Fabricators, Inc., Cincinnati, OH, pg. 1022
Michener, Sally R., Sec. & Dir.-Personnel & Pub. Rels.--Scott Specialty Gases, Inc., Plumsteadville, PA, pg. 983
Mihm, Curt, Mgr.-Human Resources--Peerless Chain Co., Winona, MN, pg. 855
Mika, W.J., V.P.-Indus. Rels.--Dan River Inc., Danville, VA, pg. 313
Miklas, Jenny, Dir.-Personnel--Henri's Food Products Co., Inc., Milwaukee, WI, pg. 530
Mikuta, John, Dir.-Personnel--Mitchel & Scot Machine Co., Inc., Indianapolis, IN, pg. 761
Milas, Joseph, Treas.--Plibrico Co., Chicago, IL, pg. 877
Miller, David R., Dir.-Human Resources--T.D. Williamson, Inc., Tulsa, OK, pg. 1192
Miller, Dean A., V.P.-Industrial Rels.--BeefAmerica Operating Co., Inc., Omaha, NE, pg. 131
Miller, Donna, Mgr.-Human Resources--Carnegie Associates, Inc., Cleveland, OH, pg. 222
Miller, Edward, V.P.-Human Resources--Tri Valley Growers Inc., San Francisco, CA, pg. 1111
Miller, Gregg P., V.P.-Indus. Rels.--Dwyer Instruments Inc., Michigan City, IN, pg. 356
Miller, Kenneth, Dir.-Personnel--Leviton Mfg. Co., Inc., Little Neck, NY, pg. 671
Miller, Linda J., V.P.-Human Resources--Dodson Group, Kansas City, MO, pg. 342
Miller, Patricia, Dir.-Human Resources--Dietrich's Milk Products, Inc., Reading, PA, pg. 337
Miller, Richard, V.P.-Human Resources--Desa International, Inc., Bowling Green, KY, pg. 331
Miller, Thomas, Mgr.-Personnel--Berger Transfer & Storage, Inc., Saint Paul, MN, pg. 141
Miller, Thomas E., Mgr.-Personnel--The C. P. Hall Company, Chicago, IL, pg. 501
Miller, Wayne O., V.P.-Personnel--Fairbanks Morse Pump Corporaton, Kansas City, KS, pg. 397
Mills, Charles A., V.P.-Human Resources--Hunt Oil Company, Dallas, TX, pg. 553
Mills, Monica, Mgr.-Human Resources--Stihl Inc., Virginia Beach, VA, pg. 1049
Mills, Nancy, Mgr.-Personnel--Stanco Metal Products, Inc., Grand Haven, MI, pg. 1035
Milton, Kent, Dir.-Personnel--Rice Food Markets Inc., Houston, TX, pg. 931
Minda, Andrew H., Dir.-Personnel--The Elwell-Parker Electric Co., Cleveland, OH, pg. 378
Minkin, Herbert E., V.P.-Human Resources--Schottenstein Stores Corporation, Columbus, OH, pg. 978
Mitchell, Becky, Dir.-Personnel--Associated Grocers of Alabama, Inc., Birmingham, AL, pg. 90
Mitchell, Elvira J., Mgr.-Personnel & Pub. Rels.--Navajo Forest Products Industries, Navajo, NM, pg. 796
Mitchell, Emily, Mgr.-Personnel--Hoffritz for Cutlery, New York, NY, pg. 538
Mitchell, Jack, Dir.-Personnel--Peter J. Schmitt Co., Inc., West Seneca, NY, pg. 977
Mitchell, James, Dir.-Personnel--Malloy Lithographing Inc., Ann Arbor, MI, pg. 703
Mitchell, Joseph, Personnel Dir.--Barnhardt Manufacturing Co., Charlotte, NC, pg. 120
Mitchell, Richard, Chief Admin. Officer & Sr. V.P.--Hy-Vee Food Stores Incorporated, Chariton, IA, pg. 556
Mitchell, Robert, V.P.-Human Resources--Central Parking Corp., Nashville, TN, pg. 234
Mitchell, Robert, V.P.-Human Resources--Central Parking Corp., Nashville, TN, pg. 234
Moffat, Kenneth M., Sr. V.P.-Personnel--Amica Mutual Insurance Co., Providence, RI, pg. 66
Mogler, Rick, Dir.-Personnel--Seigle's Home & Building Centers, Elgin, IL, pg. 987
Mohr, Christy, Personnel Dir.--Modern Equipment Co., Inc., Port Washington, WI, pg. 32
Molloy, Michelle, Mgr.-Personnel--Marcel Dekker, Inc., New York, NY, pg. 325
Montana, Mary Jo, V.P.-Admin. & Human Rels.--Keroff & Rosenberg Advertising Inc., Chicago, IL, pg. 624
Montgomery, Jennifer, Dir.-Human Resources--Holland Mark Martin, Burlington, MA, pg. 539
Montroy, Marie, Dir.-Human Resources--Ivex Packaging Corporation, Lincolnshire, IL, pg. 583
Moore, Elmer, Dir.-Human Resources--Watlow Electric Manufacturing Company, Saint Louis, MO, pg. 1167
Moore, Joe, Dir.-Human Resources--Weber-Stephen Products, Palatine, IL, pg. 1171
Moore, Julius, Dir.-Human Resources--Worsley Companies Inc., Wilmington, NC, pg. 1204
Moore, Ralph, Dir.-Human Resources--Liberty Glass Company, Sapulpa, OK, pg. 674
Moore, Ronald L., Dir.-Personnel--Reeves Southeastern Corporation, Tampa, FL, pg. 921
Moran, James G., Sr. V.P.-Human Resources--Regal Ware, Inc., Kewaskum, WI, pg. 921
Moran, M. Marcus, Jr., Treas. & Dir.-Personnel--W.E. Aubuchon Co., Inc., Westminster, MA, pg. 97
Morcone, P.M., Mgr.-Human Resources--Koehler Manufacturing Company, Marlborough, MA, pg. 639
Moreau, Leslie, Dir.-Human Res.--Elixir Industries, Gardena, CA, pg. 376
Morero, Ernie, Mgr.-Human Resources--Ruiz Food Products, Inc., Dinuba, CA, pg. 955
Morgan, Kenneth L., V.P.-Personnel--Stone & Thomas, Wheeling, WV, pg. 1051
Morgenstern, Barbara, Exec. V.P.--Nuarc Company, Inc., Niles, IL, pg. 817
Morris, Jim, Mgr.-Personnel--Sealy Mattress Company, Memphis, TN, pg. 986
Morris, Paul, V.P.-Human Resources & Controller--Arcola Wire Company, Branford, CT, pg. 81
Morrison, L. Bryan, V.P.-Human Resources--Universal Cooperatives, Inc., Minneapolis, MN, pg. 1138
Morse, Robert, V.P.-Human Resources--Spartan Stores Inc., Grand Rapids, MI, pg. 1026
Morton, Sandi, V.P.-Opers.--Visible Changes, Houston, TX, pg. 1153
Moschel, Marilyn, Dir.-Human Resources--Metro Information Services, Virginia Beach, VA, pg. 743
Mosher, Pamela, Mgr.-Pub. Rels.--Charles Dunn Company-Realtors, Los Angeles, CA, pg. 353
Mounts, Allen, V.P.-Human Resources--Keller Crescent Co., Evansville, IN, pg. 620
Mounts, Allen, V.P., Human Resources--Keller-Crescent Co., Evansville, IN, pg. 621
Mowrer, Gale, Mgr.-Human Resources--Applied Microsystems Corporation, Redmond, WA, pg. 79
Moyers, Thomas R., V.P.-Human Resources--Perdue Farms Inc., Salisbury, MD, pg. 860
Moylan, John, V.P.-Human Resources--Dayton Rogers Mfg. Co., Minneapolis, MN, pg. 321
Mueller, Helga, Controller & Personnel Mgr.--Hoechst Ceramtec North America, Inc., Mansfield, MA, pg. 537
Mueller, Marnie W., Sr. V.P.-Corp. Resources--Connecticut Mutual Life Insurance Company, Hartford, CT, pg. 274
Mullenix, Louis, Mgr.-Personnel--Penrod Drilling Corporation, Dallas, TX, pg. 859
Mullinax, Larry, Treas., Dir.-Pur., Data Processing, & Personnel--Ed Mullinax Ford, Inc., Amherst, OH, pg. 775
Mulvey, John, Dir.-Human Resources--Bill Communications, Inc., New York, NY, pg. 150
Muncy, Julie, Dir.-Human Res.--Caldwell VanRiper Inc., Indianapolis, IN, pg. 209
Munoz, Joseph, V.P.-Human Resources--Meyer Jewelers, Taylor, MI, pg. 746
Murawski, Hank, Mgr.-Human Resources--Beckwith Machinery Company, Murrysville, PA, pg. 131
Murphy, David L., Jr., V.P.-Retail Human Resources--John Hancock Mutual Life Insurance Company, Boston, MA, pg. 595
Murphy, James, Dir.-Human Resources--Educational Publishing Corporation, Oak Lawn, IL, pg. 369
Murphy, John, V.P.-Personnel--Wisconsin Dairies Cooperative, Baraboo, WI, pg. 1197
Murphy, Michael, V.P.-Personnel--Diversified Products Corporation, Opelika, AL, pg. 1193
Murphy, Patrick, Dir.-Human Resources--Western Regional Off Track Betting, Batavia, NY, pg. 1181
Murphy, Virginia, Mgr.-Human Res.--Taracorp, Inc., Atlanta, GA, pg. 1078

Murray, Cathy M., Dir.-Personnel/Insurance--McAnally Enterprises, Inc., Yucaipa, CA, pg. 726
Murray, Eugene, Dir.-Personnel--Austin Co., Inc., Greeneville, TN, pg. 98
Murray, Lee, Sr. V.P.-Personnel--The American Stock Exchange, New York, NY, pg. 62
Murray, Mary Lee, Mgr.-Personnel--Creation Windows of Indiana, Inc., Elkhart, IN, pg. 297
Murray, Michael, V.P.-Employee Benefits--MTD Products, Inc., Valley City, OH, pg. 694
Murro, John M., V.P.-Human Resources--Lebhar-Friedman, Inc., New York, NY, pg. 665
Murtaugh, Francine M., V.P.-Human Res.--Smith Pipe & Steel Co., Phoenix, AZ, pg. 1014
Murtaugh, Francine M., Dir.-Personnel--Smith Pipe & Steel Co., Phoenix, AZ, pg. 1014
Muscarrella, Betty, Dir.-Personnel--Atlantic to Pacific Bedding Corp., Bronx, NY, pg. 95
Musick, Larry, V.P.-Admin. & Human Resources--The Berkline Corporation, Morristown, TN, pg. 285
Myers, Shelly, Ass't. V.P.-Human Resources--Wasserstrom Company, Columbus, OH, pg. 1167
Myles, Debra W., Human Resources--Coca Cola Bottling Co. United, Inc., Birmingham, AL, pg. 257
Myles, Henry, V.P.-Human Resources--Communications International, Norcross, GA, pg. 269
Nagel, Thomas, Dir.-Personnel & Labor Rels.--King Kullen Grocery Co., Inc., Westbury, NY, pg. 630
Nagle, Bruce, Mgr.-Human Resources--U.S. Metalsource Corporation, Coraopolis, PA, pg. 1136
Nakaji, Sandra, Dir.-Human Res.--Integral Systems, Walnut Creek, CA, pg. 572
Nalette, Ron, Mgr.-Human Resources--ASC Incorporated, Southgate, MI, pg. 7
Napier, Margaret, V.P.-Human Resources--CPS Corporation, Franklin, TN, pg. 428
Nastasuk, Mary, Mgr.-Personnel--Jandy Industries, Novato, CA, pg. 589
Natale, Anthony G., V.P.-Human Resources--Day & Zimmermann, Inc., Radnor, PA, pg. 320
Nattier, Robert, Chief Oper. Officer, Chief Fin. Officer & Gen. Mgr.--Mid-Kansas Co-op Association, Moundridge, KS, pg. 750
Neal, Belinda, Mgr.-Personnel--Dupey Management Corp., Irving, TX, pg. 354
Neal, Ron, Dir.-Personnel--Field Packing Company, Owensboro, KY, pg. 409
Neer, Fred J., V.P.-Human Resources--Ace Hardware Corporation, Oak Brook, IL, pg. 12
Nehrkorn, William H., V.P., Sec. & Gen. Counsel--The Heil Co., Chattanooga, TN, pg. 525
Neil, Diane, Dir.-Personnel & Pur.--Dallas Peterbilt, Inc., Irving, TX, pg. 312
Nelson, Beverly, Dir.-Human Resources--Middlesex/Patriot General Insurance Companies, Concord, MA, pg. 751
Nelson, Larry, Mgr.-Personnel--Honorbuilt Industries, Inc., Minneapolis, KS, pg. 542
Nelson, Leslie, Dir.-Human Resources--National Live Stock & Meat Board, Chicago, IL, pg. 792
Nelson, Marcella, V.P.-Human Resources--The Faxon Company, Inc., Westwood, MA, pg. 404
Nelson, Scott, Dir.-Personnel--Sloan Valve Company, Franklin Park, IL, pg. 1010
Nelson, Steve, Dir.-Personnel--Davis Industries Inc., Detroit, MI, pg. 318
Nelson, Thomas, Mgr.-Personnel--TimeMed Labeling Systems, Inc., Burr Ridge, IL, pg. 1098
Nelson, Tom, Dir.-Human Resources-Springfield Div.--Associated Wholesale Grocers, Inc., Kansas City, KS, pg. 92
Nemirow, Sherri, V.P., Human Resources--Hamilton, Carver & Lee, Inc., Chicago, IL, pg. 503
Nevers, Bruce, V.P.-Human Resources--Newly Weds Foods Inc., Chicago, IL, pg. 804
Nichols, Nick, V.P.-Personnel--Fitchburg Coated Products Inc., Scranton, PA, pg. 1083
Nicholson, Ann, Mgr.-Personnel--The Buschman Co., Cincinnati, OH, pg. 196
Niedziekski, Robert, Dir.-Human Resources--Tighe Industries, Inc., York, PA, pg. 1097
Nikkel, Vernon, V.P.-Personnel--Excel Industries, Inc., Hesston, KS, pg. 392
Nimesheim, Frank, V.P.-Human Resources--Globe Glass & Mirror Co., Chicago, IL, pg. 463
Nish, William, Dir.-Personnel--Affiliated Food Distributors, Scranton, PA, pg. 23
Nolingberg, Jack M., V.P.-Indus. Rels.--Riviana Foods Inc., Houston, TX, pg. 937
Northcut, J., Dir.-Personnel--American Manufacturing Co. (TN), Chattanooga, TN, pg. 58
Nugent, Nancy, V.P.- Human Resources--Berlitz International, Inc., Princeton, NJ, pg. 142
O'Brien, Jim, Mgr.-Personnel--Danbury Printing & Lithograph, Inc., Danbury, CT, pg. 313
O'Brien, John, Dir.-Human Resources--Charles River Data Systems, Inc., Framingham, MA, pg. 240
O'Brien, John D., Mng. Partner, V.P.-Human Resources--Borg-Warner Corporation, Chicago, IL, pg. 165
O'Connell, Leonard, Mgr.-Corp. Personnel--SK Hand Tool Corp., Chicago, IL, pg. 963
O'Connell, Leonard D., Dir.-Personnel--SK Hand Tool Corp., Chicago, IL, pg. 963
O'Connor, John, Chief Fin. Officer & Controller--Marketing Communications, Lenexa, KS, pg. 709
O'Connor, Paul R., Sec., Treas. & Chief Fin. Officer--F.A. Wilhelm Construction Co., Inc., Indianapolis, IN, pg. 1189
O'Donnol, John, Dir.-Human Resources--Fairfax Lumber & Millwork Company Inc., Springfield, VA, pg. 397
O'Grady, Sharon, Dir.-Indus. Rels.--Jones Apparel Group, Inc., Bristol, PA, pg. 602
O'Hare, Sally, Dir.-Human Resources/Taren--Cole of California, Los Angeles, CA, pg. 1079
O'Kelly, Eugene, V.P.-Human Resources--Maynard Steel Casting Company, Milwaukee, WI, pg. 725
O'Leary, David C., Mng. Dir.-Human Resources--The First Boston Corporation, New York, NY, pg. 203
O'Malley, Thomas, V.P.-Indus. Rels.--Cole Business Furniture, York, PA, pg. 608
O'Neal, John T., Dir.-Personnel--Malcolm Pirnie, Inc., White Plains, NY, pg. 872
O'Neal, Patrick, Dir.-Human Resources & Personnel--The Chardon Rubber Co., Chardon, OH, pg. 239
O'Neal, Tom, V.P.-Personnel--Henco, Inc., Selmer, TN, pg. 528
O'Neil, James E., Jr., V.P.-Mfg.--Kingsbury Corporation, Keene, NH, pg. 631
O'Neill, Shirley, Personnel Dir.--BIW Cable Systems, Inc., North Dighton, MA, pg. 106
O'Reilly, Richard, V.P.-Human Recources--Sweetheart Cup Co., Inc., Chicago, IL, pg. 1067
O'Shields, Brent, Dir.-Employee Rels.--Platt Saco Lowell Corporation, Greenville, SC, pg. 876
Oatman, Carolyn, Dir.-Information Services--Harte-Hanks Communications, Inc., San Antonio, TX, pg. 513
Obele, Gary, Dir.-Human Resources--Acrometal Companies, Inc., Brainerd, MN, pg. 14
Odom, Charles, Gen. Mgr.-Personnel--Warren Distributing Corp., Raleigh, NC, pg. 1164
Oechsner, Kenneth E., Dir.-Human Resources--Mayville Metal Products Division, Mayville, WI, pg. 275
Oetzel, Brian K., V.P.-Personnel--Hart Graphics Inc., Austin, TX, pg. 513
Oliverre, Grace, Dir.-Personnel--Whaling Industries, Inc., Fall River, MA, pg. 1183
Olsewski, Paul, V.P.-Opers. & Corp. Sec.--SB Entertainment Inc., New Providence, NJ, pg. 960
Olson, Carl, V.P.-Admin. & Human Resources--J. L. Hammett Company, Braintree, MA, pg. 504
Olson, Tina, Dir.-Personnel--CRK Advertising, New York, NY, pg. 203
Ondrias, Paul, Mgr.-Personnel--Adams Extract Co., Inc., Austin, TX, pg. 16
Ontra, Beth, Human Resources--The Highland Group, Inc., Southport, CT, pg. 534
Oorlog, Richard F., V.P.-Human Resources--Snyder's Drug Stores, Inc., Minnetonka, MN, pg. 1015
Opel, Peter, V.P.-Human Resources--Whataburger, Inc., Corpus Christi, TX, pg. 1184
Oren, Beverly J., V.P.-Human Resources--Dart Transit Company, Inc., Eagan, MN, pg. 316
Orewiler, David, Mgr.-Human Resources--Robbins, Inc., Cincinnati, OH, pg. 938
Orgell, Judi, V.P.-Human Resources--Paddock Publications, Inc., Arlington Heights, IL, pg. 842
Orlich, Margie, Personnel Mgr.--Career Club Shirt Co., New York, NY, pg. 898
Orr, L. Homer, Comptroller & Personnel Dir.--S-G Metals Industries, Inc., Kansas City, KS, pg. 962
Ortlieb, John K., Personnel Dir.--Lear Siegler Seymour Corp., Seymour, IN, pg. 664
Osam, Dodie, Dir.-Personnel--Coleman Dairy Inc., Little Rock, AR, pg. 261
Osborne, Carolyn, Sec. & Dir.-Personnel--Plastigage Corporation, Jackson, MI, pg. 876
Osborne, Patrick, V.P.-Human Resources--Century Products Co., Macedonia, OH, pg. 235
Osburn, Blaine, Mgr.-Human Resources--World Title Company, Burbank, CA, pg. 1203
Ostling, Paul, Vice Chm.-Human Resources--Ernst & Young, New York, NY, pg. 387
Otero, Gilberto, Mgr.-Personnel--Goya Foods, Inc., Secaucus, NJ, pg. 474
Ott, Charlotte, Dir.-Personnel--Raymond Rosen Co., Conshohocken, PA, pg. 948
Ott, William, Controller--Pullman Industries, Inc., Madison Heights, MI, pg. 900
Otto, James, Mgr.-Human Resources--Wrought Washer Mfg., Inc., Milwaukee, WI, pg. 1205
Otto, Larry, Dir.-Personnel--Spelling Entertainment Group, Inc., Cincinnati, OH, pg. 54
Otto, Lawrence J., Mgr.-Human Resources--American Financial Corporation, Cincinnati, OH, pg. 52
Ouellette, Judy, Mgr.-Human Resources--Lawrence Pumps, Inc., Lawrence, MA, pg. 662
Ovey, Sharon, V.P.-Human Resources--Contico International, Inc., Saint Louis, MO, pg. 278
Owen, Kay, Asst. V.P.-Human Resource Devel.--Lutheran Brotherhood, Minneapolis, MN, pg. 688
Owens, Jim, Dir.-Human Rels.--Leach Corporation, Buena Park, CA, pg. 663
Owens, LaSandra, Dir.-Personnel--Pressure Systems, Hampton, VA, pg. 888
Owens, Sherry, Dir.-Personnel--Tanner Co. Inc., Rutherfordton, NC, pg. 1078
Pacchini, Carlo, V.P.-Human Resources--Nylon Corporation Of America, Manchester, NH, pg. 818
Pack, Eileen, Dir.-Personnel--Donnkenny, Inc., New York, NY, pg. 345
Page, William N., Mng. Dir.-Admin. & Sec.--Insignia Financial Group, Inc., Greenville, SC, pg. 571
Palm, Kenneth W., Dir.-Personnel--U.S. Construction Co., Inc., Columbia, SC, pg. 1135
Palmer, Diane, Dir.-Personnel--Modulite Corporation, Compton, CA, pg. 763
Palmer, Page, V.P.-Human Resources--John Hancock Mutual Life Insurance Company, Boston, MA, pg. 595
Palo, R., V.P.-Personnel--Coca-Cola Bottling Co. of Chicago, Niles, IL, pg. 257
Palumbo, Robert, V.P.-Personnel--New York City Off Track Betting Corp., New York, NY, pg. 802
Palumbo, Thomas, Dir.-Personnel--Warren Equities Inc., New York, NY, pg. 1164
Panarale, Joe, V.P.-Employee Rels.--Cummins-Allison Corp., Mount Prospect, IL, pg. 305
Panocha, Bernice, Dir.-Human Resources--Farley Candy Company, Chicago, IL, pg. 399
Papaelias, Anne, V.P.-Human Resources--Curtis Instruments, Inc., Mount Kisco, NY, pg. 305
Papke, Robert, Dir.-Personnel--Marine Travelift, Inc., Sturgeon Bay, WI, pg. 707
Paquette, Kap, Mgr.-Human Resources--Alloy Products Corporation, Waukesha, WI, pg. 41
Parish, Don, Dir.-Personnel--Arkansas Electric Cooperatives Inc., Little Rock, AR, pg. 83
Parks, Frank, Dir.-Personnel--Owen Steel Co., Inc., Columbia, SC, pg. 834
Parlee, G.A., Dir.-Human Resources--Statler Industries, Medford, MA, pg. 1041
Parpan, Donald, Mgr.-Human Resources--Troy Mills, Inc., Troy, NH, pg. 1116
Parr, Eileen, Dir.-Personnel & Office Mgr.--Capitol Metals Processing, Inc., Torrance, CA, pg. 216
Parrott, Rex, V.P.-Human Resources--Wyandot Inc., Marion, OH, pg. 1205
Parsons, Charlene, V.P.-Human Resources--Provident Mutual Life Insurance Co., Philadelphia, PA, pg. 896
Pasbrig, Dave, V.P.-Personnel--Mayville Engineering Co., Inc., Mayville, WI, pg. 725
Paschal, Annelle, Dir.-Human Resources & Pub. Rels.--U.S. Can Company, Oak Brook, IL, pg. 1134
Pasek, Mary Joe, Asst. V.P.-Admin. & Personnel--Calcot, Ltd., Bakersfield, CA, pg. 208
Patryla, Jim, Dir.-Human Resources--Golden West Broadcasters, Los Angeles, CA, pg. 467
Patten, D., Dir.-Human Resources--S & C Electric Canada Ltd., Toronto,, Canada, pg. 959
Pattison, Albert J., V.P.-Human Resources--Aloha Airgroup, Inc., Honolulu, HI, pg. 43
Pattison, Albert J., V.P.-Human Resources--Aloha Airlines, Inc., Honolulu, HI, pg. 43
Paty, JoAnne, V.P.-Human Resources--The Paty Company, Piney Flats, TN, pg. 852
Paul, Donn, Dir.-Personnel Admin.--McCarty Farms, Magee, MS, pg. 727
Paul, Pete, Admin. Services Mgr.--Standco Industries, Inc., Houston, TX, pg. 1038
Paulos, Michele, Dir.-Human Resources--Tru-Weld Grating, Inc., Wexford, PA, pg. 1117
Payne, M., Mgr.-Indus. Rels.--Estes Industries, Inc., Penrose, CO, pg. 1011
Payton, Frank, V.P. & Dir.-Human Resources--Advertising Checking Bureau Incorporated, New York, NY, pg. 21
Peacock, John, V.P.-Personnel--Standard-Thomson Corporation, Waltham, MA, pg. 1037
Pearce, James, Mgr.-Admin. & Personnel--Mississippi Lime Co., Alton, IL, pg. 760
Pearce, Robert, Principal-Human Resources--Edward D. Jones & Co., Maryland Heights, MO, pg. 603
Pearch, Norma, Dir.-Human Resources--The Inland Group, Inc., Oak Brook, IL, pg. 570
Pearcy, Robert, V.P.-Health Indus. Rels.--Blue Cross and Blue Shield of Oklahoma, Tulsa, OK, pg. 159
Pearl, Marcia, Dir.-Pur.--Lackman Food Service, Woodbury, NY, pg. 650
Peck, Stephen E., V.P.-Human Resources--Rugg Manufacturing Company, Greenfield, MA, pg. 955
Peekey, Jim, Mgr.-Human Resources--The Levolor Corporation, Sunnyvale, CA, pg. 671
Peerboom, Mary, Mgr.-Personnel--Laminaire Corporation, Rahway, NJ, pg. 652
Peffley, Donna, Mgr.-Human Res.--Hudson Valley Paper Company, Albany, NY, pg. 551
Pek, Kathleen, Dir.-Human Resources--Yankee Publishing Incorporated, Dublin, NH, pg. 1207
Pendgraft, Doug, Dir.-Human Resources--Sathers Inc., Round Lake, MN, pg. 972
Pennella, William, Sr. V.P.-Human Resources--Crowley Maritime Corporation, Oakland, CA, pg. 301
Pentaris, George, Dir.-Admin. Services & Asst. Sec.--Industrial Coatings Group, Inc., Chicago, IL, pg. 566
Pepelnjak, James F., Sec. & Dir.-Human Resources--Great Lakes Terminal & Transport Corp., Chicago, IL, pg. 482
Peppiatt, Katherine, Personnel Administrator--Del-Val Manufacturing Company, Warminster, PA, pg. 325
Perez, Rudolfo, Mgr.-Personnel--Aero Peru Corporation, Miami, FL, pg. 22
Perosio, Susanna, Personnel Mgr.--Anaheim Manufacturing Company, Anaheim, CA, pg. 71
Perry, Bill, Dir.-Personnel--Furman Lumber Company, Billerica, MA, pg. 436
Peterkin, Betsy, Mgr.-Corp. Personnel--Kelly-Moore Paint Company, Inc., San Carlos, CA, pg. 621
Peterman, Joyce, V.P.-Human Resources--Biggs Gilmore Communications, Kalamazoo, MI, pg. 149
Peters, Colleen J., V.P. & Fin. Administrator--Annabelle Candy Company, Hayward, CA, pg. 75
Peterson, Clark, V.P.-Human Resources--Utica Mutual Insurance Company, New Hartford, NY, pg. 1140
Peterson, Dave, Dir.-Personnel--Southern Minnesota Beet Sugar Cooperative, Renville, MN, pg. 1022
Peterson, Duane, Mgr.-Personnel--Wausau Homes, Inc., Rothschild, WI, pg. 1168
Peterson, J.D., Sr. V.P. & Personnel Dir.--Auto-Owners Insurance, Lansing, MI, pg. 100
Peterson, Kathy, Dir.-Human Resources--Portland Glass/American Management Group, Westbrook, ME, pg. 58
Peterson, Kim, V.P.-Human Resources--C. Brewer & Company, Limited, Honolulu, HI, pg. 174
Peterson, Nancy, V.P., Dir.-Human Resources & Admin.--Horizon Media, Inc., New York, NY, pg. 544
Peterson, Pete, V.P.-Human Resources--Quadion Corporation, Minneapolis, MN, pg. 902
Peterson, Susan, Mgr.-Personnel--D. D. Bean & Sons Co., Jaffrey, NH, pg. 129
Petrilli, Phil, Exec. Dir.-Human Resources & Admin.--Blue Cross and Blue Shield Association, Chicago, IL, pg. 159
Petro, Mike, Dir.-Human Resources--Ulbrich Stainless Steels & Special Metals, Inc., North Haven, CT, pg. 1125
Pettis, Til, Dir.-Human Resources--Pro-Line Corporation, Dallas, TX, pg. 892
Pfahler, Sam, Mgr.-Personnel--CTB Inc., Milford, IN, pg. 205

Pfister, JoAnne, Dir., Personnel, Asst. Sec.--Henderson Advertising, Inc., Greenville, SC, pg. 528
Phenix, Lee, Dir.-Personnel--Plains Cotton Co-op Association, Lubbock, TX, pg. 873
Philips, Patricia, Mgr.-Employee Rels.--Victory Markets Inc., Norwich, NY, pg. 1150
Phillips, James W., Dir.-Personnel & Investor Rels.--American Bread Company - Sunbeam Bakery, Nashville, TN, pg. 49
Phillips, Maurice, Dir.-Personnel--The Vernon Company, Newton, IA, pg. 1148
Philp, J.R., V.P.-Personnel & Admin.--Hillman Company, Pittsburgh, PA, pg. 535
Picard, Roland, Personnel Dir.--Son Chief Electrics, Inc., Winsted, CT, pg. 1018
Pickney, Darrell, Personnel Dir.--Colson Caster Corporation, Jonesboro, AR, pg. 711
Pierce, Daniel, Dir.-Personnel--Aetna Industries, Inc., Center Line, MI, pg. 23
Pierce, Gerard, Dir.-Human Resources--Wegmans Food Markets, Inc., Rochester, NY, pg. 1172
Pieroni, Gina, Dir.-Personnel--Fannie May Candy Shops, Inc., Chicago, IL, pg. 604
Pinard, Gary, Mgr.-Pur.--Granite State Manufacturing Co., Manchester, NH, pg. 476
Pinkos, Julian, V.P.-Human Resources--Hussey Seating Company, North Berwick, ME, pg. 555
Piotter, Robert, Dir.-Personnel--The Cafaro Co., Youngstown, OH, pg. 207
Pisani, Gerald B., V.P.-Human Resources--Burns & Roe Enterprises, Inc., Oradell, NJ, pg. 194
Place, E. Kay, Dir.-Personnel--Maxon Corporation, Muncie, IN, pg. 723
Plummer, Jerry L., V.P.-Human Resources--American United Life Insurance Company, Indianapolis, IN, pg. 65
Poff, Bill, Dir.-Personnel--Beutler Heating & Air Conditioning Inc., Sacramento, CA, pg. 148
Poirier, Edward, Dir.-Indus. Rels.--Kenney Manufacturing Company, Warwick, RI, pg. 623
Polma, Barbara, Dir.-Personnel--Nine West Group, Inc., Stamford, CT, pg. 807
Pomares, Jim, Sec., Treas. & Personnel Mgr.--Von Housen Motors, Sacramento, CA, pg. 1155
Popaditch, Suzanne, Dir.-Personnel--Kelsey Construction, Inc., Orlando, FL, pg. 621
Poppe, Dean, Mgr.-Personnel--Dutton-Lainson Co., Hastings, NE, pg. 356
Porter, C. Vaughn, Mgr.-Personnel--Times-World Corporation, Roanoke, VA, pg. 656
Potter, Kathi, Dir.-Human Resources--Lawson Associates Inc., Minneapolis, MN, pg. 663
Potts, Bert, Dir.-Personnel--Misener Marine Construction, Tampa, FL, pg. 759
Pounds, William, Mgr.-Personnel--Copperweld Steel Company, Warren, OH, pg. 284
Pouttu, E.E., Controller--Harwick Chemical Corp., Akron, OH, pg. 515
Powell, Tom, Personnel Mgr.--Attwood Corporation, Lowell, MI, pg. 1044
Powers, Jo, Dir.-Personnel--United Graphics, Inc., Seattle, WA, pg. 1132
Powers, Ron, Dir.-Personnel & Pub. Rels.--Ward Leonard Electric Company, Inc., Mount Vernon, NY, pg. 1127
Prater-Harvey, Peggy, V.P.-Human Resources--Memphis Light, Gas & Water, Memphis, TN, pg. 738
Pratt, Ann M., Dir.-Human Resources--Levy Security Consultants, Limited, Chicago, IL, pg. 672
Pratt, Larry, Dir.-Personnel--Akers Packaging Service Inc., Middletown, OH, pg. 28
Prendergast, Albert, Sr. V.P.-Human Resources--Mastercard International, Inc., New York, NY, pg. 720
Prendeville, Mark, Dir.-Personnel--Republic Die & Tool Company, Belleville, MI, pg. 928
Price, Dan A., Dir.-Personnel--Kaspar Wire Works, Inc., Shiner, TX, pg. 617
Price, Richard, Dir.-Personnel--American Felt & Filter, Newburgh, NY, pg. 52
Priede, Ernesto, Dir.-Personnel--Atlantic Sugar Association, Inc., Belle Glade, FL, pg. 95
Prince, J. Robert, Mgr.-Personnel--Andersen Consulting, Chicago, IL, pg. 72
Pritsker, Robert, Dir.-Personnel & Prod. Mgr.--Marquette Coppersmithing Co., Inc., Philadelphia, PA, pg. 713
Proffitt, Michael S., Dir.-Personnel--Peterson American Corp., Southfield, MI, pg. 864
Pugh, John, Dir.-Human Resources--The Regina Company, Long Beach, MS, pg. 922
Pulley, Lorraine, Dir.-Personnel--Tingley Rubber Corporation, South Plainfield, NJ, pg. 1098
Purcell, Dennis, V.P.-Human Resources--The Hennegan Company, Cincinnati, OH, pg. 529
Puszkiewicz, Esther, Mgr.-Personnel--Takatta Inc., Olympia Fields, IL, pg. 1076
Putnam, Genivieve, Mgr.-Human Res.--Plastek Group, Erie, PA, pg. 874
Quigley, Jack, Dir.-Personnel--Thetford Corporation, Ann Arbor, MI, pg. 357
Quigley, Lynn, Dir.-Personnel--Codisco Inc., Sanford, FL, pg. 258
Quinn, Bette, Mgr.-Human Resources--Pfaudler-U.S., Inc., Rochester, NY, pg. 866
Quinn, Frank, Dir.-Human Resources & Personnel Training & Devel.--Elkay Products, Inc., Shrewsbury, MA, pg. 377
Rabella, Ed, Dir.-Human Resources--Del Taco, Inc., Costa Mesa, CA, pg. 325
Radder, Jeffrey J., Dir.-Personnel--Curt G. Joa, Inc., Sheboygan Falls, WI, pg. 594
Rader, John, V.P.-Human Resources--Neenah Foundry Company, Neenah, WI, pg. 797
Radwill, Linda, V.P., Mgr.-Mktg. & Sec.--Master Appliance Corp., Racine, WI, pg. 719
Rager, Gary G., Personnel Dir.--ACF Industries, Inc., Earth City, MO, pg. 561
Ragonesi, Karin, Dir.-Human Resources--Full Circle Media Corp., Norwalk, CT, pg. 436
Rahm, Diane, Mgr.-Employment--Credit Union National Association, Madison, WI, pg. 298
Raives, Ann, V.P.-Customer Service & Corp. Communications--Montgomery Ward & Co., Inc., Chicago, IL, pg. 767
Rakow, May T., Sr. V.P.-Personnel & Sec.--Illinois Hydraulic Construction Company, South Elgin, IL, pg. 563
Ralph, David, Controller--Thermon Manufacturing Company, San Marcos, TX, pg. 1091
Ralph, Jerome W., Asst. V.P.-Personnel--Lumco Industries, Inc., Philadelphia, PA, pg. 687
Ramberg, Sue, Dir.-Personnel--DeVault Foods, Devault, PA, pg. 333
Rambo, Lewis, Sr. V.P.-Personnel--Arthur D. Little, Inc., Cambridge, MA, pg. 678
Ramirez, Rosie, Personnel--Salvati Montgomery Sakoda, Inc., Costa Mesa, CA, pg. 967
Rank, Connie, Mgr.-Human Resources--Jewelers Mutual Insurance Company, Neenah, WI, pg. 593
Ransom, Belinda, Dir.-Personnel--RII (Ricards International Inc.), Silver Spring, MD, pg. 907
Rappaport, Cy, Mgr.-Human Resources--Cyborg Systems, Inc., Chicago, IL, pg. 307
Rarey, Ray, Dir.-Personnel--A.P.S., Inc., Houston, TX, pg. 5
Rasmussen, Celeste, Personnel Admin.--Video Products Distributors, Inc., Sacramento, CA, pg. 1150
Rathbun, Kathy, V.P. & Dir.-Human Resources--Telescope Casual Furniture, Inc., Granville, NY, pg. 1085
Rausch, Rose, Dir.-Personnel--The Law Company, Inc., Wichita, KS, pg. 661
Ravencroft, Judith, Mgr.-Admin. & Personnel--Zylke & Associates, Northbrook, IL, pg. 1221
Rawlins, Corrine, Mgr.-Personnel--Cray Communications Inc., Annapolis Junction, MD, pg. 297
Ray, Windell, V.P.-Personnel--Meijer, Inc., Grand Rapids, MI, pg. 737
Raybon, A., Personnel Dir.--Dimco-Gray Company, Dayton, OH, pg. 338
Rayfield, Elizabeth, Mgr.-Personnel--Mauney Hosiery Mills, Inc., Kings Mountain, NC, pg. 722
Raymond, Dennis M., Dir.-Personnel--The Austin Company, Cleveland, OH, pg. 790
Raynow, J., Dir.-Personnel--Advance Business Graphics, Mira Loma, CA, pg. 18
Razum, Eugene, Mgr.-Human Resources--Reactive Metals & Alloys Corporation (REMACOR), West Pittsburg, PA, pg. 916
Read, Robert O., Mgr.-Plng. & Human Resources--Matthews International Corp., Pittsburgh, PA, pg. 721
Redman, Stephanie, Dir.-Human Resources--NTH Consultants, Ltd., Farmington Hills, MI, pg. 781
Redmon, Jannie, Mgr.-Human Resources & Training & Devel.--Graphic Controls, Corp., Buffalo, NY, pg. 478
Redpath, Peter A., V.P.-Personnel--Hitchcock Industries, Inc., Bloomington, MN, pg. 536
Reed, Brian, Dir.-Personnel--Kova Fertilizer Inc., Greensburg, IN, pg. 643
Reed, D.J., Personnel Dir.--Milwaukee Electric Tool Corp., Brookfield, WI, pg. 361
Reed, Sue, Dir.-Personnel--Pine State Tobacco & Candy Company, Augusta, ME, pg. 871
Reffner, Bob, Human Resources Exec.--Hardwick Clothes Inc., Cleveland, TN, pg. 508
Regan, Harold, V.P.-Personnel & Admin.--The H. W. Wilson Co., Bronx, NY, pg. 1193
Reid-Funn, Carlene, Mgr.-Human Resourse Devel.--D.C. Lottery & Charitable Games Control Board, Washington, DC, pg. 308
Reilly, Thomas E., Dir.-Human Resources--Lakeside Foods, Inc., Manitowoc, WI, pg. 651
Rein, Catherine A., Exec. V.P.-Corp. Services--Metropolitan Life Insurance Co., New York, NY, pg. 744
Reisert, Frank, Mgr.-Human Resources--Samtec Inc., New Albany, IN, pg. 968
Reiss, Stephanie, Dir.-Personnel--Jac Jacobsen Industries, Inc., Greenwich, CT, pg. 587
Reitsma, Sandy, Dir.-Personnel--Redmond Products, Inc., Chanhassen, MN, pg. 920
Remmers, Merlin J., V.P.-Personnel--Geo. H. Lehleitner & Co., Inc., Harahan, LA, pg. 666
Remoff, Gene R., V.P.-Human Resources--ARA Group, Philadelphia, PA, pg. 5
Renckley, Richard, V.P.-Human Resources--U-Haul International, Inc., Phoenix, AZ, pg. 48
Rendini, Mary G., Sr. V.P. & Human Resources Dir.--Maguire Group Inc., Foxboro, MA, pg. 701
Renken, Fred, Plant Mgr.--Renken Boat Manufacturing Co., Charleston, SC, pg. 927
Reyes, Janis, Dir.-Human Resources--Masters Inc., Gaithersburg, MD, pg. 720
Reynolds, G.H., V.P.-Corp. Rels.--RAIL Company, Towson, MD, pg. 906
Reynolds, Robert, Payroll & Benefits Supv.--Thrifty Drug Stores, Inc., Minneapolis, MN, pg. 1096
Reynolds, William, Dir.-Human Resources--Christy's Markets, Inc., Brockton, MA, pg. 249
Rhode, Christopher, Dir.-Personnel--Columbia Sussex Corporation, Fort Mitchell, KY, pg. 266
Rhodes, Bonnie, V.P.-Human Resources--Monroe Systems For Business, Inc., Morris Plains, NJ, pg. 766
Rhodes, Dusty, Dir.-Human Resources--Markair, Inc., Anchorage, AK, pg. 708
Rice, Stephen, Dir.-Human Resources--New Jersey Press, Inc., Neptune, NJ, pg. 801
Rice, Tom, Dir.-Personnel--Nemschoff Chairs, Inc., Sheboygan, WI, pg. 798
Rich, Andy, V.P.-Human Resources--Knott's Berry Farm, Buena Park, CA, pg. 637
Rich, Mark, V.P.-Personnel & Admin.--Morse Shoe, Inc., Canton, MA, pg. 772
Richards, Larry, Mgr.-Human Resources--Allied Plywood Corp., Alexandria, VA, pg. 38
Richardson, John, Dir.-Personnel--Directory Distributing Associates, Inc., Saint Louis, MO, pg. 339
Richardson, Maureen, Dir.-Personnel--Ed Taylor Construction Co., Tucker, GA, pg. 1081
Richcreek, M.J., V.P.-Human Resources--Citizens Gas & Coke Utility, Indianapolis, IN, pg. 250
Richley, John P., Dir.-Opers.--The Cafaro Co., Youngstown, OH, pg. 207
Richman, Fran, V.P.-Personnel--Carter Companies, Kansas City, MO, pg. 226
Ricker, Natt, Trainer & Adv. Mgr.--Alamo Group, Inc., La Grange, IL, pg. 29
Rickert, Rick, Dir.-Personnel--Bob Montgomery Chevrolet/ Honda, Louisville, KY, pg. 767
Ridge, Burgess D., V.P.-Admin.--Farley Industries, Chicago, IL, pg. 399
Ridge, Jayne, Dir.-Human Resources--Jazzercise, Inc., Carlsbad, CA, pg. 591
Riefke, Robert, Dir.-Personnel--Beltone Electronics Corporation, Chicago, IL, pg. 137
Riefler, Laurel, Mgr.-Personnel--CEM South, Leesburg, FL, pg. 1013
Riemer, Kenneth, V.P.-Human Resources--Children's World Learning Centers, Inc., Golden, CO, pg. 7
Riker, Glenn, Sr. V.P.-Human Resources & Sec.--Holmes Protection Group, Inc., New York, NY, pg. 540
Riley, Alice, Mgr.-Personnel--Pabst Brewing Co./Tumwater, Tumwater, WA, pg. 959
Riley, J. William, Dir.-Human Resources--Altec Industries, Inc., Birmingham, AL, pg. 45
Rinehart, Marsha, V.P.-Human Resources--Kokosing Construction Company, Inc., Fredericktown, OH, pg. 640
Ring, James, Dir.-Human Resources--Coulter Corporation, Hialeah, FL, pg. 289
Ritner, Joanne, Dir.-Personnel--Restaurant Developers Corp., Independence, OH, pg. 929
Rivera, Joanne P., V.P.-Human Resources--Tidelands Oil Production Co., Long Beach, CA, pg. 1096
Roadcap, Jerome, V.P.-Human Resources--Dairymen, Inc., Louisville, KY, pg. 311
Robb, Dee, Dir.-Personnel--Empire Southwest Co., Mesa, AZ, pg. 379
Roberson, Carmel T., V.P.-Employee Relations--Lawrence Insurance Group, Inc., New York, NY, pg. 662
Roberson, Carmel T., V.P.-Employee Rels. & Benefits--Lawrence Management Group, Inc., Albany, NY, pg. 662
Roberts, Charles, V.P.-Human Resources--Shamrock Foods Co., Phoenix, AZ, pg. 994
Roberts, H.H., Mgr.-Personnel--Blaw Knox Food & Chemical Equipment Company, Buffalo, NY, pg. 156
Roberts, Holly, Dir.-Human Resources--Duo-Fast Corporation, Franklin Park, IL, pg. 354
Roberts, Kent L., Dir.-Human Resources--Nalleys Fine Foods, Tacoma, WA, pg. 25
Roberts, Richard, Dir.-Personnel--Osco Industries Inc., Portsmouth, OH, pg. 830
Roberts, Rodney K., Dir.Personnel.--Idahoan Foods, Lewisville, ID, pg. 561
Robertson, Glenda, Asst. to Pres.--The William Bayley Co., Springfield, OH, pg. 128
Robertson, James, V.P.-Mfg. & Dir.-Personnel--Bregg Data Forms, Inc., Hauppauge, NY, pg. 173
Robertson, Michael, V.P.-Human Resources--Hub Inc., Tucker, GA, pg. 548
Robertson, William A., V.P.-Opers. & Chief Fin. Officer--Smartstar Corporation, Goleta, CA, pg. 1011
Robinson, Brenda, Dir.-Personnel & Admin. Mgr.--City Beverage Co., Atlanta, GA, pg. 251
Robinson, Dick, Dir.-Personnel--David C. Cook Publishing Co., Elgin, IL, pg. 282
Roche, Susan, V.P., Human Resources Dir.--Hill, Holliday, Connors, Cosmopulos, Inc., Boston, MA, pg. 534
Rodriguez, Charles, Sr. V.P.-Opers. & Personnel Dir.--Arnhold and S. Bleichroeder, Inc., New York, NY, pg. 84
Rodriguez, Lisa, Dir.-Personnel--Marine World Africa USA, Vallejo, CA, pg. 707
Rodriguez, Stella, Dir.-Personnel--Label-Aire Inc., Fullerton, CA, pg. 649
Roe, Gene, V.P.-Personnel--The Austin Company, Cleveland, OH, pg. 790
Roedl, Suzanne, Chief Fin. Officer--Condor D.C. Power Supplies Inc., Oxnard, CA, pg. 273
Roetzer, Sue, Mgr.-Human Resources--Adam Meldrum & Anderson Co., Inc., Buffalo, NY, pg. 16
Rogers, Ann V., Sr. V.P.-Human Resources--Texas Commerce Bancshares, Inc., Houston, TX, pg. 1089
Rogers, Charles R., Mgr.-Admin. Services--GAI Consultants, Inc., Monroeville, PA, pg. 439
Rogers, Phil, Personnel Dir.--Glosser Brothers, Inc., Johnstown, PA, pg. 978
Rohde, Paul, V.P.-Human Resources--Certified Grocers Of California, Los Angeles, CA, pg. 237
Rolek, Gary, V.P.-Human Resources--Sanborn Manufacturing Company, Springfield, MN, pg. 969
Rolfsmeyer, Jerry, Dir.-Human Resources--Walbridge Aldinger Company, Detroit, MI, pg. 1158
Roman, Jenny, Mgr.-Personnel--Dominick & Dominick, Incorporated, New York, NY, pg. 343
Romano, Joe, Mgr.-Office--Port of Galveston, Galveston, TX, pg. 881
Rondem, R.B., Mgr.-Employee Rels.--Colonial Pipeline Company, Atlanta, GA, pg. 264
Roney, John, Dir.-Personnel--Gurney Industries Inc., Gastonia, NC, pg. 495
Rook, Jim, Mgr.-Employee Benefits--Milliken & Co., Inc., Spartanburg, SC, pg. 755
Root, Stuart W., Mgr.-Personnel & Sec.--A.I. Root Company, Medina, OH, pg. 946
Roothmann, Pauline, V.P.-Personnel--I. Magnin & Co., San Francisco, CA, pg. 699
Rosa, A.F., V.P.-Human Resources--North American Refractories Company, Cleveland, OH, pg. 811
Rosansky, Victor, Sr. V.P.-Training & Devel.--ODI, Burlington, MA, pg. 818

Rosati, Joseph R., V.P.-Indus. Rels.--Edgewater Corporation, Oakmont, PA, pg. 368
Rosen, David, Mgr.-Personnel--Paul Stuart, Inc., New York, NY, pg. 1054
Rosen, Florence, Exec. V.P. & Controller--Rosen Associates Management Corp., Jericho, NY, pg. 948
Rosenfeld, Cindy, V.P., Dir. Human Resources--Korey, Kay & Partners, New York, NY, pg. 642
Rosier, Marlene, Mgr.-Human Resources--Buffelen Woodworking Company, Tacoma, WA, pg. 187
Roskin, William, Sr. V.P.-Human Resources--Viacom Broadcasting Inc., New York, NY, pg. 785
Roskin, William A., V.P.-Human Resources & Admin.--National Amusements, Inc., Dedham, MA, pg. 784
Roskin, William A., Sr. V.P.-Human Resources & Admin.--Viacom Inc., New York, NY, pg. 785
Ross, Ellen F., Dir., Human Resources--Ross Advertising, Inc., Saint Louis, MO, pg. 949
Ross, Patricia A., V.P.-Personnel & Employee Rels.--Viacom Inc., New York, NY, pg. 785
Ross, Ron, V.P.-Personnel & Corp. Grants Contact--Battenfeld Gloucester Engineering Co. Inc., Gloucester, MA, pg. 126
Rossbach, Donna, Mgr.-Personnel--Bruning Paint Company, Baltimore, MD, pg. 184
Rossi, John, Dir.-Personnel--Savemart Inc., Bronx, NY, pg. 973
Roth, Tom, V.P.-Human Resources--Pony Express Courier Corp., Charlotte, NC, pg. 166
Rowe, Larry, V.P.-Human Resources--Associated Food Stores Inc., Salt Lake City, UT, pg. 89
Roy, Nancy, Personnel Dir.--The Enro Shirt Company, Inc., Louisville, KY, pg. 78
Roy, Nancy Parks, Mgr.-Human Resources--The Apparel Group, Ltd., New York, NY, pg. 78
Rubin, William, V.P. & Mgr.-Human Resources--Phototype Color Graphics, Inc., Pennsauken, NJ, pg. 869
Ruecking, Sally, Dir.-Personnel--American Eagle Airlines, Chicago, IL, pg. 51
Ruffner, Rose, Mgr.-Personnel--Deerfield Manufacturing Co., Inc., Mason, OH, pg. 324
Rukes, Linda, Mgr.--Superior Industries of Nebraska, Inc., Omaha, NE, pg. 1063
Ruotolo, Dottie, Mgr.-Personnel--O. F. Mossberg & Sons, Inc., North Haven, CT, pg. 773
Russell, E.L., Grp. V.P. Human Res.--J.M. Huber Corporation, Edison, NJ, pg. 550
Russell, Robert, Dir.-Personnel--Cal-Maine Foods, Inc., Jackson, MS, pg. 208
Russo, Blaise, V.P.-Human Resources--Kearfott Guidance & Navigation Corp., Wayne, NJ, pg. 93
Russo, David, Dir.-Human Resources--SAS Institute Inc., Cary, NC, pg. 959
Rust, David, V.P.-Human Resources--Menasha Corporation, Neenah, WI, pg. 738
Ruth, Edward H., V.P.-Human Resources--Publix Supermarkets Inc., Lakeland, FL, pg. 898
Ruth, Richard J., V.P.-Employee Rels.--Sunnen Products Company, Saint Louis, MO, pg. 1061
Rutrough, James E., V.P.-Personnel--State Farm Mutual Automobile Insurance Company, Bloomington, IL, pg. 1041
Ruttman, David, V.P.-Human Resources--Blue Cross and Blue Shield of Oklahoma, Tulsa, OK, pg. 159
Ryan, Edward J., V.P.-Human Resources--Rich Products Corp., Buffalo, NY, pg. 932
Ryan, Elizabeth, Dir.-Personnel--Cone-Blanchard Machine Company, Windsor, VT, pg. 273
Ryan, Jan, Mgr.-Employee Rels.--Boye Needle, Chicago, IL, pg. 1205
Ryan, John, Dir.-Human Resources-PBQD, Inc.--Parsons Brinckerhoff Inc., New York, NY, pg. 850
Ryan, S.L., V.P.-Human Resources & Admin.--Guarantee Mutual Life Co., Omaha, NE, pg. 491
Ryden, Katherine, V.P.-Human Resources--Scholastic Inc., New York, NY, pg. 962
Saavides, Mario, Dir.-Human Resources--Datability, Inc., Carlstadt, NJ, pg. 316
Sadighi, Diana, Mgr.-Human Resources--RELA, Inc., Boulder, CO, pg. 924
Sadighi, Diana, Mgr.-Human Resources--RELA Product Development Div. (PDD), Boulder, CO, pg. 924
Sager, Harlin, V.P.-Personnel--Ouachita Coca-Cola Bottling Company, Monroe, LA, pg. 831
Saidman, Joan, Dir.-Personnel--SFA, Inc., Landover, MD, pg. 961
Salamon, Aaron, V.P.-Pur. & Personnel Dir.--Pic N'pay Supermarkets, Inc., Dania, FL, pg. 869
Saleh, Muhammad, V.P.-Human Res.--Timex Corporation, Middlebury, CT, pg. 1098
Salter, Cheryl, Dir.-Human Resources--The Van Metre Companies, Burke, VA, pg. 1144
Samson, Roger, Exec. V.P.-Personnel--Sterling Supply Company, Inc., Lisle, IL, pg. 1047
Samuelsen, David, Dir.-Human Resources--Danly Die Set Division, Cicero, IL, pg. 275
Sandberg, Joel, V.P, Sec., Fin. & Personnel--Jameco Industries, Inc., Wyandanch, NY, pg. 588
Sanders, C., Dir.-Personnel--Bruce Industries, Inc., Dayton, NV, pg. 183
Sanders, Donna, V.P.-Human Resources--The Union Central Life Insurance Co., Cincinnati, OH, pg. 1127
Sanders, Lynn, Dir.-Personnel--Peco Inc., Portland, OR, pg. 854
Sanderson, Mark, Dir.-Personnel--PC Distributing Inc., Mount Prospect, IL, pg. 835
Santosuosso, Vincent, Jr., Dir.-Personnel--Technical Aid Corporation, Newton Upper Falls, MA, pg. 1083
Sarasin, Donald, Mgr.-Personnel--Imperial Pearl Company, Inc., Providence, RI, pg. 564
Sardie, Dan, Dir.-Human Resources--The WBDC Group, Grand Rapids, MI, pg. 1155
Sassi, Daniel E., V.P.-Human Resources & Admin.--Arinc Inc., Annapolis, MD, pg. 82
Saternus, Robert, Dir.-Personnel--Bessin Corporation, Chicago, IL, pg. 146
Saternus, Robert, Dir.-Personnel--Best Kosher Sausage Co., Chicago, IL, pg. 146
Saudek, Karen, Dir.-Personnel--Cabot Creamery Co-Operative Inc., Cabot, VT, pg. 25
Saunders, D.P., Dir.-Personnel & Industrial Rels.--Carolina Tractor & Equipment Co., Charlotte, NC, pg. 223
Saunders, Wayne A., V.P.-Human Resources--Jack Eckerd Corporation, Largo, FL, pg. 366
Savelli, Theresa, Mgr.-Human Resources--Boston Distributors, Inc., Maple Heights, OH, pg. 167
Sawyer, Carol, V.P., Personnel Dir.--Hal Riney & Partners, Inc., San Francisco, CA, pg. 935
Sawyer, Dwight A., V.P.-Human Resources--Amway Corporation, Ada, MI, pg. 70
Sawyer, Kenny, Dir.-Human Resources--Dorsey Trailers, Inc., Atlanta, GA, pg. 347
Sayles, Helen, V.P. & Mgr.-Human Resources--Liberty Mutual Insurance Co., Boston, MA, pg. 674
Scalise, J., Mgr.-Human Resources--Econolite Control Products, Inc., Anaheim, CA, pg. 367
Scanlon, Thomas M., V.P.-Employee Rels.--The Okonite Company, Ramsey, NJ, pg. 823
Scarry, Linda, Mgr.-Human Resources--Meehan Tooker, East Rutherford, NJ, pg. 736
Schaaf, Eileen, Mgr.-Personnel--ASICS Tiger Corporation, Fountain Valley, CA, pg. 8
Schadler, Alice, Mgr.-Human Resources--The Crosset Company Inc., Cincinnati, OH, pg. 300
Schaefer, Paul, V.P.-Human Resources--Tri Valley Growers Inc., San Francisco, CA, pg. 1111
Schafer, James H., V.P.-Indus. Rels.--Seattle Times Company, Seattle, WA, pg. 986
Schaible, Gloria, Admin. Asst.--RDI, Inc., Itasca, IL, pg. 906
Schappi, John V., V.P.-Human Resources--The Bureau of National Affairs, Inc., Washington, DC, pg. 189
Schatt, Joseph F., V.P.-Human Resources--McLouth Steel, Trenton, MI, pg. 731
Schaumburg, Ron, V.P.-Human Resources--National Cooperative Refinery Association, McPherson, KS, pg. 787
Schebo, Cindy, Treas., Sec. & Dir.-Personnel--Ostarr Corporation, Chicago, IL, pg. 831
Scheel, Jeff, Dir.-Human Resources--G. Heileman Brewing Co., Inc., La Crosse, WI, pg. 526
Schefer, Richard, V.P.-Human Resources--Bay State Milling Co., Quincy, MA, pg. 127
Scheimantle, Skip, Dir.-Human Resources--McRae's, Inc., Jackson, MS, pg. 733
Schell, Sue, V.P.-Human Resources & Quality Services--Advanced Energy Industry, Fort Collins, CO, pg. 20
Scherer, Gregory, V.P.-Personnel & Mktg.--Scherer Bros. Lumber Company, Minneapolis, MN, pg. 976
Scheuermann, June, Dir.-Personnel--Holcomb & Hoke Mfg. Company, Inc., Indianapolis, IN, pg. 538
Schiefer, Marianne, Mgr.-Human Resources--Worzalla Publishing Co., Inc., Stevens Point, WI, pg. 1204
Schifano, Albert I., Sr. V.P.-Personnel--Sundt Corp., Tucson, AZ, pg. 1060
Schiff, Paula, Mgr.-Personnel--S & W Fine Foods, Inc., San Ramon, CA, pg. 1111
Schild, Harold, Dir.--Tillamook County Creamery Assn., Tillamook, OR, pg. 1097
Schimpf, Barbara, Controller & Human Resources--Scharfberg & Associates, Ltd. Adv., Jenkintown, PA, pg. 974
Schittone, John P., Jr., Dir.-Human Resources--Associated Grocers, Inc., Baton Rouge, LA, pg. 89
Schlapp, Henry T., Dir.-Personnel--Marine Construction & Design Co., Seattle, WA, pg. 707
Schleisman, James, Dir.-Safety & Mgr.-Personnel--Consolidated Co-op, Gowrie, IA, pg. 276
Schmid, James, Dir.-Personnel--Bently Nevada Corporation, Minden, NV, pg. 140
Schmidt, Edward, Mgr.-Employee Rels.--E. F. Houghton & Co., Valley Forge, PA, pg. 546
Schmidt, Janet, Sr. V.P.-Human Resources--First American Bankshares, Inc., Washington, DC, pg. 412
Schmidt, Linda G., V.P.-Human Resources--Totes Incorporated, Loveland, OH, pg. 1103
Schmitz, Larry, Corp. Admin.--B&W Co-op, Inc., Breckenridge, MI, pg. 107
Schmitz, Paul, Mgr.-Personnel--Findley Adhesives, Inc., Wauwatosa, WI, pg. 410
Schneider, Cheryl, Dir.-Personnel--Poly Pak America, Inc., Los Angeles, CA, pg. 880
Schneider, Joan, Dir.-Personnel--Edwards Brothers, Inc., Ann Arbor, MI, pg. 369
Schneider, Kathy, Dir.-Personnel--F & W Publications, Inc., Cincinnati, OH, pg. 394
Schoemaker, Roger C., V.P.-Employee & Labor Rels.--Booth Newspapers, Inc., Grand Rapids, MI, pg. 165
Schramek, Brad, Dir.-Human Resources--TSC Industries, Inc., Nashville, TN, pg. 1075
Schrot, Barbara J., V.P.-Compensation & Benefits--First Federal Savings and Loan Assn. of Rochester, Rochester, NY, pg. 413
Schrum, Nancy, Dir.-Human Resources--Carolina Mills, Inc., Maiden, NC, pg. 223
Schuett, Amy, Dir.-Human Resources--Office Electronics, Inc., Itasca, IL, pg. 821
Schuette, Georgia, Dir.-Personnel--J H Collectibles, Milwaukee, WI, pg. 584
Schulman, Pamela, Dir.-Human Resources--Thomas R. Hopson Broker, Inc., Marietta, GA, pg. 544
Schultz, James E., V.P.-Indus. Rels.--American Standard Inc., New York, NY, pg. 61
Schussler, Jerry, Dir.-Personnel--Hygeia Dairy Co., Inc., Harlingen, TX, pg. 557
Schwanke, Dean, Dir.-Human Resources--Smead Manufacturing Company, Hastings, MN, pg. 1011
Schwartz, Barbara, V.P.-Human Resources--Sid Tool Co. Inc., Plainview, NY, pg. 1002
Schwartz, Barbara, V.P.-Human Resources--MSC Industrial Supply Co., Plainview, NY, pg. 693
Schwartz, Helene, Sr. V.P.-Human Resources--M.E.D. Communications, Woodbridge, NJ, pg. 692
Schwartz, Shirley, Dir.-Personnel--Airways Rent A Car, Schiller Park, IL, pg. 934
Schweickardt, James, Dir.-Human Resources--Pacific Coast Producers, Lodi, CA, pg. 839
Schwery, Wes, Mgr.-Personnel--ACL Technologies, Santa Ana, CA, pg. 2
Scott, Allen, Dir.-Employee Rels.--Ingram Industries Inc., Nashville, TN, pg. 568
Scott, Frances, Dir.-Personnel--Crain Communications, Inc., Detroit, MI, pg. 295
Scruggs, Julian, Dir.-Human Resources--Piedmont Mechanical, Inc., Spartanburg, SC, pg. 870
Scrutton, Keith, V.P.-Personnel--Jervis B. Webb Company, Farmington Hills, MI, pg. 1170
Seaman, Thomas, Controller & Dir.-Personnel--Blauer Manufacturing Co., Inc., Boston, MA, pg. 156
Seamon, Ken L., Dir.-Personnel--Longyear Company, Salt Lake City, UT, pg. 682
Searls, Lynn, V.P.-Human Resources--Ranging, East Bloomfield, NY, pg. 300
Sears, Richard G., V.P.-Employee Rels.--Masland Industries, Carlisle, PA, pg. 717
Seay, V., Dir.-Personnel--Groendyk Mfg. Co., Inc., Buchanan, VA, pg. 480
Sechovek, Kirby, V.P.-Human Resources--Locus Computing Corp., Inglewood, CA, pg. 680
Sedwick, Linda, Dir.-Human Resources--The Stellar Group Inc., Jacksonville, FL, pg. 1046
Seeger, Geri, Mgr.-Human Resources--Industrial Electronic Engineers, Inc., Van Nuys, CA, pg. 566
Seeks, Russ, Dir.-Personnel--American Red Ball World Wide Movers, Indianapolis, IN, pg. 918
Selander, Jo, Dir.-Human Resources--Christianity Today, Inc., Carol Stream, IL, pg. 249
Sellar, Phil, Dir.-Human Resources--Blue Diamond Growers, Sacramento, CA, pg. 160
Sellers, Garry, Sr. V.P.-Personnel--DHL Corporation, Redwood City, CA, pg. 309
Sellers, Garry, V.P.-Human Resources--DHL Airways, Inc., Redwood City, CA, pg. 309
Serafini, Dan, Human Resources Coord.--Open Court Publishing Company, Chicago, IL, pg. 227
Serff, Paul, Chief Exec. Officer & Sr. V.P.-Human Resources--Tom's Foods, Columbus, GA, pg. 1101
Seritchfield, C., Dir.-Personnel--American Foundry Group, Inc., Bixby, OK, pg. 54
Serne, Marlene, Dir.-Personnel--Trendway Corporation, Holland, MI, pg. 1109
Serratore, Greg, Mgr.-Personnel--World's Finest Chocolate, Inc., Chicago, IL, pg. 1203
Sessler, Andrea, Sr. V.P., Dir. Human Resources & Pub. Rels.--Ammirati & Puris Inc., New York, NY, pg. 67
Settle, Shirley, Mgr.-Personnel--Electro Mechanical Design Services, Inc., Gaithersburg, MD, pg. 375
Setzer, Scott, Personnel Mgr.--Setzer Forest Products, Sacramento, CA, pg. 993
Severson, Ron, Dir.-Personnel--True Companies, Casper, WY, pg. 1117
Shadwick, Peggy, Personnel Dir.--Communications International, New York, NY, pg. 269
Shaffer, Don, V.P.-Human Resources--Steinbach, White Plains, NY, pg. 1045
Shaffer, Linda, Dir.-Human Res.--Metal Seal & Products, Inc., Willoughby, OH, pg. 741
Shankster, M. Garvin, V.P. & Chief Human Resources Officer--S. C. Johnson & Son, Inc., Racine, WI, pg. 599
Shannon-Yancey, Doris, V.P.-Human Resources--The Weather Channel, Atlanta, GA, pg. 654
Shannon-Yancy, Doris, V.P.-Human Resources--The Travel Channel, Atlanta, GA, pg. 654
Sharp, William, Dir.-Personnel--Tension Envelope Corp., Kansas City, MO, pg. 1088
Sharpe, Carl, Dir.-Human Resources--Binning's Building Products, Inc., Lexington, NC, pg. 151
Sharry, Paul, Mgr.-Personnel--Evening Post Publishing Co., Charleston, SC, pg. 391
Shaver, Greg, Mgr.-Personnel--Service Supply Co. Inc. of Indiana, Indianapolis, IN, pg. 992
Shaw, Murray, V.P.-Human Resources--Tracor, Inc., Austin, TX, pg. 1104
Shaw, Richard, Plant Mgr.--Faribault Woolen Mill Co., Faribault, MN, pg. 399
Shaw, Scott, V.P.-Personnel--Werthan Packaging, Inc., Nashville, TN, pg. 1176
Shea, J., V.P.-Personnel--Shure Brothers Incorporated, Evanston, IL, pg. 1001
Sheard, James L., Sr. V.P.-Human Resources--Federated Mutual Insurance Company, Owatonna, MN, pg. 405
Sheehan, Frank, V.P.-Indus. Rels.--The Bibb Company, Macon, GA, pg. 781
Sheffield, Steven, Dir.-Human Resources--Warehouse Home Furnishings Distributor, Dublin, GA, pg. 1163
Sheffield, Tyler W., Chief Fin. Officer & Treas.--Burnham Broadcasting Company, Chicago, IL, pg. 193
Shepherd, Patrick, Dir.-Personnel & Employee Benefits--Piper Aircraft Corporation, Vero Beach, FL, pg. 872
Sheppard, Betty J., V.P.-Admin. & Dir.-Personnel--Canal Insurance Co., Greenville, SC, pg. 213
Sheridan, Tom, V.P.-Human Resources--National Welders Supply Co. Inc., Charlotte, NC, pg. 794
Sherman, Richard, V.P.-Human Resources--Southern States Cooperative, Inc., Richmond, VA, pg. 1022
Sherwood, Gene F., 2nd V.P.-Human Resources--Shenandoah Life Insurance Company, Roanoke, VA, pg. 997
Shinnick, Dee, Dir.-Human Resources, Personnel Training & Devel.--Dawahares, Inc., Lexington, KY, pg. 319
Shirley, John, Mgr.-Human Resources--Sunbeam Home Comfort, Shubuta, MS, pg. 1059

Shoaf, Daniel L., Dir.-Personnel--Chicago Tube & Iron Co., Chicago, IL, pg. 246
Shoemaker, Chris, Personnel Mgr.--Frankel & Company, Chicago, IL, pg. 429
Shoemaker, Joe, Personnel Dir.--Zoeller Co., Louisville, KY, pg. 1220
Shogren, Daniel C., Natl. Dir.-Human Resources--Grant Thornton, Chicago, IL, pg. 477
Sholakh, Kariman, Mgr.-Human Resources--Nexus Plastics, Inc., Hawthorne, NJ, pg. 805
Short, Robert, Mgr.-Personnel--Pacific Hide & Fur Depot, Great Falls, MT, pg. 840
Shrader, Debbie, Admin.-Personnel--Brown & Haley, Tacoma, WA, pg. 182
Shuerman, Janice, V.P.-Admin. & Personnel--MFA Incorporated, Columbia, MO, pg. 692
Shuster, Dan, Dir.-Intl. Admin.--Amway Corporation, Ada, MI, pg. 70
Sicheri, Dick, Dir.-Human Resources--Snap-Tite, Incorporated, Erie, PA, pg. 1014
Sichko, W., V.P.-Human Resources--North American Salt Company, Overland Park, KS, pg. 812
Sidman, Bobby, Dir.-Personnel--Maywood, Inc., Amarillo, TX, pg. 725
Sierp, Kathy, Personnel Dir.--Ovation Marketing, Inc., La Crosse, WI, pg. 832
Siff, Barry, V.P.-Human Resources--ITI Marketing Services, Inc., Omaha, NE, pg. 561
Sijersen, Susan, Dir.-Personnel--Milk Specialties Company, Dundee, IL, pg. 753
Sikora, Shirley A., Dir.-Compensation, Employee Benefits & Personnel--The Edward J. DeBartolo Corporation, Youngstown, OH, pg. 323
Silver, Robert, Sr. V.P.-Human Resources--Pergament Home Centers, Inc., Melville, NY, pg. 862
Silvey, Ray, Corp. V.P.-Human Resources--Mid-America Dairymen, Inc., Springfield, MO, pg. 750
Simerson, Faye, Dir.-Personnel--The Pantry, Inc., Sanford, NC, pg. 846
Simmons, George, Dir.-Personnel--Aberdeen Mfg. Corporation, New York, NY, pg. 200
Simmons, Tom, Controller--Bongards Creameries Inc., Norwood, MN, pg. 164
Simon, Mary T., Treas. & Dir.-Personnel--J.L. Lester & Son, Inc., Rockmart, GA, pg. 668
Simon, Michael R., Sr. V.P.-Human Resources--Cumberland-Swan, Inc., Smyrna, TN, pg. 304
Simon, Wayne L., Dir.-Human Resources--Ellwood City Forge, Ellwood City, PA, pg. 378
Simons, Carey, Mgr.-Personnel--Mersman Furniture, Celina, OH, pg. 741
Simpson, Pamela, Mgr.-Personnel--Twincraft, Inc., Winooski, VT, pg. 1122
Sims, Pete, Mgr.-Human Resources--Cullman Products Corporation, Cullman, AL, pg. 304
Sims, Sam, Mgr.-Personnel--Rochester Gauges Inc. Of Texas, Dallas, TX, pg. 444
Sincoff, M.Z., V.P.-Human Resources--DIMAC Corporation, Bridgeton, MO, pg. 338
Sincoff, Michael Z., Sr. V.P., Human Resources--DIMAC DIRECT, Bridgeton, MO, pg. 338
Singer, Ethel, Dir.-Personnel--Splendor Form International Inc., Long Island City, NY, pg. 1031
Singleton, R. Keith, Mgr. -Indus. Relations--The Crystal Tissue Co., Middletown, OH, pg. 303
Singstock, Tom, Dir.-Personnel--Ludington News Co. Inc., Detroit, MI, pg. 686
Sink, Barbara J., V.P., Sec. & Dir.-Personnel--Traders Supermarkets, Inc., Berrien Springs, MI, pg. 1105
Sirny, William, Dir.-Human Resources--Rome Cable Corporation, Rome, NY, pg. 945
Sisbarro, P.R., Dir.-Personnel--Ebsco Industries, Inc., Birmingham, AL, pg. 365
Sisul, John T., V.P.-Human Resources--Wilton Corporation, Palatine, IL, pg. 1194
Siversten, Pat, Mgr.-Personnel--Rainier Brewing Co., Seattle, WA, pg. 526
Skinner, Nancy, V.P. & Dir.-Training--Biggs Gilmore Communications, Kalamazoo, MI, pg. 149
Skogerboe, Charles, Dir.-Personnel--Berkley, Inc., Spirit Lake, IA, pg. 141
Slaybaugh, Nina, Mgr.-Personnel--Neapco, Inc., Pottstown, PA, pg. 1123
Slenn, J.R., V.P.-Human Resources--SPD Technologies, Philadelphia, PA, pg. 963
Slifer, Anne M., Dir.-Personnel & Mktg.--Modern Concrete Septic Tank Company, Ottsville, PA, pg. 762
Slinkard, John, Mgr.-Human Resources--Sun-Maid Growers of California, Kingsburg, CA, pg. 1058
Sloan, Willaim, Mgr.-Personnel--R.C.A. Rubber Company, Akron, OH, pg. 906
Slocum, Rex, V.P.-Personnel--John M. Smyth Co., Downers Grove, IL, pg. 1014
Slocumbe, Elaine, Coord.-Personnel--Atlanta Beverage Co., Atlanta, GA, pg. 94
Sloneker, Richard, Dir.-Personnel--Western States Machine Co., Hamilton, OH, pg. 1181
Smalley, Phillip A., Jr., Sr. V.P.-Human Resources--Chesapeake Financial Corp., Miami Beach, FL, pg. 243
Smith, Carol, Dir.-Human Resources--Alco Health Services Corporation-Tiffin Div., Tiffin, OH, pg. 32
Smith, Craig, Dir.-Human Resources--Johnny Appleseed's, Inc., Beverly, MA, pg. 597
Smith, Cynthia, Coord.-Human Resources--Downey Designs International, Inc., Indianapolis, IN, pg. 348
Smith, Dwight, Dir.-Personnel--J. I. Kislak Inc., Miami Lakes, FL, pg. 633
Smith, Edie, Dir.-Personnel--Triple S Plastics, Inc., Vicksburg, MI, pg. 1114
Smith, Edith, Mgr.-Personnel--Fike Corporation, Blue Springs, MO, pg. 409
Smith, Felicia, V.P.-Human Resources--Modern Group Ltd., Bristol, PA, pg. 762
Smith, Gary, Dir.-Human Resources--General Binding Corporation, Northbrook, IL, pg. 656
Smith, J.E., Dir.-Personnel--Franklin Baking Co., Inc., Goldsboro, NC, pg. 429
Smith, Jan, Office Mgr.--American Fluorescent Corporation, Waukegan, IL, pg. 54
Smith, Joe, Dir.-Human Resources--Esco Corporation, Portland, OR, pg. 388
Smith, Lauren, V.P.-Human Resources--Winston Tire Company, Burbank, CA, pg. 1197
Smith, Maureen, V.P.-Human Rels.--Yardney Technical Products, Inc., Pawcatuck, CT, pg. 1207
Smith, Michael J., V.P. & Treas.--S-T Industries, Inc., Saint James, MN, pg. 964
Smith, Patricia, Dir.-Personnel Admin.--Westat Inc., Rockville, MD, pg. 1178
Smith, Richard, Dir.-Personnel--Coca-Cola Bottling Co. of the Southwest, San Antonio, TX, pg. 257
Smith, Richard A., Sr. V.P.-Admin.--Days Inns of America, Inc., Parsippany, NJ, pg. 1100
Smith, Robert W., Jr., V.P.-Human Resources--Battelle Memorial Institute, Columbus, OH, pg. 126
Smith, Ron, Dir.-Personnel--Batson-Cook Company, West Point, GA, pg. 126
Smith, Ronald, Dir.-Personnel--Martin Paint Stores, Jamaica, NY, pg. 715
Smith, Sharon Allen, Dir.-Personnel--Intech Advanced Analog, Santa Clara, CA, pg. 572
Smith, Suzanne E., Dir.-Human Resources--A. H. Hoffman, Inc., Landisville, PA, pg. 538
Snee, Joe, Mgr.-Human Resources--Artec Distributing, Inc., Shelburne, VT, pg. 86
Snyder, D.E., Dir.-Human Resources--Seco Warwick Corporation, Meadville, PA, pg. 987
Snyder, James, Dir.-Human Resources--Congoleum Corporation, Mercerville, NJ, pg. 274
Snyder, Lance, Controller--McLaughlin Mfg. Company, Greenville, SC, pg. 731
Sober, David W., V.P.-Human Res.--Performance Food Group, Inc., Nashville, TN, pg. 861
Sobyak, Larry, V.P., Treas. & Personnel Mgr.--Demco Inc., Madison, WI, pg. 328
Sochon, Lynn, Dir.-Personnel--Joyce International, Inc., New York, NY, pg. 608
Soignier, Elmo, Dir.-Personnel--Walk, Haydel & Associates, Inc., New Orleans, LA, pg. 1159
Soliani, Carol, Mgr.-Personnel--The Turner & Seymour Mfg. Company, Torrington, CT, pg. 1119
Solonica, M., Mgr.-Personnel--Prestige Stamping, Inc., Warren, MI, pg. 888
Solsbury, Kay, Mgr.-Personnel Training--Amerisure Companies, Detroit, MI, pg. 66
Soltis, William T., Mgr.-Indus. Rels.--Consolidated Industries, Inc., Cheshire, CT, pg. 276
Sonstelie, Cynthia P., V.P.-Human Resources--Simpson Investment Co., Seattle, WA, pg. 1007
Sopranos, O.J., V.P.-Personnel--Amsted Industries Incorporated, Chicago, IL, pg. 68
Sorrentino, Helen, Mgr.-Personnel--Croll-Reynolds Company, Westfield, NJ, pg. 300
Sosiak, Jack J., V.P.-Human Resources--Exide Corporation, Reading, PA, pg. 393
Soucy, Kathleen M., Dir.-Personnel--Facemate Corporation, Chicopee, MA, pg. 396
Southern, Robert E., Dir.-Personnel--Affiliated Foods Southwest, Little Rock, AR, pg. 24
Southgate-Fox, Susie, V.P.-Human Resources--Lettuce Entertain You Enterprises, Inc., Chicago, IL, pg. 668
Sparks, R.C., Dir.-Personnel--S & C Electric Company, Chicago, IL, pg. 958
Spelde, Judy, Dir.-Human Resources--Empire Airlines, Hayden Lake, ID, pg. 379
Spence, T.A., Personnel Mgr.--Franklin Steel Company, Franklin, PA, pg. 429
Sperandio, Rose Ann, Dir.-Personnel--The P.J. Carlin Construction Company, New Rochelle, NY, pg. 220
Speranza, Nickolas, V.P.-Human Resources--Cablevision Industries Corp., Liberty, NY, pg. 206
Spies, Jon, Dir.-Human Resources-Kansas City Div.--Associated Wholesale Grocers, Inc., Kansas City, KS, pg. 92
Spivack, Ilse, Dir.-Personnel--L'Ermitage Hotels, West Hollywood, CA, pg. 668
Sponseller, Ben, Dir.-Personnel--Abbott Laboratories/Ashland, Ashland, OH, pg. 9
Spradley, Elizabeth, Dir.-Personnel--The Suddath Companies, Jacksonville, FL, pg. 1055
Sprint, Julienne D., Sr. V.P. & Dir.- Human Resources--Ellerbe Becket, Inc., Minneapolis, MN, pg. 378
Squitieri, Jan, Dir.-Human Resources--B. Green & Co., Baltimore, MD, pg. 484
Srail, Mitch, Dir.-Human Services--Domino's Pizza Inc., Ann Arbor, MI, pg. 344
Stack, Charles J., Exec. V.P. & Dir.-Personnel Div.--Mutual of Omaha Insurance Company, Omaha, NE, pg. 779
Stack, Charles J., Exec. V.P. & Dir.-Personnel--Mutual of Omaha, Omaha, NE, pg. 779
Stafford, Henrietta, Mgr.-Personnel--Watkins System Inc., Concordville, PA, pg. 1167
Stafford, Mary M., V.P.-Human Resources--Margo's La Mode, Inc., Dallas, TX, pg. 373
Stanko, Barbara, Dir.-Personnel--Orix Real Estate Equities, Inc., Chicago, IL, pg. 829
Stanley, Bruce, Dir.-Personnel--Capital Industries, Inc., Seattle, WA, pg. 215
Stanton, James, V.P. & Human Resources--Capital Bancorp, Miami, FL, pg. 214
Stanton, John J., Dir.-Indus. Rels.--Utility Trailer Manufacturing Co., City of Industry, CA, pg. 1141
Stanton, Len, Dir.-Human Resources--North Atlantic Industries, Inc., Hauppauge, NY, pg. 812
Stark, Susan, Dir.-Personnel--Farnam Companies, Inc., Phoenix, AZ, pg. 403
Starley, Barbara, Controller & Dir.-Personnel--Martz & Wadas, Scottsdale, AZ, pg. 716
Staudmyer, Frederick, V.P.-Human Resources--Ziff Communications Company, New York, NY, pg. 1218
Steckel, Richard, Dir.-Employee Rels.--Elkay Manufacturing Company, Oak Brook, IL, pg. 377
Stecker, Cynthia, Personnel Dir.--National Beef Packing Company, Liberal, KS, pg. 1128
Steel, Bill, Mgr.-Human Resources--Bard Mfg. Co., Bryan, OH, pg. 119
Steele, Andrea, Dir.-Personnel--Duron, Inc., Beltsville, MD, pg. 355
Steele, Donald F., Sr. V.P.-Employee Rels.--The Hertz Corporation, Park Ridge, NJ, pg. 849
Stefanski, Peggy, Dir.-Human Resources--GenDerm Corporation, Lincolnshire, IL, pg. 448
Steinberg, Karl, V.P.-Human Resources--Encyclopaedia Britannica, Inc., Chicago, IL, pg. 381
Steinberg, Larry, V.P.-Human Resources--The Levy Organization, Chicago, IL, pg. 672
Steiner, Don, Dir.-Human Resources--Star Lumber & Supply Company, Inc., Wichita, KS, pg. 1039
Steinke, Sue, Mgr.-Human Resources--Sanborn Manufacturing Company, Springfield, MN, pg. 969
Stellingwerf, Diane, Dir.-Human Resources--Juhl Marketing Communications, Mishawaka, IN, pg. 608
Steltmann, Harry F., V.P., Chief Fin. Officer, Treas & Sec.--Eclipse, Inc., Rockford, IL, pg. 366
Stephens, Blanca M., Sr. V.P.-Human Resources & Opers.--Nelson Communications, Inc., New York, NY, pg. 797
Stephens, J. Michael, Controller, Div. Dir.-Admin. Services & Personnel Dir.--Goodwill Industries of America, Inc., Bethesda, MD, pg. 471
Stephenson, Twyla, V.P.-Human Resources--Turtle Wax, Inc., Chicago, IL, pg. 1120
Stern, Robert A., V.P.-Human Resources--The Scott Company, Marysville, OH, pg. 982
Stevens, Bill, Personnel Mgr.--J-Starr Industries, Inc., Fort Atkinson, WI, pg. 1040
Stevens, Phyllis A., Dir.-Human Resources--Rama Group of Companies, Cheektowaga, NY, pg. 910
Stevens, Robert, Corp. Dir.-Indus. Rels.--Pabst Brewing Co., San Antonio, TX, pg. 959
Stevenson, Sherry, Dir.-Personnel--Crown Holdings, Inc., Roseville, MN, pg. 302
Stewart, Dick, Dir.-Personnel--AEA, Inc., Charlotte, NC, pg. 3
Stewart, Stacy, Dir.-Human Resources--AJC International, Inc., Atlanta, GA, pg. 4
Stewart, Yvonne, Mgr.-Personnel--Chemtech Industries, Inc., Saint Louis, MO, pg. 242
Stillings, Robert, V.P.-Opers., Sls., Mktg. & Personnel Dir.--Presto Food Stores, Inc., Plant City, FL, pg. 888
Stillman, Jedd B., Treas. & Dir.-Personnel--David Michael & Co. Inc., Philadelphia, PA, pg. 747
Stinson, Ruth Ann, Treas. & Dir.-Personnel--Young Supply Company, Detroit, MI, pg. 1214
Stocker, Brian J., Dir.-Human Resources--Ultra Tool & Plastics, Inc., Amherst, NY, pg. 1125
Stocker, Phil, V.P.-Personnel--Beckley-Cardy, Inc., Duluth, MN, pg. 21
Stone, Conrad, V.P.-Personnel--Sterlite Corporation, Townsend, MA, pg. 1047
Stoup, Pat, V.P.-Human Rels.--Carlson Retail Marketing, Minneapolis, MN, pg. 221
Strachan, Wendy, V.P.-Human Resources--Hyatt International Corporation, Chicago, IL, pg. 495
Strampel, Leona, Dir.-Personnel--Omega World Travel, Inc., Falls Church, VA, pg. 826
Strassel, Gary, Dir.-Admin.--Carlisle Equipment Company, Wilder, KY, pg. 220
Street, Darnelle, Mgr.-Human Resources--Parks Sausage Company, Baltimore, MD, pg. 850
Strickland, Judy, Dir.-Personnel, Data Processing & Telecommunications--Eagle Lincoln Mercury Inc., Dallas, TX, pg. 362
Strine, R. Dean, Dir.-Personnel--The National Latex Products Co., Ashland, OH, pg. 791
Stropkai, Sylvia, Dir.-Personnel--Conair Corporation, Stamford, CT, pg. 272
Strupp, James J., Sr. V.P.-Human Resources--GAF Corporation, Wayne, NJ, pg. 438
Strupp, James J., V.P.-Human Resources--International Specialty Products, Inc., Wilmington, DE, pg. 438
Stubbs, Linda S., V.P.-Admin. & Human Resources--Dimeo Construction Company, Providence, RI, pg. 338
Stuhlmann, Eric, V.P. & Chief Fin. Officer--Shurfine-Central Corp., Northlake, IL, pg. 1001
Stump, David, Dir.-Personnel--Associated Electric Co-op Inc., Springfield, MO, pg. 89
Stumpf, Donald E., Mgr.-Personnel--Spectrum Industries, Inc., Chippewa Falls, WI, pg. 1029
Sturzl, Edward, V.P.-Personnel--Sargento Cheese Co., Plymouth, WI, pg. 971
Sturzl, Edward A., V.P.-Human Resources--Sargento Incorporated, Plymouth, WI, pg. 971
Suddarth, John, V.P.-Human Resources--Essex Group, Inc., Fort Wayne, IN, pg. 389
Sullivan, Ralph, Sr. V.P.-Personnel Training & Devel.--Juhl Marketing Communications, Mishawaka, IN, pg. 608
Sullivan, Tina, Dir.-Personnel--Petroleum Marketers, Inc., Roanoke, VA, pg. 865
Sullivan, William, Dir.-Personnel--Dietzgen Corporation, Des Plaines, IL, pg. 337
Sulliven, Edward, V.P.-Human Resources--Sullivan Paper Company, West Springfield, MA, pg. 1057
Summers, Robert, Dir.-Human Resources--Chief Industries, Inc., Grand Island, NE, pg. 247
Sunday, Harold L., V.P.-Human Resources--Collins & Aikman Textile Group, Charlotte, NC, pg. 262
Sundquist, Kathleen G., Dir.-Personnel--UFE Incorporated, Stillwater, MN, pg. 1123
Super, Mike, Dir.-Human Resources--Druther's International, Inc., Louisville, KY, pg. 350

Supple, Faith, Dir.-Human Resources--Imperial Schrade Corp., Ellenville, NY, pg. 564
Svana, Raymond E., Dir.-Personnel--Industrial Acoustics Company, Inc., Bronx, NY, pg. 565
Sveinson, Pamela, V.P.-Human Resources--Cowles Media Company, Minneapolis, MN, pg. 291
Swanson, Arnold, Dir.-Personnel--The Aarque Companies, Jamestown, NY, pg. 9
Swanson, Dale, V.P.-Human Resources--Mesirow Financial, Chicago, IL, pg. 741
Swanson, David, Mgr.-Personnel--Arrow Industries, Inc., Carrollton, TX, pg. 85
Swanson, Walter, Dir.-Employee Benefits--Willamette-Western Corporation, Portland, OR, pg. 1190
Swanzey, Robert, Sr. V.P.-Human Resources & Opers.--Century Business Credit Corporation, New York, NY, pg. 235
Sweigart, April, Dir.-Personnel--North Central Life Insurance Companies, Saint Paul, MN, pg. 813
Szymaniak, Stanley, Asst. V.P., Admn. & Human Resources Dir.--Sahara Coal Co., Chicago, IL, pg. 966
Talbot, Sherry, Mgr.-Personnel--Norbest, Inc., Midvale, UT, pg. 809
Talley, Rich, Mgr.-Personnel--Concordia Publishing House, Saint Louis, MO, pg. 272
Tamashasky, J., V.P.-Human Resources--Mosler Inc., Hamilton, OH, pg. 772
Tange, Cindy, Mgr.-Personnel--Cragar Industries, Compton, CA, pg. 761
Tangolics, Linda, Dir.-Personnel--American International Container, Inc., Miami, FL, pg. 56
Tankersley, Ed, V.P.-Personnel--Lay Packing Company Inc., Knoxville, TN, pg. 663
Tapia, JoAnn, Dir.-Human Resources--Shafer Commercial Seating Inc., Denver, CO, pg. 994
Taradash, Elliott, V.P.-Production, Sec. & Treas.--M. Grossman Son, Inc., Passaic, NJ, pg. 489
Tarajano, Jose, Gen. Counsel & Mgr.-Personnel--Pala Group, Inc., Baton Rouge, LA, pg. 843
Tavano, Donald, Mgr.-Personnel--Printed Circuit Corporation, Woburn, MA, pg. 891
Taylor, Allen C., V.P.-Labor Rels. & Human Resources--Lykes Bros. Steamship Co., Inc., New Orleans, LA, pg. 688
Taylor, Beverley, Office Mgr.--Martin Forest Industries, Healdsburg, CA, pg. 715
Taylor, James, Dir.-Human Resources--MCorp, Dallas, TX, pg. 732
Taylor, Lori, V.P., Dir. Human Resources--Ross Roy Inc., Bloomfield Hills, MI, pg. 950
Taylor, Michael, Dir.-Personnel--Homes of Merit Inc., Bartow, FL, pg. 542
Taylor, Patricia, Dir.-Personnel--Virginia State Lottery Department, Richmond, VA, pg. 1153
Teague, Becki, Personnel Mgr.--Mallory, Inc., Carson City, NV, pg. 703
Teasley, William, Dir.-Personnel--The Wm. Powell Company, Cincinnati, OH, pg. 882
Telly, Theresa, Dir.-Personnel & Admin.--Pharmacaps Inc., Elizabeth, NJ, pg. 866
Tenenbaum, Lee, Sr. V.P.-Legal/Personnel--Nationwise Automotive, Inc., Columbus, OH, pg. 795
Tennessen, Dennis, Dir.-Personnel--Thom Thumb Food Market Inc., Hastings, MN, pg. 879
Teresa Silva, Dir.-Human Resources & Sls. Supvr.--Windsor Fashions, Los Angeles, CA, pg. 1195
Terry, Martin, V.P.-Human Resources--Findlay Industries, Inc., Findlay, OH, pg. 410
Testa, Marta, Mgr.-Personnel--Bridgeport Fittings, Inc., Stratford, CT, pg. 175
Thayer, Vickey, V.P.-Human Resources--Lozier Corporation, Omaha, NE, pg. 686
Thibideau, Chuck, Sr. V.P.-Employee Rels.--Trans World Airlines, Inc., Mount Kisco, NY, pg. 561
Tholey, James M., Chief Oper. Officer, Chief Fin. Officer, & Treas.--Peirce-Phelps, Inc., Philadelphia, PA, pg. 855
Thoma, Diane, Dir.-Personnel--FDL Foods, Inc., Dubuque, IA, pg. 394
Thomas, Anita, Mgr.-Human Resources--Wells Manufacturing Company, Verdi, NV, pg. 1027
Thomas, Carter G., Reg. Dir.-Claims--Country Mutual Insurance Company, Bloomington, IL, pg. 289
Thomas, Dave, V.P.-Production--Williams-White & Co., Moline, IL, pg. 1191
Thomas, Jay, Mgr.-Human Resources--Carroll's Foods, Inc., Warsaw, NC, pg. 225
Thomas, Lee, Dir.-Personnel--California Cedar Products, Inc., Stockton, CA, pg. 209
Thomas, Russell, Sr. V.P.-Human Resources--Servistar Corporation, East Butler, PA, pg. 992
Thomas, Sue, V.P.-Human Resources--Esprit de Corp., San Francisco, CA, pg. 388
Thompson, Don, Dir.-Personnel--T.D. Williamson, Inc., Tulsa, OK, pg. 1192
Thompson, Gene, Dir.-Human Resources--Stowe-Pharr Mills, Inc., McAdenville, NC, pg. 1052
Thompson, George, Mgr.-Human Resources--Power Conversion, Inc., Saddle Brook, NJ, pg. 883
Thompson, Jack, Dir.-Indus. Rels.--The Flexible Corp., Delaware, OH, pg. 421
Thompson, Mark, Dir.-Personnel--Kesterson Food Company, Inc., Paris, TN, pg. 624
Thompson, Patricia, Dir.-Personnel--Martrade Ltd., Santa Fe Springs, CA, pg. 716
Thompson, Peggie, Dir.-Personnel & Adv.--Virginia Metal Industries, Inc., Orange, VA, pg. 1152
Thompson, Ray G., Mgr.-Employee Rels.--Justiss Oil Co., Inc., Jena, LA, pg. 610
Thompson, Stan, Dir.-Personnel--San Diego Zoo, San Diego, CA, pg. 969
Thompson, Stan, Mgr.-Personnel--San Diego Wild Animal Park, Escondido, CA, pg. 969
Thornhill, A. James, Dir.-Personnel--Allison-Erwin Co. Inc., Charlotte, NC, pg. 40
Tielborg, Peter, Dir.-Human Resources--George Lithograph, San Francisco, CA, pg. 452
Tifft, D., Mgr.-Personnel--Hardinge Brothers, Inc., Elmira, NY, pg. 508
Tingey, Delbert, Dir.-Benefits--Kaibab Industries, Phoenix, AZ, pg. 614
Tinsley, Lucy T., Mgr.-Human Resources--Builder Marts of America, Greenville, SC, pg. 187
Tisdale, Linda, Mgr.-Personnel--Advanced Circuit Technology, Nashua, NH, pg. 20
Todd, Maryann, Dir.-Human Resources--Powell Electronics Inc., Philadelphia, PA, pg. 882
Toener, John, Dir.-Personnel & Mgr.-Plant--Hudepohl-Schoenling Brewing Company, Cincinnati, OH, pg. 550
Toleno, Susan, Mgr.-Personnel--Instrument Specialties Company, Delaware Water Gap, PA, pg. 572
Tollison, Eugene, Mgr.-Personnel--Palmetto Spinning Corp., Laurens, SC, pg. 844
Tolly, David H., V.P., Sec. & Gen. Counsel--Savage Arms Inc., Westfield, MA, pg. 973
Tolson, Catherine, Asst. Dir., Human Resources--Stackig, Sanderson & White, Inc., McLean, VA, pg. 1034
Tomasko, Stephen J., V.P.-Human Resources--The Brenlin Group, Akron, OH, pg. 173
Tomerlin, John, V.P.-Human Resources--Enterprise Products Company, Houston, TX, pg. 382
Tomlin, Larry, Dir.-Human Resources--Artco-Bell Corporation, Temple, TX, pg. 86
Toms, C.R., Sec. & Personnel Dir.--Rubatex Corporation, Bedford, VA, pg. 480
Toncar, Patricia A., V.P., Dir., Human Resources--Griswold, Inc., Cleveland, OH, pg. 950
Tonkin, John B., Mgr.-Corp Services--Price Brothers Co., Dayton, OH, pg. 888
Toolen, Kathleen, Dir.-Personnel--J. C. Brock Corp., Buffalo, NY, pg. 178
Torke, Ward J., V.P.-Sls., Mktg. & Personnel Dir.--Torke Coffee Company, Inc., Sheboygan, WI, pg. 1102
Tosch, John, V.P. & Corp. Counsel--American Speedy Printing Centers, Inc., Bloomfield Hills, MI, pg. 61
Tosha, Sandra, Dir.-Employee Rels.--AP Parts Manufacturing Company, Toledo, OH, pg. 240
Townsend, Ralph N., V.P.-Personnel--Martin K. Eby Construction Company, Inc., Wichita, KS, pg. 365
Tragarz, Nancy, Mgr.-Personnel--East Moline Metal Products Company, East Moline, IL, pg. 363
Trapp, George J., Sr. V.P.-Human Resources--New York Life Insurance Company, New York, NY, pg. 802
Trella, Donald, Dir.-Human Resources--Big Y Foods Inc., Springfield, MA, pg. 149
Trelut, James, V.P.-Human Resources--Nob Hill General Store, Inc., Gilroy, CA, pg. 807
Trent, David, Mgr.-Human Resouces--King & Prince Seafood Corporation, Brunswick, GA, pg. 631
Tresca, Paul, Dir.-Personnel--After Six, Incorporated, Philadelphia, PA, pg. 24
Trial, Lisa, Mgr.-Personnel--NESLAB Instruments, Inc., Newington, NH, pg. 798
Trine, Denise, Mgr., Personnel & Payroll--Communico, Indianapolis, IN, pg. 270
Trotman, Donna, Personnel Dir.--Varel Manufacturing Co., Dallas, TX, pg. 1145
Trujillo, F. Timothy, Dir.-Personnel--Lear Siegler Telecommunications Div., Anaheim, CA, pg. 664
Trull, Kathryn, Dir.-Personnel--Fritz Chemical Company, Mesquite, TX, pg. 434
Trumble, Betty, Mgr.-Personnel--The Pro Corporation, Florence, MA, pg. 891
Tryon, Douglas, V.P.-Human Resources--P M Company, Philadelphia, PA, pg. 835
Tschirhart, Elaine, V.P.-Human Resources--Indian Head Industries Inc., Southfield, MI, pg. 565
Tucker, Roberta, Personnel Mgr.--Waring & LaRosa, Inc., New York, NY, pg. 1163
Tucker, Roi R., V.P.-Human Resources--D'Agostino Supermarkets Inc., Larchmont, NY, pg. 310
Turner, Debra G., Asst. V.P.-Human Resources--Stauffer Communications, Inc., Topeka, KS, pg. 1042
Turner, G., Dir.-Personnel--Webster Industries Inc., Tiffin, OH, pg. 1171
Turner, James A., V.P. & Dir.-Human Resources--Lester B. Knight & Associates, Inc., Chicago, IL, pg. 637
Turner, Robert J., V.P.-Human Resources--Treasure Chest Advertising Co., Inc., Glendora, CA, pg. 1108
Tussey, Randall, Dir.-Personnel--Brach Candy Company, Chattanooga, TN, pg. 177
Tvilborg, Pete, Dir.-Personnel--Syar Industries, Inc., Napa, CA, pg. 1068
Tylinski, David, Dir.-Personnel--Marathon Cheese Corp., Marathon, WI, pg. 705
Tyska, R., Personnel Mgr.--Packard Instrument Co., Inc., Meriden, CT, pg. 213
Ullom, Yvette L., V.P., Fin., Human Resources & Pur.--Fitzgerald & Company, Inc., Cranston, RI, pg. 416
Underhill, Stephen M., Chief Fin. Officer, Controller & Dir.-Personnel--Rowtronics Company Inc., Indianapolis, IN, pg. 953
Vail, Gary, Dir.-Human Resources--Hvide Shipping, Inc., Fort Lauderdale, FL, pg. 556
Van Aken, John, Sr. V.P.-Human Resources--Visa U.S.A. Inc., San Mateo, CA, pg. 1153
Van Derdys, Benjamin, Dir.-Personnel--Puerto Rico Tourism Company, New York, NY, pg. 899
Van Dolah, Gary, Dir.-Personnel--Hay & Forage Industries, Hesston, KS, pg. 4
Van Dyke, John, V.P.-Personnel--Hall Contracting Corp., Louisville, KY, pg. 501
Van Dyne, Paul, Dir.-Compensation & Benefits--Payless Cashways, Inc., Kansas City, MO, pg. 853
Van Etta, John, Dir.-Human Resources--Lake Region Manufacturing Company, Inc., Chaska, MN, pg. 651
Van Fossan, Janet, Dir.-Human Resources & Sr. Partner--Carmichael Lynch, Inc., Minneapolis, MN, pg. 222
Van Gordon, Paul, V.P.-Human Resources--Rosauer's Supermarkets, Inc., Spokane, WA, pg. 947
Van Hine, Richard, Dir.-Human Resources--Tech Industries, Inc., Woonsocket, RI, pg. 1083
Van Horn, Charlie, Dir.-Human Resources--Thomas Steel Strip Corp., Warren, OH, pg. 1094
Van Moer, Rose, Dir.-Personnel--Walman Optical Company, Minneapolis, MN, pg. 1161
Van Skyock, Jim, Dir.-Personnel--Union City Body Company, Inc., Union City, IN, pg. 1128
Vance, Nick, Dir.-Personnel--Press Enterprise Company, Riverside, CA, pg. 887
Vanderbaan, Russ, Mgr.-Human Resources--Morgan Construction Company, Worcester, MA, pg. 769
Vanderveer, Rodney, Dir.-Human Resources--Rostone Corporation, Lafayette, IN, pg. 950
Vanek, Janet, Mgr.-Human Resources--Security Mutual Life Insurance Co. of New York, Binghamton, NY, pg. 987
VanPelt, J.F., V.P.-Human Resources--Graybar Electric Company, Inc., Clayton, MO, pg. 479
Vargas, Andres, Dir.-Personnel--Cash & Carry Grocer Inc., Chicago, IL, pg. 228
Varma, Bob, V.P.-Opers.--Nathan's Famous Inc., Westbury, NY, pg. 784
Vasilopoulos, Joan, Dir.-Human Resources--Bose Corporation, Framingham, MA, pg. 167
Vaterasian, Michael, Dir.-Personnel--Kasle Steel Corporation, Dearborn, MI, pg. 617
Vaugh, Curtis, Dir.-Personnel--Peterson Industries Inc., Decatur, AR, pg. 864
Vaughan, Alan, Dir.-Human Resources--Minyard Food Stores, Coppell, TX, pg. 759
Vaughn, Ruby, Dir.-Personnel--C. B. Ragland Company, Nashville, TN, pg. 909
Venable, Richard, V.P.-Admin.--McCarty Farms, Magee, MS, pg. 727
Verdoni, Jane, Mgr.-Personnel--Bel-Ray Company, Inc., Farmingdale, NJ, pg. 133
Verhagen, Timothy J., V.P.-Human Resources & Assoc. Gen. Counsel--The Marley Company, Mission Woods, KS, pg. 710
Vetta, Karen, Mgr.-Human Resources--Tekra Corporation, New Berlin, WI, pg. 1084
Vickers, George, Asst. V.P.-Human Resources--Riceland Foods, Inc., Stuttgart, AR, pg. 931
Vickery, Dave, Dir.-Human Resources--Gordon Food Service Inc., Grand Rapids, MI, pg. 472
Victor, Kathy Higgins, V.P.-Human Resources--Northwest Airlines, Inc., Saint Paul, MN, pg. 782
Vidal, Robert G., Sr. V.P.-Human Resources--CenterMark Properties, Inc., Saint Louis, MO, pg. 231
Vidian, Sara, Dir.-Human Resources--Rainfair, Inc., Racine, WI, pg. 910
Vlach, Joseph, V.P.-Admin.--A. W. Mendenhall Co., Inc., Elk Grove Village, IL, pg. 739
Voght, Judy, V.P.-Personnel & Human Resources & Sec.--Tennelec/Nucleus, Inc., Oak Ridge, TN, pg. 1087
Volanski, John, Dir.-Personnel--Rodale Press, Inc., Emmaus, PA, pg. 942
Volino, Don, Dir.-Human Resources--Almac's Inc., East Providence, RI, pg. 1214
Volk, Pam, Mgr.-Human Resources--Idaho Supreme Company, Firth, ID, pg. 561
Vollman, David, Dir.-Data Processing--Henri's Food Products Co., Inc., Milwaukee, WI, pg. 530
Voncina, J., Mgr.-Personnel--Helmsley Enterprises, Inc., New York, NY, pg. 527
Vorreyer, Richard W., Dir.-Indus. Rels.--Lindsay Olive Growers, Lindsay, CA, pg. 676
Vukonich, Mary, Mgr.-Personnel--Vic Manufacturing, Minneapolis, MN, pg. 1149
Vukovich, Julieann, Mgr.-Human Resources--Harza Engineering Co., Chicago, IL, pg. 516
Vuolo, G., V.P.-Labor Rels.--The Grand Union Company, Wayne, NJ, pg. 476
Wachner, Barbara Jo, Exec. V.P.-Mktg., Personnel & Sec.--BGW Systems, Inc., Hawthorne, CA, pg. 106
Wade, Christeen, Dir.-Personnel--Tri-State Wholesale Associated Grocers, El Paso, TX, pg. 1111
Wade, Ed, Player Personnel Admin.--The Phillies-A Limited Partnership, Philadelphia, PA, pg. 867
Wade, Tom W., Jr., Chm. Bd. & Chief Exec. Officer--Tom Wade Co., Kenton, TN, pg. 1157
Waggoner, Jo, Mgr.-Personnel--Pacific Wood Treating Coporation, Ridgefield, WA, pg. 842
Waggoner, Peter, Dir.-Personnel--Waggoner Corp., Troy, MI, pg. 1158
Wagner, Mary, Mgr.-Indus. Rels.--Donlee Technologies Inc., York, PA, pg. 344
Wahlers, Sheila, Dir.-Employee Benefits--Butterick Company, Inc., New York, NY, pg. 197
Waldon, Cynthia, Mgr.-Human Resources--Guard Publishing Company, Eugene, OR, pg. 491
Waldron, Gregory, Sr. V.P., Worldwide Dir., Human Resources--Burson-Marsteller, New York, NY, pg. 1210
Walker, C. Denny, Sec. & Dir.-Personnel--Draper Corporation, Greensboro, NC, pg. 348
Walker, Kern, V.P.-Human Resources--Kurt Manufacturing Co. Inc., Fridley, MN, pg. 646
Walker, Mark, Dir.-Personnel--Klaussner Furniture Industry, Asheboro, NC, pg. 634
Walker, Sharon, Dir.-Admin.--Blue Coral, Inc., Cleveland, OH, pg. 159
Walker, Theresa J., Dir.-Personnel--American Systems Corporation, Chantilly, VA, pg. 63
Walkmath, Luanne T., Limited Investment Partner & Dir.-Human Resources--J. C. Bradford & Co., Nashville, TN, pg. 170
Wall, Scott, Mgr.-Personnel--Action Instruments, Inc., San Diego, CA, pg. 14
Wallace, Lynda, Dir.-Personnel--Swiss-M-Tex, L.P., Travelers Rest, SC, pg. 1068
Waller, Edeast, Dir.-Human Resources--Battelle-Institut E.V., Frankfurt/Main, Germany, pg. 126

Wallersheim, Lorrie, Mgr.-Human Resources--H. C. Miller Company, Milwaukee, WI, pg. 754
Walmsley, Linda, Dir.-Human Resources--Trinidad/Benham Corporation, Denver, CO, pg. 1113
Walsh, Edward, Sr. V.P.-Human Resources--Nutri/System Inc., Blue Bell, PA, pg. 818
Walsh, Jim, V.P.-Human Resources--Edward Don & Company of Illinois, North Riverside, IL, pg. 344
Walter, Patricia, Asst. V.P.-Human Resources--Atlas Van Lines, Inc., Evansville, IN, pg. 96
Walters, Paul, Sr. V.P.-Admin.--Detroit Diesel Corp., Detroit, MI, pg. 859
Walthen, Sandra, Dir.-Personnel--Weichert Realty, Inc., Alexandria, VA, pg. 1173
Walton, Kathy, Personnel Dir. & Admin. Office Mgr.--GWP, Inc., Los Angeles, CA, pg. 441
Walton, Thomas, Mgr.-Personnel--Schweizer Aircraft Corporation, Elmira, NY, pg. 981
Waltos, Ken, Mgr.-Personnel--United States Bakery, Portland, OR, pg. 1134
Wamser, April, Dir.-Personnel--Mark Andy, Inc., Chesterfield, MO, pg. 708
Wandschneider, J.F., V.P.-Corp. & Indus. Rels.--Bradley Corporation, Menomonee Falls, WI, pg. 170
Wantman, Kay, Dir.-Personnel--United Foam Plastics Corporation, Georgetown, MA, pg. 1132
Wanzelak, Al, V.P.-Human Resources--Farm Fresh, Inc., Norfolk, VA, pg. 401
Wanzler, Audre, Dir.-Support Services & Personnel Mgr.--Automotive Rentals, Inc., Mount Laurel, NJ, pg. 101
Ward, Craig, V.P. Admin.-Human Resources--A & E Stores, Inc., Ridgefield, NJ, pg. 1
Ward, David K., V.P.-Admin.--Ward Trucking Corp., Altoona, PA, pg. 1163
Ward, Dick, Controller--Mary Maxim, Inc., Port Huron, MI, pg. 722
Wardell, Barbara, Dir.-Personnel--The Beverly Hills Hotel, Beverly Hills, CA, pg. 148
Ware, Grady R., Dir.-Personnel--States, Inc., Breckenridge, TX, pg. 1041
Warner, Michelle, Managing Dir.-Employee Services--Ferrell Companies Inc./Ferrellgas, Liberty, MO, pg. 407
Warren, Pam, Dir.-Personnel--Contract Furnishings & Systems, Ltd., New York, NY, pg. 280
Washington, Claudith, Dir.-Personnel--Zytec Corp., Eden Prairie, MN, pg. 1221
Wasielewski, Ted, V.P.-Personnel--Baltimore Stationery Co., Baltimore, MD, pg. 116
Waters, James L., V.P.-Employee Rels.--Schnadig Corporation, Chicago, IL, pg. 977
Watkins, Dean, Mgr.-Human Resources--Taylor Machine Works, Inc., Louisville, MS, pg. 1081
Watson, William, Dir.-Human Resources--Mitek, Inc., Chesterfield, MO, pg. 762
Weary, Robert, Dir.-Human Res.--Knouse Foods Inc., Peach Glen, PA, pg. 637
Weaver, Rebecca, Mgr.-Human Resources--Weaver Popcorn Company, Inc., Van Buren, IN, pg. 1170
Webb, Tanya, Dir.-Personnel--Wallace Co. Inc., Houston, TX, pg. 1160
Weber, Gail E., Sr. V.P.-Human Resources & Corp. Serv.--The New England, Boston, MA, pg. 799
Weber, Gail E., Human Resources--The New England, Boston, MA, pg. 799
Weber, Robert, V.P.-Employee Rels.--Preformed Line Products, Cleveland, OH, pg. 886
Weber, Robinn, Dir.-Personnel & Employee Benefits--Russell Stover Candies, Inc., Kansas City, MO, pg. 957
Weber, Susan, Dir.-Human Resources--United Grocers Inc., Portland, OR, pg. 1132
Wechsler, Allan B., Mgr. & Dir.-Personnel--Brown Brothers, Harriman & Co., New York, NY, pg. 181
Wechsler, F., V.P.-Personnel--The Hartz Mountain Corp., Harrison, NJ, pg. 514
Wecker, Irwin, Sr. V.P.-Human Resources--Morse Diesel International, New York, NY, pg. 771
Weeks, George E., Mgr.-Personnel--Maryland Plastics, Inc., Federalsburg, MD, pg. 717
Weeks, George E., Mgr.-Personnel--Maryland Plastics, Inc., Federalsburg, MD, pg. 152
Weeks, Shirley, Chief Fin. Officer & Dir.-Data Processing--Bill Woeste Dealer Group, Cincinnati, OH, pg. 1198
Weeks, Tom, Mgr.-Human Resources & Safety--Coles Express, Bangor, ME, pg. 261
Weinberg, Jo Ann, Dir.-Personnel--Hardin Construction Group, Inc., Atlanta, GA, pg. 508
Weinberg, Pamela T., Sr. V.P., Human Resources--Lawrence Butner Advertising, Inc., New York, NY, pg. 197
Weintraub, Jacqueline, Dir.-Personnel--C. I. Hayes, Inc., Cranston, RI, pg. 519
Weisinger, Robert, Mgr.-Personnel--General Sportcraft Company Ltd., Bergenfield, NJ, pg. 450
Weiss, Robert, Dir.-Personnel & Pur.--Austin Sculpture, Holbrook, NY, pg. 99
Weissblatt, Rita, Mgr.-Personnel--Wechsler Coffee Corp., Moonachie, NJ, pg. 1172
Welbrock, Lynne, Dir.-Human Resources--John Blair Communications, Inc., New York, NY, pg. 155
Welch, Jennifer, Dir.-Personnel & Insurance--USA Petroleum Corporation, Santa Monica, CA, pg. 1124
Welch, Rick, Dir.-Human Resources--McNaughton & Gunn, Inc., Saline, MI, pg. 732
Welge, Rob, Dir.-Personnel--Gilster Mary Lee Corp., Chester, IL, pg. 460
Wellbrock, Lynne, Dir.-Human Resources--Blair Television, New York, NY, pg. 155
Weller, M., Mgr.-Personnel--Miller Electric Mfg. Co., Appleton, WI, pg. 754
Wells, Dave, Personnel Mgr.--Brooks Foods, Mt. Summit, IN, pg. 26
Wells, Earl, Dir.-Personnel--Anchor Industries Inc., Evansville, IN, pg. 71
Wells, Henry, Sr. V.P.-Human Resources--E.J Brach Corporation, Oakbrook Terrace, IL, pg. 169
Wells, Jack, Personnel Dir.--International Cheese Company Limited Partnership, Hinesburg, VT, pg. 575
Wemlinger, Kathy, Dir.-Human Resources--R.S. Owens, Chicago, IL, pg. 834
Wendell, Beth, Dir.-Personnel--The Great Lakes Cheese Co., Newbury, OH, pg. 481
Wenzel, Gilbert F., Dir.-Human Resources--MSI Insurance Companies, Arden Hills, MN, pg. 693
Wermeister, James R., Dir.-Indus. Rels.--Norfolk Shipbuilding & Drydock Corporation, Norfolk, VA, pg. 810
West, Russell, Dir.-Personnel--Community Cash Stores, Spartanburg, SC, pg. 270
West, Theresa, Dir.-Personnel--VV Publishing Corp., New York, NY, pg. 1142
Wetterlin, Debbie, Dir.-Personnel--Triangle Pacific Corporation, Dallas, TX, pg. 1112
Whelan, Joseph, Dir.-Personnel--A-P-A Transport Corp., North Bergen, NJ, pg. 5
Whitaker, Welty E., Dir.-Personnel--Southern Belle Dairy Company, Inc., Somerset, KY, pg. 1020
White, Carolyn M., Dir.-Personnel--Lawry's Restaurants, Inc., Los Angeles, CA, pg. 663
White, Corliss, Dir.-Human Resources--VASA Insurance Group, Inc., Indianapolis, IN, pg. 1146
White, John F., V.P.-Human Resources--Montgomery Elevator Company, Moline, IL, pg. 767
White, M.J., Dir.-Employee Rels.--Griffin Wheel Co., Chicago, IL, pg. 69
White, Michael D., Dir.-Human Resources--Gene B. Glick Company, Inc., Indianapolis, IN, pg. 462
White, Robert, V.P.-Human Resources--Hobart Brothers Co., Troy, OH, pg. 536
White, Susan, V.P.- Human Resources--MTV Networks, New York, NY, pg. 785
White, Tammy, Dir.-Personnel--Town & Country Food Markets, Inc., Wichita, KS, pg. 1103
Whitefield, Doug, Dir.-Personnel--Maze Nails, Peru, IL, pg. 725
Whiteman, Kirk, Dir.-Admin.--Bridgeport Fittings, Inc., Stratford, CT, pg. 175
Wiemeler, Patricia, Mgr.-Personnel--Stuart-Ironsides, Inc., Willowbrook, IL, pg. 1054
Wiggins, Spencer, V.P.-Human Resources--Godfather's Pizza, Inc., Omaha, NE, pg. 464
Wilborn, Janice, Human Resources Mgr.--Aetna Health Plans, San Bruno, CA, pg. 23
Wilcox, Charles, Dir.-Personnel--Kirby Building Systems, Inc., Nashville, TN, pg. 632
Wilde, Darwin, V.P.-Personnel--Our Own Hardware Company, Burnsville, MN, pg. 832
Wildenhaus, Sue, Mgr.-Personnel--A & W Restaurants, Inc., Livonia, MI, pg. 1
Wildsmith, Rose Marie, Dir.-Human Relations--Telesensory, Mountain View, CA, pg. 1085
Wilfong, Karen, Dir.-Personnel & Data Processing--Harry H. Bell & Sons, Inc., Saint Petersburg, FL, pg. 134
Wilkens, Marie, V.P.-Personnel--Oxford First Corporation, Philadelphia, PA, pg. 834
Wilkes, J.C., V.P.-Human Resources--Carus Corporation, Peru, IL, pg. 227
Wilkinson, Karl, Dir.-Personnel--The Bartell Drug Company, Seattle, WA, pg. 122
Williams, Dan, Personnel & Pur. Dir.--M.A.B. Paints, Terre Haute, IN, pg. 184
Williams, Dennis, Dir.-Personnel--Abco Markets, Inc., Phoenix, AZ, pg. 10
Williams, Judy, Mgr.-Human Resources--Time Systems, Inc., Phoenix, AZ, pg. 1097
Williams, L. Eugene, Sr. V.P.-Human Resources--Budget Rent A Car Corporation, Lisle, IL, pg. 131
Williams, Michael S., Co-Dir.-Human Resources--Herff Jones Inc., Indianapolis, IN, pg. 531
Williams, Nancy, V.P.-Personnel--Katz Communications, Inc., New York, NY, pg. 618
Williams, Richard, V.P.-Employee Rels.--Milwaukee Sentinel, Milwaukee, WI, pg. 607
Williams, Richard A., V.P.-Employee Rels.--The Milwaukee Journal, Milwaukee, WI, pg. 607
Williams, Ron, Dir.-Human Resources--Murdock, Inc., Compton, CA, pg. 776
Williams, Timothy L., Sr. V.P.-Human Resources--R. L. Polk & Co., Detroit, MI, pg. 879
Williams, Wayne, Mgr.-Personnel--Whitin Roberts Co., Sanford, NC, pg. 1187
Williamson, Karl, Dir.-Personnel--Fostoria Industries, Inc., Fostoria, OH, pg. 427
Wilseck, Joseph, Dir.-Human Resources--The ISI Manufacturing, Inc., Fraser, MI, pg. 560
Wilson, Fred, Dir.-Personnel--R.S. Young Excavating, Inc., Flint, MI, pg. 1209
Wilson, Judy, Dir.-Personnel--Turner Dairies, Inc., Covington, TN, pg. 1119
Wilson, Linda, Dir.-Personnel--U.R.M. Stores, Inc., Spokane, WA, pg. 1124
Wilson, Richard P., Sr. V.P.-Human Resources--Franchise Enterprises Inc., Rocky Mount, NC, pg. 428
Wilson, Robert K., Dir.-Personnel--Roseburg Forest Products Co., Dillard, OR, pg. 948
Wilson, Victoria, Dir.-Pub. Rels. & Personnel--American SelfCare Corporation, Columbus, GA, pg. 60
Wineland, Douglas D., V.P.-Personnel Services--W.S. Badcock Corporation, Mulberry, FL, pg. 113
Wingert, J. Robert, Dir.-Corp. Human Resources--Dentsply International Inc., York, PA, pg. 329
Winschel, Richard, Mgr.-Personnel--Ridg-U-Rak, Inc., North East, PA, pg. 933
Winslow, Emmet, Dir.-Mfg. & Personnel--Whiting Manufacturing Co., Inc., Cincinnati, OH, pg. 1187
Winston, Michael T., Dir.-Personnel--Action Equipment, Londonderry, NH, pg. 14
Winter, Patti, Dir.-Personnel--Siemer Milling Company, Teutopolis, IL, pg. 1002
Winters, Dick, V.P.-Human Resources--BJ Acquisition Corp., Charlotte, NC, pg. 107
Wirtz, Joseph, Mgr.-Personnel--Pitco Frialator Inc., Concord, NH, pg. 157
Wise, Dan, Dir.-Human Resources--Heery International, Inc., Atlanta, GA, pg. 525
Wisneski, Robyn, Dir.-Personnel--General Media Publishing Group, New York, NY, pg. 450
Witte, Linda, Mgr.-Human Resources--Servus Footwear Company, Rock Island, IL, pg. 993
Wittig, James R., V.P.-Human Resources--American Seating Company, Grand Rapids, MI, pg. 60
Wittmier, Darwin, Dir.-Personnel--Nodak Mutual Insurance Co., Fargo, ND, pg. 808
Wittmier, Darwin T., Dir.-Human Resources--Nodak Mutual Insurance Company, Fargo, ND, pg. 808
Witwer, John L., Jr., Dir.-Personnel--Lancaster Malleable Castings Company, Lancaster, PA, pg. 653
Wolcott, Barbara M., Mgr.-Human Res.--Townsend & Bottum, Inc., Ann Arbor, MI, pg. 1104
Wolf, Steven E., V.P.-Human Resources--Pueblo International, Inc., Pompano Beach, FL, pg. 899
Wolfe, Teri, Dir.-Personnel--Lost Arrow Corporation, Ventura, CA, pg. 684
Wolter, Richard, Dir.-Personnel--Symons Corporation, Des Plaines, IL, pg. 1069
Wolverton, Michael G., Dir.-Personnel--Fleer Corporation, Mount Laurel, NJ, pg. 695
Wood, Bruce, Dir.-Human Resources--Great Salt Lake Minerals & Chemicals Corp., Ogden, UT, pg. 482
Wood, C. William, V.P.-Human Resources--PacifiCare Health Systems, Inc., Cypress, CA, pg. 1127
Wood, Carol S., Treas., Sec., Controller & Chief Fin. Officer--Higginbotham-Bartlett Co., Lubbock, TX, pg. 533
Wood, Dennis, Sr. V.P., Gen. Counsel & Personnel--Atari Games Corporation, Milpitas, CA, pg. 93
Woodruff, W., V.P.-Personnel--Steuart Petroleum Company, Washington, DC, pg. 1048
Woods, John, Mgr.-Personnel--Shugart Corporation, Irvine, CA, pg. 1001
Woods, Valerie, Dir.-Human Resources--Bing Steel Inc., Detroit, MI, pg. 151
Workes, Mona, Mgr.-Personnel--Efco Corporation, Monett, MO, pg. 359
Workman, Sandra, Dir.-Personnel--Computer Sales International Inc., Saint Louis, MO, pg. 271
Worley, Ernie, Dir.-Human Resources--Automation Intelligence, Inc., Maitland, FL, pg. 101
Worobow, Robert, V.P.-Human Resources--Quill Corp., Lincolnshire, IL, pg. 905
Wortman, Dan B., V.P.-Human Resources--Bernhardt Furniture Co., Lenoir, NC, pg. 144
Wright, Frank, Dir.-Human Resources--Thompson Tractor Company, Birmingham, AL, pg. 1095
Wright, Randy, Mgr.-Personnel--Quik N Tasty Foods, Belton, MO, pg. 905
Wyle, Edwin W., Dir.-Human Resources--Coppus Engineering Corp., Millbury, MA, pg. 285
Wyles, J.R., Personnel Mgr.--Schenectady Chemicals, Inc., Schenectady, NY, pg. 975
Wyman, William Corson, Mgr.-Personnel--Electro Fiberoptics Corporation, Northborough, MA, pg. 374
Yake, Byron, Dir.-Human Resources--The Associated Press, New York, NY, pg. 91
Yanca, Larry, Dir.-Personnel--C. W. Zumbiel Company, Cincinnati, OH, pg. 1221
Yanello, Cheryl, V.P.-Human Resources--Everfresh Beverages Inc., Franklin Park, IL, pg. 391
Yarsin, A.B., Exec. V.P., Gen Mgr. & Human Resources Mgr.--Miller Products Company, Inc., North Bergen, NJ, pg. 755
Yates, Veseth, Dir.-Human Resources--Darigold, Inc., Seattle, WA, pg. 315
Yates, Vesetn, Dir.-Human Resources--Dairygold Inc., Seattle, WA, pg. 311
Yeakel, Lana, Dir.-Personnel--AMI Industries, Inc., Colorado Springs, CO, pg. 5
Yelverton, Tracey, Mgr.-Human Resources--PCI, Austin, TX, pg. 836
Yesulis, Norine, Mgr.-Personnel--Tang Industries Inc., Elk Grove Village, IL, pg. 1078
York, Larry, V.P.-Human Resources--Meadowcraft, Inc., Birmingham, AL, pg. 733
York, Mildred, V.P.-Personnel--American Arbritration Association, New York, NY, pg. 49
Young, David, Dir.-Human Resources Devel.--Friendly Ice Cream Corp., Wilbraham, MA, pg. 1087
Young, Heather, Personnel Mgr.--Boyer Bros. Inc., Altoona, PA, pg. 169
Young, William J., Sr. V.P., Human Resources Dir.--William Douglas McAdams Inc., New York, NY, pg. 726
Yount, Deborah E., Dir.-Personnel--UES, Inc., Dayton, OH, pg. 1122
Zagari, Don, Mgr.-Personnel--Cerro Copper Products Co., Sauget, IL, pg. 711
Zaloum, Basile H., V.P.-Human Resources--Interstate Resources, Inc., Rosslyn, VA, pg. 580
Zampini, Ralph, Dir.-Personnel--Krasdale Foods Inc., Bronx, NY, pg. 644
Zani, D., V.P.-Human Resources--F & M Distributors Inc., Warren, MI, pg. 393
Zdeb, Diane, Dir.-Personnel--Bentley, Barnes & Lynn, Inc., Chicago, IL, pg. 140
Zega, Robert, Personnel Dir.--AEC, Inc., Wood Dale, IL, pg. 1047
Zeller, Dudley, Dir.-Personnel & Risk Mngmt.--Golden Gem Growers Inc., Umatilla, FL, pg. 466
Zeppelin, Tom, Mgr.-Personnel--Gulf States Manufacturers, Inc., Starkville, MS, pg. 494
Zermmerman, Holly, Gen. Mgr.-Human Resources--Farmland Industries, Inc., Kansas City, MO, pg. 402

Zibell, Susan M., Asst. V.P. & Dir. Personnel--Great Lakes Financial Resources, Inc., Homewood, IL, pg. 481
Zimcosky, Jim, V.P.-Human Resources--Affiliated Food Stores, Keller, TX, pg. 23
Zimmerman, Edward, Sec., Treas. & Personnel Mgr.--Dobles Chevrolet, Inc., Manchester, NH, pg. 342
Zimmerman, Michelle, Dir.-Human Resources--Microband Companies, Inc., Fairfield, NJ, pg. 748
Zinsmeister, Rudy, V.P.-Human Resources--White Swan, Inc., Euless, TX, pg. 1156
Zitelli, Bernadette, Dir.-Human Resources--Bel-Art Products, Pequannock, NJ, pg. 133
Zuccaro, Kim, Dir.-Personnel--Seaman-Patrick Paper Company, Detroit, MI, pg. 986
Zug, Steve, Mgr.-Human Resources--Wavetek Communications Div., Indianapolis, IN, pg. 1168

PRESIDENT

Aamodt, Gary N.J., Pres. & Chief Exec. Officer--Augsburg Fortress, Publishers, Minneapolis, MN, pg. 98
Aanenson, Vernon O., Pres. & Treas.--Old Dutch Foods, Inc., Saint Paul, MN, pg. 823
Aaron, Marcus, II, Pres.--The Homer Laughlin China Company, Newell, WV, pg. 661
Aaron, Richard J., Pres. & Chief Oper. Officer--Berkeley Industries Inc., Laguna Beach, CA, pg. 141
Abbell, Joseph J., Chm. Bd. & Pres.--Abbell Associates, Chicago, IL, pg. 9
Abbey, Nelson D., III, Pres. & Chief Oper. Officer--Abbey Etna Machine Company, Perrysburg, OH, pg. 9
Abbot, Jerry, Pres.--Metro Label Corp., Garland, TX, pg. 743
Abbot, Jerry, Pres.--Metro Label Corp., Belleville, NJ, pg. 743
Abbott, Garry, Mng. Dir. & Creative Dir.--Ketchum Advertising Singapore, Singapore, Singapore, pg. 625
Abbott, John R., Pres.--J.R. Abbott Construction, Inc., Seattle, WA, pg. 9
Abdalla, Herbert A., Pres. & Chief Exec. Officer--Abdalla's Lafayette, Inc., Lafayette, LA, pg. 10
Abel, Gary V., Pres.--C.R. Daniels, Inc., Ellicott City, MD, pg. 314
Abott, Michael, Pres.--American Republic Insurance Co., Des Moines, IA, pg. 60
Abplanalp, Robert H., Chm. Bd., Pres. & Chief Exec. Officer--Precision Valve Corporation, Yonkers, NY, pg. 885
Abraham, Eugene V., Sr. Partner--Sargent & Lundy, Chicago, IL, pg. 971
Abraham, Otto W., Chm. Bd. & Pres.--Engineered Products, Inc., Pittsburgh, PA, pg. 382
Abrams, Alan R., Pres.--Abbott Glass Co., Inc., Maspeth, NY, pg. 9
Abrams, Allan, Chm. Bd. & Pres.--Arrow Fastener Co., Inc., Saddle Brook, NJ, pg. 85
Abrams, Richard, Pres.--Abrams Publishing Inc., Waterbury, CT, pg. 10
Abrams, Stephen, Pres.--Organically Grown Corporation, Los Angeles, CA, pg. 829
Abramson, David B., Pres. & Chief Exec. Officer--Abramson Ehrlich Manes, Inc., Washington, DC, pg. 10
Abramson, Earl, Chm. Bd. & Pres.--Rapid Mounting & Finishing Co., Chicago, IL, pg. 913
Abramson, Howard J., Pres.--Baron-Abramson, Inc., Medford, MA, pg. 121
Ach, Roger W., II, Pres. & Chief Exec. Officer--Chicago West Pullman Corporation, Cincinnati, OH, pg. 246
Achenbaum, Warren, Pres.--Cox & Company, Inc., New York, NY, pg. 292
Achi, Maher, Mng. Dir.--H & C, Leo Burnett, Beirut,, Lebanon, pg. 192
Acker, David, Pres.--Sleepy's The Mattress Professionals, Port Washington, NY, pg. 1010
Acker, Stanley, Chm., Pres. & Chief Exec. Officer--Pavion Ltd., Nyack on Hudson, NY, pg. 852
Acker, William L., III, Pres.--Acker Drill Co. Inc., Chinchilla, PA, pg. 12
Ackerman, Robert D., Pres. & Chief Oper. Officer--Lord, Sullivan & Yoder, Inc. Advertising, Columbus, OH, pg. 683
Ackerman, Roy A., Chm. Bd. & Chief Exec. Officer--Astre Corporate Group, Alexandria, VA, pg. 92
Acklen, Charles, Pres. & Chief Exec. Officer--Bill's Dollar Stores, Inc., Jackson, MS, pg. 150
Acomb, James C., Pres. & Chief Exec. Officer--Restaurant Company, Inc., Birmingham, AL, pg. 929
Acree, James, Pres.--G & W Electric Co., Blue Island, IL, pg. 438
Adams, Bradway B., Pres.--Arcola Wire Company, Branford, CT, pg. 81
Adams, Harold L., Chm. Bd., Pres. & Cheif Exec. Officer--RTKL Associates Inc., Baltimore, MD, pg. 908
Adams, Harry, Pres., Chief Exec. Officer, & Chief Fin. Officer--Pyttronic Industries, Inc., Montgomeryville, PA, pg. 901
Adams, John G., Pres. & Gen. Mgr.--Adams Extract Co., Inc., Austin, TX, pg. 16
Adams, John S., Pres.--Construction Management Service, Wilmington, DE, pg. 277
Adams, Kirby, Pres. & Chief Exec. Officer--Titanium Metals Corporation, Denver, CO, pg. 1109
Adams, Pelham E., Pres.--Adams Business Forms, Topeka, KS, pg. 16
Adams, Peter D., Chm. & Pres.--Adams Rite Manufacturing Co., City of Industry, CA, pg. 16
Adams, R.E., Pres.--Dixie Electric Cooperative, Union Springs, AL, pg. 341
Adams, R.L., Pres. & Chief Exec. Officer--Rubatex Corporation, Bedford, VA, pg. 480
Adams, Robert E., Pres. & Chief Exec. Officer--MidSouth Ice Co., Huntsville, AL, pg. 1030
Adams, Robert J., Pres. & Chief Exec. Officer--R. P. Adams Company, Inc., Tonawanda, NY, pg. 16
Adar, U., Pres.-North America--Zim-American Israeli Shipping Co., New York, NY, pg. 1219
Addy, Donald, Pres.--Normark Corporation, Minneapolis, MN, pg. 810
Adelman, Jason, Pres.--A & Z Hayward, Inc., East Providence, RI, pg. 1
Adelsperger, Steven L., Pres.--Union City Body Company, Inc., Union City, IN, pg. 1128
Adelstein, Stanford M., Pres.--Northwestern Engineering Co., Rapid City, SD, pg. 815
Ades, Alan, Chm., Pres. & Chief Exec. Officer--A & E Stores, Inc., Ridgefield, NJ, pg. 1
Adkins, William J., Pres.--Torrance Nissan, Inc., Torrance, CA, pg. 1102
Adler, Frederick R., Mng. Partner--Adler & Shaykin, New York, NY, pg. 17
Adler, Larry M., Pres. & Chief Exec. Officer--Adler Boschetto Peebles & Partners, Inc., New York, NY, pg. 17
Adler, Michael, Pres.--Myron Manufacturing Corporation, Maywood, NJ, pg. 780
Adler, Thomas W., Pres.--Fort Dearborn Lithograph Company, Niles, IL, pg. 425
Adolfson, David G., Chm. Bd., Pres. & Chief Exec. Officer--Adolfson & Peterson, Inc., Minneapolis, MN, pg. 18
Adrian, R., Gen. Mgr.--Central, East Central, West Central Divs., Niles, IL, pg. 817
Affleck, Mark, Pres.--California Avocado Commission, Santa Ana, CA, pg. 209
Agan, R.E., Pres. & Chief Exec. Officer--Hardinge Brothers, Inc., Elmira, NY, pg. 508
Aginian, Richard D., Pres. & Chief Exec. Officer--Suburban Communications Corp., Livonia, MI, pg. 1055
Agne, Sue Wiegmann, Pres.--E.M. Wiegmann & Company, Inc., Freeburg, IL, pg. 1188
Agresta, Michael, Pres.--Michael Stevens Ltd., Edison, NJ, pg. 1048
Agronin, R.D., Grp. V.P.--The Black Clawson Co., New York, NY, pg. 154
Aguirre, Henry J., Pres. & Treas.--Mexican Industries in Michigan, Detroit, MI, pg. 745
Ahern, Paul J., Pres.--Ahern New York, New York, NY, pg. 26
Ahrens, Jay, Chm. Bd., Pres. & Chief Exec. Officer--Holly's Inc., Grand Rapids, MI, pg. 540
Aitken, Sharon, Pres.--The Florists Assn. of Greater Cleveland, Inc., Cleveland, OH, pg. 421
Akers, James F., Pres. & Chief Exec. Officer--The Crystal Tissue Co., Middletown, OH, pg. 303
Akers, William C., Chm. Bd.--The Crystal Tissue Co., Middletown, OH, pg. 303
Akers, William C., Pres.--Akers Packaging Service Inc., Middletown, OH, pg. 28
Akins, Perry S., Pres. & Chief Exec. Officer--ELS Educational Services, Culver City, CA, pg. 56
Al-Barzinji, Jamal, Pres.--Mar-Jac Inc., Gainesville, GA, pg. 705
Alban, James C., III, Pres.--Alban Tractor Co. Inc., Baltimore, MD, pg. 30
Albarelli, Michael, Jr., Chm. Bd. & Pres.--Amloid Corporation, Saddle Brook, NJ, pg. 67
Albers, John R., Chm. Bd., Pres. & Chief Exec. Officer--Dr Pepper/Seven-Up Companies, Inc., Dallas, TX, pg. 342
Albers, Murrey R., Chm. Bd. & Pres.--United States Bakery, Portland, OR, pg. 1134
Albert, Andrew B., Pres. & Co-Chief Exec. Officer--Rittenhouse Inc., Park Ridge, IL, pg. 936
Albert, Larry, Pres.--R.L. Albert & Son, Inc., Greenwich, CT, pg. 31
Albert, Michael P., Chm. Bd. & Pres.--The Harodite Finishing Company Inc., North Dighton, MA, pg. 510
Albertson, Ed, Pres.--DSIC/TMP Worldwide, Clawson, MI, pg. 1074
Albrecht, Arlin, Pres.--Red Wing Publishing Company, Red Wing, MN, pg. 919
Albrecht, Ivan, Pres.--Gilcrest Storage, Akron, OH, pg. 31
Albrecht, Steven, Pres. & Chief Exec. Officer--The Fred W. Albrecht Grocery Co., Akron, OH, pg. 31
Alcantara, Severo, Pres.--Marketforce Advertising Philippines Inc., Manila,, Philippines, pg. 330
Alcorn, Charles S., Pres. & Chief Oper. Officer--Donlee Technologies Inc., York, PA, pg. 344
Alcorn, Terry, V.P.-North American Sls.--Connors Brunswick, Inc., South Portland, ME, pg. 275
Alcorn, Terry, V.P.-N. American Sls.--Port Clyde Foods Co., South Portland, ME, pg. 276
Aldrich, David, Pres.--Energy and Technology Management Corporation, Germantown, MD, pg. 981
Aldrich, Thomas L., Pres. & Chief Exec. Officer--Camp International, Jackson, MI, pg. 153
Aldridge, Edward C., Pres. & Chief Exec. Officer--The Aerospace Corporation, El Segundo, CA, pg. 22
Alesi, Charles, Pres.--O. S. Walker Co. Inc., Worcester, MA, pg. 1160
Alessandrini, Walter, Pres. & Chief Exec. Officer--Union Switch & Signal Inc., Pittsburgh, PA, pg. 1129
Aleu, Dr. Fernando, Pres.--Paco Rabanne Parfums, New York, NY, pg. 842
Alexander, George, Pres.--Herbal Enterprises Inc., Manchester, CT, pg. 530
Alexander, Patrick D., Pres. & Chief Exec. Officer--Cold Spring Granite Company, Minnetonka, MN, pg. 259
Alexander, Toni, Pres.--Intercommunications Inc., Newport Beach, CA, pg. 574
Aley, Paul N., Pres. & Chief Exec. Officer--National Machinery Company, Tiffin, OH, pg. 792
Alford, B.W., II, Pres.--Alford Refrigerated Warehouse, Inc., Dallas, TX, pg. 34
Alford, J. Keith, Pres. & Chief Exec. Officer--Adam Meldrum & Anderson Co., Inc., Buffalo, NY, pg. 16
Algre, Marie A., Gen. Mgr.-North America--Aero Peru Corporation, Miami, FL, pg. 22
Allard, Jean Marc, Chm. Bd., Pres. & Chief Exec. Officer--Hubbard Construction Co., Winter Park, FL, pg. 549
Allard, John R., Pres. & Chief Exec. Officer--Jewell Instruments, Inc., Manchester, NH, pg. 594
Allard, R., Pres.--Snow-Nabstedt Power Transmissions, Manchester, NH, pg. 476
Allard, Ronald A., Pres.--Granite State Manufacturing Co., Manchester, NH, pg. 476
Allbritten, G.R., Chief Oper. Officer--Ferry-Morse Seed Company, Modesto, CA, pg. 407
Allegretti, Alfred, Pres.--Bayside Fuel Oil Depot Corp., Brooklyn, NY, pg. 128
Allemeier, David, Pres., Chief Creative Officer--Noble & Associates, Springfield, MO, pg. 808
Allen, Charles S., Pres. & Chief Exec. Officer--Sloan Valve Company, Franklin Park, IL, pg. 1010
Allen, David, Chm., Pres. & Chief Exec. Officer--AMD Industries Inc., Cicero, IL, pg. 5
Allen, Delbert E., Jr., Pres.--Allen Canning Company, Siloam Springs, AR, pg. 35
Allen, Guy F., Chm. Bd. & Pres.--R.G. Meadows, Inc., Great Neck, NY, pg. 733
Allen, Harvey, Pres. & Chief Exec. Officer--M.S. Walker, Inc./Seacoast, Somerville, MA, pg. 1160
Allen, Herbert A., Pres. & Mng. Dir.--Allen & Company Incorporated, New York, NY, pg. 35
Allen, J. William Jr., Pres.--J.W. Allen & Company, Wheeling, IL, pg. 36
Allen, Kenneth L., Pres.-Homebuilding Div.--The Great Atlantic Companies, Hampton, VA, pg. 480
Allen, R. Todd, Pres. & Chief Oper. Officer--The Harry Alter Company, Chicago, IL, pg. 45
Allen, Robert M., Pres.--Allens Of Hastings, Inc., Hastings, NE, pg. 36
Allen, Robert, Jr., Pres.--Allen Steel Co., Salt Lake City, UT, pg. 36
Allen, Stanley, Pres.--Allen Foods, Inc., Saint Louis, MO, pg. 36
Allen, Terrence J., Chm. Bd. & Pres.--Pemco Die Casting Corporation, Bridgman, MI, pg. 856
Allen, Terry, Pres.-Swimwear/Taren--Cole of California, Los Angeles, CA, pg. 1079
Allen, Todd, Pres.--The Harry Alter Company, Chicago, IL, pg. 1086
Allen, William A., Pres.--Wells Mfg. Corp., Dond Du Lac, WI, pg. 1123
Allen, William B., Pres.--Republic Alloys, Inc., Charlotte, NC, pg. 927
Allison, James, Pres. & Dir.-Res. & Devel.--Taylor-Evans Seed Co., Tulia, TX, pg. 1081
Allred, Barry L., Pres., Chief Oper. Officer & Treas.--Elkins Constructors, Inc., Jacksonville, FL, pg. 377
Allsop, Ivor J., Pres.--Allsop, Inc., Bellingham, WA, pg. 43
Allsopp, Cornelius, P.E., Pres. & Treas.--Harvey Construction Company, Inc., Bedford, NH, pg. 515
Allsup, Lonnie D., Chm. Bd. & Pres.--Allsups Convenience Stores Inc., Clovis, NM, pg. 43
Alois, Edward J., Pres.--Unifoil Corporation, Passaic, NJ, pg. 1126
Alosa, Joseph R., Pres. & Treas.--Patsy's, Inc., Concord, NH, pg. 851
Alperson, Robert, Chm. Bd. & Pres.--Rolled Steel Products Corporation, Los Angeles, CA, pg. 944
Alpert, Norman R., Chm. Bd., Pres. & Chief Exec. Officer--Bio-Tek Instruments, Inc., Winooski, VT, pg. 152
Alsop, Richard D., Pres.--Bonneville Communications, Salt Lake City, UT, pg. 164
Alterman, Sidney, Pres.--Alterman Transport Lines, Inc., Opa Locka, FL, pg. 45
Altholz, Thomas I., Pres. & Chief Oper. Officer--Inlander-Steindler Paper, Vernon Hills, IL, pg. 570
Altier, Richard J., Pres. & Chief Oper. Officer--Altier & Sons Shoes Inc., Rochester, NY, pg. 45
Altman, Barry, Pres.--Smith Mailer, City of Industry, CA, pg. 210
Altobello, Daniel, Chm., Pres. & Chief Exec. Officer--Caterair International, Potomac, MD, pg. 229
Alvarez, Antonio C., Pres. & Chief Oper. Officer--Phar-Mor, Inc., Youngstown, OH, pg. 866
Alvarez, Julio, Pres.--Wolfberg, Alvarez & Associates Inc., Miami, FL, pg. 1199
Alvarez, Julius, Pres.--Nortown Oldsmobile Inc., Skokie, IL, pg. 816
Alvarez, Paul H., Chm. Bd., Pres. & Chief Exec. Officer--Ketchum Communications Inc., Pittsburgh, PA, pg. 625
Alyea, G. Mark, Pres. & Chief Oper. Officer--Alro Group, Jackson, MI, pg. 44
Ambraziunas, Ray, Pres.--Cellular Service, Inc., Glendale, CA, pg. 231
Ambrose, Michael, Pres. & Gen. Mgr.--Cottman Transmission Systems, Inc., Fort Washington, PA, pg. 288
Ament, Werner E., Chm. Bd., Pres., Chief Exec. Officer & Sec.--Milex of America, Inc., Chicago, IL, pg. 753
Ames, William, Pres.--Allied Paper Incorporated, Dayton, OH, pg. 38
Ammann, Fritz, Pres. & Chief Exec. Officer--Esprit de Corp., San Francisco, CA, pg. 388
Amore, Joe, Chm. Bd., Pres. & Chief Exec. Officer--BeefAmerica Operating Co., Inc., Omaha, NE, pg. 131
Amos, George H., III, Pres.--Tucson Realty & Trust Co., Tucson, AZ, pg. 1118
Amster, Harry S., Pres.--A S H, Inc., Phoenix, AZ, pg. 8
Anasto, John, Pres., Chief Exec. & Chief Oper. Officer--Strongheart Products, Inc., Kansas City, KS, pg. 1054
Anchel, Edward, Chm. Bd. & Pres.--Sparkomatic Corporation, Milford, PA, pg. 1025
Anchel, Edward, Chm. Bd. & Pres.--Kenco, Middlebury, IN, pg. 1025
Anchel, Edward, Chm. & Pres.--Altec Lansing Consumer Products, Milford, PA, pg. 1025
Andalcio, David, Pres.--Abbott Industrial Supply, Chicago, IL, pg. 9
Anderson, Arthur, Pres.--Lindenmeyr Munroe, Peabody, MA, pg. 233

Anderson, Barry, Mng. Dir.--Mattingly & Partners/Sydney, Crows Nest,, Australia, pg. 331
Anderson, Charles J., Pres.--Anderson Advertising, Inc., San Antonio, TX, pg. 72
Anderson, Charles M., Pres. & Chief Oper. Officer--Stamler Corporation, Millersburg, KY, pg. 1035
Anderson, Clifford I., Chm. Bd. & Pres.--Crown Holdings, Inc., Roseville, MN, pg. 302
Anderson, Craig, Pres.--The Hercules Tire & Rubber Company, Findlay, OH, pg. 531
Anderson, Craig E., Pres.--Hercules Tire & Rubber Company, Findlay, OH, pg. 531
Anderson, Davis G., Pres.--Chicago Extruded Metals Co., Cicero, IL, pg. 245
Anderson, Ernest R., Pres.--Anderson, Dusenbury & Alban, Atlanta, GA, pg. 72
Anderson, G. D., Jr., Pres. & Chief Exec. Officer--Sherley Grain Company, Bovina, TX, pg. 998
Anderson, Gordon B., Chm. Bd. & Pres.--Gordy's, Inc., Worthington, MN, pg. 472
Anderson, Harold E., Pres.--Anderson Trucking Service Inc., Saint Cloud, MN, pg. 73
Anderson, Ivan V., Jr., Pres.--Evening Post Publishing Co., Charleston, SC, pg. 391
Anderson, James D., Pres. & Chief Exec. Officer--Central DuPage Health System, Naperville, IL, pg. 232
Anderson, James R., Pres.--Concrete Technology Corp., Tacoma, WA, pg. 273
Anderson, John, Pres., Chief Exec. & Oper. Officer--Alabama Farmers Co-op, Decatur, AL, pg. 28
Anderson, John E., Pres. & Treas.--Topa Equities Ltd, Inc., Los Angeles, CA, pg. 1101
Anderson, John R., Chm. Bd. & Pres.--Anderson Industries Inc., Rockford, IL, pg. 73
Anderson, Liz, Chm. Bd.--Washington State Dairy Products Commission, Seattle, WA, pg. 1167
Anderson, Mark R., Pres. & Chief Exec. Officer--Mark Anderson Associates, Inc., Arlington Heights, IL, pg. 73
Anderson, Milada F., Pres.--F & B Manufacturing Co., Chicago, IL, pg. 393
Anderson, Norm, Pres., Chief Exec. Officer--Anderson, Rothstein & Fiqua, San Francisco, CA, pg. 73
Anderson, R. Quintus, Chm. Bd. & Pres.--The Aarque Companies, Jamestown, NY, pg. 9
Anderson, Ralph, Chm Bd., Pres., & Chief Exec. Officer--Belcan Corporation, Cincinnati, OH, pg. 133
Anderson, Richard C., Pres. & Chief Exec. Officer--Fairfield Industries, Inc., Houston, TX, pg. 397
Anderson, Richard E., Chm. Bd. & Pres.--Cadet Manufacturing Company, Vancouver, WA, pg. 207
Anderson, Richard N., Pres.--X-A Cabinet Corporation, La Mirada, CA, pg. 1206
Anderson, Richard P., Pres. & Chief Exec. Officer--The Andersons, Maumee, OH, pg. 73
Anderson, Robert, Pres.--Celebrity Boats, Inc., Benton, IL, pg. 609
Anderson, Robert, Pres.--Bruss Company, Chicago, IL, pg. 184
Anderson, Ruel L., Jr., Pres. & Chief Exec. Officer--Anco Insulations, Inc., Baton Rouge, LA, pg. 72
Anderson, Thomas L., Chm. Bd. & Pres.--Anderson Industries, Inc., Dallas, TX, pg. 72
Andis, M. L., Chm. Bd. & Pres.--Andis Company, Racine, WI, pg. 74
Andonian, Andy K., Pres.--A K H Company, Inc., Los Angeles, CA, pg. 4
Andras, O.S., Pres.--Enterprise Products Company, Houston, TX, pg. 382
Andre, Benny, Pres.--Diamond Motors Inc., Baton Rouge, LA, pg. 335
Andreas, George C., Chm. Bd. & Pres.--Lantzsch-Andreas Enterprises, Inc., Vienna, VA, pg. 658
Andreoli, James M., Pres. & Chief Exec. Officer--Baker Commodities, Inc., Los Angeles, CA, pg. 115
Andretta, Vincent J., Pres., Chief Exec. Officer & Treas.--Colony Liquor Distributors, Inc., Kingston, NY, pg. 264
Andrews, George W., Chm. Bd. & Pres.--Keco Industry, Inc., Florence, KY, pg. 619
Andrews, Mark G., Pres.--C & M Corporation, Wauregan, CT, pg. 198
Andringa, Mary, Pres. & Chief Oper. Officer--Vermeer Manufacturing Company, Pella, IA, pg. 1148
Andrus, Edward R., Pres. & Chief Exec. Officer--Premier Coatings, Inc., Elk Grove Village, IL, pg. 886
Anfankar, Haim, Pres. & Gen. Mgr.--Willoughby's, New York, NY, pg. 1193
Anfield, Frank A., Pres. & Chief Exec. Officer-Y&R New York--Young & Rubicam New York, New York, NY, pg. 1211
Angelich, Samuel M., Chm., Pres. & Chief Exec. Officer--Amelco Corporation, Gardena, CA, pg. 47
Angell, Charles T., Pres.--Newly Weds Foods Inc., Chicago, IL, pg. 804
Angelo, Ray, Pres.--Angelo Brothers Co., Philadelphia, PA, pg. 74
Anger, Randy C., Pres.--J. M. Jayson & Co., Inc., Getsville, NY, pg. 591
Anglin, Richard R., Pres. & Chief Exec. & Oper. Officer--Robertson Factories, Inc., Taunton, MA, pg. 939
Angott, Lawrence, Pres.--C.F. Burger Creamery Company, Detroit, MI, pg. 190
Anhut, Francie, Pres. & Chief Oper. Officer--MarketPulse, Cambridge, MA, pg. 884
Anschutz, Philip, Pres.--Anschutz Corporation, Denver, CO, pg. 75
Anson, Joe, Pres.--Anson-Stoner, Inc., Winter Park, FL, pg. 76
Anthony, Clary, Sr., Pres.--Anthony Forest Products Co., Inc., El Dorado, AR, pg. 77
Anthony, Don, Pres.--Lexington Co-Op Oil Co., Lexington, NE, pg. 673
Anthony, John E., Chm. Bd. & Pres.--Bearden Lumber Company, Inc., Bearden, AR, pg. 129
Antink, Grant S., Pres. & Chief Exec. Officer--Drafting Graphics, Inc., Elk Grove Village, IL, pg. 348
Anton, Karl V., Jr., Pres.--Van Son Holland Ink Corp. of America, Mineola, NY, pg. 1144
Anton, Nick, Pres.--WEN Products, Inc., Chicago, IL, pg. 1156
Antonellis, Domenic, Pres.--Stark Candy Company, Pewaukee, WI, pg. 1123
Antonellis, Domenic M., Pres. & Chief Oper. Officer--New England Confectionery Co., Cambridge, MA, pg. 1123
Antos, Joseph, Dr., Mng. Dir.--Young & Rubicam Vienna Werbegesellschaft m.b.H., Vienna,, Austria, pg. 1213
Appell, Louis J., Jr., Pres.--Susquehanna Pfaltzgraff, York, PA, pg. 1065
Apperson, R.P., Chm. Bd. & Pres.--Apperson Business Forms, Inc., Los Angeles, CA, pg. 78
Appich, Charles W., Jr., Pres.--Emrick Chevrolet Sales Corporation, Richmond, VA, pg. 380
Apple, P. Jack, Pres.--Cummins Cumberland Inc., Louisville, KY, pg. 305
Applebach, Chuck, Pres. & Chief Oper. Officer--The Polizos Agency, Norfolk, VA, pg. 879
Applebaum, Arnold N., Pres.--Solid State Devices, Inc., La Mirada, CA, pg. 1017
Appleby, Don, Pres.--The George E. Failing Company, Enid, OK, pg. 161
Applegate, L. Thomas, Pres. & Chief Oper. Officer--Surgical Appliance Industries, Inc., Cincinnati, OH, pg. 1065
Applequist, Dale M., Pres., Chief Exec. Officer & New Bus. Contact--Cash Plus, Inc., Minneapolis, MN, pg. 228
Applequist, Roy, Pres.--Great Plains Manufacturing, Inc., Assaria, KS, pg. 482
Appt, James L., Pres. Treas. & New Bus. Contact--Communications Concepts, Toledo, OH, pg. 269
Apter, Allen D., Pres.--R.A. Industries, Inc., Lansdale, PA, pg. 906
Aquilina, Benjamin, Pres.--Victoria Packing Corporation, Brooklyn, NY, pg. 1149
Aquirre, G.E., Chm. Bd. & Pres.--SaniServ, Indianapolis, IN, pg. 970
Arakelian, George H., Chm. Bd. & Pres.--Standard Manufacturing Company, Troy, NY, pg. 1037
Arbit, Bruce, Co-Mng. Dir.--A.B. Data, Ltd., Milwaukee, WI, pg. 1
Arbuckle, James E., Pres. & Chief Oper. Officer--Besser Company, Alpena, MI, pg. 146
Arcadi, John, Pres.--Depew Development Inc., Lancaster, NY, pg. 331
Arcati, Fortunato, Pres.--Champion Aluminum Corporation, Syosset, NY, pg. 238
Archer, Ward, Jr., Pres. & Chief Exec. Officer--Archer/Malmo Adv., Inc., Memphis, TN, pg. 80
Archuleta, Celestino E., Pres.--National Systems & Research Co., Colorado Springs, CO, pg. 794
Arellano, Ignacio, Pres.--Arellano/BSB Publicidad, Mexico,, Mexico, pg. 109
Arenberg, William D., Pres. & Chief Exec. Officer--Columbia Pipe & Supply Company, Chicago, IL, pg. 266
Arends, H.J., Pres.--Auto-Owners Insurance, Lansing, MI, pg. 100
Arends, H.J., Pres.--Home-Owners Insurance Co., Lansing, MI, pg. 100
Arends, H.J., Pres.--Property-Owners Insurance Co., Marion, IN, pg. 100
Arens, Richard P., Chm. Bd., Pres., Chief Exec. & Fin. Officer--Alacon, Sunnyvale, CA, pg. 29
Arlen, John R., Pres.--Thetford Corporation, Ann Arbor, MI, pg. 357
Arlen, Michael, Pres. & Creative Dir.--Arlen Advertising, Los Angeles, CA, pg. 83
Armentrout, Max, Pres.--Mongold Lumber Co., Elkins, WV, pg. 710
Armour, John, Pres.--Dormeyer Industries, Chicago, IL, pg. 346
Armstrong, Frank, III, Chm. & Pres.--National Fruit Product Company, Winchester, VA, pg. 789
Armstrong, John, Pres.--The Crocker-Fels Company, Cincinnati, OH, pg. 299
Armstrong, M.H., Pres. & Chief Exec. Officer--Armstrong International, Inc., Three Rivers, MI, pg. 83
Armstrong, Mark, Pres.--The Monarch Company, Inc., Atlanta, GA, pg. 765
Armstrong, Mark, Pres.--Dad's Root Beer, Chicago, IL, pg. 765
Armstrong, T.K., Jr., Pres. & Chief Oper. Officer--Texas Steel Co., Inc., Fort Worth, TX, pg. 1090
Army, Kenneth L., V.P.-Fin. & Opers.--National Retail Hardware Assn., Indianapolis, IN, pg. 793
Arnold, David, Pres. & Chief Exec. Officer--Pacific Northern Oil Corp., Seattle, WA, pg. 841
Arnold, David, Pres.--L. M. Scofield Company, Los Angeles, CA, pg. 982
Arnold, George L., Pres. & Chief Oper. Officer--EvansGroup, Dallas, TX, pg. 391
Arnold, Howard M., Pres. & Chief Exec. Officer--Chartway Technologies, Rockville, MD, pg. 240
Arnold, John M., Pres.--Petroleum Products Corp., Middletown, PA, pg. 865
Arnold, Steve, Pres. & Chief Exec. Officer--One Stop Supply, Tyler, TX, pg. 827
Arnold, Truman, Chm. Bd., Pres. & Chief Exec. Officer--Truman Arnold Companies, Texarkana, TX, pg. 84
Aronoff, Jack, Pres.--Gate City Beverage Distributors, San Bernardino, CA, pg. 444
Aronson, Arnold, Chm. Bd. & Chief Exec. Officer--Woodward & Lothrop/John Wanamaker, Washington, DC, pg. 1201
Aronson, Jules R., Pres.--Lumco Industries, Inc., Philadelphia, PA, pg. 687
Aronson, Maurice, Pres.--Sprayway, Inc., Addison, IL, pg. 222
Arpels, Philippe, Pres. & Chief Oper. Officer--Van Cleef & Arpels, Inc., New York, NY, pg. 1144
Arpin, David, Pres.--Paul Arpin Vanlines, Inc., East Greenwich, RI, pg. 85
Arquilla, George, III, Pres.--Burnside Construction Co., Downers Grove, WI, pg. 194
Arras, Richard K., Pres. & Chief Oper. Officer--Perkins Family Restaurants, Memphis, TN, pg. 1088
Arras, Rick, Pres.--Tennessee Restaurant Corp., Itasca, IL, pg. 1087
Arrendale, Thomas A., Jr., Pres.--Fieldale Corporation, Baldwin, GA, pg. 409
Arrington, Michael B., Pres. & Chief Exec. Officer--Arrington Travel Center Inc., Chicago, IL, pg. 85
Arst, Mike, Pres.--Goldsmiths, Inc., Wichita, KS, pg. 469
Arth, Lawrence J., Pres. & Chief Oper. Officer--Ameritas Life Insurance Corp., Lincoln, NE, pg. 66
Arthur, Thomas D., Pres.--Havatampa Incorporated, Tampa, FL, pg. 517
Arthur, Thomas D., Pres.--H.A.T. Holding Company, Tampa, FL, pg. 517
Artin, Michael, Pres.--American Mathematical Society, Inc., Providence, RI, pg. 58
Artinian, Garo, Pres.--Delta Surprenant Wire & Cable, Inc., Clinton, MA, pg. 327
Aruffo, A. James, Pres.--Zenith Products Corp., Aston, PA, pg. 1217
Asch, Peter, Pres. & Chief Exec. Officer--Twincraft, Inc., Winooski, VT, pg. 1122
Asche, Phil, Area Dir.-Australia & New Zealand--Young & Rubicam Sydney Pty. Ltd., North Sydney,, Australia, pg. 1213
Aschinger, Carl J., Jr., Chm. Bd., Pres. & Chief Exec. Officer--Columbus Show Case Company, Columbus, OH, pg. 267
Aschkenasy, Herbert, Pres.--Oregon Freeze Dry, Inc., Albany, OR, pg. 829
Ash, Carroll L., Co-Chm., Pres. & Chief Exec. Officer--Trojan Steel Co., Charleston, WV, pg. 1115
Ash, Dick, Pres.--Hunter Marine Corporation, Alachua, FL, pg. 555
Ash, Jerome M., Pres.--Perfection Automotive Products Corporation, Livonia, MI, pg. 861
Ashkenazy, Severyn, Pres.--L'Ermitage Hotels, West Hollywood, CA, pg. 668
Ashkin, Joseph, Pres.--Rugby-Darby Group Of Cos., Rockville Centre, NY, pg. 955
Ashley, Diane, Pres.--Ciociola & Company Advertising, Inc., New York, NY, pg. 250
Ashman, Raymond D., Jr., Chm. Bd. & Pres.--Ashman Enterprises, Inc., Brecksville, OH, pg. 88
Ashton, Alan C., Pres.--WordPerfect Corporation, Orem, UT, pg. 1202
Askinas, Milton, Pres.--Glen Oaks Industries, Inc., New York, NY, pg. 461
Aspland, Brian, Chm. Bd., Pres. & Chief Exec. Officer--Integral Systems, Inc., Sunnyvale, CA, pg. 573
Asplundh, Christopher, Pres.--Asplundh Tree Expert Co., Willow Grove, PA, pg. 88
Astrup, Leonard, Pres.--Astrup Drugs, Inc., Austin, MN, pg. 93
Atkins, Richard, Pres.--General Media Services, Inc., Westport, CT, pg. 450
Atkins, Steve, Pres. & New Bus. Contact--The Atkins Agency, San Antonio, TX, pg. 94
Atkinson, Basil, Pres.--Judson-Atkinson Candies, Inc., San Antonio, TX, pg. 608
Atols, Robert M., Pres.--Atols Tool and Mold Corp., Schiller Park, IL, pg. 97
Attaway, Julian J., Pres.--M M Systems Corporation, Tucker, GA, pg. 692
Atwood, Gary A., Pres.--Atwood Distributing, Inc., Enid, OK, pg. 97
Aubuchon, William E., Pres.--W.E. Aubuchon Co., Inc., Westminster, MA, pg. 97
August, James M., Pres.--Stone, August, Baker Communications Companies, Troy, MI, pg. 1050
Aukeman, Lewis, Pres.--California Milk Producers, Artesia, CA, pg. 210
Auray, Delbert L., Pres. & Treas.--Bridgeport Fittings, Inc., Stratford, CT, pg. 175
Aurichio, Joseph L., Pres. & Chief Exec. Officer--Kearney-National, Inc., White Plains, NY, pg. 357
Ausherman, Marvin E., Pres.--Ausherman Construction Company, Frederick, MD, pg. 98
Austad, Dave, Pres. & Chief Exec. Officer--The Austad Company, Sioux Falls, SD, pg. 98
Austin, George K., Jr., Pres.--A-Dec, Inc., Newberg, OR, pg. 1
Austin, John T.,Sr., Pres.--James Austin Co., Mars, PA, pg. 99
Austin, Mike, Chm. Bd. & Pres.--Austin Associates, Inc., San Jose, CA, pg. 98
Austin, Richard K., Pres.--O/E Automation, Inc., Troy, MI, pg. 819
Austin, William F., Pres., Sec. & Treas.--Starkey Laboratories, Inc., Eden Prairie, MN, pg. 1040
Autrey, David E., Pres.--Piedmont Mechanical, Inc., Spartanburg, SC, pg. 870
Autrey, H.E., Pres.--Miller Electric Company, Jacksonville, FL, pg. 754
Autry, Gene, Chm. Bd., Pres. & Chief Exec. Officer--Golden West Broadcasters, Los Angeles, CA, pg. 467
Avallone, A. Louis, Pres.--Alpha Associates, Inc., Woodbridge, NJ, pg. 43
Aves, John C., Chm., Pres. & Chief Exec. Officer--Aves Advertising, Inc., Grand Rapids, MI, pg. 102
Avigne, Gary, Pres.--Coventry Hotels Association, Saddle Brook, NJ, pg. 290
Avril, Arthur C., Pres.--Sakrete, Inc., Cincinnati, OH, pg. 967
Awad, Dennis J., Pres., Chief Exec. & Fin. Officer & Treas.--Tele-Com Products, Inc., Duarte, CA, pg. 1084
Awrey, Robert C., Chm. Bd.--Awrey Bakeries, Inc., Livonia, MI, pg. 103
Axelrad, James A., Pres. & Chief Exec. Officer--Pakula & Company, Chicago, IL, pg. 843

Axleroad, Donald, Pres.--The Food Group, New York, NY, pg. 423
Axtell, Maynard, Pres.--National Travelers Life Co., Des Moines, IA, pg. 794
Aydlotte, William Y., Pres. & Creative Dir.--Aydlotte & Cartwright, Inc., Atlanta, GA, pg. 103
Aylward, E.W., Pres. & Gen. Mgr.--Neenah Foundry Company, Neenah, WI, pg. 797
Aylward, Thomas J., Pres.--Sandusky Plastics, Inc., Sandusky, OH, pg. 383
Ayotte, R. Lee, Pres.--Insurance Intermediaries, Inc., Dublin, OH, pg. 795
Babich, N., Pres. & Chief Exec. Officer--Hitchiner Manufacturing Company, Inc., Milford, NH, pg. 536
Babyak, George, Pres.--Ohio Transmission Corporation, Columbus, OH, pg. 822
Baccari, Bernard E., Pres.--Darlene Jewelry Manufacturing Company, Pawtucket, RI, pg. 315
Bachhuber, Carl, Pres.--Mayville Engineering Co., Inc., Mayville, WI, pg. 725
Bachman, Dale L., Pres.--Bachman's, Inc., Minneapolis, MN, pg. 108
Bachman, John C., Chm. Bd., Pres., Chief Exec. & Oper. Officer--Automated Marketing Systems, Inc., Chicago, IL, pg. 100
Bachmann, John W., Mng. Principal--Edward D. Jones & Co., Maryland Heights, MO, pg. 603
Bachmann, Thomas M., Chm. Bd., Pres. & Chief Exec. Officer--Calico Cat Press, Inc., New Providence, NJ, pg. 209
Bachmann, Thomas M., Pres. & Chief Exec. Officer--SB Entertainment Inc., New Providence, NJ, pg. 960
Bacig, Louis, Pres.--Carmichael Lynch, Inc., Minneapolis, MN, pg. 222
Backer, William M., Pres. & Exec. Creative Dir.--Backer Spielvogel Bates Worldwide, Inc., New York, NY, pg. 108
Backman, William D., Jr., Pres. & Chief Exec. Officer--Aurora Casket Company, Aurora, IN, pg. 98
Badcock, Wogan S., Jr., Chm. Bd. & Pres.--W.S. Badcock Corporation, Mulberry, FL, pg. 113
Bader, Burke B., Pres.--Bader & Co., Ipava, IL, pg. 113
Bader, R.E., Pres.--Manostat Corporation, New York, NY, pg. 704
Bader, Ronald L., Pres. & Chief Exec. Officer--Bader Rutter & Assoc., Inc., Brookfield, WI, pg. 113
Badrick, John, Pres.--Glenayre Turnkey Technologies, Inc., Springfield, NJ, pg. 462
Badtke, Donald J., Chm. Bd. & Pres.--Stanley Knight Corporation, New Troy, MI, pg. 1038
Baer, Robert E., Pres.--Efficient Engineering Co., Troy, MI, pg. 371
Baer, Robert J., Pres.--Unigroup, Inc., Fenton, MO, pg. 1126
Baer, Robert J., Pres.--United Van Lines, Inc., Fenton, MO, pg. 1126
Bag, Seymour, Pres.--Apparel Industries, Inc., New York, NY, pg. 78
Baggett, W. Les, Pres. & Chief Exec. Officer--LePage's, Inc., Pittsburgh, PA, pg. 287
Baggott, George E., Pres.--Cres-Cor/Crown-X, Cleveland, OH, pg. 298
Bahrenburg, D. Claeys, Pres.--Hearst Magazines Division, New York, NY, pg. 523
Bahrenburg, D. Claeys, Pres.-Hearst Magazine Div.--Redbook, New York, NY, pg. 523
Bailey, Charles, Pres. & Chief Exec. Officer--Signet Industries, Fraser, MI, pg. 1003
Bailey, Edgar H., Chm. Bd. & Pres.--Leader Federal Bank For Savings, Memphis, TN, pg. 663
Bailey, Gordon, Pres. & Treas.--Gordon Bailey & Associates, Inc., Stone Mountain, GA, pg. 114
Bailey, John, Chm. Bd., Pres., Chief Exec. & Fin. Officer & Treas.--Cal/Emblem Labels, Inc., Fresno, CA, pg. 208
Bailey, John H., Chm. Bd., Pres., Chief Exec. & Chief Oper. Officer--The Climatic Corp., Columbia, SC, pg. 255
Bain, H., Chm. Bd. & Pres.--Homewood Corporation, Columbus, OH, pg. 542
Baines, Henry T., Pres.--Stop Shop Save, Baltimore, MD, pg. 1052
Baird, J. Allen, Pres. & Chief Exec. Officer--Mrs. Baird's Bakeries, Inc., Fort Worth, TX, pg. 760
Baird, J. Anthony, Pres.--Hydro-Mill Co., Chatsworth, CA, pg. 557
Baird, Stephen W., Pres.--Baird & Warner Inc., Chicago, IL, pg. 114
Baird, William S., Pres. & Chief Oper. Officer--Alabama Metal Industries Corporation, Birmingham, AL, pg. 28
Baird, Yvonne, Pres.--Baird Ray Nissan, Inc., Longwood, FL, pg. 114
Bak, Gene, Pres.--Mooney Chemicals, Cleveland, OH, pg. 768
Baker, Bruce, Pres.--Pachmayr Gun Works Inc., Monrovia, CA, pg. 839
Baker, Charles W., Pres. & Chief Exec. Officer--Jackson Paper Company, Jackson, MS, pg. 587
Baker, Daniel, Pres. & Chief Exec. Officer--Tate Access Floors, Inc., Jessup, MD, pg. 1080
Baker, Daniel L., Chm. Bd. & Pres.--Baker Concrete Construction, Inc., Monroe, OH, pg. 115
Baker, Douglas, Pres.--Tropitone Furniture Co. Inc., Sarasota, FL, pg. 1116
Baker, Douglas U., Pres. & Creative Dir.--Significs, Inc., Rochester, NY, pg. 1004
Baker, F.C. Buzz, Pres. & Chief Exec. Officer--Creswell, Munsell, Fultz & Zirbel, Cedar Rapids, IA, pg. 1211
Baker, Gordon, Pres. & Gen. Mgr.-Instrument Div.--Newage Industries Inc., Willow Grove, PA, pg. 803
Baker, Gordon, Pres.--Newage Industries Inc., Testing Instruments Division, Willow Grove, PA, pg. 803
Baker, H.R., Pres. & Chief Exec. Officer--Marathon Electric Manufacturing Corp., Wausau, WI, pg. 705
Baker, John, Pres.--Micro Electronics, Columbus, OH, pg. 748
Baker, Lee, Pres.--S. Gumpert Co., Inc., Columbus, OH, pg. 932
Baker, Maurice W., Pres. & Chief Exec. Officer--Madison Grocery Co., Inc., Richmond, KY, pg. 699
Baker, Raymond E., Pres.--Newage Industries Inc., Plastics Division, Willow Grove, PA, pg. 803
Baker, Robert, Pres.--The Chamberlain Group, Inc., Elmhurst, IL, pg. 350
Baker, Robert L., Pres.--Plant Maintenance Service Corporation, Memphis, TN, pg. 874
Baker, Ronald, Chm. Bd., Pres. & Chief Exec. Officer--Millmaster Onyx Group, Inc., Westport, CT, pg. 755
Baker, Ronald, Chm. & Chief Exec. Officer--Mantrose Haeuser Co., Westport, CT, pg. 756
Baker, William L., Jr., Pres.--J B Labs, Inc., Holland, MI, pg. 584
Bakke, Richard, Pres. & Chief Exec. Officer--Portland Glass/American Management Group, Westbrook, ME, pg. 58
Bakke, Richard M., Pres. & Chief Exec. Officer--American Management Group, Westbrook, ME, pg. 57
Balaz, J.K., Pres. & Chief Exec. Officer--Flinn & Dreffein Engineering Co., Northbrook, IL, pg. 419
Balcerzak, Bob, Pres.--Kokomo Spring Company, Inc., Kokomo, IN, pg. 640
Baldetti, P.G., Pres.--Burks Pumps, Inc., Piqua, OH, pg. 507
Baldetti, P.G., Pres.--Barnes Pumps, Inc., Mansfield, OH, pg. 507
Baldetti, Paul, Pres.--Prosser/Enpo Industries, Piqua, OH, pg. 507
Baldwin, Dan D., Pres. & Chief Exec. Officer--Nautilus, Independence, VA, pg. 796
Baldwin, Daryl, Acting Pres.--Super Club Music Corp., Marietta, GA, pg. 1062
Baldwin, Ed F., Chm. Bd., Pres. & Treas.--Baldwin Construction, Inc., Fort Collins, CO, pg. 115
Baldwin, Everett N., Pres. & Chief Exec. Officer--Welch's, Concord, MA, pg. 789
Baldwin, Gary E., Pres.--Buckman Laboratories, Inc., Memphis, TN, pg. 188
Baldwin, James G., Chm. Bd.--The Carbide/Graphite Group, Inc., Pittsburgh, PA, pg. 217
Baldwin, John W., Pres.--Polyvinyl Films, Inc., Sutton, MA, pg. 880
Baldwin, Sandra, Pres. & Treas.--H & H Distributing Company, Inc., West Union, IA, pg. 495
Bale, James K., Pres.--Bale Of Kentucky, Inc., Horse Cave, KY, pg. 115
Bale, James K., Pres.--Farmers Investment Company, Inc., Horse Cave, KY, pg. 115
Ball, Anna C., Pres.--Geo. J. Ball, Inc., West Chicago, IL, pg. 115
Ball, Brad A., Pres. (Odd Days), Exec. Creative Dir.--Davis, Ball & Colombatto Advertising, Inc., Los Angeles, CA, pg. 318
Ball, George, Pres.--W. Atlee Burpee Co., Warminster, PA, pg. 116
Ball, George, Jr., Pres.--Pan-American Seed Co., West Chicago, IL, pg. 116
Ball, James, Pres.--Cello Bag Company, Inc., Tukwila, WA, pg. 231
Ball, Jess, Pres. & Chief Exec. Officer--Alford Industries, Inc., Ridgefield Park, NJ, pg. 33
Ball, John K., Pres. & Chief Oper. Officer--R. M. Shoemaker Co., West Conshohocken, PA, pg. 1000
Ball, William A., Sr., Pres.--Air Power, Inc., High Point, NC, pg. 27
Ballard, Larry, Pres.--Middlesex/Patriot General Insurance Companies, Concord, MA, pg. 751
Ballard, Larry C., Chm. Bd., Pres. & Chief Exec. Officer--Sentry Insurance, A Mutual Company, Stevens Point, WI, pg. 990
Ballard, Marshall, Pres.--Penrod Drilling Corporation, Dallas, TX, pg. 859
Ballentine, Don, Pres.--H. B. Smith Co., Inc., Westfield, MA, pg. 1013
Ballhagen, Lloyd, Pres. & Chief Exec. Officer--Harris Enterprises Inc., Hutchinson, KS, pg. 511
Ballou, F. Remington, Pres.--B.A. Ballou & Co. Inc., East Providence, RI, pg. 116
Balsamo, Salvatore, Chm. Bd., Pres. & Chief Exec. Officer--Technical Aid Corporation, Newton Upper Falls, MA, pg. 1083
Balson, Patrick, Pres.--Aetna Bearing Company, Chicago, IL, pg. 23
Bancroft, Joseph C., Chm. Bd.--Croft Metal Inc., McComb, MS, pg. 300
Bandremer, Henry, Pres.--Curvcraft, Dunn, NC, pg. 306
Banducci, Barry, Pres. & Chief Exec. Officer--The Equion Corporation, New Haven, CT, pg. 385
Bandy, George, Pres.--Horner Rausch Company, Nashville, TN, pg. 544
Bandy, Susan, Pres.--Bandy Carroll Hellige Advertising, Louisville, KY, pg. 117
Bank, Morton B., Pres. & Chief Exec. Officer--Bank M F & Company, Inc., Minneapolis, MN, pg. 117
Banks, Jacob W., Chm. Bd. & Pres.--Bearing Service Company, Pittsburgh, PA, pg. 130
Bankston, James G., Pres.--W. O. Bankston Enterprises Inc., Dallas, TX, pg. 118
Bankston, William S., Pres. & Chief Exec. Officer--AmTran Corporation, Conway, AR, pg. 69
Bankuty, Geza E., Chm. Bd., Pres. & Chief Exec. Officer--New England Machinery, Inc., Bradenton, FL, pg. 800
Baracos, Leon, Pres.--Weilwood Industries, Inc., New York, NY, pg. 970
Baranski, Dennis A., Chm. Bd., Pres. & Chief Exec. Officer--Barancorp, Lecompton, KS, pg. 118
Barash, Ralph, Pres. & Chief Exec. Officer--Polarome Mfg. Co. Inc., Jersey City, NJ, pg. 878
Barbar, George E., Chm. Bd. & Pres.--The Barbar Group, Inc., Boca Raton, FL, pg. 119
Barber, Aubrey, L., Jr., Pres.--Barber Brothers Contracting Company, Baton Rouge, LA, pg. 119
Barber, Joseph J., Jr., Pres.--Cine Magnetics, Inc., Mamaroneck, NY, pg. 250
Barbour, Alfred D., Pres.--Roessing Bronze Co., Mars, PA, pg. 943
Barbour, Alfred R., Chm. Bd.--Roessing Bronze Co., Mars, PA, pg. 943
Barclay, John P., Jr., Pres. & Chief Exec. Officer--Wire Rope Corp. of America, Inc., Saint Joseph, MO, pg. 1197
Barclay, John P., Jr., Pres.--Leschen Wire Rope, Saint Joseph, MO, pg. 1197
Bard, James R., Pres.--Bard Mfg. Co., Bryan, OH, pg. 119
Bardis, Christo D., Pres.--Reynen, Bardis & Winn, Sacramento, CA, pg. 930
Bardo, Charles, Pres.--Ceramic Cooling Tower Co., Ft. Worth, TX, pg. 69
Barger, Michael E., Chief Exec. Officer--Barger Builder & Developers, Saint Petersburg, FL, pg. 119
Barker, Ed, Pres.--Instrumentarium Imaging, Inc., Milwaukee, WI, pg. 572
Barker, J.A., Pres.--Charing Cross Group, Louisville, KY, pg. 239
Barker, Robert A., Pres.--Barker Campbell & Farley, Virginia Beach, VA, pg. 120
Barletta, Frank, Pres.--A. Barletta & Sons, Hazleton, PA, pg. 120
Barlow, J. Bruce, Pres.--Macristy Industries, Inc., New Britain, CT, pg. 698
Barlow, Richard A., Pres. & Chief Exec. Officer--Bentley-Harris Manufacturing Co., Lionville, PA, pg. 140
Barlow, Witt, Chm., Pres. & Chief Exec. Officer--Great Lakes Dredge & Dock, Oak Brook, IL, pg. 481
Barnes, Donald, Jr., Pres.--Belle Tire Distributor Inc., Allen Park, MI, pg. 136
Barnes, Keith, Pres.--Farmstead Foods, Inc., Albert Lea, MN, pg. 402
Barnes, Larry B., Chm. Bd.--LB Industries Inc., Boise, ID, pg. 647
Barnes, Richard A., Pres. & Chief Oper. Officer--Republic Fastener Products Corp., Great Falls, SC, pg. 928
Barnes, Richard J., Pres.--Coastal Dairy Products, Inc., Wilson, NC, pg. 257
Barnes, Robert, Pres.--Bead Industries Inc., Bridgeport, CT, pg. 129
Barnes, Robert L., Pres. & Chief Oper. Officer--Knight Architects Engineers Planners, Inc., Chicago, IL, pg. 637
Barnes, William, Pres. & Chief Exec. Officer--Spectrulite Consortium, Inc., Madison, IL, pg. 1029
Barnett, Cecil C., Chm. Bd., Pres., Chief Exec. Officer & Treas.--Algood Food Company, Louisville, KY, pg. 34
Barnett, Daniel, Pres.--Machado & Co. Inc., New York, NY, pg. 696
Barnett, Marilyn, Pres.--Mars Advertising Co., Southfield, MI, pg. 713
Barnett, Paul S., Pres.--Barnett Millworks, Inc., Theodore, AL, pg. 120
Barnette, W. A., Jr., Pres.--Greenwood Packing Plant, Greenwood, SC, pg. 486
Barnhard, Ronald H., Pres.--Lasky Company, Millburn, NJ, pg. 660
Barnhardt, T.M. III, Pres. & Chief Exec. Officer--Barnhardt Manufacturing Co., Charlotte, NC, pg. 120
Barnhardt, T.M., III, Pres. & Chief Oper. Officer--Carolina Absorbent Cotton Co., Charlotte, NC, pg. 120
Barnhart, Jeffrey, Pres.--Creative Marketing Alliance Inc., Princeton Junction, NJ, pg. 297
Barnhart, Terry L., Pres. & Chief Oper. Officer--Barnhart Advertising, Marketing & Public Relations, Inc., Denver, CO, pg. 120
Barnhill, R.E., Jr., Pres.--Barnhill Contracting Company, Tarboro, NC, pg. 121
Barocas, Martin, Pres.--Santee Print Works, Inc., New York, NY, pg. 970
Baron, Ken, Pres. & Creative Dir.--Baron & Zaretsky Advertising, Inc., New York, NY, pg. 121
Baron, Selma, Pres.--Baron Advertising, Inc., Cleveland, OH, pg. 121
Barouh, Rich, Pres.--Baroum Eaton Allen Corporation, Brooklyn, NY, pg. 121
Barouh, Victor, Chm. & Chief Exec. Officer--Ko-Rec-Type, Brooklyn, NY, pg. 121
Barr, Donald M., Pres.--Barr & Barr, Inc., New York, NY, pg. 121
Barr, Michael, Pres. & Treas.--Barr Electric Corporation, Wheeling, IL, pg. 122
Barrans, Terry, Pres. & Chief Exec. Officer--Fisher Mills, Inc., Seattle, WA, pg. 415
Barre, Stephen A., Chm. Bd., Pres., Chief Exec. Officer & Sec.--Servo Corporation of America, Hicksville, NY, pg. 993
Barrell, Dave, Mgr.-Sls. & Mktg.--Glasteel Industrial Laminates, Duarte, CA, pg. 461
Barrera, Jess, Pres. & Chief Exec. Officer--Southern California Bancorp, Laguna Beach, CA, pg. 1020
Barrett, John F., Pres. & Chief Oper. Officer--Western & Southern Life Insurance Co., Cincinnati, OH, pg. 1181
Barriga, Mauricio, Mng. Dir.--Comunica Leo Burnett-Costa Rica, Peralta,, Costa Rica, pg. 192
Barringer, Paul B., II, Pres. & Chief Exec. Officer--Coastal Lumber Company, Weldon, NC, pg. 257
Barro, Tom, Pres.--Lamp Post Franchise Corporation, Tustin, CA, pg. 652
Barrocas, Alberto, Pres. & Treas.--Injection Footwear Corp., Miami, FL, pg. 569
Barry, H., Pres. & Dir.-Sls.--Uniflex, Inc., Hicksville, NY, pg. 1126
Barry, Ronald N., Jr., Pres.--Hopkinsville Elevator Company, Inc., Hopkinsville, KY, pg. 543
Bartell, George D., Pres.--The Bartell Drug Company, Seattle, WA, pg. 122
Barthelmes, Richard B., Publisher--Gourmet, New York, NY, pg. 19
Bartholomae, Raymond E., Exec. V.P. & G.M.--Symons Corporation, Des Plaines, IL, pg. 1069

Bartholow, Peter, Chm. Bd., Pres. & Chief Oper. Officer--MCorp, Dallas, TX, pg. 732
Bartle, Kenneth, Pres.--Hitchcock Chair Company LTD, Riverton, CT, pg. 536
Bartlett, Richard C., Pres. & Chief Oper. Officer--Mary Kay Cosmetics Inc., Dallas, TX, pg. 716
Bartlett, Robert A., Jr., Pres. & Chief Oper. Officer--The F.A. Bartlett Tree Expert Co., Stamford, CT, pg. 123
Barton, A.P., Jr., Chm. Bd., Pres. & Chief Exec. Officer--Mutual Manufacturing & Supply Co., Cincinnati, OH, pg. 778
Barton, C.J., Pres.--Dorr-Oliver Incorporated, Milford, CT, pg. 346
Barton, Max E., Pres. & Chief Exec. Officer--Groendyke Transports, Inc., Enid, OK, pg. 489
Basile, Peter A., Pres.--Peter A. Basile Sons Inc., Livonia, MI, pg. 124
Basinait, Martin C., Pres. & Chief Exec. Officer--Western Regional Off Track Betting, Batavia, NY, pg. 1181
Baska, Jim, Pres. & Chief Exec. Officer--Associated Wholesale Grocers, Inc., Kansas City, KS, pg. 92
Baskin, Scott, Pres.--Mark Shale, Willowbrook, IL, pg. 994
Bassett, William C., Pres.--The W.E. Bassett Company, Shelton, CT, pg. 125
Basso, Joseph, Pres.--Basso & Associates Inc. Adv. & Public Relations, Costa Mesa, CA, pg. 125
Bast, Charles W., Pres. & Treas.--Bast Chevrolet Inc., Seaford, NY, pg. 125
Bateman, Howard F., Pres.--Bateman Brothers Lumber Co., Inc., New Britain, PA, pg. 125
Bates, Edsel E., Pres.--W. L. Hailey & Company, Inc., Nashville, TN, pg. 500
Bates, John C., Pres.--Heidtman Steel Products, Inc., Toledo, OH, pg. 525
Bates, Robert D., Chm. Bd., Pres. & Chief Exec. Officer--Guarantee Mutual Life Co., Omaha, NE, pg. 491
Bates, Wesley, Chm. Bd. & Pres.--Stanley Steemer International, Inc., Dublin, OH, pg. 1038
Batkin, Sanford L., Pres. & Treas.--Universal Folding Box Company, Inc., Hoboken, NJ, pg. 1138
Batt, James M., Pres. & Chief Exec. Officer--Peck Spring Company, Plainville, CT, pg. 854
Battaglia, Michael S., Pres. & Chief Oper. Officer--Mosler Inc., Hamilton, OH, pg. 772
Batteast, Robert V., Chm. Bd. & Pres.--Batteast Construction Company, Inc., South Bend, IN, pg. 126
Battle, A. George, Mng. Partner-Mktg. Devel.--Andersen Consulting, Chicago, IL, pg. 72
Batz, Gary C., Pres.--Fike Corporation, Blue Springs, MO, pg. 409
Bauer, John A., Jr., Chm. Bd.--Pennock, Philadelphia, PA, pg. 858
Bauer, John P., Pres.--Basic Food International Inc., Fort Lauderdale, FL, pg. 124
Bauerle, Donald C., Jr., Pres.--Codisco Inc., Sanford, FL, pg. 258
Baugh, Robert H., Chm. Bd. & Pres.--Baugh Construction Company, Seattle, WA, pg. 127
Baugher, John O., Pres. & Treas.--Baugher Chevrolet-Buick-Geo, Inc., Waynesboro, VA, pg. 127
Baughman, George K., Pres. & Treas.--Plastomer Corp., Livonia, MI, pg. 876
Baughman, Kathy, Pres.--HLB Communications, Inc., Chicago, IL, pg. 496
Bauknight, Harry L., Pres. & Chief Oper. Officer--Palmetto Wholesale Co., Inc., Columbia, SC, pg. 844
Baum, John C., Pres.--W. A. Baum Company, Inc., Copiague, NY, pg. 127
Baum, Macy, Pres.--Lansdale, Carr & Baum, Irvine, CA, pg. 658
Bauman, B. Kent, Pres. & Chief Fin. Officer--Condon Oil Company, Inc., Ripon, WI, pg. 273
Bauman, W.A., Pres. & Treas.--Enger-Kress Company, West Bend, WI, pg. 381
Baumann, Daniel E., Pres. & Chief Oper. Officer--Paddock Publications, Inc., Arlington Heights, IL, pg. 842
Baumann, John, V.P.-Mktg.--The Swiss Colony, Monroe, WI, pg. 1068
Baur, Robert, Pres.--MNP Corp., Utica, MI, pg. 693
Bawden, John D., Pres.--Bawden Corporation, Eldridge, IA, pg. 127
Bawden, Mark, Pres.--Bawden Printing, Inc., Eldridge, IA, pg. 127
Bawden, Mike, Pres.--Bawden, Torrey & Associates, Davenport, IA, pg. 127
Baxt, Victor J., Pres.--Teknor Apex Company, Pawtucket, RI, pg. 1084
Baxter, Raymond, Pres.--Sunshine/Salerno, Inc. (NJ), Sayreville, NJ, pg. 439
Bayer, Robert, Pres.--Target Sportswear, Inc., New York, NY, pg. 1079
Bayley, Robert E., Pres.--Programmed Maintenance Services, Inc., Kirkland, WA, pg. 128
Bayley, Ronald, Pres.--Robert E. Bayley Construction, Seattle, WA, pg. 128
Bayly, George V., Pres. & Chief Exec. Officer--Ivex Packaging Corporation, Lincolnshire, IL, pg. 583
Beach, William H., Chm. Bd., Pres., Chief Exec. & Oper. Officer--Beach Mold & Tool Inc., New Albany, IN, pg. 128
Beadles, C. Victor, III, Pres.--Beadles Lumber Company, Inc., Moultrie, GA, pg. 129
Beadles, Wayne, Chm. Bd. & Pres.--Woodruff Electrical Co-Op, Forest City, AR, pg. 1200
Beale, Robert B., Pres.--Control Systems Inc., Saint Paul, MN, pg. 281
Beall, Edward S., Pres. & Chief Oper. Officer--Brix Maritime Co., Portland, OR, pg. 177
Beall, Robert M. II, Pres.--Beall's, Inc., Bradenton, FL, pg. 129
Beals, Jeffrey A., Pres.--The International Boiler Works Company, East Stroudsburg, PA, pg. 575
Bean, Delcie D., Pres., Treas. & Chief Exec. Officer--D. D. Bean & Sons Co., Jaffrey, NH, pg. 129
Bean, Doug, Partner--Eric Mower and Associates/Buffalo, Inc., Buffalo, NY, pg. 774
Bean, Ronald H., Pres.--Pizza Haven Inc., Seattle, WA, pg. 873
Bear, Lewis, Jr., Pres.--The Lewis Bear Company, Pensacola, FL, pg. 129
Bear, Richard, Pres.--The Mediscus Group, Buena Park, CA, pg. 736
Beard, A.D., Chm. Bd. & Pres.--Formation, Inc., Moorestown, NJ, pg. 424
Beard, C. Randolph, Jr., Pres.--Annin & Company, Roseland, NJ, pg. 75
Beardall, James C., Chm. Bd., Pres. & Chief Exec. Officer--Anderson Lumber Company, Ogden, UT, pg. 73
Beasley, Lawrence H., Pres.--Apache Plastics, L.P., Stockton, CA, pg. 77
Beaton, Bradford, Pres. & Chief Exec. Officer--New England Newspaper Supply Company, Inc., Millbury, MA, pg. 800
Beattie, Henry, Pres.--Super D Drug Stores, Memphis, TN, pg. 1062
Beauchamp, David F., Pres.--United States Cold Storage, Inc., Cherry Hill, NJ, pg. 1135
Beauchamp, Patrick L., Chm. Bd., Pres. & Treas.--Beauchamp Distributing Company, Compton, CA, pg. 130
Beaulieu, Paul H., Pres. & Creative Dir.--Media Concepts Corporation, Assonet, MA, pg. 734
Beaver, Donald C., Pres., Chief Exec. Officer & Treas.--Brian Center Management Corporation, Hickory, NC, pg. 175
Beban, Gary, Pres.--CB Commercial Real Estate Group, Inc., Los Angeles, CA, pg. 222
Bechen, Peter F., Chm. Bd., Pres. & Chief Oper. Officer--M & T Incorporated, Portland, OR, pg. 690
Becher, F. James, Jr., Chm. Bd. & Pres.--Geneva Corporation, Greensboro, NC, pg. 451
Bechtel, Riley, Pres.--Bechtel Group, Inc., San Francisco, CA, pg. 130
Beck, Arthur R., Pres. & Chief Oper. Officer--Precision Twist Drill Co., Crystal Lake, IL, pg. 885
Beck, Arthur R., Pres. & Chief Oper. Officer--Mohawk Tools, Crystal Lake, IL, pg. 885
Beck, J. Edward, Jr., Pres.--Bitrek Corporation, Waynesboro, PA, pg. 153
Beck, Jerry, Chm. Bd., Pres. & Chief Exec. Officer--Mighty Distributing System, Norcross, GA, pg. 752
Beck, Paul D., Pres. & Chief Exec. Officer--Tecknit, Cranford, NJ, pg. 1084
Becker, Alan, Pres.--Crown Leisure Products, Owosso, MI, pg. 200
Becker, B. Frederick, Pres. & Chief Exec. Officer--M M I Companies, Inc., Deerfield, IL, pg. 692
Becker, J., Pres.--Speedrack Products Group, Ltd., Sparta, MI, pg. 1029
Beckman, Irving, Pres.--Shoe-Town, Inc., Totowa, NJ, pg. 999
Beckner, Kerrie, Pres. & Chief Oper. Officer--Alpha One Exchange, New Providence, NJ, pg. 43
Beckwith, F. W., Chm. Bd., Pres. & Chief Exec. Officer--Fareway Stores, Inc., Boone, IA, pg. 399
Beckwith, G. Nicholas III, Pres. & Chief Exec. Officer--Beckwith Machinery Company, Murrysville, PA, pg. 131
Beckwith, Ronald, Pres.--Douglas Steel Fabricating Corporation, Lansing, MI, pg. 347
Bedell, Thomas, Pres.--Berkley, Inc., Spirit Lake, IA, pg. 141
Bedford, N. Clark, Pres.--Beckwith Elevator Co., Boston, MA, pg. 131
Beebe, Stephen, Pres.--J.R. Simplot Co.-Food Group, Boise, ID, pg. 1007
Beech, Robert A., Pres. & Chief Exec. Officer--T O Plastics, Inc., Minneapolis, MN, pg. 1074
Beecham, R. Thomas, Pres. & Chief Oper. Officer--Jernberg Industries, Inc., Chicago, IL, pg. 593
Beecker, Charles, Pres.--Automotive Plastic Technologies, Inc., Sterling Heights, MI, pg. 101
Beeler, Donald, Chm. Bd., Pres. & Chief Exec. Officer--Snyder's Drug Stores, Inc., Minnetonka, MN, pg. 1015
Beer, Anthony P., Pres.--Buhler Inc., Minneapolis, MN, pg. 187
Beer, Murray L., Chm. Bd., Pres. & Chief Exec. Officer--Globe Mortgage Company, Hackensack, NJ, pg. 464
Beers, John, Pres. & Chief Exec. Officer--Reese Finer Foods, Inc., Bloomfield, NJ, pg. 921
Beeson, Robert L., Pres.--Marley Pump Co., Mission, KS, pg. 710
Beggs, Lyman M., Chm., Pres. & Chief Exec. Officer--Sealy, Inc., Cleveland, OH, pg. 985
Beggs, Lymann M., Chm., Pres. & Chief Exec. Officer--Sealy Corporation, Cleveland, OH, pg. 985
Behan, Patrick J., Pres. & Chief Oper. Officer--Hill-Behan Lumber Company, Saint Louis, MO, pg. 534
Behary, Michael E., Pres.--Cleveland Machine Controls, Cleveland, OH, pg. 255
Behnke, Bruce, Pres. & Chief Exec. Officer--Stanley Fastening Systems, Worcester, MA, pg. 1038
Behr, Claus, Pres. & Chief Exec. Officer--Behr Stores Inc., Louisville, KY, pg. 132
Behr, Richard, Pres. & Chief Exec. Officer--Joseph Behr & Sons Inc., Rockford, IL, pg. 132
Behrakis, George D., Pres. & Treas.--Muro Pharmaceutical, Inc., Tewksbury, MA, pg. 776
Behrend, Leslie G., Pres.--Knight PMD, Inc., Barrington, IL, pg. 637
Beidas, Burhan S., Chief Exec. Officer & Mng. Partner--BSB Madco, Dubai,, United Arab Emirates, pg. 110
Beisler, Edward J., Pres.--Beisler & Associates, Inc., New York, NY, pg. 1071
Beitzel, George D., Pres.--Western Farm Credit Bank, Sacramento, CA, pg. 405
Belden, John, Pres. & Chief Exec. Officer--OCTus, San Diego, CA, pg. 818
Belgrad, D.A., Pres. & Chief Exec. Officer--Schnadig Corporation, Chicago, IL, pg. 977
Belk, Thomas M., Pres.--Belk Stores Services Inc., Charlotte, NC, pg. 134
Belkin, Steve, Chm. Bd. & Pres.--Trans National Travel, Boston, MA, pg. 1106
Bell, A. Quinn, Pres. & Chief Exec. Officer--The Suddath Companies, Jacksonville, FL, pg. 1055
Bell, C. Huston, Pres.--Vantage Companies, Dallas, TX, pg. 1145
Bell, David, Mng. Dir.--BSB Thailand, Bangkok, Thailand, pg. 110
Bell, Dennis, Pres.--Wisconsin Label Corporation, Algoma, WI, pg. 1198
Bell, Gene, Pres., Chief Exec. Officer--Union-Tribune Publishing Company, San Diego, CA, pg. 284
Bell, Harry H., Jr., Pres. & Chief Exec. Officer--Harry H. Bell & Sons, Inc., Saint Petersburg, FL, pg. 134
Bell, Jerry, Pres.--Minnesota Twins Baseball Club, Minneapolis, MN, pg. 758
Bell, John, Pres. & Chief Exec. Officer--Dixico, Inc., Dallas, TX, pg. 135
Bell, John, Jr., Chm. Bd. & Chief Exec. Officer--Bell Packaging Corporation, Marion, IN, pg. 135
Bell, Michael O., Pres.--Anthem Companies, Inc., Indianapolis, IN, pg. 90
Bell, Ray, Chm. Bd., Pres. & Chief Exec. Officer--Atex Oil Co. of Texas, Inc., Amarillo, TX, pg. 93
Bell, Ray, Pres.--Bell Construction Co. Inc., Brentwood, TN, pg. 134
Bell, Ray L., Pres. & Chief Exec. Officer--Bell Gas, Inc., Roswell, NM, pg. 134
Bell, Richard E., Pres. & Chief Exec. Officer--Riceland Foods, Inc., Stuttgart, AR, pg. 931
Bell, Robert, Pres.--Faraday, Inc., Tecumseh, MI, pg. 399
Bell, Ron, Pres.--Kanex, Cleveland, OH, pg. 616
Bell, Theodore A., Pres. & Chief Creative Officer-Leo Burnett USA--Leo Burnett Company, Inc., Chicago, IL, pg. 191
Bellacicco, Joseph, Pres.--Bellacicco & Sons, Queens Village, NY, pg. 136
Bellamy, Otis, Pres.--Bellamy Brothers, Inc., Ellenwood, GA, pg. 136
Beller, Albert, Pres.--Amsco School Publications, Inc., New York, NY, pg. 68
Bello, John J., Pres.--National Football League Properties, Inc., New York, NY, pg. 788
Belmont, Richard P., Pres.--Kings Island Company, Cincinnati, OH, pg. 53
Belot, Thomas G., Pres.--The Vollrath Company Inc., Sheboygan, WI, pg. 1154
Beltz, William A., Pres., Chief Exec. Officer & Editor-in-Chief--The Bureau of National Affairs, Inc., Washington, DC, pg. 189
Belz, Jack A., Pres. & Chief Exec. Officer--Belz Enterprises, Memphis, TN, pg. 138
Bender, Gerald, Pres. & Gen. Mgr.--Molded Fiber Glass Co., Union City, PA, pg. 764
Bender, Robert, Chm. Bd., Pres. & Chief Exec. Officer--Megas Beauty Aids, Inc., Cleveland, OH, pg. 737
Bender, Robert F., Chm. Bd., Pres. & Chief Exec. Officer--Airguard Industries Inc., Louisville, KY, pg. 27
Bender, Thomas B., Jr., Chm. Bd. & Pres.--Bender Shipbuilding & Repair Company, Mobile, AL, pg. 138
Benderson, Nathan, Pres.--Benderson Development Co., Inc., Buffalo, NY, pg. 138
Bendheim, P.E., Pres.--Mathieu Corporation, Riverdale, NJ, pg. 720
Bendheim, J.C., Pres.--Philipp Brothers Chemicals, Inc., Fort Lee, NJ, pg. 867
Benhamou, Guy, Pres.--Oroamerica, Inc., Burbank, CA, pg. 830
Benincasa, S., Pres.--Argo International Corp., New York, NY, pg. 81
Benjamin, Colin, Chm., Pres. & Chief Exec. Officer--Associated Metals & Minerals Corp., White Plains, NY, pg. 91
Benjamin, Mark, Pres. & Chief Exec. Officer--Morley Group, Santa Monica, CA, pg. 770
Benjamin, Mark E., Pres.--Benjamin Metals Company, Gardena, CA, pg. 139
Bennack, Frank A., Jr., Pres. & Chief Exec. Officer--The Hearst Corporation, New York, NY, pg. 521
Bennack, Frank A., Jr., Pres. & Chief Exec. Officer--Colonial Homes, New York, NY, pg. 523
Benner, Rick, Pres.--Sacramento Kings, Sacramento, CA, pg. 965
Bennett, Bruce, Pres.--The Hunt Corporation, Indianapolis, IN, pg. 553
Bennett, Gail Kirk, Sr., Pres.--Bennett Brothers, Inc., Chicago, IL, pg. 139
Bennett, Harold C., Pres.--Utility Trailer Manufacturing Co., City of Industry, CA, pg. 1141
Bennett, Jeffrey, Pres. & Chief Exec. Officer--Nature's Recipe Pet Foods, Corona, CA, pg. 796
Bennett, Joseph, Pres.--Trio Products Inc., Elyria, OH, pg. 1114
Bennett, Leamon J., Pres.--Puget Sound Plywood, Inc., Tacoma, WA, pg. 899
Bennett, Stanley T., Pres.--Oakhurst Dairy, Portland, ME, pg. 819
Bennett, Thomas Bert, Pres.--Wayne Dalton Corporation, Mount Hope, OH, pg. 312
Beno, Mike, Pres.--Label Products & Design Division, Green Bay, WI, pg. 608
Benoit, Steve, Pres.--Mountain States Constructors, Inc., Albuquerque, NM, pg. 773
Bensimon, Rachel, Pres. & Chief Fin. Officer--Dearden's, Inc., Los Angeles, CA, pg. 322
Benson, Donald W., Pres. & Chief Exec. Officer--Associated Grocers, Inc., Seattle, WA, pg. 90
Benson, Gerald, Chm. Bd., Pres. & Chief Exec. Officer--The Benatty Corporation, Cambridge, OH, pg. 138
Benson, Larry R., Pres.--Benson's, Inc., Bogart, GA, pg. 140

Benson, Tom, Jr., Chm. Bd. & Pres.--Benson Management Company, San Antonio, TX, pg. 140
Bent, Gardner L., Chm. Bd. & Pres.--S. Bent & Brothers, Inc., Gardner, MA, pg. 140
Benua, T.R., Jr., Pres. & Treas.--Ebco Mfg. Company, Columbus, OH, pg. 365
Benun, Ronald, Pres.--Bentex Kiddie Corporation, New York, NY, pg. 140
Benziger, Michael, Mng. Gen. Partner--Glen Ellen Winery, Glen Ellen, CA, pg. 461
Berard, Jacques, Gen. Mgr.--Levi Strauss France, S.A., Les Ulis,, France, pg. 671
Berdass, Daniel M., Pres.--Bermo, Inc., Circle Pines, MN, pg. 143
Beren, S.O., Chm. Bd., Pres. & Chief Exec. Officer--Misco Industries, Wichita, KS, pg. 759
Berenson, Paul S., Chm., Pres. & Dir.-Creative--Berenson, Isham & Partners, Inc., Boston, MA, pg. 141
Beres, Gary S., Pres.--Crafty Beaver Home Center, Skokie, IL, pg. 295
Beres, Louis H., Pres. & Chief Exec. Officer--Lou Beres & Associates, Inc., Chicago, IL, pg. 141
Beretta, David, Pres.--Amtrol Inc., West Warwick, RI, pg. 70
Berg, Harris, V.P. & Gen. Mgr.--Wick Bldg. Systems Inc. Manufactured Homes Div., Marshfield, WI, pg. 1188
Berg, Jack H., Pres. & Chief Exec. Officer--Serfilco, Ltd., Northbrook, IL, pg. 990
Berg, N.A., Pres.--American Steel Foundries, Chicago, IL, pg. 69
Berg, Ronald, Pres.--Alpha Shirt Co., Philadelphia, PA, pg. 44
Bergami, Frank, Pres.--Rolock, Inc., Fairfield, CT, pg. 944
Bergami, Samuel, Pres.--Alinabal, Inc., Milford, CT, pg. 34
Bergamo, Ron, Pres. & Gen. Mgr.--KTSP-TV--Great American Broadcasting Company, Cincinnati, OH, pg. 52
Bergan, Cole, Pres.--Smith Metal Arts Company, Inc., Buffalo, NY, pg. 1013
Berger, Steve, Pres.--Promotional Broadcast Services, Los Angeles, CA, pg. 1180
Bergeron, Edmond, Pres.--Carnrick Labs., Inc., Cedar Knolls, NJ, pg. 222
Bergeron, Edmund, Pres.--Rystan Company, Inc., Little Falls, NJ, pg. 222
Berghash, David, Pres.--Brimms Inc., Tonawanda, NY, pg. 176
Bergman, Gary C., Pres.--Superior Auctioneers & Marketing, Inc., San Antonio, TX, pg. 1063
Bergman, Robert S., Pres. & Treas.--Processed Plastic Company, Montgomery, IL, pg. 892
Bergman, Stanley M., Chm. Bd., Pres. & Chief Exec. Officer--Henry Schein, Inc., Port Washington, NY, pg. 975
Bergquist, C.R., Chm. Bd., Pres. & Chief Exec. Officer--Bergquist Company, Inc., Minneapolis, MN, pg. 141
Bergquist, David, Pres.--Northland Container Corp., Plymouth, MI, pg. 814
Bergson, Jim, Pres.--Colle & McVoy, Inc., Minneapolis, MN, pg. 261
Bergt, Mike, Pres.--Markair, Inc., Anchorage, AK, pg. 708
Beriker, Kerman, Chief Exec. Officer & Gen. Mgr.--The Beverly Hills Hotel, Beverly Hills, CA, pg. 148
Berk, Alexander, Pres.--Barton Brands, Ltd., Chicago, IL, pg. 123
Berk, Fred, Pres., Chief Exec. & Chief Oper. Officer--Huffman Koos Co., River Edge, NJ, pg. 551
Berke, Leonard, Pres.--Cincinnati Sub-Zero Products, Inc., Cincinnati, OH, pg. 250
Berkley, Allen, Pres.--Berkliff Corporation, New York, NY, pg. 142
Berkley, William, Pres. & Chief Exec. Officer--Tension Envelope Corp., Kansas City, MO, pg. 1088
Berkley, William, Pres.--Interlaken Capital, Inc., Greenwich, CT, pg. 574
Berkowitz, A.M., Pres.--J.E. Berkowitz, LP, Westville, NJ, pg. 142
Berkowitz, David H., Pres.--Central Paper Company, Newark, NJ, pg. 233
Berkowitz, Marshall L., Pres. & Chief Exec. Officer--Mohawk Distilled Products, North Miami, FL, pg. 763
Berkson, Howard, Pres.--Stanbee Company, Inc., Carlstadt, NJ, pg. 1035
Berlin, David N., Chm. Bd & Pres.--Metalloy Corporation, Hudson, MI, pg. 742
Berlin, Jack, Pres.--Potato Sales Company, Inc., Los Angeles, CA, pg. 882
Berline, Jim, Pres. & New Bus. Contact--The Berline Group Inc., Bingham Farms, MI, pg. 142
Berman, Barry H., Chm. Bd. & Pres.--CRN International, Inc., Hamden, CT, pg. 203
Berman, Barton M., Chm. Bd., Pres. & Chief Exec. Officer--Amurcon Corporation, Southfield, MI, pg. 70
Berman, Milton I., Chm. Bd., Pres. & Treas.--Avibank Mfg., Inc., Burbank, CA, pg. 102
Bermudez, Edmundo, Dir.--Rums of Puerto Rico, New York, NY, pg. 956
Bernard, Thomas E., Pres.--B & G Wholesalers, Inc., Nashville, TN, pg. 106
Bernards, Douglas, Pres.--Bernards Brothers, Inc., San Fernando, CA, pg. 143
Berndt, Dick, Sr. V.P., Mng. Dir.--Western International Media Corporation, Toronto,, Canada, pg. 1180
Berner, Philip, Pres.--Bernea Food Service, Inc., Otsego, MI, pg. 143
Bernes, I. Robert, Pres.--Triple A Specialty Company, Bedford Park, IL, pg. 1114
Bernhard, Charles R., Pres.--Bernhard Mechanical Contractor, Inc., Baton Rouge, LA, pg. 143
Bernhardt, George A., Pres.--Bernhardt Furniture Co., Lenoir, NC, pg. 144
Bernheim, Daniel S., Jr., Pres.--Bankcrafters, Inc., Philadelphia, PA, pg. 117
Bernon, Alan J., Pres.--Garelick Farms, Inc., Franklin, MA, pg. 443
Bernstein, Alfred, Pres.--Montebello Brands Inc., Baltimore, MD, pg. 767
Bernstein, Gene M., Pres.--Northville Industries Corp., Melville, NY, pg. 814
Bernstein, Harvey, Pres. & Sec.--Spirite Industries, Inc., Englewood, NJ, pg. 1031
Bernstein, Philip L., Pres.--Jacob Stern & Sons, Inc., Santa Barbara, CA, pg. 1047
Bernstein, Robert, Chm. Bd., Pres. & Chief Exec. Officer--Bernstein-Rein Advertising, Inc., Kansas City, MO, pg. 144
Bernstein, Saul H., Pres., Chief Exec. Officer & Treas.--Savoy Construction Co. Inc., Kensington, MD, pg. 973
Bernuth, Peter K., Chm. Bd., Pres. & Treas.--The Bernuth Corporation, Miami, FL, pg. 144
Berolzheimer, Philip, Pres.--California Cedar Products, Inc., Stockton, CA, pg. 209
Berolzheimer, Philip, Pres.--Duraflame, Inc., Stockton, CA, pg. 209
Berry, Claude A., Jr., Chm. Bd. & Pres.--Wehr Constructors Inc., Louisville, KY, pg. 1172
Berry, Dan W., Pres.--Seminole Manufacturing Company, Columbus, MS, pg. 989
Berry, Fred F., Jr., Pres.--Berry Companies, Inc., Wichita, KS, pg. 144
Berryman, David H., Pres.--Gibson Guitar Corporation, Inc., Nashville, TN, pg. 456
Bersoff, Edward H., Dr., Pres.--BTG, Inc., Vienna, VA, pg. 107
Berson, Paul A., Pres.--B & B Motor & Control Corporation, Long Island City, NY, pg. 105
Bertacchi, Lawrence, Pres.--Casa Di Bertacchi, Vineland, NJ, pg. 932
Bertelli, Jay, Chm. Bd., Pres. & Chief Exec. Officer--Mercury Computer Systems, Inc., Lowell, MA, pg. 740
Berthold, James K., Chm. Bd. & Pres.--Sunnen Products Company, Saint Louis, MO, pg. 1061
Bertrand, Leona C., Owner & Pres.--Bertrand Advertising Agency, Inc., Hollywood, CA, pg. 144
Bertuch, Henri L., Pres.--DVC Industries, Bay Shore, NY, pg. 310
Berwind, C. Graham, Jr., Chm. Bd., Pres., Chief Exec. & Chief Oper. Officer--Berwind Corporation, Philadelphia, PA, pg. 145
Besche, Michael, Pres.--Besche Oil Company, Inc., Waldorf, MD, pg. 145
Bess, Ron, Pres. & Chief Oper. Officer--Bayer Bess Vanderwarker Inc., Chicago, IL, pg. 128
Besse, John, Pres.--Northern Michigan Veneers, Inc., Gladstone, MI, pg. 814
Besse, Stephen, Pres.--Gravymaster Inc., Branford, CT, pg. 478
Besse, William C., Chief Exec. Officer--Sanborn Manufacturing Company, Springfield, MN, pg. 969
Best, Ron, Pres. & Chief Exec. Officer--Totes Incorporated, Loveland, OH, pg. 1103
Betagole, Robert, Pres.--Mike Albert Leasing, Inc., Cincinnati, OH, pg. 31
Bete, Channing L., Jr., Pres.--Channing L. Bete Co., Inc., South Deerfield, MA, pg. 147
Bethel, James E., Pres. & Chief Exec. Officer--Western Federal Savings & Loan Association, Marina Del Rey, CA, pg. 1179
Bettar, Michael R., Pres.--Esther Williams Swimming Pool Co., Delair, NJ, pg. 389
Bettendorf, Larry, Pres.--The Protector Corporation, Addison, IL, pg. 895
Betz, Frederic J., Pres. & Chief Exec. Officer--Nationwide Homes, Inc., Martinsville, VA, pg. 795
Bevan, L. Darrell, Pres. & Chief Exec. Officer--Vidicom, L.D. Bevan Company, Inc., Thousand Oaks, CA, pg. 1151
Bever, C.C., Jr., Chm. Bd., Pres. & Chief Oper. Officer--B & B Cash Grocery Store, Tampa, FL, pg. 105
Bevington, John F., Pres. & Chief Exec. Officer--The National Super Service Co., Toledo, OH, pg. 794
Bevis, J. Wayne, Pres. & Chief Exec. Officer--Pella Corporation, Pella, IA, pg. 856
Beyer, Larry, Pres.--ZBS Industries, Inc., Mayfield Village, OH, pg. 1215
Beyer, Sonya Z., Chm., Pres. & Chief Exec. Officer--Midco International Inc., Chicago, IL, pg. 751
Beyland, L.S., Pres. & Chief Oper. Officer--Rome Cable Corporation, Rome, NY, pg. 945
Bezak, Sharon, Pres.--Sharon Concepts, Inc., Union, NJ, pg. 995
Bhutani, Raj, Dr., Pres. & Chief Exec. Officer--Alra Laboratories, Inc., Gurnee, IL, pg. 44
Biagi, Roy, V.P.--Lee Myles Associates Corporation, Maywood, NJ, pg. 666
Bibler, James, Pres.--Bibler Brothers, Inc., Russellville, AR, pg. 148
Biblowitz, Joshua, Pres. & Chief Oper. Officer--Masters, Inc., Westbury, NY, pg. 720
Biblowitz, Joshua, Pres.--Central Textile Div., Westbury, NY, pg. 720
Bickman, James, Pres. & Treas.--Stocker & Yale, Inc., Beverly, MA, pg. 1050
Bickman, James, Pres.--MFE Instruments, Beverly, MA, pg. 1050
Biddinger, Clay M., Pres. & Chief Exec. Officer--Sun Financial Group, Inc., Tampa, FL, pg. 1058
Biddle, James, Sr, Pres. & Chief Exec. Officer--Mader Construction Group Inc., Elma, NY, pg. 699
Biddulph, Kemp, Pres.--Biddulph Oldsmobile, Glendale, AZ, pg. 149
Bidwell, F., Pres.--Malone Advertising, Inc., Akron, OH, pg. 703
Biedenharn, Hank, Pres.--Ouachita Coca-Cola Bottling Company, Monroe, LA, pg. 831
Bieger, Mike, Pres.--Perry's Ice Cream Co., Inc., Akron, NY, pg. 863
Bienenfeld, Marvin, Pres.--Bestform Foundations, Inc., Long Island City, NY, pg. 147
Bienenfeld, Marvin, Pres.--Lily of France, Inc., New York, NY, pg. 147
Bienenfeld, Marvin, Pres.--Poirette Corsets, Inc., New York, NY, pg. 147
Bienstock, David L., Pres.--Target Enterprises Ltd., Hollywood, CA, pg. 1079
Bierer, Alice, Pres. & Chief Fin. Officer--Essex Grain Products, Inc., Frazer, PA, pg. 389
Biever, Barton R., Jr., Pres.--Alpha Mills Corp., Schuylkill Haven, PA, pg. 43
Bigden, Julian V., Pres.--Fenner Manheim, Manheim, PA, pg. 406
Biggs, John H., Pres. & Chief Oper. Officer--Teachers Insurance and Annuity Association-College Retirement Equities Fund, New York, NY, pg. 1082
Bilinovich, Thomas, Pres.--Mark Machine Inc., White City, OR, pg. 708
Billeter, H.A., Pres. & Chief Exec. Officer--Johnny Appleseed's, Inc., Beverly, MA, pg. 597
Biltekoff, James, Pres.--Elan Foods, Buffalo, NY, pg. 372
Binner, Art, Acting Pres.--Mohawk Plastics, Inc., Bernardston, MA, pg. 763
Binns, James, Pres. & Chief Exec. Officer--Timex Corporation, Middlebury, CT, pg. 1098
Binsack, Herbert, Pres.--Bison Foods Company, Buffalo, NY, pg. 1140
Binswanger, John K., Pres.--The Binswanger Company, Philadelphia, PA, pg. 151
Biondi, Frank J., Jr., Pres. & Chief Exec. Officer--Viacom Inc., New York, NY, pg. 785
Birch, Ian, Editor--Us Magazine, New York, NY, pg. 1052
Birkhauser, Robert R., III, Pres.--Auto Glass Specialists, Madison, WI, pg. 100
Birle, James R., Co-Chm. & Co-Chief Exec. Officer--Collins & Aikman Group Inc., Santa Monica, CA, pg. 262
Birnaum, William, Pres.--Alexander Doll Co., Inc., New York, NY, pg. 33
Birndorf, Harold, Pres.--Atlas Lift Truck Rentals & Sales, Inc., Schiller Park, IL, pg. 96
Bisch, Damian, Pres. & Chief Exec. Officer--Damian Bisch & Partners, Inc. Advertising, New York, NY, pg. 153
Bishop, C.M., Jr., Pres. & Co-Chief Exec. Officer--Pendleton Woolen Mills, Inc., Portland, OR, pg. 857
Bishop, J. Ronald, Pres.--Electro-Wire Products, Inc., Rochester Hills, MI, pg. 375
Bishop, Thomas A., Gen. Mgr.--Arizona Auction Services, Inc., d/b/a Southwest Auto Auction, Chandler, AZ, pg. 293
Bishop, Vernon, Chm. Bd., Pres. & Chief Exec. Officer--Lebanon Chemical Corp., Lebanon, PA, pg. 665
Bishop, William L., Pres. & Chief Oper. Officer--The Western Group, Saint Louis, MO, pg. 1179
Bissell, John M., Pres.--Bissell Inc., Grand Rapids, MI, pg. 153
Bissett, William J., Pres.--Sportsystems Corporation, Buffalo, NY, pg. 326
Bither, Richard A., Pres.--Giffels Associates, Inc., Southfield, MI, pg. 457
Bitter, Adriana Scalamandre, Pres.--Scalamandre, Inc., Long Island City, NY, pg. 974
Bittinger, Larry, Pres. & Chief Oper. Officer--Prism Integrated Sanitation Management, Inc., Miami, FL, pg. 599
Bittner, Clarence J., Pres. & Chief Oper. Officer--Shook National Corporation, Dayton, OH, pg. 1000
Bittner, Clarence J., Pres. & Chief Oper. Officer--Shook, Inc., Dayton, OH, pg. 1000
Bivona, Gary, Pres.--Insulating Materials, Inc., Schenectady, NY, pg. 572
Bixler, Phyllis, Pres. & Gen. Mgr.--Ranch-Way, Inc., Fort Collins, CO, pg. 911
Bizzaro, Richard, Pres. & Chief Exec. Officer-Food Division--Weider Health & Fitness, Woodland Hills, CA, pg. 1173
Bjorkman, Joseph R., Pres.--Alkota Cleaning Systems, Inc., Alcester, SD, pg. 34
Black, Frank C., Pres.--Vogler Motor Company, Inc., Carbondale, IL, pg. 1154
Black, James, Chm. Bd. & Pres.--Johnson County Farm Bureau Co-op, Franklin, IN, pg. 598
Black, Jeff, Pres. & Treas.--Black & Co., Decatur, IL, pg. 154
Black, Scott, Pres.--Black Gillock & Langberg, Houston, TX, pg. 154
Black, W.J. II, Pres., Chief Exec. Officer & Treas.--Walter J. Black, Inc., Port Washington, NY, pg. 154
Black, William H., III, Pres.--Black Cadillac Olds, Inc., Greensboro, NC, pg. 153
Blackburn, Donald F., Pres.--American Foodservice Corp., King of Prussia, PA, pg. 54
Blacker, Stanley, Chm. Bd. & Pres.--Stanley Blacker, Inc., Philadelphia, PA, pg. 155
Blackstock, Hoyt, Pres.--J.R. Simplot Co. Food Group, Boise, ID, pg. 1007
Blackwell, Lawrence, Pres.--Mindgames, Inc., Pine Bluff, AR, pg. 756
Blagge, Timothy J., Pres. & Chief Exec. Officer--Tim & Diane Blagge Inc., Rancho Cordova, CA, pg. 155
Blair, Michael D., Pres. & Chief Exec. Officer--Cyborg Systems, Inc., Chicago, IL, pg. 307
Blair, R. Cary, Pres. & Chief Exec. Officer--Westfield Companies, Westfield Center, OH, pg. 1182
Blair, Richard M., Pres.--Young-Phillips Sales Co., Winston-Salem, NC, pg. 1210
Blake, Jerry A., Pres. & Chief Oper. Officer--Active Tool & Manufacturing Co., Inc., Roseville, MI, pg. 15
Blake, Richard F., Pres.--Transistor Devices, Inc., Cedar Knolls, NJ, pg. 1107
Blanchard, Kenneth E., Chm. Bd., Pres. & Chief Oper. Officer--Phonetics, Inc., Aston, PA, pg. 869
Blanchard, Richard F., Pres.--Wm. Blanchard Co., Springfield, NJ, pg. 155
Bland, William W., Chm. Bd. & Pres.--Bland Cadillac Company, Houston, TX, pg. 155

Blank, Richard, Chm. Bd. & Pres.--Direct Communications Corporation, Bronxville, NY, pg. 339
Blankenship, Michael F., Pres. & Creative Dir.--Porcaro Blankenship Advertising, Anchorage, AK, pg. 881
Blankenship, Truman, Pres.--Berryman Products, Inc., Arlington, TX, pg. 144
Blanton, Raymond L., Pres. & Chief Exec. Officer--Bee-Gee Shoe Div., Dayton, OH, pg. 373
Blatt, John A., Pres.--Automation Products Group, Mount Clemens, MI, pg. 560
Blatt, John A., Pres.--ISI Robotics II, Anchorville, MI, pg. 560
Blatt, L. Douglas, Pres. & Chief Exec. Officer--The ISI Manufacturing, Inc., Fraser, MI, pg. 560
Blatt, L.D., Pres.--ISI Robotics I, Fraser, MI, pg. 560
Blatt, S., Pres. & Treas.--Columbus Steel Drum Company, Blacklick, OH, pg. 267
Blattner, William H., Jr., Pres.--D.H. Blattner & Sons, Inc., Avon, MN, pg. 156
Blau, Barry, Chm. Bd. & Chief Exec. Officer--Barry Blau & Partners, Inc., Fairfield, CT, pg. 156
Blauer, Charles, Pres.--Blauer Manufacturing Co., Inc., Boston, MA, pg. 156
Blaugrund, Lee S., Pres.--American Furniture Company, Albuquerque, NM, pg. 55
Bleiweis, Raymond L., Pres.--Rocket Industries, Inc./Excel, The Exercise Company, Pico Rivera, CA, pg. 941
Blevins, J. William, Pres.--The Marble Company, Nashville, TN, pg. 156
Blevins, James W., Pres. & Chief Exec Officer--Blevins Inc., Nashville, TN, pg. 156
Blicher, Bert, Pres. & Chief Oper. Officer--Oxford First Corporation, Philadelphia, PA, pg. 834
Blinder, James F., Pres. & Treas.--Nelson Brothers Furniture Co., Chicago, IL, pg. 797
Bliss, David, Pres.--Quality Stores Inc., North Muskegon, MI, pg. 904
Bliss, James C., Pres. & Chief Exec. Officer--Telesensory, Mountain View, CA, pg. 1085
Bloch, Federico, Pres. & Chief Exec. Officer--Taca International Airlines, S. A., New Orleans, LA, pg. 1076
Block, Edward L., Pres. & Chief Exec. Officer--Block Distributing Company, San Antonio, TX, pg. 157
Block, George P., Pres.--Carstens Health Industries, Inc., Chicago, IL, pg. 225
Block, Joseph, Pres.--Block & Nardizzi, Stamford, CT, pg. 157
Block, Paul J., Pres.--Revlon International Corporation, New York, NY, pg. 696
Block, Richard, Pres.--AGI Inc., Melrose Park, IL, pg. 4
Block, Sam, Jr., Pres.--Ideal Chemical & Supply Company, Memphis, TN, pg. 562
Block, William, Jr., Pres.--Blade Communications, Inc., Toledo, OH, pg. 155
Block, William, Jr., Pres. & Co-Publr.--Toledo Blade Co., Toledo, OH, pg. 155
Blommer, Henry, Jr., Pres.--Blommer Chocolate Co., Chicago, IL, pg. 157
Blonkenmeyer, Oscar Jr., Pres.--Lasting Products, Inc., Dallas, TX, pg. 660
Bloom, Donald, Pres. & Chief Exec. Officer--Bloom Electric Services, Inc., Oklahoma City, OK, pg. 157
Bloom, Jack, Pres.--Baldi, Bloom & Whelan Advertising, New York, NY, pg. 115
Bloomgarden, Kathy, Pres.--Ruder, Finn, Inc., New York, NY, pg. 954
Blouin, Joseph, Pres.--Fabex Inc., Novi, MI, pg. 395
Blount, Dan S., Pres. & Chief Oper. Officer--Montgomery Elevator Company, Moline, IL, pg. 767
Blue, David S., Pres. & Chief Exec. Officer--Louisville Scrap Material Co., Inc., Louisville, KY, pg. 684
Bluemke, Jack, Chm. Bd.--Cream Products Co., Inc., Westchester, IL, pg. 297
Bluemke, John, Jr., Pres.--Cream Products Co., Inc., Westchester, IL, pg. 297
Bluhm, Neil, Pres.--Amfac, Inc., Chicago, IL, pg. 585
Bluhm, Neil G., Pres.--JMB Realty Corporation, Chicago, IL, pg. 584
Blum, Michael, Chm. Bd. & Pres.--Heller International, Chicago, IL, pg. 526
Blum, Richard J., Pres.--The Kirk & Blum Mfg. Co., Cincinnati, OH, pg. 633
Blum, Robert M., Pres.--Craftex Mills Inc. of Pennsylvania, Blue Bell, PA, pg. 295
Blume, Robert L., Pres. & Chief Exec. Officer--Capital Development Co., Lacey, WA, pg. 215
Blumenthal, Alan, Pres.--Radiator Specialty Company, Charlotte, NC, pg. 909
Blumenthal, Harry J., Jr., Pres.--Blumenthal Print Works, Inc., New Orleans, LA, pg. 161
Blumenthal, Robert, Pres. & Chief Exec. Officer--Penn Emblem Co., Philadelphia, PA, pg. 857
Blumenthal, Robert S., Pres.--Advance Mechanical Systems, Inc., Elk Grove Village, IL, pg. 19
Blumenthal, Thomas A., Chm. Bd. Pres. & Chief Exec. Officer--Norwalk Powdered Metals, Inc., Norwalk, CT, pg. 816
Boasberg, Howard, Chm. Bd. & Chief Exec. Officer--Boasberg Valentine-Radford, Inc., Kansas City, MO, pg. 1143
Bobinchuck, Michael, Pres.--Par Industries, inc., Medina, OH, pg. 847
Bobit, Ty, Pres.--Bobit Publishing Company, Redondo Beach, CA, pg. 161
Boccardi, Louis D., Pres. & Chief Exec. Officer--The Associated Press, New York, NY, pg. 91
Boccitto, Elio, Pres. & Chief Oper. Officer--Berlitz International, Inc., Princeton, NJ, pg. 142
Boccitto, Elio, Pres.--Berlitz Publishing Company Inc., New York, NY, pg. 142
Bock, Daniel M., Pres.--Carquest Corporation, Tarrytown, NY, pg. 224
Bocksch, David, Pres. & Chief Oper. Officer--Monroe Systems For Business, Inc., Morris Plains, NJ, pg. 766
Bodden, Max, Pres. & Chief Exec. Officer--Communications Plus, Inc., New York, NY, pg. 269
Boddie, William L., Pres.--Boddie-Noell Enterprises Inc., Rocky Mount, NC, pg. 161
Bodiford, Jake, Gen. Mgr.--Newport Div., Crosby, TX, pg. 900
Bodine, John R., Pres. & Chief Exec. Officer--Bodine Electric Company, Chicago, IL, pg. 162
Bodine, Richard P., Pres.--The Bodine Corp., Bridgeport, CT, pg. 161
Bodman, James W., Pres. & Chief Oper. Officer--Vienna Sausage Mfg. Co., Chicago, IL, pg. 1151
Bodner, Herbert, Pres. & Chief Exec. Officer--Fru-Con Construction Corporation, Ballwin, MO, pg. 435
Boedeker, Theodore R., Pres.--Tricon Industries, Inc., Downers Grove, IL, pg. 1113
Boehm, Josef F., Pres. & Chief Oper. Officer--Alaska Industrial Hardware Inc., Anchorage, AK, pg. 30
Boelter, Robert, Pres.--Advertising, Boelter & Lincoln, Madison, WI, pg. 21
Boerner, Allen, Chm. Bd. & Pres.--Cambio Equities Corp., Fullerton, CA, pg. 211
Boes, Francis X., Pres. & Chief Exec. Officer--Oriel Corporation, Stratford, CT, pg. 829
Boesen, Ulrich, Mng. Dir.--Leo Burnett Denmark, Copenhagen, Denmark, pg. 192
Boesenberg, Charles M., Pres. & Chief Oper. Officer--Central Point Software, Inc., Beaverton, OR, pg. 234
Bogan, Thomas F., Pres.--Avatar Corporation, Hopkinton, MA, pg. 101
Bogan, Tod, Pres.--Carl's Drug Company, Inc., Rome, NY, pg. 1150
Bogdovitz, Walter J., Pres.--Harza Engineering Co., Chicago, IL, pg. 516
Bogrand, Randall, Pres. & Chief Exec. Officer--Tollycraft Yachts Corp., Kelso, WA, pg. 1100
Boh, Robert H., Chm. Bd., Pres. & Chief Exec. Officer--Boh Corporation, New Orleans, LA, pg. 162
Boh, Robert H., Chm. Bd. & Pres.--Boh Brothers Construction Company, Inc., New Orleans, LA, pg. 162
Bohan, Gloria, Pres. & Chief Oper. Officer--Omega World Travel, Inc., Falls Church, VA, pg. 826
Bohbot, Allen J., Pres. & Chief Exec. Officer--Bohbot Communications, Inc., New York, NY, pg. 162
Bohrer, Thomas C., Pres.--International Specialty Products, Inc., Wilmington, DE, pg. 438
Bokor, James, Pres.--Robert James Sales Inc., Buffalo, NY, pg. 589
Bokser, Stephen R., Pres. & Chief Oper. Officer--White Rose Food, Long Island City, NY, pg. 335
Boland, David, Chm. Bd., Pres. & Chief Exec. Officer--David Boland, Inc., Titusville, FL, pg. 162
Bolin, Todd, Pres. & Chief Oper. Officer--M. R. Bolin Inc., Minneapolis, MN, pg. 162
Bollat S., Luis R., Pres.--Publimerca S.A., Guatemala City,, Guatemala, pg. 105
Bollier, Roger D., Pres.--Niagara Cutter, Inc., North Tonawanda, NY, pg. 805
Bollinger, Glenn D., Chm. Bd. & Pres.--Bollinger Industries Inc., Irving, TX, pg. 163
Bollinger, Richard, Pres.--Bollinger Machine Shop And Shipyard, Inc., Lockport, LA, pg. 163
Bolton, Thomas L., Pres.--Ivan Allen Company, Inc., Atlanta, GA, pg. 36
Boman, Lael P., Pres.--B & K Steel & Supply, Inc., Ogden, UT, pg. 105
Bomer, Robert, Pres.--Curtis C. Gunn, Inc., San Antonio, TX, pg. 494
Bomstein, Howard, Chm. Bd., Pres. & Chief Exec. Officer--The Bomstein Agency, Washington, DC, pg. 164
Bonadies, Lewis M., Pres. & Chief Exec. Officer--Willis Case Harwood, Inc., Dayton, OH, pg. 1192
Bonahoom, A. James, Jr., Pres. & Sec.--Wolverine Packing Co., Detroit, MI, pg. 1199
Bonburg, Thomas, Pres.--Winston Tire Company, Burbank, CA, pg. 1197
Boncosky, William A., Pres.--HPS, Inc., Indianapolis, IN, pg. 497
Bond, Geoff, Pres. & Chief Oper. Officer--Cooperheat, Inc., Piscataway, NJ, pg. 283
Bond, James H., Pres.--Central Parking Corp., Nashville, TN, pg. 234
Bond, James H., Pres.--Central Parking Corp., Nashville, TN, pg. 234
Bond, Jonathan, Pres.--Kirshenbaum & Bond, New York, NY, pg. 633
Bond, Roger A., Pres.--Abbott Ball Company, West Hartford, CT, pg. 9
Bone, Ronald A., Pres.--Columbia Iron & Metal Co., Cleveland, OH, pg. 265
Bones, Harvey, Pres.--Baltimore Luggage Company, Baltimore, MD, pg. 116
Bonfante, Michael, Pres. & Chief Exec. Officer--Nob Hill General Store, Inc., Gilroy, CA, pg. 807
Boniface, William, Pres.--Bonland Industries, Inc., Wayne, NJ, pg. 164
Bonn, Neal F., Pres. & Chief Exec. Officer--F.H. Bonn Company, Arlington Heights, IL, pg. 164
Bonn, Neal F., Pres. & Chief Exec. Officer--International Steel Wool Corporation, Springfield, OH, pg. 164
Bono, Vincent, Pres.--Clearpoint Research Corporation, Hopkinton, MA, pg. 254
Bonsib, Richard E., Chm. Bd. & Pres.--Bonsib Inc., Fort Wayne, IN, pg. 164
Boodjeh, Parviz, Pres. & Chief Exec. Officer--Discount Drug Mart Inc., Medina, OH, pg. 339
Booher, K.L., Pres.--Miller Electric Mfg. Co., Appleton, WI, pg. 754
Bookshester, Dennis, Pres. & Chief Exec. Officer--Bailey Banks & Biddle, Irving, TX, pg. 1215
Boone, Florence, Chm. Bd.--Pace, Arlington Heights, IL, pg. 922
Boos, William, Pres.--Gibson Wine Company, Elk Grove, CA, pg. 457
Booth, Charles H., Jr., Chm. Bd., Pres. & Chief Exec. Officer--Burrell Group, New Kensington, PA, pg. 195
Booth, John L., II, Pres. & Chief Fin. Officer--Booth American, Detroit, MI, pg. 165
Booth, Ralph H., II, Pres. & Treas.--Booth American, Detroit, MI, pg. 165
Bordages, William, Pres.--Azon Corporation, Johnson City, NY, pg. 105
Bordages, William, Pres.--Keuffel & Esser, Rockaway, NJ, pg. 105
Borden, John, Exec. V.P.--FTD/Florists' Transworld Delivery Association, Southfield, MI, pg. 395
Borden, Lorraine, Chm. Bd., Chief Exec. Officer, Chief Fin. Officer, Pres.--Great Scott Advertising Co. Inc., New York, NY, pg. 482
Borders, Bill, Pres. & Dir.-Creative Services--Borders, Perrin & Norrander, Inc., Portland, OR, pg. 165
Boren, Leland E., Chm. Bd., Pres. & Chief Exec. Officer--Avis Industrial Corporation, Upland, IN, pg. 102
Borg, Malcolm A., Chm. Bd. & Pres.--Macromedia Inc., Hackensack, NJ, pg. 698
Borghorst, Bob, Pres.--Arthur A. Pozzi Co., Inc., Portland, OR, pg. 883
Borgudd, Ake, Chief Exec. Officer--BSB Sweden, Stockholm,, Sweden, pg. 110
Borin, Arthur A., Pres.--Amalloy, Goshen, NY, pg. 46
Born, Harmon M., Pres.--Beaudry Ford, Inc., Atlanta, GA, pg. 130
Born, Ross J., Co-Pres.--Just Born, Inc., Bethlehem, PA, pg. 610
Born, Ross J., Co-Pres.--Just Born, Inc., Bethlehem, PA, pg. 610
Bornhoeft, Jack H., Pres.--Gerhardt F. Meyne Co., Chicago, IL, pg. 746
Borowsky, Ned S., Pres. & Chief Oper. Officer--North American Publishing Company, Philadelphia, PA, pg. 811
Borshoff, Thomas N., Pres. & Chief Exec. Officer--First Federal Savings and Loan Assn. of Rochester, Rochester, NY, pg. 413
Boruch, John, Pres.--Amkor Electronics, Inc., West Chester, PA, pg. 67
Bosboom, Tony J., Pres. & Chief Exec. Officer--Fabric Wholesalers, Inc., Portland, OR, pg. 396
Bosca, C.B., Pres.--Hugo Bosca Co., Inc., Springfield, OH, pg. 166
Bosco, Jerry, Pres.--Relief Printing Corporation, Baldwin Park, CA, pg. 925
Boshamer, Ulf, Pres.--Klear Knit Inc., Clover, SC, pg. 634
Bosma, Tiemen, Pres--Ad/Productions, Amsterdam,, Netherlands, pg. 1211
Boso, James, Pres. & Chief Exec. Officer--SPI Holdings, Richardson, TX, pg. 318
Bostian, Ray, Pres.--Southern Pump & Tank Co. Inc., Charlotte, NC, pg. 1022
Botkin, James I., Pres.--Cutler Manufacturing Corporation, Highland City, FL, pg. 307
Bottendorf, Larry, Pres. & Chief Exec. Officer--ECP Incorporated, Westchester, IL, pg. 317
Bottner, Irving J., Pres. & Chief Oper. Officer--Revlon-Realistic Professional Products, Inc., New York, NY, pg. 696
Botto, Robert J., Pres.--Botto, Roessner, Horne & Messinger, Inc., New York, NY, pg. 625
Botwick, Terry, Pres.--Hearst Entertainment, New York, NY, pg. 523
Bouchard, John E., III, Chm. Bd. & Pres.--John Bouchard & Sons Company, Nashville, TN, pg. 168
Bouckaert, Thomas, Pres.--Conquest Carpet Mills, Dalton, GA, pg. 276
Bouldin, Kent, Pres.--Leather Center, Inc., Carrollton, TX, pg. 664
Boulton, Samuel R., Pres. & Chief Oper. Officer--Taylor Drug Stores, Inc., Louisville, KY, pg. 1081
Bourland, Curtis F., Pres. & Chief Exec. Officer--Continental Graphics Holdings, Inc., Los Angeles, CA, pg. 279
Bourns, Gordon L., Chm. Bd.--Bourns, Inc., Riverside, CA, pg. 168
Boury, George, Chm. Bd & Pres.--Boury Incorporated, Wheeling, WV, pg. 168
Bovaird, W.J., Pres. & Chief Exec. Officer--Bovaird Supply Co., Tulsa, OK, pg. 168
Bowden, Al, Pres. & Chief Exec. Officer--Sencore, Inc., Sioux Falls, SD, pg. 989
Bowe, Richard E., Chm. Bd. & Pres.--Ellicott Machine Corp., Baltimore, MD, pg. 378
Bowen, Jeffrey A., Pres.--Flo-Pac Corporation, Minneapolis, MN, pg. 419
Bowen, Steve, Pres., Chief Exec. Officer--Geer, DuBois Inc., New York, NY, pg. 447
Bowers, Charles E., Jr., Pres.--The Fibre-Metal Products Company, Concordville, PA, pg. 408
Bowers, Peter, Pres.--Ross Roy Canada, Ltd., Toronto,, Canada, pg. 950
Bowers, Robert, Pres.--North Carolina Mutual Wholesale Drug Co., Durham, NC, pg. 813
Bowis, John, Pres.--Chevy Chase Cars & Geo, Bethesda, MD, pg. 244
Bowker, Gary, Pres.--Alloy Technology International Inc., West Nyack, NY, pg. 41
Bowling, David O., Pres.--Meldrum & Fewsmith Yellow Pages Inc., Cleveland, OH, pg. 737
Bowlus, Charles C., Pres.--Boston Distributors, Inc., Maple Heights, OH, pg. 167
Bowman, John E., Pres.--Saunders Brothers, Westbrook, ME, pg. 972
Bowman, William F., Pres.--Associated Company, Inc., Wichita, KS, pg. 89
Bowyer, Thomas S., Jr., Pres.--Schmidt Baking Co., Inc., Baltimore, MD, pg. 976
Boyan, William L., Jr., Pres. & Chief Oper. Officer--John Hancock Mutual Life Insurance Company, Boston, MA, pg. 595
Boyd, Dennis, Pres. & Chief Exec. Officer--Royal Waterbeds, Maryland Heights, MO, pg. 953

Boyd, J.A., Chm. Bd., Pres. & Chief Exec. Officer--Fish Engineering & Construction, Inc., Houston, TX, pg. 414
Boyd, James E., Pres.--Duff-Norton, Charlotte, NC, pg. 1032
Boyd, Melvin C., Pres.--Boyd, Tamney & Cross Advertising/ Marketing, Wayne, PA, pg. 169
Boyd, Morton, Jr., Pres. & Chief Exec. Officer--First National Bank of Louisville, Louisville, KY, pg. 413
Boyd, Robert A., Pres. & Chief Oper. Officer--J.H. Baxter & Company, San Mateo, CA, pg. 127
Boyd, Thomas J., Chm. Bd. & Pres.--Navajo Forest Products Industries, Navajo, NM, pg. 796
Boyd, Walter, Pres.--International Data Group, Boston, MA, pg. 576
Boyd, William W., Chmn. Bd. & Pres.--Sterling Plumbing Group, Inc., Schaumburg, IL, pg. 640
Boyden, James, Pres. & Chief Exec. Officer--Teachers Management & Investment Corporation, Newport Beach, CA, pg. 1082
Boyer, K., Pres.--Haviland/Wilbur-Ellis Agricultural, Sparta, MI, pg. 517
Boyer, Rahn, Pres. & Chief Exec. Officer--Gem-Dandy, Inc., Madison, NC, pg. 447
Boyle, Les, Chm. Bd., Pres. & Chief Exec. Officer--CRE, Inc., Indianapolis, IN, pg. 203
Boyle, P.J., Pres.--Schulze & Burch Biscuit Company, Chicago, IL, pg. 979
Boyle, R.E., Chm. Bd., Pres. & Chief Exec. Officer--Ormet Corporation, Hannibal, OH, pg. 822
Bozof, Albert, Pres.--Bozof Dinettes, Inc., Olive Branch, MS, pg. 169
Brabson, John A., Jr., Pres.--Lykes Energy, Inc., Tampa, FL, pg. 689
Braby, James R., Pres. & Chief Oper. Officer--Octagon Process Inc., Edgewater, NJ, pg. 821
Bracey, Morris W., Chm. Bd., Pres., Chief Exec. & Chief Oper. Officer--Dealers Electrical Supply Co., Waco, TX, pg. 322
Brachman, Merom, Pres.--Yenkin-Majestic Paint Corporation, Columbus, OH, pg. 1208
Bradberry, E.G., Pres.--Continental Ozark, Inc., Fayetteville, AR, pg. 280
Bradburd, Arnold W., Chm. Bd., Pres. & Chief Exec. Officer--Interstate Steel Supply Co., Philadelphia, PA, pg. 580
Bradbury, David, Chm. Bd. & Pres.--Bradbury Company, Inc., Moundridge, KS, pg. 169
Braddock, James L., Chm. Bd., Pres. & Treas.--Fastec Industrial, Elkhart, IN, pg. 403
Bradfield, Joe L., Pres.--Woodbury Business Forms, Inc., La Grange, GA, pg. 1200
Bradfield, William, Pres. & Chief Oper. Officer--Sathers Inc., Round Lake, MN, pg. 972
Bradford, Judson T., Chm. Bd. & Pres.--Bradford Company, Holland, MI, pg. 170
Bradley, David R. Jr., Pres. & Editor--News-Press & Gazette Company, St. Joseph, MA, pg. 804
Bradley, George H., Pres.--LFC Holding Corporation, Boca Raton, FL, pg. 647
Bradley, George H., Pres.--Levitz Furniture Corporation, Boca Raton, FL, pg. 647
Bradley, Kirk J., Pres.--Lee-Moore Oil Co., Inc., Sanford, NC, pg. 665
Bradley, Roberta Palm, Supt.--Seattle City Light, Seattle, WA, pg. 986
Bradley, William J., Pres. & Chief Exec. Officer--Perry & Derrick Co., Cincinnati, OH, pg. 863
Bradshaw, Raymond D., Pres. & Creative Dir.--Bradshaw Associates in Advertising, Inc., Springfield, MO, pg. 171
Brady, Barrett, Pres. & Chief Exec. Officer--Dunn Industries Inc., Kansas City, MO, pg. 354
Brady, Frank, Pres. & Chief Exec. Officer--The Brady Marketing Company, Pacheco, CA, pg. 171
Brady, John, Pres.--Brady Enterprises, Inc., East Weymouth, MA, pg. 171
Brady, John, Pres. & Chief Oper. Officer--Excelsior Manufacturing & Supply Corp., Itasca, IL, pg. 392
Brainin, Garry, Chm. Bd. & Pres.--Altair Corporation, Lincolnshire, IL, pg. 45
Brakhan, Andrew, Pres.--Sennheiser Electronic Corp., Old Lyme, CT, pg. 989
Braman, Norman, Pres.--Braman World Car Center, Miami, FL, pg. 171
Bramble, David C., Pres. & Chief Oper. Officer--David A. Bramble, Inc., Chestertown, MD, pg. 171
Bramsen, James, Pres.--Spraying Systems Co., Wheaton, IL, pg. 1032
Bramson, Edward, Pres.--Sherborne Group, Inc., New York, NY, pg. 998
Branca, Dominick, Pres.--Falcon Candy Company, Philadelphia, PA, pg. 398
Branch, William J., Jr., Pres. & Chief Exec. Officer--Masland Industries, Carlisle, PA, pg. 717
Brand, David R., Pres.--Brand, Shick & Wesley, Cleveland, OH, pg. 172
Brandon, J.D., Chm. Bd. & Pres.--The Pro-Quip Corporation, Tulsa, OK, pg. 892
Brandon, William H., Jr., Pres.--The American Bankers Association, Washington, DC, pg. 49
Bransfield, M. Declan III, Pres.--Eberle Direct Marketing Group, Inc., Vienna, VA, pg. 365
Branson, James, Pres.--Flexible Flyer Inc., West Point, MS, pg. 847
Brant, Peter, Pres.--Brant Allen Industries, Inc., Greenwich, CT, pg. 172
Brantlinger, F. Herbert, Pres. & Chief Exec. Officer--Lawrence Insurance Group, Inc., New York, NY, pg. 662
Brantlinger, F. Herbert, Pres. & Chief Exec. Officer--United Community Insurance Co., Albany, NY, pg. 662
Bras, Robert W., Pres.--Menu Foods, Inc., Pennsauken, NJ, pg. 739
Brasier, James, Pres.--Tastee Freez Intl. Inc., Utica, MI, pg. 321
Brasier, James P., Pres.--De Novo Corporation, Utica, MI, pg. 321
Braswell, Gary, Pres. & Chief Exec. Officer--MPD, Inc., Owensboro, KY, pg. 693
Braum, William H., Pres. & Chief Exec. Officer--Braum Ice Cream Stores Inc., Oklahoma City, OK, pg. 172
Braun, Curt, Pres.--Hunter Engineering Co., Inc., Riverside, CA, pg. 554
Braun, Ed, Pres. & Chief Exec. Officer--Sloan Technology, Santa Barbara, CA, pg. 1146
Braun, Edward H., Pres.--Veeco Instrumentations, Inc., Plainview, NY, pg. 1146
Braunheim, Stephen, Pres.--California Manufacturing Enterprises, City of Industry, CA, pg. 210
Braunlich, H.P., Jr., Chm. Bd., Pres. & Chief Exec. Officer--Brammer Manufacturing Company, Davenport, IA, pg. 171
Brawer, Robert A., Pres. & Chief Exec. Officer--Maidenform, Inc., New York, NY, pg. 701
Brazier, John M., Pres. & Chief Exec. Officer--Brazier Forest Industries, Inc., Seattle, WA, pg. 172
Breen, James J., Sr. V.P. & Chief Oper. Officer--Manhattan National Corporation, Cincinnati, OH, pg. 1128
Brems, Christian, Pres.--Brems Eastman Glade, Inc., Seattle, WA, pg. 173
Bren, Donald, Chm. Bd.--Irvine Company, Newport Beach, CA, pg. 582
Bren, Shirley, Pres.--Swell-Wear, Inc., New York, NY, pg. 1067
Brendel, Albert, Pres.--Sensor Developments Inc., Orion, MI, pg. 990
Brenia, Paul S., Chm., Pres. & Chief Exec. Officer--Ancra Corporation, Hawthorne, CA, pg. 72
Brennan, James M., Pres.--Penn Colour Graphics, Inc., Huntingdon Valley, PA, pg. 857
Brennan, John J., Pres.--The Vanguard Group, Inc., Wayne, PA, pg. 1145
Brennan, Norman, Pres.--Dimco-Gray Company, Dayton, OH, pg. 338
Brennan, Robert J., Pres. & Chief Oper. Officer--American Institute for Foreign Study, London, United Kingdom, pg. 56
Brenner, Frank A., Pres.--Hart Services, Inc., Chicago, IL, pg. 513
Brenner, Ronald D., Pres. & Chief Exec. Officer--Technology for Energy Corporation, Knoxville, TN, pg. 1084
Brenton, Donald L., Pres. & Chief Oper. Officer--Autoswage Products, Inc., Shelton, CT, pg. 101
Bresky, H.H., Pres.--Seaboard Corporation, Newton, MA, pg. 984
Bresky, Harry, Pres.--Seaboard Flour Corporation, Newton, MA, pg. 984
Bresnahan, William J., Pres.--Hynes Industries Inc., Youngstown, OH, pg. 557
Bresnahan, William P., Pres.--Colad Group Inc., Buffalo, NY, pg. 259
Bressanelli, Jerome P., Pres.--Canton Drop Forge, Canton, OH, pg. 214
Bressler, Irving, Pres.--Bregg Data Forms, Inc., Hauppauge, NY, pg. 173
Brestle, Daniel J., Pres.--Clinique Laboratories, Inc., New York, NY, pg. 389
Brestle, Daniel J., Pres.--Prescriptives, Inc., New York, NY, pg. 389
Breuer-Murray, Linda, Pres.--Breuer Electric Mfg. Co., Chicago, IL, pg. 174
Brewer, C. James, Pres.--Burgess-Norton Mfg. Co., Geneva, IL, pg. 69
Brewer, Mark, Pres.--Falley's Inc., Topeka, KS, pg. 1214
Brewer, Patrick, Pres.--Grandville Printing Company, Grandville, MI, pg. 476
Brewer, William C., Pres.--King Prime, Inc., Morgantown, WV, pg. 631
Brey, William, Pres.--Restonic Corporation, Chicago, IL, pg. 929
Brian, William A., Pres.--Brian Unlimited Distribution Company, Inc., Detroit, MI, pg. 175
Brice, Hal, Pres.--Heil-Brice Retail Advertising, San Clemente, CA, pg. 525
Brick, Frank E., Pres. & Chief Exec. Officer--Basic Computer, Akron, OH, pg. 124
Brickel, Jack W., Pres., Chief Exec. & Chief Oper. Officer & Dir.-Personnel--BEC Inc., Richmond, MI, pg. 106
Brickley, James A., Pres. & Chief Exec. Officer--Federal Farm Credit Banks Funding Corporation, Jersey City, NJ, pg. 404
Bridell, Robert J., Chm. Bd & Pres. & Chief Exec. Officer--American Tara Corporation, Atlanta, GA, pg. 63
Bridges, Paul, Pres.--Bridges & Company, Inc., Pittsburgh, PA, pg. 175
Brien, Louis, Chief Exec. Officer--Just Pants, Chicago, IL, pg. 610
Brierley, Harold M., Chm. Bd. & Pres.--Brierley & Partners, Dallas, TX, pg. 175
Briggs, J. Scott, Pres.--Ziff-Davis Publishing Company, New York, NY, pg. 1219
Briggs, Mikel S., Pres.--Office Electronics, Inc., Itasca, IL, pg. 821
Briggs, R. Michael, Pres. & Chief Exec. Officer--Certified Holding Corp., Everett, WA, pg. 237
Brigham, James R., Jr., Pres.--Diagraph Corporation, Earth City, MO, pg. 335
Brightbill, William, Pres. & Treas.--Ritter Bros., Inc., Harrisburg, PA, pg. 936
Brilliant, Dave, Pres.--Sporto Corp., Boston, MA, pg. 1032
Brim, A. Eugene, Chm. Bd. & Pres.--Brim, Inc., Portland, OR, pg. 176
Brindell, Charlie, Pres. & Chief Exec. Officer--Trammell Crow Company, Dallas, TX, pg. 1106
Brindle, A.W., Pres.--Wards Cove Packing Company, Seattle, WA, pg. 1163
Brindley, James M., Chm. Bd--W.A. Roosevelt Co., La Crosse, WI, pg. 946
Brink, Douglas, Pres.--Brink Electric Construction Company, Rapid City, SD, pg. 176
Brinkley, D.R., Pres. & Chief Exec. Officer--Colonial Pipeline Company, Atlanta, GA, pg. 264
Brinkmeyer, Marc A., Pres.--Riley Creek Lumber Company, Laclede, ID, pg. 935
Brinson, A. Vernon, Pres.--Royal Oldsmobile Mazda, Inc., Metairie, LA, pg. 953
Briscoe, John R., Pres. & Chief Exec. Officer--Bergelectric Corporation, Los Angeles, CA, pg. 141
Briskie, Julius, Pres.--Pace Press, Inc., New York, NY, pg. 838
Britt, Lance, Pres.--Citation Companies, Inc., Birmingham, AL, pg. 250
Britzke, Robert W., Pres.--RTW, Rogers Tool Works, Inc., Rogers, AR, pg. 908
Briukerhoff, Peter, Chm. Bd., Pres. & Chief Exec. Officer--Aqua Fab Industries, Inc., East Greenwich, RI, pg. 79
Brizzolara, Bruce J., Pres. & Chief Exec. Officer--Fisher Pen Company, Franklin Park, IL, pg. 415
Broad, John W., Chm. Bd., Pres. & Chief Exec. Officer--Broad Vogt & Conant Inc., River Rouge, MI, pg. 177
Broadhurst, James, Chm., Pres. & Chief Exec. Officer--Eat N Park Restaurants, Pittsburgh, PA, pg. 364
Brock, Kathleen K., Pres.--Broyles, Allebaugh & Davis, Inc., Englewood, CO, pg. 183
Brock, Paul K., Pres. & Chief Exec. Officer--Brock Candy Company, Chattanooga, TN, pg. 177
Brocke, George F., Jr., Pres.--George F. Brocke & Sons, Inc., Kendrick, ID, pg. 178
Brockman, Paul M., Pres.--Hamburger Hamlets Inc., Sherman Oaks, CA, pg. 1169
Brod, Irven J., Pres.--Empire Diamond Corporation, New York, NY, pg. 379
Brodbeck, William J., Pres. & Chief Exec. Officer--Brodbeck Enterprises, Inc., Platteville, WI, pg. 178
Brode, Harold, Pres. & Chief Exec. Officer--Broder Bros. Co., Plymouth, MI, pg. 178
Broderick, Fred J., Pres. & Chief Oper. Officer--Haskel, Inc., Burbank, CA, pg. 516
Brodsky, William J., Pres.--Chicago Mercantile Exchange, Chicago, IL, pg. 245
Brogan, Marcia, Mng. Partner--Brogan & Partners Advertising/Public Relations Inc, Detroit, MI, pg. 178
Brojack, William, Pres.--William Brojack Lumber Company, pg. 179
Brokaw, Donald C., Pres.--Illinois Range Company, Mount Prospect, IL, pg. 563
Bromboch, Richard, Co-Pres.--A.D. Clark, Inc., Los Angeles, CA, pg. 252
Bromley, Wayne L., Jr., Pres.--Giles & Ransome, Inc., Bensalem, PA, pg. 458
Bronson, Dave, Pres.--Bronson Leigh Weeks, Portland, OR, pg. 179
Bronstein, David G., Pres. & Chief Exec. Officer--Big V Supermarkets, Inc., Florida, NY, pg. 149
Brooks, Barlow W., Jr., Pres. & Chief Exec. Officer--Roll Forming Corporation, Shelbyville, KY, pg. 944
Brooks, Heather, Pres.--Atlas Pen & Pencil Corporation, Hollywood, FL, pg. 96
Brooks, John M., Pres.--John W. Brooks Inc., Nelsonville, OH, pg. 180
Brooks, Richard, Pres.--Component Technology Corp., Erie, PA, pg. 270
Brookshire, R. A., Pres.--Brookshire Bros., Inc., Lufkin, TX, pg. 180
Brophy, Robert, Pres.--Icicle Seafoods, Inc., Seattle, WA, pg. 561
Brosius, Andy, Pres.--Midwest Industries, Inc., Ida Grove, IA, pg. 752
Bross, Michael D., Pres.--Round Hill Foods, Inc., New Oxford, PA, pg. 952
Brost, Jay, Pres. & Chief Exec. Officer--Miniature Precision Components, Walworth, WI, pg. 757
Brotman, Phyllis B., Pres., Chief Exec. Officer & New Bus. Contact--Image Dynamics, Incorporated, Baltimore, MD, pg. 563
Broudski, Norman, Pres. & Chief Exec. Officer--City Postal, Inc., New York, NY, pg. 251
Broussard, Mark, Pres.--LINC Capital Management, Chicago, IL, pg. 648
Brower, William R., Pres.--BrowerPease, Inc., Hamilton, OH, pg. 181
Brown, Bruce W., Pres. & Chief Exec. Officer--The Hubinger Company, Keokuk, IA, pg. 550
Brown, C. Dewitt, Pres.--DBM Hatch, Inc., El Monte, CA, pg. 308
Brown, C. Terry, Chm. Bd., Pres., Chief Exec. Officer & Chief Oper. Officer--Atlas Hotels, Inc., San Diego, CA, pg. 96
Brown, Carter, Pres. & Chief Exec. Officer--Omega Performance Group, San Francisco, CA, pg. 826
Brown, Charles, Chm. Bd., Pres. & Chief Exec. Officer--Bayou State Oil Corporation, Shreveport, LA, pg. 128
Brown, D. Warren, Pres. & Chief Exec. Officer--Wyandot Inc., Marion, OH, pg. 1205
Brown, Dale, Pres. & Chief Exec. Officer--Sive/Young & Rubicam, Cincinnati, OH, pg. 1211
Brown, David C., Pres. & Chief Exec. Officer--Browns Lumber & Supply Company, Fairmont, WV, pg. 183
Brown, David S., Pres.--WYO-Ben, Inc., Billings, MT, pg. 1157
Brown, Dennis, Pres.--American Health Companies, Inc., Pittsburgh, PA, pg. 55
Brown, Dennis, Pres. & Chief Exec. Officer--Diet Center, Inc., Pittsburgh, PA, pg. 55
Brown, Edward C., Pres. & Treas.--Bill Brown Ford Inc., Livonia, MI, pg. 182
Brown, Franklin, Sr., Pres.--F.M. Brown Sons, Inc., Sinking Spring, PA, pg. 183
Brown, Glenn, Pres.--Contract Freighters, Inc., Joplin, MO, pg. 280
Brown, Irving, Pres.--Axelband & Brown & Associates Inc., Cleveland, OH, pg. 103
Brown, J.S., III, Pres.--Bruce Foods Corp., Saint Martinville, LA, pg. 183

Brown, Jerry, Pres.--Arrow Pneumatics Co. Inc., Lake Zurich, IL, pg. 85
Brown, Joe, Pres.--Black & Veatch Architects, Inc., Kansas City, MO, pg. 154
Brown, Larry L., Sr., Pres. & Chief Exec. Officer--Riverside Central Services, Inc., Natchez, MS, pg. 937
Brown, Michael S., Pres.--Wometco Enterprises, Inc., Coral Gables, FL, pg. 1199
Brown, Mike, Pres. & Exec. V.P.--City Meats & Provisions Co., Tucsan, AZ, pg. 251
Brown, Millard, Pres. & Chief Exec. Officer--Powell Electronics Inc., Philadelphia, PA, pg. 882
Brown, Milton, Pres.--Suntec Industries Inc., Rockford, IL, pg. 1062
Brown, Robert D., Pres.--Berry-Brown Advertising, Inc., Dallas, TX, pg. 144
Brown, Ronald A., Pres. & Chief Exec. Officer--Calcor Space Facility, Inc., Whittier, CA, pg. 208
Brown, Russell, Pres.--Agsco, Inc., Grand Forks, ND, pg. 4
Brown, Sam J., Pres.--Feed Service Corp., Crete, NE, pg. 405
Brown, Stephen, Mng. Dir.--BSB Malaysia Sdn. Bhd., Kuala Lumpur,, Malaysia, pg. 110
Brown, Sylvan L., Chm. Bd., Pres. & Chief Exec. Officer--Mediacomp, Inc., Houston, TX, pg. 735
Brown, Ted B., Pres.--Hibbert Group, Trenton, NJ, pg. 532
Brown, Thomas V., Pres. & Chief Exec. Officer--Caraustar Industries, Inc., Austell, GA, pg. 217
Brown, W. Melvin, Jr., Pres.--American Development Corporation, North Charleston, SC, pg. 51
Brown, W. S. IV, Pres. & Chief Exec. Officer--Daxus Corporation, Pittsburgh, PA, pg. 319
Brown, Wayne J., Pres.--Brown Evans Company, Mesa, AZ, pg. 182
Brown, William V., Pres.--American Ball Manufacturing, Carrollton, TX, pg. 890
Brown, Willis E., Jr., Pres.--Brown Motors, Toledo, OH, pg. 182
Browne, Steven B., Chm. Bd., Pres. & Chief Exec. Officer--All American Bottling Corp., Oklahoma City, OK, pg. 35
Brownell, Jon, Pres.--Monte Vista Co-Op Association, Inc., Monte Vista, CO, pg. 766
Browning, Calvin D., Pres.--Elk Supply Company, Clinton, OK, pg. 376
Browning, Frederick M., Pres.--Browning Chemical Corporation, White Plains, NY, pg. 183
Brownstein, Berny, Pres.--The Brownstein Group, Philadelphia, PA, pg. 183
Broyhill, J. Edgar II, Pres.--Edgar B. Furniture Co., Clemmons, NC, pg. 368
Brubaker, Bob, Pres.--King & Prince Seafood Corporation, Brunswick, GA, pg. 631
Brubaker, Herman, Pres.--Milk Marketing Inc., Strongsville, OH, pg. 753
Bruce, Robert, Pres.--Aladdin Petroleum Corporation, Wichita, KS, pg. 29
Bruce, Tom B., Pres.--Bruce Industries, Inc., Dayton, NV, pg. 183
Bruder, Thomas A., Jr., Pres.--M. A. Bruder & Sons, Inc., Broomall, PA, pg. 184
Bruenger, M.W., Pres.--M. Bruenger & Co., Inc., Wichita, KS, pg. 184
Bruggeman, Steven, Pres.--Diversified Dynamics Inc., Minneapolis, MN, pg. 340
Bruggeman, Steven, Pres.--Cat Pumps Corporation, Minneapolis, MN, pg. 340
Brunner, M.F., Pres.--Brunner & Lay, Inc., Franklin Park, IL, pg. 184
Brunner, Michael J., Pres. & Chief Oper. Officer--Blattner/Brunner Inc., Pittsburgh, PA, pg. 156
Bruno, Kendra Elliott, Pres.--Dixie Brewing Co., Inc., New Orleans, LA, pg. 341
Brunswick, Paul E., Pres. & Chief Oper. Officer--Stiegler, Wells & Brunswick, Inc., Bethlehem, PA, pg. 1049
Brush, Douglas, Pres.--Sentry Group, Rochester, NY, pg. 990
Brush, Wayne, Pres.--Old American Pottery Company, Howe, TX, pg. 823
Bruskrud, W.R., Pres. & Treas.--Bemco Inc., Simi Valley, CA, pg. 138
Brutger, Larry, Chm. Bd. & Pres.--Brutger Equities, Inc., Saint Cloud, MN, pg. 185
Bryan, A. Chris, II, Pres., Chief Exec. Officer, Sec. & Treas.--BA Advertising, Dallas, TX, pg. 105
Bryan, E. E., Dir.--West Virginia Lottery, Charleston, WV, pg. 1178
Bryan, F. Sibley, Jr., Pres. & Chief Exec. Officer--Chipman-Union, Inc., Union Point, GA, pg. 248
Bryant, A.W., Pres. & Treas.--Century Fence Company, Pewaukee, WI, pg. 235
Bryant, C. Edward, Jr., Pres.--Continental Conveyor & Equipment Company, Winfield, AL, pg. 798
Bryant, Harry M., Sr., Pres.--Bryant Supply Company, Inc., Gastonia, NC, pg. 185
Bryant, Matthew C., Pres.--USA--Media Buying Services Intl. Inc., New York, NY, pg. 734
Bryant, Ronald D., Pres.--Masters Inc., Gaithersburg, MD, pg. 720
Bryce, William H., Jr., Pres.--Bryce Corporation, Memphis, TN, pg. 185
Brynes, Edward G., Jr., Pres. & Chief Exec. Officer--Byrnes & Kiefer Company, Callery, PA, pg. 198
Brzoska, Michael J., Pres.--ACR Industries Inc., Mount Clemens, MI, pg. 2
Buatte, Ronald W., Pres. & Gen. Mgr.--Seabrook Foods, Inc., Fresno, CA, pg. 984
Bucci, Anthony L., Pres. & Chief Exec. Officer--Marc Advertising, Pittsburgh, PA, pg. 706
Buchalski, Marty, Pres.--A. Epstein & Sons (U.K.) Ltd., London, United Kingdom, pg. 384
Buchanan, Craig, Pres.--Walla Walla Grain Growers, Inc., Walla Walla, WA, pg. 1160
Buchanan, Robert C., Pres. & Chief Exec. Officer--Fox Valley Corporation, Appleton, WI, pg. 427
Bucher, Larry C., Pres.--Lloyd Properties, Los Angeles, CA, pg. 680
Bucher, Robert, Mgr.--Schreiber Milling Co., Saint Joseph, MO, pg. 549
Buck, Charles T., Chm. Bd., Pres. & Chief Exec. Officer--Buck Knives, Inc., El Cajon, CA, pg. 185
Buck, Dave, V.P.--AmeriData, Inc., Minneapolis, MN, pg. 66
Buckles, John, Pres.--Liberty Military Sales Co., Houston, TX, pg. 674
Buckley, Maurice, Pres. & Chief Exec. Officer--Panarco, Inc., Summit, NJ, pg. 845
Buckman, M.W., Chm. Bd. & Pres.--Bulab Holdings, Inc., Memphis, TN, pg. 188
Buckman, S.B., Pres.--Buckman Laboratories, Memphis, TN, pg. 185
Buckman, Steven B., Pres. & Chief Oper. Officer--Buckman Laboratories, International, Memphis, TN, pg. 188
Bucksbaum, Matthew, Pres., Treas. & Sec.--General Growth Companies, Inc., Des Moines, IA, pg. 449
Buckwalter, Alan R., III, Pres.--Texas Commerce Bancshares, Inc., Houston, TX, pg. 1089
Buddig, William C., Pres.--Carl Buddig & Company, Homewood, IL, pg. 186
Budig, George J., Pres.--George E. Fern Company, Cincinnati, OH, pg. 186
Budig, Otto M., Jr., Pres.--Budco Group Inc., Cincinnati, OH, pg. 186
Budig, Otto M., Jr., Pres.--O/B Leasing Company, Cincinnati, OH, pg. 186
Budig, Otto M., Jr., Pres.--Parsec, Cincinnati, OH, pg. 186
Budig, Otto M., Jr., Pres.--Piggyback Services, Inc., Cincinnati, OH, pg. 186
Buerkle, W.W., Pres.--Buerkle Buick-Honda Co., Saint Paul, MN, pg. 186
Buff, Helen, Pres.--Penny Plate, Inc., Cherry Hill, NJ, pg. 858
Buffum, Robert, Pres. & Chief Oper. Officer--Omniflight, Inc., Dallas, TX, pg. 826
Buhl, Tim, Pres. & Chief Exec. Officer--Aerco International Inc., Northvale, NJ, pg. 21
Bull, Marshall R., Chm. Bd. & Pres.--Industrial Wire Products Corporation, Pomona, CA, pg. 567
Bull, William H., Pres., Chief Exec. Officer & Treas.--McNaughton-McKay Electric Co., Madison Heights, MI, pg. 732
Bullard, Edward D., Pres.--E. D. Bullard Company, Cynthiana, KY, pg. 188
Bulloch, Juanita A., Pres., Chief Exec. Officer & Treas.--Southeastern Steel Company, Florence, SC, pg. 1020
Bullock, R.C., Chm. Bd. & Pres.--Curt Bullock Builders, Inc., Danville, IL, pg. 188
Bullock, S. Lynn, Mgr.-Reg.--Devoe Paint Corporation, Salt Lake City, UT, pg. 334
Bumby, Edward W., Pres.--Ripon Foods, Inc., Ripon, WI, pg. 935
Bundrant, Charles, Pres.--Trident Seafood Corporation, Seattle, WA, pg. 1113
Bundschuh, George A.W., Pres.--New York Life Insurance Company, New York, NY, pg. 802
Bungert, John, III, Pres.--Captive Plastics, Piscataway, NJ, pg. 216
Bungey, Michael, Chm. & Chief Exec. Officer--BSB Dorland Limited, London,, United Kingdom, pg. 109
Bunn, Arthur H., Pres. & Chief Exec. Officer--Bunn-O-Matic Corporation, Springfield, IL, pg. 188
Buns, Kenneth W., Pres.--Dualite Sales & Service, Inc., Williamsburg, OH, pg. 350
Buntin, Jeffrey W., Pres. & Creative Dir.--Buntin Advertising, Inc., Nashville, TN, pg. 188
Buonanno, Vincent, Pres.--Tempel Steel Company, Skokie, IL, pg. 1086
Burandt, Gary (NY), Pres. & Chief Exec. Officer--Dentsu, Young & Rubicam Partnerships, New York, NY, pg. 330
Burch, R.L., Chm. Bd. & Pres.--Jonathan Manufacturing Corp., Fullerton, CA, pg. 602
Burdick, Henry, Pres.--Pharmavite Corp., Mission Hills, CA, pg. 866
Burdick, Richard L., Chm., Pres., Chief Exec. & Chief Oper. Officer--Thermon Manufacturing Company, San Marcos, TX, pg. 1091
Buresh, D.A., Pres.--Kamstra Communications, Inc., Saint Paul, MN, pg. 615
Burge, Bill, Pres.--Gaston Johnston, Clifton, NJ, pg. 1159
Burge, William L., Pres.--Walco-Linck Company, Clifton, NJ, pg. 1159
Burgess, Bill, Pres. & Chief Oper. Officer--AmeriServ Food Company, Dallas, TX, pg. 66
Burgess, Charles, V.P. & Gen. Mgr.--Steffen Dairy Foods Co., Inc., Wichita, KS, pg. 884
Burgess, Malcolm S., Jr., Chm. Bd. & Pres.--Burgess Pigment Co., Sandersville, GA, pg. 190
Burgett, William Brian, Pres.--Kokosing Construction Company, Inc., Fredericktown, OH, pg. 640
Burgo, Ray, Pres.--Giant Eagle, Inc., Pittsburgh, PA, pg. 455
Burgoyne, James F., Pres.--Burgoyne, Inc., Philadelphia, PA, pg. 190
Burke, Bernard J., Pres.--Finnaren & Haley, Inc., Conshohocken, PA, pg. 411
Burke, Gary W., Pres. & Chief Exec. Officer--Burke Engineering Company, South El Monte, CA, pg. 190
Burke, J. Gary, Pres.--Truck World Inc., Hubbard, OH, pg. 1117
Burke, James A., Pres.--Twin County Grocers, Inc., Edison, NJ, pg. 1122
Burke, John, Pres. & Chief Exec. Officer--Cato Johnson-New York, New York, NY, pg. 1210
Burke, Lawrence J., II, Pres. & Chief Exec. Officer--Burke Communication Industries, Inc., Chicago, IL, pg. 190
Burke, Michael J., Pres.--Buffalo Hospital Supply Co., Inc., Amherst, NY, pg. 187
Burke, R. James, Pres.--Drive Train Industries, Denver, CO, pg. 349
Burke, Richard, Pres.--Main Brothers Oil Company, Inc., Albany, NY, pg. 702
Burke, Richard A., Pres.--Intrepid Corp., Milwaukee, WI, pg. 581
Burke, Richard A., Pres.--Trek Bicycle Corporation, Waterloo, WI, pg. 581
Burkhardt, William C., Pres. & Chief Exec. Officer--Bahlsen Inc., Cary, NC, pg. 114
Burkle, Ronald, Chm. Bd. & Partner--The Yucaipa Companies, Claremont, CA, pg. 1214
Burman, George, Pres.--D. M. Management Company, Hingham, MA, pg. 309
Burnap, David K., Pres.--David K. Burnap Advertising Agency, Inc., Dayton, OH, pg. 191
Burnes, Hugh S., Jr., Pres.--Rome Manufacturing Co., Rome, GA, pg. 945
Burnet, Roger H., Pres.--McCarthy Building Companies, Saint Louis, MO, pg. 727
Burnette, Courtney B., Pres.--Agway Petroleum Corp., De Witt, NY, pg. 25
Burnette, Larry, Pres.--Foote & Davies Inc., Atlanta, GA, pg. 423
Burns, Richard, Pres.--Central Commissary, Inc., Phoenix, AZ, pg. 287
Burns, Stephen F., Chm. Bd., Pres. & Chief Exec. Officer--Wheaton Van Lines, Inc., Indianapolis, IN, pg. 1184
Burnstad, Kirk, Chief Oper. Officer--Burnstad Brothers, Inc., Tomah, WI, pg. 194
Burnstad, Victor, Pres.--Burnstad Brothers, Inc., Tomah, WI, pg. 194
Burnstead, Frederick H., Pres.--Burnstead Construction Company, Bellevue, WA, pg. 194
Burress, Mark, Chm. Bd. & Pres.--Affiliates Group Inc., Nashville, TN, pg. 24
Burris, A.A., III, Chm. Bd. & Pres.--Burris Chemical Inc., Charleston, SC, pg. 195
Burris, J. Mark, Pres. & Chief Exec. Officer--The Burris Agency, Inc., High Point, NC, pg. 195
Burris, J.D., Pres. & Chief Oper. Officer--The Alpha Corporation Of Tennessee, Collierville, TN, pg. 43
Burris, Jerry L., Pres.--Syndicate Systems, Inc., Indianapolis, IN, pg. 1069
Burris, Robert D., Pres. & Chief Oper. Officer--Burris Foods, Inc., Milford, DE, pg. 195
Burriss, John H., Pres.--B. Burriss Companies, Columbia, SC, pg. 195
Burroughs, James R., Pres. & Chief Oper. Officer--First Gray Line Corporation, Beverly Hills, CA, pg. 413
Burrow, Grady, Pres. & Chief Exec. Officer--National Computer Print, Inc., Birmingham, AL, pg. 786
Burrows, B.S., Pres.--Haas Brothers, San Francisco, CA, pg. 498
Burrows, R.W., Jr., Chm. Bd. & Pres.--Burrows Paper Corporation, Little Falls, NY, pg. 195
Burstein, Lawrence C., Publisher--Self, New York, NY, pg. 19
Burt, John R., Chm. Bd. & Pres.--Duro-Last Roofing, Inc., Saginaw, MI, pg. 355
Burt, W. E., Chm. Bd., Pres., & Chief Exec. Officer--Dairy Fresh Corp., Greensboro, AL, pg. 310
Burtman, Charles, Pres. & Chief Exec. Officer--Burtman Iron Works, Inc., Boston, MA, pg. 195
Burton, James, Pres. & Chief Oper. Officer--Reading Tube Corp., Reading, PA, pg. 916
Burton, Raymond C., Jr., Pres. & Chief Exec. Officer--TTX Co., Chicago, IL, pg. 1075
Burtraw, Roger L., Pres.--Kingston Warren, Southfield, MI, pg. 514
Burzycki, Thomas, Pres.--The Selmer Co., Elkhart, IN, pg. 573
Busboom, Larry D., Pres. & Chief Fin. Officer--Sun Diamond Growers of California, Pleasanton, CA, pg. 1058
Busboom, Larry D., Pres.--Sun-land Products of California, Pleasanton, CA, pg. 1058
Busch, Dr. Paul L., Pres. & Chief Exec. Officer--Malcolm Pirnie, Inc., White Plains, NY, pg. 872
Busch, Sondra L., Chief Exec. Officer--Admark, Inc., Topeka, KS, pg. 18
Bush, David, Pres.--Sechrist Industries, Inc., Anaheim, CA, pg. 987
Buskirk, Ernest, Pres. & Chief Exec. Officer--Rock Hill Materials Company, Catasauqua, PA, pg. 941
Bustillo, Oscar, Jr., Pres. & Chief Oper. Officer--Republic National Bank Of Miami, Miami, FL, pg. 928
Butcher, Andrew D.W., Pres., Chief Exec. Officer--International Communications Group, Inc., Los Angeles, CA, pg. 576
Butcher, Jonathan, Chm. Bd. & Pres.--Butcher & Co., Inc., Philadelphia, PA, pg. 196
Butcko, Joseph D., Pres.--Crescive Die & Tool, Inc., Saline, MI, pg. 298
Butera, Paul, Pres.--Butera Finer Foods Inc., Elgin, IL, pg. 196
Butler, Carl E., Pres.--Holstein Association of America, Brattleboro, VT, pg. 541
Butler, Edmund R., Pres. & Chief Exec. Officer--Mississippi Valley Gas Co., Jackson, MS, pg. 1208
Butler, Frank W., Pres.--Catalina Yachts, Inc., Woodland Hills, CA, pg. 229
Butler, James M., Pres.--Mid-States Petroleum Inc., Troy, MI, pg. 750
Butler, Jo Ann, Pres.--Budget Marketing, Inc., Des Moines, IA, pg. 186
Butler, William, Chm. Bd., Pres., Chief Exec. Officer & Treas.--Corporex Companies, Inc., Covington, KY, pg. 287
Butman, Russell, Pres.--A-G Co-op Creamery, Arcadia, WI, pg. 4
Butner, Lawrence, Pres.--Lawrence Butner Advertising, Inc., New York, NY, pg. 197
Butt, Charles C., Pres. & Chief Exec. Officer--H. E. Butt Grocery Co., San Antonio, TX, pg. 197
Butterworth, Edward L., Pres. & Chief Exec. Officer--Fedco, Inc., Santa Fe Springs, CA, pg. 404
Buttle, Eugene H., Pres. & Chief Exec. Officer--American Inks & Coatings Corp., Valley Forge, PA, pg. 56

Buttress, Steve, Dir.--Nebraska Dept. of Economic Development, Lincoln, NE, pg. 796
Butz, Otto, Pres. & Chief Exec. Officer--Golden Gate University, San Francisco, CA, pg. 466
Butz, Terry, Pres.--Kelso-Burnett Company, Rolling Meadows, IL, pg. 622
Buyer, Betty R., Pres.--Buyer Advertising, Inc., Newton, MA, pg. 197
Byer, Allan G., Chm. Bd., Pres. & Chief Exec. Officer--Byer California, San Francisco, CA, pg. 197
Byers, Stan J., Pres. & Chief Oper. Officer--Bunton Company, Louisville, KY, pg. 188
Bylin, Arthur M., Pres.--Prince Manufacturing, Inc., Lawrenceville, NJ, pg. 890
Bynum, Glen, Pres.--Allied Tire Sales, Orlando, FL, pg. 40
Byrd, David M., Pres.--Southern Beverage Packers, Inc., Augusta, GA, pg. 1020
Byrd, Nathan L., Gen. Mgr.--Equity Supply Company, Kalispell, MT, pg. 385
Byrd, Robert, Pres. & Chief Exec. Officer--The Keller Manufacturing Co., Inc., Corydon, IN, pg. 621
Byrne, Arthur, Pres.--The Wiremold Company, West Hartford, CT, pg. 1197
Byrne, John F., Sr., Pres.--Jack Byrne Ford & Mercury, Inc., Mechanicville, NY, pg. 198
Byrne, Larry, Pres.--Ann Arbor Assembly Corporation, Ypsilanti, MI, pg. 368
Byrnes, Donald J., Pres. & Chief Oper. Officer--Spalding & Evenflo Companies, Inc., Tampa, FL, pg. 1024
Caballero, Dennis P., Pres.--Security Industrial Insurance Co., Inc., Donaldsonville, LA, pg. 832
Cabana, Charles, Pres.--Mark Chevrolet Inc., Wayne, MI, pg. 708
Cabianca, Vicki, Dir.--B-W Advertising Agency, Phoenix, AZ, pg. 107
Cabot, Samuel, III, Pres.--Samuel Cabot, Inc., Newburyport, MA, pg. 206
Cabral, Gilbert, Pres. & Chief Exec. Officer--MICOM Communications Corp., Simi Valley, CA, pg. 748
Cabrihna, Lawrence, Pres.--Aloha IslandAir, Honolulu, HI, pg. 43
Caccavaro, George T., Pres.--Cone-Blanchard Machine Company, Windsor, VT, pg. 273
Caddock, Richard E. Sr., Pres.--Caddock Electronics, Inc., Riverside, CA, pg. 207
Cadieux, Chester, Chm. Bd. & Pres.--QuikTrip Corporation, Tulsa, OK, pg. 905
Cafaro, Anthony M., Pres. & Chief Exec. Officer--The Cafaro Co., Youngstown, OH, pg. 207
Cafferata, Patricia A., Pres. & Chief Exec. Officer--Young & Rubicam Chicago, Chicago, IL, pg. 1211
Cafiero, Eugene A., Chm. Bd., Pres., Chief Exec. & Oper. Officer--KDI Corporation, Cincinnati, OH, pg. 612
Cahill, Larry, Pres. & Treas.--Larken Inc., Cedar Rapids, IA, pg. 659
Caiazza, D., Pres. & Chief Exec. Officer--Copperweld Steel Company, Warren, OH, pg. 284
Cain, Herman, Pres. & Chief Exec. Officer--Godfather's Pizza, Inc., Omaha, NE, pg. 464
Calabrese, Frank, Pres.--F C L Graphics, Harwood Heights, IL, pg. 394
Calabrese, P.J., Pres.--The Grieve Corporation, Round Lake, IL, pg. 486
Calafati, Gabriel R., Chm. Bd., Pres. & Treas.--Frank Briscoe Co. Inc., Roseland, NJ, pg. 176
Calandra, T.M., Pres.--Starcrest Products of California, Perris, CA, pg. 1040
Calandruccio, Robert, Pres. & Chief Oper. Officer--Vitt Media International, Inc., New York, NY, pg. 1153
Calano, James C., Pres. & Chief Exec. Officer--CareerTrack Inc., Boulder, CO, pg. 218
Calcaterra, Edward L., Pres.--J. S. Alberici Construction Co., Inc., Saint Louis, MO, pg. 31
Calcattera, Paul, Pres.--Cowtown Boot Company, El Paso, TX, pg. 291
Calder, Iain, Chm. Bd. & Pres.--The National Enquirer, Lantana, FL, pg. 788
Caldwell, John D., Chm. Bd., Pres. & Chief Exec. Officer--Borchers Bros., San Jose, CA, pg. 165
Calicchio, John, Pres.--Decal Enterprises, Inc., New York, NY, pg. 323
Calico, Ralph, Pres.--Epec, Inc., New Bedford, MA, pg. 384
Calkins, Harlan D., Chm. Bd. & Pres.--Rochester Midland Corporation, Rochester, NY, pg. 940
Calkins, James E., Chm. Bd. & Pres.--The Calkins Manufacturing Company, Spokane, WA, pg. 210
Call, William, Chm., Pres. & Chief Exec. Officer--Maverik Country Stores, Inc., Afton, WY, pg. 722
Callaghan, Howard, Pres.--Plastic Suppliers, Inc., Columbus, OH, pg. 875
Callaghan, Joseph, Pres.--Powers Pharmaceutical, Brockton, MA, pg. 236
Callahan, Frank W., Pres. & Chief Exec. Officer--McKinney Inc. Advertising & Public Relations, Philadelphia, PA, pg. 730
Callahan, Joseph, Pres.--Crawford Fittings & Co., Solon, OH, pg. 297
Callahan, Ralph W., Jr., Chm. Bd., Pres. & Chief Exec. Officer--Henderson Advertising, Inc., Greenville, SC, pg. 528
Callahan, Robert L., Pres.--Ingersoll Engineers Inc., Rockford, IL, pg. 568
Callahan, Robert M., Pres.--Channel Technologies, Inc., Santa Barbara, CA, pg. 239
Callaway, Edward C., Pres.--Crested Butte Mountain Resort, Inc., Mount Crested Butte, CO, pg. 299
Calligaris, A.E., Chm. Bd., Pres. & Chief Exec. Officer--Stebbins Engineering & Mfg. Co., Watertown, NY, pg. 1043
Calton, Kenneth J., Pres.--North Carolina Equipment Co., Raleigh, NC, pg. 812
Calvert, Steve, Pres.--Keystone Foods Corporation, Bala-Cynwyd, PA, pg. 628
Calvitti, Raymond, Pres. & Chief Exec. Officer--KDI Sylvan Pools, Inc., Doylestown, PA, pg. 612
Camacho, Ernest M., Pres.--Pacifica Services, Inc., Pasadena, CA, pg. 842
Camerlo, James P., Jr., Chm. Bd. & Pres.--Western Dairymen Cooperative, Inc., Thornton, CO, pg. 1178
Cameron, Gerald T., Jr., Pres.--Amray, Inc., Bedford, MA, pg. 68
Cameron, Walter F., Pres.--Walter F. Cameron Advertising Inc., Melville, NY, pg. 212
Caminitti, Tony, Pres.--Pedus Services, Inc., Los Angeles, CA, pg. 854
Camosy, Raymond J., Pres. & Chief Exec. Officer--Camosy, Inc., Russell, IL, pg. 212
Camp, Barry S., Pres.--Hub Inc., Tucker, GA, pg. 548
Camp, Vernon D., Pres.--Cavalier Corporation, Chattanooga, TN, pg. 229
Campbell, Argyle, Chm. Bd. & Pres.--Cambro Manufacturing Company, Huntington Beach, CA, pg. 211
Campbell, C., Pres.--SAE Engineering, Inc., Santa Clara, CA, pg. 959
Campbell, Calvin A., Jr., Chm. Bd., Pres. & Chief Exec. Officer--Goodman Equipment Corp., Bedford Park, IL, pg. 470
Campbell, Craig, Pres. & New Bus. Contact--Campbell and Wagman, Los Angeles, CA, pg. 213
Campbell, David, Pres.--MTD Products, Inc., Valley City, OH, pg. 694
Campbell, Dick, Pres. & Chief Exec. Officer--BJ Acquisition Corp., Charlotte, NC, pg. 107
Campbell, Doug, Pres.--Thermal Technology Industries, N. Kansas City, MO, pg. 1091
Campbell, John J., III, Chm. Bd. & Pres.--John J. Campbell Co., Inc., Memphis, TN, pg. 212
Campbell, Loren S., Pres.--American Gilsonite Co., Salt Lake City, UT, pg. 55
Campbell, Neil, Pres.--Bio Medic Corporation, Maywood, NJ, pg. 152
Campbell, R.S., Pres. & Chief Exec. Officer--Commercial & Architectural Products Inc., Dover, OH, pg. 268
Campbell, Richard J., Pres.--Benjamin Obdyke, Inc., Warminster, PA, pg. 819
Campbell, Robert, Pres. & Chief Exec. Officer--Pfaudler-U.S., Inc., Rochester, NY, pg. 866
Campbell, Robert M., Chm. Bd. & Pres.--The Campbell Group, Baltimore, MD, pg. 213
Campbell, Steve, Gen. Mgr.--Sudler & Hennessey, Auckland,, New Zealand, pg. 1214
Campbell, Steven B., Pres. & Chief Fin. Officer--H. S. Crocker Co., Inc., King of Prussia, PA, pg. 299
Campbell, T. Scott, Pres.--T. Bruce Sales, Inc., West Middlesex, PA, pg. 183
Campbell, William, Pres.--Allmetal Screw Products Corp., Edgewood, NY, pg. 40
Campbell, William M., Pres.--Camalloy, Inc., Washington, PA, pg. 211
Canadeo, Ernest G., Chm. Bd. & Pres.--EGC Media Group, Inc., Hicksville, NY, pg. 359
Canale, John D., Pres.--D. Canale Food Services, Inc., Memphis, TN, pg. 213
Canfield, Arthur J., III, Pres.--A. J. Canfield Co., Chicago, IL, pg. 214
Canning, Charles F., Jr., Pres.--Pine State Tobacco & Candy Company, Augusta, ME, pg. 871
Cantrell, Ron, Pres.--DeVlieg Bullard Services Group, Rockford, IL, pg. 333
Cantrell, Ronald, Pres.--Danly-Komatsu L.P., Cicero, IL, pg. 275
Capeletti, Joe, Pres.--Capeletti Bros., Inc., Miami Lakes, FL, pg. 214
Capener, Don R., Pres., Adv.--Capener, Matthews & Walcher, San Diego, CA, pg. 214
Capizzi, Anthony, Chm. Bd., Pres. & Chief Exec. Officer--Quality Food Oils, Inc., New Milford, CT, pg. 903
Caplan, James A., Chm. Bd., Pres., Treas., Prod. Mgr. & Chief Engr.--Capp, Inc., Philadelphia, PA, pg. 216
Capon, Dale E., Chm. Bd. & Pres.--Rieth-Riley Construction Co. Inc., Goshen, IN, pg. 934
Caponi, Thomas A., Pres.--Olsonite Corporation, Detroit, MI, pg. 824
Capp, Morris, Pres.--Shoe City Corporation, Montgomery, AL, pg. 382
Cappelletti, Grace E., Pres.--Putman Publishing Co., Chicago, IL, pg. 901
Cappy, Michael, Chm. Bd. & Pres.--Norcross Industries, Inc., Louisville, KY, pg. 809
Capriotti, Laurence, Pres. & Chief Exec. Officer--Intercounty Title Co. of Illinois, Chicago, IL, pg. 574
Carabini, Louis E., Chm. Bd. & Pres.--Monex International, Ltd., Newport Beach, CA, pg. 765
Carcara, P.J., Pres. & Chief Exec. Officer--Baldt, Inc., Chester, PA, pg. 115
Carcich, James J., Pres.--International Permalite, Inc., Ontario, CA, pg. 579
Carden, Gerald T., Pres.--Carden & Cherry, Inc., Nashville, TN, pg. 217
Cardenas, Francisco, Chm., Pres. & Mng. Dir.--Leo Burnett S.A. de C.V., Mexico,, Mexico, pg. 193
Carder, John, Pres.--Carder, Inc., Lamar, CO, pg. 217
Cardillo, Harry M., Pres.--Globe International Inc., Buffalo, NY, pg. 464
Cardone, Albert A., Chm. & Chief Exec. Officer--Empire Blue Cross & Blue Shield, New York, NY, pg. 379
Carey, D.J., Pres.--Noville Essential Oil Co., Inc., North Bergen, NJ, pg. 817
Carey, D.L., Pres.--Knouse Foods Inc., Peach Glen, PA, pg. 637
Carey, Francis J., Pres. & Mng. Dir.--W. P. Carey & Co., Inc., New York, NY, pg. 218
Carey, G. Cheston, Jr., Pres.--Carey Machinery & Supply Company, Baltimore, MD, pg. 218
Cargen, David, Pres. & Chief Exec. Officer--Power King Products Co., Beaver Dam, WI, pg. 883
Cargill, Don A., Pres. & Chief Exec. Officer--Cargill Detroit Corp., Clawson, MI, pg. 219
Carideo, Frank, Pres.--Fire Control Instruments, Inc., Newton, MA, pg. 411
Carl, Fred, Jr., Chm. Bd., Pres. & Chief Exec. Officer--Viking Range Corp., Greenwood, MS, pg. 1151
Carlberg, W. Charles, Pres. & Chief Exec. Officer--Rives Carlberg, Houston, TX, pg. 937
Carles, John B., Pres.--Carles Inc., New York, NY, pg. 220
Carley, S.E., Pres. & Chief Exec. Officer--Fair Lanes Inc., Hunt Valley, MD, pg. 396
Carlile, Rex, Pres.--Trim Trends, Clawson, MI, pg. 514
Carlisle, Brian, Chm. Bd. & Chief Exec. Officer--Adept Technology, Inc., San Jose, CA, pg. 17
Carlisle, L. T. III, Chm., Pres. & Chief Exec. Officer--Carlisle Retailers, Inc., Ashtabula, OH, pg. 220
Carlisle, Wayne, Pres.--Carlisle Equipment Company, Wilder, KY, pg. 220
Carlo, Nelson, Pres. & Treas.--Abbott Group Ltd., Chicago, IL, pg. 9
Carlo, Nelson, Pres. & Treas.--Abbott Products Inc., Chicago, IL, pg. 9
Carlsen, Charles, Pres. & Chief Oper. Officer--Upper Midwest Industries, Inc., Minneapolis, MN, pg. 1140
Carlson, Curtis L., Chm. Bd., Pres. & Chief Exec. Officer--Carlson Companies, Inc., Minneapolis, MN, pg. 220
Carlson, E. Jerome, Pres. & Chief Exec. Officer--The Instant Web Companies, Chanhassen, MN, pg. 571
Carlson, Gerald K., Pres., Treas. & Chief Fin. Officer--Bureau of Engraving, Minneapolis, MN, pg. 189
Carlson, Gerda, Div. Exec. V.P.--Damart/TMP Worldwide, Minneapolis, MN, pg. 1074
Carlson, Robert A., Chm. Bd. & Pres.--North Atlantic Industries, Inc., Hauppauge, NY, pg. 812
Carlson, Robert F., Jr., Pres.--Seabeam Ind., Inc., Westwood, MA, pg. 239
Carlson, Sandra, Pres. & Dir.-Creative--Carlson & Partners, Inc., New York, NY, pg. 222
Carlton, Edward, Jr., Pres. & Chief Exec. Officer--Corrugated Metals, Inc., Chicago, IL, pg. 287
Carmichael, Dan R., Pres.--The Shelby Insurance Group, Shelby, OH, pg. 90
Carmon, Max, V.P.-Mfg.--Formfit Rogers, New York, NY, pg. 78
Carmon, Max, V.P.-Mfg.--Jones New York Intimates, New York, NY, pg. 78
Carnahan, Gary, Pres.--Ecco Services, Inc., Bella Vista, AR, pg. 283
Carnevali, Fausto, Pres.--R.P. Partners SRL, Milan,, Italy, pg. 626
Carney, Peter Roy, Pres.--Superior Graphite Company, Chicago, IL, pg. 1063
Carota, Richard J., Chm., Pres. & Chief Exec. Officer--Finch, Pruyn & Co., Inc., Glens Falls, NY, pg. 410
Carpenter, David O., Pres.--Great Lakes Carbon Corp., Briarcliff Manor, NY, pg. 545
Carpenter, David O., Dr., Pres.--Horsehead Industries, Inc., New York, NY, pg. 545
Carpenter, George E., Pres.--Semac Industries Inc., Millersburg, OH, pg. 989
Carpenter, K.M., Pres.--Curtis-Toledo, Inc., Saint Louis, MO, pg. 306
Carpenter, Richard M., Pres. & Chief Exec. Officer--S. C. Johnson & Son, Inc., Racine, WI, pg. 599
Carr, Donald, Pres.--4Day Tire Stores, Irvine, CA, pg. 427
Carr, Francis J., Pres. & Chief Oper. Officer--Interstate Electric Supply Company, Inc., Chantilly, VA, pg. 580
Carr, John, III, Pres. & Chief Exec. Officer--Central Supply Co., Inc., Indianapolis, IN, pg. 234
Carr, Michael T., Pres. & Chief Exec. Officer-Publishing Division--Weider Health & Fitness, Woodland Hills, CA, pg. 1173
Carr, Patrick F., Pres. & Chief Oper. Officer--Mayflower Transit, Inc., Carmel, IN, pg. 724
Carr, Robert O., Pres.--The Oliver Carr Co., Washington, DC, pg. 225
Carrafiello, A. Louis, Pres., Treas. & Chief Exec. Officer--Carrafiello, Diehl & Associates, Inc., Irvington, NY, pg. 225
Carris, William, Pres.--Carris Reels, Inc., Rutland, VT, pg. 225
Carrol, J.E., Pres.--Thrall Car Mfg. Co., Chicago Heights, IL, pg. 350
Carroll, Richard, Pres.--Sommer & Maca Industries, Inc., Chicago, IL, pg. 1017
Carroll, Robert J., Pres. & Chief Oper. Officer--National Cleaning Contractors, Inc., New York, NY, pg. 786
Carroll, Thomas, Chm. Bd. & Pres.--CRL, Inc., Des Plaines, IL, pg. 203
Carroll, Tom, Pres. & New Bus. Contact--Weiss, Whitten, Carroll, Stagliano Inc., New York, NY, pg. 1174
Carruthers, George, Pres., Chief Exec. & Chief Fin. Officer, Controller--Polycoat Systems, Inc., Hudson Falls, NY, pg. 880
Carse, Wayne L., Pres.--Carse Oil Co. Inc., Orlando, FL, pg. 225
Carson, Bruce M., Pres.--Dot Printer, Inc., Irvine, CA, pg. 347
Carson, Charles E., Pres.--Minarik Electric Company, Glendale, CA, pg. 756
Carson, Richard L., Pres.--Henry Bacon Building Materials, Inc., Issaquah, WA, pg. 113
Carstarphen, J.M., Chm. Bd., Pres. & Chief Exec. Officer--Stowe-Pharr Mills, Inc., McAdenville, NC, pg. 1052
Carstens, Matthew, Pres.--United Steel & Wire Co., Battle Creek, MI, pg. 1137
Carstensen, David N., Pres.--Carstensen Freight Line, Inc., Clinton, IA, pg. 226
Carswell, Charles, Pres.--Lytron Incorporated, Woburn, MA, pg. 690
Carter, Arthur L., Pres.--Shepaug Corporation, New York, NY, pg. 997
Carter, Donald J., Pres., Treas. & Chief Exec. Officer--Home Interiors & Gifts, Inc., Dallas, TX, pg. 541

Carter, Jerry C., Chm. Bd., Pres. & Chief Exec. Officer--Jerry C. Carter, Inc., Gainesville, GA, pg. 226
Carter, Jud, Pres.--Bell-Carter Foods, Inc., Lafayette, CA, pg. 134
Carter, Robert E., Pres.--Ketchum, Inc., Pittsburgh, PA, pg. 626
Carter, Sam, Chm. Bd. & Pres.--Carter Companies, Kansas City, MO, pg. 226
Cartwright, James, Pres.--The Electron Corp., Littleton, CO, pg. 375
Cartwright, William Y., Pres., Chief Exec., Chief Fin. Officer & Treas.--Cartwright Communications Co., Cincinnati, OH, pg. 227
Carus, Andre W., Pres.--Open Court Publishing Company, Chicago, IL, pg. 227
Carus, M. Blouke, Chm. Bd., Pres., Chief Exec. & Chief Oper. Officer--Carus Corporation, Peru, IL, pg. 227
Caruso, Jack, Chm. Bd. & Pres.--Regency Dodge Inc., Jacksonville, FL, pg. 922
Caruso, Joseph A., Pres.--Jordan Tamraz Caruso Advertising, Inc., Chicago, IL, pg. 605
Caruthers, William A., Pres.--Greenhorne & O'Mara, Inc., Greenbelt, MD, pg. 485
Carvelli, A.J., Vice Chm. & Chief Exec. Officer--Pannier Corporation, Pittsburgh, PA, pg. 846
Casanova, Paul L., Pres., Sec. & New Bus. Contact--Casanova Pendrill Publicidad Inc., Irvine, CA, pg. 227
Casavant, S., Partner--Energy Brokers Guild, Stevensville, MI, pg. 381
Caschette, Gerard, Pres. & Treas.--Genesee Metal Stampings, Inc., West Henrietta, NY, pg. 451
Casebeer, Scott, Pres.--Capitol Chevrolet Cadillac GEO, Inc., Salem, OR, pg. 215
Casey, Brian T., Pres.--Thomas Engineering Inc., Hoffman Estates, IL, pg. 1093
Casey, Martin M., Pres. & Chief Exec. Officer--El Torito Restaurants, Inc., Irvine, CA, pg. 372
Casgrain, Timothy, Pres. & Chief Exec. Officer--SBN System Inc., Fort Wayne, IN, pg. 960
Cashbaugh, Bruce, Pres.--Juhl Marketing Communications, Mishawaka, IN, pg. 608
Cashman, Robert L., Chm. Bd., Pres. & Chief Exec. Officer--Pacific Envelope Company, Anaheim, CA, pg. 840
Casper, Charles D., Pres. & Chief Oper. Officer--The Chesapeake Life Insurance Co., Lincoln, NE, pg. 243
Cassel, John P., Pres.--Pioneer Aluminum, Inc., Los Angeles, CA, pg. 871
Cassens, Allen, Pres.--Cassens Transport Company, Edwardsville, IL, pg. 228
Cassese, Patrick J., Chm. Bd., Pres. & Chief Exec. Officer--Antares Group Inc., Cleveland, OH, pg. 76
Cassetty, Fred, Chm. Bd., Pres. & Chief Exec. Officer--Alley-Cassetty Coal Co., Nashville, TN, pg. 37
Cassis, Jorge, Mng. Dir.--Leo Burnett Chile, Santiago,, Chile, pg. 192
Cassner, Alvin B., Pres. & Chief Exec. Officer--Rotary Forms Press, Inc., Hillsboro, OH, pg. 950
Cassner, Alvin B., Pres.--Computer Stock Forms, Inc., Greenfield, OH, pg. 951
Cassner, Alvin B., Pres.--Quality Computer Forms, Inc., Ocala, FL, pg. 951
Cassner, Alvin B., Pres.--Units Sets, Inc., Wilmington, OH, pg. 951
Casteborn, Lars, Pres.--VASA Insurance Group, Inc., Indianapolis, IN, pg. 1146
Castle, Frank E., Pres. & Chief Exec. Officer--Components Corporation Of America, Dallas, TX, pg. 270
Castle, Jim, Pres.--Stuart-Ironsides, Inc., Willowbrook, IL, pg. 1054
Castonguay, Lee, Pres. & Gen. Mgr.--Hubacher Cadillac Inc., Sacramento, CA, pg. 548
Castonguay, Perry, Pres.--Kingfisher Co-Op Elevator Association, Kingfisher, OK, pg. 631
Castro, Adolfo, Chief Exec. Officer--Lowe MBAC, Barcelona,, Spain, pg. 685
Castro, Richard, Pres. & Chief Oper. Officer--Superior Fast Freight, Irwindale, CA, pg. 1063
Cataland, James R., Pres. & Chief Exec. Officer--Arthur Treacher's, Inc., Youngstown, OH, pg. 87
Cataldo, C.A., Pres. & Chief Exec. Officer--Hostmark Management Group, Rowing Meadows, IL, pg. 545
Catenacci, Carlo J., Pres.--John Carlo Inc., Mount Clemens, MI, pg. 220
Cathers, David M., Pres. & Chief Oper. Officer--Franklin Spier, Inc., New York, NY, pg. 1031
Cation, Kenneth L., Grp. Pres.--Atlas/Soundolier, Fenton, MO, pg. 64
Catsimatidis, John, Chm. Bd., Pres. & Chief Exec. Officer--Red Apple Companies, New York, NY, pg. 917
Catsimatidis, John, Chm. Bd.--United Acquisition Corporation, New York, NY, pg. 1130
Caudie, Louise Bell, Pres.--Star Food Products, Inc., Burlington, NC, pg. 1039
Causley, James F., Jr., Pres.--James Chevrolet Inc., Mount Clemens, MI, pg. 588
Causley, James Sr., Pres.--Jim Causley Pontiac GMC Inc., Mt. Clemens, MI, pg. 229
Cavalli, Caroline, Pres. & Sec.--Orbitair International Ltd., New York, NY, pg. 828
Cavanaugh, Jim, Pres.--Jani King International, Inc., Dallas, TX, pg. 589
Cavaricci, James, Pres.--Z. Cavaricci Inc., Los Angeles, CA, pg. 1215
Cavens, Leonard W., Pres.--Pease Industries, Inc., Fairfield, OH, pg. 854
Caye, C.G., Pres.--Techsteel, Inc., Atlanta, GA, pg. 230
Caye, Charles G., Jr., Pres.--W.C. Caye & Company, Inc., Atlanta, GA, pg. 230
Cecchi, Giuseppe, Pres. & Chief Exec. Officer--The IDI Group Companies, Arlington, VA, pg. 560
Ceccoli, Darryll M., Pres.--Automobile Auction Division, Atlanta, GA, pg. 293
Cei, Jay, Pres. & Chief Oper. Officer--Ulbrich Wire, Inc., North Haven, CT, pg. 1125
Ceiley, Glen, Pres.--Bisco Industries, Anaheim, CA, pg. 153
Cejka, J.B., Pres.--Ward Products Corporation, New Brunswick, NJ, pg. 1163
Celauro, John, Pres.--4C Foods Corporation, Brooklyn, NY, pg. 427
Celentano, Domenick, Chm. Bd. & Pres.--Celentano Brothers, Verona, NJ, pg. 231
Centeno, Victor Lopes, Chm. & Chief Exec. Officer--BSB Portugal, Lisbon,, Portugal, pg. 110
Chadsey, Jack, Pres., Chief Exec. & Oper. Officer--Sunglass Hut Corporation, Miami, FL, pg. 1060
Chadwick, James R., Pres.--Chadwick-Helmuth Company, Inc., El Monte, CA, pg. 237
Chadwick, Winslow, Jr., Pres. & Chief Fin. Officer--Consolidated Companies Inc. (CONCO), Metairie, LA, pg. 276
Chaffee, David S., Pres.--Chaffee Case & Partners, Providence, RI, pg. 237
Chagnon, Emile A., Jr., Pres. & Treas.--Chagnon Lumber Company, Inc., Nashua, NH, pg. 238
Chaiken, Eugene B., Chm., Pres. & Chief Exec. Officer--Almo Corp., Philadelphia, PA, pg. 43
Chaikin, Scott, Grp. Pres.--Dix & Eaton Incorporated, Cleveland, OH, pg. 341
Chalek, Mitchel J., Pres.--Chalek & Chalek, Inc., New York, NY, pg. 238
Chalfin, R. Barry, Mng. Partner--Cosmopulos Crowley Daly/CKG, Boston, MA, pg. 288
Chalk, Howard W., Pres., New Bus. Contact & Creative Dir.--Chalk & Partners, Ltd., New York, NY, pg. 238
Chalmers, David B., Chm. Bd., Pres. & Chief Exec. Officer--Coral Petroleum Corporation, Houston, TX, pg. 285
Chambers, Harry L., Pres. & Chief Exec. Officer--Kettle Restaurants, Houston, TX, pg. 626
Champagne, Jack, Pres.--Rau Fasteners, Inc., Providence, RI, pg. 913
Champion, James K., Pres.--Riverdale Chemical Co., Glenwood, IL, pg. 937
Chance, Richard G., Pres.--Chance Industries, Inc., Wichita, KS, pg. 238
Chandran, Robert, Pres.--Chemoil, San Francisco, CA, pg. 242
Chapman, Frank B., Pres.--Steelox Systems, Inc., Mason, OH, pg. 1044
Chapman, Lawrence, Pres. & Chief Exec. Officer--Manna Pro Corporation, Saint Louis, MO, pg. 704
Chapman, Peter K., Pres. & Chief Exec. Officer--Dalfort Corp., Dallas, TX, pg. 312
Chapman, R.N., Chm. Bd., Pres. & Chief Exec. Officer--Pneumatic Scale Corporation, Quincy, MA, pg. 122
Chapman, Robert H., Chm. & Pres.--Barry-Wehmiller Company, Saint Louis, MO, pg. 122
Chapman, Robert H., III, Pres.--Inman Mills, Inman, SC, pg. 570
Chapman, Steven G., Pres.--ITA Group, West Des Moines, IA, pg. 560
Chapman, Wilford, Chm. Bd. & Pres.--Idaho Supreme Company, Firth, ID, pg. 561
Chappell, Sarah S., Pres.--Spencer Oil Company, Huntsville, AL, pg. 1030
Chapple, Spencer, Pres. & Chief Oper. Officer--Avadyne, Inc., Monterey, CA, pg. 101
Charkiewicz, Thomas, Pres.--Manufacturers Technologies, Inc., West Springfield, MA, pg. 705
Charles, R., Chm. Bd. & Pres.--Hydro Group, Inc., Bridgewater, NJ, pg. 556
Charlesworth, Gary M., Gen. Mgr.--Georgia Auction Services, Inc., Atlanta, GA, pg. 293
Charlton, Chuck, Pres.--Byron's, Inc., Gallatin, TN, pg. 932
Charnas, Robert D., Pres.--CSA, Inc., Glastonbury, CT, pg. 204
Charnley, Peter, Pres.--General Tools Mfg., New York, NY, pg. 451
Charron, Theodore, J., Pres., Chief Exec. Officer & Creative Dir.--Charron, Schwartz & Partners, Inc., New York, NY, pg. 240
Charton, Steve, Chm. Bd., Pres & Chief Exec. Officer--Alex Foods, Inc., Anaheim, CA, pg. 33
Chartreau, Doyne, Pres.--Ward Manufacturing, Inc., Blassburg, PA, pg. 1163
Chase, Francis H. III, Chm. Bd., Pres., Chief Exec., Chief Fin. Officer & Treas.--F. H. Chase, Inc., Foxboro, MA, pg. 240
Chase, John W., Pres.--Chase Chevrolet Co., Stockton, CA, pg. 240
Chase, Thomas E., Pres.--Pizzagalli Construction Co., South Burlington, VT, pg. 873
Chastain, J.D., Pres.--Redburn Tire Company, Phoenix, AZ, pg. 919
Chatman, James I., Chm. Bd. & Pres.--Technology Applications, Inc., Alexandria, VA, pg. 1083
Chatt, Joseph R., Pres.--Caribe Express, Aguadilla, PR, pg. 220
Chavez, Gabriel, Pres. & Gen. Mgr.--Nova Power, Inc., Santa Ana, CA, pg. 816
Chavkin, Robert, Pres.--Biddle Sawyer Corporation, New York, NY, pg. 148
Chazanoff, Jay D., Sr. Exec. V.P. & Chief Oper. Officer--Integrated Resources, Inc., New York, NY, pg. 573
Cheatley, H.W., Pres.--Bunn-O-Matic Corp. of Canada Ltd., Aurora,, Canada, pg. 188
Cheek, Ben F., III, Chm. Bd. & Pres.--1st Franklin Corporation, Toccoa, GA, pg. 413
Cheema, Jasse, Chm. Bd. & Pres.--Theodore Barry & Associates, Los Angeles, CA, pg. 122
Chehebar, J., Chief Exec. Officer--Rainbow Apparel Distribution Center, Brooklyn, NY, pg. 910
Chen, David, Mng. Partner--Muse Cordero Chen, Inc., Los Angeles, CA, pg. 777
Chen, Jeffrey C., Chm. Bd., Pres. & Chief Exec. Officer--General Sciences Corp., Laurel, MD, pg. 981
Cheney, Tom, Pres.--The Orr Felt Company, Piqua, OH, pg. 830
Cheney, William J., Chm. Bd., Pres. & Chief Exec. Officer--Steadly Company, Carthage, MO, pg. 1043
Chenok, Philip B., Pres. & Chief Exec. Officer--American Institute of C.P.A.'s Inc., New York, NY, pg. 56
Cher, Ronald, Pres.--Elder Manufacturing Company, Creve Coeur, MO, pg. 373
Cherenson, Lee, Pres.--The Cherenson Group, Livingston, NJ, pg. 243
Cherner, Drew J., Pres.--Market Development Group, Inc., Maitland, FL, pg. 709
Chertkow, Louis, Chief Exec. Officer--Elkay Plastics Company, Inc., Los Angeles, CA, pg. 377
Cherubini, Julian, Pres.--Alimed, Inc., Dedham, MA, pg. 34
Chesebro, R.E., Jr., Pres.--Wigwam Mills, Inc., Sheboygan, WI, pg. 1189
Chesterton, James D., Pres. & Chief Exec. Officer--A.W. Chesterton Company, Stoneham, MA, pg. 244
Chestnut, E. Randall, Pres.--Beacon Mfg. Co., Swannanoa, NC, pg. 129
Cheung, C. C., Chm. Bd. & Pres.--Green Spot Packaging Inc., Claremont, CA, pg. 485
Cheyne, Craig, Pres. & Dir. Acct. Mngmt.--Decker Rickard, Glastonbury, CT, pg. 324
Child, Sheldon F., Pres.--R.C. Willey Home Furnishings, Salt Lake City, UT, pg. 1190
Childers, Bruce S., Chm., Chief Exec. Officer--Meldrum & Fewsmith Yellow Pages Inc., Cleveland, OH, pg. 737
Childers, Bruce S., Chm., Chief Exec. Officer--Excel Media Services Inc., Cleveland, OH, pg. 737
Childs, Brian D., Pres. & Chief Oper. Officer--ComputerLand Canada Ltd., Brampton,, Canada, pg. 271
Childs, Winston, Pres.--MSI Services, Inc., Washington, DC, pg. 693
Chilewich, Simon, Pres. & Chief Exec. Officer--Chilewich Partners, White Plains, NY, pg. 248
Chimenti, Ronald C., Pres. & Chief Exec. Officer--DCI Marketing, Milwaukee, WI, pg. 308
Chisholm, Samuel J., Pres.--The Mingo Group, Inc., New York, NY, pg. 757
Choate, C. Randall, Pres.--Newspaper Advertising Specialists, Inc. (N.A.S.), Chicago, IL, pg. 805
Chopra, Deepak, Chm. Bd., Pres. & Chief Exec. Officer--UDT Sensors, Inc., Hawthorne, CA, pg. 1122
Choquette, Paul J., Jr., Pres.--Gilbane Building Company, Providence, RI, pg. 457
Chorengel, Bernd, Pres.--Hyatt International Corporation, Chicago, IL, pg. 495
Chow, F. C., Pres.--Gilvin-Terrill Inc., Amarillo, TX, pg. 460
Chow, Lena, Pres. & New Bus. Contact--Lena Chow, Inc., Palo Alto, CA, pg. 248
Choy, I.J., Pres.--American Tape Corporation, North Bergen, NJ, pg. 63
Christ, Clifford C., Pres. & Gen. Mgr.--NavCom Defense Electronics, Inc., El Monte, CA, pg. 796
Christensen, Mahlon, Pres. & Chief Exec. Officer--Muska Electric Company, Saint Paul, MN, pg. 777
Christensen, Susan M., Pres., Direct Mktg. Sub.--Kupper Parker Communications Inc., Saint Louis, MO, pg. 646
Christensen, Todd, Pres.--Crest Distributing Company, Inc., Provo, UT, pg. 298
Christenson, Jerry, Pres.--Christenson, Barclay & Shaw, Inc., Overland Park, KS, pg. 248
Christian, Betty S., Chm. Bd., Pres. & Chief Exec. Officer--Central Coca-Cola Bottling Company, Inc., Richmond, VA, pg. 232
Christianson, Stanley D., Pres. & Chief Exec. Officer--Thrall Enterprises, Inc., Chicago, IL, pg. 1095
Christionson, Arthur, Pres. & Gen. Mgr.--Norpac Foods, Inc. Cooperative, Stayton, OR, pg. 810
Christison, Richard J., Pres.--Coleman & Christison, Inc., Saint Paul, MN, pg. 261
Christmas, James W., Pres. & Chief Exec. Officer--KCS Energy Inc., Edison, NJ, pg. 612
Christopher, Brian, Pres.--Christenson Electric, Inc., Portland, OR, pg. 248
Christopher, Robert A., Pres. & Chief Exec. Officer--Globe Industries, Inc., Chicago, IL, pg. 464
Christopher, Thomas, Pres.--Bookstop, Inc., Austin, TX, pg. 120
Chronis, Peter W., Pres.--Reece-Campbell, Inc., Cincinnati, OH, pg. 920
Chryst, Steven L., Pres. & Chief Exec. Officer--Anchor Financial Corporation, Myrtle Beach, SC, pg. 71
Chun, Thomas T.W., Pres.--Mutual Welding Co., Ltd, Honolulu, HI, pg. 779
Church, John F., Jr., Pres.--The Cincinnati Cordage & Paper Company, Cincinnati, OH, pg. 249
Church, Mark V., Pres.--National Media Services, Inc., Atlanta, GA, pg. 792
Church, William R., Pres. & Chief Exec. Officer--Church & Church Inc., Utica, MI, pg. 249
Cicio, Joseph, Chm. Bd. & Chief Exec. Officer--I. Magnin & Co., San Francisco, CA, pg. 699
Ciganda, Carlos, Joint Office Mgr.--BSB Publicidad S.A., Pamplona,, Spain, pg. 110
Cilurao, Joe, Pres. & Chief Exec. Officer--Mobile Technology Inc., Los Angeles, CA, pg. 762
Ciociola, Mel, Chm. & Exec. Creative Dir.--Ciociola & Company Advertising, Inc., New York, NY, pg. 250
Ciola, Tom, Pres.--National Health Products, Orlando, FL, pg. 791
Cipolla, Vin, Pres.--Ingalls, Quinn & Johnson, Boston, MA, pg. 567
Cipriani, Robert, Pres., Creative Dir.--Cipriani Kremer Design, Boston, MA, pg. 84
Circo, Dennis P., Pres. & Chief Exec. Officer--Precision Industries, Omaha, NE, pg. 885
Citron, Kirk, Pres.--Atlas Citron Haligman & Bedecarre, San Francisco, CA, pg. 96
Clain, G., Pres., Chief Exec. & Chief Oper. Officer--J. Gerber & Co. Inc., New York, NY, pg. 453
Clancy, Joseph E., Chm. Bd., Pres. & Chief Oper. Officer--Bridgeport Machines, Inc., Bridgeport, CT, pg. 175

Clapp, Larry E., Pres. & Dir.-Creative--The J.W. Moore Group, Greensboro, NC, pg. 768
Clarity, Tim B., Pres.--Clarity Coverdale Rueff Advertising, Minneapolis, MN, pg. 251
Clark, A. James, Chm. Bd., Pres. & Chief Exec. Officer--Clark Construction Group, Bethesda, MD, pg. 252
Clark, A. James, Chm. Bd. & Pres.--Clark Enterprises, Inc., Bethesda, MD, pg. 252
Clark, A. James, Chm., Pres. & Chief Exec. Officer--CEI Construction, Inc., Bethesda, MD, pg. 200
Clark, Al, Chm. Bd. & Pres.--Southeastern Investment Properties Inc., Orlando, FL, pg. 1019
Clark, Charles, Pres. & Chief Oper. Officer--Dukane Corporation, Saint Charles, IL, pg. 351
Clark, Clinton A., Pres. & Chief Exec. Officer--Jerrico, Inc., Lexington, KY, pg. 229
Clark, Clinton A., Pres. & Chief Exec. Officer--Long John Silver's, Inc., Lexington, KY, pg. 229
Clark, Cyrus, III, Pres.--Cyrus Clark Co., Inc., New York, NY, pg. 253
Clark, David R., Pres.--Thomas & Howard, Columbia, SC, pg. 1093
Clark, Don, Pres. & Chief Exec. Officer--Mid America Steel, Inc., Fargo, ND, pg. 750
Clark, Donald A., Pres.--Covington Foods, Inc., Covington, IN, pg. 290
Clark, Edwin J., Pres. & Chief Exec. Officer--Dwyer Instruments Inc., Michigan City, IN, pg. 356
Clark, Erwin, Sr. V.P.--Milk Specialties Company, Dundee, IL, pg. 753
Clark, George A., Chm. Bd., Pres. & Chief Exec. Officer--Snap-Tite, Incorporated, Erie, PA, pg. 1014
Clark, H.S., Pres. & Chief Exec. Officer--Jackson Packing Co. Inc., Jackson, MS, pg. 587
Clark, J. Thomas, Pres.--Dubin-Clark & Company, Greenwich, CT, pg. 350
Clark, James, Pres.--Tecon Pacific, Sacramento, CA, pg. 1084
Clark, John P., Pres. & Chief Exec. Officer--Industrial Coatings Group, Inc., Chicago, IL, pg. 566
Clark, Linda Carole, Pres.--Complete Interiors Inc., Altamonte Springs, FL, pg. 270
Clark, O.B., Pres.--Associated Electric Co-op Inc., Springfield, MO, pg. 89
Clark, Thomas J., Pres.--TJ Clark Advertising/PR, Hingham, MA, pg. 251
Clarkson, William E., Pres.--Clarkson Construction Companies, Kansas City, MO, pg. 253
Claudon, Ronald C., Sr., Pres. & Chief Oper. Officer--Valley Pontiac Buick GMC, Inc., Auburn, WA, pg. 1143
Clauser, Fred, Pres.--Koh-I-Noor, Inc., Bloomsbury, NJ, pg. 639
Clay, Larry D., Pres. & Chief Exec. Officer--Pacific Coast Producers, Lodi, CA, pg. 839
Clay, Larry D., Pres. & Chief Exec. Officer--Hoover Group, Inc., Alpharetta, GA, pg. 543
Clay, Robert Edwin, Pres. & Chief Oper. Officer--Pridgeon & Clay, Inc., Grand Rapids, MI, pg. 889
Clay, Robert W., Pres.--Town & Country Supermarket, Hardy, AR, pg. 1103
Clayberg, H.D., Pres.--Union Equity, Enid, OK, pg. 402
Clayton, Don, Chm. Bd. & Pres.--Professional Putters Association, Fayetteville, NC, pg. 901
Clayton, Don S., Pres.--Putt Putt Golf Courses of America, Inc., Fayetteville, NC, pg. 901
Clayton, William, Jr., Pres.--Clayton Industries Co., El Monte, CA, pg. 253
Claytor, W. Graham, Jr., Chm. Bd., Pres. & Chief Exec. Officer--Amtrak-National Railroad Passenger Corp., Washington, DC, pg. 69
Cleary, John A., Pres.--Donnelley Marketing, Inc., Stamford, CT, pg. 1011
Cleary, Mark, Pres.--Clemco Industries, Washington, MO, pg. 254
Cleary, Mark, Pres.--Clemco Industries Corp., Washington, MO, pg. 254
Cleary, Martin J., Pres. & Chief Oper. Officer--The Richard & David Jacobs Group, Westlake, OH, pg. 932
Cleberg, Harry C., Pres. & Chief Exec. Officer--Farmland Industries, Inc., Kansas City, MO, pg. 402
Clegg, James, Pres.--Sunbeam-Oster Household Products, Schaumburg, IL, pg. 1059
Clemens, Clair W., Pres. & Chief Exec. Officer--Hatfield Quality Meats, Inc., Hatfield, PA, pg. 517
Clemens, Jack S., Pres. & Chief Exec. Officer--Clemens Markets Inc., Lansdale, PA, pg. 254
Clemens, Jay, Pres. & Chief Exec. Officer--Turtledove Clemens, Inc., Portland, OR, pg. 1120
Clemens, Roni, Pres.--Roni Hicks & Associates, Inc., San Diego, CA, pg. 533
Clement, Coy, Pres. & Chief Exec. Officer--Leichtung, Inc., Cleveland, OH, pg. 666
Clement, Gale W., Chm. Bd. & Pres.--Idahoan Foods, Lewisville, ID, pg. 561
Clements, Richard H., Chm. Bd., Pres. , & Chief Fin. Officer--Clements Foods Co., Oklahoma City, OK, pg. 254
Clements, W.M., Chm. Bd., Pres. & Chief Exec. Officer--Golden Eagle Distributors, Inc., Tucson, AZ, pg. 466
Clemons, Luther F., Pres.--Associated Equipment Company, Inc., Mobile, AL, pg. 89
Cleveland, C.E. Thomas, Pres.--H.O. Penn Machinery Co. Inc., Armonk, NY, pg. 857
Cleveland, James R., Sr., Chm. Bd., Pres. & Chief Exec. Officer--Cleveland Group, Inc., Atlanta, GA, pg. 255
Cleveland, Jay W., Pres. & Treas.--Cleveland Brothers Equipment Co., Harrisburg, PA, pg. 255
Clifford, William M., Chm., Pres. & Chief Exec. Officer--St. Johnsbury Trucking Co., Inc., Holliston, MA, pg. 966
Cliggot, Richard, Pres.--Cliggot Publishing, Greenwich, CT, pg. 255
Climch, Stephen H., Pres.--The Presmet Corp., Worcester, MA, pg. 887
Cline, Morgan E., Chm. Bd. & Pres.--Cline, Davis & Mann, Inc., New York, NY, pg. 255
Clinton, Gary, Chm. Bd., Pres. & Chief Exec. Officer--United Design, Noble, OK, pg. 1131
Clinton, Jean M., Chief Oper. Officer--United Design, Noble, OK, pg. 1131
Clinton, Jerry, Chm. Bd. & Pres.--Grey Eagle Distributors Inc., Maryland Heights, MO, pg. 486
Clore, Larry, Pres.--Multi-Ad Services, Inc., Peoria, IL, pg. 775
Cloud, Bruce B., Pres. & Chief Oper. Officer--H.B. Zachry, San Antonio, TX, pg. 1215
Cloud, Bruce B., Pres.--H. B. Zachry Company, San Antonio, TX, pg. 1215
Cloud, Stephen R., Pres. & Chief Exec. Officer--IBT, Inc., Shawnee Mission, KS, pg. 558
Clow, Lee, Pres., Exec. Creative Dir.--Chiat/Day/Mojo Inc. Advertising, Venice, CA, pg. 244
Clowe, C. Tom, Pres. & Chief Exec. Officer--Central Freight Lines Inc., Waco, TX, pg. 232
Clutterbuck, Howard, Pres.--American Journal Of Nursing Company, New York, NY, pg. 57
Clymer, John A., Pres. & Chief Oper. Officer--The Minnesota Mutual Life Insurance Company, Saint Paul, MN, pg. 757
Coady, Todd M., Chm. Bd., Pres. & Chief Exec. Officer--Hicks Oil-Hicks Gas, Inc., Roberts, IL, pg. 533
Coan, Gaylord O., Pres.--Gold Kist, Inc., Atlanta, GA, pg. 465
Coates, Jean Pettijohn, Pres., Treas. & Creative Dir.--The Coates Agency, Portland, OR, pg. 257
Coath, J. Douglas, Sr., Pres. & Chief Exec. Officer--Frank W. Winne & Son, Inc., Philadelphia, PA, pg. 1196
Coatney, Doyle, Pres. & Chief Exec. Officer--Acme Truck Line, Inc., Harvey, LA, pg. 13
Cober, Richard G., Pres.--Prudential-LMI Commercial Insurance Company, Mansfield, OH, pg. 897
Coburn, Ronald, Pres. & Chief Exec. Officer--Savage Arms Inc., Westfield, MA, pg. 973
Coccari, Greg, Pres.--Teleflora, Los Angeles, CA, pg. 60
Cochill, Thomas, Pres. & Chief Exec. Officer--Webcraft Technologies, Inc., North Brunswick, NJ, pg. 1171
Cochran, Jack, Pres.--Markwood Inc., High Point, NC, pg. 710
Cochran, Jack, Pres.--Stanton Cooper, High Point, NC, pg. 710
Cochran, Jack, Pres.--Woodmark Originals, High Point, NC, pg. 710
Cochran, Perkins, Pres.--Lithograph Printing Company, Inc., Memphis, TN, pg. 678
Cochran, R.W., Pres. & Chief Exec. Officer--817
Cochrane, Jerry W., Pres.--Cochrane Furniture Co., Inc., Lincolnton, NC, pg. 258
Cockayne, Jim D., Pres.--Weiss Sheet Metal Company, Gardena, CA, pg. 1174
Coco, Lewis M., Pres.--JPS Elastomerics Corp., Northampton, MA, pg. 586
Code, Andrew W., Gen. Partner--Code, Hennessy & Simmons, Chicago, IL, pg. 258
Coffman, Gregory M., Pres.--K & G Of Wisconsin, Inc., Milwaukee, WI, pg. 610
Cogan, Marshall S., Chm. Bd., Pres. & Chief Exec. Officer--21 International Holdings, Inc., New York, NY, pg. 1121
Coggin, Luther, Pres. & Chief Exec. Officer--Coggin-O'Steen Investment Corp., Jacksonville, FL, pg. 259
Coggin, Luther, Pres. & Chief Exec. Officer--Coggin Pontiac-GMC Inc., Jacksonville, FL, pg. 259
Coggins, Lester A., Sr., Pres.--Lester Coggins Trucking, Okahumpka, FL, pg. 259
Coghlin, John F., Pres.--Dock Foundry Company, Three Rivers, MI, pg. 342
Cohan, Norman H., Pres. & Chief Exec. Officer--Security Plastics, Inc., Miami Lakes, FL, pg. 987
Cohen, Arnold, Pres.--J. Crew Group, Inc., New York, NY, pg. 584
Cohen, Donald, Chm. Bd., Pres., Chief Exec. Officer & Chief Fin. Officer--Tool King, Denver, CO, pg. 1101
Cohen, Eli D., Pres., Chief Oper. Officer & Treas.--Duane Reade, Long Island City, NY, pg. 350
Cohen, Gerald D., Pres.--Information Builders, New York, NY, pg. 567
Cohen, Harry, Pres.--First Computer Corporation, Los Angeles, CA, pg. 412
Cohen, Howard, Pres.--Host Apparel, Inc., New York, NY, pg. 545
Cohen, John K., Pres. & Chief Exec. Officer--Carlyle & Co. Jewelers, Greensboro, NC, pg. 222
Cohen, Joseph A., Chm. Bd. & Pres.--Sunweave Linen Corporation, New York, NY, pg. 1062
Cohen, Leonard, Pres. & Chief Exec. Officer--Kelly, Scott And Madison, Inc., Chicago, IL, pg. 621
Cohen, Lewis M., Pres. & Chief Exec. Officer--Acme Canvas Co., Inc., Malden, MA, pg. 13
Cohen, Lewis M., Pres. & Chief Exec. Officer--Century Products Inc., Malden, MA, pg. 13
Cohen, Louis D., Pres. & Chief Exec. Officer--Sheplers, Inc., Wichita, KS, pg. 998
Cohen, Maurice, Mng. Dir.--Artplan Publicidade, Rio de Janeiro,, Brazil, pg. 1072
Cohen, Millard S., Pres.--Nixdorff Krein Industries Inc., Saint Louis, MO, pg. 807
Cohen, Peter J., Pres. & Chief Exec. Officer--Periphonics Corp., Bohemia, NY, pg. 862
Cohen, Peter J., Exec. V.P.--Hollytex, Saddle Brook, NJ, pg. 1121
Cohen, Ralph A., Pres.--Accurate Perforating Co., Chicago, IL, pg. 11
Cohen, Richard, Pres.--C & S Wholesale Grocery Inc., Brattleboro, VT, pg. 198
Cohen, Robert, V.P.--Acme Canvas Co., Inc., Malden, MA, pg. 13
Cohen, Robert H., Chm. Bd. & Pres.--Beauty Enterprises Inc., Hartford, CT, pg. 130
Cohen, Robert L., Pres. & Chief Exec. Officer--The Hotsy Corporation, Englewood, CO, pg. 545
Cohen, Robert N., Pres.--Daycon Products Company, Inc., Capitol Heights, MD, pg. 321
Cohen, Sam, Pres.--Service Packing Company, Los Angeles, CA, pg. 992
Cohen, Steven A., Chm. Bd. & Pres.--Andy Frain Services, Inc., Chicago, IL, pg. 428
Cohen, Warren, Pres.--All-Luminum Products, Inc., Philadelphia, PA, pg. 35
Cohenca, Jacques, Pres.--Jason Industrial, Inc., Fairfield, NJ, pg. 590
Cohn, Richard, Pres.--Decorative Crafts, Inc., Greenwich, CT, pg. 324
Cohn, Richard, Pres.--Sigmund Cohn Corp., Mount Vernon, NY, pg. 259
Coker, Kenneth, Pres. of Bd. Dir.--Plains Electric Generation Transmission Co-Op, Inc., Albuquerque, NM, pg. 873
Colangelo, Larry A., Pres. & Chief Exec. Officer--SPD Technologies, Philadelphia, PA, pg. 963
Colburn, Craig P., Pres.--Dahlstrom Manufacturing Company, Inc., Jamestown, NY, pg. 310
Colby, Rick, Pres. & Creative Dir.--Larsen Colby Advertising, Los Angeles, CA, pg. 659
Cole, Alan, Pres.--The Berkline Corporation, Morristown, TN, pg. 285
Cole, Jack, Pres.--Lance Camper Manufacturing Corporation, Pacoima, CA, pg. 653
Cole, Richard, Pres.--Hygrade Metal Moulding Mfg. Corp., Farmingdale, NY, pg. 557
Colehower, William S., Pres.--Jomac, Inc., Warrington, PA, pg. 602
Coleman, James R., Pres.--Coleman Cadillac Inc., Bethesda, MD, pg. 261
Coleman, Jim, Pres. & Chief Exec. Officer--Coleman Cable Systems, Inc., North Chicago, IL, pg. 260
Coleman, Rogers K., Pres.--Blue Cross & Blue Shield of Texas, Inc., Richardson, TX, pg. 160
Coleman, Tom, Pres.--E-Z Mart Stores, Inc., Texarkana, TX, pg. 361
Coleman, Walter C., III, Pres.--Coleman Dairy Inc., Little Rock, AR, pg. 261
Colgan, Paul, Chm. Bd. & Pres.--Waldo Bros. Company, Boston, MA, pg. 1159
Colin, Lawrence, Pres. & Chief Exec. Officer--Colin Service Systems, Inc., White Plains, NY, pg. 261
Collanus, Alpo, Pres.--J & C Advertising, Helsinki,, Finland, pg. 104
Collette, Murray P., Pres. & Chief Exec. Officer--Oak Rubber Company, Ravenna, OH, pg. 819
Collier, R.M., Pres.--Brighton Foods Company, Marietta, OH, pg. 180
Colligan, Richard, Pres.--The Colligan Group, New York, NY, pg. 949
Collings, Charles L., Pres. & Chief Exec. Officer--Raley's, West Sacramento, CA, pg. 910
Collins, Bert, Pres. & Chief Exec. Officer--North Carolina Mutual Life Insurance Co., Durham, NC, pg. 813
Collins, Christopher C., Chm. Bd., Pres. & Chief Exec. Officer--Nuttall Gear Corporation, Niagara Falls, NY, pg. 818
Collins, Fulton, Chm. & Chief Exec. Officer--Liberty Glass Company, Sapulpa, OK, pg. 674
Collins, James L. S., Pres.--Chick-Fil-A, Inc., Atlanta, GA, pg. 247
Collins, John A. III, Pres.--American Marking Systems, Clifton, NJ, pg. 58
Collins, Kevin, Pres.--Collins Chevrolet, GEO, Louisville, KY, pg. 263
Collins, Marilyn, Pres. & Chief Exec. Officer--Valley Innovative Management Service, Jackson, MS, pg. 1109
Collins, Nicholas P., Pres. & Chief Exec. Officer--Esco Corporation, Portland, OR, pg. 388
Collins, Thomas A., Pres.--Southern Frozen Foods, Montezuma, GA, pg. 26
Collins, W., III, Chm. Bd. & Pres.--Warren E. Collins, Inc., Braintree, MA, pg. 263
Collins, Wayne, Pres. & Chief Exec. Officer--Pennock, Philadelphia, PA, pg. 858
Collins, William, Pres. & Chief Exec. Officer--Bill Collins Ford Inc., Louisville, KY, pg. 263
Collins, William A., Pres.--Collins Electric Company, Inc., Chicopee, MA, pg. 263
Colliver, Danielle, Pres.-Detroit/Ayer & Sr. V.P., Mng. Dir.--N W Ayer Inc., Detroit, MI, pg. 104
Collman, Nicholas, Chm., Pres. & Chief Exec. Officer--John D. Lucas Printing Company, Baltimore, MD, pg. 263
Collman, Nicholas J., Chm., Pres. & Chief Exec. Officer--Collman Graphics, Inc., Baltimore, MD, pg. 263
Colman, James A., Pres. & Chief Exec. Officer--Acme Mills Co. Inc., Detroit, MI, pg. 13
Colman, John, Chief Exec. Officer--Mother Earth News, New York, NY, pg. 773
Colomb, Gilles, Chm.--Wunderman Cato Johnson France, Boulogne,, France, pg. 1212
Colonna, Peter, Pres., Chief Exec. Officer & Mng. Dir.--Colonna Bros., Inc., North Bergen, NJ, pg. 264
Colsky, Richard A., Pres. & Chief Exec. Officer--Colsky Media, Inc., San Francisco, CA, pg. 265
Colton, Bruce L., Pres. & Chief Exec. Officer--Domestic Linen Supply & Laundry Co., Detroit, MI, pg. 343
Colucci, James, Sr. V.P.-Sls. & Mktg.--Allied Products, Fort Lauderdale, FL, pg. 276
Columbus, Shanna J., Chm. Bd., Pres. & New Bus. Contact--Price Weber Marketing Communications, Inc., Louisville, KY, pg. 889
Colway, David E., Pres. & Chief Fin. Officer--Adams Colway & Associates, Rochester, NY, pg. 16
Colwell, Thomas G., Chm. Bd., Pres. & Chief Exec. Officer--Colwell Industries, Inc., Minneapolis, MN, pg. 267
Combs, Bennett A., Pres.--Combs & Heathcott, Little Rock, AR, pg. 267

Combs, W.C., V.P. & Pres.-Potters Industries, Inc.--PQ Corporation, Valley Forge, PA, pg. 836
Combs, W.C., Pres. & Chief Exec. Officer--Potters Industries, Inc., Parsippany, NJ, pg. 837
Combs, William H., III, Pres.--Tamaqua Cable Products Corporation, Schuylkill Haven, PA, pg. 1077
Comley, John, Pres.--Clearing International, Inc., Chicago, IL, pg. 254
Comment, J.W., Pres. & Chief Oper. Officer--Helzberg's Diamond Shops, Inc., North Kansas City, MO, pg. 528
Commerot, Gerard, Pres.--CIA Ketchum, Paris,, France, pg. 625
Como, John, Sr., Pres.--Amco Folding Cartons, Inc., Towaco, NJ, pg. 47
Compton, Franklin, Pres. & New Bus. Contact--Sawyer Riley Compton Inc., Atlanta, GA, pg. 973
Compton, William, Pres., Chief Exec. Officer & Chief Oper. Officer--Tropical Garment Manufacturing Company, Tampa, FL, pg. 1116
Comstock, Harwood B., Pres.--The Cornwall & Patterson Co., Bridgeport, CT, pg. 884
Comstock, Rodger H., Pres.--Burns International Security Services, Inc., Parsippany, NJ, pg. 166
Conant, Victor, Pres. & Chief Exec. Officer--Nightingale-Conant Corp., Niles, IL, pg. 807
Concannon, Bill, Pres. & Chief Exec. Officer--Trammell Crow Company, Dallas, TX, pg. 1106
Conde, Mike, Pres. & Chief Exec. Officer--Everfresh Beverages Inc., Franklin Park, IL, pg. 391
Condict, Pete, Pres.--Magicsilk, Inc., Charlotte, NC, pg. 700
Condie, Richard, Pres. & Chief Exec. Officer--E.J. Brach Corporation, Oakbrook Terrace, IL, pg. 169
Condon, F., Pres.--F.G. Montabert, Midland Park, NJ, pg. 766
Condon, Leon J., Pres., Chief Oper. Officer & Treas.--Kennington Ltd., Inc., Los Angeles, CA, pg. 623
Cone, G. Hollis, Chm. Bd., Pres. & Chief Exec. Officer--Defender Services, Inc., Columbia, SC, pg. 324
Conese, Eugene P., Jr., Pres. & Chief Exec. Officer--Greenwich Air Services, Miami, FL, pg. 485
Confer, Richard P., Pres. & Chief Exec. Officer--Hubbard Milling Company, Mankato, MN, pg. 549
Congel, Robert J., Mng. Partner--The Pyramid Companies, Syracuse, NY, pg. 901
Coniglio, Charles E., Natl. Sls. Mgr.--RHS, Santa Fe Springs, CA, pg. 907
Conklin, Charles E., Pres. & Chief Exec. Officer--Conklin Instrument Corporation, Pleasant Valley, NY, pg. 274
Conley, Joseph H., Jr., Pres. & Chief Exec. Officer--Cook Moving Systems, Inc., Buffalo, NY, pg. 282
Connally, John H., Pres.--States, Inc., Breckenridge, TX, pg. 1041
Connell, Grover, Chm. Bd. & Pres.--Connell Rice & Sugar Co., Westfield, NJ, pg. 275
Connell, Lawrence, Pres. & Chief Exec. Officer--Society for Savings Bancorp, Inc., Hartford, CT, pg. 1016
Connell, William F., Chm. Bd. & Chief Exec. Officer--Connell Limited Partnership, Boston, MA, pg. 275
Connelly, Thomas S., Chm. Bd., Pres., Chief Exec. & Chief Oper. Officer--Connelly Containers, Inc., Bala-Cynwyd, PA, pg. 275
Conney, Timothy, Pres.--Host for Her, New York, NY, pg. 545
Connolly, Andy, Pres.--Riverside Millwork Company, Inc., Panacook, NH, pg. 937
Connor, Bruce, Pres.--Wright-Schuchart, Inc., Seattle, WA, pg. 1204
Connor, David J., Pres. & Chief Exec. Officer--Carrols Corporation, Syracuse, NY, pg. 225
Connor, Robert C., Pres.--The Union of Arkansas Corp., Little Rock, AR, pg. 1127
Connors, Chester L., Pres. & Treas.--Magneco/Metrel, Inc., Addison, IL, pg. 700
Connors, John M., Jr., Pres. & Chief Exec. Officer--Hill, Holliday, Connors, Cosmopulos, Inc., Boston, MA, pg. 534
Conrad, Bernhard, Pres.--A-B Emblem Div. of Conrad Industries, Inc., Weaverville, NC, pg. 2
Conrad, Carlton J., Jr., Pres. & Chief Exec. Officer--E. H. Titchener & Company, Binghamton, NY, pg. 1099
Conrad, Carlton J., Sr., Chm. Bd.--E. H. Titchener & Company, Binghamton, NY, pg. 1099
Conrad, Michael B., Pres. & Chief Creative Officer-Leo Burnett International--Leo Burnett Company, Inc., Chicago, IL, pg. 191
Consoli, Tom, Exec. V.P.--WGM/Hydro, South San Francisco, CA, pg. 1156
Constable, John, Partner & Exec. Art Dir.--Frankenberry, Laughlin & Constable, Inc., Milwaukee, WI, pg. 429
Constantin, Gus, Chm. Bd., Pres. & Chief Exec. Officer--Phoenix American Incorporated, San Rafael, CA, pg. 868
Constantino, Carol, Pres.--The Noteworthy Company, Amsterdam, NY, pg. 816
Contadino, Joseph, Chm. Bd., Pres. & Treas.--Del Webb's Coventry, Phoenix, AZ, pg. 1171
Conti, Edward A., Pres.--C B J Enterprises, Inc., Tustin, CA, pg. 199
Contos, Larry D., Pres.--Pay Less Super Markets, Inc., Anderson, IN, pg. 852
Contravasso, Jean, Gen. Mgr.--Rennoc Corporation, Vineland, NJ, pg. 927
Conver, Tim, Pres.--Aerovironment, Inc., Monrovia, CA, pg. 22
Conway, Robert, Pres.--Besser Canada, Ltd., Bramalea,, Canada, pg. 146
Conway, William E., Jr., Pres.--Carlyle Holding Corporation, Washington, DC, pg. 222
Cook, Bud, Chm. Bd. & Pres.--Cook Holding Corporation, Haines City, FL, pg. 282
Cook, Burren, Sr., Chm. Bd. & Pres.--B.C. Cook & Sons Enterprises, Inc., Haines City, FL, pg. 282
Cook, Carl, Chm. Bd. & Pres.--Overland Transportation System, Inc., Indianapolis, IN, pg. 832
Cook, Greg, Pres. & Chief Oper. Officer--Cook Manufacturing Corporation, Duncan, OK, pg. 282
Cook, Jack E., Pres.--National Concrete Products Company, Plymouth, MI, pg. 787
Cook, Jack P., Chm. Bd. & Pres.--Bon Ton Foods, Inc., York, PA, pg. 164
Cook, Ken W., Pres. & Chief Oper. Officer--Barry Huey, Bullock & Cook Advertising, Inc., Birmingham, AL, pg. 551
Cook, Lyndol, Pres. & Chief Exec. Officer--Polaris Pool Systems, Inc., San Marcos, CA, pg. 878
Cook, Nicholas H., Pres. & Chief Exec. Officer--Brauns Fashions, Inc., Minneapolis, MN, pg. 172
Cook, Thomas, Pres.--American Metal & Plastics, Grand Rapids, MI, pg. 58
Cooke, J.P. Blase, Pres.--Harkins Builders, Inc., Silver Spring, MD, pg. 509
Cooke, Jack Kent, Pres.--Jack Kent Cooke, Inc., Middleburg, VA, pg. 282
Coombs, Christopher E., Pres.--Cairns & Brother, Inc., Clifton, NJ, pg. 207
Coon, Miles A., Pres., Chief Oper. Officer & Treas.--Red Wing Products, Inc., Plainview, NY, pg. 919
Cooper, Anthony S., Exec. Dir.--D.C. Lottery & Charitable Games Control Board, Washington, DC, pg. 308
Cooper, Benny, Pres.--Affiliated Foods, Inc., Amarillo, TX, pg. 24
Cooper, Burton, Pres.--Green Bus Lines, Inc., Jamaica, NY, pg. 483
Cooper, H., Pres.--Delta Foremost Chemical Corp., Memphis, TN, pg. 327
Cooper, Harvey, Pres.--Maxine Of Hollywood, Inc., Los Angeles, CA, pg. 723
Cooper, Joseph V., Chm. Bd. & Pres.--C. Weaver Chevrolet, Inc., New York Mills, NY, pg. 1170
Cooper, Marshall Y., Jr., Pres., Chief Exec. Officer & Chm. Bd.--Harriet & Henderson Yarns, Inc., Henderson, NC, pg. 511
Cooper, Norton J., Pres. & Chief Exec. Officer--Charles Jacquin et Cie, Inc., Philadelphia, PA, pg. 588
Cooper, William, Pres.--Spectronics Corporation, Westbury, NY, pg. 1029
Cooper, William R., Chm. Bd. & Pres.--Paragon Group, Inc., Dallas, TX, pg. 847
Cope, Larry W., Pres. & Chief Exec. Officer--Clear Springs Foods, Inc., Buhl, ID, pg. 254
Cope, Thomas L., Pres.--John Copes Food Products, Inc., Rheems, PA, pg. 284
Copeland, Alvin C., Chm. Bd.--Church's Fried Chicken, Inc., Jefferson, LA, pg. 284
Copeland, Daniel M., Pres.--Ploof Truck Lines, Inc., Jacksonville, FL, pg. 877
Copland, James R., III, Pres., Chief Exec. Officer & Treas.--Copland Fabrics, Inc., Burlington, NC, pg. 284
Copley, David C., Pres.--The Copley Press, Inc., La Jolla, CA, pg. 284
Copley, Helen K., Publisher--Union-Tribune Publishing Company, San Diego, CA, pg. 284
Coppola, Alfred C., Pres. & Chief Oper. Officer--The Okonite Company, Ramsey, NJ, pg. 823
Coppola, Carl, Pres. & Sec.--Mark Lighting Fixture Co., Inc., Moonachie, NJ, pg. 708
Copps, Timothy J., Pres.--The Copps Corp., Stevens Point, WI, pg. 285
Corbett, James R., Pres.--Bike Athletic Co., Knoxville, TN, pg. 150
Corbett, Larry R., Pres.--Austin Co., Inc., Greeneville, TN, pg. 98
Corbin, R.B., Pres.--Metal Trades, Inc., Hollywood, SC, pg. 741
Corbin, Richard J., Pres. & Chief Exec. Officer--Forster Mfg. Co., Inc., Wilton, ME, pg. 21
Corcoran, John E., Pres.--Corcoran Trucking Company, Billings, MT, pg. 285
Cordero, Mavis, Mng. Partner--Muse Cordero Chen, Inc., Los Angeles, CA, pg. 777
Cordes, William O., Pres. & Chief Exec. Officer--Draper Corporation, Greensboro, NC, pg. 348
Cordova, Randy M., Pres.--World Dryer Corp., Berkeley, IL, pg. 1027
Cordvoa, Sam, Chm. Bd.--Cordova Enterprise, Sylmar, CA, pg. 285
Corelli, Richard, Pres.--Petals, White Plains, NY, pg. 286
Corelli, Ronald, Pres.--Corham, Inc., White Plains, NY, pg. 286
Corkin, Herbert I., Chm. Bd., Pres., Chief Exec. & Chief Oper. Officer--The Entwistle Company, Hudson, MA, pg. 383
Cormier, Harry W., Jr., Pres.--Cormier Rice Milling Company, Inc., De Witt, AR, pg. 286
Cormier, Leonard L., III, Pres.--Cormier Chevrolet Company, Inc., Long Beach, CA, pg. 286
Cornelio, Albert C., Pres. & Chief Exec. Officer--The Berkshire Life Insurance Company, Pittsfield, MA, pg. 142
Cornell, M. Keen, Pres. & Chief Exec. Officer--Cornell Iron Works, Inc., Mountaintop, PA, pg. 286
Cornell, Michael V., Pres.--Williams-White & Co., Moline, IL, pg. 1191
Cornell, Michael V., Pres.--Williams, White & Company, Moline, IL, pg. 1191
Cornellier, Victor, Pres.--TSI Industries, Inc., Landover, MD, pg. 1075
Cornish, D. Samuel, Pres.--Collegeville/Imagineering L.P., Collegeville, PA, pg. 262
Cornish, David A., Pres. & Chief Exec. Officer--Collegeville Flag Mfg. Company, Collegeville, PA, pg. 261
Cornstein, David, Pres. & Chief Exec. Officer--Finlay Enterprises, Inc., New York, NY, pg. 411
Cornwall, John R., Pres. & Chief Oper. Officer--MetLife Capital Corporation, Bellevue, WA, pg. 744
Corogin, Peter J., Pres.--Lake Erie Electric, Inc., Westlake, OH, pg. 651
Corr, Robert, Pres.--R.J. Corr Naturals, Inc., Posen, IL, pg. 287
Corr, Thomas L., Pres. & Chief Exec. Officer--George E. Warren Corp., Vero Beach, FL, pg. 1164
Corral, Frank, Pres.--Chicago Heights Steel, Chicago Heights, IL, pg. 245
Corrao, Michael J., Chm. Bd., Pres. & Chief Exec. Officer--Gingiss International, Chicago, IL, pg. 460
Correa, Juan, Pres.--Walworth Company, Houston, TX, pg. 1162
Corrigan, Dennis, Pres.--Corrigan Bros., Inc., Saint Louis, MO, pg. 287
Corsini, John M., Pres. & Chief Oper. Officer--Uncas Manufacturing Company, Providence, RI, pg. 1125
Cortesi, John, Pres.--Central Grocers Co-op, Franklin Park, IL, pg. 232
Corwin, Joe, Gen. Mgr.--Rich Products Co., Hilliard, OH, pg. 932
Cosentino, Francis J., Pres. & Chief Exec. Officer--ICE Communications, Inc., Rochester, NY, pg. 559
Cosgrave, Gary D., Chm. & Chief Exec. Officer--Pro Hardware, Inc., Englewood, CO, pg. 891
Cosgrove, Edward M., Pres.--Warren Equities Inc., New York, NY, pg. 1164
Cosgrove, T.J., Pres.--M-B Company Inc. of Wisconsin, Chilton, WI, pg. 691
Cosper, Fred, Pres.--Simmons Outdoor Corp., Miami, FL, pg. 1005
Costa, Emanuele, Pres.--Overseas Partners, Inc., New York, NY, pg. 833
Costa, Jose Maria, Pres.--JMC Creatividad Orientada/ Young & Rubicam, Caracas,, Venezuela, pg. 1213
Costello, John, Pres.--Western Diesel Services Inc., Saint Louis, MO, pg. 1179
Costello, Maureen, Pres.--Yum Yum Donut Shop, Inc., City of Industry, CA, pg. 1214
Costello, Richard N., Pres. & Chief Oper. Officer--TBWA Advertising, Inc., New York, NY, pg. 1071
Costides, Nick, Pres.--Cosco, Inc., Columbus, IN, pg. 287
Cote, John, Pres.--Waccamaw Corporation, Myrtle Beach, SC, pg. 453
Cotel, Florence, Mng. Dir.--Kobs & Draft, Courbevoie,, France, pg. 112
Cotler, Leslie B., Pres.--H. Cotler Company, New York, NY, pg. 288
Cotter, Daniel A., Pres. & Chief Exec. Officer & Dir.--Cotter & Company, Chicago, IL, pg. 288
Cottrell, Comer J., Chm. Bd. & Pres.--Pro-Line Corporation, Dallas, TX, pg. 892
Coughlin, F.X., Pres. & Treas.--F.X. Coughlin Co., Taylor, MI, pg. 289
Coughlin, Jack, Pres. & Exec. Creative Dir.--Esrock Advertising, Orland Park, IL, pg. 388
Coughlin, Michael D., Pres.--Concord Litho Co., Inc., Concord, NH, pg. 272
Coughlin, Michael J., Exec. V.P.--Brooks Beverages Inc., Columbus, OH, pg. 179
Coughter, Peter J., Jr., Pres.--Siddall, Matus & Coughter, Inc. Advertising & Public Relations, Richmond, VA, pg. 1002
Coulombe, Cecile J., Pres., Treas. & Sec.--White Rock Distilleries Inc., Lewiston, ME, pg. 1186
Coulson, Deborah, Reg. Dir.-K&D Asia--K&D Asia-Hong Kong, Wanchai,, Hong Kong, pg. 112
Coulson, Robert, Pres. & Chief Exec. Officer--American Arbitration Association, New York, NY, pg. 49
Coulter, Joseph R., Jr., Pres.--Coulter Corporation, Hialeah, FL, pg. 289
Coulter, Lionnel, Pres.--Taj International Hotels, Washington, DC, pg. 1076
Councilor, T., Pres. & Treas.--Black Millwork Co., Inc., Allendale, NJ, pg. 154
Counton, Ron, Pres.--Rice & Rice Inc., Minneapolis, MN, pg. 1143
Courbey, Patrice, Chm. Bd. & Pres.--Meridian Technology Leasing Services, Deerfield, IL, pg. 740
Cousteau, Capt. J. Y., Chm. Bd.--U.S. Divers Co., Inc., Santa Ana, CA, pg. 1135
Couvelaire, Alexandre, Pres. & Treas.--Mooney Aircraft Corporation, Kerrville, TX, pg. 768
Couzin, N.C., Pres.--Mid-Continent Screw Products Co., Lincolnwood, IL, pg. 750
Covington, Edward H., Pres.--Harriss & Covington Hosiery Mills, High Point, NC, pg. 512
Cowan, R. Douglas, Pres. & Chief Exec. Officer--The Davey Tree Expert Company, Kent, OH, pg. 317
Cowart, D.R., Pres.--The Wm. Powell Company, Cincinnati, OH, pg. 882
Cowart, D.R., Pres.--The Starflo Corporation, Orangeburg, SC, pg. 883
Cowherd, Edwin, Pres.--Congoleum Corporation, Mercerville, NJ, pg. 274
Cowin, John J., Chm. Bd., Pres. & Treas.--Cowin & Company, Inc., Birmingham, AL, pg. 291
Cowles, Alfred, Jr., Pres. & Chief Exec. Officer--Bluff City Distributing Co., Inc., Memphis, TN, pg. 161
Cox, Al, Pres.--Mannington Ceramic Tile, Lexington, NC, pg. 704
Cox, Anne H., Mng. Partner & Chief Fin. Officer--Eire Partners, Inc., Chicago, IL, pg. 372
Cox, Archibald, Jr., Pres. & Chief Exec. Officer--The First Boston Corporation, New York, NY, pg. 203
Cox, Bob, Pres. & Creative Dir.--Cox Landey and Partners, Inc., New York, NY, pg. 294
Cox, Charles, Pres. & Owner--Cox Furniture, Maxton, NC, pg. 294
Cox, David C., Pres. & Chief Exec. Officer--Cowles Media Company, Minneapolis, MN, pg. 291
Cox, Dennis F., Pres.--Godfrey Advertising, Lancaster, PA, pg. 464
Cox, Theodore, Pres.--Watt Industries, Santa Monica, CA, pg. 1168
Cox, William B., Jr., Pres.--Cox Wood Preserving Co., Orangeburg, SC, pg. 295

Coxwell, John B., Pres.--J.B. Coxwell Contract, Inc., Jacksonville, FL, pg. 295
Coyle, Bob, Principal & Mktg. Dir.--Sullivan Haas Coyle, Atlanta, GA, pg. 1056
Crabtree, James T., Pres.--SCR, Inc., Lake Oswego, OR, pg. 961
Crabtree, Tom, V.P., Adv.--Sav-Rite Advertising, Salisbury, NC, pg. 973
Cracraft, Thomas M., Pres. & Chief Exec. Officer--Computerland, Arlington, TX, pg. 271
Craddock, James Berry, Pres.--Craddock Development Co., Inc., Colorado Springs, CO, pg. 295
Craft, Jack, Pres.--Skinner Corp., Lanett, AL, pg. 1009
Craft, Stanley, Chm., Pres. & Chief Exec. Officer--Essex Group, Inc., Fort Wayne, IN, pg. 389
Craig, H. Max, Jr., Pres.--Gaston County Dyeing Machine Co., Stanley, NC, pg. 444
Craig, Hank, V.P. & Gen. Mgr.--Jacksonville Manufacturing Co., Inc., Jacksonville, AR, pg. 921
Craig, Jean, Pres. & Exec. Creative Dir.--Kresser/Craig, Santa Monica, CA, pg. 644
Craigmile, David F., Pres.--Elkay Manufacturing Company, Oak Brook, IL, pg. 377
Crain, Keith E., Publr. & Editorial Dir.--Automotive News, Detroit, MI, pg. 101
Crain, Rance, Pres. & Editor-in-Chief--Advertising Age, Chicago, IL, pg. 295
Crain, Rance E., Pres.--Crain Communications, Inc., Detroit, MI, pg. 295
Crandall, Jerry R., Commissioner--Michigan State Lottery Bureau, Lansing, MI, pg. 747
Crandell, J. Wayne, Pres.--Perry Equipment Corporation, Mineral Wells, TX, pg. 863
Crane, Dan, Pres.--Traveling Software Inc., Bothell, WA, pg. 1108
Crane, Gerald, Pres.--Decatur News Publishing Company, Inc., Decatur, GA, pg. 323
Crane, Jameson, Pres.--Crane Plastics Company, Columbus, OH, pg. 296
Crane, Jeffrey D., Pres.--Crane Construction Co., Northbrook, IL, pg. 296
Crawford, Charles, Pres. & Treas.--Adair Feed & Grain Company, Adair, IA, pg. 16
Crawford, Mike, Chm. Bd. & Pres.--McCommunications Inc., Dallas, TX, pg. 727
Crawford, William, Pres. & Chief Exec. Officer--Memphis Light, Gas & Water, Memphis, TN, pg. 738
Crawford, William F., Pres.--Standard Tool & Manufacturing Company, Lyndhurst, NJ, pg. 1037
Creach, Dale, Pres. & Chief Oper. Officer--MFA Oil Company, Columbia, MO, pg. 692
Creedon, Robert J., Pres.--Senator Ford, Sacramento, CA, pg. 989
Cregier, Fred, Pres. & Chief Exec. Officer--Danfoss Dukes Fluid Power Inc., Saint Charles, IL, pg. 314
Cress, Robert G., Pres.--J. A. Riggs Tractor Co., Little Rock, AR, pg. 934
Cretegny, Raymond, Pres.--Norfoods, Inc., Overland Park, KS, pg. 810
Cretors, Phyllis, Pres.--The Popcorn Factory, Lake Forest, IL, pg. 426
Crews, Hilliard, Chm. Bd., Pres., Chief Exec. Officer & Chief Fin. Officer--Shelby Group International, Inc., Memphis, TN, pg. 996
Crhistopher, Todd, Pres.--Taylor Medical Inc., Beaumont, TX, pg. 1081
Crider, Joe D., Pres. & Chief Oper. Officer--Reliance Steel & Aluminum Co., Los Angeles, CA, pg. 925
Crifasi, Samuel J., Pres.--Hi Nabor Supermarket Inc., Baton Rouge, LA, pg. 532
Crilly, John H., Pres. & Chief Exec. Officer--Sun Data Inc., Norcross, GA, pg. 1058
Crisafulli, Frank, Pres.--United Food Service Distributors, Inc., Albany, NY, pg. 1132
Crisp, Donald W., Pres. & Chief Exec. Officer--Caroline Hunt Trust Estate, Dallas, TX, pg. 553
Crispin, Andre A., Pres. & Chief Exec. Officer--The Crispin Company, Houston, TX, pg. 299
Crispin, Charles, Pres.--Crispin & Porter Advertising Inc., Miami, FL, pg. 299
Cristiano, Joseph P., Pres. & Chief Exec. Officer--Kelly-Moore Paint Company, Inc., San Carlos, CA, pg. 621
Crittenden, Earl M., Pres.--Silver Springs Citrus Co-op, Ocoee, FL, pg. 1004
Crockett, Bruce, Pres.--Ensoniq Corporation, Malvern, PA, pg. 382
Crockett, R.J., Pres. & Chief Exec. Officer--Dexter Company, Fairfield, IA, pg. 334
Croll, Samuel W. III, Pres.--Croll-Reynolds Company, Westfield, NJ, pg. 300
Cronin, Eugene F., Jr., Pres. & Chief Exec. Officer--CSE Corporation, San Francisco, CA, pg. 204
Cronin, Eugene F., Jr., Pres.--CSE Services Insurance Brokerage, San Francisco, CA, pg. 205
Cronin, Tim, Pres. & Chief Exec. Officer--Rumrill-Hoyt, Inc., Rochester, NY, pg. 955
Cronin, Tim, Pres.--Battery St. Enterprises, Running Gear Div., Boulder, CO, pg. 670
Cronin, William J., Jr., Pres.--Cronin & Company, Inc., Glastonbury, CT, pg. 300
Crook, Steven E., Pres. & Chief Exec. Officer--Crooks Supermarket Inc., Nashville, TN, pg. 300
Cross, Joe D., Jr., Pres.--Cross Motors Corp., Louisville, KY, pg. 300
Crossett, Donald S., Pres. & Chief Exec. Officer--IDC Services, Inc., Chicago, IL, pg. 559
Crossingham, James H., Jr., Chm. Bd. & Pres.--Spencer's Inc., Mount Airy, NC, pg. 1030
Crossman, R.E., Pres. & Gen. Mgr.--Bryant Grinder Corp., Springfield, VT, pg. 468
Crossman, Richard, Pres.--Vermont USA Machine Tool Group, North Springfield, VT, pg. 468
Croteau, Marcel, Pres.--Spiegel Meats, Inc., Miami, FL, pg. 1030
Crotty, L. William, Chm., Pres. & Chief Exec. Officer--Van Dyne-Crotty, Inc., Dayton, OH, pg. 1144
Crouch, Terry, Pres.--Jackson Products Corp., Lexington, TN, pg. 587
Crowder, Otis A., Pres. & Chief Exec. Officer--Crowder Construction Co., Charlotte, NC, pg. 301
Crowe, Byron A., Pres.--Crowe Rope Company, Warren, ME, pg. 301
Crowell, Donald W., Mng. Partner--Crowell, Weedon & Co., Los Angeles, CA, pg. 301
Crowell, Raymond E., Chm. Bd. & Pres.--Glines & Rhodes, Inc., Attleboro, MA, pg. 463
Crowl, David H., Pres-Radio Grp.--Great American Broadcasting Company, Cincinnati, OH, pg. 52
Crowley, J.J., Jr., Pres. & Chief Exec. Officer--Fuller O'Brien Paints, South San Francisco, CA, pg. 820
Crowley, Jerome J., Jr., Pres.--The O'Brien Corporation, South San Francisco, CA, pg. 820
Crowley, John, Pres.--Capitol Metals Processing, Inc., Torrance, CA, pg. 216
Crowley, Joseph J., Pres.--Crowley Webb & Associates, Buffalo, NY, pg. 301
Crowley, Ralph D., Jr., Pres.--Polar Corporation, Worcester, MA, pg. 878
Croyle, Toby N., Pres.--Maxon Marine, Inc., Tell City, IN, pg. 246
Crum, David H., Pres., Chief Exec. & Chief Fin. Officer--Crum Electric Supply Co., Inc., Casper, WY, pg. 303
Crum, Niles D., Publisher--Institutional Distribution, New York, NY, pg. 150
Crump, Harold C., Pres. & Gen. Mgr.--KSTP-TV, Saint Paul, MN, pg. 549
Cuff, William, Pres.--Diamond Walnut Growers, Inc., Stockton, CA, pg. 1058
Culbertson, James F., Jr., Pres.--Temp-Control Mechanical Corp., Portland, OR, pg. 1086
Cullen, J. Russell, Jr., Pres.--Nason and Cullen, Inc., Wayne, PA, pg. 784
Cullers, Vincent T., Pres., Chief Exec. Officer & Treas.--Vince Cullers Advertising Inc., Chicago, IL, pg. 304
Cullman, Lewis B., Pres.--Cullman Ventures, Inc., New York, NY, pg. 304
Cullum, Kenneth H., Pres. & Chief Exec. Officer--Bristol Steel & Iron Works, Inc., Bristol, VA, pg. 176
Culver, Robert H., Pres.--Culver & Associates, Inc., Omaha, NE, pg. 304
Cummings, Robert S., Pres.--SAIC Engineering, Inc., Lakeville, MA, pg. 982
Cummings, Terry M., Pres. & Chief Exec. Officer--Bremer Financial Corporation, Saint Paul, MN, pg. 173
Cummings, Thomas L., III, Pres. & Chief Oper. Officer--Cummings Inc., Nashville, TN, pg. 304
Cummins, Bob, Pres.--Wellborn - DE Corp., Albuquerque, NM, pg. 354
Cummins, Mick, Pres. & Chief Exec. Officer--EvansGroup, San Francisco, CA, pg. 391
Cummins, Robert, Chm. Bd.--Video Products Distributors, Inc., Sacramento, CA, pg. 1150
Cunnigham, John P., Pres.--Cooley, Inc., Pawtucket, RI, pg. 282
Cunningham, C. Donald, Pres.--OMCO Mould, Inc., Winchester, IN, pg. 819
Cunningham, Dennis M., Pres.--Master Collectors Inc., Atlanta, GA, pg. 719
Cunningham, Don, Pres., New Bus. Contact--CGRW Advertising, Inc., Los Angeles, CA, pg. 201
Cunningham, Peter A., Chm. Bd., Pres. & Chief Exec. Officer--INPUT, Mountain View, CA, pg. 571
Cunningham, Terence, Pres.--Arnold Machinery Company of Arizona, Laveen, AZ, pg. 85
Cuny, John D., Pres.--Anthem Health Plans of Florida Inc., Jacksonville, FL, pg. 90
Curl, Stephen, Pres.--Pasotex Corporation, El Paso, TX, pg. 851
Curran, H. Thomas, Pres.--American Systems Corporation, Chantilly, VA, pg. 63
Curran, William, Pres.--Curran Contracting Co., Crystal Lake, IL, pg. 305
Currey, Bradley, Jr., Pres. & Chief Exec. Officer--Rock-Tenn Company, Norcross, GA, pg. 941
Currey, R.J., Pres. & Chief Oper. Officer--Illinois Consolidated Telephone Co., Mattoon, IL, pg. 563
Currie, William G., Chm. Bd., Pres., Chief Exec. & Chief Oper. Officer--Universal Companies, Inc., Grand Rapids, MI, pg. 1138
Curry, Bernard F., Jr., Pres.--The Curry Corporation, Scarsdale, NY, pg. 305
Curry, Charles H., Pres. & Chief Oper. Officer--Burrell Communications Group Inc., Chicago, IL, pg. 195
Curry, Jim, Mng. Dir.--Leo Burnett Limited, Auckland,, New Zealand, pg. 193
Curry, John, Pres.--Knutson Construction Co., Minneapolis, MN, pg. 638
Curtis, Charles, Pres. & Chief Exec. Officer--Cramer Inc., Kansas City, KS, pg. 296
Curtis, Charley, Pres.--Nana Regional Corporation, Inc., Anchorage, AK, pg. 783
Curtis, Chuck, Chief Exec. Officer & Pres.--Valentine-Radford, Inc., Kansas City, MO, pg. 1142
Curtis, Donald, Pres.--Curtis Media Group Inc., Raleigh, NC, pg. 305
Curtis, Jonathan G., Pres.--CDM Federal Programs Corporation, Fairfax, VA, pg. 212
Curtis, Ken C., Pres.--John M. Smyth Co., Downers Grove, IL, pg. 1014
Curtis, Paul F., Pres., Chief Oper. Officer & Treas.--L.N. Curtis & Sons, Oakland, CA, pg. 306
Curtis, Scott H., Product Application Mgr.--Anderson Products, Worcester, MA, pg. 1194
Cutler, Jay, Pres.--Educational Insights, Inc., Dominguez Hills, CA, pg. 369
Cutter, W.R., Chm. Bd. & Pres.--Cutter Flying Service, Inc., Albuquerque, NM, pg. 307
Cypher, Victor, Pres. & Chief Exec. Officer--Caldwell Manufacturing Company, Rochester, NY, pg. 208
Czerwinski, Eugene, Pres.--Cerwin Vega, Inc., Simi Valley, CA, pg. 237
Cziraky, Debra Adray, Pres. & Chief Exec. Officer--Adray Appliance & Photo Center, Inc., Dearborn, MI, pg. 18
D'Amour, Gerald E., Chm. Bd. & Pres.--Big Y Foods Inc., Springfield, MA, pg. 149
D'Anna, Angelo N., Pres.--Mars Super Markets, Inc., Baltimore, MD, pg. 714
Dabagia, Robert C., Pres. & Chief Admin. Officer--Horizon Bancorp, Michigan City, IN, pg. 544
Dabagia, Robert C., Pres. & Chief Admin. Officer--First Citizens Bank, N.A., Michigan City, IN, pg. 544
Dabah, Haim, Pres. & Chief Exec. Officer--Gitano Group Inc., New York, NY, pg. 460
Dadourian, Alexander A., Chm. Bd.--Interroyal Corporation, Warren, PA, pg. 580
Dadourian, Haig R., Pres.--Interroyal Corporation, Warren, PA, pg. 580
Dague, Paul D., Pres.--Jones Blair Company, Dallas, TX, pg. 602
Dahl, H.D., Pres. & Chief Oper. Officer--Drummond Company, Inc., Jasper, AL, pg. 349
Dahlberg, Burton F., Pres.--Kraus-Anderson, Inc., Minneapolis, MN, pg. 644
Dahlin, John D., Pres.--Dahlin Smith White, Inc., Salt Lake City, UT, pg. 310
Dahlsten, Wanda, Pres.--Dahlsten Truck Line, Inc., Clay Center, NE, pg. 310
Daidone, John, Pres.--Daidone Electrical Inc., Newark, NJ, pg. 310
Daigle, Peter H., Pres.--The Erin Company, Bangor, ME, pg. 387
Daigle, Richard, Pres.--Daigle Oil Co., Fort Kent, ME, pg. 310
Dailanc, Jean-Marc, Pres.--Muskin Leisure Products, Inc., Wilkes-Barre, PA, pg. 777
Dailey, Charles, Pres.--Michigan Blueberry Growers Assn., Grand Junction, MI, pg. 747
Dake, William P., Pres.--Stewart's Ice Cream Co., Inc., Saratoga Springs, NY, pg. 1048
Dale, Robert V., Pres.--Windmill Corp. d/b/a Martha White Foods, Inc., Brentwood, TN, pg. 1195
Dally, Scott, Pres. & Chief Exec. Officer--Dally Advertising, Inc., Fort Worth, TX, pg. 312
Dalquist, H. David, III, Pres.--Northland Aluminum Products, Inc., Minneapolis, MN, pg. 814
Dalton, James, Jr., Pres. & Chief Exec. Officer--Quorum Health Group, Inc., Brentwood, TN, pg. 905
Daly, David G., Pres. & Chief Oper. Officer--Herff Jones Inc., Indianapolis, IN, pg. 531
Daly, Harold E., Jr., Mng. Partner--Cosmopulos Crowley Daly/CKG, Boston, MA, pg. 288
Daly, Leo A., Chm. Bd., Pres. & Treas.--Leo A. Daly Company, Omaha, NE, pg. 313
Dambra, Barton, Pres. & Chief Exec. Officer--Markin Tubing, Inc., Wyoming, NY, pg. 709
Dammeier, Brian, Pres.--Print Northwest, Fife, WA, pg. 891
Danforth, Robert, Pres.--Litecontrol Corporation, Hanson, MA, pg. 677
Dangar, James I., Pres.--Law Engineering, Inc., Atlanta, GA, pg. 661
Daniel, Larry, Pres. & Chief Exec. & Chief Fin. Officer--The Daniel Co. of Springfield, Springfield, MO, pg. 314
Daniell, James, Pres.--American Strip Steel Inc., Kearny, NJ, pg. 63
Daniels, David P., Pres. & Chief Oper. Officer--Penn-Daniels, Inc., Quincy, IL, pg. 857
Daniels, Lee S., Pres.--Daniels Printing Company, Everett, MA, pg. 314
Daniels, William A., Chm. Bd. & Pres.--Daniels Manufacturing Corporation, Orlando, FL, pg. 314
Dann, Earl, Pres.--Dann Dee Display Fixtures, Chicago, IL, pg. 314
Danuser, Jerry, Pres.--Danuser Machine Co., Fulton, MO, pg. 315
Danziger, Lawrence, Pres./ML Div.--Deare Marketing Inc./ Matthew-Lawrence Advertising & Sales Promotion Inc., New York, NY, pg. 323
Darby, Fred W., Pres.--Niagara Transformer Corp., Buffalo, NY, pg. 806
Darby, John J., Mng. Dir.--Darby & Associates, Christchurch,, New Zealand, pg. 111
Dargatz, Kenneth C., Pres. & Chief Exec. Officer--Haden, Inc., Madison Heights, MI, pg. 499
Darian, Ralph, Pres., Chief Exex. & Chief Fin. Officer--Levonian Brothers Inc., Troy, NY, pg. 671
Dariano, Leonard, Pres.--Metro Ford Sales, Inc., Schenectady, NY, pg. 743
Darien, Frank, Pres.--Darien & Kilburg, Inc., San Jose, CA, pg. 315
Darling, Albert, Jr., Pres.--Darling Envelope Corporation, Shawnee Mission, KS, pg. 315
Darling, John B., Pres.--Darling's, Bangor, ME, pg. 315
Darnell, Larry, Pres.--Lakeside Industries, Redmond, WA, pg. 651
Darouny, Roger, Mng. Dir.--AMA Leo Burnett, Giza,, Egypt, pg. 192
Dart, Robert C., Pres.--Dart Container Corp., Mason, MI, pg. 316
Darwin, Sidney, Pres.--Cardinal Inc., Port Reading, NJ, pg. 217
Darwish, Charles, Pres.--United States Realty & Investment Co., Newark, NJ, pg. 1137
Dasburg, John, Pres. & Chief Exec. Officer--Northwest Airlines, Inc., Saint Paul, MN, pg. 782
Dasburg, John H., Pres. & Chief Exec. Officer--NWA, Inc., Saint Paul, MN, pg. 782
Daugherty, Mike, Pres.--Mike Daugherty's Hurling Chevrolet, Inc., Sacramento, CA, pg. 555
Daunhauer, John R., Jr., Chm. Bd. & Pres.--Byerly Ford-Nissan Inc., Louisville, KY, pg. 198

Daus, John, Jr., Pres. & Chief Exec. Officer--Anchor Industries Inc., Evansville, IN, pg. 71
Davenport, J.T., Jr., Pres. & Treas.--J.T. Davenport & Sons, Inc., Sanford, NC, pg. 317
Davenport, R.B., IV, Pres. & Chief Oper. Officer--Krystal Company, Chattanooga, TN, pg. 645
Davey, Jim, Dir.--Oregon State Lottery, Salem, OR, pg. 829
David, Paul, Pres. & Chief Exec. Officer--Camelot Music, Inc., North Canton, OH, pg. 212
Davidson, Edward W., Jr., Pres.--Rosser Fabrap International, Atlanta, GA, pg. 950
Davidson, F. Lee, Pres. & Chief Exec. Officer--Parks Corporation, Somerset, MA, pg. 849
Davidson, Martin, Pres. & Chief Exec. Officer--Southern Pipe & Supply Co., Inc., Meridian, MS, pg. 1022
Davidson, Rick, Pres.--Sunbeam Outdoor Products Co., Neosho, MO, pg. 1059
Davidson, William, Chm., Pres., Chief Exec. & Chief Oper. Officer--Guardian Industries Corp., Northville, MI, pg. 491
Davidson, William, Pres.--Bell South Business Product Division, Atlanta, GA, pg. 136
Davies, George P., Chm. Bd. & Pres.--Trico Electric Co-Op, Tucson, AZ, pg. 1113
Davis, Alan B., Chief Oper. Officer--Princeville Corporation, Princeville, HI, pg. 890
Davis, Alan V., Pres. & Chief Oper. Officer--The Bibb Company, Macon, GA, pg. 781
Davis, Albert E., Pres.--Diemakers, Inc., Monroe City, MO, pg. 336
Davis, Allen V.C., Chm. Bd. & Pres.--Custom Control Sensors, Inc., Chatsworth, CA, pg. 306
Davis, Charles E., Sr., Chm. Bd. & Pres.--Laboratory Supply Company, Inc., Louisville, KY, pg. 649
Davis, Dick, Pres. & Chief Exec. Officer--Esco Elevators, Inc., Fort Worth, TX, pg. 388
Davis, Edgar E., Pres. & Chief Oper. Officer--West Point-Pepperell, Inc., West Point, GA, pg. 400
Davis, Edward, Pres. & Chief Oper. Officer--Advertising Checking Bureau Incorporated, New York, NY, pg. 21
Davis, Edward, Pres.--Bernard Johnson Incorporated, Houston, TX, pg. 598
Davis, George L., Pres. & Chief Exec. Officer--First American Bankshares, Inc., Washington, DC, pg. 412
Davis, Gerald, Pres.--Merchants Distributors, Inc., Hickory, NC, pg. 33
Davis, Glen, Pres.--Addison Steel Inc., Orlando, FL, pg. 17
Davis, Irvin, Chm. Bd. & Pres.--Clayton-Davis & Associates, Incorporated, Saint Louis, MO, pg. 253
Davis, J. Roy, Jr., Pres.--S&D Coffee Inc., Concord, NC, pg. 959
Davis, J.B., Pres.--Klaussner Corporation, Asheboro, NC, pg. 634
Davis, James B., Jr., Pres.--Jimmy Davis Enterprises, Inc., Madison, FL, pg. 318
Davis, Jay M., Pres. & Chief Oper. Officer--National Distributing Co., Inc., Atlanta, GA, pg. 787
Davis, Jeffrey G., Chm., Pres. & Chief Exec. Officer--Aetna Plywood, Inc., Arlington Heights, IL, pg. 23
Davis, Jeffrey J., Pres.--Joseph Davis, Inc., Buffalo, NY, pg. 318
Davis, Jerome R., Pres.--Davis & Phillips, Inc., Norfolk, VA, pg. 319
Davis, Jerry, Pres. & Chief Oper. Officer--Affiliated Foods Southwest, Little Rock, AR, pg. 24
Davis, Joanne M., Pres.--OMON, New York Ltd., New York, NY, pg. 826
Davis, Joe, Pres.--LB Industries Inc., Boise, ID, pg. 647
Davis, Joe H., Jr., Pres.--Leader Services, Inc., Memphis, TN, pg. 664
Davis, John H., Pres. & Treas.--American Saw & Manufacturing Co., East Longmeadow, MA, pg. 60
Davis, Kim E., Pres.-DATEC Ind., Inc.--Davis Industries Inc., Detroit, MI, pg. 318
Davis, Kindle, Pres.--Bud Davis Cadillac, Inc., Memphis, TN, pg. 318
Davis, Larry D., Pres.--U.S. Turbine Corporation, Maineville, OH, pg. 1137
Davis, Marvin, Pres.--Davis Companies, Los Angeles, CA, pg. 318
Davis, Richard, Chm. Bd. & Pres.-Davis Industries--Davis Industries Inc., Detroit, MI, pg. 318
Davis, Richard L., II, Pres.--Davis Industries Inc., Detroit, MI, pg. 318
Davis, Roger W., Pres.--Frank Paxton Company, Kansas City, MO, pg. 592
Davis, Ronald J., Pres. & Chief Exec. Officer--Biggs Gilmore Communications, Kalamazoo, MI, pg. 149
Davis, T. Grant, Jr., Pres.--Davis-Moore Oldsmobile, Inc., Wichita, KS, pg. 319
Davis, W.F., Jr., Pres., Chief Exec. Officer & Treas.--Palmetto Spinning Corp., Laurens, SC, pg. 844
Davis, William, Pres. & Chief Exec. Officer--Cabot Creamery Co-Operative Inc., Cabot, VT, pg. 25
Davis, William D., Pres. & Chief Exec. Officer--Merchandising Equipment Group, Arlington Heights, IL, pg. 739
Davis, William H., Pres. & Chief Oper. Officer--Gilman Paper Co., Saint Marys, GA, pg. 459
Davis, William H., Pres. & Dir.-Quality--Holland Mark Martin, Burlington, MA, pg. 539
Davis, William Jack, Chm. Bd. & Pres.--Davis Mining & Manufacturing, Colburn, VA, pg. 319
Davis, William V., Pres.--Coble Dairy Products Co-op, Lexington, NC, pg. 257
Davison, Denis, Pres.--Clear Shield National, Inc., Wheeling, IL, pg. 383
Dawahare, A.F., Pres. & Dir.-Sls. & Mktg.--Dawahares, Inc., Lexington, KY, pg. 319
Dawe, Donald, Pres.--AVA-Automatic Vendors of America, Atlanta, GA, pg. 8
Dawley, D.B., Pres.--Revco Scientific Inc., Asheville, NC, pg. 930
Dawson, Charles, Pres.--Larkin, Inc., Atlanta, GA, pg. 667
Dawson, Chuck, Pres.--Rocky Mountain Bank Note Company, Lakewood, CO, pg. 942
Day, Joseph C., Chief Exec. Officer--Freudenberg-NOK (MI), Plymouth, MI, pg. 432
Day, Timothy T., Pres. & Chief Exec. Officer--Bar-S Foods Co., Phoenix, AZ, pg. 118
Dayan, Ezra, Pres.--Lady Marlene Sales Corp., New York, NY, pg. 650
De Arment, W.S., Chief Exec. Officer--Hold-E-Zee, Ltd., Rochester, NY, pg. 239
de Caussin, Adrian X., Pres.--Fadal Engineering Company, Inc., North Hollywood, CA, pg. 396
De Deo, Joseph E., Pres., Y&R Europe--Young & Rubicam International European Hdqrs., London, United Kingdom, pg. 1213
De Forrest, Sean B., Pres.--American Lock & Supply Inc., Anaheim, CA, pg. 57
De Jesse, Paul A., Pres.--Paul A. De Jesse, Inc. Advertising, Freehold, NJ, pg. 321
De Kertanguy, Loic, Pres.--J.B. Martin Company, New York, NY, pg. 715
de Kervasdoue, Jean, Pres.--Medecine et Systemes Informatiques Intergres, Montpellier,, France, pg. 982
De Mento, Biagio, Sr., Pres. & Chief Exec. Officer--Brooks Provisions Inc., Philadelphia, PA, pg. 180
De Nooyer, James S., Pres.--De Nooyer Chevrolet Inc., Albany, NY, pg. 329
De Pasquale, John A., Chm. Bd.--The Direct Marketing Group Inc., New York, NY, pg. 339
de Plas, Pierre, Pres. & Gen. Mgr.--TBWA de Plas, Paris,, France, pg. 1072
De Sanders, Lee, Pres.--Lone Star Cadillac Co., Dallas, TX, pg. 682
De Stigter, Glenn H., Pres. & Chief Oper. Officer--The Weitz-Cohen Construction Co., Des Moines, IA, pg. 1174
De Vito, Robert A., Chm. Bd., Pres., Chief Exec. & Chief Oper. Officer--Cyber Systems, Inc., Anaheim, CA, pg. 307
De Vries, Henry, Pres.--Midwest Fasteners Corporation, Kalamazoo, MI, pg. 752
Deacon, David, Pres. & Chief Exec. Officer--Deacon Day Advertising and The McLauchlan Group, Toronto,, Canada, pg. 685
Dean, Frederick, Pres.--American Argo Corp., New York, NY, pg. 283
DeAngelo, Tom, Pres.--Clark Foodservice, Inc., Elk Grove Village, IL, pg. 252
Dearden, Douglas E., Chief Exec. Officer & Personnel Dir.--Dearden's, Inc., Los Angeles, CA, pg. 322
Deardorff, T.D., Chm. Bd. & Pres.--Deardorff-Jackson Company, Oxnard, CA, pg. 323
Deare, Jennifer, Pres./DMI--Deare Marketing Inc./Matthew-Lawrence Advertising & Sales Promotion Inc., New York, NY, pg. 323
DeArment, William S., Pres. & Gen. Mgr.--Channellock, Inc., Meadville, PA, pg. 239
Deary, Roy G., Jr., Pres.--Nor-Cal Beverage Co., Inc., West Sacramento, CA, pg. 808
Deaver, Dan, Pres. & Chief Exec. Officer--Franks Supply Company, Inc., Albuquerque, NM, pg. 429
DeBartolo, E.J., Chm. Bd.--Louisiana Downs, Bossier City, LA, pg. 323
DeBartolo, Edward J., Jr., Pres. & Chief Admin. Officer--The Edward J. DeBartolo Corporation, Youngstown, OH, pg. 323
DeBlase, Thomas E., Pres. & Chief Oper. Officer--Binkley Company, Warrenton, MO, pg. 151
Deborde, Shelby J., Jr., Pres.--Bearing Distributors, Inc., Columbia, SC, pg. 130
DeCamp, D.A., Pres. & Chief Exec. Officer--Flexfab, Inc., Hastings, MI, pg. 418
DeCardenas, Gilbert, Pres.--Cacique Cheese Co., Inc., City of Industry, CA, pg. 206
DeCarion, Philip, Pres.--Cornucopia, Inc., Irvine, CA, pg. 287
DeCarlo, Anthony J., Pres. & Chief Exec. Officer--Lumbermens Merchandising Corporation, Wayne, PA, pg. 687
DeCastro, H.L., Pres.--CAE Link Allen Division, Alexandria, VA, pg. 198
DeCastro, Howard, Pres. & Chief Exec. Officer--Northwest Aerospace Training Corporation, Saint Paul, MN, pg. 782
DeCesaris, Geaton A., Jr., Pres. & Chief Exec. Officer--Washington Homes, Inc., Landover, MD, pg. 1166
DeCesaris, Geaton A., Sr., Chm. Bd.--Washington Homes, Inc., Landover, MD, pg. 1166
Dechamps, Daniel, Pres. & Treas.--Trumpf Inc., Farmington, CT, pg. 1118
Decker, Gilbert F., Pres. & Chief Exec. Officer--Acurex Environmental Corporation, Mountain View, CA, pg. 15
Decker, Jack E., Pres. & Chief Exec. Officer--Campbell Oil Co., Massillon, OH, pg. 213
Dedert, William G., Pres.--Dedert Corporation, Olympia Fields, IL, pg. 324
Dedman, Robert H., Jr., Pres. & Chief Oper. Officer--Club Corporation International, Dallas, TX, pg. 256
Dee, Jonathan, Pres.--Ce De Candy, Inc., Union, NJ, pg. 230
Dee, Robert, Pres.--Dee Paper Company, Chester, PA, pg. 324
Deen, George C., Pres.--Deen Wholesale Meat Company, Inc., Fort Worth, TX, pg. 324
DeForest, James V., Pres.--Peckham Industries, Inc., White Plains, NY, pg. 854
DeForest, Samuel D., Pres.--Walpole Woodworkers, Inc., Walpole, MA, pg. 1161
DeFrancisci, Leonard, Pres. & Chief Exec. Officer--De Francisci Machine Corp.(Demaco), Ridgewood, NY, pg. 321
DeFusco, Ronald, Pres.--Plymouth Lamston Stores, Corp., Saddle Brook, NJ, pg. 877
DeGeorge, Lawrence J., Chm. Bd., Pres. & Chief Exec. Officer--LPL Technologies, Inc., Wallingford, CT, pg. 648
DeGrazia, Nicholas J., Pres. & Chief Oper. Officer--Lionel Trains, Inc., Chesterfield, MI, pg. 677
Dehaan, Christal, Chm. Bd., Pres. & Chief Exec. Officer--Resort Condominiums International, Indianapolis, IN, pg. 929
DeHaven, J., Pres.--Yardley Products Corporation, Yardley, PA, pg. 341
Dehmlow, Steven L., Pres. & Chief Oper. Officer--Great Lakes Terminal & Transport Corp., Chicago, IL, pg. 482
Deinhammer, Robert L., Pres.--Applied Microsystems Corporation, Redmond, WA, pg. 79
Deirlein, J.N., Pres.--Republic Contracting Corp., Columbia, SC, pg. 928
Deitsch, David, Pres.--Deitsch Plastics Company, West Haven, CT, pg. 325
DeJonge, Max, Pres.--O'Neal Steel Inc., Birmingham, AL, pg. 827
DeJoris, John Paul, Chm. Bd. & Pres.--John Paul Mitchell Systems, Beverly Hills, CA, pg. 762
Dekker, Marcel, Chm. Bd. & Pres.--Marcel Dekker, Inc., New York, NY, pg. 325
Dekko, Chester E., Chm. Bd., Pres. & Chief Exec. Officer--Group Dekko International Inc., Kendallville, IN, pg. 489
Dektas, Michael C., Pres.--Dektas & Eger, Inc., Cincinnati, OH, pg. 325
Del Dotto, Reno, Pres.--Tri-K Industries, Inc., Emerson, NJ, pg. 1110
Del Guidice, Christopher, Chm. Bd. & Pres.--Del American Properties, Inc., Maitland, FL, pg. 325
Del Mar, Bruce, Pres. & Treas.--Del Mar Avionics, Irvine, CA, pg. 325
Del Monte, Raymond, Pres. & Chief Exec. Officer--Wolff Associates, Inc., Rochester, NY, pg. 1199
DeLaguardia, Mario, Pres.--Aminco, Inc., Savannah, GA, pg. 67
DeLaguradia, Mike, Pres.--Carson Products Company, Savannah, GA, pg. 67
Delahaut, Robert J., Pres.--M K Diamond Products, Inc., Torrance, CA, pg. 692
Delaney, John W., Pres. & Chief Exec. Officer--TransCoastal Mortgage Company, Bellevue, WA, pg. 1107
Delber, David H., Pres.--Union Steel Products, Incorporated, Albion, MI, pg. 1129
DelGaldo, Joseph A., Pres. & Chief Exec. Officer--Carlson, DelGaldo, Hoag, Matthei Advertising, Inc., Stamford, CT, pg. 222
DeLibero, Shirley A., Exec. Dir.--NJ Transit, Newark, NJ, pg. 801
Dellamano, Patricia, Pres. & Chief Exec. & Chief Fin. Officer--Patson's Press, Sunnyvale, CA, pg. 851
Dellaquila, Stephen J., Pres. & Treas.--Della Construction Co. Inc., Enfield, CT, pg. 326
Dellaripa, Jim, Pres.--GNWC Wire, Cable & Network Producers, Downers Grove, IL, pg. 440
DeLoache, John S., Pres.--Shealy Electrical Wholesalers, Greenville, SC, pg. 996
Delonis, Robert J., Pres. & Chief Exec. Officer--Great Lakes Bancorp, Ann Arbor, MI, pg. 480
DeLorenzo, David A., Pres., Dole Food Co. & Exec. V.P., Dole Food Co., Inc.--Dole Food Company, Inc., Westlake Village, CA, pg. 840
Delpit, Larry, Pres.--Casey Co., Bakersfield, CA, pg. 228
Delsol, Robert J., Pres.--Pacific Steel Casting Co., Berkeley, CA, pg. 841
DeLuca, Frederick, Pres.--Subway Franchisee Advertising Fund Trust, Milford, CT, pg. 1055
DeLuca, Robert, Chm. Bd., Pres. & Chief Exec. Officer--Aero Data Metal Crafters, Bohemia, NY, pg. 22
DeMarco, Albert J., Pres. & Chief Oper. Officer--Nutri/System Inc., Blue Bell, PA, pg. 818
DeMarco, Tony, Pres.--Certified Grocers of Florida, Inc., Ocala, FL, pg. 237
DeMaria, Richard J., Pres.--DeMaria Building Co. Inc., Novi, MI, pg. 327
DeMars, Dan R., Pres.--The DeMars Corp., Indianapolis, IN, pg. 327
Dembicks, Andrew E., Pres.--Southern Case, Inc., Raleigh, NC, pg. 1020
Dembinski, Jan A., Pres., Chief Exec. Officer & Treas.--M.J. Daly & Sons, Inc., Waterbury, CT, pg. 313
Demere, Robert H., Jr., Pres. & Chief Oper. Officer--Colonial Oil Industries, Savannah, GA, pg. 263
Demetrios, Michael B., Pres.--Marine World Africa USA, Vallejo, CA, pg. 707
Demmer, William J., Pres.--Jack Demmer Ford, Inc., Wayne, MI, pg. 328
DeMoulas, Telemachus A., Pres. & Chief Exec. Officer--Demoulas Super Markets, Tewksbury, MA, pg. 328
DeMuth, Christopher, Pres.--American Enterprise Institute for Public Policy Research, Washington, DC, pg. 51
Denaro-Baucom, Betty, Pres.--E-B Advertising Display Inc., Massillon, OH, pg. 358
Denburg, Stanley M., Pres.--Barton Press, Inc., West Orange, NJ, pg. 123
Denenberg, Alfred H., Pres.--Adelphia Lamp & Shade Inc., Philadelphia, PA, pg. 17
Denis Thomas, S., Pres.--Textilease Corporation, Beltsville, MD, pg. 1090
Denise, Robert, Chm., Pres., Chief Exec. Officer & Chief Fin. Officer--Bucilla Corporation, Hazleton, PA, pg. 185
Denlinger, John M., Pres. & Gen. Mgr.--Denlinger, Inc., Paradise, PA, pg. 329
Dennis, Aaron S., Pres. & Treas.--Dennis Chemical Company, Inc., Saint Louis, MO, pg. 329
Dennis, H.C., Pres.--W.J. Dennis Co., Elgin, IL, pg. 329
Denrich, Louis, Pres.--So-Lo-Food, Inc., Baltimore, MD, pg. 1016
Dent, Frederick B., Jr., Pres.--Mayfair Mills, Inc., Arcadia, SC, pg. 724
Dent, James R., Chm. Bd & Pres.--Crosby & Overton, Inc., Long Beach, CA, pg. 300
Dentino, Karl G., Pres.--Rosenfield/Dentino, Inc., Jersey City, NJ, pg. 948
Dentner, Richard R., Pres.--Heico Inc., Lisle, IL, pg. 525
Denton, Clyde, Pres.--Zetec, Inc., Issaquah, WA, pg. 1217

Denton, John, Pres.--Myers Foods Company, Plumsteadville, PA, pg. 506
Denton, John E., Pres.--Hanover Foods Corporation, Hanover, PA, pg. 506
Denton, Leet E., Pres.--Denton Enterprises Inc., Grosse Pointe, MI, pg. 329
DePaul, John, Pres.--DDF&M Inc. Dudreck DePaul Ficco & Morgan Inc., Pittsburgh, PA, pg. 308
DePerno, James, V.P.--Dunkirk Ice Cream Co., Inc., Dunkirk, NY, pg. 353
DePriest, Ted, Pres. & Chief Oper. Officer--Pacific Sound Resources, Seattle, WA, pg. 841
Deramo, Frank, Exec. V.P.--Syroco Inc., Baldwinsville, NY, pg. 1070
Deramus, William H., Pres.--Miller & Co., Selma, AL, pg. 753
Derrey, Robert F., Pres. & Chief Exec. Officer--Barr Brothers & Co., Inc., New York, NY, pg. 121
Derst, Edward J., III, Pres. & Chief Exec. Officer--Derst Baking Company, Inc., Savannah, GA, pg. 331
DeRuiter, David, Pres.--Davlin Paint Company, Inc., Berkeley, CA, pg. 319
DeSantis, Carl, Pres.--Sundown Vitamin Co., Inc., Fort Lauderdale, FL, pg. 1060
DeSantis, Carl, Pres.--Rexall Group, Fort Lauderdale, FL, pg. 1060
DeSantis, Carl, Pres.--Thompson Nutritional Products, Fort Lauderdale, FL, pg. 1060
DeSilva, Bernard, Dr., Pres.--Lukenheimer Co., Cincinnati, OH, pg. 687
Desnoes, Peter B., Mng. Gen. Partner--Burnham Broadcasting Company, Chicago, IL, pg. 193
Desperak, Jack, Pres. & Chief Exec. Officer--Splendor Form International Inc., Long Island City, NY, pg. 1031
DesRoches, Greg, Pres.--Cornerstone, Baltimore, MD, pg. 286
Dessy, William J., Vice Chm., Pres. & Chief Exec. Officer--T.L. James & Company, Ruston, LA, pg. 588
DeStefano, Daniel A., Pres.--Deerskin Trading Post, Inc., Carlstadt, NJ, pg. 324
Deters, Roger E., Pres.--Norcostco, Inc., Minneapolis, MN, pg. 809
Dethlefsen, Walt, Acting Pres. & V.P.-Adv. & Mktg.--Network Services Company of Chicago, Mount Prospect, IL, pg. 798
DeTitta, Louis, Jr., Pres., Chief Oper. Officer--SSD&W Integrated Marketing Communications, Montville, NJ, pg. 964
Dettloff, Paul, Pres.--Color Custom, Inc., Warren, MI, pg. 264
Deutsch, Carl, Pres.--The Deutsch Company, Santa Monica, CA, pg. 333
DeVault, George H., Pres.--Egyptian Lacquer Manufacturing Company, Inc., Lafayette, IN, pg. 371
Dever, Michael L., Pres.--Automanage, Fairfield, OH, pg. 100
Devereux, John Wm., Jr., Pres.--Flowers of Hawaii, San Marino, CA, pg. 421
Deverse, Frank T., Chm. Bd., Pres., Chief Exec. Officer & Treas.--International Microcircuits, Inc., Milpitas, CA, pg. 579
DeVille, Paul, Pres.--ASA Properties Hawaii Inc., Honolulu, HI, pg. 863
Devine, Brian, Mng. Dir.--TMP/Telephone Marketing Programs, Ltd., Ilford,, United Kingdom, pg. 1074
Devine, Hugh T., Pres. & New Bus. Contact--Devine & Pearson, Inc., Quincy, MA, pg. 333
Devona, Thomas C., Pres. & Treas.--Rite-Way, Inc., Saddle Brook, NJ, pg. 936
DeVos, Richard, Pres.--Amway Corporation, Ada, MI, pg. 70
Dew, Donald F., Chm. Bd., Pres. & Chief Exec. Officer--Diemolding Corp., Canastota, NY, pg. 336
Dewberry, Sidney O., Mng. Partner--Dewberry & Davis, Fairfax, VA, pg. 334
DeWeerd, LaVerne, Pres.--Dickinson Press, Inc., Grand Rapids, MI, pg. 336
DeWitt, Gene, Pres.--DeWitt Media, Inc., New York, NY, pg. 334
DeWitt, Larry, Pres.--Cargill Flour Milling Div., Minneapolis, MN, pg. 219
DeYager, Peter W., Pres.--Foreign Candy Co., Inc., Huff, IA, pg. 424
Di Sorbo, James, Pres. & Chief Exec. Officer--Hoechst Ceramtec North America, Inc., Mansfield, MA, pg. 537
Di Zazzo, James G., Chm. Bd. & Pres.--Oomphies, Inc., Lawrence, MA, pg. 827
Diamantis, George, Pres.--National Group, Inc., Chattanooga, TN, pg. 789
Diamond, Abraham L., Pres. & Chief Exec. Officer--Diamond Chemical Co., Inc., Lyndhurst, NJ, pg. 335
Diamond, Lawrence, Chm. Bd., Pres., Chief Exec. & Chief Oper. Officer & Dir.-Pur.--Triangle Marketing Corp., New York, NY, pg. 1112
Diamond, Russell W., Pres.--Snyder-Diamond, Santa Monica, CA, pg. 1015
Diamond, Thedore L., Pres.--T.L. Diamond Company, New York, NY, pg. 335
Diaz, Gonzalo E., Pres.--Med-Lab Supply Company, Inc., Miami, FL, pg. 734
DiBattista, Raymond, Pres. & Chief Exec. Officer--United Metal Fabricators, Inc., Johnstown, PA, pg. 1133
DiBuduo, Anthony J., Pres.--Independent Insurance Agents and Brokers of California, San Francisco, CA, pg. 565
DiBui, William J., Pres., Chief Exec. & Chief Oper. Officer--Rumsey Electric Co., Philadelphia, PA, pg. 956
Diccicco, Michael, Pres.--Letven-Diccicco, Inc., Horsham, PA, pg. 669
Dickerson, Arthur J., Chm. Bd., Pres. & Chief Exec. Officer--Southwestern Petroleum Corporation, Fort Worth, TX, pg. 1024
Dickerson, John, Pres.--GPD Limited, Norcross, GA, pg. 440
Dickerson, Michael A., Pres. & Chief Exec. Officer--High Point Financial Corp., Branchville, NJ, pg. 533
Dickerson, Michael A., Vice Chm., Pres. & Chief Exec. Officer--The Pocono Bank, Milford, PA, pg. 534
Dickson, John R., Pres. & Chief Exec. Officer--Roundy's, Inc., Pewaukee, WI, pg. 952
Dickten, Erich, Chm. Bd.--Dickten & Masch Manufacturing Co., Nashotah, WI, pg. 336
DiCorpo, Louis A., Pres.--Brookfield Engineering Laboratories, Inc., Stoughton, MA, pg. 179
Didde, David D., Pres. & Chief Exec. Officer--Didde Web Press, Emporia, KS, pg. 336
Diddle, L.E., Pres.--Bulab Realty Of Missouri, Inc., Memphis, TN, pg. 188
Diddle, L.E., Pres.--Bulab Realty Of Tennessee, Inc., Memphis, TN, pg. 188
Diebel, Robert, Pres.--Diebel Manufacturing Co., Morton Grove, IL, pg. 336
Diedrick, Arthur Hill, Chm. Bd., Pres. & Chief Exec. Officer--Communications International, New York, NY, pg. 269
Diedrick, G. Vern, Chm. Bd., Chief Exec. Officer, & Pres.--Maecorp Inc., Chicago, IL, pg. 699
Diem, John R., Pres.--Southern Agricultural Insecticides, Palmetto, FL, pg. 1020
Diemer, Edmund, Pres. & Treas.--Metal Seal & Products, Inc., Willoughby, OH, pg. 741
Dierberg, Robert J., Pres., Chief Exec. Officer & Treas.--Dierbergs Markets Inc., Chesterfield, MO, pg. 337
Dietrich, Thomas W., Pres. & Chief Exec. Officer--Dietrich's Milk Products, Inc., Reading, PA, pg. 337
Dietterich, Richard, Pres.--Dorman-Roth Foods, Inc., Moonachie, NJ, pg. 346
Dietz, Alan, Pres. & Co-Creative Dir.--Ryder & Schild, Inc., Miami, FL, pg. 958
Dietz, W.R., Chm. Bd., Pres. & Chief Exec. Officer--American Savings Bank, White Plains, NY, pg. 60
DiFeo, Samuel X, Pres.--DiFeo Automotive Network, Jersey City, NJ, pg. 337
DiFillippo, Thomas A., Chm. Bd. & Pres.--DeVault Foods, Devault, PA, pg. 333
DiGioia, Anthony M., Jr., Pres.--GAI Consultants, Inc., Monroeville, PA, pg. 439
DiJohn, Joseph, Exec. Dir.--Pace, Arlington Heights, IL, pg. 922
Dikschei, Denis, Mng. Dir.--E.C. DeWitt & Company (Aust.) Pty. Ltd., Braeside,, Australia, pg. 417
Dillard, Henry, III, Pres.--Electronic Drives and Controls, Parsippany, NJ, pg. 375
Dille, Steven B., Pres. & Chief Oper. Officer--Scicom Data Services, Ltd., Minnetonka, MN, pg. 981
Dillon, Mike, Chm. Bd. & Pres.--Tom's Foods, Columbus, GA, pg. 1101
DiLorenzo, James E., Chm. Bd., Pres. & Chief Exec. Officer--Quality Pontiac, Inc., Albuquerque, NM, pg. 904
DiMeglio, S. J., Pres.--Guest Services, Inc., Fairfax, VA, pg. 493
Dineen, R.J., Pres. & Chief Exec. Officer--The Marley Company, Mission Woods, KS, pg. 710
Dinger, William S., Pres.--William H. Sadlier, Inc., New York, NY, pg. 966
Dingwell, Everett W., Pres. & Chief Exec. Officer--Certified Grocers Of California, Los Angeles, CA, pg. 237
Dingwell, Everett W., Pres.--Pacific Economy Company, Los Angeles, CA, pg. 237
Dinin, David, Pres.--Linotype-Hell Company, Hauppauge, NY, pg. 677
DiPaolo, Tony, Pres.--Jos. M. Herman Shoe Co., Greenwich, CT, pg. 531
Dippold, George J., Chm. Bd. & Pres.--Whittaker, Clark & Daniels, Inc., South Plainfield, NJ, pg. 1187
Dircks, W.R., Pres.--Berger Transfer & Storage, Inc., Saint Paul, MN, pg. 141
Dirkes, James V., Pres., Chief Exec. Officer & Treas.--Rapid Engineering Inc., Comstock Park, MI, pg. 913
Disbrow, R.E., Pres.--Ohio Valley Electric Corporation, Piketon, OH, pg. 822
Dischler, Ralph, Pres.--Maplehurst Farms, Inc., Indianapolis, IN, pg. 705
Dishinger, C.W., V.P.--Richmond Screw Anchor Company, Fort Worth, TX, pg. 933
Dishman, Charles H., Pres. & Chief Exec. Officer--Tri-City Oldsmobile Inc., Louisville, KY, pg. 1110
Dishon, James, Pres. & Chief Exec. Officer--Agripac Inc., Salem, OR, pg. 25
DiTrapano, Charles, Pres.--GPS Healthcare, Pottsville, PA, pg. 145
Dittmer, Thomas, Pres.--Refco Inc., Chicago, IL, pg. 921
Divane Jr., William T., Pres. & Treas.--Divane Bros. Electric Co., Franklin Park, IL, pg. 340
Dixon, Gene, Jr., Pres.--Kyanite Mining Corporation, Dillwyn, VA, pg. 647
Dixon, John, Pres. & Chief Oper. Officer--Columbus Mills, Inc., Columbus, GA, pg. 267
Dixon, Robert P., Pres. & Chief Exec. Officer--SF Services, North Little Rock, AR, pg. 961
Doak, William R., Pres.--Bent Tube, Inc., Fowlerville, MI, pg. 140
Doan, D.T., Pres.--Central Life Assurance Co., Des Moines, IA, pg. 232
Dobbins, Ronald, Pres. & Chief Oper. Officer--United American Healthcare Corp., Detroit, MI, pg. 826
Dobbins, Ronald R., Pres.--OmniCare Health Plan, Detroit, MI, pg. 826
Dockter, James E., Pres.--Professional Book Distributors, Inc., Alpharetta, GA, pg. 894
Doehrman, Dale F., Chm. Bd. & Chief Exec. Officer--The Medical Protective Company, Fort Wayne, IN, pg. 735
Doerr, Ronald H., Pres. & Chief Oper. Officer--National Steel Corporation, Mishawaka, IN, pg. 793
Doherty, John F., Pres. & Chief Exec. Officer--Sequentia Inc., Strongsville, OH, pg. 990
Doherty, John F., Pres. & Chief Exec. Officer--Sequentia Inc. Reinforced Plastics Div., Strongsville, OH, pg. 990
Doherty, Robert C., Pres. & Chief Exec. Officer--McKinney & Silver, Raleigh, NC, pg. 730
Doka, Michael, Pres.--Rehrig Pacific Company, Los Angeles, CA, pg. 922
Dokmo, Harold B., Jr., Chm. Bd., Pres., Treas. & Sec.--Norcraft Companies, Inc., Saint Paul, MN, pg. 809
Dokmo, Richard C., Pres.--Tape Coat Division, Evanston, IL, pg. 1072
Dolan, John F., Chm. Bd. & Pres.--Fairfax Lumber & Millwork Company Inc., Springfield, VA, pg. 397
Dolge, Alfred K., Pres.--The C.B. Dolge Co., Westport, CT, pg. 941
Dolik, Michael, Pres.--The Virtual Group, Rochester Hills, MI, pg. 1153
Dolinko, Paul, Pres.--Best Provision Co., Inc., Newark, NJ, pg. 146
Dolson, Robert A., Pres. & Chief Exec. Officer--Continental Water Company, Saint Louis, MO, pg. 280
Domashco, Rick, Pres.--Gannett Transit, New York, NY, pg. 442
Domecq, Michael, Pres. & Chief Exec. Officer--Domecq Importers Inc., Old Greenwich, CT, pg. 343
Dominioni, A.M., Pres.--Bel Paese Sales Company, Inc., Lakewood, NJ, pg. 133
Donahoe, Edward J., Chm. Bd., Pres. & Acct. Supvr.--Donahoe & Purohit, Inc., Rosemont, IL, pg. 344
Donahue, James C., Pres. & Chief Exec. Officer--Donahue, Inc., Advertising, Hartford, CT, pg. 344
Donahue, Matthew, Pres.--The Dee Howard Company, San Antonio, TX, pg. 547
Donahue, Richard J., Chm. Bd.--Great Salt Lake Minerals & Chemicals Corp., Ogden, UT, pg. 482
Donaldson, Bruce, Pres.--Donaldson Group, San Francisco, CA, pg. 344
Donaldson, Darrell, Pres., Chief Exec. & Fin. Officer--Hot Shot Delivery Inc., Houston, TX, pg. 545
Donaldson, J. Bennett, Pres., Chief Exec. Officer & Sec.--Cunningham-Limp Development Co., Troy, MI, pg. 305
Donalson, Jane, Pres.--Dexol Industries, Inc., Torrance, CA, pg. 334
Donati, Ronald H., Pres.--Zycon Corporation, Santa Clara, CA, pg. 1221
Donegan, James, Chm. Bd., Pres., Chief Exec. & Oper. Officer--Sipex Corporation, Billerica, MA, pg. 1009
Donino, Frank, Pres. & Chief Exec. Officer--Donino & Partners, Inc., Atlanta, GA, pg. 344
Donley, Terrance K., Pres. & Treas.--Donley's, Inc., Cleveland, OH, pg. 345
Donnally, Thomas, Pres.--Camping World Holdings, Inc., Bowling Green, KY, pg. 213
Donnelly, James, Pres. & Chief Exec. Officer--Baxter Hodell Donnelly Preston Inc., Cincinnati, OH, pg. 127
Donofrio, Hal, Pres. & Chief Exec. Officer--Richardson, Myers & Donofrio, Inc., Baltimore, MD, pg. 933
Donohoe, James A., III, Pres. & Chief Exec. Officer--The Donohoe Companies, Inc., Washington, DC, pg. 345
Donohoo, J.G., Chm. Bd. & Pres.--The Gibson Group Inc., Cincinnati, OH, pg. 456
Donovan, Richard P., Pres., Chief Exec. & Fin. Officer--World Jai-alai, Miami, FL, pg. 1202
Donsky, Howard, Pres.--Sterling Jewelry & Distributing Co., Dallas, TX, pg. 1047
Dooley, Lawrence W., Pres.--Engineering & Construction Division, Philadelphia, PA, pg. 320
Doonan, Wendell M., Pres.--Doonan & Sons, Inc., Great Bend, KS, pg. 346
Doran, Ralph, III, Pres.--Burkhardt & Christy Advertising, Inc., New York, NY, pg. 191
Doran, Robert J., Pres. & Treas.--Ace Doran Hauling & Rigging Company, Cincinnati, OH, pg. 346
Dorfman, Robert, Pres.--King Wire & Cable Corporation, Jamaica, NY, pg. 631
Dorman, James I., Jr., Pres.--Garney Holding Company, Inc., Kansas City, MO, pg. 443
Dorn, Edward G., Chm. Bd. & Pres.--Edward G. Dorn & Associates, Inc., Rolling Meadows, IL, pg. 346
Dorn, Ernst W., II, Pres.--Ernst W. Dorn Co., Inc., Gardena, CA, pg. 346
Dornbush, Dennis C., Pres. & Treas.--Sintel, Inc., Spring Lake, MI, pg. 1008
Dornfield, Stuart R., Pres., Creative, Radio, TV Production & New Bus. Contact--Gold Coast Advertising, Miami, FL, pg. 465
Dorris, Al, Pres. & Chief Exec. Officer--Xerxes Corporation, Minneapolis, MN, pg. 1206
Dorrity, Charles E., Pres.--Mark III Industries, Ocala, FL, pg. 708
Dorsa, Peter A., Pres.--Epoxylite Corporation, Irvine, CA, pg. 384
Dorsy, Claude, Pres.--First Florida Equities, Ltd., Miami, FL, pg. 413
Dott, Jackson Y., Pres.--Monarch Avalon, Inc., Baltimore, MD, pg. 765
Dougherty, R.E., Jr., Pres. & Treas.--Tasa Corporation, Pittsburgh, PA, pg. 1079
Dougherty, R.L., Pres.--Fischbach & Dougherty, Inc., Atlanta, GA, pg. 414
Douglas, J. Scott, Pres.--Dancker, Sellew & Douglas, Inc., New York, NY, pg. 314
Douglas, Jon A., Pres. & Chief Exec. Officer--Jon Douglas Company, Beverly Hills, CA, pg. 347
Douglas, Walter E., Chm. Bd. & Pres.--Avis Ford Inc., Southfield, MI, pg. 102
Douglass, A. Stone, Chm. Bd. & Owner--Piper Aircraft Corporation, Vero Beach, FL, pg. 872
Douma, David L., Chm. Bd. & Pres.--Theradyne Corporation, Lakeville, MN, pg. 1065
Doutre, Gerald, Pres.--Redco Foods, Inc., Windsor, CT, pg. 919
Dowell, John D., Pres.--Imperial, Inc., Green Bay, WI, pg. 564
Dowing, Lowell M., Sr., Pres.--Lowell Packing Company, Fitzgerald, GA, pg. 685
Downey, J. Michael, Pres.--Downey Printing, Waukee, IA, pg. 348

Downey, Paul, Pres., Treas. & Sec.--Advanced Circuit Technology, Nashua, NH, pg. 20
Downey, Richard T., Pres.--Hypertronics Corporation, Hudson, MA, pg. 557
Dowsett, Patrick W., Pres.--East Moline Metal Products Company, East Moline, IL, pg. 363
Doyle, King, Pres.--King Milling Company, Lowell, MI, pg. 631
Doyle, L. F. Boker, Pres.--Fiduciary Trust Co. International, New York, NY, pg. 408
Doyle, L. F. Boker, Pres.--Fiduciary Trust Company International, New York, NY, pg. 408
Doyle, W.E., Jr., Pres.--Peterson Tractor Company, San Leandro, CA, pg. 865
Draeger, Ken, Pres. & Chief Exec. Officer--Decision Data Inc., Horsham, PA, pg. 323
Drago, Franklin J., Pres.--Bison Canning Co., Inc., Angola, NY, pg. 474
Dragotta, Robert, Chm. Bd. & Pres.--National Out-of-Home Media/Metro 8; New York, NY, pg. 792
Drake, John H., Pres.--Cole Henderson Drake, Inc., Atlanta, GA, pg. 260
Drakesmith, John, Pres.--Heintzelman's Truck Center Inc., Orlando, FL, pg. 526
Drasner, Fred, Pres. & Chief Exec. Officer--U.S. News & World Report, New York, NY, pg. 1136
Dray, Patrick M., Pres.--Columbia Corporation, Brentwood, TN, pg. 265
Drebes, Charles F., Pres. & Chief Exec. Officer--Gaylord Printing, Inc., Detroit, MI, pg. 446
Drechsel, James G., Pres.--IMPO Glaztile, Burr Ridge, IL, pg. 564
Dreisbach, Mark L., Pres.--Dreisbach & Sons Cadillac Company, Detroit, MI, pg. 348
Drell, Leonard B., Chm. Bd., Pres., Chief Exec. & Chief Oper. Officer--DeMert & Dougherty, Inc., Westchester, IL, pg. 328
Drendel, Gene, Pres.--Capitol Group, Springfield, IL, pg. 215
Dresen, William, Pres.--Penda Corporation, Portage, WI, pg. 857
Dressler, Sidney, Pres.--Colfax, Inc., Pawtucket, RI, pg. 261
Dreusike, Don, Pres. & Chief Exec. Officer--Dinwiddie Construction Co., San Francisco, CA, pg. 338
Drew, Walter H., Pres. & Chief Exec. Officer--Menasha Corporation, Neenah, WI, pg. 738
Dreyer, John W., Chm. Bd., Pres. & Chief Exec. Officer--Harold M. Pitman Co., Inc., Totowa, NJ, pg. 872
Drier, William E., Pres. & Exec. Creative Dir.--McFarland & Drier, Inc., Miami, FL, pg. 729
Drinkward, Cecil W., Pres.--Hoffman Corporation, Portland, OR, pg. 537
Driver, George F., Pres. & Chief Oper. Officer--Robert F. Driver Co., Inc., San Diego, CA, pg. 349
Droesch, E. Richard, Pres.--Florence Corporation, Huntington, NY, pg. 420
Drucker, Norman, Pres.--Ain Plastics, Inc., Mount Vernon, NY, pg. 26
Drumheller, Phillip M., Pres.--Lane Press, Inc., South Burlington, VT, pg. 654
Drumm, Streuby L., Jr., Pres.--Drumm & Associates, Inc., Metairie, LA, pg. 349
Drumm, W.C., Pres.--Monarch Ware, Inc., Algoma, WI, pg. 742
Drumm, Wesley C., Chm. Bd., Pres. & Treas.--The Metal Ware Corp., Two Rivers, WI, pg. 741
Drury, Francis T., Pres.--Somerset Technologies, Inc., Somerset, NJ, pg. 1017
Drutt, William, Pres., Chief Exec. Officer & Sec.--Harris & Drutt Inc., Philadelphia, PA, pg. 511
Du, Ben R., Pres.--Flojet Corporation, Irvine, CA, pg. 419
Dub, Anthony, Pres.--CS First Boston USA, Inc., New York, NY, pg. 204
Dubin, Howard S., Pres.--Manufacturers' News, Inc., Evanston, IL, pg. 705
Dubin, Melvin, Chm. Bd. & Pres.--Slant/Fin Corporation, Greenvale, NY, pg. 1010
DuBose, S.I., Pres.--White Electrical Construction Co., Atlanta, GA, pg. 1185
Ducamp, Michel, Mng. Dir.--Leo Burnett Worldwide Inc., Brussels,, Belgium, pg. 193
Duchossois, Craig J., Pres.--Duchossois Industries, Inc., Elmhurst, IL, pg. 350
Duda, Ferdinand S., Pres.--A. Duda & Sons Inc., Oviedo, FL, pg. 351
Dudek, Walter, Pres.--Dudek & Bock Spring Manufacturing Company, Chicago, IL, pg. 351
Dudley, W. Ted, Pres.--Hypro Corporation, New Brighton, MN, pg. 557
Dudnyk, Edward K., Pres.--Dudnyk Advertising, Horsham, PA, pg. 351
Dueffent, Gary, Pres. & Treas.--Lincoln Industries, Inc., Boonville, IN, pg. 1221
Duffy, Brian, Pres. & Chief Oper. Officer--C.B. Fleet Company, Incorporated, Lynchburg, VA, pg. 417
Duffy, David A., Pres.--Duffy & Shanley, Inc., Providence, RI, pg. 351
Duffy, Richard A., Pres.--Geyer-McAllister Publications, Inc., New York, NY, pg. 455
Dugan, J. Patrick, Pres. & Chief Exec. Officer--Microband Companies, Inc., Fairfield, NJ, pg. 748
Dugan, Thomas, V.P. & Gen. Mgr.--Anaheim Manufacturing Company, Anaheim, CA, pg. 71
Duggan, Joel E., Pres.--Duggan Industries, Inc., Dallas, TX, pg. 351
Duggan, John A., M.D., Pres.--Fallon Community Health Plan, West Boylston, MA, pg. 398
Dugger, Irene, Chm. Bd., Pres., Chief Exec. Officer & Treas.--Queen Oxygen Company, Columbus, OH, pg. 904
Dujardin, Paul, Pres.--Raymond Automation Co., Inc., Norwalk, CT, pg. 915
Dukes, D.R., Pres. & Chief Oper. Officer--Ingram Micro Inc., Santa Ana, CA, pg. 569
Dukes, Hazel N., Pres.--New York City Off Track Betting Corp., New York, NY, pg. 802
duMoulin, Richard T., Chm., Pres. & Chief Exec. Officer--Marine Transport Lines, Inc., Secaucus, NJ, pg. 707
Duncan-Campagne, Gail, Pres.--Jerome-Duncan Ford, Sterling Heights, MI, pg. 593
Duncan, Melvin D. Jr., Pres.--American Red Ball World Wide Movers, Indianapolis, IN, pg. 918
Duncan, Melvin D., Jr., Pres. of American Red Ball Transit & Vice Chm. Red Ball Corp.--Red Ball Corporation, Seattle, WA, pg. 918
Duncan, Melvin D., Jr., Pres.--Red Ball Leasing, Inc., Indianapolis, IN, pg. 918
Dunham, James I., Chm. Bd. & Pres.--American Liberty Financial Corp., Baton Rouge, LA, pg. 57
Dunham, Michael D., Pres.--Effective Management Systems, Milwaukee, WI, pg. 370
Dunlap, Edward B., Chm Bd., Pres., & Chief Exec. Officer--Centimark Corporation, Bethel Park, PA, pg. 231
Dunlap, William D., Worldwide Chief Exec. Officer--CME-KHBB Advertising, Minneapolis, MN, pg. 202
Dunmire, Cyril C., Jr., Pres.--Stabler Companies, Inc., Harrisburg, PA, pg. 1034
Dunn, James, Pres.--Plaskolite Inc., Columbus, OH, pg. 874
Dunn, Jerry, Pres.--Yorktown Tool & Die Corporation, Yorktown, IN, pg. 1208
Dunn, Joseph C., Mng. Partner--Charles Dunn Company-Realtors, Los Angeles, CA, pg. 353
Dunn, Keith, Pres.--McGuffey's Restaurants, Inc., Asheville, NC, pg. 729
Dunn, Richard C., Mng. Partner--Charles Dunn Company-Realtors, Los Angeles, CA, pg. 353
Dunning, Roger, Pres. & Gen. Mgr.--North Dakota Mill & Elevator Association, Grand Forks, ND, pg. 813
Dunville, Joseph R., Chm. Bd., Pres., & Chief Exec. Officer--Idea Engineering & Fabricating, Detroit, MI, pg. 562
Dupey, Patricia, Pres.--Dupey Management Corp., Irving, TX, pg. 354
DuPont, Kent G., Pres.--G.B. DuPont Co., Inc., Troy, MI, pg. 354
Dupps, John A., Jr., Pres.--Dupps Company, Germantown, OH, pg. 354
Duque, Edite, Chief Exec. Officer--Ayer Portugal, Lisbon,, Portugal, pg. 104
Durbetaki, John, Owner--OrCAD L.P., Hillsboro, OR, pg. 828
Durfee, John, Pres.--Bethel Mills, Inc., Bethel, VT, pg. 148
Durham, G.R., Pres. & Chief Exec. Officer--Walter Industries, Inc., Tampa, FL, pg. 1161
Durham, Larry, Pres.--Durham Transportation, Inc., Austin, TX, pg. 354
Durham, Paul, Pres.--Miller Meester Advertising Inc., Minneapolis, MN, pg. 754
Durham, Timothy S., Pres. & Chief Exec. Officer--Carpenter Manufacturing, Inc., Mitchell, IN, pg. 991
Durnin, Douglas K., Pres.--A. K. Durnin Chrysler Plymouth, Inc., Baton Rouge, LA, pg. 355
Durocher, Francis W., Chm. Bd., Pres. & Treas.--Gust K. Newberg Construction Co., Chicago, IL, pg. 803
Durovsik, Thomas E., Pres.--The Franklin Mint, Franklin Center, PA, pg. 60
Durrett, William, Pres.--Cimarron American Fidelity, Cimarron, KS, pg. 52
Durrett, William E., Chm. Bd., Pres. & Chief Exec. Officer--American Fidelity Corp., Oklahoma City, OK, pg. 52
Durum, Daryl E., Pres.--All Nation Insurance Co., Saint Paul, MN, pg. 35
Dustman, Lloyd, Chm. & Pres.--CAC Microcircuits, Inc., Mount Carmel, IL, pg. 198
Duval, Betsyann, Pres.--Duval & Partners, Boston, MA, pg. 356
Duvall, Sharon B., Pres. & Chief Exec. Officer--Andre-Boudin Bakeries, Inc., San Francisco, CA, pg. 969
Dweck, Michael, Pres. & New Bus. Contact--Dweck & Campbell, Inc., New York, NY, pg. 356
Dwelle, T.A., Pres.--Nella Oil Company, Auburn, CA, pg. 797
Dworin, Steve, Pres.--Deutsch/Dworin, Inc., New York, NY, pg. 333
Dworin, Steve, Pres.--Deutsch Direct, New York, NY, pg. 333
Dworman, Alvin, Chm. Bd. & Pres.--Lee National Corporation, New York, NY, pg. 666
Dwyer, Toni A., Chm. & Pres.--Communication Trends, Inc., Atlanta, GA, pg. 269
Dye, Michael H., Pres. & Chief Oper. Officer--Post Buckley Schuh & Jernigan, Miami, FL, pg. 881
Dygus, Walter J., Pres.--D & R Advertising, Deer Park, NY, pg. 307
Dym, Morrie, Pres. & Chief Exec. Officer--Five Dollar Clothing Stores, Los Angeles, CA, pg. 416
Dyson, Robert R., Pres. & Chief Oper. Officer--The Dyson-Kissner-Moran Corporation, New York, NY, pg. 357
Each, Thomas, Pres.--Trewax Company, Santa Fe Springs, CA, pg. 159
Eacott, James H., III, Pres. & Treas.--Bartlett Brainard & Eacott, Inc., Bloomfield, CT, pg. 122
Eagle, John R., Pres. & Chief Oper. Officer--Eagle Lincoln Mercury Inc., Dallas, TX, pg. 362
Earnhardt, Hal J., III, Pres.--Earnhardt's Auto Center, Tempe, AZ, pg. 362
Earp, Donald C., Pres.--Earp Meat Company, Kansas City, KS, pg. 362
Easley, Dick L., Chm. Bd. & Pres.--Health America/CapitalCare, Inc., Lincoln, NE, pg. 779
Easley, Ronald L., Chm. Bd., Pres. & Chief Exec. Officer--System Planning Corp., Arlington, VA, pg. 1070
East, David, Mng. Dir.--Wunderman Worldwide, Sandton, South Africa, pg. 1214
East, F. Howard, Pres., Chief Oper. & Chief Fin. Officer--Bell Packaging Corporation, Marion, IN, pg. 135
Easterly, Thomas B., Pres.--Johnstown Knitting Mill Co., Johnstown, NY, pg. 602
Easterwood, Bill, Pres.--Choctaw Electric Co-Op, Hugo, OK, pg. 248
Eastham, John, Chm.--Evans/Public Relations, Seattle, WA, pg. 391
Eastland, Woods E., Pres. & Chief Exec. Officer--Staple Cotton Cooperative Association, Greenwood, MS, pg. 1038
Eaton, Bruce C., Pres.--Eaton Office Supply Co., Inc., Amherst, NY, pg. 364
Eaton, Henry F., Chm. & Chief Exec. Officer--Dix & Eaton Incorporated, Cleveland, OH, pg. 341
Eaton, Wyndham, Pres. & Chief Exec. Officer--Eaton Equipment Corp., Blasdell, NY, pg. 364
Eaves, Hayden, Pres. & Chief Exec. Officer--Trammell Crow Company, Dallas, TX, pg. 1106
Eby, Martin K., Chm. Bd. & Pres.--Eby Corporation, Wichita, KS, pg. 365
Echevarria, Angel, Pres. & Chief Exec. Officer--Echevarria Angel Co., Inc., Los Angeles, CA, pg. 365
Ecke, Paul, III, Pres.--Paul Ecke Ranch, Inc., Encinitas, CA, pg. 366
Eckerling, Sanford, Pres. & Treas.--Universal Overall Company, Chicago, IL, pg. 1139
Eckert, David, Co-Pres.--Smith Valve Corporation, Whitinsville, MA, pg. 1014
Eckert, John P., Pres. & Chief Oper. Officer--The Babcock & Wilcox Company, New Orleans, LA, pg. 107
Eckert, Wesley, Pres. & Chief Exec. Officer--Darigold, Inc., Seattle, WA, pg. 315
Eckert, Wesley, Pres.--Dairygold Inc., Seattle, WA, pg. 311
Eckhoff, Gilbert B., Pres. & Chief Exec. Officer--Henningsen Foods, Inc., White Plains, NY, pg. 629
Eckl, James F., Pres.--Gray & Kilgore, Inc., Troy, MI, pg. 950
Eckman, Harold R., Pres.--Eckman Construction Company, Bedford, NH, pg. 366
Eckstein, Erwin B., Chm. Bd., Pres. & Chief Exec. Officer--Spectrum Color Center, Golden, CO, pg. 1029
Economos, John, Pres.--Atlanta Beverage Co., Atlanta, GA, pg. 94
Eddings, J. Carson, Pres. & Chief Exec. Officer--The William Cook Agency, Inc., Jacksonville, FL, pg. 282
Eddings, J. Carson, Pres., Chief Exec. Officer--William Cook Public Relations, Inc., Jacksonville, FL, pg. 282
Eddins, Mark A., Pres. & Chief Exec. Officer--Friendly Chevrolet Co. Inc., Dallas, TX, pg. 433
Edelbrock, Victor, Chm. Bd., Pres. & Chief Exec. Officer--Edelbrock Corp., Torrance, CA, pg. 367
Edelman, Leo, Pres.--Greater New York Box Co., Clifton, NJ, pg. 483
Edelmann, Edgar S., Pres. & Mktg. Dir.--Edelmann Scott, Inc., Richmond, VA, pg. 368
Edelmann, George, Gen. Mgr.-North America--Lan-Chile Airlines, Miami, FL, pg. 653
Edelson, Kenneth J., Pres. & Chief Exec. Officer--General Sportcraft Company Ltd., Bergenfield, NJ, pg. 450
Edelson, L., Pres.--Westchester Lace, Inc., North Bergen, NJ, pg. 1178
Edelson, Norman, Pres.--Edelson & Sons Corporation, New York, NY, pg. 368
Edelstein, David, Chm. Bd. & Pres.--Edelstein Associates Advertising Inc., Seattle, WA, pg. 368
Edick, Fred W., Pres.--Dyke Industry, Inc., Little Rock, AR, pg. 356
Edleman, Lawrence, Pres.--The Universal Steel Co., Cleveland, OH, pg. 265
Edmonson, William, Pres.--ARA/Cory Refreshment Services, Inc., Mount Prospect, IL, pg. 6
Edmund, Robert M., Pres. & Chief Exec. Officer--Edmund Scientific Company, Barrington, NJ, pg. 369
Edmundson, Gary, Pres.--Silvercrest Western Home Industries Corporation, Corona, CA, pg. 1004
Edwards, Barrie, Pres.--Music Sales Corporation, New York, NY, pg. 777
Edwards, George D., II, Pres. & Chief Exec. Officer--Hottman Edwards, Baltimore, MD, pg. 545
Edwards, Jimmie R., Pres.--Vulcan Iron Works, Inc., Detroit, MI, pg. 1155
Edwards, John J., Pres. & Chief Exec. Officer--Pilot Air Freight Corp., Lima, PA, pg. 870
Edwards, Kim, Pres.--Gates Energy Products, Inc., Alachua, FL, pg. 445
Edwards, Martin H., Pres.--Edwards Brothers, Inc., Ann Arbor, MI, pg. 369
Edwards, Merle W., Jr., Pres.--Coastal Wholesale, Inc., Kinston, NC, pg. 257
Edwards, Oral W., Chm. Bd. & Pres.--GES Inc., Marianna, AR, pg. 439
Edwards, R.C., Chm. Bd. & Pres.--Edwards Engineering Corporation, Pompton Plains, NJ, pg. 370
Edwards, Terry J., Pres.--Centre Lime & Stone Co., Inc., Pleasant Gap, PA, pg. 517
Edwards, W. Linton, III, Pres.--Benjamin Ansehl Company, Saint Louis, MO, pg. 76
Edwards, Wesley, Pres. & Chief Exec. Officer--Spinnerin Yarn Co., Inc., South Hackensack, NJ, pg. 1031
Edwards, William E., III, Pres. & Chief Oper. Officer--Cardinal Aluminum Co., Louisville, KY, pg. 217
Edwards, William G., Pres.--Destiny Industry Inc., Moultrie, GA, pg. 332
Edwards, William H., Dr., Pres.--State Volunteer Mutual Insurance Co. Inc., Brentwood, TN, pg. 1041
Effler, Donald, Pres.--Houston Effler & Partners, Boston, MA, pg. 546
Egan, Gerald L., Pres. & Chief Exec. Officer--Egan Cos., Minneapolis, MN, pg. 371
Egan, Gerald L., Pres.--Egan & Sons Insulation, Minneapolis, MN, pg. 371
Egan, Gerald L., Pres.--Egan McKay Electrical Contractors, Minneapolis, MN, pg. 371
Egan, Richard W., Pres. & Chief Exec. Officer--The Levolor Corporation, Sunnyvale, CA, pg. 671
Egan, Robert, Pres.--Niagara Therapy Mfg. Corp., Stanley, NC, pg. 806
Egbert, John C., Pres. & Chief Exec. Officer--McCourt Label Co., Lewis Run, PA, pg. 727

Corporate Responsibilities Index

Eggen, Arne, Mng. Dir., Dir. os Scandinavian Opers.--Kobs & Draft, Oslo, Norway, pg. 112
Egizii, Robert, Pres. & Chief Exec. Officerf--Egizii Electric, Inc., Springfield, IL, pg. 371
Egner, Clayton W., Pres.--Schutte Lumber Company, Kansas City, MO, pg. 980
Ehler, Thomas, Pres.--Claire Manufacturing Co., Addison, IL, pg. 222
Ehlke, J. David, Pres. & Chief Oper. Officer--Segue Partners, Cambridge, MA, pg. 885
Ehrenfeld, Robert L., Pres.--Halocarbon Products Corp., River Edge, NJ, pg. 502
Ehrenthal, Herb, Pres.--Rubin Ehrenthal & Associates, New York, NY, pg. 953
Ehrlichman, Stephen M., Pres.--L. Fish Corporation, Chicago, IL, pg. 414
Eichen, Paul, Pres.--Proxima Corporation, San Diego, CA, pg. 896
Eichler, Franklin R., Pres. & Chief Exec. Officer--The Sico Company, Mount Joy, PA, pg. 1001
Eichler, Franklin R., Pres.--First Mount Joy Corporation, Mount Joy, PA, pg. 413
Eichman, Frank, Chm. Bd. & Pres.--Alcom Printing Group, Inc., Bethlehem, PA, pg. 32
Eidel, Helmuth L., Pres.--Tri-City Electrical Contractors Inc., Altamonte Springs, FL, pg. 1110
Eihusen, Robert, Pres.--Chief Industries, Inc., Grand Island, NE, pg. 247
Einstein, Ted, Pres.--Einstein Moomjy Inc., Pine Brook, NJ, pg. 371
Eisele, Ed, Pres. & Chief Exec. Officer--Holsum Bakery, Inc., Phoenix, AZ, pg. 541
Eiseman, Thomas A., Pres.--Revere Electric Supply Co., Chicago, IL, pg. 930
Eisenberg, Kenneth, Pres.--Kenwal Products Corp., Detroit, MI, pg. 624
Eisenbrey, John R., Chm. Bd., Pres. & Chief Exec. Officer--Artesian Resources Corporation, Newark, DE, pg. 86
Eisenstadt, Marvin Ernest, Pres.--Cumberland Packing Corp., Brooklyn, NY, pg. 304
Eisner, Bill, Pres., Chief Exec. Officer & Creative Dir.--William Eisner & Associates Inc., Milwaukee, WI, pg. 372
Eisner, Steven C., Pres. & Chief Exec. Officer--Eisner & Associates, Inc., Baltimore, MD, pg. 372
Eitzinger, Robert, Pres.--Mid-West Automation Systems, Buffalo Grove, IL, pg. 750
Eizenberg, Michael I., Pres.--American Council for International Studies, Boston, MA, pg. 56
Ekberg Johnson, Judith, Pres. & Chief Exec. Officer--Meyer Broadcasting Company, Bismarck, ND, pg. 746
Eklund, Wesley, Pres.--Fleet Engineers, Inc., Muskegon, MI, pg. 417
Eklund, Wesley, Pres.--Lee Industries, Muskegon, MI, pg. 417
Ekstrom, L.W., Pres.--Bingham, Mt. Prospect, IL, pg. 151
Elen, Robert W., Pres. & Creative Dir.--Robert Elen & Associates, Los Angeles, CA, pg. 376
Elias, Louis, Pres.--Elias Brothers Restaurants, inc., Warren, MI, pg. 376
Eliasek, Thomas, Pres.--Harris Steel Co., Chicago, IL, pg. 512
Eliel, Ernest L., Dr., Pres.--American Chemical Society, Washington, DC, pg. 50
Elkhatib, Hasan M., Pres.--Dena Corporation, Elk Grove Village, IL, pg. 329
Elkhatib, Hasan M., Pres. & Chief Exec. Officer--Meta International, Inc., Elk Grove Village, IL, pg. 329
Elkin, Irv, Pres.--Associated Milk Producers North Central Region, New Ulm, MN, pg. 91
Elkin, Irvin, Pres.--Associated Milk Producers, Inc., San Antonio, TX, pg. 91
Elkington, John, Pres.--Elkington Realty & Development, Memphis, TN, pg. 377
Elkman, Richard, Pres. & Chief Exec. Officer--Group Two Advertising, Inc., Philadelphia, PA, pg. 490
Ellenthal, Ira, Pres. & Publisher--The Atlantic Monthly Magazine, Boston, MA, pg. 95
Eller, David G., Pres. & Chief Exec. Officer--The Granada Group, Houston, TX, pg. 475
Ellingson, Chester W., Jr., Chm. Bd., Pres. & Chief Exec. Officer--Reese Enterprises, Inc., Rosemount, MN, pg. 920
Elliot, Marion, Pres.--Denver Wholesale Florists Company, Denver, CO, pg. 331
Elliot, Russell, Pres.--Schering-Plough Healthcare Products Advertising Corp., Liberty Corner, NJ, pg. 976
Elliott, Charles A., Chm. Bd., Pres. & Chief Exec., Officer--Crenlo, Inc., Rochester, MN, pg. 298
Elliott, Joseph E., Pres.--Encyclopaedia Britannica Educational Corporation, Chicago, IL, pg. 380
Elliott, Tim, Pres.--Earle Palmer Brown/Bethesda, Bethesda, MD, pg. 182
Ellis, Andy, Pres.--Mico, Inc., Springfield, VA, pg. 748
Ellis, James C., Pres.--Juniata Office Supplies, Altoona, PA, pg. 608
Ellis, William H., Chm. Bd., Pres. & Chief Oper. Officer--Farley Candy Company, Chicago, IL, pg. 399
Ellison, Michael R., Pres.--Michael R. Ellison Inc., Phoenix, AZ, pg. 378
Ellison, Ray, Chm. Bd. & Pres.--Rayco, San Antonio, TX, pg. 914
Ellstrom, Olof W., Jr., Pres.--Dearborn Gage Company, Garden City, MI, pg. 322
Elmburg, John R., Pres.--Blitz USA, Miami, OK, pg. 157
Elmburg, John R., Pres.--Blitz U.S.A., Inc., Miami, OK, pg. 157
Elmore, David, Chm. Bd. & Pres.--Olson-Travelworld Ltd., Manhattan Beach, CA, pg. 824
Elsberry, Howard W., Chm., Pres. & Chief Exec. Officer--Westlake Hardware, Inc., Shawnee Mission, KS, pg. 1183
Elsener, Frank, Pres. & Chief Exec. Officer--Tree Top, Inc., Selah, WA, pg. 1109
Elser, Arnold J., Pres., Dir. Creative Services--Elser & Aucone, Inc., New York, NY, pg. 378
Embry, Merle, Pres.-Multi-Plex, Inc.--Davis Industries Inc., Detroit, MI, pg. 318
Emery, Don, Pres.--Reference Software International, San Francisco, CA, pg. 921
Emison, James W., Pres.--Western Petroleum Company, Eden Prairie, MN, pg. 1181
Emmerling, John A., Chm. Bd., Pres. & Chief Exec. Officer--John Emmerling Inc., New York, NY, pg. 379
Emmerling, Paul E., V.P.-Sls. & Mktg.--American Welding & Manufacturing Co., Warren, OH, pg. 65
Emmerson, A.A., Pres.--Sierra Pacific Industries, Redding, CA, pg. 1003
Emrich, William J., Pres.--Fugro-McClelland, Inc., Houston, TX, pg. 435
Engel, Arthur, Pres. & Chief Exec. Officer--Southwest Marine, Inc., San Diego, CA, pg. 1023
Engel, Clyde W., Chm. Bd. & Pres.--Libco Corporation, Chicago, IL, pg. 674
Engel, Irving H., Pres.--Milady Brassiere & Corset Co., Inc., New York, NY, pg. 753
Engel, Irving H., Pres.--Roxanne Swim Suits Co., Inc., New York, NY, pg. 753
Engel, W.R., Pres. & Treas.--American Mutual Life Insurance Company, Des Moines, IA, pg. 58
Engelson, David, Pres. & Chief Fin. Officer--First Connecticut SBIC, Bridgeport, CT, pg. 412
England, Ed D., Pres.--C P Converters, Inc., York, PA, pg. 203
England, Ronald M., Pres.--Waldes Truarc, Inc., Somerset, NJ, pg. 1159
Englander, Roman, Pres.--Drug Guild Distributors, Inc., Secaucus, NJ, pg. 349
Engle, Clyde W., Chm. Bd., Pres. & Treas.--GSC Enterprises, Inc., Chicago, IL, pg. 440
Englefield, Benjamin B., Co-Pres.--Englefield, Inc., Newark, OH, pg. 382
Englefield, F.W., IV, Co-Pres., Chief Exec. & Chief Fin. Officer--Englefield, Inc., Newark, OH, pg. 382
Engler, Paul F., Chm. Bd. & Pres.--Cactus Feeders, Inc., Amarillo, TX, pg. 207
English, James D., Pres.--Kalamazoo Label Co., Kalamazoo, MI, pg. 615
Enichen, Robert C., Pres.--Exact Equipment Corporation, Langhorne, PA, pg. 392
Eno, Julius Ralph, Pres.--Hamamatsu Corp., Bridgewater, NJ, pg. 502
Ensles, Dave, Pres.--Garvey Grain, Wichita, KS, pg. 444
Ensor, Clyde F., Sr., Chm. Bd. & Pres.--Hesco Parts Corporation, Louisville, KY, pg. 531
Epley, Arthur, Pres.--Microwave Networks Incorporated, Houston, TX, pg. 749
Epple, John H., Pres.--University Book Store, Madison, WI, pg. 1139
Epprecht, Hans, Pres. & Chief Exec. Officer--The Great Lakes Cheese Co., Newbury, OH, pg. 481
Epstein, Abram, Pres.--A J M Packaging Corporation, Detroit, MI, pg. 4
Epstein, Herb, Pres.--Seward Luggage Company, Petersburg, VA, pg. 993
Epstein, Jerome P., Pres.--Perry Group, Inc., Hainesport, NJ, pg. 863
Epstein, Jim, Pres.--Moore, Epstein, Moore, Tampa, FL, pg. 768
Epstein, Martin, Pres., Chief Exec. & Chief Fin. Officer--Associated Machinecraft Corporation, Los Angeles, CA, pg. 90
Epstein, P., Chm. Bd.--Perry Products Corp., Hainesport, NJ, pg. 863
Epstein, Richard, Pres.--Ventura Travelware, Inc., Long Island City, NY, pg. 1147
Epstein, Richard, Chm. Bd., Pres. & Chief Exec. Officer--Vesco Oil Corp., Southfield, MI, pg. 1149
Erb, Fred A., Chm., Pres. & Chief Exec. Officer--Erb Lumber Company, Birmingham, MI, pg. 360
Erdle, William J., III, Chm. Bd. & Pres.--Erdle Perforating Co., Rochester, NY, pg. 385
Erfert, Reiner, Chm.--Michael Conrad & Leo Burnett GmbH & Co. KG, Frankfurt/Main, Germany, pg. 192
Ergul, Necdet, Pres.--Microphase Corporation, Norwalk, CT, pg. 749
Erickson, Chuck, Pres. & Chief Exec. Officer--Digital Pathways Inc., Mountain View, CA, pg. 337
Erickson, Claire L., Pres.--Erickson Oil Products, Inc., Hudson, WI, pg. 386
Erickson, Dean, Pres.--Erickson Diversified Corp., Hudson, WI, pg. 386
Erickson, Donovan, Pres. & Chief Exec. Officer--Holiday Companies, Minneapolis, MN, pg. 539
Erickson, John, Pres.--I.C. System, Inc., Vadnais Heights, MN, pg. 558
Erickson, John H., Pres.--Erickson Transport Corporation, Springfield, MO, pg. 383
Erickson, John T., Pres.--Anderson Brothers Construction Brainerd, Brainerd, MN, pg. 72
Erickson, Mel, Sr., Pres., Sec. & Treas.--Central Feed Mills, Inc., Snohomish, WA, pg. 232
Erickson, Robert K., Pres.--Donald L. Arends Inc., Oak Brook, IL, pg. 81
Ericson, James D., Pres. & Chief Oper. Officer--Northwestern Mutual Life Insurance Co., Milwaukee, WI, pg. 815
Ernst, Paul W., Pres. & Chief Exec. Officer--Carter Day Industries, Inc., Minneapolis, MN, pg. 226
Ernst, Paul W., Pres.--Hart-Carter Co., Minneapolis, MN, pg. 226
Erokan, Dennis, Pres. & Editor-in-Chief--Bam Publications, Inc., Pleasant Hill, CA, pg. 117
Erskine, John E., Jr., Pres.--Racine Federated, Inc., Racine, WI, pg. 909
Ertel, William B., Pres.--M&W Gear Company, Gibson City, IL, pg. 690
Ervin, William W., Pres. & Chief Exec. Officer--O'Neal & Prelle, Hartford, CT, pg. 827
Esak, J. Ronald, Pres. & Chief Exec. Officer--Nexus Plastics, Inc., Hawthorne, NJ, pg. 805
Escamez, Jorge, Pres.--Crisa Corporation, Plano, TX, pg. 299
Eschbach, Rudolf, Pres.--Iroquois Die & Mfg. Co., Warren, MI, pg. 582
Eskilson, Thomas T., Pres.--Dixie Dairy Company, Gary, IN, pg. 341
Espen, Robert W., Pres.--Miether Bearing Products, Inc., Odessa, TX, pg. 32
Esposito, Chris, Pres.--Four Seasons Solar Products Corp., Holbrook, NY, pg. 427
Esposito, Joseph, Pres.--Merriam-Webster, Inc., Springfield, MA, pg. 381
Esposito, Louis S., Pres.--Turnbull Enterprises, Inc., Baltimore, MD, pg. 1119
Esten, Robert, Pres.-Fox River Paper Co.--Rising Paper Company, Housatonic, MA, pg. 428
Esten, Robert L., Pres.--Fox River Paper Company, Appleton, WI, pg. 428
Estenson, Noel, Pres. & Chief Exec. Officer-Cenex Inc.--Cenex/Land O'Lakes, Inc., Saint Paul, MN, pg. 653
Estenson, Noel, Pres.--CENEX (Farmers Union Central Exchange, Inc.), Inver Grove Heights, MN, pg. 231
Estenson, Noel, Pres. & Chief Exec. Officer-Cenex Inc.--Cenex/Land O'Lakes, Inc., Saint Paul, MN, pg. 231
Estes, Alexandra H., Chm. Bd. & Pres.--Haeger Industries, Inc., Dundee, IL, pg. 499
Estes, Jon C., Pres.--New Hermes Incorporated, Norwalk, CT, pg. 801
Estes, Robey W., Jr., Pres. & Treas.--Estes Express Lines, Inc., Richmond, VA, pg. 389
Estey, John W., Pres. & Chief Oper. Officer--S & C Electric Company, Chicago, IL, pg. 958
Ethier, James B., Pres. & Chief Oper. Officer--Bush Brothers & Company, Dandridge, TN, pg. 196
Ethier, James B., Pres.--Blytheville Canning Company, Inc., Blytheville, AR, pg. 196
Ethier, James B., Pres.--Shiocton Kraut Co., Shiocton, WI, pg. 196
Ethier, James B., Pres.--Valley Canning Co., Inc., Ville Platte, LA, pg. 196
Ethier, James B., Pres.--Bush Brothers & Company, Augusta, WI, pg. 196
Ethier, James B., Pres.--Blytheville Canning Company, Inc., Muskogee, OK, pg. 196
Etteridge, Steven, Pres.--Temps & Company, Washington, DC, pg. 1086
Ettinger, Bernard, Pres.--Clay-Park Labs, Inc., Bronx, NY, pg. 253
Ettleson, Richard, Chm. Bd. & Pres.--Electro Brand, Inc., Chicago, IL, pg. 374
Eukovich, Bob, V.P.--Pullman/Holt Corp., Tampa, FL, pg. 1186
Eulich, John, Pres.--Mark Andy, Inc., Chesterfield, MO, pg. 708
Evan, Uri, Pres.--I. Rokeach & Sons, Inc., Paramus, NJ, pg. 944
Evans, David S., Pres.--CBP Resources, Inc., Greensboro, NC, pg. 199
Evans, Gary, Pres. & Chief Exec. Officer--Sioux Honey Association, Sioux City, IA, pg. 1008
Evans, Hugh, Jr., Chm. Bd.--Western Federal Savings & Loan Association, Marina Del Rey, CA, pg. 1179
Evans, Jack Jr., Pres. & Chief Oper. Officer--Tom Thumb Food & Drugs, Inc., Dallas, TX, pg. 912
Evans, Jack W., Jr., Pres.--Pages Drugs, Dallas, TX, pg. 912
Evans, James C., Pres.--CTB Inc., Milford, IN, pg. 205
Evans, Jim, Pres. & Chief Exec. Officer--Evans, Hardy & Young, Inc., Santa Barbara, CA, pg. 390
Evans, John, Pres. & Gen. Mgr.--Stu Evans Lincoln-Mercury Inc., Southgate, MI, pg. 390
Evans, John, Sr. V.P.--Al Paul Lefton Co., Inc., Public Relations, Philadelphia, PA, pg. 666
Evans, John E., Chm. Bd. & Chief Exec. Officer--Allied Mutual Insurance Company, Des Moines, IA, pg. 38
Evans, Kenneth L., Pres. & Chief Exec. Officer--Oberdorfer Industries, Inc., Syracuse, NY, pg. 819
Evans, L. Victor, Pres.--Peterson Industries Inc., Decatur, AR, pg. 864
Evans, Larry J., Pres.--Western Co-Op Electric Utility Association, Wakeeney, KS, pg. 1178
Evans, Michael, Pres.--Hopple Plastics, Inc., Florence, KY, pg. 544
Evans, R. Evan, Pres.--Eva-Tone Inc., Clearwater, FL, pg. 390
Evans, Ronald, Pres. & Chief Exec. Officer-Best Western Intl.--B-W Advertising Agency, Phoenix, AZ, pg. 107
Evans, Ronald A., Pres. & Chief Exec. Officer--Best Western International, Inc., Phoenix, AZ, pg. 146
Evans, Thomas D., Pres.--The Vagabond Inns, San Diego, CA, pg. 1142
Evans, Tom, Pres.--The Vagabond Inns, San Diego, CA, pg. 1142
Evenson, Jerry, Pres.--Northwest Pipe Fittings, Inc., Billings, MT, pg. 815
Everett, Larry, Pres. & Gen. Mgr.--JFG Coffee Company, Knoxville, TN, pg. 923
Everist, Thomas, Pres.--L. G. Everist Inc., Sioux Falls, SD, pg. 392
Evers, Charles K., Chm. Bd., Pres. & Chief Exec. Officer--American Bread Company - Sunbeam Bakery, Nashville, TN, pg. 49
Ewart, James K., III, Pres. & Chief Exec. Officer--U.S. Construction Co., Inc., Columbia, SC, pg. 1135
Ewing, Al, Pres.--Cajun Electric Power Co-op, Baton Rouge, LA, pg. 207
Ewing, George, Jr., Pres.--A. H. Hoffman, Inc., Landisville, PA, pg. 538
Ezans, Yuri, Pres.--Mother's Food Products, Newark, NJ, pg. 944

Ezell, John William, Pres.--Purity Dairies Inc., Nashville, TN, pg. 901
Faaf, Charles, Pres.--U.S. Music Corporation, New Berlin, WI, pg. 1136
Faber, L., Pres.--Willmar Manufacturing, Willmar, MN, pg. 1193
Faber, N., Pres.--Neil Faber Media Inc., New York, NY, pg. 395
Fabian, John M., Pres. & Chief Exec. Officer--Anser (Analytic Services Inc.), Arlington, VA, pg. 76
Fabick, Harry, Pres. & Chief Oper. Officer--John Fabick Tractor Company, Fenton, MO, pg. 396
Fabrizio, Anthony M., Chm. Bd., Pres. & New Bus. Contact--Multi Media Services Corp., Alexandria, VA, pg. 775
Fabrizzi, Vincent J., Pres., New Bus. Contact & Merger/Acquisitions Contact--Paradigm Communications, Tampa, FL, pg. 847
Fagan, Robert, Chm. Bd. & Pres.--Audio Specialist, Inc., Newington, CT, pg. 98
Fagel, Harold, Pres. & Chief Exec. Officer--Aurora Packing Co., Inc., North Aurora, IL, pg. 98
Fahs, John C., Pres.--California Panel & Veneer Company, Cerritos, CA, pg. 210
Fain, John H., Chm., Pres., Chief Exec. & Chief Oper. Officer--Metro Information Services, Virginia Beach, VA, pg. 743
Fairbanks, J. Nelson, Pres.--United States Sugar Corporation, Clewiston, FL, pg. 1137
Fairchild, Henry B., III, Pres.--Handy Wacks Corporation, Sparta, MI, pg. 505
Faison, F.J., Jr., Pres.--Carroll's Foods, Inc., Warsaw, NC, pg. 225
Falkowski, Michael, Pres.--The Brulin Corporation, Indianapolis, IN, pg. 184
Fallarino, John, Pres.--Metpar Corporation, Westbury, NY, pg. 742
Fallaw, Michael, Gen. Mgr.--MacLean Molded Products, Inc., Wheeling, IL, pg. 698
Faller, Robert O., Chm. Bd., Pres.--FKQ Advertising Inc., Clearwater, FL, pg. 394
Famalette, Joseph, Pres. & Chief Exec. Officer--American Crystal Sugar Company, Moorhead, MN, pg. 51
Fanjoy, Weldon S., Pres.--Plastic Packaging, Inc., Hickory, NC, pg. 875
Farago, Peter, Pres. & Creative Dir.--Farago Advertising, New York, NY, pg. 399
Farina, Robert E., Pres.& Chief Exec. Officer--Global Turnkey Systems Inc., Waldwick, NJ, pg. 463
Farkas, Thomas P., Pres.--Dynamic Controls Corp., South Windsor, CT, pg. 356
Farley, James N., Pres. & Chief Exec. Officer--FamTec International, Inc., Des Plaines, IL, pg. 398
Farley, T.M., Mng. Partner & Chief Exec. Officer--Brown Brothers, Harriman & Co., New York, NY, pg. 181
Farlow, William S., Pres.--O. A. Newton & Son Co., Bridgeville, DE, pg. 805
Farmer, Bruce J., Pres. & Chief Exec. Officer--Farmers Marine Copper Works, Galveston, TX, pg. 401
Farmer, Bruce J., Pres.--Farmer's Copper & Industrial Supply, Galveston, TX, pg. 401
Farmer, James W., Pres.--LaMaster Farmer, Et Al, Minneapolis, MN, pg. 652
Farnsworth, Jack, Pres. & Chief Exec. Officer--Daily Racing Form, Inc., Hightstown, NJ, pg. 611
Farnsworth, Jack, Pres. & Chief Oper. Officer--Daily Racing Form, Inc. Pacific, Los Angeles, CA, pg. 611
Farnsworth, Jack, Pres. & Chief Oper. Officer--Daily Racing Form, Inc. (Midwest), Chicago, IL, pg. 611
Farnsworth, Jack, Pres. & Chief Oper. Officer--Daily Racing Form, Inc. (Northwest), Seattle, WA, pg. 611
Farnsworth, Ken, Chm. Bd. & Pres.--Rhodes International, Inc., Salt Lake City, UT, pg. 931
Farnsworth, Ross N., Pres.--Farnsworth Companies, Mesa, AZ, pg. 403
Farr, Mel, Pres.--Mel Farr Ford, Inc., Oak Park, MI, pg. 403
Farrell, Catherine, Pres.--Farrell CMA, New York, NY, pg. 403
Farrell, Frank A., Jr., Chm. Bd & Pres.--Hope's Architectural Products Inc., Jamestown, NY, pg. 543
Farrell, Jay, Pres. & New Bus. Contact--Davidson Marketing, Inc., Chicago, IL, pg. 318
Farris, Edward, Pres.--E F Industries, Carson, CA, pg. 359
Farver, Herb, Chm. Bd. & Pres.--Blissfield Manufacturing Company, Blissfield, MI, pg. 157
Fassio, Virgil, V.P. & Publisher--Seattle Post-Intelligencer, Seattle, WA, pg. 524
Fattaleh, Daniel L., Chm. Bd., Pres., Chief Exec. Officer & Treas.--The Delphi Glass Corp. Delphi Stained Glass Centers, Lansing, MI, pg. 326
Faucetta, Peter, Chm. Bd., Pres. & Chief Exec. Officer--Applied Graphics Technologies, Oceanside, NY, pg. 1136
Fauntleroy, Dort, Pres.--Moline Corporation, Saint Charles, IL, pg. 764
Fausel, J.M., V.P. & Gen. Mgr.--L&J Technologies, Morton Grove, IL, pg. 647
Favre, Art E., Pres.--Performance Contractors Inc., Baton Rouge, LA, pg. 861
Favreau, Armand, Pres.--W.S. Libbey Company, Great Falls, SC, pg. 674
Fayfield, Robert, Pres., Chief Exec. Officer & Chm. Bd.--Banner Engineering Corp., Minneapolis, MN, pg. 118
Feaster, Robert K., Pres.--Abingdon Press, Nashville, TN, pg. 10
Featherstone, Harry, Pres.--The Will-Burt Company, Orrville, OH, pg. 1190
Federico, Andrew, Pres. & Chief Exec. Officer--Novar Electronics, Barberton, OH, pg. 817
Fee, Frank J., III, Pres. & Treas.--Reliable Automatic Sprinkler Co., Inc., Mount Vernon, NY, pg. 924
Fehr, Robert, Pres.--Cox Lumber Co., Saint Petersburg, FL, pg. 294
Fehrm, Albert G., Pres.--Symmons Industries Inc., Braintree, MA, pg. 1069
Fehsenfeld, Mac, Pres. & Chief Exec. Officer--Crystal Flash Petroleum Corp., Indianapolis, IN, pg. 303
Fehskens, Ken, Pres. & Chief Exec. Officer--Ventura Associates, Inc., New York, NY, pg. 1147
Feigenbaum, Jacob I., Pres.--Robby Len Fashions, New York, NY, pg. 78
Feigenbaum, Robert E., Pres.--Charmglow Industries, Inc., DuQuoin, IL, pg. 240
Feimster, Jim, Pres.--Crosman Corporation, East Bloomfield, NY, pg. 695
Feinberg, Barry, Pres.--Nationwise Automotive, Inc., Columbus, OH, pg. 795
Feinberg, Martin, Pres.--Winner Communications, Inc., New York, NY, pg. 1196
Feinberg, Robert, Pres.--Duron, Inc., Beltsville, MD, pg. 355
Feld, Kenneth, Pres.--Ice Follies & Holiday on Ice, Vienna, VA, pg. 935
Feld, Kenneth J., Pres.--Ringling Bros., Barnum & Bailey Combined Shows, Inc., Vienna, VA, pg. 935
Felder, G. Frank, Pres.--Bankhead Enterprises Inc., Atlanta, GA, pg. 117
Feldheim, Richard, Pres.--Mil-Mor Media, Inc., Richmond, VA, pg. 753
Feldheim, Richard, Pres.--John F. Murray Advertising Agency Inc., New York, NY, pg. 776
Feldman, Gerald, Pres. & Chief Exec. Officer--Allied Advertising Agency, Boston, MA, pg. 37
Feldman, Joseph, Pres. & Chief Exec. Officer--Isfel Company, Inc., Rahway, NJ, pg. 582
Feldman, Steven M., Pres.--Totsy Manufacturing Company, Inc., Holyoke, MA, pg. 1103
Felker, G. Steven, Pres., Chief Exec. Officer & Treas.--Walton Monroe Mills, Inc., Monroe, GA, pg. 1162
Feller, Raymond, Pres.--University Press of America, Inc., Lanham, MD, pg. 953
Fellers, Doyle, Pres.--Fellers & Company, Austin, TX, pg. 405
Fellman, Nelson, Pres., Sls. Promo.--Rosanio, Bailets & Talamo, Inc., Cherry Hill, NJ, pg. 947
Fellowes, James E., Pres. & Chief Oper. Officer--Fellowes Manufacturing Co., Itasca, IL, pg. 405
Felsenthal, Donald, Pres.--Earle Industries, Inc Earle, AR, pg. 362
Felton, Chuck, Gen. Mgr.--South Central Co-Op, Fairfax, MN, pg. 1019
Felts, Jeffrey E., Pres. & Chief Exec. Officer--Hamilton Mutual Insurance Company Of Cincinnati, Cincinnati, OH, pg. 503
Fenn, Douglas, Pres.--Tell City Chair Co., Tell City, IN, pg. 1085
Fenning, W.M., Pres.--Cleveland Wrecking Company, Los Angeles, CA, pg. 255
Fenster, Albert J., Pres.--Capucci Creations International, Inc., Beverly Hills, CA, pg. 216
Fenton, Frank, Pres.--Rath Manufacturing, Janesville, WI, pg. 350
Ferenbach, Richard S., Pres.--Leon-Ferenbach Company, Hoboken, NJ, pg. 667
Ference, Carol, V.P. & Publr.--House Beautiful, New York, NY, pg. 523
Ferguson, Robert, Pres.--Maccabees Mutual Life Insurance, Southfield, MI, pg. 696
Ferguson, Robert L., Pres. & Chief Exec. Officer--CenterMark Properties, Inc., Saint Louis, MO, pg. 231
Ferguson, Sam, Pres., Chief Exec. & Chief Oper. Officer--Ferguson Industries, Dallas, TX, pg. 406
Ferguson, W.A. III, Pres.--Setco Sales Company, Cincinnati, OH, pg. 993
Ferguson, Whitworth, Jr., Pres.--Ferguson Electric Construction Co., Inc., Buffalo, NY, pg. 406
Ferman, James L., Jr., Pres.--Ferman Oldsmobile, Tampa, FL, pg. 406
Fern, Sanford M., Pres.--Fern/Hanaway, Inc. Advertising/Public Relations, Warwick, RI, pg. 407
Fernandez, Carlos C., Chm., Pres. & Chief Exec. Officer--Purity, Inc., Miami, FL, pg. 901
Fernandez, Castor A., Pres. & Chief Exec. Officer--Castor Advertising Corp., New York, NY, pg. 229
Fernandez, Manuel, Pres. & Chief Exec. Officer--Gartner Group, Inc., Stamford, CT, pg. 443
Fernandez, Nestor, Pres. & Chief Exec. Officer--Digitron Tool Co., Inc., Miamisburg, OH, pg. 337
Fernee, Brian, Pres.--RNF Media Corporation Inc., Beverly Hills, CA, pg. 907
Feroe, W. Richard, Pres.--Glen Raven Mills, Inc.-Textured Yarn Group-Norlina Division, Glen Raven, NC, pg. 461
Feroe, W. Richard, Pres.-Norlina Mills--Glen Raven Mills, Inc.-Textured Yarn Group, Norlina Div., Glen Raven, NC, pg. 462
Ferran, David J., Pres. & Chief Exec. Officer--Tylan General, Inc., San Diego, CA, pg. 1122
Ferrara, Arthur V., Pres. & Chief Exec. Officer--The Guardian Life Insurance Company of America, New York, NY, pg. 492
Ferreira-Pero, Marta, Pres.--JMCT Publicidad, New York, NY, pg. 604
Ferrell, James E., Chm. Bd., Pres. & Chief Exec. Officer--Ferrell Companies Inc./Ferrellgas, Liberty, MO, pg. 407
Ferrelli, Richard Gaetano, Pres. & Acct. Services--Greengage Associates, Inc., New York, NY, pg. 485
Ferrera, Kenneth G., Pres.--James Ferrera & Sons, Inc., Canton, MA, pg. 407
Ferrigno, Emanuel, Pres.--Creative Salon Furniture Inc., Brooklyn, NY, pg. 297
Ferry, Richard M., Chm. Bd., Pres. & Chief Exec. Officer--Korn/Ferry International, Los Angeles, CA, pg. 642
Fertell, Paul A., Pres., Chief Oper. & Chief Fin. Officer--Seton Company, Norristown, PA, pg. 993
Fertitta, George A., Pres. & Chief Oper. Officer--Margeotes Fertitta & Weiss, Inc., New York, NY, pg. 706
Fesenmyer, D. Kennedy, Pres. & Chief Exec. Officer--Lobdell-Emery Manufacturing Company, Alma, MI, pg. 680
Fetridge, Clark W., Pres. & Chief Exec. Officer--The Dartnell Corporation, Chicago, IL, pg. 316
Fetter, Thompson, Pres. & Chief Exec. Officer--Kettenburg Marine Corporation, San Diego, CA, pg. 626
Fetterman, Lewis M., Jr., Pres. & Chief Exec. Officer--Lundy Packing Co. Inc., Clinton, NC, pg. 687
Feuer, Irwin, Pres. & Chief Exec. Officer--Feuer Leather Corporation, Hawthorne, NY, pg. 407
Feuerstein, Aaron, Pres. & Chief Exec. Officer--Malden Mills Industries, Inc., Lawrence, MA, pg. 702
Feury, Robert, Pres.--Allied Building Products Corporation, East Rutherford, NJ, pg. 37
Fey, Thomas, Pres.--Prince Gardner Incorporated, Saint Louis, MO, pg. 890
Feys, Allan, Pres.--H.O. Trerice Company, Oak Park, MI, pg. 1110
Ficks, Lee B., Pres., Chief Exec. Officer, & Treas.--Ficks Reed Company, Cincinnati, OH, pg. 408
Fidellow, Alan E., Pres.--Wolff & Munier, Inc., Hawthorne, NY, pg. 1199
Fiebig, Phil, Mng. Dir.--Leo Burnett Sdn. Bhd., Kuala Lumpur,, Malaysia, pg. 193
Fiederlein, G.L., Pres. & Chief Oper. Officer--R. T. Vanderbilt Company, Inc., Norwalk, CT, pg. 1144
Fiedler, Richard D., Pres.--Crown Fence Co., Pasadena, CA, pg. 302
Fiedler, Richard K., Pres.--Admiral Maintenance Service L.P., Lincolnwood, IL, pg. 18
Fiegehen, Al, Pres.--Cubix Corporation, Carson City, NV, pg. 303
Field, Kenneth W., Pres. & Chief Exec. Officer--Continental Web Press, Inc., Itasca, IL, pg. 280
Field, Lawrence, Pres. & Chief Exec. Officer--Field Container Company, L.P., Elk Grove Village, IL, pg. 409
Field, Ronald, Pres.--Consolidated Beverages, Inc., Auburn, MA, pg. 276
Fielding, Bill, Pres.--Excel Corp., Wichita, KS, pg. 219
Fields, Catherine M., Pres. & Chief Exec. Officer--P. S. International Inc., Indianapolis, IN, pg. 837
Fields, Debra, Chm. Bd., Pres. & Chief Exec. Officer--Mrs. Fields' Inc., Park City, UT, pg. 761
Fields, Debra, Pres. & Chief Exec. Officer--La Petite Boulangerie, Inc., Park City, UT, pg. 761
Fields, Debra, Pres., Chief Exec. & Chief Oper. Officer--Mrs. Fields Cookies Inc., Park City, UT, pg. 761
Fields, F.W., Pres.--The Coe Mfg. Co., Painesville, OH, pg. 258
Fierberg, Stephen J., Pres.--Day Data Systems, Radnor, PA, pg. 320
Fierko, Edward J., Pres.--Eco Water Systems, Saint Paul, MN, pg. 367
Fiery, D.E., Pres.--Miller Chemical & Fertilizer Corp., Hanover, PA, pg. 32
Fiesler, Robert E., Pres.--Fort Worth Lumber Company, Fort Worth, TX, pg. 425
Figge, Frank, Pres.--Servus Footwear Company, Rock Island, IL, pg. 993
Figurelli, J.A., Pres.--Sargent Manufacturing Company, New Haven, CT, pg. 361
Fike, John T., Pres. & Chief Exec. Officer--Northwest Paper Converting Company, Vancouver, WA, pg. 814
Fiman, Jack, Chm. Bd. & Pres.--Martin & Benedict Inc., Santa Monica, CA, pg. 714
Fimbel, Edward, Jr., Chm. Bd. & Pres.--Fimbel Door Corporation, Whitehouse, NJ, pg. 409
Finch, G.G., Pres.--Pressed Steel Tank Co., Inc., West Allis, WI, pg. 887
Finch, Sam, Pres.--Blue Grass Foods, Inc., Crescent Springs, KY, pg. 160
Findlay, Cary, Chm. Bd. & Pres.--Conso Products Company, Union, SC, pg. 276
Findlay, Walstein C., Jr., Pres.--Wally Findlay Galleries International, Chicago, IL, pg. 410
Findlay, Walstein C., Jr., Pres.--Wally Findlay Galleries, Inc., Palm Beach, FL, pg. 410
Findlay, Walstein C., Jr., Pres.--Wally Findlay Galleries, Inc., New York, NY, pg. 410
Findley, John, Pres.--Findley Adhesives, Inc., Wauwatosa, WI, pg. 410
Fine, Allan H., Co-Pres.--M. Fine & Sons Manufacturing Co., Inc., New York, NY, pg. 411
Fine, Lonnie, Pres.--Triangle Maintenance Corporation, Valley Stream, NY, pg. 1112
Fine, Martin L., Co-Pres.--M. Fine & Sons Manufacturing Co., Inc., New York, NY, pg. 411
Fine, S.A., Pres. & Chief Oper. Officer--The Biltrite Corporation, Waltham, MA, pg. 151
Fine, Stephen L., Co-Pres.--M. Fine & Sons Manufacturing Co., Inc., New York, NY, pg. 411
Finegood, David, Pres.--Good Companies, Carson, CA, pg. 470
Fineman, Bernard S., Pres. & Treas.--Caldwell Tanks, Inc., Louisville, KY, pg. 209
Finerty, Patrick, Pres. & V.P.-Fin.--Robert B. Aikens & Associates Inc., Troy, MI, pg. 26
Finesilver, Lynn, Pres. & Chief Exec. Officer--Finesilver Manufacturing Company, San Antonio, TX, pg. 411
Finger, Robert, Pres.--Finger Furniture Company, Inc., Houston, TX, pg. 411
Fingerle, John B., Pres.--Fingerle Lumber Co., Ann Arbor, MI, pg. 411
Fingerman, Edward, Pres.--The Patrician Group, New York, NY, pg. 851
Fink, David, Pres.--Guilford Transportation Industries Inc., Merrimack, NH, pg. 493
Fink, George, Pres.--Remco Enterprises, Inc., Houston, TX, pg. 926
Fink, Ruth G., Pres.--CGF Industries, Topeka, KS, pg. 201
Finkell, Donald, Pres. & Chief Exec. Officer--Standard Plywood, Inc., Clinton, SC, pg. 1037
Finkelstein, David, Pres.--Leathers Best, Melville, NY, pg. 664
Finkelstein, Marc S., Pres.--Hughes-Treitler Manufacturing Corporation, Garden City, NY, pg. 552

Finlayson, Bruce A., V.P.-Mktg.--Hawthorne Adv., Inc., Philadelphia, PA, pg. 518
Finley, Pat, Pres.--Security Products Company of Delaware, Inc., Minneapolis, MN, pg. 1138
Finley, Patrick M., Pres. & Gen. Mgr.--Universal Cooperatives, Inc., Minneapolis, MN, pg. 1138
Finley, Peggy, Pres.--American Antenna Corp, Elgin, IL, pg. 216
Finlon, Cathey M., Pres., Treas. & New Bus. Contact--McClain Finlon Advertising, Denver, CO, pg. 727
Finn, J.L., Pres.--Howden Sirocco inc., Hyde Park, MA, pg. 547
Finn, J.L., Pres.--Sturtevant Div., Boston, MA, pg. 547
Finn, Jerome, Pres.--P/A Industries, Inc., Bloomfield, CT, pg. 835
Finnegan, Lawrence J., Chm., Pres., Chief Exec. & Chief Oper. Officer--Boston Mutual Life Insurance Co., Canton, MA, pg. 167
Fiondella, Robert W., Pres. & Principal--Phoenix Home Life Mutual Insurance Company, Hartford, CT, pg. 868
Fiore, Robert J., Pres., Chief Oper. Officer & Creative Dir.--Warwick Baker & Fiore Inc., New York, NY, pg. 1165
Firestone, Sue, Pres. & Chief Exec. Officer--Design 1 Interiors, Los Angeles, CA, pg. 332
Firnhaber, Robert, Pres. & Grp. V.P.-Ambassador Brand--Ambassador Cards, Kansas City, MO, pg. 50
Fisch, Michael J., Pres. & Cheif Exec. Officer--The Bakersfield Californian, Bakersfield, CA, pg. 115
Fischer, Charlotte G., Pres. & Chief Exec. Officer--Parklane Hosiery Co., Inc., Hasbrouck Heights, NJ, pg. 849
Fischer, Stephen E., Pres.--Pharmacaps Inc., Elizabeth, NJ, pg. 866
Fishbein, Harry, Pres.--United Envelope Company, Inc., New York, NY, pg. 1131
Fisher, Alfred J., III, Pres.--General Safety Corporation, Saint Clair Shores, MI, pg. 450
Fisher, Bob, Pres.--RE/MAX International, Inc., Englewood, CO, pg. 915
Fisher, David G., Pres. & Chief Exec. Officer--Pioneer Engineering & Manufacturing Co., Warren, MI, pg. 871
Fisher, Dwayne, Pres.--The Scoular Company, Omaha, NE, pg. 983
Fisher, Henry, Pres.--Pyramid Handbags Inc., New York, NY, pg. 901
Fisher, Lawrence, Pres. & Dir.--Braun/Ketchum Public Relations, Los Angeles, CA, pg. 625
Fisher, Mike, Jr., Pres. & Chief Exec. Officer--Fisher Graphic Industries, Modesto, CA, pg. 415
Fisher, Robert E., Pres.--Plibrico Co., Chicago, IL, pg. 877
Fisher, Robert J., Pres.--Fisher Skylights, Inc., West Nyack, NY, pg. 415
Fisher, Steven, Chm. Bd., Pres. & Chief Exec. Officer--Continental Circuits Corp., Phoenix, AZ, pg. 278
Fishman, Alan H., Mng. Partner--Adler & Shaykin, New York, NY, pg. 17
Fishman, Mark, Pres.--Fishman & Tobin, Inc., Philadelphia, PA, pg. 415
Fisk, Wallace K., Pres. & Chief Exec. Officer--AmClyde Engineered Products, Inc., Saint Paul, MN, pg. 47
Fitzgerald, D.F., Pres. & Treas.--Son Chief Electrics, Inc., Winsted, CT, pg. 1018
Fitzgerald, David P., Pres.--Fitzgerald & Co., Atlanta, GA, pg. 416
Fitzgerald, Duane D., Pres. & Chief Exec. Officer--Bath Iron Works, Bath, ME, pg. 126
Fitzgerald, John W., Pres.--Bolton-Emerson, Inc., Lawrence, MA, pg. 163
Fitzgerald, Robert, Pres.--Flavor House Products, Inc., Dothan, AL, pg. 417
FitzGibbon, David A., V.P. & Chief Oper. Officer--Bardes Corp., Cincinnati, OH, pg. 119
Fitzpatrick, Gerard J., Pres.--Fitzpatrick & Weller, Inc., Ellicottville, NY, pg. 416
Fitzpatrick, Michael J., Pres.--Hamlin, Inc., Lake Mills, WI, pg. 503
FitzPatrick, Paul, Pres. & Chief Oper. Officer--The Weather Channel, Atlanta, GA, pg. 654
Fitzsimons, Michael J., Pres. & Chief Oper. Officer--Copper & Brass Sales, Inc., East Detroit, MI, pg. 284
Fladmark, O. Lars, Pres.--Beckley-Cardy, Inc., Duluth, MN, pg. 21
Flanagan, David J., Jr., Pres.--Flanagan Brothers, Bear Creek, WI, pg. 416
Flanagan, James P., Pres. & Dir.-Client Services--Tinsley Advertising, Miami, FL, pg. 1099
Flanagan, John, Pres.--Goodheart-Willcox Co., Inc., South Holland, IL, pg. 470
Flanders, Allen F., Pres. & Chief Exec. Officer--Hope Design Group, San Diego, CA, pg. 543
Flanders, Dudley K., Pres. & Chief Exec. Officer--Flanders Industries, Inc., Fort Smith, AR, pg. 416
Flaxman, Richard L., Pres.--Towne, Silverstein, Rotter Inc., New York, NY, pg. 1104
Fleenor, Roger H., Pres.--Red Apple, Inc., Ontario, OR, pg. 918
Fleischer, Morton H., Pres., Chief Exec. Officer & Treas.--Franchise Finance Corp. of America, Scottsdale, AZ, pg. 428
Fleischhacker, Joseph J., Sr., Pres.--Lake Region Manufacturing Company, Inc., Chaska, MN, pg. 651
Fleischman, Marvin H., Pres., Chief Exec. & Chief Fin. Officer--Lakeside Refining Co. Inc., Southfield, MI, pg. 651
Fleischmann, David, Pres.--Standard Manifold Company, Inc., Chicago, IL, pg. 1037
Fleming, Donald R., Pres. & Chief Oper. Officer--Zoeller Co., Louisville, KY, pg. 1220
Fleming, James B., Pres.--Triangle Distributing Company, Santa Fe Springs, CA, pg. 1111
Fleming, Kenneth, Pres. & Chief Oper. Officer--World Publishing Company, Tulsa, OK, pg. 1203
Fleming, Mark Jack, Chm. Bd., Pres. & Chief Exec. Officer--Merchants Publishing Co., Kalamazoo, MI, pg. 739
Fleming, Robert W., Pres.--Folger Nolan Fleming Douglas, Washington, DC, pg. 422
Fletcher, Andy, Pres. & Chief Exec. Officer--Fletcher Hunt Wirth Associates, Inc., Kansas City, MO, pg. 418
Fletcher, Donald J., Pres.--George S. May International Company, Park Ridge, IL, pg. 723
Fletcher, Robert, Pres.--Fletcher Enterprises, Phoenix, AZ, pg. 418
Fletcher, Susan, Chm. Bd. & Pres.--Suzannah Farms, Pennsauken, NJ, pg. 1065
Flint, H. Howard, II, Pres. & Chief Oper. Officer--Flint Ink Corp., Detroit, MI, pg. 419
Floathe, Maury, Chm. Bd. & Pres.--Floathe Johnson Associates, Inc., Kirkland, WA, pg. 419
Flock, H.H., Pres.--Tuthill Pump, Alsip, IL, pg. 1120
Flodstrom, Len, Pres.--Flodstrom Construction Co., Deerfield, IL, pg. 419
Flood, Lawrence P., Pres. & Chief Exec. Officer--Owen Steel Co., Inc., Columbia, SC, pg. 834
Flood, Peter E., Pres. & Chief Exec. Officer--The Flood Company, Hudson, OH, pg. 419
Florence, Leonard, Chm. Bd., Pres. & Chief Exec. Officer--Syratech Corporation, East Boston, MA, pg. 1070
Florence, Leonard, Pres.--Wallace International Silversmiths, Inc., East Boston, MA, pg. 1070
Florez-Estrada, Fernando, Mng. Dir.--Causa Publicidad, Lima, Peru, pg. 192
Flori, John R., Pres. & Chief. Exec. Officer--Flori Corp., Phoenix, AZ, pg. 420
Florig, Edward, Pres. & Treas.--Florig Equipment Company, Inc., Conshohocken, PA, pg. 421
Florio, Steven T., Pres. & Chief Exec. Officer--The New Yorker Magazine, New York, NY, pg. 803
Florio, Thomas, Publisher--Conde Nast Traveler, New York, NY, pg. 19
Floto, Ronald, Pres.--Kash N Karry Food Stores, Inc., Tampa, FL, pg. 617
Floum, Robert, Pres. & Chief Exec. Officer--Fishers Big Wheel Inc., New Castle, PA, pg. 415
Flowers, F.W., Jr., Pres.--Eager Beaver, Lake Wales, FL, pg. 362
Flummerfelt, J. Kent, Pres., Chief Exec. Officer & Chm.--Lechmere, Inc., Woburn, MA, pg. 665
Flynn, Robert, Pres.--Home Innovations Bed Fashions, New York, NY, pg. 541
Flynn, Terrance L., Pres. & Brdcst. Production--Flynn/Sabatino, Miamisburg, OH, pg. 421
Flynn, William J., Pres.--Mutual of America, New York, NY, pg. 777
Fogarty, Robert S., Jr., Chm. Bd. & Pres.--Kindel Furniture Company, Grand Rapids, MI, pg. 630
Fogarty, William H., Pres.--Fogarty & Klein/Winius Brandon, Houston, TX, pg. 421
Fogel, William, Pres.--Jordon Commercial Refrigerator Co., Philadelphia, PA, pg. 605
Fogg, A.S., Jr., Pres. & Chief Oper. Officer--Farm Stores, Inc., Miami, FL, pg. 401
Fogg, F.W., Pres. & Chief Exec. Officer--Southeastern Medequip, Inc., Jacksonville Beach, FL, pg. 1019
Fohrman, Neal, Pres., Chief Exec. & Chief Fin. Officer & Controller--Red Calliope & Associates, Inc., Los Angeles, CA, pg. 918
Fojtasek, Joe, Pres.--Fojtasek Companies, Inc., Irving, TX, pg. 421
Foley, Bill, Chief Exec. Officer--Greeff Fabrics, Port Chester, NY, pg. 262
Foley, Dennis J., Pres.--Lombardi FoodService, Inc., Utica, MI, pg. 681
Foley, John P., Pres.--NFM Creative Communications, Pittsburgh, PA, pg. 780
Foley, Judith K., Partner--NFM Creative Communications, Pittsburgh, PA, pg. 780
Foley, Patrick, Chm., Pres. & Chief Exec. Officer--DHL Corporation, Redwood City, CA, pg. 309
Foley, Patrick, Chm., Pres. & Chief Exec. Officer--DHL Airways, Inc., Redwood City, CA, pg. 309
Foley, Paul, Jr., Pres.--Foley Holding Company, Inc., Wichita, KS, pg. 422
Foley, Stephen X., Pres.--Steve Foley Cadillac, Northbrook, IL, pg. 422
Foley, Thomas C., Chm. Bd. & Chief Exec. Officer--NTC Group, Greenwich, CT, pg. 781
Foley, Vicky L., Chm. Bd. & Pres.--V.F. Energies, Inc., Madisonville, KY, pg. 1141
Foley, Vicky L., Pres.--Triple F Limousin Cattle, Paris, KY, pg. 1141
Foley, William A., Pres.--C&A Wallcoverings, Cleveland, OH, pg. 262
Folkert, Rod, Pres. & Chief Exec. Officer--Grocers Baking Co., Grand Rapids, MI, pg. 488
Follan, James, Pres.--First Trust Savings Bank, Jacksonville, FL, pg. 491
Follett, C.R., Pres.--Follett Library Book Co., Crystal Lake, IL, pg. 422
Follett, K.A., Pres.--Wilcox & Follett Co., Chicago, IL, pg. 422
Foltz, C. Henry, Pres. & Chief Oper. Officer--Liggett-Stashower, Inc., Cleveland, OH, pg. 675
Folz, Theodore W., Pres. & Chief Exec. Officer--Consolidated Cigar Corporation, Fort Lauderdale, FL, pg. 276
Fones, Maynard, Pres.--Fones & Mann Inc., New York, NY, pg. 422
Fontaine, George, Gen. Mgr.--Sandpiper Cove Div., Destin, FL, pg. 900
Fontaine, R. Richard, Pres. & Chief Oper. Officer--B. Dalton Bookseller, Inc., New York, NY, pg. 120
Fontenot, M.L., Chm. Bd. & Pres.--Perfect Fit Industries, Inc., Monroe, NC, pg. 861
Foot, Silas B., III, Pres.--S.B. Foot Tanning Co., Red Wing, MN, pg. 919
Foote, J.D., Pres.--Pegasus International Corporation, Pennington, NJ, pg. 855
Foran, Dave, Pres.--Equipment Manufacturing, Inc., Warren, MI, pg. 385
Forbes, Malcolm S., Jr., Pres., Chief Exec. & Editor-in-Chief--Forbes, Inc., New York, NY, pg. 423
Forbriger, Connie, Pres.--Tressa, Inc., Erlanger, KY, pg. 1110
Ford, Dennis P., Pres.--Marstrat, Inc., Chicago, IL, pg. 714
Ford, James, Pres.--Tabs Associates, Abingdon, MD, pg. 1076
Ford, Jay G., Pres.--Vindicator Corporation, Austin, TX, pg. 1152
Ford, John S., Jr., Pres.--Ford Steel Co., Inc., Maryland Heights, MO, pg. 423
Ford, William J., Pres.--National Truck Leasing System, Oakbrook Terrace, IL, pg. 794
Forde, John P., Pres. & Chief Oper. Officer--Times Fiber Communications, Inc., Wallingford, CT, pg. 648
Forester, Benjamin, Pres.--Rex Lumber Company, Acton, MA, pg. 930
Forestier, Jean-Loup le, Mng. Dir.--BSB France, Puteaux, France, pg. 109
Forgione, Anthony, Chm. Bd. & Pres.--Boyer Bros. Inc., Altoona, PA, pg. 169
Forman, Willis M., Pres., Chief Exec. Officer & Treas.--Paper Calmenson & Co., Saint Paul, MN, pg. 847
Forrest, B., Pres.--W. E. Long Company, Chicago, IL, pg. 682
Forssberg, Henrik J., Pres., Chief Exec. Officer & Creative Dir.--Hank Forssberg, Inc., Hackensack, NJ, pg. 424
Forstmann, Theodore J., Partner--Forstmann Little & Co., New York, NY, pg. 424
Forsyth, James G., III, Pres.--Moto, Inc., Belleville, IL, pg. 773
Forsythe, Gerald, Chm. Bd., Pres. & Chief Exec. Officer--Indeck Power Equipment Company, Wheeling, IL, pg. 564
Forsythe, James, Pres.--Forsythe Marcelli Johnson Advertising, Inc., Newport Beach, CA, pg. 425
Forte, I.R., Pres.--SK Hand Tool Corp., Chicago, IL, pg. 963
Forter, Rod, Pres.--The Read Corporation, Middleboro, MA, pg. 916
Fortgang, Mathew, Pres.--M. Fabrikant & Sons, Inc., New York, NY, pg. 396
Forti, Ed, Pres.--D.F.A. Advertising, New York, NY, pg. 309
Fortier, John A., Pres.--Bacco Construction Co., Iron Mountain, MI, pg. 108
Fortinberry, Glen W., Chm. & Chief Exec. Officer--Ross Roy Group, Inc., Bloomfield Hills, MI, pg. 949
Fortinberry, Glen W., Chm. Bd., Pres. & Chief Exec. Officer--Ross Roy Inc., Bloomfield Hills, MI, pg. 950
Fortson, Thomas N., Jr., Pres.--Terminix Service, Inc., Columbia, SC, pg. 1088
Fortunoff, Alan, Pres.--Fortunoff, Westbury, NY, pg. 425
Fosket, Gene, Pres.--Plasma Technology, Inc., Torrance, CA, pg. 874
Foss, Stephen W., Pres.--Foss Manufacturing Company Incorporated, Hampton, NH, pg. 426
Fossa, Ernest, Partner & Dir. Media Services--Goldberg Fossa Seid Advertising, Inc., New York, NY, pg. 465
Foster, Boyd, Pres. & Chief Exec. Officer--Arrowhead Mills, Inc., Hereford, TX, pg. 86
Foster, G. A., Jr., Pres.--Guaranty Corporation, Baton Rouge, LA, pg. 491
Foster, Gregg L., Pres.--Elyria Foundry Company, Elyria, OH, pg. 378
Foster, John, Pres.--Foster Pontiac, Inc., Milwaukee, WI, pg. 426
Foster, Lawrence H., Pres.--Foster Refrigerator Corporation, Hudson, NY, pg. 426
Foster, Neil, Pres. & Chief Exec. Officer--Star Sales Co., Inc., Knoxville, TN, pg. 1040
Foster, P. Wesley, Jr., Pres.--The Long & Foster Companies, Inc., Fairfax, VA, pg. 682
Foster, P. Wesley, Jr., Pres.--The Long & Foster Real Estate, Inc., Fairfax, VA, pg. 682
Foster, Ronald B., Pres.--Rea Magnet Wire Company, Inc., Fort Wayne, IN, pg. 915
Foster, Ronald H., Pres.--The Stellar Group Inc., Jacksonville, FL, pg. 1046
Foster, W.B., Pres.--Modern Woodmen of America, Rock Island, IL, pg. 763
Foster, Willett S., IV, Pres. & Chief Exec. Officer--Edlund Company, Inc., Burlington, VT, pg. 368
Fotouhi, Farida, Pres.--Fotouhi Alonso Inc. Advertising & Marketing, Los Angeles, CA, pg. 427
Fournier, Anne, Chm.--IG Conseil S.A., Paris,, France, pg. 625
Fournier, Daniel S., Natl. Sls. Mgr.--Sheffield Silver Co., Taunton, MA, pg. 920
Fowler, Frederick V., Jr., Chm. Bd., Pres. & Chief Exec. Officer--Fred V. Fowler Company, Inc., Newton, MA, pg. 427
Fowler, Jack, Pres.--Arcata Corporation, San Francisco, CA, pg. 80
Fowler, Jack W., Pres. & Chief Exec. Officer--Arcata Graphics Company, Baltimore, MD, pg. 80
Fowler, Mark, Pres.--Systech Computer Corporation, San Diego, CA, pg. 1071
Fowler, Theodore M., Jr., Pres. & Chief Exec. Officer--Golden Corral Corporation, Raleigh, NC, pg. 466
Fox, Herbert C., Chm. Bd., Pres., Chief Exec. Officer & Dir.-Pub. Rels.--Active Electrical Supply Company, Chicago, IL, pg. 15
Fox, John E., Jr., Pres.--Arkansas Oak Flooring, Pine Bluff, AR, pg. 83
Fox, Michael P., Pres.--Naz-Dar Company, Chicago, IL, pg. 1095
Fox, Richard B., Pres.--C.B. Fox Company, New Orleans, LA, pg. 427
Foxworth, Walter L., Pres.--Foxworth-Galbraith Lumber Co., Dallas, TX, pg. 428
Fraatz, Paul, Jr., Pres. & Treas.--Pacor, Inc., Philadelphia, PA, pg. 842

France, B.E., Pres., Chief Oper. Officer & Treas.--The H. T. Hackney Co., Knoxville, TN, pg. 498
France, William A., Jr., Pres.--J. H. France Refractories Co., Snow Shoe, PA, pg. 428
Franceschini, Donald J., Pres.--Playtex Apparel Inc., Stamford, CT, pg. 876
Francis, Thomas M., Pres.--Windsor Industries, Inc., Englewood, CO, pg. 1195
Franco, M., Pres.--Soundesign Corporation, Jersey City, NJ, pg. 1018
Frank, Cary, Pres.--Arrow Chevrolet, Inc., Midlothian, IL, pg. 85
Frank, George, Pres.--Corner Pockets of America, Billings, MT, pg. 286
Frank, Gerrie E., Pres. & Gen. Mgr.--Frank Industries, Inc., Brown City, MI, pg. 429
Frank, H. Alan, Pres., Chief Fin. Officer & Treas.--Union Industries, Inc., Providence, RI, pg. 1128
Frank, James S., Pres.--Frank Consolidated Enterprises Inc., Des Plaines, IL, pg. 428
Frank, Karl, Gen. Mgr.--Tucker Rocky Distributing, Portland, OR, pg. 1118
Frank, Mick, Pres.-Homes--Scherer Bros. Lumber Company, Minneapolis, MN, pg. 976
Frank, Richard, Pres. & Chief Oper. Officer--Monterey's Tex Mex Cafe, Irving, TX, pg. 767
Frank, Richard R., Pres.--Lawry's Restaurants, Inc., Los Angeles, CA, pg. 663
Frank, Thomas E., Pres. & Chief Exec. Officer--Hickory Farms, Inc., Maumee, OH, pg. 532
Frankel, Barry R., Pres., Chief Oper. Officer & New Bus. Contact--SJ Weinstein Associates Inc., New York, NY, pg. 1173
Frankenstein, Annabel E., Pres.--Heather Crolie, Inc., Rochester, NY, pg. 300
Franklin, E. Thomas, Chm., Pres. & Treas.--Franklin Baking Co., Inc., Goldsboro, NC, pg. 429
Franklin, Larry, Pres. & Chief Exec. Officer--Harte-Hanks Communications, Inc., San Antonio, TX, pg. 513
Franklin, Larry, Pres.--Franklin Sports Industries, Stoughton, MA, pg. 429
Franklin, R.J., Pres. & Chief Fin. Officer--McMaster Carr Supply Co. Inc., Elmhurst, IL, pg. 731
Franze, Harry, Pres.--AMF Bakery Systems, Richmond, VA, pg. 5
Franzen, Eberhard, Pres.--Presto Lock, Inc., Garfield, NJ, pg. 888
Franzone, John B., Pres. & Chief Exec. Officer--Fawn Industries, Inc., Hunt Valley, MD, pg. 404
Frascari, Dr. Giuliano, Mng. Dir.--Telephone Marketing Programs-SMET, Milan,, Italy, pg. 1074
Frascella, Anthony J., Pres.--Predco, Inc., Pennsauken, NJ, pg. 341
Fraser, Arthur W., Pres.--Peck Road Ford Truck Sales, Whittier, CA, pg. 854
Fraser, Duncan, Pres.--Interform Corporation, Bridgeville, PA, pg. 574
Frazer, Nimrod T., Chm. & Pres.--The Enstar Group, Inc., Montgomery, AL, pg. 382
Frazier, Richard M., Acting Chm. Bd. & Pres.--Hickman Williams & Co. Inc., Cincinnati, OH, pg. 532
Frazier, Warner, Pres. & Chief Exec. Officer--Simplicity Manufacturing, Inc., Port Washington, WI, pg. 1006
Frechette, Peter L., Pres. & Chief Exec. Officer--Patterson Dental Company, Minneapolis, MN, pg. 851
Frederic, Rand, Pres. & Chief Exec. Officer--Frederic Printing Company, Aurora, CO, pg. 430
Frederick, Ron, Pres.--Johnson Technology, Muskegon, MI, pg. 431
Fredericks, James, Chief Oper. Officer--Benson Corp., Weyauwega, WI, pg. 447
Fredericks, Wesley C., Jr., Pres. & Chief Oper. Officer--Manufacturers Products Company, Warren, MI, pg. 705
Frederickson, A.D., Pres.--Road Machinery Company, Phoenix, AZ, pg. 937
Fredman, Michael, Chm.--Dorland Business Communications, London,, United Kingdom, pg. 111
Fredrickson, John W., Pres.--Fredrickson Motor Express Corp., Charlotte, NC, pg. 430
Fredrickson, Joseph, Pres.--Eldorado Chemical Company, San Antonio, TX, pg. 373
Freebairn, John C., Pres. & Chief Oper. Officer--Cascino Purcell Freebairn, Atlanta, GA, pg. 227
Freed, Gloria, Pres.--Freed & Associates, Baltimore, MD, pg. 430
Freed, Joseph, Chm. Bd. & Chief Exec. Officer--Capitol Construction Group, Inc., Wheeling, IL, pg. 215
Freedland, Hymen, Pres.--Ambassador Steel Co., Detroit, MI, pg. 47
Freedland, Richard, Pres.--Freedland Industries Corporation, Dearborn, MI, pg. 430
Freedland, Sidney, Chm. Bd. & Pres.--Homemaker Shops, Inc., Southfield, MI, pg. 542
Freedman, Eugene M., Chm. Bd. & Chief Exec. Officer--Coopers & Lybrand, New York, NY, pg. 283
Freedman, Leslie, Pres. & Chief Fin. Officer--FMS Management Systems, Inc., North Miami Beach, FL, pg. 394
Freedman, Mark, Pres.--S. Freedman & Sons, Inc., Landover, MD, pg. 430
Freeland, Robert D., Pres.--Havens Steel Co., Kansas City, MO, pg. 517
Freeman, Benjamin H., II, Pres.--H. Freeman & Son, Inc., Philadelphia, PA, pg. 431
Freeman, Bruce, Pres.--Griffin Homes, Inc., Calabasas, CA, pg. 487
Freeman, Gary, Pres.--Freeman Blanshei Partners, San Francisco, CA, pg. 431
Freeman, Joshua M., Pres. & Chief Oper. Officer--Carl M. Freeman Associates, Inc., Potomac, MD, pg. 431
Freeman, Larry J., Pres. & Chief Exec. Officer--Freeman Cosmetic Corp., Los Angeles, CA, pg. 431
Freeman, Norman, Pres.--Associated Air Freight, Inc., New Hyde Park, NY, pg. 89
Freeman, Ray, Chief Oper. Officer--Remington Apparel, Inc., Wilmington, NC, pg. 926
Freeman, Walter, Pres.--Kentucky Indiana Lumber Co. Inc., Louisville, KY, pg. 623
Freeman, William A., Pres.--Watkins Associated Industries Inc., Atlanta, GA, pg. 1167
Frehner, Garth E., Pres.--Frehner Construction Company, Inc., North Las Vegas, NV, pg. 432
Frelat, B., Pres.--Rail Europe Inc., White Plains, NY, pg. 910
French, Morton R., Chm. Bd., Pres., Chief Exec. & Chief Fin. Officer--Commercial Plastics & Supplies Corp., Richmond Hill, NY, pg. 268
French, Philip, Pres. & Chief Exec. Officer--Countrymark Cooperative, Inc., Indianapolis, IN, pg. 290
French, Philip, Pres.--Countrymark Co-Op Inc., Delaware, OH, pg. 290
Frenzer, Peter, Pres.--Nationwide Life Insurance Co., Columbus, OH, pg. 795
Fresard, F. James, Pres.--Jim Fresard Pontiac Buick, Inc., Royal Oak, MI, pg. 432
Frew, Bud L., Pres. & Chief Exec Officer--MFA Incorporated, Columbia, MO, pg. 692
Frey, Chuck, Gen. Mgr.--NuArc Co., Philadelphia, PA, pg. 817
Frey, Dale F., Chm. Bd. & Pres.--General Electric Master Retirement Trust, Stamford, CT, pg. 449
Frey, John S., Chm. Bd. & Pres.--John S. Frey Enterprises, Los Angeles, CA, pg. 433
Frey, Perry, Pres. & Gen. Mgr.-WTVN-AM--Great American Broadcasting Company, Cincinnati, OH, pg. 52
Frey, Thomas W., Pres. & Chief Exec. Officer--Amano Cincinnati, Inc., Cincinnati, OH, pg. 46
Frezel, Jerrold A., Pres.--Premier Dental Products Company, Norristown, PA, pg. 886
Friberg, John R., Pres., Chief Exec. Officer & Sec.--Eastern Smelting & Refining Corporation, Lynn, MA, pg. 363
Fricchione, Henry, Pres.--Simplex Industries, Inc., Scranton, PA, pg. 1006
Fricks, John, Pres.--Fricks & Associates/Advertising Inc., Atlanta, GA, pg. 433
Fridgeirsson, M.G., Pres.--Iceland Seafood Corporation, Camp Hill, PA, pg. 561
Fried, Ben, Pres.--B.T.F. Corporation, East Rutherford, NJ, pg. 107
Fried, R., Pres.--Monarch Luggage Co. Inc., Brooklyn, NY, pg. 765
Fried, Richard, Pres. & Mngmt. Supvr.--GBF/Ayer, Los Angeles, CA, pg. 104
Frieder, L. Peter, Jr., Pres.--Gentex Optics, Inc., Simpson, PA, pg. 452
Friedheim, Louis, Pres. & Chief Exec. Officer--Cougle Commission Company, Inc., Chicago, IL, pg. 289
Friedl, Donald G., Chm. Bd., Pres. & Chief Exec. Officer--All Seasons Services, Inc., Braintree, MA, pg. 35
Friedland, Thomas S., Pres. & Chief Exec. Officer--Harper Industries, Inc., New York, NY, pg. 510
Friedlander, Jack, Pres.--Acme Continental Foods, Inc., Chicago, IL, pg. 13
Friedlander, Sam, Pres. & Chief Exec. Officer--Production Machinery Corporation, Mentor, OH, pg. 893
Friedler, Jerry, Pres.--Grocers Specialty Co., Los Angeles, CA, pg. 237
Friedler, Jerry, Pres.--Grocers General Merchandise Company, Los Angeles, CA, pg. 237
Friedman, Albert, Pres.--Banner Wholesale Grocers, Inc., Chicago, IL, pg. 118
Friedman, Ernest L., Pres.--King Koil Licensing Company Inc., Saint Paul, MN, pg. 630
Friedman, J. Roger, Pres.--Lebhar-Friedman, Inc., New York, NY, pg. 665
Friedman, Jack N., Chm. Bd., Pres. & Chief Exec. Officer--Florasynth Inc., New York, NY, pg. 420
Friedman, Mark, Pres.--S. Rothchild & Co., Inc., New York, NY, pg. 951
Friedman, Mark, Pres.--Junior Concept Div., New York, NY, pg. 951
Friedman, Robert, Pres. & Chief Exec. Officer--Loehmann's, Inc., Bronx, NY, pg. 681
Friedson, David, Pres. & Chief Exec. Officer--Freeson Advertising Agency, Miami Lakes, FL, pg. 431
Friend, Sol, Pres.--On-Cor Frozen Foods Inc., Chicago, IL, pg. 826
Friendt, Glenn, Pres. & Chief Exec. Officer--Kahler Friendt & Partners, Inc., Omaha, NE, pg. 613
Frisch, Alfred, Pres.--Beaver Street Fisheries, Inc., Jacksonville, FL, pg. 130
Fristedt, Hans, Pres. & Chief Oper. Officer--American Trading and Production Corporation, Baltimore, MD, pg. 64
Fritsch, Bill, Pres.--Christiansen & Fritsch, Inc., Seattle, WA, pg. 249
Fritz, James P., Chm. Bd., Pres. & Chief Exec. Officer--Fritz Co. Inc., Newport, MN, pg. 434
Fritz, Leonard, Pres.--Huron Valley Steel Corp., Belleville, MI, pg. 555
Fritz, Lynn C., Chm. Bd., Pres. & Chief Exec. Officer--Fritz Companies, Inc., San Francisco, CA, pg. 434
Fritz, Michael, Pres.--Rugg Manufacturing Company, Greenfield, MA, pg. 955
Fritz, William J., Pres.--Everbrite, Inc., Greenfield, WI, pg. 391
Fritze, William, Pres.--Philip Fritze & Sons, Inc., Whippany, NJ, pg. 434
Fritzke, Tom L., Pres.--Heresite Protective Coatings Inc., Manitowoc, WI, pg. 531
Froehlich, Virgil, Pres. & Gen. Mgr.--Affiliated Foods Cooperative Inc., Norfolk, NE, pg. 23
Frohlich, Peter E., Pres.--Bommer Industries, Inc., Landrum, SC, pg. 164
Frohring, Glenn H., Pres.--Newbury Industries, Inc., Newbury, OH, pg. 803
Fromm, William M., Pres.--Barkley & Evergreen Advertising, Inc., Shawnee Mission, KS, pg. 120
Fromson, Howard A., Pres.--Ano-Coil Corporation, Rockville, CT, pg. 75
Fronzoni, Alessio, Mng. Dir.--Leo Burnett Co., S.R.L., Milan,, Italy, pg. 192
Frost, Chad, Pres.--Frost Inc., Grand Rapids, MI, pg. 435
Frost, Michael, Pres.--Burner Systems International, Inc., Chattanooga, TN, pg. 357
Frost, Michael, Pres. & Chief Oper. Officer--Information Systems, Montvale, NJ, pg. 316
Frost, Mike, Pres.--Colonial Petroleum Co., Cliffside, NC, pg. 264
Frost, Stephen B., Pres.--Frost Company, Andover, MA, pg. 435
Fry, Charles F., Pres.--Fry/Hammond/Barr Incorporated, Orlando, FL, pg. 435
Fry, Jim, Pres. & Chief Oper. Officer--Tuscarora Yarns Inc., Mount Pleasant, NC, pg. 1120
Fryml, J.S., Pres. & Chief Exec. Officer--American Fast Print, Limited, Spartanburg, SC, pg. 52
Fuchs, Anne Sutherland, Publisher--Vogue Magazine, New York, NY, pg. 19
Fuchs, Bernard, Chm. Bd., Pres. & Chief Exec. Officer--Specialty Retailers, Inc., Houston, TX, pg. 1029
Fuerbach, W.F., Jr., Chm. Bd., Pres. & Treas.--S. M. Frank & Co., Inc., Peekskill, NY, pg. 429
Fugazy, Roy D., Pres. & Chief Exec. Officer--Fugazy International Corporation, New York, NY, pg. 435
Fugazy, Roy D., Chief Exec. Officer--Fugazy Travel, New York, NY, pg. 435
Fugazy, Roy D., Chief Exec. Officer--Fugazy Limousines, New York, NY, pg. 435
Fuglestad, Judy, Pres.--Gem Top Mfg., Inc., Clackamas, OR, pg. 448
Fuhrman, Robert J., Pres.--Eggland's Best, Inc., King of Prussia, PA, pg. 371
Fukunaga, Thomas I., Pres. & Chief Oper. Officer--Servco Pacific Inc., Honolulu, HI, pg. 991
Fuldner, Christopher T., Pres.--Efco Corporation, Monett, MO, pg. 359
Fuller, Jeff, Pres.--Nacoma Consolidated, Inc., Nacogdoches, TX, pg. 782
Fulton, Wm. M., Pres.--Fleming Packaging Corp., Peoria, IL, pg. 417
Fumire, R.A., Pres.--Summit Corporation of America, Thomaston, CT, pg. 1058
Funk, Albert, Pres.--Modern Hilift Equipment Co., West Conshohocken, PA, pg. 763
Funk, Tommy, Pres.--Sebastian Cotton & Grain Corp., Sebastian, TX, pg. 986
Fuqua, Jeffrey B., Pres.--Amick Construction Ltd., Orlando, FL, pg. 67
Furgal, James W., Pres.--Camillus Cutlery Co., Camillus, NY, pg. 212
Furlong, Edward, Jr., Pres. & Chief Exec. Officer--WWF Paper Corporation, Bala-Cynwyd, PA, pg. 1157
Furlong, Ralph D., Pres.--Industrial Steel & Wire Company, Chicago, IL, pg. 567
Furman, Thomas D., Jr., Pres. & Chief Oper. Officer--Camp Dresser & McKee Inc., Cambridge, MA, pg. 212
Furnari, Beverly, Pres.--Fairview Construction, Inc, Auburn Hills, MI, pg. 397
Furones, Miguel A., Pres.--Vitruvio/Leo Burnett, Madrid,, Spain, pg. 193
Furukawa, Tamotsu, Pres.--Fishking Processors, Inc., Los Angeles, CA, pg. 415
Furzer, Simon, Mng. Dir.--Chiat/Day/Mojo Pty. Ltd., Nedlands,, Australia, pg. 245
Fusco, Edmund J., Sr., Pres.--The Fusco Corporation, New Haven, CT, pg. 437
Fusz, Louis, Jr., Pres.--Lou Fusz Automotive Network, Saint Louis, MO, pg. 437
Futter, Bernard, Pres. & Chief Exec. Officer--Futter Lumber Corporation, Rockville Centre, NY, pg. 437
Futterman, Jack, Chm. Bd., Pres. & Chief Exec. Officer--Supermarkets General Corporation, Woodbridge, NJ, pg. 1064
Futterman, Jack, Chm. Bd., Pres. & Chief Exec. Officer--Pathmark, Woodbridge, NJ, pg. 1064
Fuzak, Arthur W., Pres.--Kimstock, Inc., Santa Ana, CA, pg. 630
Gabbert, James D., Chm. Bd., Pres. & Chief Exec. Officer--Gabbert's, Inc., Minneapolis, MN, pg. 441
Gace, Francis, Pres. & Chief Oper. Officer--Lewis & Gace, Inc., Fort Lee, NJ, pg. 673
Gaddy, Bob L., Pres.--Pace Industries, Inc., Fayetteville, AR, pg. 838
Gaffin, Seth, Pres. & Chief Exec. Officer--Baris Shoe Company, Inc., New York, NY, pg. 119
Gaffney, Edward J., Pres. & Treas.--Ortho-Kinetics, Inc., Waukesha, WI, pg. 830
Gaffney, Michael, Pres. & Chief Oper. Officer--The Joey Reiman Agency, Atlanta, GA, pg. 923
Gahm, W. Dwight, Chm. Bd., Pres. & Chief Exec. Officer--Kitchen Kompact, Inc., Jeffersonville, IN, pg. 634
Gaither, Ann Heafner, Chm. Bd., Pres. & Chief Exec. Officer--J. H. Heafner Co. Inc., Lincolnton, NC, pg. 520
Galanis, Terry S., Jr., Pres.--Sealing Devices Inc., Lancaster, NY, pg. 984
Galante, Eugene J., Pres. & Treas.--Tagsons Papers, Inc., Albany, NY, pg. 1076
Galesi, Francesco, Chm. Bd., Pres. & Chief Exec. Officer--Rotterdam Ventures Inc., Guilderland Center, NY, pg. 951
Galex, Martin, Pres. & Chief Exec. Officer--Therapedic Associates, Inc., Boca Raton, FL, pg. 1090
Galin, Julius, Pres.--Connecticut Spring & Stamping Corporation, Farmington, CT, pg. 275
Gallagher, Charles A., Pres.--The Cretex Companies, Elk River, MN, pg. 299
Gallagher, Edward A., IV, Pres.--George Transfer, Inc., Parkton, MD, pg. 453
Gallagher, Hugh, Jr., Pres.--Consolidated Metal Products, Inc., Cincinnati, OH, pg. 276

Gallagher, Maurice J., Jr., Pres.--WestAir Holding Inc., Fresno, CA, pg. 1178
Gallagher, Robert J., Jr., Pres.--R. J. Gallagher Co., Houston, TX, pg. 441
Galler, Anthony, Pres. & Chief Oper. Officer--Samelson-Leon Company, Inc., Memphis, TN, pg. 968
Gallivan, John P., Pres.--D. Waldner Company, Inc., Farmingdale, NY, pg. 1159
Gallo, Julio, Pres.--E & J Gallo Winery, Modesto, CA, pg. 441
Gallo, Julio, Pres.--Bartles & Jaymes, Modesto, CA, pg. 442
Gallucci, John, Chm. Bd., Pres. & Treas.--Concrete Construction Company, Columbus, OH, pg. 273
Galusha, Frank, Pres.--G & A Communications, Newport Beach, CA, pg. 438
Galuten, Jerry, Chm. Bd. & Pres.--SGD International Corp., New York, NY, pg. 962
Galvin, Greg, Chief Oper. Officer--Kroh Operating L.P., Overland Park, KS, pg. 645
Gamache, Robert, Pres.--Albert Trostel Packings, Ltd., Lake Geneva, WI, pg. 1116
Gamba, Jeanette L., Pres. & Sec.--Jordan Associates, Oklahoma City, OK, pg. 604
Gambill, Ben S., Jr., Pres.--Braid Electric Company, Nashville, TN, pg. 171
Gambill, Harry, Pres.--Trans Union Corp., Chicago, IL, pg. 712
Gambino, Joseph L., Pres. & Chief Exec. Officer--The Atlas Construction Co., Stamford, CT, pg. 96
Gamel, Thomas W., Pres.--Timpte Industries, Inc., Denver, CO, pg. 1098
Ganahl, Peter, Pres.--Ganahl Lumber Company, Anaheim, CA, pg. 442
Gando, David C., Pres.--Martin, Cole, Dando & Robertson, Memphis, TN, pg. 714
Gandrud, Robert P., Pres. & Chief Exec. Officer--Lutheran Brotherhood, Minneapolis, MN, pg. 688
Gang, James, Pres.--RI Holdings, Whippany, NJ, pg. 907
Gannaway, Michael T., Pres.-Fragrance Grp.--Charles of the Ritz Group Ltd., New York, NY, pg. 695
Gans, Leo, Pres.--Action Technology Company, Rockaway, NJ, pg. 15
Gans, Robert J., Chm. Bd. & Pres.--Gans Ink & Supply Company, Inc., Los Angeles, CA, pg. 442
Gant, Allen E., Jr., Pres. & Asst. Treas.--Glen Raven Mills, Inc., Glen Raven, NC, pg. 461
Gantz, Joseph, Pres.--Empire Brushes, Inc., Greenville, NC, pg. 379
Ganz, Susan, Pres.--Lion Brothers Company, Inc., Owings Mills, MD, pg. 677
Gaples, Harry S., Pres.--Kleinschmidt Inc., Deerfield, IL, pg. 635
Garay, Charles J., Chm. Bd. & Pres.--Laminaire Corporation, Rahway, NJ, pg. 652
Garber, George E., Pres.--The St. George Group, Inc., Pittsburgh, PA, pg. 966
Garcia, A., Pres.--North & Judd, Middletown, CT, pg. 812
Gardella, David, Pres.-The Instant Web Companies--The Instant Web Companies, Chanhassen, MN, pg. 571
Gardella, William T., Pres.--Rex Marine Center, Inc., Norwalk, CT, pg. 930
Gardiner, Scott, Chm. Bd., Pres., Chief Exec. & Chief Oper. Officer--Gardiner Metal Company, Chicago, IL, pg. 443
Gardiner, Walter A., Pres.--Imperial Schrade Corp., New York, NY, pg. 564
Gardiner, Walter A., Pres.--Imperial Schrade Corp., Ellenville, NY, pg. 564
Gardner, David E., Pres. & Sec.--Alfred Nickles Bakery, Inc., Navarre, OH, pg. 806
Gardner, Gary E., Pres. & Chief Oper. Officer--Soft Sheen Products, Inc., Chicago, IL, pg. 1016
Gardner, Jean, Pres.--Penninsular Meat Company, Inc., Tampa, FL, pg. 858
Gardner, Lewis, Pres.--Eastern Milk Producers Cooperative Assn., Inc., Syracuse, NY, pg. 363
Gardner, Oliver, Pres.--Corcoran Mfg. Co., Inc., Anaheim, CA, pg. 285
Gardner, Philip D., Pres. & Chief Exec. Officer--Findlay Industries, Inc., Findlay, OH, pg. 410
Gardner, Richard E., Pres.--Calumet Construction Corporation, Hammond, IN, pg. 211
Gardner, Robert K., Pres. & Exec. Creative Dir.--Gardner Communications, Inc., San Francisco, CA, pg. 443
Gardner, Terri, Pres.--Brainstorm Advertising & Sales Promotions, Chicago, IL, pg. 171
Gargiulo, James V., Pres.--Sofco-Mead, Inc., Scotia, NY, pg. 1016
Gargiulo, James V., Pres.--D. J. Mead-Hubbs & Howe, Buffalo, NY, pg. 1016
Garman, M. Lawrence, Pres. & Chief Exec. Officer--Daubert Industries, Inc., Westchester, IL, pg. 317
Garratt, Reginald G., Pres. & Chief Oper. Officer--Knowles Electronics, Inc., Itasca, IL, pg. 637
Garrell, Bernard, Pres.--Colonial Supply Corporation, Manchester, NH, pg. 264
Garrett, E.P., Pres.--Welco Lumber Company, Marysville, WA, pg. 1175
Garrison, John, Pres.--SBS Products, Inc., Saginaw, MI, pg. 323
Garry, William J., Editor-in-Chief--Bon Appetit Magazine, Los Angeles, CA, pg. 636
Garvens, Kent, Pres.--Electro-Coatings, Inc., Emeryville, CA, pg. 374
Garvey, John, Chm. Bd. & Chief Exec. Officer--Petroleum Inc., Wichita, KS, pg. 865
Garvey, Robert A., Pres.--North Star Steel Co., Minneapolis, MN, pg. 219
Garvey, Willard W., Chm. Bd., Pres. & Chief Exec. Officer--Garvey Industries, Inc., Wichita, KS, pg. 443
Gary, Richard M., Pres. & New Bus. Contact--The Gary Group, Culver City, CA, pg. 444
Gasaway, Dick, Pres.--Happy Holiday Tree Farms, Sheridan, MI, pg. 506
Gaskell, John, Pres.--Media Management Associates, Fort Lee, NJ, pg. 734
Gaskill, Charles, Pres.--The WBDC Group, Grand Rapids, MI, pg. 1155
Gassman, John, Pres., Chief Exec. Officer & Chief Fin. Officer--Townsend & Bottum, Inc., Ann Arbor, MI, pg. 1104
Gast, Warren E., Pres. & Gen. Mgr.--Gast Mfg. Corp., Benton Harbor, MI, pg. 444
Gatehouse, Rihcard, Pres.--Halsey Taylor, Oak Brook, IL, pg. 377
Gates, Phillip C., Chm. Bd. & Pres.--Seald-Sweet Growers, Inc., Vero Beach, FL, pg. 984
Gates, Tim J., Pres.,Treas. & Dir.-Mngmt. Info. Systems--Southern Ohio Fabricators, Inc., Cincinnati, OH, pg. 1022
Gattas, Fred P., Jr., Pres.--Fred P. Gattas Company, Inc., Memphis, TN, pg. 446
Gaunt, John C., Pres. & Chief Exec. Officer--Ellerbe Becket, Inc., Minneapolis, MN, pg. 378
Gauss, Calvin, Pres.--Playtex FP Group Incorporated, Stamford, CT, pg. 877
Gauss, Calvin J., Pres.--Playtex Family Products Corp., Stamford, CT, pg. 877
Gaver, Joseph C., Pres.--Trayer Products, Inc., Elmira, NY, pg. 1108
Gay, A.L., Jr., Pres.--The Georgia Marble Company, Kennesaw, GA, pg. 453
Gaylord, Edson I., Chm. Bd. & Chief Exec. Officer--Ingersoll International Inc., Rockford, IL, pg. 568
Gaylord, Edward L., Chm. & Pres.--Broadmoor Hotel, Inc., Colorado Springs, CO, pg. 177
Gaylord, Edward L., Pres. & Publisher--Oklahoma Publishing Company, Oklahoma City, OK, pg. 446
Gaylord, Edward L., Pres. & Publisher--The Daily & Sunday Oklahoman, Oklahoma City, OK, pg. 446
Gebert, Kenton R., Pres., Chief Exec. & Chief Oper. Officer--The Dickerson Group, Inc., Monroe, NC, pg. 335
Gebo, Brenton T., Pres.--Gebo Distributing Co., Inc., Plainview, TX, pg. 447
Gee, William, III, Pres.--Cloverhill Bakery, Chicago, IL, pg. 256
Geer, Joseph R., Pres., Chief Exec. Officer--PMC Partnership, Ltd., Westport, CT, pg. 836
Gehl, R.E., Pres.--Whisper Soft Mills Inc., New York, NY, pg. 1185
Gehret, Charles, Pres.--Premier Refractories & Chemicals Inc., King of Prussia, PA, pg. 887
Gehrig, Robert W., Pres.--Smith & Gillespie Engineers, Inc., Jacksonville, FL, pg. 1012
Geier, Hans, Pres.--Stratton Corp., South Londonderry, VT, pg. 1053
Geiger, Eugene G., Pres. & Treas.--Geiger Brothers, Lewiston, ME, pg. 447
Geiger, Ron, Pres. & Chief Exec. Officer--Harker's Inc., Le Mars, IA, pg. 509
Geiger, Thomas B., Jr., Pres.--Capital Tire, Inc., Toledo, OH, pg. 215
Geise, David N., Pres.--Furman Foods, Inc., Northumberland, PA, pg. 436
Geisler, Dick G., Pres.--Cowboy Oil Company, Pocatello, ID, pg. 290
Gelber, Phillip, Commission Chm.--New Jersey State Lottery, Trenton, NJ, pg. 801
Gelder, Robert, Pres. & Treas.--Barden & Robeson Corporation, Middleport, NY, pg. 119
Geldmacher, Jay L., V.P. & Gen. Mgr.--Synchro-Start Products, Inc., Niles, IL, pg. 638
Geller, Anthony, Pres. & Chief Exec. Officer--Union Holdings, Inc., New York, NY, pg. 1128
Geller, Larry, Pres. & Chief Exec. Officer--Rosauer's Supermarkets, Inc., Spokane, WA, pg. 947
Geller, Stephen, Pres.--Stephen L. Geller Inc., New York, NY, pg. 447
Gellerman, Jay M., Pres. & Treas.--Jaydon Incorporated, Rock Island, IL, pg. 590
Gellerstedt, L.L., III, Pres. & Chief Exec. Officer--Beers Construction Company, Atlanta, GA, pg. 132
Gellert, Jay, Pres., Chief Exec. Officer & Dir.--Aetna Health Plans, San Bruno, CA, pg. 23
Gelman, Alan, Pres. & Gen. Mgr.--American Envelope of Philadelphia, Philadelphia, PA, pg. 199
Gelpi, John J., Pres.--Industrial Metals Of The South, New Orleans, LA, pg. 566
Genasci, Bill, Pres.--Select Sires, Inc., Plain City, OH, pg. 988
Gencarelli, Louis A., Sr., Pres.--Bess Eaton Donut Flour Co., Inc., Westerly, RI, pg. 146
Gendler, Paul, Dr., Pres.--Language Institute for English (L.I.F.E.), Rutherford, NJ, pg. 142
Geneser, Joe, Pres.--The Vernon Company, Newton, IA, pg. 1148
Genovese, Rocco C., Pres. & Chief Oper. Officer--Burke Industries, Inc., San Jose, CA, pg. 191
Genovese, Rocco C., Pres. & Chief Oper. Officer--Burke Industries Inc., San Jose, CA, pg. 190
Gentine, Lawrence J., Pres.-Food Service Corp.--Sargento Incorporated, Plymouth, WI, pg. 971
Gentine, Louis P., Pres. & Chief Exec. Officer--Sargento Incorporated, Plymouth, WI, pg. 971
Gentleman, John F., Pres.--ULLICO Inc., Washington, DC, pg. 1124
Gentner, John M., Pres.--Blaw Knox Food & Chemical Equipment Company, Buffalo, NY, pg. 156
Gentry, Jack T., Chm. Bd. & Pres.--Positronic Industries, Inc., Springfield, MO, pg. 881
Gentry, Marvin D., Chm. Bd. & Pres.--New Fortis Corp., King, NC, pg. 800
Genuardi, Charles A., Pres. & Chief Exec. Officer--Genuardi Super Markets Inc., Norristown, PA, pg. 452
Geocaris, John T., Pres.--Little Lady Foods, Inc., Elk Grove Village, IL, pg. 679
George, Len, Pres.--American Buildings Co., Eufaula, AL, pg. 49
George, Mary H., Pres.--Hulman & Company, Terre Haute, IN, pg. 552
George, Michael J., Pres. & Chief Exec. Officer--Melody Foods, Inc., Farmington Hills, MI, pg. 738
George, Ross, Pres.--Simonds Industries Inc., Fitchburg, MA, pg. 1006
Georgehead, Christopher W., II, Pres. & Chief Exec. Officer--Gateway Press, Inc., Louisville, KY, pg. 446
Georgescu, Peter A., Pres.-Y&R Inc.--Young & Rubicam Inc., New York, NY, pg. 1210
Georgine, Robert A., Chm., Pres. & Chief Exec. Officer--ULLICO Inc., Washington, DC, pg. 1124
Georgoulis, Stratton, Chm. Bd., Pres. & Chief Exec. Officer--TIC United Corporation, Dallas, TX, pg. 1073
Gephardt, William E., Jr., Pres. & Chief Exec. Officer--Frontier Foundries, Inc., Titusville, PA, pg. 434
Geraci, F. Phillip, Pres.--Advertising To Women, Inc., New York, NY, pg. 21
Gerard, Stephen, Pres., Chief Exec. Officer & Treas.--Boliiger, Inc., Stamford, CT, pg. 163
Gerber, Charlie, Pres.--Alcor Envelope Co., Rochester, NY, pg. 40
Gerber, Jack, Pres. & Chief Exec. Officer--Concordia Publishing House, Saint Louis, MO, pg. 272
Gerbig, Robert L., Pres. & Chief Exec. Officer--Gerbig, Snell/Weisheimer & Assoc., Inc., Worthington, OH, pg. 454
Gerbis, Harold, Sr., Pres.--Quincy Mutual Fire Insurance Company, Quincy, MA, pg. 905
Gerchenson, Jeffery H., Pres. & Chief Oper. Officer--Alva/Amco Pharmacal Companies, Inc., Chicago, IL, pg. 46
Gerdes, Thomas R., Pres.--Plastic Moldings Corp., Cincinnati, OH, pg. 875
Gerdis, Lawrence E., Pres.--Charlie Thomas Auto World, Houston, TX, pg. 1092
Gerdy, Harvey, Chm. Bd., Pres. & Chief Exec. Officer--International Seaway Trading Corporation, Mayfield Village, OH, pg. 579
Geresi, Joseph, Pres.--Paisano Publications, Inc., Agoura, CA, pg. 843
Gerken, Edward, Chm. Bd. & Pres.--Norwalk Furniture Corporation, Norwalk, OH, pg. 816
Gerling, Paul J., Pres. & Chief Oper. Officer--American Laundry Machinery Inc., Cincinnati, OH, pg. 57
Germain, W. Robert, V.P.--Mormac Marine Transport, Inc., Stamford, CT, pg. 770
Gerrity, James F., III, Pres. & Chief Exec. Officer--Gerrity Co., Inc., Newton, MA, pg. 454
Gershoni, Reuven, Pres.--G.L. Advertising, Dumont, NJ, pg. 440
Gerson, Matthew, Pres.--Gerson & Gerson, Inc., New York, NY, pg. 454
Gerstein, David B., Pres.--Thermwell Products Co., Inc., Paterson, NJ, pg. 1092
Gerstein, Irving, Pres.--Gordon Jewelry Corporation, Irving, TX, pg. 1215
Gerstein, Irving, Pres.--Lever Mfg. Corp., Paterson, NJ, pg. 1092
Gertler, Leonard, Pres.--All American Home Center, Downey, CA, pg. 35
Gessner, David, Pres. & Treas.--Gessner Industries, Concord, NC, pg. 455
Getman, D.S., Chm. Bd. & Pres.--Getman Corporation, Bangor, MI, pg. 455
Gettlefinger, Herman E., Pres.--Kelso Oil Company, Knoxville, TN, pg. 622
Gettleman, Maurice H., Chm. Bd & Pres.--IBM Foods, Inglewood, CA, pg. 558
Getto, Barry I., Pres. & Chief Exec. Officer--Howes Leather Company, Inc., Quincy, MA, pg. 548
Getz, William A., Chm. Bd.--Williams-White & Co., Moline, IL, pg. 1191
Ghaemmaghami, Nicky, Pres.--Hydraulics International, Inc., Chatsworth, CA, pg. 556
Ghafari, Yousif B., Pres. & Chief Exec. & Chief Oper. Officer--Ghafari Associates, Inc., Dearborn, MI, pg. 455
Ghersy, Gustavo, Pres.--BSB/Ghersy-Quintero, C.A. Publicidad, Caracas,, Venezuela, pg. 109
Gherty, Jack, Pres. & Chief Exec. Officer--Land O'Lakes, Inc., Arden Hills, MN, pg. 653
Gherty, John, Pres. & Chief Exec. Officer-Land O'Lakes Inc.--Cenex/Land O'Lakes, Inc., Saint Paul, MN, pg. 653
Gherty, John, Pres. & Chief Exec. Officer-Land O'Lakes Inc.--Cenex/Land O'Lakes, Inc., Saint Paul, MN, pg. 231
Ghiz, Lewis, Pres.--Paddock Pool Construction Co., Scottsdale, AZ, pg. 842
Giaquinta, Jerry, Pres./Chief Exec. Officer--Bob Thomas & Associates, Inc. Public Relations, Venice, CA, pg. 244
Giaquinta, Jerry, Pres./Chief Exec Officer--Bob Thomas Associates, Toronto, Canada, pg. 244
Gibb, Robert, Jr., Pres.--Robert Gibb & Sons, Inc., Fargo, ND, pg. 456
Gibbons, Michael, Pres.--Krause's Sofa Factory, Inc., Brea, CA, pg. 644
Gibbs, Charles W., Pres.--Gibbs Wire & Steel Company, Inc., Southington, CT, pg. 456
Gibbs, Frank, Pres. & Chief Oper. Officer--Ryan Herco Products Corp., Burbank, CA, pg. 958
Gibby, Jerry, Pres.--Northeast Texas Farmers Co-Op, Sulphur Springs, TX, pg. 813
Gibralter, Robert, Mng. Dir.--BSB Singapore, Singapore, Singapore, pg. 110
Gibson, Daniel, Pres.--Wolcott & Lincoln, Inc., Kansas City, MO, pg. 1198
Gibson, Raymond E., Pres.--Whiting Corporation, Harvey, IL, pg. 1187
Gibson, Robert, Pres. & Chief Oper. Officer--The Medical Protective Company, Fort Wayne, IN, pg. 735
Gibson, William B., Chm., Pres. & Chief Exec. Officer--Sudler & Hennessey, New York, NY, pg. 1211
Giermak, C.F., Pres.--Eriez Magnetics, Erie, PA, pg. 386
Giesen, Richard A., Chm. Bd., Pres. & Chief Exec. Officer--American Appraisal Associates, Inc., Milwaukee, WI, pg. 48

Gietzen, Jeff, Pres.--D & W Food Centers, Inc., Grand Rapids, MI, pg. 308
Giffir, Carl, Pres.-Natl. Insurance Services--Pan-American Life Insurance Company, New Orleans, LA, pg. 845
Gigante, Paul, Pres. & Creative Dir.--Gigante Vaz & Partners Advertising, Inc., Parsippany, NJ, pg. 457
Gigas, George, Pres.--Cablewave Systems, Inc., North Haven, CT, pg. 206
Gignac, Kenneth, Chm. Bd. & Pres.--Elgin-Honey Hill Corporation, Chicago, IL, pg. 376
Gignac, Robert J., Chm. Bd.--Thunderline Corporation, Belleville, MI, pg. 1096
Gilbert, Bruce C., Pres., Chief Exec. Officer & Treas.--Great Lakes Construction Co., Cleveland, OH, pg. 481
Gilbert, Duane L., Pres. & Owner--Gilbert Mfg. Corp., Locke Mills, ME, pg. 458
Gilbert, Jeffrey, Pres.--Decor Corporation, Columbus, OH, pg. 324
Gilbert, R.P., Pres.--Richmond Technology Inc., Redlands, CA, pg. 933
Gilbert, Richard, Pres. & Sls. Promo. Mgr.--Zena Jeans, New York, NY, pg. 1217
Gilbert, Richard D., Pres.--Converse Professional Group, Inc., Pasadena, CA, pg. 281
Gilbert, Robert, Pres.--Kaukauna Cheese, Little Chute, WI, pg. 619
Gilbert, Walter F., Chm. Bd., Pres., Chief Exec. Officer & Treas.--Semco Industries, Stoughton, MA, pg. 989
Gilbert, William B., Chm. Bd. & Pres.--Lifetime Doors Inc., Farmington Hills, MI, pg. 675
Giles, Bill, Pres.--The Phillies-A Limited Partnership, Philadelphia, PA, pg. 867
Gilfenbain, Norman, Pres.--Norden Fruit Company, Inc., Los Angeles, CA, pg. 809
Gilgallon, Ed, Pres.--Career Club Shirt Co., New York, NY, pg. 898
Gill, Edward F., Jr., V.P. & Gen. Mgr.--Colson Caster Corporation, Jonesboro, AR, pg. 711
Gill, H. Ross, III, Pres.--The National Latex Products Co., Ashland, OH, pg. 791
Gill, Robert, Pres.--Border States Industries, Inc., Fargo, ND, pg. 165
Gill, Stephen E., Pres. & Chief Exec. Officer--M.C. Gill Corporation, El Monte, CA, pg. 458
Gilleland, Richard A., Chm. Bd., Pres. & Chief Exec. Officer--Kendall Healthcare Products Co., Mansfield, MA, pg. 622
Gillen, Dick, Chm. Bd., Pres. & Chief Exec. Officer--Harbor Financial Mortgage Corp., Houston, TX, pg. 506
Gillespey, Wayne, V.P.-Mfg.--Barnes Pumps, Inc., Mansfield, OH, pg. 507
Gillespie, F. Harold, Chm. & Chief Exec. Officer--Davis Mechanical Contractors, Inc., Greenville, SC, pg. 318
Gillespie, Richard J., Pres.--The Gillespie Organization, Inc., Princeton, NJ, pg. 458
Gilliam, John, Pres.--Anderson Wholesale Company, Muskogee, OK, pg. 73
Gillis, Wayne H., Chm. Bd. & Pres.--Gillis Advertising & Public Relations, Birmingham, AL, pg. 459
Gillman, R.N., Pres. & Chief Exec. Officer--Poly-Seal Corporation, Baltimore, MD, pg. 880
Gillogly, Fred D., Pres. & Treas.--Gillogly Chevrolet Inc., West Seneca, NY, pg. 459
Gilman, Bill, Pres. & Chief Oper. Officer--McLaughlin Mfg. Company, Greenville, SC, pg. 731
Gilman, Shirley J., Pres. & Treas.--Marty Gilman, Inc., Gilman, CT, pg. 459
Gilman, Steven F., Chm. Bd., Pres, & Chief Exec. Officer--Style Auto, Van Nuys, CA, pg. 1055
Gilmartin, Gene, Pres. & Chief Exec. Officer--Hoffman York & Compton, Milwaukee, WI, pg. 538
Gilmore, Howard N., Jr., Pres. & Chief Exec. Officer--Gilmore Envelope Corp., Los Angeles, CA, pg. 460
Gilpatrick, Rick, Pres.--Gilpatrick Construction Company, Riverton, WY, pg. 460
Gimbel, Robert, Gen. Mgr.--Marmon-Herrington Company, Louisville, KY, pg. 711
Gingg, Conrad, Pres. & Chief Exec. Officer--United Dairymen of Arizona, Tempe, AZ, pg. 1131
Ginsberg, Daniel, Pres.--DGWB, Inc., Irvine, CA, pg. 309
Ginsberg, David M., Pres.--Ginsberg's Institutional Foods, Inc., Hudson, NY, pg. 460
Ginsberg, Frank, Pres. & Creative Dir.--Avrett, Free & Ginsberg, Inc., New York, NY, pg. 103
Ginsberg, Jeffrey M., Pres.--Milton Samuels Advertising Agency, Inc., New York, NY, pg. 968
Ginsberg, Randolph K., Pres.--George Rice & Sons, Los Angeles, CA, pg. 931
Ginsberg, Robert I., Pres. & Chief Exec. Officer--Carol Wright Sales, Inc., Stamford, CT, pg. 1011
Ginsburg, Dan, Pres.-K&D Worldwide--Kobs & Draft Advertising, Inc., Chicago, IL, pg. 109
Ginzberg, Marc, Chm. Bd., Pres. & Chief Exec. Officer--Primary Industries Corporation, New York, NY, pg. 889
Giorgio, Robert J., Pres.--Life Sciences International, Philadelphia, PA, pg. 320
Gipson, G., Pres.--The Caxton Printers Ltd., Caldwell, ID, pg. 230
Girard, Chris, Pres. & Chief Exec. Officer--Plaid Pantries, Inc., Beaverton, OR, pg. 873
Girgenti, Steve, Pres. & New Bus. Contact--Girgenti, Hughes, Butler & McDowell, New York, NY, pg. 460
Girves, Parris, Pres. & Chief Exec. Officer--Brown Derby, Inc., Cleveland, OH, pg. 181
Gish, Dale L., Chm. Bd. & Pres.--Gish, Sherwood & Friends, Inc., Nashville, TN, pg. 460
Gittelman, Isadore, Pres.--Triumph Pet Industries, Inc., Hillburn, NY, pg. 1115
Giugni, June, Pres.--Cosmetique, Inc., Vernon Hills, IL, pg. 288
Giumarra, Sal, Pres.--Giumarra Vineyards, Bakersfield, CA, pg. 460
Giurato, Anthony J., Gen. Mgr.--Dealers Auto Auction of Dallas, Inc., Grand Prairie, TX, pg. 293
Givens, Susie, Pres. & Chief Exec. Officer--The Thompson Group Companies, Henderson, KY, pg. 1094
Givens, William, Pres.--ECRM, Tewksbury, MA, pg. 359
Gladstone, Robert, Pres.--Quadrangle Development Corporation, Washington, DC, pg. 902
Glas, Don ald A., Pres. & Chief Exec. Officer--First State Federal Savings & Loan, Hutchinson, MN, pg. 413
Glasgow, Lloyd J., Pres.--Jacques Jugeat, Inc., New York, NY, pg. 608
Glaske, Paul E., Pres. & Chief Exec. Officer--Blue Bird Corporation, Fort Valley, GA, pg. 158
Glass, Eric E., Pres.--The Taney Corporation, Taneytown, MD, pg. 1077
Glass, Walter, Chm. Bd. & Pres.--American Louver Co., Skokie, IL, pg. 57
Glass, Wilbur H., Jr., Pres.--The Auchter Company, Jacksonville, FL, pg. 98
Glasscock, Larry, Pres. & Chief Oper. Officer--First American Bank, N.A., Washington, D.C., Washington, DC, pg. 412
Glatt, Herbert, Pres.--Magla Products, Chatham, NJ, pg. 700
Glatz, Simon, Pres. & Chief Exec. Officer--Advanced Marine Enterprises, Inc., Arlington, VA, pg. 20
Glauberman, Stuart, Pres.--Malco Products, Inc., Barberton, OH, pg. 702
Glazer, Robert S., Chm. Bd., Pres. & Chief Exec. Officer--Glazers Wholesale Drug Co. Inc., Dallas, TX, pg. 461
Gleason, David M., Pres.--Austin Powder Co., Cleveland, OH, pg. 99
Gleason, Edward L., Pres.--Transammonia Inc., New York, NY, pg. 1106
Gleason, Sheldon, Chm. Bd., Pres., Chief Exec. & Chief Fin. Officer & Controller--Genie Manufacturing Corp., Rush, NY, pg. 452
Gleitsmann, R. Jr., Pres. & Chief Exec. Officer--Hardie Irrigation-Landscape Div., Carson City, NV, pg. 508
Glen, James, Pres.--Chem-Tainer Corporation, Brooklyn, NY, pg. 241
Glendenning, Jack, Pres.--Inland Printing Co., Inc., La Crosse, WI, pg. 570
Glenn, Malcolm, Regional Mng. Dir.-Asia Region--Leo Burnett Intl., Asia Hdqtrs., Hong Kong,, Hong Kong, pg. 192
Glenn, Tyler E., Jr., Pres. & Chief Oper. Officer--The Downs Group, Inc., Charlotte, NC, pg. 348
Glick, Eugene B., Pres.--Gene B. Glick Company, Inc., Indianapolis, IN, pg. 462
Glick, Joe, Div. Pres.--DSI/TMP Worldwide, Danville, IL, pg. 1074
Glick, Robert, Pres. & Chief Exec. Officer--Martin Paint Stores, Jamaica, NY, pg. 715
Glickman, Marshall L., Pres. & Chief Exec. Officer--Ruslander & Sons, Inc., Buffalo, NY, pg. 956
Glickman, Marshall L., Pres. & Chief Exec. Officer--The Jewett Refrigerator Co., Inc., Buffalo, NY, pg. 957
Glickman, Stuart, Chm., Pres. Chief Exec. & Chief Fin. Officer--Security Alarms & Fire Engineering Inc., Davie, FL, pg. 987
Glikbarg, Thomas S., Chm., Pres. & Chief Exec. Officer--Lyon's Restaurants, Inc., Foster City, CA, pg. 690
Global, Donald, Pres.--U.S. Repeating Arms Company, New Haven, CT, pg. 1137
Glockner, Wm., Pres.--O'Brien Machinery Company, Downingtown, PA, pg. 820
Glover, Edmund C., Pres.--Batson-Cook Company, West Point, GA, pg. 126
Glover, John G., Pres.--Color Graphics, Inc., Atlanta, GA, pg. 264
Glover, Keith, Pres. & Gen. Mgr.--Producers Rice Mill Inc., Stuttgart, AR, pg. 892
Gluck, Frederick, Mng. Dir.--McKinsey & Company, Inc., New York, NY, pg. 731
Gluckman, Thomas, Pres.--Fownes Brothers & Co., Inc., New York, NY, pg. 427
Glynn, William C., Pres.--Intermountain Industries, Inc., Boise, ID, pg. 575
Glynn, William C., Pres.--IGI Resources, Inc., Boise, ID, pg. 575
Godfrey, William G., Chm. Bd., Pres. & Chief Exec. Officer--Tekra Corporation, New Berlin, WI, pg. 1084
Godshall, Jonathan H., Pres.--Igloo Corporation, Houston, TX, pg. 562
Godwin, Jimmy D., Pres.--Forms & Supply, Inc., Charlotte, NC, pg. 424
Goebel, Arthur F., Pres. & Treas.--Goebel Art, Inc., Coon Rapids, MN, pg. 464
Goebel, Christopher J., Pres., Chief Exec. Officer & Chief Oper. Officer--Star Lumber & Supply Company, Inc., Wichita, KS, pg. 1039
Goebel, Robert L., Co-Chm. Bd.--Star Lumber & Supply Company, Inc., Wichita, KS, pg. 1039
Goebel, William J., Co-Chm. Bd.--Star Lumber & Supply Company, Inc., Wichita, KS, pg. 1039
Goedert, Philip H., Pres.--RNL Design, Denver, CO, pg. 907
Goefft, L. Michael, Pres.--Mandelbaum Mooney Ashley, San Francisco, CA, pg. 703
Goetsch, Warren D., Pres.--Menard Electric Cooperative, Petersburg, IL, pg. 738
Goetschel, Arthur W., Pres.--Griffin Wheel Co., Chicago, IL, pg. 69
Goetschel, Arthur W., Pres.--Griffin Canada Inc., Saint Hyacinthe,, Canada, pg. 69
Goetz, Lew, Pres. & Chief Exec. Officer--SOR Inc., Lenexa, KS, pg. 963
Gogol, Gary J., Pres. & Chief Exec. Officer--Annabelle Candy Company, Hayward, CA, pg. 75
Gohmann, J. Michael, Pres. & Chief Exec. Officer--Gohmann Asphalt & Construction Inc., Clarksville, IN, pg. 465
Goland, Martin, Pres.--Southwest Research Institute, San Antonio, TX, pg. 1023
Gold, Danny, Pres.--Kombi, Ltd., Naugatuck, CT, pg. 641
Gold, Jeffrey M., Chm. Bd. & Chief Exec. Officer--Goldmark Industries, Ltd., New York, NY, pg. 468
Gold, Martin F., Pres. & Chief Exec. Officer--Artec Distributing, Inc., Shelburne, VT, pg. 86
Gold, Stanley P., Pres.--Shamrock Holdings, Inc., Burbank, CA, pg. 994
Goldberg, Arthur, Chm. Bd., Pres. & Chief Exec. Officer--Di Giorgio Corporation, Somerset, NJ, pg. 334
Goldberg, Fred., Pres. & Chief Exec. Officer--Goldberg Moser O'Neill, San Francisco, CA, pg. 465
Goldberg, Ira, Partner & Dir. Acct. Services--Goldberg Fossa Seid Advertising, Inc., New York, NY, pg. 465
Goldberg, Leo, Pres.--Dexter Chemical Corp., Bronx, NY, pg. 334
Goldberg, Morton, Pres. & Treas.--Morton Goldberg Associates, Inc., New York, NY, pg. 465
Goldberger, Eugene, Pres.--Goldberger Doll Mfg. Company, Inc., Brooklyn, NY, pg. 466
Goldberger, Frederick, Pres.--Protimex Corporation, Studio City, CA, pg. 895
Goldblatt, Marvin, Pres.--Capitol Construction Group, Inc., Wheeling, IL, pg. 215
Golde, William, Pres.--Michael Business Machines Corporation, North Charleston, SC, pg. 747
Golden, Michael, Pres.--Stephen Gould Paper Co., Inc., Whippany, NJ, pg. 473
Goldfarb, Abraham, Pres.--National Banner Company, Dallas, TX, pg. 786
Goldfarb, Andrew, Pres. & Chief Exec. Officer--HCC Industries, Rosemead, CA, pg. 496
Goldfarb, Ellen, Pres.--House of Perfection, Inc., New York, NY, pg. 546
Goldfine, Steven B., Pres.--Northern Drug Company, Duluth, MN, pg. 814
Goldhirsh, Bernard A., Chm. Bd.--The Goldhirsh Group Inc., Boston, MA, pg. 467
Goldish, Marc, Pres.--Milton Industries, Inc., Chicago, IL, pg. 756
Goldman, Dave, Owner--Jones & Lamson Waterbury Farrel Corp., Cheshire, CT, pg. 468
Goldman, David, Pres. & Treas.--Goldman Financial Group, Boston, MA, pg. 468
Goldman, David H., Pres.--Voit Sports, Inc., Fairport, NY, pg. 1154
Goldman, David H., Pres.--Voit Corp., Fairport, NY, pg. 1154
Goldman, David L., Pres.--Interplast Universal Industries, Inc., Lodi, NJ, pg. 579
Goldman, Hal, Pres.--Elek-Tek, Inc., Skokie, IL, pg. 375
Goldman, Howard, Pres.--Gulf Distribution Inc., Miami, FL, pg. 493
Goldman, James W., Pres.--JWG Associates, Wellesley, MA, pg. 586
Goldman, Melvin, Pres.--Kores Nordic USA Corp., Summerville, SC, pg. 642
Goldman, Monte, Pres.--Eastern Canvas Products, Inc., Ward Hill, MA, pg. 363
Goldman, Myron, Pres.--Excelled Sheepskin & Leather Coat Corporation, New York, NY, pg. 392
Goldman, Samuel, Pres.--Executive Car Leasing, Inc., Los Angeles, CA, pg. 393
Goldman, Siegmund I., Chm. Bd. & Pres.--S. I. Goldman Co., Longwood, FL, pg. 467
Goldman, Steve, Pres. & Chief Exec. Officer--Power-One, Inc., Camarillo, CA, pg. 883
Goldman, Thomas, Pres.--Iowa Paint Mfg. Company, Inc., Des Moines, IA, pg. 582
Goldmeier, Alan, Pres.--Ross Bicycles USA Ltd., Farmingdale, NY, pg. 949
Goldner, Paul, Pres.--Database America Companies, Montvale, NJ, pg. 316
Goldner, Paul D., Pres.--Parker Steel Company, Toledo, OH, pg. 849
Goldress, Jerry E., Mng. Partner--Adler & Shaykin, New York, NY, pg. 17
Goldring, Allen A., Pres.--Overseas Military Sales Corporation, Woodbury, NY, pg. 833
Goldring, Norman M., Pres. & Chief Exec. Officer--CPM, Inc., Chicago, IL, pg. 203
Goldsbury, Christopher, Pres.--Pace Foods, Inc., San Antonio, TX, pg. 838
Goldsmith, Gerald, Pres. & Chief Oper. Officer--Rothschild North America Inc., New York, NY, pg. 951
Goldsmith, Gerald, Pres. & Chief Oper. Officer--Rothschild Inc., New York, NY, pg. 951
Goldsmith, Herbert, Pres.--Members Only By Europe Craft, New York, NY, pg. 738
Goldstein, Buford, J., Pres.--Hampton Print Works, Inc., Johnson City, TN, pg. 504
Goldstein, Joel G., Pres.--Joel Goldstein Marketing Communications, Santa Monica, CA, pg. 469
Goldstein, Mona, Mng. Dir.--Wunderman Worldwide, Toronto,, Canada, pg. 1213
Goldwyn, Bruce, Pres.--Culver Textile Corporation, West New York, NJ, pg. 304
Golemo, Stanley M., Jr., Chm. Bd. & Pres.--Hood & Company, Hamburg, PA, pg. 542
Golenberg, Gary, Pres. & Chief Exec. Officer--The Gibson-Homans Company, Twinsburg, OH, pg. 457
Golias, Tipton L., Pres. & Chief Exec. Officer--Helena Laboratories Corporation, Beaumont, TX, pg. 526
Golnick, Leon S., Chm. Bd.--Leon Shaffer Golnick Advertising, Inc., Fort Lauderdale, FL, pg. 469
Golteus, Hans, Pres. & Chief Oper. Officer--Norwegian Cruise Line, Coral Gables, FL, pg. 816
Golub, Eugene, Chm. Bd. & Pres.--Golub & Co., Chicago, IL, pg. 469
Golub, Neil, Pres. & Chief Oper. Officer--Price Chopper, Schenectady, NY, pg. 469
Golub, Neil M., Pres. & Chief Oper. Officer--Golub Corporation, Schenectady, NY, pg. 469
Gomez, Barry, Pres.--Ezon Products, Inc., Germantown, TN, pg. 393
Gompf, Hans E., Pres.--Arburg, Inc., Berlin, CT, pg. 79

Gonzalez, Clemente, Gen. Mgr.--Comunica Leo Burnett, Guatemala City,, Guatemala, pg. 192
Good, Richard L., Pres. & Chief Oper. Officer--NTS Corporation, Louisville, KY, pg. 781
Good, Robert W., Pres.--Wolfer Printing Company, City of Commerce, CA, pg. 1199
Good, Steven L., Pres.--Sheldon Good & Co., Inc., Chicago, IL, pg. 470
Goodall, Richard L., Pres.--Dixon Valve & Coupling Company, Chestertown, MD, pg. 341
Goodart, Tyrone G., Pres. & Chief Exec. Officer--Carus Chemical Company, Chemical Div., Ottawa, IL, pg. 227
Goodchild, John, Pres. & Chief Exec. Officer--The Weightman Group, Philadelphia, PA, pg. 1173
Gooden, C. Michael, Chm. Bd. & Pres.--Integrated Systems Analysts, Inc., Arlington, VA, pg. 573
Gooding, Terence, Dr., Pres.--Wavetek Communications Div., Indianapolis, IN, pg. 1168
Gooding, Terrance, Pres. & Chief Exec. Officer--Wavetek Corporation, San Diego, CA, pg. 1168
Goodman, Alvin, Pres.--Bonhomme Shirtmakers, Ltd., New York, NY, pg. 164
Goodman, Andrew, Pres.--Sherwood Lumber Corporation, Islandia, NY, pg. 999
Goodman, Charles S., Pres.--Syracuse China Corp., Syracuse, NY, pg. 1065
Goodman, Fredric, V.P.-Fin.--Welsbach Electric Corp., Long Island City, NY, pg. 1175
Goodman, James F., Pres. & Chief Exec. Officer--Capitol Broadcasting Co., Inc., Raleigh, NC, pg. 215
Goodman, Mark, Pres.--J. Josephson, Inc., South Hackensack, NJ, pg. 607
Goodman, Marvin, Pres.--Apparel Ventures, Inc., Gardena, CA, pg. 78
Goodman, Murray, Pres. & Treas.--Goodmans, Inc., Phoenix, AZ, pg. 471
Goodman, Robert, Pres.--Garber, Goodman Advertising, Inc., Miami, FL, pg. 443
Goodman, Ronald S., Pres.--Old Quaker Paint Co., Santa Ana, CA, pg. 823
Goodnight, James H., Chief Exec. Officer--SAS Institute Inc., Cary, NC, pg. 959
Goodrich, T.M., Pres.--BE & K, Inc., Birmingham, AL, pg. 106
Goodwill, R.E., Jr., Pres.--Layne & Bowler, Memphis, TN, pg. 710
Goodwin, D.W., Pres.--Dealers Manufacturing Company, Minneapolis, MN, pg. 322
Goodwin, Daniel L., Chm. Bd. & Chief Exec. Officer--The Inland Group, Inc., Oak Brook, IL, pg. 570
Goolsby, John L., Pres. & Chief Exec. Officer--Summa Corporation, Las Vegas, NV, pg. 1057
Goolsby, Robert, Chm. Bd. & Pres.--Goolsby Foods, Inc., Columbus, GA, pg. 471
Goossens, Edward, Pres.--Wayne Wire Cloth Products, Inc., Kalkaska, MI, pg. 1169
Gorak, Michael, Pres.--Martin Universal Design, Inc., Westland, MI, pg. 715
Gorak, Michael, Pres.--Martin F. Weber Company, Philadelphia, PA, pg. 716
Gordon, Barry J., Pres.--American Funds Advisor Inc., Garden City, NJ, pg. 55
Gordon, Dan, Pres.--Gordon Food Service Inc., Grand Rapids, MI, pg. 472
Gordon, Jerome A., Pres.--Brendamour's Sporting Goods Co., Cincinnati, OH, pg. 173
Gordon, Kenneth, Pres.--Kenneth Gordon New Orleans, Ltd., New Orleans, LA, pg. 472
Gordon, Laurence, Pres. & Chief Exec. Officer--Gordon & Smith, Inc., San Diego, CA, pg. 472
Gordon, Lloyd, Pres. & Treas.--Amcell Corporation, Watertown, MA, pg. 47
Gordon, Melvin S., Pres.--Paradise Fruit Company, Inc., Plant City, FL, pg. 847
Gordon, Michael, Pres. & Treas.--Koret Givenchy, New York, NY, pg. 642
Gordon, Michael J., Pres.-KMI Services--Kirk-Mayer, Inc., Los Angeles, CA, pg. 633
Gordon, Miles, Pres.--Financial Network Investment, Torrance, CA, pg. 410
Gore, Chester, Pres. & Creative Dir.--Chester Gore Company Inc., New York, NY, pg. 472
Gore, Jeffrey R., Pres.--Gore Graphics, Inc., Los Angeles, CA, pg. 472
Gore, Larry, Pres.--Polo/Ralph Lauren Factory Store, Carlstadt, NJ, pg. 880
Gore, Robert W., Pres. & Chief Exec. Officer--W. L. Gore & Associates, Inc., Newark, DE, pg. 472
Gorell, Frank, Pres.--Jamison Bedding, Inc., Franklin, TN, pg. 589
Gorga, Joseph L., Pres.--Elastic Fabrics of America, Greensboro, NC, pg. 202
Gorla, Barbara, Pres.--National Media Mail, Inc., Santa Ana, CA, pg. 792
Gorman, Kenneth J., Pres. & Chief Oper. Officer--Atlantic Mutual Companies, New York, NY, pg. 94
Gorman, L.A., Pres.--L.L. Bean, Inc., Freeport, ME, pg. 648
Gorman, Martin D., Co-Pres. & Chief Oper. Officer--Encore Marketing International, Lanham, MD, pg. 380
Gorman, Patrick J., Co-Pres. & Chief Exec. Officer--Encore Marketing International, Lanham, MD, pg. 380
Gorra, William, Pres.--Syndet Products, Inc., Bolton, CT, pg. 1069
Gorra, William, Pres. & Chief Exec. & Chief Fin. Officer--Chemical Specialties Corp., Springfield, MA, pg. 1069
Gorski, John A., High Chief Ranger--Catholic Order of Foresters, Naperville, IL, pg. 229
Gorsun, Barry R., Pres. & Chief Exec. Officer--Summa Four, Inc., Manchester, NH, pg. 1057
Goss, John, Pres. & Chief Oper. Officer--Supershuttle International, Los Angeles, CA, pg. 1064
Goss, Robert M., Pres., Chief Oper. Officer--Transco Inc., Chicago, IL, pg. 1106
Gosselin, W. Gerard, Pres.--Lyon Metal Products, Inc., Montgomery, IL, pg. 690
Gossett, Barry P., Pres.--The Scotsman Group, Inc., Baltimore, MD, pg. 982
Gossling, Paul, Chief Exec. Officer--Gilbert & Bennett, Georgetown, CT, pg. 457
Gossman, Robert, Pres.--MD Pneumatics, Inc., Springfield, MO, pg. 1120
Gosson, Anthony, Pres.--Swirl, Inc., New York, NY, pg. 1068
Gottlieb, Eugene V., Pres.--Quantic Industries, Inc., San Carlos, CA, pg. 904
Gottschalk, Gary, Pres. & Chief Exec. Officer--The Harter Group, Sturgis, MI, pg. 513
Gough, Thomas L., Pres. & Chief Oper. Officer--Integral Systems, Walnut Creek, CA, pg. 572
Goulazian, Peter, Pres. & Chief Exec. Officer--Katz Communications, Inc., New York, NY, pg. 618
Gould, Desmond, Brand Mgr.--The William G. Bell Company, East Weymouth, MA, pg. 171
Gould, Fredric H., Exec. Officer--Gould Investors, L.P., Great Neck, NY, pg. 473
Gould, Harry E., Jr., Chm. Bd. & Pres.--Gould Paper Corporation, New York, NY, pg. 473
Gould, Peter J., Pres. & Chief Exec. Officer--Aldine Technologies, Carlstadt, NJ, pg. 33
Gould, Steve, Pres.--Pajama Craft, Inc., New York, NY, pg. 545
Gould, Steven, Pres.--Gould Packaging, Inc., Vancouver, WA, pg. 473
Gould, William S., III, Pres.--Magnetic Analysis Corp., Mount Vernon, NY, pg. 700
Goulet, Victor, Pres. & Chief Exec. Officer--ERA Real Estate, Overland Park, KS, pg. 360
Graber, Michael, Pres. & Chief Exec. Officer--Buffalo White GMC, Inc., Buffalo, NY, pg. 187
Grabow, Steve, Pres.--Sally Lou Fashions Corporation, New York, NY, pg. 967
Grabowski, J., Pres.--Arcinco, Inc., Garfield, NJ, pg. 81
Grace, Kevin, Pres. & Chief Oper. Officer--Spring Engineers, Inc., Houston, TX, pg. 1033
Grace, W.M., Chm. Bd. & Pres.--W. M. Grace Development, Phoenix, AZ, pg. 474
Graff, Stewart, Pres.--Douglas Stephen Plastics, Inc., Paterson, NJ, pg. 347
Graham, James, Pres. & Chief Exec. Officer--Versa Services Ltd., Etobicoke,, Canada, pg. 7
Graham, John D., Chm. & Chief Exec. Officer--Fleishman Hillard Inc., Saint Louis, MO, pg. 417
Graham, Malcolm S., Pres.--Atlantic Aviation Corp., New Castle, DE, pg. 94
Graham, Ronald L., Pres.-Elect--American Mathematical Society, Inc., Providence, RI, pg. 58
Graham, Stacey, Pres. & Chief Oper. Officer--Lewis, Clark & Graham, Atlanta, GA, pg. 673
Grams, Jerry, Pres. & Chief Oper. Officer--Freeway Corporation, Cleveland, OH, pg. 432
Grandy, Jay F., Pres. & Chief Exec. Officer--Snokist Growers, Yakima, WA, pg. 1015
Granger, Gary, Pres.--Granger Construction Co., Lansing, MI, pg. 476
Granger, Jean-Yves, Mng. Dir.--Wunderman, Vincennes,, France, pg. 1212
Granik, Russell, Deputy Commissioner & Chief Oper. Officer--National Basketball Association, New York, NY, pg. 786
Grant, Berl, Pres. & Chief Exec. Officer--Seymour Manufacturing Company, Seymour, IN, pg. 994
Grant, David, Pres.--Voyager Emblems, Inc., Sanborn, NY, pg. 1155
Grant, Donald W., Pres. & Mgr.-Sls.--Western Reinsurance Brokers, Inc., Los Angeles, CA, pg. 1181
Grant, Howard C., Chm. & Pres.--Grant Marketing Communications Inc., Lafayette Hill, PA, pg. 477
Grant, Ronald, Pres.--Ziniz Inc., Louisville, KY, pg. 1220
Grant, Tone, Pres.--Refco Group Ltd., Chicago, IL, pg. 921
Grant, Walter L., Pres. & Chief Exec. Officer--Camellia Food Stores Co-op Inc., Norfolk, VA, pg. 211
Grantham, H. Varley, Pres.--Grantham Company, Orlando, FL, pg. 477
Grantham, Lloyd, V.P.-Engrng.--B & K Steel & Supply, Inc., Ogden, UT, pg. 105
Granzon, Gary W., Pres. & Chief Oper. Officer--ANGUS Chemical Company, Buffalo Grove, IL, pg. 75
Grassman, William, Pres.--Future Foam, Inc., Council Bluffs, IA, pg. 437
Grau, Juan, Chm. Bd., Pres. & Chief Exec. Officer--Bacardi Imports, Inc., Miami, FL, pg. 108
Graunke, Terence, Chm. Bd. & Pres.--U.S. Communications Corporation, Minneapolis, MN, pg. 1135
Gravenhorst, Ted, Jr., Pres.--John Boos & Company, Effingham, IL, pg. 165
Graves, Earl G., Chm. Bd., Pres. & Chief Exec. Officer--Earl G. Graves, Ltd., New York, NY, pg. 478
Graves, Herbert C., Pres.--Freedom Forge Corporation, Burnham, PA, pg. 430
Graves, Malcom, Jr., Pres.--Remarks, Inc., Dublin, OH, pg. 925
Gray, C.C. Howard, Pres. & Chief Exec. Officer--James N. Gray Construction Co., Inc., Lexington, KY, pg. 479
Gray, James H., Pres. & Chief Exec. Officer--Harbor Bancorp, Long Beach, CA, pg. 506
Gray, James R., Pres.--Gray-Pro, Inc., Boulder, CO, pg. 479
Gray, John T., Pres. & Chief Exec. Officer--The Genie Company, Alliance, OH, pg. 452
Gray, John, S., Sr., Chm. Bd. & Pres.--Jack Gray Transport, Inc., Gary, IN, pg. 479
Gray, Kerry, Pres.--Associated Advertising Agency, Inc., Wichita, KS, pg. 89
Gray, Lawrence F., Pres.--The Heil Co., Chattanooga, TN, pg. 525
Gray, Mark H., Pres.--Gray Baumgarten Layport, Inc., Pittsburgh, PA, pg. 479
Gray, R. Joseph, Pres.--Continental Eagle Corporation, Prattville, AL, pg. 278
Gray, Robert A., Pres. & Chief Exec. Officer--Gray Printing Co., Fostoria, OH, pg. 479
Gray, Roger L., Pres. & Chief Exec. Officer--Gray Kirk/VanSant Advertising, Inc., Baltimore, MD, pg. 479
Gray, Steven P., Pres.--Chi Systems, Inc., Ann Arbor, MI, pg. 244
Gray, William Don, Pres.--Ugly Duckling Rent-A-Car, Phoenix, AZ, pg. 1125
Graybill, V. Lynn, Pres.--Peerless Chain Co., Winona, MN, pg. 855
Grayson, John R., Pres.--RainSoft Water Conditioning Co., Elk Grove Village, IL, pg. 910
Greeco, Richard, Pres.--Greeco Brothers, Inc., Lawrence, MA, pg. 483
Greek, David N., Pres.--Hill & Griffith Company, Cincinnati, OH, pg. 534
Greely, William C., Pres. & Chief Exec. Officer--Keeneland Assoc., Inc., Lexington, KY, pg. 620
Green, Bernard, Pres.--B. Green & Co., Baltimore, MD, pg. 484
Green, Bernard S., Pres.--Maurice Electric Supply Company, Washington, DC, pg. 722
Green, Charles L., Chm., Pres. & Chief Exec. Officer--Ford Products Corporation, Valley Cottage, NY, pg. 423
Green, Jack, Pres.--Tallapoosa River Electric Co-Op, South Lafayette, AL, pg. 1077
Green, James M., Pres. & Chief Exec. Officer--FWD Corporation, Clintonville, WI, pg. 395
Green, James M., Pres. & Chief Exec. Officer--Seagrave Fire Apparatus, Inc., Clintonville, WI, pg. 395
Green, John, Pres. & Chief Exec. Officer--Bauerlein Inc., New Orleans, LA, pg. 127
Green, Peter J., Pres.--John E. Green Co., Highland Park, MI, pg. 484
Green, Richard K., Pres. & Chief Oper. Officer--Blistex, Inc., Oak Brook, IL, pg. 157
Green, Stanley, Pres., Chief Exec. & Chief Fin. Officer--DAQ Electronics Inc., Middlesex, NJ, pg. 308
Green, Stephen J., Chm. Bd.--E-II Holdings, Inc., New York, NY, pg. 358
Greenbaum, John, Pres. & Chief Oper. Officer--RELA, Inc., Boulder, CO, pg. 924
Greenbaum, John, Pres. & Chief Oper. Officer--RELA Product Development Div. (PDD), Boulder, CO, pg. 924
Greenbaum, John, Pres. & Chief Oper. Officer--RELA Manufacturing Division, Boulder, CO, pg. 924
Greenberg, David A., Pres.--The Clinipad Corporation, Guilford, CT, pg. 255
Greenberg, Emanuel, Pres.--Jack Greenberg Inc., Philadelphia, PA, pg. 485
Greenberg, Frank, Pres.--Baltic Linen Company, Inc., Valley Stream, NY, pg. 116
Greenberg, Nancy Ryan, Pres.--Pro Media, Inc., Needham, MA, pg. 892
Greenblatt, Sherwin, Pres. & Chief Oper. Officer--Bose Corporation, Framingham, MA, pg. 167
Greene, Joy, Pres. & Chief Oper. Officer--CYB Yasumura Design, New York, NY, pg. 1210
Greene, Randy, Chm. Bd. & Pres.--Blevins Concession Supply Co., Tampa, FL, pg. 156
Greene, Ronald D., Mng. Dir.--Devon Direct Marketing & Advertising, Inc., Berwyn, PA, pg. 334
Greene, Warren E., Pres.--Adair Greene Advertising, Atlanta, GA, pg. 16
Greenfield, Bernard, Pres.--Federal Distributing Corporation, Maspeth, NY, pg. 404
Greenfield, Dan, Pres.--Carco International, Inc., Fort Smith, AR, pg. 217
Greenfield, Harley J., Chm., Pres. & Chief Exec. Officer--Jennifer Convertibles Inc., Paramus, NJ, pg. 592
Greenfield, Steven, Pres.--Commonwealth Toy & Novelty Company, New York, NY, pg. 269
Greenhouse, Martin, Pres. & Co-Creative Dir.--Berenter Greenhouse & Webster, Inc., New York, NY, pg. 141
Greenland, Leo, Chm. & Chief Exec. Officer--Smith/Greenland, Incorporated, New York, NY, pg. 1012
Greenspun, Brian L., Pres.--Las Vegas Sun, Inc., Las Vegas, NV, pg. 659
Greenwood, John, Pres.--Micron Separations, Inc., Westborough, MA, pg. 749
Greenwood, Lorne, Pres.-Davis Tool & Engineering Co.--Davis Industries Inc., Detroit, MI, pg. 318
Greer, Carl, Pres.--Illinois Limited Partnership, Alsip, IL, pg. 715
Greer, Carl C., Pres.--Martin Exploration Management Company, Alsip, IL, pg. 715
Greer, G.M., Pres.--Radionics, Inc., Salinas, CA, pg. 909
Greer, Jack V., Sr., Pres.--Autry Greer & Sons, Inc., Prichard, AL, pg. 486
Greer, Paul, Pres.--NPS, Inc., Wayne, PA, pg. 321
Grefenstette, Carl, Pres. & Chief Exec. Officer--Hillman Company, Pittsburgh, PA, pg. 535
Gregerson, R.L., Pres.--American Excelsior Company, Arlington, TX, pg. 51
Gregg, Robert C., Pres.--Gregg Industries, Inc., El Monte, CA, pg. 486
Gregoire, Ronald, Pres.--Cerritos Ford, Inc., Cerritos, CA, pg. 236
Gregorich, Dan, Pres.--Airmaster Fan Co., Michigan Center, MI, pg. 28
Gregory, Bruce, Pres. & Chief Exec. Officer--Ready Systems, Sunnyvale, CA, pg. 916
Gregory, E. John, Sr., Chm. Bd. & Pres.--J.T. Slocomb Company, South Glastonbury, CT, pg. 1010
Gregory, James R., Pres.--Gregory & Clyburne, Inc., Stamford, CT, pg. 486
Gregory, Ralph, Pres.--Newman, Saylor & Gregory, Columbia, SC, pg. 804
Gregory, William H., Chm. Bd. & Pres.--Gregory Affiliates, Inc., Beaverton, OR, pg. 486
Gresham, Edward R., Pres. & Chief Oper. Officer--Network Real Estate of California, Inc., Soquel, CA, pg. 798

Gresham, Edward R., Pres. & Chief Oper. Officer--Network Real Estate, Inc., Soquel, CA, pg. 798
Gresham, Edward R., Pres. & Chief Oper. Officer--Network Home Services, Inc., Soquel, CA, pg. 798
Gress, Ronald D., Pres.--Gress Foods Inc., Gainesville, GA, pg. 486
Gretschel, W. Michael, Pres.--Market Development Group Inc., Washington, DC, pg. 709
Grey, Joel, Administrator--Auburn Faith Community Hospital, Auburn, CA, pg. 97
Grier, James R., III, Pres.--Martin K. Eby Construction Company, Inc., Wichita, KS, pg. 365
Griffen, Donald K., Pres. & Chief Exec. Officer--INTEGRATEC, Atlanta, GA, pg. 573
Griffin, Dennis B., Pres. & Chief Exec. Officer--Griffin Industries, Inc., Cold Spring, KY, pg. 487
Griffin, Donald, Pres.--Winko-Matic Signal Co./Multisonics Corp., Norcross, GA, pg. 1196
Griffin, George G., Chm. Bd., Pres. & Treas.--Davis Advertising Inc., Philadelphia, PA, pg. 318
Griffin, Jeff, Chm. Bd., Pres. & Chief Exec. Officer--Mountain Air Delivery, Sparks, NV, pg. 773
Griffin, John, Pres.--Sewell Village Cadillac Co., Dallas, TX, pg. 993
Griffin, John W., Pres.--Griffin Manufacturing Co., Muskogee, OK, pg. 487
Griffin, Mark E., Chm. Bd., Pres. & Chief Exec. Officer--Lewis Drug, Inc., Sioux Falls, SD, pg. 673
Griffin, Martha, Chm. Bd.--Griffin Manufacturing Co., Muskogee, OK, pg. 487
Griffis, W.I., Pres. & Chief Exec. Officer--T.J. Morris Company, Inc., Statesboro, GA, pg. 771
Griffith, Verne, Pres.--Koch Engineering Company, Inc., Akron, OH, pg. 638
Griffiths, Donald P., Sr., Pres. & Chief Exec. Officer--Colusa Elevator Co., Colusa, IL, pg. 267
Griggs, David, Pres., Chief Exec. & Chief Fin. Officer & Treas.--Jack Griggs Inc., Exeter, CA, pg. 488
Grimaud, Joseph A., Jr., Pres. & Chief Exec. Officer--Precision Tune, Inc., Leesburg, VA, pg. 885
Grimes, Thomas D., Pres. & Treas.--Puritan Bakery, Inc., Carson, CA, pg. 900
Grimmer, Park, Pres.--Grimmer Realty Co. Inc., Birmingham, AL, pg. 488
Grinberg, Efraim, Pres. & Chief Oper. Officer--North American Watch Corporation, Lyndhurst, NJ, pg. 812
Grinberg, Efraim, Pres.--Movado Watch Co., Lyndhurst, NJ, pg. 812
Grinzewitsch, George, Chm. Bd & Pres.--Von Housen Motors, Sacramento, CA, pg. 1155
Grisanti, Michael J., Pres. & Chief Exec. Officer--Grisanti, Inc., Louisville, KY, pg. 488
Griswold, Donald G., Pres.--Griswold Industries, Inc., Costa Mesa, CA, pg. 488
Griter, H.E., Pres.-Dist. Div.--Chemtech Industries, Inc., Saint Louis, MO, pg. 242
Groat, Jonathan M., Pres. & Chief Exec. Officer--Smith-Lee Co., Inc., Oneida, NY, pg. 1013
Grodd, Clifford, Pres.--Paul Stuart, Inc., New York, NY, pg. 1054
Groendyke, Jay, Pres. & Chief Exec. Officer--Dieline Corporation, Kentwood, MI, pg. 336
Groene, Stanley, Pres.--Kruse Hardware Company, Fairfield, OH, pg. 645
Groenevelt, Aat, Chm. Bd. & Pres.--Provimi Veal Corporation, Waukesha, WI, pg. 896
Grogan, David R., Chm., Pres. & Chief Exec. Officer--Toter Incorporated, Statesville, NC, pg. 1103
Gromer, Richard H., Pres. & Chief Exec. Officer--Gromer Super Markets, Inc., Elgin, IL, pg. 489
Gronda, Richard, Pres.--Farrell Lines Incorporated, New York, NY, pg. 403
Gropp, Louis, Editor-in-Chief--House Beautiful, New York, NY, pg. 523
Gropper, Edward, Chm. Bd & Pres.--Faber, Coe & Gregg, Inc., Secaucus, NJ, pg. 395
Gross, Emerick, Pres. & Chief Exec. Officer--Dan's Supreme Super Markets Inc., Hempstead, NY, pg. 314
Gross, Jack, Pres.--Gloria Vanderbilt Division, New York, NY, pg. 460
Gross, John J., Partner--John Gross & Co., Baltimore, MD, pg. 489
Gross, Myron, Pres.--Pioneer Paper Corporation, Carlstadt, NJ, pg. 872
Grossenburg, Gene C., Pres.--Grossenburg Implements, Incorporated, Winner, SD, pg. 489
Grossman, Andrew, Pres.--Jones Apparel Group, Inc., Bristol, PA, pg. 602
Grossman, David, Pres.--Grossman Iron & Steel Company, St. Louis, MO, pg. 489
Grossman, Lou, Pres.--Gillespie Public Relations, Inc., Princeton, NJ, pg. 458
Grossman, Max, Pres.--M. Grossman Son, Inc., Passaic, NJ, pg. 489
Grossman, Michael W., Pres.--Midwest Mechanical Contractors Inc., Kansas City, MO, pg. 752
Grossman, Mortimer, Pres.--International Components Corporation, Melville, NY, pg. 576
Grossman, Neil J., Chm. Bd. & Pres.--Reed Exhibition Companies, Boston, MA, pg. 920
Grossman, Steven, Pres.--Massachusetts Envelope Co., Somerville, MA, pg. 718
Grossman, Steven M., Pres.--Southern Container Corporation, Hauppauge, NY, pg. 1020
Grosvenor, Gilbert M., Chm. Bd. & Pres.--National Geographic Society, Washington, DC, pg. 789
Grot, John, Chm. Bd. & Pres.--Pascoe Building Systems, Inc., Columbus, GA, pg. 851
Grothgar, Niels, Chm. Bd. & Chief Exec. Officer--Wilkens Ayer, Hamburg,, Germany, pg. 104
Groussman, Dean, Chm., Pres. & Chief Exec. Officer--Zale Corporation, Irving, TX, pg. 1215
Grove, Richard C., Pres.--Milwaukee Electric Tool Corp., Brookfield, WI, pg. 361
Grove, Ron, Pres.--Tash, Inc., Des Plaines, IL, pg. 1080
Grover, Billy D., Pres.--Hardaway Construction Company, Inc., Nashville, TN, pg. 508
Grower, Roger, Pres.--Datamedia Corporation, Nashua, NH, pg. 316
Grua, Rudolph, Pres. & Chief Exec. Officer--General Binding Corporation, Northbrook, IL, pg. 656
Grua, Rudolph, Pres. & Chief Exec. Officer--VeloBind, Inc., Northbrook, IL, pg. 657
Grubb, David H., Pres. & Chief Oper. Officer--Swinerton & Walberg Co., San Francisco, CA, pg. 1068
Gruber, David, Pres.--MEPC American Properties Incorporated, Dallas, TX, pg. 692
Gruber, Paul, Pres.--ERM-South, Inc., Tampa, FL, pg. 360
Grubman, John, Pres.--Media Printing Corporation, Miami, FL, pg. 734
Gruner, Charles, Pres.--Rostone Corporation, Lafayette, IN, pg. 950
Grunsten, Richard, Pres.--GSP Marketing Services, Inc., Chicago, IL, pg. 441
Grutsch, R.J., Pres.-Western Division--Sithe Energies, U.S.A., Inc., San Diego, CA, pg. 1009
Grybauskas, Roland, Pres. & Creative Dir.--Grybauskas & Partners, New York, NY, pg. 490
Gualtieri, Albert L., Pres.--Powerine Oil Company Holdings, Santa Fe Springs, CA, pg. 883
Guccione, Bob, Publr.--Saturday Review Magazine, New York, NY, pg. 450
Guccione, Kathy Keeton, Pres.--Omni Publications International Ltd., New York, NY, pg. 450
Guedes, Sandra, Dir.--Montana Lottery, Helena, MT, pg. 766
Guerraro, Juan Antonio, Mng. Dir.--Final Art, Madrid,, Spain, pg. 111
Guerrero, Juan Antonio, Gen. Mgr.--Kobs & Draft S.A., Madrid,, Spain, pg. 112
Guerrieri, Alan, Pres.--Showell Farms, Inc., Showell, MD, pg. 1000
Guertler, Walter E., Jr., Chm. Bd., Pres., Chief Exec. Officer--Systems Engineering & Manufacturing Corp., Stoughton, MA, pg. 1071
Gugino, Carmelo, Jr., Pres. & Treas.--Dinaire Corp., Buffalo, NY, pg. 338
Guida, Bernadette Castro, Pres.--Castro Convertible Corporation, New Hyde Park, NY, pg. 229
Guido, Sally A., Pres.--Lee Myles Associates Corporation, Maywood, NJ, pg. 666
Gulbas, Bruce, Pres. & Chief Exec. Officer--National Restaurant Supply Company, El Paso, TX, pg. 793
Gulden, G., V.P. & Gen. Mgr.--Stonco, Union, NJ, pg. 1050
Gullickson, W.D., Jr., Pres. & Chief Exec. Officer--McLaughlin Gormley King Company, Minneapolis, MN, pg. 731
Gulling, Daniel L., Pres. & Chief Exec. Officer--Marinette Marine Corporation, Marinette, WI, pg. 707
Gunder, Stephen, Chm. Bd. & Pres.--Gunder & Associates, Inc., Dublin, OH, pg. 494
Gunderson, Richard L., Pres. & Chief Exec. Officer--Aid Association For Lutherans, Appleton, WI, pg. 26
Gunn, Robert W., Pres.--Rudel Machinery Company, Inc., Shelton, CT, pg. 954
Gunther, Herbert Chao, Pres.--Public Media Center, San Francisco, CA, pg. 898
Gupta, Gautam, Pres.--I D E Associates, Billerica, MA, pg. 560
Gupta, Gautam, Pres.--Idea Courier, Inc., Tempe, AZ, pg. 560
Gupta, Gautom, Pres.--I D E Corporation, Billerica, MA, pg. 560
Gupta, Vin, Pres.--Vinod Gupta Company, Inc., Omaha, NE, pg. 494
Gupta, Vinod, Chm., Pres., Chief Exec. Officer--American Business Information, Inc., Omaha, NE, pg. 50
Gurgold, Carl, Pres.--Tiffany Extruders, Inc., Paterson, NJ, pg. 1096
Gurin, Richard S., Pres. & Chief Exec. Officer--Binney & Smith Inc., Easton, PA, pg. 502
Gurley, Patrick J., Pres.--Gurley Motor Company, Gallup, NM, pg. 494
Gurney, Robert J., Jr., Chm. Bd., Pres. & Chief Exec. Officer--Gurney Industries Inc., Gastonia, NC, pg. 495
Gurnitz, Robert N., Pres. & Chief Exec. Officer--Northwestern Steel & Wire Co., Sterling, IL, pg. 815
Gurr, Danny, Pres.--DeWolfe & Fiske Inc., Canton, MA, pg. 237
Gurr, Danny, Pres.--Lauriat Inc., Canton, MA, pg. 237
Gussman, Marvin, Pres.--Marvin Engineering Company, Inc., Inglewood, CA, pg. 716
Gustafson, F. Edward, Pres.--Viskase Corporation, Bedford Park, IL, pg. 383
Gustafson, Mel A., Pres.--Coast Packing Company, Vernon, CA, pg. 257
Gustafsson, M., Pres.--Coldwater Seafood Corporation, Rowayton, CT, pg. 260
Gutenplan, Martin, Pres.--Mateco Electronics Corp., Brooklyn, NY, pg. 720
Guthrie, Francis J., Pres.--The Guthrie Group, Portland, ME, pg. 495
Gutterman, Arthur, Pres., Chief Oper. & Chief Exec. Officer--Jelmar Company, Lincolnwood, IL, pg. 592
Guttman, Alan R., Pres. & Treas.--The Guttman Group, Belle Vernon, PA, pg. 495
Guyer, Ray, Pres. & Merger & Acquisition Contact--PetCare Plus, Inc., Addison, IL, pg. 863
Guzik, Mitchell, Pres.--Gilda Marx Inc., Los Angeles, CA, pg. 716
Guzman, Pedro, Pres.--ETL Testing Laboratories, Inc, Cortland, NY, pg. 361
Gwaltney, John R., Chm. Bd., Pres. & Chief Exec. Officer--Forestry Suppliers, Inc., Jackson, MS, pg. 424
Gwinn, John C., Jr., Pres.--Congaree Construction Co., Inc., Columbia, SC, pg. 274
Gwosdz, James, Chm. Bd. & Pres.--Orange Grove Co-operative, Orange Grove, TX, pg. 828
Gygi, Richard W., Pres.--CPS Corporation, Franklin, TN, pg. 428
Haas, B.K., Pres.--Bud Industries, Inc., Willoughby, OH, pg. 186
Haas, Donald J., Pres.--National Band & Tag Co., Newport, KY, pg. 786
Habecker, Eugene B., Pres. & Chief Exec. Officer--American Bible Society, New York, NY, pg. 49
Habegger, Fred, Pres.--The Habegger Corporation, Cincinnati, OH, pg. 498
Haber, Barry, Gen. Mgr.--Cuisinarts Inc., Stamford, CT, pg. 272
Haberkorn, Steve, Pres. & Mgr.-Adv.--Pistol Pete's Pizza, Phoenix, AZ, pg. 872
Habermann, N.N., Pres. & Chief Exec. Officer--Restaurant Enterprises Group, Inc., Irvine, CA, pg. 929
Habernickel, Duke, Pres.--The Haband Co., Paterson, NJ, pg. 498
Hackel, Allan, Pres.--The Allan R. Hackel Organization, Newton Center, MA, pg. 498
Hacker, Joshua, Chm. Bd., Pres., Chief Exec. & Chief Fin. Officer--Seaboard Electronics Co., Carlsbad, CA, pg. 983
Hackerman, Willard, Pres. & Treas.--Whiting-Turner Contracting Co., Baltimore, MD, pg. 1187
Hackman, Daryl, Pres.--Farm & Home Oil Company, Telford, PA, pg. 401
Hackney, Robert H., Pres. & Chief Exec. Officer--Hackney Brothers, Inc., Wilson, NC, pg. 498
Hadden, E.M., Pres.--Standard Supply & Hardware, New Orleans, LA, pg. 1037
Hadfield, F.C., Chm. Bd.--Kwik-Kopy Corp., Cypress, TX, pg. 647
Hadley, Dick, Pres.--Brown & Hadley & Partners, Seattle, WA, pg. 182
Haehn, Jeffrey S., Pres.--Crystal Cabinet Works, Inc., Princeton, MN, pg. 303
Haentjens, Walter D., Pres.--Barrett Haentjens & Company, Hazleton, PA, pg. 499
Haeseker, Henry W., Pres. & Chief Exec. Officer--Boyle Engineering Corp., Newport Beach, CA, pg. 169
Haessler, John, Pres. & Chief Exec. Officer--Woodmen Accident & Life Co., Lincoln, NE, pg. 1200
Hafner, Joseph A., Pres. & Chief Exec. Officer--Riviana Foods Inc., Houston, TX, pg. 937
Haft, Alfred, Pres.--Haywin Textile Products, Inc., Brooklyn, NY, pg. 520
Hagen, John K., Jr., Pres.--George W. Auch Co., Pontiac, MI, pg. 97
Haggar, Joe, III, Pres. & Chief Exec. Officer--Haggar Apparel Company, Dallas, TX, pg. 499
Haggen, Richard R., Pres. & Chief Oper. Officer--Haggen's, Inc., Bellingham, WA, pg. 499
Haggerty, Arthur, Pres.--John R. Hollingsworth Co., Phoenixville, PA, pg. 539
Hagie, John R., Pres.--Hagie Manufacturing Co., Clarion, IA, pg. 499
Hagmeyer, R.W., Pres.--Venta Inc., Denver, CO, pg. 1147
Hagood, Benjamin A., Pres.--William M. Bird & Co., Inc., Charleston, SC, pg. 152
Hahn, George E., Pres.--J.R. Hahn Co., Inc., Indianapolis, IN, pg. 500
Hahn, Norman, Pres. & Chm. Bd.--Conestoga Wood Specialties, Inc., Earl, PA, pg. 273
Haidinger, Robert N., Chm. Bd., Pres. & Chief Exec. Officer--Jac Jacobsen Industries, Inc., Greenwich, CT, pg. 587
Haight, G.I., Div. Mgr.--Stillman Seal, Carlsbad, CA, pg. 1049
Haigis, Richard, Pres.--The Giardini/Russell Group, Watertown, MA, pg. 456
Hainen, Gene L., Pres.--The Pierce Co., Inc., Upland, IN, pg. 102
Haines, W.K., Jr., Pres.--Haines & Co., Inc., North Canton, OH, pg. 500
Hains, Guy, Pres.--Graphic Center, Inc., Bloomfield, CT, pg. 478
Hale, Guy A., Chm. Bd., Pres. & Chief Exec. Officer--The Alamo Learning Systems, Inc., San Ramon, CA, pg. 29
Hale, John, Chm. Bd. & Pres.--Telex Communications, Inc., Minneapolis, MN, pg. 1085
Hale, Rodney L., Pres. & Chief Exec. Officer--Academy Insurance Group, Inc., Atlanta, GA, pg. 11
Hales, Robert, Pres.--Deseret Management Corporation, Salt Lake City, UT, pg. 332
Haley, Clifton, Chm. Bd., Pres. & Chief Exec. Officer--Beech Holdings Corp., Chicago, IL, pg. 131
Haley, Clifton, Chm.Bd., Pres. & Chief Exec. Officer--Budget Rent A Car Corporation, Lisle, IL, pg. 131
Haley, Jane Gosiger, Pres.--Gosiger Inc., Dayton, OH, pg. 472
Haley, Mark T., Pres. & Gen. Mgr.--Brown & Haley, Tacoma, WA, pg. 182
Haley, Russell J., Chm. Bd. & Pres.--Midwest Tire & Muffler, Inc., Rapid City, SD, pg. 752
Hall, Alvin D., Pres. & Chief Exec. Officer--Miller & Smith, Inc., McLean, VA, pg. 755
Hall, Charles, Chief Oper. Officer--G.C. Thorsen, Inc., Rockford, IL, pg. 609
Hall, Edward J., Pres.--QEI, Inc., Springfield, NJ, pg. 902
Hall, K. Michael, Pres., Chief Exec. & Chief Oper. Officer--Hall Contracting Corp., Louisville, KY, pg. 501
Hall, Larry, Pres.--Hall Sign, Inc., Bloomington, IN, pg. 501
Hall, Laurence W., Jr., Pres.--Robbins Manufacturing Company, Tampa, FL, pg. 938
Hall, Richard A., Pres.--Hall, Haerr, Peterson & Harney, Inc., Peoria, IL, pg. 501
Hall, Richard N., Sr., Pres.--Tennessee Dressed Beef Company, Nashville, TN, pg. 1087
Hall, Stuart, Pres.--Hanna Car Wash International, Inc., Portland, OR, pg. 505
Hall, Willie, Pres.--Taylor Home Health Inc., Beaumont, TX, pg. 1081
Hallam, Howard, Pres. & Chief Oper. Officer--Ben E. Keith Company, Fort Worth, TX, pg. 620

Hallam, John F., Pres. & Owner--Ceiling & Partitions, Inc., Landover, MD, pg. 230
Hallcom, Terry, Pres.--The USAir Shuttle, Jackson Heights, NY, pg. 1118
Halle, Bruce T., Chm. Bd. & Pres.--Reinalt-Thomas Corp., Ann Arbor, MI, pg. 923
Hallgren, Kenneth, Pres. & Chief Oper. Officer--Hurd Millwork Company, Inc., Medford, WI, pg. 1123
Hallman, Richard, Pres.--Electronic Data Magnetics, Inc., High Point, NC, pg. 375
Halloran, John B., Pres.--Peabody Office Furniture Corporation, Boston, MA, pg. 853
Hallstedt, Fred, Pres. & V.P-Sls. & Mktg.--Sonneveldt Company, Grand Rapids, MI, pg. 1018
Halperin, Thomas C., Chm Bd., Pres. & Chief Exec. Officer--Commercial Light Company, Hillside, IL, pg. 268
Halpern, Colin, Chm. Bd. & Pres.--NPS Corporation, Elmwood Park, NJ, pg. 781
Halton, Dale F., Chm. Bd., Pres. & Chief Exec. Officer--Pepsi-Cola Bottling Company of Charlotte Inc., Charlotte, NC, pg. 860
Halvorson, William, Pres.--Prospect Motors, Inc., Jackson, CA, pg. 895
Ham, John, Exec. V.P. & Gen. Mgr.--Metabo Corporation, West Chester, PA, pg. 741
Hamblett, Stephen, Chm. Bd., Chief Exec. Officer & Publr.--Providence Journal Company, Providence, RI, pg. 895
Hamilton, Gary, Pres.--Evans Fabrication, Inc., Harvey, LA, pg. 390
Hamilton, Hal, Pres.--Market Forge Company, Everett, MA, pg. 1027
Hamilton, J.A., Pres.--PTS Electronics Corporation, Bloomington, IN, pg. 837
Hamilton, Josh, Pres.--Clinton Mills, Geneva, AL, pg. 202
Hamilton, Richard F., Pres.--Monterey Mechanical Company, Oakland, CA, pg. 767
Hamilton, Robert J. Jr., Pres.--Hamilton Equipment, Inc., Ephrata, PA, pg. 503
Hamilton, Sherman, Pres. & Chief Exec. Officer--Hamilton Sweeney Advertising, Inc., Denver, CO, pg. 503
Hamilton, Steven, Pres.--Hamilton Co., Inc., Reno, NV, pg. 503
Hamister, Mark E., Chm. Bd., Pres. & Chief Exec. Officer--National Health Care Affiliates, Inc., Buffalo, NY, pg. 791
Hamm, Jerry T., Pres.--Jerry Hamm Chevrolet Inc., Jacksonville, FL, pg. 503
Hammer, John, Pres.--Redken Laboratories, Inc., Canoga Park, CA, pg. 919
Hammerstein, Steve, Pres.--Kwik-Kopy Corp., Cypress, TX, pg. 647
Hammond, Harold E., Pres. & Chief Exec. Officer--H & H Advertising, Fort Worth, TX, pg. 496
Hammond, Joseph M., Pres. & Chief Exec. Officer--Jervis B. Webb Company, Farmington Hills, MI, pg. 1170
Hammond, Michael M., Pres.-Revlon-N. Amer.--Alexandra De Markoff, Ltd., New York, NY, pg. 695
Hammond, Michael M., Pres.--Almay, Inc., New York, NY, pg. 695
Hammond, Toby R., Pres.--Hancock Lumber, Inc., Casco, ME, pg. 504
Hampshire, Bill, Pres.--Ravenswood Aluminum Corp., Ravenswood, WV, pg. 914
Hampton, John C., Chm. Bd., Pres. & Chief Exec. Officer--Hampton Resources Inc., Portland, OR, pg. 504
Hamway, Ezra, Pres.--Remco Toys, New York, NY, pg. 926
Hancock, David, Pres.--Spectrum Industries, Inc., Chippewa Falls, WI, pg. 1029
Hancock, Robert J., Pres. & Gen. Mgr.--Intertec Publishing, Overland Park, KS, pg. 611
Handel, Samuel, Pres.--Handel & Company, Inc., Pennsauken, NJ, pg. 504
Handerhan, Kevin J., Pres.--Ellwood City Forge, Ellwood City, PA, pg. 378
Handler, Russell, Pres.--Newport/Cape Dory Yachts, Inc., Manorville, NY, pg. 804
Handler, Sheryl, Pres. & Chief Exec. Officer--Thinking Machines Corporation, Cambridge, MA, pg. 1092
Hanel, L. Sterling, Pres.--Hanel Lumber Co., Inc., Hood River, OR, pg. 505
Hanft, Adam, Pres. & Chief Oper. Officer--Slater Hanft Martin, Inc., New York, NY, pg. 1010
Haniseh, Michael, Dr., Pres.--American Barmag Co., Charlotte, NC, pg. 49
Hankins, A. Burton, Pres.--Hankins Lumber Company, Inc., Grenada, MS, pg. 505
Hanks, Bea, Assoc. Publr.--Mother Earth News, New York, NY, pg. 773
Hanlin, Russell L., Pres., Chief Exec. & Chief Oper. Officer--Sunkist Growers, Inc., Sherman Oaks, CA, pg. 1060
Hanlon, Jack, Pres. & Chief Oper. Officer--Gerber Plumbing Fixtures Corporation, Chicago, IL, pg. 454
Hanlon, Jack, Pres. & Chief Oper. Officer--Kokomo Sanitary Pottery Corp., Chicago, IL, pg. 640
Hanlon, Mark Z., Pres.--BCM Engineers Inc., Plymouth Meeting, PA, pg. 106
Hann, S.A., Chm. Bd. & Pres.--Health Care Lodges, Coffeyville, KS, pg. 520
Hanna, Allan C., Pres. & Chief Exec. Officer--Zephyr Inc., North Muskegon, MI, pg. 1217
Hanna, H.D., Pres.--Atlas Supply Company, Atlanta, GA, pg. 96
Hanna, William W., Pres. & Chief Oper. Officer--Koch Industries, Incorporated, Wichita, KS, pg. 639
Hannah, Thomas E., Pres. & Chief Exec. Officer--Collins & Aikman Textile Group, Charlotte, NC, pg. 262
Hannay, Roger A., Pres. & Chief Exec. Officer--Clifford B. Hannay & Son Inc., Westerlo, NY, pg. 505
Hannebrink, Dave, Pres. & Chief Exec. Officer--Covalent Systems Corporation, Fremont, CA, pg. 290
Hano, Frank, Pres. & Chief Exec. Officer--Technicarbon Company, Inc., Springfield, MA, pg. 1083
Hanon, John, Pres.--Berks Products Corporation, Reading, PA, pg. 142
Hansberger, James R., Pres.--RAM Golf Corporation, Melrose Park, IL, pg. 910
Hansen, Charles M., Pres. & Chief Exec. Officer--Pillowtex Corporation, Dallas, TX, pg. 870
Hansen, D.K., Pres.--Crystal Cream & Butter Company, Sacramento, CA, pg. 303
Hansen, Donald W., Chm. Bd. & Pres.--Delta Resins & Refractories, Inc., Milwaukee, WI, pg. 327
Hansen, Hal T., Pres.--Cargill Investor Services, Inc., Chicago, IL, pg. 219
Hansen, R.C., Pres.--A. L. Hansen Mfg. Co., Waukegan, IL, pg. 506
Hansen, R.W., Chm. Bd., Pres. & Chief Exec. Officer--Furnas Electric Company, Batavia, IL, pg. 437
Hansen, W.E., Chm. Bd. & Pres.--Brandywine Sports, Inc., Wilmington, DE, pg. 172
Hanson, Allan D., Pres. & Chief Exec. Officer--Harvest States Cooperatives, Saint Paul, MN, pg. 514
Hanson, George V., Chm. Bd., Pres. & Chief Exec. Officer--Old Home Foods, Inc., Saint Paul, MN, pg. 823
Hanson, J.D., Mng. Partner--Arthur Andersen & Co., London, United Kingdom, pg. 72
Hanson, Leroy, Dr., Pres. & Chief Oper. Officer--Triple F, Inc., Des Moines, IA, pg. 1114
Hanssen, Warren, Pres.--Viking Graphics, Chicago, IL, pg. 1151
Happel, F.J., Pres.--Ampco Metal Incorporated, Milwaukee, WI, pg. 67
Harary, Joe, Pres.--Jacques Moret, Inc., New York, NY, pg. 588
Harbert, Raymond J., Pres. & Chief Exec. Officer--Harbert Corporation, Birmingham, AL, pg. 506
Harbour, Patrick C., Pres.--Harbour Contractors, Inc., Naperville, IL, pg. 506
Hard, Brian, Pres.--Penske Truck Leasing Corp., Reading, PA, pg. 859
Hardage, Samuel A., Chm. Bd.--Woodfin Holding Corporation, San Diego, CA, pg. 1200
Hardcastle, Jeffrey, Pres.--Hardwoods Of Michigan, Inc., Clinton, MI, pg. 509
Harder, Ronald R., Pres. & Chief Exec. Officer--Jewelers Mutual Insurance Company, Neenah, WI, pg. 593
Hardesty, John, Pres.--Preston Energy Inc., Kingwood, WV, pg. 888
Hardesty, John, Pres.--Electro Dynamics Crystal Corporation, Overland Park, KS, pg. 374
Hardin, James, Pres.--Brookshire Grocery, Tyler, TX, pg. 180
Harding, Arthur J., Jr., Pres. & Chief Oper. Officer--PPA Industries, Inc., Dallas, TX, pg. 836
Harding, Craig K., Chm. Bd. & Pres.--Majestic Molded Products, Inc., Holbrook, NY, pg. 702
Harding, John H., Pres. & Chief Oper. Officer--National Life Insurance Company, Montpelier, VT, pg. 791
Hardison, Jerry, Pres.--Lone Star Corrugated Container Corporation, Irving, TX, pg. 682
Hardwick, Bryan D., Jr., Pres.--Bryan Hardwick Associates, Palos Verdes Estates, CA, pg. 508
Hardy, Allan J., Pres.--Gemini Aluminum Corporation, Pomona, CA, pg. 448
Hardy, Joseph A. Sr., Chm., Pres. & Chief Exec. Officer--84 Lumber Co., Eighty Four, PA, pg. 371
Hardy, Richard B., Pres., Chief Exec. & Chief Oper. Officer--Hyde Manufacturing Co., Southbridge, MA, pg. 556
Hare, Donald E., Pres. & Chief Exec. Officer--Coppus Engineering Corp., Millbury, MA, pg. 285
Haretakis, John, Pres.--Spires Restaurants Inc., Orange, CA, pg. 1031
Haritopoulos, D., Pres. & Creative Dir.--Geo-Young & Rubicam, Athens,, Greece, pg. 1212
Harker, Roger, Pres. & Chief Oper. Officer--Bently Nevada Corporation, Minden, NV, pg. 140
Harlan, John M., Chm. Bd. & Pres.--Harlan Electric Co., Southfield, MI, pg. 509
Harlan, Leonard, Pres.--Castle-Harlan, Inc., New York, NY, pg. 229
Harling, C. Gene, Chm. Bd., Pres. & Chief Exec. Officer--FirstFed Michigan Corporation, Detroit, MI, pg. 414
Harling, C. Gene, Chm. Bd., Pres. & Chief Exec. Officer--First Federal of Michigan, Detroit, MI, pg. 414
Harmon, Austin, Pres. & Chief Exec. Officer--Harmon Smith Inc., Kansas City, MO, pg. 510
Harmon, David E., Chm. Bd., Pres., Chief Exec. & Chief Oper. Officer--El Camino Resources, Ltd., Northridge, CA, pg. 372
Harmon, Lowell D., Chm. Bd. & Pres.--Progressive Driver Services, Inc., Jacksonville, FL, pg. 894
Harmon, Steven J., Pres. & Chief Exec. Officer--Twin City Die Castings Co., Minneapolis, MN, pg. 1121
Harp, Donald L., Chm. Bd. & Pres.--Harp's Food Stores, Inc., Springdale, AR, pg. 510
Harper, Dan, Pres.--Mannington Wood Floors, High Point, NC, pg. 704
Harper, Daniel R., Chm. Bd. & Pres.--Harper Bros., Inc., Fort Myers, FL, pg. 510
Harper, Richard, Pres.--Convenient Food Mart, Inc., Schaumburg, IL, pg. 281
Harrell, Edward H., Pres.--Tribune Review Publishing Co., Greensburg, PA, pg. 1112
Harrell, Samuel M., Chm. Bd., Pres. & Chief Exec. Officer--EDI International, Inc., Cincinnati, OH, pg. 359
Harrington, David, Exec. Dir.--Arkansas Industrial Development Commission, Little Rock, AR, pg. 83
Harrington, David A., Pres.--Delta Rubber Company, Danielson, CT, pg. 327
Harris, G.C., Jr., Pres. & Chief Exec. Officer--Jackson Mills, Inc., Wellford, SC, pg. 587
Harris, George, Pres.--Evenflo Juvenile Furniture Co., Piqua, OH, pg. 1024
Harris, George, Pres. & Chief Fin. Officer--Harris, Baio & McCullough Inc., Philadelphia, PA, pg. 511
Harris, Hanlon, Jr., Pres.--West Dairies, Inc., Spring City, PA, pg. 1177
Harris, James, Pres. & Chief Operating Officer--GFA Brands, Inc., Cresskill, NJ, pg. 440
Harris, Jay H., Pres. & Chief Oper. Officer--All American Industries, Inc., Boca Raton, FL, pg. 316
Harris, John C., Chm. Bd., Pres. & Chief Exec. Officer--Harris Farms, Inc., Coalinga, CA, pg. 511
Harris, Michael S., Pres. & Chief Exec. Officer--Deck House Inc., Acton, MA, pg. 324
Harris, Patrick, Pres.--K-J Distributors, Inc., Glendale, AZ, pg. 612
Harris, Richard M., Pres.--Predicasts, Cleveland, OH, pg. 1219
Harris, Robert D., Pres. & Chief Oper. Officer--Elastic Materials, Inc., Smithville, OH, pg. 372
Harris, Stan, Pres. & Dir.-Creative--Harris Drury Cohen, Fort Lauderdale, FL, pg. 511
Harrison, James I., Jr., Pres.--Harco Drug, Inc., Tuscaloosa, AL, pg. 507
Harrison, John C., Jr., Pres.--Harrison Construction Corp., Miami, FL, pg. 512
Harrison, Morton D., Pres.--MHB Inc., Williamsport, PA, pg. 692
Harrison, Thomas L., Pres.--Harrison, Star, Wiener & Beitler, Inc., New York, NY, pg. 512
Harriss, Bill, Pres.--Homes of Merit Inc., Bartow, FL, pg. 542
Hart, Alex W., Pres. & Chief Exec. Officer--Mastercard International, Inc., New York, NY, pg. 720
Hart, David, Pres.--Hart Graphics Inc., Austin, TX, pg. 513
Hart, Ronald D., Pres. & Treas.--Hart Crowser, Inc., Seattle, WA, pg. 512
Hartford, J. Lynn, Pres.--Brown & Caldwell Consulting Engineers, Pleasant Hill, CA, pg. 181
Hartke, Phillip, Pres.--Effingham-Clay Service Co., Effingham, IL, pg. 371
Hartley-Leonard, Darryl, Pres.--Hyatt Hotels Corporation, Chicago, IL, pg. 495
Hartley, Milton E., Pres. & Chief Exec. Officer--The Elder-Beerman Stores Corp., Dayton, OH, pg. 373
Hartman, Carl C., Pres., Chief Oper. & Chief Exec. Officer--Trinidad/Benham Corporation, Denver, CO, pg. 1113
Hartman, John, Pres.--Chemung Ford, Inc., Elmira, NY, pg. 242
Hartman, Mel, Pres.--Casting Material Company, Chattanooga, TN, pg. 229
Hartmann, E.J., Chm. Bd. & Pres.--Ziebart International Corporation, Troy, MI, pg. 1217
Hartnett, Robert M., Sr. V.P. & Gen. Mgr.--Bennigan's, Dallas, TX, pg. 958
Harton, T. Dean, Pres.--Hawthorne Corp., Charleston, SC, pg. 518
Harts, John, Pres.--Overly Manufacturing Co., Greensburg, PA, pg. 833
Hartshorn, Terry, Pres. & Chief Exec. Officer--PacifiCare Health Systems, Inc., Cypress, CA, pg. 1127
Hartter, Gary, Pres.--Tri-State Motor Transit Co., Joplin, MO, pg. 1111
Hartunian, Gordon, Pres.--A B C Appliance Inc., Pontiac, MI, pg. 2
Harty, John B., Pres. & Chief Exec. Officer--PBS Building Systems of America, Anaheim, CA, pg. 835
Hartzell, Robert C., Chm. Bd. & Pres.--Hartzell Corporation, Saint Paul, MN, pg. 514
Harvey, Joseph H. III, Pres. & Chief Oper. Officer--J.H. Harvey Company, Nashville, GA, pg. 515
Harvie, James, Chm. Bd., Pres. & Chief Exec. Officer--General Ship Corporation, Boston, MA, pg. 450
Harvieux, Ron, Pres. & Chief Exec. Officer--M&H Advertising, Minneapolis, MN, pg. 690
Haselow, John H., Pres.--Haselow & Associates, Inc., Cleveland, OH, pg. 516
Haselton, Philip N., Pres.--Detex Corporation, New Braunfels, TX, pg. 333
Haseotes, Demetrios B., Chm. Bd.--Cumberland Farms, Inc., Canton, MA, pg. 304
Haserjian, Harold, Pres.--Carpeteria, Inc., Valencia, CA, pg. 224
Haskins, John H., Pres.--Arrow Tank & Engineering Co., Minneapolis, MN, pg. 85
Hasler, Joseph W., Pres. & Chief Exec. Officer--Illinois Cereal Mills, Inc., Paris, IL, pg. 562
Hasley, Michael J., Pres.--Quality Control Corporation, Harwood Heights, IL, pg. 903
Hassinger, Hubert, Pres.--Perkasie Industries Corporation, Perkasie, PA, pg. 862
Hassinger, Norman M., Jr., Chm. Bd., Pres., Chief Exec. & Chief Oper. Officer--The Hassinger Companies, Itasca, IL, pg. 516
Hasslocher, Germano, Pres.--Hasslocher Enterprises, Inc., d/b/a Frontier Enterprises, San Antonio, TX, pg. 516
Hasty, Herndon, Pres. & Gen. Mgr.-KYYS-FM--Great American Broadcasting Company, Cincinnati, OH, pg. 52
Hatch, Richard, Pres.--Baxter Advertising, Inc., Minneapolis, MN, pg. 127
Hatch, Wilda G., Pres.--Standard Corporation, Ogden, UT, pg. 1036
Hatfield, Rodney B., Pres.--Blue Grass Chrysler-Plymouth, Lexington, KY, pg. 156
Hauber, H. C., Pres. & Chief Exec. Officer--Golden Sun Feeds, Inc., Estherville, IA, pg. 467
Hauber, W.M., Chm. Bd., Pres. & Chief Exec. Officer--Matthews International Corp., Pittsburgh, PA, pg. 721
Hauck, John C., Pres.--Tubular Steel Inc., Saint Louis, MO, pg. 1118
Hauck, L. Christian, Pres. & Chief Exec. Officer--Sunflower Electric Power Corporation, Hays, KS, pg. 1060
Hauck, Roger, Pres.--Marshall Erdman and Associates, Inc., Madison, WI, pg. 385
Haueisen, Charles, Pres.--Continental Forge Company, Compton, CA, pg. 279
Haversat, Robert A., Pres. & Chief Exec. Officer--ESSTAR Incorporated, New Haven, CT, pg. 361
Haversat, Robert A., Chm. Bd., Pres. & Chief Exec. Officer--Essex Industries, New Haven, CT, pg. 361

Haviland, E. Bernard, Pres.--Haviland Products--Haviland Enterprises, Grand Rapids, MI, pg. 517
Hawbaker, Danel P., Pres.--Glenn O. Hawbaker, Inc., State College, PA, pg. 517
Hawk, Elmer R., Pres.--Gertrude Hawk Chocolates, Inc., Troop, PA, pg. 517
Hawk, Richard C., Chm. Bd. & Chief Exec. Officer--Help Management Corporation, Overland Park, KS, pg. 527
Hawk, Robert, Pres. & Chief Exec. Officer--Hale-Halsell Company, Tulsa, OK, pg. 500
Hawkins, Arthur M., Pres. & Chief Exec. Officer--Exide Corporation, Reading, PA, pg. 393
Hawkins, James T., Pres.--Weasler Engineering Inc., West Bend, WI, pg. 1169
Hawkins, Kerry, Pres.--Cargill Ltd., Winnipeg,, Canada, pg. 219
Hawkins, Marvin J., Sr., Chm. Bd. & Pres.--J.D. Diffenbaugh, Inc., Riverside, CA, pg. 337
Hawkins, O.E., Pres.--Hawkins Markets, Inc., Wooster, OH, pg. 518
Haworth, Richard G., Pres. & Chief Exec. Officer--Haworth, Inc., Holland, MI, pg. 518
Haws, Terry R., Pres.--Haws Drinking Faucet Co., Berkeley, CA, pg. 518
Hawthorne, Brian, Pres. & Chief Exec. Officer--Hawthorne Lift Systems, Escondido, CA, pg. 519
Hawthorne, James T., Pres.--Hawthorne Machinery Company, San Diego, CA, pg. 519
Hawthorne, Timothy R., Chm. Bd. & Pres.--Hawthorne Communications, Inc., Fairfield, IA, pg. 518
Hay, Robert J., Pres. & Chief Oper. Officer--Foam Product Corporation, Eddystone, PA, pg. 1121
Haydel, Gerald M., Co-Chm. Bd. & Chief Exec. Officer--Walk, Haydel & Associates, Inc., New Orleans, LA, pg. 1159
Hayes, Carl I., Jr., Pres. & Treas.--C. I. Hayes, Inc., Cranston, RI, pg. 519
Hayes, Carl R., Pres.--Amlings Flowerland, Hinsdale, IL, pg. 67
Hayes, Carl R., Pres.--Amlings Landscape Co., Hinsdale, IL, pg. 67
Hayes, Dennis C., Pres.--Hayes Microcomputer Products, Inc., Norcross, GA, pg. 519
Hayes, Forrest, Pres.--Brittany Corporation, Cleveland, OH, pg. 177
Hayes, J. Michael, Pres. & Chief Exec. Officer--C. B. Ragland Company, Nashville, TN, pg. 909
Hayes, John, Pres.--The Architects Collaborative, Inc., San Francisco, CA, pg. 81
Hayes, Lacy, Pres.--Anchor Continental Incorporated, Columbia, SC, pg. 71
Hayes, Matthew, Pres., Chief Exec. Officer & Treas.--Hayes/Harwood, Stowe, VT, pg. 519
Hayes, R. Dixon, Pres. & Chief Exec. Officer--Shenango Furnace Company, Princeton, NJ, pg. 997
Hayes, Walter, Chm., Pres. & Chief Exec. Officer--Aston Martin LaGonda of North America, Inc., Stamford, CT, pg. 92
Hayesm, John, Pres.--The Architects Collaborative, Inc. (TAC), Cambridge, MA, pg. 80
Haynes, Gary, Pres., Chief Exec. Officer--Ericson Marketing Communications, Nashville, TN, pg. 386
Haynes, Stanley R., Pres.--Pacific Capital Bancorp, Salinas, CA, pg. 839
Haynes, Thomas J., Pres. & Chief Oper. Officer--HP Direct, Indianapolis, IN, pg. 497
Hays, Harry S., Pres.--Allen & Ohara, Inc., Memphis, TN, pg. 36
Hays, William, Sr., Pres. & Chief Exec. Officer--Town & Country Ford Inc., Louisville, KY, pg. 1103
Haysbert, Raymond V., Sr., Chm. Bd., Pres. & Chief Exec. Officer--Parks Sausage Company, Baltimore, MD, pg. 850
Hazen, Robert, Pres.--Hazen Paper Company, Holyoke, MA, pg. 520
Hazen, Thomas, Chief Exec. Officer & Treas.--Hazen Paper Company, Holyoke, MA, pg. 520
Head, Michael, Pres.--ELE International, Inc., Lake Bluff, IL, pg. 359
Headbloom, Gust, Jr., Pres.--Apex Broach & Machine Co., Detroit, MI, pg. 77
Heagerty, John D., Pres.--The Coakley Heagerty Companies, Ltd., San Jose, CA, pg. 256
Healey, William J., Pres. & Chief Exec. Officer--Viking Yacht Co., New Gretna, NJ, pg. 1151
Healy, Denis J., Pres.--Turtle Wax, Inc., Chicago, IL, pg. 1120
Healy, Thomas, Pres.--Owen-Ames-Kimball Co., Grand Rapids, MI, pg. 833
Healy, Tim, Pres. & Chief Oper. Officer--Kemmerer Bottling Group Inc., Joliet, IL, pg. 622
Heaney, Joe, Pres. & Chief Oper. Officer--Cornnuts Inc., Alameda, CA, pg. 286
Heard, William, Jr., Pres.--Bill Heard Enterprises, Inc., Columbus, GA, pg. 521
Hearn, John, Pres. & Chief Exec. Officer--Tennelec/ Nucleus, Inc., Oak Ridge, TN, pg. 1087
Hearn, Michael, Pres.--MBT Associates, Inc., San Francisco, CA, pg. 691
Heath, Ralph S., III, Pres.--Ovation Marketing, Inc., La Crosse, WI, pg. 832
Heath, Rodney, Pres. & Chief Exec. Officer--U.S. Enertek, Inc., Farmington, NM, pg. 1135
Heatley, Sidney, Pres.--Seymour of Sycamore, Inc., Sycamore, IL, pg. 994
Heaton, James, Pres.--UFE Cal Tec Inc., Brea, CA, pg. 1123
Heavener, Mac, Pres.-Servicenter Div.--ERA Real Estate, Overland Park, KS, pg. 360
Hebenstreit, James B., Pres.--Bartlett and Company, Kansas City, MO, pg. 122
Hebert, Lawrence I., Pres. & Chief Oper. Officer--Perpetual Corporation, Washington, DC, pg. 862
Heck, Raymond E., Pres.--Heck Enterprises, Inc., Baton Rouge, LA, pg. 524
Heck, Warren, Pres.--Greater New York Mutual Insurance Company, New York, NY, pg. 483
Hecker, Denny, Pres.--Greater Orlando Auto Auction, Orlando, FL, pg. 483
Heckler, John J., Pres.--Her Majesty, Mauldin, SC, pg. 530
Hector, P. Holcomb, V.P. & G.M.--Diamondhead Div., Bay Saint Louis, MS, pg. 900
Hedgepath, Richard L., Pres. & Gen. Mgr.--Electrical Equipment Company, Richmond, VA, pg. 374
Hedger, Richard, Dir. & Chm.-Europe--Ayer Europe, London,, United Kingdom, pg. 104
Hedlund, J.C., Chm. Bd. & Pres.--California Offset Printers, Inc., Glendale, CA, pg. 210
Hedrick, Wally, Dir.--Idaho Lottery, Boise, ID, pg. 561
Heeringa, Donald G., Chm. Bd. & Pres.--Trendway Corporation, Holland, MI, pg. 1109
Heffel, Jerry, Pres.-Southwestern Co.--Southwestern/Great American Inc., Nashville, TN, pg. 1023
Heffelbower, D.E., Pres.--Mason Company, Lexington, KY, pg. 718
Hefter, Harry O., Chm. Bd. & Pres.--The HOH Organizations, Chicago, IL, pg. 497
Heid, Markham, Pres.--Wallich Lumber Co., Detroit, MI, pg. 1161
Heide, Stan, Pres. & Chief Exec. Officer--Michigan Wheel Corporation, Grand Rapids, MI, pg. 747
Heider, David, Pres. & Chief Exec. Officer--United Hardware Distributing Co., Plymouth, MN, pg. 1132
Heidrich, James K., Jr., Chm. Bd., Pres. & Chief Exec. Officer--The Miami Margarine Co., Cincinnati, OH, pg. 746
Heily, John M., Chm. Bd., Pres. & Chief Exec. Officer--Continental Mills, Inc., Tukwila, WA, pg. 279
Heiman, Gary, Pres. & Chief Oper. Officer--Standard Textile Co., Inc., Cincinnati, OH, pg. 1037
Heimark, James, Pres.--Huntting Elevator Co., Austin, MN, pg. 555
Heine, Spencer, Pres. & Chief Exec. Officer--The Signature Group, Schaumburg, IL, pg. 768
Heineman, Nicholas A., Pres. & Chief Exec. Officer--Conway Import Co. Inc., Elmsford, NY, pg. 281
Heinen, John J., Pres. & Chief Exec. Officer--Heinen's Inc., Warrensville Heights, OH, pg. 526
Heins, Richard M., Pres. & Chief Exec. Officer--CUNA Mutual Insurance Society, Madison, WI, pg. 205
Heinson, R. Conrad, Pres.--Allied Oil & Supply, Inc., Omaha, NE, pg. 38
Heinson, R. Conrad, Pres.--Allied Tire Co., Omaha, NE, pg. 38
Heinz, James H., Pres.--Bell Flavors & Fragrances, Northbrook, IL, pg. 134
Heiser, Edward R., Pres. & Chief Exec. Officer--Wells Aluminum Corp., South Bend, IN, pg. 1175
Heisler, Emerson W., Pres. & Chief Oper. Officer--Price Brothers Co., Dayton, OH, pg. 888
Heisley, Michael E., Pres.--The Field Controls Company, Kinston, NC, pg. 525
Heitman, Frederick C., Pres.--Brooks Products, Inc., El Monte, CA, pg. 180
Helbein, Jerrold, Pres.--La France Corporation, Philadelphia, PA, pg. 649
Held, Robert, Pres.--Seely Equipment & Supply Co., Inc., Wall, NJ, pg. 763
Heldfond, Robert C., Pres.--E B 5 Corporation, Portland, OR, pg. 359
Helgason, Sigurdur, Pres. & Chief Exec. Officer--IceLandAir, New York, NY, pg. 561
Hellberg, Clifford, Chm. Bd., Pres., Chief Exec. Officer--Creative Productions, Pittsburgh, PA, pg. 297
Hellenbrand, V.J., Chm. Bd. & Pres.--Research Products Corporation, Madison, WI, pg. 928
Heller, Chester M., Sr., Chm. Bd., Pres. & Chief Exec. Officer--Marquette Coppersmithing Co., Inc., Philadelphia, PA, pg. 713
Heller, H. Robert, Pres.--Visa U.S.A. Inc., San Mateo, CA, pg. 1153
Heller, Harvey R., Pres.--Heller Bros. Packing Corp., Winter Garden, FL, pg. 526
Heller, John R., Chm. Bd. & Pres.--Heller Seasonings & Ingredients, Inc., Bedford Park, IL, pg. 526
Hellman, Bryce, Pres.--J. Hellman Produce, Inc., Los Angeles, CA, pg. 527
Hellweg, John, Pres.--Evansville Brewing Company, Evansville, IN, pg. 391
Helm, Greg J., Chief Exec. Officer--Stein Robaire Helm, Inc., Los Angeles, CA, pg. 1045
Helmick, David G., Pres.--Helmick Corporation, Fairmont, WV, pg. 527
Helms, Carol A., Pres.--Edd Helms Electrical Contracting, Miami, FL, pg. 527
Helms, M. Ronald, Pres. & Chief Exec. Officer--Roper Bros. Lumber Co., Inc., Petersburg, VA, pg. 947
Helmsley, Harry B., Chm. Bd., Pres. & Chief Exec. Officer--Helmsley Enterprises, Inc., New York, NY, pg. 527
Helpern, Joan, Pres.--Helpern Joan & David, Inc., Everett, MA, pg. 528
Helpern, Joan, Pres.--Joan & David, Inc., Everett, MA, pg. 528
Helton, Raymond E., Pres. & Chief Exec. Officer--Sterling Electric, Inc., Irvine, CA, pg. 1046
Helzer, James A., Pres. & Chief Exec. Officer--Unicover Corporation, Cheyenne, WY, pg. 1126
Hemmer, Paul W., Jr., Pres. & Chief Exec. Officer--Paul Hemmer Construction Company, Fort Mitchell, KY, pg. 528
Hemphill, Robert B., Chm., Pres. & Chief Exec. & Chief Oper. Officer--Barclay White Incorporated, Berwyn, PA, pg. 119
Hempt, George F., Pres.--Hempt Brothers, Inc., Camp Hill, PA, pg. 528
Henderson, Bruce M., Pres.--Henderson Electric Co., Inc., Louisville, KY, pg. 529
Henderson, Donald E., Pres.--Joseph J. Henderson & Son, Inc., Gurnee, IL, pg. 529
Henderson, J. C., V.P.-Construction--Davis Electrical Constructors, Inc., Greenville, SC, pg. 318
Henderson, John N., III, Pres. & Chief Exec. Officer--Mid-West Paper Products Company, Warren, MI, pg. 750
Henderson, Marvin A., Pres.--Henderson Auctioneers, Livingston, LA, pg. 528
Henderson, Max, Pres.--Panduit Company, Tinley Park, IL, pg. 845
Henderson, Richard L., Pres.--Drug Emporium of Arizona, Inc., Scottsdale, AZ, pg. 349
Henderson, Robert J., Sr., Chm. Bd., Pres. & Chief Exec. Officer--Ford Development Corporation, Cincinnati, OH, pg. 423
Henderson, Thomas J., Chief Exec. Officer--Deco Products Co., Decorah, IA, pg. 324
Hendricks, Adele, Pres.--Deans Photo Service, Inc., San Diego, CA, pg. 322
Hendricks, Kenneth A., Chm. Bd., Pres. & Chief Exec. Officer--ABC Supply Company, Inc., Beloit, WI, pg. 2
Hendrickson, Orvil J., V.P. & Sec.--Industrial Contractors, Inc., Idaho Falls, ID, pg. 566
Hendrix, Tom E., Chm. Bd., Pres. & Chief Exec. Officer--Henco, Inc., Selmer, TN, pg. 528
Heningway, John, Pres.--Stevedoring Services Of America, Seattle, WA, pg. 1048
Henkel, David R., Chm. Bd. & Pres.--Johnson & Quin, Inc., Niles, IL, pg. 599
Henley, Nixon C., Pres.--Henley Paper Company, Greensboro, NC, pg. 529
Henneke, Ben G., Jr., Pres.--Energy Fuels Development Corporation, Tulsa, OK, pg. 381
Hennessy, John M., Pres. & Chief Exec. Officer--CS First Boston Group, Inc., New York, NY, pg. 203
Hennessy, Michael, Pres.--Munro & Company, Inc., Hot Springs, AR, pg. 775
Hennessy, Michael W., Pres.--Lovejoy Inc., Downers Grove, IL, pg. 685
Henning, Peter H., Pres. & Chief Exec. Officer--Plano Molding Co., Plano, IL, pg. 874
Henning, Robert V., Pres.--Belmont Metals, Inc., Brooklyn, NY, pg. 137
Henricks, J.R. III, Pres.--Hendrick Management Corporation, Charlotte, NC, pg. 529
Henry, David A., Pres.--Henry Gill Silverman Advertising, Denver, CO, pg. 530
Henry, James C., Jr., Pres. & Chief Exec. Officer--E.P. Henry Corporation, Woodbury, NJ, pg. 530
Henry, Joe E., Pres.--Auto Crane Company, Tulsa, OK, pg. 100
Henry, Larry, Pres.--Full Circle Media Corp., Norwalk, CT, pg. 436
Henry, Peter, Gen. Mgr.--Sonoma Mission Inn & Spa, Sonoma, CA, pg. 1018
Henry, William L., Pres. & Chief Oper. Officer--The Stroh Brewery Company, Detroit, MI, pg. 1053
Henry, William L., III, Pres.--Linear Dynamics Inc., Parsippany, NJ, pg. 676
Hensley, James W., Pres.--Hensley & Co., Phoenix, AZ, pg. 530
Hensley, Thomas L., Pres. & Chief Exec. Officer--Druther's International, Inc., Louisville, KY, pg. 350
Hentges, Richard J., Pres. & Chief Oper. Officer--Foley-Belsaw Company, Minneapolis, MN, pg. 422
Herbers, Donald, Pres. & Chief Oper. Officer--Pinne/ Herbers Advertising Inc., San Francisco, CA, pg. 871
Herbert, Richard, Pres., Chief Exec. & Fin. Officer--VanDine, Humphrey, Herbert, Alber & Manges, Inc., Pittsburgh, PA, pg. 1145
Herbison, J. Steve, Pres. & Chief Exec. Officer--U.R.M. Stores, Inc., Spokane, WA, pg. 1124
Herbster, Charles, Chm. Bd. & Pres.--Conklin Co. Inc., Shakopee, MN, pg. 274
Herche, David F., Chief Exec. Officer--Enerfab Inc., Cincinnati, OH, pg. 381
Herley, John W., Pres.--Atlas Wire Corporation, Schiller Park, IL, pg. 97
Herman, Bernard, Pres.--Star Video Entertainment, L.P., Jersey City, NJ, pg. 1040
Herman, Dave, Pres.--KOB-TV, Inc., Albuquerque, NM, pg. 549
Herman, Stuart, Pres.--Herman Associates, Inc., New York, NY, pg. 531
Hermann, Ronald B., Chm. & Pres.--General Automotive Specialty Co., Inc., North Brunswick, NJ, pg. 449
Hermanson, Terry, Pres.--Mr. Christmas Inc., New York, NY, pg. 761
Hermenet, E.W., Pres.--Brooks Foods, Mt. Summit, IN, pg. 26
Hermes, Charles, Pres.--Dutton-Lainson Co., Hastings, NE, pg. 356
Hermesdorf, J., Pres. & Chief Exec. Officer--Teepak, Inc., Westchester, IL, pg. 535
Hernandez, Gus, Pres.--Precisionaire, Inc., Saint Petersburg, FL, pg. 886
Hernandez, Juan Manuel, Mng. Dir.--Leo Burnett Colombia, S.A., Bogota, Colombia, pg. 192
Hernandez, Noel, Chm. Bd., Pres. & Chief Fin. Officer--Graphic Productions Company, Miami, FL, pg. 478
Herndon, Carl M., Pres.--Black Fin Yacht Corporation, Fort Lauderdale, FL, pg. 154
Herpel, Mark, Pres.--Compel Marketing, Inc., Greensboro, NC, pg. 270
Herran, Manuel, Pres.--Real Holding Management Corp., Miami, FL, pg. 917
Herres, Robert, Gen., Pres. & Chief Oper. Officer--United Services Automobile Association (USAA), San Antonio, TX, pg. 1134
Herring, Barry E., Pres. & Chief Oper. Officer--Spatz & Co., Northbrook, IL, pg. 1026
Herring, James, Pres. & Chief Exec. Officer--Friona Industries, L.P., Amarillo, TX, pg. 434
Herring, Phil, Pres.--Herring Newman, Seattle, WA, pg. 531

Herring, Sherwin, Pres.--Southco Distributing Company, Goldsboro, NC, pg. 1019
Herschend, Jack, Chm. Bd.--Silver Dollar City, Inc., Branson, MO, pg. 1004
Hershaft, Judith, Pres.--Innovative Plastics Corporation, Orangeburg, NY, pg. 570
Hershfield, Sam, Principal & Client Services Dir.--Scott/Lancaster/Hershfield, Los Angeles, CA, pg. 982
Herslow, John H., Pres.--Sillcocks Plastics International, Inc., Berkeley Heights, NJ, pg. 1004
Herst, Douglas J., Chm. Bd. & Pres.--Peerless Lighting Corp., Berkeley, CA, pg. 855
Herter, Edward M., Pres.--Simpson Electric Co., Elgin, IL, pg. 1007
Hess, Donald E., Pres. & Chief Exec. Officer--Parisian, Inc., Birmingham, AL, pg. 848
Hess, Robert, Chm. Bd. & Pres.--Lancaster Malleable Castings Company, Lancaster, PA, pg. 653
Hess, Ronald G., Pres.--W-B Supply Co., Pampa, TX, pg. 1155
Hess, Warren J., Pres.--Triplett Electrical Instrument Corporation, Bluffton, OH, pg. 1114
Hesselroth, Warren, Pres.--Hauenstein & Burmeister, Inc., Minneapolis, MN, pg. 517
Hesser, Grant V., Pres. & Chief Exec. Officer--Maescher Industries, Inc., Cincinnati, OH, pg. 699
Hester, Donnie P., Pres.--LifeSurance Corporation, Atlanta, GA, pg. 921
Hester, Evelyn, Pres.--Dover Handbag Co., Inc., New York, NY, pg. 1048
Hester, Thomas P., Pres.--Rocky Rococo Corporation, Madison, WI, pg. 942
Hetherwick, Fred B., Chm. Bd., Pres. & Chief Exec. Officer--Plastigage Corporation, Jackson, MI, pg. 876
Heuser, George J., Pres. & Chief Oper. Officer--Metalcenter, Inc., Santa Fe Springs, CA, pg. 742
Heuser, Henry V., Jr., Pres. & Chief Exec. Officer--Henry Vogt Machine Co., Louisville, KY, pg. 1154
Hewett, Dexter B., Pres.--Sonicair, Scottsdale, AZ, pg. 1018
Hewitt, Richard, Pres.--The Tog Shop, Americus, GA, pg. 1100
Hewitt, Tomas F., Pres.--TCC, Miami, FL, pg. 1072
Heye, Donald R., Pres.--Hyspan Precision Products, Inc., Chula Vista, CA, pg. 557
Heyman, Leonard J., Chm. Bd., Pres., Chief Exec. & Chief Oper. Officer--Heyman Corporation, Niles, IL, pg. 532
Hickey, Betsy, Pres.--Mutual Benefit Financial Service Co., Providence, RI, pg. 778
Hickey, R. Michael, Pres. & Chief Exec. Officer--Bioproducts, Inc., Brecksville, OH, pg. 152
Hickey, William M., Pres. & Chief Exec. Officer--Lapham-Hickey Steel Corp., Chicago, IL, pg. 658
Hickinbotham, Ralph W., Pres.--Hickinbotham Bros., Ltd, Stockton, CA, pg. 532
Hickman, Bryan, Pres.--Liberty Tool Corporation, Rochester, NY, pg. 674
Hicks, Donald J., Chm. Bd., Pres. & Chief Exec. Officer--Hicks & Associates Inc., Coral Gables, FL, pg. 982
Hiebing, Roman G., Jr., Pres. & Mngmt. Dir.--The Hiebing Group, Inc., Madison, WI, pg. 533
Higdon, Ira, Pres.--Ira Higdon Grocery, Inc., Cairo, GA, pg. 533
Higdon, Joe, Pres.--Stones, Inc., Bainbridge, GA, pg. 1051
Higginbotham, J.L., Pres. & Chief Exec. Officer--Higginbotham-Bartlett Co., Lubbock, TX, pg. 533
Higginbotham, Steve F., Pres.--Ozark Motor Lines, Memphis, TN, pg. 835
Higgins, Frank A., Pres.--Yale Industrial Trucks Of Southern California, City of Industry, CA, pg. 1207
Higgins, Larry B., Chm. Bd., Pres. & Chief Exec. Officer--H & H Tube & Manufacturing Co., Vanderbilt, MI, pg. 495
Higgins, S.L., Chm. Bd. & Pres.--Air Industries Corporation, Garden Grove, CA, pg. 27
High, C.N., Pres.--Perfection-Schwank Inc., Waynesboro, GA, pg. 861
High, S. Dale, Chm. Bd. & Pres.--High Industries Inc., Lancaster, PA, pg. 533
Hilbert, William M., Pres. & Chief Oper. Officer--PHB Parker Die Castings, Fairview, PA, pg. 836
Hildreth, Horace A., Jr., Pres. & Sec.--Diversified Communications, Portland, ME, pg. 340
Hill, Alan, Pres.--Lawrence Paper Company, Lawrence, KS, pg. 662
Hill, Alexander R., Pres.--Building Plastics, Inc., Memphis, TN, pg. 188
Hill, D.J., Pres. & Chief Exec. Officer--Micro Component Technology Inc., Saint Paul, MN, pg. 748
Hill, EdwardG., Jr., Pres. & Chief Exec. Officer--Abco Markets, Inc., Phoenix, AZ, pg. 10
Hill, Howard, Pres.--Keysor Century Corporation, Saugus, CA, pg. 627
Hill, Robert D., Pres.--PST Vans, Inc., Salt Lake City, UT, pg. 837
Hill, Stephen R., Chm. & Pres.--Tone Commander Systems, Redmond, WA, pg. 1101
Hillerich, John A., III, Pres. & Chief Exec. Officer--Hillerich & Bradsby Co., Inc., Louisville, KY, pg. 535
Hillery, Robert R., Pres.--Gulf Exploration, Houston, TX, pg. 493
Hilsinger, Arthur R., Jr., Chm. Bd., Pres. & Treas.--The Hilsinger Corp., Plainville, MA, pg. 535
Himes, Michael B., Chm. Bd., Pres. & Chief Exec. Officer--Petroleum Traders Corporation, Fort Wayne, IN, pg. 865
Hinden, Milton, Pres.--Duro Dyne Corporation, Farmingdale, NY, pg. 355
Hindin, Richard J., Pres.--Adworks, Inc., Washington, DC, pg. 21
Hines, John P., Pres.--E. R. Moore Co., Chicago, IL, pg. 768
Hines, Lee, Pres. & Chief Exec. Officer--I Ski Ski Goggles, City of Commerce, CA, pg. 557
Hines, Milton, Chm. & Pres.--Atchison County Co-op Association, Atchison, KS, pg. 93
Hinkle, Max E., Chm. Bd., Pres., Chief Exec. Officer & Treas.--Rowtronics Company Inc., Indianapolis, IN, pg. 953
Hinman, Kirk, Pres., Chief Exec. Officer, Chief Fin. Officer & Treas.--Rome Strip Steel Co., Inc., Rome, NY, pg. 946
Hinshaw, W. Eric, Pres.--Kingsdown, Inc., Mebane, NC, pg. 632
Hinterlong, B.J., Pres. & Gen. Mgr.--Thomas Conveyor Company, Burleson, TX, pg. 1093
Hinton, Floyd G., Pres.--Dahlem Company, Inc., Louisville, KY, pg. 310
Hipkins, Kenneth A., Partner--Kalb Voorhis & Co., New York, NY, pg. 615
Hipp, Frederick R., Pres.-Casual Restaurants Div.--Gilbert/Robinson, Inc., Kansas City, MO, pg. 458
Hirota, S., Pres.--Leader Instruments Corporation, Hauppauge, NY, pg. 664
Hirsch, Alan J., Pres.--Aldan Rubber Co., Philadelphia, PA, pg. 32
Hirsch, D.M., Pres.--Pawtucket Fasteners Inc., Pawtucket, RI, pg. 852
Hirsch, Foster, Pres.--Fel Corporation, Farmingdale, NJ, pg. 405
Hirsch, Foster, Pres.--FEL Corporation, Farmingdale, NJ, pg. 394
Hirsch, Gary D., Chm., Pres., Dir., & Treas.--Grand Union Holdings Corporation, Riverside, CT, pg. 475
Hirsch, Gary D., Chm. Bd.--The Grand Union Company, Wayne, NJ, pg. 476
Hirsch, Henry C. (Harry), Pres. & Chief Oper. Officer--Wiltel Communications Systems, Inc., The Woodlands, TX, pg. 1194
Hirsch, Nathan, Pres. & Chief Exec. Officer--Junior Gallery Ltd., New York, NY, pg. 609
Hirsch, Stanley, Pres.--Structural Industries, Inc., Hicksville, NY, pg. 1054
Hirschauer, Tom F., Pres. & Chief Exec. Officer--Bloomhorst Story O'Hara Inc., Indianapolis, IN, pg. 158
Hirschfeld, David L., Pres., Chief Exec. Officer & Treas.--Hirschfeld, Inc., San Angelo, TX, pg. 536
Hirschfeld, David L., Chm. Bd. & Pres.--Hirschfeld Steel Company, Inc., San Angelo, TX, pg. 536
Hirschfeld, William, Pres.--MidCoast Mortgage Corporation, Melville, NY, pg. 751
Hirschmann, Joseph L., Pres.--First DataBank, San Bruno, CA, pg. 522
Hirschorn, Martin, Pres.--Industrial Acoustics Company, Inc., Bronx, NY, pg. 565
Hirsh, Charles, Pres.--Accurate Box Co., Inc., Paterson, NJ, pg. 11
Hirshman, K.J., Pres.--Foron International Sales Corp., Binghamton, NY, pg. 346
Hirshman, Karl J., Pres.--Doron Precision Systems, Inc., Binghamton, NY, pg. 346
Hitchcock, R. Cyrus, Pres. & New Bus. Contact--Hitchcock-Fleming & Associates, Inc., Akron, OH, pg. 536
Hitchcock, Timothy R., Pres. & Chief Exec. Officer--Hitchcock Industries, Inc., Bloomington, MN, pg. 536
Hitchock, Phillip, Pres.--Panel Processing, Inc., Alpena, MI, pg. 846
Hively, Charles, Pres., Chief Exec. Officer & Creative Dir.--The Hively Agency Inc., Houston, TX, pg. 536
Hladky, Joe, Pres. & Publr.--Gazette Company, Inc., Cedar Rapids, IA, pg. 447
Hoagland, Robert, Pres.--H. B. Ives, Wallingford, CT, pg. 583
Hobart, W.H., Chm. Bd., Pres., Chief Exec. & Chief Oper. Officer--Hobart Brothers Co., Troy, OH, pg. 536
Hobbs, Bert, Pres.--The Office of Lee Kendrick, Fairfax, VA, pg. 334
Hochfelder, James Lawrence, Pres.--Beldoch Industries Corporation, West Hempstead, NY, pg. 133
Hock, Conrad, Jr., Chm. Bd. & Pres.--Williams Foods Inc., Lenexa, KS, pg. 1191
Hockaday, Irvine O., Jr., Pres. & Chief Exec. Officer--Hallmark Cards, Inc., Kansas City, MO, pg. 501
Hockersmith, Harold, Pres. & Chief Oper. Officer--Hoffco, Inc., Richmond, IN, pg. 537
Hodes, Alan, Chm. Bd. & Pres.--Pen-Tab Industries, Inc., Glendale, NY, pg. 856
Hodes, Phillip, Pres.--Garsite/TSR, Inc., Kansas City, KS, pg. 443
Hodgekins, Barry J., Pres.--Josam Company, Michigan City, IN, pg. 607
Hodges, James R., Pres.--Royal Paper Box of California, Montebello, CA, pg. 953
Hodges, Wendell, Pres.--Town Square Furniture, Inc., Hillsboro, TX, pg. 1104
Hodgson, Marley, Chm. Bd. & Pres.--Trafalgar/Ghurka, Norwalk, CT, pg. 1105
Hodin, Joseph, Chm., Pres. & Chief Exec. Officer--Giant Markets Inc., Scranton, PA, pg. 456
Hodskins, David, Pres.--Hodskins Simone & Searls, Inc., Palo Alto, CA, pg. 537
Hoeft, William L., Pres.--Ziegler Inc., Minneapolis, MN, pg. 1218
Hoelzer, Dennis, Chm. Bd., Pres. & Chief Exec. Officer--Sentinel Computer Services Inc., Oak Brook, IL, pg. 990
Hoeper, Howard P., Chm. Bd. & Pres.--H.P.H. Industries Ltd., Lake Forest, IL, pg. 497
Hofer, Thomas W., Pres.--Spring-Green Lawn Care Corporation, Plainfield, IL, pg. 1033
Hoffer, Robert A., Sr., Pres. & Chief Exec. Officer--Hoffer Plastics Corporation, South Elgin, IL, pg. 537
Hoffman, Donald, Pres. & Treas.--Creative Playthings Ltd., Framingham, MA, pg. 297
Hoffman, Douglas A., Pres.--Electric Specialty & Supply Corp., Boston, MA, pg. 374
Hoffman, Ebba C., Chm., Pres., Chief Exec. & Chief Fin. Officer--Smead Manufacturing Company, Hastings, MN, pg. 1011
Hoffman, Harvey, Pres.--Fraenkel Company, Baton Rouge, LA, pg. 428
Hoffman, Jeffrey, Pres.--Gilmore Bros., Inc., Kalamazoo, MI, pg. 459
Hoffman, Julius, Pres.--Hoffman Brothers Packing Co., Los Angeles, CA, pg. 537
Hoffman, Mark, Pres.--A.P.S., Inc., Houston, TX, pg. 5
Hoffman, Rhonda S., Partner--The Haughey Group, Inc., Boston, MA, pg. 517
Hoffman, Robert, Pres.--Crown Prince, Inc. (CA), City of Industry, CA, pg. 302
Hoffman, Robert, Pres.--EVCON Holdings, Wichita, KS, pg. 391
Hofkin, Joseph, Pres.--Porteous, South Portland, ME, pg. 353
Hofley, Norman H., Pres.--Hofley Manufacturing Company, Warren, MI, pg. 538
Hofmann, John, Pres.--Frigid Products, Inc., Elizabeth, NJ, pg. 889
Hofmeister, George S., Chm. Bd. & Pres.--EWI, Inc., Salem, OH, pg. 361
Hogan, Frank J., Pres. & Chief Exec. Officer--Overseas Service Corporation, West Palm Beach, FL, pg. 833
Hogarty, Charles J., Pres.--Keystone Automotive Industries, Inc., Pomona, CA, pg. 627
Hogarty, Daniel J. Jr., Pres. & Chief Exec. Officer--The Troy Savings Bank, Troy, NY, pg. 1116
Hogg, Michael, Chm.--Michael Hogg-Young & Rubicam (Pvt.) Ltd., Harare,, Zimbabwe, pg. 1214
Hogg, Robert H., III, Chief Exec. Officer & Pres.--Better Brands Of Atlanta, Inc., Atlanta, GA, pg. 148
Hohlfeld, Pauline, Pres.--Tennessee Wholesale Drug Company, Nashville, TN, pg. 1088
Hohman, Theodore, Pres.--TCH Industries Inc., Grand Rapids, MI, pg. 1072
Hohmeier, John, Pres.--MTD Products Limited, Kitchener,, Canada, pg. 694
Hojnacki, Judith, Partner--Eric Mower and Associates/Buffalo, Inc., Buffalo, NY, pg. 774
Hoke, Joe, Chm., Pres. & Chief Exec. Officer--Mintz & Hoke Inc., Avon, CT, pg. 759
Hokin, Myron, Pres. & Chief Exec. Officer--Century America Corporation, Chicago, IL, pg. 234
Holas, Frank W., Pres. & Chief Exec. Officer--Rich SeaPak Corp., Saint Simons Island, GA, pg. 932
Holden, John S., Jr., Pres.--Automatic Machine Products Company, Attleboro, MA, pg. 100
Holden, Richmond Y., Jr., Pres.--J. L. Hammett Company, Braintree, MA, pg. 504
Holden, Stuart, Jr., Pres.--Keeney Manufacturing Co., Newington, CT, pg. 620
Holder, George Hugh, Pres.--Hershey Creamery Company, Harrisburg, PA, pg. 531
Holder, Thomas M., Pres.--Holder Corporation, Atlanta, GA, pg. 538
Holding, R. E., Pres. & Chief Exec. Officer--Sinclair Oil Corp., Salt Lake City, UT, pg. 1008
Holec, Kenneth, Pres. & Chief Exec. Officer--Lawson Associates Inc., Minneapolis, MN, pg. 663
Holiday, H. Roger, Pres.--Time Oil Company, Seattle, WA, pg. 1097
Holland, Richard F., Pres. & Chief Exec. Officer--AEI Holding Co., Inc., Fullerton, CA, pg. 3
Holland, Richard F., Pres. & Chief Exec. Officer--American Electronics, Inc., Fullerton, CA, pg. 3
Hollander, Ross H., Pres.--Hartford Distributors Inc., Manchester, CT, pg. 514
Holleman, Matthew, Pres.--Yazoo Investment Corporation, Jackson, MS, pg. 1207
Hollenbeck, Richard, Pres.--National Brands, Inc., Phoenix, AZ, pg. 786
Holler, Roger W., Jr., Pres.--Roger Holler Chevrolet Co., Winter Park, FL, pg. 539
Hollern, Michael P., Chm. Bd. & Pres.--Brooks Resources Corporation, Bend, OR, pg. 180
Hollest, Roger H., Exec. V.P.--Phillips Fine Art Auctioneers, New York, NY, pg. 867
Holley, Tom, Pres.--Gramex Corporation, Bridgeton, MO, pg. 475
Hollingsworth, Rodney, Pres.--Sun Bulb Company, Inc., Arcadia, FL, pg. 1058
Hollingsworth, Ronnie, Pres.--Hollingsworth Oil Co. Inc., Springfield, TN, pg. 539
Hollis, Mark C., Pres. & Chief Oper. Officer--Publix Supermarkets Inc., Lakeland, FL, pg. 898
Hollis, Samuel B., Pres.--Federal Compress & Warehouse Company, Inc., Memphis, TN, pg. 404
Hollister, Dean, Pres. & Chief Exec. Officer--Hollister Advertising, New Providence, NJ, pg. 539
Hollister, Gary, Pres.--Merle Norman Cosmetics, Inc., Los Angeles, CA, pg. 740
Hollow, Norman, Pres.--A & S Tribal Industries, Poplar, MT, pg. 1
Holm, Carl-Eric, Chm. & Chief Exec. Officer--BSB Finnad Oy, Helsinki,, Finland, pg. 109
Holman, W. H., Jr., Chm. Bd., Pres. & Chief Exec. & Oper. Officers--Jitney-Jungle Stores of America, Inc., Jackson, MS, pg. 594
Holmes, Adrian, Chm.--Lowe Howard-Spink Limited, London,, United Kingdom, pg. 685
Holmes, George B., Pres., Chief Exec. & Chief Fin. Officer--Dombrowski & Holmes, Inc., Chicago, IL, pg. 343
Holmes, Howard S., Pres.--Chelsea Milling Co., Chelsea, MI, pg. 241
Holmes, John B., Jr., Pres. & Chief Oper. Officer--Zilkha Energy Company, Houston, TX, pg. 1219
Holmes, Martin, Pres.--Belvedere Company, Belvidere, IL, pg. 138
Holmes, Ned, Chm. Bd.--Port of Houston Authority, Houston, TX, pg. 881
Holmstrom, Tom, Pres. & Chief Exec. Officer--A & E Business Products, Duluth, MN, pg. 1081
Holness, Gordon V.R., Pres.--Albert Kahn Associates, Inc., Detroit, MI, pg. 613
Holoubek, Verne R., Pres.--Holoubek Inc., Waukesha, WI, pg. 540

Holst-Knudsen, Carl T., Pres.--Thomas Publishing Co., New York, NY, pg. 1093
Holston, Craig, Pres. & Chief Exec. Officer--Charles Holston, Inc., Jennings, LA, pg. 541
Holt, David, Pres.--Wunda Weve Carpet Co., Greenville, SC, pg. 1205
Holt, Dennis F., Pres. & Chief Exec. Officer--Western International Media Corporation, Los Angeles, CA, pg. 1179
Holt, William S., Pres.--Great Salt Lake Minerals & Chemicals Corp., Ogden, UT, pg. 482
Holton, Earl, Pres.--Meijer, Inc., Grand Rapids, MI, pg. 737
Holton, John, Pres.--Holton Namiotka Jones, Inc., Lafayette Hill, PA, pg. 541
Holtz, Abel, Chm. Bd. & Pres.--Capital Bancorp, Miami, FL, pg. 214
Holtzman, Bernard, Pres.--Harve Benard Ltd. Manufacturing, Secaucus, NJ, pg. 514
Holubec, Henry, Pres.--Contractors Supplies, Inc., Lufkin, TX, pg. 280
Holzcheiter, Kenneth J., Pres. & Gen. Mgr.--A.N. Deringer, Inc., Saint Albans, VT, pg. 331
Holzer, Julian, Pres.--Holzer Watch Co., Inc., New York, NY, pg. 541
Homan, Robert W., Pres. & Treas.--Homan Lumber Mart, Inc., Elkhart, IN, pg. 541
Hommel, George A., Pres.--The Sanymetal Products Co., Inc., Vanceburg, KY, pg. 970
Hommes, Jan, Pres.--Leo Burnett Publicidade, Ltda., Sao Paulo,, Brazil, pg. 193
Honan, Terry, Pres. & Chief Exec. Officer--SAE-Pinkerton & Laws Inc., Atlanta, GA, pg. 966
Honbarrier, Archie L., Pres.--Central Transport Inc., High Point, NC, pg. 234
Honda, Takao, Pres.--Johnson Company, Ltd., Yokohama, Japan, pg. 599
Honek, J. Frank, Pres.--Connecticut Drive Shaft, Inc., Milford, CT, pg. 274
Hong, Il-hae, Pres.--Diamond Ad Ltd., Seoul,, Korea, pg. 111
Honig, John, Pres.--Anglo Fabrics Company, Inc., New York, NY, pg. 75
Honkamp, John A., Pres.--Hydrite Chemical Company, Brookfield, WI, pg. 556
Honroth, Dale K., Pres. & Chief Exec. Officer--Kendale Industries, Inc., Valley View, OH, pg. 622
Hood, Frank J., Pres. & Chief Exec. Officer--Welsh Farms, Inc., Long Valley, NJ, pg. 1175
Hood, Jeanne, Pres.--Northridge Industries, Inc., Las Vegas, NV, pg. 495
Hoof, A. C., Pres. & Owner--Hoof Products Company, Chicago, IL, pg. 543
Hoogendijk, E., Pres.--The Hartwell Corporation, Placentia, CA, pg. 514
Hoogeweegen, Boudewijn, Chm. & Chief Exec. Officer--BSB Amsterdam, Amsterdam,, Netherlands, pg. 109
Hook, James B., Pres.--V. B. Hook & Co., Inc., Columbia, SC, pg. 543
Hooker, A. Frank, Jr., Pres. & Chief Oper. Officer--Hooker Furniture Corporation, Martinsville, VA, pg. 543
Hooker, E. Stanton, Pres. & Chief Exec. Officer--Midland Paper Co., Chicago, IL, pg. 751
Hooker, Robert L., Pres.--Transnational Motors Inc., Grand Rapids, MI, pg. 1107
Hooper, Lee, Pres.--Sharon Tube Company, Sharon, PA, pg. 995
Hoover, Herbert A., Pres. & Chief Exec. Officer--Acheson Industries, Inc., Port Huron, MI, pg. 12
Hopkins, Jerry W., Pres. & Chief Oper. Officer--Texas Refinery Corp., Fort Worth, TX, pg. 1089
Hopp, B.P., Pres.--Tony Lambert Company, New York, NY, pg. 652
Hoppe, Charles W., Pres.--The Long Island Rail Road Co., Jamaica, NY, pg. 745
Hoppe, David T., Chm. Bd. & Pres.--CORS, Itasca, IL, pg. 203
Hopper, Victor D., Chm. Bd., Pres. & Chief Exec. Officer--Hopper Inc., Bakersfield, CA, pg. 543
Hopson, Steve M., Pres. & Chief Exec. Officer--Thomas R. Hopson Broker, Inc., Marietta, GA, pg. 544
Hopton, David, Pres. & Chief Exec. Officer--U.S. Metalsource Corporation, Coraopolis, PA, pg. 1136
Horan, Harrison R., Pres.--Bostrom Seating, Inc., Piedmont, AL, pg. 168
Hord, Fenton N., Pres. & Chief Exec. Officer--Carolina Builders Corporation, Raleigh, NC, pg. 223
Horlick, Dennis, Pres. & Creative Dir.--Horlick Levin Advertising Inc., Los Angeles, CA, pg. 544
Horn, Richard, Pres. & Treas.--Mulberry Metal Products, Inc., Union, NJ, pg. 775
Horn, Russell E., Jr., Co-Pres.--Pace Resources, Inc., York, PA, pg. 838
Horn, Tom L., Jr., Pres. & Chief Exec. Officer--Kanawha Steel & Equipment Co., Charleston, WV, pg. 615
Hornady, S., Pres.--Hornady Manufacturing Company, Grand Island, NE, pg. 544
Horne, Eugene B., Jr., Pres. & Chief Oper. Officer--The Pantry, Inc., Sanford, NC, pg. 846
Horne, F.L., Pres.--Gas-Fired Products, Inc., Charlotte, NC, pg. 444
Horne, Joseph A., Pres.--Rolane Corporation, Greensboro, NC, pg. 263
Hornstein, Richard, Pres.--Norel Paper Corporation, Little Ferry, NJ, pg. 810
Hornung, Donald F., Pres. & Gen. Mgr.--Crustbuster, Inc., Dodge City, KS, pg. 303
Horowitz, Barry M., Dr., Pres. & Chief Exec. & Oper. Officer--Mitre Corporation, Bedford, MA, pg. 762
Horst, David L., Pres. & Chief Oper. Officer--The Sheridan Press, Inc., Hanover, PA, pg. 998
Hort, Michael, Pres.--Enterprise Press, Inc., New York, NY, pg. 382
Horton, N.D., Jr., Pres.--Horton Homes, Inc., Eatonton, GA, pg. 545
Horton, Richard B., Pres.--Edgerton Forge, Inc., Edgerton, OH, pg. 102
Hosch, Robert F., Chm. Bd. & Pres.--Harris Mechanical Contracting Co., Saint Paul, MN, pg. 512
Host, Theodore J., Pres. & Chief Oper. Officer--The Scott Company, Marysville, OH, pg. 982
Houchens, Ruel, Pres.--Houchens Industries Inc., Bowling Green, KY, pg. 545
Houck, Peter, Pres. & Chief Exec. Officer--Houck Industries, Inc., Tulare, CA, pg. 545
Houde, K., Pres.--Calumet Photographic, Inc., Bensenville, IL, pg. 211
Hougen, Randall, Pres. & Chief Exec. Officer--Hougen Manufacturing Inc., Flint, MI, pg. 546
Hougland, J.M., Pres. & Chief Oper. Officer--F. R. Manufacturing Corporation, Stockton, CA, pg. 395
Houlihan, Lawrence, Chm. Bd., Pres., Chief Exec. & Chief Fin. Officer, Treas. & Sec.--Frank B. Ross Co. Inc., Jersey City, NJ, pg. 949
Houseman, James E., Pres. & Treas.--Harrop Industries, Inc., Columbus, OH, pg. 512
Housen, Charles B., Chm. Bd., Pres. & Chief Exec. Officer--Erving Paper Mills, Erving, MA, pg. 388
Housey, John J., Jr., Pres.--Orleans Materials & Equipment Co., Inc., New Orleans, LA, pg. 829
Housh, Allen A., Pres.--Cargill Marine & Terminal, Wayzata, MN, pg. 219
Houston, Loren W., Chm. Bd. & Pres.--Superior Container, Inc., Warrensville, OH, pg. 1063
Hovatter, Buddy, Pres. & Creative Dir.--Tallant LaPointe & Partners, Inc., San Francisco, CA, pg. 1077
Hovespian, Suren, Chm. Bd. & Pres.--Lafayette Steel Co., Detroit, MI, pg. 650
Hovland, Bruce, Pres. & Gen. Mgr.--Interstate Payco Seed Company, West Fargo, ND, pg. 580
Howalt, F. Harvey, Jr., Pres. & Chief Exec. Officer--Textile Rubber & Chemical Company, Dalton, GA, pg. 1090
Howard, Charles, Pres.--Howard Manufacturing, Kent, WA, pg. 547
Howard, Ervin W., Pres.--Plymouth Locomotive International, Inc., Plymouth, OH, pg. 877
Howard, Gary, Pres.--Bizzack Inc., Lexington, KY, pg. 153
Howard, Gerald T., Pres. & Chief Exec. Officer--D.C.I., Inc., Saint Cloud, MN, pg. 308
Howard, Kenneth, Pres.--The Columbia Mfg. Company, Inc., Westfield, MA, pg. 265
Howard, Marvin, Pres. & New Bus. Contact--Sisti, Zinbarg & Howard, Inc., Paramus, NJ, pg. 1009
Howard, Ron, Pres. & Chief Exec. Officer--Datability, Inc., Carlstadt, NJ, pg. 316
Howe, Kevin, Pres.--Dac Easy, Inc., Dallas, TX, pg. 571
Howell, Delbert, Pres.--Edmonson Wheat Growers, Inc., Edmonson, TX, pg. 369
Howell, G.T., Pres. & Chief Oper. Officer--Universal Life Insurance Company, Memphis, TN, pg. 1138
Howell, John S., Chm. Bd., Pres. & Chief Exec. Officer--Howell Instruments Corp., Fort Worth, TX, pg. 547
Howk, Richard H., Chm. Bd. & Pres.--Mathews & Boucher, Rochester, NY, pg. 720
Hoy, Thomas P., Pres. & Chief Exec. Officer--Geo. H. Lehleitner & Co., Inc., Harahan, LA, pg. 666
Hoyt, David P., Pres. & Chief Exec. Officer--Virginia Metal Industries, Inc., Orange, VA, pg. 1152
Hoyt, James E., Pres.--Midway Products Corporation, Monroe, MI, pg. 751
Hoyt, Seth, Pres. & Publr.--Cosmopolitan, New York, NY, pg. 523
Hoyt, Steven B., Pres.--Vinyl Therm, Inc., Bloomington, MN, pg. 1152
Hozik, John, Pres. & Chief Exec. Officer--The Philadelphia Bourse, Inc., Lanham, MD, pg. 866
Hradko, Joe, Chm. Bd. & Pres.--Cragar Industries, Compton, CA, pg. 761
Hroblak, Gerald, Chief Exec. Officer & Pres.--United Broadcasting Inc., Bethesda, MD, pg. 1131
Hrudka, Joseph, Chm. Bd. & Pres.--Hurst Performances, Inc., Cleveland, OH, pg. 761
Hrudka, Joseph F., Chm., Pres. & Chief Exec. Officer--Mr. Gasket Company, Cleveland, OH, pg. 761
Hubacher, John J., Pres.--Rado Watch Company, Inc., New York, NY, pg. 909
Hubbard, Henry H., III, Pres. & Chief Exec. Officer--Madigan Brothers, Inc., River Forest, IL, pg. 699
Hubbard, John D., Pres.--Hinderliter Heat Treating, Inc., Dallas, TX, pg. 535
Hubbard, R. D., Chm. Bd. & Chief Exec. Officer--Hollywood Park, Inc., Inglewood, CA, pg. 540
Hubbard, R.D., Chm. Bd., Pres. & Chief Exec. Officer--AFG Industries, Inc., Fort Worth, TX, pg. 3
Hubbard, Robert A., Chm. Bd. & Pres.--Wilbur Smith Associates, Columbia, SC, pg. 1011
Hubbard, Robert A., Gen. Mgr.--Curries Company, Mason City, IA, pg. 361
Hubbard, Samuel T., Pres. & Chief Exec. Officer--Alling & Cory Company, Rochester, NY, pg. 40
Hubbard, Stanley S., Chm., Pres., & Chief Exec. Officer--Hubbard Broadcasting, Inc., Saint Paul, MN, pg. 548
Huber, Erwin H., Pres.--Adhesive Research, Inc., Glen Rock, PA, pg. 1102
Huber, Paul, Pres.--Seco Warwick Corporation, Meadville, PA, pg. 987
Huber, Ron, Chm. Bd., Pres. & Chief Exec. Officer--Time Systems, Inc., Phoenix, AZ, pg. 1097
Huber, Ron, Chm. Bd., Pres. & Chief Exec. Officer--Time Index, Inc., Phoenix, AZ, pg. 1097
Hubler, Howard, Pres.--Hubler Chevrolet Inc., Indianapolis, IN, pg. 550
Hubner, Cornelius E., Pres. & Chief Exec. Officer--American Felt & Filter, Newburgh, NY, pg. 52
Hubner, Donald A., Pres.--Central/Shippee, Inc., Bloomingdale, NJ, pg. 234
Hubner, Donald A., Pres.--Allied Felt Group, Bloomingdale, NJ, pg. 234
Hudak, Steve, Pres.--Kool Seal, Inc., Twinsburg, OH, pg. 641
Hudetz, Peter, Pres & Chief Oper. Officer--Solar Press, Inc., Naperville, IL, pg. 1016
Hudson, Chris, Chm. Bd., Pres. & Chief Exec. Officer--Automation Intelligence, Inc., Maitland, FL, pg. 101
Hudson, James E., Pres.--Jim Hudson, Pontiac, Oldsmobile GMC, Columbia, SC, pg. 551
Hudson, M. R., Chm. Bd. & Pres.--Fisca Oil Co., Inc., Westwood, KS, pg. 414
Hudson, Paul H., Pres. & Creative Dir.--Roberts Communications Inc., East Rochester, NY, pg. 938
Hudson, Robert C., Jr., Pres. & Treas.--H.D. Hudson Manufacturing Company, Chicago, IL, pg. 551
Hudson, Stev, Pres.--Nylon Corporation Of America, Manchester, NH, pg. 818
Huemme, Richard C., Pres. & Chief Exec. Officer--Pittsburgh Tube Co., Monaca, PA, pg. 873
Huennekens, Donovan D., Pres.--The Lusk Company, Irvine, CA, pg. 687
Huether, Douglas, Pres.--Independent Can Company, Belcamp, MD, pg. 564
Huey, Barry, Chm. Bd. & Chief Exec. Officer--Barry Huey, Bullock & Cook Advertising, Inc., Birmingham, AL, pg. 551
Huey, Craig, Pres.--Creative Direct Marketing Group, Inc., Torrance, CA, pg. 297
Huffman, Neil, Pres. & Chief Oper. Officer--Neil Huffman Nissan Inc., Louisville, KY, pg. 551
Huffman, Neil, Pres.--Neil Huffman Volkswagon Mazda Suburu, Louisville, KY, pg. 551
Huffman, Neil, Pres.--Neil Huffman Chrysler Plymouth Dodge, Louisville, KY, pg. 551
Huffman, R.N., Pres. & Treas.--RAIL Company, Towson, MD, pg. 906
Huffman, Rick, Pres. & Dir.-Stores--Arnolds Interiors, Inc., San Diego, CA, pg. 85
Huges, George E., Jr., Pres.--E.H. Hughes Company, Inc., Louisville, KY, pg. 552
Huget, Larry, Pres.--Bucyrus Blades Inc., Bucyrus, OH, pg. 388
Huggins, David, Pres. & Chief Exec. Officer--RMS Techs, Inc., Marlton, NJ, pg. 907
Huggins, Frank, Pres.--Jack Lenor Larsen, Inc., New York, NY, pg. 659
Hughes, B. Wayne, Pres. & Chief Exec. Officer--Public Storage, Inc., Glendale, CA, pg. 898
Hughes, Glenn E., Pres.--Herman Hughes & Sons, Inc., North Salt Lake, UT, pg. 552
Hughes, H.D., Chm. Bd., Pres., Chief Exec. Officer & Sls. Dir.--Diversified Group, Inc., Harahan, LA, pg. 340
Hughes, Jack A., Pres. & Treas.--Hughes Advertising Inc., Saint Louis, MO, pg. 551
Hughes, Jim, Chm., Pres. & Creative Dir.--TH&M Advertising, Inc., Irvine, CA, pg. 1073
Hughes, Richard, Pres. & Chief Exec. Officer--Hinderliter Industries, Inc., McKinney, TX, pg. 535
Hughes, Roger T., Pres. & Chief Exec. Officer--DonTech, Chicago, IL, pg. 345
Hughey, B.C., Pres.--Martin Industries (AL), Florence, AL, pg. 715
Hughson, Dean, Pres.--Monark Egg Corporation, Kansas City, MO, pg. 765
Huisinga, Darrel, Pres. & Treas.--J. D. Streett & Co., Inc., Maryland Heights, MO, pg. 1053
Hull, Cordell W., Pres.--Bechtel Power Corporation, San Francisco, CA, pg. 131
Hull, Hardwood Campbell, Mng. Dir.--Leo Burnett Co., Inc. Sucursal Argentina, Buenos Aires,, Argentina, pg. 192
Hull, Rodney R., Pres.--Chernoff/Silver & Associates, Columbia, SC, pg. 243
Hullinger, G.E., V.P. & Gen. Mgr.--Borg-Warner Automotive, Inc., Control Systems, Sterling Heights, MI, pg. 166
Hulseman, R.L., Pres.--Solo Cup Company, Highland Park, IL, pg. 961
Hulseman, Robert L., Pres.--SCC Holding Co., Highland Park, IL, pg. 961
Hulsey, Neven, Pres. & Chief Exec. Officer--Earle M. Jorgensen Company, Brea, CA, pg. 605
Hultgren, Hilmer C., Pres.--Louisiana Utilities Supply Company, Baton Rouge, LA, pg. 684
Humbert, Pierre, Pres.--Direct Press Modern Litho Corporation, Huntington Station, NY, pg. 339
Hume, George H., Pres.--Basic American Foods, San Francisco, CA, pg. 124
Hummel, David, Pres.--Victor King Advertising, Virginia Beach, VA, pg. 630
Humphrey, Roy, Pres.--Shea Homes, Walnut, CA, pg. 996
Humphrey, Stephen, Pres.--Bronner Slosberg Humphrey, Boston, MA, pg. 179
Humphreys, Anderson, Pres. & Exec. Dir.-Creative--Humphreys Price/Cochran & Sanford Advertising, Memphis, TN, pg. 553
Humphreys, Henry, Pres.--National Spinning Co., Inc., New York, NY, pg. 793
Humston, William L., Pres.--Standard Electronics, Inc., Amherst, NY, pg. 1036
Hundey, Ronald L., Pres.--U.S. Furniture Industries, Inc., High Point, NC, pg. 1136
Hundley, Monty D., Pres.--Tollman/Hundley Hotels, Valhalla, NY, pg. 1100
Hung, Edward, Pres.--Caswell/Massey Co. Ltd., Edison, NJ, pg. 229
Hunger, Jack E., Chm. Bd. & Pres.--World Shipping, Inc., Lakewood, OH, pg. 1203
Hunt, Bruce W., Pres. & Chief Exec. Officer--Petro-Hunt Corporation, Dallas, TX, pg. 865
Hunt, Donald, Pres.--Bennett Ringrose Wolsfeld Jarvis, Inc., Minneapolis, MN, pg. 139
Hunt, Frank M., Chm. Bd. & Pres.--Citrus World Inc., Lake Wales, FL, pg. 251
Hunt, Joseph A., Pres.--Westat Inc., Rockville, MD, pg. 1178

Hunt, Lamar, Owner--Kansas City Chiefs Football Club, Kansas City, MO, pg. 616
Hunt, M.L., Pres. & Chief Exec. Officer--Hunt Building Corporation, El Paso, TX, pg. 553
Hunt, Terrill E., Pres.--Allied Security, International, Spokane, WA, pg. 40
Hunt, William, Chief Exec. Officer--Lundia Div. of MII, Inc., Jacksonville, IL, pg. 687
Hunter, Jerry E., Pres.--JPS Textile Group, Inc., Greenville, SC, pg. 586
Hunter, Samuel P., Pres.--T. A. Loving Company, Goldsboro, NC, pg. 685
Hurd, G. David, Chm. Bd., Pres. & Chief Exec. Officer--The Principal Financial Group, Des Moines, IA, pg. 890
Hurd, W. Russell, Pres. & Chief Exec. Officer--F.N. Burt Company, Inc., Buffalo, NY, pg. 195
Hurford, Gary T., Pres.--Hunt Oil Company, Dallas, TX, pg. 553
Hurley, Jack, Pres. & Chief Exec. Officer--Centrifugal & Mechanical Industries, Saint Louis, MO, pg. 609
Hurley, Richard T., Pres.--Maritz Performance Improvement Company, Fenton, MO, pg. 708
Hurt, Michael L., Pres. & Chief Oper. Officer--T.B. Wood's Sons Company, Chambersburg, PA, pg. 1200
Huseby, Robert, Pres.-Quorum Health Resources, Inc.--Quorum Health Group, Inc., Brentwood, TN, pg. 905
Huskey, Tommy, Pres. & Chief Exec. Officer--Carolina Mirror Company, North Wilkesboro, NC, pg. 223
Huss, Jack, Pres. & Chief Exec. Officer--Briggs Industries, Inc., Tampa, FL, pg. 175
Hussey, P.W., Jr., Pres.--Hussey Seating Company, North Berwick, ME, pg. 555
Hussey, Philip W., Jr., Pres. & Chief Exec. Officer--Hussey Corporation, North Berwick, ME, pg. 555
Hussman, Walter E., Jr., Chm. Bd., Pres. & Publr.--Wehco Media, Inc., Little Rock, AR, pg. 1172
Huston, H.M., Pres.--Rodman Industries, Marinette, WI, pg. 408
Huston, Harland W., Chm. & Pres.--Fiberesin Industries Inc., Oconomowoc, WI, pg. 408
Huston, John L., Pres.--National Live Stock & Meat Board, Chicago, IL, pg. 792
Hutchens, Jeff, Pres.--Hutchens Industries Inc., Springfield, MO, pg. 555
Hutchins, Alma A., Pres.--Hutchins Manufacturing Company, Pasadena, CA, pg. 555
Hutner, Richard, Pres.--Pelouze Scale Co., Evanston, IL, pg. 856
Hutter, Heinz F., Pres. & Chief Oper. Officer--Cargill Inc., Wayzata, MN, pg. 219
Hutton, Charles R., Pres.--Chuck Hutton Chevrolet Company, Memphis, TN, pg. 556
Hvide, J. Erik, Pres.--Hvide Shipping, Inc., Fort Lauderdale, FL, pg. 556
Hyer, Frank S., Pres.--Hyer Industries Inc./Thayer Scale, Pembroke, MA, pg. 557
Hyland, Tony, Pres.--Farnam Companies, Inc., Phoenix, AZ, pg. 403
Hylton, Tracy W., Pres.--WRM, Inc., Mabscott, WV, pg. 1156
Hyman, Steven, Pres.--Smarty Pants N Tops Too, Inc., City of Industry, CA, pg. 1011
Iacovelli, Guido, Chm. Bd. & Pres.--Chef Italia, Inc., Vestal, NY, pg. 241
Iarossi, Frank J., Chm. Bd. & Pres.--American Bureau of Shipping, New York, NY, pg. 50
Iason, John, Pres.--N. Erlanger, Blumgart & Company, Inc., New York, NY, pg. 387
Ibos, Robert J., Chm. Bd., Pres. & Chief Exec. Officer--National Engineering & Contracting Co., Strongsville, OH, pg. 788
Ibsen, Dr. Robert, Chm. Bd., Pres., Chief Exec. Officer & Treas.--Den-Mat Corporation, Santa Maria, CA, pg. 328
Icahn, Carl C., Chm. Bd. & Chief Exec. Officer--Trans World Airlines, Inc., Mount Kisco, NY, pg. 561
Iceman, T.L., Pres.--The Gerstenslager Company, Wooster, OH, pg. 454
Ielmini, John, Pres.--Patterson Frozen Foods, Inc., Patterson, CA, pg. 851
Ilaria, Peter V., Chm. Bd. & Pres.--Tropar Mfg. Co., Inc., Florham Park, NJ, pg. 1115
Ilitch, Michael, Chm. Bd. & Pres.--Little Caesar Enterprises, Inc., Detroit, MI, pg. 678
Iltis, John F., Pres.--John Iltis Associates, Chicago, IL, pg. 563
Imamura, K. Peter, Pres.--Pioneer Communications of America, Upper Saddle River, NJ, pg. 871
Imperato, Louis, Pres. & Chief Exec. Officer--American Military Arms Corporation, Jacksonville, AR, pg. 58
Imperia, Enio, Pres.--Imperia Bros., Inc., Pelham Manor, NY, pg. 563
Indursky, Harry, Chm. Bd. & Pres.--Cambridge Street Metal Co., Inc., Allston, MA, pg. 211
Ingalls, Daniel, H.H., Jr., Pres.--Virginia Hot Springs, Inc., Hot Springs, VA, pg. 1152
Ingersoll, Gary, Pres.--Graphisphere Holding Company, Des Plaines, IL, pg. 478
Ingersoll, Gary R., Pres. & Chief Exec. Officer--Bradley Printing Company, Des Plaines, IL, pg. 478
Ingham, Thomas R., Jr., Pres.-STCO--Simpson Timber Co., Shelton, WA, pg. 1007
Inglett, Terris, Chm. Bd. & Pres.--Mauna Loa Macadamia Nut Corporation, Hilo, HI, pg. 174
Ingman, Tom, Pres. & Chief Oper. Officer--Condor D.C. Power Supplies Inc., Oxnard, CA, pg. 273
Ingram, Donald C., Pres. & Chief Exec. Officer--Ingram Paper Company, City of Industry, CA, pg. 569
Ingram, E. Bronson, Pres. & Chief Exec. Officer--Ingram Industries Inc., Nashville, TN, pg. 568
Ingram, E.W., III, Pres. & Chief Exec. Officer--White Castle System, Inc., Columbus, OH, pg. 1185
Ingram, Tony, Pres.--B & B Homes Corporation, Casper, WY, pg. 105
Inman, George W., Pres.--Inman Construction Corporation, Memphis, TN, pg. 570
Inman, Gerald, Pres. & Chief Exec. Officer--Paul Inman Associates Inc., Farmington Hills, MI, pg. 570
Inman, Hugh, Pres.--Bell South Enterprises, Atlanta, GA, pg. 136
Iouse, Carmine, Pres.--Stratmar Systems, Inc., Port Chester, NY, pg. 1053
Ippolito, Pat, Pres.--Ideal Macaroni Company, Bedford Heights, OH, pg. 562
Irish, George, V.P. & Publisher--San Antonio Light, San Antonio, TX, pg. 524
Irvin, Stanton L., Pres. & Gen. Mgr.--Tri-State Wholesale Associated Grocers, El Paso, TX, pg. 1111
Irwin, John N., Mng. Dir.--Hillside Capital, Inc., New York, NY, pg. 535
Irwin, William, Pres.--Labelon Corporation, Canandaigua, NY, pg. 649
Isemoto, Toshito, Pres.--Isemoto Contracting Co. Ltd., Hilo, HI, pg. 582
Isen, Irvin, Pres. & Chief Oper. Officer--Paramount Packaging Corp., Chalfont, PA, pg. 848
Isgren, Carl E., Pres.--Owen Health Care, Houston, TX, pg. 833
Isherwood, Robert, Chm. Bd. & Pres.--Ambac International Corp., Columbia, SC, pg. 47
Ishiyama, George S., Pres., Located in Tokyo--Alaska Pulp Corporation, Seattle, WA, pg. 30
Iskra, Gary, Pres. & Chief Exec. Officer--Koolvent Aluminum Products, Inc., Pittsburgh, PA, pg. 641
Islander, Al, Pres.--CasChem Inc., Bayonne, NJ, pg. 227
Isola, Alfred, Chm. Bd. & Pres.--Silver State Disposal Service, Inc., Las Vegas, NV, pg. 1004
Israel, Robert L., Pres.--Empire National Bank, Traverse City, MI, pg. 379
Israelson, Chase, Pres.--The Dorris Lumber & Moulding Co., Sacramento, CA, pg. 347
Isseleib, Lutz, Chm., Pres. & Chief Oper. Officer--Falstaff Brewing Corporation, Vancouver, WA, pg. 959
Issleib, Lutz, Chm. Bd. & Pres.--S & P Company, Mill Valley, CA, pg. 959
Issleib, Lutz, Pres. & Chief Exec. Officer--Pabst Brewing Co./Tumwater, Tumwater, WA, pg. 959
Issleib, Lutz, Chm. Bd., Pres., Chief Exec. & Chief Oper. Officer--General Brewing Company, Vancouver, WA, pg. 959
Issleib, Lutz, Chm. Bd. & Pres.--Pearl Brewing Company, San Antonio, TX, pg. 959
Issleib, Lutz E., Chm. Bd. & Pres.--Pabst Brewing Co., San Antonio, TX, pg. 959
Issler, James E., Pres. & Chief Oper. Officer--H.H. Brown Shoe Company, Inc., Greenwich, CT, pg. 182
Italia, Carmen, Pres. & Creative Dir.--Italia/Gal Advertising, Los Angeles, CA, pg. 582
Ittner, George, Pres. & Chief Oper. Officer--New Hampton, Inc., New York, NY, pg. 801
Iverson, John S., Pres.--McCain Manufacturing Corp., Chicago, IL, pg. 726
Jackel, Steve, Pres. & Chief Oper. Officer--McCrory Stores Div., York, PA, pg. 934
Jackel, Steve, Pres.--T.G. & Y. Stores Co., York, PA, pg. 934
Jackel, Steve, Pres.--T.G. & Y. Holdings, Inc., York, PA, pg. 934
Jackman, Joseph R., Chm. Bd., Pres. & Chief Exec. Officer--Reactive Metals & Alloys Corporation (REMACOR), West Pittsburg, PA, pg. 916
Jackson, David J., Pres. & Chief Exec. Officer--Tupman Thurlow Co. Inc., New Rochelle, NY, pg. 1119
Jackson, Gene, Pres.--Gene Jackson Farms, Oxnard, CA, pg. 351
Jackson, Harold W., Pres.--Sunsweet Growers Inc., Yuba City, CA, pg. 1058
Jackson, J.R. Bryan, Pres.--Superior Machine Company Of South Carolina, Inc., Florence, SC, pg. 1064
Jackson, Margaret, Pres.--Western Pacific Data Systems, San Diego, CA, pg. 1180
Jackson, Mary Anne, Chm., Pres. & Chief Oper. Officer--My Own Meals, Inc., Deerfield, IL, pg. 779
Jackson, Parker, Pres.--Wallace Moir Co., Beverly Hills, CA, pg. 763
Jackson, Philip C., Chm. Bd., Pres. & Chief Exec. Officer--Ateron Corp., Parsippany, NJ, pg. 93
Jackson, Robert C., Pres.--Lumber Systems, Inc., Vancouver, WA, pg. 687
Jackson, W. Ronald, Chm. Bd. & Pres.--Cleveland Chair Company, Cleveland, TN, pg. 255
Jackson, William L., Chm. Bd. & Pres.--Parrish Tire Company, Inc., Winston-Salem, NC, pg. 850
Jacob, James A., Pres.--Ajax Paving Industries Inc., Madison Heights, MI, pg. 28
Jacob, Ted, Chm. Bd.--American Legend Corporate, Seattle, WA, pg. 57
Jacober, Jeffrey M., Pres. & Chief Exec. Officer--SGI Inc., Cranston, RI, pg. 962
Jacobowitz, Jeff, Pres.--Symplex Communications Corp., Ann Arbor, MI, pg. 1069
Jacobs, B.E., Pres.--Grede Transport, Inc., Milwaukee, WI, pg. 483
Jacobs, B.E., Pres.--Roberts Foundry Co., Inc., Milwaukee, WI, pg. 483
Jacobs, B.E., Pres.--Grede New Castle, Inc, Milwaukee, WI, pg. 483
Jacobs, B.E., Pres.--Grede Permcast, Inc., Milwaukee, WI, pg. 483
Jacobs, B.E., Pres.--Grede Vassar, Inc., Milwaukee, WI, pg. 483
Jacobs, Bruce E., Pres.--Grede Foundries, Inc., Milwaukee, WI, pg. 483
Jacobs, Gilbert, Pres. & Chief Exec. Officer--Planning Systems Inc., McLean, VA, pg. 874
Jacobs, Howard, Pres.--Reitman Industries, West Caldwell, NJ, pg. 924
Jacobs, Leonard J., Chm. Bd., Pres. & Chief Exec. Officer--Jet Spray Corp., Norwood, MA, pg. 593
Jacobs, Norman, Chm. Bd. & Pres.--Century Publishing Company, Evanston, IL, pg. 235
Jacobsen, Earl D., Pres. & Chief Oper. Officer--Central Data Corporation, Champaign, IL, pg. 232
Jacobsen, William R., Pres.--Jacobsen Manufacturing, Inc., Safety Harbor, FL, pg. 588
Jacobson, Fred, Pres.--Money Point Diamond Co., Chesapeake, VA, pg. 765
Jacobson, Irving, Pres.--Glencraft Lingerie, Inc., New York, NY, pg. 462
Jacobson, Marvin S., Pres.--Hallmark Advertising, Inc., Pittsburgh, PA, pg. 501
Jacobson, Mitchell, Pres., Treas. & Chief Exec. Officer--Sid Tool Co. Inc., Plainview, NY, pg. 1002
Jacobson, Mitchell, Pres. & Chief Exec. Officer--MSC Industrial Supply Co., Plainview, NY, pg. 693
Jacoff, Sydney, Pres.--Great Neck Saw Manufacturers, Inc., Mineola, NY, pg. 482
Jaeger, Joseph A., Pres.--MCC Group, Inc., Metairie, LA, pg. 691
Jaermann, Urs, Gen. Mgr.--Sigma, Zurich,, Switzerland, pg. 1212
Jaffee, Leon S., Pres.--American Printers & Lithographers, Chicago, IL, pg. 59
Jagoda, Don, Pres.--Don Jagoda Associates, Inc., Melville, NY, pg. 588
Jagoda, Leonard J., Chm., Pres. & Chief Exec. Officer--American SelfCare Corporation, Columbus, GA, pg. 60
Jahn, Richard A., Pres.--Wotco Inc., Mills, WY, pg. 1204
Jalbert, Michael E., Pres.--Penetone Corp., Tenafly, NJ, pg. 1172
Jamboretz, Glennon D., Chm. Bd., Pres. & Chief Exec. Officer--The Glennon Companies, Saint Louis, MO, pg. 462
James, Artis E., Jr., Pres. & Chief Exec. Officer--Purcell Co., Inc., Bay Saint Louis, MS, pg. 900
James, Edward R., Pres.--James Building Corporation, Northbrook, IL, pg. 588
James, Evan R., Pres. & Chief Oper. Officer--Tal Inc., Erie, PA, pg. 1077
James, Gene A., Pres. & Chief Exec. Officer--Southern States Cooperative, Inc., Richmond, VA, pg. 1022
James, Sean, Pres.--Wagner Spray Tech Corp., Minneapolis, MN, pg. 1158
Jamieson, Gordon, Pres.--La Salle County Farm Supply, Ottawa, IL, pg. 649
Jamison, C.H., Pres.--Jupiter Industries, Inc., Chicago, IL, pg. 609
Jamison, David, Pres.--Jamison, Cawdrey, Benjamin, San Francisco, CA, pg. 589
Jamison, R. Kenneth, Pres. & Chief Oper. Officer--Southern Radio Corporation, pg. 1022
Janik, Richard A., Pres. & Chief Exec. Officer--Janik & Associates, Inc., Los Angeles, CA, pg. 589
Janikies, Nicholas, Pres.--Jan-Co., Inc., Cranston, RI, pg. 589
Janisse, Roland, Gen. Dir.--Leo Burnett Company, Ltd.-Taiwan Branch, Taipei,, Taiwan, pg. 192
Janning, James C., Pres. & Chief Oper. Officer--Harbour Group Ltd., Clayton, MO, pg. 506
Jannotta, Edgar D., Mng. Partner--William Blair & Company, Chicago, IL, pg. 155
Jansen, James H., Pres., Chief Exec. & Oper. Officer--Lynden Incorporated, Seattle, WA, pg. 689
Janssen, Georg, Mng. Dir.--BSB/Taiwan Company Limited, Taipei,, Taiwan, pg. 110
Janzem, Glen N., Pres. & Chief Exec. Officer--Ranchers Cotton Oil, Fresno, CA, pg. 911
Jaquith, Richard, Pres.--Delta Industries, East Granby, CT, pg. 327
Jasper, Paul T., Pres. & Chief Exec. Officer--Shurfine-Central Corp., Northlake, IL, pg. 1001
Javier, Antero B., Pres.--Dentsu, Young & Rubicam, Alcantara/Manila, Manila, Philippines, pg. 330
Jaworski, Walter J., Chm. Bd., Pres. Chief Exec. Officer & Chief Oper. Officer--Miken Companies, Inc., Cheektowaga, NY, pg. 752
Jay, Dan, Pres., Chief Exec. & Chief Fin. Officer--Campmor Inc., Paramus, NJ, pg. 213
Jeans, J.B., Pres.--Robins Engineers & Constructors, Inc., Englewood, CO, pg. 939
Jedlinski, Ronald T., Pres.--Roman, Inc., Roselle, IL, pg. 945
Jeffer, Donald P., Pres.--Huntsinger & Jeffer, Richmond, VA, pg. 555
Jeffers, Jerry, Pres.--Abbott Electronics, Inc., Los Angeles, CA, pg. 9
Jeffers, John J., Pres.--MidWest Body Corporation, Paris, IL, pg. 752
Jefferson, William H., Pres.--General Latex & Chemical Corporation, Cambridge, MA, pg. 449
Jeffrey, Bob, Pres., Treas. & New Bus. Contact--Goldsmith/Jeffrey, Inc., New York, NY, pg. 469
Jelenic, Robert M., Pres. & Chief Exec. Officer--Journal Register Company, Trenton, NJ, pg. 608
Jelin, William, Pres.--Karnak Corporation, Clark, NJ, pg. 617
Jemison, Frank Z., Jr., Pres., Chief Exec. & Chief Oper. Officer--Jemison, Inc., Memphis, TN, pg. 592
Jenckes, A.C., Pres.--Detroit Coil Company, Ferndale, MI, pg. 333
Jenkins, Alan B., Pres.--Felton Brush Inc., Manchester, NH, pg. 406
Jenkins, D. Wayne, Pres.--Quik Print Inc., Wichita, KS, pg. 905
Jenkins, Don, Jr., Pres. & Treas.--Athens Paper Co. Inc., Nashville, TN, pg. 93
Jenkins, J. Michael, Pres. & Chief Exec. Officer--Ponderosa, Inc., Vandalia, OH, pg. 743
Jenkins, Maynard, Pres. & Chief Exec. Officer--Orchard Supply Hardware, San Jose, CA, pg. 828
Jenkins, R.E., Chm. Bd.--Bingham, Mt. Prospect, IL, pg. 151

Jenkins, Raymond H., Pres. & Treas.--Cabana Foods, Inc., Detroit, MI, pg. 206
Jennings, J.L., Jr., Pres.--Mount Vernon Mills, Inc., Greenville, SC, pg. 844
Jensen, Arne A., Chief Exec. Officer--BSB Bates-Gruppen A/S, Oslo,, Norway, pg. 109
Jensen, Bruce H., Pres.--Fotheringham & Associates, Salt Lake City, UT, pg. 427
Jensen, Colin C., Pres.--Irving F. Jensen Co., Inc., Sioux City, IA, pg. 593
Jensen, Gary A., Pres. & Sec.--Jensen Electric Company, Reno, NV, pg. 592
Jensen, Jorgen, Gen. Mgr.-North America--Austrian Airlines, White Stone, NY, pg. 100
Jensen, Linda, V.P.-Sls.--M. H. Greenebaum, Inc., Parsippany, NJ, pg. 485
Jensen, Steven, Pres. & Chief Exec. Officer--Norbest, Inc., Midvale, UT, pg. 809
Jerant, Frank, Pres.--Vintners International Company, Inc., Gonzales, CA, pg. 1152
Jerome, Jerome K., Pres. & Chief Exec. Officer--Jerome Foods Inc., Barron, WI, pg. 593
Jespersen, Keith, Pres.--Russ Reid Company, Inc., Pasadena, CA, pg. 923
Jewell, Everett G., Chm. Bd., Pres., Chief Exec. Officer & Treas.--Jewell Building Systems, Dallas, NC, pg. 594
Jewell, John B., Pres.--The Parman Corporation, Nashville, TN, pg. 850
Jewett, Edgar B., III, Pres.--Folger Adam Company, Lemont, IL, pg. 422
Jibben, Laura A., Exec. Dir.--Regional Transportation Authority (RTA), Chicago, IL, pg. 922
Jimenez, Carlos, Pres., Chief Oper. Officer & Dir.-Creative--Leslie Advertising, Greenville, SC, pg. 668
Joa, Martha F., Pres.--Curt G. Joa, Inc., Sheboygan Falls, WI, pg. 594
Joannou, Madeline, Chief Exec. Officer--G. Joannou Cycle Co. Inc., Northvale, NJ, pg. 595
Joblon, Kenneth, Pres.--Brittany Dyeing & Printing Corporation, New Bedford, MA, pg. 177
Jodnes, Jarle, Mng. Dir.--Bates Advertising A/S, Oslo,, Norway, pg. 110
Joel, Irving, Pres.--Miller Bros. Industries, Inc., Richmond, VA, pg. 753
Joel, Larry, Chm. & Pres.--D & K Optical, Inc., Louisville, KY, pg. 307
Joffrion, A.A., Pres.--Joffko International, Houston, TX, pg. 595
Johnannessen, Paul, Chm. Bd. & Pres.--Megapulse, Inc., Bedford, MA, pg. 737
Johnson, A. Stanley, Chm. Bd., Pres. & Chief Exec. Officer--Van Leunens Inc., Cincinnati, OH, pg. 1144
Johnson, Al II, Pres.--Dobson & Johnson, Inc., Nashville, TN, pg. 342
Johnson, Arthur E., Pres., Chief Oper. Officer & Gen. Mgr.--Basler Electric Company, Highland, IL, pg. 125
Johnson, Berton, Pres.--Gay Johnson's Inc., Grand Junction, CO, pg. 446
Johnson, Bob, Pres.--Leo Eisenberg & Co., Inc., Kansas City, MO, pg. 372
Johnson, Bruce W., Pres.--Geosafe Corporation, Richland, WA, pg. 126
Johnson, Carl A., Pres., Chief Exec. & Chief Oper. Officer--Berlin Steel Construction Co., Berlin, CT, pg. 142
Johnson, Christopher R., Pres.--Capital City Press, Inc., Montpelier, VT, pg. 214
Johnson, Craig, Pres. & Chief Oper. Officer--Ris Paper Company, Long Island City, NY, pg. 935
Johnson, D.A., Pres.--Al Johnson Construction Co., Minneapolis, MN, pg. 597
Johnson, Dean C., Pres.--Arcon Construction Co., Inc., Mora, MN, pg. 81
Johnson, Deborah U., Pres.--Rick Johnson & Company, Inc., Albuquerque, NM, pg. 597
Johnson, Dick, Pres. & Representative Dir.--Amway (Japan) Limited, Tokyo, Japan, pg. 71
Johnson, Douglas, Pres.--Precision Carbide Tool Company, Inc., Niles, IL, pg. 885
Johnson, Dudley, Pres.--Young & Franklin, Inc., Liverpool, NY, pg. 1209
Johnson, E. Marvin, Pres.--House of Raeford Farms, Inc., Raeford, NC, pg. 546
Johnson, Edward C., III, Chm. & Chief Exec. Officer--Fidelity Investments (FMR Corp.), Boston, MA, pg. 408
Johnson, Elmer Lee, Pres.--Bruce-Andersen Company, Inc., Belgrade, MT, pg. 183
Johnson, Ernie J., Pres.--Struthers-Dunn Inc., Pitman, NJ, pg. 693
Johnson, Gary, Business Mgr.--Missile Supply Co., Salt Lake City, UT, pg. 374
Johnson, Gary S., Pres. & Chief Exec. Officer--Superior Oil Co. Inc., Indianapolis, IN, pg. 1064
Johnson, Gilbert E., Pres. & Treas.--G.E. Johnson Construction Co., Inc., Colorado Springs, CO, pg. 597
Johnson, Glendon E., Chm. Bd., Pres. & Chief Exec. Officer--John Alden Financial Corporation, Miami, FL, pg. 32
Johnson, J.A., Pres.--Treadwell Corporation, Thomaston, CT, pg. 1108
Johnson, J.D., Pres.--Duke Manufacturing Co., Inc., Saint Louis, MO, pg. 352
Johnson, J.D., Co-Chm. Bd., Pres. & Chief Exec. Officer--G.S. Blodgett Corporation, Burlington, VT, pg. 157
Johnson, Jim, Pres.--SBN Systems Inc.-Montreal, Montreal,, Canada, pg. 960
Johnson, John, Pres.--Steuart Investment Co., Washington, DC, pg. 1048
Johnson, John B., Pres., Editor & Treas.--Johnson Newspaper Corporation, Watertown, NY, pg. 598
Johnson, John L., Chm. Bd. & Pres.--Thoroughbred Software International, Inc., Somerset, NJ, pg. 1095
Johnson, Keith E., Pres.--United Piece Dye Works, LP, Princeton Junction, NJ, pg. 1134
Johnson, Leland A., Pres.--ASCG, Inc., Portland, OR, pg. 7
Johnson, Mark, Pres. & New Bus. Contact--Cohen/ Johnson, Inc., Los Angeles, CA, pg. 259
Johnson, O.B., III, Pres.--White Star Steel, Houston, TX, pg. 784
Johnson, Okey B., Jr., Chm. Bd. & Pres.--Nashville Steel Corp., Nashville, TN, pg. 784
Johnson, Peter, Pres.--Faribault Woolen Mill Co., Faribault, MN, pg. 399
Johnson, Philip L., Pres.--Millstone Coffee, Inc., Everett, WA, pg. 756
Johnson, Ralph, Pres.--Lake County Press, Waukegan, IL, pg. 651
Johnson, Ralph D., Pres.--Johnson Storage & Moving Company, Denver, CO, pg. 600
Johnson, Randy D., Pres.--E Z Loader Boat Trailers, Inc., Spokane, WA, pg. 361
Johnson, Richard W., Pres. & Chief Exec. Officer--Johnson Bros. Corp., Litchfield, MN, pg. 597
Johnson, Rodger L., Pres. & Chief Oper. Officer--Brock Control Systems, Inc., Atlanta, GA, pg. 178
Johnson, Roger, Pres.--Pyramid Mountain Lumber, Seeley Lake, MT, pg. 901
Johnson, Ronald, Pres. & Chief Oper. Officer--Hoogovens Aluminum Corp., Secaucus, NJ, pg. 543
·Johnson, S. Ross, Pres.-Canadian Opers.--The Prudential Insurance Company of America, Newark, NJ, pg. 896
Johnson, Terry L., Pres.--Holt Hosiery Mills, Inc., Burlington, NC, pg. 541
Johnson, Thomas B., Chm. & Pres.--The Johnson Industries Corp., Urbana, OH, pg. 598
Johnson, Victor L., Pres.--JCI Data Processing, Inc., Delran, NJ, pg. 584
Johnson, Walter F., Jr., Pres.--Johnson & Towers, Inc., Mount Laurel, NJ, pg. 601
Johnson, Warren, Pres. & Chief Exec. Officer--ATI Industries, Escondido, CA, pg. 8
Johnson, Wesley S., Chm. Bd. & Pres.--Blue Boar Cafeteria Co., Louisville, KY, pg. 158
Johnson, Weston L., Chm. Bd. & Pres.--Good Stuff Food Company, Inc., Los Angeles, CA, pg. 470
Johnston, Doug, Chief Oper. Officer & Pres.--Ziebart Canada, Inc., Downsview,, Canada, pg. 1218
Johnston, Duane, Gen. Mgr.--Rugby Farmers Union Elevator Company, Rugby, ND, pg. 955
Johnston, Ernest S. III, Pres.--Ernest S. Johnston Advertising, Inc., Washington, DC, pg. 601
Johnston, Fred B., II, Pres. & Chief Exec. Officer--Fred B. Johnston Company, Inc., Chapin, SC, pg. 601
Johnston, Hampton, Pres.--Olan Mills, Inc., Chattanooga, TN, pg. 756
Johnston, Paul, Pres. & Gen. Mgr--Agri-Mark, Inc., Lawrence, MA, pg. 25
Johnston, R. W., Pres.--Norandex Inc., Macedonia, OH, pg. 809
Johnston, Sid D., Pres. & Chief Exec. Officer--Despatch Industries, Minneapolis, MN, pg. 332
Joiner, Eric J., Pres.--AJC International, Inc., Atlanta, GA, pg. 4
Joiner, Larry W., Pres.--Delta Pride Catfish, Inc., Indianola, MS, pg. 327
Joles, Everett, V.P.-Sls. & Gen. Mgr.--Foy-Johnston, Inc., Cincinnati, OH, pg. 863
Jolly, Roy H., Pres. & Chief Exec. Officer--E.C. Barton & Co., Jonesboro, AR, pg. 123
Jonas, Gary F., Pres. & Chief Oper. Officer--Earle Palmer Brown, Bethesda, MD, pg. 182
Jones, Alan C., Pres., Chief Exec. Officer & Sec.--United Grocers Inc., Portland, OR, pg. 1132
Jones, Alfred W., Jr., Chm. Bd. & Pres.--Sea Island Company, Sea Island, GA, pg. 983
Jones, Bucky, Pres.--Dairymen, Inc., Louisville, KY, pg. 311
Jones, Caroline R., Pres. & Creative Dir.--Caroline Jones Advertising, Inc., New York, NY, pg. 603
Jones, Chester, Pres. & Chief Exec. Officer--Hunter Corp., Portage, IN, pg. 554
Jones, Darlene S., Pres.--Specialized Media Services, Inc., Charlotte, NC, pg. 1027
Jones, Dave, Pres.--The Regina Company, Atlanta, GA, pg. 922
Jones, David, Pres. & Chief Oper. Officer--Gunnebo Fastening Corp., York, PA, pg. 494
Jones, G.R., Jr., Pres.--Roffe, Inc., Seattle, WA, pg. 943
Jones, Glenn R., Chm. Bd., Pres., Chief Exec. Officer & Sole Stockholder--Jones International Ltd., Englewood, CO, pg. 603
Jones, H. Douglas, Pres.--Jones, Anastasi & Birchfield, Dublin, OH, pg. 602
Jones, J. Gregory, Pres. & Chief Fin. Officer--Peck Jones Construction, Los Angeles, CA, pg. 854
Jones, J. Kevin, Pres.--Rev-A-Shelf, Louisville, KY, pg. 930
Jones, James C., Pres.--Airco Mechanical Inc., Sacramento, CA, pg. 27
Jones, James R., Pres. & Chief Oper. Officer--Dodson Group, Kansas City, MO, pg. 342
Jones, Jeffrey, Pres. & Chief Oper. Officer--Jones Chemicals, Inc., Le Roy, NY, pg. 603
Jones, Jesse N., III, Pres. & Chief Exec. Officer--Glenroy Construction Co. Inc., Indianapolis, IN, pg. 462
Jones, John W., Pres. & Chief Exec. Officer--Modern Welding Co., Inc., Owensboro, KY, pg. 763
Jones, M. Bruce, Pres.--Mannington Resilient Floors, Salem, NJ, pg. 704
Jones, M.C., Pres.--Jones Dairy Farm, Fort Atkinson, WI, pg. 603
Jones, Michael E., Pres. & Chief Oper. Officer--Capital Electric Group, Inc., Phoenix, AZ, pg. 215
Jones, Michael E., Pres.--Vegas Electric Supply, Las Vegas, NV, pg. 215
Jones, Norman T., Chief Exec. Officer--Growmark, Inc., Bloomington, IL, pg. 490
Jones, Paul W., Pres.--Greenfield Industries Inc., Evans, GA, pg. 507
Jones, Peter, Pres.--Hyman Freightways Inc., Moundsview, MN, pg. 557
Jones, Phil, Pres.--Jones & Thomas, Inc., Decatur, IL, pg. 604
Jones, Phil, Pres.--Rangen, Inc., Buhl, ID, pg. 912
Jones, Reese, Pres.--Farallon Computing, Inc., Emeryville, CA, pg. 399
Jones, Rex, Pres.--Dealers Transport Company, Inc., Memphis, TN, pg. 322
Jones, Roger, Pres.--Magic Valley Foods, Inc., Rupert, ID, pg. 700
Jones, Ronald L., Pres.--Dawn Food Products, Inc., Jackson, MI, pg. 319
Jones, Stanley, Pres., Chief Exec. Officer & Gen. Mgr.--Buhrman-Pharr Hardware Company, Texarkana, AR, pg. 187
Jones, Sydney T., III, Pres. & Treas.--Hudson Valley Paper Company, Albany, NY, pg. 551
Jones, W.L., Pres.--Gulf States Manufacturers, Inc., Starkville, MS, pg. 494
Jones, Wilbur S., Jr., Pres. & Co-Chief Exec. Officer--Stone & Thomas, Wheeling, WV, pg. 1051
Jones, William W., Jr., Pres. & Chief Exec. Officer--Baltimore Stationery Co., Baltimore, MD, pg. 116
Joplin, William F., Pres.--Oil & Gas Supply Company, Houston, TX, pg. 823
Joran, Jack, Pres. & Gen. Mgr.-Nash Canada--The Nash Engineering Company, Norwalk, CT, pg. 783
Jordan, J. Luther, Jr., Chm. Bd.--Baton Rouge Water Works Company, Baton Rouge, LA, pg. 126
Jordan, Michael K., Pres.--Small Parts, Inc., Logansport, IN, pg. 1010
Jordan, Rick, Pres.--American Sign & Marketing Services, Inc., Florence, KY, pg. 61
Jordan, W.D., Pres.--Thermalloy, Inc., Farmers Branch, TX, pg. 1091
Jordon, Melton, Jr., Pres.--Rural Electric Co-op, Lindsay, OK, pg. 956
Jordon, Roger, Pres.--Vitarine Pharmaceuticals, Inc., Springfield Gardens, NY, pg. 383
Jorgensen, Erik, Pres. & Chief Oper. Officer--Faber/Castell Corporation, Parsippany, NJ, pg. 395
Joseph, Edwin, Chm. Bd. & Pres.--The Great Atlantic Companies, Hampton, VA, pg. 480
Joseph, James, Pres.--Bandini Fertilizer Company, Los Angeles, CA, pg. 117
Joseph, Jerome, Chm. Bd., Pres. & Treas.--Uppco, Inc., Chicago, IL, pg. 1139
Joseph, Peter, Partner--Joseph, Littlejohn & Levy, New York, NY, pg. 607
Joseph, Thomas, Chm., Pres. & Chief Exec. Officer--Markdata Inc., Pittston, PA, pg. 708
Josephs, Daniel, Pres. & Chief Oper. Officer--Dominick's Finer Foods, Northlake, IL, pg. 343
Josephson, Marvin, Chm. Bd., Pres. & Chief Exec. Officer--Josephson International Inc., New York, NY, pg. 607
Joshi, Krishan K., Pres. & Chief Exec. Officer--UES, Inc., Dayton, OH, pg. 1122
Journalist, John, Gen. Mgr.--Pyle Inc., Chicago, IL, pg. 648
Juanarena, Douglas B., Pres. & Chief Exec. Officer--Pressure Systems, Hampton, VA, pg. 888
Jubelirer, Harry L., Pres.--John Reyer Company, Sharon, PA, pg. 930
Judge, Thomas J., Pres. & Chief Exec. Officer--The Austin Company, Cleveland, OH, pg. 790
Judson, Donald, Pres.--Electro Methods Inc., South Windsor, CT, pg. 375
Judy, Aubrey E., Chief Oper. Officer--Farmers Telephone Co-Op, Kingstree, SC, pg. 402
Judy, S. Wade, Pres. & Chief Exec. Officer--Woolrich, Inc., Woolrich, PA, pg. 1201
Juett, J. Lee, Chm. Bd., Pres. & Chief Exec. Officer--J. Lee Hackett Co., Farmington, MI, pg. 498
Juilfs, George, Pres. & Chief Exec. Officer--SENCORP, Newport, KY, pg. 989
Julian, Michael, Chm. Bd., Pres. & Chief Exec. Officer--Farm Fresh, Inc., Norfolk, VA, pg. 401
Juliano, Philip, Pres.--Genova Hartwick Juliano, Inc., Greenwich, CT, pg. 452
Julius, George P., Jr., Pres. & Chief Oper. Officer--Brooks Beverage Management, Inc., Holland, MI, pg. 179
Jumonville, Dan, Chm. Bd. & Pres.--Group Insurance Inc., Baton Rouge, LA, pg. 490
Jung, James D., Pres.--JII/Sales Promotion Associates, Inc., Coshocton, OH, pg. 604
Jung, Jerrold M., Pres.--Michigan Tractor And Machinery Co., Novi, MI, pg. 747
Jungquist, Jerry, Acting Pres. & Chief Exec. Officer--The King Company, Owatonna, MN, pg. 630
Junin, Juzar, Mng. Dir. & Mngmt. Supvr.--AIM Communications, Jakarta, Indonesia, pg. 192
Junkin, J.S., Pres.--California Products Corp., Cambridge, MA, pg. 210
Juodis, Walter, Pres. & Chief Exec. Officer--American Manufacturing Company, Inc. (LA), Lafayette, LA, pg. 58
Jurgens, Thomas, Pres. & Chief Exec. Officer--ODL Incorporated, Zeeland, MI, pg. 819
Jurgensen, James P., Pres.--Valley Asphalt Corporation, Cincinnati, OH, pg. 1143
Jurock, Oswald, Chm. Bd. & Chief Exec. Officer--Red Carpet Real Estate Services, Inc., San Diego, CA, pg. 918
Justiss, James F., Jr., Chm. Bd., Pres. & Chief Exec. Officer--Justiss Oil Co., Inc., Jena, LA, pg. 610
Kaczor, Walt, Sr. V.P. & Chief Fin. Officer--Professional Healthcare Systems, Inc., Los Angeles, CA, pg. 894
Kaempfer, J.W., Jr., Pres.--The Kaempfer Company, Investment Builders, Washington, DC, pg. 613
Kafka, Rick, Pres. & Dir.-Mktg.--Gosnell Builders, Phoenix, AZ, pg. 472
Kafka, Robert F., Pres.--Associated Diesel Service & Equipment Company, Wilmington, CA, pg. 89
Kahlig, Clarence J., Pres.--North Park Lincoln Mercury Inc., San Antonio, TX, pg. 813
Kahlor, Robert A., Pres.--Journal Communications Inc., Milwaukee, WI, pg. 607

Kahn, Harold, Pres.--Montgomery Ward & Co., Inc., Chicago, IL, pg. 767
Kahn, Henri, Pres.--Monico Alloys, Inc., Los Angeles, CA, pg. 765
Kahn, Henry C., Pres.--American Institute For Foreign Study, Greenwich, CT, pg. 56
Kahn, Marc, Pres.-RAO-Wholesale Div.--Rao Wholesale Tire Centers, Inc., Detroit, MI, pg. 912
Kahn, Mark, Pres.--Production Tool Supply Co., Warren, MI, pg. 893
Kahn, Myron, Pres.--Croscill, Inc., New York, NY, pg. 300
Kahn, Walter, Pres.--Empire Steel Trading Company, New York, NY, pg. 380
Kairella, Charles, Pres.--Adventure Tours USA, Inc., Dallas, TX, pg. 21
Kairys, L.M., Pres.--Lustine Oldsmobile & Buick, Inc., Hyattsville, MD, pg. 688
Kaiser, A.E., Pres.--Acme Refrigeration Of Baton Rouge Inc., Baton Rouge, LA, pg. 13
Kaiser, Benjamin, Pres.--David G. Steven, Inc., New York, NY, pg. 1048
Kaiser, John R., Pres.--Kaiser Tobacco Company, Inc., New Albany, IN, pg. 615
Kaiser, Larry, Pres.--MPO Videotronics, Inc., New York, NY, pg. 693
Kaiser, Lloyd, Pres.--Phoenix Data Incorporated, Phoenix, AZ, pg. 630
Kaiser, Marshall, Pres. & Chief Exec. Officer--Safe Harbor Water Power Corporation, Conestoga, PA, pg. 966
Kaiser, R. S., Pres.--Gallagher-Kaiser Corp., Detroit, MI, pg. 441
Kaitz, Ben B., Pres.--Palm Beach Beauty Products Co., Minneapolis, MN, pg. 843
Kalahar, T.L., Chief Exec. Officer--Camelot Communications, Inc., Dallas, TX, pg. 212
Kaldor, Lee, Pres.--Nodak Electric Co-op, Grand Forks, ND, pg. 808
Kalin, Edward L., Pres.--Kalin Enterprises, Inc., Sarasota, FL, pg. 615
Kalkhoven, Kevin, Pres.--Uniphase Corporation, San Jose, CA, pg. 1129
Kalkman, Donald A., Pres.--Mustang Manufacturing Company, Inc., Owatonna, MN, pg. 777
Kallenbach, Mary, Mktg. Mgr.--Marketing Services Unltd., Waukesha, WI, pg. 709
Kallman, Irwin, Pres.--Bookazine Company, Inc., Bayonne, NJ, pg. 164
Kaloyanides, Stephen, Pres.--New England Coffee Company, Malden, MA, pg. 800
Kalter, Alan, Pres. & Chief Oper. Officer--W.B. Doner & Company, Southfield, MI, pg. 344
Kam, Albert K.F., Pres. & Gen. Mgr.--Superior Coffee & Foods/Hawaii, Aiea, HI, pg. 174
Kamat, Ulas N., Pres.--Republic Container Corp., Jersey City, NJ, pg. 927
Kamberos, Chris, Chm. Bd., Pres. & Chief Oper. Officer--Treasure Island Foodmarts Inc., Chicago, IL, pg. 1109
Kamborian, Jacob S., Pres.--International Shoe Machine Corp., Nashua, NH, pg. 579
Kamenstein, Peter D., Vice Chm., Pres. & Chief Oper. Officer--M. Kamenstein, Inc., White Plains, NY, pg. 615
Kamins, Philip E., Pres.--PMC, Inc., Sun Valley, CA, pg. 836
Kaminski, R.S., Chm. & Pres.--Continental/Midland, Inc., Park Forest, IL, pg. 279
Kaminsky, Harry, V.P.--AmeriData, Inc., Minneapolis, MN, pg. 66
Kaminsky, Howard, Pres.-Trade Book Groups--Hearst Books/Business Publishing Group, New York, NY, pg. 521
Kaminstein, Merwin F., Chm. Bd., Pres. & Chief Exec. Officer--Brookstone Company, Inc., Peterborough, NH, pg. 180
Kamitaki, Tadami, Pres.--Maui Varieties, Ltd., Honolulu, HI, pg. 721
Kamm, Jacob O., Chm. Bd., Pres. & Chief Exec. Officer--Electric Furnace Co., Salem, OH, pg. 373
Kammer, Robert E., Pres.--United Farm Tools Speedy Mfg. Div., Oelwein, IA, pg. 1132
Kammerer, M.J., Pres.--Valve and Controls Division, The Woodlands, TX, pg. 565
Kampmeier, Donald G., Pres. & Gen. Mgr.--Central Livestock Association, Inc., South St. Paul, MN, pg. 233
Kampouris, Emmanuel A., Chm. Bd, Pres. & Chief Exec. Officer--American Standard Inc., New York, NY, pg. 61
Kanai, Noritoshi, Pres.--Mutual Trading Co., Inc., Los Angeles, CA, pg. 779
Kandel, Jerry, Pres.--Darda Inc. (USA), Baltimore, MD, pg. 315
Kane, Gary A., Pres. & Chief Oper. Officer--J. G. Hook, Inc., Philadelphia, PA, pg. 543
Kane, Gibby, Chm. Bd. & Pres.--Marden-Kane, Inc., Lake Success, NY, pg. 706
Kane, Jerry, Pres.--Sam Kane Beef Processors, Inc., Corpus Christi, TX, pg. 616
Kaneff, Howard T., Pres.--Arkay Packaging Corporation, Hauppauge, NY, pg. 83
Kaneshiro, Glenn, Pres.--Pacific Hawaiian Ltd., Hilo, HI, pg. 840
Kangas, Edward A., Mng. Partner--Deloitte & Touche, Wilton, CT, pg. 326
Kanngiesser, Tom, Pres.--Systems Parking, Inc., Pasadena, CA, pg. 1071
Kaplan, Bernard H., Pres.--BSA Advertising, Inc., New York, NY, pg. 107
Kaplan, Daniel I., Pres.--Hertz Equipment Rental Corp., Park Ridge, NJ, pg. 849
Kaplan, James, Pres.--Kaplan Electronics, Wayne, NJ, pg. 616
Kaplan, James, Pres.--Cornell Dubilier Electronics, Wayne, NJ, pg. 616
Kaplan, Robert, Pres.--Complex Industry Corporation, New York, NY, pg. 270
Kaplan, V. Jerome, Chief Exec. Officer--The Apparel Group, Ltd., New York, NY, pg. 78
Kaplan, V. Jerome, Pres.--The Enro Shirt Company, Inc., Louisville, KY, pg. 78
Kaplanek, Charles, Jr., Pres.--Floral Glass & Mirror, Inc., Hauppauge, NY, pg. 420
Kappel, Joseph J., Pres. & Chief Exec. Officer--Vectura Group, Inc., Pittsburgh, PA, pg. 1146
Kappler, George, Chm., Pres. & Chief Exec. Officer--KSG Inc., Guntersville, AL, pg. 613
Kapson, Craig, Pres.--Jordan Motors, Inc., Mishawaka, IN, pg. 605
Karabots, Nick G., Chm. Bd.--S L C Graphics, Inc., Pittston, PA, pg. 963
Karakas, Steve, Pres. & Adv. Dir.--Karakas, VanSickle Ouellette Advertising & Public Relations, Portland, OR, pg. 616
Karapetian, Vahe, Pres.--A A Cater Truck Manufacturing Company, Inc., Los Angeles, CA, pg. 1
Karchon, James, Pres.--Engineering Service, Inc., Southfield, MI, pg. 382
Karges, Edwin, Chm. Bd. & Pres.--Karges Furniture Company, Evansville, IN, pg. 616
Karler, Jess, Pres.--Karler Packing Company, Inc., Albuquerque, NM, pg. 617
Karlin, Robert, Pres.--Santa Monica Ford Company, Santa Monica, CA, pg. 970
Karlyn, William M., Pres.--Autoroll Machine Corp., Middleton, MA, pg. 101
Karman, James B., Pres.--Spaulding & Slye Company, Burlington, MA, pg. 1026
Karmazin, Mel, Pres. & Chief Exec. Officer--Infinity Broadcasting Corporation, New York, NY, pg. 567
Karol, Steven E., Pres. & Chief Exec. Officer--H M K Enterprises, Inc., Waltham, MA, pg. 497
Karp, Harvey M., Pres.--HMK Advertising, Inc., Chestnut Hill, MA, pg. 497
Karp, Jack L., Pres.--L. Karp & Sons, Inc., Elk Grove Village, IL, pg. 617
Karsten, Harry, Jr., Chm. Bd & Pres.--Golden West Homes, Santa Ana, CA, pg. 467
Kasabian, David R., Pres. & Creative Dir.--DRK Inc., Boston, MA, pg. 309
Kasch, Jeffrey C., Pres.--M.W. Kasch Company, Mequon, WI, pg. 617
Kasen, Stewart M., Pres. & Chief Oper. Officer--First Land & Development, Inc., Richmond, VA, pg. 18
Kasen, Stewart M., Co-Chm., Pres. & Chief Exec. Officer--Best Products Co., Inc., Richmond, VA, pg. 17
Kasle, Roger, Pres.--Kasle Steel Corporation, Dearborn, MI, pg. 617
Kaspar, Don G., Chm. Bd & Pres.--Kaspar Wire Works, Inc., Shiner, TX, pg. 617
Kass, David, Pres.--Muscum Boutique Intercontinental, Ltd., New York, NY, pg. 777
Kass, M.A., Pres.--Republic Industries, Inc., Harwood Heights, IL, pg. 928
Kassab, Robert L., Vice Chm., Pres. & Chief Oper. Officer--Stainless Incorporated, Deerfield Beach, FL, pg. 1035
Kassouf, James, Pres., Chief Exec. Officer & Treas.--Metropolitan Properties Inc., Cleveland, OH, pg. 745
Kastner, Johannes, Mng. Dir.--Kastner & Partner GmbH Werbeagentur, Frankfurt/Main, Germany, pg. 192
Kathwari, M. Farooq, Chm., Pres. & Chief Exec. Officer--Green Mountain Holding Corporation, Danbury, CT, pg. 485
Kathwari, M. Farooq, Chm., Pres. & Chief Exec. Officer--Ethan Allen, Inc., Danbury, CT, pg. 485
Katoh, Mr., Pres.--Colonial Beef Co., Philadelphia, PA, pg. 263
Katopodis, Louis, Pres. & Chief Oper. Officer--Fiesta Mart Inc., Houston, TX, pg. 409
Katowczik, Dennis, Pres.--Fort Pitt Acquisitions Company, Inc., Coraopolis, PA, pg. 425
Katsin, Daniel H., Pres. & New Bus. Contact--Katsin/Loeb Advertising, San Francisco, CA, pg. 618
Katz, Alvin, Pres.--Manhattan Store Interiors, Inc., Brooklyn, NY, pg. 704
Katz, James M., Pres.--Encore Shoe Corporation, Rochester, NH, pg. 380
Katz, Lewis, Pres. & Chief Exec. Officer--Kinney System, Inc., New York, NY, pg. 632
Katz, Murray L., Pres.--Empire Kosher Poultry, Inc., Mifflintown, PA, pg. 379
Katz, N., Pres. & Chief Exec. Officer--I. Appel Corporation, New York, NY, pg. 78
Katz, Robert W., Jr., Pres.--Katz, Inc., Honesdale, PA, pg. 618
Katzen, Dr. Cyrus, Pres. & Chief Exec. Officer--Mozel Development Corp., Baileys Crossroads, VA, pg. 774
Katzman, Jerry F., Pres.--William Morris Agency, Inc., Beverly Hills, CA, pg. 771
Katzman, Maurice, Pres.--Mastercraft Furniture Corp., Omaha, NE, pg. 720
Katzman, Richard, Pres.--Kaz, Inc., New York, NY, pg. 619
Kaucheck, Larry, Pres.--Fibre Glass-Evercoat Company Inc., Cincinnati, OH, pg. 408
Kaufelt, Stanley P., Chm. Bd., Pres. & Chief Exec. Officer--Mayfair Super Markets, Inc., Elizabeth, NJ, pg. 724
Kauffman, Reese, Pres.--Kauffman Products, Inc., Carmel, IN, pg. 618
Kaufman, Judith, Pres.--Media Power, Inc., Charlotte, NC, pg. 734
Kaufman, Mark, Chief Exec. Officer--Environetics, Branford, CT, pg. 383
Kaufman, Michael S., Pres.--Metromedia Steakhouses, Inc., Vandalia, OH, pg. 744
Kaufman, Richard F., Pres. & Chief Exec. Officer--Amstore Corporation, Muskegon, MI, pg. 69
Kaumeyer, Jeff, Pres. & Chief Oper. Officer--Hammond Farrell Inc., New York, NY, pg. 504
Kay, Irene, Commission Chm.--Ohio Lottery Commission, Cleveland, OH, pg. 822
Kay, John W., Pres.--Harmeson Manufacturing Company, Inc., Frankfort, IN, pg. 510
Kay, Robert F., Pres.--Woodwork Corporation of America, Chicago, IL, pg. 1201
Kazarian, Paul, Chm. & Mng. Dir.--Sunbeam-Oster Company, Inc., Providence, RI, pg. 1059
Kearney, E. James, Mng. Partner & Chief Oper. Officer--Eire Partners, Inc., Chicago, IL, pg. 372
Kearney, Joseph S., Jr., Pres.--Northwestern Industrial Piping, Niles, IL, pg. 815
Kearns, Vincent Ed., Pres.--B. H. Aircraft Co., Inc., Farmingdale, NY, pg. 106
Kearns, Walter J., Chm. Bd. & Pres.--Data Documents Holdings, Inc., Omaha, NE, pg. 316
Kearny, John, Acting Pres.--Builders Emporium, Irvine, CA, pg. 262
Keating, Daniel J., Jr., Chm. Bd., Pres. & Chief Exec. Officer--Daniel J. Keating Co., Villanova, PA, pg. 619
Keating, Robert P., Pres.--P.J. Keating Company, Lunenburg, MA, pg. 619
Kec, Robert F., Pres.--Western States Petroleum Inc., Phoenix, AZ, pg. 1181
Keehn, Robert P., Pres.--Tiernay Metals, Inc., Redondo Beach, CA, pg. 1096
Keeler, Alexander, Pres. & Treas.--Keller Motor Car Company, Inc., Latham, NY, pg. 621
Keen, J. Merrill, Pres.--Keen Compressed Gas Co., Inc., Wilmington, DE, pg. 619
Keene, Michael R., Pres.--John Roberts Company, Minneapolis, MN, pg. 938
Keener, J.W., Jr., Pres., Chief Exec. Officer & Treas.--The Chardon Rubber Co., Chardon, OH, pg. 239
Keeney, Lafayette, Chm. Bd., Pres. & Chief Exec. Officer--Sage-Allen & Co., Inc., Hartford, CT, pg. 966
Keeney, Michael D., Pres.--Walle Corporation, Jefferson, LA, pg. 1161
Keersmaeker, Charles A., Pres.--The John Johnson Co., Detroit, MI, pg. 597
Keeton, Kathy, Pres. & Chief Oper. Officer--General Media Publishing Group, New York, NY, pg. 450
Kegley, Donald R., Pres.--National Seating Co., Vonore, TN, pg. 793
Kehne, Richard M., Chm. Bd. & Pres.--Kehne Electric Company, Inc., Saint Paul, MN, pg. 620
Keikkinen, Leo V., Pres.--Elkay Products, Inc., Shrewsbury, MA, pg. 377
Keil, Carl, Pres.--EduServ, Saint Paul, MN, pg. 369
Keiler, Richard W., Pres.--Keiler & Company, Farmington, CT, pg. 620
Keiser, Michael, Pres.--Health Care Distributors of Indiana, Inc., South Bend, IN, pg. 520
Keith, Paul, Pres.--Tobacco Supply, Springfield, TN, pg. 1099
Kelb, Don E., Pres.--High Point Oil Co., Indianapolis, IN, pg. 534
Kelleher, Richard M., Pres.--Guest Quarters Suite Hotels, Boston, MA, pg. 493
Kellen, Stephen M., Pres.--Arnhold and S. Bleichroeder, Inc., New York, NY, pg. 84
Keller, Gary H., Chm. Bd. & Pres.--Landmark Hotel Corporation, Topeka, KS, pg. 656
Keller, Robert L., Chief Exec. Officer--H. P. Hood Inc., Boston, MA, pg. 25
Keller, Robert L., Pres. & Chief Exec. Officer--J. J. Keller & Associates, Inc., Neenah, WI, pg. 620
Keller, William L., III, Pres.--Keymark Corporation, Fonda, NY, pg. 627
Kelley, Gary L., Chm. Bd., Pres. & Chief Exec. Officer--Kelley Bean Co., Inc., Morrill, NE, pg. 621
Kelley, Glenn, Pres.--Kelley & Wallwork Inc., Boston, MA, pg. 621
Kelley, James E., Pres.--Warm Brothers Construction Company, Cincinnati, OH, pg. 1163
Kelley, Joseph G., Jr., Pres., Treas. & Chief Fin. Officer--Jordan's Meats, Portland, ME, pg. 605
Kelley, Terry, Pres. & Chief Oper. Officer--Team Bancshares, Inc., Dallas, TX, pg. 1082
Kelliher, Linda, Pres. & Dir.-Creative--Kelliher/Samets Marketing Communications, Burlington, VT, pg. 621
Kellman, Joseph, Chm., Pres. & Chief Exec. Officer--Globe Glass & Mirror Co., Chicago, IL, pg. 463
Kellman, Mildred, Chm. Bd. & Pres.--Globe-Amerada Glass Company, Elk Grove Village, IL, pg. 463
Kellogg, Charles T., Pres., Chief Exec. Officer & Treas.--Hubbard Hall Inc., Waterbury, CT, pg. 549
Kellogg, Martin N., Pres., Chief Oper. Officer & Corp. Sec.--UFE Incorporated, Stillwater, MN, pg. 1123
Kellum, Robert, Pres.--Alliance Management, Inc., Seattle, WA, pg. 37
Kelly, Brian, Pres.--Fitchburg Coated Products Inc., Scranton, PA, pg. 1083
Kelly, Dermot G., Gen. Mgr.--S. C. Johnson & Son, Limited, Brantford,, Canada, pg. 600
Kelly, Donald P., Chm. Bd., Pres. & Chief Exec. Officer--Envirodyne Industries, Inc., Oak Brook, IL, pg. 383
Kelly, Edmund F., Pres. & Chief Oper. Officer--Liberty Mutual Insurance Co., Boston, MA, pg. 674
Kelly, J. Fredrick, Jr., Pres. & Chief Exec. Officer--Aeroglide Corporation, Cary, NC, pg. 22
Kelly, J. Fredrick, Jr., Pres.--American Machinery Corp., Orlando, FL, pg. 22
Kelly, John, Pres. & Chief Oper. Officer--Biederman, Kelly & Shaffer, Inc., New York, NY, pg. 149
Kelly, John D., Pres. & Chief Exec. Officer--Na-Churs Plant Food Company, Marion, OH, pg. 782
Kelly, Paul E., Jr., Pres.--Cawsl Corporation, Wynnewood, PA, pg. 229
Kelly, Robert L., Pres. & Chief Exec. Officer--Kelly Michener Inc., Lancaster, PA, pg. 621
Kelly, Stephen J., Chm. Bd., Pres. & Chief Exec. Officer--South Chester Tube Co., Concordville, PA, pg. 1019
Kelly, Steven, Pres.--Southtec, Inc., Albany, NY, pg. 1019
Kelsey, Robert E., Pres.--Kelsey Construction, Inc., Orlando, FL, pg. 621
Kelso, R.W., Pres. & Chief Exec. Officer--PQ Corporation, Valley Forge, PA, pg. 836

Kemerling, James L., Pres. & Chief Exec. Officer--Shade Computer Forms Co., Green Bay, WI, pg. 994
Kemp, Edith P., Pres.--Lanman & Kemp-Barclay Co. Inc., Westwood, NJ, pg. 657
Kempf, Pat, Pres.--Moroch & Assoc., Inc., Dallas, TX, pg. 770
Kendall, Donald S., III, Chm. Bd. & Pres.--Mack Molding Company, Arlington, VT, pg. 697
Kendall, Stephen F., Pres. & Chief Exec. Officer--Aluminum Shapes, Inc., Delair, NJ, pg. 46
Kenlon, John, Pres.--Stern's Miracle-Gro Products, Inc., Port Washington, NY, pg. 1048
Kenneally, J.D., Pres.--International Systems & Controls Corp., Houston, TX, pg. 579
Kenneally, Thomas F., Sr., Pres. & Chief Exec. Officer--Town Pump, Inc., Butte, MT, pg. 1104
Kennedy, Andrew G., Chm. & Pres.--Kentile Floors Inc., South Plainfield, NJ, pg. 623
Kennedy, Bernard, Pres. & Chief Oper. Officer--King Kullen Grocery Co., Inc., Westbury, NY, pg. 630
Kennedy, Ian, Chm. Bd.--K&D Bond Direct, Surrey Hills,, Australia, pg. 112
Kennedy, James C., Chm. & Chief Exec. Officer--Cox Enterprises, Inc., Atlanta, GA, pg. 292
Kennedy, John M., Pres.--T. H. Rogers Lumber Co. Inc., Oklahoma City, OK, pg. 943
Kennedy, Karen S., Chm. Bd., Pres., Treas. & New Bus. Contact--KSK Communications, Ltd., Vienna, VA, pg. 613
Kennedy, Michael, Pres.--WinCup, Phoenix, AZ, pg. 1195
Kennedy, Peter M., III, Pres.--Dominick & Dominick, Incorporated, New York, NY, pg. 343
Kennedy, Tom, Pres.--Kennedy Associates, Richmond, VA, pg. 623
Kennedy, Tom, Pres.--APPX Software, Richmond, VA, pg. 623
Kenney, G. Dickson, Pres. & Chief Exec. Officer--Kenney Manufacturing Company, Warwick, RI, pg. 623
Kenny, James C., Pres. & Chief Exec. Officer--Harbour Industries, Inc., Shelburne, VT, pg. 507
Kent, J.H., Pres.--Varied Investments, Inc., Muscatine, IA, pg. 1145
Kent, Mark B., Pres. & Chief Opers. Officer--The Kent Manufacturing Co., Pickens, SC, pg. 623
Kentner, Pat, Gen. Mgr. & Dir.--Railway Educational Bureau, Omaha, NE, pg. 1005
Kenyon, E. Niles, Pres. & Chief Oper. Officer--The Conair Group, Inc., Pittsburgh, PA, pg. 272
Kenyon, T.R., Pres.--Ed Holderness Supplies, Tucson, AZ, pg. 538
Keplen, Paul, Pres.--LINC Capital Corporation, Chicago, IL, pg. 648
Kepler, Forrest M., Jr., Pres.--Banner Associates Inc., Laramie, WY, pg. 118
Kerbs, Charles F., Jr., Pres.--Federal Chicago Corporation, North Chicago, IL, pg. 404
Kerckhoff, Richard D., Jr., Gen. Mgr.--Pevely Dairy Company, Saint Louis, MO, pg. 884
Kerman, Harold M., Pres.--Steiner Electric Co., Elk Grove Village, IL, pg. 1045
Kern, Tom, V.P. & G.M.--Sloan Technology, Santa Barbara, CA, pg. 1146
Kernan, Margaret G., Publr.--Country Sampler, Saint Charles, IL, pg. 968
Kerner, Lester, Pres.--General Aerospace Materials Corporation, Plainview, NY, pg. 448
Kerr, Howard J., Chm. Bd., Pres. & Chief Exec. Officer--Consolidated Pipe & Supply Company, Birmingham, AL, pg. 277
Kerschen, Richard, Chm. Bd., Pres. & Chief Exec. Officer--The Law Company, Inc., Wichita, KS, pg. 661
Kersic, John T., Publisher & Pres.-Educational Publ. Grp.--Educational Publishing Corporation, Oak Lawn, IL, pg. 369
Kerstetter, Bert, Pres.--Calico Corners, Kennett Square, PA, pg. 209
Kervick, Robert B., Pres.--Kervick Enterprises, Inc., Worcester, MA, pg. 624
Kerwin, B., Pres.--Waukesha Foundry Inc., Waukesha, WI, pg. 1168
Kerz, Paul J., Chm. Bd., Pres. & Chief Exec. Officer--Health Management Systems, Inc., New York, NY, pg. 521
Kesler, Philip, Pres.--Warner Candy Company, Inc., Chicago, IL, pg. 1164
Kessler, Dennis, Pres.--Fel-Pro Incorporated, Skokie, IL, pg. 405
Kester, Jay, Pres.--The Cherokee Group, Sunland, CA, pg. 243
Kesterson, Tommy, Chm. Bd. & Pres.--Kesterson Food Company, Inc., Paris, TN, pg. 624
Keston, Michael I., Pres.--Larwin Company, Encino, CA, pg. 659
Ketchum, John W., Pres.--Loeffler Ketchum Mountjoy, Charlotte, NC, pg. 680
Kettelhut, Willis, Pres.--Reinke Manufacturing Co., Inc., Deshler, NE, pg. 924
Kettler, Clarence E., Pres.--Kettler Brothers, Inc., Montgomery Village, MD, pg. 626
Keys, Howard, Pres.--Keyes Motors, Inc., Van Nuys, CA, pg. 627
Khim, Dr. Jay W., Chm. Bd., Pres. & Chief Exec. Officer--JWK International Corp., Annandale, VA, pg. 586
Kiam, Victor, II, Chm. Bd., Pres., Chief Exec. & Chief Oper. Officer--Remington Products Inc., Bridgeport, CT, pg. 926
Kidd, James, Pres.--Engineering Technology Ltd. (E.T.), Troy, MI, pg. 382
Kidd, Kenneth, Chm. Bd. & Pres.--Superior Label Systems, Inc., Cincinnati, OH, pg. 1063
Kiefer, William C., Chm. Bd. & Pres.--Bel-Ray Company, Inc., Farmingdale, NJ, pg. 133
Kiefus, Jerry, Pres.--Big Joe Manufacturing Co., Lincolnwood, IL, pg. 149
Kiel, Douglas G., Pres.--WTMJ, Inc., Milwaukee, WI, pg. 608
Kiely, Ray, Pres.--Vernell's Candy Company, Bellevue, WA, pg. 1148
Kiepper, Alan F., Pres.--New York City Transit Authority, Brooklyn, NY, pg. 745
Kies, A.M., Pres. & Chief Exec. Officer--Erico International, Cleveland, OH, pg. 386
Kies, William S., Pres. & Chief Oper. Officer--IGA, Inc. (Independent Grocers Alliance), Chicago, IL, pg. 560
Kieseman, Joseph, Pres. & Chief Exec. Officer--Allied Mercantile Company, Philadelphia, PA, pg. 38
Kiggen, James D., Chm. Bd., Pres. & Chief Exec. Officer--Xtek, Inc., Cincinnati, OH, pg. 1206
Kilb, Jerry L., Pres. & Chief Oper. Officer--GranTree Corporation, Beaverton, OR, pg. 477
Kiley, James, Chief Exec. Officer & Gen. Mgr.--Sioux Valley Empire Electric Association, Colman, SD, pg. 1009
Kilgore, Benjamin W., III, Pres. & Chief Oper. Officer--Pine State Creamery Co., Raleigh, NC, pg. 871
Kilgore, Tom D., Pres. & Chief Exec. Officer--Oglethorpe Power Corp., Tucker, GA, pg. 822
Kilguss, Howard K., Chm. Bd., Pres. & Treas.--Excell Manufacturing Company, Providence, RI, pg. 392
Killinger, Kerry K., Chm. Bd., Chief Exec. Officer & Pres.--Washington Mutual Savings Bank, Seattle, WA, pg. 1166
Kim, Edward, Pres., Chief Oper. & Chief Exec. Officer--Ronald Hsu Construction, Capitol Heights, MD, pg. 548
Kim, John, Pres.--Inkel Technology, Fremont, CA, pg. 570
Kim, Kenneth H., Chm., Pres., Chief Exec. Officer, Corp. Sec. & Treas.--Medieval Dinner & Tournament, Inc., Buena Park, CA, pg. 735
Kimball, L. Robert, Pres. & Treas.--L. Robert Kimball & Associates, Ebensburg, PA, pg. 629
Kimbell, David A., Chm. Bd. & Pres.--Burk Royalty Co., Wichita Falls, TX, pg. 190
Kimbrell, James R., Pres. & Chief Exec. Officer--La Mesa R V Center, Inc., La Mesa, CA, pg. 649
Kimmell, Garman O., Pres.--Kimray, Inc., Oklahoma City, OK, pg. 629
Kimsey, Gary, Pres.--Gemtron Corporation, Sweetwater, TN, pg. 3
Kimsey, Gary, Pres.--Hamilton, Inc., Vincennes, IN, pg. 3
King, Charles, Pres.--Eatel Corporation, Gonzales, LA, pg. 364
King, Darryl, Pres.--A. Grace Development, Houston, TX, pg. 474
King, David, Pres.--John Hancock Mutual Funds, Boston, MA, pg. 596
King, Dennis E., Pres.--Dunlap & Co. Inc., Columbus, IN, pg. 353
King, Dennis, M., Pres.--Harley Ellington Pierce Yee Associates, Inc., Southfield, MI, pg. 509
King, Edwin D., Pres.--King Fuels Inc., Troy, NY, pg. 630
King, George F., Chm. Bd., Pres. & Chief Exec. Officer--Kirby Building Systems, Inc., Nashville, TN, pg. 632
King, Gil, Pres.--Sterling, Inc., Milwaukee, WI, pg. 1047
King, James M., Dr., Pres.--GAI Consultants, Inc., Fort Wayne, IN, pg. 439
King, Jim, Pres. & Chief Oper. Officer--Sunox, Inc., Charlotte, NC, pg. 1062
King, John D., Pres.--Walker Wire & Steel Company, Ferndale, MI, pg. 1160
King, John H., Pres. & Chief Oper. Officer--HDS Services, Farmington Hills, MI, pg. 496
King, R.L., Jr., Pres.--Mount Vernon Dryer Fabrics, Greenville, SC, pg. 845
King, Richard S., Pres.--King Industries, Inc., Norwalk, CT, pg. 630
King, Robert C., Sr., Pres.--Richmond Motor Company, Richmond, VA, pg. 933
King, Tommy, Pres. & Chief Exec. Officer--Western Trailer Equipment & Manufacturing Co., Abilene, TX, pg. 1182
King, William E., Pres.--LINC Equipment Services, Lincolnshire, IL, pg. 648
Kingele, Michael, Pres.--Hollytex Carpet Mills, Inc., Ontario, CA, pg. 540
Kingsmore, Harold D., Pres. & Chief Oper. Officer--Graniteville Co., Graniteville, SC, pg. 476
Kingston, Ellery, Pres.--Standard Industries, Inc., Salt Lake City, UT, pg. 1036
Kinlein, David, Pres.--Optic Graphics, Inc., Glen Burnie, MD, pg. 827
Kinney, Ronald F., Chm. Bd & Pres.--All-Phase Electric Supply Co. Inc., Benton Harbor, MI, pg. 35
Kinning, Rick L., Pres. & Treas.--RK Mechanical, Inc., Lakewood, CO, pg. 907
Kinzly, Robert E., Pres. & Treas.--Scipar, Buffalo, NY, pg. 982
Kiplinger, Austin H., Pres.--Kiplinger's Personal Finance Magazine, Washington, DC, pg. 632
Kiplinger, Knight A., Pres.--The Kiplinger Washington Editors, Inc., Washington, DC, pg. 632
Kipper, Barbara L., Chm. Bd.--The Charles Levy Company, Chicago, IL, pg. 672
Kipping, Arthur, Pres. & Chief Exec. Officer--Ray-Carroll County Grain Co-op, Richmond, MO, pg. 914
Kirby, Carroll R., Pres.--Hydro/Kirby Agri Service, Inc., Lancaster, PA, pg. 556
Kirby, G.E., Chm. & Pres.--Atlanta Wire Works, Inc., Jonesboro, GA, pg. 94
Kirby, George, Pres.--Benchmark Homes, Inc., Brookville, OH, pg. 138
Kirby, Mike, Pres.--Valley Onions, McAllen, TX, pg. 351
Kirby, Robert, Pres.--Castleberry's Food Company, Augusta, GA, pg. 229
Kircher, William J., Chm. Bd., Pres., Creative Dir. & Acct. Supvr.--William J. Kircher & Associates, Washington, DC, pg. 633
Kirgis, Robert, Chm. Bd. & Pres.--Farmway Co-Op Inc., Beloit, KS, pg. 402
Kirk, Jesse, Chm. Bd. & Pres.--Dallas Peterbilt, Inc., Irving, TX, pg. 312
Kirk, Milo, Pres.--MADD (Mothers Against Drunk Driving), Irving, TX, pg. 691
Kirk, Thomas L., Chm. Bd. & Pres. & Chief Exec. Office--Kirk-Mayer, Inc., Los Angeles, CA, pg. 633
Kirkpatrick, Don O., Chm. Bd. & Pres.--Quality Foods Inc., Little Rock, AR, pg. 903
Kirkpatrick, Elwood, Pres.--Michigan Milk Producers Association, Novi, MI, pg. 747
Kirkpatrick, James, Pres.--Allied Mutual Insurance Company, Des Moines, IA, pg. 38
Kirkwood, J.H., Chm., Pres. & Chief Exec. Officer--Edgewater Corporation, Oakmont, PA, pg. 368
Kirschman, Arnold, Pres.--Morris Kirschman & Company, Inc., New Orleans, LA, pg. 633
Kislak, Jay I., Chm. Bd., Pres. & Chief Exec. Officer--J. I. Kislak Inc., Miami Lakes, FL, pg. 633
Kislevitz, Joshua, Mng. Dir.--Colorforms, Ramsey, NJ, pg. 265
Kissling, Richard W., Sr., Pres.--A. C. Kissling, Inc., Philadelphia, PA, pg. 634
Kitchen, Michael B., Pres.--The Cumis Group Ltd., Burlington,, Canada, pg. 206
Kitchen, Willis M., Pres.--Gulf Coast Lead Company, Inc., Tampa, FL, pg. 493
Kittederg, Joseph B., Pres. & Exec. Oper. Officer--Tilcon, Inc., New Britain, CT, pg. 1097
Kittoe, Larry, Pres.--DeBruce Grain Inc., North Kansas City, MO, pg. 323
Kitzie, John, Pres.--Savemart Inc., Bronx, NY, pg. 973
Kitzinger, Bruce, Pres.--Waterloo Service Company, Waterloo, IA, pg. 1167
Kitzmiller, Mike, Pres.--Crest Cadillac Company, Nashville, TN, pg. 298
Klapmeier, James, Pres.--Klapmeier Management Company, Mora, MN, pg. 634
Klapmeier, James E., Pres.--Bluewater Marine, Mora, MN, pg. 161
Klas, Robert C., Jr., Pres.--Tapemark, West St. Paul, MN, pg. 1078
Klaus, Frank A., Pres.--Bristol Industries, Brea, CA, pg. 176
Klaus, L. George, Chm. Bd., Pres. & Chief Exec. Officer--Integral Systems, Walnut Creek, CA, pg. 572
Klaus, Robert, Pres. & Chief Exec. Officer--Klaus Radio Inc., Peoria, IL, pg. 634
Klausen, Jorgen, Mng. Dir.--Klausen & Partners A/S, Copenhagen, Denmark, pg. 1212
Klein, Calvin, Pres.--CRK Advertising, New York, NY, pg. 203
Klein, Calvin, Pres. & Chief Exec. Officer--Calvin Klein, Inc., New York, NY, pg. 635
Klein, Emery I., Pres.--Alaron Inc., Troy, MI, pg. 30
Klein, Frank, Pres.--Carnival Creations, New York, NY, pg. 222
Klein, John H., Pres. & Chief Exec. Officer--Zenith Laboratories, Inc., Northvale, NJ, pg. 1217
Klein, John I., Pres. & New Bus. Contact--John Klein & Assoc., Inc., Cleveland, OH, pg. 635
Klein, John Steven, Pres.--Klein Advertising Inc., Los Angeles, CA, pg. 635
Klein, Jonas B., Pres. & Treas.--Eastland Shoe Manufacturing Corporation, Freeport, ME, pg. 364
Klein, Joseph M., Pres.--CCI Corporation, Tulsa, OK, pg. 200
Klein, Ken, Gen. Mgr.--Relief Printing Corporation, Baldwin Park, CA, pg. 925
Klein, Michael S., Pres.--Sentinel Consumer Products, Inc., Mentor, OH, pg. 990
Klein, Richard T. Jr., Pres. & Chief Oper. Officer--Klein Tools Inc., Skokie, IL, pg. 635
Klemens, Roney, V.P.-Admin.--Wickes Mfg. Co., Southfield, MI, pg. 262
Klepinger, Robert, Pres.--Bailey, Klepinger & Medrich, Inc., Ann Arbor, MI, pg. 114
Klibert, Jeffery M., Pres. & Chief Exec. Officer--Lift-All Co., Inc., Manheim, PA, pg. 675
Kline, Arnold W., Chm. Bd., Pres. & Chief Oper. Officer--Boston Trading Ltd. Inc., Lynn, MA, pg. 168
Kline, Carlton E., Pres.--Atlanta Motor Lines, Inc., Conley, GA, pg. 94
Kline, Jerome C., Pres.--Kline Iron & Steel Co., Inc., Columbia, SC, pg. 635
Kline, Richard, Pres.--C B R Cement Corporation, San Mateo, CA, pg. 199
Kline, Richard G., Pres.--Gardner Publications, Inc., Cincinnati, OH, pg. 443
Kling, Thomas R., Pres.--Philadelphia Gear Corp., King of Prussia, PA, pg. 866
Klinger, Kathryn, Pres.--Georgette Klinger, Inc., New York, NY, pg. 635
Klink, Edwin H., Chm. Bd. & Pres.--E & A Industries, Inc., Indianapolis, IN, pg. 358
Klink, Edwin H., Chm. Bd. & Pres.--H & K Realty Co. Inc., Indianapolis, IN, pg. 358
Klink, Edwin H., Chm. & Pres.--Technicare Cleaning Systems Inc., Indianapolis, IN, pg. 359
Klink, Patricia W. DeBlank, Pres. & Chief Exec. Officer--Advisers Capital Management Inc., New York, NY, pg. 21
Klipsch, Fred S., Chm. Bd. & Pres.--Klipsch & Associates Inc., Hope, AR, pg. 635
Klitzky, David, Pres.--The Great Frame Up Systems, Inc., Franklin Park, IL, pg. 480
Klong, Lawrence A., Pres.--K & R Delivery, Inc., Hinsdale, IL, pg. 610
Kloster, Carol G., Pres. & Chief Exec. Officer--The Charles Levy Company, Chicago, IL, pg. 672
Klosterman, Edward, Pres.--Shield Security, Inc., Los Angeles, CA, pg. 999
Klosterman, Edward, Pres.--ESM Tech., Orange, CA, pg. 999
Klosterman, Ken Jr., Pres.--Klosterman's Baking Company, Cincinnati, OH, pg. 636
Kluener, James A., Sr., Chm. Bd. & Pres.--Kluener Packing Company, Cincinnati, OH, pg. 636
Kluge, John W., Chm. & Pres.--Metromedia Company, East Rutherford, NJ, pg. 743

Klym, Richard W., Pres. & Chief Exec. Officer--Kirkwood Industries, Inc., Cleveland, OH, pg. 633
Klym, Richard W., Pres.--Toledo Commutator Co., Owosso, MI, pg. 633
Knaebel, Joseph I., Pres.--Mid-Am Building Supply, Inc., Moberly, MO, pg. 749
Knape, Susan, Pres.--Knape & Knape, Dallas, TX, pg. 636
Knapheide, H. W. III, Pres.--The Knapheide Mfg. Co., Quincy, IL, pg. 636
Knapp, Cleon T., Chm. Bd. & Pres.--Knapp Communications Corporation, Los Angeles, CA, pg. 636
Knapp, Jules F., Chm. Bd., Pres. & Chief Exec. Officer--United Coatings, Inc., Kankakee, IL, pg. 1131
Knauss, E. William, Pres., Chief Oper. Officer & Treas.--E.W. Knauss & Son, Inc., Quakertown, PA, pg. 636
Kniberg, Alfred A., Chief Exec. Officer--The Strouse, Adler Company, New Haven, CT, pg. 1054
Knight, Theodore H., Chm. Bd. & Pres.--Misener Marine Construction, Tampa, FL, pg. 759
Knipfing, G.R., Chm., Pres. & Chief Exec. Officer--Scheduling Technology Corporation, Hopkinton, MA, pg. 975
Knobbe, Urban, Chm. Bd. & Pres.--Ag Processing Inc A Cooperative, Omaha, NE, pg. 24
Knoll, James B., Pres. & Chief Exec. Officer--Specialty Equipment Companies Inc., Belvidere, IL, pg. 1027
Knoll, Jim, Pres.--Ice Craft, Rockton, IL, pg. 1027
Knoll, Robert, Pres.--Marx/Knoll, Denight & Dodge, Inc., Portland, OR, pg. 716
Knopf, Paul R., Pres. & Chief Exec. Officer--Sheehy, Knopf & Shaver, Inc., Louisville, KY, pg. 996
Knopke, Richard J., Pres.--Contractors Supply Company, Inc., Kansas City, MO, pg. 281
Knoss, Kenneth, Pres.--School Apparel, Inc., San Francisco, CA, pg. 978
Knowles, C. Harry, Pres. & Chief Exec. Officer--Metrologic Instruments, Inc., Blackwood, NJ, pg. 743
Knowles, True H., Pres. & Chief Oper. Officer--Dr Pepper Company, Dallas, TX, pg. 342
Knox, Charles E., Jr., Chm. Bd. & Chief Exec. Officer--Knox Oil of Texas Inc., Dallas, TX, pg. 638
Knudson, Gerald, Pres. & Chief Exec. Officer--Resonex, Inc., Sunnyvale, CA, pg. 929
Knudson, Knute S., Pres. & Chief Oper. Officer--Dixson, Inc., Grand Junction, CO, pg. 341
Knuths, Leroy R., Chm. Bd., Pres. & Chief Exec. Officer--Rosco Manufacturing Co., Madison, SD, pg. 947
Kobacker, Alfred J., Pres.--The Kobacker Company & Affiliates, Columbus, OH, pg. 638
Koch, Anthony H., Chm. Bd. & Pres.--Alamo Industrial Group, San Antonio, TX, pg. 29
Koch, Anthony H., Chm. Bd. & Pres.--Alamo Iron Works, San Antonio, TX, pg. 29
Koch, G. Fred, Pres. & Treas.--Plywood Plastics Inc., Buffalo, NY, pg. 878
Koch, Robert L. II, Pres. & Chief Exec. Officer--George Koch Sons, Inc., Evansville, IN, pg. 639
Koch, William I., Pres.--Oxbow Corporation, West Palm Beach, FL, pg. 834
Kocheck, Michael, Pres.--Monarch Construction Company, Cincinnati, OH, pg. 765
Koci, Ludvik F., Pres. & Chief Oper. Officer--Detroit Diesel Corp., Detroit, MI, pg. 859
Kocourek, Wayne C., Vice Chm. & Pres.--Applied Industrial Materials Corporation, Deerfield, IL, pg. 79
Koehlein, Gregg, Pres., Chief Exec. Officer, Plant & Mfg. Mgr.--Mallory, Inc., Carson City, NV, pg. 703
Koehlinger, A.W., Pres. & Chief Exec. Officer--R. A. Jones & Co. Inc., Covington, KY, pg. 604
Koeneman, R.M., Pres.--Remcor Products Co., Glendale Heights, IL, pg. 926
Koenigsberg, William A., Pres. & Chief Exec. Officer--Horizon Media, Inc., New York, NY, pg. 544
Koenitzer, John E., Pres. & Chief Exec. Officer--Helwig Carbon Products, Inc., Milwaukee, WI, pg. 528
Koentopf, David D., Pres. & Chief Oper. Officer--Lifetouch, Inc., Bloomington, MN, pg. 675
Koerner, John, Pres.--Barq's, Inc., New Orleans, LA, pg. 121
Koerner, John, Pres.--Delaware Punch Co., New Orleans, LA, pg. 121
Koffman, Burton, Pres. & Treas.--Ben Arnold Co., Inc., Binghamton, NY, pg. 84
Koffman, Burton I., Chm. Bd. & Pres.--Great American Industries, Inc., Vestal, NY, pg. 480
Koffman, Burton I., Chm. Bd.--Apparel America, Inc., New Haven, CT, pg. 78
Koffman, Robert G., Pres. & Chief Exec. Officer--United Stores, Bay City, MI, pg. 1137
Kogen, J., Pres.--Shure Brothers Incorporated, Evanston, IL, pg. 1001
Koh, Kay Yew, Acting Pres. & Chief Fin. Officer--Shakey's Incorporated, South San Francisco, CA, pg. 994
Koh, Kay Yew, Acting Pres. & Chief Fin. Officer--Monarch Foods, Inc., Tukwila, WA, pg. 994
Kohl, Herb, Pres.--Milwaukee Bucks, Inc., Milwaukee, WI, pg. 756
Kohl, Jack, Pres.--Man-Gill Chemical Company, Cleveland, OH, pg. 703
Kohler, Freya, Chief Exec. Officer--Komplettburo GmbH, Internationale Kommunikation, Munich, Germany, pg. 625
Kohler, Herbert V., Jr., Chm. Bd., Pres., Chief Oper. & Chief Exec. Officer--Kohler Company, Kohler, WI, pg. 639
Kohn, Alvin, Pres.--Pincus Bros., Inc., Philadelphia, PA, pg. 870
Kojabashian, C., Pres.--Foster-Miller, Inc., Waltham, MA, pg. 426
Kolikof, Robert A., Pres., Chief Exec. Officer & Chief Oper. Officer--Prudential Metal Supply Corp., East Dedham, MA, pg. 898
Koller, Alois J., Jr., Pres.--Koller Enterprises, Inc., Fenton, MO, pg. 641
Kolody, John F., Pres. & Dir.-Creative--John F. Kolody Inc., Ossining, NY, pg. 641
Kolon, John S., Pres.--Kolon, Bittker & Desmond, Inc., Troy, MI, pg. 641
Kolopsky, Jerry, Chm. Bd., Pres. & Adv. Dir.--King Bear Enterprises, Inc., North Merrick, NY, pg. 630
Koltes, Clifford, Pres.--ACI Financial Corp., Minnetonka, MN, pg. 2
Kolvenbach, Donald M., Pres., Chief Exec. Officer & Chief Oper. Officer--Affiliated of Florida Inc., Tampa, FL, pg. 23
Komar, Charles E., Pres. & Chief Exec. Officer--Charles Komar & Sons, Inc., New York, NY, pg. 641
Komatsuzaki, Takashi, Div. & Branch Mgr.--Technical Instruments Div., San Jose, CA, pg. 1068
Komline, Russel M., Pres.--Komline-Sanderson Engineering Corp., Peapack, NJ, pg. 641
Konczal, Dennis R., Pres.--The Sierra Capital Companies, San Francisco, CA, pg. 1002
Kondrup, Erland, Pres.--Arthur Cheese Company, Arthur, IL, pg. 87
Konheim, B. Brad, Pres. & Chief Exec. Officer--Kobra International Ltd, New York, NY, pg. 638
Konig, Thomas, Pres. & Chief Exec. Officer--Meritcare, Inc., Pittsburgh, PA, pg. 740
Koontz, James L., Pres. & Chief Exec. Officer--Kingsbury Corporation, Keene, NH, pg. 631
Koosed, Terry, Pres.--H W Electronics, Inc., Van Nuys, CA, pg. 497
Koper, R.M., V.P. & Gen. Mgr.--Stephens-Adamson, Pittsburgh, PA, pg. 732
Kopko, Edward M., Chm. Bd., Pres., Chief Exec. & Chief Oper. Officer--Butler International, Montvale, NJ, pg. 197
Koplik, Michael, Pres.--Perry H. Koplik & Sons, New York, NY, pg. 641
Koplovitz, Kay, Pres. & Chief Exec. Officer--USA Network, New York, NY, pg. 1124
Kops, Paul F., Jr., Pres.--Pemko Manufacturing Company, Ventura, CA, pg. 856
Korallus, Horst, Pres.--Volvo Sales & Service Center, Lile, IL, pg. 1155
Korba, Robert W., Pres.--Sammons Enterprises, Inc., Dallas, TX, pg. 968
Korber, Al, Pres.--J. Korber & Company, Albuquerque, NM, pg. 641
Korkmaz, Fares F., Pres.--Interstate Resources, Inc., Rosslyn, VA, pg. 580
Korman, Berton E., Partner--Korman Co., Trevose, PA, pg. 642
Korman, Leonard I., Partner--Korman Co., Trevose, PA, pg. 642
Korman, Steven H., Partner--Korman Co., Trevose, PA, pg. 642
Korn, Mel R., Pres. & Chief Exec. Officer--Geographic Marketing Group (GMG), Philadelphia, PA, pg. 452
Kornblum, Eugene, Pres.--St. Louis Music, Inc., Saint Louis, MO, pg. 967
Korsant, Philip B., Pres.--Ziff Communications Company, New York, NY, pg. 1218
Koshizawa, Shoji, Pres., Chief Exec. Officer--Chuo Senko Advertising Co., Ltd., Tokyo, Japan, pg. 103
Kosloff, Alan, Chm. Bd., Chief Exec. Officer & Pres.--American Marketing Industries, Inc., Kansas City, MO, pg. 58
Kosloff, Alan, Pres.--Swingster Company, Kansas City, MO, pg. 58
Kosloff, Theodore L., Pres. & Treas.--Roosevelt Paper Co., Philadelphia, PA, pg. 946
Koslow, Harold, Pres.--S. P. Dunham & Co., Lawrenceville, NJ, pg. 353
Kosner, Edward, Pres. & Editor--New York Magazine Company, New York, NY, pg. 611
Kossoff, Stanley M., Pres. & Chief Exec. Officer--Lillie Rubin Affiliates Inc., Miami, FL, pg. 954
Kostantinidis, Andirriya, Chm. & Chief Exec. Officer--Repco Incorporated, Orlando, FL, pg. 927
Koster, William P., Pres.--ASM International, Materials Park, OH, pg. 8
Kostopoulos, Peter, Mng. Partner--Cosmopulos Crowley Daly/CKG, Boston, MA, pg. 288
Kotcher, Raymond L., Pres. & Chief Oper. Officer--Ketchum Public Relations/Corporate, New York, NY, pg. 625
Koth, Robert J., Pres.--API Group Inc., Saint Paul, MN, pg. 5
Kotkins, Henry L., Jr., Pres.--Skyway Luggage Co., Seattle, WA, pg. 1009
Kouleyan, Aram, Owner--Knar Gold & Silver Exchange, Los Angeles, CA, pg. 636
Kovac, F. Peter, Pres., Chief Exec. Officer--NKH&W, Inc., Kansas City, MO, pg. 781
Kovacs, George, Pres.--George Kovacs Lighting, Inc., Glendale, NY, pg. 643
Kovaleski, Charles J., Pres.--Attorney's Title Insurance Fund, Orlando, FL, pg. 97
Kowalski, Audrey, Pres. & Chief Exec. Officer--Kowalski Sausage Co., Inc., Hamtramck, MI, pg. 643
Kowaluk, R.S., Pres.--Evans Adhesive Corp., Columbus, OH, pg. 390
Kozub, Edward F., Pres.--Janlynn Corporation, Indian Orchard, MA, pg. 589
Kraft, Harold E., Chm. Bd. & Chief Exec. Officer--Ward Kraft, Inc., Fort Scott, KS, pg. 643
Kraft, Marvin E., Pres.--Lario Oil & Gas Company, Wichita, KS, pg. 658
Kraft, Roger, Pres.--Ward Kraft, Inc., Fort Scott, KS, pg. 643
Krafthefer, Kerry, Pres.--Progress Casting Group, Inc., Plymouth, MN, pg. 894
Kraines, Lawrence M., Pres.--Kraco Enterprises, Inc., Compton, CA, pg. 643
Krall, Norris E., Pres.--Thomas & Skinner, Inc., Indianapolis, IN, pg. 1093
Kramer, Arnold A., Pres. & Chief Exec. Officer--Trimfit, Inc., Philadelphia, PA, pg. 1113
Kramer, Dale, Pres. & Chief Exec. Officer--ShopKo Stores, Inc., Green Bay, WI, pg. 1000
Kramer, Gordon M., Chm. Bd., Pres. & Chief Exec. Officer--Continental Plastic Card Co., Coral Springs, FL, pg. 280
Kramer, John P., Pres. & New Bus. Contact--Media Store Inc., New York, NY, pg. 735
Kramer, Nancy, Pres.--re:Source Marketing, Columbus, OH, pg. 929
Kramer, Robert, Pres. & Treas.--John H. Graham & Co., Inc., Oradell, NJ, pg. 475
Kramers, Kraig W., Pres.--Graphic Arts Center, Portland, OR, pg. 279
Kramme, Paul E., Jr., Pres.--Ace Glass Incorporated, Vineland, NJ, pg. 11
Kranenburg, Casper, Gen. Mgr.--Kuoni Travel, Inc., New York, NY, pg. 646
Krantz, John M., Pres.--Adventure Lands of America, Inc., Des Moines, IA, pg. 21
Krasne, Charles A., Pres. & Chief Exec. Officer--Krasdale Foods Inc., Bronx, NY, pg. 644
Kratena, Jiri, Mng. Dir.--Young & Rubicam Czechoslovakia, Prague,, Czechoslovakia, pg. 1212
Krause, Jim, Dir. Client Services & New Bus. Contact--Krause, Nadurek & Eickmeyer, Dallas, TX, pg. 644
Krause, Steve, Pres.--Krause Plow Corp., Hutchinson, KS, pg. 644
Krause, Thelma, Pres.--Oakland Tool & Manufacturing Company, Fraser, MI, pg. 819
Krauss, Carl R., Pres.--Lakewood Engineering & Manufacturing Co., Chicago, IL, pg. 652
Krauss, Charles H., Pres.--Spartan International, Holt, MI, pg. 1026
Krauss, Ingo, Chm. & Chief Exec. Officer-Y & R Adv.-Europe--Young & Rubicam GmbH, Frankfurt/Main, Germany, pg. 1213
Kravetz, Stanley, Pres.--The Frye Company, Andover, MA, pg. 435
Kravitz, Edward N., Pres. & Chief Oper. Officer--The Flexible Corp., Delaware, OH, pg. 421
Krawczyk, Nancy, Pres.--Johanson Manufacturing Corporation, Boonton, NJ, pg. 595
Krebel, Albert D., Pres. & Chief Exec. Officer--Reed & Barton Corporation, Taunton, MA, pg. 920
Kreher, Thomas W., Pres.--Kreher Steel Company, Inc., Melrose Park, IL, pg. 644
Kreilick, Thomas K., Pres.--Candle Corporation of America, Oshkosh, WI, pg. 214
Kreiter, Harry, Chm. Bd. & Pres.--Castcraft Industries, Inc., Skokie, IL, pg. 228
Kreitzberg, Richard A., Pres. & Chief Exec. Officer--Microflect Company, Inc., Salem, OR, pg. 749
Krelstein, Richard, Pres.--Noma-International, Inc., Forest Park, IL, pg. 808
Krempa, Frank S., Pres.--Lenape Forge, Inc., West Chester, PA, pg. 667
Kremsdorf, Joel, Pres.--Gusso Manufacturing, Inc., Brooklyn, NY, pg. 495
Kreps, Dennis J., Chm. Bd., Pres. & Dir.-Creative--Kreps-Wise Associates, Saint Louis, MO, pg. 644
Kress, James F., Pres. & Chief Exec. Officer--Green Bay Packaging Inc., Green Bay, WI, pg. 483
Kreusch, Paul P., Pres. & Chief Exec. Officer--Leonard Kreusch, Inc., Moonachie, NJ, pg. 645
Kreusser, Richard T., Pres. & Chief Exec. Officer--Handley & Miller, Inc., Indianapolis, IN, pg. 505
Kriebel, Barry F., Pres.--Sun-Maid Growers of California, Kingsburg, CA, pg. 1058
Krier, B. Bruce, Chm. Bd. & Pres.--Krier Foods, Inc., Brown Deer, WI, pg. 645
Krieser, Kurt, Pres.--Evy Of California, Inc., Los Angeles, CA, pg. 392
Krihak, Paul R., Pres. & Treas.--Holbrook Lumber Company, Albany, NY, pg. 538
Krippaehne, William W., Jr., Pres.--Fisher Companies, Inc., Seattle, WA, pg. 414
Krissel, Robert A., Pres. & Chief Oper. Officer--Equitable Bag Company, Long Island City, NY, pg. 385
Krivkovich, Peter G., Pres. & Chief Oper. Officer--Cramer-Krasselt, Milwaukee, WI, pg. 296
Kroeger, Barney, Pres.--A & A Associates, Santa Fe Springs, CA, pg. 1220
Kroeger, Dan, Pres.--Gold Medal Products Co., Cincinnati, OH, pg. 465
Kroetch, Arthur, Chm. Bd., Pres. & Chief Exec. Officer--Scotchman Industries, Inc., Philip, SD, pg. 982
Kronick, Barry L., Pres. & Chief Exec. Officer--Furman Lumber Company, Billerica, MA, pg. 436
Kroot, Brian, Pres.--Northeastern Graphic Supply, Inc., Portland, ME, pg. 814
Kroyer, Robert W., Pres.--Ketchum Advertising/USA, New York, NY, pg. 625
Krucks, William, Chm. Bd. & Pres.--Rauland-Borg Corporation, Skokie, IL, pg. 914
Krueger, Robert A., Pres., Chief Exec. Officer & Treas.--Tri-Mark Metal Corp., Detroit, MI, pg. 1110
Krum, Frank, Pres. & Chief Exec. Officer--Golden Cat Corporation, South Bend, IN, pg. 637
Krumscheid, R.W. Jr., Pres.--Minor Rubber Co., Inc., Bloomfield, NJ, pg. 758
Krumwiede, Robert, Chm. Bd. & Pres.--C-Line Products, Inc., Des Plaines, IL, pg. 198
Krupa, Paul A., Pres.--Surgical Specialties, Reading, PA, pg. 1065
Krupsha, Andrew, Chm. Bd. & Pres.--Kleer Pak Corporation, Berwick, PA, pg. 635
Kruse, Howard W., Pres.--Blue Bell Creameries, Inc., Brenham, TX, pg. 158
Kruse, Mitchell, Pres., Chief Exec. Officer & Auctioneer--Kruse International, Auburn, IN, pg. 645
Krusha, Kenneth J., Pres. & Chief Exec. Officer--J.H. Findorff & Son, Inc., Madison, WI, pg. 411
Kruske, Ed, Pres.--Gentz Industries Inc., Warren, MI, pg. 431

Kruver, Donald R., Pres.--Hill International Inc., Willingboro, NJ, pg. 534
Kuban, William G., Pres., Chief Exec. Officer & Treas.--Kurt Manufacturing Co. Inc., Fridley, MN, pg. 646
Kubiac, Anne, Pres.--Photogenic Machine Company, Inc., Youngstown, OH, pg. 869
Kubicki, Charles, Pres.--Cincinnati United Contractors, Loveland, OH, pg. 250
Kubovic, John W., Pres. & Chief Exec. Officer--The Nash Engineering Company, Norwalk, CT, pg. 783
Kucich, John J., Pres. & Chief Exec. Officer--Dribeck Importers, Inc., Greenwich, CT, pg. 349
Kuck, Paul, Pres.--Regal Marine Industries Inc., Orlando, FL, pg. 921
Kucklick, Frederick, Pres.--Hess Engineering Inc., Niles, MI, pg. 532
Kuebler, J. Clark, Pres.--Uniflow Manufacturing Co., Erie, PA, pg. 1126
Kuehne, Carl W., Pres. & Chief Exec. Officer--American Foods Group, Inc., Minneapolis, MN, pg. 54
Kuehner, Pat, Pres.--Homes & Son Contractors, Inc., Phoenix, AZ, pg. 542
Kuhlman, Lyle S., Pres.--Argiland Company, Byron, MN, pg. 81
Kuhlman, Ronald, Pres.--Kuhlman, Inc., Menomonee Falls, WI, pg. 646
Kuhn, Brent, Pres., New Bus. Contact & Media Dir.--Bennett Kuhn Varner, Inc., Atlanta, GA, pg. 139
Kuhn, Paul J., Pres.--Park Motor Sales Company, Detroit, MI, pg. 849
Kuhn, R.J., Pres.--Reliable Castings Corporation, Cincinnati, OH, pg. 924
Kuhns, Dwight, Pres.--Arcadian Power Corp., Pleasanton, CA, pg. 80
Kuiper, Karl D., Pres.--Grindmaster Corporation, Louisville, KY, pg. 488
Kujovich, L., Pres. & Chief Exec. Officer--Dietzgen Corporation, Des Plaines, IL, pg. 337
Kukla, Robert J., Pres. & Chief Oper. Officer--Kukla Press, Inc., Elk Grove Village, IL, pg. 646
Kull, L.A., Pres. & Chief Oper. Officer--Science Applications International Corporation, San Diego, CA, pg. 981
Kull, Laurie, V.P. & Chief Oper. Officer--Lake to Lake Dairy, Kiel, WI, pg. 653
Kullberg, Gary W., Pres. & Chief Oper. Officer--Pancom International Corp., Stamford, CT, pg. 845
Kummer, Fred S., Chm., Pres., Chief Exec. Officer, Treas. & Founder--HBE Corporation, Saint Louis, MO, pg. 495
Kunkel, Ronald J., Pres.--Diamond Crystal Specialty Foods, Inc., Wilmington, MA, pg. 335
Kunz, Larry P., Pres. & Chief Oper. Officer--Payless Cashways, Inc., Kansas City, MO, pg. 853
Kunzler, Christian C., Jr., Chm. Bd. & Pres.--Kunzler & Company, Inc., Lancaster, PA, pg. 646
Kuperschmid, Bruce, Pres.--Broadcast Time, Inc., Roslyn, NY, pg. 177
Kupperman, Melvin, Pres. & Chief Exec. Officer--A. Epstein and Sons, Intl., Inc., Chicago, IL, pg. 384
Kurdziel, Joseph, Chm. Bd. & Pres.--Kurdziel Industries, Inc., Muskegon, MI, pg. 646
Kurland, Marc E., Pres.--Handy Manufacturing Co., Inc., Newark, NJ, pg. 505
Kurnit, Paul, Pres. & Chief Oper. Officer--Griffin Bacal Inc., New York, NY, pg. 486
Kuronya, Joseph, Pres.--Dynamic Metal Products Company, Manchester, CT, pg. 356
Kurtenbach, Aelred J., Dr., Pres.--Daktronics, Inc., Brookings, SD, pg. 312
Kurtz, Anthony D., Pres.--Kulite Semiconductor Products, Inc., Leonia, NJ, pg. 646
Kurtz, Robert M., Jr., Pres.--Kurtz Bros., Inc., Clearfield, PA, pg. 646
Kurtz, Virginia Hoyt, Pres.--Hoyt Corporation, Westport, MA, pg. 548
Kurtzman, Allan, Pres.--Kurtzman/Slavin/Linda, Inc., Northfield, IL, pg. 646
Kury, Mark C., Pres.--Marmac Corporation, Parkersburg, WV, pg. 710
Kussell, Paul D., Pres.--Shepard Clothing Company, New Bedford, MA, pg. 997
Kvamme, Mark D., Pres., New Bus. Contact--CKS Partners, San Francisco, CA, pg. 202
Kvetko, Edward C., Pres.--Gloria Jean's Coffee Bean Corp., Buffalo Grove, IL, pg. 470
Kwader, Alex, Pres., Chief Exec. Officer & Gen. Mgr.--Specialty Paperboard Inc., Brattleboro, VT, pg. 1027
Kwasnicki, Stanley, Pres.--Premier Metal Products Company, Bronx, NY, pg. 836
Kyle, James H., V.P. & G.M.--Spring Hill Nurseries Co., Tipp City, OH, pg. 426
Kyne, J.F., Pres.--Hauck Mfg. Co., Cleona, PA, pg. 517
La Pointe, Armand, Pres.--Western International Merchandising, Los Angeles, CA, pg. 1180
La Rosa, Michael, Pres.--La Rosa's, Inc., Cincinnati, OH, pg. 649
LaBarba, Lucian M., Pres. & Chief Exec. Officer--American Produce & Vegetable Co., Dallas, TX, pg. 59
LaBarge, Pierre III, Chm. Bd. & Pres.--LaBarge Pipe & Steel Company, Saint Louis, MO, pg. 649
LaBeau, Tim, Pres.--Aldi Inc., Batavia, IL, pg. 33
Labovitz, George H., Dr., Chm. Bd., Pres. & Chief Exec. Officer--ODI, Burlington, MA, pg. 818
LaBue, Anthony C., Pres.--Transco Inc., Wayne, MI, pg. 1107
Lackey, A. Wayne, Chm. Bd. & Pres.--Dentec Corporation, Boca Raton, FL, pg. 329
Lackman, Thomas F., Chm. Bd. & Pres.--Lackman Food Service, Woodbury, NY, pg. 650
Lacourciere, William J., Chief Exec. Officer, Chm. Bd., Pres.--Novametrix Medical Systems Inc., Wallingford, CT, pg. 817
Lacy, Andre B., Chm., Pres. & Chief Exec. Officer--LDI, Ltd., Indianapolis, IN, pg. 647
Laddin, Paul, Pres.--Laddin & Company, Inc., New York, NY, pg. 650
Ladds, H.P., Jr., Pres. & Chief Exec. Officer--Columbus McKinnon Corp., Amherst, NY, pg. 266
LaDue, Jack W., Pres. & Treas.--Gas Equipment Company, Inc., Dallas, TX, pg. 444
Laethem, Ray, Pres.--Ray Laethem Pontiac GMC Truck Co., Detroit, MI, pg. 650
Lafaye, Jean-Paul, Pres. & Chief Exec. Officer-Worldwide--Cato Johnson Worldwide, New York, NY, pg. 1210
Lafayette, Maurice, Jr., Pres. & Chief Exec. Officer--Lafayette Manufacturing, Inc., Hayward, CA, pg. 650
LaFetra, A.W., Pres.--Rain Bird Sprinkler Mfg. Corp., Glendora, CA, pg. 910
Lafleur, Georges, Chm. & Chief Exec.--Lowe Communication Group, Brussels,, Belgium, pg. 685
Lafleur, Georges, Pres. & Chief Exec. Officer--Lowe Troost S.A., Brussels,, Belgium, pg. 685
LaFlomme, Lon, Pres. & Chief Oper. Officer--EvansGroup, Seattle, WA, pg. 391
LaFond, Jerry, Chief Exec. Officer--The Asher Winer Company, Fitchburg, MA, pg. 88
LaGrone, Bobby D., Pres.--U.S. Rubber Reclaiming, Inc., Vicksburg, MS, pg. 306
Laine, R., Pres., Chief Fin. Officer & Treas.--Telechron, Inc., Ashland, MA, pg. 1085
Laird, Larrie W., Pres.--Laird & Company, Scobeyville, NJ, pg. 650
Laird, William, Pres.--Blockhouse Co., Inc., Red Lion, PA, pg. 157
Lakin, Edwin A., Pres.--Boscov's Department Stores, Inc., Reading, PA, pg. 167
Lakin, Louis, Pres.--Lakin General Corporation, Chicago, IL, pg. 652
Lam, Steve, Pres.--Para Systems Inc., Carrollton, TX, pg. 270
LaMantia, Charles R., Pres. & Chief Exec. Officer--Arthur D. Little, Inc., Cambridge, MA, pg. 678
LaMarca, James, Chm. Bd., Pres. & Chief Exec. Officer--LaMarca Group Inc., New York, NY, pg. 652
LaMarca, James, Chm. Bd & Pres.--LaMarca Direct Marketing, New York, NY, pg. 652
Lamb, Isabelle S., Chm. Bd., Pres. & Treas.--Enterprises International Inc., Hoquiam, WA, pg. 382
Lamb, Joseph S., Pres. & Chief Exec. Officer--Bank Of North Dakota, Bismarck, ND, pg. 117
Lamb, Michael R., Pres. & Mgr.-Construction--Lamb Engineering & Construction Co., Salt Lake City, UT, pg. 652
Lamb, Robert E., II, Pres.--Robert E. Lamb, Inc., Valley Forge, PA, pg. 652
Lambert, Dave, Sr., Pres.--G & L Products, Charles City, IA, pg. 438
Lambert, James L., Pres. & Chief Exec. Officer--Artecon, Inc., Carlsbad, CA, pg. 809
Lamberth, George A., Pres.--Spreckles Industries, Inc., Pleasanton, CA, pg. 1032
Lambesis, Nicholas, Pres. & Chief Exec. Officer--Lambesis Communications, San Diego, CA, pg. 652
Lamer, Gerald P., Pres.--Marine Travelift, Inc., Sturgeon Bay, WI, pg. 707
Lamm, Donald S., Chm. Bd. & Pres.--W.W. Norton & Company, Inc., New York, NY, pg. 815
Lammie, J.L., Pres. & Chief Exec. Officer--Parsons Brinckerhoff Inc., New York, NY, pg. 850
Lammie, James L., Pres.--Parsons Brinckerhoff Quade & Douglas, Inc., New York, NY, pg. 850
Lammis, Larry, Pres.--Inkel Corp., La Mirada, CA, pg. 569
Lamoreux, F. Holmes, Chm. Bd., Pres. & Chief Exec. Officer--Sabreliner Corp., Chesterfield, MO, pg. 965
Lampi, Steve, Pres.--Bridgeman's Restaurants Inc., Minneapolis, MN, pg. 175
Lampton, Leslie B., Sr., Chm. Bd & Pres.--Ergon, Inc., Jackson, MS, pg. 386
Lampton, Mason H., Pres.--The Hardaway Company, Columbus, GA, pg. 507
Lamus, Jorge Arenas, Pres.--Aser Publicidad/Y&R, Bogota,, Colombia, pg. 1213
Lan, Richard, Pres.--McCain Citrus Inc., Chicago, IL, pg. 726
Lancaster, Patrick R., III, Pres. & Chief Exec. Officer--Lantech Inc., Louisville, KY, pg. 658
Lancaster, Peggy, Principal & Creative Dir.--Scott/Lancaster/Hershfield, Los Angeles, CA, pg. 982
Landau, Roy, Chm. Bd., Pres. & Chief Exec. & Chief Fin. Officer--Landau Building Co., Wexford, PA, pg. 654
Lande, James, Pres. & Chief Oper. Officer--Quadion Corporation, Minneapolis, MN, pg. 902
Landegger, C.C., Chm. Bd.--The Black Clawson Co., New York, NY, pg. 154
Landel, Michael, Pres. & Chief Exec. Officer--Seiler Corporation, Waltham, MA, pg. 987
Landers, D. Mike, Pres.--Garvey Elevators Inc., Hutchinson, KS, pg. 443
Landers, John W., Pres.--Harold Moore & Associates, Inc., Fayetteville, TN, pg. 768
Landgraf, Thomas, General Mgr.--Cheney Company, New Berlin, WI, pg. 242
Landon, Cass, Co-Pres. & Chief Exec. Officer--Mission Industries, Santa Barbara, CA, pg. 760
Landreth, N. David, Pres.--Henco, Inc., Selmer, TN, pg. 528
Landry, Thomas H., Pres.--Alex J. Etkin, Inc., Farmington Hills, MI, pg. 389
Landsberger, David, Pres.--Bel-Art Products, Pequannock, NJ, pg. 133
Lane, Beau, Pres.--E. B. Lane & Associates, Inc., Phoenix, AZ, pg. 656
Lane, Clifford, Pres. & Chief Oper. Officer--ILC Industries, Inc., Bohemia, NY, pg. 560
Lane, David Alan, Pres.--LevLane Advertising, Inc., Bala-Cynwyd, PA, pg. 671
Lane, William N., III, Chm. Bd., Pres. & Chief Exec. Officer--Lane Industries, Inc., Northbrook, IL, pg. 656
Laney, L.C., Pres. & Chief Oper. Officer--Ingles Markets, Inc., Asheville, NC, pg. 568
Lang, Burt, Pres.--LINC Quantum Analytics, Foster City, CA, pg. 648
Lang, Ed, Pres.--General Spring, Inc., Hartsville, TN, pg. 450
Lang, G. Thomas, Pres.--Dad's Products Co., Inc., Meadville, PA, pg. 310
Lang, Henry S., Chm. Bd., Pres. & Chief Exec. Officer--Home Juice Company, Melrose Park, IL, pg. 541
Lang, Robert H., Jr., Pres. & Chief Exec. Officer--Horn Packaging Corporation, Ayer, MA, pg. 544
Langan, Kevin, Pres.--Northway Motorcar Corporation, Latham, NY, pg. 814
Lange, Chadwick S., Pres.--Owatonna Canning Company, Owatonna, MN, pg. 833
Langer, David, Pres., Chief Exec. & Chief Oper. Officer & Treas.--David Langer & Co., Inc., Hollywood, CA, pg. 657
Langmack, Peter, Pres. & New Bus. Contact--Henry Russell Bruce, Inc., Cedar Rapids, IA, pg. 530
Langston, Robert E., Pres.--Langston Companies, Memphis, TN, pg. 657
Langston, W. P., Pres. & Chief Exec. Officer--Barber Ice Cream Company, Birmingham, AL, pg. 119
Langston, W.P., Pres.--Barber Dairies, Inc., Birmingham, AL, pg. 119
Lanigan, John J., Jr., Pres.--MI-Jack Products, Inc., Hazel Crest, IL, pg. 746
Lanigan, John J., Sr., Chm. Bd. & Pres.--MI-Jack Products, Inc., Hazel Crest, IL, pg. 746
Lanigan, Robert J., Pres.--Daniel F. Young, Inc., New York, NY, pg. 1209
Lantz, James, Pres.--Flint Manufacturing Co., Burton, MI, pg. 419
Lape, Robert M., Pres. & Treas.--Neer Manufacturing Company, Lexington, OH, pg. 797
Lapeyre, J. M., Jr., Chm. & Pres.--The Laitram Corporation, Harahan, LA, pg. 650
Lapeyre, J.M., Jr., Pres.--Digicourse, Inc., Harahan, LA, pg. 651
Lapeyre, J.M., Jr., Chm. & Pres.--Intralox, Inc., Harahan, LA, pg. 651
Lapides, John S., Pres.--United Aluminum Corporation, North Haven, CT, pg. 1130
Lapides, Morton M., Chm. Bd., Pres. & Chief Exec. Officer--Alleco Inc., Cheverly, MD, pg. 35
Lapin, Byron R., Pres.--Clayton Corporation, Fenton, MO, pg. 253
Lapin, Phil, Pres.--Falcon Safety Products Inc., Branchburg, NJ, pg. 398
Laporta, Michael, Pres.--Automotive Rentals, Inc., Mount Laurel, NJ, pg. 101
LaPorte, Thomas B., Pres.--Reliance Elevator Company, Chicago, IL, pg. 925
Lappin, R. Todd, Pres.--Lappin Electric Company, Milwaukee, WI, pg. 658
Lappin, Richard C., Pres. & Chief Oper. Officer--Farley Industries, Chicago, IL, pg. 399
LaRiche, Louis, Pres.--Lou LaRiche Chevrolet-Subaru Inc., Plymouth, MI, pg. 658
Larison, H.H., Pres.--Columbia Paint Co., Spokane, WA, pg. 265
Larkin, Carl, Chm. Bd., Pres. & New Bus. Contact--Larkin Meeder & Schweidel, Dallas, TX, pg. 659
Larkin, Thomas, Pres.--Thermal American Fused Quartz Co., Louisville, KY, pg. 1091
Larned, Gardner, Chm. Bd., Pres., & Chief Exec. Officer--Berry Bearing Co., Lyons, IL, pg. 144
Laroche, Walter, Pres.--Laroche Holdings, Inc., Atlanta, GA, pg. 659
Larock, Duane W., Pres.--R.A. Mueller, Inc., Cincinnati, OH, pg. 774
Larsen, Leslie A., Pres.--Advanced Input Devices, Inc., Coeur D'Alene, ID, pg. 20
Larson, Dale, Pres.--Larson Manufacturing Company, Brookings, SD, pg. 659
Larson, Dave, Pres.--Cargill Nutrena Feed, Minneapolis, MN, pg. 219
Larson, Greg, Pres.--Demco Inc., Madison, WI, pg. 328
Lash, James A., Chm. Bd.--Reading Tube Corp., Reading, PA, pg. 916
Laskey, John L., Pres.--Laskey Associates, Fremont, CA, pg. 660
Laskin, Meyer, Pres. & Chief Oper. Officer--MacAndrews & Forbes Co., Camden, NJ, pg. 694
Lasko, John C., Chm. Bd., Pres. & Treas.--Republic Die & Tool Company, Belleville, MI, pg. 928
Lasko, Oscar, Pres.--Lasko Metal Products, Inc., West Chester, PA, pg. 660
Lasky, David, Pres.--Bresler's Industries, Inc., Des Plaines, IL, pg. 174
Lass, E. Donald, Pres., Editor & Chief Exec. Officer--New Jersey Press, Inc., Neptune, NJ, pg. 801
Lassen, J. R., Pres.--Salt River Project Agricultural Improvement and Power District, Tempe, AZ, pg. 967
Late, Frank M., Chm. Bd. & Pres.--Republic Supply Company, Dallas, TX, pg. 928
Latture, David, Gen. Mgr.--Chattanooga Choo-Choo Holiday Inn, Chattanooga, TN, pg. 241
Lau, David C., Pres.--Aunt Nellie's Farm Kitchens, Inc., Clyman, WI, pg. 98
Lauder, Leonard, Pres. & Chief Exec. Officer--Estee Lauder, Inc., New York, NY, pg. 389
Lauer, Jerry, V.P.-Info. Services--Certified Grocers Advertising Co., Los Angeles, CA, pg. 236
Lauerer, Kenneth G., Pres. & Chief Oper. Officer--Lauerer Markin Gibbs, Inc., Maumee, OH, pg. 660
Lauerman, James M., Pres. & Chief Oper. Officer--Bailey Lauerman & Associates, Inc., Lincoln, NE, pg. 114
Lauffenburger, Robert, Pres.--Rocco Turkeys, Inc., Dayton, VA, pg. 940
Laughlin, Steven L., Partner & Creative Dir.--Frankenberry, Laughlin & Constable, Inc., Milwaukee, WI, pg. 429
Laulhere, M., Pres.--Hood Corporation, Whittier, CA, pg. 542

Corporate Responsibilities Index

Launey, Robert E., Pres.--Launey, Hachmann & Harris, Inc., New York, NY, pg. 661
Lavallee, Paul, Pres.--EMS Eastern Regional Office, Foxboro, MA, pg. 370
Laverdiere, Stephen, Pres. & Chief Exec. Officer--Laverdiere's Enterprises, Winslow, ME, pg. 661
Lavidge, Arthur W., Pres. & Treas.--Lavidge & Associates Inc., Knoxville, TN, pg. 661
Lavidge, William R., Pres.--Drackett & Lavidge, Inc., Scottsdale, AZ, pg. 348
Laviers, Harry, Jr., Pres. & Chief Exec. Officer--South East Coal Co., Irvine, KY, pg. 1019
Lavine, S.E., Pres. & Chief Oper. Officer--D&H Distributing Company, Harrisburg, PA, pg. 307
Lavoie, Raymonde, Partner--RTA Advertising, Inc., Montreal,, Canada, pg. 193
Law, D. Brian, Pres.--Magline, Inc., Pinconning, MI, pg. 700
Law, Jordan, Grp. Pres. & Gen. Mgr.--Microdot Aerospace Fastening Systems Group, Fullerton, CA, pg. 749
LaWarre, William M., Pres.--Northlich Stolley LaWarre, Cincinnati, OH, pg. 814
Lawernce, W. Larry Jr., Pres. & Chief Exec. Officer--Sunline Coach Co., Inc., Denver, PA, pg. 1061
Lawin, Bruce A., Pres.--Specialty Manufacturing Company, St. Paul, MN, pg. 1027
Lawrence, Pelham B., Pres.--Perdue Farms Inc., Salisbury, MD, pg. 860
Lawrence, Richard, V.P.--New Zealand Lamb Co., Inc., Elmsford, NY, pg. 803
Lawrence, Steve, Pres.--Lawrence Metal Products, Inc., Bay Shore, NY, pg. 662
Laws, Dean R., Pres.--Eisaman, Johns & Laws Advertising, Inc., Los Angeles, CA, pg. 372
Lawsen, John, Pres.--New Balance Athletic Shoe, Inc., Boston, MA, pg. 798
Lawson, John, Plant Mgr.--United Farm Tools, Mohawk, Fitzgerald, GA, pg. 1132
Lawson, Rodney, Pres., Chief Oper. Officer & Chief Exec. Officer--Lawson Mechanical Contractors, Sacramento, CA, pg. 663
Lawson, Sam, Pres. & Chief Exec. Officer--United Farm Tools, Inc., Glasgow, KY, pg. 1131
Lawton, Norman B., Pres.--Star Cutter Co., Farmington Hills, MI, pg. 1039
Lax, Bobby A., Pres. & Gen. Mgr.--Distributors Oil Company, Inc., Baton Rouge, LA, pg. 340
Lay, Joe L., Jr., Chm. Bd., Pres. & Chief Exec. Officer--Lay Packing Company Inc., Knoxville, TN, pg. 663
Laybourne, Geraldine, Pres.--Nickelodeon/Nick At Nite, New York, NY, pg. 785
Layton, Bill, Jr., Pres. & Chief Oper. Officer--Welsco Inc., North Little Rock, AR, pg. 1175
Lazarchick, Robert, Pres.--Terre Hill Concrete Products, Inc., Terre Hill, PA, pg. 1089
Lazarus, James J., Pres.--L&R Manufacturing Co., Kearny, NJ, pg. 647
Lea, George A. Jr., Chm. Bd., Pres. & Chief Exec. Officer--The Mad Butcher, Inc., Pine Bluff, AR, pg. 699
Leach, Edwin, F., II, Pres.--Leach & Garner Company, North Attleboro, MA, pg. 663
Leaf, Ron, Pres.--First District Association, Litchfield, MN, pg. 412
Leander, Henry A., Pres.--Ford Meter Box Company, Wabash, IN, pg. 423
Lear, R.H., Pres.--Treaty Co., Greenville, OH, pg. 1109
Leary, Jack, Pres.--The Motorlease Corp., Farmington, CT, pg. 773
Leasher, Randy, Pres.--Cassano's Inc., Dayton, OH, pg. 228
Leasure, George, Pres., Chief Exec. & Chief Fin. Officer & Treas.--Ghent Manufacturing, Inc., Lebanon, OH, pg. 455
Leasure, George, Pres.--Waddell Div. of Ghent Mfg. Co., Greenfield, OH, pg. 455
Leavitt, Julian, Chm. Bd., Pres., Chief Exec. Officer & Treas.--Sweetlife Foods, Inc., Suffield, CT, pg. 1067
Lebel, Alfred J., Pres. & Chief Exec. Officer--Bates Fabrics, Inc., Lewiston, ME, pg. 125
LeBlanc, James J., Pres. & Chief Oper. Officer--K & B, Inc., New Orleans, LA, pg. 611
Lebrija, Jose Antonio, Pres.--Lebrija Rubio Publicidad S.A., Mexico,, Mexico, pg. 104
Lechmann, Ewald, Pres. & Chief Exec. Officer--Wollin Products, Inc., Stevensville, MI, pg. 1199
Leder, Ronald E., Principal--Cooper Leder Marcomm, Lake Success, NY, pg. 283
LeDonne, Peter, Pres.--LeDonne, Wilner & Weiner, Inc., New York, NY, pg. 665
Lee, Andrew, Chm. Bd., Pres. & Chief Oper. Officer--Daniel Caron Ltd., New York, NY, pg. 224
Lee, Bill, Pres.--The Children's Place Retail Stores, Inc., Pine Brook, NJ, pg. 247
Lee, Bobbie, Pres.--Superior Reprographics, Seattle, WA, pg. 1064
Lee, H. Clark, Pres.--Valley Detroit Diesel Allison, City of Industry, CA, pg. 1143
Lee, James C., III, Pres.--Buffalo Rock Company, Birmingham, AL, pg. 187
Lee, James D., Chm. Bd. & Pres.--Hamilton, Carver & Lee, Inc., Chicago, IL, pg. 503
Lee, John E., Pres. & Chief Exec. Officer--Carver, Inc., Garden City, GA, pg. 227
Lee, John E., Pres. & Chief Exec. Officer--Murray-Carver, East Bridgewater, MA, pg. 776
Lee, John J., Jr., Pres.--Ireland Gourmet Shop, Atlantic City, NJ, pg. 582
Lee, John W., Pres. & Chief Oper. Officer--Georgia Iron Works Co., Grovetown, GA, pg. 453
Lee, John, Jr., Pres. & Treas.--Ireland Coffee Tea, Inc., Pleasantville, NJ, pg. 582
Lee, John, Jr., Pres.--The Lenson Corporation, Pleasantville, NJ, pg. 582
Lee, Leighton, III, Pres.--Lee Company, Westbrook, CT, pg. 665
Lee, M.S., Pres.--Houston Fearless 76 Inc., Compton, CA, pg. 546
Lee, Patrick P., Chm. Bd. & Pres.--Enidine Incorporated, Orchard Park, NY, pg. 382
Lee, Paul M., Pres. & Chief Exec. Officer--Quik Wok Corporation, Dallas, TX, pg. 905
Lee, Preston R., Chm. Bd. & Pres.--Besteel Industries, Irvine, CA, pg. 147
Lee, Richard A., Pres.--Lee & Riley, Inc., Minneapolis, MN, pg. 666
Lee, Weldon A., Pres., Chief Exec. Officer--Atlantic Builders Group Inc., Baltimore, MD, pg. 94
Lee, William, Pres.--Lee Grocery Company, Everett, WA, pg. 665
Leebern, Donald, Jr., Pres.--Georgia Crown Distributing, Columbus, GA, pg. 453
Leebow, Steven, Chm. Bd., Pres. & Chief Exec. Officer--Pacesetter Steel Service, Inc., Marietta, GA, pg. 839
Leeds, Michael S., Pres. & Chief Exec. Officer--C M P Publications, Inc., Manhasset, NY, pg. 202
Leeds, Robert K., Chm. Bd. & Pres.--Jewelmont Corporation, Minneapolis, MN, pg. 594
Leef, James M., Pres.--Industrial Towel & Uniform, New Berlin, WI, pg. 567
Leff, Martin J., Pres.--Carole Wren, Inc., New York, NY, pg. 1204
Leff, Myron J., Pres. & Gen. Mgr.--BSB/Leff & Squicciarini, Dublin, OH, pg. 108
Leffler, Carlos R., Pres.--Carlos R. Leffler Inc., Richland, PA, pg. 666
Lefkovits, Samuel, Pres.--Roselle Paper Co., Inc., Roselle, NJ, pg. 948
Lefkowitz, Leopold, Pres.--Crystal Clear Industries Company, Ridgefield Park, NJ, pg. 303
Lefler, R. Stephen, Pres. & Chief Exec. Officer--Williamson-Dickie Mfg. Co., Fort Worth, TX, pg. 1192
Lefler, R. Stephen, Pres.--Williamson-Dickie Apparel Mfg. Co., Fort Worth, TX, pg. 1192
LeFort, Leo J., Chm., Chief Exec. Officer--Arocom Direct, Inc., Cleveland, OH, pg. 737
LeFort, Leo J., Chm., Chief Exec. Officer--Arocom Marketing Group, Inc., Cleveland, OH, pg. 737
LeFrak, Richard S., Pres.--Lefrak Organization Inc., Rego Park, NY, pg. 666
Lefton, Al Paul Jr., Pres. & Chief Exec. Officer--Al Paul Lefton Co., Inc., Philadelphia, PA, pg. 666
Legacki, Frank, Pres.--Kaepa Inc., San Antonio, TX, pg. 613
Leger, Buster, Pres.--Woolcan, Lachine,, Canada, pg. 1201
Legum, Jeffrey A., Pres.--The Park Circle Motor Co., Baltimore, MD, pg. 848
Lehman, Jonathan E., Pres. & Treas.--Georgian Press, Inc., New York, NY, pg. 453
Lehmann, Durwood C., Pres.--Brance Krachy Company, Inc., Houston, TX, pg. 171
Lehmann, Heinz R., Pres.--American Laubscher Corp., Farmingdale, NY, pg. 57
Lehmann, John, Chm. Bd., Pres. & Chief Exec. Officer--Butterick Company, Inc., New York, NY, pg. 197
Leicht, Richard F., Jr., Pres.--Eclipse Manufacturing Company, Sheboygan, WI, pg. 367
Leigh, Lynn, Pres.--Hydril Company, Los Angeles, CA, pg. 556
Leigh, Lynn L., Pres.--Hydril Company, Houston, TX, pg. 556
Leighton, Robert, Pres.--Steelite, Inc., Pittsburgh, PA, pg. 1044
Leimer, Dwight, Pres.--Jay Instrument & Specialty Co., Cincinnati, OH, pg. 590
Leinweber, John L., Pres. & Chief Exec. Officer--American Office Equipment, La Grange, IL, pg. 58
Leipsner, Stephen R., Chm., Pres. & Chief Exec. Officer--S & A Restaurant Corp., Dallas, TX, pg. 958
Leistra, Wayne, Pres.--Mendenhall & Leistra, Grand Rapids, MI, pg. 739
Leisure, Joe, Chm. & Pres.--Rush County Farm Bureau Co-op, Rushville, IN, pg. 956
Lemeunier, Anny-Claude, Pres.--Bordelais, Lemeunier & Leo Burnett, Clichy,, France, pg. 192
LeMire, Arthur J., Pres.--Kasper Machine Company, Madison Heights, MI, pg. 618
Lemke, Paul G., Sr., Chm. Bd. & Pres.--Thruway Fasteners Inc., North Tonawanda, NY, pg. 1096
Lemman, Peter R., Pres.--North Coast Electric Company, Bellevue, WA, pg. 813
Lemmons, Wayne, Dir.--Delaware Lottery, Dover, DE, pg. 326
Lenac, Ralph Z., Pres.--Lenac, Warford, Stone, Inc., Newport Beach, CA, pg. 667
Lenk, Robert E., Pres.--The Savogran Company, Norwood, MA, pg. 973
Lenker, Max V., Pres.--Racetrac Petroleum, Inc., Smyrna, GA, pg. 909
Lenox, Stan, Pres.--Jetstream Systems, Hayward, CA, pg. 122
Lenway, Fred, Pres.--Aratex Services, Inc., Schaumburg, IL, pg. 7
Leon, Thomas, Pres., Chief Exec. Officer & Creative Dir.--S. R. Leon Company, Inc., Oyster Bay, NY, pg. 667
Leonard, K. E., Pres. & Chief Exec. Officer--Leonard & Harral Packing Co., San Antonio, TX, pg. 667
Leonard, Lois, Chm. Bd. & Pres.--Young & Roehr, Inc., Portland, OR, pg. 1210
Leonard, Michael, Pres.--Harman Automotive, Southfield, MI, pg. 514
Leonard, Miller, Pres. & Creative Dir.--Goodrum Leonard & Associates, Inc., Nashville, TN, pg. 471
Leonard, Richard, Pres.--Sunstates Realty Group Inc., Raleigh, NC, pg. 1062
Leonard, Robert, Pres.--Ticketmaster Corporation, Los Angeles, CA, pg. 1096
Leonard, Thomas, Pres.-USA--Samsonite Corporation, Denver, CO, pg. 358
Leonard, Tom, Pres.--Lark Luggage Company, Inc., Denver, CO, pg. 359
Leonardi, John P., Pres.--Gilbert, Whitney & Johns, Inc., Whippany, NJ, pg. 458
Leonardini, Tony, Jr., Pres.--Artichoke Industries, Inc., Castroville, CA, pg. 87
Leone, John A., Pres. & Chief Exec. Officer--Bonney Forge Corporation, Allentown, PA, pg. 164
Leong, Jack, Chm. Bd., Pres. & Chief Exec. Officer--Mutual Distributors Ltd., Honolulu, HI, pg. 778
Leonhard, R. W., Chm. Bd., Pres. & Chief Exec. Officer--Southwestern Industries, Inc., Rancho Dominguez, CA, pg. 1023
Leonsis, Ted, Chm. Bd., Chief Exec. Officer, Pres. & New Bus. Contact--Redgate Communications Corp., Vero Beach, FL, pg. 919
Leoussis, Nicos J., Mng. Dir.--J. N. Leoussis Advertising & Marketing S.A., Athens,, Greece, pg. 1072
LePage, Bernard, Pres.--Christian Memorial Cultural Center, Rochester Hills, MI, pg. 249
Lepore, Albert, Pres.--Mulach Steel Corporation, Bridgeville, PA, pg. 775
Lepore, Alfred, Pres.--Ferrara Foods & Confections, Inc., New York, NY, pg. 407
Lepore, Guy, Pres.--Monitor Aerospace Corporation, Amityville, NY, pg. 765
Lerch, Howard D., Sr., Pres.--Mazo Lerch Company, Inc., Alexandria, VA, pg. 725
Lerner, Mike, Pres.--Marisa Christina Inc., New York, NY, pg. 707
Lervick, Rodger O., Pres.--Twin City Foods, Inc., Stanwood, WA, pg. 1122
LeSaffre, Peter, Chm. Bd. & Pres.--R.W. Electronics, Andover, MA, pg. 908
Leser, Bernard H., Pres.--The Conde Nast Publications Inc., New York, NY, pg. 19
Lesh, Charles P., Chm., Pres. & Treas.--Holcomb & Hoke Mfg. Company, Inc., Indianapolis, IN, pg. 538
Lesher, Richard, Pres.--Nation's Business, Washington, DC, pg. 794
Lessen, Frank, Pres.--Precision Plastics Inc., Columbia City, IN, pg. 885
Lesser, Stanford J., Pres.--Alba Forwarding Co., Inc., Jersey City, NJ, pg. 30
Lester, Raymond R., Pres.--J.L. Lester & Son, Inc., Rockmart, GA, pg. 668
Lester, Stan, Chm. Bd.--California Apricot Advisory Board, Walnut Creek, CA, pg. 209
Letica, Illija, Pres. & Chief Exec. Officer--Letica Corporation, Rochester Hills, MI, pg. 668
Lettmann, John W., Pres.--Malt-O-Meal Company, Minneapolis, MN, pg. 703
Letts, Charles E., Jr., Pres. & Chief Exec. Officer--Letts Industries, Inc., Detroit, MI, pg. 668
Letts, W. Jackson, Chm. Bd. & Pres.--Fairbanks Morse Pump Corporation, Kansas City, KS, pg. 397
Leum, Leonard L., Pres.--Pioneer Supermarkets, Los Angeles, CA, pg. 872
Levenson, Barbara L., Pres. & Chief Exec. Officer--Levenson & Hill, Inc., Irving, TX, pg. 670
Levering, Dennis E., Pres.--Furnival/State Machinery Co., Lancaster, PA, pg. 437
Levi, Kenneth, Pres.--Mayer Myers Paper Company, Memphis, TN, pg. 724
Levin, Jerry W., Pres. & Chief Exec. Officer--Revlon, Inc., New York, NY, pg. 696
Levin, Louis M., Pres. & Treas.--Midwest Petroleum Co., Saint Louis, MO, pg. 752
Levin, Michael S., Pres. & Chief Exec. Officer--Titan Industrial Corp., New York, NY, pg. 1099
Levin, Ralph, Pres.--Sturgis Iron & Metal Company, Inc., Sturgis, MI, pg. 1055
Levine, David, Pres.--Fashion Shop of Kentucky Inc., Louisville, KY, pg. 403
Levine, Richard, Pres. & Chief Exec. Officer--Alleson of Rochester, Inc., Rochester, NY, pg. 37
Levine, Sol, Pres.--Revlon Group Inc., New York, NY, pg. 695
Levit, Milton, Pres.--Grocers Supply Co. Inc., Houston, TX, pg. 488
Leviton, H., Pres.--Leviton Mfg. Co., Inc., Little Neck, NY, pg. 671
Levitt, Bruce, Pres. & Chief Creative Officer--Pollak Levitt Chaiet, Advertising, Atlanta, GA, pg. 879
Levitt, Michael J., Pres.--Michael's Development Company, Marlton, NJ, pg. 747
Levy, Barry W., Chm. Bd., Chief Exec. Officer & Communications Dir.--Levy Security Consultants, Limited, Chicago, IL, pg. 672
Levy, Edward C., Jr., Pres. & Treas.--Edward C. Levy Co., Inc., Detroit, MI, pg. 672
Levy, Frank L., Pres. & Chief Exec. Officer--L & L Oil Company, Inc., Metairie, LA, pg. 647
Levy, Jack, Pres.--Jack Levy Associates, Chicago, IL, pg. 672
Levy, Joel M., Pres.--Rice Food Markets Inc., Houston, TX, pg. 931
Levy, Michael R., Chm. & Pres.--Mediatex Communications Corporation, Austin, TX, pg. 735
Levy, Nessim, Pres. & Chief Exec. Officer--Level Export Sales Corp., New York, NY, pg. 670
Levy, Philip J., Pres.--Jacob Levy & Bros., Inc., Louisville, KY, pg. 672
Levy, Robert, Pres. & Chief Oper. Officer--Norman Levy Associates, Inc., Southfield, MI, pg. 672
Levy, Sam, Pres.--Schwegmann Giant Super Markets, New Orleans, LA, pg. 980
Levy, Sam, Chief Exec. Officer--Mactavish Machine Manufacturing Company, Richmond, VA, pg. 698
Levy, Walter, Pres.--Rockville Fabrics Corporation, New York, NY, pg. 942
Lewellen, William H., Pres.--Maritz Marketing Research, Inc., Fenton, MO, pg. 707
Lewin, Joseph, Chm. Bd. & Pres.--Health Vitamin Company, Inc., Yonkers, NY, pg. 521

Lewis, Byron E., Chm. & Chief Exec. Officer--Uniworld Group, Inc., New York, NY, pg. 1139
Lewis, Delbert R., Pres.--Media America Corp., Phoenix, AZ, pg. 734
Lewis, Donald D., Pres. & Chief Exec. Officer--Donald D. Lewis Advertising, Burbank, CA, pg. 672
Lewis, Eugene, Pres.--Lewis & Coker Super Markets, Houston, TX, pg. 673
Lewis, Fred H., Pres. & Treas.--Lewis Advertising Agency, Newark, NJ, pg. 672
Lewis, Jack S., Pres.--MBS Holding, Inc., Arlington, TX, pg. 691
Lewis, Jack S., Pres.--Mayfield Building Supply Co., Arlington, TX, pg. 691
Lewis, Jesse, Chm. Bd., Pres. & Chief Exec. Officer--Consumers Markets Inc., Springfield, MO, pg. 277
Lewis, John H., Jr., Chm. Bd. & Pres.--Lewis Communications, Inc., Mobile, AL, pg. 673
Lewis, Leslie B., Chm. & Pres.--Asahi/America, Inc., Malden, MA, pg. 87
Lewis, Michael A., Pres. & Chief Exec. Officer--Ticor Title Guarantee Co., New York, NY, pg. 1096
Lewis, R. Jack, Jr., Pres. & Chief Exec. Officer--Lewis Brothers Bakeries, Inc., Evansville, IN, pg. 673
Lewis, R.T., Pres.--Roydon Wear, Inc., New York, NY, pg. 283
Lewis, Richard A., Pres. & Chief Exec. Officer--Lewis Homes Management Corp., Upland, CA, pg. 673
Lewis, Richard T., Pres.--Coordinated Apparel, Inc., New York, NY, pg. 283
Lewis, Rob, Chief Oper. Officer--Perfection Company, Gering, NE, pg. 680
Lewis, Ronald E., Pres.--Vic Manufacturing, Minneapolis, MN, pg. 1149
Lewis, William, Chm. Bd., Pres. & Chief Exec. Officer--Career Blazers Inc., New York, NY, pg. 218
Lewitt, Bert, Pres.--Morley Construction Co., Inc., Santa Monica, CA, pg. 770
Lezin, Jeremy, Pres.--Salz Leathers, Inc., Santa Cruz, CA, pg. 968
Lezin, Norman S., Chm. Bd.--Salz Leathers, Inc., Santa Cruz, CA, pg. 968
Libby, Henry G., Chm. Bd. & Pres.--The Disston Co., Greensboro, NC, pg. 339
Liberman, Maurice, Pres.--Certified Corp., Brockton, MA, pg. 236
Liberman, Z., Pres.--Talk-A-Phone Co., Chicago, IL, pg. 1077
Licht, J.M., Pres. & Chief Exec. Officer--Duraco Products, Inc., Streamwood, IL, pg. 354
Lichtendahl, Kenneth, Pres.--Hudepohl-Schoenling Brewing Company, Cincinnati, OH, pg. 550
Lichtenstein, Howard, Pres. & Chief Oper. Officer--American Life Insurance Company of New York, New York, NY, pg. 778
Lichter, Robert, Pres. & Chief Exec. Officer--John Burnham & Co., San Diego, CA, pg. 194
Lida, Robert S., Pres.--Lida Advertising Company, Wichita, KS, pg. 674
Liddy, Richard A., Pres. & Chief Exec. Officer--General American Life Insurance Co., St. Louis, MO, pg. 448
Liebenow, Larry, Pres. & Chief Exec. Officer--Quaker Fabric Corporation, Fall River, MA, pg. 903
Liebenstein, John B., Pres.--The Brady Company, Menomonee Falls, WI, pg. 171
Lieberman, Mark H., Pres.--Londontown Holdings Corporation, Eldersburg, MD, pg. 681
Lieberman, Mark H., Pres.--Londontown Corporation, Eldersburg, MD, pg. 682
Lieberman, Mark T., Pres. & Chief Oper. Officer--Lieberman-Appalucci, Allentown, PA, pg. 675
Lieberman, Paul J., Pres.--Superior Linen & Drapery Company, Hackensack, NJ, pg. 1064
Lieberman, Stephen, Pres., Chief Exec. & Chief Oper. Officer--Carousel Snack Bars Of Minnesota, Minneapolis, MN, pg. 224
Liebermann, Thomas R., Chm Bd., Pres. & Chief Oper. Officer--Kaye Instruments, Inc., Bedford, MA, pg. 619
Liebman, Charles, Pres.--Coilcraft, Inc., Cary, IL, pg. 259
Liedel, G. Laurence, Pres.--The Betham Corporation, Middlesex, NJ, pg. 147
Lienau, Robert, Jr., Pres.--Trend Offset Printing Services, Los Alamitos, CA, pg. 1109
Lieppe, Charles, Pres. & Chief Exec. Officer--Pen Holdings, Inc., Brentwood, TN, pg. 856
Light, L. L., Pres. & Chief Oper. Officer--L. B. Smith, Inc., Camp Hill, PA, pg. 1013
Lightfoot, Robert, Acting Exec. Dir.--Arizona Lottery, Phoenix, AZ, pg. 82
Ligon, Ed D., Chm. Bd. & Pres.--Orbit Valve International, Inc., Little Rock, AR, pg. 828
Liimatainen, B.C., Pres.--A. Finkl & Sons Co., Chicago, IL, pg. 411
Liles, Jack D., Pres.--TVESCO, Inc., Memphis, TN, pg. 1075
Lillis, William J., Pres. & Chief Exec. Officer--Winterkorn Lillis Inc., Rochester, NY, pg. 1197
Lilly, Ed, Pres. & Chief Exec. Officer--Serta, Inc., Des Plaines, IL, pg. 991
Lilly, George D., Pres. & Treas.--SJL of Kansas Corp., Wichita, KS, pg. 962
Lima, William, Chm. Bd. & Pres.--Russell-Stanley Corporation, Red Bank, NJ, pg. 957
Lin, Leon C., Pres.--H. Salt Seafood Restaurants, Monterey Park, CA, pg. 967
Lincoln, George A., Chm. Bd. & Pres.--Lincoln Industries, Lincoln, NE, pg. 676
Lindahl, Herbert W., Pres. & Chief Oper. Officer--State Industries Inc., Ashland City, TN, pg. 1041
Lindberg, Neal R., Pres.--Peoples Electric Company, Inc., Saint Paul, MN, pg. 859
Lindbloom, Paul M., Pres.--Acrometal Companies, Inc., Brainerd, MN, pg. 14
Lindemann, D.L., Pres. & Chief Exec. Officer--Citizens Gas & Coke Utility, Indianapolis, IN, pg. 250
Lindenbach, Patrick, Pres. & Chief Exec. Officer--Nalleys Fine Foods, Tacoma, WA, pg. 25
Linder, Douglas, Pres.--Cargill Citro-America, Inc., Minneapolis, MN, pg. 219
Linder, H. Willard, Pres. & Sec.--Minnesota Electric Supply Company, Willmar, MN, pg. 757
Linder, James L., Pres.--Linder & Associates, Inc., Wichita, KS, pg. 676
Lindley, James H., Pres.--Moyer Products, Inc., Fresno, CA, pg. 774
Lindner, Keith E., Pres. & Chief Oper. Officer--Chiquita Brands International, Inc., Cincinnati, OH, pg. 53
Lindner, Keith E., Pres. & Chief Oper. Officer--Chiquita Brands, Inc., Cincinnati, OH, pg. 53
Lindner, Richard E., Jr., Pres.--Thriftway, Inc., Cincinnati, OH, pg. 1095
Lindner, Robert D., Jr., Pres.--United Dairy Farmers, Inc., Cincinnati, OH, pg. 1131
Lindner, S. Craig, Pres. & Chief Oper. Officer--Spelling Entertainment Group, Inc., Cincinnati, OH, pg. 54
Lindquist, Philip, Pres.--Rena-Ware Distributors Inc., Redmond, WA, pg. 926
Lindsay, Edward W., Jr., Pres.--Lindsay Manufacturing Inc., Ponca City, OK, pg. 676
Lindsay, Marsha, Pres. & Chief Exec. Officer--Lindsay, Stone & Briggs Advertising, Inc., Madison, WI, pg. 676
Lindsay, Mike, Pres. & Chief Exec. Officer--Cray Communications Inc., Annapolis Junction, MD, pg. 297
Lindsay, Russ, Pres.--Indeck Energy Services, Inc., Buffalo Grove, IL, pg. 564
Lindsey, Bobby, Pres.--Dixie Oil Company, Tifton, GA, pg. 341
Lindstrom, Raymond W., Pres.--Restaurants Unlimited, Seattle, WA, pg. 929
Lindstrom, Richard, Pres.--Columbia General Life Insurance Co., Laguna Hills, CA, pg. 1127
Linett, Caryl, Pres. & Creative Dir.--Linett & Harrison, Millburn, NJ, pg. 676
Ling, John, Pres. & Chief Exec. Officer--Bettcher Manufacturing Corp., Cleveland, OH, pg. 148
Lingle, Glann C., Pres.--Paramount Petroleum Corp., Paramount, CA, pg. 848
Link, Perry, Pres.--O.P. Link Handle Company, Salem, IN, pg. 676
Linkous, R.E., Pres. & Chief Exec. Officer--Linkous Construction Company, Inc., Memphis, TN, pg. 677
Linn, Randy, Pres.--Linn Products, Inc., Charlotte, MI, pg. 677
Linsmayer, J. Nicholas, Pres.--Villaume Industries, Inc., Saint Paul, MN, pg. 1151
Linzer, Morton A., Pres. & Treas.--Linzer Products Corp., Flushing, NY, pg. 677
Lionheart, Ely, Pres.--QST Industries, Inc., Chicago, IL, pg. 902
Lipari, Francis J., Pres. & Chief Exec. Officer--Communication & Design Agency Inc., Latham, NY, pg. 269
Lipeles, Richard, Pres.--PacifiCare of California, Cypress, CA, pg. 1127
Lipke, Brian J., Pres. & Chief Exec. Officer--Gibraltar Steel Corp., Buffalo, NY, pg. 456
Lipkin, Edward B., Pres.--National Property Analysts, Inc., Philadelphia, PA, pg. 792
Lipman, Ira A., Chm. & Pres.--Guardsmark, Inc., Memphis, TN, pg. 492
Lipman, Michael, Pres. & Chief Oper. Officer--Jameco Industries, Inc., Wyandanch, NY, pg. 588
Lipman, Robert S., Pres.--Lipman, Richmond, Greene, New York, NY, pg. 677
Lipner, William E., Pres. & Chief Exec. Officer--NFO Research, Inc., Greenwich, CT, pg. 780
Lipoff, Steven, Pres., Treas. & Chief Fin. Officer--Butler Foods, Inc., Philadelphia, PA, pg. 197
Lippe, George, Pres. & Chief Exec. Officer--Trammell Crow Company, Dallas, TX, pg. 1106
Lippincott, Thomas J., Pres. & Treas.--Nebraska-Iowa Supply Company, Blair, NE, pg. 796
Lipscomb, Michael S., Pres. & Chief Exec. Officer--Argo-Tech Corporation, Cleveland, OH, pg. 82
Lipsky, W. Robert, Pres.--QLM Associates, Inc., Princeton, NJ, pg. 902
Lipson, David, Pres.--Knightbridge Partners, Chicago, IL, pg. 637
Lipton, Harry, Pres. & Chief Exec. Officer--American Aircraft Parts Manufacturing Co., Dearborn, MI, pg. 48
Liquori, Marty, Pres.--Athletic Attic Properties Inc., Gainesville, FL, pg. 94
Lisherness, Harley, Chm. Bd. & Pres.--Roofing Wholesale Co., Inc., Phoenix, AZ, pg. 946
Lisi, Konrad, Pres.--Electro Fiberoptics Corporation, Northborough, MA, pg. 374
List, Donald A., Pres.--Alatec Products, Inc., North Hollywood, CA, pg. 30
List, Herbert A., Jr., Pres.--List Industries, Inc., Deerfield Beach, FL, pg. 677
Litewka, Albert, Pres. & Chief Exec. Officer--Jacobs & Gerber, Inc., Los Angeles, CA, pg. 587
Litoff, Ronald, Pres.--Ronald Litoff, Ltd., New York, NY, pg. 678
Littfin, John A., Pres.--Littfin Lumber Company, Winsted, MN, pg. 678
Little, Christopher, Pres.--Cowles Magazines, Inc., Harrisburg, PA, pg. 291
Littlejohn, B.R., III, Pres. & Chief Exec. Officer--Community Cash Stores, Spartanburg, SC, pg. 270
Littleton, David B., Pres.--American Plastic Toys Inc., Walled Lake, MI, pg. 59
Litvak, Leonard, Chm. Bd., Pres. & Chief Exec. Officer--Champion Boxed Beef, Denver, CO, pg. 238
Litzsinger, Paul R., Pres. & Chief Exec. Officer--Follett Corporation, Chicago, IL, pg. 422
Liuzzi, R.C., Pres. & Chief Exec. Officer--CF Industries, Inc., Long Grove, IL, pg. 200
Livingston, Doug, Pres.--Patriot Direct Dial Systems, Los Angeles, CA, pg. 1180
Livingston, Phil K., Pres. & Chief Exec. Officer--Citizens National Bancshares Inc., Hammond, LA, pg. 250
Livingston, Robert, Chm., Pres. & Chief Exec. Officer--Grand Banks Yachts, Ltd., Greenwich, CT, pg. 475
Livingston, Roger, Pres. & Chief Exec. Officer--Livingston & Company, Seattle, WA, pg. 679
Ljungberg, Robert, Chm. Bd., Pres., Chief Exec. & Chief Oper. Officer--Ultra Tool & Plastics, Inc., Amherst, NY, pg. 1125
Llaneza, Frank, Pres.--Villazon Company Inc., Tampa, FL, pg. 1152
Llewellyn, John S., Jr., Pres. & Chief Exec. Officer--Ocean Spray Cranberries, Inc., Lakeville, MA, pg. 820
Lloyd, Harold S., Pres.--Lloyd Controls, Inc., Mountlake Terrace, WA, pg. 679
Lobel, Henry K., Chm. Bd. & Pres.--Smith-Edwards-Dunlap Company, Philadelphia, PA, pg. 1012
Lockard, Ken, Pres.--Lockard Construction, Inc., Waterloo, IA, pg. 680
Lockhart, Freda L., Pres. & Chief Exec. Officer--Lockhart Cadillac Inc., Indianapolis, IN, pg. 680
Lockhart, Gary, Pres.--Outdoor Venture Corp., Stearns, KY, pg. 832
Lockhart, Keith E., Pres.--Lockhart & Pettus, Inc., New York, NY, pg. 680
Locks, Clifford K., Pres.--Locks Advertising Agency, East Northport, NY, pg. 680
Lockwood, Earl F., Pres. & Chief Exec. Officer--Betac International Corporation, Alexandria, VA, pg. 147
Lockwood, Robert, Pres.& Chief Exec. Officer--Our Sunday Visitor, Inc., Huntington, IN, pg. 832
Loder, Andrew, Dir.-Opers.--Walnut Grove-Nutrena Feed Div., Cargill, Inc., Atlantic, IA, pg. 219
Lodge, Thomas R., Pres.--Delaware Ribbon Manufacturers, Inc., Philadelphia, PA, pg. 326
Lodi, Giorgio, Mng. Dir.--BSB Italia, Milan,, Italy, pg. 110
Loeb, H. Richard, Pres.--Piknik Products Company, Inc., Montgomery, AL, pg. 870
Loeber, George, Pres.--Loeber Motors, Inc., Chicago, IL, pg. 680
Loeffler, Martin H., Pres.--Amphenol Corporation, Wallingford, CT, pg. 648
Loewenberg, William Ira, Pres.--Southern Leather Company, Memphis, TN, pg. 1021
Lofgren, Carlton R., Pres.--McAnally Enterprises, Inc., Yucaipa, CA, pg. 726
Loft, John D., Chm. Bd. & Pres.--Loft's Seeds, Inc., Bound Brook, NJ, pg. 681
Logan, Oran, Pres. & Chief Oper. Officer--Alamo Group, Inc., Seguin, TX, pg. 29
Logghe, Eugene A., Pres.--Logghe Stamping Company, Fraser, MI, pg. 681
Loghry, Gerald, Pres.--Fleischli Oil Company, Inc., Cheyenne, WY, pg. 417
Lohaus, Peter, Pres.--Tetko, Inc., Briarcliff Manor, NY, pg. 1089
Lohman, Gordon R., Pres. & Chief Exec. Officer--Amsted Industries Incorporated, Chicago, IL, pg. 68
Lohmeyer, Richard J., Pres.--Lohmeyer Simpson Communications, Inc., Morristown, NJ, pg. 681
Lohse, Herb, Pres.--Midwest Auto Parts Distributors, Inc., Saint Paul, MN, pg. 751
Lois, George, Chm. & Chief Exec. Officer--Lois/USA, New York, NY, pg. 681
Lom, Thomas, Pres.--William Douglas McAdams Inc., New York, NY, pg. 726
Lombard, George E., Pres. & Chief Exec. Officer--Lombard Company, Alsip, IL, pg. 681
London, Eric, Pres.--London Litho Aluminum Co., Inc., Lincolnwood, IL, pg. 681
Loney, Robert T., Pres.--Fay, Spofford & Thorndike, Inc., Lexington, MA, pg. 404
Long, Charles A. Jr., Chm. Bd. & Pres.--Sullivan Long & Hagerty, Inc., Birmingham, AL, pg. 1057
Long, David R., Pres. & Chief Exec. Officer--Rice Growers Association of California, West Sacramento, CA, pg. 931
Long, Jonathan R., Pres. & Chief Fin. Officer--J. E. Higgins Lumber Co., Concord, CA, pg. 533
Long, R. Dean, Pres.--Evanston Bank, Evanston, IL, pg. 483
Long, William D., Chm. Bd. & Pres.--Waremart Inc., Boise, ID, pg. 1163
Longsworth, Charles, Chm., Pres. & Chief Exec. Officer--Colonial Williamsburg Foundation, Williamsburg, VA, pg. 264
Longtin, George A., Pres.--Cepco, Manchester, CT, pg. 263
Lonsdorf, Joseph C., Pres.--Tausche Martin Lonsdorf, Atlanta, GA, pg. 1080
Loomis, Charles E., Jr., Pres.--Loomis Brothers, Inc., Cedar Rapids, IA, pg. 683
Looper, R.K., Pres. & Chief Oper. Officer--Cal-Maine Foods, Inc., Jackson, MS, pg. 208
Lorber, Arnold, Pres.--Lorber Industries Of California, Gardena, CA, pg. 683
Lorberbaum, Alan S., Pres.--Aladdin Mills Inc., Dalton, GA, pg. 29
Lord, Donald, Pres.--Chernin's Shoes, Chicago, IL, pg. 243
Lorn, Bernard, Pres.--Inner Secrets, Inc., Hoboken, NJ, pg. 570
Lortz, Gary, Pres. & New Bus. Contact--Lortz Direct Marketing Inc., Omaha, NE, pg. 684
LoRusso, Michael, Pres.--The Economics Press, Inc., Fairfield, NJ, pg. 367
Los, Hendric J.M., Pres.--Walker Magnetics Group, Inc., Worcester, MA, pg. 1160
Loschengruber, Albert, Mng. Dir.--BSB Frankfurt Werbeagentur GmbH, Frankfurt/Main,, Germany, pg. 109
Losurdo, Michael, Pres.--Losurdo Foods, Inc., Hackensack, NJ, pg. 684
Lougee, Alan T., Pres.--The Chicago Faucet Co., Des Plaines, IL, pg. 245

Loughlin, Richard J., Pres. & Chief Exec. Officer--Century 21 Real Estate Corp., Irvine, CA, pg. 744
Loughran, Joseph E., Pres.--Airline Hydraulics Corporation, Bensalem, PA, pg. 27
Louis, Stillman A., Pres.--Chemstone Corp., Strasburg, VA, pg. 242
Love, Donald, Pres.--Clover Financial Corporation, Merchantville, NJ, pg. 256
Love, Robert D., Pres.--Love Box Company, Inc., Wichita, KS, pg. 685
Love, Rodney, Pres.--Grocers Equipment Co., Los Angeles, CA, pg. 237
Love, Rodney, Pres.--Crown Grocers, Inc., Los Angeles, CA, pg. 237
Loveall, Gregg, Chief Rep.--Dentsu, Young & Rubicam/ Shanghai, Shanghai, People's Republic of China, pg. 330
Loveland, Peter G., Pres., Treas. & Gen. Counsel--Maze Nails, Peru, IL, pg. 725
Lovell, Gerald, Pres.--Fargo Glass & Paint Company, Fargo, ND, pg. 399
Lovitz, David D., Pres. & Chief Oper. Officer--The Hartz Mountain Corp., Harrison, NJ, pg. 514
Lovro, Elton O., Gen. Mgr.--Finley Farmers Grain Elevator Company, Finley, ND, pg. 411
Low, K. Prescott, Chm. Bd., Pres. & Publr.--George W. Prescott Publishing Co., Quincy, MA, pg. 887
Lowe, Don F., Pres. & Chief Exec. Officer--Sir Speedy, Inc., Laguna Hills, CA, pg. 613
Lowe, J.B., Jr., Chm. Bd., Pres. & Chief Exec. Officer--TD Industries Inc., Dallas, TX, pg. 1072
Lowe, Thomas P., Pres.--Lyman Lumber Company, Excelsior, MN, pg. 689
Lowe, William C., Pres., Chief Exec. & Chief Oper. Officer--Gulfstream Holdings Corporation, Savannah, GA, pg. 494
Lowenstein, Irwin L., Pres. & Chief Exec. Officer--Rhodes, Inc., Atlanta, GA, pg. 931
Lower, James, Pres.--Commercial Printers Of Connecticut, Norwich, CT, pg. 268
Lower, Martin A., Pres. & Treas.--Ludlow Textiles Co., Inc., Ludlow, MA, pg. 686
Lowrey, W.A., Chm. Bd., Pres. & Chief Exec. Officer--DDC PerTec, Tucson, AZ, pg. 308
Lowther, Mike, Chm. Bd. & Pres.--World Title Company, Burbank, CA, pg. 1203
Lowy, Rudolph, Chm. Bd., Pres. & Chief Exec. Officer--Pacific States Casualty Co., Los Angeles, CA, pg. 841
Lozelle, James R., Pres. & Chief Exec. Officer--Edgewood Tool & Manufacturing Company, Romulus, MI, pg. 368
Lubs, John, Pres. & Chief Oper. Officer--Mason Shoe Mfg. Co., Chippewa Falls, WI, pg. 718
Lubs, John, Pres. & Chief Oper. Officer--Wissota Trader & B.A. Mason, Chippewa Falls, WI, pg. 718
Lucchetti, D.J., Pres.--Pacific Coast Building Products Inc., Sacramento, CA, pg. 839
Lucchino, Lawrence, Pres.--Baltimore Orioles, Inc., Baltimore, MD, pg. 116
Luddy, Robert, Pres. & Chief Exec. Officer--Captive-Aire Systems, Inc., Youngsville, NC, pg. 216
Ludington, David, Pres. & Chief Oper. Officer--Ludington News Co. Inc., Detroit, MI, pg. 686
Ludlam, Roger J., Pres. & Chief Oper. Officer--S. J. Groves & Sons Company, Minneapolis, MN, pg. 490
Ludlow, Robert B., Pres.--Bedford Industries, Inc., Worthington, MN, pg. 131
Ludt, S.G., Pres., Chief Exec. Officer & Treas.--Columbian Rope Company, Guntown, MS, pg. 266
Ludwick, Edward, Pres.--Fairmont Homes, Inc., Nappanee, IN, pg. 397
Ludwig, Melvin, Chm. Bd. & Pres.--Eagle Electric Mfg. Co., Inc., Long Island City, NY, pg. 362
Luecke, David A., Pres. & Chief Exec. Officer--Riemeier Lumber Company, Inc., Cincinnati, OH, pg. 934
Lugar, Thomas R., Pres.--Thomas L. Green & Co., Inc., Indianapolis, IN, pg. 484
Lugbill, Charles, Chm. Bd. & Pres.--Lugbill Brothers, Inc., Archbold, OH, pg. 686
Lukenbill, Gregg, Owner & Mng. Partner--Sacramento Kings, Sacramento, CA, pg. 965
Lukens, Joseph C., II, Pres.--Insurance Management Associates, Wichita, KS, pg. 572
Luksch, James A., Pres.--Blonder-Tongue Laboratories, Inc., Old Bridge, NJ, pg. 157
Lummis, Larry, Pres.--Sherwood Corporation, Fremont, CA, pg. 570
Lund, Joe, Pres.--Farmhand, Inc., Excelsior, MN, pg. 402
Lunda, Milton A., Pres.--Phoenix Steel, Inc., Eau Claire, WI, pg. 869
Lundberg, Jack, Pres.--Denver Equipment Company, Colorado Springs, CO, pg. 331
Lundberg, Lars, Pres--Young & Rubicam Sweden AB (Holding), Stockholm,, Sweden, pg. 1213
Lundby, Eric, Pres.--Omaha Property & Casualty Co., Omaha, NE, pg. 779
Lundeen, Mark, Pres. & Chief Exec. Officer--Buzz Barton & Associates, Inc., Oak Brook, IL, pg. 123
Lundell, Ulf, Pres.--Alimak Elevator Company, Bridgeport, CT, pg. 34
Lunder, Peter, Pres., Chief Oper. Officer & Sec.--Dexter Shoe Company, Dexter, ME, pg. 334
Lunderstadt, Carl, Pres. & Chief Oper. Officer--Florida Crushed Stone Company, Leesburg, FL, pg. 420
Lundin, Sven, Pres.--Cargocaire Engineering Corporation, Amesbury, MA, pg. 220
Lundy, Richard, Jr., Pres.--Lundy Construction Co., Inc., Williamsport, PA, pg. 687
Lunenfeld, Marilyn, V.P.--Draper Daniels Media Services, Inc., Melrose Park, IL, pg. 348
Lunger, Gary, Pres.--Erie Press Systems, Erie, PA, pg. 386
Lunt, James H., Pres.--Rogers, Lunt & Bowlen Co., Greenfield, MA, pg. 943
Luntz, Andrew, Pres.--Luntz Corporation, Canton, OH, pg. 687
Lupient, James W., Pres. & Treas.--Jim Lupient Enterprises, Golden Valley, MN, pg. 687
Lurio, Lee H., Pres. & Treas.--Elbeco Incorporated, Reading, PA, pg. 372
Luscombe, Kevin, Chm. Bd. & Mng. Dir.--Luscombe and Partners Pty. Ltd., Port Melbourne,, Australia, pg. 344
Luskey, Alvin (Butch), Pres.--Luskeys Western Stores, Inc., Fort Worth, TX, pg. 688
Luskey, Louis, Chm. Bd. & Pres.--Luskeys Western Stores, Inc., Fort Worth, TX, pg. 688
Lussky, Fairleigh, Pres.--Progress Paint Mfg. Co., Louisville, KY, pg. 894
Lustbader, Edward E., Chm. Bd., Pres., Chief Exec. Officer & Treas.--The P.J. Carlin Construction Company, New Rochelle, NY, pg. 220
Luther, Jon, Pres.--Concession Air Corporation, Buffalo, NY, pg. 326
Luttman, Robert W., Pres.--Nibble with Gibble's, Inc., Chambersburg, PA, pg. 806
Lutz, Merritt, Pres. & Chief Oper. Officer--Candle Corporation, Santa Monica, CA, pg. 214
Luxion, W.T., Pres.--Wil-Freds Construction, Inc., Aurora, IL, pg. 1189
Lydick, J. Lee, Pres.--Grant-Lydick Beverage Co., San Antonio, TX, pg. 477
Lyke, A. Douglas, Pres.--Lyke Corporation, Ripon, WI, pg. 688
Lyman, James M., Pres. & Chief Exec. Officer--Industrial General Corporation, Elyria, OH, pg. 566
Lynch, John, Chm. & Pres.--Towers, Perrin, Forster & Crosby, Inc., New York, NY, pg. 1103
Lynch, John J., Pres.--Wm. E. Wright Limited Partnership, West Warren, MA, pg. 1205
Lynch, John J., Pres.--Boye Needle, Chicago, IL, pg. 1205
Lynch, William T., Pres.--Leo Burnett Company, Inc., Chicago, IL, pg. 191
Lynn, Jeffrey G., Chm. Bd., Pres. & Chief Exec. Officer--Dunham's Athleisure Corporation, Waterford, MI, pg. 353
Lynnes, R. Milton, Pres. & Chief Oper. Officer--Grant/ Jacoby, Inc., Chicago, IL, pg. 477
Lyon, James E., Chm. Bd. & Chief Exec. Officer--Ruska Instrument Corporation, Houston, TX, pg. 956
Lyons, E.M., Pres.--Conley Frog & Switch Company, Memphis, TN, pg. 274
Lyons, James E., Pres.--Rowman & Littlefield Publishers, Inc., Lanham, MD, pg. 952
Lyons, R., Pres.--Lehigh-Leopold, Burlington, IA, pg. 608
Lyons, Richard B., Pres.--Monier Roof Tile, Inc., Orange, CA, pg. 765
Lytle, L. Ben, Pres. & Chief Exec. Officer--The Associated Group, Indianapolis, IN, pg. 90
Lytle, R.D., Chm. Bd., Pres. & Chief Exec. Officer--Star Bronze Company, Alliance, OH, pg. 1039
Lytton, Don, Pres.--La-Co Industries, Inc., Chicago, IL, pg. 648
Maahs, Jerry D., Pres.--Alto Shaam Inc., Menomonee Falls, WI, pg. 46
Maas, Curtis, Pres. & Chief Exec. Officer--Lafayette Precision Products Inc., Brooklyn, NY, pg. 906
Maas, Curtis, Pres. & Chief Exec. Officer--Reichel & Drews Inc., Itasca, IL, pg. 906
Maas, Curtis N., Chm. Bd. & Chief Exec. Officer--RDI, Inc., Itasca, IL, pg. 906
Mabe, James G., Pres.--Columbia Farms Inc., Leesville, SC, pg. 265
Mabee, Larry, Pres.--Big Bear Supermarkets No. 3, San Diego, CA, pg. 149
Macaskill, Bridget, Pres. & Chief Oper. Officer--Oppenheimer Management Corp., New York, NY, pg. 719
MacConnell, Christopher J., Pres.--Thomson MacConnell Cadillac, Inc., Cincinnati, OH, pg. 1095
MacDaniels, John Scott, Chief Exec. Officer & Creative Dir.--MacDaniels, Henry & Sproul, Inc., San Francisco, CA, pg. 696
Macdonald, A. Ewan, Pres. & Chief Exec. Officer--Del Monte Foods, San Francisco, CA, pg. 325
MacDonald, Geoffrey, Pres.--American Finance Group, Boston, MA, pg. 52
MacDonald, R.V., Pres.--Butter Kernel Products, Minneapolis, MN, pg. 399
MacDonald, Reid V., Pres. & Chief Exec. Officer--Faribault Foods Inc., Minneapolis, MN, pg. 399
MacDonald, William F., Jr., Chm. Bd., Pres., Chief Exec. & Chief Oper. Officer--E. F. Houghton & Co., Valley Forge, PA, pg. 546
MacDougal, Frank, Pres.--Prudential Mortgage Capital, Newark, NJ, pg. 897
MacDougald, Jim, Pres.--AMI Industries, Inc., Colorado Springs, CO, pg. 5
Macfarlane, Iain, Pres. & Chief Exec. Officer--KNOX International Corp., Knoxville, TN, pg. 638
MacGibbon, W. Douglas, Pres., Treas. & Dir.-Creative--The In-House Agency, Weehawken, NJ, pg. 564
Machado, Gus, Pres. & Chief Exec. Officer--Gus Machado Enterprises, Hialeah, FL, pg. 696
Mack, James E., Pres.--Tyler Refrigeration Corp., Niles, MI, pg. 62
Mack, Jim, Pres.--Frankel & Company, Chicago, IL, pg. 429
Mack, Paul F., Pres.--Mack Printing Company, Easton, PA, pg. 697
Mackenna, Luis, Exec. Dir.--BSB Chile Publicidad, Santiago, , Chile, pg. 109
MacKenzie, Brian S., Pres. & Chief Oper. Officer--Builder Marts of America, Greenville, SC, pg. 187
Mackey, Richard Jr., Pres.--Oliver Oil Company, Inc., Chambersburg, PA, pg. 824
MacKinnon, M.C., Pres.--United Gilsonite Laboratories, Scranton, PA, pg. 1132
MacLean, Barry L., Chm., Pres., Chief Exec. & Chief Oper. Officer--Maclean-Fogg Co., Mundelein, IL, pg. 697
MacLeod, Malcolm W., Pres. & Chief Exec. Officer--Moran Towing & Transporation Co. Inc, Greenwich, CT, pg. 769
MacLeod, Richard, Pres.--Tapco Products Company, Plymouth, MI, pg. 1078
MacNeil, Bruce M., Pres.--Ark-Les Corporation, Watertown, MA, pg. 82
MacPherson, Angus, Pres. & Chief Exec. Officer--Breton Construction, Inc., Irvine, CA, pg. 174
MacPherson, Donald R., Pres. & Chief Exec. Officer--Red Devil Inc., Union, NJ, pg. 918
MacVittie, Paula R., Pres. & Chief Exec. Officer--Caldwell VanRiper Inc., Indianapolis, IN, pg. 209
Maddox, Fontaine A., Jr., Pres.--Tri-State Mack Distributors, Memphis, TN, pg. 1111
Maddox, James A., Pres.--Ermco, Inc., Indianapolis, IN, pg. 387
Madeod, Tom, Pres. & Chief Oper. Officer--Iams Company, Dayton, OH, pg. 561
Madison, Chris, Pres.--Madison Graham Colorgraphics, Inc., Los Angeles, CA, pg. 699
Madonna, Jon C., Chm. & Chief Exec. Officer--KPMG Peat Marwick, New York, NY, pg. 613
Magdovitz, Earl, Pres.--Imperial Manufacturing Company, Memphis, TN, pg. 564
Maged, Jack, Pres. & Chief Oper. Officer--Cox Advertising, New York, NY, pg. 292
Magee, James A., Pres.--The Magee Carpet Company, Bloomsburg, PA, pg. 700
Maghielse, Craig, Chm. Bd., Pres. & Chief Exec. Officer--Maghielse Tool Corporation, Grand Rapids, MI, pg. 700
Magid, Alfred, Pres.--Joshua Meier Corp., North Bergen, NJ, pg. 737
Magill, Larry, Pres.--Direct Response Broadcasting Network, Inc., Philadelphia, PA, pg. 339
Maglathlin, Peter, Dir.--Danbury Mint, Norwalk, CT, pg. 691
Magliocco, Antonio, Jr., Pres.--Peerless Importers, Inc., Brooklyn, NY, pg. 855
Magnano, Louis A., Pres. & Chief Exec. Officer--Blue Bird Coach Lines Inc., Olean, NY, pg. 158
Magnell, Steffen I., Pres.--Sanborn Manufacturing Company, Springfield, MN, pg. 969
Maguire, Cary M., Pres.--Maguire Oil Co., Dallas, TX, pg. 701
Maguire, Robert F., III, Mng. Partner--Maguire Thomas Partners, Los Angeles, CA, pg. 701
Maharam, Donald, Pres.--Maharam Fabric Corporation, Hauppauge, NY, pg. 701
Maharry, Anne, Pres. & Chief Fin. Officer--Bull, Inc., San Diego, CA, pg. 981
Maher, Jeffrey, Pres. & Chief Exec. Officer--MCC, Inc., Essex, CT, pg. 691
Mahler, Darrell, Pres., Gen. Mgr., Adv. & Sls. Promo. Mgr.--Blue Cross Laboratories, Saugus, CA, pg. 160
Mahler, Herbert P., Pres.--Henri's Food Products Co., Inc., Milwaukee, WI, pg. 530
Mahoney, Gerald F., Pres.--Pavey Envelope & Tag Corp., Jersey City, NJ, pg. 852
Mahoney, P. Michael, Pres.--Bankmanagers Corp., Milwaukee, WI, pg. 118
Mahoney, Stephen J., Pres. & Chief Exec. Officer--McInnes Steel Company, Corry, PA, pg. 729
Mahr, Michael, Pres.--Maryland Paper Box Company, Baltimore, MD, pg. 717
Maibach, Benjamin C., III, Pres.--Barton-Malow Enterprises, Inc., Southfield, MI, pg. 123
Maier, A., Pres.--Quality Bakers of America Cooperative, Inc., Greenwich, CT, pg. 903
Maier, Russell, Pres. & Chief Exec. Officer--Republic Engineered Steels, Inc., Massillon, OH, pg. 928
Mains, Donald A., Pres. & Treas.--Tradehome Shoe Stores, Inc., Saint Paul, MN, pg. 1105
Maintz, Antoine, Pres.--Muelhens, Inc., Orange, CT, pg. 774
Maites, Alan, Mng. Dir.--Robinson & Maites, Inc., Chicago, IL, pg. 940
Maitland, John B., Pres.--Business Information Technology, Wilmington, DE, pg. 196
Maiuccoro, John M., Pres. & Treas.--Imperial Pools, Inc., Latham, NY, pg. 564
Makhani, Madan P., Chm. Bd., Pres., Chief Oper. Officer & Chief Fin. Officer--American Foundry Group, Inc., Bixby, OK, pg. 54
Maki, Glen, Pres.--Maki Corporation, Lunenburg, MA, pg. 702
Malecha, Kenneth, Pres.--Best Brands, St. Paul, MN, pg. 146
Maley, John H.P., Pres. & Chief Exec. Officer--Chattanooga Group, Hixson, TN, pg. 241
Malfese, Mark, Pres.--Unistrut Corporation, Ann Arbor, MI, pg. 1130
Malin, Amir J., Co-Pres. & Chief Exec. Officer--October Films, Inc., New York, NY, pg. 821
Malinsky, Aaron, Pres. & Chief Exec. Officer--Victory Markets Inc., Norwich, NY, pg. 1150
Malkani, Roma, Pres. & Chief Exec. Officer--Information Systems & Network Corporation, Bethesda, MD, pg. 567
Malkin, Roger D., Chm. Bd.--Southwide, Inc., New York, NY, pg. 1024
Mallendick, Robert J., Pres. & Treas.--Empire Petroleum, Inc., Toledo, OH, pg. 379
Mallet, Robert I., Pres.--Mallet & Co., Carnegie, PA, pg. 703
Mallett, J.L., Pres.--Thomas Pipe & Steel, Inc., Baton Rouge, LA, pg. 1093
Mallott, Bryon I., Pres. & Chief Exec. Officer--Sealaska Corporation, Juneau, AK, pg. 984
Malloy, W. Manning, Pres. & Treas.--Cheraw Yarn Mills, Inc., Cheraw, SC, pg. 242
Malm, Arnold, Pres.--Office Connection, Inc., Fort Lauderdale, FL, pg. 821
Malone, Tom, Pres.--Milliken & Co., Inc., Spartanburg, SC, pg. 755
Maloos, Vic, Pres. & Chief Exec. Officer--Bovay, Houston, TX, pg. 169
Malpass, F.F., Pres.--East Jordan Iron Works, East Jordan, MI, pg. 362
Malzahn, Edwin, Chm. Bd. & Pres.--Charles Machine Works, Inc., Perry, OK, pg. 240

Manasco, David, Pres. & Chief Exec. Officer--Trina, Inc., Fall River, MA, pg. 1113
Mancini, Brooks T., Pres. & Treas.--B.T. Mancini Co., Inc., Milpitas, CA, pg. 703
Mandel, Jerome M., Pres.--Waterous Company, South Saint Paul, MN, pg. 50
Mandelbaum, Mervyn, Pres. & Chief Exec. Officer--Superba, Inc., Los Angeles, CA, pg. 1063
Mandell, Lawrence, Pres.--Key Food Stores Co-operative, Inc., Brooklyn, NY, pg. 626
Mandell, Robert A., Pres.--Greater Construction Corp., Altamonte Springs, FL, pg. 483
Mandor, Robert, Pres.--Concord Assets Group, Inc., Boca Raton, FL, pg. 272
Maness, John D., Pres.--Dick Bruhn Inc., Salinas, CA, pg. 184
Maness, Kenneth P., Sr., Pres.--Maness Industries, Inc., Long Beach, CA, pg. 703
Maness, Roy J., Pres.--W.H. Weaver Construction Co., Greensboro, NC, pg. 1170
Mang, Robert B., Pres. & Chief Oper. Officer--Woodward & Lothrop/John Wanamaker, Washington, DC, pg. 1201
Mango, Wilfred G., Jr., Pres. & Chief Exec. Officer--George A. Fuller Company, New York, NY, pg. 436
Mangum, F.L., Pres. & V.P.-Contracting Bus. Unit--Flakt Inc., Bahnson Div., Winston-Salem, NC, pg. 416
Manhold, Earl, III, Pres.--Clark Gum Company, Barrington, IL, pg. 252
Manke, Charles, Pres.--Manke Lumber Company, Inc., Tacoma, WA, pg. 704
Mann, John L., Pres.--Associated Aircraft Supply Company, Dallas, TX, pg. 89
Mann, Marcia, Dr., Sec.--The Florida Lottery, Tallahassee, FL, pg. 420
Mann, Marvin L., Chm. & Chief Exec. Officer--Lexmark International, Inc., Greenwich, CT, pg. 673
Mann, Samuel J., Pres. & Chief Exec. Officer--Inverness Corp., Fair Lawn, NJ, pg. 581
Manning, J. William, Sr., Chm. Bd. & Chief Exec. Officer--Manning Equipment, Inc., Louisville, KY, pg. 704
Manning, Thomas A., Pres.--Judd's Incorporated, Washington, DC, pg. 608
Manning, Wayne, Pres.--Bashas, Chandler, AZ, pg. 124
Mannion, John B., Exec. Dir.--American Water Works Association, Denver, CO, pg. 65
Mannlein, William J., Pres. & Chief Exec. Officer--Fleming Packaging Corp., Peoria, IL, pg. 417
Manschot, Robert, Pres. & Chief Exec. Officer--Rural Metro Corporation, Scottsdale, AZ, pg. 956
Mansfield, Michael F., Pres.--Mansfield Oil Company, Gainesville, GA, pg. 704
Mansfield, Terry, Mng. Dir.--The National Magazine Company Ltd., London, United Kingdom, pg. 524
Manzi, James, Pres. & Chief Exec. Officer--Lotus Publishing Corporation, Cambridge, MA, pg. 576
Mara, Edward J., Jr., Pres. & Chief Exec. Officer--American Fuel Cell & Coated Fabrics Co. (Amfuel), Magnolia, AR, pg. 55
Marberg, Edwin, Pres., Chief Exec. Officer & Treas.--MCM Enterprises, Inc., Crawfordsville, IN, pg. 691
Marble, Stephen C., Pres. & Chief Exec. Officer--Nielsen Construction Company, San Diego, CA, pg. 807
Marcalus, Nicholas R., Pres. & Chief Oper. Officer--Marcal Paper Mills, Inc., Elmwood Park, NJ, pg. 706
Marchesano, Carole, Pres.--Goldberg Marchesano Kohlman Inc., Washington, DC, pg. 465
Marchitto, Al, Chm. Bd. & Chief Exec. Officer--Simunico, Inc., Rutherford, NJ, pg. 1007
Marciano, Maurice, Pres.--Guess ?, Inc., Los Angeles, CA, pg. 493
Marcil, William C., Pres. & Publr.--Forum Publishing Company, Fargo, ND, pg. 426
Marclar, Al, Pres.--Trout Inc., Chelan, WA, pg. 1116
Marcucci, Louis L., Chm. Bd. & Pres.--Gonnella Baking Co., Chicago, IL, pg. 469
Marcus, Frank W., Pres.--Harold Leonard & Company, Inc., Union, NJ, pg. 667
Marcus, Jay, Pres.--Halsey Drug Co., Inc., Brooklyn, NY, pg. 502
Marcus, Martin, Pres.--Marcus Brothers Textiles, Inc., New York, NY, pg. 706
Margolin, Sam S., Pres. & Chief Exec. Officer--National Mortgage Company, Memphis, TN, pg. 792
Margolis, Terry, Pres.--Elastic Stop Nut, Union, NJ, pg. 514
Margulies, Alvin, Pres.--Leather Warehouse, Inc., East Rutherford, NJ, pg. 664
Margus, Brad, Pres.--Kitchens Of The Ocean, Inc., Deerfield Beach, FL, pg. 634
Maria, Joseph, Pres.--Wall Colmonoy Corp., Madison Heights, MI, pg. 1160
Marici, Joseph J., Pres.--Messenger Corporation, Phoenix, AZ, pg. 741
Marin, Al, Pres.--Marco Color Labs, Inc., Hawthorne, CA, pg. 706
Marine, Walter S., Pres.--Capital Pants Co., Philadelphia, PA, pg. 215
Marino, Kenneth, Pres.--Orbel Corporation, Phillipsburg, NJ, pg. 828
Marion, James P., III, Pres. & Chief Exec. Officer--Bloomsburg Mills Inc., New York, NY, pg. 158
Marischen, Robert J., Pres.--Huntco Inc., Chesterfield, MO, pg. 554
Markel, John D., Pres., Chief Exec. Officer & Treas.--Smartstar Corporation, Goleta, CA, pg. 1011
Markey, James, Chm. Bd. & Pres.--Action Manufacturing Co., Philadelphia, PA, pg. 15
Markle, Lewis E., Pres. & Chief Oper. Officer--Cowper & Siegfried, Amherst, NY, pg. 291
Markley, Buck, Gen. Mgr.--Manna Pro Partners, Denver, CO, pg. 704
Markoff, Steven, Pres.--A-Mark Financial, Santa Monica, CA, pg. 1
Marks, Julius, Jr., Pres.--Libertyville Lincoln-Mercury Sales, Inc., Libertyville, IL, pg. 674
Marks, Marilyn, Pres. & Chief Exec. Officer--Dorsey Trailers, Inc., Atlanta, GA, pg. 347
Marks, P.J., Pres.--Gomar Manufacturing Co., Inc., Linden, NJ, pg. 469
Marks, Peter, Chm. Bd. & Pres.--Weksler Instruments Corp., Freeport, NY, pg. 1174
Marks, Samuel L., Pres.--Allied Sporting Goods Inc., Louisville, KY, pg. 40
Marks, Steven L., Pres. & Chief Exec. Officer--Kettering Advertising Display Co., Englewood Cliffs, NJ, pg. 626
Markson, Ted, Pres.--Baar & Beards, New York, NY, pg. 107
Marling, Mark E., Chm. Bd. & Pres.--Ed Marling Stores, Inc., Topeka, KS, pg. 710
Marlow, Alan, Pres. & Chief Oper. Officer--Harvey Industries, Inc., Waltham, MA, pg. 515
Marlow, Raymond, Pres.--Marlow Industries, Dallas, TX, pg. 710
Marlowe, Robert, Pres.--Frazier-Williams Chevrolet GEO, Milford, OH, pg. 430
Marmis, Cary, Chm. Bd. & Pres.--Empire West Companies, Inc., Tucson, AZ, pg. 380
Marold, Ron, Pres.--Maxcor Manufacturing, Inc., Colorado Springs, CO, pg. 722
Marolda, Robert L., Pres.--Energy Minerals Corporation, Denver, CO, pg. 381
Marontate, Michael, Pres.--Marontate & Co., Auburn Hills, MI, pg. 713
Marotta, Thomas S., Chm. Bd. & Pres.--Marotta Scientific Controls, Inc., Montville, NJ, pg. 713
Marquardt, James, Pres.--Marquardt & Roche Inc., Stamford, CT, pg. 713
Marquis, Dale, Pres.--Pacifica Real Estate Group, Santa Barbara, CA, pg. 842
Marquis, Dale M., Pres.--Invest West Financial Corporation, Santa Barbara, CA, pg. 842
Marquis, Douglas P., Pres. & Chief Oper. Officer--Handgards Inc., Northbrook, IL, pg. 504
Marr, Malcolm, Pres.--Imperial Litho/Graphics, Inc., Phoenix, AZ, pg. 564
Marram, Edward P., Dr., Chm. Bd., Pres., Chief Exec. Officer & Treas.--Geo-Centers, Inc., Newton Center, MA, pg. 452
Marranzino, Pasquale, Jr., Pres.--Karsh & Hagan, Inc., Englewood, CO, pg. 617
Marriner, E. Randolph, Pres., Chief Exec. Officer--Marriner Marketing Communications, Inc., Columbia, MD, pg. 713
Mars, Forrest E., Jr., Chm. Bd. & Co-Pres.--Mars, Incorporated, McLean, VA, pg. 713
Mars, George, Pres.--Key Plastics, Inc., Livonia, MI, pg. 627
Mars, George, Pres.--Superior Division of Key Plastics, Felton, PA, pg. 627
Marsden, David, Partner--Matter Galbucci Leo Burnett, Werbeagentur, Zurich,, Switzerland, pg. 193
Marsello, Robert, Pres.--Imperial Pearl Company, Inc., Providence, RI, pg. 564
Marsh, Daniel C., Pres.--Premarc Corporation, Durand, MI, pg. 886
Marsh, G. Reid, III, Pres.--Marsh Furniture Company, High Point, NC, pg. 714
Marsh, Garry C., Pres.--Riverside Press, Inc., Dallas, TX, pg. 937
Marshall, Charles R., Pres. & Gen. Mgr.--Westlie Motor Company, Minot, ND, pg. 1183
Marshall, John L., III, Pres.--Marshall Contractors Inc., Rumford, RI, pg. 714
Marshall, Lowell R., Pres. & Chief Exec. Officer--Republic Storage Systems Company Inc., Canton, OH, pg. 928
Marshall, R.J., Pres.--R. J. Marshall Co., Southfield, MI, pg. 714
Marshall, Raymond, Pres.--Evans Brothers Company, Inc., Waukesha, WI, pg. 390
Marshall, Robin L., Pres. & Chief Exec. Officer--Great Lakes Technologies Corp., Kalamazoo, MI, pg. 482
Marshman, John C., Pres.--Sioux Falls Construction Company, Sioux Falls, SD, pg. 1008
Marsiglia, A.J., Chm. & Pres.--Responsive Marketing Communications, Inc., Schaumburg, IL, pg. 929
Marsilius, N.M. III, Pres. & Treas.--The Producto Machine Co., Bridgeport, CT, pg. 893
Marstiller, Phyllis C., Pres. & Chief Oper. Officer--Blue Cross & Blue Shield of Virginia, Richmond, VA, pg. 160
Martell, C. Ron, Chm. Bd. & Pres.--Microdynamics, Inc., Dallas, TX, pg. 749
Marteney, Lee, Pres.--Packaging Products & Design, Santa Ana, CA, pg. 842
Marti, Wayne, Pres.--Ott Food Products, Carthage, MO, pg. 831
Martin, A. Jay, Pres.--National Safety Associates, Memphis, TN, pg. 793
Martin, Bernard, Pres.--Carpenter Rigging, San Francisco, CA, pg. 224
Martin, Brian, Pres.--Refrigeration Supplies Distributors, Monterey Park, CA, pg. 921
Martin, Carlton, Pres.--Martins Abbatoir & Wholesale Meats Inc., Godwin, NC, pg. 716
Martin, Dennis K., Pres.--The Marlin Company, Springfield, MO, pg. 710
Martin, Edward, Pres.--The Dunlap Companies, Fort Worth, TX, pg. 353
Martin, Elliot, Chm. Bd., Pres. & Chief Exec. Officer--Windsor Publications, Inc., Chatsworth, CA, pg. 1196
Martin, Eugene, Pres.--FoodCraft Equipment Co., Inc., Lancaster, PA, pg. 860
Martin, Gerry L., Pres. & Chief Oper. Officer--Horizon Paper Co., Inc., New York, NY, pg. 544
Martin, Gordon, Chm. Bd., Pres. & Chief Exec. Officer--Martin Forest Industries, Healdsburg, CA, pg. 715
Martin, J. Edward, Partner--Albert C. Martin & Associates, Los Angeles, CA, pg. 714
Martin, J. Landis, Chm. Bd., Pres. & Chief Exec. Officer--Tremont Corporation, Denver, CO, pg. 1109
Martin, James R., Pres.--Meadville Forging Co., Meadville, PA, pg. 733
Martin, Joe R., Chm. Bd. & Pres.--Martin Sprocket & Gear, Inc., Arlington, TX, pg. 715
Martin, Kenneth D., Pres.--Martin Door Mfg., Inc., Salt Lake City, UT, pg. 714
Martin, Patrick, Exec. V.P.--Shelby & Shane Marketing Communications, Cincinnati, OH, pg. 996
Martin, Rex, Pres. & Chief Exec. Officer--Nibco, Inc., Elkhart, IN, pg. 806
Martin, Ruben S., III, Chm. Bd. & Pres.--Martin Gas Corporation, Kilgore, TX, pg. 715
Martin, W.G., Pres.--Nitram Energy inc., Orchard Park, NY, pg. 807
Martin, W.G., Pres.--Burgess Manning, Inc., Orchard Park, NY, pg. 807
Martin, Wayne, Pres. & Chief Exec. Officer--Plains Co-op Oil Mill, Lubbock, TX, pg. 873
Martindale, William A., Chm. Bd., Pres. & Chief Exec. Officer--Martrade Ltd., Santa Fe Springs, CA, pg. 716
Martinen, John A., Pres.--Globus-Gateway/Cosmos Tourama, Rego Park, NY, pg. 464
Martino, Anthony A., Chm. Bd. & Pres.--Maaco Enterprises Inc., King of Prussia, PA, pg. 694
Martiny, Kim R., Chm. Bd., Pres. & Chief Exec. Officer--Martiny & Company, Cincinnati, OH, pg. 716
Martire, Robert, Chm. Bd. & Pres.--Atlantic to Pacific Bedding Corp., Bronx, NY, pg. 95
Martz, Carrie, Chm. Bd. & Pres.--Martz & Wadas, Scottsdale, AZ, pg. 716
Marvell, Edward M., Pres.--Curtis Instruments, Inc., Mount Kisco, NY, pg. 305
Marvin, Frank R., Pres.--Marvin Lumber & Cedar Company, Warroad, MN, pg. 716
Marx, Arthur A., Pres. & Chief Exec. Officer--Merling, Marx & Seidman, Inc., New York, NY, pg. 741
Mascarin, Ed, Pres.--Crane Carrier Company, Tulsa, OK, pg. 296
Masek, Joseph P., Pres.--Masek Distributing Inc., Gering, NE, pg. 717
Mashburn, Harry L., Pres. & Treas.--Mashburn Construction Company, Columbia, SC, pg. 717
Maslin, Harvey L., Pres. & Chief Oper. Officer--Western Temporary Services, Inc., Walnut Creek, CA, pg. 1181
Maslow, Lester, Chm. Bd. & Pres.--Best Manufacturing, Inc., New York, NY, pg. 146
Mason, Charles T., Jr., Chm. Bd. & Pres.--Mason & Madison, Inc., New Haven, CT, pg. 718
Mason, David D. S., Pres., Chief Exec. Officer, Chief Fin. Officer & Treas.--Mason Oil Company, Ione, CA, pg. 718
Mason, Elizabeth A., Pres.--Friedman Benjamin Inc. Adv., New York, NY, pg. 433
Mason, Marc, Co-Pres. & Chief Oper. Officer-Production Sector--Flambeau Products Corp., Middlefield, OH, pg. 809
Mason, William T., Pres. & Chief Exec. Officer--Adra Systems, Inc., Lowell, MA, pg. 18
Massa, Joseph, Pres. & Gen. Mgr.--House of Bianchi, Boston, MA, pg. 546
Massaro, Carl, Pres.--Ajax Manufacturing Company, Inc., Hillsborough, NJ, pg. 28
Massey, C. Knox, Jr., Pres.--Tucker Wayne/Luckie & Company, Birmingham, AL, pg. 1118
Massey, Donald E., Pres. & Chief Exec. Officer--Don Massey Cadillac Inc., Plymouth, MI, pg. 719
Massey, Donald E., Pres.--Massey Cadillac, Inc., Orlando, FL, pg. 719
Massicott, Andre J., Pres. & Chief Oper. Officer--Heath Consultants Incorporated, Stoughton, MA, pg. 524
Massman, Henry J., IV, Pres.--Massman Construction Company, Kansas City, MO, pg. 719
Masterson, Patrick F., Pres.--Topflight Corp., York, PA, pg. 1102
Masterson, Peggy Bell, Pres. & Creative Dir.--Masterson Rothberg Advertising, New York, NY, pg. 720
Matarese, James M., Chm., Pres. & Chief Exec. Officer--Phoenix International, Inc., Beverly, NJ, pg. 868
Matathia, Ira, Pres., Chief Exec. Officer--Chiat/Day/Mojo Inc. Advertising, Toronto,, Canada, pg. 245
Mateer, Mike, Pres.--Mount Vernon Neon, Mount Vernon, IL, pg. 391
Matellini, Dante, Chm. Bd. & Pres.--Aero Peru Corporation, Miami, FL, pg. 22
Mather, William J., Pres. & Chief Exec. Officer--Lawrence Agency Corporation, Schnectady, NY, pg. 662
Mathias, James P., Pres.--JPM Company, Lewisburg, PA, pg. 586
Mathis, Catherine A., Pres.--Princeton Partners, Inc., Princeton, NJ, pg. 890
Mathis, Catherine A., Pres.--Princeton Partners, Inc., Princeton, NJ, pg. 1177
Mathis, Jennifer M., Pres.--Valley Fig Growers, Fresno, CA, pg. 1058
Mathot, Henk, Pres. & Chief Exec. Officer--Cargill Fertilizer, Inc., Riverview, FL, pg. 219
Matt, Nicholas O., Pres--The F. X. Matt Brewing Co., Utica, NY, pg. 721
Matteson, William C., Pres. & Chief Exec. Officer--Clarke Goward Fitts Matteson, Inc., Boston, MA, pg. 253
Matthaei, William L., Pres. & Chief Exec. Officer--Roman Meal Company, Tacoma, WA, pg. 945
Matthews, Clark D., Pres.--Consolidated Industrial Corporation, Birmingham, MI, pg. 276
Matthewson, Edwin, Pres. & Chief Exec. Officer--Pullman Industries, Inc., Madison Heights, MI, pg. 900
Matthias, Donald, Pres.--Little Falls Color Print, Little Falls, NY, pg. 1057
Mattingly, Thomas F., Chm. Bd. & Pres.--Metro Foods, Inc., Memphis, TN, pg. 743
Mattison, A.M., Pres.--Mattison Machine Works, Rockford, IL, pg. 721
Matts, Joseph, Jr., Chm. Bd. & Pres.--HWH Architects Engineers Planners Inc., Cleveland, OH, pg. 498
Matuja, Robert D., Pres.--Groesbeck Lumber & Supply, Inc., Warren, MI, pg. 489

Corporate Responsibilities Index

Matuszak, Mark, Pres.--Hult Fritz Matuszak & Associates, Inc., Peoria, IL, pg. 552
Matz, Monte, Pres.--Progress West, Omaha, NE, pg. 894
Matz, Robert, Pres.--Trahan, Burden & Charles, Inc., Baltimore, MD, pg. 1105
Matz, V., Pres.--Kirk & Matz Ltd., Danbury, CT, pg. 633
Maughan, Rex, Chm. Bd., Pres. & Chief Exec. Officer--Forever Living Products, Tempe, AZ, pg. 424
Mauldin, Steve, Pres. & Gen. Mgr.-WTSP-TV--Great American Broadcasting Company, Cincinnati, OH, pg. 52
Mauloff, Greg, Pres.--NWS, Inc., Chicago, IL, pg. 782
Mauney, William K., III, Pres.--Mauney Hosiery Mills, Inc., Kings Mountain, NC, pg. 722
Maupin, Robert W., Pres. & Chief Oper. Officer--Shelter Mutual Insurance Company, Columbia, MO, pg. 997
Mauren, P. Reed, Chm. Bd., Pres., & Gen. Mgr.--Galaxy Business Products, Honolulu, HI, pg. 742
Maurer, P. Reed, Chm. Bd., Chief Exec. Officer & Pres.--Metpac, Ltd., Honolulu, HI, pg. 742
Maurey, Joseph E., Chm. Bd. & Pres.--Maurey Manufacturing Corp., Chicago, IL, pg. 722
Maurin, James E., Pres.--The Maurin-Odgen Companies, New Orleans, LA, pg. 722
Maussner, Richard A., Pres.--Rama Group of Companies, Cheektowaga, NY, pg. 910
Mautz, Bernhard F., Jr., Pres.--Mautz Paint Company, Madison, WI, pg. 722
Maxon, Gene H., Pres., Chief Exec. & Chief Oper. Officer--Harley Industries, Inc., Tulsa, OK, pg. 509
Maxwell, Earle W., Jr., Pres.--Sunbeam Casual Furniture Co., Portland, TN, pg. 1059
Maxwell, R. L., Pres. & Chief Exec. Officer--The Lathrop Company, Toledo, OH, pg. 660
Maxwell, Robert G., Pres.--American Kennel Club, Inc., New York, NY, pg. 57
May, Charles, Pres.--Guardian Alarm Co., Southfield, MI, pg. 491
May, Henry L., Pres.--The May Apparel Group, Inc., Mebane, NC, pg. 723
May, Peter W., Pres. & Chief Oper. Officer--Trian Group, New York, NY, pg. 1111
May, Van, Pres. & Chief Exec. Officer--Plains Cotton Co-op Association, Lubbock, TX, pg. 873
Mayer, Cyrus, Pres.--Mayer Berkshire Corporation, Wayne, NJ, pg. 724
Mayer, Mark A., Pres.--Peter A. Mayer Advertising, Inc., New Orleans, LA, pg. 724
Mayer, Robert, Pres.--Cole Hersee Company, Boston, MA, pg. 260
Mayers, Benjamin H., Pres.--Ace Novelty Company, Inc., Bellevue, WA, pg. 12
Mayfield, John D., III, Pres. & Chief Exec. Officer--Texas Life Insurance Company, Waco, TX, pg. 745
Mayhall, David, Pres.--Tri-State Armature Electric Works, Memphis, TN, pg. 1110
Maynard, John C., Pres.--Maywood, Inc., Amarillo, TX, pg. 725
Mays, Gregg, Pres.--Almac's Inc., East Providence, RI, pg. 1214
Mays, William, Chm. Bd. & Pres.--Mays Chemical Company, Indianapolis, IN, pg. 725
Mazaika, Robert J., Chm. Bd., Pres. & Chief Exec. Officer--Uniroyal Chemical Company, Inc., Middlebury, CT, pg. 1129
Mazey, Andrew, Mng. Dir.--BSB New Zealand Limited, Wellington,, New Zealand, pg. 110
Maziarka, Donald, Pres., Chief Exec. & Chief Oper. Officer--George Sollitt Construction, Wood Dale, IL, pg. 1017
Mazzotta, Dorothy, Pres.--Friendly Holidays Inc., Lake Success, NY, pg. 433
Mc Afee, Gary, Pres.--Pete Fall Ford Inc., Elkhart, IN, pg. 398
McAdams, Brian, Chm. Bd.--McAdams, Richman & Ong, Inc., Bala-Cynwyd, PA, pg. 725
McAfee, Charles, Pres.--McAfee Consolidated Inc., Mesa, AZ, pg. 726
McAlaine, Robert, Chm. Bd. & Pres.--Namico, Inc., Philadelphia, PA, pg. 783
McAllister, Larry N., Pres.--Metal Masters Foodservice Equipment, Smyrna, DE, pg. 741
McAnally, N.A., Chm. Bd. & Chief Fin. Officer--McAnally Enterprises, Inc., Yucaipa, CA, pg. 726
McAndrews, J.J., Pres. & Chief Oper. Officer--Mona Industries, Inc., Paterson, NJ, pg. 764
McAtee, James C., Pres.--Electric Power Equipment Co., Columbus, OH, pg. 373
McAuliff, Timothy M., Pres. & Chief Exec. Officer--John Blair Communications, Inc., New York, NY, pg. 155
McAuliff, Timothy M., Pres. & Chief Exec. Officer--Blair Television, New York, NY, pg. 155
McAuliffe, John, Chm. Bd. & Pres.--Beauty Handbook Corporation, Los Angeles, CA, pg. 130
McAuliffe, John, Chm. Bd. & Pres.--Compendium Systems, New York, NY, pg. 270
McBeth, Robert D., Chm. Bd., Pres. & Chief Exec. Officer--Associated Industrial Supply, Inc., Columbia, SC, pg. 90
McBride, John H., Pres. & Chief Exec. Officer--Porcelain Metals Corp., Louisville, KY, pg. 881
McBride, Robert D., Pres. & Chief Exec. Officer--McLouth Steel, Trenton, MI, pg. 731
McCaffery, W., Pres. & Dir.-Creative Services--McCaffery & Ratner, Inc., New York, NY, pg. 726
McCaffray, S.J., Chm. Bd. & Pres.--National Frozen Foods Corp., Seattle, WA, pg. 789
McCaffrey, Jim, Pres.--Romanoff International, Inc., Charlotte, NC, pg. 945
McCaig, John C., Pres.--Quinlan Advertising, Carmel, IN, pg. 905
McCaig, Joseph J., Pres. & Chief Exec. Officer--The Grand Union Company, Wayne, NJ, pg. 476
McCall, Robert H., Pres. & Chief Exec. Officer--McCall Oil & Chemical Corp., Portland, OR, pg. 726
McCall, Terry, Chm. Bd.--Lockwood Corporation, Gering, NE, pg. 680
McCall, W. Calder, Chm. Bd.--McCall Oil & Chemical Corp., Portland, OR, pg. 726
McCallin, Daniel J., Pres.--Steel, Inc., Commerce City, CO, pg. 1044
McCallum, Elkin, Pres. & Chief Exec. Officer--Joan Fabrics Corp., Tyngsboro, MA, pg. 594
McCann, David A., V.P. & Publr.--Town & Country, New York, NY, pg. 523
McCann, James, Pres.--800-Flowers, Westbury, NY, pg. 371
McCanna, William, Pres.--Meadowcraft, Inc., Birmingham, AL, pg. 733
McCarter, William J., Pres. & Chief Exec. Officer--WTTW (Channel 11), Chicago, IL, pg. 1156
McCarthy, C. James, Pres.--Luzianne Blue Plate Foods, New Orleans, LA, pg. 923
McCarty, John R., Pres., Chief Exec. Officer & Chief Fin. Officer--McCarty Farms, Magee, MS, pg. 727
McCaskey, Raymond F., Pres. & Chief Oper. Officer--Blue Cross & Blue Shield of Illinois, Chicago, IL, pg. 160
McCauley, Arthur, Chm. & Pres.--Norwalk Co., Inc., South Norwalk, CT, pg. 816
McClain, John R., Pres.--Owen Pacific, Los Angeles, CA, pg. 834
McClellan, Richard P., Pres. & Chief Exec. Officer--Pro-Log Corporation, Monterey, CA, pg. 892
McClelland, Kent, Pres.--Shamrock Foods Co., Phoenix, AZ, pg. 994
McClelland, Mike, Pres. & Chief Exec. Officer--Hardware Wholesalers, Inc., Fort Wayne, IN, pg. 508
McClelland, Norman P., Chief Exec. Officer--Shamrock Foods Co., Phoenix, AZ, pg. 994
McClung, Gary N., Pres. & Gen. Mgr.--Midway Ford Truck Center Inc., Kansas City, MO, pg. 751
McClung, J. David, Pres. & Chief Exec. Officer--Green Holdings, Inc., Denver, CO, pg. 484
McClure, Frank L., Pres.--Holmes Tuttle Ford, Inc., Tucson, AZ, pg. 540
McClurg, Douglas G., Pres. & Chief Exec. Officer--Mossberg Industries, Inc., Cumberland, RI, pg. 772
McCluskey, Edward V., Pres.--Standard Brands of America, Inc., Pompano Beach, FL, pg. 1035
McCollister, Paul, Chm. Bd., Pres. & Chief Exec. Officer--Jackson Hole Ski Resort, Teton Village, WY, pg. 587
McCollow, Thomas J., Chm. Bd., Pres. & Chief Exec. Officer--Journal Communications Inc., Milwaukee, WI, pg. 607
McCollum, Robert, Chm. Bd. & Chief Exec. Officer--R. S. Hughes Co., Inc., Los Angeles, CA, pg. 551
McCombs, Stewart W., Pres.--Starr Seigle McCombs, Inc., Honolulu, HI, pg. 1040
McConnell, James V., Jr., Pres.--McConnell Automotive, Mobile, AL, pg. 727
McConnell, Peter, Pres.--North American Salt Company, Overland Park, KS, pg. 812
McConnell, William R., Chm. Bd. & Pres.--McConnell Cabinets, Inc., El Monte, CA, pg. 727
McCormack, John J., III, Pres. & Chief Exec. Officer--Accurate Bushing Co., Inc., Garwood, NJ, pg. 11
McCormack, Mark H., Chm. Bd., Pres. & Chief Exec. Officer--International Management Group (IMG), Cleveland, OH, pg. 578
McCormack, Maryanne, Pres.--Visible Changes, Houston, TX, pg. 1153
McCormick, E.F., Pres. & Chief Oper. Officer--Lykes Bros. Steamship Co., Inc., New Orleans, LA, pg. 688
McCormick, Jack, Pres.--J.H. McCormick, Inc., Burbank, CA, pg. 727
McCormick, Rick, Pres. & Chief Oper. Officer--Eastway Delivery Service of Dallas, Inc., Grapevine, TX, pg. 364
McCormick, Rick, Pres. & Chief Oper. Officer--Eastway Air Cartage, Inc., Houston, TX, pg. 364
McCormick, Rick M., Pres. & Chief Oper. Officer--Eastway Delivery Service of Houston, Inc., Houston, TX, pg. 364
McCormick, Stephen, Pres.--Madison National Life Insurance Co., Inc., Middleton, WI, pg. 451
McCormick, T.P., Pres.--McCormick Paint Works Company, Rockville, MD, pg. 727
McCourt, Kenneth W., Pres. & Chief Exec. Officer--Buffalo Color Corporation, Parsippany, NJ, pg. 187
McCoy, Curtis G., Chm. Bd. & Pres.--Fantastic Sam's International, Inc., Memphis, TN, pg. 398
McCoy, Duncan, Pres. & Chief Exec. Officer--New Texas Tumbleweed, Houston, TX, pg. 802
McCoy, James T., Pres. & Chief Oper. Officer--The John C. Groub Company Inc., Seymour, IN, pg. 489
McCoy, Michael A., Pres.--Associated Process Controls, Pleasanton, CA, pg. 92
McCoy, V. Glenn, Pres.--Fleetwood Aluminum Products, Corona, CA, pg. 417
McCracken, A. Keith, Pres. & Chief Exec. Officer--McCracken Brooks Communications, Inc., Minneapolis, MN, pg. 728
McCready, James P., Pres. & Chief Oper. Officer--The Brenlin Group, Akron, OH, pg. 173
McCroskey, V. Donald, Pres.--Willson Safety Products, Reading, PA, pg. 1193
McCroskey, V.D., Pres. & Chief Exec. Officer--WGM Safety Corporation, Reading, PA, pg. 1156
McCucheon, Darrell, V.P. & Exec. Mgr.--Reliable Chevrolet, Richardson, TX, pg. 924
McCullough, Bernice, Pres.--Broadcast Supply West, Tacoma, WA, pg. 177
McCullough, R.L., Pres., Chief Oper. Officer & Partner--E.H. Brown Advertising, Inc., Chicago, IL, pg. 181
McCurdy, Charles G., Pres.--K-III Communications Corporation, New York, NY, pg. 610
McCurdy, Ken, Pres. & Chief Exec. Officer--McCurdy & Co., Inc., Rochester, NY, pg. 728
McDaniel, Gary P., Chm., Chief Exec. Officer & Sec.--ROC Properties Inc., Englewood, CO, pg. 908
McDaniel, R. Leon, Pres. & Chief Oper. Officer--Pioneer Oil Company Inc., Fort Worth, TX, pg. 872
McDavid, T.J., Pres.--Concorp, Inc., Nitro, WV, pg. 272
McDermid, Edward J., Sr., Pres.--Frontier Lumber Company, Inc., Buffalo, NY, pg. 434
McDermitt, Edward A., Jr., Pres. & Chief Exec. Officer--National Bulk Carriers, Inc., New York, NY, pg. 786
McDermott, Joseph, Jr., Pres. & Chief Exec. Officer--EBM Systems, Inc., Greenbelt, MD, pg. 359
McDivitt, Kris, Pres. & Chief Exec. Officer--Lost Arrow Corporation, Ventura, CA, pg. 684
McDonald, Charles R., Chm., Pres. & Chief Exec. Officer--McDonald Equipment Co., Willoughby, OH, pg. 728
McDonald, David J., Pres. & Chief Exec. Officer--Curtice-Burns Foods, Inc., Rochester, NY, pg. 25
McDonald, Dennis, Chm. Bd.--The Meyercord Company, Carol Stream, IL, pg. 746
McDonald, J.M., III, Chm. Bd., Pres. & Chief Exec. Officer--A. Y. McDonald Industries, Inc., Dubuque, IA, pg. 728
McDonald, Kelli, Pres., Chief Oper. Officer--EvansGroup, Denver, CO, pg. 391
McDonald, Lawrence, Pres. & Chief Exec. Officer--Gai's Seattle French Baking Co., Inc., Seattle, WA, pg. 441
McDonald, Richard E., Pres. & Chief Exec. Officer--McDonald Davis & Associates, Inc., Milwaukee, WI, pg. 728
McDonald, Stuart R., Pres., Chief Exec. Officer & Treas.--Marshall & Williams Co., Greenville, SC, pg. 714
McDonnell, Dennis P., Pres. & Chief Exec. Officer--Trace Products, San Jose, CA, pg. 1104
McDonnell, Michael, Pres. & Chief Exec. Officer--West Union Corp., Memphis, TN, pg. 1177
McDonough, Patrick J., Pres.--Excel Media Services Inc., Cleveland, OH, pg. 737
McDonough, Russell B., Jr., Chm. Bd., Pres. & Chief Exec. Officer--Winrock Enterprises, Inc., Little Rock, AR, pg. 1197
McDougall, Daniel R., Pres.--McDougall Associates, Inc., Peabody, MA, pg. 728
McDow, Tom, Pres.-Great American Opportunities, Inc.--Southwestern/Great American Inc., Nashville, TN, pg. 1023
McDowell, Frank, Pres. & Chief Exec. Officer--Cardinal Realty Services Inc., Reynoldsburg, OH, pg. 218
McDowell, James, Pres.--McKay Chemical Co., Los Angeles, CA, pg. 159
McElhaney, Jack B., Pres. & Chief Exec. Officer--Ministers Life Insurance Company, Minneapolis, MN, pg. 757
McElwee, Arthur, Chm. Bd. & Pres.--Goshen Rubber Co., Inc., Goshen, IN, pg. 472
McEniry, Robert G., Pres.--Standard Welders Supply Co., Memphis, TN, pg. 1038
McEuen, Thomas, Pres. & New Bus. Contact--Kaiser McEuen Inc., Los Angeles, CA, pg. 615
McEvoy, A.P., Jr., Pres.--Western Extrusions, Carrollton, TX, pg. 1179
McEvoy, Patrick J., Pres.--Industrial Electronic Engineers, Inc., Van Nuys, CA, pg. 566
McEwen, Joseph, Pres.--Moreco Inc., Bristol, PA, pg. 763
McFall, George E., Pres. & Chief Exec. Officer--Western Linen Corp., Phoenix, AZ, pg. 1180
McFall, Tom, Chm., Pres. & Chief Exec. Officer--Weatherly Financial Group, New York, NY, pg. 1169
McFarling, Donald P., Pres. & Chief Exec. Officer--McFarling Foods, Inc., Indianapolis, IN, pg. 729
McFerson, D. Richard, Pres. & Gen. Mgr.--Nationwide Mutual Insurance Company, Columbus, OH, pg. 795
McGarry, John P., Pres. & Chief Exec. Officer-Y&R North America--Young & Rubicam New York, New York, NY, pg. 1211
McGee, Julie, Pres. & Editor-In-Chief--McDougal, Littell & Company, Evanston, IL, pg. 728
McGehee, F. Sutton, Pres.--Mac Papers, Inc., Jacksonville, FL, pg. 694
McGibney, Fredrick R., Dir.--Vermont Lottery Commission, Barre, VT, pg. 1148
McGill, James D., Pres.--United McGill Corp., Groveport, OH, pg. 1133
McGill, Jay, V.P. & Publisher--Motor Boating & Sailing, New York, NY, pg. 523
McGill, John R., Pres.--Developers Diversified, Moreland Hills, OH, pg. 333
McGinnis, Arthur J., Jr., Chm. Bd., Pres., Chief Oper. Officer--Simmons-Boardman Publishing Corp., New York, NY, pg. 1005
McGlothlin, James W., Chm. Bd. & Pres.--The United Company, Bristol, VA, pg. 1131
McGrath, David J., Jr., Pres. & Chief Exec. Officer--TAD Technical Services Corp., Cambridge, MA, pg. 1071
McGrath, E.A., Pres.--Graybar Electric Company, Inc., Clayton, MO, pg. 479
McGrath, G.J., Chm. Bd. & Pres.--Mico Inc., North Mankato, MN, pg. 748
McGrath, Michael S., V.P. & Gen. Mgr.--I.B.C. Root Beer Company, Dallas, TX, pg. 342
McGrath, Michael S., V.P. & Gen. Mgr.--Premier Beverages, Dallas, TX, pg. 342
McGrath, Patrick J., Pres.--Jordan, McGrath, Case & Taylor Inc., New York, NY, pg. 604
McGrath, Roger G., Pres. & Chief Exec. Officer--V.G.S. Corp. d/b/a Southland Oil Company, Jackson, MS, pg. 1141
McGregor, William J., Pres. & Creative Dir.--The Criterion Group, Inc., Atlanta, GA, pg. 299
McHugh, James P., Pres. & Chief Exec. Officer--James McHugh Construction Co., Chicago, IL, pg. 729
McHugh, Joe, Mgr.--Periphonics Voice Processing Systems Ltd., Camberley,, United Kingdom, pg. 862
McIlrath, James A., Pres.--Dry Storage Corporation, Des Plaines, IL, pg. 350
McIlvain, J. Gibson, III, Pres.--J. Gibson McIlvain Co., White Marsh, MD, pg. 729
McInerney, Martin J., Pres.--McInerney Inc., Oak Park, MI, pg. 729
McIntyre, Burt, Pres.--Claremont Flock Corporation, Claremont, NH, pg. 251

Corporate Responsibilities Index

McIntyre, Douglas A., Pres. & Chief Exec. Officer--Financial World Partners, New York, NY, pg. 410
McIntyre, William D., Chief Oper. Officer--American Speedy Printing Centers, Inc., Bloomfield Hills, MI, pg. 61
McIvor, Patrick J., Pres. & Chief Exec. Officer--Simms & McIvor Marketing Communications, Somerville, NJ, pg. 1005
McKay, Carl, Pres. & Chief Exec. Officer--Sioux Manufacturing Corp., Fort Totten, ND, pg. 1008
McKay, Eugene H., Jr., Pres.--Archway Cookies, Inc., Battle Creek, MI, pg. 81
McKean, Brad, Pres.--McKean Oldsmobile Company, Pittsburgh, PA, pg. 730
McKean, Gilbert R., Pres.--Breckenridge Material Company, Saint Louis, MO, pg. 173
McKee, Ellsworth, Pres. & Chief Exec. Officer--McKee Foods Corporation, Collegedale, TN, pg. 730
McKee, Frank Sr., Pres.--National Van Lines, Inc., Broadview, IL, pg. 794
McKee, Frank, Jr.; Exec. V.P.--National Van Lines, Inc., Broadview, IL, pg. 794
McKee, John, V.P.-Retail--McKee Door, Inc., Aurora, IL, pg. 730
McKee, R. Ellsworth, Pres. & Chief Exec. Officer--McKee Baking Co., Inc., Collegedale, TN, pg. 730
McKee, Ronald, Pres.--BetterBrands, Ltd., Waipahu, HI, pg. 1214
McKeel, Sam S., Pres., Chief Exec. Officer & Publr.--Chicago Sun Times, Chicago, IL, pg. 18
McKelvey, Andrew J., Chm. & Pres.--TMP Worldwide, Inc., New York, NY, pg. 1073
McKenna, Andrew J., Chm., Pres. & Chief Exec. Officer--Schwarz Paper Company, Morton Grove, IL, pg. 980
McKenna, Eugene M., Pres.--Doyle McKenna Bayer Brown, Reno, NV, pg. 348
McKenna, M.J., Pres.--Baltimore Aircoil Company, Jessup, MD, pg. 69
McKenna, Michael, Pres.--Tempo Products Company, Cleveland, OH, pg. 875
McKenna, P.W., Chm. Bd., Pres. & Chief Oper. Officer--Plasti-Kote Company Inc., Medina, OH, pg. 875
McKenna, Robert J., Pres. & Chief Oper. Officer--National Car Rental System, Inc., Minneapolis, MN, pg. 786
McKenney, J.S., Pres.--The Figaro Company, Inc., Mesquite, TX, pg. 409
McKenzie, Craig, Pres. & Chief Exec. Officer--EvansGroup, Phoenix, AZ, pg. 391
McKenzie, James, Pres.--Leo Burnett Company Ltd., Toronto,, Canada, pg. 192
McKenzie, Joe, Chm. Bd. & Chief Exec. Officer--Rangaire & Company, Cleburne, TX, pg. 912
McKenzie, L.W., Jr., Pres.--LWMCK Corporation, Effingham, IL, pg. 648
McKenzie, Mary Alice, Pres.--John McKenzie Packing Co., Inc., Burlington, VT, pg. 730
McKenzie, Michael K., Pres. & Chief Exec. Officer--GSC Enterprises, Inc., Sulphur Springs, TX, pg. 440
McKenzie, W. Guy, Jr., Chief Exec. Officer--McKenzie Tank Lines, Inc., Tallahassee, FL, pg. 730
McKeon, Gerard J., Pres.--New York Racing Association, Jamaica, NY, pg. 803
McKeown, John M., Pres.--Krommenhoek McKeown Associates, San Diego, CA, pg. 645
McKernan, R.T., Pres.--Packard Instrument Co., Inc., Meriden, CT, pg. 213
McKinlay, Douglas R., Pres.--McKinlay & Partners, Inc., Simsbury, CT, pg. 730
McKinney, William H., Pres.--The Royal China & Porcelain Companies Inc., Moorestown, NJ, pg. 953
McKinnon, T. Benson, Pres. & Chief Exec. Officer--McKinnon Bridge Co., Franklin, TN, pg. 731
McKinstry, David, Chief Exec. Officer--Young & Rubicam South Africa, Kenilworth, South Africa, pg. 1214
McKissick, A. Foster, Pres.--Heritage Lincoln-Mercury, Greenville, SC, pg. 398
McKissick, A. Foster, III, Pres.--Fairway Ford, Inc., Greenville, SC, pg. 397
McKnight, Mac, Pres.--Mac's Machinery & Supply, Boise, ID, pg. 341
McKone, Peter J., Pres.--MCKONE & CO., INC., Irving, TX, pg. 731
McLaren, Fred B., Pres.--Hughes Markets Inc., Irwindale, CA, pg. 552
McLaughlin, A.T., Jr., Pres.--Dick Corporation, Large, PA, pg. 335
McLaughlin, Harry Y., Pres.--McLaughlin Industrial Distributors, Inc., Pico Rivera, CA, pg. 731
McLaughlin, John T., Pres.--Royal Oak Ford Inc., Royal Oak, MI, pg. 953
McLean, David L., Mng. Dir.-Sydney & Australia--Sudler & Hennessey Sydney, Sydney,, Australia, pg. 1214
McLean, Gary R., Chm. Bd. & Pres.--Interstate Distributor Company, Tacoma, WA, pg. 580
McLean, James A., Jr., Pres.--McLean-Thomas Inc., Buffalo, NY, pg. 731
McLean, Lee, Jr., Pres.--McLean Enterprises, Inc., Springfield, MO, pg. 731
McLean, Robert C., Pres.--Campbell Construction Co., Sacramento, CA, pg. 213
McLean, Victor H., Pres. & Chief Exec. Officer--Davis-Newman-Payne, Knoxville, TN, pg. 319
McLean, William L., III, Chm. Bd. & Pres.--Independent Publications, Inc., Bryn Mawr, PA, pg. 565
McLellan, Robert S., Pres.--Bixby International Corp., Newburyport, MA, pg. 153
McLennan, Grant, Pres.--Alpha Electronic Signal Technologies, Inc., Elizabeth, NJ, pg. 43
McLeod, John S., Sr., Pres.--Mar-Mac Manufacturing Company, Inc., McBee, SC, pg. 705
McMahon, John J., Pres.--McWane, Inc., Birmingham, AL, pg. 733
McMahon, John J. Jr., Pres. & Chief Exec. Officer--Clow Corporation, Birmingham, AL, pg. 733
McMahon, John M., Pres. & Chief Oper. Officer--Miller & Long Co. Inc., Bethesda, MD, pg. 754
McMahon, Nelson, Jr., Pres.--The Fleetwood Company, Downers Grove, IL, pg. 417
McMahon, Patrick, Dir.--Virginia Department of Economic Development Tourism Development Group, Richmond, VA, pg. 1152
McMahon, Richard, Pres.--Minnesota Brewing Company, Saint Paul, MN, pg. 757
McManus, James R., Chm. Bd., Pres. & Chief Exec. Officer--Marketing Corp. of America, Westport, CT, pg. 709
McManus, Michael F., Jr., Pres.--Header Products Inc., Romulus, MI, pg. 520
McMennamy, Roger N., Pres. & Chief Exec. Officer--Cooper Communities, Inc., Bella Vista, AR, pg. 283
McMichael, Jim, Pres.--Axelson, Inc., Longview, TX, pg. 103
McMichael, John, Pres.--Bob Frink Chevrolet G.E.O. Management, Sacramento, CA, pg. 433
McMillan, Douglas, Pres. & Chief Oper. Officer--Allison-Erwin Co. Inc., Charlotte, NC, pg. 40
McMillan, Edward, Pres.--First Boston Asset Management Corporation, New York, NY, pg. 204
McMillen, John, Pres.--The Garber Company, Ashland, OH, pg. 442
McMillen, Karl, Pres.--Todd Pipe & Supply Hawthorne, Hawthorne, CA, pg. 1100
McMillen, Robert B., Pres. & Chief Exec. Officer--Totem Resources Corporation, Seattle, WA, pg. 1103
McMorris, Jerry, Pres. & Chief Exec. Officer--N.W. Transport Service, Inc., Commerce City, CO, pg. 781
McMullen, Thomas, Pres. & Chief Oper. Officer--Unifax, Inc., Wilkes-Barre, PA, pg. 1126
McMullin, Dan, Pres.--Mini Mart, Inc., Casper, WY, pg. 757
McMullin, John B., Jr., Pres.--Somerset Pontiac GMC Inc., Troy, MI, pg. 1017
McMurry, W.N., Pres.--Rissler & McMurry Company, Casper, WY, pg. 936
McNally, Andrew, IV, Pres. & Chief Exec. Officer--Rand McNally & Company, Skokie, IL, pg. 911
McNamara, Austin, Pres. & Chief Exec. Officer--Dinner Bell Foods, Inc., Cincinnati, OH, pg. 53
McNamara, Dennis C., Sr., Pres.--McNamara Pontiac Inc., Orlando, FL, pg. 732
McNamara, James, Pres. & Chief Exec. Officer--New World Entertainment, Inc., Los Angeles, CA, pg. 74
McNamara, John F., Chm. Bd., Pres. & Chief Exec. Officer--Alco Health Services Corporation, Malvern, PA, pg. 31
McNaughton, Robert L., Pres.--McNaughton & Gunn, Inc., Saline, MI, pg. 732
McNeel, Van L., Chm. Bd. & Chief Exec. Officer--McNeel International Corp., Tampa, FL, pg. 732
McNeeley, Bob, Pres.--Reilly Industries Inc., Indianapolis, IN, pg. 923
McNeeley, Donald R., Pres. & Chief Oper. Officer--Chicago Tube & Iron Co., Chicago, IL, pg. 246
McNeeley, Robert D., Pres.--Reilly Industries, Inc., Indianapolis, IN, pg. 923
McNeil, Gordon H., Pres. & Chief Exec. Officer--Magnetic Technologies Corporation, Rochester, NY, pg. 701
McNeil, Manford R., Pres.--Romac Industries, Inc., Seattle, WA, pg. 945
McNeil, Robert D., Pres.--Penguin Industries, Inc., Coatesville, PA, pg. 857
McNeill, Bruce, Chm. Bd., Pres. & Chief Exec. Officer--Superior Federal Bank, Fort Smith, AR, pg. 1063
McNeilus, Denzil, Pres.--McNeilus Companies, Dodge Center, MN, pg. 732
McNerney, J. Peter, Pres.--Seneca Wire & Manufacturing Co., Fostoria, OH, pg. 989
McNulty, Frank N., Pres. & Chief Oper. Officer--Parade Publications Inc., New York, NY, pg. 847
McNutt, L.W., Jr., Pres.--Collin Street Bakery, Corsicana, TX, pg. 262
McPhail, Douglas J., Pres., Chief Exec. & Fin. Officer & Treas.--Indiana Records Managers, Indianapolis, IN, pg. 565
McPhail, Robert L., Gen. Mgr.--Basin Electric Power Co-Op, Bismarck, ND, pg. 125
McPhearson, J. R., Jr., Pres.--Strachan Shipping Co., Garden City, GA, pg. 1052
McPhedrain, Willard M., Pres.--Mary Maxim, Inc., Port Huron, MI, pg. 722
McQueeny, James, Pres.--Kohm Associates, Inc., Oradell, NJ, pg. 640
McQuern, Marcia, Pres. & Exec. Editor--Press Enterprise Company, Riverside, CA, pg. 887
McRae, Richard, Jr., Pres. & Chief Exec. Officer--McRae's, Inc., Jackson, MS, pg. 733
McSparran, Robert B., Chm. Bd. & Pres.--Atlantic Dairy Cooperative, Southampton, PA, pg. 94
McSwain, Ronald, Pres.--McSwain Carpets Inc., Cincinnati, OH, pg. 733
McSweene, Michael T., Pres. & Chief Exec. Officer--DIMAC Corporation, Bridgeton, MO, pg. 338
McSweeney, Michael T., Pres. & Chief Exec. Officer--DIMAC DIRECT, Bridgeton, MO, pg. 338
McSwiney, Ben L., Pres. & Chief Exec. Officer--Whitestar Graphics, Inc., Spring Grove, IL, pg. 1186
McSwiney, Ben L., Pres. & Chief Oper. Officer--Forms Corporation Of America, Spring Grove, IL, pg. 1187
McTague, Michael, Pres. & Chief Exec. Officer--Fauber Construction Company, Inc., Lafayette, IN, pg. 403
McVaney, C. Edward, Chm. Bd., Pres. & Chief Exec. Officer--J.D. Edwards & Company, Denver, CO, pg. 370
McWilliam, Richard, Pres.--The Upper Deck Company, Carlsbad, CA, pg. 1140
McWilliams, Alexander M., Pres.--McWilliams Forge Co., Rockaway, NJ, pg. 733
Mead, William, Pres.--Rainfair, Inc., Racine, WI, pg. 910
Meade, Kenneth, Pres.--Meade Group, Inc., Detroit, MI, pg. 733
Meade, Sterling, Partner--Meade Ullman Advertising & Public Relations, Agoura Hills, CA, pg. 733
Meador, W.E., Pres. & Gen. Mgr.--Long-Airdox Company, Oak Hill, WV, pg. 711
Meads, Gary, Pres. & Chief Oper. Officer--Knoth & Meads Company, San Diego, CA, pg. 637
Meag, Jack, Pres. & Chief Exec. Officer--Schreiber Foods, Inc., Green Bay, WI, pg. 978
Meagher, Dennis T., Pres.--Wyatt Inc., Branford, CT, pg. 1205
Meagher, Joseph B., Pres. & Chief Exec. Officer--Yankee Publishing Incorporated, Dublin, NH, pg. 1207
Mealey, Donald, Pres.--Don Mealey Chevrolet Inc., Orlando, FL, pg. 733
Meany, Kevin C., Pres., Chief Exec. & New Bus. & Merger/Aquisition Contact--Partners Meany, Inc., Albany, NY, pg. 850
Mears, Paul S., Jr., Pres.--Mears Transportation Group, Orlando, FL, pg. 734
Mears, William A., Pres.--Lan-O-Sheen, Inc., Saint Paul, MN, pg. 653
Mebus, Philip K., Jr., Pres. & Treas.--Arrow Metal Products Corporation, Detroit, MI, pg. 85
Mechigian, Robert, Pres.--Bob Saks Toyota, Farmington, MI, pg. 402
Mechigian, Robert, Sr., Pres.--Farmington Hills Holding Company, Farmington, MI, pg. 402
Medary, William, Pres. & Chief Exec. Officer--Bass Enterprises Production Company, Fort Worth, TX, pg. 125
Medico, Thomas, Pres.--Medico Industries, Inc., Wilkes-Barre, PA, pg. 735
Medlin, Candice, Pres.--U.S. Creative, Inc., Austin, TX, pg. 1135
Mee, George, Chm. & Pres.--Mallery Lumber Corp., Emporium, PA, pg. 702
Meelia, Richard D., Pres.--Kendall Healthcare Products Company, Mansfield, MA, pg. 622
Meer, E. Harvey, Pres., Chief Oper. Officer & Treas.--Meer Corporation, North Bergen, NJ, pg. 736
Mehiel, Chris, Pres.--Specialty Industries, Inc., Red Lion, PA, pg. 1027
Mehlis, David L., Chm. Bd., Pres. & Chief Exec. Officer--David C. Cook Publishing Co., Elgin, IL, pg. 282
Meider, Elmer, Jr., Pres.--Highlights for Children, Inc., Columbus, OH, pg. 534
Meijer, Dirk Jan, Chm Bd--Prins, Meijer, Stamenkovits en van Walbeek/Young & Rubicam B.V., Amsterdam,, Netherlands, pg. 1212
Mele, Dennis A., Pres.--Cleaners Hanger Co., Palm Harbor, FL, pg. 254
Mellor, Rob C., Chm., Pres. & Chief Exec. Officer--Vinson Supply Co., Tulsa, OK, pg. 968
Mellott, Forrest R., Pres.--H.B. Mellott Estate, Inc., McConnellsburg, PA, pg. 738
Melloy, Robert E., Pres.--Melloy Bros. Enterprises, Albuquerque, NM, pg. 738
Melman, Richard, Pres.--Lettuce Entertain You Enterprises, Inc., Chicago, IL, pg. 668
Melnuk, Paul D., Pres. & Chief Oper. Officer--Clark Oil & Refining Corporation, Saint Louis, MO, pg. 252
Meloon, Walter N., Pres. & Chief Exec. Officer--Correct Craft, Inc., Orlando, FL, pg. 287
Meltzer, Steven, Chm. Bd. & Pres.--MI Fund Incorporated, New York, NY, pg. 692
Menapace, T. Howard, Pres.--Rico Motor Company, Gallup, NM, pg. 933
Mendell, Mark R., Pres.--Cannon, Grand Island, NY, pg. 214
Mendelson, Ira, Pres. & Chief Exec. Officer--Murry's, Inc., Forestville, MD, pg. 777
Mendelson, Ira, Pres.--Murry's, Inc., Forestville, MD, pg. 777
Mendoza, R.V., Pres. & Chief Exec. Officer--Sterling Homes Corp., Sparks, NV, pg. 1046
Menke, Peter, Pres.--Saladmaster, Arlington, TX, pg. 967
Mennen, Herbert, Pres.--Mennen Medical Inc., Clarence, NY, pg. 739
Menzer, Donald, Pres.--Marathon Cheese Corp., Marathon, WI, pg. 705
Meoni, Ronald J., Pres. & Chief Exec. Officer--The Napier Company, Meriden, CT, pg. 783
Mercandte, Frank, Pres. & Chief Exec. Officer--Franklin Federal Savings Association, Ottawa, KS, pg. 429
Mercier, Douglas, Pres.--Carlton Manufacturing, Inc., Elkhart, IN, pg. 222
Mercier, Gustavo, Pres.--Sealy Mattress Company of Puerto Rico, Rio Piedras, PR, pg. 985
Meredith, Allen, Pres. & Chief Exec. Officer--Trammell Crow Company, Dallas, TX, pg. 1106
Meredith, David, Pres. & New Business Contact--BSB Japan Ltd., Tokyo, Japan, pg. 110
Meredith, George, Pres. & Creative Dir.--Gianettino & Meredith Advertising, Short Hills, NJ, pg. 455
Meredith, Nevin W., Pres. & Chief Exec. Officer--National Oats Co., Cedar Rapids, IA, pg. 25
Merksamer, Gerald M., Pres.--De Vons Jewelers, Sacramento, CA, pg. 321
Merlav, K.A., Chm. Bd., Pres. & Chief Exec. Officer--Ottenheimer & Company, Inc., Bannockburn, IL, pg. 831
Mermelstein, Bernard, Pres. & Chief Exec. Officer--Elgin Watch International, Inc., Long Island City, NY, pg. 376
Mermelstein, David, Pres.--Croton Watch Company, New York, NY, pg. 300
Merrell, John K., Pres., Chief Exec. Officer & Chief Oper. Officer--Industrial Dielectrics, Inc., Noblesville, IN, pg. 566
Merrell, W.M., Pres. & Chief Exec. Officer--Howard, Merrell & Partners, Inc., Raleigh, NC, pg. 547
Merrill, Thomas L., Pres. & Chief Exec. Officer--Altec Industries, Inc., Birmingham, AL, pg. 45
Merritt, R.O., Pres. & Gen. Mgr.--Mrs. Alison's Cookie Company, Saint Louis, MO, pg. 760
Merritt, Stanley S., Pres. & Chief Exec. Officer--Stan Merritt Inc./Advertising, New York, NY, pg. 741
Merson, Robert, Pres. & Chief Exec. Officer--Southern Electric Supply Co., Inc., Meridian, MS, pg. 1020

Mertens, Lynne, Pres.--Warrens Waller Press, South San Francisco, CA, pg. 1165
Mertes, Wayne, Pres.--National R.V., Inc., Perris, CA, pg. 792
Merz, John Frederick, Jr., Chm. Bd., Pres. & Treas.--Scott Specialty Gases, Inc., Plumsteadville, PA, pg. 983
Mesci, Haluk, Chief Exec. Officer & Creative Dir.--Markom/Leo Burnett A.S., Istanbul,, Turkey, pg. 193
Meske, Donald E., Pres.--Deluxe Homes Of Pennsylvania, Inc., Berwick, PA, pg. 327
Mesker, Ron, Pres.--Love's Enterprises, Inc., Costa Mesa, CA, pg. 685
Metropoulos, C. Dean, Pres.--International Cheese Company Limited Partnership, Hinesburg, VT, pg. 575
Metz, Tom, Pres.--Model Glass, Inc., Anaheim, CA, pg. 762
Metzger, John U., Pres. & Chief Oper. Officer--West Coast Life Insurance Co., San Francisco, CA, pg. 795
Meyer, Bernard, Pres. & Chief Oper. Officer--Allright Corporation, Houston, TX, pg. 41
Meyer, Frederick R., Chm. Bd. & Pres.--Aladdin Industries, Incorporated, Nashville, TN, pg. 29
Meyer, H.J., Pres.--CHB Corp., Belcamp, MD, pg. 201
Meyer, Jeffrey, Pres.--Renaissance Publishing Co., Inc., Auburn, IN, pg. 926
Meyer, Kenneth, Pres.--Logan & Kanawha Coal Co., Cincinnati, OH, pg. 681
Meyer, Robert L., Pres.--Meyer & Wallis, Inc., Milwaukee, WI, pg. 746
Meyer, Robert W., Reg. V.P.--Alco Health Services Corporation-Tiffin Div., Tiffin, OH, pg. 32
Meyocks, Richard, Pres. & Chief Exec. Officer--Meyocks Benkstein Associates, Des Moines, IA, pg. 746
Meza, Gonzalo, Chm. & Pres.--BSB/Meza, Ltda., Bogota,, Colombia, pg. 110
Mezo, Linda, Pres. & Chief Oper. Officer--Keyes Martin, Springfield, NJ, pg. 627
MgGrath, Donald E., Pres.--Tyler Limited Partnership, Benson, MN, pg. 1122
Micciche, Romano, Pres.--Advanced Instruments, Inc., Needham Heights, MA, pg. 20
Michael, David, Pres.--Professional Apartment Management, Inc., Lodi, CA, pg. 893
Michael, Edward A., Pres. & Chief Exec. Officer--Diamond Brands, Inc., Cloquet, MN, pg. 335
Michael, George, Principal--Michael, Bolger, Reinschmiedt, King (MBRK), Dallas, TX, pg. 746
Michaels, J. David, Chm. Bd. & Pres.--Michaels Group Inc., Latham, NY, pg. 747
Michaels, William, Pres.--Alvey Inc., Saint Louis, MO, pg. 46
Michaels, William, Chm. Bd. & Pres.--The Buschman Co., Cincinnati, OH, pg. 196
Michalek, Edward, Pres. & Chief Exec. Officer--Advance Machine Company, Plymouth, MN, pg. 18
Michaud, Roger P., Pres.--American Stabilis, Inc., Lewiston, ME, pg. 61
Michel, George E., Pres. & Chief Exec. Officer--A & W Restaurants, Inc., Livonia, MI, pg. 1
Michelson, Alan P., Pres.--Easy Day Manufacturing Company, Inc., Holliston, MA, pg. 364
Michelson, James A., Pres.--Simons Michelson Zieve, Inc., Troy, MI, pg. 1006
Michka, A. Richard, Pres.--Dacor Corporation, Northfield, IL, pg. 310
Michod, David, Chm. Bd. & Chief Exec. Officer--Lane Limited, Tucker, GA, pg. 657
Midaly, Gabe, Pres.--The Union Fork & Hoe Co., Columbus, OH, pg. 1128
Middleton, Charles S., Chm. Bd., Pres. & Chief Exec. Officer--Cal-Air Inc., Whittier, CA, pg. 208
Middleton, Peter, Mng. Dir.--Kobs & Draft, London,, United Kingdom, pg. 112
Miglin, Marilyn, Pres.--Marilyn Miglin, Inc., Chicago, IL, pg. 752
Mihos, Christy, Pres.--Christy's Markets, Inc., Brockton, MA, pg. 249
Mikelsons, J. George, Chm. Bd., Pres. & Chief Exec. Officer--Amtran, Inc., Indianapolis, IN, pg. 69
Mikon, Arnold, Pres. & Chief Exec. Officer--The Smith Group, Inc., Detroit, MI, pg. 1012
Mikytuck, Robert, Jr., Pres.--Better Baked Foods, Inc., North East, PA, pg. 148
Milam, Milton E., Pres.--Cissell Manufacturing Company, Louisville, KY, pg. 357
Milane, John A., Pres.--Tinius Olsen Testing Machine Co., Inc., Willow Grove, PA, pg. 1098
Milavsky, Harold, Chm. Bd. & Pres.--Trizec Properties, Inc., Encino, CA, pg. 1115
Milby, J.R., Pres.--Diamond Chain Company, Indianapolis, IN, pg. 69
Miles, Frank, Pres.--Miles Sand & Gravel Company, Auburn, WA, pg. 753
Miles, John C., Pres. & Chief Oper. Officer--Dentsply International Inc., York, PA, pg. 329
Miles, Ronald William Gordon, Pres. & Gen. Mgr.--Ceras Johnson Ltda., Rio de Janeiro,, Brazil, pg. 599
Milgrim, Hale, Pres. & Chief Exec. Officer--Capitol Records, Inc., Hollywood, CA, pg. 216
Mill, Victor J., III, Pres. & Treas.--Lawrence Pumps, Inc., Lawrence, MA, pg. 662
Millar, Craig, V.P.-Broadcasting Sls.; Pres. & Gen. Mgr.-WBRC-TV--Great American Broadcasting Company, Cincinnati, OH, pg. 52
Millard, Dan, Chm. Bd., Pres., Chief Exec. & Chief Oper. Officer--Central Illinois Steel Company, Carlinville, IL, pg. 232
Millard, Suzanne T., Chm. Bd. & Pres.--Turtle & Hughes, Inc., Linden, NJ, pg. 1119
Millenson, Elliott, Pres. & Chief Exec. Officer--Pollenex Corporation, Chicago, IL, pg. 879
Millenson, Elliott, Pres.--Pollenex Corporation, Chicago, IL, pg. 821
Miller, Allyn M., Pres.--Flair Communications Agency, Inc., Chicago, IL, pg. 416
Miller, Arnold, Pres.--Matrix Essentials, Inc., Solon, OH, pg. 721
Miller, Augustus C., Chm. Bd., Pres., Chief Exec. Officer--Miller Oil Co., Inc., Norfolk, VA, pg. 754
Miller, Bernard J., III, Pres.--Columbian Advertising Inc., Chicago, IL, pg. 266
Miller, Bill, Pres., Chief Exec. & Chief Oper. Officer--Contico International, Inc., Saint Louis, MO, pg. 278
Miller, Bruce, Pres.--Suissa/Miller, Santa Monica, CA, pg. 1056
Miller, C. Preston, Pres.--American Paper Products Group, Ltd., Youngstown, OH, pg. 59
Miller, Charles H., Gen. Mgr.--Hay & Forage Industries, Hesston, KS, pg. 4
Miller, Chester R., Pres.--Herlin Press, West Haven, CT, pg. 531
Miller, Daniel, Pres.-Mktg.--Dexter Shoe Company, Dexter, ME, pg. 334
Miller, David, Pres. & Chief Exec. Officer--Columbia National Group, Inc., Cleveland, OH, pg. 265
Miller, David, Pres.--McInerney-Miller Brothers Inc., Detroit, MI, pg. 729
Miller, Don, Pres. & Chief Exec. Officer--Ederer Inc., Seattle, WA, pg. 368
Miller, Donald E., Pres. & Chief Oper. Officer--The Gates Corporation, Denver, CO, pg. 445
Miller, Donald E., Pres. & Chief Oper. Officer--The Gates Rubber Company, Denver, CO, pg. 445
Miller, Donald P., Pres.--Roppe Corp., Fostoria, OH, pg. 947
Miller, Eric, Pres.--Brooklyn Bottling Co., Milton, NY, pg. 179
Miller, Ernest M., Jr., Pres.--Arvida, Boca Raton, FL, pg. 586
Miller, Frank, Pres.--Darling-Delaware Co., Inc., Irving, TX, pg. 315
Miller, Gary, Pres. & Chief Exec. Officer--Chadwick-Miller Inc., Canton, MA, pg. 237
Miller, George D., Pres. & Chief Exec. Officer--National Fire Protection Association, Quincy, MA, pg. 788
Miller, Gerd, Chm. Bd. & Pres.--Miller Curtain Co., Inc., San Antonio, TX, pg. 754
Miller, Harvey, Pres.--Phillips, Miller, Speyer & Frost, Inc., Amityville, NY, pg. 867
Miller, Henry E., Jr., Pres.--Miller Building Corp., Wilmington, NC, pg. 753
Miller, Herbert, Chm. Bd. & Chief Exec. Officer--Western Development Corporation, Washington, DC, pg. 1179
Miller, Jack, Pres.--Quill Corp., Lincolnshire, IL, pg. 905
Miller, Jack H., Pres.--Howard Miller Clock Company, Zeeland, MI, pg. 754
Miller, James, Pres.--Brodhead-Garrett Co., Mansfield, OH, pg. 178
Miller, James A., Pres.--Dewey Corporation, Jackson, MS, pg. 334
Miller, James C., Pres.--Realty One, Cleveland, OH, pg. 917
Miller, James H., Pres. & Chief Exec. Officer--Plastics Manufacturing Company, Dallas, TX, pg. 876
Miller, Jay, Pres.--TargetCom, Inc., Chicago, IL, pg. 1079
Miller, Jaydee W., Pres.--Pyromet, Inc., Aston, PA, pg. 901
Miller, Jim, Pres. & Chief Exec. Officer--J P Foodservice, Inc., Hanover, MD, pg. 586
Miller, John, V.P.-Mktg.--Sealy Mattress Company, Memphis, TN, pg. 986
Miller, John, Pres.--Hyplains Dressed Beef, Inc., Dodge City, KS, pg. 557
Miller, John, Pres.--Eastern Flat Bed Systems, Newberry, SC, pg. 363
Miller, John, Pres.--L & R Communications, Limited, Sioux City, IA, pg. 647
Miller, John C., Pres.--Miller-St. Nazianz, Inc., Saint Nazianz, WI, pg. 755
Miller, John S., Pres. & Chief Exec. Officer--Tencarva Machinery Co., Inc., Greensboro, NC, pg. 1086
Miller, Ken, Pres.--Young Stuff Apparel Group, Inc., New York, NY, pg. 1214
Miller, Larry, Chm. Bd., Pres. & Chief Exec. Officer--Corinthian Media, Inc., New York, NY, pg. 286
Miller, Leigh B., Pres. & Chief Exec. Officer--Freedman, Gibson & White Inc., Cincinnati, OH, pg. 430
Miller, Lewis, Pres. & Chief Exec. Officer--Industrial Ceramics, Inc., Derry, PA, pg. 566
Miller, Michael J., Pres.--Miller Business Systems, Inc., Arlington, TX, pg. 753
Miller, Philip D., Exec. V.P.--Howard Miller Clock Company, Zeeland, MI, pg. 754
Miller, Richard A., Pres.--Prentiss Incorporated, Floral Park, NY, pg. 887
Miller, Richard C., Pres. & Chief Exec. Officer--YPMS/TMP Worldwide, Inc., Mequon, WI, pg. 1074
Miller, Robert, Pres.--Miller Advertising Agency Inc., New York, NY, pg. 753
Miller, Scott F., Pres.--Miller Transporters, Inc., Jackson, MS, pg. 334
Miller, Stanford, Pres.--Rosco Laboratories, Inc., Port Chester, NY, pg. 947
Miller, Stephan G., Pres.--Citizens Realty & Insurance Inc., Evansville, IN, pg. 251
Miller, Steven, Chm. Bd., Pres. & Chief Exec. Officer--Miller Personnel, Inc., North Brunswick, NJ, pg. 755
Miller, Stuart A., Pres.--Miller Products Company, Inc., North Bergen, NJ, pg. 755
Miller, Virgil, Pres.--Sauder Manufacturing Corporation, Archbold, OH, pg. 972
Miller, William F., Pres.--McKellar Developers of La Jolla, San Diego, CA, pg. 730
Millgard, V. Dennis, Pres. & Chief Exec. Officer--The Millgard Corp., Livonia, MI, pg. 755
Milligan, George, Pres.--Graham Group, Inc., Des Moines, IA, pg. 475
Millner, Guy W., Chm. & Chief Exec. Officer--Norrell Corporation, Atlanta, GA, pg. 810
Mills, John, Pres. & Chief Oper. Officer--Medline Industries, Inc., Mundelein, IL, pg. 736
Mills, Keith, Pres.--Digital Electronic Automation, Livonia, MI, pg. 337
Mills, William G., Pres.--R.W. Eaken, Inc., Leesport, PA, pg. 362
Millstein, Jack H., Jr., Pres.--Millstein Industries, Jeannette, PA, pg. 756
Milner, Dave, Pres. & Gen. Mgr.-KEX-AM--Great American Broadcasting Company, Cincinnati, OH, pg. 52
Milnor, G.S., Pres. & Chief Exec. Officer--Millers' Mutual Insurance Assn. Of Illinois, Alton, IL, pg. 755
Milnor, George I., Pres.--Millers' General Insurance Company, Alton, IL, pg. 755
Milobinski, Hans, Pres.--Keiper Recaro, Inc., Clawson, MI, pg. 620
Milovich, Mitch, Pres.--Baker Material Handling Corp., Summerville, SC, pg. 115
Milroy, Robert C., Pres.--Alexander Marketing Services, Inc., Grand Rapids, MI, pg. 33
Milstein, Howard, Chm. & Pres.--The Milford Agency, New York, NY, pg. 753
Milstein, Howard P., Chm. & Chief Exec. Officer--Douglas Elliman-Gibbons & Ives, Inc., New York, NY, pg. 347
Milton, James W., Pres.--Milton Can Co., Inc., Elizabeth, NJ, pg. 756
Mims, T.J., Pres., Chief Exec. & Chief Oper. Officer--Canal Insurance Co., Greenville, SC, pg. 213
Miniat, Ronald, Chm., Pres. & Chief Exec. Officer--Ed Miniat, Inc., Chicago, IL, pg. 757
Minihan, John M., Pres. & Chief Exec. Officer--Louisville Bedding Company, Louisville, KY, pg. 684
Minkus, Morton D., Pres.--Transilwrap Company, Inc., Chicago, IL, pg. 1107
Minnema, John, Pres. & Gen. Mgr.--Cherry Central Cooperative, Traverse City, MI, pg. 243
Minnick, Terry, Chm. Bd., Pres. & Chief Exec. Officer--The Pro Corporation, Florence, MA, pg. 891
Minor, Henry H., III, Pres.--P.W. Minor & Son, Inc., Batavia, NY, pg. 758
Miranda, Guillermo, Jr., Chm. Bd. & Chief Exec. Officer & Pres.--Gator Industries Inc., Hialeah, FL, pg. 446
Mirando, Louis, Pres. & Gen. Mgr.--Long Island Water Corporation, Lynbrook, NY, pg. 682
Misch, Donald L., Chief Exec. Officer & Gen. Mgr.--Jasper County Farm Bureau Co-op Association, Inc., Rensselaer, IN, pg. 590
Missett, Judi, Pres. & Chief Exec. Officer--Jazzercise, Inc., Carlsbad, CA, pg. 591
Mitchel, Thomas L., Chm. Bd. & Pres.--Mitchel & Scot Machine Co., Inc., Indianapolis, IN, pg. 761
Mitchell, Danny, Pres. & Chief Oper. Officer--Godwin Advertising Agency, Inc., Jackson, MS, pg. 464
Mitchell, Doug, Chm. Bd. & Pres.--Perryton Equity, Perryton, TX, pg. 863
Mitchell, Elliott, Chm. Bd., Pres. & Chief Exec. Officer--Arcade Inc., Chattanooga, TN, pg. 80
Mitchell, Emery, Pres.--Lucky Fruit & Produce, Inc., Sacramento, CA, pg. 686
Mitchell, R.B., Pres., Chief Exec. Officer--Marshall Jaccoma Mitchell Advertising, New York, NY, pg. 714
Mitchell, R.L., Pres.--Koehler Manufacturing Company, Marlborough, MA, pg. 639
Mitchell, Richard S., Jr., Pres.--Moyer Mitchell Company, Inc., Voorhees, NJ, pg. 774
Mitchell, Ronald B., Chm. Bd. & Pres.--Mitchell & Assoc., Inc., Bethesda, MD, pg. 761
Mitchell, Stephen C., Pres. & Chief Oper. Officer--Lester B. Knight & Associates, Inc., Chicago, IL, pg. 637
Mitchell, William A., Jr., Pres.--Carter, Atlanta, GA, pg. 226
Mitchell, William F., Chm. Bd., Pres. & Chief Exec. Officer--Mitchell Corporation of Owosso, Owosso, MI, pg. 761
Miyares, Marta, Pres.--Agencias USA, Chicago, IL, pg. 24
Mockley, B.A., Chm. Bd. & Pres.--Anchor Gasoline Corporation, Tulsa, OK, pg. 71
Mockley, B.A., Pres.--Canal Refining Co., Tulsa, OK, pg. 71
Mockley, B.A., Pres.--Cove Petroleum, Tulsa, OK, pg. 71
Mode, Frank, Jr., Pres.--Palmer Manufacturing Company, Malden, MA, pg. 844
Modell, Michael S., Pres.--Henry Modell & Company, Inc., Long Island City, NY, pg. 762
Moe, Henrik, Pres., Chief Oper. & Exec. Officer--DEC International, Inc., Madison, WI, pg. 308
Moeller, Eudy F., Sr., Pres.--Fessel, Siegfriedt & Moeller, Inc., Louisville, KY, pg. 407
Moeller, John, Pres.--Simmons Juvenile Products Co., Inc., New London, WI, pg. 1008
Moeller, Richard J., Pres.--Advanstar Communications, Cleveland, OH, pg. 21
Mogas, V. Louis, Pres. & Chief Exec. Officer--Mogas Industries, Inc., Houston, TX, pg. 763
Mohan, D.M., Pres. & Chief Exec. Officer--Southern Pacific Transportation Co., San Francisco, CA, pg. 75
Mohan, D.M., Pres. & Chief Exec. Officer--Southern Pacific Lines, San Francisco, CA, pg. 1022
Mohlin, C. Rick, Pres.--Carney/Mohlin & Company, Lynnfield, MA, pg. 222
Mohrman, Roy, Chm. Bd., Pres. & Chief Exec. Officer--Handling Systems Engineering, Jacksonville, FL, pg. 505
Moilanen, Thomas A., Pres. & Chief Exec. Officer--Cloverdale Equipment Co., Oak Park, MI, pg. 256
Mojden, Andrew W., Pres.--Fleetwood Systems, Inc., Countryside, IL, pg. 417
Molin, Kim E., Pres.--Molin Auto Parts Inc., Buffalo, NY, pg. 764
Moll, Ted, Pres.--Aircap Industries Corp., Verona, MS, pg. 694
Moll, William, Pres. & Gen. Mgr.-WKRC-TV--Great American Broadcasting Company, Cincinnati, OH, pg. 52
Moller, John J., Pres. & Chief Exec. Officer--USA Petroleum Corporation, Santa Monica, CA, pg. 1124
Moloney, Earl, Chm. Bd. & Chief Exec. Officer--Molon Motor & Coil Corp., Rolling Meadows, IL, pg. 764
Molsbee, Alan, Pres.--International Business Interiors Inc., Chicago, IL, pg. 575
Monahan, Tom, Pres.--Leonard Monahan Lubars & Kelly, Providence, RI, pg. 668

Monahan, William D., Pres. & Chief Exec. Officer--Edward V. Monahan Inc., Eastpointe, MI, pg. 765
Mondin, Galliano, Chief Exec. Officer--Diadora America, Inc., Kent, WA, pg 335
Monette, Edward A., Chm., Pres., Chief Exec. & Oper. Officer--St. Croix Press, Inc., New Richmond, WI, pg. 966
Monge, Dimitri, Pres. & Chief Oper. Officer--Airtex Products, Fairfield, IL, pg. 1123
Moniz, Jose Carlos Botelho, Mng. Dir.--EPG/TBWA, Lisbon, , Portugal, pg. 1072
Monjello, Donald, Pres.--American Frozen Foods, Inc., Stratford, CT, pg. 55
Monk, Albert C., III, Pres. & Chief Oper. Officer--A.C. Monk Co., Inc., Farmville, NC, pg. 766
Monk, Richard H., Jr., Pres. & Chief Oper. Officer--Avondale Mills, Inc., Sylacauga, AL, pg. 103
Monkiewicz, Ray C., Pres.--Kayem Foods, Inc., Chelsea, MA, pg. 619
Monks, Richard, Pres., Chief Exec. Officer & Chief Oper. Officer--ConTec International, Schenectady, NY, pg. 278
Montague, L.D., Jr., Pres.--B. L. Montague Co., Sumter, SC, pg. 766
Montanus, Phil, Pres.-Devel.--Towne Properties, Cincinnati, OH, pg. 1104
Montembeault, Gerald, Pres.--Dobles Chevrolet, Inc., Manchester, NH, pg. 342
Monteroso, Amalia, Pres.--Century 21 Agmont Real Estate, Inc., Chicago, IL, pg. 235
Montgomery, Robert, Pres.--Bob Montgomery Chevrolet/ Honda, Louisville, KY, pg. 767
Montgomery, Walter S., Jr., Pres., Treas., Chief Exec. & Chief Fin. Officer--Spartan Mills, Spartanburg, SC, pg. 1026
Montgomery, William, Chm. Bd., Pres., & Chief Exec. Officer--The SArgent-SOwell Company, Grand Prairie, TX, pg. 971
Montrone, Paul M., Pres.--The Henley Group, Inc., Hampton, NH, pg. 529
Montrone, Paul M., Pres. & Mng. Dir.--New Hampshire Oak, Hampton, NH, pg. 800
Mooar, William E., Pres.--Coast Manufacturing Company, Yonkers, NY, pg. 257
Moody, Maxey D., III, Pres.--M. D. Moody & Sons Inc., Jacksonville, FL, pg. 768
Mooers, John, Pres.--Wilshire Newport Inc., Burbank, CA, pg. 1193
Moon, Hangup, Pres.--Electronics Stamping Corp., Rancho Dominguez, CA, pg. 375
Moon, J.S., Pres.--Patterson Laboratories, Inc., Detroit, MI, pg. 852
Moon, Wayne, Pres. & Chief Oper. Officer--Kaiser Foundation Health & Hospitals Group, Oakland, CA, pg. 614
Moon, Willard, Pres. & Dir. Acct. Mngmt.--Point Communications, Inc., Dallas, TX, pg. 878
Mooney, James P., Chm. Bd. & Chief Exec. Officer--Mooney Chemicals, Cleveland, OH, pg. 768
Mooney, Joseph T., Jr., Pres.--Monsey Products Company, Kimberton, PA, pg. 766
Mooney, Michael A., Pres.--Mills Hall Walborn & Associates, Mayfield Heights, OH, pg. 756
Mooney, Susan, Pres. & Treas.--Daw Technologies, Inc., Salt Lake City, UT, pg. 319
Moore, Alan, Pres.--Shofar Kosher Foods, Inc., Newark, NJ, pg. 1000
Moore, Charles V., Pres.--Trainer Wortham & Company Incorporated, New York, NY, pg. 1106
Moore, Clyde R., Pres. & Chief Oper. Officer--Thomas & Betts Holdings, Inc., Memphis, TN, pg. 425
Moore, Clyde W., Pres.--Crown International, Inc., Elkhart, IN, pg. 302
Moore, Hillar C., Jr., Pres. & Chief Exec. Officer--Associated Grocers, Inc., Baton Rouge, LA, pg. 89
Moore, Jack, Pres.--Union Underwear Co., Inc., Bowling Green, KY, pg. 400
Moore, Jack, Pres.--Fruit of the Loom, Bowling Green, KY, pg. 400
Moore, James T., II, Pres. & Chief Oper. Officer--Invetech Co., Detroit, MI, pg. 581
Moore, John O., Pres. & Chief Exec. Officer--Duncan Equipment Company, Duncan, OK, pg. 352
Moore, M.H., Pres. & Chief Exec. Officer--Longyear Company, Salt Lake City, UT, pg. 682
Moore, Mark M., Pres.--Texas Metal Works, Inc., Beaumont, TX, pg. 1089
Moore, Michael, Pres.--Sun Process Converting Company, Elk Grove Village, IL, pg. 1059
Moore, Michael J., Chm. Bd. & Pres.--Southland Industries, Long Beach, CA, pg. 1023
Moore, Richard, Pres. & Chief Exec. Officer--Kingswood Advertising, Inc., Ardmore, PA, pg. 632
Moore, Stanley A., Pres.--Overton Moore & Associates, Gardena, CA, pg. 833
Moore, Steven R., Pres.--Rex Moore Electrical Contractors & Engineers, West Sacramento, CA, pg. 768
Moore, Thomas R., Pres. & Chief Exec. Officer--Remmele Engineering, Inc., Saint Paul, MN, pg. 926
Moore, Thomas W., Pres.--Sunniland Corporation, Sanford, FL, pg. 1061
Moore, Wayne R., Chm. Bd., Pres. & Chief Exec. Officer--Moore Special Tool Co., Inc., Bridgeport, CT, pg. 768
Moore, William M., Jr., Chm. Bd. & Pres.--Trident Financial Corporation, Raleigh, NC, pg. 1113
Moorman, John R., Chief Exec. Officer--Mrs. Goochs Natural Food Markets, Sherman Oaks, CA, pg. 761
Moorman, Michael F., Pres.--Peebles, Inc., South Hill, VA, pg. 855
Moos, J. Clifford, Chm., Pres. & Chief Exec. Officer--Economy Folding Box Corp., Chicago, IL, pg. 367
Moothart, William H., Pres.--Chatsworth Data Corporation, Chatsworth, CA, pg. 241
Morales, Jesus M., Pres.--Sunbeam del Peru S.A., Lima, Peru, pg. 1059
Moram, Robert J., Pres. & Chief Exec. Officer--Ludlow Composites Corporation, Fremont, OH, pg. 686
Moran, Arthur, Pres.--Art Moran Pontiac-GMC Inc., Southfield, MI, pg. 769
Moran, Gordon W., Pres. & Chief Exec. Officer--Hollingsworth & Vose Co., East Walpole, MA, pg. 539
Moran, Keenan, Pres.--Tuffy Associates Corp., Toledo, OH, pg. 1119
Moran, Patricia, Pres. & Chief Exec. Officer--JM Family Enterprises Inc., Deerfield Beach, FL, pg. 584
Morean, William, Chief Exec. Officer--Jabil Circuit Inc., Saint Petersburg, FL, pg. 587
Moree, B.E., Pres.--Pony Express Courier Corp., Charlotte, NC, pg. 166
Moreland, Donald C., Pres. & Chief Exec. Officer--Frank Paxton Company, Kansas City, MO, pg. 592
Morelli, Joseph, Chm. Bd., Pres. & Chief Exec. Officer--M. H. Rhodes, Inc., Avon, CT, pg. 931
Morgan, Alfred Y., Jr., Pres.--White Rock Products Corp., White Stone, NY, pg. 1186
Morgan, Jerry, Pres. & Chief Oper. Officer--Sargent & Greenleaf, Inc., Nicholasville, KY, pg. 971
Morgan, John S., Chm., Pres. & Chief Exec. Officer--Morgan Foods, Inc., Austin, IN, pg. 770
Morgan, Lloyd H., Pres. & Chief Oper. Officer--The Gage Company, Pittsburgh, PA, pg. 441
Morgan, Phillip R., Pres. & Chief Exec. Officer--Morgan Construction Company, Worcester, MA, pg. 769
Morgan, Robert, Pres.--Morgan Manufacturing Company, Inc., Paris, IL, pg. 770
Morgan, Robert, Chm. Bd., Pres. & Chief Exec. Officer--Morgan Industries Inc., Bala-Cynwyd, PA, pg. 770
Morgensen, Jerry L., Pres.--Hensel Phelps Construction Co., Greeley, CO, pg. 530
Moriarty, Kevin, Pres. & Chief Exec. Officer--Del Taco, Inc., Costa Mesa, CA, pg. 325
Moriarty, Kevin K., Pres. & Chief Exec. Officer--Del Taco/ Naugles, Costa Mesa, CA, pg. 325
Morin, Curtis L., Pres. & Treas.--Bennington Iron Works, Inc., Bennington, VT, pg. 139
Moritz, John D., Pres.--Moritz Cadillac-Saab Inc., Arlington, TX, pg. 770
Mork, John, Pres.--Eastern American Energy Corporation, Charleston, WV, pg. 363
Mork, P.W., Pres.--B-E Holdings Inc., South Milwaukee, WI, pg. 106
Mork, Phillip, Pres.--Bucyrus-Erie Company, South Milwaukee, WI, pg. 186
Morley, Harry T., Pres. & Chief Exec. Officer--Taylor-Morley, Inc., Saint Louis, MO, pg. 1081
Morris, Andrew, Pres. & Chief Oper. Officer--Warner, Bicking, Morris & Partners, Inc., New York, NY, pg. 1164
Morris, Charles H., Pres.--Morris Newspaper Corporation, Savannah, GA, pg. 771
Morris, Donald E., Pres.--Acorn Engineering Company, City of Industry, CA, pg. 14
Morris, G. Ronald, Pres. & Chief Exec. Officer--Western Industries, Inc., Milwaukee, WI, pg. 1179
Morris, George C., Pres.--Niagara Blower Company, Buffalo, NY, pg. 805
Morris, Glynn, Pres. & Chief Oper. Officer--Presto Food Products, Inc., City of Industry, CA, pg. 888
Morris, J.W., Pres. & Chief Exec. Officer--Gerland Corp., Houston, TX, pg. 454
Morris, John L., Pres.--Bass Pro Shops, Inc., Springfield, MO, pg. 125
Morris, Ken, Pres.--Siegel & Gale, New York, NY, pg. 1002
Morris, Leslie M., Jr., Pres.--Sands Investments, Inc., Myrtle Beach, SC, pg. 970
Morris, Marvin, V.P.-Mktg.--Alamo Group, Inc., La Grange, IL, pg. 29
Morris, Michael, Dir.--Missouri Lottery, Jefferson City, MO, pg. 760
Morris, Robert, Pres.--Harmon City, Inc., West Valley City, UT, pg. 510
Morris, T.N., Jr., Chm., Pres. & Chief Exec. Officer--Calcasieu Lumber Company, Austin, TX, pg. 208
Morris, Thomas B., Jr., Chm. Policy Committee, Mng. Ptnr. & Chief Exec. Officer)--Dechert Price & Rhoads, Philadelphia, PA, pg. 323
Morris, William C., Chm. Bd. & Pres.--J. & W. Seligman & Company, New York, NY, pg. 584
Morris, William S., III, Pres.--Shivers Trading & Operating Co., Augusta, GA, pg. 999
Morrison, J.M., Chm. Bd. & Pres.--Morrison, Inc., Hammond, IN, pg. 771
Morrison, Richard S., Pres. & Chief Exec. Officer--Molded Fiber Glass Companies, Ashtabula, OH, pg. 763
Morrison, Robert B., Pres. & New Bus. Contact--The Morrison Agency, Atlanta, GA, pg. 771
Morrissette, Arthur E., Pres.--Interstate Van Lines, Inc., Springfield, VA, pg. 581
Morrow, Charles B., Pres.--Fannie May Candy Shops, Inc., Chicago, IL, pg. 604
Morrow, David W., Chm. Bd., Pres., Chief Exec. Officer & Chief Oper. Officer--Pueblo International, Inc., Pompano Beach, FL, pg. 899
Morrow, M.R., Pres. & Gen. Mgr.--Sunbeam Corporation (Canada) Limited, Toronto, Canada, pg. 1059
Morse, Edward J., Sr., Chm. Bd. & Pres.--Morse Operations Inc., Ft. Lauderdale, FL, pg. 772
Mortenson, M.A., Jr., Chm. Bd., Chief Exec. Officer & Pres.--M. A. Mortenson Company, Minneapolis, MN, pg. 772
Mortine, Neil R., V.P., Dir. Pub. Rels.--Lord, Sullivan & Yoder/Public Relations, Columbus, OH, pg. 684
Morton, Jay W., Pres. & Chief Exec. Officer--United Engines, Inc., Oklahoma City, OK, pg. 1131
Mosack, Carl L., Pres.--Conbraco Industries Inc., Matthews, NC, pg. 272
Moscowitz, Edwin, Pres.--Peerless Umbrella Co., Inc., Harrison, NJ, pg. 855
Moseley, F.C., Pres.--Simpson Investment Co., Seattle, WA, pg. 1007
Moseley, F.C., Pres.-SICO--Simpson Timber Co., Shelton, WA, pg. 1007
Mosely, Larry, Pres.--Ingrid-Sevko, Inc., Deerfield, IL, pg. 569
Moses, Louis S., Pres. & Creative Dir.--Moses Anshell, Inc., Phoenix, AZ, pg. 76
Moshontz, Michael, Pres.--Blue Coral, Inc., Cleveland, OH, pg. 159
Mosquera, Carlos M., Chm. Bd., Pres. & Chief Exec. Officer--Cicero/BSB Publicidad S.A., Buenos Aires,, Argentina, pg. 111
Moss, Charles W., Pres.--Hickory Construction Company, Hickory, NC, pg. 532
Moss, Geo. French, Pres.--Western States Envelope Co., Butler, WI, pg. 1181
Moss, Victor, Pres. & Sec.--Tomco Auto Products, Inc., Vernon, CA, pg. 1100
Mossberg, Alan I., Pres., Chief Exec. & Chief Oper. Officer & Treas.--O. F. Mossberg & Sons, Inc., North Haven, CT, pg. 773
Most, Nathan, Pres.--Amex Commodities Corporation, New York, NY, pg. 63
Motta, Robert D., Pres.--Southwest Floor Covering Inc., San Diego, CA, pg. 1023
Moy, Maria Christina Carvalho Pinto, Pres.--Impact Comunicacoes, Sao Paulo,, Brazil, pg. 1213
Moyer, Curtis F., Pres.--Moyer Packing Company, Souderton, PA, pg. 774
Moyer, William C., Dr., Chm. Bd., Pres. & Chief Exec. Officer--SFA, Inc., Landover, MD, pg. 961
Moynihan, James J., Pres. & Chief Exec. Officer--Heery International, Inc., Atlanta, GA, pg. 525
Mucha, Horst, Pres.--Hohner/HSS Inc., Ashland, VA, pg. 538
Muck, Philip F., Pres., Chief Exec. Officer & Treas.--Munroe, Inc., Pittsburgh, PA, pg. 776
Mueller, Curt, Pres.--Mueller Sports Medicine, Inc., Prairie du Sac, WI, pg. 774
Muench, M.A., Pres.--Muench-Kreuzer Candle Company, Syracuse, NY, pg. 774
Muer, Charles A., Pres.--C. A. Muer Corp., Detroit, MI, pg. 774
Muldoon, Joe, Pres.--PC Distributing Inc., Mount Prospect, IL, pg. 835
Muldrow, Ken, Pres. & Chief Exec. Officer--Goodpasture, Inc., Brownfield, TX, pg. 471
Mulhern, Patrick M., Pres.--Mulhern Belting, Inc., Oakland, NJ, pg. 775
Mullane, Denis F., Pres. & Chief Exec. Officer--Connecticut Mutual Life Insurance Company, Hartford, CT, pg. 274
Mulle, Sherman G., Pres.--Mulle/Breen Advertising, Toluca Lake, CA, pg. 775
Mullen, David T., Pres. & New Bus. Contact--The Marketing Continuum, Inc., Dallas, TX, pg. 709
Mullen, J.J., Pres.--Apple Vacations West Inc., Elk Grove Village, IL, pg. 79
Mullen, James X., Pres. & Chief Exec. Officer--Mullen Advertising, Inc., Wenham, MA, pg. 775
Mullet, Paul, Pres.--Excel Industries, Inc., Hesston, KS, pg. 392
Mullett, D.H., Pres.--Bradley Corporation, Menomonee Falls, WI, pg. 170
Mulligan, James, Pres.--M M M Sales, Inc., City of Industry, CA, pg. 692
Mullin, Francis I., Pres. & Chief Oper. Officer--The Seven-Up Company, Dallas, TX, pg. 342
Mullinax, Charles E., Pres.--Ed Mullinax Ford, Inc., Amherst, OH, pg. 775
Mullinex, Travis, Pres. & Chief Oper. Officer--Tri Valley Growers Inc., San Francisco, CA, pg. 1111
Mullins, Roy L., Jr., Pres. & Chief Exec. Officer--Beacon Sales Corporation, Jacksonville, FL, pg. 129
Mumford, Don, Pres.--Alma Industries, High Point, NC, pg. 43
Mundinger, William D., Pres.--YSD Industries, Youngstown, OH, pg. 1207
Mundschau, Walter J., Pres.--Kalmbach Publishing Co., Milwaukee, WI, pg. 615
Mundt, G. Henry, III, Pres. & Chief Exec. Officer--Cirrus System, Inc., Westchester, IL, pg. 720
Mungo, Frank, Pres.--Temperature Equipment Corporation, Melrose Park, IL, pg. 1086
Mungo, Frank, Pres.--Bryant Mungo Division, Lansing, IL, pg. 1086
Mungo, Stewart, Pres.--Michael J. Mungo Company, Inc., Columbia, SC, pg. 775
Munigle, Charles L., Pres.--Munigle Corporation, West Hartford, CT, pg. 775
Munro, Donald, Chm. Bd., Chief Exec. Officer & Treas.--Munro & Company, Inc., Hot Springs, AR, pg. 775
Munsch, Kenneth M., Pres.--ATCOM, Inc., Research Triangle Park, NC, pg. 93
Munsen, Paul, Pres. & Chief Exec. Officer--Munsen's Discovery Enterprises, Hinsdale, IL, pg. 776
Munson, Dee, Pres.--Evans Food Group, Seattle, WA, pg. 391
Munter, Hal, Pres.--Forman Brothers, Inc., Washington, DC, pg. 424
Murakami, Kakuichi, Pres. & Reg. Dir.--Dentsu, Young & Rubicam/Tokyo, Tokyo, Japan, pg. 330
Murawski, J., Exec. V.P.--Pioneer Industrial Products Co., Willard, OH, pg. 871
Murchison, Anne, Pres.--Topcor Financial Corporation, Chicago, IL, pg. 1101
Murdock, David H., Pres. & Chief Exec. Officer--Pacific Holding Corporation, Los Angeles, CA, pg. 840
Murdock, Harold G., Jr., Pres.--Murdock, Inc., Compton, CA, pg. 776
Murphy, Bill, Chief Exec.--Lowe Luerzer GmbH, Frankfurt/ Main, Germany, pg. 685
Murphy, Dan, V.P. & Gen. Mgr.--Sauerman, Melrose Park, IL, pg. 47
Murphy, Henry, Pres.--Americo Manufacturing Co., Inc., Acworth, GA, pg. 66

Murphy, Kenneth T., Chm. Bd., Pres. & Chief Exec. Officer--First Abilene Bankshares, Inc., Abilene, TX, pg. 411
Murphy, Michael, Pres.--Kal Kan Foods, Inc., Vernon, CA, pg. 713
Murphy, Peter, Jr., Chm. Bd., Pres. & Chief Exec. Officer--Murphy Company, Eugene, OR, pg. 776
Murphy, Robert E., Pres.--California Pacific Research, Inc., Reno, NV, pg. 210
Murphy, Robert E., Pres.--Japs-Olson Company, Minneapolis, MN, pg. 590
Murphy, Wendell H., Pres.--Murphy Farms Inc., Rose Hill, NC, pg. 776
Murray, Arthur G., Pres. & Chief Oper. Officer--Sunshine Biscuits, Inc., Woodbridge, NJ, pg. 439
Murray, Charles C., Pres., Chief Exec. Officer--Apparel America, Inc., New Haven, CT, pg. 78
Murray, Gerald, Pres.--Ruder, Finn, Inc., Chicago, IL, pg. 954
Murray, James C., Pres. & Chief Exec. Officer--Utilities Construction Co., Inc. Of South Carolina, Charleston, SC, pg. 1141
Murray, John J., Pres.--Hausted, Medina, OH, pg. 1008
Murray, Martha S., Publisher--Bon Appetit Magazine, Los Angeles, CA, pg. 636
Murray, N. Leight, Pres. & Chief Exec. Officer--The Airolite Company, Marietta, OH, pg. 28
Murray, Tommy, Pres.--Snyder Potato Chips, Berlin, PA, pg. 26
Murray, Vince, Pres. & Chief Oper. Officer--Fleer Corporation, Mount Laurel, NJ, pg. 695
Muse, Albert C., Pres. & Chief Exec. Officer--Crown Coal & Coke Co. Inc., Pittsburgh, PA, pg. 302
Muselman, Arthur K., Pres.--E.P. Graphics, Inc., Berne, IN, pg. 360
Musgrove, H.B., Chm. Bd., Pres. & Chief Exec. Officer--Frantz Manufacturing Co., Sterling, IL, pg. 429
Mushkin, Albert S., Pres. & Chief Oper. Officer--Master Industries Corp., New York, NY, pg. 719
Muskat, Irwin, Chm. Bd., Pres. & Chief Exec. Officer--Granite State Packing Co., Manchester, NH, pg. 476
Must, Alan, Pres.--Detroit City Dairy, Inc., Highland Park, MI, pg. 333
Must, Joel, Pres.-Warehouse--Detroit City Dairy, Inc., Highland Park, MI, pg. 333
Muth, Richard, Pres.--Orco Block Company, Stanton, CA, pg. 828
Muti, Arthur M., Pres.--Penco Products, Oaks, PA, pg. 857
Mutz, O.U., Pres.--Sovereign Group Inc., Indianapolis, IN, pg. 1024
Myers, A. Maurice, Pres., Chief Exec. Officer & Dir.--Aloha Airgroup, Inc., Honolulu, HI, pg. 43
Myers, C.C., Pres. & Chief Exec. Officer--C. C. Myers, Inc., Rancho Cordova, CA, pg. 780
Myers, Charles C., Pres.--Superior Industries of Nebraska, Inc., Omaha, NE, pg. 1063
Myers, Douglas G., Exec. Dir.-Zoological Society--San Diego Zoo, San Diego, CA, pg. 969
Myers, Edward, Chm. Bd. & Pres.--Tillamook County Creamery Assn., Tillamook, OR, pg. 1097
Myers, Francis J., Jr., Pres.--F J M Corporation, Elk Grove Village, IL, pg. 394
Myers, Gary F., Pres.--Kocolene Oil Corp., Seymour, IN, pg. 639
Myers, Howard B., Pres. & Chief Exec. Officer--Triumph*Lor, Inc., Houston, TX, pg. 1115
Myers, Jay, Pres. & Dir.-Adv.--Andiamo, Inc., Fountain Valley, CA, pg. 74
Myers, Jerry K., Pres. & Chief Exec. Officer--Steelcase Inc., Grand Rapids, MI, pg. 1044
Myers, Joseph E., Chm. Bd. & Pres.--Collins Oldsmobile Inc., Indianapolis, IN, pg. 263
Myers, Kenneth B., Pres.--Badger Northland Inc., Kaukauna, WI, pg. 113
Myers, Kip, Pres. & Creative Dir.--Myers & Associates, Inc., Stuart, FL, pg. 780
Myers, L.G., Pres., Chief Exec. Officer & Admin. Dir.--LubeCon Systems, Inc., Fremont, MI, pg. 686
Myers, Norman S., Pres., Treas., Chief Exec. & Fin. Officers--IDM Controls, Houston, TX, pg. 560
Myerson, James Parker, Pres.--Ben Myerson Candy Company, Inc., Los Angeles, CA, pg. 780
Myhre, Larry E., Pres.--Hallidie Machinery Company, Inc., Seattle, WA, pg. 501
Myhren, Trygve, Pres. & Chief Oper. Officer--Providence Journal Company, Providence, RI, pg. 895
Myra, Harold, Chief Exec. Officer--Christianity Today, Inc., Carol Stream, IL, pg. 249
Myrick, Bobby H., Pres. & Treas.--Myrick Construction Inc., Biscoe, NC, pg. 780
Naccarato, Vincent A., Chm. Bd., Pres. & Chief Exec. Officer--Wilton Industries, Inc., Woodridge, IL, pg. 1194
Nachman, David K., Pres. & Chief Exec. Officer--The Spohn Corporation, Cleveland, OH, pg. 1032
Nachman, David K., Pres. & Chief Exec. Officer--Emerald Corporation, Cleveland, OH, pg. 378
Nacht, Stephen, Pres.--Shonac Corporation, Columbus, OH, pg. 1000
Nadel, Herbert, Pres.--Nadel Partnership, Inc., Los Angeles, CA, pg. 782
Nadel, Jack, Chm. Bd. & Pres.--Measured Marketing Services, Los Angeles, CA, pg. 734
Nadelberg, Michael, Pres.--Moorgate Advertising Agency, Boston, MA, pg. 768
Nadorf, Ben J., Pres. & Treas.--Everlast Sports Manufacturing Corp., Bronx, NY, pg. 392
Nady, John, Pres. & Chief Exec. Officer--Nady Systems, Inc., Emeryville, CA, pg. 783
Nagel, Bruce, Pres.--Cole-Layer-Trumble Company (CLT), Dayton, OH, pg. 320
Nagy, Bob, Pres. & Chief Exec. Officer--Vernay Laboratories, Inc., Yellow Springs, OH, pg. 1148
Nahey, Brian L., Pres. & Chief Exec. Officer--Venturedyne, Ltd., Milwaukee, WI, pg. 1148
Nahikian, William, Pres.--Color Arts, Inc., Racine, WI, pg. 264
Nahser, F. Byron, Pres. & Chief Exec. Officer--Frank C. Nahser Inc., Chicago, IL, pg. 783
Naify, Robert A., Pres.--The Todd-AO Corporation, San Francisco, CA, pg. 1099
Naik, Jim, Sr., Pres.--Royal Cruise Line Inc., San Francisco, CA, pg. 953
Naimo, Al, Pres.--Property Management Services, Inc., Vancouver, WA, pg. 894
Nakahara, Asuka, Pres. & Chief Exec. Officer--Trammell Crow Company, Dallas, TX, pg. 1106
Nakajima, Hide, Pres.--Atari Games Corporation, Milpitas, CA, pg. 93
Nakajima, Shunji, Pres.--ASICS Tiger Corporation, Fountain Valley, CA, pg. 8
Nakash, Joseph, Chm. Bd. & Pres.--Jordache Enterprises, Inc., New York, NY, pg. 604
Nall, P.V., Pres.--Ideal Industries, Inc., Sycamore, IL, pg. 562
Nanda, Arun, Chm. & Mng. Dir.--Rediffusion, Bombay, India, pg. 331
Nangia, Charles, V.P.-Engrng. Services--Pascoe Building Systems, Inc., Columbus, GA, pg. 851
Napolitan, John D., Pres.--M. J. Brock & Sons, Inc., Los Angeles, CA, pg. 178
Narens, Robert L., Pres.--The Akro Corporation, Canton, OH, pg. 262
Narlinger, Dennis, Chm., Pres. & Chief Exec. Officer--Shugart Corporation, Irvine, CA, pg. 1001
Nash, Merrill L., Pres.--Symons Corporation, Pasadena, CA, pg. 1069
Nash, Samuel T., Jr., Pres.--Universal Securities Corporation, Birmingham, AL, pg. 1139
Nason, Charles T., Chm. Bd., Pres. & Chief Exec. Officer--The Acacia Group, Washington, DC, pg. 10
Nason, Charles W., Chm. Bd. & Pres.--Worzalla Publishing Co., Inc., Stevens Point, WI, pg. 1204
Nason, Robert E., Exec. Partner--Grant Thornton, Chicago, IL, pg. 477
Nasser, Roland G., Pres.--Star Expansion Company, Mountainville, NY, pg. 1039
Nast, Glen M., Pres. & Treas.--Northern Wire & Cable, Inc., Troy, MI, pg. 814
Nathan, Jarrett M., Mng. Partner & Creative Dir.--Eire Partners, Inc., Chicago, IL, pg. 372
Navas, Stanley R., Pres.--Concrete Pipe & Products Co. Inc., Richmond, VA, pg. 273
Nave, Michael, Pres.--Mercury Distributing Co., Inc., Chatsworth, CA, pg. 740
Nayes, R.A., Pres.--The Gilman Company, Chattanooga, TN, pg. 603
Naylor, James, Jr., Pres.--Maleson Naylor, Owings Mills, MD, pg. 702
Neal, Gary M., Pres. & Chief Exec. Officer--Watlow Electric Manufacturing Company, Saint Louis, MO, pg. 1167
Neal, John R., Chm. Bd. & Pres.--JRN, Inc., Columbia, TN, pg. 586
Nedblake, G. Wesley, Pres.--Package Service Company, Inc., Kansas City, MO, pg. 842
Neeb, Philip, Pres.--Neeb Corporation, Bad Axe, MI, pg. 797
Needham, Tom, Chm., Pres. & Chief Exec. Officer--Allen & Hoshall, Inc., Memphis, TN, pg. 36
Needle, Edward G., Pres.--Atlantic Plumbing Supply Company, Washington, DC, pg. 95
Neely, Bill, Pres. & Chief Oper. Officer--M. B. Kahn Construction Co., Inc., Columbia, SC, pg. 614
Neely, Juanita L., Pres.--Layman Candy Company, Inc., Salem, VA, pg. 663
Nei, Gary, Pres. & Chief Exec. Officer--Eon Labs, Inc., Lake Forest, IL, pg. 383
Neighbors, Thomas H., Pres. & Chief Oper. Officer--Falcon Associates, Ltd., McLean, VA, pg. 981
Neil, John, Pres.--J-Starr Industries, Inc., Fort Atkinson, WI, pg. 1040
Neis, Arnold Hayward, Pres.--E.T. Browne Drug Co., Inc., Englewood Cliffs, NJ, pg. 183
Neisel, Peter, Chief Exec. Officer--Schwab Corp., Lafayette, IN, pg. 980
Neisewander, Ray H., Jr., Pres.--Raynor Garage Door Company, Dixon, IL, pg. 915
Nelsen, Clifford D., Chm. Bd. & Pres.--Nelsen Steel & Wire Co., Franklin Park, IL, pg. 797
Nelson, D., Chief Exec. Officer--Comlinear Corporation, Fort Collins, CO, pg. 268
Nelson, Dan, Chm. & Chief Exec. Officer--Nelson & Schmidt, Inc., Milwaukee, WI, pg. 797
Nelson, Dan, Pres.--Technical Publishing, Milwaukee, WI, pg. 797
Nelson, G. F., Pres.--Willamette-Western Corporation, Portland, OR, pg. 1190
Nelson, J. F., Jr., Pres.--Golden Gem Growers Inc., Umatilla, FL, pg. 466
Nelson, Jack, Pres. & Chief Oper. Officer--Allied Systems, Ltd., Decatur, GA, pg. 40
Nelson, James, Owner & Pres.--The Butcher Co., Marlborough, MA, pg. 196
Nelson, Jeffrey L., Gen. Mgr.--East River Electrical Power Co., Madison, SD, pg. 363
Nelson, John T., Sr., Pres.--Nelson Photo Supplies, San Diego, CA, pg. 797
Nelson, Ken, Pres.--Barrel O'Fun Snack Foods Co., Perham, MN, pg. 122
Nelson, Kenneth M., Pres.--Nelson & Small Inc., Portland, ME, pg. 798
Nelson, Kirk N., Pres. & Chief Oper. Officer--Federated Mutual Insurance Company, Owatonna, MN, pg. 405
Neman, Robert, Pres.--La Computer Center, Lawndale, CA, pg. 648
Nemanick, Richard C., Pres.--The Lorvic Corp., St. Louis, MO, pg. 684
Nemec, Jim, Pres.--Harmony Engineering Corporation, Minneapolis, MN, pg. 510
Nemetz, Jeffrey A., Pres.--Jeffrey Nemetz & Associates, Inc., Chicago, IL, pg. 798
Nemschoff, Mark, Pres., Chief Exec. Officer & Treas.--Nemschoff Chairs, Inc., Sheboygan, WI, pg. 798
Nerad, Jerry, Pres.--TimeMed Labeling Systems, Inc., Burr Ridge, IL, pg. 1098
Nerbonne, Robert A., Pres.--Pitco Frialator Inc., Concord, NH, pg. 157
Nerland, Rick, Chm. Bd., Pres. & New Bus. Contact--The Nerland Agency, Inc., Anchorage, AK, pg. 798
Nesi, Vincent, Pres.--Bugle Boy Industries, Inc., Simi Valley, CA, pg. 187
Ness, Greg, Pres.--G.L. Ness Agency, Inc., Fargo, ND, pg. 798
Netter, Edward, Chm. Bd. & Pres.--Geneve Corporation, Stamford, CT, pg. 451
Neubauer, Joseph, Chm. Bd., Pres. & Chief Exec. Officer--ARA Group, Philadelphia, PA, pg. 5
Neubauer, Joseph, Chm. Bd. & Pres.--ARA Services, Inc., Philadelphia, PA, pg. 5
Neufeld, Richard S., Pres.--U.S. Reduction Company, Munster, IN, pg. 1137
Neuhoff, James H., Chm. Bd., Pres. & Chief Exec. Officer--Valleydale Packers Inc., Bristol, VA, pg. 1143
Neukirchen, Kathy, Pres.--Media Plus, Seattle, WA, pg. 734
Neumann, Dr. Myrel, Pres. & Chief Exec. Officer--Midwest Vision Centers, Sauk Rapids, MN, pg. 752
Neumann, Frank G., Pres.--Valu Discount, Inc., Louisville, KY, pg. 1143
Neuwirth, Frank, Chm. Bd. & Pres.--Unex Conveying Systems, Inc., Jackson, NJ, pg. 1126
Nevelle, Tim, Pres.--Creation Windows of Indiana, Inc., Elkhart, IN, pg. 297
Nevers, Ronald, Pres.--D'Agostino Supermarkets Inc., Larchmont, NY, pg. 310
Neville, Patrick, Pres. & Chief Exec. Officer--Henrys, Inc., Wichita, KS, pg. 530
Neville, Robert J., Chm. Bd., Pres. & Chief Exec. Officer--The North American Manufacturing Co., Cleveland, OH, pg. 811
Nevin, John J., Pres. & Chief Exec. Officer--Broadcast Electronics, Inc., Quincy, IL, pg. 177
Newberry, Richard A., Pres. & Chief Oper. Officer--Starcraft Automotive Corp., Goshen, IN, pg. 1040
Newcomer, David W. IV, Pres. & Partner--D. W. Newcomer's Sons, Inc., Kansas City, MO, pg. 804
Newell, Byron B., Pres.--Cameron-Newell Advertising, Inc., Van Nuys, CA, pg. 212
Newell, Liz, Pres. & Chief Exec. Officer--Kragie/Newell, Des Moines, IA, pg. 643
Newgard, J. Richard, Pres. & Chief Exec. Officer--Henry Newgard & Company, Arlington Heights, IL, pg. 804
Newhart, Lawrence E., Acting Pres.--NPS Energy Services, Inc., Wayne, PA, pg. 321
Newman, Frank A., Pres. & Chief Exec. Officer--F & M Distributors Inc., Warren, MI, pg. 393
Newman, Michael, Pres. & Chief Exec. Officer--Polo/Ralph Lauren Corporation, New York, NY, pg. 879
Newman, Paul, Pres.--Newman's Own, Inc., Westport, CT, pg. 804
Newman, Ralph S., Jr., Pres. & Chief Exec. Officer--Farmers Rice Cooperative, Sacramento, CA, pg. 401
Neyer, Donald L., Chm. Bd. & Pres.--Al Neyer, Inc., Cincinnati, OH, pg. 805
Ng, James, Mng. Dir.--Dentsu, Young & Rubicam/Hong Kong, Hong Kong, Hong Kong, pg. 330
Nichoalds, Donald, Pres.--Luxor Corporation, Waukegan, IL, pg. 365
Nicholas, Peter M., Pres.--Boston Scientific Corp., Watertown, MA, pg. 167
Nichols, Harry, Pres.--Walker-Pioneer Moss, New York, NY, pg. 1160
Nichols, Victor K., Pres.--Safeguard Business Systems, Inc., Fort Washington, PA, pg. 966
Nichols, W.C., Pres. & Chief Exec. Officer--Renfro Corp., Mount Airy, NC, pg. 926
Nicholson, G. R., Pres.--E-Z Serve Corp., Houston, TX, pg. 361
Nicholson, James B., Pres. & Chief Exec. Officer--PVS Chemicals, Inc., Detroit, MI, pg. 837
Nick, Dynn, Pres. & Chief Exec. Officer--Great Lakes Sportswear Manufacturing Industries, Detroit, MI, pg. 482
Nickel, Albert G., Pres. & Chief Oper. Officer--Dorritie Lyons & Nickel, Inc., New York, NY, pg. 347
Nickel, Mark A., Chief Exec. Officer & Exec. Publr.--Sampler Publications Inc., Saint Charles, IL, pg. 968
Nickell, Bob, Pres.--Tucker-Rocky Distributing, Irving, TX, pg. 647
Nickels, Robert T., Pres. & Chief Exec. Officer--Replogle Globes, Inc., Broadview, IL, pg. 927
Nickerson, Joshua A., Jr., Chm. Bd. & Pres.--Nickerson Lumber Company, Orleans, MA, pg. 806
Nickey, Gaylen, Pres.--Washington Beef Company, Landover, MD, pg. 1165
Nicolaus, Ronald, Pres.--Plymouth Creameries, Inc., Plymouth, WI, pg. 877
Nidiffer, Ray L., Pres.--C & K Markets, Inc., Brookings, OR, pg. 198
Niebla, J. Fernando, Chm. Bd. & Chief Exec. Officer--Infotec Development, Inc., Santa Ana, CA, pg. 567
Niedermeyer, Edward C., Pres.--Pacific Wood Treating Coporation, Ridgefield, WA, pg. 842
Niehaus, Gerlad, Pres. & Chief Exec. Officer--Evana Automation, Evansville, IN, pg. 390
Nielsen, Claude B., Pres. & Chief Exec. Officer--Coca Cola Bottling Co. United, Inc., Birmingham, AL, pg. 257
Nielsen, James N., Gen. Mgr.--Maid-O-Mist, Chicago, IL, pg. 1062
Nielsen, M.A., Pres., Chief Exec. Officer & Treas.--Wesbar Corporation, West Bend, WI, pg. 1176
Nielsen, Robert, Pres.--Aramis, Inc., New York, NY, pg. 389
Nielsen, S. Christian, III, Pres.--The Nielsen Company, Cincinnati, OH, pg. 807

Niemeger, W. Phil, Exec. V.P. & Chief Exec. Officer--Nasco, Fort Atkinson, WI, pg. 452
Niemiec, Leo P., Pres. & Chief Exec. Officer--Lawnware Products, Inc., Morton Grove, IL, pg. 661
Nierenberg, Bruce, Pres. & Chief Exec. Officer--Costa Cruise Lines, N.V., Miami, FL, pg. 288
Nierenberg, Roy A., Pres.--Experience in Software, Inc., Berkeley, CA, pg. 393
Niermeyer, David A., Pres.--Stakmore Inc., Owego, NY, pg. 1035
Nies, Thomas M., Chm. Bd., Pres. & Chief Exec. Officer--Cincom Systems, Inc., Cincinnati, OH, pg. 250
Nikkel, Robert F., Pres. & Chief Fin. Officer--The Nikkel Corporation, Sacramento, CA, pg. 807
Niles, Lou, Pres.--Benson Industries, Inc., Portland, OR, pg. 139
Nimnicht, Billie N., Jr., Pres.--Nimnicht Chevrolet Company, Jacksonville, FL, pg. 807
Nissen, William, Chm. Bd. & Pres.--Apache Hose & Belting Company, Cedar Rapids, IA, pg. 77
Nixon, Geoffrey R., Pres. & Chief Oper. Officer--Austin Kelley Advertising, Inc., Atlanta, GA, pg. 99
Nixon, P. Andrews, Chm. Bd., Pres. & Chief Exec. Officer--Dead River Company, Portland, ME, pg. 321
Noble, Robert B., Chm. & Chief Exec. Officer--Noble & Associates, Springfield, MO, pg. 808
Noel, Marc, Pres. & Chief Exec. Officer--NMC of North America, Inc., Zebulon, NC, pg. 781
Noel, Rodger, Pres.--Noel Canning Corporation, Yakima, WA, pg. 808
Noel, Stacy, Pres.--Temporaries, Incorporated, Houston, TX, pg. 1086
Noel, T. Howard, Pres. & Chief Oper. Officer--Hayes, Seay, Mattern & Mattern, Inc., Roanoke, VA, pg. 519
Nolen, Chapin, Pres.--Combe Incorporated, White Plains, NY, pg. 267
Noonan, Jack, Pres. & Chief Exec. Officer--SPSS Inc., Chicago, IL, pg. 964
Noonan, Pat, Pres.--Whittenberg Construction Co., Louisville, KY, pg. 1187
Noor, Amri, Gen. Mgr.--BSB Indonesia, Jakarta,, Indonesia, pg. 110
Norbitz, Wayne, Pres. & Chief Oper. Officer--Nathan's Famous Inc., Westbury, NY, pg. 784
Norden, Roger C., Pres.--Standard Medical Imaging, Inc., Columbia, MD, pg. 1037
Nordin, Roger, Pres.--Green Spot Packaging Inc., Claremont, CA, pg. 485
Nordquist, Ove, Pres. & Chief Exec. Officer--Commodore Cruise Line, Ltd., Coral Gables, FL, pg. 269
Nordquist, Ove, Pres. & Chief Exec. Officer--Crown Cruise Line, Coral Gables, FL, pg. 269
Norheim, Oddvar, Chm. Bd. & Pres.--American Crane & Equipment Corp., Douglassville, PA, pg. 51
Norlander, John, Pres.--Radisson Hotel Corporation, Minneapolis, MN, pg. 221
Norman, Geroge J., Pres.--Norman Brothers Nissan Inc., Orlando, FL, pg. 810
Norman, K.J., Pres.--Ampco Metal Inc., Dallas Div., Garland, TX, pg. 68
Norman, Reeve, Vice-Chm., Pres. & Chief Exec. Officer--Electrical Wholesale Supply Company, Inc., Idaho Falls, ID, pg. 374
Norris, Donald R., Pres. & Gen. Mgr.--East Kentucky Power Co-op, Winchester, KY, pg. 362
Norris, Frank W., Jr., Pres.--Badger Construction Equipment Co., Insley Div., Winona, MN, pg. 113
Norris, Frank W., Jr., Pres.--Badger Equipment Company, Winona, MN, pg. 102
Norris, Michael H., Pres.--Deerfield Manufacturing Co., Inc., Mason, OH, pg. 324
Northrup, Donald, Pres.--BKM Enterprises, Inc., East Hartford, CT, pg. 107
Norton, J. Patrick, Chm. Bd., Pres. & Chief Exec. Officer--Fabreeka International, Inc., Stoughton, MA, pg. 396
Norton, James, Pres.--Muralo Co., Inc., Bayonne, NJ, pg. 776
Norton, Lawrence J., Pres.--Modern Equipment Rentals Inc., Wilmington, DE, pg. 763
Norton, Peter B., Pres. & Chief Oper. Officer--Encyclopaedia Britannica, Inc., Chicago, IL, pg. 381
Norton, Timothy C., Chm. Bd.--Norton Associates, Inc., Chicago, IL, pg. 815
Norwood, James, Pres.--Norwood Shoe Corporation, De Soto, MO, pg. 816
Noseworthy, Heber L., Pres. & Chief Oper. Officer--ACO Inc., Farmington Hills, MI, pg. 2
Noskin, Arthur, Pres.--Polymer Plastics Corporation, Hauppauge, NY, pg. 880
Nottberg, Henry, III, Chm. Bd., Pres. & Chief Exec. Officer--U.S. Engineering Company, Kansas City, MO, pg. 1135
Novak, John S., Pres.--Sokol & Company, Countryside, IL, pg. 1016
Novelly, Paul A., Pres. & Chief Exec. Officer--Apex Oil Company, Inc., Saint Louis, MO, pg. 78
Nowotny, Lutz, Pres.--Weinberger Werbehaus Ges.m.b.H & Co. KG, Vienna,, Austria, pg. 105
Noyes, James E., Pres.--MTI Vacations, Inc., Oak Brook, IL, pg. 694
Nulman, Louis, Pres. & Chief Exec. Officer--Alden Auto Parts Wholesale, Inc., Somerset, MA, pg. 32
Nulton, Karl E., Pres.--Johnson Acoustical & Supply Co., Portland, OR, pg. 597
Nunez, Elpidio, Pres. & Chief Exec. Officer--Northwestern Meats Inc., Miami, FL, pg. 815
Nunley, Richard L., Chm. Bd., Pres. & Treas.--Better Living Inc., Charlottesville, VA, pg. 148
Nusbaum, Irving, Pres. & Chief Exec. Officer--New York Carpet World Inc., Southfield, MI, pg. 802
Nusim, Joseph, Chm., Pres. & Chief Exec. Officer--Channel Home Centers Inc., Whippany, NJ, pg. 238
Nussbaum, Marlene R., Partner--The Haughey Group, Inc., Boston, MA, pg. 517
Nussbaum, Victor M., Jr., Pres.--Southern Foods, Inc., Greensboro, NC, pg. 1021
Nussdorf, Bernard, Pres.--Quality King Distributors, Ronkonkoma, NY, pg. 903
Nybo, Howard J., Pres.--Will & Baumer Incorporated, Liverpool, NY, pg. 1190
Nye, Keith, Gen. Mgr.--Country Classic Dairies, Inc., Bozeman, MT, pg. 289
O'Briain, Niall, Pres.--Fraser Paper, Ltd., Stamford, CT, pg. 430
O'Brian, Thomas, Pres.--American Decal & Mfg. Co., Chicago, IL, pg. 51
O'Brien, Charles R., Pres.--Ring Screw Works, Madison Heights, MI, pg. 935
O'Brien, Daniel W., Pres.--F.H. Stoltze Land & Lumber Company, Stillwater, MN, pg. 1050
O'Brien, F.L., III, Chm., Pres. & Chief Exec. Officer--O'Brien Energy Systems Inc., Philadelphia, PA, pg. 820
O'Brien, John F., Pres. & Chief Exec. Officer--All America Financial, Worcester, MA, pg. 34
O'Brien, John F., Pres. & Chief Exec. Officer--State Mutual Life Assurance Company of America, Worcester, MA, pg. 35
O'Brien, John F., Pres. & Chief Exec. Officer--All American Financial, Worcester, MA, pg. 34
O'Brien, John F., Chm. Bd. & Pres.--The Hanover Insurance Company, Worcester, MA, pg. 34
O'Brien, Jutus, Mng. Dir.--Leo Burnett Venezuela, C.A., Caracas,, Venezuela, pg. 193
O'Brien, Roy E., Jr., Pres.--Roy O'Brien Inc., St. Clair Shores, MI, pg. 820
O'Brien, Stephen J., Pres. & Chief Exec. Officer--Diversified Products Corporation, Opelika, AL, pg. 1193
O'Bryan, Michael L., Pres.--O'Bryan Brothers Inc., Chicago, IL, pg. 820
O'Callaghan, Kevin, Pres.--Universal Builders Supply, Inc., Mount Vernon, NY, pg. 1137
O'Connell, John, Pres. & Chief Exec. Officer--Garvin Fire Protection Systems, Orange, CA, pg. 444
O'Connell, Peter J., Exec. Dir.--Rhode Island Lottery, Cranston, RI, pg. 931
O'Connor, Ellen Cook, Pres.--O'Connor Maccioli, Inc., Dallas, TX, pg. 821
O'Connor, Neil, Pres.--George T. Schmidt, Niles, IL, pg. 976
O'Connor, Thomas D., Chm., Pres. & Chief Exec. Officer--Mohawk Paper Mills, Inc., Cohoes, NY, pg. 763
O'Connor, Thomas P., Pres.--Monitor Capital Advisors Inc., New York, NY, pg. 803
O'Daly, Fergus F., Chm. & Chief Exec. Officer--Poppe Tyson, New York, NY, pg. 880
O'Dell, Jane, Pres. & Treas.--Westfall GMC Truck Inc., North Kansas City, MO, pg. 1182
O'Donahue, Shannon, Pres.--Reid & O'Donahue Advertising, Inc., Montgomery, AL, pg. 923
O'Donnell, James E., Chm. Bd., Pres. & Chief Exec. Officer--Wheatland Tube Company, Collingswood, NJ, pg. 1184
O'Donnell, Owen, Pres. & Chief Exec. Officer--Management Dynamics, New Providence, NJ, pg. 703
O'Donoghue, Chris, Mng. Dir.--Ketchum Public Relations PLC, London,, United Kingdom, pg. 625
O'Gorman, Thomas, Pres.--Glenoit Mills, Inc., Tarboro, NC, pg. 462
O'Halloran, James J., Pres.--O'Halloran Advertising, Inc., Wilton, CT, pg. 822
O'Keeffe, William F., Pres.--O'Keeffe's, Inc., San Francisco, CA, pg. 823
O'Leary, Alice, Pres. & Chief Exec. Officer--Kaprielian/O'Leary, New York, NY, pg. 616
O'Leary, Dennis P., Chm. Bd. & Pres.--The F. D. Lawrence Electric Co., Cincinnati, OH, pg. 661
O'Leary, Patrick B., Pres.--Landau & Heyman Inc., Chicago, IL, pg. 654
O'Leary, Stephen E., Pres.--Townsend & O'Leary, Inc., Laguna Hills, CA, pg. 1104
O'Malia, Daniel J., Pres. & Chief Exec. Officer--O'Malia Food Markets Inc., Noblesville, IN, pg. 825
O'Malley, Shaun F., Co-Chm. & Sr. Partner--Price Waterhouse - U.S., New York, NY, pg. 888
O'Neil, Gary M., Pres. & Chief Exec. Officer--O'Neil Griffin & Associates, Inc., Manchester, NH, pg. 827
O'Neil, Robert L., II, Pres.--Paschen Contractors, Inc., Chicago, IL, pg. 851
O'Neil, W.E., Pres.--O'Neil Industries Inc., Chicago, IL, pg. 827
O'Neil, William J., Pres.--William O'Neil & Co., Inc., Los Angeles, CA, pg. 827
O'Neile, Charles, Pres.--Western States Machine Co., Hamilton, OH, pg. 1181
O'Neill, Donal Kieran, Chm. Bd., Pres. & Chief Exec. Officer--Ed Taylor Construction Co., Tucker, GA, pg. 1081
O'Neill, Donald, Pres.--NBS Southern, Inc., Largo, FL, pg. 960
O'Neill, Donald F., Pres. & Chief Exec. Officer--P M Company, Philadelphia, PA, pg. 835
O'Neill, John, Pres.--Berwick Bay Oil Co. Inc., Morgan City, LA, pg. 144
O'Neill, John J., Pres.--Morrison Textile Machinery Co., Fort Lawn, SC, pg. 771
O'Rahilly, Pres.--Creative Marketing International Corp., West Chicago, IL, pg. 297
O'Reilly, Charlie, Pres.--O'Reilly Auto Inc., Springfield, MO, pg. 829
O'Reilly, David, Pres.-Ozark Automotive Dist.--O'Reilly Auto Inc., Springfield, MO, pg. 829
O'Reilly, Larry, Pres.-Corp. Sls.--O'Reilly Auto Inc., Springfield, MO, pg. 829
O'Rourke, Gerald J., Pres.--A & A Manufacturing Co., New Berlin, WI, pg. 1
O'Rourke, Gordon, Pres.--Continental Coin Corporation, Van Nuys, CA, pg. 278
O'Rourke, William F., Pres.--Coca-Cola Bottling Co. of Chicago, Niles, IL, pg. 257
O'Shea, Kevin, Co-Pres.--The Myers Group (U.S) Inc., Rouses Point, NY, pg. 780
O'Sullivan, Tom, Pres. & Partner--Weller & O'Sullivan Advertising, Los Angeles, CA, pg. 1175
O'Toole, John F., Pres.--Franklin Steel Company, Franklin, PA, pg. 429
Oakes, R.K., Pres.--Aladdin Synergetics, Inc., Nashville, TN, pg. 29
Oakley, Bruce, Pres.--Bruce Oakley, Inc., North Little Rock, AR, pg. 819
Oasis, Russ, Pres.--The Ad Team Of Florida Inc., North Miami, FL, pg. 16
Oates, James, Pres. & Partner--Whitehawk Partnership, Pasadena, CA, pg. 1186
Oatway, Francis C., Pres. & Chief Exec. Officer--Hargro Enterprises, Inc., Stamford, CT, pg. 509
Oben, Walter J., Sr., Pres.--Southgate Ford Inc., Southgate, MI, pg. 1023
Obert, Mark J., Pres.--General Automotive Corporation, Ann Arbor, MI, pg. 448
Oberting, V.A., Jr., Pres.--Interstate Commodities Inc., Troy, NY, pg. 580
Oberweis, Elaine, Pres.--Oberweis Dairy, Inc., Aurora, IL, pg. 820
Ockels, Theodore S., Pres., Chief Exec. Officer, Chief Fin. Officer & Treas.--Up-Right Work Platforms Division, Selma, CA, pg. 1139
Oddy, Bill, Pres. & Chief Exec. Officer--California Electric Service, Oakland, CA, pg. 209
Odems, William, Pres. & Chief Exec. Officer--Recon/Optical, Inc., Barrington, IL, pg. 917
Oden, Clyde W., Dr., Pres. & Chief Exec. Officer--United Health Plan, Inglewood, CA, pg. 1133
Odle, Richard, Pres.--Keywell Corporation, Detroit, MI, pg. 629
Oechler, Richard, Pres.--Crown Coat, Inc., Grand Rapids, MI, pg. 609
Oelbaum, Harold, Pres.--Kane-Miller Corp., Tarrytown, NY, pg. 616
Oeltjen, Ed. J., Pres.--Consolidated Metco, Inc., Portland, OR, pg. 277
Oertli, Fred G., Jr., Pres.--Guarantee Electrical Company, Saint Louis, MO, pg. 490
Oetting, William K., Pres.--Kreonite, Inc., Wichita, KS, pg. 644
Offray, Claude, Jr., Pres. & Chief Exec. Officer--C.M. Offray & Son Inc., Chester, NJ, pg. 822
Oggs, Larry, Pres.--Crown Buick, Inc., Metairie, LA, pg. 302
Ogilvie, G., Pres.--Midwesco Filter Resources, Winchester, VA, pg. 751
Ogle, D. Clark, Chm. Bd., Pres., Chief Exec. & Chief Oper. Officer--Peter J. Schmitt Holdings, West Seneca, NY, pg. 976
Ohaus, James, Pres.--Ohaus Corporation, Florham Park, NJ, pg. 822
Ohlemeyer, K.A., Pres.--Sporlan Valve Company, Saint Louis, MO, pg. 1032
Ohlmann, Walter, Pres. & Chief Exec. Officer--Penny/Ohlmann/Neiman, Inc., Dayton, OH, pg. 858
Okumura, Nelson, Pres.--Valley Isle Produce, Inc., Kahului, HI, pg. 1143
Okwit, Sy, Pres.--LNR Communications, Hauppauge, NY, pg. 648
Olcott, Emery G., Pres. & Chief Exec. Officer--Canberra Industries, Inc., Meriden, CT, pg. 213
Oldenburg, Wayne C., Pres. & Chief Exec. Officer--The Oldenburg Group Companies, Milwaukee, WI, pg. 824
Oldham, Gareth J., Chm. & Chief Exec. Officer--BSB Hunter Advertising, Dublin, Ireland, pg. 110
Oldham, Noble, Pres. & Chief Exec. Officer--Artco-Bell Corporation, Temple, TX, pg. 86
Oleff, Paul K., Pres.--Bentley, Barnes & Lynn, Inc., Chicago, IL, pg. 140
Olesen, Victor L., Pres.--Vic Olesen & Partners, Inc., Los Angeles, CA, pg. 824
Oleson, Dr. Douglas E., Pres. & Chief Exec. Officer--Battelle Memorial Institute, Columbus, OH, pg. 126
Olin, Larry G., Pres., Chief Oper. Officer & Treas.--Humiston-Keeling, Inc., Chicago, IL, pg. 552
Olinde, J. Beauregard, Pres.--B. Olinde & Sons Company, Inc., Baton Rouge, LA, pg. 824
Oliver, Heath, Pres.--Bardons & Oliver, Inc., Cleveland, OH, pg. 119
Oliveri, Joseph F., Pres.--Interface Electronics Corporation, Hopkinton, MA, pg. 574
Ollinger, R.J., Pres.--Harris Ford, Inc., Lynnwood, WA, pg. 512
Olmstead, R.N., Chm. Bd. & Pres.--Modern Equipment Co., Inc., Port Washington, WI, pg. 32
Olsen, David A., Chm., Pres., Chief Exec. & Chief Oper. Officer--Johnson & Higgins, New York, NY, pg. 598
Olsen, George A., Pres. & Chief Exec. Officer--Kingsbury, Inc., Philadelphia, PA, pg. 632
Olsen, Joan D., Pres.--BTD/TMP Worldwide, Garden Grove, CA, pg. 1073
Olsen, Richard, Pres.--Custom Pak, Inc., Clinton, IA, pg. 306
Olsen, T. W., Pres. & Chief Exec. Officer--United A G Co-op, Inc., Omaha, NE, pg. 1130
Olson, Frank A., Chm. Bd. & Pres.--Park Ridge Corporation, Park Ridge, NJ, pg. 849
Olson, James N., Pres.--Rockford Acromatic Product Co., Rockford, IL, pg. 941
Olson, John M., Pres.--John M. Olson Company, Saint Clair Shores, MI, pg. 824
Olson, Kent F., Pres. & Chief Exec. Officer--Northwestern Drug Company, Minneapolis, MN, pg. 343
Olson, Paul, Pres.--Intercole, Inc., Washington, PA, pg. 574
Olson, Sherman V., Pres. & Treas.--Danafilms, Inc., Westborough, MA, pg. 313
Olsrud, Sherman, Pres.--Sherms Thunderbird Market, Medford, OR, pg. 998
Oltmans, Joseph O., II, Pres.--Oltmans Construction Company, Whittier, CA, pg. 824

Corporate Responsibilities Index

Oman, Jack A., Chm. Bd. & Pres.--Oman Construction Co. Inc., Nashville, TN, pg. 825
Omer, Don C., Pres.--Inland Associates, Olathe, KS, pg. 570
Omer, Don C., Chm. Bd., Pres., Chief Exec. & Fin. Officer--Inland Associates, Inc., Olathe, KS, pg. 570
Ommodt, Donald, Pres. & Chief Exec. Officer--Cass-Clay Creamery, Fargo, ND, pg. 228
Onderdonk, S.R., Pres. & Chief Exec. Officer--Econolite Control Products, Inc., Anaheim, CA, pg. 367
Onoratti, James, Pres.--McDowell Mfg. Co., Du Bois, PA, pg. 32
Onstead, R. Randall, Jr., Pres. & Chief Oper. Officer--Randall's Food Markets, Inc., Houston, TX, pg. 911
Opler, Edmond, Jr., Chm. Bd., Pres. & Chief Exec. Officer--World's Finest Chocolate, Inc., Chicago, IL, pg. 1203
Opperman, Dwight D., Pres. & Chief Exec. Officer--West Publishing Co., Eagan, MN, pg. 1177
Oram, John, Pres.--ICC Industries, Inc., New York, NY, pg. 558
Orden, Ted, Chm. Bd. & Pres.--Thrifty Oil Company, Downey, CA, pg. 1096
Ordway, Peter S., Chm., Pres. & Chief Exec. Officer--Union Pump Company, Battle Creek, MI, pg. 1128
Oren, Doandl G., Pres.--Dart Transit Company, Inc., Eagan, MN, pg. 316
Orentzel, Richard, Pres.--American White Cross Laboratories, Inc., New Rochelle, NY, pg. 65
Oringer, Howard, Chm. Bd. & Chief Exec. Officer--Telesciences Co. Systems Inc., Moorestown, NJ, pg. 1085
Orkney, David, Pres.--G.I. Joe's Inc., Wilsonville, OR, pg. 440
Orlando, Stephen, Pres.--Ortronics, Inc., Pawcatuck, CT, pg. 830
Oropeza, Frank, Pres.--Transpo Electronics, Inc., Orlando, FL, pg. 1108
Orr, Clark, Jr., Pres. & Chief Exec. Officer--Orr Safety Equipment Company, Louisville, KY, pg. 830
Orr, Donald, Pres.--The Pollock Corp., Pottstown, PA, pg. 879
Orr, Donald C., Pres.--Nashville Machine Co. Inc., Nashville, TN, pg. 784
Orrall, Roy E., Pres.--Winthrop Printing Company, Inc., Boston, MA, pg. 1197
Orrico, Eugene, Pres.--Keeners, Inc., Seattle, WA, pg. 620
Ortman, Raymond L., Pres.--Kokomo Grain Co., Inc., Kokomo, IN, pg. 640
Ortolani, Timothy S., Chm. Bd., Pres. & Chief Exec. Officer--Carton-Craft Corporation, Buffalo, NY, pg. 226
Orton, J. Roy, Pres.--National Grape Co-Op Association, Inc., Westfield, NY, pg. 789
Orullian, B. La Rae, Pres. & Chief Exec. Officer--Equitable Bankshares of Colorado, Inc., Denver, CO, pg. 385
Osborn, Joseph, Pres. & Creative Dir.--Osborn & Barr Communications, Clayton, MO, pg. 830
Osborne, Michael E., Pres. & Chief Exec. Officer--The Milnot Company, Saint Louis, MO, pg. 756
Oscherqitz, Sheldon, Pres.--Sinai 48 Kosher Foods Corp., Chicago, IL, pg. 146
Osherow, Allen J., Chm. Bd. & Pres.--Windsor Art Products, Inc., Pico Rivera, CA, pg. 1195
Oson, Tom, Pres.-Scherer Financial--Scherer Bros. Lumber Company, Minneapolis, MN, pg. 976
Ostby, Kevin C., Pres.--Davis Paint Company, Kansas City, MO, pg. 319
Ostendorf, Bob, Pres. & Chief Exec. Officer--VMC Fiberglass Products Inc., Daleville, AL, pg. 1142
Ostergard, Tonn, Pres. & Chief Exec. Officer--Crete Carrier Corp., Lincoln, NE, pg. 299
Ostermeier, Wilmer, Pres.--The Swanson Company Manufacturers, Phoenix, AZ, pg. 1066
Osterneck, Guy-Kenneth, Chm. Bd., Pres. & Treas.--The Osterneck Co. Inc., Lumberton, NC, pg. 831
Ostrom, G.J., Pres. & Gen. Mgr.--Heckethorn Mfg. Company, Dyersburg, TN, pg. 524
Ostrover, Julian, Pres.--American Fabrics Company, New York, NY, pg. 51
Ostrow, Joel J., Pres.--Ostrow Textile Co., Inc., Rock Hill, SC, pg. 831
Oswald, Robert, Pres.--Apex Corporation, Indianapolis, IN, pg. 78
Otakie, Daniel A., Chm., Pres., Chief Exec. Officer & Treas.--Futures Personnel Services, Baltimore, MD, pg. 438
Otero, Richard J., Chm., Pres. & Chief Exec. Officer--RJO Enterprises, Inc., Lanham, MD, pg. 907
Otis, William L., Jr., Chm. Bd. & Pres.--Columbia Lumber & Manufacturing Co., Columbia, SC, pg. 265
Ott, Robert B., Jr., Pres.--The Hennegan Company, Cincinnati, OH, pg. 529
Ott, William, Pres.--Brookhurst, Inc., Compton, CA, pg. 179
Otte, Stephen B., Pres. & Chief Exec. Officer--Florists' Mutual Insurance Co., Edwardsville, IL, pg. 421
Otten, Leslie B., Pres. & Treas.--Sunday River Skiway Corporation, Bethel, ME, pg. 1059
Ottke, Donald L., Pres.--Stegner Food Products Co., Cincinnati, OH, pg. 1045
Otto, Henry James, Pres. & Chief Fin. Officer--Sid Harvey Inc., Valley Stream, NY, pg. 515
Otto, Richard E., Pres.--Owners Insurance Co., Lima, OH, pg. 100
Otton, Ric, Exec. Dir.--Chiat/Day/Mojo, South Melbourne,, Australia, pg. 245
Ounjian, George E., Pres.--Careers USA Inc., Philadelphia, PA, pg. 218
Ourso, E.J., Chm., Pres. & Chief Exec. Officer--Ourso Investment Corporation, Donaldsonville, LA, pg. 832
Oustalet, A.J.M. Butch, Pres.--Butch Oustalet Ford Saab, Inc., Gulfport, MS, pg. 832
Ovadia, Jeff, Pres.--Nulaid Foods, Ripon, CA, pg. 817
Overstreet, Thomas E., Pres.--Overstreet Paving Company, Largo, FL, pg. 833
Owen, E.H., Pres.--Baton Rouge Water Works Company, Baton Rouge, LA, pg. 126
Owen, Robert E., Chm. Bd. & Pres.--Owen Industries, Inc., Carter Lake, IA, pg. 834
Owen, Robert E., Pres.--Lincoln Steel, Lincoln, NE, pg. 834
Owens, Nick, Pres.--L. R. Nelson Corporation, Peoria, IL, pg. 797
Owens, Phil, Pres. & Chief Oper. Officer--Top-Seal Corp., Phoenix, AZ, pg. 1083
Owens, Richard J., Pres. & Chief Exec. Officer--Manning & Lewis Engineering Co., Union, NJ, pg. 704
Owings, F. Miller, Pres.--Paramount Foods Inc., Louisville, KY, pg. 848
Owsley, T. Reed, Pres.--Owsley & Sons, Inc., Fort Mill, SC, pg. 834
Owzik, John, Pres.--Dickten & Masch Manufacturing Co., Nashotah, WI, pg. 336
Oyama, Shunichi, Pres.--Japan Travel Bureau International, Inc., New York, NY, pg. 590
Ozuna, Robert, Pres.--New Bedford Panoramex Corporation, Upland, CA, pg. 799
Paben, John, Pres.--Lozier Corporation, Omaha, NE, pg. 686
Paben, John M., Exec. V.P. & Gen. Mgr.--Lozier Store Fixtures, Inc., Omaha, NE, pg. 686
Pacholewski, Bob, Gen. Mgr.--The Cleveland Builders Supply Co., Cleveland, OH, pg. 1036
Pachulski, Phil, Chm. Bd. & Pres.--Prime Technology, Inc., Grand Rapids, MI, pg. 889
Packard Thomas M., Pres. & Chief Exec. Officer--Country Lake Foods, Inc., Saint Paul, MN, pg. 654
Packo, Mary Ann, Pres.--National Yellow Pages Monitor (NYPM), San Francisco, CA, pg. 781
Padnos, Jeffrey S., Pres. & Chief Oper. Officer--Louis Padnos Iron & Metal Co., Holland, MI, pg. 842
Pagano, Robert P., Pres. & New Bus. Contact--Pagano, Schenck & Kay, Inc., Providence, RI, pg. 843
Page, F. Roger, Chm. Bd., Pres., Chief Exec. & Fin. Officer--Pace Oil Co., Inc., Winston-Salem, NC, pg. 838
Page, James, Co-Pres. & Chief Oper. Officer--Mission Industries, Santa Barbara, CA, pg. 760
Page, Robert L., Pres. & Chief Exec. Officer--Replacements, Ltd., Greensboro, NC, pg. 927
Paget, Sam, Pres.--Bell Chemical Company, Chicago, IL, pg. 134
Pagliarin, Annibale, Mng. Dir.--Padova Ayer, Padova,, Italy, pg. 104
Pahidis, Gus P., Pres.--Cedar Farms Company, Inc., Philadelphia, PA, pg. 230
Pahl, Charles E., Pres. & Chief Exec. Officer--J.H. Larson Electrical Company, Golden Valley, MN, pg. 659
Paine, Thomas H., Jr., Pres.--Dana Communications, Inc., Hopewell, NJ, pg. 313
Palagonia, Joseph P., Pres.--J.M.P. Bakery Co., Inc., Brooklyn, NY, pg. 586
Palan, Robert, Pres. & Chief Exec. Officer--King Louie International, Inc., Grandview, MO, pg. 631
Paletz, Lenn, Chm., Pres., Chief Exec. & Chief Oper. Officer--The Sportsman's Guide, Inc., Eagan, MN, pg. 1032
Paley, Edward, Pres.--The Texwipe Co., Inc., Upper Saddle River, NJ, pg. 1090
Pallas, Robert M., Pres.--Pallas Advertising, Inc., San Francisco, CA, pg. 843
Palmatier, Rex, Pres.--Clark Door Co., Inc., Maryland Heights, MO, pg. 252
Palmer, A. Robert, Pres. & Chief Exec. Officer--Eastern Color Printing Company, Avon, CT, pg. 363
Palmer, Douglas E., Pres. & Chief Fin. Officer--Terminal Grain Corp., Sioux City, IA, pg. 1088
Palmer, Eldon D., Pres. & Chief Exec. Officer--Kenworth of Indianapolis Inc., Indianapolis, IN, pg. 624
Palmer, Jeffrey W., Pres.--Palmer Moving & Storage Co., Livonia, MI, pg. 844
Palmer, Jimmie R., Pres.--Triangle Electric Company, Madison Heights, MI, pg. 1112
Palmer, Richard M., Jr., Chm. Bd. & Pres.--R.M. Palmer Company, West Reading, PA, pg. 843
Palmer, Robert J., Pres.--R.J. Palmer, Inc., New York, NY, pg. 844
Palmer, Tom, Pres.--Western Diesel Services Inc., Saint Louis, MO, pg. 1179
Palmer, Wayne L., Pres.--Palmer International, Inc., Worcester, PA, pg. 844
Palmieri, Victor, Chief Exec. Officer--Mutual Benefit Life Insurance Company, Newark, NJ, pg. 778
Palmiero, Robert, Pres.--Southern Apparel Corporation, Largo, FL, pg. 1020
Pamel, James P., Pres. & Treas.--National Reproductions Corporation, Madison Heights, MI, pg. 793
Pamplin, Dr. Robert B., Jr., Pres., Chief Oper. Officer & Sec.--R. B. Pamplin Corp., Portland, OR, pg. 844
Pankow, Charles J., Jr., Pres. & Chief Exec. Officer--Charles Pankow Builders, Ltd., Altadena, CA, pg. 846
Pansini, Andrew A., Pres.--Jandy Industries, Novato, CA, pg. 589
Paolin, John, Pres.--Paolin & Sweeney, Cherry Hill, NJ, pg. 847
Papagiannacopoulos, Costas, Chm., Mng. Dir. & Chief Exec. Officer--BSB Athens Advertising S.A., Athens,, Greece, pg. 109
Paparo, Irving, Chm. Bd. & Pres.--House of Ronnie, Inc., New York, NY, pg. 546
Papera, Joseph R., Pres.--Allstate Can Corporation, Clifton, NJ, pg. 43
Papera, Robert P., Pres.--Expo Industries, Inc., San Diego, CA, pg. 393
Papleacos, T. Michael, Sr. Exec. V.P.--Platt Saco Lowell Corporation, Greenville, SC, pg. 876
Papola, William, Jr., Pres.--Network Real Estate of Central California, Inc., Soquel, CA, pg. 798
Papola, William, Jr., Pres.--Network Real Estate of Southern California, Inc., Soquel, CA, pg. 798
Papp, Gary, Pres.--Wenczel Tile Co., Trenton, NJ, pg. 1176
Pappas, Michael, Pres.--Keyes Company, Miami, FL, pg. 627
Pappas, Phil, Jr., Pres.--Univex Corporation, Salem, NH, pg. 1139
Pappenthenasi, Arthur J., Pres. & Chief Exec. Officer--Scangas Brothers Holdings, Inc., Lynn, MA, pg. 974
Para, Dan, Pres.--Seko-Air Freight, Elk Grove Village, IL, pg. 988
Parana, Gene T., Pres. & Chief Exec. Officer--Anderson Lithograph Company, Los Angeles, CA, pg. 73
Parent, Roger, Deputy Exec. Dir.--American Library Association, Chicago, IL, pg. 57
Parfet, Martha, Chm. Bd.--Gilmore Bros., Inc., Kalamazoo, MI, pg. 459
Parfit, Gavin, Pres.--Golodetz Corporation, New York, NY, pg. 469
Paridy, David, Pres.--Edelmann Div. of Stant, Inc., Deerfield, IL, pg. 368
Paridy, David R., Pres. & Chief Exec. Officer--Standard-Thomson Corporation, Waltham, MA, pg. 1037
Parisi, Joseph, Jr., Pres.--Parisi, Inc., Philadelphia, PA, pg. 848
Park, J. Leonard, Chm. Bd., Pres., Chief Exec. Officer & Treas.--George W. Park Seed Co., Inc., Greenwood, SC, pg. 849
Park, Jerry, Pres.--The Benson Music Group, Nashville, TN, pg. 140
Park, John W., Pres.--Globe Business Furniture, Inc., Hendersonville, TN, pg. 463
Park, John W., Pres.--Chairworld, Inc., City of Commerce, CA, pg. 463
Parker, Barry, Pres.--County Seat Stores, Inc., Dallas, TX, pg. 290
Parker, David H., Chm. Bd., Pres. & Chief Exec. Officer--Pelican Products, Torrance, CA, pg. 856
Parker, Jay, Pres.--HOH Associates, Alexandria, VA, pg. 882
Parker, JoAnn, Chm. Bd. & Chief Exec. Officer--Omniflight, Inc., Dallas, TX, pg. 826
Parker, John, Pres., Chief Exec. & Oper. Officer--Continental National American Real Estate Inc., San Jose, CA, pg. 280
Parker, Ken, Pres.--Therm, Inc., Ithaca, NY, pg. 1090
Parker, KennethA., Pres.--Aquidneck Data Company, Middletown, RI, pg. 320
Parker, Larry L., Pres. & Chief Exec. Officer--Leach Corporation, Buena Park, CA, pg. 663
Parker, Ronald I., Chm. Bd., Pres. & Chief Exec. Officer--Indian Head Industries Inc., Southfield, MI, pg. 565
Parker, Thomas L., Pres. & Treas.--MacKinnon-Parker, Inc., Toledo, OH, pg. 697
Parkhill, J.S., Pres.--The Stackpole Corporation, Boston, MA, pg. 1034
Parkinson, Dorn, Pres.--Washington Corporation, Missoula, MT, pg. 1165
Parkinson, Roger P., Pres. & Publisher--Star Tribune, Minneapolis-St. Paul, Minneapolis, MN, pg. 291
Parks, Delton C., Pres. & Gen. Mgr.--Country Fresh, Inc., Grand Rapids, MI, pg. 289
Parks, Raymond F., Pres. & Chief Oper. Officer--J. H. Fletcher & Co., Huntington, WV, pg. 418
Parks, Richard V., Vice Chm.--Farrell Lines Incorporated, New York, NY, pg. 403
Parks, Robert M., Chm. Bd. & Pres.--Parks Products, Inc., Hollywood, CA, pg. 850
Parmiter, Don, Pres.--Malibu Grand Prix Corporation, Canoga Park, CA, pg. 702
Parra, Tim, Pres.--F.P.A., Inc., Irving, TX, pg. 394
Parrish, John W., Chm. Bd. & Pres.--Loxcreen Company, West Columbia, SC, pg. 686
Parry, Robert A., Chm. Bd., Pres. & Chief Exec. Officer--Monroc, Inc., Salt Lake City, UT, pg. 766
Parry, Tom C., Pres. & Chief Exec. Officer--Mississippi Chemical Corporation, Yazoo City, MS, pg. 760
Parsons, Larry E., Pres.--Ken-Mac Metal, Inc., Cleveland, OH, pg. 622
Parsons, Robert F., Pres. & Chief Oper. Officer--Hajoca Corp., Ardmore, PA, pg. 500
Parten, Steve, Pres. & Chief Oper. Officer--Bromar Inc., Newport Beach, CA, pg. 179
Pascucci, Leon, Pres.--G. Leblanc Corporation, Kenosha, WI, pg. 665
Pascucci, Vito, Chm. Bd.--G. Leblanc Corporation, Kenosha, WI, pg. 665
Pascucci, Vito, Pres.--Frank Holton Co., Elkhorn, WI, pg. 665
Paskal, Joseph, Pres.--J & R Film Company, Los Angeles, CA, pg. 586
Pasquarello, Theodore, Pres. & Chief Exec. Officer--Chiswick Trading Inc., Sudbury, MA, pg. 248
Pasquerilla, Frank J., Chm. Bd. & Chief Exec. Officer--Crown American Corporation, Johnstown, PA, pg. 301
Pasquerilla, Mark E., Pres.--Crown American Corporation, Johnstown, PA, pg. 301
Passage, James T., Pres.--Harza Northwest, Inc., Bellevue, WA, pg. 516
Pastor, Irwin, Pres. & Chief Exec. Officer--W&F Manufacturing Corporation, Inc., Buffalo, NY, pg. 1155
Pastor, Todd, Pres.--W&F Manufacturing Corporation, Inc., Buffalo, NY, pg. 1155
Patch, Arthur, Pres. & Chief Exec. Officer--AppleTree Markets, Houston, TX, pg. 79
Patel, Ken N., Pres. & Chief Exec. Officer--Carrier Vibrating Equipment, Inc., Louisville, KY, pg. 225
Patel, Michael, Pres.--Magic Pan International Inc., Burlingame, CA, pg. 700
Patel, Pat, Pres.--Capsonic Group, Inc., Elgin, IL, pg. 216
Patenge, Kenneth E., Chm., Pres. & Chief Exec. Officer--Wohlert Corp., Lansing, MI, pg. 1198
Paterson, Sid, Pres. & Acct. Exec.--Sid Paterson Assoc., Inc., New York, NY, pg. 851
Paton, Judy, Sr. V.P., Mng. Dir.--Hill, Holliday/Toronto, Toronto,, Canada, pg. 534
Patrick, Stuart K., Pres. & Chief Exec. Officer--Baird, Patrick & Co., Inc., New York, NY, pg. 114

Patten, Charles R., Chm. Bd. & Pres.--Colfax Envelope Corporation, Buffalo Grove, IL, pg. 261
Patterson, Charles, Pres., Chief Exec. Officer & Chief Oper. Officer--Walman Optical Company, Minneapolis, MN, pg. 1161
Patterson, Donald S., Sr. V.P.--Edwards Baking Co., Atlanta, GA, pg. 369
Patterson, Jim, Mng. Dir.--Leo Burnett Pte. Ltd., Singapore, Singapore, pg. 193
Patterson, Pat, Pres.--McKenzie Tank Lines, Inc., Tallahassee, FL, pg. 730
Patterson, Ray, Pres.--Bell & Howell Ltd., Weston,, Canada, pg. 135
Patterson, Ray, Chief Exec. Officer--Esskay Manufacturing Co., San Antonio, TX, pg. 389
Patton, J.H., III, Chm. Bd. & Pres.--National Bedding & Furniture Industries, Memphis, TN, pg. 786
Paul, Douglas, Pres. & Chief Oper. Officer--American Learning Corp., Chicago, IL, pg. 381
Pavao, James S., Pres.--Whaling Industries, Inc., Fall River, MA, pg. 1183
Paxton, C. William, Sr. V.P.-Engineered Prods.--Bliss-Salem, Inc., Salem, OH, pg. 156
Payer, Steven, Pres.--Pratt-Read Corporation, Bridgeport, CT, pg. 884
Payne, Ronald G., Pres. & Chief Exec. Officer--Warehouse Home Furnishings Distributor, Dublin, GA, pg. 1163
Payne, Walter F., Pres. & Chief Exec. Officer--Blue Diamond Growers, Sacramento, CA, pg. 160
Peacock, J.H., Pres. & Gen. Mgr.--Perfection Hy-Test Company, Florence, SC, pg. 711
Pearce, Gary M., Vice Chm. & Pres.--Pearce Industries Inc., Houston, TX, pg. 853
Pearce, P. F., Pres.--Biddle Instruments, Blue Bell, PA, pg. 148
Peardon, Thomas, Pres. & Chief Exec. Officer--Brunschwig & Fils, Inc., White Plains, NY, pg. 184
Pearlman, Jack, Pres.--Atlite Lighting Equip, Inc., Maspeth, NY, pg. 97
Pearlstine, Edwin, Jr., Pres.--Pearlstine Distributors Inc., Charleston, SC, pg. 853
Pearson, Harry, Pres.--United Farm Bureau Family Life Insurance Co., Indianapolis, IN, pg. 1131
Pearson, John, Pres.--Ervin Industries, Inc., Ann Arbor, MI, pg. 387
Pearson, Paul H., Pres. & Chief Exec. Officer--Security Mutual Life Insurance Co. of New York, Binghamton, NY, pg. 987
Pearson, Ronald, Chm. Bd., Pres. & Chief Exec. Officer--Hy-Vee Food Stores Incorporated, Chariton, IA, pg. 556
Pearson, Ronald A., Pres.--New Mech Companies, Inc., Saint Paul, MN, pg. 802
Peavey, Melia, Pres.--Peavey Electronic Corp., Meridian, MS, pg. 854
Peck, Donald E., Pres.--Pacific Metal Company, Portland, OR, pg. 841
Peck, Julius S., Pres.--Peck Iron & Metal Company, Inc., Portsmouth, VA, pg. 854
Peck, Norm, Pres.--Ektelon Corp., San Diego, CA, pg. 890
Pedas, Ted A., Pres. & Chief Oper. Officer--The White Lily Foods Co., Knoxville, TN, pg. 1186
Peden, Jean H., Pres.--The Women's Bank, N.A., Denver, CO, pg. 385
Pederson, Kurt, Pres.--Thunderline Corporation, Belleville, MI, pg. 1096
Pedone, Michael F., Pres. & Chief Exec. Officer--Pedone & Partners Inc., New York, NY, pg. 854
Peeler, Bobby J., Pres.--Peelers Rug Company, Inc., Gaffney, SC, pg. 855
Peepas, James Z., Pres.--Selecto-Flash, Inc., West Orange, NJ, pg. 988
Peeples, Minor, Pres. & Chief Exec. Officer--Standco Industries, Inc., Houston, TX, pg. 1038
Peine, Herb, Pres.--Hastings Co-Op Creamery Company, Hastings, MN, pg. 516
Peister, Alan, Pres.--David L. Peister Co., Inc., New York, NY, pg. 856
Pellegrini, Donald P., Pres. & Chief Exec. Officer--The Spring Air Company, Des Plaines, IL, pg. 1032
Pellegrino, A. Robert, Pres.--Foster & Gallagher Inc., Peoria, IL, pg. 426
Pellegrino, John B., Pres. & Chief Exec. Offcier--Ridg-U-Rak, Inc., North East, PA, pg. 933
Pemberton, Marlin H., Chm. Bd., Pres. & Chief Exec. Officer--Acorn Building Components Inc., Detroit, MI, pg. 13
Pemble, John C., Pres. & Chief Exec. Officer--Itran Corporation, Manchester, NH, pg. 583
Pena, Luis X., Pres., Chief Exec. Officer & Chief Fin. Officer--Gulf States Asphalt Company, Inc., South Houston, TX, pg. 493
Penman, James A., Pres.--United Tectonic Industry, Harrisburg, PA, pg. 1137
Penn, Richard L., Pres.--Cummins Mid-South, Inc., Memphis, TN, pg. 305
Penney, C.Brad, Pres. & Chief Exec. Officer--Streamlight Inc., Norristown, PA, pg. 1053
Penrod, Alan, Pres.--Harford Systems, Inc., Aberdeen, MD, pg. 152
Penrod, Allen, Pres.--Maryland Plastics, Inc., Federalsburg, MD, pg. 717
Penrod, Allen, Pres.--Maryland Plastics, Inc., Federalsburg, MD, pg. 152
Penske, Richard H., Chm. Bd., Pres. & Treas.--Piercing Pagoda, Inc., Bethlehem, PA, pg. 870
Penske, Roger, Pres.--Penske Transportation Inc., Reading, PA, pg. 859
Penske, Roger S., Pres.--Penske Corporation, Detroit, MI, pg. 859
Pentecost, James, Pres.--Printco, Inc., Greenville, MI, pg. 891
Pentecost, Jim, Pres.--Power & Telephone Supply Company, Memphis, TN, pg. 883
Pentz, Paul, Pres. & Chief Exec. Officer--Servistar Corporation, East Butler, PA, pg. 992
Pepe, John M., Pres.--John S. Barnes Corp., Rockford, IL, pg. 120
Pepper, David, Pres.--Harry Pepper & Associates, Jacksonville, FL, pg. 859
Pepper, J. Stanley, Pres.--The Pepper Companies, Inc., Chicago, IL, pg. 859
Peppers, Henry, Pres.--Datron Incorporated, Hoffman Estates, IL, pg. 316
Pepys, Shirley, Chm., Pres. & Chief Exec. Officer--Noel-Joanna, Inc., Rancho Santa Margarita, CA, pg. 808
Peralta-Ramos, A.H., Pres.--Medtech Laboratories, Inc., Jackson, WY, pg. 736
Percival, Robert, Pres.--Intelligent Controls Inc., Lynnwood, WA, pg. 573
Perconti, Paul J., Pres. & Chief Exec. Officer--Thornton Oil Corp., Louisville, KY, pg. 1095
Perdomo, Luis A., Chm. Bd., Pres. & Chief Exec. Officer--Perdomo-Ted Bates/Publicidad, Lima,, Peru, pg. 112
Perel, Jonathan S., Pres.--General Services Corporation, Richmond, VA, pg. 450
Perelman, Jeffrey, Pres.--Belmont Industries, Inc., Philadelphia, PA, pg. 136
Peres, Edward J., Pres.--Century Autoline, Baltimore, MD, pg. 235
Perez, Jean-Yves, Pres. & Chief Exec. Officer--Woodward-Clyde Group, Inc., Denver, CO, pg. 1200
Perez, Jean-Yves, Pres. & Chief Exec. Officer--Woodward-Clyde International, Denver, CO, pg. 1201
Perez, John, Pres. & Chief Exec. Officer--Perez Trading Co. Inc., Miami, FL, pg. 860
Perez, Lombardo, Chm. Bd., Pres. & Chief Oper. Officer--Metro Ford Inc., Miami, FL, pg. 743
Perkins, Charles, Pres.--Cole Papers Inc., Fargo, ND, pg. 260
Perkins, Lawrence, Chm. Bd., Pres. & Treas.--Connecticut Container Corporation, North Haven, CT, pg. 274
Perkins, Leigh H., Jr., Pres.--The Orvis Company, Inc., Manchester, VT, pg. 830
Perkins, S.J., Pres.--Flexonics Inc., Bartlett, IL, pg. 419
Perkins, William, Pres.--Ketchum Advertising/New York, New York, NY, pg. 625
Perks, Douglas,, Pres. & Chief Oper. Officer--Eclipse, Inc., Rockford, IL, pg. 366
Perlbinder, Arnold, Pres.--P.D. Fashions, New York, NY, pg. 836
Perlman, Lee, Pres.--Eastern Air Devices, Inc., Dover, NH, pg. 363
Perlman, Sam, Pres.--Astro Wire & Cable Corporation, Worcester, MA, pg. 92
Perlmuter, Richard M., Pres. & Chief Exec. Officer--Perlmuter Printing Company, Cleveland, OH, pg. 862
Perott, Edward J., Pres.--Chip Supply Inc., Orlando, FL, pg. 248
Perrino, S. Ronald, Chm. Bd., Pres. & Chief Exec. Officer--S.T. Research, Newington, VA, pg. 964
Perry, Chris N., Chm., Chief Exec. Officer & Exec. Creative Dir.--Meldrum & Fewsmith Advertising Inc., Cleveland, OH, pg. 737
Perry, David H., Pres.--Detecto Scale Company, Webb City, MO, pg. 332
Perry, Egbert L., Pres. & Chief Oper. Officer--H. J. Russell Corp., Atlanta, GA, pg. 957
Persia, Raymond J., Pres.--Electro-Matic Products Inc., Farmington Hills, MI, pg. 374
Persichini, Dominic, Pres.--Air Gage Company, Livonia, MI, pg. 27
Pesch, Alan J., Chm. Bd., Pres. & Chief Exec. Officer--Ship Analytics, Inc., North Stonington, CT, pg. 999
Peslar, Norman, Pres.--Automotive Moulding Company, Warren, MI, pg. 101
Peter, Hugh M., Jr., Pres.--Peter Lumber Company, Pleasantville, NJ, pg. 864
Peters, A. Clark, Pres. & Chief Exec. Officer--LaSalle-Deitch Co., Inc., Elkhart, IN, pg. 660
Peters, A.D., Pres.--Chamberlain Health & Beauty Aids Company, Des Moines, IA, pg. 238
Peters, Donald J., Pres. & Chief Oper. Officer--American Stone-Mix, Inc., Towson, MD, pg. 63
Peters, J.E., Pres.--Delmar Studios, Charlotte, NC, pg. 279
Peters, Robert C., Pres. & Chief Oper. Officer--New World Entertainment, Inc., Los Angeles, CA, pg. 74
Peters, Robert L., Chm. Bd., Pres. & Chief Exec. Officer--Holmquist Grain & Lumber Co., Oakland, NE, pg. 540
Peters, Roger, Pres. & Chief Exec. Officer--Kold Kist Brands, Inc., Los Angeles, CA, pg. 641
Peters, Samuel L., Pres.--Miami Systems Corporation, Cincinnati, OH, pg. 746
Petersen, Allen D., Chm. Bd., Pres. & Chief Exec. Officer--American Tool Companies, Inc., Lincoln, NE, pg. 64
Petersen, Fred M., Pres., Chief Exec. Officer & Chief Oper. Officer--Omaha Public Power District, Omaha, NE, pg. 825
Petersen, John M., Pres., Chief Fin. Officer & Treas.--Erie Family Life Insurance Company, Erie, PA, pg. 386
Petersen, K.C., Pres. & Chief Oper. Officer--Schenectady Chemicals, Inc., Schenectady, NY, pg. 975
Petersen, March, Pres. & Sec.--Petersen Graphics Group, South Bend, IN, pg. 864
Petersen, Merritt, Grp. V.P.--Honeymead Products Co., Mankato, MN, pg. 542
Petersen, Mike, Pres.--Petersen Aluminum Corporation, Elk Grove Village, IL, pg. 864
Peterson, Alan, Pres.--Bergman Tool Mfg. Co., Inc., Buffalo, NY, pg. 64
Peterson, Arlo, Pres.--AEC, Anoka, MN, pg. 3
Peterson, Arthur M., Pres.--Kampgrounds of America, Inc., Billings, MT, pg. 613
Peterson, Carl, Pres. & Gen. Mgr.--Kansas City Chiefs Football Club, Kansas City, MO, pg. 616
Peterson, Charles T., Actng. Pres.--Continental Machines, Inc., Savage, MN, pg. 279
Peterson, Ellsworth L., Pres. & Gen. Mgr.--Peterson Builders, Inc., Sturgeon Bay, WI, pg. 864
Peterson, Eric, Pres.--Peterson American Corp., Southfield, MI, pg. 864
Peterson, H.A., Pres.--Minn-Dak Growers, Ltd., Grand Forks, ND, pg. 757
Peterson, Jim L., Pres. & Chief Exec. Officer--Whataburger, Inc., Corpus Christi, TX, pg. 1184
Peterson, Kristina, V.P. & Publisher-Reference & Travel--Fodor's Travel Publications, Inc., New York, NY, pg. 19
Peterson, Marvin, Pres.--Peterson Motor Company, Boise, ID, pg. 865
Peterson, Palmer G., Pres.--Bituminous Roadways, Inc., Minneapolis, MN, pg. 153
Peterson, Ralph R., Pres. & Chief Exec. Officer--CH2M Hill Companies, Ltd., Englewood, CO, pg. 202
Peterson, Roger E., Pres. & Chief Exec. Officer--Ace Hardware Corporation, Oak Brook, IL, pg. 12
Petertyl, Gary, Pres. & Creative Dir.--Sefton Associates Inc., Grand Rapids, MI, pg. 987
Petrarca, Anthony A., Pres.--The Cedarwood Companies, Akron, OH, pg. 230
Petricca, Robert W., Pres.--Petricca Industries, Inc., Pittsfield, MA, pg. 865
Petricoff, Mark, Pres.--Leshner Mills. Inc., Hamilton, OH, pg. 668
Petrocine, Thomas M., Pres. & Chief Oper. Officer--Christopher Thomas Associates Inc., Garden City, NY, pg. 249
Petsche, Thomas, Chm. Bd. & Pres.--Rocky Mountain Mechanical, Inc., Salt Lake City, UT, pg. 942
Pettey, Patrick, Pres.--Dave Syverson Truck Center, Inc., Rochester, MN, pg. 1071
Pettit, Wallace, Pres.--Polka Dot Dairy, Hastings, MN, pg. 879
Petty, John L., Pres. & Chief Exec. Officer--Mid-South Milling Company, Inc., Memphis, TN, pg. 750
Petty, William, Chief Exec. Officer--Comstock Michigan Fruit, Rochester, NY, pg. 25
Petty, William, Pres.--Evergreen Healthcare Ltd., Carmel, IN, pg. 391
Peyton, Herbert H., Chm. Bd. & Pres.--Gate Petroleum Company, Jacksonville, FL, pg. 445
Pfaff, Frederick A., Pres.--Anchor Tool & Die Company, Cleveland, OH, pg. 71
Pfeifer, David, Pres.--Gamma One, Inc., North Haven, CT, pg. 442
Pfeiffer, Richard N., Pres.--Neill-LaVielle Supply Co., Louisville, KY, pg. 797
Pflaster, Felix, Pres.--Arnold Steel Company, Inc., Lakewood, NJ, pg. 85
Phares, Elwood W., II, Chm. Bd. & Pres.--Wechco, Inc., Princeton, NJ, pg. 1172
Phares, Elwood W., II, Chm. Bd., Pres. & Chief Exec. Officer--West Chemical Products, Inc., Princeton, NJ, pg. 1172
Phelps, Ashton, Jr., Pres. & Publr.--The Times-Picayune Publishing Corp., New Orleans, LA, pg. 1098
Phelps, Isaac E., Pres. & Chief Exec. Officer--World Aerospace Corporation, Maple Grove, MN, pg. 1202
Phelps, Joe, Pres.--The Phelps Group, Los Angeles, CA, pg. 866
Phelps, Jon, Pres. & Chief Exec. Officer--Hickerson Phelps Kirtley & Associates, Kansas City, MO, pg. 532
Phelps, Norman, Pres. & Chief Exec. Officer--Valley Forge Associates, Valley Forge, PA, pg. 1143
Phelps, Norman, Pres. & Chief Exec. Officer--National Liberty, Frazer, PA, pg. 791
Phelps, Terry M., Chm. Bd., Pres. & Chief Exec. Officer--Petroleum Marketers, Inc., Roanoke, VA, pg. 865
Philip, Robert W., Pres.-Schnitzer Steel Industries, Inc.--Schnitzer Steel Industries, Inc., Portland, OR, pg. 977
Phillips, Bradford E., Pres. & Chief Exec. Officer--Jones Optical Company, Boulder, CO, pg. 1103
Phillips, David, Chm. Bd. & Chief Exec. Officer--Financial Protection Services Inc., Springfield, VA, pg. 410
Phillips, Ira H., Pres. & Chief Oper. Officer--Quoizel Inc., Hauppauge, NY, pg. 905
Phillips, John, Pres.--Technology Transfer Institute, Santa Monica, CA, pg. 1084
Phillips, Kathleen, Pres.--The Phillips Agency, Horsham, PA, pg. 867
Phillips, Kenneth H., Pres.--Plan International U.S.A., Warwick, RI, pg. 874
Phillips, Samuel, Exec. V.P. & Gen. Mgr.--E. B. Kingman Company, Leominster, MA, pg. 631
Phillips, T.B., Managing Dir.--Red L Foods, Pomfret Center, CT, pg. 1128
Phillips, Thomas L., Chm. Bd., Pres. & Chief Exec. Officer--Phillips Publishing Inc., Potomac, MD, pg. 868
Piccinini, Robert M., Chm. Bd. & Chief Exec. Officer & Pres.--Save Mart Supermarkets, Modesto, CA, pg. 973
Picini, Dan E., Chm. Bd., Pres. & Chief Oper. Officer--Duro-Test Corporation, Fairfield, NJ, pg. 355
Picken, Robert F., Chm. Bd. & Pres.--Peerless Confection Company, Chicago, IL, pg. 855
Pickering, Gordon G., Chm. Bd., Pres. & Gen. Counsel--Pickering Industries Inc., Tacoma, WA, pg. 869
Pickering, Jeff, Pres.--JAG Northwest Inc., Tacoma, WA, pg. 870
Pickett, Al, III, Pres.--Buquet & Le Blanc Inc., Baton Rouge, LA, pg. 189
Picknelly, Peter A., Jr., Pres. & Chief Exec. Officer--Peter Pan Bus Lines, Inc., Springfield, MA, pg. 864
Picou, Donald, Pres.--Picou Brothers Construction Company, Gonzales, LA, pg. 870
Piech, Timothy R., Pres. & Adv. Mgr.--U.S. Food Products, Inc., Chicago, IL, pg. 1136
Piegza, Henry J., Pres.--WSF Industries, Inc., Tonawanda, NY, pg. 1156
Pierce, Brian, Pres. & Chief Exec. Officer--Peirce-Phelps, Inc., Philadelphia, PA, pg. 855

Pierce, Frederick G., II, Chm. Bd., Pres. & Chief Exec. Officer--Niagara Envelope Company, Inc., Buffalo, NY, pg. 805
Pierce, Harvey, Pres. & Chief Oper. Officer--American Family Mutual Insurance Co., Madison, WI, pg. 51
Pierce, Pamela, Pres.--Austin Sculpture, Holbrook, NY, pg. 99
Pieri, Albert, Pres.--California Artichoke & Vegetable Growers Corp., Castroville, CA, pg. 209
Piet, Lawrence F., Pres.--Dumore Corporation, Mauston, WI, pg. 352
Pietrafesa, Richard C., Jr., Pres.--Jos. J. Pietrafesa Co., Inc., Liverpool, NY, pg. 870
Pietrini, Andrew G., Pres.--UIS, Inc., New York, NY, pg. 1123
Pietsch, James E., Pres.--Yoakum Packing Company, Yoakum, TX, pg. 1208
Piette, Edward, Pres. & Gen. Mgr.-WDAF-TV--Great American Broadcasting Company, Cincinnati, OH, pg. 52
Pigott, Richard, Pres.--Spring Arbor Distributors, Belleville, MI, pg. 1033
Pike, Larry R., Chm. Bd., Pres. & Chief Exec. Officer--The Union Central Life Insurance Co., Cincinnati, OH, pg. 1127
Pike, Matthew Lee, III, Pres.--Elite Lamp, Inc., West Memphis, AR, pg. 376
Pilafieies, Emile, Pres.--Putzmeister, Inc., Gardena, CA, pg. 901
Pilarczyk, R.R., Pres., Chief Exec. Officer & Treas.--General Computer Corp. Inc., Twinsburg, OH, pg. 449
Pindyck, Bruce E., Chm. Bd. & Chief Exec. Officer--Meridian Industries, Inc., Milwaukee, WI, pg. 740
Pingel, Paul, Chm. Bd. & Pres.--New Cooperative Inc., Fort Dodge, IA, pg. 799
Pink, Ronald A., Pres.--Distribution America, Des Plaines, IL, pg. 340
Pinkerton, C.R., Pres. & Chief Exec. Officer--Winters Welding Works, Inc., Winters, TX, pg. 1197
Pinkerton, Fred H., Jr., Pres. & Chief Exec. Officer--Allied Foods, Inc., Atlanta, GA, pg. 38
Pinto, James J., Pres. & Chief Exec. Officer--Action Instruments, Inc., San Diego, CA, pg. 14
Pinto, M. Christina Carvalho, Pres. & Creative Dir.--Young & Rubicam Brasil, Sao Paulo,, Brazil, pg. 1213
Pinzino, Thomas F., Pres.--Sunnyland Refining Co., Inc., Birmingham, AL, pg. 616
Piper, Peter A., Pres. & Chief Oper. Officer--American Eagle Airlines, Chicago, IL, pg. 51
Pirella, Emanuele, Pres.--Gariboldi Parisi Verga/Interad, Milan,, Italy, pg. 685
Pirrong, J., Pres. & Chief Exec. Officer--BIW Cable Systems, Inc., North Dighton, MA, pg. 106
Pirtle, Robert, Chm. & Pres.--General Business Services, Inc., Columbia, MD, pg. 449
Pisa, Michael A., Jr., Pres.--Continental Paper & Supply Co., Detroit, MI, pg. 280
Pisani, Anthony, Pres.--APG Security, Inc., Denver, CO, pg. 5
Pistilli, Frederick M., Pres.--Westclox, Norcross, GA, pg. 451
Pistilli, Frederick M., Chm. & Chief Exec. Officer--Seth Thomas, Norcross, GA, pg. 451
Pistulka, Louis, Gen. Mgr.--Big Horn Co-Op Marketing Association, Greybull, WY, pg. 149
Pitt, Irving E., Pres.--Murray's Discount Auto Stores, Taylor, MI, pg. 777
Pitterich, Michael P., Chm. Bd. & Pres.--Moltrup Steel Products Company, Beaver Falls, PA, pg. 764
Pittman, Gary, Chm. Bd., Pres., Chief Exec., Chief Oper. & Chief Fin. Officer--PCI, Austin, TX, pg. 836
Pixler, D., Pres.--Apple Lines, Inc., Madison, SD, pg. 79
Pizer, Larry, Pres. & New Bus. Contact--Ott Communications, Inc., Louisville, KY, pg. 831
Plamondon, William, Pres. & Chief Oper. Officer (Budget Corp.)--Budget Rent A Car Corporation, Lisle, IL, pg. 131
Planes, John, Pres.--Planes Moving And Storage, Inc., Cincinnati, OH, pg. 874
Plant, Morton B., Pres.--Samuel G. Keywell Co., Baltimore, MD, pg. 629
Plantz, Gerald, Pres.--Die Cast Products, Inc., Gardena, CA, pg. 336
Plaskett, Robert W., Pres.--Macwhyte Co., Kenosha, WI, pg. 69
Platania, Philip, Pres., Chief Exec. & Chief Fin. Officer--Andmore Sportswear Corporation, Port Jervis, NY, pg. 74
Platt, Charles, Pres. & Chief Oper. Officer--Alamo Rent-A-Car Inc., Fort Lauderdale, FL, pg. 30
Pleau, G. Steve, Pres.--Future Ford/Hugo Inc., Roseville, CA, pg. 437
Pliss, Stephen, Pres.--Stephen Associates, Inc., New York, NY, pg. 1046
Plitt, Robert A., Sr. V.P.--The Donohoe Companies, Inc., Washington, DC, pg. 345
Plotkin, B. William, Pres. & Sec.--The Fairfield Lumber & Supply Company, Fairfield, CT, pg. 397
Plotkin, Ron, Pres.--Communications Planning Corporation/TMP Worldwide, Westlake Village, CA, pg. 1073
Plowman, M.N., Pres.--D.S.U.-Peterbilt & GMC, Inc., Portland, OR, pg. 309
Plummer, Terry, Pres.--The Zippertubing Co., Los Angeles, CA, pg. 1220
Plunk, Robert, Pres. & Chief Exec. Officer--Preferred Risk Mutual Insurance, West Des Moines, IA, pg. 886
Plunkett, Robert G., Pres.--Plunkett-Webster, Inc., New Rochelle, NY, pg. 877
Pochick, Daniel T., Pres.--Rish Equipment Company, Bluefield, WV, pg. 935
Poehlmann, Karl M., Pres. & Chief Exec. Officer--George Uhe Co., Inc., Paramus, NJ, pg. 1125
Pogmore, James W., Pres.--Cramer Company, Old Saybrook, CT, pg. 296
Pogue, A. Mack, Chm. Bd., Pres. & Chief Exec. Officer--Lincoln Property Company, Dallas, TX, pg. 676
Pogue, Richard W., Mng. Partner--Jones, Day, Reavis & Pogue, Cleveland, OH, pg. 603
Pohan, Armand, Pres.--A-P-A Transport Corp., North Bergen, NJ, pg. 5
Pohlad, Carl R., Pres.--Bank Shares, Inc., Minneapolis, MN, pg. 117
Poindexter, John E., Pres.--Basic Construction Company, Newport News, VA, pg. 124
Poindexter, Larry, Pres.--Batey/Poindexter, Los Angeles, CA, pg. 126
Poiry, James R., Pres.--Harris-Kayot, Inc., Fort Wayne, IN, pg. 512
Poitevint, A.L., Chm. Bd. & Pres.--Flint River Mills, Bainbridge, GA, pg. 419
Pokarczyk, George, Pres. & Chief Oper. Officer--Duling Optical Corporation, Louisville, KY, pg. 352
Pol, Steve W., Pres.--Airtrol, Inc., Baton Rouge, LA, pg. 28
Polacheck, Isabelle, Pres.--Reliable Knitting Works, Milwaukee, WI, pg. 924
Polack, Jack, Pres.--Acme Poultry Company, Inc., Seattle, WA, pg. 13
Polera, Catherine, Pres., Chief Fin. Officer, Sec. & Treas.--Polera Building Corp., Scarsdale, NY, pg. 878
Polk, Stephen R., Pres. & Chief Oper. Officer--R. L. Polk & Co., Detroit, MI, pg. 879
Pollack, Dan, Pres.--Stock Yards Packing Co., Inc., Chicago, IL, pg. 1049
Pollack, Gerald M., Pres.--Pollack Corporation, Scarborough, ME, pg. 879
Pollak, H.M., Pres.--American Machine & Tool Company, Royersford, PA, pg. 57
Pollak, Louis M., Pres.--Injectron Corporation, Plainfield, NJ, pg. 569
Pollan, Burt, Pres.--Azcon Corp., Chicago, IL, pg. 161
Pollara, John, Pres.--Zieman Manufacturing Company, Inc., Whittier, CA, pg. 1218
Pollard, Frank, Pres. & Chief Oper. Officer--GenDerm Corporation, Lincolnshire, IL, pg. 448
Pollard, Frank, Pres.--GalenPharma, Inc., Lincolnshire, IL, pg. 448
Polley, David, Pres.--World Carpets, Inc., Dalton, GA, pg. 1202
Pollock, Elsie Frankfurt, Pres.--Page Boy Company, Inc., Dallas, TX, pg. 843
Pollock, Louis I., Chm. Bd. & Pres.--Morris Coupling Co., Erie, PA, pg. 771
Pollock, William K., Chm. Bd. & Chief Exec. Officer--Key Industries, Inc., Fort Scott, KS, pg. 627
Pomeranz, Edward, Pres.--Stanley Roberts, Inc., Lodi, NJ, pg. 939
Pons, Francisco, Chm. Bd. & Pres.--Atlantic Sugar Association, Inc., Belle Glade, FL, pg. 95
Pool, Harvey, Pres.--Pool Communications, Los Angeles, CA, pg. 880
Poole, W. David, Jr., Pres.--Y.C. Ballenger Electrical Contractors, Spartanburg, SC, pg. 116
Pope, John W., Sr., Pres.--Variety Wholesalers, Inc., Raleigh, NC, pg. 1146
Pope, Robert H., Pres.--Hancock Peanut Company, Courtland, VA, pg. 504
Pope, Robert M., Pres.--Minot Builders Supply Association, Minot, ND, pg. 758
Pope, Wendell E., Pres.--Clark & Pope, Inc., New York, NY, pg. 253
Popofsky, David, Chm. Bd., Pres. & Creative--Popofsky Advertising, Inc., New York, NY, pg. 880
Popp, John F., Chm. Bd. & Pres.--Perfection Bakeries Inc., Fort Wayne, IN, pg. 861
Poppel, Seth, Chm. Bd. & Pres.--American Vision Centers, Inc., New York, NY, pg. 65
Popple, John A., Chm. Bd., Pres. & Chief Exec. Officer--LeeWards Creative Crafts, Inc., Elgin, IL, pg. 666
Porchey, David, Chm. Bd. & Pres.--Pawnee Industries, Inc., Wichita, KS, pg. 852
Porter, Arthur, Pres.--Arthur Porter Construction, Phoenix, AZ, pg. 881
Porter, Jamie D., Gen. Mgr.--Missouri Auction Services Corp. d/b/a 166 Auto Action, Springfield, MO, pg. 293
Porter, Robert L., Pres. & Chief Oper. Officer--Oliver Products Company, Grand Rapids, MI, pg. 824
Posen, L.M., Pres.--Beltone Electronics Corporation, Chicago, IL, pg. 137
Posey, Lee, Pres. & Chief Exec. Officer--Palm Harbor Homes, Inc., Dallas, TX, pg. 843
Posinski, Frank J., Pres. & Chief Oper. Officer--Cincinnati Gear Company, Cincinnati, OH, pg. 250
Posner, Gerald D., Pres.--Electronic Measurements, Inc., Neptune, NJ, pg. 145
Posner, Peter S., Pres., Chief Oper. Officer, New Bus. Contact--Newmark, Posner & Mitchell, Inc., New York, NY, pg. 804
Posner, Victor, Chm. Bd., Pres. & Chief Exec. Officer--Chesapeake Financial Corp., Miami Beach, FL, pg. 243
Posner, Victor, Chm. Bd. & Pres.--Royal Crown Cola Co., Miami Beach, FL, pg. 243
Post, Bill, Pres.--The Levy Organization, Chicago, IL, pg. 672
Post, James R., Pres., Chief Exec. Officer, Chief Fin. Officer--Ostarr Corporation, Chicago, IL, pg. 831
Post, Ned, Pres.--Scott U.S.A., Ketchum, ID, pg. 983
Postal, Andrew, Pres.--Judy Bond, Inc., New York, NY, pg. 608
Potack, Michael R., Pres.--Coat, Apron & Linen Supply, Bronx, NY, pg. 257
Potamkin, Alan, Pres.--Potamkin Toyota, Inc., Miami, FL, pg. 882
Potamkin, Victor, Pres. & Chief Exec. Officer--Potamkin Manhattan, New York, NY, pg. 882
Potash, Jerome, Pres.--OPT Industries, Inc., Phillipsburg, NJ, pg. 819
Potkin, Harvey, Pres. & Chief Oper. Officer--National Foods Inc., Bronx, NY, pg. 788
Potter, Luther D., Pres.--Luke Potter Dodge Inc., Winter Park, FL, pg. 882
Pottinger, Don, Pres.--J.R. Simplot Co., Minerals & Chemicals Group, Pocatello, ID, pg. 1007
Pottinger, Don, Pres.--J.R. Simplot Co.-Minerals & Chemical Group, Pocatello, ID, pg. 1007
Poulnot, Edwin, III, Pres.--Kerrison Dry Goods Company, Inc., Charleston, SC, pg. 624
Poupore, John, Chm. Bd., Co-Pres. & Chief Exec. Officer--Helm, Inc., Highland Park, MI, pg. 527
Poure, James, Chm. Bd., Pres. & Chief Exec. Officer--General Alum & Chemical, Holland, OH, pg. 448
Povah, Trevor H., Pres.--Hamilton Stores, Inc., West Yellowstone, MT, pg. 503
Powell, Don G., Chm. Bd. & Pres.--American Capital Management & Research, Inc., Houston, TX, pg. 50
Powell, M. Lee, III, Pres.--Ballenger Paving Company, Inc., Taylors, SC, pg. 116
Powell, Richard M., Pres. & Chief Exec. Officer--L. Powell Co., Inc., Culver City, CA, pg. 882
Powell, Robert C., Chm. Bd. & Pres.--Robert C. Powell Developments, Incorporated, Sacramento, CA, pg. 882
Powell, T.E., III, Pres.--Carolina Biological Supply Co., Burlington, NC, pg. 222
Powell, William K., Pres.--Fred Weber Inc., Maryland Heights, MO, pg. 1171
Power, James D., III, Pres.--J.D. Power and Associates, Agoura Hills, CA, pg. 883
Power, John G., Pres.--Desert Medical Supply Inc., Phoenix, AZ, pg. 1081
Power, William, Chm., Pres. & Chief Exec. Officer-Canada--Young & Rubicam, Ltd., Toronto,, Canada, pg. 1213
Powers, Frederic B., Jr., Chm. Bd. & Pres.--The Rawlplug Company, Inc., New Rochelle, NY, pg. 914
Powers, Walter E., Pres.--Tri-Chem, Inc., Harrison, NJ, pg. 1110
Poynter, James, Pres.--Telesciences Co. Systems Inc., Moorestown, NJ, pg. 1085
Pozza, Duane C., Pres.--Bartlett Cocke Jr. Construction Co., San Antonio, TX, pg. 258
Prairie, Duane, Pres. & Chief Exec. Officer--Park Construction Company, Minneapolis, MN, pg. 848
Prange, Henry C., Chm. Bd.--H. C. Prange Company, Green Bay, WI, pg. 884
Prasse, Henry R., Chm. Bd. & Pres.--Out of Home Media Services, Inc., New York, NY, pg. 832
Pratt, Cliff W., Pres. & Treas.--Universal Molding Company, Lynwood, CA, pg. 1139
Pratt, R. George, Jr., Pres. & Treas.--Bradford Oil Company, Inc., Bradford, VT, pg. 170
Pratte, Gary D., Pres. & Treas.--E.J. Bartells Co., Renton, WA, pg. 122
Prawer, Gilbert, Owner--S.P.C. Transport, Portland, ME, pg. 963
Prechter, Heinz C., Chm. & Chief Exec. Officer--ASC Incorporated, Southgate, MI, pg. 7
Prentice, Daniel F., Pres. & Chief Oper. Officer--Generra Sportswear Company, Inc., Tukwila, WA, pg. 451
Preonas, Demetri, Gen. Mgr.--Rich Products Dayton, Dayton, OH, pg. 932
Press, Frank, Pres.--National Academy Sciences USA, Washington, DC, pg. 784
Presser, Leon, Dr., Pres.--Softool Corporation, Goleta, CA, pg. 1016
Pressman, Fred, Pres.--Barneys New York, New York, NY, pg. 120
Pressman, James R., Pres. & Chief Oper. Officer--Pressman Toy Corp., New York, NY, pg. 887
Prestenburg, H., Jr., Pres.--Intrepid Enterprises, Inc., Harvey, LA, pg. 581
Preston, Donald, Pres. & Chief Exec. Officer--Bijur Lubricating Corporation, Bennington, VT, pg. 150
Pretak, Thomas, Pres.--The Turner & Seymour Mfg. Company, Torrington, CT, pg. 1119
Previdi, Melissa, Pres. & Chief Exec. Officer--Danbury Printing & Lithograph, Inc., Danbury, CT, pg. 313
Previti, James, Chm. Bd, Pres. & Chief Exec. Officer--Forecast Mortgage Corporation, Rancho Cucamonga, CA, pg. 423
Price, John, Pres.--N. G. Gilbert Corporation, Muncie, IN, pg. 458
Price, Mary Beth, Pres.--Media That Works, Cincinnati, OH, pg. 735
Price, Thomas P., Jr., Pres. & Chief Exec. Officer--Sabin Robbins Paper Co., Cincinnati, OH, pg. 965
Price, William C., Principal--Media That Works, Cincinnati, OH, pg. 735
Priebe, Bruce, Pres.--Cargill Seed Div., Minneapolis, MN, pg. 219
Prince, John, Pres. & Gen. Mgr.--Alto Dairy Cooperative, Waupun, WI, pg. 45
Prince, R.S., Pres. & Chief Oper. Officer--Central States Diversified, Inc., Saint Louis, MO, pg. 234
Prince, Robert, Pres.--Printing House, Inc., Quincy, FL, pg. 891
Printz, Bernadine, Pres.--Commercial & Industrial Administration Co. inc, Santa Clara, CA, pg. 268
Prischak, Andrew M., Pres.--Plastek Group, Erie, PA, pg. 874
Pritchett, Mike, Pres. & Chief Exec. Officer--Evangeline Medical & X-Ray Distributors, Baton Rouge, LA, pg. 390
Pritchett, Tad, Chief Oper. Officer--Rocco Further Processing, Timberville, VA, pg. 940
Pritz, Benjamin, Pres.--Par Beverage Co., Cincinnati, OH, pg. 476
Pritz, Benjamin L., Chm. Bd., Pres. & Chief Exec. Officer--Grandpa Brands Company, Cincinnati, OH, pg. 476
Pritz, Benjamin L., Pres.--C.S. Dent & Co., Cincinnati, OH, pg. 476
Pritz, Benjamin L., Pres.--A. J. Lehman Co., Cincinnati, OH, pg. 476
Pritzker, R.A., Pres.--Fenestra Corporation, Erie, PA, pg. 711
Pritzker, Robert A., Pres. & Chief Exec. Officer--The Marmon Group, Inc., Chicago, IL, pg. 710

Pritzker, Thomas J., Pres.--Hyatt Corporation, Chicago, IL, pg. 495
Prochot, J.B., Pres.--Bruner Corporation, Milwaukee, WI, pg. 184
Proctor, Barbara G., Pres. & Chief Exec. Officer--Proctor & Gardner Advertising, Inc., Chicago, IL, pg. 892
Proctor, Thomas E., Pres.--American Technical Publishers, Inc., Homewood, IL, pg. 63
Proffitt, Brian, Pres.--Zephyr Baskets & Balloons, New Providence, NJ, pg. 1217
Profit, Joe, Pres. & Chief Exec. Officer--Communications International, Norcross, GA, pg. 269
Proies, Michael C., Pres.--Taren Holdings, Inc., Los Angeles, CA, pg. 1078
Proies, Michael C., Pres.--Catalina, Los Angeles, CA, pg. 1079
Pronko, David, Chm. Bd., Pres. & Chief Exec. Officer--PE Systems, Reston, VA, pg. 836
Prosser, Michael A., Pres.--Pacific Foods, Inc., Kent, WA, pg. 840
Prostrollo, Jerry, Pres.--Prostrollo Motor Company, Madison, SD, pg. 895
Protasio, Telmo, Chm.--Young & Rubicam (Portugal), Lisbon,, Portugal, pg. 1213
Prout, Stephen, Pres. & Chief Exec. Officer--AQHI, Inc., Colchester, CT, pg. 5
Pruim, E.G., Chm. Bd., Pres. & Chief Exec. Officer--Wrought Washer Mfg., Inc., Milwaukee, WI, pg. 1205
Pruitt, Cheryl, Exec. V.P. & Treas.--Tremont Foods, Linthicum Heights, MD, pg. 1109
Pruitt, J. Doug, Pres.--Sundt Corp., Tucson, AZ, pg. 1060
Pruitt, Robert, Chm. Bd. & Pres.--Tremont Foods, Linthicum Heights, MD, pg. 1109
Prusiewicz, Richard, Pres.--Kearney, Tucker, GA, pg. 357
Psomas, Tim, Pres.--Psomas & Associates, Santa Monica, CA, pg. 898
Puccini, Robert S., Pres. & Chief Exec. Officer--Head Sports, Inc., Boulder, CO, pg. 520
Puckett, Stephen R., Pres. & Creative Dir.--The Puckett Group, Saint Louis, MO, pg. 899
Pugh, Dave, Pres. & Gen. Mgr.-WLZR-AM-FM--Great American Broadcasting Company, Cincinnati, OH, pg. 52
Pugh, Loren, Pres.--Cummins Intermountain Diesel, Salt Lake City, UT, pg. 305
Pugh, William, Jr., Chm. Bd. & Pres.--Pugh Oil Company, Racine, WI, pg. 899
Pulitzer, Arthur C., Pres.--Wemco, Inc., New Orleans, LA, pg. 1176
Pulleyn, Chris, Partner & Mng. Dir.--Buck & Pulleyn, Inc., Rochester, NY, pg. 185
Pulliam, Larry, Pres.--AGCO Inc., Norcross, GA, pg. 4
Pulliam, Larry, Pres.--AGCO Corporation, Norcross, GA, pg. 4
Pumpelly, R. Glenn, Pres.--Pumpelly Oil, Inc., Westlake, LA, pg. 900
Purcell, Frank, Pres. & Chief Exec. Officer--Purcell International Group, Inc., Los Angeles, CA, pg. 900
Purdy, Kenneth, Pres.--Prime Tanning Co., Inc., Berwick, ME, pg. 889
Puris, Martin, Pres. & Chief Exec. Officer--Ammirati & Puris Inc., New York, NY, pg. 67
Purmort, F.W., Jr., Chm. Bd. & Pres.--Central Mutual Insurance Co., Van Wert, OH, pg. 233
Purpura, Vicnent M., Pres. & Chief Oper. Officer--D.A. Davidson & Co., Great Falls, MT, pg. 318
Pursell, J.T., Pres.--Parker Fertilizer Co., Inc., Sylacauga, AL, pg. 849
Purser, Lat W., III, Pres. & Head of Devel.--Lat Purser & Associate, Charlotte, NC, pg. 901
Purvis, J.E., Pres. & Treas.--A.C. Legg Packing Company, Inc., Birmingham, AL, pg. 666
Puschel, Gerald W., Pres. & Chief Oper. Officer--F. Schumacher & Co., New York, NY, pg. 979
Puskar, Ross, Principal--Puskar Gibbon Chapin, Inc., Dallas, TX, pg. 901
Putnam, David C., Pres.--TBV, Inc., Millbury, MA, pg. 1149
Putnam, Raymond E., Pres.--Brubaker Tool Corp., Millersburg, PA, pg. 183
Putnam, Thomas, Pres.--Markem Corporation, Keene, NH, pg. 708
Putterman, Saul, Pres. & Treas.--Milton Shoe Manufacturing Company, Inc., Milton, PA, pg. 756
Puttner, Dr. Gerhard, Chm. & Pres.--Dr. Puttner & BSB Worldwide Werbegesellschaft m.b.H., Vienna,, Austria, pg. 111
Pyle, Jerry H., Pres.--Gulf States Toyota, Houston, TX, pg. 494
Pyle, Thomas F., Chm. Bd., Pres. & Chief Exec. Officer--RAYOVAC Corporation, Madison, WI, pg. 915
Quackenbush, David S., Pres.--Quackenbush Co. Inc., Buffalo, NY, pg. 902
Quadracci, H.V., Pres. & Chief Exec. Officer--Quad/ Graphics, Inc., Pewaukee, WI, pg. 902
Quain, Robert C., Pres.--MacNaughton Einson Graphics, Fair Lawn, NJ, pg. 698
Quebedeaus, Thomas, Pres.--Quebedeaux Pontiac, Inc., Tucson, AZ, pg. 904
Quest, Robert W., Pres.--Advanced Controls, Inc., Irvine, CA, pg. 20
Quick, J. Douglas, Pres. & Chief Exec. Officer--Lakeside Foods, Inc., Manitowoc, WI, pg. 651
Quick, J. Douglas, Pres. & Chief Exec. Officer--Oceana Foods, Shelby, MI, pg. 651
Quier, Myrtle B., Chm. Bd., Pres. & Chief Exec. Officer--Reading Eagle Company, Reading, PA, pg. 916
Quillen, James R., Pres.--Thunderbird Steel Corporation, Albuquerque, NM, pg. 1096
Quinif, Edward, Chm. Bd. & Pres.--Walled Lake Door Company, Phoenix, AZ, pg. 1161
Quinlan, Donald P., Chm. Bd., Pres., Chief Exec. & Chief Oper. Officer--Graphic Controls Corporation, Buffalo, NY, pg. 478
Quinland, Donald P., Chm. Bd., Pres. & Chief Exec. Officer--Graphic Controls, Corp., Buffalo, NY, pg. 478
Quinlen, W.L., III, Pres.--Choctaw, Inc., Memphis, TN, pg. 248
Quinn, Dan, Pres.--CCC Conveyors, Inc., Dallas, TX, pg. 357
Quinn, James A., Pres.--Brokay Products, Inc., Philadelphia, PA, pg. 217
Quinn, James L., Pres.--Devlin Lumber & Supply Corp., Rockville, MD, pg. 334
Quinn, Jay, Pres. & Chief Oper. Officer--Eric Mower and Associates, Inc., Syracuse, NY, pg. 774
Quinn, Patrick M., Pres., Chief Exec. Officer & Chief Oper. Officer--Spartan Stores Inc., Grand Rapids, MI, pg. 1026
Quinn, Ralph, Pres.--United Refrigerated Services, Atlanta, GA, pg. 1134
Quinn, Roy, Pres. & Controller--Pompeian, Inc., Baltimore, MD, pg. 880
Quinn, Thomas H., Pres. & Chief Oper. Officer--Jordan Industries, Inc., Deerfield, IL, pg. 604
Quinn, William, Pres. & Chief Oper. Officer--Dana Perfumes Corp., New York, NY, pg. 313
Quinnies, Barry C., Pres. & Chief Exec. Officer--Independent Metals, Germantown, WI, pg. 565
Quirch, Guillermo, Sr., Pres.--E & G Foods, Miami, FL, pg. 358
Quirk, John E., Pres. & Chief Exec. Officer--Village Car Company, Bangor, ME, pg. 1151
Quirk, Peter R., Pres. & Chief Oper. Officer--Walk, Haydel & Associates, Inc., New Orleans, LA, pg. 1159
Rabin, Hal, Pres.-Field Support Bank Div.--Sonicair, Scottsdale, AZ, pg. 1018
Rabold, Robert E.H., Chm., Pres. & Chief Exec. Officer--Motorists Mutual Insurance Co., Columbus, OH, pg. 773
Rabun, John T. Jr., Pres.--Powers Construction Co., Inc., Florence, SC, pg. 883
Rackoff, W.H., Pres.--Asko, Inc, Homestead, PA, pg. 88
Radek, Edward, Sr., Co-Chm. Bd. & Pres.--Ready Metal Manufacturing Company, Chicago, IL, pg. 916
Radi, B.A., Pres.--Weil-McLain, Michigan City, IN, pg. 710
Radigan, Robert, Pres.--Plasti-Kote Co., Pactra Hobby, Valencia, CA, pg. 875
Radler, Louis, Chm. Bd., Pres. & Chief Exec. Officer--Chessco Industries, Inc., Westport, CT, pg. 243
Radtke, Wallace, Pres.--Fargo Clinic Ltd., Fargo, ND, pg. 399
Radu, George, Pres.--International Gear Corporation, Cleveland, OH, pg. 578
Radus, Philip, Pres. & Treas.--Ribbon Narrow Fabric Company, Secaucus, NJ, pg. 931
Radwill, Scott, Pres., Chief Exec. & Chief Oper. Officer-Export--Master Appliance Corp., Racine, WI, pg. 719
Raeder, Lorenz H., Pres.--Branch Cheese Company, Inc., Branch, WI, pg. 576
Raffo, A.J., Pres.--Chatham Manufacturing Company, Elkin, NC, pg. 202
Raftery, William, Pres.--H. Koch & Sons, Anaheim, CA, pg. 262
Ragel, Jack, Chm., Pres. & Chief Exec. Officer--Stephan & Brady, Incorporated, Madison, WI, pg. 1046
Ragland, Larry, Pres.--Woodstuff Manufacturing, Inc., Phoenix, AZ, pg. 986
Rago, Michael J., Pres.--Trumbull Corporation, West Mifflin, PA, pg. 1117
Ragsdale, T. Smith, III, Pres.--T.S. Ragsdale Company, Incorporated, Lake City, SC, pg. 910
Raimo, Thomas M., Pres. & Chief Exec. Officer--Hudson & Affiliated Co., Shawnee Mission, KS, pg. 551
Raimondo, A.F., Pres. & Chief Exec. Officer--Behlen Mfg. Co., Columbus, NE, pg. 132
Rainville, Donald, Pres. & Chief Oper. Officer--Universal Dynamics Inc., Woodbridge, VA, pg. 1138
Raisbeck, Peter, Pres. & Chief Exec. Officer--Institutional Financing Services, Benicia, CA, pg. 571
Rakolta, John, Jr., Pres., Chief Exec. Officer & Treas.--Walbridge Aldinger Company, Detroit, MI, pg. 1158
Rakow, Thomas S., Pres., Chief Exec. Officer & Treas.--Illinois Hydraulic Construction Company, South Elgin, IL, pg. 563
Rakstang, Robert, Pres.--Hanna Corporation, Chicago, IL, pg. 505
Raleigh, W.J., Pres.--Clinton Mills Sales Co., New York, NY, pg. 202
Ramella, Henry, Pres.--The Felters Company, Millbury, MA, pg. 406
Ramis, Guillermo, Pres.--McFarland & Drier International, San Juan, PR, pg. 729
Ramm, Robert, Pres.--Topsy's International Inc., Kansas City, MO, pg. 1102
Ramos, Antonio C., Pres. & Treas.--New England Stone Industries, Inc., Esmond, RI, pg. 800
Rampone, C. Frank, Pres.--Hart Engineering Corporation, Greenville, RI, pg. 512
Ramsey, J.C., Pres.--Royle Systems Group, Pompton Lakes, NJ, pg. 953
Ramsey, Jack, Pres.--Darlington Veneer Company, Darlington, SC, pg. 315
Ramsey, James K., Pres.--The William Bayley Co., Springfield, OH, pg. 128
Ramsey, John C., Pres. & Gen. Mgr.--Diamond Hill Plywood Company, Darlington, SC, pg. 316
Ramsey, K.C., Pres.--United States Bronze Powders, Inc., Flemington, NJ, pg. 1134
Rand, Ben A., Jr., Pres.--Rand's Inc., North Little Rock, AR, pg. 912
Rand, David, Pres.--Tingley Rubber Corporation, South Plainfield, NJ, pg. 1098
Randall, Dick J., Pres.--William Lyon Company, Newport Beach, CA, pg. 690
Randall, James H., Pres.--Allfast Fastening Systems, Inc., City of Industry, CA, pg. 37
Randall, Ronald F., Chm. Bd., Pres. & Chief Exec. Officer--Randall Stores, Inc., Mitchell, SD, pg. 911
Randolph, Don L., Pres.--Randolph Medical Inc., Livonia, MI, pg. 912
Rands, Tara, Pres.--Brush Research Manufacturing Company, Los Angeles, CA, pg. 184
Rankin, Claiborne, Pres. & Chief Exec. Officer--Bruning Paint Company, Baltimore, MD, pg. 184
Rankin, Thompson L., Chm., Pres. & Chief Exec. Officer--Lykes Brothers Inc. of Florida, Tampa, FL, pg. 688
Ransbottom, Richard, Pres.--Bryant Universal Roofers Inc., Phoenix, AZ, pg. 185
Ranzau, Dennis R., Pres.--Equity Fund Advisors Inc., Houston, TX, pg. 385
Rapelje, Ronald D., Pres. & Chief Exec. Officer--Ebeling & Reuss Company, Allentown, PA, pg. 365
Raper, Mark, Pres., Gen. Mgr., Pub. Rels.--Earle Palmer Brown/Richmond, Richmond, VA, pg. 182
Rapp, C.J., Pres.--The Jolt Company, Rochester, NY, pg. 602
Rapp, Horst, Chm. Bd. & Pres.--Alloway Manufacturing, Fargo, ND, pg. 41
Rapp, William M., Pres.--Vance Industries, Inc., Chicago, IL, pg. 1144
Rappaport, Dr. Allan, Chm. Bd., Pres. & Chief Exec. Officer--National Emergency Services, Inc., Tiburon, CA, pg. 788
Rappaport, Edward, Pres.--W. Braun Company, Chicago, IL, pg. 172
Rappeport, G., Pres.--Donlen Corp., Deerfield, IL, pg. 345
Rapton, Mallon, Pres.--Rapton Honda-GMC, Sacramento, CA, pg. 913
Rasband, Ronald A., Pres. & Chief Oper. Officer--Huntsman Chemical Corporation, Salt Lake City, UT, pg. 555
Rath, Frank E., Jr., Pres.--Spang & Company, Butler, PA, pg. 1025
Rathemacher, Carl P., Pres.--Modern Handling Equipment of N.J., Inc., Edison, NJ, pg. 763
Ratka, Marcia, Pres. & Broker--Wieland Realty Associates, Inc., Atlanta, GA, pg. 1189
Ratliff, Don, Pres. & Chief Oper. Officer--Gouchenour Adv., Inc., Orlando, FL, pg. 473
Ratliff, Robert J., Pres. & Chief Exec. Officer--Hesston, Norcross, GA, pg. 4
Ratner, Dennis, Pres.--Creative Hairdressers, Falls Church, VA, pg. 297
Ratner, Michael H., Pres.--Richter & Ratner Contracting Corporation, Maspeth, NY, pg. 933
Rattigan, Thomas J., Chm. Bd., Pres. & Chief Exec. Officer--G. Heileman Brewing Co., Inc., La Crosse, WI, pg. 526
Rattner, Selma, Pres.--Paragon Paint & Varnish Corp., Long Island City, NY, pg. 848
Rattray, Douglas C., Pres.--Brandt, Inc., Bensalem, PA, pg. 1111
Ratzlaff, John, Pres.--Mid-Kansas Co-op Association, Moundridge, KS, pg. 750
Rauch, C. Dixon, III, Pres. & Chief Exec. Officer--Rundel Products, Inc., Portland, OR, pg. 956
Rauch, Francis, Chm. Bd. & Pres.--M & C Specialties Company, Southampton, PA, pg. 690
Rauenhorst, Mark, Pres. & Chief Oper. Officer--OPUS Corp., Minnetonka, MN, pg. 828
Rauenhorst, Neil, Pres.--Opus South Corporation, Tampa, FL, pg. 828
Rauh, Robert B., Chm. Bd., Pres., Chief Fin. Officer & New Bus. Contact--Rauh, Good, Darlo & Barnes Advertising Associates, Inc., Los Gatos, CA, pg. 914
Ravel, Francis, Pres.--OSC Corporation d/b/a Olympic Sales Co., Los Angeles, CA, pg. 819
Ravizza, Eugene A., Chm. Bd. & Pres.--Synergism, Inc., Sunnyvale, CA, pg. 1069
Rawson, Michael J., Pres.--Kingsley Machine Co., Hollywood, CA, pg. 632
Ray, Bill F., Pres., Chief Exec. Officer & Chief Oper. Officer--Binning's Building Products, Inc., Lexington, NC, pg. 151
Ray, Floyd, Pres.--Empire Electric Association, Cortez, CO, pg. 379
Ray, Gene, Pres.--TDA, Atlanta, GA, pg. 1072
Ray, William S., Pres. & Chief Exec. Officer--Ray Communications, Inc., Elizabeth City, NC, pg. 914
Raydon, Max E., Pres. & Chief Exec. Officer--Homeland Stores, Inc., Oklahoma City, OK, pg. 542
Rayevich, Ron, Pres.--Prudential Equity Investment Div., Newark, NJ, pg. 897
Rayve, Robert G., Pres. & Chief Exec. Officer--The Spencer Turbine Co., Windsor, CT, pg. 1030
Rayve, Robert G., Pres. & Chief Exec. Officer--Spencer Turbine Co., Windsor, CT, pg. 1030
Read, R.T., Chm. Bd., Pres. & Chief Exec. Officer--Harwick Chemical Corp., Akron, OH, pg. 515
Read, Rosalie, Country Mgr.--Berlitz Schools of Languages Ltd., London, United Kingdom, pg. 143
Reading, Charles, Pres.--Capital Controls Company Inc., Colmar, PA, pg. 215
Reagan, Thomas N., Pres.--Reagan Equipment Company, Inc., Gretna, LA, pg. 917
Reardon, Warren J., III, Pres.--Daniel Green Co., Dolgeville, NY, pg. 484
Rechler, Donald, Pres.--Reckson Associates, Melville, NY, pg. 917
Recht, William, Jr., Pres.--Durex Industries Inc., Jersey City, NJ, pg. 354
Rector, Ben K., Pres.--Caltrol, Inc., Glendora, CA, pg. 211
Rector, Bruce, Mng. Gen. Partner & Winemaker--Glen Ellen Winery, Glen Ellen, CA, pg. 461
Reddy, Prasad, Chm. Bd., Pres. & Chief Exec. Officer--Freeman Shoes Company, Beloit, WI, pg. 431
Redman, Richard C., Chm. Bd., Pres. & Chief Exec. Officer--Sellen Construction Company, Seattle, WA, pg. 988
Redmon, C. Peter, Pres. & Mgr.-Adv.--W. C. Redmon Co., Peru, IN, pg. 919
Redmond, Michael W., Pres.--Witcher Construction Company, Minneapolis, MN, pg. 1198
Reed, Bill, Pres.--Royal Oak Enterprises, Inc., Atlanta, GA, pg. 953
Reed, Carol A., Pres.--Reed Grain & Bean Company, Buhl, ID, pg. 920
Reed, E.C., Pres. & Sec.--Utica Boilers Inc., Utica, NY, pg. 1140

Corporate Responsibilities Index

Reed, Frank, Pres.--AEC, Inc., Wood Dale, IL, pg. 1047
Reed, Gene, Pres.--Gene Reed Chevrolet, Charleston Heights, SC, pg. 920
Reed, Joel L., Pres. & Chief Exec. Officer--Insilco Corporation, Midland, TX, pg. 571
Reed, John L., Pres.--Reed Motors, Inc., Orlando, FL, pg. 920
Reed, Richard C., Chm Bd. & Pres.--Kova Fertilizer Inc., Greensburg, IN, pg. 643
Reed, Ward, Pres.--Science Applications International Corporation (SAIC Virgin Islands), Saint Thomas, VI, pg. 982
Reed, William D., Pres. & Chief Oper. Officer--Computer Corporation of America, Cambridge, MA, pg. 884
Reedy, L. M., Pres.--Hollymatic Corporation, Countryside, IL, pg. 539
Reemer, Steven I., Pres. & Chief Oper. Officer--Radix Corporation, Salt Lake City, UT, pg. 909
Reese, Michael R., Chm Bd., Pres. & Chief Exec. Officer--Pierce Manufacturing, Inc., Appleton, WI, pg. 870
Reeve, Richard D., Pres.--Reeve Aleutian Airways, Inc., Anchorage, AK, pg. 921
Reeves, Rebecca B., Pres. & New Bus. Contact--The Reeves Agency, Inc., Baltimore, MD, pg. 921
Reeves, Samuel T., Pres.--Dunavant Enterprises, Inc., Memphis, TN, pg. 352
Reeves, Samuel T., Pres.--Dunavant Enterprises, Fresno, CA, pg. 352
Reeves, Thomas, Pres.--Sigler & Reeves, Phoenix, AZ, pg. 1003
Regan, John, Pres. & Chief Exec. Officer--Regan Holding Corporation, Petaluma, CA, pg. 921
Regan, Lynda, Sr. V.P.-Mktg. Officer--Regan Holding Corporation, Petaluma, CA, pg. 921
Regan, Ronald J., Pres.--Argosy Electronics, Inc., Eden Prairie, MN, pg. 82
Regelbrugge, Roger R., Pres. & Chief Exec. Officer--Georgetown Industries, Inc., Charlotte, NC, pg. 453
Regian, Greg, Pres.--Regian Advertising & Public Relations, Fort Worth, TX, pg. 922
Reich, Mort, Pres. & Chief Exec. Officer--The Reich Group, Inc., Philadelphia, PA, pg. 922
Reich, Steve, Pres.--American Specialty Foods, Niles, IL, pg. 881
Reichborn, P.K., Pres. & Treas.--Goodway Tool Corporation, Stamford, CT, pg. 471
Reichenstein, Marvin, Chm. Bd. & Pres.--Reichenstein Advertising Agency, Mountainside, NJ, pg. 922
Reicher, Michael, Pres.--UDL Laboratories, Inc., Rockford, IL, pg. 1072
Reichert, Robert C., Pres.--Kings Toyota Suzuki, Cincinnati, OH, pg. 631
Reichlin, Robert J., Pres. & Chief Exec. Officer--Zuckerman-Honickman Inc., King of Prussia, PA, pg. 1221
Reichman, Wayne, Pres.--Laramie Tire Distributors Inc., Norristown, PA, pg. 658
Reichmann, Charles, Chief Exec. Officer--Dri Mark Products, Inc., Port Washington, NY, pg. 349
Reichmann, Louis, Pres.--Dri Mark Products, Inc., Port Washington, NY, pg. 349
Reichwein, John H., Jr., Pres.--Revcor, Inc., Carpentersville, IL, pg. 930
Reid, Connie, Pres. & Chief Oper. Officer--Bradley Communications, Inc., Anchorage, AK, pg. 170
Reid, Daniel S., Pres., Chief Oper. Officer--McCaffrey and McCall, New York, NY, pg. 726
Reid, James A., Pres.--Hollywood Alloy Casting Company, Compton, CA, pg. 540
Reidbord, Murray S., Pres.--Reidbord Bros., Inc., Pittsburgh, PA, pg. 923
Reidel, Arthur A., Chm. Bd. & Chief Exec. Officer--Willamette-Western Corporation, Portland, OR, pg. 1190
Reifschneider, Darrel, Chm. Bd. & Chief Exec. Officer--Manchester Tank & Equipment Company, Lynwood, CA, pg. 703
Reigle, Jeffrey A., Pres. & Chief Exec. Officer--Regal Ware, Inc., Kewaskum, WI, pg. 921
Reilly, Albert, Pres.--Rough Brothers, Inc., Cincinnati, OH, pg. 952
Reilly, Donald C., Pres.--Superior Tube Company, Collegeville, PA, pg. 1064
Reilly, Frank E., Pres.--F/S Reilly, Media +, San Francisco, CA, pg. 923
Reilly, James W., Pres.--Sherman & Reilly, Inc., Chattanooga, TN, pg. 998
Reilly, Kevin, Jr., Pres. & Chief Exec. Officer--Lamar Corporation, Baton Rouge, LA, pg. 652
Reilly, Michael K., Pres. & Chief Exec. Officer--Ziegler Coal Holding Co., Fairview Heights, IL, pg. 1218
Reilly, William F., Chm. Bd.--Soap Opera Digest, New York, NY, pg. 611
Reily, Timothy, Chm. Bd., Pres. & Chief Exec. Officer--Reily Electric Supply, Inc., Metairie, LA, pg. 923
Reily, W.B. III, Pres.--William B. Reily & Co., Inc., New Orleans, LA, pg. 923
Reiman, Stephen W., Pres. & Chief Exec. Officer--W.A. Roosevelt Co., La Crosse, WI, pg. 946
Reimel, T.L., Pres. & Treas.--Reimel Carter Advertising, Inc., Philadelphia, PA, pg. 923
Reimer, Kenneth F., Pres. & Chief Exec. Officer--Roma Holdings, Dallas, TX, pg. 945
Rein, Morrison, Pres. & Chief Exec. Officer--Standard Security Life Insurance Company of New York, New York, NY, pg. 452
Reinhart, Thomas, Chm. Bd.--The Hammerblow Corp., Wausau, WI, pg. 504
Reinig, L.P., Chm. Bd. & Pres.--Los Alamos Technical Associates, Inc., Los Alamos, NM, pg. 684
Reinken, Alan, Pres.--Homestead House Inc., Broomfield, CO, pg. 542
Reisdorf, Raymond, Pres.--L. L. Olds Seed Company, Madison, WI, pg. 824
Reiss, Richard T., Pres. & Treas.--R.C.A. Rubber Company, Akron, OH, pg. 906
Reives, Louis, Pres.--Versatech Engineering, Lexington, KY, pg. 718
Remos, Gary, Chm. Bd., Pres. & Chief Exec. Officer--Advanced Manufacturing & Development, Willits, CA, pg. 20
Remstad, Michael, Mgr.-Mktg.--Tuff-Kote Dinol, Inc., Troy, MI, pg. 1217
Remus, Dale H., Pres.--Consolidated Lumber Co., Stillwater, MN, pg. 276
Renaud, Ernest, Acting Pres.--Church's Fried Chicken, Inc., Jefferson, LA, pg. 284
Renda, Steven L., Chm. Bd., Pres. & Chief Exec. Officer--Ideal Pool Corp., Atlanta, GA, pg. 562
Renfroe, Royce, Pres. & Chief Exec. Officer--Bentley Mills, Inc., City of Industry, CA, pg. 140
Renken, Carl E., Pres. & Chief Exec. Officer--Renken Boat Manufacturing Co., Charleston, SC, pg. 927
Rennert, Ira Leon, Pres. & Chief Exec. Officer--Renco Group, New York, NY, pg. 926
Reno, William J., Chm. Bd., Pres. & Chief Exec. Officer--F.B. Wright Co., Dearborn, MI, pg. 1204
Rentenbach, T.M., Pres. & Chief Exec. Officer--Rentenbach Engineering Company, Knoxville, TN, pg. 927
Reny, L. Guy, Chm. Bd. & Pres.--Standard Duplicating Machines Corp., Andover, MA, pg. 1036
Repeta, Richard J., Pres.--Maguire Group Inc., Foxboro, MA, pg. 701
Resch, George, Pres.--Resource, Inc., Tampa, FL, pg. 929
Ressen, Frank, Pres.--Precision Plastics, Crawfordsville, IN, pg. 885
Rettig, James, Pres.--Crowley Maritime Corporation, Oakland, CA, pg. 301
Reuhl, Douglas G., Pres.--American TV & Appliance of Madison, Inc., Madison, WI, pg. 65
Reuland, Noel, Pres.--Reuland Electric Company, City of Industry, CA, pg. 930
Reuscher, Richard, Pres.--Keystone Carbon Company, Saint Marys, PA, pg. 628
Reynolds, E. Thomas, Pres.--Vitt/Reynolds Media International Limited, Toronto,, Canada, pg. 1154
Reynolds, James G., Chm. Bd. & Pres.--Portland Food Products Company, Portland, OR, pg. 881
Reynolds, John K., Pres.--F.T. Reynolds Company, Glendive, MT, pg. 930
Reynolds, Marshall T., Pres.--Chapman Printing Company, Huntington, WV, pg. 239
Reynolds, Tom, Pres.--Puritan/Churchill Chemical Company, Atlanta, GA, pg. 900
Rha, Raymond R., Pres.--Office Equipment Company Of Chicago, Chicago, IL, pg. 821
Rhea, Stephen L., Pres., New Bus. Contact & Acct. Services Mgr.--Rhea & Kaiser Advertising, Inc., Naperville, IL, pg. 930
Rhinerson, R.H., Pres.--Gaggenau USA Corporation, Norwood, MA, pg. 441
Rhoades, Jeffrey P., Pres.--Rhoades Development, Santa Ana, CA, pg. 931
Rhoades, Ralph S., Pres. & Chief Exec. Officer--Blue Cross and Blue Shield of Oklahoma, Tulsa, OK, pg. 159
Rhodes, Brent, Pres. & Chief Exec. Officer--Carter Chambers Supply, Inc., Baton Rouge, LA, pg. 226
Rhodes, Hedric E., Pres. & Chief Exec. Officer--Griffith Laboratories Worldwide, Inc., Alsip, IL, pg. 487
Ricart, Rhett, Pres.--Ricart Ford Inc., Groveport, OH, pg. 931
Riccobon, Paul J., Pres.--Riccobon & Company, Inc., Santa Fe Springs, CA, pg. 931
Riccobon, Paul J., Pres.--National Computer Supplies, Santa Fe Springs, CA, pg. 931
Rice, G.L., Pres.--Hydreco, Augusta, GA, pg. 559
Rice, Linda Johnson, Pres. & Chief Oper. Officer--Johnson Publishing Company, Inc., Chicago, IL, pg. 598
Rice, Linda Johnson, Pres.--Fashion Fair Cosmetics, Chicago, IL, pg. 599
Rice, Ronald J., Pres.--Tanning Research Labs., Inc., Ormond Beach, FL, pg. 1078
Rice, Tandy, Jr., Chm. Bd. & Chief Exec. Officer--Top Billing Inc., Nashville, TN, pg. 1101 ,
Rice, Wayne, Pres.--Farmland Foods, Inc., Kansas City, MO, pg. 402
Rich, Francis P., Jr., Chm. Bd. & Pres.--Action Equipment, Londonderry, NH, pg. 14
Rich, John W., Jr., Pres.--Reading Anthracite Co., Pottsville, PA, pg. 916
Rich, Michael, Pres.--Tenax Corporation, Danbury, CT, pg. 1086
Rich, Robert E., Jr., Pres.--Rich Products Corp., Buffalo, NY, pg. 932
Richard, Russell R., Pres. & Chief Oper. Officer--Pacific Scene Inc., San Diego, CA, pg. 841
Richards, Brian, Pres.-Residential--Gosnell Builders, Phoenix, AZ, pg. 472
Richards, Craig, Pres., Chief Oper. Officer & Treas.--Jeffrey Michael, Kirkland, WA, pg. 591
Richards, H. Lee, Pres.--Quality Chekd Dairy Products Association, Naperville, IL, pg. 903
Richards, James C., Pres.--Southwire Company, Inc., Carrollton, GA, pg. 1024
Richards, Robert J., Pres. & Chief Exec. Officer--SKR Resources, Inc., New York, NY, pg. 963
Richards, Wells E., Pres.--Richards Brothers of Mountain Grove, Mountain Grove, MO, pg. 932
Richards, William T., Pres.--Idaho Forest Industry, Inc., Coeur D'Alene, ID, pg. 561
Richardson, C. Vance, Pres.--Clayson Knitting Co. Inc., Star, NC, pg. 253
Richardson, Charles, Pres.--Richardson Strang Associates, Portland, OR, pg. 933
Richardson, James Craig, Pres.--Richco Plastics Company, Chicago, IL, pg. 933
Richardson, Jim, Pres.--Triton Inc., Doraville, GA, pg. 1114
Richardson, John S., Pres., Chief Exec. & Chief Fin. Officer--Sugar Creek Packing Co., Mason, OH, pg. 1056
Richardson, Joseph E., III, Pres.--Richardson Industries, Inc., Shaboygan Falls, WI, pg. 932
Richardson, Joseph, III, Pres.--Richardson Brothers Co., Sheboygan Falls, WI, pg. 932
Richardson, Michael C., Pres.--Air Land Forwarders, Inc., Jacksonville, FL, pg. 1056
Richardson, Ron, Pres.--Universal Vise & Tool Co., Parma, MI, pg. 103
Richardson, Thomas, Chm. Bd., Pres. & Chief Exec. Officer--Delta Education, Inc., Hudson, NH, pg. 326
Richardson, Walter H., Gen. Mgr.--Traco Advertising, Inc., Tulsa, OK, pg. 1104
Richer, Alvin, Chm., Pres. & Chief Exec. Officer--Arnold Machinery Co., Salt Lake City, UT, pg. 84
Richey, Steve, Pres.--Precision Parts Corp., Morristown, TN, pg. 885
Richey, Van L., Pres. & Chief Exec. Officer--American Cast Iron Pipe Co., Birmingham, AL, pg. 50
Richie, Rick, Pres.--Ashworth Bros., Inc., Fall River, MA, pg. 88
Richler, Franklin R., Pres.--Sisco Company, Mount Joy, PA, pg. 413
Richman, David, Pres.--S.D. Richman Sons, Inc., Philadelphia, PA, pg. 933
Richmond, A. Vernon, Pres.--W. M. Barr & Co., Inc., Memphis, TN, pg. 121
Richter, Jerome B., Vice Chm. & Pres.--Kangaroos, USA Inc., Chesterfield, MO, pg. 616
Richter, Jerome B., Pres.--Trans World Shoe Import Co., Inc., Chesterfield, MO, pg. 616
Rickman, William, Pres.--Kroch's & Brentano's, Inc., Chicago, IL, pg. 645
Riddle, H. Marvin, III, Pres.--Asbury Carbons, Inc., Asbury, NJ, pg. 87
Riddleberger, James E., Pres.--Riddleberger Brothers, Inc., Mount Crawford, VA, pg. 933
Ridella, A., Pres. & Chief Oper. Officer--Swepco Tube Corporation, Clifton, NJ, pg. 1067
Rider, C.G., Pres. & Chief Exec. Officer--AEA, Inc., Charlotte, NC, pg. 3
Rider, Chuck, Chm., Pres. & Chief Exec. Officer--Automotive Marketing Assoc., Nashville, TN, pg. 224
Rider, Gene, Pres.--Genevar Enterprises, Colorado Springs, CO, pg. 451
Ridgway, David, Pres.--Tiffany Stand & Furniture Company, St. Louis, MO, pg. 1097
Riechelmann, Thijs, Mng. Dir.--Riechelmann, Lopes Cardozo & Van Bercum B.V., Amsterdam,, Netherlands, pg. 1212
Riediger, V.D., Pres.--Nobles Industries, Inc., Saint Paul, MN, pg. 808
Riefler, Grover, Pres.--T. L. Smith Machine, Springville, NY, pg. 1013
Riefler, Grover, Pres.--CEM South, Leesburg, FL, pg. 1013
Riehl, James E., Sr., Pres.--Roseville Chrysler Plymouth Inc., Roseville, MI, pg. 949
Riemer, David, Chm. Bd., Pres. & Chief Exec. Officer--Arley Merchandise Corporation, Taunton, MA, pg. 83
Rienhard, Eric, Pres.--Pepsi-Cola Bottling Co., Denver, CO, pg. 860
Rieple, Ted, Pres.--Strategic Distribution Inc., Greenwich, CT, pg. 1053
Rieple, Ted, Pres.--SafetyMaster Corporation, Billings, MT, pg. 1053
Riesett, Don, Pres.--Doner & Company Limited, London,, United Kingdom, pg. 344
Rieson, Dean A., Pres.--Carlson Real Estate Company, Minneapolis, MN, pg. 221
Rifkin, Leonard, Chm. Bd. & Pres.--Omni Source Corporation, Fort Wayne, IN, pg. 826
Riggio, Leonard, Chm. Bd., Pres. & Chief Exec. Officer--Barnes & Noble Bookstores, Inc., New York, NY, pg. 120
Riggio, Steve, Exec. V.P. & Chief Oper. Officer--Marboro Books Inc., New York, NY, pg. 120
Riggs, Dave, Pres.--California Strawberry Advisory Board, Watsonville, CA, pg. 210
Riggs, Gwen, Mng. Dir.--Sudler & Hennessey, Melbourne,, Australia, pg. 1213
Riggs, Louis V., Pres. & Chief Exec. Officer--A. Teichert & Son, Inc., Sacramento, CA, pg. 1084
Rihm, Walter F., Pres.--Rihm Motor Company, Saint Paul, MN, pg. 934
Rijos, John, Pres.--Lane Hotels, Inc., Northbrook, IL, pg. 657
Rijsermans, Henry, Gen. Mgr.--Cato Johnson Direct Promotion, Brussels,, Belgium, pg. 1211
Riklis, Meshulam, Chm. Bd. & Pres.--Riklis Family Corporation, New York, NY, pg. 934
Riklis, Meshulam, Pres. & Chief Exec. Officer--McCrory Corporation, New York, NY, pg. 934
Riley, James V., Pres.--Weber Cohn & Riley, Inc., Chicago, IL, pg. 1171
Riley, R.C., Pres.--Independent Insurance Agents of America, Alexandria, VA, pg. 565
Riley, Richard W., Pres.--Label-Aire Inc., Fullerton, CA, pg. 649
Rilott, James H., Pres.--Atwood Industries, Inc., Rockford, IL, pg. 97
Rinard, R. E., Pres. & Chief Oper. Officer--Pacific Enterprises Oil Company (USA), Dallas, TX, pg. 840
Rinehart, Tom, Pres.--Custom Shop Shirtmakers Inc., New York, NY, pg. 306
Ring, Bob, Pres. & Chief Oper. Officer--The Coleman Company, Inc., Wichita, KS, pg. 695
Ring, Bob, Pres.--Coleman Outdoor Products, Wichita, KS, pg. 695
Ringle, Ted, Pres.--Silicon Valley Development, Santa Clara, CA, pg. 1004
Rink, Robert A., Pres. & Chief Exec. Officer--Prestige Stamping, Inc., Warren, MI, pg. 888
Rinke, Roland, Pres., Treas. & Chief Exec. Officer--Rinke Pontiac-GMC Co., Warren, MI, pg. 935

Riodan, Thomas W., Pres. & Chief Exec. Officer--Ferro Union, Inc., Torrance, CA, pg. 407
Rion, Bill, Pres. & Chief Oper. Officer--Wayn-Tex Inc., Waynesboro, VA, pg. 1169
Riordan, Michael T., Pres. & Chief Oper. Officer--Fort Howard Corporation, Green Bay, WI, pg. 425
Ripich, Terry, Pres.--American Tank & Fabricating Co., Cleveland, OH, pg. 63
Ripka, Sy, Pres., Chief Fin. Officer--The Alden Group Ltd., New York, NY, pg. 32
Ripley, Barrett F., Pres. & Chief Exec. Officer--Troy Mills, Inc., Troy, NH, pg. 1116
Ripley, William, Pres.--Silvestri Corp., Chicago, IL, pg. 1005
Risdall, Charles A., Pres.--Smith System Manufacturing Company, Shoreview, MN, pg. 1014
Risdall, John, Pres.--John Risdall Advertising, New Brighton, MN, pg. 935
Riskedal, Ken, Pres.--Interstate Producers Livestock Association, Peoria, IL, pg. 580
Riskind, Kenneth J., Pres. & Chief Exec. Officer--Fullerton Metals Co., Northbrook, IL, pg. 436
Risley, J. Stephen, Jr., Pres.--Sunrise Nissan of Orange Park, Orange Park, FL, pg. 1062
Risser, P.N., III, Pres.--Risser Oil Corp., Clearwater, FL, pg. 936
Rissman, R. O., Pres.--Tiger Electronics, Inc., Vernon Hills, IL, pg. 1097
Rist, Robert G., Pres. & Chief Exec. Officer--Warner Press, Inc., Anderson, IN, pg. 1164
Ritchie, Earl, Pres.--The Paxall Group, Inc., Skokie, IL, pg. 852
Ritchie, H.T., Pres. & Chief Oper. Officer--Ritchie Corporation, Wichita, KS, pg. 936
Ritchie, Robert D., Pres.--Ted Thomas Associates Inc., Advertising, Philadelphia, PA, pg. 1092
Ritchie, Ronald J., Pres. & Chief Exec. Officer--Arnpex Corporation, Redwood City, CA, pg. 998
Ritsema, Larry J., Pres.--Challenge Technologies, Grand Haven, MI, pg. 238
Ritter, Alan C., Pres.--Universal Photonics, Inc., Hicksville, NY, pg. 1139
Ritter, Michael J., Pres. & Chief Oper. Officer--Continental Cablevision, Boston, MA, pg. 278
Rivera, Richard, Pres. & Chief Exec. Officer--TGI Friday's, Inc., Addison, TX, pg. 221
Rivers, Philip R., Pres. & New Bus. Contact--Rivers Trainor Doyle & Walsh, Inc., Providence, RI, pg. 937
Rizzuto, Leandro P., Chm. Bd. & Pres.--Conair Corporation, Stamford, CT, pg. 272
Roach, Howard, Pres.--Howards Appliances, Inc., San Gabriel, CA, pg. 547
Road, John W., Pres.--Taylor Medical of LA, Beaumont, TX, pg. 1081
Roads, Lee, Pres.--M.A.B. Paints, Terre Haute, IN, pg. 184
Robb, D.H., Pres. & Chief Oper. Officer--Chittenden & Eastman Co., Burlington, IA, pg. 248
Robbins, Donald M., Pres.--Hollywood Park, Inc., Inglewood, CA, pg. 540
Robbins, James O., Pres.--Cable Division, Atlanta, GA, pg. 294
Robbins, L.C., Pres. & Chief Exec. Officer--Star Food Processing, Inc., San Antonio, TX, pg. 1039
Robert, Dean E., Sr., Chm. Bd. & Pres.--Roberts Foods, Inc., Springfield, IL, pg. 938
Robert, George, Pres.--Benjamin Sheridan Co., Racine, WI, pg. 300
Robert, Ralph, Pres.--Stuart Anderson's Black Angus/Cattle Company Restaurants, Los Altos, CA, pg. 60
Roberts, C. J., Jr., Pres., Chief Oper. Officer & Treas.--The Leavell Company, El Paso, TX, pg. 664
Roberts, Charles, Jr., Chm. Bd. & Pres.--Chas Roberts Air Conditioning, Inc., Phoenix, AZ, pg. 938
Roberts, Dale, V.P., Mktg.--Veda Design Group, Alexandria, VA, pg. 1146
Roberts, David, Pres. & Chief Oper. Officer--Doran Textiles Inc., Shelby, NC, pg. 346
Roberts, David, Pres. & Chief Oper. Officer--Doran Mill Co., Shelby, NC, pg. 346
Roberts, Gary, Pres., Chief Oper. Officer--Greenstone Roberts Advertising, Melville, NY, pg. 485
Roberts, Harry, Pres.--EvansGroup, Portland, OR, pg. 391
Roberts, John H., Pres. & Chief Exec. Officer--J. H. Roberts Industries Inc., Des Plaines, IL, pg. 938
Roberts, John K., Jr., Pres. & Chief Exec. Officer--Pan-American Life Insurance Company, New Orleans, LA, pg. 845
Roberts, Paul J., Pres. & Chief Oper. Officer--Carco Electronics, Menlo Park, CA, pg. 217
Roberts, Ralph, Pres.--Grandy's, Inc., Lewisville, TX, pg. 476
Roberts, Ralph L., Chm. Bd. & Pres.--Gator Freightways, Inc., Wilmington, OH, pg. 446
Roberts, Robert A., Pres. & Treas.--C.F. Haglin & Sons, Minneapolis, MN, pg. 499
Roberts, Stephen M., Pres., Chief Exec. Officer & Treas.--F. L. Roberts & Co. Inc., Springfield, MA, pg. 938
Robertson, G. Bruce, Pres. & Chief Exec. Officer--Robertson Marketing Inc., Charlotte, NC, pg. 939
Robertson, Robert G., Pres. & Chief Exec. Officer--White Hen Pantry, Inc., Elmhurst, IL, pg. 1185
Robertson, Scott V., Pres. & Chief Exec. Officer--Robertson's Auto Salvage, Wareham, MA, pg. 939
Robins, Alan, Pres.--Wallace Leisure Products, Inc., Philadelphia, PA, pg. 1160
Robins, Frank, III, Chm. Bd.--Conway Corporation, Conway, AR, pg. 281
Robinson, Bob, Pres.--Doane Products Co., Joplin, MO, pg. 342
Robinson, Bob, Pres. & Chief Exec. Officer--Doane Products Co., Branded Sales Div., Joplin, MO, pg. 342
Robinson, Charles K., Jr., Pres. & Treas.--Swayne Robinson & Company, Richmond, IN, pg. 939
Robinson, Clark, Pres. & Treas.--Streech Electric Company, Anaheim, CA, pg. 1053
Robinson, Claude D., Pres. & Chief Exec. Officer--Sivyer Steel Corporation, Bettendorf, IA, pg. 1013
Robinson, E. Montgomery, Pres. & Treas.--Top Flight, Inc., Chattanooga, TN, pg. 1101
Robinson, Frank, Pres.--Kingsbridge Media & Marketing, Inc., Van Nuys, CA, pg. 631
Robinson, Frank, Pres.--Robinson Helicopter Company, Inc., Torrance, CA, pg. 940
Robinson, H. Ivens, Pres. & Chief Exec. Officer--Robinson Lumber & Export Company, New Orleans, LA, pg. 940
Robinson, Hugh C. III, Pres.--Presto Food Stores, Inc., Plant City, FL, pg. 888
Robinson, James B., Chm. Bd. & Pres.--American Manufacturing Co. (TN), Chattanooga, TN, pg. 58
Robinson, John H., Mng. Partner--Black & Veatch, Kansas City, MO, pg. 154
Robinson, Leon, Jr., Pres.--Robinson Bus Service, Evanston, IL, pg. 939
Robinson, Murray, Pres.--Delta & Pine Land Company, Scott, MS, pg. 1024
Robinson, Richard, Chm. Bd., Pres. & Chief Exec. Officer--SI Holdings Inc., New York, NY, pg. 962
Robinson, Richard, Chm. Bd., Pres. & Chief Exec. Officer--Scholastic Inc., New York, NY, pg. 962
Robinson, Ron, Pres. & Chief Oper. Officer--Cranford Johnson Robinson Woods, Little Rock, AR, pg. 296
Robinson, Samuel G., Sr., Pres.--Robinson Lumber Company, New Orleans, LA, pg. 940
Robinson, William A., Mng. Dir.--Robinson & Maites, Inc., Chicago, IL, pg. 940
Robison, Lyle Douglas, Pres.--Cloud Corporation, Des Plaines, IL, pg. 256
Robles, Mauro, Chm. Bd. & Pres.--La Reina, Inc., Los Angeles, CA, pg. 649
Robson, Steve, Pres.--Sun Lakes Marketing, Sun Lakes, AZ, pg. 1059
Roche, Jack F., Chm. Bd., Pres. & Chief Exec. Officer--PMC Industries Inc., Wickliffe, OH, pg. 836
Roche, M.B., Pres.--Roche Constructors, Inc., Greeley, CO, pg. 940
Rocheleau, Donald, Pres.--Attwood Corporation, Lowell, MI, pg. 1044
Rochford, William F., Dir.--Maryland State Lottery, Baltimore, MD, pg. 717
Rochon, Pierre, Pres.--SLM, Inc., Gloversville, NY, pg. 963
Rodbell, Clyde A., Pres.--Apex Supply Co. Inc., Atlanta, GA, pg. 78
Roddenbery, Julien B., Jr., Pres. & Chief Exec. Officer--W. B. Roddenbery Company, Inc., Cairo, GA, pg. 942
Roddie, Anton, Pres.--Western Data Systems, Calabasas, CA, pg. 1178
Rodefeld, Charles A., Pres.--Rodefeld Co., Inc., Richmond, IN, pg. 942
Rodell, Rick, Pres. & Chief Exec. Officer--Manufacturers Consolidation Service, Memphis, TN, pg. 705
Rodgers, Dan, Chm. Bd. & Pres.--Thompson Medical Company, Inc., West Palm Beach, FL, pg. 1094
Rodgers, P.G., Pres.--Cashco, Inc., Ellsworth, KS, pg. 228
Rodgers, Ronald, Chm. Bd. & Pres.--J.B. Rodgers Mechanical Contractors, Phoenix, AZ, pg. 943
Rodriguez, Carlos, Pres.--Mason Distributors, Inc., Hialeah, FL, pg. 718
Rodriguez, Ray, Pres. & Chief Exec. Officer--Univision Holdings, Inc., New York, NY, pg. 502
Rodstein, Barbara I., Pres.--Harden Industries, Inc., Los Angeles, CA, pg. 508
Roe, David, V.P.-Publishing--Nation's Business, Washington, DC, pg. 794
Roe, K. Keith, Chm. Bd., Pres., Chief Exec. & Chief Oper. Officer--Burns & Roe Enterprises, Inc., Oradell, NJ, pg. 194
Roelofs, Pieter, Pres. & Chief Exec. Officer--Taco John's International, Inc., Cheyenne, WY, pg. 1076
Roesler, Mark, Pres. & Chief Exec. Officer--Curtis Management Group, Indianapolis, IN, pg. 306
Roessner, John K. III, Chm. Bd. & Pres.--E. J. Brooks Company, Newark, NJ, pg. 179
Roessner, John K., III, Pres.--Ekstrom Industries, Inc., Farmington Hills, MI, pg. 180
Rogan, Richard M., Pres. & Chief Exec. Officer--Burlington Motor Carriers Inc., Daleville, IN, pg. 191
Rogers, C. Jeffrey, Pres.--Bonanza Restaurants, Dallas, TX, pg. 744
Rogers, Curtis K., Pres. & New Bus. Contact--Rogers & Associates Advertising, Inc., Santa Clara, CA, pg. 943
Rogers, Desiree, Dir.--Illinois State Lottery, Springfield, IL, pg. 563
Rogers, Joe W., Jr., Pres.--Waffle House, Inc., Norcross, GA, pg. 1157
Rogers, Lloyd F., Pres. & Chief Exec. Officer--Wells Lamont, Niles, IL, pg. 712
Rogers, M. Weldon, III, Chm. Bd., Pres. & Chief Exec. Officer--EAC Corporation, Saint Louis, MO, pg. 359
Rogers, Richard A., Pres.--Wilkins-Rogers Incorporated, Ellicott City, MD, pg. 1190
Rogers, Richard R., Chm. Bd., Pres. & Chief Exec. Officer--Mary Kay Corporation, Dallas, TX, pg. 716
Rogers, William H., Pres.--Rogers Markets Inc., Fort Wayne, IN, pg. 943
Rogers, Yandell, Jr., Pres. & Gen. Counsel--YRJ Corporation, Houston, TX, pg. 1206
Rogerson, Michael, Chm. Bd., Pres. & Chief Exec. Officer--Rogerson Aircraft Corporation, Irvine, CA, pg. 943
Rogness, Kurt E., Chief Exec. Officer--Hammel, Green & Abrahamson, Inc., Minneapolis, MN, pg. 504
Rohrer, John P., Pres.--Rohrer Corporation, Wadsworth, OH, pg. 944
Rojaica, Kruno, Pres.--Lukenheimer Co.-Energo Valves, Cincinnati, OH, pg. 687
Rokop, Joseph, Jr., Pres.--Rokop Corporation, Bridgeville, PA, pg. 944
Roland, Frank H., Pres.--Halstead Industries, Inc., Greensboro, NC, pg. 502
Rolla, M.F., Pres. & Chief Oper. Officer--Gem Industries Finance Corporation, Toccoa, GA, pg. 447
Rolla, M.F., Pres. & Chief Oper. Officer--Gem Industries, Inc., Gardner, MA, pg. 447
Roller, Thomas B., Pres. & Chief Exec. Officer--Plywood Panels, Inc., New Orleans, LA, pg. 878
Rollin, Daniel J., Pres.--Heights Heating & Cooling, Auburn Hills, MI, pg. 525
Rollins, David, Pres. & Chief Exec. Officer--Nashville Wire Product Co., Nashville, TN, pg. 784
Rolwing, R.E., Pres.--Graycor, Inc., Homewood, IL, pg. 479
Rolwing, Robert, Pres.--Inland Construction Company, Homewood, IL, pg. 480
Romann, Gad, Pres.--Romann & Tannenholz Advertising, Inc., New York, NY, pg. 945
Romeo, R., Pres.--Web Food Products Corp., Jamaica, NY, pg. 1170
Romer, Klaus, Pres. & Chief Exec. Officer--McGean-Rohco, Inc., Cleveland, OH, pg. 729
Ronan, Harry A., Chm. Bd. & Pres.--Ronco Communications & Electronics Inc., Tonawanda, NY, pg. 946
Roney, Blake M., Pres.--Nu Skin International, Provo, UT, pg. 817
Roney, Dennis, Pres.--Roney Div. of Oberweis Dairy, Inc., Aurora, IL, pg. 820
Roney, Patrick E., Chm. Bd., Pres. & Chief Exec. Officer--Electro Mechanical Design Services, Inc., Gaithersburg, MD, pg. 375
Roof, R. Phil, Pres. & Chief Exec. Officer--RPR & Associates, Inc., Columbia, SC, pg. 908
Rooks, W. Howard, Pres.--Weichert Realty, Inc., Alexandria, VA, pg. 1173
Rooney, L.F., III, Pres.--Manhattan Building Companies, Tulsa, OK, pg. 703
Roop, James J., Pres. & Chief Oper. Officer--Watt, Roop & Co., Cleveland, OH, pg. 1168
Root, John A., Chm. Bd. & Pres.--A.I. Root Company, Medina, OH, pg. 946
Root, P.T., Pres.--Root Corporation, Mount Wolf, PA, pg. 946
Roper, Gerald, Pres. & Chief Exec. Officer--Chicago Convention & Tourism Bureau, Chicago, IL, pg. 245
Roper, Jarvis, Pres.--Smith Motors, Inc., Hammond, IN, pg. 1014
Roper, John L. III, Pres. & Chief Exec. Officer--Norfolk Shipbuilding & Drydock Corporation, Norfolk, VA, pg. 810
Rorie, Durwood G., Jr., Pres.--United Air Specialists, Inc., Cincinnati, OH, pg. 1130
Rosamond, Patricia A., Pres.--Rodgers Builders, Inc., Charlotte, NC, pg. 942
Rosania, William S., Pres.--Structural Foam Plastics, Inc., North Branch, NJ, pg. 1054
Rosasco, Nat G., Pres.--Northwestern Golf Company, Chicago, IL, pg. 815
Rose, Gervase R., Pres.--Roman Electric Company, Inc., Milwaukee, WI, pg. 945
Rose, Jules, Chm. Bd.--Sloans Supermarkets, Inc., New York, NY, pg. 1010
Rose, Kenneth L., Pres. & Chief Exec. Officer--Henkels & McCoy, Inc., Blue Bell, PA, pg. 529
Rose, Marshall, Exec. Officer--Gould Investors, L.P., Great Neck, NY, pg. 473
Rose, Robert, Pres. & New Bus. Contact--Marketing Magic Inc., Fort Lauderdale, FL, pg. 709
Rose, Robert C., III, Pres. & Chief Exec. Officer--Altama Delta Corp., Darien, GA, pg. 45
Rose, William R., Chm. Bd., Pres. & Chief Exec. Officer--Rose Packing Company, South Barrington, IL, pg. 947
Rosedale, Miles, Chm. Bd., Pres. & Chief Exec. Officer--Monrovia Nursery Co., Azusa, CA, pg. 766
Rosekrans, John, Pres.--Wham-O Div. of Kransco, San Gabriel, CA, pg. 644
Rosekrans, John N., Jr., Pres.--Kransco, San Francisco, CA, pg. 644
Rosemond, Bruce, Pres.--Santa Rosa Steel Forming, Inc., Santa Rosa, CA, pg. 970
Rosen, Albert L., Pres. & Gen. Mgr.--San Francisco Giants Baseball Club, San Francisco, CA, pg. 969
Rosen, Andrew, Pres.--Calvin Klein Sport, New York, NY, pg. 635
Rosen, David, Pres. & Chief Exec. Officer--CB North America, Inc., Glens Falls, NY, pg. 199
Rosen, David, Pres.--CB Sports Inc., Glens Falls, NY, pg. 199
Rosen, Edward, Pres.--Star Children's Dress Company, Inc., New York, NY, pg. 1039
Rosen, Edward, Pres.--Virginia Apparel Manufacturing Co., Inc., Amelia Court House, VA, pg. 1039
Rosen, Fred K., Pres.--Grayline Housewares, Elgin, IL, pg. 480
Rosen, Jack, Chm., Pres., Chief Exec. & Chief Oper. Officer--Hazel Bishop Corporation, Englewood Cliffs, NJ, pg. 520
Rosen, Kermit, Pres.--Alaskan Copper Companies, Seattle, WA, pg. 30
Rosen, Lawrence, Pres.--Rose Art Industries, Orange, NJ, pg. 947
Rosen, Leon, Pres.--Pace Collection, Inc., Long Island City, NY, pg. 838
Rosen, Morris, Pres.--Pearl-Pressman-Liberty Communications Group, Philadelphia, PA, pg. 853
Rosen, Nancy, Dir.-Opers.--New York City Dept. of General Services, New York, NY, pg. 802
Rosen, Robert A., Pres.--Rosen Associates Management Corp., Jericho, NY, pg. 948
Rosen, Theodore A., Pres. & Chief Oper. Officer--Raymond Rosen Co., Conshohocken, PA, pg. 948
Rosen, Thomas, Pres.--Rosens Diversified, Inc., Fairmont, MN, pg. 948
Rosenbaum, Eli, Pres.--Bruckner Machine & Tool Corp., Port Washington, NY, pg. 183
Rosenbaum, Ronnie, Pres.--Vogue & Body Shops, Inc., Jacksonville, FL, pg. 1154

Rosenberg, Alan, Pres. & Chief Exec. Officer--Seaman Furniture Co., Inc., Woodbury, NY, pg. 986
Rosenberg, Burton M., Pres.--Henry I. Siegel Company, Inc., New York, NY, pg. 1002
Rosenberg, Charles, Pres.--Rose Printing Company, Inc., Tallahassee, FL, pg. 948
Rosenberg, Michael, Pres.--Ketchum Advertising (Japan) Ltd., Tokyo, Japan, pg. 626
Rosenberg, Michael G., Pres.--Hubbs Importing Corp., Emerson, NJ, pg. 550
Rosenberg, Steven, Pres.--Arrow Industries, Inc., Carrollton, TX, pg. 85
Rosenberger, Philip E., Pres.--Jepson-Murray Advertising, Lansing, MI, pg. 593
Rosenberger, William L., Pres.--Rosenbergers Dairies, Inc., Hatfield, PA, pg. 948
Rosenblum, Lewis, Pres.--Teca Corporation, Pleasantville, NY, pg. 1082
Rosendin, Raymond J., Pres. & Treas.--Rosendin Electric, Inc., San Jose, CA, pg. 948
Rosenfeld, Laurence, Pres.--Stackig, Sanderson & White, Inc., McLean, VA, pg. 1034
Rosenfield, George, Pres.--Tasco, Miami, FL, pg. 1079
Rosenheim, Harry, III, Pres.--Philadelphia Reserve Supply Company, Croydon, PA, pg. 867
Rosenshein, Bernard J., Pres.--Rosenshein Associates, New Rochelle, NY, pg. 948
Rosenthal, George I., Chm. Bd. & Pres.--Raleigh Enterprises, Inc., Los Angeles, CA, pg. 910
Rosenthal, Marvin, Pres.--National Lumber Co., Warren, MI, pg. 792
Rosenthal, Richard H., Pres.--F & W Publications, Inc., Cincinnati, OH, pg. 394
Rosenthal, Robert, Pres.--Rosenthal Chevrolet Co., Arlington, VA, pg. 949
Rosenthal, Robert M., Pres.--Rosenthal Automotive Organization, Arlington, VA, pg. 949
Rosenthal, Stuart, Pres. & Chief Oper. Officer--Furr's Supermarkets, Albuquerque, NM, pg. 437
Roshak, Arthur J., Pres.--Colonial Dodge Inc., East Detroit, MI, pg. 263
Roska, Jon, Pres., New Bus. Contact & Creative Dir.--Roska Direct Marketing, Inc., North Wales, PA, pg. 949
Roskovensky, E.A., Pres.--Davis Wire Corporation, Irwindale, CA, pg. 319
Rosner, Richard, Pres.--Glamorise Foundations, Inc., New York, NY, pg. 460
Ross, Barry J., Pres.--Robinhood Homes, Inc., San Diego, CA, pg. 939
Ross, Bruce, Pres.--J H Collectibles, Milwaukee, WI, pg. 584
Ross, Charles M., Pres.--Charles Curtain Company, Inc., Dallas, TX, pg. 239
Ross, Darryl A., Chm. Bd. & Pres.--Ross Advertising, Inc., Saint Louis, MO, pg. 949
Ross, Edward W., Pres.--The Jupiter Corporation, Chicago, IL, pg. 609
Ross, Fred C., Vice Chm., Pres. & Chief Exec. Officer--Allied Old English, Inc., Port Reading, NJ, pg. 38
Ross, Gerald, Pres., Chief Exec. & Chief Fin. Officer & Treas.--MGR Equipment Corp., Inwood, NY, pg. 692
Ross, Jack, Pres.--Jack Ross Motors Inc., Tempe, AZ, pg. 949
Ross, Jeffrey W., Pres.--Southeastern Capital Corporation, Denver, CO, pg. 1019
Ross, Joseph, Pres. & Chief Exec. Officer--Entron Industries Limited Partnership, Glendale, NY, pg. 383
Ross, Marc S., Pres. & Chief Exec. Officer--Veda International, Inc., Alexandria, VA, pg. 1146
Ross, Marc S., Pres. & Chief Exec. Officer--Veda Incorporated, Alexandria, VA, pg. 1146
Ross, Wayne, Pres.--Micropump Corporation, Vancouver, WA, pg. 749
Rosse, James N., Pres.--Freedom Newspapers Inc., Irvine, CA, pg. 431
Rossetti, Paul, Pres.--DKM Building Enterprises, L.P., Lawrenceville, NJ, pg. 357
Rossi, Carlo, Pres. & Gen. Mgr.--Carlo Rossi Vineyards, Modesto, CA, pg. 442
Rossi, Dominick F., Jr., Pres.-Ayer USA--N W Ayer Incorporated, New York, NY, pg. 103
Rossi, Dominick F., Jr., Pres.-Ayer USA--N W Ayer Inc., New York, NY, pg. 104
Rossin, Jack, Chm. & Chief Exec. Officer--Rossin Greenberg Seronick, Boston, MA, pg. 950
Rossio, Robert D., Pres. & Chief Exec. Officer--Lindsay Olive Growers, Lindsay, CA, pg. 676
Rossio, Robert D., Pres.--Lindsay International, Lindsay, CA, pg. 676
Rosskam, Skip, III, Pres. & Chief Oper. Officer--David Michael & Co. Inc., Philadelphia, PA, pg. 747
Rossmeyer, Bruce, Pres.--Bruce Rossmeyer's Toyotaland, Longwood, FL, pg. 950
Rost, Jon, Pres.--Jacobson Rost, Inc., Sheboygan, WI, pg. 588
Rosuck, I. Donald, Pres.--Culligan International Company, Northbrook, IL, pg. 358
Rotando, Lynn Andrew, Chm., Pres. & Chief Exec. Officer--Rotando Lerch & Iafeliece Advertising, Stamford, CT, pg. 950
Roth, Ernie, Pres. & New Bus. Contact--Furman, Roth Adv., New York, NY, pg. 437
Roth, Jack, Pres. & Chief Exec. Officer--Admarketing, Inc., Los Angeles, CA, pg. 18
Roth, Michael I., Pres., Chief Oper. Officer & Chief Exec. Officer--The Mutual Life Insurance Company of New York (MONY), New York, NY, pg. 778
Roth, Robert, Pres. & Publisher--Chicago Reader, Inc., Chicago, IL, pg. 245
Roth, Robert S., Pres.--World Oil Company, South Gate, CA, pg. 1203
Roth, Stanley, Chm. Bd. & Pres.--Panorama Press, Inc., Clifton, NJ, pg. 846
Rothbaum, Michael, Pres. & Chief Exec. Officer--The Harwood Companies, Inc., New York, NY, pg. 515
Rothenberger, E.C., Pres.--Vari Tronics Company, Inc., Duarte, CA, pg. 1145
Rothfeld, Eric, Pres.--Sasson Jeans for Men, New York, NY, pg. 972
Roths, Jim, Mktg. Mgr.--Telex Hy-gain Div., Lincoln, NE, pg. 1085
Rothschild, Diane, Pres.--Grace & Rothschild, New York, NY, pg. 474
Rothschild, Loren R., Pres.--American Protection Industries, Inc., Los Angeles, CA, pg. 60
Rothwell, Brian G., Pres. & Chief Exec. Officer--Bay State Milling Co., Quincy, MA, pg. 127
Rott, Herbert F., Jr., Pres.--Des Moines Tire, Des Moines, IA, pg. 951
Roubin, Angel S., Pres. & Treas.--Roubinco, Inc., Fairfax, VA, pg. 952
Roush, David P., Chm. Bd., Pres. & Chief Exec. Officer--Rocor Transportation Companies Inc., Oklahoma City, OK, pg. 942
Roussel, Louis J., Jr., Chm. Bd., Pres. & Chief Exec. Officer--Victory Financial Group, Inc., Metairie, LA, pg. 1150
Roussy, Mark, Pres.-Relocation & Asset Mngmt. Services--RE/MAX International, Inc., Englewood, CO, pg. 915
Rovansek, Gary, Pres.--The Reliable Corp., Chicago, IL, pg. 924
Rovey, Emil, Pres.--United Producers & Consumers Co-Op, Phoenix, AZ, pg. 1134
Rowan, Frederick J., Pres. & Chief Exec. Officer--The William Carter Company, New York, NY, pg. 226
Rowe, John, Pres.--Justrite Manufacturing Company, Des Plaines, IL, pg. 610
Rowe, O. Regan, Jr., Chm. Bd & Pres.--Rowe Corp., Charlotte, NC, pg. 952
Rowe, Richard R., Chm. Bd., Pres. & Chief Exec. Officer--The Faxon Company, Inc., Westwood, MA, pg. 404
Rowell, L.J., Jr., Chm. Bd., Pres. & Chief Exec. Officer--Provident Mutual Life Insurance Co., Philadelphia, PA, pg. 896
Rowley, Ronald L., Pres.--BCP Technical Service, Inc., Gretna, LA, pg. 106
Rowse, James R., Sr., Chm. Bd.--Veryfine Products, Inc., Westford, MA, pg. 1148
Rowse, Sam B., Pres.--Veryfine Products, Inc., Westford, MA, pg. 1148
Rowsey, Paul, III, Pres. & Gen. Counsel--Rosewood Property Company, Dallas, TX, pg. 949
Royan, John, Pres.--Silicon Power Cube Corporation, Long Beach, CA, pg. 1004
Rozek, John F., Pres.--Amity Leather Products Company, West Bend, WI, pg. 67
Ruark, Roger, Pres., Chief Fin. Officer--Garrison-Lontine Advertising, Denver, CO, pg. 443
Rubenstein, Richard D., Pres. & Creative Dir.--Adamson Advertising, Inc., Saint Louis, MO, pg. 17
Rubie, Kerry, Chief Exec. Officer--Leo Burnett Limited, London,, United Kingdom, pg. 193
Rubin, Donald, Pres.--M. Rubin & Sons Inc., New York, NY, pg. 954
Rubin, Gerrold R., Pres.--Rubin Postaer & Associates, Santa Monica, CA, pg. 954
Rubin, Harold R., Pres. & Chief Exec. Officer--Stevens-Lee Company, Minneapolis, MN, pg. 1048
Rubin, Irving A., Chm. Bd., Pres. & Chief Exec. Officer--Container Products Inc., Southfield, MI, pg. 278
Rubin, Joel, Chm. Bd., Pres. & Chief Exec. Officer--Phototype Color Graphics, Inc., Pennsauken, NJ, pg. 869
Rubin, Mark A., Pres.--Shogyo International Corporation, Great Neck, NY, pg. 1000
Rubin, Michael B., Pres.--Shokai Far East Ltd., Peekskill, NY, pg. 1000
Rubin, Richard, Chm., Pres., Chief Exec. & Chief Oper. Officer--Donnkenny, Inc., New York, NY, pg. 345
Rubin, Stephen, Pres.--Vita Food Products, Inc., Chicago, IL, pg. 1153
Rubin, William S., Chm. Bd & Pres.--Rubin Response Services, Inc., Schaumburg, IL, pg. 954
Rubino, Bill, Pres.--Jofco Inc., Jasper, IN, pg. 595
Rubino, Gail M., Pres. & Chief Exec. Officer--A. Pomerantz & Co., Philadelphia, PA, pg. 880
Ruby, Ronald, Pres.--Ram Graphics, Inc., Alexandria, IN, pg. 910
Rucker, Adin H., Jr., Pres. & Treas.--Stonecutter Mills Corp., Spindale, NC, pg. 1051
Ruckriegel, Robert, Pres.--Wharfside Restaurants, Inc., Jasper, IN, pg. 1184
Ruda, Kevin, Pres.--Holsum Foods, Waukesha, WI, pg. 515
Ruddy, James P., Pres.--General Welding Supply Corporation, Westbury, NY, pg. 451
Ruddy, Thomas, Pres. & Gen. Mgr.--Circle A.W. Products, Co., Portland, OR, pg. 250
Ruden, Gerald, Pres.--Mid-South Ford Truck Sales, Inc., Memphis, TN, pg. 750
Rudin, Steven, Pres.--Koret of California, San Francisco, CA, pg. 642
Rudloff, Hans-Joerg, Chm. Bd., Pres. & Chief Exec. Officer--Financiere Credit Suisse-First Boston, Zug,, Switzerland, pg. 204
Rudloff, Hans-Jorg, Pres. & Chm. Bd.--CS First Boston Financiere, Inc., New York, NY, pg. 204
Rudolph, Frederick W., Pres.--Rudolph/Libbe, Inc., Walbridge, OH, pg. 955
Rudolph, John E., Pres.--Rudolph Foods Company, Lima, OH, pg. 954
Ruf, Dave G., Jr., Pres.--Burns & McDonnell Engineers-Architects-Consultants, Kansas City, MO, pg. 194
Ruffin, Phillip G, Pres.--Town & Country Food Markets, Inc., Wichita, KS, pg. 1103
Ruffin, Shelton, Pres.--Ruffin Building Systems, Inc., Oak Grove, LA, pg. 955
Ruhl, Frank, Pres. & Chief Exec. Officer--Ruhl Companies, Inc., Valhalla, NY, pg. 955
Ruhl, John, Sr., Gen. Mgr.--Steelcase Wood Div., Kentwood, MI, pg. 1044
Ruhlin, John, Jr., Chm. Bd., Pres. & Chief Exec. Officer--The Ruhlin Company, Sharon Center, OH, pg. 955
Ruhlman, Jon R., Pres. & Chief Exec. Officer--Preformed Line Products, Cleveland, OH, pg. 886
Ruiz, Fred, Pres. & Chief Exec. Officer--Ruiz Food Products, Inc., Dinuba, CA, pg. 955
Rule, Ronald C., Pres. & Chief Exec. Officer--The United States Playing Card Company, Cincinnati, OH, pg. 1136
Rumpeltin, Frank E., Pres.--Century Products Co., Macedonia, OH, pg. 235
Rumpf, Norman, Pres.--Apollo Colors, Inc., Northbrook, IL, pg. 78
Runk, John W., Chm. Bd. & Pres.--Directory Distributing Associates, Inc., Saint Louis, MO, pg. 339
Runk, Lee H., Pres. & Chief Oper. Officer--Harvard Industries, Inc., Farmingdale, NJ, pg. 514
Rupard, Hay, Pres.--Peake Printers, Inc., Cheverly, MD, pg. 853
Rupp, Glenn, Pres. & Chief Exec. Officer--Simmons Upholstered Furniture, Inc., Saint Louis, MO, pg. 1005
Rushen, Frank, Pres.--Instrument Specialties Company, Delaware Water Gap, PA, pg. 572
Rushing, J. Carroll, Pres.--Intex Chemical Inc., Greer, SC, pg. 581
Russell, Bob, Pres.--Russell Chevrolet Company, Sherwood, AR, pg. 957
Russell, Charles T., Chief Exec. Officer--Visa U.S.A. Inc., San Mateo, CA, pg. 1153
Russell, Chester D., Jr., Pres.--Associated Of Los Angeles, Los Angeles, CA, pg. 90
Russell, Dick, Pres. & Chief Exec. Officer--Guaranteed Products, Inc., City of Industry, CA, pg. 491
Russell, E. Wayne, Jr., Pres.--Russell Petroleum Corporation, Montgomery, AL, pg. 957
Russell, Jerome, Pres. & Gen. Mgr.--City Beverage Co., Atlanta, GA, pg. 251
Russell, John, Pres.--Days Inns of America, Inc., Parsippany, NJ, pg. 1100
Russell, John H., Pres.--Kissimmee Toyota Inc., Kissimmee, FL, pg. 633
Russell, Michael T., Pres.--STS Holdings, Inc., Northbrook, IL, pg. 964
Russell, Nancy H., Pres.--Food & Gas, Inc., Decatur, GA, pg. 423
Russell, Richard, Pres.--Unison Insurance Co., Charleston, SC, pg. 66
Russell, Robert B., Jr., Pres.--Ruscon Corp., Charleston, SC, pg. 956
Russell, Stephen P., Pres. & Chief Oper. Officer--Russell Industries, Inc., Carnegie, PA, pg. 957
Russell, Steven, Pres.--Swanson Russell Associates, Lincoln, NE, pg. 1066
Russell, Wayland, Pres.--Rainbow Home Rentals, Canfield, OH, pg. 910
Russeth, Gerald, Pres. & Chief Exec. Officer--Coken Company, Inc., Providence, RI, pg. 259
Russillo, Thomas R., Pres. & Chief Oper. Officer--Ben Venue Laboratories, Inc., Bedford, OH, pg. 138
Russo, Anthony J., Chm. Bd. & Pres.--E.C.D., Inc., Hillside, NJ, pg. 359
Russo, Paul, Co-Pres.--Smith Valve Corporation, Whitinsville, MA, pg. 1014
Russo, Peter R., Pres.--Data Instruments, Inc., Acton, MA, pg. 316
Russo, Thomas, Pres.--Fyrnetics, Inc., Roselle, IL, pg. 438
Rust, Edward B., Jr., Chm. Bd., Pres. & Chief Exec. Officer--State Farm Mutual Automobile Insurance Company, Bloomington, IL, pg. 1041
Rust, Lois, Pres. & Chief Exec. Officer--Rose Acre Farms, Seymour, IN, pg. 947
Rutherford, Clyde E., Chm. Bd. & Pres.--Dairylea Cooperative Inc., East Syracuse, NY, pg. 311
Rutherford, J. Larry, Pres. & Chief Exec. Officer--Atlantic Gulf Communities Corporation, Miami, FL, pg. 95
Rutherford, Terry, Pres.--General Marine Industries, Inc., Panama City, FL, pg. 449
Ruthman, T.R., Pres., Gen. Mgr. & Adv. Dir.--Ruthman Pump & Engineering Co., Cincinnati, OH, pg. 957
Ruting, Wayne, Pres. & Chief. Exec. Officer--Columbine Systems Inc., Golden, CO, pg. 266
Rutledge, Perry, Pres.--Farmers Mutual Hail Insurance Co., Des Moines, IA, pg. 401
Ryals, Donald L., Pres. & Chief Oper. Officer--Network Capital Group, Campbell, CA, pg. 798
Ryan, Charles P., Jr., Chm. Bd., Pres.--Charan Industries, Inc., Garden City, NY, pg. 239
Ryan, Colleen, Pres.--Ryan Oldsmobile, Billings, MT, pg. 958
Ryan, James M., Pres.--Imprint Products, L.P., Rockville Centre, NY, pg. 564
Ryan, Jim, Pres.-Ryan Construction Co.--Ryan Properties Inc., Minneapolis, MN, pg. 958
Ryan, Pat, Pres.--Ryan Properties Inc., Minneapolis, MN, pg. 958
Ryan, Philip, Pres.--Taylor Oil Co. Inc., Winston-Salem, NC, pg. 1082
Ryan, W., Pres.--New Haven Mfg. Corp., New Haven, CT, pg. 801
Ryden, John G., Dir.--Yale University Press, New Haven, CT, pg. 1207
Rygh, Ole B., Pres. & Chief Exec. Officer--IDAB International Incorporated, Hampton, VA, pg. 559
Ryman, R.L., Sr. V.P.-Sls. & Mktg.--Prince Gardner Incorporated, Saint Louis, MO, pg. 890
Ryno, Ronald P., Chm. Bd. & Pres.--Cuplex, Inc., Garland, TX, pg. 305
Rynone, Richard T., Pres.--Rynone Manufacturing Corporation, Sayre, PA, pg. 958
Rysdon, Phil, Pres.--Sioux Steel Company, Sioux Falls, SD, pg. 1008

Ryser, Frank, Chm. Bd., Pres., Chief Exec. Officer & Treas.--Ryser Brothers Inc., Chicago, IL, pg. 958
Ryzman, Zvi, Pres.--Ardell International, Inc., City of Commerce, CA, pg. 81
Sabath, Robert E., Pres. & Chief Oper. Officer--Knight/Emerson Consulting, Inc., Chicago, IL, pg. 637
Sabath, Robert E., Pres.--Knight Management Consulting, Inc., Chicago, IL, pg. 637
Sabbatino, Anthony, Pres., Chief Oper. & Chief Exec. Officer--Bogue Electric Manufacturing Co., Paterson, NJ, pg. 162
Sabbeth, Stephen J., Chm. Bd. & Pres.--Sabbeth Industries Ltd, Deer Park, NY, pg. 965
Sabourin, Rick, Pres. & Treas.--Bestop, Inc., Broomfield, CO, pg. 147
Saca, Tony, Pres.--Filco, Inc., Sacramento, CA, pg. 409
Sachnowitz, Larry, Pres. & Sr. Creative Dir.--Sachnowitz & Co., Houston, TX, pg. 965
Sachs, Louis S., Chm. Bd. & Pres.--Sachs Holding Company, Chesterfield, MO, pg. 965
Sack, Thomas F., Pres., Chief Exec. & Oper. Officer--Haddon Craftsmen, Inc., Scranton, PA, pg. 499
Sackett, Janice J., Pres.--LeGrand Johnson Construction Co., Logan, UT, pg. 598
Sackett, Neil, Pres.--Carter-Jones Lumber Company, Kent, OH, pg. 226
Sackett, Ron, Pres. & Dir. Creative Services--Case Foley Sackett, Inc., Minneapolis, MN, pg. 227
Sackin, Erwin R., V.P.--S-G Metals Industries, Inc., Kansas City, KS, pg. 962
Sacks, Leonard, Pres.--Sacks & Rosen, Inc. Advertising, New York, NY, pg. 965
Sada, Francisco, Pres.--Wisdom Imports Sales Co. Inc., Irvine, CA, pg. 1198
Sadler, R. Jackson, Rev. Dr., Pres.--Christian Children's Fund, Inc., Richmond, VA, pg. 248
Sadler, Robert A., Pres.--Monroe Printing Company, East Stroudsburg, PA, pg. 697
Sadow, Bernard D., Pres.--United States Luggage Company, Hauppauge, NY, pg. 1136
Saeys, Cas, Mng. Dir.--Wunderman Worldwide v.o.f., Amsterdam,, Netherlands, pg. 1212
Safiol, George E., Pres. & Chief Exec. Officer--General Instrument Corporation, New York, NY, pg. 425
Sage, David, Pres.--Holy Cross Electric Association, Glenwood Springs, CO, pg. 541
Sage, George, Pres.--Bonanza Bus Lines, Inc., Providence, RI, pg. 164
Sager, Robert, Pres.--Gordon Brothers, Boston, MA, pg. 471
Saginaw, David, Pres. & Chief Oper. Officer--Roytex, Inc., New York, NY, pg. 953
Sagolla, Michael, Gen. Mgr.--Tactair Fluid Controls Corp., Beverly, NJ, pg. 869
Saillant, J., Pres.--Stihl Eastern Canada Ltd., Ville Vanier,, Canada, pg. 1049
Saint-Jacques, Madeleine, Pres.--Young & Rubicam, Ltee., Montreal,, Canada, pg. 1213
Saito, Hank, Pres.--Gougler Industries, Inc., Kent, OH, pg. 473
Sakane, Masahiro, Pres. & Chief Oper. Officer--Komatsu Dresser Company, Lincolnshire, IL, pg. 565
Sakosits, Mildred, Pres. & Sec.--Hoboken Wood Flooring Corporation, Wayne, NJ, pg. 537
Saks, Alan, Pres. & Chief Exec. Officer--Saxon Paint & Home Care Centers Inc., Chicago, IL, pg. 973
Saks, Michael, Pres.--EBSC Corporation, Gary, IN, pg. 359
Salamon, Joseph, Pres.--Pic N'pay Supermarkets, Inc., Dania, FL, pg. 869
Salamone, Anthony, Pres.--Sunroc Corporation, Media, PA, pg. 1062
Salamone, Anthony A., Pres.--Telkee Inc., Media, PA, pg. 1062
Salas, Conrado, Dir.--Alas/DPP Barcelona S.A., Barcelona,, Spain, pg. 109
Saldanha, Walter, Chm. & Mng. Dir.--Chaitra Leo Burnett Advertising Private Ltd., Bombay, India, pg. 192
Saless, S.S., Pres.-WWES--WW Engineering & Science Inc., Grand Rapids, MI, pg. 1058
Sall, Hyman L., Pres.--Atlantic Metals Corporation, Philadelphia, PA, pg. 95
Salter, Michael, Pres. & Chief Oper. Officer--Beno's, Los Angeles, CA, pg. 139
Salvati, Philip J., Pres. & Chief Exec. Officer--Salvati Montgomery Sakoda, Inc., Costa Mesa, CA, pg. 967
Salvatierra, Richard, Pres.--RII (Ricards International Inc.), Silver Spring, MD, pg. 907
Salwasser, Melvin, Pres.--Salwasser Manufacturing Company, Inc., Reedley, CA, pg. 968
Samburg, A. Gene, Chm. Bd., Pres. & Chief Exec. Officer--Kastle Systems, Inc., Arlington, VA, pg. 618
Samis, Michael S., Pres. & Chief Exec. Officer--Macklanburg-Duncan Co., Oklahoma City, OK, pg. 697
Sams, Kenneth D., Pres.--Cherokee Brick & Tile Co., Macon, GA, pg. 243
Samsill, Mark, Pres. & Chief Exec. Officer--Samsill Corporation, Fort Worth, TX, pg. 968
Samson, Bernice, Chm. & Pres .--Sterling Supply Company, Inc., Lisle, IL, pg. 1047
Samuels, Allen, Pres.--Allen Samuels Chevrolet GEO, Waco, TX, pg. 969
San Jose, George L., Pres. & Exec. Creative Dir.--San Jose & Associates, Chicago, IL, pg. 969
Sanada, Takashi, Pres.--KYB Corporation of America, Lombard, IL, pg. 613
Sanborn, Bruce, Chm. Bd., Pres. & Chief Exec. Officer--North Central Life Insurance Companies, Saint Paul, MN, pg. 813
Sanborn, Bruce C., Chm. Bd., Pres. & Chief Exec. Officer--Financial Life Companies, Inc., St. Paul, MN, pg. 813
Sanchez, Fausto H., Pres. & Creative Dir.--Sanchez & Levitan, Inc., Miami, FL, pg. 970
Sandberg, A.L., Pres. & Chief Exec. Officer--Delta Sugar Corporation, Clarksburg, CA, pg. 327
Sanders, Allen H., Pres.--Bates Container, Inc., North Richland Hills, TX, pg. 125
Sanders, Charles N., Gen. Mgr.--Atlanta Auto Auction, Inc., Red Oak, GA, pg. 293
Sanders, John, Pres. & Chief Exec. Officer WW (New York & Detroit)--Wunderman Cato Johnson, New York, NY, pg. 1211
Sanders, Lewis A., Pres.--Sanford C. Bernstein & Co., Inc., New York, NY, pg. 144
Sanders, Max D., Chm. Bd. & Pres.--Ohmite Manufacturing Company, Skokie, IL, pg. 823
Sanders, O'Neil, Chm. Bd., Pres., Chief Exec. & Chief Oper. Officer--Associated Petroleum Carriers, Spartanburg, SC, pg. 91
Sanderson, Sandra B., Pres. & Chief Exec. Officer--Sanderson Plumbing Products Inc., Columbus, MS, pg. 970
Sandhu, M.S., Chm. Bd., Pres. & Chief Exec. Officer--SRS Technologies, Newport Beach, CA, pg. 964
Sandifer, Thomas N., Pres. & Chief Exec. Officer--Cain & Bultman, Inc., Jacksonville, FL, pg. 207
Sandler, Ernest, Pres. & Chief Exec. Officer--Interstate Drug Exchange, Inc., Amityville, NY, pg. 580
Sandler, Kenneth B., Pres. & New Bus. Contact--Sandler Communications Inc., New York, NY, pg. 970
Sandner, John, Pres.--Howard Industries, Inc., Milford, IL, pg. 547
Sandridge, Ken, Pres.--Maris, West & Baker, Inc., Jackson, MS, pg. 707
Sands, Louis, IV, Pres.--Sands Motor Company, Inc., Glendale, AZ, pg. 970
Sanford, Robert P., Pres.--Sanford & Hawley, Inc., Unionville, CT, pg. 970
Sanger, Frank N., Pres.--Parkway Fabricators, Inc., South Amboy, NJ, pg. 480
Sanguinetti, P.A., Pres.--Consolidated Publishing Company, Anniston, AL, pg. 277
Sanguinetti, Pat, Pres. & Chief Exec. Officer--Blue Anchor, Inc., Sacramento, CA, pg. 158
Sani, Ashok, Pres.--CGS Industries, Inc., Long Island City, NY, pg. 201
Sankes, Gary, Chm. Bd & Pres.--Scrufari Construction Co. Inc., Niagara Falls, NY, pg. 983
Sanning, Frank, Pres.--Optical Corp. of America, Louisville, KY, pg. 827
Sano, Rex M., Pres.--International Designer Accessories, Inc., Secaucus, NJ, pg. 578
Sansone, Tom, Pres.--Jabil Circuit Inc., Saint Petersburg, FL, pg. 587
Santulli, Richard T., Pres. & Chief Exec. Officer--Executive Jet Aviation, Inc., Columbus, OH, pg. 393
Sanzone, Vincent P., Pres.--Tecot Electric Supply Company, New Castle, DE, pg. 1084
Saperstein, Stan, Pres.--Kraft Hardware, Inc., New York, NY, pg. 643
Sapos, Mary Ann, Pres. & Chief Exec. Officer--Hutchins/Young & Rubicam, Rochester, NY, pg. 1211
Sargent, David K., Pres.--Up-Right, Inc., Selma, CA, pg. 1139
Sargent, John W., Pres., Treas., New Bus. Contact, Production & Research Dir.--Sargent & Potratz, Inc., Brookfield, WI, pg. 971
Sargent, Lee M., Pres. & Chief Exec. Officer--Todd & Sargent, Inc., Ames, IA, pg. 1100
Sarich, Steven N., Brewery Mgr.--Rainier Brewing Co., Seattle, WA, pg. 526
Sarkisian, Norman,, Owner, Pres. & Chief Exec. Officer--Beacon Group, Bloomfield, CT, pg. 128
Sarkisian, Robert, Pres.--Marketing Displays International, Inc., Farmington Hills, MI, pg. 709
Sarmiento, Antonio A., Chm. Bd., Pres. & Sec.--Lumas Realty, Inc., Miami, FL, pg. 687
Sarne, Yoav, Pres.--A. Epstein & Sons (Israel) Ltd., Tel Aviv, Israel, pg. 384
Sass, George G., Pres. & Creative Dir.--Sass & Associates, Annapolis, MD, pg. 972
Sasser, Billy G., Chm. Bd., Pres. & Chief Exec. Officer--Reeves Southeastern Corporation, Tampa, FL, pg. 921
Sasso, Art, Pres. & Dir.-Creative--The Jason Group, Inc., Short Hills, NJ, pg. 590
Sassos, Thomas P., Pres.--Vernon Sassos McGill, Inc., New York, NY, pg. 1148
Sastri, M.S., Pres.--Aluma Shield Industries, Inc., Daytona Beach, FL, pg. 46
Saubert, Walter E., Pres.--Red Ball Forwarders, Inc., Indianapolis, IN, pg. 918
Sauder, Maynard, Pres. & Chief Exec. Officer--Sauder Woodworking Co., Archbold, OH, pg. 972
Sauer, Mark, Pres. & Chief Exec. Officer--Pittsburgh Pirates Professional Baseball Club, Pittsburgh, PA, pg. 873
Sauey, Craig L., Pres. & Chief Exec. Officer--Flambeau Corporation, Baraboo, WI, pg. 809
Sauey, Eric W., Pres.--Seats Incorporated, Reedsburg, WI, pg. 810
Sauey, W.R., Chm. Bd., Pres. & Treas.--Nordic Group of Companies, Ltd., Baraboo, WI, pg. 809
Saul, Bill, Pres.--Beach City Chevrolet Co., Long Beach, CA, pg. 128
Saul, Charles F., Pres. & Chief Exec. Officer--Agway, Inc., De Witt, NY, pg. 25
Saul, Franklin R., Pres.--Emigrant Savings Bank, New York, NY, pg. 379
Saunders, Robert H., Jr., Pres. & Chief Exec. Officer--The J. M. Ney Company, Bloomfield, CT, pg. 805
Savage, Alfred, Exec. Dir.--Chicago Transit Authority, Chicago, IL, pg. 922
Savaiano, N.J., Chm. Bd. & Pres.--United Laboratories, Inc., Itasca, IL, pg. 1133
Savey, Jason, Co-Pres.-Mktg. & Fin. Sector--Flambeau Products Corp., Middlefield, OH, pg. 809
Savoie, Michael P., Sr., Pres.--Mike Savoie Chevrolet Inc., Troy, MI, pg. 973
Sawicz, Thomas T., Pres.--United World Life Insurance Company, Omaha, NE, pg. 779
Sawyer, David, Pres.--Tony Downs Foods Company, Saint James, MN, pg. 348
Sawyer, Herbert C., Pres. & Treas.--Potter Hazlehurst Incorporated, East Greenwich, RI, pg. 882
Saxon, Ronald, Pres.--Ron Saxon Ford, Inc., Saint Paul, MN, pg. 973
Saydah, Richard, Pres.--Cecil Saydah Company, Los Angeles, CA, pg. 973
Sayers, J. Handley, Pres.--Phoenix Enterprises Inc., Nashville, TN, pg. 868
Sayle, John G., Pres. & Treas.--The Hall China Company, East Liverpool, OH, pg. 501
Sazenski, Jim, Pres.--Jesco, Inc., Minneapolis, MN, pg. 593
Scanlan, Thomas M., Jr., Pres. & Chief Exec. Officer--The Ward Machinery Company, Cockeysville, MD, pg. 1162
Scansaroli, John M., Pres.--Electrocatalytic, Inc., Union, NJ, pg. 375
Scarborough, Jim, Pres.--Bargain Town U.S.A., Inc., Montgomery, AL, pg. 382
Scarfe, Harry Jr., Pres.--North Electric Supply, Inc., Auburn Hills, MI, pg. 813
Scarlett, Joseph, Pres. & Chief Oper. Officer--TSC Industries, Inc., Nashville, TN, pg. 1075
Schaake, Donald E., Pres. & Chief Exec. Officer--Schaake Packing Company, Inc., Ellensburg, WA, pg. 974
Schachter, Wm., Pres.--CSI International Corporation, New York, NY, pg. 205
Schad, Theodore G., Jr., Chm. Bd., Pres. & Chief Exec. Officer--Schad Industries, Inc., Lafayette, LA, pg. 974
Schad, Theodore G., Jr., Chm. Bd., Pres. & Chief Exec. Officer--Lou Ana Foods, Inc., Opelousas, LA, pg. 974
Schaedler, James D., Pres.--Schaedler Brothers, Inc., Harrisburg, PA, pg. 974
Schaefer, Gerard J., Pres.--Moss Telecommunications Services, Grand Rapids, MI, pg. 772
Schaettle, Karl, Pres.--Panel Prints, Inc., Old Forge, PA, pg. 846
Schaffer, Ian, Pres.--Gordon & Ferguson of Delaware, Inc., Plymouth, MN, pg. 471
Schaffer, Monroe, Pres.--S. Schaffer Grocery Corporation, New Rochelle, NY, pg. 974
Schaffer, Walter L., Mng. Dir.--Carnegie Associates, Inc., Cleveland, OH, pg. 222
Schaible, Paul G., Jr., Chm. Bd., Pres. & Chief Exec. Officer--Chelsea State Bank, Chelsea, MI, pg. 241
Schalhamer, Melvin A., Pres. & Treas.--Allied Chucker & Engineering Company, Jackson, MI, pg. 37
Schalk, E.N., Pres. & Chief Exec. Officer--Fostoria Industries, Inc., Fostoria, OH, pg. 427
Schaller, Christopher L., Chm., Pres. & Chief Exec. Officer--Forstmann & Company, Inc., New York, NY, pg. 424
Schamp, E.D., Pres.--Peco Inc., Portland, OR, pg. 854
Schardt, Ronald, Chm. Bd., Chief Exec. Officer & Chief Oper. Officer--Reinke Manufacturing Co., Inc., Deshler, NE, pg. 924
Scharer, Si, Pres.--Scharer Associates, Inc., Great Neck, NY, pg. 974
Scharfberg, Sheldon, Pres., Chief Exec. Officer, Treasurer & New Bus. Contact--Scharfberg & Associates, Ltd. Adv., Jenkintown, PA, pg. 974
Scharff, Werner G., Chm. Bd. & Pres.--Lanz, Inc., Culver City, CA, pg. 658
Schatz, Douglas S., Pres. & Chief Exec. Officer--Advanced Energy Industry, Fort Collins, CO, pg. 20
Schauer, Ronald, Pres.--Magnetic Data, Inc., Eden Prairie, MN, pg. 700
Schawk, David A., Pres.--Schawk, Inc., Des Plaines, IL, pg. 974
Scheele, Ken, Pres.--Crossman Corp., East Bloomfield, NY, pg. 300
Scheele, Kenneth, Pres.--Ranging, East Bloomfield, NY, pg. 300
Scheeler, Charles, Pres.--C.J. Langenfelder & Son, Inc., Baltimore, MD, pg. 657
Scheer, Wm. N., Pres.--Scheer Advertising Agency, South Orange, NJ, pg. 975
Scheideler, Albert, Pres. & Chief Exec. Officer--McNally Industries, Inc., Grantsburg, WI, pg. 731
Schein, Eliot DeY., Pres.--Schein/Blattstein Advertising, Inc., New York, NY, pg. 975
Scheinman, Tom, Pres. & Chief Exec. Officer--The Unimax Corporation, New York, NY, pg. 1127
Schell, Michael, Pres. & Creative Dir.--Schell/Mullaney, New York, NY, pg. 975
Scheller, Sanford G., Pres. & Chief Exec. Officer--Treasure Chest Advertising Co., Inc., Glendora, CA, pg. 1108
Schenk, George, Pres. & Chief Exec. Officer--J.M. Huber Corporation, Edison, NJ, pg. 550
Schenk, Tony, Chm. Bd., Pres. & Chief Exec. Officer--Enabling Technologies Company, Stuart, FL, pg. 380
Schepps, Lee M., Pres.--The Julius Schepps Co., Dallas, TX, pg. 975
Scherbing, Gordon K., Pres. & Chief Exec. Officer--Farmers Union Marketing & Processing Association, Redwood Falls, MN, pg. 402
Scherer, Gilbert, Pres.--American Passage Media Corporation, Seattle, WA, pg. 59
Scherer, Roger, Pres.--Scherer Bros. Lumber Company, Minneapolis, MN, pg. 976
Schermund, William H., Pres.--M.E.D. Communications, Woodbridge, NJ, pg. 692
Schiavone, Phillip, Pres. & Chief Exec. Officer--E. W. Howell Company, Inc., Port Washington, NY, pg. 547
Schiavone, Ronald, Pres. & Chief Exec. Officer--Schiavone Construction Co., Secaucus, NJ, pg. 976
Schichtel, Gerald F., Pres. & Chief Oper. Officer--Hilliard Corporation, Elmira, NY, pg. 535
Schiciano, Joseph S., Pres.--The Coon-De Visser Co., Royal Oak, MI, pg. 282
Schick, Joseph C., Chm. Bd., Pres., Chief Exec. Officer & Chief Oper. Officer--Raub Supply Company, Lancaster, PA, pg. 913
Schiefelbein, Tina, Partner & Client Services--RTA Advertising, Inc., Montreal,, Canada, pg. 193

Schiewetz, Richard F., Pres.--Primus Inc., Dayton, OH, pg. 890
Schiffer, Laurence A., Pres.--Love Mortgage Company, St. Louis, MO, pg. 685
Schifter, Craig R., Pres.--Squire-Cogswell Company, Northbrook, IL, pg. 1034
Schifter, Craig R., Pres.--Aeros Instruments, Inc., Northbrook, IL, pg. 1034
Schill, Anthony, Exec. V.P.--Niagara Frontier Transporation Metro System, Inc., Buffalo, NY, pg. 806
Schiller, Leonard M., Owner & Dir.-Acquisitions--The Dearborn Group, Chicago, IL, pg. 322
Schiller, Paul, Pres.--Lawrence & Schiller, Inc., Sioux Falls, SD, pg. 663
Schimmenti, Michael R., Pres. & Chief Oper. Officer--Griffin Corporation, Valdosta, GA, pg. 487
Schimpf, Glenn P., Pres. & Chief Exec. Officer--Danis Industries Corporation, Dayton, OH, pg. 314
Schirmang, William P., Pres., Treas. & Sls. Mgr.--Skokie Valley Beverage Co., Wheeling, IL, pg. 1009
Schlachter, H. J., Pres. & Chief Exec. Officer--Maxitrol Co., Southfield, MI, pg. 723
Schlagenhauf, Edward B., Pres.--Badger Truck Center, Inc., Milwaukee, WI, pg. 113
Schlatter, Donald A., Pres., Chief Exec. Officer & Gen. Counsel--Art Iron, Inc., Toledo, OH, pg. 86
Schlemmer, Robert E., Pres. & Chief Exec. Officer--United States Ceramic Tile Co., East Sparta, OH, pg. 1135
Schlessman, Lee E., Chm. Bd. & Pres.--Greeley Gas Co., Denver, CO, pg. 483
Schloemer, Jay B., Pres.--Stockton West Burkhart Inc., Cincinnati, OH, pg. 1050
Schlosser, Jeffrey P., Pres.--Schlosser Forge Company, Rancho Cucamonga, CA, pg. 976
Schlotfeldt, Walter, Pres. & Chief Exec. Officer--Badger Air Brush Company, Franklin Park, IL, pg. 113
Schlott, Richard L., Pres.--Coldwell Bankers/Schlott Realtors, Wayne, NJ, pg. 260
Schlott, Robert, Pres.--Warren Distribution, Inc., Omaha, NE, pg. 1164
Schlueter, John J., Chm. Bd. & Chief Exec. Officer--Knapp Shoes Inc., Brockton, MA, pg. 636
Schlussel, Edward, Pres.--Apex Mills Corporation, Inwood, NY, pg. 78
Schluth, Michael V., Pres.--Alstin Advertising, Inc., Philadelphia, PA, pg. 45
Schmader, M.T., Pres.--Thomas Steel Strip Corp., Warren, OH, pg. 1094
Schmell, Earl, Pres.--John Zink Co., Tulsa, OK, pg. 639
Schmermund, William H., Pres.--CHC Advertising, Woodbridge, NJ, pg. 201
Schmid, Charles W., Pres. & Chief Oper. Officer--Carlson Travel Network-Commercial, Minneapolis, MN, pg. 221
Schmid, Franz A., Pres & Gen Mgr--Sunbeam del Peru S.A., Lima, Peru, pg. 1059
Schmid, Howard G., Pres.--Nodak Mutual Insurance Company, Fargo, ND, pg. 808
Schmid, James A., Pres. & Chief Exec. Officer--Crescent Electric Supply Co., East Dubuque, IL, pg. 298
Schmidt, Arnold, Pres.--Bay Industries Inc., pg. 127
Schmidt, Jerome, Pres.--Dakco Distributors, Inc., Minot, ND, pg. 311
Schmidt, Marcus, Pres. & Chief Exec. Officer--Atlas Tool Inc., Roseville, MI, pg. 96
Schmidt, Peter G., Pres. & Chief Exec. Officer--Marine Construction & Design Co., Seattle, WA, pg. 707
Schmidt, Ronald, Pres. & Chief Exec. Officer--I B Diffusion, LP, Chicago, IL, pg. 558
Schmidt, Ronald D., Chm. Bd., Pres. & Chief Exec. Officer--Zytec Corp., Eden Prairie, MN, pg. 1221
Schmidt, William B., Chm. Bd., Pres. & Treas.--Coca-Cola Bottling Company of Elizabethtown, Elizabethtown, KY, pg. 258
Schmidtgall, William H., Pres.--DMI, Inc., Goodfield, IL, pg. 309
Schmieding, Lawrence H., Pres.--Schmieding Enterprises Inc., Springdale, AR, pg. 976
Schmitt, Thomas M., Pres.--Paul A. Schmitt Music Company, Minneapolis, MN, pg. 976
Schmitt, Tom, Pres.-Network Div.--ERA Real Estate, Overland Park, KS, pg. 360
Schmuhl, William J., Jr., Pres. & Treas.--Bristol Products, L.P., Bristol, IN, pg. 176
Schneeberger, Don R., Pres. & Treas.--Vess Beverages, Inc., Maryland Heights, MO, pg. 1149
Schneeberger, Donald G., Pres. & Chief Oper. Officer--H. C. Miller Company, Milwaukee, WI, pg. 754
Schneider, Charles R., Pres. & Chief Exec. Officer--Baker Industries, Inc., Parsippany, NJ, pg. 166
Schneider, Donald J., Pres.--Schneider National, Inc., Green Bay, WI, pg. 977
Schneider, Isidore, Pres. & Chief Exec. Officer--Schneider Mills, Inc., New York, NY, pg. 977
Schneider, Richard, Pres.--Pioneer Plastics Holding, Inc., Auburn, ME, pg. 872
Schneider, Richard, Pres.--Pioneer Plastics Corp., Auburn, ME, pg. 872
Schneiderman, David, Pres.--VV Publishing Corp., New York, NY, pg. 1142
Schneier, Lance W., Pres.--Acess Energy Corporation, Dublin, OH, pg. 12
Schnider, Joseph, Pres.--Madison Electric Co., Detroit, MI, pg. 699
Schnieber, Glenn E., Pres.--Schnieber Fine Foods, Inc., Lincoln, NE, pg. 977
Schnitzer, Kenneth L., Jr., Pres.--Park Place Motorcars, Dallas, TX, pg. 849
Schnitzlein, Albert H., Pres. & Chief Exec. Officer--Franchise Enterprises Inc., Rocky Mount, NC, pg. 428
Schoen, Charles, Pres.--Electrical Insulation Suppliers, Hillside, IL, pg. 374
Schoen, Paul, Pres.--U-Haul International, Inc., Phoenix, AZ, pg. 48
Schoenecker, Guy, Pres. & Chief Exec. Officer--Guy Schoenecker, Inc., Minneapolis, MN, pg. 977
Schoeneman, Herbert M., Pres.--Schoeneman Brothers Company, Sioux Falls, SD, pg. 978
Schofield, Ray, Gen. Mgr.--Kennedy Valve, Elmira, NY, pg. 623
Schofield, Robert, Pres. & Chief Exec. Officer--Affiliated Food Distributors, Scranton, PA, pg. 23
Scholler, Ray, Pres.--Times Printing Company, Inc., Random Lake, WI, pg. 1098
Scholnick, Harvey, Pres. & Chief Oper. Officer--Marcus Advertising, Inc., Cleveland, OH, pg. 706
Scholobhm, Roy, Pres.--National Corset Supply House, Los Angeles, CA, pg. 787
Scholtens, Michael, Chm., & Chief Exec. Officer--Nutech, Inc., San Jose, CA, pg. 817
Schoonover, Steven L., Pres. & Chief Exec. Officer--Fibrebond Corporation, Minden, LA, pg. 408
Schorr, Roger J., Pres. & Chief Exec. Officer--The Crosset Company Inc., Cincinnati, OH, pg. 300
Schott, Melvin, Pres.--Schott Brothers, Inc., Perth Amboy, NJ, pg. 978
Schott, Owen W., Pres. & Chief Exec. Officer--Schott Corporation, Wayzata, MN, pg. 978
Schottenstein, Jerome, Chm. Bd. & Pres.--Kroehler Furniture Manufacturing Company, Inc., Conover, NC, pg. 645
Schottenstein, Saul, Pres.--Schottenstein Stores Corporation, Columbus, OH, pg. 978
Schottland, Peter, V.P. & Gen. Mgr.--American Packaging Corporation, Rochester, NY, pg. 59
Schottland, S.B., Pres.--American Packaging Corporation, Philadelphia, PA, pg. 59
Schouten, Jack, Mng. Dir.--Lowe Kuiper & Schouten B.V., Amsterdam,, Netherlands, pg. 685
Schraeder, Robert, Pres.--W F I, Inc., Houston, TX, pg. 1156
Schrager, Harley, Pres. & Chief Oper. Officer--Pacesetter Corporation, Omaha, NE, pg. 839
Schramm, Howard M., Jr., Chm. Bd. & Pres.--Turner Supply Company, Mobile, AL, pg. 1119
Schrank, Mike, Pres.--Walser Automotive Corporation, Richfield, MN, pg. 1161
Schraufnagel, Harland, Pres.--Abbyland Foods, Inc., Abbotsford, WI, pg. 10
Schreiber, Raymond G., Pres.--H & D Steel Service, Inc., North Royalton, OH, pg. 495
Schreier, Bradley, Pres. & Chief Oper. Officer--Taylor Corporation, Mankato, MN, pg. 1081
Schrier, Eric, Pres.--Hippocrates Partners, San Francisco, CA, pg. 535
Schrimpf, Bill, Pres.--Piasa Motor Fuels Inc., Hartford, IL, pg. 869
Schrimpf, Bill, Pres.--Piasa Oil Transport Inc., Hartford, IL, pg. 869
Schroeder, Poul, Pres.--Finagrain, Cie Commerciale Agricole et Financiere S.A., Geneva, Switzerland, pg. 279
Schroeder, Steven B., Pres.--Atlas Refinery, Newark, NJ, pg. 96
Schron, Jack H., Jr., Pres.--Jergens Inc., Cleveland, OH, pg. 593
Schrott, John D., Jr., Chm. Bd., Pres. & Chief Exec. Officer--Reel-O-Matic Systems, Inc., Oklahoma City, OK, pg. 920
Schrum, E.P., Pres., Chief Exec. Officer & Treas.--Carolina Mills, Inc., Maiden, NC, pg. 223
Schubauer, James W., Pres.--Schumacher & Forelle, Inc., Great Neck, NY, pg. 979
Schube, Frank W., Pres. & Chief Exec. Officer--Dualite Inc., Williamsburg, OH, pg. 350
Schubert, Clayton, Pres.--Clarklift Of Minnesota, Inc., Bloomington, MN, pg. 253
Schubert, J.R., Pres.--The Springwall Mattress Co., Akron, OH, pg. 1033
Schubert, William C., Pres., Treas., & Chief Exec. Officer--Kitchell Corporation, Phoenix, AZ, pg. 634
Schuck, Jackye, Pres.--Schuck & Sons Construction Co., Glendale, AZ, pg. 979
Schudmak, Mel E., Pres.--Cora Texas Manufacturing Co., White Castle, LA, pg. 285
Schuette, John A., Pres.--Invincible Metal Furniture Co., Manitowoc, WI, pg. 582
Schuette, Marvin, Pres. & Chief Exec. Officer--Wausau Homes, Inc., Rothschild, WI, pg. 1168
Schuff, David, Pres.--Schuff Steel Co., Phoenix, AZ, pg. 979
Schuler, Michael, Pres.--Zippo Manufacturing Company, Bradford, PA, pg. 1220
Schuler, William P., Pres.--Geo. F. Schuler, Inc., Stockton, CA, pg. 979
Schull, Lee, Pres.--Building Products Inc., Watertown, SD, pg. 188
Schulman, Marc S., Pres.--Eli's Chicago's Finest, Inc., Chicago, IL, pg. 376
Schulte, Donn, Pres. & Chief Exec. Officer--World Computer Corp., Auburn Hills, MI, pg. 1202
Schulte, Fred C., Pres. & Chief Exec. Officer--Elgin National Industries, Inc., Chicago, IL, pg. 609
Schultz, David M., Pres.--Media Logic, Inc., Albany, NY, pg. 734
Schultz, James R., Pres. & Chief Exec. Officer--Great Lakes Lithograph Co., Cleveland, OH, pg. 481
Schultz, William, Pres. & Chief Exec. Officer--Fender Musical Instruments, Scottsdale, AZ, pg. 406
Schulze, Horst, Pres. & Chief Oper. Officer--W.B. Johnson Property, Inc., Atlanta, GA, pg. 598
Schumacher, Donald, Chm. Bd. & Pres.--Schumacher Electric Corporation, Chicago, IL, pg. 979
Schumacher, Donald, Pres. & Chief Exec. Officer--Spurgeon Mercantile Company, Chicago, IL, pg. 1034
Schumacher, Kenneth H., Chm. Bd. & Pres.--Paradata Computer Networks, Inc., Farmington Hills, MI, pg. 847
Schumacher, Larry, Pres.--Schumacher-Dugan Construction, West Chester, OH, pg. 979
Schuman, S. W., Jr., Chm. Bd. & Pres.--West Coast Growers & Packers, Inc., Selma, CA, pg. 1177
Schurr, Karl, Pres.--Minco Products, Inc., Minneapolis, MN, pg. 756
Schurz, Franklin D., Jr., Pres.--Schurz Communications, Inc., South Bend, IN, pg. 979
Schutte, Alden F., Pres. & Chief Exec. Officer--Schutte & Company, Buffalo, NY, pg. 979
Schwab, Samuel C., Pres. & Chief Exec. Officer--S. Schwab Company, Cumberland, MD, pg. 980
Schwabe, Ernest, Pres.--Aerotron, Inc., Raleigh, NC, pg. 22
Schwan, Geoffrey E., Pres.--Double AA Builders, Ltd., Phoenix, AZ, pg. 347
Schwan, Marvin M., Chm. Bd., Pres. & Chief Exec. Officer--Schwan's Sales Enterprises, Marshall, MN, pg. 980
Schwartz, Arthur, Pres.--Schwartz & Benjamin, Inc., New York, NY, pg. 980
Schwartz, Arthur L., Pres.--Parsons & Whittemore Enterprises, Rye Brook, NY, pg. 850
Schwartz, Curtis, Pres.--Hartz Group, New York, NY, pg. 514
Schwartz, Daniel, Pres.--Doe Spun, Inc., New York, NY, pg. 343
Schwartz, David, Pres.--J. C. Brock Corp., Buffalo, NY, pg. 178
Schwartz, Fred W., Pres.--Cable Electric Products, Inc., Providence, RI, pg. 671
Schwartz, Jack, Pres.--Jack Schwartz Shoes, Inc., New York, NY, pg. 980
Schwartz, Joel P., Pres.--Ben Schwartz Market, Inc., Peoria, IL, pg. 980
Schwartz, Kurt, Pres.--Success Advertising, Inc., Livingston, NJ, pg. 243
Schwartz, Larry, Pres.--Standard Shoe Company, Inglewood, CA, pg. 1037
Schwartz, Lou, Pres.--Toy Biz, Inc., New York, NY, pg. 1104
Schwartz, M.I., Pres.--Swivelier Co., Inc., Nanuet, NY, pg. 1068
Schwartz, M.J., Chm. Bd., Pres. & Chief Exec. Officer--Quaker City Motor Parts Company, Middletown, DE, pg. 903
Schwartz, Richard, Pres.--North American Enclosures, Inc., Central Islip, NY, pg. 811
Schwartz, Robert G., Chm. Bd., Pres. & Chief Exec. Officer--Metropolitan Life Insurance Co., New York, NY, pg. 744
Schwartz, Stanley, Pres.--Standard Garment Company, Inc., New York, NY, pg. 1036
Schwartz, Steve, Pres.--Palm Iron & Bridge Works, Inc., Sacramento, CA, pg. 843
Schwartz, William, Pres.--Kern's Bakeries, Incorporated, Knoxville, TN, pg. 624
Schwartz, William C., Pres.--Sheffield Steel Corporation-Joliet, Joliet, IL, pg. 996
Schwartzstein, Daniel, Pres.--Sebastian & Cooke, Parsippany, NJ, pg. 986
Schwartzwalder, Larry, Pres.--Tishman Realty & Construction Co., New York, NY, pg. 1099
Schwedel, Alan R., Pres. & Chief Exec. Officer--Amerbelle Corporation, Rockville, CT, pg. 47
Schweich, H.L., Pres. & Gen. Mgr.--Cerro Copper Products Co., Sauget, IL, pg. 711
Schweiner, Jerry, Chm. Bd., Pres. & Chief Exec. Officer--Benco Industries, Inc., Fort Deposit, AL, pg. 138
Schweizer, Melvin, Chm. Bd. & Pres.--Prairie Farms Dairy, Inc., Carlinville, IL, pg. 884
Schweizer, Paul H., Pres. & Treas.--Schweizer Aircraft Corporation, Elmira, NY, pg. 981
Schwesig, N.L., Pres.--Maritz Inc., Fenton, MO, pg. 707
Schwinn, E.R., Jr., Pres.--Schwinn Bicycle Company, Chicago, IL, pg. 981
Sciame, Frank, Pres., Treas., Chief Exec. & Chief Fin. Officer--F.J. Sciame Construction, New York, NY, pg. 981
Scibelli, R.M., Pres. & Chief Exec. Officer--Yardney Technical Products, Inc., Pawcatuck, CT, pg. 1207
Scopetta, John N., Chm. Bd., Pres. & Chief Exec. Officer--Power Engineering Co. Inc., Coral Gables, FL, pg. 883
Scoppechio, Debbie, Pres., New Bus. Contact & Mktg. Dir.--Creative Alliance, Inc., Louisville, KY, pg. 297
Scordato, Richard E., Pres.--Medical Laboratory Automation, Inc., Pleasantville, NY, pg. 735
Scott, Bruce, Pres.--Cotton Electric Co-Op, Walters, OK, pg. 288
Scott, Daniel T., Pres.--Scott Printing Corporation, Jersey City, NJ, pg. 983
Scott, Harry, Pres. & Chief Exec. Oper.--Corporate Travel Services, Oakland, CA, pg. 287
Scott, Louis, Pres.--Louis Scott Associates, Inc., Rochelle Park, NJ, pg. 982
Scott, Patrick, Pres. & Chief Exec. Officer--Fisher Broadcasting, Inc., Seattle, WA, pg. 415
Scott, Roland, Pres.--Whitney Blake Company of Vermont, Inc., Bellows Falls, VT, pg. 155
Scott, Roland E., Pres. & Treas.--Burt Equipment Company, Inc., Westminster Station, VT, pg. 195
Scott, Ronald F., Pres.--Machining Enterprises Inc., Warren, MI, pg. 696
Scott, Steve, Pres. & Principal--Scott/Lancaster/Hershfield, Los Angeles, CA, pg. 982
Scott, Stuart, Gen. Mgr.--Health Waters, Inc., Hackensack, NJ, pg. 968
Scott, W.G., Pres.-Green Mining--Green Holdings, Inc., Denver, CO, pg. 484
Scott, Walter, Jr., Chm. Bd. & Pres.--Peter Kiewit Sons Inc., Omaha, NE, pg. 629
Scott, William, V.P. & Gen. Mgr.--ABB Environmental Systems, Knoxville, TN, pg. 2
Scotti, Gavin A., Pres. & Chief Exec. Officer--Klemtner Advertising Inc., New York, NY, pg. 635
Scotton, William P., Pres.--Custom Decor, Inc., Dover, DE, pg. 306
Scowby, Ronald S., Pres.--Mutual of America Financial Services Corp., New York, NY, pg. 778

Scriba, Ralph D., Chm. Bd. & Chief Exec. Officer--Swift-Cor Tool Engineering, Gardena, CA, pg. 1067
Scribner, Arnold, Pres. & Chief Exec. Officer--VSI Fasteners, Inc., Stanton, CA, pg. 1142
Scroggins, Louise, Pres.-Chuck Ruhr Advertising--Chuck Ruhr Advertising, Minneapolis, MN, pg. 955
Scully, Dennis, Pres.--Cordley Temprite, Oak Brook, IL, pg. 377
Seaborn, Louis A., Pres.--Potter-Shackelford Construction Co., Greenville, SC, pg. 882
Seabrook, Charles F., II, Pres.--Seabrook Brothers & Sons, Inc., Seabrook, NJ, pg. 984
Seabrook, James H., Jr., Pres. & Chief Exec. Officer--Seabrook Wallcoverings, Inc., Memphis, TN, pg. 984
Seaman, James D., Pres.--Seaman Timber Company, Inc., Montevallo, AL, pg. 986
Seaman, Wayne, Chief Exec. Officer & Gen. Mgr.--West Central Co-op, Ralston, IA, pg. 1176
Searle, George, Pres. & Chief Exec. Officer--IA Construction Corp., Concordville, PA, pg. 558
Seaton, Kenneth M., Chm. Bd., Pres. & Chief Exec. Officer--Family Inns of America, Inc., Pigeon Forge, TN, pg. 398
Seavitt, James, Pres.--Village Ford Inc., Dearborn, MI, pg. 1151
Seay, O. Elwyn, Pres. & Chief Exec. Officer--FM Industries, Inc., Fort Worth, TX, pg. 394
Sebastian, Paul E., Pres. & Chief Fin. Officer--Jockey International, Inc., Kenosha, WI, pg. 595
Sechler, Scott I., Chm. Bd. & Pres.--Farmer's Pride, Inc., Fredericksburg, PA, pg. 401
Secrist, Richard, Chm. Bd., Pres. & Chief Exec. Officer--Blue Tee Corporation, New York, NY, pg. 161
Sedin, Ken, Natl. Sls. Mgr.--Heet Automotive, Westchester, IL, pg. 328
Sedlacek, Mark, Pres.--Prepco, Los Angeles, CA, pg. 887
Sedler, Herbert L., Pres.--Paper Enterprises, Inc., Bronx, NY, pg. 847
Seeger, John, Jr., Pres.--Dayton Rogers Mfg. Co., Minneapolis, MN, pg. 321
Seeland, Allen R., Pres.--C. S. Johnson Co., Champaign, IL, pg. 597
Seelert, Robert, Pres. & Chief Exec. Officer--Kayser-Roth Hosiery, Inc., Greensboro, NC, pg. 262
Seeley, Raynor, M., Pres.--PTA Corporation, Oxford, CT, pg. 837
Seessel, Arthur N., III, Pres.--Seessel Holdings, Inc., Memphis, TN, pg. 987
Segal, George, Pres.--Automotive Supply Assoc., Inc., Concord, NH, pg. 101
Segal, Gordon I., Pres. & Chief Exec. Officer--Euromarket Designs, Inc., Northbrook, IL, pg. 390
Segal, John, Pres.--North American Products Corp., Jasper, IN, pg. 811
Segal, Myron, Chm. Bd., Pres. & Chief Exec. Officer--Premier Mill Corp., New York, NY, pg. 887
Segal, Philip L., Pres.--American Snacks, Inc., Chelsea, MA, pg. 61
Segal, Steven F., Pres.--Sigallo, Ltd., New York, NY, pg. 1003
Segall, Samson, Chm. Bd., Pres. & Treas.--Sharon-Jay Togs, Inc., New Bedford, MA, pg. 995
Segars, Donald, Pres.--Reilly-Whiteman Inc., Conshohocken, PA, pg. 222
Segerdahl, Earl E., Chm. Bd. & Pres.--The Segerdahl Corp., Wheeling, IL, pg. 987
Seibel, Monroe, Pres.--Seibel & Stern Corp., New York, NY, pg. 987
Seibert, Fred, Pres.--Hanna-Barbera Productions, Inc., Los Angeles, CA, pg. 53
Seid, Steven, Partner & Dir. Opers.--Goldberg Fossa Seid Advertising, Inc., New York, NY, pg. 465
Seidman, Theodore M., Chm. Bd. & Pres.--Air Conditioning Co., Inc., Glendale, CA, pg. 26
Seigle, Harry J., Pres.--Seigle's Home & Building Centers, Elgin, IL, pg. 987
Seimer, Arnold B., Pres.--Sycon Corporation, Marion, OH, pg. 1069
Seitz, Melvin C., Jr., Pres., Chief Exec. Officer, Chief Oper. Officer & Controller--Service Supply Co. Inc. of Indiana, Indianapolis, IN, pg. 992
Selders, Wim, H.J., Pres. & Chief Exec. Officer--Ortel Corporation, Alhambra, CA, pg. 830
Seldin, Marc A., Pres.--Miss Elaine Inc., Saint Louis, MO, pg. 760
Seldomridge, Mark, Pres.--Cenvill Development Corp., West Palm Beach, FL, pg. 235
Self, W.M., Pres. & Chief Oper. Officer--Greenwood Mills, Inc., Greenwood, SC, pg. 485
Selig, T., Pres.--BLH Electronics, Canton, MA, pg. 107
Seligman, Scott J., Pres.--Seligman & Associates, Inc., Bloomfield Hills, MI, pg. 988
Sellers, Robert B., Pres.--Bob Sellers Pontiac GMC Truck Inc., Farmington Hills, MI, pg. 988
Sellers, Thomas D., Pres.--Dean Sellers Ford Inc., Troy, MI, pg. 988
Sellstrom, Barbara M., Pres.--Sellstrom Manufacturing Co., Palatine, IL, pg. 988
Selness, Wayne P., Pres.--Strouds, City of Industry, CA, pg. 1054
Selover, George H., Pres.--Selover Buick, Inc., Billings, MT, pg. 988
Seltzer, Edwin C., Chm. Bd. & Pres.--Roller Derby Skate Company, Litchfield, IL, pg. 944
Seltzer, Samuel M., Chm. Bd. & Pres.--Allison Corporation, Livingston, NJ, pg. 40
Selzer, William H., Pres. & Chief Exec. Officer--Cox Hobbies, Inc., Corona, CA, pg. 294
Semler, Jerry D., Chm. Bd., Pres. & Chief Exec. Officer--American United Life Insurance Company, Indianapolis, IN, pg. 65
Semmelhack, John L., Pres.--Hammacher, Schlemmer & Co., Inc., Chicago, IL, pg. 503
Semon, Joseph R., Pres.--Casket Shells, Inc., Eynon, PA, pg. 228
Sennell, Mike, Pres. & Chief Exec. Officer--Air Jamaica Ltd., Miami, FL, pg. 27
Senty, James A., Chm. Bd. & Pres.--Consolidated Midwest, Inc., La Crosse, WI, pg. 277
Senty, James A., Chm. Bd. & Pres.--Midwest Bottle Gas Company, La Crosse, WI, pg. 277
Sepanik, Edward, Pres.--Jackes-Evans Mfg. Co., Saint Louis, MO, pg. 587
Seppala, Samuel R., Pres. & Chief Exec. Officer--Seppala & AHO Construction Company, New Ipswich, NH, pg. 990
Sergerdahl, Anders, Pres.--Albert Trostel & Sons Company, Milwaukee, WI, pg. 1116
Serino, Matthew, Pres.--Serino Coyne Inc., New York, NY, pg. 991
Serio, Jay B., Pres. & New Bus. Contact--Joiner Rowland Serio Koeppel, Dallas, TX, pg. 602
Serls, David, Pres.--Colonial Metals Co., Columbia, PA, pg. 263
Serrano, Isadoro, Gen Mgr.--Comunica Leo Burnett, Guatemala City,, Guatemala, pg. 192
SerVaas, Beurt, Chm. Bd. & Pres.--The Curtis Publishing Company, Indianapolis, IN, pg. 306
Servaas, Beurt, Chm. Bd. & Pres.--Servaas, Inc., Indianapolis, IN, pg. 991
SerVaas, Cory, M.D., Chm. Bd., Pres. & Chief Exec. Officer--Benjamin Franklin Literary & Medical Society, Inc., Indianapolis, IN, pg. 139
SerVaas, Cory, M.D., Pres. & Chief Exec. Officer--The Saturday Evening Post Society, Indianapolis, IN, pg. 139
Settles, Tom, Pres. --Power Contracting & Engineering Corp., Rolling Meadows, IL, pg. 883
Setzer, G.C., Partner--Setzer Forest Products, Sacramento, CA, pg. 993
Setzer, Leonard, Pres. & Chief Exec. Officer--National Merchandise Co., Inc., Jacksonville, FL, pg. 792
Seuss, C. David, Chm., Pres., Chief Exec. Officer & Treas.--Spinnaker Software Corporation, Cambridge, MA, pg. 1031
Severe, John, Pres. & Gen. Mgr.--Western Grain, Inc., Wichita, KS, pg. 1179
Severson, R.H., Pres.--Kent Feeds Inc., Muscatine, IA, pg. 1146
Sevier, Helen, Chm. Bd., Pres., Chief Exec. & Chief Oper. Officer--B.A.S.S., Inc., Montgomery, AL, pg. 105
Seward, John E., Jr., Pres. & Chief Exec. Officer--The Paty Company, Piney Flats, TN, pg. 852
Sewell, Chris, Pres.--Lithotype Company, Inc., South San Francisco, CA, pg. 678
Sexhus, Dennis, Pres.--Peabody Myers Corp., Streator, IL, pg. 900
Sexton, Edward W., Jr., Pres. & Chief Exec. Officer--Sexton Can Co., Inc., Cambridge, MA, pg. 993
Shackelford, Craig, Pres. & Chief Exec. Officer--Wilson Pugh Inc., Portland, AR, pg. 1194
Shacklett, James, III, Chief Exec. Officer--National Label Company, Lafayette Hill, PA, pg. 791
Shade, Tom, Pres. & Chief Exec. Officer--Moorman Mfg. Company, Quincy, IL, pg. 769
Shafer, Byron A., Pres. & Chief Exec. Officer--Shafer Commercial Seating Inc., Denver, CO, pg. 994
Shafer, Ernst S., Pres., Chief Exec., Chief Oper. & Chief Fin. Officer--Smith-Shafer Oil Co., Rockford, IL, pg. 1014
Shafer, Gary, Pres. & Chief Exec. Officer--Trammell Crow Company, Dallas, TX, pg. 1106
Shaffer, David N., Co-Pres.--Just Born, Inc., Bethlehem, PA, pg. 610
Shaffer, David N., Co-Pres.--Just Born, Inc., Bethlehem, PA, pg. 610
Shaffer, James B., Pres. & Chief Exec. Officer--Guy Gannett Publishing Company, Portland, ME, pg. 442
Shaffer, Martin M., Pres.--Tru-Weld Grating, Inc., Wexford, PA, pg. 1117
Shaffer, Michael L., Pres.-U.S. Van Lines Transportation Group--Atlas Van Lines, Inc., Evansville, IN, pg. 96
Shafler, R. Scott, Pres.--Cortec Group, New York, NY, pg. 287
Shafto, Robert A., Pres. & Chief Exec. Officer--The New England, Boston, MA, pg. 799
Shah, Harry, Pres.--National Food Stores, Inc. T/A Krauszer's, Edison, NJ, pg. 788
Shah, Satish, Pres. & Chief Exec. Officer--Accra Pac Group, Elkhart, IN, pg. 11
Shaheen, George T., Mng. Partner--Andersen Consulting, Chicago, IL, pg. 72
Shaker, Anthony I., Pres.--Balco, Inc. (MA), Boston, MA, pg. 115
Shaker, Joseph G., Pres.--Shaker Advertising Agency, Oak Park, IL, pg. 994
Shames, Sidney J., Chm. Bd., Pres., CEO, COO, CFO & Treas.--Melard Manufacturing Corporation, Passaic, NJ, pg. 737
Shanahan, James P., Pres. & Chief Exec. Officer--Kranco, Inc., Houston, TX, pg. 643
Shanbar, Donald M., Partner--The Haughey Group, Inc., Boston, MA, pg. 517
Shand, Robert, Partner--Rice/Spector Inc., Venice, CA, pg. 931
Shaneour, Dwight C., Jr., Chm. Bd., Pres. & Chief Exec. Officer--The Shane Group Inc., Hillsdale, MI, pg. 995
Shank, Glen L., Pres., Chief Exec. & Oper. Officer--Duckwall-Alco Stores, Inc., Abilene, KS, pg. 351
Shankar, R. Sam, Pres.--Tork, Inc., Mount Vernon, NY, pg. 1102
Shanks, Donald K., Pres. & Chief Oper. Officer--Unigard Security Insurance Co., Bellevue, WA, pg. 596
Shanks, L.E., Pres.--The Double-Cola Company, Chattanooga, TN, pg. 347
Shannahan, Tim, Pres. & Chief Exec. Officer--Video Products Distributors, Inc., Sacramento, CA, pg. 1150
Shapell, Nathan, Chm. Bd., Pres. & Chief Exec. Officer--Shapell Industries, Inc., Beverly Hills, CA, pg. 995
Shapero, J., Chm. Bd., Pres. & Chief Exec. Officer--Quael Corp., Detroit, MI, pg. 902
Shapiro, Albert, Pres.--Commander Oil Corporation, Oyster Bay, NY, pg. 268
Shapiro, Leonard, Pres.--Shapco, Inc., Van Nuys, CA, pg. 995
Shapiro, Leonard, Pres.--Kelly Pipe Div., Van Nuys, CA, pg. 995
Shapiro, Mark, Pres. & New Bus. Contact--Louis London Advertising & Sales Promotion, Saint Louis, MO, pg. 684
Shapiro, Richard B., Chm. Bd., Pres. & Chief Exec. Officer--Charles River Data Systems, Inc., Framingham, MA, pg. 240
Shapiro, Thomas J., Pres.--Wayne Steel, Inc., Wooster, OH, pg. 1169
Shapson, Edward M., Pres., Pub. Rels. & New Bus. Contact--Shapson Gero & Sommers, Inc., Philadelphia, PA, pg. 995
Sharbel, Patrick, Pres. & Chief Exec. Officer--Humboldt Express, Inc., Nashville, TN, pg. 552
Share, Harvey, Pres. & Chief Exec. Officer--Bobst Group Inc., Roseland, NJ, pg. 161
Sharif, Yazan N., Pres.--INDRESCO, Inc., Dallas, TX, pg. 565
Sharp, David L., Pres.--Sharp Hartwig, Inc., Seattle, WA, pg. 995
Sharp, David L., Pres. & Chief Oper. Officer--Standun, Inc., Irwindale, CA, pg. 1038
Sharp, Gene, Pres. & Chief Exec. Officer--Affiliated Food Stores, Keller, TX, pg. 23
Sharp, Jack B., Pres.--Sharp Oil Company, Anthony, NM, pg. 995
Sharp, Joe, Pres.--Evergreen International Aviation, Inc., McMinnville, OR, pg. 392
Sharp, Joe, Pres.--Fairfield Electric Co-op, Winnsboro, SC, pg. 397
Sharp, Lemuel, III, Pres.--W.G. Mills, Inc., Sarasota, FL, pg. 756
Sharp, M.B., Pres.--Bush Development Corp., Williamsburg, VA, pg. 196
Sharp, Sharon, Exec. Dir.--California State Lottery, Sacramento, CA, pg. 210
Sharpe, Jack, Pres.--King Group, Inc., Fenton, MI, pg. 630
Shaughnessy, William J., Pres. & Chief Exec. Officer--Wilbur Chocolate Co., Inc., Lititz, PA, pg. 219
Shaw, Bill, Chief Exec. Officer--Earl May Seed & Nursery L.P., Shenandoah, IA, pg. 724
Shaw, James C., Pres.--Spirol International Corp., Danielson, CT, pg. 1031
Shaw, James C., Pres.--C.E.M. Div. Spirol Intl. Corp., Danielson, CT, pg. 1031
Shaw, Morris, Pres. & Gen. Mgr.--Shaw Creations, Inc., New York, NY, pg. 996
Shaw, Robert, Pres.--International Jensen Inc., Lincolnshire, IL, pg. 578
Shaw, Robert, Pres.--Spirit Cruises, Norfolk, VA, pg. 1031
Shaw, Robert A., Chm. Bd. & Pres.--Allied Plywood Corp., Alexandria, VA, pg. 38
Shaw, Ronald W., Pres. & Chief Exec. Officer--Cives Corp., Roswell, GA, pg. 251
Shaw, William H., Pres. & Chief Exec. Officer--United Foam Plastics Corporation, Georgetown, MA, pg. 1132
Shaykin, Leonard, Mng. Partner--Adler & Shaykin, New York, NY, pg. 17
Shea, Michael D., Pres.--Standard Gravure Corp./Shea Communications, Atlanta, GA, pg. 1036
Shea, Peter, Chief Oper. Officer--John Morrell & Co., Cincinnati, OH, pg. 54
Shea, William E., Pres.--Ames Safety Envelope Company, Inc., Somerville, MA, pg. 66
Shea, William E., Pres.--Ames Color File Division, Somerville, MA, pg. 66
Shearer, Jeff, Pres. & Chief Oper. Officer--Boston Chicken, Inc., Naperville, IL, pg. 167
Shearer, Jonathan, Pres.--Paine Furniture Co., Norwood, MA, pg. 843
Shearer, Martin P., Pres. & Chief Exec. Officer--Southern Belle Dairy Company, Inc., Somerset, KY, pg. 1020
Shearman, William H., Pres.--Shearman Corporation, Lake Charles, LA, pg. 996
Sheckell, Frank N., Jr., Pres.--Chivas Products Ltd., Sterling Heights, MI, pg. 248
Sheedan, Dan, Pres.--Ferguson Manufacturing & Equipment Company, Dallas, TX, pg. 406
Sheehan, David F., Mng. Partner & Chief Exec. Officer--Eire Partners, Inc., Chicago, IL, pg. 372
Sheehan, Dennis W., Chm. Bd., Pres. & Chief Exec. Officer--AXIA Incorporated, Oak Brook, IL, pg. 8
Sheehan, William J., Pres. & Chief Exec. Officer--Omni Hotels, Hampton, NH, pg. 826
Sheerr, Richard C., Chm. Bd., Pres & Chief Exec. Officer--Crown Textile Company, Blue Bell, PA, pg. 302
Sheets, Walter G., Pres. & Chief Exec. Officer--Rapid Industries, Inc., Louisville, KY, pg. 913
Sheffield, John W., Jr., Pres.--Sheffield Hardware Company, Americus, GA, pg. 996
Sheik, S.J., Jr., Pres.--Ochoco Lumber Company, Prineville, OR, pg. 821
Sheinbaum, Uri, Chm. Bd & Pres.--Calmark Investment Company, Los Angeles, CA, pg. 211
Shelby, David T., Pres.--ICM Industries, Inc., Chicago, IL, pg. 559
Sheldon, J.M., Chm. Bd., Pres. & Chief Exec. Officer--Sheldons' Inc., Antigo, WI, pg. 996
Shelford, John, Gen. Mgr.--Michigan Blueberry Growers Assn., Grand Junction, MI, pg. 747
Shellenbarger, David, Chm. Bd. & Pres.--Macro Computer Products Inc., Rochester Hills, MI, pg. 698
Shelton, John, Pres.--Texas Olefins Co., Houston, TX, pg. 1089
Shelton, Phillip, Chm. Bd & Pres.--Sunclipse, Inc., Montebello, CA, pg. 1059
Shelton, Thomas R., Pres.--Case Foods, Inc., Salisbury, MD, pg. 227
Shepard, D. C., Chm. Bd.--Menasha Corporation, Neenah, WI, pg. 738

Corporate Responsibilities Index

Shepherd, Jeff, Pres. & Chief Exec. Officer--Pic'n Pay Stores, Inc., Charlotte, NC, pg. 201
Shepherd, Donald R., Chm. Bd. & Chief Exec. Officer--Loomis, Sayles & Co., Boston, MA, pg. 799
Shepherd, J. Harold, Chief Exec. Officer--Shepherd Construction Co., Inc., Atlanta, GA, pg. 998
Shepherd, R. Craig, V.P.--Transamerican Refining Corporation, Houston, TX, pg. 1106
Shepherd, Thomas R., Chm. Bd.--Diet Center, Inc., Pittsburgh, PA, pg. 55
Sheppard, Tom, Pres.--Fischer Lime & Cement Company, Memphis, TN, pg. 414
Sheridan, Edward J., Pres. & Chief Exec. Officer--Edwin B. Stimpson Company, Inc., Bayport, NY, pg. 1049
Sheridan, R. Champlin, Chm. Bd. & Chief Exec. Officer--The Sheridan Group, Hanover, PA, pg. 998
Sherman, Floyd, Pres. & Chief Oper. Officer--Triangle Pacific Corporation, Dallas, TX, pg. 1112
Sherman, Floyd, Pres.--Bruce Hardwood Floors, Dallas, TX, pg. 1112
Sherman, Floyd, Pres.--IXL Furniture, Dallas, TX, pg. 1112
Sherman, Larry, Pres.--Lombard Lincoln-Mercury & Leasing, Inc., Lombard, IL, pg. 681
Sherman, Malcolm, Pres. & Chief Exec. Officer--Morse Shoe, Inc., Canton, MA, pg. 772
Sherrer, Robert, Pres.--Tom James Company, Arlington, TX, pg. 589
Sherry, Steve, Pres.--Wilson, Horne, McClelland & Gray, Inc., Atlanta, GA, pg. 1193
Sherwood, Lew, Pres. & Creative Dir.--Sherwood & Schneider Advertising, New York, NY, pg. 999
Sherwood, Steven, Pres.--Clayton, Williams & Sherwood, Inc., Newport Beach, CA, pg. 254
Shevack, Brett, Pres. & Chief Exec. Officer--Partners & Shevack, Inc., New York, NY, pg. 850
Shewmake, C. B., Jr., Pres.--Algernon Blair International, Montgomery, AL, pg. 155
Shidler, Jay, Pres. & Mng. Partner--The Shidler Group, San Francisco, CA, pg. 999
Shidler, Jay, Pres.--REMark Advertising, Honolulu, HI, pg. 999
Shields, Gerald N., Chm. Bd., Pres. & Chief Exec. Officer--Graymills Corp., Chicago, IL, pg. 480
Shields, John, Pres. & Chief Exec. Officer--TACT Holding, South Pasadena, CA, pg. 1076
Shiffman, Milton S., Pres. & Chief Exec. Officer--Shiffman/Fergusson/Stone Advertising Inc., Fort Lee, NJ, pg. 999
Shillestad, John G., Chm. Bd., Pres. & Chief Exec. Officer--Columbian Mutual Life Insurance Co., Binghamton, NY, pg. 266
Shillman, Norman, Pres.--Shillcraft, Inc., Baltimore, MD, pg. 999
Shilvock, Ray J., Chm. Bd.--Graham Paint and Varnish Company, Chicago, IL, pg. 475
Shine, Joel, Pres.--First Financial Group, Inc., Encino, CA, pg. 413
Shine, Sam M., Pres.--Samtec Inc., New Albany, IN, pg. 968
Shinn, Lyle B., Jr., Pres.--Chicago Lock Company, Chicago, IL, pg. 245
Shipley, William S. II, Chm. Bd., Pres. & Chief Exec. Officer--Shipley Oil Company, York, PA, pg. 999
Shiragao, Shiro F., Chm. Bd., Pres. & Chief Exec. Officer--T C Manufacturing Company, Inc., Evanston, IL, pg. 1072
Shirahata, Ko, Pres.--Pentax Precision Instruments Corp., Orangeburg, NY, pg. 859
Shirazi, Mehdi, Pres. & Chief Exec. Officer--Sigman Meat Co. Inc., Arvada, CO, pg. 1003
Shirk, James A., Pres.--Beer Nuts, Inc., Bloomington, IL, pg. 132
Shivley, John T., Pres.--Nana Development Corporation, Katzebue, AK, pg. 783
Shlomm, Boris, Pres. & Chief Exec. Officer--Amicale Industries, Inc., New York, NY, pg. 66
Shlossman, Arthur, Pres. & Chief Exec. Officer--Jersey Printing Company, Inc., Bayonne, NJ, pg. 593
Shmina, Arthur, Pres.--Shmina Construction, Inc., Livonia, MI, pg. 124
Shoaff, Victor, Dir.-Sls. & Mktg.--Magnetrol International, Downers Grove, IL, pg. 701
Shobanjo, Abiodun O., Mng. Dir.--Insight Communications Ltd., Lagos,, Nigeria, pg. 111
Shoen, E.J., Chm. Bd. & Pres.--Amerco, A Nevada Corporation, Reno, NV, pg. 47
Shondeck, David O., Pres.--Oberg Industries Co., Freeport, PA, pg. 819
Shor, Charles, Pres.--Duro Paper Bag Manufacturing Co., Ludlow, KY, pg. 355
Shore, Lawrence A., Pres.--Lawrence Group, Inc., Schenectady, NY, pg. 662
Shore, Lawrence A., Pres. & Chief Exec. Officer--United Republic Reinsurance Company, Houston, TX, pg. 662
Shore, Lawrence A., Pres.--Lawrence Management Group, Inc., Albany, NY, pg. 662
Short, Sandy, Mng. Dir.--Young & Rubicam New Zealand Ltd., Auckland,, New Zealand, pg. 1214
Shostack, G. Lynn, Chm. Bd. & Pres.--Joyce International, Inc., New York, NY, pg. 608
Shoulders, Barry, Pres. & Chief Exec. Officer--The Kartridg Pak Co., Davenport, IA, pg. 617
Shoulders, Barry W., Pres.--Kartridg Pak Co., Davenport, IA, pg. 122
Shoulders, Warren E., Pres.--Heat Controller, Inc., Jackson, MI, pg. 524
Shouldis, George, V.P.-Opers. & Fin.--Dri-Print Foils, Rahway, NJ, pg. 349
Shoushaniao, H., Pres.--Technic Incorporated, Cranston, RI, pg. 1083
Shoushaniao, H., Pres.--Technic Incorporated-Equipment Div., Pawtucket, RI, pg. 1083
Shuford, A. Pope, Pres. & Chief Exec. Officer--Shuford Mills, Inc., Hickory, NC, pg. 1001
Shuford, Harley F., Jr., Pres.--Century Furniture Industries, Hickory, NC, pg. 235
Shuford, Jim, Pres.--Bowen Brothers Fruit Co., Inc., Winter Haven, FL, pg. 169
Shukle, Janice, Pres.--Harris Advertising, Inc., Ann Arbor, MI, pg. 511
Shull, P. Doug, Pres.--Transmet Corporation, Columbus, OH, pg. 1107
Shulman, Mark, Pres.--Bon Jour International Ltd., New York, NY, pg. 164
Shultz, Gerald, Chm. Bd., Pres. & Chief Exec. Officer--Micro-Met L Corp., Indianapolis, IN, pg. 748
Shultz, Gordon W., Pres.--Schultz Steel Company, South Gate, CA, pg. 979
Shum, Vivian, Mng. Dir.--HHCC International, Inc., Wanchai,, Hong Kong, pg. 534
Shuman, Willard E., Pres. & Chief Oper. Officer--Insurance Corp. of America, Houston, TX, pg. 572
Shura, Richard, Pres.--Central States Enterprises, Inc., Heathrow, FL, pg. 234
Shure, Daniel B., Pres.--Strombecker Corporation, Chicago, IL, pg. 1054
Shurman, John, Pres.--Beverage Canners International Corp., Miami, FL, pg. 148
Shuster, George, Pres.--Cranston Print Works Company, Cranston, RI, pg. 296
Siano, Jerry J., Chm. & Chief Exec. Officer--N W Ayer Incorporated, New York, NY, pg. 103
Sibley, Earl A., Chm. Bd. & Pres.--Shannon & Wilson, Inc., Seattle, WA, pg. 995
Sibley, S. Dan, Pres. & Gen. Mgr.--Glen Raven Mills, Inc., Glen Raven, NC, pg. 461
Sicola, Tom, Chm. Bd., Pres. & New Bus. Contact--Sicola Martin Koons Frank, Inc., Austin, TX, pg. 1001
Sidrane, Michelle, Pres.--Crown Publishers, Inc., New York, NY, pg. 20
Siebel, Gretchen, Pres., Chief Oper. Officer--Siebel/Mohr, Inc., New York, NY, pg. 1002
Siebenthal, Paul, Pres.--Associated Grocers of Alabama, Inc., Birmingham, AL, pg. 90
Siegal, Michael D., Pres. & Chief Exec. & Chief Oper. Officer--Olympic Steel Inc., Bedford Heights, OH, pg. 825
Siegel, Gary M., Pres.--Lawler-Havens Inc., Cleveland, OH, pg. 661
Siegel, Mace, Pres.--The Macerich Co., Santa Monica, CA, pg. 696
Siegel, Martin D., Pres.--Siegel Corp., Fort Worth, TX, pg. 1002
Siegel, Martin D., Pres.--Legis Corporation, Ft. Worth, TX, pg. 1002
Siegel, Scott, Pres.--R.S. Owens, Chicago, IL, pg. 834
Siemer, A.B., Pres.--Air-O-Matic Power Steer Co., Marion, OH, pg. 1069
Siemer, Al, Pres.--Bellofram Corp., Newell, WV, pg. 136
Siemer, Arnold B., Chm. Bd. & Pres.--Desco Corporation, Columbus, OH, pg. 332
Siemer, Richard C., Pres.--Siemer Milling Company, Teutopolis, IL, pg. 1002
Siemer, Richard C., Pres.--Hodgson Mill, Inc., Gainesville, MO, pg. 1002
Sierra, Antonio M., Pres.--Business Mens Insurance Corporation, Miami, FL, pg. 196
Siess, Robert D., P.E., Pres. & Chief Oper. Officer--Tarlton Corporation, Saint Louis, MO, pg. 1079
Sietsema, Doug, Pres. & Chief Exec. Officer--Kolesar & Hartwell Inc., Minneapolis, MN, pg. 641
Sigel, Arthur R., Chm. Bd., Pres. & Chief Exec. Officer--Velsicol Chemical Corporation, Rosemont, IL, pg. 1147
Silberstein, Bruce Jay, Pres.--Columbus Pipe & Equipment Company, Columbus, OH, pg. 267
Silbey, S. Dan, Pres. & Gen. Mgr.--Glen Raven Mills, Inc.-Park Ave. Finishing Division, Glen Raven, NC, pg. 461
Siler, J.G., Pres.--Underground Construction Company, Inc., Benicia, CA, pg. 1125
Silk, Steven, Chief Exec. Officer--The Estee Corporation, Parsippany, NJ, pg. 389
Sill, Mitchell J., Pres.--Road Machinery & Supplies Co., Savage, MN, pg. 937
Silva, Gil, Pres.--J. A. Sexauer, Scarsdale, NY, pg. 357
Silver, Bertram R., Pres.--Jenkins Spirits Corp. Ltd., Londonderry, NH, pg. 592
Silver, Cary, Pres.--Silver's Inc., Detroit, MI, pg. 1005
Silver, J. Leonard, Chm. Bd., Pres. & Personnel Training & Devel.--Hoffritz for Cutlery, New York, NY, pg. 538
Silver, Martin, Pres., Chief Fin. Officer & Treas.--Star Liquor Dealers, Syosset, NY, pg. 1039
Silver, R. Phillip, Pres.--Silgan Corporation, Stamford, CT, pg. 1004
Silverberg, H. Gene, Pres.--Bigsby & Kruthers, Inc., Chicago, IL, pg. 150
Silverman, A.A., Chm. Bd., Pres. & Chief Exec. Officer--Vilter Manufacturing Corporation, Milwaukee, WI, pg. 1152
Silverman, Barry, Pres.--Ranir Corporation, Grand Rapids, MI, pg. 912
Silverman, Bruce, Pres. & New Bus. Contact--Asher/Gould Advertising, Inc., Los Angeles, CA, pg. 88
Silverman, Bruce, Pres. & New Business Contact--Media Buyers, Inc., Los Angeles, CA, pg. 88
Silverman, Michael D., Pres.--The Jaydor Corporation, Millburn, NJ, pg. 591
Silverman, Morris J., Pres.--Silverman Products & Textiles, New York, NY, pg. 1004
Silverstein, Elaine, Pres.--Beber Silverstein & Partners, Inc., Miami, FL, pg. 130
Silverstone, Bruce T., Pres. & Creative Dir.--Silverstone, Adkins & Breit, Inc., Stratford, CT, pg. 1005
Simeus, Dumas M., Pres. & Chief Oper. Officer--TLC Beatrice International Holdings Inc., New York, NY, pg. 1073
Simkins, L.J., Chm. Bd., Pres., Chief Exec. & Chief Oper. Officer--Simkins Industries, Inc., New Haven, CT, pg. 1005
Simmons, A.R., Pres.--Pipe Fabricating & Supply Company, Santa Fe Springs, CA, pg. 872
Simmons, D. Ramsay, Jr., Pres.--Elberta Crate & Box Company, Bainbridge, GA, pg. 372
Simmons, E.C., III, Pres., New Bus. Contact & Creative Dir.--Simmons, Durham & Associates, Saint Louis, MO, pg. 1005
Simmons, Edward M., Pres.--McIlhenny Company, Avery Island, LA, pg. 729
Simmons, Edward M., Chm. Bd. & Pres.--B. F. Trappey's Sons, Inc., New Iberia, LA, pg. 729
Simmons, Hardwick, Pres. & Chief Exec. Officer--Prudential Securities Inc., New York, NY, pg. 897
Simmons, Harold C., Chm. Bd., Pres. & Chief Exec. Officer--Contran Corporation, Dallas, TX, pg. 281
Simmons, Robert, Pres.--Atlas Power Equipment Company, Harvard, IL, pg. 96
Simon, Alan D., Chm. Bd. & Pres.--Omaha Steaks International, Omaha, NE, pg. 825
Simon, David A., Pres. & Chief Exec. Officer--Prime Hospitality Corp., Fairfield, NJ, pg. 889
Simon, Donald R., Chm. Bd., Pres. & Treas.--Contractors Steel Company, Livonia, MI, pg. 280
Simon, Donald S., Jr., Pres.--Serta Mattress Company, Vacaville, CA, pg. 991
Simon, Edward, Pres.--Eagle Button Co., Inc., Carlstadt, NJ, pg. 362
Simon, Ernie, Pres.--Ann Raskas Gourmet Confectioners, Edwardsville, KS, pg. 913
Simon, Frederick J., Chm. Bd. & Pres.--Omaha Creative Group, Omaha, NE, pg. 825
Simon, Joseph A., Sr., Chm. Bd., Pres. & Chief Exec. Officer--U.S. Manufacturing Corp., Roseville, MI, pg. 1136
Simon, Paul S., Pres. & Chief Fin. Officer--Morris Corporation, Augusta, GA, pg. 999
Simon, Peter, Pres. & Chief Exec. Officer--Simon & Associates, New Providence, NJ, pg. 1006
Simon, Phillip, Pres.--Joseph Simon & Sons, Inc., Tacoma, WA, pg. 1006
Simon, Ralph, Dr., Pres.--Quality Technologies Corporation, Sunnyvale, CA, pg. 904
Simon, Sidney, Pres.--Direct Marketing Group, Taylor, MI, pg. 879
Simone, James, Jr., Pres.--Ideal Forging Corporation, Southington, CT, pg. 562
Simons, Carl, Pres.--Gateway Apparel, Inc., Saint Louis, MO, pg. 445
Simons, James W., Pres.--Mersman Furniture, Celina, OH, pg. 741
Simpkins, Joe, Chm. Bd. & Chief Exec. Officer--Tiffany Industries, Inc., Saint Louis, MO, pg. 1097
Simpson, Jack, Chief Exec. Officer--Advance Seed Co., Fulton, KY, pg. 407
Simpson, Jack, Pres.--Perry Brothers, Inc., Lufkin, TX, pg. 862
Simpson, John, Pres. & Chief Exec. Officer--H. E. Sargent, Inc., Stillwater, ME, pg. 971
Simpson, Mike, Pres.--Carlson Retail Marketing, Minneapolis, MN, pg. 221
Simpson, William H., Pres., Pfaltzgraff Group--The Pfaltzgraff Co., York, PA, pg. 1065
Sims, R. Sanderson, Pres.--Peck Sims Mueller, Inc., Honolulu, HI, pg. 854
Simunek, Tom, Pres.--Meehan Tooker, East Rutherford, NJ, pg. 736
Sinanis, John, Pres. & Chief Exec. Officer--Hermes Automotive Manufacturing Corp., Detroit, MI, pg. 531
Sinclair, Robert J., Pres.--Sinclair Printing & Litho, Inc., Los Angeles, CA, pg. 1008
Sinclair, Stephen, Pres. & Chief Exec. Officer--Orix Real Estate Equities, Inc., Chicago, IL, pg. 829
Singer, Bernice, Pres.--Merchants Rent A Car, Inc., Hooksett, NH, pg. 739
Singer, Elliott, Pres.--Fox-Knapp Inc., New York, NY, pg. 427
Singer, Jerome, Pres.--Aetna Industries, Inc., Center Line, MI, pg. 23
Singer, Martin, Pres. & Chief Oper. Officer--Singers Supermarkets, Inc., North Bergen, NJ, pg. 1008
Singh, Ranjit, Pres.--Singh Industries, Cedar Knolls, NJ, pg. 1008
Sink, B. Vaughn, Pres.--Sullivan Higdon & Sink Incorporated, Wichita, KS, pg. 1056
Sink, Kenneth W., Pres. & Treas.--Traders Supermarkets, Inc., Berrien Springs, MI, pg. 1105
Sinnott, Walter B., Pres.--Hazen & Sawyer, New York, NY, pg. 520
Siragusa, Ross D., Jr., Pres.--Game Time, Inc., Fort Payne, AL, pg. 442
Sirotek, H. Bruce, Pres.--Illinois Auto Electric Co., Elmhurst, IL, pg. 562
Sirotkin, Paul, Pres.--Rapid Industrial Plastics Company, Jersey City, NJ, pg. 913
Sista, Shambhu V., Mng. Dir.--Sista's Private Limited, Bombay, India, pg. 112
Sitarz, Richard, Pres.--Prospect Foundry, Inc., Minneapolis, MN, pg. 895
Siteman, Alvin, Pres.--Site Oil Co. of Missouri, Clayton, MO, pg. 1009
Sitt, Eddie, Pres.--Baby Togs, Inc., New York, NY, pg. 107
Sivalls, C. Richard, Pres. & Chief Exec. Officer--Sivalls, Inc., Odessa, TX, pg. 1009
Sizemore, Mason, Pres. & Chief Oper. Officer--Seattle Times Company, Seattle, WA, pg. 986
Sjogren, Wade R., Pres.--Whibco, Inc., Leesburg, NJ, pg. 1185
Skagen, Jim, Pres.--Gordon Sign Company, Denver, CO, pg. 472
Skaggs, Gary, Pres.--Antenna Products Corp., Mineral Wells, TX, pg. 76
Skaggs, James B., Chm. Bd., Pres. & Chief Exec. Officer--Tracor, Inc., Austin, TX, pg. 1104
Skase, Christopher C., Chm. Bd.--Princeville Corporation, Princeville, HI, pg. 890

Skawski, Robert, Pres.--Motek Engineering & Manufacturing Company, Cambridge, MN, pg. 773
Skeates, William B., Pres.--Naylor Pipe Company, Chicago, IL, pg. 796
Skelley, John, Pres.--Arizona Grains Inc., Casa Grande, AZ, pg. 82
Skiles, ALlan, Pres.--The Office of Lee Kendrick, Fairfax, VA, pg. 334
Sklar, Irwin B., Chm. Bd.--Robert F. Driver Co., Inc., San Diego, CA, pg. 349
Skocypec, Russell, V.P. & Gen. Mgr.--Vacudyne Inc., Chicago Heights, IL, pg. 45
Slabe, James F., Pres. & Chief Oper. Officer--Executive Enterprises, Inc., New York, NY, pg. 393
Slane, John C., Pres.--Slane Hosiery Mills, Inc., High Point, NC, pg. 1010
Slater, Clifford D., Pres.--Maui Divers Of Hawaii, Ltd., Honolulu, HI, pg. 721
Slater, Michael, Pres.--Wechsler Coffee Corp., Moonachie, NJ, pg. 1172
Slater, Thomas F., Chm., Pres. & Chief Exec. Officer--Actron Manufacturing Company, Cleveland, OH, pg. 15
Slautterback, E.G., Pres.--Medical Analysis Systems Inc., Camarillo, CA, pg. 735
Sledd, Robert C., Pres. & Chief Exec. Officer--Performance Food Group, Inc., Nashville, TN, pg. 861
Sleeman, Robert J., Pres.--Frog Switch & Manufacturing Company, Carlisle, PA, pg. 434
Sleepeck, Michael, Pres.--Sleepeck Printing Company, Bellwood, IL, pg. 1010
Slifka, Alfred A., Pres. & Chief Exec. Officer--Global Petroleum Corp., Waltham, MA, pg. 463
Sloan, Robert B., Pres., Chief Oper. Officer & Treas.--Downey Designs International, Inc., Indianapolis, IN, pg. 348
Sloan, Temple, III, Pres.--Carquest, Andalusia, AL, pg. 224
Slocum, Christopher B., Pres.--Cornell Storefront Systems, Inc., Mountaintop, PA, pg. 286
Slone, Mary Ellen, Pres.--Meridian Communications, Lexington, KY, pg. 740
Sloss, Lynes, Pres. & Chief Exec. Officer--Bellwether Technology Corporation, New Orleans, LA, pg. 136
Slotta, Peter L., Pres. & Treas.--Pan American Trade Development Corp., New York, NY, pg. 845
Sloup, Frank B., Pres.--Pet Life Foods, Inc., Willowbrook, IL, pg. 863
Slovin, Bruce, Pres.--MacAndrews & Forbes Holdings Inc., New York, NY, pg. 694
Slovin, Bruce, Pres.--Andrews Group, Incorporated, New York, NY, pg. 74
Small, Robert, Pres. & Chief Exec. Officer--The Fairmont Hotels, San Francisco, CA, pg. 397
Smallworth, Mary, Area Pres.--Aratex Services, Lawrenceville, GA, pg. 6
Smead, H.J., Chm. Bd., Pres., Chief Exec. & Chief Fin. Officer & Sec.--Kaiser Aerospace & Electronics Corp., Foster City, CA, pg. 614
Smead, L.H., Pres.--Sasco Group, Cerritos, CA, pg. 971
Smidt, E.R., Pres.--McKee Door, Inc., Aurora, IL, pg. 730
Smillie, Charles M. III, Chm. Bd. & Pres.--Hennells, Inc., Ferndale, MI, pg. 530
Smit, James H., Pres. & Chief Exec. Officer--Spartan Oil Corp., Lansing, MI, pg. 1026
Smith, Al, Pres.--Computer Sales International Inc., Saint Louis, MO, pg. 271
Smith, Bill, Pres.--R & G Sloane Mfg. Co., Inc., Sun Valley, CA, pg. 1010
Smith, Bradley C., Pres. & Gen. Mgr.--Raymark Friction Company, Manheim, PA, pg. 914
Smith, Brian, Pres. & Chief Oper. Officer--Cole National Corporation, Cleveland, OH, pg. 260
Smith, Brian, Pres. & Chief Oper. Officer--Cole Vision Corporation, Cleveland, OH, pg. 260
Smith, Brian B., Pres.--Things Remembered, Cleveland, OH, pg. 260
Smith, Bryan, Pres.--Cole Key Corporation, Cleveland, OH, pg. 260
Smith, C. Michael, Pres., Chief Oper. Officer & Sec.--Orders Distributing Co., Greenville, SC, pg. 829
Smith, Carl W., Pres.--Smith Farms, Inc., Flatonia, TX, pg. 1012
Smith, Curtis R., Pres.--Whiting & Davis Company, Plainville, MA, pg. 236
Smith, Dale E., Chm. Bd. & Pres.--Farm Journal, Inc., Philadelphia, PA, pg. 401
Smith, Daniel F., Pres.--Smith Brothers Farms, Inc., Kent, WA, pg. 1011
Smith, Daryl D., Pres. & Chief Exec. Officer--Troy Corporation, East Hanover, NJ, pg. 1116
Smith, David M., Pres. & Chief Exec. Officer--Chemical Exchange Industries, Houston, TX, pg. 242
Smith, Derrick A.M., Pres.--Whitin Roberts Co., Sanford, NC, pg. 1187
Smith, Derrick A.M., Chm. Bd.--Whitin Roberts Mfg. Div., Sanford, NC, pg. 1187
Smith, Don, Pres.--Hygeia Dairy Co., Inc., Harlingen, TX, pg. 557
Smith, Donald N., Pres.--Friendly Ice Cream Corp., Wilbraham, MA, pg. 1087
Smith, Eric, Pres. & Chief Oper. Officer--Howe Furniture Corporation, Trumbull, CT, pg. 547
Smith, Everett G., Pres.--Albert Trostel & Sons Co., West Allis, WI, pg. 1116
Smith, Everett G., Pres.--Everett Smith Investment Co. of Delaware, Milwaukee, WI, pg. 1013
Smith, Ewing, Pres.--Aster Nut Products Inc., Newark, NJ, pg. 92
Smith, Ferdinand J., III, Chm. Bd., Pres., Chief Exec. Officer, Creative Dir.--Jay Incorporated, Rochester, NY, pg. 590
Smith, Francis C., Chm. Bd.--Burgess & Niple, Limited, Columbus, OH, pg. 190
Smith, Fred W., Pres. & Chief Exec. Officer--Donrey Media Group, Fort Smith, AR, pg. 345
Smith, Gary, Pres. & Chief Exec. Officer--Hercules Engines, Inc., Canton, OH, pg. 531
Smith, Gary K., Pres.--American Uniform Co., Cleveland, TN, pg. 1045
Smith, Gary W., Chm. Bd., Pres. & Chief Exec. Officer--Proto Systems of Atlanta, Alpharetta, GA, pg. 895
Smith, Gene R., Pres.--Nooter Corporation, Saint Louis, MO, pg. 808
Smith, George, Pres.--Drumheller Bag & Supply, Valdosta, GA, pg. 810
Smith, George E., Pres. & Chief Exec. Officer--Alco Industries, Inc., Valley Forge, PA, pg. 32
Smith, George J., Pres. & Chief Oper. Officer--Arrow Group Industries, Inc., Wayne, NJ, pg. 357
Smith, Gordon C., Pres., Chief Exec. & Chief Oper. Officer--J.R. Simplot Company, Boise, ID, pg. 1007
Smith, Gordon H., Pres.--Sargent-Fletcher Co., El Monte, CA, pg. 970
Smith, Gordon H., Chm. Bd. & Pres.--Smith Frozen Foods, Inc., Weston, OR, pg. 1012
Smith, Gregory H., Chm. Bd. & Pres.--Maine Potato Growers, Inc., Presque Isle, ME, pg. 702
Smith, H. Thompson, Pres.--Unitary Products Group-Residential, Tyler, TX, pg. 61
Smith, H. Wayne, Pres. & Treas.--Smith, Kaplan, Allen & Reynolds, Inc., Omaha, NE, pg. 1013
Smith, H.T., Pres.--The Trane Company, La Crosse, WI, pg. 62
Smith, Hal, Pres.--Ernst Home Center, Inc., Seattle, WA, pg. 387
Smith, Hal C., Pres.--H.H. Cutler Company, Grand Rapids, MI, pg. 306
Smith, Herbert, Pres.--Smith Pipe & Steel Co., Phoenix, AZ, pg. 1014
Smith, J. Morse, Chm. Bd. & Pres.--H.J. Baker & Bro., Inc., New York, NY, pg. 114
Smith, J. Neil, Chm. Bd., Pres. & Chief Exec. Officer--American Technical Services Group, Inc., Norcross, GA, pg. 63
Smith, Jack, Pres.--LSI Truck Products Corp.-Neway/Anchor Lock, Muskegon, MI, pg. 664
Smith, James A. III, Pres.--Smith & Sons Foods, Inc., Macon, GA, pg. 1014
Smith, James Keith, II, Pres.--Keith Smith Farms, Inc., Hot Springs, AR, pg. 1012
Smith, James S., Pres.--J. M. Smith Corp., Spartanburg, SC, pg. 1012
Smith, Jay L., Pres.--Smith Industries, Inc., Montgomery, AL, pg. 1013
Smith, Joe, Pres. & Chief Exec. Officer--Capitol Industries-EMI Inc., Hollywood, CA, pg. 216
Smith, John, Pres.--Modern Group Ltd., Bristol, PA, pg. 762
Smith, John F., Pres.--Material Handling Equipment Co., Bristol, PA, pg. 763
Smith, John S., Pres.--Southeastern Equipment Company, Inc., Augusta, GA, pg. 1019
Smith, Joseph H., Pres.--Omni Lens Corporation, Forty Fort, PA, pg. 826
Smith, Larry, Pres.--Phillips Plastics Corporation, Phillips, WI, pg. 867
Smith, Lee Allan, Pres. & Exec. Creative Dir.--Ackerman McQueen, Inc., Oklahoma City, OK, pg. 12
Smith, LeRoy T., Chm. Bd., Pres. & Chief Exec. Officer--S-T Industries, Inc., Saint James, MN, pg. 964
Smith, Lonnie L., Pres. & Chief Exec. Officer--Cumberland-Swan, Inc., Smyrna, TN, pg. 304
Smith, M.T., Pres.--Midwest Coast Transport L.P., Sioux Falls, SD, pg. 752
Smith, Michael, Pres., Chief Exec. Officer & Creative Dir.--J. Richard Smith, Ltd., Melville, NY, pg. 1013
Smith, Michael L., Chm., Pres. & Chief Exec. Officer--Mayflower Transit, Inc., Carmel, IN, pg. 724
Smith, Peter, Pres. & Chief Oper. Officer--W S Holding Company, Euless, TX, pg. 1156
Smith, Peter, Pres. & Chief Oper. Officer--White Swan, Inc., Euless, TX, pg. 1156
Smith, Peter W., Pres.--Peter W. Smith & Company, Inc., Chicago, IL, pg. 1011
Smith, Phil, Pres.--Golden Cat Corporation, South Bend, IN, pg. 637
Smith, Philip, Pres.--AGEMA Infrared Systems, Inc., Secaucus, NJ, pg. 24
Smith, Richard, Pres.--The Fremont Co., Fremont, OH, pg. 432
Smith, Robert J., Pres.--Smith, Badofsky & Raffel, Inc. Advertising, Chicago, IL, pg. 1011
Smith, Robin, Pres. & Chief Exec. Officer--Publishers Clearing House, Port Washington, NY, pg. 898
Smith, Roger, Gen. Mgr.--Universal Vise & Tool Co., Parma, MI, pg. 1103
Smith, Roger W., Pres.--Pawling Corporation, Pawling, NY, pg. 852
Smith, Roland, F., Pres. & Chief Exec. Officer--Jamison Door Company, Hagerstown, MD, pg. 589
Smith, Russell G., Chm. Bd. & Pres.--Collegiate Concepts Inc., Tucker, GA, pg. 262
Smith, Sanderson, Pres.--Cornell Forge Company, Chicago, IL, pg. 286
Smith, Stephen E., Chm. Bd. & Pres.--LSJ Sportswear Inc., Deerfield, WI, pg. 739
Smith, Steven N., Pres.--Universal Construction Company, Kansas City, KS, pg. 1138
Smith, T.W., Pres.--Calcot, Ltd., Bakersfield, CA, pg. 208
Smith, Terrence L., Chm. Bd., Pres. & Chief Exec. Officer--California Hardware Co., City of Industry, CA, pg. 209
Smith, Theodore B., Jr., Pres.--John Hassall, Inc., Westbury, NY, pg. 516
Smith, Thomas J., Pres.--Norwesco, Inc., Minneapolis, MN, pg. 816
Smith, W. T., Jr., Pres.--Delmar Photographic and Printing Company, Charlotte, NC, pg. 279
Smith, W.T., Pres. & Gen. Mgr.--Tidelands Oil Production Co., Long Beach, CA, pg. 1096
Smith, Wally, Pres. & Chief Exec. Officer--Recreational Equipment, Inc., Kent, WA, pg. 917
Smith, William, Pres. & Representative Dir.--Leo Burnett-Kyodo Co. Ltd., Tokyo, Japan, pg. 192
Smith, William, Pres.--Challenge Graphics Equipment Co., Grand Haven, MI, pg. 238
Smith, William D., Pres. & Chief Exec. Officer--Brown & Bigelow, Inc., Saint Paul, MN, pg. 181
Smith, William E., Pres., Chief Oper. Officer & Sec.--Fitzgerald & Company, Inc., Cranston, RI, pg. 416
Smith, William J., Chm. Bd., Pres. & Chief Exec. Officer--U.S. Can Company, Oak Brook, IL, pg. 1134
Smitson, Robert M., Pres. & Chief Exec. Officer--Maxon Corporation, Muncie, IN, pg. 723
Smola, Steve, Pres. & Chief Exec. Officer--Wheeler Brothers Grain Co., Watonga, OK, pg. 1184
Smoler, Irwin, Pres.--Wicker Park L.P., Chicago, IL, pg. 1188
Smulowitz, William, Chm., Pres. & Chief Exec. Officer--The Lion, Inc. (Gibbons-Stegmaier Brewery), Wilkes-Barre, PA, pg. 677
Smyth, Frederick, Pres. & New Bus. Contact--Smyth, Bauer & Lewis Advertising Inc., Richmond, VA, pg. 1014
Smythe, Thomas M., Chm Bd. & Pres.--Keller Crescent Co., Evansville, IN, pg. 620
Snavely, Stephen V., Pres.--Snavely Forest Products, Inc., Pittsburgh, PA, pg. 1015
Snediker, James M., Pres.--Chicago Show Printing Co., Morton Grove, IL, pg. 246
Snelling, Mark H., Pres.--The Shelburne Corporation, Shelburne, VT, pg. 996
Snelling, Mark H., Pres.--Barrecrafters, Shelburne, VT, pg. 996
Snetzer, Michael A., Pres.--Contran Corporation, Dallas, TX, pg. 281
Snoddon, Larry E., Pres. & Chief Exec. Officer--Burson-Marsteller, New York, NY, pg. 1210
Snoddy, L.O., Chm. Bd. & Pres.--Telsco Industries, Garland, TX, pg. 1085
Snodgrass, Jim, Chm. Bd. & Pres.--The Stiffel Company, Chicago, IL, pg. 1049
Snowden, David, Pres. & Chief Exec. Officer--Tarco, North Little Rock, AR, pg. 1078
Snowden, William F., Chm. Bd., Pres. & Chief Exec. Officer--Topline Imports, Inc., Bellevue, WA, pg. 1102
Snyder, Eugene, Pres. & Chief Exec. Officer--Snyder Brothers, Inc., Minneapolis, MN, pg. 1015
Snyder, Fred J., Jr., Pres. & Chief Exec. Officer--Fiske Brothers Refining Company, Newark, NJ, pg. 415
Snyder, Fred J., Jr., Pres.--Lubriplate Div. of Fiske Bros. Refining Co., Newark, NJ, pg. 416
Snyder, Gerald J., Pres.--Snyder Tank Corp., Buffalo, NY, pg. 1015
Snyder, John, Pres.--Schneider Commercial Real Estate, Orange, CA, pg. 977
Snyder, Kenneth W., Pres.--Andrews/Mautner, Inc., Milwaukee, WI, pg. 74
Snyder, Mel, Pres.--Pro Clinica Inc., New York, NY, pg. 891
Snyder, R.A., Pres.--In-N-Out Burgers, Baldwin Park, CA, pg. 564
Snyder, W. Patrick, Pres.--Cummins Southwest Inc., Phoenix, AZ, pg. 305
Sobel, Robert, Pres.--Land N Sea, Inc., New York, NY, pg. 653
Sobin, Stephen A., Pres.--State-Wide Capital Corp., Uniondale, NY, pg. 1041
Sodini, Peter, Pres.--Purity Supreme, Inc., North Billerica, MA, pg. 901
Soehnlen, Daniel, Pres.--Superior Dairy, Inc., Canton, OH, pg. 1063
Soesanto, Hendra, Chm. & Fin. Dir.--Metro, Jakarta,, Indonesia, pg. 331
Sohl, Brandon A., Pres.--Auto Driveaway Co., Chicago, IL, pg. 100
Sokolofski, Edward G., Pres.--WICO Corporation, Niles, IL, pg. 1156
Solan, George D., Pres.--S & S Graphics, Inc., Laurel, MD, pg. 959
Solda, Marc, Pres. & Treas.--Jamison Plastic Corporation, Allentown, PA, pg. 589
Solheim, Karsten, Pres.--Karsten Manufacturing Corporation, Phoenix, AZ, pg. 617
Soliman, Anwar, Pres. & Chief Exec. Officer--American Restaurant Group, Inc., Newport Beach, CA, pg. 60
Solin, Darrol B., Pres. & Chief Exec. Officer--MacNamara, Klein & Solin Inc., New York, NY, pg. 698
Sollenbarger, Stanley D., V.P.--Superior Coffee & Foods/Hawaii, Aiea, HI, pg. 174
Solloway, Erwine, Chm. Bd. & Pres.--ACR Mechanical Corporation, Orange, CA, pg. 2
Soloff, Lawrence L., Pres. & Chief Exec. Officer--Century Seafood Inc., Philadelphia, PA, pg. 235
Solombrino, Scott, Chm. Bd., Pres. & Chief Exec. Officer--Dav-El Services, Inc., New York, NY, pg. 317
Solomon, Robert, Chm. Bd., Pres. & Chief Exec. Officer--Dakin, Inc., Burlingame, CA, pg. 311
Solomon, Robert B., Chm. Bd. & Pres.--Robert Solomon & Associates Adv. Inc., Bloomfield Hills, MI, pg. 1017
Solomon, Russ, Pres.--Tower Records, West Sacramento, CA, pg. 694
Solomon, Russell S., Pres. & Chief Exec. Officer--MTS, Inc., West Sacramento, CA, pg. 694
Solomon, Russell S., Pres. & Chief Exec. Officer--Pulse Magazine, West Sacramento, CA, pg. 694
Solomon, William R., Pres.--American Fluorescent Corporation, Waukegan, IL, pg. 54
Solomon, William T., Chm. Bd., Pres. & Chief Exec. Officer--Austin Industries, Inc., Dallas, TX, pg. 99
Solomon, Zachary, Pres. & Chief Oper. Officer--Associated Merchandising Corp., New York, NY, pg. 91
Solon, Robert, Pres.--Robert Towers Advertising, Inc., New York, NY, pg. 1103
Somerset, H.R., Pres. & Chief Exec. Officer--California & Hawaiian Sugar Company, Concord, CA, pg. 210

Sommer, James, Pres., Chief Oper. & Fin. Officer & Treas.--Service Motor Company, Dale, WI, pg. 992
Sommer, Jon W., Pres. & Chief Exec. Officer--Sommer Metalcraft Corporation, Crawfordsville, IN, pg. 1018
Sommer, Jon W., Chm. Bd. & Pres.--Crown Products Co., Crawfordsville, IN, pg. 1018
Sommers, John G., Pres.--Allied Printing Services, Inc., Manchester, CT, pg. 38
Somrock, J.D., Pres. & Chief Exec. Officer--E.F. Johnson Company, Eden Prarie, MN, pg. 598
Sondhi, Vir K., Chm. Bd. & Pres.--National Solvent Corporation, Medina, OH, pg. 793
Sonnenberg, Frank K., Pres.--RMI Marketing & Advertising, Emerson, NJ, pg. 907
Sontag, Frederick B., Pres.--Unison Industries, Jacksonville, FL, pg. 1130
Sontag, Frederick B., Pres.--Unison Industries, Jacksonville, FL, pg. 1130
Soong, Leo, Pres.--Crystal Geyser, Calistoga, CA, pg. 303
Sopko, W.E., Pres.--Stamco Industries Inc., Euclid, OH, pg. 1035
Sorbo, Eugene, Pres.--Technographics, Inc., Stratton, PA, pg. 1083
Sorokwasz, Michael, Pres. & Chief Exec. Officer--TST/Impreso, Inc., Coppell, TX, pg. 1075
Soskin, David H., Pres. & Chief Oper. Officer--Communications Diversified, New York, NY, pg. 269
Sosnow, Lawrence I., Pres.--Patient Care, Inc., West Orange, NJ, pg. 851
Sossong, A.T., Pres.--Reitz Coal Company, Windber, PA, pg. 145
Sotos, George J., Joint Mng. Dir.--Industrial Acoustics Company, Ltd., Staines,, United Kingdom, pg. 566
Souder, Chuck, Pres.--DH Medical Supply Inc., West Hartford, CT, pg. 1081
Soule, Wallace, Jr., Dir.--Maine State Lottery Commission, Augusta, ME, pg. 702
Soulia, Joseph, Pres.--Infotec Development, Inc., Santa Ana, CA, pg. 567
Soultanian, Sarkis, Chm. & Pres.--National Utility Service, Inc., Park Ridge, NJ, pg. 794
Southard, Bill, Pres.--Earle Palmer Brown/New York, New York, NY, pg. 182
Southwell, Leonard, Chief Exec. Officer--Prairie Farms Dairy, Inc., Carlinville, IL, pg. 884
Southwick, R.D., Pres.--AGR International, Inc., Butler, PA, pg. 4
Sowles, Lawrence H., Pres.--L.H. Sowles Company, Inc., Minneapolis, MN, pg. 1024
Spain, W.J., Jr., Pres. & Chief Exec. Officer--Birdsong Corporation, Sulfolk, VA, pg. 153
Spang, Larry, Pres.--Ardco, Inc., Alsip, IL, pg. 81
Spangler, C. Gregory, Pres.--Spangler Candy Company, Bryan, OH, pg. 1025
Spangler, Dave, Pres.--Hooker Industries, Ontario, CA, pg. 543
Spangler, William C., Pres.--Dettra Flag Company, Oaks, PA, pg. 333
Spanos, Alex G., Chm. Bd. & Pres.--San Diego Chargers, San Diego, CA, pg. 969
Spanos, Dean A., Pres.--A. G. Spanos Development, Inc., Stockton, CA, pg. 1025
Sparler, Daniel J., Chm. Bd., Pres. & Chief Exec. Officer--Yorktowne Paper Mills, Inc., York, PA, pg. 1208
Spath, Robert, Pres.--Templeton, Kenly & Co., Inc., Broadview, IL, pg. 1086
Spaulding, Susan, Pres.--Market Directions, Inc., Kansas City, MO, pg. 1143
Speakman, D., Mng. Dir.--The Campaign Palace, Melbourne,, Australia, pg. 111
Speakman, W.A. III, Pres. & Chief Exec. Officer--Speakman Company, Wilmington, DE, pg. 1027
Spear, Kenneth H., Chm. Bd., Pres. & Chief Exec. Officer--Del-Val Manufacturing Company, Warminster, PA, pg. 325
Spears, Richard F., Pres.--Chicago, Chicago, IL, pg. 656
Spector, Don, Pres.--Rice/Spector Inc., Venice, CA, pg. 931
Spector, Michael J., Chm. Bd. & Pres., & Chief Exec. Officer--Margo Nursery Farms, Inc., Miami, FL, pg. 706
Speek, Peter V., Pres. & Treas.--Fremont Forest Products, Whittier, CA, pg. 432
Speh, Albert J., Jr., Chm. Bd. & Pres.--May & Speh, Inc., Downers Grove, IL, pg. 724
Speicher, Donald E., Pres.--Ross Engineering Co., Inc., Leola, PA, pg. 949
Speier, Stephen, Pres. & Chief Oper. Officer--Penny & Speier Inc., Houston, TX, pg. 858
Speiser, John P., Pres.--Diehl Specialties Intl., Defiance, OH, pg. 336
Speiser, John P., Pres.--Diehl, Inc., Defiance, OH, pg. 336
Spelde, M.E., Chm. Bd., Pres. & Chief Exec. Officer--Empire Airlines, Hayden Lake, ID, pg. 379
Spence, Jeffrey E., Chm. Bd., Pres., Controller & Chief Exec. & Fin. Officer--Controlled Systems of Wisconsin, Inc., Nashotah, WI, pg. 281
Spence, Paula, Pres.--Hameroff/Milenthal/Spence, Inc., Columbus, OH, pg. 503
Spence, Robert L., Pres. & Chief Exec. Officer--Pacific Lumber & Shipping Co., Seattle, WA, pg. 840
Spence, Roy, Pres.--GSD&M, Austin, TX, pg. 441
Spencer, G.W., Pres.--Spencer Industries, Inc., New Brunswick, NJ, pg. 1030
Spencer, Gordon W., Chm. Bd.--Casual Sportswear Co., Inc., Dunmore, PA, pg. 1030
Spencer, Guy J., Jr., Chm. Bd., Pres. & Chief Exec. Officer--Spencer Companies Inc., Huntsville, AL, pg. 1030
Spencer, Ronald E., Pres.--Faber Enterprises, Inc., Canoga Park, CA, pg. 395
Spenlinhauer, John, III, Pres.--Spencer Press, Inc., Wells, ME, pg. 1030
Sperber, Burton S., Chm. Bd., Pres. , & Chief Exec. Officer--Environmental Industries, Inc., Calabasas, CA, pg. 383
Sperber, Martin, Chm. Bd. & Pres.--Schein Pharmaceutical, Inc., Port Washington, NY, pg. 975
Sperling, Gay, Pres. & New Bus. Contact--Sperling, New Orleans, LA, pg. 1030
Spertell, Alayne, Pres.--Smith's Personnel Service, Inc., New York, NY, pg. 1014
Speyer, Stuart W., Pres.--Tennsco Corporation, Dickson, TN, pg. 1088
Spidalette, Lou, Pres.--LINC Medical Imaging, Newport Beach, CA, pg. 648
Spiegel, Joel R., Pres.--Deutsch, Shea & Evans, Inc., South San Francisco, CA, pg. 333
Spiegel, Morton L., Pres. & Treas.--Southwark Metal Manufacturing Company, Philadelphia, PA, pg. 1023
Spiegel, Si, Pres.--Hudson Valley Tree, Inc., Newburgh, NY, pg. 551
Spiegelman, Edmond, Pres. & Dir.-Mktg.--General Metalcraft, Inc., Dover, DE, pg. 450
Spiewak, Michael, Pres. & Chief Exec. Officer--I. Spiewak & Sons, Inc., New York, NY, pg. 1031
Spigai, Daniel J., Chief Exec. Officer--Howard Needles Tammen & Bergendoff, Kansas City, MO, pg. 547
Spires, Keith, Pres. & Chief Exec. Officer--Osco Industries Inc., Portsmouth, OH, pg. 830
Spitalnick, Dennis, Pres.--Wellmade Industries, Inc., New York, NY, pg. 1175
Spitzer, Joseph, Pres.--Perfect Pearl Company, Inc., New York, NY, pg. 861
Spoehof, John, Pres.--Prince Corporation, Holland, MI, pg. 890
Spokane, Jules, Pres.--Hamburg Brothers Inc., Pittsburgh, PA, pg. 502
Sponsler, James R., Pres. & Chief Oper. Officer--Rustco Products Company, Denver, CO, pg. 957
Spoor, John, Pres.--State Electric Supply Co., Huntington, WV, pg. 1040
Sport, Michael C., Chm. Bd., Pres. & Chief Exec. Officer--Production Management Companies, Inc., Harvey, LA, pg. 893
Spradley, James W., Jr., Pres. & Chief Exec. Officer--Standard Candy Co., Inc., Nashville, TN, pg. 1035
Spradlin, Robert, Pres. & Chief Exec. Officer--Contract Interiors Inc., Southfield, MI, pg. 280
Spraetz, Kenneth, Pres.--Performance Contracting Group, Charlotte, NC, pg. 861
Spranger, Hanno W., Pres. & Chief Exec. Officer--Netzsch, Inc., Exton, PA, pg. 798
Spring, Chris, Pres.--Spring, O'Brien & Co. Inc., New York, NY, pg. 1033
Springborn, Robert C., Chm. Bd., Pres. Chief Exec. Officer--Springborn Laboratories, Inc., Enfield, CT, pg. 1033
Sprole, Robert R., II, Chm. Bd. & Pres.--Therm, Inc., Ithaca, NY, pg. 1090
Sprott, H.B., Jr., Pres. & Chief Exec. Officer--Sprott Oil Co., Inc., Manning, SC, pg. 1034
Spurck, Fredric C., Pres. & Chief Exec. Officer--Webster Industries Inc., Tiffin, OH, pg. 1171
Spurrier, Hal, Pres. & Chief Opers. Offcier--Snyder Industries, Inc., Lincoln, NE, pg. 1015
Squier, Robert C., Pres.--Curtis Screw Co., Inc., Buffalo, NY, pg. 306
St. John, Dan J., Pres.--Robinson & St. John Advertising & Public Relations, Inc., Jacksonville, FL, pg. 940
St. John, Dan J., Pres.--Robinson & St. John Advertising & Public Relations, Public Relations Div., Jacksonville, FL, pg. 940
Staab, Gary, Pres.--Spangler, Inc., Kansas City, KS, pg. 1025
Staab, Walter, Chm. & Pres.--SFM Media Corporation, New York, NY, pg. 962
Stabler, Donald B., Chm. Bd.--Stabler Companies, Inc., Harrisburg, PA, pg. 1034
Stabler, Donald B., Chm. Bd. & Pres.--Stabler Construction Company, Harrisburg, PA, pg. 1034
Stadelman, Pete, Pres., Chief Exec. & Fin. Officer--Stadelman Fruit Inc., Yakima, WA, pg. 1034
Stadelman, Russell C. II, Pres.--Russell Stadelman & Company, Germantown, TN, pg. 1034
Staff, Chris, Pres.--White Stag Manufacturing Company, Van Nuys, CA, pg. 1186
Stafford, Randy, Pres. & Chief Exec. Officer--The Court Company, Memphis, TN, pg. 290
Stager, D., Pres.--Tri-Mark Inc., Piqua, OH, pg. 537
Stager, Donald K., Chm. Bd., Pres. & Chief Exec. Officer--Dillingham Construction Corporation, Pleasanton, CA, pg. 337
Stahel, Kurt, Pres.--Trimtex Co. Inc., Williamsport, PA, pg. 1113
Staheli, Donald L., Pres. & Chief Exec. Officer--Continental Grain Company, New York, NY, pg. 279
Stahl, Charles, Pres.--ISI FLuid Power, Inc., Fraser, MI, pg. 560
Stahl, Edward, Pres.--Piper Industries, Inc., Dallas, TX, pg. 872
Stahlke, William R., Pres.--Executive Capital Corp., Big Rock, IL, pg. 392
Stahmann, Wayne R., Pres.--Stahmann Farms, Inc., Las Cruces, NM, pg. 1034
Stamatakis, Alex, Chm. & Pres.--Construction Machinery Company, Waterloo, IA, pg. 277
Stamm, James A., Pres.-Specialized Transportation Group--Atlas Van Lines, Inc., Evansville, IN, pg. 96
Stamp, William M., Jr., Pres.--Farm Family Mutual Insurance Co., Glenmont, NY, pg. 401
Standen, Michael, Chm., Pres. & Chief Exec. Officer--Metallurg, Inc., New York, NY, pg. 742
Standish, Victor J., Pres. & Treas.--York Barbell Co., Inc., York, PA, pg. 1208
Standley, Martin, Mng. Dir.--Standley Burridge Collings Ltd., London, United Kingdom, pg. 112
Stanek, Dr. Edward J., Commissioner--Iowa Lottery, Des Moines, IA, pg. 582
Stanke, Mary, Pres. & Sec.--JS&A Advertising, Las Vegas, NV, pg. 586
Stanke, Mary, Pres.--JS&A Group, Inc., Las Vegas, NV, pg. 586
Stanko, Gary, Pres., Chief Exec. Officer--Marketing Alternatives, Inc., Arlington Heights, IL, pg. 709
Stanley, Elmar, Pres.--Takatta Inc., Olympia Fields, IL, pg. 1076
Stanley, Fred C., Pres.--Stanley Stores Inc., Bay City, TX, pg. 1038
Stanley, John R., Chm. Bd. & Pres.--Transamerican Refining Corporation, Houston, TX, pg. 1106
Stanley, John W., Jr., Pres., Chief Exec. Officer & Sec.--Blue Ridge Transfer Co., Roanoke, VA, pg. 161
Stanley, Lowell, Pres.--Brown Wood Preserving Company, Louisville, KY, pg. 183
Stanley, Richard H., Pres.--SC Companies, Inc., Muscatine, IA, pg. 960
Stanley, Theodore R., Pres.--MBI Inc., Norwalk, CT, pg. 691
Stansberry, Warren H., III, Pres. & Treas.--Stanco Metal Products, Inc., Grand Haven, MI, pg. 1035
Stansfield, Elaine, Pres. & Chief Oper. Officer--The Sunflower Group, Overland Park, KS, pg. 1060
Stanton, Myron E., Pres.--Recording & Statistical Corporation, Norwalk, CT, pg. 917
Stanzak, Adam, Pres.--Key Cadillac, Inc., Edina, MN, pg. 626
Stark, Bill, Chm. Bd. & Pres.--Semco, Inc., Houston, TX, pg. 989
Stark, V., Gen. Mgr.--Hiniker Company, Mankato, MN, pg. 535
Starr, Lawrence D., Pres.--Koch Supplies Inc., Kansas City, MO, pg. 639
Starr, Louis E., Jr., Pres.--Windermere Communications, Inc., Bala-Cynwyd, PA, pg. 1195
Starr, Max J., Pres.--General Automation, Inc., Skokie, IL, pg. 448
Starrett, Frederick D., III, Pres., Treas., Sls. & Mktg.--Penobscot Frozen Foods, Inc., Belfast, ME, pg. 858
Starvel, Frank A., Pres. & Chief Exec. Officer--New England Dairies, Inc., Hartford, CT, pg. 800
Starwalt, Ronald, Pres.--Grand Prairie Co-op, Inc., Tolono, IL, pg. 475
Stastny, Wayne, Gen. Mgr.--Harig Products, Elgin, IL, pg. 175
Statham, Carl E., Pres.--Southside Ford Truck Sales Inc., Chicago, IL, pg. 1023
Statton, Philip J., Pres.--Statton Furniture Manufacturing Company, Hagerstown, MD, pg. 1042
Stauch, Manfred R., Pres. & Adv.--Stauch Vetromile & Mitchell Advertising, Inc., East Providence, RI, pg. 1042
Stauffer, Conrad, Exec. Dir.--Pennsylvania State Lottery, Middletown, PA, pg. 858
Stauffer, John H., Chm. Bd. & Pres.--Stauffer Communications, Inc., Topeka, KS, pg. 1042
Stavis, Frank, Pres.--Blue Bell/King Koil, Inc., Windsor, CT, pg. 158
Stawasz, Cherie, Pres.--Stawasz Public Relations, New York, NY, pg. 605
Stayer, Ralph C., Pres. & Chief Exec. Officer--Johnsonville Foods, Inc., Kohler, WI, pg. 601
Steakley, John W., Pres.--Steakley Chevrolet Subaru Inc., Dallas, TX, pg. 1043
Stearns, Neele E., Jr., Pres. & Chief Exec. Officer--CC Industries, Inc., Chicago, IL, pg. 199
Stearns, Richard, Pres.--Prudential Institutional Investment Management Div., Newark, NJ, pg. 897
Stearns, Robert P., Pres.--SCS Engineers, Long Beach, CA, pg. 961
Steck, Raymond, Pres.--A.B.P. Midwest, Inc., Madison, WI, pg. 2
Steedman, Donald, Chm. Bd. & Pres.--Littleford Day, Taylor-Stiles Division, Florence, KY, pg. 679
Steele, Harold, Pres.--H S Die & Engineering, Inc., Grand Rapids, MI, pg. 497
Steele, Loren, Vice Chm., Chief Exec. Officer & Pres.--Super 8 Motels, Inc., Aberdeen, SD, pg. 1062
Steele, Marvin, Pres.--Sterling Lumber & Investment Co., Denver, CO, pg. 1047
Steeley, Charles B., Pres. & Chief Exec. Officer--United Graphics, Inc., Seattle, WA, pg. 1132
Steenberg, W.D., Chm. Bd. & Pres.--Steenberg Homes, Inc., Fond du Lac, WI, pg. 1045
Stefanic, David, Pres. & Chief Exec. Officer--TV Host Inc., Harrisburg, PA, pg. 1075
Stefano, Michael, Pres.--Dove International, Inc., Burr Ridge, IL, pg. 713
Stegemiller, David C., Pres.--Cast Products, Jackson, MI, pg. 514
Stegner, Edward J., Chm. Bd. & Chief Exec. Officer--Stegner Food Products Co., Cincinnati, OH, pg. 1045
Steil, Gordon E., Pres. & Chief Exec. Officer--Harrington & King, Chicago, IL, pg. 511
Stein, Gerald, Pres.--Zilber, Ltd., Milwaukee, WI, pg. 1219
Stein, Joseph L., Pres.--General Refractories Co., U. S. Refractories Div., Pittsburgh, PA, pg. 136
Stein, Larry, Pres.--Crown Foods Inc., Saint Louis, MO, pg. 302
Stein, Lester, Pres.--Charles River Foods, Inc., Boston, MA, pg. 240
Stein, Martin, Pres. & Chief Exec. Officer--Dawn Joy Fashions, Inc., New York, NY, pg. 319
Stein, Martin, Pres.--Sherri Martin, New York, NY, pg. 319
Stein, Martin, Pres. & Treas.--Sterling Paper Co., Philadelphia, PA, pg. 1047
Stein, Martin E., Jr., Pres. & Chief Exec. Officer--Regency Group Inc., Jacksonville, FL, pg. 922
Stein, Michael Alan, Pres. & Chief Oper. Officer--Electro-Science Laboratories, Inc., King of Prussia, PA, pg. 375
Stein, Steven B., Pres. & Chief Oper. Officer--Allied Security, Inc., Pittsburgh, PA, pg. 39
Stein, Thomas, Pres & New Bus. Contact--Stein, Killpatrick & Rogan Advertising, New York, NY, pg. 1045
Stein, William E., Pres. & Chief Oper. Officer--McConnaughy Stein Schmidt Brown, Chicago, IL, pg. 727
Steinbach, James, Pres.--MSD, Inc., Darlington, SC, pg. 693

Steinbarth, Ralph, Pres.--La Preferida, Inc., Chicago, IL, pg. 649
Steinberg, Irwin, Mng. Partner--Friedman, Eisenstein, Raemer & Schwartz, Chicago, IL, pg. 433
Steinberg, Lawrence, Pres. & Chief Exec. Officer--Unisystems, Inc., New York, NY, pg. 1130
Steinberg, Marc H., Pres.--Pennsylvania Petroleum Product Company, Southhampton, PA, pg. 858
Steinberg, S. Ty, Pres. & Chief Exec. Officer--M. Buten & Sons Inc., Philadelphia, PA, pg. 196
Steiner, Cy, Pres., Admin. & Acct. Services--Steiner/Bressler Advertising, Birmingham, AL, pg. 1045
Steiner, Edward S., Pres.--Steiner & Company, Milford, DE, pg. 1045
Steiner, Lawrence G., Pres. & Chief Exec. Officer--American Linen Supply Company, Minneapolis, MN, pg. 57
Steiner, Richard R., Pres. & Chief Exec. Officer--Steiner Corporation, Salt Lake City, UT, pg. 1045
Steiner, Thomas, Pres.--Advance Business Graphics, Mira Loma, CA, pg. 18
Steinert, Jan Allan, Pres. & Chief Exec. Officer--Steinert & Associates, Inc., New York, NY, pg. 1045
Steinhauer, Frederick C., Chm. Bd. & Pres.--Madison Dairy Produce Company, Madison, WI, pg. 699
Steinman, Mark, Pres.--Chorus Line, Inc., Vernon, CA, pg. 591
Steiny, Susan, Pres.--Steiny & Company, Inc., Los Angeles, CA, pg. 1049
Steitz, William N., Pres.--Sauer Industries, Inc., Pittsburgh, PA, pg. 972
Stemen, Milton, Pres.--R & B Machine Tool Co., Saline, MI, pg. 906
Stepanian, Stephen, Pres. & Chief Oper. Officer--Printed Circuit Corporation, Woburn, MA, pg. 891
Stephan, E.W., Pres.--Royal Caribbean Cruises Ltd., Miami, FL, pg. 953
Stephan, Walter, Pres. & Chief Exec. Officer--Uvex Safety, Inc., Smithfield, RI, pg. 1141
Stephen, George, Sr., Pres.--Weber-Stephen Products, Palatine, IL, pg. 1171
Stephen, Phillip L., Pres. & Chief Oper. Officer--Aid Auto Stores, Inc., Westbury, NY, pg. 26
Stephens, J.M., Pres. & Chief Exec. Officer--Davis Electrical Constructors, Inc., Greenville, SC, pg. 318
Stephens, J.T., Pres., Chief Exec. Officer & Chief Oper. Officer--Ebsco Industries, Inc., Birmingham, AL, pg. 365
Stephens, James H., Pres.--Tribble & Stephens Co., Houston, TX, pg. 1112
Stephens, Phillip K., Pres., New Bus. Contact & Acct. Supvr.--Neal & Stephens Advertising, Inc., Kettering, OH, pg. 796
Stephens, Richard T., Pres. & Chief Oper. Officer--Delaware North Companies, Inc., Buffalo, NY, pg. 326
Stephens, W. Lackey, Pres.--R.L. Ziegler Co. Inc., Tuscaloosa, AL, pg. 1218
Stephens, Warren A., Pres. & Chief Exec. Officer--Stephens, Inc., Little Rock, AR, pg. 1046
Stephenson, G.W., Jr., Pres. & Treas.--Stephenson, Inc., Alexandria, VA, pg. 1046
Stephenson, James M. Jr., Chm. Bd. & Pres.--Kinetic Systems Corporation, Lockport, IL, pg. 630
Stephenson, Joseph E., Pres. & Chief Exec. Officer--Shenandoah Life Insurance Company, Roanoke, VA, pg. 997
Sterling, John R., Pres.--John Sterling Corporation, Richmond, IL, pg. 1046
Stern, Arnold, Pres.--Jarchem Industries, Inc., Newark, NJ, pg. 590
Stern, David J., Commissioner--National Basketball Association, New York, NY, pg. 786
Stern, M.L., Pres.--M.L. Stern & Company, Inc., Beverly Hills, CA, pg. 1047
Stern, Rodolfo, Pres.--Real Estate Corp. of Florida, Kissimmee, FL, pg. 917
Stern, William J., Pres.--Stern Advertising, Inc., Pepper Pike, OH, pg. 1047
Sternberg, Sheldon, Pres.--Bessin Corporation, Chicago, IL, pg. 146
Sternberg, Sheldon, Chm. Bd. & Pres.--Best Kosher Sausage Co., Chicago, IL, pg. 146
Sterner, Dr. Frank, Pres.--E.R. Wagner Mfg. Co. Wagner Prods. Div., Hustisford, WI, pg. 1158
Sternheimer, Mark A., Pres.--Sternheimer Brothers Inc., Sandston, VA, pg. 1048
Stetson, John B., Pres.--Transportation & Distribution Associates, Radnor, PA, pg. 320
Stevens, Andrew E., Chm. Bd., Pres., Mktg. & Pub. Rel. Dir.--GWP, Inc., Los Angeles, CA, pg. 441
Stevens, Bruce, Pres.--Rollex Corporation, Elk Grove Village, IL, pg. 944
Stevens, Bruce A., Pres.--Steinway Musical Properties, Inc., Waltham, MA, pg. 1045
Stevens, Bruce A., Pres.--Steinway & Sons, Long Island City, NY, pg. 1046
Stevens, Claude, Pres. & Chief Exec. Officer--Haworth Group Inc., Minnetonka, MN, pg. 518
Stevens, Edward M., Group Pres.--Dix & Eaton Incorporated, Cleveland, OH, pg. 341
Stevens, Elizabeth, Pres.--Cold Heading Co., Detroit, MI, pg. 259
Stevens, Frank D., Pres.--International Cold Storage Co., Inc., Andover, KS, pg. 576
Stevens, Frank P., Chm. Bd., Pres., Treas., Chief Exec. Officer & Chief Fin. Officer--Professional Travel, Inc., Dalton, GA, pg. 894
Stevens, Gus, Pres. & Chief Oper. Officer--Cyberex, Inc., Mentor, OH, pg. 307
Stevens, James, Pres. & Chief Exec. Officer--Big Cheese Pizza Corporation, Wichita, KS, pg. 464
Stevens, Jim J., Pres.--Lincoln Provision Company, Inc., Chicago, IL, pg. 676
Stevens, Meri, Pres.-Waverly Fabrics--F. Schumacher & Co., New York, NY, pg. 979
Stevens, Meri, Pres.--Waverly Fabrics, New York, NY, pg. 979
Stevens, Philip L., Pres. & Chief Exec. Officer--Gerber Advertising, Portland, OR, pg. 453
Stevenson, Charles E., Jr., Chm., Pres. & Chief Exec. Officer--CEBCOR (Consolidated Employment Benefits Corp.), Chicago, IL, pg. 230
Stevenson, Robert L., Pres. & Treas.--Eastman Machine Co., Buffalo, NY, pg. 364
Steves, Sam Bel, II, Pres. & Chief Oper. Officer--Steves & Sons, San Antonio, TX, pg. 1048
Steward, Robert H., Jr., Pres.--York Building Products Co., Inc., York, PA, pg. 1208
Stewart, Andrew K., Chm. Bd., Pres. & Chief Exec. Officer--Computer Methods Corporation, Livonia, MI, pg. 271
Stewart, Charles W., Pres. & Chief Oper. Offier--Blue Shield of California, San Francisco, CA, pg. 161
Stewart, George, Pres.--Sunbeam Home Comfort, Shubuta, MS, pg. 1059
Stewart, James, Chm. Bd. & Pres.--Consolidated Co-op, Gowrie, IA, pg. 276
Stewart, Richard, Chm., Pres. & Chief Exec. Officer--Praxis International Inc., Cambridge, MA, pg. 884
Stewart, Robert, Pres. & Partner--Meade Ullman Advertising & Public Relations, Agoura Hills, CA, pg. 733
Stewart, Robert L., Chm. Bd. & Pres.--Honorbuilt Industries, Inc., Minneapolis, KS, pg. 542
Stewart, Terry, Pres.--Marvel Entertainment Group, New York, NY, pg. 695
Stickler, Ivan, Pres.--Mid-America Dairymen, Inc., Springfield, MO, pg. 750
Stiefel, W.K., Chm. & Pres.--Stiefel Laboratories, Inc., Coral Gables, FL, pg. 1048
Stiefel, W.K., Pres. & Chief Exec. Officer--Stiefel Laboratories, Inc., Oak Hill, Oak Hill, NY, pg. 1048
Stiegelmeyer, Jim, Pres.-Oliver Trucking Co.-Indianapolis, In.--Queens Group, Inc., Long Island City, NY, pg. 904
Stiff, P. Enoch, Pres. & Chief Exec. Officer--Trak International, Inc., Port Washington, WI, pg. 1106
Stiles, Terry, Pres.--Stiles Corporation, Fort Lauderdale, FL, pg. 1049
Stilitano, Carl P., Pres.--Babcock Lumber Company, Pittsburgh, PA, pg. 107
Stillman, Walter R., Chm. Bd. & Pres.--Stillman & Hoag, Inc., Englewood, NJ, pg. 1049
Stimpson, Fred T., Pres. & Chief Exec. Officer--Gulf Lumber Company, Inc., Mobile, AL, pg. 493
Stinson, Frank, Pres.--Roundtree Automotive Group, Shreveport, LA, pg. 952
Stipp, John S., Chm. Bd. & Chief Exec. Officer--District Petroleum Products, Inc., Sandusky, OH, pg. 340
Stipp, Scott L., Pres.--District Petroleum Products, Inc., Sandusky, OH, pg. 340
Stirling, James R., Pres.--Bell & Howell Phillipsburg Company, Lehigh Valley, PA, pg. 135
Stobie, J. Morgan, V.P.--Reliance Medical Products, Inc., Mason, OH, pg. 925
Stockham, Herbert, Pres. & Chief Exec. Officer--Stockham Valves & Fittings, Inc., Birmingham, AL, pg. 1050
Stoddard, Nathaniel C., Pres. & Chief Oper. Officer--Garden Way, Inc., Troy, NY, pg. 443
Stoehr, James H., Jr., Pres. & Chief Exec. Officer--Robbins, Inc., Cincinnati, OH, pg. 938
Stogel, Lawrence, Pres.--The Stogel Companies Inc., New York, NY, pg. 1050
Stokes, Curt, Pres. & Chief Exec. Officer--Dean Operations Inc., Kansas City, MO, pg. 322
Stollenwerck, Richard, Pres./Latin America--Wunderman Cato Johnson, New York, NY, pg. 1211
Stollenwerk, John J., Pres.--Allen-Edmonds Shoe Corp., Port Washington, WI, pg. 36
Stoller, Seymour, Pres.--General Drug Co., Chicago, IL, pg. 449
Stolmeier, Robert C., Pres.--KCL Corporation, Shelbyville, IN, pg. 611
Stone, Albert, Pres. & Chief Exec. Officer--Sterlite Corporation, Townsend, MA, pg. 1047
Stone, Andrew L., Chm. Bd., Pres. & Chief Exec. Officer--K-D Lamp Company, Cincinnati, OH, pg. 612
Stone, Charles G., Chm., Pres. & Chief Exec. Officer--Stone & Simons Advertising, Inc., Southfield, MI, pg. 1051
Stone, Charles Rivers, Pres.--Stone Manufacturing Company, Inc., Greenville, SC, pg. 1051
Stone, Don, Pres.--Don Stone Associates Inc., Mamaroneck, NY, pg. 1050
Stone, Elliot, Pres.--West Coast National Video, Philadelphia, PA, pg. 1177
Stone, Elliot, Pres. & Chief Exec. Officer--National Video, Inc., Philadelphia, PA, pg. 1177
Stone, George E., Chm.--Jackson Mills, Inc., Wellford, SC, pg. 587
Stone, Howard S., Pres. & Sec.--Bake-Line Products, Inc., Des Plaines, IL, pg. 114
Stone, James L., Pres.--Mercer Transportation Co., Louisville, KY, pg. 739
Stone, Jeffrey, Pres.--Formu-3 International, Inc., Canton, OH, pg. 424
Stone, Roger, Pres.--Stone Advertising, New York, NY, pg. 1050
Stone, Ron, Pres.--Stone August Baker Public Relations, Troy, MI, pg. 1051
Storhoff, Donald, Pres.--Wisconsin Dairies Cooperative, Baraboo, WI, pg. 1197
Stork, J.M., Pres.--Stonhard, Inc., Maple Shade, NJ, pg. 1051
Storm, John A., Pres.--Storm Products Company, Inc., Inglewood, CA, pg. 1052
Storms, Charles D., Pres. & Chief Exec. Officer--Red Spot Paint & Varnish Co., Evansville, IN, pg. 918
Stout, D.R., Pres.--Marion Power Shovel Division, Marion, OH, pg. 565
Stout, Everett E., Pres., Chief Exec. Officer, Chief Fin. Officer & Controller--Metaltech, Inc., Kirkwood, MO, pg. 742
Stout, Jack T., Pres.--NDC Distributors, Inc., Los Angeles, CA, pg. 787
Stowers, James E., Pres.--Twentieth Century Companies, Kansas City, MO, pg. 1121
Stowers, James E., Pres.--Twentieth Century Investors, Inc., Kansas City, MO, pg. 1121
Strack, R., Pres.--Global Steel Products Corporation, Deer Park, NY, pg. 463
Strader, Haywood, Pres. & Chief Oper. Officer--Hopkinsville Milling Co., Hopkinsville, KY, pg. 543
Strahman, Herman, Jr., Chm. Bd. & Pres.--Strahman Valves, Inc., Florham Park, NJ, pg. 1052
Strang, Stephen E., Pres. & Publisher--Strang Communications Company, Lake Mary, FL, pg. 1052
Strange, Don E., Pres. & Chief Oper. Officer--Schneller, Inc., Kent, OH, pg. 977
Strange, Peter S., Pres.--Frank Messer & Sons Construction Co., Cincinnati, OH, pg. 741
Straschnoy, Dario, Pres.--Young & Rubicam Argentina, Buenos Aires,, Argentina, pg. 1213
Strassberg, Gerrson, Pres.--Anglers Roslyn Group Ltd., Flushing, NY, pg. 75
Stratakos, John, Pres.--ENI, Rochester, NY, pg. 360
Stratton, James W., Chm. Bd., Pres. & Chief Exec. Officer--Stratton Management Company, Plymouth Meeting, PA, pg. 1053
Stratton, Peter, Pres.--Kendall-Futuro Company, Newport, KY, pg. 622
Stratton, Terry A., Pres.--Aviation Constructors, Inc., Atlanta, GA, pg. 255
Straub, Gary F., Pres. & Chief Oper. Officer--Fine Organics Corp., Lodi, NJ, pg. 411
Straub, Kenneth, Pres.--Par Enterprises, Inc., Wheeling, WV, pg. 847
Strauce, David, Chm. Bd. & Pres.--Key Container Corporation, Pawtucket, RI, pg. 626
Straus, Roger W., Jr., Pres. & Chief Exec. Officer--Farrar, Straus & Giroux, Inc., New York, NY, pg. 403
Strauss, Richard H., Pres.--Advance Packaging Corporation, Grand Rapids, MI, pg. 19
Straut, Charles, Mng. Dir.--Hillside Capital, Inc., New York, NY, pg. 535
Street, Gordon P., Jr., Chm. Bd., Pres. & Chief Exec. & Chief Oper. Officer--North American Royalties, Inc., Chattanooga, TN, pg. 811
Streur, Wayne A., Pres.--Castex Industries Inc., Holland, MI, pg. 228
Strickler, Charles O., Pres.--Rocco Inc., Harrisonburg, VA, pg. 940
Strike, Anthony, Pres.--One Hour Martinizing Dry Cleaning Franchise (System), Cincinnati, OH, pg. 826
Strite, L. Gerald, Pres.--Shenandoah Mfg. Co. Inc., Harrisonburg, VA, pg. 997
Strobel, Oren J., Pres. & Treas.--O. J. Strobel Oil & Tire Co., Inc., Summerville, SC, pg. 1053
Strom, Robert B., Pres.--Foulds Inc., Libertyville, IL, pg. 427
Stromberg, Hank, Pres.--Stromberg-Connors Communications, Rye Brook, NY, pg. 1054
Strong, Dennis, Pres.--Formac Corporation, Minneapolis, MN, pg. 424
Strong, Warren R., Chief Exec. Officer, Chief Oper. Officer, & Pres.--Macco Constructors, Inc., Paramount, CA, pg. 696
Stropes, Larry, Pres., Chief Exec. Officer & New Bus. Contact--Fabianac, Stropes & Armstrong, Inc., San Francisco, CA, pg. 395
Strubel, Richard P., Pres. & Chief Exec. Officer--MICRODOT, Inc., Chicago, IL, pg. 749
Strum, Brian J., Pres.--Prudential Development & Retail Div., Newark, NJ, pg. 897
Strum, Lonny, Pres.--Earle Palmer Brown & Spiro, Philadelphia, PA, pg. 182
Strumbos, George, Pres.--Washers, Inc., Livonia, MI, pg. 1165
Stryker, C. Samuel, Jr., Chief Oper. Officer, Exec. V.P., New Bus. Contact--PMC Partnership, Ltd., Westport, CT, pg. 836
Studer, R.T., Pres.--HPM Corporation, Mount Gilead, OH, pg. 497
Studley, Dennis, Dir.-Opers.--Claud S. Gordon Company, Richmond, IL, pg. 1167
Studstill, Dan, Pres.--All Pro, Inc., Andalusia, AL, pg. 224
Stuhr, Ed, Pres.--Stuhr Enterprises Inc., Wilton, IA, pg. 1055
Stull, Roger, Chm. Bd. & Pres.--Penhall International, Anaheim, CA, pg. 857
Stumpf, Charles T., Chm. Bd., Pres., Chief Exec. Officer & Treas.--Financial Associates, Overland Park, KS, pg. 410
Stumpf, R., Gen. Mgr.--VisiRecord Systems, Inc., South Norwalk, CT, pg. 1153
Stupak, Bob, Pres. & New Bus. Contact--Dine Out Advertising Corp., Las Vegas, NV, pg. 338
Sturgess, Thomas, Pres.--Redman Industries, Inc., Dallas, TX, pg. 919
Sturm, Arthur C., Jr., Chm. Bd. & Pres.--The Sturm Communications Group, Inc., Chicago, IL, pg. 1055
Stusser, Leslie E., Pres.--Stusser Electric Company, Seattle, WA, pg. 1055
Subilia, Maurice H., Pres.--Fiber Materials, Inc., Biddeford, ME, pg. 408
Suchor, Lawrence F., Pres.--Larrys, Inc., Gillette, WY, pg. 659
Sudiura, Go, Pres. & Owner--Miller Fluid Power Corp., Bensenville, IL, pg. 754
Sugahara, Kaytaro G., Pres.--Fairfield Maxwell Ltd., New York, NY, pg. 397
Sugahara, Kaytaro G., Pres.--Fairfield International Corporation, New York, NY, pg. 397
Sugarman, Leonard, Chm. Bd., Pres. & Chief Exec. Officer--Statler Industries, Medford, MA, pg. 1041
Suhowatsky, Stephen J., Pres. & Chief Exec. Officer--Syracuse Supply Company, Syracuse, NY, pg. 1070
Suitt, T. Howard, Pres. & Chief Exec. Officer--Suitt Construction Company, Inc., Greenville, SC, pg. 1056

Suknow, Irving, Pres.--Reading Body Works, Inc., Reading, PA, pg. 916
Sullivan, C., Pres.--Gem, Incorporated, Byhalia, MS, pg. 447
Sullivan, Dan J., Jr., Pres.--Sullivan & Cozart Inc., Louisville, KY, pg. 1056
Sullivan, Harold, III, Pres.--Payson Casters, Inc., Gurnee, IL, pg. 853
Sullivan, James, Chm. Bd., Pres. & Chief Exec. Officer--Sullivan Holding Company, Brentwood, TN, pg. 1056
Sullivan, Jerry, Principal & Co-Creative Dir.--Sullivan Haas Coyle, Atlanta, GA, pg. 1056
Sullivan, Kenneth R., Pres. & Chief Exec. Officer--Sullivan Oil Company, Baton Rouge, LA, pg. 1057
Sullivan, Michael J., Pres.--Hano Business Forms, Inc., Springfield, MA, pg. 505
Sullivan, Michael L., Pres.--Dunmore Corporation, Newtown, PA, pg. 353
Sullivan, Paul J., Pres.--Sullivan & Brownell, Inc., Randolph, VT, pg. 1056
Sullivan, Rhonda L., Pres.--Lavelle Industries Inc., Burlington, WI, pg. 661
Sullivan, Thomas C., Pres. & Chief Fin. Officer--Sullivan Paper Company, West Springfield, MA, pg. 1057
Sullivan, Walter, Pres.--VJ Growers, Inc., Apopka, FL, pg. 1141
Sulpizio, Robert, Pres.--Roberts & Raymond Assoc., Inc., Bala-Cynwyd, PA, pg. 939
Sulprizio, Ray R., Pres.--United Engine & Machine Company, Carson City, NV, pg. 1131
Sult, Erroll, Pres.--National Welders Supply Co. Inc., Charlotte, NC, pg. 794
Suma, Charles M., Pres. & Chief Oper. Officer--Piper Aircraft Corporation, Vero Beach, FL, pg. 872
Summer, Kenneth, Pres.--Propper Manufacturing Co., Inc., Long Island City, NY, pg. 895
Summer, Roland C., Pres.--A. J. Hollander Co., Inc., New York, NY, pg. 539
Summerfield, Arthur E., Jr., Chm. Bd. & Pres.--Summerfield Truck Co. Inc., Portage, IN, pg. 1057
Summerlin, Glenn W., Pres.--Grizzard Advertising, Inc., Atlanta, GA, pg. 488
Summers, Cary, Pres. & Chief Exec. Officer--Silver Dollar City, Inc., Branson, MO, pg. 1004
Summers, Toby, Pres. & Chief Oper. Officer--Coca-Cola Bottling Co. of the Southwest, San Antonio, TX, pg. 257
Sumner, Richard, Pres.--Ershigs, Inc., Bellingham, WA, pg. 387
Sun, David, Pres. & Chief Exec. Officer--Sun Computers, Inc., Carson, CA, pg. 1058
Sunderland, James P., Chm. Bd.--Ash Grove Cement Company, Overland Park, KS, pg. 87
Sundet, Johnson, Pres. & Chief Exec. Officer--Rollerblade, Inc., Minnetonka, MN, pg. 944
Sundman, David M., Pres.--Littleton Coin Co., Inc., Littleton, NH, pg. 679
Super, A. Charles, Pres.--Franklin Press, San Bernardino, CA, pg. 279
Surber, Don, Pres.--Accurate Threaded Fasteners, Inc., Lincolnwood, IL, pg. 11
Sutherland, William P., Pres. & Chief Exec. Officer--Chapman Direct Advertising, New York, NY, pg. 1210
Sutika, James M., Pres. & Treas.--Van Pelt Corporation, Detroit, MI, pg. 1144
Sutter, Carl F., Jr., Pres.--Fisheries Supply Company, Seattle, WA, pg. 415
Sutter, Lynn R., Chm. Bd. & Pres.--Sutter/Martin, Inc., Buffalo Grove, IL, pg. 1065
Sutter, Robert J., Pres.--Minstar, Inc., Minneapolis, MN, pg. 758
Sutter, Robert J., Pres. & Chief Oper. Officer--Genmar Industries, Inc., Minneapolis, MN, pg. 759
Sutton, D. R., Sec.--Tillamook County Creamery Assn., Tillamook, OR, pg. 1097
Sutton, J. Keith, Pres.--Arocom Direct, Inc., Cleveland, OH, pg. 737
Sutton, Roy V., Pres. & Chief Exec. Officer--W. B. Goode Company, Inc., Richmond, VA, pg. 470
Suzio, Len, Pres. & Chief Exec. Officer--New England Corporation, Hamden, CT, pg. 800
Svare, Allen O., Pres. & Gen. Mgr.--Dakota Drug, Inc., Minot, ND, pg. 311
Swaffar, Billy J., Pres.--First Electric Cooperative, Jacksonville, AR, pg. 412
Swallen, Donald, Chm. Bd., Pres.& Chief Exec. Officer--Swallen's, Inc., Cincinnati, OH, pg. 1066
Swan, Donald H., Pres.--Waldorf Corporation, Saint Paul, MN, pg. 1159
Swan, Frank, Pres.--Nationwide Beef, Inc., Chicago, IL, pg. 795
Swaner, Gary, Pres.--Swaner Hardwood Company, Inc., Burbank, CA, pg. 1066
Swanson, Roger W., Pres.--Champion Business Forms, Glendale Heights, IL, pg. 238
Swartz, Benjamin P., Pres.--David Brett, Inc., Easton, MA, pg. 174
Swartz, Edward, Pres.--Aiken Electric Cooperative Inc., Aiken, SC, pg. 26
Swayne, Keith, Pres.--Case-Swayne Co. Inc., Santa Ana, CA, pg. 228
Swearingen, Robert K., Pres.--Maritz Travel Co., Fenton, MO, pg. 708
Sweasy, William J., Pres.--Red Wing Shoe Co., Inc., Red Wing, MN, pg. 919
Swedback, James M., Pres.--Pioneer Mutual Life Insurance Company, Fargo, ND, pg. 872
Sweebe, Richard C., Pres.--Mid America International Trucks, Inc., Memphis, TN, pg. 750
Sweeney, Harry A., Jr., Pres.--Dorland Sweeney Jones, Philadelphia, PA, pg. 346
Sweeney, Jacob B., Jr., Pres.--Jake Sweeney Automotive Inc., Cincinnati, OH, pg. 1067
Sweeney, James, Pres.--McGaw, Inc., Irvine, CA, pg. 729
Sweeney, Mary S., Pres. & Dir.-Adv.--Jake Sweeney Auto Leasing Inc., Cincinnati, OH, pg. 1066
Sweeney, Mary S., Pres. & Dir.-Adv.--Jake Sweeney Auto Leasing, Inc., Cincinnati, OH, pg. 1067
Swift, Charles O., Chm. Bd. & Pres.--Swift Dodge Rolls Royce Inc., Sacramento, CA, pg. 1067
Swift, Humphrey H., Pres. & Adv. Mgr.--Swift Instruments, Inc., Dorchester, MA, pg. 1068
Swift, M. Allen, Chm. Bd., Pres. & Treas.--M. Swift & Sons Inc., Hartford, CT, pg. 1068
Swift, Vincent, Mng. Dir. & New Bus. Contact--Leo Burnett Ltd., Quarry Bay,, Hong Kong, pg. 193
Swinehart, Keith, II, Pres.--Vanguard Plastics, Inc., McPherson, KS, pg. 1145
Swisher, John R., Pres. & Chief Exec. Officer--United Feeds, Inc., Sheridan, IN, pg. 1132
Switzenbaum, Samuel, Pres. & Chief Exec. Officer--Strouse Greenberg & Co., Inc., Philadelphia, PA, pg. 1054
Swoboda, Ralph, Pres.--Credit Union National Association, Madison, WI, pg. 298
Swope, Richard S., Pres.--Swope Automotive Group, Inc., Louisville, KY, pg. 1068
Syar, James M., Pres. & Chief Oper. Officer--Syar Industries, Inc., Napa, CA, pg. 1068
Sybrius, Gerhard, Pres.--Precision Roll Grinders, Inc., Allentown, PA, pg. 885
Synott, Lee, Chm. Bd., Pres. & Chief Exec. Officer--Ingram Book Company, La Vergne, TN, pg. 569
Syverson, David B., Pres.--Dave Syverson Lincoln Mercury, Albert Lea, MN, pg. 1071
Sze, Andy, Pres. & Chief Exec. Officer--Clipper Exxpress Co., Lemont, IL, pg. 256
T.C. Fitzgerald, Pres.--Griffin Pipe Products Co., Downers Grove, IL, pg. 69
Tabachneck, Avrum, Pres.--Trading Port, Inc., Albany, NY, pg. 1105
Tabart, John E., Pres. & Chief Exec. Officer--Princeville Corporation, Princeville, HI, pg. 890
Tabor, Jon K., Chm. Bd., Pres. & Chief Exec. Officer--Allied Mineral Products, Inc., Columbus, OH, pg. 38
Tacony, Kenneth, Pres.--Tacony Corporation, Fenton, MO, pg. 1076
Taddei, Armando, Chm. Bd., Pres. & Treas.--Hunter Contracting Company, Gilbert, AZ, pg. 554
Taft, Gary F., Pres.--Morflex, Inc., Greensboro, NC, pg. 923
Tait, John E., Chm. Bd., Pres. & Chief Exec. Officer--The Penn Mutual Life Insurance Company, Philadelphia, PA, pg. 858
Tait, Stewart R., Pres.--Narrow Fabric Industries, Inc., West Reading, PA, pg. 783
Takahashi, Ken, Pres.--Japan Directory Advertising Company, Ltd. (JDAC), Tokyo, Japan, pg. 1074
Tako, Anthony, Chm. Bd. & Pres.--Gerrard and Company, Des Plaines, IL, pg. 454
Talbert, John B., Jr., Pres.--Hanes Companies, Inc., Winston-Salem, NC, pg. 505
Talge, H. Stephen, Pres.--Dazey Corporation, Industrial Airport, KS, pg. 321
Talley, Willie, Chm. Bd., Pres. & Chief Exec. Officer--ColorTyme, Inc., Athens, TX, pg. 265
Tallichet, David C., Jr., Chm. Bd., Pres. & Chief Exec. Officer--Specialty Restaurants Corporation, Anaheim, CA, pg. 1027
Tamaroff, Jeffrey L., Pres.--Jeffrey Buick-Nissan Inc., Roseville, MI, pg. 591
Tamaroff, Marvin, Pres.--Tamaroff Buick Inc., Southfield, MI, pg. 1077
Tamski, Thomas J., Pres. & Chief Exec. Officer--Global Marketing Resources, New York, NY, pg. 463
Tanaka, Akira, Pres.--Dentsu, Sudler & Hennessey, Tokyo, Japan, pg. 330
Tananbaum, Andrew, Pres. & Chief Fin. Officer--Century Business Credit Corporation, New York, NY, pg. 235
Tancred, Grace M., Pres.--Northwest Tobacco & Candy Co., Fayetteville, AR, pg. 815
Tang, Cyrus, Chm. Bd., Pres., & Chief Exec. Officer--Tang Industries Inc., Elk Grove Village, IL, pg. 1078
Tang, Oscar L., Chm. & Pres.--KOA Holdings, New York, NY, pg. 612
Tang, Patrick, Pres.--Anderson Die Castings, Inc., Wheeling, IL, pg. 72
Tang, Tom Y.C., Pres.--Tekni-Plex, Inc., Brooklyn, NY, pg. 1084
Taniguchi, Barry, Pres.--Puna Plantation Hawaii Ltd., Hilo, HI, pg. 900
Tanimoto, Douglas, Dr., Pres. & Chief Oper. Officer--Laser Power Corporation, San Diego, CA, pg. 660
Tanklage, Robert C., Pres.--La Victoria Foods, Inc., City of Industry, CA, pg. 649
Tannenberg, Dieter E.A., Pres. & Chief Exec. Officer--Bell & Howell Document Management Products Company, Chicago, IL, pg. 135
Tanner, Arthur A., Pres.--Standard-Knapp, Inc., Portland, CT, pg. 1036
Tanner, James T., Pres. & Chief Exec. Officer--Tanner Co. Inc., Rutherfordton, NC, pg. 1078
Tarajano, Ana M., Pres.--Pala Group, Inc., Baton Rouge, LA, pg. 843
Taratoot, Louis J., Chm., Pres. & Chief Exec. Officer--Taracorp, Inc., Atlanta, GA, pg. 1078
Targett, William J., Pres. & Chief Exec. Officer--Meier Metal Service Centers, Inc., Hazel Park, MI, pg. 737
Tarica, James, Pres.--Jimlar Corporation, Great Neck, NY, pg. 594
Tarlow, Arthur S., Jr., Pres.--Alden Shoe Co., Inc., Middleboro, MA, pg. 33
Tarlow, Dick, Pres., New Bus. Contact & Creative Dir.--Tarlow Advertising, New York, NY, pg. 1079
Tarlton, Peter W., Pres.--Wheelock Inc., Long Branch, NJ, pg. 1185
Tarorick, Felix, Pres.--Quaker Industries Limited, Antioch, IL, pg. 903
Tarrant, R. Lane, Chm. Bd., Pres. & Chief Exec. Officer--Tarrant Service Agency, Inc., Louisville, KY, pg. 1079
Tarroja, Vincent C., Exec. V.P. & Gen. Mgr.--San Miguel (U.S.A.) Inc., San Mateo, CA, pg. 969
Tarzian, Thomas, Chm. Bd.--Sarkes Tarzian, Incorporated, Bloomington, IN, pg. 1079
Tase, D., Pres.-Wienerschnitzel Div. & Orig. Hamburger Stand--Galardi Group, Inc., Newport Beach, CA, pg. 441
Tassani, Sally M., Pres. & Chief Exec. Officer--Tassani Communications, Chicago, IL, pg. 1080
Tate, G.M., Pres.--Hardaway Concrete Co., Inc., Columbia, SC, pg. 507
Tate, Gene, Pres.--Merchants Truck Line, Inc., New Albany, MS, pg. 740
Tate, Jay, Pres.--Dale Industries Inc., Dearborn, MI, pg. 312
Tatman, Richard M., Chm. Bd. & Pres.--Acme Foundry, Inc., Coffeyville, KS, pg. 13
Tattenbaum, Donald, Pres.--Pergament Home Centers, Inc., Melville, NY, pg. 862
Tattersall, Keith, Chm. Bd., Pres. & Chief Exec. Officer--Amperif Corporation, Chatsworth, CA, pg. 68
Tatum, Ray, Pres.--Royal Jeep Eagle Chrysler Plymouth, Inc., Casselberry, FL, pg. 953
Tatum, Ray M., Pres.--Royal Jeep Eagle & Chrysler Plymouth, Casselberry, FL, pg. 953
Tatum, Roger, Partner--Tatum Toomey & Whicker, High Point, NC, pg. 1080
Tatum, W.L., Pres.--Tatum Farms, Dawsonville, GA, pg. 1080
Tauber, Orner J., Jr., Pres. & Chief Exec. Officer--Tauber Oil Company, Houston, TX, pg. 1080
Tauscher, William Y., Pres. & Chief Exec. Officer--ComputerLand Corporation, Pleasanton, CA, pg. 271
Tavel, Mark K., Pres. & Chief Investment Officer--Rothchild Asset Management Inc., New York, NY, pg. 951
Tawil, Morris E., Pres.--Tawil Associates Inc., Carteret, NJ, pg. 1080
Taxe, Howard, Pres.--RS Electronics, Livonia, MI, pg. 908
Taylor-Gordon, Elaine, Pres.--Taylor-Gordon/Widmann & Co., Inc., New York, NY, pg. 1081
Taylor, Andrew C., Pres. & Treas.--Enterprise Rent-A-Car Company, Saint Louis, MO, pg. 382
Taylor, Bruce W., Pres. & Chief Oper. Officer--Cole Taylor Bank, Chicago, IL, pg. 260
Taylor, Dale, Pres. & Chief Exec. Officer--Abelson-Taylor, Inc., Chicago, IL, pg. 10
Taylor, David, Pres.--Velcon Filters, Inc., San Jose, CA, pg. 1146
Taylor, Dick, Pres.--Plantation Foods Inc., Waco, TX, pg. 874
Taylor, George, Pres.--CFB Industries, Inc., Chicago, IL, pg. 201
Taylor, Harry, Chm. Bd. & Pres.--Republic Telcom Systems Corporation, Boulder, CO, pg. 928
Taylor, J. Curtiss, Pres.--George Lithograph, San Francisco, CA, pg. 452
Taylor, James W., Pres. & Chief Exec. Officer--Nelson A. Taylor Co., Inc., Gloversville, NY, pg. 1080
Taylor, Jay, Pres. & Creative Dir.--Taylor Advertising, Inc., Tucson, AZ, pg. 1080
Taylor, Jerry, V.P. & Dir.-Adv. & Mktg.--Jordache Advertising, New York, NY, pg. 604
Taylor, Jim, Pres.--QDI, Inc., Denver, CO, pg. 82
Taylor, Kenneth M., Pres.--Producers Co-op Association, Inc., Girard, KS, pg. 892
Taylor, Mark D., Pres. & Chief Exec. Officer--Tyndale House Publishers, Inc., Carol Stream, IL, pg. 1122
Taylor, Merle, Pres.--Wasco Products, Inc., Sanford, ME, pg. 1165
Taylor, Paul, Pres.--Southeastern Freight Lines, Inc., Columbia, SC, pg. 1019
Taylor, Ronald S., Pres.--Capital Industries, Inc., Seattle, WA, pg. 215
Taylor, Stephen D., Pres. & Chief Exec. Officer--American Savings of Florida, ESB, Miami, FL, pg. 382
Taylor, Thomas H., Jr., Pres. & Chief Exec. Officer--Ohio Machinery Co., Cleveland, OH, pg. 822
Taylor, W.A., III, Pres.--Taylor Machine Works, Inc., Louisville, MS, pg. 1081
Taylor, William, Pres. & Chief Exec. Officer--S. E. Huffman Corp., Clover, SC, pg. 551
Taylor, William W., Chm. Bd. & Pres.--Midcoast Industrial Services Corporation, Cedar Rapids, IA, pg. 751
Teague, Robert M., Pres. & Chief Exec. Officer--Thermo Industries Inc., Charlotte, NC, pg. 1091
Teague, Thomas L., Pres. & Chief Oper. Officer--Salem National Corporation, Winston-Salem, NC, pg. 967
Teasley, Larkin, Pres. & Chief Exec. Officer--Golden State Mutual Life Insurance Company, Los Angeles, CA, pg. 467
Teel, Bill, Pres.--T. J. Cinnamons Ltd., Kansas City, MO, pg. 1073
Teel, E. Gerald, Pres. & Chief Oper. Officer--Vita-Milk Dairy, Inc., Seattle, WA, pg. 1153
Teets, John B., Pres. & Chief Exec. Officer--Dunn-Edwards Corporation, Los Angeles, CA, pg. 353
Teller, Louis L., Vice Chm. & Chief Exec. Officer--Octagon Process Inc., Edgewater, NJ, pg. 821
Temkin, Steven, Pres.--Temkin & Temkin, Northbrook, IL, pg. 1086
Temple, John, Pres. & Chief Exec. Officer--Guideposts Associates, Inc., Carmel, NY, pg. 493
Temple, Thomas C., Pres.--U.S. Oil & Refining Co., Tacoma, WA, pg. 1097
Tenenbaum, Harold, Pres.--A. Tenenbaum Co. Inc., North Little Rock, AR, pg. 1087
Tennenhouse, Donald, V.P., Mktg. & Bus. Devel.--Adplan Associates, Evansville, IN, pg. 18
Tenny, Morton, Pres.--Union Pen Company, Greenwich, CT, pg. 1128
Tepas, Gary L., Pres. & Chief Exec. Officer--Emkay, Inc., Itasca, IL, pg. 379
Terborgh, Eliot, Pres. & Chief Exec. Officer--Selectone Corporation, Hayward, CA, pg. 988
Terlato, Anthony, Pres. & Chief Exec. Officer--Paterno Imports Limited, Chicago, IL, pg. 851
Terlato, Anthony, Pres.--Pacific Wine Co., Chicago, IL, pg. 851

Terlizzi, Alfred, Pres.--Ballet Makers, Inc., Totowa, NJ, pg. 116
Terlizzi, Alfred, Pres.--Capezio Ballet Makers, Inc., New York, NY, pg. 116
Terral, Thomas F., Pres. & Chief Exec. Officer--Terral-Norris Seed Co., Inc., Lake Providence, LA, pg. 1088
Terrell, Charles, Pres., Treas. & Chief Exec. Officer--New Haven Savings Bank, New Haven, CT, pg. 801
Terrell, James R., Pres. & Chief Oper. Officer-TV Stations--Gaylord Broadcasting Co., Dallas, TX, pg. 446
Teruya, Mark, Pres.--Armstrong Produce Ltd., Honolulu, HI, pg. 84
Terwillger, Dennis, Chm. Bd. & Pres.--Condere Corporation, Hamden, CT, pg. 273
Tescher, John, Pres.--Grove Valve & Regulator Company, Oakland, CA, pg. 490
Teshinsky, Fred, Pres.--Tulip Corporation, Los Angeles, CA, pg. 1119
Teslow, Paul, Pres. & Chief Exec. Officer--UniHealth America, Burbank, CA, pg. 1126
Tessereau, Herbert L., Vice Chm. & Chief Exec. Officer--Doane Products Co., Joplin, MO, pg. 342
Tessmer, Raymond R., Pres.--Jefferson Chevrolet Co., Detroit, MI, pg. 591
Testwuide, Thomas R., Pres. & Chief Exec. Officer--Schreier Malting Co., Sheboygan, WI, pg. 978
Teufel, Robert J., Pres. & Chief Oper. Officer--Rodale Press, Inc., Emmaus, PA, pg. 942
Tewksbury, Harold V., Pres.--Solon Manufacturing Company, Solon, ME, pg. 1017
Thach, John, Pres.--Lavelle Aircraft Company, Philadelphia, PA, pg. 661
Thain, Clare, Mng. Partner & New Bus. Contact--Ronald James Direct, Los Angeles, CA, pg. 946
Thames, C.E., Pres.--Enco Materials, Inc., Nashville, TN, pg. 380
Tharp, James T., Chm. Bd. & Pres.--McCrory Construction Co., Inc., Columbia, SC, pg. 728
Thayer, Lester R., Chm. Bd. & Pres.--Multiple Allied Services, Inc., Hayward, CA, pg. 775
Thayer, Ty, Pres.--Cargill Salt, Newark, CA, pg. 219
Thayer, Tyrone, Pres.--Cargill Salt Division, Minneapolis, MN, pg. 219
Theis, Stephen, Pres.--Simonds-Shields-Theis Grain Co., Kansas City, MO, pg. 1006
Theisen, Claude I., Pres. & Chief Exec. Officer--T & S Brass & Bronze Works, Inc., Travelers Rest, SC, pg. 1074
Theiss, George B., Pres. & Chief Operating Officer--Arthur Murray Intl., Inc., Coral Gables, FL, pg. 776
Thenappan, Vis, Pres. & Chief Exec. Officer--San Angelo Electric Service Company, San Angelo, TX, pg. 969
Theofilos, Steve P., Chm. Bd., Pres. & Chief Exec. Officer--Theochem Labs., Inc., Tampa, FL, pg. 1090
Thibert, Tom, Pres.-Mktg.--AP Parts Manufacturing Company, Toledo, OH, pg. 240
Thiel, Wilbert, Pres.--Chicorp, Inc., Chicago, IL, pg. 247
Thigpen, John C., Pres. & Chief Oper. Officer--Westgate Inc., Port Allen, LA, pg. 1182
Thom, William C., Pres.--Harmony House Records & Tapes, Troy, MI, pg. 510
Thomas, Berl M., Pres.--Speedling Incorporated, Sun City, FL, pg. 1029
Thomas, Bryan, Chm. Bd., Pres. & New Bus. Contact--Thomas & Perkins, Denver, CO, pg. 1093
Thomas, G. N., Chm. Bd., Pres., Chief Exec. Officer, Chief Fin. Officer & Treas.--A. Levy & J. Zentner Co., Sacramento, CA, pg. 671
Thomas, Gary, Pres. & Chief Oper. Officer--RTMX-Uniflex Inc., Chapel Hill, NC, pg. 908
Thomas, Howard, Pres. & Chief Exec. Officer--Hubert Company, Harrison, OH, pg. 550
Thomas, Ira D., Pres.--Ira Thomas Associates, Inc., Youngstown, OH, pg. 1092
Thomas, James A., Mng. Partner--Maguire Thomas Partners, Los Angeles, CA, pg. 701
Thomas, John E., Pres. & Chief Exec. Officer--Tippins Incorporated, Pittsburgh, PA, pg. 1099
Thomas, John W., III, Pres.--Thomas Built Buses, Inc., High Point, NC, pg. 1092
Thomas, Joseph, Pres.--Cummins-American Corp., Mount Prospect, IL, pg. 304
Thomas, Mark, Pres. & Chief Exec. Officer--Standard Communications Corporation, Carson, CA, pg. 1036
Thomas, Newton B., Chm. Bd. & Pres.--Newtron Group Inc., Baton Rouge, LA, pg. 805
Thomas, Raymond L., Pres.--Frederick Trading Company, Frederick, MD, pg. 430
Thomas, Robert L., Pres. & Treas.--Saul Bros. & Company, Inc., Norcross, GA, pg. 972
Thomas, S. Denis, Pres. & Chief Exec. Officer--Berol Corporation, Brentwood, TN, pg. 856
Thomas, Terence W., Chm. Bd. & Pres.--Arizona Wholesale Supply Company, Phoenix, AZ, pg. 82
Thomasson, G.B., V.P. & Gen. Mgr.--Brainard Strapping, Warren, OH, pg. 171
Thompson, Bryan E., Chm. Bd. & Pres.--Quintron Systems, Inc., Santa Maria, CA, pg. 905
Thompson, C.H., Jr., Pres. & Treas.--Burlington Basket Co., Burlington, IA, pg. 191
Thompson, Dan, Pres.--Border States Paving, Inc., Fargo, ND, pg. 165
Thompson, Frank, Pres. & Treas.--C.F. Thompson Group, Inc., Windsor, CT, pg. 1094
Thompson, James R., Pres.--T & R Electric Supply Company, Inc., Colman, SD, pg. 1071
Thompson, John R., Pres.--Thompson Advertising Productions, Inc., Farmington Hills, MI, pg. 1094
Thompson, Kenneth W., Chm. Bd. & Pres.--Thompson/Marince Advertising, San Antonio, TX, pg. 1094
Thompson, Michael D., Pres. & Chief Exec. Officer--Thompson Tractor Company, Birmingham, AL, pg. 1095
Thompson, Michael H., Pres. & Creative Dir.--Thompson & Company, Memphis, TN, pg. 1094
Thompson, Paul, Pres.--DEC/Bou-Matic, Madison, WI, pg. 309
Thompson, R.K., Pres.--Xebec Corporation, Kansas City, MO, pg. 1206
Thompson, Ralph L., Pres. & Chief Oper. Officer--Fahlgren Martin, Inc., Parkersburg, WV, pg. 396
Thompson, Richard K., Pres.--DIT-MCO Intl., Kansas City, MO, pg. 1206
Thompson, Robert M., Pres. & Chief Exec. Officer--Thompson-McCully Co., Belleville, MI, pg. 1094
Thompson, Roger K., Pres.--Kennedy Manufacturing Company, Van Wert, OH, pg. 623
Thompson, Ronald J., Pres.--Fitzgerald Advertising Inc., New Orleans, LA, pg. 416
Thompson, Scott, Chm. Bd., Pres., Chief Exec. & Chief Oper. Officer--Advanced Technology, Inc., Reston, VA, pg. 20
Thompson, Scott, Pres.--Thompson Enterprises Inc., Minnetonka, MN, pg. 1094
Thompson, Virl, Pres.--Georgie Boy Manufacturing, Inc., Edwardsburg, MI, pg. 453
Thompson, Wayne, Pres. & Treas.--Tank Service, Inc., Knoxville, TN, pg. 526
Thoms, Robert, Pres. & Chief Oper. Officer--Fortifiber Corporation, Los Angeles, CA, pg. 425
Thomsen, Paul A., Pres.--Schaeps Ice Cream Company, Madison, WI, pg. 974
Thomson, Donald, Pres.--Precision Arc Co., Bridgeport, CT, pg. 1013
Thomson, James A., Pres. & Chief Exec. Officer--RAND, Santa Monica, CA, pg. 911
Thomson, Robert H., Pres. & Chief Exec. Officer--Construction Specialties, Inc., Cranford, NJ, pg. 277
Thorbeck, John, Chief Exec. Officer & Pres.--Geo. E. Keith Company, Bridgewater, MA, pg. 620
Thornburg, H.A., Chief Exec. Officer--Bridgewater Resources Corporation, Beverly Hills, CA, pg. 175
Thorne, John D., Pres.--Archibald Candy Company, Chicago, IL, pg. 604
Thornton, John C., Pres.--American Rug Craftsmen Inc., Sugar Valley, GA, pg. 60
Thornton, Neil, Pres. & Chief Exec. Officer--American Industries Inc., Portland, OR, pg. 55
Thornton, Peter B., Pres.--Stern & Stern Industries Inc., New York, NY, pg. 1048
Thornton, T.D., II, Pres. & Treas.--Progress Printing Company, Lynchburg, VA, pg. 894
Thorson, Kenneth W., Dir.--Virginia State Lottery Department, Richmond, VA, pg. 1153
Thorson, Tom, V.P., Dir. Adv.--Electro Ad Agency, Inc., Culver City, CA, pg. 374
Thrall, Oliver, Pres.--Windsor Shade Tobacco Company, Inc., Hartford, CT, pg. 1196
Threshie, R. David, Jr., Publisher--The Orange County Register, Santa Ana, CA, pg. 431
Throgmartin, Jerry, Pres.--Gregg Appliances Inc., Indianapolis, IN, pg. 486
Thursam, Wally, Pres.--Y&R/Wunderman Worldwide/Detroit, Detroit, MI, pg. 1211
Thybony, James D., Pres.--Thybony Wall Coverings Co., Chicago, IL, pg. 1096
Tibball, George, Pres.--STG Marketing Communications, Inc., Fairfield, CT, pg. 964
Tideman, Philip, Chm. Bd., Pres. & Chief Exec. Officer--United Power Association, Elk River, MN, pg. 1134
Tierney, Richard D., Pres.--Cole Business Furniture, York, PA, pg. 608
Tierney, Thomas T., Pres.--Vitatech International, Inc., Tustin, CA, pg. 1153
Tietjen, James J., Pres. & Chief Exec. Officer--SRI International, Menlo Park, CA, pg. 964
Tietjen, Mary, Pres.--Wendt Advertising, Inc., Great Falls, MT, pg. 1176
Tiffin, Robert A., Jr., Pres.--Tiffin Motor Homes, Inc., Red Bay, AL, pg. 1097
Tikkanen, Paul, Pres.--Frank Ix & Sons, Inc., New York, NY, pg. 584
Tilley, William H., Pres. & Owner--Jacmar Companies, Inc., Alhambra, CA, pg. 587
Tills, James J., Pres.--J.F.P. & Associates of Florida, Inc., Sanford, FL, pg. 584
Timbi, Sidney, Chief Exec. Officer--Covington Industries, Atlanta, GA, pg. 290
Timbi, Sidney, Pres.--Game Winner, Inc., Atlanta, GA, pg. 290
Timble, James N., Pres. & Chief Exec. Officer--Headco Industries, Inc., Broadview, IL, pg. 520
Timperman, Ernest J., Pres. & Chief Exec. Officer--Random Corporation, Cincinnati, OH, pg. 912
Tinberg, Richard W., Pres. & Chief Exec. Officer--Bradford Exchange Ltd., Niles, IL, pg. 170
Tindal, Charles H., Chm. Bd., Pres. & Chief Exec. Officer--Palmer Electric Co., Winter Park, FL, pg. 843
Tiseo, Benedict, Pres.--NTH Consultants, Ltd., Farmington Hills, MI, pg. 781
Titus, Roy W., Pres.--Minuteman Press International, Farmingdale, NY, pg. 759
Tobelmann, P.A., Chm. Bd. & Chief Exec. Officer--Swepco Tube Corporation, Clifton, NJ, pg. 1067
Tober, Lester V., Pres. & Chief Exec. Officer--Tober Industries, Inc., Saint Louis, MO, pg. 1099
Toberman, Walter I., Pres.--Toberman, Saint Louis, MO, pg. 1099
Tobey, Joel N., Pres. & Chief Exec. Officer--Amica Mutual Insurance Co., Providence, RI, pg. 66
Tobias, Gerald, Pres.--Rogerson Hiller Corporation, Port Angeles, WA, pg. 944
Tobiason, Ralph, Pres.--Fenton Press, Inc., Addison, IL, pg. 406
Tobin, Bernard, Pres.--Torino Fashions, Inc., New York, NY, pg. 1102
Tobin, John J., Pres.--Molesphini & Tobin, Inc., New York, NY, pg. 764
Tobin, Thomas J., Jr., Pres.--L.F. Driscoll Co., Bala-Cynwyd, PA, pg. 349
Todd, A.J., III, Pres.--A.M. Todd Company, Kalamazoo, MI, pg. 1100
Todd, J. L., Chm. Bd. & Pres.--J. L. Todd Auction Co., Rome, GA, pg. 1099
Todd, Paul, Jr., Pres.--Kalamazoo Holdings, Inc., Kalamazoo, MI, pg. 615
Tofany, Vincent L., Pres.--NBS Imaging Systems, Inc., Fort Wayne, IN, pg. 960
Tointon, Robert G., Pres.--Phelps Tointon Inc., Greeley, CO, pg. 866
Tolaney, Murly, Pres. & Chief Exec. Officer--James M. Montgomery Consulting Engineers, Pasadena, CA, pg. 767
Tolkan, Norman N., Chm. Bd. & Pres.--Door Store, Inc., Washington, DC, pg. 346
Tolkin, Marvin, Pres.--Jennifer Dale, Inc., New York, NY, pg. 592
Tolone, Thomas A., Pres. & Chief Oper. Officer--Paoli, Inc., Paoli, IN, pg. 846
Tombras, Charles P., Jr., Chm. Bd. & Pres.--Charles Tombras Advertising, Inc., Knoxville, TN, pg. 1100
Tomjack, Thomas J., Chm Bd. & Pres.--North Pacific Lumber Company, Portland, OR, pg. 813
Tomlin, Eugene B., Pres. & Chief Exec. Officer--I. H. French & Co. Inc., Champaign, IL, pg. 432
Tomlinson, John W., Pres.--Monumental Millwork, Inc., Westminster, MD, pg. 768
Tompkins, Richard, Pres.--Diamond Electronics, Inc., Lancaster, OH, pg. 335
Tompkins, States D., Pres. & Chief Exec. Officer--Cresmer, Woodward, O'Mara & Ormsbee, New York, NY, pg. 298
Toms, Nick, Pres.--Edwardstone & Company, Inc., New York, NY, pg. 370
Tomsich, Robert J., Chm.--NESCO, Inc., Mayfield Heights, OH, pg. 798
Tongen, Richard W., Pres. & Chief Exec. Officer--American Hardware Mutual Insurance Co., Minnetonka, MN, pg. 55
Toombs, Eugene M., Pres.--Mitek, Inc., Chesterfield, MO, pg. 762
Toomey, Richard, Partner--Tatum Toomey & Whicker, High Point, NC, pg. 1080
Toresco, Donald, Pres.--Ocean Chevrolet, Inc., Toms River, NJ, pg. 820
Torinus, John B., Jr., Chm. Bd. & Chief Exec. Officer--Serigraph, Inc., West Bend, WI, pg. 991
Torke, Elwood F., Pres.--Torke Coffee Company, Inc., Sheboygan, WI, pg. 1102
Torras, Joseph H., Chm. Bd. & Pres.--Eastern Fine Paper, Incorporated, Brewer, ME, pg. 363
Torrey, George B., Pres. & Chief Oper. Officer--G. R. Herberger's, Inc., Saint Cloud, MN, pg. 530
Torstenson, Robert H., Chm. Bd. & Pres.--Duo-Fast Corporation, Franklin Park, IL, pg. 354
Tortoriello, Anthony M., Chm. Bd. & Pres.--Torco Oil, Chicago, IL, pg. 1102
Tosto, Leo R., Pres.--Trerice Tosto International, Bingham Farms, MI, pg. 1110
Toth, Al, Pres.--PBM Publishing, Independence, OH, pg. 835
Toth, Alex S., Chm. Bd., Pres. & Chief Exec. Officer--PBM Office Products, Cleveland, OH, pg. 835
Toth, John A., Pres.--Key Manufacturing Group, Inc., Royal Oak, MI, pg. 627
Totten, David, Pres.--Totten Tubes, Inc., Los Angeles, CA, pg. 1103
Touhey, Carl E., Pres. & Treas.--Orange Motor Company Inc., Albany, NY, pg. 828
Toulmin, H.A., Jr., Pres. & Treas.--Central Pharmaceuticals, Inc., Seymour, IN, pg. 234
Townsend, D., Pres. & Gen. Mgr.--Simpson Dura-Vent Co., Inc., Vacaville, CA, pg. 1007
Townsend, Ted, Pres.--Townsend Engineering Co., Des Moines, IA, pg. 1104
Towson, S.K., Jr., Pres.--The Elwell-Parker Electric Co., Cleveland, OH, pg. 378
Trachtenberg, Joseph M., Pres. & Chief Oper. Officer--Victaulic Company of America, Easton, PA, pg. 1149
Trad, Raja, Chief Exec. Officer--Radius Leo Burnett U.A.E, Dubai., United Arab Emirates, pg. 193
Traeger-Rado, Jacqueline, Pres.--Plastoid Corporation, Hamburg, NJ, pg. 876
Traeger, Peter, Pres.--Artistic Carton Company, Elgin, IL, pg. 87
Trainor, James J., Pres.--Federal Business Products, Inc., Clifton, NJ, pg. 404
Trapp, Donald, Pres.--Leson Chevrolet Company, Inc., Harvey, LA, pg. 668
Traub, Andrew, Pres.--Block Industries, Inc., Wilmington, NC, pg. 157
Trauscht, Donald C., Pres. & Chief Exec. Officer--Borg-Warner Corporation, Chicago, IL, pg. 165
Traut, R.M., Pres.--Follett Service Corporation, Chicago, IL, pg. 422
Trauth, David E., Jr., Pres. & Chief Exec. Officer--Trauth Dairy Inc., Newport, KY, pg. 1108
Travis, Daryl, Pres.--Arian, Lowe, Travis & Gusick, Inc., Chicago, IL, pg. 82
Travis, James D., Pres. & Chief Oper. Officer--Hal Riney & Partners, Inc., San Francisco, CA, pg. 935
Trawick, Jack, Pres.--STRAFCO, Inc., San Antonio, TX, pg. 1052
Traylor, Thomas W., Pres.--Traylor Brothers, Inc., Evansville, IN, pg. 1108
Traylor, W. Leroy, Jr., Pres. & Chief Exec. Officer--Traylor Chemical & Supply Co., Orlando, FL, pg. 1108
Tredenick, Wm. T., Pres.--Resco Products, Inc., Conshohocken, PA, pg. 928
Tredennick, W.T., Pres.--North State Pyrophyllite, Greensboro, NC, pg. 928
Trees, Michael, Chief Exec. Officer--B&W Co-op, Inc., Breckenridge, MI, pg. 107

Treffiletti, Carmen D., Pres.--J. Treffiletti & Sons, Inc., Albany, NY, pg. 1109
Treguer, Jean-Paul, Pres.--MGTB Ayer, Paris,, France, pg. 104
Treiber, Walter G., Jr., Pres. & Chief Oper. Officer--Chicago White Metal Casting, Inc., Bensenville, IL, pg. 246
Treis, Donald J., Pres. & Chief Oper. Officer--Arandell-Schmidt Corporation, Menomonee Falls, WI, pg. 79
Tremaine, B.G., III, Pres.--Miller Company, Meriden, CT, pg. 754
Tremaine, B.G., Jr., Chm. Bd.--Miller Company, Meriden, CT, pg. 754
Trenkamp, Robert, Pres. & Chief Exec. Officer--Varityper, Inc., East Hanover, NJ, pg. 1146
Treonis, Norm, Pres.-Inland Property Management Group, Inc.--The Inland Group, Inc., Oak Brook, IL, pg. 570
Tresnowski, Bernard R., Pres.--Blue Cross and Blue Shield Association, Chicago, IL, pg. 159
Trevvett, Herbert E., Pres. & Chief Exec. Officer--Commercial Travelers Mutual Insurance Company, Utica, NY, pg. 269
Tribull, Christoph, Chm. Bd., Pres., Chief Exec. & Chief Oper. Officer--Sierracin Corporation, Sylmar, CA, pg. 1003
Trick, Mike, Pres.--Southland Flooring Supplies of Louisville, Inc., Louisville, KY, pg. 1023
Trimble, William S., Jr., Pres.--Wm. S. Trimble Company, Inc., Knoxville, TN, pg. 1113
Trinchero, Roger J., Pres.--Sutter Home Winery, Inc., Saint Helena, CA, pg. 1065
Trinkle, Robert C., Pres.--Trinkle Sales, Inc., Cherry Hill, NJ, pg. 1114
Trisler, James, Pres.--Paramount Fitness Equipment Corp., Los Angeles, CA, pg. 848
Trofholz, LeRoy, Pres. & Chief Exec. Officer--Wagner Mills Inc., Schuyler, NE, pg. 1158
Troger, Jay R., Pres. & Chief Exec. Officer--Hackney & Sons, Inc., Washington, NC, pg. 498
Troha, Dennis, Pres.--Boat Transit, Inc., Costa Mesa, CA, pg. 609
Troha, Dennis, Pres.--Jupiter Corp. Transportation System, Kenosha, WI, pg. 609
Troncalli, Charles D., Pres.--Troncalli Motors, Inc., Decatur, GA, pg. 1115
Trone, Oliver S. (Lee), III, Pres.--Trone Advertising, Inc., Greensboro, NC, pg. 1115
Trotter, J. Don, Pres. & Chief Exec. Officer--SCT Yarns, Inc., Chattanooga, TN, pg. 961
Trotter, John J., Pres.--Alloy Products Corporation, Waukesha, WI, pg. 41
Trotter, Phillip, Pres. & Chief Exec. Officer--Vanguard Energy Corp., Houston, TX, pg. 1145
Trotter, W.M., Pres. & Chief Exec. Officer--Consolidated Systems, Inc., Columbia, SC, pg. 277
Trowbridge, Paul, Chm. Bd., Pres. & Chief Exec. Officer--H.M. Smyth Co., Saint Paul, MN, pg. 1014
Troyer, Clifford, Pres.--Dan Dee Pretzel & Potato Chip Co., Waterford, PA, pg. 313
Truchi, David, Pres. & Chief Exec. Officer--Trucchis Markets, Raynham, MA, pg. 1117
Trucksess, William, Pres.--Philadelphia Sign Company, Palmyra, NJ, pg. 867
True, H.A., Jr., Pres. & Chief Exec. Officer--True Companies, Casper, WY, pg. 1117
True, S.M., Jr., Pres.--Southern Farm Bureau Casualty Insurance Company, Ridgeland, MS, pg. 1021
Truesdell, J. E., Jr., Pres. & Sec.--J. Austin Oil Co., Flint, MI, pg. 99
Trullinger, F.L., Pres.--The Chas. H. Lilly Co., Portland, OR, pg. 675
Trump, Donald J., Pres.--Trump Organization, New York, NY, pg. 1118
Trump, Eddie, Pres.--The Trump Group, New York, NY, pg. 1117
Trunk, de Paul, Pres.--Trunk & Associates, Inc., Montclair, NJ, pg. 1118
Tryon, Robert, Pres.--Tactair Fluid Controls Corp., Beverly, NJ, pg. 869
Tsai, Francis, Pres.--American Mitac Corporation, Fremont, CA, pg. 58
Tscheulin, Frederick R., Chm. Bd., Pres. & Chief Exec. Officer--The Highland Group, Inc., Southport, CT, pg. 534
Tucker, A.G., Pres.--Haulpak Division, Komatsu Dresser Company, Peoria, IL, pg. 565
Tucker, F. Louis, Jr., Pres.--Mustang Tractor & Equip. Co., Houston, TX, pg. 777
Tucker, Richard B.C., Chm. Bd. & Pres.--Wm. T. Burnett & Co., Inc., Baltimore, MD, pg. 191
Tucker, Robert D., Pres.--Scherer Scientific, Ltd., Atlanta, GA, pg. 976
Tuckerman, Donald M., Pres. & Chief Exec. Officer--Elkman Advertising & Public Relations, Bala-Cynwyd, PA, pg. 377
Tuckerman, Donald M., Pres. & Chief Exec. Officer--Elkman Advertising, Public Relations Div., Bala-Cynwyd, PA, pg. 378
Tuckerman, Dr. Steven A., Pres.--Tuckerman Optical Co., Columbus, OH, pg. 1118
Tudor, Robert B., Jr., Pres.--Tudor Inc., Alexandria, LA, pg. 1118
Tulley, John E., Pres.--Tulley Buick-Pontiac Company, Inc., Nashua, NH, pg. 1119
Tully, John M., Pres.--Anderson-Tully Co., Memphis, TN, pg. 73
Tunick, Barry, Pres. & Gen. Mgr.--Estes Industries, Inc., Penrose, CO, pg. 1011
Tunmore, E. Roger, Pres. & Sec.--Tunmore Oldsmobile Inc., Buffalo, NY, pg. 1119
Turco, Lou, Pres.--Freeman Manufacturing & Supply Company, Cleveland, OH, pg. 431
Turcotte, Norman J., Pres. & Chief Exec. Officer--Associated Grocers of New England, Inc., Manchester, NH, pg. 90
Turk, Allen, Pres. & Chief Oper. Officer--S. E. Huffman Corp., Clover, SC, pg. 551
Turk, Stanley M., Pres. & New Bus. Contact--CDA/Turk Group, Irvington-on-Hudson, NY, pg. 200
Turley, Robert W., Pres. & Chief Exec. Officer--Intermountain Farmers Association, Salt Lake City, UT, pg. 575
Turley, Stewart, Chm. Bd., Pres. & Chief Exec. Officer--Jack Eckerd Corporation, Largo, FL, pg. 366
Turner, Charles R., Pres.--Cincinnati Incorporated, Harrison, OH, pg. 250
Turner, David B., Pres.--Scott Lumber Company, Bridgeport, OH, pg. 983
Turner, Edward T., Jr., Chm. Bd. & Pres.--Weston Paper & Manufacturing Co., Terre Haute, IN, pg. 1183
Turner, Eric M., Exec. Dir.--Massachusetts State Lottery, Braintree, MA, pg. 719
Turner, George, Dir.--Colorado Lottery, Denver, CO, pg. 265
Turner, Joseph A., III, Pres.--Sigal Construction, Washington, DC, pg. 1003
Turner, Lawrence O., Jr., Pres.--Backus Turner & Partners, Inc., Miami, FL, pg. 112
Turner, Peter Alexander, Pres.--Turner Dairies, Inc., Covington, TN, pg. 1119
Turner, Richard E., Jr., Pres.--Falconer Glass Industries, Inc., Falconer, NY, pg. 492
Turner, Roger, Pres., Chief Exec. & Fin. Officer--Western Controls, North Salt Lake, UT, pg. 1178
Turner, Ronald D.V., Pres. & Chief Oper. Officer--Elliott Company, Jeannette, PA, pg. 378
Turner, Tom, Pres. & Chief Exec. Officer--Associated Druggists, Wichita, KS, pg. 304
Turner, W.B., Jr., Pres. & Chief Oper. Officer--W. C. Bradley Co., Columbus, GA, pg. 170
Turner, William, Chm. Bd., Pres., Chief Exec. & Chief Oper. Officer--The Pullman Company, Livingston, NJ, pg. 899
Turner, William, Chm. Bd., Pres., Chief Exec. & Chief Oper. Officer--Lear Siegler Diversified Holdings Corp., Livingston, NJ, pg. 424
Turner, William J., Chm. Bd., Pres. & Chief Exec. Officer--Lear Siegler Diversified Holdings Corp., Livingston, NJ, pg. 664
Turner, William J., Chm. Bd., Pres. & Chief Exec. Officer--Lear Siegler Diversified Holdings Corp., Livingston, NJ, pg. 424
Turrell, Clifford, Pres., Chief Exec. Officer & Chief Fin. Officer--Cogifer Inc., Cincinnati, OH, pg. 259
Turriff, Thomas J., Chm. Bd., Pres. & Treas.--Tab Chemicals, Inc., Chicago, IL, pg. 1075
Tusher, Thomas W., Pres. & Chief Oper. Officer--Levi Strauss & Co., San Francisco, CA, pg. 670
Tushman, Earl, Pres.--Orleans International, Inc., Bloomfield Hills, MI, pg. 829
Tushman, Larry, Mng. Partner--Sherwood Food Distributors, Detroit, MI, pg. 998
Tustin, Doris, Pres.--Hal Langerman Co., Blue Bell, PA, pg. 657
Tuthill, James G., Jr., Pres. & Chief Exec. Officer--Tuthill Corporation, Hinsdale, IL, pg. 1120
Tutor, Ronald N., Pres. & Chief Exec. Officer--Tutor-Saliba Corporation, Sylmar, CA, pg. 1120
Tuttle, J.L., Pres. & Chief Exec. Officer--Ohio Gas Company, Bryan, OH, pg. 822
Tway, Robert C., III, Pres. & Chief Exec. Officer--Kentucky Manufacturing Co., Louisville, KY, pg. 624
Tway, Robert C., III, Pres.--R.C. Tway Coal Company, Louisville, KY, pg. 1120
Tweddle, Michael E., Chm. Bd. & Pres.--Tweddle Litho Company, St. Clair Shores, MI, pg. 1120
Tweten, James, Pres.--Magnolia Hi-Fi, Inc., Seattle, WA, pg. 701
Twigg-Smith, Thurston, Chm., Pres. & Chief Exec. Officer--Persis Corporation, Honolulu, HI, pg. 863
Tyler, James, Pres.--El Dorado Tire Co., Troy, MI, pg. 372
Tyler, Robert, Pres. & Gen. Mgr.--Nabholz Construction Corp., Conway, AR, pg. 782
Tyrrell, Thomas, Pres. & Chief Exec. Officer--American Steel & Wire Corporation, Cuyahoga Heights, OH, pg. 246
Tyson, Dr. Thomas J., Chm. Bd., Pres. & Chief Exec. Officer--Energy & Environmental Research Corp., Irvine, CA, pg. 381
Uddenberg, A. Keith, Pres.--Keith Uddenberg, Inc., Gig Harbor, WA, pg. 1125
Uehlinger, Robert E., Pres.--Johnson Supply & Equipment Corp., Houston, TX, pg. 601
Uhl, Richard J., Pres. & Chief Exec. Officer--Chicago Holdings, Inc., Pittsburgh, PA, pg. 245
Uhlman, Steve, Pres.--Tech Poulson, Inc., Scottsdale, AZ, pg. 1083
Uhlmann, John W., Pres.--The Uhlmann Co., Kansas City, MO, pg. 1125
Uhlmann, Steve, Pres.--The Tech Group, Scottsdale, AZ, pg. 1082
Ulbrich, Frederick C., Jr., Chm. Bd., Pres. & Chief Exec. Officer--Ulbrich Stainless Steels & Special Metals, Inc., North Haven, CT, pg. 1125
Ullenberg, Ronald T., Pres.--Ullenberg Corp., Chattanooga, TN, pg. 1125
Ullman, David, Partner--Meade Ullman Advertising & Public Relations, Agoura Hills, CA, pg. 733
Ullman, Myron E., III, Co-Chm. & Co- Chief Exec. Officer--R. H. Macy & Co., Inc., New York, NY, pg. 698
Ullmark, Hana, Pres.--Anderson & Lembke Inc., New York, NY, pg. 73
Ulrich, Dean, Pres.--Ventura Coastal Corporation, Ventura, CA, pg. 1147
Ulrich, Lloyd, Pres. & Chief Exec. Officer--Chicago Mechanical, Inc., Chicago, IL, pg. 245
Umans, A.R., Pres., Chief Exec. Officer & Treas.--RHC/Spacemaster Corporation, Melrose Park, IL, pg. 906
Umphenour, Russ, Chm., Pres. & Chief Exec. Officer--Mrs. Winner's Chicken & Biscuit Restaurants, Atlanta, GA, pg. 761
Umphenour, Russell, Jr., Chm. Bd., Pres. & Chief Exec. Officer--R.T.M. Winners, Atlanta, GA, pg. 908
Unanue, Joseph, Pres.--Goya Foods, Inc., Secaucus, NJ, pg. 474
Unbehagen, John, Chm. Bd.--Port of Galveston, Galveston, TX, pg. 881
Undercofler, J. Clayton, III, Chm. Bd.--Southeastern Pennsylvania Transportation Authority, Philadelphia, PA, pg. 1020
Underwood, Charlie, Pres.--Egg Harbor Yacht Co., Inc., Egg Harbor City, NJ, pg. 371
Underwood, James, Jr., Pres.--Shepard Niles, Inc., Montour Falls, NY, pg. 997
Unger, David, Pres.--Midwesco Inc., Niles, IL, pg. 751
Unger, Gerald F., Pres. & Chief Exec. Officer--Unger Company, Cleveland, OH, pg. 1126
Unger, James J., Pres.--ACF Industries, Inc., Earth City, MO, pg. 561
Unger, Les, Pres. & Chief Exec. Officer--Bufkor, Inc., Clearwater, FL, pg. 187
Unger, Phillip W., Chm. Bd. & Pres.--Alliance America, Norcross, GA, pg. 37
Ungerman, Robert T., Pres.--Lampert Yards, Inc., Saint Paul, MN, pg. 653
Unipan, John T., Pres. & Chief Exec. Officer--Continental American Life Insurance Co., Newark, DE, pg. 896
Unrine, Tom, Pres. & Chief Oper. Officer--Margo's La Mode, Inc., Dallas, TX, pg. 373
Unroe, Brad, Pres. & Chief Exec. Officer--Communico, Indianapolis, IN, pg. 270
UnSheid, Henry, Pres.--Texas Electric Cooperatives, Inc., Austin, TX, pg. 1089
Upton, Herbert H., Jr., Pres.--Malloy Lithographing Inc., Ann Arbor, MI, pg. 703
Uray, Harold, Pres.--Pulliam Motor Company, Columbia, SC, pg. 899
Urquahrt, Richard A. III, Pres. & Treas.--SS Restaurant Corporation, Raleigh, NC, pg. 466
Urrutia, Mike, Chm. Bd. & Pres.--Producers Livestock, North Salt Lake, UT, pg. 892
Urschel, Robert R., Pres.--Urschel Labs Inc., Valparaiso, IN, pg. 1140
Uselton, J.C., Pres.--Sverdrup Investments, Inc., Maryland Heights, MO, pg. 1066
Usibelli, Joseph E., Jr., Pres.--Usibelli Coal Mine, Inc., Healy, AK, pg. 1140
Usinger, Fritz, Pres.--Fred Usinger, Inc., Milwaukee, WI, pg. 1140
Ussery, Dave, Pres. & Representative Dir.--Amway Korea, Ltd., Seoul,, Korea, pg. 71
Uytengsu, Wilfred, Pres.--GF Industries, Inc., Oakland, CA, pg. 439
Vaagen, Duane, Pres.--Vaagen Brothers Lumber, Inc., Colville, WA, pg. 1142
Vahl, Jay, Pres.--Payless Car Rental System, Inc., Saint Petersburg, FL, pg. 853
Vaira, Dale, V.P. & Gen. Mgr.--Winter Volvo & Lincoln Mercury, Sacramento, CA, pg. 1197
Vakil, Usman U., Chm. Bd., Pres. & Treas.--Lights Of America, Inc., Walnut, CA, pg. 675
Valade, Robert C., Pres. & Chief Exec. Officer--Carhartt, Inc., Dearborn, MI, pg. 220
Valby, Mary Jane, Dir.-Sls. & Mktg.--Lucca Packing Div., Nalley's Fine Foods, South San Francisco, CA, pg. 25
Valentine, Joseph C., Chm. Bd., Pres. & Chief Exec. Officer--Lubrication Engineers, Inc., Fort Worth, TX, pg. 686
Valentine, Joseph P., Pres.--Consolidated Industries, Inc., Cheshire, CT, pg. 276
Valentine, Michael, Pres.--Mele Manufacturing Co., Inc., Utica, NY, pg. 737
Valentine, Victor V., Pres.--Triple S Technologies, Inc., Vicksburg, MI, pg. 1114
Valentino, Daniel J., Mng. Dir.-North America--Gemini Consulting, Morristown, NJ, pg. 448
Valentino, Harry, Pres. & Chief Oper. Officer--Fresh Mark, Inc., Massillon, OH, pg. 432
Valk, Ted P., Pres.--Valk Manufacturing Company, New Kingstown, PA, pg. 1143
Vallan, Ronald L., Pres.--Young Supply Company, Detroit, MI, pg. 1214
Vallejo, Gustavo, Gen. Mgr.--VIP Publicidad, Quito,, Ecuador, pg. 112
Vallely, Mark J., Pres.--A.T. Clayton & Company, Inc., New York, NY, pg. 253
Vallerie, Donald E., Sr., Pres.--Vallerie's Transport Service, Inc., Norwalk, CT, pg. 1143
Vallozzi, Andrew A., Pres. & Treas.--FCN Advertising, Milwaukee, WI, pg. 394
Valois, Denis, Pres.--L & L Nursery Supply, Inc., Chino, CA, pg. 647
Valva, George, Pres.--Dugan, Valva Associates, Morristown, NJ, pg. 351
Van Anderson, E., V.P.--Grit Publishing Company, Williamsport, PA, pg. 1043
Van Buren, David, Pres. & Chief Exec. Officer--Applied Solar Energy Corporation, City of Industry, CA, pg. 79
van Cuylenberg, Peter, Pres. & Chief Oper. Officer--Next, Inc., Redwood City, CA, pg. 805
Van Denburgh, Frank, Pres.--American Fence Co. of Midwest, Phoenix, AZ, pg. 52
Van Denburgh, John P., Jr., Chm. Bd., Pres. & Chief Exec. Officer--American Fence Company, Phoenix, AZ, pg. 52
Van Dyck, Robert G., Pres.--Bradner Central Company, Chicago, IL, pg. 170
Van Faasen, William, Pres.--Blue Cross and Blue Shield of Massachusetts, Boston, MA, pg. 159
Van Forsythe, H., Pres.--Belgrave Industries, Santa Ana, CA, pg. 133
Van Fossen, Jack, Pres. & Chief Exec. Officer--Red Roof Inns, Inc., Hilliard, OH, pg. 918
Van Gorder, Terry, Pres. & Chief Exec. Officer--Knott's Berry Farm, Buena Park, CA, pg. 637

Van Houten, James F., Pres. & Chief Exec. Officer--MSI Insurance Companies, Arden Hills, MN, pg. 693
Van Hulst, Jack, Pres. & Chief Exec. Officer--Pennex Products Co., Inc., Verona, PA, pg. 858
Van Kanegan, Roy W., Jr., Pres., Treas. & Sec.--Target Stamped Products Corp., Kinsman, OH, pg. 1079
Van Matre, Harry C., Pres.--Dimeo Construction Company, Providence, RI, pg. 338
Van Melis, Charles, Pres.--Key Handling Systems, Inc., Hackensack, NJ, pg. 627
Van Metre, Albert G., Sr., Chm. & Pres.--The Van Metre Companies, Burke, VA, pg. 1144
Van Mollenberg, H., Chm. Bd., Pres. & Chief Exec. Officer--Mollenberg-Betz Inc., Buffalo, NY, pg. 764
Van Ort, Dale, Pres. & Chief Oper. Officer--Freeman Decorating Co., Dallas, TX, pg. 431
Van Pelt, Donald C., Chm. Bd., Pres. & Chief Exec. Officer--Plymouth Tube Company, Warrenville, IL, pg. 877
Van Steenkiste, Dwight P., Pres.--Genova Products, Inc., Davison, MI, pg. 452
Van Tuyl, Cecil L., Chm. Bd., Pres. & Chief Exec. Officer--V.T. Inc., Merriam, KS, pg. 1142
Van Winkle, Fritz, Chm. Bd. & Pres.--Van Winkle & Associates, Inc., Atlanta, GA, pg. 1144
Van Wyk, Brooke, Pres. & Chief Exec. Officer--Pace International Corporation, Kirkland, WA, pg. 838
Vance, Don K., Pres.--Country Home Bakery, Inc., Bridgeport, CT, pg. 290
Vandail, Allan, Chm. Bd.--U.S. Graphite, Inc., Saginaw, MI, pg. 1136
Vander Boon, Orie, Pres.--Ada Beef, Inc., Ada, MI, pg. 16
Vanderbeck, Joan, Pres.--Service Web Offset Corporation, Chicago, IL, pg. 992
Vandergriff, Victor, Pres.--Vandergriff Chevrolet GEO, Arlington, TX, pg. 1144
Vanderminden, Henry J.W., III, Pres.--Telescope Casual Furniture, Inc., Granville, NY, pg. 1085
Vandervelde, Dave, Pres.--Corn States Hybrid Service, Incorporated, Des Moines, IA, pg. 286
Vangelos, Allen J., Pres. & Chief Exec. Officer--Calavo Growers of California, Tustin, CA, pg. 208
Vann, James A., Jr., Pres. & Chief Oper. Officer--Alabama Electric Cooperative, Inc., Andalusia, AL, pg. 28
Vann, James M., Jr., Chm. Bd. & Chief Exec. Officer--Rea Magnet Wire Company, Inc., Fort Wayne, IN, pg. 915
Varacchi, John, Pres.--Furniture Consultants, New York, NY, pg. 437
Varel, Daniel W., Chm. Bd., Pres. & Gen. Mgr.--Varel Manufacturing Co., Dallas, TX, pg. 1145
Varella, Dan, Pres.--Life Line Nutritionals, Inc., Hayward, CA, pg. 675
Vargas, Arnulfo, Pres., Chief Exec. Officer & Investor Rels. Dir.--Cash & Carry Grocer Inc., Chicago, IL, pg. 228
Vasselli, Joseph F., Pres.--Houston Foods Company, Chicago, IL, pg. 547
Vassiliadis, Billy, Pres.--R & R Advertising, Las Vegas, NV, pg. 906
Vaudo, Anthony S., Pres.--Pawnee Extrusions, Grand Prairie, TX, pg. 852
Vaughan, Beverly, Pres.--PSI Group of Companies, Memphis, TN, pg. 837
Vaughn, A., Pres. & Chief Exec. Officer--Maryland & Virginia Milk Producers Association, Reston, VA, pg. 717
Vaughn, Ronald H., Pres.--Neapco, Inc., Pottstown, PA, pg. 1123
Vazquez, Jorge, Mng. Dir.--Ayer Vazquez S.A. de Publicidad, Buenos Aires,, Argentina, pg. 104
Vazzana, John D., Chm. Bd., Pres. & Chief Exec. Officer--NRM-Steelastic, Akron, OH, pg. 781
Veghte, Robert I., Pres. & Chief Exec. Officer--Wheaton Inc., Millville, NJ, pg. 1184
Veino, Gerald F., Pres.--The Blodgett Oven Co., Inc., Burlington, VT, pg. 157
Veit, Werner, Pres.--Booth Newspapers, Inc., Grand Rapids, MI, pg. 165
Veith, Edwin T., Pres.--Carver Boat Corp., Pulaski, WI, pg. 758
Velasquez, ArthurR., Pres. & Chief Exec. Officer--Azteca Foods, Incorporated, Chicago, IL, pg. 105
Velasquez, Luis Guillermo, Pres.--Banana Services Inc., Coral Gables, FL, pg. 117
Veloz, Robert, Pres.--J. C. Carter Company, Inc., Costa Mesa, CA, pg. 226
Venberg, Walter W., Pres.--Homes By Dave Brown, Tempe, AZ, pg. 542
Venet, Zal, Chm. Bd., Pres. & Chief Exec. Officer--The Venet Companies, Inc., Union, NJ, pg. 1147
Vensel, John, Chm. Bd., Pres. & Chief Exec. Officer--Crucible Materials Corp., Syracuse, NY, pg. 302
Ventre, Martin, Pres.--Ventre Packing Company, Inc., Syracuse, NY, pg. 1147
Ventura, Jules C., Pres.--Durlacher & Co., Inc., Long Island City, NY, pg. 354
Venturini, Martin, Sr. V.P.-Mktg.--Convenient Food Mart, Inc., Schaumburg, IL, pg. 281
Vera, Alan D., Pres. & Chief Exec. Officer--The Quest Business Agency, Inc., Houston, TX, pg. 904
Verbeke, Pierre J., Pres.--Econocom-USA Inc., Memphis, TN, pg. 367
Verble, C. Michael, Pres. & Chief Exec. Officer--North American Roofing Company, Inc., Carmel, IN, pg. 811
Verby, William, Pres.--Anton Smit & Co., Inc., Deer Park, NY, pg. 1011
Verdoorn, Sid, Pres., Chief Exec. & Chief Oper. Officer--C. H. Robinson Co. Inc., Eden Prairie, MN, pg. 939
Verebay, Leonard J., Pres.--Queens Group, Inc., Long Island City, NY, pg. 904
Vereen, W.J., Pres., Treas., & Chief Exec. Officer--Riverside Manufacturing Co., Moultrie, GA, pg. 937
Verhassel, Jean-Pierre, Pres.--Serono Baker Diagnostics, Allentown, PA, pg. 991
Verkuil, Paul R., Pres.--American Automobile Association, National Travel Department, Heathrow, FL, pg. 49
Vermeer, Gary J., Founder--Vermeer Manufacturing Company, Pella, IA, pg. 1148
VerMerris, R.C., Chm. Bd. & Pres.--Radix Wire Company, Cleveland, OH, pg. 909
Vermylen, Paul A., Pres.--A. Zeregas Sons, Inc., Fair Lawn, NJ, pg. 1217
Vermylen, Paul A., Jr., Pres., Treas. & Sec.--Meenan Oil Co. Limited Partnership, Syosset, NY, pg. 736
Verner, James R., Pres. & Chief Oper. Officer--Acousti Engineering Co. of Florida, Orlando, FL, pg. 14
Verni, Ralph F., Pres. & Chief Exec. Officer, New England Investment Companies--The New England, Boston, MA, pg. 799
Veroni, Clive, Pres.--Stringer Veroni Ketchum, Toronto,, Canada, pg. 626
Verrette, William C., Pres.--Champion, Inc., Iron Mountain, MI, pg. 238
Veru, Theodore D., Co-Chm. & Chief Oper. Officer--Lois/USA, New York, NY, pg. 681
Vesey, Deyna, Co-Pres., Creative Dir. & New Bus. Contact--Kidvertiser, New York, NY, pg. 629
Vetterli, John E., Pres.--The Flecto Co., Inc., Oakland, CA, pg. 417
Veziris, Anthony, Pres.--Steinbach, White Plains, NY, pg. 1045
Vickers, David, Pres. & Chief Oper. Officer--H.G. Fenton Material Company, San Diego, CA, pg. 406
Vickers, David, Pres. & Chief Oper. Officer--Pre-Mix Concrete Co., San Diego, CA, pg. 406
Vierling, Ed, Pres.--Jerell, Inc., Dallas, TX, pg. 593
Vilani, Semin, Pres.--1st Family Travelers Hawaii, Honolulu, HI, pg. 412
Vile, Joel, D., Chm. Bd. & Pres.--Vile-Goller, Fine Art Printing & Lithography, Kansas City, KS, pg. 1151
Vilett, J.M., Jr., Pres.--Northland Electric Supply Company, Minneapolis, MN, pg. 814
Villani, Edmond D., Pres.--Scudder, Stevens & Clark, Inc., New York, NY, pg. 983
Vincent, Burton J., Chm. Bd, Pres. & Chief Exec. Officer--Vincent Food Industries, Inc., Chicago, IL, pg. 1152
Vincent, G.A., Chm. Bd., Pres., Chief Exec. Officer & Chief Oper. Officer--The C. P. Hall Company, Chicago, IL, pg. 501
Vincent, Philip S., Pres. & Chief Oper. Officer--Southern Mills, Inc., Union City, GA, pg. 1021
Vincent, Robert A., Pres.--David Clark Company, Inc., Worcester, MA, pg. 252
Vinciquerra, R.E., Pres.--Tyler Elevator Products, Inc., Valley View, OH, pg. 1122
Vinson, Carol D., Pres. & Chief Oper. Officer--Insignia Financial Group, Inc., Greenville, SC, pg. 571
Vinyard, Leon E., Pres. & Chief Exec. Officer--Intermatic Inc., Spring Grove, IL, pg. 575
Viola, Harry, Pres.--Harry Viola Advertising, Lyndhurst, NJ, pg. 1152
Virvo, Alexander, Pres. & New Bus. Contact--ADV Marketing Group, Inc., Stamford, CT, pg. 2
Vitale, Alberto, Chm., Pres. & Chief Exec. Officer--Random House, Inc., New York, NY, pg. 19
Vitale, Alberto, Pres.--Alfred A. Knopf, Inc., New York, NY, pg. 20
Vitale, Damon S., Pres. & Chief Oper. Officer--Desa International, Inc., Bowling Green, KY, pg. 331
Vitale, Kenneth, Pres.--Rotary Multiforms, Inc., Detroit, MI, pg. 951
Vitale, Louis, Pres.--Los Angeles Smoking Curing Company, Los Angeles, CA, pg. 684
Vitale, Pietro, Pres.--Oh Boy Corporation, San Fernando, CA, pg. 822
Vitner, William A., Pres.--C.J. Vitner & Co., Inc., Chicago, IL, pg. 1153
Vitullo, Don, Plant Mgr.--Andes Candies, Inc., Delavan, WI, pg. 169
Vitus, Maurice, Jr., Pres.--Vitus Electrical Supply Company, Eugene, OR, pg. 1154
Vives, Mauricio, Gen. Mgr.--Young & Rubicam de Chile Ltda., Santiago,, Chile, pg. 1213
Vivian, Harry M., Pres.--Vivian Millworks, Forty Fort, PA, pg. 1154
Viviano, Anthony J., Pres.--Sterling Heights Dodge, Inc., Sterling Heights, MI, pg. 1046
Vizzi, C.J., Pres.--York Wallcoverings Inc., York, PA, pg. 1208
Vlahakis, Bernard, Pres. & Chief Exec. Officer--Trailer Wheel & Frame Company, Houston, TX, pg. 1105
Vlamis, Ted A., Pres.--Continental American Corp. d/b/a Pioneer Balloon Company, Wichita, KS, pg. 278
Vlasich, Bill, Pres.--Power Conversion, Inc., Saddle Brook, NJ, pg. 883
Vlcek, Don, Pres.--Domino's Pizza Distribution Corp., Ann Arbor, MI, pg. 344
Vogel, Dick, Pres.--America Outdoors Ltd, Thiensville, WI, pg. 48
Vogel, Michael, Pres. & Chief Oper. Officer--Acme Boot Co., Inc., Clarksville, TN, pg. 400
Vogel, T.N., Pres.--Nutech, Inc., San Jose, CA, pg. 817
Vogel, William C., Pres. & New Bus. Contact--The Vogel Communications Group, Los Angeles, CA, pg. 1154
Vogl, Alex J., Chm. Bd. & Pres.--Wilton Corporation, Palatine, IL, pg. 1194
Vold, R.S., Pres.--Timesavers Inc., Minneapolis, MN, pg. 1098
Volgenau, Ernst, Dr., Pres.--Systems Research And Applications Corporation, Arlington, VA, pg. 1071
Volk, John, Pres.--The John Volk Company, Chicago, IL, pg. 1154
Volkert, Arthur, Pres.--Dakota Electric Association, Farmington, MN, pg. 312
Vollrath, Walter III, Pres. & Chief Exec. Officer--Polar Ware Company, Sheboygan, WI, pg. 878
Von Arx, George, Pres.--Jorgensen Steel & Aluminum, Brea, CA, pg. 605
Von Hamm, Gunther, Pres. & Treas.--G. Von Hamm Textiles, Inc., Honolulu, HI, pg. 1155
von Trapp, Johannes, Pres.--Trapp Family Lodge, Inc., Stowe, VT, pg. 1108
Vor Broker, Robert S., Pres.--Edward Don & Company of Illinois, North Riverside, IL, pg. 344
Vorhauer, Eduardo, Pres.--Young & Rubicam, S.A. de C.V., Mexico,, Mexico, pg. 1213
Vortmann, R.H., Pres. & Chief Exec. Officer--National Steel & Shipbuilding Company, San Diego, CA, pg. 794
Vosburg, N.E., Pres. & Chief Exec. Officer--Pacific Hide & Fur Depot, Great Falls, MT, pg. 840
Voss, Michael D., Chm. Bd. & Chief Exec. Officer--Meehan Tooker, East Rutherford, NJ, pg. 736
Voss, Michael P., Pres.--Birdsall Voss & Kloppenburg, Inc., Mequon, WI, pg. 152
Voss, William J., Pres.--Voss Industries, Inc., Cleveland, OH, pg. 1155
Vosseller, Jim, Pres.--Everpure Inc., Westmont, IL, pg. 358
Voves, Joseph, Pres.--Metric & Multistandard Components, Hawthorne, NY, pg. 743
Vrancart, Al, Pres.--NBS Card Services, Inc., South Plainfield, NJ, pg. 960
Vrydagh, Andre, Mng. Dir.--BSB Brussels SA/NV, Brussels,, Belgium, pg. 109
Wabiszewski, Edmund D., Pres.--Maynard Steel Casting Company, Milwaukee, WI, pg. 725
Wachner, Brian Gary, Chm. Bd. & Pres.--BGW Systems, Inc., Hawthorne, CA, pg. 106
Wachstein, Barbara, Pres. & Chief Exec. Officer--Great Lakes Recreation Co., Livonia, MI, pg. 481
Wachter, Russell, S., Pres.--Maryland Virginia Milk Producers Association, Inc., Reston, VA, pg. 717
Wacker, Fred G., III, Pres.--Liquid Controls Corporation, Lake Bluff, IL, pg. 677
Waddell, R. Scott, Pres. & Treas.--Standard Locknut & Lockwasher, Carmel, IN, pg. 1037
Wade, Jim, Adv. Mgr.--National Machinery Adv. Services, Tiffin, OH, pg. 792
Wade, Tom W., Jr., Chm. Bd. & Chief Exec. Officer--Tom Wade Co., Kenton, TN, pg. 1157
Wadsworth, Maurice A., Chm. & Pres.--Gannett Fleming Affiliates, Inc., Harrisburg, PA, pg. 442
Wadsworth, Samuel T., Pres.--United Parking, Inc., Atlanta, GA, pg. 1134
Wadsworth, Stanley, Chm. Bd., Pres. & Chief Exec. Officer--Golf Hosts, Inc., Palm Harbor, FL, pg. 469
Wagener, John H., Pres.--Barge-Wagener, Inc., Atlanta, GA, pg. 119
Waggoner, William, Pres. & Treas.--Waggoner Corp., Troy, MI, pg. 1158
Wagner, D. Keith, Pres.--Charles Town Races, Inc., Charles Town, WV, pg. 240
Wagner, Daniel J., Pres.--Logistics Systems Architects, Sacramento, CA, pg. 982
Wagner, Jack, Pres. & Chief Exec. Officer--Hiross Inc., Niagara Falls, NY, pg. 536
Wagner, Jacqueline, Pres.--Creative Marketing Resource, Inc., Chicago, IL, pg. 297
Wagner, Jim, Pres.--White County Farm Bureau Co-Op Association, Monticello, IN, pg. 1185
Wagner, John R., Pres.--City Machine Tool & Die Company, Muncie, IN, pg. 251
Wagner, Michael R., Pres.--First Worthing, Dallas, TX, pg. 414
Wagner, Roger P., Pres. & Chief Oper. Officer--Trump's Castle Casino Resort, Atlantic City, NJ, pg. 1118
Wagstaff, W., Pres.--Wagstaff Eastern, Hebron, KY, pg. 1158
Wagstaff, William G., Pres.--Wagstaff Inc., Spokane, WA, pg. 1158
Wahl, Eugene R., Pres.--Vibra Screw Inc., Totowa, NJ, pg. 1149
Wahl, John F., Pres. & Chief Exec. Officer--Wahl Clipper Corp., Sterling, IL, pg. 1158
Wahl, William Sr., Pres.--Wahl Instruments, Culver City, CA, pg. 1158
Wahlert, Robert H., Chm. Bd., Pres. & Chief Exec. Officer--FDL Foods, Inc., Dubuque, IA, pg. 394
Wahtola, Charles, Pres.--Woodward-Clyde Federal Services, Denver, CO, pg. 1201
Wahtola, Charles, Pres. & Chief Exec. Officer--Woodward-Clyde Consultants, Denver, CO, pg. 1201
Waingrow, F.R., Pres.--Petersen Publishing Company, Los Angeles, CA, pg. 864
Waite, Harley Jr., Chm. Bd., Pres. & Chief Exec. Officer--Eastern Technologies Ltd, Amesbury, MA, pg. 364
Waitt, Ted, Pres.--Gateway 2000, Sioux City, SD, pg. 446
Wake, Richard, Co-Pres.--Eby Brown Co., Aurora, IL, pg. 365
Wake, Tom, Co-Pres.--Eby Brown Co., Aurora, IL, pg. 365
Wakeham, Carl, Mng. Dir.--Cato Johnson Cape Town, Kenilworth, South Africa, pg. 1214
Wakley, James T., Pres.--Colonial Millwork, Inc., Beverley, WV, pg. 710
Walborn, George A., Pres.--Windsor Service, Inc., Reading, PA, pg. 1196
Walcher, Jack, Chm., Pres. & Chief Exec. Officer--Eddins-Walcher Company, Midland, TX, pg. 367
Walcott, Larry, Pres.--Knoxville Journal Corporation, Maryville, TN, pg. 863
Waldbillig, William J., Pres. & Chief Exec. Officer--Waldbillig & Besteman, Inc., Madison, WI, pg. 1159
Waldman, William C., Pres.--Meldrum & Fewsmith Advertising Inc., Cleveland, OH, pg. 737
Waldorf, Robert, Chm. Bd & Pres.--Idea Man, Inc., Los Angeles, CA, pg. 562
Walken, George, Actg. Pres.--Anthem Life Insurance Companies, Inc., Dallas, TX, pg. 90
Walkenshaw, Philip S., Pres., Chief Exec. Officer & Treas.--The Townsend Agency, Ltd., Rosemont, IL, pg. 1104
Walker, D.T., V.P. & Gen. Mgr.--Acheson Colloids Company, Port Huron, MI, pg. 12
Walker, Deloss, Chm. Bd. & Pres.--Walker & Associates, Inc., Memphis, TN, pg. 1159

Walker, J. Henry, Pres.--Dundee Mills, Inc., Griffin, GA, pg. 352
Walker, James A., Jr., Pres.--Jones Company, Inc., Waycross, GA, pg. 603
Walker, Jimmy, Pres.--Fuel South, Inc., Hazlehurst, GA, pg. 435
Walker, John T., Chm. Bd., Pres. & Chief Exec. Officer--St. Paul Metalcraft, Inc., Saint Paul, MN, pg. 967
Walker, Lewis R., Pres.--Woodcraft Industries, Inc., Saint Cloud, MN, pg. 1200
Walker, M. Chris, Chief Exec. Officer--Walker & Associates, Inc., Welcome, NC, pg. 1159
Walker, Philip R., Pres. & Chief Exec. Officer--Tennessee Farmers Co-op, La Vergne, TN, pg. 1087
Walker, Robert H., Pres. & Treas.--Walker Die Casting, Inc., Lewisburg, TN, pg. 1160
Walker, Ronald E., Pres. & Sec.--Lyon Conklin & Company, Baltimore, MD, pg. 690
Walker, Ronald F., Pres. & Chief Oper. Officer--American Financial Corporation, Cincinnati, OH, pg. 52
Walker, Susan L., Exec. Dir.--South Dakota Lottery, Pierre, SD, pg. 1019
Walker, W. T., Pres.--Somerset Refinery Inc., Somerset, KY, pg. 1017
Wall, Gloria, Pres.--Al Larson Boat Shop, Inc., Terminal Island, CA, pg. 659
Wall, John Lyndon, Chm. Bd. & Pres.--Bryant Electric Company, Inc., High Point, NC, pg. 185
Wall, Michael, Pres.--Premier Industries, Inc., Tacoma, WA, pg. 887
Wall, Ronald-Randolph, Pres.--Ross Roy Communications/ N.Y., New York, NY, pg. 950
Wallace, C.S., Jr., Pres.--Wallace Co. Inc., Houston, TX, pg. 1160
Wallace, Cliff, Pres.--Thrifty Drug Stores, Inc., Minneapolis, MN, pg. 1096
Wallace, Floyd, Chief Exec. Officer--Cooper Instrument Corp., Middlefield, CT, pg. 283
Wallace, H.K., Pres.--Lazy Days R V Center, Inc., Tampa, FL, pg. 663
Wallace, Juanita, Pres., Chief Fin. Officer, Treas. & Sec.--Wallace & Wallace Fuel Oil, St. Albans, NY, pg. 1160
Wallace, Robert, Pres.--Delta Life Corporation, Memphis, TN, pg. 327
Wallace, Thomas T., Pres.--Johnston, Lemon & Co. Inc., Washington, DC, pg. 601
Wallach, James G., Pres. & Chief Exec. Officer--Central National-Gottesman Inc., Purchase, NY, pg. 233
Wallen, Ernest, Pres.--Heat Bath Park Metallurgical, Inc., Indian Orchard, MA, pg. 524
Wallenfelsz, James D., Pres.--Interplastic Corp., Saint Paul, MN, pg. 579
Waller, Bob, Pres.--Evergreen Mills Inc., Ada, OK, pg. 1145
Waller, Jim, Chief Exec. Officer--Ithaca Industries Inc., Wilkesboro, NC, pg. 582
Waller, Leslie P., Pres.--Scientific Corporation, Fort Pierce, FL, pg. 535
Wallis, Norma, Pres. & Chief Exec. Officer--Livernois Engineering Company, Dearborn, MI, pg. 679
Walliser, Carl J., Pres.--Print-O-Tape, Mundelein, IL, pg. 891
Wallwork, W.W., III, Pres.--W.W. Wallwork, Inc., Fargo, ND, pg. 1161
Walmsley, Gregory H., Pres.--Norweco, Inc., Spokane, WA, pg. 816
Walpert, H.E., Chm. Bd., Pres. & Chief Exec. Officer--Ed Walpert & Associates, Rancho Mirage, CA, pg. 1161
Walsh, Daniel J., Pres.--Walsh Construction Co. of Illinois, Chicago, IL, pg. 1161
Walsh, David G., Pres.--Long MFG. NC, Inc., Tarboro, NC, pg. 682
Walsh, John, Pres.--La Marche Mfg. Co., Des Plaines, IL, pg. 649
Walsh, Michael, Pres.--Ocean Properties, Ltd., Boynton Beach, FL, pg. 820
Walsworth, Don O., Pres. & Chief Exec. Officer--Walsworth Publishing Company, Inc., Marceline, MO, pg. 1161
Walter, Bruce C., Chm. Bd., Pres. & Mktg. Dir.--Multi-Media Marketing Communications, Inc. (M.M.M.C., Inc.), Seal Beach, CA, pg. 775
Walter, Curtis, Pres.--Bongards Creameries Inc., Norwood, MN, pg. 164
Walter, Paul F., Chm. Bd., Pres. & Chief Exec. Officer--Thermo Electric Co., Inc., Saddle Brook, NJ, pg. 1091
Walters, Floyd G., Pres.--D&Z, Inc., Philadelphia, PA, pg. 320
Walters, Richard, Pres.--Olson Rug Company, Chicago, IL, pg. 824
Walters, Roger A., Chm. Bd. & Pres.--Harrison Paint Corporation, Canton, OH, pg. 512
Walters, W. Lindsey, Chm. Bd. & Pres.--Flexel, Inc., Atlanta, GA, pg. 418
Waltersdorf, John M., Pres.--Tristate Electrical Supply Co., Inc., Hagerstown, MD, pg. 1114
Walton, Charles W., Pres. & Chief Exec. Officer--Dempster, Inc., Toccoa, GA, pg. 328
Walton, Frank H., Pres.--Combustion Power Company, Menlo Park, CA, pg. 267
Walts, Harry P., Pres. & Chief Exec. Officer--Winston Steel Products Co., Detroit, MI, pg. 1197
Walzman, Mark, Pres.--Mark Fabricks, Inc., Los Angeles, CA, pg. 708
Wang, David, Pres.--Tech Industries, Inc., Woonsocket, RI, pg. 1083
Wang, Robert, Pres.--Wang's International, Inc., Memphis, TN, pg. 1162
Wantock, Richard C., Pres.--Watkins Incorporated, Winona, MN, pg. 1167
Ward, David K., Pres.--Ward Trucking Corp., Altoona, PA, pg. 1163
Ward, Louis L., Chm. Bd., Pres. & Chief Oper. Officer--Russell Stover Candies, Inc., Kansas City, MO, pg. 957
Ward, Patrick J., Chm. Bd., Pres. & Chief Exec. Officer--Caltex Petroleum Corporation, Irving, TX, pg. 211
Ward, Robert A., Jr., Chm. Bd., Pres., Dir. Client Services--Carelli, Glynn & Ward, Butler, NJ, pg. 218
Ward, Robert L., Pres.--Wray-Ward-Laseter Advertising, Charlotte, NC, pg. 1204
Ward, Stewart R., Pres. & Gen. Mgr.--Brad Foote Gear Works, Inc., Cicero, IL, pg. 169
Ward, William, Pres.--Ashley F. Ward, Inc., Cincinnati, OH, pg. 1162
Wardell, Jay, Exec. V.P.--Beef Industry Council, Chicago, IL, pg. 792
Wardrop, Jack, Pres.--Wardrop Murtaugh Temple, Chicago, IL, pg. 1163
Ware, Donald G., Pres.--Harris and Love, Inc., Salt Lake City, UT, pg. 512
Warehime, Michael, Pres.--Snyder's of Hanover, Inc., Hanover, PA, pg. 1015
Warlick, Anderson, Pres. & Chief Oper. Officer--Parkdale Mills, Gastonia, NC, pg. 849
Warmington, James P., Pres.--Warmington Homes, Costa Mesa, CA, pg. 1164
Warmoth, Frank J., Pres. & Chief Oper. Officer--B. L. Montague Co., Sumter, SC, pg. 766
Warn, Michael T., Pres. & Chief Exec. Officer--Warn Industries, Inc., Milwaukie, OR, pg. 1164
Warner, Charles N., Pres.--The U.S. Baird Corporation, Stratford, CT, pg. 114
Warner, Charles N., Pres.--The A. H. Nilson Machine Co., Stratford, CT, pg. 114
Warner, D. Gill, Pres., Chief Exec. Officer & Gen Mgr.--Associated Food Stores Inc., Salt Lake City, UT, pg. 89
Warner, F., Pres.--Laubeck Corporation/Cross, Carbondale, PA, pg. 660
Warner, Fred, Pres.--Beckley Perforating Co., Springfield, NJ, pg. 660
Warner, James J., Pres.--Warner Vineyards, Paw Paw, MI, pg. 1164
Warner, Jon, Pres. & Chief Oper. Officer--Gulf States Paper Corporation, Tuscaloosa, AL, pg. 494
Warp, Harold G., Pres.--Flex-O-Glass, Inc., Chicago, IL, pg. 418
Warp, Harold G., Pres.--Warp Brothers, Chicago, IL, pg. 418
Warren, Frank M., Jr., Pres. & Chief Exec. Officer--Rogers Group Inc., Nashville, TN, pg. 943
Warren, Frank Raymond, Pres.--Warren Properties, Rancho Santa Fe, CA, pg. 1165
Warren, Gene A., Pres. & Chief Exec. Officer--Anson Industries, Inc., Melrose Park, IL, pg. 76
Warren, James, Pres.--Kinko's Corporation, Ventura, CA, pg. 632
Warren, James R., Pres.--Cameron & Barkley Company, Inc., Charleston Heights, SC, pg. 212
Warren, Jim, Pres. & Chief Exec. Officer--Solvay Pharmaceuticals, Inc., Marietta, GA, pg. 1017
Warren, Paul B., Chm. Bd & Pres.--UVP, Inc., San Gabriel, CA, pg. 1124
Warren, Peter, Pres.--Warren/Kremer/CMP/Advertising/ Inc., New York, NY, pg. 1165
Warren, Robert S., Jr., Pres.--Warren Distributing Corp., Raleigh, NC, pg. 1164
Warrenfeltz, Steven, Pres. & Chief Exec. Officer--Old World Industries, Inc., Northbrook, IL, pg. 823
Warzell, Peter, Pres.--United Artists Theatre Circuit, Inc., Englewood, CO, pg. 1130
Waskiewicz, David F., Pres.--Rodney Hunt Company, Orange, MA, pg. 553
Wasserman, Gerald, Pres. & Chief Exec. Officer--Weider Health & Fitness, Woodland Hills, CA, pg. 1173
Wasserstrom, Rodney, Pres. & Chief Exec. Officer--Wasserstrom Company, Columbus, OH, pg. 1167
Wassmer, Richard, Pres.--Swiss-M-Tex, L.P., Travelers Rest, SC, pg. 1068
Wassner, Leonard, Pres.--Arnav Industries, Inc., New York, NY, pg. 84
Wasylowsky, Walter P., Pres.--Magna-Pow'r Inc., Franklin Park, IL, pg. 559
Watanabe, Keizo, Pres.--Scripto-Tokai, Inc., Fontana, CA, pg. 983
Waters, Dan H., Pres.--Leader Leasing, Inc., Memphis, TN, pg. 664
Waters, George B., Pres. & Publisher--Rome Sentinel Co., Rome, NY, pg. 946
Waters, Martin C., Pres. & Chief Exec. Officer--Locus Computing Corp., Inglewood, CA, pg. 680
Watkins, Edward G., Chm. Bd., Pres. & Chief Exec. Officer--Simplex Time Recorder Co., Gardner, MA, pg. 1006
Watkins, George E., Co-Pres.--Watkins System Inc., Concordville, PA, pg. 1167
Watkins, Ronald W., Pres. & Chief Exec. Officer--Nebraska Public Power District, Columbus, NE, pg. 796
Watkins, Wallace H., Pres.--Utica Mutual Insurance Company, New Hartford, NY, pg. 1140
Watson, Albert O., Pres.--Watson's Quality Turkey Products, Inc., Turnersville, NJ, pg. 1168
Watson, David, Pres.--Advanced DZign Systems, Reading, PA, pg. 320
Watson, Don, Pres./Chief Exec. Officer-New York--Chiat/ Day/Mojo/New York, New York, NY, pg. 244
Watson, Donald, Pres.--Griffin Envelope, Inc., Seattle, WA, pg. 487
Watson, James F., Pres.--Skyway Freight Systems, Inc., Watsonville, CA, pg. 1009
Watson, John, Chm. Bd.--VMC Fiberglass Products Inc., Daleville, AL, pg. 1142
Watson, John D., Pres. & Chief Exec. Officer--Display Technologies, Inc., Elgin, IL, pg. 339
Watson, Malcolm Lee, Pres.--Watson Electric Supply Inc., Dallas, TX, pg. 1168
Watson, Paul, Chm., Pres. & Chief Exec. Officer--Farmers Co-op Market Inc., Frisco City, AL, pg. 401
Watson, R.L., Jr., Pres.--Watson Food Service Industries, Dallas, TX, pg. 1156
Watts, Ken, Pres.--Chase Chrysler/Plymouth, Stockton, CA, pg. 240
Waxenberg, Alan M., V.P. & Publisher--Good Housekeeping, New York, NY, pg. 523
Waxman, Jerry, Pres.--Alan Lithograph, Inc., Inglewood, CA, pg. 30
Weaber, Galen G., Pres.--Walter H. Weaber Sons, Inc., Lebanon, PA, pg. 1169
Weatherby, Ed, Chm. Bd. & Pres.--Weatherby, Inc., South Gate, CA, pg. 1169
Weathersby, William C., Pres.--American Safety Razor Company, Verona, VA, pg. 604
Weaver, Charles S., Pres.--Peerless Pottery, Inc., Rockport, IN, pg. 855
Weaver, Michael E., Pres., Chief Exec. Officer & Chief Oper. Officer--Weaver Popcorn Company, Inc., Van Buren, IN, pg. 1170
Weaver, Wayne, Pres. & Chief Exec. Officer--Nine West Group, Inc., Stamford, CT, pg. 807
Webb, Harley D., Chm. Bd. & Pres.--WBH Industries, Inc., Arlington, TX, pg. 1155
Webb, J. Fred, Pres. & Chief Exec. Officer--Fred Webb Inc., Greenville, NC, pg. 1170
Webb, J.J., Pres. & Chief Exec. Officer--Atlantic Steel Company, Atlanta, GA, pg. 95
Webb, James R., Pres.--Uncle Ben's, Inc., Houston, TX, pg. 713
Webb, O. Glenn, Chm. Bd. & Pres.--Growmark, Inc., Bloomington, IL, pg. 490
Webb, R.M., Pres. & Chief Exec. Officer--Webb, Murray & Associates, La Porte, TX, pg. 1170
Webber, Patricia Redmond, Pres.--Redmond Products, Inc., Chanhassen, MN, pg. 920
Webber, Randall M., Pres.--Humphrey Products Company, Kalamazoo, MI, pg. 553
Webber, Robert E., Pres.--Osmose Wood Preserving Co., Buffalo, NY, pg. 830
Weber, Alex, Pres.--Caravan Products Company, Inc., Totowa, NJ, pg. 217
Weber, Alex, Pres.--Carpro, Inc., Totowa, NJ, pg. 217
Weber, Franz Kent, Chm. Bd., Pres. & Chief Exec. Officer--Modulite Corporation, Compton, CA, pg. 763
Weber, James, Pres.--Coleman Spas, Inc., Chandler, AZ, pg. 695
Weber, Joseph A., Jr., Pres.--Weber Marking Systems, Inc., Arlington Heights, IL, pg. 1171
Weber, Robin, Chm. Bd. & Pres.--Elastomeric Technologies, Inc., Hatboro, PA, pg. 372
Wedel, Jan, Pres.--Stolper-Fabralloy Co., Waukesha, WI, pg. 1050
Wedell, Dorrance R., Pres. & Chief Oper. Officer--United States Pipe & Foundry Company, Birmingham, AL, pg. 1162
Wedgworth, George H., Pres.--Sugar Cane Growers Cooperative of Florida, Belle Glade, FL, pg. 1056
Weeberg, Lynn, Controller--American Wyott Corporation, Cheyenne, WY, pg. 65
Weed, Mark A., Pres. & Chief Exec. Officer--Fisher Properties Inc., Seattle, WA, pg. 415
Weekly, John W., Pres. & Chief Oper. Officer--Mutual of Omaha Insurance Company, Omaha, NE, pg. 779
Weeks, Ralph W., Pres. & Chief Exec. Officer--Quality Petroleum Corp., Lakeland, FL, pg. 903
Wegman, Daniel R., Pres.--Wegmans Food Markets, Inc., Rochester, NY, pg. 1172
Wegner, Charles T., IV, Pres. & Chief Oper. Officer--The Jel Sert Co., West Chicago, IL, pg. 591
Wehlke, Bob, Pres.-Towne Properties Asset Management Co.--Towne Properties, Cincinnati, OH, pg. 1104
Wehrle, Henry B. III, Pres. & Chief Oper. Officer--McJunkin Corporation, Charleston, WV, pg. 730
Wehrung, Vernon, Pres.--Modern Concrete Septic Tank Company, Ottsville, PA, pg. 762
Weibel, Fred E., Pres.--Weibel Vineyards, Mission San Jose, CA, pg. 1173
Weichert, James M., Pres.--Weichert Company, Morris Plains, NJ, pg. 1173
Weidaw, Robert F., Pres. & Chief Oper. Officer--Cogentrix Incorporated, Charlotte, NC, pg. 258
Weider, Eric, Pres. & Chief Exec. Officer-Equipment Division--Weider Health & Fitness, Woodland Hills, CA, pg. 1173
Weil, David S., Pres., Chief Exec. & Chief Oper. Officer--Ampacet Corporation, Tarrytown, NY, pg. 67
Weil, Gilbert, Pres.--Bigg's Hyper Shoppes Ohio, Inc., Milford, OH, pg. 150
Weil, Grilbert, Pres.--Bigg's Hyper Shoppes, Inc., Milford, OH, pg. 150
Weil, John D., Pres. & Chief Exec. Officer--American Envelope Company, Chicago, IL, pg. 199
Weil, Robert S., II, Pres.--Weil Brothers Cotton Inc., Montgomery, AL, pg. 1173
Weiler, Gerhard, Pres. & Chief Exec. Officer--Automatic Liquid Packaging, Inc., Woodstock, IL, pg. 100
Weinbach, Lawrence A., Mng. Partner & Chief Exec. Officer--Arthur Andersen & Co., S.C., New York, NY, pg. 72
Weinberg, Rhona, Pres.--Coast Grain Company, Inc., Ontario, CA, pg. 256
Weinberger, Alan D., Chm., Pres. & Chief Exec. Officer--The ASCII Group, Inc., Bethesda, MD, pg. 8
Weinberger, Leon J., Pres. & Chief Exec. Officer--Employers Insurance of Wausau a Mutual Co., Wausau, WI, pg. 380
Weinberger, Leon J., Pres. & Chief Exec. Officer--Employers Insurance of Wausau a Mutual Co., Wausau, WI, pg. 795
Weiner, David L., Pres.--Marketing Support, Incorporated, Chicago, IL, pg. 709
Weiner, Sol B., Pres.--Weiners Enterprises, Inc., Houston, TX, pg. 1173
Weinfeld, Larry, Pres.--Wally Frank, Ltd., Middle Village, NY, pg. 429
Weingarten, John, Pres.--DeWeese Inc., Los Angeles, CA, pg. 334

Weinhart, James J., Pres.--Master Molded Products Corporation, Elgin, IL, pg. 720
Weins, Leo M., Pres. & Treas.--The H. W. Wilson Co., Bronx, NY, pg. 1193
Weinstein, Harvey, Pres.--West Mill Clothes, Inc., Woodside, NY, pg. 1177
Weinstein, Howard J., Chm., Pres. & Chief Exec. Officer--Adams Wine Co., Atlanta, GA, pg. 17
Weinstein, Jerry L., Pres.--UC Industries, Inc., Parsippany, NJ, pg. 1122
Weinstein, Joan, Pres.--Ultimo Ltd., Chicago, IL, pg. 1125
Weinstein, Leo, Pres.--Levlad, Inc., Chatsworth, CA, pg. 671
Weinstein, Stephen, Pres.--Weinstein Otterman & Associates, New York, NY, pg. 1173
Weinstein, Stephen G., Pres.--Logistix, Fremont, CA, pg. 681
Weinstock, Ronald D., Pres.--Weinstock, White & Associates, Memphis, TN, pg. 1174
Weintraub, Robert, Pres. & Creative Dir.--Weintraub and Associates, Inc., Saint Louis, MO, pg. 1174
Weir, David A., Pres.--Pepsi-Cola Albany Bottling Co., Inc., Latham, NY, pg. 860
Weis, Dick, Pres. & Chief Exec. Officer--Food Services of America, Seattle, WA, pg. 423
Weisberg, Jeff, Pres.--A & W Foods, Inc., Cleveland, OH, pg. 1
Weisberg, Larry, Pres. & Chief Oper. Officer--Waring & LaRosa, Inc., New York, NY, pg. 1163
Weisberge, Michael, Pres.--General Textiles, Chula Vista, CA, pg. 451
Weisblum, Bernard, Pres.--Advisors Advertising, Fort Lauderdale, FL, pg. 21
Weisend, C. Frederick, Chm. Bd., Pres. & Chief Exec. Officer--Fritz Chemical Company, Mesquite, TX, pg. 434
Weisiger, Ed, Jr., Pres.--Carolina Tractor & Equipment Co., Charlotte, NC, pg. 223
Weisman, Henry, Pres. & Treas.--Nuarc Company, Inc., Niles, IL, pg. 817
Weisman, Stephen, Pres.--Plainville Stock Company, Inc., Plainville, MA, pg. 874
Weisner, Robert, Pres.--Robbins Auto Parts, Inc., Dover, NH, pg. 938
Weiss, Arnold, Pres.--Cosmos Communications, Inc., Long Island City, NY, pg. 288
Weiss, Donald, Pres.--White Storage & Retrieval Systems, Inc., Kenilworth, NJ, pg. 1186
Weiss, Kenneth, Pres.--North Atlantic Industries Systems Division, Columbia, MD, pg. 812
Weiss, Larry, Chm. Bd., Pres., Chief Exec. Officer & Sec.--Save More Food Mart, Inc., Hobart, IN, pg. 973
Weiss, Wilfred A., Pres.--Weiss Packing Co., Inc., Donora, PA, pg. 1174
Weissman, Jerrold, Pres.--Carl Weissman & Sons, Inc., Great Falls, MT, pg. 1174
Weitz, Fred W., Chm. Bd. & Pres.--The Weitz Corporation, Des Moines, IA, pg. 1174
Weitzel, John P., Pres. & Chief Oper. Officer--Bankers Systems Inc., Saint Cloud, MN, pg. 117
Weitzman, Alan R., Pres. & Chief Exec. Officer--Weitzman/ /Livingston, Inc., Bethesda, MD, pg. 1174
Welch, Brent J., Pres.--ITI Marketing Services, Inc., Omaha, NE, pg. 561
Welch, Ed, Pres.--The Clarinda Company, Clarinda, IA, pg. 1187
Welch, James, Pres.--Vecta, Grand Prairie, TX, pg. 1044
Welch, Joseph F., Chm., Pres. & Chief Exec. Officer--Bachman Company, Reading, PA, pg. 108
Welch, Phil, Mng. Dir.--Bungey Medical, London,, United Kingdom, pg. 111
Welch, Stuart, Pres.--Emery Waterhouse Company, Portland, ME, pg. 379
Weldon, Stephen N., Pres.--Makers Of Kal, Inc., Woodland Hills, CA, pg. 702
Welge, Donald E., Pres. & Gen. Mgr.--Gilster Mary Lee Corp., Chester, IL, pg. 460
Welk, Donald, Pres.--Patch Communications, Titusville, FL, pg. 851
Wellens, Leroy, Chm. Bd., Pres., Chief Exec. & Chief Fin. Officer & Treas.--Wellens & Co., Inc., Minneapolis, MN, pg. 1175
Weller, Jim, Partner & Creative Dir.--Weller & O'Sullivan Advertising, Los Angeles, CA, pg. 1175
Welles, D.K., Jr., Pres. & Chief Exec. Officer--Therma-Tru Corp., Maumee, OH, pg. 1090
Wellington, Richard, Pres.--Wellington Industries Inc., Paterson, NJ, pg. 1175
Wellington, Richard, Pres.--Wellington Home Products, Paterson, NJ, pg. 1175
Wellnitz, Barbara, Pres.-PHI Public Relations--Potter Hazlehurst Incorporated, East Greenwich, RI, pg. 882
Wells, George M., Pres.--Ash Grove Cement Company, Overland Park, KS, pg. 87
Wells, Wallace J., Pres.--International Chemical Company, Tulsa, OK, pg. 576
Wells, William, Pres.--Delaware Electric Co-Op, Greenwood, DE, pg. 325
Welsh, A.D., Jr., Pres.--Welsh Company, Saint Louis, MO, pg. 1175
Welsh, Robert J., Pres.--Welsh Graphics, Pasadena, CA, pg. 1176
Welter, Edward P., Pres. & Chief Oper. Officer--Fabwel Inc., Elkhart, IN, pg. 396
Weltin, Larry, Pres.--R.F. Broadus & Associates, Inc., Atlanta, GA, pg. 177
Welty, Stanley R., Jr., Pres.--The Wooster Brush Company, Wooster, OH, pg. 1202
Wendell, Earl W., Pres. & Chief Exec. Officer--Gaylord Entertainment Co., Nashville, TN, pg. 446
Wendland, Robert, Pres.--The F. Dohmen Company, Germantown, WI, pg. 343
Wendler, Glenn, Chm. Bd. & Pres.--Amana Society, Amana, IA, pg. 46
Wendt, Roderick, Pres. & Treas.--Jeld-Wen, Inc., Klamath Falls, OR, pg. 591
Wenger, Jerry, Chm. Bd. & Pres.--Wenger Corporation, Owatonna, MN, pg. 1176
Wenner, Jann S., Chm. Bd.--Straight Arrow Publishers, Inc., New York, NY, pg. 1052
Wenner, Jann S., Chm. Bd.--Rolling Stone Magazine, New York, NY, pg. 1052
Wenstrand, Thomas W., Co-Pres. & Sec.--Hawkeye Steel Products, Inc., Houghton, IA, pg. 518
Wenstrand, Thomas W., Pres.--Brower Equipment, Houghton, IA, pg. 518
Wenstrup, H.D., Pres. & Chief Exec. Officer--CHEMCENTRAL Corporation, Bedford Park, IL, pg. 241
Wergeles, Donald S., Pres.--Calet, Hirsch & Ferrell, Inc., New York, NY, pg. 949
Werner, Marc, Pres. & Chief Exec. Officer--Amarlite Architectural Products, Atlanta, GA, pg. 47
Werra, Robert, Chm., Pres. & Chief Exec. Officer--Amrecorp Realty Inc., Dallas, TX, pg. 68
Werthan, Bernard, Jr., Pres. & Chief Exec. Officer--Werthan Packaging, Inc., Nashville, TN, pg. 1176
Werts, Lucille, Pres.--Erin Group Administrators, Inc., Lancaster, PA, pg. 387
Wescott, Paul A., Pres.--Howell Laboratories, Inc., Bridgton, ME, pg. 548
Wesley, James W., Pres.--Summit Communications, Inc., Atlanta, GA, pg. 1057
West, Benjamin B., Pres. & Chief Exec. Officer--West & Company Marketing & Advertising, Tampa, FL, pg. 1177
West, Charles, Pres.--Delagra Corporation, Bridgeville, DE, pg. 325
West, G. Vincent, Pres.--West Lumber Co., Atlanta, GA, pg. 1177
West, John A., Pres.--Cimlinc Inc., Itasca, IL, pg. 249
West, W.G., Pres.--Stanchem Inc., East Berlin, CT, pg. 1035
West, Walter, Pres.--Couristan Inc., Fort Lee, NJ, pg. 290
West, William K., Pres. & Creative Dir.--West, Pausback & Vaughan, Inc., Durham, NC, pg. 1177
Westerberg, John R., Pres.--Nelson Westerberg, Inc., Elk Grove Village, IL, pg. 1178
Westerdahl, Edward G., II, Pres.--The Schmidt/Westerdahl Group Ltd., Portland, OR, pg. 976
WEsterfield, Robert, Pres.--Full Service Beverage Company, Wichita, KS, pg. 436
Westerman, William, Pres. & Chief Oper. Officer--Cogsdill Tool Products, Inc., Lugoff, SC, pg. 259
Westhoff, Joseph J., Pres.--Atlantic Concrete Products, Inc., Tullytown, PA, pg. 94
Westin, Richard S., Chm. Bd., Pres. & Chief Exec. Officer--Westin, Inc., Omaha, NE, pg. 1183
Westlake, Wayne S., Pres.--Difco, Inc., Findlay, OH, pg. 337
Westmore, Byron, Pres.--The Lane Construction Corp., Meriden, CT, pg. 656
Weston, J., Pres.--Mellon Corporation, New York, NY, pg. 738
Westphal, Byron, Chm. Bd., Pres. & Chief Exec. Officer--Integrated Energy Controls Corp., Minneapolis, MN, pg. 573
Wetsel, Cecil, Jr., Pres. & Treas.--Wetsel-Oviatt Lumber Company, Folsom, CA, pg. 1183
Wexler, David, Pres.--Tourneau Inc., New York, NY, pg. 1103
Wexner, Alfred B., Pres.--Wexner & Jacobson, Inc., Memphis, TN, pg. 1183
Weyforth, Frank G., Jr., Chm. Bd., Chief Exec. Officer & Pres.--Marketing Resources of America, Inc., Overland Park, KS, pg. 709
Weyl, Tom, Pres. & Chief Creative Officer--Martin Williams Advertising Inc., Minneapolis, MN, pg. 1191
Weyrens, J., Pres. & Chief Exec. Officer--Our Own Hardware Company, Burnsville, MN, pg. 832
Whalen, John D., Pres. & Chief Exec. Officer--Pennsylvania Crusher Corp., Broomall, PA, pg. 858
Whaling, George, Pres. & Chief Exec. Officer--Petty Company, Inc., Effingham, IL, pg. 866
Wheatley, Charles N., Pres. & Chief Exec. Officer--Sahara Coal Co., Chicago, IL, pg. 966
Wheaton, Robert E., Chm. Bd., Pres., Chief Exec. & Chief Fin. Officer--The Bekins Company, Glendale, CA, pg. 132
Wheeler, Irving, Pres.--Haines City Citrus Growers Association, Haines City, FL, pg. 500
Wheeler, Richard, Pres.--Wyoming Machine Company, Casper, WY, pg. 1206
Wheeler, Thomas, Pres.--Electro-Wire Products, Inc., Dearborn, MI, pg. 375
Wheeler, Thomas B., Pres. & Chief Exec. Officer--Massachusetts Mutual Life Insurance Co., Springfield, MA, pg. 718
Whelan, Robert, Pres.--Buff Whelan Chevrolet & GEO, Inc., Sterling Heights, MI, pg. 1185
Whelan, William A., Pres. & Chief Exec. Officer--Roseburg Forest Products Co., Dillard, OR, pg. 948
Whicker, Burton, Partner--Tatum Toomey & Whicker, High Point, NC, pg. 1080
Whillock, Carl S., Pres.--Arkansas Electric Cooperatives Inc., Little Rock, AR, pg. 83
Whipps, Pauline, Pres.--Whipps, Athol, MA, pg. 1185
Whisenhunt, Andrew, Pres. & Chief Exec. Officer--Arkansas Farm Bureau Federation, Little Rock, AR, pg. 83
Whitaker, Gary, Chm., Pres. & Chief Exec. Officer--Curtis Mathes Corporation, Athens, TX, pg. 720
White, Ann S., Pres.--White, Good & Co., Lebanon, PA, pg. 1185
White, Bob, Pres. & Chief Exec. Officer--Marketing Communications, Lenexa, KS, pg. 709
White, Charles Y., Pres. & Chief Oper. Officer--Mississippi Lime Co., Alton, IL, pg. 760
White, Donald J., Pres. & Chief Oper. Officer--The Saugatuck Marketing Group, Westport, CT, pg. 972
White, E. James, Chm. Bd. & Pres.--E. James White Company, Herndon, VA, pg. 1185
White, Ed, Pres.--Vallet Food Serv Inc., Dubuque, IA, pg. 1143
White, Eliot C., Pres., Treas. & Publr.--The Record-Journal Publishing Company, Meriden, CT, pg. 917
White, George, Gen. Mgr.--Abbott Laboratories/Ashland, Ashland, OH, pg. 9
White, John Hazen, Pres.--Taco Inc., Cranston, RI, pg. 1076
White, John, Jr., Pres.--Country Companies Insurance Group, Bloomington, IL, pg. 289
White, Michael H., Pres. & Chief Exec. Officer--Rite-Hite Corporation, Milwaukee, WI, pg. 936
White, Michael H., Pres.--Rite-Hite Corporation (IA), Dubuque, IA, pg. 936
White, Phillip, Pres.--Sweetheart Cup Co., Inc., Chicago, IL, pg. 1067
White, Raymond W., Pres. & Chief Oper. Officer--Christie Electric Corporation, Gardena, CA, pg. 249
White, Robert C., Pres. & Chief Exec. Officer--Industrial Rubber Products Company, Charleston, WV, pg. 566
White, Robert G., Chm. Bd., Pres. & Chief Exec. Officer--New England Frozen Foods, Southborough, MA, pg. 800
White, Susan H., Lottery Unit Chief--Connecticut State Lottery, Newington, CT, pg. 275
White, T.H., Pres. & Chief Oper. Officer--Byron Weston Paper Co., Dalton, MA, pg. 296
White, Thomas A., Pres. & Chief Exec. Officer--Crane & Co., Inc., Dalton, MA, pg. 296
White, William J., Chm. Bd., Pres. & Chief Exec. Officer--Bell & Howell Company, Skokie, IL, pg. 134
Whiteford, Russell E., Pres. & Chief Exec. Officer--Buxton Company, Chicopee, MA, pg. 197
Whitehouse, William L., III, Pres.--Chelsea Moore Company, Cincinnati, OH, pg. 241
Whitemyer, Donald E., Pres.--Whitemyer Advertising, Inc., Zoar, OH, pg. 1186
Whitfield, Bill, Pres.--Century Boats By General Marine Industries, Panama City, FL, pg. 450
Whitfield, Frank G., Pres. & Chief Exec. Officer--Whitfield Foods, Inc., Montgomery, AL, pg. 1187
Whitfield, J.D., Pres.--Sverdrup Corporation, Maryland Heights, MO, pg. 1065
Whitfield, Willaim, Chm. Bd. & Pres.--GMI, Inc.-Glasstream, Panama City, FL, pg. 450
Whiting, R. Bruce, Pres. & Chief Oper. Officer--Kaibab Industries, Phoenix, AZ, pg. 614
Whiting, Richard T., Pres. & Chief Exec. Officer--Whiting Manufacturing Co., Inc., Cincinnati, OH, pg. 1187
Whitman, Christine, Pres.--CVC Products, Inc., Rochester, NY, pg. 206
Whitney, Haynes, Jr., Pres.--Democrat Printing & Lithograph Company, Little Rock, AR, pg. 328
Whitney, John K., Chm.--Gaymar Industries, Inc., Orchard Park, NY, pg. 447
Whitney, Michael A., Pres.--The Robert E. Morris Company, Farmington, CT, pg. 771
Whitsell, William A., Pres.--Copeland Lumber Yard, Inc., Portland, OR, pg. 284
Whitson, James N., Pres.--Mountain Valley Spring Company, Hot Springs, AR, pg. 968
Whitt, David, Pres. & Chief Oper. Officer--Elixir Industries, Gardena, CA, pg. 376
Whitten, Lowell, Pres. & Gen. Mgr.--Cutter Flying Service, Inc., Albuquerque, NM, pg. 307
Whittenberg, Joseph, Pres. & Chief Exec. Officer--Kurfees Coatings, Inc., Louisville, KY, pg. 646
Whittle, John J., Chm. Bd., Pres. & Chief Exec. Officer--Farmers and Traders Life Insurance Co., Syracuse, NY, pg. 401
Whittle, Robert L., Pres.--Williams Whittle Associates, Inc., Alexandria, VA, pg. 1191
Whyte, Fred, Pres.--Stihl Inc., Virginia Beach, VA, pg. 1049
Whyte, George C., Jr., Chm. Bd., Pres. & Chief Exec. Officer--Dakotah, Inc., Webster, SD, pg. 312
Wiatt, James, Pres.--International Creative Management, Inc., Los Angeles, CA, pg. 607
Wick, Jeff, Pres. & Chief Oper. Officer--Wick Building Systems, Mazomanie, WI, pg. 1188
Wickens, Donald L., Chm. & Pres.--The Benham Group, Oklahoma City, OK, pg. 138
Wickersham, John, Pres. & Chief Exec. Officer--Bill Communications, Inc., New York, NY, pg. 150
Wickett, John, Pres.--Seaman-Patrick Paper Company, Detroit, MI, pg. 986
Wickham, William A., Pres.--SBC Advertising, Columbus, OH, pg. 960
Wickland, John A. III, Pres.--Wickland Corporation, Sacramento, CA, pg. 1188
Widmer, Bruno, Pres.--Advico Young & Rubicam AG, Zurich,, Switzerland, pg. 1211
Wiedemer, Richard A. Jr., Pres.--Hinkley Lighting Inc., Cleveland, OH, pg. 535
Wieden, Dan G., Pres. & Creative Dir.--Wieden & Kennedy, Inc., Portland, OR, pg. 1188
Wiedenbeck, Roger D., Chm. Bd. & Pres.--The Johnson Corporation, Three Rivers, MI, pg. 597
Wieland, John F., Chm. Bd., Pres. & Chief Exec. Officer--John Wieland Homes Inc., Atlanta, GA, pg. 1188
Wiener, Louis P., Pres.--Standard Chlorine Chemical Company, Kearny, NJ, pg. 1035
Wiersma, W.R., Pres.--Rutt Custom Cabinetry, Goodville, PA, pg. 957
Wiesemes, Rhoda, Pres. & Treas.--Quality Packaging Products, Inc., Benton Harbor, MI, pg. 903
Wigand, Emeric, Pres.--Wigand Corporation, Colorado Springs, CO, pg. 1189
Wiggins, Clarence R., Chm. Bd., Pres. & Chief Exec. Officer--Century Data Systems, Raleigh, NC, pg. 235
Wiggins, William H., Pres. & Chief Oper. Officer--Thiele Kaolin Co., Sandersville, GA, pg. 1092
Wilbur, Brayton Jr., Pres. & Chief Exec. Officer--Wilbur-Ellis Company & Connell Brothers Company, San Francisco, CA, pg. 1189
Wilcha, J., Pres.--Wild's Baking Company, Englewood, NJ, pg. 1189

Wilcox, David, Pres.--Mountain States Pipe & Supply Company, Colorado Springs, CO, pg. 773
Wilcox, S. C., Pres.--Star-Parts Inc., Hazleton, PA, pg. 1039
Wild, Floyd, Pres.--Lyon County Co-op Oil Co., Marshall, MN, pg. 690
Wildauer, Werner K., Chm. Bd. & Pres.--Leupold & Stevens, Inc., Beaverton, OR, pg. 669
Wilder, Duane, Chm. Bd., Pres. & Treas.--WDP, Inc., New York, NY, pg. 1156
Wilder, Robert O., Chm. Bd., Pres. & Chief Exec. Officer--National Forge Company, Irvine, PA, pg. 788
Wildman, Donald C., Pres.--Scoville Press, Inc., Minneapolis, MN, pg. 983
Wilen, Don, Pres.--Computer Instruments Corporation, Westbury, NY, pg. 271
Wilen, Joseph, Pres.--Wilen Manufacturing Company, Inc., Atlanta, GA, pg. 1189
Wiley, George, Pres.--Swede Sportswear Company, Inc., Los Angeles, CA, pg. 1066
Wilhelm, James M., Pres. & Chief Exec. Officer--F.A. Wilhelm Construction Co., Inc., Indianapolis, IN, pg. 1189
Wilhoit, Joseph W., Pres.--Phoenix Fuel Company, Inc., Phoenix, AZ, pg. 868
Wilke, William P., IV, Pres.--Hammond Lead Products, Inc., Hammond, IN, pg. 504
Wilkes, John, Pres.--John Dusenbery Co., Inc., Randolph, NJ, pg. 355
Wilkie, Michael L., Chm. Bd., Pres., Chief Exec. & Chief Oper. Officer--DoAll Company, Des Plaines, IL, pg. 341
Wilkins, David G., Pres. & Chief Oper. Officer--Doe-Anderson Advertising Agency, Inc., Louisville, KY, pg. 342
Wilkins, W.N. (Bill), Pres.--Wilkins Outdoor Network, Inc., Atlanta, GA, pg. 1189
Wilkinson, Jay G., Pres.--Pebsco Inc., Columbus, OH, pg. 795
Willard, Jane, Pres.--Willard Grain & Feed, Inc., Celina, TX, pg. 1190
Willemarck, Patrick, Gen. Mgr.--Young & Rubicam Belgium S.A., Brussels,, Belgium, pg. 1212
Willert, William D., Pres. & Treas.--Willert Home Products, Inc., Saint Louis, MO, pg. 1190
Williams, Bruce E., Pres., Chief Exec. Officer & Treas.--Williams Company Of Orlando, Inc., Orlando, FL, pg. 1190
Williams, Charles T., Pres.--Echo Design Group, Inc., New York, NY, pg. 365
Williams, Dan, Pres. & Chief Exec. Officer--DMI The Healthcare Agency, Chicago, IL, pg. 309
Williams, David A., Pres. & Gen. Mgr.--Regency Lincoln Mercury, Dallas, TX, pg. 922
Williams, David J., Chm. Bd., Pres. & Chief Exec. Officer--Power Process Piping, Inc., Plymouth, MI, pg. 883
Williams, Don E., Chm. Bd., Pres. & Chief Exec. Officer--Don E. Williams Co., Rock Island, IL, pg. 1190
Williams, Donald H., Jr., Pres.--Lewis Advertising, Inc., Rocky Mount, NC, pg. 673
Williams, E. Roger, Pres.--The Travel Channel, Atlanta, GA, pg. 654
Williams, Fred G., Jr., Pres.--Coakley & Williams Inc., Greenbelt, MD, pg. 256
Williams, George T., Pres. & Chief Exec. Officer--Clinton Mills Inc., Clinton, SC, pg. 202
Williams, J. McDonald, Pres. & Chief Exec. Officer--Trammell Crow Company, Dallas, TX, pg. 1106
Williams, J.L., Pres.--Minyard Food Stores, Coppell, TX, pg. 759
Williams, James A., Pres. & Chief Oper. Officer--Petroleum Inc., Wichita, KS, pg. 865
Williams, James C., Pres.--Williams Distributing Company, Grand Rapids, MI, pg. 1190
Williams, James E., Pres. & Chief Exec. Officer--Golden State Foods Corp., Pasadena, CA, pg. 466
Williams, Joe V. III, Pres. & Treas.--Hardwick Clothes Inc., Cleveland, TN, pg. 508
Williams, John A., Pres.--Memphis Group, Inc., Memphis, TN, pg. 738
Williams, John D., Jr., Pres.--Williams International Industries, Inc., Richmond, VA, pg. 1191
Williams, John F., Chm. Bd., Pres. & New Bus. Contact--John Williams & Associates, Ltd., Sausalito, CA, pg. 1190
Williams, John T., Pres.--Berkshire Industries, Inc., Westfield, MA, pg. 142
Williams, Kathleen, Pres. & Chief Exec. Officer--Williams Television Time, Inc., Santa Monica, CA, pg. 1191
Williams, Larry E., Pres. & Chief Exec. Officer--National Cooperative Refinery Association, McPherson, KS, pg. 787
Williams, Lorraine, Pres.--TSR, Inc., Lake Geneva, WI, pg. 1075
Williams, Mark, Pres.--Carr Gottstein Foods, Anchorage, AK, pg. 225
Williams, R.L., Pres. & Chief Oper. Officer--Dan River Inc., Danville, VA, pg. 313
Williams, Robert, Pres.--Vengroff Williams & Associates, Inc., Centerpoint, NY, pg. 1147
Williams, Robert, Pres.--Topline Advertising, Ronkonkoma, NY, pg. 1102
Williams, Robert J., Sr., Chm. Bd. & Chief Exec. Officer--Cadillac Products, Inc., Troy, MI, pg. 207
Williams, Robert M., Pres. & Treas.--Williams Patent Crusher and Pulverizer Co., Saint Louis, MO, pg. 1191
Williams, Ronald, Pres. & Chief Exec. Officer--The Gary-Williams Company, Denver, CO, pg. 444
Williams, Ronald, Pres. & Chief Exec. Officer--Gary-Williams Energy Corporation, Denver, CO, pg. 444
Williams, Sam A., Pres.--Atlanta Market Center, Atlanta, GA, pg. 94
Williams, Sam B., Pres. & Chief Exec. Officer--Williams International, Walled Lake, MI, pg. 1191
Williams, Terry, Pres.--Day Products, Bridgeport, NJ, pg. 320
Williams, Thomas M., Pres. & Chief Exec. Officer--The Bates Mfg. Co., Hackettstown, NJ, pg. 125
Williams, Tim J., Pres.--Williams & Rockwood, Salt Lake City, UT, pg. 1191
Williamson, Gilbert, Pres.--Champion Pneumatic Machinery Co., Inc., Princeton, IL, pg. 238
Williamson, Hugh H., III, Chm. Bd., Pres. & Chief Exec. Officer--Carolina Steel Corporation, Greensboro, NC, pg. 223
Williamson, Ralph, Pres.--Airline Manufacturing Company, Inc., Columbus, MS, pg. 27
Williamson, Richard B., Pres. & Chief Exec. Officer--T.D. Williamson, Inc., Tulsa, OK, pg. 1192
Willies, Douglas, Pres.--Keith Clark, Sidney, NY, pg. 304
Willingham, Thomas K., Pres.--Kex Products, Inc., La Vergne, TN, pg. 145
Willingham, Tom, Pres. & Chief Exec. Officer--Interstate Distributors Inc., Norcross, GA, pg. 580
Willink, Wayne L., Pres.--Dairyland Power Cooperative, La Crosse, WI, pg. 311
Willis, RobertF., Pres. & Chief Exec. Officer--Maine Printing & Business Forms Co., Portland, ME, pg. 702
Willis, William F., Sr. Exec. V.P.--Tennessee Valley Authority, Knoxville, TN, pg. 1088
Willix, Carmen, Pres. & Chief Exec. Officer--Metropolitan Sunday Newspapers, Inc., New York, NY, pg. 745
Willix, Carmen, Pres. & Chief Exec. Officer--Metro-Puck Comics Network, New York, NY, pg. 745
Willnow, Rod, Pres.& Gen. Mgr.--Matls. Handling Div.--Hoover Group, Inc., Alpharetta, GA, pg. 543
Willoch, Ray, Pres.--Georgia Duck & Cordage Mills, Scottdale, GA, pg. 453
Wills, J. Blacklock, Jr., Pres.--Wills Group, Inc., La Plata, MD, pg. 1193
Wills, R. Scott, Pres.--Wills and Evans, New York, NY, pg. 1193
Wills, Robert, Pres.--Journal/Sentinel Inc., Milwaukee, WI, pg. 607
Wills, Robert, Pres.--Milwaukee Sentinel, Milwaukee, WI, pg. 607
Wills, Robert, Pres.--The Milwaukee Journal, Milwaukee, WI, pg. 607
Wilmot, Thomas C., Pres. & Chief Exec. Officer--Wilmorite Inc., Rochester, NY, pg. 1193
Wilsey, Michael W., Chm. Bd. & Pres.--Wilsey Bennett Co., San Francisco, CA, pg. 1193
Wilson, Clifford D., Pres. & Chief Exec. Officer--Ritchie Industries, Inc., Conrad, IA, pg. 936
Wilson, David, Pres. & Gen. Mgr.--Wilson Products Co., Salt Lake City, UT, pg. 1194
Wilson, David H., Pres.--Goddess Bra Company, East Boston, MA, pg. 464
Wilson, Dean G., Chm. Bd., Pres. & Chief Exec. Officer--Blaw Knox Corp., Pittsburgh, PA, pg. 156
Wilson, Fred, Pres.--The Ingersoll Milling Machine Co., Rockford, IL, pg. 568
Wilson, Harold, Pres.--SICO INC., Minneapolis, MN, pg. 1001
Wilson, Ian R., Chm. Bd., Pres., & Chief Exec. Officer--Windmill Holdings Corp., San Francisco, CA, pg. 1195
Wilson, J.S., Jr., Pres. & Chief Exec. Officer--Conwood Company L.P., Memphis, TN, pg. 281
Wilson, Jim, Pres.--Jim Wilson & Associates, Montgomery, AL, pg. 1193
Wilson, John F., Pres.--Courtesy Chevrolet & Imports Inc., Ithaca, NY, pg. 290
Wilson, Lawrence A., Pres. & Chief Exec. Officer--HCB Contractors, Dallas, TX, pg. 496
Wilson, Mark, Pres. & Chief Exec. Officer--Ace Office Products, Rolling Meadows, IL, pg. 12
Wilson, Mark, Pres.--Spotnails Inc., Rolling Meadows, IL, pg. 1032
Wilson, Ralph C., Jr., Chm. Bd. & Pres.--Ralph C. Wilson Enterprises, Detroit, MI, pg. 1194
Wilson, Rich Jr., Chm. Bd. & Pres.--Heavy Machines, Inc., Memphis, TN, pg. 524
Wilson, Riley, Pres., Treas., Sec. & Controller--Rapid Power Technologies, Inc., Brookfield, CT, pg. 913
Wilson, Ronald D., Pres.--Philadelphia Coca-Cola Bottling Co., Philadelphia, PA, pg. 866
Wilson, Spence, Pres.--Kemmons Wilson Companies, Memphis, TN, pg. 1194
Wilson, Steven A., Pres. & Chief Oper. Officer--The Bases Group, Covington, KY, pg. 124
Wilson, Terry, Pres.--Kilsby-Roberts, Brea, CA, pg. 606
Wilson, Tim, Pres.--Ernest Paper Products, Inc., Los Angeles, CA, pg. 387
Wilson, Valarie M., Chm. & Chief Exec. Officer--Wilson Sculley Associates, Saint Louis, MO, pg. 1194
Wilson, Wallace S., Chm. Bd., Pres. & Chief Exec. Officer--Wilson Industries Inc., Houston, TX, pg. 1193
Wilson, William, Pres. & Chief Exec. Officer--Pioneer/Eclipse Corp., Sparta, NC, pg. 871
Wilthew, Robert M., Pres.--Greer Steel Co., Dover, OH, pg. 486
Wimberly, Joseph J., III, Chm. Bd. & Pres.--I. C. Thomasson Associates, Inc., Nashville, TN, pg. 1094
Wimsatt, James E., Exec. Dir.--New Hampshire Sweepstakes Commission, Concord, NH, pg. 801
Winch, John J., Pres.--The Minster Machine Company, Minster, OH, pg. 759
Windell, Steve A., Mng. Partner & Chief Fin. Officer--R. W. Beck & Associates, Inc., Seattle, WA, pg. 131
Windemuller, Edward, Pres.--Windemuller Electric Inc., Grandville, MI, pg. 1195
Windham, Robert T., Sr., Chm. Bd., Pres. & Chief Exec. Officer--The Windham Company, Pensacola, FL, pg. 1195
Wine, Norman Lee, Pres. & Chief Exec. Officer--Wine & Schulz Inc., Louisville, KY, pg. 1196
Wing, Sam A., Jr., Chm. Bd., Pres. & Chief Exec. Officer--Wing Industries, Inc., Dallas, TX, pg. 1196
Wink, William J., III, Pres.--Bill Wink Chevrolet & GEO, Dearborn, MI, pg. 1196
Winkelmann, Joe, Chm. Bd., Pres. & Chief Exec. Officer--Greenstripe Media, Inc., Newport Beach, CA, pg. 485
Winkler, Agnieszka, Pres.--Winkler McManus, San Francisco, CA, pg. 1196
Winkler, Herbert, Pres.--Jonbil Inc., Chase City, VA, pg. 602
Winkler, Sheri, Pres.--American Marketing Works & International Corporation, Gardena, CA, pg. 58
Winn, Elwood, Pres. & Chief Exec. Officer--Certified Grocers Midwest, Inc., Hodgkins, IL, pg. 236
Winninghoff, Albert, Chm.--Noorderviiet & Winninghoff/Leo Burnett B.V., Amsterdam,, Netherlands, pg. 193
Winship, Blanton C., Pres. & Chief Exec. Officer--Transus Inc., Atlanta, GA, pg. 1108
Winspear, William W., Pres.--Associated Materials Inc., Dallas, TX, pg. 91
Winston, Ronald, Pres.--Harry Winston, Inc., New York, NY, pg. 1197
Winter, William R., Jr., Pres. & Chief Oper. Officer--Williams Steel & Hardware Company, Minneapolis, MN, pg. 1191
Winters, Steve D., Pres. & Chief Exec. Officer--Bepco, Inc., Winston-Salem, NC, pg. 141
Wirt, John, Pres.--Brown-Minneapolis Tank & Fabricating Co., Eagan, MN, pg. 182
Wirta, Ray, Pres. & Chief Oper. Officer--Koll Co., Newport Beach, CA, pg. 641
Wishnack, Marshall B., Pres.--Wheat, First Securities Inc., Richmond, VA, pg. 1184
Wisne, Lawrence A., Pres. & Chief Exec. Officer--Progressive Tool & Industries Co., Southfield, MI, pg. 894
Wissler, Robert C., Pres. & Chief Oper. Officer--Comprehensive Business Services Inc., Carlsbad, CA, pg. 612
Wistisen, Martin, Pres. & Chief Exec. Officer--AgriNorthwest, Inc., Kennewick, WA, pg. 25
Withall, David W., Pres.--Miner Enterprises Inc., Geneva, IL, pg. 756
Witherwax, Jeffrey T., Pres. & Treas.--Naugatuck Glass Company, Naugatuck, CT, pg. 796
Witkowski, John, Pres.--Home Innovations, Inc., New York, NY, pg. 541
Witmer, Thomas H., Pres. & Chief Exec. Officer--Medrad, Inc., Pittsburgh, PA, pg. 736
Witowski, John, Pres.--Home Curtain Corporation, New York, NY, pg. 541
Witt, Barry, Pres.--Westgate Fabrics, Inc., Grand Prairie, TX, pg. 1182
Witt, Howard, Pres.--Littelfuse, Inc., Des Plaines, IL, pg. 678
Witt, Ray H., Pres.--CMI International Inc., Southfield, MI, pg. 202
Wittersheim, James, Pres.--Semblex Corporation, Elmhurst, IL, pg. 989
Wittig, Richard E., Pres.--Preservative Paint Company, Seattle, WA, pg. 887
Witwer, Richard P., Pres.--Kalas Manufacturing, Inc., Denver, PA, pg. 615
Wodrich, Dan, Controller & Chief Exec. Officer--Greenway Co-Op Service, Rochester, MN, pg. 485
Woeste, Bill F., Jr., Pres. & Dir.-Pur.--Bill Woeste Dealer Group, Cincinnati, OH, pg. 1198
Woithe, Robert, Pres.--Stevens Home Fashions, New York, NY, pg. 400
Wojcik, Frederick W., Pres.--Cheyenne Outfitters, Inc., Cheyenne, WY, pg. 244
Wojnowich, Saul, Pres. & Chief Exec. Officer--Highland Mills Inc., Charlotte, NC, pg. 534
Wolande, Charles, Pres. & Chief Fin. Officer--Comark, Bloomingdale, IL, pg. 267
Wolchansky, Charles L., Pres.--Security Van Lines, Inc., Kenner, LA, pg. 987
Wolcott, James D., Jr., Pres.--Weldon, Williams & Lick, Inc., Fort Smith, AR, pg. 1175
Wolf, Dale, Pres.--Wolf Blumberg Krody Inc., Cincinnati, OH, pg. 1199
Wolf, Lawrence, Pres., Chief Exec. Officer, Sec. & Treas.--Leonard Wholesale, Inc., Elizabeth, NJ, pg. 668
Wolf, Leland A., Pres. & Chief Exec. Officer--Leland A. Wolf & Associates, Foster City, CA, pg. 1199
Wolf, Mark E., Pres.--Wolf Manufacturing Company, Waco, TX, pg. 1199
Wolf, Michael A., Pres. & Chief Oper. Officer--Hobart Brothers Co., Troy, OH, pg. 536
Wolf, Robert C., Pres.--Wilkata Packaging Corporation, Kearny, NJ, pg. 1189
Wolfe, John F., Pres., Chief Exec. Officer & Publisher--The Dispatch Printing Company, Columbus, OH, pg. 339
Wolfe, Mike, Pres.--Century Computer Marketing, Marina Del Rey, CA, pg. 235
Wolfe, Ronald J., Pres. & Chief Exec. Officer--Restaurant Developers Corp., Independence, OH, pg. 929
Wolfe, Sterling H., Jr., Pres.--S.W. Jr. Enterprises, Inc., Santa Ana Heights, CA, pg. 965
Wolff, Eike, Mng. Dir.--Wolff & Partner, Stuttgart,, Germany, pg. 112
Wolff, Jerry, Pres.--Total Communications Group, New York, NY, pg. 1102
Wolfington, John F., Pres.--Wolfington Body Company, Exton, PA, pg. 1199
Wolford, David G., Pres., Chief Exec. Officer & Publr.--Commtek Communications, Vienna, VA, pg. 269
Wolfson, B.J., Pres. & Chief Oper. Officer--Flexible Products Company, Marietta, GA, pg. 418
Wolken, Hal, Pres. & Chief Exec. Officer--A. W. Mendenhall Co., Inc., Elk Grove Village, IL, pg. 739
Wolstein, Bert L., Chief Exec. Officer--Developers Diversified, Moreland Hills, OH, pg. 333
Wong, George R., Pres.--Bel Air Markets, Sacramento, CA, pg. 133
Wong, John E., Pres.--Duary/J.F. Duncan Industries, Inc., Downey, CA, pg. 350
Wong, Peter, Pres.--Peter Wong & Associates, Inc., Richmond, VA, pg. 1199
Woo, Bon Hyung, Pres.--Dentsu, Young & Rubicam/Seoul, Seoul,, Korea, pg. 330

Wood, Bruce, Pres. & Chief Exec. Officer--Lockwood Corporation, Gering, NE, pg. 680
Wood, David E., Vice Chm. & Chief Oper. Officer--Harris Farms, Inc., Coalinga, CA, pg. 511
Wood, Jack T., Pres. & Chief Exec. Officer--Straw Hat Cooperative Corp., Dublin, CA, pg. 1053
Wood, R. Ray, Chm., Pres., Chief Exec. & Chief Oper. Officer--Rockford Products Corp., Rockford, IL, pg. 941
Wood, R.B., Pres. & Treas.--Timec Company, Vallejo, CA, pg. 1097
Wood, Richard P., Jr., Pres.--Wawa, Inc., Wawa, PA, pg. 1169
Wood, Robert J., Pres.--CBM Industries, Inc., Minneapolis, MN, pg. 199
Wood, Thomas L., Pres.--CSI Advertising Inc., Atlanta, GA, pg. 205
Wood, W. Barton III, Pres.--The W.B. Wood Company, New Providence, NJ, pg. 1199
Wood, W.G., Pres.--Tolleson Lumber Company, Inc., Perry, GA, pg. 1100
Woodard, James, Jr., Pres.--Woodward Direct, Inc., Skokie, IL, pg. 1201
Woodbeck, Milford E., Jr., Pres.--Overhead Conveyor Co., Ferndale, MI, pg. 832
Woodfin, Ira J., Pres.--Woodfin-Smith Pontiac, Inc., Baton Rouge, LA, pg. 1200
Woodford, D.H., Pres.--PTC Aerospace, Inc., Litchfield, CT, pg. 837
Woodhall, J.A., Jr., Chm. Bd., Pres. & Chief Exec. Officer--Central Allied Enterprises, Canton, OH, pg. 232
Woodrow, Barry, Pres.--Evans Industries, Inc., Detroit, MI, pg. 390
Woodruff, Paul H., Chm. Bd., Pres. & Chief Exec. Officer--The ERM Group, Exton, PA, pg. 360
Woods, Alfred, Pres.--R & S Strauss, Inc., South River, NJ, pg. 1053
Woods, Gregory R., Pres. & Chief Exec. Officer--Science & Engineering Associates, Albuquerque, NM, pg. 982
Woods, Joe E., Pres.--Joe E. Woods, Inc., Mesa, AZ, pg. 1200
Woodson, Glen, II, Pres. & Chief Oper. Officer--Crouch Supply Company, Inc., Fort Worth, TX, pg. 301
Woodson, Melinda, Pres.--Wholesale Electronic Supply, Dallas, TX, pg. 1188
Woodward, Craig, Pres.--Gillis Public Relations, Inc., Birmingham, AL, pg. 459
Woodward, Stephen, Chief Exec. Officer--Ayer Ltd., London,, United Kingdom, pg. 104
Woodworth, Pat, Chm. Bd., Pres. & Chief Exec. Officer--Winona Knits, Winona, MN, pg. 1196
Woodworth, Peter, Pres.--Winona Knitting Mills, Inc., Winona, MN, pg. 1196
Wooldridge, Ray W., Pres.--Space Master International, Atlanta, GA, pg. 1024
Woolverton, Fred T., Jr., Pres.--Woolverton Oldsmobile-G.M.C. Truck, Inc., Jacksonville, FL, pg. 1201
Woolworth, Richard, Chm. Bd. & Pres.--Blue Cross & Blue Shield of Oregon, Portland, OR, pg. 160
Woomer, James A., Jr., Pres.--Small Tube Products Co., Inc., Altoona, PA, pg. 1010
Wootton, Bill, Pres.--C-B Corporation, Charlotte, NC, pg. 198
Workman, M.C., Pres.--Benjamin Moore & Co., Montvale, NJ, pg. 139
Workman, R.E., Pres.--Tru-Fit Products Corp., Medina, OH, pg. 1117
Wornick, Ronald C., Chm. Bd. & Pres.--The Wornick Company, Burlingame, CA, pg. 1203
Worrell, Terry N., Pres. & Chief Exec. Officer--Sound Warehouse, Inc., Dallas, TX, pg. 1018
Worrell, Thomas E., Jr., Chm. Bd. & Pres.--Worrell Enterprises, Inc., Boca Raton, FL, pg. 1203
Worsley, Walter C., Jr., Chm. Bd. & Pres.--Worsley Companies Inc., Wilmington, NC, pg. 1204
Wortell, Brent, Pres.--Triton Industries, Inc., Chicago, IL, pg. 1114
Wortman, J. John, Pres. & Chief Exec. Officer--Amerisure Companies, Detroit, MI, pg. 66
Wozniak, Edward F., Pres. & Chief Exec. Officer--Wozniak Industries, Inc., Oakbrook Terrace, IL, pg. 1204
Wratten, John, Pres. & Chief Exec. Officer--Seattle Lighting Fixture Co., Seattle, WA, pg. 986
Wrede, Harold, Pres.--Battenfeld Gloucester Engineering Co. Inc., Gloucester, MA, pg. 126
Wreede, Paul G., Pres.--The Commercial Bank, Delphos, OH, pg. 268
Wright, Carl M., Sr. V.P.--Construction Machinery Company, Waterloo, IA, pg. 277
Wright, Curtis, Pres.--Battenberg, Fillhardt & Wright, Inc., San Jose, CA, pg. 126
Wright, Edmund S., Pres. & Chief Exec. Officer--North American Refractories Company, Cleveland, OH, pg. 811
Wright, Edward S., Pres.--John R. Lyman Company, Chicopee, MA, pg. 689
Wright, Jeff, Pres.--Kauffman Stewart Advertising, Minneapolis, MN, pg. 618
Wright, Jerry, Pres. & Chief Exec. Officer--Placid Oil Company, Dallas, TX, pg. 873
Wright, Merrill W., Jr., Chm. Bd. & Pres.--G.F. Wright Steel & Wire Company, Worcester, MA, pg. 1205
Wright, Michael W., Chm.--ShopKo Stores, Inc., Green Bay, WI, pg. 1000
Wright, Nina, Pres.--Arts & Communications Counselors, Inc., Toronto,, Canada, pg. 954
Wright, Patrick E., Pres.--Owensboro Grain Co., Inc., Owensboro, KY, pg. 834
Wright, Robert L., Pres.--Wright Brand Foods, Inc., Vernon, TX, pg. 1204
Wright, T., Chief Oper. Officer--Spalding Canada, Concord,, Canada, pg. 1025
Wright, Tim, Pres.--Keystone Coffee, San Jose, CA, pg. 628
Wrobel, John, Pres.--Hewitt-Robins Corp., West Caldwell, NJ, pg. 532
Wulf, Jerold W., Pres. & Chief Exec. Officer--Andersen Windows Inc., Bayport, MN, pg. 72
Wurm, Robert, Chm. Bd. & Chief Exec. Officer--La Belle Industries, Inc., Oconomowoc, WI, pg. 648
Wurz, Albert, Pres.--Accu-Sort Systems, Inc., Telford, PA, pg. 11
Wurzburg, Richard, Pres.--Wurzburg, Inc., Memphis, TN, pg. 1205
Wurzel, Tom, Chm. Bd., Pres. & Chief Exec. Officer--ACL Technologies, Santa Ana, CA, pg. 2
Wyatt, John W., Pres.--Venchurs Packaging, Inc., Adrian, MI, pg. 1147
Wyatt, Peter F., Pres.--N E D Corp., Worcester, MA, pg. 780
Wyckaerk, Luke, Chm. Bd., Pres. & Chief Exec. Officer--Intertrade Industries, Huntington Beach, CA, pg. 581
Wydman, Marcy, Pres.--Witt Company, Cincinnati, OH, pg. 1198
Wyler, Jeff, Pres.--Jeff Wyler Dealer Group, Inc., Cincinnati, OH, pg. 1206
Wylie, Rick, Pres.--Beutler Heating & Air Conditioning Inc., Sacramento, CA, pg. 148
Wynne, John O., Pres.--Landmark Communications, Inc., Norfolk, VA, pg. 654
Wyse, Lois, Pres.--Wyse Advertising, Inc., Cleveland, OH, pg. 1206
Wyse, Sam, Pres.--Field Packing Company, Owensboro, KY, pg. 409
Yacenda, Richard, Pres.--Moss and Company, Inc., New York, NY, pg. 772
Yaffe, Fred, Chm. Bd. & Chief Exec. Officer--Yaffe & Co., Southfield, MI, pg. 1207
Yager, Vincent C., Pres. & Chief Exec. Officer--Great Lakes Financial Resources, Inc., Homewood, IL, pg. 481
Yaguda, Jerome D., Pres. & Chief Exec. Officer--Wakefern Food Corporation, Elizabeth, NJ, pg. 1158
Yahn, Clarence H., Pres. & Chief Oper. Officer--Blount Lumber Company, Lacona, NY, pg. 158
Yaklich, Frank J., Jr., Pres. & Chief Exec. Officer--CF&I Steel Corporation, Pueblo, CO, pg. 201
Yamakoshi, Warren, Pres.--Nobart, Inc., Chicago, IL, pg. 808
Yamaura, Shun, Pres. & Chief Exec. Officer--PhoneMate, Inc., Torrance, CA, pg. 869
Yanke, Ron, Pres. & Owner--Nashua Homes of Idaho Inc., Boise, ID, pg. 784
Yared, Paul, Pres. & Chief Exec. Officer--McNeil & NRM., Inc., Akron, OH, pg. 732
Yarmark, Murray B., Pres.--Triboro Electric Corp., Warminster, PA, pg. 1112
Yarnall, John, Pres.--Nuhahn, Inc., Gardena, CA, pg. 817
Yates, Frances R., V.P. & Gen. Mgr.--Graves-Humphreys Company, Roanoke, VA, pg. 592
Yates, Jim E., Pres.--Yates Enterprises Inc., Texarkana, TX, pg. 1207
Yeargan, Edmund L., Jr., Pres.--Battey Machinery Company, Rome, GA, pg. 127
Yen, Dominic F., Pres.--Adec International Automation Corp., Cleveland, OH, pg. 17
Yerant, Gene S., Chm. & Pres.--Transport Insurance Co., Dallas, TX, pg. 54
Yerger, John R., Chm. Bd. & Pres.--Yerger Bros., Inc., Lititz, PA, pg. 1208
Yesawich, Peter C., Ph.D., Pres. & Chief Exec. Officer--Robinson, Yesawich & Pepperdine, Orlando, FL, pg. 940
Yeshoua, Jack, Pres.--Lucky Winner, Inc., New York, NY, pg. 686
Yocom, John, Div. Pres.--NDAP/TMP Worldwide, Toronto,, Canada, pg. 1074
Yoder, Allen, Jr., Pres.--Jayco Inc., Middlebury, IN, pg. 590
Yoder, Kent, Pres., Chief Exec. Officer, Chief Fin. Officer & Treas.--Yoder Oil Company Inc., Elkhart, IN, pg. 1208
Yoh, Harold L., Jr., Chm. Bd., Pres. & Chief Exec. Officer--Day & Zimmermann, Inc., Radnor, PA, pg. 320
York, Michael L., Pres.--Vortec Corporation, Cincinnati, OH, pg. 246
York, Susan, Partner--Rice/Spector Inc., Venice, CA, pg. 931
Young, Alan V., Pres. & Chief Exec. Officer--Young Automotive Group, Indianapolis, IN, pg. 1209
Young, Barton, Pres.--Speer, Young & Hollander, Inc., Los Angeles, CA, pg. 1030
Young, Charles, Pres. & Chief Oper. Officer--Affiliated Computer Services, Inc., Dallas, TX, pg. 23
Young, Daniel, Pres.--Federal Data Corporation, Bethesda, MD, pg. 404
Young, David, Chm. Bd. & Pres.--Young & Laramore, Indianapolis, IN, pg. 1209
Young, Dennis, Pres.--International Airline Support Group, Inc., Miami, FL, pg. 575
Young, Dr. C.B.F., Chm. Bd. & Pres.--Young Refining Corp., Douglasville, GA, pg. 1210
Young, E.V., Jr., Pres.--George W. Cochran Co., Inc., Washington, DC, pg. 258
Young, F.M., Jr., Pres.--Young Radiator Company, Racine, WI, pg. 1210
Young, J. Givens, Chm. Bd. & Pres.--Young Pecan Shelling Co., Inc., Florence, SC, pg. 1209
Young, Jack, Chm. Bd., Pres., Chief Exec. & Chief Fin. Officer--Jack Young Associates, Hazleton, PA, pg. 1209
Young, Jill, Pres.--Muhlhauser & Young, San Francisco, CA, pg. 774
Young, John A., Jr., Pres.--Burd & Fletcher Company, Kansas City, MO, pg. 189
Young, Michael T., Pres.--Young Electric Sign Company, Salt Lake City, UT, pg. 1209
Young, Richard F., Chm. Bd., Pres. & Chief Exec. Officer--Sues, Young & Brown Inc., Baldwin Park, CA, pg. 1056
Young, Robert S., Pres.--R.S. Young Excavating, Inc., Flint, MI, pg. 1209
Young, William C., Pres.--Plastipak Packaging Inc., Plymouth, MI, pg. 876
Young, William D., Sr., Pres. & Chief Exec. Officer--General Wholesale Company, Inc., Atlanta, GA, pg. 451
Younger, Gordon M., Pres.--Seattle Packaging Corporation, Seattle, WA, pg. 986
Yu, Eleanor N., Pres.--AdLand Advertising, Inc., San Francisco, CA, pg. 17
Yu, Jeffrey, Mng. Dir.--BSB Hong Kong, Hong Kong,, Hong Kong, pg. 110
Yung, Richard, Pres.--MCRB Service Bureau, Inc., North Hollywood, CA, pg. 691
Yung, William J., Pres. & Chief Exec. Officer--Columbia Sussex Corporation, Fort Mitchell, KY, pg. 266
Zack, Christine, Chm. Bd. & Pres.--Zack Company, Chicago, IL, pg. 1215
Zacky, Robert, Pres. & Sec.--Zacky Farms, Inc., South El Monte, CA, pg. 1215
Zahn, Andrew, Pres.--Mama Tish's Italian Specialties, Chicago, IL, pg. 703
Zaks, Rodnay, Pres. & Chief Exec. Officer--Sybex Group, Alameda, CA, pg. 1069
Zaleski, Stephen C., Pres.--New York Systems Exchange Corp., Melville, NY, pg. 1070
Zall, Lawrence, Pres.--Paris Presents, Gurnee, IL, pg. 848
Zambito, Steven, Pres. & Chief Exec. Officer--Talon, Inc., Meadville, PA, pg. 1077
Zamoiski, C. J., Jr., Chm. Bd., Pres. & Chief Exec. Officer--The Zamoiski Co., Baltimore, MD, pg. 1216
Zander, Paul H., Pres.--Zander's Creamery Inc., Cross Plains, WI, pg. 1216
Zanotti, John P., Pres. & Chief Oper. Officer--Great American Broadcasting Company, Cincinnati, OH, pg. 52
Zantop, Duane A., Chm. Bd., Pres. & Chief Exec. Officer--Zantop International Airlines, Inc., Ypsilanti, MI, pg. 1216
Zanville, Joel, Pres.--Advance Steel Co., Detroit, MI, pg. 20
Zapiecki, Michael, Chm. & Chief Exec. Officer--Zapiecki & Partners Inc., Toledo, OH, pg. 1216
Zappa, R., Chief Exec. Officer--Zappa Plastics, Phillipsburg, NJ, pg. 1216
Zaransky, Michael, Pres. & Sec.--Ridgeview Motors, Inc., Schiller Park, IL, pg. 934
Zaransky, Michael H., Pres.--Airways Rent A Car, Schiller Park, IL, pg. 934
Zaremba, Walter, Pres. & Chief Exec. Officer--Zaremba Corporation, Lakewood, OH, pg. 1216
Zaricki, Tom, Pres. & Chief Exec. Officer--Arizona Supermarkets, Inc., Phoenix, AZ, pg. 82
Zarrow, Henry, Pres. & Chief Exec. Officer--Sooner Pipe & Supply Corp., Tulsa, OK, pg. 1018
Zattosky, S.M., Pres., Chief Exec. Officer & Treas.--Cortland Line Co., Inc., Cortland, NY, pg. 287
Zebrack, Herbert, Pres.--Lithographix, Inc., Los Angeles, CA, pg. 678
Zec, Boyana, Pres.--A. Epstein & Sons (France) Inc., Aubervilliers, France, pg. 384
Zechman, Jan E., Pres. & Dir.-Creative--Zechman & Associates Adv. Inc., Chicago, IL, pg. 1216
Zedella, Jim, Pres.--Nutrition World, Des Plaines, IL, pg. 818
Zekaria, Maurice, Pres.--Windsor Fashions, Los Angeles, CA, pg. 1195
Zelazo, Dr. R.E., Pres.--Astronautics Corp. of America, Milwaukee, WI, pg. 93
Zelazo, Dr. R.E., Pres. & Chief Exec. Officer--Kearfott Guidance & Navigation Corp., Wayne, NJ, pg. 93
Zell, Samuel, Chm. Bd. & Pres.--Equity Group Investments, Chicago, IL, pg. 385
Zeller, M.C., Pres.--Zeller Corp., Defiance, OH, pg. 1216
Zellner, R.W., Pres.--The Rotor Tool Company, Cleveland, OH, pg. 951
Zelmo, David, Pres.--Publix Group, New York, NY, pg. 898
Zeman, A.L., Pres.--The Wyco Tool Co., Racine, WI, pg. 909
Zemenick, Carl, Pres. & Chief Exec. & Chief Oper. Officer--GF Office Furniture Ltd., Gallatin, TN, pg. 439
Zemenick, Carl, Pres.--GF Office Furniture, Youngstown, OH, pg. 439
Zemsky, Howard, Pres.--Zemco Industries, Inc., Buffalo, NY, pg. 1217
Zenegy, Louis, Chm. Bd., Pres. & Chief Exec. Officer--Polymer Development Laboratories, Inc., Orange, CA, pg. 880
Zenie, Francis H., Pres.--Zymark Corporation, Hopkinton, MA, pg. 1221
Zeratsky, J.G., Pres.--National Rivet & Manufacturing Company, Waupun, WI, pg. 793
Zeratsky, J.G., Pres.--The Shaler Company, Waupun, WI, pg. 793
Zeus, William, Jr., Pres. & Chief Exec. Officer--National Tool & Manufacturing Company, Kenilworth, NJ, pg. 794
Ziccardi, Donald P., Pres. & Chief Exec. Officer--The Sussman/Ziccardi Group, New York, NY, pg. 1065
Zickler, Leo E., Pres. & Chief Exec. Officer--Oxford Realty Services Corp., Bethesda, MD, pg. 835
Zieger, Claus D., Pres. & Treas.--Interbath, Inc., City of Industry, CA, pg. 574
Ziegler, Gordon S., Jr., Pres. & Chief Oper. Officer--Ziegler Chemical & Mineral Corp., Jericho, NY, pg. 1218
Ziegler, Harold, Jr., Pres.--Ziegler Tire & Supply Company, Inc., Canton, OH, pg. 1218
Ziegler, Ronald L., Pres.--Westco Products, Inc., Pico Rivera, CA, pg. 1178
Zien, Richard, Pres.--Mendelsohn/Zien Advertising, Inc., Los Angeles, CA, pg. 739
Zierke, David L., Mgr.-Mktg. & Sls.--Cotta Transmission Company, Rockford, IL, pg. 1062
Zifferer, Morton F., Jr., Pres. & Chief Exec. Officer--New Standard Corporation, Mount Joy, PA, pg. 802
Zildjian, Armand, Pres.--Avedis Zildjian Company, Norwell, MA, pg. 1219
Zimand, Gerald, Pres.--Plascal Corporation, Farmingdale, NY, pg. 874
Zimdar, Dorothy L., Pres.--Zimdar Enterprises, Wyoming, MI, pg. 1220
Zimet, I.M., Pres.--ATAPCO Office Products Group, Saint Louis, MO, pg. 64
Zimmer, Karl, III, Pres. & Chief Oper. Officer--Zimmer Paper Products Inc., Indianapolis, IN, pg. 1220

Zimmerli, Kurt, Chm. Bd., Pres., Chief Exec. Officer & Chief Oper. Officer--Zima Corp., Spartanburg, SC, pg. 1219
Zimmerman, Alan K., Pres.--Marval Industries, Inc., Mamaroneck, NY, pg. 716
Zimmerman, Martin E., Pres. & Chief Exec. Officer--The LINC Group, Inc., Chicago, IL, pg. 648
Zimmerman, William R., Chm. Bd., Pres. & Chief Exec. Officer--Zimmerman Holdings, Inc., San Marino, CA, pg. 1220
Zimmermann, F.N., Chm. Bd. & Pres.--March Manufacturing Inc., Glenview, IL, pg. 706
Zinbarg, Benson, Pres., Chief Exec. & Chief Fin. Officer & Treas.--Sun Hill Industries, Stamford, CT, pg. 1059
Zinn, Thomas R., Pres. & Sec.--Stearns Enterprises, Inc., Lexington, KY, pg. 1043
Ziols, Gregory J., Pres.--Bloomfield Industries, Chicago, IL, pg. 1027
Zito, Paul M., Pres. & Chief Exec. Officer--Bacharach Inc., Pittsburgh, PA, pg. 108
Zitterkopf, Irvin L., Pres. & Chief Exec. Officer--Southern Minnesota Beet Sugar Cooperative, Renville, MN, pg. 1022
Zlotnik, Arnold, Pres.--Surco Products, Inc., Braddock, PA, pg. 1065
Zobel, Richard, Reg. Mng. Dir.--Leo Burnett Ltd., Europe/ Middle East Hdqtrs., London,, United Kingdom, pg. 193
Zoidis, Thomas D., Pres.--Butcher & Singer, Philadelphia, PA, pg. 1184
Zoll, Lawrence, Pres.--Kassel & Zoll Provisions, Inc., Chicago, IL, pg. 618
Zollars, Robert L., Pres. & Chief Oper. Officer--Huitt-Zollars, Inc., Dallas, TX, pg. 552
Zoltak, John, Pres.--Support Systems Associates, Inc., Hauppauge, NY, pg. 1064
Zubizarreta, Teresa A., Pres.--Zubi Advertising Services, Inc., Miami, FL, pg. 1221
Zuckerman, Shelton, Pres.--Sigal/Zuckerman Co., Chevy Chase, MD, pg. 1003
Zuckerwar, Richard J., Chm. Bd. & Pres.--The Grandoe Corporation, Gloversville, NY, pg. 476
Zugay, Michael, Pres.--Atlas Car Div., Bliss-Salem Inc., Salem, OH, pg. 157
Zugay, Michael J., Pres.--Bliss-Salem, Inc., Salem, OH, pg. 156
Zuk, Ben, Chm. Bd. & Pres.--Plastic Reel Corp. of America, Lyndhurst, NJ, pg. 875
Zukerman, Allan B., Pres. & Chief Oper. Officer--Montgomery, Zukerman, Davis, Inc., Indianapolis, IN, pg. 768
Zumbiel, Robert W., Pres.--C. W. Zumbiel Company, Cincinnati, OH, pg. 1221
Zurilla, Tom, Pres. & Chief Exec. Officer--G B Stores, Johnstown, PA, pg. 978
Zygulski, Robert, Pres. & Chief Opers. Officer--South Bend Plastics, Inc., Mishawaka, IN, pg. 1019
Zylke, Ralph B., Pres.--Zylke & Associates, Northbrook, IL, pg. 1221

PRINCIPALS

Abbell, Joseph J., Chm. Bd. & Pres.--Abbell Associates, Chicago, IL, pg. 9
Abbey, Nelson D., III, Pres. & Chief Oper. Officer--Abbey Etna Machine Company, Perrysburg, OH, pg. 9
Abbot, Jerry, Pres.--Metro Label Corp., Belleville, NJ, pg. 743
Abelson, Marv, Chm. Bd.--Abelson-Taylor, Inc., Chicago, IL, pg. 10
Abraham, Lee, Chm. Bd. & Chief Exec. Officer--Associated Merchandising Corp., New York, NY, pg. 91
Acheson, A M., Exec. Partner--Black & Veatch, Kansas City, MO, pg. 154
Ackerman, Robert D., Pres. & Chief Oper. Officer--Lord, Sullivan & Yoder, Inc. Advertising, Columbus, OH, pg. 683
Ackerman, Roy A., Chm. Bd. & Chief Exec. Officer--Astre Corporate Group, Alexandria, VA, pg. 92
Adam, P.J., Asst. Mng. Partner--Black & Veatch, Kansas City, MO, pg. 154
Adelman, Sheldon G., Chm. Bd. & Chief Exec. Officer--Blue Coral, Inc., Cleveland, OH, pg. 159
Adelson, Andrew S., Sr. V.P.--Sanford C. Bernstein & Co., Inc., New York, NY, pg. 144
Adelstein, Bruce S., Exec. V.P. & Sec.--Olympic Steel Inc., Bedford Heights, OH, pg. 825
Ades, Alan, Chm., Pres. & Chief Exec. Officer--A & E Stores, Inc., Ridgefield, NJ, pg. 1
Adkins, Marshall, Sec. & Treas.--United Feeds, Inc., Sheridan, IN, pg. 1132
Agee, Robert D., V.P.-Sls.--Artco-Bell Corporation, Temple, TX, pg. 86
Agin, Frank, Exec. Dir.--Burgess & Niple, Limited, Columbus, OH, pg. 190
Akers, Herbert H., Vice Chm.--Lithograph Printing Company, Inc., Memphis, TN, pg. 678
Alban, James C., III, Pres.--Alban Tractor Co. Inc., Baltimore, MD, pg. 30
Alberici, Gabriel J., Chm. Bd. & Treas.--J. S. Alberici Construction Co., Inc., Saint Louis, MO, pg. 31
Alberici, John S., Chief Fin. Officer, Sr. V.P. & Sec.--J. S. Alberici Construction Co., Inc., Saint Louis, MO, pg. 31
Albert, Andrew B., Pres. & Co-Chief Exec. Officer--Rittenhouse Inc., Park Ridge, IL, pg. 936
Albert, Michael P., Chm. Bd. & Pres.--The Harodite Finishing Company Inc., North Dighton, MA, pg. 510
Albert, Rachel F., Treas.--The Harodite Finishing Company Inc., North Dighton, MA, pg. 510
Albertelli, George J., Sr. V.P. & Sec.--The Stellar Group Inc., Jacksonville, FL, pg. 1046
Albrecht, Fred I., Chm. Bd.--The Fred W. Albrecht Grocery Co., Akron, OH, pg. 31
Albrecht, Randal A., Chm. Bd.--DEC International, Inc., Madison, WI, pg. 308
Alesso, Dominick, Sec. & Gen. Counsel--A-P-A Transport Corp., North Bergen, NJ, pg. 5
Alexander, Norman E., Chm. Bd.--Ampacet Corporation, Tarrytown, NY, pg. 67
Allard, Gerald R., Chm. Bd.--Jewell Instruments, Inc., Manchester, NH, pg. 594
Allbritton, Joe L., Chm. Bd. & Chief Exec. Officer--Perpetual Corporation, Washington, DC, pg. 862
Allegretti, Alfred, Pres.--Bayside Fuel Oil Depot Corp., Brooklyn, NY, pg. 128
Allegretti, Victor, V.P.--Bayside Fuel Oil Depot Corp., Brooklyn, NY, pg. 128
Allen, Charles S., Pres. & Chief Exec. Officer--Sloan Valve Company, Franklin Park, IL, pg. 1010
Allen, Floyd E., Chm. Bd.--Mid-West Paper Products Company, Warren, MI, pg. 750
Allen, Kathleen, Sec.--California Panel & Veneer Company, Cerritos, CA, pg. 210
Allen, Robert B., Sr., Chm. Bd.--Allen Steel Co., Salt Lake City, UT, pg. 36
Allen, Thomas G., V.P.-Sls. & Mktg.--Effective Management Systems, Milwaukee, WI, pg. 370
Allsup, Barbara J., V.P., Sec. & Treas.--Allsups Convenience Stores Inc., Clovis, NM, pg. 43
Allsup, Lonnie D., Chm. Bd. & Pres.--Allsups Convenience Stores Inc., Clovis, NM, pg. 43
Allsup, Mark A., V.P.--Allsups Convenience Stores Inc., Clovis, NM, pg. 43
Alpert, Norman R., Chm. Bd., Pres. & Chief Exec. Officer--Bio-Tek Instruments, Inc., Winooski, VT, pg. 152
Alpert, Warren, Chm. Bd.--Warren Equities Inc., New York, NY, pg. 1164
Alter, James M., Chm. Bd. & Chief Exec. Officer--The Harry Alter Company, Chicago, IL, pg. 45
Alterman, Richard, V.P.--Alterman Transport Lines, Inc., Opa Locka, FL, pg. 45
Alterman, Sidney, Pres.--Alterman Transport Lines, Inc., Opa Locka, FL, pg. 45
Altier, Richard J., Pres. & Chief Oper. Officer--Altier & Sons Shoes Inc., Rochester, NY, pg. 45
Altier, Richard L., Chm. Bd.--Altier & Sons Shoes Inc., Rochester, NY, pg. 45
Amant, Charles, Chm. Bd.--Alkota Cleaning Systems, Inc., Alcester, SD, pg. 34
Ames, Richard S., Chm. & Chief Exec. Officer--Command Plastic Corporation, Akron, OH, pg. 268
Ammirati, Ralph, Chm. & Creative Dir.--Ammirati & Puris Inc., New York, NY, pg. 67
Amore, Joe, Chm. Bd., Pres. & Chief Exec. Officer--BeefAmerica Operating Co., Inc., Omaha, NE, pg. 131
Anastasi, Joseph A., Exec. V.P., Creative Dir.--Jones, Anastasi & Birchfield, Dublin, OH, pg. 602
Anderson, Bruce, Exec. V.P., Treas. & Dir.-Mfg. & Quality Control--Integrated Energy Controls Corp., Minneapolis, MN, pg. 573
Anderson, Bruce S., V.P.--Gordy's, Inc., Worthington, MN, pg. 472
Anderson, E. Dean, Chm. Bd. & Chief Exec. Officer--Leslie Advertising, Greenville, SC, pg. 668
Anderson, Gordon B., Chm. Bd. & Pres.--Gordy's, Inc., Worthington, MN, pg. 472
Anderson, Harold E., Pres.--Anderson Trucking Service Inc., Saint Cloud, MN, pg. 73
Anderson, James T., Chm.--Anderson Wholesale Company, Muskogee, OK, pg. 73
Anderson, John R., Chm. Bd. & Pres.--Anderson Industries Inc., Rockford, IL, pg. 73
Anderson, Mark R., Pres. & Chief Exec. Officer--Mark Anderson Associates, Inc., Arlington Heights, IL, pg. 73
Anderson, Robert W., Jr., Pres.-Development Co.--Cogentrix Incorporated, Charlotte, NC, pg. 258
Anderson, Thomas G., Chief Oper. Officer, Chief Fin. Officer & V.P.--Gordy's, Inc., Worthington, MN, pg. 472
Andonian, Andy K., Pres.--A K H Company, Inc., Los Angeles, CA, pg. 4
Andonian, George, V.P.--A K H Company, Inc., Los Angeles, CA, pg. 4
Andonian, Hratch K., Exec. V.P., Sec. & Treas.--A K H Company, Inc., Los Angeles, CA, pg. 4
Andonian, John, Exec. V.P.--A K H Company, Inc., Los Angeles, CA, pg. 4
Andre, Benny, Pres.--Diamond Motors Inc., Baton Rouge, LA, pg. 335
Andreas, George C., Chm. Bd. & Pres.--Lantzsch-Andreas Enterprises, Inc., Vienna, VA, pg. 658
Andreas, Ursula E., Exec. V.P.--Lantzsch-Andreas Enterprises, Inc., Vienna, VA, pg. 658
Andrews, Mark, Jr., Chm. Bd.--Mark Andy, Inc., Chesterfield, MO, pg. 708
Anson, Joe, Pres.--Anson-Stoner, Inc., Winter Park, FL, pg. 76
Anthony, Beryl, Sr., Chm. Bd.--Anthony Forest Products Co., Inc., El Dorado, AR, pg. 77
Anthony, Clary, Sr., Pres.--Anthony Forest Products Co., Inc., El Dorado, AR, pg. 77
Anthony, James Norman, Exec. V.P.--Bearden Lumber Company, Inc., Bearden, AR, pg. 129
Anthony, John E., Chm. Bd. & Pres.--Bearden Lumber Company, Inc., Bearden, AR, pg. 129
Appell, Louis J., Jr., Pres.--Susquehanna Pfaltzgraff, York, PA, pg. 1065
Apperson, R.P., Chm. Bd. & Pres.--Apperson Business Forms, Inc., Los Angeles, CA, pg. 78
Applebaum, David, V.P.-Mfg.--Triangle Marketing Corp., New York, NY, pg. 1112
Aquilino, Vincent, Sec.--Graymills Corp., Chicago, IL, pg. 480
Archard, Phillip, V.P. & Controller--Bridgeport Machines, Inc., Bridgeport, CT, pg. 175
Arens, Joel, Exec. V.P., Treas. & Sec.--Alacon, Sunnyvale, CA, pg. 29
Arens, Richard P., Chm. Bd., Pres., Chief Exec. & Fin. Officer--Alacon, Sunnyvale, CA, pg. 29
Armstrong, John, Pres.--The Crocker-Fels Company, Cincinnati, OH, pg. 299
Armstrong, L.F., Chm. Bd.--Armstrong International, Inc., Three Rivers, MI, pg. 83
Armstrong, M.H., Pres. & Chief Exec. Officer--Armstrong International, Inc., Three Rivers, MI, pg. 83
Armstrong, Ronald, Chm. Bd. & Creative Dir.--Fabianac, Stropes & Armstrong, Inc., San Francisco, CA, pg. 395
Arnhold, Henry H., Chm. Bd.--Arnhold and S. Bleichroeder, Inc., New York, NY, pg. 84
Arnold, H.G., Chm. Bd. & Chief Fin. Officer--Venta Inc., Denver, CO, pg. 1147
Arnold, Steve, Pres. & Chief Exec. Officer--One Stop Supply, Tyler, TX, pg. 827
Aro, Jeanne, V.P.-Fin & Admin.--Mini Mart, Inc., Casper, WY, pg. 757
Aronson, Arnold, Chm. Bd. & Chief Exec. Officer--Woodward & Lothrop/John Wanamaker, Washington, DC, pg. 1201
Arpin, David, Pres.--Paul Arpin Vanlines, Inc., East Greenwich, RI, pg. 85
Arpin, Paul G., Chief Exec. Officer--Paul Arpin Vanlines, Inc., East Greenwich, RI, pg. 85
Arquilla, George, III, Pres.--Burnside Construction Co., Downers Grove, WI, pg. 194
Arquilla, George, Jr., Chm. Bd.--Burnside Construction Co., Downers Grove, WI, pg. 194
Arrington, Michael B., Pres. & Chief Exec. Officer--Arrington Travel Center Inc., Chicago, IL, pg. 85
Asher, Harold, Chm.-Exec. Committee--Asher/Gould Advertising, Inc., Los Angeles, CA, pg. 88
Ashmore, R.C., V.P. & Asst. Sec.--Ballenger Paving Company, Inc., Taylors, SC, pg. 116
Ashton, Alan C., Pres.--WordPerfect Corporation, Orem, UT, pg. 1202
Attaway, Julian J., Pres.--M M Systems Corporation, Tucker, GA, pg. 692
Attaway, Michael H., Asst. Treas.--M M Systems Corporation, Tucker, GA, pg. 692
Attig, Ron, V.P.-Heavy Division--M. A. Mortenson Company, Minneapolis, MN, pg. 772
Auch, Frederick J., Jr., Chm. Bd. & Chief Exec. Officer--George W. Auch Co., Pontiac, MI, pg. 97
Auch, G. William, III, Chief Oper. Officer & V.P.--George W. Auch Co., Pontiac, MI, pg. 97
Auray, Delbert L., Pres. & Treas.--Bridgeport Fittings, Inc., Stratford, CT, pg. 175
Auriemma, Louis, Exec. V.P.--Haddon Craftsmen, Inc., Scranton, PA, pg. 499
Austad, Dave, Pres. & Chief Exec. Officer--The Austad Company, Sioux Falls, SD, pg. 98
Austad, Oscar, Chm. Bd.--The Austad Company, Sioux Falls, SD, pg. 98
Avery, John C., Partner--Roney & Co., Detroit, MI, pg. 946
Avrett, John G., Chm. & Chief Exec. Officer--Avrett, Free & Ginsberg, Inc., New York, NY, pg. 103
Awad, Dennis J., Pres., Chief Exec. & Fin. Officer & Treas.--Tele-Com Products, Inc., Duarte, CA, pg. 1084
Axelrad, James A., Pres. & Chief Exec. Officer--Pakula & Company, Chicago, IL, pg. 843
Axelrad, Milton S., Chm. Bd.--Pakula & Company, Chicago, IL, pg. 843
Ayers, D. Tom, V.P.--MBT Associates, Inc., San Francisco, CA, pg. 691
Azar, Cyrus, Sec.--Symplex Communications Corp., Ann Arbor, MI, pg. 1069
Azrak, Marvin, Owner--Remco Toys, New York, NY, pg. 926
Bachhuber, Carl, Pres.--Mayville Engineering Co., Inc., Mayville, WI, pg. 725
Bachhuber, Robert, V.P.-MEC--Mayville Engineering Co., Inc., Mayville, WI, pg. 725
Bachhuber, Ted J., Chm. Bd.--Mayville Engineering Co., Inc., Mayville, WI, pg. 725
Bacig, Louis, Pres.--Carmichael Lynch, Inc., Minneapolis, MN, pg. 222
Badcock, Wogan S., Jr., Chm. Bd. & Pres.--W.S. Badcock Corporation, Mulberry, FL, pg. 113
Bader, Ronald L., Pres. & Chief Exec. Officer--Bader Rutter & Assoc., Inc., Brookfield, WI, pg. 113
Baer, Robert E., Pres.--Efficient Engineering Co., Troy, MI, pg. 371
Baer, Robert J., Pres.--United Van Lines, Inc., Fenton, MO, pg. 1126
Bailey, Coley L., Chm. Bd.--Mississippi Chemical Corporation, Yazoo City, MS, pg. 760
Bailey, Gordon, Pres. & Treas.--Gordon Bailey & Associates, Inc., Stone Mountain, GA, pg. 114
Bailey, Jack, V.P. & Treas.--Smith-Lee Co., Inc., Oneida, NY, pg. 1013
Bailey, John H., Chm. Bd., Pres., Chief Exec. & Chief Oper. Officer--The Climatic Corp., Columbia, SC, pg. 255
Baird, John W., Chm. Bd.--Baird & Warner Inc., Chicago, IL, pg. 114
Baker, Douglas, Pres.--Tropitone Furniture Co. Inc., Sarasota, FL, pg. 1116
Baker, Raymond E., Chm. Bd.--Newage Industries Inc., Willow Grove, PA, pg. 803
Baker, Robert, Chief Exec. Officer--Skyway Freight Systems, Inc., Watsonville, CA, pg. 1009
Baldwin, Ed F., Chm. Bd., Pres. & Treas.--Baldwin Construction, Inc., Fort Collins, CO, pg. 115
Baldwin, Sandra, Pres. & Treas.--H & H Distributing Company, Inc., West Union, IA, pg. 495
Ballard, Larry C., Chm. Bd., Pres. & Chief Exec. Officer--Sentry Insurance, A Mutual Company, Stevens Point, WI, pg. 990
Balson, Patrick, Pres.--Aetna Bearing Company, Chicago, IL, pg. 23
Bankston, James G., Pres.--W. O. Bankston Enterprises Inc., Dallas, TX, pg. 118
Bankston, William O., Chm. Bd.--W. O. Bankston Enterprises Inc., Dallas, TX, pg. 118
Baranski, Dennis A., Chm. Bd., Pres. & Chief Exec. Officer--Barancorp, Lecompton, KS, pg. 118

Barbar, Anthony K.G., Exec. V.P.--The Barbar Group, Inc., Boca Raton, FL, pg. 119
Barbar, George E., Chm. Bd. & Pres.--The Barbar Group, Inc., Boca Raton, FL, pg. 119
Barbour, Alfred D., Pres.--Roessing Bronze Co., Mars, PA, pg. 943
Barbour, Alfred R., Chm. Bd.--Roessing Bronze Co., Mars, PA, pg. 943
Barclay, H. Douglas, Chm. Bd.--Syracuse Supply Company, Syracuse, NY, pg. 1070
Bardis, Christo D., Pres.--Reynen, Bardis & Winn, Sacramento, CA, pg. 930
Barge, John M., Chief Exec. Officer--Barge-Wagener, Inc., Atlanta, GA, pg. 119
Barger, Michael E., Chief Exec. Officer--Barger Builder & Developers, Saint Petersburg, FL, pg. 119
Bargull, Raymond C., Exec. V.P.-Real Estate Officer & Chief Fin. Officer--Sundt Corp., Tucson, AZ, pg. 1060
Barker, Paul, Chm. Bd.--McLaughlin Mfg. Company, Greenville, SC, pg. 731
Barletta, Frank, Pres.--A. Barletta & Sons, Hazleton, PA, pg. 120
Barnes, James, V.P., Treas. & Chief Fin. Officer--Wohlert Corp., Lansing, MI, pg. 1198
Barnett, Cecil C., Chm. Bd., Pres., Chief Exec. Officer & Treas.--Algood Food Company, Louisville, KY, pg. 34
Barnett, Charles E., Chm. Bd.--Barnett Millworks, Inc., Theodore, AL, pg. 120
Barnett, Paul S., Pres.--Barnett Millworks, Inc., Theodore, AL, pg. 120
Barnhard, Sherwood A., Chm. Bd.--Lasky Company, Millburn, NJ, pg. 660
Barnhardt, James H., Sr., Chm. Bd.--Barnhardt Manufacturing Co., Charlotte, NC, pg. 120
Barnhill, R.E., Chm. Bd.--Barnhill Contracting Company, Tarboro, NC, pg. 121
Barnhill, R.E., Jr., Pres.--Barnhill Contracting Company, Tarboro, NC, pg. 121
Barr, Thomas A., Chm. Bd.--Barr & Barr, Inc., New York, NY, pg. 121
Barro, Tom, Pres.--Lamp Post Franchise Corporation, Tustin, CA, pg. 652
Barry, Richard F. III, Vice Chm.--Landmark Communications, Inc., Norfolk, VA, pg. 654
Bartlett, Paul D., Jr., Chm. Bd.--Bartlett and Company, Kansas City, MO, pg. 122
Basha, Edward N., Jr., Chm. Bd.--Bashas, Chandler, AZ, pg. 124
Baskin, Scott, Pres.--Mark Shale, Willowbrook, IL, pg. 994
Baskin, Shale, Chm. Bd.--Mark Shale, Willowbrook, IL, pg. 994
Basler, William L., Chm. Bd., Chief Exec. Officer & Treas.--Basler Electric Company, Highland, IL, pg. 125
Bass, Sid R., Chm. Bd.--Bass Enterprises Production Company, Fort Worth, TX, pg. 125
Bastian, Bruce W., Chm. Bd.--WordPerfect Corporation, Orem, UT, pg. 1202
Batten, Frank, Chm. Bd.--Landmark Communications, Inc., Norfolk, VA, pg. 654
Baugh, Thomas E., Jr., Sec.--Sands Investments, Inc., Myrtle Beach, SC, pg. 970
Baugher, Claude O., Chm. Bd.--Baugher Chevrolet-Buick-Geo, Inc., Waynesboro, VA, pg. 127
Baugher, John O., Pres. & Treas.--Baugher Chevrolet-Buick-Geo, Inc., Waynesboro, VA, pg. 127
Baughman, Kathy, Pres.--HLB Communications, Inc., Chicago, IL, pg. 496
Baum, Robert H., Vice Chm. & Gen. Counsel--The Inland Group, Inc., Oak Brook, IL, pg. 570
Bauman, Richard A., Exec. V.P.-Fin. & Admin.--LaBarge Pipe & Steel Company, Saint Louis, MO, pg. 649
Bayer, Gary R., Chm. & Chief Exec. Officer--Bayer Bess Vanderwarker Inc., Chicago, IL, pg. 128
Bayley, Robert E., Chm. Bd. & Chief Exec. Officer--Robert E. Bayley Construction, Seattle, WA, pg. 128
Beale, Robert B., Pres.--Control Systems Inc., Saint Paul, MN, pg. 281
Bear, Lewis, Jr., Pres.--The Lewis Bear Company, Pensacola, FL, pg. 129
Beauchamp, Jim, V.P.--The Jolt Company, Rochester, NY, pg. 602
Beaver, Donald C., Pres., Chief Exec. Officer & Treas.--Brian Center Management Corporation, Hickory, NC, pg. 175
Bechtler, Andreas H., Vice Chm.--Pneumafil Corp., Charlotte, NC, pg. 878
Beck, Arthur R., Pres. & Chief Oper. Officer--Precision Twist Drill Co., Crystal Lake, IL, pg. 885
Becker, A. Carl, V.P.-Pur. & Engrng.--Nuttall Gear Corporation, Niagara Falls, NY, pg. 818
Beckwith, James S. III, Chm. Bd.--Beckwith Machinery Company, Murrysville, PA, pg. 131
Beddor, William N., Chm. Bd.--Japs-Olson Company, Minneapolis, MN, pg. 590
Beeler, Donald, Chm. Bd., Pres. & Chief Exec. Officer--Snyder's Drug Stores, Inc., Minnetonka, MN, pg. 1015
Beer, Murray L., Chm. Bd., Pres. & Chief Exec. Officer--Globe Mortgage Company, Hackensack, NJ, pg. 464
Behrens, Peter, Vice Chm.--Great Salt Lake Minerals & Chemicals Corp., Ogden, UT, pg. 482
Belden, John, Pres. & Chief Exec. Officer--OCTus, San Diego, CA, pg. 818
Belk, John M., Chm. Bd. & Chief Exec. Officer--Belk Stores Services Inc., Charlotte, NC, pg. 134
Bell, John, Jr., Chm. Bd. & Chief Exec. Officer--Bell Packaging Corporation, Marion, IN, pg. 135
Bell, Ray, Pres.--Bell Construction Co. Inc., Brentwood, TN, pg. 134
Bell, Richard E., Pres. & Chief Exec. Officer--Riceland Foods, Inc., Stuttgart, AR, pg. 931
Belz, Jack A., Pres. & Chief Exec. Officer--Belz Enterprises, Memphis, TN, pg. 138
Benavides, Patrick R., V.P.-Engrng.--Bonney Forge Corporation, Allentown, PA, pg. 164
Benbow, David, V.P.--Timpte Industries, Inc., Denver, CO, pg. 1098
Bender, Robert L., Exec. V.P. & Treas.--Lord, Sullivan & Yoder, Inc. Advertising, Columbus, OH, pg. 683
Bendzin, Leonard J., Exec. V.P. & Chief Oper. Officer--Globe Mortgage Company, Hackensack, NJ, pg. 464
Benjamin, Harry, Partner--Roney & Co., Detroit, MI, pg. 946
Bennack, Frank A., Jr., Pres. & Chief Exec. Officer--The Hearst Corporation, New York, NY, pg. 521
Bennett, Joseph, Pres.--Trio Products Inc., Elyria, OH, pg. 1114
Benson, Jerome, V.P.--Benson Management Company, San Antonio, TX, pg. 140
Benson, Tom, Jr., Chm. Bd. & Pres.--Benson Management Company, San Antonio, TX, pg. 140
Berenter, Bill, Chm. Bd. & Co-Creative Dir.--Berenter Greenhouse & Webster, Inc., New York, NY, pg. 141
Berg, Adolph, Chief Fin. Officer--Alpha Shirt Co., Philadelphia, PA, pg. 44
Berg, Jack H., Pres. & Chief Exec. Officer--Serfilco, Ltd., Northbrook, IL, pg. 990
Berg, Ronald, Pres.--Alpha Shirt Co., Philadelphia, PA, pg. 44
Bergman, David R., Exec. V.P. & Sec.--Processed Plastic Company, Montgomery, IL, pg. 892
Bergman, Robert S., Pres. & Treas.--Processed Plastic Company, Montgomery, IL, pg. 892
Berkes, Judith C., Program Mgr.-Exports--Deck House Inc., Acton, MA, pg. 324
Berman, Barry H., Chm. Bd. & Pres.--CRN International, Inc., Hamden, CT, pg. 203
Bernard, Norman, Chm. Bd. & Chief Exec. Officer--Master Industries Corp., New York, NY, pg. 719
Berner, Philip, Pres.--Bernea Food Service, Inc., Otsego, MI, pg. 143
Bernes, I. Robert, Pres.--Triple A Specialty Company, Bedford Park, IL, pg. 1114
Bernstein, Arthur, V.P.-Pur., Sportswear--Milady Brassiere & Corset Co., Inc., New York, NY, pg. 753
Bernstein, S.J., Chm. Bd. & Chief Exec. Officer--The Biltrite Corporation, Waltham, MA, pg. 151
Bernstein, Sheldon, Sec. & Treas.--Milady Brassiere & Corset Co., Inc., New York, NY, pg. 753
Bernstein, Zalman C., Chm. & Chief Exec. Officer--Sanford C. Bernstein & Co., Inc., New York, NY, pg. 144
Berolzheimer, Philip, Pres.--California Cedar Products, Inc., Stockton, CA, pg. 209
Berry, Robert E., Chm. Bd.--Berry-Brown Advertising, Inc., Dallas, TX, pg. 144
Bertelsen, Anita M., Sec.--Waldorf Corporation, Saint Paul, MN, pg. 1159
Bertrand, Frederic H., Chm. Bd. & Chief Exec. Officer--National Life Insurance Company, Montpelier, VT, pg. 791
Berwind, C. Graham, Jr., Chm. Bd., Pres., Chief Exec. & Chief Oper. Officer--Berwind Corporation, Philadelphia, PA, pg. 145
Bess, Ron, Pres. & Chief Oper. Officer--Bayer Bess Vanderwarker Inc., Chicago, IL, pg. 128
Besse, Robert, Sr. V.P.--Sanborn Manufacturing Company, Springfield, MN, pg. 969
Besse, William C., Chief Exec. Officer--Sanborn Manufacturing Company, Springfield, MN, pg. 969
Best, Ron, Pres. & Chief Exec. Officer--Totes Incorporated, Loveland, OH, pg. 1103
Betagole, Robert, Pres.--Mike Albert Leasing, Inc., Cincinnati, OH, pg. 31
Bete, Channing L., Jr., Pres.--Channing L. Bete Co., Inc., South Deerfield, MA, pg. 147
Beutler, Gary, Chm. Bd.--Beutler Heating & Air Conditioning Inc., Sacramento, CA, pg. 148
Bevan, L. Darrell, Pres. & Chief Exec. Officer--Vidicom, L.D. Bevan Company, Inc., Thousand Oaks, CA, pg. 1151
Bever, C.C., Jr., Chm. Bd., Pres. & Chief Oper. Officer--B & B Cash Grocery Store, Tampa, FL, pg. 105
Bever, J. Andrew, Vice Chm. & Dir.-Real Estate--B & B Cash Grocery Store, Tampa, FL, pg. 105
Beyer, Larry, Pres.--ZBS Industries, Inc., Mayfield Village, OH, pg. 1215
Biblowitz, Joshua, Pres. & Chief Oper. Officer--Masters, Inc., Westbury, NY, pg. 720
Biblowitz, Louis, Chm. Bd.--Masters, Inc., Westbury, NY, pg. 720
Biblowitz, Max, Vice Chm.--Masters, Inc., Westbury, NY, pg. 720
Bieber, William F., Chief Exec. Officer--Acrometal Companies, Inc., Brainerd, MN, pg. 14
Biederman, Barry, Chm. Bd. & Creative Dir.--Biederman, Kelly & Shaffer, Inc., New York, NY, pg. 149
Biederman, Wayne, Exec. V.P.--Northern Wire & Cable, Inc., Troy, MI, pg. 814
Bieri, Leon, Exec. V.P. & Gen. Mgr.--RJO Enterprises, Inc., Lanham, MD, pg. 907
Billig, Peter, V.P.--Chilewich Partners, White Plains, NY, pg. 248
Birkhauser, Robert R., Chm.--Auto Glass Specialists, Madison, WI, pg. 100
Bisbee, Lyndell, Gen. Mgr.--Sunnyland Foods, Inc., Thomasville, GA, pg. 1061
Bishop, B.H., Chm. Bd. & Co-Chief Exec. Officer--Pendleton Woolen Mills, Inc., Portland, OR, pg. 857
Bishop, C.M., Jr., Pres. & Co-Chief Exec. Officer--Pendleton Woolen Mills, Inc., Portland, OR, pg. 857
Bishop, Thomas, Exec. V.P.--Alaron Inc., Troy, MI, pg. 30
Bishop, Vernon, Chm. Bd., Pres. & Chief Exec. Officer--Lebanon Chemical Corp., Lebanon, PA, pg. 665
Bissell, John M., Pres.--Bissell Inc., Grand Rapids, MI, pg. 153
Bixby, B.C., Chm. Bd.--Bixby International Corp., Newburyport, MA, pg. 153
Bjorkman, Joseph R., Pres.--Alkota Cleaning Systems, Inc., Alcester, SD, pg. 34
Black, Stuart M., Chm. Bd.--Black & Co., Decatur, IL, pg. 154
Black, T.M., Jr., Sec. & Dir.-Research--Walter J. Black, Inc., Port Washington, NY, pg. 154
Black, T.M., Sr., Chm. Bd. & Editor-in-Chief--Walter J. Black, Inc., Port Washington, NY, pg. 154
Black, W.J. II, Pres., Chief Exec. Officer & Treas.--Walter J. Black, Inc., Port Washington, NY, pg. 154
Black, William H., II, Chm. Bd.--Black Cadillac Olds, Inc., Greensboro, NC, pg. 153
Black, William H., III, Pres.--Black Cadillac Olds, Inc., Greensboro, NC, pg. 153
Blackburn, Donald F., Pres.--American Foodservice Corp., King of Prussia, PA, pg. 54
Blacker, Stanley, Chm. Bd. & Pres.--Stanley Blacker, Inc., Philadelphia, PA, pg. 155
Blackwell, Charles E., Chm. Bd.--Piedmont Mechanical, Inc., Spartanburg, SC, pg. 870
Blagaich, Alvin, V.P.-Sls. & Mktg.--Fenton Press, Inc., Addison, IL, pg. 406
Blair, Michael D., Pres. & Chief Exec. Officer--Cyborg Systems, Inc., Chicago, IL, pg. 307
Blanchard, Craig A., Chief Fin. Officer, Treas. & Controller--Sheldons' Inc., Antigo, WI, pg. 996
Blanchard, Kirk F., Chm. Bd.--Wyatt Inc., Branford, CT, pg. 1205
Blanchard, Richard F., Pres.--Wm. Blanchard Co., Springfield, NJ, pg. 155
Blanchard, Roger, Chm. Bd.--ACR Industries Inc., Mount Clemens, MI, pg. 2
Blanchard, William C., Sec. & Treas.--Wm. Blanchard Co., Springfield, NJ, pg. 155
Bland, William W., Chm. Bd. & Pres.--Bland Cadillac Company, Houston, TX, pg. 155
Blank, Jeffrey, Sec. & Dir.-Mktg.--Elastic Materials, Inc., Smithville, OH, pg. 372
Blattner, Simon J., Jr., Co-Chief Exec. Officer--Rittenhouse Inc., Park Ridge, IL, pg. 936
Blevins, James W., Pres. & Chief Exec Officer--Blevins Inc., Nashville, TN, pg. 156
Blinder, James F., Pres. & Treas.--Nelson Brothers Furniture Co., Chicago, IL, pg. 797
Block, Annabelle, Chm. Bd.--Annabelle Candy Company, Hayward, CA, pg. 75
Bloomfield, Coleman, Chm. Bd. & Chief Exec. Officer--The Minnesota Mutual Life Insurance Company, Saint Paul, MN, pg. 757
Blue, David S., Pres. & Chief Exec. Officer--Louisville Scrap Material Co., Inc., Louisville, KY, pg. 684
Boccardi, Louis D., Pres. & Chief Exec. Officer--The Associated Press, New York, NY, pg. 91
Boddie, Ben Mayo, Chm. Bd. & Chief Exec. Officer--Boddie-Noell Enterprises Inc., Rocky Mount, NC, pg. 161
Boddie, Nick B., Vice Chm.--Boddie-Noell Enterprises Inc., Rocky Mount, NC, pg. 161
Bodine, Paul J., Chm. Bd.--Bodine Electric Company, Chicago, IL, pg. 162
Boehm, Josef F., Pres. & Chief Oper. Officer--Alaska Industrial Hardware Inc., Anchorage, AK, pg. 30
Boersma, Bernie, Mgr.-Natl. Sls. & Export--LubeCon Systems, Inc., Fremont, MI, pg. 686
Boh, Robert H., Chm. Bd., Pres. & Chief Exec. Officer--Boh Corporation, New Orleans, LA, pg. 162
Boh, Robert H., Chm. Bd. & Pres.--Boh Brothers Construction Company, Inc., New Orleans, LA, pg. 162
Bohan, Daniel P., Exec. V.P., Treas. & Sec.--Omega World Travel, Inc., Falls Church, VA, pg. 826
Bohan, Gloria, Pres. & Chief Oper. Officer--Omega World Travel, Inc., Falls Church, VA, pg. 826
Bohm, Friedrich K.M., Mng. Partner--NBBJ, Columbus, OH, pg. 780
Bokor, James, Pres.--Robert James Sales Inc., Buffalo, NY, pg. 589
Boland, David, Chm. Bd., Pres. & Chief Exec. Officer--David Boland, Inc., Titusville, FL, pg. 162
Bolen, David E., Chief Oper. Officer--LeeWards Creative Crafts, Inc., Elgin, IL, pg. 666
Bollier, Roger D., Pres.--Niagara Cutter, Inc., North Tonawanda, NY, pg. 805
Bollinger, Bob, Chief Exec. Officer--Bollinger Industries Inc., Irving, TX, pg. 163
Bollinger, Donald T., Chm. Bd., Chief Exec. Officer & Dir.-Fin.--Bollinger Machine Shop And Shipyard, Inc., Lockport, LA, pg. 163
Bollinger, Glenn D., Chm. Bd. & Pres.--Bollinger Industries Inc., Irving, TX, pg. 163
Bonham, Donald L., Chm. Bd. & Chief Exec. Officer--Fiesta Mart Inc., Houston, TX, pg. 409
Borck, George, Exec. V.P.-Mktg.--Leather Center, Inc., Carrollton, TX, pg. 664
Borders, Bill, Pres. & Dir.-Creative Services--Borders, Perrin & Norrander, Inc., Portland, OR, pg. 165
Boren, Leland E., Chm. Bd., Pres. & Chief Exec. Officer--Avis Industrial Corporation, Upland, IN, pg. 102
Bork, Steven E., Exec. V.P.--Mark Anderson Associates, Inc., Arlington Heights, IL, pg. 73
Bouchez, Jacques, V.P. & Chief Oper. Officer--The Crispin Company, Houston, TX, pg. 299
Bouldin, Kent, Pres.--Leather Center, Inc., Carrollton, TX, pg. 664
Bourns, Gordon L., Chm. Bd.--Bourns, Inc., Riverside, CA, pg. 168
Boury, George, Chm. Bd. & Pres.--Boury Incorporated, Wheeling, WV, pg. 168
Boury, Michael, Vice Chm.--Boury Incorporated, Wheeling, WV, pg. 168
Bovaird, W.J., Pres. & Chief Exec. Officer--Bovaird Supply Co., Tulsa, OK, pg. 168
Bovis, George S., Sr. V.P.-Mktg. Devel. & Growth Plng.--White Hen Pantry, Inc., Elmhurst, IL, pg. 1185
Bowers, Bruce, V.P.--Chilewich Partners, White Plains, NY, pg. 248
Bowers, Paul D., Jr., Chm. Bd.--The WBDC Group, Grand Rapids, MI, pg. 1155
Bowling, Gene H., V.P.-Mktg. & Sls.--Alkota Cleaning Systems, Inc., Alcester, SD, pg. 34

Bowlus, Charles C., Pres.--Boston Distributors, Inc., Maple Heights, OH, pg. 167
Boyden, James, Pres. & Chief Exec. Officer--Teachers Management & Investment Corporation, Newport Beach, CA, pg. 1082
Braatz, Clay R., Sr. V.P.-Personnel--Western Reinsurance Brokers, Inc., Los Angeles, CA, pg. 1181
Bradford, James C., Jr., Sr. Partner--J. C. Bradford & Co., Nashville, TN, pg. 170
Bradley, Joseph A., V.P.--Foulds Inc., Libertyville, IL, pg. 427
Brady, Frank, Pres. & Chief Exec. Officer--The Brady Marketing Company, Pacheco, CA, pg. 171
Brant, Murray, Chm. Bd.--Brant Allen Industries, Inc., Greenwich, CT, pg. 172
Brant, Peter, Pres.--Brant Allen Industries, Inc., Greenwich, CT, pg. 172
Bratt, John A., Chm. Bd.--Yorktown Tool & Die Corporation, Yorktown, IN, pg. 1208
Braunheim, Stephen, Pres.--California Manufacturing Enterprises, City of Industry, CA, pg. 210
Bray, John J., Chm.-Forum Europe Ltd.--The Forum Corporation, Boston, MA, pg. 425
Bray, Stan, Controller--Bizzack Inc., Lexington, KY, pg. 153
Brendel, Albert, Pres.--Sensor Developments Inc., Orion, MI, pg. 990
Brennan, David L., Chm. Bd. & Chief Exec. Officer--The Brenlin Group, Akron, OH, pg. 173
Brenner, Ronald D., Pres. & Chief Exec. Officer--Technology for Energy Corporation, Knoxville, TN, pg. 1084
Bresky, Harry, Pres.--Seaboard Flour Corporation, Newton, MA, pg. 984
Brick, Frank E., Pres. & Chief Exec. Officer--Basic Computer, Akron, OH, pg. 124
Brickel, Jack W., Pres., Chief Exec. & Chief Oper. Officer & Dir.-Personnel--BEC Inc., Richmond, MI, pg. 106
Brickel, Mary L., Chm. Bd.--BEC Inc., Richmond, MI, pg. 106
Bricker, Marvin, Co-Pres. & Treas.--Hawkeye Steel Products, Inc., Houghton, IA, pg. 518
Briegel, Jack, V.P.--McNaughton & Gunn, Inc., Saline, MI, pg. 732
Brightbill, William, Pres. & Treas.--Ritter Bros., Inc., Harrisburg, PA, pg. 936
Brindle, A.W., Pres.--Wards Cove Packing Company, Seattle, WA, pg. 1163
Brindle, Harold A., V.P. & Sec.--Wards Cove Packing Company, Seattle, WA, pg. 1163
Brinton, Garrison W., Chm. Bd.--Label-Aire Inc., Fullerton, CA, pg. 649
Brock, Paul K., Pres. & Chief Exec. Officer--Brock Candy Company, Chattanooga, TN, pg. 177
Brode, Harold, Pres. & Chief Exec. Officer--Broder Bros. Co., Plymouth, MI, pg. 178
Brojack, William, Pres.--William Brojack Lumber Company, pg. 179
Bromley, Wayne L., Jr., Pres.--Giles & Ransome, Inc., Bensalem, PA, pg. 458
Brooks, Gloria J., V.P.--John W. Brooks Inc., Nelsonville, OH, pg. 180
Brooks, John M., Pres.--John W. Brooks Inc., Nelsonville, OH, pg. 180
Brooks, John W., Chm. Bd.--John W. Brooks Inc., Nelsonville, OH, pg. 180
Brookshire, Bruce G., Chm. & Chief Exec. Officer--Brookshire Grocery, Tyler, TX, pg. 180
Brostoff, George, Chm. Bd. & Treas.--Symplex Communications Corp., Ann Arbor, MI, pg. 1069
Broudski, Norman, Pres. & Chief Exec. Officer--City Postal, Inc., New York, NY, pg. 251
Brouillette, Donald G., Pres. & Chief Exec. Officer--Demeter, Inc., Fowler, IN, pg. 328
Brower, William R., Pres.--BrowerPease, Inc., Hamilton, OH, pg. 181
Brown, A. Worley, Chm. Bd.--Rock-Tenn Company, Norcross, GA, pg. 941
Brown, D. Warren, Pres. & Chief Exec. Officer--Wyandot Inc., Marion, OH, pg. 1205
Brown, J.S., III, Pres.--Bruce Foods Corp., Saint Martinville, LA, pg. 183
Brown, Kimberly, Sec.--Field Container Company, L.P., Elk Grove Village, IL, pg. 409
Brown, Larry L., Sr., Pres. & Chief Exec. Officer--Riverside Central Services, Inc., Natchez, MS, pg. 937
Brown, Michael S., Pres.--Wometco Enterprises, Inc., Coral Gables, FL, pg. 1199
Brown, Norman S., V.P.--Bruce Foods Corp., Saint Martinville, LA, pg. 183
Brown, Robert D., Pres.--Berry-Brown Advertising, Inc., Dallas, TX, pg. 144
Brown, Wayne J., Pres.--Brown Evans Company, Mesa, AZ, pg. 182
Brown, Willis E., Jr., Pres.--Brown Motors, Toledo, OH, pg. 182
Brownstein, Howard N., Chm. Bd.--National Property Analysts, Inc., Philadelphia, PA, pg. 792
Broyhill, J. Edgar II, Pres.--Edgar B. Furniture Co., Clemmons, NC, pg. 368
Bruce, Frank B., Chm. Bd.--Bruce Industries, Inc., Dayton, NV, pg. 183
Bruce, Tom B., Pres.--Bruce Industries, Inc., Dayton, NV, pg. 163
Bruder, Thomas A., Jr., Pres.--M. A. Bruder & Sons, Inc., Broomall, PA, pg. 184
Bruenger, Leona, Chm. Bd.--M. Bruenger & Co., Inc., Wichita, KS, pg. 184
Bruenger, M.W., Pres.--M. Bruenger & Co., Inc., Wichita, KS, pg. 184
Brutger, Larry, Chm. Bd. & Pres.--Brutger Equities, Inc., Saint Cloud, MN, pg. 185
Bryant, Ronald D., Pres.--Masters Inc., Gaithersburg, MD, pg. 720
Brzustewicz, Robert, Chief Exec. Officer & Sec.--Northern Wire & Cable, Inc., Troy, MI, pg. 814
Buchan, John, Exec. V.P.--Cloverdale Equipment Co., Oak Park, MI, pg. 256
Bucksbaum, Martin, Chm. Bd. & Chief Exec. & Info. Officer--General Growth Companies, Inc., Des Moines, IA, pg. 449
Bucksbaum, Matthew, Pres., Treas. & Sec.--General Growth Companies, Inc., Des Moines, IA, pg. 449
Buddig, John C., Treas.--Carl Buddig & Company, Homewood, IL, pg. 186
Buddig, Thomas R., V.P.-Sls. & Mktg.--Carl Buddig & Company, Homewood, IL, pg. 186
Buddig, William C., Pres.--Carl Buddig & Company, Homewood, IL, pg. 186
Budig, George J., V.P., Sec. & Treas.--Budco Group Inc., Cincinnati, OH, pg. 186
Budig, Otto M., Jr., Pres.--Budco Group Inc., Cincinnati, OH, pg. 186
Buehler, David G., V.P.--Wharfside Restaurants, Inc., Jasper, IN, pg. 1184
Buehler, Judith Stetter, Sec.--Wharfside Restaurants, Inc., Jasper, IN, pg. 1184
Buettner, Milton B., Chm. Bd.--Western Reinsurance Brokers, Inc., Los Angeles, CA, pg. 1181
Bull, Marshall R., Chm. Bd. & Pres.--Industrial Wire Products Corporation, Pomona, CA, pg. 567
Bumby, Edward W., Pres.--Ripon Foods, Inc., Ripon, WI, pg. 935
Bumby, John E., Chm. Bd.--Ripon Foods, Inc., Ripon, WI, pg. 935
Burdick, Richard L., Chm., Pres., Chief Exec. & Chief Oper. Officer--Thermon Manufacturing Company, San Marcos, TX, pg. 1091
Burgess, Malcolm S., Jr., Chm. Bd. & Pres.--Burgess Pigment Co., Sandersville, GA, pg. 190
Burke, John J., Jr., Partner--Roney & Co., Detroit, MI, pg. 946
Burkle, Ronald, Chm. Bd. & Partner--The Yucaipa Companies, Claremont, CA, pg. 1214
Burnes, Hugh S., Jr., Pres.--Rome Manufacturing Co., Rome, GA, pg. 945
Burrow, Grady, Pres. & Chief Exec. Officer--National Computer Print, Inc., Birmingham, AL, pg. 786
Burrow, Ray, Sr. V.P.-Opers. & Fin.--National Computer Print, Inc., Birmingham, AL, pg. 786
Burt, John R., Chm. Bd. & Pres.--Duro-Last Roofing, Inc., Saginaw, MI, pg. 355
Bush, Raymond T., Sr. V.P. & Chief Fin. Officer--Maguire Group Inc., Foxboro, MA, pg. 701
Butera, Paul, Pres.--Butera Finer Foods Inc., Elgin, IL, pg. 196
Butt, Charles C., Pres. & Chief Exec. Officer--H. E. Butt Grocery Co., San Antonio, TX, pg. 197
Byer, Allan G., Chm. Bd., Pres. & Chief Exec. Officer--Byer California, San Francisco, CA, pg. 197
Byer, Marian, Treas. & Sec.--Byer California, San Francisco, CA, pg. 197
Byrne, John F., Sr., Pres.--Jack Byrne Ford & Mercury, Inc., Mechanicville, NY, pg. 198
Cabana, Bill, Mgr.-New Car Sls.--Mark Chevrolet Inc., Wayne, MI, pg. 708
Cabana, Charles, Pres.--Mark Chevrolet Inc., Wayne, MI, pg. 708
Cabot, Samuel, III, Pres.--Samuel Cabot, Inc., Newburyport, MA, pg. 206
Cafaro, Anthony M., Pres. & Chief Exec. Officer--The Cafaro Co., Youngstown, OH, pg. 207
Cafaro, William M., Chm. Bd.--The Cafaro Co., Youngstown, OH, pg. 207
Cahill, Kenneth, V.P. & Sec.--Larken Inc., Cedar Rapids, IA, pg. 659
Cahill, Larry, Pres. & Treas.--Larken Inc., Cedar Rapids, IA, pg. 659
Calabrese, P.J., Pres.--The Grieve Corporation, Round Lake, IL, pg. 486
Calafati, Gabriel R., Chm. Bd., Pres. & Treas.--Frank Briscoe Co. Inc., Roseland, NJ, pg. 176
Calano, James C., Pres. & Chief Exec. Officer--CareerTrack Inc., Boulder, CO, pg. 218
Calcaterra, Edward L., Pres.--J. S. Alberici Construction Co., Inc., Saint Louis, MO, pg. 31
Caldwell, John D., Chm. Bd., Pres. & Chief Exec. Officer--Borchers Bros., San Jose, CA, pg. 165
Call, Val, V.P., Sec. & Treas.--Maverik Country Stores, Inc., Afton, WY, pg. 722
Call, William, Chm., Pres. & Chief Exec. Officer--Maverik Country Stores, Inc., Afton, WY, pg. 722
Camp, Barry S., Pres.--Hub Inc., Tucker, GA, pg. 548
Camp, Ben H., Chm. Bd. & Chief Exec. Officer--Hub Inc., Tucker, GA, pg. 548
Campbell, C., Pres.--SAE Engineering, Inc., Santa Clara, CA, pg. 959
Campbell, Chester K., Chm. Bd.--Campbell Oil Co., Massillon, OH, pg. 213
Campbell, Robert E., Exec. V.P.--T. Bruce Sales, Inc., West Middlesex, PA, pg. 183
Campbell, T. Scott, Pres.--T. Bruce Sales, Inc., West Middlesex, PA, pg. 183
Canfield, Arthur, Sr., Chm. Bd.--A. J. Canfield Co., Chicago, IL, pg. 214
Capizzi, Anthony, Chm. Bd., Pres. & Chief Exec. Officer--Quality Food Oils, Inc., New Milford, CT, pg. 903
Capizzi, Frank, V.P. & Chief Oper. Officer--Quality Food Oils, Inc., New Milford, CT, pg. 903
Caplan, James A., Chm. Bd., Pres., Treas., Prod. Mgr. & Chief Engr.--Capp, Inc., Philadelphia, PA, pg. 216
Carcara, P.J., Pres. & Chief Exec. Officer--Baldt, Inc., Chester, PA, pg. 115
Carden, Gerald T., Pres.--Carden & Cherry, Inc., Nashville, TN, pg. 217
Cardin, Judge Meyer, Chm. Bd.--B. Green & Co., Baltimore, MD, pg. 484
Carey, D.L., Pres.--Knouse Foods Inc., Peach Glen, PA, pg. 637
Carey, William P., Chm. Bd. & Mng. Dir.--W. P. Carey & Co., Inc., New York, NY, pg. 218
Carlson, Curtis L., Chm. Bd., Pres. & Chief Exec. Officer--Carlson Companies, Inc., Minneapolis, MN, pg. 220
Carlson, Robert S., V.P.--The Atlas Construction Co., Stamford, CT, pg. 96
Carlson, Robert W., Jr., Chm. & Chief Exec. Officer--Quadion Corporation, Minneapolis, MN, pg. 902
Carnahan, John M., Sec. & Treas.--Woodfin-Smith Pontiac, Inc., Baton Rouge, LA, pg. 1200
Carpender, Gary, Exec. V.P.--American International Container, Inc., Miami, FL, pg. 56
Carpenter, Judith, Chm. Bd.--National Welders Supply Co. Inc., Charlotte, NC, pg. 794
Carr, Oliver, Chm. Bd.--The Oliver Carr Co., Washington, DC, pg. 225
Carstens, Donald D., Chm. Bd.--Pullman Industries, Inc., Madison Heights, MI, pg. 900
Carter, Donald J., Pres., Treas. & Chief Exec. Officer--Home Interiors & Gifts, Inc., Dallas, TX, pg. 541
Carter, Jud, Pres.--Bell-Carter Foods, Inc., Lafayette, CA, pg. 134
Carter, Sam, Chm. Bd. & Pres.--Carter Companies, Kansas City, MO, pg. 226
Carter, Tim, Chm. Bd. & Chief Exec. Officer--Bell-Carter Foods, Inc., Lafayette, CA, pg. 134
Carus, M. Blouke, Chm. Bd., Pres., Chief Exec. & Chief Oper. Officer--Carus Corporation, Peru, IL, pg. 227
Carus, Paul, Exec. V.P. & Treas.--Carus Corporation, Peru, IL, pg. 227
Caruso, Jack, Chm. Bd. & Pres.--Regency Dodge Inc., Jacksonville, FL, pg. 922
Caruso, John G., Exec. V.P., Loan Admin. & Sec.--Globe Mortgage Company, Hackensack, NJ, pg. 464
Caruthers, William A., Pres.--Greenhorne & O'Mara, Inc., Greenbelt, MD, pg. 485
Casey, Richard T., Co-Pres.--The Myers Group (U.S) Inc., Rouses Point, NY, pg. 780
Casey, William R., Chm. Bd. & Chief Exec. Officer--The Myers Group (U.S) Inc., Rouses Point, NY, pg. 780
Cashman, G. E., V.P.--Pacific Envelope Company, Anaheim, CA, pg. 840
Cashman, Robert L., Chm. Bd., Pres. & Chief Exec. Officer--Pacific Envelope Company, Anaheim, CA, pg. 840
Cashwell, Henry V., Sec. & Treas.--Tencarva Machinery Co., Inc., Greensboro, NC, pg. 1086
Cassels, W. Tobin, Jr., Chm. Bd.--Southeastern Freight Lines, Inc., Columbia, SC, pg. 1019
Cassese, Patrick J., Chm. Bd., Pres. & Chief Exec. Officer--Antares Group Inc., Cleveland, OH, pg. 76
Cassner, Alice E., V.P.--Rotary Forms Press, Inc., Hillsboro, OH, pg. 950
Cassner, Alvin B., Pres. & Chief Exec. Officer--Rotary Forms Press, Inc., Hillsboro, OH, pg. 950
Cassner, Jon H., Sec. & Treas.--Rotary Forms Press, Inc., Hillsboro, OH, pg. 950
Casty, David, Chm. Bd.--American Snacks, Inc., Chelsea, MA, pg. 61
Cataldo, C.A., Pres. & Chief Exec. Officer--Hostmark Management Group, Rowing Meadows, IL, pg. 545
Cataldo, Robert J., Exec. V.P.-Opers.--Hostmark Management Group, Rowing Meadows, IL, pg. 545
Catsimatidis, John, Chm. Bd., Pres. & Chief Exec. Officer--Red Apple Companies, New York, NY, pg. 917
Cervenka, Robert, Chief Exec. Officer--Phillips Plastics Corporation, Phillips, WI, pg. 867
Chalmers, David B., Chm. Bd., Pres. & Chief Exec. Officer--Coral Petroleum Corporation, Houston, TX, pg. 285
Chambers, Merle, Chm. of the Exec. Committee--Clipper Exxpress Co., Lemont, IL, pg. 256
Chamblin, Dale, Exec. V.P. & Sec.--California Electric Service, Oakland, CA, pg. 209
Chan, David M., V.P. & Chief Fin. Officer--Quik Wok Corporation, Dallas, TX, pg. 905
Chapman, D.B., Chm. Bd--Columbian Rope Company, Guntown, MS, pg. 266
Chapman, David F., V.P. & Reg. Mgr.-Southwest--Gilbane Building Company, Providence, RI, pg. 457
Chapoton, David, Chm. Bd.--De Novo Corporation, Utica, MI, pg. 321
Chappell, Sarah S., Sr. V.P.-Personnel--Spencer Companies Inc., Huntsville, AL, pg. 1030
Charlton, Peter A.M., Partner, Creative Dir.--Kupper Parker Communications Inc., Saint Louis, MO, pg. 646
Chase, William K., Chm. of Bd.--Chase Chevrolet Co., Stockton, CA, pg. 240
Chenoweth, Nick, V.P. & Gen. Counsel--Empire Airlines, Hayden Lake, ID, pg. 379
Chernick, Aubrey G., Chm. Bd. & Chief Exec. Officer--Candle Corporation, Santa Monica, CA, pg. 214
Chesson, Dave, Exec. V.P.-Opers. & Sec.--Leslie Advertising, Greenville, SC, pg. 668
Chester, Teresa, V.P.--Design 1 Interiors, Los Angeles, CA, pg. 332
Chicca, Thomas, V.P.-Eastern Region--Greenhorne & O'Mara, Inc., Greenbelt, MD, pg. 485
Chilewich, Simon, Pres. & Chief Exec. Officer--Chilewich Partners, White Plains, NY, pg. 248
Christensen, Lee R., Chief Fin. Officer & V.P.--Moran Towing & Transportation Co. Inc., Greenwich, CT, pg. 769
Christian, Betty S., Chm. Bd., Pres. & Chief Exec. Officer--Central Coca-Cola Bottling Company, Inc., Richmond, VA, pg. 232
Christianson, Warren G., Chm. Bd.--Despatch Industries, Minneapolis, MN, pg. 332
Chun, Rupert K., Exec. V.P.--Mutual Welding Co., Ltd, Honolulu, HI, pg. 779
Chun, Tai Vee, V.P.-Prod.--Mutual Welding Co., Ltd, Honolulu, HI, pg. 779
Chun, Thomas T.W., Pres.--Mutual Welding Co., Ltd, Honolulu, HI, pg. 779

Church, John F., Jr., Pres.--The Cincinnati Cordage & Paper Company, Cincinnati, OH, pg. 249
Clancy, Joseph E., Chm. Bd., Pres. & Chief Oper. Officer--Bridgeport Machines, Inc., Bridgeport, CT, pg. 175
Clanton, Fred, V.P.-Opers.--Colfax Envelope Corporation, Buffalo Grove, IL, pg. 261
Clark, Edward, Chm. Bd.--American Seating Company, Grand Rapids, MI, pg. 60
Clark, Edwin J., Pres. & Chief Exec. Officer--Dwyer Instruments Inc., Michigan City, IN, pg. 356
Clark, J. Thomas, Pres.--Dubin-Clark & Company, Greenwich, CT, pg. 350
Clark, Lester, Chm. Bd.--States, Inc., Breckenridge, TX, pg. 1041
Clark, Linda Carole, Pres.--Complete Interiors Inc., Altamonte Springs, FL, pg. 270
Clark, William J., Chm. Bd.--Massachusetts Mutual Life Insurance Co., Springfield, MA, pg. 718
Clayton, David, Exec. V.P.--Andy Frain Services, Inc., Chicago, IL, pg. 428
Clements, Edward B., V.P. & Chief Exec. Officer--Clements Foods Co., Oklahoma City, OK, pg. 254
Clements, Richard H., Chm. Bd., Pres. , & Chief Fin. Officer--Clements Foods Co., Oklahoma City, OK, pg. 254
Clements, Robert H., V.P.--Clements Foods Co., Oklahoma City, OK, pg. 254
Cleveland, James R., Sr., Chm. Bd., Pres. & Chief Exec. Officer--Cleveland Group, Inc., Atlanta, GA, pg. 255
Cleveland, L. W., Sr., Chm. Emeritus--Cleveland Group, Inc., Atlanta, GA, pg. 255
Cleveland, Louie W., Jr., V.P.--Cleveland Group, Inc., Atlanta, GA, pg. 255
Cleveland, Van, Sec.--Cleveland Group, Inc., Atlanta, GA, pg. 255
Cline, Lynn, Chief Fin. Officer--Rudolph Foods Company, Lima, OH, pg. 954
Cloud, Forrest R., Chm. Bd.--IBT, Inc., Shawnee Mission, KS, pg. 558
Cloud, Stephen R., Pres. & Chief Exec. Officer--IBT, Inc., Shawnee Mission, KS, pg. 558
Cocke, Bartlett, Jr., Chm. Bd. & Chief Exec. Officer--Bartlett Cocke Jr. Construction Co., San Antonio, TX, pg. 258
Cohan, Norman H., Pres. & Chief Exec. Officer--Security Plastics, Inc., Miami Lakes, FL, pg. 987
Cohen, Boris, Chm. Bd.--All-Luminum Products, Inc., Philadelphia, PA, pg. 35
Cohen, Howard, Pres.--Host Apparel, Inc., New York, NY, pg. 545
Cohen, Ian N., Partner, Acct. Services--Kupper Parker Communications Inc., Saint Louis, MO, pg. 646
Cohen, Irving, Chm. Bd.--Host Apparel, Inc., New York, NY, pg. 545
Cohen, Lewis M., Pres. & Chief Exec. Officer--Acme Canvas Co., Inc., Malden, MA, pg. 13
Cohen, Peter J., Pres. & Chief Exec. Officer--Periphonics Corp., Bohemia, NY, pg. 862
Cohen, Philip E., Chief Oper. Officer & Dir.-Client Services--Harris Drury Cohen, Fort Lauderdale, FL, pg. 511
Cohen, Steven, Exec. V.P.--Host Apparel, Inc., New York, NY, pg. 545
Cohen, Steven A., Chm. Bd. & Pres.--Andy Frain Services, Inc., Chicago, IL, pg. 428
Cohen, Warren, Pres.--All-Luminum Products, Inc., Philadelphia, PA, pg. 35
Cole, Catherine P., Chief Oper. Oficer & Sec.--Columbine Systems Inc., Golden, CO, pg. 266
Cole, George, V.P.-Mktg.--Periphonics Corp., Bohemia, NY, pg. 862
Cole, Jeffrey A., Chm. Bd. & Chief Exec. Officer--Cole National Corporation, Cleveland, OH, pg. 260
Coleman, Walter C., III, Pres.--Coleman Dairy Inc., Little Rock, AR, pg. 261
Coleman, Walter C., Jr., Chm. Bd.--Coleman Dairy Inc., Little Rock, AR, pg. 261
Collins, Christopher C., Chm. Bd., Pres. & Chief Exec. Officer--Nuttall Gear Corporation, Niagara Falls, NY, pg. 818
Collins, Kevin, Pres.--Collins Chevrolet, GEO, Louisville, KY, pg. 263
Colman, Bob, Owner--Colman Toyota, Baton Rouge, LA, pg. 263
Coma, Robert S., Chief Admin. Officer--Howard Needles Tammen & Bergendoff, Kansas City, MO, pg. 547
Como, John, Jr., V.P., Sec. & Treas.--Amco Folding Cartons, Inc., Towaco, NJ, pg. 47
Como, John, Sr., Pres.--Amco Folding Cartons, Inc., Towaco, NJ, pg. 47
Compton, William, Pres., Chief Exec. Officer & Chief Oper. Officer--Tropical Garment Manufacturing Company, Tampa, FL, pg. 1116
Cone, G. Hollis, Chm. Bd., Pres. & Chief Exec. Officer--Defender Services, Inc., Columbia, SC, pg. 324
Congel, Robert J., Mng. Partner--The Pyramid Companies, Syracuse, NY, pg. 901
Connell, William F., Chm. Bd. & Chief Exec. Officer--Connell Limited Partnership, Boston, MA, pg. 275
Connon, Dana, Grp. V.P.--Welsh Company, Saint Louis, MO, pg. 1175
Connor, Robert C., Pres.--The Union of Arkansas Corp., Little Rock, AR, pg. 1127
Constantino, Joseph M., Exec. V.P.--The Atlas Construction Co., Stamford, CT, pg. 96
Contos, Larry D., Pres.--Pay Less Super Markets, Inc., Anderson, IN, pg. 852
Converse, Stephen, Dir.-Mktg.--Keller Construction Company Ltd., El Monte, CA, pg. 620
Cook, C. Larry, Vice Chm.--Overland Transportation System, Inc., Indianapolis, IN, pg. 832
Cook, Carl, Chm. Bd. & Pres.--Overland Transportation System, Inc., Indianapolis, IN, pg. 832
Cook, Daniel L., V.P. & Chief Fin. Officer--Overland Transportation System, Inc., Indianapolis, IN, pg. 832
Cook, Greg, Pres. & Chief Oper. Officer--Cook Manufacturing Corporation, Duncan, OK, pg. 282
Cook, James D., Chm. Bd. & Chief Exec. Officer--Concord Litho Co., Inc., Concord, NH, pg. 272
Cook, Samuel R., Chm. Bd. & Chief Exec. Officer--Broughton Foods Company, Marietta, OH, pg. 180
Cook, Stephen A., V.P. & Chief Oper. Officer--Overland Transportation System, Inc., Indianapolis, IN, pg. 832
Coomer, Ralph, Treas. & Sec.--Ziniz Inc., Louisville, KY, pg. 1220
Cooper, Norton J., Pres. & Chief Exec. Officer--Charles Jacquin et Cie, Inc., Philadelphia, PA, pg. 588
Coopersmith, Marvin, Exec. V.P.-Opers.--Ranir Corporation, Grand Rapids, MI, pg. 912
Copland, James R., III, Pres., Chief Exec. Officer & Treas.--Copland Fabrics, Inc., Burlington, NC, pg. 284
Copland, Ronald G., V.P. & Sec.--Copland Fabrics, Inc., Burlington, NC, pg. 284
Copley, Helen K., Chm. Bd. & Chief Exec. Officer--The Copley Press, Inc., La Jolla, CA, pg. 284
Copps, Donald C., V.P.-Mdsg.--The Copps Corp., Stevens Point, WI, pg. 285
Copps, Frederick C., Exec. V.P.-Wholesale--The Copps Corp., Stevens Point, WI, pg. 285
Copps, Michael W., Chm. Bd. & Chief Exec. Officer--The Copps Corp., Stevens Point, WI, pg. 285
Copps, Thomas R., V.P.-Pub. Rels.--The Copps Corp., Stevens Point, WI, pg. 285
Copps, Timothy J., Pres.--The Copps Corp., Stevens Point, WI, pg. 285
Cormier, Harry W., Jr., Pres.--Cormier Rice Milling Company, Inc., De Witt, AR, pg. 286
Cornell, M. Keen, Pres. & Chief Exec. Officer--Cornell Iron Works, Inc., Mountaintop, PA, pg. 286
Cornwell, Terry, V.P.--Macro Computer Products Inc., Rochester Hills, MI, pg. 698
Cosenza, G. Joseph, Vice Chm.--The Inland Group, Inc., Oak Brook, IL, pg. 570
Cosgrave, Gary D., Chm. & Chief Exec. Officer--Pro Hardware, Inc., Englewood, CO, pg. 891
Cosgrove, Hazel, Vice Chm., Treas., & Corp. Sec.--Pro Hardware, Inc., Englewood, CO, pg. 891
Costa, Emanuele, Pres.--Overseas Partners, Inc., New York, NY, pg. 833
Cothren, H. Bobby, Sr. V.P.--The Stellar Group Inc., Jacksonville, FL, pg. 1046
Cotter, Daniel A., Pres. & Chief Exec. Officer & Dir.--Cotter & Company, Chicago, IL, pg. 288
Cotton, John L., Dir.-Mktg.--Howard Needles Tammen & Bergendoff, Kansas City, MO, pg. 547
Coulombe, Cecile J., Pres., Treas. & Sec.--White Rock Distilleries Inc., Lewiston, ME, pg. 1186
Coulombe, Raymond R., Chm. & Chief Exec. Officer--White Rock Distilleries Inc., Lewiston, ME, pg. 1186
Courtney, Lawrence, V.P.-Southeast Region--Greenhorne & O'Mara, Inc., Greenbelt, MD, pg. 485
Cowin, John J., Chm. Bd., Pres. & Treas.--Cowin & Company, Inc., Birmingham, AL, pg. 291
Cowin, Peter G., V.P.--Cowin & Company, Inc., Birmingham, AL, pg. 291
Cowles, Alfred, Jr., Pres. & Chief Exec. Officer--Bluff City Distributing Co., Inc., Memphis, TN, pg. 161
Cowles, Glen, V.P.-Pur.--Bluff City Distributing Co., Inc., Memphis, TN, pg. 161
Cox, Charles, Pres. & Owner--Cox Furniture, Maxton, NC, pg. 294
Coyne, Nancy, Chm. Bd., Chief Exec. Officer & Dir.-Creative Services--Serino Coyne Inc., New York, NY, pg. 991
Crabtree, James T., Pres.--SCR, Inc., Lake Oswego, OR, pg. 961
Craddock, James Berry, Pres.--Craddock Development Co., Inc., Colorado Springs, CO, pg. 295
Craft, Donald B., Exec. V.P.--Wyatt Inc., Branford, CT, pg. 1205
Crane, Jeffrey D., Pres.--Crane Construction Co., Northbrook, IL, pg. 296
Crawford, Bernard K., Chm. Bd.--Standard Tool & Manufacturing Company, Lyndhurst, NJ, pg. 1037
Crawford, Jerry, Chm. Bd.--Rome Manufacturing Co., Rome, GA, pg. 945
Crawford, William F., Pres.--Standard Tool & Manufacturing Company, Lyndhurst, NJ, pg. 1037
Cretors, Phyllis, Pres.--The Popcorn Factory, Lake Forest, IL, pg. 426
Crispin, Andre A., Pres. & Chief Exec. Officer--The Crispin Company, Houston, TX, pg. 299
Crispin, Charles, Pres.--Crispin & Porter Advertising Inc., Miami, FL, pg. 299
Crosby, Samuel C., Chief Oper. Officer--Astre Corporate Group, Alexandria, VA, pg. 92
Cross, Joe D., Jr., Pres.--Cross Motors Corp., Louisville, KY, pg. 300
Cross, Joe D., Sr., Chm.--Cross Motors Corp., Louisville, KY, pg. 300
Crowley, Malvern D., V.P.-Fin. & Treas.--Drug Emporium of Arizona, Inc., Scottsdale, AZ, pg. 349
Crowley, Thomas B., Chm. Bd. & Chief Exec. Officer--Crowley Maritime Corporation, Oakland, CA, pg. 301
Crowser, John C., Chief Exec. Officer--Hart Crowser, Inc., Seattle, WA, pg. 512
Cuff, Harry, Treas.--Kampgrounds of America, Inc., Billings, MT, pg. 613
Culbertson, James F., Jr., Pres.--Temp-Control Mechanical Corp., Portland, OR, pg. 1086
Cullen, J. Russell, Jr., Pres.--Nason and Cullen, Inc., Wayne, PA, pg. 784
Cullen, John B., Chm. Bd. & Chief Exec. Officer--King Kullen Grocery Co., Inc., Westbury, NY, pg. 630
Cullers, Marian B., Exec. V.P. & Sec.--Vince Cullers Advertising Inc., Chicago, IL, pg. 304
Cullers, Vincent T., Pres., Chief Exec. Officer & Treas.--Vince Cullers Advertising Inc., Chicago, IL, pg. 304
Cummings, R. C., Sec. & Gen. Counsel--Smith-Lee Co., Inc., Oneida, NY, pg. 1013
Currey, Bradley, Jr., Pres. & Chief Exec. Officer--Rock-Tenn Company, Norcross, GA, pg. 941
Cutler, Burton, Chm. Bd.--Educational Insights, Inc., Dominguez Hills, CA, pg. 369
Cutler, Jay, Pres.--Educational Insights, Inc., Dominguez Hills, CA, pg. 369
d'Abo, Richard, Partner--The Yucaipa Companies, Claremont, CA, pg. 1214
Dabbs, Karl, V.P.-Fin., Treas. & Sec.--B.A.S.S., Inc., Montgomery, AL, pg. 105
Daley, James E., Co-Chm.--Price Waterhouse - U.S., New York, NY, pg. 888
Daly, Harold E., Jr., Mng. Partner--Cosmopulos Crowley Daly/CKG, Boston, MA, pg. 288
Daly, Michael J., Treas.--Chessco Industries, Inc., Westport, CT, pg. 243
Damonte, John J., Jr., V.P.--MBT Associates, Inc., San Francisco, CA, pg. 691
Daniel, Larry, Pres. & Chief Exec. & Chief Fin. Officer--The Daniel Co. of Springfield, Springfield, MO, pg. 314
Daniel, Ron, V.P., Dir.-Personnel & Sec.--The Daniel Co. of Springfield, Springfield, MO, pg. 314
Daniel, William, Sec. & Dir.-Art--Equinox Advertising, Inc., Chicago, IL, pg. 384
Daniels, David P., Pres. & Chief Oper. Officer--Penn-Daniels, Inc., Quincy, IL, pg. 857
Daniels, Richard A., Sr. V.P.-Sls.--Periphonics Corp., Bohemia, NY, pg. 862
Daniels, Steven L., AIA, V.P.-Operations--Ritter Bros., Inc., Harrisburg, PA, pg. 936
Daniels, William D., Chm. Bd. & Chief Exec. Officer--Penn-Daniels, Inc., Quincy, IL, pg. 857
Darwish, Charles, Pres.--United States Realty & Investment Co., Newark, NJ, pg. 1137
Daunhauer, John R., Jr., Chm. Bd. & Pres.--Byerly Ford-Nissan Inc., Louisville, KY, pg. 198
Davidson, Kerry S., V.P.--Universal Securities Corporation, Birmingham, AL, pg. 1139
Davis, Allen S., Sr. V.P.-Opers.--White Hen Pantry, Inc., Elmhurst, IL, pg. 1185
Davis, Charles E., Sr., Chm. Bd. & Pres.--Laboratory Supply Company, Inc., Louisville, KY, pg. 649
Davis, Greg, Chm.--Ravenswood Aluminum Corp., Ravenswood, WV, pg. 914
Davis, Harold, Chm.--Electrical Wholesale Supply Company, Inc., Idaho Falls, ID, pg. 374
Davis, Jim, Group V.P.--B.A.S.S., Inc., Montgomery, AL, pg. 105
Davis, Mark D., Pres. (Even Days)--Davis, Ball & Colombatto Advertising, Inc., Los Angeles, CA, pg. 318
Davis, W. Jack, Chm. Bd.--Austin Powder Co., Cleveland, OH, pg. 99
Davis, W. Jack, Chm. Bd.--Rish Equipment Company, Bluefield, WV, pg. 935
Davis, Warren A., Exec. V.P. & Chief Fin. Officer--Gateway Apparel, Inc., Saint Louis, MO, pg. 445
Davis, William, V.P.--Remarks, Inc., Dublin, OH, pg. 925
Day, Timothy T., Pres. & Chief Exec. Officer--Bar-S Foods Co., Phoenix, AZ, pg. 118
De Mento, Biagio, Sr., Pres. & Chief Exec. Officer--Brooks Provisions Inc., Philadelphia, PA, pg. 180
De Pasquale, John A., Chm. Bd.--The Direct Marketing Group Inc., New York, NY, pg. 339
Dearden, Douglas E., Chief Exec. Officer & Personnel Dir.--Dearden's, Inc., Los Angeles, CA, pg. 322
DeBartolo, Edward J., Chm. Bd. & Chief Exec. Officer--The Edward J. DeBartolo Corporation, Youngstown, OH, pg. 323
DeBartolo, Edward J., Jr., Pres. & Chief Admin. Officer--The Edward J. DeBartolo Corporation, Youngstown, OH, pg. 323
DeBlasio, Carl, Exec. V.P.--Planes Moving And Storage, Inc., Cincinnati, OH, pg. 874
DeCamp, D.A., Pres. & Chief Exec. Officer--Flexfab, Inc., Hastings, MI, pg. 418
Dedman, Robert H., Jr., Pres. & Chief Oper. Officer--Club Corporation International, Dallas, TX, pg. 256
Dedman, Robert H., Sr., Chm. Bd. & Chief Exec. Officer--Club Corporation International, Dallas, TX, pg. 256
DeGrazia, Nicholas J., Pres. & Chief Oper. Officer--Lionel Trains, Inc., Chesterfield, MI, pg. 677
DeHahn, Mary L., Partner, Production & Pub. Rels.--Kupper Parker Communications Inc., Saint Louis, MO, pg. 646
Dehmlow, Steven L., Pres. & Chief Oper. Officer--Great Lakes Terminal & Transport Corp., Chicago, IL, pg. 482
Dekko, Chester E., Chm. Bd., Pres. & Chief Exec. Officer--Group Dekko International Inc., Kendallville, IN, pg. 489
Dellinger, J.B., III, V.P.-Fin.--Rodgers Builders, Inc., Charlotte, NC, pg. 942
Delman, Jacob J., Chm. Bd. & Chief Oper. Officer--Splendor Form International Inc., Long Island City, NY, pg. 1031
Denrich, Louis, Pres.--So-Lo-Food, Inc., Baltimore, MD, pg. 1016
Denrich, Stephen, Chief Exec. Officer--So-Lo-Food, Inc., Baltimore, MD, pg. 1016
DePaul, John, Pres.--DDF&M Inc. Dudreck DePaul Ficco & Morgan Inc., Pittsburgh, PA, pg. 308
Deramus, William H., Pres.--Miller & Co., Selma, AL, pg. 753
DeRuiter, David, Pres.--Davlin Paint Company, Inc., Berkeley, CA, pg. 319
DeSantis, Carl, Pres.--Sundown Vitamin Co., Inc., Fort Lauderdale, FL, pg. 1060
DeSantis, Damon, Exec. V.P.--Sundown Vitamin Co., Inc., Fort Lauderdale, FL, pg. 1060
Desnoes, Peter B., Mng. Gen. Partner--Burnham Broadcasting Company, Chicago, IL, pg. 193
Desperak, Jack, Pres. & Chief Exec. Officer--Splendor Form International Inc., Long Island City, NY, pg. 1031
Devine, Steve, Dir.-Mktg.--Whitmire Distribution, Folsom, CA, pg. 1187
DeVos, Richard, Pres.--Amway Corporation, Ada, MI, pg. 70

Dew, B. Jarvis, Vice Chm.--Diemolding Corp., Canastota, NY, pg. 336
Dew, Bruce J., Sec.--Diemolding Corp., Canastota, NY, pg. 336
Dew, Donald F., Chm. Bd., Pres. & Chief Exec. Officer--Diemolding Corp., Canastota, NY, pg. 336
Dezelan, Annette G., V.P.--Gohmann Asphalt & Construction Inc., Clarksville, IN, pg. 465
Di Zazzo, James G., Chm. Bd. & Pres.--Oomphies, Inc., Lawrence, MA, pg. 827
Diamond, Lawrence, Chm. Bd., Pres., Chief Exec. & Chief Oper. Officer & Dir.-Pur.--Triangle Marketing Corp., New York, NY, pg. 1112
Dick, Donald W., Treas.--Overseas Partners, Inc., New York, NY, pg. 833
Dick, Dorsey W., Chm. Bd.--Dick Corporation, Large, PA, pg. 335
Dick, Douglas P., Sr. V.P.-Sls. & Mktg.--Dick Corporation, Large, PA, pg. 335
Dickerson, Arthur J., Chm. Bd., Pres. & Chief Exec. Officer--Southwestern Petroleum Corporation, Fort Worth, TX, pg. 1024
Dickten, Erich, Chm. Bd.--Dickten & Masch Manufacturing Co., Nashotah, WI, pg. 336
Didde, Carl, Chm. Bd.--Didde Web Press, Emporia, KS, pg. 336
Didde, David D., Pres. & Chief Exec. Officer--Didde Web Press, Emporia, KS, pg. 336
Diebel, Robert, Pres.--Diebel Manufacturing Co., Morton Grove, IL, pg. 336
Diehl, William A., Chm. Bd.--Diehl Specialties Intl., Defiance, OH, pg. 336
Digges, J.J., Exec. V.P.--Bush Development Corp., Williamsburg, VA, pg. 196
DiGioia, Anthony M., Jr., Pres.--GAI Consultants, Inc., Monroeville, PA, pg. 439
DiJulius, Paul, Chm. Bd.--Lavelle Aircraft Company, Philadelphia, PA, pg. 661
DiMatteo, Dominick, Chm. Bd.--Dominick's Finer Foods, Northlake, IL, pg. 343
DiMatteo, James, Vice Chm. & Chief Exec. Officer--Dominick's Finer Foods, Northlake, IL, pg. 343
Dimeo, Thomas P., Chm. Bd.--Dimeo Construction Company, Providence, RI, pg. 338
Divane Jr., William T., Pres. & Treas.--Divane Bros. Electric Co., Franklin Park, IL, pg. 340
Dockter, James E., Pres.--Professional Book Distributors, Inc., Alpharetta, GA, pg. 894
Doermer, Richard T., Vice Chm.--Avis Industrial Corporation, Upland, IN, pg. 102
Dokmo, Harold B., Jr., Chm. Bd., Pres., Treas. & Sec.--Norcraft Companies, Inc., Saint Paul, MN, pg. 809
Dolan, John F., Chm. Bd. & Pres.--Fairfax Lumber & Millwork Company Inc., Springfield, VA, pg. 397
Domash, Norman, Sr. V.P.--Conway Import Co. Inc., Elmsford, NY, pg. 281
Donahue, Richard J., Chm. Bd.--Great Salt Lake Minerals & Chemicals Corp., Ogden, UT, pg. 482
Donaldson, Bill, Partner--Vic Olesen & Partners, Inc., Los Angeles, CA, pg. 824
Donati, Ronald H., Pres.--Zycon Corporation, Santa Clara, CA, pg. 1221
Donelan, Francis P., V.P., Sec. & Gen. Counsel--George A. Fuller Company, New York, NY, pg. 436
Donohoo, J.G., Chm. Bd. & Pres.--The Gibson Group Inc., Cincinnati, OH, pg. 456
Donovan, Thomas D., V.P.--GAI Consultants, Inc., Monroeville, PA, pg. 439
Doolittle, Robert S., Partner & Dir.-Corp. Fin.--J. C. Bradford & Co., Nashville, TN, pg. 170
Doran, Robert J., Pres. & Treas.--Ace Doran Hauling & Rigging Company, Cincinnati, OH, pg. 346
Dorf, Noel, V.P.-Sls & Mktg.--The Harwood Companies, Inc., New York, NY, pg. 515
Dorn, Ernst W., II, Pres.--Ernst W. Dorn Co., Inc., Gardena, CA, pg. 346
Dorsy, Claude, Pres.--First Florida Equities, Ltd., Miami, FL, pg. 413
Dortch, David D., Sr., Chm. Bd.--Humboldt Express, Inc., Nashville, TN, pg. 552
Dortch, David W., Dir.-Pur.--Humboldt Express, Inc., Nashville, TN, pg. 552
Dostov, Steven, Treas.--New England Coffee Company, Malden, MA, pg. 800
Douglas, Walter E., Chm. Bd. & Pres.--Avis Ford Inc., Southfield, MI, pg. 102
Douglass, A. Stone, Chm. Bd. & Owner--Piper Aircraft Corporation, Vero Beach, FL, pg. 872
Douglass, Don, Chm. Bd.--Alamo Group, Inc., Seguin, TX, pg. 29
Dowie, Sandra L., Sec.--Freeman Decorating Co., Dallas, TX, pg. 431
Dowing, Lowell M., Sr., Pres.--Lowell Packing Company, Fitzgerald, GA, pg. 685
Downing, Lowell Morris, Jr., V.P.--Lowell Packing Company, Fitzgerald, GA, pg. 685
Downs, Ryan A., V.P.-Sls. & Mktg.--Flanagan Brothers, Bear Creek, WI, pg. 416
Drake, Ann M., Chief Exec. Officer--Dry Storage Corporation, Des Plaines, IL, pg. 350
Drake, Larry R., V.P.-Human Resources & Information Services--Graphic Controls Corporation, Buffalo, NY, pg. 478
Drell, Leonard B., Chm. Bd., Pres., Chief Exec. & Chief Oper. Officer--DeMert & Dougherty, Inc., Westchester, IL, pg. 328
Drendel, Lee S., Chm. Bd.--Capitol Group, Springfield, IL, pg. 215
Dresen, William, Pres.--Penda Corporation, Portage, WI, pg. 857
Drewry, John T., V.P., Chief Oper. & Chief Fin. Officer & Treas.--Advanced Marine Enterprises, Inc., Arlington, VA, pg. 20
Drier, William E., Pres. & Exec. Creative Dir.--McFarland & Drier, Inc., Miami, FL, pg. 729
Drinkall, W.H., Chm. Bd. & Chief Exec. Officer--South Bend Plastics, Inc., Mishawaka, IN, pg. 1019
Driscoll, Gordon, V.P.-Fin.--Bolton-Emerson, Inc., Lawrence, MA, pg. 163
Driver, Robert F., Chm. Bd. Emeritus--Robert F. Driver Co., Inc., San Diego, CA, pg. 349
Drower, Herbert M., V.P.--Transilwrap Company, Inc., Chicago, IL, pg. 1107
Drucker, Norman, Pres.--Ain Plastics, Inc., Mount Vernon, NY, pg. 26
Drumm, Streuby L., Jr., Pres.--Drumm & Associates, Inc., Metairie, LA, pg. 349
Drummond, E.A., Vice Chm.--Drummond Company, Inc., Jasper, AL, pg. 349
Drummond, Garry N., Chief Exec. Officer--Drummond Company, Inc., Jasper, AL, pg. 349
Drury, John R., Chief Exec. Officer--Harris Drury Cohen, Fort Lauderdale, FL, pg. 511
Drutt, William, Pres., Chief Exec. Officer & Sec.--Harris & Drutt Inc., Philadelphia, PA, pg. 511
Dubin, Ronald N., Chm. Bd.--Dubin-Clark & Company, Greenwich, CT, pg. 350
Dudreck, Albert W., Chm. Bd. & Chief Exec. Officer--DDF&M Inc. Dudreck DePaul Ficco & Morgan Inc., Pittsburgh, PA, pg. 308
Dueser, Fred F., Chief Exec. Officer--States, Inc., Breckenridge, TX, pg. 1041
Dugan, Francis R., Chm. & Chief Exec. Officer--Dugan & Meyers Interests, Inc., Cincinnati, OH, pg. 351
Dugger, Irene, Chm. Bd., Pres., Chief Exec. Officer & Treas.--Queen Oxygen Company, Columbus, OH, pg. 904
Dumke, William E., V.P.-Fin. & Chief Fin. Officer--Henningsen Foods, Inc., White Plains, NY, pg. 629
Dummer, Eugene R., V.P.--Valu Discount, Inc., Louisville, KY, pg. 1143
Duncan-Campagne, Gail, Pres.--Jerome-Duncan Ford, Sterling Heights, MI, pg. 593
Duncan, Melvin D., Jr., Pres. of American Red Ball Transit & Vice Chm. Red Ball Corp.--Red Ball Corporation, Seattle, WA, pg. 918
Duncan, Richard J., Chm. Bd.--Jerome-Duncan Ford, Sterling Heights, MI, pg. 593
Dunham, Cynthia Harris, Owner, Treas. & Sec.--K-J Distributors, Inc., Glendale, AZ, pg. 612
Dunham, James I., Chm. Bd. & Pres.--American Liberty Financial Corp., Baton Rouge, LA, pg. 57
Dunham, Michael D., Pres.--Effective Management Systems, Milwaukee, WI, pg. 370
Dunlap, Roy R., Chm. Bd.--SOR Inc., Lenexa, KS, pg. 963
Dunn, Joseph C., Mng. Partner--Charles Dunn Company-Realtors, Los Angeles, CA, pg. 353
Dunn, Richard C., Mng. Partner--Charles Dunn Company-Realtors, Los Angeles, CA, pg. 353
Dupey, Michael, Chm. Bd. & Chief Exec. Officer--Dupey Management Corp., Irving, TX, pg. 354
Dupey, Patricia, Pres.--Dupey Management Corp., Irving, TX, pg. 354
Dusenbery, John F., Chief Exec. Officer--John Dusenbery Co., Inc., Randolph, NJ, pg. 355
Dykstra, Thomas M., V.P. & Treas.--Effective Management Systems, Milwaukee, WI, pg. 370
Dziadkowicz, Edward, V.P.--Western Reinsurance Brokers, Inc., Los Angeles, CA, pg. 1181
Eagle, John R., Pres. & Chief Oper. Officer--Eagle Lincoln Mercury Inc., Dallas, TX, pg. 362
Eagle, Robert M., Chm. Bd. & Chief Exec. Officer--Eagle Lincoln Mercury Inc., Dallas, TX, pg. 362
Easley, Ronald L., Chm. Bd., Pres. & Chief Exec. Officer--System Planning Corp., Arlington, VA, pg. 1070
Easterly, Clark, Chm. Bd.--Johnstown Knitting Mill Co., Johnstown, NY, pg. 602
Easterly, Thomas B., Pres.--Johnstown Knitting Mill Co., Johnstown, NY, pg. 602
Easterly, Virginia, V.P.--Johnstown Knitting Mill Co., Johnstown, NY, pg. 602
Eaton, Bruce C., Pres.--Eaton Office Supply Co., Inc., Amherst, NY, pg. 364
Eberle, Bruce, Chm. Bd. & Chief Exec. Officer--Eberle Direct Marketing Group, Inc., Vienna, VA, pg. 365
Echevarria, Angel, Pres. & Chief Exec. Officer--Echevarria Angel Co., Inc., Los Angeles, CA, pg. 365
Echevarria, Michael, Chief Oper. Officer & Exec. V.P.--Echevarria Angel Co., Inc., Los Angeles, CA, pg. 365
Echlin, Lewis H., III, Partner--Roney & Co., Detroit, MI, pg. 946
Eckerling, Sanford, Pres. & Treas.--Universal Overall Company, Chicago, IL, pg. 1139
Eckman, Amy, V.P. & Gen. Counsel--Eckman Construction Company, Bedford, NH, pg. 366
Eckman, Harold R., Pres.--Eckman Construction Company, Bedford, NH, pg. 366
Edelbrock, Victor, Chm. Bd., Pres. & Chief Exec. Officer--Edelbrock Corp., Torrance, CA, pg. 367
Edelstein, Sidney M., Dr., Chm. Bd.--Dexter Chemical Corp., Bronx, NY, pg. 334
Edwards, Oral W., Chm. Bd. & Pres.--GES Inc., Marianna, AR, pg. 439
Edwards, Steve, Chief Oper. Officer & V.P.--GES Inc., Marianna, AR, pg. 439
Edwards, William C., Chm. Bd.--Acurex Environmental Corporation, Mountain View, CA, pg. 15
Egner, Clayton W., Pres.--Schutte Lumber Company, Kansas City, MO, pg. 980
Eidel, Helmuth L., Pres.--Tri-City Electrical Contractors Inc., Altamonte Springs, FL, pg. 1110
Eidel, Paula, Exec. V.P.--Tri-City Electrical Contractors Inc., Altamonte Springs, FL, pg. 1110
Eiseman, Michael P., Exec. V.P., Treas. & Information Systems Dir.--Revere Electric Supply Co., Chicago, IL, pg. 930
Eiseman, Thomas A., Pres.--Revere Electric Supply Co., Chicago, IL, pg. 930
Ekstrom, L.W., Pres.--Bingham, Mt. Prospect, IL, pg. 151
Elias, Fred, Chm. Bd.--Elias Brothers Restaurants, Inc., Warren, MI, pg. 376
Elias, Louis, Pres.--Elias Brothers Restaurants, Inc., Warren, MI, pg. 376
Elkhatib, Hasan M., Pres.--Dena Corporation, Elk Grove Village, IL, pg. 329
Elkington, John, Pres.--Elkington Realty & Development, Memphis, TN, pg. 377
Elkman, Stanley, Chm. Bd.--Elkman Advertising & Public Relations, Bala-Cynwyd, PA, pg. 377
Ellis, Carol Cormier, Sec. & Treas.--Cormier Rice Milling Company, Inc., De Witt, AR, pg. 286
Ellis, Frank P., IV, Chm. Bd.--Associated Equipment Company, Inc., Mobile, AL, pg. 89
Ellis, William H., Chm. Bd., Pres. & Chief Oper. Officer--Farley Candy Company, Chicago, IL, pg. 399
Ellstrom, Elmer, Jr., Chm. Bd. & Chief Exec. Officer--Dearborn Gage Company, Garden City, MI, pg. 322
Ellstrom, Olof W., Exec. V.P.--Dearborn Gage Company, Garden City, MI, pg. 322
Ellstrom, Olof W., Jr., Pres.--Dearborn Gage Company, Garden City, MI, pg. 322
Ellstrom, Richard, V.P.--Dearborn Gage Company, Garden City, MI, pg. 322
Elmburg, John R., Pres.--Blitz USA, Miami, OK, pg. 157
Elmburg, Linda T., Sec.--Blitz USA, Miami, OK, pg. 157
Elsperman, Robert P., P.E., Chm. Bd. & Chief Exec. Officer--Tarlton Corporation, Saint Louis, MO, pg. 1079
Emison, James W., Pres.--Western Petroleum Company, Eden Prairie, MN, pg. 1181
Engel, Sandor J., V.P.--Milady Brassiere & Corset Co., Inc., New York, NY, pg. 753
English, James D., Pres.--Kalamazoo Label Co., Kalamazoo, MI, pg. 615
Enichen, Robert C., Pres.--Exact Equipment Corporation, Langhorne, PA, pg. 392
Epstein, Alan L., Partner, Media Services--Kupper Parker Communications Inc., Saint Louis, MO, pg. 646
Erani, Albert, Exec. V.P. & Sec.--A & E Stores, Inc., Ridgefield, NJ, pg. 1
Erani, Dennis, Exec. V.P. & G.M.--A & E Stores, Inc., Ridgefield, NJ, pg. 1
Erb, Fred A., Chm., Pres. & Chief Exec. Officer--Erb Lumber Company, Birmingham, MI, pg. 360
Erdle, William J., III, Chm. Bd. & Pres.--Erdle Perforating Co., Rochester, NY, pg. 385
Erickson, Dean, Pres.--Erickson Diversified Corp., Hudson, WI, pg. 386
Erickson, Mel, Sr., Pres., Sec. & Treas.--Central Feed Mills, Inc., Snohomish, WA, pg. 232
Erokan, Dennis, Pres. & Editor-in-Chief--Bam Publications, Inc., Pleasant Hill, CA, pg. 117
Esposito, Chris, Pres.--Four Seasons Solar Products Corp., Holbrook, NY, pg. 427
Esposito, Joseph, Exec. V.P.--Four Seasons Solar Products Corp., Holbrook, NY, pg. 427
Estes, Alexandra H., Chm. Bd. & Pres.--Haeger Industries, Inc., Dundee, IL, pg. 499
Ettinger, Bernard, Pres.--Clay-Park Labs, Inc., Bronx, NY, pg. 253
Ettinger, Steven, V.P.--Clay-Park Labs, Inc., Bronx, NY, pg. 253
Evans, Robert A., V.P. & Gen. Mgr.-Information Prods.--Graphic Controls Corporation, Buffalo, NY, pg. 478
Evans, Sue, Sec.--Jergens Inc., Cleveland, OH, pg. 593
Evers, Charles K., Chm. Bd., Pres. & Chief Exec. Officer--American Bread Company - Sunbeam Bakery, Nashville, TN, pg. 49
Faaf, Charles, Pres.--U.S. Music Corporation, New Berlin, WI, pg. 1136
Faber, N., Pres.--Neil Faber Media Inc., New York, NY, pg. 395
Fabick, Harry, Pres. & Chief Oper. Officer--John Fabick Tractor Company, Fenton, MO, pg. 396
Fabick, John, Chm. Bd.--John Fabick Tractor Company, Fenton, MO, pg. 396
Fagel, Harold, Pres. & Chief Exec. Officer--Aurora Packing Co., Inc., North Aurora, IL, pg. 98
Fahs, John C., Pres.--California Panel & Veneer Company, Cerritos, CA, pg. 210
Fain, John H., Chm., Pres., Chief Exec. & Chief Oper. Officer--Metro Information Services, Virginia Beach, VA, pg. 743
Fairchild, Henry B., III, Pres.--Handy Wacks Corporation, Sparta, MI, pg. 505
Fairchild, Marcia, Chm. Bd.--Handy Wacks Corporation, Sparta, MI, pg. 505
Falkowski, Michael, Pres.--The Brulin Corporation, Indianapolis, IN, pg. 184
Farley, James N., Pres. & Chief Exec. Officer--FamTec International, Inc., Des Plaines, IL, pg. 398
Farley, William F., Chm. Bd. & Chief Exec. Officer--Farley Industries, Chicago, IL, pg. 399
Farnsworth, Ross N., Pres.--Farnsworth Companies, Mesa, AZ, pg. 403
Farr, Mel, Pres.--Mel Farr Ford, Inc., Oak Park, MI, pg. 403
Farrell, Neal F., Mng. Partner, V.P., Gen. Counsel & Chief Fin. Officer--Borg-Warner Corporation, Chicago, IL, pg. 165
Favre, Art E., Pres.--Performance Contractors Inc., Baton Rouge, LA, pg. 861
Fedrick, C. Richard, Vice Chm.--Sundt Corp., Tucson, AZ, pg. 1060
Fegert, Donald R., V.P.--Tri-Mark Metal Corp., Detroit, MI, pg. 1110
Fehsenfeld, Frank B., Chm. Bd.--Crystal Flash Petroleum Corp., Indianapolis, IN, pg. 303
Fehsenfeld, Fred M., V.P. & Treas.--Crystal Flash Petroleum Corp., Indianapolis, IN, pg. 303
Fehsenfeld, Mac, Pres. & Chief Exec. Officer--Crystal Flash Petroleum Corp., Indianapolis, IN, pg. 303

Feinberg, Barry, Pres.--Nationwise Automotive, Inc., Columbus, OH, pg. 795
Felber, John, Partner & Dir.-Options--J. C. Bradford & Co., Nashville, TN, pg. 170
Feles, Gust, Exec. V.P. & Sec.--Carhartt, Inc., Dearborn, MI, pg. 220
Fellin, Edward, Treas.--Economy Folding Box Corp., Chicago, IL, pg. 367
Fennessy, William J., V.P.-Fin. & Treas.--LDI, Ltd., Indianapolis, IN, pg. 647
Fernandez, Carlos C., Chm., Pres. & Chief Exec. Officer--Purity, Inc., Miami, FL, pg. 901
Ferrara, Arthur V., Pres. & Chief Exec. Officer--The Guardian Life Insurance Company of America, New York, NY, pg. 492
Ferrell, James E., Chm. Bd., Pres. & Chief Exec. Officer--Ferrell Companies Inc./Ferrellgas, Liberty, MO, pg. 407
Ferrera, Harold, Chief Exec. Officer--James Ferrera & Sons, Inc., Canton, MA, pg. 407
Fetridge, Clark W., Pres. & Chief Exec. Officer--The Dartnell Corporation, Chicago, IL, pg. 316
Fetter, Jane T., Chm. Bd. & Sec.--Kettenburg Marine Corporation, San Diego, CA, pg. 626
Fetter, Thompson, Pres. & Chief Exec. Officer--Kettenburg Marine Corporation, San Diego, CA, pg. 626
Ficks, Lee B., Pres., Chief Exec. Officer, & Treas.--Ficks Reed Company, Cincinnati, OH, pg. 408
Field, Eli, Chm. Bd.--Field Container Company, L.P., Elk Grove Village, IL, pg. 409
Field, Lawrence, Pres. & Chief Exec. Officer--Field Container Company, L.P., Elk Grove Village, IL, pg. 409
Field, Ronald, Pres.--Consolidated Beverages, Inc., Auburn, MA, pg. 276
Fike, John T., Pres. & Chief Exec. Officer--Northwest Paper Converting Company, Vancouver, WA, pg. 814
Fimiano, Andrew, Exec. V.P.--Southland Industries, Long Beach, CA, pg. 1023
Findlay, Walstein C., Jr., Pres.--Wally Findlay Galleries International, Chicago, IL, pg. 410
Fine, Allan H., Co-Pres.--M. Fine & Sons Manufacturing Co., Inc., New York, NY, pg. 411
Fine, Leo, Chm. Bd.--M. Fine & Sons Manufacturing Co., Inc., New York, NY, pg. 411
Fine, Martin L., Co-Pres.--M. Fine & Sons Manufacturing Co., Inc., New York, NY, pg. 411
Fine, S.A., Pres. & Chief Oper. Officer--The Biltrite Corporation, Waltham, MA, pg. 151
Fine, Stephen L., Co-Pres.--M. Fine & Sons Manufacturing Co., Inc., New York, NY, pg. 411
Finegood, Daniel, First V.P.--Good Companies, Carson, CA, pg. 470
Finegood, David, Pres.--Good Companies, Carson, CA, pg. 470
Finegood, Freddi Sue, Sec.--Good Companies, Carson, CA, pg. 470
Finger, Robert, Pres.--Finger Furniture Company, Inc., Houston, TX, pg. 411
Fingerle, John B., Pres.--Fingerle Lumber Co., Ann Arbor, MI, pg. 411
Fingerle, Larry, Sec. & Treas.--Fingerle Lumber Co., Ann Arbor, MI, pg. 411
Fingerle, Mark M., V.P. & Dir.-Pur.--Fingerle Lumber Co., Ann Arbor, MI, pg. 411
Finkel, Nathan, V.P. & Sec.--FMS Management Systems, Inc., North Miami Beach, FL, pg. 394
Finkl, Charles W., Chm. Bd.--A. Finkl & Sons Co., Chicago, IL, pg. 411
Finnegan, Lawrence J., Chm., Pres., Chief Exec. & Chief Oper. Officer--Boston Mutual Life Insurance Co., Canton, MA, pg. 167
Firestone, Steve, V.P.--Design 1 Interiors, Los Angeles, CA, pg. 332
Firestone, Sue, Pres. & Chief Exec. Officer--Design 1 Interiors, Los Angeles, CA, pg. 332
Fischer, James M., Jr., Chm. Bd.--Standard Candy Co., Inc., Nashville, TN, pg. 1035
Fish, Milton, Jr., V.P. & Sec.--L. Fish Corporation, Chicago, IL, pg. 414
Fisher, Bob, Pres.--RE/MAX International, Inc., Englewood, CO, pg. 915
Fisher, Joseph N., V.P.--Fisher Skylights, Inc., West Nyack, NY, pg. 415
Fisher, Mike, Jr., Pres. & Chief Exec. Officer--Fisher Graphic Industries, Modesto, CA, pg. 415
Fisher, Mike, Sr., Chm. Bd.--Fisher Graphic Industries, Modesto, CA, pg. 415
Fisher, Paul C., Chm. Bd.--Fisher Pen Company, Franklin Park, IL, pg. 415
Fisher, Robert J., Pres.--Fisher Skylights, Inc., West Nyack, NY, pg. 415
Fisher, Steven, Chm. Bd., Pres. & Chief Exec. Officer--Continental Circuits Corp., Phoenix, AZ, pg. 278
Fisher, Thomas J., Exec. V.P.--Fisher Skylights, Inc., West Nyack, NY, pg. 415
Fisher, Thomas Scott, Chm. Bd. & Chief Exec. Officer--Samelson-Leon Company, Inc., Memphis, TN, pg. 968
Fitzgerald, D.F., Pres. & Treas.--Son Chief Electrics, Inc., Winsted, CT, pg. 1018
Fitzgerald, Hope, Sec. & Sls. Admin.--Son Chief Electrics, Inc., Winsted, CT, pg. 1018
Fitzgerald, John W., Pres.--Bolton-Emerson, Inc., Lawrence, MA, pg. 163
Fitzpatrick, Dana G., Mgr.-Intl.--Fitzpatrick & Weller, Inc., Ellicottville, NY, pg. 416
Fitzpatrick, Gerard J., Pres.--Fitzpatrick & Weller, Inc., Ellicottville, NY, pg. 416
Flanagan, David D., V.P.-Production--Flanagan Brothers, Bear Creek, WI, pg. 416
Flanagan, David J., Jr., Pres.--Flanagan Brothers, Bear Creek, WI, pg. 416
Flanders, Margie S., V.P. & Asst. Treas.--Paddock Publications, Inc., Arlington Heights, IL, pg. 842
Flood, Earl F., Chm. Bd.--The Flood Company, Hudson, OH, pg. 419
Flood, Peter E., Pres. & Chief Exec. Officer--The Flood Company, Hudson, OH, pg. 419
Flood, Thomas, V.P.-Admin. & Fin. & Treas.--TSC Industries, Inc., Nashville, TN, pg. 1075
Flori, Robert D., Chm. Bd. & Treas.--Flori Corp., Phoenix, AZ, pg. 420
Fogarty, William H., Pres.--Fogarty & Klein/Winius Brandon, Houston, TX, pg. 421
Foley, Thomas H., Chm. Bd.--The Bibb Company, Macon, GA, pg. 781
Foley, Vicky L., Chm. Bd. & Pres.--V.F. Energies, Inc., Madisonville, KY, pg. 1141
Follett, Robert J., Chm. Bd.--Follett Corporation, Chicago, IL, pg. 422
Folts, John B., Exec. V.P., Sec. & Treas.--Hargro Enterprises, Inc., Stamford, CT, pg. 509
Forbes, Malcolm S., Jr., Pres., Chief Exec. & Editor-in-Chief--Forbes, Inc., New York, NY, pg. 423
Forbriger, Bill, V.P.--Tressa, Inc., Erlanger, KY, pg. 1110
Forbriger, Connie, Pres.--Tressa, Inc., Erlanger, KY, pg. 1110
Forkner, Thomas F., Vice Chm.--Waffle House, Inc., Norcross, GA, pg. 1157
Forstmann, Nicholas C., Partner--Forstmann Little & Co., New York, NY, pg. 424
Forstmann, Theodore J., Partner--Forstmann Little & Co., New York, NY, pg. 424
Fortinberry, Glen W., Chm. & Chief Exec. Officer--Ross Roy Group, Inc., Bloomfield Hills, MI, pg. 949
Fortson, Thomas N., Jr., Pres.--Terminix Service, Inc., Columbia, SC, pg. 1088
Foster, L.B., Chm. Bd.--Summit Corporation of America, Thomaston, CT, pg. 1058
Foster, Ronald B., Pres.--Rea Magnet Wire Company, Inc., Fort Wayne, IN, pg. 915
Foster, Ronald H., Pres.--The Stellar Group Inc., Jacksonville, FL, pg. 1046
Foster, Thomas, Chm. Bd. & Chief Exec. Officer--Foster & Gallagher Inc., Peoria, IL, pg. 426
Fowler, Frederick V., Jr., Chm. Bd., Pres. & Chief Exec. Officer--Fred V. Fowler Company, Inc., Newton, MA, pg. 427
Fowlie, Robert G., V.P.-Opers.--Brush Research Manufacturing Company, Los Angeles, CA, pg. 184
Fox, Herbert C., Chm. Bd., Pres., Chief Exec. Officer & Dir.-Pub. Rels.--Active Electrical Supply Company, Chicago, IL, pg. 15
Fox, Raymond A., V.P., Chief Oper. Officer & Sec.--Active Electrical Supply Company, Chicago, IL, pg. 15
Fox, Wayne F., Chm. Bd. & Chief Exec. Officer--Triple F, Inc., Des Moines, IA, pg. 1114
Frandsen, Dennis, Chm. Bd. & Owner--Plastech Corporation, Forest Lake, MN, pg. 874
Frank, H. Alan, Pres., Chief Fin. Officer & Treas.--Union Industries, Inc., Providence, RI, pg. 1128
Frank, Harley, V.P. & Sec.--Union Industries, Inc., Providence, RI, pg. 1128
Frank, James S., Pres.--Frank Consolidated Enterprises Inc., Des Plaines, IL, pg. 428
Franklin, Larry, Pres. & Chief Exec. Officer--Harte-Hanks Communications, Inc., San Antonio, TX, pg. 513
Franz, Victor, V.P. & Sec.--Fenton Press, Inc., Addison, IL, pg. 406
Frederic, Rand, Pres. & Chief Exec. Officer--Frederic Printing Company, Aurora, CO, pg. 430
Frederick, David M., V.P.-International--Velsicol Chemical Corporation, Rosemont, IL, pg. 1147
Fredericks, Wesley C., Jr., Pres. & Chief Oper. Officer--Manufacturers Products Company, Warren, MI, pg. 705
Freedland, Hymen, Pres.--Ambassador Steel Co., Detroit, MI, pg. 47
Freedland, Michael, Treas. & Sec.--Ambassador Steel Co., Detroit, MI, pg. 47
Freedman, Leslie, Pres. & Chief Fin. Officer--FMS Management Systems, Inc., North Miami Beach, FL, pg. 394
Freedman, Martin B., V.P. & Treas.--FMS Management Systems, Inc., North Miami Beach, FL, pg. 394
Freeman, D.S., Jr., Chm. Bd. & Chief Exec. Officer--Freeman Decorating Co., Dallas, TX, pg. 431
Frem, Antoine N., Vice Chm.--Interstate Resources, Inc., Rosslyn, VA, pg. 580
Frem, George N., Chm. Bd. & Chief Exec. Office--Interstate Resources, Inc., Rosslyn, VA, pg. 580
Frey, Eugene U., Chm. Bd. & Chief Exec. Officer--Waldorf Corporation, Saint Paul, MN, pg. 1159
Fried, Richard, Pres. & Mngmt. Supvr.--GBF/Ayer, Los Angeles, CA, pg. 104
Friedman, Albert, Pres.--Banner Wholesale Grocers, Inc., Chicago, IL, pg. 118
Friedman, Irwin, Asst. Sec.--Banner Wholesale Grocers, Inc., Chicago, IL, pg. 118
Frost, Chad, Pres.--Frost Inc., Grand Rapids, MI, pg. 435
Fuldner, Christopher T., Pres.--Efco Corporation, Monett, MO, pg. 359
Fumagali, Luigi, Chm. Bd.--The Dee Howard Company, San Antonio, TX, pg. 547
Furlong, Edward, Jr., Pres. & Chief Exec. Officer--WWF Paper Corporation, Bala-Cynwyd, PA, pg. 1157
Gabay, Alex, V.P.--Ain Plastics, Inc., Mount Vernon, NY, pg. 26
Gable, Robert E., Chm. Bd.--Stearns Enterprises, Inc., Lexington, KY, pg. 1043
Galesi, Francesco, Chm. Bd., Pres. & Chief Exec. Officer--Rotterdam Ventures Inc., Guilderland Center, NY, pg. 951
Galler, Anthony, Pres. & Chief Oper. Officer--Samelson-Leon Company, Inc., Memphis, TN, pg. 968
Gallivan, James F., Partner & Acct. Exec.--J. C. Bradford & Co., Nashville, TN, pg. 170
Gallivan, John P., Pres.--D. Waldner Company, Inc., Farmingdale, NY, pg. 1159
Gallo, Ernest, Chm. Bd.--E & J Gallo Winery, Modesto, CA, pg. 441
Gallo, Julio, Pres.--E & J Gallo Winery, Modesto, CA, pg. 441
Galvez, Matthew S., Chief Fin. Officer--Manufacturers Products Company, Warren, MI, pg. 705
Gambino, Joseph L., Pres. & Chief Exec. Officer--The Atlas Construction Co., Stamford, CT, pg. 96
Gamel, Thomas W., Pres.--Timpte Industries, Inc., Denver, CO, pg. 1098
Ganahl, Peter, Pres.--Ganahl Lumber Company, Anaheim, CA, pg. 442
Gant, Allen E., Jr., Pres & Asst. Treas.--Glen Raven Mills, Inc., Glen Raven, NC, pg. 461
Gaples, Harry S., Pres.--Kleinschmidt Inc., Deerfield, IL, pg. 635
Garbarini, Rose, Sec.--Los Angeles Smoking Curing Company, Los Angeles, CA, pg. 684
Garcia, Frank, V.P.-Mktg.--Good Companies, Carson, CA, pg. 470
Gardiner, Scott, Chm. Bd., Pres., Chief Exec. & Chief Oper. Officer--Gardiner Metal Company, Chicago, IL, pg. 443
Gargiulo, James V., Pres.--D. J. Mead-Hubbs & Howe, Buffalo, NY, pg. 1016
Gasaway, Dick, Pres.--Happy Holiday Tree Farms, Sheridan, MI, pg. 506
Gaskill, Charles, Pres.--The WBDC Group, Grand Rapids, MI, pg. 1155
Gates, William C., V.P., Treas. & Chief Fin. Officer--Graphic Controls Corporation, Buffalo, NY, pg. 478
Gavinski, C. Martin, Chief Fin. Officer--Penda Corporation, Portage, WI, pg. 857
Geisselbrecht, Elvin, Treas. & Sec.--YRJ Corporation, Houston, TX, pg. 1206
Genello, Bob, Grp. Acct. Dir.--Carmichael Lynch, Inc., Minneapolis, MN, pg. 222
Genkin, I. Stephen, Treas.--Triangle Marketing Corp., New York, NY, pg. 1112
Gentine, Leonard A., Sr., Chm. Bd.--Sargento Incorporated, Plymouth, WI, pg. 971
Gentine, Louis P., Pres. & Chief Exec. Officer--Sargento Incorporated, Plymouth, WI, pg. 971
George, Ernest, Chm. Bd.--Southern California Bancorp, Laguna Beach, CA, pg. 1020
George, Leslie, Sr., V.P.--King Group, Inc., Fenton, MI, pg. 630
Gerard, Antonia, Exec. V.P., Chief Fin. & Oper. Officer, Sec. & Controller--Bolliger, Inc., Stamford, CT, pg. 163
Gerard, Stephen, Pres., Chief Exec. Officer & Treas.--Bolliger, Inc., Stamford, CT, pg. 163
Gerchenson, Emile H., Chm. Bd. & Chief Exec. Officer--Alva/Amco Pharmacal Companies, Inc., Chicago, IL, pg. 46
Gerchenson, Jeffery H., Pres. & Chief Oper. Officer--Alva/Amco Pharmacal Companies, Inc., Chicago, IL, pg. 46
Geresi, Joseph, Pres.--Paisano Publications, Inc., Agoura, CA, pg. 843
Gerrity, J. Frank, II, Chm. Bd. & Treas.--Gerrity Co., Inc., Newton, MA, pg. 454
Gerrity, James F., III, Pres. & Chief Exec. Officer--Gerrity Co., Inc., Newton, MA, pg. 454
Gerstein, David M., Chief Exec. Officer--K & R Delivery, Inc., Hinsdale, IL, pg. 610
Ghafari, Yousif B., Pres. & Chief Exec. & Chief Oper. Officer--Ghafari Associates, Inc., Dearborn, MI, pg. 455
Gherty, Jack, Pres. & Chief Exec. Officer--Land O'Lakes, Inc., Arden Hills, MN, pg. 653
Giannotti, Richard, V.P.-Tech. Services--Periphonics Corp., Bohemia, NY, pg. 862
Giarrusso, Raymond J., Sec. & Treas.--GAI Consultants, Inc., Monroeville, PA, pg. 439
Gibbs, Benjamin, Treas.--Pine State Creamery Co., Raleigh, NC, pg. 871
Gibbs, Charles F., Chm.--Gibbs Wire & Steel Company, Inc., Southington, CT, pg. 456
Gibbs, Charles W., Pres.--Gibbs Wire & Steel Company, Inc., Southington, CT, pg. 456
Gibson, Daniel, Pres.--Wolcott & Lincoln, Inc., Kansas City, MO, pg. 1198
Gilbane, Jean A., Asst. Treas--Gilbane Building Company, Providence, RI, pg. 457
Gilbane, Robert V., Sec.--Gilbane Building Company, Providence, RI, pg. 457
Gilbane, Thomas F., Jr., Exec. V.P.--Gilbane Building Company, Providence, RI, pg. 457
Gilbane, William J., Chm. Bd.--Gilbane Building Company, Providence, RI, pg. 457
Gilbert, Duane L., Pres. & Owner--Gilbert Mfg. Corp., Locke Mills, ME, pg. 458
Gill, Merwyn C., Chm. Bd.--M.C. Gill Corporation, El Monte, CA, pg. 458
Gill, Phillip C., V.P.-Mktg.--M.C. Gill Corporation, El Monte, CA, pg. 458
Gill, Stephen E., Pres. & Chief Exec. Officer--M.C. Gill Corporation, El Monte, CA, pg. 458
Gillespie, Richard J., Pres.--The Gillespie Organization, Inc., Princeton, NJ, pg. 458
Gillis, Wayne H., Chm. Bd. & Pres.--Gillis Advertising & Public Relations, Birmingham, AL, pg. 459
Gilman, Howard, Chm. Bd. & Chief Exec. Officer--Gilman Paper Co., Saint Marys, GA, pg. 459
Gilman, Neil, V.P. & Sec.--Marty Gilman, Inc., Gilman, CT, pg. 459
Gilman, Shirley J., Pres. & Treas.--Marty Gilman, Inc., Gilman, CT, pg. 459
Gilmore, Howard N., Jr., Pres. & Chief Exec. Officer--Gilmore Envelope Corp., Los Angeles, CA, pg. 460
Ginsberg, David M., Pres.--Ginsberg's Institutional Foods, Inc., Hudson, NY, pg. 460
Ginsberg, Frank, Pres. & Creative Dir.--Avrett, Free & Ginsberg, Inc., New York, NY, pg. 103
Ginsberg, Ira M., V.P. & Sec.--Ginsberg's Institutional Foods, Inc., Hudson, NY, pg. 460
Ginsberg, Morton A., Chm. Bd.--Ginsberg's Institutional Foods, Inc., Hudson, NY, pg. 460

Glass, Sherwin, Chm. Bd.--Warehouse Home Furnishings Distributor, Dublin, GA, pg. 1163
Glatz, Simon, Pres. & Chief Exec. Officer--Advanced Marine Enterprises, Inc., Arlington, VA, pg. 20
Glickman, Stuart, Chm., Pres. Chief Exec. & Chief Fin. Officer--Security Alarms & Fire Engineering Inc., Davie, FL, pg. 987
Glidden, Robert D., Jr., V.P.-Fin. & Treas.--Robert James Sales Inc., Buffalo, NY, pg. 589
Godchaux, Charles R., Vice Chm.--Riviana Foods Inc., Houston, TX, pg. 937
Godchaux, Frank A., III, Chm. Bd.--Riviana Foods Inc., Houston, TX, pg. 937
Godfrey, Mark, Mgr.-Opers.--Felton Brush Inc., Manchester, NH, pg. 406
Godfrey, Richard H., Chm. Bd.--Felton Brush Inc., Manchester, NH, pg. 406
Goebel, Arthur F., Pres. & Treas.--Goebel Art, Inc., Coon Rapids, MN, pg. 464
Goebel, Margaret E., Sec.--Goebel Art, Inc., Coon Rapids, MN, pg. 464
Goedert, Philip H., Pres. & Dir.--RNL Facilities Corporation, Denver, CO, pg. 907
Gohmann, J. Michael, Pres. & Chief Exec. Officer--Gohmann Asphalt & Construction Inc., Clarksville, IN, pg. 465
Gohmann, John R., V.P., Chief Oper. Officer, Sec. & Dir.-Pur.--Gohmann Asphalt & Construction Inc., Clarksville, IN, pg. 465
Gold, Martin F., Pres. & Chief Exec. Officer--Artec Distributing, Inc., Shelburne, VT, pg. 86
Goldberg, Howard D., Corp. Sec.--Artec Distributing, Inc., Shelburne, VT, pg. 86
Goldberger, Eugene, Pres.--Goldberger Doll Mfg. Company, Inc., Brooklyn, NY, pg. 466
Golden, Dale, Exec. V.P.--Stephen Gould Paper Co., Inc., Whippany, NJ, pg. 473
Golden, John, Exec. V.P.--Stephen Gould Paper Co., Inc., Whippany, NJ, pg. 473
Golden, Michael, Pres.--Stephen Gould Paper Co., Inc., Whippany, NJ, pg. 473
Goldman, Myron, Pres.--Excelled Sheepskin & Leather Coat Corporation, New York, NY, pg. 392
Goldmeier, Alan, Pres.--Ross Bicycles USA Ltd., Farmingdale, NY, pg. 949
Goldner, Paul, Pres.--Database America Companies, Montvale, NJ, pg. 316
Golenberg, Gary, Pres. & Chief Exec. Officer--The Gibson-Homans Company, Twinsburg, OH, pg. 457
Golodetz, Michele, Chm. Bd.--Golodetz Corporation, New York, NY, pg. 469
Golub, Eugene, Chm. Bd. & Pres.--Golub & Co., Chicago, IL, pg. 469
Goodman, Cary C., Chief Exec. Officer--Howard Needles Tammen & Bergendoff, Kansas City, MO, pg. 547
Goodman, Lawrence B., Chm. Bd. & Treas.--The Ormond Shops, Inc., North Bergen, NJ, pg. 830
Goodman, Richard F., V.P.-Real Estate--The Ormond Shops, Inc., North Bergen, NJ, pg. 830
Goodrich, T.M., Pres.--BE & K, Inc., Birmingham, AL, pg. 106
Goodwin, Daniel L., Chm. Bd. & Chief Exec. Officer--The Inland Group, Inc., Oak Brook, IL, pg. 570
Gordon, Harry, Chm. Bd. & Controller--Saul Bros. & Company, Inc., Norcross, GA, pg. 972
Gordon, Peter, Chm. Bd.--Crystal Geyser, Calistoga, CA, pg. 303
Gore, Chester, Pres. & Creative Dir.--Chester Gore Company Inc., New York, NY, pg. 472
Gore, Gerie, V.P., Admin.--Chester Gore Company Inc., New York, NY, pg. 472
Gosnell, Robert A., Chief Exec. Officer--Gosnell Builders, Phoenix, AZ, pg. 472
Goss, Howard S., Chm., Chief Exec. Officer & Treas.--Transco Inc., Chicago, IL, pg. 1106
Gouchenour, C. Lee, Chm. & Chief Exec. Officer--Gouchenour Adv., Inc., Orlando, FL, pg. 473
Gould, Morley, Chm. Bd.--Asher/Gould Advertising, Inc., Los Angeles, CA, pg. 88
Gould, Peter J., Pres. & Chief Exec. Officer--Aldine Technologies, Carlstadt, NJ, pg. 33
Goulooze, Gene D., Vice Chm. & Chief Exec. Officer--Sonneveldt Company, Grand Rapids, MI, pg. 1018
Grace, John R., Chief Exec. Officer--Spring Engineers, Inc., Houston, TX, pg. 1033
Granger, Alton L., Chm. & Chief Exec. Officer--Granger Construction Co., Lansing, MI, pg. 476
Granger, Glenn, V.P.--Granger Construction Co., Lansing, MI, pg. 476
Granger, Jerry, V.P.--Granger Construction Co., Lansing, MI, pg. 476
Grant, Donald W., Pres. & Mgr.-Sls.--Western Reinsurance Brokers, Inc., Los Angeles, CA, pg. 1181
Graves, Earl G., Chm. Bd., Pres. & Chief Exec. Officer--Earl G. Graves, Ltd., New York, NY, pg. 478
Graves, Malcom, Jr., Pres.--Remarks, Inc., Dublin, OH, pg. 925
Gray, C.C. Howard, Pres. & Chief Exec. Officer--James N. Gray Construction Co., Inc., Lexington, KY, pg. 479
Gray, Franklin N., Exec. V.P.--James N. Gray Construction Co., Inc., Lexington, KY, pg. 479
Gray, James P., II, Chief Oper. Officer--James N. Gray Construction Co., Inc., Lexington, KY, pg. 479
Gray, Lois Howard, Chm. Bd.--James N. Gray Construction Co., Inc., Lexington, KY, pg. 479
Gray, Melvin, Chm. & Chief Exec. Officer--Graycor, Inc., Homewood, IL, pg. 479
Gray, Richard E., Sr. V.P.--GAI Consultants, Inc., Monroeville, PA, pg. 439
Gray, Robert A., Pres. & Chief Exec. Officer--Gray Printing Co., Fostoria, OH, pg. 479
Gray, Thomas M., Chm. Bd.--Gray Printing Co., Fostoria, OH, pg. 479
Green, Benjamin L., Exec. V.P.--B. Green & Co., Baltimore, MD, pg. 484
Green, Bernard, Pres.--B. Green & Co., Baltimore, MD, pg. 484
Green, Charles, V.P.--B. Green & Co., Baltimore, MD, pg. 484
Green, Leonard, Partner--Leonard Green & Partners, Los Angeles, CA, pg. 485
Greenberg, David A., Pres.--The Clinipad Corporation, Guilford, CT, pg. 255
Greenblatt, Maurice, Chm. Bd.--United Van Lines, Inc., Fenton, MO, pg. 1126
Greene, Randy, Chm. Bd. & Pres.--Blevins Concession Supply Co., Tampa, FL, pg. 156
Greenstone, Ronald, Chm. & Chief Exec. Officer--Greenstone Roberts Advertising, Melville, NY, pg. 485
Greer, Carl C., Pres.--Martin Exploration Management Company, Alsip, IL, pg. 715
Gregory, E. John, Sr., Chm. Bd. & Pres.--J.T. Slocomb Company, South Glastonbury, CT, pg. 1010
Grieve, G.P., Chm. Bd.--The Grieve Corporation, Round Lake, IL, pg. 486
Griffin, Rutledge A., Jr., Chief Exec. Officer--Griffin Corporation, Valdosta, GA, pg. 487
Griffith, Dan L., Chief Fin. Officer & Exec. V.P.--Bridgeport Machines, Inc., Bridgeport, CT, pg. 175
Griggs, David, Pres., Chief Exec. & Chief Fin. Officer & Treas.--Jack Griggs Inc., Exeter, CA, pg. 488
Griggs, Forest, III, V.P.--Jack Griggs Inc., Exeter, CA, pg. 488
Griggs, Forest, Jr., Sec.--Jack Griggs Inc., Exeter, CA, pg. 488
Grimaud, Joseph A., Jr., Pres. & Chief Exec. Officer--Precision Tune, Inc., Leesburg, VA, pg. 885
Groat, Jonathan M., Pres. & Chief Exec. Officer--Smith-Lee Co., Inc., Oneida, NY, pg. 1013
Grogan, David R., Chm., Pres. & Chief Exec. Officer--Toter Incorporated, Statesville, NC, pg. 1103
Grossman, Michael W., Pres.--Midwest Mechanical Contractors Inc., Kansas City, MO, pg. 752
Grzyb, Steve J., Partner, Brdcst. Consulting--Kupper Parker Communications Inc., Saint Louis, MO, pg. 646
Gubler, Gayla J., Dir.-Leasing--Regency Associates Limited Partnership, Evansville, IN, pg. 922
Gugino, Carmelo, Jr., Pres. & Treas.--Dinaire Corp., Buffalo, NY, pg. 338
Gutenplan, Martin, Pres.--Mateco Electronics Corp., Brooklyn, NY, pg. 720
Gygi, Richard W., Pres.--CPS Corporation, Franklin, TN, pg. 428
Hacker, Joshua, Chm. Bd., Pres., Chief Exec. & Chief Fin. Officer--Seaboard Electronics Co., Carlsbad, CA, pg. 983
Hackney, Robert H., Pres. & Chief Exec. Officer--Hackney Brothers, Inc., Wilson, NC, pg. 498
Hackney, Thomas J., Jr., Chm. Bd.--Hackney Brothers, Inc., Wilson, NC, pg. 498
Hadfield, Neil, Chm. Bd., Chief Fin. Officer & Sec.--Western Pacific Data Systems, San Diego, CA, pg. 1180
Hagie, R.W., Chm. Bd.--Hagie Manufacturing Co., Clarion, IA, pg. 499
Hagmeyer, R.W., Pres.--Venta Inc., Denver, CO, pg. 1147
Hahn, George E., Pres.--J.R. Hahn Co., Inc., Indianapolis, IN, pg. 500
Hahn, Warren E., Chm. Bd.--J.R. Hahn Co., Inc., Indianapolis, IN, pg. 500
Haines, W.K., Jr., Pres.--Haines & Co., Inc., North Canton, OH, pg. 500
Haines, W.K., Sr., Chm. Bd.--Haines & Co., Inc., North Canton, OH, pg. 500
Hale, Judson D., Sr., Sr. V.P.--Yankee Publishing Incorporated, Dublin, NH, pg. 1207
Hall, Donald J., Chm. Bd.--Hallmark Cards, Inc., Kansas City, MO, pg. 501
Hall, K. Michael, Pres., Chief Exec. & Chief Oper. Officer--Hall Contracting Corp., Louisville, KY, pg. 501
Hall, Kenneth E., Chm. Bd.--Hall Contracting Corp., Louisville, KY, pg. 501
Hallstedt, Fred, Pres. & V.P-Sls. & Mktg.--Sonneveldt Company, Grand Rapids, MI, pg. 1018
Halperin, D.R., Dir.-Media--Commercial Light Company, Hillside, IL, pg. 268
Halperin, P.J., Mgr.-Systems--Commercial Light Company, Hillside, IL, pg. 268
Halperin, Thomas C., Chm Bd., Pres. & Chief Exec. Officer--Commercial Light Company, Hillside, IL, pg. 268
Halvorson, Frank E., V.P.--Prospect Motors, Inc., Jackson, CA, pg. 895
Halvorson, William, Pres.--Prospect Motors, Inc., Jackson, CA, pg. 895
Hamister, George E., Sr. V.P.-Asset Mngmt.--National Health Care Affiliates, Inc., Buffalo, NY, pg. 791
Hamister, Mark E., Chm. Bd., Pres. & Chief Exec. Officer--National Health Care Affiliates, Inc., Buffalo, NY, pg. 791
Hamister, Oliver C., V.P.-Admin., Treas. & Sec.--National Health Care Affiliates, Inc., Buffalo, NY, pg. 791
Hamm, Jerry T., Pres.--Jerry Hamm Chevrolet Inc., Jacksonville, FL, pg. 503
Hampel, Robert E., Sr. Exec. Chief Fin. Officer, Treas. & Sec.--Keller Crescent Co., Evansville, IN, pg. 620
Hanel, L. Sterling, Pres.--Hanel Lumber Co., Inc., Hood River, OR, pg. 505
Hanman, Gary, Chief Exec. Officer--Mid-America Dairymen, Inc., Springfield, MO, pg. 750
Hano, Frank, V.P.--Hano Business Forms, Inc., Springfield, MA, pg. 505
Hano, Philip III, V.P. & Sec.--Hano Business Forms, Inc., Springfield, MA, pg. 505
Hansen, Donald E., Chm. Bd.--H & H Distributing Company, Inc., West Union, IA, pg. 495
Hansen, J.G., Sec.--Furnas Electric Company, Batavia, IL, pg. 437
Hansen, R.W., Chm. Bd., Pres. & Chief Exec. Officer--Furnas Electric Company, Batavia, IL, pg. 437
Hanson, Charles, V.P.-Environmental--Velsicol Chemical Corporation, Rosemont, IL, pg. 1147
Hanson, George V., Chm. Bd., Pres. & Chief Exec. Officer--Old Home Foods, Inc., Saint Paul, MN, pg. 823
Hanson, Leroy, Dr., Pres. & Chief Oper. Officer--Triple F, Inc., Des Moines, IA, pg. 1114
Hardaway, L. H., Jr., Chm. Bd.--Hardaway Construction Company, Inc., Nashville, TN, pg. 508
Harding, John H., Pres. & Chief Oper. Officer--National Life Insurance Company, Montpelier, VT, pg. 791
Hardten, R.D., Exec. Partner--Black & Veatch, Kansas City, MO, pg. 154
Haretakis, John, Pres.--Spires Restaurants Inc., Orange, CA, pg. 1031
Harmon, David E., Chm. Bd., Pres., Chief Exec. & Chief Oper. Officer--El Camino Resources, Ltd., Northridge, CA, pg. 372
Harmon, Lowell D., Chm. Bd. & Pres.--Progressive Driver Services, Inc., Jacksonville, FL, pg. 894
Harrell, Samuel M., Chm. Bd., Pres. & Chief Exec. Officer--EDI International, Inc., Cincinnati, OH, pg. 359
Harris, Geoffrey, Exec. V.P.--Silvestri Corp., Chicago, IL, pg. 1005
Harris, June C., V.P. & Sec.--Old Home Foods, Inc., Saint Paul, MN, pg. 823
Harris, Michael, Sr. V.P.--K-J Distributors, Inc., Glendale, AZ, pg. 612
Harris, Patrick, Pres.--K-J Distributors, Inc., Glendale, AZ, pg. 612
Harris, Robert D., Pres. & Chief Oper. Officer--Elastic Materials, Inc., Smithville, OH, pg. 372
Harris, Stan, Pres. & Dir.-Creative--Harris Drury Cohen, Fort Lauderdale, FL, pg. 511
Hart, Dorothy, V.P.-Fin. & Admin.--McNaughton & Gunn, Inc., Saline, MI, pg. 732
Hart, Ronald D., Pres. & Treas.--Hart Crowser, Inc., Seattle, WA, pg. 512
Harte, Houston H., Chm. Bd.--Harte-Hanks Communications, Inc., San Antonio, TX, pg. 513
Hartke, Phillip, Pres.--Effingham-Clay Service Co., Effingham, IL, pg. 371
Hartman, Lawrence M., Chief Fin. Officer & Exec. V.P.--Velsicol Chemical Corporation, Rosemont, IL, pg. 1147
Hartmann, E.J., Chm. Bd. & Pres.--Ziebart International Corporation, Troy, MI, pg. 1217
Hartunian, Gordon, Pres.--A B C Appliance Inc., Pontiac, MI, pg. 2
Hartzell, Robert C., Chm. Bd. & Pres.--Hartzell Corporation, Saint Paul, MN, pg. 514
Haskell, Charles L., Exec. V.P.-Fin. & Legal--Lettuce Entertain You Enterprises, Inc., Chicago, IL, pg. 668
Hassinger, Norman M., Jr., Chm. Bd., Pres., Chief Exec. & Chief Oper. Officer--The Hassinger Companies, Itasca, IL, pg. 516
Hatch, Wilda G., Pres.--Standard Corporation, Ogden, UT, pg. 1036
Hatt, Peter M., Chm. & Chief Exec. Officer--Borders, Perrin & Norrander, Inc., Portland, OR, pg. 165
Hauber, W.M., Chm. Bd., Pres. & Chief Exec. Officer--Matthews International Corp., Pittsburgh, PA, pg. 721
Hawk, Richard C., Chm. Bd. & Chief Exec. Officer--Help Management Corporation, Overland Park, KS, pg. 527
Hawkins, Arthur M., Pres. & Chief Exec. Officer--Exide Corporation, Reading, PA, pg. 393
Hawkins, Marvin J., Sr., Chm. Bd. & Pres.--J.D. Diffenbaugh, Inc., Riverside, CA, pg. 337
Hawkins, O.E., Pres.--Hawkins Markets, Inc., Wooster, OH, pg. 518
Hawley, Gary, V.P.-Fin. & Chief Fin. Officer--Snyder's Drug Stores, Inc., Minnetonka, MN, pg. 1015
Haworth, G.W., Chm. Bd.--Haworth, Inc., Holland, MI, pg. 518
Haworth, Richard G., Pres. & Chief Exec. Officer--Haworth, Inc., Holland, MI, pg. 518
Haydel, Agatha M., Treas.--Walk, Haydel & Associates, Inc., New Orleans, LA, pg. 1159
Haydel, Gerald M., Co-Chm. Bd. & Chief Exec. Officer--Walk, Haydel & Associates, Inc., New Orleans, LA, pg. 1159
Hayden, Donald C., Chief Exec. Officer--Transco Inc., Wayne, MI, pg. 1107
Hayes, Carl R., Pres.--Amlings Flowerland, Hinsdale, IL, pg. 67
Hayes, Dennis C., Pres.--Hayes Microcomputer Products, Inc., Norcross, GA, pg. 519
Hayesm, John, Pres.--The Architects Collaborative, Inc. (TAC), Cambridge, MA, pg. 80
Hazlehurst, Thomas E., Chm. Bd.--Potter Hazlehurst Incorporated, East Greenwich, RI, pg. 882
Healey, Robert T., Chm. Bd.--Viking Yacht Co., New Gretna, NJ, pg. 1151
Healey, William J., Pres. & Chief Exec. Officer--Viking Yacht Co., New Gretna, NJ, pg. 1151
Healy, Denis J., Pres.--Turtle Wax, Inc., Chicago, IL, pg. 1120
Healy, Sondra A., Chm. Bd.--Turtle Wax, Inc., Chicago, IL, pg. 1120
Hearn, Michael, Pres.--MBT Associates, Inc., San Francisco, CA, pg. 691
Heath, Milton W., Jr., Chm. Bd., Chief Exec. Officer & Treas.--Heath Consultants Incorporated, Stoughton, MA, pg. 524
Hecht, David, V.P.--Niagara Envelope Company, Inc., Buffalo, NY, pg. 805
Hecht, Len, V.P.-Mktg.--Queens Group, Inc., Long Island City, NY, pg. 904
Hecker, Denny, Pres.--Greater Orlando Auto Auction, Orlando, FL, pg. 483
Hedinger, Howard, Chm. Bd. & Treas.--American Industries Inc., Portland, OR, pg. 55
Heil, Joseph F., Jr., Chm. Bd. & Chief Exec. Officer--The Heil Co., Chattanooga, TN, pg. 525
Heiman, Mark, Exec. V.P.--Standard Textile Co., Inc., Cincinnati, OH, pg. 1037

Heiman, Paul, Chm. Bd. & Chief Exec. Officer--Standard Textile Co., Inc., Cincinnati, OH, pg. 1037
Heineman, Brett D., Sec. & Mgr.-East Reg. Sls.--Conway Import Co. Inc., Elmsford, NY, pg. 281
Heineman, Nicholas A., Pres. & Chief Exec. Officer--Conway Import Co. Inc., Elmsford, NY, pg. 281
Heinman, Gregg J., V.P.-Opers., Sec. & Treas.--Conway Import Co. Inc., Elmsford, NY, pg. 281
Heitman, Frederick C., Pres.--Brooks Products, Inc., El Monte, CA, pg. 180
Heller, Andrew T., Exec. V.P.--Marquette Coppersmithing Co., Inc., Philadelphia, PA, pg. 713
Heller, C.M., Jr., Vice Chm. & Treas.--Marquette Coppersmithing Co., Inc., Philadelphia, PA, pg. 713
Heller, Chester M., Sr., Chm. Bd., Pres. & Chief Exec. Officer--Marquette Coppersmithing Co., Inc., Philadelphia, PA, pg. 713
Heller, Cyrus, V.P.-Pur.--Marquette Coppersmithing Co., Inc., Philadelphia, PA, pg. 713
Heller, Rodney D., Comptroller--Marquette Coppersmithing Co., Inc., Philadelphia, PA, pg. 713
Helms, Carol A., Pres.--Edd Helms Electrical Contracting, Miami, FL, pg. 527
Helms, W. Edd, Jr., Chm.--Edd Helms Electrical Contracting, Miami, FL, pg. 527
Helzberg, Barnett C., Jr., Chm. Bd. & Chief Exec. Officer--Helzberg's Diamond Shops, Inc., North Kansas City, MO, pg. 528
Henderson, C. Max, Chm. Bd. & Chief Exec. Officer--Laroche Holdings, Inc., Atlanta, GA, pg. 659
Henderson, Donald E., Pres.--Joseph J. Henderson & Son, Inc., Gurnee, IL, pg. 529
Henderson, John N., III, Pres. & Chief Exec. Officer--Mid-West Paper Products Company, Warren, MI, pg. 750
Henderson, Marilyn, Sec.--Joseph J. Henderson & Son, Inc., Gurnee, IL, pg. 529
Henderson, Richard L., Pres.--Drug Emporium of Arizona, Inc., Scottsdale, AZ, pg. 349
Hendricks, Diane M., V.P. & Sec.--ABC Supply Company, Inc., Beloit, WI, pg. 2
Hendricks, Kenneth A., Chm. Bd., Pres. & Chief Exec. Officer--ABC Supply Company, Inc., Beloit, WI, pg. 2
Hendricks, Ruth Ann, Corp. Sec.--Rose Acre Farms, Seymour, IN, pg. 947
Hendrix, Tom E., Chm. Bd., Pres. & Chief Exec. Officer--Henco, Inc., Selmer, TN, pg. 528
Henley, A.B., Jr., Chm. Bd.--Henley Paper Company, Greensboro, NC, pg. 529
Henley, Nixon C., Pres.--Henley Paper Company, Greensboro, NC, pg. 529
Hennesy, Thomas J., Chm. Bd. & Chief Exec. Officer--TSC Industries, Inc., Nashville, TN, pg. 1075
Henning, William W., Sr. V.P.-Sls.--Toter Incorporated, Statesville, NC, pg. 1103
Henningsen, Victor W., Jr., Chm.--Henningsen Foods, Inc., White Plains, NY, pg. 629
Henricks, J.R. III, Pres.--Hendrick Management Corporation, Charlotte, NC, pg. 529
Henry, A. Shafer, Sr. V.P.--E.P. Henry Corporation, Woodbury, NJ, pg. 530
Henry, J.C., II, Exec. V.P.--E.P. Henry Corporation, Woodbury, NJ, pg. 530
Henry, James C., Jr., Pres. & Chief Exec. Officer--E.P. Henry Corporation, Woodbury, NJ, pg. 530
Herndon, Carl M., Pres.--Black Fin Yacht Corporation, Fort Lauderdale, FL, pg. 154
Herring, Barry E., Pres. & Chief Oper. Officer--Spatz & Co., Northbrook, IL, pg. 1026
Hertog, Roger, Exec. V.P.--Sanford C. Bernstein & Co., Inc., New York, NY, pg. 144
Hertz, Arthur, Chm. Bd. & Chief Exec. Officer--Wometco Enterprises, Inc., Coral Gables, FL, pg. 1199
Hess, Marshall, Chm. Bd.--Fishers Big Wheel Inc., New Castle, PA, pg. 415
Hetherwick, Fred B., Chm. Bd., Pres. & Chief Exec. Officer--Plastigage Corporation, Jackson, MI, pg. 876
Hettrick, John L., Chm. Bd. & Chief Exec. Officer--WSF Industries, Inc., Tonawanda, NY, pg. 1156
Hewett, Dexter B., Pres.--Sonicair, Scottsdale, AZ, pg. 1018
Hickey, William III, V.P.-Mktg. & Sls.--H.M. Smyth Co., Saint Paul, MN, pg. 1014
Hicks, Linda G., Sec.--Gardiner Metal Company, Chicago, IL, pg. 443
High, Calvin G., Sr. V.P.--High Industries Inc., Lancaster, PA, pg. 533
High, S. Dale, Chm. Bd. & Pres.--High Industries Inc., Lancaster, PA, pg. 533
Hildreth, Horace A., Jr., Pres. & Sec.--Diversified Communications, Portland, ME, pg. 340
Hill, Edward D., Partner & Dir.-Sls. & Mktg.--J. C. Bradford & Co., Nashville, TN, pg. 170
Hill, George J., III, Chm.--Hill, Holliday, Connors, Cosmopulos, Inc., Boston, MA, pg. 534
Hill, Richard H., Exec. V.P.--Alexander Marketing Services, Inc., Grand Rapids, MI, pg. 33
Hill, Stephen R., Chm. & Pres.--Tone Commander Systems, Redmond, WA, pg. 1101
Hilsinger, Arthur R., Jr., Chm. Bd., Pres. & Treas.--The Hilsinger Corp., Plainville, MA, pg. 535
Hinden, Milton, Pres.--Duro Dyne Corporation, Farmingdale, NY, pg. 355
Hindman, Don J., Chm. Bd. & Chief Exec. Officer--Clark Foodservice, Inc., Elk Grove Village, IL, pg. 252
Hinkle, Max E., Chm. Bd., Pres., Chief Exec. Officer & Treas.--Rowtronics Company Inc., Indianapolis, IN, pg. 953
Hitchcock, Gregory T., Chm. Bd.--Hitchcock Industries, Inc., Bloomington, MN, pg. 536
Hitchcock, Timothy R., Pres. & Chief Exec. Officer--Hitchcock Industries, Inc., Bloomington, MN, pg. 536
Hochfelder, J. Gene, Chm. & Chief Exec. Officer--Beldoch Industries Corporation, West Hempstead, NY, pg. 133
Hochfelder, James Lawrence, Pres.--Beldoch Industries Corporation, West Hempstead, NY, pg. 133
Hochfelder, Thomas G., Sr. V.P. & Treas.--Beldoch Industries Corporation, West Hempstead, NY, pg. 133
Hockaday, Irvine O., Jr., Pres. & Chief Exec. Officer--Hallmark Cards, Inc., Kansas City, MO, pg. 501
Hockaday, Peter S., Sr. V.P.--MBT Associates, Inc., San Francisco, CA, pg. 691
Hodes, Alan, Chm. Bd. & Pres.--Pen-Tab Industries, Inc., Glendale, NY, pg. 856
Hodin, Joseph, Chm., Pres. & Chief Exec. Officer--Giant Markets Inc., Scranton, PA, pg. 456
Hodin, William, V.P.--Giant Markets Inc., Scranton, PA, pg. 456
Hoeper, Howard P., Chm. Bd. & Pres.--H.P.H. Industries Ltd., Lake Forest, IL, pg. 497
Hoffman, Ebba C., Chm., Pres., Chief Exec. & Chief Fin. Officer--Smead Manufacturing Company, Hastings, MN, pg. 1011
Hofley, Norman H., Pres.--Hofley Manufacturing Company, Warren, MI, pg. 538
Hogan, Robert L., V.P.--Clover Financial Corporation, Merchantville, NJ, pg. 256
Hohman, Theodore, Pres.--TCH Industries Inc., Grand Rapids, MI, pg. 1072
Holder, Robert M., Jr., Chm. Bd.--Holder Corporation, Atlanta, GA, pg. 538
Holmes, George B., Pres., Chief Exec. & Chief Fin. Officer--Dombrowski & Holmes, Inc., Chicago, IL, pg. 343
Holmes, Harold, Co-Chm. Bd.--Taco John's International, Inc., Cheyenne, WY, pg. 1076
Holoubek, Verne R., Pres.--Holoubek Inc., Waukesha, WI, pg. 540
Holt, William S., Pres.--Great Salt Lake Minerals & Chemicals Corp., Ogden, UT, pg. 482
Honek, Andrew P., V.P.--Connecticut Drive Shaft, Inc., Milford, CT, pg. 274
Honek, J. Frank, Pres.--Connecticut Drive Shaft, Inc., Milford, CT, pg. 274
Honek, Joseph A., Chm. Bd.--Connecticut Drive Shaft, Inc., Milford, CT, pg. 274
Hoppe, David T., Chm. Bd. & Pres.--CORS, Itasca, IL, pg. 203
Horlick, Dennis, Pres. & Creative Dir.--Horlick Levin Advertising Inc., Los Angeles, CA, pg. 544
Hough, Richard T., Chm. Bd.--CHEMCENTRAL Corporation, Bedford Park, IL, pg. 241
Housen, Charles B., Chm. Bd., Pres. & Chief Exec. Officer--Erving Paper Mills, Erving, MA, pg. 388
Houston, Loren W., Chm. Bd. & Pres.--Superior Container, Inc., Warrensville, OH, pg. 1063
Howard, Charles, Pres.--Howard Manufacturing, Kent, WA, pg. 547
Howell, John S., Chm. Bd., Pres. & Chief Exec. Officer--Howell Instruments Corp., Fort Worth, TX, pg. 547
Hoyt, Bruce K., Chm. Bd.--Vinyl Therm, Inc., Bloomington, MN, pg. 1152
Hoyt, Carol A., V.P.-Human Resources--Advance Packaging Corporation, Grand Rapids, MI, pg. 19
Hoyt, James, Gen. Partner--The Hoyt Group, Shawnee Mission, KS, pg. 548
Hoyt, Steven B., Pres.--Vinyl Therm, Inc., Bloomington, MN, pg. 1152
Hribar, John A., V.P.--GAI Consultants, Inc., Monroeville, PA, pg. 439
Hubbard, Stanley S., Chm., Pres., & Chief Exec. Officer--Hubbard Broadcasting, Inc., Saint Paul, MN, pg. 548
Huber, Judy, Exec. V.P., Treas. & Sec.--Time Systems, Inc., Phoenix, AZ, pg. 1097
Huber, Ron, Chm. Bd., Pres. & Chief Exec. Officer--Time Systems, Inc., Phoenix, AZ, pg. 1097
Huberman Goldberg, Marilyn, Sr. V.P.--Muscum Boutique Intercontinental, Ltd., New York, NY, pg. 777
Hubler, Howard, Pres.--Hubler Chevrolet Inc., Indianapolis, IN, pg. 550
Hudson, Chris, Chm. Bd., Pres. & Chief Exec. Officer--Automation Intelligence, Inc., Maitland, FL, pg. 101
Hudson, Christopher, V.P.-Bus. Devel.--Automation Intelligence, Inc., Maitland, FL, pg. 101
Huebner, Donald F., Chief Fin. Officer, Treas. & Controller--Active Electrical Supply Company, Chicago, IL, pg. 15
Huettl, Thomas R., Sr. V.P., Chief Oper. Officer, Treas. & Sec.--Steenberg Homes, Inc., Fond du Lac, WI, pg. 1045
Hughes, Roger K., Chm. Bd.--Hughes Markets Inc., Irwindale, CA, pg. 552
Hulsey, Nona Jean, Chm. Emeritus--Macklanburg-Duncan Co., Oklahoma City, OK, pg. 697
Humphrey, John W., Chm. Bd.--The Forum Corporation, Boston, MA, pg. 425
Hunger, Jack E., Chm. Bd. & Pres.--World Shipping, Inc., Lakewood, OH, pg. 1203
Hunt, Robert C., Chm. Bd. & Chief Exec. Officer--The Hunt Corporation, Indianapolis, IN, pg. 553
Hunter, Glen, V.P.--Moss Telecommunications Services, Grand Rapids, MI, pg. 772
Huntsman, Jon M., Chm. Bd. & Chief Exec. Officer--Huntsman Chemical Corporation, Salt Lake City, UT, pg. 555
Huskey, John M., Pres.-Calmark Devel.--Calmark Investment Company, Los Angeles, CA, pg. 211
Idelman, Sheri, Chief Oper. Officer--ITI Marketing Services, Inc., Omaha, NE, pg. 561
Idelman, Steven A., Chm. Bd.--ITI Marketing Services, Inc., Omaha, NE, pg. 561
Ielmini, Angelo, Exec. V.P.--Patterson Frozen Foods, Inc., Patterson, CA, pg. 851
Ielmini, John, Pres.--Patterson Frozen Foods, Inc., Patterson, CA, pg. 851
Iglar, Michael J., Treas.--Brad Foote Gear Works, Inc., Cicero, IL, pg. 169
Ilitch, Marian, Sec. & Treas.--Little Caesar Enterprises, Inc., Detroit, MI, pg. 678
Ilitch, Michael, Chm. Bd. & Pres.--Little Caesar Enterprises, Inc., Detroit, MI, pg. 678
Imperatore, Arthur E., Chm. Bd.--A-P-A Transport Corp., North Bergen, NJ, pg. 5
Ingman, Tom, Pres. & Chief Oper. Officer--Condor D.C. Power Supplies Inc., Oxnard, CA, pg. 273
Ingram, Richard E., Chm. Bd., Chief Exec. & Chief Fin. Officer--Builder Marts of America, Greenville, SC, pg. 187
Ingram, Robert, Exec. V.P.--Corinthian Media, Inc., New York, NY, pg. 286
Ireton, John F., Chm. Bd.--American Foodservice Corp., King of Prussia, PA, pg. 54
Isen, Harold, Chm. Bd. & Chief Exec. Officer--Paramount Packaging Corp., Chalfont, PA, pg. 848
Isen, Irvin, Pres. & Chief Oper. Officer--Paramount Packaging Corp., Chalfont, PA, pg. 848
Ishbia, Earl D., Mng. Partner--Sherwood Food Distributors, Detroit, MI, pg. 998
Ivey, Reef C., III, Gen. Counsel--Nutri/System Inc., Blue Bell, PA, pg. 818
Jackson, J.R. Bryan, Pres.--Superior Machine Company Of South Carolina, Inc., Florence, SC, pg. 1064
Jackson, Margaret, Pres.--Western Pacific Data Systems, San Diego, CA, pg. 1180
Jacobowitz, Jeff, Pres.--Symplex Communications Corp., Ann Arbor, MI, pg. 1069
Jacobs, Bruce E., Pres.--Grede Foundries, Inc., Milwaukee, WI, pg. 483
Jacobs, Burleigh E., Chm. Bd.--Grede Foundries, Inc., Milwaukee, WI, pg. 483
Jacobs, Jeremy M., Chm. & Chief Exec. Officer--Delaware North Companies, Inc., Buffalo, NY, pg. 326
Jacobs, K.J., Chm. Bd.--E.J. Brach Corporation, Oakbrook Terrace, IL, pg. 169
Jacobs, Leonard J., Chm. Bd., Pres. & Chief Exec. Officer--Jet Spray Corp., Norwood, MA, pg. 593
Jacobson, Arnold E., Treas. & Dir.-Data Processing--Goddess Bra Company, East Boston, MA, pg. 464
Jacobson, Mitchell, Pres. & Chief Exec. Officer--MSC Industrial Supply Co., Plainview, NY, pg. 693
Jacobson, Robert N., V.P.-Fin., Treas., Sec. & Chief Fin. Officer--The Atlas Construction Co., Stamford, CT, pg. 96
Jacobson, Sidney, Chm. Bd.--MSC Industrial Supply Co., Plainview, NY, pg. 693
Jacobson, William, V.P.--Goddess Bra Company, East Boston, MA, pg. 464
Jacoby, J.E.M., Exec. V.P.--Stephens, Inc., Little Rock, AR, pg. 1046
Jaffee, Leon S., Pres.--American Printers & Lithographers, Chicago, IL, pg. 59
James, Edward R., Pres.--James Building Corporation, Northbrook, IL, pg. 588
James, Jeanne, Sr. V.P.--Design 1 Interiors, Los Angeles, CA, pg. 332
James, John H., Chm. Bd.--Texas Steel Co., Inc., Fort Worth, TX, pg. 1090
Jamison, R. Kenneth, Pres. & Chief Oper. Officer--Southern Radio Corporation, pg. 1022
Jamison, Thomas J., Chm. Bd. & Chief Exec. Officer--Southern Radio Corporation, pg. 1022
Jaworski, Pauline, V.P.-Personnel--Miken Companies, Inc., Cheektowaga, NY, pg. 752
Jaworski, Walter J., Chm. Bd., Pres. Chief Exec. Officer & Chief Oper. Officer--Miken Companies, Inc., Cheektowaga, NY, pg. 752
Jayson, Joseph M., Chm. Bd. & Chief Exec. Officer--J. M. Jayson & Co., Inc., Getsville, NY, pg. 591
Jedlinski, Ronald T., Pres.--Roman, Inc., Roselle, IL, pg. 945
Jeffers, John J., Pres.--MidWest Body Corporation, Paris, IL, pg. 752
Jemison, Frank Z., Jr., Pres., Chief Exec. & Chief Oper. Officer--Jemison, Inc., Memphis, TN, pg. 592
Jemison, Frank Z., Sr., Chm. Bd.--Jemison, Inc., Memphis, TN, pg. 592
Jenkins, Alan B., Pres.--Felton Brush Inc., Manchester, NH, pg. 406
Jenkins, R.E., Chm. Bd.--Bingham, Mt. Prospect, IL, pg. 151
Jensen, Colin C., Pres.--Irving F. Jensen Co., Inc., Sioux City, IA, pg. 593
Jensen, Elizabeth D., V.P. & Chief Exec. Officer--Jensen Electric Company, Reno, NV, pg. 592
Jensen, Erik M., Exec. V.P.--Irving F. Jensen Co., Inc., Sioux City, IA, pg. 593
Jensen, Gary A., Pres. & Sec.--Jensen Electric Company, Reno, NV, pg. 592
Jerome, Jerome K., Pres. & Chief Exec. Officer--Jerome Foods Inc., Barron, WI, pg. 593
Jesperson, Daryl, Sr. V.P.--RE/MAX International, Inc., Englewood, CO, pg. 915
Jessup, Stewart E., Chm. Bd.--Riceland Foods, Inc., Stuttgart, AR, pg. 931
Jimenez, Carlos, Pres., Chief Oper. Officer & Dir.-Creative--Leslie Advertising, Greenville, SC, pg. 668
Joa, Curt G., Chm. Bd.--Curt G. Joa, Inc., Sheboygan Falls, WI, pg. 594
Joa, Martha F., Pres.--Curt G. Joa, Inc., Sheboygan Falls, WI, pg. 594
Joel, Andrew, V.P.--Miller Bros. Industries, Inc., Richmond, VA, pg. 753
Joel, Irving, Pres.--Miller Bros. Industries, Inc., Richmond, VA, pg. 753
Joel, Larry, Chm. Bd.--Duling Optical Corporation, Louisville, KY, pg. 352
Joffrion, A.A., Pres.--Joffko International, Houston, TX, pg. 595
Johnson, A. Stanley, Chm. Bd., Pres. & Chief Exec. Officer--Van Leunens Inc., Cincinnati, OH, pg. 1144
Johnson, Berton, Pres.--Gay Johnson's Inc., Grand Junction, CO, pg. 446
Johnson, Carl I., Jr., Exec. V.P.--Johnson Supply & Equipment Corp., Houston, TX, pg. 601
Johnson, Catherine C., V.P. & Sec.--Johnson Newspaper Corporation, Watertown, NY, pg. 598
Johnson, D., Mgr.-Mktg.--Felton Brush Inc., Manchester, NH, pg. 406

Corporate Responsibilities Index

Johnson, E. Peter, Sr. V.P. & Gen. Counsel--Sundt Corp., Tucson, AZ, pg. 1060
Johnson, George D., V.P. & Treas.--Ballenger Paving Company, Inc., Taylors, SC, pg. 116
Johnson, Gilbert E., Pres. & Treas.--G. E. Johnson Construction Co., Inc., Colorado Springs, CO, pg. 597
Johnson, John B., Pres., Editor & Treas.--Johnson Newspaper Corporation, Watertown, NY, pg. 598
Johnson, John H., Chm. Bd. & Chief Exec. Officer--Johnson Publishing Company, Inc., Chicago, IL, pg. 598
Johnson, LaRee K., Chm. Bd.--LeGrand Johnson Construction Co., Logan, UT, pg. 598
Johnson, Orville D., Chm. Bd. & Chief Exec. Officer--UFE Incorporated, Stillwater, MN, pg. 1123
Johnson, Philip R., V.P.--Johnson Bros. Corp., Litchfield, MN, pg. 597
Johnson, Randy D., Pres.--E Z Loader Boat Trailers, Inc., Spokane, WA, pg. 361
Johnson, Richard W., Pres. & Chief Exec. Officer--Johnson Bros. Corp., Litchfield, MN, pg. 597
Johnson, Stewart H., V.P. & Sec.--Ballenger Paving Company, Inc., Taylors, SC, pg. 116
Johnson, Thomas B., Chm. & Pres.--The Johnson Industries Corp., Urbana, OH, pg. 598
Johnson, Walter D., Exec. V.P., Chief Fin. Officer & Sec.--Johnson Bros. Corp., Litchfield, MN, pg. 597
Johnston, Fred B., II, Pres. & Chief Exec. Officer--Fred B. Johnston Company, Inc., Chapin, SC, pg. 601
Johnston, Jim, V.P.-Pur.--Fred B. Johnston Company, Inc., Chapin, SC, pg. 601
Johnston, Sid D., Pres. & Chief Exec. Officer--Despatch Industries, Minneapolis, MN, pg. 332
Jones, Barbara R., Chm. Bd.--Baltimore Stationery Co., Baltimore, MD, pg. 116
Jones, Bucky, Pres.--Dairymen, Inc., Louisville, KY, pg. 311
Jones, Charles J., Treas.--Metallurg, Inc., New York, NY, pg. 742
Jones, Glenn W., Jr., Partner--J. C. Bradford & Co., Nashville, TN, pg. 170
Jones, H. Douglas, Pres.--Jones, Anastasi & Birchfield, Dublin, OH, pg. 602
Jones, J. Gregory, Pres. & Chief Fin. Officer--Peck Jones Construction, Los Angeles, CA, pg. 854
Jones, J. Kevin, Exec. V.P.-Mktg.--Peck Jones Construction, Los Angeles, CA, pg. 854
Jones, James C., Jr., Chm. Bd. & Chief Exec. Officer--Jones Company, Inc., Waycross, GA, pg. 603
Jones, Jerve M., Chief Exec. Officer--Peck Jones Construction, Los Angeles, CA, pg. 854
Jones, Joann K., Chm. Bd.--Capital Electric Group, Inc., Phoenix, AZ, pg. 215
Jones, John E., Chm. Bd.--Cummins-American Corp., Mount Prospect, IL, pg. 304
Jones, Michael E., Pres. & Chief Oper. Officer--Capital Electric Group, Inc., Phoenix, AZ, pg. 215
Jones, William W., Jr., Pres. & Chief Exec. Officer--Baltimore Stationery Co., Baltimore, MD, pg. 116
Jons, Otto P., V.P.-Engrng.--Advanced Marine Enterprises, Inc., Arlington, VA, pg. 20
Jordan, Charles A., V.P. & Sec.--Jordan Tamraz Caruso Advertising, Inc., Chicago, IL, pg. 605
Jordan, J. Luther, Jr., Chm. Bd.--Baton Rouge Water Works Company, Baton Rouge, LA, pg. 126
Jordan, John W. II, Chm. Bd. & Chief Exec. Officer--Jordan Industries, Inc., Deerfield, IL, pg. 604
Jorgensen, Erik, Pres. & Chief Oper. Officer--Faber/Castell Corporation, Parsippany, NJ, pg. 395
Joseph, Edwin, Chm. Bd. & Pres.--The Great Atlantic Companies, Hampton, VA, pg. 480
Joseph, Peter, Partner--Joseph, Littlejohn & Levy, New York, NY, pg. 607
Joseph, Thomas, Chm., Pres. & Chief Exec. Officer--Markdata Inc., Pittston, PA, pg. 708
Joshi, Krishan K., Pres. & Chief Exec. Officer--UES, Inc., Dayton, OH, pg. 1122
Juanarena, Douglas B., Pres. & Chief Exec. Officer--Pressure Systems, Hampton, VA, pg. 888
Jumonville, Dan, Chm. Bd. & Pres.--Group Insurance Inc., Baton Rouge, LA, pg. 490
Justiss, James F., Jr., Chm. Bd., Pres. & Chief Exec. Officer--Justiss Oil Co., Inc., Jena, LA, pg. 610
Kaempfer, J.W., Jr., Pres.--The Kaempfer Company, Investment Builders, Washington, DC, pg. 613
Kagan, Michael, Exec. V.P. & Chief Fin. Officer--Tropical Garment Manufacturing Company, Tampa, FL, pg. 1116
Kahlig, Clarence J., Pres.--North Park Lincoln Mercury Inc., San Antonio, TX, pg. 813
Kahn, Alan, Chm. Bd.--M. B. Kahn Construction Co., Inc., Columbia, SC, pg. 614
Kaitz, Ben B., Pres.--Palm Beach Beauty Products Co., Minneapolis, MN, pg. 843
Kaitz, Miriam Collins, Sec. & Treas.--Palm Beach Beauty Products Co., Minneapolis, MN, pg. 843
Kaitz, Richard A., Exec. V.P.--Palm Beach Beauty Products Co., Minneapolis, MN, pg. 843
Kaloyanides, Stephen, Pres.--New England Coffee Company, Malden, MA, pg. 800
Kalt, S. Richard, Exec. V.P.--CRN International, Inc., Hamden, CT, pg. 203
Kaltman, Eric, Chief Exec. Officer--Queens Group, Inc., Long Island City, NY, pg. 904
Kamberos, Chris, Chm. Bd., Pres. & Chief Oper. Officer--Treasure Island Foodmarts Inc., Chicago, IL, pg. 1109
Kamberos, Frank, V.P.--Treasure Island Foodmarts Inc., Chicago, IL, pg. 1109
Kamitaki, Tadami, Pres.--Maui Varieties, Ltd., Honolulu, HI, pg. 721
Kamm, Jacob O., Chm. Bd., Pres. & Chief Exec. Officer--Electric Furnace Co., Salem, OH, pg. 373
Kanai, Noritoshi, Pres.--Mutual Trading Co., Inc., Los Angeles, CA, pg. 779
Kane, Robert J., Chm. Bd.--Western Regional Off Track Betting, Batavia, NY, pg. 1181
Kaplan, James, Pres.--Kaplan Electronics, Wayne, NJ, pg. 616
Kappler, George, Chm., Pres. & Chief Exec. Officer--KSG Inc., Guntersville, AL, pg. 613
Karmanos, Peter, Jr., Chm. Bd. & Chief Exec. Officer--Compuware Corporation, Farmington Hills, MI, pg. 271
Karp, Jack L., Pres.--L. Karp & Sons, Inc., Elk Grove Village, IL, pg. 617
Karsten, Harry, Jr., Chm. Bd. & Pres.--Golden West Homes, Santa Ana, CA, pg. 467
Katz, Morton, V.P. & Treas.--Clay-Park Labs, Inc., Bronx, NY, pg. 253
Kaufman, Donald L., Pres. & Dir.-Sls. & Mktg., Alside Div.--Associated Materials Inc., Dallas, TX, pg. 91
Kazmarek, Robert, Vice Chm.--ACR Industries Inc., Mount Clemens, MI, pg. 2
Keating, Daniel J., III, Chief Oper. Officer--Daniel J. Keating Co., Villanova, PA, pg. 619
Keating, Daniel J., Jr., Chm. Bd., Pres. & Chief Exec. Officer--Daniel J. Keating Co., Villanova, PA, pg. 619
Keener, Wayne, Chief Exec. Officer--Keeners, Inc., Seattle, WA, pg. 620
Keeton, Kathy, Pres. & Chief Oper. Officer--General Media Publishing Group, New York, NY, pg. 450
Keeton, Thomas, Chief Oper. Officer--Keller Construction Company Ltd., El Monte, CA, pg. 620
Kehne, Richard M., Chm. Bd. & Pres.--Kehne Electric Company, Inc., Saint Paul, MN, pg. 620
Keiser, Michael, Pres.--Health Care Distributors of Indiana, Inc., South Bend, IN, pg. 520
Kellen, Stephen M., Pres.--Arnhold and S. Bleichroeder, Inc., New York, NY, pg. 84
Kellman, Joseph, Chm., Pres. & Chief Exec. Officer--Globe Glass & Mirror Co., Chicago, IL, pg. 463
Kellogg, Martin N., Pres., Chief Oper. Officer & Corp. Sec.--UFE Incorporated, Stillwater, MN, pg. 1123
Kelly, Paul E., Sr., Chm. Bd.--Superior Tube Company, Collegeville, PA, pg. 1064
Kelly, R.J., III, Partner--Roney & Co., Detroit, MI, pg. 946
Kelly, Tom, Art Dir.--Cappelli Miles Wiltz & Kelly, Portland, OR, pg. 216
Kemerling, James L., Pres. & Chief Exec. Officer--Shade Computer Forms Co., Green Bay, WI, pg. 994
Kennedy, Andrew G., Chm. & Pres.--Kentile Floors Inc., South Plainfield, NJ, pg. 623
Kennedy, Bernard, Pres. & Chief Oper. Officer--King Kullen Grocery Co., Inc., Westbury, NY, pg. 630
Kennedy, T.C., Chm. Bd.--BE & K, Inc., Birmingham, AL, pg. 106
Kent, Warren T., Chm. & Chief Exec. Officer--The Kent Manufacturing Co., Pickens, SC, pg. 623
Kerz, Paul J., Chm. Bd., Pres. & Chief Exec. Officer--Health Management Systems, Inc., New York, NY, pg. 521
Kiam, Victor, II, Chm. Bd., Pres., Chief Exec. & Chief Oper. Officer--Remington Products Inc., Bridgeport, CT, pg. 926
Kilgore, Benjamin W., III, Pres. & Chief Oper. Officer--Pine State Creamery Co., Raleigh, NC, pg. 871
Kim, James J., Chm. & Chief Exec. Officer--Amkor Electronics, Inc., West Chester, PA, pg. 67
Kindseth, Gary A., Exec. V.P.--Faribault Foods Inc., Minneapolis, MN, pg. 399
King, Dennis E., Pres.--Dunlap & Co. Inc., Columbus, IN, pg. 353
King, George F., Chm. Bd., Pres. & Chief Exec. Officer--Kirby Building Systems, Inc., Nashville, TN, pg. 632
King, Jim, Pres. & Chief Oper. Officer--Sunox, Inc., Charlotte, NC, pg. 1062
King, John, Chm. & Chief Exec. Officer--Sunox, Inc., Charlotte, NC, pg. 1062
King, Robert C., Sr., Pres.--Richmond Motor Company, Richmond, VA, pg. 933
Kinne, Morris, V.P. & Gen. Counsel--Bar-S Foods Co., Phoenix, AZ, pg. 118
Kinning, Rick L., Pres. & Treas.--RK Mechanical, Inc., Lakewood, CO, pg. 907
Kiplinger, Austin H., Chm. Bd.--The Kiplinger Washington Editors, Inc., Washington, DC, pg. 632
Kiplinger, Knight A., Pres.--The Kiplinger Washington Editors, Inc., Washington, DC, pg. 632
Kiplinger, Todd L., V.P.-Investments--The Kiplinger Washington Editors, Inc., Washington, DC, pg. 632
Kipper, Barbara L., Chm. Bd.--The Charles Levy Company, Chicago, IL, pg. 672
Kirby, Carroll R., Pres.--Hydro/Kirby Agri Service, Inc., Lancaster, PA, pg. 556
Kirk, Thomas L., Chm. Bd. & Pres. & Chief Exec. Office--Kirk-Mayer, Inc., Los Angeles, CA, pg. 633
Kitch, Fred, Exec. V.P.--Keller Crescent Co., Evansville, IN, pg. 620
Kitchell, Samuel F., Chm. Bd.--Kitchell Corporation, Phoenix, AZ, pg. 634
Kitchen, Douglas O., Partner & Dir.-Futures--J. C. Bradford & Co., Nashville, TN, pg. 170
Kizer, William L., V.P.-Georgia Interior Construction Div.--Ed Taylor Construction Co., Tucker, GA, pg. 1081
Kleban, Albert J., Sec. & Gen. Counsel--Chessco Industries, Inc., Westport, CT, pg. 243
Klein, Bernard, Chm. Bd., Sec. & Treas.--Alaron Inc., Troy, MI, pg. 30
Klein, Calvin, Pres. & Chief Exec. Officer--Calvin Klein, Inc., New York, NY, pg. 635
Klein, Emery I., Pres.--Alaron Inc., Troy, MI, pg. 30
Klein, Michael S., Chm. Bd. & Chief Exec. Officer--Klein Tools Inc., Skokie, IL, pg. 635
Kleinman, Mel, V.P.-Sls.--El Camino Resources, Ltd., Northridge, CA, pg. 372
Kleinrock, Dr. Leonard, Chm. Bd. & Chief Exec. Officer--Technology Transfer Institute, Santa Monica, CA, pg. 1084
Klevay, Walter S., Sr., Chm. & Chief Exec. Officer--Kleco Corp., Brecksville, OH, pg. 634
Kline, Arnold W., Chm. Bd., Pres. & Chief Oper. Officer--Boston Trading Ltd. Inc., Lynn, MA, pg. 168
Kling, John J., Chm. Bd.--Southern Ohio Fabricators, Inc., Cincinnati, OH, pg. 1022
Klink, Edwin H., Chm. Bd. & Pres.--E & A Industries, Inc., Indianapolis, IN, pg. 358
Klong, Lawrence A., Pres.--K & R Delivery, Inc., Hinsdale, IL, pg. 610
Kloster, Carol G., Pres. & Chief Exec. Officer--The Charles Levy Company, Chicago, IL, pg. 672
Kluener, James A., Sr., Chm. Bd. & Pres.--Kluener Packing Company, Cincinnati, OH, pg. 636
Knapheide, H. W. III, Pres.--The Knapheide Mfg. Co., Quincy, IL, pg. 636
Knapp, Jules F., Chm. Bd., Pres. & Chief Exec. Officer--United Coatings, Inc., Kankakee, IL, pg. 1131
Knight, Robert B., Sr. V.P.-Admin. & Treas.--White Hen Pantry, Inc., Elmhurst, IL, pg. 1185
Knox, Marion A., Jr., V.P., Treas. & Sec.--Terminix Service, Inc., Columbia, SC, pg. 1088
Knox, Marion A., Sr., Vice Chm.--Terminix Service, Inc., Columbia, SC, pg. 1088
Knox, T.P, Jr., Chm. Bd.--Terminix Service, Inc., Columbia, SC, pg. 1088
Knuths, Leroy R., Chm. Bd., Pres. & Chief Exec. Officer--Rosco Manufacturing Co., Madison, SD, pg. 947
Koch, Robert L. II, Pres. & Chief Exec. Officer--George Koch Sons, Inc., Evansville, IN, pg. 639
Koerner, John, Pres.--Barq's, Inc., New Orleans, LA, pg. 121
Kohler, Herbert V., Jr., Chm. Bd., Pres., Chief Oper. & Chief Exec. Officer--Kohler Company, Kohler, WI, pg. 639
Kohls, Gary, Dir.-Research--Effective Management Systems, Milwaukee, WI, pg. 370
Kolkebeck, W. Charles, V.P.-Mktg. & Sls.--Nuttall Gear Corporation, Niagara Falls, NY, pg. 818
Koll, Donald M., Chm. Bd. & Chief Exec. Officer--Koll Co., Newport Beach, CA, pg. 641
Kolon, John S., Pres.--Kolon, Bittker & Desmond, Inc., Troy, MI, pg. 641
Komen, Richard B., Chm. Bd.--Restaurants Unlimited, Seattle, WA, pg. 929
Korman, Berton E., Partner--Korman Co., Trevose, PA, pg. 642
Korman, Leonard I., Partner--Korman Co., Trevose, PA, pg. 642
Korman, Steven H., Partner--Korman Co., Trevose, PA, pg. 642
Kossoff, Stanley M., Pres. & Chief Exec. Officer--Lillie Rubin Affiliates Inc., Miami, FL, pg. 954
Kouleyan, Aram, Owner--Knar Gold & Silver Exchange, Los Angeles, CA, pg. 636
Kozakis, Achilles, Chm. Bd. & Mng. Dir.--Joffko International, Houston, TX, pg. 595
Kramer, Arnold A., Pres. & Chief Exec. Officer--Trimfit, Inc., Philadelphia, PA, pg. 1113
Kramer, Gordon M., Chm. Bd., Pres. & Chief Exec. Officer--Continental Plastic Card Co., Coral Springs, FL, pg. 280
Kramer, Martin B., Chm. Bd.--Trimfit, Inc., Philadelphia, PA, pg. 1113
Krause, Jim, Dir. Client Services & New Bus. Contact--Krause, Nadurek & Eickmeyer, Dallas, TX, pg. 644
Krauss, Carl W., Chm. Bd.--Lakewood Engineering & Manufacturing Co., Chicago, IL, pg. 652
Kretsch, Jerold, Chm. Bd.--Sanborn Manufacturing Company, Springfield, MN, pg. 969
Kreusch, Paul P., Pres. & Chief Exec. Officer--Leonard Kreusch, Inc., Moonachie, NJ, pg. 645
Krommenhoek, William, Chief Exec. Officer--Krommenhoek McKeown Associates, San Diego, CA, pg. 645
Krucks, William, Chm. Bd. & Pres.--Rauland-Borg Corporation, Skokie, IL, pg. 914
Krueger, Robert A., Pres., Chief Exec. Officer & Treas.--Tri-Mark Metal Corp., Detroit, MI, pg. 1110
Krupa, Paul A., Pres.--Surgical Specialties, Reading, PA, pg. 1065
Krupsha, Andrew, Chm. Bd. & Pres.--Kleer Pak Corporation, Berwick, PA, pg. 635
Kruse, Mitchell, Pres., Chief Exec. Officer & Auctioneer--Kruse International, Auburn, IN, pg. 645
Kughn, Richard P., Chm. Bd. & Chief Exec. Officer--Lionel Trains, Inc., Chesterfield, MI, pg. 677
Kuiper, Karl D., Pres.--Grindmaster Corporation, Louisville, KY, pg. 488
Kupper, Bruce D., Mng. Partner--Kupper Parker Communications Inc., Saint Louis, MO, pg. 646
Kurdziel, Joseph, Chm. Bd. & Pres.--Kurdziel Industries, Inc., Muskegon, MI, pg. 646
Kurdziel, Theodore, V.P.-Prod. & Treas.--Kurdziel Industries, Inc., Muskegon, MI, pg. 646
Kurdziel, Walter J., Exec. V.P.-Production--Kurdziel Industries, Inc., Muskegon, MI, pg. 646
Kvetko, Gloria Jean, Owner--Gloria Jean's Coffee Bean Corp., Buffalo Grove, IL, pg. 464
LaBarge, Pierre III, Chm. Bd. & Pres.--LaBarge Pipe & Steel Company, Saint Louis, MO, pg. 649
Labovitz, George H., Dr., Chm. Bd., Pres. & Chief Exec. Officer--ODI, Burlington, MA, pg. 818
Lackman, Thomas F., Chm. Bd. & Pres.--Lackman Food Service, Woodbury, NY, pg. 650
LaCrosse, Jim, Chm. Bd.--NWS, Inc., Chicago, IL, pg. 782
Lacy, Andre B., Chm., Pres. & Chief Exec. Officer--LDI, Ltd., Indianapolis, IN, pg. 647
Lacy, Roane, Chm. Bd.--Plantation Foods Inc., Waco, TX, pg. 874
Lacy, Roane, Jr., Chief Exec. Officer--Plantation Foods Inc., Waco, TX, pg. 874
LaFond, Jerry, Chief Exec. Officer--The Asher Winer Company, Fitchburg, MA, pg. 88
LaGrega, Andrew T., Sr. V.P.-Sls., Mktg., Adv. & Human Resources--Wilder Management Associates, Waltham, MA, pg. 1189
Lakin, James E., Chm. Bd.--Timpte Industries, Inc., Denver, CO, pg. 1098
Lamb, James R., Exec. V.P.--Lamb Engineering & Construction Co., Salt Lake City, UT, pg. 652

Lamb, Michael R., Pres. & Mgr.-Construction--Lamb Engineering & Construction Co., Salt Lake City, UT, pg. 652
Lamb, Robert E., II, Pres.--Robert E. Lamb, Inc., Valley Forge, PA, pg. 652
LaMonica, Michael, V.P.-Sls. & Mktg.--Bridgeport Machines, Inc., Bridgeport, CT, pg. 175
Lane, Daniel, V.P. & Chief Fin. Officer--Quality Food Oils, Inc., New Milford, CT, pg. 903
Lange, Chadwick S., Pres.--Owatonna Canning Company, Owatonna, MN, pg. 833
Lange, Stephens J., Chm. Bd.--Owatonna Canning Company, Owatonna, MN, pg. 833
Langer, David, Pres., Chief Exec. & Chief Oper. Officer & Treas.--David Langer & Co., Inc., Hollywood, CA, pg. 657
Lapeyre, J. M., Jr., Chm. & Pres.--The Laitram Corporation, Harahan, LA, pg. 650
Lapin, Aaron S., Chm. Bd.--Clayton Corporation, Fenton, MO, pg. 253
Lapin, Byron R., Pres.--Clayton Corporation, Fenton, MO, pg. 253
Larkin, Frank, Chm. Bd. & Investor Rels. Dir.--North Shore Movers, Northbrook, IL, pg. 813
Larned, Gardner, Chm. Bd., Pres., & Chief Exec. Officer--Berry Bearing Co., Lyons, IL, pg. 144
Laskey, John L., Pres.--Laskey Associates, Fremont, CA, pg. 660
Lasko, John C., Chm. Bd., Pres. & Treas.--Republic Die & Tool Company, Belleville, MI, pg. 928
Lasko, Oscar, Pres.--Lasko Metal Products, Inc., West Chester, PA, pg. 660
Lauerer, Kenneth G., Pres. & Chief Oper. Officer--Lauerer Markin Gibbs, Inc., Maumee, OH, pg. 660
Laufer, Hans K., V.P.-Opers.--Superior Machine Company Of South Carolina, Inc., Florence, SC, pg. 1064
Lauren, Ralph, Chm. Bd.--Polo/Ralph Lauren Corporation, New York, NY, pg. 879
Lawson, Archie, V.P.-Admin.--Lawson Mechanical Contractors, Sacramento, CA, pg. 663
Lawson, Rodney, Pres., Chief Oper. Officer & Chief Exec. Officer--Lawson Mechanical Contractors, Sacramento, CA, pg. 663
Lawton, Bradley L., Exec. V.P.--Star Cutter Co., Farmington Hills, MI, pg. 1039
Lawton, Norman B., Pres.--Star Cutter Co., Farmington Hills, MI, pg. 1039
Layden, A.J., Chm. Bd. & Chief Exec. Officer--Allright Corporation, Houston, TX, pg. 41
LaZebnik, Robert, Owner--Airmaster Fan Co., Michigan Center, MI, pg. 28
Lebau, Joseph P., Exec. V.P.--Ben Schwartz Market, Inc., Peoria, IL, pg. 980
Lee, James C., III, Pres.--Buffalo Rock Company, Birmingham, AL, pg. 187
Lee, James C., Jr., Chm. Bd.--Buffalo Rock Company, Birmingham, AL, pg. 187
Lee, Paul M., Pres. & Chief Exec. Officer--Quik Wok Corporation, Dallas, TX, pg. 905
Lee, Rhoady R., Jr., Chm. Bd. & Chief Exec. Officer--Lakeside Industries, Redmond, WA, pg. 651
Lee, Richard, Dr., Chm. Bd.--The Apparel Group, Ltd., New York, NY, pg. 78
Lee, Robert R., Exec. V.P.--Progressive Driver Services, Inc., Jacksonville, FL, pg. 894
Lee, Thomas H., Chm. Bd.--Chadwick-Miller Inc., Canton, MA, pg. 237
Leebow, Steven, Chm. Bd., Pres. & Chief Exec. Officer--Pacesetter Steel Service, Inc., Marietta, GA, pg. 839
Leeds, Daniel H., V.P.--C M P Publications, Inc., Manhasset, NY, pg. 202
Leeds, Gerard G., Co-Chm. Bd.--C M P Publications, Inc., Manhasset, NY, pg. 202
Leeds, Lilo J., Co-Chm. Bd.--C M P Publications, Inc., Manhasset, NY, pg. 202
Leeds, Michael S., Pres. & Chief Exec. Officer--C M P Publications, Inc., Manhasset, NY, pg. 202
Leff, Joseph, Chm. Bd.--National Spinning Co., Inc., New York, NY, pg. 793
Leffler, Carlos R., Pres.--Carlos R. Leffler Inc., Richland, PA, pg. 666
Lehmer, Thomas W., Chief Exec. Officer--Prepco, Los Angeles, CA, pg. 887
Leibman, Lee, Sr. V.P., Promo.--Asher/Gould Advertising, Inc., Los Angeles, CA, pg. 88
Leinweber, John L., Pres. & Chief Exec. Officer--American Office Equipment, La Grange, IL, pg. 58
Lemon, James H., Jr., Chm. Bd. & Chief Exec. Officer--Johnston, Lemon & Co. Inc., Washington, DC, pg. 601
Lenderman, Gaynell, Sec.--Gay Johnson's Inc., Grand Junction, CO, pg. 446
Lenhart, Miles L., V.P.-Fin., Treas. & Sec.--Reeves Southeastern Corporation, Tampa, FL, pg. 921
Lennox, Jeffery, Controller--Niagara Envelope Company, Inc., Buffalo, NY, pg. 805
Lenz, Randolph W., Chm. Bd.--FWD Corporation, Clintonville, WI, pg. 395
Leon, Juan, Exec. V.P.-Mfg.--Leather Center, Inc., Carrollton, TX, pg. 664
Leone, John A., Pres. & Chief Exec. Officer--Bonney Forge Corporation, Allentown, PA, pg. 164
LePage, Bernard, Pres.--Christian Memorial Cultural Center, Rochester Hills, MI, pg. 249
Lerch, Howard D., Sr., Pres.--Mazo Lerch Company, Inc., Alexandria, VA, pg. 725
Leu, Dennis, V.P.-Mktg. & Sls.--Velsicol Chemical Corporation, Rosemont, IL, pg. 1147
Leum, Leonard L., Pres.--Pioneer Supermarkets, Los Angeles, CA, pg. 872
Levi, Kenneth, Pres.--Mayer Myers Paper Company, Memphis, TN, pg. 724
Levi, Malcolm, Sr., Chm. Bd.--Mayer Myers Paper Company, Memphis, TN, pg. 724
Levin, Ralph, Pres.--Sturgis Iron & Metal Company, Inc., Sturgis, MI, pg. 1055
Levin, Ronald J., Chm.--Horlick Levin Advertising Inc., Los Angeles, CA, pg. 544
Levy, Allan, V.P., Controller, Sec. & Data Processing Dir.--Level Export Sales Corp., New York, NY, pg. 670
Levy, Barry W., Chm. Bd., Chief Exec. Officer & Communications Dir.--Levy Security Consultants, Limited, Chicago, IL, pg. 672
Levy, Edward C., Jr., Pres. & Treas.--Edward C. Levy Co., Inc., Detroit, MI, pg. 672
Levy, Isaac A., Chm. Bd.--Level Export Sales Corp., New York, NY, pg. 670
Levy, Martin, Exec. V.P.--Landau & Heyman Inc., Chicago, IL, pg. 654
Levy, Nessim, Pres. & Chief Exec. Officer--Level Export Sales Corp., New York, NY, pg. 670
Levy, Paul, Partner--Joseph, Littlejohn & Levy, New York, NY, pg. 607
Levy, Sam, Pres.--Schwegmann Giant Super Markets, New Orleans, LA, pg. 980
Levy, Saul, Chm. Bd.--Nationwise Automotive, Inc., Columbus, OH, pg. 795
Lewis, George T., Chm. Bd. & Chief Exec. Officer--Cogentrix Incorporated, Charlotte, NC, pg. 258
Lewis, James E., Sr. V.P.-Opers.--Cogentrix Incorporated, Charlotte, NC, pg. 258
Lewis, William, Chm. Bd., Pres. & Chief Exec. Officer--Career Blazers Inc., New York, NY, pg. 218
Lewkowitz, Martin, Vice Chm.--Ranir Corporation, Grand Rapids, MI, pg. 912
Lieberman, David, Treas.--Carousel Snack Bars Of Minnesota, Minneapolis, MN, pg. 224
Lieberman, Stephen, Pres., Chief Exec. & Chief Oper. Officer--Carousel Snack Bars Of Minnesota, Minneapolis, MN, pg. 224
Liedel, G. Laurence, Pres.--The Betham Corporation, Middlesex, NJ, pg. 147
Lifton, Robert, Chm. Bd.--American Printers & Lithographers, Chicago, IL, pg. 59
Linbeck, Leo E., Jr., Chm. Bd. & Chief Exec. Officer--Linbeck Corp., Houston, TX, pg. 675
Lincoln, George A., Chm. Bd. & Pres.--Lincoln Industries, Lincoln, NE, pg. 676
Lind, Ralph, Corp. Sec. & Controller--St. Croix Press, Inc., New Richmond, WI, pg. 966
Lindahl, Herbert W., Pres. & Chief Oper. Officer--State Industries Inc., Ashland City, TN, pg. 1041
Lindahl, John, Chm. Bd. & Chief Exec. Officer--State Industries Inc., Ashland City, TN, pg. 1041
Lindquist, Dean, Mgr.-Sls.--St. Croix Press, Inc., New Richmond, WI, pg. 966
Lindsay, James W., Chief Exec. Officer--Ag Processing Inc A Cooperative, Omaha, NE, pg. 24
Liniger, Dave, Chm. Bd.--RE/MAX International, Inc., Englewood, CO, pg. 915
Liniger, Gail, Chief Exec. Officer--RE/MAX International, Inc., Englewood, CO, pg. 915
Linn, Randy, Pres.--Linn Products, Inc., Charlotte, MI, pg. 677
Lintz, Robert H., Chm. Bd.--Sterling Homes Corp., Sparks, NV, pg. 1046
Lipke, Brian J., Pres. & Chief Exec. Officer--Gibraltar Steel Corp., Buffalo, NY, pg. 456
Lipke, Neil E., Exec. V.P.--Gibraltar Steel Corp., Buffalo, NY, pg. 456
Lipkin, Edward B., Pres.--National Property Analysts, Inc., Philadelphia, PA, pg. 792
Lipton, Harry, Pres. & Chief Exec. Officer--American Aircraft Parts Manufacturing Co., Dearborn, MI, pg. 48
Little, William Brian, Partner--Forstmann Little & Co., New York, NY, pg. 424
Littlejohn, Angus, Partner--Joseph, Littlejohn & Levy, New York, NY, pg. 607
Litvak, Leonard, Chm. Bd., Pres. & Chief Exec. Officer--Champion Boxed Beef, Denver, CO, pg. 238
Litzsinger, Paul R., Pres. & Chief Exec. Officer--Follett Corporation, Chicago, IL, pg. 422
Liuzzi, R.C., Pres. & Chief Exec. Officer--CF Industries, Inc., Long Grove, IL, pg. 200
Ljungberg, Robert, Chm. Bd., Pres., Chief Exec. & Chief Oper. Officer--Ultra Tool & Plastics, Inc., Amherst, NY, pg. 1125
Llewellyn, John S., Jr., Pres. & Chief Exec. Officer--Ocean Spray Cranberries, Inc., Lakeville, MA, pg. 820
Lobisser, George, Dir.--Pace International Corporation, Kirkland, WA, pg. 838
Lockhart, Keith E., Pres.--Lockhart & Pettus, Inc., New York, NY, pg. 680
Lockwood, Earl F., Pres. & Chief Exec. Officer--Betac International Corporation, Alexandria, VA, pg. 147
Logan, Oran, Pres. & Chief Oper. Officer--Alamo Group, Inc., Seguin, TX, pg. 29
Lombard, George E., Pres. & Chief Exec. Officer--Lombard Company, Alsip, IL, pg. 681
Lorenz, Horzt, Chm. Bd.--Kanex, Cleveland, OH, pg. 616
LoStocco, Ralph J., V.P.-Admin.--Bridgeport Machines, Inc., Bridgeport, CT, pg. 175
Lotter, John G.H., Chm. Bd. & Chief Exec. Officer--H. C. Miller Company, Milwaukee, WI, pg. 754
Love, Donald, Pres.--Clover Financial Corporation, Merchantville, NJ, pg. 256
Lowery, Everet, Controller--Conbraco Industries Inc., Matthews, NC, pg. 272
Lozelle, James R., Pres. & Chief Exec. Officer--Edgewood Tool & Manufacturing Company, Romulus, MI, pg. 368
Ludington, Ivan, Jr., Chm Bd. & Chief Exec. Officer--Ludington News Co. Inc., Detroit, MI, pg. 686
Lurie, Robert A., Chm. Bd.--San Francisco Giants Baseball Club, San Francisco, CA, pg. 969
Lustbader, Brian G., Exec. V.P., Gen. Counsel & Sec.--The P.J. Carlin Construction Company, New Rochelle, NY, pg. 220
Lustbader, Edward E., Chm. Bd., Pres., Chief Exec. Officer & Treas.--The P.J. Carlin Construction Company, New Rochelle, NY, pg. 220
Lynch, Hal, Sec.--Sunrise Nissan of Orange Park, Orange Park, FL, pg. 1062
Lynch, Kevin, Exec. V.P.--HLB Communications, Inc., Chicago, IL, pg. 496
Lynch, Leland T., Chm. & Chief Exec. Officer--Carmichael Lynch, Inc., Minneapolis, MN, pg. 222
Lyon, William, Chm. Bd.--William Lyon Company, Newport Beach, CA, pg. 690
Lyons, William P., Chm. Bd.--Pennex Products Co., Inc., Verona, PA, pg. 858
Mabee, Betty L., Sr. V.P.--Big Bear Supermarkets No. 3, San Diego, CA, pg. 149
Mabee, John C., Chm. Bd.--Big Bear Supermarkets No. 3, San Diego, CA, pg. 149
Mabee, Larry, Pres.--Big Bear Supermarkets No. 3, San Diego, CA, pg. 149
MacConnell, Christopher J., Pres.--Thomson MacConnell Cadillac, Inc., Cincinnati, OH, pg. 1095
MacCready, Paul, Dr., Chm. Bd. & Chief Exec. Officer--Aerovironment, Inc., Monrovia, CA, pg. 22
MacDonald, Reid V., Pres. & Chief Exec. Officer--Faribault Foods Inc., Minneapolis, MN, pg. 399
MacDonald, William F., Jr., Chm. Bd., Pres., Chief Exec. & Chief Oper. Officer--E. F. Houghton & Co., Valley Forge, PA, pg. 546
Mace, Mike E., V.P. & Asst. Sec.--Ballenger Paving Company, Inc., Taylors, SC, pg. 116
Machado, Gus, Pres. & Chief Exec. Officer--Gus Machado Enterprises, Hialeah, FL, pg. 696
Mack, Paul F., Pres.--Mack Printing Company, Easton, PA, pg. 697
MacLean, Barry L., Chm., Pres., Chief Exec. & Chief Oper. Officer--Maclean-Fogg Co., Mundelein, IL, pg. 697
MacLeod, Malcolm W., Pres. & Chief Exec. Officer--Moran Towing & Transportation Co. Inc, Greenwich, CT, pg. 769
Magnano, Louis A., Pres. & Chief Exec. Officer--Blue Bird Coach Lines Inc., Olean, NY, pg. 158
Maguire, Cary M., Pres.--Maguire Oil Co., Dallas, TX, pg. 701
Maguire, Robert F., III, Mng. Partner--Maguire Thomas Partners, Los Angeles, CA, pg. 701
Mahon, Daniel J., V.P.-Fin.--Thermo Electric Co., Inc., Saddle Brook, NJ, pg. 1091
Mahoney, P. Michael, Pres.--Bankmanagers Corp., Milwaukee, WI, pg. 118
Mahr, Malcolm, Chm. Bd.--Maryland Paper Box Company, Baltimore, MD, pg. 717
Mahr, Michael, Pres.--Maryland Paper Box Company, Baltimore, MD, pg. 717
Mailow, Anders E., V.P.-New Devel.--Graphic Controls Corporation, Buffalo, NY, pg. 478
Makhani, Madan P., Chm. Bd., Pres., Chief Oper. Officer & Chief Fin. Officer--American Foundry Group, Inc., Bixby, OK, pg. 54
Maki, Glen, Pres.--Maki Corporation, Lunenburg, MA, pg. 702
Malkani, Roma, Pres. & Chief Exec. Officer--Information Systems & Network Corporation, Bethesda, MD, pg. 567
Mallen, David J., Chief Fin. Officer & Sr. V.P.-Employee Benefits--Wilder Management Associates, Waltham, MA, pg. 1189
Mallett, J.L., Pres.--Thomas Pipe & Steel, Inc., Baton Rouge, LA, pg. 1093
Mallott, Bryon I., Pres. & Chief Exec. Officer--Sealaska Corporation, Juneau, AK, pg. 984
Malott, Charles T., Partner & Dir.-Admin.--J. C. Bradford & Co., Nashville, TN, pg. 170
Maltzman, Donald, Chm. Bd.--Tomco Auto Products, Inc., Vernon, CA, pg. 1100
Mango, Wilfred G., Jr., Pres. & Chief Exec. Officer--George A. Fuller Company, New York, NY, pg. 436
Marberg, Edwin, Pres., Chief Exec. Officer & Treas.--MCM Enterprises, Inc., Crawfordsville, IN, pg. 691
Margalith, Ethan Harold, Chm. Bd., Chief Exec. Officer & Treas.--Starving Students, Inc., Los Angeles, CA, pg. 1040
Margolis, Milton J., Vice Chm.--Host Apparel, Inc., New York, NY, pg. 545
Marinucci, Lisa W., Sec.--Marquette Coppersmithing Co., Inc., Philadelphia, PA, pg. 713
Marion, James P., Jr., Chm. Bd.--Bloomsburg Mills Inc., New York, NY, pg. 158
Marischen, Robert J., Pres.--Huntco Inc., Chesterfield, MO, pg. 554
Markin, William R., Chm. & Chief Exec. Officer--Lauerer Markin Gibbs, Inc., Maumee, OH, pg. 660
Markos, Dennis, Chief Exec. Officer--Penda Corporation, Portage, WI, pg. 857
Marks, Marilyn, Pres. & Chief Exec. Officer--Dorsey Trailers, Inc., Atlanta, GA, pg. 347
Marks, Peter, Contact-Mergers & Acquisitions & Dir.-Plng. & Devel.--Weksler Instruments Corp., Freeport, NY, pg. 1174
Marks, Sam, Exec. V.P., Corp. Sec. & Dir.-Pur.--Triangle Marketing Corp., New York, NY, pg. 1112
Marlett, Glen C., V.P.--St. Croix Press, Inc., New Richmond, WI, pg. 966
Marmis, Cary, Chm. Bd. & Pres.--Empire West Companies, Inc., Tucson, AZ, pg. 380
Marshall, Richard J., V.P.-Opers. & Legal Counsel--Maverik Country Stores, Inc., Afton, WY, pg. 722
Marsilius, N.M. III, Pres. & Treas.--The Producto Machine Co., Bridgeport, CT, pg. 893
Marsilius, Philip R., Chm. Bd.--The Producto Machine Co., Bridgeport, CT, pg. 893
Martin O'Neill, Chm. Bd.--Bata Shoe Co., Inc., Belcamp, MD, pg. 201
Martin, Gordon, Chm. Bd., Pres. & Chief Exec. Officer--Martin Forest Industries, Healdsburg, CA, pg. 715
Martindale, William A., Chm. Bd., Pres. & Chief Exec. Officer--Martrade Ltd., Santa Fe Springs, CA, pg. 716
Martire, Robert, Chm. Bd. & Pres.--Atlantic to Pacific Bedding Corp., Bronx, NY, pg. 95

Masek, Fred F., Chm. Bd.--Masek Distributing Inc., Gering, NE, pg. 717
Massman, Henry J., IV, Pres.--Massman Construction Company, Kansas City, MO, pg. 719
Mathis, Jim, V.P.-Mktg., Sec. & Treas.--Precision Parts Corp., Morristown, TN, pg. 885
Matthews Arthur, Carol, V.P.--Carroll's Foods, Inc., Warsaw, NC, pg. 225
Matthews, James, V.P.--Carroll's Foods, Inc., Warsaw, NC, pg. 225
Matthews, Jeffrey, V.P.--Carroll's Foods, Inc., Warsaw, NC, pg. 225
Matthews, Joyce Carroll, Chm. Bd., Sec. & Treas.--Carroll's Foods, Inc., Warsaw, NC, pg. 225
Mattison, A.M., Pres.--Mattison Machine Works, Rockford, IL, pg. 721
Mattison, P.L., Jr., V.P. & Sec.--Mattison Machine Works, Rockford, IL, pg. 721
Matz, V., Pres.--Kirk & Matz Ltd., Danbury, CT, pg. 633
Maughan, Rex, Chm. Bd., Pres. & Chief Exec. Officer--Forever Living Products, Tempe, AZ, pg. 424
Mauldin, W. Crayton, Sr. V.P. & Controller--Leslie Advertising, Greenville, SC, pg. 668
Mauloff, Greg, Pres.--NWS, Inc., Chicago, IL, pg. 782
Mauney, Charles F., Exec. V.P. & Chief Oper. Officer--Mauney Hosiery Mills, Inc., Kings Mountain, NC, pg. 722
Mauney, William K., III, Pres.--Mauney Hosiery Mills, Inc., Kings Mountain, NC, pg. 722
Mauney, William K., Jr., Chm. Bd.--Mauney Hosiery Mills, Inc., Kings Mountain, NC, pg. 722
Maurey, Joseph E., Chm. Bd. & Pres.--Maurey Manufacturing Corp., Chicago, IL, pg. 722
Maurin, James E., Pres.--The Maurin-Odgen Companies, New Orleans, LA, pg. 722
Mautz, Bernhard F., Jr., Pres.--Mautz Paint Company, Madison, WI, pg. 722
Maxwell, Joseph D., V.P.-Mktg.--TSC Industries, Inc., Nashville, TN, pg. 1075
Maxwell, R. L., Pres. & Chief Exec. Officer--The Lathrop Company, Toledo, OH, pg. 660
May, Henry L., Pres.--The May Apparel Group, Inc., Mebane, NC, pg. 723
May, John, Chm. Bd.--The May Apparel Group, Inc., Mebane, NC, pg. 723
Maynard, John C., Pres.--Maywood, Inc., Amarillo, TX, pg. 725
Mays, William, Chm. Bd. & Pres.--Mays Chemical Company, Indianapolis, IN, pg. 725
McAdams, H. Hall, III, Chm. Bd.--The Union of Arkansas Corp., Little Rock, AR, pg. 1127
McAtee, James C., Pres.--Electric Power Equipment Co., Columbus, OH, pg. 373
McCaffery, W., Pres. & Dir.-Creative Services--McCaffery & Ratner, Inc., New York, NY, pg. 726
McCain, William B., Chm. Bd.--McCain Manufacturing Corp., Chicago, IL, pg. 726
McCall, Ronald L., Vice Chm., Chief Exec. Officer, Chief Fin. Officer & Treas.--M. B. Kahn Construction Co., Inc., Columbia, SC, pg. 614
McCarter, John N., Jr., Sr. V.P.--Defender Services, Inc., Columbia, SC, pg. 324
McCarthy, Michael M., Chm. Bd.--McCarthy Building Companies, Saint Louis, MO, pg. 727
McCleary, James K., Chief Exec. Officer--AmeriData, Inc., Minneapolis, MN, pg. 66
McCormick, Rick M., Pres. & Chief Oper. Officer--Eastway Delivery Service of Houston, Inc., Houston, TX, pg. 364
McCormick, Robert, Exec. V.P.--Abelson-Taylor, Inc., Chicago, IL, pg. 10
McCoy, Duncan, Pres. & Chief Exec. Officer--New Texas Tumbleweed, Houston, TX, pg. 802
McCoy, Michael A., Pres.--Associated Process Controls, Pleasanton, CA, pg. 92
McCullough, R. Michael, Sr. Partner--Booz Allen & Hamilton Inc., New York, NY, pg. 165
McDonald, Charles R., Chm., Pres. & Chief Exec. Officer--McDonald Equipment Co., Willoughby, OH, pg. 728
McDonald, Thomas C., Chm. Bd.--Grindmaster Corporation, Louisville, KY, pg. 488
McDougal, Alfred L., Chief Exec. Officer--McDougal, Littell & Company, Evanston, IL, pg. 728
McDowell, James W., Exec. V.P. & Chief Exec. Officer--Dairymen, Inc., Louisville, KY, pg. 311
McElwee, Arthur, Chm. Bd. & Pres.--Goshen Rubber Co., Inc., Goshen, IN, pg. 472
McEvoy, A.P., Jr., Pres.--Western Extrusions, Carrollton, TX, pg. 1179
McFarland, Howard C., III, Chief Oper. Officer & Chief Fin. Officer--Mid-West Paper Products Company, Warren, MI, pg. 750
McFarland, William C., Chm. Bd. & Treas.--McFarland & Drier, Inc., Miami, FL, pg. 729
McGehee, Frank S., Co-Chm. Bd.--Mac Papers, Inc., Jacksonville, FL, pg. 694
McGehee, Thomas R., Co-Chm Bd. & Chief Exec. Officer--Mac Papers, Inc., Jacksonville, FL, pg. 694
McGill, James D., Pres.--United McGill Corp., Groveport, OH, pg. 1133
McGill, Jayne F., Sec.--United McGill Corp., Groveport, OH, pg. 1133
McGlothlin, James W., Chm. Bd. & Pres.--The United Company, Bristol, VA, pg. 1131
McGovern, Patrick J., Chm. Bd.--International Data Group, Boston, MA, pg. 576
McGrath, Brent P., Chief Fin. Officer, Treas. & Sec.--Mico Inc., North Mankato, MN, pg. 748
McGrath, Daniel S., V.P.-Sls.--Mico Inc., North Mankato, MN, pg. 748
McGrath, G.J., Chm. Bd. & Pres.--Mico Inc., North Mankato, MN, pg. 748
McGrath, J. Brian, Chm. Bd.--Executive Enterprises, Inc., New York, NY, pg. 393
McGuinan, Mr., Chm.--Baker & McKenzie International, Chicago, IL, pg. 115
McIlhenny, Paul C.P., V.P. & Sec.--McIlhenny Company, Avery Island, LA, pg. 729
McIlrath, James A., Pres.--Dry Storage Corporation, Des Plaines, IL, pg. 350
McIvor, Patrick J., Pres. & Chief Exec. Officer--Simms & McIvor Marketing Communications, Somerville, NJ, pg. 1005
McKee, Ellsworth, Pres. & Chief Exec. Officer--McKee Foods Corporation, Collegedale, TN, pg. 730
McKee, Jack C., Exec. V.P. & Chief Oper. Officer--McKee Foods Corporation, Collegedale, TN, pg. 730
McKee, O.D., Chm. Bd.--McKee Foods Corporation, Collegedale, TN, pg. 730
McKenna, P.W., Chm. Bd., Pres. & Chief Oper. Officer--Plasti-Kote Company Inc., Medina, OH, pg. 875
McKeown, John M., Pres.--Krommenhoek McKeown Associates, San Diego, CA, pg. 645
McKinnon, T. Benson, Pres. & Chief Exec. Officer--McKinnon Bridge Co., Franklin, TN, pg. 731
McKissick, A. Foster, III, Pres.--Fairway Ford, Inc., Greenville, SC, pg. 397
McKittrick, Leo, V.P.--PSI Group of Companies, Memphis, TN, pg. 837
McLean, Lee, Jr., Pres.--McLean Enterprises, Inc., Springfield, MO, pg. 731
McLeod, John S., Jr., V.P.-Mktg.--Mar-Mac Manufacturing Company, Inc., McBee, SC, pg. 705
McLeod, John S., Sr., Pres.--Mar-Mac Manufacturing Company, Inc., McBee, SC, pg. 705
McMichael, John, Pres.--Bob Frink Chevrolet G.E.O. Management, Sacramento, CA, pg. 433
McMullen, Walter P., Sr., Chm. Bd. & Chief Exec. Officer--Lithograph Printing Company, Inc., Memphis, TN, pg. 678
McNally, John, Exec. V.P.--JM Family Enterprises Inc., Deerfield Beach, FL, pg. 584
McNaughton, Robert L., Pres.--McNaughton & Gunn, Inc., Saline, MI, pg. 732
McVaney, C. Edward, Chm. Bd., Pres. & Chief Exec. Officer--J.D. Edwards & Company, Denver, CO, pg. 370
McWilliams, Alexander M., Pres.--McWilliams Forge Co., Rockaway, NJ, pg. 733
McWilliams, Timothy C., Exec. V.P.--McWilliams Forge Co., Rockaway, NJ, pg. 733
Medary, William, Pres. & Chief Exec. Officer--Bass Enterprises Production Company, Fort Worth, TX, pg. 125
Medler, Albert, Vice Chm.--Plastigage Corporation, Jackson, MI, pg. 876
Meehan, Terry, V.P. & Dir.-Software Devel.--Periphonics Corp., Bohemia, NY, pg. 862
Meissner, Harold C., Vice Chm.--Andersen Windows Inc., Bayport, MN, pg. 72
Mele, Edward V., Chm. Bd.--Mele Manufacturing Co., Inc., Utica, NY, pg. 737
Mele, Joseph E., V.P.--Mele Manufacturing Co., Inc., Utica, NY, pg. 737
Melman, Richard, Pres.--Lettuce Entertain You Enterprises, Inc., Chicago, IL, pg. 668
Meloon, Ralph C., Sr., Chm. Bd.--Correct Craft, Inc., Orlando, FL, pg. 287
Meloon, Walter O., Treas.--Correct Craft, Inc., Orlando, FL, pg. 287
Mendenhall, O.C., Vice Chm.--Fiesta Mart Inc., Houston, TX, pg. 409
Meng, J., Chief Fin. Officer--David Langer & Co., Inc., Hollywood, CA, pg. 657
Mertes, Wayne, Pres.--National R.V., Inc., Perris, CA, pg. 792
Meyer, Bernard, Pres. & Chief Oper. Officer--Allright Corporation, Houston, TX, pg. 41
Meyer, Joseph, V.P.-Vegetable Oil & Export Soybean Meal--Ag Processing Inc A Cooperative, Omaha, NE, pg. 24
Meyer, Robert L., Pres.--Meyer & Wallis, Inc., Milwaukee, WI, pg. 746
Meyer, Ronald, Exec. V.P.-Opers.--Gateway Apparel, Inc., Saint Louis, MO, pg. 445
Meyers, Robert G., Sr. V.P.--Defender Services, Inc., Columbia, SC, pg. 324
Michael, David, Pres.--Professional Apartment Management, Inc., Lodi, CA, pg. 893
Michael, Joseph, Chm.--Professional Apartment Management, Inc., Lodi, CA, pg. 893
Michaels, John H., V.P.--Michaels Group Inc., Latham, NY, pg. 747
Michelson, James A., Pres.--Simons Michelson Zieve, Inc., Troy, MI, pg. 1006
Michelson, Lawrence J., V.P.--Simons Michelson Zieve, Inc., Troy, MI, pg. 1006
Mikon, Arnold, Pres. & Chief Exec. Officer--The Smith Group, Inc., Detroit, MI, pg. 1012
Milenthal, David, Chm. Bd.--Hameroff/Milenthal/Spence, Inc., Columbus, OH, pg. 503
Milenthal, Richard K., Exec. V.P.--Hameroff/Milenthal/Spence, Inc., Columbus, OH, pg. 503
Miles, Rod, Chief Fin. Officer--Cappelli Miles Wiltz & Kelly, Portland, OR, pg. 216
Miles, Ronald, V.P.-Property Mngmt.--Regency Associates Limited Partnership, Evansville, IN, pg. 922
Millard, Suzanne T., Chm. Bd. & Pres.--Turtle & Hughes, Inc., Linden, NJ, pg. 1119
Millenson, Elliott, Pres.--Pollenex Corporation, Chicago, IL, pg. 821
Miller, Arnold, Treas.--Quill Corp., Lincolnshire, IL, pg. 905
Miller, Augustus C., Chm. Bd., Pres., Chief Exec. Officer--Miller Oil Co., Inc., Norfolk, VA, pg. 754
Miller, Bill, Pres., Chief Exec. & Chief Oper. Officer--Contico International, Inc., Saint Louis, MO, pg. 278
Miller, Don, Pres. & Chief Exec. Officer--Ederer Inc., Seattle, WA, pg. 368
Miller, Harvey L., Sec.--Quill Corp., Lincolnshire, IL, pg. 905
Miller, Jack, Pres.--Quill Corp., Lincolnshire, IL, pg. 905
Miller, John C., Pres.--Miller-St. Nazianz, Inc., Saint Nazianz, WI, pg. 755
Miller, Larry, Chm. Bd., Pres. & Chief Exec. Officer--Corinthian Media, Inc., New York, NY, pg. 286
Miller, Lester, Chm. Bd.--Contico International, Inc., Saint Louis, MO, pg. 278
Miller, Opha H., Chm. Bd.--Miller & Co., Selma, AL, pg. 753
Miller, Robert S., Chm. Bd. & Chief Exec. Officer--Better Baked Foods, Inc., North East, PA, pg. 148
Miller, Stuart A., Pres.--Miller Products Company, Inc., North Bergen, NJ, pg. 755
Milroy, Robert C., Pres.--Alexander Marketing Services, Inc., Grand Rapids, MI, pg. 33
Miniat, Edmund, Chief Fin. Officer & Treas.--Ed Miniat, Inc., Chicago, IL, pg. 757
Miniat, Edmund, Jr., Exec. V.P.--Ed Miniat, Inc., Chicago, IL, pg. 757
Miniat, Ronald, Chm., Pres. & Chief Exec. Officer--Ed Miniat, Inc., Chicago, IL, pg. 757
Minkus, Morton D., Pres.--Transilwrap Company, Inc., Chicago, IL, pg. 1107
Minnick, Terry, Chm. Bd., Pres. & Chief Exec. Officer--The Pro Corporation, Florence, MA, pg. 891
Minyard, Bob L., Chm. Exec. Committee--Minyard Food Stores, Coppell, TX, pg. 759
Minyard, Lisbeth, Co-Chm. Bd. & Treas.--Minyard Food Stores, Coppell, TX, pg. 759
Miska, Steven M., Chm. Bd. & Chief Exec. Officer--Generra Sportswear Company, Inc., Tukwila, WA, pg. 451
Mitchel, Michael M., V.P.--Economy Folding Box Corp., Chicago, IL, pg. 367
Mitchell, William F., Chm. Bd., Pres. & Chief Exec. Officer--Mitchell Corporation of Owosso, Owosso, MI, pg. 761
Mitchum, Billy E., Sec. & Treas.--Defender Services, Inc., Columbia, SC, pg. 324
Moeller, Richard J., Pres.--Advanstar Communications, Cleveland, OH, pg. 21
Moilanen, Thomas A., Pres. & Chief Exec. Officer--Cloverdale Equipment Co., Oak Park, MI, pg. 256
Moloney, Earl, Chm. Bd. & Chief Exec. Officer--Molon Motor & Coil Corp., Rolling Meadows, IL, pg. 764
Molz, Otis, Chm. Bd.--Farmland Industries, Inc., Kansas City, MO, pg. 402
Monaghan, Thomas S., Chm. Bd., Pres. & Chief Exec. Officer--Domino's Pizza Inc., Ann Arbor, MI, pg. 344
Monette, Edward A., Chm., Pres., Chief Exec. & Oper. Officer--St. Croix Press, Inc., New Richmond, WI, pg. 966
Monkiewicz, Ray C., Pres.--Kayem Foods, Inc., Chelsea, MA, pg. 619
Montanus, Phil, Pres.-Devel.--Towne Properties, Cincinnati, OH, pg. 1104
Montgomery, Christian, Exec. V.P.-Mktg.--Andy Frain Services, Inc., Chicago, IL, pg. 428
Montgomery, William, Chm. Bd., Pres., & Chief Exec. Officer--The SArgent-SOwell Company, Grand Prairie, TX, pg. 971
Moody, Maxey D., III, Pres.--M. D. Moody & Sons Inc., Jacksonville, FL, pg. 768
Moody, T.B., V.P.--M. D. Moody & Sons Inc., Jacksonville, FL, pg. 768
Mooney, Edward P., V.P. & Chief Oper. Officer--Monsey Products Company, Kimberton, PA, pg. 766
Mooney, Joseph T., Jr., Pres.--Monsey Products Company, Kimberton, PA, pg. 766
Moore, Harold, Chm. Bd.--Harold Moore & Associates, Inc., Fayetteville, TN, pg. 768
Moore, Michael, Pres.--Sun Process Converting Company, Elk Grove Village, IL, pg. 1059
Moore, Michael J., Chm. Bd. & Pres.--Southland Industries, Long Beach, CA, pg. 1023
Moore, Steven R., Pres.--Rex Moore Electrical Contractors & Engineers, West Sacramento, CA, pg. 768
Moore, William E., Chm. Bd.--Kelly-Moore Paint Company, Inc., San Carlos, CA, pg. 621
Moos, J. Clifford, Chm., Pres. & Chief Exec. Officer--Economy Folding Box Corp., Chicago, IL, pg. 367
Moran, James M., Chm. Bd.--JM Family Enterprises Inc., Deerfield Beach, FL, pg. 584
Moran, James M., Jr., Exec. V.P.-Mktg.--JM Family Enterprises Inc., Deerfield Beach, FL, pg. 584
Moran, Patricia, Pres. & Chief Exec. Officer--JM Family Enterprises Inc., Deerfield Beach, FL, pg. 584
Moran, Thomas E., Chm. Bd.--Moran Towing & Transporation Co. Inc, Greenwich, CT, pg. 769
Morgan, John S., Chm., Pres. & Chief Exec. Officer--Morgan Foods, Inc., Austin, IN, pg. 770
Morgan, Robert, Pres.--Morgan Manufacturing Company, Inc., Paris, IL, pg. 770
Morgan, V. Harley, Exec. V.P. & Sec.--Northwest Paper Converting Company, Vancouver, WA, pg. 814
Morgensen, Jerry L., Pres.--Hensel Phelps Construction Co., Greeley, CO, pg. 530
Morris, Andrew, Pres. & Chief Oper. Officer--Warner, Bicking, Morris & Partners, Inc., New York, NY, pg. 1164
Morris, Ann P., Sec.--Peirce-Phelps, Inc., Philadelphia, PA, pg. 855
Morris, Leslie M., Jr., Pres.--Sands Investments, Inc., Myrtle Beach, SC, pg. 970
Morrison, Richard S., Pres. & Chief Exec. Officer--Molded Fiber Glass Companies, Ashtabula, OH, pg. 763
Morse, Edward J., Jr., V.P.--Morse Operations Inc., Ft. Lauderdale, FL, pg. 772
Morse, Edward J., Sr., Chm. Bd. & Pres.--Morse Operations Inc., Ft. Lauderdale, FL, pg. 772
Mosack, Carl L., Pres.--Conbraco Industries Inc., Matthews, NC, pg. 272
Moscowitz, Edwin, Pres.--Peerless Umbrella Co., Inc., Harrison, NJ, pg. 855
Moseley, F.C., Pres.--Simpson Investment Co., Seattle, WA, pg. 1007
Moshontz, Michael, Pres.--Blue Coral, Inc., Cleveland, OH, pg. 159
Moss, Cruse W., Chm. Bd. & Chief Exec. Officer--General Automotive Corporation, Ann Arbor, MI, pg. 448

Moss, Victor, Pres. & Sec.--Tomco Auto Products, Inc., Vernon, CA, pg. 1100
Mossberg, Alan I., Pres., Chief Exec. & Chief Oper. Officer & Treas.--O. F. Mossberg & Sons, Inc., North Haven, CT, pg. 773
Motta, Robert D., Pres.--Southwest Floor Covering Inc., San Diego, CA, pg. 1023
Mount, Gary, Mgr.-Production--Alkota Cleaning Systems, Inc., Alcester, SD, pg. 34
Moyer, William C., Dr., Chm. Bd., Pres. & Chief Exec. Officer--SFA, Inc., Landover, MD, pg. 961
Mueller, John S., Chm. & Chief Exec. Officer--Laidlaw Corporation, Scottsdale, AZ, pg. 650
Mueller, Judy, Dir.-Opers.--Times Printing Company, Inc., Random Lake, WI, pg. 1098
Muer, Charles A., Pres.--C. A. Muer Corp., Detroit, MI, pg. 774
Mulligan, James, Pres.--M M M Sales, Inc., City of Industry, CA, pg. 692
Mulligan, Robert J., Vice Chm. & Chief Admin. Officer--Woodward & Lothrop/John Wanamaker, Washington, DC, pg. 1201
Mullins, Roy L., Jr., Pres. & Chief Exec. Officer--Beacon Sales Corporation, Jacksonville, FL, pg. 129
Mullis, Wayne, Chm. Bd.--Bryant Universal Roofers Inc., Phoenix, AZ, pg. 185
Murdock, David H., Pres. & Chief Exec. Officer--Pacific Holding Corporation, Los Angeles, CA, pg. 840
Muro, Roy A., Chm. & Chief Exec. Officer--Vitt Media International, Inc., New York, NY, pg. 1153
Murphy, Robert E., Pres.--Japs-Olson Company, Minneapolis, MN, pg. 590
Murray, Norman J., Chm. Bd.--The Airolite Company, Marietta, OH, pg. 28
Muse, Albert C., Pres. & Chief Exec. Officer--Crown Coal & Coke Co. Inc., Pittsburgh, PA, pg. 302
Muse, Charles H., Jr., Treas. & Chief Fin. Officer--Crown Coal & Coke Co. Inc., Pittsburgh, PA, pg. 302
Mushkin, Albert S., Pres. & Chief Oper. Officer--Master Industries Corp., New York, NY, pg. 719
Musick, Gary D., V.P.-Sls.--Houston Foods Company, Chicago, IL, pg. 547
Must, Alan, Pres.--Detroit City Dairy, Inc., Highland Park, MI, pg. 333
Must, Joel, Pres.-Warehouse--Detroit City Dairy, Inc., Highland Park, MI, pg. 333
Must, Meyer, Chm. Bd.--Detroit City Dairy, Inc., Highland Park, MI, pg. 333
Mutz, O.U., Pres.--Sovereign Group Inc., Indianapolis, IN, pg. 1024
Muzyczko, T., Exec. V.P.--Bingham, Mt. Prospect, IL, pg. 151
Myers, C.C., Pres. & Chief Exec. Officer--C. C. Myers, Inc., Rancho Cordova, CA, pg. 780
Myers, Francis J., Jr., Pres.--F J M Corporation, Elk Grove Village, IL, pg. 394
Myers, John, V.P.--F J M Corporation, Elk Grove Village, IL, pg. 394
Myers, Joseph E., Chm. Bd. & Pres.--Collins Oldsmobile Inc., Indianapolis, IN, pg. 263
Myers, L.G., Pres., Chief Exec. Officer & Admin. Dir.--LubeCon Systems, Inc., Fremont, MI, pg. 686
Nady, John, Pres. & Chief Exec. Officer--Nady Systems, Inc., Emeryville, CA, pg. 783
Najjar, William K., Chm. Bd.--Ranir Corporation, Grand Rapids, MI, pg. 912
Nash, Amelia J., Exec. V.P.--Universal Securities Corporation, Birmingham, AL, pg. 1139
Nash, Samuel T., Jr., Pres.--Universal Securities Corporation, Birmingham, AL, pg. 1139
Nason, Walton H., Jr., Chm. Bd.--Nason and Cullen, Inc., Wayne, PA, pg. 784
Nast, Glen M., Pres. & Treas.--Northern Wire & Cable, Inc., Troy, MI, pg. 814
Natale, M.A., V.P.--The Betham Corporation, Middlesex, NJ, pg. 147
Naumann, George F., Chm. Bd. & Chief Exec. Officer--Victaulic Company of America, Easton, PA, pg. 1149
Neal, John R., Chm. Bd. & Pres.--JRN, Inc., Columbia, TN, pg. 586
Needham, Tom, Chm., Pres. & Chief Exec. Officer--Allen & Hoshall, Inc., Memphis, TN, pg. 36
Neely, Bill, Pres. & Chief Oper. Officer--M. B. Kahn Construction Co., Inc., Columbia, SC, pg. 614
Nelsen, C. Davis, II, Exec. V.P.--Nelsen Steel & Wire Co., Franklin Park, IL, pg. 797
Nelsen, Clifford D., Chm. Bd. & Pres.--Nelsen Steel & Wire Co., Franklin Park, IL, pg. 797
Nelsen, Leif A., Treas.--Nelsen Steel & Wire Co., Franklin Park, IL, pg. 797
Nelson, Dan, Chm. & Chief Exec. Officer--Nelson & Schmidt, Inc., Milwaukee, WI, pg. 797
Nelson, James, Owner & Pres.--The Butcher Co., Marlborough, MA, pg. 196
Nelson, Stuart K., Sr. V.P. & Gen. Counsel--Sanford C. Bernstein & Co., Inc., New York, NY, pg. 144
Nemschoff, Leonard, Chm. Bd. & Sec.--Nemschoff Chairs, Inc., Sheboygan, WI, pg. 798
Nemschoff, Mark, Pres., Chief Exec. Officer & Treas.--Nemschoff Chairs, Inc., Sheboygan, WI, pg. 798
Nerad, Jerry, Pres.--TimeMed Labeling Systems, Inc., Burr Ridge, IL, pg. 1098
Nerby, Dennis, Exec. V.P.--PSI Group of Companies, Memphis, TN, pg. 837
Nesler, Robert, V.P.-DG Trim--Indian Head Industries Inc., Southfield, MI, pg. 565
Neumann, Dr. Myrel, Pres. & Chief Exec. Officer--Midwest Vision Centers, Sauk Rapids, MN, pg. 752
Neumann, Frank G., Pres.--Valu Discount, Inc., Louisville, KY, pg. 1143
Newcomer, David W. IV, Pres. & Partner--D. W. Newcomer's Sons, Inc., Kansas City, MO, pg. 804
Newcomer, F. Peter, Partner--D. W. Newcomer's Sons, Inc., Kansas City, MO, pg. 804
Newcomer, Frank III, Partner--D. W. Newcomer's Sons, Inc., Kansas City, MO, pg. 804
Newell, Jack, Dir.-Mktg., Communications & Adv.--The ERM Group, Exton, PA, pg. 360
Newgard, J. Richard, Pres. & Chief Exec. Officer--Henry Newgard & Company, Arlington Heights, IL, pg. 804
Newgard, James H., Sec. & Treas.--Henry Newgard & Company, Arlington Heights, IL, pg. 804
Newhouse, Samuel I., Jr., Chm. Bd. & Chief Exec. Officer--Advance Publications Inc., Staten Island, NY, pg. 19
Newkirk, Gerry, Exec. V.P.--TSC Industries, Inc., Nashville, TN, pg. 1075
Newman, Edward G., V.P.--Chilewich Partners, White Plains, NY, pg. 248
Newman, Stephen C., Treas. & Dir.--RNL Facilities Corporation, Denver, CO, pg. 907
Nicholson, James B., Pres. & Chief Exec. Officer--PVS Chemicals, Inc., Detroit, MI, pg. 837
Nickels, William C., Chm. Bd.--Replogle Globes, Inc., Broadview, IL, pg. 927
Nickerson, J.T., V.P.-Mfg.--Southern Ohio Fabricators, Inc., Cincinnati, OH, pg. 1022
Nierenberg, Roy A., Pres.--Experience in Software, Inc., Berkeley, CA, pg. 393
Niermeyer, David A., Pres.--Stakmore Inc., Owego, NY, pg. 1035
Noland, L.U., Jr., Chm. Bd.--Basic Construction Company, Newport News, VA, pg. 124
Norman, Reeve, Vice-Chm., Pres. & Chief Exec. Officer--Electrical Wholesale Supply Company, Inc., Idaho Falls, ID, pg. 374
Nunley, Richard L., Chm. Bd., Pres. & Treas.--Better Living Inc., Charlottesville, VA, pg. 148
O'Brien, John D., Mng. Partner, V.P.-Human Resources--Borg-Warner Corporation, Chicago, IL, pg. 165
O'Brien, Kevin, V.P.-Fin.--Periphonics Corp., Bohemia, NY, pg. 862
O'Bryan, Michael L., Pres.--O'Bryan Brothers Inc., Chicago, IL, pg. 820
O'Bryan, Stephen F., V.P.--O'Bryan Brothers Inc., Chicago, IL, pg. 820
O'Connor, Laurence P., Chm. Bd. & Chief Exec. Officer--Unigard Security Insurance Co., Bellevue, WA, pg. 596
O'Donnell, Owen, Pres. & Chief Exec. Officer--Management Dynamics, New Providence, NJ, pg. 703
O'Malia, George Joe, Chm. Bd.--O'Malia Food Markets Inc., Noblesville, IN, pg. 825
O'Mara, A. James, Chm. Bd. & Chief Exec. Officer--Greenhorne & O'Mara, Inc., Greenbelt, MD, pg. 485
O'Neil, W.E., Pres.--O'Neil Industries Inc., Chicago, IL, pg. 827
O'Neill, Donal Kieran, Chm. Bd., Pres. & Chief Exec. Officer--Ed Taylor Construction Co., Tucker, GA, pg. 1081
O'Neill, John, Pres.--Berwick Bay Oil Co. Inc., Morgan City, LA, pg. 144
O'Neill, W. McKerall, Jr., Chm. Bd.--Berwick Bay Oil Co. Inc., Morgan City, LA, pg. 144
O'Rourke, Gerald J., Pres.--A & A Manufacturing Co., New Berlin, WI, pg. 1
O'Rourke, Ruth E., Chm. & Treas.--A & A Manufacturing Co., New Berlin, WI, pg. 1
O'Shaughnessy, John, Treas.--Consolidated Beverages, Inc., Auburn, MA, pg. 276
O'Shea, Kevin, Co-Pres.--The Myers Group (U.S) Inc., Rouses Point, NY, pg. 780
Oates, James, Pres. & Partner--Whitehawk Partnership, Pasadena, CA, pg. 1186
Oatway, Francis C., Pres. & Chief Exec. Officer--Hargro Enterprises, Inc., Stamford, CT, pg. 509
Oberweis, Elaine, Pres.--Oberweis Dairy, Inc., Aurora, IL, pg. 820
Oberweis, Marie, Sec.--Oberweis Dairy, Inc., Aurora, IL, pg. 820
Oertli, Charles W., Chm. Bd.--Guarantee Electrical Company, Saint Louis, MO, pg. 490
Oertli, Fred G., Jr., Pres.--Guarantee Electrical Company, Saint Louis, MO, pg. 490
Oertli, Fred J., Chm. Exec. Committee--Guarantee Electrical Company, Saint Louis, MO, pg. 490
Ogden, Roger H., Chm. Bd.--The Maurin-Odgen Companies, New Orleans, LA, pg. 722
Ohaus, James, Pres.--Ohaus Corporation, Florham Park, NJ, pg. 822
Oldham, Noble, Pres. & Chief Exec. Officer--Artco-Bell Corporation, Temple, TX, pg. 86
Olesen, Victor L., Pres.--Vic Olesen & Partners, Inc., Los Angeles, CA, pg. 824
Oleson, Dr. Douglas E., Pres. & Chief Exec. Officer--Battelle Memorial Institute, Columbus, OH, pg. 126
Ollinger, R.J., Pres.--Harris Ford, Inc., Lynnwood, WA, pg. 512
Olsen, David A., Chm., Pres., Chief Exec. & Chief Oper. Officer--Johnson & Higgins, New York, NY, pg. 598
Olsen, Fred, Chm. Bd.--Timex Corporation, Middlebury, CT, pg. 1098
Olsson, Walter S., Partner--Roney & Co., Detroit, MI, pg. 946
Omer, Don C., Pres.--Inland Associates, Olathe, KS, pg. 570
Onstead, R. Randall, Jr., Pres. & Chief Oper. Officer--Randall's Food Markets, Inc., Houston, TX, pg. 911
Opler, Edmond, Jr., Chm. Bd., Pres. & Chief Exec. Officer--World's Finest Chocolate, Inc., Chicago, IL, pg. 1203
Oren, John R., Chm. Bd. & Chief Exec. Officer--Eastway Delivery Service of Houston, Inc., Houston, TX, pg. 364
Orrico, Eugene, Pres.--Keeners, Inc., Seattle, WA, pg. 620
Ortiz, Ralph, Office Mgr.--Rabco Health Service, New York, NY, pg. 908
Osterneck, Guy-Kenneth, Chm. Bd., Pres. & Treas.--The Osterneck Co. Inc., Lumberton, NC, pg. 831
Osterneck, Myles, V.P.-Sls.--The Osterneck Co. Inc., Lumberton, NC, pg. 831
Otakie, Daniel A., Chm., Pres., Chief Exec. Officer & Treas.--Futures Personnel Services, Baltimore, MD, pg. 438
Otero, Richard J., Chm., Pres. & Chief Exec. Officer--RJO Enterprises, Inc., Lanham, MD, pg. 907
Ott, Robert B., Chm. Bd.--The Hennegan Company, Cincinnati, OH, pg. 529
Oudt, John, Chm. Bd.--Barq's, Inc., New Orleans, LA, pg. 121
Ouimet, Emil R., Chm. Bd. & Treas.--Ouimet Industries, West Wareham, MA, pg. 831
Ounjian, Marilyn J., Chm. Bd. & Chief Exec. Officer--Careers USA Inc., Philadelphia, PA, pg. 218
Ourso, E.J., Chm., Pres. & Chief Exec. Officer--Ourso Investment Corporation, Donaldsonville, LA, pg. 832
Owen, Dian G., Chm. Bd.--Owen Health Care, Houston, TX, pg. 833
Owen, E.H., Pres.--Baton Rouge Water Works Company, Baton Rouge, LA, pg. 126
Owings, Frank, Jr., Exec. V.P., Mng. Dir., Sec. & Treas.--Service Supply Co. Inc. of Indiana, Indianapolis, IN, pg. 992
Owsley, T. Reed, Pres.--Owsley & Sons, Inc., Fort Mill, SC, pg. 834
Pachulski, Phil, Chm. Bd. & Pres.--Prime Technology, Inc., Grand Rapids, MI, pg. 889
Paddock, R. Y., Vice Chm.--Paddock Publications, Inc., Arlington Heights, IL, pg. 842
Paddock, S. R., Jr., Chm., Chief Exec. Officer & Publr.--Paddock Publications, Inc., Arlington Heights, IL, pg. 842
Padula, William R., Mgr.-Engine Div.--Carolina Tractor & Equipment Co., Charlotte, NC, pg. 223
Page, Doris B., Treas. & Sec.--Pace Oil Co., Inc., Winston-Salem, NC, pg. 838
Page, F. Roger, Chm. Bd., Pres., Chief Exec. & Fin. Officer--Pace Oil Co., Inc., Winston-Salem, NC, pg. 838
Page, Jack L., Chm. Bd.--Kalamazoo Label Co., Kalamazoo, MI, pg. 615
Pamplin, Dr. Robert B., Jr., Pres., Chief Oper. Officer & Sec.--R. B. Pamplin Corp., Portland, OR, pg. 844
Pamplin, Robert B., Sr., Chm. Bd. & Chief Exec. Officer--R. B. Pamplin Corp., Portland, OR, pg. 844
Pansini, Andrew A., Pres.--Jandy Industries, Novato, CA, pg. 589
Pansini, Andrew L., Chm. Bd.--Jandy Industries, Novato, CA, pg. 589
Paparo, Irving, Chm. Bd. & Pres.--House of Ronnie, Inc., New York, NY, pg. 546
Papiernick, Donald, Treas. & Controller--The Harwood Companies, Inc., New York, NY, pg. 515
Park, James C., Chm. Bd. & Chief Exec. Officer--Besser Company, Alpena, MI, pg. 146
Park, John W., Pres.--Globe Business Furniture, Inc., Hendersonville, TN, pg. 463
Parker, B.L., Chm. Bd.--MacKinnon-Parker, Inc., Toledo, OH, pg. 697
Parker, Larry L., Mng. Partner--Kupper Parker Communications Inc., Saint Louis, MO, pg. 646
Parker, Ronald I., Chm. Bd., Pres. & Chief Exec. Officer--Indian Head Industries Inc., Southfield, MI, pg. 565
Parker, Thomas L., Pres. & Treas.--MacKinnon-Parker, Inc., Toledo, OH, pg. 697
Parks, Robert M., Chm. Bd. & Pres.--Parks Products, Inc., Hollywood, CA, pg. 850
Parra, Tim, Pres.--F.P.A., Inc., Irving, TX, pg. 394
Parry, Tom C., Pres. & Chief Exec. Officer--Mississippi Chemical Corporation, Yazoo City, MS, pg. 760
Partridge, Fred, Exec. V.P. & Chief Fin. Officer--Smith-Emery Company, Los Angeles, CA, pg. 1012
Partridge, George F., Chm. Bd.--Smith-Emery Company, Los Angeles, CA, pg. 1012
Partridge, James E., Pres.--Smith-Emery Company, Los Angeles, CA, pg. 1012
Pasquerilla, Frank J., Chm. Bd. & Chief Exec. Officer--Crown American Corporation, Johnstown, PA, pg. 301
Passaro, Lanny A., Chm. Bd.--MidWest Body Corporation, Paris, IL, pg. 752
Patel, Jay, V.P.-Res. & Devel.--Periphonics Corp., Bohemia, NY, pg. 862
Patenge, Kenneth E., Chm., Pres. & Chief Exec. Officer--Wohlert Corp., Lansing, MI, pg. 1198
Patten, Charles R., Chm. Bd. & Pres.--Colfax Envelope Corporation, Buffalo Grove, IL, pg. 261
Patterson, Kent E., Chief Oper. Officer--The ERM Group, Exton, PA, pg. 360
Patton, J.L., Exec. Partner--Black & Veatch, Kansas City, MO, pg. 154
Paturzo, Michael R., Treas. & Sec.--Henningsen Foods, Inc., White Plains, NY, pg. 629
Paty, John C., Jr., Chm. Bd.--The Paty Company, Piney Flats, TN, pg. 852
Peabody, Jonathan C., V.P. & Treas.--Peabody Office Furniture Corporation, Boston, MA, pg. 853
Peabody, Lester C., Chm. Bd.--Peabody Office Furniture Corporation, Boston, MA, pg. 853
Peavey, Hartley D., Chief Exec. Officer--Peavey Electronic Corp., Meridian, MS, pg. 854
Peavey, Melia, Pres.--Peavey Electronic Corp., Meridian, MS, pg. 854
Peck, Richard, Exec. V.P.--Ranir Corporation, Grand Rapids, MI, pg. 912
Peiss, Karen G., Exec. V.P.--Gardiner Metal Company, Chicago, IL, pg. 443
Pellegrini, Donald P., Pres. & Chief Exec. Officer--The Spring Air Company, Des Plaines, IL, pg. 1032
Pemberton, Marlin H., Chm. Bd., Pres. & Chief Exec. Officer--Acorn Building Components Inc., Detroit, MI, pg. 13
Pepper, Richard S., Chief Exec. Officer--The Pepper Companies, Inc., Chicago, IL, pg. 859
Pepys, Shirley, Chm., Pres. & Chief Exec. Officer--Noel-Joanna, Inc., Rancho Santa Margarita, CA, pg. 808
Perel, Jonathan S., Pres.--General Services Corporation, Richmond, VA, pg. 450

Perelman, Raymond G., Chm. Bd. & Chief Exec. Officer--Belmont Industries, Inc., Philadelphia, PA, pg. 136
Perelman, Ronald O., Chm. Bd. & Chief Exec. Officer--MacAndrews & Forbes Holdings Inc., New York, NY, pg. 694
Perez, Lombardo, Chm. Bd., Pres. & Chief Oper. Officer--Metro Ford Inc., Miami, FL, pg. 743
Perks, A. Campbell, Chm. Bd. & Chief Exec. Officer--Eclipse, Inc., Rockford, IL, pg. 366
Perks, Douglas,, Pres. & Chief Oper. Officer--Eclipse, Inc., Rockford, IL, pg. 366
Perrier, Art, Exec. V.P., Treas. & Sec.--Maryland Paper Box Company, Baltimore, MD, pg. 717
Perry, D., Sec.--Perry Equipment Corporation, Mineral Wells, TX, pg. 863
Perry, Dale, Co-Chm. Bd.--Perry's Ice Cream Co., Inc., Akron, NY, pg. 863
Perry, M. Dunman, Jr., Chm. Bd. & Chief Exec. Officer--Perry Equipment Corporation, Mineral Wells, TX, pg. 863
Pesch, Robert C., V.P.-Opers. & Prod. Devel.--Houston Foods Company, Chicago, IL, pg. 547
Peters, A. Clark, Pres. & Chief Exec. Officer--LaSalle-Deitch Co., Inc., Elkhart, IN, pg. 660
Peters, J.L., Jr., Vice Chm. & Treas.--Fairfax Lumber & Millwork Company Inc., Springfield, VA, pg. 397
Peters, Robert L., Chm. Bd., Pres. & Chief Exec. Officer--Holmquist Grain & Lumber Co., Oakland, NE, pg. 540
Peterson, Arthur M., Pres.--Kampgrounds of America, Inc., Billings, MT, pg. 613
Petsche, Thomas, Chm. Bd. & Pres.--Rocky Mountain Mechanical, Inc., Salt Lake City, UT, pg. 942
Pettus, Theodore D., Exec. V.P.--Lockhart & Pettus, Inc., New York, NY, pg. 680
Pfaff, Edward, Chm. Bd.--Anchor Tool & Die Company, Cleveland, OH, pg. 71
Phelps, Joe, V.P.--Phelps Tointon Inc., Greeley, CO, pg. 866
Phelps, Terry M., Chm. Bd., Pres. & Chief Exec. Officer--Petroleum Marketers, Inc., Roanoke, VA, pg. 865
Phillips, Edward E., Chm. Bd.--The New England, Boston, MA, pg. 799
Pickering, Gordon G., Chm. Bd., Pres. & Gen. Counsel--Pickering Industries Inc., Tacoma, WA, pg. 869
Picknelly, Peter A., Jr., Pres. & Chief Exec. Officer--Peter Pan Bus Lines, Inc., Springfield, MA, pg. 864
Picou, Donald, Pres.--Picou Brothers Construction Company, Gonzales, LA, pg. 870
Picou, Richard, V.P., Sec. & Treas.--Picou Brothers Construction Company, Gonzales, LA, pg. 870
Piegza, Henry J., Pres.--WSF Industries, Inc., Tonawanda, NY, pg. 1156
Pierce, Brian, Pres. & Chief Exec. Officer--Peirce-Phelps, Inc., Philadelphia, PA, pg. 855
Pierce, Frederick G., II, Chm. Bd., Pres. & Chief Exec. Officer--Niagara Envelope Company, Inc., Buffalo, NY, pg. 805
Pierce, James, Exec. V.P.--Cyborg Systems, Inc., Chicago, IL, pg. 307
Pierce, Willard G., Chm. Bd.--Flexfab, Inc., Hastings, MI, pg. 418
Pieri, Albert, Pres.--California Artichoke & Vegetable Growers Corp., Castroville, CA, pg. 209
Pikovsky, Eugene, Chm. & Chief Exec. Officerr--Hyman Freightways Inc., Moundsview, MN, pg. 557
Pincus, David, Chm. Bd. & Chief Exec. Officer--Pincus Bros., Inc., Philadelphia, PA, pg. 870
Pitt, Irving E., Pres.--Murray's Discount Auto Stores, Taylor, MI, pg. 777
Planes, John, Pres.--Planes Moving And Storage, Inc., Cincinnati, OH, pg. 874
Plas, Raymond C., Exec. V.P.-Mktg. & Mdsg.--Gateway Apparel, Inc., Saint Louis, MO, pg. 445
Poehlmann, Karl M., Pres. & Chief Exec. Officer--George Uhe Co., Inc., Paramus, NJ, pg. 1125
Pohan, Armand, Pres.--A-P-A Transport Corp., North Bergen, NJ, pg. 5
Pohlad, Carl, Owner--Minnesota Twins Baseball Club, Minneapolis, MN, pg. 758
Poindexter, John E., Pres.--Basic Construction Company, Newport News, VA, pg. 124
Pollnow, Charles, Chm. Bd., Chief Exec. & Oper. Officer--The Brulin Corporation, Indianapolis, IN, pg. 184
Pope, J. Mathews, V.P.--Hancock Peanut Company, Courtland, VA, pg. 504
Pope, Robert H., Pres.--Hancock Peanut Company, Courtland, VA, pg. 504
Popek, Gerald J., Chm. Bd.--Locus Computing Corp., Inglewood, CA, pg. 680
Poppert, Claris, Chm. Bd. & Chief Exec. Officer--Benson Industries Inc., Portland, OR, pg. 139
Popple, John A., Chm. Bd., Pres. & Chief Exec. Officer--LeeWards Creative Crafts, Inc., Elgin, IL, pg. 666
Porter, Arthur, Pres.--Arthur Porter Construction, Phoenix, AZ, pg. 881
Porter, Charles, Chm. & Dir.-Creative--Crispin & Porter Advertising Inc., Miami, FL, pg. 299
Posner, Steven, Vice Chm.--Graniteville Co., Graniteville, SC, pg. 476
Posner, Victor, Chm. Bd. & Chief Exec. Officer--Graniteville Co., Graniteville, SC, pg. 476
Posner, Victor, Chm. Bd., Pres. & Chief Exec. Officer--Chesapeake Financial Corp., Miami Beach, FL, pg. 243
Post, James R., Pres., Chief Exec. Officer, Chief Fin. Officer--Ostarr Corporation, Chicago, IL, pg. 831
Powell, Harold H., Chm. Bd.--Powell Electronics Inc., Philadelphia, PA, pg. 882
Powell, M. Lee, III, Pres.--Ballenger Paving Company, Inc., Taylors, SC, pg. 116
Powers, Christopher W., V.P.-Subsidiary Opers.--The Rawlplug Company, Inc., New Rochelle, NY, pg. 914
Powers, Frederic B., Jr., Chm. Bd. & Pres.--The Rawlplug Company, Inc., New Rochelle, NY, pg. 914
Powers, Jeffrey R., V.P.-Mktg.--The Rawlplug Company, Inc., New Rochelle, NY, pg. 914
Pratten, Robert, Chief Fin. Officer--Regency Associates Limited Partnership, Evansville, IN, pg. 922
Prendergast, M. Raymond, Chm. Bd. & Chief Exec. Officer--Boston Distributors, Inc., Maple Heights, OH, pg. 167
Prentice, Daniel F., Pres. & Chief Oper. Officer--Generra Sportswear Company, Inc., Tukwila, WA, pg. 451
Preonas, Demetri, Gen. Mgr.--Rich Products Dayton, Dayton, OH, pg. 932
Pressman, Fred, Pres.--Barneys New York, New York, NY, pg. 120
Pressman, Gene, V.P. & Chief Exec. Officer--Barneys New York, New York, NY, pg. 120
Pressman, Robert, V.P. & Chief Oper. Officer--Barneys New York, New York, NY, pg. 120
Prinzo, Felix J., Sr. V.P. & Chief Fin. Officer--Laroche Holdings, Inc., Atlanta, GA, pg. 659
Pritz, Benjamin L., Chm. Bd., Pres. & Chief Exec. Officer--Grandpa Brands Company, Cincinnati, OH, pg. 476
Pritzker, Jay A., Chm. Bd.--Hyatt Corporation, Chicago, IL, pg. 495
Pritzker, Thomas J., Pres.--Hyatt Corporation, Chicago, IL, pg. 495
Proffitt, Brian, Pres.--Zephyr Baskets & Balloons, New Providence, NJ, pg. 1217
Profit, Joe, Pres. & Chief Exec. Officer--Communications International, Norcross, GA, pg. 269
Pruim, E.G., Chm. Bd., Pres. & Chief Exec. Officer--Wrought Washer Mfg., Inc., Milwaukee, WI, pg. 1205
Pruitt, Robert, Chm. Bd. & Pres.--Tremont Foods, Linthicum Heights, MD, pg. 1109
Pucheu, John, Jr., Chm. Bd.--Calcot, Ltd., Bakersfield, CA, pg. 208
Pumpelly, R. Glenn, Pres.--Pumpelly Oil, Inc., Westlake, LA, pg. 900
Pumpelly, Robert J., Chm. Bd.--Pumpelly Oil, Inc., Westlake, LA, pg. 900
Pumpelly, Vida, V.P.--Pumpelly Oil, Inc., Westlake, LA, pg. 900
Puris, Martin, Pres. & Chief Exec. Officer--Ammirati & Puris Inc., New York, NY, pg. 67
Quinif, Edward, Chm. Bd. & Pres.--Walled Lake Door Company, Phoenix, AZ, pg. 1161
Quinlan, Donald P., Chm. Bd., Pres., Chief Exec. & Chief Oper. Officer--Graphic Controls Corporation, Buffalo, NY, pg. 478
Quinn, Thomas H., Pres. & Chief Oper. Officer--Jordan Industries, Inc., Deerfield, IL, pg. 604
Quinnies, Barry C., Pres. & Chief Exec. Officer--Independent Metals, Germantown, WI, pg. 565
Raab, Max L., Chm. Bd. & Chief Exec. Officer--J. G. Hook, Inc., Philadelphia, PA, pg. 543
Radler, Louis, Chm. Bd., Pres. & Chief Exec. Officer--Chessco Industries, Inc., Westport, CT, pg. 243
Radwill, Alvera, Chm. Bd., Chief Fin. Officer & Treas.--Master Appliance Corp., Racine, WI, pg. 719
Radwill, Linda, V.P., Mgr.-Mktg. & Sec.--Master Appliance Corp., Racine, WI, pg. 719
Radwill, Scott, Pres., Chief Exec. & Chief Oper. Officer-Export--Master Appliance Corp., Racine, WI, pg. 719
Ragsdale, Charles S., V.P.--T.S. Ragsdale Company, Incorporated, Lake City, SC, pg. 910
Ragsdale, T. Smith, III, Pres.--T.S. Ragsdale Company, Incorporated, Lake City, SC, pg. 910
Raines, J.R., Chm. Bd.--San Angelo Electric Service Company, San Angelo, TX, pg. 969
Rakolta, John, Jr., Pres., Chief Exec. Officer & Treas.--Walbridge Aldinger Company, Detroit, MI, pg. 1158
Rakolta, John, Sr., Chm. Bd. & Sec.--Walbridge Aldinger Company, Detroit, MI, pg. 1158
Rakow, May T., Sr. V.P.-Personnel & Sec.--Illinois Hydraulic Construction Company, South Elgin, IL, pg. 563
Rakow, Thomas S., Pres., Chief Exec. Officer & Treas.--Illinois Hydraulic Construction Company, South Elgin, IL, pg. 563
Ramey, William F., Chm. Bd.--Jasper County Farm Bureau Co-op Association, Inc., Rensselaer, IN, pg. 590
Randall, Ronald F., Chm. Bd., Pres. & Chief Exec. Officer--Randall Stores, Inc., Mitchell, SD, pg. 911
Rands, Mary, Sec. & Treas.--Brush Research Manufacturing Company, Los Angeles, CA, pg. 184
Rands, Tara, Pres.--Brush Research Manufacturing Company, Los Angeles, CA, pg. 184
Rankin, Stuart, Treas. & New Bus. Contact--Equinox Advertising, Inc., Chicago, IL, pg. 384
Ransome, Ernest L., III, Chm. Bd.--Giles & Ransome, Inc., Bensalem, PA, pg. 458
Ransome, Percy A., III, Vice Chm.--Giles & Ransome, Inc., Bensalem, PA, pg. 458
Rapp, C.J., Pres.--The Jolt Company, Rochester, NY, pg. 602
Rapp, William M., Pres.--Vance Industries, Inc., Chicago, IL, pg. 1144
Rappaport, Stanley, Exec. V.P.--House of Ronnie, Inc., New York, NY, pg. 546
Rappeport, Don, Chm. Bd. & Chief Exec. Officer--Donlen Corp., Deerfield, IL, pg. 345
Rath, Frank E., Chm. Bd.--Spang & Company, Butler, PA, pg. 1025
Rath, Frank E., Jr., Pres.--Spang & Company, Butler, PA, pg. 1025
Rath, Robert, Vice Chm.--Spang & Company, Butler, PA, pg. 1025
Ratner, Charles, Chm. Bd.--Richter & Ratner Contracting Corporation, Maspeth, NY, pg. 933
Ratner, Michael H., Pres.--Richter & Ratner Contracting Corporation, Maspeth, NY, pg. 933
Ratner, S., Chm. Bd. & Dir-Acct. Services--McCaffery & Ratner, Inc., New York, NY, pg. 726
Rau, Howard C., Chm. Bd.--Edwin B. Stimpson Company, Inc., Bayport, NY, pg. 1049
Rauch, C. Dixon, III, Pres. & Chief Exec. Officer--Rundel Products, Inc., Portland, OR, pg. 956
Ravizza, Eugene A., Chm. Bd. & Pres.--Synergism, Inc., Sunnyvale, CA, pg. 1069
Rayner, Mitch A., V.P., Chief Oper. Officer & Sec.--Performance Contractors Inc., Baton Rouge, LA, pg. 861
Ready, James, Exec. V.P.--Ready Systems, Sunnyvale, CA, pg. 916
Reber, Stanley R., Exec. V.P. & Chief Investment Officer--Provident Mutual Life Insurance Co., Philadelphia, PA, pg. 896
Redman, Richard C., Chm. Bd., Pres. & Chief Exec. Officer--Sellen Construction Company, Seattle, WA, pg. 988
Redmond, Michael W., Pres.--Witcher Construction Company, Minneapolis, MN, pg. 1198
Redmond, Thomas, Sr., Chm. Bd.--Redmond Products, Inc., Chanhassen, MN, pg. 920
Reed, Alan C., Chm. Bd. & Chief Exec. Officer--Radix Corporation, Salt Lake City, UT, pg. 909
Reed, E.C., Pres. & Sec.--Utica Boilers Inc., Utica, NY, pg. 1140
Reed, Robert E., Chm. Bd.--Utica Boilers Inc., Utica, NY, pg. 1140
Regal, Melvyn, Vice Chm.--Foster & Gallagher Inc., Peoria, IL, pg. 426
Reid, George, Dir.-Computer Opers.--Sanford C. Bernstein & Co., Inc., New York, NY, pg. 144
Reid, James A., Pres.--Hollywood Alloy Casting Company, Compton, CA, pg. 540
Reilly, Donald C., Pres.--Superior Tube Company, Collegeville, PA, pg. 1064
Reinig, L.P., Chm. Bd. & Pres.--Los Alamos Technical Associates, Inc., Los Alamos, NM, pg. 684
Reiss, Clifford E. II, Sec. & Asst. To Pres.--R.C.A. Rubber Company, Akron, OH, pg. 906
Reiss, Richard T., Pres. & Treas.--R.C.A. Rubber Company, Akron, OH, pg. 906
Remos, Gary, Chm. Bd., Pres. & Chief Exec. Officer--Advanced Manufacturing & Development, Willits, CA, pg. 20
Rendini, Mary G., Sr. V.P. & Human Resources Dir.--Maguire Group Inc., Foxboro, MA, pg. 701
Reno, William J., Chm. Bd., Pres. & Chief Exec. Officer--F.B. Wright Co., Dearborn, MI, pg. 1204
Rentenbach, T.J., Chm. Bd.--Rentenbach Engineering Company, Knoxville, TN, pg. 927
Rentenbach, T.M., Pres. & Chief Exec. Officer--Rentenbach Engineering Company, Knoxville, TN, pg. 927
Repeta, Richard J., Pres.--Maguire Group Inc., Foxboro, MA, pg. 701
Resnick, Mark, Partner--The Yucaipa Companies, Claremont, CA, pg. 1214
Resnick, Stewart, Chm. Bd.--American Protection Industries, Inc., Los Angeles, CA, pg. 60
Reynen, John D., Treas. & Sec.--Reynen, Bardis & Winn, Sacramento, CA, pg. 930
Reynolds, Donald W., Chm. Bd.--Donrey Media Group, Fort Smith, AR, pg. 345
Ricardo, Jose, Chm. Bd. & Chief Exec. Officer--RII (Ricards International Inc.), Silver Spring, MD, pg. 907
Rice, Joyce, V.P.-Training & Co-founder--T. J. Cinnamons Ltd., Kansas City, MO, pg. 1073
Rice, Ted, Chm. Bd. & Co-founder--T. J. Cinnamons Ltd., Kansas City, MO, pg. 1073
Rich, Francis P., Jr., Chm. Bd. & Pres.--Action Equipment, Londonderry, NH, pg. 14
Rich, Robert E., Chm. Bd.--Rich Products Corp., Buffalo, NY, pg. 932
Rich, Robert E., Jr., Pres.--Rich Products Corp., Buffalo, NY, pg. 932
Richardson, James Craig, Pres.--Richco Plastics Company, Chicago, IL, pg. 933
Richey, Steve, Pres.--Precision Parts Corp., Morristown, TN, pg. 885
Richmond James A., Exec. V.P.-Mortgate Loans--Globe Mortgage Company, Hackensack, NJ, pg. 464
Richter, James A., Mng. Partner--Roney & Co., Detroit, MI, pg. 946
Richter, Jerome B., Vice Chm. & Pres.--Kangaroos, USA Inc., Chesterfield, MO, pg. 616
Rider, C.G., Pres. & Chief Exec. Officer--AEA, Inc., Charlotte, NC, pg. 3
Riley, Richard W., Pres.--Label-Aire Inc., Fullerton, CA, pg. 649
Risk, J. Fred, Chm. Bd.--Sovereign Group Inc., Indianapolis, IN, pg. 1024
Risley, J. Stephen, Jr., Pres.--Sunrise Nissan of Orange Park, Orange Park, FL, pg. 1062
Risser, P.N., III, Pres.--Risser Oil Corp., Clearwater, FL, pg. 936
Ritchie, H.T., Pres. & Chief Oper. Officer--Ritchie Corporation, Wichita, KS, pg. 936
Ritchie, Hale D., Jr., Chm. Bd. & Chief Exec. Officer--Ritchie Corporation, Wichita, KS, pg. 936
Ritchie, Robert D., Pres.--Ted Thomas Associates Inc., Advertising, Philadelphia, PA, pg. 1092
Rivett, Ron, Chm. Bd.--Super 8 Motels, Inc., Aberdeen, SD, pg. 1062
Rizzuto, Leandro P., Chm. Bd. & Pres.--Conair Corporation, Stamford, CT, pg. 272
Roberson, Gregg C., Sr. V.P. & Chief Oper. Officer--Drug Emporium of Arizona, Inc., Scottsdale, AZ, pg. 349
Roberts, Charles, Jr., Chm. Bd. & Pres.--Chas Roberts Air Conditioning, Inc., Phoenix, AZ, pg. 938
Roberts, John H., Pres. & Chief Exec. Officer--J. H. Roberts Industries Inc., Des Plaines, IL, pg. 938
Roberts, Ralph L., Chm. Bd. & Pres.--Gator Freightways, Inc., Wilmington, OH, pg. 446
Robertson, Ellen, V.P.--Robertson Marketing Inc., Charlotte, NC, pg. 939
Robertson, G. Bruce, Pres. & Chief Exec. Officer--Robertson Marketing Inc., Charlotte, NC, pg. 939
Robertson, Robert G., Pres. & Chief Exec. Officer--White Hen Pantry, Inc., Elmhurst, IL, pg. 1185
Robins, Gerald, Chm. Bd.--Roland International Corporation, Coconut Grove, FL, pg. 944
Robinson, E. Montogmery, Pres. & Treas.--Top Flight, Inc., Chattanooga, TN, pg. 1101

Robinson, Harry T., Jr., Chm. Bd. & Sec.--Top Flight, Inc., Chattanooga, TN, pg. 1101
Robinson, J.H., Jr., Exec. Partner--Black & Veatch, Kansas City, MO, pg. 154
Robinson, John H., Mng. Partner--Black & Veatch, Kansas City, MO, pg. 154
Robinson, Leon, Jr., Pres.--Robinson Bus Service, Evanston, IL, pg. 939
Robinson, Robert J., Exec. V.P. & Chief Oper. Officer--AXIA Incorporated, Oak Brook, IL, pg. 8
Roche, M.B., Pres.--Roche Constructors, Inc., Greeley, CO, pg. 940
Rocke, Richard, V.P.--Sterling, Inc., Milwaukee, WI, pg. 1047
Rockwell, Stuart, Pur. Agent--Felton Brush Inc., Manchester, NH, pg. 406
Rodbell, Clyde A., Pres.--Apex Supply Co. Inc., Atlanta, GA, pg. 78
Roddenbery, Julien B., Jr., Pres. & Chief Exec. Officer--W. B. Roddenbery Company, Inc., Cairo, GA, pg. 942
Roddie, Anton, Pres.--Western Data Systems, Calabasas, CA, pg. 1178
Rodefeld, Charles A., Pres.--Rodefeld Co., Inc., Richmond, IN, pg. 942
Rodgers, B.D., Chm. Bd.--Rodgers Builders, Inc., Charlotte, NC, pg. 942
Rogers, Joe W., Jr., Pres.--Waffle House, Inc., Norcross, GA, pg. 1157
Rogers, Richard R., Chm. & Chief Exec. Officer--Mary Kay Cosmetics Inc., Dallas, TX, pg. 716
Rogers, Yandell, Jr., Pres. & Gen. Counsel--YRJ Corporation, Houston, TX, pg. 1206
Rogerson, Michael, Chm. Bd., Pres. & Chief Exec. Officer--Rogerson Aircraft Corporation, Irvine, CA, pg. 943
Rohn, Robert J., V.P.-Field Opers. Mgr.--Double AA Builders, Ltd., Phoenix, AZ, pg. 347
Rokop, Joseph, Chm. Bd.--Rokop Corporation, Bridgeville, PA, pg. 944
Rokop, Judith, Exec. V.P.-Pur.--Rokop Corporation, Bridgeville, PA, pg. 944
Rokop, Nik, V.P.-Engrng.--Rokop Corporation, Bridgeville, PA, pg. 944
Rolla, M.F., Pres. & Chief Oper. Officer--Gem Industries, Inc., Gardner, MA, pg. 447
Rones, James, Chm. Bd.--Americo Manufacturing Co., Inc., Acworth, GA, pg. 66
Roney, William C., III, Partner--Roney & Co., Detroit, MI, pg. 946
Roob, R., Chm. Bd.--Benjamin Moore & Co., Montvale, NJ, pg. 139
Rooks, W. Howard, Pres.--Weichert Realty, Inc., Alexandria, VA, pg. 1173
Roos, Mark D., V.P., Treas. & Chief Fin. Officer--The Airolite Company, Marietta, OH, pg. 28
Root, L.D., Jr., Chm. Bd.--Root Corporation, Mount Wolf, PA, pg. 946
Root, P.T., Pres.--Root Corporation, Mount Wolf, PA, pg. 946
Roper, Leroy B., Chm. Bd.--Roper Bros. Lumber Co., Inc., Petersburg, VA, pg. 947
Rosamond, Patricia A., Pres.--Rodgers Builders, Inc., Charlotte, NC, pg. 942
Rose, Gervase R., Pres.--Roman Electric Company, Inc., Milwaukee, WI, pg. 945
Rose, Mike, V.P.--Marketing Communications, Lenexa, KS, pg. 709
Rosen, David, Pres.--CB Sports Inc., Glens Falls, NY, pg. 199
Rosen, Edward H., Chm. & Chief Exec. Officer--Raymond Rosen Co., Conshohocken, PA, pg. 948
Rosen, Florence, Exec. V.P. & Controller--Rosen Associates Management Corp., Jericho, NY, pg. 948
Rosen, Robert A., Pres.--Rosen Associates Management Corp., Jericho, NY, pg. 948
Rosen, Theodore A., Pres. & Chief Oper. Officer--Raymond Rosen Co., Conshohocken, PA, pg. 948
Rosenbaum, Eli, Pres.--Bruckner Machine & Tool Corp., Port Washington, NY, pg. 183
Rosenbaum, Marlon, Treas.--Bruckner Machine & Tool Corp., Port Washington, NY, pg. 183
Rosenbaum, Robert, Exec. V.P.--Bruckner Machine & Tool Corp., Port Washington, NY, pg. 183
Rosenberg, Harold, Chm. Bd.--Octagon Process Inc., Edgewater, NJ, pg. 821
Rosenberg, Marvin, Chm. Bd. & Sec.--Towne Properties, Cincinnati, OH, pg. 1104
Rosenblit, Donald, Sr. Exec. V.P., Dir. Acct. Services--Elkman Advertising & Public Relations, Bala-Cynwyd, PA, pg. 377
Rosendin, Bertha C., Chm. Bd.--Rosendin Electric, Inc., San Jose, CA, pg. 948
Rosendin, Louis M., Exec. V.P. & Sec.--Rosendin Electric, Inc., San Jose, CA, pg. 948
Rosendin, Raymond J., Pres. & Treas.--Rosendin Electric, Inc., San Jose, CA, pg. 948
Rosenfield, Estelle, Treas.--Tasco, Miami, FL, pg. 1079
Rosenfield, George, Pres.--Tasco, Miami, FL, pg. 1079
Rosenfield, Sheryl, Exec. V.P.--Tasco, Miami, FL, pg. 1079
Rosenthal, Richard H., Pres.--F & W Publications, Inc., Cincinnati, OH, pg. 394
Ross, Audrey, Treas.--J H Collectibles, Milwaukee, WI, pg. 584
Ross, Bruce, Pres.--J H Collectibles, Milwaukee, WI, pg. 584
Ross, Jack, Pres.--Jack Ross Motors Inc., Tempe, AZ, pg. 949
Ross, Joseph, Pres. & Chief Exec. Officer--Entron Industries Limited Partnership, Glendale, NY, pg. 383
Ross, Kenneth, Chm. & Chief Exec. Officer--J H Collectibles, Milwaukee, WI, pg. 584
Ross, Marc S., Pres. & Chief Exec. Officer--Veda Incorporated, Alexandria, VA, pg. 1146
Ross, Robert L., Chm. Bd.--Black Fin Yacht Corporation, Fort Lauderdale, FL, pg. 154
Ross, Thomas, V.P.-Sls. & Admin.--Jack Ross Motors Inc., Tempe, AZ, pg. 949
Rossmeyer, Bruce, Pres.--Bruce Rossmeyer's Toyotaland, Longwood, FL, pg. 950
Roth, Bernard B., Chm. Bd. & Chief Exec. Officer--World Oil Company, South Gate, CA, pg. 1203
Roth, Robert S., Pres.--World Oil Company, South Gate, CA, pg. 1203
Rothbaum, Michael, Pres. & Chief Exec. Officer--The Harwood Companies, Inc., New York, NY, pg. 515
Rothwell, Bernard J., III, Chm. Bd.--Bay State Milling Co., Quincy, MA, pg. 127
Rothwell, Brian G., Pres. & Chief Exec. Officer--Bay State Milling Co., Quincy, MA, pg. 127
Rotter, Steve H., Chm. Bd.--Towne, Silverstein, Rotter Inc., New York, NY, pg. 1104
Rotunno, J.R., Chm. Bd.--O'Neil Industries Inc., Chicago, IL, pg. 827
Roussel, Louis J., Jr., Chm. Bd., Pres. & Chief Exec. Officer--Victory Financial Group, Inc., Metairie, LA, pg. 1150
Rowell, L.J. , Jr., Chm. Bd., Pres. & Chief Exec. Officer--Provident Mutual Life Insurance Co., Philadelphia, PA, pg. 896
Rubin, Arlene, V.P., Fin.--Rubin Response Services, Inc., Schaumburg, IL, pg. 954
Rubin, Georgette, Treas. & Sec.--Lillie Rubin Affiliates Inc., Miami, FL, pg. 954
Rubin, Gerrold R., Pres.--Rubin Postaer & Associates, Santa Monica, CA, pg. 954
Rubin, Howard, Exec. V.P.--Shogyo International Corporation, Great Neck, NY, pg. 1000
Rubin, Joel, Chm. Bd., Pres. & Chief Exec. Officer--Phototype Color Graphics, Inc., Pennsauken, NJ, pg. 869
Rubin, Mark A., Pres.--Shogyo International Corporation, Great Neck, NY, pg. 1000
Rubin, Richard, Chm., Pres., Chief Exec. & Chief Oper. Officer--Donnkenny, Inc., New York, NY, pg. 345
Rubin, William S., Chm. Bd. & Pres.--Rubin Response Services, Inc., Schaumburg, IL, pg. 954
Ruckriegel, Lovella, Treas.--Wharfside Restaurants, Inc., Jasper, IN, pg. 1184
Ruckriegel, Robert, Pres.--Wharfside Restaurants, Inc., Jasper, IN, pg. 1184
Rudolph, James E., V.P.-Opers.--Rudolph Foods Company, Lima, OH, pg. 954
Rudolph, John E., Pres.--Rudolph Foods Company, Lima, OH, pg. 954
Rudolph, Richard M., V.P.-Mktg.--Rudolph Foods Company, Lima, OH, pg. 954
Ruhr, Charles F., Chm. Bd. & Chief Exec. Officer--Chuck Ruhr Advertising, Minneapolis, MN, pg. 955
Ruisch, R.G., Exec. Partner--Black & Veatch, Kansas City, MO, pg. 154
Ruiz, Fred, Pres. & Chief Exec. Officer--Ruiz Food Products, Inc., Dinuba, CA, pg. 955
Ruiz, Louis, Chm. Bd.--Ruiz Food Products, Inc., Dinuba, CA, pg. 955
Runk, John W., Chm. Bd. & Pres.--Directory Distributing Associates, Inc., Saint Louis, MO, pg. 339
Russo, Robert S., V.P.--American Technical Services Group, Inc., Norcross, GA, pg. 63
Rust, Edward B., Jr., Chm. Bd., Pres. & Chief Exec. Officer--State Farm Mutual Automobile Insurance Company, Bloomington, IL, pg. 1041
Rust, Lois, Pres. & Chief Exec. Officer--Rose Acre Farms, Seymour, IN, pg. 947
Rutherford, Clyde E., Chm. Bd. & Pres.--Dairylea Cooperative Inc., East Syracuse, NY, pg. 311
Rutherford, Jack D., Chm. & Chief Exec. Officer--ICM Industries, Inc., Chicago, IL, pg. 559
Ruting, Wayne, Chm. Bd.--Columbine Systems Inc., Golden, CO, pg. 266
Rutland, Guy W., III, Vice Chm.--Allied Systems, Ltd., Decatur, GA, pg. 40
Rutland, Robert J., Chm. Bd. & Chief Exec. Officer--Allied Systems, Ltd., Decatur, GA, pg. 40
Rychlinski, Victor Z., Dir.-Engrng.--Brad Foote Gear Works, Inc., Cicero, IL, pg. 169
Rynone, Richard T., Pres.--Rynone Manufacturing Corporation, Sayre, PA, pg. 958
Rynone, William J., Sec. & Treas.--Rynone Manufacturing Corporation, Sayre, PA, pg. 958
Sabbatino, Anthony, Pres., Chief Oper. & Chief Exec. Officer--Bogue Electric Manufacturing Co., Paterson, NJ, pg. 162
Sack, Thomas F., Pres., Chief Exec. & Oper. Officer--Haddon Craftsmen, Inc., Scranton, PA, pg. 499
Sackett, Janice J., Pres.--LeGrand Johnson Construction Co., Logan, UT, pg. 598
Sahm, Roland R., Chm. Bd. & Chief Exec. Officer--Elixir Industries, Gardena, CA, pg. 376
Sakosits, John J., Chm. Bd., Chief Exec. & Chief Oper. Officer--Hoboken Wood Flooring Corporation, Wayne, NJ, pg. 537
Sakosits, Mildred, Pres. & Sec.--Hoboken Wood Flooring Corporation, Wayne, NJ, pg. 537
Saks, Alan, Pres. & Chief Exec. Officer--Saxon Paint & Home Care Centers Inc., Chicago, IL, pg. 973
Saliba, Naseeb M., Exec. V.P. & Sec.--Tutor-Saliba Corporation, Sylmar, CA, pg. 1120
Saltzman, Irving, Treas.--Banner Wholesale Grocers, Inc., Chicago, IL, pg. 118
Saltzman, Richard, Asst. Treas.--Banner Wholesale Grocers, Inc., Chicago, IL, pg. 118
Saltzman, Shirley, Sec.--Banner Wholesale Grocers, Inc., Chicago, IL, pg. 118
Salvatierra, Richard, Pres.--RII (Ricards International Inc.), Silver Spring, MD, pg. 907
Salver, Henry A., V.P.-Corp. Devel.--GAI Consultants, Inc., Monroeville, PA, pg. 439
Samuels, Allen, Pres.--Allen Samuels Chevrolet GEO, Waco, TX, pg. 969
Samuelson, F.A., Exec. V.P.-Creative Services--Keller Crescent Co., Evansville, IN, pg. 620
Sanchez, Fernando, Exec. V.P.-Fin. & Admin.--Leather Center, Inc., Carrollton, TX, pg. 664
Sanders, Don, V.P.--Midwest Mechanical Contractors Inc., Kansas City, MO, pg. 752
Sanders, Gerald, V.P.--Queens Group, Inc., Long Island City, NY, pg. 904
Sanders, Lewis A., Pres.--Sanford C. Bernstein & Co., Inc., New York, NY, pg. 144
Sanders, Max D., Chm. Bd. & Pres.--Ohmite Manufacturing Company, Skokie, IL, pg. 823
Sankes, Gary, Chm. Bd. & Pres.--Scrufari Construction Co. Inc., Niagara Falls, NY, pg. 983
Sarckowsky, Herman, Chm. Bd.--Pace International Corporation, Kirkland, WA, pg. 838
Sarkisian, Norman,, Owner, Pres. & Chief Exec. Officer--Beacon Group, Bloomfield, CT, pg. 128
Sasser, Billy G., Chm. Bd., Pres. & Chief Exec. Officer--Reeves Southeastern Corporation, Tampa, FL, pg. 921
Saterbo, Bryan, Sr. V.P. & Treas.--Colorado Boxed Beef Co., Auburndale, FL, pg. 265
Saterbo, Stephen, Sr. V.P.-Sls. & Mktg.--Colorado Boxed Beef Co., Auburndale, FL, pg. 265
Saubert, Walter E., Owner--Red Ball Corporation, Seattle, WA, pg. 918
Sauey, W.R., Chm. Bd., Pres. & Treas.--Nordic Group of Companies, Ltd., Baraboo, WI, pg. 809
Saunders, Manuel, Chm. Bd.--Be-Lo Markets Inc., Norfolk, VA, pg. 212
Savaiano, N.J., Chm. Bd. & Pres.--United Laboratories, Inc., Itasca, IL, pg. 1133
Saxon, Ronald, Pres.--Ron Saxon Ford, Inc., Saint Paul, MN, pg. 973
Scanlan, Thomas M., Jr., Pres. & Chief Exec. Officer--The Ward Machinery Company, Cockeysville, MD, pg. 1162
Scarlett, Joseph, Pres. & Chief Oper. Officer--TSC Industries, Inc., Nashville, TN, pg. 1075
Schackow, Gerald D., Chm. Bd.--Athletic Attic Properties Inc., Gainesville, FL, pg. 94
Schaefer, Gerard J., Pres.--Moss Telecommunications Services, Grand Rapids, MI, pg. 772
Scharff, Werner G., Chm. Bd. & Pres.--Lanz, Inc., Culver City, CA, pg. 658
Schecter, Leroy, Chm. Bd. & Chief Exec. Officer--American Strip Steel Inc., Kearny, NJ, pg. 63
Schield, Lawrence R., Jr., Partner--Whitehawk Partnership, Pasadena, CA, pg. 1186
Schifano, Albert I., Sr. V.P.-Personnel--Sundt Corp., Tucson, AZ, pg. 1060
Schiller, Leonard M., Owner & Dir.-Acquisitions--The Dearborn Group, Chicago, IL, pg. 322
Schiller, Phil, Owner--The Dearborn Group, Chicago, IL, pg. 322
Schinman, H.L., Chm. Bd., Treas., Sec. & Gen. Counsel--Bogue Electric Manufacturing Co., Paterson, NJ, pg. 162
Schirmang, Anton T., V.P.--Skokie Valley Beverage Co., Wheeling, IL, pg. 1009
Schirmang, Barbara P., V.P.--Skokie Valley Beverage Co., Wheeling, IL, pg. 1009
Schirmang, William A., V.P.-Data Processing & Sec.--Skokie Valley Beverage Co., Wheeling, IL, pg. 1009
Schirmang, William P., Pres., Treas. & Sls. Mgr.--Skokie Valley Beverage Co., Wheeling, IL, pg. 1009
Schlatter, Donald A., Pres., Chief Exec. Officer & Gen. Counsel--Art Iron, Inc., Toledo, OH, pg. 86
Schlatter, H.H., Chm. Bd.--Art Iron, Inc., Toledo, OH, pg. 86
Schlobohm, Jon, Sec. & Treas.--National Corset Supply House, Los Angeles, CA, pg. 787
Schlueter, John J., Chm. Bd. & Chief Exec. Officer--Knapp Shoes Inc., Brockton, MA, pg. 636
Schmidt, Peter G., Pres. & Chief Exec. Officer--Marine Construction & Design Co., Seattle, WA, pg. 707
Schneeberger, Donald G., Pres. & Chief Oper. Officer--H. C. Miller Company, Milwaukee, WI, pg. 754
Schneeberger, R. Louis, V.P. & Chief Fin. Officer--Olympic Steel Inc., Bedford Heights, OH, pg. 825
Schnitzer, Kenneth L., Jr., Pres.--Park Place Motorcars, Dallas, TX, pg. 849
Schnuck, Craig, Chm. Bd. & Chief Exec. Officer--Schnuck Markets, Inc., Maryland Heights, MO, pg. 977
Schnuck, Scott, Pres. & Chief Oper. Officer--Schnuck Markets, Inc., Maryland Heights, MO, pg. 977
Scholler, Bernice, Sec. & Treas.--Times Printing Company, Inc., Random Lake, WI, pg. 1098
Scholler, James, Dir.-Pur.--Times Printing Company, Inc., Random Lake, WI, pg. 1098
Scholler, John, V.P.-Prod.--Times Printing Company, Inc., Random Lake, WI, pg. 1098
Scholler, Ray, Pres.--Times Printing Company, Inc., Random Lake, WI, pg. 1098
Scholobhm, Roy, Pres.--National Corset Supply House, Los Angeles, CA, pg. 787
Scholtens, Michael, Chm., & Chief Exec. Officer--Nutech, Inc., San Jose, CA, pg. 817
Schonberger, Phillip, Chm. Bd.--Landau & Heyman Inc., Chicago, IL, pg. 654
Schottland, S.B., Pres.--American Packaging Corporation, Philadelphia, PA, pg. 59
Schrandt, Brian, V.P.-Detroit Gasket--Indian Head Industries Inc., Southfield, MI, pg. 565
Schraufnagel, Harland, Pres.--Abbyland Foods, Inc., Abbotsford, WI, pg. 10
Schroeder, Bradley A., V.P.-Fin.--Houston Foods Company, Chicago, IL, pg. 547
Schron, Jack H. Sr., Chm. Bd.--Jergens Inc., Cleveland, OH, pg. 593
Schron, Jack H., Jr., Pres.--Jergens Inc., Cleveland, OH, pg. 593
Schubert, William C., Pres., Treas., & Chief Exec. Officer--Kitchell Corporation, Phoenix, AZ, pg. 634
Schudmak, Mel E., Pres.--Cora Texas Manufacturing Co., White Castle, LA, pg. 285

Schuenke, Donald J., Chm. Bd. & Chief Exec. Officer--Northwestern Mutual Life Insurance Co., Milwaukee, WI, pg. 815
Schull, Johanna, Sec. & Treas.--Building Products Inc., Watertown, SD, pg. 188
Schull, Lee, Pres.--Building Products Inc., Watertown, SD, pg. 188
Schull, Lester, Exec. V.P.--Building Products Inc., Watertown, SD, pg. 188
Schulte, J., Chief Fin. Officer & V.P.--Nelson A. Taylor Co., Inc., Gloversville, NY, pg. 1080
Schultz, Jay, Treas. & Sec.--ZBS Industries, Inc., Mayfield Village, OH, pg. 1215
Schumacher, Kenneth H., Chm. Bd. & Pres.--Paradata Computer Networks, Inc., Farmington Hills, MI, pg. 847
Schurz, Franklin D., Jr., Pres.--Schurz Communications, Inc., South Bend, IN, pg. 979
Schurz, James M., Sr. V.P.--Schurz Communications, Inc., South Bend, IN, pg. 979
Schurz, Mary, V.P. & Sec.--Schurz Communications, Inc., South Bend, IN, pg. 979
Schurz, Scott C., V.P.--Schurz Communications, Inc., South Bend, IN, pg. 979
Schwab, Richard D., Chm. Bd.--S. Schwab Company, Cumberland, MD, pg. 980
Schwab, Samuel C., Pres. & Chief Exec. Officer--S. Schwab Company, Cumberland, MD, pg. 980
Schwan, Geoffrey E., Pres.--Double AA Builders, Ltd., Phoenix, AZ, pg. 347
Schwartz, Barry, Chm. Bd. & Chief Exec. Officer--Doe Spun, Inc., New York, NY, pg. 343
Schwartz, Barry K., Chm. Bd. & Chief Oper. Officer--Calvin Klein, Inc., New York, NY, pg. 635
Schwartz, Joel P., Pres.--Ben Schwartz Market, Inc., Peoria, IL, pg. 980
Schwartz, M.I., Pres.--Swivelier Co., Inc., Nanuet, NY, pg. 1068
Schwartz, Steven, Chief Oper. Officer--Doe Spun, Inc., New York, NY, pg. 343
Schwegmann, John, Chief Exec. Officer & Chm.--Schwegmann Giant Super Markets, New Orleans, LA, pg. 980
Scobie, William M., Chm. Bd., Chief Exec. & Legal Officer--Mason Shoe Mfg. Co., Chippewa Falls, WI, pg. 718
Scobie, William M., Chm. Bd., Chief Exec. & Legal Officer--Wissota Trader & B.A. Mason, Chippewa Falls, WI, pg. 718
Scott, Gary L., V.P.-Natl. Sls. Mgr. & Corp. Sec.--Alkota Cleaning Systems, Inc., Alcester, SD, pg. 34
Scott, Hugh, III, Chief Exec. Officer--Western Diesel Services Inc., Saint Louis, MO, pg. 1179
Scott, James A., Mgr.-Adv.--Alkota Cleaning Systems, Inc., Alcester, SD, pg. 34
Scott, James R., Partner & Dir.-Municipal Bonds--J. C. Bradford & Co., Nashville, TN, pg. 170
Scudder, Charles D., Chm. Bd. & Chief Exec. Officer--Charing Cross Group, Louisville, KY, pg. 239
Scudder, Richard B., Chm. Bd.--MediaNews Group Inc., Houston, TX, pg. 735
Seabrook, Charles F., II, Pres.--Seabrook Brothers & Sons, Inc., Seabrook, NJ, pg. 984
Seabrook, James M., Chm. Bd. & Chief Exec. Officer--Seabrook Brothers & Sons, Inc., Seabrook, NJ, pg. 984
Seabrook, James M., Jr., V.P. & Gen. Mgr.--Seabrook Brothers & Sons, Inc., Seabrook, NJ, pg. 984
Seaton, Kenneth M., Chm. Bd., Pres. & Chief Exec. Officer--Family Inns of America, Inc., Pigeon Forge, TN, pg. 398
Seay, Catherine, Sr. V.P., Creative Dir.--Williams Whittle Associates, Inc., Alexandria, VA, pg. 1191
Secrist, Richard, Chm. Bd., Pres. & Chief Exec. Officer--Blue Tee Corporation, New York, NY, pg. 161
Sedler, Herbert L., Pres.--Paper Enterprises, Inc., Bronx, NY, pg. 847
Sedler, Jordan B., V.P., Sec. & Treas.--Paper Enterprises, Inc., Bronx, NY, pg. 847
Segerdahl, Earl E., Chm. Bd. & Pres.--The Segerdahl Corp., Wheeling, IL, pg. 987
Seidman, Theodore M., Chm. Bd. & Pres.--Air Conditioning Co., Inc., Glendale, CA, pg. 26
Seigle, Harry J., Pres.--Seigle's Home & Building Centers, Elgin, IL, pg. 987
Seipel, Paul E., V.P.-Sls. & Mktg.--Brad Foote Gear Works, Inc., Cicero, IL, pg. 169
Seitz, Edgar C., III, Exec. V.P.-Pur., Import & Export--Service Supply Co. Inc. of Indiana, Indianapolis, IN, pg. 992
Seitz, Edgar C., Jr., Chm. Bd. & Exec. V.P.-Pur.--Service Supply Co. Inc. of Indiana, Indianapolis, IN, pg. 992
Seitz, Melvin C., Jr., Pres., Chief Exec. Officer, Chief Oper. Officer & Controller--Service Supply Co. Inc. of Indiana, Indianapolis, IN, pg. 992
Seitz, Tadd C., Chm. Bd. & Chief Exec. Officer--The Scott Company, Marysville, OH, pg. 982
Self, Robert E., V.P.--The WBDC Group, Grand Rapids, MI, pg. 1155
Serino, Matthew, Pres.--Serino Coyne Inc., New York, NY, pg. 991
Sevier, Helen, Chm. Bd., Pres., Chief Exec. & Chief Oper. Officer--B.A.S.S., Inc., Montgomery, AL, pg. 105
Sewell, I.F., Chm. Bd.--Lithotype Company, Inc., South San Francisco, CA, pg. 678
Shafer, Phil, V.P.-Sls.--United Feeds, Inc., Sheridan, IN, pg. 1132
Shaheen, David, Vice Chm. & Chief Exec. Officer--World Carpets, Inc., Dalton, GA, pg. 1202
Shaheen, John, Chm. Bd.--World Carpets, Inc., Dalton, GA, pg. 1202
Shaheen, Piera, Vice Chm.--World Carpets, Inc., Dalton, GA, pg. 1202
Shannahan, Tim, Pres. & Chief Exec. Officer--Video Products Distributors, Inc., Sacramento, CA, pg. 1150
Shapell, David, Exec. V.P.--Shapell Industries, Inc., Beverly Hills, CA, pg. 995
Shapell, Nathan, Chm. Bd., Pres. & Chief Exec. Officer--Shapell Industries, Inc., Beverly Hills, CA, pg. 995
Shapero, J., Chm. Bd., Pres. & Chief Exec. Officer--Quael Corp., Detroit, MI, pg. 902
Shapiro, Albert, Pres.--Commander Oil Corporation, Oyster Bay, NY, pg. 268
Shapiro, Harold D., Exec. V.P.--Commander Oil Corporation, Oyster Bay, NY, pg. 268
Shapiro, Joseph G., Exec. V.P.--Commander Oil Corporation, Oyster Bay, NY, pg. 268
Sharp, M.B., Pres.--Bush Development Corp., Williamsburg, VA, pg. 196
Sharpe, Jack, Pres.--King Group, Inc., Fenton, MI, pg. 630
Shaw, R.W., Chm. Bd.--American Inks & Coatings Corp., Valley Forge, PA, pg. 56
Shea, Michael, Partner & Dir.-Corp. & Govt. Bonds--J. C. Bradford & Co., Nashville, TN, pg. 170
Shea, Michael D., Pres.--Standard Gravure Corp./Shea Communications, Atlanta, GA, pg. 1036
Shearer, Martin P., Pres. & Chief Exec. Officer--Southern Belle Dairy Company, Inc., Somerset, KY, pg. 1020
Shearer, Max A., V.P.-Opers.--Southern Belle Dairy Company, Inc., Somerset, KY, pg. 1020
Shearman, William H., Pres.--Shearman Corporation, Lake Charles, LA, pg. 996
Sheehan, Dennis W., Chm. Bd., Pres. & Chief Exec. Officer--AXIA Incorporated, Oak Brook, IL, pg. 8
Sheets, Mary J., Sec. & Treas.--Rapid Industries, Inc., Louisville, KY, pg. 913
Sheets, Walter G., Pres. & Chief Exec. Officer--Rapid Industries, Inc., Louisville, KY, pg. 913
Sheinbaum, Uri, Chm. Bd. & Pres.--Calmark Investment Company, Los Angeles, CA, pg. 211
Shelby, David T., Pres.--ICM Industries, Inc., Chicago, IL, pg. 559
Sheldon, A.L., V.P.--Sheldons' Inc., Antigo, WI, pg. 996
Sheldon, J.M., Chm. Bd., Pres. & Chief Exec. Officer--Sheldons' Inc., Antigo, WI, pg. 996
Shell, Earl L., Chm. Bd. & Chief Exec. Officer--Hardin Construction Group, Inc., Atlanta, GA, pg. 508
Shellenbarger, David, Chm. Bd. & Pres.--Macro Computer Products Inc., Rochester Hills, MI, pg. 698
Shelley, Tully, III, V.P.--MBT Associates, Inc., San Francisco, CA, pg. 691
Shelton, Thomas R., Pres.--Case Foods, Inc., Salisbury, MD, pg. 227
Sheridan, Edward J., Pres. & Chief Exec. Officer--Edwin B. Stimpson Company, Inc., Bayport, NY, pg. 1049
Sheridan, R. Champlin, Chm. Bd. & Chief Exec. Officer--The Sheridan Group, Hanover, PA, pg. 998
Sherwood, Steven, Pres.--Clayton, Williams & Sherwood, Inc., Newport Beach, CA, pg. 254
Shields, Gerald N., Chm. Bd., Pres. & Chief Exec. Officer--Graymills Corp., Chicago, IL, pg. 480
Shillman, Norman, Pres.--Shillcraft, Inc., Baltimore, MD, pg. 999
Shirazi, Mehdi, Pres. & Chief Exec. Officer--Sigman Meat Co. Inc., Arvada, CO, pg. 1003
Shirk, Betty J., Treas. & Sec.--Beer Nuts, Inc., Bloomington, IL, pg. 132
Shirk, James A., Pres.--Beer Nuts, Inc., Bloomington, IL, pg. 132
Shiver, Roy D., Exec. V.P.-Opers.--Defender Services, Inc., Columbia, SC, pg. 324
Shuford, A. Pope, Pres. & Chief Exec. Officer--Shuford Mills, Inc., Hickory, NC, pg. 1001
Shultz, Gerald, Chm. Bd., Pres. & Chief Exec. Officer--Micro-Met L Corp., Indianapolis, IN, pg. 748
Shura, Richard, Pres.--Central States Enterprises, Inc., Heathrow, FL, pg. 234
Shure, S.N., Chm. Bd.--Shure Brothers Incorporated, Evanston, IL, pg. 1001
Sibley, Harold O., Exec. V.P.--The WBDC Group, Grand Rapids, MI, pg. 1155
Siegal, Michael D., Pres. & Chief Exec. & Chief Oper. Officer--Olympic Steel Inc., Bedford Heights, OH, pg. 825
Siegel, Owen R., Chm. Bd. & Chief Exec. Officer--R.S. Owens, Chicago, IL, pg. 834
Siemer, Arnold B., Chm. Bd. & Pres.--Desco Corporation, Columbus, OH, pg. 332
Siemer, Richard C., Pres.--Siemer Milling Company, Teutopolis, IL, pg. 1002
Sigel, Arthur R., Chm. Bd., Pres. & Chief Exec. Officer--Velsicol Chemical Corporation, Rosemont, IL, pg. 1147
Sigman, Benjamin L., V.P. & Sec.--B. Green & Co., Baltimore, MD, pg. 484
Silverman, Alan, V.P. & Sec.--Silverman Products & Textiles, New York, NY, pg. 1004
Silverman, Barry, Pres.--Ranir Corporation, Grand Rapids, MI, pg. 912
Silverman, Bruce, Pres. & New Bus. Contact--Asher/Gould Advertising, Inc., Los Angeles, CA, pg. 88
Silverman, Glen, V.P.--Silverman Products & Textiles, New York, NY, pg. 1004
Silverman, Lester, V.P. & Treas.--Silverman Products & Textiles, New York, NY, pg. 1004
Simon, Donald S., Jr., Pres.--Serta Mattress Company, Vacaville, CA, pg. 991
Simon, Donald, Sr., Chm. Bd.--Serta Mattress Company, Vacaville, CA, pg. 991
Simon, Laurence P., Sr. V.P.--Health Management Systems, Inc., New York, NY, pg. 521
Simon, Melvin, Chief Exec. Officer--Melvin Simon & Associates, Indianapolis, IN, pg. 1006
Simons, Carl, Pres.--Gateway Apparel, Inc., Saint Louis, MO, pg. 445
Simons, Leonard N., V.P.--Simons Michelson Zieve, Inc., Troy, MI, pg. 1006
Simons, W. Lucas, Mng. Partner--J. C. Bradford & Co., Nashville, TN, pg. 170
Singleton, William Dean, Vice Chm. & Chief Exec. Officer--MediaNews Group Inc., Houston, TX, pg. 735
Sink, Barbara J., V.P., Sec. & Dir.-Personnel--Traders Supermarkets, Inc., Berrien Springs, MI, pg. 1105
Sink, Kenneth W., Pres. & Treas.--Traders Supermarkets, Inc., Berrien Springs, MI, pg. 1105
Sirkin, Samuel, Sec.--Clay-Park Labs, Inc., Bronx, NY, pg. 253
Sirotek, H. Bruce, Pres.--Illinois Auto Electric Co., Elmhurst, IL, pg. 562
Sirotek, Jonathan R., Grp. V.P.--Illinois Auto Electric Co., Elmhurst, IL, pg. 562
Sirotek, R. Gordon, Grp. V.P.--Illinois Auto Electric Co., Elmhurst, IL, pg. 562
Sirotek, Robert L., Chm. Bd.--Illinois Auto Electric Co., Elmhurst, IL, pg. 562
Siskin, David, Partner--CKS Partners, San Francisco, CA, pg. 202
Sklar, Irwin B., Chm. Bd.--Robert F. Driver Co., Inc., San Diego, CA, pg. 349
Slabe, James F., Pres. & Chief Oper. Officer--Executive Enterprises, Inc., New York, NY, pg. 393
Sloan, William E. II, Exec. V.P., Treas. & Sec.--Sloan Valve Company, Franklin Park, IL, pg. 1010
Slovin, Bruce, Pres.--MacAndrews & Forbes Holdings Inc., New York, NY, pg. 694
Smith, Bradley C., Pres. & Gen. Mgr.--Raymark Friction Company, Manheim, PA, pg. 914
Smith, David L., Chm. Bd. & Owner--Homestead House Inc., Broomfield, CO, pg. 542
Smith, Francis C., Chm. Bd.--Burgess & Niple, Limited, Columbus, OH, pg. 190
Smith, Gary W., Chm. Bd., Pres. & Chief Exec. Officer--Proto Systems of Atlanta, Alpharetta, GA, pg. 895
Smith, J. Neil, Chm. Bd., Pres. & Chief Exec. Officer--American Technical Services Group, Inc., Norcross, GA, pg. 63
Smith, LeRoy T., Chm. Bd., Pres. & Chief Exec. Officer--S-T Industries, Inc., Saint James, MN, pg. 964
Smith, Richard P., Exec. V.P. & Chief Exec. Officer--Dairylea Cooperative Inc., East Syracuse, NY, pg. 311
Smith, Robert C., Sr. V.P., Sec. & Gen. Counsel--White Hen Pantry, Inc., Elmhurst, IL, pg. 1185
Smith, Stan, V.P.-Opers. & Pur. Dir.--Exact Equipment Corporation, Langhorne, PA, pg. 392
Smith, T.W., Pres.--Calcot, Ltd., Bakersfield, CA, pg. 208
Smith, William J., Chm. Bd., Pres. & Chief Exec. Officer--U.S. Can Company, Oak Brook, IL, pg. 1134
Smitson, Robert M., Pres. & Chief Exec. Officer--Maxon Corporation, Muncie, IN, pg. 723
Smyth, Anthony, Sec.--John M. Smyth Co., Downers Grove, IL, pg. 1014
Smyth, John M., Chm. Bd.--John M. Smyth Co., Downers Grove, IL, pg. 1014
Smyth, Robert W., V.P.--John M. Smyth Co., Downers Grove, IL, pg. 1014
Smythe, Thomas M., Chm Bd. & Pres.--Keller Crescent Co., Evansville, IN, pg. 620
Snediker, R.R., Chm. Bd.--Chicago Show Printing Co., Morton Grove, IL, pg. 246
Snelling, Andrew P., Treas. & Sec.--The Shelburne Corporation, Shelburne, VT, pg. 996
Snelling, Mark H., Pres.--The Shelburne Corporation, Shelburne, VT, pg. 996
Snoddy, L.O., Chm. Bd. & Pres.--Telsco Industries, Garland, TX, pg. 1085
Snowden, William F., Chm. Bd., Pres. & Chief Exec. Officer--Topline Imports, Inc., Bellevue, WA, pg. 1102
Snyder, Richard W., Chm. Bd. & Chief Exec. Officer--SnyderGeneral Corporation, Dallas, TX, pg. 1015
Solombrino, Scott, Chm. Bd., Pres. & Chief Exec. Officer--Dav-El Services, Inc., New York, NY, pg. 317
Solomon, Jerry L., Chm. Bd.--American Fluorescent Corporation, Waukegan, IL, pg. 54
Solomon, William R., Pres.--American Fluorescent Corporation, Waukegan, IL, pg. 54
Sommer, Adrian, V.P.--Service Motor Company, Dale, WI, pg. 992
Sommer, James, Pres., Chief Oper. & Fin. Officer & Treas.--Service Motor Company, Dale, WI, pg. 992
Sondhi, Vir K., Chm. Bd. & Pres.--National Solvent Corporation, Medina, OH, pg. 793
Songy, Gerald E., Exec. V.P.--The Maurin-Odgen Companies, New Orleans, LA, pg. 722
Soong, Leo, Pres.--Crystal Geyser, Calistoga, CA, pg. 303
Spanos, Alex G., Chm. Bd.--A. G. Spanos Development, Inc., Stockton, CA, pg. 1025
Spanos, Dean A., Pres.--A. G. Spanos Development, Inc., Stockton, CA, pg. 1025
Spanos, George G., Legal Counsel--A. G. Spanos Development, Inc., Stockton, CA, pg. 1025
Spatz, Wendy, V.P.-Design & Promo.--Spatz & Co., Northbrook, IL, pg. 1026
Spelde, M.E., Chm. Bd., Pres. & Chief Exec. Officer--Empire Airlines, Hayden Lake, ID, pg. 379
Spence, Andrew R., Partner--Roney & Co., Detroit, MI, pg. 946
Spence, Paula, Pres.--Hameroff/Milenthal/Spence, Inc., Columbus, OH, pg. 503
Spencer, Guy J. III, V.P.--Spencer Companies Inc., Huntsville, AL, pg. 1030
Spencer, Guy J., Jr., Chm. Bd., Pres. & Chief Exec. Officer--Spencer Companies Inc., Huntsville, AL, pg. 1030
Speyer, Lester D., Chm. Bd.--Tennsco Corporation, Dickson, TN, pg. 1088
Speyer, Stuart W., Pres.--Tennsco Corporation, Dickson, TN, pg. 1088
Spiewak, Gerald, Chm. Bd.--I. Spiewak & Sons, Inc., New York, NY, pg. 1031
Spiewak, Michael, Pres. & Chief Exec. Officer--I. Spiewak & Sons, Inc., New York, NY, pg. 1031
Spigai, Daniel J., Chief Exec. Officer--Howard Needles Tammen & Bergendoff, Kansas City, MO, pg. 547
Sport, Michael C., Chm. Bd., Pres. & Chief Exec. Officer--Production Management Companies, Inc., Harvey, LA, pg. 893

Spradley, James W., Jr., Pres. & Chief Exec. Officer--Standard Candy Co., Inc., Nashville, TN, pg. 1035
Springborn, Robert C., Chm. Bd., Pres. Chief Exec. Officer--Springborn Laboratories, Inc., Enfield, CT, pg. 1033
Sprott, H.B., Jr., Pres. & Chief Exec. Officer--Sprott Oil Co., Inc., Manning, SC, pg. 1034
St. Jacques, Robert, Chm. Bd.--Ocean Spray Cranberries, Inc., Lakeville, MA, pg. 820
Stadelman, Pete, Pres., Chief Exec. & Fin. Officer--Stadelman Fruit Inc., Yakima, WA, pg. 1034
Stadelman, Russell C. II, Pres.--Russell Stadelman & Company, Germantown, TN, pg. 1034
Stadelman, Russell C., Sr., Chm. Bd. & Treas.--Russell Stadelman & Company, Germantown, TN, pg. 1034
Stadelman, Shirley M., Sec.--Russell Stadelman & Company, Germantown, TN, pg. 1034
Stahl, Jack, Treas.--Boston Trading Ltd. Inc., Lynn, MA, pg. 168
Standen, Michael, Chm., Pres. & Chief Exec. Officer--Metallurg, Inc., New York, NY, pg. 742
Stanley, John R., Chm. Bd. & Pres.--Transamerican Refining Corporation, Houston, TX, pg. 1106
Stanton, Laura, V.P., Sec. & Treas.--Dunlap & Co. Inc., Columbus, IN, pg. 353
Stasior, William F., Chm. Bd. & Chief Exec. Officer--Booz Allen & Hamilton Inc., New York, NY, pg. 165
Steakley, John W., Pres.--Steakley Chevrolet Subaru Inc., Dallas, TX, pg. 1043
Stearns, Neele E., Jr., Pres. & Chief Exec. Officer--CC Industries, Inc., Chicago, IL, pg. 199
Steele, Loren, Vice Chm., Chief Exec. Officer & Pres.--Super 8 Motels, Inc., Aberdeen, SD, pg. 1062
Steen, A.B., Chm Bd.--T.D. Williamson, Inc., Tulsa, OK, pg. 1192
Steenberg, W.D., Chm. Bd. & Pres.--Steenberg Homes, Inc., Fond du Lac, WI, pg. 1045
Steinberg, S. Ty, Pres. & Chief Exec. Officer--M. Buten & Sons Inc., Philadelphia, PA, pg. 196
Steiner, Robert, Treas.--Grandpa Brands Company, Cincinnati, OH, pg. 476
Steinhart, Conrad, Treas. & Sec.--Happy Holiday Tree Farms, Sheridan, MI, pg. 506
Steiny, John O., Chm. Bd.--Steiny & Company, Inc., Los Angeles, CA, pg. 1049
Steiny, Susan, Pres.--Steiny & Company, Inc., Los Angeles, CA, pg. 1049
Stephen, George, Sr., Pres.--Weber-Stephen Products, Palatine, IL, pg. 1171
Stephens, Elton B., Chm. Bd.--Ebsco Industries, Inc., Birmingham, AL, pg. 365
Stephens, J.T., Pres., Chief Exec. Officer & Chief Oper. Officer--Ebsco Industries, Inc., Birmingham, AL, pg. 365
Stephens, Warren A., Pres. & Chief Exec. Officer--Stephens, Inc., Little Rock, AR, pg. 1046
Stern, Fred, Legal Officer--David Langer & Co., Inc., Hollywood, CA, pg. 657
Stern, H. Peter, Chm. Bd.--Star Expansion Company, Mountainville, NY, pg. 1039
Stern, Leonard N., Chm. Bd. & Chief Exec. Officer--The Hartz Mountain Corp., Harrison, NJ, pg. 514
Stevens, Frank P., Chm. Bd., Pres., Treas., Chief Exec. Officer & Chief Fin. Officer--Professional Travel, Inc., Dalton, GA, pg. 894
Stevens, Philip L., Pres. & Chief Exec. Officer--Gerber Advertising, Portland, OR, pg. 453
Stewart, Andrew K., Chm. Bd., Pres. & Chief Exec. Officer--Computer Methods Corporation, Livonia, MI, pg. 271
Stewart, Robert A., Owner & Chief Exec. Officer--Advance Steel Co., Detroit, MI, pg. 20
Stewart, Robert M., Sr., Chm. Bd. & Chief Exec. Officer--Remarks, Inc., Dublin, OH, pg. 925
Stickler, Ivan, Pres.--Mid-America Dairymen, Inc., Springfield, MO, pg. 750
Stipp, John S., Chm. Bd. & Chief Exec. Officer--District Petroleum Products, Inc., Sandusky, OH, pg. 340
Stoehr, James H., Jr., Pres. & Chief Exec. Officer--Robbins, Inc., Cincinnati, OH, pg. 938
Stoge, Robert, Dir.-Pur.--Keller Construction Company Ltd., El Monte, CA, pg. 620
Stollenwerk, John J., Pres.--Allen-Edmonds Shoe Corp., Port Washington, WI, pg. 36
Stone, Charles G., Chm., Pres. & Chief Exec. Officer--Stone & Simons Advertising, Inc., Southfield, MI, pg. 1051
Stone, John McWilliams, Jr., Chm. Bd. & Chief Exec. Officer--Dukane Corporation, Saint Charles, IL, pg. 351
Stoner, Mike, Exec. V.P.--Anson-Stoner, Inc., Winter Park, FL, pg. 76
Stork, H. Donald, Chm. Bd.--Stonhard, Inc., Maple Shade, NJ, pg. 1051
Story, Kendra A., Treas. & Controller--ABC Supply Company, Inc., Beloit, WI, pg. 2
Strauss, Richard H., Pres.--Advance Packaging Corporation, Grand Rapids, MI, pg. 19
Street, Gordon P., Jr., Chm. Bd., Pres. & Chief Exec. & Chief Oper. Officer--North American Royalties, Inc., Chattanooga, TN, pg. 811
Streur, Wayne A., Pres.--Castex Industries Inc., Holland, MI, pg. 228
Strickler, Charles O., Pres.--Rocco Inc., Harrisonburg, VA, pg. 940
Strickler, R.H., Chm. Bd.--Rocco Inc., Harrisonburg, VA, pg. 940
Strike, George L., Chm. Bd.--American Laundry Machinery Inc., Cincinnati, OH, pg. 57
Stroh, Peter W., Chm. Bd. & Chief Exec. Officer--The Stroh Brewery Company, Detroit, MI, pg. 1053
Strom, Peter, Vice Chm.--Polo/Ralph Lauren Corporation, New York, NY, pg. 879
Strom, Robert B., Pres.--Foulds Inc., Libertyville, IL, pg. 427
Stropes, Larry, Pres., Chief Exec. Officer & New Bus. Contact--Fabianac, Stropes & Armstrong, Inc., San Francisco, CA, pg. 395
Strubel, Richard P., Pres. & Chief Exec. Officer--MICRODOT, Inc., Chicago, IL, pg. 749
Stumpf, Charles T., Chm. Bd., Pres., Chief Exec. Officer & Treas.--Financial Associates, Overland Park, KS, pg. 410
Styslinger, Lee J., Jr., Chm. Bd.--Altec Industries, Inc., Birmingham, AL, pg. 45
Suard, Andrea Bollinger, Sec.--Bollinger Machine Shop And Shipyard, Inc., Lockport, LA, pg. 163
Suddath, Stephen M., Chm. Bd.--The Suddath Companies, Jacksonville, FL, pg. 1055
Suess, Mary M.T., V.P.--Midcoast Industrial Services Corporation, Cedar Rapids, IA, pg. 751
Suhowatsky, Stephen J., Pres. & Chief Exec. Officer--Syracuse Supply Company, Syracuse, NY, pg. 1070
Suitt, T. Howard, Pres. & Chief Exec. Officer--Suitt Construction Company, Inc., Greenville, SC, pg. 1056
Sullivan, Glenda D., Sec.--Sullivan Oil Company, Baton Rouge, LA, pg. 1057
Sullivan, Kenneth R., Pres. & Chief Exec. Officer--Sullivan Oil Company, Baton Rouge, LA, pg. 1057
Sullivan, Richard S., Chm. Bd.--Sullivan Paper Company, West Springfield, MA, pg. 1057
Sullivan, Robert E., Chm. & Chief Exec. Officer--Lord, Sullivan & Yoder, Inc. Advertising, Columbus, OH, pg. 683
Sullivan, Thomas C., Pres. & Chief Fin. Officer--Sullivan Paper Company, West Springfield, MA, pg. 1057
Sulprizio, Deuta, V.P. & Treas.--United Engine & Machine Company, Carson City, NV, pg. 1131
Sulprizio, Ray R., Pres.--United Engine & Machine Company, Carson City, NV, pg. 1131
Summerfield, Arthur E., Jr., Chm. Bd. & Pres.--Summerfield Truck Co. Inc., Portage, IN, pg. 1057
Sunderland, James P., Chm. Bd.--Ash Grove Cement Company, Overland Park, KS, pg. 87
Sunderland, Robert, Chm. Bd.--Ash Grove Cement Company, Overland Park, KS, pg. 87
Sundman, David M., Pres.--Littleton Coin Co., Inc., Littleton, NH, pg. 679
Sundman, Maynard, Founder--Littleton Coin Co., Inc., Littleton, NH, pg. 679
Sutton, Roy V., Pres. & Chief Exec. Officer--W. B. Goode Company, Inc., Richmond, VA, pg. 470
Sweeney, Jacob B., Jr., Pres.--Jake Sweeney Automotive Inc., Cincinnati, OH, pg. 1067
Swidler, Michael, Sr. V.P. & Dir.-Client Services--Keroff & Rosenberg Advertising Inc., Chicago, IL, pg. 624
Swift, Charles O., Chm. Bd. & Pres.--Swift Dodge Rolls Royce Inc., Sacramento, CA, pg. 1067
Swigert, Henry T., Chm. Bd.--Esco Corporation, Portland, OR, pg. 388
Swisher, John R., Pres. & Chief Exec. Officer--United Feeds, Inc., Sheridan, IN, pg. 1132
Sytsma, Fred, Exec. V.P.-OEM Sls.--Frost Inc., Grand Rapids, MI, pg. 435
Syverson, David B., Pres.--Dave Syverson Lincoln Mercury, Albert Lea, MN, pg. 1071
Taddei, Armando, Chm. Bd., Pres. & Treas.--Hunter Contracting Company, Gilbert, AZ, pg. 554
Taddei, Mirian H., Sec.--Hunter Contracting Company, Gilbert, AZ, pg. 554
Tait, John E., Chm. Bd., Pres. & Chief Exec. Officer--The Penn Mutual Life Insurance Company, Philadelphia, PA, pg. 858
Talge, H. Stephen, Pres.--Dazey Corporation, Industrial Airport, KS, pg. 321
Tallichet, David C., Jr., Chm. Bd., Pres. & Chief Exec. Officer--Specialty Restaurants Corporation, Anaheim, CA, pg. 1027
Talmage, Frank B., Chm. Bd. & Chief Exec. Officer--Superior Reprographics, Seattle, WA, pg. 1064
Tang, Cyrus, Chm. Bd., Pres., & Chief Exec. Officer--Tang Industries Inc., Elk Grove Village, IL, pg. 1078
Tang, Patrick, Pres.--Anderson Die Castings, Inc., Wheeling, IL, pg. 72
Tang, Tom Y.C., Pres.--Tekni-Plex, Inc., Brooklyn, NY, pg. 1084
Tanis, Beth, Exec. V.P. & Chief Oper. Officer--Zephyr Baskets & Balloons, New Providence, NJ, pg. 1217
Tanner, James T., Pres. & Chief Exec. Officer--Tanner Co. Inc., Rutherfordton, NC, pg. 1078
Tanner, Michael S., Exec. V.P.--Tanner Co. Inc., Rutherfordton, NC, pg. 1078
Tanner, Simpson B., III, Chm. Bd.--Tanner Co. Inc., Rutherfordton, NC, pg. 1078
Tarantino, Dominic A., Co-Chm.--Price Waterhouse - U.S., New York, NY, pg. 888
Tarte, Bernard J., Jr., V.P. & Treas.--Bradner Central Company, Chicago, IL, pg. 170
Tarzian, Thomas, Chm. Bd.--Sarkes Tarzian, Incorporated, Bloomington, IN, pg. 1079
Tatman, Richard M., Chm. Bd. & Pres.--Acme Foundry, Inc., Coffeyville, KS, pg. 13
Tattersall, Keith, Chm. Bd., Pres. & Chief Exec. Officer--Amperif Corporation, Chatsworth, CA, pg. 68
Tauber, David, Exec. V.P.--Tauber Oil Company, Houston, TX, pg. 1080
Tauber, Orner J., Jr., Pres. & Chief Exec. Officer--Tauber Oil Company, Houston, TX, pg. 1080
Tauber, Richard, Exec. V.P.--Tauber Oil Company, Houston, TX, pg. 1080
Tauscher, William Y., Chm. Bd.--Regency Lincoln Mercury, Dallas, TX, pg. 922
Tawil, Morris E., Pres.--Tawil Associates Inc., Carteret, NJ, pg. 1080
Taylor, Dale, Pres. & Chief Exec. Officer--Abelson-Taylor, Inc., Chicago, IL, pg. 10
Taylor, David P. Jr., V.P.-Mktg.--Capital Industries, Inc., Seattle, WA, pg. 215
Taylor, J. Curtiss, Pres.--George Lithograph, San Francisco, CA, pg. 452
Taylor, James H., Jr., Partner, Chief Fin. Officer--Kupper Parker Communications Inc., Saint Louis, MO, pg. 646
Taylor, Ronald S., Pres.--Capital Industries, Inc., Seattle, WA, pg. 215
Taylor, William W., Chm. Bd. & Pres.--Midcoast Industrial Services Corporation, Cedar Rapids, IA, pg. 751
Teel, Bill, Pres.--T. J. Cinnamons Ltd., Kansas City, MO, pg. 1073
Terteniz, Oyton, V.P.-Mid Atlantic Region--Greenhorne & O'Mara, Inc., Greenbelt, MD, pg. 485
Theofilos, Steve P., Chm. Bd., Pres. & Chief Exec. Officer--Theochem Labs., Inc., Tampa, FL, pg. 1090
Thielman, David, Chief Exec. Officer--E Z Loader Boat Trailers, Inc., Spokane, WA, pg. 361
Thigpen, John C., Pres. & Chief Oper. Officer--Westgate Inc., Port Allen, LA, pg. 1182
Thomas, James A., Mng. Partner--Maguire Thomas Partners, Los Angeles, CA, pg. 701
Thomas, John E., Pres. & Chief Exec. Officer--Tippins Incorporated, Pittsburgh, PA, pg. 1099
Thomas, John W., Jr., Chm. Bd. & Chief Exec. Officer--Thomas Built Buses, Inc., High Point, NC, pg. 1092
Thomas, Robert L., Pres. & Treas.--Saul Bros. & Company, Inc., Norcross, GA, pg. 972
Thomas, Terence W., Chm. Bd. & Pres.--Arizona Wholesale Supply Company, Phoenix, AZ, pg. 82
Thompson, Jack, L., V.P.-Heavy Tech.--J.D. Edwards & Company, Denver, CO, pg. 370
Thompson, Scott, Chm. Bd., Pres., Chief Exec. & Chief Oper. Officer--Advanced Technology, Inc., Reston, VA, pg. 20
Throgmartin, William G., Chief Exec. Officer--Gregg Appliances Inc., Indianapolis, IN, pg. 486
Thurston, Ray, Chm. Bd. & Chief Exec. Officer--Sonicair, Scottsdale, AZ, pg. 1018
Tinsley, Sandra C., Chm. Bd.--Tinsley Advertising, Miami, FL, pg. 1099
Tippins, George W., Chm. Bd.--Tippins Incorporated, Pittsburgh, PA, pg. 1099
Tishman, John L., Chm.--Tishman Realty & Construction Co., New York, NY, pg. 1099
Toberman, David, Treas. & Sec.--Toberman, Saint Louis, MO, pg. 1099
Toberman, Walter I., Pres.--Toberman, Saint Louis, MO, pg. 1099
Tobiason, Ralph, Pres.--Fenton Press, Inc., Addison, IL, pg. 406
Tointon, Robert G., Pres.--Phelps Tointon Inc., Greeley, CO, pg. 866
Tolone, Thomas A., Pres. & Chief Oper. Officer--Paoli, Inc., Paoli, IN, pg. 846
Tomlin, Eugene B., Pres. & Chief Exec. Officer--I. H. French & Co. Inc., Champaign, IL, pg. 432
Tomsick, Frank, Chm. & Chief Exec. Officer--MBT Associates, Inc., San Francisco, CA, pg. 691
Torinus, John B., Jr., Chm. Bd. & Chief Exec. Officer--Serigraph, Inc., West Bend, WI, pg. 991
Torstenson, Robert H., Chm. Bd. & Pres.--Duo-Fast Corporation, Franklin Park, IL, pg. 354
Tosto, Leo R., Pres.--Trerice Tosto International, Bingham Farms, MI, pg. 1110
Toth, Alex S., Chm. Bd., Pres. & Chief Exec. Officer--PBM Office Products, Cleveland, OH, pg. 835
Trauscht, Donald C., Pres. & Chief Exec. Officer--Borg-Warner Corporation, Chicago, IL, pg. 165
Trauth, Andrew, V.P.-Engrng.--Trauth Dairy Inc., Newport, KY, pg. 1108
Trauth, David E., Jr., Pres. & Chief Exec. Officer--Trauth Dairy Inc., Newport, KY, pg. 1108
Trauth, Louis J., Jr., Chm. Bd.--Trauth Dairy Inc., Newport, KY, pg. 1108
Trauth, Steven A., V.P.-Prod. & Sec.--Trauth Dairy Inc., Newport, KY, pg. 1108
Tremaine, B.G., Jr., Chm. Bd.--Miller Company, Meriden, CT, pg. 754
Trerice, Byron W., Jr., Chm. Bd. & Chief Exec. Officer--Trerice Tosto International, Bingham Farms, MI, pg. 1110
Trick, Mark, V.P.--Southland Flooring Supplies of Louisville, Inc., Louisville, KY, pg. 1023
Trick, Mike, Pres.--Southland Flooring Supplies of Louisville, Inc., Louisville, KY, pg. 1023
Trinkle, Robert C., Pres.--Trinkle Sales, Inc., Cherry Hill, NJ, pg. 1114
Trowbridge, Paul, Chm. Bd., Pres. & Chief Exec. Officer--H.M. Smyth Co., Saint Paul, MN, pg. 1014
True, H.A., Jr., Pres. & Chief Exec. Officer--True Companies, Casper, WY, pg. 1117
Truesdell, J. E. III, Treas.--J. Austin Oil Co., Flint, MI, pg. 99
Truesdell, J. E., Jr., Pres. & Sec.--J. Austin Oil Co., Flint, MI, pg. 99
Trump, Eddie, Pres.--The Trump Group, New York, NY, pg. 1117
Trump, Julius, Chm. Bd. & Chief Exec. Officer--The Trump Group, New York, NY, pg. 1117
Trusheim, H. Edwin, Chm. Bd.--General American Life Insurance Co., St. Louis, MO, pg. 448
Tubis, Sandy, Sr. V.P.--Design 1 Interiors, Los Angeles, CA, pg. 332
Tuckerman, Donald M., Pres. & Chief Exec. Officer--Elkman Advertising & Public Relations, Bala-Cynwyd, PA, pg. 377
Tuckerman, Dr. Steven A., Pres.--Tuckerman Optical Co., Columbus, OH, pg. 1118
Tudor, Michael S., Sec. & Gen. Counsel--Tudor Inc., Alexandria, LA, pg. 1118
Tudor, Robert B., Jr., Pres.--Tudor Inc., Alexandria, LA, pg. 1118
Tully, John M., Pres.--Anderson-Tully Co., Memphis, TN, pg. 73
Turk, Edward, V.P.--PSI Group of Companies, Memphis, TN, pg. 837
Turner, James A., III, Vice Chm.--National Welders Supply Co. Inc., Charlotte, NC, pg. 794
Turner, James A., Jr., Chief Exec. Officer--National Welders Supply Co. Inc., Charlotte, NC, pg. 794
Tushman, Larry, Mng. Partner--Sherwood Food Distributors, Detroit, MI, pg. 998

Tutor, Albert G., Exec. V.P. & Treas.--Tutor-Saliba Corporation, Sylmar, CA, pg. 1120
Tutor, Ronald N., Pres. & Chief Exec. Officer--Tutor-Saliba Corporation, Sylmar, CA, pg. 1120
Tweten, James, Pres.--Magnolia Hi-Fi, Inc., Seattle, WA, pg. 701
Tweten, Leonard M., Chm. Bd.--Magnolia Hi-Fi, Inc., Seattle, WA, pg. 701
Uddenberg, A. Keith, Pres.--Keith Uddenberg, Inc., Gig Harbor, WA, pg. 1125
Uddenberg, Eugenia M., Sec. & Treas.--Keith Uddenberg, Inc., Gig Harbor, WA, pg. 1125
Uddenberg, R. Keith, V.P.--Keith Uddenberg, Inc., Gig Harbor, WA, pg. 1125
Uhl, R.W., V.P.-Fin.--Bar-S Foods Co., Phoenix, AZ, pg. 118
Uicker, Joseph B., Sr. V.P.--The Smith Group, Inc., Detroit, MI, pg. 1012
Ulbrich, Frederick C., III, Pres.-Service Ctr. Grp.--Ulbrich Stainless Steels & Special Metals, Inc., North Haven, CT, pg. 1125
Ulbrich, Frederick C., Jr., Chm. Bd., Pres. & Chief Exec. Officer--Ulbrich Stainless Steels & Special Metals, Inc., North Haven, CT, pg. 1125
Ulbrich, Richard J., Vice Chm.--Ulbrich Stainless Steels & Special Metals, Inc., North Haven, CT, pg. 1125
Uzolins, Uldis, Chief Fin. Officer & V.P.--Fred V. Fowler Company, Inc., Newton, MA, pg. 427
Vahlsing, Donald W., V.P. & Sec.--Effective Management Systems, Milwaukee, WI, pg. 370
Valade, Robert C., Pres. & Chief Exec. Officer--Carhartt, Inc., Dearborn, MI, pg. 220
Van Andel, Jay, Chm. Bd.--Amway Corporation, Ada, MI, pg. 70
Van Hulst, Jack, Pres. & Chief Exec. Officer--Pennex Products Co., Inc., Verona, PA, pg. 858
Van Luven, G.A., Vice Chm., Chief Fin. Officer, Treas. & Controller--The Gage Company, Pittsburgh, PA, pg. 441
Van Metre, Albert G., Sr., Chm. & Pres.--The Van Metre Companies, Burke, VA, pg. 1144
Van Slyke, Peter, Exec. V.P.--Stephen Gould Paper Co., Inc., Whippany, NJ, pg. 473
Van Tuyl, Cecil L., Chm. Bd., Pres. & Chief Exec. Officer--V.T. Inc., Merriam, KS, pg. 1142
Van Wyk, Brooke, Pres. & Chief Exec. Officer--Pace International Corporation, Kirkland, WA, pg. 838
Vann, James M., Jr., Chm. Bd. & Chief Exec. Officer--Rea Magnet Wire Company, Inc., Fort Wayne, IN, pg. 915
Varblow, Carl R., Chm. Bd. & Chief Fin. Officer--Veda Incorporated, Alexandria, VA, pg. 1146
Vargas, Arnulfo, Pres., Chief Exec. Officer & Investor Rels. Dir.--Cash & Carry Grocer Inc., Chicago, IL, pg. 228
Varnadore, Lon, Exec. V.P.--Western Reinsurance Brokers, Inc., Los Angeles, CA, pg. 1181
Vasselli, Joseph F., Pres.--Houston Foods Company, Chicago, IL, pg. 547
Vaughan, Beverly, Pres.--PSI Group of Companies, Memphis, TN, pg. 837
Vavasis, Andrew S., Exec. V.P. & Chief Oper. Officer--Vance Industries, Inc., Chicago, IL, pg. 1144
Veazie, Richard, V.P.--PSI Group of Companies, Memphis, TN, pg. 837
Verebay, Leonard J., Pres.--Queens Group, Inc., Long Island City, NY, pg. 904
Vereen, W.J., Pres., Treas., & Chief Exec. Officer--Riverside Manufacturing Co., Moultrie, GA, pg. 937
Vetter, Jean, Mgr.-Data Processing--Times Printing Company, Inc., Random Lake, WI, pg. 1098
Vinyard, Leon E., Pres. & Chief Exec. Officer--Intermatic Inc., Spring Grove, IL, pg. 575
Vitale, Louis, Pres.--Los Angeles Smoking Curing Company, Los Angeles, CA, pg. 684
Vittek, Louis, V.P.-Mfg.--Artco-Bell Corporation, Temple, TX, pg. 86
Vlick, Robert P., Sr. V.P.-Bldg. System Services Group--Air Conditioning Co., Inc., Glendale, CA, pg. 26
Vogel, Jack H., Chief Fin. Officer--Clay-Park Labs, Inc., Bronx, NY, pg. 253
Vogel, T.N., Pres.--Nutech, Inc., San Jose, CA, pg. 817
von Luhrte, Richard L., Exec. V.P., Sec. & Dir.--RNL Facilities Corporation, Denver, CO, pg. 907
Vora, S.B., Sec.--The Smith Group, Inc., Detroit, MI, pg. 1012
Voss, Michael D., Chm. Bd. & Chief Exec. Officer--Meehan Tooker, East Rutherford, NJ, pg. 736
Wabiszewski, Edmund D., Pres.--Maynard Steel Casting Company, Milwaukee, WI, pg. 725
Wade, Tom W., Jr., Chm. Bd. & Chief Exec. Officer--Tom Wade Co., Kenton, TN, pg. 1157
Wagener, John H., Pres.--Barge-Wagener, Inc., Atlanta, GA, pg. 119
Waggoner, Donald E., Chm. Bd.--Waggoner Corp., Troy, MI, pg. 1158
Waggoner, William, Pres. & Treas.--Waggoner Corp., Troy, MI, pg. 1158
Wagner, Michael R., Pres.--First Worthing, Dallas, TX, pg. 414
Wahl, John F., Pres. & Chief Exec. Officer--Wahl Clipper Corp., Sterling, IL, pg. 1158
Wahl, Robert L., Chm. Bd.--Wahl Clipper Corp., Sterling, IL, pg. 1158
Wahlert, Robert H., Chm. Bd., Pres. & Chief Exec. Officer--FDL Foods, Inc., Dubuque, IA, pg. 394
Wake, Richard, Co-Pres.--Eby Brown Co., Aurora, IL, pg. 365
Wake, Tom, Co-Pres.--Eby Brown Co., Aurora, IL, pg. 365
Walcher, Jack, Chm., Pres. & Chief Exec. Officer--Eddins-Walcher Company, Midland, TX, pg. 367
Waldner, Stephen, Chief Exec. Officer--D. Waldner Company, Inc., Farmingdale, NY, pg. 1159
Waldorf, Robert, Chm. Bd. & Pres.--Idea Man, Inc., Los Angeles, CA, pg. 562
Walk, Consuelo F., Sec.--Walk, Haydel & Associates, Inc., New Orleans, LA, pg. 1159
Walk, Frank H., Co-Chm. Bd. & Chief Exec. Officer--Walk, Haydel & Associates, Inc., New Orleans, LA, pg. 1159
Walker, John T., Chm. Bd., Pres. & Chief Exec. Officer--St. Paul Metalcraft, Inc., Saint Paul, MN, pg. 967
Walliser, Doug, V.P.--Timpte Industries, Inc., Denver, CO, pg. 1098
Wallwork, W.W., III, Pres.--W.W. Wallwork, Inc., Fargo, ND, pg. 1161
Walsh, Daniel J., Pres.--Walsh Construction Co. of Illinois, Chicago, IL, pg. 1161
Walsh, Mathew, Jr., Chm. Bd.--Walsh Construction Co. of Illinois, Chicago, IL, pg. 1161
Walter, Paul F., Chm. Bd., Pres. & Chief Exec. Officer--Thermo Electric Co., Inc., Saddle Brook, NJ, pg. 1091
Walters, Victor, V.P. & Dir.-Flight--Empire Airlines, Hayden Lake, ID, pg. 379
Waltzer, Julius, V.P. & Treas.--Jack Young Associates, Hazleton, PA, pg. 1209
Ward, Ashley F., Chm. Bd.--Ashley F. Ward, Inc., Cincinnati, OH, pg. 1162
Ward, David K., Pres.--Ward Trucking Corp., Altoona, PA, pg. 1163
Ward, G. William, Chm. Bd.--Ward Trucking Corp., Altoona, PA, pg. 1163
Ward, Louis L., Chm. Bd., Pres. & Chief Oper. Officer--Russell Stover Candies, Inc., Kansas City, MO, pg. 957
Ward, Stewart R., Pres. & Gen. Mgr.--Brad Foote Gear Works, Inc., Cicero, IL, pg. 169
Ward, William, Pres.--Ashley F. Ward, Inc., Cincinnati, OH, pg. 1162
Warner, Charles N., Pres.--The U.S. Baird Corporation, Stratford, CT, pg. 114
Warner, John E., Chm. Bd., Chief Exec. Officer & Creative Dir.--Warner, Bicking, Morris & Partners, Inc., New York, NY, pg. 1164
Warog, Thomas, V.P.--Scrufari Construction Co. Inc., Niagara Falls, NY, pg. 983
Warry, Lowrance, Chm. Bd. & Treas.--AEA, Inc., Charlotte, NC, pg. 3
Washington, Bernard, Dir.-Creative--Equinox Advertising, Inc., Chicago, IL, pg. 384
Waters, George B., Pres. & Publisher--Rome Sentinel Co., Rome, NY, pg. 946
Waters, Shirley B., V.P. & Sec.--Rome Sentinel Co., Rome, NY, pg. 946
Waters, Stephen, V.P. & Gen. Mgr.--Rome Sentinel Co., Rome, NY, pg. 946
Watkins, Joe, V.P. & Controller--McLean Enterprises, Inc., Springfield, MO, pg. 731
Watson, James F., Pres.--Skyway Freight Systems, Inc., Watsonville, CA, pg. 1009
Watt, William A., V.P.-Sls.--Moran Towing & Transporation Co. Inc, Greenwich, CT, pg. 769
Weasler, Anthony V., Chm. Bd.--Weasler Engineering Inc., West Bend, WI, pg. 1169
Weaver, W.N., Jr., Sec.--GSC Enterprises, Inc., Chicago, IL, pg. 440
Webb, George H., Chm. Bd.--Jervis B. Webb Company, Farmington Hills, MI, pg. 1170
Webb, Jervis C., Chm. Bd. Emeritus--Jervis B. Webb Company, Farmington Hills, MI, pg. 1170
Webb, Max, Sr. V.P.--Shapell Industries, Inc., Beverly Hills, CA, pg. 995
Webbe, Scotson, Chm. Bd.--Handgards Inc., Northbrook, IL, pg. 504
Weckworth, Rodney R., Exec. V.P.--Rex Moore Electrical Contractors & Engineers, West Sacramento, CA, pg. 768
Wehberg, Joyce, Chief Oper. Officer & Dir.-Pur.--Shillcraft, Inc., Baltimore, MD, pg. 999
Weider, Joseph, Chm. Bd.--Weider Health & Fitness, Woodland Hills, CA, pg. 1173
Weil, Adolph, Jr., Chm. Bd.--Weil Brothers Cotton Inc., Montgomery, AL, pg. 1173
Weil, David S., Pres., Chief Exec. & Chief Oper. Officer--Ampacet Corporation, Tarrytown, NY, pg. 67
Weil, Robert S., II, Pres.--Weil Brothers Cotton Inc., Montgomery, AL, pg. 1173
Weingardt, Ronald, Exec. V.P.--Sun Process Converting Company, Elk Grove Village, IL, pg. 1059
Weinstein, Harvey, Pres.--West Mill Clothes, Inc., Woodside, NY, pg. 1177
Weinstein, Joan, Pres.--Ultimo Ltd., Chicago, IL, pg. 1125
Weisbart, Graig, Chm. Bd.--Sigman Meat Co. Inc., Arvada, CO, pg. 1003
Weisberg, Arthur, Chm. Bd.--State Electric Supply Co., Huntington, WV, pg. 1040
Weisenberg, Robert, Gen. Mgr.--Effective Management Systems, Milwaukee, WI, pg. 370
Weisend, C. Frederick, Chm. Bd., Pres. & Chief Exec. Officer--Fritz Chemical Company, Mesquite, TX, pg. 434
Weisiger, Ed, Jr., Pres.--Carolina Tractor & Equipment Co., Charlotte, NC, pg. 223
Weiss, Larry, Chm. Bd., Pres., Chief Exec. Officer & Sec.--Save More Food Mart, Inc., Hobart, IN, pg. 973
Weissman, S.J., Vice Chm.--Lasky Company, Millburn, NJ, pg. 660
Weitz, Fred W., Chm. Bd. & Pres.--The Weitz Corporation, Des Moines, IA, pg. 1174
Welsh, A.D., Jr., Pres.--Welsh Company, Saint Louis, MO, pg. 1175
Welter, Edward P., Pres. & Chief Oper. Officer--Fabwel Inc., Elkhart, IN, pg. 396
Wenger, Jerry, Chm. Bd. & Pres.--Wenger Corporation, Owatonna, MN, pg. 1176
Wenner, Jann S., Chm. Bd.--Straight Arrow Publishers, Inc., New York, NY, pg. 1052
Wenstrand, Thomas W., Co-Pres. & Sec.--Hawkeye Steel Products, Inc., Houghton, IA, pg. 518
Werra, Robert, Chm., Pres. & Chief Exec. Officer--Amrecorp Realty Inc., Dallas, TX, pg. 68
Werthan, Bernard, Jr., Pres. & Chief Exec. Officer--Werthan Packaging, Inc., Nashville, TN, pg. 1176
West, Charles B., Chm. Bd.--West Lumber Co., Atlanta, GA, pg. 1177
Western, James, V.P.--Macro Computer Products Inc., Rochester Hills, MI, pg. 698
Westphal, Byron, Chm. Bd., Pres. & Chief Exec. Officer--Integrated Energy Controls Corp., Minneapolis, MN, pg. 573
Westreich, Murray, Exec. V.P., Sec. & Treas.--West Mill Clothes, Inc., Woodside, NY, pg. 1177
Wheaton, Robert E., Chm. Bd., Pres., Chief Exec. & Chief Fin. Officer--The Bekins Company, Glendale, CA, pg. 132
Wheeler, Thomas B., Pres. & Chief Exec. Officer--Massachusetts Mutual Life Insurance Co., Springfield, MA, pg. 718
White, Bob, Pres. & Chief Exec. Officer--Marketing Communications, Lenexa, KS, pg. 709
White, Ed, Pres.--Vallet Food Serv Inc., Dubuque, IA, pg. 1143
White, Michael H., Pres.--Rite-Hite Corporation (IA), Dubuque, IA, pg. 936
Whiteman, John O., Pres.-Empire Machinery--Empire Southwest Co., Mesa, AZ, pg. 379
Whitfield, Frank G., Pres. & Chief Exec. Officer--Whitfield Foods, Inc., Montgomery, AL, pg. 1187
Whitfield, L. B. III, Chm. Bd.--Whitfield Foods, Inc., Montgomery, AL, pg. 1187
Whiting, C. Ross, Chm. Bd.--Whiting Manufacturing Co., Inc., Cincinnati, OH, pg. 1187
Whiting, Richard T., Pres. & Chief Exec. Officer--Whiting Manufacturing Co., Inc., Cincinnati, OH, pg. 1187
Whitney, John K., Chm.--Gaymar Industries, Inc., Orchard Park, NY, pg. 447
Whittle, Robert L., Pres.--Williams Whittle Associates, Inc., Alexandria, VA, pg. 1191
Wiedenmayer, Christopher M., Chm. Bd. & Chief Exec. Officer--Faber/Castell Corporation, Parsippany, NJ, pg. 395
Wieland, John F., Chm. Bd., Pres. & Chief Exec. Officer--John Wieland Homes Inc., Atlanta, GA, pg. 1188
Wilcox, David, Pres.--Mountain States Pipe & Supply Company, Colorado Springs, CO, pg. 773
Wilder, Joel B., Chm. Bd.--Wilder Management Associates, Waltham, MA, pg. 1189
Wilder, Thomas, V.P.--Wilder Management Associates, Waltham, MA, pg. 1189
Wiley, Thomas L., Principal--Dewberry & Davis, Fairfax, VA, pg. 334
Wilhelm, James M., Pres. & Chief Exec. Officer--F.A. Wilhelm Construction Co., Inc., Indianapolis, IN, pg. 1189
Wilhoit, Joseph W., Pres.--Phoenix Fuel Company, Inc., Phoenix, AZ, pg. 868
Wilhoit, T.A., Sec.--Phoenix Fuel Company, Inc., Phoenix, AZ, pg. 868
Wilkens, Dennis, V.P.--Davlin Paint Company, Inc., Berkeley, CA, pg. 319
Willert, August W., Jr., Chm. Bd.--Willert Home Products, Inc., Saint Louis, MO, pg. 1190
Willert, William D., Pres. & Treas.--Willert Home Products, Inc., Saint Louis, MO, pg. 1190
Willert, Willimae C., V.P. & Sec.--Willert Home Products, Inc., Saint Louis, MO, pg. 1190
Williams, Alan, Sr. V.P.--MBT Associates, Inc., San Francisco, CA, pg. 691
Williams, Byron, Chm. Bd. & Sec.--Clayton, Williams & Sherwood, Inc., Newport Beach, CA, pg. 254
Williams, D. Anderson, Chm. Bd.--Williams Whittle Associates, Inc., Alexandria, VA, pg. 1191
Williams, David A., Pres. & Gen. Mgr.--Regency Lincoln Mercury, Dallas, TX, pg. 922
Williams, Don E., Chm. Bd., Pres. & Chief Exec. Officer--Don E. Williams Co., Rock Island, IL, pg. 1190
Williams, Gretchen, Co-Chm. Bd. & Sec.--Minyard Food Stores, Coppell, TX, pg. 759
Williams, James C., Pres.--Williams Distributing Company, Grand Rapids, MI, pg. 1190
Williams, Jimmie D., Exec. V.P., Chief Fin. Officer, Treas. & Sec.--Belz Enterprises, Memphis, TN, pg. 138
Williams, Richard John, Legal Officer--Handgards Inc., Northbrook, IL, pg. 504
Williams, Robert T., Chm. Bd.--Williams Distributing Company, Grand Rapids, MI, pg. 1190
Williams, Robert T., Jr., V.P.-Opers.--Williams Distributing Company, Grand Rapids, MI, pg. 1190
Williamson, Richard B., Pres. & Chief Exec. Officer--T.D. Williamson, Inc., Tulsa, OK, pg. 1192
Wilsey, Michael W., Chm. Bd. & Pres.--Wilsey Bennett Co., San Francisco, CA, pg. 1193
Wilson, Arnold B., V.P.--Goddess Bra Company, East Boston, MA, pg. 464
Wilson, David H., Pres.--Goddess Bra Company, East Boston, MA, pg. 464
Wilson, Eric, V.P.--Hensel Phelps Construction Co., Greeley, CO, pg. 530
Wilson, John F., Pres.--Courtesy Chevrolet & Imports Inc., Ithaca, NY, pg. 290
Wilson, Kemmons, Jr., Exec. V.P.--Kemmons Wilson Companies, Memphis, TN, pg. 1194
Wilson, Kemmons, Sr., Chm. Bd. & Owner--Kemmons Wilson Companies, Memphis, TN, pg. 1194
Wilson, Robert, Exec. V.P.--Kemmons Wilson Companies, Memphis, TN, pg. 1194
Wilson, Spence, Pres.--Kemmons Wilson Companies, Memphis, TN, pg. 1194
Wilson, William, Pres. & Chief Exec. Officer--Pioneer/Eclipse Corp., Sparta, NC, pg. 871
Wiltz, Kathy, Dir., Client Services & Acct. Supvr.--Cappelli Miles Wiltz & Kelly, Portland, OR, pg. 216
Winkler, Herbert, Pres.--Jonbil Inc., Chase City, VA, pg. 602
Winship, Blanton C., Pres. & Chief Exec. Officer--Transus Inc., Atlanta, GA, pg. 1108
Winspear, William W., Pres.--Associated Materials Inc., Dallas, TX, pg. 91
Winston, Sam, Chm. Bd. & Chief Exec. Officer--Winston Tire Company, Burbank, CA, pg. 1197

Winters, Robert C., Chm. Bd. & Chief Exec. Officer--The Prudential Insurance Company of America, Newark, NJ, pg. 896
Winterson, Keith J., V.P.-Fin.--Bonney Forge Corporation, Allentown, PA, pg. 164
Witmer, James, Chief Fin. Officer--Avis Ford Inc., Southfield, MI, pg. 102
Wlodarski, Arthur, V.P.-Pur.--Houston Foods Company, Chicago, IL, pg. 547
Woeste, Bill F., Jr., Pres. & Dir.-Pur.--Bill Woeste Dealer Group, Cincinnati, OH, pg. 1198
Woeste, Cynthia, V.P. & Sec.--Bill Woeste Dealer Group, Cincinnati, OH, pg. 1198
Wolf, Lawrence, Pres., Chief Exec. Officer, Sec. & Treas.--Leonard Wholesale, Inc., Elizabeth, NJ, pg. 668
Wolford, David G., Pres., Chief Exec. Officer & Publr.--Commtek Communications, Vienna, VA, pg. 269
Wolfort, David, V.P.--Olympic Steel Inc., Bedford Heights, OH, pg. 825
Wolfs, David, V.P.-Mktg.--El Camino Resources, Ltd., Northridge, CA, pg. 372
Wong, Albert, Treas.--Bel Air Markets, Sacramento, CA, pg. 133
Wong, Gene, Controller--Bel Air Markets, Sacramento, CA, pg. 133
Wong, George R., Pres.--Bel Air Markets, Sacramento, CA, pg. 133
Wood, Guy, Exec. V.P.--Gloria Jean's Coffee Bean Corp., Buffalo Grove, IL, pg. 464
Woodbeck, Milford E., Chm. Bd.--Overhead Conveyor Co., Ferndale, MI, pg. 832
Woodbeck, Milford E., Jr., Pres.--Overhead Conveyor Co., Ferndale, MI, pg. 832
Woodfin, Ira J., Pres.--Woodfin-Smith Pontiac, Inc., Baton Rouge, LA, pg. 1200
Woodruff, Paul H., Chm. Bd., Pres. & Chief Exec. Officer--The ERM Group, Exton, PA, pg. 360
Woodson, James, Co-Chm. Bd.--Taco John's International, Inc., Cheyenne, WY, pg. 1076
Woolverton, Fred T., Jr., Pres.--Woolverton Oldsmobile-G.M.C. Truck, Inc., Jacksonville, FL, pg. 1201
Workman, C.E., Chm. Bd. & Chief Exec. Officer--Tru-Fit Products Corp., Medina, OH, pg. 1117
Workman, M.C., Pres.--Benjamin Moore & Co., Montvale, NJ, pg. 139
Workman, R.E., Pres.--Tru-Fit Products Corp., Medina, OH, pg. 1117
Worrell, Thomas E., Jr., Chm. Bd. & Pres.--Worrell Enterprises, Inc., Boca Raton, FL, pg. 1203
Worsley, Walter C., Jr., Chm. Bd. & Pres.--Worsley Companies Inc., Wilmington, NC, pg. 1204
Wurz, Albert, Pres.--Accu-Sort Systems, Inc., Telford, PA, pg. 11
Wurz, Jane, Sec. & Treas.--Accu-Sort Systems, Inc., Telford, PA, pg. 11
Wurzburg, Reginald, Chief Exec. Officer--Wurzburg, Inc., Memphis, TN, pg. 1205
Wurzburg, Richard, Pres.--Wurzburg, Inc., Memphis, TN, pg. 1205
Wurzel, Tom, Chm. Bd., Pres. & Chief Exec. Officer--ACL Technologies, Santa Ana, CA, pg. 2
Wyler, Jeff, Pres.--Jeff Wyler Dealer Group, Inc., Cincinnati, OH, pg. 1206
Yarmark, Martin J., Exec. V.P.--Triboro Electric Corp., Warminster, PA, pg. 1112
Yarmark, Murray B., Pres.--Triboro Electric Corp., Warminster, PA, pg. 1112
Yee, Robert, V.P.--MBT Associates, Inc., San Francisco, CA, pg. 691
Yoder, Bruce, V.P.-Plng. Div.--Greenhorne & O'Mara, Inc., Greenbelt, MD, pg. 485
Yoh, Harold L., Jr., Chm. Bd., Pres. & Chief Exec. Officer--Day & Zimmermann, Inc., Radnor, PA, pg. 320
Yohman, Edward J., Chm. Bd. & Chief Exec. Officer--Cyberex, Inc., Mentor, OH, pg. 307
Yondo, Donald C., V.P.--Advance Packaging Corporation, Grand Rapids, MI, pg. 19
York, Marie Denise DeBartolo, Exec. V.P.-Corp. Mktg. & Communications--The Edward J. DeBartolo Corporation, Youngstown, OH, pg. 323
Youmans, Peter, Owner & Chief Exec. Officer--Connecticut Spring & Stamping Corporation, Farmington, CT, pg. 275
Young, Alan V., Pres. & Chief Exec. Officer--Young Automotive Group, Indianapolis, IN, pg. 1209
Young, Dan E., Chm. Bd.--Young Automotive Group, Indianapolis, IN, pg. 1209
Young, Dr. C.B.F., Chm. Bd. & Pres.--Young Refining Corp., Douglasville, GA, pg. 1210
Young, E.V., Jr., Pres.--George W. Cochran Co., Inc., Washington, DC, pg. 258
Young, F.M., Jr., Pres.--Young Radiator Company, Racine, WI, pg. 1210
Young, Jack, Chm. Bd., Pres., Chief Exec. & Chief Fin. Officer--Jack Young Associates, Hazleton, PA, pg. 1209
Young, R.J., V.P.--George W. Cochran Co., Inc., Washington, DC, pg. 258
Young, Richard F., Chm. Bd., Pres. & Chief Exec. Officer--Sues, Young & Brown Inc., Baldwin Park, CA, pg. 1056
Young, W.E., Sec. & Treas.--George W. Cochran Co., Inc., Washington, DC, pg. 258
Young, William A., V.P.--Young Automotive Group, Indianapolis, IN, pg. 1209
Yraceburu, Vatinia, Sec.--United Engine & Machine Company, Carson City, NV, pg. 1131
Zachrich, C.S., Sec.--Haeger Industries, Inc., Dundee, IL, pg. 499
Zachry, H.B., Jr., Chm. Bd. & Chief Exec. Officer--H.B. Zachry, San Antonio, TX, pg. 1215
Zalkind, Steve, V.P.--Clover Financial Corporation, Merchantville, NJ, pg. 256
Zenie, Francis H., Pres.--Zymark Corporation, Hopkinton, MA, pg. 1221
Zenner, Merrill, Chm. Bd.--The Reliable Corp., Chicago, IL, pg. 924
Zeratsky, J.G., Pres.--National Rivet & Manufacturing Company, Waupun, WI, pg. 793
Zickler, Leo E., Pres. & Chief Exec. Officer--Oxford Realty Services Corp., Bethesda, MD, pg. 835
Ziegler, Allen S., Chm. Bd.--Westco Products, Inc., Pico Rivera, CA, pg. 1178
Ziegler, Douglas, Sec. & Treas.--Westco Products, Inc., Pico Rivera, CA, pg. 1178
Ziegler, Gordon S., Jr., Pres. & Chief Oper. Officer--Ziegler Chemical & Mineral Corp., Jericho, NY, pg. 1218
Ziegler, Ronald L., Pres.--Westco Products, Inc., Pico Rivera, CA, pg. 1178
Zieve, Morton, Chm. Bd.--Simons Michelson Zieve, Inc., Troy, MI, pg. 1006
Ziff, William B., Jr., Chm. Bd.--Ziff Communications Company, New York, NY, pg. 1218
Zifferer, Morton F., Jr., Pres. & Chief Exec. Officer--New Standard Corporation, Mount Joy, PA, pg. 802
Zilkha, Ezra, Chm. Bd.--Union Holdings, Inc., New York, NY, pg. 1128
Zilkha, Selim K., Chm. Bd. & Chief Exec. Officer--Zilkha Energy Company, Houston, TX, pg. 1219
Zimdar, Dorothy L., Pres.--Zimdar Enterprises, Wyoming, MI, pg. 1220
Zimdar, William L., V.P. & Chief Fin. Officer--Zimdar Enterprises, Wyoming, MI, pg. 1220
Zimmerli, Kurt, Chm. Bd., Pres., Chief Exec. Officer & Chief Oper. Officer--Zima Corp., Spartanburg, SC, pg. 1219
Zimmerman, William R., Chm. Bd., Pres. & Chief Exec. Officer--Zimmerman Holdings, Inc., San Marino, CA, pg. 1220
Zylke, Ralph B., Pres.--Zylke & Associates, Northbrook, IL, pg. 1221
Zylstra, Stan, Chm. Bd.--Land O'Lakes, Inc., Arden Hills, MN, pg. 653

PUBLIC RELATIONS

Aamodt, Jeanne, Dir.-Pub. Rels.--Ellerbe Becket, Inc., Minneapolis, MN, pg. 378
Abbott, Barbara, Mgr.-Pub. Rels.--Wenczel Tile Co., Trenton, NJ, pg. 1176
Abels, Mark, V.P.-Corp. Communications--NWA, Inc., Saint Paul, MN, pg. 782
Abels, Mark E., V.P.-Corp. Communications--Northwest Airlines, Inc., Saint Paul, MN, pg. 782
Abood, Mary E., Dir.-Pub. Rels.--Advanstar Communications, Cleveland, OH, pg. 21
Acerson, Jeff, Dir.-Corp. Communications--WordPerfect Corporation, Orem, UT, pg. 1202
Ackerman, Stephanie C., Dir.-Corp. Communications of Aloha--Aloha Airgroup, Inc., Honolulu, HI, pg. 43
Ackerman, Stephanie C., Dir.-Corp. Communications--Aloha Airlines, Inc., Honolulu, HI, pg. 43
Adams, Ann, Dir.-Pub. Rels.--Jordan Associates, Oklahoma City, OK, pg. 604
Adams, Mary, Mgr.-Customer Service--Sunbeam Home Comfort, Shubuta, MS, pg. 1059
Adams, Richard, Mgr.-Mktg. & Pub. Rels.--Great Lakes Dredge & Dock, Oak Brook, IL, pg. 481
Adduci, Liane, V.P. & Dir.-Corp. Communications--Bayer Bess Vanderwarker Inc., Chicago, IL, pg. 128
Adriaenssens, Kristel, Pub. Rels. Dir.--Bordelais, Lemeunier & Leo Burnett, Clichy,, France, pg. 192
Ahlersmeyer, Amy S., Pub. Rels. Mgr.--Bonsib Inc., Fort Wayne, IN, pg. 164
Aiken, Barry H., Dir.-Human Res. & Public Affairs--Johnson Wax Limited, Camberley,, United Kingdom, pg. 600
Albertini, Stephen, Sr. V.P., Gen. Mgr., Pub. Rel.--Earle Palmer Brown & Spiro, Philadelphia, PA, pg. 182
Alcouloumre, Henry, Dir.-Pub. Rels.--CCI Corporation, Tulsa, OK, pg. 200
Alexander, Bob, V.P.-Customer Service--Republic Telcom Systems Corporation, Boulder, CO, pg. 928
Alexander, Don M., V.P.-Publicity--Adam Meldrum & Anderson Co., Inc., Buffalo, NY, pg. 16
Alfonto, Amelia, Dir.-Pub. Rels.--Baar & Beards, New York, NY, pg. 107
Allen, Joseph, Dir.-Communications--Borg-Warner Corporation, Chicago, IL, pg. 165
Allen, Joseph C., Dir.-Pub. Rels.--Baker Industries, Inc., Parsippany, NJ, pg. 166
Allendorf, Donald, Dir.-Mktg. Communications & Res.--The Gates Rubber Company, Denver, CO, pg. 445
Altman, Frances, Mgr.-Pub. Rels.--Teepak, Inc., Westchester, IL, pg. 535
Amaral, Fatima, Liason Officer--BSB Portugal, Lisbon,, Portugal, pg. 110
Andersen, David C., V.P.-Public Affairs--Cable Division, Atlanta, GA, pg. 294
Andersen, Douglas, V.P.-Adv., Pub. Rels. & Mktg.--Allied Mutual Insurance Company, Des Moines, IA, pg. 38
Anderson, Candyce, Mgr.-Indus. Rels.--Lone Star Brewing, San Antonio, TX, pg. 526
Anderson, Curtis W., V.P.-Member & Pub. Rels.--Sunkist Growers, Inc., Sherman Oaks, CA, pg. 1060
Anderson, Scott, Mgr.-Communications--Clark Oil & Refining Corporation, Saint Louis, MO, pg. 252
Anthony, Susan, Exec. V.P., Pub. Rels.--Richardson, Myers & Donofrio, Inc., Baltimore, MD, pg. 933
Arbige, Stephanie, Dir., Pub. Rels.--MCC, Inc., Essex, CT, pg. 691
Arias, Alfredo, Pub. Rels. Dir.--San Jose & Associates, Chicago, IL, pg. 969
Arnold, Richard K., Mgr.-Corp. Communications--Agway, Inc., De Witt, NY, pg. 25
Atkinson, Stella, Pub. Rels.--Wilshire Newport Inc., Burbank, CA, pg. 1193
Attenborough, Louisa, Mgr.-Pub. Rel.--Veryfine Products, Inc., Westford, MA, pg. 1148
Autry, Charles T., Sr. V.P.-Governmental Affairs & Gen. Counsel--Oglethorpe Power Corp., Tucker, GA, pg. 822
Bachler, Bud, V.P.-Mktg./Communications--Winona Knits, Winona, MN, pg. 1196
Bachman, Pat, Sr. V.P.-Customer Rels.--Tollycraft Yachts Corp., Kelso, WA, pg. 1100
Baddish, Laura, Dir.-Pub. Rels.--The Alden Group Ltd., New York, NY, pg. 32
Badesch, Roger, Dir.-Adv. & Pub. Rels.--Gloria Jean's Coffee Bean Corp., Buffalo Grove, IL, pg. 464
Baer, Linda A., Dir.-Communications--The Spring Air Company, Des Plaines, IL, pg. 1032
Bahdaw, Carol, Dir.-Mktg. & Pub. Rels.--Van Cleef & Arpels, Inc., New York, NY, pg. 1144
Bailey, Barbara, Mgr.-Mktg./Communications--Robert E. Lamb, Inc., Valley Forge, PA, pg. 652
Bailey, Jan, Dir.-Communications--Furnival/State Machinery Co., Lancaster, PA, pg. 437
Baisley, Sarah, Dir.-Publicity & Pub. Rels.--Hanna-Barbera Productions, Inc., Los Angeles, CA, pg. 53
Baker, Larry, V.P.-Human Rels.--National Machinery Company, Tiffin, OH, pg. 792
Ball, Jim, V.P.-Communications--Dr Pepper/Seven-Up Companies, Inc., Dallas, TX, pg. 342
Ball, Vern, Dir.-Fulfillment Services--Petersen Publishing Company, Los Angeles, CA, pg. 864
Ballard, Margaret B., Dir.-Corp. Communications--Hayes Microcomputer Products, Inc., Norcross, GA, pg. 519
Ballin, Scott, Dir., Communications--Milton Samuels Advertising Agency, Inc., New York, NY, pg. 968
Ballinger, Tim, Mgr.-Mktg. Communications--Sloan Technology, Santa Barbara, CA, pg. 1146
Balte, Cindy, Coord.-Pub. Rels.--Gordon Bailey & Associates, Inc., Stone Mountain, GA, pg. 114
Bankers, Gene, V.P.-Communications & Investor Rels.--ShopKo Stores, Inc., Green Bay, WI, pg. 1000
Barber, Peggy, Assoc. Exec. Dir.-Communications--American Library Association, Chicago, IL, pg. 57
Barchus, Patti, Corp. Communications Dir.--American Family Mutual Insurance Co., Madison, WI, pg. 51
Barmmer, Russ, V.P.-Pub. Rels.--Burkhardt & Christy Advertising, Inc., New York, NY, pg. 191
Barnard, Nancy, Coord.-Pub. Rels.--Computer Dynamics, Inc., Virginia Beach, VA, pg. 271
Barnes, Roy, V.P., Pub. Rels.--Stone, August, Baker Communications Companies, Troy, MI, pg. 1050
Barnes, Roy, V.P., Pub. Rels.--R. J. Baker Advertising, Inc., Troy, MI, pg. 1051
Baron, Myrna, V.P., Pub. Rels. Dir.--Baron & Zaretsky Advertising, Inc., New York, NY, pg. 121
Barone, Richard, V.P.-Mktg. & Pub. Rels.--New York Racing Association, Jamaica, NY, pg. 803
Baronowski, Susan, Pub. Rels.--White, Good & Co., Lebanon, PA, pg. 1185
Barr, P.C., Dir.-Pub. Rels.--Illinois Consolidated Telephone Co., Mattoon, IL, pg. 563
Barringer, David W., Dir.-Communications--Goodwill Industries of America, Inc., Bethesda, MD, pg. 471
Batsilas, Mgr.-Pub. Rels. & Mktg.--Austin Sculpture, Holbrook, NY, pg. 99
Baxter, Harry, V.P. & Dir.-Public Rels.--Jackson Hole Ski Resort, Teton Village, WY, pg. 587
Bean, Barbara, Dir.-Communications--Kitchell Corporation, Phoenix, AZ, pg. 634
Beard, Christel, Pub. Rels. Assoc.--Speer, Young & Hollander, Inc., Los Angeles, CA, pg. 1030
Beck, Deborah A., V.P.-New Bus.--Northwestern Mutual Life Insurance Co., Milwaukee, WI, pg. 815
Beck, Denise, Pub. Rels. Mgr.--Arnold Fortuna Lawner & Cabot, Portland, ME, pg. 84
Becker, Deborah, Sr. V.P., Pub. Rels. Dir.--Colle & McVoy, Inc., Minneapolis, MN, pg. 261
Beemer, Kathleen, Dir.-Pub. Affairs--Recreational Equipment, Inc., Kent, WA, pg. 917
Beggs, Robert W., Sr. V.P. & Sec.--Society for Savings Bancorp, Inc., Hartford, CT, pg. 1016
Beiro, M. Mark, Dir.-Pub. Rels.--Tampa Jai-Alai, Tampa, FL, pg. 1203
Beisel, Philipp J., V.P.-Information--R. H. Macy & Co., Inc., New York, NY, pg. 698
Belinger, Harry, V.P.-Pub. Affairs--ARA Group, Philadelphia, PA, pg. 5
Bell, Robert C., Mgr.-Communications & Dir.-Internal Art, Meetings Plng. & Video--Battenfeld Gloucester Engineering Co. Inc., Gloucester, MA, pg. 126
Benkstein, Ken, Exec. V.P. & Pub. Rels. Dir.--Meyocks Benkstein Associates, Des Moines, IA, pg. 746
Bennett, Judith A., V.P.-Mktg. & Pub. Rels.--Fabric Wholesalers, Inc., Portland, OR, pg. 396
Bennett, Tevis, Dir.-Pub. Rels.--Rapid Industries, Inc., Louisville, KY, pg. 913
Bentelspacher, Fred, Sr. V.P.-Gen. Mdsg.--Hess's Department Stores, Inc., Allentown, PA, pg. 302
Berger, Joy, Pub. Rels. Dir.--RTA Advertising, Inc., Montreal,, Canada, pg. 193
Bergh, Gloria, Mgr.-Pub. Rels.--Modern Woodmen of America, Rock Island, IL, pg. 763
Bergmann, Richard, Mgr.-Distr. & Customer Service--Findley Adhesives, Inc., Wauwatosa, WI, pg. 410
Bernett, Paula, Mgr.-Pub. Rels.--Guideposts Associates, Inc., Carmel, NY, pg. 493
Berrier, Roy, Personnel Dir.--Mannington Ceramic Tile, Lexington, NC, pg. 704
Best, Kenneth G., V.P.-Cargo, Sls. & Services of Aloha--Aloha Airgroup, Inc., Honolulu, HI, pg. 43
Beverly, Stephen, Mgr.-Pub. Rels.--Warner Press, Inc., Anderson, IN, pg. 1164
Bevilagua, D., Mgr.-Indus. Rels.--American Welding & Manufacturing Co., Warren, OH, pg. 65
Billingsley, Grant, Mgr.-Pub. Affairs--Insilco Corporation, Midland, TX, pg. 571
Binck, Walter, Mgr.-Customer Service--Howe Furniture Corporation, Trumbull, CT, pg. 547
Bird, Thomas S., Jr., Dir.-Communications--Cole Business Furniture, York, PA, pg. 608
Black, Pamela, Sr. V.P., Pub. Rels.--Stephan & Brady, Incorporated, Madison, WI, pg. 1046

Black, Ralph, Dir.-Human Resources--Christian Children's Fund, Inc., Richmond, VA, pg. 248
Black, Vince, Mgr.-Imports--Zephyr Baskets & Balloons, New Providence, NJ, pg. 1217
Blackburn, Mike, Dir., Pub. Rels.--Peter Wong & Associates, Inc., Richmond, VA, pg. 1199
Blair, Betty, Dir.-Customer Service--Seattle City Light, Seattle, WA, pg. 986
Blickens, George, Dir.-Personnel--Haddon Craftsmen, Inc., Scranton, PA, pg. 499
Blomberg, Joe, V.P.-Personnel--Microdot Aerospace Fastening Systems Group, Fullerton, CA, pg. 749
Blount, Girard M., V.P.-Pub. Rels.--Sands Investments, Inc., Myrtle Beach, SC, pg. 970
Boasberg, Eve, Pub. Rels. Mgr.--Sperling, New Orleans, LA, pg. 1030
Bodi, Mark M., V.P., Pub. Rels.--O'Neil Griffin & Associates, Inc., Manchester, NH, pg. 827
Bodie, Carolyn, V.P., Pub. Rels.--Gray Kirk/VanSant Advertising, Inc., Baltimore, MD, pg. 479
Bodoskky, Louis, V.P.-Mdse. Info.--Steinbach, White Plains, NY, pg. 1045
Boesch, Elizabeth L., Mgr.-Communications & Community Rels.--Nebraska Public Power District, Columbus, NE, pg. 796
Bogart, Judith, Dir., Pub. Rels.--Sive/Young & Rubicam, Cincinnati, OH, pg. 1211
Bogunia, Sandra, Pub. Rels. Dir.--Lou Beres & Associates, Inc., Chicago, IL, pg. 141
Bogus, Ron, Mgr.-Pub. Affairs--Nebraska Public Power District, Columbus, NE, pg. 796
Boissonneault, Martha, Dir.-Corp. Communications--Summa Four, Inc., Manchester, NH, pg. 1057
Bolling, Pat, Pub. Rels. Dir.--The Puckett Group, Saint Louis, MO, pg. 899
Borden, Richard, Mgr.-Mktg. Communications--MICOM Communications Corp., Simi Valley, CA, pg. 748
Borden, Richard, Mgr.-Pub. Rels.--MICOM Communications Corp., United Kingdom, pg. 748
Boren, Karen, Mgr.-Pub. Rels. & Media--Atlantic Gulf Communities Corporation, Miami, FL, pg. 95
Borgen, Larry W., Mgr.-Adv.--American Hardware Mutual Insurance Co., Minnetonka, MN, pg. 55
Boston, Dorothy, Dir.-Community Affairs--Ziff Communications Company, New York, NY, pg. 1218
Bottega, Debra, Mktg. Coord.--Flexel, Inc., Atlanta, GA, pg. 418
Boulais, Dee, Mgr.-Sls. & Service--Lan-O-Sheen, Inc., Saint Paul, MN, pg. 653
Boulton, Richard, Dir.-Communications--DonTech, Chicago, IL, pg. 345
Bourgeois, Bob, Dir.- Pub. Rels.--Meyer & Wallis, Inc., Milwaukee, WI, pg. 746
Bowden, Margo R., V.P.-Pub. Rels.--Johnson & Higgins, New York, NY, pg. 598
Bowen, LaRita R., V.P.-Pub. Rels.--Avis Industrial Corporation, Upland, IN, pg. 102
Bowman, Clarinda, Publicity & Promo. Coord.--Abingdon Press, Nashville, TN, pg. 10
Bowman, Joaquin, Dir.-Pub. Rels.--Southeastern Pennsylvania Transportation Authority, Philadelphia, PA, pg. 1020
Boyce, Raymond A., Sr. V.P.-Corp. Rels.--Viacom Inc., New York, NY, pg. 785
Boyle, Kevin, V.P.-Pub. Rels.--Zena Jeans, New York, NY, pg. 1217
Boyter, J. Earle, V.P.-Mktg. & Sls.--Piper Aircraft Corporation, Vero Beach, FL, pg. 872
Braatz, Clay R., Sr. V.P.-Personnel--Western Reinsurance Brokers, Inc., Los Angeles, CA, pg. 1181
Bradley, Connie, V.P.-Human Resourses--Kalmbach Publishing Co., Milwaukee, WI, pg. 615
Bradley, Tom, Assoc. Dir.-Pub. Rels.--Mintz & Hoke Inc., Avon, CT, pg. 759
Brafman, Leon, Dir.-Mdsg. & Adv.--B. Green & Co., Baltimore, MD, pg. 484
Brancoli, David, Dir.-Pub. Rels.--Visa U.S.A. Inc., San Mateo, CA, pg. 1153
Bratnick, Michael, V.P., Acct. Supvr., Pub. Rels.--Gilbert, Whitney & Johns, Inc., Whippany, NJ, pg. 458
Bratz, Keith, Dir.-Communications--Provident Mutual Life Insurance Co., Philadelphia, PA, pg. 896
Braun, Norman, V.P.-Pub. Affairs--Encyclopaedia Britannica, Inc., Chicago, IL, pg. 381
Brazier, David A., V.P., Dir. Bus. Affairs--Creswell, Munsell, Fultz & Zirbel, Cedar Rapids, IA, pg. 1211
Brender, Kristin, Dir.-Pub. Rels.--American Speedy Printing Centers, Inc., Bloomfield Hills, MI, pg. 61
Brett, Derwood, Corp. Communications--Arkansas Electric Cooperatives Inc., Little Rock, AR, pg. 83
Brewer, Marilyn, Dir.-Corp. Communications--Woodward-Clyde Group, Inc., Denver, CO, pg. 1200
Breya, Marge, V.P., Pub. Rels.--Karakas, VanSickle Ouellette Advertising & Public Relations, Portland, OR, pg. 616
Brightman, Patrick, Pub. Rels. Mgr.--SSD&W Integrated Marketing Communications, Montville, NJ, pg. 964
Briick, Gerald, Dir.-Mfg. & Customer Services-Midwest--W. Braun Company, Chicago, IL, pg. 172
Brinkmoeller, Tom, V.P.- Pub. Rels.--Gouchenour Adv., Inc., Orlando, FL, pg. 473
Briscoe, Andy, Dir.-Natl. Pub. Affairs--MADD (Mothers Against Drunk Driving), Irving, TX, pg. 691
Britton, Tracy T., Dir.-Promos.--Straight Arrow Publishers, Inc., New York, NY, pg. 1052
Brower, Paul G., V.P.-Communications--Gold Kist, Inc., Atlanta, GA, pg. 465
Brown, Carolyn, Pub. Rels.--Image Dynamics, Incorporated, Baltimore, MD, pg. 563
Brown, Cathy, Customer Service--Flexible Flyer Inc., West Point, MS, pg. 847
Brown, Garry, Communications & Pub. Information Coord.--Highlights for Children, Inc., Columbus, OH, pg. 534
Brown, Herbert R., V.P.-Community Affairs--Western & Southern Life Insurance Co., Cincinnati, OH, pg. 1181
Brown, Kathleen, Natl. Pub. Rels. Mngmt.--Sperling, New Orleans, LA, pg. 1030
Brown, Malcolm P., Sr. V.P.-Mktg. & Communications--The Binswanger Company, Philadelphia, PA, pg. 151
Brown, Mary Rose, V.P., Pub. Rels. Services--The Atkins Agency, San Antonio, TX, pg. 94
Brown, Pauline, Mgr.-Pub. Rels. & Adv.--Arrow Pneumatics Co. Inc., Lake Zurich, IL, pg. 85
Brown, Robert W., Dir.-Pub. Rels.--Baltimore Orioles, Inc., Baltimore, MD, pg. 116
Brown, Tim, Pub. Rels. Dir.--Fotheringham & Associates, Salt Lake City, UT, pg. 427
Brownstein, Beverly, Exec. V.P., Pub. Rels. Dir.--The Brownstein Group, Philadelphia, PA, pg. 183
Bru, Alfred, Mgr.-Adv. & Pub. Rels.--Komatsu Dresser Company, Lincolnshire, IL, pg. 565
Bruno, Jim, Pub. Rels. Dir.--Roska Direct Marketing, Inc., North Wales, PA, pg. 949
Bruyn, Kimberly, Mgr.-Pub. Rels.--Amway Corporation, Ada, MI, pg. 70
Bryan, J.L., Dir.-Communications & Pub. Rels.--Sverdrup Corporation, Maryland Heights, MO, pg. 1065
Bryant, Jennifer, Natl. Pub. Rels. Dir.--Young & Rubicam Sydney Pty. Ltd., North Sydney,, Australia, pg. 1213
Buckley, E.W., Dir.-Corp. Services--Decision Data Inc., Horsham, PA, pg. 323
Buffington, Dorothy, Dir.-Communications--The ERM Group, Exton, PA, pg. 360
Burge, Susan, Dir.-Pub. Rels.--Schwegmann Giant Super Markets, New Orleans, LA, pg. 980
Burgher, Pam, Mgr.-Pub. Rels.--Moran Industries, Inc., Midlothian, IL, pg. 769
Burkhardt, Sheila, Dir.-Member Rels.--Michigan Milk Producers Association, Novi, MI, pg. 747
Burkhart, David, Pub. Rels. Supvr.--Lenac, Warford, Stone, Inc., Newport Beach, CA, pg. 667
Burkhart, Ronald R., V.P.-Communications--IGA, Inc. (Independent Grocers Alliance), Chicago, IL, pg. 560
Burns, Edward V., V.P.-Human Resources--Penske Truck Leasing, Chesterfield, MO, pg. 859
Burris, Mary Ellen, Dir.-Consumer Affairs--Wegmans Food Markets, Inc., Rochester, NY, pg. 1172
Calek, Terry A., V.P. & Dir.-Pub. Affairs--Mutual of Omaha Insurance Company, Omaha, NE, pg. 779
Calek, Terry A., V.P. & Dir.-Pub. Affairs--Mutual of Omaha, Omaha, NE, pg. 779
Calhoun, Merrell, Pres.-Pub. Rels.--Sullivan Haas Coyle, Atlanta, GA, pg. 1056
Callahan, Howard M., Mgr.-Communications--McArdle Printing Co., Inc., Upper Marlboro, MD, pg. 189
Calvert, Nancy A., Dir.-Adv. & Pub. Rels.--Shure Brothers Incorporated, Evanston, IL, pg. 1001
Cameron, John J., Dir.-Corp. Communications--Ace Hardware Corporation, Oak Brook, IL, pg. 12
Cameron, Marsha, Exec. V.P.-Pub. Rels.--Archer/Malmo Adv., Inc., Memphis, TN, pg. 80
Camp, Diane M., Dir.-Adv. & Pub. Rels.--Hooker Industries, Ontario, CA, pg. 543
Campbell, DeeAnn, V.P.-Communications--Del Monte Foods, San Francisco, CA, pg. 325
Campbell, H. Reid, Specialist-Customer Services--Tennessee Valley Authority, Knoxville, TN, pg. 1088
Cantele, Chris, Pub. Rels. Dir., New Bus. Contact--Creative Marketing International Corp., West Chicago, IL, pg. 297
Cantin, Robert L., Dir.-Communications--Karsten Manufacturing Corporation, Phoenix, AZ, pg. 617
Carley, Robin, Pub. Rels. Dir.--Sisti, Zinbarg & Howard, Inc., Paramus, NJ, pg. 1009
Carlson, Duane R., V.P.-Communications--Blue Cross and Blue Shield Association, Chicago, IL, pg. 159
Carlson, George W., Publicity Dir.--Saratoga Harness Racing, Inc., Saratoga Springs, NY, pg. 970
Carney, Ed, Dir.-Pub. Rels.--Western Regional Off Track Betting, Batavia, NY, pg. 1181
Carr Locke, Robin, Dir.-Communications--San Francisco Giants Baseball Club, San Francisco, CA, pg. 969
Carr, Gail A., Coord.-Mktg. Service--Microdot Aerospace Fastening Systems Group, Fullerton, CA, pg. 749
Carroll, Delphine, Dir.-Pub. Rels.--Nutri/System Inc., Blue Bell, PA, pg. 818
Cartwright, Marie Izzo, Asst. V.P.-Corp. Mktg. & Communications--The Edward J. DeBartolo Corporation, Youngstown, OH, pg. 323
Cartwright, Mary L., Sr. V.P.-Communications & Employee Devel.--Tennessee Valley Authority, Knoxville, TN, pg. 1088
Case, Brian, Mgr.-Pub. Rels.--BCM Engineers Inc., Plymouth Meeting, PA, pg. 106
Cashen, Susan, V.P., Pub. Rels. Dir.--Leonard Monahan Lubars & Kelly, Providence, RI, pg. 668
Castaldi, Thomas E., V.P.-Communications--Essex Group, Inc., Fort Wayne, IN, pg. 389
Cates, Max, Dir.-Mktg. Communications--Associated Electric Co-op Inc., Springfield, MO, pg. 89
Cation, Kenneth L., Grp. Pres.--Atlas/Soundolier, Fenton, MO, pg. 64
Cattaneo, Joseph, Sr. V.P., Pub. Rels.--Gunder & Associates, Inc., Dublin, OH, pg. 494
Cauble, Toni M., Dir.-Corp. Communications--West Point-Pepperell, Inc., West Point, GA, pg. 400
Causing, Amy, Dir.-Pub. Rels. & Publ.--Weider Health & Fitness, Woodland Hills, CA, pg. 1173
Cavsey, Diana, Dir.-Pub. Rels.--Sammons Enterprises, Inc., Dallas, TX, pg. 968
Cecil, Allan V., V.P.-Pub. Affairs--National Gypsum Company, Charlotte, NC, pg. 790
Ceneceros, Claudia, Pub. Rels. Dir.--Pinne/Herbers Advertising Inc., San Francisco, CA, pg. 871
Chadwick, Clarence, Dir.-Human Rels.--Grocers Supply Co. Inc., Houston, TX, pg. 488
Chadwick, Doyia, Pub. Rels. Dir.--Young & Laramore, Indianapolis, IN, pg. 1209
Chafe, H. David, Matls. Info. Dir.--ASM International, Materials Park, OH, pg. 8
Chapman, Kim, Mgr.-Pub. Rels.--Matrix Essentials, Inc., Solon, OH, pg. 721
Charatzi, Dimitra, Public Rels. Dir.--J. N. Leoussis Advertising & Marketing S.A., Athens,, Greece, pg. 1072
Chase, David J., V.P.-Govt. & Pub. Rels.--Lennox International Inc., Richardson, TX, pg. 667
Chatham, Mary, Communications Specialist--Bourns, Inc., Riverside, CA, pg. 168
Chaves, D. Doc, Asst. V.P.-Corp. Communications--Ameritas Life Insurance Corp., Lincoln, NE, pg. 66
Chess, Paul, Mgr.-Mktg. Communications--Schwinn Bicycle Company, Chicago, IL, pg. 981
Child, Laura, Member Communications Coord.--Michigan Milk Producers Association, Novi, MI, pg. 747
Chmel, Valentine, V.P.-Communications--West Coast Life Insurance Co., San Francisco, CA, pg. 795
Choate, Carl, V.P.-Corp. Services--Pillowtex Corporation, Dallas, TX, pg. 870
Christensen, Duane D., Sr. V.P.-Corp. Communications--Maritz Inc., Fenton, MO, pg. 707
Christian, John, V.P.-Customer Service & Engineering--Del Mar Avionics, Irvine, CA, pg. 325
Christon, Dean, Mgr.-Pub. Rels.--DHL Corporation, Redwood City, CA, pg. 309
Christon, Dean, Mgr.-Mktg. Communications--DHL Airways, Inc., Redwood City, CA, pg. 309
Chura, Kyle P., Mgr.-Corp. Rels.--ASC Incorporated, Southgate, MI, pg. 7
Cleary, Kate, Public Rels. Mgr.--DonTech, Chicago, IL, pg. 345
Clement, Ilaina, V.P., Pub. Rels.--Decker Rickard, Glastonbury, CT, pg. 324
Clouser, Christopher E., Sr. V.P.-Communications & Adv.--Northwest Airlines, Inc., Saint Paul, MN, pg. 782
Coalter, Rick, Dir.-Mktg. Communications--J. A. Sexauer, Scarsdale, NY, pg. 357
Cobb, Robert D., V.P.-Communications--B.A.S.S., Inc., Montgomery, AL, pg. 105
Cochran, Jack W., 2nd V.P.-Customer Services--Shenandoah Life Insurance Company, Roanoke, VA, pg. 997
Cochran, Mary M., Dir.-Corp. Communications--Amtran, Inc., Indianapolis, IN, pg. 69
Cody, Steve, Sr. V.P., Pub. Rels. Dir.--Earle Palmer Brown/ New York, New York, NY, pg. 182
Coffey, Suzanne, Mgr.-Public Relations--Tri Valley Growers Inc., San Francisco, CA, pg. 1111
Cohen, Peter, Sr. V.P., Pub. Rels.--Ingalls, Quinn & Johnson, Boston, MA, pg. 567
Cole, Ken, V.P.-Public Affairs--Memphis Light, Gas & Water, Memphis, TN, pg. 738
Coleman, Claire, Pub. Rels. Asst.--CHF Industries, Inc., New York, NY, pg. 200
Collins, Dan F., Mgr.-Pub. Rels.--Andersen Consulting, Chicago, IL, pg. 72
Collins, Scott, V.P., Pub. Rels.--Haselow & Associates, Inc., Cleveland, OH, pg. 516
Collins, Wendell Wood, Dir.-Corp. Communications--The Associated Press, New York, NY, pg. 91
Collinsworth, Daisy, Dir.-Pub. Rels.--Buck & Pulleyn, Inc., Rochester, NY, pg. 185
Colvin, Clark T., V.P.-External Affairs--Cajun Electric Power Co-op, Baton Rouge, LA, pg. 207
Colvin, Tom, Mgr.-Customer Service--RDI, Inc., Itasca, IL, pg. 906
Condit, Hilary, V.P.-Corp. Rels.--Viacom Inc., New York, NY, pg. 785
Condon, Mark, Asst. V.P.-Communications--Credit Union National Association, Madison, WI, pg. 298
Confer, William C., V.P.-Industry & Customer Rels.--Roundy's, Inc., Pewaukee, WI, pg. 952
Conley, James, V.P., Dir. Pub. Rels.--Arnold Fortuna Lawner & Cabot, Boston, MA, pg. 84
Conlin, E.J., Acct. Supvr., Pub. Rels.--Arnold Fortuna Lawner & Cabot, Hartford, CT, pg. 84
Connors, William, Pub. Rels. Dir.--IceLandAir, New York, NY, pg. 561
Conroy, James T., V.P.-Public Affairs--Revlon Group Inc., New York, NY, pg. 695
Contos Wilson, Dixie, Dir.-Pub. Rels.--Pay Less Super Markets, Inc., Anderson, IN, pg. 852
Coplan, Ben, Dir.-Pub. Rels.--Holstein Association of America, Brattleboro, VT, pg. 541
Copps, Thomas R., V.P.-Pub. Rels.--The Copps Corp., Stevens Point, WI, pg. 285
Cosgrove, Howard, V.P., Pub. Rels.--Lindsay, Stone & Briggs Advertising, Inc., Madison, WI, pg. 676
Cotton, Bruce C., Sr. V.P.-Pub. Affairs--Jerrico, Inc., Lexington, KY, pg. 229
Cotton, Bruce C., Sr. V.P.-Pub. Affairs--Long John Silver's, Inc., Lexington, KY, pg. 229
Cowell, Carin, Coord.-Communications--IDAB International Incorporated, Hampton, VA, pg. 559
Cowell, John F., III, Mng. Dir. & Grp. Comm. Officer--CS First Boston Group, Inc., New York, NY, pg. 203
Cox, Dorothy, Mktg. Communications Coord.--Westclox, Norcross, GA, pg. 451
Cox, Dorothy, Mktg. Communications Coord.--Seth Thomas, Norcross, GA, pg. 451
Cox, Kitty, Dir.-Mktg. Communications--Greenwood Mills, Inc., New York, NY, pg. 486
Craft, Christine, Dir.-Pub. Rels.--Brim, Inc., Portland, OR, pg. 176
Crawford, Jerriann, Dir.-Pub. Rels.--Keller Crescent Co., Irving, TX, pg. 621
Crawford, Richard C., Mgr.-Transmission & Customer Services--Tennessee Valley Authority, Knoxville, TN, pg. 1088
Cremin, Judith, Pub. Rels.--Greengage Associates, Inc., New York, NY, pg. 485
Crowley, Kathleen, Dir.-Pub. Rels.--Polar Corporation, Worcester, MA, pg. 878

Corporate Responsibilities Index

Cruickshank, Jim, V.P.-Communications--Fender Musical Instruments, Scottsdale, AZ, pg. 406
Crystal, Jay, Mgr.-Pub. Rels.--Imperia Bros., Inc., Pelham Manor, NY, pg. 563
Cullen, David A., 2nd V.P.-Customer Service--Boston Mutual Life Insurance Co., Canton, MA, pg. 167
Cullen, Karon, Dir.-Corp. Communications--W.B. Johnson Property, Inc., Atlanta, GA, pg. 598
Cullers, Carmelita R., Dir.-Pub. Rels. & Special Events Coord.--Vince Cullers Advertising Inc., Chicago, IL, pg. 304
Cunningham, Jim, V.P.-Customer Service--Blue Cross & Blue Shield of Texas, Inc., Richardson, TX, pg. 160
Curran, Thomas, V.P.-Customer Service--The Wm. Powell Company, Cincinnati, OH, pg. 882
Czupor, James, V.P., Pub. Rels.--Thomas & Perkins, Denver, CO, pg. 1093
D'Alessio, Alice, Dir.-Communications--Marshall Erdman and Associates, Inc., Madison, WI, pg. 385
D'Amour, Claire M., V.P.-Corp. Affairs--Big Y Foods Inc., Springfield, MA, pg. 149
Dages, W.E., Dir.-Pub. Rels.--The F.A. Bartlett Tree Expert Co., Stamford, CT, pg. 123
Daggett, John, Dir.-Pub. Rels.--RAYOVAC Corporation, Madison, WI, pg. 915
Davern, Erin, Pub. Rels., Acct Exec.--Lenac, Warford, Stone, Inc., Newport Beach, CA, pg. 667
Davies, Mitzi, Dir.-Adv. & Pub. Rels.--Roffe, Inc., Seattle, WA, pg. 943
Davis, J.D., Dir.-Communications & Pub. Rels.--Borg-Warner Automotive, Inc., Livonia, MI, pg. 166
Davis, Jeff, Dir.-Communications--Universal Companies, Inc., Grand Rapids, MI, pg. 1138
Davis, Mitch, V.P.-Pub. Rels.--C & S Wholesale Grocery Inc., Brattleboro, VT, pg. 198
Davis, Philip, Pub. Rels. Dir.--Waldbillig & Besteman, Inc., Madison, WI, pg. 1159
Dawshare, Harding E., V.P. & Dir.-Pub. Rels.--Dawahares, Inc., Lexington, KY, pg. 319
Deaver, William, Dir.-Adv. & Promo.--United States Savings Bonds Division, Treasury Department, Washington, DC, pg. 1137
DeGood, Paul W., Mgr.-Mktg. Services--M.C. Gill Corporation, El Monte, CA, pg. 458
DeHahn, Mary L., Partner, Production & Pub. Rels.--Kupper Parker Communications Inc., Saint Louis, MO, pg. 646
Del Col, Dante V., V.P.-Adv. & Promo.--Random House, Inc., New York, NY, pg. 19
Del Pozzo, Lisa, Dir.-Pub. Rels.--Marketing Magic Inc., Fort Lauderdale, FL, pg. 709
Delano, Kate, Pub. Rels.--Sass & Associates, Annapolis, MD, pg. 972
Delgado, Alicia, Mgr.-Pub. Rels.--Aero Peru Corporation, Miami, FL, pg. 22
DeLo, Tina R., Coord.-Mktg. Communications--Decision Data Inc., Horsham, PA, pg. 323
DeLora, Charles A., Sr. V.P.-Sls., Mktg., Adv. & Pub. Rels.--Service Supply Co. Inc. of Indiana, Indianapolis, IN, pg. 992
DeLuca, Rosanne, Dir., Bus. Devel. & Pub. Rels.--Waring & LaRosa, Inc., New York, NY, pg. 1163
Delude, Gary, Pub. Rels. & Acct. Exec.--Mark Anderson Associates, Inc., Scottsdale, AZ, pg. 73
Dennig, Loretta, Dir.-Pub. Rels.--Minyard Food Stores, Coppell, TX, pg. 759
Densen, Rob, Dir.-Pub. Affairs--Oppenheimer Management Corp., New York, NY, pg. 719
Dent, Joan, Dir.-Pub. Rels. Info.--American Water Works Association, Denver, CO, pg. 65
Deogracias, Sandy, V.P., Pub. Rels.--Martiny & Company, Cincinnati, OH, pg. 716
Dervales, R.J., V.P.-Indus. Rels.--Atlantic Steel Company, Atlanta, GA, pg. 95
Desch, Theodore E., Sr. V.P.-Law & Corp. Affairs--Blue Cross & Blue Shield of Illinois, Chicago, IL, pg. 160
Detjen, Dale, Mgr.-Member Services--Dakota Electric Association, Farmington, MN, pg. 312
Deutsch, Dayna, Dir.-Public Affairs--KSTP-TV, Saint Paul, MN, pg. 549
Devine, Bridgette, Dir.-Pub. Rels. & Adv.--Harry Winston, Inc., New York, NY, pg. 1197
Diamantis, Diane G., Dir.-Mktg. Communications--Stiles Corporation, Fort Lauderdale, FL, pg. 1049
Dietrich, Frank, Supervisor-Pub. Rels.--Tassani Communications, Chicago, IL, pg. 1080
Dilorio, Joe, Dir.-Client Devel.--DeMaria Building Co. Inc., Novi, MI, pg. 327
Dilcango-Crowel, Elaine, V.P., Pub. Rels.--Winterkorn Lillis Inc., Rochester, NY, pg. 1197
Dillihunt, Curtis L., V.P.-Customer Service & Mktg.--Memphis Light, Gas & Water, Memphis, TN, pg. 738
Dillon, John, V.P., Pub. Rels.--Speer, Young & Hollander, Inc., Los Angeles, CA, pg. 1030
DiLouie, Craig, Mgr.-Communications, Indus. & Commercial--Creative Marketing Alliance Inc., Princeton Junction, NJ, pg. 297
DiMaso, Donna, Mgr.-Cust. Rels.--Shurfine-Central Corp., Northlake, IL, pg. 1001
Dimon, Wanda, Mgr.-Adv., Mktg. Promo. & Pub. Rels.--Crested Butte Mountain Resort, Inc., Mount Crested Butte, CO, pg. 299
Disney, Jack, Media Rels. Dir.--Hollywood Park, Inc., Inglewood, CA, pg. 540
Dockter, Dell, Mgr.-Pub. Rels.--CUNA Mutual Insurance Society, Madison, WI, pg. 205
Dodson, Cindi, Dir.-Pub. Rels.--Leo Eisenberg & Co., Inc., Kansas City, MO, pg. 372
Dolan, Brian P., Exec. Dir.-Pub. Affairs--The Long Island Rail Road Co., Jamaica, NY, pg. 745
Doltor, Julie, Mgr.-Customer Service--Servus Footwear Company, Rock Island, IL, pg. 993
Domeshek, David, V.P., Pub. Rels.--Duval & Partners, Boston, MA, pg. 356
Domingo, Marie, Pub. Rels. Coord.--Speer, Young & Hollander, Inc., Los Angeles, CA, pg. 1030
Donehue, J. Douglas, Dir.-Corp. Communications--Evening Post Publishing Co., Charleston, SC, pg. 391
Donnellon, Kenneth P., V.P.-Adv. & Communications--John Blair Communications, Inc., New York, NY, pg. 155
Donnellon, Kenneth P., V.P.-Adv. & Communications--Blair Television, New York, NY, pg. 155
Donoghue, Ken, Dir.-Pub. Rels.--Keiler & Company, Farmington, CT, pg. 620
Dorn, Linda, Pub. Rels. Dir.--Edward G. Dorn & Associates, Inc., Rolling Meadows, IL, pg. 346
Douglas, Richard, Sr. V.P.-Corp. Affairs--Sun Diamond Growers of California, Pleasanton, CA, pg. 1058
Downie, Timothy, V.P.-Customer Service--Uforma Shelby Business Forms, Shelby, OH, pg. 746
Downing, Ann, Dir.-Corp. Communications--Harte-Hanks Communications, Inc., San Antonio, TX, pg. 513
Downs, Jennifer, Dir.-Pub. Consumer Affairs--Meijer, Inc., Grand Rapids, MI, pg. 737
Doyal, Steve, Mgr.-Corp. Media Rels.--Hallmark Cards, Inc., Kansas City, MO, pg. 501
Doyal, Steve, Dir.-Media Rels.--Ambassador Cards, Kansas City, MO, pg. 502
Doyle, Matthew, V.P.-U.S. Service--Ampex Corporation, Redwood City, CA, pg. 998
Drabowicz, Barbara, Mgr., Pub. Rels.--Thompson & Company, Memphis, TN, pg. 1094
Drohan, Terri Dutton, Dir., Pub. Rels.--Stern Advertising, Inc., Pepper Pike, OH, pg. 1047
Droz, Kenneth, Promo. & Pub. Rels. Dir.--Robert Solomon & Associates Adv. Inc., Bloomfield Hills, MI, pg. 1017
Drum, Jack, Mgr., Pub. Rels.--The Highland Group, Inc., Southport, CT, pg. 534
Duer, Rodger, Dir.-Pub. Rels.--Monrovia Nursery Co., Azusa, CA, pg. 766
Dunn, Robert H., V.P.-Corp. Communications & Community Affairs--Levi Strauss & Co., San Francisco, CA, pg. 670
Dunnirvine, R., Controller--Telechron, Inc., Ashland, MA, pg. 1085
Durante, Sheila, V.P. Pub. Rels.--MCKONE & CO., INC., Irving, TX, pg. 731
Duvall, Martine, Mgr.-Adv. & Public Rels.--Showell Farms, Inc., Showell, MD, pg. 1000
Dye, Robert, V.P.-Communications--Journal Communications Inc., Milwaukee, WI, pg. 607
Eaglefield, Ray, Mgr.-Service--Norman Brothers Nissan Inc., Orlando, FL, pg. 810
Easter, Steven, V.P.-Govt. Member Rels. & Sec.--Blue Diamond Growers, Sacramento, CA, pg. 160
Ebert, Carol J., Dir.-Mktg. Communications & Pub. Rels.--Gates Energy Products, Inc., Alachua, FL, pg. 445
Eccleston, John, Sr. V.P., Pub. Rels.--Block & Nardizzi, Stamford, CT, pg. 157
Eck, Eileen, V.P.-Communications--Damian Bisch & Partners, Inc. Advertising, New York, NY, pg. 153
Eckardt, Eleanor P., V.P.-Consumer Rels.--Levitz Furniture Corporation, Boca Raton, FL, pg. 647
Eddy, Rusty, Dir.-Pub. Rels.--Glen Ellen Winery, Glen Ellen, CA, pg. 461
Edwards, Diane, V.P.& Assoc. Dir.-Pub. Rels.--Mintz & Hoke Inc., Avon, CT, pg. 759
Edwards, Karen K., Dir.-Mktg, Sls. Promo., Mdse. & Communications--Applied Microsystems Corporation, Redmond, WA, pg. 79
Edwards, Mason, Jr., Mgr.-Customer Rels.--Ventura Travelware, Inc., Long Island City, NY, pg. 1147
Ellis, Jeff, V.P.-Personal Lines--VASA North Atlantic Insurance Company, Indianapolis, IN, pg. 1146
Emerson, Nedwin, V.P. & Dir.-Adv. & Pub. Rels.--The Troy Savings Bank, Troy, NY, pg. 1116
England, Laura E., Mgr.-Pub. Rels.--Atlantic Dairy Cooperative, Southampton, PA, pg. 94
Ensweiler, Richard L., Sr. V.P.-Corp. & Public Rels.--CUNA Mutual Insurance Society, Madison, WI, pg. 205
Epstein, Marvin M., Dir.-Pub. Rels. & Adv.--The Austin Company, Cleveland, OH, pg. 790
Erickson, Conroy, Dir.-Pub. Rels.--Rand McNally & Company, Skokie, IL, pg. 911
Erskine, Terry, V.P.-Labor Rels.--Northwest Airlines, Inc., Saint Paul, MN, pg. 782
Erwin, Carol E., Dir.-Public Affairs--Kohler Company, Kohler, WI, pg. 639
Esposito, Sharyn, V.P., Bus. Affairs--Griffin Bacal Inc., New York, NY, pg. 486
Etheredge, Nancy, Dir., Pub. Rels., A.P.R.--Culver & Associates, Inc., Omaha, NE, pg. 304
Eulich, Karis, Mgr.-Pub. Rels.--C. R. Anthony Company, Oklahoma City, OK, pg. 77
Evans, Susan, Dir.-Public Rels.--Viacom Cable, Pleasanton, CA, pg. 785
Everett, Carol, Adv. & Public Rels. Exec.--Scheduling Technology Corporation, Hopkinton, MA, pg. 975
Eves, Jeffrey P., V.P.-Pub. Affairs--Fort Howard Corporation, Green Bay, WI, pg. 425
Extract, Barbara Royce, Dir.-Corp. & Public Rels.--Environmental Industries, Inc., Calabasas, CA, pg. 383
Fabro, Louis V., Dir.-Media Rels.--Nationwide Mutual Insurance Company, Columbus, OH, pg. 795
Fabro, Louis V., Dir.-Media Rels.--Nationwide Corporation, Columbus, OH, pg. 795
Fader, L., Dir.-Sls. Promo.--Lensclean, Inc., Carlstadt, NJ, pg. 33
Fader, Liz, Mgr.-Pub. Rels. & Adv.--Aldine Technologies, Carlstadt, NJ, pg. 33
Fader, Liz, Mgr.-Pub. Rels. & Adv.--Lensclean, Inc., Carlstadt, NJ, pg. 33
Falck, Susan, Mgr.-Pub. Rels.--Pip Printing, Agoura Hills, CA, pg. 616
Falcone, Kathy, V.P., Pub. Rels.--Fletcher Hunt Wirth Associates, Inc., Kansas City, MO, pg. 418
Farrel, Mary, V.P.-Corp. Communications--Amfac, Inc., Chicago, IL, pg. 585
Farrell, Dorothy, Dir.-Communications--Sargento Cheese Co., Plymouth, WI, pg. 971
Farrell, Earl, V.P.-Pub. Rels.--Walker & Associates, Inc., Memphis, TN, pg. 1159
Farrell, Laurie, Mgr.-Pub. Rels.--International Jensen Inc., Lincolnshire, IL, pg. 578
Farrell, Mary, Dir.-Corp. Communication--JMB Realty Corporation, Chicago, IL, pg. 584
Faulkner, Jim, Dir.-Public Rels.--Trans World Airlines, Inc., Mount Kisco, NY, pg. 561
Feagans, Elizabeth W., V.P.-Mktg. & Communications--The Royal China & Porcelain Companies Inc., Moorestown, NJ, pg. 953
Feld, Larry, Pub. Rels.--Carelli, Glynn & Ward, Butler, NJ, pg. 218
Fellman, Nelson, Pres., Sls. Promo.--Rosanio, Bailets & Talamo, Inc., Cherry Hill, NJ, pg. 947
Fenimore, George W., Sr. V.P.-Pub. Affairs--Peck Jones Construction, Los Angeles, CA, pg. 854
Fenton, Bette, Dir.-Pub. Rels. & Communications--Star Tribune, Minneapolis-St. Paul, Minneapolis, MN, pg. 291
Ferguson, Carolyn, Mgr.-Natl. Mktg.--Columbus Show Case Company, Columbus, OH, pg. 267
Ferris, Deborah A., Dir.-Pub. Rels.--Giffels Associates, Inc., Southfield, MI, pg. 457
Fetter, Jane T., Chm. Bd. & Sec.--Kettenburg Marine Corporation, San Diego, CA, pg. 626
Fetterer, Peter J., Mgr.-Media & Civic Services--Kohler Company, Kohler, WI, pg. 639
Fey, David, Dir.-Pub. Rels.--Ellerbe Becket, Inc., Minneapolis, MN, pg. 378
Fick, William J., Creative Dir.--Lyon Metal Products, Inc., Montgomery, IL, pg. 690
Fiden, Elizabeth M., Mktg. Communications Mgr.--Dukane Corporation, Saint Charles, IL, pg. 351
Fie, Julie, Dir.-Publicity--Sacramento Kings, Sacramento, CA, pg. 965
Figueras, Luis G., V.P.- Consumer Promos./Pub. Rels.--GS&B-Lintas Advertising, Coral Gables, FL, pg. 440
Fitzgerald, Margaret, Sr. V.P., Dir. Community Rels.--Hill, Holliday, Connors, Cosmopulos, Inc., Boston, MA, pg. 534
Fitzmaurice, Robert, Mgr.-Indus. Rel.--Target Sportswear, Inc., New York, NY, pg. 1079
Fiuczynski, Hans, Dir.-External Rels.--Mars, Incorporated, McLean, VA, pg. 713
Fjalstad, Sherm, Mgr.-Communications & Indus. Rels.--Federated Mutual Insurance Company, Owatonna, MN, pg. 405
Flaherty, David, Dir.-Pub. Affairs--ARA Group, Philadelphia, PA, pg. 5
Flaherty, David, Dir.-Public Affairs--ARA Services, Inc., Philadelphia, PA, pg. 5
Fleeger, David, Dir. Pub. Rels.--Blattner/Brunner Inc., Pittsburgh, PA, pg. 156
Flick, Earl D., Head-Office Pub. Affairs--The Aerospace Corporation, El Segundo, CA, pg. 22
Florence, A.A., V.P.-Communications & Plng.--Union Switch & Signal Inc., Pittsburgh, PA, pg. 1129
Flores, Rosa M., Dir.-Communications--American International Container, Inc., Miami, FL, pg. 56
Flynn, Margaret, Communications Coordinator--Guy Gannett Publishing Company, Portland, ME, pg. 442
Flynn, T.G., Sr. V.P. & Mgr.-Pub. Rels.--Bechtel Group, Inc., San Francisco, CA, pg. 130
Foley, Ricky D., Mgr.-Sls. Promo. & Pub. Rels.--V.F. Energies, Inc., Madisonville, KY, pg. 1141
Folkes, S., Dir.-Mktg. Communications--General Binding Corporation, Northbrook, IL, pg. 656
Forgione, Deborah, Dir.-Mktg.--Boyer Bros. Inc., Altoona, PA, pg. 169
Forsyth, Steve, V.P., Pub. Rels. Dir.--Stephan & Brady, Incorporated, Madison, WI, pg. 1046
Fortier, Ed, Dir.-Customer Service--Varityper, Inc., East Hanover, NJ, pg. 1146
Foster, Jeannie, Mgr.-Customer Service-Rupture Discs--Fike Corporation, Blue Springs, MO, pg. 409
Foster, Judith M., Corp. Customer Liaison--Gilbert Mfg. Corp., Locke Mills, ME, pg. 458
Fox, Connie, Dir.-Corp. Affairs--Delta Queen Steamboat Company, New Orleans, LA, pg. 385
Fox, Laura, Dir.-Pub. Rels. & Mktg.--Williams Television Time, Inc., Santa Monica, CA, pg. 1191
Franco, Harry, Sr. V.P. & Dir.-Communications--Soundesign Corporation, Jersey City, NJ, pg. 1018
Franco, Thomas S., V.P.-Corp. Communications--The Berkshire Life Insurance Company, Pittsfield, MA, pg. 142
Franks, Allan, Dir.-Environmental Pub. Rels.--Hameroff/Milenthal/Spence, Inc., Columbus, OH, pg. 503
Franks, Donna, Communications Mgr.--Advanced Technology, Inc., Reston, VA, pg. 20
Frantz, David E., Dir.-Mktg. & Pub. Rels.--Developers Diversified, Moreland Hills, OH, pg. 333
Frautschi, Deanna L., V.P.-Communications & Human Resources--Country Companies Insurance Group, Bloomington, IL, pg. 289
Frautschi, Deanna L., V.P.-Communications & Human Resources--Country Life Insurance Company, Bloomington, IL, pg. 289
Frautschi, Deanna L., V.P.-Communications & Human Resources--Country Mutual Insurance Company, Bloomington, IL, pg. 289
Frawley, Jim, V.P., Pub. Rels. Dir.--Mason & Madison, Inc., New Haven, CT, pg. 718
Fredo, Peter W., V.P.-Customer Communications & Adv.--United Parcel Service of America, Inc., Atlanta, GA, pg. 1133
French, Richard, V.P., Pub. Rels. Dir.--Rockett, Burkhead, Lewis & Winslow, Raleigh, NC, pg. 941
Frey, Charles, V.P.-Pub. Rels.--Nelson & Schmidt, Inc., Milwaukee, WI, pg. 797
Frey, Geraldine R., Dir.-Pub. Rels.--John S. Frey Enterprises, Los Angeles, CA, pg. 433

Friedman, Ray, Dir.-Mktg. Communications--San Francisco French Bread Company, Oakland, CA, pg. 969
Friesen, Janis M., Dir., Pub. Rels.--Sullivan Higdon & Sink Incorporated, Wichita, KS, pg. 1056
Frisbie, Steve, Dir.-Mdse. & Pub. Rels.--Godfather's Pizza, Inc., Omaha, NE, pg. 464
Frohock, Anne, Dir.-Pub. Rels.--Sachs Holding Company, Chesterfield, MO, pg. 965
Futuran, Marge, Dir.-Pub. Rels.--Clayton-Davis & Associates, Incorporated, Saint Louis, MO, pg. 253
Gahm, Tom, Sr. V.P.-Pub. Rels.--Miller Meester Advertising Inc., Minneapolis, MN, pg. 754
Gajevski, Linda, V.P.-Bus. Devel. & Publ. Rels.--Meldrum & Fewsmith Communications Inc., Cleveland, OH, pg. 737
Galanou, Dina, Public Rels. Dir.--Leo Burnett S.A., Athens,, Greece, pg. 193
Gallone, Larry, Mgr.-Mktg. Communications--Powell Electronics Inc., Philadelphia, PA, pg. 882
Garbs, Cindy Crane, Dir.-Public Affairs--Randall's Food Markets, Inc., Houston, TX, pg. 911
Garrison, Karen, Dir.-Communications--Payless Cashways, Inc., Kansas City, MO, pg. 853
Garson, William Donald, Dir.-Corp. Communications--Forbes, Inc., New York, NY, pg. 423
Gass, Jerry H., Dir.-Communications & Govt. Affairs--Southern States Cooperative, Inc., Richmond, VA, pg. 1022
Gavigan, Peter, Dir.-Pub. Rels.--The Cherenson Group, Livingston, NJ, pg. 243
Gazzola, John M., Jr., Pub. Rels. Mgr.--Virginia Hot Springs, Inc., Hot Springs, VA, pg. 1152
Geiselman, R.D., Mgr.-Mktg. Services, Communications & Adv.--E. F. Houghton & Co., Valley Forge, PA, pg. 546
Geismar, Penelope A., Mgr.-Corp. Communications--Crain Communications, Inc., Detroit, MI, pg. 295
George, Ed, Dir.-Communications--The Florida Lottery, Tallahassee, FL, pg. 420
Georgeson, Cynthia, Environmental Communications Mgr.--S. C. Johnson & Son, Inc., Racine, WI, pg. 599
Geraci, Michael, Pub. Rels. Dir.--VanDine, Humphrey, Herbert, Alber & Manges, Inc., Pittsburgh, PA, pg. 1145
Gerbig, Stephanie, Corp. Communications Coord.--Atlas Van Lines, Inc., Evansville, IN, pg. 96
Gerchenson, Jeffery H., Pres. & Chief Oper. Officer--Alva/Amco Pharmacal Companies, Inc., Chicago, IL, pg. 46
Gerstein, Mel, Treas. & Dir.-Mktg., Adv. & Pub. Rels.--Thermwell Products Co., Inc., Paterson, NJ, pg. 1092
Gerstl, Tibor, V.P.-Mktg. Communications--Leviton Mfg. Co., Inc., Little Neck, NY, pg. 671
Gerstle, May, Dir.-Community Rels.--Seattle City Light, Seattle, WA, pg. 986
Giannuzzi, Bernadette, Press & Public Rels. Dir.--Ayer Vazquez S.A. de Publicidad, Buenos Aires,, Argentina, pg. 104
Gibson, Roberta J., V.P.-Adv. & Pub. Rels.--Hill-Behan Lumber Company, Saint Louis, MO, pg. 534
Gibson, Susan, Communications Specialist--Schnuck Markets, Inc., Maryland Heights, MO, pg. 977
Gibson, Tom, Mgr.-Pub. Rels.--Financial World Partners, New York, NY, pg. 410
Giesen, Laurie, Mgr.-Pub. Rels.--American Appraisal Associates, Inc., Milwaukee, WI, pg. 48
Gifford, Samuel L. II, V.P.-Pub. Affairs & Adv.--Delaware North Companies, Inc., Buffalo, NY, pg. 326
Gilbertson, David, V.P., Pub. Rels.--EvansGroup, Phoenix, AZ, pg. 391
Gillespie, Thomas J., Jr., Asst. V.P.-Govt. & Pub. Affairs--Amtrak-National Railroad Passenger Corp., Washington, DC, pg. 69
Gittere, Tracey, Dir.-Communications--800-Flowers, Westbury, NY, pg. 371
Glenn, Lyn, Dir.-Communications--Kaibab Industries, Phoenix, AZ, pg. 614
Glick, Muriel, V.P., Dir. Pub. Rels.--Frankel & Company, Chicago, IL, pg. 429
Glover, Kim, Pub. Rels. Dir.--The Criterion Group, Inc., Atlanta, GA, pg. 299
Glover, Norman, Mgr.-Customer Service--Kingsbury Corporation, Keene, NH, pg. 631
Gnatzig, Bill, V.P., Agricultural Pub. Rels.--Colle & McVoy Public Relations, Minneapolis, MN, pg. 261
Godfrey, Mark, Dir.-Mktg.--Micro Component Technology Inc., Saint Paul, MN, pg. 748
Golatka, B.J., Dir.-Customer Services & Admin.--AP Parts Manufacturing Company, Toledo, OH, pg. 240
Goldsmith, Danae A., Dir.-Corp. Communications--Fru-Con Construction Corporation, Ballwin, MO, pg. 435
Gorham, Christine, Dir.-Press & Publicity/MTV Europe--MTV Networks, New York, NY, pg. 785
Gorski, Ann, V.P.-Corp. Communications--Goldman, Sachs & Co., New York, NY, pg. 468
Gorski, Ann, V.P.-Corp. Communications--Goldman Sachs, New York, NY, pg. 468
Gould, Mark, Dir.-Pub. Rels.--Paterno Imports Limited, Chicago, IL, pg. 851
Gould, Mark, Dir.-Pub. Rels.--Pacific Wine Co., Chicago, IL, pg. 851
Grace, Gary W., Dir.-Adv.--RJO Enterprises, Inc., Lanham, MD, pg. 907
Graebner, Linda S., V.P.-Mktg. Communications--Dole Food Company, Inc., Westlake Village, CA, pg. 840
Gray, Carol, Dir. Pub. Rels.--Gray Baumgarten Layport, Inc., Pittsburgh, PA, pg. 479
Green, Cathy O., V.P.-Pub. Affairs--H.B. Zachry, San Antonio, TX, pg. 1215
Green, William J., V.P.-Govt. Rels.--MacAndrews & Forbes Co., Camden, NJ, pg. 694
Greene, Pat Ryan, Sr. Pub. Rels. Specialist--MSI Insurance Companies, Arden Hills, MN, pg. 693
Greitzer, Betty, Dir.-Pub. Affairs--Pathmark, Woodbridge, NJ, pg. 1064
Grenda, Kay, Dir.-Personnel--Energy & Environmental Research Corp., Irvine, CA, pg. 381
Groner, J., Mgr.-Communications--General Binding Corporation, Northbrook, IL, pg. 656
Gross, Julie, Dir.-Pub. Rels.--Plan International U.S.A., Warwick, RI, pg. 874
Grossman, James, V.P., Pub. Rels.--Stone, August, Baker Communications Companies, Troy, MI, pg. 1050
Grossman, James, V.P., Pub. Rels., Promo. & Special Events--Stone August Baker Public Relations, Troy, MI, pg. 1051
Gruenwald, Jan, Mgr.-Pub. Rels.--Candle Corporation, Santa Monica, CA, pg. 214
Guenther, Curt, V.P.-Pub. Rels.--Humphreys Price/Cochran & Sanford Advertising, Memphis, TN, pg. 553
Guerrero, Regulo, Exec. V.P., Pub. Rels.--JMC Creatividad Orientada/Young & Rubicam, Caracas,, Venezuela, pg. 1213
Guion, William, 2nd V.P.-Communications--Pan-American Life Insurance Company, New Orleans, LA, pg. 845
Gura, Jerry, Dir.-Pub. Affairs--Amsted Industries Incorporated, Chicago, IL, pg. 68
Guthrie, Catherine, Integrated Communications Dir.--Leo Burnett Ltd., Quarry Bay,, Hong Kong, pg. 193
Gutmann, Gunter, Dir.-Public Rels.--Battelle-Institut E.V., Frankfurt/Main, Germany, pg. 126
Hagen, Richard, Mgr.-Communications Services--Lutheran Brotherhood, Minneapolis, MN, pg. 688
Halfmann, Adeline A., Mgr.-Mktg. Communications--Regal Ware, Inc., Kewaskum, WI, pg. 921
Hall, Dane, Dir.-Pub. Rels.--General Media Publishing Group, New York, NY, pg. 450
Hall, Dane, Dir.-Pub. Rels.--Omni Publications International Ltd., New York, NY, pg. 450
Hall, Edward C., Exec. V.P.-Client Services--The New England, Boston, MA, pg. 799
Hamby, Bill, V.P., Dir. Pub. Rels.--Siddall, Matus & Coughter, Inc. Advertising & Public Relations, Richmond, VA, pg. 1002
Hank, Ron, Dir.-Corp. Rels.--Cincom Systems, Inc., Cincinnati, OH, pg. 250
Hannah, Gail, Pub. Rels. Dir., Acct. Exec.--Brems Eastman Glade, Inc., Seattle, WA, pg. 173
Hapeman, Carolyn, Pub. Rels.--Partners Meany, Inc., Albany, NY, pg. 850
Harden, Milano, Mgr.-Adv. & Pub. Rels.--CEBCOR (Consolidated Employment Benefits Corp.), Chicago, IL, pg. 230
Hardgrove, Maureen, Pub. Rels. Coord.--RE/MAX International, Inc., Englewood, CO, pg. 915
Hardwick, Ron, Dir.-Pub. Rels. & Personnel--Miniature Precision Components, Walworth, WI, pg. 757
Harkness, Brian, Sr. V.P., Dir. Pub. Rels.--SBC Advertising, Columbus, OH, pg. 960
Harr, Lucy, V.P.-Communications--Credit Union National Association, Madison, WI, pg. 298
Harrad, Mark A., V.P.-Corp. Rels.--Viacom Inc., New York, NY, pg. 785
Harrell, Pamela A., Dir.-Mktg.--Seaboard Electronics Co., Carlsbad, CA, pg. 983
Harrelson, Mike, Mgr.-Pub. Rels.--Lost Arrow Corporation, Ventura, CA, pg. 684
Harrington, Peter N., V.P.-Public Rels.--The New England, Boston, MA, pg. 799
Harris-Stewart, Fran, Public Affairs Specialist--D.C. Lottery & Charitable Games Control Board, Washington, DC, pg. 308
Harrison, Cynthia, V.P.-Corp. Communication--Scholastic Inc., New York, NY, pg. 962
Harrison, Thomas, Sr. V.P., Pub. Rels.--Russ Reid Company, Inc., Pasadena, CA, pg. 923
Harrison, Walter, Mgr.-Pub. Rels.--Delta Pride Catfish, Inc., Indianola, MS, pg. 327
Hartlage, C. Daniel, V.P., Pub. Rels.--Fessel, Siegfriedt & Moeller, Inc., Louisville, KY, pg. 407
Hartmann, Richard J., Mgr.-Mktg. Communications--Elkay Manufacturing Company, Oak Brook, IL, pg. 377
Hartup, Nan, Mgr.-Client Services--National Media Services, Inc., Atlanta, GA, pg. 792
Haskell, Robert G., V.P.-Pub. Affairs--Pacific Mutual Life Insurance Company, Newport Beach, CA, pg. 841
Hawley, C. Scott, Dir.-Pub. Rels.--Carlson & Partners, Inc., New York, NY, pg. 222
Hawley, Rusty, Dir.-Communications--National Football League Properties, Inc., New York, NY, pg. 788
Haworth, Keri, Pub. Rel. Asst.--Thompson Advertising Productions, Inc., Farmington Hills, MI, pg. 1094
Hayden, Anne E., V.P.-Human Resources--Metropolitan Life Insurance Co., New York, NY, pg. 744
Haymaker, Kate, Mgr.-Pub. Rels.--Chicago Convention & Tourism Bureau, Chicago, IL, pg. 245
Haynes, Lisa, Mgr.-Pub. Rels.--Heil-Brice Retail Advertising, San Clemente, CA, pg. 525
Heaton, Richard L., V.P.-Communications--L. Robert Kimball & Associates, Ebensburg, PA, pg. 629
Heerman, William R., Sr. V.P.-Law & Communications, Sec. & Gen. Counsel--Aid Association For Lutherans, Appleton, WI, pg. 26
Heffner, Michael, Sr. V.P.-Pub. Rels.--Al Paul Lefton Co., Inc., Philadelphia, PA, pg. 666
Heffner, Michael, Sr. V.P., Pub. Rel.--Al Paul Lefton Co., Inc., Public Relations, Philadelphia, PA, pg. 666
Heithaus, Walter, V.P., Pub. Rels.--Reed Exhibition Companies, Boston, MA, pg. 920
Heller, John, Dir.-Opers.--The IDI Group Companies, Arlington, VA, pg. 560
Helme, Monte, V.P.-Pub. Info.--Century 21 Real Estate Corp., Irvine, CA, pg. 744
Hermeling, Tim, Mgr.-Pub. Rels.--Budget Rent A Car Corporation, Lisle, IL, pg. 131
Hermeling, Timothy, Mgr.-Public Rel.--Beech Holdings Corp., Chicago, IL, pg. 131
Herndon, Jennifer, Communications Dir.--John Zink Co., Tulsa, OK, pg. 639
Herron, James W., Mgr.-Customer Service--Georgia Iron Works Co., Grovetown, GA, pg. 453
Hershman, Mark E., V.P.-Corp. Communications & Admin. Services--VASA Insurance Group, Inc., Indianapolis, IN, pg. 1146
Herzog, Robert, V.P.-Indus. Rels.--Hollytex, Saddle Brook, NJ, pg. 1121
Hetherington, James R., V.P.-Corp. Communications--American United Life Insurance Company, Indianapolis, IN, pg. 65
Heuberger, Mark, Supvr.-Communications--Memphis Light, Gas & Water, Memphis, TN, pg. 738
Heying, Mary Beth, Mgr.-Pub. Rels.--Edward D. Jones & Co., Maryland Heights, MO, pg. 603
Hickman, Sue, Dir.-Personnel & Indus. Rels.--American Wyott Corporation, Cheyenne, WY, pg. 65
Hier, Mark, Dir.-Pub. Rels. & Adv.--The Minnesota Mutual Life Insurance Company, Saint Paul, MN, pg. 757
Higbee, Ann G., Pres.-EMA Pub. Rels. Services--Eric Mower and Associates, Inc., Syracuse, NY, pg. 774
Higgins, John A., Dir.-Pub. Rels.--KPMG Peat Marwick, New York, NY, pg. 613
Highsmith, Frances Paddock, V.P.-Consumer Affairs--Jones Dairy Farm, Fort Atkinson, WI, pg. 603
Hildebrandt, Jeffrey A., Mgr.-Corp. Communications--CareerTrack Inc., Boulder, CO, pg. 218
Hill, Denise, Pub. Rels. Mgr.--Rosanio, Bailets & Talamo, Inc., Cherry Hill, NJ, pg. 947
Hill, Whitney, Trade Rels. Dir.--M&M/Mars, Hackettstown, NJ, pg. 713
Hillman, Sandra S., Exec. V.P., Pub. Rels. Dir.--Trahan, Burden & Charles, Inc., Baltimore, MD, pg. 1105
Hinton, Bruce, Dir.-Communications--Long John Silver's, Inc., Lexington, KY, pg. 229
Hirano, Steven S., Grp. V.P.-Hawaiin Adv. & Pub. Rels.--Servco Pacific Inc., Honolulu, HI, pg. 991
Hiznay, Paul, Sr. V.P.-Sls. & Mdsg.--Mona Industries, Inc., Paterson, NJ, pg. 764
Hock, Stanley, Dir.-Pub. Rels.--Sutter Home Winery, Inc., Saint Helena, CA, pg. 1065
Hocklander, Daniel, Dir.-Pub. Rels.--D. W. Newcomer's Sons, Inc., Kansas City, MO, pg. 804
Hodges, Charles, V.P./Pub. Rels.--Larkin Meeder & Schweidel, Dallas, TX, pg. 659
Hoefer, Stephen H., Dir.-Govt. Rels. & Transportation--Agway, Inc., De Witt, NY, pg. 25
Hoefle, John G., V.P. & Chief Information Officer--Overland Transportation System, Inc., Indianapolis, IN, pg. 832
Hoenig, Cynthia, V.P. & Dir.-Pub. Rels.--Eric Mower and Associates/Rochester, Inc., Rochester, NY, pg. 774
Hoffer, Imogene J., Dir.-Publications--UES, Inc., Dayton, OH, pg. 1122
Hofmeister, Stephanie, PR Coordinator--Costa Cruise Lines, N.V., Miami, FL, pg. 288
Hogan, Susan, V.P.-Communications & Adv.--AGCO Corporation, Norcross, GA, pg. 4
Hogan, Susan, V.P.-Communications--Hesston, Norcross, GA, pg. 4
Holferty, Kenneth J., V.P.-Client Services--Dodson Group, Kansas City, MO, pg. 342
Hollingsworth, E.C., Pub. Affairs Asst.--Phoenix Home Life Mutual Insurance Company, Hartford, CT, pg. 868
Hood, Melinda Brewer, Mgr.-Corp. Communications--Mississippi Chemical Corporation, Yazoo City, MS, pg. 760
Hood, Melinda Brewer, Mgr.-Communications--Newsprint South, Inc., Yazoo City, MS, pg. 760
Hoopes, James L., V.P.-Sls. & Pub. Rels.--Dayton Rogers Mfg. Co., Minneapolis, MN, pg. 321
Hoover, Harry, Dir. Pub. Rels.--Loeffler Ketchum Mountjoy, Charlotte, NC, pg. 680
Hopperton, Richard H., Dir.-Pub. Rels.--Alexander Marketing Services, Inc., Grand Rapids, MI, pg. 33
Horne, Charles E., III, V.P.-Adv. & Communications--Amica Mutual Insurance Co., Providence, RI, pg. 66
Hoskins, Kenneth R., V.P., Mng. Dir.-Pub. Rels.--Doe-Anderson Advertising Agency, Inc., Louisville, KY, pg. 342
Houdret, J., Dir.-Communications--Decision Data Inc., Horsham, PA, pg. 323
Hoult, Martha, Dir.-Pub. Rels.--Recon/Optical, Inc., Barrington, IL, pg. 917
House, Edith, V.P., Pub. Rels.--Trahan, Burden & Charles, Inc., Baltimore, MD, pg. 1105
House, James P., Pub. Rels. Dir.--Broyles, Allebaugh & Davis, Inc., Englewood, CO, pg. 183
House, James P., Pub. Rels. Dir.--EvansGroup, Denver, CO, pg. 391
House, Mary Helen, Dir.-Mktg., Adv., Art, Audio/Visual & Communication Services--Gold Medal Products Co., Cincinnati, OH, pg. 465
Howard, Dick, V.P.-Pub. Affairs--Blue Cross and Blue Shield of Oklahoma, Tulsa, OK, pg. 159
Howard, Richard M., Dir.-Mktg.--Shafer Commercial Seating Inc., Denver, CO, pg. 994
Howk, Paula, Dir., Pub. Rels.--Jay Incorporated, Rochester, NY, pg. 590
Howman, Stacey, Pub. Rels. Dir.--TTA/Newport, Inc., Newport Beach, CA, pg. 1092
Hucker, Charles W., Div. V.P.-Pub. Affairs & Communications--Hallmark Cards, Inc., Kansas City, MO, pg. 501
Huffman, William V., V.P.-Communications--Farmers Rice Cooperative, Sacramento, CA, pg. 401
Hughes, Betty A., Dir.-Consumer Affairs--Weber-Stephen Products, Palatine, IL, pg. 1171
Hughes, David, Dir., Pub. Rels.--Fern/Hanaway, Inc. Advertising/Public Relations, Warwick, RI, pg. 407
Hughes, Ray, Adv. Mgr. & Communications Dir.--Varel Manufacturing Co., Dallas, TX, pg. 1145
Hynson, Carroll H., Deputy Dir.-Public Affairs--Maryland State Lottery, Baltimore, MD, pg. 717
Iacunato, Debby, V.P.-Corp. Communications--PacifiCare Health Systems, Inc., Cypress, CA, pg. 1127
Iannaci, Debra, Editor & Pub. Rels. Coord.--Ad-Tech Communications, Miami Lakes, FL, pg. 16

Imre, David, Sr. V.P., Pub. Rels.--Image Dynamics, Incorporated, Baltimore, MD, pg. 563
Inderman, Bob, Dir.-Pub. Rels.--Marketing Resources of America, Inc., Overland Park, KS, pg. 709
Ingle, Don, V.P., Dir. Pub. Rels.--Cramer-Krasselt, Milwaukee, WI, pg. 296
Ingram, Martha, Dir.-Pub. Affairs--Ingram Industries Inc., Nashville, TN, pg. 568
Inman, Anne B., V.P., Pub. Rels. Services--LevLane Advertising, Inc., Bala-Cynwyd, PA, pg. 671
Inserra, Tracy, Acct. Coord./Pub. Rels. Asst.--Deare Marketing Inc./Matthew-Lawrence Advertising & Sales Promotion Inc., New York, NY, pg. 323
Isen, Tina, Pub. Rels.--Scharfberg & Associates, Ltd. Adv., Jenkintown, PA, pg. 974
Ivice, Lin, Mgr.-Pub. Rels.--Quill Corp., Lincolnshire, IL, pg. 905
Jackson, James, Jr., Dir.-Human Resources--OmniCare Health Plan, Detroit, MI, pg. 826
Jacobs, Ruth, Mgr.-Pub. Rels.--Mosler Inc., Hamilton, OH, pg. 772
Jaquett, Zachary, Dir.-Communications--Industrial Acoustics Company, Inc., Bronx, NY, pg. 565
Jardine, Thomas D., V.P.-Pub. Rels. & Pub. Affairs--Carlson Companies, Inc., Minneapolis, MN, pg. 220
Jardine, Tom, V.P.-Pub. Rels.--Radisson Hotel Corporation, Minneapolis, MN, pg. 221
Jefferson, Jeffield, Mgr.-Communications--Port of Houston Authority, Houston, TX, pg. 881
Jellen, Steve, Mgr.-Service--Fairway Ford, Inc., Greenville, SC, pg. 397
Jennings, Donna, Dir.-Communications--Velsicol Chemical Corporation, Rosemont, IL, pg. 1147
Jennings, Duffy, V.P.-Pub. Rels.--San Francisco Giants Baseball Club, San Francisco, CA, pg. 969
Jennings, Madeline, Dir.-Mktg.& Communications--Sellstrom Manufacturing Co., Palatine, IL, pg. 988
Jennings, Mary, Dir.-Promo.--Parade Publications Inc., New York, NY, pg. 847
Jensen, Debra J., Mgr.-Community Rels.--The Principal Financial Group, Des Moines, IA, pg. 890
Jernigan, Paul, Dir.-Adv. & Public Rels.--Gibson Guitar Corporation, Inc., Nashville, TN, pg. 456
Jhaveri, Chand, V.P.-Res. & Devel.--Central Pharmaceuticals, Inc., Seymour, IN, pg. 234
Johns, Anne, Dir., Pub. Rels.--Cramer-Krasselt, Phoenix, AZ, pg. 296
Johnson, Frederick H., V.P.-Dir. of Newspaper Rels.--Parade Publications Inc., New York, NY, pg. 847
Johnson, Lori, Mgr.-Pub. Rels.--Cargill Salt, Newark, CA, pg. 219
Johnson, Mike, Dir.-Communications--G. Leblanc Corporation, Kenosha, WI, pg. 665
Johnson, Roger J., Sr. V.P.-Corp. Info. Services, Chief Fin. Officer & Treas.--Aid Association For Lutherans, Appleton, WI, pg. 26
Johnston, Bill, Dir.-Pub. Rels.--San Diego Chargers, San Diego, CA, pg. 969
Johnstone, Stephen F., Sr. V.P., Pub. Rels. Dir.--Andrews/Mautner, Inc., Milwaukee, WI, pg. 74
Joly, John, Dir.-Public Affairs--Seattle Post-Intelligencer, Seattle, WA, pg. 524
Jones, Emory M., V.P.-Pub. Rels.--Cascino Purcell Freebairn, Atlanta, GA, pg. 227
Jones, Jon, V.P.-Distr. & Customer Services--Igloo Corporation, Houston, TX, pg. 562
Jones, Mary Ann, Dir.-Customer Rels.--Publix Supermarkets Inc., Lakeland, FL, pg. 898
Jones, Susan, Editro--Alimed, Inc., Dedham, MA, pg. 34
Jones, Susan S., Mgr.-Communications--BNA Software, Washington, DC, pg. 189
Jones, T., V.P.-Tech./Customer Service--Telechron, Inc., Ashland, MA, pg. 1085
Junkin, Zella, Dir.-Pub. Rels.--Wilton Industries, Inc., Woodridge, IL, pg. 1194
Kahn, Bette, Mgr.-Pub. Rels. & Community Affairs--Euromarket Designs, Inc., Northbrook, IL, pg. 390
Kaminski, T., Mgr.-Pub. Rels.--E.J. Brach Corporation, Oakbrook Terrace, IL, pg. 169
Kampfe, Jill, Dir., Pub. Rels.--Aydlotte & Cartwright, Inc., Atlanta, GA, pg. 103
Kanner, Abraham P., Sr. V.P.-Corp. Affairs--Maidenform, Inc., New York, NY, pg. 701
Kaplan, Jerry, Natl. Sls. Mgr.--Duncan Toys Company, Middlefield, OH, pg. 810
Karch, Cheri, Dir.-Corp. Rels.--Worzalla Publishing Co., Inc., Stevens Point, WI, pg. 1204
Karporal, Cathy, Dir.-Consumer Affairs--Weaver Popcorn Company, Inc., Van Buren, IN, pg. 1170
Kaufmann, Harry, Dir.-Pub. Rels. & Adv.--Sea Island Company, Sea Island, GA, pg. 983
Kavoukian, Jack C., Dir.-Mktg. Communications & Adv.--Hohner/HSS Inc., Ashland, VA, pg. 538
Kazmark, Karen, V.P., Investor & Pub. Rels.--KSK Communications, Ltd., Vienna, VA, pg. 613
Kearney, Edward R., V.P.-Investor Rels. & Communications--General Instrument Corporation, New York, NY, pg. 425
Kearney, Susan M., Mgr.-Sls. & Mktg. Communications--Life Sciences International, Philadelphia, PA, pg. 320
Keim, Lewis P., V.P.-Pub. Rels.--The Gates Corporation, Denver, CO, pg. 445
Keithley, Don, Partner & Dealer Rels.--J.D. Power and Associates, Agoura Hills, CA, pg. 883
Keller, Jacqueline, Sr. V.P.-Mktg. & Communications--Mayfair Super Markets, Inc., Elizabeth, NJ, pg. 724
Kelley, Kathleen, Public Relations Rep.--In-N-Out Burgers, Baldwin Park, CA, pg. 564
Kelley, Marian, Mgr.-Pub. Rels.--Tracor, Inc., Austin, TX, pg. 1104
Kelley, Paul J., Dir.-Govt. & Pub. Rels.--U-Haul International, Inc., Phoenix, AZ, pg. 48
Kellogg, Molly, Dir.-Communications--Hubbard Hall Inc., Waterbury, CT, pg. 549
Kelly, Dorothy R., Dir.-Employee Communications--Metropolitan Life Insurance Co., New York, NY, pg. 744
Kelly, James P., Sr. V.P.-Labor Rels.--United Parcel Service of America, Inc., Atlanta, GA, pg. 1133
Kelly, Ronna, Dir.-Community Rels.--The Orange County Register, Santa Ana, CA, pg. 431
Kelly, Tim, V.P.-Pub. Rels.--Paolin & Sweeney, Cherry Hill, NJ, pg. 847
Kennedy, K.E., Dir.-Communications--Coopers & Lybrand, New York, NY, pg. 283
Kenville, Mark, Dir.-Member Relations & Communications--Dairylea Cooperative Inc., East Syracuse, NY, pg. 311
Kepler, Gary, Mgr.-Customer Service--Sargent & Greenleaf, Inc., Nicholasville, KY, pg. 971
Kerrigan, Janet, Mgr.-Pub. Rels.--Lettuce Entertain You Enterprises, Inc., Chicago, IL, pg. 668
Key, James A., V.P.-Adv., Pub. Rels. & Sls. Promo.--Continental Conveyor & Equipment Company, Winfield, AL, pg. 798
Kilgore, Joe, Mgr.-Mktg. & Pub. Rels.--Chattanooga Choo-Choo Holiday Inn, Chattanooga, TN, pg. 241
Killian, Ray A., Sr., Exec. V.P.-Human Resources & Pub. Rels.--Belk Stores Services Inc., Charlotte, NC, pg. 134
King, Joyce, V.P., Community Rels.--Hill, Holliday, Connors, Cosmopulos, Inc., Boston, MA, pg. 534
Kingsbaker, Tony, Asst. Dir., Pub. Rels.--Cramer-Krasselt, Phoenix, AZ, pg. 296
Kinimoth, Barbara, V.P.-Corp. Communications--The Hassinger Companies, Itasca, IL, pg. 516
Kintner, Michael, V.P.-Pub. Rels.--O'Neal & Prelle, Hartford, CT, pg. 827
Kirk, Donald A., V.P.-American Communications--American Systems Corporation, Chantilly, VA, pg. 63
Klarfeld, John M., Press Officer--Oxbow Corporation, West Palm Beach, FL, pg. 834
Klein, Carol J., V.P.-Corp. Affairs--Dole Food Company, Inc., Westlake Village, CA, pg. 840
Klein, Keith, Dir. of Pub. Rels.--Milton Samuels Advertising Agency, Inc., New York, NY, pg. 968
Klein, Mark, Pub. Rels. News Dir.--The Coakley Heagerty Companies, Ltd., San Jose, CA, pg. 256
Klien, Connie, Mgr.-Mktg. Services--Brown & Haley, Tacoma, WA, pg. 182
Koek, Anita, Mgr.-Media Buying & Pub. Rels.--Intralox, Inc., Harahan, LA, pg. 651
Koff, Michael, V.P., Pub. Rels. Dir.--The St. George Group, Inc., Pittsburgh, PA, pg. 966
Konig, Helmut, Public Rels.--Michael Conrad & Leo Burnett GmbH & Co. KG, Frankfurt/Main, Germany, pg. 192
Korologos, Mike, Exec. V.P., Dir. Pub. Rels.--EvansGroup, Salt Lake City, UT, pg. 391
Kosick, David, V.P., Pub. Rels.-Consumer--The St. George Group, Inc., Pittsburgh, PA, pg. 966
Kosmicki, Richard, Sr. V.P., Dir. Pub. Rel.--Pancom International Corp., Stamford, CT, pg. 845
Koupal, Pam, Dir.-Communications--Missouri Lottery, Jefferson City, MO, pg. 760
Kovacik, Rob, Mgr.-Customer Service--Hollymatic Corporation, Countryside, IL, pg. 539
Kovacs, Ken, Dir.-Pub. Rels. & Adv.--Golden Gate University, San Francisco, CA, pg. 466
Kowal, John A., Dir.-Pub. Rels.--Zylke & Associates, Northbrook, IL, pg. 1221
Kowalczyk, Mary, Dir., Pub. Affairs--The John Volk Company, Chicago, IL, pg. 1154
Kroft, Gina, Mgr.-Pub. Rels. & Special Events--Crested Butte Mountain Resort, Inc., Mount Crested Butte, CO, pg. 299
Krumrine, Jane, V.P.-Corp. Communications--Johnson & Higgins, New York, NY, pg. 598
Kubiak, Rick, Mgr.-Mktg. & Communications--Carver Boat Corp., Pulaski, WI, pg. 758
Kuhn, Kelly L., Mgr.-Pub. Rels.--Arrington Travel Center Inc., Chicago, IL, pg. 85
Kunklier, J. Patrick, Dir., Pub. Rels.--Hitchcock-Fleming & Associates, Inc., Akron, OH, pg. 536
Kushner, Denise D., Mgr.-Communications--L. M. Scofield Company, Los Angeles, CA, pg. 982
Kyle, Kurt, Sls. & Mktg. Coord.--McNeil & NRM., Inc., Akron, OH, pg. 732
LaBree, Sandra E., Mgr.-Adv. Communications--Simonds Industries Inc., Fitchburg, MA, pg. 1006
Lachima, Jim, Dir.-Media Rels.--Pittsburgh Pirates Professional Baseball Club, Pittsburgh, PA, pg. 873
Lagomarsino, Missy, Dir.-Pub. Rels.--Martz & Wadas, Scottsdale, AZ, pg. 716
Lally, Ann, V.P., Communications--Tucker Wayne/Luckie & Company, Atlanta, GA, pg. 1118
Lamneck, William C., Dir.-Communications--Nationwide Mutual Insurance Company, Columbus, OH, pg. 795
Lancaster, Whitney C., Asst. V.P. & Mgr.-Adv. & Pub. Rels.--Liberty Mutual Insurance Co., Boston, MA, pg. 674
Lane, Diane, Pub. Rels. Dir.--E. B. Lane & Associates, Inc., Phoenix, AZ, pg. 656
Lane, Kathleen, Mgr.-Pub. Rels.--The Weather Channel, Atlanta, GA, pg. 654
Lane, Lynda, Sr. V.P.-Admin. Corp. Communications--Koll Co., Newport Beach, CA, pg. 641
Langner, S., Dir.-Pub. Rels.--Benjamin Moore & Co., Montvale, NJ, pg. 139
Lanigan, William J., V.P.-Regional Services--MI-Jack Products, Inc., Hazel Crest, IL, pg. 746
Lanouette, Jane, Dir.-Pub. Rels.--Allied Advertising Agency, Boston, MA, pg. 37
Lanter, D.M., Dir.-Communications--Black & Veatch, Kansas City, MO, pg. 154
LaPorte, Joseph J., V.P.-Corp. Rels.--General Binding Corporation, Northbrook, IL, pg. 656
Larance, Larry, V.P.-Pub. Rels. & Human Resources--General American Life Insurance Co., St. Louis, MO, pg. 448
Lassers, Pam, V.P.-Adv. & Public Rels.--Marilyn Miglin, Inc., Chicago, IL, pg. 752
Laughton, Barbara, V.P. & Dir.-Pub. Rels.--ICE Communications, Inc., Rochester, NY, pg. 559
Lautzenheiser, Karen R., V.P.-Communications--Day & Zimmermann, Inc., Radnor, PA, pg. 320
Lauzzana, Gail A., Mgr.-Corp. Communications--Peterson American Corp., Southfield, MI, pg. 864
Lawlor, John, Mgr.-Pub. Rels.--Ocean Spray Cranberries, Inc., Lakeville, MA, pg. 820
Lawson, Lisa B., Dir.-Mktg. Communications--Mosler Inc., Hamilton, OH, pg. 772
Lawyer, Jean B., Dir.-Corp. Communications--Country Companies Insurance Group, Bloomington, IL, pg. 289
Lawyer, Jean B., Dir.-Corp. Rels.--Country Life Insurance Company, Bloomington, IL, pg. 289
Lawyer, Jean B., Dir.-Communications--Country Mutual Insurance Company, Bloomington, IL, pg. 289
Lawyer, Jean B., Dir.-Corp. Communications--CC Services, Bloomington, IL, pg. 289
Lee, Mary T., V.P.-Customer Rels.--Red Devil Inc., Union, NJ, pg. 918
Lee, R.C., V.P.-Personnel & Community Affairs--United States Sugar Corporation, Clewiston, FL, pg. 1137
Lehnhard, Mary Nell, V.P.-Office of Govt. Rels.--Blue Cross and Blue Shield Association, Chicago, IL, pg. 159
Leider, Debbie, Dir.-Pub. Rels.--Grant/Jacoby, Inc., Chicago, IL, pg. 477
Leigeber, Mgr.-Customer Service--Cullman Products Corporation, Cullman, AL, pg. 304
Leitzinger, Joseph, V.P.-Pub. Affairs--Simpson Investment Co., Seattle, WA, pg. 1007
Lemmon, David, Dir.-Pub. Rels. & Adv.--World Jai-alai, Miami, FL, pg. 1202
Lemmon, David, Dir.-Pub. Rels.--Miami Jai-Alai, Miami, FL, pg. 1203
Lenart, Nina, Dir.-Pub. Rels.--Freeman Cosmetic Corp., Los Angeles, CA, pg. 431
Leonard, Joseph, Exec. V.P.-Customer Services--Northwest Airlines, Inc., Saint Paul, MN, pg. 782
LePla, Joe, Gen. Mgr., Pub. Rels.--Floathe Johnson Associates, Inc., Kirkland, WA, pg. 419
Lester, William C., V.P.-Member, Pub. Rels. & Security--Ag Processing Inc A Cooperative, Omaha, NE, pg. 24
Levenson, Stanley R., Chief Exec. Officer & Dir.-Pub. Rels.--Levenson & Hill, Inc., Irving, TX, pg. 670
Leventhal, JoAnne, Asst. V.P.-Public Affairs--Phoenix Home Life Mutual Insurance Company, Hartford, CT, pg. 868
Levitan, Aida, Exec. V.P., Pub. Rels. Dir.--Sanchez & Levitan, Inc., Miami, FL, pg. 970
Levy, Barry W., Chm. Bd., Chief Exec. Officer & Communications Dir.--Levy Security Consultants, Limited, Chicago, IL, pg. 672
Levy, Jay, Communications Mgr.--AGEMA Infrared Systems, Inc., Secaucus, NJ, pg. 24
Lewis-Phillips, Susan, Pub. Rels. Dir.--Bailey, Klepinger & Medrich, Inc., Ann Arbor, MI, pg. 114
Lewis, Jennifer, Pub. Rels.--Joel Goldstein Marketing Communications, Santa Monica, CA, pg. 469
Lewis, Mary, Mgr.-Mktg. Communications--The Ingersoll Milling Machine Co., Rockford, IL, pg. 568
Liddell, Gail, Mgr.-Communications--New Hermes Incorporated, Norwalk, CT, pg. 801
Lieberman, Cindy, Dir., Corp. Communications--BEC Advertising, Chicago, IL, pg. 106
Lieberman, Cindy S., Dir.-Corp. Communications--Beltone Electronics Corporation, Chicago, IL, pg. 137
Lief, Fred, Dir.-Promo.--New York Racing Association, Jamaica, NY, pg. 803
Lindell, Edward A., Sr. V.P.-External Affairs--Lutheran Brotherhood, Minneapolis, MN, pg. 688
Lippincott, Procter, Sr. V.P., Acct. Dir. & Pub. Rels.--Spring, O'Brien & Co. Inc., New York, NY, pg. 1033
Liscik, Raymond, V.P.-Adv., Mktg., Sls. & Pub. Rels.--JCI Data Processing, Inc., Delran, NJ, pg. 584
Lloyd, Rodie, Mgr.-Pub. Rels.--L.L. Bean, Inc., Freeport, ME, pg. 648
Lodge, James E., Exec. Dir.-Communications & Corp. American Banking--The American Bankers Association, Washington, DC, pg. 49
Loewenberg, Harry L., Dir.-Customer Service--Southern Leather Company, Memphis, TN, pg. 1021
Loewenherz, Nancy, Dir.-Pub. Rels.--Commodore Cruise Line, Ltd., Coral Gables, FL, pg. 269
Logan, Lacey, Dir.-Communications & Pub. Rels.--The Stroh Brewery Company, Detroit, MI, pg. 1053
Long, Nancy B., Acct. Supvr.-Pub. Rels.--Dorland Sweeney Jones, Philadelphia, PA, pg. 346
Lordi, Georgette, Pub. Rels.--Chester Gore Company Inc., New York, NY, pg. 472
Lose, Linnea, V.P., Pub. Rels. Dir.--Wolf Blumberg Krody Inc., Cincinnati, OH, pg. 1199
Loughlin, Richard, V.P.-Indus. Rels.--Holiday Companies, Minneapolis, MN, pg. 539
Louw, Susanne, Mng. Dir., Pub. Rels., Client Service/Acct. Dir.--Wunderman Worldwide A/S, Copenhagen, Denmark, pg. 1212
Loux, Michael, Dir.-Mkt. Research--Jervis B. Webb Company, Farmington Hills, MI, pg. 1170
Lovejoy, Kellie, Dir.-Adv. & Pub. Rels.--Cole of California, Los Angeles, CA, pg. 1079
Loverd, William T., V.P. & Dir.-Publicity--Alfred A. Knopf, Inc., New York, NY, pg. 20
Lucke, Susan, Pub. Rels. Dir.--The Coates Agency, Portland, OR, pg. 257
Lueck, Guada, Mgr.-Adv. & Pub. Rels.--Post Buckley Schuh & Jernigan, Miami, FL, pg. 881
Luginbuhl, Dan R., V.P.-Communications--Penske Corporation, Detroit, MI, pg. 859
Lunceford, Michael, V.P.-Corp. Affairs--Mary Kay Cosmetics Inc., Dallas, TX, pg. 716
Luongo, Lucille, Sr. V.P.-Corp. Communications--Katz Communications, Inc., New York, NY, pg. 618
Lynch, Carol, Mgr.-Mktg. Communications, Consumer Prods.--Leviton Mfg. Co., Inc., Little Neck, NY, pg. 671

Lynes, Judy, V.P., Dir. Pub. Rels.--The Phelps Group, Los Angeles, CA, pg. 866
Lyon, Jennifer, Pub. Rels.--Bryan Hardwick Associates, Palos Verdes Estates, CA, pg. 508
Lyons, Harry, Dir.-Special Projects--DDC PerTec, Tucson, AZ, pg. 308
Macius, Mindy, Dir.-Adv. & Pub. Rels.--Houston Foods Company, Chicago, IL, pg. 547
MacKay, Gordon D., Sr. V.P.-Pub. Affairs/Pub. Rels.--The New England, Boston, MA, pg. 799
MacLellan, Erin, Pub. Rels. Dir.--Chernoff/Silver & Associates, Columbia, SC, pg. 243
MacNamara, Frank W., Vice Chm., Dir., Media & Communications--MacNamara, Klein & Solin Inc., New York, NY, pg. 698
Madaras, William, Mgr.-Pub. Rels.--Information Builders, New York, NY, pg. 567
Maddrey, Judi, V.P., Grp. Mngmt. Supvr. & Pub. Rels.--Rives Carlberg, Houston, TX, pg. 937
Maher, Cindi, Communications Supvr.--ANGUS Chemical Company, Buffalo Grove, IL, pg. 75
Maitland, Angus, Vice Chm., Corp. Communications (London)--Burson-Marsteller, New York, NY, pg. 1210
Malinowski, Felix, V.P.-Pub. Rels.--Marontate & Co., Auburn Hills, MI, pg. 713
Malloy, Jim, Dir.-Mktg. & Sls.--Advanced Controls, Inc., Irvine, CA, pg. 20
Malone, Donald P., Mgr.-Publications--The Long Island Rail Road Co., Jamaica, NY, pg. 745
Maltby, Sara, Dir.-Pub. Rels.--Kragie/Newell, Des Moines, IA, pg. 643
Manahan, Dave, Dir.-Pub. Rels.--The Jason Group, Inc., Short Hills, NJ, pg. 590
Marcus, Bruce T., Sr. V.P.-Corp. Mktg. & Communications--WTTW (Channel 11), Chicago, IL, pg. 1156
Marino, Alfonse, Sr. V.P., Creative Dir.--Warren/Kremer/CMP/Advertising/Inc., New York, NY, pg. 1165
Martin, Aimee, Dir., Pub. Rels.--Rick Johnson & Company, Inc., Albuquerque, NM, pg. 597
Martin, Andrew, Dir.-Publicity--Crown Publishers, Inc., New York, NY, pg. 20
Martin, Phil, Pres., Ericson Pub. Rels.--Ericson Marketing Communications, Nashville, TN, pg. 386
Martin, Roger L., V.P.-Human Resources & Community Rels.--Steelcase Inc., Grand Rapids, MI, pg. 1044
Martinez, Alicia, Dir.-Mktg. & Corp. Communications--Metropolitan Transportation Authority, New York, NY, pg. 745
Martinsen, Jim, Dir.-Adv. & Pub. Rels.--Sheldons' Inc., Antigo, WI, pg. 996
Mascio, Joan L., Asst. Mgr.-Pub. Rels. & Adv.--The Austin Company, Cleveland, OH, pg. 790
Maselli, Michelle, Mgr.-Consumer Affairs--Mayfair Super Markets, Inc., Elizabeth, NJ, pg. 724
Masnik, Carol, Mgr.-Pub. Rels.--Rainier Brewing Co., Seattle, WA, pg. 526
Mason, Debbie, V.P.-Corp. Communications--JM Family Enterprises Inc., Deerfield Beach, FL, pg. 584
Mastalski, Stanley, Mgr.-Customer Service--H. Freeman & Son, Inc., Philadelphia, PA, pg. 431
Maston, Roger, Dir.-Client Rels.--Leon Shaffer Golnick Advertising, Inc., Fort Lauderdale, FL, pg. 469
Mata, Vikki, Acting Dir.-Communications--Sealaska Corporation, Juneau, AK, pg. 984
Matassoni, William L., Dir.-Communications--McKinsey & Company, Inc., New York, NY, pg. 731
Mathias, Larry L., V.P.-Human Resources & Pub. Rels.--American Crystal Sugar Company, Moorhead, MN, pg. 51
Matteson, Bill, V.P.-Pub. Affairs--Farmland Industries, Inc., Kansas City, MO, pg. 402
Mattich, Mario, Mgr.-Pub. Rels.--Leviton Mfg. Co., Inc., Little Neck, NY, pg. 671
Matusik, Valerie, V.P.-Pub. Rels.--Kokosing Construction Company, Inc., Fredericktown, OH, pg. 640
Maurano, Steven, V.P., Pub. Rels.--Duffy & Shanley, Inc., Providence, RI, pg. 351
May, James P., Corp. Pub. Rels. Mgr.--S. C. Johnson & Son, Inc., Racine, WI, pg. 599
May, Pat, Dir.-Pub. Rels.--Rocco Inc., Harrisonburg, VA, pg. 940
May, Patricia, Dir.-Pub. Rels.--Rocco Further Processing, Timberville, VA, pg. 940
May, Patricia L., Dir.-Pub. Rels.--Rocco Turkeys, Inc., Dayton, VA, pg. 940
Mayfield, Barry, Mgr.-Public Affairs--East Kentucky Power Co-op, Winchester, KY, pg. 362
Mayne, Courtney, Customer Service Dir.--National Oats Co., Cedar Rapids, IA, pg. 25
Mayo, Susan T., V.P.-Pub. Rels. & Consumer Affairs--Farm Fresh, Inc., Norfolk, VA, pg. 401
McAfee, Floydetta M., V.P., Pub. Rels. Dir.--Caroline Jones Advertising, Inc., New York, NY, pg. 603
McAiley, Ron, Mgr.-Customer Service--Arcata Graphics Kingsport, Kingsport, TN, pg. 80
McArdle, John E., V.P.-Communications--George S. May International Company, Park Ridge, IL, pg. 723
McCarthy, Eric, Dir.-Corp. Communications--Walter Industries, Inc., Tampa, FL, pg. 1161
McCarthy, Loretta, Sr. V.P.-Mktg. & Communications--Oppenheimer Management Corp., New York, NY, pg. 719
McClain, Thomas E., Dir.-Communications--Battelle Memorial Institute, Columbus, OH, pg. 126
McClusky, Marianne, Dir., Pub. Rels.--Zapiecki & Partners Inc., Toledo, OH, pg. 1216
McCollister, Holly, V.P. & Personnel Dir.--Jackson Hole Ski Resort, Teton Village, WY, pg. 587
McCormick, Dawn, Dir.-Corp. Communications--Irvine Company, Newport Beach, CA, pg. 582
McCray, Beth, Pub. Rels. & Acct. Mgr.--Huntsinger & Jeffer, Richmond, VA, pg. 555
McCue, Bill, Pub. Rels. Mgr.--Sir Speedy, Inc., Laguna Hills, CA, pg. 613
McCutchan, Anne, Pub. Rels. Dir.--Cappelli Miles Wiltz & Kelly, Portland, OR, pg. 216
McDermott, Bob, Dir.-Pub. Rels.--Publix Supermarkets Inc., Lakeland, FL, pg. 898
McDermott, Ruth N., Mgr.-Personnel & Communications--Distribution America, Des Plaines, IL, pg. 340
McDevitt, Michael, V.P.-Western Mgr.-Newspaper Rels.--Parade Publications Inc., New York, NY, pg. 847
McDonald, Ken J., Dir.-Communications--Amway Corporation, Ada, MI, pg. 70
McDonnell, Frances, Mgr.-Pub. Rels.--Massachusetts State Lottery, Braintree, MA, pg. 719
McDonough, Katherine A., V.P.-Pub. Affairs--Barnes & Noble Bookstores, Inc., New York, NY, pg. 120
McGeehan, George, Dir.-Pub. Rels.--The Binswanger Company, Philadelphia, PA, pg. 151
McGinnity, Dan, Mgr.-Corp. Communications--Sentry Insurance, A Mutual Company, Stevens Point, WI, pg. 990
McGlothlin, Kathryn, V.P.-Claims--VASA North Atlantic Insurance Company, Indianapolis, IN, pg. 1146
McGovern, Sue, Pub. Rels. Dir.--McDougall Associates, Inc., Peabody, MA, pg. 728
McGowan, Richard, Sr. V.P., Dir. Communications--Young & Rubicam Inc., New York, NY, pg. 1210
McGraw, Joseph M., Dir.-Adv. & Pub. Rels.--United Gilsonite Laboratories, Scranton, PA, pg. 1132
McGreevy, Rebecca C., Sr. V.P.-Pub. Rels.--Estee Lauder, Inc., New York, NY, pg. 389
McHugh, John J., Mgr.-Literature Prod.--S & C Electric Company, Chicago, IL, pg. 958
McIlwaine, Charles B., V.P.-Communications--The Coleman Company, Inc., Wichita, KS, pg. 695
McKee, Ruth, V.P.-Customer Service, Ground--Northwest Airlines, Inc., Saint Paul, MN, pg. 782
McKenzie, Ken, Communications Dir.--Morning Glory Farms Region, Shawano, WI, pg. 770
McLain-Johnson, Marian, Media Rels.--The Minnesota Mutual Life Insurance Company, Saint Paul, MN, pg. 757
McLaughlin, Lisa, Dir.-Corp. Communications--Encyclopaedia Britannica, Inc., Chicago, IL, pg. 381
McLaughlin, Mike, Dir.-Adv. & Pub. Rels.--North Central Life Insurance Companies, Saint Paul, MN, pg. 813
McLennan, Rebecca, Dir.-Pub. Rels.--Kolon, Bittker & Desmond, Inc., Troy, MI, pg. 641
McMahon, Margaret, Dir.-Pub. Rels. & Personnel--Shonac Corporation, Columbus, OH, pg. 1000
McNabb, Joanne, Dir.-Pub. Affairs--California State Lottery, Sacramento, CA, pg. 210
Meador, Janice, V.P.-Corp. Services & Personnel Dir.--Kwik-Kopy Corp., Cypress, TX, pg. 647
Medina, Sylvia, Mgr.-Customer Service--Caribe Express, Aguadilla, PR, pg. 220
Mehrhof, Ken, Adv. & Pub. Rels. Consultant--Somerset Technologies, Inc., Somerset, NJ, pg. 1017
Meir, Charlene, Mgr.-Customer Service--Eli's Chicago's Finest, Inc., Chicago, IL, pg. 376
Meissner, Dan, Dir.-Corp. Communications--Gulf States Paper Corporation, Tuscaloosa, AL, pg. 494
Meissner, Marlene, Mgr.-Pub. Rels.--Oregon State Lottery, Salem, OR, pg. 829
Melillo, Anthony, Mgr.-Customer Service--Eastern Color Printing Company, Avon, CT, pg. 363
Melley, Maura L., V.P.-Govt. Affairs--Phoenix Home Life Mutual Insurance Company, Hartford, CT, pg. 868
Menaugh, Steve, Dir.-Corp. Communications--The Marley Company, Mission Woods, KS, pg. 710
Menna, Christine, V.P.-Pub. Rels.--Crown American Corporation, Johnstown, PA, pg. 301
Menouar, Najad, Pub. Rels. Dir.--Lowe Troost S.A., Brussels,, Belgium, pg. 685
Mercer, Laura, Sr. V.P., Dir. Pub. Rels.--Price/McNabb, Inc., Asheville, NC, pg. 888
Merrell, Jerry, V.P.-Corp. Communications--Motorists Mutual Insurance Co., Columbus, OH, pg. 773
Merritt, Terry, Asst. Corp. Sec. & Pub. Rels. Coord.--Walbridge Aldinger Company, Detroit, MI, pg. 1158
Metcalf, Mary Kay, Mgr.-Communications & Bus.-to-Bus.--Creative Marketing Alliance Inc., Princeton Junction, NJ, pg. 297
Metson, Sigrid, Corp. Communications Mgr.--Reference Software International, San Francisco, CA, pg. 921
Metts, M. C., Dir.-Telecommunications--Nutech, Inc., San Jose, CA, pg. 817
Meyer, John A., V.P.-Midwest Mgr.-Newspaper Rels.--Parade Publications Inc., New York, NY, pg. 847
Meyerson, Mort, Natl. Dir.-Pub. Communications--Ernst & Young, New York, NY, pg. 387
Michaelson, Marc, V.P., Pub. Rels. Dir.--Weber Cohn & Riley, Inc., Chicago, IL, pg. 1171
Michelson, Gertrude G., Sr. V.P.-External Affairs--R. H. Macy & Co., Inc., New York, NY, pg. 698
Michener, Sally R., Sec. & Dir.-Personnel & Pub. Rels.--Scott Specialty Gases, Inc., Plumsteadville, PA, pg. 983
Middleton, Robert, Sr. Pub. Affairs Rep.--Port of Oakland, Oakland, CA, pg. 881
Milkovich, Bob, Mgr.-Public Rels.--Pabst Brewing Co., San Antonio, TX, pg. 959
Miller, Bill, Dir.-Pub. Rels.--The United Company, Bristol, VA, pg. 1131
Miller, Dalene, Dir.-Public Rels.--D.A. Davidson & Co., Great Falls, MT, pg. 318
Miller, Dean A., V.P.-Industrial Rels.--BeefAmerica Operating Co., Inc., Omaha, NE, pg. 131
Miller, Debra, Pub. Rels., Fashion & Special Events--Woodward & Lothrop/John Wanamaker, Washington, DC, pg. 1201
Miller, Gregg P., V.P.-Indus. Rels.--Dwyer Instruments Inc., Michigan City, IN, pg. 356
Miller, Mark, V.P.-Corp. Rels.--Solvay Pharmaceuticals, Inc., Marietta, GA, pg. 1017
Miller, Mary Ann, Pub. Rels. Dir.--DDF&M Inc. Dudreck DePaul Ficco & Morgan Inc., Pittsburgh, PA, pg. 308
Miller, Monica, Mgr.-Pub. Rels. & Res.--Taco John's International, Inc., Cheyenne, WY, pg. 1076
Miller, Nadine, Pub. Rels. Mgr.--Lake to Lake Dairy, Kiel, WI, pg. 653
Minasian, Peter F., Dir.-Pub. Rels.--H. P. Hood Inc., Boston, MA, pg. 25
Misdom, Janine, Mgr.-Communications--Ballet Makers, Inc., Totowa, NJ, pg. 116
Miskinis, E. W., V.P.-Human Resources--Jeffrey Division, Columbus, OH, pg. 565
Mitchell, Elvira J., Mgr.-Personnel & Pub. Rels.--Navajo Forest Products Industries, Navajo, NM, pg. 796
Mitchell, Howard, V.P.-Public Rels.--Keller Crescent Co., Evansville, IN, pg. 620
Mitchell, Howard, V.P., Pub. Rels.--Keller-Crescent Co., Evansville, IN, pg. 621
Mizanin, Susan M., Mktg. Communications Specialist--Dukane Corporation, Saint Charles, IL, pg. 351
Mock, Paul, Public Rels. Mgr.--The Selmer Co., Elkhart, IN, pg. 573
Monsen, Erik, Dir.-Pub. Rels. & Safety--Applied Solar Energy Corporation, City of Industry, CA, pg. 79
Monson, Catherine, Grp. V.P.-Mktg. & Training--Sir Speedy, Inc., Laguna Hills, CA, pg. 613
Montgomery, Megan, Dir.-Pub. Rels.--Lost Arrow Corporation, Ventura, CA, pg. 684
Moody, Jay, Dir.-Pub. Rels.--Gregory & Clyburne, Inc., Stamford, CT, pg. 486
Moore, Bill, Mgr.-Customer Service--Hackney & Sons, Inc., Washington, NC, pg. 498
Moore, Bob, Dir.-Pub. Rels.--Kansas City Chiefs Football Club, Kansas City, MO, pg. 616
Morales, Deborah, Mgr.-Pub. Rels.--Hammacher, Schlemmer & Co., Inc., Chicago, IL, pg. 503
Morgan, William H., Exec. V.P. & Dir.-Communications--Elias Brothers Restaurants, Inc., Warren, MI, pg. 376
Moriarty, Daniel, Sr. V.P.-Pub. Rels.--Revlon, Inc., New York, NY, pg. 696
Moriles, Amador P., Public Rels. Dir.--Hemisphere-Leo Burnett, Inc., Metro Manila,, Philippines, pg. 192
Morrison, Andrew, Asst. V.P.-Pub. Affairs--Pacific Mutual Life Insurance Company, Newport Beach, CA, pg. 841
Morrison, Kathryn D., V.P., Sec., Treas. & Pub. Rels. Dir.--The Morrison Agency, Atlanta, GA, pg. 771
Morrissey, Madeleine, Dir.-Adv. & Pub. Rels.--Dana Perfumes Corp., New York, NY, pg. 313
Morrow, Susan, Dir.-Communications--Dac Easy, Inc., Dallas, TX, pg. 571
Morse, Raymond G., Mgr.-Customer Service--Cone-Blanchard Machine Company, Windsor, VT, pg. 273
Mortensen, Deb, Dir.-Pub. Rels.--South Dakota Lottery, Pierre, SD, pg. 1019
Mortine, Neil R., V.P., Dir. Pub. Rels.--Lord, Sullivan & Yoder/Public Relations, Columbus, OH, pg. 684
Mosack-Lee, Carole, Dir.-Adv. & Communications--Conbraco Industries Inc., Matthews, NC, pg. 272
Moss, Barbara Aumann, Dir.- Pub. Rels.--Grant Marketing Communications Inc., Lafayette Hill, PA, pg. 477
Mounts, Sandy Lesko, Deputy Dir.-Pub. Rels.--Ohio Lottery Commission, Cleveland, OH, pg. 822
Muckleroy, Jim, Dir.-Public Rels.--Brookshire Grocery, Tyler, TX, pg. 180
Mudar, Demetria, Dir.-Pub. Rels.--Avis, Inc., Garden City, NY, pg. 102
Mueller, Terri F., Dir.-Corp. Communications--ERA Real Estate, Overland Park, KS, pg. 360
Muldoon Roberts, Cate, Dir.-Pub. Rels.--Roni Hicks & Associates, Inc., San Diego, CA, pg. 533
Mullally, Lee, Pub. Rels. Dir.--Ovation Marketing, Inc., La Crosse, WI, pg. 832
Mullen, Sarah C. Luke, Sr. V.P.-Communications--The American Stock Exchange, New York, NY, pg. 62
Mullins, Steve, Dir., Pub. Rels.--A.B. Data, Ltd., Milwaukee, WI, pg. 1
Mumma, J.S., Sr.-V.P.-Mktg. & Pub. Rels.--Atlas Van Lines, Inc., Evansville, IN, pg. 96
Murray, Margaret, Dir.-Adv. & Pub. Rels.--Crosman Corporation, East Bloomfield, NY, pg. 695
Murray, William, Dir.-Corp. Communications--Atlantic Mutual Companies, New York, NY, pg. 94
Myers, Ronald W., V.P.-Fin. & Admin. & Chief Fin. Officer--GF Office Furniture Ltd., Gallatin, TN, pg. 439
Myers, Truman, Sr. V.P.-Pub. Rels.--Robinson, Yesawich & Pepperdine, Orlando, FL, pg. 940
Myland, Larry, Mgr.-Corp. Communications--Humphrey Products Company, Kalamazoo, MI, pg. 553
Nagel, Thomas, Dir.-Personnel & Labor Rels.--King Kullen Grocery Co., Inc., Westbury, NY, pg. 630
Nagle, Terry, Dir.-Communications--Land O'Lakes, Inc., Arden Hills, MN, pg. 653
Nally, G.M., Dir.-Communications--Hobart Brothers Co., Troy, OH, pg. 536
Nashe, Carol, V.P.-Community Rels.--Blue Cross and Blue Shield of Massachusetts, Boston, MA, pg. 159
Nathan, Joy, Sr. V.P., Pub. Rels.--Williams Whittle Associates, Inc., Alexandria, VA, pg. 1191
Natz, Daryl C., V.P.-Public Affairs--Continental Grain Company, New York, NY, pg. 279
Naught, Donald, V.P.-Communications & Training--Long John Silver's, Inc., Lexington, KY, pg. 229
Neader, Margie, Media Coord.--G. Heileman Brewing Co., Inc., La Crosse, WI, pg. 526
Neely, Susan K., Sr. V.P., Gen. Mgr., Pub. Rels.--Creswell, Munsell, Fultz & Zirbel, Washington, DC, pg. 1211
Nelson, Benjamin, Dir.-Indus. Mkt. Rels.--Markem Corporation, Keene, NH, pg. 708
Nelson, Peter J., V.P.-Corp. Information--Public Storage, Inc., Glendale, CA, pg. 898
Nelson, Rebecca, Dir.-Pub. Rels.--Lida Advertising Company, Wichita, KS, pg. 674
Nelson, W. Mike, V.P.-Human Resources & Legal--Brooks Beverages Inc., Columbus, OH, pg. 179
Nenninger, B., Mgr.-Pub. Rels.--Welsh Company, Saint Louis, MO, pg. 1175

Nestor, David L., Dir.-Natl Pub. Rels.--Coopers & Lybrand, New York, NY, pg. 283
Neumann, Vivian F., Special Projects Coord.--St. Paul Metalcraft, Inc., Saint Paul, MN, pg. 967
Newell, Jack, Dir.-Mktg., Communications & Adv.--The ERM Group, Exton, PA, pg. 360
Newton, Karen L., Mgr.-Public Rels. & Communications--Ziebart International Corporation, Troy, MI, pg. 1217
Nichol, David W., V.P., Pub. Rels.--Lewis Communications, Inc., Mobile, AL, pg. 673
Nickell, Dennis, Dir.- Pub. Rels.--Penny/Ohlmann/Neiman, Inc., Dayton, OH, pg. 858
Nickerson, Greg, V.P., Pub. Rels.--Bader Rutter & Assoc., Inc., Brookfield, WI, pg. 113
Nicoll, Rob, Dir.-Mktg. Communications--JPS Elastomerics Corp., Northampton, MA, pg. 586
Nixon, Don, Dir.-Customer Service--Croft Metal Inc., McComb, MS, pg. 300
Noble, Raymond, Mgr.-Pub. Rels.--Avis, Inc., Garden City, NY, pg. 102
Nolan, Robert, V.P.-Pub. Rels.--First Federal Savings and Loan Assn. of Rochester, Rochester, NY, pg. 413
Nolte, Brenda, Pub. Affairs Officer--Payless Cashways, Inc., Kansas City, MO, pg. 853
Norris, Christopher M.F., Dir.-Corp. Communications--Compuware Corporation, Farmington Hills, MI, pg. 271
Noto, Peggy, Dir.-Pub. Rels.--Control Systems Inc., Saint Paul, MN, pg. 281
Novotny, Bruce, Dir.-Video & Communications--Harmon Smith Inc., Kansas City, MO, pg. 510
Nurray, Maureen, Dir.-Pub. Rels.--North Atlantic Industries, Inc., Hauppauge, NY, pg. 812
Nusbaum, Dave, V.P.-Adv. & Pub. Rels. & Dir.-Mktg.--Kampgrounds of America, Inc., Billings, MT, pg. 613
Nusz, June, Mgr.-Communications--Hypro Corporation, New Brighton, MN, pg. 557
O'Brien, Richard J., Sr. V.P.- Pub. Rels.--Mutual of America, New York, NY, pg. 777
O'Callaghan, Mary Lou, V.P.-Media Rels.--USA Network, New York, NY, pg. 1124
O'Connell, Richard F., V.P.-Pub. Affairs--Blue Cross & Blue Shield of Illinois, Chicago, IL, pg. 160
O'Connor, Lisa Ayr, Media Coord.--Howe Furniture Corporation, Trumbull, CT, pg. 547
O'Donnell, James F., Dir.-Corp. Communications--The Hearst Corporation, New York, NY, pg. 521
O'Donnell, James F., Dir.-Communications--Hearst Magazines Division, New York, NY, pg. 523
O'Hara, J.D.M., Dir.-Corp. Communications--Collins & Aikman Textile Group, Charlotte, NC, pg. 262
O'Herron, Mary J., Dir.-Pub. Rels.--Marine World Africa USA, Vallejo, CA, pg. 707
O'Keefe, Mary, Mgr.-Media Rels.--The Principal Financial Group, Des Moines, IA, pg. 890
O'Meara, Mary K., Dir.-Adv.--Sargent Manufacturing Company, New Haven, CT, pg. 361
Oakes, Ella, Mgr.-Customer Service--Quality Technologies Corporation, Sunnyvale, CA, pg. 904
Oatman, Carolyn, Dir.-Information Services--Harte-Hanks Communications, Inc., San Antonio, TX, pg. 513
Oddy, Julie, Public Rels. Dir.--Paul Stuart, Inc., New York, NY, pg. 1054
Ogburn, Fred, Mgr.-Corp. Communications--Cogsdill Tool Products, Inc., Lugoff, SC, pg. 259
Oldberg, Carol A., Dir.-Communications--Gingiss International, Chicago, IL, pg. 460
Oliver, Al, Customer Rels.--Formex, Inc. - Permanent Steel Forms, Richmond, VA, pg. 470
Olsen, Michael J., V.P.-Communications--National Car Rental System, Inc., Minneapolis, MN, pg. 786
Opolko, Phyllis, Dir.-Mktg. & Pub. Rels.--Monarch Avalon, Inc., Baltimore, MD, pg. 765
Orio, Paul, Dir.-Affiliate Rels.--CRN International, Inc., Hamden, CT, pg. 203
Orlando, Mary, Customer Service--Narrow Fabric Industries, Inc., West Reading, PA, pg. 783
Orlicki, Suzanne F., Dir.-Corp. Communications--R. L. Polk & Co., Detroit, MI, pg. 879
Orr, John, V.P. & Mgr.-Pub. Rels.--Al Paul Lefton Co., Inc., Philadelphia, PA, pg. 666
Orr, John, V.P. & Mgr., Pub. Rel. Dept.--Al Paul Lefton Co., Inc., Public Relations, Philadelphia, PA, pg. 666
Orr, Tommy, Sr. V.P.--Harbor Financial Mortgage Corp., Houston, TX, pg. 506
Osborn, Townes, V.P.-Pub. Rels.--Lavidge & Associates Inc., Knoxville, TN, pg. 661
Otis, Annette, Dir.-Business Rels.--Associated Grocers, Inc., Seattle, WA, pg. 90
Otto, Paula, Dir.-Pub. Info.--Virginia State Lottery Department, Richmond, VA, pg. 1153
Pace, Melinda, Pub. Rels. Mgr.--The Food Group, New York, NY, pg. 423
Pacini, Martha, Dir.-Corp. Communications--Heery International, Inc., Atlanta, GA, pg. 525
Painter, Larry, Sr. V.P., Pub. Rels.--Maris, West & Baker, Inc., Jackson, MS, pg. 707
Palazzolo, Barbara, Partner & Pub. Rels.--Brogan & Partners Advertising/Public Relations Inc, Detroit, MI, pg. 178
Palmer, Edward M., Dir.-Customer Service--Finch, Pruyn & Co., Inc., Glens Falls, NY, pg. 410
Palmer, Heidi, Mgr.-Pub. Rels.--Avatar Corporation, Hopkinton, MA, pg. 101
Paluszek, John L., Pres., Pub. Affairs--Ketchum Public Relations/Corporate, New York, NY, pg. 625
Pamerleau, W.C., Mgr.-Communications--Auto-Owners Insurance, Lansing, MI, pg. 100
Panczak, William, Sr. V.P.-Customer & Trade Rels.--Advertising Checking Bureau Incorporated, New York, NY, pg. 21
Parker, Joan, Sr. V.P., Pub. Rels.--Ayer Public Relations, New York, NY, pg. 104
Parker, Martha, Sr. V.P., Pub. Rels.--Fitzgerald & Company, Inc., Cranston, RI, pg. 416
Parker, Nancy W., Dir.-Pub. Rels.--Artesian Resources Corporation, Newark, DE, pg. 86
Parker, Nancy W., Dir.-Pub. Rels.--Artesian Water Company, Inc., Newark, DE, pg. 86
Parker, S. Victoria, V.P.-Corp. Rels. & Human Resources--John Wieland Homes Inc., Atlanta, GA, pg. 1188
Parrish, David, Corp. V.P.-Member Rels. & Admin.--Mid-America Dairymen, Inc., Springfield, MO, pg. 750
Parrish, Glenn E., V.P.-Customer Service E. & W.--Tennessee Valley Authority, Knoxville, TN, pg. 1088
Paschal, Annelle, Dir.-Human Resources & Pub. Rels.--U.S. Can Company, Oak Brook, IL, pg. 1134
Pasternak, Irene, Dir., Community Affairs--Bernstein-Rein Advertising, Inc., Kansas City, MO, pg. 144
Patarino, Vincent, V.P.-Customer Service--Queens Group Indiana, Inc., Indianapolis, IN, pg. 904
Paternack, Irene, Dir.-Mktg. Communications--Applied Microsystems Corporation, Redmond, WA, pg. 79
Patrick, Barbara A., Asst. Mgr.-Communications--Tax Management, Inc., Washington, DC, pg. 190
Patterson, Bill, V.P.-Corp. Communications--Hameroff/Milenthal/Spence, Inc., Columbus, OH, pg. 503
Patterson, J.R., Sr. V.P.-Customer Service--Atlas Van Lines, Inc., Evansville, IN, pg. 96
Patterson, Jeff, Pub. Rels. Spec.--Swanson Russell Associates, Lincoln, NE, pg. 1066
Patton, Francie, Dir.-Pub. Rels.--Hudepohl-Schoenling Brewing Company, Cincinnati, OH, pg. 550
Patton, Michael J., Dir., Pub. Rels.--TJ Clark Advertising/PR, Hingham, MA, pg. 251
Pawlick, Thomas, Dir.-Mktg. Communications--Medline Industries, Inc., Mundelein, IL, pg. 736
Payne, Ronald G., Pres. & Chief Exec. Officer--Warehouse Home Furnishings Distributor, Dublin, GA, pg. 1163
Peck, Don, Asst. Dir.-Tourism Services--Kentucky Department of Travel Development, Frankfort, KY, pg. 623
Pelly, Jerry D., V.P.-Sls. , Customer Service & Sec.--Forestry Suppliers, Inc., Jackson, MS, pg. 424
Pelton, Carole Allaway, Dir.-Adv.--Rain Bird Sprinkler Mfg. Corp., Glendora, CA, pg. 910
Penza, Gloria Jean, Dir.-Information--Long Island Water Corporation, Lynbrook, NY, pg. 682
Peralta, Lila, Dir.-Communications--Harris Drury Cohen, Fort Lauderdale, FL, pg. 511
Perlow, Gail R., V.P.-Media--Combe Incorporated, White Plains, NY, pg. 267
Perron, John T., V.P.-Admin.--AmClyde Engineered Products, Inc., Saint Paul, MN, pg. 47
Perrone, Donna, Mgr.-Adv. & Communications--Kearney, Tucker, GA, pg. 357
Perry, Lisa, Pub. Rels. Coord.--Sheffield Silver Co., Taunton, MA, pg. 920
Pestovic, Edward J., Adv. Dir.--Steinbach, White Plains, NY, pg. 1045
Peters, Alexandra, Pub. Rels. & Adv.--Phillips Fine Art Auctioneers, New York, NY, pg. 867
Peters, Douglas S., Sr. V.P.-Representation & Public Affairs--Blue Cross and Blue Shield Association, Chicago, IL, pg. 159
Peters, Rich, 2nd V.P.-Mktg. Services & Pub. Rels.--Woodmen Accident & Life Co., Lincoln, NE, pg. 1200
Peterson, Sarah H., V.P.-Pub. Rels.--Texas Commerce Bancshares, Inc., Houston, TX, pg. 1089
Peterson, Terry, Customer Services Mgr.--Wagner Spray Tech Corp., Minneapolis, MN, pg. 1158
Petridis, Eileen, Acct. Mgr., Pub. Rels., New Bus. Contact--Brand, Shick & Wesley, Cleveland, OH, pg. 172
Petrini, Vincent, Dir.-Communications--Regional Transportation Authority (RTA), Chicago, IL, pg. 922
Petti, Ken, Pub. Rels. Mgr.--Gitano Group Inc., New York, NY, pg. 460
Pfeifer, Ellen W., Mgr.-Marcom Communications--Central Point Software, Inc., Beaverton, OR, pg. 234
Phillips, John C., Jr., Mng. Dir.-Client Rels.--Copley Real Estate Advisors, Inc., Boston, MA, pg. 799
Phillips, Rebecca, V.P.-Communications & Bus. Devel.--Indian Head Industries Inc., Southfield, MI, pg. 565
Pickford, Lori, Pub. Rels.--Provident Mutual Life Insurance Co., Philadelphia, PA, pg. 896
Pilk, Emily, Mgr.-Communications--The Bureau of National Affairs, Inc., Washington, DC, pg. 189
Pineda, Dixie, V.P.-Pub. Rels.--Levenson & Hill, Inc., Irving, TX, pg. 670
Pippin, Marilyn, V.P., Pub. Rels.--Michael, Bolger, Reinschmiedt, King (MBRK), Dallas, TX, pg. 746
Pittman, Dan, V.P., Pub. Rels. Dir.--Salvati Montgomery Sakoda, Inc., Costa Mesa, CA, pg. 967
Pittman, Joseph E., Pub. Rels. Coord.--Mutual of Omaha Insurance Company, Omaha, NE, pg. 779
Pitzer, Randy, Mgr.-Mktg. Communications--SPSS Inc., Chicago, IL, pg. 964
Plazak, Kathryn F., 2nd V.P.-Community Rels.--The New England, Boston, MA, pg. 799
Polito, Paula, V.P., Communications--Hill, Holliday, Connors, Cosmopulos, Inc., Boston, MA, pg. 534
Pollino, Patrick A., V.P.-Corp. Communications--Arthur D. Little, Inc., Cambridge, MA, pg. 678
Pope, John, Dir.-Corp. Rels.--Compuadd Corporation, Austin, TX, pg. 271
Potratz, Dean C., Exec. V.P., Sec. & Pub. Rels. Dir.--Sargent & Potratz, Inc., Brookfield, WI, pg. 971
Potts, Marilyn, Pub. Rels. Dir.--Associated Advertising Agency, Inc., Wichita, KS, pg. 89
Powell, MaryAnn, V.P.-Communications--Medieval Dinner & Tournament, Inc., Buena Park, CA, pg. 735
Power, John, Sr. V.P., Mngmt. Rep. & Communications Mgr.--Vitt Media International, Inc., New York, NY, pg. 1153
Powers, Rob, Pub. Rels. Dir.--R & R Advertising, Las Vegas, NV, pg. 906
Powers, Ron, Dir.-Personnel & Pub. Rels.--Ward Leonard Electric Company, Inc., Mount Vernon, NY, pg. 1127
Prather, Susan, V.P., Dir. Pub. Rels.--Cramer-Krasselt, Chicago, IL, pg. 296
Pratt, Claire, Pub. Rels. & Acct. Exec.--TJ Clark Advertising/PR, Hingham, MA, pg. 251
Pred, Marilyn, Dir., Pub. Rels.--Omaha Creative Group, Omaha, NE, pg. 825
Pred, Marilyn, Dir.-Pub. Rels.--Omaha Steaks International, Omaha, NE, pg. 825
Prescott, Joan, V.P., Pub. Rels. Mgr.--Barker Campbell & Farley, Virginia Beach, VA, pg. 120
Prescott, Stephanie, Corp. Communications Supvr.--SnyderGeneral Corporation, Dallas, TX, pg. 1015
Pretko, Paul, Mgr.-Customer Service--Sweetheart Cup Co., Inc., Chicago, IL, pg. 1067
Price, Joliene, V.P.-Communications--Atlanta Market Center, Atlanta, GA, pg. 94
Priore, Cathy, Dir.-Customer Service--Formfit Rogers, New York, NY, pg. 78
Priore, Cathy, Dir.-Customer Service--Jones New York Intimates, New York, NY, pg. 78
Pulizzi, Louise E., Dir.-Corp. Communications--Clark Construction Group, Bethesda, MD, pg. 252
Pullman, David, Dir.-Communications & Adv.--The Cincinnati Cordage & Paper Company, Cincinnati, OH, pg. 249
Quinn, Joellyn, V.P.-Corp. Rels. & Asst. Sec.--Credit Union National Association, Madison, WI, pg. 298
Raab, Henry R., V.P., Pub. Rels.--Stiegler, Wells & Brunswick, Inc., Bethlehem, PA, pg. 1049
Radtke, R.C., V.P.-Pub. Rels.--CUNA Mutual Insurance Society, Madison, WI, pg. 205
Radwill, Linda, V.P., Mgr.-Mktg. & Sec.--Master Appliance Corp., Racine, WI, pg. 719
Raeder, Caroline, Dir.-Communications--Cirrus System, Inc., Westchester, IL, pg. 720
Raffa, Louise M., V.P.-Corp. Communications & Adv.--Molded Fiber Glass Co., Union City, PA, pg. 764
Ragenovich, Alice, Mgr.-Pub. Rels.--Kal Kan Foods, Inc., Vernon, CA, pg. 713
Raives, Ann, V.P.-Customer Service & Corp. Communications--Montgomery Ward & Co., Inc., Chicago, IL, pg. 767
Ramsey, Karen, Dir.-Pub. Rels.--Harp's Food Stores, Inc., Springdale, AR, pg. 510
Randall, Kay, External Rels.--Mars Confectionery, Slough, United Kingdom, pg. 713
Randazzo, May C., Mgr.-Pub. Affairs/Communication--Graphic Controls, Corp., Buffalo, NY, pg. 478
Randazzo, May C., Mgr.-Pub. Affairs & Communication--Graphic Controls Corporation, Buffalo, NY, pg. 478
Ranhart, Daniel M., Mgr.-Communications--Tax Management, Inc., Washington, DC, pg. 190
Rankin, Amy, Dir.-Pub. Rels.--Robinson & St. John Advertising & Public Relations, Inc., Jacksonville, FL, pg. 940
Raper, Mark, Pres., Gen. Mgr., Pub. Rels.--Earle Palmer Brown/Richmond, Richmond, VA, pg. 182
Rasak, Jane, Asst. Dir., Pub. Rels.--Mulle/Breen Advertising, Toluca Lake, CA, pg. 775
Rasuli, Darryl, Mgr.-Pub. Rels.--Niagara Frontier Transportation Metro System, Inc., Buffalo, NY, pg. 806
Ratay, Leslie J., Mgr.-Corp. Communications--Quad/Graphics, Inc., Pewaukee, WI, pg. 902
Rattner, Judy, Pub. Rels. Specialist--Information Builders, New York, NY, pg. 567
Rau, Lisa, Mgr.-Publicity--Silver Dollar City, Inc., Branson, MO, pg. 1004
Raustein, Horst, Mgr.-Quality Assurance--Code-A-Phone Corp., Clackamas, OR, pg. 258
Reddy, Tom, Dir., Newsp. Rels.--The Sunflower Group, Overland Park, KS, pg. 1060
Redford, Elenor, Customer Rels.--Formex, Inc. - Permanent Steel Forms, Richmond, VA, pg. 470
Reed, Bill J., V.P.-Communications & Pub. Affairs--Riceland Foods, Inc., Stuttgart, AR, pg. 931
Reed, J.M., Mgr.-Corp. Communications--PQ Corporation, Valley Forge, PA, pg. 836
Reilly, Liz, Dir.-Communications--The Kiplinger Washington Editors, Inc., Washington, DC, pg. 632
Reilly, Liz, Dir.-Communications--Kiplinger's Personal Finance Magazine, Washington, DC, pg. 632
Reiser, Carol L., Pub. Rels. Specialist--Communication & Design Agency Inc., Latham, NY, pg. 269
Rekoff, Richard E., Dir.-Service--McNamara Pontiac Inc., Orlando, FL, pg. 732
Renken, Ed, Dir.-Mktg.--Renken Boat Manufacturing Co., Charleston, SC, pg. 927
Repa, Janine, Dir.-Pub. Rels.--Trump Organization, New York, NY, pg. 1118
Repa, Jeanine, Exec. Dir.-Adv. & Pub. Rels.--Trump's Castle Casino Resort, Atlantic City, NJ, pg. 1118
Reusing, Vincent P., Sr. V.P.-External Rels.--Metropolitan Life Insurance Co., New York, NY, pg. 744
Revell-Pechar, Ann, Pub. Rels. Mgr.--Sharp Hartwig, Inc., Seattle, WA, pg. 995
Reynolds, Gail A., Mgr.-Investor & Public Relations--Lawrence Insurance Group, Inc., New York, NY, pg. 662
Reynolds, Gail A., Mgr.-Pub. Rels., Investor Rels. & Adv.--Lawrence Management Group, Inc., Albany, NY, pg. 662
Reynolds, Jack, V.P.-Client Services--Emkay, Inc., Itasca, IL, pg. 379
Reznor, J.V., V.P.-Dealer Relations--Lumbermens Merchandising Corporation, Wayne, PA, pg. 687
Rhodes, George R., V.P.-Corp. Communications & Professional Rels.--Dentsply International Inc., York, PA, pg. 329
Ricci, Elaine, Dir.-External Rels.--Lechmere, Inc., Woburn, MA, pg. 665
Rice, Howard H., V.P.-Pub. Rels.--Alexander Marketing Services, Inc., Grand Rapids, MI, pg. 33
Richards, Sally, Dir.-Public Rels.--Ventura Travelware, Inc., Long Island City, NY, pg. 1147
Richer, Linda, Mgr.-Customer Service--The Protector Corporation, Addison, IL, pg. 895

Richley, J. Phillip, V.P.-Devel., Dir.-Pub. Rels. & Media Dir.--The Cafaro Co., Youngstown, OH, pg. 207
Richmond, Martha Crawford, V.P., Pub. Rels.--The Schmidt/Westerdahl Group Ltd., Portland, OR, pg. 976
Riddle, Virginia, Dir.-Pub. Rels.--Allen-Edmonds Shoe Corp., Port Washington, WI, pg. 36
Riechers, Jeanette, V.P., Pub. Rels.--Stephan & Brady, Incorporated, Madison, WI, pg. 1046
Riechers, Jeanette, Acct. Supvr., Pub. Rel.--Stephan & Brady, Incorporated, Madison, WI, pg. 1046
Rieger, Catherine, Dir., Pub. Rels.--Rockett, Burkhead, Lewis & Winslow, Raleigh, NC, pg. 941
Riesterer, Tim, Dir., Pub. Rels.--The Brady Company, Menomonee Falls, WI, pg. 171
Riffle, JoLaine, Dir.-Communications--The Lathrop Company, Toledo, OH, pg. 660
Ripley, Clinton E., V.P.-Customer Service--Advance Packaging Corporation, Grand Rapids, MI, pg. 19
Rish, Stephen A., V.P.-Pub. Rels.--Nationwide Mutual Insurance Company, Columbus, OH, pg. 795
Riste, LaDonna, Community Rels. Coord.--Dakota Electric Association, Farmington, MN, pg. 312
Robb, Jane W., Dir.-Corp. Rels.--National Life Insurance Company, Montpelier, VT, pg. 791
Roberson, Donald, Dir.-Mktg. & Sls.--Theradyne Corporation, Lakeville, MN, pg. 1065
Robertson, Dave, Dir. Pub. Rels.--Kahler Friendt & Partners, Inc., Omaha, NE, pg. 613
Robinson, Carole, V.P.-Press Rels., MTV--MTV Networks, New York, NY, pg. 785
Robinson, Carole, Sr. V.P.-Press Rels.--MTV: Music Television, New York, NY, pg. 785
Robinson, Chris, Integrated Communications Dir.--Leo Burnett S.A. de C.V., Mexico,, Mexico, pg. 193
Rodriguez, Jenne, Dir.-Community Devel. Div.--Nebraska Dept. of Economic Development, Lincoln, NE, pg. 796
Rogers, Charlie, V.P.-Customer Rels.--Globe Glass & Mirror Co., Chicago, IL, pg. 463
Rogers, Sam, Exec. V.P., Pub. Rels. Dir.--Elkman Advertising & Public Relations, Bala-Cynwyd, PA, pg. 377
Rogers, Sam, Exec. V.P., Pub. Rels. Dir.--Elkman Advertising, Public Relations Div., Bala-Cynwyd, PA, pg. 378
Rohan, Mary, Dir.-Pub. Rels.--George Kovacs Lighting, Inc., Glendale, NY, pg. 643
Rollins, Lori, Mgr.-Communications--Morrison Textile Machinery Co., Fort Lawn, SC, pg. 771
Roman, Anne, Sr. Pub. Rels. Counsel--Lauerer Markin Gibbs Public Relations Group, Maumee, OH, pg. 661
Romano, Julia A., V.P.-Information Systems & Services--New York Life Insurance Company, New York, NY, pg. 802
Romeo, Carol, Dir.-Pub. Rels.--Warner, Bicking, Morris & Partners, Inc., New York, NY, pg. 1164
Romig, Mark, Pub. Rels. & Acct. Supvr.--Peter A. Mayer Advertising, Inc., New Orleans, LA, pg. 724
Rood, Mary Ann, Dir.-Communications--Ocean Spray Cranberries, Inc., Lakeville, MA, pg. 820
Ropes, John S., V.P.-Grower Rels.--Ocean Spray Cranberries, Inc., Lakeville, MA, pg. 820
Rosati, Janet, Dir.-Consumer Relations--Fruit of the Loom, Bowling Green, KY, pg. 400
Roseman, Mary, Dir.-Consumer Nutrition Information--Long John Silver's, Inc., Lexington, KY, pg. 229
Rosen, Michael, Exec. V.P., Client Services--Sacks & Rosen, Inc. Advertising, New York, NY, pg. 965
Rosenberg, Marc, Dir., Pub. Rels., Promo. & Affiliate Rels.--Bohbot Communications, Inc., New York, NY, pg. 162
Ross, Georgette, Mgr.-Customer Service--C M P Publications, Inc., Manhasset, NY, pg. 202
Roush, Ella M., Dir.-Pub. Rels.--Moyer Packing Company, Souderton, PA, pg. 774
Rowe, Marilyn, V.P., Bus. Affairs Dir.--Backer Spielvogel Bates, Inc., Irvine, CA, pg. 108
Rowe, Reg, Sr. Pub. Rels. Supvr.--NKH&W, Inc., Kansas City, MO, pg. 781
Rudgers, Lisa, Pub. Rels. Dir.--Media Logic, Inc., Albany, NY, pg. 734
Ruff, Jim, Dir.-Human Resources--Concordia Publishing House, Saint Louis, MO, pg. 272
Rugen, Karen, V.P.-Pub. Rels.--Hyatt Hotels Corporation, Chicago, IL, pg. 495
Rusk, Becky, Dir.-Pub. Rels.--Kuhn & Wittenborn, Inc., Kansas City, MO, pg. 646
Russell, Charles, Gen. Mgr. & Pub. Rels.--Karsh & Hagan, Inc., Englewood, CO, pg. 617
Russo, Joseph M., V.P.-Pub. Affairs--The Hertz Corporation, Park Ridge, NJ, pg. 849
Russo, Lori M., Asst. Sec.--The First Boston Corporation, New York, NY, pg. 203
Ruth, Richard J., V.P.-Employee Rels.--Sunnen Products Company, Saint Louis, MO, pg. 1061
Rutman, Marc, V.P., Pub. Rels.--Launey, Hachmann & Harris, Inc., New York, NY, pg. 661
Ryan, Kristine, Pub. Rels. Specialist--McCommunications Inc., Dallas, TX, pg. 727
Sabin, David, Customer Services Mgr.--Harig Products, Elgin, IL, pg. 175
Sacco, Jodi, Dir.-Mktg. Communications--Western Data Systems, Calabasas, CA, pg. 1178
Sachse, Anne, Mgr.-Adv. & Pub. Rels.--Rite-Hite Corporation, Milwaukee, WI, pg. 936
Sacks, Richard, Pub. Rels. Dir.--Poppe Tyson, New York, NY, pg. 880
Sajkowski, Debra, Adv. Mgr.--Milwaukee Electric Tool Corp., Brookfield, WI, pg. 361
Sanborn, Sally, Dir.-P.R.--Save Mart Supermarkets, Modesto, CA, pg. 973
Sand, D.R., V.P.-Customer Rels.--Bunn-O-Matic Corporation, Springfield, IL, pg. 188
Sandberg, Kristin, Mgr.-Pub. Rels.--Hyatt International Corporation, Chicago, IL, pg. 495
Sander, Gail, Dir.-Pub. Rels.--Harris and Love, Inc., Salt Lake City, UT, pg. 512
Sanders, William H., V.P.-Customer Service--The Coleman Company, Inc., Wichita, KS, pg. 695
Satmary, Susan, Dir., Pub. Rels.--Goldberg Moser O'Neill, San Francisco, CA, pg. 465
Saul, Ida, Mgr.-Human Resources--Struthers-Dunn Inc., Pitman, NJ, pg. 693
Saurer, D.W., Mgr.-Public Rels.--Lord Corporation, Erie, PA, pg. 683
Savage, M., Dir.-Pub. Rels.--Abdalla's Lafayette, Inc., Lafayette, LA, pg. 10
Sawyer, Kelley, Dir.-Asst. Pub. Rels.--Avondale Mills, Inc., Sylacauga, AL, pg. 103
Sawyer, Lauralee, Pub. Rels. Dir.--Freedman, Gibson & White Inc., Cincinnati, OH, pg. 430
Saxton, Cliff, Dir.-Pub. Rels.--Unigroup, Inc., Fenton, MO, pg. 1126
Sayer, David C., Exec. Dir.-Adv. & Pub. Rels.--Publishers Clearing House, Port Washington, NY, pg. 898
Saylor, Beth, Promo. Coord.--JII/Sales Promotion Associates, Inc., Coshocton, OH, pg. 604
Scaife, Richard M., Dir.-Pub.Rels.--Tribune Review Publishing Co., Greensburg, PA, pg. 1112
Schakel, Wayne, V.P., Pub. Rels. Dir.--Axelband & Brown & Associates Inc., Cleveland, OH, pg. 103
Schanz, Geri, V.P., Dir. Pub. Rels.--G & A Communications, Newport Beach, CA, pg. 438
Schellie, Ken, V.P.-Corp. Communications--United Parcel Service of America, Inc., Atlanta, GA, pg. 1133
Scher, Dag M., Exec. V.P.-Corp. Communications--Rail Europe Inc., White Plains, NY, pg. 910
Schmidt, Delmore, Dir.-Communications--Harvest States Cooperatives, Saint Paul, MN, pg. 514
Schmidt, Donna, Dir.-Pub. Rels.--National Live Stock & Meat Board, Chicago, IL, pg. 792
Schneider, Maggie, Dir.-Pub. Rels.--National Cleaning Contractors, Inc., New York, NY, pg. 786
Schoeniger, Mary, Pub. Rels. Coord.--Cres-Cor/Crown-X, Cleveland, OH, pg. 298
Schofield, Sheila, Dir.-Adv. & Pub. Rels.--Omni Hotels, Hampton, NH, pg. 826
Schollenberger, Charles, V.P., Pub. Rels.--Christenson, Barclay & Shaw, Inc., Overland Park, KS, pg. 248
Schoolfield, Susan, Pub. Rels. Dir.--Regian Advertising & Public Relations, Fort Worth, TX, pg. 922
Schott Lawrence, Jennifer, Mgr.-Pub. Rels.--Costa Cruise Lines, N.V., Miami, FL, pg. 288
Schreiber, Mark, Pub. Rels. Dir.--Pennsylvania State Lottery, Middletown, PA, pg. 858
Schuetz, Michael, Dir.-Corp. Communications--The Texwipe Co., Inc., Upper Saddle River, NJ, pg. 1090
Schulman, Maureen, Dir.-Pub. Rels.--Eli's Chicago's Finest, Inc., Chicago, IL, pg. 376
Schultz, Matt, Dir. of Pub. Rels.--Jacobson Rost, Inc., Sheboygan, WI, pg. 588
Schultz, Wayne, Dir.-Customer Service--The Flecto Co., Inc., Oakland, CA, pg. 417
Schulze, Laura, Mgr.-Adv. & Pub. Rels.--Furman Lumber Company, Billerica, MA, pg. 436
Schumacher, Susan, V.P.-Pub. Rels.--Mullen Advertising, Inc., Wenham, MA, pg. 775
Schwalbe, R. Kelly, Pub. Rels. Supvr.--Harmon Smith Inc., Kansas City, MO, pg. 510
Schweikher, Karen, Dir.-Corp. Communications--Ampex Corporation, Redwood City, CA, pg. 998
Scisson, V.P. & Dir.-Pub. Rels.--Cranford Johnson Robinson Woods, Little Rock, AR, pg. 296
Scruby, Brian C., Sr. V.P., Dir. Pub. Rels.--The Quest Business Agency, Inc., Houston, TX, pg. 904
Seal, Paul, Dir.-Human Rels.--The William Carter Company, New York, NY, pg. 226
Seamans, Sandra, Mgr.-Communications--Trammell Crow Company, Dallas, TX, pg. 1106
Searcy, Diane L., Asst. to the Pres.--MFA Oil Company, Columbia, MO, pg. 692
Searls, David, V.P., Dir. Pub. Rels.--Hodskins Simone & Searls, Inc., Palo Alto, CA, pg. 537
Sears, Robert D., Dir.-Member Rels.--Agway, Inc., De Witt, NY, pg. 25
Seheley, Christine, Pub. Rels. Specialist--The Acacia Group, Washington, DC, pg. 10
Seidner, Fred, Mgr.-Pub. Rels.--Airways Rent A Car, Schiller Park, IL, pg. 934
Seifert, Charles, Pub. Rels. Dir.--MacDaniels, Henry & Sproul, Inc., San Francisco, CA, pg. 696
Seltzer, Sherwin, V.P.-Gen. Sls. Mgr., Adv. Mgr., Sls. Promo. Mgr. & Pub. Rels.--Villazon Company Inc., Tampa, FL, pg. 1152
Sergott, Pat, Sr. V.P., Pub. Rels.--Farago Advertising, New York, NY, pg. 399
Sessler, Andrea, Sr. V.P., Dir. Human Resources & Pub. Rels.--Ammirati & Puris Inc., New York, NY, pg. 67
Sette, Michael, Pub. Rels. Mgr.--Silverstone, Adkins & Breit, Inc., Stratford, CT, pg. 1005
Settles, Craig, Mgr.-Public Rels.--Experience in Software, Inc., Berkeley, CA, pg. 393
Sevcik, Fran, Dir.-Pub. Rels.--Norwegian Cruise Line, Coral Gables, FL, pg. 816
Sewell, Steve, V.P., Pub. Rels.--Godwin Advertising Agency, Inc., Jackson, MS, pg. 464
Sexer, Leslie, Dir.-Pub. Rels.--Jacques Moret, Inc., New York, NY, pg. 588
Sexton, Bob, Mgr.-Circulation--Country Sampler, Saint Charles, IL, pg. 968
Shapson, Edward M., Pres., Pub. Rels. & New Bus. Contact--Shapson Gero & Sommers, Inc., Philadelphia, PA, pg. 995
Shattuck, C. Jonathan, Sr. V.P.-Health Care Affairs--Blue Cross & Blue Shield of Illinois, Chicago, IL, pg. 160
Shaw, Cliff, Dir.-Cust. Services--California Offset Printers, Inc., Glendale, CA, pg. 210
Shaw, Daniel G., Dir.-Corp. Communications--Dairymen, Inc., Louisville, KY, pg. 311
Shaw, G. Martin, Dir.-Public Rels.--Rock-Tenn Company, Norcross, GA, pg. 941
Sheahan, William W., V.P., Adv. & Pub. Rels.--Andrews/Mautner, Inc., Milwaukee, WI, pg. 74
Shedaker, Budd A., Dir.-Equity Communications--Equity Services, Inc., Montpelier, VT, pg. 791
Sheehan, Jan, Pub. Rels. Dir.--Hughes Advertising Inc., Saint Louis, MO, pg. 551
Shelton, Bill, Mgr.-Communication--Lykes Energy, Inc., Tampa, FL, pg. 689
Shenk, Larry, V.P.-Pub. Rels.--The Phillies-A Limited Partnership, Philadelphia, PA, pg. 867
Shepard, Katherine L., Mgr.-Communications--H. P. Hood Inc., Boston, MA, pg. 25
Sherman, James, Mgr.-Mktg. Communications, Electrical Distr.--Leviton Mfg. Co., Inc., Little Neck, NY, pg. 671
Shields, Linda L., V.P.-Communications--Graymills Corp., Chicago, IL, pg. 480
Shippley, Dave, Pub. Rels.--The USAir Shuttle, Jackson Heights, NY, pg. 1118
Shirley, Philip, Sr. V.P., Pub. Rels.--Godwin Advertising Agency, Inc., Jackson, MS, pg. 464
Shoffner, Harry, Dir.-Mktg. & Pub. Rels.--Carolina Biological Supply Co., Burlington, NC, pg. 222
Shore, Laura, Mgr.-Communications & Promo. Services--Mohawk Paper Mills, Inc., Cohoes, NY, pg. 763
Shore, Toni, Publicity Dir.--N. Erlanger, Blumgart & Company, Inc., New York, NY, pg. 387
Siegel, Mark S., Exec. V.P., Communications & Media Grp.--Shamrock Holdings, Inc., Burbank, CA, pg. 994
Silvers, Steven, V.P., Pub. Rels.--Knape & Knape, Dallas, TX, pg. 636
Simmelink, Tom, V.P., Pub. Rels.--Whitemyer Advertising, Inc., Zoar, OH, pg. 1186
Simmons, Bobbi, V.P., Dir. Pub. Rels.--Caldwell VanRiper Inc., Indianapolis, IN, pg. 209
Simon, Arnold, Dir.-Pub. Rels.--Gulf Distribution Inc., Miami, FL, pg. 493
Simpson, Dick, V.P.-Mktg. & Pub. Rels.--Crowley Maritime Corporation, Oakland, CA, pg. 301
Simpson, Patricia, Dir.-Pub. Rels.--W.B. Doner & Company, Southfield, MI, pg. 344
Sinclair, Barbara, Mgr.-Corp. Communications--United Farm Bureau Family Life Insurance Co., Indianapolis, IN, pg. 1131
Sinclair, H.M., Dir.-Pub. Rels.--Allright Corporation, Houston, TX, pg. 41
Skinnarland, Kirvil, Dir.-Enviromental Affairs--Seattle City Light, Seattle, WA, pg. 986
Slade, Steven J., V.P.-Govt. Affairs--Trans World Airlines, Inc., Mount Kisco, NY, pg. 561
Slaybaugh, David, Mgr.-Consumer Pub. Rels.--The Scott Company, Marysville, OH, pg. 982
Slizewski, Bea, Dir.-Corp. Communications--Curtice-Burns Foods, Inc., Rochester, NY, pg. 25
Sloan, Robert B., V.P. & Dir.-Human Rels.--J. C. Bradford & Co., Nashville, TN, pg. 170
Slocum, Judy, Mgr.-Pub. Rels.--Port of Galveston, Galveston, TX, pg. 881
Small, Richard, Sr. V.P., Grp. Pub. Rels. Dir.--Gilbert, Whitney & Johns, Inc., Whippany, NJ, pg. 458
Smart, Lee, Dir.-Adv., Pub. Rels. & Mktg. Services--Martin Industries (AL), Florence, AL, pg. 715
Smetts, Stewart, Dir.-Mktg.--La Rosa's, Inc., Cincinnati, OH, pg. 649
Smigel, Diane B., V.P.-Corp. Information Services--John Hancock Mutual Life Insurance Company, Boston, MA, pg. 595
Smith, Brian M., Managing Dir.-Mktg. & Communications--Ferrell Companies Inc./Ferrellgas, Liberty, MO, pg. 407
Smith, Carol J., Dir.-Adv. & Pub. Rels.--Hoffco, Inc., Richmond, IN, pg. 537
Smith, Carol J., Dir.-Adv. & Pub. Rels.--Comet Industries, Richmond, IN, pg. 537
Smith, Cynthia, Mgr., Pub. Rels.--EGC Media Group, Inc., Hicksville, NY, pg. 359
Smith, Guy S., Pub. Rels. & Acct. Exec.--Jay Incorporated, Rochester, NY, pg. 590
Smith, Iris H., V.P.-Consumer Affairs--J.H. Harvey Company, Nashville, GA, pg. 515
Smith, J. Sam, Sr. V.P., Pub. Rels.--Combs & Heathcott, Little Rock, AR, pg. 267
Smith, Maggie, V.P. & Dir.-Pub. Rels.--Juhl Marketing Communications, Mishawaka, IN, pg. 608
Smith, Mary Beth, Asst. Mgr.-Mktg. Communications--Duo-Fast Corporation, Franklin Park, IL, pg. 354
Smith, Sean, Acct. Mgr., Pub. Rels.--Gray Baumgarten Layport, Inc., Pittsburgh, PA, pg. 479
Smith, Sherry, Pub. Rels. Dir.--Sperling, New Orleans, LA, pg. 1030
Smith, Susannah G., V.P.-Corp. Communications--Ringling Bros., Barnum & Bailey Combined Shows, Inc., Vienna, VA, pg. 935
Smock, Richard F., Dir.-Corp. Communications--Industrial Coatings Group, Inc., Chicago, IL, pg. 566
Snyder, J. Phil, Asst. V.P.-Communications Services--Aid Association For Lutherans, Appleton, WI, pg. 26
Sok, Ronald, Mgr.-Adv. & Pub. Rels.--Timex Corporation, Middlebury, CT, pg. 1098
Solomon, Dan, Communications Dir.--Bartles & Jaymes, Modesto, CA, pg. 442
Sorensen, Paul, Dir.-Corp. Communications--Camp Dresser & McKee Inc., Cambridge, MA, pg. 212
Sparkman, William E., V.P.-Customer Dealer Rels.--W.S. Badcock Corporation, Mulberry, FL, pg. 113
Spear, Edward M., Sr. V.P.-Customer Support--NRM-Steelastic, Akron, OH, pg. 781
Spector, David, Dir.-Pub. Rels.--Paradigm Communications, Tampa, FL, pg. 847
Spellman, Leo, Dir.-Adv. & Pub. Rels.--Steinway Musical Properties, Inc., Waltham, MA, pg. 1045
Spellman, Leo, Dir.-Adv. & Pub. Rels.--Steinway & Sons, Long Island City, NY, pg. 1046

Spencer, Olga, Dir.-Pub. Rels.--Gerber Advertising, Portland, OR, pg. 453
Spiegel, Marilyn, V.P. & Dir.-Communications--After Six, Incorporated, Philadelphia, PA, pg. 24
Spinks, Richard M., Dir.-Corp. Pub. Affairs--S. C. Johnson & Son, Inc., Racine, WI, pg. 599
Spong, Doug, Dir.-Pub. Rels. & Mng. Partner--Carmichael Lynch, Inc., Minneapolis, MN, pg. 222
Stake, R.J., Mgr.-Mktg. Communications--Weber Marking Systems, Inc., Arlington Heights, IL, pg. 1171
Stamm, Harriet, Creative, Art & Pub. Rel. Dir.--REMark Advertising, Honolulu, HI, pg. 999
Staniar, Linda B., V.P.-Pub. Rels., Adv. & Video Systems--New York Life Insurance Company, New York, NY, pg. 802
Stanton, Barbara, Mgr.-Customer Service--Tagsons Papers, Inc., Albany, NY, pg. 1076
Stanton, J., V.P., Pub. Rels.--Kamstra Communications, Inc., Saint Paul, MN, pg. 615
Stanton, Mark, V.P., Pub. Rels. Mgr.--Hutchins/Young & Rubicam, Rochester, NY, pg. 1211
Starnes, Robert H., V.P.-Adv. & Public Rels.--Western & Southern Life Insurance Co., Cincinnati, OH, pg. 1181
Stayskal, Gary, Dir.-Personnel--Ritchie Industries, Inc., Conrad, IA, pg. 936
Steck, Rich, Mgr.-Public Rels.--Royal Caribbean Cruises Ltd., Miami, FL, pg. 953
Steckel, Richard, Dir.-Employee Rels.--Elkay Manufacturing Company, Oak Brook, IL, pg. 377
Stefanski, Stan, Exec. V.P., Dir., Bus. Affairs-WW--Young & Rubicam Inc., New York, NY, pg. 1210
Stefanski, Stan, Exec. V.P., Dir. Bus. Affairs-WW--Young & Rubicam Inc., New York, NY, pg. 1210
Steger, Martha, Dir.-Pub. Rels.--Virginia Department of Economic Development Tourism Development Group, Richmond, VA, pg. 1152
Steinkamp, Mark, Coord.-Pub. Rels & Adv.--Daktronics, Inc., Brookings, SD, pg. 312
Steinweg, Bernard, Sr. V.P.-Govt. & Trade Policy--Continental Grain Company, New York, NY, pg. 279
Stern, Patti, Dir., Pub. Rels.--Cronin & Company, Inc., Glastonbury, CT, pg. 300
Sternfels, Daniel, Dir.-Passenger Service--Taca International Airlines, S. A., New Orleans, LA, pg. 1076
Stessel, Francine, Dir.-Communications--Redken Laboratories, Inc., Canoga Park, CA, pg. 919
Stevens, Andrew E., Chm. Bd., Pres., Mktg. & Pub. Rel. Dir.--GWP, Inc., Los Angeles, CA, pg. 441
Stevens, Kathleen, V.P.-Client Services--Professional Healthcare Systems, Inc., Los Angeles, CA, pg. 894
Stevenson, Elizabeth, Pub. Rels. Dir.--Brock Control Systems, Inc., Atlanta, GA, pg. 178
Stewart, Lynda J., Dir.-Communications--Cox Enterprises, Inc., Atlanta, GA, pg. 292
Stiffler, Carolyn S., Pres. & Chief Exec. Officer--Classic Markets Corp., Norcross, GA, pg. 253
Stiles, Mitchell P., V.P. Pub. Rels. Dir.--W.S. Badcock Corporation, Mulberry, FL, pg. 113
Stoael, Chuck, Sports Editor/Writer--The Stogel Companies Inc., New York, NY, pg. 1050
Stowe, Sherry, Consumer Affairs--Tom Thumb Food & Drugs, Inc., Dallas, TX, pg. 912
Stoy, Jay, Dir.-Adv. & Communications--Furnas Electric Company, Batavia, IL, pg. 437
Strandberg, Debra, Communications Asst.--Vecta, Grand Prairie, TX, pg. 1044
Strickland, James H., Dir.-Pub. Rels.--Drummond Company, Inc., Jasper, AL, pg. 349
Striegel, Dave, Dir.-Mktg. Services--Growmark, Inc., Bloomington, IL, pg. 490
Stronach, Robert, Mgr.-Communications--Eastern Milk Producers Cooperative Assn., Inc., Syracuse, NY, pg. 363
Strubel, Ella, Exec. V.P. & Dir.-Corp. Affairs & Client Pub. Relations--Leo Burnett Company, Inc., Chicago, IL, pg. 191
Sullivan, Daniel J., Mgr.-Customer Service--Dunmore Corporation, Newtown, PA, pg. 353
Swanson, John, Dir.-Adv. & Pub. Rels.--Larken Inc., Cedar Rapids, IA, pg. 659
Swanson, Neal, Mktg. Communications Mgr.--Standard Duplicating Machines Corp., Andover, MA, pg. 1036
Swanston, David, Pres.-Pub. Rels. Div.--Stackig, Sanderson & White, Inc., McLean, VA, pg. 1034
Swartz, Cynthia L., Mgr.-Corp. Communications--Jones Spacelink, Ltd., Englewood, CO, pg. 603
Swaysland, Janet, V.P. & Assoc. Dir.-Pub. Rels.--Mullen Advertising, Inc., Wenham, MA, pg. 775
Sweeney, Mark, V.P.-Sls., Mktg. & Pub. Rels.--Black Fin Yacht Corporation, Fort Lauderdale, FL, pg. 154
Swenson, Mike, Pres., Pub. Rels.--Barkley & Evergreen Advertising, Inc., Shawnee Mission, KS, pg. 120
Sykes, Lisa, Dir.-Pub. Rels.--Homeland Stores, Inc., Oklahoma City, OK, pg. 542
Symington, Mikki, Dir.-Pub. Affairs & Community Rels.--Roni Hicks & Associates, Inc., San Diego, CA, pg. 533
Szwed, Rose, Dir.-Pub. Rels.--Stone & Simons Advertising, Inc., Southfield, MI, pg. 1051
Tabora, Cristina, Dir.-Mktg. Communications--Hyatt International Corporation, Chicago, IL, pg. 495
Takekawa, Neil, V.P.-Customer Service--Aloha Airlines, Inc., Honolulu, HI, pg. 43
Takekawa, Neil M., V.P.-Customer Service--Aloha Airgroup, Inc., Honolulu, HI, pg. 43
Tallant, Richard L., V.P.-Customer Service N. & S.--Tennessee Valley Authority, Knoxville, TN, pg. 1088
Tarney, Julie, Sr. V.P., Pub. Rels.--Frankenberry, Laughlin & Constable, Inc., Milwaukee, WI, pg. 429
Tattar, Scott D., V.P., Dir. Pub. Rels.--Dudnyk Advertising, Horsham, PA, pg. 351
Taylor-Willis, Cindy, Assoc. Mgr.-Public Rels.--Dewberry & Davis, Fairfax, VA, pg. 334
Taylor, Jerry, V.P. & Dir.-Adv. & Publicity--Jordache Enterprises, Inc., New York, NY, pg. 604
Taylor, Peggy, Media & Communications Coord.--Thompson Advertising Productions, Inc., Farmington Hills, MI, pg. 1094
Taylor, R., Pub. Rels. Mgr.--Howden Sirocco inc., Hyde Park, MA, pg. 547
Tecco, Betsy Dru, Dir.-Pub. Rels.--Boyd, Tamney & Cross Advertising/Marketing, Wayne, PA, pg. 169
Templeton, Harry R., Mgr.-Mktg. Communications & Publications--Battelle Memorial Institute, Columbus, OH, pg. 126
Tenenbaum, Bob, Dir.-Pub. Rels.--Hameroff/Milenthal/Spence, Inc., Columbus, OH, pg. 503
Testino, Tony, Telecommunications--The William Cook Agency, Inc., Jacksonville, FL, pg. 282
Thielen, Lenore J., Mgr.-Mktg. & Pub. Rels.--Dillingham Construction Corporation, Pleasanton, CA, pg. 337
Thiem, Carl W., V.P.-Customer Service--Schneider National, Inc., Green Bay, WI, pg. 977
Thies-Pate, Cherie, V.P., Telemarketing Services--Ruppman National Yellow Pages Service (RNYPS), Peoria, IL, pg. 956
Thomas, Gary W., Dir.-Mktg. & Community Rels.--Fallon Community Health Plan, West Boylston, MA, pg. 398
Thomas, Gretlyn Z., Mgr.-Public Rels.--Great American Communications Company, Cincinnati, OH, pg. 53
Thomas, Gretlyn Z., Mgr.-Pub. Rels.--Great American Broadcasting Company, Cincinnati, OH, pg. 52
Thomas, Melissa, Mgr.-Communications--Arkansas Industrial Development Commission, Little Rock, AR, pg. 83
Thompson, Vince, V.P., Pub. Rels. Group--Barry Huey, Bullock & Cook Advertising, Inc., Birmingham, AL, pg. 551
Tindall, Don R., Asst. Dir.-Communications, Sr. Editor & Publr.-Cooperative Pub.--Southern States Cooperative, Inc., Richmond, VA, pg. 1022
Tinnen, J. David, V.P., Dir. Pub. Rels.--NKH&W, Inc., Kansas City, MO, pg. 781
Todd, Doris, Communications. Mgr.--Vecta, Grand Prairie, TX, pg. 1044
Toliver, Harold, Dir.-Mktg. & Public Rels.--Golden State Mutual Life Insurance Company, Los Angeles, CA, pg. 467
Toombs, Emmett, V.P.-Admin.--Hardaway Construction Company, Inc., Nashville, TN, pg. 508
Toothman, Bob, Dir.-Communications--National Steel Corporation, Mishawaka, IN, pg. 793
Torello, Judy, Sr. V.P., Dir. Corp. Communications--Backer Spielvogel Bates Worldwide, Inc., New York, NY, pg. 108
Torello, Judy, Sr. V.P., Dir. Corp. Communications--Backer Spielvogel Bates, Inc., New York, NY, pg. 108
Toro, Ralph, Dir.-Pub. Rels.--Goya Foods, Inc., Secaucus, NJ, pg. 474
Torralva, Maria Elena, Dir.-Community Rels.--San Antonio Light, San Antonio, TX, pg. 524
Townsend, David L., V.P.-Pub. Rels.--Walter Industries, Inc., Tampa, FL, pg. 1161
Trabue, Lucinda T., V.P.-Pub. Affairs--Buntin Advertising, Inc., Nashville, TN, pg. 188
Trager, Doreen, Dir. of Communications--Congoleum Corporation, Mercerville, NJ, pg. 274
Trebour, Burton, V.P.-Labor & Admin.--A-P-A Transport Corp., North Bergen, NJ, pg. 5
Trelut, Lynda, V.P.-Adv. & Pub. Rels.--Nob Hill General Store, Inc., Gilroy, CA, pg. 807
Tremayne, William H., Sr. V.P.-Pub. Affairs--The Prudential Insurance Company of America, Newark, NJ, pg. 896
Trepal, Gil, Dir.-Adv. & Pub. Rel.--American Laundry Machinery Inc., Cincinnati, OH, pg. 57
Trevis, James, V.P., Agri-Business Pub. Rel. Mgr.--Colle & McVoy Public Relations, Minneapolis, MN, pg. 261
Tringale, Steven, V.P.-Pub. Affairs--Blue Cross and Blue Shield of Massachusetts, Boston, MA, pg. 159
Tripp, Steve, Mgr.-Media Relations--Best Western International, Inc., Phoenix, AZ, pg. 146
Tromba, Ray, Dir.-Pub. Rels. & Mktg.--Louisiana Downs, Bossier City, LA, pg. 323
Troups, Charlotte B., Treas. & Dir.-Mdsg. & Adv.--Bollinger Machine Shop And Shipyard, Inc., Lockport, LA, pg. 163
Trumble, David, V.P., Pub. Rels.--Taylor Advertising, Inc., Tucson, AZ, pg. 1080
Tucker, Thomas J., V.P.-Corp. Services--American Bureau of Shipping, New York, NY, pg. 50
Upshaw, Kim, Dir.-Mktg., Sls., Adv. & Pub. Rels.--Empire Airlines, Hayden Lake, ID, pg. 379
Vachon, Brian, V.P.-Communications--National Life Insurance Company, Montpelier, VT, pg. 791
Vahejos, Ricardo, Dir., Intl. Communications--Lee & Riley, Inc., Minneapolis, MN, pg. 666
Vaillancourt, Donald C., V.P.-Communications--The Grand Union Company, Wayne, NJ, pg. 476
Valencia, Fernando, V.P., Client Services--BSB/Meza, Ltda., Bogota,, Colombia, pg. 110
Valentine, D.J., Div. Mgr.-External Affairs--Nebraska Public Power District, Columbus, NE, pg. 796
Van Andel, Nan, V.P.-Catalog & Communications--Amway Corporation, Ada, MI, pg. 70
Vance, David, Dir.-Corp. Mktg. & Communications--Austin Industries, Inc., Dallas, TX, pg. 99
VanHandof, Donna, Dir.-Customer Service--Grandpa Brands Company, Cincinnati, OH, pg. 476
VanNandorf, Donna, Customer Service--A. J. Lehman Co., Cincinnati, OH, pg. 476
VanSickle, Sharon, Treas. & Dir. Pub. Rels.--Karakas, VanSickle Ouellette Advertising & Public Relations, Portland, OR, pg. 616
VanTassel, Daniel R., Dir.-Corp. Communications--CF Industries, Inc., Long Grove, IL, pg. 200
Vastyan, John, Dir., Pub. Rels.--Godfrey Advertising, Lancaster, PA, pg. 464
Vaughn, Roy, Pres.-Buntin Pub. Rels. Co.--Buntin Advertising, Inc., Nashville, TN, pg. 188
Veal, Charlotte, Dir.-Pub. Rels.--Hearst Magazines Division, New York, NY, pg. 523
Velverde, Beryl, Pub. Rels. Acct. Supvr.--Arnold Fortuna Lawner & Cabot, Portland, ME, pg. 84
Venturelli, Margherita, Pub. Rels. Dir., New Bus. Contact & External Rels. Dir.--BSB Italia, Milan,, Italy, pg. 110
Vernet, Serge, Exec. V.P.-Investor Rels.--Vernay Laboratories, Inc., Yellow Springs, OH, pg. 1148
Vetromile, Robert W., Pres., Pub. Rels. & Creative Dir.--Stauch Vetromile & Mitchell Advertising, Inc., East Providence, RI, pg. 1042
Vetter, Richard, V.P., Media Svcs./Pub. Rels.--The Food Group, New York, NY, pg. 423
Vincent, Robert K., Sr. V.P., Pub. Rels.--Rivers Trainor Doyle & Walsh, Inc., Providence, RI, pg. 937
Vinueza, Claudia, Pub. Rels.--CSA, Inc., Glastonbury, CT, pg. 204
Virgets, Thomas L., V.P.-Customer Rels.--Anco Insulations, Inc., Baton Rouge, LA, pg. 72
Von Ruden, Martin, V.P.-Press Rels./Nickelodeon & Nick at Nite--MTV Networks, New York, NY, pg. 785
Voorhees, Bret, Communications Coord.--Iowa Lottery, Des Moines, IA, pg. 582
Vooss, M.L., Dir.-Adv. & Corp. Rels.--Lykes Bros. Steamship Co., Inc., New Orleans, LA, pg. 688
Vorce, Betsy, Sr. V.P.-Pub. Rels.--Viacom Entertainment, New York, NY, pg. 785
Vorce, Betsy, V.P.-Pub. Rels.--Viacom Broadcasting Inc., New York, NY, pg. 785
Wahlstrom, Fred, Pub. Rels. Specialist--J.D. Edwards & Company, Denver, CO, pg. 370
Waite, Karen, Mgr.-Pub. Rels.--Eastern Technologies Ltd, Amesbury, MA, pg. 364
Wakefield, Jeffrey, Dir.-Pub. Rels.--Kelliher/Samets Marketing Communications, Burlington, VT, pg. 621
Walcher, Laura, Pres., Pub. Rels. Div.--Capener, Matthews & Walcher, San Diego, CA, pg. 214
Walcott, Eustis, V.P.-Corp. Communications & Grants Contact--Massachusetts Mutual Life Insurance Co., Springfield, MA, pg. 718
Walker, Allen, V.P.-Customer Services--Dac Easy, Inc., Dallas, TX, pg. 571
Wall, Steve F., Mgr.-Pub. Rels.--Broadcast Electronics, Inc., Quincy, IL, pg. 177
Wallace, James M., Mgr.-Corp. Communications--Cargill Inc., Wayzata, MN, pg. 219
Wallace, Susan, Pub. Rels. Acct. Mgr.--Decker Rickard, Glastonbury, CT, pg. 324
Walsh, Thomas E., Sr. V.P., Pub. Rels. Services--Rivers Trainor Doyle & Walsh, Inc., Providence, RI, pg. 937
Walsh, Walter J., V.P.-Corp. Rels.--The Principal Financial Group, Des Moines, IA, pg. 890
Walters, Alice, V.P., Dir. Pub. Rels.--Gunder & Associates, Inc., Dublin, OH, pg. 494
Ward, Arthur B., Mgr.-Corp. Communications--The Nash Engineering Company, Norwalk, CT, pg. 783
Warner, Carin, Exec. V.P.-Pub. Rels.--Mullen Advertising, Inc., Wenham, MA, pg. 775
Water, Linda, V.P. & Sr. Pub. Rels. Consultant--Sefton Associates Inc., Grand Rapids, MI, pg. 987
Watkins, Marilyn, Dir.-Adv. & Pub. Rels.--Blue Anchor, Inc., Sacramento, CA, pg. 158
Watson, Donna, Dir.-Promo. & Special Services--New York City Off Track Betting Corp., New York, NY, pg. 802
Wax, Mel, Dir.-Pub. Affairs--Port of Oakland, Oakland, CA, pg. 881
Weaver, Lauren, Mgr.-Sls. Promo. & Pub. Rels.--Security Mutual Life Insurance Co. of New York, Binghamton, NY, pg. 987
Webster, Doug, Dir.-Communications--Keiler & Company, Farmington, CT, pg. 620
Webster, Guy N., Mgr.-Corp. Communication--Auto Glass Specialists, Madison, WI, pg. 100
Weidman, James III, V.P.-Corp. Communications--National Grape Co-Op Association, Inc., Westfield, NY, pg. 789
Weidman, James III, V.P.-Corp. Communications--Welch's, Concord, MA, pg. 789
Weinberg, Kay, Customer Service Mgr.--Perfection Hy-Test Company, Florence, SC, pg. 711
Weisberg, R., Dir.-Pub. Rels.--Technic Incorporated, Cranston, RI, pg. 1083
Weisert, Marvin, Sr. V.P.-Member Services--Growmark, Inc., Bloomington, IL, pg. 490
Weiss, Sally, Sr. V.P., Pub. Rels. Dir.--R.G. Meadows, Inc., Great Neck, NY, pg. 733
Weitzel, Jim, V.P., Media, Market Research & Pub. Rels--Keller-Crescent Co., Evansville, IN, pg. 621
Welch, Marion, Mgr.-Admin.--Walpole Woodworkers, Inc., Walpole, MA, pg. 1161
Wells, Susan, Pub. Rels. Dir.--Roberts Communications Inc., East Rochester, NY, pg. 938
Wemhoff, Anne, Mgr.-Pub. Rels.--Trone Advertising, Inc., Greensboro, NC, pg. 1115
Westbrook, Mary Nell, Dir.-Pub. Rels.--McCommunications Inc., Dallas, TX, pg. 727
Westerbeck, David F., V.P., Sec. & Gen. Counsel--The Union Central Life Insurance Co., Cincinnati, OH, pg. 1127
Westerfield, Terry, Mgr.-Pub. Rels.--Delta Queen Steamboat Company, New Orleans, LA, pg. 385
Whaley, Christine, Mgr.-Pub. Rels. Promo.--Perdue Farms Inc., Salisbury, MD, pg. 860
Whalley, William, Communications Consultant--Lexmark International, Inc., Greenwich, CT, pg. 673
Whitaker, Carole, Dir.-Pub. Rels.--Hayes/Harwood, Stowe, VT, pg. 519
White, W. Ward, V.P.-Communications--Northwestern Mutual Life Insurance Co., Milwaukee, WI, pg. 815
Whitehair, B.Q., Mgr.-Adv. & Mktg. Communications--Lord Corporation, Erie, PA, pg. 683
Whitesell, Phil, Dir., Pub. Rels.--Wray-Ward-Laseter Advertising, Charlotte, NC, pg. 1204
Whittington, Connie, Sr. V.P., Corp. Communications--Earle Palmer Brown, Bethesda, MD, pg. 182
Wible, David, V.P.-Mktg. & Pub. Rels.--Red Roof Inns, Inc., Hilliard, OH, pg. 918

Wilder, Walter R., V.P.-Public & Govt. Rels.--Mississippi Valley Gas Co., Jackson, MS, pg. 1208
Wildermuth, Tom, Sr. Mgr.-Adv. & Promo.--J. J. Keller & Associates, Inc., Neenah, WI, pg. 620
Wilkie, Jack, V.P.-Corp. Communications--The Franklin Mint, Franklin Center, PA, pg. 60
Williams, Betty, Mgr.-Public Rels.--Metrologic Instruments, Inc., Blackwood, NJ, pg. 743
Williams, Dawn M., Dir.-Admin. & Sec.--Erving Paper Mills, Erving, MA, pg. 388
Williams, Janice, V.P., Pub. Rels.--Dally Advertising, Inc., Fort Worth, TX, pg. 312
Williams, R. James, Dir.-Publicity--Keeneland Assoc., Inc., Lexington, KY, pg. 620
Williams, Richard, Mgr.-Consumer Communications--FTD/ Florists' Transworld Delivery Association, Southfield, MI, pg. 395
Willinsky, Dan, Mgr., Pub. Rels.--Bernstein-Rein Advertising, Inc., Kansas City, MO, pg. 144
Willis, Barbara, Dir.-Communications Program--Metropolitan Life Insurance Co., New York, NY, pg. 744
Willmann, Michael, Exec. V.P., Pub. Rels., Mktg. & Res. Dir., New Bus. Contact--Rosanio, Bailets & Talamo, Inc., Cherry Hill, NJ, pg. 947
Willmot, Robert, Dir.-Corp. Communications--Carus Chemical Company, Chemical Div., Ottawa, IL, pg. 227
Willmot, Robert J., Dir.-Corp. Communications--Carus Corporation, Peru, IL, pg. 227
Wilmot, Paul, Mgr.-Pub Rels.--Calvin Klein, Inc., New York, NY, pg. 635
Wilson, Allan, V.P.-Sls. & Cust. Service--Western Data Systems, Calabasas, CA, pg. 1178
Wilson, Holly, Adv. Mgr.--Michael Business Machines Corporation, North Charleston, SC, pg. 747
Wilson, Victoria, Dir.-Pub. Rels. & Personnel--American SelfCare Corporation, Columbus, GA, pg. 60
Wineland, Betty, V.P.-Communications--First Pyramid Life Insurance Company of America, Little Rock, AR, pg. 1150
Winograd, Polly R., Dir.-Communications--Jacques Jugeat, Inc., New York, NY, pg. 608
Winters, Gene, Mgr.-Adv. Promo.--Hauck Mfg. Co., Cleona, PA, pg. 517
Witzel, Terry, V.P.-Corp. Relations--Tri Valley Growers Inc., San Francisco, CA, pg. 1111
Woodrum, Robert, V.P.-Pub. Rels. & Dir.-Media--Korn/Ferry International, Los Angeles, CA, pg. 642
Woods, Richard, Sr. V.P. & Dir.-Pub. Rels.--Mastercard International, Inc., New York, NY, pg. 720
Woodward, Craig, Dir.-Pub. Rels.--Gillis Advertising & Public Relations, Birmingham, AL, pg. 459
Wooldridge, Natalie, Mgr.-Pub. Rels.--Carpeteria, Inc., Valencia, CA, pg. 224
Woolman, Ann, Dir.-Pub. Rels.--CRE, Inc., Indianapolis, IN, pg. 203
Woolman, Patti, Dir.-Promo.--Standard Corporation, Ogden, UT, pg. 1036
Workman, Ron, Mgr.-Mktg. Communications--Ready Systems, Sunnyvale, CA, pg. 916
Worthy, Bonnie, Pub. Rels. Acct. Supvr.--The Morrison Agency, Atlanta, GA, pg. 771
Wren, William, V.P.-Corp. Rels.--Northwest Airlines, Inc., Saint Paul, MN, pg. 782
Wright, Donald G., Dir.-Pub. Information--Nebraska Dept. of Economic Development, Lincoln, NE, pg. 796
Wyatt, Mary C., Sr. V.P., Pub. Rels.--Chaffee Case & Partners, Providence, RI, pg. 237
Yanchek, David, Customer Service Mgr.--American Wyott Corporation, Cheyenne, WY, pg. 65
Yarborough, Lesley, Mgr.-Communications--C B R Cement Corporation, San Mateo, CA, pg. 199
Yingling, Edward L., Exec. Dir.-Govt. Rels.--The American Bankers Association, Washington, DC, pg. 49
York, Anne, Dir.-Pub. Rels.--Combe Incorporated, White Plains, NY, pg. 267
York, Marie Denise DeBartolo, Exec. V.P.-Corp. Mktg. & Communications--The Edward J. DeBartolo Corporation, Youngstown, OH, pg. 323
Yost, Dick, V.P.-Customer Service--Georgie Boy Manufacturing, Inc., Edwardsburg, MI, pg. 453
Young, Patricia, V.P.-Pub. Rels.--Delta Queen Steamboat Company, New Orleans, LA, pg. 385
Yudys, Kathy, V.P.-Customer Service--Colfax Envelope Corporation, Buffalo Grove, IL, pg. 261
Yurkewitz, K.J., Public Rels. Coord.--Comlinear Corporation, Fort Collins, CO, pg. 268
Zagorac, Michael, V.P.-Pub. Affairs--Jack Eckerd Corporation, Largo, FL, pg. 366
Zalkin, Isadore, Sr. V.P.-Labor Rels.--Pathmark, Woodbridge, NJ, pg. 1064
Zeiss, Timothy P., Mgr.-Pub. Rels.--New Jersey Press, Inc., Neptune, NJ, pg. 801
Zerbe, Jim, Dir.-Mktg. Communications & Adv. Mgr.--Automotive Rentals, Inc., Mount Laurel, NJ, pg. 101
Zerza, Fred, Dir.-Pub. Rels. & Adv.--J.R. Simplot Company, Boise, ID, pg. 1007
Zielinski, Bella P., Dir.-Mktg. Communications--The Inland Group, Inc., Oak Brook, IL, pg. 570
Ziff, Mary, Dir.-Customer Service--W. Braun Co., Westlake, OH, pg. 172
Zinn, Chester A., Jr., V.P., Sec. & Gen. Counsel--MSI Insurance Companies, Arden Hills, MN, pg. 693
Zinngrabe, Mary, Mgr.-Communications--Apple Vacations West Inc., Elk Grove Village, IL, pg. 79
Zins, Al, Pub. Rels.--Advertising, Boelter & Lincoln, Madison, WI, pg. 21
Zlotnik, Arnold, Pres.--Surco Products, Inc., Braddock, PA, pg. 1065
Zweck, Brad, Mgr.-Pub. Rels.--Employers Insurance of Wausau a Mutual Co., Wausau, WI, pg. 380
Zweck, Brad, Mgr.-Pub. Rels.--Employers Insurance of Wausau a Mutual Co., Wausau, WI, pg. 795
Zwick, Lisa, Dir.-Pub. Rels.--TH&M Advertising, Inc., Irvine, CA, pg. 1073

PURCHASING

Aaron, Marvin, Pur. Agent--Creative Productions, Pittsburgh, PA, pg. 297
Abercrombie, Steve, Dir.-Pur.--T & S Brass & Bronze Works, Inc., Travelers Rest, SC, pg. 1074
Abram, Alfred, Dir.-Pur.--Lamb Engineering & Construction Co., Salt Lake City, UT, pg. 652
Abramowitz, Sandy, Pur. Dir.--Best Kosher Sausage Co., Chicago, IL, pg. 146
Ackerman, Roger, Pur. Dir.--Menasha Corporation, Neenah, WI, pg. 738
Adam, Michael, Pur. Agent--General American Door Company, Montgomery, IL, pg. 739
Adams, Frank, Mgr.-Corp. Pur.--SK Hand Tool Corp., Chicago, IL, pg. 963
Adams, Franklin J., Dir.-Pur.--SK Hand Tool Corp., Chicago, IL, pg. 963
Adams, Karen, Mgr.-Plant & Pur.--Grindmaster Corporation, Louisville, KY, pg. 488
Adams, Lafayette, Pur. Agent--Premier Metal Products Company, Bronx, NY, pg. 836
Adams, Tony, Dir.-Pur.--C. A. Muer Corp., Detroit, MI, pg. 774
Addessi, Michael, Dir.-Pur.--Ellwood City Forge, Ellwood City, PA, pg. 378
Adkins, David, Dir.-Pur.--Doehler-Jarvis, Toledo, OH, pg. 559
Adkins, Maureen, Pur. Agent--Applied Solar Energy Corporation, City of Industry, CA, pg. 79
Adler, Fred, Dir.-Pur.--Thrifty Oil Company, Downey, CA, pg. 1096
Agnew, Charles D., V.P.-Pur. & Sec.--National Savings Life Insurance Company, Murfreesboro, TN, pg. 1150
Aiken, Paul, Pur. Agent--McDowell Mfg. Co., Du Bois, PA, pg. 32
Aitken, Susan, Pur. Agent--International Designer Accessories, Inc., Secaucus, NJ, pg. 578
Albertonni, Jim, V.P.-Pur.--Kendale Industries, Inc., Valley View, OH, pg. 622
Albright, Gary, Pur. Agent--Sunnyland Foods, Inc., Thomasville, GA, pg. 1061
Alexander, Ed, Dir.-Pur.--U.S. Construction Co., Inc., Columbia, SC, pg. 1135
Alfaro, Gilbert, Pur. Agent--San Antonio Light, San Antonio, TX, pg. 524
Alisauskas, Chas. E., Pur. Agent--Macwhyte Co., Kenosha, WI, pg. 69
Alleback, Donald, Pur. Agent--American Envelope of Philadelphia, Philadelphia, PA, pg. 199
Allen, Bob, Dir.-Pur.--Team Bank, Fort Worth, TX, pg. 1082
Allen, Douglas, Pur. Agent--J.W. Allen & Company, Wheeling, IL, pg. 36
Allen, Mary, V.P.-Pur.--Positronic Industries, Inc., Springfield, MO, pg. 881
Allison, Monti, Mgr.-Pur.--Glen Raven Mills, Inc., Glen Raven, NC, pg. 461
Allison, Paul, Mgr.-Bus. Services--San Antonio Light, San Antonio, TX, pg. 524
Alsup, Gary, Mgr.-Pur.--Blue Anchor, Inc., Sacramento, CA, pg. 158
Alterman, Joe, Dir.-Pur.--Alterman Transport Lines, Inc., Opa Locka, FL, pg. 45
Aluise, David A., V.P.-Logistics--Pease Industries, Inc., Fairfield, OH, pg. 854
Amburger, Joyce, Mgr.-Pur.--CSE Corporation, San Francisco, CA, pg. 204
Ammons, D.L., Mgr.-Pur.--Lyon Metal Products, Inc., Montgomery, IL, pg. 690
Anderson, Eloise, Pur. Agent--Smith Enterprises, Rock Hill, SC, pg. 1012
Anderson, Gary, Dir.-Pur.--Arrow Tank & Engineering Co., Minneapolis, MN, pg. 85
Anderson, K. Barr, Mgr.-Purch.--Daw Technologies, Inc., Salt Lake City, UT, pg. 319
Anderson, Mark, Pur. Agent--Reading Body Works, Inc., Reading, PA, pg. 916
Anderson, Michael J., V.P.-Opers. & Pur.--Andys Rental Inc., La Mirada, CA, pg. 1206
Anderson, Robert, V.P.-Pur. Opers.--C.J. Vitner & Co., Inc., Chicago, IL, pg. 1153
Anderson, Robert C., V.P. & Pur. Agent--Transco Inc., Chicago, IL, pg. 1106
Anderson, William, Mgr.-Pur.--Tech Industries, Inc., Woonsocket, RI, pg. 1083
Andrade, Art, Pur. Agent--Calcor Space Facility, Inc., Whittier, CA, pg. 208
Andrasko, Nancy M., V.P.-Sls. & Pur.--Star-Parts Inc., Hazleton, PA, pg. 1039
Andrus, Newton, Dir.-Pur. & Property Services--WordPerfect Corporation, Orem, UT, pg. 1202
Anglin, Carol, Dir.-Pur.--Group Insurance Inc., Baton Rouge, LA, pg. 490
Angus, Alyn, Pur. Agent--Dakota Electric Association, Farmington, MN, pg. 312
Ankerson, Perry, Pres.-Point of Pur. Div.--Everbrite, Inc., Greenfield, WI, pg. 391
Antonucci, Gus, Dir.-Pur.--Quaker Fabric Corporation, Fall River, MA, pg. 903
Argus, Jean, Mgr.-Pur.--Young & Franklin, Inc., Liverpool, NY, pg. 1209
Arlt, Tom, Dir.-Pur.--Gulf States Asphalt Company, Inc., South Houston, TX, pg. 493
Armlay, Anthony, Pur. Agent--Triplett Electrical Instrument Corporation, Bluffton, OH, pg. 1114
Armstrong, Murray, Import Buyer--Ace Hardware Corporation, Oak Brook, IL, pg. 12
Aronson, David, Exec. V.P.-Sls. & Pur.--Lumco Industries, Inc., Philadelphia, PA, pg. 687
Ash, Robert, Div. Mgr.-Procurement--Metra, Commuter Rail Service Board, Chicago, IL, pg. 922
Ashkar, Caren, Pur. Agent--D. J. Mead-Hubbs & Howe, Buffalo, NY, pg. 1016
Asplundh, Carl, Jr., Exec. V.P.-Equip.--Asplundh Tree Expert Co., Willow Grove, PA, pg. 88
Atkin, David, Pur. Agent--H. B. Smith Co., Inc., Westfield, MA, pg. 1013
Attaway, Steve, Dir.-Pur.--J.D. Edwards & Company, Denver, CO, pg. 370
Aubuchon, Peter J., Sr., V.P.-Pur.--W.E. Aubuchon Co., Inc., Westminster, MA, pg. 97
Augustyne, Joe, Dir.-Pur.--Martin Universal Design, Inc., Westland, MI, pg. 715
Austi, Stella, V.P.-Pur.--Mateco Electronics Corp., Brooklyn, NY, pg. 720
Austin, Jack, Gen. Mgr.--Surco Products, Inc., Braddock, PA, pg. 1065
Austin, Jay, Mgr.-Pur. & Video--Artec Distributing, Inc., Shelburne, VT, pg. 86
Avans, Rebecca, Dir.-Pur.--Peebles, Inc., South Hill, VA, pg. 855
Avant, DeWitt, Pur. Agent--Burgess Pigment Co., Sandersville, GA, pg. 190
Ayers, James, Dir.-Pur.--Spencer's Inc., Mount Airy, NC, pg. 1030
Bachrach, Ted, Dir.-Prod. & Pur.-Raw Materials--Old Quaker Paint Co., Santa Ana, CA, pg. 823
Baez, Lyle, Mgr.-Pur.--Credit Union National Association, Madison, WI, pg. 298
Baez, Lyle, Pur. Mgr.--CUNA Service Group, Inc., Madison, WI, pg. 298
Bagwell, Charles F., V.P. & Dir.-Mfg. & Pur.--The Kent Manufacturing Co., Pickens, SC, pg. 623
Bailey, Joel, Dir.-Pur.--Worsley Companies Inc., Wilmington, NC, pg. 1204
Bailly, R. Jeffrey, Dir.-Pur.--United Foam Plastics Corporation, Georgetown, MA, pg. 1132
Bairos, Jose S., Pur. Mgr.--Arthur D. Little, Inc., Cambridge, MA, pg. 678
Bake, Trent, Dir.-Pur.--Wilson Products Co., Salt Lake City, UT, pg. 1194
Baker, Allan, Dir.-Pur.--Hyde Manufacturing Co., Southbridge, MA, pg. 556
Baker, Jim, Dir.-Pur.--UniHealth America, Burbank, CA, pg. 1126
Baker, Noel W., V.P.-Pur. Opers.--Interstate Electric Supply Company, Inc., Chantilly, VA, pg. 580
Balh, Jackie, Pur. Mgr.--Instrumentarium Imaging, Inc., Milwaukee, WI, pg. 572
Balis, Eugene, Pur. Agent--Processed Plastic Company, Montgomery, IL, pg. 892
Bangs, Michael, Dir.-Pur.--Great Lakes Lithograph Co., Cleveland, OH, pg. 481
Banko, Cyril, V.P.-Pur.--Bachman Company, Reading, PA, pg. 108
Barber, Herbert F., Dir.-Pur.--McAnally Enterprises, Inc., Yucaipa, CA, pg. 726
Barclay, James, Dir.-Adv.--Standard Corporation, Ogden, UT, pg. 1036
Barekman, Cheryl, Dir.-Pur.--Bass Enterprises Production Company, Fort Worth, TX, pg. 125
Barg, Joni, Mgr.-Pur.--MSI Insurance Companies, Arden Hills, MN, pg. 693
Barker, Harold, V.P.-Pur.--Star Bronze Company, Alliance, OH, pg. 1039
Barker, Larry, Dir.-Pur.--Sigman Meat Co. Inc., Arvada, CO, pg. 1003
Barnes, Barbara, Mgr.-Materials--Despatch Industries, Minneapolis, MN, pg. 332
Barnett, Joseph C., Dir.-Pur.--Henkels & McCoy, Inc., Blue Bell, PA, pg. 529
Barnett, Keith, Dir.-Purch.--Alamo Industrial Group, San Antonio, TX, pg. 29
Barney, Michael, Dir.-Pur.--Peoples Gas System, Inc., Tampa, FL, pg. 689
Barr, Robert, Mgr.-Pur.--Dacor Corporation, Northfield, IL, pg. 310
Barrasso, James, V.P.-Pur.--Perkins Family Restaurants, Memphis, TN, pg. 1088
Barrell, Tom, Pur. Agent--Air Gage Company, Livonia, MI, pg. 27
Barresi, C., Dir.-Pur.--Monarch Luggage Co. Inc., Brooklyn, NY, pg. 765
Bartelt, Robert, Pur. Agent--Dearborn Gage Company, Garden City, MI, pg. 322
Bartholemew, Gary, Mgr.-Pur.--L. R. Nelson Corporation, Peoria, IL, pg. 797
Bartholemew, Kevin, Mgr.-Pur.--Rundel Products, Inc., Portland, OR, pg. 956
Bartolozzi, R., Dir.-Pur.--American Felt & Filter, Newburgh, NY, pg. 52
Bason, Murray, Dir.-Pur.--Levlad, Inc., Chatsworth, CA, pg. 671
Batha, Dianna, Pur. Agent--Centrifugal & Mechanical Industries, Saint Louis, MO, pg. 609
Bathke, John, Pur. Agent--Smith System Manufacturing Company, Shoreview, MN, pg. 1014
Bathke, Jon, Mgr.-Pur.--Harmony Engineering Corporation, Minneapolis, MN, pg. 510
Batliner, Doug, Dir.-Production & Pur.--Beach Mold & Tool Inc., New Albany, IN, pg. 128
Battoe, E., Pur. Mgr.--Brooks Foods, Mt. Summit, IN, pg. 26
Bauer, Jerry, Mgr.-Pur.--Harris Steel Co., Chicago, IL, pg. 512
Bauer, John, Dir.-Pur.--Graymills Corp., Chicago, IL, pg. 480
Baum, Eric, Dir.-Pur.--Squire-Cogswell Company, Northbrook, IL, pg. 1034
Baum, Floyd, V.P.--Elyria Foundry Company, Elyria, OH, pg. 378
Beaird, Mike, Dir.-Pur.--Dr Pepper/Seven-Up Companies, Inc., Dallas, TX, pg. 342
Bean, Norman, Pur. Agent--Estes Industries, Inc., Penrose, CO, pg. 1011
Bearak, Sid, Dir.-Pur.--Admiral Maintenance Service L.P., Lincolnwood, IL, pg. 18
Beasley, Charles, V.P.-Pur.--Top Flight, Inc., Chattanooga, TN, pg. 1101

Beatty, Lois, Dir.-Pub.--Ward Leonard Electric Company, Inc., Mount Vernon, NY, pg. 1127
Beauchamp, Mel, Mgr.-Pur.--Unigroup, Inc., Fenton, MO, pg. 1126
Beaumier, Deborah, Dir.-Pur.--Sipex Corporation, Billerica, MA, pg. 1009
Beck, Bob, Dir.-Mdsg. & Mktg.--Farm Fresh, Inc., Norfolk, VA, pg. 401
Beck, Mark, V.P.-Metals--Essex Group, Inc., Fort Wayne, IN, pg. 389
Beck, William C., V.P.-Pur.--Precisionaire, Inc., Saint Petersburg, FL, pg. 886
Becker, A. Carl, V.P.-Pur. & Engrng.--Nuttall Gear Corporation, Niagara Falls, NY, pg. 818
Becker, Janie, Dir.-Pur.--Neill-LaVielle Supply Co., Louisville, KY, pg. 797
Becker, Sharon, Pur. Agent--Eagle Zinc Co., Hillsboro, IL, pg. 335
Becker, William, Pur. Agent--Quill Corp., Lincolnshire, IL, pg. 905
Beckett, Rick, Pur. Agent--Williams Patent Crusher and Pulverizer Co., Saint Louis, MO, pg. 1191
Beckman, Judy, Pur. Agent--Houck Industries, Inc., Tulare, CA, pg. 545
Beckmann, James, Dir.-Pur.--Acrometal Companies, Inc., Brainerd, MN, pg. 14
Bedell, Neil, Dir.-Pur.--Molin Auto Parts Inc., Buffalo, NY, pg. 764
Beigel, David, Mgr.-Pur.--Recon/Optical, Inc., Barrington, IL, pg. 917
Beigel, David, Mgr.-Pur.--CAI, Barrington, IL, pg. 917
Belinge, Wayne, Dir.-Pur.--First Electric Cooperative, Jacksonville, AR, pg. 412
Bell, C.R., Pur. Agent--Ampco Metal Incorporated, Milwaukee, WI, pg. 67
Bell, Paul, Dir.-Pur.--Radiator Specialty Company, Charlotte, NC, pg. 909
Bell, Randy J., Sr. V.P. & Controller--Levy Security Consultants, Limited, Chicago, IL, pg. 672
Bell, Sharon, Dir.-Pur.--PSI Group of Companies, Memphis, TN, pg. 837
Bellissimo, Kimberly, Dir.-Pur.--Eberle Direct Marketing Group, Inc., Vienna, VA, pg. 365
Bement, Jerry, Pur. Agent--Ederer Inc., Seattle, WA, pg. 368
Bender, Phyllis, Dir.-Pur.--Automation Intelligence, Inc., Maitland, FL, pg. 101
Beneson, Paul A., V.P.-Pur.--Stevens-Lee Company, Minneapolis, MN, pg. 1048
Benjamin, F.L., V.P.-Pur., Opers., Personnel & Data Processing--Morris Kirschman & Company, Inc., New Orleans, LA, pg. 633
Benjamin, Wayne, V.P. & Pur. Agent--The Times-Picayune Publishing Corp., New Orleans, LA, pg. 1098
Benner, John, Pur. Agent--Snokist Growers, Yakima, WA, pg. 1015
Bennett, Morris, V.P.-Mfg.--George Kovacs Lighting, Inc., Glendale, NY, pg. 643
Bennett, Robert, Dir.-Pur.--Pioneer Communications of America, Upper Saddle River, NJ, pg. 871
Bennett, Shirley, Mgr.-Pur. & Traffic--Witt Company, Cincinnati, OH, pg. 1198
Benoit, Louis, Agt.- Purch.--Carver, Inc., Garden City, GA, pg. 227
Benson, Don, V.P.-Pur.--Harris-Kayot, Inc., Fort Wayne, IN, pg. 512
Benson, Paul, Mgr.-Pur.--Orbit Valve Co., Little Rock, AR, pg. 828
Benzing, Lance, Mgr.-Pur.--Game Time, Inc., Fort Payne, AL, pg. 442
Berchem, Allen R., V.P.-Fin. & Pur.--Torke Coffee Company, Inc., Sheboygan, WI, pg. 1102
Berger, Ron, Pur. Agent--Alloway Manufacturing, Fargo, ND, pg. 41
Berkey, Gene, Dir.-Purch.--Red Spot Paint & Varnish Co., Evansville, IN, pg. 918
Berkowitz, Ira, V.P.-Pur.--Melard Manufacturing Corporation, Passaic, NJ, pg. 737
Bermudez, Irma, Dir.-Pur.--American International Container, Inc., Miami, FL, pg. 56
Bernardi, Michael, Sr. Buyer--Charles River Data Systems, Inc., Framingham, MA, pg. 240
Berner, Dave, Mgr.-Pur./Inventory--Case-Swayne Co. Inc., Santa Ana, CA, pg. 228
Berner, Dave, V.P.-Matls.--Ambac International Corp., Columbia, SC, pg. 47
Bernstein, Arthur, V.P.-Pur., Sportswear--Milady Brassiere & Corset Co., Inc., New York, NY, pg. 753
Berowitz, Ira, V.P.-Pur.--Melard Plastics Inc., Passaic, NJ, pg. 737
Berry, Carl, Dir.-Pur.--Recon/Optical, Inc., Barrington, IL, pg. 917
Best, Tim, Mgr.-Pur.--Kraco Enterprises, Inc., Compton, CA, pg. 643
Beth, T.D., Dir.-Pur.--L.N. Curtis & Sons, Oakland, CA, pg. 306
Betts, Bruce, Pur. Agent--Target Stamped Products Corp., Kinsman, OH, pg. 1079
Beyer, Steven C., Pur. Agent--Peter Kiewit Sons Inc., Omaha, NE, pg. 629
Biela, Dan, Mgr.-Pur.--Sweeney & Company Division, San Antonio, TX, pg. 440
Bielski, Eugene, Pur. Agent--Diebel Manufacturing Co., Morton Grove, IL, pg. 336
Bienefeld, George, Pur. Agent--Rolled Steel Products Corporation, Los Angeles, CA, pg. 944
Bigliamo, E., Pur. Agent--Edwards Engineering Corporation, Pompton Plains, NJ, pg. 370
Biolsi, Kathy, Pur. Agent--Piercing Pagoda, Inc., Bethlehem, PA, pg. 870
Biron, W., Mgr.-Matls.--Kenney Manufacturing Company, Warwick, RI, pg. 623
Bisbing, Ed, Dir.-Pur.--Advanced Circuit Technology, Nashua, NH, pg. 20
Bishop, Tom, Buyer--Timesavers Inc., Minneapolis, MN, pg. 1098
Bixler, Bruce, Mgr.-Matls.--Mack Molding Company, Arlington, VT, pg. 697
Bjalobok, Frank A., Jr., Pur. Agent--James Austin Co., Mars, PA, pg. 99
Black, J., Pur. Agent--Digitec, Marion, OH, pg. 1069
Black, J., Pur. Agent--Air-O-Matic Power Steer Co., Marion, OH, pg. 1069
Black, Jeanne, Pur. Agent--Sycon Corporation, Marion, OH, pg. 1069
Black, Vince, Mgr.-Imports--Zephyr Baskets & Balloons, New Providence, NJ, pg. 1217
Blackwell, Robert, Dir.-Pur.--Richco Plastics Company, Chicago, IL, pg. 933
Blagg, Patricia L., Pur. Dir.--Lynden Incorporated, Seattle, WA, pg. 689
Blair, S.E., Mgr.-Pur.--Wheland Foundry Div.--North American Royalties, Inc., Chattanooga, TN, pg. 811
Blair, S.E., Mgr.-Pur.--The Wheland Foundry Div., Chattanooga, TN, pg. 812
Blalock, Bill, Dir.-Pur.--Norwesco Components Div., Gastonia, NC, pg. 816
Blank, Art, V.P.-Pur. & Mfg.--All-Luminum Products, Inc., Philadelphia, PA, pg. 35
Blasucci, J., Pur. Agent--Swivelier Co., Inc., Nanuet, NY, pg. 1068
Blasucci, J., Pur. Agent--Point Electric, Nanuet, NY, pg. 1068
Blessing, E.F., Mgr.-Pur.--PQ Corporation, Valley Forge, PA, pg. 836
Bliss, Wilbur, Dir.-Pur.--Capital City Press, Inc., Montpelier, VT, pg. 214
Bloom, Anita, Mgr.-Pur.--Avatar Corporation, Hopkinton, MA, pg. 101
Blough, John, V.P.-Pur.--Snyder Potato Chips, Berlin, PA, pg. 26
Blulm, F.W., V.P.-Pur.--Stebbins Engineering & Mfg. Co., Watertown, NY, pg. 1043
Blumberg, Chris, V.P.-Pur.--Southern Pump & Tank Co. Inc., Charlotte, NC, pg. 1022
Blutstein, Morton, Exec. V.P. & Pur. Mgr.--Halper Bros., Milwaukee, WI, pg. 925
Bobby, W., Dir.-Pur.--Hardinge Brothers, Inc., Elmira, NY, pg. 508
Bobroski, Lance, Pur. Agent--Turnbull Enterprises, Inc., Baltimore, MD, pg. 1119
Boike, Steve, Buyer--The Flecto Co., Inc., Oakland, CA, pg. 417
Boing, J.D., Sr. V.P.-Pur. & Production--Sporlan Valve Company, Saint Louis, MO, pg. 1032
Boitz, Randall D., Dir.-Pur.--Turtle Wax, Inc., Chicago, IL, pg. 1120
Bolding, Ron, Dir.-Mdsg. & Pur.--United Health Plan, Inglewood, CA, pg. 1133
Bolduc, Kathy, Supvr.-Pur.--Summa Four, Inc., Manchester, NH, pg. 1057
Bolton, George C., Sr. V.P. & Dir.-Pur. & Sls.--The Law Company, Inc., Wichita, KS, pg. 661
Bond, Gene P., V.P.-Matls.--Hehr International Inc., Los Angeles, CA, pg. 525
Bond, Richard, Pur. Agent--Surgical Specialties, Reading, PA, pg. 1065
Boneck, Michael, Pur. Agent--Lasko Metal Products, Inc., West Chester, PA, pg. 660
Bonen, James J., Chief Fin. Officer--Sonicair, Scottsdale, AZ, pg. 1018
Booth, Jim, V.P.-Pur.--Bourns, Inc., Riverside, CA, pg. 168
Boothby, Stan, Pur. Dir.--Standard Duplicating Machines Corp., Andover, MA, pg. 1036
Boratko,E., Dir.-Mfg.--Detex Corporation, New Braunfels, TX, pg. 333
Borchert, James, Mgr.-Pur.--Riceland Foods, Inc., Stuttgart, AR, pg. 931
Borgeson, Ruth, Mgr.-Pur.--D. Waldner Company, Inc., Farmingdale, NY, pg. 1159
Borsaglia, Barry, Dir.-Pur.--Bell-Carter Foods, Inc., Lafayette, CA, pg. 134
Bose, P., Pur. Agent--Economy Folding Box Corp., Chicago, IL, pg. 367
Boston, Donna M., Mgr.-Pur.--Kaye Instruments, Inc., Bedford, MA, pg. 619
Bouche, Ron, Dir.-Pur.--American Foods Group, Inc., Minneapolis, MN, pg. 54
Boulianne, Roslyn, Mgr.-Pur.--Executive Car Leasing Company, Los Angeles, CA, pg. 393
Bourgeois, A.J., Dir.-Pur.--Schenectady Chemicals, Inc., Schenectady, NY, pg. 975
Bourgeois, Rick, Mgr.-Pur.--Performance Contractors Inc., Baton Rouge, LA, pg. 861
Bourke, Jean, Pur. Agent--Arrow Pneumatics Co. Inc., Lake Zurich, IL, pg. 85
Bourque, Larry, Dir.-Pur.--Triumph*Lor, Inc., Houston, TX, pg. 1115
Bowden, William, Dir.-Matl. Mngmt.--Dacor Corporation, Northfield, IL, pg. 310
Bowen, Walter E., Mgr.-Matls.--McInnes Steel Company, Corry, PA, pg. 729
Bower, Wayne, Pur. Dir.--Security Plastics, Inc., Miami Lakes, FL, pg. 987
Bowles, Bob, Mgr.-Pur.--Haws Drinking Faucet Co., Berkeley, CA, pg. 518
Bowser, Lillian, Dir.-Pur.--North Carolina Mutual Life Insurance Co., Durham, NC, pg. 813
Boyd, Jim, Dir.-Pur.--Collins Oldsmobile Inc., Indianapolis, IN, pg. 263
Boyd, John, Pur. Agent--John Bouchard & Sons Company, Nashville, TN, pg. 168
Boyd, Robert, Pur. Agent--Dana Perfumes Corp., New York, NY, pg. 313
Boyer, Kris, Dir.-Pur.--Flori Corp., Phoenix, AZ, pg. 420
Boykin, C. Dave, Pur. Agent--Power & Telephone Supply Company, Memphis, TN, pg. 883
Boyle, Wilma, Dir.-Pur.--Meadville Forging Co., Meadville, PA, pg. 733
Boytano, Fran, Dir.-Pur.--Forest Atwood Paper Company-New York, New York, NY, pg. 1157
Boyum, Jerry, Dir.-Pur.--M&W Gear Company, Gibson City, IL, pg. 690
Brace, Greg, Pur. Agent--Miller-St. Nazianz, Inc., Saint Nazianz, WI, pg. 755
Bracey, Robert, Dir.-Pur.--Modern Drop Forge Co., Blue Island, IL, pg. 762
Braden, James, V.P.-Sls. & Pur. & Chief Estimator--Concrete Construction Company, Columbus, OH, pg. 273
Bradley, William J., Pres. & Chief Exec. Officer--Perry & Derrick Co., Cincinnati, OH, pg. 863
Brady, Kris, Mgr.-Pur.--IPMC, Inc.-Detroit, Detroit, MI, pg. 583
Bramble, Jody, Supvr.-Pur.--PST Vans, Inc., Salt Lake City, UT, pg. 837
Brandt, Bret, Dir.-Pur.--Pacific Envelope Company, Anaheim, CA, pg. 840
Brant, Dennis, Matls. Mgr.--Airtex Products, Fairfield, IL, pg. 1123
Brattin, Gary, Pur. Mgr.--Sunbeam Outdoor Products Co., Neosho, MO, pg. 1059
Bratton, Donald, Dir.-Pur.--Lampert Yards, Inc., Saint Paul, MN, pg. 653
Brehm, Tim, Pur. Agent--A & A Manufacturing Co., New Berlin, WI, pg. 1
Bremmer, John, V.P.-Estimating & Pur.--R. M. Shoemaker Co., West Conshohocken, PA, pg. 1000
Brennan, Bill, Mgr.-Pur. & Maintenance--Fair Lanes Inc., Hunt Valley, MD, pg. 396
Brennan, Brendan, Dir.-Pur.--Pathmark, Woodbridge, NJ, pg. 1064
Brenton, David, Pur. Agent--Autoswage Products, Inc., Shelton, CT, pg. 101
Bressi, Joseph R., Sr. V.P.-Pur. & Mktg.--Camelot Music, Inc., North Canton, OH, pg. 212
Bretall, William W., Dir.-Pur.--Associated Electric Co-op Inc., Springfield, MO, pg. 89
Brewer, Bill, Pur. Agent--Carolina Absorbent Cotton Co., Charlotte, NC, pg. 120
Brewer, Lois, Pur. Mgr.--Finishline Industries Inc. of Georgia, Conyers, GA, pg. 433
Brewster, Bob, Dir.-Pur.--Prime Tanning Co., Inc., Berwick, ME, pg. 889
Bridges, Jackie, Dir.-Pur.--Freeman Decorating Co., Dallas, TX, pg. 431
Briggs, John V., V.P.-Matls.--Bard Mfg. Co., Bryan, OH, pg. 119
Briggs, Kurt, V.P.-Pur.--The Hotsy Corporation, Englewood, CO, pg. 545
Brill, Richard, Dir.-Pur.--The Okonite Company, Ramsey, NJ, pg. 823
Brininger, Dave, V.P.-Pur.--Interstate Distributors Inc., Norcross, GA, pg. 580
Brisendine, Harley, Pur. Agent--Rochester Gauges Inc. Of Texas, Dallas, TX, pg. 444
Britton, Michael, Pur. Agent--La Marche Mfg. Co., Des Plaines, IL, pg. 649
Brockmann, L.H., Asst. Gen. Mgr.--Walter J. Black, Inc., Port Washington, NY, pg. 154
Broman, D. Edward, V.P.-Procurement--Robinson Helicopter Company, Inc., Torrance, CA, pg. 940
Bromley, Ann, Mgr.-Mdse.--The Popcorn Factory, Lake Forest, IL, pg. 426
Bronstein, George, Dir.-Pur.--House of Bianchi, Boston, MA, pg. 546
Brooks, Barry, Mgr.-Pur.--Snyder's of Hanover, Inc., Hanover, PA, pg. 1015
Brooks, Steve B., Dir.-Pur.--Hollingsworth & Vose Co., East Walpole, MA, pg. 539
Brown, Alan, Pur. Agent--Martin F. Weber Company, Philadelphia, PA, pg. 716
Brown, C.W., V.P.-Pur.--Motor Wheel Corporation, Lansing, MI, pg. 773
Brown, Harold, Dir.-Pur.--Hart-Carter Co., Minneapolis, MN, pg. 226
Brown, J., Dir.-Pur.--Texas Steel Co., Inc., Fort Worth, TX, pg. 1090
Brown, James, Dir.-Pur.--Codisco Inc., Sanford, FL, pg. 258
Browne, Avis, Dir.-Pur.--Hydrite Chemical Company, Brookfield, WI, pg. 556
Browne, Robert, Mgr.-Pur. & Properties--The Davey Tree Expert Company, Kent, OH, pg. 317
Browning, Howard, Pur. Agent--King & Prince Seafood Corporation, Brunswick, GA, pg. 631
Brua, Denny, V.P.-Pur.--84 Lumber Co., Eighty Four, PA, pg. 371
Bruce, R., Dir.-Pur. & Gen. Services--Giffels Associates, Inc., Southfield, MI, pg. 457
Bruemmer, Arlon W., V.P.-Pur.--Bartlett Cocke Jr. Construction Co., San Antonio, TX, pg. 258
Brumfield, Donald L., V.P.-Pur. & Engrng.--Treasure Chest Advertising Co., Inc., Glendora, CA, pg. 1108
Brundage, Gary L., Dir.-Pur.--Golden Gem Growers Inc., Umatilla, FL, pg. 466
Brunskrud, Melinda, Pur. Agent--Bemco Inc., Simi Valley, CA, pg. 138
Bryan, Bob, Dir.-Pur.--Rocket Industries, Inc./Excel, The Exercise Company, Pico Rivera, CA, pg. 941
Buch, Dennis, Pur. Agent--The ISI Manufacturing, Inc., Fraser, MI, pg. 560
Buchan, John, Exec. V.P.--Cloverdale Equipment Co., Oak Park, MI, pg. 256
Buchholz, Eugene, Pur. Agent--The Shaler Company, Waupun, WI, pg. 793
Buckler, Stephen, Dir.-Pur.--R.W. Electronics, Andover, MA, pg. 908
Buckley, Dave, Mgr.-Purchasing--St. Johnsbury Trucking Co., Inc., Holliston, MA, pg. 966
Budani, Joseph, Pur. Agent--The Guardian Life Insurance Company of America, New York, NY, pg. 492

Corporate Responsibilities Index

Bullions, Kathy, Mgr.-Pur.--Black Box Corporation, Lawrence, PA, pg. 748
Bumbalo, R., Pur. Agent--Robins Engineers & Constructors, Inc., Englewood, CO, pg. 939
Bumgarner, Glenda, Mgr.-Pur.--Gaston County Dyeing Machine Co., Stanley, NC, pg. 444
Bunn, Michael, Controller--Monroc, Inc., Salt Lake City, UT, pg. 766
Burback, Ed, Pur. Agent--Uppco, Inc., Chicago, IL, pg. 1139
Burch, Jack, Mgr.-Matl.--Milliken & Co., Inc., Spartanburg, SC, pg. 755
Burck, Bruce, Pur. Agent--Mulberry Metal Products, Inc., Union, NJ, pg. 775
Burdette, Arnold E., V.P.-Pur.--Union Boiler Co., Nitro, WV, pg. 273
Burgard, Harold M., V.P.-Pur.--C.R. Daniels, Inc., Ellicott City, MD, pg. 314
Burge, Henry, Dir.-Pur.--Mississippi Valley Gas Co., Jackson, MS, pg. 1208
Burger, Leslie, Dir.-Pur.--Farnam Companies, Inc., Phoenix, AZ, pg. 403
Burgess, Gary, V.P., Treas. & Pur. Agent--Equipment Manufacturing, Inc., Warren, MI, pg. 385
Burgess, Ray, Pur. Dir.--Frank Industries, Inc., Brown City, MI, pg. 429
Burgoyne, Paul, Mgr.-Mdsg. & Adv.--Edward Don & Company of Illinois, North Riverside, IL, pg. 344
Burk, Norman W., Matls. Mgr.--Borg-Warner-Spring/ Brummer Division, Bellwood, IL, pg. 166
Burke, Anne, Dir.-Pur.--F. H. Chase, Inc., Foxboro, MA, pg. 240
Burke, John, Dir.-Pur.--Masters Inc., Gaithersburg, MD, pg. 720
Burke, John M., V.P.-Pur.--Osco Industries Inc., Portsmouth, OH, pg. 830
Burke, Pat, Dir.-Pur.--The Buschman Co., Cincinnati, OH, pg. 196
Burke, Robert K., Mgr.-Pur.--Allied Mineral Products, Inc., Columbus, OH, pg. 38
Burkhart, Verland, Dir.-Pur.--Ed Miniat, Inc., Chicago, IL, pg. 757
Burks, Bob, Mgr.-Purch.--The SArgent-SOwell Company, Grand Prairie, TX, pg. 971
Burks, Roger, Sr. V.P.-Mdsg. & Pur.--The Mad Butcher, Inc., Pine Bluff, AR, pg. 699
Burnes, Angela, Pur. Agent--Oak Rubber Company, Ravenna, OH, pg. 819
Burnham, Bruce, V.P.-Procurement--Service America Corporation, Stamford, CT, pg. 992
Burns, Corinne, Pur. Dir.--Aratex Services, Lawrenceville, GA, pg. 6
Burns, E., Dir.-Pur.--Quality Bakers of America Cooperative, Inc., Greenwich, CT, pg. 903
Burns, Scott, Pur. Agent--Cashco, Inc., Ellsworth, KS, pg. 228
Burr, Nathan, Pur. Agent--Cogsdill Tool Products, Inc., Lugoff, SC, pg. 259
Burris, Bruce M., V.P.-Pur. & Traffic--Burris Chemical Inc., Charleston, SC, pg. 195
Burton, Bob, Dir.-Pur.--Andersen Consulting, Chicago, IL, pg. 72
Burzynski, James, Pur. Agent--James Steel & Tube Company, Madison Heights, MI, pg. 102
Buscemi, Ethel, Dir.-Purch.--The Harodite Finishing Company Inc., North Dighton, MA, pg. 510
Butcher, Randye, Pur. Agent-Office Supplies--Southern States Cooperative, Inc., Richmond, VA, pg. 1022
Butt, Lois, Dir.-Pur.--The Union Central Life Insurance Co., Cincinnati, OH, pg. 1127
Butzan, Kathy, Pur. Dir.--AEC, Inc., Wood Dale, IL, pg. 1047
Byers, Candace, Mgr.-Pur.--Planning Systems Inc., McLean, VA, pg. 874
Bynum, Marilyn, Pur. Agent--Fashion Fair Cosmetics, Chicago, IL, pg. 599
Byrnes, Thomas, V.P., Sec. & Pur. Agent--Byrnes & Kiefer Company, Callery, PA, pg. 198
Bytnar, Robert, Dir.-Pur.--Replogle Globes, Inc., Broadview, IL, pg. 927
Caci, Mary, Dir.-Pur. & Personnel--Erin Group Administrators, Inc., Lancaster, PA, pg. 387
Caglione, John, Pur. Dir.--QEI, Inc., Springfield, NJ, pg. 902
Cahir, Thomas H., V.P.-Pur.--The O'Brien Corporation, South San Francisco, CA, pg. 820
Calzia, Donald G., Mgr.-Pur.--Presto Food Products, Inc., City of Industry, CA, pg. 888
Camic, William, Mgr.-Pur.--Zimmer Paper Products Inc., Indianapolis, IN, pg. 1220
Camp, Brenda, Dir.-Pur.--Cavalier Corporation, Chattanooga, TN, pg. 229
Campbell, Ike, Pur. Agent--Ward Manufacturing, Inc., Blassburg, PA, pg. 1163
Campbell, Scott, Dir.-Pur.--Eastern Color Printing Company, Avon, CT, pg. 363
Campbell, Susan, Pur. Agent--Bennington Iron Works, Inc., Bennington, VT, pg. 139
Campbell, Todd, Pur. Agent--Ohio Gas Company, Bryan, OH, pg. 822
Canady, W. Parker, V.P.-Pur. & Engrng.--Myrick Construction Inc., Biscoe, NC, pg. 780
Canales, Lou, Mgr.-Pur.--South Bend Plastics, Inc., Mishawaka, IN, pg. 1019
Cannady, Elane, Pur. Agent--Michigan Wheel Corporation, Grand Rapids, MI, pg. 747
Cannon, J. Gregory, Mgr.-Pur.--Blaw Knox Food & Chemical Equipment Company, Buffalo, NY, pg. 156
Cantrell, Jim, V.P.-Pur.--Hutchens Industries Inc., Springfield, MO, pg. 555
Cantwell, James, Pur. Agent--Reading Anthracite Co., Pottsville, PA, pg. 916
Caouette, Paula, Mgr.-Pur.--Elkay Products, Inc., Shrewsbury, MA, pg. 377
Caple, Mona, Pur. Agent--American Electronics, Inc., Fullerton, CA, pg. 3
Caponigro, Leonard, V.P.-Mfg. & Personnel & Dir.-Pur.--Tork, Inc., Mount Vernon, NY, pg. 1102
Caprio, Dorothy, Pur. Dir.--Brokay Products, Inc., Philadelphia, PA, pg. 217
Carey, Dan, Mgr.-Pur.--Structural Foam Plastics, Inc., North Branch, NJ, pg. 1054
Carlew, Jerry, Dir.-Pur.--Klipsch & Associates Inc., Hope, AR, pg. 635
Carlin, M., Pur. Agent--Eagle Electric Mfg. Co., Inc., Long Island City, NY, pg. 362
Carlson, Kevin, Pur. Agent--Specialty Manufacturing Company, St. Paul, MN, pg. 1027
Carlucci, Thomas, V.P.-Pur. & Maintenance--Fair Lanes Inc., Hunt Valley, MD, pg. 396
Carlucci, Thomas R., V.P.-Pur. & Maintenance--Fair Lane Bowling Div., Baltimore, MD, pg. 396
Carofalo, Sam, Mgr.-Pur.--Acrison, Inc., Moonachie, NJ, pg. 14
Carothers, Toni, Dir.-Pur.--Crosby & Overton, Inc., Long Beach, CA, pg. 300
Carper, Robert G., V.P.-Wholesale Pur.--Fareway Stores, Inc., Boone, IA, pg. 399
Carrier, Jim, Dir.-Pur.--World Carpets, Inc., Dalton, GA, pg. 1202
Carrier, Teresa, Pur. Agent--The Thompson Group Companies, Henderson, KY, pg. 1094
Carroll, Charles J., Pur. Agent--Milton Can Co., Inc., Elizabeth, NJ, pg. 756
Carswell, Rita, Pur. Agent--Automotive Moulding Company, Warren, MI, pg. 101
Carter, Donald J., Pres., Treas. & Chief Exec. Officer--Home Interiors & Gifts, Inc., Dallas, TX, pg. 541
Carter, Kelly, Admin. Asst.--ICM Industries, Inc., Chicago, IL, pg. 559
Carty, Tim, V.P.-Pur.--U-Haul International, Inc., Phoenix, AZ, pg. 48
Caruso, Carlton, Dir.-Pur.--Hickory Hill Furniture Corporation, Valdese, NC, pg. 816
Casciere, Frank, Mgr.-Pur.--Better Baked Foods, Inc., North East, PA, pg. 148
Casey, Colleen, Dir.-Pur. & Office Mgr.--Alliance Management, Inc., Seattle, WA, pg. 37
Casey, Hugh, Dir.-Pur.--Ziegler Chemical & Mineral Corp., Jericho, NY, pg. 1218
Cassidy, C. Maxwell, Pur. Agent--J. H. Fletcher & Co., Huntington, WV, pg. 418
Caudill, A.W., Dir.-Pur.--Morrison Textile Machinery Co., Fort Lawn, SC, pg. 771
Cavanaugh, J.C., Pur. Agent--Jones & Lamson Waterbury Farrel Corp., Cheshire, CT, pg. 468
Cefarati, Michael, Dir.-Pur.--The Great Lakes Cheese Co., Newbury, OH, pg. 481
Celentano, Domenick, Chm. Bd. & Pres.--Celentano Brothers, Verona, NJ, pg. 231
Cesta, Anthony, Pur. Agent--Ace Glass Incorporated, Vineland, NJ, pg. 11
Chambo, William, V.P.-Admin.--Gaylord Printing, Inc., Detroit, MI, pg. 446
Champe, Ronald, V.P.-Pur.--Eat N Park Restaurants, Pittsburgh, PA, pg. 364
Champion, Jackie, Mgr.-Pur.--UDL Laboratories, Inc., Rockford, IL, pg. 1072
Chance, Earl, V.P.-Pur.--Werthan Packaging, Inc., Nashville, TN, pg. 1176
Chance, Earl, Dir.-Pur.--Werthan Packaging, Inc., Nashville, TN, pg. 1176
Chandler, Jay, Dir.-Pur., Doors--Thomas R. Hopson Broker, Inc., Marietta, GA, pg. 544
Chapman, Richard, Pur. Agent--Telescope Casual Furniture, Inc., Granville, NY, pg. 1085
Chapman, Vondel, Dir.-Pur.--Idaho Supreme Company, Firth, ID, pg. 561
Chappel, Jim, Pur. Agent--Jones Chemicals, Inc., Le Roy, NY, pg. 603
Charpentier, Sandy, Pur. Dir.--Robby Len Fashions, New York, NY, pg. 78
Chaudhry, Mahmud, Mgr.-Gen. Services--Sacramento Municipal Utility District, Sacramento, CA, pg. 965
Cheesebro, Joe, Dir.-Pur.--Mayville Engineering Co., Inc., Mayville, WI, pg. 725
Chestnut, Gary, Mgr.-Pur.--Ag Processing Inc A Cooperative, Omaha, NE, pg. 24
Chewning, Debbie, Dir.-Pur.--Coastal Wholesale, Inc., Kinston, NC, pg. 257
Chicknoski, Alexander, V.P.-Pur.--Atlantic Builders Group Inc., Baltimore, MD, pg. 94
Chisholm, K.J., Pur. Agent--Symmons Industries Inc., Braintree, MA, pg. 1069
Choronzuk, Bob, Mgr.-Pur.--Bar-S Foods Co., Phoenix, AZ, pg. 118
Christensen, Ron, Dir.-Pur.--Associated Food Stores Inc., Salt Lake City, UT, pg. 89
Christian, Art, Mgr.-Pur.--American Econo-Therm, Tulsa, OK, pg. 865
Christiansen, Beric, Sr. V.P.-Distr. & Real Estate--Northern Automotive Corporation, Phoenix, AZ, pg. 1118
Christie, Dianne, Mgr.-Pur.--Neer Manufacturing Company, Lexington, OH, pg. 797
Chronowski, Larry, Dir.-Pur.--Dann Dee Display Fixtures, Chicago, IL, pg. 314
Church, Linda, V.P.-Pur.--Alban Tractor Co. Inc., Baltimore, MD, pg. 30
Ciavardini, Andrew, Mgr.-Pur.--Rynone Manufacturing Corporation, Sayre, PA, pg. 958
Cicaglao, Ross, V.P.-Pur.--Handy Manufacturing Co., Inc., Newark, NJ, pg. 505
Cicchese, William, Sr. V.P.-Sls. & Pur.--New England Frozen Foods, Southborough, MA, pg. 800
Ciecko, Andrew S., Dir.-Pur.--MNP Corp., Utica, MI, pg. 693
Cillo, James, Dir.-Pur.--Hoogovens Aluminum Corp., Secaucus, NJ, pg. 543
Claeys, Edgar, Dir.-Pur.--American Aircraft Parts Manufacturing Co., Dearborn, MI, pg. 48
Clark, Joe, Pur. Agent--Advance Mechanical Systems, Inc., Elk Grove Village, IL, pg. 19
Clark, William J., Pur. Agent--Abbey Etna Machine Company, Perrysburg, OH, pg. 9
Clarke, Wallace G., Dir.-Pur.--Mona Industries, Inc., Paterson, NJ, pg. 764
Clary, Doug, Pur. Agent--Triple S Plastics, Inc., Vicksburg, MI, pg. 1114
Clement, Gerald A., Mgr.-Pur.--The Van Metre Companies, Burke, VA, pg. 1144
CLement, Martin, Dir.-Pur.--Regal Marine Industries Inc., Orlando, FL, pg. 921
Clemmer, Terry, Dir.-Pur.--Whitin Roberts Co., Sanford, NC, pg. 1187
Clerke, William E., Dir.-Pur.--Cogentrix Incorporated, Charlotte, NC, pg. 258
Cleveland, D., Pur. Agent--J.M. Huber, Engineered Carbons Div., Borger, TX, pg. 550
Clifton, T., Pur. Agent--J.M. Huber, Flow Control Div., Tomball, TX, pg. 550
Clock, Bill, Dir.-Pur.--Bernea Food Service, Inc., Otsego, MI, pg. 143
Cobis, James, Pur. Agent--Systems Engineering & Manufacturing Corp., Stoughton, MA, pg. 1071
Coble, Joe, Dir.-Pur.--Decorative Fabrics - Mastercraft, Spindale, NC, pg. 262
Coelho, Cheryl, Mgr.-Matls.--E.C.D., Inc., Hillside, NJ, pg. 359
Coffee, John R., V.P.-Pur.--Rosendin Electric, Inc., San Jose, CA, pg. 948
Cogan, Hank, Mgr.-Pur.--The Stiffel Company, Chicago, IL, pg. 1049
Cogburn, Jerry, Pur. Agent--Maywood, Inc., Amarillo, TX, pg. 725
Cohen, Al, Sportswear Buyer--A & E Stores, Inc., Ridgefield, NJ, pg. 1
Cohn, Norman, V.P.-Piece Goods--Jerell, Inc., Dallas, TX, pg. 593
Coit, R.F., Pur. Agent--Stuart-Ironsides, Inc., Willowbrook, IL, pg. 1054
Colasurdo, John, Dir.-Pur.--Giles & Ransome, Inc., Bensalem, PA, pg. 458
Colasurdo, Richard, Pur. Agent--Blonder-Tongue Laboratories, Inc., Old Bridge, NJ, pg. 157
Cole, Donald E., V.P.-Pur.-Northwest--A.M. Todd Company, Kalamazoo, MI, pg. 1100
Coleman, Al, Mgr.-Pur.--Ancra Corporation, Hawthorne, CA, pg. 72
Coleman, Earl E., Pur. Agent--American United Life Insurance Company, Indianapolis, IN, pg. 65
Coleman, Monica, Pur. Agent-Services--SGD International Corp., New York, NY, pg. 962
Colker, Pam, Dir.-Pur.--Time Products, Inc., Atlanta, GA, pg. 1090
Colling, John, Dir.-Pur. & Traffic--Rama Group of Companies, Cheektowaga, NY, pg. 910
Collins, Colin, V.P.-Pur.--Massachusetts Mutual Life Insurance Co., Springfield, MA, pg. 718
Collins, Ken, Dir.-Materials--Taylor Machine Works, Inc., Louisville, MS, pg. 1081
Collins, Thomas, Pur. Agent--Dazey Corporation, Industrial Airport, KS, pg. 321
Colmer, Buddy, Dir.-Pur.--Brookshire Bros., Inc., Lufkin, TX, pg. 180
Colson, Carl, Pur. Agent--Kayem Foods, Inc., Chelsea, MA, pg. 619
Colvin, Art, V.P.-Pur. Dir.--Georgie Boy Manufacturing, Inc., Edwardsburg, MI, pg. 453
Compton, David D., Dir.-Opers.--Central Coca-Cola Bottling Company, Inc., Richmond, VA, pg. 232
Compton, Doug, Asst. to V.P. of Pur.--Overland Transportation System, Inc., Indianapolis, IN, pg. 832
Conley, Morgan, Pur. Agent--Western Extrusions, Carrollton, TX, pg. 1179
Connolly, Jim, Dir.-Pur.--Tidelands Oil Production Co., Long Beach, CA, pg. 1096
Connor, G., Dir.-Pur.--Peterson American Corp., Southfield, MI, pg. 864
Conrad, Audrey, Pur. Agent--Mary Maxim, Inc., Port Huron, MI, pg. 722
Conrad, Thomas, Dir.-Pur.--Denver Equipment Company, Colorado Springs, CO, pg. 331
Cook, Greg, Pres. & Chief Oper. Officer--Cook Manufacturing Corporation, Duncan, OK, pg. 282
Cooper, Bill, Pur. Agent--Sioux Steel Company, Sioux Falls, SD, pg. 1008
Cooper, William, Mgr.-Traffic & Pur. Agent--Mutual Welding Co., Ltd, Honolulu, HI, pg. 779
Corbin, James E., III, Pur. Agent--Metal Trades, Inc., Hollywood, SC, pg. 741
Corenthal, Sol, Sr. V.P.-Sls. & Pur.--Best Manufacturing, Inc., New York, NY, pg. 146
Cornell, Terry, Dir.-Pur.--Central Data Corporation, Champaign, IL, pg. 232
Corrazzo, Mike, Mgr.-Pur.--Micro Component Technology Inc., Saint Paul, MN, pg. 748
Corrigan, Alan, Mgr.-Pur.--Wahl Clipper Corp., Sterling, IL, pg. 1158
Corrigan, Thomas, Dir.-Pur.--Bridgeport Machines, Inc., Bridgeport, CT, pg. 175
Corroon, Joe, Pur. Agent--Printed Circuit Corporation, Woburn, MA, pg. 891
Corsetto, Michael, Pur. Agent--Hoboken Wood Flooring Corporation, Wayne, NJ, pg. 537
Cortney, William, Dir.-Pur.--Lincoln Electric Systems, Lincoln, NE, pg. 675
Coseglia, Fred, Dir.-Pur.--Moran Towing & Transporation Co. Inc, Greenwich, CT, pg. 769
Cosentino, Maria, Shoe Buyer--A & E Stores, Inc., Ridgefield, NJ, pg. 1
Cosgrove, John J., Dir.-Pur.-PBQD, Inc.--Parsons Brinckerhoff Inc., New York, NY, pg. 850
Cosgrove, Pat, V.P. & Pur. Agent--Ardell Industries inc., Union, NJ, pg. 604

Costello, J.A., Pur. Agent--Bell Chemical Company, Chicago, IL, pg. 134
Coughlin, Michelle, Dir.-Pur.--Bradley Printing Company, Des Plaines, IL, pg. 478
Coulombe, Raymond R., Chm. & Chief Exec. Officer--White Rock Distilleries Inc., Lewiston, ME, pg. 1186
Court, Arthur, Dir.-Pur.--Reed & Barton Corporation, Taunton, MA, pg. 920
Courtney, P., Pur. Mgr.--PTC Aerospace, Inc., Litchfield, CT, pg. 837
Cowles, Glen, V.P.-Pur.--Bluff City Distributing Co., Inc., Memphis, TN, pg. 161
Coxall, John A., V.P.-Pur.--Dimeo Construction Company, Providence, RI, pg. 338
Crabb, Larry, Mdsg. & Pur. Mgr.--Battery St. Enterprises, Running Gear Div., Boulder, CO, pg. 670
Craft, Richard, Dir.-Pur.--Swallen's, Inc., Cincinnati, OH, pg. 1066
Cramer, Carl, Pur. Agent--Lumber Systems, Inc., Vancouver, WA, pg. 687
Cramer, Ron, Pur. Agent--Monrovia Nursery Co., Azusa, CA, pg. 766
Crank, Thomas, Dir.-Pur.--Maritz Inc., Fenton, MO, pg. 707
Crews, Ron, Pur. Agent--Hooker Furniture Corporation, Martinsville, VA, pg. 543
Crider, Joe D., Pres. & Chief Oper. Officer--Reliance Steel & Aluminum Co., Los Angeles, CA, pg. 925
Crigger, Dick, Dir.-Pur.--Gebo Distributing Co., Inc., Plainview, TX, pg. 447
Crispin, George, V.P.-Procurement & Co-pack--Agripac Inc., Salem, OR, pg. 25
Crocker, William G., Mgr.-Pur.--Lee Company, Westbrook, CT, pg. 665
Cronon, Richard N., Treas. & Pur. Agent--Automatic Machine Products Company, Attleboro, MA, pg. 100
Crooks, Robert, Dir.-Pur.--Tippins Incorporated, Pittsburgh, PA, pg. 1099
Cross, Anastasia, Pur. Agent--Federal Chicago Corporation, North Chicago, IL, pg. 404
Cross, John R., V.P.-Sls. & Sec.--The Chardon Rubber Co., Chardon, OH, pg. 239
Crossland, Paul, Dir.-Pur.--Bergelectric Corporation, Los Angeles, CA, pg. 141
Crosthwait, Kent, V.P.-Sls. & Pur.--Neill-LaVielle Supply Co., Louisville, KY, pg. 797
Crum, Tom, Pur. Agent--Challenge Technologies, Grand Haven, MI, pg. 238
Crumley, Ron, Dir.-Pur.--J.L. Lester & Son, Inc., Rockmart, GA, pg. 668
Crumley, Ron, Head Buyer--J.L. Lester & Son, Inc., Rockmart, GA, pg. 668
Crump, Don, Mgr.-Purch.--Gibbs Diecasting Aluminum Corp., Henderson, KY, pg. 639
Cummings, Paul, Dir.-Pur.--Astro Wire & Cable Corporation, Worcester, MA, pg. 92
Currie, Bruce, Pur. Agent--Sparkomatic Corporation, Milford, PA, pg. 1025
Currie, Bruce, Matls. Mgr.--Altec Lansing Consumer Products, Milford, PA, pg. 1025
Curtin, J., Dir.-Pur.--Dietzgen Corporation, Des Plaines, IL, pg. 337
Curtis, Jim, Dir.-Pur.--Marshall Erdman and Associates, Inc., Madison, WI, pg. 385
Cust, Allen, Pur. Agent--H. E. Sargent, Inc., Stillwater, ME, pg. 971
Custer, Douglas R., Dir.-Procurement--American Tool Companies, Inc., Lincoln, NE, pg. 64
Custer, Janice, Mgr.-Plant--Laird & Company, Scobeyville, NJ, pg. 650
Czernia, Norbert, Pur. Agent--Midway Products Corporation, Monroe, MI, pg. 751
Czysz, Laura A., Office Mgr.--Federal Farm Credit Banks Funding Corporation, Jersey City, NJ, pg. 404
D'Angelo, John, Dir.-Sls., Mktg., Purch.--Pyttronic Industries, Inc., Montgomeryville, PA, pg. 901
Dahlstrom, N.A., V.P.-Admin. & Pur.--Alva/Amco Pharmacal Companies, Inc., Chicago, IL, pg. 46
Daleo, Mike, Pur. Agent--Sokol & Company, Countryside, IL, pg. 1016
Dalrymple, Willard H., Pur. Agent--Racine Federated, Inc., Racine, WI, pg. 909
Daly, Christopher W., Pur. Agent--The Berkshire Life Insurance Company, Pittsfield, MA, pg. 142
Damato, Samuel J., Mgr.-Pur.--Fine Organics Corp., Lodi, NJ, pg. 411
Daniel, Jeanette, Dir.-Admin. & Opers. & Pur.--Integrated Energy Controls Corp., Minneapolis, MN, pg. 573
Danziger, L., Dir.-Pur.--Isfel Company, Inc., Rahway, NJ, pg. 582
Darrold, Peck, Pur. Agent--Bedford Industries, Inc., Worthington, MN, pg. 131
Davenport, Hal, Pur. Agent--The Electron Corp., Littleton, CO, pg. 375
Davenport, Patsy, Mgr.-Pur.--Thomas & Skinner, Inc., Indianapolis, IN, pg. 1093
Davi, S., Pur. Agent--Sargent Manufacturing Company, New Haven, CT, pg. 361
Davis, Diana, Dir.-Pur.--Tri-K Industries, Inc., Emerson, NJ, pg. 1110
Davis, Glenn, Dir.-Pur.--O'Neal Steel Inc., Birmingham, AL, pg. 827
Davis, Glenn, Gen. Mgr.--Majestic Molded Products, Inc., Holbrook, NY, pg. 702
Davis, Gregory, Pur. Agent--BLH Electronics, Canton, MA, pg. 107
Davis, Lynn, V.P.-Sls., Mktg., Pur. & Mfg.--Lithotype Company, Inc., South San Francisco, CA, pg. 678
Davis, Mike, Pur. Agent--Jacobsen Manufacturing, Inc., Safety Harbor, FL, pg. 588
Davison, Dave, V.P.-Pur.--McLouth Steel, Trenton, MI, pg. 731
Deakin, H.E., Mgr.-Pur.--AP Parts Manufacturing Company, Toledo, OH, pg. 240
Dean, Andrew, Dir.-Pur.--Takatta Inc., Olympia Fields, IL, pg. 1076
Dean, Terry, Dir.-Pur.--Reliable Castings Corporation, Cincinnati, OH, pg. 924
Dease, Robert, Dir.-Pur.--Miller & Co., Selma, AL, pg. 753
DeAutremont, S.C., Dir.-Admin.--CH2M Hill Companies, Ltd., Englewood, CO, pg. 202
DeBelly, Dean, Dir.-Pur.--Southern Minnesota Beet Sugar Cooperative, Renville, MN, pg. 1022
DeBiasse, Ron, V.P.-Pur. & Real Estate--GAF Corporation, Wayne, NJ, pg. 438
Decker, Jack E., Pres. & Chief Exec. Officer--Campbell Oil Co., Massillon, OH, pg. 213
Decker, Richard, V.P.-Pur.--Dealers Electrical Supply Co., Waco, TX, pg. 322
Decker, Thomas, Dir.-Pur.--Dynamic Metal Products Company, Manchester, CT, pg. 356
Decker, Tim, Pur. Mgr.--Kennedy Valve, Elmira, NY, pg. 623
Defilipo, Bob, Dir.-Pur.--Hunter Marine Corporation, Alachua, FL, pg. 555
Degilio, Helen, Dir.-Pur.--S L C Graphics, Inc., Pittston, PA, pg. 963
Deig, Helen, Dir.-Purch.--George Koch Sons, Inc., Evansville, IN, pg. 639
DelBuono, Ron, Mgr.-Matls.--Streamlight Inc., Norristown, PA, pg. 1053
Delfini, Douglas, Pur. Agent--Connecticut Spring & Stamping Corporation, Farmington, CT, pg. 275
Della Rocca, Frank, Dir.-Pur.--Saratoga Harness Racing, Inc., Saratoga Springs, NY, pg. 970
Deller, Paul, Dir.-Pur.--Edward C. Levy Co., Inc., Detroit, MI, pg. 672
Demas, J., Dir.-Pur.--Periphonics Corp., Bohemia, NY, pg. 862
Dembiczak, Anita, V.P.-Pur.--Sun Hill Industries, Stamford, CT, pg. 1059
Dement, R., Dir.-Pur.--Galaxy Business Products, Honolulu, HI, pg. 742
DeMinck, Eugene, Mgr.-Purch.--American Crystal Sugar Company, Moorhead, MN, pg. 51
Denges, James, V.P.-Mktg. & Pur.--Central Grocers Co-op, Franklin Park, IL, pg. 232
Dermyer, William, V.P.--Omaha Public Power District, Omaha, NE, pg. 825
Deschenes, Clement, Head Buyer--Associated Grocers of New England, Inc., Manchester, NH, pg. 90
Desmond, William, Dir.-Pur.--Coilcraft, Inc., Cary, IL, pg. 259
Devers, Terry, Dir.-Pur.--Hoffco, Inc., Richmond, IN, pg. 537
DeVersa, Rod, Pur. Agent--Transamerican Refining Corporation, Houston, TX, pg. 1106
Devine, Donald, Chief Fin. Officer--Harris Farms, Inc., Coalinga, CA, pg. 511
Devore, Rob, Pur. Agent--Massman Construction Company, Kansas City, MO, pg. 719
DeVos, Dan, V.P.-Pacific Liason--Amway Corporation, Ada, MI, pg. 70
Dewey, Carol, Mgr.-Matl. Control--Code-A-Phone Corp., Clackamas, OR, pg. 258
Diamond, Lawrence, Chm. Bd., Pres., Chief Exec. & Chief Oper. Officer & Dir.-Pur.--Triangle Marketing Corp., New York, NY, pg. 1112
DiBiase, Dominick, Mgr.-Pur.--Coulter Corporation, Hialeah, FL, pg. 289
Dickerson, Robin, Pur. Agent--Metal Masters Foodservice Equipment, Smyrna, DE, pg. 741
Dickerson, Robin C., Mgr.-Pur.--Metal Masters Foodservice Equipment, Smyrna, DE, pg. 741
DiDonato, Joe, Pur. Dir.-Aerospace--Tracor, Inc., Austin, TX, pg. 1104
DiDonato, Joseph, Dir.-Procurement--Tracor Aerospace, Inc., Austin, TX, pg. 1105
Dieter, Betty, Pur. Dir.--The Gilman Company, Chattanooga, TN, pg. 603
Dilnnel, Nick, Pur. Agent--Triboro Electric Corp., Warminster, PA, pg. 1112
Dillner, Pat, Pur. Agent--Manning & Lewis Engineering Co., Union, NJ, pg. 704
Dillon, Doyle G., V.P.-Pur.--Roppe Corp., Fostoria, OH, pg. 947
Dimartini, F.M., V.P.-Prod. Devel, Raw Matls. & Pur.--Frank Ix & Sons, Inc., New York, NY, pg. 584
Dime, Jim, Dir.-Pur.--Moore Company, Westerly, RI, pg. 768
DiMiglio, Lucile, Dir.-Personnel & Pur.--Norwalk Powdered Metals, Inc., Norwalk, CT, pg. 816
Dionne, Norm, Pur. Agent--MSD, Inc., Darlington, SC, pg. 693
DiOrio, John, Pur. Agent--Cullman Products Corporation, Cullman, AL, pg. 304
Dirr, Eugene C., Mgr.-Pur.--R. A. Jones & Co. Inc., Covington, KY, pg. 604
Disbrow, D.E., Dir.-Pur.--Black & Veatch, Kansas City, MO, pg. 154
Dismukes, Alan, Buyer--Anderson Wholesale Company, Muskogee, OK, pg. 73
Dittmar, Larry, Pur. Agent--John Hassall, Inc., Westbury, NY, pg. 516
Ditto, Tom E., Pur. Agent--Kasper Machine Company, Madison Heights, MI, pg. 618
Dittrich, Michael, Pur. Agent--Hopple Plastics, Inc., Florence, KY, pg. 544
Dixon, Lance, Dir.-Pur.--Bose Corporation, Framingham, MA, pg. 167
Dlugos, R., Pur. Agent--Miller Company, Meriden, CT, pg. 754
Dlugos, Richard, Pur. Agent--Connecticut Drive Shaft, Inc., Milford, CT, pg. 274
Doarn, Michael, Dir.-Pur.--County Seat Stores, Inc., Dallas, TX, pg. 290
Dobbs, D., Dir.-Pur.--Remcor Products Co., Glendale Heights, IL, pg. 926
Dobrin, Arnold, Dir.-Pur.--Stevens-Lee Company, Minneapolis, MN, pg. 1048
Dobson, Thomas, Pur. Agent--Airline Hydraulics Corporation, Bensalem, PA, pg. 27
Doe, Randy, Dir.-Pur.--Pullman Industries, Inc., Madison Heights, MI, pg. 900
Doedoerlein, Debbie, Dir.-Pur.--Nic Sand, Cleveland, OH, pg. 159
Dolan, Ted, Pur. Agent--Ames Safety Envelope Company, Inc., Somerville, MA, pg. 66
Dollison, Dan, Mgr.-Pur.--Bruner Corporation, Milwaukee, WI, pg. 184
Domanski, Fred, Dir.-Pur.--Snyder Tank Corp., Buffalo, NY, pg. 1015
Donaldson, Holland, Mgr.-Pur.--U.S. Metalsource Corporation, Coraopolis, PA, pg. 1136
Donham, Paul, Dir.-Pur.--Quik Print Inc., Wichita, KS, pg. 905
Donnelly, Ton, V.P.-Human Resources--Everbrite, Inc., Greenfield, WI, pg. 391
Dooley, Ron, Pur. Agent--Danuser Machine Co., Fulton, MO, pg. 315
Dorio, Gail, Dir.-Pur.--Schott Brothers, Inc., Perth Amboy, NJ, pg. 978
Dorn, Rick, Dir.-Pur.--Information Systems & Network Corporation, Bethesda, MD, pg. 567
Dorris, Jack, Dir.-Pur.--Creative Publications, Oak Lawn, IL, pg. 369
Dorsey, Wayne J., Mgr.-Pur.--Miller Electric Mfg. Co., Appleton, WI, pg. 754
Dortch, David W., Dir.-Pur.--Humboldt Express, Inc., Nashville, TN, pg. 552
Dosta, William, Buyer--Kettenburg Marine Corporation, San Diego, CA, pg. 626
Dostal, Juanita, Pur. Dir.--Grandy's, Inc., Lewisville, TX, pg. 476
Dougherty, Dan, Pur. Agent--Bush Brothers & Company, Dandridge, TN, pg. 196
Douglas, Carl E., Pur. Agent--Henry Vogt Machine Co., Louisville, KY, pg. 1154
Douglas, Judy, Pur. Agent--KCL Corporation, Shelbyville, IN, pg. 611
Douthitt, Jerry D., Pur. Agent--Kartridg Pak Co., Davenport, IA, pg. 122
Downer, John F., Jr., Mgr.-Pur.--The Bureau of National Affairs, Inc., Washington, DC, pg. 189
Dozler, Alan, Dir.-Purch.--Norpac Foods, Inc. Cooperative, Stayton, OR, pg. 810
Draffin, Ken, Pur. Agent--Wurzburg, Inc., Memphis, TN, pg. 1205
Drake, Ronald C., Pur. Agent--H & H Tube & Manufacturing Co., Vanderbilt, MI, pg. 495
Dreesen, P.D., Dir.-Pur.--Science Applications International Corporation, San Diego, CA, pg. 981
Dresner, Arthur, V.P.-Advanced Matls.--International Specialty Products, Inc., Wilmington, DE, pg. 438
Driever, Jim, Pur. Agent--J.R. Simplot Co., Minerals & Chemicals Group, Pocatello, ID, pg. 1007
Driver, Daryle, V.P.-Matls. Mngmnt.--Management Dynamics, New Providence, NJ, pg. 703
Drotos, Steve, Pur. Dir.--Flambeau Products Corp., Middlefield, OH, pg. 809
Drumm, Curtis W., Pur. Agent--The Metal Ware Corp., Two Rivers, WI, pg. 741
Drushel, Don, Dir.-Pur.--WinCup, Phoenix, AZ, pg. 1195
Ducklow, Deb, Mgr.-Pur.--St. Croix Press, Inc., New Richmond, WI, pg. 966
Dudek, R.T., V.P. & Pur. Mgr.--Modern Equipment Co., Inc., Port Washington, WI, pg. 32
Duerr, Theodore J., Jr., V.P.-Pur.--Kitchen Kompact, Inc., Jeffersonville, IN, pg. 634
Duffy, David E., Dir.-Adv. & Pur.--McKee Door, Inc., Aurora, IL, pg. 730
Dugan, Bob, Dir.-Purch.--Alcom Printing Group, Inc., Bethlehem, PA, pg. 32
Duke, Joseph P., Mgr.-Pur.--Dunmore Corporation, Newtown, PA, pg. 353
Dulude, Jim, V.P.-Pur. & MIS--Quaker Fabric Corporation, Fall River, MA, pg. 903
Dumais, John, Dir.-Pur.--Beckley-Cardy, Inc., Duluth, MN, pg. 21
Dunigan, James, Dir.-Pur.--Bommer Industries, Inc., Landrum, SC, pg. 164
Dunn, Howard, Dir.-Pur.--B. Green & Co., Baltimore, MD, pg. 484
Dupps, Fred, Dir.-Pur.--Jofco Inc., Jasper, IN, pg. 595
Durelli, Al, V.P.-Distr.--Schwinn Bicycle Company, Chicago, IL, pg. 981
Durham, David, Dir.-Pur.--Cerro Copper Products Co., Sauget, IL, pg. 711
Dwyer, Larry, Asst. Mgr. & Pur. Mgr.--Deco Products Co., Decorah, IA, pg. 324
Dykstra, Henry, Dir.-Procurement--Howard Miller Clock Company, Zeeland, MI, pg. 754
Easler, Ken, Pur. Agent--Conso Products Company, Union, SC, pg. 276
Eckam, Robert C., Pur. Agent--WSF Industries, Inc., Tonawanda, NY, pg. 1156
Eckland, Gary, Pur. Dir.--Abrasive Engineering & Manufacturing Div., Olathe, KS, pg. 14
Edwards, C., Dir.-Pur.--The Gerstenslager Company, Wooster, OH, pg. 454
Edwards, John, Pur. Mgr.--American Manufacturing Co. (TN), Chattanooga, TN, pg. 58
Edwards, Richard, Pur. Agent--Plant Maintenance Service Corporation, Memphis, TN, pg. 874
Edwards, W., V.P.-Pur.--The Hubinger Company, Keokuk, IA, pg. 550
Eenhuls, Loretta, Treas. & Data Processing Dir.--Westin, Inc., Omaha, NE, pg. 1183
Egan, Jerry, Dir.-Pur.--Illinois Cereal Mills, Inc., Paris, IL, pg. 562
Egner, Bill, Pur. Agent--Schutte Lumber Company, Kansas City, MO, pg. 980
Eichenberger, Robert, Dir.-Opers.--Cubix Corporation, Carson City, NV, pg. 303
Eichenlaub, Hubert, Pur. Agent--White Storage & Retrieval Systems, Inc., Kenilworth, NJ, pg. 1186

Eichhorn, Robert E., Dir.-Pur.--Argo-Tech Corporation, Cleveland, OH, pg. 82
Eichman, James, Dir.-Pur.--Auburn Faith Community Hospital, Auburn, CA, pg. 97
Eickenberry, William, V.P.-Pur.--Sussen, Inc., Cleveland, OH, pg. 225
Eilers, Jerry, Mgr.-Pur.--BeefAmerica Operating Co., Inc., Omaha, NE, pg. 131
Eisel, Mike, Controller & Mgr.-Pur.--Little Lady Foods, Inc., Elk Grove Village, IL, pg. 679
Eisenhooth, Edward E., Mgr.-Pur.--Yerger Bros., Inc., Lititz, PA, pg. 1208
Eisner, C., V.P.-Pur.--Eagle Electric Mfg. Co., Inc., Long Island City, NY, pg. 362
Eldridge, Fred R., Mgr.-Pur.--Cargill Detroit Corp., Clawson, MI, pg. 219
Elesenbast, Dave, Dir.-Pur.--Milk Specialties Company, Dundee, IL, pg. 753
Ellingsen, Ken, V.P.-Mdse.--Leichtung, Inc., Cleveland, OH, pg. 666
Ellington, Virginia, Buyer--Davis Paint Company, Kansas City, MO, pg. 319
Elliot, Paul, Pur. Agent--Albert Trostel Packings, Ltd., Lake Geneva, WI, pg. 1116
Elliott, Morris J., Dir.-Pur.--Kohler Company, Kohler, WI, pg. 639
Ellis, Homer, Dir.-Pur.--Delta Queen Steamboat Company, New Orleans, LA, pg. 385
Ellis, Jeff, Mgr.-Pur.--Tagsons Papers, Inc., Albany, NY, pg. 1076
Ellis, Jim, Pur. Dir.--Zoeller Co., Louisville, KY, pg. 1220
Ellison, Olif, Pur. Agent--Ballenger Paving Company, Inc., Taylors, SC, pg. 116
Ellwood, David, Dir.-Pur.--Duron, Inc., Beltsville, MD, pg. 355
Elvin, Joseph, V.P.-Pur.--Marcal Paper Mills, Inc., Elmwood Park, NJ, pg. 706
Emery, Darlene, Mgr.-Pur.--Moss Telecommunications Services, Grand Rapids, MI, pg. 772
Emery, Earl, Dir.-Pur. & Traffic--CF&I Steel Corporation, Pueblo, CO, pg. 201
Emperor, June, Buyer--Bissell Inc., Grand Rapids, MI, pg. 153
Endick, Murray, Dir.-Pur.--Aberdeen Mfg. Corporation, New York, NY, pg. 200
Englander, Joseph, V.P.-Personnel & Pur.--Central Paper Company, Newark, NJ, pg. 233
Engle, Joe, V.P.-Pur.--SnyderGeneral Corporation, Dallas, TX, pg. 1015
Engstrom, Paul, Dir.-Pur.--St. Paul Metalcraft, Inc., Saint Paul, MN, pg. 967
Ensminger, Sharon, Dir.-Pur.--Visible Changes, Houston, TX, pg. 1153
Erdman, Steve, Pur. Agent--Federated Mutual Insurance Company, Owatonna, MN, pg. 405
Erdrich, Howard, Dir.-Msdg. & Pur.--Reliable Stores, Inc., Columbia, MD, pg. 925
Erickson, Bill, Pur. Agent--Continental/Midland, Inc., Park Forest, IL, pg. 279
Erickson, Charles D., Mgr.-Equipment--Bacco Construction Co., Iron Mountain, MI, pg. 108
Erwin, B.W., Pur. Agent--American Cast Iron Pipe Co., Birmingham, AL, pg. 50
Eskridge, Mark, Dir.-Pur. & Mgr.-Sls. & Mdsg., Market Res.--Hoffritz for Cutlery, New York, NY, pg. 538
Eskridge, Mark, Dir.-Sls. & Pur.--Hoffritz International, New York, NY, pg. 538
Esses, Jack, Dir.-Pur.--The Children's Place Retail Stores, Inc., Pine Brook, NJ, pg. 247
Etzinger, Robert, Dir.-Pur.--Gray Printing Co., Fostoria, OH, pg. 479
Evans, Dave, Pur. Agent--Gold Medal Products Co., Cincinnati, OH, pg. 465
Evans, Jerry, Pur. Agent--Peterson Tractor Company, San Leandro, CA, pg. 865
Evans, Junior, Mgr.-Pur.--The Gradall Co., New Philadelphia, OH, pg. 559
Evans, Richard S., Mgr.-Pur.--Hynes Industries Inc., Youngstown, OH, pg. 557
Everett, Donald S., V.P.-Pur.--Interstate Steel Supply Co., Philadelphia, PA, pg. 580
Everett, Jim, V.P.-Procurement--Long John Silver's, Inc., Lexington, KY, pg. 229
Ewing, Joe, Dir.-Personnel & Services--Mississippi Chemical Corporation, Yazoo City, MS, pg. 760
Faber, John, Dir.-Pur.--Moline Corporation, Saint Charles, IL, pg. 764
Fagan, Michael, Dir.-Pur.--Action Manufacturing Co., Philadelphia, PA, pg. 15
Fahrenkrog, Wint, Dir.-Procurement--Sathers Inc., Round Lake, MN, pg. 972
Fairclothe, Mac, Dir.-Pur.--The Field Controls Company, Kinston, NC, pg. 525
Falcon, A., Dir.-Purch.--Gator Industries Inc., Hialeah, FL, pg. 446
Falconer, Bob, Dir.-Pur.--Bradley Corporation, Menomonee Falls, WI, pg. 170
Faller, Gene, V.P.-Pur.--Union Underwear Co., Inc., Bowling Green, KY, pg. 400
Fallon, Anne, Dir.-Natl. Pur.--Allied Old English, Inc., Port Reading, NJ, pg. 38
Fallstich, Jay, Pur. Agent--Great Neck Saw Manufacturers, Inc., Mineola, NY, pg. 482
Fann, Raymond, Pur. Agent--Mission Industries, Santa Barbara, CA, pg. 760
Farias, Debbie, Mgr.-Pur.--Clifford Metal, Providence, RI, pg. 658
Farmer, Jim, Dir.-Pur.--Hazel Bishop Corporation, Englewood Cliffs, NJ, pg. 520
Farmwald, Ed, Dir.-Pur.--Jayco Inc., Middlebury, IN, pg. 590
Farrar, Lynn, V.P.-Pur.--C.B. Fleet Company, Incorporated, Lynchburg, VA, pg. 417
Faulkner, Sam, Dir.-Pur.--Tom's Foods, Columbus, GA, pg. 1101
Faux, Robert, Dir.-Pur.--Idea Man, Inc., Los Angeles, CA, pg. 562
Febbraio, George, Dir.-Pur.--Paper Enterprises, Inc., Bronx, NY, pg. 847
Fegert, Lawrence M., Dir.-Pur.--Tri-Mark Metal Corp., Detroit, MI, pg. 1110
Feiler, Fred V., Dir.-Pur.--Edgewood Tool & Manufacturing Company, Romulus, MI, pg. 368
Feinstein, Jack, Dir.-Sls., Pur. & Adv.--Universal Overall Company, Chicago, IL, pg. 1139
Felix, Edward R., V.P.-Warehouse Distr.--Bashas, Chandler, AZ, pg. 124
Felix, W.S., Dir.-Pur.--Miller Chemical & Fertilizer Corp., Hanover, PA, pg. 32
Feller, Bruce A., V.P.-Pur.--Metropolitan Life Insurance Co., New York, NY, pg. 744
Feltner, Homer, Dir.-Pur.--Quality Foods Inc., Little Rock, AR, pg. 903
Fenske, William, Dir.-Pur.--Lorsch Creative Network, Los Angeles, CA, pg. 684
Fenton, David, Dir.-Pur.--Mohawk Paper Mills, Inc., Cohoes, NY, pg. 763
Ferguson, Mac, Dir.-Pur.--Markair, Inc., Anchorage, AK, pg. 708
Ferguson, Phil, Pur. Agent--Valleydale Packers Inc., Bristol, VA, pg. 1143
Ferguson, W., Dir.-Pur.--Wilkinson Company, Inc., Stow, OH, pg. 373
Ferguson, Will, Dir.-Admin., Opers., Pur. & Import--Pace International Corporation, Kirkland, WA, pg. 838
Ferguson, William, Dir.-Pur.--Electric Furnace Co., Salem, OH, pg. 373
Ferrante, Anthony, Pur. Agent--Star Cutter Co., Farmington Hills, MI, pg. 1039
Ferraro, Vincent, Pur. Dir.--Dimco-Gray Company, Dayton, OH, pg. 338
Ferrotti, Gerald T., Mgr.-Pur.--Imperia Bros., Inc., Pelham Manor, NY, pg. 563
Fetzer, Brian R., V.P.-Procurement & Production--NRM Corporation, Columbiana, OH, pg. 781
Fezatte, Fred, V.P.-Pur.--Land O'Lakes, Inc., Arden Hills, MN, pg. 653
Fibbe, R.E., Sec. & Pur. Agent--The Kirk & Blum Mfg. Co., Cincinnati, OH, pg. 633
Fidanzi, Mario, V.P.-Pur.--Rand McNally & Company, Skokie, IL, pg. 911
Fields, Theresa, Pur. Mgr.--The Toy Factory, Elizabeth, NJ, pg. 889
Figler, D., Pur. Agent--Weber Marking Systems, Inc., Arlington Heights, IL, pg. 1171
Fingerle, Mark M., V.P. & Dir.-Pur.--Fingerle Lumber Co., Ann Arbor, MI, pg. 411
Fink, William, Sr. V.P.-Supply--Sinclair Oil Corp., Salt Lake City, UT, pg. 1008
Finlayson, Don, Pur. Dir.--McGuffey's Restaurants, Inc., Asheville, NC, pg. 729
Finley, Roy, Dir.-Pur.--Gold Kist, Inc., Atlanta, GA, pg. 465
Finnegan, Bob, Dir.-Pur.--The Shelburne Corporation, Shelburne, VT, pg. 996
Fischer, Jack, Pur. Agent--Al Larson Boat Shop, Inc., Terminal Island, CA, pg. 659
Fischer, Karin, Dir.-Pur.--North Central Life Insurance Companies, Saint Paul, MN, pg. 813
Fish, Terry, Dir.-Pur.--Maecorp Inc., Chicago, IL, pg. 699
Fisher, Allan, Mgr.-Pur.--Gast Mfg. Corp., Benton Harbor, MI, pg. 444
Fisher, David, Pur. Agent--The Miami Margarine Co., Cincinnati, OH, pg. 746
Fisher, Micael, Pur. Agent & Expediter--Fisher Skylights, Inc., West Nyack, NY, pg. 415
Fisher, R.W., Pur. Agent--Wurzburg, Inc., Memphis, TN, pg. 1205
Fisher, Robert, Pur. Mgr.--Conbraco Industries Inc., Matthews, NC, pg. 272
Fisher, Robert, Mgr.-Matls.--GMI, Inc.-Glasstream, Panama City, FL, pg. 450
Fisher, Tom, Pur. Mgr.--Big Joe Manufacturing Co., Lincolnwood, IL, pg. 149
Fisk, Sharon, Mgr.-Pur.--Interplastic Corp., Saint Paul, MN, pg. 579
Fissasloo, Bill, Dir.-Pur., Sec. & Treas.--Gress Foods Inc., Gainesville, GA, pg. 486
Fitzgerald, Thomas, Mgr.-Pur.--Tropar Mfg. Co., Inc., Florham Park, NJ, pg. 1115
Fitzsimmons, Jerry, Pur. Agent--Arrow Fastener Co., Inc., Saddle Brook, NJ, pg. 85
Fix, L., Pur. Agent--Century Fence Company, Pewaukee, WI, pg. 235
Flasco, John, Dir.-Pur.--The Akro Corporation, Canton, OH, pg. 262
Fleming, Tammy, Dir.-Pur.--Globe-Amerada Glass Company, Elk Grove Village, IL, pg. 463
Fleming, William, Buyer--Prestige Stamping, Inc., Warren, MI, pg. 888
Flood, Jack, Mgr.-Pur.--La France Corporation, Philadelphia, PA, pg. 649
Flowers, R.D., Mgr.-Pur.--Flakt Inc., Bahnson Div., Winston-Salem, NC, pg. 416
Foate, Jack L., Dir.-Pur.--Utility Trailer Manufacturing Co., City of Industry, CA, pg. 1141
Footer, Harris, V.P.-Pur.--Easy Day Manufacturing Company, Inc., Holliston, MA, pg. 364
Ford, Joe, V.P.-Pur.--Pollenex Corporation, Chicago, IL, pg. 821
Ford, Paul, Dir.-Pur.--Tenax Corporation, Danbury, CT, pg. 1086
Ford, Peter, Mgr.-Pur.--Just Born, Inc., Bethlehem, PA, pg. 610
Ford, Peter, Mgr.-Pur.--Just Born, Inc., Bethlehem, PA, pg. 610
Forsythe, Homer, V.P.-Opers.--White Swan, Inc., Euless, TX, pg. 1156
Fortney, Donald, Pur. Agent--Brunner & Lay, Inc., Franklin Park, IL, pg. 184
Fortune, Richard, Dir.-Pur.--Molded Fiber Glass Companies, Ashtabula, OH, pg. 763
Fortune, Richard, Dir.-Pur.--Molded Fiber Glass Co., Ashtabula, OH, pg. 764
Fossum, Jeffrey J., V.P. & Chief Fin. Officer--Effective Management Systems, Milwaukee, WI, pg. 370
Foster, James, Pur. Dir.--The Fibre-Metal Products Company, Concordville, PA, pg. 408
Foster, Michael, Dir.-Pur.--Hopper Inc., Bakersfield, CA, pg. 543
Fournier, Donald, Pur. Agent--Peck Spring Company, Plainville, CT, pg. 854
Fox, Joseph, Pur. Agent--Arkansas Oak Flooring, Pine Bluff, AR, pg. 83
Fox, Patricia, Dir.-Pur.--Cragar Industries, Compton, CA, pg. 761
Fox, Raymond A., V.P., Chief Oper. Officer & Sec.--Active Electrical Supply Company, Chicago, IL, pg. 15
Foxx, M.J., V.P. & Treas., Gen. Mgr. & Dir.-Pur.--Handgards Inc., Northbrook, IL, pg. 504
Fraker, Gary, V.P.-Pur. & Food Service--Delaware North Companies, Inc., Buffalo, NY, pg. 326
Fraker, Gary, V.P.-Pur.--Concession Air Corporation, Buffalo, NY, pg. 326
Fraker, Gary, V.P.-Pur.--Sportservice Corporation, Buffalo, NY, pg. 326
Francis, Marion, Pur. Agent--Anchor Continental Incorporated, Columbia, SC, pg. 71
Frank, Ray, Mgr.-Matls.--The Betham Corporation, Middlesex, NJ, pg. 147
Frantz, Dave, Mgr.-Pur.--Algood Food Company, Louisville, KY, pg. 34
Franz, Bill, Dir.-Pur.--Robert James Sales Inc., Buffalo, NY, pg. 589
Franz, Thomas J., Dir.-Pur.--Fru-Con Construction Corporation, Ballwin, MO, pg. 435
Fraser, William R., V.P.-Pur.--Friendly Ice Cream Corp., Wilbraham, MA, pg. 1087
Frazee, Ann, Dir.-Pur.--Harbor Financial Mortgage Corp., Houston, TX, pg. 506
Frazier, Charles, Buyer--Anderson Wholesale Company, Muskogee, OK, pg. 73
Frazier, Gene, Dir.-Pur.--United Farm Tools, Inc., Glasgow, KY, pg. 1131
Frazier, Jerry, Dir.-Pur. & Mdsg.--Anderson Wholesale Company, Muskogee, OK, pg. 73
Frazier, Mark, Mgr.-Matls. Control--Avatar Corporation, Hopkinton, MA, pg. 101
Frechette, Mark, Pur. Agent--National Computer Print, Inc., Birmingham, AL, pg. 786
Freeman, Steve, Dir.-Pur.--Warner Press, Inc., Anderson, IN, pg. 1164
Freiburg, Kathy, Dir.-Pur.--Rural Metro Corporation, Scottsdale, AZ, pg. 956
Fricchione, Patrick, Jr., Dir.-Pur.--Simplex Industries, Inc., Scranton, PA, pg. 1006
Friedman, Reuben, Pres. & Chief Exec. Officer--Arrow Typographers, Inc., Newark, NJ, pg. 326
Fromm, James, Mgr.-Pur. & Inventory Control--Lutheran Brotherhood, Minneapolis, MN, pg. 688
Frye, Greg, Dir.-Pur.--Professional Apartment Management, Inc., Lodi, CA, pg. 893
Fuller, Lauren, Admin./Opers. & Pur.--R.F. Broadus & Associates, Inc., Atlanta, GA, pg. 177
Fullerton, Volly W., Dir.-Pur.--Steadly Company, Carthage, MO, pg. 1043
Furey, Edward C., Dir.-Materials Mngmt.--S. C. Johnson & Son, Inc., Racine, WI, pg. 599
Gabory, Margy, Pur. Agent--Western Reinsurance Brokers, Inc., Los Angeles, CA, pg. 1181
Galindo, Maria, Mgr.-Pur.--Wahl Instruments, Culver City, CA, pg. 1158
Gallagher, George, Pur. Agent--Atlantic Metals Corporation, Philadelphia, PA, pg. 95
Gallaher, James A., V.P.-Pub. Affairs/Pub. Rels. & Sec.--The New England, Boston, MA, pg. 799
Gallo, Francine, Dir.-Office Admin.--American Institute of C.P.A.'s Inc., New York, NY, pg. 56
Gamache, J.A., Mgr.-Pur.--J.M. Huber, Printing Ink Div., Edison, NJ, pg. 550
Gamble, Judy, Mgr.-Customer Service--ACL Technologies, Santa Ana, CA, pg. 2
Gandhi, Ranesh, Dir.-Pur.--AMD Industries Inc., Cicero, IL, pg. 5
Gannon, David, Pur. Agent--The George E. Failing Company, Enid, OK, pg. 161
Garcia, J., Pur. Agent--Spirite Industries, Inc., Englewood, NJ, pg. 1031
Gardner, Grant, Dir.-Pur.--Delta Education, Inc., Hudson, NH, pg. 326
Gardner, Robert, Pur. Agent--Kulite Semiconductor Products, Inc., Leonia, NJ, pg. 646
Garmeau, Darlene, Dir.-Pur.--FaceMate Pond Lilt Great Falls, Somersworth, NH, pg. 396
Garrett, Lewis, V.P.-Pur.--Camelot Music, Inc., North Canton, OH, pg. 212
Garrison, Craig, Pur. Agent--The Johnson Corporation, Three Rivers, MI, pg. 597
Gash, Larry, Pur. Agent--Navajo Forest Products Industries, Navajo, NM, pg. 796
Gass, Bob, Pur. Agent--Meco Corporation, Greeneville, TN, pg. 734
Gatewood, James, Mgr.-Pur.--Bunton Company, Louisville, KY, pg. 188
Gaul, Joseph, Pur. Agent--Coppus Engineering Corp., Millbury, MA, pg. 285
Gauthier, Nelson, Dir.-Pur.--MFE Instruments, Beverly, MA, pg. 1050
Gaylor, Leonard, Pur. Agent--Republic Die & Tool Company, Belleville, MI, pg. 928
Gaynord, Thomas, Dir.-Pur.--Haddon Craftsmen, Inc., Scranton, PA, pg. 499
Geary, Frank E., Pur. Agent--Tinius Olsen Testing Machine Co., Inc., Willow Grove, PA, pg. 1098

Gebauer, Al, Mgr.-Pur.--Havens Steel Co., Kansas City, MO, pg. 517
Gedwill, Bill, Mgr.-Pur.--Chicago Lock Company, Chicago, IL, pg. 245
Gee, Senn, Mgr.-Pur.--World's Finest Chocolate, Inc., Chicago, IL, pg. 1203
Gehl, Tom, Mgr.-Pur.--Tekra Corporation, New Berlin, WI, pg. 1084
Geib, M.A., Mgr.-Matls.--Raymark Friction Company, Manheim, PA, pg. 914
Geib, Walter, Dir.-Procurement--Kearfott Guidance & Navigation Corp., Wayne, NJ, pg. 93
Geiger, Kenneth C., V.P. & Mgr.-Materials--Geiger Brothers, Lewiston, ME, pg. 447
Gelarden, Joe, Purchasing Supvr.--Keller Crescent Co., Evansville, IN, pg. 620
Gelarden, Joe, Pur. Supvr.--Keller-Crescent Co., Evansville, IN, pg. 621
Gelber, C., Dir.-Pur.--A. Finkl & Sons Co., Chicago, IL, pg. 411
Gelvin, John, Pur. Agent--The Harter Group, Sturgis, MI, pg. 513
Gemmel, Jane, Pur. Agent--Standard Tool & Manufacturing Company, Lyndhurst, NJ, pg. 1037
Gencius, Valentine, Dir.-Pur.--Goodman Equipment Corp., Bedford Park, IL, pg. 470
Gentile, Thomas G., Mgr.-Pur.--General Ship Corporation, Boston, MA, pg. 450
Gentle, R.M., Mgr.-Matls.--M M Systems Corporation, Tucker, GA, pg. 692
Gentry, Gary, Dir.-Pur.--Howell Instruments Corp., Fort Worth, TX, pg. 547
Gentry, Richard S., Dir.-Mfg. & Pur.--CTB Inc., Milford, IN, pg. 205
George, Donald, Dir.-Pur.--Sentinel Consumer Products, Inc., Mentor, OH, pg. 990
Gerber, James L., V.P.-Mktg. & Distr.--Nickles Bakery, Inc., Martins Ferry, OH, pg. 807
Gerchenson, Jeffery H., Pres. & Chief Oper. Officer--Alva/Amco Pharmacal Companies, Inc., Chicago, IL, pg. 46
Gerhold, John, Mgr.-Pur.--Yenkin-Majestic Paint Corporation, Columbus, OH, pg. 1208
Gertz, Dick, Mgr.-Pur.--R.S. Owens, Chicago, IL, pg. 834
Giannelli, Robert, Dir.-Pur.--Mader Construction Group Inc., Elma, NY, pg. 699
Gilbert, Harold D., V.P.-Pur.--Brock Candy Company, Chattanooga, TN, pg. 177
Gill, Pam W., Pur. Agent--Evening Post Publishing Co., Charleston, SC, pg. 391
Gillespie, Robert, Pur. Agent--Southern Ohio Fabricators, Inc., Cincinnati, OH, pg. 1022
Gillmer, Wayne, Buyer--Genova Products, Inc., Davison, MI, pg. 452
Ginsberg, Andy, Pur. Agent--Manostat Corporation, New York, NY, pg. 704
Ginsberg, Jerry, V.P.-Pur.--Milton Industries, Inc., Chicago, IL, pg. 756
Gipson, D., V.P. & Pur. Dir.-Comml. Printing--The Caxton Printers Ltd., Caldwell, ID, pg. 230
Girardi, Michael, Pur. Agent--Hilliard Corporation, Elmira, NY, pg. 535
Giuliani, Jon, Dir.-Pur.--Rite-Hite Corporation (IA), Dubuque, IA, pg. 936
Givan, Bud, Dir.-Pur.--Nashville Wire Product Co., Nashville, TN, pg. 784
Glaub, Robert, Pur. Agent--Dennis Chemical Company, Inc., Saint Louis, MO, pg. 329
Gleistein, Art, Pur. Agent--Solar Press, Inc., Naperville, IL, pg. 1016
Glenn, William E., Jr., V.P.-Pur.--J. Gibson McIlvain Co., White Marsh, MD, pg. 729
Glosup, Ed, V.P.-Pur.--Ryan Herco Products Corp., Burbank, CA, pg. 958
Gluck, Kurt, Dir.-Pur.--Franklin Sports Industries, Stoughton, MA, pg. 429
Gniffke, Bruce, Mgr.-Purch.--Zytec Corp., Eden Prairie, MN, pg. 1221
Godwin, Steve, Mgr.-Pur.--T.S. Ragsdale Company, Incorporated, Lake City, SC, pg. 910
Goering, George L., V.P.-Pur.--Weasler Engineering Inc., West Bend, WI, pg. 1169
Goerlich, K., Pur. Agent--J.M. Huber, Calcium Carbonate Div., Quincy, IL, pg. 550
Gohmann, John R., V.P., Chief Oper. Officer, Sec. & Dir.-Pur.--Gohmann Asphalt & Construction Inc., Clarksville, IN, pg. 465
Goin, Robert, Dir.-Pur.--Pickering Industries Inc., Tacoma, WA, pg. 869
Goldberg, Mark, Dir.-Data Processing & Pur.--Condor D.C. Power Supplies Inc., Oxnard, CA, pg. 273
Goldman, Charlie, V.P.-Pur.--Tollman/Hundley Hotels, Valhalla, NY, pg. 1100
Goldman, Greta, Pur. Agent--TimeMed Labeling Systems, Inc., Burr Ridge, IL, pg. 1098
Goldman, Irwin, Pur. Agent--Publix Group, New York, NY, pg. 898
Goldman, Irwin, Pur. Agent--Career Club Shirt Co., New York, NY, pg. 898
Goldstein, Sheldon, Pur. Agent--Cummins-Allison Corp., Mount Prospect, IL, pg. 305
Golubic, John, Dir.-Pur.--YSD Industries, Youngstown, OH, pg. 1207
Gomez, C.J., Dir.-Pur.--The U.S. Baird Corporation, Stratford, CT, pg. 114
Gomez, C.J., Dir.-Pur.--The A. H. Nilson Machine Co., Stratford, CT, pg. 114
Goncalves, Dolores, Pur. Agent--Merriam-Webster, Inc., Springfield, MA, pg. 381
Gonzalez, C., Sec., Treas. & Pur. Agent--Villazon Company Inc., Tampa, FL, pg. 1152
Goodell, K., Dir.-Pur.--Hofley Manufacturing Company, Warren, MI, pg. 538
Goodman, Milton L., Dir.-Pur.--Air Conditioning Co., Inc., Glendale, CA, pg. 26
Goodwin, Dave, V.P.-Adv. & Pur.--Waremart Inc., Boise, ID, pg. 1163
Goodwins, Robert, Dir.-Pur.--Seacoast Electric Company, Rye, NY, pg. 370
Goodwins, Robert W., Dir.-Pur.--Manhattan Electric Cable Corporation, Rye, NY, pg. 370
Goold, Leon, Dir.-Pur.--Servus Footwear Company, Rock Island, IL, pg. 993
Gordon, J., Mgr.-Matls.--Faber/Castell Corporation, Parsippany, NJ, pg. 395
Gordon, John, V.P.-Pur.--Muelhens, Inc., Orange, CT, pg. 774
Gordon, K., Dir.-Pur.--Motek Engineering & Manufacturing Company, Cambridge, MN, pg. 773
Gordon, Richard, Dir.-Pur.--Rogers Markets Inc., Fort Wayne, IN, pg. 943
Gore, Katie, Dir.-Pur.--Clayton Industries Co., El Monte, CA, pg. 253
Gorka, Barbara, Pur. Mgr.--Newbury Industries, Inc., Newbury, OH, pg. 803
Goss, Allan J., Pur. Agent--Penco Products, Oaks, PA, pg. 857
Gotro, James, Pur. Agent--Gaymar Industries, Inc., Orchard Park, NY, pg. 447
Gould, Wayne, Dir.-Pur.--Hale-Halsell Company, Tulsa, OK, pg. 500
Graber, D.K., Dir.-Pur.--Harwick Chemical Corp., Akron, OH, pg. 515
Graczyk, Terry, Pur. Agent--The Wyco Tool Co., Racine, WI, pg. 909
Graf, Gary, Dir.-Procurement--Dorman-Roth Foods, Inc., Moonachie, NJ, pg. 346
Graham, Evelyn, Dir.-Pur.--American Foundry Group, Inc., Bixby, OK, pg. 54
Graham, Jack, Dir.-Pur.--AEA, Inc., Charlotte, NC, pg. 3
Graham, L., Pur. Agent--Commercial & Architectural Products Inc., Dover, OH, pg. 268
Grant, Leonard, Pur. Agent--B. H. Aircraft Co., Inc., Farmingdale, NY, pg. 106
Grasse, John, Sr. V.P.-Pur. & Quality Control--Serigraph, Inc., West Bend, WI, pg. 991
Graves, Michael, Mgr.-Pur.--Nuttall Gear Corporation, Niagara Falls, NY, pg. 818
Gray, Charles, Dir.-Pur.--Kastle Systems, Inc., Arlington, VA, pg. 618
Gray, Ellen M., Sr. V.P.-Admin. Services & Dir.-Human Resources--Stephens, Inc., Little Rock, AR, pg. 1046
Grayson, Sandra, Dir.-Pur.--Power Conversion, Inc., Saddle Brook, NJ, pg. 883
Greaney, Dennis, V.P.-Matl. Control--Mary Kay Cosmetics Inc., Dallas, TX, pg. 716
Green, Bud, Dir.-Pur.--Supermarkets General Corporation, Woodbridge, NJ, pg. 1064
Green, John, V.P.-Pur.--Mississippi Lime Co., Alton, IL, pg. 760
Green, Steve, Dir.-Pur.--Richard Young Office Products, Inc., Deerfield Beach, FL, pg. 535
Greene, Ed, V.P.-Pur.--Ponderosa, Inc., Vandalia, OH, pg. 743
Greene, Michale, V.P.-Pur.--The Stellar Group Inc., Jacksonville, FL, pg. 1046
Gregory, Harry L., V.P.-Matls. Mngmt--Northwest Airlines, Inc., Saint Paul, MN, pg. 782
Gregory, Steve, Dir.-Pur.--Horton Homes, Inc., Eatonton, GA, pg. 545
Gresian, J., Pur. Agent--Telechron, Inc., Ashland, MA, pg. 1085
Gribas, John, Dir.-Pur.--Midland Grocery, Westville, IN, pg. 952
Griffin, Jay, Mgr.-Pur.--Asko, Inc, Homestead, PA, pg. 88
Griffin, Mike, Dir.-Matls. & Human Resources--GF Office Furniture Ltd., Gallatin, TN, pg. 439
Griffin, Mike, Dir.-Matls. & Human Resources--GF Office Furniture, Youngstown, OH, pg. 439
Griffith, Dwight, Pur. Agent--Gem Top Mfg., Inc., Clackamas, OR, pg. 448
Griffith, Floyd, Mgr.-Pur.--Allison Corporation, Livingston, NJ, pg. 40
Griffiths, James J., Dir.-Pur.--Randolph Medical Inc., Livonia, MI, pg. 912
Griffiths, Mary Ellen, Pur. Agent--American Mathematical Society, Inc., Providence, RI, pg. 58
Grip, Herman W., V.P.-Pur. & Distribution--J. L. Hammett Company, Braintree, MA, pg. 504
Gross, John, Mgr.-Matls. & Procurement--Niagara Frontier Transporation Metro System, Inc., Buffalo, NY, pg. 806
Gross, Kevin, Dir.-Pur.--Formu-3 International, Inc., Canton, OH, pg. 424
Grove, Alan I., Pur. Agent--E. R. Moore Co., Chicago, IL, pg. 768
Grubbs, Don, Pur. Mgr.-Petroleum--The Parman Corporation, Nashville, TN, pg. 850
Gruber, Charles, Pur. Agent--Advance Business Graphics, Mira Loma, CA, pg. 18
Gu, Suqi, Pur. Agent--Harold Leonard & Company, Inc., Union, NJ, pg. 667
Guadagho, Lou, Pur. Agent--Dothan Underwear, New York, NY, pg. 545
Gubotosi, Diane, Dir.-Pur.--Donnkenny, Inc., New York, NY, pg. 345
Guertin, E., Pur. Agent--Cable Electric Products, Inc., Providence, RI, pg. 671
Guetens, Jack, Pur. Agent--O. F. Mossberg & Sons, Inc., North Haven, CT, pg. 773
Gum, Sherwood, Mgr.-Pur.--Instrument Specialties Company, Delaware Water Gap, PA, pg. 572
Gunn, H.A., Dir.-Pur.--Standard Lafarge, Canfield, OH, pg. 1036
Gunn, John, Dir.-Corp. Pur.--Collins & Aikman Textile Group, Charlotte, NC, pg. 262
Gunning, Frank, Pur. Agent--Del Mar Avionics, Irvine, CA, pg. 325
Gunther, Edward, Mgr.-Pur.--Precision Valve Corporation, Yonkers, NY, pg. 885
Gunzelman, Deborah, Dir.-Matls. Mgmnt.--New Hermes Incorporated, Norwalk, CT, pg. 801
Guresky, Candy, Corp. Pur.--L'Ermitage Hotels, West Hollywood, CA, pg. 668
Gurin, Ron, V.P.-Pur. & Prod. Devel.--Pressman Toy Corp., New York, NY, pg. 887
Gustin, Laura, Dir.-Pur.--The Garber Company, Ashland, OH, pg. 442
Guyer, Steve, V.P.-Mfg.--Red Calliope & Associates, Inc., Los Angeles, CA, pg. 918
Haas, Bob, Pur. Agent--Martin Forest Industries, Healdsburg, CA, pg. 715
Haas, Frank, Dir.-Pur.--Grede Foundries, Inc., Milwaukee, WI, pg. 483
Haas, G. A., Mgr.-Pur.--Bud Industries, Inc., Willoughby, OH, pg. 186
Haas, Gerald, Mgr.-Pur.--W.A. Roosevelt Co., La Crosse, WI, pg. 946
Haas, Norman, Buyer--Fritz Chemical Company, Mesquite, TX, pg. 434
Haas, Terry, Mgr.-Pur.--Alco Health Services Corp.-Paducah Div., Paducah, KY, pg. 31
Haber, Bertram M., Pur. Agent--Hearst Magazines Division, New York, NY, pg. 523
Hacker, W. Joe, V.P.-Pur.--Arrowhead Mills, Inc., Hereford, TX, pg. 86
Hada, Russ, Dir.-Pur.--American Industries Inc., Portland, OR, pg. 55
Hadden, Scott, Dir.-Purch.--Keystone Automotive Industries, Inc., Pomona, CA, pg. 627
Haddock, Lee, Mgr.-Pur.--Heaters Engineering, Inc., North Webster, IN, pg. 489
Hagerty, Bruce, Dir.-Pur.--Hubbard Broadcasting, Inc., Saint Paul, MN, pg. 548
Hagerty, Bruce, Dir.-Pur.--KSTP-TV, Saint Paul, MN, pg. 549
Haggerty, Dean, Mgr.-Pur.--Plastoid Corporation, Hamburg, NJ, pg. 876
Hahn, Douglas E., V.P.-Mktg., Pur. & Adv.--J.R. Hahn Co., Inc., Indianapolis, IN, pg. 500
Hall, Brian, Mgr.-Pur.--Thetford Corporation, Ann Arbor, MI, pg. 357
Hall, Joseph, Dir.-Pur.--Westgate Inc., Port Allen, LA, pg. 1182
Hall, Lou, Gen. Mgr.-Pur.--Spartan Stores Inc., Grand Rapids, MI, pg. 1026
Hall, Ruby T., Pur. Agent--Johnson Supply & Equipment Corp., Houston, TX, pg. 601
Hall, William, Mgr.-Pur.--United Aluminum Corporation, North Haven, CT, pg. 1130
Halyn, Walter, Pur. Agent--The Coe Mfg. Co., Painesville, OH, pg. 258
Hamann, Jim, Pur. Agent--Wausau Homes, Inc., Rothschild, WI, pg. 1168
Hamister, Oliver C., V.P.-Admin., Treas. & Sec.--National Health Care Affiliates, Inc., Buffalo, NY, pg. 791
Hammann, Vada, Dir.-Pur.--Perry & Derrick Co., Cincinnati, OH, pg. 863
Hamowy, Albert, V.P.-Domestic Pur.--Soundesign Corporation, Jersey City, NJ, pg. 1018
Hampton, Kristopher D., Sr. Mgr.-Pur.--Auto Glass Specialists, Madison, WI, pg. 100
Hand, Ruth, Mgr.-Pur.--Bruce Industries, Inc., Dayton, NV, pg. 183
Handwerker, William, Sr. V.P.--Nathan's Famous Inc., Westbury, NY, pg. 784
Hanes, Dick, Dir.-Pur.--Aldan Rubber Co., Philadelphia, PA, pg. 32
Haney, Bill, Pur. Agent--MacAndrews & Forbes Co., Camden, NJ, pg. 694
Hankins, Charles, Mgr.-Pur.--Columbian Rope Company, Guntown, MS, pg. 266
Hanley, Joe, Pur. Agent--Bolton-Emerson, Inc., Lawrence, MA, pg. 163
Hanley, R.D., Pur. Agent--J.M. Huber, Oil & Gas Div., Houston, TX, pg. 550
Hannigan, Kristin, Mgr.-Pur.--Epec, Inc., New Bedford, MA, pg. 384
Hannula, Michael, Pur. Agent--Carl Weissman & Sons, Inc., Great Falls, MT, pg. 1174
Hanrahan, David, Pur. Agent--Fiber Materials, Inc., Biddeford, ME, pg. 408
Hansel, Clark, Dir.-Pur.--Dutton-Lainson Co., Hastings, NE, pg. 356
Hansen, Blair, Dir.-Pur.--Celestial Seasonings, Boulder, CO, pg. 231
Hanson, Paul, Pur. Agent--Toledo Commutator Co., Owosso, MI, pg. 633
Hanson, Robert, Pur. Dir.--Augsburg Fortress, Publishers, Minneapolis, MN, pg. 98
Hanyok, Mary, Pur.--Paradigm Communications, Tampa, FL, pg. 847
Haranga, Steven, Dir.-Pur.--Cumberland Farms, Inc., Canton, MA, pg. 304
Hardy, Mike, Mgr.-Matls.--Reichel & Drews Inc., Itasca, IL, pg. 906
Hargis, Doyle, Asst. V.P.-Pur. & Leasing--Unigard Security Insurance Co., Bellevue, WA, pg. 596
Hargy, Deborah R., Dir.-Pur.--Phonetics, Inc., Aston, PA, pg. 869
Harper, Charles, Dir.-Matl. Procurement--Duo-Fast Corporation, Franklin Park, IL, pg. 354
Harper, William, Mgr.-Pur.--Sargent-Fletcher Co., El Monte, CA, pg. 970
Harrah, Charles, Pur. Agent--Deerfield Manufacturing Co., Inc., Mason, OH, pg. 324
Harrelson, Allen, Dir.-Pur.--Gilman Paper Co., Saint Marys, GA, pg. 459
Harrelson, Rod, Dir.-Pur.--Pascoe Building Systems, Inc., Columbus, GA, pg. 851
Harrington, Chrystal, Pur. Agent--Bijur Lubricating Corporation, Bennington, VT, pg. 150
Harris, David J., Dir.-Pur.--The Flood Company, Hudson, OH, pg. 419

Harris, J., Pur. Agent--Hypertronics Corporation, Hudson, MA, pg. 557
Harris, K.L., Sr. V.P.-Pur. & Distr.--Restaurant Enterprises Group, Inc., Irvine, CA, pg. 929
Harris, Lynn, Mgr.-Pur.--Integral Systems, Inc., Sunnyvale, CA, pg. 573
Harris, Tom, Dir.-Pur.--Stonecutter Mills Corp., Spindale, NC, pg. 1051
Harrison, Roger, Pur. Agent--Diagraph Corporation, Earth City, MO, pg. 335
Hart, Darrell, Dir.-Pur. & Traffic--Macklanburg-Duncan Co., Oklahoma City, OK, pg. 697
Hart, John, Pur. Dir.--Scotchman Industries, Inc., Philip, SD, pg. 982
Hartley, Vincent, Dir.-Pur.--Health Management Systems, Inc., New York, NY, pg. 521
Hartman, Max, Pur. Agent--Flexel, Inc., Atlanta, GA, pg. 418
Hartman, R.S., Dir.-Pur.--Ludlow Composites Corporation, Fremont, OH, pg. 686
Harvey, Robert, Dir.-Pur.--Warner Press, Inc., Anderson, IN, pg. 1164
Harvey, Wilson, Mgr.-Pur.--Mississippi Chemical Corporation, Yazoo City, MS, pg. 760
Hashimoto, Wayne, Dir.-Pur.--Pacific Hawaiian Ltd., Hilo, HI, pg. 840
Hasskamp, Paul, Mgr.-Pur.--Poly-Seal Corporation, Baltimore, MD, pg. 880
Hastidt, Linda, Dir.-Pur.--Ranir Corporation, Grand Rapids, MI, pg. 912
Hathaway, Monty, Dir.-Pur.--Mersman Furniture, Celina, OH, pg. 741
Hauer, Oscar, V.P.-Pur.--Fleer Corporation, Mount Laurel, NJ, pg. 695
Hauser, Steve, Dir.-Pur.--Round Hill Foods, Inc., New Oxford, PA, pg. 952
Haut, Dan, V.P. & Chief Resource Officer--Glico Harmony Foods Corporation, Santa Cruz, CA, pg. 462
Hawes, Bob, Purchasing Mgr.--Willamette-Western Corporation, Portland, OR, pg. 1190
Hawkins, Joey, Dir.-Pur.--Young Pecan Shelling Co., Inc., Florence, SC, pg. 1209
Hawn, Clyde, Pur. Dir.-Supplies--Carolina Mills, Inc., Maiden, NC, pg. 223
Hay, Sue, Mgr.-Pur.--Microdot Aerospace Fastening Systems Group, Fullerton, CA, pg. 749
Hayden, Louis, Dir.-Procurement--Victaulic Company of America, Easton, PA, pg. 1149
Hayden, Tom, Pur. Agent--Fel Corporation, Farmingdale, NJ, pg. 405
Hayes, C.A., Dir.-Pur., Adv. & Mktg.--Blevins Inc., Nashville, TN, pg. 156
Haynes, Charles, Pur. Agent--National Life Insurance Company, Montpelier, VT, pg. 791
Hazuda, Pat, Pur. Agent--Royle Systems Group, Pompton Lakes, NJ, pg. 953
Head, Mickey, Dir.-Pur.--Southern Frozen Foods, Montezuma, GA, pg. 26
Head, Richard, Dir.-Pur.--Cummings Inc., Nashville, TN, pg. 304
Hearns, Chuck, Mgr.-Pur.--Capital Electric Group, Inc., Phoenix, AZ, pg. 215
Heath, Robert, Pur. Agent--Ford Meter Box Company, Wabash, IN, pg. 423
Hebert, Patrick, Pur. Agent--American Plastic Toys Inc., Walled Lake, MI, pg. 59
Heiman, Mark, Exec. V.P.--Standard Textile Co., Inc., Cincinnati, OH, pg. 1037
Heinig, Kirk, Pur. Agent--Richardson Brothers Co., Sheboygan Falls, WI, pg. 932
Heinrich, Les, Mgr.-Pur.--McNeil & NRM., Inc., Akron, OH, pg. 732
Heinz, William, Pur. Agent & Plant Mgr.--Charles Jacquin et Cie, Inc., Philadelphia, PA, pg. 588
Helal, E., Dir.-Pur.--Abbott Laboratories/Ashland, Ashland, OH, pg. 9
Helbley, W.C., Dir.-Pur.--Thomas Steel Strip Corp., Warren, OH, pg. 1094
Heller, Cyrus, V.P.-Pur.--Marquette Coppersmithing Co., Inc., Philadelphia, PA, pg. 713
Helnes, Bill, Mgr.-Pur.--Pneumafil Corp., Charlotte, NC, pg. 878
Hemminger, Al, Mgr.-Pur.--Hausted, Medina, OH, pg. 1008
Henderson, S.H., Dir.-Pur.--J.M. Huber, Clay Div., Macon, GA, pg. 550
Henderson, William, Dir.-Pur.--Kingsbury Corporation, Keene, NH, pg. 631
Hendler, D., Grp. V.P.-Distr.--Leviton Mfg. Co., Inc., Little Neck, NY, pg. 671
Henrioet, Sharon, Pur. Agent--Aunt Nellie's Farm Kitchens, Inc., Clyman, WI, pg. 98
Henry, Bill W., V.P.-Raw Matls. Pur.--Avondale Mills, Inc., Sylacauga, AL, pg. 103
Hensley, Herman, Sr. V.P.-Distr.--Certified Grocers Of California, Los Angeles, CA, pg. 237
Hepner, S., Pur. Agent--Bruning Paint Company, Baltimore, MD, pg. 184
Hermann, Norman, Pur. Mgr.--Andis Company, Racine, WI, pg. 74
Herold, Lad, Mgr.-Pur.--H.B. Zachry, San Antonio, TX, pg. 1215
Herr, D.R., Dir.-Pur.--Nooter Corporation, Saint Louis, MO, pg. 808
Herrenbruck, Ronald, Dir.-Pur. & Terminal Services--Atlas Van Lines, Inc., Evansville, IN, pg. 96
Herrenbruck, Stanley, Dir.-Pur.--Medicalodges, Inc., Coffeyville, KS, pg. 520
Hertzog, Mark, Dir.-Pur.--American Welding & Manufacturing Co., Warren, OH, pg. 65
Hesbon, Bruce, Pur. Agent--Everfresh Beverages Inc., Franklin Park, IL, pg. 391
Hesmond, Thomas, Dir.-Pur.--National Engineering & Contracting Co., Strongsville, OH, pg. 788
Hess, Don, Pur. Agent--Rutt Custom Cabinetry, Goodville, PA, pg. 957
Hess, Donald F., V.P.-Pur.--Hillerich & Bradsby Co., Inc., Louisville, KY, pg. 535
Hetzman, Steve, Dir.-Pur.--Duro-Last Roofing, Inc., Saginaw, MI, pg. 355
Heubel, Lucia, Dir.-Pur.--Magnetic Analysis Corp., Mount Vernon, NY, pg. 700
Heveran, James L., Mgr.-Pur.--Gerrard and Company, Des Plaines, IL, pg. 454
Hibrant, Richard, Pur. Agent--Williams, White & Company, Moline, IL, pg. 1191
Hickerson, Noble, Jr., Mgr.-Pur.--Laboratory Supply Company, Inc., Louisville, KY, pg. 649
Hicks, Ralph, Mgr.-Pur. & Inventory--Time Systems, Inc., Phoenix, AZ, pg. 1097
Higdon, Lawrence, V.P.-Pur.--Morgan Foods, Inc., Austin, IN, pg. 770
Hilbrant, Richard, Pur. Agent--Williams-White & Co., Moline, IL, pg. 1191
Hildebrand, Ron, Dir.-Pur. Hotels--Crown American Hotel Division, Johnstown, PA, pg. 302
Hill, Jim, Dir.-Pur.--Key Cadillac, Inc., Edina, MN, pg. 626
Hill, Robert, Purchasing Dir.--National Beef Packing Company, Liberal, KS, pg. 1128
Hiller, Judy, Buyer--McLaughlin Mfg. Company, Greenville, SC, pg. 731
Himpelmann, Joel, Mgr.-Pur.--Beech Holdings Corp., Chicago, IL, pg. 131
Hineman, James, Dir.-Pur.--Tri-City Electrical Contractors Inc., Altamonte Springs, FL, pg. 1110
Hines, Robert, Dir.-Pur.--Academy Insurance Group, Inc., Atlanta, GA, pg. 11
Hirsch, Jamie, V.P.-Mfg. & Pur.--Structural Industries, Inc., Hicksville, NY, pg. 1054
Hitch, Ronnie E., Div. Mgr.-Pur.--Nebraska Public Power District, Columbus, NE, pg. 796
Ho, Steven, Pur. Agent--VSI Fasteners, Inc., Stanton, CA, pg. 1142
Hodes, Jim, Mgr.-Pur.--Fairbanks Morse Pump Corporaton, Kansas City, KS, pg. 397
Hodges, Robert, Pur. Dir.--Sommer Metalcraft Corporation, Crawfordsville, IN, pg. 1018
Hodges, Robert, Pur. Dir.--Crown Products Co., Crawfordsville, IN, pg. 1018
Hoedeman, K. A., Dir.-Purchasing--Nutech, Inc., San Jose, CA, pg. 817
Hoffman, Bob, Dir.-Pur.--Netzsch, Inc., Exton, PA, pg. 798
Hoffman, James, Dir.-Pur.--Hubbard Milling Company, Mankato, MN, pg. 549
Hoffman, Paul, Mgr.-Matls.--John S. Barnes Corp., Rockford, IL, pg. 120
Hoffman, R.J., Mgr.-Pur.--Seagrave Fire Apparatus, Inc., Clintonville, WI, pg. 395
Hoffman, Robert, Mgr.-Pur.--FWD Corporation, Clintonville, WI, pg. 395
Hoffman, S., Pur. Agent--American Crane & Equipment Corp., Douglassville, PA, pg. 51
Hogan, Kevin, V.P.-Corp. Pur.--Montgomery Elevator Company, Moline, IL, pg. 767
Holden, John, Mgr.-Pur. & Adv.--Northland Container Corp., Plymouth, MI, pg. 814
Holland, Harry, Pur. Agent--Xerxes Corporation, Minneapolis, MN, pg. 1206
Holland, Steve, Dir.-Pur., Stair Parts--Thomas R. Hopson Broker, Inc., Marietta, GA, pg. 544
Holman, John, Mgr.-Matls.--Spangler Candy Company, Bryan, OH, pg. 1025
Holmes, Roland, Pur. Agent--Metalloy Corporation, Hudson, MI, pg. 742
Holt, Billy, Pur. Agent--Carroll's Foods, Inc., Warsaw, NC, pg. 225
Holtman, Danny S., Pur. Agent--Hirschfeld Steel Company, Inc., San Angelo, TX, pg. 536
Holzapfel, Nolan, Dir.-Pur.--Jabil Circuit Inc., Saint Petersburg, FL, pg. 587
Hoover, David J., Mgr.-Pur.--Union Pump Company, Battle Creek, MI, pg. 1128
Hopkins, James, V.P.-Pur.--Southern Electric Supply Co., Inc., Meridian, MS, pg. 1020
Hopper, Charles, V.P.-Pur.--Macklanburg-Duncan Co., Oklahoma City, OK, pg. 697
Hopper, Chuck, Dir.-Pur.--Macklanburg-Duncan Co., Oklahoma City, OK, pg. 697
Hopper, Frank, Asst. Dir.-Procurement--NJ Transit, Newark, NJ, pg. 801
Horan, Sean, V.P.-Pur.--Aster Nut Products Inc., Newark, NJ, pg. 92
Horensky, Tom, Mgr.-Pur.--Steelite, Inc., Pittsburgh, PA, pg. 1044
Horsfall, Jana, Mgr.-Pur.--Sunflower Electric Power Corporation, Hays, KS, pg. 1060
Horsman, Thomas H., V.P.-Pur. & Inventory Mngmt.--Williams & Company, Inc., Pittsburgh, PA, pg. 230
Horwich, David G., Mgr.-Pur.--Independent Metals, Germantown, WI, pg. 565
Hoskins, Kelly, V.P.-Pur.--California Hardware Co., City of Industry, CA, pg. 209
Housey, Daniel H., V.P. & Dir.-Pur.--Orleans Materials & Equipment Co., Inc., New Orleans, LA, pg. 829
Howard, Lisa, Dir.-Pur.--The Levy Organization, Chicago, IL, pg. 672
Howe, Linda, Pur. Agent--Roffe, Inc., Seattle, WA, pg. 943
Howell, John, Mgr. Pur.--Electrical Insulation Suppliers, Hillside, IL, pg. 374
Huck, Gary J., Dir.-Materials--Crenlo, Inc., Rochester, MN, pg. 298
Hudgins, Angie, Pur. Agent-Raw. Matls.--W. M. Barr & Co., Inc., Memphis, TN, pg. 121
Hudson, Sandy, Dir.-Pur.--VASA Insurance Group, Inc., Indianapolis, IN, pg. 1146
Huff, Robert J., Gen. Mgr.-Pur.--Steelox Systems, Inc., Mason, OH, pg. 1044
Huffman, H., Mgr.-Matls.--American Welding & Manufacturing Co., Warren, OH, pg. 431
Huffman, Wes, Pur. Agent--Lee Grocery Company, Everett, WA, pg. 665
Hughes, J., Dir.-Pur.--Guest Services, Inc., Fairfax, VA, pg. 493
Hughes, Jim, Pur. Agent--Arkansas Electric Cooperatives Inc., Little Rock, AR, pg. 83
Hughs, Bill, Dir.-Pur.--Troy Corporation, East Hanover, NJ, pg. 1116
Hulings, Henry B., Pur. Agent--McCourt Label Co., Lewis Run, PA, pg. 727
Hull, Frank, Dir.-Pur.--BE & K, Inc., Birmingham, AL, pg. 106
Hummerding, Richard, Mgr.-Pur.--National Machinery Company, Tiffin, OH, pg. 792
Humphries, R.A., Buyer-Raw Matls.--American Welding & Manufacturing Co., Warren, OH, pg. 431
Hunter, Harold, Dir.-Pur.--Cheraw Yarn Mills, Inc., Cheraw, SC, pg. 242
Hurst, Louis, Mgr.-Pur.--Universal Dynamics Inc., Woodbridge, VA, pg. 1138
Hurst, Louis, Mgr.-Pur.--Universal Dynamics, Inc., Woodbridge, VA, pg. 1138
Hurt, J., Dir.-Pur.--Hercules Tire & Rubber Company, Findlay, OH, pg. 531
Huschke, Wolfram, Dir.-Purchasing--Zappa Plastics, Phillipsburg, NJ, pg. 1216
Husk, Doc, Dir.-Pur.--Precision Parts Corp., Morristown, TN, pg. 885
Husk, Jim, V.P.-Pur.--Al Copeland Enterprises, Inc., Jefferson, LA, pg. 283
Husk, Jim, V.P.-Pur.--Church's Fried Chicken, Inc., Jefferson, LA, pg. 284
Hutchinson, Milt, Dir.-Pur.--Modern Equipment Rentals Inc., Wilmington, DE, pg. 763
Hutchinson, R., Dir.-Contracts & Pur.--Applied Solar Energy Corporation, City of Industry, CA, pg. 79
Hutslar, Joe, Pur. Agent-Supplies--Paoli, Inc., Paoli, IN, pg. 846
Hutton, Nancy, Sec., Treas. & Controller--Crustbuster, Inc., Dodge City, KS, pg. 303
Ibach, Thomas, Pur. Agent--Western States Envelope Co., Butler, WI, pg. 1181
Ibraham, Nestor, Dir.-Pur.--Stainless Incorporated, Deerfield Beach, FL, pg. 1035
Ignasiak, Gordon K., Mgr.-Pur.--Rapid Engineering Inc., Comstock Park, MI, pg. 913
Ihrake, Steve, Dir.-Pur.--Krier Foods, Inc., Brown Deer, WI, pg. 645
Imel, Cindy,, Mgr.-Pur.--Caddock Electronics, Inc., Riverside, CA, pg. 207
Ingle, Herston, Dir.-Pur.--Affiliated Foods Southwest, Little Rock, AR, pg. 24
Ingleby, Eva Marie, Pur. Agent-Rocky Mountain--Rocky Mountain Mechanical, Inc., Salt Lake City, UT, pg. 942
Iorio, Robert, V.P.-Pur.--Gibbs Wire & Steel Company, Inc., Southington, CT, pg. 456
Iozzo, Virginia, Dir.-Pur.--Sigmund Cohn Corp., Mount Vernon, NY, pg. 259
Irish, Steve, Dir.-Pur.--Capital Industries, Inc., Seattle, WA, pg. 215
Irizarry, Henry, Dir.-Pur.--Hinkley Lighting Inc., Cleveland, OH, pg. 535
Isacsson, Paul, Exec. V.P., Dir. Brdcst. Programming & Pur.--Young & Rubicam New York, New York, NY, pg. 1211
Isenberg, Gary, Pur. Agent--Larson Manufacturing Company, Brookings, SD, pg. 659
Jackson, Riley, V.P.-Mktg., Pur. & Adv.--Federal Savings Bank, Fort Smith, AR, pg. 1194
Jackson, Sandy, Pur. Agent-Equipment--SGD International Corp., New York, NY, pg. 962
Jacobs, Barbara, Mgr.-Pur.--Dean Operations Inc., Kansas City, MO, pg. 322
Jacobs, Eli, Dir.-Pur.--Nuarc Company, Inc., Niles, IL, pg. 817
Jacobusse, David, V.P.-Purchasing--Sonneveldt Company, Grand Rapids, MI, pg. 1018
Jaffe, Gerald, Dir.-Matls. Mngmt.--Velsicol Chemical Corporation, Rosemont, IL, pg. 1147
James, Warren, Pur. Mgr.--Cramer Company, Old Saybrook, CT, pg. 296
Jancewicz, Frank, Pur. Agent--The Meyercord Company, Carol Stream, IL, pg. 746
Janego, William, Dir.-Pur.--Mitchell Corporation of Owosso, Owosso, MI, pg. 761
Jansen, J.K., Pur. Dir.--Electric Power Equipment Co., Columbus, OH, pg. 373
Jarmen, Donald, Dir.-Pur.--World's Finest Chocolate Australia Pty. Ltd., Stanmore,, Australia, pg. 1203
Jarnigan, Don, Pur. Agent--JFG Coffee Company, Knoxville, TN, pg. 923
Jaus, Lothar, Pur. Dir.--Thoroughbred RD-COM GmbH, Herrenberg,, Germany, pg. 1095
Jenkins, Charles, Mgr.-Pur.--Talon, Inc., Meadville, PA, pg. 1077
Jenkins, Mary, Sec. & Treas.--Coral Petroleum Corporation, Houston, TX, pg. 285
Jensen, Jack, Dir.-Pur.--Lawson Mechanical Contractors, Sacramento, CA, pg. 663
Jensen, Peggy, Dir.-Pur.--American Antenna Corp, Elgin, IL, pg. 216
Jensen, Robert, V.P.-Human Resources & Pur.--Shape Inc., Biddeford, ME, pg. 995
Jepsen, Edward, Exec. V.P. & Chief Fin. Officer--Times Fiber Communications, Inc., Wallingford, CT, pg. 648
Jerin, J, Pur. Agent--Laubeck Corporation/Cross, Carbondale, PA, pg. 660
Jerred, Maryann, Pur. Mgr.--Waldbillig & Besteman, Inc., Madison, WI, pg. 1159
Jessup, John A., V.P.-Matls. Mngmt. & Contract Services--Trans World Airlines, Inc., Mount Kisco, NY, pg. 561
Johnson, Charles, V.P.-Pur.--Indian Head Industries Inc., Southfield, MI, pg. 565
Johnson, Claudie, Mgr.-Matls.--Sunbeam Home Comfort, Shubuta, MS, pg. 1059

Johnson, D., Pur. Mgr.--Bryant Grinder Corp., Springfield, VT, pg. 468
Johnson, Darrel, Mgr.-Pur.--Olympic Steel Inc., Bedford Heights, OH, pg. 825
Johnson, David, Dir.-Pur. & Telecommunications--Heery International, Inc., Atlanta, GA, pg. 525
Johnson, David, Dir.-Pur.--Restaurants Unlimited, Seattle, WA, pg. 929
Johnson, Don, Pur. Dir.--Sloan Technology, Santa Barbara, CA, pg. 1146
Johnson, George, Dir.-Pur.--Long MFG. NC, Inc., Tarboro, NC, pg. 682
Johnson, George, Dir.-Pur.--Long Equipment Co., Tarboro, NC, pg. 682
Johnson, George, Mgr.-Pur.--Marotta Scientific Controls, Inc., Montville, NJ, pg. 713
Johnson, Greg, Mgr.-Pur.--Steinbach, White Plains, NY, pg. 1045
Johnson, Jerry, Dir.-Pur.--C.B. Fleet Company, Incorporated, Lynchburg, VA, pg. 417
Johnson, Junior, Pur. Agent--American Fast Print, Limited, Spartanburg, SC, pg. 52
Johnson, Lee R., Chief Fin. Officer--Gator Freightways, Inc., Wilmington, OH, pg. 446
Johnson, Ron, V.P.-Procurement--Chief Industries, Inc., Grand Island, NE, pg. 247
Johnson, Sue, Mgr.-Pur.--Agripac Inc., Salem, OR, pg. 25
Johnston, Jim, Mgr.-Pur.--Morse Shoe, Inc., Canton, MA, pg. 772
Johnston, Jim, V.P.-Pur.--Fred B. Johnston Company, Inc., Chapin, SC, pg. 601
Johnstone, Glen, Dir.-Pur.--United States Ceramic Tile Co., East Sparta, OH, pg. 1135
Jones, Bob, Pur. Agent--Neapco, Inc., Pottstown, PA, pg. 1123
Jones, Bruce, Pur. Dir.--The Berkline Corporation, Morristown, TN, pg. 285
Jones, Don, Dir.-Pur.--Malloy Lithographing Inc., Ann Arbor, MI, pg. 703
Jones, F.T., Dir.-Pur.--Ebco Mfg. Company, Columbus, OH, pg. 365
Jones, Glen, Buyer--General Refractories Co., U. S. Refractories Div., Pittsburgh, PA, pg. 136
Jones, Glenda, Pur. Agent--American Manufacturing Company, Inc. (LA), Lafayette, LA, pg. 58
Jones, Harry, Mgr.-Pur.--Printing House, Inc., Quincy, FL, pg. 891
Jones, Jo Ann, Pur. Mgr.--RTW, Rogers Tool Works, Inc., Rogers, AR, pg. 908
Jones, Ken, V.P.-Pur. & Matls. Control--Columbus Show Case Company, Columbus, OH, pg. 267
Jones, Linda, Sec. & Sr. Buyer--Cumberland-Swan, Inc., Smyrna, TN, pg. 304
Jones, Robbie, Mgr.-Pur.--Memphis Publishing Company, Memphis, TN, pg. 738
Jordan, Diane, Pur. Dir.--Union-Tribune Publishing Company, San Diego, CA, pg. 284
Jorgensen, Robert, Pur. Agent--Pemco Die Casting Corporation, Bridgman, MI, pg. 856
Jouza, Rick, Dir.-Personnel & Pur. Agent--Just Pants, Chicago, IL, pg. 610
Joyce, Gerald P., Mgr.-Pur.--Sunroc Corporation, Media, PA, pg. 1062
Joyce, Jerry, Pur. Agent--Telkee Inc., Media, PA, pg. 1062
Jozwiakowski, James, Dir.-Pur.--Clark Oil & Refining Corporation, Saint Louis, MO, pg. 252
Jubinville, Mike, Pur. Agent--Esco Corporation, Portland, OR, pg. 388
Judge, Frank, Sr. Buyer--American Welding & Manufacturing Co., Warren, OH, pg. 65
Kachur, J.M., Pur. Agent--The Hall China Company, East Liverpool, OH, pg. 501
Kagan, Jeff, Mgr.-Pur.--Vidicom, L.D. Bevan Company, Inc., Thousand Oaks, CA, pg. 1151
Kahrhoff, Paula, Dir.-Pur.--Siemer Milling Company, Teutopolis, IL, pg. 1002
Kaloyanides, Steve, Jr., Dir.-Pur.--New England Coffee Company, Malden, MA, pg. 800
Kamm, J.O., II, Dir.-Pur.--Electric Furnace Co., Salem, OH, pg. 373
Kanalley, Tom, Pur. Agent--Cortland Line Co., Inc., Cortland, NY, pg. 287
Kanelos, Art, Pur. Agent--Andes Candies, Inc., Delavan, WI, pg. 169
Kaplan, Dave, V.P.-Pur.--Magnolia Hi-Fi, Inc., Seattle, WA, pg. 701
Kaplan, J., Dir.-Pur. & Traffic--Good Companies, Carson, CA, pg. 470
Kaplan, Samuel, Pres., Chief Exec. Officer, Sec. & Dir.-Sls. & Pur.--Admiration Hosiery Mills, Inc., Charlotte, NC, pg. 534
Karger, Bruce, Pur. Agent--Louis Padnos Iron & Metal Co., Holland, MI, pg. 842
Kass, Guenter C., V.P.-Pur.--The Elder-Beerman Stores Corp., Dayton, OH, pg. 373
Kass, Guenter C., V.P.-Pur.--Elder-Beerman Stores Div., Dayton, OH, pg. 373
Kazarian, Charles, Dir.-Pur.--L&J Technologies, Morton Grove, IL, pg. 647
Keck,Jack, Dir.-Pur.--First Federal Savings and Loan Assn. of Rochester, Rochester, NY, pg. 413
Keddem, Ruth, Pur. Mgr.-Canton--Grindmaster Corporation, Louisville, KY, pg. 488
Kegler, Gary, Pur. Agent--Sealing Devices Inc., Lancaster, NY, pg. 984
Keith, Neil, Dir.-Pur.--FDL Foods, Inc., Dubuque, IA, pg. 394
Kellerman, Joan, Mgr.-Pur. & Contracts--Townsend & Bottum, Inc., Ann Arbor, MI, pg. 1104
Kelley, Davis, Pur. Agent--Taylor Machine Works, Inc., Louisville, MS, pg. 1081
Kells, R.L., V.P.-Pur.--Flexible Products Company, Marietta, GA, pg. 418
Kelly, Arnold, Dir.-Purchasing--Western Regional Off Track Betting, Batavia, NY, pg. 1181
Kelly, Gregory A., Pur. Agent--The F. D. Lawrence Electric Co., Cincinnati, OH, pg. 661
Kelly, Janet, Pur. Agent--Kirkwood Industries, Inc., Cleveland, OH, pg. 633
Kelly, Michael, Pur. Agent--Litecontrol Corporation, Hanson, MA, pg. 677
Kelly, Ray, Sr. Buyer--Leupold & Stevens, Inc., Beaverton, OR, pg. 669
Kelps, Charlotte, Mgr.-Pur.--G. Leblanc Corporation, Kenosha, WI, pg. 665
Kelsch, Mike, Dir.-Import--E & A Industries, Inc., Indianapolis, IN, pg. 358
Kelso, Earl F., Pur. Agent--Continental Forge Company, Compton, CA, pg. 279
Kemerer, Floyd L., Dir.-Pur.--Amtrak-National Railroad Passenger Corp., Washington, DC, pg. 69
Kempinsky, James, Mgr.-Pur.--Serfilco, Ltd., Northbrook, IL, pg. 990
Kendrick, Ralph, Pur. Dir.--Fibres--Carolina Mills, Inc., Maiden, NC, pg. 223
Kenney, James W., Mgr.-Pur.--Crown Holdings, Inc., Roseville, MN, pg. 302
Kenney, James W., III, Pur. Agent--Crown Iron Works Company, Roseville, MN, pg. 302
Kenyon, Kerry, Pur. Agent--Peterson Industries Inc., Decatur, AR, pg. 864
Kern, Mark E., V.P.-Pur.--Overland Transportation System, Inc., Indianapolis, IN, pg. 832
Kerper, David, Dir.-Pur.--Flavor House Products, Inc., Dothan, AL, pg. 417
Kerr, Rich, Dir.-Pur.--Ivex Packaging Corporation, Lincolnshire, IL, pg. 583
Kertesz, Lou, V.P.-Produce Mdsg. & Procurement--Pueblo International, Inc., Pompano Beach, FL, pg. 899
Kertz, Robert, Pur. Agent & Office Mgr.--Anton Smit & Co., Inc., Deer Park, NY, pg. 1011
Kessler, Frank, Pur. Agent--Carver Boat Corp., Pulaski, WI, pg. 758
Kettlewell, Jim, V.P.-Pur.--Nickles Bakery, Inc., Martins Ferry, OH, pg. 807
Kiang, Nai-Wen, Dir.-Pur.--Schwinn Bicycle Company, Chicago, IL, pg. 981
Kibiloski, John, Dir.-Pur.--Trendway Corporation, Holland, MI, pg. 1109
Kiggins, Joe, Pur. Agent--Mele Manufacturing Co., Inc., Utica, NY, pg. 737
Kilander, R., Dir.-Pur.--Great Lakes Dredge & Dock, Oak Brook, IL, pg. 481
Kilderbran, Sandy, Pur. Agent--Steffen Dairy Foods Co., Inc., Wichita, KS, pg. 884
King, F., Pur. Agent--Layne & Bowler, Memphis, TN, pg. 710
King, George, Pur. Agent--Presto Lock, Inc., Garfield, NJ, pg. 888
King, Kerrie, Dir.-Pur.--Cowden Metal Specialties, Inc., Chino, CA, pg. 291
King, Preston B., Dir.-Pur.--Trojan Steel Co., Charleston, WV, pg. 1115
King, Steve, Dir.-Pur.--Tyler Elevator Products, Inc., Valley View, OH, pg. 1122
Kinney, Charles, Dir.-Materials--JPM Company, Lewisburg, PA, pg. 586
Kintopf, Jim, Supvr.-Pur.--Marine Travelift, Inc., Sturgeon Bay, WI, pg. 707
Kintopf, Jim, Supvr.-Pur.--MTI Leasing, Ltd., Sturgeon Bay, WI, pg. 707
Kintopf, Jim, Supvr.-Pur.--Shuttlelift, Inc., Sturgeon Bay, WI, pg. 707
Kirby, Patrick T., V.P.-Pur.--Amsco School Publications, Inc., New York, NY, pg. 68
Kirk, Danny, Pur. Mgr.--Madison, Inc., Tulsa, OK, pg. 433
Kirk, Richard, Mgr.-Traffic & Pur. Agent--American Bread Company - Sunbeam Bakery, Nashville, TN, pg. 49
Kitterman, Paul, Pur. Agent--The Keller Manufacturing Co., Inc., Corydon, IN, pg. 621
Kittle, Ronald F., Mgr.-Pur.--Amstore Corporation, Muskegon, MI, pg. 69
Kitto, William, V.P.-Crude Oil Pur.--Time Oil Co., Los Angeles, CA, pg. 1097
Klaas, Kurt, Dir.-Pur.--Kampgrounds of America, Inc., Billings, MT, pg. 613
Klaassen, Marvin, Pur. Agent--Furman Foods, Inc., Northumberland, PA, pg. 436
Klehm, Marlin, Dir.-Pur.--Hagie Manufacturing Co., Clarion, IA, pg. 499
Klinger, Scott, Pur. Agent--J. H. France Refractories Co., Snow Shoe, PA, pg. 428
Kloese, Leroy, Pur. Agent--Kaspar Wire Works, Inc., Shiner, TX, pg. 617
Kloop, Edward, Dir.-Pur.--Dale Industries Inc., Dearborn, MI, pg. 312
Klotnia, Joseph, V.P.-Pur. & Transportation--Hobart Brothers Co., Troy, OH, pg. 536
Klutz, Kim, Mgr.-Pur.--Acorn Engineering Company, City of Industry, CA, pg. 14
Knaub, Hank, Mgr.-Pur.--Trak International, Inc., Port Washington, WI, pg. 1106
Knauer, R.T., Dir.-Pur.--Benjamin Moore & Co., Montvale, NJ, pg. 139
Knight, Paul, Dir.-Pur.--Pfaudler-U.S., Inc., Rochester, NY, pg. 866
Knipper, P.A., V.P.-Pur.--Hub Inc., Tucker, GA, pg. 548
Knowles, Janet, V.P.-Admin. & Dir.-Pur.--Metrologic Instruments, Inc., Blackwood, NJ, pg. 743
Kobold, Jerome J., Pur. Agent--Maze Nails, Peru, IL, pg. 725
Koch, J., Dir.-Pur.--S-T Industries, Inc., Saint James, MN, pg. 964
Koehle, William, Mgr.-Pur.--Plastek Group, Erie, PA, pg. 874
Koelle, David A., Dir.-Pur.--Boyer Bros. Inc., Altoona, PA, pg. 169
Koenig, Elmer, Pur. Agent--The United States Playing Card Company, Cincinnati, OH, pg. 1136
Koerber, Alan, V.P.-Pur.--Star Food Processing, Inc., San Antonio, TX, pg. 1039
Koger, Charles, V.P.-Pur.--AmTran Corporation, Conway, AR, pg. 69
Kohan, Regina, Dir.-Pur.--Weksler Instruments Corp., Freeport, NY, pg. 1174
Kohlmeier, Fred, Plant Mgr.--Sheldons' Inc., Antigo, WI, pg. 996
Kokinda, Wayne, Mgr.-Materials--Sentry Group, Rochester, NY, pg. 990
Kolo, Henry, Pur. Agent--Perfection Automotive Products Corporation, Livonia, MI, pg. 861
Kolp, Nancy, Dir.-Pur.--The National Latex Products Co., Ashland, OH, pg. 791
Kominsky, John, Pur. Dir.--Bloomfield Industries, Chicago, IL, pg. 1027
Koonce, Terry, Dir.-Pur.--Austin Co., Inc., Greeneville, TN, pg. 98
Koopman, Robert, Dir.-Mdse.--Health Care Distributors of Indiana, Inc., South Bend, IN, pg. 520
Koppemolle, Keith, Pur. & Supply Dir.--American Family Mutual Insurance Co., Madison, WI, pg. 51
Korst, Noni, Mgr.-Pur.--Ferrell Companies Inc./Ferrellgas, Liberty, MO, pg. 407
Kough, Gene, Dir.-Pur.--American Fluorescent Corporation, Waukegan, IL, pg. 54
Kowalkowski, Sonia, Pur. Agent--Microphase Corporation, Norwalk, CT, pg. 749
Kowalski, H., Pur. Agent--H. Koch & Sons, Anaheim, CA, pg. 262
Kowieski, Ronald, Dir.-Pur.--Farley Candy Company, Chicago, IL, pg. 399
Kozell, Joseph, Pur. Agent & Stock Mgr.--Rite-Way, Inc., Saddle Brook, NJ, pg. 936
Kraemer, R.J., Dir.-Pur.--United States Bronze Powders, Inc., Flemington, NJ, pg. 1134
Krahn, Gerald, Dir.-Pur.--Marvin Lumber & Cedar Company, Warroad, MN, pg. 716
Kralik, Patricia, Dir.-Pur.--George S. May International Company, Park Ridge, IL, pg. 723
Kramer, Walt, V.P. & Pur.-Paper--Duro Paper Bag Manufacturing Co., Ludlow, KY, pg. 355
Kramp, William, Buyer--Stock Yards Packing Co., Inc., Chicago, IL, pg. 1049
Krantzow, M., Opers. Mgr.--Bogue Electric Manufacturing Co., Paterson, NJ, pg. 162
Krause, B. Leonard, V.P.-Pur.--D. D. Bean & Sons Co., Jaffrey, NH, pg. 129
Kreitzberg, Michael, Pur. Agent--Microflect Company, Inc., Salem, OR, pg. 749
Krell, Larry, Pur. Agent--Marcus Brothers Textiles, Inc., New York, NY, pg. 706
Kremer, Jerry, Pur. Mgr.--Michigan Bulb Company, Grand Rapids, MI, pg. 638
Kretsch, Clayton, Buyer--Sanborn Manufacturing Company, Springfield, MN, pg. 969
Kretsch, Lynn, Dir.-Pur.--A. L. Hansen Mfg. Co., Waukegan, IL, pg. 506
Kringen, Stu, Dir.-Sls. & Purch.--Bongards Creameries Inc., Norwood, MN, pg. 164
Kripal, Josef, V.P. & Dir.-Pur.--Reinke Manufacturing Co., Inc., Deshler, NE, pg. 924
Kroening, H.A., Dir.-Pur.--Helwig Carbon Products, Inc., Milwaukee, WI, pg. 528
Kroll, Gary, Dir.-Purch.--F & B Manufacturing Co., Chicago, IL, pg. 393
Kroll, Gary, V.P.-Pur.--Filko/Cobra, Inc., Chicago, IL, pg. 393
Kropfl, Richard, Pur. Dir.--Puritan/Churchill Chemical Company, Atlanta, GA, pg. 900
Krough, Marty, Dir-Pur--WEN Products, Inc., Chicago, IL, pg. 1156
Krzykowski, Kenneth, Dir.-Pur.--Wrought Washer Mfg., Inc., Milwaukee, WI, pg. 1205
Kubacka, Rick, Dir.-Pur.--Paradata Computer Networks, Inc., Farmington Hills, MI, pg. 847
Kucharik, D., Pur. Agent--American Inks & Coatings Corp., Valley Forge, PA, pg. 56
Kuchler, Louis, V.P.-Pur.--Angelo Brothers Co., Philadelphia, PA, pg. 74
Kufahl, Jerry, Pur. Dir.--Morning Glory Farms Region, Shawano, WI, pg. 770
Kuhne, Wayne F., Pur. Agent--Atlanta Wire Works, Inc., Jonesboro, GA, pg. 94
Kulakosky, Eugene B., Sr. V.P.-Grocery & Non-Food Buying--Victory Markets Inc., Norwich, NY, pg. 1150
Kumar, Atill, Dir.-Pur.--The Beverly Hills Hotel, Beverly Hills, CA, pg. 148
Kusche, Jeffrey, Dir.-Pur.--Rich Products Corp., Buffalo, NY, pg. 932
Kuse, Jon, V.P.-Matls. Mngmt.--Penda Corporation, Portage, WI, pg. 857
Kuykendall, S., Mgr.-Pur.--Pacific Enterprises Oil Company (USA), Dallas, TX, pg. 840
Kuyper, Dale, Dir.-Pur.--Wenger Corporation, Owatonna, MN, pg. 1176
Kvidera, John, Dir.-Pur.--Kurt Manufacturing Co. Inc., Fridley, MN, pg. 646
Kwiatek, Joe, Dir.-Pur.--First American Metro Corp., McLean, VA, pg. 412
Kwiatkowski, Donald, Mgr.-Pur.--Scipar, Buffalo, NY, pg. 982
Kwizema, Everett, Pur. Agent--Dickinson Press, Inc., Grand Rapids, MI, pg. 336
Kyle, Dick, Pur. Agent--Plasti-Kote Company Inc., Medina, OH, pg. 875
L'Heureux, Gilbert N., Pur. Agent--Wasco Products, Inc., Sanford, ME, pg. 1165
Laber, Richard, Dir.-Pur.--Flint Ink Corp., Detroit, MI, pg. 419
Laflame, David, Mgr.-Pur.--Keeney Manufacturing Co., Newington, CT, pg. 620
LaGore, Janet, Dir.-Pur.--Intex Chemical Inc., Greer, SC, pg. 581

LaGrega, Andrew T., Sr. V.P.-Sls., Mktg., Adv. & Human Resources--Wilder Management Associates, Waltham, MA, pg. 1189
Laird, Vern, Pur. Dir.--Larkin, Inc., Atlanta, GA, pg. 667
Laird, Vern, Pur. Dir.--Heatcraft, Inc., Stone Mountain, GA, pg. 667
Lamb, Tom, Dir.-Materials Mngmt.--Binning's Building Products, Inc., Lexington, NC, pg. 151
Lambert, J.D., Mgr.-Pur.--Wells Manufacturing Company, Verdi, NV, pg. 1027
Lampert, Joseph E., Dir.-Pur. & Mgr. Gen. Services--Boston Mutual Life Insurance Co., Canton, MA, pg. 167
Lamuth, Carolyn, Mgr.-Admin. Services, Pur. & Dir.-Telecommunications--Ministers Life Insurance Company, Minneapolis, MN, pg. 757
Lanard, Tom, Pur. Agent--Univex Corporation, Salem, NH, pg. 1139
Lancaster, Stan, Dir.-Pur.--Colonial Oil Industries, Savannah, GA, pg. 263
Landry, W., Pur. Agent--Jonathan Manufacturing Corp., Fullerton, CA, pg. 602
Landsfra, Steven W., Dir.-Pur.--Monsey Products Company, Kimberton, PA, pg. 766
Landwehr, Joseph, Dir.-Pur.--Walk, Haydel & Associates, Inc., New Orleans, LA, pg. 1159
Lane, Calvin, Mgr.-Pur.--McKay Chemical Co., Los Angeles, CA, pg. 159
Lane, Homer, Pur. Agent--Enco Materials, Inc., Nashville, TN, pg. 380
Lane, William, Pur. Agent--West Point-Pepperell, Inc., West Point, GA, pg. 400
Lane, William A., Gen. Pur. Agent--Home Fashions Div., New York, NY, pg. 400
Lane, William A., Gen. Pur. Agent--Custom Fabrics Div., West Point, GA, pg. 400
Lang, Ernest, Ass't. V.P.-Pur.--Wasserstrom Company, Columbus, OH, pg. 1167
Lang, William, V.P. & Buyer--Homemaker Shops, Inc., Southfield, MI, pg. 542
Langdon, Stanley, Dir.-Pur.--J. Austin Oil Co., Flint, MI, pg. 99
Langston, Dudley I., Dir.-Pur., Personnel, Fin. & Sec.--Langston Companies, Memphis, TN, pg. 657
Lanier, Donald S., V.P.-Pur.--Bryant Supply Company, Inc., Gastonia, NC, pg. 185
Lankargo, John, Mgr.-Pur.--The Pro Corporation, Florence, MA, pg. 891
Lanman, K.W., Mgr.-Pur.--Colonial Pipeline Company, Atlanta, GA, pg. 264
Lantz, Frank, Pur. Agent--Ruhl Companies, Inc., Valhalla, NY, pg. 955
Lapin, Gene, Dir.-Pur.--Clayton Corporation, Fenton, MO, pg. 253
Larson, Brian K., Mgr.-Pur.--American Learning Corp., Chicago, IL, pg. 381
Lassman, Phil, Mgr.-Pur.--Wallace Leisure Products, Inc., Philadelphia, PA, pg. 1160
Laub, David, Mgr.-Pur.--NESLAB Instruments, Inc., Newington, NH, pg. 798
Lauer, David, Dir.-Purchasing--Inland Associates, Inc., Olathe, KS, pg. 570
Lavery, Brian K., Controller--Geo-Centers, Inc., Newton Center, MA, pg. 452
Lavin, Joseph, Pur. Agent--Anderson Products, Worcester, MA, pg. 1194
Lawenda, James, Assoc. Dir., Media Pur.--Schering-Plough Healthcare Products Advertising Corp., Liberty Corner, NJ, pg. 976
Lawrence, Charles, Dir.-Pur.--Sauder Woodworking Co., Archbold, OH, pg. 972
Lawrence, Morgan, Mgr.-Pur.--Chemifax, City of Commerce, CA, pg. 159
Lazerow, David, Pur. Agent--Southwark Metal Manufacturing Company, Philadelphia, PA, pg. 1023
Lazev, Ben, Dir.-Pur.--Yardney Technical Products, Inc., Pawcatuck, CT, pg. 1207
Lear, William A., Pur. Agent--Champion Laboratories, Inc., Albion, IL, pg. 1123
Lease, Jim, Mgr.-Pur.--Universal Molding Company, Lynwood, CA, pg. 1139
Leatherman, Bill, Pur. Agent--Mannington Ceramic Tile, Lexington, NC, pg. 704
Leckie, Bruce, Mgr.-Pur.--Schumacher Electric Corporation, Chicago, IL, pg. 979
Lee, George, Pur. Agent--Hollymatic Corporation, Countryside, IL, pg. 539
Lee, Gregg, Dir.-Import & Pur.--Carolina Biological Supply Co., Burlington, NC, pg. 222
Lee, Linda, Pur. Agent--Mallory, Inc., Carson City, NV, pg. 703
Lehman, Dean, Pur. Agent--Northwest Pipe Fittings, Inc., Billings, MT, pg. 815
Lein, Shane, Mgr.-Pur. & Materials--Penrod Drilling Corporation, Dallas, TX, pg. 859
Leiser, W.J., V.P.-Procurement & Intl. Opers.--Wells Lamont, Niles, IL, pg. 712
Lekram, Frank, Dir.-Pur.--Everlast Sports Manufacturing Corp., Bronx, NY, pg. 392
Lemberg, David C., Mgr.-Pur.--Formac Corporation, Minneapolis, MN, pg. 424
Leon, Paula, Pur. Agent--Amerisure Companies, Detroit, MI, pg. 66
Leonard, John, Pur. Agent--Red Devil Inc., Union, NJ, pg. 918
Leppla, Michael, Mgr.-Computer Information Systems--Austin Powder Co., Cleveland, OH, pg. 99
Lerch, Howard D., Jr., V.P.--Mazo Lerch Company, Inc., Alexandria, VA, pg. 725
Lesage, Roy, Mgr.-Pur.--Electro Fiberoptics Corporation, Northborough, MA, pg. 374
Leskin, Ralph, Dir.-Pur.--Miken Companies, Inc., Cheektowaga, NY, pg. 752
Levicoff, Louis, Pur. Agent--Pearl-Pressman-Liberty Communications Group, Philadelphia, PA, pg. 853
Levine, Melvin, V.P.-Pur.--Wallace International Silversmiths, Inc., East Boston, MA, pg. 1070
Levine, Melvin L., Dir.-Pur.--Syratech Corporation, East Boston, MA, pg. 1070
Lewandowski, R., Dir.-Pur.--Broad Vogt & Conant Inc., River Rouge, MI, pg. 177
Lewis, Janice, Dir.-Pur.--Butterick Company, Inc., New York, NY, pg. 197
Lewis, Kenneth R., Treas. & Mgr.-Bus.--RTMX-Uniflex Inc., Chapel Hill, NC, pg. 908
Lewis, Mary, Mgr.-Pur.--Candle Corporation, Santa Monica, CA, pg. 214
Lewis, Ron, Dir.-Pur.--Hyplains Dressed Beef, Inc., Dodge City, KS, pg. 557
Libengood, Harry H., Jr., Pur. Agent--Roessing Bronze Co., Mars, PA, pg. 943
Liddy, T A. III, Pur. Agent--Lubriplate Div. of Fiske Bros. Refining Co., Newark, NJ, pg. 416
Liggett, William, Dir.-Pur.--Philadelphia Gear Corp., King of Prussia, PA, pg. 866
Lilley, Marvin, V.P.-Matls.--Marathon Electric Manufacturing Corp., Wausau, WI, pg. 705
Lim, T., Pur. Agent--Santa Rosa Steel Forming, Inc., Santa Rosa, CA, pg. 970
Linakis, John S., Sr. V.P.-Transporation & Pur.--American Institute For Foreign Study, Greenwich, CT, pg. 56
Linakis, John S., Sr. V.P.-Transportation & Pur.--American Institute for Foreign Study, London, United Kingdom, pg. 56
Lind, William, Mgr.-Produce--Affiliated Foods Southwest, Little Rock, AR, pg. 24
Lindenauer, Abraham, V.P.-Matls. Mngmt.--International Specialty Products, Inc., Wilmington, DE, pg. 438
Linser, Marge, Mgr.-Pur.--Kennedy Manufacturing Company, Van Wert, OH, pg. 623
Linskens, Sherry, Mgr.-Matls.--Wohlert Corp., Lansing, MI, pg. 1198
Lipes, R., Mgr.-Pur.--Groendyk Mfg. Co., Inc., Buchanan, VA, pg. 480
Lippetti, Aldo, V.P.-Pur.--Silver State Disposal Service, Inc., Las Vegas, NV, pg. 1004
Lippincott, Frank, Mgr.-Pur.--Bachmann Industries, Inc., Philadelphia, PA, pg. 108
Lipscomb, Samuel, V.P.-Milk Procurement--Broughton Foods Company, Marietta, OH, pg. 180
Lira, Teri, Dir.-Pur.--Brush Research Manufacturing Company, Los Angeles, CA, pg. 184
Lisa, V.J., Pur. Dir.--Rubatex Corporation, Bedford, VA, pg. 480
Lisker, Harvey, V.P.-Pur.--Antwerp Diamond Distributors Inc., New York, NY, pg. 77
Littfin, Jack, Mgr.-Mktg. & Pur.--Littfin Lumber Company, Winsted, MN, pg. 678
Loe, Tim, Pur. Agent--Mico Inc., North Mankato, MN, pg. 748
Loeffler, Curt, Pur. Agent--Nasco, Fort Atkinson, WI, pg. 452
Lofgren, Paul, Buyer--The Bartell Drug Company, Seattle, WA, pg. 122
Logghe, John, Pur. Agent--Logghe Stamping Company, Fraser, MI, pg. 681
Lohman, Charles J., Sr. V.P.-Pur.--Louisville Bedding Company, Louisville, KY, pg. 684
Lohr, Kathi, Dir.-Pur.--Newage Industries Inc., Testing Instruments Division, Willow Grove, PA, pg. 803
Lombardi, Robert, Pur. Agent--Alloy Products Corporation, Waukesha, WI, pg. 41
Long, Frederick, Dir.-Pur.--Pridgeon & Clay, Inc., Grand Rapids, MI, pg. 889
Long, Sam, Mgr.-Pur.--Madison Industries Inc. of Arizona, Phoenix, AZ, pg. 433
Loose, Charles, Pur. Agent--Welsh Company, Saint Louis, MO, pg. 1175
Loprest, Jay, Asst. V.P.-Mfg. & Purchasing--Naz-Dar Company, Chicago, IL, pg. 1095
Lorch, Frank, Dir.-Non-Resale Pur.--Golub Corporation, Schenectady, NY, pg. 469
Lorenzo, Bart, Pur. Agent--M. A. Bruder & Sons, Inc., Broomall, PA, pg. 184
Lovejoy, Joan, Mgr.-Pur.--Action Instruments, Inc., San Diego, CA, pg. 14
Lovely, James B., Mgr.-Pur.--Allied Chucker & Engineering Company, Jackson, MI, pg. 37
Lowder, Dewey, Dir.-Pur.--Pic'n Pay Stores, Inc., Charlotte, NC, pg. 201
Lowe, Art, Pur. Agent--Spectronics Corporation, Westbury, NY, pg. 1029
Lowe, Phyllis, Dir.-Pur.--Schuff Steel Co., Phoenix, AZ, pg. 979
Lowell, Roger, V.P.-Pur.--Hussey Seating Company, North Berwick, ME, pg. 555
Luber, Jack, Sr. V.P.-Purch.--Murry's, Inc., Forestville, MD, pg. 777
Lucia, Dwight, Dir.-Pur.--Field Container Company, L.P., Elk Grove Village, IL, pg. 409
Ludlow, Eric, Dir.-Pur.--Pavion Ltd., Nyack on Hudson, NY, pg. 852
Luke, Al W., V.P.-Systems Supply--ASC Incorporated, Southgate, MI, pg. 7
Luke, Joseph C., V.P.-Construction Materials--Gate Petroleum Company, Jacksonville, FL, pg. 445
Lukes, Brett J., Mgr.-Materials--Vidicom, L.D. Bevan Company, Inc., Thousand Oaks, CA, pg. 1151
Luppachino, Dominick, Pur. Agent--Alpha Q, Inc., Colchester, CT, pg. 5
Luppino, J.E., Dir.-Pur.--J.M. Huber, Chemicals Division, Havre de Grace, MD, pg. 550
Luse, Wendell, V.P.-Pur. & Sls.--Acme Poultry Company, Inc., Seattle, WA, pg. 13
Lustig, Mark, Dir.-Matls. Mngmt.--Allen-Edmonds Shoe Corp., Port Washington, WI, pg. 36
Luxem, Paul, Pur. Agent--Berger Transfer & Storage, Inc., Saint Paul, MN, pg. 141
Lynch, Ann Marie, Pur. Agent--Whiting & Davis Company, Plainville, MA, pg. 236
Lynch, Pat, Dir.-Pur.--Showell Farms, Inc., Showell, MD, pg. 1000
Lyon, Andrea, Mgr.-Pur.--Charter House Incorporated, Holland, MI, pg. 1035
Lyons, Jim, Dir.-Pur.--Rex Moore Electrical Contractors & Engineers, West Sacramento, CA, pg. 768
Lyons, R.L., V.P.-Pur.--Conley Frog & Switch Company, Memphis, TN, pg. 274
Lyons, Richard, V.P.-Procurement--King & Prince Seafood Corporation, Brunswick, GA, pg. 631
Lyons, Robert, Pur. Agent--C. W. Zumbiel Company, Cincinnati, OH, pg. 1221
Lyrla, Louis, Dir.-Pur.--Vita Food Products, Inc., Chicago, IL, pg. 1153
Lytle, Jim, Mgr.-Pur.--The Union Fork & Hoe Co., Columbus, OH, pg. 1128
Mabie, Dan, Pur. Agent--Hamlin, Inc., Lake Mills, WI, pg. 503
MacDonald, Donald, V.P.-Pur. & Engrng.--Amway Corporation, Ada, MI, pg. 70
Maceda, Joe, Dir.-Pur.--Theochem Labs., Inc., Tampa, FL, pg. 1090
Machann, Thomas, Mgr.-Pur.--Semco, Inc., Houston, TX, pg. 989
Mackey, Randy, Mgr.-Pur.--Efco Corporation, Monett, MO, pg. 359
MacKinnis, Frank, Dir.-Pur.--Perdue Farms Inc., Salisbury, MD, pg. 860
MacLellan, James S., V.P.-Materials--Binkley Company, Warrenton, MO, pg. 151
Madaffari, John, Dir.-Pur.--Western States Machine Co., Hamilton, OH, pg. 1181
Madison, Robert, Dir.-Pur.--Webcraft Technologies, Inc., North Brunswick, NJ, pg. 1171
Madrinich, Gabe, Dir.-Pur.--Waterous Company, South Saint Paul, MN, pg. 50
Magden, Ralph, Dir.-Pur.--Edelmann Div. of Stant, Inc., Deerfield, IL, pg. 368
Mager, Norbert, Dir.-Pur.--RHC/Spacemaster Corporation, Melrose Park, IL, pg. 906
Magnano, Joe, Pur. Agent--Arrow Fluid Power, Broadview, IL, pg. 85
Magnano, Joe, Pur. Agent--Arrow Fluid Power, Broadview, IL, pg. 85
Magnuson, Dale, Mgr.-Pur.--Reading Tube Corp., Reading, PA, pg. 916
Main, Barbara, V.P.-Pur.--Texas Refinery Corp., Fort Worth, TX, pg. 1089
Maker, Mac, Dir.-Pur.--Granite State Packing Co., Manchester, NH, pg. 476
Maki, Ken, Pur. Agent--Young Supply Company, Detroit, MI, pg. 1214
Malcolm, William, V.P.-Pur.--Tristate Electrical Supply Co., Inc., Hagerstown, MD, pg. 1114
Malee, Kris, Pur. Supvr.--Uniflow Manufacturing Co., Erie, PA, pg. 1126
Malin, S., Dir.-Pur.--The F.A. Bartlett Tree Expert Co., Stamford, CT, pg. 123
Manchester, Robert, Dir.-Pur.--Multiple Allied Services, Inc., Hayward, CA, pg. 775
Mann, Michael R., V.P.-Pur.--Colonial Metals Co., Columbia, PA, pg. 263
Manning, Charles, Pur. Agent--K-D Lamp Company, Cincinnati, OH, pg. 612
Manning, John, Pur. Dir.--BIW Cable Systems, Inc., North Dighton, MA, pg. 106
Manoni, Dave, Mgr.-Purch.--Hudson Valley Paper Company, Albany, NY, pg. 551
Mansfield, Fred, Pur. Agent--Karnak Corporation, Clark, NJ, pg. 617
Mares, R.J., Pur. Agent--The Cleveland Builders Supply Co., Cleveland, OH, pg. 1036
Mari, Dennis, Dir.-Pur.--La Victoria Foods, Inc., City of Industry, CA, pg. 649
Mariani, Dan, Pur. Agent--Strahman Valves, Inc., Florham Park, NJ, pg. 1052
Marion, W. Arthur, Mgr.-Matls.--American Paper Products Group, Ltd., Youngstown, OH, pg. 59
Markheim, Randy, Mgr.-Pur.--Lockwood Corporation, Gering, NE, pg. 680
Markl, Michael, Dir.-Pur.--Photogenic Machine Company, Youngstown, OH, pg. 869
Marks, Neal, Dir.-Pur.--Five Dollar Clothing Stores, Los Angeles, CA, pg. 416
Marks, Sam, Exec. V.P., Corp. Sec. & Dir.-Pur.--Triangle Marketing Corp., New York, NY, pg. 1112
Marlowe, Terry, Sr. Pur. Agent--Sentry Group, Rochester, NY, pg. 990
Marotta, Martin, Pur. Agent--Philadelphia Sign Company, Palmyra, NJ, pg. 867
Marowski, Larry, Pur. Agent--CVC Products, Inc., Rochester, NY, pg. 206
Marr, Ronda, Matls. Mgr.--Crown Leisure Products, Owosso, MI, pg. 200
Marsh, Carl P., V.P.-Mfg. & Pur.--Maui Divers Of Hawaii, Ltd., Honolulu, HI, pg. 721
Marsh, Debi, Dir.-Pur.--B. Green & Co., Baltimore, MD, pg. 484
Marsh, Joe, Dir.-Pur.--Group Dekko International Inc., Kendallville, IN, pg. 489
Martin, Ed, Pur. Agent--Diamond Crystal Specialty Foods, Inc., Wilmington, MA, pg. 335
Martin, Joseph G., V.P.-Pur.--Starcraft Automotive Corp., Goshen, IN, pg. 1040
Martin, Leonard T., Dir.-Pur.--Georgia Iron Works Co., Grovetown, GA, pg. 453
Martin, Robert W., V.P.-Pur.--Northwestern Steel & Wire Co., Sterling, IL, pg. 815
Martin, T.A., V.P.-Matls.--Miller Electric Mfg. Co., Appleton, WI, pg. 754
Martin, W.C., Jr., Dir.-Pur.--Martins Abbatoir & Wholesale Meats Inc., Godwin, NC, pg. 716

Mashburn, Phil, Dir.-Pur.--Magic Circle Manufacturing Div., Coffeyville, KS, pg. 13
Masheech, Jack, Mgr.-Pur.--International Permalite, Inc., Ontario, CA, pg. 579
Mason, Clarence, Mgr.-Purchase--National Forge Company, Irvine, PA, pg. 788
Mason, Fred, Treas., Sec. & Mgr.-Pur.--J.B. Rodgers Mechanical Contractors, Phoenix, AZ, pg. 943
Mason, Pat, Admin./Opers., Purchasing, Personnel Training & Devel.--Scharfberg & Associates, Ltd. Adv., Jenkintown, PA, pg. 974
Masson, Petur, Dir.-Mktg.--Coldwater Seafood Corporation, Rowayton, CT, pg. 260
Masten, Herb, Dir.-Pur.--1st Franklin Corporation, Toccoa, GA, pg. 413
Masters, Fran, Dir.-Pur.--Mar-Mac Manufacturing Company, Inc., McBee, SC, pg. 705
Masters, Mardell, Pur. Agent--Levlad, Inc., Chatsworth, CA, pg. 671
Mateer, Curt, Pur. Agent--Gordon Sign Company, Denver, CO, pg. 472
Matherne, Flo, Dir.-Pur.--Bollinger Machine Shop And Shipyard, Inc., Lockport, LA, pg. 163
Mathews, Candace M., Dir.-Pur.--Vitatech International, Inc., Tustin, CA, pg. 1153
Mathey, Tom, Mgr.-Mdse. & Purch.--O'Malia Food Markets Inc., Noblesville, IN, pg. 825
Mathias, Rita, Dir.-Pur.--Wenczel Tile Co., Trenton, NJ, pg. 1176
Mattas, Clair, Pur. Agent--Woolrich, Inc., Woolrich, PA, pg. 1201
Matthews, David J., Sr. V.P.-Pur. & Gen. Mdse.--Hill-Behan Lumber Company, Saint Louis, MO, pg. 534
Matthews, William A., Jr., Mgr.-Pur.--Pannier Corporation, Pittsburgh, PA, pg. 846
Mattingly, John, Mgr.-Pur.--Piper Aircraft Corporation, Vero Beach, FL, pg. 872
Mattingly, Pam, Pur. Agent--SFA, Inc., Landover, MD, pg. 961
Matura, Raymond, Produce Buyer--Stanley Stores Inc., Bay City, TX, pg. 1038
Maule, William, Dir.-Pur.--Roseburg Forest Products Co., Dillard, OR, pg. 948
Mauney, Eddie, Dir.-Pur.--Mauney Hosiery Mills, Inc., Kings Mountain, NC, pg. 722
Mawhinney, C., Mgr.-Pur.--Cairns & Brother, Inc., Clifton, NJ, pg. 207
May, Jack, Dir.-Pur.--Ortel Corporation, Alhambra, CA, pg. 830
Mazany, Stanley J., II, Mgr.-Matl. Control, Dir.-Pur.--Besser Company, Alpena, MI, pg. 146
Mazurek, Stanley, Pur. Agent--Peerless Confection Company, Chicago, IL, pg. 855
Mazzone, Pat, Sr. Buyer--Acoustic Research, Canton, MA, pg. 578
McAuliffe, Jack, V.P.--Bolliger, Inc., Stamford, CT, pg. 163
McBride, John, Dir.-Pur.--Prince Manufacturing, Inc., Lawrenceville, NJ, pg. 890
McCabe, Ken, Pur. Agent--Burks Pumps, Inc., Piqua, OH, pg. 507
McCabe, Ken, Pur. Mgr.--Prosser/Enpo Industries, Piqua, OH, pg. 507
McCabe, Ken, Purchasing Mgr.--Barnes Pumps, Inc., Mansfield, OH, pg. 507
McCabe, Ken, Pur. Mgr.--AMW Industries Inc., Conway, AR, pg. 507
McCabe, Ron, Mgr.-Pur.--Cajun Electric Power Co-op, Baton Rouge, LA, pg. 207
McCarter, James W., V.P.-Pur.--Tennessee Valley Authority, Knoxville, TN, pg. 1088
McCarthy, Donald J., Dir.-Pur.--Petro Chem Development Company, New York, NY, pg. 865
McClurg, Lester, Pur.--Uniworld Group, Inc., New York, NY, pg. 1139
McCluskey, Phillip, Mgr.-Pur.--Airguard Industries Inc., Louisville, KY, pg. 27
McCollum, Wayne E., V.P.-Mdse.--Quality Stores Inc., North Muskegon, MI, pg. 904
McCool, Jim, Mgr.-Pur.--The Spencer Turbine Co., Windsor, CT, pg. 1030
McCool, Jim, Mgr.-Pur.--Spencer Turbine Co., Windsor, CT, pg. 1030
McCord, Larry, Pur. Agent--Hydreco, Augusta, GA, pg. 559
McCormack, Thomas, Mgr.-Pur. & Stores--Memphis Light, Gas & Water, Memphis, TN, pg. 738
McCurry, Rick, Mgr.-Pur.--Ruiz Food Products, Inc., Dinuba, CA, pg. 955
McDaniel, Terry, Pur. Mgr.--The Pierce Co., Inc., Upland, IN, pg. 102
McDevitt, William J., Dir.-Pur.--John Hancock Mutual Life Insurance Company, Boston, MA, pg. 595
McDonald, Robert M., Dir.-Pur.--Beckwith Machinery Company, Murrysville, PA, pg. 131
McDonough, James, Dir.-Pur.--Ocean Spray Cranberries, Inc., Lakeville, MA, pg. 820
McElwee, A. Joseph, Pur. Agent--Zenith Products Corp., Aston, PA, pg. 1217
McFarland, Jackie, Mgr.-Pur.--The Sportsman's Guide, Inc., Eagan, MN, pg. 1032
McGloin, Charles, Mgr.-Pur.--Jet Spray Corp., Norwood, MA, pg. 593
McGovern, Kay, Mgr.-Pur.--Ace Office Products, Rolling Meadows, IL, pg. 12
McGowan, Robert, Dir.-Pur.--Tension Envelope Corp., Kansas City, MO, pg. 1088
McHugh, Peter, Mgr.-Property & Pur. Agent--Trapp Family Lodge, Inc., Stowe, VT, pg. 1108
McIntosh, Julia, Pur. Agent--Ghent Manufacturing, Inc., Lebanon, OH, pg. 455
McKenna, Thomas, Mgr.-Pur.--Parisi, Inc., Philadelphia, PA, pg. 848
McKenzie, D.E., V.P. & Dir.-Pur.--R. L. Polk & Co., Detroit, MI, pg. 879
McKeown, John C., Dir.-Pur.--Mitchel & Scot Machine Co., Inc., Indianapolis, IN, pg. 761
McKinnery, Jim, Dir.-Pur.--Brim, Inc., Portland, OR, pg. 176
McLaughlin, Kathie, Pur. Agent--Morris Coupling Co., Erie, PA, pg. 771
McLemore, Ersley, Dir.-Pur., Plng. & Inventory Control--Heckethorn Mfg. Company, Dyersburg, TN, pg. 524
McLeod, Nancie, Pur. Agent--Proto Systems of Atlanta, Alpharetta, GA, pg. 895
McMahon, Mark, Pur. Agent--Tell City Chair Co., Tell City, IN, pg. 1085
McMahon, Virginia, Pur. Agent--Syracuse China Corp., Syracuse, NY, pg. 1065
McMavish, Richard, Mgr.-Pur.--Interform Corporation, Bridgeville, PA, pg. 574
McMillan, Robert, Pur. Agent-Accessories--W. M. Barr & Co., Inc., Memphis, TN, pg. 121
McNallie, L., Mgr.-Pur.--Dahlstrom Manufacturing Company, Inc., Jamestown, NY, pg. 310
McNew, Eddie D., V.P.-Pur.--Davis Walker Corp., Irwindale, CA, pg. 525
McStay, Maureen, Pur. Agent--LeeWards Creative Crafts, Inc., Elgin, IL, pg. 666
McVay, John, Pur. Agent--The Ingersoll Milling Machine Co., Rockford, IL, pg. 568
Meabon, Mark, Dir.-Pur.--Hanover Foods Corporation, Hanover, PA, pg. 506
Means, Rod, Dir.-Pur.--Omniflight, Inc., Dallas, TX, pg. 826
Medros, Susan, Dir.-Pur.--Powers Pharmaceutical, Brockton, MA, pg. 236
Meeks, Cathy, Pur. Agent--Wurzburg, Inc., Memphis, TN, pg. 1205
Meglio, L.D., Dir.-Pur. & Office Mgr.--Norwalk Powdered Metals, Inc., Norwalk, CT, pg. 816
Meloon, Gary, Pur. Agent--Correct Craft, Inc., Orlando, FL, pg. 287
Meltzer, Samuel, Dir.-Pur.--Gusso Manufacturing, Inc., Brooklyn, NY, pg. 495
Melus, John, Pur. Agent--Nelson Brothers Furniture Co., Chicago, IL, pg. 797
Menezes, Charles, Dir.-Pur.--Purity, Inc., Miami, FL, pg. 901
Meng, J., Chief Fin. Officer--David Langer & Co., Inc., Hollywood, CA, pg. 657
Menzel, Leigh, Dir.-Pur.--Perry's Ice Cream Co., Inc., Akron, NY, pg. 863
Merchant, Steve, Dir.-Pur.--Griswold Industries, Inc., Costa Mesa, CA, pg. 488
Merilott, Sandie, Dir.-Pur.--Sundt Corp., Tucson, AZ, pg. 1060
Merkef, Donald O., V.P., Sec. & Dir.-Pur. & Data Processing--E.W. Knauss & Son, Inc., Quakertown, PA, pg. 636
Merrell, Lucy, Pur. Agent & Credit Mgr.--Nimnicht Chevrolet Company, Jacksonville, FL, pg. 807
Meske, Dan, V.P.-Pur.--Deluxe Homes Of Pennsylvania, Inc., Berwick, PA, pg. 327
Metheny, Randy, Dir.-Pur.--El Torito Restaurants, Inc., Irvine, CA, pg. 929
Meydell, Stephen, V.P.-Pur.--Hypro Corporation, New Brighton, MN, pg. 557
Meyer, Glenn, Mgr.-Pur.--Wavetek Communications Div., Indianapolis, IN, pg. 1168
Meyer, Sara, Dir.-Pur.--Lyke Corporation, Ripon, WI, pg. 688
Michaelis, Leo, Dir.-Pur.--Russell Stover Candies, Inc., Kansas City, MO, pg. 957
Michaels, Joe, Dir.-Pur.--Elias Brothers Restaurants, Inc., Warren, MI, pg. 376
Michard, Joseph, Dir.-Pur.--Greenhorne & O'Mara, Inc., Greenbelt, MD, pg. 485
Michelson, Maurice, Sr. V.P., Chief Fin. Officer, & Dir.-Admin. & Pur.--Burkhardt & Christy Advertising, Inc., New York, NY, pg. 191
Mickels, Ken, Pur. Agent--Hanna Car Wash International, Inc., Portland, OR, pg. 505
Migliozzi, M., Mgr.-Procurement--Standard-Thomson Corporation, Waltham, MA, pg. 1037
Mikula, M., Pur. Dir.--Conklin Instrument Corporation, Pleasant Valley, NY, pg. 274
Militano, Jerry, V.P.-Pur.--Leonard Wholesale, Inc., Elizabeth, NJ, pg. 668
Milkie, Robert, Dir.-Pur.--Aetna Bearing Company, Chicago, IL, pg. 23
Miller, B., Pur. Agent--Advance Seed Co., Fulton, KY, pg. 407
Miller, Bob, Dir.-Pur.--Safeguard Business Systems, Inc., Fort Washington, PA, pg. 966
Miller, David, Pur. Agent--Kimstock, Inc., Santa Ana, CA, pg. 630
Miller, Dolores, Dir.-Pur.--Rosen Associates Management Corp., Jericho, NY, pg. 948
Miller, F.N., V.P. & Gen. Mgr.-Cora Div. & Dir.-Pur.--Teepak, Inc., Westchester, IL, pg. 535
Miller, Gary, Dir.-Pur.--Hill & Griffith Company, Cincinnati, OH, pg. 534
Miller, George, Mgr.-Pur.--Therm, Inc., Ithaca, NY, pg. 1090
Miller, John, Dir.-Pur.--Ulbrich Stainless Steels & Special Metals, Inc., North Haven, CT, pg. 1125
Miller, Keith, Dir.-Pur.--United Grocers Inc., Portland, OR, pg. 1132
Miller, Nora, Dir.-Pur.--The Vagabond Inns, San Diego, CA, pg. 1142
Miller, Richard, Dir.-Pur.--Urschel Labs Inc., Valparaiso, IN, pg. 1140
Miller, Rory, Pur. Agent--Facemate Corporation, Chicopee, MA, pg. 396
Miller, Terri, Dir.-Pur.--Pitco Frialator Inc., Concord, NH, pg. 157
Millichamp, John, Dir.-Matl. Control--Hydreco, Augusta, GA, pg. 559
Milliron, Frank, Dir.-Pur.--Mountain States Pipe & Supply Company, Colorado Springs, CO, pg. 773
Mills, H., Pur. Agent--Phoenix Data Incorporated, Phoenix, AZ, pg. 630
Milton, Donald S., Dir.-Matls.--Baker Knapp & Tubbs Inc., Grand Rapids, MI, pg. 640
Minor, Briggs, Pur. Agent--Industrial Contractors, Inc., Idaho Falls, ID, pg. 566
Mitchelities, Cathy, Pur. Agent--Edlund Company, Inc., Burlington, VT, pg. 368
Mitchell, Karen, Dir.-Pur.--Telsco Industries, Garland, TX, pg. 1085
Mitchell, Troy, Dir.-Pur.--Dewberry & Davis, Fairfax, VA, pg. 334
Mitzner, Dennis, Pur. Agent--La-Co Industries, Inc., Chicago, IL, pg. 648
Mix, S., Purchasing--Turner Machine Company, Salem, OH, pg. 373
Modaffari, John, Pur. Agent--Moltrup Steel Products Company, Beaver Falls, PA, pg. 764
Moloney, Maurice, Pur. Agent--Breuer Electric Mfg. Co., Chicago, IL, pg. 174
Monahan, Connie, Dir.-Pur.--Acurex Environmental, Mountain View, CA, pg. 16
Monkell, Roy, Mgr.-Matl.--Clifford B. Hannay & Son Inc., Westerlo, NY, pg. 505
Monroe, R., Dir.-Pur.--L. B. Smith, Inc., Camp Hill, PA, pg. 1013
Montgomery, Bob, Dir.-Pur.--Renken Boat Manufacturing Co., Charleston, SC, pg. 927
Montri, Dave, Dir.-Pur.--Active Tool & Manufacturing Co., Inc., Roseville, MI, pg. 15
Moore, Barbara, Dir.-Pur.--Queen Oxygen Company, Columbus, OH, pg. 904
Moore, J.W., Mgr.-Pur.--Pace Industries, Inc., Fayetteville, AR, pg. 838
Moorman, Thomas, Buyer--Citizens Gas & Coke Utility, Indianapolis, IN, pg. 250
Moors, Russ, Pur. Agent-Findings--Eastland Shoe Manufacturing Corporation, Freeport, ME, pg. 364
Moran, John J., V.P. & Asst. Controller--Anchor Financial Corporation, Myrtle Beach, SC, pg. 71
Morgan, Paul, Dir.-Pur.--Allied Plywood Corp., Alexandria, VA, pg. 38
Morley, Bob, Pur. Dir.-Tire Div.--STRAFCO, Inc., San Antonio, TX, pg. 1052
Morrison, Steve, Parts Mgr.--D.S.U.-Peterbilt & GMC, Inc., Portland, OR, pg. 309
Morrow, John, Pur. Supvr.--Gates, McDonald & Co., Columbus, OH, pg. 795
Morrow, Sally, Dir.-Pur.--Magnasync Moviola Corporation, Hollywood, CA, pg. 586
Motyka, Dave, Dir.-Pur.--Oakland Tool & Manufacturing Company, Fraser, MI, pg. 819
Moucka, Milada, Dir.-Pur.--Alto Shaam Inc., Menomonee Falls, WI, pg. 46
Moulton, John, Dir.-Pur.--Southwestern/Great American Inc., Nashville, TN, pg. 1023
Moyer, B.L., Dir.-Pur.--Norfolk Shipbuilding & Drydock Corporation, Norfolk, VA, pg. 810
Moyer, Joyce, Dir.-Pur.--Ready Systems, Sunnyvale, CA, pg. 916
Mrock, Tom, Mgr.-Pur.--Chicago White Metal Casting, Inc., Bensenville, IL, pg. 246
Mrozinski, JoAnn, Pur. Agent--Facemate Corporation, Chicopee, MA, pg. 396
Mudge, Gary, Dir.-Pur.--Vegas Electric Supply, Las Vegas, NV, pg. 215
Mudloff, Robert, Dir.-Pur.--General Safety Corporation, Saint Clair Shores, MI, pg. 450
Mueller, Barbara, Mgr.-Pur.--The Minnesota Mutual Life Insurance Company, Saint Paul, MN, pg. 757
Mullinax, Larry, Treas., Dir.-Pur., Data Processing, & Personnel--Ed Mullinax Ford, Inc., Amherst, OH, pg. 775
Mulvihill, Kevin, Dir.-Pur.--Cello Bag Company, Inc., Tukwila, WA, pg. 231
Mundell, Mick, Dir.-Pur.--Specialty Paperboard Inc., Brattleboro, VT, pg. 1027
Mundell, Mick, Mgr.-Matls.--Specialty Paperboard Inc., Brattleboro, VT, pg. 1027
Murland, J., Pur. Agent--Pennsylvania Petroleum Product Company, Southhampton, PA, pg. 858
Murphy, Don, Pur. Mgr.--DEC/Bou-Matic, Madison, WI, pg. 309
Murphy, Kenneth, Dir.-Pur.--Chiswick Trading Inc., Sudbury, MA, pg. 248
Murrin, Tim, Pres.-Pur.--White Castle System, Inc., Columbus, OH, pg. 1185
Murrin, Tim., Dir.-Pur.--PSB Co., Columbus, OH, pg. 1185
Murry, Bob, Pur. Dir.--John Zink Co., Tulsa, OK, pg. 639
Myer, David F., V.P.-Distr.--Ace Hardware Corporation, Oak Brook, IL, pg. 12
Myers, Ben N., Pur. Agent--Batson-Cook Company, West Point, GA, pg. 126
Myers, Edwin I., Pur. Agent--York Building Products Co., Inc., York, PA, pg. 1208
Myers, Larry, Mgr.-Pur.--Richmond Technology Inc., Redlands, CA, pg. 933
Myers, Richard, Dir.-Pur.--March Manufacturing Inc., Glenview, IL, pg. 706
Nagle, Cliff, Dir.-Pur.--Tri Valley Growers Inc., San Francisco, CA, pg. 1111
Nagler, Yaacov, Sr. V.P.-Pur.--Murry's, Inc., Forestville, MD, pg. 777
Nahre, Earl, Pur. Agent--United Farm Bureau Family Life Insurance Co., Indianapolis, IN, pg. 1131
Nanney, Bob, Pur. Agent--Evergreen Mills Inc., Ada, OK, pg. 1145
Nantz, Calvin J., Dir.-Pur.--Cochrane Furniture Co., Inc., Lincolnton, NC, pg. 258
Napier, Tom, Mgr.-Pur.--The Florida Lottery, Tallahassee, FL, pg. 420
Naquin, Gasper K., Sec. & Treas.--Intrepid Enterprises, Inc., Harvey, LA, pg. 581
Nash, Gary, Pur. Agent--C. I. Hayes, Inc., Cranston, RI, pg. 519
Nasher, Manfred, Pur. Agent--Hickey-Mitchell Company, Saint Louis, MO, pg. 795

Nathan, Albert, Assoc. Head-Contract Procurement--Sargent & Lundy, Chicago, IL, pg. 971
Naughton, Dan, Mgr.-Pur.--Master Appliance Corp., Racine, WI, pg. 719
Neal, David G., V.P.-Opers.--JRN, Inc., Columbia, TN, pg. 586
Neidhardt, Richard J., V.P.-Pur.--Newly Weds Foods Inc., Chicago, IL, pg. 804
Neil, Diane, Dir.-Personnel & Pur.--Dallas Peterbilt, Inc., Irving, TX, pg. 312
Nelson, Ed, Dir.-Pur.--Holoubek Inc., Waukesha, WI, pg. 540
Nelson, Jack, Pur. & Export Mgr.--Hennells, Inc., Ferndale, MI, pg. 530
Nelson, Patti, Buyer--Radix Corporation, Salt Lake City, UT, pg. 909
Nelson, R.E., Pur. Agent--American Welding & Manufacturing Co., Warren, OH, pg. 431
Nelson, Steve, Dir.-Materials--OCTus, San Diego, CA, pg. 818
Nelson, Tom, Dir.-Pur.--Plastigage Corporation, Jackson, MI, pg. 876
Nelson, Tony, Pur. Agent--Vic Manufacturing, Minneapolis, MN, pg. 1149
Nerren, Elizabeth, Pur. Agent--Farmers Marine Copper Works, Galveston, TX, pg. 401
Neubeck, Ken, Mgr.-Matls.--Dealers Manufacturing Company, Minneapolis, MN, pg. 322
Neumann, Nick, Pur. Agent--Townsend Engineering Co., Des Moines, IA, pg. 1104
Neumiester, Jane, Pur. Agent--Ain Plastics, Inc., Mount Vernon, NY, pg. 26
Newman, Dave, V.P.-Pur.--Druther's International, Inc., Louisville, KY, pg. 350
Nicholas, Linda, Mgr.-Pur.--Myers Foods Company, Plumsteadville, PA, pg. 506
Nicholas, Steve, Pur. Agent--Topflight Corp., York, PA, pg. 1102
Nicholes, J., Dir.-Pur.--Battenfeld Gloucester Engineering Co. Inc., Gloucester, MA, pg. 126
Nichols, Pam, Pur. Agent--HLC Industries, Farmington Hills, MI, pg. 496
Nickels, William F., V.P.-Pur.--Replogle Globes, Inc., Broadview, IL, pg. 927
Nix, David, Dir.-Pur.--Century Boats By General Marine Industries, Panama City, FL, pg. 450
Nix, David, Pur. Dir.--GMI, Inc.-Glasstream, Panama City, FL, pg. 450
Nobile, Lois, Supvr.-Pur.--Pacific Optical Division, Torrance, CA, pg. 917
Nokovich, Joseph, Mgr.-Matl.--Hempt Brothers, Inc., Camp Hill, PA, pg. 528
Nolan, Tim, Dir.-Pur.--Smith Metal Arts Company, Inc., Buffalo, NY, pg. 1013
Norlington, Larry, Pur. Agent--Weil-McLain, Michigan City, IN, pg. 710
Normandin, Jim, Pur. Agent--Beauty Enterprises Inc., Hartford, CT, pg. 130
Norton, Curt, Dir.-Pur.--Essex Group, Inc., Fort Wayne, IN, pg. 389
Norton, Douglas, V.P.-Mfg. & Distr.--Portland Glass/American Management Group, Westbrook, ME, pg. 58
Novacek, Art, Mgr.-Opers. & Mktg.--The Harry Alter Company, Chicago, IL, pg. 1086
Novak, Joe, Pur. Agent--Leyse, Kewaunee, WI, pg. 1155
Null, O.D., Dir.-Pur.--Frantz Manufacturing Co., Sterling, IL, pg. 429
Null, R. Dean, Dir.-Pur.--Higginbotham-Bartlett Co., Lubbock, TX, pg. 533
O'Brien, Jerry, V.P.-Pur.--Raynor Garage Door Company, Dixon, IL, pg. 915
O'Brien, M.O., Dir.-Pur.--Atwood Industries, Inc., Rockford, IL, pg. 97
O'Connell, Jerry, Pur. Agent--Seymour of Sycamore, Inc., Sycamore, IL, pg. 994
O'Connor, Frank, Mgr.-Materials Procurement & Pur.--Vance Industries, Inc., Chicago, IL, pg. 1144
O'Donnell, Joyce, Mgr.-Pur.--Electro Methods Inc., South Windsor, CT, pg. 375
O'Reilly, Tim, Mgr.-Sundry Pur.--Kelly-Moore Paint Company, Inc., San Carlos, CA, pg. 621
O'Rourke, Michael, Dir.-Pur.--Naylor Pipe Company, Chicago, IL, pg. 796
O'Shea, Pat, V.P.-Pur.--Glazers Wholesale Drug Co. Inc., Dallas, TX, pg. 461
O'Sullivan, Peter F., V.P.-Pur. & Production Coordination--G. Heileman Brewing Co., Inc., La Crosse, WI, pg. 526
O'Toole, Rita, Dir.-Pur.--Educational Publishing Corporation, Oak Lawn, IL, pg. 369
O'Toole, Rita, Dir.-Pur.--Ideal School Supply Company, Oak Lawn, IL, pg. 369
Oakley, Donald E., V.P.--J.M. Huber, Polymer Services Div., Orange, TX, pg. 550
Obendorfer, Jim, Pur. Agent--Cooperheat, Inc., Piscataway, NJ, pg. 283
Obrzut, Don, V.P.-Mktg.--National Food Stores, Inc. T/A Krauszer's, Edison, NJ, pg. 788
Ocelus, Edward, Pur. Agent--Florig Equipment Company, Inc., Conshohocken, PA, pg. 421
Oday, Mike, Dir.-Pur. & Opers.--Roofing Wholesale Co., Inc., Phoenix, AZ, pg. 946
Odell, Alan, Mgr.-Pur.--The Children's Place Retail Stores, Inc., Pine Brook, NJ, pg. 247
Olinde, Frank, Dir.-Pur.--Pala Group, Inc., Baton Rouge, LA, pg. 843
Olinger, Donald E., V.P.-Procurement--Totes Incorporated, Loveland, OH, pg. 1103
Oliva, Carlo J., Opers. Officer-Pur. Dir.--Fiduciary Trust Co. International, New York, NY, pg. 408
Oliver, D.A., V.P.-Supply & Distr.--Gulf Oil, Westborough, MA, pg. 304
Oliver, Ray, V.P.-Opers. & Pur. & Comptroller--Tatum Farms, Dawsonville, GA, pg. 1080
Olson, John, Dir.-Pur.--M. Buten & Sons Inc., Philadelphia, PA, pg. 196
Olson, Jon, V.P.-Pur. & Food Devel.--Lyon's Restaurants, Inc., Foster City, CA, pg. 690
Orman, Ray, Buyer--Anderson Wholesale Company, Muskogee, OK, pg. 73
Orpe, Carole, Pur. Agent--The Zippertubing Co., Los Angeles, CA, pg. 1220
Ory, Robert, Dir.-Pur.--Wilton Industries, Inc., Woodridge, IL, pg. 1194
Ossam, Seymour, Pur. Agent--Hoffritz for Cutlery, New York, NY, pg. 538
Osteen, M.S., Dir.-Pur.--Perfection-Schwank Inc., Waynesboro, GA, pg. 861
Ostroski, Matthew, V.P.-Pur.--Globe Industries, Inc., Chicago, IL, pg. 464
Oswalt, Bob, Procurement Mgr.--Flexible Flyer Inc., West Point, MS, pg. 847
Ott, Richard, Dir.-Pur.--The Brulin Corporation, Indianapolis, IN, pg. 184
Overacker, Donna, V.P.-Pur.--Vienna Sausage Mfg. Co., Chicago, IL, pg. 1151
Owczarski, Dan, Dir.-Pur.--Woodwork Corporation of America, Chicago, IL, pg. 1201
Owen, Craig, Pur. Agent--Lawrence Pumps, Inc., Lawrence, MA, pg. 662
Owens, Ron, Dir.-Pur.--Stanley Stores Inc., Bay City, TX, pg. 1038
Ownby, O. Gene, V.P.-Supplies--Ivan Allen Company, Inc., Atlanta, GA, pg. 36
Ozanic, T., Dir.-Pur.--Rauland-Borg Corporation, Skokie, IL, pg. 914
Ozgowicz, M.M., Matls. Mgr.--Dukane Corporation, Saint Charles, IL, pg. 351
Pace, Kevin, Dir.-Pur.--Megas Beauty Aids, Inc., Cleveland, OH, pg. 737
Pacek, Tom, Mgr.-Materials--Wayne Steel, Inc., Wooster, OH, pg. 1169
Page, Robert, V.P.-Corp. Pur. & Services--Northwest Airlines, Inc., Saint Paul, MN, pg. 782
Page, William, Dir.-Pur.--Thiele Kaolin Co., Sandersville, GA, pg. 1092
Paige, Ben, Dir.-Central Pur.--Basler Electric Company, Highland, IL, pg. 125
Palko, John, Pur. Agent--Rapid Industries, Inc., Louisville, KY, pg. 913
Palmer, Fred, Dir.-Maintenance--Lester Coggins Trucking, Okahumpka, FL, pg. 259
Palmer, Richard, Mgr.-Pur.--Porcelain Metals Corp., Louisville, KY, pg. 881
Panagopulos, John, Dir.-Pur.--Arinc Inc., Annapolis, MD, pg. 82
Panbianco, Sonny, Pur. Agent--Palmer Manufacturing Company, Malden, MA, pg. 844
Pappa, Jack, Head-Matl. Dept.--The Aerospace Corporation, El Segundo, CA, pg. 22
Paquette, A., Pur. Agent--Eastern Air Devices, Inc., Dover, NH, pg. 363
Parham, W. Howard, Exec. V.P.-Pur. & Mfg.--Columbus Mills, Inc., Columbus, GA, pg. 267
Parker, Douglas, Dir.-Pur. & Mktg.--Camellia Food Stores Co-op Inc., Norfolk, VA, pg. 211
Parker, Jane, Dir.-Pur.--DeMert & Dougherty, Inc., Westchester, IL, pg. 328
Parker, Michael, Pur. Agent--Savage Arms Inc., Westfield, MA, pg. 973
Parks, Ken, Mgr.-Pur.--R. J. Gallagher Co., Houston, TX, pg. 441
Parr, Douglas H., V.P. & Dir.-Materials Procurement & Mngmt.--Mutual of Omaha, Omaha, NE, pg. 779
Partlow, Ken, Pur. Agent--Allsop, Inc., Bellingham, WA, pg. 43
Paskal, Marv, Pur. Agent--J & R Film Company, Los Angeles, CA, pg. 586
Patel, Raj, Mgr.-Pur.--Brown & Haley, Tacoma, WA, pg. 182
Paterson, Sue, Dir.-Pur.--Jandy Industries, Novato, CA, pg. 589
Patrick, Michael, Dir.-Pur.--Flojet Corporation, Irvine, CA, pg. 419
Pavlovich, Judy, Pur. Agent--Allied Old English, Inc., Port Reading, NJ, pg. 38
Pawloski, Mary, Dir.-Pur.--Comstock Michigan Fruit, Rochester, NY, pg. 25
Payne, Bonnie, Mgr.-Pur.--Smith Pipe & Steel Co., Phoenix, AZ, pg. 1014
Pearman, William P., Dir.-Pur.--Franklin Baking Co., Inc., Goldsboro, NC, pg. 429
Pearson, John, V.P.-Mdsg.--TSC Industries, Inc., Nashville, TN, pg. 1075
Pedigo, Gil, Mgr.-Pur.--The Apparel Group, Ltd., New York, NY, pg. 78
Pedigo, Gil, Pur.& Traffic, Mgr.--The Enro Shirt Company, Inc., Louisville, KY, pg. 78
Pence, Jay, V.P.-Pur.--Kirby Building Systems, Inc., Nashville, TN, pg. 632
Penner, Phillip, Adv. Mgr. & Pur. Agent--Accurate Perforating Co., Chicago, IL, pg. 11
Pepkin, Martin, Exec. V.P. & Dir.-Pur.--Martin Paint Stores, Jamaica, NY, pg. 715
Perez, Andy, Sr. V.P.-Pur.--National Cleaning Contractors, Inc., New York, NY, pg. 786
Perez, Joseph, Dir.-Pur.--Goya Foods, Inc., Secaucus, NJ, pg. 474
Perrone, Peggy, Pur. Agent--Waggoner Corp., Troy, MI, pg. 1158
Perry, J., Mgr.-Pur.--Wesbar Corporation, West Bend, WI, pg. 1176
Petac, Jerry, Pur. Dir.--Cres-Cor/Crown-X, Cleveland, OH, pg. 298
Peters, Don, Dir.-Pur.--S.W. Jr. Enterprises, Inc., Santa Ana Heights, CA, pg. 965
Petersen, Dale L., Pur. Agent--Henningsen Foods, Inc., White Plains, NY, pg. 629
Peterson, Dan, Mgr.-Pur.--Forms Corporation Of America, Spring Grove, IL, pg. 1187
Peterson, Darwin, Dir.-Matls. Mngmt.--RAYOVAC Corporation, Madison, WI, pg. 915
Peterson, James G., V.P.-Construction & Pur.--The Austin Company, Cleveland, OH, pg. 790
Peterson, Mike, Pur. Agent--Brown-Minneapolis Tank & Fabricating Co., Eagan, MN, pg. 182
Peterson, Paul, V.P.-Procurement--Doane Products Co., Joplin, MO, pg. 342
Peterson, R.F., Pur. Agent--Research Products Corporation, Madison, WI, pg. 928
Peterson, Robert, Pur. Agent--Yorktown Tool & Die Corporation, Yorktown, IN, pg. 1208
Peterson, Ronald, Sr. V.P.-Mktg.--Jack Eckerd Corporation, Largo, FL, pg. 366
Petkus, Janet, Pur. Agent--N W Ayer Incorporated, New York, NY, pg. 103
Petkus, Janet, V.P., Pur. Dir.--N W Ayer Inc., New York, NY, pg. 104
Petry, Max, Dir.-Pur. & Traffic Mgr.--Beach Mold & Tool Inc., New Albany, IN, pg. 128
Pettis, Chris, Dir.-Pur.--Narrow Fabric Industries, Inc., West Reading, PA, pg. 783
Pfaff, Mark, Dir.-Pur.--The Gibson-Homans Company, Twinsburg, OH, pg. 457
Phelps, G.N., Dir.-Pur.--Armstrong International, Inc., Three Rivers, MI, pg. 83
Phillips, Larry, Dir.-Pur.--Parkdale Mills, Gastonia, NC, pg. 849
Phillips, Robert L., Dir.-Pur.--Ash Grove Cement Company, Overland Park, KS, pg. 87
Phillips, W., Pur. Agent--United Gilsonite Laboratories, Scranton, PA, pg. 1132
Picard, David, Dir.-Pur.--Russell Harrington Cutlery Inc., Southbridge, MA, pg. 556
Picard, Martin, Dir.-Matls.--Rodney Hunt Company, Orange, MA, pg. 553
Picard, Walter, Mgr.-Matls.--Hart Graphics Inc., Austin, TX, pg. 513
Pickett, Jerry, Sr. V.P.-Plng., Pur. & Distr.--Tropical Garment Manufacturing Company, Tampa, FL, pg. 1116
Pickett, Jerry, V.P.-Pur.--Tropical Garment Manufacturing Company, Tampa, FL, pg. 1116
Pielach, Henry, Mgr.-Pur.--Beltone Electronics Corporation, Chicago, IL, pg. 137
Pierce, Edwin, Treas. & Mgr.-Pur.--Tolleson Lumber Company, Inc., Perry, GA, pg. 1100
Pietrangeli, Joseph J., Dir.-Pur.--Jervis B. Webb Company, Farmington Hills, MI, pg. 1170
Pifer, Glenn A., Treas. & Sec.--Allied Security, Inc., Pittsburgh, PA, pg. 39
Pigaty, Charles, Mgr.-Pur.--Bridgeport Fittings, Inc., Stratford, CT, pg. 175
Pinard, Gary, Mgr.-Pur.--Granite State Manufacturing Co., Manchester, NH, pg. 476
Pinendo, Sherry, Pur. Mgr.--Replacements, Ltd., Greensboro, NC, pg. 927
Pippin, Terry, Dir.-Mktg. & Pur.--Maverik Country Stores, Inc., Afton, WY, pg. 722
Pippine, Howard, Head Buyer--The Crosset Company Inc., Cincinnati, OH, pg. 300
Pirkey, Wil, Mgr.-Pur.--RJO Enterprises, Inc., Lanham, MD, pg. 907
Pittman, Gary, Chm. Bd., Pres., Chief Exec., Chief Oper. & Chief Fin. Officer--PCI, Austin, TX, pg. 836
Pitts, John, Pur. Agent--Sugar Cane Growers Cooperative of Florida, Belle Glade, FL, pg. 1056
Pitts, Richard, Dir.-Pur.--F.B. Wright Co., Dearborn, MI, pg. 1204
Plowman, Peter, Dir.-Pur.--Emery Waterhouse Company, Portland, ME, pg. 379
Pohlman, David, Dir.-Pur.--Crouch Supply Company, Inc., Fort Worth, TX, pg. 301
Polczynski, Tom, Pur. Agent--Oberg Industries Co., Freeport, PA, pg. 819
Polera, Anthony, Chief Exec., Chief Oper. & Info. Officer--Polera Building Corp., Scarsdale, NY, pg. 878
Politt, Dave, Dir.-Pur.--Ireland Coffee Tea, Inc., Pleasantville, NJ, pg. 582
Pollack, John, Dir.-Pur.--West Chemical Products, Inc., Princeton, NJ, pg. 1172
Pollack, John, Dir.-Pur.--Penetone Corp., Tenafly, NJ, pg. 1172
Pollack, Nick, Pur. Agent--Brian Center Management Corporation, Hickory, NC, pg. 175
Poquette, Gale, Dir.-Pur.--Dumore Corporation, Mauston, WI, pg. 352
Poreda, Elaine, Pur. Agent--New York Racing Association, Jamaica, NY, pg. 803
Portaro, F., Pur. Agent--J.M. Huber, Printing Ink Div., Edison, NJ, pg. 550
Porter, James E., Pur. Agent--Plano Molding Co., Plano, IL, pg. 874
Porter, Wayne, Dir.-Pur.--Kentile Floors Inc., South Plainfield, NJ, pg. 623
Potts, J., Dir.-Pur.--Astronautics Corp. of America, Milwaukee, WI, pg. 93
Potts, John, Mfg. Mgr. & Pur. Dir.--World Dryer Corp., Berkeley, IL, pg. 1027
Potts, Wayne, Pur. Agent--Sexton Can Co., Inc., Cambridge, MA, pg. 993
Powers, Herman L., Mgr.-Pur.--Pennsylvania Crusher Corp., Broomall, PA, pg. 858
Powers, Steve, Pur. Agent--Market Forge Company, Everett, MA, pg. 1027
Powers, Wayne, Pur. Agent--E. B. Kingman Company, Leominster, MA, pg. 631
Prader, John, Dir.-Pur.--Southeastern Pennsylvania Transportation Authority, Philadelphia, PA, pg. 1020
Pralle, Ed, Pur. Agent--Broadmoor Hotel, Inc., Colorado Springs, CO, pg. 177
Preiss, Emil, Pur. Mgr.--Axelson, Inc., Longview, TX, pg. 103

Prejean, E.J., Dir.-Pur.--Quintana Petroleum Corp., Houston, TX, pg. 905
Price, Daniel, Dir.-Purch.--The Crystal Tissue Co., Middletown, OH, pg. 303
Price, Jules, V.P.-Pur.--The P.J. Carlin Construction Company, New Rochelle, NY, pg. 220
Price, Robert J., V.P., Treas. & Pur. Mgr.--The Suddath Companies, Jacksonville, FL, pg. 1055
Prior, Dennis, Dir.-Pur.--Cranston Print Works Company, Cranston, RI, pg. 296
Pritz, Benjamin L., Chm. Bd., Pres. & Chief Exec. Officer--Grandpa Brands Company, Cincinnati, OH, pg. 476
Privott, Tom, Pur. Agent--National Welders Supply Co. Inc., Charlotte, NC, pg. 794
Pryor, Phillip, Dir.-Pur.--Progress Printing Company, Lynchburg, VA, pg. 894
Puderbaugh, T.K., Dir.-Pur.--Union City Body Company, Inc., Union City, IN, pg. 1128
Pupello, Nick, Mgr.-Pur.--Spiegel Meats, Inc., Miami, FL, pg. 1030
Purdue, Pat, Pur. Agent--Gem-Dandy, Inc., Madison, NC, pg. 447
Purvis, Gary, V.P.-Pur.--RK Mechanical, Inc., Lakewood, CO, pg. 907
Purvis, R., Pur. Agent--J.M. Huber, Wood Products Div., Charlotte, NC, pg. 550
Putman, Ben, Dir.-Pur.--Carolina Tractor & Equipment Co., Charlotte, NC, pg. 223
Putnum, Charles, Pur. Agent--S. Bent & Brothers, Inc., Gardner, MA, pg. 140
Puttrich, Paul M., V.P. & Pur. Agent--Crafty Beaver Home Center, Skokie, IL, pg. 295
Quasey, Richard L., Dir.-Pur.--The Edward J. DeBartolo Corporation, Youngstown, OH, pg. 323
Queen, Jerry, Dir.-Pur.--J. C. Brock Corp., Buffalo, NY, pg. 178
Quinter, Kathleen, Mgr.-Pur.--Hawthorne Adv., Inc., Philadelphia, PA, pg. 518
Raap, Patricka, Mgr.-Facilities--Stark Candy Company, Pewaukee, WI, pg. 1123
Racer, Marvin, V.P., Pur.--Don Jagoda Associates, Inc., Melville, NY, pg. 588
Radant, James, Mgr.-Pur.--Badger Northland Inc., Kaukauna, WI, pg. 113
Radcliff, Mark, Dir.-Pur.--Beutler Heating & Air Conditioning Inc., Sacramento, CA, pg. 148
Radziewicz, John, Dir.-Pur.--Trumpf Inc., Farmington, CT, pg. 1118
Rafter, Chuck, Pur. Agent--Cablewave Systems, Inc., North Haven, CT, pg. 206
Ragland, Al, Dir.-Pur.--Aladdin Industries, Incorporated, Nashville, TN, pg. 29
Rahn, Steve, Dir.-Pur.--The Vollrath Company Inc., Sheboygan, WI, pg. 1154
Raimondi, Frank, Pur. Agent--Carstens Health Industries, Inc., Chicago, IL, pg. 225
Rainville, Robert, Dir.-Pur.--SGI Inc., Cranston, RI, pg. 962
Ramclam, Jeff, Mgr.-Pur.--Harrison Div., Burbank, CA, pg. 1003
Ramsey, Jim, Dir.-Pur.--Chance Operations, Inc., Wichita, KS, pg. 238
Randolph, E.P., Pur. Agent--Luzianne Blue Plate Foods, New Orleans, LA, pg. 923
Randolph, Richard L., Dir.-Pur.--Cumberland-Swan, Inc., Smyrna, TN, pg. 304
Rankin, J. Martin, Pur. Agent--Lift-All Co., Inc., Manheim, PA, pg. 675
Ranly, Robert, Dir.-Pur.--Artco-Bell Corporation, Temple, TX, pg. 86
Rassouli, Hoss, V.P.-Pur.--Elixir Industries, Gardena, CA, pg. 376
Raup, Thomas S., Mgr.-Pur.--American Systems Corporation, Chantilly, VA, pg. 63
Rave, Roger, V.P.-Pur.--Heller Seasonings & Ingredients, Inc., Bedford Park, IL, pg. 526
Rawls, Ken, Dir.-Pur.--American Fuel Cell & Coated Fabrics Co. (Amfuel), Magnolia, AR, pg. 55
Ray, David, V.P.-Mktg. & Pur.--Baird Ray Nissan, Inc., Longwood, FL, pg. 114
Ray, E. Wayne, Jr., V.P.-Fin.--Riviana Foods Inc., Houston, TX, pg. 937
Raymer, Jim, V.P.-Pur.--State Industries Inc., Ashland City, TN, pg. 1041
Raynsford, Peter, Pur. Agent--Harden Furniture Company, McConnellsville, NY, pg. 508
Rea, Jane, Dir.-Pur. & Corp. Travel Planner--B.A.S.S., Inc., Montgomery, AL, pg. 105
Rea, Jane, Dir.-Pur.--Bassmaster Magazine, Montgomery, AL, pg. 105
Read, John R., Mgr.-Production Matls. Pur.--Moorman Mfg. Company, Quincy, IL, pg. 769
Ready, M., Pur. Agent--Integra Technologies Corp., Waltham, MA, pg. 572
Reddy, Bill, Dir.-Pur.--Castex Industries Inc., Holland, MI, pg. 228
Redmond, M.L., V.P.-Pur.--S & C Electric Company, Chicago, IL, pg. 958
Redwine, Jerry, V.P.-Pur.--Crane Carrier Company, Tulsa, OK, pg. 296
Reece, Bill, Mgr.-Pur.--Niagara Cutter, Inc., North Tonawanda, NY, pg. 805
Reed, Dave, Dir.-Pur.--PhoneMate, Inc., Torrance, CA, pg. 869
Reed, Todd, Dir.-Pur.--Kova Fertilizer Inc., Greensburg, IN, pg. 643
Reeder, Duane, Dir.-Pur.--Nor-Cal Beverage Co., Inc., West Sacramento, CA, pg. 808
Reese, Elaine, Mgr.-Pur.--Halocarbon Products Corp., River Edge, NJ, pg. 502
Rehme, Robert, Dir.-Pur.--Swinerton & Walberg Co., San Francisco, CA, pg. 1068
Reichert, Gene, Pur. Agent--Mersman Furniture, Celina, OH, pg. 741
Reidenhour, Gary, Pur. Agent--Berks Products Corporation, Reading, PA, pg. 142
Reilly, Jeffry, Mgr.-Corp. Pur.--Gibbs Wire & Steel Company, Inc., Southington, CT, pg. 456
Reilly, Pat, Dir.-Data Processing & Pur.--Farnsworth Development Co., Mesa, AZ, pg. 403
Rein, Catherine A., Exec. V.P.-Corp. Services--Metropolitan Life Insurance Co., New York, NY, pg. 744
Reinecke, Ted, Pur. Agent--Stanco Metal Products, Inc., Grand Haven, MI, pg. 1035
Reiss, Richard T., II, Pur. Agent--R.C.A. Rubber Company, Akron, OH, pg. 906
Remy, Jerald C., V.P.-Pur.--Auto Glass Specialists, Madison, WI, pg. 100
Rentel, Richard O., Dir.-Pur.--Marine Construction & Design Co., Seattle, WA, pg. 707
Rexroad, Arnold L., Mgr.-Pur.--The Acacia Group, Washington, DC, pg. 10
Reynolds, James F., Treas. & Dir.-Pur.--Croll-Reynolds Company, Westfield, NJ, pg. 300
Rhein, Shirley, Pur. Dir.--Brencal Contractors Inc., Detroit, MI, pg. 106
Rhoads, John, Mgr.-Adv. & Pub. Rels.--Heat Controller, Inc., Jackson, MI, pg. 524
Rhodes, Barry, Chief Oper. Officer--Turner Machine Company, Salem, OH, pg. 373
Rhodes, Rick, Pur. Agent--Continental Eagle Corporation, Prattville, AL, pg. 278
Rhodes, W.P., Pur. Agent--Franklin Steel Company, Franklin, PA, pg. 429
Richard, Robert, Dir.-Pur.--Reactive Metals & Alloys Corporation (REMACOR), West Pittsburg, PA, pg. 916
Richards, Joseph, Pur. Agent--Stephenson, Inc., Alexandria, VA, pg. 1046
Richards, R., Pur. Agent--Stocker & Yale, Inc., Beverly, MA, pg. 1050
Richardson, Frank, Mgr.-Pur.--Heath Consultants Incorporated, Stoughton, MA, pg. 524
Richter, Earl, Dir.-Purchasing--Pacesetter Corporation, Omaha, NE, pg. 839
Ridewood, Chip, Pur. Agent--Phototype Color Graphics, Inc., Pennsauken, NJ, pg. 869
Riggs, James L., Pur. Agent--The Wooster Brush Company, Wooster, OH, pg. 1202
Riggs, Terry W., V.P.-Pur.--Harry H. Bell & Sons, Inc., Saint Petersburg, FL, pg. 134
Riley, Bruce, Sr. Property Admin.--The Cafaro Co., Youngstown, OH, pg. 207
Riley, Dalton, V.P.-Pur.--Cardinal Aluminum Co., Louisville, KY, pg. 217
Riley, David, V.P.-Pur.--Alro Group, Jackson, MI, pg. 44
Rinella, Gus, Dir.-Pur.--Freeway Corporation, Cleveland, OH, pg. 432
Riner, Bill, Dir.-Pur.--Crown American Corporation, Johnstown, PA, pg. 301
Risley, Jim, V.P.-Pur.--Certified Grocers Midwest, Inc., Hodgkins, IL, pg. 236
Ritenour, Jim, Dir.-Pur.--Best Western International, Inc., Phoenix, AZ, pg. 146
Ritter, Kevin, Dir.-Pur.--Allied Foods, Inc., Atlanta, GA, pg. 38
Roady, Art, Mgr.-Pur.--East Moline Metal Products Company, East Moline, IL, pg. 363
Robb, Jerry, V.P.-Procurement/Prod. Control--Sargento Cheese Co., Plymouth, WI, pg. 971
Robbins, Jeff, Mgr.-Pur.--Daktronics, Inc., Brookings, SD, pg. 312
Robbins, Richard D., V.P.-Matls.--Goshen Rubber Co., Inc., Goshen, IN, pg. 472
Roberson, Billy, Pur. Agent--Wurzburg, Inc., Memphis, TN, pg. 1205
Roberti, Jackie, Pur. Agent--Accurate Threaded Fasteners, Inc., Lincolnwood, IL, pg. 11
Roberts, J.C., Pur. Agent--AVEX Electronics, Inc., Huntsville, AL, pg. 550
Roberts, Joseph, Dir.-Pur.--Field Packing Company, Owensboro, KY, pg. 409
Roberts, Leland D., Sec. & Dir.-Pur.--Elgin-Honey Hill Corporation, Chicago, IL, pg. 376
Robertson, Art, Dir.-Pur.--Blitz USA, Miami, OK, pg. 157
Robertson, R., Mgr.-Pur.--Venchurs Packaging, Inc., Adrian, MI, pg. 1147
Robinson, Ian, Dir.-Pur.--Conwood Company L.P., Memphis, TN, pg. 281
Robinson, Jerry D., Chief Fin. Officer, V.P. & Treas.--SFA, Inc., Landover, MD, pg. 961
Robinson, Rob, Dir.-Pur.--Davis Electrical Constructors, Inc., Greenville, SC, pg. 318
Robison, Jim, Dir.-Pur.--Henco, Inc., Selmer, TN, pg. 528
Robison, S., Pur. Agent--Port of Galveston, Galveston, TX, pg. 881
Rockwell, Stuart, Pur. Agent--Felton Brush Inc., Manchester, NH, pg. 406
Rodgers, W.E., Jr., Dir.-Pur.--Dan River Inc., Danville, VA, pg. 313
Rodriguez, M., Pur. Agent--Mid-Continent Screw Products Co., Lincolnwood, IL, pg. 750
Rodriguez, Manuel, V.P.-Grocery & Dairy--Pueblo International, Inc.-P.R. Div., Carolina, PR, pg. 899
Rogers, Gary, Pur. Agent--Palm Iron & Bridge Works, Inc., Sacramento, CA, pg. 843
Rogers, Rocky, Mgr.-Pur.--Carpeteria, Inc., Valencia, CA, pg. 224
Rogus, Jeri, Pur. Agent--Plibrico Co., Chicago, IL, pg. 877
Rokop, Judith, Exec. V.P.-Pur.--Rokop Corporation, Bridgeville, PA, pg. 944
Rombach, Klaus, Pur. Agent--Press Enterprise Company, Riverside, CA, pg. 887
Romero, C.V., Pur. Agent--Sunkist Growers, Inc., Sherman Oaks, CA, pg. 1060
Ronge, Joe, V.P.-Central Pur.--Super 8 Motels, Inc., Aberdeen, SD, pg. 1062
Rooths, Karen M., Procurement Officer--D.C. Lottery & Charitable Games Control Board, Washington, DC, pg. 308
Rosa, Bruno, V.P.-Engrng. & Pur.--AP Parts Manufacturing Company, Toledo, OH, pg. 240
Rosati, Joseph R., V.P.-Indus. Rels.--Edgewater Corporation, Oakmont, PA, pg. 368
Rose, Dave, Dir.-Pur.--Cargill Salt, Newark, CA, pg. 219
Rose, Dave, Pur. Agent--Cargill Salt, Newark, CA, pg. 219
Rosen, Carol, V.P.-Pur., Facilities Plng. & Office Services--Katz Communications, Inc., New York, NY, pg. 618
Rosenbaum, Stuart, Dir.-Pur.--David Michael & Co. Inc., Philadelphia, PA, pg. 747
Rosenberger, Richard, Mgr.-Matls.--Elastomeric Technologies, Inc., Hatboro, PA, pg. 372
Rosencutter, Sharon, Mgr.-Pur.--SAE Engineering, Inc., Santa Clara, CA, pg. 959
Rosengarten, Zev, V.P.-Pur.--Crystal Clear Industries Company, Ridgefield Park, NJ, pg. 303
Ross, D.L., Pur. Agent--Eriez Magnetics, Erie, PA, pg. 386
Ross, Ron, Dir.-Pur.--Hvide Shipping, Inc., Fort Lauderdale, FL, pg. 556
Ross, William E., Dir.-Matls. & Pur.--The Airolite Company, Marietta, OH, pg. 28
Rowland, Al, Pur. Dir.--Rosco Manufacturing Co., Madison, SD, pg. 947
Roy, Catherine, Dir.-Pur.--Coleman Cable Systems, Inc., North Chicago, IL, pg. 260
Rozewicz, James, Pur. Agent--Roman Electric Company, Inc., Milwaukee, WI, pg. 945
Ruble, Bob, Pur. Agent--Faber Enterprises, Inc., Canoga Park, CA, pg. 395
Ruby, Robert L., Pur. Agent--Jamison Door Company, Hagerstown, MD, pg. 589
Rudin, Frank, Mgr.-Pur.--United Engine & Machine Company, Carson City, NV, pg. 1131
Ruehle, Guenter, Dir.-Pur.--Pabst Brewing Co., San Antonio, TX, pg. 959
Ruggeri, Anthony, Pur. Agent--The Sanymetal Products Co., Inc., Vanceburg, KY, pg. 970
Rumney, F., Mgr.-Domestic Pur.--Shure Brothers Incorporated, Evanston, IL, pg. 1001
Runyon, Mike, Dir.-Pur.--North American Salt Company, Overland Park, KS, pg. 812
Ruoff, Ed, Mgr.-Pur.--J.T. Slocomb Company, South Glastonbury, CT, pg. 1010
Rupert, Joseph, Dir.-Pur.--Cablevision Industries Corp., Liberty, NY, pg. 206
Rush, Margurite, Mgr.-Pur.--Doron Precision Systems, Inc., Binghamton, NY, pg. 346
Rusoff, Richard, Pur. Agent--Accu-Sort Systems, Inc., Telford, PA, pg. 11
Russ, Dean, Pur. Agent--Star Bronze Company, Alliance, OH, pg. 1039
Russell, Joyce, Dir.-Pur.--The Suddath Companies, Jacksonville, FL, pg. 1055
Russell, Peg, Pur. Agent--SBS Products, Inc., Saginaw, MI, pg. 323
Rutz, Dale, Dir.-Pur. Magnetics--Basler Electric Company, Highland, IL, pg. 125
Ryan, Brigid, Mgr.-Mfg. & Pur.--American Technical Publishers, Inc., Homewood, IL, pg. 63
Ryan, H., Pur. Dir.--The Canadian Coleman Co., Ltd., Toronto,, Canada, pg. 695
Ryan, Thomas R., V.P.-Pur.--Hershey Creamery Company, Harrisburg, PA, pg. 531
Ryder, R.W., Mgr.-Pur.--AGR International, Inc., Butler, PA, pg. 4
Rywe, Joe, Pur. Agent--Columbia Sussex Corporation, Fort Mitchell, KY, pg. 266
Saari, Stuart, Dir.-Pur.--H.O. Trerice Company, Oak Park, MI, pg. 1110
Sabal, Jerry, Mgr.-Pur.--Luxor Corporation, Waukegan, IL, pg. 365
Sabatino, J.T., Mgr.-Pur.--Thrall Car Mfg. Co., Chicago Heights, IL, pg. 350
Sad, Angela, Supvr.-Pur.--Compuware Corporation, Farmington Hills, MI, pg. 271
Salamon, Aaron, V.P.-Pur. & Personnel Dir.--Pic N'pay Supermarkets, Inc., Dania, FL, pg. 869
Salisbury, D., Pur. Agent--J.M. Huber, Calcium Carbonate Div., Quincy, IL, pg. 550
Salit, F., Pur. Agent--Interstate Drug Exchange, Inc., Amityville, NY, pg. 580
Samaco, Joe, Pur. Agent--Command Plastic Corporation, Akron, OH, pg. 268
Sampson, G., Pur. Dir.--Furnas Electric Company, Batavia, IL, pg. 437
Sanderson, Jim, Dir.-Pur.--Berryman Products, Inc., Arlington, TX, pg. 144
Sanford, Frank W., V.P.-Pur. & Mktg.--Sanford & Hawley, Inc., Unionville, CT, pg. 970
Sansom, Walter R., Pur. Agent--Chapman Printing Company, Huntington, WV, pg. 239
Santaniello, Joe, V.P.-Pur. System & Admin.--BJ Acquisition Corp., Charlotte, NC, pg. 107
Santisi, J.J., Jr., Pur. Agent--Cole Hersee Company, Boston, MA, pg. 260
Saratella, Joseph, Pur. Agent-Supplies--4C Foods Corporation, Brooklyn, NY, pg. 427
Saszlow, Roberta, Dir.-Pur.--Southern Container Corporation, Hauppauge, NY, pg. 1020
Sather, Steve, Mgr.-Pur.--Peco Inc., Portland, OR, pg. 854
Savage, Sue, Dir.-Pur.--Hougen Manufacturing Inc., Flint, MI, pg. 546
Sawyer, Lou, Pur. Agent--Hyer Industries Inc./Thayer Scale, Pembroke, MA, pg. 557
Scanlan, J., V.P.-Pur.--National Oats Co., Cedar Rapids, IA, pg. 25
Scanlan, Janette, Chief Fin. Officer & Dir.-Pur.--Fowler Tools of Canada, Kitchener,, Canada, pg. 427
Scaperdine, Donald, Pur. Agent--Commercial Light Company, Hillside, IL, pg. 268

Corporate Responsibilities Index

Schaedler, Henry, V.P.-Pur.--Schaedler Brothers, Inc., Harrisburg, PA, pg. 974
Schafer, Alan, V.P.-Mfg. & Distr.--Financial World Partners, New York, NY, pg. 410
Schasane, Donald, Dir.-Pur.--Continental Circuits Corp., Phoenix, AZ, pg. 278
Schauch, S., Pur. Agent--Harco Technologies Corporation, Medina, OH, pg. 507
Schecshel, William, Pur. Mgr.--Amity Leather Products Company, West Bend, WI, pg. 67
Scheide, Bob, Mgr.-Pur.--Darda Inc. (USA), Baltimore, MD, pg. 315
Scheiderman, L., Pur. Dir.--Lehigh-Leopold, Burlington, IA, pg. 608
Schelter, Marcia, Pur. Agent--American Plastic Toys Inc., Walled Lake, MI, pg. 59
Scherb, Joan, V.P.-Pur. & Plng.--Universal Folding Box Company, Inc., Hoboken, NJ, pg. 1138
Scherer, Robert, Dir.-Pur.--Gates Canada Inc., Brantford,, Canada, pg. 445
Schickler, Joanne, Pur. Agent--Triangle Maintenance Corporation, Valley Stream, NY, pg. 1112
Schirmang, Kenneth C., V.P.-Pur.--Skokie Valley Beverage Co., Wheeling, IL, pg. 1009
Schlicting, T., Dir.-Pur.--Swepco Tube Corporation, Clifton, NJ, pg. 1067
Schlitt, Mike, Mgr.-Pur.--Eco Water Systems, Saint Paul, MN, pg. 367
Schlosser, Rita, Pur. Agent--Channellock, Inc., Meadville, PA, pg. 239
Schmall, Tony, Mgr.-Pur.--Midwest Industries, Inc., Ida Grove, IA, pg. 752
Schmidlapp, C.J., III, V.P.-Pur.--Medtech Laboratories, Inc., Jackson, WY, pg. 736
Schmidt, Gary, Pur. Agent--Aurora Casket Company, Aurora, IN, pg. 98
Schmidt, R.J., Pur. Agent--Fish Engineering & Construction, Inc., Houston, TX, pg. 414
Schmitt, Norman, Mgr.-Pur.--Illinois Auto Electric Co., Elmhurst, IL, pg. 562
Schnegg, Gene, Dir.-Pur.--Dinner Bell Foods, Inc., Cincinnati, OH, pg. 53
Schneider, Rudy, Dir.-Pur.--Wyandot Inc., Marion, OH, pg. 1205
Schoanvel, Barry, Dir.-Pur.--Sierracin/Sylmar Corporation, Sylmar, CA, pg. 1003
Scholler, James, Dir.-Pur.--Times Printing Company, Inc., Random Lake, WI, pg. 1098
Schonowsky, Herbert, Mgr.-Purch.--Zyntec GmbH, Vienna,, Austria, pg. 1221
Schrader, Wayne, Dir.-Pur.--Shugart Corporation, Irvine, CA, pg. 1001
Schrader, Wayne, Dir.-Pur.--Kennedy Company, Irwindale, CA, pg. 1001
Schrager, Herb, Pur. Dir.--Revere Electric Supply Co., Chicago, IL, pg. 930
Schrieks, Jim, Dir.-Pur.--Atlas Hotels, Inc., San Diego, CA, pg. 96
Schroer, Bill, Pur. Agent--Dualite Inc., Williamsburg, OH, pg. 350
Schubert, Barbara, Pur. Agent--Crosman Corporation, East Bloomfield, NY, pg. 695
Schuchs, C., Dir.-Pur.--Riverside Central Services, Inc., Natchez, MS, pg. 937
Schuck, Bruce, V.P.-Production & Pur.--E. F. Houghton & Co., Valley Forge, PA, pg. 546
Schuck, Larry, Dir.-Pur.--Staveley Sensors, Inc., East Hartford, CT, pg. 1043
Schuenemann, Arthur, Dir.-Pur.--Intermatic Inc., Spring Grove, IL, pg. 575
Schwarzmann, Ervin, V.P.-Pur.--National Foods Inc., Bronx, NY, pg. 788
Sciascia, Roslyn, Mgr.-Pur.--Brimms Inc., Tonawanda, NY, pg. 176
Scidillo, Carol, Pur. Agent--M. Grossman Son, Inc., Passaic, NJ, pg. 489
Scolavino, Michael, Dir.-Pur. & Sls.--Furman Lumber Company, Billerica, MA, pg. 436
Scott, Bruce, V.P.-Pur.--Golden Sun Feeds, Inc., Estherville, IA, pg. 467
Scott, Gary, Mgr.-Pur.--The Dispatch Printing Company, Columbus, OH, pg. 339
Scott, Glenn, Mgr.-Matls.--RELA Product Development Div. (PDD), Boulder, CO, pg. 924
Scott, Lisa, Buyer--The Bartell Drug Company, Seattle, WA, pg. 122
Scott, Pat, Mgr.-Pur.--Mark Andy, Inc., Chesterfield, MO, pg. 708
Scott, R., Pur. Agent--Mellon Corporation, New York, NY, pg. 738
Scott, Raymond, V.P.-Pur.--Sullivan Paper Company, West Springfield, MA, pg. 1057
Scott, Steven P., Mgr.-Pur.--Morgan Construction Company, Worcester, MA, pg. 769
Scribner, Jim, Pur. Agent--Pizza Haven Inc., Seattle, WA, pg. 873
Scully, Edward A., Mgr.-Pur.--Whiting Corporation, Harvey, IL, pg. 1187
Scurto, James, Dir.-Pur.--Sentinel Computer Services Inc., Oak Brook, IL, pg. 990
Sears, R.W., Pur. Agent--Peerless Pottery, Inc., Rockport, IN, pg. 855
Sease, Gary, V.P.-Data Processing & Inventory Control--Servistar Corporation, East Butler, PA, pg. 992
Seaver, James M., V.P.-Parts Distr.--Hesston, Norcross, GA, pg. 4
Sedar, Donald, Mgr.-Pur.--Utica Boilers Inc., Utica, NY, pg. 1140
Sedlacek, Mary, Mgr.-Pur.--J H Collectibles, Milwaukee, WI, pg. 584
Seery, Christina, Dir.-Mfg. & Pur.--Imprint Products, L.P., Rockville Centre, NY, pg. 564
Seery, Tina, Mgr.-Opers. & Pur.--Imprint Products, L.P., Rockville Centre, NY, pg. 564
Sega, Kathy, Mgr.-Pur.--Rome Cable Corporation, Rome, NY, pg. 945
Seitz, Edgar C., III, Exec. V.P.-Pur., Import & Export--Service Supply Co. Inc. of Indiana, Indianapolis, IN, pg. 992
Seitz, Edgar C., Jr., Chm. Bd. & Exec. V.P.-Pur.--Service Supply Co. Inc. of Indiana, Indianapolis, IN, pg. 992
Sekscinski, Susan E., Dir.-Pur.--Spang & Company, Butler, PA, pg. 1025
Self, Joe, Dir.-Pur.--Affiliated Foods, Inc., Amarillo, TX, pg. 24
Self, Mickey, Pur. Agent--Tennsco Corporation, Dickson, TN, pg. 1088
Sencal, Ernie, Pur. Dir.--International Cheese Company Limited Partnership, Hinesburg, VT, pg. 575
Senn, Stepfen, Dir.-Pur.--The National Super Service Co., Toledo, OH, pg. 794
Sesholtz, Walter J., V.P.-Pur.--The Hartz Mountain Corp., Harrison, NJ, pg. 514
Setton, Murry, V.P.-Opers.--A & E Stores, Inc., Ridgefield, NJ, pg. 1
Sevier, John, Production Mgr.--Moeller Marine Products, Goodlettsville, TN, pg. 768
Sewell, Lewis, Mgr.-Meats--Affiliated Foods Southwest, Little Rock, AR, pg. 24
Shafer, H. Randall, Buyer--Consolidated Wholesale Company Division, Oklahoma City, OK, pg. 440
Shafer, Robert, Pur. Agent--T.D. Williamson, Inc., Tulsa, OK, pg. 1192
Shaffer, M. Todd, Dir.-Pur. & Mfg. Services--Tru-Weld Grating, Inc., Wexford, PA, pg. 1117
Shane, Jerry, V.P.-Pur.--Mac Papers, Inc., Jacksonville, FL, pg. 694
Sharber, Robert, Dir.-Pur.--Nashville Machine Co. Inc., Nashville, TN, pg. 784
Sharpe, James, Mgr.-Pur.--Mutual Manufacturing & Supply Co., Cincinnati, OH, pg. 778
Shaver, Jerry, V.P.-Parts--Swift Dodge Rolls Royce Inc., Sacramento, CA, pg. 1067
Shawlis, Bruce, Dir.-Pur.--Craftex Mills Inc. of Pennsylvania, Blue Bell, PA, pg. 295
Shealy, Joseph, Dir.-Pur.--Palmetto Wholesale Co., Inc., Columbia, SC, pg. 844
Shearer, Sandra, Pur. Agent--Accu-Sort Systems, Inc., Telford, PA, pg. 11
Sheets, David, Dir.-Pur.--SafetyMaster Corporation, Billings, MT, pg. 1053
Sheldon, John A., V.P.-Pur.--Finch, Pruyn & Co., Inc., Glens Falls, NY, pg. 410
Sheldon, Richard, Exec. V.P. & Dir.-Pur.--Champion Boxed Beef, Denver, CO, pg. 238
Shelton, Carter, Dir.-Pur.--AFG Industries, Inc., Fort Worth, TX, pg. 3
Shelton, T., Pur. Agent--Kyanite Mining Corporation, Dillwyn, VA, pg. 647
Sheppard, Betty J., V.P.-Admin. & Dir.-Personnel--Canal Insurance Co., Greenville, SC, pg. 213
Sherman, Mikrel, Dir.-Pur.--Coble Dairy Products Co-op, Lexington, NC, pg. 257
Sherman, Robert, Dir.-Pur.--East Kentucky Power Co-op, Winchester, KY, pg. 362
Sherman, Robert, Supvr.-Pur.--East Kentucky Power Co-op, Winchester, KY, pg. 362
Shiavo, Anthony, V.P.-Pur.--J. A. Sexauer, Scarsdale, NY, pg. 357
Shields, Hank, Dir.-Buying/Mktg.--Associated Grocers of Alabama, Inc., Birmingham, AL, pg. 90
Shimon, Cathy, Pur. Agent--Lake to Lake Dairy, Kiel, WI, pg. 653
Shirley, Steven, Mgr.-Mtls.--J. H. Fletcher & Co., Huntington, WV, pg. 418
Shiverick, D.H., Pur. Agent--Crane & Co., Inc., Dalton, MA, pg. 296
Shore, Doug, Dir.-Pur.--Unex Conveying Systems, Inc., Jackson, NJ, pg. 1126
Siddall, Dennis, Pur. Agent--Northland Aluminum Products, Inc., Minneapolis, MN, pg. 814
Siegel, Gary, V.P.-Pur.-Women's Shoes--Chernin's Shoes, Chicago, IL, pg. 243
Siegert, Doug, Pur. Agent--Haviland Enterprises, Grand Rapids, MI, pg. 517
Siepert, Karina, Mgr.-Pur.--Williamson-Dickie Mfg. Co., Fort Worth, TX, pg. 1192
Silva, Barbara, Asst. Pur. Agent--Acoustic Research, Canton, MA, pg. 578
Silva, Sarmento J., Mgr.-Pur.--Hazen Paper Company, Holyoke, MA, pg. 520
Simmons, Janet, V.P.-Pur.--Del Taco, Inc., Costa Mesa, CA, pg. 325
Simon, Bruce, V.P.-Pur.--Omaha Steaks International, Omaha, NE, pg. 825
Simons, Yvonne, Sr. Buyer--Avadyne, Inc., Monterey, CA, pg. 101
Simonson, Cory, V.P.-Pur. Mens' Shoes--Chernin's Shoes, Chicago, IL, pg. 243
Simpson, James, V.P.-Matls.--Continental Conveyor & Equipment Company, Winfield, AL, pg. 798
Simpson, Jim, Pur. Agent--Harig Products, Elgin, IL, pg. 175
Singer, Burton, Dir.-Pur.--Splendor Form International Inc., Long Island City, NY, pg. 1031
Sirianni, O., Pur. Agent--The Homer Laughlin China Company, Newell, WV, pg. 661
Sirt, Jeff, Dir.-Pur.--PC Distributing Inc., Mount Prospect, IL, pg. 835
Sitar, Ed, Intl. Procurement Dir.--Dukane Corporation, Saint Charles, IL, pg. 351
Sitzler, Keith, Pur. Agent--Gemtron Corporation, Sweetwater, TN, pg. 3
Skarbinski, Jay, Pur. Agent--Electric Specialty & Supply Corp., Boston, MA, pg. 374
Skelton, Larry, Pur. Agent--Traylor Chemical & Supply Co., Orlando, FL, pg. 1108
Skobel, C., Dir.-Pur.--Pyle Inc., Chicago, IL, pg. 648
Skoien, Kathy, Pur. Agent--Windsor Art Products, Inc., Pico Rivera, CA, pg. 1195
Skramovsky, Carla, Dir.-Pur.--Ritchie Industries, Inc., Conrad, IA, pg. 936
Slater, Gail, Pur. Agent--E.J. Bartells Co., Renton, WA, pg. 122
Slough, James, Dir.-Pur.--Wheaton Glass Co., Millville, NJ, pg. 1184
Smith, Bob, Pur. Agent--Sheffield Steel Corporation-Joliet, Joliet, IL, pg. 996
Smith, David, Dir.-Pur.--Toledo Blade Co., Toledo, OH, pg. 155
Smith, Harlan, V.P.-Pur.--Kroch's & Brentano's, Inc., Chicago, IL, pg. 645
Smith, Jerry, V.P.-Agriculture--Cornnuts Inc., Alameda, CA, pg. 286
Smith, Joyce, Pur. Agent--Southern Mills, Inc., Union City, GA, pg. 1021
Smith, Ken A., Dir.-Material Control--Troy Mills, Inc., Troy, NH, pg. 1116
Smith, Mary, V.P.-Res., Devel. & Pur.--A & W Restaurants, Inc., Livonia, MI, pg. 1
Smith, Nancy, Dir.-Pur.--Edelbrock Corp., Torrance, CA, pg. 367
Smith, Pam, Mgr.-Pur.--Magnedyne Div., Carlsbad, CA, pg. 1003
Smith, Rich, V.P. & Dir.-Pur.--Hurst Performances, Inc., Cleveland, OH, pg. 761
Smith, Robert, V.P.-Matls.--Foote & Davies Inc., Atlanta, GA, pg. 423
Smith, Ron, Dir.-Materials Mgmnt.--ASC Incorporated, Southgate, MI, pg. 7
Smith, Ron, Pur. Agent--Fitchburg Coated Products Inc., Scranton, PA, pg. 1083
Smith, Stan, V.P.-Opers. & Pur. Dir.--Exact Equipment Corporation, Langhorne, PA, pg. 392
Smith, Steve, Dir.-Pur.--Berkley, Inc., Spirit Lake, IA, pg. 141
Smith, Steve, Pur. Agent--United Farm Tools, Mohawk, Fitzgerald, GA, pg. 1132
Smith, T., Dir.-Pur.--Econolite Control Products, Inc., Anaheim, CA, pg. 367
Smith, Thomas, V.P.-Pur.--Merle Norman Cosmetics, Inc., Los Angeles, CA, pg. 740
Smith, Troy, Mgr.-Pur.--Blissfield Manufacturing Company, Blissfield, MI, pg. 157
Sneed, Gary, Dir.-Matls.--Hay & Forage Industries, Hesston, KS, pg. 4
Snyder, Craig, Dir.-Pur.--Adams Business Forms, Topeka, KS, pg. 16
Snyder, Richard J., Mgr.-Pur.--The C. P. Hall Company, Chicago, IL, pg. 501
Sober, David W., V.P.-Human Res.--Performance Food Group, Inc., Nashville, TN, pg. 861
Sokup, Bernard J., Pur. Agent--Spectrum Industries, Inc., Chippewa Falls, WI, pg. 1029
Solan, Debra, V.P.-Pur.--Deerskin Trading Post, Inc., Carlstadt, NJ, pg. 324
Solda, Cesar, Pur. Agent--Jamison Plastic Corporation, Allentown, PA, pg. 589
Solecitto, Frank, Pur. Agent--Carnival Creations, New York, NY, pg. 222
Sorensen, Ken, Dir.-Pur.--Intermountain Farmers Association, Salt Lake City, UT, pg. 575
Sotek, Ray, Pur. Dir.--Nelmor Co., Inc., No. Uxbridge, MA, pg. 1047
Sour, Jared, V.P.-Opers.--AmeriData, Inc., Minneapolis, MN, pg. 66
Sowizral, Gloria, Dir.-Pur.--Stephen Gould Paper Co., Inc., Whippany, NJ, pg. 473
Soza, Marti, Office Pur.-Buyer--Empire Southwest Co., Mesa, AZ, pg. 379
Spadaccino, Sandra, V.P.-Sls. & Pur.--Philadelphia Reserve Supply Company, Croydon, PA, pg. 867
Spade, Merle, Mgr.-Pur.--Carco Electronics, Menlo Park, CA, pg. 217
Speers, David, Supvr.-Pur.--Adams Rite Manufacturing Co., City of Industry, CA, pg. 16
Sperry, Tracy, Dir.-Pur.--United Design, Noble, OK, pg. 1131
Spurrell, Bruce, Dir.-Pur.--Calavo Growers of California, Tustin, CA, pg. 208
Squarci, Lorraine, Mgr.-Pur.--Hudson Valley Tree, Inc., Newburgh, NY, pg. 551
Squillante, Judith, V.P.-Pur. & Employee Benefits--Post Buckley Schuh & Jernigan, Miami, FL, pg. 881
St. Romain, Nevin, Dir.-Distr. & Pur.--Sound Warehouse, Inc., Dallas, TX, pg. 1018
Stace, Rick, Dir.-Pur.--Sun Computers, Inc., Carson, CA, pg. 1058
Stackhouse, Brenda M., V.P.-Pur.--Thornton Oil Corp., Louisville, KY, pg. 1095
Stadt, Alexis, Mgr.-Pur.--Wozniak Industries, Inc., Oakbrook Terrace, IL, pg. 1204
Stahl, Jack, Treas.--Boston Trading Ltd. Inc., Lynn, MA, pg. 168
Stahl, Jack, V.P.-Pur.--Boston Traders Div., Lynn, MA, pg. 168
Stamper, J.W., V.P.-Pur. & Distr.--The White Lily Foods Co., Knoxville, TN, pg. 1186
Standen, B., Dir.-Pur.--Abbott Electronics, Inc., Los Angeles, CA, pg. 9
Stang, Charles, Jr., Dir.-Pur.--Maxitrol Co., Southfield, MI, pg. 723
Stansell, Tim, Dir.-Pur.--Avondale Mills, Inc., Sylacauga, AL, pg. 103
Stanton, William E., Dir.-Pur.--Clinton Mills Inc., Clinton, SC, pg. 202
Stark, John, Dir.-Pur. & Mdsg.--Affiliated of Florida Inc., Tampa, FL, pg. 23
Stautberg, Jim, Mgr.-Matls.--American Laundry Machinery Inc., Cincinnati, OH, pg. 57
Stawizynski, Steven, Dir.-Pur.--J. S. Alberici Construction Co., Inc., Saint Louis, MO, pg. 31
Steed, Larry, Dir.-Pur.--Delta Pride Catfish, Inc., Indianola, MS, pg. 327

Steele, John, Dir.-Pur.--The Uhlmann Co., Kansas City, MO, pg. 1125
Steelman, Bob, Mgr.-Pur.--Carolina Steel Corporation, Greensboro, NC, pg. 223
Stefanchik, Randy, Pur. Agent--Tekni-Plex, Inc., Brooklyn, NY, pg. 1084
Steil, Mark E., V.P.-Pur.--Harrington & King, Chicago, IL, pg. 511
Steinbarth, Richard, V.P.-Pur.--La Preferida, Inc., Chicago, IL, pg. 649
Stenger, John P., V.P.-Pur.--Westgate Fabrics, Inc., Grand Prairie, TX, pg. 1182
Stenzel, Gary, Mgr.-Pur.--Peerless Chain Co., Winona, MN, pg. 855
Stephen, George A., Jr., V.P.-Pur.--Weber-Stephen Products, Palatine, IL, pg. 1171
Stephens, Robert, Mgr.-Pur.--Plastic Suppliers, Inc., Columbus, OH, pg. 875
Stephens, Rod, Dir.-Pur. & Production Plng.--Sun-Maid Growers of California, Kingsburg, CA, pg. 1058
Stephens, Ron, Dir.-Pur.--Petro-Hunt Corporation, Dallas, TX, pg. 865
Stepner, Allen, Mgr.-Pur.--David Brett, Inc., Easton, MA, pg. 174
Stern, Joan, Mgr.-Pur.--Dri Mark Products, Inc., Port Washington, NY, pg. 349
Sterpka, Carol, Pur. Agent--Hitchcock Chair Company LTD, Riverton, CT, pg. 536
Stevens, Brad, Dir.-Purch.--Prime Technology, Inc., Grand Rapids, MI, pg. 889
Stevens, Duane A., Pur. Agent--Curt G. Joa, Inc., Sheboygan Falls, WI, pg. 594
Stewart, Emmett, Mgr.-Pur.--Fike Corporation, Blue Springs, MO, pg. 409
Stewart, Fred, Mgr.-Pur.--Associated Company, Inc., Wichita, KS, pg. 89
Stewart, Jim, Pur. Dir.-Textbooks--The Caxton Printers Ltd., Caldwell, ID, pg. 230
Stewart, Kathy, Pur. Agent--Stark Candy Company, Pewaukee, WI, pg. 1123
Stewart, Larry R., Dir.-Pur.--ACF Industries, Inc., Earth City, MO, pg. 561
Stier, John K., Dir.-Pur.--Production Tool Supply Co., Warren, MI, pg. 893
Stine, David, Mgr.-Matls.--Dial Tube Company, Bedford Park, IL, pg. 939
Stites, Samuel H., V.P.-Pur.--The Fred W. Albrecht Grocery Co., Akron, OH, pg. 31
Stivers, Lonnie L., Dir.-Pur.--Moyer Products, Inc., Fresno, CA, pg. 774
Stoge, Robert, Dir.-Pur.--Keller Construction Company Ltd., El Monte, CA, pg. 620
Stokes, Raymond, Mgr.-Pur.--Montgomery Ward & Co., Inc., Chicago, IL, pg. 767
Stone, Daciano, Mgr.-Pur.--Whaling Industries, Inc., Fall River, MA, pg. 1183
Strange, Bob, Dir.-Pur.--Fawn Industries, Inc., Hunt Valley, MD, pg. 404
Strohmeyer, Ted, Mgr.-Pur.--Foley-PLP Company, Rochester, NY, pg. 422
Struble, Spencer, V.P. & Div. Mgr.-Supplies--Markem Corporation, Keene, NH, pg. 708
Stuart, J., Pur. Agent--Valcor Engineering Corp., Springfield, NJ, pg. 1142
Stuber, Elton A., Pur. Agent--W. C. Redmon Co., Peru, IN, pg. 919
Studebaker, Dan, Mgr.-Mdsg. & Pur.--Van Dyne-Crotty, Inc., Dayton, OH, pg. 1144
Sugerman, Michael, Pur. Mgr.--Union Industries, Inc., Providence, RI, pg. 1128
Sullivan, Christine M., Pur. Agent--Quintron Systems, Inc., Santa Maria, CA, pg. 905
Sullivan, Donald J., Dir.-Pur. & Personnel Training & Devel.--Wharfside Restaurants, Inc., Jasper, IN, pg. 1184
Sullivan, Gary, Mgr.-Pur.--Capitol Group, Springfield, IL, pg. 215
Sullivan, John, V.P.-Matls.--Tamaqua Cable Products Corporation, Schuylkill Haven, PA, pg. 1077
Sullivan, Kenneth, V.P.-Facilities Mngmt.--Viacom Inc., New York, NY, pg. 785
Summerall, Fraizer, Mgr.-Pur.--Smith Industries, Inc., Montgomery, AL, pg. 1013
Sundt, Dan, Pur. Mgr.--Littelfuse, Inc., Des Plaines, IL, pg. 678
Supeau, Gary, Mgr.-Pur.--Cooper Instrument Corp., Middlefield, CT, pg. 283
Sussman, Marvin, Exec. V.P.-Pur.--Philipp Brothers Chemicals, Inc., Fort Lee, NJ, pg. 867
Sutten, Laurence, Mgr.-Pur.--Andersen Windows Inc., Bayport, MN, pg. 72
Sutton, James, Dir.-Pur.--J.H. Harvey Company, Nashville, GA, pg. 515
Svenson, Dick, Mgr.-Pur.--Lytron Incorporated, Woburn, MA, pg. 690
Swan, D.L., Pur. Agent--Dexter Company, Fairfield, IA, pg. 334
Swan, Harry, Mgr.-Pur.--Gilbert Mfg. Corp., Locke Mills, ME, pg. 458
Swanson, R.N., Pur. Agent--United States Pipe & Foundry Company, Birmingham, AL, pg. 1162
Swanson, Robert, Pur. Agent--The Chicago Faucet Co., Des Plaines, IL, pg. 245
Swanzey, Robert, Sr. V.P.-Human Resources & Opers.--Century Business Credit Corporation, New York, NY, pg. 235
Sweeney, Wayne, Pur. Agent--Vibra Screw Inc., Totowa, NJ, pg. 1149
Sweet, Jack, V.P.-Pur.--Apache Hose & Belting Company, Cedar Rapids, IA, pg. 77
Swenson, Carl, Pur. Agent--Harlan Electric Co., Southfield, MI, pg. 509
Swenson, Paul, Exec.V.P. & Chief Oper. Officer--Aetna Health Plans, San Bruno, CA, pg. 23
Swenson, Ron, Dir.-Pur.--The Dartnell Corporation, Chicago, IL, pg. 316
Switzer, Robert, Pur. Agent--Diehl Specialties Intl., Defiance, OH, pg. 336
Swoards, Charles, Pur. Agent--Detroit Coil Company, Ferndale, MI, pg. 333
Syvertsen, Kurt, Pur. Dir.--Aerco International Inc., Northvale, NJ, pg. 21
Tabet, Kenneth, Dir.-Pur.--The Hennegan Company, Cincinnati, OH, pg. 529
Tallent, Clyde A., Dir., Pur.--Grizzard Advertising, Inc., Atlanta, GA, pg. 488
Tallia, Sheila, Pur. Agent--Citizens National Bank, Hammond, LA, pg. 251
Talmon, Douglas E., Pur. Agent--Schultz Steel Company, South Gate, CA, pg. 979
Tango, William A., Dir.-Pur.--Production Machinery Corporation, Mentor, OH, pg. 893
Tank, M.O., Dir.-Pur.--Barber Dairies, Inc., Birmingham, AL, pg. 119
Tanselle, Tom, Dir.-Pur.--Manning Equipment, Inc., Louisville, KY, pg. 704
Tarver, Joe, V.P.-Pur.--Minyard Food Stores, Coppell, TX, pg. 759
Taylor, Charles, Mgr.-Pur.--Yorktowne, Inc., Red Lion, PA, pg. 1208
Taylor, Jerry, Pur. Agent--Paramount Foods Inc., Louisville, KY, pg. 848
Taylor, Robert, Mgr.-Pur.--Symons Corporation, Des Plaines, IL, pg. 1069
Terwilliger, Mary, Dir.-Acctg. & Pur.--Spreckles Industries, Inc., Pleasanton, CA, pg. 1032
Teteak, Charles A., Pur. Agent--Invincible Metal Furniture Co., Manitowoc, WI, pg. 582
Tharrington, Harold, Pur. Agent--Hackney Brothers, Inc., Wilson, NC, pg. 498
Thigpen, John, Assoc. Dir.-Pur.--Soft Sheen Products, Inc., Chicago, IL, pg. 1016
Thomas, Brad, Pur. Agent--Thomas Built Buses, Inc., High Point, NC, pg. 1092
Thomas, Crystal, Pur. Mgr.--Madison Industries, Los Angeles, CA, pg. 433
Thomas, Gerry, Mgr.-Pur.--Murdock, Inc., Compton, CA, pg. 776
Thomas, Jesse G., Treas., Sec., Chief Fin. & Chief Information Officer--Allen & Hoshall, Inc., Memphis, TN, pg. 36
Thomas, John, Dir.-Pur.--Dettra Flag Company, Oaks, PA, pg. 333
Thomas, Karen, Dir.-Pur.--Erdle Perforating Co., Rochester, NY, pg. 385
Thomas, Peter, Dir.-Pur.--National R.V., Inc., Perris, CA, pg. 792
Thomas, Roger, Pur. Agent--J.E. Berkowitz, LP, Westville, NJ, pg. 142
Thompson, B.W., Jr., Dir.-Fuel Procurement--Alabama Electric Cooperative, Inc., Andalusia, AL, pg. 28
Thompson, Glenn, Pur. Dir.--C.F. Thompson Group, Inc., Windsor, CT, pg. 1094
Thompson, John, Pur. Mgr.--Sargent & Greenleaf, Inc., Nicholasville, KY, pg. 971
Thompson, Joyce E., Dir.-Pur.--The J. M. Ney Company, Bloomfield, CT, pg. 805
Thompson, K., Pur. Agent--The Bodine Corp., Bridgeport, CT, pg. 161
Thompson, Roy, Mgr.-Purch.--Thomas Engineering Inc., Hoffman Estates, IL, pg. 1093
Thormann, Fred, V.P.-Corp. Resources--The Conde Nast Publications Inc., New York, NY, pg. 19
Thorner, Liz, Dir.-Pur.--Style Auto, Van Nuys, CA, pg. 1055
Tidwell, W.H., Dir.-Pur.--B & B Cash Grocery Store, Tampa, FL, pg. 105
Tipping, Paul, V.P.-Pur.--Grocery Supply Company Division, Sulphur Springs, TX, pg. 440
Tipton, Harrell, Pur. Dir.-Automotive Div.--STRAFCO, Inc., San Antonio, TX, pg. 1052
Titus, Lynn, Pur. Agent--Lasting Products, Inc., Dallas, TX, pg. 660
Titus, William, Sec. & Pur. Agent--Panel Prints, Inc., Old Forge, PA, pg. 846
Tobias, Paula, Pur. Agent--All Seasons Services, Inc., Braintree, MA, pg. 35
Tolaio, Mark, Pur. Agent--Salz Leathers, Inc., Santa Cruz, CA, pg. 968
Tomlinson, Larry, Mgr.-Matls.--M.C. Gill Corporation, El Monte, CA, pg. 458
Toomey, Rodger, V.P.-Mdsg. & Pur.--Food Services of America, Seattle, WA, pg. 423
Toone, Craig, Pur. Dir.--Flying J. Inc., Brigham City, UT, pg. 421
Torres, Eileen, Buyer--Tasco, Miami, FL, pg. 1079
Traup, Robert, Mgr.-Materials--New Standard Corporation, Mount Joy, PA, pg. 802
Traviglini, D., Pur. Agent--Munroe, Inc., Pittsburgh, PA, pg. 776
Treadaway, Roger, Dir.-Pur.--Days Inns of America, Inc., Atlanta, GA, pg. 1100
Treen, Ray, V.P.-Pur.-Bldg. Prods.--Hardware Wholesalers, Inc., Fort Wayne, IN, pg. 508
Treffiletti, Joseph, Pur. Agent--J. Treffiletti & Sons, Inc., Albany, NY, pg. 1109
Troutman, Kim, Pur. Agent--Pennsylvania State Lottery, Middletown, PA, pg. 858
Trouy, Gene, Pur. Agent--Sealy Mattress Company, Memphis, TN, pg. 986
Trumbull, David, Mgr.-Pur.--Nelson A. Taylor Co., Inc., Gloversville, NY, pg. 1080
Tschanen, W. F., V.P.-Opers.--American Office Equipment, La Grange, IL, pg. 58
Tucker, Janet, Mgr.-Pur.--Oklahoma Publishing Company, Oklahoma City, OK, pg. 446
Tucker, Larry, Dur.-Pur.--Empire Airlines, Hayden Lake, ID, pg. 379
Tucker, V.L., Pur. Agent--Anderson-Tully Co., Memphis, TN, pg. 73
Turf, Barbara, Exec. V.P.--Euromarket Designs, Inc., Northbrook, IL, pg. 390
Turkington, Brent, Sr. V.P.-Pur., Styrene Monomer SLs.--Huntsman Chemical Corporation, Salt Lake City, UT, pg. 555
Turpin, Joe, Pur. Agent--Sturgis Iron & Metal Company, Inc., Sturgis, MI, pg. 1055
Turton, Tim, Dir.-Pur.--McNaughton & Gunn, Inc., Saline, MI, pg. 732
Twohig, James F., Pur. Agent--General Latex & Chemical Corporation, Cambridge, MA, pg. 449
Tyson, Robert, Pur. Dir.-School Supplies--The Caxton Printers Ltd., Caldwell, ID, pg. 230
Uher, Roger, Dir.-Pur.--Farmland Industries, Inc., Kansas City, MO, pg. 402
Ulberg, J., Mgr.-Pur.--Hydraulics International, Inc., Chatsworth, CA, pg. 556
Ullmann, Rose, Pur. Agent--Theradyne Corporation, Lakeville, MN, pg. 1065
Ullom, Yvette L., V.P., Fin., Human Resources & Pur.--Fitzgerald & Company, Inc., Cranston, RI, pg. 416
Underwood, John, Mgr.-Pur.--Darigold, Inc., Seattle, WA, pg. 315
Urachez, Laslo Y., Pur. Agent--Technic Incorporated, Cranston, RI, pg. 1083
Urbina, Lisa, Supvr.-Pur.--Integral Systems, Walnut Creek, CA, pg. 572
Vaaler, Bernie, Mgr.-Procurement--Certified Grocers Of California, Los Angeles, CA, pg. 237
Vaillancourt, Paul, V.P.-Pur.--Buxton Company, Chicopee, MA, pg. 197
Vakil, Iqbal U., V.P.-Pur.--Lights Of America, Inc., Walnut, CA, pg. 675
Valone, Anthony J., V.P.-Pur.--Leviton Mfg. Co., Inc., Little Neck, NY, pg. 671
Van Pelt, George, Mgr.-Pur.--Rumsey Electric Co., Philadelphia, PA, pg. 956
Van Pelt, Robert J., Dir.-Pur.--Ginsberg's Institutional Foods, Inc., Hudson, NY, pg. 460
Van Stadt, Paul, Mgr.-Pur.--Humiston-Keeling, Inc., Chicago, IL, pg. 552
VanBesien, Leonard, Pur. Agent--Brammer Manufacturing Company, Davenport, IA, pg. 171
Vanco, Richard, Mgr.-Pur.--Columbia National Group, Inc., Cleveland, OH, pg. 265
Vander Woude, Hugh, Pur. Agent--Bissell Inc., Grand Rapids, MI, pg. 153
Vanoss, Frank, Dir.-Pur.--Vilter Manufacturing Corporation, Milwaukee, WI, pg. 1152
Vanzant, Richard, Dir.-Pur.--Rotary Forms Press, Inc., Hillsboro, OH, pg. 950
VanzenBergen, K., Pur. Agent--Waukesha Foundry Inc., Waukesha, WI, pg. 1168
Varani, Gene, Pur. Agent--L&R Manufacturing Co., Kearny, NJ, pg. 647
Varda, Bob, Mgr.-Pur.--Blue Coral, Inc., Cleveland, OH, pg. 159
Varda, Robert P., Dir.-Pur.--Simoniz Canada Ltd., Cleveland, OH, pg. 159
Varel, Daniel, Jr., Pur. Dir.--Varel Manufacturing Co., Dallas, TX, pg. 1145
Vargas, Alex, V.P., Chief Oper. Officer & Pur. Dir.--Cash & Carry Grocer Inc., Chicago, IL, pg. 228
Varteresian, Charles, V.P.-Procurement--Baker Commodities, Inc., Los Angeles, CA, pg. 115
Vasquez, Larry, Pur. Agent--Colonial Beef Co., Philadelphia, PA, pg. 263
Vasquez, Linda, Mgr.-Pur.--Mercury Computer Systems, Inc., Lowell, MA, pg. 740
Vasquez, M.J., Mgr.-Pur.--Duraco Products, Inc., Streamwood, IL, pg. 354
Vaughn, Randal, Dir.-Pur.--KSG Inc., Guntersville, AL, pg. 613
Vega, Randi, Buyer--Tasco, Miami, FL, pg. 1079
Verbout, Mel, V.P.-Milk Procurement--Cass-Clay Creamery, Fargo, ND, pg. 228
Verbraska, Wes, Pur. Agent--Imperial Pools, Inc., Latham, NY, pg. 564
Verst, Leo R., V.P.-Pur.--Kluener Packing Company, Cincinnati, OH, pg. 636
Vetsch, Bruce, Dir.-Pur.--Palm Beach Beauty Products Co., Minneapolis, MN, pg. 843
Vickerman, Ruth, Dir.-Pur. Agent--E.A. Sween Company, Eden Prairie, MN, pg. 1066
Vidas, Robert, Mgr.-Matls.--Cornell Forge Company, Chicago, IL, pg. 286
Vincent, Barbara L., Dir.-Pur. & Security Officer--UES, Inc., Dayton, OH, pg. 1122
Vinson, Walter, Pur. Dir. & Asst. Treas.--Basic Construction Company, Newport News, VA, pg. 124
Vinyard, Keith, Mgr.-Parts Distr.--Alamo Group, Inc., Seguin, TX, pg. 29
Virgine, Jane, Pur. Agent--Norweco, Inc., Spokane, WA, pg. 816
Vleck, Rudolph, Mgr.-Pur.--Mark Lighting Fixture Co., Inc., Moonachie, NJ, pg. 708
Vogel, Evelyn, Pur. Agent--U.S. Graphite, Inc., Saginaw, MI, pg. 1136
Vogel, John, Pur. Agent--General American Life Insurance Co., St. Louis, MO, pg. 448
Vogt, Sue, Dir.-Pur.--Carousel Snack Bars Of Minnesota, Minneapolis, MN, pg. 224
Voithofer, J., Pur. Agent--VJ Growers, Inc., Apopka, FL, pg. 1141
Volkening, James, Dir.-Pur.--Eclipse, Inc., Rockford, IL, pg. 366
Voltz, Amy, V.P.-Pur.--Judson-Atkinson Candies, Inc., San Antonio, TX, pg. 608
Von Bargen, Merlyn, Pur. Agent--Watkins Incorporated, Winona, MN, pg. 1167
Von Beetz, Harry, Pur. Agent--Indeck Power Equipment Company, Wheeling, IL, pg. 564

Von Hinueber, Charles, Pur. Agent--Tapemark, West St. Paul, MN, pg. 1078
Vosekas, Cathy, Buyer--Tasco, Miami, FL, pg. 1079
Wabiszewski, Edmund E. Jr., Plant Mgr. & Pur. Mgr.--Maynard Steel Casting Company, Milwaukee, WI, pg. 725
Wachtel, Jim, Dir.-Pur.--Ferguson Electric Construction Co., Inc., Buffalo, NY, pg. 406
Wagener, Tom, Mgr.-Pur.--Reliable Automatic Sprinkler Co., Inc., Mount Vernon, NY, pg. 924
Wagner, Cynthia, Dir.-Pur.--Contractors Steel Company, Livonia, MI, pg. 280
Wagner, Don, V.P.-Corp. Distr.--Mary Kay Cosmetics Inc., Dallas, TX, pg. 716
Wagner, Max, V.P.-Pur.--Bestform Foundations, Inc., Long Island City, NY, pg. 147
Wahl, William, Dir.-Pur.--American Printers & Lithographers, Chicago, IL, pg. 59
Wahlstrom, Robert P., V.P.-Pur.--Specialty Restaurants Corporation, Anaheim, CA, pg. 1027
Walden, Sam, Mgr.-Materials--Vernay Laboratories, Inc., Yellow Springs, OH, pg. 1148
Waleke, Paul, V.P.-Pur.--Northern Wire & Cable, Inc., Troy, MI, pg. 814
Walker, Ron, Dir.-Pur.--Aeros Instruments, Inc., Northbrook, IL, pg. 1034
Walker, Shawn, Dir.-Pur.--Awrey Bakeries, Inc., Livonia, MI, pg. 103
Walker, Thomas W., Pur. Agent--Bardons & Oliver, Inc., Cleveland, OH, pg. 119
Wallace, Brenda G., Pur. Agent--Hurd Lock & Manufacturing Co., Greeneville, TN, pg. 102
Wallace, Catherine A., Mgr.-Pur.--Newage Industries Inc., Willow Grove, PA, pg. 803
Wallace, Catherine A., Mgr.-Pur. & Dir.-Import--Newage Industries Inc., Plastics Division, Willow Grove, PA, pg. 803
Wallace, William, Dir.-Pur.--Malco Products, Inc., Barberton, OH, pg. 702
Waller, Jeff, Pur. Agent--Lodal, Inc., Kingsford, MI, pg. 680
Walsh, R., Pur. Agent--Foster Refrigerator Corporation, Hudson, NY, pg. 426
Walthal, Bud, Dir.-Pur.--Bearden Lumber Company, Inc., Bearden, AR, pg. 129
Ward, B., Mgr.-Pur.--McLaughlin Gormley King Company, Minneapolis, MN, pg. 731
Ward, Bob, Pur. Mgr.--Electronic Measurements, Inc., Neptune, NJ, pg. 145
Ward, Martin, Pur. Agent--Lawrence Paper Company, Lawrence, KS, pg. 662
Ward, Mike, Dir.-Pur.--Baker Concrete Construction, Inc., Monroe, OH, pg. 115
Warmflash, Howard, Dir.-Pur.--I. Spiewak & Sons, Inc., New York, NY, pg. 1031
Warren, Richard L., Dir.-Corp. Pur.--Country Home Bakery, Inc., Bridgeport, CT, pg. 290
Waska, Len, Mgr.-Pur.--Port of Houston Authority, Houston, TX, pg. 881
Waters, Patrick J., V.P.-Pur.--Industrial Acoustics Company, Inc., Bronx, NY, pg. 565
Watkins, Reave J., Mgr.-Office--Hillman Company, Pittsburgh, PA, pg. 535
Watson, David E., Pur. Agent--Dixie Electric Cooperative, Union Springs, AL, pg. 341
Watson, Tammy, Dir.-Pur.--Iowa Lottery, Des Moines, IA, pg. 582
Wattel, Bob, Exec. V.P.-Pur. & Opers.--Lettuce Entertain You Enterprises, Inc., Chicago, IL, pg. 668
Watters, Don, Pur. Agent--Oil & Gas Supply Company, Houston, TX, pg. 823
Watts, Denise, Dir.-Pur.--Tim & Diane Blagge Inc., Rancho Cordova, CA, pg. 155
Watts, R.D., V.P.-Industrial & Commodity--Riviana Foods Inc., Houston, TX, pg. 937
Weatherhead, W., Pur. Agent--J.M. Huber, Wood Products Div., Charlotte, NC, pg. 550
Weaver, Bruce, Dir.-Pur.--Microwave Networks Incorporated, Houston, TX, pg. 749
Webelhuth, Ron, Dir.-Purch. & Construction Res.--Tarlton Corporation, Saint Louis, MO, pg. 1079
Weber, Ed, Pur. Agent--Dormeyer Industries, Chicago, IL, pg. 346
Weber, George, Pur. Agent--E. J. Brooks Company, Newark, NJ, pg. 179
Weber, Leroy H., Pur. Agent--E.M. Wiegmann & Company, Inc., Freeburg, IL, pg. 1188
Webster, Richard, Pur. Agent--Electrical Wholesale Supply Company, Inc., Idaho Falls, ID, pg. 374
Weeks, Shirley, Chief Fin. Officer & Dir.-Data Processing--Bill Woeste Dealer Group, Cincinnati, OH, pg. 1198
Wegner, Ken, Dir.-Pur.--The Jel Sert Co., West Chicago, IL, pg. 591
Wehberg, Joyce, Chief Oper. Officer & Dir.-Pur.--Shillcraft, Inc., Baltimore, MD, pg. 999
Wehman, Jeffrey T., Pur. Agent--Pittsburgh Tube Co., Monaca, PA, pg. 873
Weidmann, C., Mgr.-Pur.--Capital Controls Company Inc., Colmar, PA, pg. 215
Weiland, Larry, Dir.-Sls.--Sterling Supply Company, Inc., Lisle, IL, pg. 1047
Weinbach, Myron, V.P.-Pur.--M.W. Kasch Company, Mequon, WI, pg. 617
Weingarten, Ed, Pur. Agent--Universal Photonics, Inc., Hicksville, NY, pg. 1139
Weinstein, Beryl, V.P.-Procurement--Pueblo International, Inc., Pompano Beach, FL, pg. 899
Weisberg, Jeff, Dir.-Pur.--Modern Concrete Septic Tank Company, Ottsville, PA, pg. 762
Weiss, Jeff, Dir.-Pur.--Malden Mills Industries, Inc., Lawrence, MA, pg. 702
Weiss, Robert, Dir.-Personnel & Pur.--Austin Sculpture, Holbrook, NY, pg. 99
Weissner, Alex, Pur. Agent--Ohmite Manufacturing Company, Skokie, IL, pg. 823
Weith, John, Buyer--The Bartell Drug Company, Seattle, WA, pg. 122
Welbo, Steven, Dir.-Pur.--Willoughby's, New York, NY, pg. 1193
Welch, Jim, Pur. Agent--Great Plains Manufacturing, Inc., Assaria, KS, pg. 482
Welch, Ron, Pur. Agent--Bates Container, Inc., North Richland Hills, TX, pg. 125
Welcome, Craig, Dir.-Pur.--CB North America, Inc., Glens Falls, NY, pg. 199
Wells, Connie, Mgr.-Pur.--Mayfair Mills, Inc., Arcadia, SC, pg. 724
Welshons, John, Dir.-Pur.--Smead Manufacturing Company, Hastings, MN, pg. 1011
Wendrof, Chris, Pur. Agent--L. L. Olds Seed Company, Madison, WI, pg. 824
Wentzell, Steven, Dir.-Pur.--The Entwistle Company, Hudson, MA, pg. 383
Werner, Ralph, Mgr.-Pur.--North American Products Corp., Jasper, IN, pg. 811
Wertenberger, Orlow, V.P.-Pur.--Red Roof Inns, Inc., Hilliard, OH, pg. 918
West, Robert, Pur. Agent--Marketing Displays International, Inc., Farmington Hills, MI, pg. 709
Westcott, Ronald E., V.P.-Pur.--Fabric Wholesalers, Inc., Portland, OR, pg. 396
Westerfield, Roger, Dir.-Pur.--Esco Elevators, Inc., Fort Worth, TX, pg. 388
Westley, Deborah, Dir.-Pur.--Henri's Food Products Co., Inc., Milwaukee, WI, pg. 530
Westover, David, Dir.-Pur.--American Metal & Plastics, Grand Rapids, MI, pg. 58
Wetherill, J.B., Pur. Agent--Fostoria Industries, Inc., Fostoria, OH, pg. 427
Wetmore, Richard, Pur. Agent--Blue Diamond Growers, Sacramento, CA, pg. 160
Whaley, R., Dir.-Pur.--Suitt Construction Company, Inc., Greenville, SC, pg. 1056
Wheeler, Carl, V.P.-Pur.--Super D Drug Stores, Memphis, TN, pg. 1062
Whetstone, dean, Mgr.-Matls.--National Cooperative Refinery Association, McPherson, KS, pg. 787
Whitaker, Ron, Dir.-Pur.--Schwegmann Giant Super Markets, New Orleans, LA, pg. 980
White, John, Dir.-Natl. Pur.--Safeguard Business Systems, Inc., Fort Washington, PA, pg. 966
White, Ray, Dir.-Pur.--W-B Supply Co., Pampa, TX, pg. 1155
White, Ron, Dir.-Pur.--Kasle Steel Corporation, Dearborn, MI, pg. 617
Whitfield, Frank G., Pres. & Chief Exec. Officer--Whitfield Foods, Inc., Montgomery, AL, pg. 1187
Whitley, Gene, Pur. Mgr.--Madison Industries Inc. of Georgia, Conyers, GA, pg. 433
Whitley, Ken, Pur. Agent--Antenna Products Corp., Mineral Wells, TX, pg. 76
Whitman, E.R., Dir.-Pur.--Lewis Brothers Bakeries, Inc., Evansville, IN, pg. 673
Whitton, Dale, Sr. V.P.-Grocery Pur.--Brookshire Grocery, Tyler, TX, pg. 180
Wholey, Rick, Dir.-Intl. Sourcing--Rockford International Group, Rockford, IL, pg. 942
Wick, Richard, Pur. Agent--E.R. Wagner Mfg. Co. Wagner Prods. Div., Hustisford, WI, pg. 1158
Wickman, Beverly, Dir.-Pur.--Attwood Corporation, Lowell, MI, pg. 1044
Wiencek, Donald, Dir.-Mfg. & Pur.--Continental Web Press, Inc., Itasca, IL, pg. 280
Wiener, Larry, Pur. Mgr.--Alimed, Inc., Dedham, MA, pg. 34
Wightman, Lynn, Dir.-Pur.--Perlmuter Printing Company, Cleveland, OH, pg. 862
Wilber, Kenneth H., Pur. Agent--The Columbia Corporation, Chatham, NY, pg. 1209
Wilcox, Anne, Mgr.-Pur.--The Kiplinger Washington Editors, Inc., Washington, DC, pg. 632
Wild, David L., Mgr.-Pur.--Northwestern Mutual Life Insurance Co., Milwaukee, WI, pg. 815
Wilhoite, Dennis, V.P.-Pur.--The Starflo Corporation, Orangeburg, SC, pg. 883
Wilk, Darla S., Mgr.-Pur.--Cleveland Machine Controls, Cleveland, OH, pg. 255
Wilk, John M., Pur. Agent--Acker Drill Co. Inc., Chinchilla, PA, pg. 12
Wilke, Bruce, Sr. V.P.-Distribution Opers.--Mary Kay Cosmetics Inc., Dallas, TX, pg. 716
Wilkes, Gary, Mgr.-Pur.--Findley Adhesives, Inc., Wauwatosa, WI, pg. 410
Wilkey, Donald, Dir.-Pur.--Growmark, Inc., Bloomington, IL, pg. 490
Willeford, S., Mgr.-Pur.--Besser/APPCO, San Antonio, TX, pg. 146
Willhoite, Dennis, V.P.-Pur.--The Wm. Powell Company, Cincinnati, OH, pg. 882
Williams, Dan, Personnel & Pur. Dir.--M.A.B. Paints, Terre Haute, IN, pg. 184
Williams, Doug, Dir.-Pur.--CAE Link Allen Division, Alexandria, VA, pg. 198
Williams, Jim, Pur. Agent--Maghielse Tool Corporation, Grand Rapids, MI, pg. 700
Williams, Leo, Pur. Agent--Staple Cotton Cooperative Association, Greenwood, MS, pg. 1038
Williams, Marjory, Pur. Agent--Olsonite Corporation, Detroit, MI, pg. 824
Williams, Phil, Pur. Agent--Martin Industries (AL), Florence, AL, pg. 715
Williams, Ronald O., Dir.-Pur. & Property--Transus Inc., Atlanta, GA, pg. 1108
Wilmore, Ken, V.P.-Sourcing & Acquisitions--Globe Business Furniture, Inc., Hendersonville, TN, pg. 463
Wilson, Alvis, Dir.-Pur.--HDS Services, Farmington Hills, MI, pg. 496
Wilson, Bruce, Mgr.-Procurement & Transportation--Waldorf Corporation, Saint Paul, MN, pg. 1159
Wilson, Charles, V.P.-Prod.--McKee Foods Corporation, Collegedale, TN, pg. 730
Wilson, Ray, Pur. Agent--McLaughlin Industrial Distributors, Inc., Pico Rivera, CA, pg. 731
Winkel, Mark, Dir.-Pur.--GNWC Wire, Cable & Network Producers, Downers Grove, IL, pg. 440
Winkey, Larry, Pur. Agent--United Farm Tools, Inc., Oelwein, Oelwein, IA, pg. 1132
Winn, David, Pur. Agent--Republic Industries, Inc., Harwood Heights, IL, pg. 928
Winston, Jeri, Sr. V.P.-Admin.--General Media Publishing Group, New York, NY, pg. 450
Winter, Mark, Dir.-Pur.--Robert F. Driver Co., Inc., San Diego, CA, pg. 349
Wise, Kevin, Pur. Agent--Ross Engineering Co., Inc., Leola, PA, pg. 949
Witkowski, Paul, Dir.-Pur.--North Atlantic Industries, Inc., Hauppauge, NY, pg. 812
Witt, Edward E., Sr. V.P.-Pur. & Sls.--Miller Electric Company, Jacksonville, FL, pg. 754
Witte, Jay, Dir.-Pur.--Hackney & Sons, Inc., Washington, NC, pg. 498
Wittenberg, Robert, Sr. V.P.-Sls., Mktg. & Pur.--Video Products Distributors, Inc., Sacramento, CA, pg. 1150
Wittum, Chuck, Mgr.-Pur.--Standard Locknut & Lockwasher, Carmel, IN, pg. 1037
Witzel, John A., Controller--The Dispatch Printing Company, Columbus, OH, pg. 339
Wlodarski, Arthur, V.P.-Pur.--Houston Foods Company, Chicago, IL, pg. 547
Woelkers, David C., Dir.-Pur.--Hatfield Quality Meats, Inc., Hatfield, PA, pg. 517
Woeste, Bill F., Jr., Pres. & Dir.-Pur.--Bill Woeste Dealer Group, Cincinnati, OH, pg. 1198
Wolf, Ned, V.P.-Pur.-Hardware--Hardware Wholesalers, Inc., Fort Wayne, IN, pg. 508
Wolfer, Judy, Mgr.-Pur.--Cambridge Associates, Boston, MA, pg. 316
Wolfinger, John, Pur. Agent--Johnson & Towers, Inc., Mount Laurel, NJ, pg. 601
Wood, Donald, Dir.-Pur.--Serono Baker Diagnostics, Allentown, PA, pg. 991
Wood, Dorothy, Pur. Agent--Ce De Candy, Inc., Union, NJ, pg. 230
Wood, James, Pur. Agent--Fimbel Door Corporation, Whitehouse, NJ, pg. 409
Wood, Lyn, Pur. Agent--Wingfoot Films Corporation, Carrollton, OH, pg. 555
Wood, Wayne, Dir.-Pur.--VMC Fiberglass Products Inc., Daleville, AL, pg. 1142
Woodard, Melvin, Dir.-Pur.--Holcomb & Hoke Mfg. Company, Inc., Indianapolis, IN, pg. 538
Woodruff, Peter, Dir.-Pur.--Falcon Candy Company, Philadelphia, PA, pg. 398
Woods, Jim, Pur. Agent--Lloyd Controls, Inc., Mountlake Terrace, WA, pg. 679
Wooten, David, Dir.-Pur.--Pioneer/Eclipse Corp., Sparta, NC, pg. 871
Worso, Ray, Dir.-Pur.--George W. Cochran Co., Inc., Washington, DC, pg. 258
Wright, Becky, Pur. Agent--Quality Control Corporation, Harwood Heights, IL, pg. 903
Wright, Bill, Pur. Agent--The Vernon Company, Newton, IA, pg. 1148
Wright, Doug, Mgr.-Pur.--Hamilton Co., Inc., Reno, NV, pg. 503
Wright, Thomas H., Mgr.-Pur.--Keystone Carbon Company, Saint Marys, PA, pg. 628
Wroldson, Holly, Pur. Agent--Petricca Industries, Inc., Pittsfield, MA, pg. 865
Wunsch, Joe, Dir.-Pur.--The Bibb Company, Macon, GA, pg. 781
Wurzler, Douglas, Mgr.-Personnel--Wenczel Tile Co., Trenton, NJ, pg. 1176
Wykoff, Jeffery S., Dir.-Pur.--HPS, Inc., Indianapolis, IN, pg. 497
Wyman, J., V.P.-Pur.--R & B Machine Tool Co., Saline, MI, pg. 906
Yaeger, Chris, Mgr.-Pur. & Traffic--Ficks Reed Company, Cincinnati, OH, pg. 408
Yasuo, Katsumata, Dir.-Pur.--Mutual Trading Co., Inc., Los Angeles, CA, pg. 779
Yates, Rene, Pur. Agent--B.A. Ballou & Co. Inc., East Providence, RI, pg. 116
Yeager, Dennis A., Mgr.-Pur.--PMC Industries Inc., Wickliffe, OH, pg. 836
Yeagle, Don, Pur. Mgr.--The William Bayley Co., Springfield, OH, pg. 128
Yeakle, Neil, Dir.-Pur.--B. Green & Co., Baltimore, MD, pg. 484
Yeargan, William, Pur. Agent--Jones Blair Company, Dallas, TX, pg. 602
Yoas, Russell E., Mgr.-Pur. & Production--Yorktowne Paper Mills, Inc., York, PA, pg. 1208
Yonkers, Henry, Pur. Agent--Rose Printing Company, Inc., Tallahassee, FL, pg. 948
Yost, Bruce, V.P.-Pur.--Industrial Wire Products Corporation, Pomona, CA, pg. 567
Yost, Dale C., Pur. Dir.--Lear Siegler Plastics Corp., Mendon, MI, pg. 664
Young, Dick, Mgr.-Materials--Zippo Manufacturing Company, Bradford, PA, pg. 1220
Young, Les, Pur. Agent--First District Association, Litchfield, MN, pg. 412
Yu, Johnson, Mgr.-Pur.--Paramount Fitness Equipment Corp., Los Angeles, CA, pg. 848
Yurco, T J., V.P.-Matls. Mngmt. & Logistics--U.S. Can Company, Oak Brook, IL, pg. 1134
Zanga, Lawrence A., Dir.-Pur.--Erving Paper Mills, Erving, MA, pg. 388
Zantop, Duane G., V.P.-Pur.--Zantop International Airlines, Inc., Ypsilanti, MI, pg. 1216
Zehnder, Mark, Mgr.-Pur.--Igloo Corporation, Houston, TX, pg. 562
Zekaria, Alice, Sec. & Mgr.-Gen. Mdse.--Windsor Fashions, Los Angeles, CA, pg. 1195

Zelinski, Mark, Mgr.-Pur.--Reliable Knitting Works, Milwaukee, WI, pg. 924
Zelinski, Mark, Pur. Mgr.--Penthouse Knitting Mills, Milwaukee, WI, pg. 925
Zeman, Bruce, Dir.-Pur.--A-P-A Transport Corp., North Bergen, NJ, pg. 5
Zenger, Corey, Pur. Agent--Smith Frozen Foods, Inc., Weston, OR, pg. 1012
Zeratsky, Drew, Pur. Agent--National Rivet & Manufacturing Company, Waupun, WI, pg. 793
Zicherman, Stan, Pur. Mgr.--Empire Brushes, Inc., Greenville, NC, pg. 379
Ziebel, Kitch, Dir.-Pur.--Precision Twist Drill Co., Crystal Lake, IL, pg. 885
Ziebel, Kitch, Dir.-Pur.--Mohawk Tools, Crystal Lake, IL, pg. 885
Ziebel, Kitch, Pur. Dir.--Triumph Twist Drill Co., Crystal Lake, IL, pg. 885
Zimet, Dean, Dir.-Pur.--DVC Industries, Bay Shore, NY, pg. 310
Zimmerman, E.B., Pur. Agent--Lancaster Malleable Castings Company, Lancaster, PA, pg. 653
Zink, Thomas, Dir.-Pur.--Equitable Bag Company, Long Island City, NY, pg. 385
Zitomer, Bernard, V.P.-Pur.--Sunshine Biscuits, Inc., Woodbridge, NJ, pg. 439
Zlotnik, A., Pres.--Odomaster Canada, Mississauga,, Canada, pg. 1065
Zoldos, Jerry, Mgr.-Pur.--Donlee Technologies Inc., York, PA, pg. 344
Zuckerman, Henry, V.P.-Pur.--Zuckerman-Honickman Inc., King of Prussia, PA, pg. 1221
Zuckero, Carl, Sr. V.P.-Pur.--Tweddle Litho Company, St. Clair Shores, MI, pg. 1120
Zuehlke, T.L., Mgr.-Pur.--Wells Mfg. Corp., Dond Du Lac, WI, pg. 1123
Zuendel, Steve, V.P.-Matls.--Ritchie Corporation, Wichita, KS, pg. 936
Zumbach, Norma, Dir.-Pur.--The Elwell-Parker Electric Co., Cleveland, OH, pg. 378
Zurawski, Mary, Supvr.-Pur.--Worzalla Publishing Co., Inc., Stevens Point, WI, pg. 1204

SALES

Abbatiello, Virgil, V.P.-Sls.--Dribeck Importers, Inc., Greenwich, CT, pg. 349
Abbott, Tim, V.P.-Sls. & Gen. Mgr.--Electro Dynamics Crystal Corporation, Overland Park, KS, pg. 374
Abernethy, J.W., III, V.P.-Sls.--Carolina Glove Co., Newton, NC, pg. 223
Abernethy, James S., V.P.-Sls.--Carolina Glove Co., Newton, NC, pg. 223
Abrahamson, Lee, V.P.-Sls.-OEM--Ko-Rec-Type, Brooklyn, NY, pg. 121
Abrams, Donald J., Mgr.-Sls., Drain Valves--Strahman Valves, Inc., Florham Park, NJ, pg. 1052
Abramson, Jules, V.P.-Sls.--Academy Entertainment Inc., Beverly Hills, CA, pg. 86
Abruzzo, Chris, Mgr.-Sls.--Great Lakes Technologies Corp., Kalamazoo, MI, pg. 482
Abu-Ghazold, Noel, Dir.-Sls.--The ASCII Group, Inc., Bethesda, MD, pg. 8
Accola, Richard M., V.P.-Sls. & Mktg.--Gravymaster Inc., Branford, CT, pg. 478
Accola, Richard M., V.P.-Sls. & Mktg.--Dryden & Palmer Company, Branford, CT, pg. 479
Achtner, S., Mgr.-Sls.--Burns & Roe Enterprises, Inc., Oradell, NJ, pg. 194
Acker, Claud, Asst. V.P.-Domestic Sls.--Calcot, Ltd., Bakersfield, CA, pg. 208
Acker, Jack, V.P.-Sls. & Gen. Mgr.--Sleepy's The Mattress Professionals, Port Washington, NY, pg. 1010
Ackerman, Marty, Mgr.-Sls.--Hoboken Wood Flooring Corporation, Wayne, NJ, pg. 537
Ackermann, Joe, Sr. V.P.-Sls.--Gateway Press, Inc., Louisville, KY, pg. 446
Adams, D. Scott, Natl. Sls. Mgr.--Deck House Inc., Acton, MA, pg. 324
Adams, Dale, Dir.-Sls.--Regency Lincoln Mercury, Dallas, TX, pg. 922
Adams, Ed, Dir.-Natl. Sls.--National Football League Properties, Inc., New York, NY, pg. 788
Adams, Ernest R., Dir.-Sls. & Mktg.--Evening Post Publishing Co., Charleston, SC, pg. 391
Adams, Henry, V.P.-Sls., Mktg., Adv. & Tech. Services--Norwalk Powdered Metals, Inc., Norwalk, CT, pg. 816
Adams, John, Mgr.-S.E. Distr. Sls.--King & Prince Seafood Corporation, Brunswick, GA, pg. 631
Adams, Leslie, V.P., Sls. & New Business Contact--The Phillips Agency, Horsham, PA, pg. 867
Adams, Richard B., Gen. Sls. Mgr.--R. P. Adams Company, Inc., Tonawanda, NY, pg. 16
Adams, Robert, Dir.-Specialty Sls.--Hydrite Chemical Company, Brookfield, WI, pg. 556
Adams, Roger, Pres.-Trade Sls.--Fuller O'Brien Paints, South San Francisco, CA, pg. 820
Adamson, Kristin, Mkt. Res. Analyst & Sls. Co-ordinator--W&F Manufacturing Corporation, Inc., Buffalo, NY, pg. 1155
Addis, James, Mgr.-Sls.--Gregg Industries, Inc., El Monte, CA, pg. 486
Addison, Ron, Natl. Sls. Mgr.--Battery St. Enterprises, Running Gear Div., Boulder, CO, pg. 670
Adelman, Joel, Mgr.-Sls.--Blue Coral, Inc., Cleveland, OH, pg. 159
Adelman, Steve, V.P.-Sls.--David Brett, Inc., Easton, MA, pg. 174
Aders, Thomas D., V.P.-Sls.--Ficks Reed Company, Cincinnati, OH, pg. 408
Adler, Howard, Sr. V.P.-Sls. Promo. & Mktg.--R. H. Macy & Co., Inc., New York, NY, pg. 698
Adler, Richard J., V.P.-Sls. & Sec.--Fort Dearborn Lithograph Company, Niles, IL, pg. 425
Agee, Robert D., V.P.-Sls.--Artco-Bell Corporation, Temple, TX, pg. 86
Agin, Jerry, V.P.-Sls.--Hill & Griffith Company, Cincinnati, OH, pg. 534
Aguirre, Greg, V.P.-Sls.--SaniServ, Indianapolis, IN, pg. 970
Ahern, James, Mgr.-Natl. Sls.--Precision Carbide Tool Company, Inc., Niles, IL, pg. 885
Ahlquist, A., V.P.-Sls.--Schnadig Corporation, Chicago, IL, pg. 977
Ahlstrom, Craig, Dir.-Adv., Mktg., Opers. & Sls.--Farnsworth Development Co., Mesa, AZ, pg. 403
Albert, Gene, Mgr.-Sls. Admin.--Bostrom Seating, Inc., Piedmont, AL, pg. 168
Alcorn, Terry, V.P.-North American Sls.--Connors Brunswick, Inc., South Portland, ME, pg. 275
Alcorn, Terry, V.P.-N. American Sls.--Port Clyde Foods Co., South Portland, ME, pg. 276
Alexander, Dale, V.P.-Sls. Training--Mary Kay Cosmetics Inc., Dallas, TX, pg. 716
Alexander, George, V.P.-Sls. & Mktg.--Thermon Manufacturing Company, San Marcos, TX, pg. 1091
Alexander, Lee, V.P.-Sls.--Amco Folding Cartons, Inc., Towaco, NJ, pg. 47
Alexander, Lynn E., V.P.-Mktg. & Sales--Thoroughbred Software International, Inc., Somerset, NJ, pg. 1095
Alexy, R. James, Sr. V.P.-Mktg./Sls.--The Stearns & Foster Bedding Company, Cleveland, OH, pg. 985
Alexy, R. James, Sr. V.P.-Mktg. & Sls.--Sealy, Inc., Cleveland, OH, pg. 985
Alexy, R. James, Sr. V.P.-Mktg./Sls.--Stearns & Foster Upholstery Furniture Co., Pontotoc, MS, pg. 985
Alleman, A.J., Mgr.-Sls. Service & Export--National Frozen Foods Corp., Seattle, WA, pg. 789
Allen, Alma, Mgr.-Sls. Admin.--Code-A-Phone Corp., Clackamas, OR, pg. 258
Allen, Bill, Western Circulation Mgr.--Daily Racing Form, Inc. Pacific, Los Angeles, CA, pg. 611
Allen, Calhoun, Sr. V.P., Dir.-Mktg. Services/Opers.--The Atkins Agency, San Antonio, TX, pg. 94
Allen, D., V.P.-Sls.--North & Judd, Middletown, CT, pg. 812
Allen, Dennis, Dir.-Sls.--Continental Web Press, Inc., Itasca, IL, pg. 280
Allen, James, Dir.-Corp. Sls.--Seabrook Wallcoverings, Inc., Memphis, TN, pg. 984
Allen, Joel, V.P.-Sls., Mktg. & Adv.--Allen Foods, Inc., Saint Louis, MO, pg. 36
Allen, John C., V.P.-Sls. & Mktg.--Wrought Washer Mfg., Inc., Milwaukee, WI, pg. 1205
Allen, Larry, Dir.-Sls.--Ace Office Products, Rolling Meadows, IL, pg. 12
Allen, Ralph, V.P.-Sls.--Custom Fabrics Div., West Point, GA, pg. 400
Allen, Richard, V.P.-Sls.--Allen Foods, Inc., Saint Louis, MO, pg. 36
Allen, Thomas G., V.P.-Sls. & Mktg.--Effective Management Systems, Milwaukee, WI, pg. 370
Allen, Wayne, V.P.-Sls. & Mktg. & Sec.--Idaho Supreme Company, Firth, ID, pg. 561
Allison, Bill, V.P.-Retail Sls.--Allen Canning Company, Siloam Springs, AR, pg. 35
Allman, James, Mgr.-Sls. & Mktg.--The Computer Patch of Joplin, Joplin, MO, pg. 1043
Allsop, James D., V.P.-Sls., Product Div.--Allsop, Inc., Bellingham, WA, pg. 43
Allsopp, J.E., Jr., V.P.-Sls.--Florida Crushed Stone Company, Leesburg, FL, pg. 420
Almond, Paul, Sls. Mgr.--CEM South, Leesburg, FL, pg. 1013
Alperin, Stuart A., V.P.-Sls.--Eastern Smelting & Refining Corporation, Lynn, MA, pg. 363
Alpert, Reva, Mgr.-Direct Sls.--Manostat Corporation, New York, NY, pg. 704
Alt, Claudia J., V.P.-State Sls.--Blue Cross & Blue Shield of Illinois, Chicago, IL, pg. 160
Altberg, Marla, V.P., Sls. & Mktg.--Ventura Associates, Inc., New York, NY, pg. 1147
Althoff, Victor, V.P.-Internal Sls.--American Office Equipment, La Grange, IL, pg. 58
Altmayer, L., Sls. Mgr.-Automotive Aftermarket--Littelfuse, Inc., Des Plaines, IL, pg. 678
Alves, John J., Mgr.-Findings Sls.--B.A. Ballou & Co. Inc., East Providence, RI, pg. 116
Alwardt, Fred, Mgr.-Sls.-Admin.--MidWest Body Corporation, Paris, IL, pg. 752
Alyn, A., Jr., Mgr.-Sls.--Mellon Corporation, New York, NY, pg. 738
Amabile, Ralph J., Jr., V.P.-Sls., Asian--Prime Tanning Co., Inc., Berwick, ME, pg. 889
Amos, Steve, V.P.-Sls. & Mktg.--The Blodgett Oven Co., Inc., Burlington, VT, pg. 157
Anacone, Robert B., V.P.-Mktg. & Sls.--Serono Baker Diagnostics, Allentown, PA, pg. 991
Anders, Mary, Dir.-Sls.--Levlad, Inc., Chatsworth, CA, pg. 671
Andersen, Rick, Mgr.-Sls.--Russell-Stanley West, Inc., Rancho Cucamonga, CA, pg. 957
Anderson, Bill, Mgr.-Sls. & Mktg.--Snyder Industries, Inc., Lincoln, NE, pg. 1015
Anderson, Gary, V.P.-Sls.--Mannington Mills, Inc., Salem, NJ, pg. 704
Anderson, Gene R., Grp. V.P.-Sls. & Mktg.--Southern States Cooperative, Inc., Richmond, VA, pg. 1022
Anderson, James, Dir.-Sls.--Sunkist Growers, Processed Products, Ontario, CA, pg. 1061
Anderson, John T., Mgr.-Sls.--BrowerPease, Inc., Hamilton, OH, pg. 181
Anderson, Larry, Gen. Sls. Mgr.--KSL Radio, Salt Lake City, UT, pg. 332
Anderson, Mal, Sls. Dir.--Carlson Retail Marketing, Minneapolis, MN, pg. 221
Anderson, Michael, Sls. Mgr.--Waterous Company, South Saint Paul, MN, pg. 50
Anderson, Mike, V.P.-Sls. & Mktg.--H.P.H. Industries Ltd., Lake Forest, IL, pg. 497
Anderson, Orren, V.P. & Mgr.-Sls.--Dakota Drug, Inc., Minot, ND, pg. 311
Anderson, Robert I., Exec. V.P.-Sls.--Gould Paper Corporation, New York, NY, pg. 473
Anderson, Robin, V.P.-Sls. & Mktg.--The Metal Ware Corp., Two Rivers, WI, pg. 741
Anderson, Sally, Mgr.-Adv. & Sls. Promo.--The Chamberlain Group, Inc., Elmhurst, IL, pg. 350
Anderson, Warren, Ntl. Sls. Mgr.--Dukane Communications Systems Div., Saint Charles, IL, pg. 352
Andrasko, Nancy M., V.P.-Sls. & Pur.--Star-Parts Inc., Hazleton, PA, pg. 1039
Andreas, Robert A., V.P.-Sls.--Flinn & Dreffein Engineering Co., Northbrook, IL, pg. 419
Andrews, Al, Pres.-Retail & Tanner Div.--Tanner Co. Inc., Rutherfordton, NC, pg. 1078
Andrews, Todd, V.P.-Eastern Sls.--Shade Foods, Inc., Union City, CA, pg. 810
Andrews, William H., Dir.-Sls.--The Great Lakes Cheese Co., Newbury, OH, pg. 481
Andrus, M.R., Natl. Sls. Mgr.--Duke Manufacturing Co., Inc., Saint Louis, MO, pg. 352
Aniballi, Douglas F., Sr. V.P.-Stores & Sls.--Amlings Flowerland, Hinsdale, IL, pg. 67
Annas, Carl, Consumer Sls. Mgr.--Willson Safety Products, Reading, PA, pg. 1193
Annel, John, V.P.-Sls.--The Segerdahl Corp., Wheeling, IL, pg. 987
Annexstad, A.T., Sr. V.P.-Sls.--Federated Mutual Insurance Company, Owatonna, MN, pg. 405
Antinoff, P., V.P.-Sls.--Aluminum Shapes, Inc., Delair, NJ, pg. 46
Anton, Joe, Mgr.-Sls.--Scherer Bros. Lumber Company, Minneapolis, MN, pg. 976
Antonaidis, George, V.P.-Grocery Sls.--Farley Candy Company, Chicago, IL, pg. 399
Apperson, C.A., Exec. V.P.-Sls.--Apperson Business Forms, Inc., Los Angeles, CA, pg. 78
Applebaum, Jim, V.P.-Field Sales--Costa Cruise Lines, N.V., Miami, FL, pg. 288
Appledy, Victor, Exec. V.P.-Sls. & Mktg.--Tollman/Hundley Hotels, Valhalla, NY, pg. 1100
Arbon, Gary K., V.P.-Sls.--Intermountain Farmers Association, Salt Lake City, UT, pg. 575
Arciero, Joan, Dir.-Sls.--Hitchcock Chair Company LTD, Riverton, CT, pg. 536
Arcuri, Lou, Exec. V.P.-Sls.--E.C.D., Inc., Hillside, NJ, pg. 359
Arenth, Thomas R., V.P.-East Coast Sls.--Fannie May Candy Shops, Inc., Chicago, IL, pg. 604
Arentzen, Peter, V.P.-Sls.--Tenax Corporation, Danbury, CT, pg. 1086
Aretakis, A.M., Mgr.-Mktg. & Sls.--Yardney Technical Products, Inc., Pawcatuck, CT, pg. 1207
Argeroudis, Nick, V.P.-Sls. & Mktg., Distr.--Tekra Corporation, New Berlin, WI, pg. 1084
Armagno, Mike, Mgr.-Sls.--Nic Sand, Cleveland, OH, pg. 159
Armbruster, Phil, V.P.-Mktg. Devel.--Hillerich & Bradsby Co., Inc., Louisville, KY, pg. 535
Armstrong, Darryl, V.P.-Sls.--Granite State Packing Co., Manchester, NH, pg. 476
Armstrong, Darryl, Dir.-Sls.& Mktg.--Granite State Packing Co., Manchester, NH, pg. 476
Armstrong, Federick, V.P.-Sls. & Mktg.--Pannier Corporation, Pittsburgh, PA, pg. 846
Armstrong, James, Mgr.-Sls.--B & G Wholesalers, Inc., Nashville, TN, pg. 106
Armstrong, Rich, Mgr.-Natl. Sls.--King & Prince Seafood Corporation, Brunswick, GA, pg. 631
Armstrong, Thomas E., V.P.-Sls.--Brant Allen Industries, Inc., Greenwich, CT, pg. 172
Arnau, C.R., Mgr.-Sls.--Benjamin Moore & Co., Montvale, NJ, pg. 139
Arnaudet, Larry, V.P.-Sls.--Freeman Decorating Co., Dallas, TX, pg. 431
Arnold, Ben, V.P.-Sls. & Mktg.--Chance Rides, Inc., Wichita, KS, pg. 238
Arnold, Bill, V.P., Sls. & Intl. Mktg.--Garvey International, Inc., St. Charles, IL, pg. 444
Arnold, David P., V.P.-Sls.--Preformed Line Products, Cleveland, OH, pg. 886
Arnold, Dennis, Dir.-Nat'l. Acct. Sls.--Globe Business Furniture, Inc., Hendersonville, TN, pg. 463
Arnold, Dennis P., V.P.-Sls.--Avibank Mfg., Inc., Burbank, CA, pg. 102
Arntzen, Sandra, V.P.-Retail Sls.--Maui Divers Of Hawaii, Ltd., Honolulu, HI, pg. 721
Arollado, Jim, Natl. Sls. Mgr.--Pen-Tab Industries, Inc., Glendale, NY, pg. 856
Aronin, Judy, Mgr.-Natl. Sls.--Sun Hill Industries, Stamford, CT, pg. 1059
Aronson, David, Exec. V.P.-Sls. & Pur.--Lumco Industries, Inc., Philadelphia, PA, pg. 687
Arredondo, Dan, V.P.-Sls.--Air Industries Corporation, Garden Grove, CA, pg. 27
Arthaud, John, Dir.-Sls.--Amana Society, Amana, IA, pg. 46
Arthur, Ralph W., Sr. V.P.-Mktg. & Sls.--Burlington Motor Carriers Inc., Daleville, IN, pg. 191
Arwady, Joseph, Dir.-Sls. & Mktg.--Burns International Security Services, Inc., Parsippany, NJ, pg. 166
Asbill, Robert, Mgr.-Sls.--Jones Blair Company, Dallas, TX, pg. 602
Ash, Lowell, V.P.-Sls.--Gould Paper Corporation, New York, NY, pg. 473
Ash, Rich, Mgr.-Inside Sls.--Associated Process Controls, Pleasanton, CA, pg. 92
Ashby, Dennis, Gen. Sls. Mgr.--James Steel & Tube Company, Madison Heights, MI, pg. 102
Asher, R., V.P.-Sls.--Faber/Castell Corporation, Parsippany, NJ, pg. 395
Ashley, Dan, Mgr.-Industrial Prods. Sls.--Ivex Packaging Corporation-Visalia, Visalia, CA, pg. 583

Asmus, Gerald H., V.P.-Sls.--Niagara Transformer Corp., Buffalo, NY, pg. 806
Aspinall, C. Craig, District Sls. Mgr.--Humphrey Fluid Power Ltd., Markham,, Canada, pg. 553
Astafan, Charles, Mgr.-Shredder Sls.--Columbus McKinnon Corp., Amherst, NY, pg. 266
Astorino, Michael, V.P.-Mktg. & Sls.--Kex Products, Inc., La Vergne, TN, pg. 145
Atkins, Charles, V.P.-Sls.--Tennessee Farmers Co-op, La Vergne, TN, pg. 1087
Atkins, Chuck, V.P.-Intl. Sls.--Advance Seed Co., Fulton, KY, pg. 407
Atkinson, John, Mgr.-Natl. Sls.--Kaepa Inc., San Antonio, TX, pg. 613
Aucutt, Larry, Dir.-Sls.--Noel Canning Corporation, Yakima, WA, pg. 808
Augustyn, Richard, V.P.-Mktg. & Sls.--King Group, Inc., Fenton, MI, pg. 630
Auslander, D.L., V.P.-Sls. & Mktg.--Medtech Laboratories, Inc., Jackson, WY, pg. 736
Austin, Glen, Sls. Mgr.--Alloway Manufacturing, Fargo, ND, pg. 41
Austin, Harry G., III, V.P.-Sls.--James Austin Co., Mars, PA, pg. 99
Austin, Peter, Mgr.-Sls. & Mktg.--Kingsbury Assembly Machine Div., Keene, NH, pg. 632
Averill, Richard, Natl. Sls. Mgr.--Deco Products Co., Decorah, IA, pg. 324
Avinger, Wade, Mgr.-Sls.--Holoubek Inc., Waukesha, WI, pg. 540
Axtell, Dean R., Chm. Bd. & Dir.-Intl. Sls.--Trak International, Inc., Port Washington, WI, pg. 1106
Aycack, E.C., Natl. Sls. Mgr.--Carolina Absorbent Cotton Co., Charlotte, NC, pg. 120
Ayers, Rollie, Dir.-Sls.--The Vagabond Inns, San Diego, CA, pg. 1142
Ayers, Stan, Natl. Sls. Mgr.--Clear Springs Foods, Inc., Buhl, ID, pg. 254
Aygard, George, Sr. Exec. V.P.-Sls.--Management Dynamics, New Providence, NJ, pg. 703
Aylward, A., V.P.-Sls. & Mktg.--Neenah Foundry Company, Neenah, WI, pg. 797
Baas, Roger, Mgr.-Sls.--Prince Corporation, Holland, MI, pg. 890
Babiarz, James, Mgr.-Sls.--Sensor Developments Inc., Orion, MI, pg. 990
Babrowski, Mike, Dir.-Mktg. & Sls.--Zoeller Co., Louisville, KY, pg. 1220
Bachmann, Jim, Mgr.-Sls.--Ivex Packaging Corporation-Floral and Nursery Products, Grant Park, IL, pg. 583
Bachtell, Bradley A., Dir.-Sls. & Opers.--Central Coca-Cola Bottling Company, Inc., Richmond, VA, pg. 232
Bacon, Vicky, V.P.-Mktg. & Service Oper.--Christenson Electric, Inc., Portland, OR, pg. 248
Baden, Marvin, V.P.-Mktg. & Sls., Sec. & Treas.--Producers Rice Mill Inc., Stuttgart, AR, pg. 892
Badenhop, Urban, Mgr.-Farm Equip. Sls.--Midwest Industries, Inc., Ida Grove, IA, pg. 752
Bagel, Milan, Sls. Mgr.-Electronics--Littelfuse, Inc., Des Plaines, IL, pg. 678
Bagley, Orval, Sls. Rep.--Triumph/LOR, Inc., Oklahoma City, OK, pg. 1115
Baida, Marvin, V.P.-Sls.--Idea Man, Inc., Los Angeles, CA, pg. 562
Baiden, Tim, V.P.-Mktg. & Sls.--Polar Ware Company, Sheboygan, WI, pg. 878
Baietti, Carlo, Mgr.-Sls.--The IDI Group Companies, Arlington, VA, pg. 560
Bailey, Charles, Jr., V.P.-Sls.--Signet Industries, Fraser, MI, pg. 1003
Bailey, Elaine, V.P.-Sls.--Locus Computing Corp., Inglewood, CA, pg. 680
Bailey, Tim, V.P.-Sls.--Yardley Products Corporation, Yardley, PA, pg. 341
Baillie, Brian, Dir.-Adv. & Sls. Promo.--Fort Howard Corporation, Green Bay, WI, pg. 425
Baine, John, V.P.-Sls.--Penetone Corp., Tenafly, NJ, pg. 1172
Bair, Daran, Dir.-Sls. & Mktg.--Martin Universal Design, Inc., Westland, MI, pg. 715
Baird, Dan, V.P.-Sls.--Duralam, Inc., Appleton, WI, pg. 971
Baittinger, Kenneth, Sr. V.P.-Sls. & Mktg.--Automotive Rentals, Inc., Mount Laurel, NJ, pg. 101
Bajko, Robert P., V.P.-Sls. & Mktg.--Cleveland Machine Controls, Cleveland, OH, pg. 255
Bak, Joseph, Dir.-Sls. & Service--Interform Corporation, Bridgeville, PA, pg. 574
Baker, Gene, Mgr.-Sls.--Welco Lumber Company, Marysville, WA, pg. 1175
Baker, Jim, Dir.-Sls.--Alliance Automation Systems, Rochester, NY, pg. 37
Baker, Martha, Dir.-Mktg. & Sls.--San Diego Zoo, San Diego, CA, pg. 969
Baker, Martha, Dir.-Sls. & Mktg.--San Diego Wild Animal Park, Escondido, CA, pg. 969
Baker, Michael, Mgr.-Sls--Rynone Manufacturing Corporation, Sayre, PA, pg. 958
Baker, Rob, Natl. Sls. Mgr.--Burks Pumps, Inc., Piqua, OH, pg. 507
Baker, Walt, Sr. V.P., Dir. Client Services--Ericson Marketing Communications, Nashville, TN, pg. 386
Baldo, Jim, V.P.-Sls. & Mktg.--Zippo Manufacturing Company, Bradford, PA, pg. 1220
Ballard, Jerry, V.P.-Sls. & Mktg.--Sunox, Inc., Charlotte, NC, pg. 1062
Ballen, Martin, V.P.-Auto Sls.--Troy Mills, Inc., Troy, NH, pg. 1116
Balluff, Fred, Sr. V.P.-Sls.--Gould Paper Corporation, New York, NY, pg. 473
Balogh, Edward A., Mgr.-Mktg. & Sls.--Pyro Chem, Inc., Boonton, NJ, pg. 166
Balsdon, Robert, V.P.-Sls. & Mktg.--Pioneer/Eclipse Corp., Sparta, NC, pg. 871
Bambrick, James E., Exec. V.P.--Farrell Lines Incorporated, New York, NY, pg. 403
Bamman, Sam, V.P.-Sls.--Binning's Building Products, Inc., Lexington, NC, pg. 151
Bancer, Jack D., Dir.-Natl. Comml. Sls.--Hickory Farms, Inc., Maumee, OH, pg. 532
Bankes, James, V.P.-Sls. & Mktg.--Samsill Corporation, Fort Worth, TX, pg. 968
Bankos, Ronald, Dir.-Sls.--Universal Dynamics Inc., Woodbridge, VA, pg. 1138
Banks, Dennis, Mgr.-Distribution Sls.--Interform Corporation, Bridgeville, PA, pg. 574
Bannon, Larry C., V.P.-Export Sls.--Thomas Built Buses, Inc., High Point, NC, pg. 1092
Bantsolas, N., Mgr.-Sls.--Screw Conveyor Corp., Hammond, IN, pg. 983
Banzaca, R., Sls. Mgr.--Practical Automation, Inc., Shelton, CT, pg. 34
Baracat, Anthony F., V.P.-Sls.--Interstate Van Lines, Inc., Springfield, VA, pg. 581
Baratelli, Sergio, Client Services Dir.--BSB Italia, Milan,, Italy, pg. 110
Barber, J., Mgr.-Sls.--Sexton Can Co., Inc., Cambridge, MA, pg. 993
Barber, Jack C., V.P.-Midwest Retail Sls.--Fannie May Candy Shops, Inc., Chicago, IL, pg. 604
Barber, James, Mgr.-New Car Sls.--Kissimmee Toyota Inc., Kissimmee, FL, pg. 633
Barber, Peter, V.P. & Sls. Dir.--Accurate Perforating Co., Chicago, IL, pg. 11
Barefoot, Gerald, V.P.-Sls.--Globe Industries, Inc., Chicago, IL, pg. 464
Barendsen, Bud, Mgr.-Natl. Sls.--Rochester Gauges Inc. Of Texas, Dallas, TX, pg. 444
Barhite, James T., V.P.-Sls. & Mktg.--Interface Electronics Corporation, Hopkinton, MA, pg. 574
Barnes, Martin, Dir.-Major Projects--Ellicott Machine Corp., Baltimore, MD, pg. 378
Barnes, Mary Jean, Mgr.-Sls. Services--Thomas Register, New York, NY, pg. 1093
Barnes, Steven, Dir.-Sls.--L'Ermitage Hotels, West Hollywood, CA, pg. 668
Barnett, Dennis, V.P.-Sls.--The Julius Schepps Co., Dallas, TX, pg. 975
Barnett, P., Exec. V.P.-Sls.--Hirsh Company, Skokie, IL, pg. 258
Barney, Carlton, V.P.-Ready-Made Sls.--Robertson Factories, Inc., Taunton, MA, pg. 939
Barnhill, John W., Jr., Exec. V.P. & Gen. Sls. Mgr.--Blue Bell Creameries, Inc., Brenham, TX, pg. 158
Barone, Moshe, V.P.-Sls. & Mktg.--Mennen Medical Inc., Clarence, NY, pg. 739
Barr, Constance, Asst. V.P.-Sls. & Mktg.--Siemer Milling Company, Teutopolis, IL, pg. 1002
Barraza, Billy, Mgr.-Sls.--Taca International Airlines, S. A., New Orleans, LA, pg. 1076
Barrell, Dave, Mgr.-Sls. & Mktg.--Glasteel Industrial Laminates, Duarte, CA, pg. 461
Barrett, David G., 2nd V.P.-Individual Sls.--Shenandoah Life Insurance Company, Roanoke, VA, pg. 997
Barrise, Joesph, Dir.-Sls.--J.M.P. Bakery Co., Inc., Brooklyn, NY, pg. 586
Barron, William, V.P.-Sls. & Mktg.--Littelfuse, Inc., Des Plaines, IL, pg. 678
Barry, Deanne, Asst. Mgr.-Sls. Promo.--Automotive News, Detroit, MI, pg. 101
Barry, Ed, Sr. V.P.-Sls.--Freudenberg-NOK (MI), Plymouth, MI, pg. 432
Barry, Frank, V.P.-Sls. & Mktg.--Inland Printing Co., Inc., La Crosse, WI, pg. 570
Barry, H., Pres. & Dir.-Sls.--Uniflex, Inc., Hicksville, NY, pg. 1126
Barry, J., Dir.-Sls.--Dwyer Instruments Inc., Michigan City, IN, pg. 356
Barry, James P., V.P.-Sls. & Mktg.--Remcor Products Co., Glendale Heights, IL, pg. 926
Barth, Jim, Mgr.-Sls.--World Aerospace Corporation, Maple Grove, MN, pg. 1202
Bartholomew, Allan, Natl. Sls. Mgr.-Non Foods Div.--Malco Products, Inc., Barberton, OH, pg. 702
Bartholomew, Allan, Sls. Mgr.--Whiz Automotive Chemicals Div., Barberton, OH, pg. 702
Bartlett, Gene, Sr. V.P.-Sls.--Freeman Cosmetic Corp., Los Angeles, CA, pg. 431
Bartlett, Phil, Natl. Sls. Mgr.--Russell-Stanley Corporation, Red Bank, NJ, pg. 957
Barto, William, V.P.-Sls.--Robert James Sales Inc., Buffalo, NY, pg. 589
Bartsch, Fran, Dir.-Sls., Tires--Cragar Industries, Compton, CA, pg. 761
Bartsch, Jeff, V.P.-Sls.-Eastern Reg.--Columbia Paint Co., Spokane, WA, pg. 265
Bascetta, Richard, V.P.-Sls.--Furniture Consultants, New York, NY, pg. 437
Baseman, Robert L., Exec. V.P.-Sls.--EB (NA), Chicago, IL, pg. 381
Basinger, Kirt, V.P.-Sls.--Kingsdown, Inc., Mebane, NC, pg. 632
Bass, Tommy, V.P.-Sls.-Farms--McCarty Farms, Magee, MS, pg. 727
Bass, Tommy, V.P.-Sls.--McCarty Processors, Inc., Jackson, MS, pg. 727
Batdorff, Tom, V.P.-Sls.--Dexol Industries, Inc., Torrance, CA, pg. 334
Bate, Michael, Mng. Dir.--Totes U.K. Limited, Billericay,, United Kingdom, pg. 1103
Bates, Charles, V.P.-Sls. & Mktg.--Quality Technologies Corporation, Sunnyvale, CA, pg. 904
Battles, Richard A., Gen. Sls. Mgr.--Lapham-Hickey Steel Corp., Chicago, IL, pg. 658
Bauer, Thaddeus, Dir.-Sls. & Mktg.--The Presmet Corp., Worcester, MA, pg. 887
Bauer, Tom, V.P.-Sls.--Kirkwood Industries, Inc., Cleveland, OH, pg. 633
Baugh, Jerry, Mgr.-Sls. Service--Bush Brothers & Company, Dandridge, TN, pg. 196
Bauman, Richard F., V.P.-Mktg. & Sls. Acetylenes--International Specialty Products, Inc., Wilmington, DE, pg. 438
Baumgarner, Wayne, V.P.-Sls.-Eastern Grp.--Key Industries, Inc., Fort Scott, KS, pg. 627
Baxter, Arthur P., Sr. V.P.-Mktg.--First American Bank of Georgia, N.A., Atlanta, GA, pg. 412
Baxter, John T., V.P.-Sls. & Mktg.--Alpha Associates, Inc., Woodbridge, NJ, pg. 43
Baxter, William, Mgr.-Sls. Devel.--Bruner Corporation, Milwaukee, WI, pg. 184
Bayer, Manfred, Dir.-Intl. Sls.--Jet Spray Corp., Norwood, MA, pg. 593
Baylor, Janet, Sls. Service Mgr.--E-B Advertising Display Inc., Massillon, OH, pg. 358
Beach, John W., Jr., Mgr.-Sls.--Chadwick-Helmuth Company, Inc.. El Monte, CA, pg. 237
Bear, Craig, Mgr.-Mktg. & Sls.--Alloy Products Corporation, Waukesha, WI, pg. 41
Bearb, Malcolm, Sls. Mgr.-Lafayette District--Triumph-LOR, Inc., Lafayette, LA, pg. 1115
Beard, Don, Mgr.-Fertilizer Sls.--B&W Co-op, Inc., Breckenridge, MI, pg. 107
Beard, Karen, V.P.-Sls.--Alamo Rent-A-Car Inc., Fort Lauderdale, FL, pg. 30
Beasley, Barbara, Sr. V.P.-Sls. Group--Mary Kay Cosmetics Inc., Dallas, TX, pg. 716
Beattie, Andy, Mgr.-Natl. Sls.--Cole of California, Los Angeles, CA, pg. 1079
Beattie, C. Glen, Pres. & Dir.-Sls., Amercable Div.--Associated Materials Inc., Dallas, TX, pg. 91
Beattie, David, V.P.-Sls. & Mktg.--McNaughton-McKay Electric Co., Madison Heights, MI, pg. 732
Beattie, James S., Sls. Mgr.--Crown International, Inc., Elkhart, IN, pg. 302
Beauchine, Fay, V.P.-Reservation Sls. & Services--Northwest Airlines, Inc., Saint Paul, MN, pg. 782
Becher, Hans, V.P.-Sls.--Stark Candy Company, Pewaukee, WI, pg. 1123
Becht, Rudolph, V.P.-Sls. & Mdsg.--King Kullen Grocery Co., Inc., Westbury, NY, pg. 630
Beck, Irv, Mgr.-Sls.--H. Cotler Company, New York, NY, pg. 288
Beck, Randy, Natl. Sls. Mgr.--Triumph Twist Drill Co., Crystal Lake, IL, pg. 885
Beck, Robert V., V.P.-Sls. & Mktg.--Precisionaire, Inc., Saint Petersburg, FL, pg. 886
Beck, Sue, Adv. Sls. Dir.--Shearman Corporation, Lake Charles, LA, pg. 996
Becker, Russ, Dir.-Sls. & Mktg.--Hobart Brothers Co., Troy, OH, pg. 536
Beckmann, Robert, Dir.-Sls.--Steiner Electric Co., Elk Grove Village, IL, pg. 1045
Beckstead, James H., V.P.-Sls.--E. D. Bullard Company, Cynthiana, KY, pg. 188
Beckwith, Brian, Dir.-Circulation--Soap Opera Digest, New York, NY, pg. 611
Beckwith, Robert, V.P.-Intl. Sls.--Sun Diamond Growers of California, Pleasanton, CA, pg. 1058
Bedell, R.A., V.P.-Intl. Sls.--DoAll Company, Des Plaines, IL, pg. 341
Bedford, Robert C., V.P.-Sls.--Intermatic Inc., Spring Grove, IL, pg. 575
Beebe, Bob, V.P.-Sls.--Sentinel Consumer Products, Inc., Mentor, OH, pg. 990
Beebe, Larry L., V.P.-U.S. Consumer Prods. Sls.--S. C. Johnson & Son, Inc., Racine, WI, pg. 599
Beecher, D.J., V.P.-Sls.--Globe International Inc., Buffalo, NY, pg. 464
Beers, Robert, V.P.-Sls. & Mktg.--Microdot Aerospace Fastening Systems Group, Fullerton, CA, pg. 749
Beeskow, John, V.P.-Sls.--American Plastic Toys Inc., Walled Lake, MI, pg. 59
Behle, Ted, Sls. Mgr.-Lawn Chief & Snow Chief--General Power Equipment Co., Harvard, IL, pg. 288
Behling, Roy, V.P.-Sls. & Mktg.--McNally Wellman Company, Pittsburgh, PA, pg. 732
Behnke, Robert, Sls. Mgr.--Leyse, Kewaunee, WI, pg. 1155
Behringer, Kyle, V.P.-Industrial Prods. Sls.--Ivex Packaging Corporation-Bridgeview, Bridgeview, IL, pg. 583
Beier, Peter, V.P.-Mktg. & Sls.--Cole Business Furniture, York, PA, pg. 608
Beketic, Ralph, Div. V.P.--Roundy's Inc., Milwaukee Div., Milwaukee, WI, pg. 952
Belcher, Lawrence, V.P.-Sls.--Roper Bros. Lumber Co., Inc., Petersburg, VA, pg. 947
Belger, J.H., Mgr.-Sls.--Harrop Industries, Inc., Columbus, OH, pg. 512
Bell, David C., Sr. V.P.-Sls.--J. Gibson McIlvain Co., White Marsh, MD, pg. 729
Bell, Lowell, Mgr.-Sls.--Keystone Automotive Industries, Inc. - Linthicum, Linthicum Heights, MD, pg. 628
Bell, Richard, V.P.-Sls. & Mktg.--Cornnuts Inc., Alameda, CA, pg. 286
Bellamy, Michael, V.P.-Sls.--Fashion Fair Cosmetics, Chicago, IL, pg. 599
Bellizi, David P., V.P.-Sls.--Palm Beach Beauty Products Co., Minneapolis, MN, pg. 843
Bello, Paulo de Souza, Dir.-Sls.--Ceras Johnson Ltda., Rio de Janeiro,, Brazil, pg. 599
Bellows, Charles C., Sr. V.P.-Mktg. & Sls.--Medieval Dinner & Tournament, Inc., Buena Park, CA, pg. 735
Benedict, Monica L., Dir.-Sls. & Mktg.--Booth Newspapers, Inc., Grand Rapids, MI, pg. 165
Benge, Kent, Sls. Rep.--Triumph-LOR, Inc., Spiro, OK, pg. 1115
Benison, John E., Exec. V.P.-Sls. Mktg. & Prod. Devel.--The Napier Company, Meriden, CT, pg. 783
Benitez, Adan, Dir.-Sls. Fin.--C.I.C.S.A., Mexico,, Mexico, pg. 723
Benitez, Victor, V.P., Gen. Mgr. & Mgr.-Sls.--Gus Machado Enterprises, Hialeah, FL, pg. 696

Benjamin, Martin, V.P.-Sls. & Mktg.--Pueblo International, Inc.-P.R. Div., Carolina, PR, pg. 899
Bennett, Craig, Chief Oper. Officer & V.P.-Sls. & Mktg.--Utility Trailer Manufacturing Co., City of Industry, CA, pg. 1141
Bennett, Pete, V.P.-Sls.--Pony Express Courier Corp., Charlotte, NC, pg. 166
Bennett, R. M., V.P.-Sls. & Mktg.--Smith & Sons Foods, Inc., Macon, GA, pg. 1014
Bennett, Richard R., Mgr.-Sls.--Northeastern Regional Office, Waltham, MA, pg. 233
Benninger, Brian, V.P.-Sls. & Engrng.--Kingston Warren, Southfield, MI, pg. 514
Benrey, Marc, Mgr.-Intl. Sls.--Vidicom, L.D. Bevan Company, Inc., Thousand Oaks, CA, pg. 1151
Bensimon, Ron, Mgr.-Sls.--Dearden's, Inc., Los Angeles, CA, pg. 322
Benson, Bill, Natl. Sls. Mgr.-Automotive After Mkt.--Rockford International Group, Rockford, IL, pg. 942
Benson, Ed, Gen. Sls. Mgr.--Caldwell Manufacturing, Kearney, NE, pg. 247
Benson, Steven, V.P.-Sls. & Mktg.--The Prudential Asset Management Co., Inc., Florham Park, NJ, pg. 897
Benson, Tom, Mgr.-Sls.--Thermal-Care Div., Niles, IL, pg. 751
Benstein, Robert, V.P.-Sls. & Mktg.--SCC Holding Co., Highland Park, IL, pg. 961
Benun, Eli, Mgr.-Sls.--Bentex Kiddie Corporation, New York, NY, pg. 140
Benyo, Joseph, V.P.-Sls.--John Dusenbery Co., Inc., Randolph, NJ, pg. 355
Beran, Don, V.P.-Sls. & Mktg.--Honorbuilt Industries, Inc., Minneapolis, KS, pg. 542
Berg, George, V.P.-Sls.--Na-Churs Plant Food Company, Marion, OH, pg. 782
Berger, Vin, Dir.-Sls.--Application Engineering Corporation, Wood Dale, IL, pg. 1047
Berger, Vincent, Gen. Sls. Mgr.--Whitlock, Inc., Wood Dale, IL, pg. 1047
Berges, Emil H., V.P.-Sls.--Abbott Ball Company, West Hartford, CT, pg. 9
Berglund, Jon, 1st V.P. & Dir.-Claims--Federated Mutual Insurance Company, Owatonna, MN, pg. 405
Berhang, Charles A., Dir.-Sls.--Camp International, Jackson, MI, pg. 153
Berkowitz, Donald A., Exec. V.P.-Sls. & Mktg.--Central Paper Company, Newark, NJ, pg. 233
Berkson, Michael, Eastern Reg. Mgr.--Stanbee Company, Inc., Carlstadt, NJ, pg. 1035
Berlinger, Liz, V.P.-Sls.--Jordache Enterprises, Inc., New York, NY, pg. 604
Berman, Dan, Dir.-Sls. & Mktg.--TST/Impreso, Inc., Coppell, TX, pg. 1075
Bernstein, James, V.P.-Sls.--New Hermes Incorporated, Norwalk, CT, pg. 801
Berry, Lawrence R., V.P.-Sls. & Engrng.--Georgia Iron Works Co., Grovetown, GA, pg. 453
Berryman, Al, Dir.-Sls.--Tighe Industries, Inc., York, PA, pg. 1097
Bertera, Bill, Mgr.-Sls.-Pontiac--Bob Sellers Pontiac GMC Truck Inc., Farmington Hills, MI, pg. 988
Bertges, Gerhard, Sls. Dir.--Berlitz Schools of Languages GmbH, Frankfurt/Main, Germany, pg. 143
Berthold, Howard M., V.P.-Sls.--Carus Chemical Company, Chemical Div., Ottawa, IL, pg. 227
Bertoli, L.J., Mgr.-Sls.--The Kirk & Blum Mfg. Co., Cincinnati, OH, pg. 633
Best, Kenneth G., V.P.-Cargo, Sls. & Services of Aloha--Aloha Airgroup, Inc., Honolulu, HI, pg. 43
Best, Kenneth G., V.P.-Cargo Sls. & Service--Aloha Airlines, Inc., Honolulu, HI, pg. 43
Best, Page, V.P.-Sls.--Eastern Fine Paper, Incorporated, Brewer, ME, pg. 363
Bethea, John, V.P.-Sls.--O'Brien Powder Products, Inc., Houston, TX, pg. 820
Betts, Dave, Mgr.-Retail Sls.--Furman Foods, Inc., Northumberland, PA, pg. 436
Betush, E.T., Jr., V.P.-Sls. & Mktg.--Pennex Products Co., Inc., Verona, PA, pg. 858
Betz, F. Lee, Sr. V.P.-Latin American Div.--Lykes Bros. Steamship Co., Inc., New Orleans, LA, pg. 688
Bevers, Jerry, Exec. V.P.-Sls.--Team Bank, Fort Worth, TX, pg. 1082
Bevington, Kim, Mgr.-Sls.--Elyria Foundry Company, Elyria, OH, pg. 378
Bevington, Mark, V.P.-Sls. & Mktg.--The National Super Service Co., Toledo, OH, pg. 794
Bezouska, A., V.P.-Architectural Sls.--Woodwork Corporation of America, Chicago, IL, pg. 1201
Bial, Scott, V.P.-Sls. & Mktg.--Wallace International Silversmiths, Inc., East Boston, MA, pg. 1070
Bidwell, A.K., Dir-Sls. Admin. & Adv. Mgr.--Fraser Paper, Ltd., Stamford, CT, pg. 430
Bienenfeld, Carol, Sls. & Mktg. Admin.--Admiral Packaging, Inc., Providence, RI, pg. 1128
Biermann, Charles H., Sr. V.P.-Sls.--Northwestern Steel & Wire Co., Sterling, IL, pg. 815
Biermann, Syl, V.P.-Sls.--RS Electronics, Livonia, MI, pg. 908
Bigda, Lynda, Mgr.-Sls.--My Own Meals, Inc., Deerfield, IL, pg. 779
Biggers, Jay, Mgr.-Gen. Sls.--W. B. Goode Company, Inc., Richmond, VA, pg. 470
Billman, Ted, V.P.-Sls.--General American Door Company, Montgomery, IL, pg. 739
Billmeyer, H. Duane, Dir.-Sls.--Roney & Co., Detroit, MI, pg. 946
Billmon, Paula, Mgr.-Mktg. & Sls. Support--Liberty Tool Corporation, Rochester, NY, pg. 674
Billot, Michael, Gen. Sls. Mgr.--W F I, Inc., Houston, TX, pg. 1156
Binder, Irving, Sr. V.P., Sls. Promo.--Warren/Kremer/CMP/Advertising/Inc., New York, NY, pg. 1165
Biondi, Scott, Mgr.-Sls. U.S.--Capital Controls Company Inc., Colmar, PA, pg. 215
Birkenmeier, Bill, Mgr.-Sls.--Welsh Company, Saint Louis, MO, pg. 1175
Birmingham, John H., V.P.-Customer Supports--Automation Intelligence, Inc., Maitland, FL, pg. 101
Birnbaum, Marc, Exec. V.P.-Sls. & Mktg.--Hazel Bishop Corporation, Englewood Cliffs, NJ, pg. 520
Biscombe, Barry, Mgr.-Outside Sls.--Wohlert Corp., Lansing, MI, pg. 1198
Bishop, C.M., III, Mgr.-Women's Mdse.--Pendleton Woolen Mills, Inc., Portland, OR, pg. 857
Bishop, Daniel, V.P.-Sls.-Flat Bed--Anderson Trucking Service Inc., Saint Cloud, MN, pg. 73
Bishop, Don, Grp. V.P.-Sls. & Mktg.--Gulf States Toyota, Houston, TX, pg. 494
Bitner, Bob, Sr. V.P.-Sls.--Guest Quarters Suite Hotels, Boston, MA, pg. 493
Bittker, Ron, Mgr.-Sls.--National Lumber Co., Warren, MI, pg. 792
Biviano, Michael A., V.P. & Reg. Mgr.--Carrols Corporation, Syracuse, NY, pg. 225
Bixby, B.C., Chm. Bd.--Bixby International Corp., Newburyport, MA, pg. 153
Black, Barbara, Dir.-Sls. Promo.--Abdalla's Lafayette, Inc., Lafayette, LA, pg. 10
Black, Doug, Dir.-N. American Sls.--The Thompson Group Companies, Henderson, KY, pg. 1094
Black, Randy, V.P.-Sls. & Mktg.--Bike Athletic Co., Knoxville, TN, pg. 150
Black, Walter, Mgr.-Natl. Sls.--Sunnen Products Company, Saint Louis, MO, pg. 1061
Black, Wayne, Loan Officer--Wieland Financial Services, Inc., Atlanta, GA, pg. 1188
Blackburn, F. Scott, V.P.-Sls.--Clemco Industries Corp., Washington, MO, pg. 254
Blackburn, George, Dir.-Sls.--Greenfield Industries Inc., Evans, GA, pg. 507
Blackburn, John, Area V.P.-Northeast Ohio--Basic Computer, Akron, OH, pg. 124
Blackburn, Scott, V.P.-Sls.--Clemco Industries, Washington, MO, pg. 254
Blackwell, Katrina, V.P.-Sls. & Mktg.--American Red Ball World Wide Movers, Indianapolis, IN, pg. 918
Blagaich, Alvin, V.P.-Sls. & Mktg.--Fenton Press, Inc., Addison, IL, pg. 406
Blaha, Bill, Pres.-Sls.--Pacesetter Corporation, Omaha, NE, pg. 839
Blaha, Hugh A., V.P.-Export & Govt. Sls.--C.R. Daniels, Inc., Ellicott City, MD, pg. 314
Blainey, Peter D., Dir.-Natl. Sls.--Executive Telecom Systems, Inc., Indianapolis, IN, pg. 189
Blair, Bob, Mgr.-Natl. Sls.--Pachmayr Gun Works Inc., Monrovia, CA, pg. 839
Blair, Bryce H., V.P.-Retail Sls.--Reed & Barton Corporation, Taunton, MA, pg. 920
Blais, Russell A., V.P.-Mktg. & Sls.--Naylor Pipe Company, Chicago, IL, pg. 796
Blake, Dennis, V.P.-Sls.--VSI Fasteners, Inc., Stanton, CA, pg. 1142
Blake, Jerry R., V.P.-Sls.--L & L Oil Company, Inc., Metairie, LA, pg. 647
Blake, Ron, Regional Sls. Mgr.--Prime Technology, Inc., Greenwood, IN, pg. 889
Blake, Shirley, V.P.-Sls.-Dunbar--State Electric Supply Co., Huntington, WV, pg. 1040
Blalock, David D., Exec. V.P.-Sls.--Dundee Mills, Inc., Griffin, GA, pg. 352
Blanchard, J., V.P.-Sls.--Norandex Inc., Macedonia, OH, pg. 809
Bland, Greg, Dir.-Sls.--Tasco, Miami, FL, pg. 1079
Blankendaal, Cor, Area Sls. Mgr.-Benelux & France--Bourns Benelux B.V., Voorburg,, Netherlands, pg. 168
Blankendaal, Cor, Area Sls. Mgr.--Bourns-Ohmic S.A., Paris, , France, pg. 168
Blankenship, Tim, Mgr.-Circulation--Hillsdale Daily News, Hillsdale, MI, pg. 1042
Blauser, Gary, V.P.-Sls.-Western Div.--Open Court Publishing Company, Chicago, IL, pg. 227
Blauvelt, Brian, Natl. Sls. Mgr.--Edlon Products, Inc., Avondale, PA, pg. 866
Blizard, W., Mgr.-Field Sls.-Hoist & Chain--Columbus McKinnon Corp., Amherst, NY, pg. 266
Blood, Charles, Dir.-Sls. Admin.--New England Confectionery Co., Cambridge, MA, pg. 1123
Bloom, Allen J., Exec. V.P.-Mktg & Sls.--Ringling Bros., Barnum & Bailey Combined Shows, Inc., Vienna, VA, pg. 935
Bloom, Allen J., Sr. V.P.-Mktg. & Sls.--Ice Follies & Holiday on Ice, Vienna, VA, pg. 935
Bloom, Richard A., Gen. Mgr.-Sls. & Mktg.--Bloom Electric Services, Inc., Oklahoma City, OK, pg. 157
Bloom, T., V.P.-Mktg. & Sls.--Elastic Stop Nut, Union, NJ, pg. 514
Bloomstein, Edward, Natl. Sls. Mgr.--Sterlite Corporation, Townsend, MA, pg. 1047
Blumberg, Thomas A., Grp. V.P.-Mktg. & Sls.--Leviton Mfg. Co., Inc., Little Neck, NY, pg. 671
Blumenthal, Martin, Mgr.-Sls.--Florig Equipment Company, Inc., Conshohocken, PA, pg. 421
Blumstein, Jerry, V.P. & Asst. Sls. Mgr.--Gould Paper Corporation, New York, NY, pg. 473
Blutstein, Mark, Mgr.-Sls.--Reliable Knitting Works, Milwaukee, WI, pg. 924
Blythe, Ronald, V.P.-Consumer Sls.--Stanley Fastening Systems, Worcester, MA, pg. 1038
Bochatyn, Roseanne, Dir.-Inside Sls.--Production Tool Supply Co., Warren, MI, pg. 893
Bodmer, Bill, Sr. V.P.-Adv. & Sls.--Pathmark, Woodbridge, NJ, pg. 1064
Boen, Mike, Station & Sls. Mgr.--KSTP-AM, Inc., Maplewood, MN, pg. 549
Boersma, Bernie, Mgr.-Natl. Sls. & Export--LubeCon Systems, Inc., Fremont, MI, pg. 686
Bogart, Richard P., Asst. V.P.-Sls.--Central Regional Office, Van Wert, OH, pg. 233
Boggs, Marvin K., V.P.-Sls.--Derst Baking Company, Inc., Savannah, GA, pg. 331
Boisbrun, George W., Gen. Sls. Mgr.--Philadelphia Gear Corp., King of Prussia, PA, pg. 866
Bolland, Larry, V.P.-Sls.--Gibson Guitar Corporation, Inc., Nashville, TN, pg. 456
Bolling, Fred W., V.P.-Sls.--Mid-West Company, Burr Ridge, IL, pg. 939
Bollinger, Tom, Mgr.-Sls. & Treas.--The John C. Groub Company Inc., Seymour, IN, pg. 489
Bolt, James W., V.P. & Natl. Sls. Mgr.--Bunn-O-Matic Corporation, Springfield, IL, pg. 188
Bolton, George C., Sr. V.P. & Dir.-Pur. & Sls.--The Law Company, Inc., Wichita, KS, pg. 661
Bonadio, Michael, Dir.-Sls. Promo.--Fruit of the Loom, Bowling Green, KY, pg. 400
Bond, Vince, Mgr.-Sls.--Watson's Quality Turkey Products, Inc., Turnersville, NJ, pg. 1168
Bond, William, V.P.-Sls.--Benjamin Ansehl Company, Saint Louis, MO, pg. 76
Bont, William J., V.P.-Sls.--The WBDC Group, Grand Rapids, MI, pg. 1155
Booker, Noel, Mgr.-Trade Sls.--Progress Paint Mfg. Co., Louisville, KY, pg. 894
Boone, Mitchell D., Mgr.-Sls.--Navajo Forest Products Industries, Navajo, NM, pg. 796
Boop, Ted, V.P.-Sls.--Bliss-Salem, Inc., Salem, OH, pg. 156
Boop, Ted, V.P.-Sls.--Atlas Car Div., Bliss-Salem Inc., Salem, OH, pg. 157
Booth, James E., V.P.-Sls.--McCormick Paint Works Company, Rockville, MD, pg. 727
Booth, Neil, V.P.-Sls. & Mktg.--Brown & Haley, Tacoma, WA, pg. 182
Booth, Timothy M., V.P.-Sls.--Frontier Foundries, Inc., Titusville, PA, pg. 434
Boozer, Larry, Mgr.-Mktg. & Sls.--Lancaster Malleable Castings Company, Lancaster, PA, pg. 653
Bordelon, Clarence J., V.P.-Sls. & Admin.--Tyler Elevator Products, Inc., Valley View, OH, pg. 1122
Borges, Bill, V.P.-Sls. & Mktg.--Ventura Coastal Corporation, Ventura, CA, pg. 1147
Borke, Stan, Mgr.-Sls.--Totsy Manufacturing Company, Inc., Holyoke, MA, pg. 1103
Bosch, Larry, Export Sls. Mgr.--Celestial Seasonings, Boulder, CO, pg. 231
Boshears, Robert, Mgr.-Sls.--Welsco Inc., North Little Rock, AR, pg. 1175
Bosken, Lidy, Sls. Dir.--Berlitz Schools of Languages B.V., Amsterdam,, Netherlands, pg. 143
Bost, Larry, Dir.-Sls.--Macklanburg-Duncan Co., Oklahoma City, OK, pg. 697
Boswell, J.W., V.P.-Sls.--Seco Warwick Corporation, Meadville, PA, pg. 987
Boswell, James, Jr., V.P.-Sls.--Lou Ana Foods, Inc., Opelousas, LA, pg. 974
Bouck, Robert, Dir.-Fleet & Leasing--CC Services, Bloomington, IL, pg. 289
Boulais, Dee, Mgr.-Sls. & Service--Lan-O-Sheen, Inc., Saint Paul, MN, pg. 653
Bourne, Art, V.P.-Sls./National Acct.--Kingsdown, Inc., Mebane, NC, pg. 632
Bourtsos, Costas T., Dir.-Intl. Mktg. & Export--Whiting Corporation, Harvey, IL, pg. 1187
Bovaird, B.H., Mgr.-Sls. & Quality Assurance--Bovaird Supply Co., Tulsa, OK, pg. 168
Bowen, Mary, Dir.-Mktg. & Intl. Sls.--Power & Telephone Supply Company, Memphis, TN, pg. 883
Bowling, Gene H., V.P.-Mktg. & Sls.--Alkota Cleaning Systems, Inc., Alcester, SD, pg. 34
Bowman, Bruce H., Dir.-Sls.--Arburg, Inc., Berlin, CT, pg. 79
Bowyer, Charles, Sr. V.P.-Sls.--Schmidt Baking Co., Inc., Baltimore, MD, pg. 976
Boyce, Hugh, Dir.-Sls. & Mktg.--Flexfab, Inc., Hastings, MI, pg. 418
Boyce, James, Mgr.-Sls.--Trapp Family Lodge, Inc., Stowe, VT, pg. 1108
Boychieder, Robert, V.P.-Sls. & Alternative Channels--Colad Group Inc., Buffalo, NY, pg. 259
Boyd, D.E., V.P.-Mktg. & Sls., Pre-contract--ABB Environmental Systems, Knoxville, TN, pg. 2
Boyd, Deb, Sls. Coord. & Travel Planner--Star Bronze Company, Alliance, OH, pg. 1039
Boyd, Doug, Mgr.-Sls.--Nexus Plastics, Inc., Hawthorne, NJ, pg. 805
Boyd, R. Wayne, Pres.-Sls.--Dundee Mills, Inc., Griffin, GA, pg. 352
Boyd, Stan, V.P.-Sls. & Mktg.--The Fairmont Hotels, San Francisco, CA, pg. 397
Boyer, Charles, Sls. Coord.--Suzannah Farms, Pennsauken, NJ, pg. 1065
Boyer, Robert A., V.P.-Sls. & Mktg.--Amarlite Architectural Products, Atlanta, GA, pg. 47
Boyle, C., Gen. Sls. Mgr.--Farrell Lines Incorporated, New York, NY, pg. 403
Boyle, Eric M., Sr. V.P.-Intl. Sls. & Mktg.--Lindsay Olive Growers, Lindsay, CA, pg. 676
Boyle, Eric M., V.P.-Intl. Sls.--Lindsay International, Lindsay, CA, pg. 676
Boynton, Richard, V.P.-Sls.--Sunbeam-Oster Household Products, Schaumburg, IL, pg. 1059
Boyter, J. Earle, V.P.-Mktg. & Sls.--Piper Aircraft Corporation, Vero Beach, FL, pg. 872
Bozof, Danny, V.P.-Sls.--Bozof Dinettes, Inc., Olive Branch, MS, pg. 169
Bozza, Anthony, Sls. Mgr.--Premier Metal Products Company, Bronx, NY, pg. 836
Brabham, Arthur, V.P.-Sls.--Pearlstine Distributors Inc., Charleston, SC, pg. 853
Bradbury, Phil E., Mgr.-Mktg.--Bradbury Company, Inc., Moundridge, KS, pg. 169
Bradely, Mildred, Dir.-Mktg.--Centimark Corporation, Bethel Park, PA, pg. 231

Braden, James, V.P.-Sls. & Pur. & Chief Estimator--Concrete Construction Company, Columbus, OH, pg. 273
Bradley, Rex, V.P.-Amateur Bat Sls.--Hillerich & Bradsby Co., Inc., Louisville, KY, pg. 535
Brady, Gregory A., Sr. V.P. & Gen. Mgr.-US Sls.--RAYOVAC Corporation, Madison, WI, pg. 915
Brady, Michael, V.P.-Sls. & Mktg.--M.S. Walker, Inc./Seacoast, Somerville, MA, pg. 1160
Brady, Robert E., Exec. V.P. & Dir.-Sls. & Mktg.--Kirkpatrick Pettis, Omaha, NE, pg. 779
Brady, Robert W., Exec. V.P.-Sls. & Mktg.--American Tool Companies, Inc., Lincoln, NE, pg. 64
Brainard, Chuck, Mgr.-Sls.--Village Ford Inc., Dearborn, MI, pg. 1151
Branca, Pasquale, V.P.-Sls.--Falcon Candy Company, Philadelphia, PA, pg. 398
Branton, Robert, V.P.-Sls. & Mktg.--United Hardware Distributing Co., Plymouth, MN, pg. 1132
Braun, Ed, Mgr.-Sls.--Beltone Electronics Corporation, Chicago, IL, pg. 137
Bray, John C., Exec. V.P.-Sls.--Dundee Mills, Inc., Griffin, GA, pg. 352
Breda, William E., Jr., Sr. V.P. & Gen. Sls. Mgr.--Blair Television, New York, NY, pg. 155
Breen, Don, V.P.-Sls. & Mktg.--John Morrell & Co., Cincinnati, OH, pg. 54
Breen, Robert, Asst. Sls. Mgr.--Hugo Bosca Co., Inc., Springfield, OH, pg. 166
Breezer, Harlon, V.P.- Custom Sls.--Penda Corporation, Portage, WI, pg. 857
Breisblatt, Martin A., V.P.-Sls.--The Franklin Mint, Franklin Center, PA, pg. 60
Breit, Catherine, V.P., Sls.--Shaker Advertising Agency, Oak Park, IL, pg. 994
Brenkman, R.L., V.P.-Sls.--Haulpak Division, Komatsu Dresser Company, Peoria, IL, pg. 565
Brennan, Andrew J., V.P.-Sls. & Mktg.--Everfresh Beverages Inc., Franklin Park, IL, pg. 391
Brennan, Joseph T., V.P.-Sls.--Quaker City Motor Parts Company, Middletown, DE, pg. 903
Brennan, Kevin, Mgr.-Sls.--Accurate Threaded Fasteners, Inc., Lincolnwood, IL, pg. 11
Brenner, Harry, Sr. V.P.-Sls.--Cumberland Farms, Inc., Canton, MA, pg. 304
Brenny, Mike, Dir.-Sls.--Berkley, Inc., Spirit Lake, IA, pg. 141
Brewer, Ned, Gen. Sls. Mgr.--McDowell Mfg. Co., Du Bois, PA, pg. 32
Brewster, Graham, Sr. V.P.-Sls. & Mktg.--The Napier Company, Meriden, CT, pg. 783
Briggs, Mick L., V.P.-Sls.--The National Latex Products Co., Ashland, OH, pg. 791
Briggs, Roby, V.P.-Sls.--H. B. Ives, Wallingford, CT, pg. 583
Brigham, Sharon A., Asst. Sls. Mgr.--Rodman Industries, Marinette, WI, pg. 408
Bringert, Goran, Dir.-Intl. Sls.--Kaye Instruments, Inc., Bedford, MA, pg. 619
Brisben, Frank, Exec. V.P.-Sls.--GenDerm Corporation, Lincolnshire, IL, pg. 448
Briscoe, Don L., V.P.-Sls.--Bergelectric Corporation, Los Angeles, CA, pg. 141
Britenbach, Bill, V.P.-Sls. & Mktg.--Tom's Foods, Columbus, GA, pg. 1101
Brittingham, James L., V.P.-Sls.--Rollex Corporation, Elk Grove Village, IL, pg. 944
Broadhurst, Frank, Mgr.-Sls.--Precision Parts Corp., Morristown, TN, pg. 885
Broadman, Robert, Mgr.-Sls.--Sussen, Inc., Cleveland, OH, pg. 225
Broch, Diane, Dir., Retail Sls.--Dimac Direct, San Francisco, CA, pg. 338
Brock, Milton L. Jr., Sr. V.P. & Dir.-Agency Sls.--Mutual of Omaha Insurance Company, Omaha, NE, pg. 779
Brock, Milton L., Jr., Sr. V.P. & Dir.-Agency Sls.--Mutual of Omaha, Omaha, NE, pg. 779
Brogan, Ed, V.P.-Sls.--Pollenex Corporation, Chicago, IL, pg. 879
Brokaw, A. Allen, V.P.-Mktg. & Sls.--The Airolite Company, Marietta, OH, pg. 28
Bronaugh, John, Mgr.-Sls.--Haws Drinking Faucet Co., Berkeley, CA, pg. 518
Brook, John T., Mgr.-Sls. & Mktg.--Overly Manufacturing Co., Greensburg, PA, pg. 833
Brook, Robert, Asst. Dir.-US Sls.--The ASCII Group, Inc., Bethesda, MD, pg. 8
Brooks, Bob, V.P.-Sls. & Mktg.--The Bureau of National Affairs, Inc., Washington, DC, pg. 189
Brooks, Bob, V.P.-Sls.--Henco, Inc., Selmer, TN, pg. 528
Brooks, David A., V.P.-Sls. & Mktg.--General Chemical Corporation, Parsippany, NJ, pg. 801
Brooks, Lauren, Sr. Mgr.-Apparel Sls. & Mktg.--ASICS Tiger Corporation, Fountain Valley, CA, pg. 8
Brooks, Stanley, V.P.-Sls.--Perry Group, Inc., Hainesport, NJ, pg. 863
Brophy, Joseph, Exec. V.P.-Sls.--William H. Sadlier, Inc., New York, NY, pg. 966
Brosovich, Lance, Mgr.-Intl. Sls.--Accu-Sort Systems, Inc., Telford, PA, pg. 11
Browder, J.W., V.P.-Natl. Accts.--Rangaire & Company, Cleburne, TX, pg. 912
Brown, A., V.P.-Sls.--E.J. Brach Corporation, Oakbrook Terrace, IL, pg. 169
Brown, Bill, V.P.-Sls.--Emery Waterhouse Company, Portland, ME, pg. 379
Brown, Chris, Sls. Mgr.--Madison Industries Inc. of Georgia, Conyers, GA, pg. 433
Brown, Daniel, Sr. V.P.-Sls.--J. H. Heafner Co. Inc., Lincolnton, NC, pg. 520
Brown, Dee, Mgr.-Sls.--Ritchie Industries, Inc., Conrad, IA, pg. 936
Brown, Doyle, Mgr.-Sls.--Takatta Inc., Olympia Fields, IL, pg. 1076
Brown, Glenn W., Jr., Exec. V.P.-Sls.--Sherman & Reilly, Inc., Chattanooga, TN, pg. 998
Brown, Holly, Dir.-Sls.--DeVault Foods, Devault, PA, pg. 333
Brown, James A., V.P.-Sls.--Standard Locknut & Lockwasher, Carmel, IN, pg. 1037
Brown, Jason, Natl. Sls. Mgr.--Capsonic Group, Inc., Elgin, IL, pg. 216
Brown, Jeffrey, Dir.-Sls. & Mktg.--P M Company, Philadelphia, PA, pg. 835
Brown, Jerry, Mgr.-Sls.--All-Luminum Products, Inc., Philadelphia, PA, pg. 35
Brown, Kenneth, Mgr.-Sls.--Trimtex Co. Inc., Williamsport, PA, pg. 1113
Brown, Loretta, Sls. & Mktg.--Boyer Bros. Inc., Altoona, PA, pg. 169
Brown, Louis R., V.P.-Tent Sls.--Anchor Industries Inc., Evansville, IN, pg. 71
Brown, Mike, Mgr.-Sls.--Wayne Wire Cloth Products, Inc., Kalkaska, MI, pg. 1169
Brown, Randy, V.P.-Sls. & Mktg.--Agsco, Inc., Grand Forks, ND, pg. 4
Brown, Renee C., V.P.-Mktg. & Sls.--Pro-Line Corporation, Dallas, TX, pg. 892
Brown, Stu, Mgr.-Sls.--Wahl Instruments, Culver City, CA, pg. 1158
Brown, T.G., V.P.-Sls.--Standard Lafarge, Canfield, OH, pg. 1036
Browne, Ron, Sls. Mgr.--Pacific Forge, Inc., Fontana, CA, pg. 102
Browne, William T., Jr., Sr. V.P.-Mktg. & Sls.--Marotta Scientific Controls, Inc., Montville, NJ, pg. 713
Brownstein, Martin, V.P.-Sls. & Adv. Specialty--Uniflex, Inc., Hicksville, NY, pg. 1126
Bruce, Joe, V.P.-Merchant Sls.--Calcot, Ltd., Bakersfield, CA, pg. 208
Bruggeman, Ron, Dir.-Sls.--Gourmet Foods Div., Omaha, NE, pg. 825
Brunini, Ken, V.P. & Reg. Sls. Mgr.-Consumer Prods. Div.--Glen Raven Marketing Corporation, New York, NY, pg. 461
Bruno, J. Michael, Natl. Sls. Mgr.--Dixie Brewing Co., Inc., New Orleans, LA, pg. 341
Bruno, T., Gen. Mgr.-Sls.--Peerless Importers, Inc., Brooklyn, NY, pg. 855
Brush, James, Exec. V.P.-Sls. & Mktg.--Sentry Group, Rochester, NY, pg. 990
Brwon, Richard, Mgr.-Sls.--Bell Gas, Inc., Roswell, NM, pg. 134
Bryan, Michael B., V.P.-Sls. & Mktg.--Graham Magnetics, Inc., Bedford, TX, pg. 475
Bryans, Philip, Sls. Promo. Mgr.--Dayton Rogers Mfg. Co., Minneapolis, MN, pg. 321
Bryant, Mike, Sr. V.P.-Sls.--Altec Industries, Inc., Birmingham, AL, pg. 45
Bryant, Tom, V.P.-Sls.--Evansville Brewing Company, Evansville, IN, pg. 391
Buccola, Tony, V.P.-Sls. & Mktg.--Cumberland Packing Corp., Brooklyn, NY, pg. 304
Buckingham, Lewis J., Jr., Gen. Sls. Mgr.--Old Dutch Foods, Inc., Saint Paul, MN, pg. 823
Buddig, Thomas R., V.P.-Sls. & Mktg.--Carl Buddig & Company, Homewood, IL, pg. 186
Buehler, Bob, Mgr.-Feed Mktg. & Specialty Sls.--Southern States Cooperative, Inc., Richmond, VA, pg. 1022
Bugas, Tim, Dir.-Sls.--Virginia Hot Springs, Inc., Hot Springs, VA, pg. 1152
Bukowsky, R.C., Natl. Sls. Mgr.--Ideal Industries, Inc., Sycamore, IL, pg. 562
Bull, David R., Mgr.-Natl. Sls.--Heath Consultants Incorporated, Stoughton, MA, pg. 524
Bullins, Jerry, V.P-Sls.--Klaussner Furniture Industry, Asheboro, NC, pg. 634
Bullock, Jack, V.P.-Mktg. & Sls.--Powers Pharmaceutical, Brockton, MA, pg. 236
Bullock, Thomas, V.P.-Retail Sls.--Ocean Spray Cranberries, Inc., Lakeville, MA, pg. 820
Bullus, Phillip, Area Sls. Mgr.--Bourns Electronics, Ltd., Camberley,, United Kingdom, pg. 168
Bunn, Jacob, Mgr.-Sls.--Bunn-O-Matic Corporation, Springfield, IL, pg. 188
Bunnell, Dale, V.P.-Sls.--Mark Andy, Inc., Chesterfield, MO, pg. 708
Burbacher, Susan, Asst. Sls. Mgr.--Evans Adhesive Corp., Columbus, OH, pg. 390
Burbick, Ron L., V.P.-Mktg. & Sls.--Schneller, Inc., Kent, OH, pg. 977
Burdick, Curtis, V.P.-Sls. & Sls. Promo--Distribution America, Des Plaines, IL, pg. 340
Burge, Stuart, V.P.-Sls.--The Brady Marketing Company, Pacheco, CA, pg. 171
Burgener, Jim, V.P.-Sls.--Casual Sportswear Co., Inc., Dunmore, PA, pg. 1030
Burgess, Steve, Sr. V.P.-Retail Sls.--Krause's Sofa Factory, Inc., Brea, CA, pg. 644
Burgher, Tom, Mgr.-Sls.--Welsh Company, Saint Louis, MO, pg. 1175
Buri, Gayle, V.P.-Sls.--Krause Plow Corp., Hutchinson, KS, pg. 644
Buric, Allyn C., Dir.-Natl. Sls.--Justrite Manufacturing Company, Des Plaines, IL, pg. 610
Burk, William, V.P.-Sls.--Monumental Millwork, Inc., Westminster, MD, pg. 768
Burke, Doug, V.P.-Intl Sls.--A.W. Chesterton Company, Stoneham, MA, pg. 244
Burke, John, V.P.-Sls. & Mktg.--Trek Bicycle Corporation, Waterloo, WI, pg. 581
Burke, William J., V.P.-Sls.--Osco Industries Inc., Portsmouth, OH, pg. 830
Burks, T., V.P.-Intl. Mktg. & Sls.--Shure Brothers Incorporated, Evanston, IL, pg. 1001
Burnhart, George, Mgr.-Natl. Mktg.--Longyear Company, Salt Lake City, UT, pg. 682
Burns, Jim, Mgr.-Used Car Sls.--Fairway Ford, Inc., Greenville, SC, pg. 397
Burns, Raymond E., V.P.-Sls.--Mack Molding Company, Arlington, VT, pg. 697
Burns, Robert, Mgr.-Sls. Promotion & Food Service Mktg.--Tri Valley Growers Inc., San Francisco, CA, pg. 1111
Burns, Robert D., V.P.-Sls. & Mktg.--Conway Import Co. Inc., Franklin Park, IL, pg. 281
Burns, Samuel D., V.P.-Mktg.--New Fortis Corp., King, NC, pg. 800
Burns, Tim, Sls. Dir.--Old World Automotive Products, Northbrook, IL, pg. 824
Burr, R., V.P.-Sls.--General Metalcraft, Inc., Dover, DE, pg. 450
Burris, Tom, Mgr.-Export Sls.--Stihl Inc., Virginia Beach, VA, pg. 1049
Burris, William, V.P.-Sls.--Watson Food Service Industries, Dallas, TX, pg. 1156
Burrough, Ken, Asst. V.P.-Intl. Sls.--MICOM Communications Corp., United Kingdom, pg. 748
Burton, Richard I., Dir.-Sls. & Mktg.--Twin City Die Castings Co., Minneapolis, MN, pg. 1121
Burton, Robert, Sls. & Mktg. Dir.--Sterling Homes Corp., Sparks, NV, pg. 1046
Burton, Robert, Dir.-Sls. & Mktg.--Sterling Builders, Inc., Irvine, CA, pg. 1047
Busby, Robert B., Exec. V.P. & Dir.-Sls.--Pawling Corporation, Pawling, NY, pg. 852
Busca, G.P., Sr. V.P.-Sls. & Mktg. & Chief Oper. Officer--Energy Brokers Guild, Stevensville, MI, pg. 381
Bush, Brent, Dir.-Sls.--Business Mens Insurance Corporation, Miami, FL, pg. 196
Bush, William C., V.P.-Sls., Western Region--Donlen Corp., Deerfield, IL, pg. 345
Bushy, Brian, Reg. Mgr.-Sls.--Kowalski Sausage Co., Inc., Hamtramck, MI, pg. 643
Buskirk, Jeffrey, Mgr.-Sls.--Rock Hill Materials Company, Catasauqua, PA, pg. 941
Bussing, Dave, Gen. Sls. Mgr.--M.A.B. Paints, Terre Haute, IN, pg. 184
Butler, Andrew, Dir.-Sls.--Butler Automatic, Inc., Canton, MA, pg. 197
Butler, Bill, Reg. Sls. Mgr.--Evenflo Juvenile Furniture Co., Piqua, OH, pg. 1024
Butler, Charles, Mgr.-Sls.-Custom--Maryland Plastics, Inc., Federalsburg, MD, pg. 717
Butler, Charles, Sls. Mgr.-Custom--Maryland Plastics, Inc., Federalsburg, MD, pg. 152
Butler, Norman D., V.P.-Sls. & Mktg., Service Parts Div.--Foley-PLP Company, Rochester, NY, pg. 422
Butler, Tom, V.P., Sales--The Sunflower Group, Overland Park, KS, pg. 1060
Buxbaum, E., V.P.-Sls. & Mktg.--The Akro Corporation, Canton, OH, pg. 262
Bybee, Steve, Dir.-Sls. & Mktg.--The Knapheide Mfg. Co., Quincy, IL, pg. 636
Bynon W. Lee, Mgr.-Natl. Sls.--Daniel Green Co., Dolgeville, NY, pg. 484
Bynon, W. Lee, V.P.-Sls.--Daniel Green Co., Dolgeville, NY, pg. 484
Byrne, Tom, V.P.-Sls.--A. Pomerantz & Co., Philadelphia, PA, pg. 880
Byrnes, Thomas, V.P.-Sls.--Avis, Inc., Garden City, NY, pg. 102
Cabana, Bill, Mgr.-New Car Sls.--Mark Chevrolet Inc., Wayne, MI, pg. 708
Cabral, G., Mgr.-Sls.--Plymkraft Inc., Newport News, VA, pg. 266
Cagney, Art, V.P.-Sls.--Nitram Energy inc., Orchard Park, NY, pg. 807
Calabrese, Clement A., V.P.-Retail Sls.--Sunshine Biscuits, Inc., Woodbridge, NJ, pg. 439
Calabrese, F.P., Mgr.-Sls.--The Grieve Corporation, Round Lake, IL, pg. 486
Caldera, Jerry, V.P.-Sls.--Pharmavite Corp., Mission Hills, CA, pg. 866
Caldwell, Dale, V.P.-Mktg.--Edwards Baking Co., Atlanta, GA, pg. 369
Caldwell, Robert, Natl. Sls. Mgr.--Spencer's Inc., Mount Airy, NC, pg. 1030
Calio, Joseph, V.P.-Sls. & Mktg.--Exide Corporation, Reading, PA, pg. 393
Call, Mike, Mgr.-Sls.--Samelson-Leon Company, Inc., Memphis, TN, pg. 968
Callahan, Daniel V., V.P.-Sls.--Integral Systems, Walnut Creek, CA, pg. 572
Callas, Chris, Chief Oper. Officer & Dir.-Sls. & Mktg.--Time Products, Inc., Atlanta, GA, pg. 1090
Calvano, Robert J., Gen. Sls. Mgr.--Uncas Manufacturing Company, Providence, RI, pg. 1125
Camarda, Bernard, V.P.-Sls. & Mktg.--Merchandising Equipment Group, Arlington Heights, IL, pg. 739
Campbell, Bernard, V.P.-Sls.--Connelly Containers, Inc., Bala-Cynwyd, PA, pg. 275
Campbell, Cecil, Mgr.-Natl. Sls.--Fritz Chemical Company, Mesquite, TX, pg. 434
Campbell, Don, V.P. & Controller--Western Diesel Services Inc., Saint Louis, MO, pg. 1179
Campbell, John, Sls. Dir.--Setzer Forest Products, Sacramento, CA, pg. 993
Campbell, Michael, V.P.-Sls.--Luzianne Blue Plate Foods, New Orleans, LA, pg. 923
Campbell, Thomas, V.P.-Mktg. & Sls.--KNOX International Corp., Knoxville, TN, pg. 638
Campbell, Thomas, V.P.-Sls. & Mktg.--Ranging, East Bloomfield, NY, pg. 300
Campbell, Thomas G., Mgr.-Reg. Sls.--Elastomeric Technologies, Inc., Hatboro, PA, pg. 372
Cancienne, Ron, Mgr.-Sls.--Standard Supply & Hardware, New Orleans, LA, pg. 1037
Canfield, Susan, Mgr.-Sls. Coord. & Adv.--LubeCon Systems, Inc., Fremont, MI, pg. 686
Canning, John N., V.P.-Sls. & Mktg.--Pine State Tobacco & Candy Company, Augusta, ME, pg. 871
Cannon, Robert E., V.P.-Sls. & Mktg.--Channellock, Inc., Meadville, PA, pg. 239
Cansler, E.T., V.P.-Domestic Sls.--Platt Saco Lowell Corporation, Greenville, SC, pg. 876

Canter, Richard, Sr. V.P.-Sls.--Pillowtex Corporation, Dallas, TX, pg. 870
Cantor, Lee, Natl. Sls. Mgr.--Uniflex, Inc., Hicksville, NY, pg. 1126
Cantore, Tamra, Eastern Div. Affiliate Sls. Dir.--The Weather Channel, Inc.-Atlanta Sales Office, Atlanta, GA, pg. 654
Cantrell, Mike, Mgr.-F & I Sls.--Fairway Ford, Inc., Greenville, SC, pg. 397
Cantwell, Keith, Mgr.-Sls.--Kern's Bakeries, Incorporated, Knoxville, TN, pg. 624
Canzanese, Raymond, Mgr.-Sls.--Southtec, Inc., Albany, NY, pg. 1019
Capalbo, Francis A., V.P.-Sls.--G.F. Wright Steel & Wire Company, Worcester, MA, pg. 1205
Capo, Barbara, Mgr.-Natl. Accts. & Foreign Sls.--Arrow Group Industries, Inc., Wayne, NJ, pg. 357
Capone, Donald W., Mgr.-Sls.--Munroe, Inc., Pittsburgh, PA, pg. 776
Cappa, Arthur P., V.P.-Sls.--DVC Industries, Bay Shore, NY, pg. 310
Cappadocia, Ronald, Sr. V.P.-Mktg. & Sls.--Farley Candy Company, Chicago, IL, pg. 399
Caputo, Steve, Deputy Dir.--Oregon State Lottery, Salem, OR, pg. 829
Caramela, Laurence M., Dir.-Sls. & Mktg., Bottle/Can--Central Coca-Cola Bottling Company, Inc., Richmond, VA, pg. 232
Cardillo, Robert, V.P.-Sls. & Mktg.--Avis, Inc., Garden City, NY, pg. 102
Cardinale, Rosemarie, Dir.-Sls. Promo.--Victoria Packing Corporation, Brooklyn, NY, pg. 1149
Cardona, Joseph, Dir.-Sls.--Caribe Express, Aguadilla, PR, pg. 220
Carey, Michael, Mgr.-Sls.--Muralo Co., Inc., Bayonne, NJ, pg. 776
Cariolo, Cosimo, Dir.-Sls. & Mktg.--Warren E. Collins, Inc., Braintree, MA, pg. 263
Cark, Veda, V.P.-Mktg. & Sls.--Litecontrol Corporation, Hanson, MA, pg. 677
Carlino, Jim, Mgr.-Sls.--Microband Companies, Inc., Fairfield, NJ, pg. 748
Carlisle, Larry, Loan Officer--Wieland Financial Services, Inc., Atlanta, GA, pg. 1188
Carlson, Arthur C., Reg. Mgr.-Sls.--Serfilco, Ltd., Northbrook, IL, pg. 990
Carlson, Russ, Dir.-Sls.--Victaulic International, Easton, PA, pg. 1149
Carlton, Thomas J., V.P.-Sls. & Mktg.--Corrugated Metals, Inc., Chicago, IL, pg. 287
Carmichael, Brian, Dir.-Retail--The Austad Company, Sioux Falls, SD, pg. 98
Carney, Larry, V.P.-Sls. & Mktg.-Royalle Div.--Prince Gardner Incorporated, Saint Louis, MO, pg. 890
Carnival, John, V.P. & Dir.-Sls., Mktg., Direct Mktg., Adv. & Media--Weksler Instruments Corp., Freeport, NY, pg. 1174
Carpenter, Mike, V.P.-Sls. & Mktg.--The Vollrath Company Inc., Sheboygan, WI, pg. 1154
Carr, Alan, V.P.-United States Sls.--Port Clyde Foods Co., South Portland, ME, pg. 276
Carrig, Wayne K., Mgr.-Sls.--Sealing Devices Inc., Lancaster, NY, pg. 984
Carrigan, Tim, V.P.-Sls.--Ivex Packaging Corporation-Food Packaging Division, Lincolnshire, IL, pg. 583
Carrigan, Tom, Dir.-Sls.--P/A Industries, Inc., Bloomfield, CT, pg. 835
Carrocia, M., Natl. Sls. Dir.--Pyle Inc., Chicago, IL, pg. 648
Carroll, John, V.P.-Sls.--Ranir Corporation, Grand Rapids, MI, pg. 912
Carroll, Kevin, Mgr.-Sls.--Strahman Valves, Inc., Florham Park, NJ, pg. 1052
Carson, Jim, Mgr.-Outside Sls.--Associated Process Controls, Pleasanton, CA, pg. 92
Carter, Dan, V.P.-Sls.--Tech Industries, Inc., Woonsocket, RI, pg. 1083
Carter, Jerry, V.P.-Sls.-North Eastern Region--PST Vans, Inc., Salt Lake City, UT, pg. 837
Carter, John M., Chm. Bd., & Chief Exec. Officer--Carco Electronics, Menlo Park, CA, pg. 217
Carter, Nick, V.P. & Natl. Sls. Dir.--Nightingale-Conant Div., Chicago, IL, pg. 807
Carter, Randy, Gen. Mgr.-Sls.--Peck Road Ford Truck Sales, Whittier, CA, pg. 854
Cartier, Chuck, Dir.-Sls. & Mktg.--The Beverly Hills Hotel, Beverly Hills, CA, pg. 148
Cartwright, Ken, Loan Officer--Wieland Financial Services, Inc., Atlanta, GA, pg. 1188
Cascino, J., Sr. V.P.-Sls.--Institutional Financing Services, Benicia, CA, pg. 571
Case, George, Mgr.-Natl. Sls.--Pony Sports & Leisure Inc., Warren, NJ, pg. 880
Casella, Billie, Mgr.-Circulation--Pittsburg Morning Sun, Pittsburg, KS, pg. 1042
Casey, J. Phillip, V.P.-Mktg. & Sls.--JII/Sales Promotion Associates, Inc., Coshocton, OH, pg. 604
Casey, Joseph H., Intl. Sls. Mgr.--Allied Mineral Products, Inc., Columbus, OH, pg. 38
Caspall, Ken, V.P.-Sls.--MFA Oil Company, Columbia, MO, pg. 692
Cassano, William, V.P.-Mktg. & Sls.--Whaling Industries, Inc., Fall River, MA, pg. 1183
Cassell, Lewis, Dir.-Sls.--United Piece Dye Works, LP, Princeton Junction, NJ, pg. 1134
Cassella, V.J., Mgr.-Sls.--Specialty Chemicals Div., Valley Forge, PA, pg. 837
Cassidy, Brian, Dir.-Incentive Mkt. Sls.--Hyatt Hotels Corporation, Chicago, IL, pg. 495
Cassin, Thomas C., V.P.-Mktg.--Pitco Frialator Inc., Concord, NH, pg. 157
Castle, Edward, Sls. Mgr.--Coastal Dairy Products, Inc., Wilson, NC, pg. 257
Catterall, Phil, V.P.-Sls.--Central Point Software, Inc., Beaverton, OR, pg. 234
Caudle, Morris W., V.P.-Sls.--Data Documents, Inc., Omaha, NE, pg. 316
Cavalier, Clark, V.P.-Sls.--Southern Farm Bureau Casualty Insurance Company, Ridgeland, MS, pg. 1021
Cavuto, Anthony, V.P.-Sls.--Cornell Dubilier Electronics, Wayne, NJ, pg. 616
Cepa, Dan, Mgr.-Sls.--Replogle Globes, Inc., Broadview, IL, pg. 927
Chadwick, George W., Natl. Sls. Mgr.--New England Confectionery Co., Cambridge, MA, pg. 1123
Chalifour, Marcel O., V.P.-Sls. & Mktg.--Associated Grocers of New England, Inc., Manchester, NH, pg. 90
Chambers, J.W., Sr. V.P.-Sls. & Mktg.--The Hartwell Corporation, Placentia, CA, pg. 514
Champion, Charles F., Sr. V.P.-Adv. Sls. & Mktg.--Chicago Sun Times, Chicago, IL, pg. 18
Chandler, Ron, V.P.-Sls.--Antenna Products Corp., Mineral Wells, TX, pg. 76
Chaney, Mark, Mgr.-Circulation--The Grand Island Daily Independent, Grand Island, NE, pg. 1042
Channel, Frank, Gen. Sls. Mgr.--Your Man Tours, Inc., Inglewood, CA, pg. 1214
Chaplin, Cliff, Sr. V.P.-Sls.--Gould Paper Corporation, New York, NY, pg. 473
Chapman, Ray, Natl. Sls. Mgr.--Branch Cheese Company, Inc., Branch, WI, pg. 576
Chapman, S.N., Mgr.-Sls. & Mktg.--Hall Sign, Inc., Bloomington, IN, pg. 501
Chapman, Tom, Gen. Sls. Mgr.--WIFC-FM, Wausau, WI, pg. 608
Chapman, Tom, Gen. Sls. Mgr.--WSAU-AM, Wausau, WI, pg. 608
Charas, Ethan, Dir.-Sls. Admin.--Stratmar Systems, Inc., Port Chester, NY, pg. 1053
Charles, William, V.P.-Sls.--The Hennegan Company, Cincinnati, OH, pg. 529
Charpia, Mack, Mgr.-Vehicle Sls.--Fairway Ford, Inc., Greenville, SC, pg. 397
Chartier, Charles, Mgr.-Sls.--Spotnails Inc., Rolling Meadows, IL, pg. 1032
Cheatham, J. Gilliam, V.P.-Sls.--Dundee Mills, Inc., Griffin, GA, pg. 352
Check, Robert, V.P.-Sls. Auto Div.--Joan Fabrics Corp., Tyngsboro, MA, pg. 594
Chenoweth, David A., V.P.-Sls. & Mktg.--The Paxall Group, Inc., Skokie, IL, pg. 852
Chenoweth, Rick, Dir.-Sls.--Rocco Turkeys, Inc., Dayton, VA, pg. 940
Childress, T.H., V.P.-Sls. & Opers.--Asbury Ferst, Inc., Atlanta, GA, pg. 87
Childs, Bill, Mgr.-Sls.--Pulliam Motor Company, Columbia, SC, pg. 899
Childs, Jack, V.P.-Sls.--Parisi, Inc., Philadelphia, PA, pg. 848
Chilton, Roger, V.P.-Domestic Sls.--Thomas Built Buses, Inc., High Point, NC, pg. 1092
Chiostergi, Bob, V.P.-Mktg. & Sls.--Southern Mills, Inc., Union City, GA, pg. 1021
Chisholm, Larry, Natl. Sls. Mgr.--U.S. Divers, Santa Ana, CA, pg. 1135
Choate, Claude, V.P.-Natl. Sls. & Consumer Prods.--National Oats Co., Cedar Rapids, IA, pg. 25
Choquette, Roger, V.P. & Gen. Sls. Mgr.-Southern Area--Steelcase Inc., Grand Rapids, MI, pg. 1044
Chown, Fred L., V.P.-Sls.--Lampert Yards, Inc., Saint Paul, MN, pg. 653
Chozick, Henry, V.P.-Sls.--Plascal Corporation, Farmingdale, NY, pg. 874
Christensen, Gary, Sr. V.P.-Mktg. & Sls.--Pella Corporation, Pella, IA, pg. 856
Christensen, Richard, Dir.-Standard Prod. Sls.--Cyberex, Inc., Mentor, OH, pg. 307
Christian, Michael, V.P.-Midwest Sls.--Frank Consolidated Enterprises Inc., Des Plaines, IL, pg. 428
Christopher, David, Sr. V.P.-Mktg. & Sls.--Commodore Cruise Line, Ltd., Coral Gables, FL, pg. 269
Christopher, Ken, Sls. Mgr.--JFG Coffee Company, Knoxville, TN, pg. 923
Christy, Robert, Mgr.-Sls.--Mautz Paint Company, Madison, WI, pg. 722
Chura, D.E., Gen. Mgr.-Sls.--Sporlan Valve Company, Saint Louis, MO, pg. 1032
Cianelli, Paul, V.P.-Sls.--Columbus Show Case Company, Columbus, OH, pg. 267
Cicchese, William, Sr. V.P.-Sls. & Pur.--New England Frozen Foods, Southborough, MA, pg. 800
Ciccone, Jim, Sls. Mgr.-East--ATAPCO Office Products Group, Saint Louis, MO, pg. 64
Cilley, C. S., V.P.-Sls.--Home Fashions Div., New York, NY, pg. 400
Cimbolo, Salvatore, V.P.-Sls. & Mktg.--Monroe Systems For Business, Inc., Morris Plains, NJ, pg. 766
Claassen, James G., Sr. V.P.-Mktg. & Sls.--Montgomery Elevator Company, Moline, IL, pg. 767
Clagg, Brian, Sr. Sls. Engr.--Apex Corporation, Indianapolis, IN, pg. 78
Clancy, Kevin, V.P.-Sls. & Mktg.--Homes of Merit Inc., Bartow, FL, pg. 542
Clark, James, V.P.-Circulation--The Milwaukee Journal, Milwaukee, WI, pg. 607
Clark, Lamar, Mgr.-Sls.--Binning's Building Products, Inc., Lexington, NC, pg. 151
Clark, Mike, V.P.-Sls.--Man-Gill Chemical Company, Cleveland, OH, pg. 703
Clark, W.P., Jr., V.P.-Sls. & Mktg.--Wall Colmonoy Corp., Madison Heights, MI, pg. 1160
Clarke, Christine, Asst. to Dir.-Adv. & Creative Services--CRK Advertising, New York, NY, pg. 203
Clarke, S., V.P.-Sales--Blaw Knox - Duraloy Division, Scottdale, PA, pg. 156
Clarkson, Paul, V.P.-Div. Sls.--Bradley Corporation, Menomonee Falls, WI, pg. 170
Clausing, Gordon, V.P.-Mktg. & Sls.--Times Printing Company, Inc., Random Lake, WI, pg. 1098
Clawson, Kerry A., NY Sls. Mgr.--Parade Publications Inc., New York, NY, pg. 847
Clayton, James, V.P.-Sls.--AP Parts Manufacturing Company, Toledo, OH, pg. 240
Clayton, S.R., Sr. V.P.-Tobacco Sls.--T.S. Ragsdale Company, Incorporated, Lake City, SC, pg. 910
Clayton, Ted, Mgr.-Natl. School Bus. Sls.--Thomas Built Buses, Inc., High Point, NC, pg. 1092
Cleaver, John W., V.P. & Sls. Mgr.--Gibbs Wire & Steel Company, Inc., Southington, CT, pg. 456
Cleland, Thomas G., V.P. & Gen. Sls. Mgr.-Eastern Area--Steelcase Inc., Grand Rapids, MI, pg. 1044
Clemen, Sharon A., Mgr.-Sls.--Advance Packaging Corporation, Grand Rapids, MI, pg. 19
Clement, Frank, Mgr.-Natl. Sls.--Joshua Meier Corp., North Bergen, NJ, pg. 737
Clements, Edward, Mgr.-Sls.--Clements Foods Co., Oklahoma City, OK, pg. 254
Clements, Tom, V.P.-Sls.--Brock Control Systems, Inc., Atlanta, GA, pg. 178
Cliett, Dewayne, Mgr.-Sls.--B.C. Cook & Sons Enterprises, Inc., Haines City, FL, pg. 282
Cline, Edward S., Sls. Mgr.--Carbidie Corporation, Irwin, PA, pg. 1032
Cline, Jerome, V.P.-Sls.--Zinc Corporation of America, Monaca, PA, pg. 545
Cloran, J.H., Mgr.-Bus. Devel.--The Kirk & Blum Mfg. Co., Cincinnati, OH, pg. 633
Cloutier, M.N., Factory Sls. Admin.--Badger Construction Equipment Co., Insley Div., Winona, MN, pg. 113
Clowdis, Chuck, V.P.-Sls. & Opers.--Merchants Truck Line, Inc., New Albany, MS, pg. 740
Clunk, James, Mgr.-Sls.--The Hall China Company, East Liverpool, OH, pg. 501
Coakley, Mark, Mgr.-Sls.--C.E.M. Div. Spirol Intl. Corp., Danielson, CT, pg. 1031
Coburn, William, Natl. Sls. Mgr.--Beauty Retail Products, Westchester, IL, pg. 328
Cochran, Terry, Mgr.-Circulation & Adv.--Dodge City Daily Globe, Dodge City, KS, pg. 1042
Cochrane, Joel, Natl. Sls. Mgr.-Case Div.--Cochrane Furniture Co., Inc., Lincolnton, NC, pg. 258
Cochrane, William, Mgr.-Sls.--Caldwell Manufacturing Company, Rochester, NY, pg. 208
Coe, Frederick A., Jr., Mgr.-Natl. Sls.--Koehler Manufacturing Company, Marlborough, MA, pg. 639
Coenson, Barbara, Mktg. Coord.--American Automobile Association, National Travel Department, Heathrow, FL, pg. 49
Cogen, Mitch, Mgr.-Sls.--Pyramid Handbags Inc., New York, NY, pg. 901
Cohen, Gary, Dir.-Sls.--Boston Trading Ltd. Inc., Lynn, MA, pg. 168
Cohen, Mark J., V.P.-Sls. & Mktg.--All-Luminum Products, Inc., Philadelphia, PA, pg. 35
Cohen, Robert, V.P.-Sls.-East Coast--Schnadig Corporation, Chicago, IL, pg. 977
Cohen, Warren, V.P.-Sls. & Mktg.--Eagle Electric Mfg. Co., Inc., Long Island City, NY, pg. 362
Coia, J., Mgr.-Sls.--Perry Products Corp., Hainesport, NJ, pg. 863
Coker, Joyce, Inside Sls. Supvr.--Triumph-Lor, Inc., Houston, TX, pg. 1115
Colbert,Gary, V.P.-Sls.--Clipper Exxpress Co., Lemont, IL, pg. 256
Colboch, Craig, Mgr.-Sls.--WIBW-TV AM & FM, Topeka, KS, pg. 1043
Cole, B. A., Mgr.-Gen. Sls.--Dinner Bell Foods, Inc., Cincinnati, OH, pg. 53
Cole, Donald, V.P.-Sls.--Mountain States Pipe & Supply Company, Colorado Springs, CO, pg. 773
Cole, James L., V.P.-Sls.--Southern Radio Corporation, pg. 1022
Coleman, J.L., Gen. Sls. Mgr.--Rubatex Corporation, Bedford, VA, pg. 480
Coleman, Walter B., Dir.-Sls.--Guth Lighting Company, Saint Louis, MO, pg. 588
Coles, B.R., V.P.-Sls.--Sunbeam Corporation (Canada) Limited, Toronto, Canada, pg. 1059
Colker, Jeff, Dir.-Sls. & Mktg.--Apollo Industries, Smyrna, GA, pg. 1090
Collier, Bryan, V.P.-Sls.--JM Clipper Corporation d/b/a Acadia, Roanoke, VA, pg. 507
Collins, Dave, V.P.-Franchise Sls.--Sir Speedy, Inc., Laguna Hills, CA, pg. 613
Collins, Ed, V.P., Mgr. Reg. Field Opers.--Hill, Holliday/Los Angeles, Marina Del Rey, CA, pg. 534
Colls, Brian, V.P.-European Sls.--United Air Specialists, Inc., Cincinnati, OH, pg. 1130
Colucci, James, Sr. V.P. Sls. & Mktg.--Consolidated Cigar Corporation, Fort Lauderdale, FL, pg. 276
Colucci, James, Sr. V.P.-Sls. & Mktg.--Allied Products, Fort Lauderdale, FL, pg. 276
Colucco, Robert, V.P.-Sls.--Gould Paper Corporation, New York, NY, pg. 473
Commito, Thomas F., Sr. V.P.-Mktg.--National Life Insurance Company, Montpelier, VT, pg. 791
Compagno, Robert L., V.P.-Sls.--Fellowes Manufacturing Co., Itasca, IL, pg. 405
Compton, Pam, V.P.-Sls.--Bollinger Health Care, Lubbock, TX, pg. 163
Conarroe, Richard, Mgr.-Sls. & Mktg. Devel.--Coleman International Operation, Wichita, KS, pg. 695
Condon, Sean, Mgr.-Industrial Sls.--Ivex Packaging Corporation-Grove City, Grove City, PA, pg. 583
Conley, John W., Dir.-WW Sls. & Services--LSI Truck Products Corp.-Neway/Anchor Lock, Muskegon, MI, pg. 664
Conlon, John A., Jr., Mgr. Dir.-Sls.--Rothschild Inc., New York, NY, pg. 951
Connelly, Brian, V.P.-Sls. & Mktg.--Emson Research, Inc., Bridgeport, CT, pg. 380
Connelly, Michael, Gen. Mgr.-Sls. & Mktg.--Rea Magnet Wire Company, Inc., Fort Wayne, IN, pg. 915

Corporate Responsibilities Index

Conner, John, V.P.-Sls.--Rau Fasteners, Inc., Providence, RI, pg. 913
Connon, Dana, Grp. V.P.--Welsh Company, Saint Louis, MO, pg. 1175
Connor, Barry C., Mgr.-Natl. Sls.--The Noteworthy Company, Amsterdam, NY, pg. 816
Conover, Clay, V.P.-Adv. Specialty--Keith Clark, Sidney, NY, pg. 304
Considine, Paul, V.P.-Sls. & Mktg.--American Fuel Cell & Coated Fabrics Co. (Amfuel), Magnolia, AR, pg. 55
Consorti, Steve, Dir.-Sls.--Mission Industries, Santa Barbara, CA, pg. 760
Constable, Trevor, V.P.-Sls. & Mktg.--Systech Computer Corporation, San Diego, CA, pg. 1071
Contu, Norean, Mgr.-Sls.--A. I. Root Co., San Antonio, TX, pg. 946
Converse, James P., V.P. & Gen. Sls. Mgr.--Sues, Young & Brown Inc., Baldwin Park, CA, pg. 1056
Conway, Barry, Exec. V.P.-Sls. & Mktg.--Adams Business Forms, Topeka, KS, pg. 16
Cook, Lynda, Export Sls. Mgr.--Gibson Wine Company, Elk Grove, CA, pg. 457
Cook, Michael, V.P.-Sls.--American Metal & Plastics, Grand Rapids, MI, pg. 58
Cook, Tad, V.P.-Sls.--Noma-International, Inc., Forest Park, IL, pg. 808
Cook, Terry M., V.P.-Sls.--C.J. Vitner & Co., Inc., Chicago, IL, pg. 1153
Cook, Tim, V.P.-Sls.--Orders Distributing Co., Greenville, SC, pg. 829
Cook, William R., Sls. Mgr.--The Shaler Company, Waupun, WI, pg. 793
Cooke, John W., V.P.-Sls.--Easy Day Manufacturing Company, Inc., Holliston, MA, pg. 364
Cooksey, Thomas M., V.P.-Mktg. & Sls.--Bruner Corporation, Milwaukee, WI, pg. 184
Cooksey, William K., V.P.-Sls. & Mktg.--U.S. Manufacturing Corp., Roseville, MI, pg. 1136
Cooper, Alan, Natl. Sls. Mgr.--Martin F. Weber Company, Philadelphia, PA, pg. 716
Cooper, Daryle, V.P.-Mktg. & Sls.--Eastern Air Devices, Inc., Dover, NH, pg. 363
Cooper, Glenn, Sls. Dir.--American Automobile Association, National Travel Department, Heathrow, FL, pg. 49
Cooper, Jonathan, V.P.-Sls. & Mktg.--Spectronics Corporation, Westbury, NY, pg. 1029
Cooper, Larry, V.P.-Sls.--Columbus Mills, Inc., Columbus, GA, pg. 267
Cooper, Ray, V.P.-Sls.--Gaston County Dyeing Machine Co., Stanley, NC, pg. 444
Cooper, Richard B., V.P.-Sls. Worldwide--Amalloy, Goshen, NY, pg. 46
Cooper, William, Dir.-Sls. & Mktg.--Atlas Van Lines, Inc., Evansville, IN, pg. 96
Corbett, E.M., Jr., V.P.-Sls.--Harwick Chemical Corp., Akron, OH, pg. 515
Corbett, Frank, Mgr.-Sls., Special Tran. Grp.--Atlas Specialized Transportation, Evansville, IN, pg. 97
Corbett, James, Dir.-Sls. & Mktg.--Crown Prince, Inc. (CA), City of Industry, CA, pg. 302
Corbett, Martin, Mgr.-Sls. & Adv.--Harold Leonard & Company, Inc., Union, NJ, pg. 667
Corbin, Brad, V.P.-Sls.--G.C. Thorsen, Inc., Rockford, IL, pg. 609
Corenthal, Sol, Sr. V.P.-Sls. & Pur.--Best Manufacturing, Inc., New York, NY, pg. 146
Corey, Arnold G., V.P.-Sls.--Southern Belle Dairy Company, Inc., Somerset, KY, pg. 1020
Corizzo, Joseph, V.P.-Sls.--Barq's, Inc., New Orleans, LA, pg. 121
Corizzo, Joseph, V.P.-Sls.--Delaware Punch Co., New Orleans, LA, pg. 121
Cornelison, Dave, Mgr.-Mktg. & Natl. Sls.--M & C Specialties Company, Southampton, PA, pg. 690
Cornelius, Jim, V.P.-Sls.--Edward Don & Company of Illinois, North Riverside, IL, pg. 344
Cornell, Allan, Mgr.-Sls.--Gertrude Hawk Chocolates, Inc., Troop, PA, pg. 517
Cornish, Steven, Mgr.-Sls.--Collegeville Flag Mfg. Company, Collegeville, PA, pg. 261
Cornwell, Brad, Asst. V.P.--Wieland Financial Services, Inc., Atlanta, GA, pg. 1188
Coronado, Alex, Dir.-New Prod. Devel. & Natl. Sls. Mgr.--R.J. Corr Naturals, Inc., Posen, IL, pg. 287
Corson, James, Sr. V.P.-Sls.--R & B Machine Tool Co., Saline, MI, pg. 906
Cosmo, Sallyann, Mgr.-Reg. Sls.--Agway Petroleum Corp., De Witt, NY, pg. 25
Costa, Roseann, Sls. & Mktg. Admin.--Toy Biz, Inc., New York, NY, pg. 1104
Coston, Willis D., Exec. V.P.-Sls.--Whataburger, Inc., Corpus Christi, TX, pg. 1184
Cotes, John, Mgr.-Nuclear & Military Sls.--W F I, Inc., Houston, TX, pg. 1156
Cottier, John C., V.P.-Sls.--Paul Arpin Vanlines, Inc., East Greenwich, RI, pg. 85
Cotton, John L., Dir.-Mktg.--Howard Needles Tammen & Bergendoff, Kansas City, MO, pg. 547
Cotton, Judy, V.P.-Sls. & Mktg.--The Charles Levy Company, Chicago, IL, pg. 672
Cotuno, Ken, V.P.-Natl. Accounts & Specialty Sls.--Edward Don & Company of Illinois, North Riverside, IL, pg. 344
Coughlin, G. Jay, Exec. V.P.-Sls.--Northern Drug Company, Duluth, MN, pg. 814
Coughlin, Neil P., V.P.-Sls. & Mktg.--Kingsbury Corporation, Keene, NH, pg. 631
Coulter, David, Mgr.-Sls., Special Tran. Grp.--Atlas Specialized Transportation, Evansville, IN, pg. 97
Coulton, Sally B., Mgr.-Sls. & Mktg.--BNA PLUS, Washington, DC, pg. 189
Cousins, John, Mgr.-Natl. Sls. Specialty Printing--Ivex Packaging Corporation-Troy, Troy, OH, pg. 583
Couture, George, Station & Sls. Mgr.--WDIO-TV, Duluth, MN, pg. 549
Couzin, Mark S., V.P. & Dir.-Sls.--Mid-Continent Screw Products Co., Lincolnwood, IL, pg. 750
Covey, Jim, Dir.-Communications--CMI Lloyds, Irving, TX, pg. 233
Covey, Roger, V.P.-Sls.--Perdue Farms Inc., Salisbury, MD, pg. 860
Cowell, Carin, Coord.-Communications--IDAB International Incorporated, Hampton, VA, pg. 559
Cox, Gary L., Mgr.-Mktg. & Sls.--Mitchel & Scot Machine Co., Inc., Indianapolis, IN, pg. 761
Cox, Glen, V.P.-Sls., Exhaust & Off-Road--Cragar Industries, Compton, CA, pg. 761
Cox, Mark, Mgr.-Eastern Sls.--Efco Corporation, Monett, MO, pg. 359
Coyne, J.R., Mgr.-Western Sls.--Sloan Valve Company, Franklin Park, IL, pg. 1010
Coyne, Michael, V.P.-Sls.--Royal Crown Cola Co., Miami Beach, FL, pg. 243
Craig, Donald M., V.P.-Sls.--Morgan Foods, Inc., Austin, IN, pg. 770
Crain, Bob, Dir.-Mktg. & Sls.--Steelcase Wood Div., Kentwood, MI, pg. 1044
Crain, Michael, V.P.-Sls.--Preferred Risk Mutual Insurance, West Des Moines, IA, pg. 886
Cramer, Conrad C., V.P.-Sls. & Mktg.--Pressed Steel Tank Co., Inc., West Allis, WI, pg. 887
Cramer, Richard, V.P.-Mktg. & Sls.--The Milnot Company, Saint Louis, MO, pg. 756
Crandell, Billy, Sls. Rep.--Triumph-LOR, Inc., Spiro, OK, pg. 1115
Crandell, Robert, V.P.-Sls. & Mktg.--Baker Material Handling Corp., Summerville, SC, pg. 115
Crane, C.M., V.P.-Sls.--Williamson-Dickie Mfg. Co., Fort Worth, TX, pg. 1192
Crawford, David, V.P.-Sls.--DoAll Company, Des Plaines, IL, pg. 341
Crawford, John, V.P.-Sls.--Collin Street Bakery, Corsicana, TX, pg. 262
Craycraft, H.W., Sls. Mgr.-South--ATAPCO Office Products Group, Saint Louis, MO, pg. 64
Creadon, Vince, Sr. V.P.-Sls. & Mktg.--Baker Knapp & Tubbs Inc., Grand Rapids, MI, pg. 640
Crichton, Ian S., Sr. Exec. V.P.-Sls.--G. Heileman Brewing Co., Inc., La Crosse, WI, pg. 526
Crimmins, Robert J., Exec. V.P.-Personal Insurance--Metropolitan Life Insurance Co., New York, NY, pg. 744
Cripps, Howard D., V.P.-Sls.--Kalamazoo Holdings, Inc., Kalamazoo, MI, pg. 615
Cripps, Howard D., V.P.-Sls.--Kalsec, Inc., Kalamazoo, MI, pg. 615
Crisp, William, Sls. Mgr.--Knurlet Tool Co., Warren, MI, pg. 618
Crist, J. Richard, V.P.-Field Sls.--The Coleman Company, Inc., Wichita, KS, pg. 695
Crittenden, Zack, V.P.-Sls. & Gen. Mgr.--Miller & Co., Selma, AL, pg. 753
Crnko, Tim, Mgr.-Natl. Sls.--Watlow Electric Manufacturing Company, Saint Louis, MO, pg. 1167
Cromer, Domald, Mktg. Rep.--Erin Group Administrators, Inc., Lancaster, PA, pg. 387
Cronovich, David N., V.P.-Auto. & OEM Sls.--MNP Corp., Utica, MI, pg. 693
Crook, Tony, Mgr.-Sls.--Ultra Tool & Plastics, Inc., Amherst, NY, pg. 1125
Croom, Paul, Sr. V.P.-Sls.--S&D Coffee Inc., Concord, NC, pg. 959
Crorey, David, Exec. V.P.-Sls. & Mktg.--The ISI Manufacturing, Inc., Fraser, MI, pg. 560
Crosby, Jeff, Mgr.-Sls.--Capital Electric Group, Inc., Phoenix, AZ, pg. 215
Crosby, Peter G., Sr. V.P.-Mktg. & Sls.--Belvedere Company, Belvidere, IL, pg. 138
Cross, John R., V.P.-Sls. & Sec.--The Chardon Rubber Co., Chardon, OH, pg. 239
Crossan, Barbara, Dir.-Sls.--Reynen, Bardis & Winn, Sacramento, CA, pg. 930
Crosthwait, Kent, V.P.-Sls. & Pur.--Neill-LaVielle Supply Co., Louisville, KY, pg. 797
Crotty, Don, Sls.& Cost Analyst--Takatta Inc., Olympia Fields, IL, pg. 1076
Crow, Phillip W., V.P.-Sls.--Dawn Food Products, Inc., Jackson, MI, pg. 319
Crowe, Bob, Mgr.-Sls.-New Car--Future Ford/Hugo Inc., Roseville, CA, pg. 437
Crowley, Stephen, V.P.-Mktg. & Sls.--Rome Cable Corporation, Rome, NY, pg. 945
Crowley, William G., Dir.-Sls.--Metron Steel Corp., Chicago, IL, pg. 744
Crump, Randy, V.P.-Sls.--Swift Dodge Rolls Royce Inc., Sacramento, CA, pg. 1067
Crylen, Ed, Sls. Mgr.--Midwesco Mechanical, Niles, IL, pg. 751
Cuddeback, Ron, Mgr.-Sls./New Cars--McNamara Pontiac Inc., Orlando, FL, pg. 732
Culdert, William, V.P.-Sls.- John Roberts Company, Minneapolis, MN, pg. 938
Culkin, William L., V.P.-Sls.--Amtran, Inc., Indianapolis, IN, pg. 69
Cullis, Don, V.P.-Sls.--DHL Corporation, Redwood City, CA, pg. 309
Culver, John A., Dir.-Sls. & Mktg. & Adv. Mgr.--Giumarra Vineyards, Bakersfield, CA, pg. 460
Cummings, Robert, Dir.-Sls. & Mktg.--Wisconsin Label Corporation, Algoma, WI, pg. 1198
Cummings, Thomas M., Mgr.-Sls.--The Columbia Corporation, Chatham, NY, pg. 1209
Cunningham, Aldo, V.P.-Sls.--Goya Foods, Inc., Secaucus, NJ, pg. 474
Cunningham, Tom, Sr. V.P.-Sls. & Mktg.--The Berkline Corporation, Morristown, TN, pg. 285
Cupples, Kenneth, V.P.-Sls.--Central States Enterprises, Inc., Heathrow, FL, pg. 234
Curry, Bill, Mgr.-Sls.--Art Moran Pontiac-GMC Inc., Southfield, MI, pg. 769
Curtin, Dan, V.P.-Sls.--McCain Citrus Inc., Chicago, IL, pg. 726
Curtin, John F., V.P.-Sls.--Paul Hemmer Construction Company, Fort Mitchell, KY, pg. 528
Curtis, F. Roger, V.P.-Sls.--Peerless Confection Company, Chicago, IL, pg. 855
Curtis, James J., V.P.-Sls. & Mktg.--United Graphics, Inc., Seattle, WA, pg. 1132
Curtis, Joe, V.P.-Sls. & Mktg.--United Farm Tools, Inc., Glasgow, KY, pg. 1131
Curtis, Joe, V.P.-Sls. & Mktg.--United Farm Tools, Mohawk, Fitzgerald, GA, pg. 1132
Curtis, Joe, V.P.-Sls. & Mktg.--United Farm Tools, Kentucky Div., Glasgow, KY, pg. 1132
Curtis, Kevin L., V.P.-Sls. & Mktg.--Besser Company, Alpena, MI, pg. 146
Cusanello, Elizabeth, Dir.-Sls. Admin.--Electro Fiberoptics Corporation, Northborough, MA, pg. 374
Custer, Kelly, Mgr.-Sls.--Linn Products, Inc., Charlotte, MI, pg. 677
Cwieka, W.J., V.P.-Sls.--United States Bronze Powders, Inc., Flemington, NJ, pg. 1134
Cymrot, Andrew, V.P.-Sls.--Austin Sculpture, Holbrook, NY, pg. 99
Czyzewski, Ken, Mgr.-Sls.--A & A Manufacturing Co., New Berlin, WI, pg. 1
D'Agostino, I. Steven, V.P.-Sls. & Mdse.--D'Agostino Supermarkets Inc., Larchmont, NY, pg. 310
D'Angelo, John, Dir.-Sls., Mktg., Purch.--Pyttronic Industries, Inc., Montgomeryville, PA, pg. 901
Da Puzzo, Dennis, Dir.-Sls.--Colonna Bros., Inc., North Bergen, NJ, pg. 264
Dabin, Adam, V.P.-Sls.--Elgin Watch International, Inc., Long Island City, NY, pg. 376
Dahlager, Ken, V.P.-Sls. & Mkgt.--Smith System Manufacturing Company, Shoreview, MN, pg. 1014
Dahle, W.B., V.P.-Sls.--Sokol & Company, Countryside, IL, pg. 1016
Dahm, Don, Dir.-Sls.--Squire-Cogswell Company, Northbrook, IL, pg. 1034
Dakin, Dennis, V.P.-Sls.-Vending & Food Service--Veryfine Products, Inc., Westford, MA, pg. 1148
Dakin, Don, V.P.-Contract Sls.--Tom's Foods, Columbus, GA, pg. 1101
Dalbey, Pat, Mgr.-Sls.--KMIZ-TV, Columbia, MO, pg. 1043
Dale, Tony, Dir.-Sls. & Admin.--Lion Brothers Company, Inc., Owings Mills, MD, pg. 677
Dalfo, Chris, Mgr.-Sls.--Port Saint Lucie, Port Saint Lucie, FL, pg. 95
Dallas, George W., Sls. Mgr.--Newbury Industries, Inc., Newbury, OH, pg. 803
Dally, Dick, V.P.-Sls.--Socks Division, Greensboro, NC, pg. 263
Dalrymple, E., Mgr.-Sls.--Hypertronics Corporation, Hudson, MA, pg. 557
Dalton, James S., V.P.-Sls.--Bardons & Oliver, Inc., Cleveland, OH, pg. 119
Daly, E.P., V.P.-Trade Sls. Opers.--Fuller O'Brien Paints, South San Francisco, CA, pg. 820
Damery, David, V.P. & Mgr.-Sls.--Rugg Manufacturing Company, Greenfield, MA, pg. 955
Dammeier, Kurt B., V.P.-Sls. & Mktg.--Print Northwest, Fife, WA, pg. 891
Damveld, Gary, Exec. V.P.-Sls.--Pabst Brewing Co., San Antonio, TX, pg. 959
Daniel, Albro D., Sr. V.P.-Sls.--Ford Meter Box Company, Wabash, IN, pg. 423
Daniels, Richard A., Sr. V.P.-Sls.--Periphonics Corp., Bohemia, NY, pg. 862
Danko, Debra, Dir.-Sls & Bus. Support--Candle Corporation, Santa Monica, CA, pg. 214
Dann, George, V.P.-Sls.--Northern Wire & Cable, Inc., Troy, MI, pg. 814
Danner, Bill, Mgr.-Sls. & Training--Warehouse Home Furnishings Distributor, Dublin, GA, pg. 1163
Danser, James, V.P.-Sls. & Mktg.--Topflight Corp., York, PA, pg. 1102
Danzig, Martin, V.P.-Sls.--Greeco Brothers, Inc., Lawrence, MA, pg. 483
Darian, Ralph, Pres., Chief Exec. & Chief Fin. Officer--Levonian Brothers Inc., Troy, NY, pg. 671
Darling, Bill, V.P.-Sls.-Foods--McCarty Farms, Magee, MS, pg. 727
Darling, Bill, V.P.-Sls.--McCarty Foods, Inc., Jackson, MS, pg. 727
Darwin, Gary, V.P.-Sls.--Cardinal Inc., Port Reading, NJ, pg. 217
Daubert, Wayne, Mgr.-Sls.--Crustbuster, Inc., Dodge City, KS, pg. 303
Dausey, W., V.P.-Sls. & Mktg.--PTC Aerospace, Inc., Litchfield, CT, pg. 837
Davidman, Evan, Dir.-Sls.--AJC International, Inc., Atlanta, GA, pg. 4
Davids, Michael, Natl. Sls. & Mktg. Mgr.--Koch Engineering Company, Inc., Akron, OH, pg. 638
Davidson, Harry, Mgr.-Sls. North America--Magline, Inc., Pinconning, MI, pg. 700
Davidson, Howard, V.P.-Sls.--Burrows Paper Corporation, Little Falls, NY, pg. 195
Davies, Raymond A., V.P.-Sls. & Mktg.--Duff-Norton, Charlotte, NC, pg. 1032
Davis, Al Andy, V.P.-Reg. Sls. & Gen. Mgr.--Tom's Foods, Columbus, GA, pg. 1101
Davis, Bill, Mgr.-Reg. Sls. Western--Ivex Packaging Corporation-Visalia, Visalia, CA, pg. 583
Davis, Clare E., NY Sls. Mgr.--Parade Publications Inc., New York, NY, pg. 847
Davis, D., Mgr.-Sls.--Dunlop Manufacturing Co., Unionville, MO, pg. 1148
Davis, Don, Mgr.-Sls.--Harris Ford, Inc., Lynnwood, WA, pg. 512
Davis, Fran, Mgr.-Sls.--KTVS-TV, Sterling, CO, pg. 1043
Davis, Gary, V.P.-Sls.--Funeral Security Plans, Inc., Kansas City, MO, pg. 804

Davis, Grady, V.P.-Sls. & Mktg.--Tolleson Lumber Company, Inc., Perry, GA, pg. 1100
Davis, John, Dir.-Sls. & Mktg.--Simpson Dura-Vent Co., Inc., Vacaville, CA, pg. 1007
Davis, John, V.P.-Sls.--Road Machinery & Supplies Co., Savage, MN, pg. 937
Davis, Lynn, V.P.-Sls., Mktg., Pur. & Mfg.--Lithotype Company, Inc., South San Francisco, CA, pg. 678
Davis, Philip, V.P.-Sls. & Mktg.--Stusser Electric Company, Seattle, WA, pg. 1055
Davis, Ron, Dir.-Sls.--Kanex, Cleveland, OH, pg. 616
Davis, Steve, V.P.-Sls. & Mktg.--Calavo Growers of California, Tustin, CA, pg. 208
Davis, Thomas C., V.P.-Sls. & Mktg.--The Ward Machinery Company, Cockeysville, MD, pg. 1162
Davy, Glenn, Mgr.-Spare Parts--McNeil & NRM., Inc., Akron, OH, pg. 732
Dawahare, A.F., Pres. & Dir.-Sls. & Mktg.--Dawahares, Inc., Lexington, KY, pg. 319
Dawson, John, Gen. Sls. Mgr.--WALA-TV, Mobile, AL, pg. 194
Day, Bob, Mgr.-Sls.--Hubler Chevrolet Inc., Indianapolis, IN, pg. 550
Day, Kim, V.P.-Sls. & Adv.--Zenith Products Corp., Aston, PA, pg. 1217
Day, Steve, V.P.-Parts, Opers. & Sls.--Komatsu Dresser Company, Lincolnshire, IL, pg. 565
Dayan, Bernard, Gen. Mgr. & Sls. Mgr.--Lady Marlene Sales Corp., New York, NY, pg. 650
De Sousa, Richard, Sr. V.P.-Sls. & Mdsg.--Seminole Manufacturing Company, Columbus, MS, pg. 989
Deakins, John, Sr. V.P.-Sls.--The William Carter Company, New York, NY, pg. 226
Dean, Ed, V.P.-Sls.--Angelo Brothers Co., Philadelphia, PA, pg. 74
Deardorff, W.W., Jr., Mgr.-Sls. & Sec.--Deardorff-Jackson Company, Oxnard, CA, pg. 323
Deats, Richard, Dir.-Sls.-Ticket Opers.--The Phillies-A Limited Partnership, Philadelphia, PA, pg. 867
DeCesaro, Arthur F., Jr., Exec. V.P.-Mktg.& Nat'l. Sls.--Jockey International, Inc., Kenosha, WI, pg. 595
Decker, John, Natl. Sls. Mgr.--Ridg-U-Rak, Inc., North East, PA, pg. 933
Deering, Bill, Mgr.-Sls.--Village Car Company, Bangor, ME, pg. 1151
DeFabbio, Arthur, Mgr.-Sls.--Autoswage Products, Inc., Shelton, CT, pg. 101
Defalco, Louis, V.P.-Brand Devel.--NWS, Inc., Chicago, IL, pg. 782
Deichl, John, V.P.-Mktg. & Sls.--Simpson Electric Co., Elgin, IL, pg. 1007
Del Sesto, Richard, V.P.-Sls. & Mktg.--Red Devil Inc., Union, NJ, pg. 918
Delaney, Kevin, Mgr.-Sls.--R.A. Mueller, Inc., Cincinnati, OH, pg. 774
DeLang, J.R., Dir.-Sls. & Mktg.--The Todd-AO Corporation, San Francisco, CA, pg. 1099
Delatte, Jerry A., Gen. Sls. Mgr.-Edible Oils--Riceland Foods, Inc., Stuttgart, AR, pg. 931
DelBalso, Jerry, Dir.-Sls. & Technical Services--Better Baked Foods, Inc., North East, PA, pg. 148
DelFranco, Ray, Sr. V.P.-Retail Opers.--AppleTree Markets, Houston, TX, pg. 79
Delgado, Edwardo, V.P.-Sls., Military Prods. U.S.--North Atlantic Industries, Inc., Hauppauge, NY, pg. 812
DelGozzo, A.M., V.P.-Sls.--AP Parts Manufacturing Company, Toledo, OH, pg. 240
Deliberato, Carmine J., Dir.-Mktg. & Sls.--Lavelle Aircraft Company, Philadelphia, PA, pg. 661
Dellamano, Mark, Mgr.-Sls. & Data Processing--Patson's Press, Sunnyvale, CA, pg. 851
DeLora, Charles A., Sr. V.P.-Sls., Mktg., Adv. & Pub. Rels.--Service Supply Co. Inc. of Indiana, Indianapolis, IN, pg. 992
Delp, Fred, Dir.-Int'l Sls.--North Atlantic Industries, Inc., Hauppauge, NY, pg. 812
Delp, Mark, V.P.-Mktg. & Sls.--Gemtron Corporation, Sweetwater, TN, pg. 3
Delzio, Gerry, V.P.-Sls. & Mktg.--Bolliger, Inc., Stamford, CT, pg. 163
Demarco, Joe, Dir.-Franchise Sls.--The Athlete's Foot Group, Inc., Kennesaw, GA, pg. 94
DeMarco, Richard, V.P.-Sls.--Electric Specialty & Supply Corp., Boston, MA, pg. 374
DeMarino, Louis T., Sr. V.P.-Sls. & Mktg.--The Jaydor Corporation, Millburn, NJ, pg. 591
DeMasso, Joseph, Mgr.-Natl. Sls.--Eva-Tone Inc., Clearwater, FL, pg. 390
Deming, Derrell, Dir.-Sls. & Mktg.--Thom Thumb Food Market Inc., Hastings, MN, pg. 879
Demond, John, V.P.-Sls. & Mktg.--TSC Carbide Co., Crystal Lake, IL, pg. 885
DeMond, John E., V.P.-Mktg. & Sls.--Precision Twist Drill Co., Crystal Lake, IL, pg. 885
Demond, John E., V.P.-Mktg. & Sls.--Mohawk Tools, Crystal Lake, IL, pg. 885
Demorotski, R.C., V.P.-Mining Sls.--Road Machinery Company, Phoenix, AZ, pg. 937
Dempsey, David, Dir.-Sales & Mktg.--Union Pump Company, Battle Creek, MI, pg. 1128
Denburg, Edmund, V.P.-Sls.--Barton Press, Inc., West Orange, NJ, pg. 123
Deneny, Sean, V.P. & Gen. Sls. Mgr.-First Run--Viacom Enterprises, New York, NY, pg. 785
Denham, Tom J., Sr. V.P.-Sls.--Blue Cross & Blue Shield of Illinois, Chicago, IL, pg. 160
Denis, John, V.P.-Consumer Toiletries Sls.--Conair Corporation, Stamford, CT, pg. 272
Denison, William, V.P.-Sls. & Mktg.--Milk Specialties Company, Dundee, IL, pg. 753
Denny, Robert L., Dir.-Agency Sls., Devel. & Promo. Services--State Farm Mutual Automobile Insurance Company, Bloomington, IL, pg. 1041
DePalma, J., V.P.-Sls.--Zim-American Israeli Shipping Co., New York, NY, pg. 1219
Deptulski, J., Mgr.-Sls.--Peerless Importers, Inc., Brooklyn, NY, pg. 855
Derasmo, Jack, V.P. Mktg. & Sls. Mgr.--Glen Raven Mills Marketing Corp., Pearl River, NY, pg. 461
Derasmo, Jack, V.P.-Mktg. & Sls. Mgr.--Glen Raven Marketing Corporation, Pearl River, NY, pg. 461
Derby, Shelley, V.P., Acct. Services--HMK Advertising, Inc., Chestnut Hill, MA, pg. 497
Deroche, William, Dir.-Sls.--Bud Industries, Inc., Willoughby, OH, pg. 186
Derringer, J. Charles, Mgr.-Natl. Sls.--Trio Products Inc., Elyria, OH, pg. 1114
Derum, Michael, V.P.-Sls.--Kores Nordic USA Corp., Summerville, SC, pg. 642
Desmarteau, Mike, V.P.-Franchise Sls.--Red Carpet Real Estate Services, Inc., San Diego, CA, pg. 918
DeTata, R.A., V.P.-Indus. Prod. Sls.--California & Hawaiian Sugar Company, Concord, CA, pg. 210
Dettmann, Robert J., V.P.-Sls. & Mktg.--Action Technology Company, Rockaway, NJ, pg. 15
Deuchars, Colin M., V.P.--Holmes Protection Group, Inc., New York, NY, pg. 540
Deutsch, Richard J., V.P.-Adv. & Sls.--IMPO Glaztile, Burr Ridge, IL, pg. 564
Devillier, William, V.P.-Contracting--Anco Insulations, Inc., Baton Rouge, LA, pg. 72
Devilline, F.D., V.P.-Sls. & Mktg.--Columbus McKinnon Corp., Amherst, NY, pg. 266
DeWalters, E. J., Mgr.-Sls.--Edwin B. Stimpson Company, Inc., Bayport, NY, pg. 1049
Dezek, R.J., Dir.-Sls. & Mktg.--Young Radiator Company, Racine, WI, pg. 1210
Di Pasca, Bob, N.E. Sls. Mgr.--The Jolt Company, Rochester, NY, pg. 602
Dianich, Bev, Mgr.-Sls. & Mktg.--Pacific Wood Treating Coporation, Ridgefield, WA, pg. 842
Diaz, Ydalia, Mgr.-Adv.--Fox-Knapp Inc., New York, NY, pg. 427
Dicchetti, Don, Asst. Intl. Sls. Mgr.--McCain Manufacturing Corp., Chicago, IL, pg. 726
Dick, Douglas P., Sr. V.P.-Sls. & Mktg.--Dick Corporation, Large, PA, pg. 335
Dick, M., Sales--Canefco Limited, Scarborough,, Canada, pg. 373
Dickhoff, Bill, Dir.-Sls., Mktg. & Adv.--Roofing Wholesale Co., Inc., Phoenix, AZ, pg. 946
Diederich, Joseph J., V.P.-Sls.--Bucyrus Blades Inc., Bucyrus, OH, pg. 388
Dietlin, Paul, Mgr.-Sls.--E. J. Brooks Company, Newark, NJ, pg. 179
Dietz, Dave, V.P.-Sls. & Mktg.--Hardware Wholesalers, Inc., Fort Wayne, IN, pg. 508
Dilcher, R., Mgr.-Sls.--Patterson Laboratories, Inc., Detroit, MI, pg. 852
Dillingham, John, Sr. V.P.-Sls. & Mktg.--Garney Holding Company, Inc., Kansas City, MO, pg. 443
Dillon, Jim, V.P.-Sls. & Mktg.--Foster Refrigerator Corporation, Hudson, NY, pg. 426
Dillon, Mike, V.P.-Sls.--Varityper, Inc., East Hanover, NJ, pg. 1146
Dineen, Larry, Mgr.-Natl. Sls.--Kennedy Manufacturing Company, Van Wert, OH, pg. 623
Dinkins, Greg, Sls. Mgr.--RAM Golf Corporation, Melrose Park, IL, pg. 910
DiNucci, Elaine, Sls. Coordinator--Code-A-Phone Corp., Clackamas, OR, pg. 258
Diohep, John L., V.P.-Sls.--Symmons Industries Inc., Braintree, MA, pg. 1069
DiPietro, Peter, Natl. Sls. Mgr.--Interplastic Corp., Saint Paul, MN, pg. 579
Dippel, Clem, Dir.-Sls. & Adv.--Fishing Tackle Retailer, Montgomery, AL, pg. 105
Dircks, R.J., Exec. V.P.-Mktg., Sls. & Adv.--Berger Transfer & Storage, Inc., Saint Paul, MN, pg. 141
Ditka, Ashton L., V.P.-Mktg. & Sls.--United Refining Company, Warren, PA, pg. 1130
Dittman, William, Dir.-Sls. & Mktg.--A. H. Hoffman, Inc., Landisville, PA, pg. 538
Dittmar, Ray, Dir.-Sls.--Greeff Fabrics, Port Chester, NY, pg. 262
Divine, Steven J., V.P.-Mktg.--Amfac Health Care, Folsom, CA, pg. 585
Dix, Ron, Sr. V.P.-Mktg. & Sls.--Bush Brothers & Company, Dandridge, TN, pg. 196
Dixon, Jerry, V.P.-Sls. & Mktg.--Alma Industries, High Point, NC, pg. 43
Dixon, W.R., Deputy Dir.-Devel.--Christian Children's Fund, Inc., Richmond, VA, pg. 248
Dobbins, John J., V.P.-Sls.--Menu Foods, Inc., Pennsauken, NJ, pg. 739
Docherty, Bill, V.P.-Sls.--Aircap Industries Corp., Verona, MS, pg. 694
Doddridge, Tom, Mgr.-Sls.--Power & Telephone Supply Company, Memphis, TN, pg. 883
Dodge, Michael, V.P.-Mktg. & Sls.--Alleson of Rochester, Inc., Rochester, NY, pg. 37
Dodson, Julie, Corp. Sls. Mgr.--Chattanooga Choo-Choo Holiday Inn, Chattanooga, TN, pg. 241
Doell, Don, Mgr.-Natl. Sls.--Pfaudler-U.S., Inc., Rochester, NY, pg. 866
Doering, Roy, V.P.-Sls. & Mktg.--Hurd Millwork Company, Inc., Medford, WI, pg. 1123
Doherty, John, Natl. Sls. Mgr.-Finishing--Standard Duplicating Machines Corp., Andover, MA, pg. 1036
Dolan, Jack, Div. Mgr.-Sls.--The Jel Sert Co., West Chicago, IL, pg. 591
Dolgin, Bernard, Mgr.-Sls.--Bestform Foundations, Inc., Long Island City, NY, pg. 147
Dolim, Mark, Dir.-Sls.--L.N. Curtis & Sons, Oakland, CA, pg. 306
Dollman, Walt, Mgr.-Sls. N.A.--Hoechst Ceramtec North America, Inc., Mansfield, MA, pg. 537
Dolori, Philip Dei, Natl. Sls. Mgr.--Pitco Frialator Inc., Concord, NH, pg. 157
Domenech, Miguel A., Exec. Dir.--Puerto Rico Tourism Company, New York, NY, pg. 899
Dominue, Randy, Mgr.-Sls.--Woodfin-Smith Pontiac, Inc., Baton Rouge, LA, pg. 1200
Donahue, Elise, Dir.-Sls. Devel.--Thompson Medical Company, Inc., West Palm Beach, FL, pg. 1094
Donahue, Jerry, Mgr.-Sls.--Atlantic Concrete Products, Inc., Tullytown, PA, pg. 94
Donegan, James, V.P.-Sls.--The Estee Corporation, Parsippany, NJ, pg. 389
Donegan, Jerry, Dir.-Natl. Sls.--Avedis Zildjian Company, Norwell, MA, pg. 1219
Donlon, Timothy, Dir.-Domestic Sls.--Jet Spray Corp., Norwood, MA, pg. 593
Donnelly, David H., V.P. & Gen. Sls. Mgr.-Western Area--Steelcase Inc., Grand Rapids, MI, pg. 1044
Donnelly, Gerald, V.P.--Steelcase Inc., Grand Rapids, MI, pg. 1044
Donnelly, Susan, Sls. Mgr.--Yale University Press, New Haven, CT, pg. 1207
Donner, D.A., Gen. Sls. Mgr. & Adv. Mgr.--Modern Equipment Co., Inc., Port Washington, WI, pg. 32
Donour, Deborah, Gen. Sls. Mgr.--WLTY-FM, Norfolk, VA, pg. 655
Donour, Deborah, Gen. Sls. Mgr.--WTAR-AM, Norfolk, VA, pg. 655
Doodson, K., Mgr.-Sls. & Mktg.--Metro Foods, Inc., Memphis, TN, pg. 743
Doonan, James L., Natl. Sls. Mgr.--Carlson Retail Marketing, Minneapolis, MN, pg. 221
Dooner, Peter S., Jr., V.P.-Electrical Sls.--Wheatland Tube Company, Collingswood, NJ, pg. 1184
Dorato, John, V.P.-Sls.--Tiffany Stand & Furniture Company, St. Louis, MO, pg. 1097
Dorf, Noel, V.P.-Sls & Mktg.--The Harwood Companies, Inc., New York, NY, pg. 515
Dorman, Ned, V.P.-Food Service-Mktg. & Sls.--Dorman-Roth Foods, Inc., Moonachie, NJ, pg. 346
Dornbierer, Daniel, Regional Sls. Mgr., Australia, Switzerland & Germany--Thoroughbred Europe Ltd., Romford,, United Kingdom, pg. 1095
DosSantos, Anthony, V.P.-Sls. & Mktg.--Pacific Optical Division, Torrance, CA, pg. 917
Dotson, W.J., V.P.-Auto Aftermarket Hardware Sls.--The Gates Rubber Company, Denver, CO, pg. 445
Dougherty, Dan, V.P.-Sls.--Cargill Flour Milling Div., Minneapolis, MN, pg. 219
Dougherty, Tom, Mgr.-Sls.--Detroit Coil Company, Ferndale, MI, pg. 333
Douglas, James, V.P.-Sls.--Kauffman Products, Inc., Carmel, IN, pg. 618
Douglas, Patrick J., Mgr.-Sls.--Wards Cove Packing Company, Seattle, WA, pg. 1163
Doukas, John, Dir.-Intl. Sales--Forstmann & Company, Inc., New York, NY, pg. 424
Dove, Kenneth J., V.P.-Agency--Central-United Life Insurance Co., Sioux City, IA, pg. 233
Dow, Gregory, V.P.-Sls.--Riverside Millwork Company, Inc., Panacook, NH, pg. 937
Dowell, Michael, Mgr.-National Fleet Sls.--Ziebart International Corporation, Troy, MI, pg. 1217
Dowling, Dave, Mgr.-Sls.--Pacific Foods, Inc., Kent, WA, pg. 840
Downs, Ryan A., V.P.-Sls. & Mktg.--Flanagan Brothers, Bear Creek, WI, pg. 416
Dowse, M., V.P.-Sls.--R.A. Industries, Inc., Lansdale, PA, pg. 906
Doyle, Brian, V.P., Gen. Mgr, Treas. & Dir.-Sls.--King Milling Company, Lowell, MI, pg. 631
Doyle, Daniel, Gen. Mgr.-Sls.--Kowalski Sausage Co., Inc., Hamtramck, MI, pg. 643
Doyle, David, Sls. Mgr.--Beauty-Professional, Westchester, IL, pg. 328
Drabik, Robert, Dir.-Sls.--Teca Corporation, Pleasantville, NY, pg. 1082
Drafts, G. R., V.P.-Sls.--Loxcreen Company, West Columbia, SC, pg. 686
Drago, Greg F., Mgr.-Sls.--Bison Canning Co., Inc., Angola, NY, pg. 474
Drake, Jeff, Mgr.-Sls.--Collins Oldsmobile Inc., Indianapolis, IN, pg. 263
Dreier, Richard L., V.P.-Domestic Sls.--Abbey Etna Machine Company, Perrysburg, OH, pg. 9
Drennan, George V., V.P.-Sls. & Mktg.--Hiross Inc., Niagara Falls, NY, pg. 536
Drescher, Ken, Mgr.-Natl. Sls.--The Regina Company, Atlanta, GA, pg. 922
Dress, Stan, V.P.-Sls. & Mktg.--Rex Lumber Company, Acton, MA, pg. 930
Drew, Carol, Dir.-Sls.--The Levy Organization, Chicago, IL, pg. 672
Drew, Jan, Mgr.-Special Sls.--Buck Knives, Inc., El Cajon, CA, pg. 185
Driver, Maurice, Dir.-Catalog Sls.--Globe Business Furniture, Inc., Hendersonville, TN, pg. 463
Drozdow, Steve, V.P.-Sls. & Mktg.--Ohaus Corporation, Florham Park, NJ, pg. 822
Dryden, Will, Mgr.-Gen. Sls.--Jones Blair Company, Dallas, TX, pg. 602
Drypen, William A., V.P.-Steel & Wire Sls.--MNP Corp., Utica, MI, pg. 693
Duane, Ray H., V.P.-Sls.--Combe Incorporated, White Plains, NY, pg. 267
Dube, Bill, Mgr.-Natl. Sls.--Brown & Haley, Tacoma, WA, pg. 182
Dube, Michael, V.P.-Sls.--Rapid Power Technologies, Inc., Brookfield, CT, pg. 913
Dubler, Gary, Mgr.-Sls.--Mallery Lumber Corp., Emporium, PA, pg. 702
DuBois, Ron, V.P.-Sls.--Crankshaft Machine Company, Jackson, MI, pg. 102

Corporate Responsibilities Index

Dues, David L., V.P.-Sls.--Caldwell Tanks, Inc., Louisville, KY, pg. 209
Duffy, Brian, Mgr.-Sls.--Keystone New England Warehouse - Norwood, Norwood, MA, pg. 628
Duggan, Michael, Exec. V.P.-Sls.--Melard Manufacturing Corporation, Passaic, NJ, pg. 737
Dukes, Marvin, Gen. Mgr.-Sls.--Capitol Chevrolet Cadillac GEO, Inc., Salem, OR, pg. 215
Dunbar, Edward, Gen. Sls. Mgr.--The U.S. Baird Corporation, Stratford, CT, pg. 114
Dunbar, Edward, Sls. Mgr.--The A. H. Nilson Machine Co., Stratford, CT, pg. 114
Duncan, Bill, V.P., Gen. Mgr. & Sls.--C.F. Thompson Group, Inc., Windsor, CT, pg. 1094
Duncan, David L., V.P.-Sls.--Gaylord Printing, Inc., Detroit, MI, pg. 446
Duncan, Steve, V.P.-Sls. & Mktg.--Cold Spring Granite Company, Minnetonka, MN, pg. 259
Duncheon, Charles S., V.P.-Mktg. & Sls.--Adept Technology, Inc., San Jose, CA, pg. 17
Dunn, Richard G., V.P.-Sls. & Mktg.--McIlhenny Company, Avery Island, LA, pg. 729
Dunning, John, Sr. V.P.-Sls.--Zycon Corporation, Santa Clara, CA, pg. 1221
Dupuis, Alan, V.P.-Sls. & Mktg.--Quaker Industries Limited, Antioch, IL, pg. 903
Duray, Gerald W., Dir.-Sls. & Mktg.--Power Contracting & Engineering Corp., Rolling Meadows, IL, pg. 883
Durden, Jeff, Dir.-Mktg. & Sls.--Dairymen, Inc., Louisville, KY, pg. 311
Durden, Listor, V.P.-Mktg. & Sls.--Viking Range Corp., Greenwood, MS, pg. 1151
Durocher, William G., V.P.-Sls. & Dir.-Mktg. & Intl. Sls.--Briggs Industries, Inc., Tampa, FL, pg. 175
Dwyer, Robert, Mgr.-Sls., S.E.--Mountain Valley Spring Company, Hot Springs, AR, pg. 968
Eagan, Todd, Mgr.-Sls.--Dekko Wire Div., Kendallville, Kendallville, IN, pg. 489
Eagan, Todd, Mgr.-Sls.--Albion Wire, Inc., Albion, IN, pg. 489
Earl, Eric, Mgr.-Sls. & Mkt. Research--Haviland Enterprises, Grand Rapids, MI, pg. 517
Easley, Richard, Mgr.-Sls.--Trout Inc., Chelan, WA, pg. 1116
Easterly, William, V.P.-Cloth, Bleach & Dyeing Sls.--Johnstown Knitting Mill Co., Johnstown, NY, pg. 602
Eaton, Mark, Mgr.-Natl. Sls. & Mktg.--Consolidated Metco, Inc., Portland, OR, pg. 277
Eaton, Victor, V.P.-Yearbook Sls.--Walsworth Publishing Company, Inc., Marceline, MO, pg. 1161
Eaton, W. Thompson, Exec. V.P.-Sls.--Eaton Equipment Corp., Blasdell, NY, pg. 364
Eavey, R.R., V.P.-Vending Sls.--Bahlsen Inc., Cary, NC, pg. 114
Ebeck, Bill, Mgr.-Reg. Sls. & Mktg.--Ivex Packaging Corporation-Grove City, Grove City, PA, pg. 583
Eckstein, Bruce W., V.P.-Sls.--Production Machinery Corporation, Mentor, OH, pg. 893
Ecleberry, Ronald, V.P.-Sls.--Modern Welding Co., Inc., Owensboro, KY, pg. 763
Eddy, Lane, Dir.-Sls.--Iowa Assemblies, Inc., Osceola, IA, pg. 490
Eden, Charles H., V.P.-Sls.--Russell Harrington Cutlery Inc., Southbridge, MA, pg. 556
Edgerly, Lee, Managing Dir.-Intl. Sls.--Redmond Products, Inc., Chanhassen, MN, pg. 920
Edwards, A.L., Dir.-Mktg. & Sls.--Borg-Warner Automotive, Inc., Control Systems, Sterling Heights, MI, pg. 166
Edwards, Chuck, Mgr.-Sls.--Jones Blair Company, Dallas, TX, pg. 602
Edwards, Dean, V.P.-Irrigation Sls.--Lockwood Corporation, Gering, NE, pg. 680
Edwards, Donny E., V.P.-Sls.--Destiny Industry Inc., Moultrie, GA, pg. 332
Edwards, Joe, Dir.-Sls.--Vienna Biscuit Co., Emerson, NJ, pg. 550
Edwards, Karen K., Dir.-Mktg, Sls. Promo., Mdse. & Communications--Applied Microsystems Corporation, Redmond, WA, pg. 79
Edwards, Thomas, Mgr.-Mktg. Services--Linotype-Hell Company, Hauppauge, NY, pg. 677
Edwards, Wendell, Mgr.-Sls.--The C.P. Hall Company, Memphis, TN, pg. 501
Egan, Peter, V.P.-Eastern Sls.--Frank Consolidated Enterprises Inc., Des Plaines, IL, pg. 428
Egle, Carol, V.P.-Sls.--Muench-Kreuzer Candle Company, Syracuse, NY, pg. 774
Eglinton, Dave, Mgr.-Sls. & Mktg.--L. R. Nelson Corporation, Peoria, IL, pg. 797
Eible, Kate, Mgr.-Sls. Admin. & Personnel--Furniture Consultants, New York, NY, pg. 437
Eichenbaum, Henry, Sr. V.P.-Sls.--Her Majesty, Mauldin, SC, pg. 530
Eichler, Larry, V.P.-Sls. & Mktg.--Prentiss Incorporated, Floral Park, NY, pg. 887
Eichman, Frank, Chm. Bd. & Pres.--Alcom Printing Group, Inc., Bethlehem, PA, pg. 32
Eidel, Charles J., V.P.-Sls.--Tri-City Electrical Contractors Inc., Altamonte Springs, FL, pg. 1110
Einhorn, Ryan, V.P.-Sls.-East--The Berkline Corporation, Morristown, TN, pg. 285
Einseidler, E., Gen. Mgr.-Sls.--Peerless Importers, Inc., Brooklyn, NY, pg. 855
Einziger, Ronald, V.P.-Direct Mail Sls.--Federal Distributing Corporation, Maspeth, NY, pg. 404
Eipper, Michael G., V.P.-Sls.--Pillowtex Corporation, Dallas, TX, pg. 870
Eisenberg, Morton, V.P.-Sls.--Gould Paper Corporation, New York, NY, pg. 473
Eisenhauer, Pat, V.P.-Sales & Mktg.--Crum Electric Supply Co., Inc., Casper, WY, pg. 303
Eisenman, Roger, Natl. Sls. Mgr.--WIFC-FM, Wausau, WI, pg. 608
Eisenman, Roger, Natl. Sls. Mgr.--WSAU-AM, Wausau, WI, pg. 608
Elberg, Dale, Sr. V.P.-Sls. & Mktg.--Royal Oak Enterprises, Inc., Atlanta, GA, pg. 953
Elert, Robert A., V.P.-Sls.--Trewax Company, Santa Fe Springs, CA, pg. 159
Elian, George, V.P.-Sls.--National Reproductions Corporation, Madison Heights, MI, pg. 793
Ellen, Don, Mgr.-Sls.--Peterson Industries Inc., Decatur, AR, pg. 864
Elliot, Mike, V.P.-Sls.--Alex Foods, Inc., Anaheim, CA, pg. 33
Elliott, Tom, Sr. V.P.-Sls. & Mktg.--Wiltel Communications Systems, Inc., The Woodlands, TX, pg. 1194
Elliott, W.P., V.P.-Sls.--The Selmer Co., Elkhart, IN, pg. 573
Ellis, Gary P., V.P.-Sls. & Mktg.--Crenlo, Inc., Rochester, MN, pg. 298
Ellis, Jim, Natl. Sls. Mgr.--Diamond Crystal Specialty Foods, Inc., Wilmington, MA, pg. 335
Ellison, Norman, Dir.-Sls.--Kinetic Systems Corporation, Lockport, IL, pg. 630
Elmaleh, Joseph, V.P.-Intl. Mktg. & Sls.--Eagle Electric Mfg. Co., Inc., Long Island City, NY, pg. 362
Emary, Don, V.P.-Sls.--Millstone Coffee, Inc., Everett, WA, pg. 756
Emerson, Dennis, Sr. V.P.-Sls.-West--Viacom Enterprises, New York, NY, pg. 785
Emery, Dennis, V.P.-Sls.--Dualite Inc., Williamsburg, OH, pg. 350
Emery, Dennis, V.P.-Sls.--Dualite Sales & Service, Inc., Williamsburg, OH, pg. 350
Emmerling, Paul E., V.P.-Sls. & Mktg.--American Welding & Manufacturing Co., Warren, OH, pg. 65
Emmerling, Paul E., V.P.-Sls. & Mktg.--American Welding & Manufacturing Co., Warren, OH, pg. 431
Emmert, Fred, V.P.-Sls. & Mktg.--Georgie Boy Manufacturing, Inc., Edwardsburg, MI, pg. 453
England, Jim, Dir.-Mktg. & Sls.--Diversified Products Corporation, Opelika, AL, pg. 1193
Engle, Charles, V.P.-Sls.--IXL Furniture, Dallas, TX, pg. 1112
Engle, Charles A., V.P.-Sls.--Triangle Pacific Corporation, Dallas, TX, pg. 1112
Englert, Stan, Dir.-Mktg. & Sls.--Jofco Inc., Jasper, IN, pg. 595
Englert, Stan, Mgr.-Reg. Sls.--Jofco Inc., Jasper, IN, pg. 595
English, Mollie, Dir.-Sls.--Marine World Africa USA, Vallejo, CA, pg. 707
Enos, Barry, Mgr.-Sls.--New Standard Corporation, Mount Joy, PA, pg. 802
Enos, Joyce, Mgr.-Intl. Sls.--Avatar Corporation, Hopkinton, MA, pg. 101
Ensman, Dan, Sls. Mgr.--Madison Industries, Los Angeles, CA, pg. 433
Entrekin, Terry, V.P.-Sls.--Jameco Industries, Inc., Wyandanch, NY, pg. 588
Epp, William H., Mgr.-Mktg. & Sls.--Penco Products, Oaks, PA, pg. 857
Erickson, Bill, Sr. V.P.-Sls. & Mktg.--Wellcraft Marine, Sarasota, FL, pg. 759
Erikson, Liz, V.P.-Convention Sls.--The Fairmont Hotels, San Francisco, CA, pg. 397
Erol, Robert R., V.P.-Sls. & Mktg.--Reading Tube Corp., Reading, PA, pg. 916
Erridge, Ian, V.P.-Sls. & Mktg.--Blue Diamond Growers, Sacramento, CA, pg. 160
Ervin, Mike, Dir.-Mktg. & Sls.--Hercules Engines, Inc., Canton, OH, pg. 531
Eskelson, Randy J., V.P.-Comml. Sls.--Schuff Steel Co., Phoenix, AZ, pg. 979
Eskridge, Mark, Dir.-Sls. & Pur.--Hoffritz International, New York, NY, pg. 538
Esposito, Dennis, Mgr.-Customer Service--Fine Organics Corp., Lodi, NJ, pg. 411
Esposito, George, Dir.-Sls.--Howe Furniture Corporation, Trumbull, CT, pg. 547
Essaf, Mike, Mgr.-Sls.--Cedar Farms Company, Inc., Philadelphia, PA, pg. 230
Essenberg, Donald A., V.P.-Corp. Sls.--The Berkline Corporation, Morristown, TN, pg. 285
Esser, R.W., V.P.-Sls.--Knouse Foods Inc., Peach Glen, PA, pg. 637
Esses, Michael, V.P.-Sls. & Mktg.--Pioneer Press Newspapers Inc., Wilmette, IL, pg. 18
Eubank, Cary, V.P.-Field Sls. East--Empire Brushes, Inc., Greenville, NC, pg. 379
Evans, G., V.P.-Sls. & Mktg.--Waukesha Foundry Inc., Waukesha, WI, pg. 1168
Evans, Jim, Sr. V.P.-Sls.--Hyatt Hotels Corporation, Chicago, IL, pg. 495
Evans, John A., Natl. Sls. Mgr.--Champion Laboratories, Inc., Albion, IL, pg. 1123
Evans, R.M., V.P.-Sls. & Service--Medrad, Inc., Pittsburgh, PA, pg. 736
Evans, Richard, V.P.-Sls.--Johnstown Corporation, Johnstown, PA, pg. 601
Evans, Ronald C., V.P.-Sls.--Nationwide Homes, Inc., Martinsville, VA, pg. 795
Evans, Thomas, Mgr.-Sls. & Mktg.-Indus. Div.--Dumore Corporation, Mauston, WI, pg. 352
Evans, William, Gen. Sls. Mgr.--Overland Transportation System, Inc., Indianapolis, IN, pg. 832
Evans, William M., V.P.-Sls., Adv. & Mktg.--Evans Brothers Company, Inc., Waukesha, WI, pg. 390
Ewing, Ted, V.P.-Sls.--Bawden Printing, Inc., Eldridge, IA, pg. 127
Fader, John D., Natl. Sls. Mgr.--Daxus Corporation, Pittsburgh, PA, pg. 319
Fagan, Joe, V.P.-Sls.--Vile-Goller, Fine Art Printing & Lithography, Kansas City, KS, pg. 1151
Fahey, Frank, Mgr.-Admin. Sls.--Cardinal Inc., Port Reading, NJ, pg. 217
Fair, Richard, Sls. Mgr.-Rotolast--McNeil & NRM., Inc., Akron, OH, pg. 732
Fair, Roger, Gen. Sls. Mgr.--Western States Machine Co., Hamilton, OH, pg. 1181
Falduto, Dennis, V.P.-Sls.--Amco Folding Cartons, Inc., Towaco, NJ, pg. 47
Falk, Doug, Exec. V.P.-Sls. & Mktg.--Norwegian Cruise Line, Coral Gables, FL, pg. 816
Fall, David, V.P.-Sls.--Fisher Pen Company, Franklin Park, IL, pg. 415
Faller, Siegfried, Sls. Catering & Conferences Dir.--Broadmoor Hotel, Inc., Colorado Springs, CO, pg. 177
Famulare, James, V.P.-Sls.--Jos. M. Herman Shoe Co., Greenwich, CT, pg. 531
Fandl, Joe, Sls. Mgr.--Keystone Automotive Industries, Inc. - Chicago, Chicago, IL, pg. 627
Farace, Vince, Dir.-Sls. & Mktg.--B. Green & Co., Baltimore, MD, pg. 484
Farber, Bernard, Sr. V.P.-Mktg. & Sls.--West Mill Clothes, Inc., Woodside, NY, pg. 1177
Faria, Anthony J., V.P.-Mktg. & Sls.--Samuel Cabot, Inc., Newburyport, MA, pg. 206
Farland, Jim, V.P.-Sls. & Mktg.--The Union Fork & Hoe Co., Columbus, OH, pg. 1128
Farley, Jim, Mgr.-Natl. Sls.--Solon Manufacturing Company, Solon, ME, pg. 1017
Farmer, Kevin, V.P., Sales & Mktg.--Adams Colway & Associates, Rochester, NY, pg. 16
Farnsworth, Harold R., V.P.-Sls.--E.J. Bartells Co., Renton, WA, pg. 122
Farris, Mark, V.P.-Mktg. & Sls.--E F Industries, Carson, CA, pg. 359
Farver, Pat, V.P.-Sls.--Blissfield Manufacturing Company, Blissfield, MI, pg. 157
Fasano, Tony, V.P.-Mktg. & Sls.--Neer Manufacturing Company, Lexington, OH, pg. 797
Fasbender, David L., V.P.-Sls.--Smead Manufacturing Company, Hastings, MN, pg. 1011
Fauntleroy, David, Mgr.-Sls.-Castings--Moline Corporation, Saint Charles, IL, pg. 764
Favazza, Steve, V.P.-Sls./NorthernDiv.--Schmidt Baking Co., Inc., Baltimore, MD, pg. 976
Fay, Gary, V.P.-Sls.--Pearl-Pressman-Liberty Communications Group, Philadelphia, PA, pg. 853
Fazio, Gary, V.P.-Sls.--Sealy Corporation, Cleveland, OH, pg. 985
Fee, Michael R., V.P.-Sls. Opers.--Reliable Automatic Sprinkler Co., Inc., Mount Vernon, NY, pg. 924
Feely, M., Natl. Sls. Mgr.--ECP Incorporated, Westchester, IL, pg. 317
Feerer, Homer L., V.P.-Sls. & Mktg.--Finch, Pruyn & Co., Inc., Glens Falls, NY, pg. 410
Fegely, Glenn, Dir.-Intl. Sls.--Ellwood City Forge, Ellwood City, PA, pg. 378
Feiereisen, Lee E., V.P.-Sls.--Independent Metals, Germantown, WI, pg. 565
Feigelson, Harold, V.P.-Sls.--Koret Givenchy, New York, NY, pg. 642
Feinstein, Jack, Dir.-Sls., Pur. & Adv.--Universal Overall Company, Chicago, IL, pg. 1139
Feit, Saul, Mgr.-Natl. Sls., Retail Div.--Sun Hill Industries, Stamford, CT, pg. 1059
Feldman, Don, V.P.-Sls.--Evy Of California, Inc., Los Angeles, CA, pg. 392
Feldman, Paul, V.P.-Sls.--Duro Paper Bag Manufacturing Co., Ludlow, KY, pg. 355
Feldstein, Steve, V.P.-Sls. & Service--Cray Communications Inc., Annapolis Junction, MD, pg. 297
Feller, Allan, Pres.-Sls.--Butterick Company, Inc., New York, NY, pg. 197
Fellner, Peter, Mgr. Sls. & Mktg.--Zyntec GmbH, Vienna,, Austria, pg. 1221
Ferbert, D., Sls. Mgr.-Power Fuse--Littelfuse, Inc., Des Plaines, IL, pg. 678
Ferguson, Carolyn, Mgr.-Natl. Mktg.--Columbus Show Case Company, Columbus, OH, pg. 267
Ferguson, Gerry H., V.P.-Mktg. & Sls.--Binning's Building Products, Inc., Lexington, NC, pg. 151
Ferguson, J. Robert, Mgr.-Adv. & Sls. Promo.--Dualite Sales & Service, Inc., Williamsburg, OH, pg. 350
Ferguson, Mike, Exec. V.P.-Sls. & Mktg.--Colad Group Inc., Buffalo, NY, pg. 259
Ferguson, Sam Jr., Exec. V.P. & Dir.-Sls. & Mktg.--Ferguson Industries, Dallas, TX, pg. 406
Fernandez, Carlos, V.P.-Sls.--Acorn Building Components Inc., Detroit, MI, pg. 13
Fernandez, Carlos, V.P.-Sls.--Acorn Distributing Co., Detroit, MI, pg. 14
Fernsler, John W., V.P.-Sls.--Sargento Cheese Co., Plymouth, WI, pg. 971
Ferrara, F., Mgr.-Sls.--Peerless Importers Inc., Brooklyn, NY, pg. 855
Few, Gary, V.P.-Sls.--Medecore Div., Mundelein, IL, pg. 736
Field, David, V.P.-Sls. & Mktg.--Trendway Corporation, Holland, MI, pg. 1109
Field, Mike, V.P.-Sls.--The Disston Co., Greensboro, NC, pg. 339
Fields, Gerald, V.P.-Engrng & OEM Sls.--Champion Laboratories, Inc., Albion, IL, pg. 1123
Fife, Michael, Mgr.-Sls.--Fairfax Lumber & Millwork Company Inc., Springfield, VA, pg. 397
Figan, John, Sls. Mgr.-Testing & Measurement Prods.--Bacharach Inc., Pittsburgh, PA, pg. 108
Fighter, Robert D., V.P.-Sls. & Mktg.--The Crocker-Fels Company, Cincinnati, OH, pg. 299
Filippelli, Peter, V.P.-Mktg. & Sls.--Eli's Chicago's Finest, Inc., Chicago, IL, pg. 376
Finch, David B., V.P.-Sls.--ATCOM, Inc., Research Triangle Park, NC, pg. 93
Fine, David, V.P.--M. Fine & Sons Manufacturing Co., Inc., New York, NY, pg. 411
Fines, Robert, Mgr.-Natl. Sls.--TimeMed Labeling Systems, Inc., Burr Ridge, IL, pg. 1098
Fink, James A., V.P.-Sls.--Strombecker Corporation, Chicago, IL, pg. 1054
Finley, R.L., V.P.-Sls.--Williams & Company, Inc., Pittsburgh, PA, pg. 230

Fint, Linda, V.P.-Reg. Sls.--Lifetime Television, Astoria, NY, pg. 523
Fiordaliso, Arthur R., V.P.-Sls.--Advertising Checking Bureau Incorporated, New York, NY, pg. 21
Firenze, Richard, V.P.-Sls.--Franklin Sports Industries, Stoughton, MA, pg. 429
Firle, David R., Mgr.-Sls. Services--The Hammerblow Corp., Wausau, WI, pg. 504
Fischer, Dale, Dir.-Intl. Sls. & Mktg.--Metrologic Instruments, Inc., Blackwood, NJ, pg. 743
Fischer, Louis, Sr. V.P.-Sls.--IVI Travel, Northbrook, IL, pg. 428
Fisher, Bruce, V.P.-Ag. Sls.--Lockwood Corporation, Gering, NE, pg. 680
Fisher, George, V.P.-Distributor Sales--Ballantine Books, New York, NY, pg. 19
Fisher, John, Dir.-Sls.--Valley Forest Resources Co., Marcell, MN, pg. 1152
Fisher, Randy, V.P.-Sls.--John J. Campbell Co., Inc., Memphis, TN, pg. 212
Fisher, Warren F., V.P.-Sls.--Moeller Marine Products, Goodlettsville, TN, pg. 768
Fishman, James H., V.P.-Sls.--Yankee Publishing Incorporated, Dublin, NH, pg. 1207
Fiss, Victor, Mgr.-Gen. Sls.--Beauchamp Distributing Company, Compton, CA, pg. 130
Fitzgerald, Colt, Dir.-Sls.--A. L. Hansen Mfg. Co., Waukegan, IL, pg. 506
Fitzgerald, Deborah, Mktg. & Sls. Specialist--Cooper Instrument Corp., Middlefield, CT, pg. 283
Fitzgerald, Doug, Mgr.-Sls.--KSTF-TV, Scottsbluff, NE, pg. 1043
Fitzgerald, Hope, Sec. & Sls. Admin.--Son Chief Electrics, Inc., Winsted, CT, pg. 1018
Fitzgerald, Jean, Asst. Sec. & Loan Officer--Wieland Financial Services, Inc., Atlanta, GA, pg. 1188
FitzGerald, Kristin Dean, Sr. V.P.-Sls.--Lifetime Television, Astoria, NY, pg. 523
Fitzsimmons, John, V.P.-Sls.--Xebec Corporation, Kansas City, MO, pg. 1206
Fitzwilson, John, Sls. Mgr.--Madison, Inc., Tulsa, OK, pg. 433
Flaherty, Richard, F., V.P.-Sls.--Dixon Valve & Coupling Company, Chestertown, MD, pg. 341
Flanagan, Frank, Sr. V.P.-Sls.-East--Viacom Enterprises, New York, NY, pg. 785
Flanagan, Kathleen, V.P.-Sls. & Mktg.--American Management Group, Westbrook, ME, pg. 57
Flanagan, Kathleen, V.P. Sls.--Portland Glass/American Management Group, Westbrook, ME, pg. 58
Flanagan, Terry, V.P.-Sls.--ELE International, Inc., Lake Bluff, IL, pg. 359
Flannigan, Cyndi, Dir.-Sls.--Hornady Manufacturing Company, Grand Island, NE, pg. 544
Flannigan, Mike, V.P.-Sls.--Dixico, Inc., Dallas, TX, pg. 135
Flaster, S.R., Sr. V.P.-Sls.--Ingram Book Company, La Vergne, TN, pg. 569
Fleet, Dave, Mgr.-Sls.--IPMC, Inc.-Detroit, Detroit, MI, pg. 583
Fleischer, Barry, V.P.-Sls. & Mktg.--Aldan Rubber Co., Philadelphia, PA, pg. 32
Fleming, Bill, V.P.-Sls. & Mdsg.--Pay Less Super Markets, Inc., Anderson, IN, pg. 852
Fleming, Buzz, V.P.-Sls.--M. B. Kahn Construction Co., Inc., Columbia, SC, pg. 614
Fleming, Craig, V.P.-Sls.--Silvercrest Western Home Industries Corporation, Corona, CA, pg. 1004
Fleming, D.N., Mgr.-Natl. Sls.--Industrial Chemicals Div., Valley Forge, PA, pg. 837
Fleming, Ed, Dir.-Sls.--Turner Dairies, Inc., Covington, TN, pg. 1119
Fleming, R.G., V.P.-Sls. & Mktg.--Sturtevant Div., Boston, MA, pg. 547
Fleming, Robin G., V.P.-Sls. & Mktg.--Howden Sirocco inc., Hyde Park, MA, pg. 547
Flesner, David, Sr. V.P.-Sls.--Simmons Upholstered Furniture, Inc., Saint Louis, MO, pg. 1005
Fletcher, E.E., V.P.-Sls.--National Rivet & Manufacturing Company, Waupun, WI, pg. 793
Fletcher, William, Sls. Mgr.--Wilson Machine Knife Co., Inc., Dayville, CT, pg. 556
Flick, Rocky, V.P.-Sls. & Mktg.--Blitz USA, Miami, OK, pg. 157
Flick, Rocky, V.P.-Mktg., Sls., Adv. & Export--Blitz U.S.A., Inc., Miami, OK, pg. 157
Floth, Karl, Sls. Mgr.--Davis Paint Company, Kansas City, MO, pg. 319
Flowers, William L., Mgr.-Sls.--BNA Communications, Inc., Rockville, MD, pg. 189
Floyd, Jeff, Mgr.-Comml. Sls.--Sullivan Oil Company, Baton Rouge, LA, pg. 1057
Flynn, Patrick A., Mgr.-Sls.--Standard Gravure d/b/a Oklahoma Graphics, Oklahoma City, OK, pg. 1036
Fodor, Random E., Mgr.-Sls.(Steel Division.)--Smith Pipe & Steel Co., Phoenix, AZ, pg. 1014
Foggl, R., V.P.-Sls.--Ottenheimer & Company, Inc., Bannockburn, IL, pg. 831
Foley, James, V.P.-Sls.--Mutual Manufacturing & Supply Co., Cincinnati, OH, pg. 778
Folk, James C., V.P.-Mktg. & Sls.--Jewell Instruments, Inc., Manchester, NH, pg. 594
Fontini, George, Exec. V.P.-Sls.--Zena Jeans, New York, NY, pg. 1217
Foote, Nathan, V.P.-Sls. & Mktg.--Blount Lumber Company, Lacona, NY, pg. 158
Footer, Eli, V.P.-Sls. & Mktg.--Schwartz & Benjamin, Inc., New York, NY, pg. 980
Forassiepi, Lido J., Sales Mgr.--Wellsville Fire Brick Company, Wellsville, MO, pg. 201
Forbes, Jim, V.P.-Sls.--Weber-Stephen Products, Palatine, IL, pg. 1171
Ford, Bill, Mgr.-Sls.--Bland Cadillac Company, Houston, TX, pg. 155
Ford, Jack, Natl. Sls. Mgr.--Evans Adhesive Corp., Columbus, OH, pg. 390
Ford, John, V.P.-Mktg. & Sls.--UDL Laboratories, Inc., Rockford, IL, pg. 1072
Ford, William J., Mgr.-Natl. Sls.--Harold M. Pitman Co., Inc., Totowa, NJ, pg. 872
Forgione, Deborah, Dir.-Mktg.--Boyer Bros. Inc., Altoona, PA, pg. 169
Forhan, Phillip, Dir.-Sls.--Active Tool & Manufacturing Co., Inc., Roseville, MI, pg. 15
Forman, Geoff, V.P.-Sls.--Wayne Dalton Corporation, Mount Hope, OH, pg. 312
Fornell, Karen, Mgr.-Catalog--The Popcorn Factory, Lake Forest, IL, pg. 426
Forney, Paul, V.P.-Sls.--Beverage Canners International Corp., Miami, FL, pg. 148
Forrest, Dave, Reg. Sls. Mgr.--Micro-Aire Surgical Instruments, Inc., Valencia, CA, pg. 711
Forshee, T.M., V.P.-Sls.--Riviana Foods Inc., Houston, TX, pg. 937
Fortier, Francis J., Mgr.-Distr. Sls.--Hano Business Forms, Inc., Springfield, MA, pg. 505
Fortini, Paul, V.P.-Sls.--Sullivan Paper Company, West Springfield, MA, pg. 1057
Fortna, Allen W., Mgr.-Distr. Sls.--T.B. Wood's Sons Company, Chambersburg, PA, pg. 1200
Fortune, A.H., V.P.-Sls.--Molded Fiber Glass Co., Union City, PA, pg. 764
Forward, K.C., V.P.-Adv. Sls.--U.S. News & World Report, New York, NY, pg. 1136
Foster, Ethan G., V.P.-Sls.--Soft Sheen Products, Inc., Chicago, IL, pg. 1016
Foster, Jim, V.P.-Sls. & Mktg.--Tweddle Litho Company, St. Clair Shores, MI, pg. 1120
Foster, John, V.P.-Sls.--John Roberts Company, Minneapolis, MN, pg. 938
Foster, Thomas, V.P.-Circulation--Chicago Sun Times, Chicago, IL, pg. 18
Foule, Mary, Mgr.-Sls.--Rihm Motor Company, Saint Paul, MN, pg. 934
Fountain, Jack W., V.P.-Intl. Sls.--Klipsch & Associates Inc., Hope, AR, pg. 635
Fournier, Daniel S., Natl. Sls. Mgr.--Sheffield Silver Co., Taunton, MA, pg. 920
Fowler, Don, Sales Mgr.--WPTF, Raleigh, NC, pg. 306
Fowler, Phil, V.P.-Sls. & Mktg.--Hatteras Yachts, High Point, NC, pg. 758
Fox, Bob, V.P.-Pharmaceutical Sls.--John D. Lucas Printing Company, Baltimore, MD, pg. 263
Fox, Debbie, V.P.-Sls.--Crested Butte Mountain Resort, Inc., Mount Crested Butte, CO, pg. 299
Fox, Frederick, Mgr.-Sls.--Arkansas Oak Flooring, Pine Bluff, AR, pg. 83
Fox, Mickey, Mgr.-Adv.--Thomas Built Buses, Inc., High Point, NC, pg. 1092
Fox, Mona, Sls. Admin.--Tollycraft Yachts Corp., Kelso, WA, pg. 1100
Fox, Robert, V.P.-Pharmaceutical Sls.--Collman Graphics, Inc., Baltimore, MD, pg. 263
Foxen, Tracy, Dir.-Opers. & Sls.--CORS, Itasca, IL, pg. 203
Francis, Robert J., Sr. V.P.-Sls.--Lane Press, Inc., South Burlington, VT, pg. 654
Francis, T. Sanford, Mgr.-Mktg.--Windsor Industries, Inc., Englewood, CO, pg. 1195
Franck, Dick, Sls. Mgr.--Jordan's Foods-Caribou Division, Caribou, ME, pg. 605
Franick, Ken, Dir.-Surimi Sls.--Icicle Seafoods, Inc., Seattle, WA, pg. 561
Frank, Tricia, V.P.-Sls. & Mktg.--American Eagle Airlines, Chicago, IL, pg. 51
Franke, Charlie, Mgr.-Natl. Sls.--The Chamberlain Group, Inc., Elmhurst, IL, pg. 350
Frankel, Norman, V.P.-Sls. & Mktg.--Standard Textile Co., Inc., Cincinnati, OH, pg. 1037
Franklin, James R., V.P.-Sls.--Sellstrom Manufacturing Co., Palatine, IL, pg. 988
Franklin, Joann, Mgr.-Circulation--The Hannibal Courier-Post, Hannibal, MO, pg. 1042
Franklin, Tony, Mgr.-Used Truck Sls.--Fairway Ford, Inc., Greenville, SC, pg. 397
Franks, Mike, Sls. Promo. Mgr.--Sunbeam Outdoor Products Co., Neosho, MO, pg. 1059
Frankum, Darwin, Dir.-Sls. & Mktg.--Macklanburg-Duncan Co., Oklahoma City, OK, pg. 697
Franzem, Joseph, Sr. V.P.-Sls. & Admin.--The Stroh Brewery Company, Detroit, MI, pg. 1053
Frazho, Paul R., Mgr.-Sls. & Admin.--Fastcut Tool Corporation, Troy, MI, pg. 183
Frazier, Barbara, Mgr.-Whsle. Admin.--Contract Interiors Inc., Southfield, MI, pg. 280
Frazier, Eric, Dir.-Sls.--Tab Chemicals, Inc., Chicago, IL, pg. 1075
Frazier, James H., Exec. V.P.-Sls.--Building Plastics, Inc., Memphis, TN, pg. 188
Frazier, Randel, Mgr.-National Sls.--RELA, Inc., Boulder, CO, pg. 924
Frazier, Roger, Dir.-Intl. Sls.--Gold Medal Products Co., Cincinnati, OH, pg. 465
Frazier, Russ, V.P.-Sls.--Video Products Distributors, Inc., Sacramento, CA, pg. 1150
Frazier, Walter, V.P.-Sls. & Mktg.--Roller Derby Skate Company, Litchfield, IL, pg. 944
Fred, David W., V.P.-Sls.--SK Hand Tool Corp., Chicago, IL, pg. 963
Freed, John, Mgr.-Sls.--Mettowee Lumber & Plastic Co., Inc., Granville, NY, pg. 1085
Freeman, Mark S., Sec. & Dir.-Intl. Sls. & Mktg.--Freeman Cosmetic Corp., Los Angeles, CA, pg. 431
Freiling, Walt, Dir.-Sls. & Mktg.--Jordon Commercial Refrigerator Co., Philadelphia, PA, pg. 605
French, Eddie, Natl. Sls. & Mktg. Mgr.--American Ball Manufacturing, Carrollton, TX, pg. 890
Frey, Barry, Mng. Dir.-Intl. Sls.--USA Network, New York, NY, pg. 1124
Frey, Lawrence D., V.P.-Sls.--The Buschman Co., Cincinnati, OH, pg. 196
Frey, T.J., Dir.-Sls.--Austin Consulting, Rosemont, IL, pg. 790
Frick, Terry R., Mgr.-Sls.--Precision Roll Grinders, Inc., Allentown, PA, pg. 885
Friedgood, Alan, Dir.-Sls.--United States Luggage Company, Hauppauge, NY, pg. 1136
Friedman, Reuben, Pres. & Chief Exec. Officer--Arrow Typographers, Inc., Newark, NJ, pg. 326
Friel, John P., V.P.-Sls. & Mktg.--Medrad, Inc., Pittsburgh, PA, pg. 736
Friend, Howard, Exec. V.P.-Sls. & Mktg.--On-Cor Frozen Foods Inc., Chicago, IL, pg. 826
Friend, Kent, Sr. V.P.-Sls. & Mktg.--Kraco Enterprises, Inc., Compton, CA, pg. 643
Friesen, Robert, Mgr.-Mktg. & Sls.--S-T Industries, Inc., Saint James, MN, pg. 964
Fritch, Leo, Asst. V.P.-Sls.-S.W. Reg.--Benco Industries, Inc., Fort Deposit, AL, pg. 138
Fritz, Bill, V.P.-Sls. & Mktg.--Illinois Auto Electric Co., Elmhurst, IL, pg. 562
Fritz, Wayne, V.P.-Sls.--Saladmaster, Arlington, TX, pg. 967
Froelich, Craig, Mgr.-Sls.--Young & Franklin, Inc., Liverpool, NY, pg. 1209
Fromm, Lori, Mgr.-Sls. Devel.--Seventeen Magazine, New York, NY, pg. 611
Fross, Vern, Sr. V.P.-Sls. & Mktg.--Ingram Entertainment Inc., La Vergne, TN, pg. 569
Frost, Dick, Dir.-Sls., Power--Proxima Corporation, San Diego, CA, pg. 896
Fry, Tom, V.P.-Sls., Wheel Access.--Cragar Industries, Compton, CA, pg. 761
Fuerst, Norma, Sls. Mgr.--Shofar Kosher Foods, Inc., Newark, NJ, pg. 1000
Fujimoto, Dale, V.P.-Sls. & Mktg.--KNOX International Corp., Knoxville, TN, pg. 638
Fulmer, Joseph S., V.P.-Sls.--Marshall & Williams Co., Greenville, SC, pg. 714
Fundora, Ray, Mgr.-Export Sls.--Dacor Corporation, Northfield, IL, pg. 310
Furman, Joel R., V.P.-Sls. & Mktg.--Furman Foods, Inc., Northumberland, PA, pg. 436
Futrell, Rick, Exec. V.P.-Sls.--Century Boats By General Marine Industries, Panama City, FL, pg. 450
Futrell, Rick, V.P.-Sls.--GMI, Inc.-Glasstream, Panama City, FL, pg. 450
Gabe, Jon, V.P.-Sls. & Mktg.--Fred Usinger, Inc., Milwaukee, WI, pg. 1140
Gable, Lindsay, V.P.-Video Sls.--Shape Inc., Biddeford, ME, pg. 995
Gabor, Dick, Adv. Mgr.--Sommer & Maca Industries, Inc., Chicago, IL, pg. 1017
Gaev, Louis, Dir.-Sls.--Russell-Stanley Corporation, Red Bank, NJ, pg. 957
Gage, Nevin, Sls. Mgr.--Atlas Power Equipment Company, Harvard, IL, pg. 96
Gage, Nevin I., Sls. Mgr.-Atlas & Wheeler Div.--General Power Equipment Co., Harvard, IL, pg. 288
Gage, Robert, Dir.-Sls.--Fidelity Express Money Order Company Division, Sulphur Springs, TX, pg. 440
Gagliardi, Michel, Sls. Coordinator-Intl. Div.--Penetone Corp., Tenafly, NJ, pg. 1172
Gagnassola, J.L., V.P.--Hydro Group, Inc., Bridgewater, NJ, pg. 556
Gahm, Gordon, Dir.-Sls.--Kitchen Kompact, Inc., Jeffersonville, IN, pg. 634
Gaines, A., Mgr.-Natl. Sls.--Richmond Screw Anchor Company, Fort Worth, TX, pg. 933
Gainsforth, R.H., V.P.-Sls.--Chittenden & Eastman Co., Burlington, IA, pg. 248
Galbraith, J. C., III, V.P.-Sls. & Adv.--Foxworth-Galbraith Lumber Co., Dallas, TX, pg. 428
Gale, Nelson, V.P.-Mtkg. & Sls.--Interstate Distributors Inc., Norcross, GA, pg. 580
Gall, Robert E., V.P.-Sls. & Mktg.--Amtrak-National Railroad Passenger Corp., Washington, DC, pg. 69
Gallagher, James, V.P.-Sls.--Datability, Inc., Carlstadt, NJ, pg. 316
Gallagher, Ralph, V.P.-Agency & Client Rels.--The National Enquirer, Lantana, FL, pg. 788
Gallagher, Tom, V.P.-Sls.--Michael Business Machines Corporation, North Charleston, SC, pg. 747
Gallagher, William J., V.P.-Sls.--George Transfer, Inc., Parkton, MD, pg. 453
Gallo, Joseph, V.P.-Sls.--Binkley Company, Warrenton, MO, pg. 151
Galloni, J., Sls. Mgr.-Printed Prods. Grp.--The Meyercord Company, Carol Stream, IL, pg. 746
Galvin, James, Dir.-Adv. & Mktg. & Mgr.-Sls.--Media America Corp., Phoenix, AZ, pg. 734
Gamache, Brian, Dir.-Resort Div. Sls. & Mktg.--Hyatt Hotels Corporation, Chicago, IL, pg. 495
Gamble, Richard, Dir.-Sls.--J.T. Slocomb Company, South Glastonbury, CT, pg. 1010
Gandy, Jim, Dir.-Sls.--Coble Dairy Products Co-op, Lexington, NC, pg. 257
Ganskopp, C. Robert, V.P.-Sls. & Mktg.--South Chester Tube Co., Concordville, PA, pg. 1019
Gantt, Phillip L., Dir.-Sls. & Mktg.--Vidicom, L.D. Bevan Company, Inc., Thousand Oaks, CA, pg. 1151
Ganzhorn, Carl, Mgr.-Sls.--Plymouth Locomotive International, Inc., Plymouth, OH, pg. 877
Garafalo, Art, V.P.-Sls.--Avatar Corporation, Hopkinton, MA, pg. 101
Garbriz, Mike, Exec. V.P.-Sls.--Handy Wacks Corporation, Sparta, MI, pg. 505
Garcia, Jose, V.P.-Sls.--Smartstar Corporation, Goleta, CA, pg. 1011
Garcia, L., V.P.-Engrng. & Sls.--Besser/APPCO, San Antonio, TX, pg. 146
Gardiner, Mark, Dir.-Sls. & Mktg.--Hinkley Lighting Inc., Cleveland, OH, pg. 535

Gardner, Gary W., Mgr.-Pulp & Paper Industry Sls.--Superior Machine Company Of South Carolina, Inc., Florence, SC, pg. 1064
Gardner, Jack, Mgr.-Sls.--Harden Furniture Company, McConnellsville, NY, pg. 508
Gardner, Ken, V.P.-Sls.--Diagraph Corporation, Earth City, MO, pg. 335
Garfield, Craig, Sls. & Mktg. Mgr.--Brodhead-Garrett Co., Mansfield, OH, pg. 178
Garland, Frank, V.P.-Adv. Sls.--The Weather Channel, Atlanta, GA, pg. 654
Garland, Frank, Central/Western Div. Adv. Sls. mgr.--The Weather Channel, Inc.-Chicago Sales Office, Chicago, IL, pg. 654
Garret, F.D., Dir.-Intl. Sls.--Milk Specialties Company, Dundee, IL, pg. 753
Garrett, Daniel, V.P.-Sls.--Ensoniq Corporation, Malvern, PA, pg. 382
Garrity, Robert, Mktg. Dir.--Commodore Cruise Line, Ltd., Coral Gables, FL, pg. 269
Garrott, John, Mgr.-Sls.--Delta Industries, East Granby, CT, pg. 327
Gartner, Rosalie, Mgr.-Sls.--Tricon Brazing Alloys & Chemical Products Div., Downers Grove, IL, pg. 1113
Garuckas, Joseph, V.P. & Natl. Sls. Mgr.--Mohawk Distilled Products, North Miami, FL, pg. 763
Gasaway, Dick, Pres.--Happy Holiday Tree Farms, Sheridan, MI, pg. 506
Gasmovic, Dave J., Exec. V.P. & Mgr.-Natl. Sls.--McLaughlin Mfg. Company, Greenville, SC, pg. 731
Gasparini, Donald V., Mgr.-Sls. Promo.--Sullivan Paper Company, West Springfield, MA, pg. 1057
Gasparini, Peter, Mgr.-Natl. Sls.--Heat Controller, Inc., Jackson, MI, pg. 524
Gassel, Jerry, V.P.-Sls.--Guarantee Electrical Company, Saint Louis, MO, pg. 490
Gauger, A. Gary, Mgr.-Sls.--Walbridge Aldinger Company, Detroit, MI, pg. 1158
Gaul, David, Mgr.-Sls. & Adv.--Denver Wholesale Florists Company, Denver, CO, pg. 331
Gausnell, Jack, Dir.-Sls., PDP--Proxima Corporation, San Diego, CA, pg. 896
Gawriluk, Susie, Dir.-Travel Industry Sls.--Hyatt Hotels Corporation, Chicago, IL, pg. 495
Gay, Glen, V.P.-Sls., Mktg. & Export--Pace International Corporation, Kirkland, WA, pg. 838
Gedelman, Anne, Mgr.-Sls. Promo.--Eco Water Systems, Saint Paul, MN, pg. 367
Gee, Robert, V.P.-Sls.--Cloverhill Bakery, Chicago, IL, pg. 256
Geedey, Harry, Mgr.-Sls.--Empire Kosher Poultry, Inc., Mifflintown, PA, pg. 379
Geesa, Gilbert, V.P.-Sls.--Ft. Dearborn Lithograph Graphic Arts Division, Fort Worth, TX, pg. 425
Geeslin, Jim, V.P. Sls.--Century Products Co., Macedonia, OH, pg. 235
Geheran, John J., V.P.-Sls.--Bose Corporation, Framingham, MA, pg. 167
Gehring, Mike, Sls. Dir.--WTOG-TV, Inc., St. Petersburg, FL, pg. 549
Geiger, Peter E., V.P.-Mktg. & Sls.--Geiger Brothers, Lewiston, ME, pg. 447
Geiserman, Otto, Dir.-Mktg. & Mgr.-Reg. Sls.--Digital Electronic Automation, Livonia, MI, pg. 337
Geissbuhler, R.L., Exec. V.P.-Domestic Sls.--Miller Electric Mfg. Co., Appleton, WI, pg. 754
Gelb, Mike, Sr. V.P.-Sls.--Crystal Clear Industries Company, Ridgefield Park, NJ, pg. 303
Gelina, Stanley, Mgr.-Sls.--Berkshire Industries, Inc., Westfield, MA, pg. 142
Gelini, Floyd J., Sr. V.P. & Dir.-Reg. Sls.--Blair Television, New York, NY, pg. 155
Gemmel, Kari, Mktg. & Intl. Sls. Dir.--Jackson Hole Ski Resort, Teton Village, WY, pg. 587
Genovese, Frank, V.P. & Gen. Sls. Mgr.--The Jaydor Corporation, Millburn, NJ, pg. 591
Gensheimer, Karl, V.P. & Dir.-Sls.--KSTP-TV, Saint Paul, MN, pg. 549
Gentili, Gene, Dir.-Sls. Foodservice Natl. Accounts--Ivex Packaging Corporation-Food Packaging Division, Lincolnshire, IL, pg. 583
Gentry, Denise, Sls. Asst.--Leupold & Stevens, Inc., Beaverton, OR, pg. 669
Genuser, Steve, V.P.-Mktg. & Sls.--Shugart Corporation, Irvine, CA, pg. 1001
Genuser, Steve, V.P.-Mktg. & Sls.--Kennedy Company, Irwindale, CA, pg. 1001
George, Douglas A., V.P.-Sls.--W.H. Weaver Construction Co., Greensboro, NC, pg. 1170
George, Elmer, V.P.-Sls.--Electronic Data Magnetics, Inc., High Point, NC, pg. 375
George, Richard, V.P.-Sls.--Standard Tool & Manufacturing Company, Lyndhurst, NJ, pg. 1037
George, Robert, V.P.-Sls.--Melody Foods, Inc., Farmington Hills, MI, pg. 738
Georgells, Nicholas, V.P.-Sls.--Walter H. Weaber Sons, Inc., Lebanon, PA, pg. 1169
Geraci, James, Dir.-Sls.--Brimms Inc., Tonawanda, NY, pg. 176
Gerber, Suzanne, Sls. Mgr.--Cornnuts Inc., Alameda, CA, pg. 286
Gerhard, Bill, Mgr.-Natl. Sls.--Dormeyer Industries, Chicago, IL, pg. 346
Gerlach, Fred, Mgr.-Natl. Sls.--Technical Instruments Div., San Jose, CA, pg. 1068
Gershaw, Gerald, Pres.-Intl. Div.--Therapedic Associates, Inc., Boca Raton, FL, pg. 1090
Gerstein, Mel, Treas. & Dir.-Mktg., Adv. & Pub. Rels.--Thermwell Products Co., Inc., Paterson, NJ, pg. 1092
Getto, Judith, Mgr.-Sls.--Hazen Paper Company, Holyoke, MA, pg. 520
Giamo, Kathy, Dir.-Sls. & Mktg.--Reckson Associates, Melville, NY, pg. 917
Giangiullo, Randall C., Sr. V.P.-Grp. Sls.--Phoenix Home Life Mutual Insurance Company, Hartford, CT, pg. 868
Giannestras, James, V.P.-Mktg. & Sls.--Cherry Central Cooperative, Traverse City, MI, pg. 243
Gibbons, E.A., V.P.-Mktg. & Food Service Sls.--Presto Food Products, Inc., City of Industry, CA, pg. 888
Gibbs, Donald, V.P.-Sls. & Mktg.--Lawson Mechanical Contractors, Sacramento, CA, pg. 663
Gibson, Betsy, Sls. Mgr.--Shape South, Inc., Dadeville, AL, pg. 995
Gieler, Brian P., Western Reg. Sls. Mgr.--Simpson Electric Co., Elgin, IL, pg. 1007
Gieseke, Carlton, Mgr.-Sls. Promo--Fiberesin Industries Inc., Oconomowoc, WI, pg. 408
Gilbert, Gerry, Mgr.-Sls.--Port Charlotte, Port Charlotte, FL, pg. 95
Gilchrist, Charles, Dir.-Sls.--Acme Foundry, Inc., Coffeyville, KS, pg. 13
Gill, John E., V.P.-Sls. & Mktg.--American Paper Products Group, Ltd., Youngstown, OH, pg. 59
Gillece, Rich, Mgr.-Natl. Sls.--All-Luminum Products, Inc., Philadelphia, PA, pg. 35
Gilleece, John, V.P.-Sls.--Goshen Rubber Co., Inc., Goshen, IN, pg. 472
Gilleland, Robert L., V.P.-Sls. & Adv. Dir.--LaBarge Pipe & Steel Company, Saint Louis, MO, pg. 649
Gillespie, Dennis G., Pres.-Worldwide Mktg. & Domestic Sls.--Viacom Enterprises, New York, NY, pg. 785
Gilliam, Doyle, V.P.-Sls. & Mktg.--E.C. Barton & Co., Jonesboro, AR, pg. 123
Gilliland, Wes, Sls. Mgr.--Ullenberg Corp., Chattanooga, TN, pg. 1125
Gillice, Sondra, V.P.-Sls.--Guest Services, Inc., Fairfax, VA, pg. 493
Gillman, Kenneth, V.P.-Sls.--Moldcraft Plastics Inc., Baltimore, MD, pg. 880
Gillman, Kenneth M., V.P.-Sls.--Poly-Seal Corporation, Baltimore, MD, pg. 880
Gillon, Peter, V.P.-Sls.--Harris-Kayot, Inc., Fort Wayne, IN, pg. 512
Gilman, Geoffrey, Mgr.-Sls.--Marty Gilman, Inc., Gilman, CT, pg. 459
Gilsdorf, Paul E., V.P.-Sls. & Mktg.--A-B Emblem Div. of Conrad Industries, Inc., Weaverville, NC, pg. 2
Gilson, James A., V.P.-Sls. & Adv.--Transistor Devices, Inc., Cedar Knolls, NJ, pg. 1107
Gilson, R., Dir.-Sls.--Miller Electric Mfg. Co., Appleton, WI, pg. 754
Ginley, John, Sls. Mgr.-Malco Automotive Div.--Malco Products, Inc., Barberton, OH, pg. 702
Ginsberg, Herb, V.P.-Sls.--Bel-Art Products, Pequannock, NJ, pg. 133
Giordano, Alex, Sr. V.P.-Sls.--Standard Security Life Insurance Company of New York, New York, NY, pg. 452
Giordano, Gene, V.P.-Sls.--Wilkata Packaging Corporation, Kearny, NJ, pg. 1189
Giovingo, Vic, Natl. Sls. Mgr.-Electronic Distr.--G.C. Thorsen, Inc., Rockford, IL, pg. 609
Gipson, Beverly, Mktg. Sls. Mgr.--American Water Works Association, Denver, CO, pg. 65
Girard, Peter, Dir.-Sls.--Swiss-M-Tex, L.P., Travelers Rest, SC, pg. 1068
Girkins, Ralph C., V.P.-Sales Mgr.--Abbey Etna Machine Company, Perrysburg, OH, pg. 9
Gish, A., V.P.-Consumer Sls.--Eagle Electric Mfg. Co., Inc., Long Island City, NY, pg. 362
Gitelman, Sheldon, V.P.-Sls.--Gilster Mary Lee Corp., Chester, IL, pg. 460
Gittens, Gregg, V.P.-Sls. & Mktg.--Labelon Corporation, Canandaigua, NY, pg. 649
Given, Cecil, V.P.-Sls.--The Flood Company, Hudson, OH, pg. 419
Givens, Donald, V.P.-Mktg. & Sls.--Standco Industries, Inc., Houston, TX, pg. 1038
Glabman, Chick, Pres.-Specialty Prod. Sls.--Duro Paper Bag Manufacturing Co., Ludlow, KY, pg. 355
Glaser, Jack, Mgr.-Food Ingredients/Industrial Sls.--Oregon Freeze Dry, Inc., Albany, OR, pg. 829
Glatts, George III, Mgr.-Eastern Reg. Sls. Engrng.--Elastomeric Technologies, Inc., Hatboro, PA, pg. 372
Glazer, Mark, V.P.-Sls. & Mktg.--Crisa Corporation, Plano, TX, pg. 299
Gleason, Daniel S., V.P.-Sls.--Aloha Airlines, Inc., Honolulu, HI, pg. 43
Gleason, T.P., V.P.-Sls.--Willert Home Products, Inc., Saint Louis, MO, pg. 1190
Gleaves, Leon R., V.P.-Mktg. & Sls.--Wilkins-Rogers Incorporated, Ellicott City, MD, pg. 1190
Glenn, Robert, Gen. Sls. Mgr.--Colson Caster Corporation, Jonesboro, AR, pg. 711
Glickman, Joseph L., Mgr.-Sls.--The Jewett Refrigerator Co., Inc., Buffalo, NY, pg. 957
Glickson, Tom, Sls. Mgr.-Used Cars--Roger Holler Chevrolet Co., Winter Park, FL, pg. 539
Glover, Charles, V.P.-Gen. Mfg. Sls.--W. M. Barr & Co., Inc., Memphis, TN, pg. 121
Godfrey, William T., V.P.-Mfg. & Mktg.--Morris Coupling Co., Erie, PA, pg. 771
Goer, Randy, V.P.-Sls.--Goer Manufacturing Co., Charleston, SC, pg. 907
Goetz, Wayne, Mgr.-Natl. Sls.--Voyager Emblems, Inc., Sanborn, NY, pg. 1155
Goff, Rick, Natl. Sls. Mgr.--Stanley Fastening Systems, Worcester, MA, pg. 1038
Goit, Whitney, II, Exec. V.P.-Sls. & Mktg.--Arts & Entertainment Network, New York, NY, pg. 523
Gold, Arnold, Gen. Sls. Mgr.--Benson Management Company, San Antonio, TX, pg. 140
Goldberg, Lewis, Sls. Mgr.--Fine Organics Corp., Lodi, NJ, pg. 411
Goldberg, Morton, V.P.-Sls.--Bregg Data Forms, Inc., Hauppauge, NY, pg. 173
Goldfarb, Al, Sr. V.P.-Sls.--Gould Paper Corporation, New York, NY, pg. 473
Goldfarb, Marc, V.P. & Natl. Sls. Mgr.--National Banner Company, Dallas, TX, pg. 786
Goldstein, Seymour, Mgr.-Sls.--P.D. Fashions, New York, NY, pg. 836
Goldstein, William L., V.P.-Mktg. & Sls.--Wheelock Inc., Long Branch, NJ, pg. 1185
Golomb, Dick, Gen. Sls. Mgr.--Grove Valve & Regulator Company, Oakland, CA, pg. 490
Goman, Stan, Sr. V.P.-Sls.--Tower Records, West Sacramento, CA, pg. 694
Gomeau, Mary Ellen, V.P.-Sls. & Mktg.--Phonetics, Inc., Aston, PA, pg. 869
Gonia, W.J., V.P.-Sls. & Mktg.--Flexonics Inc., Bartlett, IL, pg. 419
Good, Randy O., V.P.-Sls.--Windsor Service, Inc., Reading, PA, pg. 1196
Goodlad, Jim, Sls. Mgr.--WVUE-TV, New Orleans, LA, pg. 194
Goodlund, Dave, Mgr.-Sls.--Nemschoff Chairs, Inc., Sheboygan, WI, pg. 798
Goodman, Marvin, V.P.-Sls. & Mktg.--Plastic Suppliers, Inc., Columbus, OH, pg. 875
Goodwin, Doug, Mgr.-Sls./New Cars--McNamara Pontiac Inc., Orlando, FL, pg. 732
Goodwin, Doug, Mgr.-Gen. Sls.--Royal Jeep Eagle & Chrysler Plymouth, Casselberry, FL, pg. 953
Goold, Peter, Dir.-Mktg. & Sls.--Just Born, Inc., Bethlehem, PA, pg. 610
Gordon, Mark, V.P.-Mktg. & Sls.--Lionel Trains, Inc., Chesterfield, MI, pg. 677
Gordy, Mike, V.P.-Retail Sls.--Sargento Cheese Co., Plymouth, WI, pg. 971
Gore, Larry, Mgr.-Sls. Office--AMF Bakery Systems, Richmond, VA, pg. 5
Gorman, D., Exec. V.P.-Sls.--R. T. Vanderbilt Company, Inc., Norwalk, CT, pg. 1144
Gorman, Steve, Mgr.-Sls.--North Dakota Mill & Elevator Association, Grand Forks, ND, pg. 813
Gorski, Richard F., V.P.-O.E. Sls.--ASC Incorporated, Southgate, MI, pg. 7
Gorsky, Alec, Mgr.-Govt. Sls.--Victaulic Company of America, Easton, PA, pg. 1149
Gosselin, Raymond, V.P.-Sls.--Palmer Manufacturing Company, Malden, MA, pg. 844
Gottlieb, Allen, Mgr.-Sls.--City Postal, Inc., New York, NY, pg. 251
Gould, Peter, Dir.-Mktg. & Sls.--Just Born, Inc., Bethlehem, PA, pg. 610
Gould, William, Sls. Mgr.--Brady Enterprises, Inc., East Weymouth, MA, pg. 171
Gouwens, Bob, V.P.-Sls.--La Preferida, Inc., Chicago, IL, pg. 649
Gower, Myron T., V.P.-Engrng. Sls.--Miller Electric Company, Jacksonville, FL, pg. 754
Grabia, Leonard, V.P.-Sls.--Pascoe Building Systems, Inc., Columbus, GA, pg. 851
Grad, P., Intl. Sls. Mgr.--Data Instruments, Inc., Acton, MA, pg. 316
Grader, R.H., V.P.-Sls.--National Frozen Foods Corp., Seattle, WA, pg. 789
Graft, Jim, V.P.-Sls.--Sanborn Manufacturing Company, Springfield, MN, pg. 969
Graham, Michael, Sr. V.P.-Sls. & Mktg.--Pittsburgh Brewing Company, Pittsburgh, PA, pg. 873
Graham, Thomas, Dir.-Sls.--The Pierce Co., Inc., Upland, IN, pg. 102
Graham, Tim, Mgr. Sls.-Auto.--Meadville Forging Co., Meadville, PA, pg. 733
Grandinetti, Michael A., V.P.-Sls. & Mktg.--Tylan General, Inc., San Diego, CA, pg. 1122
Grant, Christopher, V.P.-Sls.--Christianity Today, Inc., Carol Stream, IL, pg. 249
Grant, Dan, Mgr.-Natl. Sls.--Just Born, Inc., Bethlehem, PA, pg. 610
Grant, Dan, Mgr.-Natl. Sls.--Just Born, Inc., Bethlehem, PA, pg. 610
Grant, Donald W., Pres. & Mgr.-Sls.--Western Reinsurance Brokers, Inc., Los Angeles, CA, pg. 1181
Grass, Harry, Dir.-Sls. & Mktg.--Gordon Sign Company, Denver, CO, pg. 472
Graves, Dianne, Mgr.-Circulation--Capper's, Topeka, KS, pg. 1043
Graves, Earl G., Jr., Sr. V.P.-Sls. & Mktg.--Earl G. Graves, Ltd., New York, NY, pg. 478
Gray, Brian, Mgr.-Sls./Intl. Sls. & Exports--United Aluminum Corporation, North Haven, CT, pg. 1130
Gray, Dave, V.P.-Sls., Dairy Food--Land O'Lakes, Inc., Arden Hills, MN, pg. 653
Gray, Eric L., V.P.-Sls.--F. H. Chase, Inc., Foxboro, MA, pg. 240
Gray, Jeff, Dir.-Mktg. & Sls.--W. B. Roddenbery Company, Inc., Cairo, GA, pg. 942
Gray, Richard, V.P.-Sls. & Mktg.--Rochester-Midland ICL, Omaha, NE, pg. 941
Gray, Scott A., V.P.-Sls. & Mktg.--Gray Printing Co., Fostoria, OH, pg. 479
Green, Donald, Chm. Bd. & Sr. V.P. & Gen. Mgr.--Menu Foods, Inc., Pennsauken, NJ, pg. 739
Green, Les, V.P.-Sls.--Filko/Cobra, Inc., Chicago, IL, pg. 393
Greenawalt, Jon, V.P.-Sls. & Mktg.--Lyon's Restaurants, Inc., Foster City, CA, pg. 690
Greenberg, E., Exec. V.P.-Sls. & Mktg.--Randolph Medical Inc., Livonia, MI, pg. 912
Greenberg, Fred, Exec. V.P., Sec. & Sls. Mgr.--Jack Greenberg Inc., Philadelphia, PA, pg. 485
Greenberg, Sidney, Sr. V.P.-Sls.--Jameco Industries, Inc., Wyandanch, NY, pg. 588
Greenbert, Irwin, V.P.-Natl. Acct. Sls.--Universal Folding Box Company, Inc., Hoboken, NJ, pg. 1138
Greene, Cecil L., V.P.-Sls.-Utility Div.--Shealy Electrical Wholesalers, Greenville, SC, pg. 996

Greene, Harold, V.P.-Sls.--Forever Living Products, Tempe, AZ, pg. 424
Greenisen, G.J., Mgr.-Sls.--Electric Furnace Co., Salem, OH, pg. 373
Greenisen, Phil, Mktg.--Turner Machine Company, Salem, OH, pg. 373
Greenlaw, Douglas, Exec. V.P.-Adv. Sls.--MTV Networks, New York, NY, pg. 785
Greenlee, Roy, Mgr.-Circulation--Shawnee News-Star, Shawnee, OK, pg. 1042
Greer, David, Dir.-Universe Sls. & Mktg.--Charles River Data Systems, Inc., Framingham, MA, pg. 240
Greer, Robert, Mgr.-Sls. & Mdsg.--Lee Grocery Company, Everett, WA, pg. 665
Gregg, Karen, Mgr.-Sls. & Mktg. Services--Shade Computer Forms Co., Green Bay, WI, pg. 994
Gregory, Charlie, V.P.-Mktg. & Sls.--Buck Knives, Inc., El Cajon, CA, pg. 185
Gresack, Martin, Mgr.-Sls.--Glamorise Foundations, Inc., New York, NY, pg. 460
Gress, Peter, V.P.-Intl. Sls.--Gress Foods Inc., Gainesville, GA, pg. 486
Grey, Joe, Jr., V.P.-Sls.--Riverside Press, Inc., Dallas, TX, pg. 937
Griessel, Richard, V.P.-Mktg. & Sls.--National Fire Protection Association, Quincy, MA, pg. 788
Griesser, Ralph, Natl. Sls. Mgr.--Nautilus, Independence, VA, pg. 796
Griffin, Alfred, Sls. Mgr.-Western--Atlanta Mfg. Facility, Douglasville, GA, pg. 982
Griffin, Clay, Mgr.-Sls. & Mktg.--Rustco Products Company, Denver, CO, pg. 957
Griffin, Shawn, Natl. Sls. Mgr.--Gates Energy Products, Inc., Alachua, FL, pg. 445
Griggs, Ron, V.P.-Sls.--G. Leblanc Corporation, Kenosha, WI, pg. 665
Griggs, Tom, Dir.-Sls., Wheels--Cragar Industries, Compton, CA, pg. 761
Grimaldi, Richard, Mgr.-Sls.--Somerset Pontiac GMC Inc., Troy, MI, pg. 1017
Grimm, J.E., Mgr.-Sls.-OEM--Sporlan Valve Company, Saint Louis, MO, pg. 1032
Grimm, Robert, Mgr.-Sls.--Applied Graphics Technologies, Oceanside, NY, pg. 1136
Groefsema, Bruce, Sr. V.P.-Sls.--Calcot, Ltd., Bakersfield, CA, pg. 208
Grogan, Ken, V.P. & Mgr.-Gen. Sls.--National Brands, Inc., Phoenix, AZ, pg. 786
Gross, Glenn J., Sr. V.P.-Sls.--Kransco, San Francisco, CA, pg. 644
Grossenburg, Rodney, Mgr.-Sls.--Grossenburg Implements, Incorporated, Winner, SD, pg. 489
Grossman, Bernard, V.P.-Sls., Mktg. & Fin.--M. Grossman Son, Inc., Passaic, NJ, pg. 489
Grossman, Rick, Dir.-Sls.--Optyl Eyewear Fashion International Corp., Norwood, NJ, pg. 828
Grost, Mike, V.P.-Sls.--Barrecrafters, Shelburne, VT, pg. 996
Grozelle, L., Natl. Sales Dir.-Group I--The Canadian Coleman Co., Ltd., Toronto,, Canada, pg. 695
Grywalski, Jim, Mgr.-Grp. Retail Support--Ace Hardware Corporation, Oak Brook, IL, pg. 12
Grzesiak, Arlene, Mgr.-Natl. Sls.--Grayline Housewares, Elgin, IL, pg. 480
Gudger, Charles, V.P.-Sls. & Mktg.--Universal Match Corp., Kenner, LA, pg. 335
Guenin, Greg, Mgr.-Circulation--Brainerd Daily Dispatch, Brainerd, MN, pg. 1042
Guerra, Peter M., Grp. V.P.--W&F Manufacturing Corporation, Inc., Buffalo, NY, pg. 1155
Guerrieri, Scott, V.P.-Further Processed Sls.--Showell Farms, Inc., Showell, MD, pg. 1000
Guggenheimer, Charles, Mgr.-Natl. Sls.--Lanz, Inc., Culver City, CA, pg. 658
Guido, Robert E., Dir.-Natl. Acct. Sls.--Distribution America, Des Plaines, IL, pg. 340
Gupton, Milton C., V.P.-Sls.--Kenney Manufacturing Company, Warwick, RI, pg. 623
Gurgold, Steven, Dir.-Sls.--Tiffany Extruders, Inc., Paterson, NJ, pg. 1096
Gushwa, Charles, V.P.-Mktg. & Sls.--Atlas/Soundolier, Fenton, MO, pg. 64
Guthaund, Rex, Gen. Sls. Mgr.--Willmar Manufacturing, Willmar, MN, pg. 1193
Guttas, Fred, Natl. Sls. Mgr.--Precision Twist Drill Co., Crystal Lake, IL, pg. 885
Gyenes, Ed, V.P.-Sls. & Mktg.--Beckley-Cardy, Inc., Duluth, MN, pg. 21
Haack, Bob, V.P.-Sls.--City Machine Tool & Die Company, Muncie, IN, pg. 251
Haas, Willima, V.P.-Sls.--Sweetheart Cup Co., Inc., Chicago, IL, pg. 1067
Hackett, Joseph, V.P.-Mktg. & Sls.--American Safety Razor Company, Verona, VA, pg. 604
Hackett, William F., Exec. V.P. & Natl. Sls. Mgr.--Barton Beers, Ltd., Chicago, IL, pg. 123
Hackman, Roger D., V.P.-Mktg. & Sls.--Seymour Manufacturing Company, Seymour, IN, pg. 994
Hackney, C., Sr. V.P.--Crooks Supermarket Inc., Nashville, TN, pg. 300
Hackney, R. Hodges, Exec. V.P.--Hackney & Sons, Inc., Washington, NC, pg. 498
Hadd, Dennis, V.P. & Gen. Sls. Mgr.--McNamara Pontiac Inc., Orlando, FL, pg. 732
Hadley, Jacquelyn, Chief Exec. Officer--Caswell/Massey Co. Ltd., Edison, NJ, pg. 229
Hadley, Karen, Mgr.-Sls.--Electro Dynamics Crystal Corporation, Overland Park, KS, pg. 374
Haerle, Karen, Mgr.-Sls. & Mktg.--Rose Printing Company, Inc., Tallahassee, FL, pg. 948
Haffner, Harry T., Jr., V.P.-Sls.--Swope Automotive Group, Inc., Louisville, KY, pg. 1068
Hagen, Billy, Dir.-Data Processing & Software Sls.--The Climatic Corp., Columbia, SC, pg. 255
Hagen, Cliff, V.P.-Sls.--Cass-Clay Creamery, Fargo, ND, pg. 228
Hagen, R.A., Mgr.-Sls./Construction Div.--Neenah Foundry Company, Neenah, WI, pg. 797
Hagman, Erland, V.P.-Sls.--Curtis Instruments, Inc., Mount Kisco, NY, pg. 305
Hague, Sam, V.P.-Sls.--Blaw Knox Rolls Division, Wheeling, WV, pg. 156
Hagy, Terry, Mgr.-Natl. Sls.--The Jel Sert Co., West Chicago, IL, pg. 591
Hahn, Kenneth A., V.P.-Sls.--The Wyco Tool Co., Racine, WI, pg. 909
Hahn, Michael, V.P.-Sls.-Western Grp.--Key Industries, Inc., Fort Scott, KS, pg. 627
Hahn, Michael, V.P.-Sls.--Bessin Corporation, Chicago, IL, pg. 146
Hairston, Jim, Dir.-Sls. & Mktg.--Hooker Industries, Ontario, CA, pg. 543
Hajek, Frank, V.P.-Retail Sls.-Chicago Div.--Hill-Behan Lumber Company, Saint Louis, MO, pg. 534
Hake, George, Mgr.-Sls. & Cost Analysis--Ultra Tool & Plastics, Inc., Amherst, NY, pg. 1125
Hall, Anthony, V.P.-Mktg. & Sls.--Crown Textile Company, Blue Bell, PA, pg. 302
Hall, Bob, V.P.-Builder Sls.--Erb Lumber Company, Birmingham, MI, pg. 360
Hall, Carroll, Sls. Dir.-RTC--Superior Auctioneers & Marketing, Inc., San Antonio, TX, pg. 1063
Hall, David, Sr. V.P.-Sls. & Mktg.--Time Systems, Inc., Phoenix, AZ, pg. 1097
Hall, Kenneth D., V.P.-Mktg.--Carson Products Company, Savannah, GA, pg. 67
Hall, R.A., V.P.-Sls. & Gen. Mgr.--Vilter Manufacturing Corporation, Milwaukee, WI, pg. 1152
Halliday, Rich, V.P.-Mktg.--Palm Beach Beauty Products Co., Minneapolis, MN, pg. 843
Hallstedt, Fred, Pres. & V.P-Sls. & Mktg.--Sonneveldt Company, Grand Rapids, MI, pg. 1018
Halverson, Mike, Dir.-Mktg.--Sathers Inc., Round Lake, MN, pg. 972
Hamati, Bill, Sr. V.P.-Branch Sls.--Vienna Sausage Mfg. Co., Chicago, IL, pg. 1151
Hamer, Frederick G., V.P.-Sls. & Distr.--E.F. Johnson Company, Eden Prarie, MN, pg. 598
Hamilton, Ernie, Mgr.-Sls.--Whiting Equipment Canada, Inc., Welland,, Canada, pg. 1187
Hamilton, Kenny, Gen. Mgr.-Sls.--Colman Toyota, Baton Rouge, LA, pg. 263
Hamilton, Lee, Sls. Mgr.--Triple A Specialty Company, Bedford Park, IL, pg. 1114
Hamm, John, Dir.-Sls. & Mktg.--Codisco Inc., Sanford, FL, pg. 258
Hammond, Barbara, Sr. V.P.-Sls.--Home Interiors & Gifts, Inc., Dallas, TX, pg. 541
Hampton, Charles, V.P.-Sls.--Richmond Technology Inc., Redlands, CA, pg. 933
Hamrick, R.L., Mgr.-Gen. Sls.--Champion Pneumatic Machinery Co., Inc., Princeton, IL, pg. 238
Hand, Robert, V.P.-Sls.--Arrow Fastener Co., Inc., Saddle Brook, NJ, pg. 85
Handlon, Steve, Mgr.-Sls.--Whitfield Foods, Inc., Montgomery, AL, pg. 1187
Hange, Robert, V.P.-Sls. & Mktg.--Signet Systems, Inc., Harrodsburg, KY, pg. 385
Hann, David, V.P.-Mktg. & Sls.--Micron Separations, Inc., Westborough, MA, pg. 749
Hanna, David E., Mgr.-Sls. & Mktg.--Owatonna Canning Company, Owatonna, MN, pg. 833
Hannay, Scott R., Dir.-Natl. Sls.--Clifford B. Hannay & Son Inc., Westerlo, NY, pg. 505
Hanney, Michael, Dir.-Parking Sls.-Cincinnati Brand--Amano Cincinnati, Inc., Cincinnati, OH, pg. 46
Hansbury, Ben, Dir.-Sls. & Mktg.--The Read Corporation, Middleboro, MA, pg. 916
Hansen, R.M., V.P.-Mktg. & Sls.--Pyle Inc., Chicago, IL, pg. 648
Hansill, Karen, V.P.-Sls.-Eastern Div.--Open Court Publishing Company, Chicago, IL, pg. 227
Hanson, Donald, Mgr.-Sls. (Rigid Box Div.)--F.N. Burt Company, Inc., Buffalo, NY, pg. 195
Hanson, Roberta, Mgr.-Sls.--Wieland Realty Associates, Inc., Atlanta, GA, pg. 1189
Harbaugh, William L., V.P.-Mktg. & Sls.--Burrell Group, New Kensington, PA, pg. 195
Harbuck, John G., V.P., Sls. & Mktg.--Citation Companies, Inc., Birmingham, AL, pg. 250
Hardin, Allan, Reg. Sls. Mgr.--The Benson Music Group, Nashville, TN, pg. 140
Hardin, Greg B., V.P.-Sls.--Starcraft Automotive Corp., Goshen, IN, pg. 1040
Hardinge, Thomas H., III, V.P.-Sls. & Mktg., Treas. & Sec.--Statton Furniture Manufacturing Company, Hagerstown, MD, pg. 1042
Hardison, Trafton T., Asst. V.P.-Sls.--Estes Express Lines, Inc., Richmond, VA, pg. 389
Hardy, Charles, Dir.-Mktg. & Sls.--Bollinger Machine Shop And Shipyard, Inc., Lockport, LA, pg. 163
Hardy, David, Asst. Mgr.-Sls.--Frederick Trading Company, Frederick, MD, pg. 430
Hare, Lori, V.P.-Sls. & Mktg.--Streamlight Inc., Norristown, PA, pg. 1053
Hare, R., V.P.-Sls.--Packaging Products & Design, Santa Ana, CA, pg. 842
Hare, Stan, Dir.-Indus. Sls.--Pioneer Industrial Products Co., Willard, OH, pg. 871
Hargesheimer, Don, Natl. Acct. Mgr.--Diamond Crystal Specialty Foods, Inc., Wilmington, MA, pg. 335
Harker, Gary, Exec. V.P.-Sls.--California Panel & Veneer Company, Cerritos, CA, pg. 210
Harkman, Ray, Mgr.-Sls.--Economy Folding Box Corp., Chicago, IL, pg. 367
Harl, James L., Sls. & Mktg. Mgr.--Dimco-Gray Company, Dayton, OH, pg. 338
Harlan, David M., V.P.-Natl. Sls. & Mktg.--United States Cold Storage, Inc., Cherry Hill, NJ, pg. 1135
Harland, William A., Dir.-Domestic Sls.--Broadcast Electronics, Inc., Quincy, IL, pg. 177
Harman, Michael J., Exec. V.P.-Sls. & Mktg.--Consolidated Metco, Inc., Portland, OR, pg. 277
Harmin, Steve, Mgr.-Sls.--Sid Tool Co. Inc., Plainview, NY, pg. 1002
Harmon, C.R., Gen. Sls. Mgr.--Ebco Mfg. Company, Columbus, OH, pg. 365
Harms, Jed, V.P.-Mktg. & Sls.--Triple F, Inc., Des Moines, IA, pg. 1114
Harnish, Dale, V.P.-Sls.--Engineered Polymers Corporation, Mora, MN, pg. 507
Harper, R. Steve, V.P.-Sls.--Cabot Creamery Co-Operative Inc., Cabot, VT, pg. 25
Harpold, Frank, V.P.-Sls.--J.R. Hahn Co., Inc., Indianapolis, IN, pg. 500
Harrell, Pamela A., Dir.-Mktg.--Seaboard Electronics Co., Carlsbad, CA, pg. 983
Harrington, David, Mgr.-Sls.--Central Michigan Container Corporation, Jackson, MI, pg. 19
Harrington, Denice, Mgr.-Automated Fueling Sls.--Sullivan Oil Company, Baton Rouge, LA, pg. 1057
Harrington, Ken, Gen. Mgr.-Sls.--Small Tube Products Co., Inc., Altoona, PA, pg. 1010
Harrington, Paul, Dir.-Dealer Devel.--Bluewater, Mora, MN, pg. 161
Harris, Albert, V.P.-Mktg. & Sls.--Johnson & Towers, Inc., Mount Laurel, NJ, pg. 601
Harris, Gene, Mgr.-Sls.--The Alpha Corporation Of Tennessee, Collierville, TN, pg. 43
Harris, George, V.P.-Pipeline Sls.--Tape Coat Division, Evanston, IL, pg. 1072
Harris, James, Pres. & Chief Operating Officer--GFA Brands, Inc., Cresskill, NJ, pg. 440
Harris, Regina, Dir.-Intl. Sls.--Laramie Tire Distributors Inc., Norristown, PA, pg. 658
Harris, Richard L., V.P.-Sls.--American Baler Co., Bellevue, OH, pg. 102
Harrison, William P., Mgr.-Sls.--Charles Dunn Company-Realtors, Los Angeles, CA, pg. 353
Harrod, James, Principal-Sls. Training--Edward D. Jones & Co., Maryland Heights, MO, pg. 603
Hartan, Richard K., Mgr.-Sls., Mktg. & Adv.--E.W. Knauss & Son, Inc., Quakertown, PA, pg. 636
Hartenstein, A., Dir.-Sls.--Monarch Luggage Co. Inc., Brooklyn, NY, pg. 765
Hartge, Paul E., V.P.-Sls. & Mktg.--Wayne Corporation, Richmond, IN, pg. 1169
Harting, Tom, V.P.-Sls.--Mrs. Alison's Cookie Company, Saint Louis, MO, pg. 760
Hartman, Susan, V.P.-Sls.--Hess's Department Stores, Inc., Allentown, PA, pg. 302
Harvey, Larry Z., V.P.-Sls. & Mktg.--The Electron Corp., Littleton, CO, pg. 375
Harvey, Larry Z., V.P.-Sls. & Mktg.--Electron Corp., Blackwell, OK, pg. 375
Harward, Dennis, Mgr.-Western Reg. Sls.--L & R Communications, Limited, Sioux City, IA, pg. 647
Haselton, Fred, Sr. Sls. Admin.--Bolton-Emerson Machine Knife Div., Lawrence, MA, pg. 163
Hassell, Martin, V.P.-Sls.--Yenkin-Majestic Paint Corporation, Columbus, OH, pg. 1208
Haste, John, Dir.-Field Mktg.--Pro Hardware, Inc., Englewood, CO, pg. 891
Hatch, Greg, Dir. Mktg.-Trade Sls.--Fuller O'Brien Paints, South San Francisco, CA, pg. 820
Hauck, Chester, V.P.-Indus. Sls.--Yenkin-Majestic Paint Corporation, Columbus, OH, pg. 1208
Hauck, Dick, Mgr.-Sls., Ribbon Film--Phillips-Joanna, Inc., Ladd, IL, pg. 566
Haugom, Robert, V.P.-Sls.--The Hennegan Company, Cincinnati, OH, pg. 529
Haugsby, Gary, V.P.-Sls.--Wyandot Inc., Marion, OH, pg. 1205
Haukos, Carol, Dir.-Mktg. & Human Resources--First State Federal Savings & Loan, Hutchinson, MN, pg. 413
Haun, James, Mgr.-Sls.--Cal/Emblem Labels, Inc., Fresno, CA, pg. 208
Hauser, Lawrence P., V.P.-Sls. & Mktg.--Cavalier Corporation, Chattanooga, TN, pg. 229
Hausler, Robert J., V.P.-Sls. & Mktg.--Mark Lighting Fixture Co., Inc., Moonachie, NJ, pg. 708
Haver, Dale, V.P.-Sls. & Mktg.--Ajax Paving Industries Inc., Madison Heights, MI, pg. 28
Hawkin, Nancy, Mgr.-Special Events--The Florida Lottery, Tallahassee, FL, pg. 420
Hawkins, Arthur L., V.P.-Sls.--U.S. Rubber Reclaiming, Inc., Vicksburg, MS, pg. 306
Hawkins, Patti, Mgr.-Sls.--Computer Dynamics, Inc., Virginia Beach, VA, pg. 271
Hawkinson, Lynn, Mgr.-Sls. Promo.--Michigan Blueberry Growers Assn., Grand Junction, MI, pg. 747
Hawley, F.J., Mgr.-Export & Eastern Sls.--Sloan Valve Company, Franklin Park, IL, pg. 1010
Haws, Larry, Mgr.-Retail Sls.--Idaho Supreme Company, Firth, ID, pg. 561
Hawthorne, D.J., Dir.-Sls. Admin.--Danly-Komatsu L.P., Cicero, IL, pg. 275
Hay, Bill, V.P.-Sls.--Larson Manufacturing Company, Brookings, SD, pg. 659
Hayden, Greg, V.P.-Sls.--Transport Insurance Co., Dallas, TX, pg. 54
Hayes, Jerry W., Sr. V.P.-Opers. & Instituional Sls.--Marquette Bank Minneapolis, National Association, Minneapolis, MN, pg. 117
Hayes, Lucy, Sls. Mgr.--American Water Works Association, Denver, CO, pg. 65
Hayes, Rellen, Mgr.-Sls. & Opers.--Shade Computer Forms Co., Green Bay, WI, pg. 994
Hayman, Thomas, Natl. Sls. Mgr.--CRP Hose Division, Charlotte, NC, pg. 909

Haywood, Carolyn, Sls. Admin.--Wolfer Printing Company, City of Commerce, CA, pg. 1199
Hazinga, Ad, Sls. Mgr.-Automotive OE--Littelfuse, Inc., Des Plaines, IL, pg. 678
Headley, T., V.P.-Sls.--Midwesco Filter Resources, Winchester, VA, pg. 751
Healy, James, Gen. Sls. Mgr.--Application Automation, Inc., Wood Dale, IL, pg. 1047
Heaney, Joe, Pres. & Chief Oper. Officer--Cornnuts Inc., Alameda, CA, pg. 286
Hearn, Thomas, V.P.-Sls. U.S. Domestic--American Tool Companies, Inc., Lincoln, NE, pg. 64
Heastrup, Jed C., Mgr.-Zero Product Sls.--Clemco Industries Corp., Washington, MO, pg. 254
Heazlitt, Michael, V.P.-Sls. & Mktg.--Paoli, Inc., Paoli, IN, pg. 846
Hebner, Al, Dir.-Adv. & Natl. Sls.--Osmose Wood Preserving Co., Buffalo, NY, pg. 830
Heeringa, James P., Exec. V.P.-Sls.--Trendway Corporation, Holland, MI, pg. 1109
Heerlyn, Henry, Mgr.-Sls.--Atlantic Dairy Cooperative, Southampton, PA, pg. 94
Hefley, Jim, Mgr.-Circulation--The Ardmore Daily Ardmoreite, Ardmore, OK, pg. 1042
Heilig, Michael, Dir.-Sls. & Mktg.--Flakt Inc., Bahnson Div., Winston-Salem, NC, pg. 416
Heineman, Brett D., Sec. & Mgr.-East Reg. Sls.--Conway Import Co. Inc., Elmsford, NY, pg. 281
Heinrich, Joe, V.P.-Sls.--Walworth Company, Houston, TX, pg. 1162
Heinrich, Thomas P., Mgr.-Sls.--Apex Broach & Machine Co., Detroit, MI, pg. 77
Heitzman, Michael, V.P.-Sls.--Russell Stadelman & Company, Germantown, TN, pg. 1034
Helgason, Harvey, V.P.-Sls.--Service Supply Co. Inc. of Indiana, Indianapolis, IN, pg. 992
Helland, Bruce, Mgr.-Mktg. & Sls., Garden Div.--Specialty Manufacturing Company, St. Paul, MN, pg. 1027
Hellender, Mark, V.P.-Sls. & Mktg.--Kaiser Foundation Health & Hospitals Group, Oakland, CA, pg. 614
Helweg, Brian, Mgr.-Wire Prod. Sls.--Kaspar Wire Works, Inc., Shiner, TX, pg. 617
Hemker, Harold, Mgr.-Sls.-Electric--W.A. Roosevelt Co., La Crosse, WI, pg. 946
Hemmings, Wm. M., V.P.-Sls. & Mktg. & Corp. Sec.--Enger-Kress Company, West Bend, WI, pg. 381
Henderson, C.H., V.P.-Sls.-East--Centrifugal & Mechanical Industries, Saint Louis, MO, pg. 609
Henderson, James, Dir.-Sls. & Mktg.--Fasfax Corporation, Nashua, NH, pg. 579
Henderson, Merrel, V.P.-Sls.--Somerset Refinery Inc., Somerset, KY, pg. 1017
Henderson, william, V.P.-Home Furnishing--Trimtex Co. Inc., Williamsport, PA, pg. 1113
Hendren, George, Mgr.-Sls.--Harmony Engineering Corporation, Minneapolis, MN, pg. 510
Hendricks, Gerald, V.P.-Sls.--Fargo Glass & Paint Company, Fargo, ND, pg. 399
Hendricks, Jerry P., V.P.-Sls.--Weldon, Williams & Lick, Inc., Fort Smith, AR, pg. 1175
Heneghan, Frank M., V.P.-Sls. & Mktg.--McArdle Printing Co., Inc., Upper Marlboro, MD, pg. 189
Heniff, Dave, Mgr.-Retail Sls.--Agripac Inc., Salem, OR, pg. 25
Henke, Gary, Natl. Sls. Mgr.--Foulds Inc., Libertyville, IL, pg. 427
Henkel, Greg, Mgr.-Sls.--Oregon State Lottery, Salem, OR, pg. 829
Henley, Ken, Reg. Sls. Mgr.-Gulf Coast--U.S. Enertek, Inc., Farmington, NM, pg. 1135
Hennessey, R.J., V.P.-Sls. & Mktg.--Kentile Floors Inc., South Plainfield, NJ, pg. 623
Henning, William W., Sr. V.P.-Sls.--Toter Incorporated, Statesville, NC, pg. 1103
Henningsen, Christopher K., V.P.-Sls.--Henningsen Foods, Inc., White Plains, NY, pg. 629
Hennington, Rolf, V.P.-Sls. & Mktg.--Industrial Coatings Group, Inc., Chicago, IL, pg. 566
Henry, David C., V.P.-Customer Service & Logistics Mngmt.--S. C. Johnson & Son, Inc., Racine, WI, pg. 599
Henry, J.C., III, Exec. V.P.-Sls. & Mktg.--E.P. Henry Corporation, Woodbury, NJ, pg. 530
Henry, Phil, Reg. Sls. Mgr.--Stonco, Union, NJ, pg. 1050
Henry, Steven, V.P.-Sls.--Alan Lithograph, Inc., Inglewood, CA, pg. 30
Hentges, Roger, V.P.-Sls.--Mid America Steel, Inc., Fargo, ND, pg. 750
Heraty, Daniel P., V.P.-Travelift Sls.--MI-Jack Products, Inc., Hazel Crest, IL, pg. 746
Hermann, Jesse, V.P.-Sls. & Mktg.--General Automotive Specialty Co., Inc., North Brunswick, NJ, pg. 449
Hermes, Pete, V.P.-Sls.--Duraflame, Inc., Stockton, CA, pg. 209
Hermonson, C.E., V.P.-Sls.--Biddulph Oldsmobile, Glendale, AZ, pg. 149
Hern, Walter, V.P.-Sls.--Alfred Nickles Bakery, Inc., Navarre, OH, pg. 806
Heroes, Daniel, Sales Mgr.--N.V. Maxon International S.A., Vilvoorde,, Belgium, pg. 723
Herrmann, John, V.P.-Sls. & Mktg.--O. A. Newton & Son Co., Bridgeville, DE, pg. 805
Herrmann, Ken, V.P.-Sls.--Blue Coral, Inc., Cleveland, OH, pg. 159
Hershman, Robert, Mgr. Sls.--American Library Association, Chicago, IL, pg. 57
Hershner, A., Dir.-Sls.--Shure Brothers Incorporated, Evanston, IL, pg. 1001
Herzog, John, V.P.-Sls.--Remmele Engineering, Inc., Saint Paul, MN, pg. 926
Hess, James T., V.P.-Sls.--Williams Steel & Hardware Company, Minneapolis, MN, pg. 1191
Hess, Phil, Dir.-Ticket Sls.--Sacramento Kings, Sacramento, CA, pg. 965
Hess, Williamrald A., Sr. V.P.-Mktg. & Sls.--Farmers and Traders Life Insurance Co., Syracuse, NY, pg. 401
Hester, Mark A., 2nd V.P. & Dir.-Sls. Service--Western & Southern Life Insurance Co., Cincinnati, OH, pg. 1181
Hewgley, William M., Jr., V.P.-Sls. & Mktg.--American Manufacturing Co. (TN), Chattanooga, TN, pg. 58
Heyne, William, V.P. & Gen. Sls. Mgr.-Central Area--Steelcase Inc., Grand Rapids, MI, pg. 1044
Hickey, William III, V.P.-Mktg. & Sls.--H.M. Smyth Co., Saint Paul, MN, pg. 1014
Hicks, Frank, Mgr.-Sls.--Dettra Flag Company, Oaks, PA, pg. 333
Higgins, George, V.P.-Sls.--McCain Manufacturing Corp., Chicago, IL, pg. 726
Higgins, Walter R., V.P.-Mktg. & Sls.--Delta Sugar Corporation, Clarksburg, CA, pg. 327
Highberg, Peter, V.P.-Sls. & Mktg.--Black Box Corporation, Lawrence, PA, pg. 748
Highberger, Steve K., Dir.-Sls.--SOR Inc., Lenexa, KS, pg. 963
Higuera, Gilbert, V.P.-Whlse. Sls.--Maui Divers Of Hawaii, Ltd., Honolulu, HI, pg. 721
Hildebrand, James, V.P.-Sls. & Mktg.--GF Office Furniture Ltd., Gallatin, TN, pg. 439
Hildebrand, James, V.P.-Sls. & Mktg.--GF Office Furniture, Youngstown, OH, pg. 439
Hildebrandt, David, V.P.-Intl. Sls.--Starcraft Automotive Corp., Goshen, IN, pg. 1040
Hilker, Harold, Dir.-Industrial Sls.--Sun-Maid Growers of California, Kingsburg, CA, pg. 1058
Hill, Dan, Sls.-Service Mgr.--Arcata Graphics Fairfield Inc., Fairfield, PA, pg. 80
Hill, David W., Mgr.-Sls.--Production Machinery Corporation, Mentor, OH, pg. 893
Hill, Edward D., Partner & Dir.-Sls. & Mktg.--J. C. Bradford & Co., Nashville, TN, pg. 170
Hill, Howard, Mgr.-Sls.--National Welders Supply Co. Inc., Charlotte, NC, pg. 794
Hill, Larry D., V.P.-Canned Sls.--Icicle Seafoods, Inc., Seattle, WA, pg. 561
Hill, Timothy L., Dir.-Consumer Mktg. & Sls.--Gates Energy Products, Inc., Alachua, FL, pg. 445
Hillman, Charles F., V.P.-Sls.--Berryman Products, Inc., Arlington, TX, pg. 144
Hillman, Douglas C., Exec. V.P.-Mktg. & Sls.--Londontown Corporation, Eldersburg, MD, pg. 682
Hilmoe, Karen, V.P.-Intl. Sls. & Mktg.--Code-A-Phone Corp., Clackamas, OR, pg. 258
Hilt, Jack R., Mgr.-Sls.--Fastcut Tool Corporation, Troy, MI, pg. 183
Hilton, D. Andy, Sr. V.P.-Sls. & Mktg.--Tropical Garment Manufacturing Company, Tampa, FL, pg. 1116
Hinch, Ron, Mgr.-Natl. Sls.--Abbyland Foods, Inc., Abbotsford, WI, pg. 10
Hindenburg, Marion, Sr. V.P.-Sls.--Gould Paper Corporation, New York, NY, pg. 473
Hinkle, Jane K., V.P.-Sls. & Mktg.--Octagon Process Inc., Edgewater, NJ, pg. 821
Hinner, John, Dir.-Sls. & Mktg.--Master Molded Products Corporation, Elgin, IL, pg. 720
Hinshaw, Dan, V.P.-Mktg. & Sls.--The Levolor Corporation, Sunnyvale, CA, pg. 671
Hinshe, Sue, Gen. Sls. Mgr.--Golden West Broadcasters, Los Angeles, CA, pg. 467
Hintermeister, Howard, Mgr.-Export Sls.--Electrical Insulation Suppliers, Hillside, IL, pg. 374
Hinton, Hollis, Exec. V.P.-Sls.--Union Underwear Co., Inc., Bowling Green, KY, pg. 400
Hinton, Hollis, Exec. V.P.-Sls.--Fruit of the Loom, Bowling Green, KY, pg. 400
Hipwell, Roger, Sr. V.P.-Sls. & Mktg.--Bay State Milling Co., Quincy, MA, pg. 127
Hiramoto, Steve, Sls. Mgr.--KHON-TV, Honolulu, HI, pg. 194
Hiraoka, Tony, Dir.-Parking Sls.-Amano Brand--Amano Cincinnati, Inc., Cincinnati, OH, pg. 46
Hird, Charles E., V.P.-Sls. & Mktg.--Bostrom Seating, Inc., Piedmont, AL, pg. 168
Hirsch, Julius, V.P.-Sls.--Power-One, Inc., Camarillo, CA, pg. 883
Hirsch, Robert, V.P.-Sls.--Vengroff Williams & Associates, Inc., Centerpoint, NY, pg. 1147
Hirsh, Joe, Sr. V.P. & Dir.-Sls.--NDC Distributors, Inc., Los Angeles, CA, pg. 787
Hitchcock, Roger A., Natl. Sls. Mgr.--Barcolene Penn Champ, East Butler, PA, pg. 153
Hiznay, Paul, Sr. V.P.-Sls. & Mdsg.--Mona Industries, Inc., Paterson, NJ, pg. 764
Hoak, Scott, Mgr.-Sls.--Gee Cee Cap Company, Grant City, MO, pg. 1148
Hobscheid, Fred J., Sls. Mgr.-Natl. Food Service--Lindsay International, Lindsay, CA, pg. 676
Hodges, Martina J., V.P.-Sls.--Thiele Kaolin Co., Sandersville, GA, pg. 1092
Hoff, Richard K., V.P.-Sls.--Broughton Foods Company, Marietta, OH, pg. 180
Hoffer, William, V.P.-Sls.--Hoffer Plastics Corporation, South Elgin, IL, pg. 537
Hoffman, Bob, V.P.-Sls.--Taylor Corporation, Mankato, MN, pg. 1081
Hoffman, Gary, V.P.-Sls.--Carlisle Equipment Company, Wilder, KY, pg. 220
Hoffman, Joe, Dir.-Sls.--Hale-Halsell Company, Tulsa, OK, pg. 500
Hoffman, Phyllis, V.P.-Sls. & Mktg.--Summa Four, Inc., Manchester, NH, pg. 1057
Hofmann, John, V.P.-Sls. & Mktg.--Pride Products, Inc., Elizabeth, NJ, pg. 889
Hogan, Gerald, V.P.-Consumer Appliance Sls.--Conair Corporation, Stamford, CT, pg. 272
Hogan, Jack, Reg. Sls. Mgr.--Micro-Aire Surgical Instruments, Inc., Valencia, CA, pg. 711
Hogan, Mary, Western Div. Affiliate Sls. Dir.--The Weather Channel, Inc.-Los Angeles Sales Office, Los Angeles, CA, pg. 654
Hoggard, Bret, Loan Officer--Wieland Financial Services, Inc., Atlanta, GA, pg. 1188
Hoisington, Donald W., V.P.-Intl. & Govt. Sls.--Hercules Engines, Inc., Canton, OH, pg. 531
Holbrook, Russ, Sr. V.P.-Sls.--Pillowtex Corporation, Dallas, TX, pg. 870
Holcomb, John T., 1st V.P.-Sls.--Berlin Steel Construction Co., Berlin, CT, pg. 142
Holcombe, Hubert, Jr., Exec. V.P.-Sls. & Chief Oper. Officer--Arrowhead Mills, Inc., Hereford, TX, pg. 86
Holder, Thomas M., V.P.-Sls.--Hershey Creamery Company, Harrisburg, PA, pg. 531
Holenbaugh, Robert, V.P.-Sls.--John W. Brooks Inc., Nelsonville, OH, pg. 180
Holland, William, V.P.-Sls.--AEI Holding Co., Inc., Fullerton, CA, pg. 3
Holland, William, V.P.-Sls.--American Electronics, Inc., Fullerton, CA, pg. 3
Hollander, Fritz, Dir.-Intl. Sls.--A. J. Hollander Co., Inc., New York, NY, pg. 539
Hollister, Howard, V.P.-Food Services Sls. & Mktg.--Awrey Bakeries, Inc., Livonia, MI, pg. 103
Holm, Reagan, Dir.-Sls. & Mktg.--ATAPCO Office Products Group, Saint Louis, MO, pg. 64
Holman, W.H., III, Sr. V.P.-Mktg.--Jitney-Jungle Stores of America, Inc., Jackson, MS, pg. 594
Holmes, Forest, Mgr.-Mktg. & Sls., Valves Div.--Specialty Manufacturing Company, St. Paul, MN, pg. 1027
Holmes, Harry, Mgr.-Sls.--The Vernon Company, Newton, IA, pg. 1148
Holmes, Norman, V.P.-Sls.--Service America Corporation, Stamford, CT, pg. 992
Holmes, Ronald P., V.P.-Sls.--Weston Paper & Manufacturing Co., Terre Haute, IN, pg. 1183
Holmes, Victoria, Mgr.-Intl. Sls.--Diagraph Corporation, Earth City, MO, pg. 335
Holodnak, John, Mgr.-Sls., Church Candles--A.I. Root Company, Medina, OH, pg. 946
Holsinger, J.F., V.P.-Sls. & Mktg.--The Hubinger Company, Keokuk, IA, pg. 550
Holzberg, Joel M., V.P.-Mktg. & Sls.--Unifoil Corporation, Passaic, NJ, pg. 1126
Hood, Dave, V.P.-Sls.--Diamond Hill Plywood Company, Darlington, SC, pg. 316
Hood, Richard, Mgr.-Natl. Sls.--Case-Swayne Co. Inc., Santa Ana, CA, pg. 228
Hoogerwerf, Richard, V.P.-Corp. Sls.--Alro Group, Jackson, MI, pg. 44
Hooker, Robert, Exec. V.P.-Sls.--Purity, Inc., Miami, FL, pg. 901
Hooper, Robert W., Sr. V.P.-Sls.--Ploof Truck Lines, Inc., Jacksonville, FL, pg. 877
Hoopes, James L., V.P.-Sls. & Pub. Rels.--Dayton Rogers Mfg. Co., Minneapolis, MN, pg. 321
Hoopingarner, Dana, Dir.-Branch Sls.--Sun Computers, Inc., Carson, CA, pg. 1058
Hoover, Robert, V.P.-Mktg. & Sls.--Iowa Industrial Hydraulics, Inc., Pocahontas, IA, pg. 559
Hoover, T.J., V.P.-Sls.--Wilkinson Company, Inc., Stow, OH, pg. 373
Hopkinson, Edwin, V.P.-Pipe Sls.--Wheatland Tube Company, Collingswood, NJ, pg. 1184
Hoppe, Ben, Mgr.-Sls.--FWD Corporation, Clintonville, WI, pg. 395
Hoppe, Ben, Mgr.-Sls.--Seagrave Fire Apparatus, Inc., Clintonville, WI, pg. 395
Hopper, Doug, Gen. Sls. Mgr.--Benjamin Metals Company, Gardena, CA, pg. 139
Horn, Carl J., Sr. V.P.-Sls.--Lykes Bros. Steamship Co., Inc., New Orleans, LA, pg. 688
Horne, Walter, Dir.-Sls. Admin.--Empire Brushes, Inc., Greenville, NC, pg. 379
Horner, John, V.P.-Sls.--Hoover Group, Inc., Alpharetta, GA, pg. 543
Hornik, P., V.P.-Natl. Sls.--F.G. Montabert, Midland Park, NJ, pg. 766
Hotchkin, W.F., Dir.-Mktg. & Sls.--Stamco Industries Inc., Euclid, OH, pg. 1035
Hougland, J.M., Pres. & Chief Oper. Officer--F. R. Manufacturing Corporation, Stockton, CA, pg. 395
Howard, Jim, V.P.-Sls.--Howard Manufacturing, Kent, WA, pg. 547
Howard, Thomas J., Exec. V.P.-Specialty Sls.--Young Pecan Shelling Co., Inc., Florence, SC, pg. 1209
Howe, Tommy, V.P.-Sls.--FM Industries, Inc., Fort Worth, TX, pg. 394
Howell, Robert, V.P.-Sls. & Mktg.--Wollin Products, Inc., Stevensville, MI, pg. 1199
Howell, Steve, Mgr.-Sls.--Hankins Lumber Company, Inc., Grenada, MS, pg. 505
Howle, Dwayne, Reg. Sls. Mgr.-Mid Continent--U.S. Enertek, Inc., Farmington, NM, pg. 1135
Hoyt, Richard H., V.P.-Sls. & Service--Gates, McDonald & Co., Columbus, OH, pg. 795
Hrabe, Duke, Natl. Sls. Mgr.-H/P Div.--Farnam Companies, Inc., Phoenix, AZ, pg. 403
Hrabina, Michael, V.P.-Sls. & Mktg.--Accu-Sort Systems, Inc., Telford, PA, pg. 11
Hrach, D., V.P.-Sls.--Anchor Tool & Die Company, Cleveland, OH, pg. 71
Hubbard, Gary, V.P.-Sls. & Mktg.--PacifiCare of Oregon, Inc., Lake Oswego, OR, pg. 1127
Hubbard, Theodore, Sr. V.P.-Sls.--Whittaker, Clark & Daniels, Inc., South Plainfield, NJ, pg. 1187
Huber, Phred, V.P.-Sls.--Edgar B. Furniture Co., Clemmons, NC, pg. 368
Hudson, Randy J., V.P.-Sls. & Mktg.--Transus Inc., Atlanta, GA, pg. 1108
Huesca, Rene, V.P.-Construction Sls.--Robbins Manufacturing Company, Tampa, FL, pg. 938
Huff, Joe, International Sls. Mgr.--Diehl Specialties Intl., Defiance, OH, pg. 336
Huffines, Lawrence, V.P.-Mktg. & Sls.--Pickering Industries Inc., Tacoma, WA, pg. 869

Huffman, Royce, Mgr.-Mktg. Communications--Cerro Copper Products Co., Sauget, IL, pg. 711
Hughes, Allen, Dir.-Sls.--Superior Auctioneers & Marketing, Inc., San Antonio, TX, pg. 1063
Hughes, Bill, Sls. & Mktg. Mgr.--La Belle Industries, Inc., Oconomowoc, WI, pg. 648
Hughes, H.D., Chm. Bd., Pres., Chief Exec. Officer & Sls. Dir.--Diversified Group, Inc., Harahan, LA, pg. 340
Hughes, James J., V.P.-Sls. & Mktg.--Morse Shoe Leased Div., Canton, MA, pg. 772
Hughes, Jim, V.P.-Sls. & Mktg.--Star Container, Inc., Phoenix, AZ, pg. 1082
Hughes, John S., Jr., V.P.-Sls.--Bissell Inc., Grand Rapids, MI, pg. 153
Hughey, Julie, Mgr.-Distributor Sls.--Forms Corporation Of America, Spring Grove, IL, pg. 1187
Hull, Randy L., V.P.-Sls. & Mktg. Admin.--G. Heileman Brewing Co., Inc., La Crosse, WI, pg. 526
Humphrey, Lorraine, V.P.-Sls. & Mktg.--Hollytex Carpet Mills, Inc., Ontario, CA, pg. 540
Humphrey, Robert P., V.P.-Mktg. & Sls.--Humphrey Products Company, Kalamazoo, MI, pg. 553
Hundsdorfer, Rainer, V.P.-Mktg. & Sls.--Trumpf Inc., Farmington, CT, pg. 1118
Hundt, Paul, Mgr.-Sls.-Refrigeration & Mktg. Coord.--W.A. Roosevelt Co., La Crosse, WI, pg. 946
Huneke, Howard, V.P.-Sls.--American SelfCare Corporation, Columbus, GA, pg. 60
Huneke, Howard, Sls. Dir.--American Health & Security Insurance Co., Inc., Columbus, GA, pg. 61
Hunter, Jim, Sls. Coord.--The Thompson Group Companies, Henderson, KY, pg. 1094
Hunters, Cathleen, Coord.-Sls. & Mktg.--The Vagabond Inns, San Diego, CA, pg. 1142
Huntington, Tom, V.P.-Sls.--The Climatic Corp., Columbia, SC, pg. 255
Hupp, Michael G., V.P.-Mktg. & Sls.--Warner Press, Inc., Anderson, IN, pg. 1164
Hupp, William T., V.P.-Sls.--Estes Express Lines, Inc., Richmond, VA, pg. 389
Hurley, Jack, Pres. & Chief Exec. Officer--Centrifugal & Mechanical Industries, Saint Louis, MO, pg. 609
Hurley, Kenneth B., V.P.-Mktg. & Sls.--Kaye Instruments, Inc., Bedford, MA, pg. 619
Hurst, Charles W., V.P.-Sls. & Mktg.--Lay Packing Company Inc., Knoxville, TN, pg. 663
Hurt, Calvin, V.P.-Sls.--American Frozen Foods, Inc., Stratford, CT, pg. 55
Hurtibuse, Al, Mgr.-Sls.--Northern Michigan Veneers, Inc., Gladstone, MI, pg. 814
Husak, Ted, V.P.-Sls.--Cloud Corporation, Des Plaines, IL, pg. 256
Huser, Larry, V.P.-Sls. & Mktg.--Mayville Metal Products Division, Mayville, WI, pg. 275
Husinger, Rich, Dir.-Sls.--WinCup, Phoenix, AZ, pg. 1195
Huskins, Harold L., Mgr.-Sls.--Marion Machine Company Division, Marion, NC, pg. 1064
Husko, Charles E., Mgr.-Indus. Div.--Bel-Ray Company, Inc., Farmingdale, NJ, pg. 133
Hussey, Elizabeth, Dir.-Retail Adv.--CRK Advertising, New York, NY, pg. 203
Huston, C., V.P.-Mktg. & Sls.--Dixson, Inc., Grand Junction, CO, pg. 341
Huth, J.F., Jr., Dir.-Sls.--Spang & Company, Butler, PA, pg. 1025
Hyde, Charles R., Sr., Mgr.-Sls.--Swayne Robinson & Company, Richmond, IN, pg. 939
Hyle, Dave, V.P.-Sls.--Jack Schwartz Shoes, Inc., New York, NY, pg. 980
Hynes, Mike, Natl. Sls. Mgr.--Samtec Inc., New Albany, IN, pg. 968
Iannuzzi, V., Natl. Sls. Mgr.--Manning & Lewis Engineering Co., Union, NJ, pg. 704
Igo, Mike, Mgr.-Circulation--Glenwood Post, Glenwood Springs, CO, pg. 1042
Ilaria, Peter E., Dir.-Mktg. & Sls.--Tropar Mfg. Co., Inc., Florham Park, NJ, pg. 1115
Illg, Karl, Sls. Engr.--Apex Corporation, Indianapolis, IN, pg. 78
Imus, Russ, V.P.-Sls.--Efficient Engineering Co., Troy, MI, pg. 371
Indyk, William, V.P.-Sls.--White Rock Products Corp., White Stone, NY, pg. 1186
Ingmanson, Lance, Dir.-Sls. & Mktg.--Malibu Grand Prix Corporation, Canoga Park, CA, pg. 702
Ingram, O.H., II, Asst. V.P.-Liquid Sls. & Customer Service--Ingram Barge Company, Nashville, TN, pg. 569
Ingram, Robert, V.P.-Sls.--Covington Industries, Atlanta, GA, pg. 290
Ingram, Robert F., V.P.-Sls. & Mktg.--Game Winner, Inc., Atlanta, GA, pg. 290
Inzillo, Lou, V.P.-Sls.--Aster Nut Products Inc., Newark, NJ, pg. 92
Ippolito, Gary, V.P.-Natl. Sls.--E & J Gallo Winery, Modesto, CA, pg. 441
Irwin, Rick, Sr. V.P. Sls. & Gen. Mgr. Publication Papers Div.--Gould Paper Corporation, New York, NY, pg. 473
Isaac, Gregory, V.P.-Sls.--Corcoran Mfg. Co., Inc., Anaheim, CA, pg. 285
Isham, Lance, Sr. V.P.-Sls.--Polo/Ralph Lauren Corporation, New York, NY, pg. 879
Isham, Noel H., Mgr.-Nat'l Sls.-Deco Products--O'Brien Powder Products, Inc., Houston, TX, pg. 820
Israel, John, V.P.-Mktg. & Sls. Support--Safeguard Business Systems, Inc., Fort Washington, PA, pg. 966
Ivey, Roxanne M., V.P.-Metropolitan Sls.--Blue Cross & Blue Shield of Illinois, Chicago, IL, pg. 160
Iwasyszyn, Ted, V.P.-Sls.-West--Centrifugal & Mechanical Industries, Saint Louis, MO, pg. 609
Jacino, John, 1st V.P.-Sls. & Mktg.--Wetsel-Oviatt Lumber Company, Folsom, CA, pg. 1183
Jackino, Dan, Sr. V.P.-Sls.--Gould Paper Corporation, New York, NY, pg. 473
Jackman, Neil W., V.P.-Sls. & Human Resources--Pease Industries, Inc., Fairfield, OH, pg. 854
Jacobi, C.M., V.P.-Sls. & Mktg.-World Wide--Timex Corporation, Middlebury, CT, pg. 1098
Jacobs, April, V.P.-Sls. & Mktg.--Mueller Sports Medicine, Inc., Prairie du Sac, WI, pg. 774
Jacobs, Daniel F., Dir.-Sls. & Mktg.--Albert C. Martin & Associates, Los Angeles, CA, pg. 714
Jacobs, Norman, Mgr.-Natl. Sls.--Eastern Canvas Products, Inc., Ward Hill, MA, pg. 363
Jacobs, Sol, Mgr.-Natl. Sls.--I. Spiewak & Sons, Inc., New York, NY, pg. 1031
Jacobs, Susan, Natl. Dir.-Travel Industry Sls.--The Fairmont Hotels, San Francisco, CA, pg. 397
Jacobson, Jack C., Sr. V.P.-Sls.--LePage's, Inc., Pittsburgh, PA, pg. 287
Jaeger, Jim, Mgr.-Sls.--Kluener Packing Company, Cincinnati, OH, pg. 636
Jaffe, Bob, Natl. Sls. Mgr., Missy Zena II--Zena Jeans, New York, NY, pg. 1217
Jakab, Joseph J., Gen. Sls. Mgr.--Moore Special Tool Co., Inc., Bridgeport, CT, pg. 768
James, Beau, V.P.-Sls.--Alexander Doll Co., Inc., New York, NY, pg. 33
James, Jack, V.P.-Sls.--American Bread Company - Sunbeam Bakery, Nashville, TN, pg. 49
James, John E., V.P.-Mktg. & Sls.--Doehler-Jarvis, Toledo, OH, pg. 559
Janes, Robert, V.P.-Sls.--Collman Graphics, Inc., Baltimore, MD, pg. 263
Janik, Leon L., V.P.-Sls.--New England Tap Corporation (NETCO), Foxboro, MA, pg. 183
Janowski, James F., Mgr.-Natl. Sls.--Thetford Corporation, Ann Arbor, MI, pg. 357
Jansen, Jim, Dir.-Adv.--Farm Fresh, Inc., Norfolk, VA, pg. 401
Jarus, Jim, V.P.-Food Service Sls.--King & Prince Seafood Corporation, Brunswick, GA, pg. 631
Jasken, R.J., Mgr.-Sls.--Spring Engineers, Inc., Houston, TX, pg. 1033
Jaye, Edward, V.P.-Mktg. & Sls.--Elkay Products, Inc., Shrewsbury, MA, pg. 377
Jefferis, Larry, V.P.-Sls.--Schulze & Burch Biscuit Company, Chicago, IL, pg. 979
Jeffrey, Richard, V.P.-Sls.-Parkersburg--State Electric Supply Co., Huntington, WV, pg. 1040
Jenkins, James L., Exec. V.P.-Retail Sls. & Mktg.--Curtis Mathes Corporation, Athens, TX, pg. 720
Jenkins, John M., V.P.-Sls.--Imperial Schrade Corp., New York, NY, pg. 564
Jensen, Chris, Mgr.-Sls. & Mktg.--Jensen Electric Company, Reno, NV, pg. 592
Jensen, Linda, V.P.-Sls.--M. H. Greenebaum, Inc., Parsippany, NJ, pg. 485
Jensen, Robert, Mgr.-Sls.--Sioux Steel Company, Sioux Falls, SD, pg. 1008
Jeoffroy, Jim R., V.P.-Sls.--Esco Elevators, Inc., Fort Worth, TX, pg. 388
Jerrigan, Al, V.P.-Sls.--Curtis-Toledo, Inc., Saint Louis, MO, pg. 306
Jeschelnig, Richard J., V.P.-Sls. & Engrng.--PMC Industries Inc., Wickliffe, OH, pg. 836
Jesinoski, Marvin, Mgr.-Sls.--Northwestern Drug Company, Minneapolis, MN, pg. 343
Jessop, R., Natl. Sls. Mgr.-Family Products Div.--Playtex Apparel Canada, Ltd., Malton,, Canada, pg. 876
Jesukaitis, Tom, Mgr.-Gen. Sls.--Cross Motors Corp., Louisville, KY, pg. 300
Jeter, Kevin, Exec. V.P.-Sls. & Mktg.--Days Inns of America, Inc., Atlanta, GA, pg. 1100
Jinks, Gary, Natl. Dir.-Sls. Devel.--Mary Kay Cosmetics Inc., Dallas, TX, pg. 716
John D. Hedges, Dir.-Mktg. & Sls.--Hoffco, Inc., Richmond, IN, pg. 537
John, Frank E. III, V.P.-Sls.--United Gilsonite Laboratories, Scranton, PA, pg. 1132
John, Stephen, Mgr.-Gen. Sls.--Magnolia Hi-Fi, Inc., Seattle, WA, pg. 701
Johnson, Bruce, Dir.-Sls., Western Region--Digital Pathways Inc., Mountain View, CA, pg. 337
Johnson, Carla, Circulation Dir.--Architectural Digest, Los Angeles, CA, pg. 636
Johnson, Chuck, V.P.-Sls.--Spirit Cruises, Norfolk, VA, pg. 1031
Johnson, Cliff, V.P.-Sls.--Tyndale House Publishers, Inc., Carol Stream, IL, pg. 1122
Johnson, Dave, V.P.-Sls. & Mktg.--Del Mar Avionics, Irvine, CA, pg. 325
Johnson, Dave, V.P.-Sls.--Kampgrounds of America, Inc., Billings, MT, pg. 613
Johnson, David, Exec. V.P.-Sls.--SLM, Inc., Gloversville, NY, pg. 963
Johnson, Dick, V.P.-Sls.--Cargill Seed Div., Minneapolis, MN, pg. 219
Johnson, Don, Mgr.-Sls. & Mktg.--Juno Tool & Plastic Corporation, Minnetonka, MN, pg. 299
Johnson, Donald D., Mgr.-Natl. Sls.--Eco Water Systems, Saint Paul, MN, pg. 367
Johnson, Eric, V.P.-Sls.--John Boos & Company, Effingham, IL, pg. 165
Johnson, J.B., Dir.-sls.--Birdsong Peanuts, Suffolk, VA, pg. 153
Johnson, James L., V.P.-Sls.--Martin Sprocket & Gear, Inc., Arlington, TX, pg. 715
Johnson, Jane L., Mgr.-Sls. Promo.--Marine World Africa USA, Vallejo, CA, pg. 707
Johnson, Jim, Mgr.-Circulation--Lake Wales Daily Highlander, Lake Wales, FL, pg. 1042
Johnson, Jim, Mgr.-Circulation--Winter Haven News Chief, Winter Haven, FL, pg. 1042
Johnson, Jim, Mgr.-Circulation--Auburndale Star, Auburndale, FL, pg. 1042
Johnson, Jim, Mgr.-Circulation--Haines City Herald & Ridge Shopper, Haines City, FL, pg. 1042
Johnson, Jim, Mgr.-Circulation--Shopper Publishing Group, Lakeland, FL, pg. 1042
Johnson, Jim, V.P.-Sls. & Mktg.--Midwest Mutual Insurance Co., West Des Moines, IA, pg. 886
Johnson, Keith A., Mgr.-Natl. Sls.--Clear Shield National, Inc., Wheeling, IL, pg. 383
Johnson, Larry, V.P.-Sls.--Grindmaster Corporation, Louisville, KY, pg. 488
Johnson, Lee K., Sr. V.P.-Engrng., Mktg. & Sls.--Thrall Car Mfg. Co., Chicago Heights, IL, pg. 350
Johnson, Michelle, Sls. Communication Specialist--MSI Insurance Companies, Arden Hills, MN, pg. 693
Johnson, Mike, V.P.-Sls.--Continental Machines, Inc., Savage, MN, pg. 279
Johnson, N.R., V.P.-Mktg. & Sls.--Kettering Advertising Display Co., Englewood Cliffs, NJ, pg. 626
Johnson, Rob, V.P.-Sls. & Mktg.--Sunbeam Outdoor Products Co., Neosho, MO, pg. 1059
Johnson, Wayne, Dir.-Sls.--Rockford Products Corp., Rockford, IL, pg. 941
Johnston, Jeffrey D., V.P.-Intl. Sls. & Mktg.--The Jewett Refrigerator Co., Inc., Buffalo, NY, pg. 957
Joles, Everett, V.P.-Sls. & Mktg.--Perry & Derrick Co., Cincinnati, OH, pg. 863
Jollie, Mark, Gen. Sls. Mgr.--WLUK-TV, Green Bay, WI, pg. 194
Jonap, Scott T., V.P.-Sls. & Mktg., Consumer Prods. Div.--Foley-PLP Company, Rochester, NY, pg. 422
Jones, Bob, Reg. Sls. Mgr.-Rocky Mt. North--U.S. Enertek, Inc., Farmington, NM, pg. 1135
Jones, Debra B., Sr. V.P.-Mktg.--Buxton Company, Chicopee, MA, pg. 197
Jones, J.B., V.P.-Sls. & Mktg.--Coldwater Seafood Corporation, Rowayton, CT, pg. 260
Jones, James, Sr. V.P.-Sls. & Mktg.--Mersman Furniture, Celina, OH, pg. 741
Jones, Jim, Dir.-Sls. Devel.--Hyatt Hotels Corporation, Chicago, IL, pg. 495
Jones, John H., Exec. V.P.-Sls.--Webcraft Technologies, Inc., North Brunswick, NJ, pg. 1171
Jones, Philip B., V.P.-Tube Core Opers.--Yorktowne Paper Mills, Inc., York, PA, pg. 1208
Jones, Richard, Dir.-Sls.--Edgewood Tool & Manufacturing Company, Romulus, MI, pg. 368
Jones, T. Roy, V.P.-Sls.--American Uniform Co., Cleveland, TN, pg. 1045
Jones, W., V.P.-Sls.--Acker Drill Co. Inc., Chinchilla, PA, pg. 12
Jordan, Nick, V.P.-Sls.--CPS Corporation, Franklin, TN, pg. 428
Jordan, Robert, V.P.-Sls.--I.C. System, Inc., Vadnais Heights, MN, pg. 558
Jorgensen, Rickey, Mgr.-Sls./New Cars--McNamara Pontiac Inc., Orlando, FL, pg. 732
Jorstad, Roy, V.P.-Sls.--The Butcher Co., Marlborough, MA, pg. 196
Joseph, Justin, Mgr.-Sls.--Uppco, Inc., Chicago, IL, pg. 1139
Jostedt, Dan, Mgr.-Sls.--Jandy Industries, Novato, CA, pg. 589
Jovanovski, Jovan, Dir.-Sls. & Intl. Mktg.--The Stroh Brewery Company, Detroit, MI, pg. 1053
Joyce, Kevin E., V.P.-Sls.--Naylor Pipe Company, Chicago, IL, pg. 796
Joyce, Tony, Mgr.-Sls.--K & R Delivery, Inc., Hinsdale, IL, pg. 610
Juchem, Robert, V.P.-Sls. & Mktg.--Pyttronic Industries, Inc., Montgomeryville, PA, pg. 901
Juett, Christopher G., Mgr.-Sls.--J. Lee Hackett Co., Farmington, MI, pg. 498
Juhnke, Bruce, Dir.-Intl. Mktg. & Sls.--Behlen Mfg. Co., Columbus, NE, pg. 132
Junk, Robert L., Mgr.-Sls./Private Label--Doane Products Co., Branded Sales Div., Joplin, MO, pg. 342
Just, Mark, V.P.-Sls.--Graphisphere Holding Company, Des Plaines, IL, pg. 476
Just, Mark, V.P.-Sls.--Bradley Printing Company, Des Plaines, IL, pg. 478
Jutzi, Robert, Asst. Mgr.-Sls.--Bommer Industries, Inc., Landrum, SC, pg. 164
Kabbaz, Bill, Natl. Sls. Mgr.--Barnes Pumps, Inc., Mansfield, OH, pg. 507
Kacmarynski, John, Dir.-Sls.--Marine Travelift, Inc., Sturgeon Bay, WI, pg. 707
Kacmarynski, John, Dir.-Sls.--Kewaunee Engineering Corp., Kewaunee, WI, pg. 707
Kacmarynski, John, Dir.-Sls.--MTI Leasing, Ltd., Sturgeon Bay, WI, pg. 707
Kacmarynski, John, Dir.-Sls.--Shuttlelift, Inc., Sturgeon Bay, WI, pg. 707
Kacvinsky, Ray C., V.P.-Mktg. & Sls.--Marathon Electric Manufacturing Corp., Wausau, WI, pg. 705
Kagan, Dan F., Mgr.-Sls.--Talk-A-Phone Co., Chicago, IL, pg. 1077
Kagan, Norman, Sr. V.P.-Sls.--Revlon-Realistic Professional Products, Inc., New York, NY, pg. 696
Kageler, David, Mgr.-Sls. & Service--NuArc Co., Houston, TX, pg. 817
Kahn, Judy, Mgr.-Indus. Sls.--Algood Food Company, Louisville, KY, pg. 34
Kahn, Linda, Sr. V.P.-Intl. Program Sls.--Nickelodeon/Nick At Nite, New York, NY, pg. 785
Kaiser, Mark, V.P.-Sls. & Mktg. Services--J P Foodservice, Inc., Hanover, MD, pg. 586
Kaiser, Robert J., Sr. V.P.- Sls.--Emkay, Inc., Itasca, IL, pg. 379
Kalberer, Don, Gen. Sls. Mgr.--Truck Equipment Div., Tishomingo, MS, pg. 525
Kalil, A.J., V.P.-Sls. & Mktg.--PHB Parker Die Castings, Fairview, PA, pg. 836
Kall, Terry J., V.P.-Sls. & Mktg.--Hollytex, Saddle Brook, NJ, pg. 1121
Kallman, Gary, V.P.-Sls.--Radionics, Inc., Salinas, CA, pg. 909

Corporate Responsibilities Index

Kalmuck, John, V.P.-Sls. & Mktg.--La Marche Mfg. Co., Des Plaines, IL, pg. 649
Kamauff, Bob, Mgr.-Sls./Used Cars--McNamara Pontiac Inc., Orlando, FL, pg. 732
Kaminsky, Thomas, V.P. & Natl. Sls. Mgr.--Domecq Importers Inc., Old Greenwich, CT, pg. 343
Kammersgard, Dana W., V.P.-Sls. & Mktg.--Artecon, Inc., Carlsbad, CA, pg. 809
Kampman, Kevin, Mgr.-Circulation--The Independence Examiner, Independence, MO, pg. 1042
Kampman, Kevin, Mgr.-Circulation--Blue Springs Examiner, Blue Springs, MO, pg. 1042
Kanas, Tom, V.P.-Sls. & Mktg.--Alto Shaam Inc., Menomonee Falls, WI, pg. 46
Kane, Donald, V.P.-Sls.--Alford Industries, Inc., Ridgefield Park, NJ, pg. 33
Kaplan, Jerry, Natl. Sls. Mgr.--Duncan Toys Company, Middlefield, OH, pg. 810
Kaplan, Jerry, V.P.-Yarn Sls.--Amicale Industries, Inc., New York, NY, pg. 66
Kaplan, Michael M., V.P.-Sls. & Mktg.--Life Sciences International, Philadelphia, PA, pg. 320
Kaplan, Samuel, Pres., Chief Exec. Officer, Sec. & Dir.-Sls. & Pur.--Admiration Hosiery Mills, Inc., Charlotte, NC, pg. 534
Kaplan, Steven, V.P.-Sls., Domestic--Prime Tanning Co., Inc., Berwick, ME, pg. 889
Karanauskas, E., V.P.-Sls.--Jack Lenor Larsen, Inc., New York, NY, pg. 659
Karas, Richard, V.P.-Sls., Fin. Svcs.--Nationwide Life Insurance Co., Columbus, OH, pg. 795
Karleski, Thomas, Dir.-Sls. & Mktg.--Catholic Order of Foresters, Naperville, IL, pg. 229
Karper, Donald J., V.P.-Sls. & Mktg.--Alva/Amco Pharmacal Companies, Inc., Chicago, IL, pg. 46
Kaspar, David C., Mgr.-Rack & Wire Prod. Sls.--Kaspar Wire Works, Inc., Shiner, TX, pg. 617
Kasteler, Jon, Mgr.-Sls.--Schneider Commercial Real Estate, Orange, CA, pg. 977
Katz, Alan, V.P.-Mktg. & Sls.--Empire Kosher Poultry, Inc., Mifflintown, PA, pg. 379
Katz, Alan, V.P.-Sls.--CGS Industries, Inc., Long Island City, NY, pg. 201
Katz, Harry, Exec. V.P.-Sls. & Sec.--Stock Yards Packing Co., Inc., Chicago, IL, pg. 1049
Katz, Simon, Mgr.-Intl. Sls.--Colonial Beef Co., Philadelphia, PA, pg. 263
Katzman, Michael, V.P.-Mktg. & Sls.--Mastercraft Furniture Corp., Omaha, NE, pg. 720
Kaufenberg, Ronald M., V.P.-Sls.--The Instant Web Companies, Chanhassen, MN, pg. 571
Kaufman, Bob, V.P.-Sls. & Mktg.--Mogas Industries, Inc., Houston, TX, pg. 763
Kaufman, Donald L., Pres. & Dir.-Sls. & Mktg., Alside Div.--Associated Materials Inc., Dallas, TX, pg. 91
Kaufman, L.C., V.P.-Field Sls.--AFG Industries, Inc., Fort Worth, TX, pg. 3
Kaufmann, Michael, Dir.-Sls. & Mktg.--Ford Products Corporation, Valley Cottage, NY, pg. 423
Kay, Bart, Mgr.-Western Sls.--Efco Corporation, Monett, MO, pg. 359
Kay, Carroll, V.P.-Sls., Adv. & Traffic--Kyanite Mining Corporation, Dillwyn, VA, pg. 647
Kazlo, John, Mgr.-Sls.--Consolidated Beverages, Inc., Auburn, MA, pg. 276
Kazmierczak, Leon J., Mgr.-Export Sls.--General Refractories Co., U. S. Refractories Div., Pittsburgh, PA, pg. 136
Kearins, Michael, V.P.-Sls.--Triangle Pacific Corporation, Dallas, TX, pg. 1112
Kearins, Mike, V.P.-Sls.--Bruce Hardwood Floors, Dallas, TX, pg. 1112
Keating, John J., V.P.-Sls., Mktg. & Fin.--P.J. Keating Company, Lunenburg, MA, pg. 619
Keating, Paul J., II, Dir.-Sls. & Mktg. & Treas.--P.J. Keating Company, Lunenburg, MA, pg. 619
Keating, Thomas, V.P.-Sls.--Crown Leisure Products, Owosso, MI, pg. 200
Keaton, David, V.P.-Commercial Sls.--SRI International, Menlo Park, CA, pg. 964
Keefe, Steve, Mgr.-Natl. Sls.--Flambeau Products-Columbus, Columbus, IN, pg. 810
Keefer, Ray, Sls. Mgr.--The Homer Laughlin China Company, Newell, WV, pg. 661
Keenan, James, Mgr.-Sls.--Bregg Data Forms, Inc., Hauppauge, NY, pg. 173
Kehoe, Kim, Dir.-Sls.--PC Distributing Inc., Mount Prospect, IL, pg. 835
Keiper, Douglas, Mgr.-Sls.--Lundy Construction Co., Inc., Williamsport, PA, pg. 687
Kelgey, David, V.P.-Sls.--Blue Grass Foods, Inc., Crescent Springs, KY, pg. 160
Keller, Clark, Dir.-Domestic Sls.--Applied Microsystems Corporation, Redmond, WA, pg. 79
Kelley, Bernie, V.P.-Sls.--Wang's International, Inc., Memphis, TN, pg. 1162
Kelley, Dave, Circulation Mgr.--Advertising Age, Chicago, IL, pg. 295
Kelliher, Kevin, Natl. Sls. Mgr.--Elkay Products, Inc., Shrewsbury, MA, pg. 377
Kellman, Jack, Exec. V.P.-Mktg. & Sls.--Globe Glass & Mirror Co., Chicago, IL, pg. 463
Kellogg, Jeanette, Dir.-Sls. & Mktg.--Genova Products, Inc., Davison, MI, pg. 452
Kelly, Brian, Natl. Sls. Mgr.--House of Bianchi, Boston, MA, pg. 546
Kelly, John M., V.P.-Mktg. & Sls.--Desa International, Inc., Bowling Green, KY, pg. 331
Kelly, Kevin, Mgr.-Intl. Sls.--Tekra Corporation, New Berlin, WI, pg. 1084
Kelly, Patrick T., V.P.-Sls. & Mktg.--Haws Drinking Faucet Co., Berkeley, CA, pg. 518
Kelly, Robert D., Mgr.-Sls.--The F. X. Matt Brewing Co., Utica, NY, pg. 721
Kelly, S.W., Dir.-Sls. & Mktg.--The Crystal Tissue Co., Middletown, OH, pg. 303
Kelly, Tom, Mgr.-Sls.--Bill Wink Chevrolet & GEO, Dearborn, MI, pg. 1196
Kemler, David, V.P.-Sls. & Mktg.--Information Builders, New York, NY, pg. 567
Kemp, Patricia Dent, San Francisco Sls. Mgr.--Parade Publications Inc., New York, NY, pg. 847
Kempster, Michael, Sr. V.P.-Sls. & Mktg.--Weber-Stephen Products, Palatine, IL, pg. 1171
Kennedy, Brian J., Exec. V.P.-Sls. & Mktg.--The Hertz Corporation, Park Ridge, NJ, pg. 849
Kennedy, Duane, Dir.-Consumer Sls.--Parker Fertilizer Co., Inc., Sylacauga, AL, pg. 849
Kennedy, Joan, Reg. Sls. Mgr.--Micro-Aire Surgical Instruments, Inc., Valencia, CA, pg. 711
Kennedy, Russell E., V.P.-Sls. & Mktg.--GAF Building Materials Corporation, Wayne, NJ, pg. 438
Kennedy, Thomas, V.P.-Central Sls.--North American Products Corp., Jasper, IN, pg. 811
Kennedy, Tom, Gen. Sls. Mgr.-East--Milwaukee Electric Tool Corp., Brookfield, WI, pg. 361
Kenny, Peter S., Mgr.-Natl. Sls.--Harbour Industries, Inc., Shelburne, VT, pg. 507
Kent, John, V.P.-Natl. Sls. Admin.--Barton Brands, Ltd., Chicago, IL, pg. 123
Kerans, R.W., Mgr.-Commercial Paper Sls.--Crane & Co., Inc., Dalton, MA, pg. 296
Kerkhoff, Daniel W., V.P.-Mktg. & Sls.--The Pro Corporation, Florence, MA, pg. 891
Kern, Ed, Mgr.-Export Sls.--SK Hand Tool Corp., Chicago, IL, pg. 963
Kerr, Jill, Chief Oper. Officer & V.P.-Sls. & Mktg.--The ASCII Group, Inc., Bethesda, MD, pg. 8
Kersten, Keith D., V.P.-Sls. & Food Processing--Byerly's Inc., Edina, MN, pg. 198
Kessler, Bruce, Mgr.-Sls., N.E.--Mountain Valley Spring Company, Hot Springs, AR, pg. 968
Kesterson, Danny, Exec. V.P.-Sls. & Mktg.--Kesterson Food Company, Inc., Paris, TN, pg. 624
Ketchmark, James, Mgr.-Sls.--Hoof Products Company, Chicago, IL, pg. 543
Keyes, John J., Jr., V.P.-Sls.--The Napier Company, Meriden, CT, pg. 783
Kibbe, Roy, Mgr.-Gen. Sls.--Duo-Fast Corporation, Franklin Park, IL, pg. 354
Kicey, Margaret, Mgr.-Simoniz Canada--Simoniz Canada Ltd., Cleveland, OH, pg. 159
Kick, Alan, V.P.-Sls. & Mktg.--Dynamic Metal Products Company, Manchester, CT, pg. 356
Kiedinger, Keith, V.P.-Pkgng. Sls & Natl. Sls. Mgr.--Queens Group, Inc., Long Island City, NY, pg. 904
Kilbourn, Gary, Mgr.-Sls.--Dick Bruhn Inc., Salinas, CA, pg. 184
Kilbourne, James G., Dir.-Single Copy Sls.--Petersen Publishing Company, Los Angeles, CA, pg. 864
Kilduff, Frank, Gen. Mgr.-Sls.--Southside Ford Truck Sales Inc., Chicago, IL, pg. 1023
Kilduff, John M., Sr. V.P.-Sls.--Dr Pepper Company, Dallas, TX, pg. 342
Kiley, Thomas M., V.P.-Sls.--Victaulic Company of America, Easton, PA, pg. 1149
Killough, Jerry, V.P.-Reg. Sls. & Gen. Mgr.--Tom's Foods, Columbus, GA, pg. 1101
Kilpatrick, Charlie, V.P.-Sls.--Dac Easy, Inc., Dallas, TX, pg. 571
Kilpatrick, G.H., V.P.-Sls.--Welch's, Concord, MA, pg. 789
Kilpatrick, Michael, Dir.-Sls.--California State Lottery, Sacramento, CA, pg. 210
Kilper, Bob, Distr. Sls.--Hart-Carter Co., Minneapolis, MN, pg. 226
Kimball, Don, V.P.-Sls. & Mktg.--Alex Foods, Inc., Anaheim, CA, pg. 33
Kimball, Kent, V.P.-Sls.--Advanced Input Devices, Inc., Coeur D'Alene, ID, pg. 20
Kimber, Robert W., V.P.--Bradford Company, Holland, MI, pg. 170
Kimicata, Art, V.P.-Sls. & Mktg.--Sun Data Inc., Norcross, GA, pg. 1058
Kinel, John P. Jr., V.P.-Industrial Sls.--The Spencer Turbine Co., Windsor, CT, pg. 1030
Kinel, John P., Jr., V.P.-Industrial Sls.--Spencer Turbine Co., Windsor, CT, pg. 1030
King, Alan, V.P.-Sls. & Mktg.--Carbide International Inc., Chicago, IL, pg. 507
King, Alan, V.P.-Sls. & Mktg.--Rogers Tool Works, Inc., Rogers, AR, pg. 507
King, H. Alan, V.P.-Sls. & Mktg.--RTW, Rogers Tool Works, Inc., Rogers, AR, pg. 908
King, J.E., Dir.-Sls.--Viskase Corporation, Bedford Park, IL, pg. 383
King, Larry, Dir.-Sls. & Mktg.--Ryan Herco Products Corp., Burbank, CA, pg. 958
King, Mack, Div. Mgr.-Sls.--The Jel Sert Co., West Chicago, IL, pg. 591
Kinnebrew, Jim, Asst. V.P.-Domestic Sls.--MICOM Communications Corp., Simi Valley, CA, pg. 748
Kinsley, Rick, V.P.-Sls. & Mktg.--Pfaudler-U.S., Inc., Rochester, NY, pg. 866
Kipnis, Steve, V.P.-Adv. & Sls. Dir.--GWP, Inc., Los Angeles, CA, pg. 441
Kippen, John, V.P.-Sls.--Plano Molding Co., Plano, IL, pg. 874
Kirby, John H., V.P.-Sls.--The Double-Cola Company, Chattanooga, TN, pg. 347
Kirkland, Thurman, V.P.-Sls. & Mktg.--Long MFG. NC, Inc., Tarboro, NC, pg. 682
Kirkland, Thurman, V.P.-Sls. & Mktg.--Long Equipment Co., Tarboro, NC, pg. 682
Kirkman, Paul, Exec. V.P.-Mktg. & Sls.--Beverage Canners International Corp., Miami, FL, pg. 148
Kirkner, Robert E., Dir.-Sls.--John D. Lucas Printing Company, Baltimore, MD, pg. 263
Kitch, Fred, Exec. V.P.--Keller Crescent Co., Evansville, IN, pg. 620
Kizor, Juanita, Sls. Mgr.-West--ATAPCO Office Products Group, Saint Louis, MO, pg. 64
Klackle, Michael, Dir.-Fresh Sls.--Michigan Blueberry Growers Assn., Grand Junction, MI, pg. 747
Klain, Richard M., Mgr.-Latin American Sls.--Victaulic International, Easton, PA, pg. 1149
Klapholz, Sam, V.P.-Sls.--Jerell, Inc., Dallas, TX, pg. 593
Klasell, T.A., Sls. Mgr.--Rodman Industries, Marinette, WI, pg. 408
Klauber, James, V.P.-Sls.--Linotype-Hell Company, Hauppauge, NY, pg. 677
Kledzik, M., V.P.-Sls.--The Van Metre Companies, Burke, VA, pg. 1144
Klein, James B., V.P.-Sls.--Eastland Shoe Manufacturing Corporation, Freeport, ME, pg. 364
Klein, Mitch, Gen. Sls. Mgr.--Dahlstrom Manufacturing Company, Inc., Jamestown, NY, pg. 310
Klein, Robert, Natl. Sls. Mgr.--Monarch Ware, Inc., Algoma, WI, pg. 742
Klein, Steven, Sls. Coord.--Kenco, Middlebury, IN, pg. 1025
Kleinheider, Paul, V.P.-Sls.--Buxton Company, Chicopee, MA, pg. 197
Kleinheinz, Jim, Dir.-Sls.--Health Care Distributors of Indiana, Inc., South Bend, IN, pg. 520
Kleinman, Mel, V.P.-Sls.--El Camino Resources, Ltd., Northridge, CA, pg. 372
Klemmer, Randy R., Exec. V.P.-Opers. & Sls.--Fritz Chemical Company, Mesquite, TX, pg. 434
Klenner, Arthur J., V.P.-Sls.--Petron Corporation, New Berlin, WI, pg. 1172
Klima, Mike, Dir.-Sls.--Cogifer Inc., Cincinnati, OH, pg. 259
Kloman, Larry, V.P.-Mktg. & Sls.--PhoneMate, Inc., Torrance, CA, pg. 869
Klompmaker, D.O., Mgr.-Sls.-Automotive Div.--Young Radiator Company, Racine, WI, pg. 1210
Klong, Lawrence A., Pres.--K & R Delivery, Inc., Hinsdale, IL, pg. 610
Klonne, Michael, V.P.-Mktg. & Sls.--Findley Adhesives, Inc., Wauwatosa, WI, pg. 410
Kloos, Roger, Dir.-Sls. & Mktg.--Conestoga Wood Specialties, Inc., Earl, PA, pg. 273
Kloss, D.R., Exec. V.P.-Sls.--The Fleetwood Company, Downers Grove, IL, pg. 417
Klueter, R.V., Mgr.-Adv.--Fostoria Industries, Inc., Fostoria, OH, pg. 427
Klug, William A., V.P. & Grp. Exec.-Unitary Prods. Grp.--American Standard Inc., New York, NY, pg. 61
Knape, Stephen, Mgr.-Circulation--The Holland Sentinel, Holland, MI, pg. 1042
Knapp, S.R., V.P.-Sls. & Mktg.--R. A. Jones & Co. Inc., Covington, KY, pg. 604
Kness, Rocky, Mgr.-Sls.-Used Car--Future Ford/Hugo Inc., Roseville, CA, pg. 437
Knight, Chandler, Mgr.-Sls.--Fimbel Door Corporation, Whitehouse, NJ, pg. 409
Knoblauch, D.H., Mgr.-Central Reg. Sls.--Ludlow Composites Corporation, Fremont, OH, pg. 686
Knoll, Steve, Loan Officer--Wieland Financial Services, Inc., Atlanta, GA, pg. 1188
Knopf, Tom, Sls. Mgr.--Manna Pro Partner L.P. (Limited Partnership), Denver, CO, pg. 704
Knorr, C.G., V.P.-Sls.--Ano-Coil Corporation, Rockville, CT, pg. 75
Knott, Doug, V.P.-Sls.--Brooks Foods, Mt. Summit, IN, pg. 26
Knox, Leslie H., Sr. V.P.-Sls. & Mktg.--Abco Markets, Inc., Phoenix, AZ, pg. 10
Kobran, Mitch, V.P.-Sls.--Leonard Wholesale, Inc., Elizabeth, NJ, pg. 668
Koch, Clint, Dir.-Sls.--Modern Equipment Rentals Inc., Wilmington, DE, pg. 763
Koch, Frank, Exec. V.P.-Sls.--Nature's Recipe Pet Foods, Corona, CA, pg. 796
Koch, Paul, V.P.-Sls.--Republic Container Corp., Jersey City, NJ, pg. 927
Koehle, Keith A., Mgr.-Natl. Sls.--Proto Systems of Atlanta, Alpharetta, GA, pg. 895
Koejte, Mark, Gen. Mgr.-Sls.--Prime Technology Inc., Southfield, MI, pg. 889
Koenig, Richard, V.P.-Sls.--Sun Lakes Marketing, Sun Lakes, AZ, pg. 1059
Koeniger, James K., V.P.-Sls. & Mktg.--Atlas Refinery, Newark, NJ, pg. 96
Koenitzer, J.G., Mgr.-Sls.--Helwig Carbon Products, Inc., Milwaukee, WI, pg. 528
Koenitzer, John E., Pres. & Chief Exec. Officer--Helwig Carbon Products, Inc., Milwaukee, WI, pg. 528
Koeppen, Ron, Mgr.-Sls.--Kendale Industries, Inc., Valley View, OH, pg. 622
Koetje, Jack, Sr. V.P.-Retail Opers.--Meijer, Inc., Grand Rapids, MI, pg. 737
Koetje, Mark, Gen. Sls. Mgr.--Prime Technology, Inc., Grand Rapids, MI, pg. 889
Koetter, James, V.P.-Sls.--Jeffersonville Distribution Center, Jeffersonville, IN, pg. 832
Kogerup, Alan G., Gen. Sls. Mgr.--Carstens Health Industries, Inc., Chicago, IL, pg. 225
Kohlmann, Bob, Mgr.-Intl. Sls.--Bruner Corporation, Milwaukee, WI, pg. 184
Kohlmeyer, Tex, Sls. Mgr.--United Farm Tools, Inc., Oelwein, Oelwein, IA, pg. 1132
Kolkebeck, W. Charles, V.P.-Mktg. & Sls.--Nuttall Gear Corporation, Niagara Falls, NY, pg. 818
Kondos, Jack, Dir.-Sls., Sls. Promo. & Adv.--Specialty Paperboard Inc., Brattleboro, VT, pg. 1027
Koner, Larry, Sls. Mgr.--Shokai Far East Ltd., Peekskill, NY, pg. 1000
Kontney, J., Mgr.-Trade Shows/Artist Rels.--Shure Brothers Incorporated, Evanston, IL, pg. 1001
Koop, Marline, Sls. Office Mgr.--Dinner Bell Foods, Inc., Cincinnati, OH, pg. 53

Kopin, Sheldon A., V.P.-Retail Opers.--Totes Incorporated, Loveland, OH, pg. 1103
Kops, Charles T., Mgr.-Natl. Sls.--Pemko Manufacturing Company, Ventura, CA, pg. 856
Korkosz, M., V.P. & Sls. Mgr.--Woodwork Corporation of America, Chicago, IL, pg. 1201
Korman, Hal, Natl. Sls. Mgr.--UDL Laboratories, Inc., Rockford, IL, pg. 1072
Kornfeld, Marvin, Mgr.-Sls.--Deitsch Plastics Company, West Haven, CT, pg. 325
Korrafel, Peter, Sec. & Treas.--Carquest Corporation, Tarrytown, NY, pg. 224
Korris, Michael, V.P.-Sls.--Hoboken Wood Flooring Corporation, Wayne, NJ, pg. 537
Korthals, Doug, Mgr.-Natl. Sls. & Service--Bunton Company, Louisville, KY, pg. 188
Kosier, Truman, Mgr.-Sls. & Mktg.--Schweizer Aircraft Corporation, Elmira, NY, pg. 981
Kosta, John, V.P.-Sls.--Advance Business Graphics, Mira Loma, CA, pg. 18
Kotubey, Michael J., V.P.-Construction Sls.--Balco, Inc. (MA), Boston, MA, pg. 115
Kovich, Ronald H., V.P.-Sls.--Blistex, Inc., Oak Brook, IL, pg. 157
Kowske, Robert, Sls. Dir.--Kropp Forge Co., Chicago, IL, pg. 1073
Kozlowicz, Robert, V.P.-Sls.--Kal Kan Foods, Inc., Vernon, CA, pg. 713
Kozlowski, Ken, Mgr.-Natl. Sls.--Symons Corporation, Des Plaines, IL, pg. 1069
Kozub, John F., Mgr.-Sls.--Janlynn Corporation, Indian Orchard, MA, pg. 589
Kraft, Neil, Sr. V.P., Dir.-Adv. & Creative Services--CRK Advertising, New York, NY, pg. 203
Kraines, Steve, Sr. V.P.-Sls.--Kraco Enterprises, Inc., Compton, CA, pg. 643
Kralstein, Irwin, V.P.-Sls.--I. Rokeach & Sons, Inc., Paramus, NJ, pg. 944
Kramer, Dale, Mgr.-Sls.--John H. Graham & Co., Inc., Oradell, NJ, pg. 475
Kramer, Joel, Dir.-Sls.--Dee Paper Company, Chester, PA, pg. 324
Kramer, Larry, V.P.-Sls. & Adv. Mgr.--Wilson Products Co., Salt Lake City, UT, pg. 1194
Kramer, Pete, Mgr.-Sls.--Gillogly Chevrolet Inc., West Seneca, NY, pg. 459
Krampert, Carl M., V.P.-Detroit Sls. Mgr.--Parade Publications Inc., New York, NY, pg. 847
Kratz, John C., Dir.-Sls.--Pearl Brewing Company, San Antonio, TX, pg. 959
Krause, Gary W., V.P.-Sls.--Laird & Company, Scobeyville, NJ, pg. 650
Krause, Mike, Mgr.-Sls.--Buffelen Woodworking Company, Tacoma, WA, pg. 187
Krause, Richard A., V.P.-Retail Sls.--J. L. Hammett Company, Braintree, MA, pg. 504
Krecl, Bob L., V.P.-Mktg. & Sls.--General Time Corp., Norcross, GA, pg. 451
Kreger, James, V.P.-Sls.--Seats Incorporated, Reedsburg, WI, pg. 810
Krempasky, Richard, Mgr.-Truck Prods.-Seat--National Seating Co., Vonore, TN, pg. 793
Krenmayer, Richard, V.P.-Sls.--Hoyt Corporation, Westport, MA, pg. 548
Krezo, Steve, Natl. Sls. Mgr.--Gem Top Mfg., Inc., Clackamas, OR, pg. 448
Krieg, T.J., Dir.-Sls.--J.M. Huber, Chemicals Division, Havre de Grace, MD, pg. 550
Krikorian, Charles, Natl. Sls. Mgr.--Printed Circuit Corporation, Woburn, MA, pg. 891
Kringen, Stu, Dir.-Sls. & Purch.--Bongards Creameries Inc., Norwood, MN, pg. 164
Kritzer, Sheldon, Dir.-Sls.--Poly Pak America, Inc., Los Angeles, CA, pg. 880
Krizik, Kent, Mgr.-Sls.--Cambridge Associates, Boston, MA, pg. 316
Kroetch, Jerry, V.P.-Sls. & Mktg.--Scotchman Industries, Inc., Philip, SD, pg. 982
Kronenberg, Norman, Sr. V.P.-Sls.--Totes Incorporated, Loveland, OH, pg. 1103
Kruger, Robert, Mgr. Sls.-Distribution--MidWest Body Corporation, Paris, IL, pg. 752
Krulik, Bob, Mgr.-Sls., Deco Candles--A.I. Root Company, Medina, OH, pg. 946
Krumwiede, James, V.P.-Sls. & Mktg.--C-Line Products, Inc., Des Plaines, IL, pg. 198
Kruse, Dean V., Dir.-Sls. & Auctioneer--Kruse International, Auburn, IN, pg. 645
Kruse, M., V.P.-Sls.--Heidtman Steel Products, Inc., Toledo, OH, pg. 525
Krzyzanski, Victor, V.P.-Sls.--McCain Manufacturing Corp., Chicago, IL, pg. 726
Kugler, William O., V.P.-Personnel & Wholesale Programs--Pro Hardware, Inc., Englewood, CO, pg. 891
Kuhn, Harold, V.P. & Sls. Mgr.--Park Motor Sales Company, Detroit, MI, pg. 849
Kuhns, Stephen, Dir.-Sls.--Newage Industries Inc., Willow Grove, PA, pg. 803
Kuhns, Stephen, Dir.-Sls.--Newage Industries Inc., Plastics Division, Willow Grove, PA, pg. 803
Kuli, Alex, V.P.-Worldwide Sls.--Candle Corporation, Santa Monica, CA, pg. 214
Kulik, Paul, Dir.-Sls., Mktg. & Adv.--Hennells, Inc., Ferndale, MI, pg. 530
Kullbom, Bill, V.P.-Sls.--Hawkeye Steel Products, Inc., Houghton, IA, pg. 518
Kumler, Myron, V.P.-Sls.--Farmers Mutual Hail Insurance Co., Des Moines, IA, pg. 401
Kuperus, Gaylen, Mgr.-Sls.--Hagie Manufacturing Co., Clarion, IA, pg. 499
Kurkjy, Neil, Dir.-Sls. & Mktg.--Rapid Power Technologies, Inc., Brookfield, CT, pg. 913
Kurtenbach, Frank, Mgr.-Sls.--Daktronics, Inc., Brookings, SD, pg. 312
Kuter, Ken, Sls. Mgr.--Action Technology Company, Rockaway, NJ, pg. 15
Kwiatkowski, Elaine, V.P.-Sls.--Blue Bird Coach Lines Inc., Olean, NY, pg. 158
Kyle, Kurt, Sls. & Mktg. Coord.--McNeil & NRM., Inc., Akron, OH, pg. 732
La Dolche, Gary, Div. Mgr.-Sls.--The Jel Sert Co., West Chicago, IL, pg. 591
LaBadie, Jim, Dir.-Sls. & Mktg.--Lancaster Host Resort, Lancaster, PA, pg. 653
LaCalamita, Tony, Mgr.-Regional Sls. & Mktg.--Wayne Corporation, Richmond, IN, pg. 1169
Lackley, Steve, V.P.-Sls.--Precisionaire, Inc., Saint Petersburg, FL, pg. 886
Lacny, Paul J., V.P.-State Sls.--Blue Cross & Blue Shield of Illinois, Chicago, IL, pg. 160
Lacon, Henson, Dir.-Subscription Sls.--Petersen Publishing Company, Los Angeles, CA, pg. 864
Lacoste, Roy, V.P.-Grocery Sls.--Schwegmann Giant Super Markets, New Orleans, LA, pg. 980
Lacy, Bert, V.P.-Circulation--Ziff-Davis Publishing Company, New York, NY, pg. 1219
Lacy, George T., V.P.-Grp. Field Sls.--General American Life Insurance Co., St. Louis, MO, pg. 448
Ladoucer, Lori, Mgr.-Sls.--Cutler Manufacturing Corporation, Highland City, FL, pg. 307
Lagano, Paul G. Lagano, V.P.-Sls. & Mktg.--Global Turnkey Systems Inc., Waldwick, NJ, pg. 463
LaGrega, Andrew T., Sr. V.P.-Sls., Mktg., Adv. & Human Resources--Wilder Management Associates, Waltham, MA, pg. 1189
LaMancuso, John, Mgr.-Sls./Distr.--Interroyal Corporation, Warren, PA, pg. 580
Lamb, Rick, Mgr.-Sls.--Franks Supply Company, Inc., Albuquerque, NM, pg. 429
Lamer, Allan J., V.P.-Sls.--Marine Travelift, Inc., Sturgeon Bay, WI, pg. 707
Lamie, John, Sr. V.P.-Sls.--Paco Rabanne Parfums, New York, NY, pg. 842
Lammot, Brooke, Dir.-Sls.--Clayton Manufacturing Div., Dynamic Equipment, Southfield, MI, pg. 254
Lamond, Dennis, V.P.-Sls.--Briggs Industries, Inc., Tampa, FL, pg. 175
LaMonica, Michael, V.P.-Sls. & Mktg.--Bridgeport Machines, Inc., Bridgeport, CT, pg. 175
Lanahan, Christopher, V.P.-Sls. & Mktg., MRO--Carey Machinery & Supply Company, Baltimore, MD, pg. 218
Lancashire, Scott, V.P.-Sls.--Cosco, Inc., Columbus, IN, pg. 287
Lancaster, Bill, V.P.-Sls.--Associated Wholesale Grocers, Inc., Kansas City, KS, pg. 92
Lance, Greg, V.P.-Sls.--Mark III Industries, Ocala, FL, pg. 708
Lancellotti, Ralph, Exec. V.P.-Sls.--Pressman Toy Corp., New York, NY, pg. 887
Lanctot, Edmund W., Jr., V.P.-Sls. & Mktg.--J.W. Window Components, Inc., Tampa, FL, pg. 1162
Landa, Terri, Dir.-Sls.--Sampler Publications Inc., Saint Charles, IL, pg. 968
Landa, Terri, Mgr.-Natl. Sls.--Country Sampler, Saint Charles, IL, pg. 968
Landau, Richard, Exec. V.P.-Sls.--Fruit of the Loom, Bowling Green, KY, pg. 400
Landess, James, Mgr.-Intl. Sls.--Macklanburg-Duncan Co., Oklahoma City, OK, pg. 697
Landolfi, Tony, Dir.-Mktg. & Mgr.-Natl. Sls.--4C Foods Corporation, Brooklyn, NY, pg. 427
Landry, Bob, V.P.-Sls. & Marketing--Pioneer Aluminum, Inc., Los Angeles, CA, pg. 871
Landy, Thomas, V.P.-Sls. & Mktg.--World Dryer Corp., Berkeley, IL, pg. 1027
Lane, Edwin, Mgr. Sls.-Eastern Reg.--W. Braun Co., Lyndhurst, NJ, pg. 172
Lang, D.J., V.P.-Sls.--Fox River Paper Company, Appleton, WI, pg. 428
Lang, Richard A., Jr., V.P.-Adv., Sls. & Mktg.--Dad's Products Co., Inc., Meadville, PA, pg. 310
Langbein, Karen, Promotion Mgr.--Iowa Lottery, Des Moines, IA, pg. 582
Lange, John, Sls. Mgr.-Whlse.--GPD Limited, Norcross, GA, pg. 440
Langenberger, Conrad, V.P.-N. American Sls. & Mktg.--Simplicity Manufacturing, Inc., Port Washington, WI, pg. 1006
Langenecker, Gene, Sls. Admin. Mgr.--Wells Mfg. Corp., Dond Du Lac, WI, pg. 1123
Langla, Leslye, Dir.-Sls. & Mktg.--Markair, Inc., Anchorage, AK, pg. 708
Langley, E.J., Mgr.-Sls.--Anthony Forest Products Co., Inc., El Dorado, AR, pg. 77
Lanigan, Michael, Exec. V.P.-Sls.--MI-Jack Products, Inc., Hazel Crest, IL, pg. 746
Lanigan, Patrick, V.P.-Indus. Sls.--MI-Jack Products, Inc., Hazel Crest, IL, pg. 746
Lantz, Richard K., V.P.-Mfg. & Special Sls.--Shenandoah Mfg. Co. Inc., Harrisonburg, VA, pg. 997
Lantz, Tom, V.P., Natl. Sales Mgr.--The Sunflower Group, Overland Park, KS, pg. 1060
Laos, A.G., Dir.-Mktg. & Sls.--Carter Day Co., Minneapolis, MN, pg. 226
Laos, A.G., Dir.-Sls. & Mktg.--Carter Day International, Inc., Minneapolis, MN, pg. 226
LaPlante, David, V.P.-Sls. & Mdse.--Shurfine-Central Corp., Northlake, IL, pg. 1001
LaPorte, Dennis, Dir.-Sls.--Superior Reprographics, Seattle, WA, pg. 1064
LaQuintano, T., V.P.-Sls. & Mktg.--Dietzgen Corporation, Des Plaines, IL, pg. 337
Larime, Michael W., V.P.-Sls. & Mktg.--Thetford Corporation, Ann Arbor, MI, pg. 357
Larkin, C., V.P.-Sls.--Medline Industries, Inc., Mundelein, IL, pg. 736
Larkin, James A., Sr. Exec. V.P.-Sales--North Shore Movers, Northbrook, IL, pg. 813
Larkin, James L., V.P.-Sls.--Romac Industries, Inc., Seattle, WA, pg. 945
Larkin, Steve, V.P.-Mktg. & Sls. Mgr.--Kluener Foods Co., Cincinnati, OH, pg. 636
Larranaga, Al, Reg. Sls. Mgr.--Union-Tribune Publishing Company, San Diego, CA, pg. 284
Larson, Allan G., Reg. Sls. Mgr.--Cramer Company, Old Saybrook, CT, pg. 296
Larson, Bob, Sls. Dir.--Lapeyre Stair, Inc., Harahan, LA, pg. 651
Larson, Dan, Sls. Mgr.--Robinson Industries, Huntley, IL, pg. 975
Larson, James, Gen. Sls. Mgr.--The Bureau of National Affairs, Inc., Washington, DC, pg. 189
Larsson, Sten, Dir.-European Sls.--Pan-American Seed Co., West Chicago, IL, pg. 116
Lasko, J., Prod. Mgr.-Chain Div.--Bead Industries Inc., Bridgeport, CT, pg. 129
Latigo, Dominick P., Dir.-Sls., U.S. & Canada--George S. May International Company, Park Ridge, IL, pg. 723
Latourette, Everett, Reg. Sls. & Adv. Mgr.--Cramer Company, Old Saybrook, CT, pg. 296
Lattanzi, Art, V.P.-Sls.--Copperweld Steel Company, Warren, OH, pg. 284
Laughridge, W.J. III, Mgr.-Natl. Sls.--Bommer Industries, Inc., Landrum, SC, pg. 164
Laurenson, C.P., Sr. V.P.-Sls.--A. Finkl & Sons Co., Chicago, IL, pg. 411
Lauter, Nancy A., Sr. V.P.-Mkt. Devel. & Intl. Sls.--McDougal, Littell & Company, Evanston, IL, pg. 728
Lauterbach, R., V.P.-Intl. Sls.--Perry Equipment Corporation, Mineral Wells, TX, pg. 863
Lauterborn, JoAnn, Mgr.-Special Sls. Accts.--Kaukauna Cheese, Little Chute, WI, pg. 619
Lavelle, Pat, Mgr.-Natl. Sls.--The Protector Corporation, Addison, IL, pg. 895
Lavey, Mike, Sls. Mgr.--Stocker & Yale, Inc., Beverly, MA, pg. 1050
Lavigne, Randolphe G., Mgr.-Sls. Proposals--Kingsbury Corporation, Keene, NH, pg. 631
Lavino, Sandy, Gen. Sls. Mgr.--J.H. Baxter & Company, San Mateo, CA, pg. 127
Law, Cindy, Sr. Sls. Rep. & Export Mgr.--Streamlight Inc., Norristown, PA, pg. 1053
Law, Jerry, V.P.-Sls.--Central Commissary, Inc., Phoenix, AZ, pg. 287
Law, R.L., V.P.-Sls.--Tru-Fit Products Corp., Medina, OH, pg. 1117
Lawrence, James, V.P.-Piece Goods Sls.--Woolrich, Inc., Woolrich, PA, pg. 1201
Lawrence, Ken, Mgr.-Indus. Sls.--Progress Paint Mfg. Co., Louisville, KY, pg. 894
Lawrence, Ralph G., Sr. V.P.-Sls. & Mktg.--Hyde Manufacturing Co., Southbridge, MA, pg. 556
Lawrence, Richard, Mgr.-Sls.--Anthony Forest Products Co., Inc., El Dorado, AR, pg. 77
Lawrence, Tom, Sr. V.P.-Sls. & Mktg.--Taco Inc., Cranston, RI, pg. 1076
Lax, David, Mgr.-Natl. Sls.--John Hassall, Inc., Westbury, NY, pg. 516
Lazzari, John, Mgr.-Sls.--Aeroclo Metal Products, Yonkers, NY, pg. 886
Lazzari, John, Mgr.-Sls.--Tiros Plastics Div., Yonkers, NY, pg. 886
Le Gaux, Les, Mgr.-Sls.--Martin Forest Industries, Healdsburg, CA, pg. 715
Le Petere, Carol, Dir.-Sls.--Kiplinger's Personal Finance Magazine, Washington, DC, pg. 632
Leach, Barry, Mgr.-Natl. Field Sls.--Star Expansion Company, Mountainville, NY, pg. 1039
Leach, Ronald W., V.P. & Deputy Dir.-Agency Sls. Div.--Mutual of Omaha, Omaha, NE, pg. 779
Leach, Thomas ., Dir.-Sls. & Mktg.--Horton Homes, Inc., Eatonton, GA, pg. 545
Leafstone, Howard, Mgr.-Natl. Sls.--On-Cor Frozen Foods Inc., Chicago, IL, pg. 826
Leatherman, Arthur, V.P.-Plant Oper.--La Victoria Foods, Inc., City of Industry, CA, pg. 649
LeBlanc, Paul C., Mgr.-New Prods. Sls.--Crane & Co., Inc., Dalton, MA, pg. 296
Lebo, K., Prod. Mgr.-Electronics--Bead Industries Inc., Bridgeport, CT, pg. 129
Lecker, Harvey, V.P.-Sls.--Protimex Corporation, Studio City, CA, pg. 895
Lee, Tan, Sls. Mgr.--G. Heileman Brewing Co., Inc., La Crosse, WI, pg. 526
Leech, Ronald, V.P.-Sls.--C P Converters, Inc., York, PA, pg. 203
Leeser, M.B., Sr. V.P.-Sls. & Mktg.--Thrall Car Mfg. Co., Chicago Heights, IL, pg. 350
Lefcovich, Raul, Pres.-International Sls.--Viacom Enterprises, New York, NY, pg. 785
LeFebvre, Timothy, V.P.-Domestic Sls. & Mktg.--NESLAB Instruments, Inc., Newington, NH, pg. 798
LeFevre, Robert M., Sr. V.P.-Mktg. & Sls.--The United States Playing Card Company, Cincinnati, OH, pg. 1136
Leff, Jeffrey, V.P.-Sls.--Carole Wren, Inc., New York, NY, pg. 1204
Leffler, David L., Sr. V.P.-Sls.--Century Furniture Industries, Hickory, NC, pg. 235
Legge, Jerry, Sls. Mgr.--Gibson Wine Company, Elk Grove, CA, pg. 457
LeGrande, Doug, V.P.-U.S. Sls.--Lexmark International, Inc., Greenwich, CT, pg. 673
Lehmann, G.J., Mgr.-Sls. & Mktg.--Electronic Measurements, Inc., Neptune, NJ, pg. 145
Lehnartz, David, V.P.-Sls.--National Merchandise Co., Inc., Jacksonville, FL, pg. 792
Lehnert, Sherry, Mgr.-Sls.--Kool Seal, Inc., Twinsburg, OH, pg. 641
LeHocky, Robert, V.P.-Sls.--Howard Miller Clock Company, Zeeland, MI, pg. 754
Leistritz, John P., V.P.-Mktg.--Paul Arpin Vanlines, Inc., East Greenwich, RI, pg. 85

Leman, Jim, Dir.-Sls. & Mktg.--Meridian Technology Leasing Services, Deerfield, IL, pg. 740

Lemberger, Mark, V.P.-Sls.--Western States Envelope Co., Butler, WI, pg. 1181

Lembo, D., Mgr.-Sls.--National Spinning Co., Inc., New York, NY, pg. 793

Lemery, Lisa, Dir.-Sls.--Kobra International Ltd, New York, NY, pg. 638

Lemin, J., V.P.-Cameron Machine--Somerset Technologies, Inc., Somerset, NJ, pg. 1017

Lemoyne, Herb, V.P.-Sls. & Mktg.--H.H. Brown Shoe Company, Inc., Greenwich, CT, pg. 182

Lenarth, Rick, V.P.-Sls.--Polymer Development Laboratories, Inc., Orange, CA, pg. 880

Lendecke, August, Mgr.-Sls.--The C.P. Hall Company, Stow, OH, pg. 501

Lenz, Edward R., Sr. V.P.-Distr.--Alamo Industrial Group, San Antonio, TX, pg. 29

Leon, Daniel S., Sr. V.P., Client Services--S. R. Leon Company, Inc., Oyster Bay, NY, pg. 667

Leonard, Glen, V.P.-Retail Sls.--La Victoria Foods, Inc., City of Industry, CA, pg. 649

Leone, Rick, Mgr.-Sls.--Bonney Forge Corporation, Allentown, PA, pg. 164

Leong, James, V.P.-Sls., Mktg. & Adv.--Mutual Distributors Ltd., Honolulu, HI, pg. 778

LePage, Rebecca, V.P. & Mgr.-Sls.--Christian Memorial Cultural Center, Rochester Hills, MI, pg. 249

Lepcio, Ted, V.P.-Corp. Accts.--St. Johnsbury Trucking Co., Inc., Holliston, MA, pg. 966

Lepore, John, Mktg., Sls. & Adv. Mgr.--MFE Instruments, Beverly, MA, pg. 1050

LePrevost, Larry, Natl. Sls. Mgr.--Johnson Manufacturing Co., Princeton, IA, pg. 443

Leroy, Tim, V.P.-Sls. (Mass Mkt.)--Meadowcraft, Inc., Birmingham, AL, pg. 733

Lervick, R.M., V.P.-Sls.--Ziegler Inc., Minneapolis, MN, pg. 1218

Lescoe, Daniel, V.P.-Sls. & Mktg.--Big Y Foods Inc., Springfield, MA, pg. 149

Leshiniski, Bruce A., V.P.-Sls. & Mktg.--Newly Weds Foods Inc., Chicago, IL, pg. 804

Letourneau, Peter D., V.P.-Sls. Service--Geiger Brothers, Lewiston, ME, pg. 447

Letten, Brian, Grp. V.P.-Mktg. & Sls.--Bata Shoe Co., Inc., Belcamp, MD, pg. 201

Letterman, Ron, Pres.-Carlson Travel Network-Retail--Carlson Travel Network-Commercial, Minneapolis, MN, pg. 221

Lettie, Ben, Sls. Mgr.-Mass Mdse. & Hardware--Frederick Trading Company, Frederick, MD, pg. 430

Leu, Dennis, V.P.-Mktg. & Sls.--Velsicol Chemical Corporation, Rosemont, IL, pg. 1147

Leuther, Peter, Area Sls. Mgr.--Bourns, GmbH, Stuttgart, Germany, pg. 168

Levene, David, V.P.-Sls.--Commodore Cruise Line, Ltd., Coral Gables, FL, pg. 269

Levenick, Tom, Dir.-Mktg. & Sls.--Brooks Beverages Inc., Columbus, OH, pg. 179

Levin, Alan, V.P.-Sls.--NDAP/TMP Worldwide, Toronto,, Canada, pg. 1074

Levis, Marcia, V.P.-Mktg./Sls.--Muelhens, Inc., Orange, CT, pg. 774

Levitt, Warren, Sr. V.P.-Sls.--Apparel Fabrics Div., New York, NY, pg. 400

Levy, Bruce, Dir.-Sls.--National Cleaning Contractors, Inc., New York, NY, pg. 786

Levy, Donald, V.P.-Sls.--Esther Williams Swimming Pool Co., Delair, NJ, pg. 389

Levy, Harold, Sr. V.P.-Sls.--Asko, Inc, Homestead, PA, pg. 88

Levy, Harold L., Sr. V.P.-Sls. & Mktg. & New Bus. Contact--TMP Worldwide, Inc., New York, NY, pg. 1073

Levy, R., Exec. V.P.-Sls. & Mdsg.--B. Levy & Sons, Scranton, PA, pg. 672

Levy, Rick, Sr. V.P.-Syndication Sls.--MTV Networks, New York, NY, pg. 785

Lewis, Bill, V.P.-Sls.--Forever Living Products, Tempe, AZ, pg. 424

Lewis, Brad, V.P.-Sls. & Mktg.--Crystal Cabinet Works, Inc., Princeton, MN, pg. 303

Lewis, David, Mgr.-Natl. Sls.--Bellofram Corp., Newell, WV, pg. 136

Lewis, Jim, V.P.-Field Sls. West--Empire Brushes, Inc., Greenville, NC, pg. 379

Lewis, Lisa, Dir.-Sls, Mktg. & Adv.--Music Sales Corporation, New York, NY, pg. 777

Lewis, Michael E., Mgr.-Sls. & Mktg.--Ekstrom Industries, Inc., Farmington Hills, MI, pg. 180

Lewis, Norman, Mgr.-Sls.--Kasper Machine Company, Madison Heights, MI, pg. 618

Lewis, Paul J., V.P.-Sls. & Mktg.--Telesensory, Mountain View, CA, pg. 1085

Lewis, Randy, Dir.-Mktg. & Sls.--RTMX-Uniflex Inc., Chapel Hill, NC, pg. 908

Lewkowitz, Bill, Natl. Sls. Dir.--Jackson Hole Ski Resort, Teton Village, WY, pg. 587

Libbe, Scott Wm., V.P.-Sls.--Rudolph/Libbe, Inc., Walbridge, OH, pg. 955

Liberatore, R., V.P.-Corp. Sls. & Mktg.--Formation, Inc., Moorestown, NJ, pg. 424

Libou, Bernie, V.P.-Sls.--Remco Toys, New York, NY, pg. 926

Lich, Terry, Mgr.-Sls.--Raynor Garage Door Company, Dixon, IL, pg. 915

Lichtenberger, R., Mgr.-Intl. Sls.--Graymills Corp., Chicago, IL, pg. 480

Lichtenderger, Lauren, Acting Sls. Field Mgr.--New Jersey State Lottery, Trenton, NJ, pg. 801

Liesem, Paul, V.P.-Sls.--Ohio Machinery Co., Cleveland, OH, pg. 822

Lifson, Al, V.P.-Sls. & Mktg.--Standard Chlorine Chemical Company, Kearny, NJ, pg. 1035

Lincer, Walt, V.P.-Sls. & Mktg.--Citrus World Inc., Lake Wales, FL, pg. 251

Lincoln, Stephen B., Jr., V.P.-Sls.--Garelick Farms, Inc., Franklin, MA, pg. 443

Lind, Ted. C., V.P.-Sls. & Mktg.--Hull Corporation, Hatboro, PA, pg. 552

Lindahl, John, Jr., V.P.-Sls.--State Industries Inc., Ashland City, TN, pg. 1041

Linde, Ken, Sls. Dir.--Phase Linear, Lincolnshire, IL, pg. 578

Lindeman, Gary, Dir.-Mktg. & Sls.--Microband Companies, Inc., Fairfield, NJ, pg. 748

Lindley, Peter, V.P.-Sls. & Mktg.--Sunroc Corporation, Media, PA, pg. 1062

Lindley, Peter M., V.P.-Sls. & Mktg.--Telkee Inc., Media, PA, pg. 1062

Lindquist, Dean, Mgr.-Sls.--St. Croix Press, Inc., New Richmond, WI, pg. 966

Lindroth, John G., Sr. V.P.-Domestic Sls.--General Binding Corporation, Northbrook, IL, pg. 656

Lindsay, Mark, V.P.-Sls. & Mktg.--George Lithograph, San Francisco, CA, pg. 452

Lindsey, Terrence R., V.P.-Sls.--Associated Company, Inc., Wichita, KS, pg. 89

Linduska, Paul S., Mgr.-Sls. & Mktg.--Andersen Windows Inc., Bayport, MN, pg. 72

Lines, Bruce, V.P.-Sls.--Pacific Sound Resources, Seattle, WA, pg. 841

Linet, Dale, V.P.-Sls.--Rudolph Foods Company, Lima, OH, pg. 954

Lingelbach, Tom, V.P.-Sls.--American Business Information, Inc., Omaha, NE, pg. 50

Linham, Steve, V.P.-Sls.--Renaissance Publishing Co., Inc., Auburn, IN, pg. 926

Linner, Robert, Sr. V.P.-Prod. Sls. Opers.--E.A. Sween Company, Eden Prairie, MN, pg. 1066

Linsemeyer, Bob, Mgr.-Sls.--Oil & Gas Supply Company, Houston, TX, pg. 823

Linville, D.C., Exec. V.P.-Mktg.--Chattanooga Group, Hixson, TN, pg. 241

Lipp, Ed, V.P.-Sls. Projects--Perlmuter Printing Company, Cleveland, OH, pg. 862

Lippitz, Richard, V.P.-Sls.--Allison Payment Systems Div., Indianapolis, IN, pg. 305

Lipscomb, William, V.P.-Sls. & Mktg.--Plastic Packaging, Inc., Hickory, NC, pg. 875

Liscik, Raymond, V.P.-Adv., Mktg., Sls. & Pub. Rels.--JCI Data Processing, Inc., Delran, NJ, pg. 584

List, R.S., Mgr.-Trade Sls.--Hyde Manufacturing Co., Southbridge, MA, pg. 556

Little, Tillman, Dir.-Sls.--Hankins Lumber Company, Inc., Grenada, MS, pg. 505

Littlefield, Robert, V.P.-Retail Sls.--Veryfine Products, Inc., Westford, MA, pg. 1148

Livingstone, William, Gen. Sls. Mgr.--M.S. Walker, Inc./Seacoast, Somerville, MA, pg. 1160

Llerandi, Rene, V.P.-Sls.--Margo Farms Del Caribe, Inc., Dorado, PR, pg. 706

LLona, Tom, Mgr.-Intl. Sls. & Mktg.--Code-A-Phone Corp., Clackamas, OR, pg. 258

Lloyd, Chuck, V.P.-Sls.--Maurey Manufacturing Corp., Chicago, IL, pg. 722

Lloyd, T.D., Dir.-Sls.--McLaughlin Gormley King Company, Minneapolis, MN, pg. 731

Locascio, Kenneth, Mgr.-Natl. Sls.--LSI Truck Products Corp.-Neway/Anchor Lock, Muskegon, MI, pg. 664

Loch, Doug, Mgr.-Sls.--First District Association, Litchfield, MN, pg. 412

Lochridge, John, Sr. V.P., Acct. Service--Starr Seigle McCombs, Inc., Honolulu, HI, pg. 1040

Lockhart, Gregory M., V.P.-Sls.--Lockhart Cadillac Inc., Indianapolis, IN, pg. 680

Lockner, Jack, Sr. V.P.-Sls. & Mktg.--Bankers Systems Inc., Saint Cloud, MN, pg. 117

Lodanski, Ed, Dir.-Sls., Caging Systems--Harford Systems, Inc., Aberdeen, MD, pg. 152

Lofgren, R., Dir.-Sls./Electrical Distr.--Eagle Electric Mfg. Co., Inc., Long Island City, NY, pg. 362

Logan, Bill, V.P.-Sls.--Makers Of Kal, Inc., Woodland Hills, CA, pg. 702

Logan, Bob, V.P.-Sls.--Megas Beauty Aids, Inc., Cleveland, OH, pg. 737

Lohr, D.G., V.P. & Dir.-Mktg. & Sls.-Paints--California Products Corp., Cambridge, MA, pg. 210

London, Mike, Sr. V.P. & Gen. Mktg. Mgr.--Lechmere, Inc., Woburn, MA, pg. 665

Long, Bob, Mgr.-Sls.--Old Home Foods, Inc., Saint Paul, MN, pg. 823

Long, Jack, Dir.-Sls.--Holsum Bakery, Inc., Phoenix, AZ, pg. 541

Looney, Ken, Dir.-Sls.--National Banner Company, Dallas, TX, pg. 786

Lopez, Art, Mgr.-Sls. & Service--NuArc Co., South San Francisco, CA, pg. 817

Lopez, Ray, Intl. Sls. Rep.--Triumph*Lor, Inc., Houston, TX, pg. 1115

Lopez, Ray, Intl. Acct. Rep.--Triumph-Lor, Inc., Houston, TX, pg. 1115

Lopus, Jerry, V.P.-Sls.--Peterson Tractor Company, San Leandro, CA, pg. 865

Lorbecki, David, V.P.-Sls.--Sargento Food Service Corp., Plymouth, WI, pg. 971

Lorenz, A., Natl. Sls. Mgr.--EvsWater Industrial Systems, Middletown, OH, pg. 712

Lorenz, Gerald, Dir.-Sales & Mktg.--Electro-Science Laboratories, Inc., King of Prussia, PA, pg. 375

Lotich, Rick, V.P.-Sls.--ITA Group, West Des Moines, IA, pg. 560

Lotker, Jack M., Sr. V.P.-Natl. Sls.--Homeland Stores, Inc., Oklahoma City, OK, pg. 542

Lott, Dean, V.P.-N.A. Sls.--Kreonite, Inc., Wichita, KS, pg. 644

Louden, James A., V.P.-Sls.--Komline-Sanderson Engineering Corp., Peapack, NJ, pg. 641

Louvrier, F., Sales Dir.-Consumer Prods.--N.V. Johnson Wax Belgium S.A., Groot-Bijgaarden,, Belgium, pg. 600

Love, Randolph D., Sr., V.P.-Sls.--Love Box Company, Inc., Wichita, KS, pg. 685

Lovejoy, Rita, V.P.-Sls.--American Antenna Corp, Elgin, IL, pg. 216

Lovett, Carol, Mgr.-Sls.--Rotary Forms Press, Inc., Hillsboro, OH, pg. 950

Loving, G., V.P.-Sls.--E. R. Carpenter Co., Richmond, VA, pg. 224

Lovold, Norton, Dir.-Sls.--Tone Commander Systems, Redmond, WA, pg. 1101

Lowe, David, Mgr.-Sls.--Kesterson Food Company, Inc., Paris, TN, pg. 624

Lowrey, Peter, V.P.-Natl. Sls.--A.W. Chesterton Company, Stoneham, MA, pg. 244

Loxley, Dick, Sr. V.P., Sls.--E-B Advertising Display Inc., Massillon, OH, pg. 358

Loyd, Bill, V.P.-Sls. & Mktg.--Burks Prosser/Enpo Industries, Inc., Decatur, IL, pg. 507

Loyd, Bill, V.P.-Mktg. & Sls.--Burks Pumps, Inc., Piqua, OH, pg. 507

Loyd, Bill, V.P.-Sls. & Mktg.--Prosser/Enpo Industries, Piqua, OH, pg. 507

Loyd, Bill, V.P.-Sales & Mktg.--Barnes Pumps, Inc., Mansfield, OH, pg. 507

Loyd, Bill, V.P.-Sales & Mktg.--AMW Industries Inc., Conway, AR, pg. 507

Lucas, Bill, Dir.-Sls.--Beltone Electronics Corporation, Chicago, IL, pg. 137

Lucas, Dave, Mgr.-Sls.--Roney Div. of Oberweis Dairy, Inc., Aurora, IL, pg. 820

Lucas, Don, V.P.-Sls.--Century Fence Company, Pewaukee, WI, pg. 235

Luchs, Kenneth, V.P.-Mktg., Sls. & Adv.--Reliable Stores, Inc., Columbia, MD, pg. 925

Luckadoo, John, V.P.-Natl. Accts. & Traffic--Fredrickson Motor Express Corp., Charlotte, NC, pg. 430

Ludak, Matt, Sr. V.P.-Sls.--SLM, Inc., Gloversville, NY, pg. 963

Ludlow, Ted, V.P.-Sls. & Mktg.--Bedford Industries, Inc., Worthington, MN, pg. 131

Ludwig, Bill, Dir.-Sls. & Mktg.--Polka Dot Dairy, Hastings, MN, pg. 879

Luedke, Donald A., V.P.-Sls.--Consolidated Industries, Inc., Cheshire, CT, pg. 276

Luedke, Keith, V.P.-Sls.--Field Packing Company, Owensboro, KY, pg. 409

Lueken, Tom, Mgr.-Sls. & Mktg., Retail Div.--R.S. Owens, Chicago, IL, pg. 834

Luitjens, Steve, Mgr.-Natl. Sls.--Sathers Inc., Round Lake, MN, pg. 972

Lukaszyk, William R., V.P.-Material Handling Sls.--Universal Dynamics Inc., Woodbridge, VA, pg. 1138

Lukitsh, Walt, Mgr.-Sls.--Arrow Fluid Power, Broadview, IL, pg. 85

Lund, J., Mgr.-Sls. & Mktg.--Simmons Juvenile Products Co., Inc., New London, WI, pg. 1008

Lund, Robert, Mgr.-Intl. Sls. & Mktg.--Hamilton Co., Inc., Reno, NV, pg. 503

Lundy, Dee, Dir.-Sls. & Mktg.--Family Inns of America, Inc., Pigeon Forge, TN, pg. 398

Lunt, George C. II, V.P.-Sls.--Rogers, Lunt & Bowlen Co., Greenfield, MA, pg. 943

Luongo, Daniel, Dir.-Sls.--Modern Handling Equipment Co., Bristol, PA, pg. 763

Luse, Wendell, V.P.-Pur. & Sls.--Acme Poultry Company, Inc., Seattle, WA, pg. 13

Lussier, Maureen, Gen. Mgr.--W.L.M. Bensdorp Company, Westborough, MA, pg. 139

Lussky, William, V.P.-Sls.--Progress Paint Mfg. Co., Louisville, KY, pg. 894

Lutfy, E.C., Natl. Sls. Mgr.--Data Instruments, Inc., Acton, MA, pg. 316

Lutz, Dave, Mgr.-Industrial Prods. Sls.--Ivex Packaging Corporation-Hillside, Hillside, IL, pg. 583

Lykins, B. C., V.P.-Sls.--Valley Asphalt Corporation, Cincinnati, OH, pg. 1143

Lynch, Bill, V.P.-Sls. & Mktg.--Dukane Ultrasonics Div., Saint Charles, IL, pg. 352

Lynch, Edward, V.P.-Sls. & Intl. Mktg.--Ames Safety Envelope Company, Inc., Somerville, MA, pg. 66

Lynch, Jack, V.P.-Sls.-General Freight Car Prods.--Thrall Car Mfg. Co., Chicago Heights, IL, pg. 350

Lynch, Kevin, V.P.-Eastern Sls. Opers.--Integral Systems, Walnut Creek, CA, pg. 572

Lynch, Pat, V.P.-Sls. & Mktg.--IDAB International Incorporated, Hampton, VA, pg. 559

Lynch, Tim, Natl. Sls. Mgr.--RHC/Spacemaster Corporation, Melrose Park, IL, pg. 906

Lynn, Ralph, V.P.-Western Reg. Sls.--Toter Incorporated, Statesville, NC, pg. 1103

Lynne, Mara, Sls. Dir.--Smith's Personnel Service, Inc., New York, NY, pg. 1014

Lytle, Robert, V.P.-Sls. & Mktg.--Allied Paper Incorporated, Dayton, OH, pg. 38

Lytton, Richard, Asst. V.P.-Natl. & Govt. Acct. Sls.--Monroe Systems For Business, Inc., Morris Plains, NJ, pg. 766

Maas, Robert A., V.P.-Sls. & Mktg.--Kalmbach Publishing Co., Milwaukee, WI, pg. 615

MacConnell, Daniel R., V.P.-Sls.--Thomson MacConnell Cadillac, Inc., Cincinnati, OH, pg. 1095

MacDonald, Michael, V.P.-Sls.--Beech Holdings Corp., Chicago, IL, pg. 131

MacDonald, R.R., Dir.-Sls.--Detex Corporation, New Braunfels, TX, pg. 333

MacEachern, Jack, Sr. V.P.-Sls.--The William Carter Company, New York, NY, pg. 226

Macfarlane, Bud, V.P.-Sls. & Mktg.--Innovative Plastics Corporation, Orangeburg, NY, pg. 570

MacGregor, John A., Jr., V.P.-Sls. & Mktg.--The Kent Manufacturing Co., Pickens, SC, pg. 623

Machado, Gonzalo, Client Svcs. Dir.--Ayer Vazquez S.A. de Publicidad, Buenos Aires,, Argentina, pg. 104

Machamer, Lamont, V.P.-Sls. & Mktg.--Dyatron/Bondo Corporation, Atlanta, GA, pg. 356
MacKay, Iain, Sls. Dir.--Adams Rite (Europe) Ltd., Swanley,, United Kingdom, pg. 17
MacKenzie, Scott, Mgr.-Natl. Sls.--Jennifer Dale, Inc., New York, NY, pg. 592
MacKenzie, Warren, V.P.-Sls. & Mktg.--Pittsburgh Tube Co., Monaca, PA, pg. 873
Mackin, Mike, Mgr.-Sls.--Hanel Lumber Co., Inc., Hood River, OR, pg. 505
Mackinnon, G., Mgr.-Sls.--Bloomfield Industries Canada Ltd., Mississauga,, Canada, pg. 1027
Maddox, J.A., V.P.-Mktg. & Sls.--Wilbur Chocolate Co., Inc., Lititz, PA, pg. 219
Maddox, Richard, V.P.-Sls. & Mktg.--Bachmann Industries, Inc., Philadelphia, PA, pg. 108
Maddox, Richard, V.P.-Sls.--Blue Bird Corporation, Fort Valley, GA, pg. 158
Madsen, Richard, Dir.-Sls.--Little Lady Foods, Inc., Elk Grove Village, IL, pg. 679
Maez, Felix, V.P.-Sls.--Celestial Seasonings, Boulder, CO, pg. 231
Maggetti, Robert, V.P.-Sls.--After Six, Incorporated, Philadelphia, PA, pg. 24
Maglio, Louis A., V.P.-Sls.--Walpole Woodworkers, Inc., Walpole, MA, pg. 1161
Magnacca, Scott, Mgr.-Sls./Mktg.--SBN Systems Inc.-Canadian Operations, Mississauga,, Canada, pg. 960
Magri, Bill, V.P.-Sls. Los Angeles Div.--Vienna Sausage Mfg. Co., Chicago, IL, pg. 1151
Magyaros, J.M., Mgr.-Intl. Sls.--Electric Furnace Co., Salem, OH, pg. 373
Mahar, Joe, Dir.-Sls.--ITS: Intertrade Scientific, Inc., Vernon, CT, pg. 748
Maher, William, V.P.-Sls. Admin.--Equitable Bag Company, Long Island City, NY, pg. 385
Mahon, Robert, Central Reg. Adv. Sls. Mgr.--The Weather Channel, Inc.-Chicago Sales Office, Chicago, IL, pg. 654
Mahoney, Dave, V.P.-Sls.--Rainier Brewing Co., Seattle, WA, pg. 526
Mahoney, David S., V.P.-Sls.-West Region--G. Heileman Brewing Co., Inc., La Crosse, WI, pg. 526
Mahoney, Michael, Mgr.- Sls.--Wallich Lumber Co., Detroit, MI, pg. 1161
Mahorney, William R., V.P.-Sls., Western Reg.--Ash Grove Cement Company, Overland Park, KS, pg. 87
Maier, Ed, V.P.-Sls.--ENI, Rochester, NY, pg. 360
Mairorino, Kim, Sales Acct. Rep.--Patriot Direct Dial Systems, Los Angeles, CA, pg. 1180
Maiuccoro, Gary, Dir.-Sls. & Mktg.--Imperial Pools, Inc., Latham, NY, pg. 564
Maki, Jack, V.P.-Sls.--Tape Coat Division, Evanston, IL, pg. 1072
Males, Ron, V.P.-Sls.--QuikTrip Corporation, Tulsa, OK, pg. 905
Mallett, Jeff, V.P.-Sls. & Mktg.--Reference Software International, San Francisco, CA, pg. 921
Mallett, Jill, Mgr.-Sls.--Thomas Pipe & Steel, Inc., Baton Rouge, LA, pg. 1093
Malloy, Bill, Mgr.-Sls.--Cheraw Yarn Mills, Inc., Cheraw, SC, pg. 242
Malloy, Jim, Dir.-Mktg. & Sls.--Advanced Controls, Inc., Irvine, CA, pg. 20
Maloley, Charles, Mgr.-Sls.--Humiston-Keeling, Inc., Chicago, IL, pg. 552
Malone, Kevin, V.P.-Customer Service & Sls.--Advanced Input Devices, Inc., Coeur D'Alene, ID, pg. 20
Maloney, Donal P., V.P.-ESS Sls. & Mktg.--Elliott Company, Jeannette, PA, pg. 378
Maloney, Michael M., V.P.-Sls. & Mktg.--American Envelope Company, Chicago, IL, pg. 199
Manby, Joel, Sr. V.P.-Mktg. & Sls.--Spring Arbor Distributors, Belleville, MI, pg. 1033
Manchem, Craig, Exec. V.P.-Sls. & Mktg.--Hurst Performances, Inc., Cleveland, OH, pg. 761
Manchester, Bruce, Mgr.-Intl. Sls.--NESLAB Instruments, Inc., Newington, NH, pg. 798
Mandell, Alan, V.P.-Sls. & Mktg.--S. E. Huffman Corp., Clover, SC, pg. 551
Manelin, Bradley A., Sr. V.P.-Sls.--North Pacific Lumber Company, Portland, OR, pg. 813
Mangi, Jack, V.P.-Sls.--Pace Press, Inc., New York, NY, pg. 838
Mangold, Fred, Dir.-Sls.--Jake Sweeney Automotive Inc., Cincinnati, OH, pg. 1067
Mangrum, Curtis R., V.P.-Sls.--Excelsior Manufacturing & Supply Corp., Itasca, IL, pg. 392
Manis, Mike, Sls. Mgr.--N. Erlanger, Blumgart & Company, Inc., New York, NY, pg. 387
Mankamyer, Dick, Mktg. & Sls.--The Springwall Mattress Co., Akron, OH, pg. 1033
Mann, Barry, Dir.-Sls. & Mktg.--Enidine Incorporated, Orchard Park, NY, pg. 382
Mann, Carl A., V.P.-Sls.--Presto Lock, Inc., Garfield, NJ, pg. 888
Mann, Christopher, V.P.-Sls. & Mktg.--CVC Products, Inc., Rochester, NY, pg. 206
Mann, Donald, Sr. V.P.--World's Finest Chocolate, Inc., Chicago, IL, pg. 1203
Mann, Lou, V.P.-Sls.--Capitol Records, Inc., Hollywood, CA, pg. 216
Mannarino, J., Mgr.-O.E.M. Sls.--Eagle Electric Mfg. Co., Inc., Long Island City, NY, pg. 362
Manno, Ted, Sls. & Mktg. Admin.--Delaware Lottery, Dover, DE, pg. 326
Marano, Jim, Natl. Sls. Mgr.--Sillcocks Plastics International, Inc., Berkeley Heights, NJ, pg. 1004
Marceaux, Charles G., Mgr.-Sls.--Westgate Inc., Port Allen, LA, pg. 1182
Marck, Andy, Div. Mgr.-Sls.--The Jel Sert Co., West Chicago, IL, pg. 591
Marco-Koehler, Antionette, Administrator-Sls. & Mktg.--Octagon Process Inc., Edgewater, NJ, pg. 821
Marcoe, Joe, Mgr.-Sls.--KCOY-TV, Santa Maria, CA, pg. 1043
Marcozzi, John, Dir.-Direct Sls.--ASC Incorporated, Southgate, MI, pg. 7
Marfuggi, Eugene, Exec. V.P.-Natl. Sls., Mktg. & Adv.--Ferrara Foods & Confections, Inc., New York, NY, pg. 407
Marin, Peter, V.P.-Sls.--William O'Neil & Co., Inc., Los Angeles, CA, pg. 827
Marinello, David, V.P.-Sls. & Mktg.-Branded Prods.--International Jensen Inc., Lincolnshire, IL, pg. 578
Marini, Jeff, Natl. Sls. Mgr.--Autoroll Machine Corp., Middleton, MA, pg. 101
Markham, Bob, Sls. Mgr.-RCA/GE Video--Arizona Wholesale Supply Company, Phoenix, AZ, pg. 82
Markham, Paul, V.P.-Sls.--ECRM, Tewksbury, MA, pg. 359
Marks, Ted, V.P.-Sls.--Gould Paper Corporation, New York, NY, pg. 473
Marks, Walter A., V.P.-Sls.--G.B. DuPont Co., Inc., Troy, MI, pg. 354
Marmion, Bridget, V.P. & Dir.-Mktg. & Sls.--Farrar, Straus & Giroux, Inc., New York, NY, pg. 403
Marquart, Stan, Dir.-Sls.--Cenex/Land O'Lakes, Inc., Saint Paul, MN, pg. 653
Marquart, Stan, Dir.-Sls.--Cenex/Land O'Lakes, Inc., Saint Paul, MN, pg. 231
Marr, A.G., V.P.-Mining Sls.--Road Machinery Company, Phoenix, AZ, pg. 937
Marr, Clifford T., V.P.-Mktg. & Sls.--Pioneer Plastics Corp., Auburn, ME, pg. 872
Marra, Dan, Mgr.-Reg. Sls. Mgr. Southeast--Ivex Packaging Corporation-Madison, Madison, GA, pg. 583
Mars, Ann, Mgr.-Sls. & Mktg.--The Flood Company, Hudson, OH, pg. 419
Marsh, G., Mgr.-Sls. Admin.--Kentile Floors Inc., South Plainfield, NJ, pg. 623
Marshall, Duff, Mgr.-Sls., Mktg. & Adv.--Marvin Lumber & Cedar Company, Warroad, MN, pg. 716
Marshall, Michael J., V.P.-Sls.--Zymark Corporation, Hopkinton, MA, pg. 1221
Martens, D. A., V.P.-Sls. & Mktg.--West Coast Growers & Packers, Inc., Selma, CA, pg. 1177
Martin, Dan T., V.P.-Sls. & Customer Service Dry Bulk--Ingram Barge Company, Nashville, TN, pg. 569
Martin, John, V.P.-Residential Mktg.--Irvine Company, Newport Beach, CA, pg. 582
Martin, Lawrence M., V.P.-Mktg. & Sls.--Hitchcock Industries, Inc., Bloomington, MN, pg. 536
Martin, M., V.P.-Natl. Acct. Sls.--F.G. Montabert, Midland Park, NJ, pg. 766
Martin, Richard, V.P.-Sls. & Mktg., C&L--Tekra Corporation, New Berlin, WI, pg. 1084
Martin, Tilden, V.P.-Sls.--Better Brands Of Atlanta, Inc., Atlanta, GA, pg. 148
Martinello, Tony, Mgr.-Premium Sls.--Holoubek Inc., Waukesha, WI, pg. 540
Martinez, Paul, V.P.-Sls. & Mktg.--Label-Aire Inc., Fullerton, CA, pg. 649
Martino, Nick, Mgr.-Natl. Sls.--Metrologic Instruments, Inc., Blackwood, NJ, pg. 743
Mason, Everett L., V.P.-Sls.--W. B. Roddenbery Company, Inc., Cairo, GA, pg. 942
Mason, Steve, V.P.-Retail Opers.--Homeland Stores, Inc., Oklahoma City, OK, pg. 542
Mason, Tom, Dir.-Sls. & Mktg.--Wausau Homes, Inc., Rothschild, WI, pg. 1168
Massalone, Daniel, V.P.-Sls.--Eastway Delivery Service of Houston, Inc., Houston, TX, pg. 364
Masyada, Donald S., V.P.-Electrode Sls.--The Carbide/Graphite Group, Inc., Pittsburgh, PA, pg. 217
Mathews, Ken, Mgr.-Sls.--L & L Nursery Supply, Inc., Chino, CA, pg. 647
Mathews, Richard, Mgr.-Mktg. & Sls.--Vacudyne Inc., Chicago Heights, IL, pg. 45
Matsen, Jack, V.P.-Sls., Western Region--Wm. E. Wright Limited Partnership, West Warren, MA, pg. 1205
Matsumoto, Bob, V.P.-Sls., N. America--Danly-Komatsu L.P., Cicero, IL, pg. 275
Matthews, Ted, V.P.-Sls., Southern Area--Steelcase Inc., Grand Rapids, MI, pg. 1044
Mattingly, James, V.P.-Sls.--O'Bryan Brothers Inc., Chicago, IL, pg. 820
Mattox, Robert F., Western Reg. Sls. Mgr.--General Refractories Co., U. S. Refractories Div., Pittsburgh, PA, pg. 136
Maussnar, Melissa M., Dir.-Sls. Promo.--Rama Group of Companies, Cheektowaga, NY, pg. 910
Maxim, Hilda, Asst. Dir.-US Sls.--The ASCII Group, Inc., Bethesda, MD, pg. 8
Maxwell, Harold, Mgr.-Sls.--Hempt Brothers, Inc., Camp Hill, PA, pg. 528
Maxwell, John, V.P.-Sls. & Mktg.--Ivex Packaging Corporation-Polymerization and Extrusion Division, Hazleton, PA, pg. 583
Maxwell, Larry L., V.P.-Sls.--Charmglow Industries, Inc., DuQuoin, IL, pg. 240
Mayhew, John M., V.P.-Sls.--Sunshine Biscuits, Inc., Woodbridge, NJ, pg. 439
Mazurco, Frank, V.P.-Sls. & Mktg.--Steinway & Sons, Long Island City, NY, pg. 1046
Mazziotti, Robert, Reg. V.P.-Franchise Sls.--Little Caesar Enterprises, Inc., Detroit, MI, pg. 678
Mazzola, Ronald A., Exec. Dir.-Mktg. & Sls.--McNaughton & Gunn, Inc., Saline, MI, pg. 732
Mc Creery, Tom, Sls. Dir.--Tecknit, Cranford, NJ, pg. 1084
McAdam, Robert C., Sr. V.P.-Mktg. & Sls.--Facemate Corporation, Chicopee, MA, pg. 396
McAfee, Felicia, Dir.-Sls.--Pro-Line Corporation, Dallas, TX, pg. 892
McAlister, Gary, Mgr.-New Ford Sls.--Fairway Ford, Inc., Greenville, SC, pg. 397
McBain, W.P., V.P.-Sls. & Mktg.--Daubert Coated Products, Inc., Westchester, IL, pg. 317
McBride, Richard L., Mgr.-Sls.--T. Bruce Sales, Inc., West Middlesex, PA, pg. 183
McCabe, R., Dir.-Sls.--Lensclean, Inc., Carlstadt, NJ, pg. 33
McCall, John A., V.P. & Circulation Mgr.--Seattle Times Company, Seattle, WA, pg. 986
McCall, Tim, Mgr.-Intl. Sls.--Mico Inc., North Mankato, MN, pg. 748
McCalla, Hal, V.P.-Sls.--Tennsco Corporation, Dickson, TN, pg. 1088
McCamish, Bernie, V.P.-Sls. & Mktg.--Ward Leonard Electric Company, Inc., Mount Vernon, NY, pg. 1127
McCandless, William, V.P.-Sls.--Key Handling Systems, Inc., Hackensack, NJ, pg. 627
McCarthy, Charles, V.P.-Sls. & Mktg.--Syroco Inc., Baldwinsville, NY, pg. 1070
McCarthy, Francis J., V.P.-Mktg. & Sls.--A. Duda & Sons Inc., Oviedo, FL, pg. 351
McCarthy, Patrick M., Grp. V.P.-Sls. & Mktg.--Ocean Spray Cranberries, Inc., Lakeville, MA, pg. 820
McCaughey, R. James, Exec. V.P.-Sls.--Jaydon Incorporated, Rock Island, IL, pg. 590
McCaughey, Robert, Gen. Sls. Mgr.--WPRI-TV, East Providence, RI, pg. 783
McClay, Wayne, V.P.-Sls.--PowerForce Company, Inc., Chicago, IL, pg. 560
McClure, Jim, V.P.-Sls. & Mfg.--International Cold Storage Co., Inc., Andover, KS, pg. 576
McClure, R.C., Mgr.-Sls. & Mktg., Hwy. Prods.--Potters Industries, Inc., Parsippany, NJ, pg. 837
McCollum, Bruce, Exec. V.P.--Tingley Rubber Corporation, South Plainfield, NJ, pg. 1098
McConner, Sam, Sr. V.P.-Sls.--Acme Boot Co., Inc., Clarksville, TN, pg. 400
McCook, George M., V.P.-Sls.--Purcell Co., Inc., Bay Saint Louis, MS, pg. 900
McCord, Paul, Sr., Sls. Mgr.--Security Van Lines, Inc., Kenner, LA, pg. 987
McCord, R.L., Mgr.-Sls.--American Welding & Manufacturing Co., Warren, OH, pg. 431
McCormack, J.W., V.P.-Sls.--Wheaton Van Lines, Inc., Indianapolis, IN, pg. 1184
McCormack, Jack, V.P.-Sls. & Mktg.--Mission Industries, Santa Barbara, CA, pg. 760
McCormack, T.F., V.P.-Sls.--Conwood Company L.P., Memphis, TN, pg. 281
McCormick, Joan, V.P.-Tire Equipment Sls.--McNeil & NRM., Inc., Akron, OH, pg. 732
McCormick, John L., Sr. V.P.-Tire Equip. & Sls.--NRM-Steelastic, Akron, OH, pg. 781
McCormick, Mark A., Gen. Mgr.-Sls.--Illinois Auto Electric Midwest Engine Warehouse Div., Elmhurst, IL, pg. 562
McCort, John, V.P.-Sls.--Santa Rosa Steel Forming, Inc., Santa Rosa, CA, pg. 970
McCory, John, Jr., V.P.-Sls.--TSR, Inc., Lake Geneva, WI, pg. 1075
McCoun, Kenneth N., Jr., Sr. V.P.-Sls.--North Pacific Lumber Company, Portland, OR, pg. 813
McCown, Fred E., V.P.-Sls. & Mktg.--ATAPCO Office Products Group, Saint Louis, MO, pg. 64
McCoy, John, District Mgr.--ATAPCO Globe-Weis/Kosciusko, Kosciusko, MS, pg. 64
McCracken, Jay, V.P.-Sls.--The Upper Deck Company, Carlsbad, CA, pg. 1140
McCrary, John, V.P.-Sls.--Grocery Supply Company Division, Sulphur Springs, TX, pg. 440
McCrobie, Ronald N., V.P.-Procurement--Tri-State Wholesale Associated Grocers, El Paso, TX, pg. 1111
McCullom, William, Mgr.-Sls.--United Aluminum Corporation, North Haven, CT, pg. 1130
McCullough, Brian, Mgr.-Sls.--Douglas Stephen Plastics, Inc., Paterson, NJ, pg. 347
McCullough, K.P., V.P.-Sls.--Havens Steel Co., Kansas City, MO, pg. 517
McCurdy, Robert, Dir.-Engrng. & Sls.--Holcomb & Hoke Mfg. Company, Inc., Indianapolis, IN, pg. 538
McCutheon, William, Jr., V.P.-Sls.--Cairns & Brother, Inc., Clifton, NJ, pg. 207
McDaniel, John L., V.P.-Sls. & Mktg.--Sunbeam Casual Furniture Co., Portland, TN, pg. 1059
McDole, Kevin, Natl. Sls. Mgr.--The Miami Margarine Co., Cincinnati, OH, pg. 746
McDonald, Becky, Dir.-Sls.--Keiper Recaro, Inc., Clawson, MI, pg. 620
McDonald, Frank, Dir.-Sls., Bioclean Systems--Harford Systems, Inc., Aberdeen, MD, pg. 152
McDonald, Rod, V.P. & Dir. European Sls.--J.D. Edwards & Company, Denver, CO, pg. 370
McDonell, Ken, Dir.-Specialty Prod. Sls.--Thomas Built Buses, Inc., High Point, NC, pg. 1092
McDonough, Bob, Sls. Mgr.--Larkin, Inc., Atlanta, GA, pg. 667
McDonough, Bob, Sls. Mgr.--Heatcraft, Inc., Stone Mountain, GA, pg. 667
McDougall, Douglas, Mgr.-Sls. & Consumer Promotion--Luzianne Blue Plate Foods, New Orleans, LA, pg. 923
McDowell, J. Douglas, Mgr.-Jewelry Sls.--B.A. Ballou & Co. Inc., East Providence, RI, pg. 116
McEwen, Kevin B., Sls. Coord.--Steffen Dairy Foods Co., Inc., Wichita, KS, pg. 884
McFadden, Miriam, Mgr.-Circulation--The Oak Ridger, Oak Ridge, TN, pg. 1042
McFarling, Robert E., V.P.-Sls. & Treas.--McFarling Foods, Inc., Indianapolis, IN, pg. 729
McGaha, Ray, V.P.-Sls. & Engrng.--Continental Conveyor & Equipment Company, Winfield, AL, pg. 798
McGaha, Tom, Mgr.-Sls.--Adams Extract Co., Inc., Austin, TX, pg. 16
McGarry, Richard D., Mgr.-Sls.--Southwark Metal Manufacturing Company, Philadelphia, PA, pg. 1023
McGavin, T.J., Exec. V.P., Mktg. & Sls.--Furnas Electric Company, Batavia, IL, pg. 437
McGinnis, Bill, V.P.-Sls.--Delta Education, Inc., Hudson, NH, pg. 326

Corporate Responsibilities Index

McGinnis, Tom, Gen. Mgr.-Sls.--Meadville Forging Co., Meadville, PA, pg. 733
McGinty, Paul, Exec. V.P.-Sls.--Tri Valley Growers Inc., San Francisco, CA, pg. 1111
McGlade, Tom, V.P.-Chicagoland Sls.--Vienna Sausage Mfg. Co., Chicago, IL, pg. 1151
McGonagle, William, V.P.-Sls.--Crowe Rope Company, Warren, ME, pg. 301
McGowen, Fred, Intl. Sls. Mgr.--Dukane Ultrasonics Div., Saint Charles, IL, pg. 352
McGrath, Daniel S., V.P.-Sls.--Mico Inc., North Mankato, MN, pg. 748
McGrath, John M., Sr. V.P.-Mktg. & Sls.--F.G. Montabert, Midland Park, NJ, pg. 766
McGready, James, V.P.-Sls.--Owen Steel Co., Inc., Columbia, SC, pg. 834
McGregor, Rob, V.P.-Sls. & Adv.--Brookfield Engineering Laboratories, Inc., Stoughton, MA, pg. 179
McGuiness, Lee, V.P.-Merchant Sls.--Ivex Packaging Corporation-Industrial Products Division, Newton, MA, pg. 583
McGuire, Thomas F., V.P.-Sls.--Carlisle Equipment Company, Louisville, KY, pg. 220
McHale, John, V.P.-Sls.--Maxitrol Co., Southfield, MI, pg. 723
McHeffey, Peter, Dir.-Sls.--Motor Boating & Sailing, New York, NY, pg. 523
McHenry, Brian, V.P.-Sls. & Mktg.--La France Corporation, Philadelphia, PA, pg. 649
McHugh, Craig L., V.P.-Sls.--Trace Products, San Jose, CA, pg. 1104
McHugh, Larry, Southern Reg. Adv. Sls. Mgr.--The Weather Channel, Inc.-Atlanta Sales Office, Atlanta, GA, pg. 654
McHugh, Robert E., V.P.-Mktg.--Alco Health Services Corporation, Malvern, PA, pg. 31
McInerney, J. Barrett, V.P.-Mktg. & Sls.--Crane & Co., Inc., Dalton, MA, pg. 296
McInerney, John J., V.P.-Sls. & Mktg.--McInerney Inc., Oak Park, MI, pg. 729
McInnis, Louisa, Mgr.-Sls.--Noel-Joanna, Inc., Rancho Santa Margarita, CA, pg. 808
McIntyre, Joseph E., V.P.-Sls.--Dettra Flag Company, Oaks, PA, pg. 333
McKay, Donald, Dir.-Sls. & Mktg.--Colonial Beef Co., Philadelphia, PA, pg. 263
McKee, John, V.P.-Retail--McKee Door, Inc., Aurora, IL, pg. 730
McKee, Sharon, Dir.-Sls. Devel.--The Goldhirsh Group Inc., Boston, MA, pg. 467
McKelvey, Steve, Mgr.-Sls.--Palmetto Wholesale Co., Inc., Columbia, SC, pg. 844
McKenna, Andrew J., Jr., V.P-Sls.--Schwarz Paper Company, Morton Grove, IL, pg. 980
McKenna, K., Mgr.-Natls. Sls.--ATAPCO Office Products Group, Saint Louis, MO, pg. 64
McKeon, Patrick E., Exec. V.P.-Sls. & Mktg.--Spectrum Industries, Inc., Chippewa Falls, WI, pg. 1029
McKimmey, Chuck, V.P.-Sls. & Mktg.--Jayco Inc., Middlebury, IN, pg. 590
McKinney, Robert G., Mgr.-Sls.--Chapman Printing Company, Huntington, WV, pg. 239
McKinney, Ronald L., V.P.-Sls.--Specialty Industries, Inc., Red Lion, PA, pg. 1027
McKissick, Larry, Mgr.-Natl. Sls.--Brunner & Lay, Inc., Franklin Park, IL, pg. 184
McKnight, Ron, Exec. V.P.-Sls.--United States Bakery, Portland, OR, pg. 1134
McLain, Scott A., V.P.-Natl. Sls. & Mktg.--Superior Industries of Nebraska, Inc., Omaha, NE, pg. 1063
McLaughlin, Hugh C., V.P.-Sls.--Tubular Steel Inc., Saint Louis, MO, pg. 1118
McLaughlin, Joseph, Dir.-Sales--Berlitz Publishing Company Inc., New York, NY, pg. 142
McLaughlin, Larry, V.P.-Sls.--Kendale Industries, Inc., Valley View, OH, pg. 622
McLean, Earle W., Southeast Reg. Sls. Mgr.--General Refractories Co., U. S. Refractories Div., Pittsburgh, PA, pg. 136
McLean, Edward J., V.P.-Sls.--Advance Packaging Corporation, Grand Rapids, MI, pg. 19
McLean, Steve, V.P.-Sls.--The Savogran Company, Norwood, MA, pg. 973
McLeod, Lorn E., Mgr.-Sls./Grocery Div.--Doane Products Co., Branded Sales Div., Joplin, MO, pg. 342
McMahan, John, V.P.-Sls.--The George E. Failing Company, Enid, OK, pg. 161
McMenany, W.J., Gen. Sls. Mgr.--Nimnicht Chevrolet Company, Jacksonville, FL, pg. 807
McMillan, Gloria, V.P.-Sls. & Mktg.--Kimstock, Inc., Santa Ana, CA, pg. 630
McMillan, H.J., Gen. & Sls. Mgr.--Groendyk Mfg. Co., Inc., Buchanan, VA, pg. 480
McMilliam, Terry, Mgr.-Sls. Devel.--Great Lakes Lithograph Co., Cleveland, OH, pg. 481
McMullin, Tom, Gen. Sls. Mgr.--McInnes Steel Company, Corry, PA, pg. 729
McNab, Peter, Dir.-Admin. & Sls.--Selecto-Flash, Inc., West Orange, NJ, pg. 988
McNabb, James, Dir.-Sls. & Mktg.--Associated Electric Co-op Inc., Springfield, MO, pg. 89
McNeill, Don, Mgr.-Sls.--Air Gage Company, Livonia, MI, pg. 27
McNichol, Paul, Mgr.-Sls.--L&R Manufacturing Co., Kearny, NJ, pg. 647
McPherson, James, V.P.-Sls.--Rodefeld Co., Inc., Richmond, IN, pg. 942
McPike, Dave, Mgr.-Sls.--Kokomo Spring Company, Inc., Kokomo, IN, pg. 640
McQueen, Edwin D., Exec. V.P.-Sls.--Steelox Systems, Inc., Mason, OH, pg. 1044
McQuilkin, Allan, Natl. Sls. Mgr.--Alimak Elevator Company, Bridgeport, CT, pg. 34
McRae, Joel, Mgr.-Sls.--Lamb Engineering & Construction Co., Salt Lake City, UT, pg. 652
McWilliams, Brent N., V.P.-Sls.--Laidlaw Corporation, Scottsdale, AZ, pg. 650
McWilliams, Gary A., Mgr.-Sls.--McWilliams Forge Co., Rockaway, NJ, pg. 733
McWilliams, Timothy C., Exec. V.P.--McWilliams Forge Co., Rockaway, NJ, pg. 733
Meacham, Ronald G., V.P.-Sls. & Mktg.--Bachman Company, Reading, PA, pg. 108
Mead, Jennifer, V.P.-Sls.--Echo Design Group, Inc., New York, NY, pg. 365
Mead, Sherman, Mgr.-Natl. Sls.--Laubeck Corporation/Cross, Carbondale, PA, pg. 660
Meadows, Phillip, Dir.-Sls.--Sunnyland Foods, Inc., Thomasville, GA, pg. 1061
Meany, William C., Mgr.-Sls.--Lindenmeyr Munroe, Rutherford, NJ, pg. 233
Mechanick, Marty, V.P.-Sls.--Code-A-Phone Corp., Clackamas, OR, pg. 258
Mechling, Robert, V.P.-Sls.--Midco International Inc., Chicago, IL, pg. 751
Medved, Pat, V.P.-Sls.--Broadcast Supply West, Tacoma, WA, pg. 177
Mehtlan, David L., V.P.-Sls. & Mktg.--American Stone-Mix, Inc., Towson, MD, pg. 63
Meier, Victor G., Exec. V.P.-Sls.--Premier Coatings, Inc., Elk Grove Village, IL, pg. 886
Meir, George, Natl. Sls. Mgr.--American Optical Corp., Greenwich, CT, pg. 59
Meisel, Jules, V.P.-Sls.--Gould Paper Corporation, New York, NY, pg. 473
Meisenheimer, W., Distr. Mgr.-Sls.--The Jel Sert Co., West Chicago, IL, pg. 591
Mekus, Thomas, Dir.-Sls. & Mktg.--Diehl Specialties Intl., Defiance, OH, pg. 336
Mekus, Thomas A., Mgr.-Sls. & Mktg.--Diehl, Inc., Defiance, OH, pg. 336
Melchoir, James, Dir.-Agency Sls.--MSI Insurance Companies, Arden Hills, MN, pg. 693
Melhuish, James P., Mgr.-Retail Sls.--Algood Food Company, Louisville, KY, pg. 34
Melhuish, Nicolas B., Mgr.-Export & Food Svc. Sls.--Algood Food Company, Louisville, KY, pg. 34
Mellecker, Kirk, V.P.-Sls.--Holsum Foods, Waukesha, WI, pg. 515
Meller, Mike, Mgr.-Sls.--Chemifax, City of Commerce, CA, pg. 159
Mellilo, George, V.P.-Sls.--Solvay Pharmaceuticals, Inc., Marietta, GA, pg. 1017
Melum, R.S., Gen. Mgr.-Mktg.--Atlantic Steel Company, Atlanta, GA, pg. 95
Menconi, Larry, V.P.-Sls.--Midwest Litho Arts, Des Plaines, IL, pg. 478
Mendelson, Lewis A., Exec. V.P.-Mktg.--Dazey Corporation, Industrial Airport, KS, pg. 321
Mendoza, Andy, Mgr.-Sls.--Nor-Cal Beverage Co., Inc., West Sacramento, CA, pg. 808
Merante, Joseph, Sr. V.P.-Mktg. & Sls.-No. America--Zim-American Israeli Shipping Co., New York, NY, pg. 1219
Mercer, Bruce K., Mgr.-Natl. Sls.--Swift Instruments, Inc., Dorchester, MA, pg. 1068
Mercer, Reuben E., V.P.-Credit & Sls.--Carlyle & Co. Jewelers, Greensboro, NC, pg. 222
Mercier, Gil, Gen. Sls. Mgr.--Plasti-Kote Co., Pactra Hobby, Valencia, CA, pg. 875
Merrick, George A., Exec. V.P.-Mktg., Sls. & Service--Ampex Corporation, Redwood City, CA, pg. 998
Merwise, Norm, Mgr.-Natl. Sls.--Scripto-Tokai, Inc., Fontana, CA, pg. 983
Mesa, Hernan, Dir.-Sls.--Banana Services Inc., Coral Gables, FL, pg. 117
Messer, George, V.P.-Media Sls.--Multi-Ad Services, Inc., Peoria, IL, pg. 775
Messer, James, Dir.-Sls.--E & D Grain Marketing Co, Cincinnati, OH, pg. 359
Messer, Jim, Loan Officer--Wieland Financial Services, Inc., Atlanta, GA, pg. 1188
Metcalf, Virgil L., V.P.-Sls. & Mktg.--Waldes Truarc, Inc., Somerset, NJ, pg. 1159
Metkzer, Pat, Sls. Mgr.--Mister Twister, Minden, LA, pg. 997
Metz, Gene, V.P.-Sls. & Mktg.--Sauder Woodworking Co., Archbold, OH, pg. 972
Metzler, E., V.P.-Sls.--Maghielse Tool Corporation, Grand Rapids, MI, pg. 700
Meyer, Ken, Mgr.-Sls.--Ivex Packaging Corporation-Mill Division, Joliet, IL, pg. 583
Meyer, Mark, Dir.-Sls.--South Dakota Lottery, Pierre, SD, pg. 1019
Meyer, Stephen, V.P. & Asst. Sls.Mgr.--Gould Paper Corporation, New York, NY, pg. 473
Miale, Richard, V.P.-Sls.--Industrial Wire Products Corporation, Pomona, CA, pg. 567
Michael, Dennis M., V.P.-Sls.--Frederick Trading Company, Frederick, MD, pg. 430
Michaelis, Dana, V.P.-Affiliated Sls.--The Travel Channel, Atlanta, GA, pg. 654
Michard, Laura, Dir.-Sls. & Mktg.--Beltone Electronics Corporation, Chicago, IL, pg. 137
Mickle, Robert, V.P.-Sls. & Mktg.--Wing Industries, Inc., Dallas, TX, pg. 1196
Midili, John E., Dir.-Sls.-Western Region--Union Switch & Signal Inc., Pittsburgh, PA, pg. 1129
Mikulina, Tom, V.P.-Mktg. & Sls.--The Trane Company, La Crosse, WI, pg. 62
Milbourn, G.B., V.P.-Sls.--The Coe Mfg. Co., Painesville, OH, pg. 258
Milburn, Robert, Mgr.-Sls. Office--Rudel Machinery Company, Inc., Shelton, CT, pg. 954
Miles, Marc, Dir.-Sls.-Southern Div.--Altec Industries, Inc., Birmingham, AL, pg. 45
Milito, Donna, Mgr.-Telemarketing--Thoroughbred Software International, Inc., Somerset, NJ, pg. 1095
Millar, Craig, V.P.-Broadcasting Sls.; Pres. & Gen. Mgr.-WBRC-TV--Great American Broadcasting Company, Cincinnati, OH, pg. 52
Miller, Alton Wayne, Dir.-Sls. & Mktg.--Affiliated Foods Southwest, Little Rock, AR, pg. 24
Miller, Bob, Dr.-Sls.--Tomco Auto Products, Inc., Vernon, CA, pg. 1100
Miller, Calvin, Mgr.-Sls.--Republic Die & Tool Company, Belleville, MI, pg. 928
Miller, Carl E., V.P.-Sls. & Mktg.--Butler Automatic, Inc., Canton, MA, pg. 197
Miller, Charles, Mgr.-Sls.--Beach Mold & Tool Inc., New Albany, IN, pg. 128
Miller, Dick, Gen. Sls. Mgr.--RS Electronics, Livonia, MI, pg. 908
Miller, Don, Sls. Mgr.--Alessi Incorporated, Irvine, CA, pg. 352
Miller, Donald F., V.P.-Sls.--Merriam-Webster, Inc., Springfield, MA, pg. 381
Miller, Frank W., V.P.-Mktg. & Sls.--The H. W. Wilson Co., Bronx, NY, pg. 1193
Miller, George, Exec. V.P. & Supvr.-Mngmt.--Proctor & Gardner Advertising, Inc., Chicago, IL, pg. 892
Miller, George, Mgr.-Sls.--Mark Lighting Fixture Co., Inc., Moonachie, NJ, pg. 708
Miller, Glenna A., Dir.-Mktg. & Sls.--Thermal American Fused Quartz Co., Louisville, KY, pg. 1091
Miller, J.J., Sr. V.P. & Chief Mktg. Officer--Western & Southern Life Insurance Co., Cincinnati, OH, pg. 1181
Miller, Jim, Exec. V.P.-Sls. & Mktg.--Sutter Home Winery, Inc., Saint Helena, CA, pg. 1065
Miller, Ken, V.P.-Sls.--Artec Distributing, Inc., Shelburne, VT, pg. 86
Miller, Larry, Dir.-Sls.--The Chas. H. Lilly Co., Portland, OR, pg. 675
Miller, LeRoy, Mgr.-Sls.--California Artichoke & Vegetable Growers Corp., Castroville, CA, pg. 209
Miller, Martha, Mgr.-Govt. Sls.--S-T Industries, Inc., Saint James, MN, pg. 964
Miller, Richard A., V.P.-Retail Sls.-St. Louis Div.--Hill-Behan Lumber Company, Saint Louis, MO, pg. 534
Miller, William M.C., V.P.-Adv. Sls.--U.S. News & World Report, New York, NY, pg. 1136
Mills, Fred, Dir.-Sls.--Lamb Engineering & Construction Co., Salt Lake City, UT, pg. 652
Mills, Lea Ann, Dir.-Sls. & Mktg.--Replacements, Ltd., Greensboro, NC, pg. 927
Milne, Dick, Sls. Mgr.-New Cars--James Chevrolet Inc., Mount Clemens, MI, pg. 588
Mindala, James J., V.P.-Sls.--General Computer Corp. Inc., Twinsburg, OH, pg. 449
Miner, Richard, Sr. V.P.-Sls.--Gould Paper Corporation, New York, NY, pg. 473
Minis, Henry H., V.P.-Sls.--Carson Products Company, Savannah, GA, pg. 67
Minor, Michelle, Sls. Promo. Mgr.--Automotive News, Detroit, MI, pg. 101
Minton, James A., V.P.-Sls.--Lovejoy Inc., Downers Grove, IL, pg. 685
Minutolo, Michael V., V.P.-Sls.--F. H. Chase, Inc., Foxboro, MA, pg. 240
Miranda, Ron, Dir.-Sls.--Paper Enterprises, Inc., Bronx, NY, pg. 847
Mirisch, Don, V.P.-Bus. Affairs--Hanna-Barbera Productions, Inc., Los Angeles, CA, pg. 53
Mirmina, Andrew D., Mgr.-Sls.--Connecticut Drive Shaft, Inc., Milford, CT, pg. 274
Mitacek, Pamela, Mgr.-Sls.--Replogle Globes, Inc., Broadview, IL, pg. 927
Mitchell, Doug, Sls. Rep.--American Journal Of Nursing Company, New York, NY, pg. 57
Mitchell, Harvey, V.P.-Sls.--Sentinel Consumer Products, Inc., Mentor, OH, pg. 990
Mitchell, James, V.P.-Sls.--Standard Gravure Corp./Shea Communications, Atlanta, GA, pg. 1036
Mitchell, JoBeth, Sls. Rep.--American Journal Of Nursing Company, New York, NY, pg. 57
Mitchell, Randy, Dir.-Sls.--Pioneer Express Inc., Indianapolis, IN, pg. 833
Mitchell, Vincent, Exec. V.P.-Sls. & Mktg.--Falcon Candy Company, Philadelphia, PA, pg. 398
Mitchell, William E., Dir.-Sls.--Renken Boat Manufacturing Co., Charleston, SC, pg. 927
Mix, Laurie, Mgr.-Sls. Co-ordinating--Softool Corporation, Goleta, CA, pg. 1016
Mizrachi, David, V.P.-Institutional Sls.--Leshner Mills. Inc., Hamilton, OH, pg. 668
Moehling, Paul, Sls. Mgr.--Crown Products Co., Crawfordsville, IN, pg. 1018
Moehling, Paul M., Gen. Sls. Mgr.--Sommer Metalcraft Corporation, Crawfordsville, IN, pg. 1018
Moeller, Wayne, V.P.-Sls. & Mktg.--Lozier Corporation, Omaha, NE, pg. 686
Moeller, Wayne A., V.P.-Sls. & Mktg.--Lozier Store Fixtures, Inc., Omaha, NE, pg. 686
Moerck, Rudi, Dr., V.P.-Mktg. & Sls.--Troy Corporation, East Hanover, NJ, pg. 1116
Mogan, James, Sr. V.P.-Sls. & Mdsg.--Maidenform, Inc., New York, NY, pg. 701
Mogavero, Pete, V.P.-Sls.--Anchor Industries Inc., Evansville, IN, pg. 71
Mohler, Daniel A., Western Region Adv. Sls. Mgr.--The Weather Channel, Inc.-Los Angeles Sales Office, Los Angeles, CA, pg. 654
Molinari, Phillip, Exec. V.P.-Sls.--Bugle Boy Industries, Inc., Simi Valley, CA, pg. 187
Moloney, A. Michael, Sr. V.P.-Sls.--Fraser Paper, Ltd., Stamford, CT, pg. 430
Momper, Jerry, V.P.-Natl. Sls.--Whiting Manufacturing Co., Inc., Cincinnati, OH, pg. 1187
Monahan, John P., V.P.-Sls.--Titanium Metals Corporation, Denver, CO, pg. 1109
Monahan, William G., V.P.-Sls.--Gould Paper Corporation, Stoughton, MA, pg. 473
Mongeon, Emil, V.P.-Mass Market Sls.--Empire Berol U.S.A., Brentwood, TN, pg. 856

Monhollen, Ken, Mgr.-Service--Kissimmee Toyota Inc., Kissimmee, FL, pg. 633
Moniaci, Sam, Natl. Sls. Mgr.--Redmond Products, Inc., Chanhassen, MN, pg. 920
Monroe, Thomas O., Jr., V.P.-Intl. Sls.--The Johnson Corporation, Three Rivers, MI, pg. 597
Montesano, Nick, V.P.-Sls., Mktg. & Mdse.--Quill Corp., Lincolnshire, IL, pg. 905
Moon, Alan, Mgr.-Intl. Sls.--Duo-Fast Corporation, Franklin Park, IL, pg. 354
Mooney, Greg, Mgr.-Sls.--Buck Knives, Inc., El Cajon, CA, pg. 185
Mooradian, Erich, V.P.-Sls.--Johnstown Knitting Mill Co., Johnstown, NY, pg. 602
Moore, Arnold, Mgr.-Sls. & Mktg.--State Electric Supply Co., Huntington, WV, pg. 1040
Moore, Arthur, Mgr.-Sls.--Schaedler Brothers, Inc., Harrisburg, PA, pg. 974
Moore, Bill, Mgr.-Grp. Retail Support--Ace Hardware Corporation, Oak Brook, IL, pg. 12
Moore, Bill, V.P.-Sls.--Servus Footwear Company, Rock Island, IL, pg. 993
Moore, Bruce, V.P., Sls.--E-B Advertising Display Inc., Massillon, OH, pg. 358
Moore, Carl, Mgr.-Sls.--Heidtman Steel Products, Inc., Toledo, OH, pg. 525
Moore, Dan, Mgr.-Sls.--Target Stamped Products Corp., Kinsman, OH, pg. 1079
Moore, David D., V.P.-Sls.--Minnesota Twins Baseball Club, Minneapolis, MN, pg. 758
Moore, Dorothea, V.P.-Sls.--Moore Company, Westerly, RI, pg. 768
Moore, Johnny, V.P.-Sls.--Wisdom Imports Sales Co. Inc., Irvine, CA, pg. 1198
Moore, Lester W.B., Sr. V.P., Sec. & Sls.-Fast Food Service--E.A. Sween Company, Eden Prairie, MN, pg. 1066
Moore, Mack A., Sales Mgr.--WQDR, Raleigh, NC, pg. 306
Moore, Marvin R., Natl. Sls. Mgr.--Riverdale Chemical Co., Glenwood, IL, pg. 937
Moore, Patricia, Mgr.-Sls.--Cox Hobbies, Inc., Corona, CA, pg. 294
Moore, Randy, Natl. Sls. Mgr.--John Boos & Company, Effingham, IL, pg. 165
Moore, Terry, Sls. Mgr.--Massachusetts Container Corporation, Marlborough, MA, pg. 274
Moore, Theodore K., V.P.-Sls. & Mktg.--The Chicago Faucet Co., Des Plaines, IL, pg. 245
Moore, Walter E., V.P. & Dir.-Sls.--Collegiate Concepts Inc., Tucker, GA, pg. 262
Moorhead, J.R., V.P.-Sls.--Airline Hydraulics Corporation, Bensalem, PA, pg. 27
Moran, John J., V.P. & Asst. Controller--Anchor Financial Corporation, Myrtle Beach, SC, pg. 71
Morano, Jerry, V.P.-Mktg. & Sls.--Quality Bakers of America Cooperative, Inc., Greenwich, CT, pg. 903
Morehouse, Max, Mgr.-Sls.--Sheldons' Inc., Antigo, WI, pg. 996
Moreley, Thomas S., V.P.-Sls. & Mktg.--Harrington & King, Chicago, IL, pg. 511
Morgan, Avon, Dir.-Sls.--Central Data Corporation, Champaign, IL, pg. 232
Morgan, Bill, Dir.-Sls. Admin.--Pneumatic Scale Corporation, Quincy, MA, pg. 122
Morgan, H., Dir.-Teleconferencing Mktg. & Sls.--Shure Brothers Incorporated, Evanston, IL, pg. 1001
Morgan, J. Harley, V.P.-Sls.--Pac Paper, Inc., Vancouver, WA, pg. 815
Morgan, Stanley, Mgr.-Sls.--St. Louis Music, Inc., Saint Louis, MO, pg. 967
Morgan, W. Tommy III, Exec. V.P.-Adv., Mktg. & Sls.--H.A.T. Holding Company, Tampa, FL, pg. 517
Morgan, W. Tommy, III, Exec. V.P.-Adv., Mktg. & Sls.--Havatampa Incorporated, Tampa, FL, pg. 517
Morgis, Tony, V.P., Sls.--Global Marketing Resources, New York, NY, pg. 463
Morison, John, III, V.P.-Mktg. & Sls.--Hitchiner Manufacturing Company, Inc., Milford, NH, pg. 536
Morrill, Thomas, Dir.-Sls. & Mktg.--Atchison County Co-op Association, Atchison, KS, pg. 93
Morris, J.M., Mgr.-Intl. Sls.--American Excelsior Company, Arlington, TX, pg. 51
Morris, Jerry, Mgr.-Sls.--Beer Nuts, Inc., Bloomington, IL, pg. 132
Morris, Jerry, Sr. V.P.-Sls.--P M Company, Philadelphia, PA, pg. 835
Morrison, Anthony, V.P.-Intl. Sls.--Ford Steel Co., Inc., Maryland Heights, MO, pg. 423
Morrison, Fed E., Sls.-Mgr.--Williams-White & Co., Moline, IL, pg. 1191
Morrison, Fred E., Mgr.-Sls.--Williams, White & Company, Moline, IL, pg. 1191
Morrow, David, V.P.-Sls.--Sanderson Plumbing Products Inc., Columbus, MS, pg. 970
Morrow, David, V.P.-Sls.--Magnolia Division, Columbus, MS, pg. 970
Morrow, Melynda, Dir.-Sls.--Atlas Van Lines, Inc., Evansville, IN, pg. 96
Morse, Kenneth, Dir.-Sls.--Muro Pharmaceutical, Inc., Tewksbury, MA, pg. 776
Morse, Tom, Mgr.-Sls.--Southgate Ford Inc., Southgate, MI, pg. 1023
Morsillo, J.V., Dir.-Sls., West--AP Parts Manufacturing Company, Toledo, OH, pg. 240
Morton, Larry, Natl. Sls. & Mktg. Mgr.--Scott U.S.A., Ketchum, ID, pg. 983
Mosack, Cal C., V.P.-Sls.--Conbraco Industries Inc., Matthews, NC, pg. 272
Moser, Sam, V.P.-Adv. Sls.--Nickelodeon/Nick At Nite, New York, NY, pg. 785
Moser, Scott, V.P.-Sls.--Horsehead Resource Development Company, Inc., Palmerton, PA, pg. 545
Mosey, S., Natl. Sls. Mgr.--K-D Lamp Company, Cincinnati, OH, pg. 612
Mosier, George O., V.P.-Sls. & Mktg., Intl. Div.--Foley-PLP Company, Rochester, NY, pg. 422
Mosier, Steve, Gen. Mgr.-Sls.--Westco Products, Inc., Pico Rivera, CA, pg. 1178
Moss, Margie, Dir.-Sls. Admin.--Colorforms, Ramsey, NJ, pg. 265
Moss, Wendell, Dir.-Sls.-SCAT TRAK Loaders--Trak International, Inc., Port Washington, WI, pg. 1106
Mossburg, Michael, V.P.-Sls.--Wheaton Glass Co., Millville, NJ, pg. 1184
Motsay, John M., V.P.-Sls. & Mktg.--Canton Drop Forge, Canton, OH, pg. 214
Mott, Arthur J., Mgr.-Intl. Sls.--B.A. Ballou & Co. Inc., East Providence, RI, pg. 116
Mottley, M.L., V.P.-Sls. & Mktg., Compressors--Carey Machinery & Supply Company, Baltimore, MD, pg. 218
Mougey, Charles L., Chm. Bd., Treas. & Mgr.-Sls.--Puget Sound Plywood, Inc., Tacoma, WA, pg. 899
Mowchan, Pat, V.P.-Sls.--Freeway Corporation, Cleveland, OH, pg. 432
Mowry, Ronald C., Dir.-Sls.--C. I. Hayes, Inc., Cranston, RI, pg. 519
Mozes, David, Sls. Devel.--Corinthian Media, Inc., New York, NY, pg. 286
Mroz, Alex R., Mgr.-Natl. Key Accts.--Lane Limited, Tucker, GA, pg. 657
Muche, Don R., Natl. Sls. Mgr.--Maruchan Inc., Irvine, CA, pg. 716
Mudd, Charles W., V.P.-Sls. & Mktg.--Dorsey Trailers, Inc., Atlanta, GA, pg. 347
Mudge, M.K., V.P.-Sls.--Alban Tractor Co. Inc., Baltimore, MD, pg. 30
Mudge, Rick, V.P.-Mktg. & Sls.--Cramer Inc., Kansas City, KS, pg. 296
Mudgeft, Bill, V.P.-Sls.--Regal Marine Industries Inc., Orlando, FL, pg. 921
Mueller, Brett, V.P.-Sls. & Mktg.--Mueller Sports Medicine, Inc., Prairie du Sac, WI, pg. 774
Mueller, Gerald C., Dir.-Sls. & Mktg.--Wenczel Tile Co., Trenton, NJ, pg. 1176
Mueller, Lawrence A., Exec. V.P.-Worldwide Sls. & Mktg.--J.D. Edwards & Company, Denver, CO, pg. 370
Mueller, Richard E., Exec. V.P.-Sls.--Mulberry Metal Products, Inc., Union, NJ, pg. 775
Mulhern, Matthew T., V.P.-Sls.--Mulhern Belting, Inc., Oakland, NJ, pg. 775
Mull, Richard, Exec. V.P. & Mgr.-Sls.--Walsworth Publishing Company, Inc., Marceline, MO, pg. 1161
Mullen, D., Exec. V.P.-Food Service--Comstock Michigan Fruit, Rochester, NY, pg. 25
Mullen, Larry J., V.P.-Sls., Sec. & Treas.--Terral-Norris Seed Co., Inc., Lake Providence, LA, pg. 1088
Mullins, Michael, Mgr.-Sls.--Salz Leathers, Inc., Santa Cruz, CA, pg. 968
Mulllins, Bob, V.P.-Sls.--Gator Freightways, Inc., Wilmington, OH, pg. 446
Mullock, Paul S., Sr. V.P.-Sls.--Alliance America, Norcross, GA, pg. 37
Mundt, Bud, V.P.-Sls. & Mktg.--Miller Business Systems, Inc., Arlington, TX, pg. 753
Munnis, Joseph W., V.P.-Sls. & Mktg.--Henkels & McCoy, Inc., Blue Bell, PA, pg. 529
Munroe, John T., V.P.-Sls. Services & Physical Distr.--Steelcase Inc., Grand Rapids, MI, pg. 1044
Muntone, James J., V.P.-Sls.--Reading Anthracite Coal Co., Pottsville, PA, pg. 916
Murnin, Michael, V.P.-Sls. & Mktg.--Up-Right, Inc., Selma, CA, pg. 1139
Murphy, Bill, Mgr.-Sls.--Piping Resources, Houston, TX, pg. 169
Murphy, Frank, V.P.-Sls. & Mktg.--Cerro Copper Products Co., Sauget, IL, pg. 711
Murphy, Larry, Dir.-Inside Sls.--McKee Door, Inc., Aurora, IL, pg. 730
Murphy, Larry M., V.P.-Sls. & Mktg.--R & G Sloane Mfg. Co., Inc., Sun Valley, CA, pg. 1010
Murphy, Lee, V.P. & Sls. Mgr.--Evergreen Mills Inc., Ada, OK, pg. 1145
Murphy, Max M., V.P.-Sls.--J.H. Harvey Company, Nashville, GA, pg. 515
Murphy, Robert, V.P.-Sls.--Philadelphia Gear Corp., King of Prussia, PA, pg. 866
Murphy, Tom, Natl. Sls. Mgr.--Cameo Curtains, New York, NY, pg. 200
Murphy, Tom, Exec. V.P.-Sls. & Mktg.--Meehan Tooker, East Rutherford, NJ, pg. 736
Murray, Asa G., V.P.-Sls. & Mktg.--Philadelphia Coca-Cola Bottling Co., Philadelphia, PA, pg. 866
Murray, Edward A., V.P.-Sls. & Mktg.--Koh-I-Noor, Inc., Bloomsbury, NJ, pg. 639
Murray, H. David, V.P.-Sls.--Lotus Carpet Division, Columbus, GA, pg. 267
Murray, James E., V.P.-Sls.--Cyberex, Inc., Mentor, OH, pg. 307
Murray, O.W., Mgr.-Intl. Sls.--Doron Precision Systems, Inc., Binghamton, NY, pg. 346
Murry, Alan, V.P.-Sls.--Pollenex Corporation, Chicago, IL, pg. 821
Murzinski, Edward, V.P.-Mktg. & Sls.--Revcor, Inc., Carpentersville, IL, pg. 930
Muselman, Roger, V.P.-Sls.--E.P. Graphics, Inc., Berne, IN, pg. 360
Musick, Gary D., V.P.-Sls.--Houston Foods Company, Chicago, IL, pg. 547
Mussbaun, Bob, V.P.-Sls. & Mktg.--Ireland Coffee Tea, Inc., Pleasantville, NJ, pg. 582
Musselwhite, John, Mgr.-Sls.--J.T. Davenport & Sons, Inc., Sanford, NC, pg. 317
Mutchnick, Jerry, V.P.-Sls.--Gould Paper Corporation, New York, NY, pg. 473
Muter, Shirley, Asst. Mgr.-Sls.--North & Judd, Middletown, CT, pg. 812
Myers, Dennis A., Exec. V.P.-Sls.--Nalleys Fine Foods, Tacoma, WA, pg. 25
Myers, Ed, Mgr.-Sls.--Round Hill Foods, Inc., New Oxford, PA, pg. 952
Myers, James H., V.P.-Intl. Sls. & Product Mngmt.--Simplicity Manufacturing, Inc., Port Washington, WI, pg. 1006
Myers, Robert W., Mgr.-Sls. & Mktg.--Morris Coupling Co., Erie, PA, pg. 771
Myrick, Charles, V.P.-Sls.--Myrick Construction Inc., Biscoe, NC, pg. 780
Naftaly, Gary, Mgr.-Sls.--Spectronics Corporation, Westbury, NY, pg. 1029
Nagayama, Ed, Mgr.-Accts.--J. E. Higgins Lumber Co., Concord, CA, pg. 533
Nagle, James, Natl. Sls. Mgr.--American Journal Of Nursing Company, New York, NY, pg. 57
Nahmias, R., V.P.-Sls.--Gentex Optics, Inc., Simpson, PA, pg. 452
Nall, Tom, V.P.-Sls. & Mktg.--Caliente Chili, Inc., Austin, TX, pg. 923
Nance, Alvin Y., V.P.-Sls.--Northwestern Meats Inc., Miami, FL, pg. 815
Nance, David, Sls. Mgr.--World's Finest Chocolate Australia Pty. Ltd., Stanmore,, Australia, pg. 1203
Nance, Doug, Dir.-Sls.--Grindmaster Corporation, Louisville, KY, pg. 488
Napoleon, Dan, Sls. Mgr.-New Cars--Roger Holler Chevrolet Co., Winter Park, FL, pg. 539
Napolitano, Frank, Mgr.-Sls.--Leschen Wire Rope, Saint Joseph, MO, pg. 1197
Narrow, Louis, V.P.-Sls.--Pyttronic Industries, Inc., Montgomeryville, PA, pg. 901
Nasalroad, Jim, Dir.-Sls.--Maddak Inc., Pequannock, NJ, pg. 133
Nash, D., Bus. Mgr.-Uniforms Fabrics--Milliken & Co., Inc., Spartanburg, SC, pg. 755
Nass, James, Mgr.-Sls.--Graham Paint and Varnish Company, Chicago, IL, pg. 475
Nay, Kelly, Gen. Mgr.-Sls.--Rea Magnet Wire Company, Inc., Fort Wayne, IN, pg. 915
Neal, Normand, Exec. V.P.-Sls. & Mktg.--J H Collectibles, Milwaukee, WI, pg. 584
Nealeigh, Bob, Dir.-Sls.--Warner Press, Inc., Anderson, IN, pg. 1164
Nebhut, Eileen, Coord.-Bilk Sls.--Marcel Dekker, Inc., New York, NY, pg. 325
Neff, Harry, V.P.-Sls. & Mktg.--Uvex Safety, Inc., Smithfield, RI, pg. 1141
Neifeld, Steven, Mgr.-Sls.--Altama Delta Corp., Darien, GA, pg. 45
Neill, Joseph, V.P.-Sls.--Gould Paper Corporation, New York, NY, pg. 473
Neitzel, R.E., V.P.-Sls.--Hypro Corporation, New Brighton, MN, pg. 557
Nelso, Kim, Mgr.-Sls.--Standard Restaurant Equipment Co., Las Vegas, NV, pg. 1036
Nelson, Carl, V.P.-Sls.--Nelson Photo Supplies, San Diego, CA, pg. 797
Nelson, G.L., V.P.-Sls. & Mktg.--Ampco Metal Incorporated, Milwaukee, WI, pg. 67
Nelson, Glen, V.P.-Sls. & Mktg.--Roll Forming Corporation, Shelbyville, KY, pg. 944
Nelson, James R., V.P.-Sls. & Adv.--Central/Shippee, Inc., Bloomingdale, NJ, pg. 234
Nelson, Jim, V.P.-Sls.--Allied Felt Group, Bloomingdale, NJ, pg. 234
Nelson, Jim, Dir.-Sls. & Mktg.--Ederer Inc., Seattle, WA, pg. 368
Nelson, Jim, Dir.-Sls. & Mktg.--Ederer Cranes, Seattle, WA, pg. 368
Nelson, Jim, Dir.-Sls. & Mktg.--Washington Cranes, Seattle, WA, pg. 368
Nelson, Jim, Dir.-Sls. & Mktg.--Star Cranes, Seattle, WA, pg. 368
Nelson, John L., V.P.-Sls. & Mktg.--Marlow Industries, Dallas, TX, pg. 710
Nelson, P., V.P.-Sls.--Midwest Coast Transport L.P., Sioux Falls, SD, pg. 752
Nelson, Pam, Natl. Sls. Mgr.--Reliance Medical Products, Inc., Mason, OH, pg. 925
Nelson, Rodney E., V.P.-Mktg. & Sls.--Magnetic Data, Inc., Eden Prairie, MN, pg. 700
Nelson, Scott, Dir.-Sls.--Davis Industries Inc., Detroit, MI, pg. 318
Nelson, Terry, V.P.-Sls.--Barrel O'Fun Snack Foods Co., Perham, MN, pg. 122
Nelson, Vern, Mgr.-Natl. Sls.--Crestliner, Inc., Little Falls, MN, pg. 758
Neuman, Milt, Sls. Mgr.--World's Finest Chocolate Canada Ltd., Campbellford,, Canada, pg. 1203
Neumann, Jerry, V.P.-Sls.--Rite-Hite Corporation, Milwaukee, WI, pg. 936
Neverman, Ken, Mgr.-Regional Sls. & Mktg.--Wayne Corporation, Richmond, IN, pg. 1169
Nevison, G., Sr. V.P.-Mktg. & Sls.--Eastern Technologies Ltd, Amesbury, MA, pg. 364
Newcombe, Arthur R., V.P.-Sls. & Mktg.--Parkdale Mills, Gastonia, NC, pg. 849
Newman, Larry, V.P.-Sls.--Spencer Industries, Inc., New Brunswick, NJ, pg. 1030
Newsome, Jon, Mgr.-Sls.--Custom Pak, Inc., Clinton, IA, pg. 306
Newton, Larry, V.P.-Sls.--C & S Wholesale Grocery Inc., Brattleboro, VT, pg. 198
Nibbe, Warner, Dir.-Sls. & Mktg.--Paper Calmenson & Co., Saint Paul, MN, pg. 847
Nicas, Anthony, V.P.-Sls. & Mktg.--Security Products Company of Delaware, Inc., Minneapolis, MN, pg. 1138
Nicas, Pete, V.P.-Mktg. & Sls.-Security Prods.--Universal Cooperatives, Inc., Minneapolis, MN, pg. 1138
Nicas, Pete, V.P.-Sls. & Mktg.--Security Products Company, Minneapolis, MN, pg. 1138
Nichol, Dan, Intl. Sls. Rep.--Triumph*Lor, Inc., Houston, TX, pg. 1115

Stearns, Doug, Dir.-Sls. & Mktg.--Seneca Wire & Manufacturing Co., Fostoria, OH, pg. 989
Stearns, J.B., Exec. V.P.-Intl. Sls.--Miller Electric Mfg. Co., Appleton, WI, pg. 754
Steed, Frank, V.P.-Sls. & Mktg.--Samsonite Corporation, Denver, CO, pg. 358
Steel, John M., V.P.-Mktg. & Sls.--Zytec Corp., Eden Prairie, MN, pg. 1221
Steele, Darryl, Natl. Sls. Mgr.--KSL Radio, Salt Lake City, UT, pg. 332
Steele, Donald K., V.P.-Sls. & Sec.--Industrial Dielectrics, Inc., Noblesville, IN, pg. 566
Steele, Jack F., V.P.-Sls. & Mktg.--Grede Foundries, Inc., Milwaukee, WI, pg. 483
Steele, K., Mgr.-Sls.--Sexton Can Co., Inc., Cambridge, MA, pg. 993
Steffens, Lowell G., V.P.-Sls. & Adv.--Equipment Manufacturing, Inc., Warren, MI, pg. 385
Stehle, T., Mgr.-Intl. Sls.--Hollingsworth & Vose Co., East Walpole, MA, pg. 539
Steider, Dave, V.P.-Sls.--Urschel Labs Inc., Valparaiso, IN, pg. 1140
Steidle, S., Dir.-Sls.--Specialty Paperboard Inc., Brattleboro, VT, pg. 1027
Steidle, Stephen, Dir.-Sls.--Specialty Paperboard Inc., Brattleboro, VT, pg. 1027
Stein, Jon, Mgr. Sls.-Women's Wear--Pendleton Woolen Mills, Inc., Portland, OR, pg. 857
Stein, Larry, V.P.-Sls.--D. C. Taylor Co., Cedar Rapids, IA, pg. 751
Steinberg, Bob, Dir.-Sls.--Dormeyer Industries, Chicago, IL, pg. 346
Steininger, Chris, Natl. Sls. Mgr.--Hamilton, Inc., Vincennes, IN, pg. 3
Steinkamp, Kelli, Sls. Rep.--American Journal Of Nursing Company, New York, NY, pg. 57
Steinman, Andrew, Dir.-Mktg. & Sls.--Falcon Safety Products Inc., Branchburg, NJ, pg. 398
Stepakoff, Joel, V.P.-Natl. Accts.--The Berkline Corporation, Morristown, TN, pg. 285
Stepenson, William A., V.P.-Sls.--Templeton, Kenly & Co., Inc., Broadview, IL, pg. 1086
Stephani, Jim, Mgr.-Natl. Sls.-Institution Div.--Polar Ware Company, Sheboygan, WI, pg. 878
Stephenson, Jim, Mgr.-Sls. & Service--NuArc Co., Cleveland, OH, pg. 817
Stepnowski, Thomas, Mgr.-Direct Sls.--Hano Business Forms, Inc., Springfield, MA, pg. 505
Stern, David, V.P.-Sls.--E.T. Browne Drug Co., Inc., Englewood Cliffs, NJ, pg. 183
Sterner, F. Parker, V.P.-Natl. Sls.--Mathews & Boucher, Rochester, NY, pg. 720
Stevens, Joel, Mgr.-Grp. Retail Support--Ace Hardware Corporation, Oak Brook, IL, pg. 12
Stevens, Robert, Mgr.-Sls.--Tricon Electromechanical Div., Downers Grove, IL, pg. 1113
Stevens, Robert W., Mgr.-Natl. Sls.--C.B. Fleet Company, Incorporated, Lynchburg, VA, pg. 417
Stevens, Wilma, V.P.-Sls.--Mastercraft Corporation, Winnsboro, IA, pg. 759
Stevenson, Lloyd, V.P.-Mktg. & Sls.--Abbott Ball Company, West Hartford, CT, pg. 9
Steward, Toby, V.P.-Sls. & Mktg.--AMF Bakery Systems, Richmond, VA, pg. 5
Stewart, Duncan, Dir.-Intl. Sls.--Kingsbury Corporation, Keene, NH, pg. 631
Stewart, Rob, Dir.-Sls.--Stadelman Fruit Inc., Yakima, WA, pg. 1034
Stewart, Sandy, Mgr.-Sls.--James Ferrera & Sons, Inc., Canton, MA, pg. 407
Stibich, Ron, Sr. V.P.-Mktg. & Sls.--Fibre Glass-Evercoat Company Inc., Cincinnati, OH, pg. 408
Stichman, Robert, Dir.-Sls.--WYO-Ben, Inc., Billings, MT, pg. 1157
Stick, Michael, V.P.-Sls.--Hanover Foods Corporation, Hanover, PA, pg. 506
Stick, Mike, V.P.-Sls.--Myers Foods Company, Plumsteadville, PA, pg. 506
Stickler, Don, Dir. of Sls.-Plumbing & Refrigeration--Cerro Copper Products Co., Sauget, IL, pg. 711
Stieger, Michael J., Sr. V.P-Sls.--Del Monte Foods, San Francisco, CA, pg. 325
Stiegler, Bob, Mgr.-Sls.--Kansas City Royals Radio Network, Kansas City, MO, pg. 1043
Still, Annie, Dir.-Sls.--Chattanooga Choo-Choo Holiday Inn, Chattanooga, TN, pg. 241
Stillablower, George, Dir.-Sls.--Vernay Laboratories, Inc., Yellow Springs, OH, pg. 1148
Stillings, Robert, V.P.-Opers., Sls., Mktg. & Personnel Dir.--Presto Food Stores, Inc., Plant City, FL, pg. 888
Stine, John, Mgr.-Circulation--The Yankton Press & Dakotan, Yankton, SD, pg. 1042
Stine, Richard, Dir.-Sls.--Hehr International Inc., Los Angeles, CA, pg. 525
Stinson, David N., Dir.-Govt. Sls.--Nemschoff Chairs, Inc., Sheboygan, WI, pg. 798
Stipancic, Charles E., Dir.-Sls. Headquarters-Transit--Union Switch & Signal Inc., Pittsburgh, PA, pg. 1129
Stitt, T.P., Mgr.-Sls.--Bell Chemical Company, Chicago, IL, pg. 134
Stock, John, Sls. Mgr.--Western Metal Finishing Division, South Gate, CA, pg. 1073
Stoewsand, Bob, V.P.-Sls. Admin.--Alaron Inc., Troy, MI, pg. 30
Stokes, Terry G., V.P.-Sls., Plumbing Hardware--Radiator Specialty Company, Charlotte, NC, pg. 909
Stolarz, Mike, V.P.-Sls. & Adv.--Twin County Grocers, Inc., Edison, NJ, pg. 1122
Stollsteimer, G.R., Mgr.-Sls.--Reuland Electric Company, City of Industry, CA, pg. 930
Stolz, Ed, Mgr.-Sls.--Wieland Realty Associates, Inc., Atlanta, GA, pg. 1189
Stone, Dan, Field Sls. Mgr.--Remarks Co., Indianapolis, IN, pg. 926
Stone, Harold, Jr., V.P.-Sls. & Mktg.--Renfro Corp., Mount Airy, NC, pg. 926
Stone, Harry J., V.P.-Sls.--The Royal China & Porcelain Companies Inc., Moorestown, NJ, pg. 953
Stoneking, Randall, V.P.-Agribusiness Sls.--MSI Insurance Companies, Arden Hills, MN, pg. 693
Stonestreet, Bill, Mgr.-Sls.--Sunniland Corporation, Sanford, FL, pg. 1061
Stonestrom, Steve, V.P.-Sls.--D.C.I., Inc., Saint Cloud, MN, pg. 308
Stor, Richard, Dir.-Mktg., Sls. & Adv.--Atlantic Builders Group Inc., Baltimore, MD, pg. 94
Stormont, James, V.P.-Sls.--Bodine Electric Company, Chicago, IL, pg. 162
Story, Jim, Mgr.-Sls.--Bandini Fertilizer Company, Los Angeles, CA, pg. 117
Story, Ned, Dir.-Construction & Equipment Sls.--Carolina Tractor & Equipment Co., Charlotte, NC, pg. 223
Stotzer, W.H., Mgr.-Sls.--Frantz Manufacturing Co., Sterling, IL, pg. 429
Stouffer, Spencer R., V.P.-Sls. & Adv.--Miller & Smith, Inc., McLean, VA, pg. 755
Stout, Mike, Dir.-Sls.--Gregg Appliances Inc., Indianapolis, IN, pg. 486
Stover, Don, Mgr.-Natl. Sls.--Rolock, Inc., Fairfield, CT, pg. 944
Stover, Larry, V.P.-Sls.--Bradley Corporation, Menomonee Falls, WI, pg. 170
Stover, Robert W., Mgr.-Sls.--Kunzler & Company, Inc., Lancaster, PA, pg. 646
Stowers, J. Ron, Mgr.-Sls.--North State Pyrophyllite, Greensboro, NC, pg. 928
Strafalace, Daniel, V.P.-Sls.--Bacharach Inc., Pittsburgh, PA, pg. 108
Strait, Rick E., Exec. V.P.--Netzsch, Inc., Exton, PA, pg. 798
Stratton, Mames, V.P.-Sls.--John Roberts Company, Minneapolis, MN, pg. 938
Strecker, Al, Mgr.-Sls.--Bradbury Company, Inc., Moundridge, KS, pg. 169
Strickland, Ben, Mgr.-Sls., Food Service--Beaver Street Fisheries, Inc., Jacksonville, FL, pg. 130
Strong, Dave, Dir.-Sls. & Mktg.--Integrated Energy Controls Corp., Minneapolis, MN, pg. 573
Strong, Kent S., V.P.-Sls. & Tech. Services--ANGUS Chemical Company, Buffalo Grove, IL, pg. 75
Strong, William, V.P.-Circulation--Crain Communications, Inc., Detroit, MI, pg. 295
Strouber, Murray, V.P.-Consumer Mktg. & Dir.-Sls.--Leviton Mfg. Co., Inc., Little Neck, NY, pg. 671
Strouse, Denise, Mgr.-Sls.--McCourt Label Co., Lewis Run, PA, pg. 727
Strunk, Gary, V.P.-Sls.--Peterson American Corp., Southfield, MI, pg. 864
Stuart, Robert, V.P.-Sls.--Polaris Pool Systems, Inc., San Marcos, CA, pg. 878
Stuart, William, V.P.-Mktg. & Sls.--Schulze & Burch Biscuit Company, Chicago, IL, pg. 979
Stubbe, Allen, Mgr.-Sls. & Mktg.--E.R. Wagner Mfg. Co. Wagner Prods. Div., Hustisford, WI, pg. 1158
Studebaker, Michael, V.P.-Sls. Devel.--Pebsco Inc., Columbus, OH, pg. 795
Studzinski, Keith, Mgr.-Sls.--Mike Savoie Chevrolet Inc., Troy, MI, pg. 973
Stuhr, David, Mgr.-Sls.--Minnesota Electric Supply Company, Willmar, MN, pg. 757
Sturgis, Robert, V.P.-Sls.--Lakeside Industries, Redmond, WA, pg. 651
Sugg, D., V.P.-Sls.--Stacoswitch, Inc., Costa Mesa, CA, pg. 270
Suits, Reggis, Sls. Mgr.--American Uniform Co., Cleveland, TN, pg. 1045
Sulick, E., Gen. Sls. Mgr.-Medical--Graphic Controls, Corp., Buffalo, NY, pg. 478
Sulick, E., Gen. Sls. Mgr.-Medical--Graphic Controls Corporation, Buffalo, NY, pg. 478
Sullens, Doug, Mgr.-Sls.--KGNC-AM & FM, Amarillo, TX, pg. 1043
Sullivan, Charles F., V.P.-Sls.--Pepsi-Cola Bottling Company of Charlotte Inc., Charlotte, NC, pg. 860
Sullivan, David, Reg. Sls. Mgr.-Midwest--New England Confectionery Co., Cambridge, MA, pg. 1123
Sullivan, Diana, V.P.-Custom & Made-to-Measure Sls.--Robertson Factories, Inc., Taunton, MA, pg. 939
Sullivan, E., Mgr.-Sls.--Peerless Importers, Inc., Brooklyn, NY, pg. 855
Sullivan, George E., V.P.-Sls. & Leasing--ACF Industries, Inc., Earth City, MO, pg. 561
Sullivan, George R., V.P.-Sls.--Sullivan Paper Company, West Springfield, MA, pg. 1057
Sullivan, Michael, Mgr.-Natl. Sls.--The Zippertubing Co., Los Angeles, CA, pg. 1220
Sullivan, Mike, V.P.-Sls. & Mgr.-Adv.--Lawrence Paper Company, Lawrence, KS, pg. 662
Sullivan, Mike, Dir.-Sls.--Intech Advanced Analog, Santa Clara, CA, pg. 572
Sullivan, Paul J., V.P.-Sls. & Mktg.--Lavelle Industries Inc., Burlington, WI, pg. 661
Sullivan, Paul K., Jr., Mgr.-Natl. Sls.--King Koil Licensing Company Inc., Saint Paul, MN, pg. 630
Sullivan, Sissy, V.P.-Sls.-Western Zone--Delta Pride Catfish, Inc., Indianola, MS, pg. 327
Sullivan, T.W., Dir.-Parts Sls. & Opers.--Bucyrus-Erie Company, South Milwaukee, WI, pg. 186
Sullivan, Terrence M., V.P.-Ordinary Sls.--The Minnesota Mutual Life Insurance Company, Saint Paul, MN, pg. 757
Sullivan, Timothy J., V.P.-Sls. & Mktg.--North American Salt Company, Overland Park, KS, pg. 812
Summerlin, James, V.P.-Sls.--Vindicator Corporation, Austin, TX, pg. 1152
Summers, David L., V.P.-Telemarketing--Koch Supplies Inc., Kansas City, MO, pg. 639
Suninski, Gerard, V.P.-Sls. Southern Div.--Schmidt Baking Co., Inc., Baltimore, MD, pg. 976
Surbaugh, Gary, V.P.-Natl. Sls.--Tension Envelope Corp., Kansas City, MO, pg. 1088
Suscavage, Mike, V.P., Sls.--Global Marketing Resources, New York, NY, pg. 463
Susen, Dale, Exec. V.P.- Sls.--Super 8 Motels, Inc., Aberdeen, SD, pg. 1062
Sussman, Dennis, Sr. V.P.-Sls.-Lighting Div.--Crystal Clear Industries Company, Ridgefield Park, NJ, pg. 303
Sutherland, Peter, Mgr.-Intl. Sls.--Bel-Art Products, Pequannock, NJ, pg. 133
Suttles, Karen, Mgr.-Tour & Travel Sls.--Chattanooga Choo-Choo Holiday Inn, Chattanooga, TN, pg. 241
Swaim, Ed, Mgr.-Saf-T-Liner Sls.--Thomas Built Buses, Inc., High Point, NC, pg. 1092
Swanson, Eric, V.P.-Sls.--The O'Brien Corporation, South San Francisco, CA, pg. 820
Swanson, Norman P., V.P.-Sls.--The Stroh Brewery Company, Detroit, MI, pg. 1053
Swanson, Tim, Mgr.-Sls.--KGWC-TV, Casper, WY, pg. 1043
Swartz, Dan, V.P.-Private Label Packing--4C Foods Corporation, Brooklyn, NY, pg. 427
Sweeney, Mark, V.P.-Sls., Mktg. & Pub. Rels.--Black Fin Yacht Corporation, Fort Lauderdale, FL, pg. 154
Swenson, Brent, Exec. V.P. & V.P. Sls.--Linzer Products Corp., Flushing, NY, pg. 677
Swenson, Richard, V.P.-Sls.--Wagner Spray Tech Corp., Minneapolis, MN, pg. 1158
Swerdlow, Al, Mgr.-Sls.--Miller Curtain Co., Inc., San Antonio, TX, pg. 754
Swift, Alison C., Asst. Sls. Mgr.--Technical Instruments Div., San Jose, CA, pg. 1068
Swiger, George, Mgr.-Retail Sls.--Voyager Emblems, Inc., Sanborn, NY, pg. 1155
Swingle, Edward R., V.P.-Sls.--Hesston, Norcross, GA, pg. 4
Syberg, Kevin M., V.P.-Sls.--Dualite Sales & Service, Inc., Williamsburg, OH, pg. 350
Sydnor, Sam, Mgr.-Gen. Sls.--Parks Sausage Company, Baltimore, MD, pg. 850
Sylvester, Tom, Dir.-Sls.--Modern Handling Equipment of N.J., Inc., Edison, NJ, pg. 763
Sytsma, Fred, Exec. V.P.-OEM Sls.--Frost Inc., Grand Rapids, MI, pg. 435
Szmigiel, Rick, Nissan Sls. Mgr.-New Cars--Jeffrey Buick-Nissan Inc., Roseville, MI, pg. 591
Szostak, Michael J., Dir.-Mktg. & Sls.--Douglas Steel Fabricating Corporation, Lansing, MI, pg. 347
Taber, James, V.P.-Sls.--Miller Fluid Power Corp., Bensenville, IL, pg. 754
Tabet, Maroun, V.P.-Sls.--Manufacturers Products Company, Warren, MI, pg. 705
Tague, John, Sr. V.P.-Mktg. & Sls.--Amtran, Inc., Indianapolis, IN, pg. 69
Tamberelli, Paul, V.P.-Sls.--Altec Lansing Consumer Products, Milford, PA, pg. 1025
Tang, Patrick, Pres.--Anderson Die Castings, Inc., Wheeling, IL, pg. 72
Tanner, Allan, V.P.-Sls.--Americo Manufacturing Co., Inc., Acworth, GA, pg. 66
Tapscott, Judy, Asst. Sls. Dir.--National Banner Company, Dallas, TX, pg. 786
Tarantino, Ronald M., V.P.-Sls.--Diamond Crystal Specialty Foods, Inc., Wilmington, MA, pg. 335
Tarlo, Jay, Mgr.-Sls.--Brush Research Manufacturing Company, Los Angeles, CA, pg. 184
Tarr, Gary, V.P.-Sls.--Cyborg Systems, Inc., Chicago, IL, pg. 307
Tarver, Van, Sr. V.P.-Retail--Thrifty Oil Company, Downey, CA, pg. 1096
Tasker, John, V.P.-Mktg. & Sls.--Frog Switch & Manufacturing Company, Carlisle, PA, pg. 434
Tate, John S., V.P.-Sls.--Monex International, Ltd., Newport Beach, CA, pg. 765
Tate, Mike, Ntl. Sls. Mgr.--Advance Seed Co., Fulton, KY, pg. 407
Tattersfield, George, V.P.-Sls.--Congoleum Corporation, Mercerville, NJ, pg. 274
Tatum, Jim, Dir.-Sls.--North Park Lincoln Mercury Inc., San Antonio, TX, pg. 813
Taub, David, Mgr.-Intl. Sls.--Spectronics Corporation, Westbury, NY, pg. 1029
Taugher, Steve, V.P.-Sls.--Attwood Corporation, Lowell, MI, pg. 1044
Taus, D., Mgr.-Sls. Admin.--Alva/Amco Pharmacal Companies, Inc., Chicago, IL, pg. 46
Taussig, Richard, Sr. V.P.-Sls.--Superba, Inc., Los Angeles, CA, pg. 1063
Taverna, Richard, V.P.--Par Industries, inc., Medina, OH, pg. 847
Taylor, Donald D., Sr. V.P.-Sls.--Wolverine Massachusetts Corporation, Merrimac, MA, pg. 1199
Taylor, Douglas, Sr. V.P.-Sls. & Mktg.--Spangler Candy Company, Bryan, OH, pg. 1025
Taylor, H.J., V.P.-Sls.--Peco Inc., Portland, OR, pg. 854
Taylor, Hal, Mgr.-Natl. Sls.-Retail--Weaver Popcorn Company, Inc., Van Buren, IN, pg. 1170
Taylor, Marcia, Mgr.-Sls.--Shaw Creations, Inc., New York, NY, pg. 996
Taylor, Mike, V.P.-Intl. Sls.--Atari Games Corporation, Milpitas, CA, pg. 93
Taylor, N.G., Sr. V.P.-Industrial Sls. & Mktg.--North American Refractories Company, Cleveland, OH, pg. 811
Taylor, R.B., V.P.-Sls. & Mktg.--Velcon Filters, Inc., San Jose, CA, pg. 1146
Taylor, Steve, Mgr.-Sls., Midwest--Mountain Valley Spring Company, Hot Springs, AR, pg. 968
Teeple, Andrew R., V.P.-Sls. & Mktg.--Haddon Craftsmen, Inc., Scranton, PA, pg. 499
Tellus, James, Mgr.-Promo.--SJL of Kansas Corp., Wichita, KS, pg. 962
Telsey, Mel, Dir.-Sls. & Mktg.--Peerless Importers, Inc., Brooklyn, NY, pg. 855
Temple, John, V.P.-Sales--Northwest Airlines, Inc., Saint Paul, MN, pg. 782

Temple, Wick, V.P. & Dir.-Newspaper Membership--The Associated Press, New York, NY, pg. 91
Tenura, David, Dir.-Sls. & Mktg.--Echevarria Angel Co., Inc., Los Angeles, CA, pg. 365
Teresa Silva, Dir.-Human Resources & Sls. Supvr.--Windsor Fashions, Los Angeles, CA, pg. 1195
Terpak, John, Jr., V.P.-Sls.--York Barbell Co., Inc., York, PA, pg. 1208
Terrill, R., Mgr.-Intl. Sls.--PMC Industries Inc., Wickliffe, OH, pg. 836
Tesh, Theresa, Asst. Dir.-Sales & Mktg.--SAS Institute Inc., Cary, NC, pg. 959
Thalmann, Craig, V.P.-Mktg. & Sls.--National Utility Service, Inc., Park Ridge, NJ, pg. 794
Tharp, Jim, Mgr.-Sls. & Service--NuArc Co., Kansas City, MO, pg. 817
Theesfeld, Donald A., Exec. V.P.-Sls. & Mktg.--Kettle Restaurants, Houston, TX, pg. 626
Thein, Dusty, Mgr.-Sls.--KGWN-TV, Cheyenne, WY, pg. 1043
Theriot, Scott, Dir.-Sls. & Mktg.--Algiers Iron Works & Dry Dock, Inc., New Orleans, LA, pg. 163
Theut, Joel, Mgr.-New Car Sls.--Jefferson Chevrolet Co., Detroit, MI, pg. 591
Thomas, D.T., V.P.-Sls. & Mktg.--Ball Seed Co., West Chicago, IL, pg. 116
Thomas, Griff, Dir.-Sls. & Customer Service--Telescope Casual Furniture, Inc., Granville, NY, pg. 1085
Thomas, John, V.P.-Sls.--Dempster, Inc., Toccoa, GA, pg. 328
Thomas, Pat, Reg. Sls. Mgr.--Evenflo Juvenile Furniture Co., Piqua, OH, pg. 1024
Thomason, Carl, Sls. Mgr.--Brock-McVey Company, Lexington, KY, pg. 728
Thompson, Aubrey A., V.P.-Mktg. & Sls.--Graybar Electric Company, Inc., Clayton, MO, pg. 479
Thompson, Bert, Dir.-Sls. & Mktg.--Genmar Industries, Inc., Minneapolis, MN, pg. 759
Thompson, Brent, V.P.-Sls.--Yuba Heat Transfer Division, Tulsa, OK, pg. 275
Thompson, Don, Dir.-Mktg. & Sls.--Telsco Industries, Garland, TX, pg. 1085
Thompson, Don Jr., V.P.-Sls.--The Thompson Group Companies, Henderson, KY, pg. 1094
Thompson, Gary, Mgr.-Sls.--Pak-Sher Co., Kilgore, TX, pg. 1072
Thompson, Hugh O., Mgr.-Sls.--H & H Tube & Manufacturing Co., Vanderbilt, MI, pg. 495
Thompson, James, V.P.-Natl. Sls.--Haggar Apparel Company, Dallas, TX, pg. 499
Thompson, John, V.P.-Sls. & Mktg.--Mays Chemical Company, Indianapolis, IN, pg. 725
Thompson, L., Mgr.-Sls.--Coilcraft, Inc., Cary, IL, pg. 259
Thompson, Richard, Natl. Sls. Mgr.--Slant/Fin Corporation, Greenvale, NY, pg. 1010
Thompson, William, V.P.-Sls.--Kreher Steel Company, Inc., Melrose Park, IL, pg. 644
Thornburg, Dick, V.P.-Sls., Custom Forms--Adams Business Forms, Topeka, KS, pg. 16
Thornley, James, V.P.-Mktg. & Sls.--Talon, Inc., Meadville, PA, pg. 1077
Thornton, Daniel P., Sr. V.P.-Sls. & Mktg.--Progress Printing Company, Lynchburg, VA, pg. 894
Thornton, Kathy, Mgr.-Classifieds--VV Publishing Corp., New York, NY, pg. 1142
Thrau, Brad, V.P.-Sls.--Border States Industries, Inc., Fargo, ND, pg. 165
Thurber, Bob, Dir.-Consumer Sls.--Wahl Clipper Corp., Sterling, IL, pg. 1158
Thurman, David, V.P.-Sls.-Plus Div.--Spinnaker Software Corporation, Cambridge, MA, pg. 1031
Thurstone, Peter, Sls. Mgr.--Radix Wire Company, Cleveland, OH, pg. 909
Thybony, James D., Pres.--Thybony Wall Coverings Co., Chicago, IL, pg. 1096
Tiffany, A. L., V.P.-Sls. & Mktg.--KYB Corporation of America, Lombard, IL, pg. 613
Tighe, Matthew, Mgr.-Sls.--Ace Glass Incorporated, Vineland, NJ, pg. 11
Tillis, Arlen, V.P.-Sls. & Mktg.--Cox Lumber Co., Saint Petersburg, FL, pg. 294
Tilzer, James, V.P.-Sls.--Paper Enterprises, Inc., Bronx, NY, pg. 847
Timko, Joseph R., V.P.-Mktg. & Circulation--Yankee Publishing Incorporated, Dublin, NH, pg. 1207
Tippit, Raymond, V.P.-Natl. Railroad Sls.--MI-Jack Products, Inc., Hazel Crest, IL, pg. 746
Tirschek, Joe, Sls. Mgr.--Rough Brothers, Inc., Cincinnati, OH, pg. 952
Tobin, James, Sr. V.P.-Sls. & Mktg.--The Spring Air Company, Des Plaines, IL, pg. 1032
Tobin, Linda, Dir.-Intl. Sls. Admin.--Worldvision Enterprises, New York, NY, pg. 54
Tokuhisa, Roy T., Grp. V.P.-W/S Allied Sls.--Servco Pacific Inc., Honolulu, HI, pg. 991
Tolifson, Robert, Dir.-Retail Opers.--San Francisco Giants Baseball Club, San Francisco, CA, pg. 969
Tolkin, David, Dir.-Sls., Import & Export--Jennifer Dale, Inc., New York, NY, pg. 592
Tolkin, Larry, V.P.-Sls.--Jennifer Dale, Inc., New York, NY, pg. 592
Toll, Ann, V.P. & Mgr. Sls.--Buyer Advertising, Inc., Newton, MA, pg. 197
Tollett, Gary, Mgr.-Sls.--Southwide, Inc.-Western Div., Casa Grande, AZ, pg. 1024
Toma, Tony, Dir.-Sls.--March Manufacturing Inc., Glenview, IL, pg. 706
Tomao, D.F., Dir.-Sls.-Aftermarket & Original Equipment--Raymark Friction Company, Manheim, PA, pg. 914
Tomaszewski, James M., Exec. V.P.-Retail Opers.--Lechmere, Inc., Woburn, MA, pg. 665
Tomek, Warren, V.P.-Mktg. & Law Enforcement Sls.--O. F. Mossberg & Sons, Inc., North Haven, CT, pg. 773
Tompkins, Tom, Sls. Mgr.--Eager Beaver, Lake Wales, FL, pg. 362
Toms, Michael, Catering Sls. & Dir.-Mktg.--Master Foods, Kings Lynn,, United Kingdom, pg. 713
Tonelson, Leon, Exec. V.P.-Sls.--Union Underwear Co., Inc., Bowling Green, KY, pg. 400
Tonelson, Leon, Exec. V.P.-Sls.--Fruit of the Loom, Bowling Green, KY, pg. 400
Took, Jack L., 2nd V.P.-Grp. Sls. & Mktg.--Ameritas Life Insurance Corp., Lincoln, NE, pg. 66
Tooker, DAve, Exec. V.P.-Sls. & Mktg.--Golden Cat Corporation, South Bend, IN, pg. 637
Tookey, Robert, V.P.-Sls.--Sharon Tube Company, Sharon, PA, pg. 995
Toole, Charles E., V.P.-Whlse. Sls.--Fannie May Candy Shops, Inc., Chicago, IL, pg. 604
Toomey, Kevin, V.P.-Sls.--Sheer Hosiery Div., Greensboro, NC, pg. 263
Toran, Daniel J., Exec. V.P.-Agency Opers. Admin.--The New England, Boston, MA, pg. 799
Torke, Ward J., V.P.-Sls., Mktg. & Personnel Dir.--Torke Coffee Company, Inc., Sheboygan, WI, pg. 1102
Totten, Tracy, V.P.-Sls. & Mktg.--Totten Tubes, Inc., Los Angeles, CA, pg. 1103
Towle, John, V.P.-Sls.--Edelbrock Corp., Torrance, CA, pg. 367
Townsend, Jack, V.P.-Sls. & Mktg.--Martin Industries (AL), Florence, AL, pg. 715
Tozun, Orhan, V.P.-Mktg., Sls. & Engrng.--International Microcircuits, Inc., Milpitas, CA, pg. 579
Tracy, J., Natl. Sls. Mgr.--Cable Electric Products, Inc., Providence, RI, pg. 671
Tracy, Robert, Dir.-Sls.--Joanna, Charlotte, NC, pg. 200
Tracy, Steve, Assoc. V.P.-Mktg. & Sls. Promo.--Post Buckley Schuh & Jernigan, Miami, FL, pg. 881
Traidman, Michael, V.P.-Sls. & Mktg.--Printco, Inc., Greenville, MI, pg. 891
Trakselis, Katharine, Mgr.-Sls.--Replogle Globes, Inc., Broadview, IL, pg. 927
Trapp, Robert, V.P.-Sls.-North Eastern Region--PST Vans, Inc., Salt Lake City, UT, pg. 837
Trask, Jim, V.P.-Sls.--Southern Frozen Foods, Montezuma, GA, pg. 26
Trastek, Victor, V.P.-Adv. & Sls.--Monarch Ware, Inc., Algoma, WI, pg. 742
Trastek, Victor F., V.P.-Adv. & Sls.--The Metal Ware Corp., Two Rivers, WI, pg. 741
Traut, Clem, Reg. Mgr.-Sls.--Serfilco, Ltd., Northbrook, IL, pg. 990
Tredinnick, David, Natl. Sls. Mgr.--Miether Bearing Products, Inc., Odessa, TX, pg. 32
Treicher, Steven J., V.P.-Sls.--PBS Building Systems of America, Anaheim, CA, pg. 835
Tremba, Dee, V.P., Sls.--E-B Advertising Display Inc., Massillon, OH, pg. 358
Tremble, Mark, Dir.-Sls.--J. J. Keller & Associates, Inc., Neenah, WI, pg. 620
Trent, Jim, V.P.-Sls.--Hurst Performances, Inc., Cleveland, OH, pg. 761
Treptow, Ben, Mgr.-Sls.--Bentley-Harris Manufacturing Co., Lionville, PA, pg. 140
Treriot, Scott, Dir.-Sls.--Bollinger Machine Shop And Shipyard, Inc., Lockport, LA, pg. 163
Triana, Victor, Mgr.-Natl. Sls.--VSI Fasteners, Inc., Stanton, CA, pg. 1142
Trigg, Phil, Dir.-Franchise Sls.--Precision Tune, Inc., Leesburg, VA, pg. 885
Trottman, Lanny, V.P.-Sls. & Mktg.--Desoto Hardwood Flooring Company, Memphis, TN, pg. 786
Troup, Daniel, V.P.-Mktg. & Sls.--National Fruit Product Company, Winchester, VA, pg. 789
Troyer, Daryl, V.P.-Sls.--Dan Dee Pretzel & Potato Chip Co., Waterford, PA, pg. 313
Truant, Vincent, V.P.-Natl. Acct. Sls.--Sweetheart Cup Co., Inc., Chicago, IL, pg. 1067
Trudel, Brian, M., Mgr.-Sls.--Carrier Vibrating Equipment, Inc., Louisville, KY, pg. 225
Trudell, Richard, Mgr.-Sls.-Northern New England--The Robert E. Morris Company, Farmington, CT, pg. 771
Truesdale, Bill, V.P.-Sls.--Maplehurst Farms, Inc., Indianapolis, IN, pg. 705
Tucci, Anthony, V.P.-Sls., Juice Prods.--Beverage Canners International Corp., Miami, FL, pg. 148
Tucci, Carlo, Sales Dir.--Levi Strauss & Co. (Canada), Inc., Markham,, Canada, pg. 670
Tucker, A.F., V.P. & Dir.-Mktg. & Sls.-Sports Surfaces--California Products Corp., Cambridge, MA, pg. 210
Tucker, James E., V.P.-Sls. & Mktg.--R.M. Palmer Company, West Reading, PA, pg. 843
Tucker, L.W., V.P.-Sls. & Mktg.--Thermalloy, Inc., Farmers Branch, TX, pg. 1091
Tueffel, Helen, Mgr.-Sls. Promo. & Adv.--J.D. Edwards & Company, Denver, CO, pg. 370
Tufts, Carl R., Mgr.-Sls. & Mktg.--Thomas & Skinner, Inc., Indianapolis, IN, pg. 1093
Tunnessen, James, V.P. & Reg. Mgr.--Carrols Corporation, Syracuse, NY, pg. 225
Turin, George, Dir.-Indus. Sls.--Frigid Products, Inc., Elizabeth, NJ, pg. 889
Turnbull, Joel, Dir.-Retail Sls.--Veryfine Products, Inc., Westford, MA, pg. 1148
Turner, D.G., V.P.-Sls.--Voyager Emblems, Inc., Sanborn, NY, pg. 1155
Turner, David, Dir.-Sls. & Mktg.--Dobles Chevrolet, Inc., Manchester, NH, pg. 342
Turner, Donald E., Exec. V.P.-Sls.--Lumber Systems, Inc., Vancouver, WA, pg. 687
Turner, Peter, Mgr.-Sls.--C.R. Daniels, Inc., Ellicott City, MD, pg. 314
Turner, Steve, V.P.-Sls. & Mktg.--Micro Component Technology Inc., Saint Paul, MN, pg. 748
Turpin, Jeff, Dir.-Sls.--Bearden Lumber Company, Inc., Bearden, AR, pg. 129
Turrentine, Tom, V.P.-Sls.--Lone Star Corrugated Container Corporation, Irving, TX, pg. 682
Tuschoff, Clay, Mgr.-Retail Sls.--Sullivan Oil Company, Baton Rouge, LA, pg. 1057
Twichell, E.S., Sls. Mgr.--Eriez Magnetics, Erie, PA, pg. 386
Tyrrell, George, V.P.-Sls.--Beauty Enterprises Inc., Hartford, CT, pg. 130
Uhlig, Kevin, V.P.-Machine Tool Sls.--The Producto Machine Co., Bridgeport, CT, pg. 893
Umans, Craig, V.P.-Sls.--RHC/Spacemaster Corporation, Melrose Park, IL, pg. 906
Umbenhower, Lonnie K., Sr. V.P.-Sls.--Capital Bank of California, Los Angeles, CA, pg. 214
Underweiner, H., V.P.-Mktg. & Sls.--Farrell Lines Incorporated, New York, NY, pg. 403
Underwood, Jeanne, V.P.-Natl. Accts.--Royal Cruise Line Inc., San Francisco, CA, pg. 953
Unger, Richard, V.P.-Mktg. & Sls.--H. C. Prange Company, Green Bay, WI, pg. 884
Upshaw, Kim, Dir.-Mktg., Sls., Adv. & Pub. Rels.--Empire Airlines, Hayden Lake, ID, pg. 379
Upton, Joseph H., Asst. Sls. Mgr.--Malloy Lithographing Inc., Ann Arbor, MI, pg. 703
Ur, Joseph, Dir.-Sls. & Mktg.--Bison Foods Company, Buffalo, NY, pg. 1140
Urbani, Alexander M., V.P.-Sls. & Mktg.--Penske Truck Leasing, Chesterfield, MO, pg. 859
Urice, James M., V.P. & Midwest Sls. Mgr.--Parade Publications Inc., New York, NY, pg. 847
Urquhart, G.I., V.P.-Mktg. & Sls.--Bolton-Emerson, Inc., Lawrence, MA, pg. 163
Urquhart, Glenn I., V.P.-Mktg. & Sls.--Converting Machinery Div., Lawrence, MA, pg. 163
Urrutia, Bob, Mgr.-Export Sls.--Sentry Group, Rochester, NY, pg. 990
Urschel, Ned, V.P.-Sls.--Sargent & Greenleaf, Inc., Nicholasville, KY, pg. 971
Urso, Joseph, Mgr.-Sls.--Steelite, Inc., Pittsburgh, PA, pg. 1044
Vaagen, Dennis E., Mgr.-Sls. & Mktg.--Vaagen Brothers Lumber, Inc., Colville, WA, pg. 1142
Vabder Heiden, Jim, Dir.-Sls. & Mktg.--Sanitas Healthcare Div., Hastings, NE, pg. 356
Vakil, Ishaq U., V.P.-Sls.--Lights Of America, Inc., Walnut, CA, pg. 675
Valasek, Jack, V.P.-Sls.--Schlosser Forge Company, Rancho Cucamonga, CA, pg. 976
Valby, Mary Jane, Dir.-Sls. & Mktg.--Lucca Packing Div., Nalley's Fine Foods, South San Francisco, CA, pg. 25
Valdes, T.A., V.P.-Sls.--Bacardi Imports, Inc., Miami, FL, pg. 108
Valeiras, Luis, V.P.-Sls. , Mktg. & Adv., Dir.- Corp.Travel--Gator Industries Inc., Hialeah, FL, pg. 446
Valenti, Marc, Sr. V.P. & Sls. Mgr.--Gannett Transit, New York, NY, pg. 442
Vallan, Louis D., Exec. V.P.-Sls.--Young Supply Company, Detroit, MI, pg. 1214
Vam, Kenneth Rock, Sls. Mgr.-Dehydrated Dairy Prods. Div.--Associated Milk Producers North Central Region, New Ulm, MN, pg. 91
Van Arsdale, Dan, Dir.-Sls.--Aeros Instruments, Inc., Northbrook, IL, pg. 1034
Van Dine, James, Mgr.-Sls.--Tactair Fluid Controls Corp., Beverly, NJ, pg. 869
van Hartesvelt, Mark, Sr. V.P.-Sls. & Mktg.--Guest Quarters Suite Hotels, Boston, MA, pg. 493
Van Horne, Dave, V.P.-Sls.--Norcraft Companies, Inc., Saint Paul, MN, pg. 809
Van Peit, Charles, Dir.-Sls.--Thomas R. Hopson Broker, Inc., Marietta, GA, pg. 544
Van Riper, Allen, Mgr.-Natl. Sls.--Marley Pump Co., Mission, KS, pg. 710
Van Sickle, Walter, Inside Sls. Mgr.--Clifford Metal, Providence, RI, pg. 658
Van Tosh, David J., Exec. V.P.-Sls.--EB (NA), Chicago, IL, pg. 381
Van Wormer, Sheri, Sls. Admin.--Sudbury Consumer Products Company, Phoenix, AZ, pg. 403
Vance, Richard G., V.P.-Sls. & Mktg.--Bon Ton Foods, Inc., York, PA, pg. 164
Vanderbeck, Ed, Jr., V.P.-Sls.--Black Millwork Co., Inc., Allendale, NJ, pg. 154
VanderKooi, David, Dir.-Govt. Sls.--Trendway Corporation, Holland, MI, pg. 1109
Vanderminden, Henry, IV, Mgr.-Sls.--Telescope Casual Furniture, Inc., Granville, NY, pg. 1085
VanLanen, Charles, Mgr.-Reg. Sls.--Interstate Steel Supply Co. of Maryland, Baltimore, MD, pg. 581
Vann, Gary, V.P.-Sls. & Mktg.--Mighty Distributing System, Norcross, GA, pg. 752
Vanwinkle, Windy, Mgr.-Sls.--Integral Systems, Inc., Sunnyvale, CA, pg. 573
Varakian, Robert, Sr. V.P.-Sls. & Mktg.--M. Kamenstein, Inc., White Plains, NY, pg. 615
Varvel, Russell E., Sr. V.P.-Sls.--Delta Queen Steamboat Company, New Orleans, LA, pg. 385
Vaughn, Pete, Mgr.- Ice Cream Div. Sls.--Trauth Dairy Inc., Newport, KY, pg. 1108
Veale, Ernest, V.P.-Sls., Mktg., Mdse. & Adv.--The Stellar Group Inc., Jacksonville, FL, pg. 1046
Veck, Allen, Mgr.-Sls.--T Shirt Graphics, Des Moines, IA, pg. 1148
Veidemanis, I.E., Natl. Sls. Mgr.--The William Bayley Co., Springfield, OH, pg. 128
Veirs, William, V.P.-Sls. & Mktg.--Sonneveldt Company, Grand Rapids, MI, pg. 1018
Venitelli, Mike, Natl. Sls. Mgr.--Michael Business Machines Corporation, North Charleston, SC, pg. 747
Ver Shaw, Marty, Mgr.-Inside Sls.--Country Sampler, Saint Charles, IL, pg. 968
Verduin, Cal, V.P.-Sls.--Transnational Motors Inc., Grand Rapids, MI, pg. 1107
Vernon, Glenn E., V.P.-Sls.--Adams Business Forms, Topeka, KS, pg. 16

Vernon, Kim, Dir.- Adv. Admin.--CRK Advertising, New York, NY, pg. 203
Vertun, Steve, V.P.-Sls.--Shugart Corporation, Irvine, CA, pg. 1001
Vesey, Ken, Gen. Sls. Mgr.-OEM--AP Parts Manufacturing Company, Toledo, OH, pg. 240
Vetowich, Peter C., Exec. V.P., Dir. Retail Opers.--Ross Roy Inc., Bloomfield Hills, MI, pg. 950
Vevoda, Jodi, Los Angeles Sls. Mgr.--Parade Publications Inc., New York, NY, pg. 847
Victor, Tom, V.P.-Domestic Sls.--John Fabick Tractor Company, Fenton, MO, pg. 396
Vieira, Gil, V.P.-Sls.--Ektelon Corp., San Diego, CA, pg. 890
Vincent, James, V.P.-Sls.--Cream Products Co., Inc., Westchester, IL, pg. 297
Vincent, Michael C., V.P.-Sls. & Mktg.--Interstate Electric Supply Company, Inc., Chantilly, VA, pg. 580
Vinsko, William, Mgr.-Sls.--Medico Industries, Inc., Wilkes-Barre, PA, pg. 735
Vitalo, Celena, Mgr.-Natl. Sls.--M. Kamenstein, Inc., White Plains, NY, pg. 615
Vito, James M., V.P.-Sls.--Giles & Ransome, Inc., Bensalem, PA, pg. 458
Vivian, Frank, Mgr.-Sls.--Chief E-Z Breaker, Inc., Grand Island, NE, pg. 247
Vivian, Joyce, Mgr.-Sls.--Captive Plastics, Piscataway, NJ, pg. 216
Vizcarra, Mike, Mgr.-Standard Sls.--O'Keeffe's, Inc., San Francisco, CA, pg. 823
Vizzina, Tom, Dir.-Sls. & Mktg., Mgr.-Natl. Sls.--Theochem Labs., Inc., Tampa, FL, pg. 1090
Vlaeminck, Ben, Regional Sls. Mgr., Benelux & France--Thoroughbred Europe Ltd., Romford,, United Kingdom, pg. 1095
Voelkert, Joel, V.P.-Sls.--American Buildings Co., Eufaula, AL, pg. 49
Vogelsang, Christopher, Mgr.-Sls.--Smith Metal Arts Company, Inc., Buffalo, NY, pg. 1013
Voisin, Bret, Dir.-Sls. & Mktg.--Mears Transportation Group, Orlando, FL, pg. 734
Voisin, Russell, V.P.-Intl. Sls. Publishing--Rand McNally & Company, Skokie, IL, pg. 911
Voland, Paul, Mgr.-Natl. Accts.--Howe Furniture Corporation, Trumbull, CT, pg. 547
Voltz, Steve, Sls. Mgr.--Judson-Atkinson Candies, Inc., San Antonio, TX, pg. 608
Voors, Jerry, Mgr.-Sls. & Mktg.--Cheney Company, New Berlin, WI, pg. 242
Vos, Denny, Natl. Sls. Mgr.--Vermeer Manufacturing Company, Pella, IA, pg. 1148
Voshant, James, Mgr.-Sls.-Plumbing--W.A. Roosevelt Co., La Crosse, WI, pg. 946
Voyle, Jim, Mgr.-Sls.-New Cars--Roseville Chrysler Plymouth Inc., Roseville, MI, pg. 949
Vr, Joe, Dir.-Sls. & Mktg.--Upstate Milk Cooperatives Inc., Le Roy, NY, pg. 1140
Vucovich, Doug, Mgr.-Gen. Mktg. & Sls.--Wingfoot Films Corporation, Carrollton, OH, pg. 555
Vuillet, Robert, Sr. V.P.-Natl. Sls.--North American Watch Corporation, Lyndhurst, NJ, pg. 812
Vukmanic, Frank, Sr. V.P.-Sls. & Mktg.--Amperif Corporation, Chatsworth, CA, pg. 68
Wade, Jim, V.P.-Sls. & Mktg.--Crane Carrier Company, Tulsa, OK, pg. 296
Wadsworth, Carl, Dir.-Sls.--Franklin Baking Co., Inc., Goldsboro, NC, pg. 429
Wagner, Bill, Dir.-Sls. Promo.--Penn-Daniels, Inc., Quincy, IL, pg. 857
Wagner, Grant, Dir.-Sls.--Lindsay Olive Growers, Lindsay, CA, pg. 676
Wagner, Kenneth E., Mgr.-Sls.--Carton-Craft Corporation, Buffalo, NY, pg. 226
Wagner, William L., Jr., Sr. V.P.-New Bus.--National Life Insurance Company, Montpelier, VT, pg. 791
Wahl, Jim, V.P.-Sls.--Wahl Clipper Corp., Sterling, IL, pg. 1158
Wainwright, Julie, V.P.-Intl. Sls. & Mktg.--Spinnaker Software Corporation, Cambridge, MA, pg. 1031
Wajer, Thomas, V.P.-Natl. Accts.--St. Johnsbury Trucking Co., Inc., Holliston, MA, pg. 966
Walborn, Robert L., V.P.-Sls.--Farmer's Pride, Inc., Fredericksburg, PA, pg. 401
Walch, James W., III, V.P.-Sls.--Jackson Mills, Inc., Wellford, SC, pg. 587
Walchirk, Irving, Gen. Sls. Mgr.--Sinai 48 Kosher Foods Corp., Chicago, IL, pg. 146
Waldoch, Michael, Sls. Mgr.--Waterous Company, South Saint Paul, MN, pg. 50
Waldron, Dan, v.P.-Sls. & Mktg.--Rangaire & Company, Cleburne, TX, pg. 912
Waldrop, R.E., V.P.-Sls.--Edwards Engineering Corporation, Pompton Plains, NJ, pg. 370
Walker, C.G., V.P.-Sls.--Harriet & Henderson Yarns, Inc., Henderson, NC, pg. 511
Walker, John, Western Reg. Mgr.--Stanbee Company, Inc., Carlstadt, NJ, pg. 1035
Walker, Roger, Mgr.-Natl. Sls.--Allied Paper Incorporated, Dayton, OH, pg. 38
Walker, Scott, Dir.-Western Div. Sls. & Mktg.--Hyatt Hotels Corporation, Chicago, IL, pg. 495
Walker, Wayne F., V.P.-Sls., Steel Industry--Superior Machine Company Of South Carolina, Inc., Florence, SC, pg. 1064
Wall, Edward F., V.P.-Sls.--Fredrickson Motor Express Corp., Charlotte, NC, pg. 430
Wall, John, V.P.-Sls.--Owsley & Sons, Inc., Fort Mill, SC, pg. 834
Wallace, Kenneth W., V.P.-Adv. Sls.--Parade Publications Inc., New York, NY, pg. 847
Wallake, Randy, V.P.-Pension Div.--The Minnesota Mutual Life Insurance Company, Saint Paul, MN, pg. 757
Wallin, Richard, V.P.-Sls.--Kurt Manufacturing Co. Inc., Fridley, MN, pg. 646
Wallis, John, V.P.-Sls. & Mktg.--Hyatt International Corporation, Chicago, IL, pg. 495
Wallis, Robert, V.P.-Sls.--Laubeck Corporation/Cross, Carbondale, PA, pg. 660
Walraven, Ben, V.P.-Sls.--Pan-American Seed Co., West Chicago, IL, pg. 116
Walsh, James, Sls. Mgr.-Butter Div.--Associated Milk Producers North Central Region, New Ulm, MN, pg. 91
Walsh, Richard A., Mgr.-Natl. Sls.--Newage Industries Inc., Testing Instruments Division, Willow Grove, PA, pg. 803
Walsh, Robert, V.P.-Mktg. & Sls.--Rocco Inc., Harrisonburg, VA, pg. 940
Walsh, Robert, Dir.-Mktg. & Sls.--Rocco Further Processing, Timberville, VA, pg. 940
Walsh, William C., V.P.-Sls.--Wells Fargo Alarm Services, King of Prussia, PA, pg. 166
Walter, Alan, V.P.-Mktg.--G.C. Thorsen, Inc., Rockford, IL, pg. 609
Walters, George, V.P.-Sls.--Wurzburg, Inc., Memphis, TN, pg. 1205
Waltersdorf, John G., Exec. V.P.-Sls.--Tristate Electrical Supply Co., Inc., Hagerstown, MD, pg. 1114
Walther, Lee, Dir.-Mktg. & Sls.--Piper Aircraft Corporation, Vero Beach, FL, pg. 872
Walton, Mark, Dir.-Mktg. & Sls.--Arrington Travel Center Inc., Chicago, IL, pg. 85
Walton, Mike, Mgr.-Sls.--Reichel & Drews Inc., Itasca, IL, pg. 906
Wankmiller, Albert, V.P.-Sls. & Mktg.--Print-O-Stat, Inc., York, PA, pg. 839
Wanthal, Theodore R., V.P.-Sls.--Maxon Corporation, Muncie, IN, pg. 723
Waples, Jim, Dir.-Intl. Sls.--Marine Travelift, Inc., Sturgeon Bay, WI, pg. 707
Ward, Brian P., V.P.-Sls. & Mktg.--Cortland Line Co., Inc., Cortland, NY, pg. 287
Ward, Gregory, V.P.-Sls. & Mktg.--ACL Technologies, Santa Ana, CA, pg. 2
Ward, James E.H., Sr. V.P. & Chief Mktg. Officer--Blue Cross & Blue Shield of Texas, Inc., Richardson, TX, pg. 160
Ward, R. Noel, V.P.-Sls.--Nationwide Homes, Inc., Martinsville, VA, pg. 795
Ward, R.J., V.P. & Sls. Mgr.--Difco, Inc., Findlay, OH, pg. 337
Ward, Richard, V.P.-Sls.--Aunt Nellie's Farm Kitchens, Inc., Clyman, WI, pg. 98
Ward, Richard, V.P.-Sls.--LePage's, Inc., Pittsburgh, PA, pg. 287
Ward, Robert A., Jr., Chm. Bd., Pres., Dir. Client Services--Carelli, Glynn & Ward, Butler, NJ, pg. 218
Warner, Drew, Dir.-Sls.--Okla Homer Smith Furniture Co., Fort Smith, AR, pg. 235
Warner, Glen, Dir.-Sls.--Molded Fiber Glass Co., Ashtabula, OH, pg. 764
Warren, Walter, Mgr.-Sls. & Mktg.--Salwasser Manufacturing Company, Inc., Reedley, CA, pg. 968
Warren, Yancey E., Mgr.-Sls. Support--Hackney & Sons, Inc., Washington, NC, pg. 498
Wasil, Tony, Mgr.-Sls.--Lou LaRiche Chevrolet-Subaru Inc., Plymouth, MI, pg. 658
Waterman, Win, Dir.-Sls.--Ace Office Products, Rolling Meadows, IL, pg. 12
Waters, Bud, Mgr.-Natl. Sls.--Atlas/Soundolier, Fenton, MO, pg. 64
Watkins, Jim, Mgr.-Custom Sls.--O'Keeffe's, Inc., San Francisco, CA, pg. 823
Watley, Dennis, Dir.-Sls. & Promo.--Kansas City Chiefs Football Club, Kansas City, MO, pg. 616
Watt, William A., V.P.-Sls.--Moran Towing & Transporation Co. Inc, Greenwich, CT, pg. 769
Waugh, John, Dir.-Sls. & Mktg.--Porcelain Metals Corp., Louisville, KY, pg. 881
Weatherford, Jack, Reg. Sls. Mgr.-Rocky Mt. South--U.S. Enertek, Inc., Farmington, NM, pg. 1135
Webb, Don, V.P.-Sls. & Mktg.--Central Transport Inc., High Point, NC, pg. 234
Webb, Ed, V.P.-Sls.--Peake Printers, Inc., Cheverly, MD, pg. 853
Webb, R.B., V.P.-Sls.--Atlantic Steel Company, Atlanta, GA, pg. 95
Webb, R.D., V.P.-Sls.-Eastern--A.M. Todd Company, Kalamazoo, MI, pg. 1100
Webb, Robert, V.P.-Sls. & Mktg.--Saunders Brothers, Westbrook, ME, pg. 972
Webb, Susan, Dir.-Sls. Support & Mktg.--Varityper, Inc., East Hanover, NJ, pg. 1146
Webber, Milton C., Gen. Sls. Mgr.--Hapco/American Div., Abingdon, VA, pg. 357
Weber, Bob, Natl. Sls. Mgr.-Hand Tools/Automotive--G.C. Thorsen, Inc., Rockford, IL, pg. 609
Weber, Carol, Dir.-Sls. & Mktg.--Crown Textile Company, Blue Bell, PA, pg. 302
Weber, Dick H., V.P.-Sls. & Mktg.--Doane Products Co., Branded Sales Div., Joplin, MO, pg. 342
Weber, James B., Mgr.-Sls.--Manufacturers Products Company, Warren, MI, pg. 705
Weber, John, V.P.-Govt. Contract Sls.--Anchor Industries Inc., Evansville, IN, pg. 71
Weber, Steven, Mgr.-Sls.--Logan & Kanawha Coal Co., Cincinnati, OH, pg. 681
Weber, Thomas J., Exec. V.P.-Sls. & Mktg.--Automation Intelligence, Inc., Maitland, FL, pg. 101
Webster, Don, Mgr.-Sls.--The Crosset Company Inc., Cincinnati, OH, pg. 300
Wedin, Rob, Dir.-Avocado Opers. & Intl. Mktg.--Calavo Growers of California, Tustin, CA, pg. 208
Weed, Andrew, Mgr.-Gen. Sls.--Tension Envelope Corp., Kansas City, MO, pg. 1088
Weeks, Robert, V.P.-Sls. & Mktg.--Battenfeld Gloucester Engineering Co. Inc., Gloucester, MA, pg. 126
Wegelius, Curt, V.P.-Sls. & Mktg.--Roosevelt Paper Co., Philadelphia, PA, pg. 946
Weger, David J., Dir.-Sls.--Gusso Manufacturing, Inc., Brooklyn, NY, pg. 495
Wegner, Jackie, Dir.-Natl. Accts.-Military Sls.--Pabst Brewing Co., San Antonio, TX, pg. 959
Wegner, John, Div. Mgr.-Sls.--The Jel Sert Co., West Chicago, IL, pg. 591
Wehrle, S.D., Sr. V.P.-Sls.--McJunkin Corporation, Charleston, WV, pg. 730
Weigel, Mark, V.P.-Sls.--Perry's Ice Cream Co., Inc., Akron, NY, pg. 863
Weiland, Larry, Dir.-Sls.--Sterling Supply Company, Inc., Lisle, IL, pg. 1047
Weiler, Robert, Sr. V.P.-Mktg. & Sls.--Lotus Publishing Corporation, Cambridge, MA, pg. 576
Weill, Sheldon, V.P.-Mktg. & Sls.--Universal Folding Box Company, Inc., Hoboken, NJ, pg. 1138
Weinstein, Hank, Mgr.-Sls.--American FoodService, Dallas, TX, pg. 60
Weinstein, Steve, Natl. Sls. Mgr.--Ventre Packing Company, Inc., Syracuse, NY, pg. 1147
Weinstock, Donna, Dir.-Distr. Sls.--Hydrite Chemical Company, Brookfield, WI, pg. 556
Weinsz, Dave, Sls. Dir.--Frank Industries, Inc., Brown City, MI, pg. 429
Weirback, Terry, Mgr.-Sls. & Mktg.--Perkasie Industries Corporation, Perkasie, PA, pg. 862
Weisman, Marcia, Mgr.-Sls.--Ce De Candy, Inc., Union, NJ, pg. 230
Weiss, Andrew J., V.P.-Sls. & Mktg.--Stebbins Engineering & Mfg. Co., Watertown, NY, pg. 1043
Weiss, Lynn, Exec. V.P. & Chief Oper. Officer--Spinnaker Software Corporation, Cambridge, MA, pg. 1031
Weiss, Marty, Sr. V.P.-Natl. Sls.--Bestform Foundations, Inc., Long Island City, NY, pg. 147
Weitz, Eric I., V.P.-Mktg. & Sls.--Robby Len Fashions, New York, NY, pg. 78
Welch, Bill, V.P.-Sls. Services--Arkansas Electric Cooperatives Inc., Little Rock, AR, pg. 83
Welch, Charles, Mgr.-Sls.--Bates Container, Inc., North Richland Hills, TX, pg. 125
Welch, Norman H., Jr., Exec. V.P.-Audio Sls.--Eva-Tone Inc., Clearwater, FL, pg. 390
Welch, P.P., V.P.-Sls.--Furnas Electric Company, Batavia, IL, pg. 437
Weldy, Joel, Mgr.-Sls.--Triplett Electrical Instrument Corporation, Bluffton, OH, pg. 1114
Weldy, Owen, V.P.-Sls.--Dieline Corporation, Kentwood, MI, pg. 336
Welfelt, Dave, Dir.-Sls. & Mktg.--Excel Industries, Inc., Hesston, KS, pg. 392
Welk, Tom, Dir.-Sls. & Mktg.--Lyke Corporation, Ripon, WI, pg. 688
Wellan, Wayne, V.P.-Indus. Sls.--Carter Day Industries, Inc., Minneapolis, MN, pg. 226
Wellman, Mike, V.P.-Sls. & Mktg.--Wolfer Printing Company, City of Commerce, CA, pg. 1199
Wells, G.L., Dir.-Sls. & Mktg.--Claud S. Gordon Company, Richmond, IL, pg. 1167
Wells, John, Dir.-Sls. & Mktg.--The Bakersfield Californian, Bakersfield, CA, pg. 115
Wells, Jonathan, Mgr.-Sls.--Stone & Hoover Contracting, Inc., Lorton, VA, pg. 470
Wells, Richard, V.P.-Sls.--Hardaway Concrete Co., Inc., Columbia, SC, pg. 507
Welsh, Francis John, Mgr.-Sls.--Apache Plastics, L.P., Stockton, CA, pg. 77
Wendorf, Thomas, Natl. Sls. Mgr.--Restonic Corporation, Chicago, IL, pg. 929
Wennemer, Mike, Mgr.-Sls.--Bestpak, Inc., Grove City, PA, pg. 583
Werbrouck, Eric, Sls. Dir.--Berlitz Schools of Languages of Benelux S.A., Brussels,, Belgium, pg. 143
Werner, Douglas, Dir.-Sls.--Kold Kist Brands, Inc., Los Angeles, CA, pg. 641
Werner, Lori, Sls. Communication Specialist--MSI Insurance Companies, Arden Hills, MN, pg. 693
Wesley, Charles, V.P.-Sls. & Mktg.--Hyer Industries Inc./ Thayer Scale, Pembroke, MA, pg. 557
West, J.R., V.P.-Sls.--S & C Electric Company, Chicago, IL, pg. 958
West, John R., Sls. Mgr.-Aftermarket--Cole Hersee Company, Boston, MA, pg. 260
West, Lawrence, V.P.-Sls., Processed Fruit--Snokist Growers, Yakima, WA, pg. 1015
West, W. Casey, V.P.-Sls. & Mktg.--Stanchem Inc., East Berlin, CT, pg. 1035
Wetherton, Norman C., V.P.-Special Sls.--Rose Packing Company, South Barrington, IL, pg. 947
Wetterauer, Michael, Sr. V.P.-Sls. & Mktg.--Case-Swayne Co. Inc., Santa Ana, CA, pg. 228
Wheaton, Paul, V.P.-Propane Sls.--Carlos R. Leffler Inc., Richland, PA, pg. 666
Wheeler, Ron, V.P. & Dir.-Retail Sls.--Bush Brothers & Company, Dandridge, TN, pg. 196
Whistler, Richard, Mgr.-Sls.--Genesee Metal Stampings, Inc., West Henrietta, NY, pg. 451
White, Austin, Sls. Advisor--B & G Wholesalers, Inc., Nashville, TN, pg. 106
White, B., V.P.-Sls.--Ventura Travelware, Inc., Long Island City, NY, pg. 1147
White, Betty, Mgr.-Sls.--Schutte Lumber Company, Kansas City, MO, pg. 980
White, Gordon, V.P.-Sls.--Cogsdill Tool Products, Inc., Lugoff, SC, pg. 259
White, Matthew, V.P.-Sls.--Thybony Wall Coverings Co., Chicago, IL, pg. 1096
White, Stanley, V.P.-Sls./Eastern Reg.--Wm. E. Wright Limited Partnership, West Warren, MA, pg. 1205
Whitehouse, Bevi, Dir.-Sls.--Paisano Publications, Inc., Agoura, CA, pg. 843
Whitlinger, Jack, V.P.-Sls.--The Cleveland Builders Supply Co., Cleveland, OH, pg. 1036
Whitman, Al, Dir.-Trade Sls.--Millmaster Onyx Group, Inc., Westport, CT, pg. 755

Whitman, Al, Dir.-Trade Sls.--Mantrose Haeuser Co., Westport, CT, pg. 756
Whitman, R., V.P.-Sls.--MacAndrews & Forbes Co., Camden, NJ, pg. 694
Whitney, Jim, V.P.-Sls. & Mktg.--Educational Insights, Inc., Dominguez Hills, CA, pg. 369
Whitt, John R., V.P.-Sls. & Sec.--Sherman & Reilly, Inc., Chattanooga, TN, pg. 998
Whittingham, Thomas G., V.P.-Sls.--McLouth Steel, Trenton, MI, pg. 731
Whittington, Jeff, Mgr.-Sls.--Flex-O-Glass, Inc., Chicago, IL, pg. 418
Wholihan, Steve E., V.P.-Sls. & Mktg.--Jones Dairy Farm, Fort Atkinson, WI, pg. 603
Wicks, Sidney, V.P.-Sls. Publ.--Collman Graphics, Inc., Baltimore, MD, pg. 263
Wicks, Sidney, V.P.-Publ. Sls.--John D. Lucas Printing Company, Baltimore, MD, pg. 263
Wiebusch, Jerry, Mgr.-Natl. Sls.--Lyon Metal Products, Inc., Montgomery, IL, pg. 690
Wiegand, John, Dir.-Sls.--PAC Manufacturing & Distributing Co., Winchester, VA, pg. 885
Wienholz, Ken, V.P.-Sls & Mktg.--Bell-Carter Foods, Inc., Lafayette, CA, pg. 134
Wiesemes, Kurt, V.P.-Mktg. & Sls.--Quality Packaging Products, Inc., Benton Harbor, MI, pg. 903
Wiggans, John, Dir.-Sls.--PTC Aerospace, Garden Grove, CA, pg. 837
Wiggins, Ernie, Reg. Sls. Mgr.--Snyder Bakery, Yakima, WA, pg. 1134
Wiig, Jon J., Mgr.-Sls.--Kalas Manufacturing, Inc., Denver, PA, pg. 615
Wilber, John S., Natl. Sls. Mgr.--Harry H. Bell & Sons, Inc., Saint Petersburg, FL, pg. 134
Wilbur, Jim, Mgr.-F & I Sls.--Fairway Ford, Inc., Greenville, SC, pg. 397
Wilderotter, Maggie, V.P.-Sls.--U.S. Computer Services, Rancho Cordova, CA, pg. 1135
Wiles, Ron, V.P.-Sls. & Mktg.--Therma-Tru Corp., Maumee, OH, pg. 1090
Wiley, Marvin, Mgr.-Sls., Field--Jeffersonville Distribution Center, Jeffersonville, IN, pg. 832
Wilhelm, Dick, Gen. Sls. Mgr.-West--Milwaukee Electric Tool Corp., Brookfield, WI, pg. 361
Wilhelm, Steven, Dir.-Mktg. & Resources--Woodcraft Industries, Inc., Saint Cloud, MN, pg. 1200
Wilkes, Anthony, Dir. Sls.--Berlitz de Mexico, S.A. de C.V., Mexico,, Mexico, pg. 142
Willer, Paul A., V.P.-Sls.--Wm. E. Wright Limited Partnership, West Warren, MA, pg. 1205
Williams, Al, Sls. Mgr.-Promo.--Frederick Trading Company, Frederick, MD, pg. 430
Williams, Carol C., Sls. Dir.--Abingdon Press, Nashville, TN, pg. 10
Williams, Cliff, V.P.-Mktg. & Sls.--DAQ Electronics Inc., Middlesex, NJ, pg. 308
Williams, Craig, Sls. Mgr.--Tool & Engineering Co., Chicago, IL, pg. 400
Williams, D.J., Jr., V.P.-Mktg. & Sls.--The Producto Machine Co., Bridgeport, CT, pg. 893
Williams, David, V.P.-Sls.--The Gradall Co., New Philadelphia, OH, pg. 559
Williams, Don, Dir.-Sls.--Hankins Lumber Company, Inc., Grenada, MS, pg. 505
Williams, Frank, V.P.-Sls.--Action Instruments, Inc., San Diego, CA, pg. 14
Williams, James, V.P.-Sls.--Univex Corporation, Salem, NH, pg. 1139
Williams, Joe, Dir.-Sls. & Mktg.--The Uhlmann Co., Kansas City, MO, pg. 1125
Williams, Larry, Dir.-Sls.--Moorman Mfg. Company, Quincy, IL, pg. 769
Williams, Phil, Mgr.-Intl. Sls.--George Koch Sons, Inc., Evansville, IN, pg. 639
Williams, Phillip C., Dir.-Regional Sls. & Mktg.--Wayne Corporation, Richmond, IN, pg. 1169
Williams, Stan, Mgr.-Sls.--Ain Plastics, Inc., Mount Vernon, NY, pg. 26
Williams, Thomas A., V.P.-Sls.--Bard Mfg. Co., Bryan, OH, pg. 119
Williamson, David, V.P.-Mktg. & Sls.-Office Prods. Div.--Keith Clark, Sidney, NY, pg. 304
Williamson, Jack L., V.P.-Sls.--Kearney, Tucker, GA, pg. 357
Williamson, James, Dir.-Sls.--Ventre Packing Company, Inc., Syracuse, NY, pg. 1147
Willig, Jack, V.P.-Sls.--Amsco School Publications, Inc., New York, NY, pg. 68
Willinger, Gregory, Sls. Rep.--American Journal Of Nursing Company, New York, NY, pg. 57
Wilsdorf, Hilda, V.P.-Customer Service--State Industries Inc., Ashland City, TN, pg. 1041
Wilson, Allan, V.P.-Sls. & Cust. Service--Western Data Systems, Calabasas, CA, pg. 1178
Wilson, Anthony, V.P.-Sls. & Mktg.--Tippins Incorporated, Pittsburgh, PA, pg. 1099
Wilson, Don, Mng. Dir.--Totes Canada Ltd., Etobicoke,, Canada, pg. 1103
Wilson, Gary, Mgr.-Gen. Sls.--Eagle Lincoln Mercury Inc., Dallas, TX, pg. 362
Wilson, Gary E., V.P.-Major Acct. Sls.--RAYOVAC Corporation, Madison, WI, pg. 915
Wilson, Gerry, Dir.-Adv. Sls.--Union-Tribune Publishing Company, San Diego, CA, pg. 284
Wilson, James D., V.P.-Sls.--Lappin Electric Company, Milwaukee, WI, pg. 658
Wilson, James L., Dir.-Mktg. & Sales--First DataBank, San Bruno, CA, pg. 522
Wilson, Jerry, Dir.-Grocery Sls.--J.L. Lester & Son, Inc., Rockmart, GA, pg. 668
Wilson, Jerry, Mgr.-Sls.--J.L. Lester & Son, Inc., Rockmart, GA, pg. 668
Wilson, John, Sls. Mgr.-Indus. Div.--Seymour of Sycamore, Inc., Sycamore, IL, pg. 994
Wilson, Larry, Mgr.-Sls.--National Machinery Company, Tiffin, OH, pg. 792
Wilson, Martin, V.P.-Sls.-West. Reg.--Columbia Paint Co., Spokane, WA, pg. 265
Wilson, Mike, Sls. Mgr.--Splitfire, Inc., Northbrook, IL, pg. 824
Wilson, Paul, V.P.-Sls.--Continental Eagle Corporation, Prattville, AL, pg. 278
Wilson, T.J., V.P.-Grocery Prod. Sls.--California & Hawaiian Sugar Company, Concord, CA, pg. 210
Wilson, Thomas, V.P.-Sls.--Tollman/Hundley Hotels, Valhalla, NY, pg. 1100
Wiltshire, Dennis, V.P.-Sls.--Klosterman's Baking Company, Cincinnati, OH, pg. 636
Wimbish, Schaffer B., Jr., V.P.-Sls.--Colonial Oil Industries, Savannah, GA, pg. 263
Winer, Robert, Exec. V.P.-Sls.--Soundesign Corporation, Jersey City, NJ, pg. 1018
Wing, Dudley F., V.P.-Adv. Sls.--U.S. News & World Report, New York, NY, pg. 1136
Wing, Elizabeth, Intl. Sls. Admin.--Brimms Inc., Tonawanda, NY, pg. 176
Winkler, Bob, V.P.-Sls.--Jackes-Evans Mfg. Co., Saint Louis, MO, pg. 587
Wionski, Gerd, Client Services Dir.--BSB Frankfurt Werbeagentur GmbH, Frankfurt/Main,, Germany, pg. 109
Wipf, Allen R., Midwest Reg Sls. Mgr.--General Refractories Co., U. S. Refractories Div., Pittsburgh, PA, pg. 136
Wirtanen, Phil, V.P. & Dir.-Sls.--Employers Insurance of Wausau a Mutual Co., Wausau, WI, pg. 380
Wirtanen, Phil, V.P. & Dir.-Sls.--Employers Insurance of Wausau a Mutual Co., Wausau, WI, pg. 795
Wise, Ronald, Exec. V.P.-Sls. & Mktg.--Continental Mills, Inc., Tukwila, WA, pg. 279
Wisnewski, Patti, Intl. Sls. Coordinator--Triumph*Lor, Inc., Houston, TX, pg. 1115
Witek, S.A., V.P.-Sls.--A. Finkl & Sons Co., Chicago, IL, pg. 411
Witt, Edward E., Sr. V.P.-Pur. & Sls.--Miller Electric Company, Jacksonville, FL, pg. 754
Witt, Gerald, V.P.-Sls., Central Region--Donlen Corp., Deerfield, IL, pg. 345
Wittenberg, Robert, Sr. V.P.-Sls., Mktg. & Pur.--Video Products Distributors, Inc., Sacramento, CA, pg. 1150
Witting, Paul H., Sr. V.P. & Gen. Sls. Mgr.--Steelcase Inc., Grand Rapids, MI, pg. 1044
Wittry, Jim, Sr. V.P.-Sls.--Ingram Micro Inc., Santa Ana, CA, pg. 569
Woessner, Tom, V.P.-Mktg. & sls.--Excelsior Manufacturing & Supply Corp., Itasca, IL, pg. 392
Wohl, Melissa, V.P.-Intl. Sls. & Co-Prod.--WTTW (Channel 11), Chicago, IL, pg. 1156
Wohlfeil, J.H., V.P.-Sls.--Millers' Mutual Insurance Assn. Of Illinois, Alton, IL, pg. 755
Wolf, E. Brian, V.P.-Natl. Sls.--Burke Engineering Company, South El Monte, CA, pg. 190
Wolf, Hans, Mgr.-Sls.--Howard Industries, Inc., Milford, IL, pg. 547
Wolf, Michael, V.P. & Dir.-Sls. & Mdsg.--International Seaway Trading Corporation, Mayfield Village, OH, pg. 579
Wolf, William H., Mgr.-Sls.--Consolidated Wholesale Company Division, Oklahoma City, OK, pg. 440
Wolfe, D.J., Dir.-Sls.--Solo Cup Company, Highland Park, IL, pg. 961
Wolfe, Jerry, V.P.-Sls.--Central Pharmaceuticals, Inc., Seymour, IN, pg. 234
Wolff, John, V.P.-Sls. & Mktg.--Crane Plastics Company, Columbus, OH, pg. 296
Wolk, Doug, Mgr.-Natl. Sls.--Sentry Group, Rochester, NY, pg. 990
Wollberg, Royal, Natl. Sls. Mgr.--Liquid Controls Corporation, Lake Bluff, IL, pg. 677
Wombacher, Gerald T., Sr. V.P.-Sls.--Fleming Packaging Corp., Peoria, IL, pg. 417
Wontka, Rick, Exec. V.P.-Human Resources--Stanley Fastening Systems, Worcester, MA, pg. 1038
Wood, Kenneth, Mgr.-Sls.--Tri-City Oldsmobile Inc., Louisville, KY, pg. 1110
Wood, Sharon, Yellow Pages Supvr.--Keller-Crescent Co., Evansville, IN, pg. 621
Wood, Thomas L., Natl. Sls. Mgr.--Challenge Technologies, Grand Haven, MI, pg. 238
Woodard, Ken, Dir.-Sls.--Southern Outdoors Magazine, Montgomery, AL, pg. 105
Woodard, Ken, Dir.-Sls.--Bassmaster Magazine, Montgomery, AL, pg. 105
Woodard, Ken, Dir.-Sls.--Southern Saltwater Magazine, Montgomery, AL, pg. 106
Woodman, John, V.P.-Mktg. & Sls.--Florig Equipment Company, Inc., Conshohocken, PA, pg. 421
Woodrick, Rob, Exec. V.P.-Sls. & Mktg.--D & W Food Centers, Inc., Grand Rapids, MI, pg. 308
Woodruff, Don, Jr., Mgr.-Sls.-Dealers--Taylor Machine Works, Inc., Louisville, MS, pg. 1081
Woods, Don, Dir.-Sls.--Delaware Punch Co., New Orleans, LA, pg. 121
Woods, Douglas K., V.P.-Sls.--Liberty Tool Corporation, Rochester, NY, pg. 674
Woods, Mary, Mgr.-Sls.--Sun Process Converting Company, Elk Grove Village, IL, pg. 1059
Woods, Mike, Mgr.-Natl. Sls.--National R.V., Inc., Perris, CA, pg. 792
Woodside, Alan, V.P.-Retail Sls.--Faribault Woolen Mill Co., Faribault, MN, pg. 399
Woolf, David, Exec. V.P.-Sls.--Ardell International, Inc., City of Commerce, CA, pg. 81
Wooten, Sidney C., Jr., V.P.-Mktg. & Sls.--Lane Limited, Tucker, GA, pg. 657
Worcester, Bob, Mgr.-Sls.--Dickinson Press, Inc., Grand Rapids, MI, pg. 336
Worrell, John K., V.P.-Sls.--Igloo Corporation, Houston, TX, pg. 562
Wrabel, George, V.P.-Sls. & Mktg.--N.B. Jackets Division, Marietta, GA, pg. 135
Wright, Archer, Sr. V.P., Sls.--E-B Advertising Display Inc., Massillon, OH, pg. 358
Wright, John W., Grp. V.P.-Employee Benefits Sls. & Mktg.--The New England, Boston, MA, pg. 799
Wright, L. C., V.P.-Sls. & Mktg.--Union City Body Company, Inc., Union City, IN, pg. 1128
Wright, William, Dir.-Distr.--Nationwide Financial Services, Inc., Columbus, OH, pg. 795
Wright, Yates, V.P.-Sls. & Mktg.--Kirby Building Systems, Inc., Nashville, TN, pg. 632
Wroblewski, Norbert J., Mgr.-Sls.--Plastek Group, Erie, PA, pg. 874
Wrona, Remi L., Pres.-Intl. Sls.--Sunnen Products Company, Saint Louis, MO, pg. 1061
Wurster, Hans C., Exec. V.P.-Mktg. & Sls.--Kaukauna Cheese, Little Chute, WI, pg. 619
Wurzburg, Warren S., Jr., V.P.-Labels Sls.--Wurzburg, Inc., Memphis, TN, pg. 1205
Wyckoff, Paul, Exec. V.P.-Sls. & Mktg.--Maharam Fabric Corporation, Hauppauge, NY, pg. 701
Wyman, Robert, Jr., Mgr.-Adv., Mktg., Sls. & Sls. Promo.--Mallory, Inc., Carson City, NV, pg. 703
Yakshe, Stephen, Mgr.-Sls.--Pressure Systems, Hampton, VA, pg. 888
Yargis, Dick, V.P.-Sls.--Tell City Chair Co., Tell City, IN, pg. 1085
Yarnall, Jane, Natl. Sls. Dir.--Luxor Corporation, Waukegan, IL, pg. 365
Yeager, Truman, V.P.-Sls., Fresh Fruit--Snokist Growers, Yakima, WA, pg. 1015
Yellig, C.B., V.P.-Mktg. & Sls.--Reliable Castings Corporation, Cincinnati, OH, pg. 924
Yetter, Thomas, Mgr.-Sls.--Tapemark, West St. Paul, MN, pg. 1078
Yezbak, Jim, V.P.-Sls., Consumer Prods.--The Genie Company, Akron, OH, pg. 452
Yin, Sook, Dir.-Sls. & Gen. Sls. Mgr.--Technic Incorporated, Cranston, RI, pg. 1083
Yoder, John, Dir.-Mktg. & European Sls.--Sauder Woodworking Co., Archbold, OH, pg. 972
Yorio, Frank, Sr. V.P.-Mktg. & Sls.--La Victoria Foods, Inc., City of Industry, CA, pg. 649
York, Brett, Mgr.-Reg. Sls. Central--Ivex Packaging Corporation-Grant Park, Grant Park, IL, pg. 583
Yost, Marvin, V.P.-Sls.-West--The Berkline Corporation, Morristown, TN, pg. 285
Young, Al, Dir.-Sls.--Oakland Tool & Manufacturing Company, Fraser, MI, pg. 819
Young, Dave, Mgr.-Sls.-Small Accts.--The Robert E. Morris Company, Farmington, CT, pg. 771
Young, Donald E., V.P.-Mktg. & Sls.--E. H. Titchener & Company, Binghamton, NY, pg. 1099
Young, Jim, Sls. Mgr.--Franklin Steel Company, Franklin, PA, pg. 429
Young, John, V.P.-Sls. & Mktg.--Diamond Brands, Inc., Cloquet, MN, pg. 335
Yrigoyan, Daniel, Sr. V.P.-Sls. & Mktg.--Delta Resins & Refractories, Inc., Milwaukee, WI, pg. 327
Yudis, Charles S., Exec. V.P.-Sls. & Mktg.--Capp, Inc., Philadelphia, PA, pg. 216
Yurjevich, Glen S., V.P.-Sls. & Mktg.--Shade Computer Forms Co., Green Bay, WI, pg. 994
Zachar, Karel, V.P.-Intl. Sls.--National Oats Co., Cedar Rapids, IA, pg. 25
Zachary, John, V.P.-Sls. & Retail Opers.--Affiliated Food Stores, Keller, TX, pg. 23
Zador, William, V.P.-Sls. & Mktg.--Sunbeam Home Comfort, Shubuta, MS, pg. 1059
Zager, Tom V., Mgr.-Sls. & Mktg.--Metron Steel Corp., Chicago, IL, pg. 744
Zakrzewski, Ed, V.P.-P.O. Sls.--Key Handling Systems, Inc., Hackensack, NJ, pg. 627
Zakrzewski, Mike, Natl. Sls. Mgr.--Ohaus Corporation, Florham Park, NJ, pg. 822
Zangardi, J. Michael, Dir.-Sls. & Mktg.--Simplex Industries, Inc., Scranton, PA, pg. 1006
Zarembo, Mark, V.P.-Intl. Sls. & Mktg.--NESLAB Instruments, Inc., Newington, NH, pg. 798
Zarling, Robert S., Exec. V.P.-Direct Sls.--Regal Ware, Inc., Kewaskum, WI, pg. 921
Zeifman, Les, V.P.-Sls.--Straight Arrow Publishers, Inc., New York, NY, pg. 1052
Zeigler, R.H., Dir.-Sls.--The Gerstenslager Company, Wooster, OH, pg. 454
Zelen, Bob, Sr. V.P.-Sls.--Doe Spun, Inc., New York, NY, pg. 343
Zeller, Norm, East-Central Div. Adv. Sls. Office--The Weather Channel, Inc.-Detroit Sales Office, Roseville, MI, pg. 654
Zeller, Norman, V.P.-Natl. Adv. Sls. Mgr.--The Travel Channel, Atlanta, GA, pg. 654
Zemick, M., Exec. V.P.-Sls. & Mktg.--Industrial Steel & Wire Company, Chicago, IL, pg. 567
Zeno, Paul L., Sr. V.P., Mktg. & Sls.--Global Marketing Resources, New York, NY, pg. 463
Zettel, Pat, Dir.-Sls.--Minnesota Brewing Company, Saint Paul, MN, pg. 757
Zeus, William, Jr., Pres. & Chief Exec. Officer--National Tool & Manufacturing Company, Kenilworth, NJ, pg. 794
Ziebell, Richard, Mgr.-Sls./Indus. Div.--Neenah Foundry Company, Neenah, WI, pg. 797
Zieger, Ari, Mgr.-Sls.--Interbath, Inc., City of Industry, CA, pg. 574
Ziegler, Larry, V.P.-Mfg. & Sls.--Multi-Ad Services, Inc., Peoria, IL, pg. 775
Ziel, C. D., V.P.-Sls.--Roessing Bronze Co., Mars, PA, pg. 943
Zielinski, Gary J., V.P.-Sls. & Mktg.--Heller Seasonings & Ingredients, Inc., Bedford Park, IL, pg. 526
Zierke, David L., Mgr.-Mktg. & Sls.--Cotta Transmission Company, Rockford, IL, pg. 1062

Zierton, Lee, Mgr.-Sls. & Mktg.--Imperial Litho/Graphics, Inc., Phoenix, AZ, pg. 564
Zikmund, Donald, V.P.-Sls.--Stonhard, Inc., Maple Shade, NJ, pg. 1051
Zimmerman, Bob, Mgr.-Seed & Chemical Sls.--B&W Co-op, Inc., Breckenridge, MI, pg. 107
Zimmerman, Faye, Coord.-Sls. & Mktg.--Ferguson Manufacturing & Equipment Company, Dallas, TX, pg. 406
Zimmerman, Howard, Dir.-Sls.--Nady Systems, Inc., Emeryville, CA, pg. 783
Zimmerman, Ken, Dir.-Sls.--Lund Boats, New York Mills, MN, pg. 759
Zimmerman, Ron, V.P.-Sls. & Mktg.--Leach Corporation, Buena Park, CA, pg. 663
Zimmermann, Keith, Jr., Mgr.-Natl. Sls.--Whitney Blake Company of Vermont, Inc., Bellows Falls, VT, pg. 155
Zipper, Gary, Sr. V.P.-Sls.--Gould Paper Corporation, New York, NY, pg. 473
Zirke, S., Dir.-Sls.--Borg-Warner Automotive, Inc., Transmission Systems, Muncie, IN, pg. 166
Zizkuhr, Clyde, V.P.-Sls. & Mktg.--The Crocker-Fels Company, Cincinnati, OH, pg. 299
Zlotnik, A., Pres.--Odomaster Canada, Mississauga,, Canada, pg. 1065
Zoeller, H.A., V.P.-Sls.--Kennedy Manufacturing Company, Van Wert, OH, pg. 623
Zografos, Dino, Sls. Mgr.--Newhouse Newspapers Metro-Suburbia, Inc., New York, NY, pg. 19
Zucker, Gary, Sls. Mgr.-Midwest--ATAPCO Office Products Group, Saint Louis, MO, pg. 64
Zuckerman, Benjamin R., V.P.-Sls.--Zuckerman-Honickman Inc., King of Prussia, PA, pg. 1221
Zuercher, Chris, Mgr.-Sls.--Columbian Rope Company, Guntown, MS, pg. 266
Zuppardo, Dan, V.P.-Sls., Eastern Div.--Meridian Technology Leasing Services, Deerfield, IL, pg. 740
Zurawski, Daryl T., V.P.-Buflovak Sls. & Engrng.--Blaw Knox Food & Chemical Equipment Company, Buffalo, NY, pg. 156
Zurich, Richard, Mgr.-Sls.--KCL Corporation, Shelbyville, IN, pg. 611
Zygulski, Robert, Pres. & Chief Opers. Officer--South Bend Plastics, Inc., Mishawaka, IN, pg. 1019

SENIOR VICE PRESIDENT

Abbott, Robert, Sr. V.P.--Purcell International Group, Inc., Los Angeles, CA, pg. 900
Abbott, Rohn D., Sr. V.P.--Shannon & Wilson, Inc., Seattle, WA, pg. 995
Abdalla, Evelina, Sr. V.P.--Abdalla's Lafayette, Inc., Lafayette, LA, pg. 10
Abdalla, Irma B., Sr. V.P.--Abdalla's Lafayette, Inc., Lafayette, LA, pg. 10
Abdell, George, Sr. V.P.--Admarketing, Inc., Los Angeles, CA, pg. 18
Abrams, Archie, Sr. V.P.--Pan American Trade Development Corp., New York, NY, pg. 845
Adams, Charles, Sr. V.P.-Intl. Div.--Trans World Airlines, Inc., Mount Kisco, NY, pg. 561
Adams, Kenneth, Sr. V.P.--The Milwaukee Journal, Milwaukee, WI, pg. 607
Adcock, Aubrey, Sr. V.P.--Huitt-Zollars, Inc., Dallas, TX, pg. 552
Adelson, Andrew S., Sr. V.P.--Sanford C. Bernstein & Co., Inc., New York, NY, pg. 144
Adelsperger, John W., Sr. V.P.--Union City Body Company, Inc., Union City, IN, pg. 1128
Adornato, Paul D., Sr. V.P.--Massachusetts Mutual Life Insurance Co., Springfield, MA, pg. 718
Aelis, Gary, Sr. V.P. & Chief Fin. Officer--Consolidated Cigar Corporation, Fort Lauderdale, FL, pg. 276
Affleck, John A., Sr. V.P.--Stratton Management Company, Plymouth Meeting, PA, pg. 1053
Aggarwal, Uma N., Sr. V.P.--AXIA Incorporated, Oak Brook, IL, pg. 8
Aiello, Robert J., Sr. V.P., Assoc. Dir.--Ketchum Public Relations/Pittsburgh, Pittsburgh, PA, pg. 625
Akin, Paul N., Sr. V.P.--Inman Construction Corporation, Memphis, TN, pg. 570
Akins, James H., Jr., V.P.-Pension Contracts & Compliance--American United Life Insurance Company, Indianapolis, IN, pg. 65
Alberg, Edward G., Sr. V.P.--Falley's Inc., Topeka, KS, pg. 1214
Aldrich, Lance L., Sr. V.P., Assoc. Creative Dir.--Ross Roy Inc., Bloomfield Hills, MI, pg. 950
Alexander, Bernadette, Exec. V.P., Res. Dir.--Elkman Advertising & Public Relations, Bala-Cynwyd, PA, pg. 377
Alexander, Michael P., Sr. V.P., Prod. Devel.--ASC Incorporated, Southgate, MI, pg. 7
Allen, Don, Sr. V.P. & Trust Officer--First National Bank of Sweetwater, Sweetwater, TX, pg. 412
Allen, Donald F., Jr., Sr. V.P.--I Ski Ski Goggles, City of Commerce, CA, pg. 557
Allison, William E., Sr. V.P.-Structural--The Benham Group, Oklahoma City, OK, pg. 138
Allran, Robert R., Sr. V.P.-Opers.--Detroit Diesel Corp., Detroit, MI, pg. 859
Aloian, D. Pike, Sr. V.P.--Rothschild Inc., New York, NY, pg. 951
Alpern, Marvin D., Sr. V.P. & Chief Info. Officer--American Hardware Mutual Insurance Co., Minnetonka, MN, pg. 55
Alves, G.W., Sr. V.P.--Fish Engineering & Construction, Inc., Houston, TX, pg. 414
Alyward, Scott, Sr. V.P., Grp. Supvr.--Fogarty & Klein/Winius Brandon, Houston, TX, pg. 421
Amelia, Margot A., Sr. V.P., Acct. Admin.--Gray Kirk/VanSant Advertising, Inc., Baltimore, MD, pg. 479
Amershadian, Paul, Sr. V.P.--R.G. Meadows, Inc., Great Neck, NY, pg. 733
Anderson, Gerald L., Sr. V.P., Dir. Signal Grp.--Creswell, Munsell, Fultz & Zirbel, Cedar Rapids, IA, pg. 1211
Anderson, John, Sr. V.P.--Judd's Incorporated, Washington, DC, pg. 608
Anderson, Richard T., Sr. V.P.--Rothschild Inc., New York, NY, pg. 951
Anderson, Richard T., Sr. V.P.--Rothschild Asset Management Inc., New York, NY, pg. 951
Anderson, Walter, Sr. V.P. & Editor--Parade Publications Inc., New York, NY, pg. 847
Andre, Stan, Sr. V.P.-Mktg.--Nulaid Foods, Ripon, CA, pg. 817
Angell, J. Steven, Sr. V.P.--STS Holdings, Inc., Northbrook, IL, pg. 964
Apple, John, V.P.-Floor Covering--William M. Bird & Co., Inc., Charleston, SC, pg. 152
Arceci, R.E., Sr. V.P.--Southern Pump & Tank Co. Inc., Charlotte, NC, pg. 1022
Arnholt, John, Sr. V.P., Chief Fin. Officer--McFarland & Drier, Inc., Miami, FL, pg. 729
Arnold, W. Jerry, Sr. V.P.-Estimating--SAE-Pinkerton & Laws Inc., Atlanta, GA, pg. 966
Aronson, Steven J., Sr. V.P.--ODI, Burlington, MA, pg. 818
Asche, Phil, Exec. V.P., Dir.-Y&R Adv., Area Dir.-Australia/New Zealand--Young & Rubicam Inc., New York, NY, pg. 1210
Ashkenazy, Arnold, Sr. V.P.--L'Ermitage Hotels, West Hollywood, CA, pg. 668
Ashurst, Mike, Sr. V.P.-Comml. Div. Head--Tucson Realty & Trust Co., Tucson, AZ, pg. 1118
Asplundh, Paul, Sr. V.P.--Asplundh Tree Expert Co., Willow Grove, PA, pg. 88
Auerbach, Chuck, Sr. V.P.--Lipman, Richmond, Greene, New York, NY, pg. 677
Auguston, Sally, Sr. V.P., Acct. Services Dir.--Gerber Advertising, Portland, OR, pg. 453
Azzam, Atef A., Sr. V.P.--Shannon & Wilson, Inc., Seattle, WA, pg. 995
Babian, Walter, Sr. V.P.--Eli's Chicago's Finest, Inc., Chicago, IL, pg. 376
Bacon, Richard A., Sr. V.P. & Gen. Counsel--John Wieland Homes Inc., Atlanta, GA, pg. 1188
Bader, Mark, Sr. V.P.--Shapell Industries, Inc., Beverly Hills, CA, pg. 995
Badyna, Barbara, Sr. V.P., Dir. Casting--Young & Rubicam New York, New York, NY, pg. 1211
Bahnsen, Peter F., Sr. V.P.-Bus. & Tech. Devel.--Betac International Corporation, Alexandria, VA, pg. 147
Baiden, Arthur H., III, Sr. V.P.--Potter-Shackelford Construction Co., Greenville, SC, pg. 882
Baier, Richard, Sr. V.P.--Leo Eisenberg & Co., Inc., Kansas City, MO, pg. 372
Bailey, Robert L., Sr. V.P.--NTH Consultants, Ltd., Farmington Hills, MI, pg. 781
Baker, Robert J., Sr. V.P. & Chief Oper. Officer--DKM Building Enterprises, L.P., Lawrenceville, NJ, pg. 357
Balara, James, Sr. V.P.--Hibbert Group, Trenton, NJ, pg. 532
Balazs, Csaba S., Sr. V.P.-Architecture--L. Robert Kimball & Associates, Ebensburg, PA, pg. 629
Baldassarri, Albert, Sr. V.P.--Pan American Trade Development Corp., New York, NY, pg. 845
Ball, Keith, V.P. & Dir.-Editorial--Paisano Publications, Inc., Agoura, CA, pg. 843
Ball, Leonard F., Sr. V.P., Gen. Counsel & Asst. Sec.--HTB, Inc., Oklahoma City, OK, pg. 497
Ballantyne, John R., Sr. V.P.--Liggett-Stashower, Inc., Cleveland, OH, pg. 675
Barber, Fred, Sr. V.P.-TV--Capitol Broadcasting Co., Inc., Raleigh, NC, pg. 215
Barbre, John H., Sr. V.P.-Individual Div.--American United Life Insurance Company, Indianapolis, IN, pg. 65
Barkan, Lee, Sr. V.P., Sec. & Gen. Counsel--American Vision Centers, Inc., New York, NY, pg. 65
Barnes, Gary L., Sr. V.P.--Topa Thrift & Loan Association, Los Angeles, CA, pg. 1101
Barnett, Marcella, Sr. V.P.--Kanawha Steel & Equipment Co., Charleston, WV, pg. 615
Barr, Nancy P., Sr. V.P. & Dir.-Client Services--Lord, Sullivan & Yoder, Inc. Advertising, Columbus, OH, pg. 683
Barr, Pamela S., Sr. V.P.--Watt, Roop & Co., Cleveland, OH, pg. 1168
Barron, Jeffrey, Sr. V.P.--Levy Real Estate Partners, Chicago, IL, pg. 672
Barton, Sharon, Sr. V.P.--R.T.M. Winners, Atlanta, GA, pg. 908
Bastin, Norman, Sr. V.P. & Gen. Mgr.--Compton's New Media Inc., Chicago, IL, pg. 381
Bates, Robert M., Sr. V.P.--Southwest Marine, Inc., San Diego, CA, pg. 1023
Battaglia, Anthony D., Sr. V.P.--Chiquita Brands, Inc., Cincinnati, OH, pg. 53
Bauer, Elaine, Sr. V.P. & Gen. Mdsg. Mgr.-RTW--John Wanamaker, Philadelphia, Philadelphia, PA, pg. 1201
Baxter, Waldo, Sr. V.P.--Hereford State Bank, Hereford, TX, pg. 412
Beard, David R., Sr. V.P.--RTKL Associates Inc., Baltimore, MD, pg. 908
Beaulieu, John, Sr. V.P.-Human Resources--Beech Holdings Corp., Chicago, IL, pg. 131
Becce, Nick, Sr. V.P., Mngmt. Supvr.--Cato Johnson-New York, New York, NY, pg. 1210
Becker, Mitchel, Sr. V.P. & Gen. Counsel--Morse Diesel International, New York, NY, pg. 771
Bedosky, J.J., Sr. V.P.--The F.A. Bartlett Tree Expert Co., Stamford, CT, pg. 123
Beeson, Fred E., Sr. V.P.--Ketchum, Inc., Pittsburgh, PA, pg. 626
Beggs, Robert W., Sr. V.P. & Sec.--Society for Savings Bancorp, Inc., Hartford, CT, pg. 1016
Beldon, Sanford, Sr. V.P.--Rodale Press, Inc., Emmaus, PA, pg. 942
Bell, Kenneth D., Sr. V.P.-Retail Banking Div.--First Federal Savings and Loan Assn. of Rochester, Rochester, NY, pg. 413
Bell, Rosemary, Sr. V.P.--Pro Media, Inc., Needham, MA, pg. 892
Bellafronto, Bob, Sr. V.P.-Folding Carton Opers.--Waldorf Corporation, Saint Paul, MN, pg. 1159
Beltrametti, Marie, Sr. V.P., Mngmt. Supvr.--TBWA Advertising, Inc., New York, NY, pg. 1071
Ben-Eli, Marcia, Sr. V.P.--Lipman, Richmond, Greene, New York, NY, pg. 677
Bendzin, Leonard J., Exec. V.P. & Chief Oper. Officer--Globe Mortgage Company, Hackensack, NJ, pg. 464
Benjamin, G.R., Sr. V.P.--Champion, Inc., Iron Mountain, MI, pg. 238
Benskin, O.B., Sr. V.P.--Robert Elen & Associates, Los Angeles, CA, pg. 376
Benton, Lura, Sr. V.P.--The William Cook Agency, Inc., Jacksonville, FL, pg. 282
Berberich, William J., Sr. V.P.--Allied Systems, Ltd., Decatur, GA, pg. 40
Berger, Arnie, Sr. V.P., Grp. Dir.--Griffin Bacal Inc., New York, NY, pg. 486
Bergler, Gerald, Exec. V.P.--American Speedy Printing Centers, Inc., Bloomfield Hills, MI, pg. 61
Berkowitz, Paul, Sr. V.P.--Mohawk Distilled Products, North Miami, FL, pg. 763
Bermay, Raymond, Sr. V.P.--Estee Lauder, Intl., New York, NY, pg. 389
Bertsch, Douglas, Sr. V.P. & Mdsg.--Associated Merchandising Corp., New York, NY, pg. 91
Berumen, Michael, Sr. V.P.--PM Group Life Insurance Company, Fountain Valley, CA, pg. 841
Beskow, Craig, Sr. V.P. & Cashier--First National Bank in Cleburne, Cleburne, TX, pg. 412
Besse, Robert, Sr. V.P.--Sanborn Manufacturing Company, Springfield, MN, pg. 969
Betts, Jack, Sr. V.P.--Vinod Gupta Company, Inc., Omaha, NE, pg. 494
Biebelberg, David, Sr. V.P., Grp. Dir.--Griffin Bacal Inc., New York, NY, pg. 486
Billings, Bob, Sr. V.P.-Pharmacy--Super D Drug Stores, Memphis, TN, pg. 1062
Birchfield, Cynthia, Sr. V.P., Acct. Exec.--Jones, Anastasi & Birchfield, Dublin, OH, pg. 602
Birnbaum, Norma, Sr. V.P., Research Dir.--Sudler & Hennessey Consumer Group, New York, NY, pg. 1211
Birnberg, Gustave, Sr. V.P.--Gitano Group Inc., New York, NY, pg. 460
Bishop, Larry, Sr. V.P.--Conklin Instrument Corporation, Pleasant Valley, NY, pg. 274
Bisset, Davies W., Sr. V.P.-Underwriting--Amica Mutual Insurance Co., Providence, RI, pg. 66
Bitman, Aaron, Sr. V.P.--Penn Emblem Co., Philadelphia, PA, pg. 857
Blackman, Joyce, Sr. V.P.-Admin. Support--Memphis Light, Gas & Water, Memphis, TN, pg. 738
Blackmon, Charles, Sr. V.P.--North Carolina Mutual Life Insurance Co., Durham, NC, pg. 813
Blake, John, Sr. V.P.-Properties & Facilities--The Hertz Corporation, Park Ridge, NJ, pg. 849
Blanton, Raymond, Sr. V.P.--The Elder-Beerman Stores Corp., Dayton, OH, pg. 373
Blease, Doug, Sr. V.P.-Opers.--D & W Food Centers, Inc., Grand Rapids, MI, pg. 308
Blish, Jeff, Sr. V.P., Dir.-Plng.--Chiat/Day/Mojo Inc. Advertising, Venice, CA, pg. 244
Blucher, Vicki, Sr. V.P., Dir., Brdcst. Production--McCaffrey and McCall, New York, NY, pg. 726
Boch, William J., Sr. V.P., Assoc. Creative Dir.--Arnold Fortuna Lawner & Cabot, Boston, MA, pg. 84
Bodine, Edward F., Chm. Bd. & Treas.--The Bodine Corp., Bridgeport, CT, pg. 161
Boebinger, Charles, Sr. V.P.--Realty One, Cleveland, OH, pg. 917
Boeck, Phil, Sr. V.P.--Block Distributing Company, San Antonio, TX, pg. 157
Boggs, Dave, Sr. V.P.--Lyon Conklin & Company, Baltimore, MD, pg. 690
Bolin, James H., Sr. V.P.--Rural Metro Corporation, Scottsdale, AZ, pg. 956
Bond, Larry R., Sr. V.P.--Washington Mutual Savings Bank, Seattle, WA, pg. 1166
Bonds, Jack W., Sr. V.P.--Variety Wholesalers, Inc., Raleigh, NC, pg. 1146
Bonicatto, L.P., Sr. V.P.--Champion, Inc., Iron Mountain, MI, pg. 238
Bonnville, John W., Sr. V.P.--Wilbur Smith Associates, Columbia, SC, pg. 1011
Boone, R.E., Sr. V.P.--Versa Services Ltd., Etobicoke,, Canada, pg. 7
Booth, Louise, Sr. V.P.--Booth American, Detroit, MI, pg. 165
Borovay, Jeff, Sr. V.P.--Sterling Jewelry & Distributing Co., Dallas, TX, pg. 1047
Borshadel, Jules, Sr. V.P.--Supermarkets General Corporation, Woodbridge, NJ, pg. 1064
Bortman, W.J., Sr. V.P.--Commercial Light Company, Hillside, IL, pg. 268
Bott, D. Ron, Sr. V.P., Acct. Service--Flynn/Sabatino, Miamisburg, OH, pg. 421
Bourgon, George M., Jr., Sr. V.P. & Dir.-Personnel--First Federal of Michigan, Detroit, MI, pg. 414
Bowden, Gary A., Sr. V.P.--RTKL Associates Inc., Baltimore, MD, pg. 908
Bower, Paul, Sr. V.P.--Allen & Ohara, Inc., Memphis, TN, pg. 36
Bowman, Richard, Sr. V.P.-WTTW/Channel Broadcast Center--WTTW (Channel 11), Chicago, IL, pg. 1156
Boykin, James W., Sr. V.P.--Codisco Inc., Sanford, FL, pg. 258
Boyle, Jan, Sr. V.P., Grp. Dir.--Ammirati & Puris Inc., New York, NY, pg. 67

Boyle, Patrick, Sr. V.P.-Pension--New York Life Insurance Company, New York, NY, pg. 802
Bozzi, Harvey J., Jr., Sr. V.P., Mngmt. Supvr.--Hutchins/Young & Rubicam, Rochester, NY, pg. 1211
Brady, Francis P., Sr. V.P. & Pres.-Television Div.--Viacom Broadcasting Inc., New York, NY, pg. 785
Brady, Thomas, Sr. V.P.--Barton-Malow Company, Detroit, MI, pg. 123
Brady, Thomas M., Sr. V.P.--Barton-Malow Enterprises, Inc., Southfield, MI, pg. 123
Brady, Walter M., Sr. V.P.-Agency--New York Life Insurance Company, New York, NY, pg. 802
Bralower, Steven N., Sr. V.P.-Leasing--The Oliver Carr Co., Washington, DC, pg. 225
Brashears, Don, Sr. V.P.--Cramer-Krasselt, Chicago, IL, pg. 296
Braun, Neil S., Sr. V.P. & Chm. & Chief Exec. Officer-Viacom Entertainment--Viacom Inc., New York, NY, pg. 785
Brauner, Richard, Sr. V.P.--Lipman, Richmond, Greene, New York, NY, pg. 677
Brenick, Lonnie, Sr. V.P.--Sundt Corp., Tucson, AZ, pg. 1060
Brenton, Timothy, Sr. V.P., Mngmt. Supvr.--Arnold Fortuna Lawner & Cabot, Boston, MA, pg. 84
Bresky, Otto, Jr., Sr. V.P.--Seaboard Corporation, Newton, MA, pg. 984
Breslin, William J., Sr. V.P.--Prudential-LMI Commercial Insurance Company, Mansfield, OH, pg. 897
Breyer, Allan D., Sr. V.P. & Mgr.-Mngmt. Information Systems--First Federal of Michigan, Detroit, MI, pg. 414
Brierre, William V., Sr. V.P.-Washington--Lykes Bros. Steamship Co., Inc., New Orleans, LA, pg. 688
Brinberg, Simeon, Sr. V.P. & Sec.--Georgetown Partners, Inc., Great Neck, NY, pg. 473
Brine, Kevin R., Sr. V.P.--Sanford C. Bernstein & Co., Inc., New York, NY, pg. 144
Brinkerhoff, John, Sr. V.P. & Dir.-Creative--Lord, Sullivan & Yoder, Inc. Advertising, Columbus, OH, pg. 683
Broderick, Matt, Sr. V.P.--Coldwell Bankers/Schlott Realtors, Wayne, NJ, pg. 260
Broderick, Timothy W., V.P.--The El-Bee Chargit Corp., Dayton, OH, pg. 373
Broeker, Richard, Sr. V.P. & Chief Development Officer--Ellerbe Becket, Inc., Minneapolis, MN, pg. 378
Bronstein, Liane, Sr. V.P.--Mutual of America, New York, NY, pg. 777
Brooks, Raymond C., Sr. V.P.--Johnson & Higgins, New York, NY, pg. 598
Brooks, Ronald C., Sr. V.P.--Summa Corporation, Las Vegas, NV, pg. 1057
Brosh, Amnon, Sr. V.P.--Kulite Semiconductor Products, Inc., Leonia, NJ, pg. 646
Browing, Nicole, Sr. V.P.-Affil. Sls.--MTV Networks, New York, NY, pg. 785
Brown, Crispin R.W., Sr. Partner--Ingersoll Engineers Inc., Rockford, IL, pg. 568
Brown, John, Sr. V.P. & Chief Creative Officer--Eric Mower and Associates/Rochester, Inc., Rochester, NY, pg. 774
Brown, Michael, Sr. V.P.--W&F Manufacturing Corporation, Inc., Buffalo, NY, pg. 1155
Brown, Michael, Sr. V.P.--Capitol Construction Group, Inc., Wheeling, IL, pg. 215
Brown, Rod, Sr. V.P. & Gen. Mgr.--Newsprint South, Inc., Yazoo City, MS, pg. 760
Bruce, Douglas A., Sr. V.P., Dir. Consumer HealthCare Grp.--Klemtner Advertising Inc., New York, NY, pg. 635
Bruckheimer, Allen J., Sr. V.P. & Asst. Treas.--Mutual of America, New York, NY, pg. 777
Bucci, Marshall, Sr. V.P., Grp. Dir.--Sherwood & Schneider Advertising, New York, NY, pg. 999
Buchbinder, L.W., V.P. & Treas.--Panorama Press, Inc., Clifton, NJ, pg. 846
Buchwald, Lee E., Sr. V.P.--Rothschild Inc., New York, NY, pg. 951
Buck, Jay K., Sr. V.P.--Chicago Corp., Chicago, IL, pg. 247
Buckel, Harry J., Sr. V.P.--Harte-Hanks Communications, Inc., San Antonio, TX, pg. 513
Buckland, Michael, Sr. V.P.--LevLane Advertising, Inc., Bala-Cynwyd, PA, pg. 671
Bucklew, Emmett, Sr. V.P.-Furniture Dept.--Schottenstein Stores Corporation, Columbus, OH, pg. 978
Buckley, Robert E., Sr. V.P., Dir. Signal Grp.--Creswell, Munsell, Fultz & Zirbel, Cedar Rapids, IA, pg. 1211
Buda, T.J., Sr. V.P., Sec. & Gen. Counsel--Auto-Owners Insurance, Lansing, MI, pg. 100
Budd, Michael T., Sr. V.P.--Western Petroleum Company, Eden Prairie, MN, pg. 1181
Budkey, Barry, Sr. V.P.--Centimark Corporation, Bethel Park, PA, pg. 231
Buechner, Barry L., Sr. V.P.-Bus. Plng. & Systems--Day & Zimmermann, Inc., Radnor, PA, pg. 320
Bulandr, Peter J., Sr. V.P.--STS Holdings, Inc., Northbrook, IL, pg. 964
Bullett, David B., Sr. V.P.--Teachers Insurance and Annuity Association-College Retirement Equities Fund, New York, NY, pg. 1082
Bullock, Don, Sr. V.P.--The Dunlap Companies, Fort Worth, TX, pg. 353
Burch, Harold R., Sr. V.P.-Claims--State Volunteer Mutual Insurance Co. Inc., Brentwood, TN, pg. 1041
Burch, Phil, Sr. V.P.-Retail Opers.--Hickory Farms, Inc., Maumee, OH, pg. 532
Burcin, Doug, Sr. V.P., Grp. Supvr.--Sudler & Hennessey, New York, NY, pg. 1211
Burd, Larry W., Sr. V.P.--Kreonite, Inc., Wichita, KS, pg. 644
Burden, Laurance T., Sr. V.P. & Chief Information Officer--S. C. Johnson & Son, Inc., Racine, WI, pg. 599
Burkard, J. THomas, Sr. V.P.-Special Markets--Mutual of America, New York, NY, pg. 777
Burns, Don R., Sr. V.P.-Outdoor T.V. & Cable--Donrey Media Group, Fort Smith, AR, pg. 345
Burns, Vincent B., Sr. V.P.--Independence Investment Associates, Inc., Boston, MA, pg. 596
Burrows, Dennis A., Sr. V.P. & Sec.--Roper Bros. Lumber Co., Inc., Petersburg, VA, pg. 947
Burton, David I., Sr. V.P.-Specialty Derivitive Chemicals--International Specialty Products, Inc., Wilmington, DE, pg. 438
Burton, Edwin T., Sr. V.P.--Rothschild Inc., New York, NY, pg. 951
Burton, Keith, Sr. V.P., Dir.--Ketchum Public Relations/Chicago, Chicago, IL, pg. 625
Burton, William J., Sr. V.P.--Massachusetts Mutual Life Insurance Co., Springfield, MA, pg. 718
Bussell, Lee, Sr. V.P., Acct. Services--Newman, Saylor & Gregory, Columbia, SC, pg. 804
Byrd, Doyle, Sr. V.P.-Human Resources & Devel.--Central Freight Lines Inc., Waco, TX, pg. 232
Byrne, James, Sr. V.P.--G. Von Hamm Textiles, Inc., Honolulu, HI, pg. 1155
Cain, Harry P., II, Sr. V.P.-Federal Programs--Blue Cross and Blue Shield Association, Chicago, IL, pg. 159
Calabrese, Julia J., Sr. V.P.-Property Mngmt.--The Kaempfer Company, Investment Builders, Washington, DC, pg. 613
Calafati, Peter G., V.P.--Frank Briscoe Co. Inc., Roseland, NJ, pg. 176
Caliendo, O'Neal, Sr. V.P., Production Services--Responsive Marketing Communications, Inc., Schaumburg, IL, pg. 929
Callas, Maria, Sr. V.P.--Theochem Labs., Inc., Tampa, FL, pg. 1090
Camens, Bernard, Sr. V.P.-Sls- Lighting Div.--Crystal Clear Industries Company, Ridgefield Park, NJ, pg. 303
Cameron, Donald D., Sr. V.P.--Massachusetts Mutual Life Insurance Co., Springfield, MA, pg. 718
Campbell, John, Sr. V.P.--Penske Truck Leasing, Chesterfield, MO, pg. 859
Campbell, John J., Sr. V.P.--Elbeco Incorporated, Reading, PA, pg. 372
Campbell, John R., Sr. V.P. & Publisher--Financial World Partners, New York, NY, pg. 410
Campbell, Ronald E., Sr. V.P.--The Troy Savings Bank, Troy, NY, pg. 1116
Canfield, Alan B., Sr. V.P.--A. J. Canfield Co., Chicago, IL, pg. 214
Cannelli, John, Sr. V.P.-Music & Talent--MTV: Music Television, New York, NY, pg. 785
Cappo, Joe, Sr. V.P. & Grp. Publisher--Crain Communications, Inc., Detroit, MI, pg. 295
Cappo, Joe, Sr. V.P.-Publishing Dir.--Advertising Age, Chicago, IL, pg. 295
Cardwell, Kenneth D., Sr. V.P.--Massachusetts Mutual Life Insurance Co., Springfield, MA, pg. 718
Carlin, Gabriel S., Sr. V.P.--Ko-Rec-Type, Brooklyn, NY, pg. 121
Carlson, Kelly, Sr. V.P.-Career Organizations--Phoenix Home Life Mutual Insurance Company, Hartford, CT, pg. 868
Carlucci, John F., Sr. V.P.--Carrafiello, Diehl & Associates, Inc., Irvington, NY, pg. 225
Carroll, Ray, Sr. V.P.--Kroch's & Brentano's, Inc., Chicago, IL, pg. 645
Cash, James M., Jr., Sr. V.P.-Corp. Services--Pan-American Life Insurance Company, New Orleans, LA, pg. 845
Cassidy, William L., Sr. V.P.-Service--National Life Insurance Company, Montpelier, VT, pg. 791
Castilla, Craig K., Sr. V.P.--Rothschild Inc., New York, NY, pg. 951
Cato, Tom, Sr. V.P.-Logistics & Prod. Service--Montgomery Ward & Co., Inc., Chicago, IL, pg. 767
Cauble, Lorraine, Sr. V.P.-Regional Opers.--Fantastic Sam's International, Inc., Memphis, TN, pg. 398
Caudill, James, Sr. V.P., Assoc. Dir.--Ketchum Public Relations/San Francisco, San Francisco, CA, pg. 625
Caufield, William E., Sr. V.P.-Grp. Benefit Opers.--John Hancock Mutual Life Insurance Company, Boston, MA, pg. 595
Causey, Alan, Sr. V.P., Dir. Social Analysis & Forecasts--Ammirati & Puris Inc., New York, NY, pg. 67
Cavin, Terry, Sr. V.P., Chief Oper. Officer--Russ Reid Company, Inc., Pasadena, CA, pg. 923
Cayo, Dale J., Sr. V.P.--Mason Shoe Mfg. Co., Chippewa Falls, WI, pg. 718
Cerrato, Anthony, Sr. V.P.--Vitt Media Direct, New York, NY, pg. 1154
Cerrato, John, Sr. V.P.-Corp. Services--Mutual of America, New York, NY, pg. 777
Chait, Arthur, Sr. V.P.-Bus. & Policy Grp.--SRI International, Menlo Park, CA, pg. 964
Champagne, Steve, Sr. V.P.--Harbor Financial Mortgage Corp., Houston, TX, pg. 506
Chapel, Burdette, Sr. V.P.--Capital Development Co., Lacey, WA, pg. 215
Chappell, Sarah S., Sr. V.P.-Personnel--Spencer Companies Inc., Huntsville, AL, pg. 1030
Chautin, Marlene, Sr. V.P., Assoc. Dir. Local Brdcst.--Young & Rubicam New York, New York, NY, pg. 1211
Chen, Terry, Chief Fin. Officer & Sr. V.P.--Allright Corporation, Houston, TX, pg. 41
Chensoff, Gary V., Sr. V.P.--JMB Realty Corporation, Chicago, IL, pg. 584
Cheshire, Bob, Sr. V.P.--Bernard Johnson Incorporated, Houston, TX, pg. 598
Cheskis, Herbert L., Sr. V.P.-Northeastern Agencies--New York Life Insurance Company, New York, NY, pg. 802
Chiara, Robert, Sr. V.P.--Geyer-McAllister Publications, Inc., New York, NY, pg. 455
Childers, James H., Sr. V.P.--Health Care Lodges, Coffeyville, KS, pg. 520
Chitwood, Frank W., Sr. V.P., Asst. Sec. & Mng. Principal-HTB/Tulsa--HTB, Inc., Oklahoma City, OK, pg. 497
Chomakos, James, Sr. V.P. & Mgr.-Mktg. Admin.--First Federal of Michigan, Detroit, MI, pg. 414
Christopher, Eugene N., Sr. V.P.--TAD Technical Services Corp., Cambridge, MA, pg. 1071
Cincauage, Ramond J., Sr. V.P.--Wyatt Inc., Branford, CT, pg. 1205
Cippinger, William G., Sr. V.P.--Southland Industries, Long Beach, CA, pg. 1023
Clark, John F., Sr. V.P.--Mark Lipman Div., Memphis, TN, pg. 493
Clark, John F., Jr., Sr. V.P.--Guardsmark, Inc., Memphis, TN, pg. 492
Clark, Roger L., Sr. V.P.-Mediterranean Services--Lykes Bros. Steamship Co., Inc., New Orleans, LA, pg. 688
Clark, Steve, Sr. V.P.-Church's--Church's Fried Chicken, Inc., Jefferson, LA, pg. 284
Clarke, James, Sr. V.P.--EvansGroup, Seattle, WA, pg. 391
Clausen, Ned, Sr. V.P., Grp. Dir.--Griffin Bacal Inc., New York, NY, pg. 486
Clements, Bruce W., Sr. V.P., Productivity & Organization--ASC Incorporated, Southgate, MI, pg. 7
Clements, James F., Sr. V.P.--George Rice & Sons, Los Angeles, CA, pg. 931
Clemmons, Kerry D., Sr. V.P.--John Alden Financial Corporation, Miami, FL, pg. 32
Cline, George W., Sr. V.P., Grp. Dir.--Griswold, Inc., Cleveland, OH, pg. 950
Clouser, Christopher E., Sr. V.P.-Communications & Adv.--Northwest Airlines, Inc., Saint Paul, MN, pg. 782
Coatney, Michael, Sr. V.P.--Acme Truck Line, Inc., Harvey, LA, pg. 13
Coats, Hector A., Sr. V.P.--Keystone Foods Corporation, Bala-Cynwyd, PA, pg. 628
Cody, Steve, Sr. V.P., Pub. Rels. Dir.--Earle Palmer Brown/New York, New York, NY, pg. 182
Coe, Paul E., Jr., Sr. V.P.--MCC Group, Inc., Metairie, LA, pg. 691
Coffman, Roy, Sr. V.P.--Christianity Today, Inc., Carol Stream, IL, pg. 249
Cohen, Carol, Sr. V.P.--The Levy Organization, Chicago, IL, pg. 672
Cohen, Carol, Sr. V.P.--Levy Restaurants, Chicago, IL, pg. 672
Cohen, Edward, Sr. V.P.--Carrafiello, Diehl & Associates, Inc., Irvington, NY, pg. 225
Cohen, Ronald E., Sr. V.P.--Duane Reade, Long Island City, NY, pg. 350
Cole, Anne, Sr. V.P.--Cole of California, Los Angeles, CA, pg. 1079
Collett, Kathryn H., Deputy Chm. & Sr. V.P.--Montgomery Elevator Company, Moline, IL, pg. 767
Collier, Joe, Sr. V.P.--Allied Systems, Ltd., Decatur, GA, pg. 40
Colliver, Danielle, Pres.-Detroit/Ayer & Sr. V.P., Mng. Dir.--N W Ayer Inc., Detroit, MI, pg. 104
Comardello, Nicholas P., Sr. V.P.-Residential Mortgage Lending Div.--First Federal Savings and Loan Assn. of Rochester, Rochester, NY, pg. 413
Condit, Tim, Sr. V.P.-Space Frame Grp.--Unistrut Corporation, Ann Arbor, MI, pg. 1130
Conly, Michael J., Sr. V.P.--Harte-Hanks Communications, Inc., San Antonio, TX, pg. 513
Conn, John, Sr. V.P.--J. L. Todd Auction Co., Rome, GA, pg. 1099
Connelly, John, Exec. V.P. & Dir-Creative/Writer--ICE Communications, Inc., Rochester, NY, pg. 559
Conroy, James T., Sr. V.P.-Corp. Affairs--MacAndrews & Forbes Holdings Inc., New York, NY, pg. 694
Constantino, Joseph M., Exec. V.P.--The Atlas Construction Co., Stamford, CT, pg. 96
Conti, Richard, Sr. V.P., Grp. Dir.--Griffin Bacal Inc., New York, NY, pg. 486
Conway, William C., Sr. V.P.--Mutual of America, New York, NY, pg. 777
Conyers, Rita, Sr. V.P.-Corp. Communications & Exec. Training--Mutual of America, New York, NY, pg. 777
Cooke, Berkley, Sr. V.P.--Cramer-Krasselt, Phoenix, AZ, pg. 296
Cooper, Dennis E., Sr. V.P.--R.T.M. Winners, Atlanta, GA, pg. 908
Cooper, Jerry, Sr. V.P.--W&F Manufacturing Corporation, Inc., Buffalo, NY, pg. 1155
Cooper, Sally, Sr. V.P.-C&E Group--Wholesale Electronic Supply, Dallas, TX, pg. 1188
Coover, James, Sr. V.P.--Avadyne, Inc., Monterey, CA, pg. 101
Coppola, Edward, Sr. V.P.--The Macerich Co., Santa Monica, CA, pg. 696
Cornick, Jack A., Sr. V.P.--Washington Mutual Savings Bank, Seattle, WA, pg. 1166
Cory, M. Thomas, V.P.-Plumbing Div.--Radiator Specialty Company, Charlotte, NC, pg. 909
Costa, Michael A., Sr. V.P.--Calmark Development Corp., Los Angeles, CA, pg. 211
Costigan, Alexander, Sr. V.P.--Henri's Food Products Co., Inc., Milwaukee, WI, pg. 530
Costlow, Curtis C., Sr. V.P.-Property Management--Crown American Corporation, Johnstown, PA, pg. 301
Cothren, H. Bobby, Sr. V.P.--The Stellar Group Inc., Jacksonville, FL, pg. 1046
Cotter, Clifton C., Sr. V.P.--M.J. Daly & Sons, Inc., Waterbury, CT, pg. 313
Coulson, Deb, Sr. V.P., Reg. Dir.-K&D Asia--Kobs & Draft Advertising, Inc., Chicago, IL, pg. 109
Cowan, Roy, Sr. V.P.--Davis, Ball & Colombatto Advertising, Inc., Los Angeles, CA, pg. 318
Cox, Garvin, Sr. V.P.--Texas Refinery Corp., Fort Worth, TX, pg. 1089
Cox, Jerry A., Sr. V.P.--Union City Body Company, Inc., Union City, IN, pg. 1128
Coyne, Kevin, Sr. V.P., Media Dir.--Backer Spielvogel Bates, Inc., Irvine, CA, pg. 108
Craig, Robert, Sr. V.P., Yellow Pages Mgr.--Hutchins/Young & Rubicam, Rochester, NY, pg. 1211
Creadon, Vince, Sr. V.P.-Sls. & Mktg.--Baker Knapp & Tubbs Inc., Grand Rapids, MI, pg. 640
Croft, Jerry L., Sr. V.P.--Century Publishing Company, Evanston, IL, pg. 235
Cron, Richard M., Sr. V.P.-Devel.--Farley Industries, Chicago, IL, pg. 399

Crosby, Lindsey L., Sr. V.P.--The Bibb Company, Macon, GA, pg. 781
Cross, John P., Sr. V.P.--STS Holdings, Inc., Northbrook, IL, pg. 964
Crouch, Robert F., Sr. V.P.--The Copley Press, Inc., La Jolla, CA, pg. 284
Crowder, Otis P., Sr. V.P.--Crowder Construction Co., Charlotte, NC, pg. 301
Crowder, W.T., Sr. V.P.--Crowder Construction Co., Charlotte, NC, pg. 301
Crowell, Peter, Sr. V.P., Grp. Media Dir.--Arnold Fortuna Lawner & Cabot, Boston, MA, pg. 84
Cruikshank, Ronald, Sr. V.P., Gen. Counsel--Ketchum Communications Inc., Pittsburgh, PA, pg. 625
Cumming, Virgil H., Sr. V.P.--Teachers Insurance and Annuity Association-College Retirement Equities Fund, New York, NY, pg. 1082
Cunningham, Gary, Sr. V.P., Dir. Print Services--Avrett, Free & Ginsberg, Inc., New York, NY, pg. 103
Cunningham, Michael, Sr. V.P. & Exec. Dir.-Creative--Eric Mower and Associates, Inc., Syracuse, NY, pg. 774
Curling, David, Sr. V.P.--The William Cook Agency, Inc., Jacksonville, FL, pg. 282
Custodio, Eduardo R., Sr. V.P.--Hemisphere-Leo Burnett, Inc., Metro Manila,, Philippines, pg. 192
D'Amour, Donald H., Sr. V.P. & Chief Exec. Officer--Big Y Foods Inc., Springfield, MA, pg. 149
Daboul, Peter, Sr. V.P.--Massachusetts Mutual Life Insurance Co., Springfield, MA, pg. 718
Dalimonte, Alfred A., Sr. V.P.--Microband Companies, Inc., Fairfield, NJ, pg. 748
Daly, Denis J., Sr. V.P.--Hubbard Milling Company, Mankato, MN, pg. 549
Dana, Nicholas, Sr. V.P.--Douglas Elliman-Gibbons & Ives, Inc., New York, NY, pg. 347
Dane, Peter, Sr. V.P.--Allright Corporation, Houston, TX, pg. 41
Dane, Richard, Sr. V.P.--Allright Corporation, Houston, TX, pg. 41
Danuff, Ilene, Sr. V.P., Grp. Media Dir.--McCaffrey and McCall, New York, NY, pg. 726
Darazsdi, Frank J., Sr. Partner--Ingersoll Engineers Inc., Rockford, IL, pg. 568
Darazsdi, James J., Chief Exec. Officer & Sr. V.P.--Rocco Inc., Harrisonburg, VA, pg. 940
Dargis, Leon A., Sr. V.P. & Chief Trust Officer--Horizon Bancorp, Michigan City, IN, pg. 544
Darien, Frank, Sr., Exec. V.P.--Darien & Kilburg, Inc., San Jose, CA, pg. 315
Davenport, Robin, Sr. V.P., Assoc. Creative Dir.-Copy--Sudler & Hennessey, New York, NY, pg. 1211
Davis, David H., Sr. V.P.--Johnston, Lemon & Co. Inc., Washington, DC, pg. 601
Davis, Dwight, Sr. V.P.-Western Division--Employers Insurance of Wausau a Mutual Co., Wausau, WI, pg. 380
Davis, Dwight, Sr. V.P.-Western Division--Employers Insurance of Wausau a Mutual Co., Wausau, WI, pg. 795
Davis, Garland A., Sr. V.P.--Fritz Chemical Company, Mesquite, TX, pg. 434
Davis, Marvin, Sr. V.P., Grp. Dir.--Sherwood & Schneider Advertising, New York, NY, pg. 999
Davis, Mike, Sr. V.P.--Purcell International Group, Inc., Los Angeles, CA, pg. 900
Davis, Paula, Ph.D., Sr. V.P.-Scientific Services--M.E.D. Communications, Woodbridge, NJ, pg. 692
Davis, Thomas, Sr. V.P.--John Morrell & Co., Cincinnati, OH, pg. 54
Daykin, Leonard, Sr. V.P.--Don Jagoda Associates, Inc., Melville, NY, pg. 588
Dean, Jay, Sr. V.P., Consumer Res. Dir.--Young & Rubicam San Francisco, San Francisco, CA, pg. 1211
DeArmond, Richard L., Sr. V.P.--Idaho Forest Industry, Inc., Coeur D'Alene, ID, pg. 561
Dearth, Robert A., Jr., Sr. V.P.-Chiquita Tropical Products Grp.--Chiquita Brands International, Inc., Cincinnati, OH, pg. 53
Debrecht, Donald R., Sr. V.P., Treas. & Controller--Hill-Behan Lumber Company, Saint Louis, MO, pg. 534
DeCius, Dennis A., Chief Fin. Officer & Sr. V.P.--First National Bank of Central California, Salinas, CA, pg. 839
DeGisa, Patrick J., V.P. & Gen Mgr.--George W. Prescott Publishing Co., Quincy, MA, pg. 887
deGraffenreid, James T., Sr. V.P.--Phillips Publishing Inc., Potomac, MD, pg. 868
Deisinger, Robert, Sr. V.P.--American Technical Publishers, Inc., Homewood, IL, pg. 63
Del Priore, Michael J., Sr. V.P. & Mng. Dir.--J. & W. Seligman & Company, New York, NY, pg. 584
DeLeo, Jack S., Sr. V.P.--Hitchcock-Fleming & Associates, Inc., Akron, OH, pg. 536
Dembrow, Jon, Sr. V.P.--Young Stuff Apparel Group, Inc., New York, NY, pg. 1214
DeMeno, William P., Sr. V.P.-Bus Opers.--Nationwide Mutual Insurance Company, Columbus, OH, pg. 795
DeMilt, William A., Sr. V.P. & Treas.--Mutual of America, New York, NY, pg. 777
Denny, C. Patterson, Sr. V.P.-The Television Production Center--WTTW (Channel 11), Chicago, IL, pg. 1156
Deshmukh, A.R., Sr. V.P.-Advanced Programs--Anser (Analytic Services Inc.), Arlington, VA, pg. 76
Desimon, Edward, Sr. V.P., Land Devel.--Kettler Brothers, Inc., Montgomery Village, MD, pg. 626
Dessen, Stanley B., Sr. V.P.-Taxation--Revlon, Inc., New York, NY, pg. 696
Devine, Matthew, Sr. V.P.--Devine & Pearson, Inc., Quincy, MA, pg. 333
Devine, Thomas, Sr. V.P.--Devine & Pearson, Inc., Quincy, MA, pg. 333
DeVino, Frank, Sr. V.P. & Graphics Dir.--Omni Publications International Ltd., New York, NY, pg. 450
Di Liberto, John G., Sr. V.P.-Claims--Utica Mutual Insurance Company, New Hartford, NY, pg. 1140
Di Santo, Carol, Sr. V.P., Dir. Proworx--Cline, Davis & Mann, Inc., New York, NY, pg. 255
Dial, Michael C., Sr. V.P.-Fin.--Cooper Communities, Inc., Bella Vista, AR, pg. 283
DiCanio, Gerard, Sr. V.P.-Fin.--Viacom Productions Inc., Universal City, CA, pg. 785
Dick, Lee, Sr. V.P.--Davis, Ball & Colombatto Advertising, Inc., Los Angeles, CA, pg. 318
Dickerson, Robert E., Exec. V.P.-Lubricants--Southwestern Petroleum Corporation, Fort Worth, TX, pg. 1024
Dickinson, Don, Sr. V.P.--Gerber Advertising, Portland, OR, pg. 453
Dickson, Nickie, Sr. V.P., Admin. & Fin.--Newman, Saylor & Gregory, Columbia, SC, pg. 804
Dill, Donald W., Sr. V.P.--Certified Grocers Advertising Co., Los Angeles, CA, pg. 236
Dinicoli, Joe, Sr. V.P.--Payless Car Rental System, Inc., Saint Petersburg, FL, pg. 853
Dinkler, Vincent J., Sr. V.P.--Macco Constructors, Inc., Paramount, CA, pg. 696
DiPietro, Al, Chief Fin. Officer & Sr. V.P.--LaMarca Group Inc., New York, NY, pg. 652
Dixon, Andrew, Sr. V.P. -Human Resources--Continental Cablevision, Boston, MA, pg. 278
Dobson, John, Sr. V.P.--Owen Industries, Inc., Carter Lake, IA, pg. 834
Dodd, Steve, Sr. V.P., Acct. Supvr.--EvansGroup, Dallas, TX, pg. 391
Doelger, Frank W., Sr. V.P.--Douglas Elliman-Gibbons & Ives, Inc., New York, NY, pg. 347
Dolci, Louis, Sr. V.P.--Torcon, Inc., Westfield, NJ, pg. 1102
Domash, Norman, Sr. V.P.--Conway Import Co. Inc., Elmsford, NY, pg. 281
Donaldson, John, Sr. V.P.--Capital Development Co., Lacey, WA, pg. 215
Donovan, John J., Jr., Sr. V.P.-Leasing--The Oliver Carr Co., Washington, DC, pg. 225
Donsbach, Dale, Sr. V.P.--Petty Company, Inc., Effingham, IL, pg. 866
Donsky, Abe H., Sr. V.P.--Sterling Jewelry & Distributing Co., Dallas, TX, pg. 1047
Donsky, Nathan, Sr. V.P.--Sterling Jewelry & Distributing Co., Dallas, TX, pg. 1047
Dooley, C. Terry, Sr. V.P.--Morley Group, Santa Monica, CA, pg. 770
Doran, Carl, Sr. V.P.-Export--Ford Meter Box Company, Wabash, IN, pg. 423
Dorman, Alan J., Sr. V.P.--Washington Mutual Savings Bank, Seattle, WA, pg. 1166
Douglas, Murray, Sr. V.P.--Brunschwig & Fils, Inc., White Plains, NY, pg. 184
Douglas, W. Leslie, Sr. V.P.--Folger Nolan Fleming Douglas, Washington, DC, pg. 422
Downham, Richard J., Sr. V.P.-Claims--American Hardware Mutual Insurance Co., Minnetonka, MN, pg. 55
Downing, Robert B., Sr. V.P.--Oxford Realty Services Corp., Bethesda, MD, pg. 835
Doyle, Dennis M., Sr. V.P.--Chiquita Brands, Inc., Cincinnati, OH, pg. 53
Drake, Gerald L., Sr. V.P.--Wilbur Smith Associates, Columbia, SC, pg. 1011
Draper, John, Sr. V.P., Acct. Supvr.--Sudler & Hennessey Consumer Group, New York, NY, pg. 1211
Dull, Charles W., Sr. V.P.-Corp. Staff Services & Chief Quality Officer--Aid Association For Lutherans, Appleton, WI, pg. 26
Dunlap, Ira G., Sr. V.P.--The Dunlap Companies, Fort Worth, TX, pg. 353
Dunlop, W. Wayne, Sr. V.P.--Barclay White Incorporated, Berwyn, PA, pg. 119
Dunn, Toby, Sr. V.P., Mngmt. Supvr.--Avrett, Free & Ginsberg, Inc., New York, NY, pg. 103
Dunning, John A., Grp. Sr. V.P.--Horizon Media, Inc., New York, NY, pg. 544
Durbin, Ed, Sr. V.P.--Kaiser Aerospace & Electronics Corp., Foster City, CA, pg. 614
Dutil, Mark, Sr. V.P. & Dir.-Creative--Goldfarb & Company Advertising, Southfield, MI, pg. 467
Dutta, Sanat, Sr. V.P.-Opers.--Ingram Micro Inc., Santa Ana, CA, pg. 569
Earls, Clifford D., Sr. V.P.--Knight/Emerson Consulting, Inc., Chicago, IL, pg. 637
Eastment, George T., III, Sr. V.P.--The Long & Foster Companies, Inc., Fairfax, VA, pg. 682
Eastment, George T., III, Sr. V.P.--The Long & Foster Real Estate, Inc., Fairfax, VA, pg. 682
Echevarria, Michael, Chief Oper. Officer & Exec. V.P.--Echevarria Angel Co., Inc., Los Angeles, CA, pg. 365
Edney, John, Sr. V.P.--Durham Transportation, Inc., Austin, TX, pg. 354
Ehlers, Lyle, Sr. V.P.--Camosy, Inc., Russell, IL, pg. 212
Ehrlich, Jerome MD, Sr. V.P., Medical Dir.--Sudler & Hennessey, New York, NY, pg. 1211
Eisenstein, Lois, Sr. V.P.-Business Affairs & Gen. Counsel--MTV Networks, New York, NY, pg. 785
Eisenstein, Lois Peel, Sr. V.P.-Bus. Affairs & Gen. Counsel-MTV Networks--Viacom Inc., New York, NY, pg. 785
Eitel, Stephen W., Sr. V.P.--Illinois Cereal Mills, Inc., Paris, IL, pg. 562
Ekse, Bill, Sr. V.P.--The Schmidt/Westerdahl Group Ltd., Portland, OR, pg. 976
Elberson, Charlie, Sr. V.P.--Price/McNabb, Inc., Asheville, NC, pg. 888
Eldrige, George Thomas, Sr. V.P.-Services--Central Life Assurance Co., Des Moines, IA, pg. 232
Elledge, E. Ben, Sr. V.P.--Coral Petroleum Corporation, Houston, TX, pg. 285
Endemann, Carlton, Jr., Sr. V.P.--Pepsi-Cola Albany Bottling Co., Inc., Latham, NY, pg. 860
Engel, David R., Sr. V.P.--Southwest Marine, Inc., San Diego, CA, pg. 1023
Engel, Doug, Sr. V.P. & Exec. Dir.-Creative--Miller Meester Advertising Inc., Minneapolis, MN, pg. 754
Ennis, Robert, Sr. V.P.-Mfg.--Havatampa Incorporated, Tampa, FL, pg. 517
Ervin, Jon D., Sr. V.P.--Acess Energy Corporation, Dublin, OH, pg. 12
Essner, Warren A., Sr. V.P. & Auditor--Mutual of America, New York, NY, pg. 777
Evans, Gary, Sr. V.P., TV Production--Russ Reid Company, Inc., Pasadena, CA, pg. 923
Evans, John, Sr. V.P.--Al Paul Lefton Co., Inc., Philadelphia, PA, pg. 666
Evans, Thomas R., Sr. V.P.--U.S. News & World Report, New York, NY, pg. 1136
Evans, Wayne C., Sr. V.P. (Salt Lake City) & Dir.--EvansGroup, Salt Lake City, UT, pg. 390
Faems, Michael J., Sr. V.P., Exec. Creative Dir.--Young & Rubicam Chicago, Chicago, IL, pg. 1211
Fain, Jonathan D., Sr. V.P.--Teknor Apex Company, Pawtucket, RI, pg. 1084
Fairfield, Derrell, Sr. V.P.--Shamrock Foods Co., Phoenix, AZ, pg. 994
Falvo, Janet, Sr. V.P., Fin. Services--Chapman Direct Advertising, New York, NY, pg. 1210
Farkas, Joseph R., Sr. V.P.--The Bodine Corp., Bridgeport, CT, pg. 161
Farrell, Frank, Sr. V.P.--Admarketing, Inc., Los Angeles, CA, pg. 18
Fasilis, James G., Sr. V.P.--Griswold, Inc., Cleveland, OH, pg. 950
Feinberg, Mel J., Sr. V.P.--Koolvent Aluminum Products, Inc., Pittsburgh, PA, pg. 641
Feinerman, Judith, Sr. V.P., Dir. Brdcst. Services--Backer Spielvogel Bates, Inc., New York, NY, pg. 108
Felder, Stan, Sr. V.P.--Biggs Gilmore Communications, Kalamazoo, MI, pg. 149
Feldman, Steve, Sr. V.P., Sr. Art Dir.--TBWA Advertising, Inc., New York, NY, pg. 1071
Feniger, Judith A., Sr. V.P.-PROCONSUL--The Jayme Organization, Inc., Cleveland, OH, pg. 591
Fenimore, George W., Sr. V.P.-Pub. Affairs--Peck Jones Construction, Los Angeles, CA, pg. 854
Fenno, Harold, Sr. V.P.--Atlantic Gulf Communities Corporation, Miami, FL, pg. 95
Ferguson, Charles L., Sr. V.P.--Granite State Manufacturing Co., Manchester, NH, pg. 476
Fero, James F. Jr., Sr. V.P.--Davis Mechanical Contractors, Inc., Greenville, SC, pg. 318
Ferrara, Roger C., Sr. V.P.-Fin. Advisory Services--Mutual of America, New York, NY, pg. 777
Fiderer, Martin, Sr. V.P., Acct. Services--Pancom International Corp., Stamford, CT, pg. 845
Field, Fiske, Sr. V.P.- National Accts.--Mutual of America, New York, NY, pg. 777
Field, Paul, Sr. V.P.--Richardson, Myers & Donofrio, Inc., Baltimore, MD, pg. 933
Figenshu, William R., Sr. V.P. & Pres.-Radio Div.--Viacom Broadcasting Inc., New York, NY, pg. 785
Fine, Mark L., Sr. V.P.--Summa Corporation, Las Vegas, NV, pg. 1057
Fink, Terry, Sr. V.P., Media Dir.--Edelmann Scott, Inc., Richmond, VA, pg. 368
Finley, Peter S., Sr. V.P.--Harbour Group Ltd., Clayton, MO, pg. 506
Finley, Russell G., Sr. V.P., Mktg./Media--John Emmerling Inc., New York, NY, pg. 379
Firth, Donald, Sr. V.P.-Logistics--Pathmark, Woodbridge, NJ, pg. 1064
Fischer, Donald, Sr. V.P.-Intl. Systems--United Parcel Service of America, Inc., Atlanta, GA, pg. 1133
Fisher, C. Douglas, Sr. V.P. & Dir.-Creative--Lord, Sullivan & Yoder, Inc. Advertising, Columbus, OH, pg. 683
Fisher, J.W., Sr. V.P.-Underwriting--Auto-Owners Insurance, Lansing, MI, pg. 100
Fitzgerald, Daniel J., Sr. V.P. & Actuary--Massachusetts Mutual Life Insurance Co., Springfield, MA, pg. 718
Fitzgerald, Walter D., Sr. V.P.--Chicago Corp., Chicago, IL, pg. 247
Fitzhugh, Ed, Sr. V.P.--First National Bank in Cleburne, Cleburne, TX, pg. 412
Fitzpatrick, Pat, Sr. V.P.-California Region--United States Cold Storage, Inc., Cherry Hill, NJ, pg. 1135
Fitzpatrick, Paul, Sr. V.P.--I. Magnin & Co., San Francisco, CA, pg. 699
Flack, John, Sr. V.P.--Geneve Corporation, Stamford, CT, pg. 451
Flaherty, Edward III, Sr. V.P.--The St. George Group, Inc., Pittsburgh, PA, pg. 966
Flaherty, Robert, Sr. V.P., Assoc. Dir.--Ketchum Public Relations/New York, New York, NY, pg. 625
Flaster, S.R., Sr. V.P.-Sls.--Ingram Book Company, La Vergne, TN, pg. 569
Fleischer, Stuart, Sr. V.P.--Communications Diversified, New York, NY, pg. 269
Fleishman, Ernest, Sr. V.P.-Magazine Grp.--Scholastic Inc., New York, NY, pg. 962
Flesh, Robert T., Sr. V.P.--Thrifty Oil Company, Downey, CA, pg. 1096
Flint, Mark, Sr. V.P. & Chief Fin. Officer--Peter J. Schmitt Holdings, West Seneca, NY, pg. 976
Flood, Thomas J., Sr. V.P.--Capital Bancorp, Miami, FL, pg. 214
Flores, Armando B., Sr. V.P.-Admin.--Amfac Distribution Corporation, Folsom, CA, pg. 585
Flowers, Robert J., Sr. V.P.--Washington Mutual Savings Bank, Seattle, WA, pg. 1166
Fojtasek, Richard, V.P.--Fojtasek Companies, Inc., Irving, TX, pg. 421
Foley Murphy, Kathy, Sr. V.P., Dir.-Acct. Services--Young & Rubicam San Francisco, San Francisco, CA, pg. 1211
Follick, Wayne, Sr. V.P.--N.W. Transport Service, Inc., Commerce City, CO, pg. 781
Forbes, Matthew, Sr. V.P., Assoc. Creative Dir.--Lipman, Richmond, Greene, New York, NY, pg. 677
Forebaugh, Jack, Sr. V.P.--Keywell Corporation, Detroit, MI, pg. 629
Foreman, Sue, Sr. V.P., Creative Dir./Consumer Products--William Douglas McAdams Inc., New York, NY, pg. 726

Foster, Walter, Sr. V.P.--The Stellar Group Inc., Jacksonville, FL, pg. 1046
Foti, Samuel J., Exec. V.P.-Insurance Opers.--The Mutual Life Insurance Company of New York (MONY), New York, NY, pg. 778
Fountain, Mike, Exec. V.P. & Dir.-Creative--ICE Communications, Inc., Rochester, NY, pg. 559
Fox, Roy, Sr. V.P.-Hotel Services--Commodore Cruise Line, Ltd., Coral Gables, FL, pg. 269
Foy, John B., Sr. V.P.-Information Systems & Services--New York Life Insurance Company, New York, NY, pg. 802
Fradkin, S., Sr. V.P.--Eagle Electric Mfg. Co., Inc., Long Island City, NY, pg. 362
Fraizer, Kathy, Sr. V.P. & Gen. Mgr.-Accessories--John Wanamaker, Philadelphia, PA, pg. 1201
Franck, Donald G., Sr. V.P. & Mgr.-Commercial Real Estate Loans--First Federal of Michigan, Detroit, MI, pg. 414
Francke, Julia A., Sr. V.P., Grp. Acct. Supvr.--Ross Roy Inc., Bloomfield Hills, MI, pg. 950
Francomano, George, Sr. V.P.--Teachers Insurance and Annuity Association-College Retirement Equities Fund, New York, NY, pg. 1082
Frankel, S. Leroy, Sr. V.P.--Reitman Industries, West Caldwell, NJ, pg. 924
Franklin, Jeffrey B., Sr. V.P.--Franklin Baking Co., Inc., Goldsboro, NC, pg. 429
Frechette, Robert M., Sr. V.P.-Merchant Acceptance--Mastercard International, Inc., New York, NY, pg. 720
Freeman, Jeff E., Sr. V.P.-Fin., Sec. & Treas.--Havatampa Incorporated, Tampa, FL, pg. 517
Freeman, Paula, Sr. V.P.--Davis, Ball & Colombatto Advertising, Inc., Los Angeles, CA, pg. 318
Freiborg, A., Sr. V.P.--Marquette Bank Rochester, Rochester, MN, pg. 117
Freimuth, Steven J., Sr. V.P.--Washington Mutual Savings Bank, Seattle, WA, pg. 1166
Friedlander, Gary, Sr. V.P.--Rice Food Markets Inc., Houston, TX, pg. 931
Friedlander, Lindy J., Sr. V.P.--Washington Mutual Savings Bank, Seattle, WA, pg. 1166
Friedlander, Tom, Sr. V.P.--Rice Food Markets Inc., Houston, TX, pg. 931
Friedman, Dean, Sr. V.P. & Grp. Mgmt. Supvr.--W.B. Doner & Company, Southfield, MI, pg. 344
Friedman, Norman, Sr. V.P.--Kingsley Machine Co., Hollywood, CA, pg. 632
Frindt, Dwight, Sr. V.P.--Clayton, Williams & Sherwood, Inc., Newport Beach, CA, pg. 254
Fritsch, Al, Chief Oper. Officer & V.P.--Flair Communications Agency, Inc., Chicago, IL, pg. 416
Frost, Bruce A., Sr. V.P.-Indus.--Fru-Con Construction Corporation, Ballwin, MO, pg. 435
Fruedenthal, Frank, Sr. V.P. & Gen. Mgr.-Midwest Div.--Altec Industries, Inc., Birmingham, AL, pg. 45
Fulton, Robert, Sr. V.P.--Centimark Corporation, Bethel Park, PA, pg. 231
Gaffney, John, Sr. V.P., Natl. Media Dir.--Arnold Fortuna Lawner & Cabot, Boston, MA, pg. 84
Gahm, Tom, Sr. V.P.-Pub. Rels.--Miller Meester Advertising Inc., Minneapolis, MN, pg. 754
Gajda, Joseph, Sr. V.P. & Gen. Mgr.--Morse Shoe, Inc., Canton, MA, pg. 772
Gallagher, Patrick J., Sr. V.P.--San Francisco Giants Baseball Club, San Francisco, CA, pg. 969
Gandhi, Bharat, Sr. V.P.--The Pepper Companies, Inc., Chicago, IL, pg. 859
Garneau, Benjamin P., Sr. V.P.-Compliance--The Women's Bank, N.A., Denver, CO, pg. 385
Garretson, Michael, Sr. V.P.--Atlantic Gulf Communities Corporation, Miami, FL, pg. 95
Gasper, James W., Sr. V.P. & Gen. Mgr.--PBS Building Systems of America, Anaheim, CA, pg. 835
Gaswhala, Sid A., Sr. V.P.--Knight Architects Engineers Planners, Inc., Chicago, IL, pg. 637
Gaudet, Kenneth J., Sr. V.P.--TCC, Miami, FL, pg. 1072
Gear, Ronald J., Sr. V.P.--Stanley Consultants, Inc., Muscatine, IA, pg. 961
Gearhart, Lloyd E., Sr. V.P.--John Alden Financial Corporation, Miami, FL, pg. 32
Geary, Thomas, Sr. V.P.--S L C Graphics, Inc., Pittston, PA, pg. 963
Gebben, D.J., Sr. V.P.--WW Engineering & Science Inc., Grand Rapids, MI, pg. 1058
Gehring, Roger, Sr. V.P.--WGM Safety Corporation, Reading, PA, pg. 1156
George, Alvin, Sr. V.P.--Lipman, Richmond, Greene, New York, NY, pg. 677
George, Henry, Sr. V.P., Retail Grp.--Hughes Advertising Inc., Saint Louis, MO, pg. 551
Gereaue, Michael, Sr. V.P.-Pensions--Pan-American Life Insurance Company, New Orleans, LA, pg. 845
Germer, R. E., Sr. V.P.--Flying J. Inc., Brigham City, UT, pg. 421
Gerschick, Julie A., Sr. V.P.-Control & Compliance--Great Lakes Bancorp, Ann Arbor, MI, pg. 480
Gershel, George F., Jr., Sr. V.P.-Tobacco--Consolidated Cigar Corporation, Fort Lauderdale, FL, pg. 276
Gershman, Mark, Sr. V.P., Assoc. Creative Dir.--Avrett, Free & Ginsberg, Inc., New York, NY, pg. 103
Gertz, William, Sr. V.P.-Mktg.--American Institute For Foreign Study, Greenwich, CT, pg. 56
Giacini, Vivian P., Sr. V.P.-Human Resources--Mutual of America, New York, NY, pg. 777
Gibney, Charles W., Sr. V.P. & Chief Fin. Officer--Macromedia Inc., Hackensack, NJ, pg. 698
Gilbert, John O., Sr. V.P.-Member Insurance Services--Aid Association For Lutherans, Appleton, WI, pg. 26
Gilbert, T.L., Sr. V.P.-Individual Div.--Guarantee Mutual Life Co., Omaha, NE, pg. 491
Gilles, Jerry, Sr. V.P.--Mills Hall Walborn & Associates, Mayfield Heights, OH, pg. 756
Gillespie, Doy, Sr. V.P.--Molded Fiber Glass Companies, Ashtabula, OH, pg. 763
Gillespie, John B., Sr. V.P.--John Wieland Homes Inc., Atlanta, GA, pg. 1188
Gilliam, Thomas, Sr. V.P.- Technical Opers.--Mutual of America, New York, NY, pg. 777
Ginsberg, Saul, Sr. V.P.--Lipman, Richmond, Greene, New York, NY, pg. 677
Giroux, Donald K., Sr. V.P. & Dir.-Opers--Harley Ellington Pierce Yee Associates, Inc., Southfield, MI, pg. 509
Gissler, Sig, Sr. V.P.--The Milwaukee Journal, Milwaukee, WI, pg. 607
Glenn, Alan, Sr. V.P.--Drug Guild Distributors, Inc., Secaucus, NJ, pg. 349
Glenn, Clyde A., Sr. V.P.--Potter-Shackelford Construction Co., Greenville, SC, pg. 882
Glosser, Paul L., Sr. V.P.--G B Stores, Johnstown, PA, pg. 978
Glosser, Paul L., Sr. V.P.--Glosser Brothers, Inc., Johnstown, PA, pg. 978
Glover, William J., Jr., Sr. V.P. & Clerk--Fay, Spofford & Thorndike, Inc., Lexington, MA, pg. 404
Goddard, John W., Sr. V.P., Pres. & Chief Exec. Officer/ Viacom Cable--Viacom Inc., New York, NY, pg. 785
Gold, Joseph, Sr. V.P.--Spirit Cruises, Norfolk, VA, pg. 1031
Gold, Joshua S., Sr. V.P.-Port Folio Acquisition--Oxford First Corporation, Philadelphia, PA, pg. 834
Goldberg, Al, Sr. V.P.--Jordache Enterprises, Inc., New York, NY, pg. 604
Golden, Richard I., Sr. V.P., Dir. Devel. Labs--N W Ayer Inc., New York, NY, pg. 104
Goldenberg, Len, Sr. V.P., Mng. Dir., WW Communications--N W Ayer Inc., New York, NY, pg. 104
Goldfinger, Sam, Sr. V.P.-Individual Life--New York Life Insurance Company, New York, NY, pg. 802
Goldman, Mark, Sr. V.P., Mng. Dir.--The Criterion Group, Inc., Atlanta, GA, pg. 299
Goldman, Richard, Sr. V.P., Controller--TBWA Advertising, Inc., New York, NY, pg. 1071
Goldstein, Laurie, Sr. V.P.-Production Mngmt.--MTV Networks, New York, NY, pg. 785
Golnick, Greg, Sr. V.P.--Leon Shaffer Golnick Advertising, Inc., Fort Lauderdale, FL, pg. 469
Goodwin, Warren, Sr. V.P.--Herman Associates, Inc., New York, NY, pg. 531
Gordon, Steven, Sr. V.P.-Devel./Drama--Viacom Productions Inc., Universal City, CA, pg. 785
Gordon, William R., Sr. V.P.-Agricultural Investment--John Hancock Mutual Life Insurance Company, Boston, MA, pg. 595
Gottehrer, Barry, Sr. V.P.--Massachusetts Mutual Life Insurance Co., Springfield, MA, pg. 718
Gould, Matthew J., Sr. V.P.--Georgetown Partners, Inc., Great Neck, NY, pg. 473
Graber, Martin, Sr. V.P.--National Mortgage Company, Memphis, TN, pg. 792
Graddy, H.T., Sr. V.P.--Inman Construction Corporation, Memphis, TN, pg. 570
Graef, Russell, Sr. V.P.--World Shipping, Inc., Lakewood, OH, pg. 1203
Graf, Mark G., Sr. V.P.--Griswold, Inc., Cleveland, OH, pg. 950
Grant, Everett L., III, Sr. V.P.-Spec. Asst. to Chm.-Fin.--TLC Beatrice International Holdings Inc., New York, NY, pg. 1073
Graves, Earl G., Jr., Sr. V.P.-Sls. & Mktg.--Earl G. Graves, Ltd., New York, NY, pg. 478
Graves, Robert W., Sr. V.P.--Topa Thrift & Loan Association, Los Angeles, CA, pg. 1101
Gray, Richard E., Sr. V.P.--GAI Consultants, Inc., Monroeville, PA, pg. 439
Green, David, Sr. V.P.--Miller Advertising Agency Inc., New York, NY, pg. 753
Green, Doug, Sr. V.P. & Gen. Counsel--Ellerbe Becket, Inc., Minneapolis, MN, pg. 378
Greene, Gordon, Sr. V.P.--Sheldon Good & Co., Inc., Chicago, IL, pg. 470
Greenfield, Peter R., Sr. V.P.--Guardsmark, Inc., Memphis, TN, pg. 492
Greenfield, Rachel, Sr. V.P.--Ziff-Davis Publishing Company, New York, NY, pg. 1219
Greenfield, Robert, Sr. V.P.-Bus. Admin.--Viacom Productions Inc., Universal City, CA, pg. 785
Greenfield, Ronnie, Sr. V.P., Acct. Service--EvansGroup, Los Angeles, CA, pg. 391
Greenshields, Jack, Sr. V.P.-Mill Opers.--Waldorf Corporation, Saint Paul, MN, pg. 1159
Greenwood, Donald J., Sr. V.P. & Dir.-Res. & Devel.--Monarch Avalon, Inc., Baltimore, MD, pg. 765
Greer, Wilbur C., Sr. V.P.--Law Engineering, Inc., Atlanta, GA, pg. 661
Griffin, Gloria, Sr. V.P.--Griffin Homes, Inc., Calabasas, CA, pg. 487
Griffin, J.E., Sr. V.P.-Window Treatment Prods.--Allison-Erwin Co. Inc., Charlotte, NC, pg. 40
Griffin, R.E., Sr. V.P.--Sivalls, Inc., Odessa, TX, pg. 1009
Groessl, David, Sr. V.P.--Wisconsin Label Corporation, Algoma, WI, pg. 1198
Groskopt, John, Sr. V.P.--M M I Companies, Inc., Deerfield, IL, pg. 692
Gross, Neil G., Sr. V.P.--Acme Mills Co. Inc., Detroit, MI, pg. 13
Grossman, Harold, Sr. V.P., Mktg. Research--Sudler & Hennessey, New York, NY, pg. 1211
Growick, Phil, Sr. V.P.--Warren/Kremer/CMP/Advertising/ Inc., New York, NY, pg. 1165
Guenther, John S., Sr. V.P.--Geo. J. Ball, Inc., West Chicago, IL, pg. 115
Gugel, Craig, Sr. V.P., Dir. Media Res. & Tech.--Backer Spielvogel Bates, Inc., New York, NY, pg. 108
Guiver, Dennis, Sr. V.P.--Harris and Love, Inc., Salt Lake City, UT, pg. 512
Gullickson, Betsy, Sr. V.P., Assoc. Dir.--Ketchum Public Relations/San Francisco, San Francisco, CA, pg. 625
Gundlach, Paul, Sr. V.P., Acct. Supvr.--Sudler & Hennessey Consumer Group, New York, NY, pg. 1211
Guthrie, Alan S., Sr. V.P.--Horizon Paper Co., Inc., New York, NY, pg. 544
Gutierrez, Ruben, Sr. V.P., Program Dir.--Sudler & Hennessey Consumer Group, New York, NY, pg. 1211
Haberern, John, Sr. V.P.--Rodale Press, Inc., Emmaus, PA, pg. 942
Hafner, Kenneth O., Sr. V.P.--Johnson Bros. Corp., Litchfield, MN, pg. 597
Hagan, Bernard F., Chief Oper. Officer & Sr. V.P.--Henkels & McCoy, Inc., Blue Bell, PA, pg. 529
Haggard, Rick, Sr. V.P.-Comml. Loans--Federal Savings Bank, Fort Smith, AR, pg. 1194
Haight, Allen M., Sr. V.P.-Grp. Dept.--The Prudential Insurance Company of America, Newark, NJ, pg. 896
Haire, James R., Sr. V.P.--Ameritas Life Insurance Corp., Lincoln, NE, pg. 66
Hall, David B., Sr. V.P.--Shamrock Foods Co., Phoenix, AZ, pg. 994
Hall, Joe, Chief Oper. Officer & Sr. V.P.-Opers.--Central Freight Lines Inc., Waco, TX, pg. 232
Hall, John B., Sr. V.P. & Sec.--Norbest, Inc., Midvale, UT, pg. 809
Hallmark, Robert J., Sr. V.P.-Claims & Gen. Counsel--Insurance Corp. of America, Houston, TX, pg. 572
Halperin, Richard E., Sr. V.P.--MacAndrews & Forbes Holdings Inc., New York, NY, pg. 694
Hamersley, Gordon, Sr. V.P.--Douglas Elliman, Inc., Southampton, NY, pg. 347
Hammond, Barbara, Sr. V.P.-Sls.--Home Interiors & Gifts, Inc., Dallas, TX, pg. 541
Hampton, John W., Sr. V.P. & Controller--NTS Corporation, Louisville, KY, pg. 781
Hancock, Joyce K., Sr. V.P. & Controller--First Federal of Michigan, Detroit, MI, pg. 414
Hancock, Steve, Sr. V.P., Plng. Dir.--Chiat/Day/Mojo/New York, New York, NY, pg. 244
Handa, Nar, Sr. V.P.--Plastek Group, Erie, PA, pg. 874
Handwerker, William, Sr. V.P.--Nathan's Famous Inc., Westbury, NY, pg. 784
Handy, Tom, Sr. V.P., Assoc. Dir. Bus. Affairs & Admin.--Young & Rubicam New York, New York, NY, pg. 1211
Hanover, Jerome A., Sr. V.P.--Belz Enterprises, Memphis, TN, pg. 138
Hansen, Paul, Sr. V.P., Mngmt. Supvr.--William Douglas McAdams Inc., New York, NY, pg. 726
Hansen, Richard A., Sr. V.P.-Mutual Funds Investments--New York Life Insurance Company, New York, NY, pg. 802
Haper, Charles, Sr. V.P.--Windsor Industries, Inc., Englewood, CO, pg. 1195
Hargreaves, Kenneth L., Sr. V.P.--Massachusetts Mutual Life Insurance Co., Springfield, MA, pg. 718
Harley, Larry, Exec. V.P.-Distr. Group--Mary Kay Cosmetics Inc., Dallas, TX, pg. 716
Harpole, D. Jack, Chief Admin. Officer & Sr. V.P.--Cajun Electric Power Co-op, Baton Rouge, LA, pg. 207
Harrington, Leigh, Sr. V.P.-Actuary--West Coast Life Insurance Co., San Francisco, CA, pg. 795
Harris, Joseph, Sr. V.P. & Treas.--Powell Electronics Inc., Philadelphia, PA, pg. 882
Harris, Lloyd F., Sr. V.P.--First National Bank of Sweetwater, Sweetwater, TX, pg. 412
Harris, Michael, Sr. V.P.--K-J Distributors, Inc., Glendale, AZ, pg. 612
Harrison, Thomas, Sr. V.P., Pub. Rels.--Russ Reid Company, Inc., Pasadena, CA, pg. 923
Hart, David L., V.P. & Asst to Pres.--Ohio Valley Electric Corporation, Piketon, OH, pg. 822
Hartberg, Craig F., Sr. V.P. & Reg. Mgr.-Private Banking--Team Bancshares, Inc., Dallas, TX, pg. 1082
Hartley, Milton E., Sr. V.P.--H. C. Prange Company, Green Bay, WI, pg. 884
Hartnett, Robert M., Sr. V.P. & Gen. Mgr.-Bennagins--S & A Restaurant Corp., Dallas, TX, pg. 958
Hartsell, Larry W., Sr. V.P.--Fredrickson Motor Express Corp., Charlotte, NC, pg. 430
Hassell, Les, Sr. V.P.--Didde Web Press, Emporia, KS, pg. 336
Havel, Rick, Sr. V.P.--Petty Company, Inc., Effingham, IL, pg. 866
Havens, Samuel H., Sr. V.P.-Grp. Dept.--The Prudential Insurance Company of America, Newark, NJ, pg. 896
Hawk, Gerald A., Sr. V.P.--Cole Taylor Bank, Chicago, IL, pg. 260
Hawkes, Thomas, Sr. V.P.-Gen. Counsel--Beech Holdings Corp., Chicago, IL, pg. 131
Hawkins, Stephen A., Sr. V.P.--Massachusetts Mutual Life Insurance Co., Springfield, MA, pg. 718
Hayer, John, Sr. V.P.--Kulite Semiconductor Products, Inc., Leonia, NJ, pg. 646
Hayes, Raymond J., Sr. V.P.-Real Estate Mngmt.--Mutual of America, New York, NY, pg. 777
Haysbert, Reginald G., Sr. V.P.--Parks Sausage Company, Baltimore, MD, pg. 850
Hayward, Cynthia, Sr. V.P.--Chi Systems, Inc., Ann Arbor, MI, pg. 244
Head, Jim, Sr. V.P., Co-Dir.--Grant/Jacoby, Inc., Chicago, IL, pg. 477
Headrick, Jon C., Sr. V.P.--Ameritas Life Insurance Corp., Lincoln, NE, pg. 66
Heartsell, Gordon L., Sr. V.P.--Russell Petroleum Corporation, Montgomery, AL, pg. 957
Hebb, Walter M., Sr. V.P.-Office Products Group--General Binding Corporation, Northbrook, IL, pg. 656
Hechtman, Henry, Sr. V.P. & Dir.-Creative--Keroff & Rosenberg Advertising Inc., Chicago, IL, pg. 624
Heckman, George, Sr. V.P.-Capital Projects--Oglethorpe Power Corp., Tucker, GA, pg. 822
Hedblom, Lawrence, Sr. V.P.--Financial World Partners, New York, NY, pg. 410
Heffernan, Gerard E., Sr. V.P.--Stratton Management Company, Plymouth Meeting, PA, pg. 1053
Heffner, Michael, Sr. V.P., Pub. Rel.--Al Paul Lefton Co., Inc., Public Relations, Philadelphia, PA, pg. 666

Heimbach, Paul A., Sr. V.P.-Engrng./Viacom Networks--Viacom Inc., New York, NY, pg. 785
Heinz, James J., Exec. V.P., Consumer Div. Mgr.--Colle & McVoy, Inc., Minneapolis, MN, pg. 261
Hellams, Howard, Sr. V.P., Creative Services--Newman, Saylor & Gregory, Columbia, SC, pg. 804
Hellberg, S.W., Sr. V.P.--Creative Productions, Pittsburgh, PA, pg. 297
Henderson, W. A. Fred, Sr. V.P.--Spencer Companies Inc., Huntsville, AL, pg. 1030
Hendra, Tom, Sr. V.P.-Mdsg.--ShopKo Stores, Inc., Green Bay, WI, pg. 1000
Hendrickson, Warren J., Sr. V.P.--Knight Architects Engineers Planners, Inc., Chicago, IL, pg. 637
Henry, A. Shafer, Sr. V.P.--E.P. Henry Corporation, Woodbury, NJ, pg. 530
Henry, Robert J., Sr. V.P.--Golden West Homes, Santa Ana, CA, pg. 467
Henry, Roger, Sr. V.P.--Swingster Company, Kansas City, MO, pg. 58
Herman, Joan E., Sr. V.P.-Group Ins.--Phoenix Home Life Mutual Insurance Company, Hartford, CT, pg. 868
Hershberger, Larry D., Sr. V.P.--Teachers Insurance and Annuity Association-College Retirement Equities Fund, New York, NY, pg. 1082
Hertzberg, Mike, Sr. V.P.--JMB Realty Corporation, Chicago, IL, pg. 584
Herzog, Douglas, Sr. V.P.-Programming--MTV: Music Television, New York, NY, pg. 785
Hess, Andy, Sr. V.P.-Corp. Apparel Mdse.--Fishers Big Wheel Inc., New Castle, PA, pg. 415
Hickman, Milton, Sr. V.P.-Specialty Label Div.--Haggar Apparel Company, Dallas, TX, pg. 499
Hickson, Richard, Chief Oper. Officer, Sr. V.P. & Dir.--Holmes Protection Group, Inc., New York, NY, pg. 540
Higashiomori, Hiro, Sr. V.P.--Scripto-Tokai, Inc., Fontana, CA, pg. 983
High, Calvin G., Sr. V.P.--High Industries Inc., Lancaster, PA, pg. 533
Hilker, Louis M., Sr. V.P.-Coord. Scheduling--J.E. Dunn Construction Co., Kansas City, MO, pg. 354
Hill, Colin, Sr. V.P.-Casting Grp.--Esco Corporation, Portland, OR, pg. 388
Hill, G. Stanley, Sr. V.P.-Mktg. & Customer Service--Oglethorpe Power Corp., Tucker, GA, pg. 822
Hill, George E., Sr. V.P.--Golden State Mutual Life Insurance Company, Los Angeles, CA, pg. 467
Hill, Joe, Sr. V.P.--Sullivan Long & Hagerty, Inc., Birmingham, AL, pg. 1057
Hilliard-Jones, Amy, Sr. V.P. & Dir. Integrated Mktg. Services--Burrell Communications Group Inc., Chicago, IL, pg. 195
Himmel, Jeffrey S., Sr. V.P.--Rothschild Inc., New York, NY, pg. 951
Hinchey, Keith, Sr. V.P.--HTB, Inc., Oklahoma City, OK, pg. 497
Hinckley, Edwin N., Sr. V.P.--Tucker Wayne/Luckie & Company, Atlanta, GA, pg. 1118
Hinrichs, Horst, Sr. V.P.-Transportation Prods.--American Standard Inc., New York, NY, pg. 61
Hirsch, Marvin, Sr. V.P.--Goldfarb & Company Advertising, Southfield, MI, pg. 467
Hirschman, Susan C., Sr. V.P. & Editor-in Chief-Greenwillow Books--William Morrow & Co., Inc., New York, NY, pg. 521
Hochberger, Stuart C., Sr. V.P.-Investment--Fiduciary Trust Co. International, New York, NY, pg. 408
Hochhauser, Richard M., Sr. V.P.--Harte-Hanks Communications, Inc., San Antonio, TX, pg. 513
Hockaday, Peter S., Sr. V.P.--MBT Associates, Inc., San Francisco, CA, pg. 691
Hockensmith, James T., Sr. V.P.-Environmental Services--L. Robert Kimball & Associates, Ebensburg, PA, pg. 629
Hoffhines, William A., Sr. V.P. & Mgr. Grand Rapids Div.--First Federal of Michigan, Detroit, MI, pg. 414
Hoffman, Edward N., Sr. V.P.--Miller Advertising Agency Inc., New York, NY, pg. 753
Hoffman, Henry, Sr. V.P.--Tri-State Motor Transit Co., Joplin, MO, pg. 1111
Hogg, Jack B., Sr. V.P.--Better Brands Of Atlanta, Inc., Atlanta, GA, pg. 148
Holland, Louisa, Sr. V.P., Program Dir.--Sudler & Hennessey Consumer Group, New York, NY, pg. 1211
Hollander, Bruce, Sr. V.P.--Don Jagoda Associates, Inc., Melville, NY, pg. 588
Holley, Arthur D., Sr. V.P.--M M I Companies, Inc., Deerfield, IL, pg. 692
Holloway, Douglas, Sr. V.P.-Affiliate Rels.--USA Network, New York, NY, pg. 1124
Holt, Robert D., Sr. V.P.--Ugly Duckling Rent-A-Car, Phoenix, AZ, pg. 1125
Holtgreive, Robert J., Sr. V.P.--Hercules Engines, Inc., Canton, OH, pg. 531
Holton, Donna D., Sr. V.P.--The Penn Mutual Life Insurance Company, Philadelphia, PA, pg. 858
Holtz, Daniel M., Sr. V.P.--Capital Bancorp, Miami, FL, pg. 214
Honbarrier, G. L., V.P.--Central Transport Inc., High Point, NC, pg. 234
Hood, Robert, Sr. V.P. & Chief Fin. Officer--Crowley Maritime Corporation, Oakland, CA, pg. 301
Hooe, Bill, Sr. V.P.--Biggs Gilmore Communications, Kalamazoo, MI, pg. 149
Hooke, T.M., Sr. V.P.--Camelot Communications, Inc., Dallas, TX, pg. 212
Hopp, James A., Sr. V.P. & Gen. Mdsg. Mgr.-Women's Apparel--Elder-Beerman Stores Div., Dayton, OH, pg. 373
Horne, Bob, Sr. V.P., Grp. Dir.--Griffin Bacal Inc., New York, NY, pg. 486
Horowitz, Edward D., Sr. V.P.--National Amusements, Inc., Dedham, MA, pg. 784
Horowitz, Edward D., Sr. V.P.-Tech. & Opers.--Viacom Inc., New York, NY, pg. 785
Horton, Adelaide, Sr. V.P., Chief Opers. Officer-Worldwide--Chiat/Day/Mojo/New York, New York, NY, pg. 244
Horvath, Gary, Sr. V.P.-Recreation--Service America Corporation, Stamford, CT, pg. 992
Hoskins, Kelly L., Sr. V.P., Entertainment Div.--TBWA Kerlick Switzer, Saint Louis, MO, pg. 1071
Hotchner, Ursula, Sr. V.P.--Newman's Own, Inc., Westport, CT, pg. 804
Hothorn, Peter, Sr. V.P.-Food & Beverage--Omni Hotels, Hampton, NH, pg. 826
Housam, Charles, Sr. V.P., Dir.-Plng. & Opers.--Ketchum Advertising/Philadelphia, Philadelphia, PA, pg. 625
Housley, Douglas, G., Sr. V.P.--Topa Thrift & Loan Association, Los Angeles, CA, pg. 1101
Howe, James, Sr. V.P.--Freeman Decorating Co., Dallas, TX, pg. 431
Hoysradt, Jean E., Sr. V.P.-Investment--New York Life Insurance Company, New York, NY, pg. 802
Huber, Charles B., Sr. V.P.--Code-A-Phone Corp., Clackamas, OR, pg. 258
Huberman Goldberg, Marilyn, Sr. V.P.--Muscum Boutique Intercontinental, Ltd., New York, NY, pg. 777
Hudetz, Joseph, Sr. V.P. & Chief Devel. Officer--Solar Press, Inc., Naperville, IL, pg. 1016
Hudson, Jean, Sr. V.P., Media Dir.-Retail--Arnold Fortuna Lawner & Cabot, Boston, MA, pg. 84
Huff, Donald R., Sr. V.P.-Underwriting & Asst. Sec.--Federated Mutual Insurance Company, Owatonna, MN, pg. 405
Hufford, Eugene S., Sr. V.P.--D.A. Davidson & Co., Great Falls, MT, pg. 318
Hughes, Lawrence, Sr. V.P.-Airline & Hub Opers.--DHL Corporation, Redwood City, CA, pg. 309
Hull, Robert W., Sr. V.P.--Harbour Group Ltd., Clayton, MO, pg. 506
Hunt, William G., Jr., Sr. V.P.-Ordinary Agencies Dept.--The Prudential Insurance Company of America, Newark, NJ, pg. 896
Hunter, Barry, Sr. V.P.--Keywell Corporation, Detroit, MI, pg. 629
Hunter, Thomas C., Sr. V.P.--Law Engineering, Inc., Atlanta, GA, pg. 661
Hurley, Skip, Sr. V.P.-Computer Graphic Services--M.E.D. Communications, Woodbridge, NJ, pg. 692
Hussa, Robert R., Sr. V.P.--Rothschild Inc., New York, NY, pg. 951
Hutchins, B., Sr. V.P., Acct. Dir.--Leo Burnett Company Ltd., Toronto,, Canada, pg. 192
Hutchison, J.H., Sr. V.P.--Serigraph, Inc., West Bend, WI, pg. 991
Hyman, Alan, Sr. V.P., Los Angeles--Vitt Media International, Inc., New York, NY, pg. 1153
Hyman, Alan, Sr. V.P.--Vitt Media International, Inc. - Los Angeles, Los Angeles, CA, pg. 1154
Iacono, George, Sr. V.P. & Gen. Mdse. Mgr.-Dept. Store Div.--Schottenstein Stores Corporation, Columbus, OH, pg. 978
Iler, Robert C., Sr. V.P.--Sheehy, Knopf & Shaver, Inc., Louisville, KY, pg. 996
Imbroglio, Joseph A., Sr. V.P.--Strouds, City of Industry, CA, pg. 1054
Isaacson, Scott, Sr. V.P.-Mktg.--Employers Insurance of Wausau a Mutual Co., Wausau, WI, pg. 380
Isaacson, Scott, Sr. V.P.-Mktg.--Employers Insurance of Wausau a Mutual Co., Wausau, WI, pg. 795
Ishee, George, Sr. V.P.--Ergon, Inc., Jackson, MS, pg. 386
Isidore, Tony, Exec. V.P., Creative Dir.--Warwick Baker & Fiore Inc., New York, NY, pg. 1165
Jacobs, Herbert V., Sr. V.P.--Rothschild Inc., New York, NY, pg. 951
Jacobs, Randy, Sr. V.P., Quad City Mgr.--Henry Russell Bruce, Inc., Cedar Rapids, IA, pg. 530
Jahn, David R., Sr. V.P.-South Central Division--Employers Insurance of Wausau a Mutual Co., Wausau, WI, pg. 380
Jahn, David R., Sr. V.P.-South Central Division--Employers Insurance of Wausau a Mutual Co., Wausau, WI, pg. 795
Jain, Naresh, Sr. V.P.--Pincus Bros., Inc., Philadelphia, PA, pg. 870
James, Jeanne, Sr. V.P.--Design 'I Interiors, Los Angeles, CA, pg. 332
James, Roger, Sr. V.P.-Opers.--Sealy Corporation, Cleveland, OH, pg. 985
James, Roger J., Sr. V.P.-Opers.--Ohio-Sealy Mattress Mfg. Co., Inc., Randolph, MA, pg. 985
James, Roger J., Sr. V.P.-Opers.--Ohio-Sealy Mattress Manufacturing Co.-Fort Worth, Richland Hills, TX, pg. 985
James, Roger J., Sr. V.P.-Opers.--Ohio-Sealy Mattress Manufacturing Co.-Houston, Brenham, TX, pg. 985
James, Roger J., Sr. V.P.-Opers.--The Stearns & Foster Bedding Company, Cleveland, OH, pg. 985
James, Roger J., Sr. V.P.-Opers.--The Stearns & Foster Upholstery Furniture Company, Cleveland, OH, pg. 985
James, Roger J., Sr. V.P.-Opers.--Sealy Mattress Company of Albany, Inc., Albany, NY, pg. 985
James, Roger J., Sr. V.P.-Opers.--Sealy of Minnesota, Inc., Saint Paul, MN, pg. 985
James, Roger J., Sr. V.P.-Opers.--Sealy Connecticut, Inc., Oakville, CT, pg. 985
James, Roger J., Sr. V.P.-Opers.--Sealy Mattress Company of Illinois, Batavia, IL, pg. 985
James, Roger J., Sr. V.P.-Opers.--Sealy Mattress Company of Kansas City, Inc., Kansas City, KS, pg. 985
James, Roger J., Sr. V.P.-Opers.--Sealy Mattress Company of Memphis, Memphis, TN, pg. 985
James, Roger J., Sr. V.P.-Opers.--Sealy Mattress Company of Michigan, Inc., Taylor, MI, pg. 985
Jamison, C.H., Sr. V.P.--The Jupiter Corporation, Chicago, IL, pg. 609
Janssen, Dan W., Chm. & Sr. V.P., Canada--Ziebart International Corporation, Troy, MI, pg. 1217
Janz, James F., Sr. V.P.--Zilber, Ltd., Milwaukee, WI, pg. 1219
Jarman, Dan, Sr. V.P. of Phone Div.--Midwest Motel Supply, Aberdeen, SD, pg. 1063
Jarrard, C. Farnham, Jr., Sr. V.P.--Bristol Steel & Iron Works, Inc., Bristol, VA, pg. 176
Jernigan, Jeff, Sr. V.P.--SAE-Pinkerton & Laws Inc., Atlanta, GA, pg. 966
Jeske, Robert, Sr. V.P.-Specialized Transportation Grp.--Atlas Specialized Transportation, Evansville, IN, pg. 97
Jesperson, Daryl, Sr. V.P.--RE/MAX International, Inc., Englewood, CO, pg. 915
Johnson Morris, Rule, Sr. V.P., Dir.-MIS--Ammirati & Puris Inc., New York, NY, pg. 67
Johnson-Becklin, Katherine, Sr. V.P., Acct. Dir.--Stephan & Brady, Incorporated, Madison, WI, pg. 1046
Johnson, Frank M., Sr. V.P.-Retail Mktg.--Associated Grocers, Inc., Seattle, WA, pg. 90
Johnson, James E., Sr. V.P.-Group Div.--The Minnesota Mutual Life Insurance Company, Saint Paul, MN, pg. 757
Johnson, Jim, Sr. V.P.- Creative Services--Cranford Johnson Robinson Woods, Little Rock, AR, pg. 296
Johnson, L. Eugene, Jr., Sr. V.P.--Blue Boar Cafeteria Co., Louisville, KY, pg. 158
Johnson, Michael B., Sr. V.P.--First American Bankshares, Inc., Washington, DC, pg. 412
Johnson, Morris, Sr. V.P. & Exec. Dir.-Art--Goldfarb & Company Advertising, Southfield, MI, pg. 467
Johnson, Peter, Sr. V.P.--MEPC American Properties Incorporated, Dallas, TX, pg. 692
Johnson, Peter N., Sr. V.P.-Chief Oper. Officer--Artesian Resources Corporation, Newark, DE, pg. 86
Johnson, Peter N., Sr. V.P.-Chief Oper. Officer--Artesian Water Company, Inc., Newark, DE, pg. 86
Johnson, Peter N., Sr. V.P.--The Southwood Company, Newark, DE, pg. 87
Johnson, Phil, Sr. V.P., Agribusiness--Colle & McVoy, Inc., Minneapolis, MN, pg. 261
Johnson, Timothy L., V.P. & Mktg. Dir.--MetLife Capital Corporation, Bellevue, WA, pg. 744
Johnson, Victor, Sr. V.P.--Plywood Panels, Inc., New Orleans, LA, pg. 878
Johnston, William M., Sr. V.P.--Southwest Marine, Inc., San Diego, CA, pg. 1023
Johr, R.C., Sr. V.P.--WW Engineering & Science Inc., Grand Rapids, MI, pg. 1058
Jones, Arthur L., Sr. V.P.-Retail Devel.--Associated Grocers, Inc., Seattle, WA, pg. 90
Jones, Bobby L., Sr. V.P.--United American Healthcare Corp., Detroit, MI, pg. 826
Jones, Donald M., Sr. V.P.--Owen Health Care, Houston, TX, pg. 833
Jones, James, Sr. V.P.--Ergon, Inc., Jackson, MS, pg. 386
Jones, Jerry L., Sr. V.P.-Human Res.--Jitney-Jungle Stores of America, Inc., Jackson, MS, pg. 594
Jones, Ron, Sr. V.P.-Distr.--Unistrut Corporation, Ann Arbor, MI, pg. 1130
Jones, Thomas C., Sr. V.P.--High School Division, Boston, MA, pg. 56
Jordon, Preston, Sr. V.P.-Business Support--Blue Cross and Blue Shield Association, Chicago, IL, pg. 159
Joseph, Jerome L., Sr. V.P.--Homes By Dave Brown, Tempe, AZ, pg. 542
Joseph, John, Sr. V.P., Dir.--Ketchum Directory Advertising/Chicago, Chicago, IL, pg. 625
Judd, D.E., Sr. V.P.--Camelot Communications, Inc., Dallas, TX, pg. 212
Judge, Gregg, Sr. V.P.--Ellerbe Becket Construction Services, Minneapolis, MN, pg. 378
June, David M., Sr. V.P. & Controller--Omni Hotels, Hampton, NH, pg. 826
Kahler, Harry, Sr. V.P.--RMS Techs, Inc., Marlton, NJ, pg. 907
Kalelkar, Ashok S., Sr. V.P. & Grp. Officer--Arthur D. Little, Inc., Cambridge, MA, pg. 678
Kalhorn, Gene, Sr. V.P.--Watlow Electric Manufacturing Company, Saint Louis, MO, pg. 1167
Kamer, Joel Y., Sr. V.P.-Retail Distr. Fin. Services--John Hancock Mutual Life Insurance Company, Boston, MA, pg. 595
Kandle, Sally I., Sr. V.P., Casting Dir.--N W Ayer Inc., New York, NY, pg. 104
Kane, John H., Sr. V.P.--Carrafiello, Diehl & Associates, Inc., Irvington, NY, pg. 225
Kanies, Henry, Sr. V.P.--Chattanooga Group, Hixson, TN, pg. 241
Kantor, Bob, Sr. V.P., Grp. Dir.--Griffin Bacal Inc., New York, NY, pg. 486
Karam, Edmund P., Sr. V.P. & Grp. Pres.-General Commodities--Continental Grain Company, New York, NY, pg. 279
Kato, Alex F., Sr. V.P.-Corp. Lending--Great Lakes Bancorp, Ann Arbor, MI, pg. 480
Kato, Norman, Sr. V.P.-Opers.--Nob Hill General Store, Inc., Gilroy, CA, pg. 807
Katz, Enid, Sr. V.P., Dir. Comml. Production--Young & Rubicam Chicago, Chicago, IL, pg. 1211
Katz, Mariam, Sr. V.P.--Katz, Inc., Honesdale, PA, pg. 618
Kauffman, Irv, Sr. V.P.--Sachnowitz & Co., Houston, TX, pg. 965
Kaufman, Arthur, Sr. V.P., Art Grp. Head--Sudler & Hennessey, New York, NY, pg. 1211
Kaufmann, Karl, Sr. V.P., Client Devel.--McCracken Brooks Communications, Inc., Minneapolis, MN, pg. 728
Kay, Herbert, Sr. V.P.--Prime Hospitality Corp., Fairfield, NJ, pg. 889
Keach, G.S., Sr. V.P.--Rodgers Builders, Inc., Charlotte, NC, pg. 942
Keating, Edmund J., Sr. V.P., Grp. Dir.--Griffin Bacal Inc., New York, NY, pg. 486
Keenan, Michael, Sr. V.P., Mng. Dir.--Western International Media Corporation, New York, NY, pg. 1180
Keenan, Steven L., Sr. V.P., Grp. Dir.--Young & Rubicam Chicago, Chicago, IL, pg. 1211
Keim, William, G., Sr. V.P., CLient Services--MCC, Inc., Essex, CT, pg. 691

Keiser, Robert T., Sr. V.P.--Geneve Corporation, Stamford, CT, pg. 451
Keller, Larry J., Sr. V.P.--HTB, Inc., Oklahoma City, OK, pg. 497
Kelley, A. Robert, Sr. V.P.--Allen & Hoshall, Inc., Memphis, TN, pg. 36
Kelley, Jim, Sr. V.P.--Orders Distributing Co., Greenville, SC, pg. 829
Kellman, John, V.P.-Retail Div.--Globe-Amerada Glass Company, Elk Grove Village, IL, pg. 463
Kellman, Michael, V.P.-Natl. Auto Glass Replacement Program--Globe-Amerada Glass Company, Elk Grove Village, IL, pg. 463
Kellman, Robert, V.P.-Auto Glass--Globe-Amerada Glass Company, Elk Grove Village, IL, pg. 463
Kelly, J.M., Sr. V.P.-Mngmt. Information Services--Ingram Micro Inc., Santa Ana, CA, pg. 569
Kelly, Jack, Sr. V.P.-Comml. Mktg.--Preferred Risk Mutual Insurance, West Des Moines, IA, pg. 886
Kelly, Joseph A., Sr. V.P.--LaMarca Group Inc., New York, NY, pg. 652
Kelly, Michael, Sr. V.P., Assoc. Dir.--Ketchum Public Relations/Pittsburgh, Pittsburgh, PA, pg. 625
Kelly, Michael J., Sr. V.P. & Treas.--N W Ayer Incorporated, New York, NY, pg. 103
Kennedy, David O., Sr. V.P.--Lester B. Knight Cast Metals, Inc., Chicago, IL, pg. 637
Kennedy, Marguerite E., Sr. V.P., Media Dir.--Carrafiello, Diehl & Associates, Inc., Irvington, NY, pg. 225
Kenny, Bernard, Sr. V.P.-Southern Div.--Pathmark, Woodbridge, NJ, pg. 1064
Keone, L. Michael, Sr. V.P.-Pacific Agencies--New York Life Insurance Company, New York, NY, pg. 802
Kerry, Alan E., Sr. V.P.--American Trading Real Estate Properties, Inc., Baltimore, MD, pg. 65
Keshner, Fred, Sr. V.P.--Glenoit Mills, Inc., Tarboro, NC, pg. 462
Kessel, Barry, Sr. V.P., Exec. Creative Dir.--Chapman Direct Advertising, New York, NY, pg. 1210
Kevorkian, Aram T., Sr. V.P.--Rochester Midland Corporation, Rochester, NY, pg. 940
Kidder, Norman, Sr. V.P.--Rauland-Borg Corporation, Skokie, IL, pg. 914
Kiefer, John W., Sr. V.P.--Capital Bancorp, Miami, FL, pg. 214
Killeffer, Louis, Sr. V.P., Grp. Dir.--Ammirati & Puris Inc., New York, NY, pg. 67
Killough, James, Sr. V.P.--Post Buckley Schuh & Jernigan, Miami, FL, pg. 881
Kim, Samuel, Sr. V.P., Intl.--Diamond Ad Ltd., Seoul,, Korea, pg. 111
King, Albert R., Sr. V.P. & Mgr.-Mortgage Opers.--First Federal of Michigan, Detroit, MI, pg. 414
King, Ronald F., Sr. V.P.-Information Services--Blue Cross and Blue Shield of Oklahoma, Tulsa, OK, pg. 159
Kingery, Thomas K., Sr. V.P. & Dir.-Stores--Elder-Beerman Stores Div., Dayton, OH, pg. 373
Kingsley, Alfred D., Sr. V.P.--Icahn & Co., Inc., Mount Kisco, NY, pg. 561
Kirk, Wally, Sr. V.P.--Condere Corporation, Hamden, CT, pg. 273
Kirklin, Max F., Sr. V.P.--Allied Security, International, Spokane, WA, pg. 40
Kirkpatrick, Mark, Sr. V.P.--Tucker Wayne/Luckie & Company, Atlanta, GA, pg. 1118
Kirman, Roger, Sr. V.P.-Business Affairs--Viacom Productions Inc., Universal City, CA, pg. 785
Kirsch, Joel, Sr. V.P.-Amity--Amity Leather Products Company, West Bend, WI, pg. 67
Kirschner, Gerold, Sr. V.P.--Glamorise Foundations, Inc., New York, NY, pg. 460
Kislevitz, David, Sr. V.P.--Colorforms, Ramsey, NJ, pg. 265
Kittner, Marc R., Sr. V.P. & Corp. Counsel--Washington Mutual Savings Bank, Seattle, WA, pg. 1166
Klaus, Peter R., Sr. V.P.--Pan American Trade Development Corp., New York, NY, pg. 845
Klee, Marc H., Sr. V.P.--American Funds Advisor Inc., Garden City, NJ, pg. 55
Kleeblatt, James R., Sr. V.P.--Johnston, Lemon & Co. Inc., Washington, DC, pg. 601
Klein, Rochelle, Sr. V.P., Exec. Creative Dir.--Hal Riney & Partners, Inc., New York, NY, pg. 935
Kleinman, Ira J., Sr. V.P.--The Prudential Insurance Company of America, Newark, NJ, pg. 896
Kleva, Gregory A., Jr., Sr. V.P. & Deputy Gen. Counsel--Mutual of America, New York, NY, pg. 777
Klocke, Delmar D., Sr. V.P.--Linder & Associates, Inc., Wichita, KS, pg. 676
Klotz, William H., Sr. V.P.--Cummins-American Corp., Mount Prospect, IL, pg. 304
Kluger, Barry, Sr. V.P.-Media & Network Talent Rels./VH-1--MTV Networks, New York, NY, pg. 785
Kluger, Barry, Sr. V.P.-Media & Network Talent Rels.--VH-1/Video Hits One, New York, NY, pg. 785
Knopf, Robert J., Sr. V.P.-Development--Quadrangle Development Corporation, Washington, DC, pg. 902
Koehn, Ronald M., Sr. V.P.-College Program Devel.--American Institute For Foreign Study, Greenwich, CT, pg. 56
Koffman, Richard E., Sr. V.P.--Great American Industries, Inc., Vestal, NY, pg. 480
Kolar, Susan, Sr. V.P. & Chief Fin. Officer--Viacom Entertainment, New York, NY, pg. 785
Kolius, Donna Ramsdell, Sr. V.P.-Portfolio Services Div.--CB Commercial Real Estate Group Central Division, Houston, TX, pg. 222
Kopas, Kenneth, Sr. V.P., Media Dir.--Sudler & Hennessey Consumer Group, New York, NY, pg. 1211
Koppele, Gary S., Sr. V.P.--Big V Supermarkets, Inc., Florida, NY, pg. 149
Korff, Ira A., Sr. V.P.--Viacom Inc., New York, NY, pg. 785
Kostka, Lauson, Sr. V.P.--Ellerbe Becket Construction Services, Minneapolis, MN, pg. 378
Kramer, C. David, Sr. V.P.--Godfrey Advertising, Lancaster, PA, pg. 464
Kreisle, William, Sr. V.P.--Warmington Homes, Costa Mesa, CA, pg. 1164
Kreisler, Mark, Sr. V.P.-Whirlpool Div.--Hamburg Brothers Inc., Pittsburgh, PA, pg. 502
Kreitzer, Roderick G., Pres. & Chief Exec. Officer--Baker Knapp & Tubbs Inc., Grand Rapids, MI, pg. 640
Kremer, Abraham, Sr. V.P.--Warren/Kremer/CMP/Advertising/Inc., New York, NY, pg. 1165
Krieger, James F., Sr. V.P.--Standard Medical Imaging, Inc., Columbia, MD, pg. 1037
Kring, Gail, Sr. V.P.--Plains Co-op Oil Mill, Lubbock, TX, pg. 873
Krissoff, Robert, Sr. V.P.-Consumer Div.--Murry's, Inc., Forestville, MD, pg. 777
Kronen, Eric, Sr. V.P.-Puget Sound--Viacom Cable, Pleasanton, CA, pg. 785
Kronenberger, Robert, Chief Fin. Officer, Sr. V.P. & Treas.--Petty Company, Inc., Effingham, IL, pg. 866
Kronfeld, Gary H., Sr. V.P.--Spirite Industries, Inc., Englewood, NJ, pg. 1031
Kruse, Jim, V.P.--Schneider Commercial Real Estate, Orange, CA, pg. 977
Kubas, S.L., Sr. V.P.--WW Engineering & Science Inc., Grand Rapids, MI, pg. 1058
La Blina, William, Sr. V.P.--Helmsley Enterprises, Inc., New York, NY, pg. 527
La Rose, Peter, Sr. V.P.-Electronics--Nelson & Small Inc., Portland, ME, pg. 798
LaBastie, James G., Sr. V.P.--Law Engineering, Inc., Atlanta, GA, pg. 661
Lacey, L.A., Jr., Sr. V.P.--Ingram Distribution Group Inc., La Vergne, TN, pg. 569
LaFontaine, Louis J., Sr. V.P.-Corp. Affairs--The Mutual Life Insurance Company of New York (MONY), New York, NY, pg. 778
Lambert, Mary-Ann, Sr. V.P.--MacNamara, Klein & Solin Inc., New York, NY, pg. 698
Lamm, Kenneth R., Sr. V.P.--Cramer-Krasselt, Milwaukee, WI, pg. 296
Lance, James A., Sr. V.P.--The Elder-Beerman Stores Corp., Dayton, OH, pg. 373
Lance, Walter C., Sr. V.P., Controller & Asst. Sec.--N W Ayer Incorporated, New York, NY, pg. 103
Lanchner, Bertrand M., Sr. V.P., Legal & Sec.--N W Ayer Incorporated, New York, NY, pg. 103
Landi, Val, Sr. V.P.--CW Publishing, Inc., Framingham, MA, pg. 576
Langford, Frederick K., Sr. V.P.-Intl. Aerosol--Precision Valve Corporation, Yonkers, NY, pg. 885
Langmead, Jeffrey P., Sr. V.P. & Chief Oper. Officer--Blue Cross & Blue Shield of Texas, Inc., Richardson, TX, pg. 160
Lanzano, Steven, Sr. V.P., Group Media Dir.--Ammirati & Puris Inc., New York, NY, pg. 67
LaRocca, Robert, Sr. V.P.--Carrafiello, Diehl & Associates, Inc., Irvington, NY, pg. 225
Larson, Dale F., Sr. V.P. & Grp. Pres.-World Milling Industries--Continental Grain Company, New York, NY, pg. 279
Larson, Lloyd J., Sr. V.P.--Stanley Consultants, Inc., Muscatine, IA, pg. 961
Lasalandra, Peter, Sr. V.P.-Fin.--American Institute For Foreign Study, Greenwich, CT, pg. 56
Lasday, Louis, Sr. V.P.--Hallmark Advertising, Inc., Pittsburgh, PA, pg. 501
Lastihenos, Jerry, Sr. V.P.--Hazen & Sawyer, New York, NY, pg. 520
Laughinghouse, Gary J., Sr. V.P. & Gen. Mgr.--Phoenix Home Life Mutual Insurance Company, Hartford, CT, pg. 868
Lauren, Jerry, Sr. V.P.-Mens Design--Polo/Ralph Lauren Corporation, New York, NY, pg. 879
Lautensack Jr., Robert G., Sr. V.P.--Phoenix Home Life Mutual Insurance Company, Hartford, CT, pg. 868
Lauterbach, Dennis, Sr. V.P.-Branch Oper.--Montgomery Elevator Company, Moline, IL, pg. 767
Laval, Larry, V.P.-Carpets--William M. Bird & Co., Inc., Charleston, SC, pg. 152
Lavelle, Timothy E., Sr. V.P. & Mng. Dir.--Trident Financial Corporation, Raleigh, NC, pg. 1113
Layfield, Debbi B., Sr. V.P.--Grizzard Advertising, Inc., Atlanta, GA, pg. 488
Laytin, William M., Sr. V.P. & Legal Counsel--The Hassinger Companies, Itasca, IL, pg. 516
Leadingham, Deanna R., V.P.--The El-Bee Chargit Corp., Dayton, OH, pg. 373
Leahy, Robert B., Sr. V.P.--Folger Nolan Fleming Douglas, Washington, DC, pg. 422
LeCroy, Edwin P., Jr., Sr. V.P.--Durham Transportation, Inc., Austin, TX, pg. 354
Lee, Rhoady R., Sr., Sr. V.P.--Lakeside Industries, Redmond, WA, pg. 651
Leedom, John N., Jr., Sr. V.P.--Wholesale Electronic Supply, Dallas, TX, pg. 1188
Leeds, Dale, Sr. V.P.--Zapiecki & Partners Inc., Toledo, OH, pg. 1216
Lemons, Richard M., Sr. V.P.--Knight Architects Engineers Planners, Inc., Chicago, IL, pg. 637
Lesman, Howard, Sr. V.P., Grp. Dir.--Ammirati & Puris Inc., New York, NY, pg. 67
Less, Theodore D., Sr. V.P.--Frank Consolidated Enterprises Inc., Des Plaines, IL, pg. 428
Leung, Robert, Sr. V.P.--Carrafiello, Diehl & Associates, Inc., Irvington, NY, pg. 225
Levenson, Al, Sr. V.P.--Ostrow Textile Co., Inc., Rock Hill, SC, pg. 831
Levi, Malcolm, Jr., Sr. V.P.--Mayer Myers Paper Company, Memphis, TN, pg. 724
Levin, Larry, Sr. V.P.-Special Projects--New World Entertainment, Inc., Los Angeles, CA, pg. 74
Levine, Joan, Sr. V.P.--Concord Assets Group, Inc., Boca Raton, FL, pg. 272
Levy, Glenn, Sr. V.P., Creative Supvr.--Sudler & Hennessey Consumer Group, New York, NY, pg. 1211
Levy, Larry, Sr. V.P.-Electronics Div.--Hamburg Brothers Inc., Pittsburgh, PA, pg. 502
Lewis, David J., Sr. V.P.-Environmental--Cogentrix Incorporated, Charlotte, NC, pg. 258
Lewis, James E., Sr. V.P.--First American Bankshares, Inc., Washington, DC, pg. 412
Lewis, Richard, Sr. V.P., Mngmt. Supvr.--TBWA Advertising, Inc., New York, NY, pg. 1071
Lewis, Stanley R., Sr. V.P.--HTB, Inc., Oklahoma City, OK, pg. 497
Libera, John J., Sr. V.P.--Massachusetts Mutual Life Insurance Co., Springfield, MA, pg. 718
Lick, David, Chief Fin. Officer & Sr. V.P.--Western Development Corporation, Washington, DC, pg. 1179
Liebgold, Peter, Sr. V.P.--Pan American Trade Development Corp., New York, NY, pg. 845
Linakis, John S., Sr. V.P.-Transporation & Pur.--American Institute For Foreign Study, Greenwich, CT, pg. 56
Lindroth, John G., Sr. V.P.-Domestic Sls.--General Binding Corporation, Northbrook, IL, pg. 656
Lineback, Charles D., Sr. V.P.-Reinsurance Div.--American United Life Insurance Company, Indianapolis, IN, pg. 65
Lintner, Richard P., Sr. V.P.--Weaver Popcorn Company, Inc., Van Buren, IN, pg. 1170
Lipeles, Richard, Sr. V.P. & Pres.-Pacificare California--PacifiCare Health Systems, Inc., Cypress, CA, pg. 1127
Lippman, Stacey, Sr. V.P., Corp. Media Dir.--Chiat/Day/Mojo/New York, New York, NY, pg. 244
Lipton, Sy, Sr. V.P.--Warren/Kremer/CMP/Advertising/Inc., New York, NY, pg. 1165
Lister, Harry J., Sr. V.P.--Johnston, Lemon & Co. Inc., Washington, DC, pg. 601
Little, S.W., Sr. V.P.-Book Prod. Group--Ingram Book Company, La Vergne, TN, pg. 569
Lloyd, Eugene W., Sr. V.P.--Torcon, Inc., Westfield, NJ, pg. 1102
Lloyd, Peter, Sr. V.P.--Price/McNabb, Inc., Asheville, NC, pg. 888
Lockwood, D.E., Sr. V.P.--Fish Engineering & Construction, Inc., Houston, TX, pg. 414
Loev, Gerald, Sr. V.P.--The Prudential Insurance Company of America, Newark, NJ, pg. 896
Loftus, William A., Sr. V.P.--Ace Hardware Corporation, Oak Brook, IL, pg. 12
Lombardo, P.M., Sr. V.P.--Del American Properties, Inc., Maitland, FL, pg. 325
Long, Phil, Exec. V.P.--Biggs Gilmore Communications, Kalamazoo, MI, pg. 149
Long, Robert E., Sr. V.P. & Admin.--Park Bank, Milwaukee, WI, pg. 118
Long, Wm. J., Sr. V.P.--Sullivan Long & Hagerty, Inc., Birmingham, AL, pg. 1057
Longmoore, John T., Sr. V.P.-Group Pensions--John Hancock Mutual Life Insurance Company, Boston, MA, pg. 595
Looney, Vincent J., Sr. V.P. & Reg. Office Admin.--Utica Mutual Insurance Company, New Hartford, NY, pg. 1140
Lopez, John M., Sr. V.P.--Philadelphia Sign Company, Palmyra, NJ, pg. 867
Losee, Thomas P., Jr., Sr. V.P. & Publishing Dir.--Knapp Communications Corporation, Los Angeles, CA, pg. 636
Losee, Tom, Sr. V.P. & Publishing Dir.--Architectural Digest, Los Angeles, CA, pg. 636
Losee, Tom, Sr. V.P. & Publishing Dir.--Bon Appetit Magazine, Los Angeles, CA, pg. 636
Louis, Kenneth C., Sr. V.P.-Individual Markets--Ameritas Life Insurance Corp., Lincoln, NE, pg. 66
Love, Jimmy, Sr. V.P. & Sec.--T.L. James & Company, Ruston, LA, pg. 588
Lovett, M.F., Chief Fin. Officer & Sr. V.P.--Ingram Book Company, La Vergne, TN, pg. 569
Lowe, Scott, Sr. V.P., Assoc. Dir. Local Brdcst.--Young & Rubicam New York, New York, NY, pg. 1211
Lowenfels, Fred, Sr. V.P. & Gen. Counsel--Transammonia Inc., New York, NY, pg. 1106
Lozier, Mark, Sr. V.P.--Keywell Corporation, Detroit, MI, pg. 629
Lucas, Bill L., Sr. V.P.--Human Resources--Associated Merchandising Corp., New York, NY, pg. 91
Lucien, Kent T., Sr. V.P. & Treas.--Ka'u Agribusiness Co., Inc., Pahala, HI, pg. 174
Luckie, Bob, III, Sr. V.P.--Tucker Wayne/Luckie & Company, Birmingham, AL, pg. 1118
Luckwaldt, Herbert, Sr. V.P.-Oper.--Beech Holdings Corp., Chicago, IL, pg. 131
Luckwaldt, Herbert, Sr. V.P.-Oper.--Budget Rent A Car Corporation, Lisle, IL, pg. 131
Lunde, Mark R., Sr. V.P., Internal Services-Des Moines--Creswell, Munsell, Fultz & Zirbel, Cedar Rapids, IA, pg. 1211
Lunt, Dan, Sr. V.P.--WordPerfect Corporation, Orem, UT, pg. 1202
Lutz, Wayne, V.P.-Corp. Affairs--Taco John's International, Inc., Cheyenne, WY, pg. 1076
Lydic, John R., Sr. V.P., Dir.-Fin. & Controller--Harley Ellington Pierce Yee Associates, Inc., Southfield, MI, pg. 509
Mabee, Betty L., Sr. V.P.--Big Bear Supermarkets No. 3, San Diego, CA, pg. 149
MacKinnon, Malcolm D., Sr. V.P.-IIS & A--The Prudential Insurance Company of America, Newark, NJ, pg. 896
MacLeod, Robert, Sr. V.P. & Publr.-Teen--Petersen Publishing Company, Los Angeles, CA, pg. 864
MacWilliams, Kenneth E., Sr. V.P.-Gateway Investors--The Prudential Insurance Company of America, Newark, NJ, pg. 896
Madia, Daniel R., Sr. V.P., Asst. to the Pres.--Ketchum Communications Inc., Pittsburgh, PA, pg. 625
Madia, Dr. William J., Sr. V.P.--Battelle Memorial Institute, Columbus, OH, pg. 126
Madison, David J., Sr. V.P.--YPMS/TMP Worldwide, Inc., Mequon, WI, pg. 1074

Magalska, J.M., Sr. V.P., Grp. & Retire Oper.--Employers Insurance of Wausau a Mutual Co., Wausau, WI, pg. 380
Magalska, J.M., Sr. V.P., Grp. & Retire Oper.--Employers Insurance of Wausau a Mutual Co., Wausau, WI, pg. 795
Magee, Stephen J., Sr. V.P., Creative Supvr.--N W Ayer Inc., New York, NY, pg. 104
Magnolia, Rudy N., Sr. V.P.--YPMS/TMP Worldwide, Inc., Mequon, WI, pg. 1074
Maher, Frank, Sr. V.P., Gen. Mgr.--Ayer Chicago, Chicago, IL, pg. 104
Maier, Carl, Sr. V.P.--Advertising To Women, Inc., New York, NY, pg. 21
Malcolm, A. Carlton, Jr., Sr. V.P.--Tucker Wayne/Luckie & Company, Atlanta, GA, pg. 1118
Maleu, Gordon, Sr. V.P.--Holsum Foods, Waukesha, WI, pg. 515
Malone, Joe N., Sr. V.P. & Chief Oper. Officer--Sound Warehouse, Inc., Dallas, TX, pg. 1018
Mancuso, Richard, Sr. V.P. & Chief Fin. Officer--Associated Merchandising Corp., New York, NY, pg. 91
Manfredi, Robert R., Sr. V.P.--RTKL Associates Inc., Baltimore, MD, pg. 908
Manion, F. William, Sr. V.P. & Mgr.-Branch Opers.--First Federal of Michigan, Detroit, MI, pg. 414
Manley, John E., Sr. V.P.-Fin. Advisory Services--Mutual of America, New York, NY, pg. 777
Mann, Donald, Sr. V.P.--World's Finest Chocolate, Inc., Chicago, IL, pg. 1203
Manning, Michael P., Sr. Exec. V.P. & Chief Investment Officer--Mutual of Omaha Fund Management Co., Omaha, NE, pg. 779
Mantel, Wendy, Sr. V.P., Acct. Supvr.--Sudler & Hennessey, New York, NY, pg. 1211
Manukas, George, Sr. V.P. & Chief Fin. Officer--DKM Building Enterprises, L.P., Lawrenceville, NJ, pg. 357
Marcus, H. Gwen, Sr. V.P. & Gen. Counsel-Showtime Networks-Viacom Inc., New York, NY, pg. 785
Maresco, Richard, Sr. V.P.--Robinson Export-Import Corporation, Springfield, VA, pg. 748
Marginsm, Bill, Sr. V.P.-West Territory--Montgomery Ward & Co., Inc., Chicago, IL, pg. 767
Marhefka, Roger P., Sr. V.P.-Mktg.--Rothschild Inc., New York, NY, pg. 951
Marine, Jack J., Sr. V.P.--Capital Pants Co., Philadelphia, PA, pg. 215
Markell, Andrew S., Sr. V.P.--League General Insurance Co., Detroit, MI, pg. 205
Marklin, George, Sr. V.P.--Watlow Electric Manufacturing Company, Saint Louis, MO, pg. 1167
Markoul, John, Sr. V.P.--National Reproductions Corporation, Madison Heights, MI, pg. 793
Marks, Gordon W., Sr. V.P.--Swinerton & Walberg Co., San Francisco, CA, pg. 1068
Marks, Jeff, Sr. V.P., Grp. Dir.--Griffin Bacal Inc., New York, NY, pg. 486
Marlatt, M. Andy, Sr. V.P.--Owen Health Care, Houston, TX, pg. 833
Marlow, James, Sr. V.P. & Chief Fin. Officer--Varityper, Inc., East Hanover, NJ, pg. 1146
Maron, Gerard F., Sr. V.P.-Mid-Atlantic Region--United States Cold Storage, Inc., Cherry Hill, NJ, pg. 1135
Marr, Richard A., Sr. V.P.--Stanley Consultants, Inc., Muscatine, IA, pg. 961
Marteney, Virginia, Sr. V.P.--Packaging Products & Design, Santa Ana, CA, pg. 842
Martin, Jim, Sr. V.P., Acct. Services--MCKONE & CO., INC., Irving, TX, pg. 731
Martin, Julian, Sr. V.P., Acct. Dir.--Chiat/Day/Mojo, London, United Kingdom, pg. 245
Martin, Ray, Sr. V.P.--Bernard Johnson Incorporated, Houston, TX, pg. 598
Martin, Ronald, Sr. V.P. & Chief Fin. Officer--Mayflower Transit, Inc., Carmel, IN, pg. 724
Martincic, Joseph, Sr. V.P.-Admin.--Blue Cross & Blue Shield of Oregon, Portland, OR, pg. 160
Martinez, Gary W., Sr. V.P.--Phoenix American Incorporated, San Rafael, CA, pg. 868
Martinez, Luis, Sr. V.P., Grp. Acct. Supvr.--Ross Roy Inc., Bloomfield Hills, MI, pg. 950
Martinez, Robert T., Sr. V.P.-Intermodal--Lykes Bros. Steamship Co., Inc., New Orleans, LA, pg. 688
Martocchie, James, Sr. V.P.--Graphic Center, Inc., Bloomfield, CT, pg. 478
Marziano, Peter, Sr. V.P.--H. Freeman & Son, Inc., Philadelphia, PA, pg. 431
Masket, Steven N., Sr. V.P. & Gen. Counsel--Maidenform, Inc., New York, NY, pg. 701
Mason, Paul, Sr. V.P.-Productions--Viacom Productions Inc., Universal City, CA, pg. 785
Mathison, Robert J., Sr. V.P.--Washington Mutual Savings Bank, Seattle, WA, pg. 1166
Matteo, Anthony, Sr. V.P.--The Kobacker Company & Affiliates, Columbus, OH, pg. 638
Matthews, Harold, Sr. V.P.--Allright Corporation, Houston, TX, pg. 41
Matthews, Jerry, Sr. V.P.-Fin.--D & W Food Centers, Inc., Grand Rapids, MI, pg. 308
Maull, Robert W., Sr. V.P. & Actuary--Mutual of America, New York, NY, pg. 777
Mauro, Scott, Sr. V.P.-Arts & Entertainment Div.--Great Scott Advertising Co. Inc., New York, NY, pg. 482
Maycock, Ian D., Sr. V.P.--Hunt Oil International Exploration-Fountain Place, Dallas, TX, pg. 554
Maycock, Jan D., Sr. V.P.-Intl. Exploration--Hunt Oil Company, Dallas, TX, pg. 553
Mayer, Karl, Sr. V.P.--Oxford Realty Services Corp., Bethesda, MD, pg. 835
Mayo, A.R., Sr. V.P.-Sugar Houses--United States Sugar Corporation, Clewiston, FL, pg. 1137
Mayorek, John, Sr. V.P.--Conair Corporation, Stamford, CT, pg. 272
Mazur, Daniel, Sr. V.P.-Branded Goods--Topco Associates, Inc., Skokie, IL, pg. 1101
McAlpine, Kingsley, Sr. V.P.--Lily of France, Inc., New York, NY, pg. 147
McCarter, John N., Jr., Sr. V.P.--Defender Services, Inc., Columbia, SC, pg. 324
McCarthy, Francis F., Sr. V.P.--McCarthy Building Companies, Saint Louis, MO, pg. 727
McCarthy, Ruth L., Sr. V.P.--Carrafiello, Diehl & Associates, Inc., Irvington, NY, pg. 225
McClellan, Bill T., Sr. V.P.--The Paty Company, Piney Flats, TN, pg. 852
McClellan, Robert E., Jr., Sr. V.P.--Florists' Mutual Insurance Co., Edwardsville, IL, pg. 421
McClelland, Dave, Sr. V.P.--Pacifica Services, Inc., Pasadena, CA, pg. 842
McClun, Jerry, Sr. V.P., Media--Russ Reid Company, Inc., Pasadena, CA, pg. 923
McCrone, Carol, Sr. V.P.--Warren/Kremer/CMP/Advertising/Inc., New York, NY, pg. 1165
McDiarmid, Robert, Sr. V.P.--Della Construction Co. Inc., Enfield, CT, pg. 326
McDonald, John, Sr. V.P.--Christy's Markets, Inc., Brockton, MA, pg. 249
McElmurray, William T., Sr. V.P.--Massachusetts Mutual Life Insurance Co., Springfield, MA, pg. 718
McEvoy, Dan, Sr. V.P.-Residental--Tucson Realty & Trust Co., Tucson, AZ, pg. 1118
McGreevy, M. Kenneth, Sr. V.P.--Prudential-LMI Commercial Insurance Company, Mansfield, OH, pg. 897
McGregor, Gerald L., Sr. V.P.-Claims--Farm Family Mutual Insurance Co., Glenmont, NY, pg. 401
McIntosh, Robert, Sr. V.P. & Dir.-Service Mngmt.--Omni Hotels, Hampton, NH, pg. 826
McIntyre, William D., Chief Oper. Officer--American Speedy Printing Centers, Inc., Bloomfield Hills, MI, pg. 61
McKenna, Jim, Sr. V.P.--Davis, Ball & Colombatto Advertising, Inc., Los Angeles, CA, pg. 318
McKeon, James C., Sr. V.P.--Massachusetts Mutual Life Insurance Co., Springfield, MA, pg. 718
McKernan, Richard, Sr. V.P.--Canberra Industries, Inc., Meriden, CT, pg. 213
McLaughlin, Michael J., Sr. V.P. & Deputy Gen. Counsel--New York Life Insurance Company, New York, NY, pg. 802
McLellan, Kenneth H., Jr., Sr. V.P.--Chicago Corp., Chicago, IL, pg. 247
McMahon, C.J., Sr. V.P.--Villaume Industries, Inc., Saint Paul, MN, pg. 1151
McMillan, J.H., Sr. V.P.-Construction--Esco Elevators, Inc., Fort Worth, TX, pg. 388
McNamara, Maureen, Sr. V.P., Dir. Strategic Plng. & Media Services--Arnold Fortuna Lawner & Cabot, Boston, MA, pg. 84
McNeil, Gary L., Sr. V.P.--ASCG, Inc., Portland, OR, pg. 7
McPhee, Ronald P., Sr. V.P.--Teachers Insurance and Annuity Association-College Retirement Equities Fund, New York, NY, pg. 1082
McQueeney, Thomas, Sr. V.P., Dir. Bus. Affairs & Admin.--Young & Rubicam New York, New York, NY, pg. 1211
McReynolds, Richard, Sr. V.P.--Tucker Wayne/Luckie & Company, Atlanta, GA, pg. 1118
McShane, Kevin, Sr. V.P., Creative Dir./Copy--William Douglas McAdams Inc., New York, NY, pg. 726
McShulkis, Joseph, Sr. V.P.--Atlantic Aviation Corp., New Castle, DE, pg. 94
Mears, James, Sr. V.P.--Mears Transportation Group, Orlando, FL, pg. 734
Meeks, James E., Sr. V.P., Acctg. Dir., Special Projects--Creswell, Munsell, Fultz & Zirbel, Cedar Rapids, IA, pg. 1211
Megna, Michael S., Sr. V.P.--American Appraisal Associates, Inc., Milwaukee, WI, pg. 48
Mendelson, Stuart, Sr. V.P.-Food Service--Murry's, Inc., Forestville, MD, pg. 777
Mendelson, Stuat, Sr. V.P.-Food Service--Murry's, Inc., Forestville, MD, pg. 777
Mennen, Barnett, M.D., Sr. V.P., Medical & Mktg. Dir.--William Douglas McAdams Inc., New York, NY, pg. 726
Merk, Rick, Sr. V.P.--Hancock Lumber, Inc., Casco, ME, pg. 504
Merkert, Tighe, Sr. V.P.--Service America Corporation, Stamford, CT, pg. 992
Merrill, Keniston P., Sr. V.P. & Chief Investment Officer--National Life Insurance Company, Montpelier, VT, pg. 791
Merriman, Mark, Sr. V.P., Grp. Supvr.--Sudler & Hennessey, New York, NY, pg. 1211
Metzner, R.H., Sr. V.P.--Brierley & Partners, Dallas, TX, pg. 175
Mevorah, Sam, Sr. V.P.--Heyman Corporation, Niles, IL, pg. 532
Meyer, William A., Sr. V.P.--Great Lakes Lithograph Co., Cleveland, OH, pg. 481
Meyers, Robert G., Sr. V.P.--Defender Services, Inc., Columbia, SC, pg. 324
Michael, Robert W., Sr. V.P. & Grp. Exec.--Walter Industries, Inc., Tampa, FL, pg. 1161
Miksis-Zivic, Rosemarie, Sr. V.P. & Assoc. Dir.-Creative--Towne, Silverstein, Rotter Inc., New York, NY, pg. 1104
Milam, Christopher, Sr. V.P.--Golub & Co., Chicago, IL, pg. 469
Miles, Richard, Exec. V.P.--CSE Corporation, San Francisco, CA, pg. 204
Millas, Tim, Exec. V.P., Creative Dir.-CMC--Sudler & Hennessey, New York, NY, pg. 1211
Miller, Chris, Sr. V.P. & Gen. Mgr. Popeyes--Al Copeland Enterprises, Inc., Jefferson, LA, pg. 283
Miller, Chris, Sr. V.P.-Popeye's--Church's Fried Chicken, Inc., Jefferson, LA, pg. 284
Miller, Elaine, Sr. V.P., Media & Support--Gerber Advertising, Portland, OR, pg. 453
Miller, Harlan, Sr. V.P.--Marcus Advertising, Inc., Cleveland, OH, pg. 706
Miller, Raymond P., Sr. V.P.--Shannon & Wilson, Inc., Seattle, WA, pg. 995
Milliken, George, Sr. V.P.--Davis, Ball & Colombatto Advertising, Inc., Los Angeles, CA, pg. 318
Milne, Malcolm R., Sr. V.P. & Treas.--First Federal of Michigan, Detroit, MI, pg. 414
Minihan, Robert, Sr. V.P., Assoc. Creative Dir.--Arnold Fortuna Lawner & Cabot, Boston, MA, pg. 84
Mische, Eric F., Sr. V.P.--Brown & Caldwell Consulting Engineers, Pleasant Hill, CA, pg. 181
Mitchell, Richard A., Sr. V.P.--Cresmer, Woodward, O'Mara & Ormsbee, New York, NY, pg. 298
Mitchell, Sandy, Sr. V.P., Admin. Mgr., Consumer Res.--Young & Rubicam New York, New York, NY, pg. 1211
Moix, M.H., Jr., Sr. V.P.--Nabholz Construction Corp., Conway, AR, pg. 782
Montague, C.H., Sr. V.P.--Peoples Gas System, Inc., Tampa, FL, pg. 689
Moody, Joe R., Sr. V.P.-Electrical--The Benham Group, Oklahoma City, OK, pg. 138
Moon, Franklin, Sr. V.P.--Bernard Johnson Incorporated, Houston, TX, pg. 598
Moore, Alan, Sr. V.P.-No. Asian Region--Dentsu Wunderman Direct Inc., Tokyo,, Japan, pg. 1213
Moore, David, Sr. V.P.-Grp. Ins.--Ameritas Life Insurance Corp., Lincoln, NE, pg. 66
Moore, Howard, Sr. V.P.--Century Business Credit Corporation, New York, NY, pg. 235
Moore, J.L., Jr., Sr. V.P. & Dir.--Bechtel Group, Inc., San Francisco, CA, pg. 130
Moore, Michael, Sr. V.P.--Atlantic Gulf Communities Corporation, Miami, FL, pg. 95
Moore, P.J., Sr. V.P., Chief Oper. Officer, Chief Fin. Officer, Sec. & Treas.--Green Holdings, Inc., Denver, CO, pg. 484
Moore, P.J., Sr. V.P., Chief Fin. Officer, Sec. & Treas.--Green International, Inc., Denver, CO, pg. 484
Moore, P.J., Sr. V.P., Sec. & Treas.--Green Mining, Inc., Denver, CO, pg. 484
Moore, P.J., Sr. V.P., Treas. & Sec.--C.C. Conley & Sons, Inc., Denver, CO, pg. 484
Moore, P.J., Sr. V.P., Sec. & Treas.--Green International-Guyana, Inc., Denver, CO, pg. 484
Moore, P.J., Sr. V.P.--Northland Alaska, Inc., Anchorage, AK, pg. 484
Moore, T.M., Sr. V.P.-Insurance Oper.--Millers' Mutual Insurance Assn. Of Illinois, Alton, IL, pg. 755
Moores, Ronald, Sr. V.P.--Kulite Semiconductor Products, Inc., Leonia, NJ, pg. 646
Morais, Robert J., Sr. V.P.--Carrafiello, Diehl & Associates, Inc., Irvington, NY, pg. 225
Morano, Barbara, Sr. V.P., Dir. Media Plng. & Dev.--Sudler & Hennessey, New York, NY, pg. 1211
Morgan, Donald, Sr. V.P., Acct. Group Supvr.--William Douglas McAdams Inc., New York, NY, pg. 726
Morgan, James L., Sr. V.P.-Surveying & Mapping--L. Robert Kimball & Associates, Ebensburg, PA, pg. 629
Morgan, Michele, Sr. V.P.--Juhl Marketing Communications, Mishawaka, IN, pg. 608
Morgan, Ross L., Sr. V.P.--UES, Inc., Dayton, OH, pg. 1122
Morketter, Ronald C., Sr. V.P.-Engrng. & Tech.--Harley Ellington Pierce Yee Associates, Inc., Southfield, MI, pg. 509
Morong, C. Oscar, Jr., Sr. V.P.--Teachers Insurance and Annuity Association-College Retirement Equities Fund, New York, NY, pg. 1082
Morris, Edward J., Sr. V.P.--Rothschild Inc., New York, NY, pg. 951
Morris, James V., Sr. V.P.--Security Industrial Insurance Co., Inc., Donaldsonville, LA, pg. 832
Morris, Joseph D., Sr. V.P.--Sullivan Long & Hagerty, Inc., Birmingham, AL, pg. 1057
Morrisey, Dolores J., Sr. V.P.--Mutual of America, New York, NY, pg. 777
Morrison, Robert E., Sr. V.P.--Summa Corporation, Las Vegas, NV, pg. 1057
Morton, Mary, Sr. V.P., Grp. Mngmt. Supvr.--Chiat/Day/Mojo/New York, New York, NY, pg. 244
Moser, Bill, Sr. V.P., Vehicle Systems--Marketing Resources of America, Inc., Overland Park, KS, pg. 709
Moskowitz, Lori, Sr. V.P. & Dir., Acct. Services--Frankfurt Gips Balkind, Advertising, New York, NY, pg. 429
Mottier, Bradley D., Sr. V.P.--Unison Industries, Jacksonville, FL, pg. 1130
Mottier, Bradley D., Sr. V.P.--Unison Industries, Jacksonville, FL, pg. 1130
Moxhan, A.J., Sr. V.P.--Pacific Scene Inc., San Diego, CA, pg. 841
Mueller, Edward L., Sr. V.P.-Estimating--Baker Concrete Construction, Inc., Monroe, OH, pg. 115
Mullen, George J., Jr., Sr. V.P.--Fiduciary Trust Company International, New York, NY, pg. 408
Mullins, Tom, Sr. V.P.--Western International Media Corporation, Los Angeles, CA, pg. 1179
Mullock, Paul S., Sr. V.P.-Sls.--Alliance America, Norcross, GA, pg. 37
Murphy, David, Sr. V.P. & Gen. Mgr.--Fayva--Morse Shoe, Inc., Canton, MA, pg. 772
Murphy, David G., Sr. V.P.--Washington Mutual Savings Bank, Seattle, WA, pg. 1166
Murphy, Michael A., Sr. V.P. & Mng. Dir.--Trident Financial Corporation, Raleigh, NC, pg. 1113
Murphy, Mike, Sr. V.P.--Tucker Wayne/Luckie & Company, Birmingham, AL, pg. 1118
Murray, Cornelius A., Sr. V.P.--Ira Thomas Associates, Inc., Youngstown, OH, pg. 1092
Murtaugh, Phil, Sr. V.P.--Wardrop Murtaugh Temple, Chicago, IL, pg. 1163
Myers, Gregor W., Sr. V.P.-Retail Banking--Charter Oak Financial Corporation, Cincinnati, OH, pg. 491
Nadel, George J., Sr. V.P.--Loehmann's, Inc., Bronx, NY, pg. 681
Nadler, Lynn M., Sr. V.P.-Technical Services--Mutual of America, New York, NY, pg. 777
Nakagawa, Jean H., Sr. V.P.--Servco Pacific Inc., Honolulu, HI, pg. 991

Nakamura, Yoshi, Sr. V.P.-Orix Real Estate Equities, Inc., Chicago, IL, pg. 829
Napoleon, Roger F., Sr. V.P. & Assoc. Gen. Counsel--Mutual of America, New York, NY, pg. 777
Nauman, Dan, Sr. V.P.-Nuclear Generation--Tennessee Valley Authority, Knoxville, TN, pg. 1088
Needham, Gretchen F., Sr. V.P.-Communications--LaSalle Partners, Chicago, IL, pg. 660
Neeley, Joseph A., Sr. V.P.-Mechanical Elec. Service--George A. Fuller Company, New York, NY, pg. 436
Nehrig, Ralph, Sr. V.P.--NESCO, Inc., Mayfield Heights, OH, pg. 798
Nelson, Gerald, Sr. V.P.-Southern Region--United States Cold Storage, Inc., Cherry Hill, NJ, pg. 1135
Nelson, Lloyd, Sr. V.P., Dir.-Admin. & Asst. Sec.--Federated Mutual Insurance Company, Owatonna, MN, pg. 405
Nelson, Robert, Sr. V.P., Dir. Brdcst. Production--TBWA Advertising, Inc., New York, NY, pg. 1071
Newman, Cary, Sr. V.P.-Worldwide Opers.--Redken Laboratories, Inc., Canoga Park, CA, pg. 919
Newman, Laurence R., Sr. V.P.-Worldwide Service Businesses & Corp. Devel.--S. C. Johnson & Son, Inc., Racine, WI, pg. 599
Newman, Michael H., Sr. V.P.--Golub & Co., Chicago, IL, pg. 469
Newton, Gary, V.P.-Consumer Loans--Federal Savings Bank, Fort Smith, AR, pg. 1194
Niederman, Ted A., Sr. V.P.--RTKL Associates Inc., Baltimore, MD, pg. 908
Nimtz, Richard H., Sr. V.P.--Giant Eagle, Inc., Pittsburgh, PA, pg. 455
Nissman, Arthur, Sr. V.P.--Batey/Poindexter, Los Angeles, CA, pg. 126
Noell, Nicholas A., Sr. V.P. & Treas.--PMC Partnership, Ltd., Westport, CT, pg. 836
Nolan, Patrick J., Sr. V.P., Chief Fin. Officer & Treas.--LFC Holding Corporation, Boca Raton, FL, pg. 647
Noon, Margaret, Sr. V.P., Assoc. Creative Dir.-Art--Sudler & Hennessey, New York, NY, pg. 1211
Nordeen, Peggy, Sr. V.P.--Grant/Jacoby, Inc., Chicago, IL, pg. 477
Nordgren, Bradley J., Sr. V.P. & Chief Fin. Officer--EvansGroup, Salt Lake City, UT, pg. 390
Norris, David A., Sr. V.P.--Ketchum, Inc., Pittsburgh, PA, pg. 626
Nowak, Edward, Sr. V.P.--Chaffee Case & Partners, Providence, RI, pg. 237
Nutter, Bob, Sr. V.P.--Nabholz Construction Corp., Conway, AR, pg. 782
O'Brien, Richard J., Sr. V.P.- Pub. Rels.--Mutual of America, New York, NY, pg. 777
O'Bryan, Kevin M., Sr. V.P.--The Troy Savings Bank, Troy, NY, pg. 1116
O'Connell, John, Jr., Sr. V.P.--Freeman Decorating Co., Dallas, TX, pg. 431
O'Donnell, Duane, Sr. V.P.--Jack Gray Transport, Inc., Gary, IN, pg. 479
O'Hara, Eugene M., Sr. V.P., Comptroller & Chief Fin. Officer--The Prudential Insurance Company of America, Newark, NJ, pg. 896
O'Hare, Stephen T., Sr. V.P.-Corp. Services--Pacific Mutual Life Insurance Company, Newport Beach, CA, pg. 841
O'Neal, Jack, Sr. V.P.--Atlantic Gulf Communities Corporation, Miami, FL, pg. 95
O'Neil, A.F., Sr. V.P.--O'Neil Industries Inc., Chicago, IL, pg. 827
O'Neill, James J., Sr. V.P.--Rothschild Inc., New York, NY, pg. 951
O'Rourke, Dennis, Sr. V.P. & Chief Fin. Officer--Goldberg Moser O'Neill, San Francisco, CA, pg. 465
O'Toole, Michael B., Sr. V.P.-Retail Information Services--John Hancock Mutual Life Insurance Company, Boston, MA, pg. 595
Oakley, Andrew C., Sr. V.P. & Dir.-Engrng.--Huitt-Zollars, Inc., Dallas, TX, pg. 552
Obermeyer, Joe, Sr. V.P., Grp. Head--Wolf Blumberg Krody Inc., Cincinnati, OH, pg. 1199
Okonow, Dale, Chief Fin. Officer & Sr. V.P.--H M K Enterprises, Inc., Waltham, MA, pg. 497
Oliver, E. Victor, Sr. V.P.--ComputerLand Canada Ltd., Brampton,, Canada, pg. 271
Olivero, Martin, Sr. V.P., Client Services & Acct. Exec.--Wilshire Newport Inc., Burbank, CA, pg. 1193
Olson, Vernon C., Sr. V.P.--Summa Corporation, Las Vegas, NV, pg. 1057
Opila, Andy, Sr. V.P.--Watt, Roop & Co., Cleveland, OH, pg. 1168
Oppenheimer, Deanna W., Sr. V.P.--Washington Mutual Savings Bank, Seattle, WA, pg. 1166
Osgood, R.W., Sr. V.P.--Kirby Building Systems, Inc., Nashville, TN, pg. 632
Oshry, Elliott S., Sr. V.P.--Ketchum, Inc., Pittsburgh, PA, pg. 626
Osterhoust, Raymond, Sr. V.P.-Investments--Farm Family Mutual Insurance Co., Glenmont, NY, pg. 401
Otto, Jo, Sr. V.P.--Concord Assets Group, Inc., Boca Raton, FL, pg. 272
Overlock, Bill, Sr. V.P. & Chief Fin. Officer--Western International Media Corporation, Los Angeles, CA, pg. 1179
Owens, C. Richard, Sr. V.P. & Chief Fin. Officer--DKM, Ltd., New York, NY, pg. 357
Owens, Carroll W., Jr., Sr. V.P.--Johnston, Lemon & Co. Inc., Washington, DC, pg. 601
Pacana, Robert, Sr. V.P.--Dudek & Bock Spring Manufacturing Company, Chicago, IL, pg. 351
Paczkowski, Donald P., Sr. V.P.--Massachusetts Mutual Life Insurance Co., Springfield, MA, pg. 718
Pagano, M.J., Sr. V.P.-Reinsurance Assumed--Unigard Security Insurance Co., Bellevue, WA, pg. 596
Pagilese, Ernest, Sr. V.P., Mngmt. Supvr.--Arnold Fortuna Lawner & Cabot, Boston, MA, pg. 84
Painter, Richard O., Sr. V.P.-Southeastern Agencies--New York Life Insurance Company, New York, NY, pg. 802
Paley, Florence, Sr. V.P.--The Texwipe Co., Inc., Upper Saddle River, NJ, pg. 1090
Pallotta, John J., Jr., Sr. V.P.-Grp. Insurance--The Guardian Life Insurance Company of America, New York, NY, pg. 492
Palmer, Donald H., Sr. V.P. & Dir.-Exports & Imports--WWF Paper Corporation, Bala-Cynwyd, PA, pg. 1157
Palmer, Kenneth A., Sr. V.P.-Information Services--Western & Southern Life Insurance Co., Cincinnati, OH, pg. 1181
Pappas, Nicholas J., Sr. V.P.--Fay, Spofford & Thorndike, Inc., Lexington, MA, pg. 404
Parisi, Peter, Sr. V.P.--Warren/Kremer/CMP/Advertising/Inc., New York, NY, pg. 1165
Parker, Michael, Sr. V.P.--Trader Joes Co., South Pasadena, CA, pg. 1076
Parker, Robert A., Sr. V.P.--Macco Constructors, Inc., Paramount, CA, pg. 696
Parker, Ronald W., Sr. V.P.-Franchise Opers.--Bonanza Restaurants, Dallas, TX, pg. 744
Parkinson, Jon, Sr. V.P., Creative Dir.--Hal Riney & Partners, Inc., New York, NY, pg. 935
Parks, Peter, Sr. V.P., Pres.-Helix Div.--William Douglas McAdams Inc., New York, NY, pg. 726
Parry, Vincent, Sr. V.P., Creative Dir.-Copy--Sudler & Hennessey, New York, NY, pg. 1211
Parsons, Edward H., Sr. V.P.--Cole Taylor Bank, Chicago, IL, pg. 260
Parsons, Jeff, Sr. V.P., Chief Fin. Officer--Redgate Communications Corp., Vero Beach, FL, pg. 919
Patanio, Salvatore P., Sr. V.P.--Rothschild Inc., New York, NY, pg. 951
Pate, S.R., Sr. V.P.--Sverdrup Corporation, Maryland Heights, MO, pg. 1065
Patmore, Holly, Sr. V.P.--HMK Advertising, Inc., Chestnut Hill, MA, pg. 497
Paton, Robert, Sr. V.P.-Central Div.--Pathmark, Woodbridge, NJ, pg. 1064
Patterson, Michael, Sr. V.P.--Petty Company, Inc., Effingham, IL, pg. 866
Paul, Lyle R., Sr. V.P.-Agency--New York Life Insurance Company, New York, NY, pg. 802
Paulson, Paul, Exec. V.P.--Warwick Baker & Fiore Inc., New York, NY, pg. 1165
Paulus, Michael S., Sr. V.P.-Jayme Advertising--The Jayme Organization, Inc., Cleveland, OH, pg. 591
Paumi, Joseph, Sr. V.P., Creative Dir.-Art--Sudler & Hennessey, New York, NY, pg. 1211
Pautzke, Donavon, Sr. V.P.--Malt-O-Meal Company, Minneapolis, MN, pg. 703
Pavelle, Elizabeth Jane, Sr. V.P.--The Lipsitt Design Group, New York, NY, pg. 950
Peacock, Oren, Sr. V.P.--Eckerd Drug Co., Garland, TX, pg. 366
Pearsall, Dennis E., Sr. V.P.-Retail Banking--Great Lakes Bancorp, Ann Arbor, MI, pg. 480
Pedranti, James, Sr. V.P.--Sparkomatic Corporation, Milford, PA, pg. 1025
Pedranti, Jim, Sr. V.P.--Kenco, Middlebury, IN, pg. 1025
Peek, Ron, Sr. V.-.-Opers.--Ingram Merchandising Service Inc., La Vergne, TN, pg. 569
Pelino, Tino, Sr. V.P., Dir. Print Services--Backer Spielvogel Bates, Inc., New York, NY, pg. 108
Penczak, Bill, Sr. V.P., Grp. Supvr.--Fogarty & Klein/Winius Brandon, Houston, TX, pg. 421
Pepperdine, James, Sr. V.P.--Robinson, Yesawich & Pepperdine, Orlando, FL, pg. 940
Perez, Michael G., Sr. V.P.--Stainless Incorporated, Deerfield Beach, FL, pg. 1035
Perkins, Harry, Sr. V.P.--Connecticut Container Corporation, North Haven, CT, pg. 274
Perpich, William M., Sr. V.P.--STS Holdings, Inc., Northbrook, IL, pg. 964
Perry, Jim, Sr. V.P.--United Coatings, Inc., Kankakee, IL, pg. 1131
Peterson, C.T., Sr. V.P.--DoAll Company, Des Plaines, IL, pg. 341
Peterson, Raymond C., Sr. V.P.-Systems--Mutual of America, New York, NY, pg. 777
Petrequin, Scott O., Sr. V.P.--Mohawk Paper Mills, Inc., Cohoes, NY, pg. 763
Petrosian, Peter, Sr. V.P.--Service America Corporation, Stamford, CT, pg. 992
Pflugk, Peter, Sr. V.P.--Estee Lauder, Intl., New York, NY, pg. 389
Pfursich, Edwin, Sr. V.P.-Agencies--Lutheran Brotherhood, Minneapolis, MN, pg. 688
Philip, Craig, Chief Oper. Officer & Sr. V.P.--Ingram Barge Company, Nashville, TN, pg. 569
Philipps, Edward W., Sr. V.P.--American Savings Bank, White Plains, NY, pg. 60
Phillips, Donald J.M., Sr. V.P.--Ted Thomas Associates Inc., Advertising, Philadelphia, PA, pg. 1092
Phillips, Gary, Sr. V.P.-Springfield Div.--Associated Wholesale Grocers, Inc., Kansas City, KS, pg. 92
Phillips, John A., Sr. V.P.--McKee Foods Corporation, Collegedale, TN, pg. 730
Phillips, Robert L., Sr. V.P.--Huitt-Zollars, Inc., Dallas, TX, pg. 552
Phillips, Robert M., Sr. V.P.-Services--General Computer Corp. Inc., Twinsburg, OH, pg. 449
Picha, Marlene, Sr. V.P., Client Services--Responsive Marketing Communications, Inc., Schaumburg, IL, pg. 929
Pickler, W.H., III, Sr. V.P.-Mngmt. Information Systems--Ingram Book Company, La Vergne, TN, pg. 569
Picknelly, Paul, Sr. V.P.--Peter Pan Bus Lines, Inc., Springfield, MA, pg. 864
Piehler, Robert, Sr. V.P.-Corp. Communications & Planning--R. L. Polk & Co., Detroit, MI, pg. 879
Pillers, Robert H., Sr. V.P.--Petty Company, Inc., Effingham, IL, pg. 866
Pinckes, Michael A., Sr. V.P., Grp. Acct. Supvr.--Ross Roy Inc., Bloomfield Hills, MI, pg. 950
Pineda, Prudencio, Sr. V.P.-Distr.--Minyard Food Stores, Coppell, TX, pg. 759
Pipia, John F., Sr. V.P.-Credit Policy--First American Bankshares, Inc., Washington, DC, pg. 412
Pitelka, David L., Sr. V.P. & Controller--First American Bankshares, Inc., Washington, DC, pg. 412
Pizzo, Tom, Sr. V.P.-New Business Factoring--Century Business Credit Corporation, New York, NY, pg. 235
Plante, Arnold, Sr. V.P.--Keywell Corporation, Detroit, MI, pg. 629
Poad, William J., Sr. V.P.--Lester B. Knight & Associates, Inc., Chicago, IL, pg. 637
Poad, William J., Sr. V.P.--Knight Architects Engineers Planners, Inc., Chicago, IL, pg. 637
Pohl, C. Chandler, Sr. V.P.--Carlson, DelGaldo, Hoag, Matthei Advertising, Inc., Stamford, CT, pg. 222
Polacheck, Bob, Sr. V.P.--George Sollitt Construction, Wood Dale, IL, pg. 1017
Polack, Valerie, Sr. V.P.--Acme Poultry Company, Inc., Seattle, WA, pg. 13
Polizzi, James V., Sr. V.P., Dir. Adv. Services--Gilbert, Whitney & Johns, Inc., Whippany, NJ, pg. 458
Ponder, Daniel S., Sr. V.P., Chief Fin. Officer--Anthony M. Franco Inc., Detroit, MI, pg. 950
Pool, Edson K., Sr. V.P., Grp. Dir.--Young & Rubicam Detroit, Detroit, MI, pg. 1211
Porter, Bill, Sr. V.P., Media Services--Richardson, Myers & Donofrio, Inc., Baltimore, MD, pg. 933
Porter, Clyde, Sr. V.P.--Allen & Ohara, Inc., Memphis, TN, pg. 36
Potter, Randy, Exec. V.P.--Bankers Systems Inc., Saint Cloud, MN, pg. 117
Potter, Robert L., Sr. V.P.-Special Projects--Nason and Cullen, Inc., Wayne, PA, pg. 784
Powell, H.E., Sr. V.P.-Claims--Auto-Owners Insurance, Lansing, MI, pg. 100
Prensky, David, Sr. V.P. & Gen. Mgr.-Men's--John Wanamaker, Philadelphia, Philadelphia, PA, pg. 1201
Presser, Abe, Sr. V.P.--Softool Corporation, Goleta, CA, pg. 1016
Preston, Mike, Sr. V.P.--A.P.S., Inc., Houston, TX, pg. 5
Price, I. Edward, Sr. V.P.-Individual Ins. Systems & Admin.--The Prudential Insurance Company of America, Newark, NJ, pg. 896
Price, R.H., Sr. V.P.--Kirby Building Systems, Inc., Nashville, TN, pg. 632
Prillman, Bob M., Sr. V.P.--Caraustar Industries, Inc., Austell, GA, pg. 217
Prinzo, Felix J., Sr. V.P. & Chief Fin. Officer--Laroche Holdings, Inc., Atlanta, GA, pg. 659
Promoff, David, Sr. V.P.--Capital Bancorp, Miami, FL, pg. 214
Prosch, Tim, Sr. V.P., Mng. Dir., Client Services--Ayer Chicago, Chicago, IL, pg. 104
Prowse, W. James, Sr. V.P.-MIS, Human Resources & Recruiting--Compuware Corporation, Farmington Hills, MI, pg. 271
Puglisi, John, Sr. V.P., Mngmt. Supvr.--William Douglas McAdams Inc., New York, NY, pg. 726
Puglisi, Kenneth F., Sr. V.P.-Bank Research--Chicago Corp., Chicago, IL, pg. 247
Pyle, Judith D., Vice Chm. & Sr. V.P.--RAYOVAC Corporation, Madison, WI, pg. 915
Quereau, James Van Dyke, Sr. V.P.--Stratton Management Company, Plymouth Meeting, PA, pg. 1053
Quigley, James E., III, Sr. V.P.--Rothschild Inc., New York, NY, pg. 951
Rabar, Peter, Sr. V.P.--Wunderman Cato Johnson, New York, NY, pg. 1211
Racer, James H., Sr. V.P.--SENCORP, Newport, KY, pg. 989
Radam, Janice, Sr. V.P., Media Dir.--William Douglas McAdams Inc., New York, NY, pg. 726
Raimer, Fred, Sr. V.P., Dir. Fin.--The Joey Reiman Agency, Atlanta, GA, pg. 923
Raitt, Gene, Sr. V.P.--The Reich Group, Inc., Philadelphia, PA, pg. 922
Rakers, Al J., Sr. V.P.--Tubular Steel Inc., Saint Louis, MO, pg. 1118
Rankin, Michael, Sr. V.P.--Camosy, Inc., Russell, IL, pg. 212
Rasco, John, Sr. V.P.--Fellers & Company, Austin, TX, pg. 405
Rathmann, Jerry, Sr. V.P.--Foster & Gallagher Inc., Peoria, IL, pg. 426
Readon, James, Sr. V.P.--Johnson & Higgins, New York, NY, pg. 598
Reddy, Govi C., Sr. V.P. & Pres.-Film Prod. Div.--General Binding Corporation, Northbrook, IL, pg. 656
Rediske, R.R., Sr. V.P.--WW Engineering & Science Inc., Grand Rapids, MI, pg. 1058
Redmon, Mike, Sr. V.P.-Building Prods.--Southwestern Petroleum Corporation, Fort Worth, TX, pg. 1024
Reed, James W., Sr. V.P.--Marcus Advertising, Inc., Cleveland, OH, pg. 706
Reeder, James S., Jr., Sr. V.P.--Tucker Wayne/Luckie & Company, Atlanta, GA, pg. 1118
Rees, William, Sr. V.P.--Huron Valley Steel Corp., Belleville, MI, pg. 555
Reeves, Michael W., Sr. V.P.-Western Agencies--New York Life Insurance Company, New York, NY, pg. 802
Rein, James O., Sr. V.P.--Harbert Corporation, Birmingham, AL, pg. 506
Reinstein, Stephen I., Sr. V.P.--Summa Corporation, Las Vegas, NV, pg. 1057
Reisler, Charles, Sr. V.P., Acct. Mngmt.--Siegel & Gale, New York, NY, pg. 1002
Remley, Richard, Sr. V.P.--Greeley Gas Co., Denver, CO, pg. 483
Rennaker, Wayne, Sr. V.P.--Ford Meter Box Company, Wabash, IN, pg. 423
Rense, Paige, Sr. V.P. & Editor-in-Chief--Knapp Communications Corporation, Los Angeles, CA, pg. 636
Reshkin, S.J., Sr. V.P.--E.H. Brown Advertising, Inc., Chicago, IL, pg. 181

Reyhons, Dennis L., Sr. V.P.--Massachusetts Mutual Life Insurance Co., Springfield, MA, pg. 718
Reynolds, Ronald E., Sr. V.P.-Flight Opers.--Trans World Airlines, Inc., Mount Kisco, NY, pg. 561
Rhind, Jamie, Sr. V.P., Assoc. Media Dir.--Avrett, Free & Ginsberg, Inc., New York, NY, pg. 103
Rice, Adrian, Sr. V.P. & Gen. Mgr.-Home Store--John Wanamaker, Philadelphia, Philadelphia, PA, pg. 1201
Richardson, James A., Sr. V.P.-Member Field Services--Aid Association For Lutherans, Appleton, WI, pg. 26
Richey, Leonard, Sr. V.P.--George W. Park Seed Co., Inc., Greenwood, SC, pg. 849
Rife, Teresa A., Chief Fin. Officer & Sr. V.P.--Roma Holdings, Dallas, TX, pg. 945
Riker, Harland A., Jr., Sr. V.P. & Grp. Officer--Arthur D. Little, Inc., Cambridge, MA, pg. 678
Riley, Ron, Sr. V.P.--W. M. Barr & Co., Inc., Memphis, TN, pg. 121
Rinaldi, John, Sr. V.P., Grp. Supvr.--Sudler & Hennessey, New York, NY, pg. 1211
Ringel, Jordan, Sr. V.P., Bus. Affairs--SFM Media Corporation, New York, NY, pg. 962
Riso, Daniel R., Sr. V.P.--Robinson Export-Import Corporation, Springfield, VA, pg. 748
Rivas, Joyce, Sr. V.P., Mngmt. Supvr.--Earle Palmer Brown & Spiro, Philadelphia, PA, pg. 182
Roach, Larry, Sr. V.P.-Civil--The Benham Group, Oklahoma City, OK, pg. 138
Roberson, Richard, Sr. V.P.-Eckerd Vision Grp.--Jack Eckerd Corporation, Largo, FL, pg. 366
Roberts, E.D., Jr., Sr. V.P. & Treas.--Parish Water Company, Inc., Baton Rouge, LA, pg. 126
Roberts, Fred, Sr. V.P.--The National Bank of Sussex County, Branchville, NJ, pg. 534
Roberts, William R., Sr. V.P.--American Systems Corporation, Chantilly, VA, pg. 63
Robertson, Bill, Sr. V.P., Acct. Grp. Supvr.--William Douglas McAdams Inc., New York, NY, pg. 726
Robinson, Bert, Sr. V.P.--Ballet Makers, Inc., Totowa, NJ, pg. 116
Robinson, Harry J., Sr. V.P.--The Troy Savings Bank, Troy, NY, pg. 1116
Robinson, Peter, Sr. V.P.--Hazen & Sawyer, New York, NY, pg. 520
Robinson, Thomas E., Sr. V.P. & Sec.--The Entwistle Company, Hudson, MA, pg. 383
Roces, Evelyn, Sr. V.P., Acct. Supvr.--Sudler & Hennessey, New York, NY, pg. 1211
Rock, Robert D., Sr. V.P.-Individual Annuity--New York Life Insurance Company, New York, NY, pg. 802
Roddy, Russell Jr., Sr. V.P.--Harza Engineering Co., Chicago, IL, pg. 516
Rode, Albert, Sr. V.P.--Pan American Trade Development Corp., New York, NY, pg. 845
Roden, John, Sr. V.P. & Gen. Mgr.--Colorado Boxed Beef Co., Auburndale, FL, pg. 265
Rodgers, Gordon K., Sr. V.P.-Agency--Canal Insurance Co., Greenville, SC, pg. 213
Rodler, John, Sr. V.P.--Folger Nolan Fleming Douglas, Washington, DC, pg. 422
Rodriguez, Raoul, Sr. V.P., Dir.-Hispanic Services--GSD&M, Austin, TX, pg. 441
Rogenstein, Lucy, Sr. V.P.--Taylor-Gordon/Widmann & Co., Inc., New York, NY, pg. 1081
Rogers, Sam, Exec. V.P., Pub. Rels. Dir.--Elkman Advertising & Public Relations, Bala-Cynwyd, PA, pg. 377
Rogers, Sam, Exec. V.P., Pub. Rels. Dir.--Elkman Advertising, Public Relations Div., Bala-Cynwyd, PA, pg. 378
Rogers, Stephen, Sr. Exec. V.P.--Black Gillock & Langberg, Houston, TX, pg. 154
Rogoski, Patricia D., Sr. V.P.--Peoplemark, Inc., Memphis, TN, pg. 493
Rolander, John, Sr. V.P.--M A C Group (Japan), Inc., Tokyo, Japan, pg. 448
Romine, Frederick H., Sr. V.P.--Leader Federal Bank For Savings, Memphis, TN, pg. 663
Rootberg, Philip, Sr. V.P.-Corp. Devel.--Jupiter Industries, Inc., Chicago, IL, pg. 609
Rosenberg, Michael, Sr. V.P.--Keywell Corporation, Detroit, MI, pg. 629
Rosenfeld, Arnold, Sr. V.P.--Cox Enterprises Newspaper Division, Atlanta, GA, pg. 292
Rosenthal, Robert, Sr. V.P., Mngmt. Supvr.--TBWA Advertising, Inc., New York, NY, pg. 1071
Rosenzweig, Israel, Sr. V.P.--Georgetown Partners, Inc., Great Neck, NY, pg. 473
Rosoff, Lyn, Sr. V.P., Mngmt. Supvr.--Arnold Fortuna Lawner & Cabot, Boston, MA, pg. 84
Ross, David E., Sr. V.P.--SCS Engineers, Long Beach, CA, pg. 961
Ross, Donald L., Sr. V.P.--Enterprise Rent-A-Car Company, Saint Louis, MO, pg. 382
Ross, Leonard, Sr. V.P., Production--Chapman Direct Advertising, New York, NY, pg. 1210
Ross, Mason G., Sr. V.P.-Real Estate--Northwestern Mutual Life Insurance Co., Milwaukee, WI, pg. 815
Rossi, Chuck, Sr. V.P.--Goldfarb & Company Advertising, Southfield, MI, pg. 467
Roth, Steven, Sr. V.P.--Carrafiello, Diehl & Associates, Inc., Irvington, NY, pg. 225
Rothman, Allan, Sr. V.P.--National Out-of-Home Media/Metro 8, New York, NY, pg. 792
Rourke, James G., Sr. V.P. & Temp. Clerk--Fay, Spofford & Thorndike, Inc., Lexington, MA, pg. 404
Rowe, Kenneth D., Sr. V.P.--Coleman & Christison, Inc., Saint Paul, MN, pg. 261
Rowland, Michael, Sr. V.P. & Supvr.-Mngmt.--Kirshenbaum & Bond, New York, NY, pg. 633
Rubin, Marc, Sr. V.P., Assoc. Creative Dir.--Cox Advertising, New York, NY, pg. 292
Rubinstein, John, Sr. V.P.--Leo Eisenberg & Co., Inc., Kansas City, MO, pg. 372
Rudd, Nicholas, Sr. V.P., Chief Info. Officer-Y&R Inc.--Young & Rubicam Inc., New York, NY, pg. 1210
Ruff, Donald W., Sr. V.P. & Mgr.-Corp. Opers & Auditing--First Federal of Michigan, Detroit, MI, pg. 414
Ruffin, Bruce E., Sr. V.P. & Community Investment Officer--First Federal of Michigan, Detroit, MI, pg. 414
Rugaber, D.A., Sr. V.P.--AGR International, Inc., Butler, PA, pg. 4
Ruggles, Gordon, Sr. V.P.--Hazen & Sawyer, New York, NY, pg. 520
Ruiz, Eugene, Sr. V.P.--Rotterdam Ventures Inc., Guilderland Center, NY, pg. 951
Russell, L.G., Sr. V.P.-Opers.--Ingram Book Company, La Vergne, TN, pg. 569
Russell, Michael, Sr. V.P.--The William Cook Agency, Inc., Jacksonville, FL, pg. 282
Russinko, Richard, Sr. V.P., Assoc. Creative Dir.-Art--Sudler & Hennessey, New York, NY, pg. 1211
Rutledge, D.W., Sr. V.P.-Admin.--Ingram Micro Inc., Santa Ana, CA, pg. 569
Rutledge, William A., Sr. V.P. & Sec.--Farmers Mutual Hail Insurance Co., Des Moines, IA, pg. 401
Ruzicka, Leonard R., Sr. V.P., Sec. & Gen. Counsel--Fru-Con Construction Corporation, Ballwin, MO, pg. 435
Ryan, Patrick C., Sr. V.P.--Johnston, Lemon & Co. Inc., Washington, DC, pg. 601
Ryder, M. Lynn, Sr. V.P.--Washington Mutual Savings Bank, Seattle, WA, pg. 1166
Saba, Robert J., Sr. V.P.-No. Region--The Grand Union Company, Wayne, NJ, pg. 476
Sackett, Richard, Sr. V.P.--LeGrand Johnson Construction Co., Logan, UT, pg. 598
Sage, Ron, V.P.-Custom Pack Sls.--Nalleys Fine Foods, Tacoma, WA, pg. 25
Sakoff, Edward A., Sr. V.P.--Buzz Barton & Associates, Inc., Oak Brook, IL, pg. 123
Sakurai, George S., Sr. V.P.-Gen. Auto. Opers.--Servco Pacific Inc., Honolulu, HI, pg. 991
Sall, John P., Sr. V.P.--SAS Institute Inc., Cary, NC, pg. 959
Salley, J. Ronald, Sr. V.P.--Shannon & Wilson, Inc., Seattle, WA, pg. 995
Salton, Linda M., Sr. V.P. & Reg. Mgr.-Trust Banking--Team Bancshares, Inc., Dallas, TX, pg. 1082
Sama, Ralph, Sr. V.P.--Hancock Lumber, Inc., Casco, ME, pg. 504
Sampson, Ronald, Sr. V.P.--Burrell Communications Group Inc., Chicago, IL, pg. 195
Sanchez, Robert, Sr. V.P., Dir. New Business--AyerDirect, Direct Response, New York, NY, pg. 104
Sanders, Calvin, Sr. V.P.--Dealers Electrical Supply Co., Waco, TX, pg. 322
Sanders, Gerald, V.P.--Queens Group, Inc., Long Island City, NY, pg. 904
Sanfilippo, James A., Exec. V.P., Mngmt. Supvr.--Backer Spielvogel Bates, Inc., Irvine, CA, pg. 108
Santi, Peter, Sr. V.P.--Lipman, Richmond, Greene, New York, NY, pg. 677
Santillo, Carl J., Exec. V.P.-Opers.--Employers Insurance of Wausau a Mutual Co., Wausau, WI, pg. 380
Santillo, Carl J., Exec. V.P.-Opers.--Employers Insurance of Wausau a Mutual Co., Wausau, WI, pg. 795
Sapp, G. David, Sr. V.P.-Investments--American United Life Insurance Company, Indianapolis, IN, pg. 65
Sarcone, Anthony, Sr. V.P.--Century Business Credit Corporation, New York, NY, pg. 235
Saterbo, Bryan, Sr. V.P. & Treas.--Colorado Boxed Beef Co., Auburndale, FL, pg. 265
Sauders, Roy Jr., Sr. V.P.--Central Mutual Insurance Co., Van Wert, OH, pg. 233
Scannell, Herb, Sr. V.P.-Programming--Nickelodeon/Nick At Nite, New York, NY, pg. 785
Schaible, John E., III, Sr. V.P.-Opers. & Business Devel.--Rich Products Corp., Buffalo, NY, pg. 932
Scheer, Norman J., Sr. V.P.--Scheer Advertising Agency, South Orange, NJ, pg. 975
Schenker, Leo, Sr. Exec. V.P.--Central National-Gottesman Inc., Purchase, NY, pg. 233
Schifrin, Mark E., Sr. V.P.--Oxford Realty Services Corp., Bethesda, MD, pg. 835
Schilling, Ernest, Sr. V.P.-Midwest & West--Powell Electronics Inc., Philadelphia, PA, pg. 882
Schinner, E., Sr. V.P.--Baltimore Aircoil Company, Jessup, MD, pg. 69
Schleicher, Gerald, Sr. V.P.--Boasberg Valentine-Radford, Inc., Kansas City, MO, pg. 1143
Schleiff, Henry S., Sr. V.P.--National Amusements, Inc., Dedham, MA, pg. 784
Schmid, Al, Sr. V.P.--Springer Schmid Group, Beachwood, OH, pg. 1033
Schmidt, Robert, Sr. V.P. & Chief Fin. Officer--The Charles Levy Company, Chicago, IL, pg. 672
Schoenberg, Lester L., Sr. V.P.-Individual Policy Services--New York Life Insurance Company, New York, NY, pg. 802
Schor, Edward N., Sr. V.P. & Gen. Counsel/Communications--Viacom Broadcasting Inc., New York, NY, pg. 785
Schor, Edward N., Sr. V.P., Gen. Counsel/Communications--Viacom Cable, Pleasanton, CA, pg. 785
Schoun, Andy, Sr. V.P.-Music Programming & Promotions--MTV: Music Television, New York, NY, pg. 785
Schuldt, Jerry, Sr. V.P.--Affiliated of Florida Inc., Tampa, FL, pg. 23
Schullman, A.H., Sr. V.P.--E.H. Brown Advertising, Inc., Chicago, IL, pg. 181
Schurz, James M., Sr. V.P.--Schurz Communications, Inc., South Bend, IN, pg. 979
Schwartz, Roy, Sr. V.P.--Newmark, Posner & Mitchell, Inc., New York, NY, pg. 804
Scott, E. Michael, Sr. V.P.--Ted Thomas Associates Inc., Advertising, Philadelphia, PA, pg. 1092
Scott, John, Sr. V.P.--MacNamara, Klein & Solin Inc., New York, NY, pg. 698
Scott, W.G., Sr. V.P.--Green International, Inc., Denver, CO, pg. 484
Scribner, Raymond, Sr. V.P.--Telescope Casual Furniture, Inc., Granville, NY, pg. 1085
Sculti, Leon, Sr. V.P.--Torcon, Inc., Westfield, NJ, pg. 1102
Seay, Doug, Sr. V.P., Dir. Brdcst. Programming--Hal Riney & Partners, Inc., New York, NY, pg. 935
Sebastian, Ron L., Sr. V.P.-Mortgage Banking--Charter Oak Financial Corporation, Cincinnati, OH, pg. 491
Sehlin, A.A., Sr. V.P.-Structures--Johnson Bros. Corp., Litchfield, MN, pg. 597
Seigel, Howard, Sr. V.P.--Talent & Residuals, Inc., Burbank, CA, pg. 560
Selzer, Arthur, Vice Chm.--Amana Society, Amana, IA, pg. 46
Seminara, Vito, Sr. V.P.--Panorama Press, Inc., Clifton, NJ, pg. 846
Serraglio, Raymond, Sr. V.P.--Mills Hall Walborn & Associates, Mayfield Heights, OH, pg. 756
Setzer, Lewis F., Sr. V.P.--Hickory Printing Group, Inc., Hickory, NC, pg. 533
Seward, John E., Sr., Sr. V.P.--The Paty Company, Piney Flats, TN, pg. 852
Shalack, Theodore J., Sr. V.P.-Insurance Opers.--The Mutual Life Insurance Company of New York (MONY), New York, NY, pg. 778
Shalibo, Donald, Sr. V.P.--Barton-Malow Enterprises, Inc., Southfield, MI, pg. 123
Shalibo, Donald L., Sr. V.P.--Barton-Malow Company, Detroit, MI, pg. 123
Shanahan, James P., Sr. V.P.-Pension Div.--American United Life Insurance Company, Indianapolis, IN, pg. 65
Shannon, Gerald T., Sr. V.P.--Marmon Corporation, Chicago, IL, pg. 711
Shannon, William G., Sr. V.P.-Individual Fin. Plng.--Mutual of America, New York, NY, pg. 777
Sharman, John, Sr. V.P.--Vitt Media International, Inc., New York, NY, pg. 1153
Sharman, John, Sr. V.P.--Vitt Media International, Inc., New York, NY, pg. 1153
Sharpe, John, Sr. V.P. & Dir.-Client Services--Buntin Advertising, Inc., Nashville, TN, pg. 188
Sharretts, David K., Sr. V.P.--David A. Bramble, Inc., Chestertown, MD, pg. 171
Shartle, Frank, Sr. V.P.--EBM Systems, Inc., Greenbelt, MD, pg. 359
Shaw, Henry D., Sr. V.P.-Individual Insurance Prods.--John Hancock Mutual Life Insurance Company, Boston, MA, pg. 595
Shaw, Richard C., Sr. V.P.--Phoenix Home Life Mutual Insurance Company, Hartford, CT, pg. 868
Shea, Kevin, Sr. V.P. & Chief Fin. Officer--Beech Holdings Corp., Chicago, IL, pg. 131
Shea, Thomas G., Sr. V.P.--Carrafiello, Diehl & Associates, Inc., Irvington, NY, pg. 225
Sheetz, Ralph, Sr. V.P.--Carlos R. Leffler Inc., Richland, PA, pg. 666
Sheiffer, Arnold, Sr. V.P. & Chief Oper. Officer--Katz Communications, Inc., New York, NY, pg. 618
Shellabarger, Phil, Sr. V.P. & Compliance Officer--Stephens, Inc., Little Rock, AR, pg. 1046
Shemin, Barry L., Sr. V.P.-Retirement Security--John Hancock Mutual Life Insurance Company, Boston, MA, pg. 595
Shepard, Stephen E., Sr. V.P.-Special Projects--Huitt-Zollars, Inc., Dallas, TX, pg. 552
Sherry, Robert, Sr. V.P.--Rotterdam Ventures Inc., Guilderland Center, NY, pg. 951
Shirck, Bruce, Sr. V.P.-Opers.--Lyon's Restaurants, Inc., Foster City, CA, pg. 690
Shortlidge, Thomas A., Sr. V.P., Exec. Creative Dir.--Young & Rubicam Chicago, Chicago, IL, pg. 1211
Shriver, Jack, Sr. V.P.--SAE-Pinkerton & Laws Inc., Atlanta, GA, pg. 966
Shuford, A. Alex, Sr. V.P.-Upholstery Div.--Century Furniture Industries, Hickory, NC, pg. 235
Siefker, John, Sr. V.P.--PacifiCare Health Systems, Inc., Cypress, CA, pg. 1127
Siegel, Barry, Sr. V.P., Dir. Mktg. Research--Sudler & Hennessey, New York, NY, pg. 1211
Siegel, Howard, Sr. V.P.--Entertainment Partners, Burbank, CA, pg. 560
Siegel, Howard, Sr. V.P.--Production Payments, Inc., Burbank, CA, pg. 560
Silberman, Ira, Sr. V.P.--Diversified Products Corporation, Opelika, AL, pg. 1193
Silverberg, Edward L., Sr. V.P.--Keystone Foods Corporation, Bala-Cynwyd, PA, pg. 628
Silverman, Joyce, Sr. V.P.--Lipman, Richmond, Greene, New York, NY, pg. 677
Simon, Martin S., Sr. V.P.--Connell Rice & Sugar Co., Westfield, NJ, pg. 275
Simons, Beverly, Sr. V.P., Pres.-McAdams PR--William Douglas McAdams Inc., New York, NY, pg. 726
Simpson, David, Sr. V.P.--SAE-Pinkerton & Laws Inc., Atlanta, GA, pg. 966
Sims, Robert, Sr. V.P.--National Geographic Society, Washington, DC, pg. 789
Singerman, Steve, Sr. V.P., Assoc. Dir.--Ketchum Public Relations/Chicago, Chicago, IL, pg. 625
Singleton, Richard R., Sr. V.P.--Oxford Realty Services Corp., Bethesda, MD, pg. 835
Skiles, James, Sr. V.P.--American Finance Group, Boston, MA, pg. 52
Skillins, Gunar, Sr. V.P., Assoc. Creative Dir.--Avrett, Free & Ginsberg, Inc., New York, NY, pg. 103
Slabaugh, Raymond M., III, Sr. V.P.--Blue Cross & Blue Shield of Virginia, Richmond, VA, pg. 160
Slade, James L., Sr. V.P.--HTB, Inc., Oklahoma City, OK, pg. 497
Slavich, D.M., Sr. V.P. & Dir.--Bechtel Group, Inc., San Francisco, CA, pg. 130
Sloan, Harold, Sr. V.P.--Southern Pump & Tank Co. Inc., Charlotte, NC, pg. 1022

Slosburg, Bernice, Sr. V.P.--Letven-Diccicco, Inc., Horsham, PA, pg. 669
Slotkin, Todd J., Sr. V.P.--MacAndrews & Forbes Holdings Inc., New York, NY, pg. 694
Slovin, Bruce, Sr. V.P.--Alexandra De Markoff, Ltd., New York, NY, pg. 695
Small, John G., Sr. V.P.-New Bus. Service Admin.--The New England, Boston, MA, pg. 799
Smith, Alan E., Sr. V.P.--Keller & Gannon, San Francisco, CA, pg. 637
Smith, Dane, Sr. V.P.--The Macerich Co., Santa Monica, CA, pg. 696
Smith, E. Berry, Sr. V.P.-Broadcasting--Schurz Communications, Inc., South Bend, IN, pg. 979
Smith, Elizabeth M., Exec. V.P., Media Dir.--Gillis Advertising & Public Relations, Birmingham, AL, pg. 459
Smith, Gaylon, Sr. V.P.-Franchising--Arby's, Inc., Miami Beach, FL, pg. 243
Smith, George S., Sr. V.P. & Chief Fin. Officer--Viacom International Inc., New York, NY, pg. 785
Smith, James, Sr. V.P.--Bromar Inc., Newport Beach, CA, pg. 179
Smith, John M., Sr. V.P.-Equity Prods.--The Guardian Life Insurance Company of America, New York, NY, pg. 492
Smith, Larry L., Sr. V.P.-Health Indus. Rels.--Blue Cross and Blue Shield of Oklahoma, Tulsa, OK, pg. 159
Smith, Leon P., Sr. V.P.--American Merchants Life Insurance Co., Minnetonka, MN, pg. 55
Smith, Matthew, Sr. V.P. & Chief Fin. Officer--CW Publishing, Inc., Framingham, MA, pg. 576
Smoke, Jacki, Sr. V.P. & Mgr.-Opers.--Goldfarb & Company Advertising, Southfield, MI, pg. 467
Snyder, Garland O., Sr. V.P.-Design/Sls.--Contract Interiors Inc., Southfield, MI, pg. 280
Snyder, John H., Sr. V.P. & Dir. -Stores--Elder-Beerman Stores Div., Dayton, OH, pg. 373
Snyder, Joseph A., Sr. V.P.--Union City Body Company, Inc., Union City, IN, pg. 1128
Snyder, Richard, Sr. V.P.-Mktg.--Unistrut Corporation, Ann Arbor, MI, pg. 1130
Soehner, Richard O., Sr. V.P.--Cassano's Inc., Dayton, OH, pg. 228
Solay, Dick, Sr. V.P., Grp. Supvr.--Poppe Tyson, New York, NY, pg. 880
Solomon, Andrew, Sr. V.P.--Sterling Jewelry & Distributing Co., Dallas, TX, pg. 1047
Somers, John A., Sr. V.P.--Teachers Insurance and Annuity Association-College Retirement Equities Fund, New York, NY, pg. 1082
Somerville, John E., Vice Chm.--James M. Montgomery Consulting Engineers, Pasadena, CA, pg. 767
Sommer, Larry, Sr. V.P. & Pres.-Prange Way--H. C. Prange Company, Green Bay, WI, pg. 884
Sourdiff, Jerald, Sr. V.P. & Controller--Lutheran Brotherhood, Minneapolis, MN, pg. 688
Southwell, Donald G., Sr. V.P.-District Agencies--The Prudential Insurance Company of America, Newark, NJ, pg. 896
Sparks, David, Sr. V.P.-Mrktg & Sls.--Beech Holdings Corp., Chicago, IL, pg. 131
Spector, Howard B., Sr. V.P.--Guardsmark, Inc., Memphis, TN, pg. 492
Spellman, Richard A., Sr. V.P., Gen. Counsel & Sec.--Guarantee Mutual Life Co., Omaha, NE, pg. 491
Spence, William, Sr. V.P.--Coral Petroleum Corporation, Houston, TX, pg. 285
Spencer, Mac, Sr. V.P.--Wellcraft Marine, Sarasota, FL, pg. 759
Sperduto, Tony, Sr. V.P.-Fin. & Admin.--Optyl Eyewear Fashion International Corp., Norwood, NJ, pg. 828
Spillane, Robert, Sr. V.P. & Treas.--Donnelley Marketing, Inc., Stamford, CT, pg. 1011
Spitze, James, Sr. V.P.-Information Systems--Tri Valley Growers Inc., San Francisco, CA, pg. 1111
Spitzer, Morton E., Sr. V.P.-District Agencies--The Prudential Insurance Company of America, Newark, NJ, pg. 896
Sprague, John, Sr. V.P.-Sls.--Kettering Advertising Display Co., Englewood Cliffs, NJ, pg. 626
Sprint, Julienne D., Sr. V.P. & Dir.- Human Resources--Ellerbe Becket, Inc., Minneapolis, MN, pg. 378
Sproule, Martha S., Sr. V.P.--Rothschild Inc., New York, NY, pg. 951
St. George, Anthony A., Vice Chm. & Sr. V.P.--Advanced Technology, Inc., Reston, VA, pg. 20
Stackpole, Earle, Sr. V.P.--New York Carpet World Inc., Southfield, MI, pg. 802
Stalder, Dennis, Sr. V.P.-Wholesale Opers.--Associated Grocers, Inc., Seattle, WA, pg. 90
Stalenhoef, Jos P., Sr. V.P.-North America, Chiquita Tropical Products Grp.--Chiquita Brands International, Inc., Cincinnati, OH, pg. 53
Stalenhoef, Jos P., Sr. V.P.--Chiquita Brands, Inc., Cincinnati, OH, pg. 53
Stamatis, Jim, Sr. V.P.--W. M. Grace Development, Phoenix, AZ, pg. 474
Stangler, Kevin J., Sr. V.P., Chief Oper. & Fin. Officer & Treas.--Ministers Life Insurance Company, Minneapolis, MN, pg. 757
Stanner, H. Kent, Sr. V.P.--International Management Group (IMG), Cleveland, OH, pg. 578
Steele, James E., Sr. V.P. & Controller--Landmark Hotel Corporation, Topeka, KS, pg. 656
Stefanski, Stan, Exec. V.P., Dir. Bus. Affairs-WW--Young & Rubicam Inc., New York, NY, pg. 1210
Stefanski, Stan, Sr. V.P., Dir. Bus. Affairs & Admin.--Young & Rubicam New York, New York, NY, pg. 1211
Stegner, M.J., Sr. V.P.--Bovay, Houston, TX, pg. 169
Steman, Michael W., Sr. V.P.-Store Plng.--R. H. Macy & Co., Inc., New York, NY, pg. 698
Stepanik, Dennis S., Sr. V.P.--Owen Health Care, Houston, TX, pg. 833
Stephens, G. Martin, Sr. V.P.--Golden Gem Growers Inc., Umatilla, FL, pg. 466
Sternberg, Jeff, Sr. V.P., Mngmt. Supvr.--Anson-Stoner, Inc., Winter Park, FL, pg. 76
Stewart, David O., Sr. V.P.--Christianity Today, Inc., Carol Stream, IL, pg. 249
Stickley, Kent, Sr. V.P.-Mdse.--Nationwise Automotive, Inc., Columbus, OH, pg. 795
Stine, Darrell W., Sr. V.P.-NY Region--The Grand Union Company, Wayne, NJ, pg. 476
Stocksdale, ThomasA., Sr. V.P.--Macco Constructors, Inc., Paramount, CA, pg. 696
Stogel, Yale, Sr. V.P.--The Stogel Companies Inc., New York, NY, pg. 1050
Stone, David K., Sr. V.P. & Dir.-Opers.--Fiduciary Trust Company International, New York, NY, pg. 408
Stone, Monty, Sr. V.P.--Allright Corporation, Houston, TX, pg. 41
Stonehocker, Keith, Sr. V.P.--Christianity Today, Inc., Carol Stream, IL, pg. 249
Stoner, Alan J., Sr. V.P.-Opers.--Whataburger, Inc., Corpus Christi, TX, pg. 1184
Storm, Phil, Sr. V.P.-After Market Div.--Freudenberg-NOK (MI), Plymouth, MI, pg. 432
Stotler, John L., Sr. V.P. & Gen. Counsel--National Life Insurance Company, Montpelier, VT, pg. 791
Strang, Duncan, Sr. V.P.--Richardson Strang Associates, Portland, OR, pg. 933
Strickland, Bruce, Sr. V.P.-Land Acquisitions--Forecast Mortgage Corporation, Rancho Cucamonga, CA, pg. 423
Strom, Dennis, Sr. V.P.--UniHealth America, Burbank, CA, pg. 1126
Stromberg, J.C., Sr. V.P.--Bechtel Group, Inc., San Francisco, CA, pg. 130
Stryk, Manfred, Sr. V.P. & Dir.-Corp. Admin.--Harley Ellington Pierce Yee Associates, Inc., Southfield, MI, pg. 509
Stryker, Elsebeth Sexton, Sr. V.P. & Sec.--PMC Partnership, Ltd., Westport, CT, pg. 836
Styslinger, Lee J., III, Sr. V.P.-Corp. Group--Altec Industries, Inc., Birmingham, AL, pg. 45
Sukalo, Paul, Sr. V.P.--Washington Homes, Inc., Landover, MD, pg. 1166
Sullivan, Ralph, Sr. V.P.-Personnel Training & Devel.--Juhl Marketing Communications, Mishawaka, IN, pg. 608
Sullivan, Stephen W., Sr. V.P.--Harte-Hanks Communications, Inc., San Antonio, TX, pg. 513
Sumner, Paul, Sr. V.P.--The Upper Deck Company, Carlsbad, CA, pg. 1140
Sundquist, Mark J., Sr. V.P.--STS Holdings, Inc., Northbrook, IL, pg. 964
Sung, Kihong, Sr. V.P. & Chief Actuary--The Mutual Life Insurance Company of New York (MONY), New York, NY, pg. 778
Sussman, Dennis, Sr. V.P.-Sls.-Lighting Div.--Crystal Clear Industries Company, Ridgefield Park, NJ, pg. 303
Sutphin, Christopher F., Sr. V.P.--General Instrument Corporation, New York, NY, pg. 425
Sutter, Suzanne, Sr. V.P.--Cole Key Corporation, Cleveland, OH, pg. 260
Sutton, Debbie, Sr. V.P.-Acct. Services--Towne, Silverstein, Rotter Inc., New York, NY, pg. 1104
Swafford, John, Sr. V.P.--Mueller Sports Medicine, Inc., Prairie du Sac, WI, pg. 774
Swanson, Brenda, Sr. V.P., Dir. Opers.--Haworth Group Inc., Minnetonka, MN, pg. 518
Swanson, John, Sr. V.P.--The Levy Organization, Chicago, IL, pg. 672
Swanson, John, Sr. V.P.--Levy Restaurants, Chicago, IL, pg. 672
Swanson, Michael, Sr. V.P.--Plywood Panels, Inc., New Orleans, LA, pg. 878
Sweed, Phyllis, Sr. V.P.--Geyer-McAllister Publications, Inc., New York, NY, pg. 455
Sweeney, Anne, Sr. V.P.-Program Enterprises--Nickelodeon/Nick At Nite, New York, NY, pg. 785
Sweeney, Joseph, Sr. V.P.--Advertising To Women, Inc., New York, NY, pg. 21
Sweet, Frederic H., Sr. V.P.-Govt. Rels.--Northwestern Mutual Life Insurance Co., Milwaukee, WI, pg. 815
Swick, Norman H., Sr. V.P.--Washington Mutual Savings Bank, Seattle, WA, pg. 1166
Swicord, Earl, Sr. V.P.--King & Prince Seafood Corporation, Brunswick, GA, pg. 631
Swift, Stephen H., Sr. V.P.--Swift Instruments, Inc., Dorchester, MA, pg. 1068
Sykes, Guy, Sr. V.P.--Peter J. Schmitt Holdings, West Seneca, NY, pg. 976
Synott, Lee, Sr. V.P.--Ingram Distribution Group Inc., La Vergne, TN, pg. 569
Tackett, Bill D., Sr. V.P.-Northern Region--United States Cold Storage, Inc., Cherry Hill, NJ, pg. 1135
Takeda, Tom, Sr. V.P.-Seals Div.--Freudenberg-NOK (MI), Plymouth, MI, pg. 432
Taloni, Adam R., Pres.-Nash Europe--The Nash Engineering Company, Norwalk, CT, pg. 783
Tamcsin, Dennis, Sr. V.P.-Agencies--Northwestern Mutual Life Insurance Co., Milwaukee, WI, pg. 815
Tarpley, Joe, Sr. V.P.--J. L. Todd Auction Co., Rome, GA, pg. 1099
Tarrant, Johnny, Sr. V.P.--Quik Print Inc., Wichita, KS, pg. 905
Taylor, J.L., Sr. V.P.--Ingram Distribution Group Inc., La Vergne, TN, pg. 569
Taylor, Joe W., Sr. V.P.--Eastland National Bank, Eastland, TX, pg. 412
Taylor, Mark, Sr. V.P.--Taracorp, Inc., Atlanta, GA, pg. 1078
Taylor, Michael E., Sr. V.P.--Topa Savings Bank, Los Angeles, CA, pg. 1101
Taylor, N.G., Sr. V.P.-Industrial Sls. & Mktg.--North American Refractories Company, Cleveland, OH, pg. 811
Taylor, Richard L., Sr. V.P., Center Mngmt.--CenterMark Properties, Inc., Saint Louis, MO, pg. 231
Taylor, S.R., Sr. V.P.-Distribution--Ingram Book Company, La Vergne, TN, pg. 569
Taylor, Thomas A., Sr. V.P.-Claims--Amica Mutual Insurance Co., Providence, RI, pg. 66
Teague, Henry H., Sr. V.P.--Rosser Fabrap International, Atlanta, GA, pg. 950
Teichman, James, Sr. V.P.--Phar-Mor, Inc., Youngstown, OH, pg. 866
Temple, William N., Sr. V.P. & Grp. Exec.--Walter Industries, Inc., Tampa, FL, pg. 1161
Thomas, Barbara, Sr. V.P.--Tribble & Stephens Co., Houston, TX, pg. 1112
Thomas, Buddy, Sr. V.P.-Export--Southwestern Petroleum Corporation, Fort Worth, TX, pg. 1024
Thompson, Gerry, Sr. V.P.--College Division, Greenwich, CT, pg. 56
Thompson, L. Dan, Chief Oper. Officer & Sr. V.P.--Schad Industries, Inc., Lafayette, LA, pg. 974
Thompson, L. Don, Chief Oper. Officer & Sr. V.P.--Lou Ana Foods, Inc., Opelousas, LA, pg. 974
Thompson, Terrie J., Sr. V.P.--AmClyde Engineered Products, Inc., Saint Paul, MN, pg. 47
Thorell, C. Scott, Sr. V.P.--Integrated Systems Analysts, Inc., Arlington, VA, pg. 573
Tidwell, Sam, Sr. V.P.--Edwards Baking Co., Atlanta, GA, pg. 369
Tierney, John, 1st Sr. V.P.--Mars Advertising Co., Southfield, MI, pg. 713
Tietjen, Hugh, Sr. V.P.--Ziff Communications Company, New York, NY, pg. 1218
Tips, Bradley, Sr. V.P.--Cramer-Krasselt, Chicago, IL, pg. 296
Toffler, Van, Sr. V.P.-Entertainment & Bus. Devel.--MTV: Music Television, New York, NY, pg. 785
Tokarczyk, George, Sr. V.P.--D & K Optical, Inc., Louisville, KY, pg. 307
Tolar, Thomas, Sr. V.P.--Sarkes Tarzian, Incorporated, Bloomington, IN, pg. 1079
Tong, Bryant J., Sr. V.P.--Phoenix American Incorporated, San Rafael, CA, pg. 868
Toomey, Christopher, Sr. V.P.-Equip.--Della Construction Co. Inc., Enfield, CT, pg. 326
Torgersen, Donald B., Sr. V.P.-Food Grp.--Rich Products Corp., Buffalo, NY, pg. 932
Towry, Terence N., Sr. V.P.--Phoenix Home Life Mutual Insurance Company, Hartford, CT, pg. 868
Tracey, Vinnie, Sr. V.P.--RE/MAX International, Inc., Englewood, CO, pg. 915
Traub, Wayne, Sr. V.P., Acct. Supvr.--Sudler & Hennessey, New York, NY, pg. 1211
Trigg, Donald C., Sr. V.P.-Sec. & Gen. Counsel--The Associated Group, Indianapolis, IN, pg. 90
Trikaminas, Peter A., Sr. V.P.--Teachers Insurance and Annuity Association-College Retirement Equities Fund, New York, NY, pg. 1082
Trumbore, John, Sr. V.P., Mktg. Research--Harris, Baio & McCullough Inc., Philadelphia, PA, pg. 511
Trusk, John, Sr. V.P., Mng. Dir., Creative Services--Ayer Chicago, Chicago, IL, pg. 104
Tubis, Sandy, Sr. V.P.--Design 1 Interiors, Los Angeles, CA, pg. 332
Tucker, John J., Sr. V.P.--Kingswood Advertising, Inc., Ardmore, PA, pg. 632
Tuney, John, Sr. V.P.--JMB Realty Corporation, Chicago, IL, pg. 584
Turk, Stanley M., Sr. V.P.--Carrafiello, Diehl & Associates, Inc., Irvington, NY, pg. 225
Turnbull, James II, Sr. V.P., Creative Dir.--Y&R/Wunderman Worldwide/Detroit, Detroit, MI, pg. 1211
Turner, G.L., Sr. V.P.--Fish Engineering & Construction, Inc., Houston, TX, pg. 414
Turner, John, Sr. V.P.--Davis, Ball & Colombatto Advertising, Inc., Los Angeles, CA, pg. 318
Tutt, William B., Sr. V.P.--Broadmoor Hotel, Inc., Colorado Springs, CO, pg. 177
Uicker, Joseph B., Sr. V.P.--The Smith Group, Inc., Detroit, MI, pg. 1012
Underhill, Robert L., Chief Oper. Officer & Sr. V.P.--Channing L. Bete Co., Inc., South Deerfield, MA, pg. 147
Underwood, Eugene, Sr. V.P.--Dana Communications, Inc., Hopewell, NJ, pg. 313
Upright, David, Sr. V.P., Creative Supvr.--Sudler & Hennessey Consumer Group, New York, NY, pg. 1211
Urankar, John, Sr. V.P.-Claims--Transport Insurance Co., Dallas, TX, pg. 54
Urbanic, Joseph, Sr. V.P.--Centimark Corporation, Bethel Park, PA, pg. 231
Urey, Joe, Sr. V.P.--Price/McNabb, Inc., Asheville, NC, pg. 888
Urstadt, Jeffery, Sr. V.P.--Douglas Elliman-Gibbons & Ives, Inc., New York, NY, pg. 347
Usher, F. Barrie, Sr. V.P.-Canada--New York Life Insurance Company, New York, NY, pg. 802
Vail, Robert E., Sr. V.P.--Godfrey Advertising, Lancaster, PA, pg. 464
Valentine, D.E., Sr. V.P.--Camelot Communications, Inc., Dallas, TX, pg. 212
Vamos, James E., Sr. V.P.-Real Estate--McGean-Rohco, Inc., Cleveland, OH, pg. 729
Van Erp, Dirk, Sr. V.P.--Knight Architects Engineers Planners, Inc., Chicago, IL, pg. 637
Vandenbergh, Robert A., Sr. V.P. & Chief Lending Officer--The National Bank of Sussex County, Branchville, NJ, pg. 534
Vander Zwaag, Donald D., Sr. V.P. & Treas.--Bradford Company, Holland, MI, pg. 170
VanderWeele, Julie, Sr. V.P.-Mktg.--Mesirow Financial, Chicago, IL, pg. 741
VanDine, Harold F., Sr. V.P.-Architecture & Design--Harley Ellington Pierce Yee Associates, Inc., Southfield, MI, pg. 509
Varage, Thomas J., Sr. V.P. & Chief Investment Officer--Mutual of America, New York, NY, pg. 777
Varel, Mark, Sr. V.P.--Varel Manufacturing Co., Dallas, TX, pg. 1145

Vargo, Geoffrey, Sr. V.P.--Sarkes Tarzian, Incorporated, Bloomington, IN, pg. 1079
Varvara, Peter, Sr. V.P., Exec. Acct. Dir.--N W Ayer Inc., New York, NY, pg. 104
Veltrop, Jon A., Sr. V.P.--Harza Engineering Co., Chicago, IL, pg. 516
Verdon, William, Sr. V.P. & Gen. Counsel--Crowley Maritime Corporation, Oakland, CA, pg. 301
Verlizzo, Frank, Sr. V.P., Art Dir.--LeDonne, Wilner & Weiner, Inc., New York, NY, pg. 665
Vignola, Nancy, Sr. V.P.-Home Collection Design--Polo/Ralph Lauren Corporation, New York, NY, pg. 879
Vlick, Robert P., Sr. V.P.-Bldg. System Services Group--Air Conditioning Co., Inc., Glendale, CA, pg. 26
Vogel, Allen, Sr. V.P.-New Business Accounts Receivable Financing--Century Business Credit Corporation, New York, NY, pg. 235
Vogian, Peter J., Sr. V.P.--Massachusetts Mutual Life Insurance Co., Springfield, MA, pg. 718
Von Forell, Kenneth J., Jr., Sr. V.P.--Florists' Mutual Insurance Co., Edwardsville, IL, pg. 421
Vorce, Betsy, Sr. V.P.-Pub. Rels.--Viacom Entertainment, New York, NY, pg. 785
Vouvakis, Jim, Sr. V.P.-Yellow Pages--Western International Media Corporation, Los Angeles, CA, pg. 1179
Vouvakis, Jim, Sr. V.P.--U.S. Yellow Pages, Los Angeles, CA, pg. 1180
Wachtel, James R., Sr. V.P.-Atlantic--Lykes Bros. Steamship Co., Inc., New Orleans, LA, pg. 688
Wages, Randy P., Sr. V.P.--Breton Construction, Inc., Irvine, CA, pg. 174
Wagner, Daniel E., Sr. V.P., Grp. Dir.--Young & Rubicam Detroit, Detroit, MI, pg. 1211
Wahlberg, Sarah J., Sr. V.P.--First National Bank of Blue Island, Blue Island, IL, pg. 481
Walden, Tunnie, Sr. V.P.--Southeastern Equipment Company, Inc., Augusta, GA, pg. 1019
Waldrup, Ira E., Sr. V.P.--Guardsmark, Inc., Memphis, TN, pg. 492
Walker, Daniel W., Sr. V.P.--Kokosing Construction Company, Inc., Fredericktown, OH, pg. 640
Walker, Gerald T., Sr. V.P.-Grp. Div.--American United Life Insurance Company, Indianapolis, IN, pg. 65
Walker, Kim, Sr. V.P.-Multinatl. Bus. Devel.--Backer Spielvogel Bates Worldwide, Inc., New York, NY, pg. 108
Walker, T.P., Sr. V.P. & Sec.--Stonecutter Mills Corp., Spindale, NC, pg. 1051
Wall, Richard A., Sr. V.P.-Special Projects--R. H. Macy & Co., Inc., New York, NY, pg. 698
Wallach, Kenneth L., Sr. V.P.--Central National-Gottesman Inc., Purchase, NY, pg. 233
Wallis, W. Budge, Sr. V.P. & Gen. Mgr.-Book Div.--F & W Publications, Inc., Cincinnati, OH, pg. 394
Wang, Rosa, Sr. V.P.--Bugle Boy Industries, Inc., Simi Valley, CA, pg. 187
Ward, Bill, Sr. V.P., Sec. & Treas.--N.W. Transport Service, Inc., Commerce City, CO, pg. 781
Warr, A. Joe, Sr. V.P.--Gary-Williams Energy Corporation, Denver, CO, pg. 444
Waters, John E., Sr. V.P.-Environment--Gannett Fleming Affiliates, Inc., Harrisburg, PA, pg. 442
Watts, Robert H., Sr. V.P.--John Hancock Advisers, Inc., Boston, MA, pg. 596
Waxler, Burton, Sr. V.P. & Treas.--National Cleaning Contractors, Inc., New York, NY, pg. 786
Waxman, Norman, Sr. V.P.--Schnadig Corporation, Chicago, IL, pg. 977
Wealand, Tommy, Sr. V.P., Gen. Mgr.--Marketing Resources of America, Inc., Overland Park, KS, pg. 709
Webb, Max, Sr. V.P.--Shapell Industries, Inc., Beverly Hills, CA, pg. 995
Webb, Robert D., Sr. V.P. & Treas.--Knight Architects Engineers Planners, Inc., Chicago, IL, pg. 637
Webb, Scott, Sr. V.P. & Dir.-Creative--Nickelodeon/Nick At Nite, New York, NY, pg. 785
Wechsler, Alfred E., Sr. V.P. & Chief Professional Officer--Arthur D. Little, Inc., Cambridge, MA, pg. 678
Wechter, Rochelle, Sr. V.P.--ELS Educational Services, Culver City, CA, pg. 56
Wecker, Irwin, Sr. V.P.-Human Resources--Morse Diesel International, New York, NY, pg. 771
Wecker, Richard A., Sr. V.P.-Mktg.--New York Life Insurance Company, New York, NY, pg. 802
Weed, Gregory, Sr. V.P., Acct. Supvr.--Sudler & Hennessey Consumer Group, New York, NY, pg. 1211
Weeden, Walter W., Jr., Sr. V.P.-Transportation Prods. & Gen. Mgr.--Servo Corporation of America, Hicksville, NY, pg. 993
Weinert, Eileen, Sr. V.P.--Media That Works, Cincinnati, OH, pg. 735
Weingarden, Earl, Sr. V.P., Exec. Creative Dir.--Lou Beres & Associates, Inc., Chicago, IL, pg. 141
Weinstein, Daniel, Sr. V.P.--Keywell Corporation, Detroit, MI, pg. 629
Weinstein, Mark M., Sr. V.P. & Gen. Counsel--Viacom Inc., New York, NY, pg. 785
Weinstein, Mark M., Sr. V.P. & Gen. Counsel--Viacom International Inc., New York, NY, pg. 785
Weintraub, Irving J., Chief Fin. Officer & Sr. V.P.--William Morris Agency, Inc., Beverly Hills, CA, pg. 771
Weiser, John W., Sr. V.P. & Gen. Counsel--Bechtel Group, Inc., San Francisco, CA, pg. 130
Weistling, William M., Sr., Sr. V.P.--The Donohoe Companies, Inc., Washington, DC, pg. 345
Welch, Edward A., Sr. V.P.--Fay, Spofford & Thorndike, Inc., Lexington, MA, pg. 404
Welch, Robin B., Sr. V.P.-Grp. Ins. Dept.--New York Life Insurance Company, New York, NY, pg. 802
Welsh, John, Sr. V.P., Assoc. Creative Dir.--Arnold Fortuna Lawner & Cabot, Boston, MA, pg. 84
Welsh, Michael T., Sr. V.P. & Sec.--First Federal of Michigan, Detroit, MI, pg. 414
Welsh, Paul J., Exec. V.P.--NKH&W, Inc., Kansas City, MO, pg. 781
Wendorf, Nile, Sr. V.P.-Bus. Devel.--Kemmerer Bottling Group Inc., Joliet, IL, pg. 622
Wendt, Edward G., Jr., Sr. V.P.-Grp. Dept. Ins.--New York Life Insurance Company, New York, NY, pg. 802
Wengler, Roman, Sr. V.P.--Harza Engineering Co., Chicago, IL, pg. 516
Werner, Jon B., Sr. V.P.--Pacific Scene Inc., San Diego, CA, pg. 841
Wheeler, David, Sr. V.P.--LaMarca Group Inc., New York, NY, pg. 652
Whicker, Dennis R., Sr. V.P., Fin. Services--EvansGroup, Salt Lake City, UT, pg. 390
Whitcome, James P., Sr. V.P.-Capitol Improvements--CenterMark Properties, Inc., Saint Louis, MO, pg. 231
White, Eldridge W., Exec. V.P. & Partner--Donino & Partners, Inc., Atlanta, GA, pg. 344
White, Jeff, Sr. V.P.--Biggs Gilmore Communications, Kalamazoo, MI, pg. 149
White, Lisa, Sr. V.P., Acct. Services Dir.--The Joey Reiman Agency, Atlanta, GA, pg. 923
White, William R., Sr. V.P.-Corp. Communications--Mutual of America, New York, NY, pg. 777
Whitehouse, David, Sr. V.P. & Sec.--Ellerbe Becket Construction Services, Minneapolis, MN, pg. 378
Whitely, George, Sr. V.P., Acct. Dir.--Stephan & Brady, Incorporated, Madison, WI, pg. 1046
Whittaker, Arlynn, Sr. V.P.--Admarketing, Inc., Los Angeles, CA, pg. 18
Wickett, Richard, Sr. V.P.--Investor Rels.--Post Buckley Schuh & Jernigan, Miami, FL, pg. 881
Wilbur, D. Elliott, Sr. V.P.--Arthur D. Little, Inc., Cambridge, MA, pg. 678
Wilcox, Mack, Sr. V.P.--Atlantic Gulf Communities Corporation, Miami, FL, pg. 95
Wiley, Dr. William R., Sr. V.P.--Battelle Memorial Institute, Columbus, OH, pg. 126
Wiley, William, Sr. V.P.--Tri-State Motor Transit Co., Joplin, MO, pg. 1111
Wilke, Bruce, Sr. V.P.-Distribution Opers.--Mary Kay Cosmetics Inc., Dallas, TX, pg. 716
Williams, Alan, Sr. V.P.--MBT Associates, Inc., San Francisco, CA, pg. 691
Williams, Eldridge M., Sr. V.P.--Universal Life Insurance Company, Memphis, TN, pg. 1138
Williams, Lonnie, Sr. V.P.--Nabholz Construction Corp., Conway, AR, pg. 782
Williams, Timothy L., Sr. V.P.-Human Resources--R. L. Polk & Co., Detroit, MI, pg. 879
Williams, Tom, Sr. V.P.-Kansas City Div.--Associated Wholesale Grocers, Inc., Kansas City, KS, pg. 92
Williams, W. Peter, Sr. V.P.--Chicago Corp., Chicago, IL, pg. 247
Williamson, L., Sr. V.P., Corp. Devel.--Leo Burnett Company Ltd., Toronto,, Canada, pg. 192
Wilson, David G., Sr. V.P. & Grp. Mgr.-Comml. Banking--Team Bancshares, Inc., Dallas, TX, pg. 1082
Wilson, Paul, Sr. V.P.--Biggs Gilmore Communications, Kalamazoo, MI, pg. 149
Windley, Kathryn, Sr. V.P., Assoc. Creative Dir.--Hal Riney & Partners, Inc., New York, NY, pg. 935
Wisdorf, Douglas G., Sr. V.P. & Controller--Washington Mutual Savings Bank, Seattle, WA, pg. 1166
Wisely, Richard, Sr. V.P.--Sundown Vitamin Co., Inc., Fort Lauderdale, FL, pg. 1060
Wissell, Donald E., Sr. V.P.-Admin. Services--Mutual of America, New York, NY, pg. 777
Witt, Robert B., Sr. V.P.--Tristate Electrical Supply Co., Inc., Hagerstown, MD, pg. 1114
Wohadlo, Leonard R., Sr. V.P.--Harbert Corporation, Birmingham, AL, pg. 506
Wolf, James A., Sr. V.P.--Teachers Insurance and Annuity Association-College Retirement Equities Fund, New York, NY, pg. 1082
Wolf, Robert D., Sr. V.P.--Bee-Gee Shoe Div., Dayton, OH, pg. 373
Wolfe, Deloris, Sr. V.P.--First National Bank in Cleburne, Cleburne, TX, pg. 412
Wolfe, J.G., Jr., Sr. V.P.--Zenith Div.--Allison-Erwin Co. Inc., Charlotte, NC, pg. 40
Wolfson, Susan, Sr. V.P.--Stawasz Public Relations, New York, NY, pg. 605
Wolthausen, Reed, Sr. V.P. & Chief Fin. Officer--Burke Industries Inc., San Jose, CA, pg. 190
Wood, C. Courtney, Sr. V.P.--Independent Insurance Agents of America, Alexandria, VA, pg. 565
Woodfield, Marion, Sr. V.P., Acctg. Services--EvansGroup, Salt Lake City, UT, pg. 390
Woods, Wayne, Sr. V.P.--Cranford Johnson Robinson Woods, Little Rock, AR, pg. 296
Wordsworth, Iris B., Sr. V.P. & Dir.-Corp. Rels.--First American Bankshares, Inc., Washington, DC, pg. 412
Wormwood, Ronadl, Sr. V.P.--Hancock Lumber, Inc., Casco, ME, pg. 504
Wright, Carl B., Sr. V.P.--The Union Central Life Insurance Co., Cincinnati, OH, pg. 1127
Wright, Charles, V.P.-Agency--State Farm Mutual Automobile Insurance Company, Bloomington, IL, pg. 1041
Wright, James W., Sr. V.P. & Cashier--Park Bank, Milwaukee, WI, pg. 118
Wright, Jerry, Sr. V.P., Acct. Services--GBF/Ayer, Los Angeles, CA, pg. 104
Wright, Lonnie R., Sr. V.P.-Fin. Institutions--John Alden Financial Corporation, Miami, FL, pg. 32
Wright, Virgil W., Sr. V.P.--McArdle Printing Co., Inc., Upper Marlboro, MD, pg. 189
Wynne, Arthur, Sr. V.P.--Lawry's Restaurants, Inc., Los Angeles, CA, pg. 663
Wynne, Nancy R., Sr. V.P., Dir. Real Estate--Young & Rubicam Inc., New York, NY, pg. 1210
Yaeger, Phil, Sr. V.P.--Price/McNabb, Inc., Asheville, NC, pg. 888
Yarrington, Hugh J., Sr. V.P. & Exec. Editor--The Bureau of National Affairs, Inc., Washington, DC, pg. 189
Yeatman, Robert, Sr. V.P.--Washington Homes, Inc., Landover, MD, pg. 1166
Yorio, Frank, Sr. V.P.-Mktg. & Sls.--La Victoria Foods, Inc., City of Industry, CA, pg. 649
Young, Mark, Sr. V.P.-Animation Devel.--Hanna-Barbera Productions, Inc., Los Angeles, CA, pg. 53
Young, Stephen N., Sr. V.P.--The Clinipad Corporation, Guilford, CT, pg. 255
Young, William J., Sr. V.P., Human Resources Dir.--William Douglas McAdams Inc., New York, NY, pg. 726
Youngblood, Larry, Sr. V.P.--E.A. Sween Company, Eden Prairie, MN, pg. 1066
Younggren, David, Sr. V.P.--The Gary-Williams Company, Denver, CO, pg. 444
Younggren, David, Sr. V.P.--Gary-Williams Energy Corporation, Denver, CO, pg. 444
Youngmark, Roy, Sr. V.P. & Dir.-Creative--Goldfarb & Company Advertising, Southfield, MI, pg. 467
Zach, Bob, Sr. V.P., Media Dir.--Chiat/Day/Mojo/New York, New York, NY, pg. 244
Zackson, David, M.D., Sr. V.P., Medical Dir.--William Douglas McAdams Inc., New York, NY, pg. 726
Zamoiski, John, Sr. V.P.--Don Jagoda Associates, Inc., Melville, NY, pg. 588
Zapisek, John R., Sr. V.P., Chief Fin. Officer & Treas.--Utica Mutual Insurance Company, New Hartford, NY, pg. 1140
Zehner, Arnie, Sr. V.P.-Energy--Fru-Con Construction Corporation, Ballwin, MO, pg. 435
Zeiger, Thomas, Sr. V.P.--Shapell Industries, Inc., Beverly Hills, CA, pg. 995
Zerrer, Jeffery, Sr. V.P.--American Finance Group, Boston, MA, pg. 52
Zimet, I.M., Sr. V.P.--American Trading and Production Corporation, Baltimore, MD, pg. 64
Zimmerman, Hiram, Sr. V.P., Dir. Typographic Services--Sudler & Hennessey, New York, NY, pg. 1211
Zimmerman, Michael, Sr. V.P.--Watt, Roop & Co., Cleveland, OH, pg. 1168
Zingle, Mark, Sr. V.P. & Chief Actuary--Ministers Life Insurance Company, Minneapolis, MN, pg. 757
Zorio, John W., Sr. V.P.-No. Central Agencies--New York Life Insurance Company, New York, NY, pg. 802
Zoss, Howard, Sr. V.P.--Marcus Advertising, Inc., Cleveland, OH, pg. 706
Zost, Edward D., Sr. V.P.--Owen Health Care, Houston, TX, pg. 833
Zwirecki, John, Sr. V.P.--Washington Homes, Inc., Landover, MD, pg. 1166
Zyboyovsky, James F., Sr. V.P.--Kearney-National, Inc., White Plains, NY, pg. 357

TREASURER

Aanenson, Vernon O., Pres. & Treas.--Old Dutch Foods, Inc., Saint Paul, MN, pg. 823
Abair,Daniel, Sec. & Treas.--Park Motor Sales Company, Detroit, MI, pg. 849
Abbey, Richard, Sec. & Treas.--Automotive Moulding Company, Warren, MI, pg. 101
Abbot, Patricia, Treas. & Sec.--Metro Label Corp., Garland, TX, pg. 743
Abdalla Black, Barbara, V.P. & Treas.--Abdalla's Lafayette, Inc., Lafayette, LA, pg. 10
Abernathy, Shawan, V.P. & Treas.--Nacoma Consolidated, Inc., Nacogdoches, TX, pg. 782
Abetamarco, Vincent, Treas.--The Stroh Brewery Company, Detroit, MI, pg. 1053
Abrahamson, Mary Jo, Sr. V.P., Chief Fin. Officer & Treas.--Zapiecki & Partners Inc., Toledo, OH, pg. 1216
Abrams, Jerry, Treas. & Chief Fin. Officer--Hoogovens Aluminum Corp., Secaucus, NJ, pg. 543
Abramson, Larry, V.P. & Treas.--Keyes Motors, Inc., Van Nuys, CA, pg. 627
Abramson, Mike, Treas.--Microband Companies, Inc., Fairfield, NJ, pg. 748
Abroms, Harold L., Chief Oper. Officer, Exec. V.P., Treas. & Sec.--Parisian, Inc., Birmingham, AL, pg. 848
Accardo, Jack P., V.P. & Chief Fin. Officer, Treas. & Sec.--Kasper Machine Company, Madison Heights, MI, pg. 618
Acton, Elizabeth S., V.P. & Asst. Treas.--Park Ridge Corporation, Park Ridge, NJ, pg. 849
Adams, Joe, Exec. V.P., Treas.--Creative Alliance, Inc., Louisville, KY, pg. 297
Adams, John S., V.P. & Treas.--Hatzel & Buehler, Inc., Wilmington, DE, pg. 277
Adams, Lyle, Treas.--Gregory Affiliates, Inc., Beaverton, OR, pg. 486
Adamski, Richard J., V.P. & Treas.--Teachers Insurance and Annuity Association-College Retirement Equities Fund, New York, NY, pg. 1082
Adelstein, Bruce S., Exec. V.P. & Sec.--Olympic Steel Inc., Bedford Heights, OH, pg. 825
Adessi, Alfred, Treas. & Sec.--Mossberg Industries, Inc., Cumberland, RI, pg. 772
Adkins, Tony K., Treas.--Chapman Printing Company, Huntington, WV, pg. 239
Agemian, Charles A., Treas.--Macromedia Inc., Hackensack, NJ, pg. 698
Aguirre, Henry J., Pres. & Treas.--Mexican Industries in Michigan, Detroit, MI, pg. 745
Ahlin, Thomas, Sec. & Treas.--Fargo Clinic Ltd., Fargo, ND, pg. 399
Ahrens, Pamela A., Treas.--Roche Constructors, Inc., Greeley, CO, pg. 940
Akaraguian, Anoush, V.P. & Treas.--Organically Grown Corporation, Los Angeles, CA, pg. 829
Akin, Richard L., V.P. & Treas.--Golf Hosts, Inc., Palm Harbor, FL, pg. 469
Akins, Edwin E., Treas., Sec. & Dir.-Personnel--T.J. Morris Company, Inc., Statesboro, GA, pg. 771
Albarelli, Joseph, Exec. V.P. & Treas.--Amloid Corporation, Saddle Brook, NJ, pg. 67

Alberici, Gabriel J., Chm. Bd. & Treas.--J. S. Alberici Construction Co., Inc., Saint Louis, MO, pg. 31
Albert, Billie, Treas. & Sec.--Farmway Co-Op Inc., Beloit, KS, pg. 402
Albert, Insulinde, Treas. & Sec.--R.L. Albert & Son, Inc., Greenwich, CT, pg. 31
Albert, Rachel F., Treas.--The Harodite Finishing Company Inc., North Dighton, MA, pg. 510
Alberts, Robert J., Corp. Sec. & Treas.--Templeton, Kenly & Co., Inc., Broadview, IL, pg. 1086
Albrecht, Fred, Exec. V.P.-Fin.--First Worthing, Dallas, TX, pg. 414
Alderson, Wayne, Treas.--Crescent Electric Supply Co., East Dubuque, IL, pg. 298
Alderton, Susan E., V.P.-Fin. & Treas.--Tremont Corporation, Denver, CO, pg. 1109
Alessi, Laurie, Treas.--Interstate Commodities Inc., Troy, NY, pg. 580
Alexander, Bill, V.P., Treas. & Chief Fin. Officer--Purcell Co., Inc., Bay Saint Louis, MS, pg. 900
Alexander, James C., V.P., Sec. & Treas.--General Homes Corporation, Houston, TX, pg. 449
Alflen, J., Treas. & Sec.--Torrance Nissan, Inc., Torrance, CA, pg. 1102
Alford, Fred F., Jr., Treas.--Alford Refrigerated Warehouse, Inc., Dallas, TX, pg. 34
Alford, M.L., V.P. & Treas.--Staple Cotton Cooperative Association, Greenwood, MS, pg. 1038
Allard, Maurice E., Treas. & Controller--Granite State Manufacturing Co., Manchester, NH, pg. 476
Allen, Clinton G., Sec. & Treas.--Bill Heard Chevrolet Inc., Columbus, GA, pg. 521
Allen, Gordon, Treas. & Controller--Crown Fence Co., Pasadena, CA, pg. 302
Allen, Joseph, Exec. V.P., Treas. & Sec.--Brant Allen Industries, Inc., Greenwich, CT, pg. 172
Allen, Rick, V.P.- Fin., Admin. & Chief Fin. Officer--J.D. Edwards & Company, Denver, CO, pg. 370
Allen, Robert J., Treas. & Sec.--Mason Shoe Mfg. Co., Chippewa Falls, WI, pg. 718
Allen, Robert J., Sec. & Treas.--Wissota Trader & B.A. Mason, Chippewa Falls, WI, pg. 718
Allen, Tom R., V.P.-Fin. & Treas.--Harriet & Henderson Yarns, Inc., Henderson, NC, pg. 511
Allen, Tucker, Treas.--JM Family Enterprises Inc., Deerfield Beach, FL, pg. 584
Allen, W. Dean, Chief Fin. Officer & Treas.--Expo Industries, Inc., San Diego, CA, pg. 393
Allgyer, James D., Controller--Masland Industries, Carlisle, PA, pg. 717
Allred, Barry L., Pres., Chief Oper. Officer & Treas.--Elkins Constructors, Inc., Jacksonville, FL, pg. 377
Allsopp, Cornelius, P.E., Pres. & Treas.--Harvey Construction Company, Inc., Bedford, NH, pg. 515
Allsup, Barbara J., V.P., Sec. & Treas.--Allsups Convenience Stores Inc., Clovis, NM, pg. 43
Allsup, Jay M., Chief Fin. Officer & Treas.--Standun, Inc., Irwindale, CA, pg. 1038
Alongi, Linda, Sec. & Treas.--American Furniture Company, Albuquerque, NM, pg. 55
Alosa, Joseph R., Pres. & Treas.--Patsy's, Inc., Concord, NH, pg. 851
Alperson, Steven, V.P. & Treas.--Rolled Steel Products Corporation, Los Angeles, CA, pg. 944
Altmaier, Chris, Treas.--Southern Belle Dairy Company, Inc., Somerset, KY, pg. 1020
Amato, Larry, Chief Fin. Officer, Treas. & Sec.--Elkay Products, Inc., Shrewsbury, MA, pg. 377
Ambrose, William A., Exec. V.P., Treas. & Dir.-Investor Rels.--Worsley Companies Inc., Wilmington, NC, pg. 1204
Ames, J.W., V.P.-Fin., Treas. & Sec.--Milwaukee Electric Tool Corp., Brookfield, WI, pg. 361
Amster, Kirk, V.P., Treas. & Sec.--A S H, Inc., Phoenix, AZ, pg. 8
Amsterdam, J., Chm. Bd.--Leviton Mfg. Co., Inc., Little Neck, NY, pg. 671
Amsterdam, M., Sec. & Treas.--General Metalcraft, Inc., Dover, DE, pg. 450
Anderson, Bruce, Exec. V.P., Treas. & Dir.-Mfg. & Quality Control--Integrated Energy Controls Corp., Minneapolis, MN, pg. 573
Anderson, Carroll, Treas.--Iowa Paint Mfg. Company, Inc., Des Moines, IA, pg. 582
Anderson, Charles W., V.P. & Asst. Treas.--Anderson Industries, Inc., Dallas, TX, pg. 72
Anderson, Eric, Exec. V.P. & Treas.--The Conde Nast Publications Inc., New York, NY, pg. 19
Anderson, Eric, Controller & Treas.--Spurgeon Mercantile Company, Chicago, IL, pg. 1034
Anderson, Florence J., Treas.--Anderson Advertising, Inc., San Antonio, TX, pg. 72
Anderson, Gary, Treas. & Sec.--X-A Cabinet Corporation, La Mirada, CA, pg. 1206
Anderson, Gerald L., V.P.-Fin. & Treas.--Georgetown Industries, Inc., Charlotte, NC, pg. 453
Anderson, James R., V.P.-Fin., Sec. & Treas.--The Austin Company, Cleveland, OH, pg. 790
Anderson, John E., Pres. & Treas.--Topa Equities Ltd, Inc., Los Angeles, CA, pg. 1101
Anderson, Jon, V.P. & Treas.--Gulf States Paper Corporation, Tuscaloosa, AL, pg. 494
Anderson, Reid, Treas.--Grand Prairie Co-op, Inc., Tolono, IL, pg. 475
Anderson, Robert, Asst. Treas.--Channel Home Centers Inc., Whippany, NJ, pg. 238
Anderson, Robert W., Sec., Treas. & Comptroller--Superior Oil Co. Inc., Indianapolis, IN, pg. 1064
Anderson, William, V.P. & Treas.--Wilsey Bennett Co., San Francisco, CA, pg. 1193
Anderson, William J., Sec. & Treas.--Pella Corporation, Pella, IA, pg. 856
Andonian, Hratch K., Exec. V.P., Sec. & Treas.--A K H Company, Inc., Los Angeles, CA, pg. 4
Andre, Wayne, Treas. & Sec.--Roseville Chrysler Plymouth Inc., Roseville, MI, pg. 949
Andres, P.J., V.P. & Treas.--U.S. Can Company, Oak Brook, IL, pg. 1134
Andretta, Vincent J., Pres., Chief Exec. Officer & Treas.--Colony Liquor Distributors, Inc., Kingston, NY, pg. 264
Andrews, Donald L., Treas.--SRI International, Menlo Park, CA, pg. 964
Andrews, Sheri L., V.P. & Treas.--Lozier Corporation, Omaha, NE, pg. 686
Anguish, J. Edward, V.P. & Treas.--John Hancock Networking Insurance Agency, Boston, MA, pg. 596
Ankeney, Daniel, Treas.--Menasha Corporation, Neenah, WI, pg. 738
Annello, Larry, V.P.-Fin.--Audio Specialist, Inc., Newington, CT, pg. 98
Ansted, James P., Chief Fin. Officer, Treas., Sec.--Plastic Suppliers, Inc., Columbus, OH, pg. 875
Antaman, John, Treas.--Barneys New York, New York, NY, pg. 120
Anthony, Aubra, Jr., Treas., Sec. & Counsel--Anthony Forest Products Co., Inc., El Dorado, AR, pg. 77
Anthony, Gordon C., Exec. V.P. & Treas.--The Flood Company, Hudson, OH, pg. 419
Antonopoulou, X., Treas.--Geo-Young & Rubicam, Athens,, Greece, pg. 1212
Appelwick, Karen K., Sec. & Treas.--Apple Lines, Inc., Madison, SD, pg. 79
Appich, Donald L., V.P. & Treas.--Emrick Chevrolet Sales Corporation, Richmond, VA, pg. 380
Appt, James L., Pres. Treas. & New Bus. Contact--Communications Concepts, Toledo, OH, pg. 269
Arakelian, Dorothy J., Treas. & Sec.--Standard Manufacturing Company, Troy, NY, pg. 1037
Arana, Cherly, Treas. & Sec.--Chase Chevrolet Co., Stockton, CA, pg. 240
Arboneaux, Jesse P., V.P., Chief Fin. Officer, Treas. & Sec.--Ourso Investment Corporation, Donaldsonville, LA, pg. 832
Arcadi, Vincent, Sec. & Treas.--Depew Development Inc., Lancaster, NY, pg. 331
Archer, Ophelia, Treas. & Sec.--Stahmann Farms, Inc., Las Cruces, NM, pg. 1034
Archibald, Kathy R., Sec. & Treas.--Printing House, Inc., Quincy, FL, pg. 891
Arciello, M.J., V.P.-Fin. & Treas.--Nickles Bakery, Inc., Martins Ferry, OH, pg. 807
Arends, Martha O., Treas.--Donald L. Arends Inc., Oak Brook, IL, pg. 81
Arens, Joel, Exec. V.P., Treas. & Sec.--Alacon, Sunnyvale, CA, pg. 29
Arfmann, Bruce, Chief Fin. Officer & Treas.--RELA, Inc., Boulder, CO, pg. 924
Arita, Don T., Treas.--Silicon Valley Development, Santa Clara, CA, pg. 1004
Armentrout, Steve, Assoc. Treas.--American Mathematical Society, Inc., Providence, RI, pg. 58
Armstrong, Donald, Treas.--Carl Weissman & Sons, Inc., Great Falls, MT, pg. 1174
Arnold, Barbara M., Treas.--Petroleum Products Corp., Middletown, PA, pg. 865
Arrigo, Joseph F., V.P., Treas. & Sec.--UIS, Inc., New York, NY, pg. 1123
Arsenault, James, Treas. & Controller--The Asher Winer Company, Fitchburg, MA, pg. 88
Artz, Frederick A., Treas.--Spang & Company, Butler, PA, pg. 1025
Asch, David, Exec. V.P.-Treas. & Sec.--Twincraft, Inc., Winooski, VT, pg. 1122
Asche, Ron D., Controller, Treas. & Div. Mgr.-Fin. & Acct.--Nebraska Public Power District, Columbus, NE, pg. 796
Aschinger, Carl J., Jr., Chm. Bd., Pres. & Chief Exec. Officer--Columbus Show Case Company, Columbus, OH, pg. 267
Ashby, Ralph, Treas. & Sec.--United Producers & Consumers Co-Op, Phoenix, AZ, pg. 1134
Ashkin, Anna, Sec. & Treas.--Rugby-Darby Group Of Cos., Rockville Centre, NY, pg. 955
Ashley, Charles L., V.P. & Treas.--A. Duda & Sons Inc., Oviedo, FL, pg. 351
Ashley, Kenneth, Chief Fin. Officer, Sec. & Treas.--National R.V., Inc., Perris, CA, pg. 792
Ashman, Stephen N., Treas.--Capital Bancorp, Miami, FL, pg. 214
Astle, Frederic C., V.P.-Fin. & Treas.--A-P-A Transport Corp., North Bergen, NJ, pg. 5
Aston, James A., Mng. Dir.-Investment Banking & Treas.--Insignia Financial Group, Inc., Greenville, SC, pg. 571
Astrowsky, Barry, V.P.-Fin.--Brandt, Inc., Bensalem, PA, pg. 1111
Astrup, Corrine, Treas. & Sec.--Astrup Drugs, Inc., Austin, MN, pg. 93
Atkins, Pat, Corp. Sec., Treas.--The Atkins Agency, San Antonio, TX, pg. 94
Attardi, Charles, Jr., Sec. & Treas.--North Carolina Equipment Co., Raleigh, NC, pg. 812
Attaway, Michael H., Asst. Treas.--M M Systems Corporation, Tucker, GA, pg. 692
Attebury, Ronald L., Chief Fin. Officer & Treas.--Norbest, Inc., Midvale, UT, pg. 809
Atwood, Fern, Asst. Sec. & Treas.--Atwood Distributing, Inc., Enid, OK, pg. 97
Auray, Delbert L., Pres. & Treas.--Bridgeport Fittings, Inc., Stratford, CT, pg. 175
Aurnou, Michael W., Treas.--Yenkin-Majestic Paint Corporation, Columbus, OH, pg. 1208
Austin, Joan D., Exec. V.P. & Treas.--A-Dec, Inc., Newberg, OR, pg. 1
Austin, Laurence, V.P.-Fin., Sec. & Treas.--Miniature Precision Components, Walworth, WI, pg. 757
Autry, Jacqueline, Exec. V.P., Treas. & Chief Fin. Officer--Golden West Broadcasters, Los Angeles, CA, pg. 467
Avellino, Ann Marie, V.P., Controller--Stackig, Sanderson & White, Inc., McLean, VA, pg. 1034
Avery, James, Treas. & Sec.--Schumacher-Dugan Construction, West Chester, OH, pg. 979
Avery, Ken, Sr. V.P.-Finance--Yardney Technical Products, Inc., Pawcatuck, CT, pg. 1207
Avery, O. Keith, Sec. & Treas.--Presto Food Stores, Inc., Plant City, FL, pg. 888
Avril, Mary J., V.P. & Treas.--Sakrete, Inc., Cincinnati, OH, pg. 967
Awad, Dennis J., Pres., Chief Exec. & Fin. Officer & Treas.--Tele-Com Products, Inc., Duarte, CA, pg. 1084
Bacciocco, James S., Treas.--Kendall Healthcare Products Co., Mansfield, MA, pg. 622
Bachman, Lee W., V.P.-Fin. & Treas.--Bachman's, Inc., Minneapolis, MN, pg. 108
Bachmeier, Ronald M., V.P.-Fin., Chief Fin. Officer & Treas.--Xerxes Corporation, Minneapolis, MN, pg. 1206
Bacigalupo, John W., Chief Exec. Officer--Kelly-Moore Paint Company, Inc., San Carlos, CA, pg. 621
Baden, Marvin, V.P.-Mktg. & Sls., Sec. & Treas.--Producers Rice Mill Inc., Stuttgart, AR, pg. 892
Bailey, Gordon, Pres. & Treas.--Gordon Bailey & Associates, Inc., Stone Mountain, GA, pg. 114
Bailey, John, Chm. Bd., Pres., Chief Exec. & Fin. Officer & Treas.--Cal/Emblem Labels, Inc., Fresno, CA, pg. 208
Bailey, R. T., Treas.--Century Data Systems, Raleigh, NC, pg. 235
Bailie, John, Treas.--Eaton Equipment Corp., Blasdell, NY, pg. 364
Baioni, Louis, Exec. V.P. & Treas.--Dunavant Enterprises, Inc., Memphis, TN, pg. 352
Bair, A.D., Treas.--Root Corporation, Mount Wolf, PA, pg. 946
Baird, Donn, Treas.--Kalamazoo Holdings, Inc., Kalamazoo, MI, pg. 615
Baird, M. Rex, Sr. V.P., Treas. & Chief Fin. Officer--Summa Corporation, Las Vegas, NV, pg. 1057
Bakalar, John S., Exec. V.P. & Treas.--Rand McNally & Company, Skokie, IL, pg. 911
Baker, Dennis W., Treas.--CF Industries, Inc., Long Grove, IL, pg. 200
Baker, Jack, Treas.--Thomas R. Hopson Broker, Inc., Marietta, GA, pg. 544
Baker, James E., V.P.-Fin. & Treas.--Guy Gannett Publishing Company, Portland, ME, pg. 442
Baker, John E., Chief Fin. Officer, Treas. & Controller--Steuart Investment Co., Washington, DC, pg. 1048
Baker, Richard J., Exec. V.P., Treas.--The Highland Group, Inc., Southport, CT, pg. 534
Baker, T.F., Sr. V.P.-Fin., Treas. & Chief Fin. Officer--Harvest States Cooperatives, Saint Paul, MN, pg. 514
Baker, Thomas J., Treas.--BCM Engineers Inc., Plymouth Meeting, PA, pg. 106
Baker, W. Kendall, V.P., Treas., Chief Fin. & Acctg. Officer--Jim Walter Homes, Inc., Tampa, FL, pg. 1162
Balaban, Jay, Treas. & Sec.--Chorus Line, Inc., Vernon, CA, pg. 591
Balasi, Barbara, Treas.--DMI The Healthcare Agency, Chicago, IL, pg. 309
Baldwin, Ed F., Chm. Bd., Pres. & Treas.--Baldwin Construction, Inc., Fort Collins, CO, pg. 115
Baldwin, Sandra, Pres. & Treas.--H & H Distributing Company, Inc., West Union, IA, pg. 495
Ball, Alice, Treas. & Sec.--Air Power, Inc., High Point, NC, pg. 27
Ball, Donald L., V.P. & Treas.--Blissfield Manufacturing Company, Blissfield, MI, pg. 157
Ball, M.Z., Treas.--Bush Development Corp., Williamsburg, VA, pg. 196
Ballance, T. S., V.P.-Fin. & Treas.--Somerset Refinery Inc., Somerset, KY, pg. 1017
Ballantine, J. C., V.P., Sec. & Treas.--Miller Building Corp., Wilmington, NC, pg. 753
Banig, L.C., V.P.-Fin. & Treas.--Actron Manufacturing Company, Cleveland, OH, pg. 15
Banks, Glen, Sr. V.P. & Treas.--Forever Living Products, Tempe, AZ, pg. 424
Banquer, C.S., Treas. & Controller--Acme Refrigeration Of Baton Rouge Inc., Baton Rouge, LA, pg. 13
Barber, Dan, Sec. & Treas.--Barnett Millworks, Inc., Theodore, AL, pg. 120
Barber, George W., Jr., Chm. Bd., Chief Fin. Officer & Treas.--Barber Dairies, Inc., Birmingham, AL, pg. 119
Barden, William, V.P.-Fin. & Admin.--Langston Companies, Memphis, TN, pg. 657
Barefoot, Wayne, Treas.--Victaulic Company of America, Easton, PA, pg. 1149
Barg, David W., Treas.--Finger Furniture Company, Inc., Houston, TX, pg. 411
Baris, Sylvia, Treas.--Baris Shoe Company, Inc., New York, NY, pg. 119
Barker, D.W., Treas. & Chief Fin. Officer--Maescher Industries, Inc., Cincinnati, OH, pg. 699
Barker, Roger, V.P. & Treas.--Buffalo Rock Company, Birmingham, AL, pg. 187
Barlow, Carol Ann, Sec. & Treas.--Macristy Industries, Inc., New Britain, CT, pg. 698
Barlow, Felton W., Treas.--T.L. James & Company, Ruston, LA, pg. 588
Barnard, Michael, V.P. & Treas.--Amtran, Inc., Indianapolis, IN, pg. 69
Barnes, James, V.P., Treas. & Chief Fin. Officer--Wohlert Corp., Lansing, MI, pg. 1198
Barnes, R. B., Jr., Sec. & Treas.--Austin Co., Inc., Greeneville, TN, pg. 98
Barnett, Cecil C., Chm. Bd., Pres., Chief Exec. Officer & Treas.--Algood Food Company, Louisville, KY, pg. 34
Barnhardt, Sadler H., Sec. & Treas.--Barnhardt Manufacturing Co., Charlotte, NC, pg. 120
Barnhill, Richard D., Chief Fin. Officer, Treas. & Sec.--Idea Engineering & Fabricating, Detroit, MI, pg. 562
Barocas, Leon, V.P., Treas. & Sec.--Santee Print Works, Inc., New York, NY, pg. 970
Barone, Elaine, V.P., Sec. & Treas.--Coken Company, Inc., Providence, RI, pg. 259

Barow, Stanley, Treas.--Cortec Group, New York, NY, pg. 287
Barr, Michael, Pres. & Treas.--Barr Electric Corporation, Wheeling, IL, pg. 122
Barr, Thomas D., Treas.--Barr & Barr, Inc., New York, NY, pg. 121
Barrett, Fred C., Treas. & Sec.--Ryan Oldsmobile, Billings, MT, pg. 958
Barrett, JoAnn, Treas.--Bingham, Mt. Prospect, IL, pg. 151
Barrett, Paul, Sr. V.P.-Fin., Treas., & Chief Fin. Officer--Bill's Dollar Stores, Inc., Jackson, MS, pg. 150
Barrocas, Alberto, Pres. & Treas.--Injection Footwear Corp., Miami, FL, pg. 569
Barrott, John C., Sec. & Asst. Treas.--Aurora Casket Company, Aurora, IN, pg. 98
Barry, John F., Treas.--Oakhurst Dairy, Portland, ME, pg. 819
Bartenstein, Jeff C., Sec., Treas. & Controller--Alaska Industrial Hardware Inc., Anchorage, AK, pg. 30
Bartik, John G., Treas.--Sealy Corporation, Cleveland, OH, pg. 985
Bartlett, Noel, Treas.--Helena Laboratories Corporation, Beaumont, TX, pg. 526
Basco, E.M., Treas.--Fish Engineering & Construction, Inc., Houston, TX, pg. 414
Basile, Peter A., Pres.--Peter A. Basile Sons Inc., Livonia, MI, pg. 124
Basler, William L., Chm. Bd., Chief Exec. Officer & Treas.--Basler Electric Company, Highland, IL, pg. 125
Basquin, Peter, Chm. Bd., Sec. & Treas.--Harmeson Manufacturing Company, Inc., Frankfort, IN, pg. 510
Bass, Norma, Treas. & Sec.--The Parman Corporation, Nashville, TN, pg. 850
Bast, Charles W., Pres. & Treas.--Bast Chevrolet Inc., Seaford, NY, pg. 125
Batarseh, Gabriel, Sec. & Treas.--Filco, Inc., Sacramento, CA, pg. 409
Bateman, Kevin P., Treas.--Bateman Brothers Lumber Co., Inc., New Britain, PA, pg. 125
Bates, Dorothy G., Sec. & Treas.--Ring Technologies, Inc., Warren, MI, pg. 935
Bates, Maxine, Treas.--Bates Container, Inc., North Richland Hills, TX, pg. 125
Batkin, Sanford L., Pres. & Treas.--Universal Folding Box Company, Inc., Hoboken, NJ, pg. 1138
Battaglia, Thomas S., V.P. & Treas.--American Standard Inc., New York, NY, pg. 61
Battan, Thomas A., Treas. & Comptroller--W. L. Hailey & Company, Inc., Nashville, TN, pg. 500
Bauer, Elmer, Treas.--Dettra Flag Company, Oaks, PA, pg. 333
Bauer, James P., V.P.-Fin. & Treas.--Small Parts, Inc., Logansport, IN, pg. 1010
Bauer, Mimi, Treas. & Sec.--Basic Food International Inc., Fort Lauderdale, FL, pg. 124
Baugher, John O., Pres. & Treas.--Baugher Chevrolet-Buick-Geo, Inc., Waynesboro, VA, pg. 127
Baughman, George K., Pres. & Treas.--Plastomer Corp., Livonia, MI, pg. 876
Baum, W.A., Sec. & Treas.--W. A. Baum Company, Inc., Copiague, NY, pg. 127
Bauman, W.A., Pres. & Treas.--Enger-Kress Company, West Bend, WI, pg. 381
Baumann, Albert F., Treas.--Encore Marketing International, Lanham, MD, pg. 380
Baumann, Keith, Treas.--Shepard Niles, Inc., Montour Falls, NY, pg. 997
Baumgarte, Virginia, Sec. & Treas.--E.M. Wiegmann & Company, Inc., Freeburg, IL, pg. 1188
Bavougian, Vartan, Treas.--Winston Tire Company, Burbank, CA, pg. 1197
Bayer, William J., V.P. & Treas.--W S Holding Company, Euless, TX, pg. 1156
Bayley, Joanne, Treas. & Sec.--Robert E. Bayley Construction, Seattle, WA, pg. 128
Bazaire, Keith, Treas.--Grocers Baking Co., Grand Rapids, MI, pg. 488
Beach, Juanita, Sec. & Treas.--Beach Mold & Tool Inc., New Albany, IN, pg. 128
Bean, Delcie D., Pres., Treas. & Chief Exec. Officer--D. D. Bean & Sons Co., Jaffrey, NH, pg. 129
Beans, Stephen, Treas.--The Swanson Company Manufacturers, Phoenix, AZ, pg. 1066
Beard, Karen E., Sec. & Treas.--N. G. Gilbert Corporation, Muncie, IN, pg. 458
Beard, Thomas, Sr. V.P., Chief Fin. Officer, Treas. & Controller--Petroleum Inc., Wichita, KS, pg. 865
Beard, Thomas G., V.P.-Admin., Treas., Controller & Sec.--Palmer Electric Co., Winter Park, FL, pg. 843
Beauch, Steve, Sec. & Treas.--Veda Design Group, Alexandria, VA, pg. 1146
Beauchamp, Patrick L., Chm. Bd., Pres. & Treas.--Beauchamp Distributing Company, Compton, CA, pg. 130
Beaudoin, Marc, Sec. & Treas.--Hancock Lumber, Inc., Casco, ME, pg. 504
Beaulieu, Jon C., Treas.--Anderson Trucking Service Inc., Saint Cloud, MN, pg. 73
Beaver, Donald C., Pres., Chief Exec. Officer & Treas.--Brian Center Management Corporation, Hickory, NC, pg. 175
Beaver, Patricia, Treas.--Brian Center Management Corporation, Hickory, NC, pg. 175
Beck, Thomas E., V.P. & Treas.--Bitrek Corporation, Waynesboro, PA, pg. 153
Becker, James, Treas.--Red Wing Publishing Company, Red Wing, MN, pg. 919
Becker, Michael, Treas.--National Car Rental System, Inc., Minneapolis, MN, pg. 786
Becker, Paul, V.P., Sec., Treas. & Gen. Counsel--Cosco Industries, Spring Valley, NY, pg. 288
Becker, Robert, Sec. & Treas.--Ershigs, Inc., Bellingham, WA, pg. 387
Beckett, Steven J., Treas.--American Optical Corp., Greenwich, CT, pg. 59
Beckman, Martin, V.P. & Treas.--Hauenstein & Burmeister, Inc., Minneapolis, MN, pg. 517
Beda, Bruce A., V.P., Treas., Chief Fin. Officer & Sec.--Venturedyne, Ltd., Milwaukee, WI, pg. 1148
Bedford, Henry, Treas.--Southwestern/Great American Inc., Nashville, TN, pg. 1023
Bedford, Norman C., Treas.--Beckwith Elevator Co., Boston, MA, pg. 131
Behner, Barbara, Chief Fin. Officer, Sec. & Treas.--Harmon Smith Inc., Kansas City, MO, pg. 510
Behrakis, George D., Pres. & Treas.--Muro Pharmaceutical, Inc., Tewksbury, MA, pg. 776
Beil, Leo, V.P. & Treas.--C. A. Muer Corp., Detroit, MI, pg. 774
Belitsky, Lee J., V.P., Treas. & Comptroller--Morse Shoe, Inc., Canton, MA, pg. 772
Bell, Dennis, Controller & Treas.--Vernay Laboratories, Inc., Yellow Springs, OH, pg. 1148
Bell, Donald C., V.P. & Treas.--SENCORP, Newport, KY, pg. 989
Bell, George, Treas.--AJC International, Inc., Atlanta, GA, pg. 4
Bell, Kayden, V.P., Sec. & Treas.--Arnold Machinery Co., Salt Lake City, UT, pg. 84
Bell, Robert, Treas.--American Foundry Group, Inc., Bixby, OK, pg. 54
Beller, Laurence, Treas.--Amsco School Publications, Inc., New York, NY, pg. 68
Bellina, Gerald, Treas.--DAQ Electronics Inc., Middlesex, NJ, pg. 308
Bellis, W.J., Treas. & Controller--AGR International, Inc., Butler, PA, pg. 4
Bellora, Terry C., V.P.-Fin. & Treas.--Pace Industries, Inc., Fayetteville, AR, pg. 838
Belsly, J. Robert, Treas.--Nodak Mutual Insurance Company, Fargo, ND, pg. 808
Belsly, J. Robert, Treas.--Nodak Mutual Insurance Co., Fargo, ND, pg. 808
Bender, Michael, Treas., Controller & Chief Accountant--Lewis Drug, Inc., Sioux Falls, SD, pg. 673
Bender, Rita M., Treas.--Airguard Industries Inc., Louisville, KY, pg. 27
Bender, Robert L., Exec. V.P. & Treas.--Lord, Sullivan & Yoder, Inc. Advertising, Columbus, OH, pg. 683
Benedict, Shirley, V.P.-Fin.--Winona Knits, Winona, MN, pg. 1196
Benfield, James, Treas.--Transammonia Inc., New York, NY, pg. 1106
Bennett, G. Kirk, Jr., V.P. & Treas.--Bennett Brothers, Inc., Chicago, IL, pg. 139
Bennett, James D., Chief Fin. Officer & Treas.--V.G.S. Corp. d/b/a Southland Oil Company, Jackson, MS, pg. 1141
Bennett, Nancy, Treas.--Nature's Recipe Pet Foods, Corona, CA, pg. 796
Benson, Betty, Treas. & Sec.--Delaware Electric Co-Op, Greenwood, DE, pg. 325
Benson, James O., V.P. & Treas.--PHB Parker Die Castings, Fairview, PA, pg. 836
Bentcover, Bruce, Treas.--Hallmark Cards, Inc., Kansas City, MO, pg. 501
Bentley, Alan, Sec. & Treas.--National Merchandise Co., Inc., Jacksonville, FL, pg. 792
Bentley, Rita P., Treas.--Daniel F. Young, Inc., New York, NY, pg. 1209
Benton, Don R., Treas.--Farm Family Mutual Insurance Co., Glenmont, NY, pg. 401
Benton, Murray, Dir.-Personnel & Treas.--Mid South Sales, Helena, AR, pg. 750
Benton, Virgil, II., Vice Chm. & Treas.--Keystone Automotive Industries, Inc., Pomona, CA, pg. 627
Benua, T.R., Jr., Pres. & Treas.--Ebco Mfg. Company, Columbus, OH, pg. 365
Benz, Edward, Asst. Treas. & Controller--Wheaton Van Lines, Inc., Indianapolis, IN, pg. 1184
Berardi, John F., V.P.-Fin. & Treas.--Farmland Industries, Inc., Kansas City, MO, pg. 402
Berdass, Margo, V.P. & Treas.--Bermo, Inc., Circle Pines, MN, pg. 143
Beren, Eugene J., Treas.--Merchant Capital Group Ltd, Chicago, IL, pg. 739
Berg, W. Robert, Vice Chm., Treas. & Sec.--Bartlett and Company, Kansas City, MO, pg. 122
Bergan, John W., V.P. & Treas.--Morgan Construction Company, Worcester, MA, pg. 769
Berger, Bryan, Sec. & Treas.--Smith Farms, Inc., Flatonia, TX, pg. 1012
Bergman, Robert S., Pres. & Treas.--Processed Plastic Company, Montgomery, IL, pg. 892
Bergum, Richard, Treas.--The Scott Company, Marysville, OH, pg. 982
Berkley, Herbert R., Sec. & Treas.--Berkliff Corporation, New York, NY, pg. 142
Berkley, Richard L., Sec. & Treas.--Tension Envelope Corp., Kansas City, MO, pg. 1088
Berkson, Stanley, Sec. & Treas.--Stanbee Company, Inc., Carlstadt, NJ, pg. 1035
Berlin, Alan, Treas. & Sec.--Potato Sales Company, Inc., Los Angeles, CA, pg. 882
Berlin, Marvin, Sec. & Treas.--New York Carpet World Inc., Southfield, MI, pg. 802
Berman, Milton I., Chm. Bd., Pres. & Treas.--Avibank Mfg., Inc., Burbank, CA, pg. 102
Berman, Robert, Sec. & Treas.--Metpar Corporation, Westbury, NY, pg. 742
Bernard, Ann, Treas.--B & G Wholesalers, Inc., Nashville, TN, pg. 106
Bernard, Walter, Treas.--La Salle County Farm Supply, Ottawa, IL, pg. 649
Bernardy, Raymond L., Treas.--Bankers Systems Inc., Saint Cloud, MN, pg. 117
Bernhardt, Robert I., Treas.--Joseph J. Henderson & Son, Inc., Gurnee, IL, pg. 529
Bernstein, Brian A., Chief Fin. Officer & Treas.--American Chemical Society, Washington, DC, pg. 50
Bernstein, Jonathan, V.P., Treas. & Sec.--National Foods Inc., Bronx, NY, pg. 788
Bernstein, Saul H., Pres., Chief Exec. Officer & Treas.--Savoy Construction Co. Inc., Kensington, MD, pg. 973
Bernstein, Sheldon, Sec. & Treas.--Milady Brassiere & Corset Co., Inc., New York, NY, pg. 753
Bernuth, Peter K., Chm. Bd., Pres. & Treas.--The Bernuth Corporation, Miami, FL, pg. 144
Berra, Phillip, Treas.--Hercules Tire & Rubber Company, Findlay, OH, pg. 531
Berry, Anna, Treas.--Southwire Company, Inc., Carrollton, GA, pg. 1024
Bersoff, Marilyn, Sec. & Treas.--BTG, Inc., Vienna, VA, pg. 107
Bertolini, Arthur G., Sr. V.P.-Fin. & Admin., Treas. & Sec.--Rocor Transportation Companies Inc., Oklahoma City, OK, pg. 942
Besse, Melissa, Treas.--Northern Michigan Veneers, Inc., Gladstone, MI, pg. 814
Besse, Robert, Sr. V.P.--Sanborn Manufacturing Company, Springfield, MN, pg. 969
Beutler, Tom, Sec., Treas. & Controller--Beutler Heating & Air Conditioning Inc., Sacramento, CA, pg. 148
Bevis, Douglas A., Treas.--CH2M Hill Companies, Ltd., Englewood, CO, pg. 202
Bialt, B., Gen. Mgr. & Treas.--Cofinco, Inc., New York, NY, pg. 810
Biber, Michael, Treas.--Fabex Inc., Novi, MI, pg. 395
Bibler, Laurie, Treas. & Sec.--Bibler Brothers, Inc., Russellville, AR, pg. 148
Bickelhaupt, Herbert E., Treas.--Curt G. Joa, Inc., Sheboygan Falls, WI, pg. 594
Bickford, John H., Chm. Bd. & Treas.--Transistor Devices, Inc., Cedar Knolls, NJ, pg. 1107
Billings, George, Treas.--Greater Construction Corp., Altamonte Springs, FL, pg. 483
Billings, K.W., Sec. & Treas.--Ranchers Cotton Oil, Fresno, CA, pg. 911
Binder, Susan A., V.P. & Treas.--ICC Industries, Inc., New York, NY, pg. 558
Bishop, J. Randall, Sec. & Treas.--Cameron & Barkley Company, Inc., Charleston Heights, SC, pg. 212
Bishop, P.S., Treas. & Sec.--Rissler & McMurry Company, Casper, WY, pg. 936
Bittker, David, Treas.--National Lumber Co., Warren, MI, pg. 792
Bixby, Allan B., Jr. V.P. & Treas.--Massachusetts Mutual Life Insurance Co., Springfield, MA, pg. 718
Bixler, C.K., Treas.--Ranch-Way, Inc., Fort Collins, CO, pg. 911
Black, David R., Controller & Treas.--Jitney-Jungle Stores of America, Inc., Jackson, MS, pg. 594
Black, Jeff, Pres. & Treas.--Black & Co., Decatur, IL, pg. 154
Black, W.J. II, Pres., Chief Exec. Officer & Treas.--Walter J. Black, Inc., Port Washington, NY, pg. 154
Blackmore, David, V.P. & Treas.--Cardinal Realty Services Inc., Reynoldsburg, OH, pg. 218
Blackwell, Daisy S., Treas. & Sec.--Yazoo Investment Corporation, Jackson, MS, pg. 1207
Blackwell, Don W., Chief Fin. Officer, V.P. & Treas.--VASA Insurance Group, Inc., Indianapolis, IN, pg. 1146
Blackwell, Don W., Treas.--Brougher Agency, Inc., Indianapolis, IN, pg. 1146
Blagge, Diane L., V.P. & Treas.--Tim & Diane Blagge Inc., Rancho Cordova, CA, pg. 155
Blair, Gary J., V.P.-Admin. & Treas.--Blade Communications, Inc., Toledo, OH, pg. 155
Blair, Gary J., V.P.-Admin. & Treas.--Toledo Blade Co., Toledo, OH, pg. 155
Blanchard, William C., Sec. & Treas.--Wm. Blanchard Co., Springfield, NJ, pg. 155
Blanton, Robert L., V.P.-Fin. & Asst. Treas.--Keystone Automotive Industries, Inc., Pomona, CA, pg. 627
Blatt, S., Pres. & Treas.--Columbus Steel Drum Company, Blacklick, OH, pg. 267
Blattner, Stephen C., Sec., Treas. & Chief Fin. Officer--D.H. Blattner & Sons, Inc., Avon, MN, pg. 156
Blazer, Dennis, Treas.--Plastic Moldings Corp., Cincinnati, OH, pg. 875
Blethen, William, Treas.--Seattle Times Company, Seattle, WA, pg. 986
Blickens, Robert, V.P.-Fin., Treas. & Comptroller--Komline-Sanderson Engineering Corp., Peapack, NJ, pg. 641
Blinder, James F., Pres. & Treas.--Nelson Brothers Furniture Co., Chicago, IL, pg. 797
Blodgett, John H., Treas.--Detex Corporation, New Braunfels, TX, pg. 333
Blommer, Joseph, Treas.--Blommer Chocolate Co., Chicago, IL, pg. 157
Blonkenmeyer, Gerald G., Treas. & Sec.--Lasting Products, Inc., Dallas, TX, pg. 660
Blount, Jimmie, Sec., Treas. & Controller--Delta Pride Catfish, Inc., Indianola, MS, pg. 327
Blumberg, Jerome, Treas.--The Jaydor Corporation, Millburn, NJ, pg. 591
Boardman, Allan J., Grp. V.P.-Admin. & Treas.--The Aerospace Corporation, El Segundo, CA, pg. 22
Bodifor, Lowell, Sec. & Treas.--Fort Worth Lumber Company, Fort Worth, TX, pg. 425
Bodine, Edward F., Chm. Bd. & Treas.--The Bodine Corp., Bridgeport, CT, pg. 161
Bodnar, Joseph L., Chief Fin. Officer & Treas.--Standard Tool & Manufacturing Company, Lyndhurst, NJ, pg. 1037
Boehnke, Carrol, Treas.--Central Livestock Association, Inc., South St. Paul, MN, pg. 233
Boersma, Max D., V.P. & Treas.--Transnational Motors Inc., Grand Rapids, MI, pg. 1107
Boeshart, Frank, V.P., Treas. & Controller--Terminal Grain Corp., Sioux City, IA, pg. 1088
Bogan, Robert, Treas.--Buquet & Le Blanc Inc., Baton Rouge, LA, pg. 189

Boggess, Jerry W., Treas.--HCB Contractors, Dallas, TX, pg. 496
Boh, Stephen H., Treas.--Boh Corporation, New Orleans, LA, pg. 162
Boh, Stephen H., Treas.--Boh Brothers Construction Company, Inc., New Orleans, LA, pg. 162
Bohan, Daniel P., Exec. V.P., Treas. & Sec.--Omega World Travel, Inc., Falls Church, VA, pg. 826
Bohman, Terrance, V.P.-Fin.--Universal Cooperatives, Inc., Minneapolis, MN, pg. 1138
Bohn, James J., Treas.--United Gilsonite Laboratories, Scranton, PA, pg. 1132
Bohn, Vincent, Treas.--Shepaug Corporation, New York, NY, pg. 997
Bohn, Vincent A., Treas.--The Unimax Corporation, New York, NY, pg. 1127
Boland, Michael, Sec. & Treas.--David Boland, Inc., Titusville, FL, pg. 162
Bollinger, Tom, Mgr.-Sls. & Treas.--The John C. Groub Company Inc., Seymour, IN, pg. 489
Bolt, C.S., Jr., Treas.--Dan River Inc., Danville, VA, pg. 313
Bomberger, D.L., Sr. V.P. & Treas.--Guarantee Mutual Life Co., Omaha, NE, pg. 491
Bonebrake, Merrill, Treas.--M.A.B. Paints, Terre Haute, IN, pg. 184
Boner, Jim, Treas.--Deardorff-Jackson Company, Oxnard, CA, pg. 323
Bonifaci, John, Treas. & Controller--Old Home Foods, Inc., Saint Paul, MN, pg. 823
Bonn, Allan, Treas. & Sec.--F.H. Bonn Company, Arlington Heights, IL, pg. 164
Bonner, Jerry, Treas.--Paragon Group, Inc., Dallas, TX, pg. 847
Bonney, David R., Sr. V.P., Treas.--Sage-Allen & Co., Inc., Hartford, CT, pg. 966
Bonsall, Mark B., Assoc. Gen. Mgr.--Salt River Project Agricultural Improvement and Power District, Tempe, AZ, pg. 967
Bonsib, Gretchen A., Sr. V.P., Sec. & Treas.--Bonsib Inc., Fort Wayne, IN, pg. 164
Boone, Jim, Treas.--PCI, Austin, TX, pg. 836
Booth, Ralph H., II, Pres. & Treas.--Booth American, Detroit, MI, pg. 165
Bootz, Howard W., Treas. & Corp. Sec.--Red Spot Paint & Varnish Co., Evansville, IN, pg. 918
Boppe, Larry, Chief Fin. Officer & V.P.-Opers.--Toter Incorporated, Statesville, NC, pg. 1103
Borazanian, Barbara, Treas.--Realty One, Cleveland, OH, pg. 917
Borgman, Jerry, Treas. & Controller--Lyon's Restaurants, Inc., Foster City, CA, pg. 690
Borkhoder, Lloyd, Sec. & Controller--Pete Fall Ford Inc., Elkhart, IN, pg. 398
Born, J. Ivan, V.P., Sec. & Treas.--Beaudry Ford, Inc., Atlanta, GA, pg. 130
Bos, Gerald, Corp. V.P.-Acctg. & Fin. & Asst. Treas.--Mid-America Dairymen, Inc., Springfield, MO, pg. 750
Bos, John, Treas.--California Milk Producers, Artesia, CA, pg. 210
Bosch, Joel, Treas. & Sec.--Minot Builders Supply Association, Minot, ND, pg. 758
Boslievac, Bill, Treas.--Garnac Grain Co., Inc., Overland Park, KS, pg. 810
Bossle, R.D., Treas.--Lyon Conklin & Company, Baltimore, MD, pg. 690
Bostwick, Tony, V.P. & Treas.--Braum Ice Cream Stores Inc., Oklahoma City, OK, pg. 172
Botte, Sam, Chief Fin. Officer, V.P.-Fin., Treas. & Controller--Raub Supply Company, Lancaster, PA, pg. 913
Boucher, Andre A., Treas.--Burke Engineering Company, South El Monte, CA, pg. 190
Bouillon, D.J., Treas. & Chief Fin. Officer--Fostoria Industries, Inc., Fostoria, OH, pg. 427
Bouise, Crag, Treas. & Controller--Thermal Technology Industries, N. Kansas City, MO, pg. 1091
Bouknight, John L., V.P.-Assets--The Climatic Corp., Columbia, SC, pg. 255
Bouland, Harold, V.P. & Treas.--E.C. Barton & Co., Jonesboro, AR, pg. 123
Bowden, C.E., V.P.-Grain/Traffic, Sec., & Treas.--Fisher Mills, Inc., Seattle, WA, pg. 415
Bowen, George, Treas.--Oppenheimer Management Corp., New York, NY, pg. 719
Bowen, Terry, Treas.--Therm, Inc., Ithaca, NY, pg. 1090
Bowland, Charlotte, Treas.--Petro-Hunt Corporation, Dallas, TX, pg. 865
Bowles, Larry D., V.P. & Treas.--Jerrico, Inc., Lexington, KY, pg. 229
Boyd, John, V.P.-Fin. & Treas.--American Eagle Airlines, Chicago, IL, pg. 51
Boyd, Julius, Sec. & Treas.--Fairway Ford, Inc., Greenville, SC, pg. 397
Boyd, Julius, Sec. & Treas.--Heritage Lincoln-Mercury, Greenville, SC, pg. 398
Boyet, Charles, Controller & Treas.--Sigmund Cohn Corp., Mount Vernon, NY, pg. 259
Boyle, David F., Treas.--HLC Industries, Farmington Hills, MI, pg. 496
Boyle, Pamela, Treas.--Schnieber Fine Foods, Inc., Lincoln, NE, pg. 977
Boyle, Robert K., Sec. & Treas.--The Lewis Bear Company, Pensacola, FL, pg. 129
Boyle, Sandra, Treas. & Acct. Mgr.--CRE, Inc., Indianapolis, IN, pg. 203
Brace, James, V.P.-Treasurer & CFO--Littelfuse, Inc., Des Plaines, IL, pg. 678
Bracken, Charles H., Jr., Treas.--Hillman Company, Pittsburgh, PA, pg. 535
Braddock, James L., Chm. Bd., Pres. & Treas.--Fastec Industrial, Elkhart, IN, pg. 403
Bradley, D. Scott, Treas.--CC Industries, Inc., Chicago, IL, pg. 199
Bradley, Robert J., V.P., Treas.--Cramer-Krasselt, Milwaukee, WI, pg. 296
Bradley, Scott, Treas.--American Envelope Company, Chicago, IL, pg. 199
Bradly, Charles E., Treas. & Controller--Fabreeka International, Inc., Stoughton, MA, pg. 396
Brady, C.F., V.P. & Treas.--Hunt Oil Company, Dallas, TX, pg. 553
Brady, John T., Exec. V.P. & Treas.--Worldvision Enterprises, New York, NY, pg. 54
Branca, Carmela, Treas.--Falcon Candy Company, Philadelphia, PA, pg. 398
Branch, Kenneth A., Sec., Treas. & Controller--Randall's Food Markets, Inc., Houston, TX, pg. 911
Brand, Robert, Treas. & Sec.--Performance Contracting Group, Charlotte, NC, pg. 861
Brand, Robert, Treas. & Sec.--Performance Contracting, Inc., Charlotte, NC, pg. 861
Brandin, Seymour, Chief Fin. Officer & Treas.--Heyman Corporation, Niles, IL, pg. 532
Brandon, Lynda, Sec. & Treas.--John J. Campbell Co., Inc., Memphis, TN, pg. 212
Brands, James E., Exec. V.P., Sec. & Treas.--Scherer Scientific, Ltd., Atlanta, GA, pg. 976
Brannan, Michael, V.P. & Treas.--Meridian Technology Leasing Services, Deerfield, IL, pg. 740
Brannen, John T., Treas. & Sec.--Mid America International Trucks, Inc., Memphis, TN, pg. 750
Brantlinger, F. Herbert, Asst. Treas.--Global Insurance Company, Houston, TX, pg. 662
Brauer, Robert I., Treas.--Menard Electric Cooperative, Petersburg, IL, pg. 738
Brecht, Warren F., V.P., Treas. & Sec.--Butler International, Montvale, NJ, pg. 197
Breen, John, Treas.--Foster Medical Supply, Inc., Waltham, MA, pg. 426
Breiner, James M., Chm. Bd. & Treas.--First Connecticut SBIC, Bridgeport, CT, pg. 412
Brennan, John M., Sr. V.P. & Treas.--Capitol Broadcasting Co., Inc., Raleigh, NC, pg. 215
Brennan, Walter, Sec. & Treas.--American Fabrics Company, New York, NY, pg. 51
Brenner, William G., Treas.--The Union Central Life Insurance Co., Cincinnati, OH, pg. 1127
Brenzia, John, Treas.--Elliott Company, Jeannette, PA, pg. 378
Bretza, Thomas, Exec. V.P.-Fin. & Treas.--Krier Foods, Inc., Brown Deer, WI, pg. 645
Brewer, Stan, V.P.-Opers., Sec. & Treas.--Associated Food Stores Inc., Salt Lake City, UT, pg. 89
Brewton, R. Gerald, Sec. & Treas.--Jerry Hamm Chevrolet Inc., Jacksonville, FL, pg. 503
Brice, Joni, Chief Exec. Officer--Heil-Brice Retail Advertising, San Clemente, CA, pg. 525
Bricker, J.W., V.P. & Treas.--White Castle System, Inc., Columbus, OH, pg. 1185
Bricker, Marvin, Co-Pres. & Treas.--Hawkeye Steel Products, Inc., Houghton, IA, pg. 518
Bridges, Laura, Treas.--Stones, Inc., Bainbridge, GA, pg. 1051
Bridges, Maxine L., Sec., Treas. & Dir.-Personnel & Investor Rels.--Sterling Homes Corp., Sparks, NV, pg. 1046
Briggs, K. Douglas, V.P., Treas. & Sec.--Quincy Mutual Fire Insurance Company, Quincy, MA, pg. 905
Brightbill, William, Pres. & Treas.--Ritter Bros., Inc., Harrisburg, PA, pg. 936
Brinkman, Harry H., Treas.--Columbus Pipe & Equipment Company, Columbus, OH, pg. 267
Brinton, G.W., Treas.--Label-Aire Inc., Fullerton, CA, pg. 649
Brittelli, Brenda S., Chief Fin. Officer, Sec.,Treas. & Controller--Adams Wine Co., Atlanta, GA, pg. 17
Brix, Robert H., Treas.--Northwestern Drug Company, Minneapolis, MN, pg. 343
Brock, Frank E., Sec. & Treas.--Williamson-Dickie Mfg. Co., Fort Worth, TX, pg. 1192
Brock, Tony, Exec. V.P. & Treas.--Beadles Lumber Company, Inc., Moultrie, GA, pg. 129
Brocke, Dean, Treas.--George F. Brocke & Sons, Inc., Kendrick, ID, pg. 178
Brocksher, Jean, Sec. & Asst. Treas.--Allright Corporation, Houston, TX, pg. 41
Brocoff, Robert R., Sr. V.P.-Fin.--Kraco Enterprises, Inc., Compton, CA, pg. 643
Brod, Spencer, Sec. & Treas.--Empire Diamond Corporation, New York, NY, pg. 379
Brode, Michael, V.P. & Treas.--Broder Bros. Co., Plymouth, MI, pg. 178
Broderick, John J., V.P., Sec. & Treas.--Judd's Incorporated, Washington, DC, pg. 608
Brodt, John D., Treas. & Sec.--Ohio Valley Electric Corporation, Piketon, OH, pg. 822
Brogan, Mary, Treas.--Monroe Printing Company, East Stroudsburg, PA, pg. 697
Broll, Arthur G., Jr., Chm. Bd., Chief Fin. Officer & Treas.--Geographic Marketing Group (GMG), Philadelphia, PA, pg. 452
Bronell, Joel, Treas.--Walsworth Publishing Company, Inc., Marceline, MO, pg. 1161
Brooks, J.B., Sec. & Treas.--Flexel, Inc., Atlanta, GA, pg. 418
Brooks, Winfrey, Treas.--General Services Corporation, Richmond, VA, pg. 450
Broughton, John R., Treas.--Broughton Foods Company, Marietta, OH, pg. 180
Brown, Allen, Sec. & Treas.--Riverside Central Services, Inc., Natchez, MS, pg. 937
Brown, C. Merrill, Treas.--F.M. Brown Sons, Inc., Sinking Spring, PA, pg. 183
Brown, Edward C., Pres. & Treas.--Bill Brown Ford Inc., Livonia, MI, pg. 182
Brown, Gail, Sec. & Treas.--Mayfield Building Supply Co., Arlington, TX, pg. 691
Brown, Gayle, Treas.--Sammons Enterprises, Inc., Dallas, TX, pg. 968
Brown, Gordon S., Sec. & Treas.--Bruce Foods Corp., Saint Martinville, LA, pg. 183
Brown, Hubbell H., Treas.--Windsor Shade Tobacco Company, Inc., Hartford, CT, pg. 1196
Brown, Jack, Treas.--Myers Foods Company, Plumsteadville, PA, pg. 506
Brown, Jack, Treas.--Dedert Corporation, Olympia Fields, IL, pg. 324
Brown, Katherine, Treas. & Sec.--Troncalli Motors, Inc., Decatur, GA, pg. 1115
Brown, Keith A., Exec. V.P. & Treas.--General Ship Corporation, Boston, MA, pg. 450
Brown, Nancy, Treas. & Sec.--Heintzelman's Truck Center Inc., Orlando, FL, pg. 526
Brown, Susan, Chief Fin. Officer & Treas.--American Tara Corporation, Atlanta, GA, pg. 63
Brown, William K., V.P. & Treas.--ELS Educational Services, Culver City, CA, pg. 56
Browning, Jean, Treas. & Sec.--Browning Chemical Corporation, White Plains, NY, pg. 183
Broz, James F., Controller & Asst. Treas.--Office Electronics, Inc., Itasca, IL, pg. 821
Brubaker, Jerry L., Sec. & Treas.--Schneller, Inc., Kent, OH, pg. 977
Bruckheimer, Allen J., Sr. V.P. & Asst. Treas.--Mutual of America, New York, NY, pg. 777
Bruens, John, Treas. & Sec.--WRM, Inc., Mabscott, WV, pg. 1156
Brumby, Jane, Treas.--Pumpelly Oil, Inc., Westlake, LA, pg. 900
Brumleue, David L., Treas. & Sec.--Hodgson Mill, Inc., Gainesville, MO, pg. 1002
Brumleve, David, Chief Fin. Officer, Treas., & Sec.--Siemer Milling Company, Teutopolis, IL, pg. 1002
Brummond, Brad, Chief Fin. Officer & Treas.--Super 8 Motels, Inc., Aberdeen, SD, pg. 1062
Bruskrud, W.R., Pres. & Treas.--Bemco Inc., Simi Valley, CA, pg. 138
Brustein, Lawrence, Chief Fin. Officer, Sec. & Treas.--Henry Modell & Company, Inc., Long Island City, NY, pg. 762
Bryan, A. Chris, II, Pres., Chief Exec. Officer, Sec. & Treas.--BA Advertising, Dallas, TX, pg. 105
Bryan, Charles R., Exec. V.P., Sec. & Treas.--AVA-Automatic Vendors of America, Atlanta, GA, pg. 8
Bryant, A.W., Pres. & Treas.--Century Fence Company, Pewaukee, WI, pg. 235
Bryant, Geraldine D., Treas. & Sec.--Lowell Packing Company, Fitzgerald, GA, pg. 685
Bryant, Richard J., Sec. & Treas.--Bryant Supply Company, Inc., Gastonia, NC, pg. 185
Buchanan, Mary Jane, Sec. & Treas.--Heights Heating & Cooling, Auburn Hills, MI, pg. 525
Buchbinder, L.W., V.P. & Treas.--Panorama Press, Inc., Clifton, NJ, pg. 846
Buchbiner, Henry M., Chm. Bd. & Treas.--Ardco, Inc., Alsip, IL, pg. 81
Buckelew, L. Nick, Treas.--Trico Electric Co-Op, Tucson, AZ, pg. 1113
Buckingham, Douglas A., Treas. & Controller--WYO-Ben, Inc., Billings, MT, pg. 1157
Buckley, Alan, Chief Fin. Officer, Sec., Treas. & Legal Officer--Pease Industries, Inc., Fairfield, OH, pg. 854
Buckman, M.W., Treas. & Asst. Sec.--Bulab Holdings, Inc., Memphis, TN, pg. 188
Bucksbaum, Matthew, Pres., Treas. & Sec.--General Growth Companies, Inc., Des Moines, IA, pg. 449
Buddig, John C., Treas.--Carl Buddig & Company, Homewood, IL, pg. 186
Budig, George J., V.P., Sec. & Treas.--Budco Group Inc., Cincinnati, OH, pg. 186
Buettner, William P., V.P. & Controller--The Austin Company, Cleveland, OH, pg. 790
Buiter, Michael R., V.P. & Treas.--Dr Pepper/Seven-Up Companies, Inc., Dallas, TX, pg. 342
Bull, William H., Pres., Chief Exec. Officer & Treas.--McNaughton-McKay Electric Co., Madison Heights, MI, pg. 732
Bulloch, Juanita A., Pres., Chief Exec. Officer & Treas.--Southeastern Steel Company, Florence, SC, pg. 1020
Burgess, Gary, V.P., Treas. & Pur. Agent--Equipment Manufacturing, Inc., Warren, MI, pg. 385
Burgoyne, Mary Louise, Sec. & Treas.--Burgoyne, Inc., Philadelphia, PA, pg. 190
Burguieres, Robert N., V.P.-Fin. & Treas.--Precision Tune, Inc., Leesburg, VA, pg. 885
Burke, Charles G., Sr. V.P.-Admin., Treas., & Asst. Sec.--Joan Fabrics Corp., Tyngsboro, MA, pg. 594
Burke, Patrick, V.P., Controller & Treas.--Ziff Communications Company, New York, NY, pg. 1218
Burkett, Thomas L., V.P. & Treas.--Golden Gem Growers Inc., Umatilla, FL, pg. 466
Burkey, Michelle, Controller & Treas.--Edgerton Forge, Inc., Edgerton, OH, pg. 102
Burns, John W., Exec. V.P., Sec. & Treas.--Consolidated Industrial Corporation, Birmingham, MI, pg. 276
Burns, Martha, Treas.--The Polizos Agency, Norfolk, VA, pg. 879
Burns, Ralph A., Treas.--Urschel Labs Inc., Valparaiso, IN, pg. 1140
Burnstead, Joan, Sec. & Treas.--Burnstead Construction Company, Bellevue, WA, pg. 194
Burris, Steven Y., Sec. & Treas.--Burris Chemical Inc., Charleston, SC, pg. 195
Burrow, Ray, Sr. V.P.-Opers. & Fin.--National Computer Print, Inc., Birmingham, AL, pg. 786
Burson, Glenda, Treas.--McWane, Inc., Birmingham, AL, pg. 733
Busby, Mike, Chief Fin. Officer, Treas. & Controller--Crested Butte Mountain Resort, Inc., Mount Crested Butte, CO, pg. 299
Buskirk, Glen, Sec. & Treas.--Rock Hill Materials Company, Catasauqua, PA, pg. 941
Buss, Cal, V.P., Sec. & Treas.--Vallet Food Serv Inc., Dubuque, IA, pg. 1143

Buste, Wendy, Treas.--Dyke Industry, Inc., Little Rock, AR, pg. 356
Butcko, Mae Alice, Sec. & Treas.--Crescive Die & Tool, Inc., Saline, MI, pg. 298
Buten, Max, V.P.-Fin. & Treas.--M. Buten & Sons Inc., Philadelphia, PA, pg. 196
Butler, John M., Sr. V.P. & Treas.--John Hancock Leasing Corporation, Boston, MA, pg. 596
Butler, William, Chm. Bd., Pres., Chief Exec. Officer & Treas.--Corporex Companies, Inc., Covington, KY, pg. 287
Butler, William, Treas.--Litecontrol Corporation, Hanson, MA, pg. 677
Butterfield, Mark, Sec. & Treas.--Ausherman Construction Company, Frederick, MD, pg. 98
Bybee, O. Lynn, Treas. & Controller--Wick Building Systems, Mazomanie, WI, pg. 1188
Byer, Marian, Treas. & Sec.--Byer California, San Francisco, CA, pg. 197
Byer, P. Roger, V.P.-Fin. & Treas.--KDI Corporation, Cincinnati, OH, pg. 612
Byers, Dennis W., Chief Fin. Officer, V.P.-Fin. & Treas.--Quality Stores Inc., North Muskegon, MI, pg. 904
Byrnes, Leo, Treas.--Dairyland Power Cooperative, La Crosse, WI, pg. 311
Byrum, Barbara, Sr. V.P., Opers., Sec. & Treas.--Gunder & Associates, Inc., Dublin, OH, pg. 494
Cagenello, Donald L., Sec. & Treas.--Graphic Center, Inc., Bloomfield, CT, pg. 478
Cahill, J. Michael, Exec. V.P. & Treas.--Channing L. Bete Co., Inc., South Deerfield, MA, pg. 147
Cahill, Larry, Pres. & Treas.--Larken Inc., Cedar Rapids, IA, pg. 659
Calafati, Gabriel R., Chm. Bd., Pres. & Treas.--Frank Briscoe Co. Inc., Roseland, NJ, pg. 176
Calcagno, J., Treas.--E.J. Brach Corporation, Oakbrook Terrace, IL, pg. 169
Call, Val, V.P., Sec. & Treas.--Maverik Country Stores, Inc., Afton, WY, pg. 722
Callegari, Don, V.P.-Fin. & Acting Treas.--R. J. Gallagher Co., Houston, TX, pg. 441
Cameron, William, Sr. V.P., Treas.--Ketchum Communications Inc., Pittsburgh, PA, pg. 625
Camimer, Carol, Treas.--Efficient Engineering Co., Troy, MI, pg. 371
Camp, William C., Treas. & Chief Fin. Officer--Science & Engineering Associates, Albuquerque, NM, pg. 982
Campbell, Andrew, Chief Fin. Officer, V.P., Treas. & Sec.--Simmons Upholstered Furniture, Inc., Saint Louis, MO, pg. 1005
Campbell, J.H., Jr., Chief Fin. Officer, Treas. & Legal Counsel--Associated Grocers, Inc., Baton Rouge, LA, pg. 89
Campbell, Jack T., Treas., Asst. Sec. & Chief Fin. Officer--The Kent Manufacturing Co., Pickens, SC, pg. 623
Campbell, Larry, Exec. V.P., Sec. & Treas.--Farm Journal, Inc., Philadelphia, PA, pg. 401
Campbell, Lela, Treas. & Sec.--Choctaw Electric Co-Op, Hugo, OK, pg. 248
Campbell, Newton A., Chm. Bd. & Treas.--Burns & McDonnell Engineers-Architects-Consultants, Kansas City, MO, pg. 194
Campney, Robert, V.P. & Treas.--Pacesetter Corporation, Omaha, NE, pg. 839
Canalchio, James F., V.P. & Treas.--Dixon Valve & Coupling Company, Chestertown, MD, pg. 341
Canale, Chris W., Treas.--D. Canale Food Services, Inc., Memphis, TN, pg. 213
Cantlin, John, V.P.-Fin.--Stockham Valves & Fittings, Inc., Birmingham, AL, pg. 1050
Caplan, James A., Chm. Bd., Pres., Treas., Prod. Mgr. & Chief Engr.--Capp, Inc., Philadelphia, PA, pg. 216
Caputo, Carmen M., Chief Fin. Officer, V.P.-Fin. & Treas.--Tork, Inc., Mount Vernon, NY, pg. 1102
Caram, Edward J., Treas.--Lombardi FoodService, Inc., Utica, MI, pg. 681
Cardarelli, Donald P., V.P. & Treas.--Agway, Inc., De Witt, NY, pg. 25
Carelli, Gloria A., Exec. V.P., Dir. Creative Services & Treas.--Carelli, Glynn & Ward, Butler, NJ, pg. 218
Caricofe, Ronald L., Treas.--Concrete Pipe & Products Co. Inc., Richmond, VA, pg. 273
Caridi, Thomas, Sr. V.P., Fin. & Treas.--Reed Exhibition Companies, Boston, MA, pg. 920
Carlborg, John, Jr., Treas.--Burnside Construction Co., Downers Grove, WI, pg. 194
Carli, Raymond, Asst. Treas.--The First Boston Corporation, New York, NY, pg. 203
Carlo, Nelson, Pres. & Treas.--Abbott Group Ltd., Chicago, IL, pg. 9
Carlo, Nelson, Pres. & Treas.--Abbott Products Inc., Chicago, IL, pg. 9
Carlos, Andrew C., Exec. V.P. & Treas.--National Distributing Co., Inc., Atlanta, GA, pg. 787
Carlovatto, Jeff, Treas. & Controller--QST Industries, Inc., Chicago, IL, pg. 902
Carlson, Gerald K., Pres., Treas. & Chief Fin. Officer--Bureau of Engraving, Minneapolis, MN, pg. 189
Carlson, Jane, Sec. & Treas.--Midcoast Industrial Services Corporation, Cedar Rapids, IA, pg. 751
Carlson, Lawrence S., Sec. & Treas.--Fleetwood Systems, Inc., Countryside, IL, pg. 417
Carlson, Robert F., Sr., Chm. Bd., Chief Exec. Officer & Treas.--Channel Technologies, Inc., Santa Barbara, CA, pg. 239
Carlson, Ronald A., Sec. & Treas.--Helwig Carbon Products, Inc., Milwaukee, WI, pg. 528
Carlton, Dorothy, Sec. & Treas.--Corrugated Metals, Inc., Chicago, IL, pg. 287
Carlucci, John D., V.P., Asst. Treas.--N W Ayer Inc., New York, NY, pg. 104
Carmany, Dave, V.P.-Fin., Treas. & Controller--Castleberry's Food Company, Augusta, GA, pg. 229
Carnes, Candace, Treas.--Badger Air Brush Company, Franklin Park, IL, pg. 113
Carney, Dennis, Treas.--Midwest Mutual Insurance Co., West Des Moines, IA, pg. 886
Carney, Richard, Treas.--Chuck Hutton Chevrolet Company, Memphis, TN, pg. 556
Carns, Charles E., Jr., V.P., Treas. & Chief Fin. Officer--Mears Transportation Group, Orlando, FL, pg. 734
Caroll, Chuck, Treas., Controller & Chief Fin. Officer--South East Coal Co., Irvine, KY, pg. 1019
Carpenter, Clark, V.P. & Treas.--Elkay Manufacturing Company, Oak Brook, IL, pg. 377
Carpenter, Ransom A., Treas. & Controller--Mauney Hosiery Mills, Inc., Kings Mountain, NC, pg. 722
Carr, Jack R., Treas.--Russell Stover Candies, Inc., Kansas City, MO, pg. 957
Carr, Tim, V.P. & Treas.--Domino's Pizza Inc., Ann Arbor, MI, pg. 344
Carrafiello, A. Louis, Pres., Treas. & Chief Exec. Officer--Carrafiello, Diehl & Associates, Inc., Irvington, NY, pg. 225
Carrier, Arthur, Sec. & Treas.--Associated Electric Co-op Inc., Springfield, MO, pg. 89
Carroll, Jim, Treas., Chief Fin. Officer & Sec.--The Chicago Faucet Co., Des Plaines, IL, pg. 245
Carroll, Robert, Sr. V.P.-East--Powell Electronics Inc., Philadelphia, PA, pg. 882
Carrozzino, Donald J., V.P.-Fin. & Treas.--Pennsylvania Crusher Corp., Broomall, PA, pg. 858
Carrus, G., Co.-Chm. & Treas.--Infinity Broadcasting Corporation, New York, NY, pg. 567
Carse, Jimmie L., Sec. & Treas.--Carse Oil Co. Inc., Orlando, FL, pg. 225
Carstensen, James A., Treas.--Carstensen Freight Line, Inc., Clinton, IA, pg. 226
Carter, Donald J., Pres., Treas. & Chief Exec. Officer--Home Interiors & Gifts, Inc., Dallas, TX, pg. 541
Carter, Nelson, Treas. & Chief Fin. Officer--Jerry C. Carter, Inc., Gainesville, GA, pg. 226
Carter, Sam R., Chief Fin. Officer & Treas.--Farmers Co-op Market Inc., Frisco City, AL, pg. 401
Cartwright, William Y., Pres., Chief Exec., Chief Fin. Officer & Treas.--Cartwright Communications Co., Cincinnati, OH, pg. 227
Carus, Paul, Exec. V.P. & Treas.--Carus Corporation, Peru, IL, pg. 227
Caruso, Jo Ann, Sec. & Treas.--Regency Dodge Inc., Jacksonville, FL, pg. 922
Cary, Harold, V.P. & Treas.--Harold Moore & Associates, Inc., Fayetteville, TN, pg. 768
Casanova, Barbara, Treas.--Casanova Pendrill Publicidad Inc., Irvine, CA, pg. 227
Caschette, Gerard, Pres. & Treas.--Genesee Metal Stampings, Inc., West Henrietta, NY, pg. 451
Casey, Karen L., Sec. & Treas.--Libertyville Lincoln-Mercury Sales, Inc., Libertyville, IL, pg. 674
Cash, Robert, V.P. & Treas.--Seattle Pacific Industries, Inc., Seattle, WA, pg. 986
Cashman, Georgia, Treas.--Pacific Envelope Company, Anaheim, CA, pg. 840
Cashman, Maurice J., Treas.--National Forge Company, Irvine, PA, pg. 788
Cashwell, Henry V., Sec. & Treas.--Tencarva Machinery Co., Inc., Greensboro, NC, pg. 1086
Cassano, James, Treas. & Chief Fin. Officer--Hill International Inc., Willingboro, NJ, pg. 534
Cassens, Kay, Sec. & Treas.--Cassens Transport Company, Edwardsville, IL, pg. 228
Cassreino, Charles W., Treas.--MCC Group, Inc., Metairie, LA, pg. 691
Castiglione, Philip, Sec. & Treas.--Ray Laethem Pontiac GMC Truck Co., Detroit, MI, pg. 650
Caston, Debra, Treas. & Media Buyer--McCommunications Inc., Dallas, TX, pg. 727
Castro, Dorothy, Sr. V.P., Treas. & Sec.--Superior Fast Freight, Irwindale, CA, pg. 1063
Casty, Ronald, Treas.--American Snacks, Inc., Chelsea, MA, pg. 61
Cathey, O.D., Sec. & Treas.--Bearden Lumber Company, Inc., Bearden, AR, pg. 129
Caton, Robert J., Sr. V.P. & Treas.--Fay, Spofford & Thorndike, Inc., Lexington, MA, pg. 404
Cauley, Robert N., Jr., Sr. V.P., Treas.--Houston Effler & Partners, Boston, MA, pg. 546
Cavender, William, Treas. & Sec.--Hallidie Machinery Company, Inc., Seattle, WA, pg. 501
Ceithaml, Carl, Chief Fin. Officer--The Harter Group, Sturgis, MI, pg. 513
Cejka, F.V., Treas. & Sec.--Ward Products Corporation, New Brunswick, NJ, pg. 1163
Celentano, Leslie, Treas.--Celentano Brothers, Verona, NJ, pg. 231
Cernahouz, Ralph, Chief Fin. Officer & Treas.--Schumacher Electric Corporation, Chicago, IL, pg. 979
Chadwick, Norman, Treas.--The Hercules Tire & Rubber Company, Findlay, OH, pg. 531
Chagnon, Emile A., Jr., Pres. & Treas.--Chagnon Lumber Company, Inc., Nashua, NH, pg. 238
Chan, Paul, Sec. & Treas.--Generra Sportswear Company, Inc., Tukwila, WA, pg. 451
Charlestein, Gary, Chief Exec. Officer & Treas.--Premier Dental Products Company, Norristown, PA, pg. 886
Charron, Carol, Sec. & Treas.--Art Moran Pontiac-GMC Inc., Southfield, MI, pg. 769
Charron, Marjorie, Treas. & Gen. Mgr--Charron, Schwartz & Partners, Inc., New York, NY, pg. 240
Charwath, Walter, V.P. & Treas.--Faber/Castell Corporation, Parsippany, NJ, pg. 395
Chase, Francis H. III, Chm. Bd., Pres., Chief Exec., Chief Fin. Officer & Treas.--F. H. Chase, Inc., Foxboro, MA, pg. 240
Chase, Harry, V.P.-Fin., Treas. & Admin.--Elgin National Industries, Inc., Chicago, IL, pg. 609
Cheatham, C.L., Treas.--Brierley & Partners, Dallas, TX, pg. 175
Checchia, John, V.P., Treas., & Mgr.-Personnel & Data Processing--Media Printing Corporation, Miami, FL, pg. 734
Chen, Dr. Lily C., Exec. V.P., Treas. & Chief Fin. Officer--General Sciences Corp., Laurel, MD, pg. 981
Cheney, Jeffrey P., Treas.--Kohler Company, Kohler, WI, pg. 639
Chin, John, Treas.--Henry I. Siegel Company, Inc., New York, NY, pg. 1002
Cho, Dan, Dir.-Fin.--Sun Computers, Inc., Carson, CA, pg. 1058
Choksi, Paritosh K., Sr. V.P., Chief Fin. Officer & Treas.--Phoenix American Incorporated, San Rafael, CA, pg. 868
Choksi, Umesh, Asst. Treas.--ACF Industries, Inc., Earth City, MO, pg. 561
Chopra, Beera, V.P.-Opers. & Treas.--Family Inns of America, Inc., Pigeon Forge, TN, pg. 398
Chraime, C., Sr. V.P. & Treas.--Soundesign Corporation, Jersey City, NJ, pg. 1018
Christel, Henry, V.P.-Treas.--William H. Sadlier, Inc., New York, NY, pg. 966
Christensen, Dallis, Treas. & Chief Information Officer--Daw Technologies, Inc., Salt Lake City, UT, pg. 319
Christo, Stephen R., Treas.--Mustang Tractor & Equip. Co., Houston, TX, pg. 777
Chrzanowski, Rebecca, Sec. & Treas.--Aldi Inc., Batavia, IL, pg. 33
Chung, Ray, Exec. V.P., Chief Fin. Officer & Treas.--Windmill Holdings Corp., San Francisco, CA, pg. 1195
Church, R.D., Sec. & Treas.--Erico International, Cleveland, OH, pg. 386
Chynoweth, Robert, Treas. & Sec.--Wyoming Machine Company, Casper, WY, pg. 1206
Cicotte, Thomas, Sec. & Treas.--Shmina Construction, Inc., Livonia, MI, pg. 124
Cistone, Daniel, Treas.--MtC Remco Tape Products Co., North Hollywood, CA, pg. 690
Clancy, Paul G., Treas.--Diversified Communications, Portland, ME, pg. 340
Clanin, Bob, Mgr.-Treasury--United Parcel Service of America, Inc., Atlanta, GA, pg. 1133
Clark, Ann, Dir.-Fin. & Admin.--Alliance Automation Systems, Rochester, NY, pg. 37
Clark, David C., V.P. & Treas.--Jervis B. Webb Company, Farmington Hills, MI, pg. 1170
Clark, George A., Chm. Bd., Pres. & Chief Exec. Officer--Snap-Tite, Incorporated, Erie, PA, pg. 1014
Clark, George P., V.P. & Treas.--Snap-Tite, Incorporated, Erie, PA, pg. 1014
Clark, James A., Chief Fin. Officer & Treas.--Integral Systems, Walnut Creek, CA, pg. 572
Clark, Margaret, Treas. & Sec.--Covington Foods, Inc., Covington, IN, pg. 290
Clark, Scott W., Sec. & Treas.--Construction Management Service, Wilmington, DE, pg. 277
Clark, Susan, V.P., Treas. & Asst. Sec.--HTB, Inc., Oklahoma City, OK, pg. 497
Clarke, Edwin R., Chief Fin. Officer, Treas. & Sec.--Letts Industries, Inc., Detroit, MI, pg. 668
Clarke, Lois A., Treas.--Virginia Metal Industries, Inc., Orange, VA, pg. 1152
Clarke, Ted, Chief Fin. Officer, Treas. & Controller--Hynes Industries Inc., Youngstown, OH, pg. 557
Clarke, Thomas W., V.P.-Fin. & Treas.--Flint Ink Corp., Detroit, MI, pg. 419
Clary, Tom, Treas.--Green Construction of Indiana, Inc., Oaktown, IN, pg. 484
Claunch, Joe Howard, Sec. & Treas.--Somerset Refinery Inc., Somerset, KY, pg. 1017
Clay, B.J., Treas.--The Hardaway Company, Columbus, GA, pg. 507
Clay, Frank, Treas. & Controller--Pacific Hawaiian Ltd., Hilo, HI, pg. 840
Clements, Norman F., V.P., Sec. & Treas.--EAC Corporation, Saint Louis, MO, pg. 359
Cleveland, Jay W., Pres. & Treas.--Cleveland Brothers Equipment Co., Harrisburg, PA, pg. 255
Click, James E., Treas., Chief Exec. Officer & Sec.--Maryland & Virginia Milk Producers Association, Reston, VA, pg. 717
Clifton, Harold, Treas., Sec. & Chief Fin. Officer--Hopper Inc., Bakersfield, CA, pg. 543
Clinton, Robert, V.P.-Fin.--United Design, Noble, OK, pg. 1131
Clock, Joe, Treas.--Cawsl Corporation, Wynnewood, PA, pg. 229
Clyburne, Evelyn, Sec. & Treas.--Gregory & Clyburne, Inc., Stamford, CT, pg. 486
Coakley, Neil T., Chm. Bd., Sec. & Treas.--Coakley & Williams Inc., Greenbelt, MD, pg. 256
Coates, Jean Pettijohn, Pres., Treas. & Creative Dir.--The Coates Agency, Portland, OR, pg. 257
Coats, W. John, V.P.-Fin.--Nutri/System Inc., Blue Bell, PA, pg. 818
Cobb, Larry, V.P.-Fin., Treas. & Sec.--Ed Taylor Construction Co., Tucker, GA, pg. 1081
Cochran, Deryl E., Sec. & Treas.--Plastics Manufacturing Company, Dallas, TX, pg. 876
Cockrell, Mel, Chief Fin. Officer, Treas., Controller & Sec.--Ben E. Keith Company, Fort Worth, TX, pg. 620
Coffey, Larry R., Pres. & Treas.--Landmark Community Newspapers, Inc., Shelbyville, KY, pg. 655
Coggins, Lester, Jr., Sec. & Treas.--Lester Coggins Trucking, Okahumpka, FL, pg. 259
Cohan, Robert, Treas.--Dean Operations Inc., Kansas City, MO, pg. 322
Cohen, Alan H., Chief Fin. Officer & Treas.--George Uhe Co., Inc., Paramus, NJ, pg. 1125
Cohen, Arvin, Exec. V.P. & Treas.--Snyder Brothers, Inc., Minneapolis, MN, pg. 1015
Cohen, Benjamin H., Treas.--The First Boston Corporation, New York, NY, pg. 203

Cohen, Eli D., Pres., Chief Oper. Officer & Treas.--Duane Reade, Long Island City, NY, pg. 350
Cohen, Ezra, V.P., Sec. & Treas.--Sunweave Linen Corporation, New York, NY, pg. 1062
Cohen, Harry, Chief Fin. Officer, Treas. & Sec.--Mozel Development Corp., Baileys Crossroads, VA, pg. 774
Cohen, Irving, Treas. & Chief Fin. Officer--Acme Canvas Co., Inc., Malden, MA, pg. 13
Cohen, Isaac, Treas. & Sec.--First Computer Corporation, Los Angeles, CA, pg. 412
Cohen, Larry, Treas.--Service Packing Company, Los Angeles, CA, pg. 992
Cohen, Lewis, Treas. & Controller--Kastle Systems, Inc., Arlington, VA, pg. 618
Cohen, Robert B., V.P. & Treas.--Federal Compress & Warehouse Company, Inc., Memphis, TN, pg. 404
Cohen, Warren, V.P., Sec. & Treas.--Unisystems, Inc., New York, NY, pg. 1130
Cohn, Carol, Treas. & Sec.--Decorative Crafts, Inc., Greenwich, CT, pg. 324
Colby, Albert A., Jr., V.P. & Treas.--International Chemical Company, Tulsa, OK, pg. 576
Colcord, William, Treas.--Kayem Foods, Inc., Chelsea, MA, pg. 619
Cole, Ann, Treas.--Hygrade Metal Moulding Mfg. Corp., Farmingdale, NY, pg. 557
Cole, Catherine P., Chief Oper. Oficer & Sec.--Columbine Systems Inc., Golden, CO, pg. 266
Cole, Madison F., Jr., Treas.--Norrell Corporation, Atlanta, GA, pg. 810
Cole, W.P., Treas.--American Buildings Co., Eufaula, AL, pg. 49
Collings, Glenn M., V.P.-Fin. & Treas.--Moore Special Tool Co., Inc., Bridgeport, CT, pg. 768
Collins, Catherine L., Treas.--Whiting Corporation, Harvey, IL, pg. 1187
Collins, Donald F., Treas. & Sec.--Collins Electric Company, Inc., Chicopee, MA, pg. 263
Collins, Lawrence A., Sec. & Treas.--J. H. Roberts Industries Inc., Des Plaines, IL, pg. 938
Collins, T.R., V.P.-Fin. & Treas.--Motor Wheel Corporation, Lansing, MI, pg. 773
Collins, Tim, Chief Fin. Officer, Treas. & Controller--Capital Electric Group, Inc., Phoenix, AZ, pg. 215
Collins, William K., Treas.--Bill Collins Ford Inc., Louisville, KY, pg. 263
Colnes, Martin B., Sec. & Treas.--Engineered Products, Inc., Pittsburgh, PA, pg. 382
Colton, Leonard H., Treas.--Domestic Linen Supply & Laundry Co., Detroit, MI, pg. 343
Colucci, Elena, Treas.--Laminaire Corporation, Rahway, NJ, pg. 652
Colwell, Jerry, Treas. & Chief Fin. Officer--Advanced Manufacturing & Development, Willits, CA, pg. 20
Comas, Louis G., V.P. & Treas.--Londontown Corporation, Eldersburg, MD, pg. 682
Combs, Kevin, Treas., Chief Fin. Officer & Sec.--Symons Corporation, Pasadena, CA, pg. 1069
Comfort, Eugene C., V.P. & Treas.--Pacific Metal Company, Portland, OR, pg. 841
Commisso, Rocco, Exec. V.P. & Chief Fin. Officer--Cablevision Industries Corp., Liberty, NY, pg. 206
Como, John, Jr., V.P., Sec. & Treas.--Amco Folding Cartons, Inc., Towaco, NJ, pg. 47
Conder, Patrick, Treas.--Owensboro Grain Co., Inc., Owensboro, KY, pg. 834
Condon, Leon J., Pres., Chief Oper. Officer & Treas.--Kennington Ltd., Inc., Los Angeles, CA, pg. 623
Conforti, Sam, Sec. & Treas.--Bentley, Barnes & Lynn, Inc., Chicago, IL, pg. 140
Connaughton, Michael, Treas.--Dahlem Company, Inc., Louisville, KY, pg. 310
Connell, Terry, Sr. V.P. & Treas.--Connell Rice & Sugar Co., Westfield, NJ, pg. 275
Connor, John J., Treas.--Polyvinyl Films, Inc., Sutton, MA, pg. 880
Connors, Chester L., Pres. & Treas.--Magneco/Metrel, Inc., Addison, IL, pg. 700
Constantinides, Ellen, Exec. V.P. & Treas.--Coordinated Apparel, Inc., New York, NY, pg. 283
Contadino, Joseph, Chm. Bd., Pres. & Treas.--Del Webb's Coventry, Phoenix, AZ, pg. 1171
Conway, Frederick F., Treas.--Thompson Steel Co., Inc., Canton, MA, pg. 1094
Conway, Robert D., Treas. & Sec.--Schneider National, Inc., Green Bay, WI, pg. 977
Cook, Debbie, Sec. & Treas.--Cook Manufacturing Corporation, Duncan, OK, pg. 282
Cook, Donald L., Chief Fin. Officer & Treas.--Shuford Mills, Inc., Hickory, NC, pg. 1001
Cook, George, Treas.--Mid America Steel, Inc., Fargo, ND, pg. 750
Cook, J.M., V.P., Chief Fin. Officer & Treas.--American Cast Iron Pipe Co., Birmingham, AL, pg. 50
Cook, John, Treas.--Marontate & Co., Auburn Hills, MI, pg. 713
Cook, Marsha Weir, Treas. & Sec.--Mediatex Communications Corporation, Austin, TX, pg. 735
Cook, Mike, Sec. & Treas.--Collins Oldsmobile Inc., Indianapolis, IN, pg. 263
Cookson, John S., V.P.-Fin., Treas., Chief Fin. Officer, Sec. & Dir.-Investor Rels.--Kingsbury Corporation, Keene, NH, pg. 631
Cool, Janet, Treas.--Daniel Green Co., Dolgeville, NY, pg. 484
Coombe, V. Anderson, Chm. Bd., Chief Exec. Officer, & Treas.--The Wm. Powell Company, Cincinnati, OH, pg. 882
Coombs, E.D., Jr., V.P. & Treas.--Anderson-Tully Co., Memphis, TN, pg. 73
Coon, Miles A., Pres., Chief Oper. Officer & Treas.--Red Wing Products, Inc., Plainview, NY, pg. 919
Cooney, Edward, Sr. V.P. & Treas.--Amtrol Inc., West Warwick, RI, pg. 70
Coopee, Tom, Treas.--Merriam-Webster, Inc., Springfield, MA, pg. 381
Cooper, David, V.P. & Treas.--Dole Food Company, Inc., Westlake Village, CA, pg. 840
Cooper, Maxine, Sec. & Treas.--Maxine Of Hollywood, Inc., Los Angeles, CA, pg. 723
Cooperman, Michael, Chief Fin. Officer, V.P. & Treas.--Josephson International Inc., New York, NY, pg. 607
Copland, James R., III, Pres., Chief Exec. Officer & Treas.--Copland Fabrics, Inc., Burlington, NC, pg. 284
Corbett, Keith, Treas.--North Carolina Mutual Life Insurance Co., Durham, NC, pg. 813
Corbin, Richard F., Sec. & Treas.--Metal Trades, Inc., Hollywood, SC, pg. 741
Cordek, Lawrence D., Chief Fin. Officer & Corp. Sec.--G B Stores, Johnstown, PA, pg. 978
Cordle, Audra, Chief Fin. Officer, Treas. & Controller--Consolidated Co-op, Gowrie, IA, pg. 276
Corelli, Christopher, Treas. & Sec.--Corham, Inc., White Plains, NY, pg. 286
Cornell, G.L., V.P.-Acctng. & Real Estate & Treas.--Auto-Owners Insurance, Lansing, MI, pg. 100
Cornewll, Ed, Treas. & Asst. Sec.--U.S. Furniture Industries, Inc., High Point, NC, pg. 1136
Cornish, H.L., Jr., Sr. V.P., Treas. & Sec.--Carson Products Company, Savannah, GA, pg. 67
Corogin, John S., Chm. Bd., Sec. & Treas.--Lake Erie Electric, Inc., Westlake, OH, pg. 651
Cosbey, J.R., V.P., Sec. & Treas.--Daubert Industries, Inc., Westchester, IL, pg. 317
Cosgrove, Hazel, Vice Chm., Treas., & Corp. Sec.--Pro Hardware, Inc., Englewood, CO, pg. 891
Cote, Gilman, Sec. & Treas.--Connecticut Spring & Stamping Corporation, Farmington, CT, pg. 275
Cote, Rick, Treas.--Ivex Packaging Corporation, Lincolnshire, IL, pg. 583
Cotton, Owen L., V.P.-Fin. & Treas.--J. R. Norton Company, Phoenix, AZ, pg. 816
Couch, James A., V.P.-Fin., Treas. & Chief Fin. Officer--Clark Foodservice, Inc., Elk Grove Village, IL, pg. 252
Coughlin, F.X., Pres. & Treas.--F.X. Coughlin Co., Taylor, MI, pg. 289
Coughlin, John, V.P.-Fin. & Treas.--Caldwell Manufacturing Company, Rochester, NY, pg. 208
Coulombe, Cecile J., Pres., Treas. & Sec.--White Rock Distilleries Inc., Lewiston, ME, pg. 1186
Coulombe, Cecile J., V.P. & Treas.--Nuyens Liquor Importing, Inc., Syosset, NY, pg. 1186
Coulonbe, James D., Chief Fin. Officer& Treas.--American Foods Group, Inc., Minneapolis, MN, pg. 54
Councilor, T., Pres. & Treas.--Black Millwork Co., Inc., Allendale, NJ, pg. 154
Countryman, Peter J., Chief Fin. Officer, Treas. & Controller--Sabin Robbins Paper Co., Cincinnati, OH, pg. 965
Couri, Ronald J., Treas.--Couristan Inc., Fort Lee, NJ, pg. 290
Couvelaire, Alexandre, Pres. & Treas.--Mooney Aircraft Corporation, Kerrville, TX, pg. 768
Covey, Harold D., Exec. V.P., Treas. & Chief Admin. Officer--State Farm Fire and Casualty Co., Bloomington, IL, pg. 1041
Covey, Harold D., Exec. V.P., Treas. & Chief Admin. Officer--State Farm General Insurance Co., Bloomington, IL, pg. 1041
Cowan, Richard, Sec., Treas., Controller & Chief Fin. Officer--Wheeler Brothers Grain Co., Watonga, OK, pg. 1184
Cowgill, F. Brooks, V.P. & Treas.--The New England, Boston, MA, pg. 799
Cowin, John J., Chm. Bd., Pres & Treas.--Cowin & Company, Inc., Birmingham, AL, pg. 291
Cowles, H.B., Chief Fin. Officer, Treas. & Controller--Bluff City Distributing Co., Inc., Memphis, TN, pg. 161
Cox, Arthur, Sec. & Treas.--The Knapheide Mfg. Co., Quincy, IL, pg. 636
Cox, Craig M., Treas.--Diehl Specialties Intl., Defiance, OH, pg. 336
Cox, Samuel J., V.P. & Treas.--Mars Super Markets, Inc., Baltimore, MD, pg. 714
Coxwell, Frances, Sec. & Treas.--J.B. Coxwell Contract, Inc., Jacksonville, FL, pg. 295
Coyne, Paul L., Treas.--Taren Holdings, Inc., Los Angeles, CA, pg. 1078
Crabtree, William B., Sec. & Treas.--SCR, Inc., Lake Oswego, OR, pg. 961
Craft, Ronald K., V.P.-Fin., Treas. & Controller--CF&I Steel Corporation, Pueblo, CO, pg. 201
Craig, Tom, V.P.-Fin. & Treas.--Wagner Spray Tech Corp., Minneapolis, MN, pg. 1158
Crain, Mary Kay, Treas.--Crain Communications, Inc., Detroit, MI, pg. 295
Crane, Mary Louise, Treas. & Sec.--Decatur News Publishing Company, Inc., Decatur, GA, pg. 323
Crawford, Charles, Pres. & Treas.--Adair Feed & Grain Company, Adair, IA, pg. 16
Crawford, Donna M., Sec.--The American Companies, Inc., Topeka, KS, pg. 50
Crawford, James, Treas.--J.R. Simplot Company, Boise, ID, pg. 1007
Crawford, Larry L., V.P.-Fin. & Treas.--Talon, Inc., Meadville, PA, pg. 1077
Creagh, Richard P., Controller, Treas. & Chief Fin. Officer--Hoffman Brothers Packing Co., Los Angeles, CA, pg. 537
Creel, W.E., Treas. & Sec.--Michigan Tractor And Machinery Co., Novi, MI, pg. 747
Crews, Robert, V.P.--Fisca Oil Co., Inc., Westwood, KS, pg. 414
Cribbs, Francis J., Exec. V.P., Chief Fin. Officer & Treas.--Lloyd Properties, Los Angeles, CA, pg. 680
Crifasi, James, Sec. & Treas.--Hi Nabor Supermarket Inc., Baton Rouge, LA, pg. 532
Cripe, Richard L., Treas.--Gohmann Asphalt & Construction Inc., Clarksville, IN, pg. 465
Crisafulli, Robert, Jr., Treas.--Baltimore Orioles, Inc., Baltimore, MD, pg. 116
Crisanti, John, Treas.--The U.S. Baird Corporation, Stratford, CT, pg. 114
Crisanti, John, Treas.--The A. H. Nilson Machine Co., Stratford, CT, pg. 114
Crocker, Frederick G., Jr., V.P. & Chief Fin. Officer & Treas.--Springborn Laboratories, Inc., Enfield, CT, pg. 1033
Cronen, Vin, Sec. & Treas.--Whittaker, Clark & Daniels, Inc., South Plainfield, NJ, pg. 1187
Cronon, Richard N., Treas. & Pur. Agent--Automatic Machine Products Company, Attleboro, MA, pg. 100
Cross, Richard M., V.P. & Treas.--First Land & Development, Inc., Richmond, VA, pg. 18
Crosta, Edward A., Sr. V.P. & Treas.--West Lumber Co., Atlanta, GA, pg. 1177
Crotty, Thomas, Exec. V.P., Treas.--Sudler & Hennessey, New York, NY, pg. 1211
Crowe, Kenneth, Treas.--Cinamerica Theatres, L.P., Los Angeles, CA, pg. 249
Crowell, Ralph, Exec. V.P. & Treas.--Glines & Rhodes, Inc., Attleboro, MA, pg. 463
Crowley, Denis M., Treas.--Polar Corporation, Worcester, MA, pg. 878
Crowley, Malvern D., V.P.-Fin. & Treas.--Drug Emporium of Arizona, Inc., Scottsdale, AZ, pg. 349
Crowley, Timothy R., Treas. & Sec.--Health Care Lodges, Coffeyville, KS, pg. 520
Cruickshank, James E., Treas.--John Hancock Capital Corporation, Boston, MA, pg. 596
Crum, Mary M., Treas. & Sec.--Crum Electric Supply Co., Inc., Casper, WY, pg. 303
Cruncleton, Barbara A., Treas., Sec. & Dir.--John S. Frey Enterprises, Los Angeles, CA, pg. 433
Crutcher, Richard E., Treas. & Sec.--East Kentucky Power Co-op, Winchester, KY, pg. 362
Crutcher, Shirley, Treas. & Sec.--Fojtasek Companies, Inc., Irving, TX, pg. 421
Crvarich, Gene, V.P., Sec. & Treas.--Al Larson Boat Shop, Inc., Terminal Island, CA, pg. 659
Crystal, Lynn, Treas.--Finesilver Manufacturing Company, San Antonio, TX, pg. 411
Csepella, John, Treas.--Color Arts, Inc., Racine, WI, pg. 264
Cubberly, Walter A., Chm. Bd. & Treas.--Kalas Manufacturing, Inc., Denver, PA, pg. 615
Cudzewicz, Alexander, Dir.-Fin., Treas. & Chief Fin. Officer--Sargent & Lundy, Chicago, IL, pg. 971
Cuff, Harry, Treas.--Kampgrounds of America, Inc., Billings, MT, pg. 613
Culbreth, Robert, Chief Fin. Officer, Treas. & Controller--Skinner Corp., Lanett, AL, pg. 1009
Cullers, Vincent T., Pres., Chief Exec. Officer & Treas.--Vince Cullers Advertising Inc., Chicago, IL, pg. 304
Cunningham, A., V.P. & Treas.--Fishers Big Wheel Inc., New Castle, PA, pg. 415
Currier, Ronald, Sec. & Treas.--Gilpatrick Construction Company, Riverton, WY, pg. 460
Curry, Barbara A., Treas.--The Curry Corporation, Scarsdale, NY, pg. 305
Curtis, Paul F., Pres., Chief Oper. Officer & Treas.--L.N. Curtis & Sons, Oakland, CA, pg. 306
Curtis, Stan, Asst. Sec. & Treas.--Continental Forge Company, Compton, CA, pg. 279
Curto, Anthony, Treas. & Sec.--LaMarca Group Inc., New York, NY, pg. 652
Curto, Anthony, Sec. & Treas.--LaMarca Direct Marketing, New York, NY, pg. 652
Czarnecki, Walter P., Exec. V.P.--Penske Corporation, Detroit, MI, pg. 859
Czerwinski, Connie, V.P., Sec. & Treas.--Cerwin Vega, Inc., Simi Valley, CA, pg. 237
D'Haeze, T.M., V.P.-Fin. & Acctg., Treas. & Sec.--Dwyer Instruments Inc., Michigan City, IN, pg. 356
Daane, Charles, Treas.--Trio Products Inc., Elyria, OH, pg. 1114
Dabbs, Karl, V.P.-Fin., Treas. & Sec.--B.A.S.S., Inc., Montgomery, AL, pg. 105
Dabney, D., Sec. & Treas.--Chevy Chase Cars & Geo, Bethesda, MD, pg. 244
Dale, Jimmy, Treas. & Mgr.-Acct.--Oman Construction Co. Inc., Nashville, TN, pg. 825
Daley, Vincent, Dir.-Fin.--Guideposts Associates, Inc., Carmel, NY, pg. 493
Dallal, Fortunate, V.P.-Personnel & Treas.--Windsor Fashions, Los Angeles, CA, pg. 1195
Daly, Kathleen C., Treas. & Sec.--Frank Messer & Sons Construction Co., Cincinnati, OH, pg. 741
Daly, Leo A., Chm. Bd., Pres. & Treas.--Leo A. Daly Company, Omaha, NE, pg. 313
Daly, Michael J., Treas.--Chessco Industries, Inc., Westport, CT, pg. 243
Dancy, Richard H., Jr., V.P. & Treas.--The John Johnson Co., Detroit, MI, pg. 597
Dandurand, Don, V.P. & Treas.--Jewell Instruments, Inc., Manchester, NH, pg. 594
Dangelo, Jacqueline, Controller & Treas.--The Tobin Corporation, North Ridgeville, OH, pg. 102
Daniel, Carole J., V.P. & Asst. Treas.--National Group, Inc., Chattanooga, TN, pg. 789
Daniel, Michael, Sec., Treas. & Controller--Field Packing Company, Owensboro, KY, pg. 409
Daniels, Stephen D., V.P. & Treas.--Lane Industries, Inc., Northbrook, IL, pg. 656
Danisewicz, Mark, Treas.--American Systems Corporation, Chantilly, VA, pg. 63
Darnell, W. Reid, Sec. & Treas.--Florida Crushed Stone Company, Leesburg, FL, pg. 420
Darrah, Rodney C., V.P.-Treas.--UES, Inc., Dayton, OH, pg. 1122
Daugherty, Timothy, Treas.--Darling's, Bangor, ME, pg. 315

Davenport, Earl M., Treas.--Smith Brothers Farms, Inc., Kent, WA, pg. 1011
Davenport, J.T., Jr., Pres. & Treas.--J.T. Davenport & Sons, Inc., Sanford, NC, pg. 317
Davenport, Lynn E., V.P. & Treas.--The Edward J. DeBartolo Corporation, Youngstown, OH, pg. 323
Davey, Bruce J., V.P. & Treas.--New York Life Insurance Company, New York, NY, pg. 802
Davidson, David A., Treas.--CB Commercial Real Estate Group, Inc., Los Angeles, CA, pg. 222
Davis, Adrienne, Sec. & Treas.--Clayton-Davis & Associates, Incorporated, Saint Louis, MO, pg. 253
Davis, Bonnie, Sec. & Treas.--O.P. Link Handle Company, Salem, IN, pg. 676
Davis, Charles E., Jr., Sec. & Treas.--Laboratory Supply Company, Inc., Louisville, KY, pg. 649
Davis, Clyde P., Exec. V.P., Treas. & Creative Dir.--Cline, Davis & Mann, Inc., New York, NY, pg. 255
Davis, Edna R., Sec. & Treas.--South States Inc., Shreveport, LA, pg. 340
Davis, Gary K., Treas. & Sec.--Bud Davis Cadillac, Inc., Memphis, TN, pg. 318
Davis, John H., Pres. & Treas.--American Saw & Manufacturing Co., East Longmeadow, MA, pg. 60
Davis, Lucy A., Treas.--The Pierce Co., Inc., Upland, IN, pg. 102
Davis, Martha O., Sec. & Treas.--Jimmy Davis Enterprises, Inc., Madison, FL, pg. 318
Davis, Melinda, Treas.--Allen Canning Company, Siloam Springs, AR, pg. 35
Davis, Robert, Treas.--S L C Graphics, Inc., Pittston, PA, pg. 963
Davis, Robert M., Chm., Sec. & Treas.--Davis, Ball & Colombatto Advertising, Inc., Los Angeles, CA, pg. 318
Davis, Robert W. II, Sr. V.P.-Acct. & Fin. & Treas.--Sarkes Tarzian, Incorporated, Bloomington, IN, pg. 1079
Davis, W.F., Jr., Pres., Chief Exec. Officer & Treas.--Palmetto Spinning Corp., Laurens, SC, pg. 844
Dawahare, Martin, Sec. & Treas.--Dawahares, Inc., Lexington, KY, pg. 319
Dawkins, George, Treas. & Sec.--Austin Industries, Inc., Dallas, TX, pg. 99
Dawson, Timothy A., Treas.--Mississippi Chemical Corporation, Yazoo City, MS, pg. 760
Dawson, Timothy A., V.P.-Fin. & Treas.--Newsprint South, Inc., Yazoo City, MS, pg. 760
Day, R. James, V.P. & Treas.--Simpson Investment Co., Seattle, WA, pg. 1007
Day, Robert J., V.P. & Treas.-SICO--Simpson Timber Co., Shelton, WA, pg. 1007
Day, Sharon, Treas. & Sec.--Catalina Yachts, Inc., Woodland Hills, CA, pg. 229
Day, Susan, Treas.--North American Salt Company, Overland Park, KS, pg. 812
de Caussin, Larry F., Treas.--Fadal Engineering Company, Inc., North Hollywood, CA, pg. 396
Dean, John S., Sec. & Treas.--Oglethorpe Power Corp., Tucker, GA, pg. 822
DeAngelo, Joseph A., Treas.--Moran Towing & Transporation Co. Inc, Greenwich, CT, pg. 769
Deborde, W. Paul, Sr., V.P. & Treas.--Bearing Distributors, Inc., Columbia, SC, pg. 130
DeBow, Al, Treas.--Chicago Heights Steel, Chicago Heights, IL, pg. 245
Debrecht, Donald R., Sr. V.P., Treas. & Controller--Hill-Behan Lumber Company, Saint Louis, MO, pg. 534
Dechamps, Daniel, Pres. & Treas.--Trumpf Inc., Farmington, CT, pg. 1118
Deckard, Dean, Asst. Treas.--H. E. Butt Grocery Co., San Antonio, TX, pg. 197
Deckle, N.H., Treas.--American Liberty Financial Corp., Baton Rouge, LA, pg. 57
Dee, Jay, Treas. & Sec.--Dee Paper Company, Chester, PA, pg. 324
Deel, Daryl, Exec. V.P. & Treas.--Tri-State Motor Transit Co., Joplin, MO, pg. 1111
Deen, Nancy, Sec. & Treas.--Deen Wholesale Meat Company, Inc., Fort Worth, TX, pg. 324
Deeney, Gerald D., V.P., Chief Fin. Officer & Treas.--Hubbard Broadcasting, Inc., Saint Paul, MN, pg. 548
DeGregory, Alfred D., V.P.-Fin., Treas. & Chief Fin. Officer--Blue Diamond Growers, Sacramento, CA, pg. 160
Del Mar, Bruce, Pres. & Treas.--Del Mar Avionics, Irvine, CA, pg. 325
Delaloye, John F., V.P., Sec. & Treas.--Hickey-Mitchell Company, Saint Louis, MO, pg. 795
Delfini, Joseph, Sec. & Treas.--Colonial Beef Co., Philadelphia, PA, pg. 263
Delia, Richard J., Treas.--Redken Laboratories, Inc., Canoga Park, CA, pg. 919
Delisle, Ken, Treas.--B.A. Ballou & Co. Inc., East Providence, RI, pg. 116
Dellaquila, Stephen J., Pres. & Treas.--Della Construction Co. Inc., Enfield, CT, pg. 326
Delman, Richard, Chief Fin. Officer, Treas., Sec. & Controller--Splendor Form International Inc., Long Island City, NY, pg. 1031
DeLorenzo, Ralph, Controller--Red Devil Inc., Union, NJ, pg. 918
DeLuca, John, V.P. & Treas.--National Engineering & Contracting Co., Strongsville, OH, pg. 788
Demarest, John D., Chief Fin. Officer, V.P. & Treas.--Production Management Companies, Inc., Harvey, LA, pg. 893
Dembinski, Jan A., Pres., Chief Exec. Officer & Treas.--M.J. Daly & Sons, Inc., Waterbury, CT, pg. 313
DeMeo, Donald A., V.P. & Treas.--Joseph Davis, Inc., Buffalo, NY, pg. 318
DeMilt, William A., Sr. V.P. & Treas.--Mutual of America, New York, NY, pg. 777
Denaro, J., V.P., Chief Fin. Officer & Treas.--R. T. Vanderbilt Company, Inc., Norwalk, CT, pg. 1144
Denburg, Sheldon, V.P. & Treas.--Barton Press, Inc., West Orange, NJ, pg. 123
Denker, Michael, Sec. & Treas.--Arcon Construction Co., Inc., Mora, MN, pg. 81
Dennis, Aaron S., Pres. & Treas.--Dennis Chemical Company, Inc., Saint Louis, MO, pg. 329
Dennis, David M., Sr. V.P., Chief Fin. Officer & Treas.--SBC Advertising, Columbus, OH, pg. 960
Dennis, John N., V.P.-Sls. Dept.--Annin & Company, Roseland, NJ, pg. 75
Dent, Robert L., Exec. V.P. & Treas.--Crosby & Overton, Inc., Long Beach, CA, pg. 300
Denton, David, Treas. & Sec.--Bale Of Kentucky, Inc., Horse Cave, KY, pg. 115
Depolo, Robert A., Mgr.-Personnel, Treas. & Sec.--Monterey Mechanical Company, Oakland, CA, pg. 767
DePopas, Michael, Treas.--Carolina Steel Corporation, Greensboro, NC, pg. 223
DeSabatino, Fred, Treas. & Sec.--Capital Pants Co., Philadelphia, PA, pg. 215
Deutchman, Howard, V.P., Sec. & Treas.--Mark Fabricks, Inc., Los Angeles, CA, pg. 708
Devanney, William J., V.P., Sec. & Treas.--Meier Metal Service Centers, Inc., Hazel Park, MI, pg. 737
Devareaux, Vance A., Exec. V.P., Sec., Treas. & Chief Fin. Officer--Arrowhead Mills, Inc., Hereford, TX, pg. 86
Deverse, Frank T., Chm. Bd., Pres., Chief Exec. Officer & Treas.--International Microcircuits, Inc., Milpitas, CA, pg. 579
Devine, Jack M., Sec. & Treas.--Associated Diesel Service & Equipment Company, Wilmington, CA, pg. 89
Dhole, Gulab, Treas.--Petron Corporation, New Berlin, WI, pg. 1172
Dhole, Gulab S., V.P.-Fin. & Admin.--Penetone Corp., Tenafly, NJ, pg. 1172
Diamond, Clare W., Sec. & Treas.--T.L. Diamond Company, New York, NY, pg. 335
Diamond, David A., Treas.--Nationwide Corporation, Columbus, OH, pg. 795
Diamond, Frederic, Exec. V.P., Sec. & Treas.--Diamond Chemical Co., Inc., Lyndhurst, NJ, pg. 335
Diamond, Isadore, Chm. Bd., Treas. & Chief Fin. & Chief Acctg. Officer--Magnetic Technologies Corporation, Rochester, NY, pg. 701
Diamond, Walter S., Sec. & Treas.--Snyder-Diamond, Santa Monica, CA, pg. 1015
Diaz, Gonzalo A., V.P. & Treas.--Med-Lab Supply Company, Inc., Miami, FL, pg. 734
Dibble, L.E., Treas.--Buckman Laboratories, Memphis, TN, pg. 185
Dibble, L.E., Treas. & Asst. Sec.--Bulab Holdings, Inc., Memphis, TN, pg. 188
DiChello, Joseph, Treas.--New England Log Homes, Inc., Hamden, CT, pg. 800
Dick, Donald W., Treas.--Overseas Partners, Inc., New York, NY, pg. 833
Dickinson, Royce, Sec., Treas. & Controller--Power Process Piping, Inc., Plymouth, MI, pg. 883
Dickler, Herbert, Treas. & Sec.--Bankcrafters, Inc., Philadelphia, PA, pg. 117
Dickman, Jack, V.P. & Asst. Treas.--E & J Gallo Winery, Modesto, CA, pg. 441
Diedrich, John C., Chief Fin. Officer & Treas.--Cummins-American Corp., Mount Prospect, IL, pg. 304
Diehl, Harrison L., Treas.--First Mount Joy Corporation, Mount Joy, PA, pg. 413
Diehl, Harrison L., Treas.--Sisco Company, Mount Joy, PA, pg. 413
Diehl, Harrison, Jr., Treas.--The Sico Company, Mount Joy, PA, pg. 1001
Diekemper, Greg, Treas.--Guarantee Electrical Company, Saint Louis, MO, pg. 490
Diem, Linda L., Sec. & Treas.--Southern Agricultural Insecticides, Palmetto, FL, pg. 1020
Diemer, Edmund, Pres. & Treas.--Metal Seal & Products, Inc., Willoughby, OH, pg. 741
Dierberg, Robert J., Pres., Chief Exec. Officer & Treas.--Dierbergs Markets Inc., Chesterfield, MO, pg. 337
Dieschbourg, Edward J., V.P. & Treas.--Replogle Globes, Inc., Broadview, IL, pg. 927
Dietrich, Kerry, Chief Fin. Officer & Treas.--Dietrich's Milk Products, Inc., Reading, PA, pg. 337
Dietz, D., Treas.--Stacoswitch, Inc., Costa Mesa, CA, pg. 270
Dietz, Walter, V.P. & Treas.--Thriftway, Inc., Cincinnati, OH, pg. 1095
Dilland, John, Dir.-Fin. & Asst. Treas.--Michigan Milk Producers Association, Novi, MI, pg. 747
Dillard, Joe, Treas.--Continental American Corp. d/b/a Pioneer Balloon Company, Wichita, KS, pg. 278
Dille, Guy, V.P.-Fin. & Treas.--Williams & Company, Inc., Pittsburgh, PA, pg. 230
Dillenschneider, John J., Treas.--Penny Plate, Inc., Cherry Hill, NJ, pg. 858
Diracles, John M., Jr., V.P. & Treas.--Carlson Companies, Inc., Minneapolis, MN, pg. 220
Dirkes, James V., Pres., Chief Exec. Officer & Treas.--Rapid Engineering Inc., Comstock Park, MI, pg. 913
Divane Jr., William T., Pres. & Treas.--Divane Bros. Electric Co., Franklin Park, IL, pg. 340
Diver, J. Edmond, V.P. & Treas.--Metropolitan Insurance & Annuity Co., New York, NY, pg. 744
Diver, J. Edmond, V.P. & Treas.--Metropolitan Tower Life Insurance Co., New York, NY, pg. 744
Dockter, Rebecca L., Treas. & Sec.--Professional Book Distributors, Inc., Alpharetta, GA, pg. 894
Dodge, Larry W., V.P. & Treas.--Mayflower Transit, Inc., Carmel, IN, pg. 724
Dodson, Bill D., V.P.-Fin., Services & Treas.--Marathon Electric Manufacturing Corp., Wausau, WI, pg. 705
Dodson, Richard, Treas.--Berks Products Corporation, Reading, PA, pg. 142
Dohler, D. Gary, Chief Fin. Officer--Atlantic Builders Group Inc., Baltimore, MD, pg. 94
Dokmo, Harold B., Jr., Chm. Bd., Pres., Treas. & Sec.--Norcraft Companies, Inc., Saint Paul, MN, pg. 809
Dolan, Bernard P., Sr. V.P., Treas.--Backer Spielvogel Bates, Inc., New York, NY, pg. 108
Dolan, Kevin, V.P.-Fin. & Treas.--Cajun Electric Power Co-op, Baton Rouge, LA, pg. 207
Dolan, Robert L., V.P. & Treas.--The Acacia Group, Washington, DC, pg. 10
Doll, David J., Chief Fin. Officer & Sr. V.P.--Bodine Electric Company, Chicago, IL, pg. 162
Doll, Mark G., V.P. & Treas.--Northwestern Mutual Life Insurance Co., Milwaukee, WI, pg. 815
Dolle, Jerome H., Treas.--George Transfer, Inc., Parkton, MD, pg. 453
Dominijanni, Joseph, Treas. & V.P.-Finance--EWI, Inc., Salem, OH, pg. 361
Donahoe, Michael P., V.P., Chief Fin. Officer & Treas.--Perkins Family Restaurants, Memphis, TN, pg. 1088
Donahue, Robert F., V.P. & Treas.--Paddock Publications, Inc., Arlington Heights, IL, pg. 842
Donaldson, George, Sec. & Treas.--Henco, Inc., Selmer, TN, pg. 528
Donavan, Doug, Chief Fin. & Info. Officer, Treas., Controller & Sec.--Campbell Oil Co., Massillon, OH, pg. 213
Donley, Terrance K., Pres. & Treas.--Donley's, Inc., Cleveland, OH, pg. 345
Donohoo, William G., V.P. & Treas.--The Gibson Group Inc., Cincinnati, OH, pg. 456
Donohue, Connie, Treas.--R & R Advertising, Las Vegas, NV, pg. 906
Donohue, Leonard, Treas. & Sec.--Steiner & Company, Milford, DE, pg. 1045
Donovan, Gordon S., Treas.--Envirodyne Industries, Inc., Oak Brook, IL, pg. 383
Dooley, Jo Ann C., V.P., Sec. & Treas.--Gardner Publications, Inc., Cincinnati, OH, pg. 443
Dooley, Thomas E., V.P.-Fin. & Treas.--National Amusements, Inc., Dedham, MA, pg. 784
Dopkins, Leonard A., Chm. Bd., Treas. & Sec.--Standard Electronics, Inc., Amherst, NY, pg. 1036
Doran, Michael W., Treas. & Sec.--Midway Ford Truck Center Inc., Kansas City, MO, pg. 751
Doran, Robert J., Pres. & Treas.--Ace Doran Hauling & Rigging Company, Cincinnati, OH, pg. 346
Dorn, Cecilia A., Sec. & Treas.--Edward G. Dorn & Associates, Inc., Rolling Meadows, IL, pg. 346
Dornbush, Dennis C., Pres. & Treas.--Sintel, Inc., Spring Lake, MI, pg. 1008
Doster, Robert E., Treas. & Sec.--Lift-All Co., Inc., Manheim, PA, pg. 675
Dostov, Steven, Treas.--New England Coffee Company, Malden, MA, pg. 800
Dougherty, R.E., Jr., Pres. & Treas.--Tasa Corporation, Pittsburgh, PA, pg. 1079
Douglas, Ruth, Treas.--Warner Candy Company, Inc., Chicago, IL, pg. 1164
Douthit, R. E., V.P., Sec. & Treas.--Smith & Sons Foods, Inc., Macon, GA, pg. 1014
Downey, Paul, Pres., Treas. & Sec.--Advanced Circuit Technology, Nashua, NH, pg. 20
Downs, Beverly B., Vice Chm., Chief Exec. Officer & Treas.--The Downs Group, Inc., Charlotte, NC, pg. 348
Downs, Marie F., Treas.--Flanagan Brothers, Bear Creek, WI, pg. 416
Downs, Richard S., V.P. & Treas.--American Foodservice Corp., King of Prussia, PA, pg. 54
Dowsett, Connie, Chief Fin. Officer & Treas.--East Moline Metal Products Company, East Moline, IL, pg. 363
Doyle, Brian, V.P., Gen. Mgr, Treas. & Dir.-Sls.--King Milling Company, Lowell, MI, pg. 631
Doyle, Daniel P., Treas.--Publishers Clearing House, Port Washington, NY, pg. 898
Doyle, Michael M., Exec. V.P., Treas. & Fin.--Rivers Trainor Doyle & Walsh, Inc., Providence, RI, pg. 937
Dragoo, Nina, V.P., Treas. & Chief Fin. Officer--California Hardware Co., City of Industry, CA, pg. 209
Dreisbach, Albert J., Treas.--Ekstrom Industries, Inc., Farmington Hills, MI, pg. 180
Drescher, Donald, Sec. & Treas.--Dazey Corporation, Industrial Airport, KS, pg. 321
Dressler, Michael B., Treas.--Colfax, Inc., Pawtucket, RI, pg. 261
Drettmann, Henry, Chm. Bd., Chief Exec. Officer & Treas.--Active Tool & Manufacturing Co., Inc., Roseville, MI, pg. 15
Drewry, John T., V.P., Chief Oper. & Chief Fin. Officer & Treas.--Advanced Marine Enterprises, Inc., Arlington, VA, pg. 20
Driscoll, Edward C., Chm. Bd., Chief Exec. Officer & Treas.-L.F. Driscoll Co., Bala-Cynwyd, PA, pg. 349
Drobot, Joseph, Treas.--Wall Colmonoy Corp., Madison Heights, MI, pg. 1160
Drucker, N., V.P.-Fin., Treas. & Sec.--Weber Marking Systems, Inc., Arlington Heights, IL, pg. 1171
Drumm, Wesley C., Chm. Bd., Pres. & Treas.--The Metal Ware Corp., Two Rivers, WI, pg. 741
Drury, Daniel, Treas. & Controller--Liquid Controls Corporation, Lake Bluff, IL, pg. 677
Drutt, Diane, V.P., Treas. & Media Dir.--Harris & Drutt Inc., Philadelphia, PA, pg. 511
Dryer, Ned, Sec. & Treas.--National Brands, Inc., Phoenix, AZ, pg. 786
Du, Carmela, Treas.--Flojet Corporation, Irvine, CA, pg. 419
Dubner, Miriam, Sec. & Treas.--Gerson & Gerson, Inc., New York, NY, pg. 454
Dubrowski, Jerome, V.P., Treas. & Chief Fin. Officer--Louis Dreyfus Corporation, Wilton, CT, pg. 348
Duckworth, James, Exec. V.P.-Fin. & Treas.--Quaker City Motor Parts Company, Middletown, DE, pg. 903
Duckworth, William D., V.P., Corp. Treas. & Asst. Sec.--Stauffer Communications, Inc., Topeka, KS, pg. 1042
Dueffent, Gary, Pres. & Treas.--Lincoln Industries, Inc., Boonville, IN, pg. 1221
Duersch, Charles A., Treas.--Western States Machine Co., Hamilton, OH, pg. 1181

Dugan, Joel H., Sr. V.P.-Fin. & Admin.; Sec. & Treas.--Rhodes, Inc., Atlanta, GA, pg. 931
Duggan, Joe D., V.P. & Treas.--Duggan Industries, Inc., Dallas, TX, pg. 351
Dugger, Irene, Chm. Bd., Pres., Chief Exec. Officer & Treas.--Queen Oxygen Company, Columbus, OH, pg. 904
Dula, C. Stephen, Sec.-Treas. & Chief Fin. Officer--Salem National Corporation, Winston-Salem, NC, pg. 967
Dulany, Charles R., Treas.--Ocean Spray Cranberries, Inc., Lakeville, MA, pg. 820
Dulin, Ann, Treas.--Gerbig, Snell/Weisheimer & Assoc., Inc., Worthington, OH, pg. 454
Dumbacher, Robert J., V.P.-Fin. & Treas.--Racetrac Petroleum, Inc., Smyrna, GA, pg. 909
Dunaway, Amy M., Treas. & Controller--The Enstar Group, Inc., Montgomery, AL, pg. 382
Duncan, Willis P., Jr., V.P.-Fin. & Treas.--Thomas Built Buses, Inc., High Point, NC, pg. 1092
Dunham, Cynthia Harris, Owner, Treas. & Sec.--K-J Distributors, Inc., Glendale, AZ, pg. 612
Dunleavy, Karen, Treas.--Gould Investors, L.P., Great Neck, NY, pg. 473
Dunler, Don, Treas. & Gen. Mgr.--Perryton Equity, Perryton, TX, pg. 863
Dunn, Gary, V.P. & Treas.--Arrow Chevrolet, Inc., Midlothian, IL, pg. 85
Dupps, David M., Treas. & Sec.--Dupps Company, Germantown, OH, pg. 354
Dupree, J. W., Jr., Treas.--Mac Papers, Inc., Jacksonville, FL, pg. 694
Dupuis, Lenore, Treas.--Your Man Tours, Inc., Inglewood, CA, pg. 1214
Durfee, Barbara, Treas. & Sec.--Bethel Mills, Inc., Bethel, VT, pg. 148
Durgin, William, V.P. & Treas.--Nickerson Lumber Company, Orleans, MA, pg. 806
Durham, B.W., Jr., Exec. V.P., Treas.--Simmons, Durham & Associates, Saint Louis, MO, pg. 1005
Durnin, Jerry L., Sec. & Treas.--A. K. Durnin Chrysler Plymouth, Inc., Baton Rouge, LA, pg. 355
Durocher, Francis W., Chm. Bd., Pres. & Treas.--Gust K. Newberg Construction Co., Chicago, IL, pg. 803
Duval, William D., V.P. & Treas.--Masters Inc., Gaithersburg, MD, pg. 720
Duwe, John, Sec. & Treas.--United States Bakery, Portland, OR, pg. 1134
Dvorak, William F., Treas.--Great Lakes Terminal & Transport Corp., Chicago, IL, pg. 482
Dwyer, Dean P., Treas.--The Copley Press, Inc., La Jolla, CA, pg. 284
Dyer, Darrell, V.P. & Treas.--Telex Communications, Inc., Minneapolis, MN, pg. 1085
Dyer, Ron, V.P.-Admin. & Treas.--K & B, Inc., New Orleans, LA, pg. 611
Dykstra, Thomas M., V.P. & Treas.--Effective Management Systems, Milwaukee, WI, pg. 370
Dykstra, William, Sr. V.P., Treas. & Investor Rels. Dir.--Reed & Barton Corporation, Taunton, MA, pg. 920
Dyros, Joe, Treas.--Kervick Enterprises, Inc., Worcester, MA, pg. 624
Eacott, James H., III, Pres. & Treas.--Bartlett Brainard & Eacott, Inc., Bloomfield, CT, pg. 122
Eagel, M.J., Sec. & Treas.--Pipe Fabricating & Supply Company, Santa Fe Springs, CA, pg. 872
Eagin, Mary, Treas.--Hoffer Plastics Corporation, South Elgin, IL, pg. 537
Eaken, Barbara J., Sec., Treas. & Comptroller--R.W. Eaken, Inc., Leesport, PA, pg. 362
Earnhardt, Jim Babe, Sec. & Treas.--Earnhardt's Auto Center, Tempe, AZ, pg. 362
Earp, Marie, Sec. & Treas.--Earp Meat Company, Kansas City, KS, pg. 362
Easterly, Clark, Jr., Treas.--Johnstown Knitting Mill Co., Johnstown, NY, pg. 602
Eaton, Robert L., Sec. & Treas.--Invincible Metal Furniture Co., Manitowoc, WI, pg. 582
Eaton, Sandra, Treas.--Rand's Inc., North Little Rock, AR, pg. 912
Eaton, Scott, Sec. & Treas.--Sasco/Valley Electric, Mountain View, CA, pg. 972
Eccles, J.E., Treas.--Millers' Mutual Insurance Assn. Of Illinois, Alton, IL, pg. 755
Eck, Dale F., V.P. & Treas.--The Entwistle Company, Hudson, MA, pg. 383
Eck, Joseph, Treas. & Controller--King Kullen Grocery Co., Inc., Westbury, NY, pg. 630
Eckenrod, Jeannie, Treas. & Sec.--FKG Oil Company, Belleville, IL, pg. 773
Eckerling, Sanford, Pres. & Treas.--Universal Overall Company, Chicago, IL, pg. 1139
Edelman, Mitchell, Treas.--Greater New York Box Co., Clifton, NJ, pg. 483
Eder, Dennis, V.P.-Treasury--UniHealth America, Burbank, CA, pg. 1126
Edreich, Jack, Treas. & Sec.--Brittany Dyeing & Printing Corporation, New Bedford, MA, pg. 177
Edwards, G. Gail, V.P.-Finance & Treas.--Delaware North Companies, Inc., Buffalo, NY, pg. 326
Edwards, Jerry, Sr. V.P, Sec. & Treas.--Berry Companies, Inc., Wichita, KS, pg. 144
Edwards, Lily, Treas. & Office Mgr.--Bertrand Advertising Agency, Inc., Hollywood, CA, pg. 144
Edwards, Mike, Treas.--Cargill Detroit Corp., Clawson, MI, pg. 219
Edwards, R.L., Treas.--The Spencer Turbine Co., Windsor, CT, pg. 1030
Edwards, Richard L., Treas.--Spencer Turbine Co., Windsor, CT, pg. 1030
Edwards, William F., Sec. & Treas.--Pilot Air Freight Corp., Lima, PA, pg. 870
Eenhuls, Loretta, Treas. & Data Processing Dir.--Westin, Inc., Omaha, NE, pg. 1183
Effstrom, Carroll E., Sec. & Treas.--Farmers Marine Copper Works, Galveston, TX, pg. 401
Eggert, Ulrich, Treas.--Kowalski Sausage Co., Inc., Hamtramck, MI, pg. 643
Ehret, A.D., V.P., Sec. & Treas.--Dexter Company, Fairfield, IA, pg. 334
Ehrlich, Henry, Sec. & Treas.--Bregg Data Forms, Inc., Hauppauge, NY, pg. 173
Eigendorf, Richard, V.P. & Asst. Treas.--Viacom Inc., New York, NY, pg. 785
Einstein, Ernst, Sec. & Treas.--Einstein Moomjy Inc., Pine Brook, NJ, pg. 371
Eiseman, Michael P., Exec. V.P., Treas. & Information Systems Dir.--Revere Electric Supply Co., Chicago, IL, pg. 930
Eisenberg, Craig, Chief Fin. Officer & Treas.--American Strip Steel Inc., Kearny, NJ, pg. 63
Eisenberg, Donald, Treas.--Master Industries Corp., New York, NY, pg. 719
Eisenmayer, Mildred F., Sec. & Asst. Treas.--Cullman Ventures, Inc., New York, NY, pg. 304
Eisenstadt, Ruth, Treas. & Office Mgr.--Pike & Fischer, Bethesda, MD, pg. 190
Eisenstein, Joshua J., Treas.--Central National-Gottesman Inc., Purchase, NY, pg. 233
Eitze, William O., V.P.-Fin., Chief Fin. Officer, Controller & Treas.--Carl M. Freeman Associates, Inc., Potomac, MD, pg. 431
Eitzinger, Gisela, Treas. & Sec.--Mid-West Automation Systems, Buffalo Grove, IL, pg. 750
Eklund, Louis, E., Jr., Chm. & Treas.--Fleet Engineers, Inc., Muskegon, MI, pg. 417
Elder, Thomas L., V.P. & Treas.--R.C. Tway Coal Company, Louisville, KY, pg. 1120
Ellis, Carol Cormier, Sec. & Treas.--Cormier Rice Milling Company, Inc., De Witt, AR, pg. 286
Ellis, Edward H., Treas.--Gaylord Entertainment Co., Nashville, TN, pg. 446
Ellison, Susan, Sec. & Treas.--Michael R. Ellison Inc., Phoenix, AZ, pg. 378
Elyea, Mike, V.P. & Treas.--Burk Royalty Co., Wichita Falls, TX, pg. 190
Emmett, Denis L., Treasurer--Erving Paper Mills, Erving, MA, pg. 388
Endsley, Woody P., V.P. & Treas.--Tracor, Inc., Austin, TX, pg. 1104
Eng, Richard, Treas.--Lifetouch, Inc., Bloomington, MN, pg. 675
Engel, W.R., Pres. & Treas.--American Mutual Life Insurance Company, Des Moines, IA, pg. 58
Engelman, Wayne, Sr. V.P., Sec. & Treas.--Colle & McVoy, Inc., Minneapolis, MN, pg. 261
Engle, Clyde W., Chm. Bd., Pres. & Treas.--GSC Enterprises, Inc., Chicago, IL, pg. 440
English, Chris, Chief Fin. Officer & Treas.--Webster Industries Inc., Tiffin, OH, pg. 1171
Ennis, E. L., Chief Fin. Officer, Treas. & Controller--Strachan Shipping Co., Garden City, GA, pg. 1052
Ennis, Richard A., V.P.-Fin. & Admin. & Treas.--Associated Grocers of New England, Inc., Manchester, NH, pg. 90
Ensinger, James, Treas. & Sec.--Rudel Machinery Company, Inc., Shelton, CT, pg. 954
Entrono, Joseph A., Treas.--H.J. Baker & Bro., Inc., New York, NY, pg. 114
Epprecht, John W., V.P., Sec. & Treas.--The Great Lakes Cheese Co., Newbury, OH, pg. 481
Epstein, Lawrence, Sec. & Treas.--A J M Packaging Corporation, Detroit, MI, pg. 4
Epstein, Mary K., Asst. Treas.--Perry Group, Inc., Hainesport, NJ, pg. 863
Erb, George L., Treas. & Sec.--Erb Lumber Company, Birmingham, MI, pg. 360
Erdman, Lee, V.P. Fin. & Treas.--YSI Incorporated, Yellow Springs, OH, pg. 1207
Erera, Larence E., Sec. & Treas.--American Funds Advisor Inc., Garden City, NJ, pg. 55
Erickson, David, Treas.--Deans Photo Service, Inc., San Diego, CA, pg. 322
Erickson, Leif V., Treas. & Sec.--Erickson Transport Corporation, Springfield, MO, pg. 386
Erickson, Mel, Sr., Pres., Sec. & Treas.--Central Feed Mills, Inc., Snohomish, WA, pg. 232
Erickson, S.K., Exec. V.P. & Treas.--Ziegler Inc., Minneapolis, MN, pg. 1218
Eskilson, Arnold J., Sec. & Treas.--Dixie Dairy Company, Gary, IN, pg. 341
Esposito, Thomas R., Treas.--High Industries Inc., Lancaster, PA, pg. 533
Essenburg, Kim, Treas.--The Brulin Corporation, Indianapolis, IN, pg. 184
Estes, Robey W., Jr., Pres. & Treas.--Estes Express Lines, Inc., Richmond, VA, pg. 389
Etteridge, Timothy, Sec. & Treas.--Temps & Company, Washington, DC, pg. 1086
Etterling, Robert, Treas. & Sec.--Simonds-Shields-Theis Grain Co., Kansas City, MO, pg. 1006
Eubanks, John T., V.P. & Treas.--Anderson Industries, Inc., Dallas, TX, pg. 72
Evans, Andrew J., Treas. & Sec.--Harrison Paint Corporation, Canton, OH, pg. 512
Evans, Gregg, Treas. & Sec.--Shield Security, Inc., Los Angeles, CA, pg. 999
Evans, Jody, Sec. & Treas.--Bell Construction Co. Inc., Brentwood, TN, pg. 134
Everhart, Michael, Treas.--Parrish Tire Company, Inc., Winston-Salem, NC, pg. 850
Ewens, James J., Treas.--Quad/Graphics, Inc., Pewaukee, WI, pg. 902
Ezerski, Ronald E., V.P.-Fin. & Treas.--Patterson Dental Company, Minneapolis, MN, pg. 851
Ezratty, Joseph, Treas.--The Benatty Corporation, Cambridge, OH, pg. 138
Ezzell, Brewer M., Treas.--Murphy Farms Inc., Rose Hill, NC, pg. 776
Fagan, Larry, Gen. Mgr., Corp. Sec. & Treas.--Associated Machinecraft Corporation, Los Angeles, CA, pg. 90
Fagel, Marvin, V.P.-Investor Rels. & Sec.--Aurora Packing Co., Inc., North Aurora, IL, pg. 98
Faiella, John, Treas.--Gilman Paper Co., Saint Marys, GA, pg. 459
Faklaris, John R., Treas.--DMI, Inc., Goodfield, IL, pg. 309
Falchook, Adam, V.P. & Treas.--Jennifer Convertibles Inc., Paramus, NJ, pg. 592
Falconi, Robert, Chief Fin. Officer, Treas. & Sec.--Planning Systems Inc., McLean, VA, pg. 874
Falksen, Jerry, V.P. & Treas.--Nobles Industries, Inc., Saint Paul, MN, pg. 808
Fankhauser, James R., Sr. Fin. Partner, Sec. & Treas.--Fahlgren Martin, Inc., Parkersburg, WV, pg. 396
Fantich, Lawrence, Treas. & Sec.--Tool King, Denver, CO, pg. 1101
Farady, John T., V.P. & Treas.--John Hancock Mutual Life Insurance Company, Boston, MA, pg. 595
Farley, A. Palmer, Exec. V.P., Treas.--Barker Campbell & Farley, Virginia Beach, VA, pg. 120
Farlik, Terry, Sec. & Treas.--Seco Warwick Corporation, Meadville, PA, pg. 987
Farquharson, Donald E., Treas.--Cambridge Street Metal Co., Inc., Allston, MA, pg. 211
Fato, Martha, Sec. & Treas.--Par Enterprises, Inc., Wheeling, WV, pg. 847
Fattaleh, Daniel L., Chm. Bd., Pres., Chief Exec. Officer & Treas.--The Delphi Glass Corp. Delphi Stained Glass Centers, Lansing, MI, pg. 326
Faussemagne, Jack, J., Treas.--W.B. Johnson Property, Inc., Atlanta, GA, pg. 598
Fay, Thomas F., Treas. & Sec.--Overhead Conveyor Co., Ferndale, MI, pg. 832
Fee, Frank J., III, Pres. & Treas.--Reliable Automatic Sprinkler Co., Inc., Mount Vernon, NY, pg. 924
Feldman, Shirley, Sec. & Treas.--Isfel Company, Inc., Rahway, NJ, pg. 582
Felhofer, G., Treas.--Stolper-Fabralloy Co., Waukesha, WI, pg. 1050
Felker, G. Steven, Pres., Chief Exec. Officer & Treas.--Walton Monroe Mills, Inc., Monroe, GA, pg. 1162
Fellenstein, Mike, Sec., Treas. & Comptroller--Biddulph Oldsmobile, Glendale, AZ, pg. 149
Fellin, Edward, Treas.--Economy Folding Box Corp., Chicago, IL, pg. 367
Felsh, Nicholas, V.P. & Treas.--Frederick Trading Company, Frederick, MD, pg. 430
Feltes, John, Sec. & Treas.--Automatic Liquid Packaging, Inc., Woodstock, IL, pg. 100
Fenendael, Lee F., Treas.--Condon Oil Company, Inc., Ripon, WI, pg. 273
Fennessy, William J., V.P.-Fin. & Treas.--LDI, Ltd., Indianapolis, IN, pg. 647
Fenster, Fred A., Treas. & Sec.--Capucci Creations International, Inc., Beverly Hills, CA, pg. 216
Fentress, Kenneth P., Treas. & Sec.--L & R Communications, Limited, Sioux City, IA, pg. 647
Ferguson, Bruce, Treas.--Macro Computer Products Inc., Rochester Hills, MI, pg. 698
Ferguson, Kevin R., Asst. Treas.--Illinois Consolidated Telephone Co., Mattoon, IL, pg. 563
Ferman, Martha S., Sec. & Treas.--Ferman Oldsmobile, Tampa, FL, pg. 406
Fermano,Joseph, Chief Fin. Officer--Blue Cross and Blue Shield of Massachusetts, Boston, MA, pg. 159
Fernandez, Nancy, Treas.--Digitron Tool Co., Inc., Miamisburg, OH, pg. 337
Ferrera, Alfred, Asst. Treas.--James Ferrera & Sons, Inc., Canton, MA, pg. 407
Ferrera, James J., Controller & Treas.--James Ferrera & Sons, Inc., Canton, MA, pg. 407
Ficks, Lee B., Pres., Chief Exec. Officer, & Treas.--Ficks Reed Company, Cincinnati, OH, pg. 408
Field, Diane, V.P. & Treas.--Continental Web Press, Inc., Itasca, IL, pg. 280
Fields, Barb, Treas. & Dir.-Accounting--Jackson Hole Ski Resort, Teton Village, WY, pg. 587
Fields, William, Treas. & Controller--Sherborne Group, Inc., New York, NY, pg. 998
Fierle, R., V.P., Treas. & Sec.--Quackenbush Co. Inc., Buffalo, NY, pg. 902
Figuerelli, David C., Treas.--Essex Industries, New Haven, CT, pg. 361
Figurelli, David C., Treas.--ESSTAR Incorporated, New Haven, CT, pg. 361
Fikejs, John W., Treas. & Sec.--Plymouth Tube Company, Warrenville, IL, pg. 877
Filippine, Larry L., Treas.--McLouth Steel, Trenton, MI, pg. 731
Filler, Elaine, V.P. & Treas.--The Pocono Bank, Milford, PA, pg. 534
Fincher, Larry, Exec. V.P., Sec. & Treas.--Truman Arnold Companies, Texarkana, TX, pg. 84
Fineman, Bernard S., Pres. & Treas.--Caldwell Tanks, Inc., Louisville, KY, pg. 209
Fineman, Evan L., Treas. & Chief Fin. Officer--Atlantic Dairy Cooperative, Southampton, PA, pg. 94
Fingerle, Larry, Sec. & Treas.--Fingerle Lumber Co., Ann Arbor, MI, pg. 411
Finkelstein, Ronald W., Sec. & Treas.--Multi Media Services Corp., Alexandria, VA, pg. 775
Finlon, Cathey M., Pres., Treas. & New Bus. Contact--McClain Finlon Advertising, Denver, CO, pg. 727
Finn, Larry, Treas.--Stark Candy Company, Rewaukee, WI, pg. 1123
Finn, Lawrence J., Treas.--New England Confectionery Co., Cambridge, MA, pg. 1123
Finney, Charles, Chief Fin. Officer & Treas.--Computer Methods Corporation, Livonia, MI, pg. 271
Fiore, Donald A., Treas. & Mgr.-Personnel--Palmer Manufacturing Company, Malden, MA, pg. 844
Fischer, Jerome, Sec. & Treas.--Buerkle Buick-Honda Co., Saint Paul, MN, pg. 186

Corporate Responsibilities Index

Fischer, Philip, Treas. & Sec.--Torcon, Inc., Westfield, NJ, pg. 1102
Fishbein, Robert, Exec. V.P. & Treas.--United Envelope Company, Inc., New York, NY, pg. 1131
Fisher, G.O., V.P. & Treas.--Fisher Companies, Inc., Seattle, WA, pg. 414
Fisher, Harold, Sec. & Treas.--Hillerich & Bradsby Co., Inc., Louisville, KY, pg. 535
Fisher, Lloyd B., Jr., Treas.--Quael Corp., Detroit, MI, pg. 902
Fisher, Martha, Controller & Asst. Treas.--Prudential Metal Supply Corp., East Dedham, MA, pg. 898
Fisher, Norma Joe, Treas., Controller & Chief Fin. Officer--Fisher Graphic Industries, Modesto, CA, pg. 415
Fissasloo, Bill, Dir.-Pur., Sec. & Treas.--Gress Foods Inc., Gainesville, GA, pg. 486
Fitch, Thomas R., Treas.--Rugg Manufacturing Company, Greenfield, MA, pg. 955
Fitzgerald, D.F., Pres. & Treas.--Son Chief Electrics, Inc., Winsted, CT, pg. 1018
FitzGerald, Denis J., M.D., Treas.--Fallon Community Health Plan, West Boylston, MA, pg. 398
Fitzgerald, William J., V.P. & Treas.--H M K Enterprises, Inc., Waltham, MA, pg. 497
Fitzpatrick, Gregory J., V.P. & Treas.--Fitzpatrick & Weller, Inc., Ellicottville, NY, pg. 416
Flagg, John E., Treas.--David Clark Company, Inc., Worcester, MA, pg. 252
Flanders, Margie S., V.P. & Asst. Treas.--Paddock Publications, Inc., Arlington Heights, IL, pg. 842
Flanigan, D., Exec. V.P. & Treas.--J.D. Diffenbaugh, Inc., Riverside, CA, pg. 337
Flanigan, Michael, Treas. & Comptroller--Jones Blair Company, Dallas, TX, pg. 602
Flegger, Allen, Treas. & Controller--Southern Apparel Corporation, Largo, FL, pg. 1020
Fleischer, Morton H., Pres., Chief Exec. Officer & Treas.--Franchise Finance Corp. of America, Scottsdale, AZ, pg. 428
Fleischhacker, V.M., Treas.--Lake Region Manufacturing Company, Inc., Chaska, MN, pg. 651
Fleischman, Donald, V.P.-Fin., Treas. & Chief Fin. Officer--Ampacet Corporation, Tarrytown, NY, pg. 67
Fleming, Gordon, Sec. & Treas.--Brock Candy Company, Chattanooga, TN, pg. 177
Fleming, T. Clifford, Treas.--Batteast Construction Company, Inc., South Bend, IN, pg. 126
Fletcher, Emory, V.P. & Treas.--Martin Sprocket & Gear, Inc., Arlington, TX, pg. 715
Fleury, Thomas J., Treas.--Beckwith Machinery Company, Murrysville, PA, pg. 131
Flodstrom, Majken, Sec. & Treas.--Flodstrom Construction Co., Deerfield, IL, pg. 419
Flood, Thomas, V.P.-Admin. & Fin. & Treas.--TSC Industries, Inc., Nashville, TN, pg. 1075
Flori, Robert D., Chm. Bd. & Treas.--Flori Corp., Phoenix, AZ, pg. 420
Florig, Edward, Pres. & Treas.--Florig Equipment Company, Inc., Conshohocken, PA, pg. 421
Floyd, Robert K., V.P.-Fin. & Chief Fin. Officer--Tracor, Inc., Austin, TX, pg. 1104
Floyd, Thomas A., Sr. V.P.-Fin., Treas. & Admin.--Martin Exploration Management Company, Alsip, IL, pg. 715
Fluegeman, Raymond W., Chief Fin. Officer, Treas., Controller & Dir.-Data Processing--Robbins, Inc., Cincinnati, OH, pg. 938
Flynn, Gary, Exec. V.P., Treas. & Sec.--Rotary Multiforms, Inc., Detroit, MI, pg. 951
Fobes, Clyde R., V.P. & Treas.--Desco Corporation, Columbus, OH, pg. 332
Foecking, Leland R., Treas., Controller & Sec.--Joseph Behr & Sons Inc., Rockford, IL, pg. 132
Fok, Angela, Treas.--The Berline Group Inc., Bingham Farms, MI, pg. 142
Folts, John B., Exec. V.P., Sec. & Treas.--Hargro Enterprises, Inc., Stamford, CT, pg. 509
Folwell, Jean, Chief Fin. Officer & Asst. Treas.--MADD (Mothers Against Drunk Driving), Irving, TX, pg. 691
Fong, Dean, Sec. & Treas.--Lucky Fruit & Produce, Inc., Sacramento, CA, pg. 686
Foradori, Beth, V.P. & Treas.--The Motorlease Corp., Farmington, CT, pg. 773
Forbes, Clyde R., V.P. & Treas.--Sycon Corporation, Marion, OH, pg. 1069
Forbes, Karen, V.P.-Fin. & Treas.--Kettenburg Marine Corporation, San Diego, CA, pg. 626
Forgione, Dennis, Corp. Sec.--Boyer Bros. Inc., Altoona, PA, pg. 169
Forman, Willis M., Pres., Chief Exec. Officer & Treas.--Paper Calmenson & Co., Saint Paul, MN, pg. 847
Fortmuller, George A., Chief Fin. Officer, Treas. & Sec.--Edwin B. Stimpson Company, Inc., Bayport, NY, pg. 1049
Fortunoff, Helene, Sec. & Treas.--Fortunoff, Westbury, NY, pg. 425
Foss, Jean, Treas.--Foss Manufacturing Company Incorporated, Hampton, NH, pg. 426
Foster, James, Treas.--Foster Pontiac, Inc., Milwaukee, WI, pg. 426
Foster, Mayson H., Sec. & Treas.--Citizens National Bancshares Inc., Hammond, LA, pg. 250
Foster, Phillip W., V.P.-Fin. & Treas.--Remmele Engineering, Inc., Saint Paul, MN, pg. 926
Foster, R.A., Treas./Controller--United States Bronze Powders, Inc., Flemington, NJ, pg. 1134
Foster, Robert J., V.P.-Fin.--National Machinery Company, Tiffin, OH, pg. 792
Foster, Stephen P., V.P. & Treas.--Edlund Company, Inc., Burlington, VT, pg. 368
Fox, Harold, Exec. V.P.-Fin. & Treas.--Del Taco/Naugles, Costa Mesa, CA, pg. 325
Fox, John, Sec. & Treas.--Presto Lock, Inc., Garfield, NJ, pg. 888
Fox, Marvin, Treas.--El Dorado Tire Co., Troy, MI, pg. 372
Fox, Randolph, V.P.-Fin., Treas. & Sec.--Metal Masters Foodservice Equipment, Smyrna, DE, pg. 741
Fox, Richard, Treas.--American Laubscher Corp., Farmingdale, NY, pg. 57
Foxworthy, Clarence N., Treas.--NKH&W, Inc., Kansas City, MO, pg. 781
Foxx, M.J., V.P. & Treas., Gen. Mgr. & Dir.-Pur.--Handgards Inc., Northbrook, IL, pg. 504
Foytek, Francis, Treas.--Mediacomp, Inc., Houston, TX, pg. 735
Fraatz, Paul, Jr., Pres. & Treas.--Pacor, Inc., Philadelphia, PA, pg. 842
Fraedrich, David S., V.P., Sec. & Treas.--John W. Brooks Inc., Nelsonville, OH, pg. 180
Fralick, Millie, Sec. & Asst. Treas.--Behr Stores Inc., Louisville, KY, pg. 132
France, B.E., Pres., Chief Oper. Officer & Treas.--The H. T. Hackney Co., Knoxville, TN, pg. 498
Francht, Joseph E., Sr. V.P.-Fin. & Treas.--NWA, Inc., Saint Paul, MN, pg. 782
Francht, Joseph E., Jr., Sr. V.P. & Treas.--Northwest Airlines, Inc., Saint Paul, MN, pg. 782
Francine, John, V.P., Sec. & Treas.--Aetna Plywood, Inc., Arlington Heights, IL, pg. 23
Francis, Kent, Chief Fin. Officer & Treas.--O'Malia Food Markets Inc., Noblesville, IN, pg. 825
Franco, Frank J., Treas. & Sec.--Peckham Industries, Inc., White Plains, NY, pg. 854
Frank, George, Exec. V.P., Chief Oper. Officer & Treas.--Sicola Martin Koons Frank, Inc., Austin, TX, pg. 1001
Frank, H. Alan, Pres., Chief Fin. Officer & Treas.--Union Industries, Inc., Providence, RI, pg. 1128
Frank, Wally, Treas.--Wally Frank, Ltd., Middle Village, NY, pg. 429
Franke , Kenneth, V.P & Treas.--Riemeier Lumber Company, Inc., Cincinnati, OH, pg. 934
Frankel, Ernst D., Chief Fin. Officer, Treas., Controller & Sec.--Standard Textile Co., Inc., Cincinnati, OH, pg. 1037
Franklin, Alice, Treas. & Sec.--Hickory Construction Company, Hickory, NC, pg. 532
Franklin, E. Thomas, Chm., Pres. & Treas.--Franklin Baking Co., Inc., Goldsboro, NC, pg. 429
Franklin, Irving H., Chm. Bd. & Treas.--Franklin Sports Industries, Stoughton, MA, pg. 429
Fraser, D.A., Treas.--All American Home Center, Downey, CA, pg. 35
Frazen, Mary A., Exec. V.P., Sec. & Treas.--Ed Marling Stores, Inc., Topeka, KS, pg. 710
Frederick, Scott, Chief Fin. Officer & Treas.--American Appraisal Associates, Inc., Milwaukee, WI, pg. 48
Freedland, Michael, Treas. & Sec.--Ambassador Steel Co., Detroit, MI, pg. 47
Freedland, Ruth, Treas.--Freedland Industries Corporation, Dearborn, MI, pg. 430
Freedman, Martin B., V.P. & Treas.--FMS Management Systems, Inc., North Miami Beach, FL, pg. 394
Freeman, Jeff E., Sr. V.P.-Fin., Sec. & Treas.--Havatampa Incorporated, Tampa, FL, pg. 517
Freeman, Jeff E., Sr. V.P.-Fin., Sec. & Treas.--H.A.T. Holding Company, Tampa, FL, pg. 517
Freeman, John, Chief Fin. Officer, V.P., Treas. & Sec.--Robert F. Driver Co., Inc., San Diego, CA, pg. 349
Freeman, Patricia, Treas.--Freeman Blanshei Partners, San Francisco, CA, pg. 431
Freeman, Peter C., Treas.--Dillingham Construction Corporation, Pleasanton, CA, pg. 337
Freeman, William, V.P.-Treas.--Seymour of Sycamore, Inc., Sycamore, IL, pg. 994
Freilich, Joseph, Treas. & Sec.--Icahn & Co., Inc., Mount Kisco, NY, pg. 561
Freimark, Jeffrey P., Exec. V.P., Chief Fin. Officer & Gen. Counsel & Sec.--Pueblo International, Inc., Pompano Beach, FL, pg. 899
French, Morton R., Jr., V.P. & Treas.--Commercial Plastics & Supplies Corp., Richmond Hill, NY, pg. 268
French, R.G., Treas. & Controller--Sunkist Growers, Inc., Sherman Oaks, CA, pg. 1060
Frey, Susanne, Treas.--The Habegger Corporation, Cincinnati, OH, pg. 498
Fridl, Richard J., Treas.--The Heil Co., Chattanooga, TN, pg. 525
Fried, Peter A., Treas. & Sec.--Rothschild North America Inc., New York, NY, pg. 951
Fried, Richard, Treas.--Stiefel Laboratories, Inc., Oak Hill, Oak Hill, NY, pg. 1048
Frieden, John C., V.P. & Treas.--CTB Inc., Milford, IN, pg. 205
Friedman, Jerry, Exec. V.P., Treas. & Sec.--Marvin Engineering Company, Inc., Inglewood, CA, pg. 716
Friedman, Louis, Treas.--E & J Gallo Winery, Modesto, CA, pg. 441
Friedman, Mark H., Exec. V.P., Treas. & Chief Fin. Officer--Style Auto, Van Nuys, CA, pg. 1055
Friedman, Marty, Chief Fin. Officer, Treas, & Controller--Power Contracting & Engineering Corp., Rolling Meadows, IL, pg. 883
Friesen, David, Treas. & Asst. Sec.--Clemens Markets Inc., Lansdale, PA, pg. 254
Frisch, Benjamin P., V.P., Sec. & Treas.--Beaver Street Fisheries, Inc., Jacksonville, FL, pg. 130
Fritsch, Allan J., Treas.--The Nielsen Company, Cincinnati, OH, pg. 807
Frost, George, Chief Fin. Officer & Treas.--UFE Incorporated, Stillwater, MN, pg. 1123
Frye, Darrell, V.P.-Fin. & Sec.--Harriss & Covington Hosiery Mills, High Point, NC, pg. 512
Fuchs, William, Treas.--S. Rothchild & Co., Inc., New York, NY, pg. 951
Fudge, Dorothy, Treas. & Sec.--Tom James Of Atlanta, Inc., Atlanta, GA, pg. 589
Fuefing, Klans, Sec. & Treas.--American Barmag Co., Charlotte, NC, pg. 49
Fuerbach, W.F., Jr., Chm. Bd., Pres. & Treas.--S. M. Frank & Co., Inc., Peekskill, NY, pg. 429
Fujiki, Yoichi, Treas.--Argo-Tech Corporation, Cleveland, OH, pg. 82
Fuller, Alan B., Treas.--Galardi Group, Inc., Newport Beach, CA, pg. 441
Fullerton, William A., V.P. & Treas.--Coca-Cola Bottling Co. of Chicago, Niles, IL, pg. 257
Furlong, Daniel R., Exec. V.P., Treas.--Paradigm Communications, Tampa, FL, pg. 847
Furman, William W., Jr., Treas. & Data Processing Mgr.--Furman Foods, Inc., Northumberland, PA, pg. 436
Furrer, Ron, Treas. & Controller--Darigold, Inc., Seattle, WA, pg. 315
Furrer, Ronald, Treas.--Dairygold Inc., Seattle, WA, pg. 311
Furst, Rafael, Sr. V.P. & Treas.--The Elder-Beerman Stores Corp., Dayton, OH, pg. 373
Fusaro, Angelo, V.P.-Corp. Affairs--The Apparel Group, Ltd., New York, NY, pg. 78
Fusz, Martha, Treas.--Lou Fusz Automotive Network, Saint Louis, MO, pg. 437
Futter, Kenneth, Sec. & Treas.--Futter Lumber Corporation, Rockville Centre, NY, pg. 437
Gabbard, W. Ray, Treas.--Orbit Valve International, Inc., Little Rock, AR, pg. 828
Gabriel, Doug, V.P., Treas. & Controller--Apperson Business Forms, Inc., Los Angeles, CA, pg. 78
Gabrys, Gerard, V.P.-Fin. & Treas.--Guest Services, Inc., Fairfax, VA, pg. 493
Gaglioti, Joseph, V.P. & Treas.--Cole National Corporation, Cleveland, OH, pg. 260
Gaglioti, Joseph, V.P. & Treas.--Cole Key Corporation, Cleveland, OH, pg. 260
Gaglioti, Joseph, Treas.--Things Remembered, Cleveland, OH, pg. 260
Gaglitoti, Joseph, V.P. & Treas.--Cole Vision Corporation, Cleveland, OH, pg. 260
Gahm, Walter D., Jr., V.P. & Treas.--Kitchen Kompact, Inc., Jeffersonville, IN, pg. 634
Gainer, Arthur, Treas. & Sec.--Champaign Landmark, Urbana, OH, pg. 238
Galante, A., Sr. V.P. & Treas.--Noville Essential Oil Co., Inc., North Bergen, NJ, pg. 817
Galante, Eugene J., Pres. & Treas.--Tagsons Papers, Inc., Albany, NY, pg. 1076
Gallagher, Cindy, Sec. & Treas.--Jim Fresard Pontiac Buick, Inc., Royal Oak, MI, pg. 432
Gallagher, Frank W., Chief Fin. Officer & Treas.--Paramount Packaging Corp., Chalfont, PA, pg. 848
Gallagher, Jack, Treas.--Peterson Tractor Company, San Leandro, CA, pg. 865
Gallucci, John, Chm. Bd., Pres. & Treas.--Concrete Construction Company, Columbus, OH, pg. 273
Galuten, Sandra L., Treas.--SGD International Corp., New York, NY, pg. 962
Gancarz, Robert A., Treas.--Creative Marketing International Corp., West Chicago, IL, pg. 297
Gann, Sam H., Sec., Treas. & Dir.-Opers.--Pioneer Oil Company Inc., Fort Worth, TX, pg. 872
Gannon, Thomas A., Treas. & Controller--Reading Eagle Company, Reading, PA, pg. 916
Gant, Harry, Chief Fin. Officer, Treas. & Sec.--Young Radiator Company, Racine, WI, pg. 1210
Gantt, G. Russell, V.P., Treas. & Asst. Sec.--Glen Raven Mills, Inc., Glen Raven, NC, pg. 461
Garceau, Albert A., V.P., Chief Fin. Officer & Treas.--Mr. Gasket Company, Cleveland, OH, pg. 761
Garcema, Albert, Chief Fin. Officer & Treas.--Cragar Industries, Compton, CA, pg. 761
Garcia, Randy, V.P. & Treas.--Simmons Oil Corp., Phoenix, AZ, pg. 1005
Gardiner, Scott, Chm. Bd., Pres., Chief Exec. & Chief Oper. Officer--Gardiner Metal Company, Chicago, IL, pg. 443
Gardner, John, Treas.--General Parts, Inc., Raleigh, NC, pg. 224
Garibaldi, John L., Sr. V.P.-Fin., Chief Fin. Officer & Treas.--Aloha Airgroup, Inc., Honolulu, HI, pg. 43
Garibaldi, John L., Sr. V.P.-Fin., Chief Fin. Officer & Treas.--Aloha Airlines, Inc., Honolulu, HI, pg. 43
Garrity, William E., Treas. & Dir.-Data Processing--Capital Industries, Inc., Seattle, WA, pg. 215
Gash, C. Ray, Chief Fin. Officer, Sr. V.P., Treas. & Sec.--Stephens, Inc., Little Rock, AR, pg. 1046
Gasparelli, Adeline, Sec. & Treas.--Wyse Advertising, Inc., Cleveland, OH, pg. 1206
Gaster, Pattie L., V.P.-Fin. & Treas.--Lee-Moore Oil Co., Inc., Sanford, NC, pg. 665
Gasthalter, Robert, V.P. & Treas.--Gulf Distribution Inc., Miami, FL, pg. 493
Gately, James E., Treas.--Daniels Printing Company, Everett, MA, pg. 314
Gates, Tim J., Pres.,Treas. & Dir.-Mngmt. Info. Systems--Southern Ohio Fabricators, Inc., Cincinnati, OH, pg. 1022
Gates, William C., Chief Fin. Officer, V.P. & Treas.--Graphic Controls, Corp., Buffalo, NY, pg. 478
Gates, William C., V.P., Treas. & Chief Fin. Officer--Graphic Controls Corporation, Buffalo, NY, pg. 478
Gatta, Rosanne, Asst. V.P. & Treas.--Provident Mutual Life Insurance Co., Philadelphia, PA, pg. 896
Gattas, Andrew D., Treas. & Sec.--Fred P. Gattas Company, Inc., Memphis, TN, pg. 446
Gau, Jack, Sec. & Treas.--G. R. Herberger's, Inc., Saint Cloud, MN, pg. 530
Gaughier, Albert R., Controller & Treas.--Oliver Products Company, Grand Rapids, MI, pg. 824
Gaughran, Raymond H., Treas.--Entron Industries Limited Partnership, Glendale, NY, pg. 383
Gauthier, Leon, V.P.-Fin. & Treas.--Microphase Corporation, Norwalk, CT, pg. 749
Gaw, Ed, Chief Fin. Officer, Treas. & Sec.--Griffin Corporation, Valdosta, GA, pg. 487
Gaylord, Thomas M., Sec. & Treas.--Mack Molding Company, Arlington, VT, pg. 697
Gazarek, Celeste, V.P.-Fin. & Treas.--National Frozen Foods Corp., Seattle, WA, pg. 789

Gebo, L. Evelyn, V.P., Sec. & Treas.--Gebo Distributing Co., Inc., Plainview, TX, pg. 447
Gee, Edward, Treas. & Sec.--Cloverhill Bakery, Chicago, IL, pg. 256
Geiger, Eugene G., Pres. & Treas.--Geiger Brothers, Lewiston, ME, pg. 447
Geisselbrecht, Elvin, Treas. & Sec.--YRJ Corporation, Houston, TX, pg. 1206
Gejoff, Louis, Treas., Controller, Sec. & Chief Fin. Officer--Carver, Inc., Garden City, GA, pg. 227
Gejoff, Louis, Chief Fin. Officer, Treas., Controller & Sec.--Murray-Carver, East Bridgewater, MA, pg. 776
Gelder, Robert, Pres. & Treas.--Barden & Robeson Corporation, Middleport, NY, pg. 119
Geller, Judith, Treas. & Asst. Sec.--Union Holdings, Inc., New York, NY, pg. 1128
Gellerman, Jay M., Pres. & Treas.--Jaydon Incorporated, Rock Island, IL, pg. 590
Gelstharp, Peter, Treas.--Industrial Acoustics Company, Ltd., Staines,, United Kingdom, pg. 566
Genkin, I. Stephen, Treas.--Triangle Marketing Corp., New York, NY, pg. 1112
Genuardi, Dominic, Treas.--Genuardi Super Markets Inc., Norristown, PA, pg. 452
George, Dennis A., Treas. & Sec.--Sharon Tube Company, Sharon, PA, pg. 995
George, Leslie, Jr., Treas. & Sec.--King Group, Inc., Fenton, MI, pg. 630
George, Thomas A., Sec. & Treas.--Melody Foods, Inc., Farmington Hills, MI, pg. 738
Geraghty, Larry, Treas.--Trident Seafood Corporation, Seattle, WA, pg. 1113
Gerard, Stephen, Pres., Chief Exec. Officer & Treas.--Bolliger, Inc., Stamford, CT, pg. 163
Geren, Tracey, Treas. & Sec.--Weldon, Williams & Lick, Inc., Fort Smith, AR, pg. 1175
Gernert, John, Treas.--Systems Parking, Inc., Pasadena, CA, pg. 1071
Gerrity, J. Frank, II, Chm. Bd. & Treas.--Gerrity Co., Inc., Newton, MA, pg. 454
Gersten, F.S., V.P. & Treas.--J.M. Huber Corporation, Edison, NJ, pg. 550
Gerstman, Henry, Sec., Treas. & Controller--Century Business Credit Corporation, New York, NY, pg. 235
Gerstman, Henry, Treas.--Century Data Services, Inc., New York, NY, pg. 235
Gessner, David, Pres. & Treas.--Gessner Industries, Concord, NC, pg. 455
Gettlegfinger, Herman E., Chief Fin. Officer, Treas. & Sec.--Pride Oil Co., Inc., Knoxville, TN, pg. 622
Gezon, Lucinda, Treas.--The WBDC Group, Grand Rapids, MI, pg. 1155
Ghazaleh, Sam, Treas.--Ebeling & Reuss Company, Allentown, PA, pg. 365
Giarrusso, Raymond J., Sec. & Treas.--GAI Consultants, Inc., Monroeville, PA, pg. 439
Gibb, Bradley, Sec. & Treas.--Robert Gibb & Sons, Inc., Fargo, ND, pg. 456
Gibbons, Tom, Treas.--Del Monte Foods, San Francisco, CA, pg. 325
Gibbs, Benjamin, Treas.--Pine State Creamery Co., Raleigh, NC, pg. 871
Gibbs, David H., Treas.--Owen-Ames-Kimball Co., Grand Rapids, MI, pg. 833
Gibson, M.L., V.P. & Treas.--Hardinge Brothers, Inc., Elmira, NY, pg. 508
Giglia, John, Sr. V.P. & Treas.--White Rose Food, Long Island City, NY, pg. 335
Gignac, Kenneth, Chm. Bd. & Pres.--Elgin-Honey Hill Corporation, Chicago, IL, pg. 376
Gilbert, Bruce C., Pres., Chief Exec. Officer & Treas.--Great Lakes Construction Co., Cleveland, OH, pg. 481
Gilbert, Walter, Treas.--Cora Texas Manufacturing Co., White Castle, LA, pg. 285
Gilbert, Walter F., Chm. Bd., Pres., Chief Exec. Officer & Treas.--Semco Industries, Stoughton, MA, pg. 989
Gilboy, Thomas V., Chief Fin. Officer & V.P.-Fin.--Troy Corporation, East Hanover, NJ, pg. 1116
Gill, Harry R., II, Chm. Bd.--The National Latex Products Co., Ashland, OH, pg. 791
Gillespie, Larry, Controller & Treas.--HLB Communications, Inc., Chicago, IL, pg. 496
Gillette, James R., Sr. V.P.-Fin., Treas. & Chief Fin. Officer--Swinerton & Walberg Co., San Francisco, CA, pg. 1068
Gillogly, Fred D., Pres. & Treas.--Gillogly Chevrolet Inc., West Seneca, NY, pg. 459
Gilman, Shirley J., Pres. & Treas.--Marty Gilman, Inc., Gilman, CT, pg. 459
Gilmore, Russell, Treas. & Controller--Hamilton Sweeney Advertising, Inc., Denver, CO, pg. 503
Ginzberg, David, Treas.--Golodetz Corporation, New York, NY, pg. 469
Giordullo, Tony, Sec. & Treas.--Frazier-Williams Chevrolet GEO, Milford, OH, pg. 430
Girtman, William L., V.P.-Fin. & Treas.--W.S. Badcock Corporation, Mulberry, FL, pg. 113
Gittelman, Milton, V.P, Treas. & Sec.--Triumph Pet Industries, Inc., Hillburn, NY, pg. 1115
Giuliani, John, Treas. & Sec.--Lodal, Inc., Kingsford, MI, pg. 680
Glass, William, Chief Fin. Officer--Advanced Controls, Inc., Irvine, CA, pg. 20
Glazer, Ira, Sr. V.P.-Fin. & Treas.--Maidenform, Inc., New York, NY, pg. 701
Gleason, Jean, V.P. & Treas.--Genie Manufacturing Corp., Rush, NY, pg. 452
Glenn, G. Lee, Chief Fin. Officer, V.P. & Treas.--Kelley Bean Co., Inc., Morrill, NE, pg. 621
Glenn, Jerry, V.P.-Fin. & Treas.--Consolidated Group, Inc., Charlotte, NC, pg. 357
Glenn, Jerry, V.P.-Fin. & Treas.--Consolidated Engravers-East, Inc., Charlotte, NC, pg. 357
Glenn, Jerry, V.P.-Fin. & Treas.--Consolidated Screen-Makers, Inc., Charlotte, NC, pg. 357
Glickman, M.P., Treas.--Strombecker Corporation, Chicago, IL, pg. 1054
Glickman, Stanley, Chm. Bd. & Treas.--Red Calliope & Associates, Inc., Los Angeles, CA, pg. 918
Glickstein, Neil A., V.P.-Fin.--Binney & Smith Inc., Easton, PA, pg. 502
Glidden, Robert D., Jr., V.P.-Fin. & Treas.--Robert James Sales Inc., Buffalo, NY, pg. 589
Glotzon, Martin, Treas. & Sec.--PC Distributing Inc., Mount Prospect, IL, pg. 835
Gluth, R.C., V.P. & Treas.--Fenestra Corporation, Erie, PA, pg. 711
Gluth, Robert C., Chief Fin. Officer--The Marmon Group, Inc., Chicago, IL, pg. 710
Glynn, John J., Sec. & Treas.--Baird, Patrick & Co., Inc., New York, NY, pg. 114
Glynn, Terry, Treas. & Sec.--A. J. Canfield Co., Chicago, IL, pg. 214
Godfrey, Robert, Sec. & Treas.--Central States Enterprises, Inc., Heathrow, FL, pg. 234
Goebel, Arthur F., Pres. & Treas.--Goebel Art, Inc., Coon Rapids, MN, pg. 464
Goebel, Michael G., Exec. V.P.-Mdsg.--Star Lumber & Supply Company, Inc., Wichita, KS, pg. 1039
Goeggel, Richard A., Treas.--AppleTree Markets, Houston, TX, pg. 79
Goguen, Paul A., Exec. V.P., Sec. & Treas.--Sexton Can Co., Inc., Cambridge, MA, pg. 993
Goldberg, Arthur, Chief Fin. Officer, V.P.-Fin & Treas.--Forster Mfg. Co., Inc., Wilton, ME, pg. 21
Goldberg, Lawrence G., V.P. & Treas.--Monitor Aerospace Corporation, Amityville, NY, pg. 765
Goldberg, Morton, Pres. & Treas.--Morton Goldberg Associates, Inc., New York, NY, pg. 465
Goldberger, Seymour, Treas. & Adv. Dir.--Goldberger Doll Mfg. Company, Inc., Brooklyn, NY, pg. 466
Golden, David, Chief Fin. Officer, Treas. & Sec.--Stephen Gould Paper Co., Inc., Whippany, NJ, pg. 473
Golden, J.M., V.P.-Fin.--Hub Inc., Tucker, GA, pg. 548
Goldenberg, Victoria, Sec. & Treas.--Fashion Shop of Kentucky Inc., Louisville, KY, pg. 403
Goldfine, Manley, Treas.--Northern Drug Company, Duluth, MN, pg. 814
Goldman, David, Pres. & Treas.--Goldman Financial Group, Boston, MA, pg. 468
Goldman, Marilyn S., Exec. V.P., Sec. & Treas.--S. I. Goldman Co., Longwood, FL, pg. 467
Goldman, Zachary C., Exec. V.P., Treas. & Sec.--Londontown Holdings Corporation, Eldersburg, MD, pg. 681
Goldstein, Barbara, Exec. V.P., Treas.--Media Power, Inc., Charlotte, NC, pg. 734
Goldstein, Mark L., Treas. & Sec.--Dexter Chemical Corp., Bronx, NY, pg. 334
Goldstein, Norman R., V.P., Treas. & Asst. Sec.--Barton Brands, Ltd., Chicago, IL, pg. 123
Goldstein, Norman R., Asst. Sec. & Asst. Treas.--Barton Beers, Ltd., Chicago, IL, pg. 123
Goldstein, Samuel R., Chm. Bd. & Treas.--Apex Oil Company, Inc., Saint Louis, MO, pg. 78
Gonda, Robert, Treas.--Restaurant Enterprises Group, Inc., Irvine, CA, pg. 929
Gonnelli, Pat, V.P. & Treas.--The Franklin Mint, Franklin Center, PA, pg. 60
Good, W.C., Treas.--Fairfield Electric Co-op, Winnsboro, SC, pg. 397
Goodman, Lawrence B., Chm. Bd. & Treas.--The Ormond Shops, Inc., North Bergen, NJ, pg. 830
Goodman, Murray, Pres. & Treas.--Goodmans, Inc., Phoenix, AZ, pg. 471
Goodman, Phillip, Treas.--Burtman Iron Works, Inc., Boston, MA, pg. 195
Goodman, Rhea, Sec. & Treas.--Bonhomme Shirtmakers, Ltd., New York, NY, pg. 164
Goodrich, Bradley, V.P.-Fin. & Treas.--Electro Fiberoptics Corporation, Northborough, MA, pg. 374
Gordon, Flem, Treas.--V.F. Energies, Inc., Madisonville, KY, pg. 1141
Gordon, John M., Chief Fin. Officer, Treas., Sec.--Gordon Food Service Inc., Grand Rapids, MI, pg. 472
Gordon, Lloyd, Pres. & Treas.--Amcell Corporation, Watertown, MA, pg. 47
Gordon, Michael, Pres. & Treas.--Koret Givenchy, New York, NY, pg. 642
Gordonson, Robert, Treas. & Chief Fin. Officer--Masters, Inc., Westbury, NY, pg. 720
Gore, Dr. Genevieve W., Treas. & Sec.--W. L. Gore & Associates, Inc., Newark, DE, pg. 472
Gorenflo, Karen L., Fin. Mgr. & Treasurer--FKQ Advertising Inc., Clearwater, FL, pg. 394
Goss, Howard S., Chm., Chief Exec. Officer & Treas.--Transco Inc., Chicago, IL, pg. 1106
Gossett, Darrell, Exec. V.P., Sec. & Treas.--Ermco, Inc., Indianapolis, IN, pg. 387
Gossett, Howard B., V.P.-Fin. & Credit Mgr.--Dundee Mills, Inc., Griffin, GA, pg. 352
Gottschalk, Eldon W., Co-Chm., Sec. & Treas.--Jack Lawlor Advertising, Inc., Pasadena, CA, pg. 661
Gould, H. Joshua, Treas.--Interplan, Denver, CO, pg. 907
Graeff, Rodney J., V.P.-Fin. & Treas.--Walter H. Weaber Sons, Inc., Lebanon, PA, pg. 1169
Graf, Gary, V.P. & Treas.--Parisi, Inc., Philadelphia, PA, pg. 848
Graff, M., Treas. & Sec.--Douglas Stephen Plastics, Inc., Paterson, NJ, pg. 347
Graff, Margaret A., Sr. V.P. & Treas.--Atlantic Gulf Communities Corporation, Miami, FL, pg. 95
Graham, David, Treas.--Aston Martin LaGonda of North America, Inc., Stamford, CT, pg. 92
Graham, Jack W., Chm. Bd., Sec. & Treas.--Petty Company, Inc., Effingham, IL, pg. 866
Graham, Russell, Treas.--Standard Duplicating Machines Corp., Andover, MA, pg. 1036
Grandle, Susan, Mgr.-Human Resources & Treas.--Tricon Industries, Inc., Downers Grove, IL, pg. 1113
Granicher, John W., Sr. V.P. & Sec. & Treas.--Keller & Gannon, San Francisco, CA, pg. 637
Granlund, Leland R., V.P., Treas. & Chief Fin. Officer--Western Petroleum Company, Eden Prairie, MN, pg. 1181
Grant, Shirley, Sec. & Treas.--Grant Marketing Communications Inc., Lafayette Hill, PA, pg. 477
Grantham, Linda, Treas.--Grantham Company, Orlando, FL, pg. 477
Grasso, Frank, Treas.--Parsons & Whittemore Enterprises, Rye Brook, NY, pg. 850
Grathwohl, Joseph A., Treas.--Jake Sweeney Auto Leasing, Inc., Cincinnati, OH, pg. 1067
Graunke, Scott, Sr. V.P. & Treas.--Amlings Flowerland, Hinsdale, IL, pg. 67
Graver, Patrick J., Treas.--Bell & Howell Company, Skokie, IL, pg. 134
Gray, Dale, V.P. & Treas.--Dutton-Lainson Co., Hastings, NE, pg. 356
Gray, Jim, Treas.--Superior Federal Bank, Fort Smith, AR, pg. 1063
Green, John, Treas.--Omaha Public Power District, Omaha, NE, pg. 825
Green, John R., Sec. & Treas.--John E. Green Co., Highland Park, MI, pg. 484
Green, Velmar, Treas.--Michigan Milk Producers Association, Novi, MI, pg. 747
Greene, Jerry W., Sec. & Treas.--Hanes Companies, Inc., Winston-Salem, NC, pg. 505
Greenfield, Barry, Treas.--Opus South Corporation, Tampa, FL, pg. 828
Greengard, Michael, V.P., Sec. & Treas.--Thompson Enterprises Inc., Minnetonka, MN, pg. 1094
Greenhalgh, F.A., V.P. & Treas.--Day & Zimmermann, Inc., Radnor, PA, pg. 320
Greening, Bruce C., Treas.--ASC Incorporated, Southgate, MI, pg. 7
Greenspun, Barbara, Publr. & Treas.--Las Vegas Sun, Inc., Las Vegas, NV, pg. 659
Greer, Jack, V.P. & Treas.--Autry Greer & Sons, Inc., Prichard, AL, pg. 486
Gregerson, Richard E., V.P.-Fin.--The Equion Corporation, New Haven, CT, pg. 385
Gregory, Carl, Chief Fin. Officer, V.P.-Fin. & Treas.--Preformed Line Products, Cleveland, OH, pg. 886
Gregory, Jack, V.P. & Treas.--Santa Rosa Steel Forming, Inc., Santa Rosa, CA, pg. 970
Gregory, Russell, Chief Fin. Officer & Treas.--The Ruhlin Company, Sharon Center, OH, pg. 955
Grietzer, Roland, Controller & Treas.--Alcom Printing Group, Inc., Bethlehem, PA, pg. 32
Griffin, Earl, Treas.--Miller Bros. Industries, Inc., Richmond, VA, pg. 753
Griffin, George G., Chm. Bd., Pres. & Treas.--Davis Advertising Inc., Philadelphia, PA, pg. 318
Griffin, L.B., Treas.--Allison-Erwin Co. Inc., Charlotte, NC, pg. 40
Griffith, Mike, Treas. & Sec.--Southern Radio Corporation, pg. 1022
Griffith, Robert, V.P., Sec. & Treas.--The Chas. H. Lilly Co., Portland, OR, pg. 675
Griffiths, Phyllis J., Treas.--Colusa Elevator Co., Colusa, IL, pg. 267
Griggs, David, Pres., Chief Exec. & Chief Fin. Officer & Treas.--Jack Griggs Inc., Exeter, CA, pg. 488
Grimes, Thomas D., Pres. & Treas.--Puritan Bakery, Inc., Carson, CA, pg. 900
Grimley, Robert, Sec. & Treas.--Duo-Fast Corporation, Franklin Park, IL, pg. 354
Grimm, Jeffrey, V.P.-Fin. & Treas.--Portland Food Products Company, Portland, OR, pg. 881
Grimmer, Susan L., V.P. & Treas.--Grimmer Realty Co. Inc., Birmingham, AL, pg. 488
Grissom, S.L., Treas.--Illinois Consolidated Telephone Co., Mattoon, IL, pg. 563
Griswold, Richard, V.P. & Treas.--Loos & Co., Inc., Pomfret, CT, pg. 683
Grogg, Mary, Sec. & Treas.--Mike Savoie Chevrolet Inc., Troy, MI, pg. 973
Gross, Donald, V.P., Treas. & Sec.--Dan's Supreme Super Markets Inc., Hempstead, NY, pg. 314
Gross, Leonard, V.P. & Treas.--Shapco, Inc., Van Nuys, CA, pg. 995
Grossman, Edgar, Treas.--Massachusetts Envelope Co., Somerville, MA, pg. 718
Grossman, Melvin, V.P., Sec. & Treas.--Lithographix, Inc., Los Angeles, CA, pg. 678
Grossman, Morton, Chief Fin. Officer & Treas.--Waring & LaRosa, Inc., New York, NY, pg. 1163
Groth, John F., Treas.--Baker Concrete Construction, Inc., Monroe, OH, pg. 115
Grotti, Erich, Treas.--Trayco of S.C., Inc., Florence, SC, pg. 358
Grover, Rich, Sr. V.P. & Treas.--BeefAmerica Operating Co., Inc., Omaha, NE, pg. 131
Gruenberg, Craig L., Exec. V.P., Chief Oper. Officer--William Eisner & Associates Inc., Milwaukee, WI, pg. 372
Gruhl, Robert H., Chief Fin. Officer, Sr. V.P. & Treas.--Liberty Mutual Insurance Co., Boston, MA, pg. 674
Grunnah, Judith, Treas.--Reliance Elevator Company, Chicago, IL, pg. 925
Grupka, Richard A., Sec. & Treas.--John W. Danforth Co., Buffalo, NY, pg. 314
Gryn, Len, Exec. V.P.--Weber-Stephen Products, Palatine, IL, pg. 1171
Guccione, Anthony, Sec. & Treas.--General Media Publishing Group, New York, NY, pg. 450
Guenther, John S., Sr. V.P.--Geo. J. Ball, Inc., West Chicago, IL, pg. 115
Guenther, Thomas P., Exec. V.P. & Treas.--Dickten & Masch Manufacturing Co., Nashotah, WI, pg. 336

Guercio, Thomas R., V.P., Treas. & Chief Fin. Officer--Reliable Stores, Inc., Columbia, MD, pg. 925
Guest, Christine M., Treas.--Allens Of Hastings, Inc., Hastings, NE, pg. 36
Gugino, Carmelo, Jr., Pres. & Treas.--Dinaire Corp., Buffalo, NY, pg. 338
Gulbas, Jacqueline, Sec. & Treas.--National Restaurant Supply Company, El Paso, TX, pg. 793
Gunder, Peter, Treas.--M M I Companies, Inc., Deerfield, IL, pg. 692
Gurewitz, Lorrie, Sec. & Treas.--Poly Pak America, Inc., Los Angeles, CA, pg. 880
Guriel, Florian, Asst. Sec. & Treas.--Whiting Equipment Canada, Inc., Welland,, Canada, pg. 1187
Gusick, Dennis, V.P.-Fin., Treas. & Sec.--Helm, Inc., Highland Park, MI, pg. 527
Gutierrez, A., V.P.-Fin. & Treas.--Dietzgen Corporation, Des Plaines, IL, pg. 337
Gutowski, David T., Treas.--Glenshaw Glass Co. Inc., Glenshaw, PA, pg. 462
Gutterson, Gerald, Chief Fin. Officer, Treas. & Sec.--Martin Paint Stores, Jamaica, NY, pg. 715
Guttman, Alan R., Pres. & Treas.--The Guttman Group, Belle Vernon, PA, pg. 495
Haag, Stephen, V.P. & Treas.--Swaner Hardwood Company, Inc., Burbank, CA, pg. 1066
Haas, David, Treas.--Keen Compressed Gas Co., Inc., Wilmington, DE, pg. 619
Haas, Fred Jr., Sec. & Treas.--National Band & Tag Co., Newport, KY, pg. 786
Haas, Joseph S., Treas. & Controller--CRL, Inc., Des Plaines, IL, pg. 203
Haddix, David D., Treas.--Therma-Tru Corp., Maumee, OH, pg. 1090
Haentjens, R.P., Exec. V.P. & Treas.--Barrett Haentjens & Company, Hazleton, PA, pg. 499
Haft, Julie, Sec. & Treas.--Haywin Textile Products, Inc., Brooklyn, NY, pg. 520
Hagadorn, Robert E., Exec. V.P., Treas. & Sec.--Hazen & Sawyer, New York, NY, pg. 520
Hagedorn, H., Treas.--Don Stone Associates Inc., Mamaroneck, NY, pg. 1050
Hagen, Doug, Treas.--American Foods Group, Inc., Minneapolis, MN, pg. 54
Hager, Jean, Sec. & Treas.--Air Industries Corporation, Garden Grove, CA, pg. 27
Hager, Teresa, Treas.--Madison Grocery Co., Inc., Richmond, KY, pg. 699
Hagler, Billie S., Treas.--Georgia Iron Works Co., Grovetown, GA, pg. 453
Hagood D. Maybank, V.P. & Treas.--William M. Bird & Co., Inc., Charleston, SC, pg. 152
Hahnfeldt, Alfred, V.P. & Treas.--H.O. Penn Machinery Co. Inc., Armonk, NY, pg. 857
Haigh, Robert B., Chm., Chief Exec. Officer & Treas.--Chicago Tube & Iron Co., Chicago, IL, pg. 246
Haines, A.L., V.P., Treas., Controller & Chief Fin. Officer--CHEMCENTRAL Corporation, Bedford Park, IL, pg. 241
Hall, David C., Treas.--Columbine Systems Inc., Golden, CO, pg. 266
Hall, Delvis A., V.P., Treas., Sec. & Gen. Mgr.--Lone Star Cadillac Co., Dallas, TX, pg. 682
Hall, John L., V.P.-Fin., Treas. & Chief Fin. Officer--Schwab Corp., Lafayette, IN, pg. 980
Hall, Michael J., Sr. V.P., Treas., Chief Fin. & Admin. Officer--T.D. Williamson, Inc., Tulsa, OK, pg. 1192
Hall, William A., Sec. & Treas.--Tennessee Dressed Beef Company, Nashville, TN, pg. 1087
Hall, William T., Treas.--John Bouchard & Sons Company, Nashville, TN, pg. 168
Hallberg, Charles, Treas.--First District Association, Litchfield, MN, pg. 412
Haller, W. E., V.P.-Fin., Chief Fin. Officer & Treas.--The Deutsch Company, Santa Monica, CA, pg. 333
Halterman, Darlene F., Asst. Treas. & Sec.--The Sico Company, Mount Joy, PA, pg. 1001
Halterman, Darlene F., Sec. & Asst. Treas.--First Mount Joy Corporation, Mount Joy, PA, pg. 413
Halverson, Nancy, Treas.--Ovation Marketing, Inc., La Crosse, WI, pg. 832
Halvorson, Lorraine, Sec. & Treas.--Prospect Motors, Inc., Jackson, CA, pg. 895
Hamilton, D. Steven, Treas.--Rish Equipment Company, Bluefield, WV, pg. 935
Hamilton, Doug, Controller & Treas.--Spinnerin Yarn Co., Inc., South Hackensack, NJ, pg. 1031
Hamister, Oliver C., V.P.-Admin., Treas. & Sec.--National Health Care Affiliates, Inc., Buffalo, NY, pg. 791
Hammel, Robert E., Chief Fin. Officer, Treas. & Sec.--Ohio Machinery Co., Cleveland, OH, pg. 822
Hammond, Jerry, V.P., Treas. & Sec.--Cargill Fertilizer, Inc., Riverview, FL, pg. 219
Hammond, John, Treas.--Hardware Wholesalers, Inc., Fort Wayne, IN, pg. 508
Hammond, Michael, V.P.,Treas., & Sec.--H & H Advertising, Fort Worth, TX, pg. 496
Hamor, Robert, Treas.--Denlinger, Inc., Paradise, PA, pg. 329
Hampel, Robert E., Sr. Exec. Chief Fin. Officer, Treas. & Sec.--Keller Crescent Co., Evansville, IN, pg. 620
Hamrick, H. R., Sec., Treas. & Data Processing Mgr.--Haines City Citrus Growers Association, Haines City, FL, pg. 500
Hamwey, Emile J., Sr. V.P. & Asst. Treas.--Fay, Spofford & Thorndike, Inc., Lexington, MA, pg. 404
Hanaway, James F., Jr., Exec. V.P., Treas.--Fern/Hanaway, Inc. Advertising/Public Relations, Warwick, RI, pg. 407
Hancock, John C., Treas. & Sec.--Stanley Stores Inc., Bay City, TX, pg. 1038
Hand, Francis J., Treas.--Brunschwig & Fils, Inc., White Plains, NY, pg. 184
Hanel, William W., Treas.--Hanel Lumber Co., Inc., Hood River, OR, pg. 505
Hanhart, Scott E., Asst. Treas.--Remarks, Inc., Dublin, OH, pg. 925
Hanigan, Brian, Treas.--Farley Industries, Chicago, IL, pg. 399
Hanin, Francine, Treas. & Sec.--Allied Tire Sales, Orlando, FL, pg. 40
Hanlon, T.P., Treas.--L. B. Smith, Inc., Camp Hill, PA, pg. 1013
Hannon, John C., Asst. Treas.--Wilbur-Ellis Company & Connell Brothers Company, San Francisco, CA, pg. 1189
Hano, Phillip, V.P. & Treas.--Technicarbon Company, Inc., Springfield, MA, pg. 1083
Hanson, Dale S., Chief Fin. Officer, V.P.-Fin. & Treas.--C. H. Robinson Co. Inc., Eden Prairie, MN, pg. 939
Hanson, John R., Treas.--Pala Group, Inc., Baton Rouge, LA, pg. 843
Hanson, Yvonne, V.P. & Treas.--Bridgeport Machines, Inc., Bridgeport, CT, pg. 175
Harding, Marvin E., Sec. & Treas.--Artesian Resources Corporation, Newark, DE, pg. 86
Harding, Marvin E., V.P., Chief Fin. Officer, Treas. & Sec.--Artesian Development Corporation, Newark, DE, pg. 86
Hardinge, Thomas H., III, V.P.-Sls. & Mktg., Treas. & Sec.--Statton Furniture Manufacturing Company, Hagerstown, MD, pg. 1042
Hardwick, Robert, Sec., Controller & Treas.--Axelson, Inc., Longview, TX, pg. 103
Hardy, Sophia, Sec. & Treas.--Barnhill Contracting Company, Tarboro, NC, pg. 121
Harkey, Mark, Treas.--Valley Innovative Management Service, Jackson, MS, pg. 1109
Harlan, Maureen, Treas.--Stainless Incorporated, Deerfield Beach, FL, pg. 1035
Harmon, Linda L., Chief Fin. Officer & Treas.--Progressive Driver Services, Inc., Jacksonville, FL, pg. 894
Harms, Carol, V.P. & Treas.--Montgomery Ward & Co., Inc., Chicago, IL, pg. 767
Harp, Gerald L., V.P.-Opers., Sec. & Treas.--Harp's Food Stores, Inc., Springdale, AR, pg. 510
Harper, Anne M., Treas.--Harper Bros., Inc., Fort Myers, FL, pg. 510
Harrell, Paul, Jr., Sec. & Treas.--Long MFG. NC, Inc., Tarboro, NC, pg. 682
Harrell, Thomas L., V.P. & Treas.--Glenoit Mills, Inc., Tarboro, NC, pg. 462
Harrington, John A., Sec. & Asst. Treas.--Geo. J. Ball, Inc., West Chicago, IL, pg. 115
Harrington, Laurence P., Treas.--Amray, Inc., Bedford, MA, pg. 68
Harris, Cecily, Sec. & Treas.--GFA Brands, Inc., Cresskill, NJ, pg. 440
Harris, H. David, Asst. Treas. & Controller--Transus Inc., Atlanta, GA, pg. 1108
Harris, Jay, Chief Fin. Officer & Treas.--Aetna Health Plans, San Bruno, CA, pg. 23
Harris, John G., Treas. & Sec.--Harris Enterprises Inc., Hutchinson, KS, pg. 511
Harris, Joseph, Sr. V.P. & Treas.--Powell Electronics Inc., Philadelphia, PA, pg. 882
Harris, L.E., V.P. & Treas.--Dukane Corporation, Saint Charles, IL, pg. 351
Harris, Lucious T., Asst. Treas.--Capital Bancorp, Miami, FL, pg. 214
Harris, Marc F., V.P. & Treas.--CCC Conveyors, Inc., Dallas, TX, pg. 357
Harris, Rick L., Treas.& Controller--Bader & Co., Ipava, IL, pg. 113
Harrison, Douglas M., V.P.-Fin., Chief Fin. Officer & Treas.--Lyon Metal Products, Inc., Montgomery, IL, pg. 690
Harrison, J. Steven, Treas.--Columbia Pipe & Supply Company, Chicago, IL, pg. 266
Harrison, Peggie T., Treas. & Sec.--Harco Drug, Inc., Tuscaloosa, AL, pg. 507
Harrsion, Arthur, Treas.--MHB Inc., Williamsport, PA, pg. 692
Hart, Dorothy, V.P.-Fin. & Admin.--McNaughton & Gunn, Inc., Saline, MI, pg. 732
Hart, Ronald D., Pres. & Treas.--Hart Crowser, Inc., Seattle, WA, pg. 512
Hartline, Lee, Treas. & Controller--Greer Steel Co., Dover, OH, pg. 486
Hartman, Pete, Treas. & Sec.--Chemung Ford, Inc., Elmira, NY, pg. 242
Hartman, Robert J., V.P. & Treas.--Central-United Life Insurance Co., Sioux City, IA, pg. 233
Hartog, Larry, V.P. & Treas.--Kentucky Manufacturing Co., Louisville, KY, pg. 624
Hartog, Larry, Sec. & Asst. Treas.--R.C. Tway Coal Company, Louisville, KY, pg. 1120
Hartsig, Harold, V.P. & Treas.--Pennock, Philadelphia, PA, pg. 858
Hartunian, Martin, Treas.--A B C Appliance Inc., Pontiac, MI, pg. 2
Harvatine, John, V.P.-Fin. & Treas.--AmeriData, Inc., Minneapolis, MN, pg. 66
Harvey, Jean, Sec. & Treas.--Combs & Heathcott, Little Rock, AR, pg. 267
Harvey, Nancy J., Treas.--J.H. Harvey Company, Nashville, GA, pg. 515
Haserjian, Bryan, Exec. V.P. & Treas.--Carpeteria, Inc., Valencia, CA, pg. 224
Haskins, Stephen, V.P.-Fin., Treas. & Admin. Mgr.--The Barbar Group, Inc., Boca Raton, FL, pg. 119
Haslam, George, Treas. & Sec.--Caltrol, Inc., Glendora, CA, pg. 211
Hasper, Robert P., Treas.--Advance Packaging Corporation, Grand Rapids, MI, pg. 19
Hassinger, Douglas, Treas. & Sec.--Perkasie Industries Corporation, Perkasie, PA, pg. 862
Hastings, F. Curtis, V.P. & Treas.--J.H. Findorff & Son, Inc., Madison, WI, pg. 411
Hatch, George C., Treas.--Standard Corporation, Ogden, UT, pg. 1036
Haueisen, Margaret A., Treas.--Continental Forge Company, Compton, CA, pg. 279
Haupt, J. P., Corp. Sec., Treas. & Chief Fin. & Exec. Officer--Juniata Office Supplies, Altoona, PA, pg. 608
Hauser, F.J., Sec. & Treas.--Conley Frog & Switch Company, Memphis, TN, pg. 274
Haveman, Kenneth, Sec. & Asst. Treas.--Binkley Company, Warrenton, MO, pg. 151
Haver, Kenneth, Treas.--Basic Computer, Akron, OH, pg. 124
Hawbaker, Alan, Sec. & Treas.--Glenn O. Hawbaker, Inc., State College, PA, pg. 517
Hawes, Michael S., V.P.-Fin. & Treas.--The Coleman Company, Inc., Wichita, KS, pg. 695
Hawk, Louise, Sec. & Treas.--Gertrude Hawk Chocolates, Inc., Troop, PA, pg. 517
Hawkey, Robert H., V.P.-Fin. & Admin.--Precision Valve Corporation, Yonkers, NY, pg. 885
Hawkins, Cleve, Treas.--Miller & Co., Selma, AL, pg. 753
Hawkins, Robert E., Chief Fin. Officer, Treas., Controller & Sec.--West Union Corp., Memphis, TN, pg. 1177
Hawkins, W.F., V.P.-Fin. & Treas.--Newsprint South Sales Company, Dallas, TX, pg. 760
Hawthorne, Nancy, Sr. V.P. & Treas.--Continental Cablevision, Boston, MA, pg. 278
Hayes, Carl I., Jr., Pres. & Treas.--C. I. Hayes, Inc., Cranston, RI, pg. 519
Hays, Don L., Chief Fin. Officer & Treas.--Diemakers, Inc., Monroe City, MO, pg. 336
Hays, Helen C., Treas. & Sec.--Press Enterprise Company, Riverside, CA, pg. 887
Hazen, Thomas, Chief Exec. Officer & Treas.--Hazen Paper Company, Holyoke, MA, pg. 520
Heacock, Richard, V.P.-Fin., Treas., Sec. & Controller--Apache Hose & Belting Company, Cedar Rapids, IA, pg. 77
Heagney, Larry, Sec. & Treas.--Milliken & Co., Inc., Spartanburg, SC, pg. 755
Healey, E. Peter, V.P. & Treas.--Zale Corporation, Irving, TX, pg. 1215
Heaney, T.J., Treas.--Acker Drill Co. Inc., Chinchilla, PA, pg. 12
Heath, Frederick G., V.P., Sec. & Treas.--Brown Wood Preserving Company, Louisville, KY, pg. 183
Heath, Milton W., Jr., Chm. Bd., Chief Exec. Officer & Treas.--Heath Consultants Incorporated, Stoughton, MA, pg. 524
Hedinger, Howard, Chm. Bd. & Treas.--American Industries Inc., Portland, OR, pg. 55
Heery, Joseph, V.P. & Chief Fin. Officer--Cyborg Systems, Inc., Chicago, IL, pg. 307
Heffelfinger, Roger, Treas.--Summit Communications, Inc., Atlanta, GA, pg. 1057
Hegarty, Joe, Treas.--Webcraft Technologies, Inc., North Brunswick, NJ, pg. 1171
Heil, M., Sec. & Treas.--American Excelsior Company, Arlington, TX, pg. 51
Heil, Nelson, Treas. & Sec.--Ray-Carroll County Grain Co-op, Richmond, MO, pg. 914
Heilig, William W., V.P. & Treas.--Berwind Corporation, Philadelphia, PA, pg. 145
Heinman, Gregg J., V.P.-Opers., Sec. & Treas.--Conway Import Co. Inc., Elmsford, NY, pg. 281
Heintjes, Charlotte, V.P.-Fin. & Treas.--Roytex, Inc., New York, NY, pg. 953
Heist, Gary A., Chief Fin. Officer & Treas.--Continental Machines, Inc., Savage, MN, pg. 279
Heit, Stephen A., Chief Fin. Officer & Treas.--Pavion Ltd., Nyack on Hudson, NY, pg. 852
Heldman, Barbara, Sec., Treas.--Northlich Stolley LaWarre, Cincinnati, OH, pg. 814
Heller, C.M., Jr., Vice Chm. & Treas.--Marquette Coppersmithing Co., Inc., Philadelphia, PA, pg. 713
Hellman, Murray, V.P., Treas. & Sec.--Pressman Toy Corp., New York, NY, pg. 887
Hellman, Tracy, Sec. & Treas.--J. Hellman Produce, Inc., Los Angeles, CA, pg. 527
Helman, Herb, Treas.--Murry's, Inc., Forestville, MD, pg. 777
Helmer, W., Treas. & Controller--Republic Industries, Inc., Harwood Heights, IL, pg. 928
Helmick, Louis G., III, V.P. & Treas.--Helmick Corporation, Fairmont, WV, pg. 527
Helpern, David M., Treas.--Joan & David, Inc., Everett, MA, pg. 528
Helwig, Curtis, Treas.--CFB Industries, Inc., Chicago, IL, pg. 201
Helzer, H. Albert, Treas.--Unicover Corporation, Cheyenne, WY, pg. 1126
Helzing, Carl, Sec. & Treas.--Premier Coatings, Inc., Elk Grove Village, IL, pg. 886
Hemmer, Donald M., Treas. & Sec.--Paul Hemmer Construction Company, Fort Mitchell, KY, pg. 528
Hempt, Gerald L., Sec. & Treas.--Hempt Brothers, Inc., Camp Hill, PA, pg. 528
Henady, Phillis M., Treas.--Demeter, Inc., Fowler, IN, pg. 328
Henderson, Jeffery, Sec. & Treas.--Henderson Auctioneers, Livingston, LA, pg. 528
Henderson, Richard, Treas.--Johnson County Farm Bureau Co-op, Franklin, IN, pg. 598
Hendley, Guy W., Exec. V.P.-Corp. Fin. & Treas.--Owen Steel Co., Inc., Columbia, SC, pg. 834
Hendry, William J., Treas.--Citrus World Inc., Lake Wales, FL, pg. 251
Hennessy, Dennis J., Chief Fin. Officer, Treas. & V.P.-Fin.--The Nash Engineering Company, Norwalk, CT, pg. 783
Henquinet, Wayne K., Sec. & Treas.--New Mech Companies, Inc., Saint Paul, MN, pg. 802
Henry, Joseph C., V.P., Treas. & Chief Fin. Officer--The Hanover Insurance Company, Worcester, MA, pg. 34
Henss, Laurence R., V.P., Treas. & Controller--Industrial Dielectrics, Inc., Noblesville, IN, pg. 566

Hentges, Richard J., Treas.--Foley-PLP Company, Rochester, NY, pg. 422
Herald, James, V.P.-Fin., Sec & Treas.--Morgan Foods, Inc., Austin, IN, pg. 770
Herbert, Richard, Pres., Chief Exec. & Fin. Officer--VanDine, Humphrey, Herbert, Alber & Manges, Inc., Pittsburgh, PA, pg. 1145
Hergenrader, Sallt, Treas.--Cummins Mid-South, Inc., Memphis, TN, pg. 305
Herley, Virlyn, Treas.--Atlas Wire Corporation, Schiller Park, IL, pg. 97
Herman, W. A., III, Sec. & Treas.--Morris Corporation, Augusta, GA, pg. 999
Herman, W.A., III, Treas. & Sec.--Shivers Trading & Operating Co., Augusta, GA, pg. 999
Hernandez, Louis R., V.P., Treas. & Asst. Sec.--W. P. Carey & Co., Inc., New York, NY, pg. 218
Herran, Jose, Treas.--Real Holding Management Corp., Miami, FL, pg. 917
Hersh, Gene, Treas.--California Manufacturing Enterprises, City of Industry, CA, pg. 210
Herstein, Harvey, Sr. V.P. & Treas.--Kenneth Gordon New Orleans, Ltd., New Orleans, LA, pg. 472
Heuer, Duane, Sec. & Treas.--Bongards Creameries Inc., Norwood, MN, pg. 164
Hewett, Jack A., Sr. V.P.-Admin., Chief Fin. Officer & Treas.--VASA North Atlantic Insurance Company, Indianapolis, IN, pg. 1146
Hiatt, David A., Sec. & Treas.--The National Super Service Co., Toledo, OH, pg. 794
Hickey, James J., V.P. & Treas.--Smith Valve Corporation, Whitinsville, MA, pg. 1014
Hicks, Maude H., Sec. & Treas.--Horton Homes, Inc., Eatonton, GA, pg. 545
Higgins, Katherine, Treas.--Edelbrock Corp., Torrance, CA, pg. 367
Hilger, Kenneth, Treas. & Chief Fin. Officer--Gardiner Metal Company, Chicago, IL, pg. 443
Hill, Dorsey, Treas. & Sec.--Tallapoosa River Electric Co-Op, South Lafayette, AL, pg. 1077
Hill, R.E., Sec. & Treas.--Democrat Printing & Lithograph Company, Little Rock, AR, pg. 328
Hill, Robert M., Sec. & Treas.--First Electric Cooperative, Jacksonville, AR, pg. 412
Hilliard, John A., V.P.-Fin., Treas. & Chief Fin. Officer--American Linen Supply Company, Minneapolis, MN, pg. 57
Hilsinger, Arthur R., Jr., Chm. Bd., Pres. & Treas.--The Hilsinger Corp., Plainville, MA, pg. 535
Hilton, Richard H., Treas.--Utica Boilers Inc., Utica, NY, pg. 1140
Hilton, Ronald G., Corp. Treas. & Sec.--Inlander-Steindler Paper, Vernon Hills, IL, pg. 570
Hinderer, H. William III, Chief Fin. Officer & V.P.-Fin. & Admin.--Tacony Corporation, Fenton, MO, pg. 1076
Hindman, Robert A., Sr. V.P.-Fin., Treas. & Sec.--Brix Maritime Co., Portland, OR, pg. 177
Hines, Edward J., V.P., Treas. & Sec.--Wolverine Massachusetts Corporation, Merrimac, MA, pg. 1199
Hinkle, Kenneth A. III, Sr. V.P.-Fin. & Treas.--Hess's Department Stores, Inc., Allentown, PA, pg. 302
Hinman, Kirk, Pres., Chief Exec. Officer, Chief Fin. Officer & Treas.--Rome Strip Steel Co., Inc., Rome, NY, pg. 946
Hinton, Betty, Sec. & Treas.--Blue Grass Chrysler-Plymouth, Lexington, KY, pg. 156
Hirman, Arland E., V.P., Sec. & Treas.--Advanstar Communications, Cleveland, OH, pg. 21
Hirsch, Gary D., Chm., Pres., Dir., & Treas.--Grand Union Holdings Corporation, Riverside, CT, pg. 475
Hirschfeld, David L., Pres., Chief Exec. Officer & Treas.--Hirschfeld, Inc., San Angelo, TX, pg. 536
Hishmeh, Basem L., Chm. Bd. & Treas.--Aerco International Inc., Northvale, NJ, pg. 21
Hitchen, Harold, Jr., Sr. V.P. & Treas.--Amica Mutual Insurance Co., Providence, RI, pg. 66
Hlavac, Bernard, V.P. & Treas.--Sentry Insurance, A Mutual Company, Stevens Point, WI, pg. 990
Hochfelder, Thomas G., Sr. V.P. & Treas.--Beldoch Industries Corporation, West Hempstead, NY, pg. 133
Hochstedler, Kevin, Controller & Asst. Treas.--Bristol Products, L.P., Bristol, IN, pg. 176
Hodges, Charles, Treas. & Controller--Colonial Oil Industries, Savannah, GA, pg. 263
Hodges, Mark H., Treas.--Hancock Peanut Company, Courtland, VA, pg. 504
Hodgman, Frank H., III, V.P. & Treas.--Troy Mills, Inc., Troy, NH, pg. 1116
Hoelterhoff, Ernest R., Treas. & Chief Fin. Officer--Harza Engineering Co., Chicago, IL, pg. 516
Hoerner, Douglas A., Treas.--Mechanical Heat & Cold, Inc., Farmington, MI, pg. 734
Hoff, Carl D., Treas. & Controller--Rice Growers Association of California, West Sacramento, CA, pg. 931
Hoffman, Bradley, Treas.--Putman Publishing Co., Chicago, IL, pg. 901
Hoffman, Donald, Pres. & Treas.--Creative Playthings Ltd., Framingham, MA, pg. 297
Hoffman, Frank P., Treas.--Wolcott & Lincoln, Inc., Kansas City, MO, pg. 1198
Hoffman, William H., Sec. & Treas.--Jeffrey Buick-Nissan Inc., Roseville, MI, pg. 591
Hogan, Robert F., Jr., V.P. & Treas.--Associated Materials Inc., Dallas, TX, pg. 91
Hogg, G. Scott, Sec. & Treas.--Better Brands Of Atlanta, Inc., Atlanta, GA, pg. 148
Hoke, Michael, V.P. & Treas.--Argosy Electronics, Inc., Eden Prairie, MN, pg. 82
Holcomb, Robert J., Sec. & Treas.--V.T. Inc., Merriam, KS, pg. 1142
Holiday, Bob, Treas.--Ravenswood Aluminum Corp., Ravenswood, WV, pg. 914
Hollander, Jules A., Chm. Bd. & Treas.--Hartford Distributors Inc., Manchester, CT, pg. 514
Holleman, Matthew L., Exec. V.P & Treas.--Mississippi Valley Gas Co., Jackson, MS, pg. 1208
Holmes, John, Exec. V.P., Mktg. Dir. & Sec.--Paradigm Communications, Tampa, FL, pg. 847
Holmes, Mary B., Treas.--Chelsea Milling Co., Chelsea, MI, pg. 241
Holte, William T., Treas.--Road Machinery & Supplies Co., Savage, MN, pg. 937
Holter, Peter, V.P. & Treas.--Peter Lumber Company, Pleasantville, NJ, pg. 864
Holtz, Robert, Treas.--Modern Group Ltd., Bristol, PA, pg. 762
Holtzman, Morton, V.P., Sec. & Treas.--Harve Benard Ltd. Manufacturing, Secaucus, NJ, pg. 514
Holzhause, Don, V.P.-Finance--Spangler Candy Company, Bryan, OH, pg. 1025
Homan, Robert W., Pres. & Treas.--Homan Lumber Mart, Inc., Elkhart, IN, pg. 541
Homes, Gerald, Sec. & Treas.--Big Bear Supermarkets No. 3, San Diego, CA, pg. 149
Homes, Pat, V.P., Treas. & Sec.--Homes & Son Contractors, Inc., Phoenix, AZ, pg. 542
Homrich, Chris, Asst. Treas.-Intl.--Ingram Industries Inc., Nashville, TN, pg. 568
Honbarrier, Louise B., Sec. & Treas.--Central Transport Inc., High Point, NC, pg. 234
Hooker, Bruce, Sr. V.P. & Chief Fin. Officer--Amperif Corporation, Chatsworth, CA, pg. 68
Hooker, Tom, V.P.-Opers. & Treas.--Townsend Engineering Co., Des Moines, IA, pg. 1104
Hopkins, Pearl, Sec. & Treas.--A & S Tribal Industries, Poplar, MT, pg. 1
Hoppe, Dennis J., V.P., Treas. & Plng.--Hamilton, Carver & Lee, Inc., Chicago, IL, pg. 503
Horan, Don, Sr. V.P.-Fin., Chief Fin. Officer, Sec. & Treas.--Macklanburg-Duncan Co., Oklahoma City, OK, pg. 697
Horowitz, Florence, Treas.--Molesphini & Tobin, Inc., New York, NY, pg. 764
Horton, Gary, Treas.--U-Haul International, Inc., Phoenix, AZ, pg. 48
Horton, Gary B., Treas.--Amerco, A Nevada Corporation, Reno, NV, pg. 47
Horvat, Peter D., V.P., Sec. & Treas.--Lenape Forge, Inc., West Chester, PA, pg. 667
Horwitz, Alan, Treas.--Blumenthal Print Works, Inc., New Orleans, LA, pg. 161
Hoshizaki, Kotaro, Treas. & Sec.--Mutual Trading Co., Inc., Los Angeles, CA, pg. 779
Hottman, William A., V.P., Treas.--Hottman Edwards, Baltimore, MD, pg. 545
House, Randall, Sec. & Treas.--U.S. Creative, Inc., Austin, TX, pg. 1135
Household, Peter R., Treas. & Mgr.-Data Processing--Quality Control Corporation, Harwood Heights, IL, pg. 903
Housen, Charles B., Chm. Bd., Pres. & Chief Exec. Officer--Erving Paper Mills, Erving, MA, pg. 388
Houston, Jeanne A., Treas.--Superior Container, Inc., Warrensville, OH, pg. 1063
Houston, Norman A., Treas.--Golden State Mutual Life Insurance Company, Los Angeles, CA, pg. 467
Hov, Donald, Treas.--Anderson & Lembke Inc., New York, NY, pg. 73
Hovde, Robert, Treas.--Long Prairie Packing Co., Long Prairie, MN, pg. 948
Hovde, Robert A., Treas.--Rosens Diversified, Inc., Fairmont, MN, pg. 948
Hovde, Signe, V.P.-Fin. & Treas.--Alpha One Exchange, New Providence, NJ, pg. 43
Howard, Annie W., Sec. & Treas.--Mercer Transportation Co., Louisville, KY, pg. 739
Howse, P.C., Treas.--Superior Tube Company, Collegeville, PA, pg. 1064
Howse, P.C., Treas.--Anchor Darling Industries Inc., Rosemont, PA, pg. 230
Hubbard, Sonja, Controller, Treas & Sec.--E-Z Mart Stores, Inc., Texarkana, TX, pg. 361
Huber, Judy, Exec. V.P., Treas. & Sec.--Time Systems, Inc., Phoenix, AZ, pg. 1097
Hubling, Robert E., V.P. & Treas.--Steelcase Inc., Grand Rapids, MI, pg. 1044
Hubner, Eric, Treas.--Allied Felt Group, Bloomingdale, NJ, pg. 234
Hudson, Dean, Sr. V.P. & Treas.--Federal Savings Bank, Fort Smith, AR, pg. 1194
Hudson, Robert C., Jr., Pres. & Treas.--H.D. Hudson Manufacturing Company, Chicago, IL, pg. 551
Hudson, Robert S., Exec. V.P., Fin. & Treas.--Price Weber Marketing Communications, Inc., Louisville, KY, pg. 889
Huebner, Donald F., Chief Fin. Officer, Treas. & Controller--Active Electrical Supply Company, Chicago, IL, pg. 15
Huether, Richard, Treas.--Independent Can Company, Belcamp, MD, pg. 564
Huettl, Thomas R., Sr. V.P., Chief Oper. Officer, Treas. & Sec.--Steenberg Homes, Inc., Fond du Lac, WI, pg. 1045
Huffman, Kip, Sec. & Treas.--Neil Huffman Nissan Inc., Louisville, KY, pg. 551
Huffman, R.N., Pres. & Treas.--RAIL Company, Towson, MD, pg. 906
Hufford, Jack E., Treas.--American United Life Insurance Company, Indianapolis, IN, pg. 65
Hughes, David, Treas.--Central Supply Co., Inc., Indianapolis, IN, pg. 234
Hughes, Edward E. III, Treas.--Landau Building Co., Wexford, PA, pg. 654
Hughes, Jack A., Pres. & Treas.--Hughes Advertising Inc., Saint Louis, MO, pg. 551
Hughes, W. Alan, Treas. & Sec.--Fleischli Oil Company, Inc., Cheyenne, WY, pg. 417
Huguley, William H., IV, Exec. V.P. & Treas.--Batson-Cook Company, West Point, GA, pg. 126
Huisinga, Darrel, Pres. & Treas.--J. D. Streett & Co., Inc., Maryland Heights, MO, pg. 1053
Huitt, E. Larry, Chm. Bd., Sec. & Treas.--Huitt-Zollars, Inc., Dallas, TX, pg. 552
Humbert, Jose, Sec. & Treas.--Direct Press Modern Litho Corporation, Huntington Station, NY, pg. 339
Humphreys, Robert K., Sec. & Treas.--Valley Detroit Diesel Allison, City of Industry, CA, pg. 1143
Hunger, John E., Chief Fin. Officer & Treas.--World Shipping, Inc., Lakewood, OH, pg. 1203
Hunt, Bill, Sec. & Treas.--Keith Smith Farms, Inc., Hot Springs, AR, pg. 1012
Hunt, William, V.P. & Treas.--C.E.M. Div. Spirol Intl. Corp., Danielson, CT, pg. 1031
Hunter, Renee, Treas.--American Systems Engineering Corporation, Virginia Beach, VA, pg. 981
Hunter, Timothy, Treas.--McInnes Steel Company, Corry, PA, pg. 729
Hureau, Philip H., Exec. V.P., Treas.--McDougall Associates, Inc., Peabody, MA, pg. 728
Hutson, Richard D., V.P. & Asst. Treas.--North Pacific Lumber Company, Portland, OR, pg. 813
Hutter, Marilyn, Treas.--Industrial Metals Of The South, New Orleans, LA, pg. 566
Hutton, Nancy, Sec., Treas. & Controller--Crustbuster, Inc., Dodge City, KS, pg. 303
Hyde, Douglas W., Sr. V.P., Asst. Sec. & Mng. Princpial-HTB/WDC--HTB, Inc., Oklahoma City, OK, pg. 497
Hyde, Kenneth R., Jr., Exec. V.P., Chief Opers. Officer & Treas.--Hackney Brothers, Inc., Wilson, NC, pg. 498
Hyland, Richard, Treas.--The Vanguard Group, Inc., Wayne, PA, pg. 1145
Hyland, Robert J., Chief Fin. Officer & Treas.--Barclay White Incorporated, Berwyn, PA, pg. 119
Hyman, David, Treas.--Smarty Pants N Tops Too, Inc., City of Industry, CA, pg. 1011
Hymas, Scott L., Treas.--R.C. Willey Home Furnishings, Salt Lake City, UT, pg. 1190
Hyzy, Brian, Controller--Hammacher, Schlemmer & Co., Inc., Chicago, IL, pg. 503
Iacovelli, David, Sec. & Treas.--Chef Italia, Inc., Vestal, NY, pg. 241
Ianello, Angelo, V.P.-Fin. & Treas.--Contract Freighters, Inc., Joplin, MO, pg. 280
Ibsen, Dr. Robert, Chm. Bd., Pres., Chief Exec. Officer & Treas.--Den-Mat Corporation, Santa Maria, CA, pg. 328
Iglar, Michael J., Treas.--Brad Foote Gear Works, Inc., Cicero, IL, pg. 169
Ilitch, Marian, Sec. & Treas.--Little Caesar Enterprises, Inc., Detroit, MI, pg. 678
Imperia, Joseph, Sec. & Treas.--Imperia Bros., Inc., Pelham Manor, NY, pg. 563
Ingram, Betty, Sec. & Treas.--B & B Homes Corporation, Casper, WY, pg. 105
Ingram, Glenn, Treas.--Fieldale Corporation, Baldwin, GA, pg. 409
Ingram, Richard, Treas. & Sec.--T. A. Loving Company, Goldsboro, NC, pg. 685
Ioos, George E., Treas. & Sec.--Shipley Oil Company, York, PA, pg. 999
Iorio, Frank, V.P., Treas. & Sec.--Torino Fashions, Inc., New York, NY, pg. 1102
Isaias, Estefano, Treas.--Republic National Bank Of Miami, Miami, FL, pg. 928
Isom, Donna, Treas. & Sec.--Quality Foods Inc., Little Rock, AR, pg. 903
Istre, Keith A., Treas.--Lamar Corporation, Baton Rouge, LA, pg. 652
Itkin, Lawrence, Treas.--Furniture Consultants, New York, NY, pg. 437
Jablonsky, Allan J., Treas. & Controller--Trak International, Inc., Port Washington, WI, pg. 1106
Jackson, Carter, Treas.--Holy Cross Electric Association, Glenwood Springs, CO, pg. 541
Jackson, Jesse, Treas. & Controller--Cumberland-Swan, Inc., Smyrna, TN, pg. 304
Jackson, Richard, Treas. & Chief Fin. Officer--Moorman Mfg. Company, Quincy, IL, pg. 769
Jackson, Robert, V.P. & Treas.--Funk & Wagnalls Corp., Mahwah, NJ, pg. 611
Jackson, Terry, Asst. Treas.--Mary Kay Cosmetics Inc., Dallas, TX, pg. 716
Jackson, Wayne, Treas. & Sec.--G.I. Joe's Inc., Wilsonville, OR, pg. 440
Jacobs, Edward, Treas. & Dir.-Fin. Services--Glico Harmony Foods Corporation, Santa Cruz, CA, pg. 462
Jacobs, Jerry, V.P.-Fin., Treas. & Sec.--Pioneer Aluminum, Inc., Los Angeles, CA, pg. 871
Jacobs, Malcolm, Treas.--Atlantic Plumbing Supply Company, Washington, DC, pg. 95
Jacobs, Wynne, V.P. & Treas.--Southern Farm Bureau Casualty Insurance Company, Ridgeland, MS, pg. 1021
Jacobson, Arnold E., Treas. & Dir.-Data Processing--Goddess Bra Company, East Boston, MA, pg. 464
Jacobson, Harvey, Sec. & Treas.--Glencraft Lingerie, Inc., New York, NY, pg. 462
Jacobson, Mitchell, Pres., Treas. & Chief Exec. Officer--Sid Tool Co. Inc., Plainview, NY, pg. 1002
Jacobson, Phyllis, Treas.--Hallmark Advertising, Inc., Pittsburgh, PA, pg. 501
Jacobson, Robert N., V.P.-Fin., Treas., Sec. & Chief Fin. Officer--The Atlas Construction Co., Stamford, CT, pg. 96
Jacoby, Edwin A., Sr. V.P. & Treas.--United Parcel Service of America, Inc., Atlanta, GA, pg. 1133
Jacquette, R. Preston, Treas.--David A. Bramble, Inc., Chestertown, MD, pg. 171
Jaehn, Carole, Treas.--Goodway Tool Corporation, Stamford, CT, pg. 471
Jaggers, Gene, V.P.-Fin. & Treas.--Crucible Materials Corp., Syracuse, NY, pg. 302
James, David, V.P.-Fin. & Treas.--Joe E. Woods, Inc., Mesa, AZ, pg. 1200
James, David, Sec. & Treas.--Price Woods, Inc., Mesa, AZ, pg. 1200

Corporate Responsibilities Index

Jamieson, Michael A., V.P. & Treas.--Collins & Aikman Group Inc., Santa Monica, CA, pg. 262
Janikies, Margaret R., Treas.--Jan-Co., Inc., Cranston, RI, pg. 589
Jansen, James, V.P. & Treas.--John Fabick Tractor Company, Fenton, MO, pg. 396
Jarchon, Edward R., V.P. & Treas.--Barton-Malow Company, Detroit, MI, pg. 123
Jarchow, Edward R., V.P. & Treas.--Barton-Malow Enterprises, Inc., Southfield, MI, pg. 123
Jardine, Thomas V., V.P.-Legal & Treas.--Atlas Refinery, Newark, NJ, pg. 96
Jarvela, Larry J., V.P.-Fin. & Treas.--Jerome Foods Inc., Barron, WI, pg. 593
Jeanmougin, Paul, Treas.--Mosler Inc., Hamilton, OH, pg. 772
Jeffrey, Bob, Pres., Treas. & New Bus. Contact--Goldsmith/Jeffrey, Inc., New York, NY, pg. 469
Jeffrey, D.J., V.P.-Fin. & Treas.--Idaho Forest Industry, Inc., Coeur D'Alene, ID, pg. 561
Jeffries, B., Treas.--Mellon Corporation, New York, NY, pg. 738
Jehlen, Mary E., Sec. & Treas.--Arkansas Oak Flooring, Pine Bluff, AR, pg. 83
Jeko, Leslie J., V.P.--Chemical Exchange Industries, Houston, TX, pg. 242
Jenc, John E., Treas.--The Bureau of National Affairs, Inc., Washington, DC, pg. 189
Jenkins, Don, Jr., Pres. & Treas.--Athens Paper Co. Inc., Nashville, TN, pg. 93
Jenkins, Gary E., Chief Fin. Officer & Treas.--Academy Insurance Group, Inc., Atlanta, GA, pg. 11
Jenkins, Mary, Sec. & Treas.--Coral Petroleum Corporation, Houston, TX, pg. 285
Jenkins, Raymond H., Pres. & Treas.--Cabana Foods, Inc., Detroit, MI, pg. 206
Jenofsky, Mark, V.P. & Treas.--Struthers-Dunn Inc., Pitman, NJ, pg. 693
Jensen, D.M., Sec. & Treas.--Jensen Electric Company, Reno, NV, pg. 592
Jensen, Gordon E., V.P.-Comptroller, Treas. & Asst. Sec.--Omaha Property & Casualty, Omaha, NE, pg. 779
Jensen, Gordon E., V.P., Treas., Comptroller & Asst. Sec.--Omaha Property & Casualty Co., Omaha, NE, pg. 779
Jensen, Irving F., Jr., Chm., Treas. & Sec.--Irving F. Jensen Co., Inc., Sioux City, IA, pg. 593
Jensen, Jon, Controller & Treas.--Philadelphia Gear Corp., King of Prussia, PA, pg. 866
Jensen, Owen, Treas. & Controller--M. A. Mortenson Company, Minneapolis, MN, pg. 772
Jerneycic, Frank, Sec. & Treas.--F & M Distributors Inc., Warren, MI, pg. 393
Jersky, Stanley, Treas.--Faber, Coe & Gregg, Inc., Secaucus, NJ, pg. 395
Jewell, Doris, V.P.-Fin, Treas. & Sec.--Wholesale Electronic Supply, Dallas, TX, pg. 1188
Jewell, Everett G., Chm. Bd., Pres., Chief Exec. Officer & Treas.--Jewell Building Systems, Dallas, NC, pg. 594
Jimenez, Lita K., V.P. & Treas.--Garvey International, Inc., St. Charles, IL, pg. 444
Jindia, Girish K., Sr. V.P.-Fin., Treas. & Chief Fin. Officer--Advanced Technology, Inc., Reston, VA, pg. 20
Jiritano, Andrew, Tresurer--Acme Visible Records, Crozet, VA, pg. 13
Joanne Gonzalez, Treas.--The Jayme Organization, Inc., Cleveland, OH, pg. 591
Johann, J.E., Treas.--S & C Electric Company, Chicago, IL, pg. 958
Johnsey, Walter, Exec. V.P.-Admin., Chief Fin. Officer & Treas.--Drummond Company, Inc., Jasper, AL, pg. 349
Johnson, Carolyn, Treas.--La Victoria Foods, Inc., City of Industry, CA, pg. 649
Johnson, Chris, Sec. & Treas.--Fritz Co. Inc., Newport, MN, pg. 434
Johnson, Deanne, Treas. & Sec.--Elk Supply Company, Clinton, OK, pg. 376
Johnson, Eunice W., Treas. & Sec.--Johnson Publishing Company, Inc., Chicago, IL, pg. 598
Johnson, George, Treas.--Consolidated Pipe & Supply Company, Birmingham, AL, pg. 277
Johnson, George D., V.P. & Treas.--Ballenger Paving Company, Inc., Taylors, SC, pg. 116
Johnson, Gilbert E., Pres. & Treas.--G. E. Johnson Construction Co., Inc., Colorado Springs, CO, pg. 597
Johnson, Greg A., Treas. & Controller--F.H. Stoltze Land & Lumber Company, Stillwater, MN, pg. 1050
Johnson, James D., V.P. & Treas.--Cox Wood Preserving Co., Orangeburg, SC, pg. 295
Johnson, John B., Pres., Editor & Treas.--Johnson Newspaper Corporation, Watertown, NY, pg. 598
Johnson, Lee R., Chief Fin. Officer--Gator Freightways, Inc., Wilmington, OH, pg. 446
Johnson, Marc D., Treas.--E Z Loader Boat Trailers, Inc., Spokane, WA, pg. 361
Johnson, Michael, Treas.--Alco Properties, Inc., Memphis, TN, pg. 592
Johnson, Michael, V.P.-Fin. & Treas.--Alco Management, Inc., Memphis, TN, pg. 592
Johnson, Patricia M., Dir.-Fin., Treas. & Sec.--Tony Downs Foods Company, Saint James, MN, pg. 348
Johnson, RichardA., V.P.-Fin.--Illinois Auto Electric Co., Elmhurst, IL, pg. 562
Johnson, Robert K., Treas.--Century Furniture Industries, Hickory, NC, pg. 235
Johnson, Roger J., Sr. V.P.-Corp. Info. Services, Chief Fin. Officer & Treas.--Aid Association For Lutherans, Appleton, WI, pg. 26
Johnson, Ronald L., Treas.--Johnson Bros. Corp., Litchfield, MN, pg. 597
Johnson, Terrence M., Dir.-Fin.--Anderson Brothers Construction Brainerd, Brainerd, MN, pg. 72
Johnson, Victor, Chief Fin. Officer, V.P.-Fin. & Treas.--Reinke Manufacturing Co., Inc., Deshler, NE, pg. 924
Johnston, Jack W., Treas.--Primus Inc., Dayton, OH, pg. 890
Johnston, Richard C., Sec. & Treas.--Haden, Inc., Madison Heights, MI, pg. 499
Johnston, Richard C., Sec. & Treas.--Haden Equity, Ltd., Madison Heights, MI, pg. 499
Johnston, Richard C., Sec. & Treas.--Haden Investment, Ltd., Madison Heights, MI, pg. 499
Johnston, Terry, Controller & Treas.--Sioux Manufacturing Corp., Fort Totten, ND, pg. 1008
Joliff, Robert A., Treas.--The Babcock & Wilcox Company, New Orleans, LA, pg. 107
Jones, Alan P., Jr., V.P., Chief Fin. Officer & Treas.--Jones Dairy Farm, Fort Atkinson, WI, pg. 603
Jones, Ben, Vice Chm., Treas. & Chief Fin. Officer--Kasle Steel Corporation, Dearborn, MI, pg. 617
Jones, Carol Ann, Sec. & Treas.--Dealers Electrical Supply Co., Waco, TX, pg. 322
Jones, Charles J., Treas.--Metallurg, Inc., New York, NY, pg. 742
Jones, Dayton A., Treas.--Research Products Corporation, Madison, WI, pg. 928
Jones, Gary, Treas. & Sec.--Rural Electric Co-op, Lindsay, OK, pg. 956
Jones, James H., Treas.--Fannie May Candy Shops, Inc., Chicago, IL, pg. 604
Jones, Kenneth, Exec. V.P., Chief Fin. Officer, Sec. & Treas.--Hatfield Quality Meats, Inc., Hatfield, PA, pg. 517
Jones, Russell B., Sr. V.P.-Fin., Treas., Chief Fin. Officer & Sec.--GranTree Corporation, Beaverton, OR, pg. 477
Jones, Sydney T., III, Pres. & Treas.--Hudson Valley Paper Company, Albany, NY, pg. 551
Joplin, Jean, Treas. & Sec.--Oil & Gas Supply Company, Houston, TX, pg. 823
Jordan, J.E., Jr., Treas.--Young Refining Corp., Douglasville, GA, pg. 1210
Jordan, Leon, Treas. & Controller--Harbor Financial Mortgage Corp., Houston, TX, pg. 506
Joseph, Jerome, Chm. Bd., Pres. & Treas.--Uppco, Inc., Chicago, IL, pg. 1139
Josephs, Albert, V.P. & Treas.--Standard Garment Company, Inc., New York, NY, pg. 1036
Joslin, Roger, Sr. V.P. & Treas.--State Farm Mutual Automobile Insurance Company, Bloomington, IL, pg. 1041
Juanarena, Sue, Treas.--Pressure Systems, Hampton, VA, pg. 888
Jubelirer, Steven W., Treas.--John Reyer Company, Sharon, PA, pg. 930
Judge, Hugh G., Treas.--Longyear Company, Salt Lake City, UT, pg. 682
Jumonville, Francis, Sec. & Treas.--Airtrol, Inc., Baton Rouge, LA, pg. 28
Jurasek, Kris, V.P. & Treas.--Miner Enterprises Inc., Geneva, IL, pg. 756
Jurek, Stephen, Treas.--JFC Inc., Saint Cloud, MN, pg. 584
Kabay, John K., Sr. V.P., Chief Fin. Officer & Treas.--Calvin Klein, Inc., New York, NY, pg. 635
Kahlig, Sandra, Treas. & Sec.--North Park Lincoln Mercury Inc., San Antonio, TX, pg. 813
Kahn, Stanley, V.P., Sec. & Treas.--Croscill, Inc., New York, NY, pg. 300
Kaiser, Van, Exec. V.P., Treas. & Creative Dir.--Rhea & Kaiser Advertising, Inc., Naperville, IL, pg. 930
Kaitz, Miriam Collins, Sec. & Treas.--Palm Beach Beauty Products Co., Minneapolis, MN, pg. 843
Kallen, Thomas E., Chm. Bd. & Treas.--Bake-Line Products, Inc., Des Plaines, IL, pg. 114
Kallmeyer, L.B., Treas.--The Kirk & Blum Mfg. Co., Cincinnati, OH, pg. 633
Kam, Samuel, V.P. & Treas.--Farrar, Straus & Giroux, Inc., New York, NY, pg. 403
Kamm, C.P., Mgr.-Pension Admin. & Risk Mngmt.--Electric Furnace Co., Salem, OH, pg. 373
Kandris, Michael D., Sr. V.P.-Fin. & Treas.--Burlington Motor Carriers Inc., Daleville, IN, pg. 191
Kane, Aranka, Treas.--Sam Kane Beef Processors, Inc., Corpus Christi, TX, pg. 616
Kane, Robert, V.P. & Treas.--Canberra Industries, Inc., Meriden, CT, pg. 213
Kane, William, V.P., Sec., Treas. & Chief Fin. Officer--Molded Fiber Glass Companies, Ashtabula, OH, pg. 763
Kanim, Elvira, Sec. & Treas.--Miss Elliette, Inc., Los Angeles, CA, pg. 760
Kaplan, Leonard D., Chm. & Treas.--Prime Tanning Co., Inc., Berwick, ME, pg. 889
Kaplanek, Rosemary, Sec. & Treas.--Floral Glass & Mirror, Inc., Hauppauge, NY, pg. 420
Kapson, Betty, Sec. & Tres.--Jordan Motors, Inc., Mishawaka, IN, pg. 605
Karp, E., Treas.--L. Karp & Sons, Inc., Elk Grove Village, IL, pg. 617
Karp, Leonard, V.P., Chief Exec. Officer & Treas.--Best Provision Co., Inc., Newark, NJ, pg. 146
Karr, David M., Sec. & Treas.--Norpac Foods, Inc. Cooperative, Stayton, OR, pg. 810
Karsten, Robert W., Vice Chm. & Treas.--Panel Processing, Inc., Alpena, MI, pg. 846
Karwacki, Thomas J., Sec. & Treas.--The Park Circle Motor Co., Baltimore, MD, pg. 848
Kasavan, William, Chief Fin. Analyst--Forecast Mortgage Corporation, Rancho Cucamonga, CA, pg. 423
Kassouf, James, Pres., Chief Exec. Officer & Treas.--Metropolitan Properties Inc., Cleveland, OH, pg. 745
Kastner, Robert, V.P. & Treas.--S.B. Foot Tanning Co., Red Wing, MN, pg. 919
Katz, Morton, V.P. & Treas.--Clay-Park Labs, Inc., Bronx, NY, pg. 253
Katz, S., Sec. & Treas.--Manhattan Store Interiors, Inc., Brooklyn, NY, pg. 704
Katz, Stanley, V.P.-Adv. & Treas.--Stock Yards Packing Co., Inc., Chicago, IL, pg. 1049
Katzenstein, Joseph, Treas.--Philipp Brothers Chemicals, Inc., Fort Lee, NJ, pg. 867
Katzman, Lawrence, Chm. Bd. & Chief Exec. Officer--Kaz, Inc., New York, NY, pg. 619
Kauffman, Britt, Treas.--Hart Graphics Inc., Austin, TX, pg. 513
Kauffman, Jeffery R., Asst. Treas. & Asst. Sec.--Lift-All Co., Inc., Manheim, PA, pg. 675
Kaufmann, Joseph L., Chief Fin. Officer & Treas.--FWD Corporation, Clintonville, WI, pg. 395
Kaufmann, Joseph L., Treas. & Chief Fin. Officer--Seagrave Fire Apparatus, Inc., Clintonville, WI, pg. 395
Kautzman, Edward J., Treas.--Meyer Broadcasting Company, Bismarck, ND, pg. 746
Kavanaugh, Edward F., V.P., Treas., Controller & Mng. Dir.--New Hampshire Oak, Hampton, NH, pg. 800
Kawasaki, Roger, Treas.--Puna Plantation Hawaii Ltd., Hilo, HI, pg. 900
Kay, Walter A., V.P. & Treas.--Vance Publishing Corporation, Lincolnshire, IL, pg. 1144
Kazmierczak, Kenneth J., Treas., Controller & Sec.--Schreier Malting Co., Sheboygan, WI, pg. 978
Kean, James, Comptroller & Treas.--Henderson Electric Co., Inc., Louisville, KY, pg. 529
Kean, Michael G., Asst. Treas.--Allied Mutual Insurance Company, Des Moines, IA, pg. 38
Kearney, George, Exec. V.P. & Treas.--Northwestern Industrial Piping, Niles, IL, pg. 815
Keating, Paul J., II, Dir.-Sls. & Mktg. & Treas.--P.J. Keating Company, Lunenburg, MA, pg. 619
Kedrowski, Len W., Chief Fin. Officer, Treas. & Controller--Andersen Windows Inc., Bayport, MN, pg. 72
Keegan, R.Y., Treas.--Tri-Chem, Inc., Harrison, NJ, pg. 1110
Keeler, Alexander, Pres. & Treas.--Keller Motor Car Company, Inc., Latham, NY, pg. 621
Keeler, Robert D., V.P.-Fin. & Treas.--Cuplex, Inc., Garland, TX, pg. 305
Keene, Robert A., Chm. Bd., Sec. & Treas.--John Roberts Company, Minneapolis, MN, pg. 938
Keener, J.W., Jr., Pres., Chief Exec. Officer & Treas.--The Chardon Rubber Co., Chardon, OH, pg. 239
Kees, Ray, Chief Fin. Officer, Corp. Sec. & Tres.--Gem-Dandy, Inc., Madison, NC, pg. 447
Kehoe, Gerard, V.P. & Treas.--Dancker, Sellew & Douglas, Inc., New York, NY, pg. 314
Keilman, David W., Treas. & Controller--Comark, Bloomingdale, IL, pg. 267
Kelleher, Joseph, Treas.--Candle Corporation of America, Oshkosh, WI, pg. 214
Keller, Chris, Controller & Treasurer--Darda Inc. (USA), Baltimore, MD, pg. 315
Keller, James E., Treas. & Controller--Rapid Mounting & Finishing Co., Chicago, IL, pg. 913
Keller, Joe, Treas.--Blue Bird Coach Lines Inc., Olean, NY, pg. 158
Keller, John, Chm. & Treas.--Meadville Forging Co., Meadville, PA, pg. 733
Keller, Thomas C., Treas. & Sec.--Schad Industries, Inc., Lafayette, LA, pg. 974
Keller, Thomas C., Treas. & Sec.--Lou Ana Foods, Inc., Opelousas, LA, pg. 974
Kelley, Joseph G., Jr., Pres., Treas. & Chief Fin. Officer--Jordan's Meats, Portland, ME, pg. 605
Kelley, Nancy, V.P.-Fin.--Executive Car Leasing Company, Los Angeles, CA, pg. 393
Kellhofer, Don, Sec. & Treas.--Efco Corporation, Monett, MO, pg. 359
Kellogg, Charles T., Pres., Chief Exec. Officer & Treas.--Hubbard Hall Inc., Waterbury, CT, pg. 549
Kelly, Don, Chief Fin. Officer & Treas.--KSG Inc., Guntersville, AL, pg. 613
Kelly, Michael, Sr. V.P., Treas.--N W Ayer Inc., New York, NY, pg. 104
Kelly, Michael J., Sr. V.P. & Treas.--N W Ayer Incorporated, New York, NY, pg. 103
Kelly, Paul, Chief Fin. Officer & Treas.--Quaker Fabric Corporation, Fall River, MA, pg. 903
Kelly, Tricia, Treasury Analyst--Ivex Packaging Corporation, Lincolnshire, IL, pg. 583
Kenneally, Jennifer, Asst. Treas. & Mgr.-Treas. Services--Golub Corporation, Schenectady, NY, pg. 469
Kennedy, Brian A., V.P. & Treas.--Blue Cross & Blue Shield of Illinois, Chicago, IL, pg. 160
Kennedy, Charles G., Treas.--Henley Paper Company, Greensboro, NC, pg. 529
Kennedy, Karen S., Chm. Bd., Pres., Treas. & New Bus. Contact--KSK Communications, Ltd., Vienna, VA, pg. 613
Kennedy, T.N., V.P. & Treas.--Matthews International Corp., Pittsburgh, PA, pg. 721
Kennell, Gerald, V.P. & Treas.--Avis, Inc., Garden City, NY, pg. 102
Kenny, James C., Pres. & Chief Exec. Officer--Harbour Industries, Inc., Shelburne, VT, pg. 507
Keolker, Ronald H., Chief Fin. Officer, V.P., Treas. & Controller--Twin City Foods, Inc., Stanwood, WA, pg. 1122
Kerley, Marsha L., Treas. & Asst. Sec.--Peterson Builders, Inc., Sturgeon Bay, WI, pg. 864
Kern, Edward B., Treas.--WGM Safety Corporation, Reading, PA, pg. 1156
Kersten, Walt, Treas.--Golden State Foods Corp., Pasadena, CA, pg. 466
Ketsdever, Matthew, Treas.--Service Assets Corp., Newport Beach, CA, pg. 179
Keuler, Lloyd J., Treas. & Sec.--Turner Supply Company, Mobile, AL, pg. 1119
Keyes, T.L., Asst. Treas. & Admin. Asst.--Mississippi Valley Gas Co., Jackson, MS, pg. 1208
Khim, Millie, Treas.--JWK International Corp., Annandale, VA, pg. 586
Khoury, E.R., Treas. & Controller--Morrison Textile Machinery Co., Fort Lawn, SC, pg. 771
Khoury, Richel G., Vice Chm., Sec. & Treas.--Pacific Scene Inc., San Diego, CA, pg. 841

Kiburz, William L., V.P. & Treas.--American Tool Companies, Inc., Lincoln, NE, pg. 64
Kick, John V., Treas. & Sec.--Barr Brothers & Co., Inc., New York, NY, pg. 121
Kieffer, D.A., Sec./Treas.--GWC Properties, Inc., Portland, OR, pg. 727
Kieffer, D.A., V.P.-Fin., Sec. & Treas.--McCall Oil & Chemical Corp., Portland, OR, pg. 726
Kieffer, D.A., Sec./Treas.--McCall Properties, Inc., Portland, OR, pg. 727
Kieffer, D.A., Sec. & Treas.--McCall Oil Real Estate Corporation, Portland, OR, pg. 727
Kilgannon, Memma S., Sec. & Treas.--Amkor Electronics, Inc., West Chester, PA, pg. 67
Kilguss, Howard K., Chm. Bd., Pres. & Treas.--Excell Manufacturing Company, Providence, RI, pg. 392
Kim, Kenneth H., Chm., Pres., Chief Exec. Officer, Corp. Sec. & Treas.--Medieval Dinner & Tournament, Inc., Buena Park, CA, pg. 735
Kimball, L. Robert, Pres. & Treas.--L. Robert Kimball & Associates, Ebensburg, PA, pg. 629
King, F., Sec. & Treas.--Baird Ray Nissan, Inc., Longwood, FL, pg. 114
King, Harvey, Vice Chm., Fin. & Sec.--Brookshire Grocery, Tyler, TX, pg. 180
King, John, Sec. & Treas.--Greenway Co-Op Service, Rochester, MN, pg. 485
King, Lawrence E., Treas.--King Fuels Inc., Troy, NY, pg. 630
King, Mark C., V.P.-Fin. & Treas.--The Pantry, Inc., Sanford, NC, pg. 846
King, Paul L., Exec. V.P.-Fin. & Treas.--American Family Mutual Insurance Co., Madison, WI, pg. 51
King, William O., Treas.--King Industries, Inc., Norwalk, CT, pg. 630
Kinkade, Wallace R., Sec. & Treas.--Nashville Machine Co. Inc., Nashville, TN, pg. 784
Kinneson, Danny, Sec. & Treas.--DBM Hatch, Inc., El Monte, CA, pg. 308
Kinning, Rick L., Pres. & Treas.--RK Mechanical, Inc., Lakewood, CO, pg. 907
Kintz, Bob, Treas.--Breckenridge Material Company, Saint Louis, MO, pg. 173
Kinzer, Donald M., Treas.--Old Dominion Life Insurance Co., Roanoke, VA, pg. 997
Kinzly, Robert E., Pres. & Treas.--Scipar, Buffalo, NY, pg. 982
Kirby, Shelby J., Chief Fin. Officer, Treas. & Controller--T.S. Ragsdale Company, Incorporated, Lake City, SC, pg. 910
Kirk, J., Sec. & Treas.--Exact Equipment Corporation, Langhorne, PA, pg. 392
Kirkpatrick, J. Mark, Treas.--Redman Industries, Inc., Dallas, TX, pg. 919
Kirkwood, Jaimie, V.P. & Treas.--IDAB International Incorporated, Hampton, VA, pg. 559
Kiser, Jimmy, V.P.-Fin.--Kesterson Food Company, Inc., Paris, TN, pg. 624
Kistler, Fred L., V.P. & Treas.--Meijer, Inc., Grand Rapids, MI, pg. 737
Kitchens, Orman L., Treas. & Controller--Capeletti Bros., Inc., Miami Lakes, FL, pg. 214
Kittredge, Charles C., Treas.--National Life Insurance Company, Montpelier, VT, pg. 791
Kitz, Edward G., V.P. & Treas.--Roundy's, Inc., Pewaukee, WI, pg. 952
Klaasen, John, Chief Fin. Officer, V.P.-Fin. & Treas.--DoAll Company, Des Plaines, IL, pg. 341
Klas, William L., Sec. & Treas.--Tapemark, West St. Paul, MN, pg. 1078
Klaszky, Carl W., Sec. & Treas.--A.N. Deringer, Inc., Saint Albans, VT, pg. 331
Kleczka, John, Sr. V.P.-Fin. & Treas.--Bradley Corporation, Menomonee Falls, WI, pg. 170
Klein, Bernard, Chm. Bd., Sec. & Treas.--Alaron Inc., Troy, MI, pg. 30
Klein, Jonas B., Pres. & Treas.--Eastland Shoe Manufacturing Corporation, Freeport, ME, pg. 364
Klein, Martin, Sec. & Treas.--Plascal Corporation, Farmingdale, NY, pg. 874
Klein, Richard I., Treas.--Amtrak-National Railroad Passenger Corp., Washington, DC, pg. 69
Kleinmanns, Robert, V.P., Sec. & Treas.--The Economics Press, Inc., Fairfield, NJ, pg. 367
Klusendorf, James R., V.P. & Treas.--The C. P. Hall Company, Chicago, IL, pg. 501
Knaebel, Richard L., Treas.--Mid-Am Building Supply, Inc., Moberly, MO, pg. 749
Knauss, E. William, Pres., Chief Oper. Officer & Treas.--E.W. Knauss & Son, Inc., Quakertown, PA, pg. 636
Knedlik, Ronald, Chief Fin. Officer, Treas. & Sec.--Alex Lee, Inc., Hickory, NC, pg. 33
Kneissl, William L., Sr. V.P., Sec. & Treas.--The Troy Savings Bank, Troy, NY, pg. 1116
Knight, Robert B., Sr. V.P.-Admin. & Treas.--White Hen Pantry, Inc., Elmhurst, IL, pg. 1185
Knispel, Isabel, Treas. & Sec.--Arrow Fastener Co., Inc., Saddle Brook, NJ, pg. 85
Knoss, Bernice B., Treas.--School Apparel, Inc., San Francisco, CA, pg. 978
Knox, Richard, Exec. V.P., Sec. & Treas.--Knox Oil of Texas Inc., Dallas, TX, pg. 638
Knueven, Gerald R., Chief Fin. Officer, Treas. & Controller--Harold M. Pitman Co., Inc., Totowa, NJ, pg. 872
Kobulsky, Joseph, Treas.--The Phillips Agency, Horsham, PA, pg. 867
Koch, Elizabeth, Treas.--Plywood Plastics Inc., Buffalo, NY, pg. 878
Koch, G. Fred, Pres. & Treas.--Plywood Plastics Inc., Buffalo, NY, pg. 878
Koch, Jerome, Treas. & Sec.--Miles Sand & Gravel Company, Auburn, WA, pg. 753
Kochannek, Juergen, Sr. V.P. & Treas.--Fru-Con Construction Corporation, Ballwin, MO, pg. 435
Kocourek, Edward J., V.P., Sec. & Treas.--Egan Cos., Minneapolis, MN, pg. 371
Koehn, Donald L., Exec. V.P., Treas. & Sec.--Bradbury Company, Inc., Moundridge, KS, pg. 169
Koffman, Burton, Pres. & Treas.--Ben Arnold Co., Inc., Binghamton, NY, pg. 84
Koffman, Milton, Exec. V.P., Sec. & Treas.--Great American Industries, Inc., Vestal, NY, pg. 480
Kogen, Howard, V.P. & Treas.--JMB Realty Corporation, Chicago, IL, pg. 584
Kogod, Marvin, Treas. & Sec.--Maurice Electric Supply Company, Washington, DC, pg. 722
Kogovsek, Conrad J., Treas.--Keystone Carbon Company, Saint Marys, PA, pg. 628
Kohl, Edwin J., Dir.-Fin.--Electro-Science Laboratories, Inc., King of Prussia, PA, pg. 375
Kohlscheen, Russel, Sec. & Treas.--Allen Samuels Chevrolet GEO, Waco, TX, pg. 969
Kohn, Herbert, Treas. & Gen. Counsel--Bernstein-Rein Advertising, Inc., Kansas City, MO, pg. 144
Kolesar, Michael, Treas.--Gartner Group, Inc., Stamford, CT, pg. 443
Kolikof, Robert A., Pres., Chief Exec. Officer & Chief Oper. Officer--Prudential Metal Supply Corp., East Dedham, MA, pg. 898
Kolish, Thomas E., V.P. & Treas.--Thomas & Skinner, Inc., Indianapolis, IN, pg. 1093
Kolkhorst, Steven, V.P., Sec. & Treas.--Hussey Corporation, North Berwick, ME, pg. 555
Koller, Marie, Treas. & Sec.--Koller Enterprises, Inc., Fenton, MO, pg. 641
Konas, Theodore V., Controller & Asst. Treas.--Yerger Bros., Inc., Lititz, PA, pg. 1208
Kondritzer, Gerald R., V.P. & Treas.--Chiquita Brands International, Inc., Cincinnati, OH, pg. 53
Konn-McCormick, Susan, Treas.--SI Holdings Inc., New York, NY, pg. 962
Kontich, Michael J., Chief Fin. Officer & Treas.--Leupold & Stevens, Inc., Beaverton, OR, pg. 669
Koosed, Gentille, Treas.--H W Electronics, Inc., Van Nuys, CA, pg. 497
Kopitke, Robert, Treas.--TST/Impreso, Inc., Coppell, TX, pg. 1075
Kopp, Joseph T., Treas. & Sec.--Massman Construction Company, Kansas City, MO, pg. 719
Korber, Libby, Controller, Treas. & Sec.--J. Korber & Company, Albuquerque, NM, pg. 641
Korpela, Richard A., Sr. V.P., Sec. & Treas.--Lynden Incorporated, Seattle, WA, pg. 689
Korrafel, Peter, Sec. & Treas.--Carquest Corporation, Tarrytown, NY, pg. 224
Kosek, Dave, Treas. & Sec.--Asplundh Tree Expert Co., Willow Grove, PA, pg. 88
Koshiba, Mike, Treas.--Pioneer Communications of America, Upper Saddle River, NJ, pg. 871
Kostek, J.R., V.P., Sec. & Treas.--Kelso-Burnett Company, Rolling Meadows, IL, pg. 622
Koval, Thomas J., Treas. & Controller--Radiator Specialty Company, Charlotte, NC, pg. 909
Kovalefsky, Edward W., Asst. Treas.--Global Insurance Company, Houston, TX, pg. 662
Kowaleski, David L., Treas.--American Baler Co., Bellevue, OH, pg. 102
Kowaluk, R.S., Pres.--Evans Adhesive Corp., Columbus, OH, pg. 390
Kozlowski, Edward C., Treas.--ACR Industries Inc., Mount Clemens, MI, pg. 2
Kozma, M.J., Treas. & Controller--Maxitrol Co., Southfield, MI, pg. 723
Kramer, Cynthia S., Comptroller & Treas.--Seabrook Brothers & Sons, Inc., Seabrook, NJ, pg. 984
Kramer, Robert, Pres. & Treas.--John H. Graham & Co., Inc., Oradell, NJ, pg. 475
Kramer, Worth A., V.P., Treas. & Corp. Sec.--Watlow Electric Manufacturing Company, Saint Louis, MO, pg. 1167
Kramme, Richard G., V.P. & Treas.--Ace Glass Incorporated, Vineland, NJ, pg. 11
Krantz, John F., Chief Exec. Officer & Treas.--Adventure Lands of America, Inc., Des Moines, IA, pg. 21
Krause, Peter, Treas.--Carhartt, Inc., Dearborn, MI, pg. 220
Krauss, Helen, Sec. & Treas.--Spartan International, Holt, MI, pg. 1026
Krausz, K.J., Treas.--CHEMCENTRAL Corporation, Bedford Park, IL, pg. 241
Kreisman, Herbert, Chm. Bd. & Treas.--Advance Mechanical Systems, Inc., Elk Grove Village, IL, pg. 19
Kreiter, Ned, Chief Oper. Officer, Treas. & Gen. Mgr.--Castcraft Industries, Inc., Skokie, IL, pg. 228
Krejca, Jack E., Treas.--Curran Contracting Co., Crystal Lake, IL, pg. 305
Kremin, Alan F., Treas.--The Inland Group, Inc., Oak Brook, IL, pg. 570
Krempa, Robert W., V.P. & Treas.--John Hancock Networking Insurance Agency, Boston, MA, pg. 596
Kremsdorf, Wendy, Treas.--Gusso Manufacturing, Inc., Brooklyn, NY, pg. 495
Krengel, Barry M., V.P.-Fin. & Treas.--Fairbanks Morse Pump Corporaton, Kansas City, KS, pg. 397
Kretschmer, William, V.P. & Chief Fin. Officer--Save Mart Supermarkets, Modesto, CA, pg. 973
Kreuger, Wes, Treas.--Superior Graphite Company, Chicago, IL, pg. 1063
Krihak, Paul R., Pres. & Treas.--Holbrook Lumber Company, Albany, NY, pg. 538
Kristal, Samuel, Treas.--Key Food Stores Co-operative, Inc., Brooklyn, NY, pg. 626
Kromer, Dennis R., Chief Fin. Officer, Treas. & Controller--Dunn-Edwards Corporation, Los Angeles, CA, pg. 353
Kronenberger, Robert, Chief Fin. Officer, Sr. V.P. & Treas.--Petty Company, Inc., Effingham, IL, pg. 866
Kronfeld, Fred N., Chief Exec. & Chief Fin. Officer & Treas.--Spirite Industries, Inc., Englewood, NJ, pg. 1031
Krucks, Kenneth R., Asst. Treas.--Rauland-Borg Corporation, Skokie, IL, pg. 914
Krucks, William, Chm. Bd. & Pres.--Rauland-Borg Corporation, Skokie, IL, pg. 914
Krueger, Robert A., Pres., Chief Exec. Officer & Treas.--Tri-Mark Metal Corp., Detroit, MI, pg. 1110
Krugman, James, V.P. & Treas.--QEI, Inc., Springfield, NJ, pg. 902
Krugman, Mark, Chief Fin. Officer, V.P. & Treas.--Lee National Corporation, New York, NY, pg. 666
Krull, Charles, Treas.--Albert Trostel Packings, Ltd., Lake Geneva, WI, pg. 1116
Krull, Charles D., Treas.--Albert Trostel & Sons Co., West Allis, WI, pg. 1116
Krull, Charles D., V.P. & Treas.--Albert Trostel & Sons Company, Milwaukee, WI, pg. 1116
Kruml, Robert J., Chief Fin. Officer & Treas.--Health America/CapitalCare, Inc., Lincoln, NE, pg. 779
Krush, Terrence, Treas.--General Binding Corporation, Northbrook, IL, pg. 656
Kuban, William G., Pres., Chief Exec. Officer & Treas.--Kurt Manufacturing Co. Inc., Fridley, MN, pg. 646
Kuhlman, Mike, Treas.--Argiland Company, Byron, MN, pg. 81
Kuk, Tom, Treas.--Clayton, Williams & Sherwood, Inc., Newport Beach, CA, pg. 254
Kummer, Fred S., Chm., Pres., Chief Exec. Officer, Treas. & Founder--HBE Corporation, Saint Louis, MO, pg. 495
Kundert, Thomas G., Treas.--Anschutz Corporation, Denver, CO, pg. 75
Kunihara, O., Treas.--KYB Corporation of America, Lombard, IL, pg. 613
Kuntzler, Paul, Treas.--D.C. Lottery & Charitable Games Control Board, Washington, DC, pg. 308
Kunzman, Joe, V.P. & Treas.--G. Leblanc Corporation, Kenosha, WI, pg. 665
Kurdziel, Theodore, V.P.-Prod. & Treas.--Kurdziel Industries, Inc., Muskegon, MI, pg. 646
Kurtz, Dean, Treas. & Sec.--Midwest Tire & Muffler, Inc., Rapid City, SD, pg. 752
Kurtz, Stephen, Sec. & Treas.--Kulite Semiconductor Products, Inc., Leonia, NJ, pg. 646
Kurucz, Donald M., V.P. & Treas.--Walter Industries, Inc., Tampa, FL, pg. 1161
Kusche, Herbert R., Exec. V.P. & Treas.--Rich Products Corp., Buffalo, NY, pg. 932
Kusiak, Phil, Treas. & Sec.--Marsh Furniture Company, High Point, NC, pg. 714
Kusler, Kim, Controller--Joel Goldstein Marketing Communications, Santa Monica, CA, pg. 469
Kutner, Ben, Chief Fin. Officer, Treas. & Sec.--VATEX America, Inc., Richmond, VA, pg. 1141
Kutsop, Joseph, Treas.--Affiliated Food Distributors, Scranton, PA, pg. 23
Kutys, James, Sec., Treas. & Controller--IA Construction Corp., Concordville, PA, pg. 558
LaBarba, James A., Treas.--American Produce & Vegetable Co., Dallas, TX, pg. 59
Lablond, Ann, Dir.-Fin.--Clifford Metal, Providence, RI, pg. 658
Labowe, Ronald, Sec. & Treas.--Trend Offset Printing Services, Los Alamitos, CA, pg. 1109
Lacy, Roane, Jr., Chief Exec. Officer--Plantation Foods Inc., Waco, TX, pg. 874
Laddin, Howard, Sec., Treas.--Laddin & Company, Inc., New York, NY, pg. 650
LaDue, Jack W., Pres. & Treas.--Gas Equipment Company, Inc., Dallas, TX, pg. 444
Lagrange, Webber, Treas.--HP Direct, Indianapolis, IN, pg. 497
Lahr, Angela, Treas, Controller, Chief Exec. & Fin. Officer--CAC Microcircuits, Inc., Mount Carmel, IL, pg. 198
Laine, R., Pres., Chief Fin. Officer & Treas.--Telechron, Inc., Ashland, MA, pg. 1085
Lair, Raleigh, Treas.--Block Distributing Company, San Antonio, TX, pg. 157
Laird, James Jr., Treas.--Nationwide Financial Services, Inc., Columbus, OH, pg. 795
Laird, Marg E., Sec. & Treas.--Blockhouse Co., Inc., Red Lion, PA, pg. 157
Lalor, Michael, Treas.--State Industries Inc., Ashland City, TN, pg. 1041
LaMarche, Gary D., Treas. & Controller--Welco Lumber Company, Marysville, WA, pg. 1175
Lamb, Dwight, Jr., V.P., Treas. & Production Mgr.-Post--Benjamin Franklin Literary & Medical Society, Inc., Indianapolis, IN, pg. 139
Lamb, Isabelle S., Chm. Bd., Pres. & Treas.--Enterprises International Inc., Hoquiam, WA, pg. 382
Lamb, Janice B., Sec. & Treas.--Lamb Engineering & Construction Co., Salt Lake City, UT, pg. 652
Lancaster, J. Thomas, V.P. & Treas.--Western & Southern Life Insurance Co., Cincinnati, OH, pg. 1181
Lancaster, Tom, Treas. & Sec.--Atex Oil Co. of Texas, Inc., Amarillo, TX, pg. 93
Lancaster, Tom, Treas. & Sec.--Bell Gas, Inc., Roswell, NM, pg. 134
Lancaster, Wallace, Sec. & Treas.--Crown Buick, Inc., Metairie, LA, pg. 302
Landgraf, Jeanne, Asst. Treas.--Korman Co., Trevose, PA, pg. 642
Landrigan, Dan, V.P. & Treas.--The Medical Protective Company, Fort Wayne, IN, pg. 735
Langer, David, Pres., Chief Exec. & Chief Oper. Officer & Treas.--David Langer & Co., Inc., Hollywood, CA, pg. 657
Langley, W.B., Treas.--Electric Power Equipment Co., Columbus, OH, pg. 373
Langman, Allen, Sr. V.P. & Treas.--Arnhold and S. Bleichroeder, Inc., New York, NY, pg. 84
Langner, Tom, Dir.-Creative & Sls. Promo.--Grant/Jacoby, Inc., Chicago, IL, pg. 477
Lanterman, A., Kirk, Treas. & Sec.--Usibelli Coal Mine, Inc., Healy, AK, pg. 1140

Corporate Responsibilities Index

Lanuti, Joseph E., V.P.-Fin. & Treas.--Lettuce Entertain You Enterprises, Inc., Chicago, IL, pg. 668
Lape, Robert M., Pres. & Treas.--Neer Manufacturing Company, Lexington, OH, pg. 797
LaPeters, Norman, Treas.--Burton-Dixie of Blacksburg Inc., Blacksburg, SC, pg. 200
Lapin, Philip L., Asst. Sec. & Asst. Treas.--Barton Brands, Ltd., Chicago, IL, pg. 123
Lapin, Philip L., Asst. Sec. & Asst. Treas.--Barton Beers, Ltd., Chicago, IL, pg. 123
LaPorte, Milton G., V.P. & Treas.--Brance Krachy Company, Inc., Houston, TX, pg. 171
Large, Robert O., V.P.-Fin., Sec. & Treas.--International Cold Storage Co., Inc., Andover, KS, pg. 576
Larkin, Linda, Treas.--North Shore Movers, Northbrook, IL, pg. 813
LaRocca, John Steven, Treas. & Sec.--Roberts Foods, Inc., Springfield, IL, pg. 938
Larr, James D., V.P.-Fin. & Treas.--Atlas Lederer Co., Cleveland, OH, pg. 265
Larr, James D., V.P.-Fin. & Treas.--Columbia Iron & Metal Co., Cleveland, OH, pg. 265
Larr, James D., V.P.-Fin. & Treas.--Grant Steel Corp., Pittsburgh, PA, pg. 265
Larr, James D., V.P.-Fin. & Treas.--The Universal Steel Co., Cleveland, OH, pg. 265
Larsen, Tom, Treas.--Todd & Sargent, Inc., Ames, IA, pg. 1100
Larson, Bruce, Treas.--Meyocks Benkstein Associates, Des Moines, IA, pg. 746
Larson, Janet, Treas. & Sec.--United A G Co-op, Inc., Omaha, NE, pg. 1130
Larson, Karen, Treas.--Cowles Media Company, Minneapolis, MN, pg. 291
Larson, Larry, Chief Fin. Officer, Treas., Sec. & Controller--Holmquist Grain & Lumber Co., Oakland, NE, pg. 540
Larson, Patricia, Treas.--Larson Manufacturing Company, Brookings, SD, pg. 659
Laubach, E. Randall, V.P.-Fin., Chief Fin. Officer, Treas. & Admin.--The Crystal Tissue Co., Middletown, OH, pg. 303
Lauder, R. William, Treas. & Controller--Concrete Construction Company, Columbus, OH, pg. 273
Laulhere, Larry, Sec. & Treas.--Hood Corporation, Whittier, CA, pg. 542
Laurent, Louise, Treas. & Sec.--Custom Pak, Inc., Clinton, IA, pg. 306
Lavidge, Arthur W., Pres. & Treas.--Lavidge & Associates Inc., Knoxville, TN, pg. 661
Lavigne, Laurier J., Treas.--Finch, Pruyn & Co., Inc., Glens Falls, NY, pg. 410
Law, Betty J., V.P.-Treas. & Sec.--Broadcast Supply West, Tacoma, WA, pg. 177
Law, Carol, Treas.--Hygeia Dairy Co., Inc., Harlingen, TX, pg. 557
Lawrence, Albert W., Treas.--Lawrence Group, Inc., Schenectady, NY, pg. 662
Lawrence, Craig, V.P., Sec. & Treas.--Lawrence & Schiller, Inc., Sioux Falls, SD, pg. 663
Lay, Betty, Sec. & Treas.--San Angelo Electric Service Company, San Angelo, TX, pg. 969
Lay, F. Edwin, Jr., Chief Fin. Officer & Treas.--Lay Packing Company Inc., Knoxville, TN, pg. 663
Laybourne, Linda, Treas. & Chief Fin. Officer--Sues, Young & Brown Inc., Baldwin Park, CA, pg. 1056
Leasure, George, Pres., Chief Exec. & Chief Fin. Officer & Treas.--Ghent Manufacturing, Inc., Lebanon, OH, pg. 455
Leavitt, Julian, Chm. Bd., Pres., Chief Exec. Officer & Treas.--Sweetlife Foods, Inc., Suffield, CT, pg. 1067
Lebens, Jeffrey K., V.P., Treas. & Chief Fin. Officer--Intermountain Industries, Inc., Boise, ID, pg. 575
Lebens, Jeffrey K., Sr. V.P.-Fin., Admin. & Treas.--Intermountain Gas Co., Boise, ID, pg. 575
Lebens, Jeffrey K., V.P., Treas. & Chief Fin. Officer--IGI Resources, Inc., Boise, ID, pg. 575
Lee, David, V.P., Treas., Sec. & Controller--Dinwiddie Construction Co., San Francisco, CA, pg. 338
Lee, Jeanne Marie, Sec. & Treas.--Lakeside Industries, Redmond, WA, pg. 651
Lee, John, Jr., Pres. & Treas.--Ireland Coffee Tea, Inc., Pleasantville, NJ, pg. 582
Lee, Mei, Treas., Controller & Chief Fin. Officer--Ronald Hsu Construction, Capitol Heights, MD, pg. 548
Lee, Robert H., Sec. & Treas.--Wagstaff Inc., Spokane, WA, pg. 1158
Leeds, Teresa, Treas.--Jewelmont Corporation, Minneapolis, MN, pg. 594
Leef, Donald N., V.P., Chief Fin. Officer & Treas.--BIW Cable Systems, Inc., North Dighton, MA, pg. 106
Leef, Ruth L., Treas. & Sec.--Industrial Towel & Uniform, New Berlin, WI, pg. 567
Leenerts, G.R., Gen. Mgr. & Treas.--Hopkinsville Elevator Company, Inc., Hopkinsville, KY, pg. 543
Leeti, John A., V.P. & Treas.--Knouse Foods Inc., Peach Glen, PA, pg. 637
Leffler, Darryl, Treas. & Asst. Sec.--National Cooperative Refinery Association, McPherson, KS, pg. 787
Leffler, Donald, Treas. & Sec.--Redburn Tire Company, Phoenix, AZ, pg. 919
Leffler, Dorothy, Treas.--T O Plastics, Inc., Minneapolis, MN, pg. 1074
Leffler, Georgiana E., Treas.--Carlos R. Leffler Inc., Richland, PA, pg. 666
Lefkovits, Bernard, Treas.--Roselle Paper Co., Inc., Roselle, NJ, pg. 948
Lehman, Harold L., V.P. & Treas.--Chicago Holdings, Inc., Pittsburgh, PA, pg. 245
Lehman, Jonathan E., Pres. & Treas.--Georgian Press, Inc., New York, NY, pg. 453
Lehmann, Ralph, Treas. & Controller--Barq's, Inc., New Orleans, LA, pg. 121
Lehrmitt, Susan, Treas.--Jack Lenor Larsen, Inc., New York, NY, pg. 659
Lempke, R. Michael, Treas.--Fort Howard Corporation, Green Bay, WI, pg. 425
Lenhart, Miles L., V.P.-Fin., Treas. & Sec.--Reeves Southeastern Corporation, Tampa, FL, pg. 921
Lenschow, William, Treas.--Associated Milk Producers, Inc., San Antonio, TX, pg. 91
Leonard, Craig, Treas. & Sec.--Associated Company, Inc., Wichita, KS, pg. 89
Leone, William, Sr. V.P. & Treas.--Topa Insurance Company, Los Angeles, CA, pg. 1101
Leong, Edith, Treas. & Sec.--Mutual Distributors Ltd., Honolulu, HI, pg. 778
Lesh, Charles P., Chm., Pres. & Treas.--Holcomb & Hoke Mfg. Company, Inc., Indianapolis, IN, pg. 538
Lester, Sandy, Sec.-Treas.--First Abilene Bankshares, Inc., Abilene, TX, pg. 411
Letica, Gudrun, Sec. & Treas.--Letica Corporation, Rochester Hills, MI, pg. 668
Levin, Louis M., Pres. & Treas.--Midwest Petroleum Co., Saint Louis, MO, pg. 752
Levine, Paul, Treas.--Magnetic Analysis Corp., Mount Vernon, NY, pg. 700
Levins, E.E., Treas.--Credit Union National Association, Madison, WI, pg. 298
Levit, Gerald, Sec. & Treas.--Grocers Supply Co. Inc., Houston, TX, pg. 488
Levitan, Edward N., Sr. V.P.-Fin & Admin.--Costa Cruise Lines, N.V., Miami, FL, pg. 288
Levy, Edward C., Jr., Pres. & Treas.--Edward C. Levy Co., Inc., Detroit, MI, pg. 672
Levy, Steven A., Exec. V.P. & Treas.--Titan Industrial Corp., New York, NY, pg. 1099
Lewis, Edwin A., V.P. & Treas.--The Hearst Corporation, New York, NY, pg. 521
Lewis, Fred H., Pres. & Treas.--Lewis Advertising Agency, Newark, NJ, pg. 672
Lewis, Ila J., Treas.--Gerber Plumbing Fixtures Corporation, Chicago, IL, pg. 454
Lewis, Ila J., Treas.--Kokomo Sanitary Pottery Corp., Chicago, IL, pg. 640
Lewis, J.A., Sr. V.P.-Fin.--Standard Lafarge, Canfield, OH, pg. 1036
Lewis, Jim, V.P., Chief Fin. Officer, Sec. & Treas.--Hale-Halsell Company, Tulsa, OK, pg. 500
Lewis, Kenneth R., Treas. & Mgr.-Bus.--RTMX-Uniflex Inc., Chapel Hill, NC, pg. 908
Lewis, Susan, Mgr.-Fin. Services & Treas.--Waldorf Corporation, Saint Paul, MN, pg. 1159
Libbe, Allan J., Sec., Treas. & Controller--Rudolph/Libbe, Inc., Walbridge, OH, pg. 955
Librizzi, Joseph, V.P. & Treas.--Thompson Medical Company, Inc., West Palm Beach, FL, pg. 1094
Lickert, W.R., Treas. & Sec.--Mason Company, Lexington, KY, pg. 718
Lieberg, Eric N., Chief Fin. Officer & Exec. V.P.--Rundel Products, Inc., Portland, OR, pg. 956
Lieberman, David, Treas.--Carousel Snack Bars Of Minnesota, Minneapolis, MN, pg. 224
Light, Daniel T., Sec. & Treas.--Belle Tire Distributor Inc., Allen Park, MI, pg. 136
Lilly, George D., Pres. & Treas.--SJL of Kansas Corp., Wichita, KS, pg. 962
Lindberg, Dennis N., Treas.--Chicago West Pullman Heavy Industries, Cincinnati, OH, pg. 246
Linder, Donald O., Treas.--Minnesota Electric Supply Company, Willmar, MN, pg. 757
Lindgerg, Dennis N., Treas.--Chicago West Pullman Transportation Corporation, Chicago, IL, pg. 246
Lindway, Bernard S., V.P.-Fin., Treas. & Sec.--Sussen, Inc., Cleveland, OH, pg. 225
Link, Ray, V.P. & Chief Fin. Officer--Hubbard Construction Co., Winter Park, FL, pg. 549
Linkous, Clare, Treas. & Sec.--Linkous Construction Company, Inc., Memphis, TN, pg. 677
Linnen, Thomas E., V.P.-Fin., Treas. & Sec.--Continental Circuits Corp., Phoenix, AZ, pg. 278
Linton, Richard A., Controller & Asst. Treas.--Consolidated Midwest, Inc., La Crosse, WI, pg. 277
Linzer, Morton A., Pres. & Treas.--Linzer Products Corp., Flushing, NY, pg. 677
Lipoff, Lawrence, Office Mgr. & Treas.--Butler Foods, Inc., Philadelphia, PA, pg. 197
Lippincott, Thomas J., Pres. & Treas.--Nebraska-Iowa Supply Company, Blair, NE, pg. 796
Lipschultz, William H., V.P. & Treas.--Bremer Financial Corporation, Saint Paul, MN, pg. 173
Lisker, Lawrence, Chief Exec. Officer & Treas.--Antwerp Diamond Distributors Inc., New York, NY, pg. 77
List, David J., Treas.--List Industries, Inc., Deerfield Beach, FL, pg. 677
List, Ruth, Sec. & Treas.--Alatec Products, Inc., North Hollywood, CA, pg. 30
Litoff, Carol, Treas. & Sec.--Ronald Litoff, Ltd., New York, NY, pg. 678
Littell, Bettie, Sec. & Treas.--Metalcenter, Inc., Santa Fe Springs, CA, pg. 742
Little, Richard K., Treas.--Rosser Fabrap International, Atlanta, GA, pg. 950
Livingston, Dewitt, Treas.--Aiken Electric Cooperative Inc., Aiken, SC, pg. 26
Livingston, Lorton S., V.P. & Treas.--Avondale Mills, Inc., Sylacauga, AL, pg. 103
Ljungberg, Maryanne, Treas.--Ultra Tool & Plastics, Inc., Amherst, NY, pg. 1125
Lloyd, Richard, Treas.--Waterous Company, South Saint Paul, MN, pg. 50
Lobel, Edith, Treas.--Smith-Edwards-Dunlap Company, Philadelphia, PA, pg. 1012
Lobel, Leonard J., Exec. V.P., Sec. & Treas.--Almo Corp., Philadelphia, PA, pg. 43
Lockard, Verne, V.P. & Treas.--Treasure Chest Advertising Co., Inc., Glendora, CA, pg. 1108
Lodovic, Joseph, Treas.--MediaNews Group Inc., Houston, TX, pg. 735
Loeb, Carl, Treas. & Sec.--Piknik Products Company, Inc., Montgomery, AL, pg. 870
Loeber, Paul, Sec. & Treas.--Loeber Motors, Inc., Chicago, IL, pg. 680
Loeffler, William G., Chm. & Treas.--Loeffler Ketchum Mountjoy, Charlotte, NC, pg. 680
Loeuis, Ingrid, V.P., Treas.--John F. Murray Advertising Agency Inc., New York, NY, pg. 776
Loew, James P., V.P.-Fin. & Controller & Treas.--Modern Concrete Septic Tank Company, Ottsville, PA, pg. 762
Lofgren, Frederick, Chief Fin. Officer, Treas., Sec. & V.P.-Fin. & Admin.--Hitchiner Manufacturing Company, Inc., Milford, NH, pg. 536
Loftin, Jerry, V.P.-Treas. & Controller--National Bedding & Furniture Industries, Memphis, TN, pg. 786
Loftis, Harry E., V.P. & Chief Fin. Officer--Riceland Foods, Inc., Stuttgart, AR, pg. 931
Lofton, Darrell W., V.P., Treas. & Controller--Donrey Media Group, Fort Smith, AR, pg. 345
Loher, Brian H., Treas., Sec. & Dir.-Investor Rels.--Hall Contracting Corp., Louisville, KY, pg. 501
Lohman, Paul J., Treas. & Asst. Sec.--Sands Investments, Inc., Myrtle Beach, SC, pg. 970
Lohr, William J., Treas.--Citizens Insurance Company of America, Howell, MI, pg. 35
Lomen, A.J., V.P., Treas. & Chief Fin. Officer--Genmar Industries, Inc., Minneapolis, MN, pg. 759
Lomen, Arlyn J., V.P., Treas. & Chief Fin. Officer--Minstar, Inc., Minneapolis, MN, pg. 758
Loomis, Lois, Treas.--Loomis Brothers, Inc., Cedar Rapids, IA, pg. 683
Lorenz, Donald N., Chief Fin. Officer & V.P.-Fin.--Price Brothers Co., Dayton, OH, pg. 888
Lorinc, John, V.P., Sec. & Treas.--Grossman Iron & Steel Company, St. Louis, MO, pg. 489
Lortz, Nadine, Treas.--Lortz Direct Marketing Inc., Omaha, NE, pg. 684
Losurdo, Maria, Treas.--Losurdo Foods, Inc., Hackensack, NJ, pg. 684
Loth, Gerald, Treas. & Sec.--Richardson Industries, Inc., Shaboygan Falls, WI, pg. 932
Louery, James M., Treas. & Sec.--Moto, Inc., Belleville, IL, pg. 773
Lovejoy, David W., V.P. & Treas.--All World Travel Service, Inc., Dayton, OH, pg. 373
Lovelace, Belle, Treas. & Sec.--Mar-Mac Manufacturing Company, Inc., McBee, SC, pg. 705
Loveland, Peter G., Pres., Treas. & Gen. Counsel--Maze Nails, Peru, IL, pg. 725
Lovvorn, Joseph, Treas. & Controller--Alabama Farmers Co-op, Decatur, AL, pg. 28
Lowe, Clifford, Treas. & Sec.--Star Food Processing, Inc., San Antonio, TX, pg. 1039
Lowe, Walter A., V.P. & Treas.--JRN, Inc., Columbia, TN, pg. 586
Lowell, Wayne, Sr. V.P., Chief Fin. Officer & Treas.--PacifiCare Health Systems, Inc., Cypress, CA, pg. 1127
Lower, Martin A., Pres. & Treas.--Ludlow Textiles Co., Inc., Ludlow, MA, pg. 686
Lozier, Jackie, Treas.--Washington Homes, Inc., Landover, MD, pg. 1166
Lubbars, Steve, V.P. & Treas.--Castex Industries Inc., Holland, MI, pg. 228
Lucas, William J., Treas.--R.M. Palmer Company, West Reading, PA, pg. 843
Lucash, Max, Asst. Treas.--Kane-Miller Corp., Tarrytown, NY, pg. 616
Lucien, Kent T., V.P. & Treas.--Mauna Loa Macadamia Nut Corporation, Hilo, HI, pg. 174
Lucien, Kent T., V.P. & Treas.--Mauna Kea Agribusiness Co., Inc., Papaikou, HI, pg. 174
Lucien, Kent T., V.P. & Treas.--Olokele Sugar Co., Limited, Kaumakani, HI, pg. 174
Lucien, Kent T., V.P. & Treas.--Wailuku Agribusiness Co., Inc., Wailuku, HI, pg. 175
Lucien, Kent T., V.P. & Treas.--HT&T Company, Inc., Hilo, HI, pg. 174
Lucien, Kent T., V.P. & Treas.--Kilauea Agronomics, Inc., Kilauea, HI, pg. 174
Lucien, Kent T., V.P. & Treas.--Mauna Loa Resources Inc., Honolulu, HI, pg. 174
Lucien, Kent T., V.P. & Treas.--Superior Coffee & Foods/ Hawaii, Aiea, HI, pg. 174
Ludt, S.G., Pres., Chief Exec. Officer & Treas.--Columbian Rope Company, Guntown, MS, pg. 266
Ludwick, Arthur, Treas.--Rain Bird Sprinkler Mfg. Corp., Glendora, CA, pg. 910
Luebberman, Thomas M., V.P. & Treas.--Seppala & AHO Construction Company, New Ipswich, NH, pg. 990
Luhrs, Randy, Treas.--Muska Electric Company, Saint Paul, MN, pg. 777
Lukash, Donna, Treas.--Dahlsten Truck Line, Inc., Clay Center, NE, pg. 310
Lukens, Norman, V.P. & Treas.--C-Line Products, Inc., Des Plaines, IL, pg. 198
Lundquist, Bruce, Controller--Tillamook County Creamery Assn., Tillamook, OR, pg. 1097
Lunn, Thomas L., V.P. & Treas.--Ingram Industries Inc., Nashville, TN, pg. 568
Luntz, Gregory W., Chief Fin. Officer & Treas.--Luntz Corporation, Canton, OH, pg. 687
Lupient, James W., Pres. & Treas.--Jim Lupient Enterprises, Golden Valley, MN, pg. 687
Lupton, Rudea, Treas.--Associated Advertising Agency, Inc., Wichita, KS, pg. 89
Lurio, Lee H., Pres. & Treas.--Elbeco Incorporated, Reading, PA, pg. 372
Lurus, Steven A., Chief Fin. Officer & Dir.-Fin., Treas.--Metro Information Services, Virginia Beach, VA, pg. 743
Lustbader, Edward E., Chm. Bd., Pres., Chief Exec. Officer & Treas.--The P.J. Carlin Construction Company, New Rochelle, NY, pg. 220
Luzum, James A., Chief Fin. Officer, Treas. & Controller--Villaume Industries, Inc., Saint Paul, MN, pg. 1151

Lyke, Audrey R., Chief Fin. Officer & Treas.--Lyke Corporation, Ripon, WI, pg. 688
MacConnell, Cynthia S., Sec. & Treas.--Bill Woeste Dealer Group, Cincinnati, OH, pg. 1198
MacConnell, Timothy J., Treas.--Thomson MacConnell Cadillac, Inc., Cincinnati, OH, pg. 1095
Macdonald, Malcolm, Exec. V.P. & Treas.--Park Ridge Corporation, Park Ridge, NJ, pg. 849
MacGibbon, W. Douglas, Pres., Treas. & Dir.-Creative--The In-House Agency, Weehawken, NJ, pg. 564
Mack, Ann Baker, Treas.--Guard Publishing Company, Eugene, OR, pg. 491
MacKnight, Paul D., Sec. & Asst. Treas.--The Record-Journal Publishing Company, Meriden, CT, pg. 917
MacNeil, Norman E., Chm. Bd. & Treas.--Ark-Les Corporation, Watertown, MA, pg. 82
MacPherson, Donald, V.P.-Fin.--Thomas Publishing Co., New York, NY, pg. 1093
Madden, Mary Jo, Treas.--Tressa, Inc., Erlanger, KY, pg. 1110
Madlinger, Steven R., V.P., Chief Fin. Officer & Treas.--GreatBanc, Inc., Aurora, IL, pg. 482
Magdol, Michael O., Vice Chm.-Chief Fin. Officer--Fiduciary Trust Co. International, New York, NY, pg. 408
Magdovitz, Joe, Chm. Bd., Sec. & Treas.--Imperial Manufacturing Company, Memphis, TN, pg. 564
Maginn, John L., Sr. Exec. V.P., Chief Investment Officer & Treas.--Mutual of Omaha Insurance Company, Omaha, NE, pg. 779
Maginn, John L., Sr. Exec. V.P., Chief Investment Officer & Treas.--Mutual of Omaha, Omaha, NE, pg. 779
Maher, Thomas, Treas.--Garden Way, Inc., Troy, NY, pg. 443
Mahler, Glenn, V.P., Sec. & Treas.--Blue Cross Laboratories, Saugus, CA, pg. 160
Mahler, Henrietta E., Chm. Bd. & Treas.--Henri's Food Products Co., Inc., Milwaukee, WI, pg. 530
Mahn, Thomas E., Treas.--Perdue Farms Inc., Salisbury, MD, pg. 860
Mahon, Dave, Sec. & Treas.--Alro Group, Jackson, MI, pg. 44
Mahoney, Melvin M., Treas.--ARA Group, Philadelphia, PA, pg. 5
Maise, Paul P., Chief Fin. Officer & Treas.--Transco Inc., Wayne, MI, pg. 1107
Maiuccoro, John M., Pres. & Treas.--Imperial Pools, Inc., Latham, NY, pg. 564
Malik, Helen, Sec. & Treas.--Mitchell Corporation of Owosso, Owosso, MI, pg. 761
Malkani, Roma, Pres. & Chief Exec. Officer--Information Systems & Network Corporation, Bethesda, MD, pg. 567
Mallendick, Robert J., Pres. & Treas.--Empire Petroleum, Inc., Toledo, OH, pg. 379
Mallory, Richard, Treas. & Sec.--C. Weaver Chevrolet, Inc., New York Mills, NY, pg. 1170
Malloy, W. Manning, Pres. & Treas.--Cheraw Yarn Mills, Inc., Cheraw, SC, pg. 242
Maloney, Joseph J., Treas. & Sec.--Daniel J. Keating Co., Villanova, PA, pg. 619
Mancini, Brooks T., Pres. & Treas.--B.T. Mancini Co., Inc., Milpitas, CA, pg. 703
Mandeville, Robert, Chief Fin. Officer & Treas.--Cranston Print Works Company, Cranston, RI, pg. 296
Manganella, Frank, Treas.--Uniroyal Chemical Company, Inc., Middlebury, CT, pg. 1129
Maniscalco, Diane, Chief Fin. Officer-Admin./Opers.-Sec. & Treas.--Colonna Bros., Inc., North Bergen, NJ, pg. 264
Manke, James, Treas.--Manke Lumber Company, Inc., Tacoma, WA, pg. 704
Mann, Edmund S., Treas. & Corp. Sec.--Thermo Industries Inc., Charlotte, NC, pg. 1091
Mansfield, Fred W., Sec. & Treas.--Great Lakes Financial Resources, Inc., Homewood, IL, pg. 481
Manso, Esther, Comptroller, Sec. & Treas.--Metro Ford Inc., Miami, FL, pg. 743
Manukas, George, V.P., Treas. & Asst. Sec.--DKM Properties Corporation, Lawrenceville, NJ, pg. 357
Manz, Terry K., V.P., Sec. & Treas.--Cactus Feeders, Inc., Amarillo, TX, pg. 207
Marach, Roger, Chief Fin. Officer & Treas.--FamTec International, Inc., Des Plaines, IL, pg. 398
Maracino, Art, Exec. Vice Pres.--T. L. Smith Machine, Springville, NY, pg. 1013
Marberg, Edwin, Pres., Chief Exec. Officer & Treas.--MCM Enterprises, Inc., Crawfordsville, IN, pg. 691
Marcucci, George, Chief Fin. Officer & Treas.--Gonnella Baking Co., Chicago, IL, pg. 469
Marcus, Harriet, Sec. & Treas.--Harold Leonard & Company, Inc., Union, NJ, pg. 667
Marcus, Seymour, Vice Chm. & Treas.--Halsey Drug Co., Inc., Brooklyn, NY, pg. 502
Marek, Alan J., Treas. & Chief Fin. Officer--Vincent Food Industries, Inc., Chicago, IL, pg. 1152
Maresca, Robert, Sr. V.P. & Treas.--Metromedia Company, East Rutherford, NJ, pg. 743
Margalith, Ethan Harold, Chm. Bd., Chief Exec. Officer & Treas.--Starving Students, Inc., Los Angeles, CA, pg. 1040
Maris, Edward G., Sr. V.P. & Chief Fin. Officer--Northwestern Steel & Wire Co., Sterling, IL, pg. 815
Mark, Carol, Sec., Treas., Sr. Art Dir.--Marketing Magic Inc., Fort Lauderdale, FL, pg. 709
Markel, John D., Pres., Chief Exec. Officer & Treas.--Smartstar Corporation, Goleta, CA, pg. 1011
Markey, A.F., V.P. & Treas.--E. R. Carpenter Co., Richmond, VA, pg. 224
Markey, Thomas, V.P., Treas. & Sec.--National Spinning Co., Inc., New York, NY, pg. 793
Markus, Theodore, Asst. Treas.--Dickinson Press, Inc., Grand Rapids, MI, pg. 336
Marlowe, S.L., Treas.--Asko, Inc, Homestead, PA, pg. 88
Marman, Charles, Sec. & Treas.--F.T. Reynolds Company, Glendive, MT, pg. 930
Marousis, Jim, Treas.--American Decal & Mfg. Co., Chicago, IL, pg. 51
Marquardt, R.R., Chief Fin. Officer, Sec. & Treas.--Miller Electric Mfg. Co., Appleton, WI, pg. 754
Marram, Edward P., Dr., Chm. Bd., Pres., Chief Exec. Officer & Treas.--Geo-Centers, Inc., Newton Center, MA, pg. 452
Marriner, Mary E., Exec. V.P. & Treas.--Marriner Marketing Communications, Inc., Columbia, MD, pg. 713
Marshall, Gordon B., V.P.-Fin. & Treas.--The Pepper Companies, Inc., Chicago, IL, pg. 859
Marshall, Joan, V.P. & Treas.--R. J. Marshall Co., Southfield, MI, pg. 714
Marsilius, N.M. III, Pres. & Treas.--The Producto Machine Co., Bridgeport, CT, pg. 893
Martel, Frances E., Treas.--Harvey Industries, Inc., Waltham, MA, pg. 515
Martens, Willard, V.P.-Fin., Treas. & Chief Oper. Officer--TSR, Inc., Lake Geneva, WI, pg. 1075
Martin, Bill, Treas. & Sec.--I. C. Thomasson Associates, Inc., Nashville, TN, pg. 1094
Martin, Clarence, Exec. V.P., Treas. & Sec.--State Electric Supply Co., Huntington, WV, pg. 1040
Martin, Clifford R., Treas.--Prince Manufacturing, Inc., Lawrenceville, NJ, pg. 890
Martin, Dale, Treas.--Davis Industries Inc., Detroit, MI, pg. 318
Martin, George D., V.P. & Treas.--The Associated Group, Indianapolis, IN, pg. 90
Martin, Lynell, Treas. & Sec.--Martins Abbatoir & Wholesale Meats Inc., Godwin, NC, pg. 716
Martin, Roy C., Jr., V.P.-Fin. & Treas.--Triangle Electric Company, Madison Heights, MI, pg. 1112
Martin, Sarah, Treas.--Stone & Simons Advertising, Inc., Southfield, MI, pg. 1051
Martin, Terri, Treas. & Sec.--Martin Forest Industries, Healdsburg, CA, pg. 715
Martin, Virginia H., Sec. & Treas.--Martin Door Mfg., Inc., Salt Lake City, UT, pg. 714
Martin, Willie, V.P. & Treas.--Amurcon Corporation, Southfield, MI, pg. 70
Martinelli, R.M., Treas. & Controller--MPO Videotronics, Inc., New York, NY, pg. 693
Martiny, Lynn, Sec. & Treas.--Martiny & Company, Cincinnati, OH, pg. 716
Martorelli, Anna M., Treas.--Lawry's Restaurants, Inc., Los Angeles, CA, pg. 663
Marza, Yaqub, Dr., Treas.--Mar-Jac Processing, Inc., Gainesville, GA, pg. 705
Masco, Matt S., Exec. V.P., Treas. & Sec.--Pacific Wood Treating Coporation, Ridgefield, WA, pg. 842
Mashburn, Harry L., Pres. & Treas.--Mashburn Construction Company, Columbia, SC, pg. 717
Mashburn, Troy, Jr., Sec. & Treas.--Choctaw, Inc., Memphis, TN, pg. 248
Mason, David D. S., Pres., Chief Exec. Officer, Chief Fin. Officer & Treas.--Mason Oil Company, Ione, CA, pg. 718
Matarese, Betty H., Sr. V.P. & Sec.--Phoenix International, Inc., Beverly, NJ, pg. 868
Mathieu, Raymond M., Chief Fin. Officer & Treas.--Narragansett Capital Inc., Providence, RI, pg. 783
Mathis, Jim, V.P.-Mktg., Sec. & Treas.--Precision Parts Corp., Morristown, TN, pg. 885
Matthew, W.F., V.P. & Treas.--Wemco, Inc., New Orleans, LA, pg. 1176
Matthews, Joyce Carroll, Chm. Bd., Sec. & Treas.--Carroll's Foods, Inc., Warsaw, NC, pg. 225
Matthews, Roy S., V.P.-Fin. & Treas.--George S. May International Company, Park Ridge, IL, pg. 723
Matthis, Doris L., Sec. & Treas.--Kentucky Indiana Lumber Co. Inc., Louisville, KY, pg. 623
Mattingly, Barbara A., Treas. & Sec.--Metro Foods, Inc., Memphis, TN, pg. 743
Mattingly, Mike, Treas., Controller & Chief Fin. Officer--The Court Company, Memphis, TN, pg. 290
Mattison, Ben, V.P. & Treas.--Malloy Lithographing Inc., Ann Arbor, MI, pg. 703
Matyn, Harold L., Treas.--Roy O'Brien Inc., St. Clair Shores, MI, pg. 820
Mauk, Patricia, Treas. & Sec.--Dudek & Bock Spring Manufacturing Company, Chicago, IL, pg. 351
Maurer, Joseph, V.P. & Treas.--Levi Strauss & Co., San Francisco, CA, pg. 670
Maurer, Richard A., V.P. & Treas.--Van Dyne-Crotty, Inc., Dayton, OH, pg. 1144
May, Jane Ballenger, Sec. & Treas.--Y.C. Ballenger Electrical Contractors, Spartanburg, SC, pg. 116
Mayberry, Jean C., Treas. & Data Processing Mgr.--Asbury Carbons, Inc., Asbury, NJ, pg. 87
Mayer, Sylvia, Sec. & Treas.--Mayer Berkshire Corporation, Wayne, NJ, pg. 724
Mayers, Lois E., Sec. & Treas.--Ace Novelty Company, Inc., Bellevue, WA, pg. 12
Maynard, James H., Chm. Bd., Chief Exec. Officer & Treas.--Investor's Management Corp., Raleigh, NC, pg. 581
Mazzarino, Michael C., Sr. V.P.-Fin. & Treas.--Marcal Paper Mills, Inc., Elmwood Park, NJ, pg. 706
McAfee, Nancy G., V.P., Treas. & Controller--Thrall Enterprises, Inc., Chicago, IL, pg. 1095
McAtee, Larry, Treas.--Kimray, Inc., Oklahoma City, OK, pg. 629
McCaigue, Dan, Chief Fin. Officer--Showell Farms, Inc., Showell, MD, pg. 1000
McCall, Ronald L., Vice Chm., Chief Exec. Officer, Chief Fin. Officer & Treas.--M. B. Kahn Construction Co., Inc., Columbia, SC, pg. 614
McCall, W.A., Sec., Treas., Controller & Data Processing Mgr.--Dixie Oil Company, Tifton, GA, pg. 341
McCartney, W Earl, Treas.--Peter J. Schmitt Co., Inc., West Seneca, NY, pg. 977
McCartney, W. Earl, V.P. & Treasurer--Peter J. Schmitt Holdings, West Seneca, NY, pg. 976
McCausland, George J., Treas. & Controller--Ash Grove Cement Company, Overland Park, KS, pg. 87
McClelland, Frances H., Treas., Sec. & Chief Fin. Officer--Shamrock Foods Co., Phoenix, AZ, pg. 994
McCluskey, R.T., V.P. & Treas.--Fiske Brothers Refining Company, Newark, NJ, pg. 415
McConnell, Donald A., V.P., Treas. & Controller--RTKL Associates Inc., Baltimore, MD, pg. 908
McCormick, Gerald, Treas.--J.H. McCormick, Inc., Burbank, CA, pg. 727
McCoy, Janice, Sec. & Treas.--Fleetwood Aluminum Products, Corona, CA, pg. 417
McCoy, Mike, V.P., Treas. & Chief Fin. Officer--FDL Foods, Inc., Dubuque, IA, pg. 394
McCracken, Alan L., Comptroller & Treas.--Baltimore Stationery Co., Baltimore, MD, pg. 116
McCraine, Alice B., Sec. & Treas.--Bernhard Mechanical Contractor, Inc., Baton Rouge, LA, pg. 143
McCrory, Kelly L., Sec. & Treas.--Steakley Chevrolet Subaru Inc., Dallas, TX, pg. 1043
McCudden, Bernie, V.P.-Fin.--Harris Steel Co., Chicago, IL, pg. 512
McCuish, Mike, Treas.--The Smith Group, Inc., Detroit, MI, pg. 1012
McCullough, Bob, Exec. V.P., Sec. & Treas.--Harris, Baio & McCullough Inc., Philadelphia, PA, pg. 511
McDaniel, Elmer G., Sec. & Treas.--Alabama Electric Cooperative, Inc., Andalusia, AL, pg. 28
McDermid, Edward J., Jr., Treas.--Frontier Lumber Company, Inc., Buffalo, NY, pg. 434
McDonald, J.M., III, Chm. Bd., Pres., Treas. & Chief Exec. Officer--Brock-McVey Company, Lexington, KY, pg. 728
McDonald, Stuart R., Pres., Chief Exec. Officer & Treas.--Marshall & Williams Co., Greenville, SC, pg. 714
McDonald, Thomas, Chief Fin. Officer & Treas.--Jernberg Industries, Inc., Chicago, IL, pg. 593
McDonley, Anne M., V.P. & Treas.--First Signature Bank & Trust Co., Portsmouth, NH, pg. 596
McDonnell, Terry, Treas.--Lane Press, Inc., South Burlington, VT, pg. 654
McDougald, JoeD., Treas.--Quintana Petroleum Corp., Houston, TX, pg. 905
McDowell, George E., V.P., Sec. & Treas.--Clayton Corporation, Fenton, MO, pg. 253
McElhinny, David, Treas.--Rogers, Lunt & Bowlen Co., Greenfield, MA, pg. 943
McElroy, Edmund G., Jr., Treas.--The Dyson-Kissner-Moran Corporation, New York, NY, pg. 357
McElroy, Edmund G., Jr., Treas.--Centre Foundry & Machine Co., Wheeling, WV, pg. 357
McEvoy, Thomas P., Treas. & Controller--New Standard Corporation, Mount Joy, PA, pg. 802
McFarland, Roger, Treas.--Cornucopia, Inc., Irvine, CA, pg. 287
McFarland, William C., Chm. Bd. & Treas.--McFarland & Drier, Inc., Miami, FL, pg. 729
McFarling, Robert E., V.P.-Sls. & Treas.--McFarling Foods, Inc., Indianapolis, IN, pg. 729
McGafferty, Patrick J., Sec., Treas. & Chief Fin. Officer--Grisanti, Inc., Louisville, KY, pg. 488
McGill, James D., Pres.--United McGill Corp., Groveport, OH, pg. 1133
McGill, William, V.P. & Treas.--Belk Stores Services Inc., Charlotte, NC, pg. 134
McGivney, Kevin, Sr. V.P. & Treas.--Compendium Systems, New York, NY, pg. 270
McGonigle, W., Treas.--Samuel Cabot, Inc., Newburyport, MA, pg. 206
McGough, Tom, Treas.--Thompson Tractor Company, Birmingham, AL, pg. 1095
McGrath, Brent P., Chief Fin. Officer, Treas. & Sec.--Mico Inc., North Mankato, MN, pg. 748
McGuire, Patricia, Treas.--Regional Transportation Authority (RTA), Chicago, IL, pg. 922
McGurn, Robert E., Treas.--Contractors Supply Company, Inc., Kansas City, MO, pg. 281
McHugh, Joseph P., V.P. & Treas.--Howes Leather Company, Inc., Quincy, MA, pg. 548
McHugh, M. Joseph, Sr. Exec. V.P.-Fin., Admin. & Treas.--Triangle Pacific Corporation, Dallas, TX, pg. 1112
McHugh, M. Joseph, Treas.--MADD (Mothers Against Drunk Driving), Irving, TX, pg. 691
McInnis, Judy, Sec. & Treas.--Southern Electric Supply Co., Inc., Meridian, MS, pg. 1020
McIntyre, Richard A., V.P.-Fin., Treas. & Sec.--Blaw Knox Corp., Pittsburgh, PA, pg. 156
McInvale, Willie K., Jr., Sec. & Treas.--McNamara Pontiac Inc., Orlando, FL, pg. 732
McKay, Calvin, Sr. V.P. & Treas.--Acme Boot Co., Inc., Clarksville, TN, pg. 400
McKay, Dwight, Asst. Treas.--Weston Paper & Manufacturing Co., Terre Haute, IN, pg. 1183
McKenney, M.P., Sec. & Treas.--The Figaro Company, Inc., Mesquite, TX, pg. 409
McKeon, H.F., Jr., V.P. & Treas.--The Biltrite Corporation, Waltham, MA, pg. 151
McKinney, Bert, Sec. & Treas.--Contractors Supplies, Inc., Lufkin, TX, pg. 280
McKinney, Hiram Y., Sr. V.P., Sec., Treas. & Controller--Sullivan Long & Hagerty, Inc., Birmingham, AL, pg. 1057
McLaughlin, E.H., III, Exec. V.P., Treas. & Asst. Sec.--McLaughlin Industrial Distributors, Inc., Pico Rivera, CA, pg. 731
McLean, Douglas C., Treas.--Interstate Distributor Company, Tacoma, WA, pg. 580
McMahon, Robert B., Chm. Bd.,Chief Exec. Officer, Treas., & Sec.--City Meats & Provisions Co., Tucsan, AZ, pg. 251
McMann, Robert S., V.P. & Treas.--John Hancock Insurance Company of Bermuda Ltd., Hamilton, Bermuda, pg. 596
McMillan, Carl, Treas. & Gen. Mgr.--Town & Country Supermarket, Hardy, AR, pg. 1103

McNamara, Michael, V.P. & Treas.--Schwinn Bicycle Company, Chicago, IL, pg. 981
McNamara, William B., Chief Fin. Officer, Treas. & Asst. Sec.--Air Conditioning Co., Inc., Glendale, CA, pg. 26
McNeil, Steven, Treas.--Smith Pipe & Steel Co., Phoenix, AZ, pg. 1014
McNulty, Lillian, Treas.--Rocket Industries, Inc./Excel, The Exercise Company, Pico Rivera, CA, pg. 941
McPhail, Douglas J., Pres., Chief Exec. & Fin. Officer & Treas.--Indiana Records Managers, Indianapolis, IN, pg. 565
McSweeney, John J., Treas.--Metropolitan Property & Casualty Insurance Co.(Met P&C), Warwick, RI, pg. 744
Meador, M.E., Treas.--Glenroy Construction Co. Inc., Indianapolis, IN, pg. 462
Meagher, Ellen, Chief Fin. Officer & Treas.--Paisano Publications, Inc., Agoura, CA, pg. 843
Meckfessel, William R., Chief Fin. Officer--Carco Electronics, Menlo Park, CA, pg. 217
Medico, Lawrence, Treas.--Medico Industries, Inc., Wilkes-Barre, PA, pg. 735
Meehan, Gregory W.A., V.P., Chief Fin. Officer & Treas.--High Point Financial Corp., Branchville, NJ, pg. 533
Meek, David, Treas.--R. B. Pamplin Corp., Portland, OR, pg. 844
Meek, David C., V.P. & Treas.--Mount Vernon Mills, Inc., Greenville, SC, pg. 844
Meer, E. Harvey, Pres., Chief Oper. Officer & Treas.--Meer Corporation, North Bergen, NJ, pg. 736
Mees, Sandra, Treas.--Rex Marine Center, Inc., Norwalk, CT, pg. 930
Meilahn, J.E., Sr. V.P. & Chief Fin. Officer & Treas.--Federated Mutual Insurance Company, Owatonna, MN, pg. 405
Meinkoth, Richard K., Treas. & Controller--Contico International, Inc., Saint Louis, MO, pg. 278
Mellgren, Hank, Treas.--Northwest Pipe Fittings, Inc., Billings, MT, pg. 815
Mellody, Joe, Treas.--Capital Controls Company Inc., Colmar, PA, pg. 215
Mellos, Steven P., Chief Fin. Officer, V.P. & Treas.--Invetech Co., Detroit, MI, pg. 581
Mellott, John C., Treas.--Cox Enterprises, Inc., Atlanta, GA, pg. 292
Melloy, Patrick C., V.P., Sec. & Treas.--Melloy Bros. Enterprises, Albuquerque, NM, pg. 738
Melnick, Jack, Sec. & Treas.--Young Stuff Apparel Group, Inc., New York, NY, pg. 1214
Melo, James, Chm. Bd. & Treas.--Dynamic Metal Products Company, Manchester, CT, pg. 356
Meloon, Walter O., Treas.--Correct Craft, Inc., Orlando, FL, pg. 287
Mendello, William L., Exec. V.P., Sec. & Treas.--Fender Musical Instruments, Scottsdale, AZ, pg. 406
Menke, Gerald T., Treas. & Sec.--The F. D. Lawrence Electric Co., Cincinnati, OH, pg. 661
Menzies, Gregg L., Treas.--RDI, Inc., Itasca, IL, pg. 906
Mercer, Harold B., Exec. V.P. & Treas.--Swift Instruments, Inc., Dorchester, MA, pg. 1068
Mercer, Harold B., Treas.--Technical Instruments Div., San Jose, CA, pg. 1068
Mercer, James G., Asst. Treas.--Swift Instruments, Inc., Dorchester, MA, pg. 1068
Merker, Lorrie Ford, Treas.--Michigan Blueberry Growers Assn., Grand Junction, MI, pg. 747
Merton, Pond, Treas.--Interstate Producers Livestock Association, Peoria, IL, pg. 580
Meschler, Paul, Exec. V.P. & Treas.--Norfoods, Inc., Overland Park, KS, pg. 810
Messick, Alan, Sec. & Treas.--Palm Iron & Bridge Works, Inc., Sacramento, CA, pg. 843
Messmore, Larry, Sec. & Treas.--Curt Bullock Builders, Inc., Danville, IL, pg. 188
Metcalf, Robert, Sec. & Treas.--Smyth, Bauer & Lewis Advertising Inc., Richmond, VA, pg. 1014
Meth, Joseph, Treas. & Chief Fin. Officer--F. Schumacher & Co., New York, NY, pg. 979
Metro, Joseph, Treas.--The LINC Group, Inc., Chicago, IL, pg. 648
Meurice, Gilles, Chief Fin. Officer & Treas.--Seiler Corporation, Waltham, MA, pg. 987
Mevs, Tracy P., Treas. & Corp. Sec.--Zilkha Energy Company, Houston, TX, pg. 1219
Meyer, David L., V.P. & Treas.--Greeley Gas Co., Denver, CO, pg. 483
Meyer, Howard E., V.P. & Treas.--Koch Supplies Inc., Kansas City, MO, pg. 639
Meyer, Verna, Treas.--Great American Broadcasting Company, Cincinnati, OH, pg. 53
Meyers, Richard, Exec. V.P., Dir. Fin. & Treas.--Kobs & Draft Advertising, Inc., Chicago, IL, pg. 109
Miceli, Frank, Asst. Treas.--Amway Corporation, Ada, MI, pg. 70
Michaels, Marion D., Treas.--The Hiebing Group, Inc., Madison, WI, pg. 533
Michas, William, Treas.--Twin County Grocers, Inc., Edison, NJ, pg. 1122
Michel, Gary, Treas. & Sec.--Todd Pipe & Supply Hawthorne, Hawthorne, CA, pg. 1100
Michell, C.R., Vice Chm. Bd. & Treas.--EduServ, Saint Paul, MN, pg. 369
Michie, Bob, Chief Fin. Officer, Treas. & Sec.--Archer/Malmo Adv., Inc., Memphis, TN, pg. 80
Middlekauff, Dina B., Treas.--Bender Shipbuilding & Repair Company, Mobile, AL, pg. 138
Miehl, Peter C., V.P.-Fin. & Treas.--DeMert & Dougherty, Inc., Westchester, IL, pg. 328
Miffleton, Robert B., Exec. V.P. & Treas.--Forestry Suppliers, Inc., Jackson, MS, pg. 424
Miglin, Marilyn, Treas.--Chicago Convention & Tourism Bureau, Chicago, IL, pg. 245
Miike, Patrick T., Treas.--Amelco Corporation, Gardena, CA, pg. 47
Mikovich, Fran, Sec. & Treas.--Orleans Materials & Equipment Co., Inc., New Orleans, LA, pg. 829
Milano, Sandro, Sec. & Treas.--Butera Finer Foods Inc., Elgin, IL, pg. 196
Milas, Joseph, Treas.--Plibrico Co., Chicago, IL, pg. 877
Mill, Victor J., III, Pres. & Treas.--Lawrence Pumps, Inc., Lawrence, MA, pg. 662
Miller, Andrew, V.P. & Treas.--Miller Advertising Agency Inc., New York, NY, pg. 753
Miller, Arnold, Treas.--Quill Corp., Lincolnshire, IL, pg. 905
Miller, Brian W., Treas.--Star Bronze Company, Alliance, OH, pg. 1039
Miller, Catherine D., Treas.--Derst Baking Company, Inc., Savannah, GA, pg. 331
Miller, Charles T., Treas.--Hammond Lead Products, Inc., Hammond, IN, pg. 504
Miller, Donald, Treas. & Sec.--Lee Grocery Company, Everett, WA, pg. 665
Miller, Donald L., V.P.-Fin. & Treas.--Weston Paper & Manufacturing Co., Terre Haute, IN, pg. 1183
Miller, Floyd H., Sec. & Treas.--Valley Pontiac Buick GMC, Inc., Auburn, WA, pg. 1143
Miller, G.G., V.P.-Fin., Chief Fin. Officer & Treas.--AFG Industries, Inc., Fort Worth, TX, pg. 3
Miller, Gary, Treas.--Gemtron Corporation, Sweetwater, TN, pg. 3
Miller, Jay, V.P.-Fin., Treas. & Sec.--Perfection Bakeries Inc., Fort Wayne, IN, pg. 861
Miller, Jeffrey B., Treas.--Columbian Advertising Inc., Chicago, IL, pg. 266
Miller, John, Chief Fin. Officer, Treas. & Controller--RJO Enterprises, Inc., Lanham, MD, pg. 907
Miller, Katherine, Sec. & Treas.--Pyromet, Inc., Aston, PA, pg. 901
Miller, Kenneth I., Chief Fin. Officer, Treas. & Sr. V.P.--Johnston, Lemon & Co. Inc., Washington, DC, pg. 601
Miller, Lloyd A., V.P., Treas. & Sec.--Midway Products Corporation, Monroe, MI, pg. 751
Miller, Max, Chm. Bd. & Treas.--McInerney-Miller Brothers Inc., Detroit, MI, pg. 729
Miller, Mike, V.P.-Fin.--Silver Dollar City, Inc., Branson, MO, pg. 1004
Miller, Neal D., V.P., Treas. & Sec.--Hasslocher Enterprises, Inc., d/b/a Frontier Enterprises, San Antonio, TX, pg. 516
Miller, Richard L., Exec. V.P., Treas. & Sec.--Miller Transporters, Inc., Jackson, MS, pg. 334
Miller, Robert N., V.P.-Fin. & Treas.--Prentiss Incorporated, Floral Park, NY, pg. 887
Miller, Ross, Treas. & Sec.--Harris Steel Co., Chicago, IL, pg. 512
Miller, Ruth P., Treas.--Schultz Steel Company, South Gate, CA, pg. 979
Miller, Steven, Chief Fin. Officer, Treas. & Controller--Resort Condominiums International, Indianapolis, IN, pg. 929
Miller, William, Controller & Treas.--Merle Norman Cosmetics, Inc., Los Angeles, CA, pg. 740
Mills, Dean, Chief Fin. Officer & Treas.--Brooks Products, Inc., El Monte, CA, pg. 180
Mills, Olan, II, Chm. Exec. Committee--Olan Mills, Inc., Chattanooga, TN, pg. 756
Mills, Walter G., Chm. Bd., Chief Exec. Officer & Treas.--W.G. Mills, Inc., Sarasota, FL, pg. 756
Milne, Malcolm R., Sr. V.P. & Treas.--First Federal of Michigan, Detroit, MI, pg. 414
Mineart, Carol J., Chief Fin. Officer & Treasurer--Avis Industrial Corporation, Upland, IN, pg. 102
Miniat, Edmund, Chief Fin. Officer & Treas.--Ed Miniat, Inc., Chicago, IL, pg. 757
Minich, Lawrence, V.P. & Treas.--Blue Coral, Inc., Cleveland, OH, pg. 159
Minnich, Donald E., Sr. V.P. & Treas.--United Tectonic Industry, Harrisburg, PA, pg. 1137
Minnick, Robert, V.P. & Treas.--Shelter Mutual Insurance Company, Columbia, MO, pg. 997
Minyard, Lisbeth, Co-Chm. Bd. & Treas.--Minyard Food Stores, Coppell, TX, pg. 759
Miranda, Ray, Controller--Cerwin Vega, Inc., Simi Valley, CA, pg. 237
Misumi, Yoshio, Treas.--Pioneer/Eclipse Corp., Sparta, NC, pg. 871
Mitchel, Stephen, V.P., Sec. & Treas.--Mitchel & Scot Machine Co., Inc., Indianapolis, IN, pg. 761
Mitchell, Robert J., Treas.--Trans World Airlines, Inc., Mount Kisco, NY, pg. 561
Mitchell, Robert J., Treas. & Asst. Sec.--ACF Industries, Inc., Earth City, MO, pg. 561
Mitchell, Ted, Treas. & Sec.--Columbia Sussex Corporation, Fort Mitchell, KY, pg. 266
Mitchell, Winston, Treas.--Durham Transportation, Inc., Austin, TX, pg. 354
Mitchum, Billy E., Sec. & Treas.--Defender Services, Inc., Columbia, SC, pg. 324
Mitlyng, Errol P., Sr. V.P.-Fin., Treas. & Chief Fin. Officer--The Marley Company, Mission Woods, KS, pg. 710
Mize, E.J., Jr., V.P.-Fin., Treas., Chief Fin. & Acctg. Officer--United States Pipe & Foundry Company, Birmingham, AL, pg. 1162
Mize, Mike, V.P.-Corp. Plng. & Devel., Chief Fin. Officer, Sec. & Treas.--GSC Enterprises, Inc., Sulphur Springs, TX, pg. 440
Mizoguchi, Paul, Treas.--Maui Varieties, Ltd., Honolulu, HI, pg. 721
Moix, Norbert, Sec. & Treas.--Nabholz Construction Corp., Conway, AR, pg. 782
Molin, Carl E., III, Treas.--Molin Auto Parts Inc., Buffalo, NY, pg. 764
Money, Jack W., V.P.-Fin. & Treas.--North American Royalties, Inc., Chattanooga, TN, pg. 811
Monk, William C., Chm. Bd., Chief Exec. Officer & Treas.--A.C. Monk Co., Inc., Farmville, NC, pg. 766
Montgomery, R.L., Chief Fin. Officer, Exec. V.P. & Treas.--Columbus McKinnon Corp., Amherst, NY, pg. 266
Montgomery, Walter S., Jr., Pres., Treas., Chief Exec. & Chief Fin. Officer--Spartan Mills, Spartanburg, SC, pg. 1026
Mood, Alfred, Treas. & Sec.--Pyramid Mountain Lumber, Seeley Lake, MT, pg. 901
Moon, Floyd, Treas. & Asst. Sec.--Deseret Management Corporation, Salt Lake City, UT, pg. 332
Mooney, Susan, Pres. & Treas.--Daw Technologies, Inc., Salt Lake City, UT, pg. 319
Moore, B. A., Treas.--Bepco, Inc., Winston-Salem, NC, pg. 141
Moore, Brant R., Chief Fin. Officer, Treas. & Sec.--I. H. French & Co. Inc., Champaign, IL, pg. 432
Moore, James O., V.P.-Fin., Treas. & Asst. Sec.--Cullman Ventures, Inc., New York, NY, pg. 304
Moore, Kevin, Sec. & Treas.--Allsop, Inc., Bellingham, WA, pg. 43
Moore, P.J., Sr. V.P., Chief Oper. Officer, Chief Fin. Officer, Sec. & Treas.--Green Holdings, Inc., Denver, CO, pg. 484
Moore, P.J., Sr. V.P., Chief Fin. Officer, Sec. & Treas.--Green International, Inc., Denver, CO, pg. 484
Moore, P.J., Sr. V.P., Sec. & Treas.--Green Mining, Inc., Denver, CO, pg. 484
Moore, P.J., Sr. V.P., Treas. & Sec.--C.C. Conley & Sons, Inc., Denver, CO, pg. 484
Moore, P.J., Sr. V.P., Sec. & Treas.--Green International-Guyana, Inc., Denver, CO, pg. 484
Moore, Roy, Treas.--Ott Food Products, Carthage, MO, pg. 831
Moran, M. Marcus, Jr., Treas. & Dir.-Personnel--W.E. Aubuchon Co., Inc., Westminster, MA, pg. 97
Moran, Richard, V.P.-Treas.--Irvine Company, Newport Beach, CA, pg. 582
Morden, Ronald P., Sr. V.P. & Treas.--American Republic Insurance Co., Des Moines, IA, pg. 60
Morell, Curtis W., V.P. & Treas.--American Capital Management & Research, Inc., Houston, TX, pg. 50
Moreno, William F., Treas.--Machado & Co. Inc., New York, NY, pg. 696
Morgan, Paul, Treas. & Sec.--F.P.A., Inc., Irving, TX, pg. 394
Moriarity, Fredrick, Treas.--Holstein Association of America, Brattleboro, VT, pg. 541
Moriarity, Fredrick, Treas.--Holstein-Friesian Services, Inc., Brattleboro, VT, pg. 541
Morin, Curtis L., Pres. & Treas.--Bennington Iron Works, Inc., Bennington, VT, pg. 139
Morral, William G., V.P.-Fin. & Treas.--Moyer Packing Company, Souderton, PA, pg. 774
Morris, Byron, Treas.--Southeastern Equipment Company, Inc., Augusta, GA, pg. 1019
Morris, Kathryn L., Sec. & Treas.--Acorn Engineering Company, City of Industry, CA, pg. 14
Morris, Melvin, Treas. & Sec.--Mountain States Constructors, Inc., Albuquerque, NM, pg. 773
Morris, Paul F., Treas.--The Fusco Corporation, New Haven, CT, pg. 437
Morrison, Gene, Treas.--Certified Grocers of Florida, Inc., Ocala, FL, pg. 237
Morrison, Kathryn D., V.P., Sec., Treas. & Pub. Rels. Dir.--The Morrison Agency, Atlanta, GA, pg. 771
Morrison, William, Sr. V.P. & Treas.--J. H. Heafner Co. Inc., Lincolnton, NC, pg. 520
Morton, Grant, Sec. & Treas.--E.H. Hughes Company, Inc., Louisville, KY, pg. 552
Mosher, Vance C., Treas.--Cadet Manufacturing Company, Vancouver, WA, pg. 207
Moss, Richard J., Mgr.-Fin. & Treas.--Hawthorne Machinery Company, San Diego, CA, pg. 519
Mossberg, Alan I., Pres., Chief Exec. & Chief Oper. Officer & Treas.--O. F. Mossberg & Sons, Inc., North Haven, CT, pg. 773
Mossholder, J., Treas.--American Packaging Corporation, Philadelphia, PA, pg. 59
Motch, Arthur E., Jr., Chm. Bd.--R. A. Jones & Co. Inc., Covington, KY, pg. 604
Mougey, Charles L., Chm. Bd., Treas. & Mgr.-Sls.--Puget Sound Plywood, Inc., Tacoma, WA, pg. 899
Mount, Brian D., Exec. V.P., Creative Dir., Sec. & Treas.--Young & Roehr, Inc., Portland, OR, pg. 1210
Moyers, Donald L., Treas., Sec. & Controller--Riddleberger Brothers, Inc., Mount Crawford, VA, pg. 933
Muck, Philip F., Pres., Chief Exec. Officer & Treas.--Munroe, Inc., Pittsburgh, PA, pg. 776
Mudd, Thomas A., Sec. & Treas.--Doe-Anderson Advertising Agency, Inc., Louisville, KY, pg. 342
Mueller, Dorothy, Sec. & Treas.--Lombard Lincoln-Mercury & Leasing, Inc., Lombard, IL, pg. 681
Mueller, O.P., Treas.--Mueller Sports Medicine, Inc., Prairie du Sac, WI, pg. 774
Mueller, Warren A., Chm. Bd. & Treas.--C & M Corporation, Wauregan, CT, pg. 198
Mueller, William, Treas.--Berlitz International, Inc., Princeton, NJ, pg. 142
Mueser, Alan, Treas.--Heavy Machines, Inc., Memphis, TN, pg. 524
Mulkey, John, Treas.--The Zamoiski Co., Baltimore, MD, pg. 1216
Mullen, Larry J., V.P.-Sls., Sec. & Treas.--Terral-Norris Seed Co., Inc., Lake Providence, LA, pg. 1088
Mullenbach, Gerald, V.P. & Treas.--Harris Mechanical Contracting Co., Saint Paul, MN, pg. 512
Muller, Richard D., V.P. & Treas.--Honorbuilt Industries, Inc., Minneapolis, KS, pg. 542
Mullett, Paul, Treas.--Blue Boar Cafeteria Co., Louisville, KY, pg. 158
Mullinax, Larry, Treas., Dir.-Pur., Data Processing, & Personnel--Ed Mullinax Ford, Inc., Amherst, OH, pg. 775
Mullins, Kay J., Treas. & Sec.--Rockford Acromatic Product Co., Rockford, IL, pg. 941
Mumford, C.G., Exec. V.P., Treas. & Chief Fin. Officer--Arcata Corporation, San Francisco, CA, pg. 80

Muncy, Darlene, V.P., Dir. Acctg., Sec. & Treas.--Caldwell VanRiper Inc., Indianapolis, IN, pg. 209
Mungo, Robert, V.P. & Treas.--Temperature Equipment Corporation, Melrose Park, IL, pg. 1086
Munier, Robert S.C., Exec. V.P. & Treas.--Wolff & Munier, Inc., Hawthorne, NY, pg. 1199
Munro, Donald, Chm. Bd., Chief Exec. Officer & Treas.--Munro & Company, Inc., Hot Springs, AR, pg. 775
Murdock, Jack C., V.P.-Fin., Sec. & Treas.--Transus Inc., Atlanta, GA, pg. 1108
Muretta, Bruce D., Treas.--Wechco, Inc., Princeton, NJ, pg. 1172
Murillo, Jess, V.P., Treas., Controller & Chief Fin. Officer--Graham Group, Inc., Des Moines, IA, pg. 475
Murphy, C. I., Treas.--South Chester Tube Co., Concordville, PA, pg. 1019
Murphy, Genevieve, Treas.--The Food Group, New York, NY, pg. 423
Murphy, George E., V.P. & Treas.--The Jupiter Corporation, Chicago, IL, pg. 609
Murphy, James F., V.P., Asst. Treas.--N W Ayer Inc., New York, NY, pg. 104
Murphy, Kathleen A., V.P. & Treas.--Connell Limited Partnership, Boston, MA, pg. 275
Murphy, Kevin, V.P. & Treas.--Murphy Company, Eugene, OR, pg. 776
Murphy, Kevin M., Chief Fin. Officer & Treas.--Rama Group of Companies, Cheektowaga, NY, pg. 910
Murphy, Thomas, Treas.--Schneider Mills, Inc., New York, NY, pg. 977
Murray, D.D., Treas. & Asst. Sec.--Green Holdings, Inc., Denver, CO, pg. 484
Murray, Edward, Treas.--Ken-Mac Metal, Inc., Cleveland, OH, pg. 622
Murray, Howard R., Treas.--Amsted Industries Incorporated, Chicago, IL, pg. 68
Murray, John J., V.P.-Fin., Sec. & Treas.--Electro-Wire Products, Inc., Rochester Hills, MI, pg. 375
Murray, John T., Treas. & Sec.--Tinius Olsen Testing Machine Co., Inc., Willow Grove, PA, pg. 1098
Murray, Ronald, Treas.--Advance Machine Company, Plymouth, MN, pg. 18
Murtaugh, J. R., V.P.-Fin., Sec. & Treas.--Anser (Analytic Services Inc.), Arlington, VA, pg. 76
Muse, Charles H., Jr., Treas. & Chief Fin. Officer--Crown Coal & Coke Co. Inc., Pittsburgh, PA, pg. 302
Must, Mary, Treas.--Detroit City Dairy, Inc., Highland Park, MI, pg. 333
Myers, Joe N., Treas. & Sec.--T. H. Rogers Lumber Co. Inc., Oklahoma City, OK, pg. 943
Myers, Larry F., Sr. V.P., Chief Fin. Officer, Sec. & Treas.--Mitre Corporation, Bedford, MA, pg. 762
Myers, Martin, Chief Fin. Officer & Treas.--Agripac Inc., Salem, OR, pg. 25
Myers, Norman S., Pres., Treas., Chief Exec. & Fin. Officers--IDM Controls, Houston, TX, pg. 560
Myers, Robert M., Treas.--Tri-State Mack Distributors, Memphis, TN, pg. 1111
Myers, Ronald W., V.P.-Fin. & Admin. & Chief Fin. Officer--GF Office Furniture Ltd., Gallatin, TN, pg. 439
Myers, William, Treas.--Dart Container Corp., Mason, MI, pg. 316
Myerson, James, Treas. & Sec.--Ben Myerson Candy Company, Inc., Los Angeles, CA, pg. 780
Myhre, Douglas E., Treas.--Adolfson & Peterson, Inc., Minneapolis, MN, pg. 18
Myhre, Paul, V.P. & Treas.--Wright-Schuchart, Inc., Seattle, WA, pg. 1204
Myrick, Bobby H., Pres. & Treas.--Myrick Construction Inc., Biscoe, NC, pg. 780
Nagaike, Howard, Treas.--Komatsu Dresser Company, Lincolnshire, IL, pg. 565
Nakash, Ralph, Treas. & Sec.--Jordache Enterprises, Inc., New York, NY, pg. 604
Napoli, Eleanor, Asst. Treas. & Controller--Carelli, Glynn & Ward, Butler, NJ, pg. 218
Naquin, Gasper K., Sec. & Treas.--Intrepid Enterprises, Inc., Harvey, LA, pg. 581
Nash, James S., Treas., Chief Fin. Officer & Controller--E.P. Henry Corporation, Woodbury, NJ, pg. 530
Nast, Glen M., Pres. & Treas.--Northern Wire & Cable, Inc., Troy, MI, pg. 814
Natali, Jodi, Treas.--The Allan R. Hackel Organization, Newton Center, MA, pg. 498
Navoy, Michael, Treas.--Epec, Inc., New Bedford, MA, pg. 384
Nazarian, Gregory L., Treas.--Levonian Brothers Inc., Troy, NY, pg. 671
Neal, Jasper T., V.P. & Treas.--Cooper Communities, Inc., Bella Vista, AR, pg. 283
Nebuloni, Angelo J., V.P.-Fin.--Allen Foods, Inc., Saint Louis, MO, pg. 36
Nedblake, Jeff, V.P. & Treas.--Package Service Company, Inc., Kansas City, MO, pg. 842
Neis, Arthur V., Chief Fin. Officer & Treas.--Life Care Services Corporation, Des Moines, IA, pg. 1174
Neis, Arthur V., Treas.--The Weitz-Cohen Construction Co., Des Moines, IA, pg. 1174
Nellis, Kirk, Controller, Treas. & Sec.--Harley Industries, Inc., Tulsa, OK, pg. 509
Nelsen, Leif A., Treas.--Nelsen Steel & Wire Co., Franklin Park, IL, pg. 797
Nelson, C.J., Treas.--Koch Industries, Incorporated, Wichita, KS, pg. 639
Nelson, J.B., Treas.--Colonial Pipeline Company, Atlanta, GA, pg. 264
Nelson, Paula, Treas.--Kolesar & Hartwell Inc., Minneapolis, MN, pg. 641
Nemschoff, Mark, Pres., Chief Exec. Officer & Treas.--Nemschoff Chairs, Inc., Sheboygan, WI, pg. 798
Nerren, Gene H., Exec. V.P. & Treas.--Brookshire Bros., Inc., Lufkin, TX, pg. 180
Neskey, David A., Chief Fin. Officer & Sr. V.P.-Fin.--Spaulding & Slye Company, Burlington, MA, pg. 1026
Nesvet, Andrew M., V.P. & Treas.--Spaulding & Slye Company, Burlington, MA, pg. 1026
Netzsch, Wolfgang, Sec. & Treas.--Netzsch, Inc., Exton, PA, pg. 798
Neu, K., Treas.--McLaughlin Gormley King Company, Minneapolis, MN, pg. 731
Neu, Richard W., Treas.--FirstFed Michigan Corporation, Detroit, MI, pg. 414
Neuman, Ronald W., Treas. & Controller--Allen-Edmonds Shoe Corp., Port Washington, WI, pg. 36
Neumann, Janet, Treas.--Valu Discount, Inc., Louisville, KY, pg. 1143
Neville, James D., Exec. V.P., Chief Fin. Officer, Treas. & Sec.--The North American Manufacturing Co., Cleveland, OH, pg. 811
Neville, Ronald A., Treas.--Twentieth Century Companies, Kansas City, MO, pg. 1121
Neville, Ronald A., Treas.--Twentieth Century Investors, Inc., Kansas City, MO, pg. 1121
Newgard, James H., Sec. & Treas.--Henry Newgard & Company, Arlington Heights, IL, pg. 804
Newhall, R.E., V.P. & Treas.--MI-Jack Products, Inc., Hazel Crest, IL, pg. 746
Newman, Stephen C., Treas. & Dir.--RNL Facilities Corporation, Denver, CO, pg. 907
Newman, Stephen C., Treas.--RNL Design, Denver, CO, pg. 907
Newman, Van, Chm. Bd. & Treas.--Newman, Saylor & Gregory, Columbia, SC, pg. 804
Newsted, Rich, V.P.-Fin. & Treas.--National Steel Corporation, Mishawaka, IN, pg. 793
Newton, Stanley B., V.P., Treas. & Sec.--Holmes Tuttle Ford, Inc., Tucson, AZ, pg. 540
Neyer, Dan, V.P. & Asst. Treas.--Al Neyer, Inc., Cincinnati, OH, pg. 805
Neyer, Thomas, Exec. V.P. & Treas.--Al Neyer, Inc., Cincinnati, OH, pg. 805
Nicastro, Frank, V.P. & Treas.--The Grand Union Company, Wayne, NJ, pg. 476
Nichols, Jacques B., Treas. & Sec.--Fabric Wholesalers, Inc., Portland, OR, pg. 396
Nichols, Larry, Treas.--Calcot, Ltd., Bakersfield, CA, pg. 208
Nicholson, Pat, Treas.--Sunrise Nissan of Orange Park, Orange Park, FL, pg. 1062
Nicholson, Paul, V.P.-Fin. & Treas.--Pay Less Super Markets, Inc., Anderson, IN, pg. 852
Nickerson, Guy, V.P.-Fin. & Treas.--Anderson Lumber Company, Ogden, UT, pg. 73
Nickles, R., Treas. & Sec.--The Dickerson Group, Inc., Monroe, NC, pg. 335
Nicola, Shirley, Sec., Treas. & Office Mgr.--Penny & Speier Inc., Houston, TX, pg. 858
Nicolaus, Penny, Sec. & Treas.--Plymouth Creameries, Inc., Plymouth, WI, pg. 877
Nidiffer, M. June, Treas. & Sec.--C & K Markets, Inc., Brookings, OR, pg. 198
Niedens, Douglas, Sec. & Treas.--Universal Construction Company, Kansas City, KS, pg. 1138
Nielsen, M.A., Pres., Chief Exec. Officer & Treas.--Wesbar Corporation, West Bend, WI, pg. 1176
Nielson, Doug, Treas.--Plaskolite Inc., Columbus, OH, pg. 874
Nielson, Norman, Treas.--Grossenburg Implements, Incorporated, Winner, SD, pg. 489
Nies, Charles, Chief Fin. Officer & Treas.--Dal-Tile Corp., Dallas, TX, pg. 312
Nikkel, Margarita, Sec. & Treas.--The Nikkel Corporation, Sacramento, CA, pg. 807
Nilsen, James P., Chief Fin. Officer & Treas.--The Fred W. Albrecht Grocery Co., Akron, OH, pg. 31
Nimnicht, Ann, Controller, Treas. & Sec.--Nimnicht Chevrolet Company, Jacksonville, FL, pg. 807
Nitsche, John, Chief Fin. Officer, V.P. & Treas.--United Hardware Distributing Co., Plymouth, MN, pg. 1132
Noell, Nicholas A., Sr. V.P. & Treas.--PMC Partnership, Ltd., Westport, CT, pg. 836
Nohra, Joseph S., V.P. & Treas.--The Cafaro Co., Youngstown, OH, pg. 207
Nolan, Patrick J., Sr. V.P., Chief Fin. Officer & Treas.--LFC Holding Corporation, Boca Raton, FL, pg. 647
Nole, R.J., Treas.--Foron International Sales Corp., Binghamton, NY, pg. 346
Nole, Robert J., Treas. & Mgr.-Mngmt. Information Systems--Doron Precision Systems, Inc., Binghamton, NY, pg. 346
Nonn, James C., Sec. & Treas.--Pemko Manufacturing Company, Ventura, CA, pg. 856
Nonnenkamp, Donald H., Treas.--Clark Oil & Refining Corporation, Saint Louis, MO, pg. 252
Noonan, Patrick, Corp. Treas.--SnyderGeneral Corporation, Dallas, TX, pg. 1015
Norberg, Joseph, Chief Fin. Officer & Treas.--Hill, Holliday, Connors, Cosmopulos, Inc., Boston, MA, pg. 534
Norman, James G., Sec. & Treas.--Norman Brothers Nissan Inc., Orlando, FL, pg. 810
Norris, Francis J., Treas. & Sec.--Mannington Mills, Inc., Salem, NJ, pg. 704
North, Richard J., V.P., Sec. & Treas.--Miller & Smith, Inc., McLean, VA, pg. 755
Norton, James G., V.P. & Treas.--Farrell Lines Incorporated, New York, NY, pg. 403
Null, Lester H., Sr., Treas. & Sec.--ULLICO Inc., Washington, DC, pg. 1124
Numme, Kaare, Treas. & Controller--American White Cross Laboratories, Inc., New Rochelle, NY, pg. 65
Nunley, Richard L., Chm. Bd., Pres. & Treas.--Better Living Inc., Charlottesville, VA, pg. 148
Nussdorf, Lawrence, Chief Fin. Officer & Treas.--CEI Construction, Inc., Bethesda, MD, pg. 200
Nussdorf, Lawrence C., Exec. V.P. & Treas.--Clark Enterprises, Inc., Bethesda, MD, pg. 252
Nutt, Frank, Treas.--North Electric Supply, Inc., Auburn Hills, MI, pg. 813
O'Brien, Patrick, V.P., Treas. & Dir.-Strategic Plng.--The Associated Press, New York, NY, pg. 91
O'Brien, Patrick, V.P., Treas. & Dir.-Strategic Planning--Wide World Photos, Inc., New York, NY, pg. 92
O'Brien, Richard M., Sec. & Treas.--Gibraltar Steel Corp., Buffalo, NY, pg. 456
O'Brien, Thomas H., Treas.--Scudder, Stevens & Clark, Inc., New York, NY, pg. 983
O'Connor, Daniel, V.P.-Fin.--Bostrom Seating, Inc., Piedmont, AL, pg. 168
O'Donahue, Claudia, Exec. V.P., Sec. & Treas.--Reid & O'Donahue Advertising, Inc., Montgomery, AL, pg. 923
O'Donnell, Patrick J., Chief Oper. Officer, Treas. & Gen. Mgr.--National Grape Co-Op Association, Inc., Westfield, NY, pg. 789
O'Halloran, Lynn, V.P., Treas.--O'Halloran Advertising, Inc., Wilton, CT, pg. 822
O'Leary, John, V.P.-Fin., Treas. & Sec.--Republic Storage Systems Company Inc., Canton, OH, pg. 928
O'Neal, Joy, V.P. & Treas.--Key Industries, Inc., Fort Scott, KS, pg. 627
O'Neil, P.A., Treas. & Sec.--O'Neil Industries Inc., Chicago, IL, pg. 827
O'Neill, Dan, Treas.--Levi Strauss & Co. (Canada), Inc., Markham,, Canada, pg. 670
O'Neill, James E., Treas.--Henkels & McCoy, Inc., Blue Bell, PA, pg. 529
O'Neill, Patrick L., Treas.--Novar Electronics, Barberton, OH, pg. 817
O'Rourke, Ruth E., Chm. & Treas.--A & A Manufacturing Co., New Berlin, WI, pg. 1
O'Shaughnessy, John, Treas.--Consolidated Beverages, Inc., Auburn, MA, pg. 276
O'Steen, Harold S., V.P. & Treas.--Coggin-O'Steen Investment Corp., Jacksonville, FL, pg. 259
O'Steen, Harold S., V.P. & Treas.--Coggin Pontiac-GMC Inc., Jacksonville, FL, pg. 259
Obelgoner, Russell, V.P. & Treas.--Yoakum Packing Company, Yoakum, TX, pg. 1208
Oberembet, Jerome J., Sec. & Treas.--Consolidated Lumber Co., Stillwater, MN, pg. 276
Oberman, Sigmund, Treas.--Aster Nut Products Inc., Newark, NJ, pg. 92
Obst, J.C., Treas.--Schenectady Chemicals, Inc., Schenectady, NY, pg. 975
Ockels, Theodore S., Pres., Chief Exec. Officer, Chief Fin. Officer & Treas.--Up-Right Work Platforms Division, Selma, CA, pg. 1139
Ohl, Glen J., Treas. & Chief Fin. Officer--Great Lakes Bancorp, Ann Arbor, MI, pg. 480
Okeleberry, Clair, Chief Exec. Officer, Treas. & Gen. Mgr.--Producers Livestock, North Salt Lake, UT, pg. 892
Okumura, Lorrane, Treas.--Valley Isle Produce, Inc., Kahului, HI, pg. 1143
Olin, Larry G., Pres., Chief Oper. Officer & Treas.--Humiston-Keeling, Inc., Chicago, IL, pg. 552
Olinde, Humphrey T., Jr., Treas. & Sec.--B. Olinde & Sons Company, Inc., Baton Rouge, LA, pg. 824
Oliveri, Elena, V.P., Sec. & Treas.--Alleson of Rochester, Inc., Rochester, NY, pg. 37
Oliveri, Theodore A., Sec. & Treas.--Penn Colour Graphics, Inc., Huntingdon Valley, PA, pg. 857
Olofson, Roy L., Treas.--Fedco, Inc., Santa Fe Springs, CA, pg. 404
Olsen, Lawrence G., V.P., Treas. & Chief Fin. Officer--Golub Corporation, Schenectady, NY, pg. 469
Olson, Bruce L., Vice Chm. & Treas.--Help Management Corporation, Overland Park, KS, pg. 527
Olson, David, V.P.-Treas., Sec. & Data Processing--Jesco, Inc., Minneapolis, MN, pg. 593
Olson, R.F., V.P., Treas. & Sec.--Treadwell Corporation, Thomaston, CT, pg. 1108
Olson, R.J., Treas.--Atlas Van Lines, Inc., Evansville, IN, pg. 96
Olson, Raymond R., Treas.--Flo-Pac Corporation, Minneapolis, MN, pg. 419
Olson, Richard F., Sec. & Treas.--Elometa Corporation, Moonachie, NJ, pg. 1108
Olson, Sherman V., Pres. & Treas.--Danafilms, Inc., Westborough, MA, pg. 313
Olson, Steven, Treas.--Head Sports, Inc., Boulder, CO, pg. 520
Olson, T.R., Treas.--Unigard Security Insurance Co., Bellevue, WA, pg. 596
Olson, T.R., Treas.--Unigard Indemnity Co., Raleigh, NC, pg. 596
Olson, T.R., Treas.--Unigard Insurance Co., Seattle, WA, pg. 596
Olson, T.R., Treas.--Unigard Service Corp., Seattle, WA, pg. 596
Olswang, Richard R., V.P. & Treas.--Crafty Beaver Home Center, Skokie, IL, pg. 295
Omer, Joyce, Treas.--Inland Associates, Inc., Olathe, KS, pg. 570
Omlor, Jack, Chief Fin. Officer & Treas.--P M Company, Philadelphia, PA, pg. 835
Oneto, Thomas, Treas.--Bromar Inc., Newport Beach, CA, pg. 179
Onraet, Robert, Chief Fin. Officer--Telesciences Co. Systems Inc., Moorestown, NJ, pg. 1085
Opdyke, Howard, Treas.--Philadelphia Reserve Supply Company, Croydon, PA, pg. 867
Oppenheimer, Adele, Treas.--Harper Industries, Inc., New York, NY, pg. 510
Opper, Lewis, Treas. & Sec.--Jacob Levy & Bros., Inc., Louisville, KY, pg. 672
Orders, William H., Chm. Bd., Chief Exec. Officer & Treas--Orders Distributing Co., Greenville, SC, pg. 829
Orlando, Ida L., Treas. & Sec.--Ortronics, Inc., Pawcatuck, CT, pg. 830
Ormsby, Clarence, V.P., Sec. & Treas.--Servaas, Inc., Indianapolis, IN, pg. 991
Orn, Gerald, Exec. V.P. & Treas.--Central Allied Enterprises, Canton, OH, pg. 232

Orrall, J. Peter, Treas.--Winthrop Printing Company, Inc., Boston, MA, pg. 1197
Ortman, Elizabeth J., Treas. & Sec.--Kokomo Grain Co., Inc., Kokomo, IN, pg. 640
Ortolani, Thecly L., Sec. & Treas.--Carton-Craft Corporation, Buffalo, NY, pg. 226
Oshinski, Jerry P., Exec. V.P., Treas. & Sec.--Hunter Corp., Portage, IN, pg. 554
Oshiro, Hank, Treas.--Sillcocks Plastics International, Inc., Berkeley Heights, NJ, pg. 1004
Oshita, Hosen, V.P., Sec. & Treas.--Newly Weds Foods Inc., Chicago, IL, pg. 804
Oshrin, Martin, Sec. & Treas.--Junior Gallery Ltd., New York, NY, pg. 609
Ossmann, Robert E., Chief Fin. Officer, Treas. & Sec.--Heller Seasonings & Ingredients, Inc., Bedford Park, IL, pg. 526
Ostdiek, Glen R., Sec. & Treas.--Tuthill Corporation, Hinsdale, IL, pg. 1120
Osterneck, Guy-Kenneth, Chm. Bd., Pres. & Treas.--The Osterneck Co. Inc., Lumberton, NC, pg. 831
Ostroff, Arthur J., Treas. & Controller--Standard Medical Imaging, Inc., Columbia, MD, pg. 1037
Otakie, Daniel A., Chm., Pres., Chief Exec. Officer & Treas.--Futures Personnel Services, Baltimore, MD, pg. 438
Otremba, Edward, Treas.--Bituminous Roadways, Inc., Minneapolis, MN, pg. 153
Otten, Gerald J., Treas.--Binkley Company, Warrenton, MO, pg. 151
Ouimet, Emil R., Chm. Bd. & Treas.--Ouimet Industries, West Wareham, MA, pg. 831
Ouimet, Emil R., Chm. Bd. & Treas.--Ouimet Corp., Nashville, TN, pg. 831
Ovenden, J.A., Chief Fin. Officer & Treas.--Clinton Mills Inc., Clinton, SC, pg. 202
Overly, Dale L., V.P.-Opers. & Treas.--Yerger Bros., Inc., Lititz, PA, pg. 1208
Owen, David, Treas.--Essex Group, Inc., Fort Wayne, IN, pg. 389
Owen, Dolores, Sec. & Treas.--Owen Industries, Inc., Carter Lake, IA, pg. 834
Owen, Sharyl, Sec., Treas. & Chief Fin. Officer--Power-One, Inc., Camarillo, CA, pg. 883
Owings, Frank, Jr., Exec. V.P., Mng. Dir., Sec. & Treas.--Service Supply Co. Inc. of Indiana, Indianapolis, IN, pg. 992
Ozag, John W., Treas.--Justrite Manufacturing Company, Des Plaines, IL, pg. 610
Ozuna, Rosemary, Treas. & Sec.--New Bedford Panoramex Corporation, Upland, CA, pg. 799
Pace, Loran, Treas.--Pacific Northern Oil Corp., Seattle, WA, pg. 841
Pachulski, Phil, Chm. Bd. & Pres.--Prime Technology, Inc., Grand Rapids, MI, pg. 889
Packard, Scott D., Sec. & Treas.--Cloverdale Equipment Co., Oak Park, MI, pg. 256
Paddack, William, Sr. V.P.--Countrymark Cooperative, Inc., Indianapolis, IN, pg. 290
Padveen, Harry K., Treas.--Ernst W. Dorn Co., Inc., Gardena, CA, pg. 346
Page, Doris B., Treas. & Sec.--Pace Oil Co., Inc., Winston-Salem, NC, pg. 838
Page, Larry A., Treas.--Allright Corporation, Houston, TX, pg. 41
Page, V.J., Sec. & Treas.--Kalamazoo Label Co., Kalamazoo, MI, pg. 615
Painter, Benjamin D., Sec. & Treas.--Borchers Bros., San Jose, CA, pg. 165
Palladini, Frank J., V.P. & Treas.--J.W. Window Components, Inc., Tampa, FL, pg. 1162
Pallat, Daniel J., Chief Fin. Officer, V.P., Treas. & Sec.--Home Juice Company, Melrose Park, IL, pg. 541
Palmer, David, Treas. & Sec.--Farnsworth Companies, Mesa, AZ, pg. 403
Palombo, Tony, Treas.--Cleaners Hanger Co., Palm Harbor, FL, pg. 254
Pamel, James P., Pres. & Treas.--National Reproductions Corporation, Madison Heights, MI, pg. 793
Pampush, Robert, Treas. & Asst. Sec.--The Sanymetal Products Co., Inc., Vanceburg, KY, pg. 970
Pangan, Alex, Sec. & Treas.--Santa Monica Ford Company, Santa Monica, CA, pg. 970
Panko, George J., Jr., Asst. Treas.--Woolrich, Inc., Woolrich, PA, pg. 1201
Panschar, Edward G., V.P., Treas. & Chief Fin. Officer--Automated Marketing Systems, Inc., Chicago, IL, pg. 100
Pansini, David, Treas. & Sec.--Jandy Industries, Novato, CA, pg. 589
Papai, Jacki, Chief Fin. Officer, Sec. & Treas.--Ventre Packing Company, Inc., Syracuse, NY, pg. 1147
Papera, Gabriel, Treas.--Allstate Can Corporation, Clifton, NJ, pg. 43
Papiernick, Donald, Treas. & Controller--The Harwood Companies, Inc., New York, NY, pg. 515
Parfet, Ray T., Jr., Sec. & Treas.--Gilmore Bros., Inc., Kalamazoo, MI, pg. 459
Paris, Donald J., V.P.-Fin. & Treas.--Condere Corporation, Hamden, CT, pg. 273
Park, J. Leonard, Chm. Bd., Pres., Chief Exec. Officer & Treas.--George W. Park Seed Co., Inc., Greenwood, SC, pg. 849
Park, John J., V.P., Dir.-Res. & Asst. Treas.--W. P. Carey & Co., Inc., New York, NY, pg. 218
Parker, Arlene F., Treas.--Pelican Products, Torrance, CA, pg. 856
Parker, Carter, Treas. & Sec.--Louisiana Utilities Supply Company, Baton Rouge, LA, pg. 684
Parker, Dennis J., V.P.-Fin., Chief Fin. Officer & Treas.--Nibco, Inc., Elkhart, IN, pg. 806
Parker, Ron C., Treas., Sec. & Chief Fin. Officer--Roseburg Forest Products Co., Dillard, OR, pg. 948
Parker, Thomas L., Pres. & Treas.--MacKinnon-Parker, Inc., Toledo, OH, pg. 697
Parks, A.L., Sec. & Treas.--Parks Products, Inc., Hollywood, CA, pg. 850
Parrish, Henry N., V.P. & Treas.--Berwick Freight Car Co., Berwick, PA, pg. 246
Parrish, Henry N., V.P. & Treas.--Maxon Marine, Inc., Tell City, IN, pg. 246
Parrish, Sterlin, Treas.--U.S. Oil & Refining Co., Tacoma, WA, pg. 1097
Pas, Greg, V.P., Chief Fin. Officer & Treas.--Squire-Cogswell Company, Northbrook, IL, pg. 1034
Pate, Anne W., V.P. & Treas.--Roper Bros. Lumber Co., Inc., Petersburg, VA, pg. 947
Patterson, Barry, Treas.--McKee Foods Corporation, Collegedale, TN, pg. 730
Patterson, Barry, Chief Fin. Officer & Treas.--McKee Baking Co., Inc., Collegedale, TN, pg. 730
Patterson, L. Leon, Treas.--The American Bankers Association, Washington, DC, pg. 49
Patterson, William, Treas.--Neapco, Inc., Pottstown, PA, pg. 1123
Paturzo, Michael R., Treas. & Sec.--Henningsen Foods, Inc., White Plains, NY, pg. 629
Paukstis, Charles A., V.P.-Fin. & Treas.--Suburban Communications Corp., Livonia, MI, pg. 1055
Paul, Melvyn, Treas.--Garsite/TSR, Inc., Kansas City, KS, pg. 443
Paul, Steven M., Treas.--Price Brothers Co., Dayton, OH, pg. 888
Paullin, Arthur, V.P. & Treas.--Capitol Construction Group, Inc., Wheeling, IL, pg. 215
Pave, Gary D., Treas.--Rodale Press, Inc., Emmaus, PA, pg. 942
Pavony, William, Exec. V.P.-Admin. & Treas.--The Kobacker Company & Affiliates, Columbus, OH, pg. 638
Pawlowski, Walter, Treas. & Controller--H. B. Smith Co., Inc., Westfield, MA, pg. 1013
Peabody, Carol, V.P. & Treas.--Sundt Corp., Tucson, AZ, pg. 1060
Peabody, Jonathan C., V.P. & Treas.--Peabody Office Furniture Corporation, Boston, MA, pg. 853
Pearce, Stephen R., V.P. & Treas.--Pearce Industries Inc., Houston, TX, pg. 853
Pearl, Manny, Sec. & Treas.--Pearl-Pressman-Liberty Communications Group, Philadelphia, PA, pg. 853
Pearlman, Ted, V.P., Sec. & Treas.--Atlite Lighting Equip, Inc., Maspeth, NY, pg. 97
Pease, Claudia H., Treas.--Caraustar Industries, Inc., Austell, GA, pg. 217
Peck, Aaron M., Treas. & Sec.--Peck Iron & Metal Company, Inc., Portsmouth, VA, pg. 854
Peck, Stephen D., Sr. V.P., Chief Fin. Officer & Treas.--Phillips Publishing Inc., Potomac, MD, pg. 868
Peckham, Rod, V.P. & Treas.--Forstmann & Company, Inc., New York, NY, pg. 424
Pedersen, Gary, Chief Fin. Officer--Gabbert's, Inc., Minneapolis, MN, pg. 441
Peeler, Nancy Carole, Treas. & Sec.--Peelers Rug Company, Inc., Gaffney, SC, pg. 855
Peiffer, Matt, Treas.--Wyatt Cafeterias Inc., Dallas, TX, pg. 1205
Pelkowski, Larry, Treas.--John Wieland Homes of Charleston, Inc., Mount Pleasant, SC, pg. 1189
Pelkowski, Lawrence J., Treas.--John Wieland Homes Inc., Atlanta, GA, pg. 1188
Peltier, Wes, V.P.-Fin. & Treas.--Polar Ware Company, Sheboygan, WI, pg. 878
Pemberton, Alan, V.P. & Treas.--Anderson Lithograph Company, Los Angeles, CA, pg. 73
Pena, John, V.P. & Treas.--Gurley Motor Company, Gallup, NM, pg. 494
Pender, John H., Sr. V.P., Chief Invest. Officer & Member Invest. Services--Aid Association For Lutherans, Appleton, WI, pg. 26
Pendrey, J.C., Jr., Sr. V.P., Chief Fin. Officer, Sec. & Treas.--Holder Corporation, Atlanta, GA, pg. 538
Penner, W. Robert, Sr. V.P., Chief Fin. Officer & Asst. Treas.--Century 21 Real Estate Corp., Irvine, CA, pg. 744
Penno, D. Bruce, Chief Fin. Officer & Treas.--Pridgeon & Clay, Inc., Grand Rapids, MI, pg. 889
Penske, Richard H., Chm. Bd., Pres. & Treas.--Piercing Pagoda, Inc., Bethlehem, PA, pg. 870
Penz, William F., Exec. V.P. & Treas.--Ludington News Co. Inc., Detroit, MI, pg. 686
Peotter, D.L., Treas.--Fox River Paper Company, Appleton, WI, pg. 428
Pepys, Eric C., Sec. & Treas.--Dot Printer, Inc., Irvine, CA, pg. 347
Peraldo, Leo, V.P.-Fin., Treas. & Sec.--Klaussner Corporation, Asheboro, NC, pg. 634
Peraldo, Leo, V.P.-Fin., Treas. & Sec.--Klaussner Furniture Industry, Asheboro, NC, pg. 634
Percival, Sylvia, Treas.--Intelligent Controls Inc., Lynnwood, WA, pg. 573
Peritz, Abraham, Exec. V.P. & Treas.--Ruder, Finn, Inc., New York, NY, pg. 954
Perkins, Lawrence, Chm. Bd., Pres. & Treas.--Connecticut Container Corporation, North Haven, CT, pg. 274
Perlmuter, Bruce, Sec., Treas. & V.P.-Opers.--Perlmuter Printing Company, Cleveland, OH, pg. 862
Perrier, Art, Exec. V.P., Treas. & Sec.--Maryland Paper Box Company, Baltimore, MD, pg. 717
Perry, Carmen, Sec., Treas. & Controller--Outdoor Venture Corp., Stearns, KY, pg. 832
Perry, Christopher, Asst. Treasurer--Ocean Spray Cranberries, Inc., Lakeville, MA, pg. 820
Perry, Harold, V.P. & Treas.--Plant Maintenance Service Corporation, Memphis, TN, pg. 874
Perry, Jay, Sec., Treas. & Controller--Steiny & Company, Inc., Los Angeles, CA, pg. 1049
Perry, Marion E., Sec. & Treas.--Detecto Scale Company, Webb City, MO, pg. 332
Peske, Milian, Treas. & Sec.--Metric & Multistandard Components, Hawthorne, NY, pg. 743
Peter, James, Treas.--Christy's Markets, Inc., Brockton, MA, pg. 249
Peters, J.L., Jr., Vice Chm. & Treas.--Fairfax Lumber & Millwork Company Inc., Springfield, VA, pg. 397
Peters, Philip, Treas.--Long Island Water Corporation, Lynbrook, NY, pg. 682
Peters, Phillip H., Treas. & Comptroller--Continental Water Company, Saint Louis, MO, pg. 280
Peters, Richard J., V.P. & Treas.--Penske Corporation, Detroit, MI, pg. 859
Petersen, Eric, Chm. Bd. & Treas.--Petersen Graphics Group, South Bend, IN, pg. 864
Petersen, John M., Pres., Chief Fin. Officer & Treas.--Erie Family Life Insurance Company, Erie, PA, pg. 386
Petersen, John M., Pres., Chief Fin. Officer & Treas.--Erie Insurance Group, Erie, PA, pg. 386
Petersen, John M., Pres., Chief Fin. Officer & Treas.--Erie Indemnity Company, Erie, PA, pg. 386
Petersen, John M., Pres., Chief Fin. Officer & Treas.--Erie Insurance Exchange, Erie, PA, pg. 386
Peterson, Franklin, Treas.--American Mathematical Society, Inc., Providence, RI, pg. 58
Peterson, Jean, Treas. & Sec.--Peterson Motor Company, Boise, ID, pg. 865
Petit, Charles E., Exec. V.P., Chief Fin. Officer & Treas.--Fitzgerald & Company, Inc., Cranston, RI, pg. 416
Petrarca, Lenora, Treas.--The Cedarwood Companies, Akron, OH, pg. 230
Petricca, Virginia R., Treas.--Petricca Industries, Inc., Pittsfield, MA, pg. 865
Petry, Paul E., Exec. V.P., Chief Fin. Officer & Treas.--Connecticut Mutual Life Insurance Company, Hartford, CT, pg. 274
Pettey, John, Treas. & Chief Fin. Officer--Kemmons Wilson Companies, Memphis, TN, pg. 1194
Pettit, Scott, Treas. & Asst. Sec.--Globe Glass & Mirror Co., Chicago, IL, pg. 463
Pettygrove, Sharon, Asst. Treas.--O'Malia Food Markets Inc., Noblesville, IN, pg. 825
Pfeifer, Greg, Treas. & Chief Fin. Officer--Rochester-Midland ICL, Omaha, NE, pg. 941
Pfeil, Robert J., Sr. V.P., Chief Fin. Officer & Treas.--H. C. Prange Company, Green Bay, WI, pg. 884
Pfinsgraff, Martin, V.P. & Treas.--The Prudential Insurance Company of America, Newark, NJ, pg. 896
Pfister, Terry W., V.P.-Fin., Chief Fin. Officer, Sec. & Treas.--Enerfab Inc., Cincinnati, OH, pg. 381
Phagans, T. M., Sec. & Treas.--Addison Steel Inc., Orlando, FL, pg. 17
Phillips, Dayton, Sec. & Treas.--Fischer Lime & Cement Company, Memphis, TN, pg. 414
Phillips, James R., Treas.--American Management Group, Westbrook, ME, pg. 57
Phillips, Randy, Treas.--Portland Glass/American Management Group, Westbrook, ME, pg. 58
Phillis, Thomas J., V.P.-Fin. & Treas.--Burrell Group, New Kensington, PA, pg. 195
Phipps, Robecca, Treas.--Anchor Industries Inc., Evansville, IN, pg. 71
Piani, Brian, V.P.-Fin. & Treas.--Yankee Publishing Incorporated, Dublin, NH, pg. 1207
Pickering, Allen, Chief Exec. Officer, Treas. & Sec.--Pickering Industries Inc., Tacoma, WA, pg. 869
Pickert, Richard, Treas.--The National Enquirer, Lantana, FL, pg. 788
Picknelly, Peter A., Jr., Pres. & Chief Exec. Officer--Peter Pan Bus Lines, Inc., Springfield, MA, pg. 864
Picon, John, Chief Fin. Officer & Treas.--RE/MAX International, Inc., Englewood, CO, pg. 915
Picou, Richard, V.P., Sec. & Treas.--Picou Brothers Construction Company, Gonzales, LA, pg. 870
Piel, William G., V.P. & Treas.--John Alden Financial Corporation, Miami, FL, pg. 32
Pierce, A. Kenneth, Jr., V.P. & Chief Fin. Officer--The Dispatch Printing Company, Columbus, OH, pg. 339
Pierce, Edwin, Treas. & Mgr.-Pur.--Tolleson Lumber Company, Inc., Perry, GA, pg. 1100
Piercy, William H., Sec. & Treas.--Dunmore Corporation, Newtown, PA, pg. 353
Pieri, Albert, V.P., Sec. & Treas.--Artichoke Industries, Inc., Castroville, CA, pg. 87
Pierpont, Wilbur K., Treas.--R & B Machine Tool Co., Saline, MI, pg. 906
Pifer, Glenn A., Treas. & Sec.--Allied Security, Inc., Pittsburgh, PA, pg. 39
Pike, Jim, V.P. & Treas.--Mobile Technology Inc., Los Angeles, CA, pg. 762
Pike, Mary Anne, Treas. & Sec.--Elite Lamp, Inc., West Memphis, AR, pg. 376
Piluso, Richard E., Treas.--American Institute of C.P.A.'s Inc., New York, NY, pg. 56
Pingree, Gary, Treas.--Strongheart Products, Inc., Kansas City, KS, pg. 1054
Piranian, Poozant, Treas.--Interroyal Corporation, Warren, PA, pg. 580
Pirillo, Joseph A., V.P. & Treas.--Budget Marketing, Inc., Des Moines, IA, pg. 186
Pirtle, Lee, V.P., Fin., Sec. & Treas.--Responsive Marketing Communications, Inc., Schaumburg, IL, pg. 929
Pisani, Patricia, Sec. & Treas.--APG Security, Inc., Denver, CO, pg. 5
Pisarski, Pat, Treas.--Airways Rent A Car, Schiller Park, IL, pg. 934
Pitts, Jayne M., Treas.--The Lane Construction Corp., Meriden, CT, pg. 656
Pizel, Ken, Chief Fin. Officer & Treas.--Wenger Corporation, Owatonna, MN, pg. 1176
Place, Lee, V.P. & Treas.--Pullman Industries, Inc., Madison Heights, MI, pg. 900
Plack, Jeff, Treas., Controller & Corp. Sec.--Orix Real Estate Equities, Inc., Chicago, IL, pg. 829
Pleau, Gene, Sec. & Treas.--Future Ford/Hugo Inc., Roseville, CA, pg. 437

Plunkett, Rick, V.P., Sec. & Treas.--Ivan Allen Company, Inc., Atlanta, GA, pg. 36
Polera, Catherine, Pres., Chief Fin. Officer, Sec. & Treas.--Polera Building Corp., Scarsdale, NY, pg. 878
Pollack, Stanley C., Treas.--Pollack Corporation, Scarborough, ME, pg. 879
Pollard, Boyd A., Sec. & Treas.--Power & Telephone Supply Company, Memphis, TN, pg. 883
Pollock, B.R., Sec. & Treas.--Morris Coupling Co., Erie, PA, pg. 771
Pollock, Maurice, V.P., Treas. & Controller--Collin Street Bakery, Corsicana, TX, pg. 262
Pomeranz, Harold, Chm. Bd., Treas. & Sec.--Stanley Roberts, Inc., Lodi, NJ, pg. 939
Pona, Vincent, Treas.--Cyberex, Inc., Mentor, OH, pg. 307
Poole, John, Sec. & Treas.--Daycon Products Company, Inc., Capitol Heights, MD, pg. 321
Poole, Norman A., Sr. V.P.-Fin. & Treas.--L.L. Bean, Inc., Freeport, ME, pg. 648
Porteous, L. Robert, Jr., Chm. Bd., Sec. & Treas.--Porteous, South Portland, ME, pg. 353
Porter, David, Treas.--Dreisbach & Sons Cadillac Company, Detroit, MI, pg. 348
Porter, Marc A., Chief Fin. Officer, V.P. & Treas.--The Law Company, Inc., Wichita, KS, pg. 661
Portsmore, Dennis M., V.P., Treas. & Dir.-Data Processing--Reitman Industries, West Caldwell, NJ, pg. 924
Posner, Kenneth R., V.P. & Treas.--Dalfort Corp., Dallas, TX, pg. 312
Posner, Sidney, Chm. Bd., Chief Exec. Officer, Treas.--Newmark, Posner & Mitchell, Inc., New York, NY, pg. 804
Potamkin, Allen, Treas.--Potamkin Manhattan, New York, NY, pg. 882
Potter, Carl, Treas.--Dakota Electric Association, Farmington, MN, pg. 312
Potter, Donald K., Treas.--Columbia Farms Inc., Leesville, SC, pg. 265
Potts, W. L., Jr., Chief Fin. Officer, Treas. & Controller--Nutech, Inc., San Jose, CA, pg. 817
Potwin, Peter V., Treas.--Benson Industries, Inc., Portland, OR, pg. 139
Pou, William K., Sr., Exec. V.P. & Asst. Sec. & Treas.--W.S. Badcock Corporation, Mulberry, FL, pg. 113
Poulos, Lori J., V.P., Treas., Controller & Sec.--Bridgewater Resources Corporation, Beverly Hills, CA, pg. 175
Pourciau, Susan, Treas.--Fraenkel Company, Baton Rouge, LA, pg. 428
Prather, Robert L., Exec. V.P., Sec. & Treas.--Kocolene Oil Corp., Seymour, IN, pg. 639
Pratt, Cliff W., Pres. & Treas.--Universal Molding Company, Lynwood, CA, pg. 1139
Pratt, R. George, Jr., Pres. & Treas.--Bradford Oil Company, Inc., Bradford, VT, pg. 170
Pratt, Sharon, Sec. & Treas.--Lou LaRiche Chevrolet-Subaru Inc., Plymouth, MI, pg. 658
Pratte, Gary D., Pres. & Treas.--E.J. Bartells Co., Renton, WA, pg. 122
Presto, Mark A., Treas.--GAF Corporation, Wayne, NJ, pg. 438
Preston, Kevin L., Treas.--United Republic Reinsurance Company, Houston, TX, pg. 662
Price, Christopher L., Treas.--W. O. Bankston Enterprises Inc., Dallas, TX, pg. 118
Price, Frank W., Treas.--American Development Corporation, North Charleston, SC, pg. 51
Price, Gary L., Treas. & Comptroller--Ben Venue Laboratories, Inc., Bedford, OH, pg. 138
Price, Gordon, Controller, Treas. & Sec.--Coleman Cadillac Inc., Bethesda, MD, pg. 261
Price, James R., Treas.--Lewis Homes Management Corp., Upland, CA, pg. 673
Price, Jeffrey, Treas.--Countrymark Co-Op Inc., Delaware, OH, pg. 290
Pride, Robert M., V.P. & Treas.--Converse Professional Group, Inc., Pasadena, CA, pg. 281
Prieto, Angelo, Sr. V.P.-Fin. & Treas.--Globe Mortgage Company, Hackensack, NJ, pg. 464
Printz, Victoria, Sec. & Treas.--Somerset Pontiac GMC Inc., Troy, MI, pg. 1017
Prischak, Isabel J., Treas.--Plastek Group, Erie, PA, pg. 874
Propst, John, Treas.--Charles Town Races, Inc., Charles Town, WV, pg. 240
Proudfit, Debe, Sec. & Treas.--Vanport Manufacturing, Inc., Boring, OR, pg. 1145
Purvis, Darwin W., Treas.--Hoffman Corporation, Portland, OR, pg. 537
Purvis, J.E., Pres. & Treas.--A.C. Legg Packing Company, Inc., Birmingham, AL, pg. 666
Putnam, Thomas, Pres.--Markem Corporation, Keene, NH, pg. 708
Putterman, Saul, Pres. & Treas.--Milton Shoe Manufacturing Company, Inc., Milton, PA, pg. 756
Puvalowski, Gary O., Treas.--R. L. Polk & Co., Detroit, MI, pg. 879
Qualls, Robert, Treas.--Haggar Apparel Company, Dallas, TX, pg. 499
Quebedeaux, Carol, V.P., Sec. & Treas.--Quebedeaux Pontiac, Inc., Tucson, AZ, pg. 904
Quicksall, Doug, V.P., Chief Fin. Officer & Treas.--Central Freight Lines Inc., Waco, TX, pg. 232
Quirch, Eduardo, Treas.--E & G Foods, Miami, FL, pg. 358
Rabin, Erwin, Sec. & Treas.--Nationwide Beef, Inc., Chicago, IL, pg. 795
Rachey, Loren, Treas.--API Group Inc., Saint Paul, MN, pg. 5
Racibozynski, Frank, Treas. & Fin.--Metra, Commuter Rail Service Board, Chicago, IL, pg. 922
Radwill, Alvera, Chm. Bd., Chief Fin. Officer & Treas.--Master Appliance Corp., Racine, WI, pg. 719
Rafanello, Richard A., Treas. & Sec.--E.C.D., Inc., Hillside, NJ, pg. 359
Raffel, William D., Exec. V.P., Treas.--Smith, Badofsky & Raffel, Inc. Advertising, Chicago, IL, pg. 1011
Raines, Bobby J., V.P. & Treas.--Cal-Maine Foods, Inc., Jackson, MS, pg. 208
Rainville, Donald, Pres. & Chief Oper. Officer--Universal Dynamics, Inc., Woodbridge, VA, pg. 1138
Rakolta, John, Jr., Pres., Chief Exec. Officer & Treas.--Walbridge Aldinger Company, Detroit, MI, pg. 1158
Rakow, Thomas S., Pres., Chief Exec. Officer & Treas.--Illinois Hydraulic Construction Company, South Elgin, IL, pg. 563
Raley, Ruth, Sec. & Treas.--The Thompson Group Companies, Henderson, KY, pg. 1094
Ralph, Marvin G., Sec. & Treas.--Lumco Industries, Inc., Philadelphia, PA, pg. 687
Ramadei, John A., V.P.-Fin. & Treas.--Novametrix Medical Systems Inc., Wallingford, CT, pg. 817
Ramos, Antonio C., Pres. & Treas.--New England Stone Industries, Inc., Esmond, RI, pg. 800
Ramsey, Paul, Treas.--Milk Marketing Inc., Strongsville, OH, pg. 753
Ramsey, Stewart P., Treas. & Sec.--LSJ Sportswear Inc., Deerfield, WI, pg. 739
Ramus, David W., V.P., Controller, Treas. & Chief Fin. Officer--M & T Incorporated, Portland, OR, pg. 690
Rands, L. William, Chief Fin. Officer, V.P. & Treas.--Monroc, Inc., Salt Lake City, UT, pg. 766
Rands, Mary, Sec. & Treas.--Brush Research Manufacturing Company, Los Angeles, CA, pg. 184
Rank, David L., V.P.-Fin. & Treas.--Nibble with Gibble's, Inc., Chambersburg, PA, pg. 806
Rankin, Stuart, Treas. & New Bus. Contact--Equinox Advertising, Inc., Chicago, IL, pg. 384
Rao, Kenneth, Treas.--Rao Wholesale Tire Centers, Inc., Detroit, MI, pg. 912
Rapaport, Jonathan, Chief Fin. Officer, V.P. & Treas.--Pacesetter Steel Service, Inc., Marietta, GA, pg. 839
Rapp, Ronald J., Treas.--Jabil Circuit Inc., Saint Petersburg, FL, pg. 587
Raschke, Carl, Treas.--Mark III Industries, Ocala, FL, pg. 708
Rasmussen, Thomas, V.P. & Treas.--Tiernay Metals, Inc., Redondo Beach, CA, pg. 1096
Rasole, V.C., Treas.--American Trading Transportation Co., Inc., New York, NY, pg. 65
Ratcliff, G.A., Treas.--Rentenbach Engineering Company, Knoxville, TN, pg. 927
Ravino, James, Treas.--Creative Salon Furniture Inc., Brooklyn, NY, pg. 297
Rawson, Arthur, Treas.--United Broadcasting Inc., Bethesda, MD, pg. 1131
Ray, E. Wayne, Jr., V.P.-Fin.--Riviana Foods Inc., Houston, TX, pg. 937
Raymonds, Catherine, Treas.--Captive Plastics, Piscataway, NJ, pg. 216
Reardon, Leonard, V.P.-Fin. & Treas., Chief Fin. Officer--Hobart Brothers Co., Troy, OH, pg. 536
Record, John F., Sr. V.P. & Treas.--International Communications Group, Inc., Los Angeles, CA, pg. 576
Redden, W. Glenn, Mgr.-Fin. & Opers.--Associated Process Controls, Pleasanton, CA, pg. 92
Redler, Joel B., V.P. & Treas.--Forbes, Inc., New York, NY, pg. 423
Reed, Brad, Chief Oper. Officer, Sec. & Treas.--Kova Fertilizer Inc., Greensburg, IN, pg. 643
Reed, James J., V.P. & Treas.--The Davey Tree Expert Company, Kent, OH, pg. 317
Reed, Raymond, Treas. & Gen. Sls. Mgr.--Reed Motors, Inc., Orlando, FL, pg. 920
Reed, Ted, Sr. V.P.-Investments & Treas.--Silver Dollar City, Inc., Branson, MO, pg. 1004
Reed, Ward, Treas.--Science Applications International Corporation, San Diego, CA, pg. 981
Reeder, Jeff, V.P. & Treas.--Gerland Corp., Houston, TX, pg. 454
Reese, Willis, Treas.--Affiliated Food Stores, Keller, TX, pg. 23
Reeve, Michael, Asst. Treas.--Malden Mills Industries, Inc., Lawrence, MA, pg. 702
Reeves, Charles, Chief Fin. Officer & Treas.--Tennessee Farmers Co-op, La Vergne, TN, pg. 1087
Reeves, John, Treas.--The Reeves Agency, Inc., Baltimore, MD, pg. 921
Regala, John, Treas. & Chief Fin. Officer--Antares Group Inc., Cleveland, OH, pg. 76
Regan, Tim, Treas.--The Scoular Company, Omaha, NE, pg. 983
Regan, William J., Sr. V.P. & Treas.--United Services Automobile Association (USAA), San Antonio, TX, pg. 1134
Rege, Thomas J., Chief Fin. Officer, Sec., Treas. & Controller--Chartway Technologies, Rockville, MD, pg. 240
Regenbogen, Howard, Treas.--North American Watch Corporation, Lyndhurst, NJ, pg. 812
Register, John R., Sr. V.P., Chief Fin. Officer & Treas.--Technology Applications, Inc., Alexandria, VA, pg. 1083
Reidbord, Gilda P., Exec. V.P., Sec. & Treas.--Reidbord Bros., Inc., Pittsburgh, PA, pg. 923
Reif, David P., Chief Fin. Officer--Stonhard, Inc., Maple Shade, NJ, pg. 1051
Reihman, Shirley, Treas.--Amana Society, Amana, IA, pg. 46
Reilly, J.G., Exec. V.P. & Treas.--The Fairfield Lumber & Supply Company, Fairfield, CT, pg. 397
Reilly, William A., V.P. & Treas.--Cross & Brown Company, New York, NY, pg. 744
Reimel, T.L., Pres. & Treas.--Reimel Carter Advertising, Inc., Philadelphia, PA, pg. 923
Reinhart, J.W., Controller & Asst. Treas.--Logan & Kanawha Coal Co., Cincinnati, OH, pg. 681
Reinschmidt, George H., V.P. & Treas.--Freeman Decorating Co., Dallas, TX, pg. 431
Reiss, Richard T., Pres. & Treas.--R.C.A. Rubber Company, Akron, OH, pg. 906
Replogle, Dan, Treas.--Wheaton Inc., Millville, NJ, pg. 1184
Restivo, Joseph, Asst. Treas.--Blade Communications, Inc., Toledo, OH, pg. 155
Retcher, M.F., Chief Fin. Officer & Treas.--Art Iron, Inc., Toledo, OH, pg. 86
Retman, Richard, Treas.--General Safety Corporation, Saint Clair Shores, MI, pg. 450
Reyes, Nora, Sec./Treas.--Communications Plus, Inc., New York, NY, pg. 269
Reynolds, James F., Treas. & Dir.-Pur.--Croll-Reynolds Company, Westfield, NJ, pg. 300
Rhudy, Huey J., Treas. & Sec.--STRAFCO, Inc., San Antonio, TX, pg. 1052
Rhyne, Neal H., V.P.-Fin., Sec. & Treas.--Cochrane Furniture Co., Inc., Lincolnton, NC, pg. 258
Riccione, Mitch, Treas.--Ranging, East Bloomfield, NY, pg. 300
Rice, Andrew L., Asst. Treas.--Estes Express Lines, Inc., Richmond, VA, pg. 389
Rice, Bernard J., Jr., Sec. & Treas.--Blue Grass Foods, Inc., Crescent Springs, KY, pg. 160
Rice, D.A., V.P. & Treas.--American Plastic Toys Inc., Walled Lake, MI, pg. 59
Rice, Roberta, V.P., Treas. & Sec.--Western Linen Corp., Phoenix, AZ, pg. 1180
Rich, Brad, V.P.-Opers. & Treas.--Rena-Ware Distributors Inc., Redmond, WA, pg. 926
Richard, R.P., Treas.--The Florists Assn. of Greater Cleveland, Inc., Cleveland, OH, pg. 421
Richards, Dave, Treas. & Controller--Pacific Hide & Fur Depot, Great Falls, MT, pg. 840
Richards, G.A., Treas.--Ohio Gas Company, Bryan, OH, pg. 822
Richardson, Thomas, V.P., Sec., Treas. & Controller--Aladdin Petroleum Corporation, Wichita, KS, pg. 29
Richert, Edward, V.P.-Fin. & Admin., & Treas.--Office Electronics, Inc., Itasca, IL, pg. 821
Richter, Lyle H., V.P., Treas. & Sec.--Fox Valley Corporation, Appleton, WI, pg. 427
Ricke, Beatrice, Sec. & Treas.--Motek Engineering & Manufacturing Company, Cambridge, MN, pg. 773
Ricketts, Barrie, V.P.-Fin. & Treas.--Geo. J. Ball, Inc., West Chicago, IL, pg. 115
Ridenour, Mark, Exec. V.P. & Treas.--Heidtman Steel Products, Inc., Toledo, OH, pg. 525
Rider, Robert F., Chm., Chief Exec. Officer & Treas.--O. A. Newton & Son Co., Bridgeville, DE, pg. 805
Ridgway, Jeanne, V.P.-Fin. & Treas.--Mullen Advertising, Inc., Wenham, MA, pg. 775
Riederer, D.E., Treas.--Welch's, Concord, MA, pg. 789
Riely, Sandra, Sec. & Treas.--Hood Communications, Inc., Grand Terrace, CA, pg. 543
Rieman, Stephen R., Sec. & Treas.--Bard Mfg. Co., Bryan, OH, pg. 119
Riffert, Dennis, Controller & Treas.--Citizens Realty & Insurance Inc., Evansville, IN, pg. 251
Rigoni, Douglas R., Treas.--Bacco Construction Co., Iron Mountain, MI, pg. 108
Riha, Frances, Sec. & Treas.--Office Equipment Company Of Chicago, Chicago, IL, pg. 821
Riley, James, V.P., Chief Fin. Officer & Treas.--Republic Engineered Steels, Inc., Massillon, OH, pg. 928
Rillings, Robert, V.P. & Asst. Treas.--Park Ridge Corporation, Park Ridge, NJ, pg. 849
Rillings, Robert H., Treas.--The Hertz Corporation, Park Ridge, NJ, pg. 849
Ringley, Edward M., Treas.--Consolidated Systems, Inc., Columbia, SC, pg. 277
Ritacco, John A., V.P. & Treas.--G.F. Wright Steel & Wire Company, Worcester, MA, pg. 1205
Ritchie, H.D., Treas.--Ritchie Corporation, Wichita, KS, pg. 936
Rittershaus, Fred J., V.P. & Treas.--Banner Associates Inc., Laramie, WY, pg. 118
Robb, Mary Susan, Corp. Sec. & Treas.--Blue Cross and Blue Shield of Oklahoma, Tulsa, OK, pg. 159
Robbins, Stanley, Treas.--Robbins Auto Parts, Inc., Dover, NH, pg. 938
Roberson, James E., Sec. & Treas.--Merchants Truck Line, Inc., New Albany, MS, pg. 740
Roberts, C. J., Jr., Pres., Chief Oper. Officer & Treas.--The Leavell Company, El Paso, TX, pg. 664
Roberts, E.D., Jr., Sr. V.P. & Treas.--Parish Water Company, Inc., Baton Rouge, LA, pg. 126
Roberts, Michael D., 1st V.P., Controller & Asst. Treas.--W. P. Carey & Co., Inc., New York, NY, pg. 218
Roberts, Michael V., V.P.-Fin. & Treas.--Soft Sheen Products, Inc., Chicago, IL, pg. 1016
Roberts, Raymond J., Treas.--Coilcraft, Inc., Cary, IL, pg. 259
Roberts, Robert A., Pres. & Treas.--C.F. Haglin & Sons, Minneapolis, MN, pg. 499
Roberts, Seth, V.P. & Asst. Treas.--F. L. Roberts & Co. Inc., Springfield, MA, pg. 938
Roberts, Stephen M., Pres., Chief Exec. Officer & Treas.--F. L. Roberts & Co. Inc., Springfield, MA, pg. 938
Roberts, Xenia, Sec. & Treas.--Chas Roberts Air Conditioning, Inc., Phoenix, AZ, pg. 938
Robertson, I. Howard, Jr., Treas. & Chief Fin. Officer--Robertson's Auto Salvage, Wareham, MA, pg. 939
Robertson, Richard A., Treas.--G.B. DuPont Co., Inc., Troy, MI, pg. 354
Robinette, Douglas C., V.P. & Treas.--Nationwide Mutual Insurance Company, Columbus, OH, pg. 795
Robins, R. Steven, Sec., Treas., Controller & Cash Mgr.--Builder Marts of America, Greenville, SC, pg. 187
Robinson, Barbara, Chief Fin. Officer & Treas.--Robinson Helicopter Company, Inc., Torrance, CA, pg. 940
Robinson, Fran, Chief Fin. Officer & Treas.--National Mortgage Company, Memphis, TN, pg. 792
Robinson, Jerry D., Chief Fin. Officer, V.P. & Treas.--SFA, Inc., Landover, MD, pg. 961
Robinson, John R., V.P. & Treas.--Purity Dairies Inc., Nashville, TN, pg. 901

Robinson, Richard, Treas.--William Lyon Company, Newport Beach, CA, pg. 690
Robinson, Timothy C., Asst. Treas.--The Kobacker Company & Affiliates, Columbus, OH, pg. 638
Robles, Estela, Sec. & Treas.--La Reina, Inc., Los Angeles, CA, pg. 649
Robson, Jack, Treas.--John Carlo Inc., Mount Clemens, MI, pg. 220
Rocush, Peter, Sec. & Treas.--Gerrard and Company, Des Plaines, IL, pg. 454
Rodbell, Paul N., V.P. & Treas.--Apex Supply Co. Inc., Atlanta, GA, pg. 78
Rodd, Allan K., Treas. & Asst. Sec.--The Wooster Brush Company, Wooster, OH, pg. 1202
Rode, Emmy, Treas.--Remarks, Inc., Dublin, OH, pg. 925
Rodriguez, Juana, Treas.--Mason Distributors, Inc., Hialeah, FL, pg. 718
Rodriguez, Ulijes E., Treas. & Sec.--Power Engineering Co. Inc., Coral Gables, FL, pg. 883
Roedl, Suzanne, Chief Fin. Officer--Condor D.C. Power Supplies Inc., Oxnard, CA, pg. 273
Roepkey, Marianne, Treas.--Twentieth Century Investors, Kansas City, MO, pg. 1121
Rogalski, Don, V.P.-Fin. & Admin. & Treas.--The Stiffel Company, Chicago, IL, pg. 1049
Rogers, A. B., Jr., Treas.--Guaranty Corporation, Baton Rouge, LA, pg. 491
Rogers, James, Treas.--Times Fiber Communications, Inc., Wallingford, CT, pg. 648
Rogers, James P., V.P. & Treas.--International Specialty Products, Inc., Wilmington, DE, pg. 438
Rogers, James P., Treas.--LPL Technologies, Inc., Wallingford, CT, pg. 648
Rogers, John, Treas. & Controller--Mallery Lumber Corp., Emporium, PA, pg. 702
Rogers, John Baird, Chief Fin. Officer, V.P. & Treas.--Zytec Corp., Eden Prairie, MN, pg. 1221
Rogoski, Patricia D., Sr. V.P., Treas. & Chief Fin. Officer--Guardsmark, Inc., Memphis, TN, pg. 492
Rohanna, John, Sec. & Treas.--Lumbermens Merchandising Corporation, Wayne, PA, pg. 687
Rohde, Stephen L., V.P.-Fin. & Treas.--MSI Insurance Companies, Arden Hills, MN, pg. 693
Rohrbacker, Raymond B., V.P., Sec. & Treas.--Nooter Corporation, Saint Louis, MO, pg. 808
Rold, Stephen K., V.P., Treas., Sec. & Controller--Roofing Wholesale Co., Inc., Phoenix, AZ, pg. 946
Romano, D.V., Treas.--Wakefern Food Corporation, Elizabeth, NJ, pg. 1158
Romig, Michael V., V.P. & Chief Fin. Officer--Marine Construction & Design Co., Seattle, WA, pg. 707
Romney, Frank M., Asst. Sec. & Treas.--Associated Food Stores Inc., Salt Lake City, UT, pg. 89
Rone, Charles C., Jr., V.P.-Fin. & Treas.--Loxcreen Company, West Columbia, SC, pg. 686
Ronzo, Robert, Treas.--Stephen L. Geller Inc., New York, NY, pg. 447
Roos, John, V.P.-Fin. & Treas.--D & K Optical, Inc., Louisville, KY, pg. 307
Roos, Mark D., V.P., Treas. & Chief Fin. Officer--The Airolite Company, Marietta, OH, pg. 28
Roque, Romeo, Treas.--Savemart Inc., Bronx, NY, pg. 973
Rosania, John, Treas. & Sec.--Structural Foam Plastics, Inc., North Branch, NJ, pg. 1054
Rose, Estelle, Chief Fin. Officer--Kobra International Ltd, New York, NY, pg. 638
Rosen, Alan J., Treas.--Alaskan Copper Companies, Seattle, WA, pg. 30
Rosen, Barry A., V.P., Treas. & Chief Fin. Officer--Schnitzer Steel Industries, Inc., Portland, OR, pg. 977
Rosenbaum, Marlon, Treas.--Bruckner Machine & Tool Corp., Port Washington, NY, pg. 183
Rosenberg, Donald M., Exec. V.P., Treas. & Chief Fin. Officer--Oxford First Corporation, Philadelphia, PA, pg. 834
Rosenberg, Kenneth B., Exec. V.P.-Fin. & Treas.--Eastern Smelting & Refining Corporation, Lynn, MA, pg. 363
Rosenberger, Marcus L., Treas. & Sec.--Rosenbergers Dairies, Inc., Hatfield, PA, pg. 948
Rosenbloom, Sidney, V.P., Chief Fin. Officer & Treas.--McCurdy & Co., Inc., Rochester, NY, pg. 728
Rosenfield, Estelle, Treas.--Tasco, Miami, FL, pg. 1079
Rosenmeier, W.C., Jr., Sec. & Treas.--Geo. H. Lehleitner & Co., Inc., Harahan, LA, pg. 666
Rosenthal, Benjamin, Sec. & Treas.--Madison Electric Co., Detroit, MI, pg. 699
Rosner, Erwin, Treas. & Sec.--Boscov's Department Stores, Inc., Reading, PA, pg. 167
Ross, Audrey, Treas.--J H Collectibles, Milwaukee, WI, pg. 584
Ross, Judy, Sec. & Treas.--Layman Candy Company, Inc., Salem, VA, pg. 663
Ross, R.L., Sec., Treas. & Controller--Edgewater Corporation, Oakmont, PA, pg. 368
Rossa, Glynn M., V.P. & Treas.--RAYOVAC Corporation, Madison, WI, pg. 915
Rossen, James R., V.P.-Fin. & Treas.--Union Pump Company, Battle Creek, MI, pg. 1128
Rossler, John, V.P.-Fin., Treas. & Asst. Sec.--Shonac Corporation, Columbus, OH, pg. 1000
Roth, Robert, V.P., Treas.--Admarketing, Inc., Los Angeles, CA, pg. 18
Rothenberger, Eva, Sec. & Treas.--Vari Tronics Company, Inc., Duarte, CA, pg. 1145
Rothstein, Stanley, V.P.-Fin., Treas. & Asst. Sec.--Bestform Foundations, Inc., Long Island City, NY, pg. 147
Rott, Herbert, Jr., V.P., Sec. & Treas.--Rott-Keller Supply Co., Fargo, ND, pg. 951
Rotz, Violeta B., Asst. Treas.--MICRODOT, Inc., Chicago, IL, pg. 749
Roubin, Angel S., Pres. & Treas.--Roubinco, Inc., Fairfax, VA, pg. 952
Rouse, M. Brent, Treas.--Hamilton Mutual Insurance Company Of Cincinnati, Cincinnati, OH, pg. 503
Roverts, Edward D., Jr., Sr. V.P. & Treas.--Baton Rouge Water Works Company, Baton Rouge, LA, pg. 126
Rowe, John E., Treas. & Sec.--Oltmans Construction Company, Whittier, CA, pg. 824
Rowland, Chip, Treas., Media Dir.--Joiner Rowland Serio Koeppel, Dallas, TX, pg. 602
Roy, Norman E., Sr. V.P.-Fin. & Treas.--Gilbane Building Company, Providence, RI, pg. 457
Roys, Hal, Treas.--Henry Bacon Building Materials, Inc., Issaquah, WA, pg. 113
Rubenstein, Leonard M., Exec. V.P. & Treas.--General American Life Insurance Co., St. Louis, MO, pg. 448
Rubin, Benjamin H., Sec. & Treas.--Stevens-Lee Company, Minneapolis, MN, pg. 1048
Rubin, Burton, Treas.--Philadelphia Coca-Cola Bottling Co., Philadelphia, PA, pg. 866
Rubin, David M., Gen. Counsel & Sec.--American Envelope Company, Chicago, IL, pg. 199
Rucker, Adin H., Jr., Pres. & Treas.--Stonecutter Mills Corp., Spindale, NC, pg. 1051
Ruckriegel, Lovella, Treas.--Wharfside Restaurants, Inc., Jasper, IN, pg. 1184
Rud, John, Treas.--Arcadia Fryers, Arcadia, WI, pg. 80
Rud, John, Treas.--A-G Co-op Creamery, Arcadia, WI, pg. 4
Rudzik, John A., Sr. V.P.-Fin., Chief Fin. Officer, & Treas.--Centimark Corporation, Bethel Park, PA, pg. 231
Rueckel, Wallace L., Treas.--Guardian Industries Corp., Northville, MI, pg. 491
Ruffin, Pat, V.P., Treas. & Sec.--Ruffin Building Systems, Inc., Oak Grove, LA, pg. 955
Ruhkala, Peter D., Treas.--Nor-Cal Beverage Co., Inc., West Sacramento, CA, pg. 808
Ruiz, Rodolfo, V.P.-Fin. & Chief Fin. Officer--Bacardi Imports, Inc., Miami, FL, pg. 108
Ruland, James, Treas. & Sec.--H.G. Fenton Material Company, San Diego, CA, pg. 406
Runge, Scott, Treas.--Calavo Growers of California, Tustin, CA, pg. 208
Runk, Fred J., V.P. & Treas.--American Financial Corporation, Cincinnati, OH, pg. 52
Runk, Fred J., V.P., Treas. & Chief Fin. Officer--Spelling Entertainment Group, Inc., Cincinnati, OH, pg. 54
Ruscher, Stephen, V.P., Treas. & Controller--Columbia National Group, Inc., Cleveland, OH, pg. 265
Ruslander, Harold L., Sr. V.P. & Treas.--The Jewett Refrigerator Co., Inc., Buffalo, NY, pg. 957
Russell, George Earl, Treas. & Sec.--Russell Petroleum Corporation, Montgomery, AL, pg. 957
Russell, John, V.P. & Treas.--Russell Industries, Inc., Carnegie, PA, pg. 957
Russell, Richard C., Sr. V.P., Chief Fin. Officer & Treas.--Danis Industries Corporation, Dayton, OH, pg. 314
Russell, Robert J., V.P. & Treas.--Main Line Management Services, Inc., Mount Laurel, NJ, pg. 246
Russell, T. Alan, Exec. V.P., Sec. & Treas.--Illinois Cereal Mills, Inc., Paris, IL, pg. 562
Russo, Stephen J., Treas.--Western Temporary Services, Inc., Walnut Creek, CA, pg. 1181
Rutkowski, Cynthia K., Treas.--Bankmanagers Corp., Milwaukee, WI, pg. 118
Ryan, John J., V.P. & Treas.--Charan Industries, Inc., Garden City, NY, pg. 239
Ryan, Kenneth, V.P.-Fin.--The Van Metre Companies, Burke, VA, pg. 1144
Ryan, Philip, Pres.--Taylor Oil Co. Inc., Winston-Salem, NC, pg. 1082
Ryan, Robert W., Treas.--Wally Findlay Galleries International, Chicago, IL, pg. 410
Ryan, Russell J., V.P.-Sec. & Treas.--Ryan Construction Company Of Minnesota, Hibbing, MN, pg. 958
Ryan, Russell R., V.P., Treas. & Sec.--Ryan Properties Inc., Minneapolis, MN, pg. 958
Rynn, John A., V.P. & Treas.--Pen Holdings, Inc., Brentwood, TN, pg. 856
Rynn, John A., V.P. & Treas.--Berol Corporation, Brentwood, TN, pg. 856
Rynone, William J., Sec. & Treas.--Rynone Manufacturing Corporation, Sayre, PA, pg. 958
Ryser, Frank, Chm. Bd., Pres., Chief Exec. Officer & Treas.--Ryser Brothers Inc., Chicago, IL, pg. 958
Saari, Paul, Treas. & Asst. Sec.--Rock-Tenn Company, Norcross, GA, pg. 941
Sabourin, Rick, Pres. & Treas.--Bestop, Inc., Broomfield, CO, pg. 147
Sackett, Sydney J., Treas.--LeGrand Johnson Construction Co., Logan, UT, pg. 598
Sacks, Louis, Treas. & Sec.--S. Freedman & Sons, Inc., Landover, MD, pg. 430
Saffelle, Robert L., Jr., Treas.--Carolina Biological Supply Co., Burlington, NC, pg. 222
Sajeski, Edmund, Jr., Sec., Treas. & Controller--A. H. Hoffman, Inc., Landisville, PA, pg. 538
Sakoda, Kenneth, Exec. V.P., Treas. & Creative Dir.--Salvati Montgomery Sakoda, Inc., Costa Mesa, CA, pg. 967
Salamon, Robert, V.P., Sec. & Treas.--Pic N'pay Supermarkets, Inc., Dania, FL, pg. 869
Salisbury, James, Treas. & Asst. Sec.--Tri Valley Growers Inc., San Francisco, CA, pg. 1111
Salmon, John L., Chm. Bd., Sec. & Treas.--TVESCO, Inc., Memphis, TN, pg. 1075
Salomon, William, V.P. & Treas.--The Hartz Mountain Corp., Harrison, NJ, pg. 514
Saltzman, Irving, Treas.--Banner Wholesale Grocers, Inc., Chicago, IL, pg. 118
Saltzman, Richard, Asst. Treas.--Banner Wholesale Grocers, Inc., Chicago, IL, pg. 118
Salyer, Robert, V.P. & Treas.--The Paty Company, Piney Flats, TN, pg. 852
Samsill, Loretta, Exec. V.P., Sec. & Treas.--Samsill Corporation, Fort Worth, TX, pg. 968
Sanborn, David, Sec. & Treas.--Financial Life Companies, Inc., St. Paul, MN, pg. 813
Sanchez, Eugene, Treas.--Distributors Oil Company, Inc., Baton Rouge, LA, pg. 340
Sanchez, Fernando, Exec. V.P.-Fin. & Admin.--Leather Center, Inc., Carrollton, TX, pg. 664
Sanchez, Raymond, Controller, Treas. & Asst. Sec.--Hunter Engineering Co., Inc., Riverside, CA, pg. 554
Sander, Richard, Treas.--Leshner Mills. Inc., Hamilton, OH, pg. 668
Sanders, Jim, Treas. & Asst. Sec.--Hickman Williams & Co. Inc., Cincinnati, OH, pg. 532
Sanderson, Glenn, Treas.--Holman Enterprises, Pennsauken, NJ, pg. 540
Sanford, Robert W., Treas.--Sanford & Hawley, Inc., Unionville, CT, pg. 970
Sanford, Willard C., V.P. & Treas.--Employers Insurance of Wausau a Mutual Co., Wausau, WI, pg. 380
Sanford, Willard C., V.P. & Treas.--Employers Insurance of Wausau a Mutual Co., Wausau, WI, pg. 795
Santacroce, John, V.P.-Fin.--Decal Enterprises, Inc., New York, NY, pg. 323
Sapp, James, Treas.--Affiliated of Florida Inc., Tampa, FL, pg. 23
Sapyta, Michael, Treas.--Smith Enterprises, Rock Hill, SC, pg. 1012
Sarai, Andre, V.P., Treas. & Sec.--Weiss Sheet Metal Company, Gardena, CA, pg. 1174
Sarcia, James F., Treas.--Boston Mutual Life Insurance Co., Canton, MA, pg. 167
Sargent, John W., Pres., Treas., New Bus. Contact, Production & Research Dir.--Sargent & Potratz, Inc., Brookfield, WI, pg. 971
Sarkisian, Pamela Rose, Treas.--Beacon Group, Bloomfield, CT, pg. 128
Sarno, Chuck, Treas.--Knight Equipment Corp., Costa Mesa, CA, pg. 636
Sarrail, J.L., Sec. & Treas.--McConnell Cabinets, Inc., El Monte, CA, pg. 727
Sartori, Linda, Treas. & Dir.-Data Processing--Lithotype Company, Inc., South San Francisco, CA, pg. 678
Saterbo, Bryan, Sr. V.P. & Treas.--Colorado Boxed Beef Co., Auburndale, FL, pg. 265
Sauey, W.R., Chm. Bd., Pres. & Treas.--Nordic Group of Companies, Ltd., Baraboo, WI, pg. 809
Saul, Les, Treas. & Sec.--Beach City Chevrolet Co., Long Beach, CA, pg. 128
Saunders, Beulah, Sec. & Treas.--Dakco Distributors, Inc., Minot, ND, pg. 311
Saunders, Joanna, V.P. & Treas.--Oakland Tool & Manufacturing Company, Fraser, MI, pg. 819
Savitt, David, V.P. & Treas.--Pace Press, Inc., New York, NY, pg. 838
Savona, Marco, Treas.--Abbott Ball Company, West Hartford, CT, pg. 9
Sawyer, Herbert C., Pres. & Treas.--Potter Hazlehurst Incorporated, East Greenwich, RI, pg. 882
Sayle, John G., Pres. & Treas.--The Hall China Company, East Liverpool, OH, pg. 501
Scaccia, Carmelo A., V.P. & Treas.--Adam Meldrum & Anderson Co., Inc., Buffalo, NY, pg. 16
Scales, Gene, Treas. & Sec.--Allied Plywood Corp., Alexandria, VA, pg. 38
Scangas, Christopher A., Exec. V.P. & Treas.--Scangas Brothers Holdings, Inc., Lynn, MA, pg. 974
Scanlan, Arthur G., III, V.P., Sec. & Treas.--Eatel Corporation, Gonzales, LA, pg. 364
Scarberrym, Daniel K., Treas.--American Bible Society, New York, NY, pg. 49
Schalhamer, Melvin A., Pres. & Treas.--Allied Chucker & Engineering Company, Jackson, MI, pg. 37
Schall, Fred, Sec. & Treas.--Delair Group, Inc., Delair, NJ, pg. 46
Schaum, J. Michael, V.P., Sec. & Treas.--Calumet Construction Corporation, Hammond, IN, pg. 211
Schautz, Carol A., Sr. V.P., Treas.--Wunderman Cato Johnson, New York, NY, pg. 1211
Schebo, Cindy, Treas., Sec. & Dir.-Personnel--Ostarr Corporation, Chicago, IL, pg. 831
Schecter, Scott M., Sr. V.P., Chief Fin. Officer & Treas.--American Vision Centers, Inc., New York, NY, pg. 65
Scheer, Steven E., Sr. V.P., Sec. & Treas.--Scheer Advertising Agency, South Orange, NJ, pg. 975
Schefelker, Wayne F., Sec. & Treas.--Fiberesin Industries Inc., Oconomowoc, WI, pg. 408
Schein, Ester, Sec. & Treas.--Henry Schein, Inc., Port Washington, NY, pg. 975
Schelhas, Peter M., V.P.-Sls., Sec. & Treas.--Chicago White Metal Casting, Inc., Bensenville, IL, pg. 246
Scher, Gerald J., Chm. Bd., Treas. & Sec.--Westchester Lace, Inc., North Bergen, NJ, pg. 1178
Scherle, Arthur J., Sec. & Treas.--The Lorvic Corp., St. Louis, MO, pg. 684
Scherr, Ted, Sec. & Treas.--Dakota Drug, Inc., Minot, ND, pg. 311
Schier, Gary W., Treas.--Ferrous Processing & Trading Co., Detroit, MI, pg. 407
Schildge, George, Treas.--Precision Roll Grinders, Inc., Allentown, PA, pg. 885
Schilling, Rod, V.P.-Fin. & Sec.--Continental Coin Corporation, Van Nuys, CA, pg. 278
Schindler, David R., Treas.--Lykes Brothers Inc. of Florida, Tampa, FL, pg. 688
Schinman, H.L., Chm. Bd., Treas., Sec. & Gen. Counsel--Bogue Electric Manufacturing Co., Paterson, NJ, pg. 162
Schipall, Duane, Sec. & Treas.--Bawden Corporation, Eldridge, IA, pg. 127
Schippers, Tom, V.P. & Treas.--Brooks Beverage Management, Inc., Holland, MI, pg. 179
Schlagenhauf, John, Treas.--Badger Truck Center, Inc., Milwaukee, WI, pg. 113
Schleif, Lyle, Sec. & Treas.--AEC, Anoka, MN, pg. 3
Schlobohm, Jon, Sec. & Treas.--National Corset Supply House, Los Angeles, CA, pg. 787
Schlosser, Elaine, M., Treas. & Sec.--Schlosser Forge Company, Rancho Cucamonga, CA, pg. 976
Schlosser, P., Sec. & Treas.--Robins Engineers & Constructors, Inc., Englewood, CO, pg. 939

Schluter, John, Treas.--Warren Distribution, Inc., Omaha, NE, pg. 1164
Schmalzer, Victor, Treas.--W.W. Norton & Company, Inc., New York, NY, pg. 815
Schmid, Allyn G., Sr. V.P. & Treas.--Fleming Packaging Corp., Peoria, IL, pg. 417
Schmid, Daniel J., Jr., Exec. V.P.-Fin., Treas. & Asst. Sec.--G. Heileman Brewing Co., Inc., La Crosse, WI, pg. 526
Schmidt, Dennis, Treas.--Traylor Brothers, Inc., Evansville, IN, pg. 1108
Schmidt, H.J., Sec. & Treas.--L. G. Everist Inc., Sioux Falls, SD, pg. 392
Schmidt, Lawrence, V.P. & Treas.--Sellstrom Manufacturing Co., Palatine, IL, pg. 988
Schmidt, Steven K., Chm. Bd. & Treas.--Rogers & Associates Advertising, Inc., Santa Clara, CA, pg. 943
Schmidt, William B., Chm. Bd., Pres. & Treas.--Coca-Cola Bottling Company of Elizabethtown, Elizabethtown, KY, pg. 258
Schmuhl, William J., Jr., Pres. & Treas.--Bristol Products, L.P., Bristol, IN, pg. 176
Schneeberger, Don R., Pres. & Treas.--Vess Beverages, Inc., Maryland Heights, MO, pg. 1149
Schneible, William F., Sec. & Treas.--Brooklyn Bottling Co., Milton, NY, pg. 179
Schneider, Henrietta, Treas.--Atlas Pen & Pencil Corporation, Hollywood, FL, pg. 96
Schneider, Richard A., V.P.-Fin., Sec. & Treas.--North Atlantic Industries, Inc., Hauppauge, NY, pg. 812
Schocke, Robert P., Chief Fin. Officer, Treas., Controller & Sec.--Greenhorne & O'Mara, Inc., Greenbelt, MD, pg. 485
Schoeber, Eldon, V.P., Sec. & Treas.--Site Oil Co. of Missouri, Clayton, MO, pg. 1009
Schoeneman, Cecil, Treas. & Sec.--Schoeneman Brothers Company, Sioux Falls, SD, pg. 978
Schoenfeld, Richard, Treas.--Tomco Auto Products, Inc., Vernon, CA, pg. 1100
Scholz, Gelaine, Treas. & Sec.--Walser Automotive Corporation, Richfield, MN, pg. 1161
Schordock, R.A., Chief Fin. Officer, Treas. & Controller--Radix Wire Company, Cleveland, OH, pg. 909
Schou, Adele, Treas.--Lafayette Manufacturing, Inc., Hayward, CA, pg. 650
Schoultz, Deborah A., Treas.--The Fibre-Metal Products Company, Concordville, PA, pg. 408
Schroeder, Amy, Treas.--The Levy Organization, Chicago, IL, pg. 672
Schroeder, Vernon, Treas. & Sec.--Big Cheese Pizza Corporation, Wichita, KS, pg. 464
Schrum, E.P., Pres., Chief Exec. Officer & Treas.--Carolina Mills, Inc., Maiden, NC, pg. 223
Schubert, Ron, V.P. & Treas.--Nationwise Automotive, Inc., Columbus, OH, pg. 795
Schubert, William C., Pres., Treas., & Chief Exec. Officer--Kitchell Corporation, Phoenix, AZ, pg. 634
Schubert, William L., V.P.-Fin. & Treas.--SCS Engineers, Long Beach, CA, pg. 961
Schueler, T.M., Asst. Treas.--Evans Adhesive Corp., Columbus, OH, pg. 390
Schull, Johanna, Sec. & Treas.--Building Products Inc., Watertown, SD, pg. 188
Schulman, Esther, Treas.--Eli's Chicago's Finest, Inc., Chicago, IL, pg. 376
Schultz, Robert J., Chief Fin. Officer, Treas. & Sec.--Great Lakes Lithograph Co., Cleveland, OH, pg. 481
Schumacher, D.A., Chief Fin. Officer & Treas.--The Cretex Companies, Elk River, MN, pg. 299
Schumacher, Roy J., Chief Fin. Officer, V.P.-Fin., Treas.--Fair Lanes Inc., Hunt Valley, MD, pg. 396
Schumpert, Melissa, V.P. & Treas.--Hardaway Concrete Co., Inc., Columbia, SC, pg. 507
Schussler, Sam, Treas.--Primary Industries Corporation, New York, NY, pg. 889
Schwartz, Daniel L., V.P., Sec. & Treas.--Schwartz & Benjamin, Inc., New York, NY, pg. 980
Schweizer, Paul H., Pres. & Treas.--Schweizer Aircraft Corporation, Elmira, NY, pg. 981
Schwinke, Arlen, Treas.--Mid-America Dairymen, Inc., Springfield, MO, pg. 750
Schwitters, Eugene, Treas.--Southern Minnesota Beet Sugar Cooperative, Renville, MN, pg. 1022
Sciame, Frank, Pres., Treas., Chief Exec. & Chief Fin. Officer--F.J. Sciame Construction, New York, NY, pg. 981
Sciberras, M., Sec., Treas. & Comptroller--Dearborn Gage Company, Garden City, MI, pg. 322
Scier, Edward J., Treas. & Controller--Camalloy, Inc., Washington, PA, pg. 211
Scott, James T., Chm. Bd., Chief Exec. Officer & Treas.--Norcostco, Inc., Minneapolis, MN, pg. 809
Scott, Milton C., Sec., Treas. & Exec. Office Mgr.--Georgia Duck & Cordage Mills, Scottdale, GA, pg. 453
Scott, Roland E., Pres. & Treas.--Burt Equipment Company, Inc., Westminster Station, VT, pg. 195
Scott, Sherry, Sec. & Treas.--Texas Metal Works, Inc., Beaumont, TX, pg. 1089
Scott, William R., Treas.--Moore Company, Westerly, RI, pg. 768
Seagraves, Marilyn, Asst. Treas.-Cash Mgmt.--Ingram Industries Inc., Nashville, TN, pg. 568
Sealy, Carol T., Sec. & Treas.--Lewis Communications, Inc., Mobile, AL, pg. 673
Seaman, Janet W., Sec. & Treas.--Seaman Timber Company, Inc., Montevallo, AL, pg. 986
Searfoss, David W., Sr. V.P., Chief Fin. Officer & Treas.--Phoenix Home Life Mutual Insurance Company, Hartford, CT, pg. 868
Sebastian, Jack, Chief Fin. Officer & Treas.--Plains Co-op Oil Mill, Lubbock, TX, pg. 873
Sebastian, Paul E., Sr. Exec. V.P.-Fin. & Sec.--Jockey International, Inc., Kenosha, WI, pg. 595
Sedler, Jordan B., V.P., Sec. & Treas.--Paper Enterprises, Inc., Bronx, NY, pg. 847
Seelbach, Kurt H., Sr. V.P. & Treas.--Florists' Mutual Insurance Co., Edwardsville, IL, pg. 421
Seeley, Paul J., Treas., Sec. & Controller--Lindsay Manufacturing Inc., Ponca City, OK, pg. 676
Seeling, Randolph L., Treas.--Fitzgerald Advertising Inc., New Orleans, LA, pg. 416
Seery, Patrick, Chief Fin. Officer, Treas. & Controller--James McHugh Construction Co., Chicago, IL, pg. 729
Segale, David S., Sec. & Treas.--Rapton Honda-GMC, Sacramento, CA, pg. 913
Segall, Samson, Chm. Bd., Pres. & Treas.--Sharon-Jay Togs, Inc., New Bedford, MA, pg. 995
Segerson, Roger L., Treas. & Controller--Sterling Lumber & Investment Co., Denver, CO, pg. 1047
Seibold-Dietl, Jutta, Dr., Treas.--Knight Wendling AG, Zurich,, Switzerland, pg. 637
Seiden, William S., Treas.--Topcor Financial Corporation, Chicago, IL, pg. 1101
Selden, William S., Exec. V.P. & Treas.--United Exposition Service Company, Chicago, IL, pg. 1102
Seligman, Irving R., Chm. Bd. & Treas.--Seligman & Associates, Inc., Bloomfield Hills, MI, pg. 988
Selover, Patricia W., Sec. & Treas.--Selover Buick, Inc., Billings, MT, pg. 988
Sensing, Janice, Sec. & Treas.--Phoenix Enterprises Inc., Nashville, TN, pg. 868
Senty, John L., V.P., Sec. & Treas.--Midwest Bottle Gas Company, La Crosse, WI, pg. 277
Seppala, Paul, Chief Fin. Officer--S. J. Groves & Sons Company, Minneapolis, MN, pg. 490
Sereta, P.L., Treas.--Thrall Car Mfg. Co., Chicago Heights, IL, pg. 350
Sergiano, Cheryl, Asst. Treas.--Moss and Company, Inc., New York, NY, pg. 772
Sessa, Linda S., Treas.--1st Franklin Corporation, Toccoa, GA, pg. 413
Sessa, Linda S., Treas.--First Franklin Financial Corp., Toccoa, GA, pg. 413
Seuss, C. David, Chm., Pres., Chief Exec. Officer & Treas.--Spinnaker Software Corporation, Cambridge, MA, pg. 1031
Severino, Beverly, Sec. & Treas.--Great Scott Advertising Co. Inc., New York, NY, pg. 482
Severson, Ron, Dir.-Personnel--True Companies, Casper, WY, pg. 1117
Sevey, Gary, Treas.--Lockard Construction, Inc., Waterloo, IA, pg. 680
Sevick, Daniel M., Chief Fin. Officer & Treas.--The ERM Group, Exton, PA, pg. 360
Seyle, Jeanann, Sec. & Treas.--Mike Daugherty's Hurling Chevrolet, Inc., Sacramento, CA, pg. 555
Shaeffer, Stanley, Treas.--Automotive Rentals, Inc., Mount Laurel, NJ, pg. 101
Shafer, Evelyn, Sec. & Treas.--Shafer Commercial Seating Inc., Denver, CO, pg. 994
Shaffer, Jack M., Treas.--Just Born, Inc., Bethlehem, PA, pg. 610
Shaffer, Jim, Treas. & Dir.-Investor Rels.--Allied Mutual Insurance Company, Des Moines, IA, pg. 38
Shaffer, John A., V.P. & Chief Fin. Officer--Finch, Pruyn & Co., Inc., Glens Falls, NY, pg. 410
Shaffet, Michael, Treas.--M. Fabrikant & Sons, Inc., New York, NY, pg. 396
Shames, Sidney J., Chm. Bd., Pres., CEO, COO, CFO & Treas.--Melard Manufacturing Corporation, Passaic, NJ, pg. 737
Shanes, Abraham, Chm. Bd. & Treas.--Talk-A-Phone Co., Chicago, IL, pg. 1077
Shank, Robert K., Sec. & Asst. Treas.--Sisco Company, Mount Joy, PA, pg. 413
Shanks, Earl C., V.P. & Dir.-Taxes--Farley Industries, Chicago, IL, pg. 399
Sharp, J.A., Treas.--Alvey Inc., Saint Louis, MO, pg. 46
Sharp, Jack, Treas.--Aladdin Mills Inc., Dalton, GA, pg. 29
Sharp, Vivian A., Sec. & Treas.--Texas Refinery Corp., Fort Worth, TX, pg. 1089
Sharpe, Ronald A., Treas.--HPS, Inc., Indianapolis, IN, pg. 497
Shavelson, Kenneth, Chief Fin. Officer, Exec. V.P., Dir.-Intl. Fin. & Treas.--Weksler Instruments Corp., Freeport, NY, pg. 1174
Shaw, Ned W., V.P.-Fin., Treas. & Chief Fin. Officer--Bristol Steel & Iron Works, Inc., Bristol, VA, pg. 176
Shaw, Roslyn, Treas.--Direct Communications Corporation, Bronxville, NY, pg. 339
Shay, Joseph F., Treas.--House of Bianchi, Boston, MA, pg. 546
Shea, Douglas P., Treas.--Donahue, Inc., Advertising, Hartford, CT, pg. 344
Shea, James F., Jr., Treas.--Fairmont Homes, Inc., Nappanee, IN, pg. 397
Shea, Michael J., V.P.-Logistics--Ocean Spray Cranberries, Inc., Lakeville, MA, pg. 820
Sheets, Mary J., Sec. & Treas.--Rapid Industries, Inc., Louisville, KY, pg. 913
Sheffield, Langdon C., V.P. & Treas.--Sheffield Hardware Company, Americus, GA, pg. 996
Sheffield, Tyler W., Chief Fin. Officer & Treas.--Burnham Broadcasting Company, Chicago, IL, pg. 193
Sheils, John F., Treas.--Steve Foley Cadillac, Northbrook, IL, pg. 422
Sheldon, Danley K., Treas.--Ferrell Companies Inc./Ferrellgas, Liberty, MO, pg. 407
Shelley, V. Dale, V.P. & Treas.--Misco Industries, Wichita, KS, pg. 759
Shelton, James, Sec. & Treas.--Apex Corporation, Indianapolis, IN, pg. 78
Shelton, Michael, V.P. & Treas.--Directory Distributing Associates, Inc., Saint Louis, MO, pg. 339
Shepard, Robert L., Chief Fin. Officer, Dir.-Mngmt. Info. Systems, Sec. & Treas.--Acme Foundry, Inc., Coffeyville, KS, pg. 13
Shepherd, William Clyde, Jr., Sec. & Treas.--Shepherd Construction Co., Inc., Atlanta, GA, pg. 998
Sheppard, Lynne S., Treas.--Thiele Kaolin Co., Sandersville, GA, pg. 1092
Sherbow, Susan, V.P.-Corp. Communications--Little Caesar Enterprises, Inc., Detroit, MI, pg. 678
Sherrill, John, Treas. & Sec.--Howards Appliances, Inc., San Gabriel, CA, pg. 547
Sherwood, Maryellen, Treas.--McInerney Inc., Oak Park, MI, pg. 729
Shevchik, Daniel R., V.P. & Treas.--Malcolm Pirnie, Inc., White Plains, NY, pg. 872
Shiben, Taj, Treas.--Chernoff/Silver & Associates, Columbia, SC, pg. 243
Shine, Loretta, Treas. & Sec.--First Financial Group, Inc., Encino, CA, pg. 413
Shinn, William R., Treas. & Sec.--Chicago Lock Company, Chicago, IL, pg. 245
Shirk, Betty J., Treas. & Sec.--Beer Nuts, Inc., Bloomington, IL, pg. 132
Shneider, Jerry, Treas. & Controller--Kelly, Scott And Madison, Inc., Chicago, IL, pg. 621
Shoemaker, Kevin, V.P.-Fin., Sec. & Treas.--Seneca Wire & Manufacturing Co., Fostoria, OH, pg. 989
Shore, Lawrence A., Treas.--Lawrence Insurance Group, Inc., New York, NY, pg. 662
Shore, Lawrence A., Treas.--United Community Insurance Co., Albany, NY, pg. 662
Shorey, Ginger, Sec. & Treas.--Magnolia Hi-Fi, Inc., Seattle, WA, pg. 701
Shuford, Arlene, Sec. & Treas.--Bowen Brothers Fruit Co., Inc., Winter Haven, FL, pg. 169
Shuldiner, Arthur, Treas.--Durlacher & Co., Inc., Long Island City, NY, pg. 354
Sides, Gordon, Treas.--MPD, Inc., Owensboro, KY, pg. 693
Siecgrist, Linda L., Sr. V.P., Sec. & Treas.--Landmark Hotel Corporation, Topeka, KS, pg. 656
Siegel, Charles J., Chief Fin. Officer & Treas.--Topa Thrift & Loan Association, Los Angeles, CA, pg. 1101
Siegel, S.L., Treas. & Sec.--R.S. Owens, Chicago, IL, pg. 834
Signori, J., Chief Fin. Officer & Treas.--Galaxy Business Products, Honolulu, HI, pg. 742
Signorini, J.E., Exec. V.P., Treas. & Chief Fin. Officer--The F.A. Bartlett Tree Expert Co., Stamford, CT, pg. 123
Siler, Tom, V.P.-Fin. & Treas.--Michigan Wheel Corporation, Grand Rapids, MI, pg. 747
Silles, Victor, Chief Fin. Officer & Treas.--Thetford Corporation, Ann Arbor, MI, pg. 357
Sills, A. Nelson, Treas.--American Kennel Club, Inc., New York, NY, pg. 57
Silva, Ed, V.P.-Fin. & Treas.--Cincinnati Incorporated, Harrison, OH, pg. 250
Silver, Martin, Pres., Chief Fin. Officer & Treas.--Star Liquor Dealers, Syosset, NY, pg. 1039
Silver, Ralph D., V.P. & Treas.--Barton Beers, Ltd., Chicago, IL, pg. 123
Silverman, Edward, Treas.--Estee Lauder, Inc., New York, NY, pg. 389
Silverman, Harvey, Sec., Treas., Controller & Dir.-Mngmt. Information Systems--MI Fund Incorporated, New York, NY, pg. 692
Silverman, Lester, V.P. & Treas.--Silverman Products & Textiles, New York, NY, pg. 1004
Simmons, Clarence G., V.P. & Treas.--First Federal Savings and Loan Assn. of Rochester, Rochester, NY, pg. 413
Simmons, D. Ramsay, III, V.P., Sec. & Treas.--Elberta Crate & Box Company, Bainbridge, GA, pg. 372
Simon, Arthur, Chm. Bd. & Treas.--Eagle Button Co., Inc., Carlstadt, NJ, pg. 362
Simon, Donald R., Chm. Bd., Pres. & Treas.--Contractors Steel Company, Livonia, MI, pg. 280
Simon, Martin T., V.P.- Treas. & Asst. Gen. Mgr.--Affiliated Foods Cooperative Inc., Norfolk, NE, pg. 23
Simon, Mary T., Treas. & Dir.-Personnel--J.L. Lester & Son, Inc., Rockmart, GA, pg. 668
Simon, Norman, V.P., Sec. & Treas.--Joseph Simon & Sons, Inc., Tacoma, WA, pg. 1006
Simpson, Brainard, Treas.--United Health Plan, Inglewood, CA, pg. 1133
Simpson, Joe B., Jr., V.P.-Fin., Chief Fin. Officer & Treas.--The Alpha Corporation Of Tennessee, Collierville, TN, pg. 43
Sinagra, Jack G., Sr. V.P. & Asst. Treas.--Turtle & Hughes, Inc., Linden, NJ, pg. 1119
Sinanis, Stylianos, V.P. & Treas.--Hermes Automotive Manufacturing Corp., Detroit, MI, pg. 531
Singer, Max E., Chief Fin. Officer, V.P. & Treas.--U.S. Engineering Company, Kansas City, MO, pg. 1135
Sink, Jimmie B., Treas.--Coble Dairy Products Co-op, Lexington, NC, pg. 257
Sink, Kenneth W., Pres. & Treas.--Traders Supermarkets, Inc., Berrien Springs, MI, pg. 1105
Sirignano, David, Treas.--Owen Pacific, Los Angeles, CA, pg. 834
Sirotkin, Mark, Treas.--Rapid Industrial Plastics Company, Jersey City, NJ, pg. 913
Skaff, Ramez G., Sec. & Treas.--Interstate Resources, Inc., Rosslyn, VA, pg. 580
Skelton, Wesley M., Treas.--Martin Gas Corporation, Kilgore, TX, pg. 715
Skinner, Karen, Treas.--Headco Industries, Inc., Broadview, IL, pg. 520
Skokan, Ralph J., Treas.--Pawling Corporation, Pawling, NY, pg. 852
Skrobola, A.W., Sr. V.P.-Fin., Sec. & Treas.--Thomas Steel Strip Corp., Warren, OH, pg. 1094
Slaten, Paul E., Treas.--Sunnen Products Company, Saint Louis, MO, pg. 1061
Slaughter, Ken, V.P. & Treas.--Gazette Company, Inc., Cedar Rapids, IA, pg. 447
Slavin, Barry, Treas.--Kurtzman/Slavin/Linda, Inc., Northfield, IL, pg. 646
Slifka, Richard, Chief Fin. Officer & Treas.--Global Petroleum Corp., Waltham, MA, pg. 463

Sloan, Dale R., Treas.--Rochester Midland Corporation, Rochester, NY, pg. 940
Sloan, Kerry, V.P.-Fin., Treas. & Chief Fin. Officer--Hardaway Construction Company, Inc., Nashville, TN, pg. 508
Sloan, Patricia L., Sec. & Treas.--Stratton Growth Fund, Inc., Plymouth Meeting, PA, pg. 1053
Sloan, Patricia L., Sec. & Treas.--Stratton Monthly Dividend Shares, Inc., Plymouth Meeting, PA, pg. 1053
Sloan, Robert B., Pres., Chief Oper. Officer & Treas.--Downey Designs International, Inc., Indianapolis, IN, pg. 348
Sloan, William E. II, Exec. V.P., Treas. & Sec.--Sloan Valve Company, Franklin Park, IL, pg. 1010
Slotta, Peter L., Pres. & Treas.--Pan American Trade Development Corp., New York, NY, pg. 845
Slotten, Nancy, Exec. V.P. & Treas.--Border States Paving, Inc., Fargo, ND, pg. 165
Smagley, Norman, Treas., Sec. & Risk Mngmt.--GenDerm Corporation, Lincolnshire, IL, pg. 448
Small, David L., Treas.--Nelson & Small Inc., Portland, ME, pg. 798
Small, J.R., Sec. & Treas.--Atlas Supply Company, Atlanta, GA, pg. 96
Small, Jim, Treas.--Friona Industries, L.P., Amarillo, TX, pg. 434
Smeenge, James J., Sec., Treas. & Comptroller--Amick Construction Ltd., Orlando, FL, pg. 67
Smilowitz, Bernard, Sec. & Treas.--Allied Building Products Corporation, East Rutherford, NJ, pg. 37
Smith, Allen, Chief Fin. Officer, Treas. & Sec.--The Benham Group, Oklahoma City, OK, pg. 138
Smith, Bruce, Treas.--Illinois Cereal Mills, Inc., Paris, IL, pg. 562
Smith, Calvin Doyle, V.P.-Fin. & Treas.--Kettle Restaurants, Houston, TX, pg. 626
Smith, Charles Drane, Treas.--Flint River Mills, Bainbridge, GA, pg. 419
Smith, Charles F., Sr. V.P.-Fin. & Treas.--Ringling Bros., Barnum & Bailey Combined Shows, Inc., Vienna, VA, pg. 935
Smith, Clifford G. II, Treas.--The Chesapeake Life Insurance Co., Lincoln, NE, pg. 243
Smith, Donna, V.P. & Treas.--Transport Insurance Co., Dallas, TX, pg. 54
Smith, Ed, Treas. & Sec.--Martin & Bayley Inc., Carmi, IL, pg. 714
Smith, Frederick D., Treas. & Chief Fin. Officer--Construction Specialties, Inc., Cranford, NJ, pg. 277
Smith, Gary, Treas.--The Andersons, Maumee, OH, pg. 73
Smith, Gary V., Sec. & Treas.--Herman Hughes & Sons, Inc., North Salt Lake, UT, pg. 552
Smith, Glenn, Treasurer, Chief Fin. Officer--Haworth Group Inc., Minnetonka, MN, pg. 518
Smith, Glenn A., V.P. & Treas.--Blue Tee Corporation, New York, NY, pg. 161
Smith, H. Wayne, Pres. & Treas.--Smith, Kaplan, Allen & Reynolds, Inc., Omaha, NE, pg. 1013
Smith, J. Michael, V.P. & Treas.--First Citizens Bank, N.A., Michigan City, IN, pg. 544
Smith, John B., Treas.--Duncan Equipment Company, Duncan, OK, pg. 352
Smith, Judy, Asst. Treas. & Coord.-Employee Benefits--PVS Chemicals, Inc., Detroit, MI, pg. 837
Smith, Kathi, Treas.--Whitin Roberts Co., Sanford, NC, pg. 1187
Smith, Les, Treas. & Sec.--Buhrman-Pharr Hardware Company, Texarkana, AR, pg. 187
Smith, Lois M., Sec. & Treas.--Davis-Moore Oldsmobile, Inc., Wichita, KS, pg. 319
Smith, Matt, Treas.--H & D Steel Service, Inc., North Royalton, OH, pg. 495
Smith, Michael J., V.P. & Treas.--S-T Industries, Inc., Saint James, MN, pg. 964
Smith, Mike, Sec. & Treas.--Kelsey Construction, Inc., Orlando, FL, pg. 621
Smith, Patty J., Asst. V.P.-Fin. & Treas.--VASA Brougher, Inc., Indianapolis, IN, pg. 1146
Smith, R.L., Asst. Treas.--Tasa Corporation, Pittsburgh, PA, pg. 1079
Smith, Richard C., V.P. & Treas.--SC Companies, Inc., Muscatine, IA, pg. 960
Smith, Richard C., Treas.--Stanley Consultants, Inc., Muscatine, IA, pg. 961
Smith, Robert, Asst. Treas.--Berlin Steel Construction Co., Berlin, CT, pg. 142
Smith, Robert Lewis, Treas., Sec. & Controller--Hankins Lumber Company, Inc., Grenada, MS, pg. 505
Smith, Thomas, V.P., Treas. & Gen. Counsel--Dry Storage Corporation, Des Plaines, IL, pg. 350
Smith, Thomas C., Exec. V.P.-Fin.--Jonbil Inc., Chase City, VA, pg. 602
Smith, William, Chief Fin. Officer, Treas. & Controller--Hoffritz for Cutlery, New York, NY, pg. 538
Smith, William M., Treas.--McKenzie Tank Lines, Inc., Tallahassee, FL, pg. 730
Smith, William N., Treas. & Sec.--Tell City Chair Co., Tell City, IN, pg. 1085
Smits, R. James, Treas.--Green Bay Packaging Inc., Green Bay, WI, pg. 483
Smoak, Joseph F., V.P., Gen. Mgr. & Treas.--Evening Post Publishing Co., Charleston, SC, pg. 391
Smoak, Robert R., V.P., Sec. & Treas.--Bernhardt Furniture Co., Lenoir, NC, pg. 144
Snapp, Robert B., Jr., Asst. Sec. & Treas.--Clarkson Construction Companies, Kansas City, MO, pg. 253
Snediker, M.B., Treas.--Chicago Show Printing Co., Morton Grove, IL, pg. 246
Snelling, Andrew P., Treas. & Sec.--The Shelburne Corporation, Shelburne, VT, pg. 996
Snelling, Guy, Sec. & Treas.--Edmonson Wheat Growers, Inc., Edmonson, TX, pg. 369
Sny, Sharon, Chief Fin. Officer & Treas.--Duro-Last Roofing, Inc., Saginaw, MI, pg. 355
Snyder, E.L., Treas. & Sec.--In-N-Out Burgers, Baldwin Park, CA, pg. 564
Snyder, Lance, Controller--McLaughlin Mfg. Company, Greenville, SC, pg. 731
Snyder, Ross B., Sr. V.P. & Chief Fin. Officer--Blue Cross & Blue Shield of Texas, Inc., Richardson, TX, pg. 160
Sobel, Stanton, Vice Chm. & Treas.--Taracorp, Inc., Atlanta, GA, pg. 1078
Sokira, David J., V.P. & Treas.--The Okonite Company, Ramsey, NJ, pg. 823
Solan, Tom, Treas.--S & S Graphics, Inc., Laurel, MD, pg. 959
Solberg, Jeffrey M., Treas.--Growmark, Inc., Bloomington, IL, pg. 490
Solda, Marc, Pres. & Treas.--Jamison Plastic Corporation, Allentown, PA, pg. 589
Solomon, Steven L., V.P. Fin., Chief Fin. Officer & Treas.--Elixir Industries, Gardena, CA, pg. 376
Somer, S., Treas.--Neil Faber Media Inc., New York, NY, pg. 395
Sommer, James, Pres., Chief Oper. & Fin. Officer & Treas.--Service Motor Company, Dale, WI, pg. 992
Sorden, Michael R., Sec. & Treas.--Commercial Light Company, Hillside, IL, pg. 268
Sorheim, Dennis, Sec. & Treas.--Peoples Electric Company, Inc., Saint Paul, MN, pg. 859
Sorrentino, Stanley L., Chm. Bd., Chief Exec. Officer & Treas.--Uncas Manufacturing Company, Providence, RI, pg. 1125
Sorrentino, Ubaldo, V.P.-Fin. & Treas.--Krasdale Foods Inc., Bronx, NY, pg. 644
Sorzano, Carl L., Treas.--DeVault Foods, Devault, PA, pg. 333
Sosnoski, Donald S., Chief Fin. Officer, V.P. & Treas.--PVS Chemicals, Inc., Detroit, MI, pg. 837
Southard, J. James, V.P., Controller & Treas.--Hoover Group, Inc., Alpharetta, GA, pg. 543
Souza, Stephen M., V.P. & Asst. Treas.--Trans World Airlines, Inc., Mount Kisco, NY, pg. 561
Spacht, David B., Chief Fin. Officer & Asst. Treas.--Artesian Resources Corporation, Newark, DE, pg. 86
Spacht, David B., Chief Fin. Officer & Asst. Treas.--Artesian Water Company, Inc., Newark, DE, pg. 86
Spahn, David T., Treas. & Asst.Sec.--Emerald Corporation, Cleveland, OH, pg. 378
Spaman, Robert, Chief Fin. Officer & Treas.--Aves Advertising, Inc., Grand Rapids, MI, pg. 102
Sparks, William B., V.P., Sec. & Treas.--Macco Constructors, Inc., Paramount, CA, pg. 696
Spartz, Marvin, Treas.--Northland Electric Supply Company, Minneapolis, MN, pg. 814
Spector, Morton, V.P. & Treas.--D&H Distributing Company, Harrisburg, PA, pg. 307
Spector, Russell N., Asst. Treas.--International Marine Holdings, Inc., Stamford, CT, pg. 579
Speek, Peter V., Pres. & Treas.--Fremont Forest Products, Whittier, CA, pg. 432
Spence, Ann, Treas.--Controlled Systems of Wisconsin, Inc., Nashotah, WI, pg. 281
Spencer, Marilyn, Sec. & Treas.--Faber Enterprises, Inc., Canoga Park, CA, pg. 395
Sperling, Jac, V.P., Treas.--Sperling, New Orleans, LA, pg. 1030
Speyer, Robert, Treas.--Tennsco Corporation, Dickson, TN, pg. 1088
Spiegel, Morton L., Pres. & Treas.--Southwark Metal Manufacturing Company, Philadelphia, PA, pg. 1023
Spiewak, Robert, Treas.--I. Spiewak & Sons, Inc., New York, NY, pg. 1031
Spillane, Robert, Sr. V.P. & Treas.--Donnelley Marketing, Inc., Stamford, CT, pg. 1011
Spitalnick, Andrea, Sec. & Treas.--Wellmade Industries, Inc., New York, NY, pg. 1175
Spitz, Arnold J., Exec. V.P., Sec. & Treas.--International Seaway Trading Corporation, Mayfield Village, OH, pg. 579
Spitz, Randy J., Treas., Sec. & Controller--Hicks Oil-Hicks Gas, Inc., Roberts, IL, pg. 533
Spitzer, Albert, V.P. & Treas.--Perfect Pearl Company, Inc., New York, NY, pg. 861
Spohn, David T., Treas.--The Spohn Corporation, Cleveland, OH, pg. 1032
Spokowski, David, Treas.--Specialty Paperboard Inc., Brattleboro, VT, pg. 1027
Spradley, James W., Jr., Pres. & Chief Exec. Officer--Standard Candy Co., Inc., Nashville, TN, pg. 1035
Spratling, B.B., Jr., Sec. & Treas.--Dixie Electric Cooperative, Union Springs, AL, pg. 341
Sprik, Harlan, V.P.-Fin., Treas. & Sec.--Trendway Corporation, Holland, MI, pg. 1109
Springer, Branch J., V.P., Chief Fin. Officer, Treas. & Sec.--Abbey Etna Machine Company, Perrysburg, OH, pg. 9
Springer, Clyde H., Treas.--Unigroup, Inc., Fenton, MO, pg. 1126
Springer, Clyde H., Treas.--United Van Lines, Inc., Fenton, MO, pg. 1126
Springer, June, Sec. & Treas.--Smith Motors, Inc., Hammond, IN, pg. 1014
Spruyt, Michael, V.P., Treas. & Chief Fin. Officer--Bloomsburg Mills Inc., New York, NY, pg. 158
St. Cyr, Henry P., V.P. & Treas.--All America Financial, Worcester, MA, pg. 34
St. Cyr, Henry P., V.P. & Treas.--State Mutual Life Assurance Company of America, Worcester, MA, pg. 35
Stablein, L.R., V.P. & Treas.--Quintana Petroleum Services, Houston, TX, pg. 905
Stabler, Donald B., Chm. Bd.--Stabler Companies, Inc., Harrisburg, PA, pg. 1034
Stadelman, Russell C., Sr., Chm. Bd. & Treas.--Russell Stadelman & Company, Germantown, TN, pg. 1034
Staelens, Peter, Treas. & Asst. Sec.--Dawn Food Products, Inc., Jackson, MI, pg. 319
Stafford, Rose Ann, Sec. & Treas.--Equity Supply Company, Kalispell, MT, pg. 385
Stahl, Jack, Treas.--Boston Trading Ltd. Inc., Lynn, MA, pg. 168
Stahl, Ronald, Treas.--Sid Harvey Inc., Valley Stream, NY, pg. 515
Stahl, Sharon, Treas.--The Austad Company, Sioux Falls, SD, pg. 98
Staley, Larry E., Treas.--Bunn-O-Matic Corporation, Springfield, IL, pg. 188
Stalzer, Robert J., Sr. V.P. Admin., Fin., Treas. & Asst. Sec.--Servo Corporation of America, Hicksville, NY, pg. 993
Stamp, Robert L., V.P.-Fin., Treas. & Controller--The Gates Corporation, Denver, CO, pg. 445
Stamper, Conner, Treas.--States, Inc., Breckenridge, TX, pg. 1041
Standish, Victor J., Pres. & Treas.--York Barbell Co., Inc., York, PA, pg. 1208
Standridge, W.L., Chief Fin. Officer, Treas. & Sec.--Spencer Companies Inc., Huntsville, AL, pg. 1030
Stanley, Ira H., V.P.-Fin. & Treas.--Gosiger Inc., Dayton, OH, pg. 472
Stanley, Peter, Treas.--Cornell Forge Company, Chicago, IL, pg. 286
Stansberry, Warren H., III, Pres. & Treas.--Stanco Metal Products, Inc., Grand Haven, MI, pg. 1035
Stanton, Laura, V.P., Sec. & Treas.--Dunlap & Co. Inc., Columbus, IN, pg. 353
Staples, William, V.P., Treas. & Controller--Rodney Hunt Company, Orange, MA, pg. 553
Stapleton, R.D., Exec. V.P.-Fin. & Admin., Sec. & Gen. Counsel--The Lane Construction Corp., Meriden, CT, pg. 656
Starcevich, John, Treas.--Jupiter Industries, Inc., Chicago, IL, pg. 609
Starrett, Frederick D., III, Pres., Treas., Sls. & Mktg.--Penobscot Frozen Foods, Inc., Belfast, ME, pg. 858
Statile, Ronald J., V.P. & Treas.--Horsehead Industries, Inc., New York, NY, pg. 545
Statz, J.J., V.P. & Treas.--National Rivet & Manufacturing Company, Waupun, WI, pg. 793
Stauff, Michael F., V.P.-Fin. & Chief Fin. Officer--International Marine Holdings, Inc., Stamford, CT, pg. 579
Stayer, Alice, V.P., Sec. & Treas.--Johnsonville Foods, Inc., Kohler, WI, pg. 601
Stebbins, Richard G., Controller--Ohaus Corporation, Florham Park, NJ, pg. 822
Stein, Martin, Pres. & Treas.--Sterling Paper Co., Philadelphia, PA, pg. 1047
Steiner, Kevin K., V.P.-Fin. & Treas.--Steiner Corporation, Salt Lake City, UT, pg. 1045
Steiner, Robert, Treas.--Grandpa Brands Company, Cincinnati, OH, pg. 476
Steinhart, Conrad, Treas. & Sec.--Happy Holiday Tree Farms, Sheridan, MI, pg. 506
Steinhauer, Gary, Sec. & Treas.--Madison Dairy Produce Company, Madison, WI, pg. 699
Steinhilber, Jeff R., Treas., Fin. Mgr. & Chief Fin. Officer--Austin Powder Co., Cleveland, OH, pg. 99
Steltmann, Harry F., V.P., Chief Fin. Officer, Treas & Sec.--Eclipse, Inc., Rockford, IL, pg. 366
Stenger, James W., Treas.--Alling & Cory Company, Rochester, NY, pg. 40
Stephenson, G.W., Jr., Pres. & Treas.--Stephenson, Inc., Alexandria, VA, pg. 1046
Sterakian, Robert, Treas.--Sunbeam-Oster Company, Inc., Providence, RI, pg. 1059
Sterbenz, Joanne, Chief Fin. Officer & Treas.--Olson-Travelworld Ltd., Manhattan Beach, CA, pg. 824
Stern, Edwardo, Treas.--Real Estate Corp. of Florida, Kissimmee, FL, pg. 917
Sternberg, Ronald I., Exec. V.P. & Treas.--Paramount Foods Inc., Louisville, KY, pg. 848
Sterner, Gene E., Sec. & Treas.--Jordon Commercial Refrigerator Co., Philadelphia, PA, pg. 605
Sternheimer, Ross, Treas. & Sec.--Sternheimer Brothers Inc., Sandston, VA, pg. 1048
Stevens, Frank P., Chm. Bd., Pres., Treas., Chief Exec. Officer & Chief Fin. Officer--Professional Travel, Inc., Dalton, GA, pg. 894
Stevens, Jim J., Jr., Treas. & Sec.--Lincoln Provision Company, Inc., Chicago, IL, pg. 676
Stevenson, Robert L., Pres. & Treas.--Eastman Machine Co., Buffalo, NY, pg. 364
Stewart, John C., Treas.--Pizzagalli Construction Co., South Burlington, VT, pg. 873
Stillman, Jedd B., Treas. & Dir.-Personnel--David Michael & Co. Inc., Philadelphia, PA, pg. 747
Stilper, Frank, Chief Fin. Officer & Treas.--Cummins Intermountain Diesel, Salt Lake City, UT, pg. 305
Stimer, Donald B., V.P. & Treas.--Simplex Time Recorder Co., Gardner, MA, pg. 1006
Stimpson, Gordon S., Treas. & Sec.--Gulf Lumber Company, Inc., Mobile, AL, pg. 493
Stimpson, James R., Treas., Controller & Sec.--Channellock, Inc., Meadville, PA, pg. 239
Stinchcomb, G.M., Treas.--Gaylord Broadcasting Co., Dallas, TX, pg. 446
Stinchcomb, Glenn M., V.P. & Treas.--Oklahoma Publishing Company, Oklahoma City, OK, pg. 446
Stockhausen, John, Treas.--Snavely Forest Products, Inc., Pittsburgh, PA, pg. 1015
Stoegbauer, William J., Treas.--Jewelers Mutual Insurance Company, Neenah, WI, pg. 593
Stogel, Florence S., Treas.--The Stogel Companies Inc., New York, NY, pg. 1050
Stone, David, Chief Fin. Officer & Treas.--Tylan General, Inc., San Diego, CA, pg. 1122
Stone, Kathy, V.P., Treas. & Sec.--Ergon, Inc., Jackson, MS, pg. 386
Stone, Martin S., Treas. & Sec.--Helmsley Enterprises, Inc., New York, NY, pg. 527
Stone, S. Reagan, Treas.--Sebastian Cotton & Grain Corp., Sebastian, TX, pg. 986

Stone, Thomas, Treas.--Nutri/System Inc., Blue Bell, PA, pg. 818
Stoots, Ron, V.P. & Treas.--Manhattan Building Companies, Tulsa, OK, pg. 703
Story, Kendra A., Treas. & Controller--ABC Supply Company, Inc., Beloit, WI, pg. 2
Stout, Judith, Treas.--Metaltech, Inc., Kirkwood, MO, pg. 742
Stout, Paul D., Jr., V.P., Chief Fin. Officer & Treas.--McArdle Printing Co., Inc., Upper Marlboro, MD, pg. 189
Stover, F. Gary, Treas.--Laird & Company, Scobeyville, NJ, pg. 650
Strahman, Richard D., V.P. & Treas.--Strahman Valves, Inc., Florham Park, NJ, pg. 1052
Strambi, Michael, Asst. Treas.--Sun Diamond Growers of California, Pleasanton, CA, pg. 1058
Strasburg, William E., V.P. & Treas.--Independent Publications, Inc., Bryn Mawr, PA, pg. 565
Stratton, Arlene E., Treas.--Stratton Management Company, Plymouth Meeting, PA, pg. 1053
Stromberg, Kurt, Treas.--Artistic Carton Company, Elgin, IL, pg. 87
Stromberg, Kurt, Treas.--White Pigeon Paper Company, White Pigeon, MI, pg. 87
Strumbos, George, V.P. & Treas.--Alpha Bolt Company, Madison Heights, MI, pg. 1165
Stubbs, Thomas, Treas.--Bell South Enterprises, Atlanta, GA, pg. 136
Stubbs, Thomas H., Treas.--Stevens Graphics, Inc., Atlanta, GA, pg. 136
Stubs, Thomas, Treas.--Bell South Business Product Division, Atlanta, GA, pg. 136
Stuhlmann, Eric, V.P. & Chief Fin. Officer--Shurfine-Central Corp., Northlake, IL, pg. 1001
Stulik, Bruce, Treas.--Woodwork Corporation of America, Chicago, IL, pg. 1201
Stumb, W. Thomas, Treas.--KNOX International Corp., Knoxville, TN, pg. 638
Stumb, W. Thomas, Treas.--Rockwood Gardens, Ltd., Rockwood,, Canada, pg. 638
Stumb, W. Thomas, Treas.--Michigan Bulb Company, Grand Rapids, MI, pg. 638
Stumpf, Charles T., Chm. Bd., Pres., Chief Exec. Officer & Treas.--Financial Associates, Overland Park, KS, pg. 410
Sturm, Gregory W., V.P. & Treas.--Jofco Inc., Jasper, IN, pg. 595
Suchor, Leo, Sec. & Treas.--Larrys, Inc., Gillette, WY, pg. 659
Sugarman, Paul, Treas.--Statler Industries, Medford, MA, pg. 1041
Sugarman, Wendy, Treas.--JS&A Group, Inc., Las Vegas, NV, pg. 586
Suitt, T. Howard, Pres. & Chief Exec. Officer--Suitt Construction Company, Inc., Greenville, SC, pg. 1056
Suitt, T.H., Jr., V.P. & Treas.--Suitt Construction Company, Inc., Greenville, SC, pg. 1056
Sukalski, Terrence P., Chief Fin. Officer--Raymond Rosen Co., Conshohocken, PA, pg. 948
Sullivan, Barbara, Sec. & Treas.--Hesco Parts Corporation, Louisville, KY, pg. 531
Sullivan, D. Harold, V.P., Treas. & Chief Fin. Officer--Demoulas Super Markets, Tewksbury, MA, pg. 328
Sullivan, John L., Treas., Sec. & Controller--Totsy Manufacturing Company, Inc., Holyoke, MA, pg. 1103
Sullivan, John P., Treas.--Ashworth Bros., Inc., Fall River, MA, pg. 88
Sulprizio, Deuta, V.P. & Treas.--United Engine & Machine Company, Carson City, NV, pg. 1131
Sumerton, William, Dir.-Fin.--Digital Electronic Automation, Livonia, MI, pg. 337
Summerfield, Maxine, Treas.--Summerfield Truck Co. Inc., Portage, IN, pg. 1057
Summers, T.F., V.P. & Treas.--Lykes Bros. Steamship Co., Inc., New Orleans, LA, pg. 688
Sumrall, O. Malcolm, Chief Fin. Officer, Sec. & Treas.--Associated Equipment Company, Inc., Mobile, AL, pg. 89
Sun, R., Treas.--National Bulk Carriers, Inc., New York, NY, pg. 786
Suprise, Lou, Asst. Treas.--Curt G. Joa, Inc., Sheboygan Falls, WI, pg. 594
Susack, Lon, Treas.--Dick Corporation, Large, PA, pg. 335
Susco, John A., Sec. & Treas.--Ideal Forging Corporation, Southington, CT, pg. 562
Sutherland, Jerry, Sr. V.P., Treas. & Sec.--Consumers Markets Inc., Springfield, MO, pg. 277
Sutika, James M., Pres. & Treas.--Van Pelt Corporation, Detroit, MI, pg. 1144
Sutter, Ruth A., Treas.--Fisheries Supply Company, Seattle, WA, pg. 415
Sutterfield, Howard, Treas.--Brink Electric Construction Company, Rapid City, SD, pg. 176
Sutton, Max R., Treas.--Goldsmiths, Inc., Wichita, KS, pg. 469
Sutton, Woodrow A., Treas.--Encyclopaedia Britannica, Inc., Chicago, IL, pg. 381
Swadener, Mark, Treas.--Traco Advertising, Inc., Tulsa, OK, pg. 1104
Swallen, Bruce, Treas.--Swallen's, Inc., Cincinnati, OH, pg. 1066
Swallen, Jay, Sec. & Treas.--Haines & Co., Inc., North Canton, OH, pg. 500
Swanson, Craig, Treas.--Upper Midwest Industries, Inc., Minneapolis, MN, pg. 1140
Swanson, Robert, Treas.--Park Construction Company, Minneapolis, MN, pg. 848
Swanson, Stanley, Sec. & Treas.--Minuteman Press International, Farmingdale, NY, pg. 759
Swanson, William, Treas.--Bose Corporation, Framingham, MA, pg. 167
Swearings, Thomas F., Dir.-Fin. & Treas.--Hammel, Green & Abrahamson, Inc., Minneapolis, MN, pg. 504
Sweat, Gene, Treas.--Arkansas Electric Cooperatives Inc., Little Rock, AR, pg. 83
Sweeney, Brian J., Treas.--Dahlstrom Manufacturing Company, Inc., Jamestown, NY, pg. 310
Sweeney, Patty, Treas.--Aquidneck Data Company, Middletown, RI, pg. 320
Sweeney, Paul L., Sr. V.P. & Treas.--John Hancock Property and Casualty Holding Co., Boston, MA, pg. 596
Sweeney, Robert, Treas.--American Felt & Filter, Newburgh, NY, pg. 52
Sweeney, Tom, Treas. & Controller--Aetna Industries, Inc., Center Line, MI, pg. 23
Swenson, Gordon, V.P.-Fin., Treas. & Sec.--The Odom Corporation, Seattle, WA, pg. 821
Swift, M. Allen, Chm. Bd., Pres. & Treas.--M. Swift & Sons Inc., Hartford, CT, pg. 1068
Swift, Robert P., Exec. V.P. & Treas.--Swift Dodge Rolls Royce Inc., Sacramento, CA, pg. 1067
Switzer, Richard J., Sec. & Treas.--Drive Train Industries, Denver, CO, pg. 349
Swords, L. Frank, V.P., Treas. & Sec.--National Safety Associates, Memphis, TN, pg. 793
Sykes, Barbara, Treas. & Sec.--Sebastian & Cooke, Parsippany, NJ, pg. 986
Sykes, Darrell, Treas.--Ellerbe Becket Construction Services, Minneapolis, MN, pg. 378
Sylvia, Joseph, Treas. & Dir.-Fin.--Simonds Industries Inc., Fitchburg, MA, pg. 1006
Sytsema, Gerald D., Gen. Mgr. & Treas.--Maine Potato Growers, Inc., Presque Isle, ME, pg. 702
Szekely, Steven, Sec. & Treas.--Monarch Avalon, Inc., Baltimore, MD, pg. 765
Szulman-Jones, Marilyn, Sec. & Treas.--Airco Mechanical Inc., Sacramento, CA, pg. 27
Tabor, Edward, Treas.--Deck House Inc., Acton, MA, pg. 324
Tack, Kim P., Sec. & Treas.--Kartridg Pak Co., Davenport, IA, pg. 122
Tacony, Emily, Treas.--Tacony Corporation, Fenton, MO, pg. 1076
Tadda, Thomas A., Chief Fin. Officer & V.P.-Fin.--Interform Corporation, Bridgeville, PA, pg. 574
Taddei, Armando, Chm. Bd., Pres. & Treas.--Hunter Contracting Company, Gilbert, AZ, pg. 554
Takacs, W., Treas.--Hydro Group, Inc., Bridgewater, NJ, pg. 556
Takashima, Kenji, V.P., Sec., & Treas.--Pentax Precision Instruments Corp., Orangeburg, NY, pg. 859
Tang, Jane Y., Treas. & Corp. Sec.--Tekni-Plex, Inc., Brooklyn, NY, pg. 1084
Tanzey, Gene, Treas.--M M M Sales, Inc., City of Industry, CA, pg. 692
Tappan, James, Chief Fin. Officer & Treas.--United Dairymen of Arizona, Tempe, AZ, pg. 1131
Tapscott, James T., Sec. & Treas.--Columbus Mills, Inc., Columbus, GA, pg. 267
Tarlow, Thelma H., Asst. Treas.--Alden Shoe Co., Inc., Middleboro, MA, pg. 33
Tarnay, Dennis, Chief Fin. Officer & Treas.--Lake Erie Electric, Inc., Westlake, OH, pg. 651
Tarte, Bernard J., Jr., V.P. & Treas.--Bradner Central Company, Chicago, IL, pg. 170
Tassel, Gerard, Treas.--H. E. Sargent, Inc., Stillwater, ME, pg. 971
Tassi, Michael J., Chief Fin. Officer & Treas.--Torco Oil, Chicago, IL, pg. 1102
Taulbee, William, Treas.--Kluener Packing Company, Cincinnati, OH, pg. 636
Taylor, Andrew C., Pres. & Treas.--Enterprise Rent-A-Car Company, Saint Louis, MO, pg. 382
Taylor, Arnold, Treas. & Sec.--Heather Crolie, Inc., Rochester, NY, pg. 300
Taylor, Beatrice V., Treas.--Bankhead Enterprises Inc., Atlanta, GA, pg. 117
Taylor, Don R., Sr., Chief Fin. Officer, Treas. & Sec.--Homeland Stores, Inc., Oklahoma City, OK, pg. 542
Taylor, John E., Treas.--Nelson A. Taylor Co., Inc., Gloversville, NY, pg. 1080
Taylor, Jonathan W., Treas.--George E. Warren Corp., Vero Beach, FL, pg. 1164
Taylor, Mike, Sec. & Treas.--White Electrical Construction Co., Atlanta, GA, pg. 1185
Taylor, R.T., V.P., Sec. & Asst. Treas.--Al Johnson Construction Co., Minneapolis, MN, pg. 597
Taylor, William, Sr. V.P. & Treas.--Taylor-Morley, Inc., Saint Louis, MO, pg. 1081
Teeple, William W., V.P., Chief Fin. Officer & Treas.--The Stackpole Corporation, Boston, MA, pg. 1034
Teichman, Thomas D., V.P. & Treas.--Nova Power, Inc., Santa Ana, CA, pg. 816
Tell, Martin T., Chief Fin. Officer & Treas.--Jac Jacobsen Industries, Inc., Greenwich, CT, pg. 587
Tellier, James P., Sec. & Treas.--Jefferson Chevrolet Co., Detroit, MI, pg. 591
Tengelly, Owen, Treas. & Controller--Walled Lake Door Company, Phoenix, AZ, pg. 1161
Tepoorten, Harold V., Treas. & Sec.--Steel, Inc., Commerce City, CO, pg. 1044
Terminato, Marian, Dir.-Acctg. & Treas.--Octagon Process Inc., Edgewater, NJ, pg. 821
Termine, David G., Mgr.-Acct. & Asst. Treas--W. P. Carey & Co., Inc., New York, NY, pg. 218
Terrell, Charles, Pres., Treas. & Chief Exec. Officer--New Haven Savings Bank, New Haven, CT, pg. 801
Terrell, E.P., III, Exec. V.P. & Treas.--McIlhenny Company, Avery Island, LA, pg. 729
Terrell, Eddie, Sec. & Treas.--B. F. Trappey's Sons, Inc., New Iberia, LA, pg. 729
Terry, Nicole, Treas.--Precision Carbide Tool Company, Inc., Niles, IL, pg. 885
Terwin, Bob, V.P. & Treas.--National Concrete Products Company, Plymouth, MI, pg. 787
Teske, Gerald P., Exec. V.P. & Treas.--Meridian Industries, Inc., Milwaukee, WI, pg. 740
Tew, Richard, V.P. & Treas.--Predco, Inc., Pennsauken, NJ, pg. 341
Thatcher, Gerald D., Sr. V.P., Chief Fin. Officer & Treas.--Central Mutual Insurance Co., Van Wert, OH, pg. 233
Thau, Ronald R., Treas.--Thomas & Betts Holdings, Inc., Memphis, TN, pg. 425
Theofilos, Kathy S., Treas.--Theochem Labs., Inc., Tampa, FL, pg. 1090
Thewes, Thomas, Vice Chm. & Exec. V.P.-Finance--Compuware Corporation, Farmington Hills, MI, pg. 271
Thiel, Wilbert, Exec. V.P. & Treas.--Chicago Corp., Chicago, IL, pg. 247
Thieman, Ronald G., Treas.--KCL Corporation, Shelbyville, IN, pg. 611
Thiesfeld, Debra Heinson, Treas.--Allied Oil & Supply, Inc., Omaha, NE, pg. 38
Thois, William, Chief Fin. Officer, Treas., Sec. & Dir.-Admin. & Opers.--Empire Airlines, Hayden Lake, ID, pg. 379
Tholey, James M., Chief Oper. Officer, Chief Fin. Officer, & Treas.--Peirce-Phelps, Inc., Philadelphia, PA, pg. 855
Thomas, Addie Joe, Sec. & Treas.--V. B. Hook & Co., Inc., Columbia, SC, pg. 543
Thomas, Charles, Comptroller--Cello Bag Company, Inc., Tukwila, WA, pg. 231
Thomas, G. N., Chm. Bd., Pres., Chief Exec. Officer, Chief Fin. Officer & Treas.--A. Levy & J. Zentner Co., Sacramento, CA, pg. 671
Thomas, Helen, Treas. & Sec.--Camino Real Chevrolet, Monterey Park, CA, pg. 212
Thomas, Jesse G., Treas., Sec., Chief Fin. & Chief Information Officer--Allen & Hoshall, Inc., Memphis, TN, pg. 36
Thomas, Robert L., Pres. & Treas.--Saul Bros. & Company, Inc., Norcross, GA, pg. 972
Thomas, Thomas L., Treas.--Ferro Union, Inc., Torrance, CA, pg. 407
Thompson, C.H., Jr., Pres. & Treas.--Burlington Basket Co., Burlington, IA, pg. 191
Thompson, David, V.P.-Admin. Opers. & Treas.--Kennedy Manufacturing Company, Van Wert, OH, pg. 623
Thompson, Frank, Pres. & Treas.--C.F. Thompson Group, Inc., Windsor, CT, pg. 1094
Thompson, H.D., Chief Fin. Officer, V.P., Treas. & Sec.--Our Own Hardware Company, Burnsville, MN, pg. 832
Thompson, Pam, Treas. & Sec.--Key Cadillac, Inc., Edina, MN, pg. 626
Thompson, Rene C., Treas.--Universal Securities Corporation, Birmingham, AL, pg. 1139
Thompson, Steve, V.P., Gen. Mgr. & Treas.--Burlington Basket Co., Burlington, IA, pg. 191
Thomsen, Walter L., Sec. & Treas.--Schaeps Ice Cream Company, Madison, WI, pg. 974
Thorne, Daniel, V.P.-Fin. & Treas.--Pacific Enterprises Oil Company (USA), Dallas, TX, pg. 840
Thornton, A.J., Sec. & Treas.--Consolidated Publishing Company, Anniston, AL, pg. 277
Thornton, Keith, Sec. & Treas.--Farmington Hills Holding Company, Farmington, MI, pg. 402
Thornton, T.D., II, Pres. & Treas.--Progress Printing Company, Lynchburg, VA, pg. 894
Thurlow, Robin T., V.P., Chief Fin. Officer, Treas. & Sec.--Artesian Laboratories, Inc., Newark, DE, pg. 86
Tichenor, John A., Chief Fin. Officer, Treas. & Sec.--Allied Sporting Goods Inc., Louisville, KY, pg. 40
Tiffin, R. Alex, Sr., Treas. & Sec.--Tiffin Motor Homes, Inc., Red Bay, AL, pg. 1097
Tillotson, Neil E., Treas.--Textile Rubber & Chemical Company, Dalton, GA, pg. 1090
Timma, Michael C., V.P.-Fin., Sec. & Treas.--M M Systems Corporation, Tucker, GA, pg. 692
Timmons, Charles M., V.P. & Treas.--Canal Insurance Co., Greenville, SC, pg. 213
Timmons, William R., Jr., Grp. V.P. & Treas.--Canal Insurance Co., Greenville, SC, pg. 213
Tinius, Barry, Treas. & Sec.--Love Box Company, Inc., Wichita, KS, pg. 685
Tobler, Ernest W., Treas.--Cincom Systems, Inc., Cincinnati, OH, pg. 250
Todd, Jack, Mgr.-Fin.--Grocers Supply Co. Inc., Houston, TX, pg. 488
Tolkan, Victor K., Sec. & Treas.--Door Store, Inc., Washington, DC, pg. 346
Tomeker, Jay, V.P. & Treas.--Wisconsin Label Corporation, Algoma, WI, pg. 1198
Tomoff, Billie, V.P., Agency Opers. & Treas.--Haselow & Associates, Inc., Cleveland, OH, pg. 516
Tompkins, Polly, Sec. & Treas.--Burgess Pigment Co., Sandersville, GA, pg. 190
Tonkin, William H., Treas. & Sec.--Safe Harbor Water Power Corporation, Conestoga, PA, pg. 966
Torres, Vera Trinchero, Sec. & Treas.--Sutter Home Winery, Inc., Saint Helena, CA, pg. 1065
Torres, William J., V.P., Sec., Treas., Legal Officer & Telecommunications Dir.--Gibbs Wire & Steel Company, Inc., Southington, CT, pg. 456
Tortora, Dennis J., Controller & Asst. Treas.--Steinway & Sons, Long Island City, NY, pg. 1046
Totten, Jeffrey, V.P. & Treas.--Totten Tubes, Inc., Los Angeles, CA, pg. 1103
Tottino, Les, Treas. & Asst. Sec.--California Artichoke & Vegetable Growers Corp., Castroville, CA, pg. 209
Touhey, Carl E., Pres. & Treas.--Orange Motor Company Inc., Albany, NY, pg. 828
Trabucco, Robert, Sr. V.P., Chief Fin. Officer, & Treas.--Lechmere, Inc., Woburn, MA, pg. 665
Tracy, James A., Treas.--Sacramento Municipal Utility District, Sacramento, CA, pg. 965
Tran, Khahn T., V.P. & Treas.--Pacific Mutual Life Insurance Company, Newport Beach, CA, pg. 841
Trapp, Walter, V.P.-Treas.--Mary Kay Cosmetics Inc., Dallas, TX, pg. 716
Travers, Richard H., Treas.--Fred Weber Inc., Maryland Heights, MO, pg. 1171
Tremer-Huey, Lori, Treas.--Kenco, Middlebury, IN, pg. 1025
Trewin, John E., V.P. & Treas.--The O'Brien Corporation, South San Francisco, CA, pg. 820

Treynor, Sam, Sec., Treas. & Controller--Peck Road Ford Truck Sales, Whittier, CA, pg. 854
Trimakas, Harry S., V.P.-Fin. & Treas.--Pneumafil Corp., Charlotte, NC, pg. 878
Trinkle, Betty L., Treas.--Trinkle Sales, Inc., Cherry Hill, NJ, pg. 1114
Tronson, Keith, Chief Fin. Officer & Treas.--Raley's, West Sacramento, CA, pg. 910
Troups, Charlotte B., Treas. & Dir.-Mdsg. & Adv.--Bollinger Machine Shop And Shipyard, Inc., Lockport, LA, pg. 163
Trout, Jim, Treas.--Davis Mechanical Contractors, Inc., Greenville, SC, pg. 318
Troutman, W. Wilson, Controller & Asst. Treas.--Industrial Coatings Group, Inc., Chicago, IL, pg. 566
Truchi, James, Chief Fin. Officer, Treas. & Controller--Trucchis Markets, Raynham, MA, pg. 1117
Truesdell, J. E. III, Treas.--J. Austin Oil Co., Flint, MI, pg. 99
Truitt, Jim, Treas. & Sec.--Martin Industries (AL), Florence, AL, pg. 715
Truran, Francie, Asst. Treas.--Geographic Marketing Group (GMG), Philadelphia, PA, pg. 452
Tschumper, Delwin, Treas.--Badger Equipment Company, Winona, MN, pg. 102
Tsudis, Carol Cochran, Corp. Sec. & Treas.--817
Tucker, Hubert, Treas.--Bell Packaging Corporation, Marion, IN, pg. 135
Tucker, James D., Sec./Treas.--Network Real Estate of California, Inc., Soquel, CA, pg. 798
Tucker, James D., Sec./Treas.--Network Real Estate, Inc., Soquel, CA, pg. 798
Tulley, Mark M., Treas.--Tulley Buick-Pontiac Company, Inc., Nashua, NH, pg. 1119
Tullis, J. Robert, Treas.--Clear Springs Foods, Inc., Buhl, ID, pg. 254
Tully, Herbert B., Treas.--Wilbur-Ellis Company & Connell Brothers Company, San Francisco, CA, pg. 1189
Turco, Ann, V.P., Controller--The Weightman Group, Philadelphia, PA, pg. 1173
Turcotte, Bruce, Treas.--The Columbia Mfg. Company, Inc., Westfield, MA, pg. 265
Turner, C.O., III, Sec. & Treas.--Manufacturers Consolidation Service, Memphis, TN, pg. 705
Turner, Elizabeth, Treas.--The Fuller Brush Company, Great Bend, KS, pg. 436
Turner, Pearl, V.P. & Treas.--C M P Publications, Inc., Manhasset, NY, pg. 202
Turner, W. Thomas, Jr., Treas.--Funeral Security Plans, Inc., Kansas City, MO, pg. 804
Turriff, Thomas J., Chm. Bd., Pres. & Treas.--Tab Chemicals, Inc., Chicago, IL, pg. 1075
Tushar, C.P., Treas. & Controller--Oak Rubber Company, Ravenna, OH, pg. 819
Tutor, Albert G., Exec. V.P. & Treas.--Tutor-Saliba Corporation, Sylmar, CA, pg. 1120
Tutt, R. Thayer, Jr., V.P. & Treas.--Broadmoor Hotel, Inc., Colorado Springs, CO, pg. 177
Tuttle, Brian J., Treas.--Griffith Laboratories Worldwide, Inc., Alsip, IL, pg. 487
Tuttle, Howard G., Treas.--Lee Company, Westbrook, CT, pg. 665
Tyler, Beatrice B., Treas.--Cain & Bultman, Inc., Jacksonville, FL, pg. 207
Tyll, Betty, Treas. & Sec.--Sterling Heights Dodge, Inc., Sterling Heights, MI, pg. 1046
Typermass, Arthur G., Sr. V.P. & Treas.--Metropolitan Life Insurance Co., New York, NY, pg. 744
Uemura, Ken, Treas.--Persis Corporation, Honolulu, HI, pg. 863
Uenishi, Shoji, Treas.--Takatta Inc., Olympia Fields, IL, pg. 1076
Uhl, R.W., V.P.-Fin.--Bar-S Foods Co., Phoenix, AZ, pg. 118
Umans, A.R., Pres., Chief Exec. Officer & Treas.--RHC/Spacemaster Corporation, Melrose Park, IL, pg. 906
Underwood, Allen J., V.P. & Treas.--Amalloy, Goshen, NY, pg. 46
Underwood, David W., Treas.--Curries Company, Mason City, IA, pg. 361
Upson, James W., V.P., Treas.--Liggett-Stashower, Inc., Cleveland, OH, pg. 675
Urquahrt, Richard A. III, Pres. & Treas.--SS Restaurant Corporation, Raleigh, NC, pg. 466
Utz, Danny, V.P.-Fin. & Treas.--The Keller Manufacturing Co., Inc., Corydon, IN, pg. 621
Vaccarello, Chuck, Treas.--Moline Corporation, Saint Charles, IL, pg. 764
Vagnini, K.L., V.P., Sec. & Treas.--The Gerstenslager Company, Wooster, OH, pg. 454
Vahey, Dan, Treas.--Seigle's Home & Building Centers, Elgin, IL, pg. 987
Vakil, Usman U., Chm. Bd., Pres. & Treas.--Lights Of America, Inc., Walnut, CA, pg. 675
Valdes, Alfredo, V.P.-Fin., Opers., Corp. Sec. & Treas.--Domecq Importers Inc., Old Greenwich, CT, pg. 343
Valentine, T.M., V.P.-Fin. & Treas.--Formation, Inc., Moorestown, NJ, pg. 424
Valenzuela, Victor, Treasurer--Aero Peru Corporation, Miami, FL, pg. 22
Vallozzi, Andrew A., Pres. & Treas.--FCN Advertising, Milwaukee, WI, pg. 394
Van Den Blink, N. Mooers, Chm. Bd., Chief Exec. Officer, & Treas.--Hilliard Corporation, Elmira, NY, pg. 535
Van Denburgh, John, III, Treas.--American Fence Company, Phoenix, AZ, pg. 52
Van Kanegan, Roy W., Jr., Pres., Treas. & Sec.--Target Stamped Products Corp., Kinsman, OH, pg. 1079
Van Luven, G.A., Vice Chm., Chief Fin. Officer, Treas. & Controller--The Gage Company, Pittsburgh, PA, pg. 441
Van Rijn, Bernard, Chief Fin. Officer, Treas. & Sec.--Kirk-Mayer, Inc., Los Angeles, CA, pg. 633
Van Tiem, James D., Chief Fin. Officer & Treas.--The Brenlin Group, Akron, OH, pg. 173
Van, Sue, Treas.--Coulter Corporation, Hialeah, FL, pg. 289
Vanaharam, Jagu, Sr. V.P.-Finance, Accounting & Treas.--OmniCare Health Plan, Detroit, MI, pg. 826
Vanaharam, Jagu, V.P.-Fin., Accounting & Treas.--United American Healthcare Corp., Detroit, MI, pg. 826
Vandenbergh, Henry J., Jr., Chief Fin. Officer & Treas.--Rose Packing Company, South Barrington, IL, pg. 947
Vander Boon, John, Sec. & Treas.--Ada Beef, Inc., Ada, MI, pg. 16
Vander Zwaag, Donald D., Sr. V.P. & Treas.--Bradford Company, Holland, MI, pg. 170
Vanderah, Philip, Treas. & Sec.--Preferred Risk Mutual Insurance, West Des Moines, IA, pg. 886
Vanderminden, Robert D., Pres. & Treas.--Mettowee Lumber & Plastic Co., Inc., Granville, NY, pg. 1085
Vanderstelt, Mark J., Chief Fin. Officer & Treas.--Maxon Corporation, Muncie, IN, pg. 723
VanderVorst, Gary D., V.P. Fin. & Treas.--Erickson Oil Products, Inc., Hudson, WI, pg. 386
Vansant, John, Treas.--Bellamy Brothers, Inc., Ellenwood, GA, pg. 136
VanSickle, Sharon, Treas. & Dir. Pub. Rels.--Karakas, VanSickle Ouellette Advertising & Public Relations, Portland, OR, pg. 616
Vantil, Frank, Treas.--Central Grocers Co-op, Franklin Park, IL, pg. 232
Vaporciyan, Harutun, Grp. V.P. & Treas.--Giffels Associates, Inc., Southfield, MI, pg. 457
Vargo, James D., Sec. & Treas.--Daniels Manufacturing Corporation, Orlando, FL, pg. 314
Vasel, Gregory M., V.P. & Treas.--Schiavone Construction Co., Secaucus, NJ, pg. 976
Vass, William H., V.P.-Fin. & Treas.--Publix Supermarkets Inc., Lakeland, FL, pg. 898
Vaughn, Robert E., Treas., Sec. & Gen. Mgr.--Maryland Virginia Milk Producers Association, Inc., Reston, VA, pg. 717
Vaupel, Marcelyn, Treas.--Union City Body Company, Inc., Union City, IN, pg. 1128
Vavruska, Gail, V.P., Corp. Treas.--Rick Johnson & Company, Inc., Albuquerque, NM, pg. 597
Veligan, Daniel, V.P.-Fin., Sec. & Treas.--The Johnson Industries Corp., Urbana, OH, pg. 598
Verebay, Max, Treas.--Queens Group, Inc., Long Island City, NY, pg. 904
Vereen, Donald G., V.P.-Fin. & Treas.--The Bibb Company, Macon, GA, pg. 781
Vereen, W.J., Pres., Treas., & Chief Exec. Officer--Riverside Manufacturing Co., Moultrie, GA, pg. 937
Vermylen, Paul A., Jr., Pres., Treas. & Sec.--Meenan Oil Co. Limited Partnership, Syosset, NY, pg. 736
Vernon, Shirley A., Sec. & Treas.--Gilvin-Terrill Inc., Amarillo, TX, pg. 460
Verville, N.J., Chief Fin. Officer & Treas.--Bucyrus-Erie Company, South Milwaukee, WI, pg. 186
Verville, N.J., V.P., Treas. & Controller--B-E Holdings Inc., South Milwaukee, WI, pg. 106
Vestrand, Donald A., Sec. & Treas.--Holmatic, Inc., Norcross, GA, pg. 122
Vetali, Vicki M., Treas. & Controller--Excelsior Manufacturing & Supply Corp., Itasca, IL, pg. 392
Vetter, Philip L., Treas.--Osco Industries Inc., Portsmouth, OH, pg. 830
Vetter, Sandra, Sec. & Treas.--Better Baked Foods, Inc., North East, PA, pg. 148
Viall, Peter H., Asst. Treas.--Park Ridge Corporation, Park Ridge, NJ, pg. 849
Vikander, R. A., Chief Fin. Officer, V.P. & Treas.--Lapham-Hickey Steel Corp., Chicago, IL, pg. 658
Vinje, Ronald, Treas. & Sec.--Psomas & Associates, Santa Monica, CA, pg. 898
Vinson, Walter, Pur. Dir. & Asst. Treas.--Basic Construction Company, Newport News, VA, pg. 124
Vinzant, R. Lee, V.P. & Treas.--Sloss Industries Corporation, Birmingham, AL, pg. 1162
Vitale, Frank, Treas.--Waldes Truarc, Inc., Somerset, NJ, pg. 1159
Vitus, Felicia J., V.P., Sec. & Treas.--Vitus Electrical Supply Company, Eugene, OR, pg. 1154
Vogl, Charles, V.P., Treas. & Pres.-Winchester Grp.--Wilton Corporation, Palatine, IL, pg. 1194
Vogt, Doreen, Sec. & Treas.--De Nooyer Chevrolet Inc., Albany, NY, pg. 329
Vogt, H. John, V.P.-Fin. & Treas.--AXIA Incorporated, Oak Brook, IL, pg. 8
Vogt, R.W., Treas. & Chief Fin. Officer--Garvey Elevators Inc., Hutchinson, KS, pg. 443
Vollenweider, Lester, Treas.--Reily Electric Supply, Inc., Metairie, LA, pg. 923
Vollmer, John E., III, V.P., Chief Fin. Officer & Treas.--Sound Warehouse, Inc., Dallas, TX, pg. 1018
Volovic, Robert C., V.P. & Treas.--Kurtz Bros., Inc., Clearfield, PA, pg. 646
Von Hamm, Gunther, Pres. & Treas.--G. Von Hamm Textiles, Inc., Honolulu, HI, pg. 1155
von Luhrte, Richard L., Sec. & Treas.--RNL Technical Services, Denver, CO, pg. 908
von Luhrte, Richard L., Sec. & Treas.--Space Management Systems, Denver, CO, pg. 908
VonBon, Jim, Treas.--Triple F, Inc., Des Moines, IA, pg. 1114
Vondriska, Donald, Treas. & Controller--Bioproducts, Inc., Brecksville, OH, pg. 152
Voss, Marianne, Treas. & Sec.--Voss Industries, Inc., Cleveland, OH, pg. 1155
Vranek, William, Chief Fin. Officer--Coleman Cable Systems, Inc., North Chicago, IL, pg. 260
Vumbaco, James, Treas.--The Napier Company, Meriden, CT, pg. 783
Waddell, R. Scott, Pres. & Treas.--Standard Locknut & Lockwasher, Carmel, IN, pg. 1037
Wade, Donnie, Controller, Treas. & Sec.--Goodpasture, Inc., Brownfield, TX, pg. 471
Waggoner, Jerry A., Treas.--Steuart Petroleum Company, Washington, DC, pg. 1048
Wagner, Bertram, Treas.--General Aerospace Materials Corporation, Plainview, NY, pg. 448
Wagner, James D., V.P. & Treas.--Landmark Communications, Inc., Norfolk, VA, pg. 654
Wagner, Ken, Treas.--Perry & Derrick Co., Cincinnati, OH, pg. 863
Wagner, M.J., Sec. & Treas.--American Inks & Coatings Corp., Valley Forge, PA, pg. 56
Wagner, Stanley, Treas.--Publix Group, New York, NY, pg. 898
Wahl, C. Richard, Sr. V.P., Treas. & Sec.--Wheatland Tube Company, Collingswood, NJ, pg. 1184
Wahl, Ellen, Treas.--Vibra Screw Inc., Totowa, NJ, pg. 1149
Wai, Sam, Treas.--American Crystal Sugar Company, Moorhead, MN, pg. 51
Wakeland, Ralph, Exec. V.P.-Fin. & Treas.--Union Underwear Co., Inc., Bowling Green, KY, pg. 400
Walden, Susan L., Asst. Sec. & Treas.--Miller Electric Company, Jacksonville, FL, pg. 754
Waldman, Morris, Controller--Windsor Art Products, Inc., Pico Rivera, CA, pg. 1195
Waldorf, Toby, Treas. & Corp. Sec.--Idea Man, Inc., Los Angeles, CA, pg. 562
Walker, Anita, Treas.& Sec.--Fritz Chemical Company, Mesquite, TX, pg. 434
Walker, Baker, Treas., Controller, Sec. & Chief Fin. Officer--C. B. Ragland Company, Nashville, TN, pg. 909
Walker, John D., Sec. & Treas.--Anco Insulations, Inc., Baton Rouge, LA, pg. 72
Walker, Kandee Jo, Sec. & Treas.--Eldorado Chemical Company, San Antonio, TX, pg. 373
Walker, Max N., Treas. & Sec.--Gaston County Dyeing Machine Co., Stanley, NC, pg. 444
Walker, Robert H., Pres. & Treas.--Walker Die Casting, Inc., Lewisburg, TN, pg. 1160
Walker, Solomon, Treas.--Gulf Coast Lead Company, Inc., Tampa, FL, pg. 493
Wall, Kay D., Sec. & Treas.--Bryant Electric Company, Inc., High Point, NC, pg. 185
Wallace, Juanita, Pres., Chief Fin. Officer, Treas. & Sec.--Wallace & Wallace Fuel Oil, St. Albans, NY, pg. 1160
Walsh, Brendan, Treas. & Controller--Monsey Products Company, Kimberton, PA, pg. 766
Walsh, Evelyn, Treas.--Mohawk Plastics, Inc., Bernardston, MA, pg. 763
Walsh, Mark, Treas.--Ocean Properties, Ltd., Boynton Beach, FL, pg. 820
Walter, Coleen D., Treas.--Multi-Media Marketing Communications, Inc. (M.M.M.C., Inc.), Seal Beach, CA, pg. 775
Waltzer, Julius, V.P. & Treas.--Jack Young Associates, Hazleton, PA, pg. 1209
Waltzer, Julius, Treas.--Pocono Knits, Inc., Hazleton, PA, pg. 1209
Wandre, Bruce, Treas. & Controller--Crown Iron Works Company, Roseville, MN, pg. 302
Wandrei, Bruce A., Treas.--Crown Holdings, Inc., Roseville, MN, pg. 302
Ward, Bill, Sr. V.P., Sec. & Treas.--N.W. Transport Service, Inc., Commerce City, CO, pg. 781
Ward, J. Richard, Sec. & Treas.--Ward Trucking Corp., Altoona, PA, pg. 1163
Ward, Paul F., Treas.--Hollingsworth & Vose Co., East Walpole, MA, pg. 539
Wardle, D. Duane, V.P.-Fin. & Treas.--Young Electric Sign Company, Salt Lake City, UT, pg. 1209
Warford, David, V.P., Sec. & Treas.--Lenac, Warford, Stone, Inc., Newport Beach, CA, pg. 667
Wark, Dale A., V.P.-Fin., Chief Fin. Officer, Treas. & Sec.--R. M. Shoemaker Co., West Conshohocken, PA, pg. 1000
Warm, Stuart, Exec. V.P. & Treas.--Warm Brothers Construction Company, Cincinnati, OH, pg. 1163
Warmington, Carole, Sec. & Treas.--Complete Interiors Inc., Altamonte Springs, FL, pg. 270
Warnecke, Dennis C., Treas.--Kennedy Manufacturing Company, Van Wert, OH, pg. 623
Warner, Kathy, V.P.-Chief Fin. Officer--American SelfCare Corporation, Columbus, GA, pg. 60
Warner, Lynne, Treas. & Sec.--Warner Vineyards, Paw Paw, MI, pg. 1164
Warnick, Kenneth L., V.P.-Admin., Sec. & Treas.--Great Salt Lake Minerals & Chemicals Corp., Ogden, UT, pg. 482
Warren, Robert S. III, Sec. & Treas.--Warren Distributing Corp., Raleigh, NC, pg. 1164
Warren, Sidney L., Treas.--Fredrickson Motor Express Corp., Charlotte, NC, pg. 430
Warry, Lowrance, Chm. Bd. & Treas.--AEA, Inc., Charlotte, NC, pg. 3
Wassenaar, John, Treas.--Fareway Stores, Inc., Boone, IA, pg. 399
Wasserstrom, Alan, Treas.--Wasserstrom Company, Columbus, OH, pg. 1167
Waters, Russ, Treas.--Sunroc Corporation, Media, PA, pg. 1062
Waters, Russ, Treas.--Telkee Inc., Media, PA, pg. 1062
Watkins, Joe, Asst. Treas.--Watkins System Inc., Concordville, PA, pg. 1167
Watkins, Rhonda, Treas.--Charles Holston, Inc., Jennings, LA, pg. 541
Watson, Houston B., Chm. Bd., Chief Exec. Officer, Chief Fin. Officer & Treas.--Watson Electric Supply Inc., Dallas, TX, pg. 1168
Watson, T. Mitchell, Chief Fin. Officer & Treas.--B. L. Montague Co., Sumter, SC, pg. 766
Watters, Robert L., Treas.--J. Gibson McIlvain Co., White Marsh, MD, pg. 729
Waxler, Burton, Sr. V.P. & Treas.--National Cleaning Contractors, Inc., New York, NY, pg. 786
Waxman, Joanne, Treas.--Associated Metals & Minerals Corp., White Plains, NY, pg. 91
Weathers, W. Kent, Treas.--The Lusk Company, Irvine, CA, pg. 687
Weathers, W. Kent, Treas.--Lusk Interiors, Inc., Irvine, CA, pg. 688

Weaver. Neal C., V.P. & Treas.--Bourns, Inc., Riverside, CA, pg. 168
Weaver, Sandy, Treas.--Pacific States Casualty Co., Los Angeles, CA, pg. 841
Webb, E. Lynn, V.P.-Treas.--Dualite Sales & Service, Inc., Williamsburg, OH, pg. 350
Webb, Gregg, Treas.--Hawkins Markets, Inc., Wooster, OH, pg. 518
Webb, Jerry, V.P.-Fin.--Tekra Corporation, New Berlin, WI, pg. 1084
Webb, Michael W., V.P., Controller & Asst. Treas.--Margo's La Mode, Inc., Dallas, TX, pg. 373
Webb, Robert D., Sr. V.P. & Treas.--Knight Architects Engineers Planners, Inc., Chicago, IL, pg. 637
Webb, Robert D., Treas.--Knight/Emerson Consulting, Inc., Chicago, IL, pg. 637
Webb, Robert D., Sec. & Treas.--Knight PMD, Inc., Barrington, IL, pg. 637
Webb, Robert D., Treas.--Knight Management Consulting, Inc., Chicago, IL, pg. 637
Webb, Sandra, Treas. & Sec.--Delagra Corporation, Bridgeville, DE, pg. 325
Webber, John, Treas.--Modulite Corporation, Compton, CA, pg. 763
Weber, Douglas, Treas.--Edwards Brothers, Inc., Ann Arbor, MI, pg. 369
Weber, Robert T., Exec. V.P.-Fin.--Cresmer, Woodward, O'Mara & Ormsbee, New York, NY, pg. 298
Webster, Gordon J., Sec. & Treas.--Cleveland Wrecking Company, Los Angeles, CA, pg. 255
Wehrle, Michael H., Chief Fin. Officer & Treas.--McJunkin Corporation, Charleston, WV, pg. 730
Wehrle, T.E., Treas.--Sverdrup Corporation, Maryland Heights, MO, pg. 1065
Weiner, Paul, Treas.--Riklis Family Corporation, New York, NY, pg. 934
Weinhart, Martin, Chm. Bd., Chief Exec. Officer & Treas.--Master Molded Products Corporation, Elgin, IL, pg. 720
Weinman, Thomas F., Treas.--Bar-S Foods Co., Phoenix, AZ, pg. 118
Weins, Leo M., Pres. & Treas.--The H. W. Wilson Co., Bronx, NY, pg. 1193
Weinstein, Gerald, V.P.-Treas.--Lefrak Organization Inc., Rego Park, NY, pg. 666
Weis, Dan, Treas.--Jim Causley Pontiac GMC Inc., Mt. Clemens, MI, pg. 229
Weisberg, A.A., Chm. Bd. & Treas.--Technic Incorporated, Cranston, RI, pg. 1083
Weisman, Henry, Pres. & Treas.--Nuarc Company, Inc., Niles, IL, pg. 817
Weisman, Robert, Treas.--Plainville Stock Company, Inc., Plainville, MA, pg. 874
Weiss, Gerald, Treas.--Cosmos Communications, Inc., Long Island City, NY, pg. 288
Weiss, James A., Sec. & Treas.--James Chevrolet Inc., Mount Clemens, MI, pg. 588
Weiss, Selwyn M., Chm. Bd. & Treas.--Weiss Packing Co., Inc., Donora, PA, pg. 1174
Weiss, Stanley, Jr., Chief Exec. Officer & Treas.--Charles River Foods, Inc., Boston, MA, pg. 240
Welch, Kathryn, Treas.--Ervin Industries, Inc., Ann Arbor, MI, pg. 387
Weldon, Robert W., V.P.-Fin. & Treas.--Country Companies Insurance Group, Bloomington, IL, pg. 289
Weldon, Robert W., V.P.-Fin. & Treas.--Country Mutual Insurance Company, Bloomington, IL, pg. 289
Weldon, Robert W., V.P.-Fin. & Treas.--CC Services, Bloomington, IL, pg. 289
Welge, Michael W., Exec. V.P., Sec., Treas. & Comptroller--Gilster Mary Lee Corp., Chester, IL, pg. 460
Wellman, Lynda, Sec./Treas.--International Airline Support Group, Inc., Miami, FL, pg. 575
Wells, Clyde, Controller & Treas.--Vestal Manufacturing, Sweetwater, TN, pg. 1162
Wells, Gregory A., Treas. & Controller--Executive Telecom Systems, Inc., Indianapolis, IN, pg. 189
Wells, Marsha McCarty, Treas.--McCarty Farms, Magee, MS, pg. 727
Wells, Virgil, Treas.--Ebsco Industries, Inc., Birmingham, AL, pg. 365
Wendt, Roderick, Pres. & Treas.--Jeld-Wen, Inc., Klamath Falls, OR, pg. 591
Wenning, Theodore W., V.P. & Treas.--Belmont Metals, Inc., Brooklyn, NY, pg. 137
Wermerskirchen, James, Sec. & Treas.--Huntting Elevator Co., Austin, MN, pg. 555
Werschky, Bob, V.P. & Treas.--Maxcor Manufacturing, Inc., Colorado Springs, CO, pg. 722
West, G. W., Chief Fin. Officer, Corp. Sec. & Treas.--Alley-Cassetty Coal Co., Nashville, TN, pg. 37
West, Stephen O., Treas.--Gold Kist, Inc., Atlanta, GA, pg. 465
Westbrock, Leon, Sec. & Treas.--Universal Cooperatives, Inc., Minneapolis, MN, pg. 1138
Westfall, Virginia N., Treas.--Hershey Creamery Company, Harrisburg, PA, pg. 531
Westlie, James H., Treas. & Sec.--Westlie Motor Company, Minot, ND, pg. 1183
Westphal, Gordon E., Sr. V.P. & Treas.--Western States Envelope Co., Butler, WI, pg. 1181
Westreich, Murray, Exec. V.P., Sec. & Treas.--West Mill Clothes, Inc., Woodside, NY, pg. 1177
Westrich, R. Jane, Treas.--American Protection Industries, Inc., Los Angeles, CA, pg. 60
Wetsel, Cecil, Jr., Pres. & Treas.--Wetsel-Oviatt Lumber Company, Folsom, CA, pg. 1183
Whaley, Ronald L., Chief Fin. Officer, V.P. & Treas.--SCC Holding Co., Highland Park, IL, pg. 961
Wheeler, Mike, Chief Fin. Officer, V.P. & Treas.--Hy-Vee Food Stores Incorporated, Chariton, IA, pg. 556
Whiddon, Thomas E., V.P. & Treas.--Jack Eckerd Corporation, Largo, FL, pg. 366
White, Billy, Treas.--Foxworth-Galbraith Lumber Co., Dallas, TX, pg. 428
White, Bruce D., Exec. V.P., Treas.--Media Concepts Corporation, Assonet, MA, pg. 734
White, Donald G., Treas.--Wasco Products, Inc., Sanford, ME, pg. 1165
White, Eliot C., Pres., Treas. & Publr.--The Record-Journal Publishing Company, Meriden, CT, pg. 917
White, George A., Jr., Treas.--N E D Corp., Worcester, MA, pg. 780
White, H.G., V.P.-Fin.--Howell Instruments Corp., Fort Worth, TX, pg. 547
White, Jim, V.P., Treas. & Chief Fin. Officer--Tele-Trip Co., Omaha, NE, pg. 779
White, John W., Chief Fin. Officer & Asst. Treas.--United Grocers Inc., Portland, OR, pg. 1132
White, Larry, Treas.--Metromedia Steakhouses, Inc., Vandalia, OH, pg. 744
White, Rock E., Chief Fin. Officer & Treas.--Rome Cable Corporation, Rome, NY, pg. 945
White, Turner, Treas. & Sec.--Positronic Industries, Inc., Springfield, MO, pg. 881
White, Virginia L., Treas. & Sec.--Perpetual Corporation, Washington, DC, pg. 862
White, Virginia L., Sec. & Treas.--Allbritton Communications Company, Washington, DC, pg. 862
White, Virginia L., Sec. & Treas.--WJLA-TV, Washington, DC, pg. 862
White, William K., V.P. & Dir.-Fin. Plng. & Asst. Treas.--Ponderosa, Inc., Vandalia, OH, pg. 743
Whiteman, Jon, V.P. & Treas.--VASA North Atlantic Insurance Company, Indianapolis, IN, pg. 1146
Whiting, Paul L., Sr. V.P. & Chief Fin. Officer--Spalding & Evenflo Companies, Inc., Tampa, FL, pg. 1024
Whitney, Robert C., Sec. & Treas.--Frehner Construction Company, Inc., North Las Vegas, NV, pg. 432
Whitsell, Helen J., Chm. Bd., Chief Exec. Officer & Treas.--Copeland Lumber Yard, Inc., Portland, OR, pg. 284
Whitten, Earl, Chief Fin. Officer, Treas. & Controller--Sherley Grain Company, Bovina, TX, pg. 998
Widdop, James T., Treas.--Montgomery Elevator Company, Moline, IL, pg. 767
Wiedemer, Richard A. Sr., V.P. & Treas.--Hinkley Lighting Inc., Cleveland, OH, pg. 535
Wiege, Lloyd, V.P., Sec. & Treas.--Baugh Construction Company, Seattle, WA, pg. 127
Wiell, Tim, V.P., Treas. & Controller--American Bread Company - Sunbeam Bakery, Nashville, TN, pg. 49
Wiers, C. Edward, Treas.--Challenge Technologies, Grand Haven, MI, pg. 238
Wiesemes, Rhoda, Pres. & Treas.--Quality Packaging Products, Inc., Benton Harbor, MI, pg. 903
Wigchers, Arthur W., Jr., V.P. & Treas.--Zilber, Ltd., Milwaukee, WI, pg. 1219
Wiggin, Erma N., Treas.--Advanced Instruments, Inc., Needham Heights, MA, pg. 20
Wilcox, Jane T., Treas. & Sec.--Mountain States Pipe & Supply Company, Colorado Springs, CO, pg. 773
Wilcox, Terry, Treas. & Sec.--Charles Machine Works, Inc., Perry, OK, pg. 240
Wild, Richard D., Sr. V.P.-Fin. & Opers.--McDougal, Littell & Company, Evanston, IL, pg. 728
Wilkerson, Bill, Treas., Controller & Sec.--Greenwood Packing Plant, Greenwood, SC, pg. 486
Wilkerson, George S., V.P. & Treas.--Material Handling Equipment Co., Bristol, PA, pg. 763
Wilkerson, O.A., III, Sr. V.P. & Treas.--Smith Industries, Inc., Montgomery, AL, pg. 1013
Wilkes, Corbin M., V.P.-Fin. & Treas.--The Kiplinger Washington Editors, Inc., Washington, DC, pg. 632
Wilkinson, George S., V.P. & Treas.--Modern Handling Equipment of N.J., Inc., Edison, NJ, pg. 763
Wilkinson, George S., V.P. & Treas.--Moreco Inc., Bristol, PA, pg. 763
Wilkinson, George S., V.P. & Treas.--Seely Equipment & Supply Co., Inc., Wall, NJ, pg. 763
Willard, Kathy, Treas.--Willard Grain & Feed, Inc., Celina, TX, pg. 1190
Willard, Ken, V.P. & Treas.--Oxford Realty Services Corp., Bethesda, MD, pg. 835
Willbrant, Rick, V.P. & Treas.--Ambac International Corp., Columbia, SC, pg. 47
Willett, Daniel J., V.P. & Treas.--Continental Grain Company, New York, NY, pg. 279
Willging, Jerry, Sec. & Treas.--Baxter Hodell Donnelly Preston Inc., Cincinnati, OH, pg. 127
Williams, Belton R., Chief Fin. Officer, Treas. & Sec.--George W. Auch Co., Pontiac, MI, pg. 97
Williams, Edward J., Mgr. & Treas.--Brown Brothers, Harriman & Co., New York, NY, pg. 181
Williams, Faye M., Treas. & Sec.--Northwest Tobacco & Candy Co., Fayetteville, AR, pg. 815
Williams, Gregory O., Sr. V.P., Sec. & Treas.--Rothchild Asset Management Inc., New York, NY, pg. 951
Williams, Jay, Chief Fin. Officer & Treas.--Pacific Lumber & Shipping Co., Seattle, WA, pg. 840
Williams, Jerry D., Treas. & Sec.--Cajun Electric Power Co-op, Baton Rouge, LA, pg. 207
Williams, Jimmie D., Exec. V.P., Chief Fin. Officer, Treas. & Sec.--Belz Enterprises, Memphis, TN, pg. 138
Williams, John, Chief Fin. Officer--Rocco Inc., Harrisonburg, VA, pg. 940
Williams, Marie, Treas.--Solid State Devices, Inc., La Mirada, CA, pg. 1017
Williams, Melvin, Sec. & Treas.--Besche Oil Company, Inc., Waldorf, MD, pg. 145
Williams, P. Greggory, V.P.-Investments & Treas.--Shenandoah Life Insurance Company, Roanoke, VA, pg. 997
Williams, Robert J., Jr., Chief Fin. Officer--Cadillac Products, Inc., Troy, MI, pg. 207
Williams, Robert M., Chm., Chief Exec. Officer & Treas.--Genova Products, Inc., Davison, MI, pg. 452
Williams, Roger K., Treas.--Cadillac Products, Inc., Troy, MI, pg. 207
Williams, Rogers, V.P., Treas. & Controller--White Stag Manufacturing Company, Van Nuys, CA, pg. 1186
Williams, Steven D., Treas. & Controller--Coca Cola Bottling Co. United, Inc., Birmingham, AL, pg. 257
Williams, T.A., V.P.-Sec. & Treas.--E. F. Houghton & Co., Valley Forge, PA, pg. 546
Williams, Tami, Treas.--Humphreys Price/Cochran & Sanford Advertising, Memphis, TN, pg. 553
Williams, Timothy, V.P., Treas. & Sec.--Spring Arbor Distributors, Belleville, MI, pg. 1033
Williams, Victor J., Sec. & Treas.--Select Sires, Inc., Plain City, OH, pg. 988
Williams, Wgonda, Treas. & Controller--Handling Systems Engineering, Jacksonville, FL, pg. 505
Williamson, Daphne, Sec. & Treas.--Airline Manufacturing Company, Inc., Columbus, MS, pg. 27
Williamson, James C., Sr., Exec. V.P. & Treas.--Smith & Gillespie Engineers, Inc., Jacksonville, FL, pg. 1012
Williges, Allison, Mgr.-Treasury Opers.--St. Johnsbury Trucking Co., Inc., Holliston, MA, pg. 966
Willinger, Louis A., Treas.--Cummins Cumberland Inc., Louisville, KY, pg. 305
Willis, Gary, V.P.-Fin., Chief Fin. Officer & Treas.--Eddins-Walcher Company, Midland, TX, pg. 367
Willis, J.C., Treas. & Sec.--Cormier Chevrolet Company, Inc., Long Beach, CA, pg. 286
Willis, Rita S., Treas.--Maine Printing & Business Forms Co., Portland, ME, pg. 702
Willison, Charles, Treas.--Reactive Metals & Alloys Corporation (REMACOR), West Pittsburg, PA, pg. 916
Wills, R.J., Sec. & Treas.--A. Tenenbaum Co. Inc., North Little Rock, AR, pg. 1087
Wilson, Dan, Treas. & Dir.-Data Processing--Parkdale Mills, Gastonia, NC, pg. 849
Wilson, James E., V.P. & Treas.--Peerless Confection Company, Chicago, IL, pg. 855
Wilson, Jesse M., Sr., Treas.--Apollo Colors, Inc., Northbrook, IL, pg. 78
Wilson, Jimmy, Chief Fin. Officer, Treas. & Controller--J. M. Smith Corp., Spartanburg, SC, pg. 1012
Wilson, Lowell, Treas. & Sec.--Ag Processing Inc A Cooperative, Omaha, NE, pg. 24
Wilson, Riley, Pres., Treas., Sec. & Controller--Rapid Power Technologies, Inc., Brookfield, CT, pg. 913
Wilson, Rob, Sec. & Treas.--Hubler Chevrolet Inc., Indianapolis, IN, pg. 550
Wilson, Ross M., III, Asst. Treas.--American Chemical Society, Washington, DC, pg. 50
Wilson, Stephen R., Sr. V.P. & Chief Fin. Officer--CF Industries, Inc., Long Grove, IL, pg. 200
Winiarski, Victor A., Treas. & Sec.--Progressive Tool & Industries Co., Southfield, MI, pg. 894
Winkels, Thomas, Sec. & Treas.--McNeilus Companies, Dodge Center, MN, pg. 732
Winkler, William F., Chief Oper. Officer, Sec. & Treas.--Ackerman McQueen, Inc., Oklahoma City, OK, pg. 12
Winn, Elwood F., Sec., Treas. & Chief Fin. Officer--Certified Grocers Midwest, Inc., Hodgkins, IL, pg. 236
Winslow, Richard H., Chief Fin. Officer, V.P.-Fin., Controller & Treas.--Norfolk Shipbuilding & Drydock Corporation, Norfolk, VA, pg. 810
Winter, Dennis, Treas.--Hydril Company, Los Angeles, CA, pg. 556
Winter, Robert, Sec. & Treas.--Hastings Co-Op Creamery Company, Hastings, MN, pg. 516
Winters, John, Treas.--Bernea Food Service, Inc., Otsego, MI, pg. 143
Wise, Bruce S., Sec. & Treas.--Global Insurance Company, Houston, TX, pg. 662
Wise, Ronald L., Treas. & Sec.--E & A Industries, Inc., Indianapolis, IN, pg. 358
Wise, Ronald L., Sec. & Treas.--H & K Realty Co. Inc., Indianapolis, IN, pg. 358
Wise, Ronald L., Sec. & Treas.--Car Brite, Inc., Indianapolis, IN, pg. 358
Wisgerhof, Jerry G., Treas.--The Principal Financial Group, Des Moines, IA, pg. 890
Wismer, Stephen H., Exec. V.P. & Treas.--Crane & Co., Inc., Dalton, MA, pg. 296
Wisniewski, Henry G., Exec. V.P. & Treas.--Tash, Inc., Des Plaines, IL, pg. 1080
Wisotsky, Jerry, Chm. Bd., Sec. & Treas.--Imperial Litho/Graphics, Inc., Phoenix, AZ, pg. 564
Witherwax, Jeffrey T., Pres. & Treas.--Naugatuck Glass Company, Naugatuck, CT, pg. 796
Witzel, John A., Controller--The Dispatch Printing Company, Columbus, OH, pg. 339
Woerner, Otto H., Vice Chm. & Treas.--H.H. Brown Shoe Company, Inc., Greenwich, CT, pg. 182
Wojnowich, Simon, Treas.--Highland Mills Inc., Charlotte, NC, pg. 534
Wojnowski, Leon A., Sec., Treas. & Chief Fin. Officer--Connelly Containers, Inc., Bala-Cynwyd, PA, pg. 275
Wolf, J.W., V.P. & Treas.--Graybar Electric Company, Inc., Clayton, MO, pg. 479
Wolf, M.D., Treas.--Al Johnson Construction Co., Minneapolis, MN, pg. 597
Wolf, Norman, Sec. & Treas.--Carole Wren, Inc., New York, NY, pg. 1204
Wolf, Timothy W., Sec., Treas.--Fessel, Siegfriedt & Moeller, Inc., Louisville, KY, pg. 407
Wong, Albert, Treas.--Bel Air Markets, Sacramento, CA, pg. 133
Wong, Jennifer, Treas. & Controller--Peter Wong & Associates, Inc., Richmond, VA, pg. 1199
Wonowich, Boris, Treas.--Admiration Hosiery Mills, Inc., Charlotte, NC, pg. 534
Wood, Carol S., Treas., Sec., Controller & Chief Fin. Officer--Higginbotham-Bartlett Co., Lubbock, TX, pg. 533
Wood, Kurt, Treas.--CBM Industries, Inc., Minneapolis, MN, pg. 199
Wood, Robert C., Chief Fin. Officer, Treas. & Sec.--Xtek, Inc., Cincinnati, OH, pg. 1206

Wood, Robert L., Treas., Sec. & Chief Fin. Officer--Justiss Oil Co., Inc., Jena, LA, pg. 610
Woodard, James, Treas.--Tom James Company, Arlington, TX, pg. 589
Woodhatch, Maynard, Sec. & Treas.--Shearman Corporation, Lake Charles, LA, pg. 996
Woodward, David A., Sec. & Treas.--Certified Grocers Of California, Los Angeles, CA, pg. 237
Wozniak, Richard E., Treas.--Church & Church Inc., Utica, MI, pg. 249
Wright, Carl, Treas.--Times-World Corporation, Roanoke, VA, pg. 656
Wright, Clancy, Exec. V.P., Treas. & Sec.--Bawden Printing, Inc., Eldridge, IA, pg. 127
Wright, Jean C., Treas.--John R. Lyman Company, Chicopee, MA, pg. 689
Wright, Leyton E., Treas.--Allen & Ohara, Inc., Memphis, TN, pg. 36
Wright, Robert, Sec. & Treas.--W. C. Bradley Co., Columbus, GA, pg. 170
Wright, Roy W., Treas.--Cloud Corporation, Des Plaines, IL, pg. 256
Wright, Terry, V.P., Sec. & Treas.--Fones & Mann Inc., New York, NY, pg. 422
Wright, Wayne C., Chief Fin. Officer, Treas. & Sec.--Copper & Brass Sales, Inc., East Detroit, MI, pg. 284
Wu, Esther, Chief Fin. Officer, Treas. & Controller--Visible Changes, Houston, TX, pg. 1153
Wu, James W., Treas.--McKinsey & Company, Inc., New York, NY, pg. 731
Wurst, William, Sec. & Treas.--Tamaroff Leasing Co., Southfield, MI, pg. 1077
Wurz, Jane, Sec. & Treas.--Accu-Sort Systems, Inc., Telford, PA, pg. 11
Wyant, Clyde, Exec. V.P.-Fin. & Treas.--Lennox International Inc., Richardson, TX, pg. 667
Wyckaerk, Veronica M., Chief Fin. Officer & Treas.--Intertrade Industries, Huntington Beach, CA, pg. 581
Wynn, Jane M., Exec. V.P., Sec. & Treas.--Miller Electric Company, Jacksonville, FL, pg. 754
Wysinski, Robert, Treas.--Schottenstein Stores Corporation, Columbus, OH, pg. 978
Wysong, Phil, V.P. & Treas.--Fuel South, Inc., Hazlehurst, GA, pg. 435
Wysong, Phil, V.P.-Treas. & Sec.--Jones Company, Inc., Waycross, GA, pg. 603
Yacisin, Michael P., Treas.--Arinc Inc., Annapolis, MD, pg. 82
Yagi, Clyde H., Dir.-Data Processing, Sec. & Treas.--Mutual Welding Co., Ltd, Honolulu, HI, pg. 779
Yamauchi, Margaret S., Treas.--Armstrong Produce Ltd., Honolulu, HI, pg. 84
Yannes, Bob, Treas.--Ensoniq Corporation, Malvern, PA, pg. 382
Yates, Robert L., V.P. & Treas.--Tennessee Valley Authority, Knoxville, TN, pg. 1088
Yax, Vincent, Sr. V.P. & Treas.--Fairfield Maxwell Ltd., New York, NY, pg. 397
Yax, Vincent, V.P., Controller & Treas.--Fairfield International Corporation, New York, NY, pg. 397
Yeager, Leah B., Chief Fin. Officer, Treas. & Controller--Automation Intelligence, Inc., Maitland, FL, pg. 101
Yeargan, Victor B., Jr., Sec. & Treas.--Battey Machinery Company, Rome, GA, pg. 127
Yeung, William, Sec. & Treas.--Kroch's & Brentano's, Inc., Chicago, IL, pg. 645
Yoda, David, Sec. & Treas.--Trader Joes Co., South Pasadena, CA, pg. 1076
Yoder, Thomas, Treas. & Adv. Dir.--Chicago Reader, Inc., Chicago, IL, pg. 245
Yoo, Paul J., V.P.-Fin. & Treas.--Jockey International, Inc., Kenosha, WI, pg. 595
Yordy, William R., Controller & Treas.--Brian Unlimited Distribution Company, Inc., Detroit, MI, pg. 175
York, W. L., Chief Fin. Officer & Treas.--Dairy Fresh Corp., Greensboro, AL, pg. 310
Yorke, Frederick, III, V.P. & Treas.--Fiduciary Trust Company International, New York, NY, pg. 408
Yorke, Fredrick, III, V.P. & Treas.--Fiduciary Trust Co. International, New York, NY, pg. 408
Yost, Jan, Treas. & Sec.--D.S.U.-Peterbilt & GMC, Inc., Portland, OR, pg. 309
Yost, William H., Treas. & Controller--Maguire Group Inc., Foxboro, MA, pg. 701
Young, Dale, Treas.--Kansas City Chiefs Football Club, Kansas City, MO, pg. 616
Young, Fred, Jr., Treas.--Concorp, Inc., Nitro, WV, pg. 272
Young, James G., Jr., Chief Fin. Officer & Treas.--Schurz Communications, Inc., South Bend, IN, pg. 979
Young, Joy, Treas.--Precision Twist Drill Co., Crystal Lake, IL, pg. 885
Young, Mary E., Treas.--Plastipak Packaging Inc., Plymouth, MI, pg. 876
Young, Peter A., Sec. & Treas.--Burd & Fletcher Company, Kansas City, MO, pg. 189
Young, W.E., Sec. & Treas.--George W. Cochran Co., Inc., Washington, DC, pg. 258
Youngchild, Linda L., Corp. Sec. & Asst. Treas.--The Metal Ware Corp., Two Rivers, WI, pg. 741
Younggren, David, Sr. V.P.--The Gary-Williams Company, Denver, CO, pg. 444
Yu, Kenneth P., Exec. V.P., Treas. & Res. Dir.--AdLand Advertising, Inc., San Francisco, CA, pg. 17
Yuen, William, V.P.-Fin., Sec. & Treas.--J.H. Baxter & Company, San Mateo, CA, pg. 127
Yunes, Marci L., V.P.-Fin. & Treas.--Pueblo International, Inc., Pompano Beach, FL, pg. 899
Zabinski, A. F., Jr., Chief Fin. Officer, Treas. & Controller--George Sollitt Construction, Wood Dale, IL, pg. 1017
Zaccaria, Nicholas, Treas.--Gemini Consulting, Morristown, NJ, pg. 448
Zaffe, Gwen, Treas.--Myron Manufacturing Corporation, Maywood, NJ, pg. 780
Zahn, Jack, Treas.--Uniseal, Inc., Evansville, IN, pg. 639
Zahner, Josephine, Sec. & Treas.--Carey Machinery & Supply Company, Baltimore, MD, pg. 218
Zakutney, Ray, Treas. & Sec.--McConnell Automotive, Mobile, AL, pg. 727
Zalieckas, Joseph, Treas.--Hyde Manufacturing Co., Southbridge, MA, pg. 556
Zall, Betty, Treas. & Sec.--Paris Presents, Gurnee, IL, pg. 848
Zapisek, John R., Sr. V.P., Chief Fin. Officer & Treas.--Utica Mutual Insurance Company, New Hartford, NY, pg. 1140
Zary, Jerome E., V.P., Sec., Chief Fin. Officer & Treas.--Frog Switch & Manufacturing Company, Carlisle, PA, pg. 434
Zattosky, S.M., Pres., Chief Exec. Officer & Treas.--Cortland Line Co., Inc., Cortland, NY, pg. 287
Zeinger, Henry, Treas. & Sec.--King Wire & Cable Corporation, Jamaica, NY, pg. 631
Zeman, Anton L., Exec. V.P. & Treas.--Racine Federated, Inc., Racine, WI, pg. 909
Zemanek, Louis M., Sec. & Treas.--Gate Petroleum Company, Jacksonville, FL, pg. 445
Zennedjian, Violet, Sec. & Treas.--Adray Appliance & Photo Center, Inc., Dearborn, MI, pg. 18
Zeus, William, Jr., Pres. & Chief Exec. Officer--National Tool & Manufacturing Company, Kenilworth, NJ, pg. 794
Ziegler, Douglas, Sec. & Treas.--Westco Products, Inc., Pico Rivera, CA, pg. 1178
Ziegler, William C., Treas. & Sec.--Ziegler Tire & Supply Company, Inc., Canton, OH, pg. 1218
Zigmundt, Robert V., Sec. & Treas.--Kunzler & Company, Inc., Lancaster, PA, pg. 646
Ziller, Barbara, Treas.--The F. Dohmen Company, Germantown, WI, pg. 343
Zimmerman, Edward, Sec., Treas. & Personnel Mgr.--Dobles Chevrolet, Inc., Manchester, NH, pg. 342
Zimmerman, Frank, Treas., Controller & Chief Fin. Officer--Hudson & Affiliated Co., Shawnee Mission, KS, pg. 551
Zimmerman, Joyce I., Sec. & Treas.--Marval Industries, Inc., Mamaroneck, NY, pg. 716
Zimmerman, Lon D., Exec. V.P., Treas. & New Bus. Contact--Adamson Advertising, Inc., Saint Louis, MO, pg. 17
Zimmermann, W.K., Treas. & Sec.--March Manufacturing Inc., Glenview, IL, pg. 706
Zinbarg, Benson, Pres., Chief Exec. & Chief Fin. Officer & Treas.--Sun Hill Industries, Stamford, CT, pg. 1059
Znamenacek, Karel, Exec. V.P. & Treas.--Crete Carrier Corp., Lincoln, NE, pg. 299
Zoeller, Kenneth M., V.P. & Treas.--Alco Health Services Corporation, Malvern, PA, pg. 31
Zolla, Frederick J., V.P. & Treas.--Globe Industries, Inc., Chicago, IL, pg. 464
Zone, Jeff, V.P. & Treas.--Cecil Saydah Company, Los Angeles, CA, pg. 973
Zook, Randall, Treas.--Oliver Oil Company, Inc., Chambersburg, PA, pg. 824
Zucker, Murray J., V.P., Chief Fin. Officer & Treas.--The RAL Corporation, Fairfield, NJ, pg. 357
Zuckerwar, Jane, Treas.--The Grandoe Corporation, Gloversville, NY, pg. 476